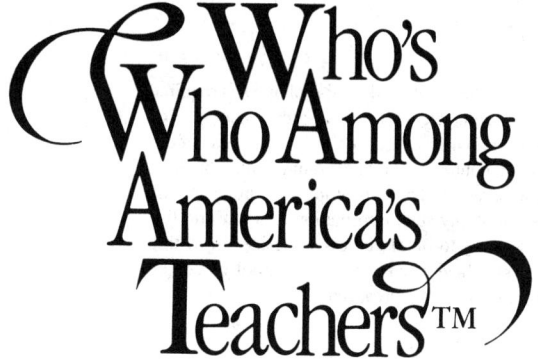

Who's Who Among America's Teachers™

The Best Teachers in America
Selected by the Best Students™

First Edition
1990

Educational Communications, Inc.
721 N. McKinley Road
Lake Forest, Illinois 60045

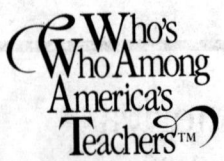

Table of Contents

Preface

It's amazing what youngsters will tell you if you ask. We asked the top 5% of our nation's high school and college students, those listed in WHO's WHO AMONG AMERICAN HIGH SCHOOL STUDENTS ® and THE NATIONAL DEAN's LIST ® to select the best teachers they ever had, those who truly made a difference in their lives and they responded . . . a lot.

Within the pages of this book you will find biographical profiles of approximately 25,000 outstanding teachers, each of whom was selected by one or more of their former students. These teachers were remembered by their students, sometimes more than ten years after they were together. The enthusiasm of the students to honor and recognize their former teachers was overwhelming. Many of their comments were memorable, but in essence what they said was, "this teacher was special."

On a personal level, over and over again students wrote us about teachers who treated them as individuals, cared about them as individuals and were able to "push the right buttons" to make their individuality emerge and/or thrive. In some cases the teachers appear to have turned around troubled students, but in most cases the teachers were credited with a consistency of caring which motivated the students to be consistently responsive.

Academically, the students were quick to recognize teachers who knew and loved their subject matter and communicated their enthusiasm to the students. We have all been in classrooms that come alive with the energy good teachers and their students produce — it is a great, but too often rare experience. Yet, the teachers in this book produce this energy often, and their students have been touched by their experience, probably for a lifetime.

Since 1967 our company has produced fine reference and recognition publications. We have won several reference book awards and have always been committed to the highest standards in our selection process. Nevertheless, I can't recall a project that has been more fun and satisfying than publishing this book. What I've learned or had confirmed from working on this publication is this:

> Good or great teachers do well because they love what they're doing and they genuinely care about kids and education. They don't seem to covet recognition and other awards, but they sure deserve them. Good students (and probably all students), on the other hand, know good teachers when they have them, and the value these teachers impart is retained long after the subject matter has grown fuzzy.

So, this book is a tribute to 25,000 outstanding teachers from the best judges of good teaching, the ultimate consumers of education, their former, grateful students. We hope this book will inspire some students to become good teachers and maybe even motivate some teachers who are not in this book to try a little harder, reach a little higher, care a little more. We will make certain that this book becomes a valuable reference resource for school boards and others in education who want to know who the best teachers are and where they can be found.

So, to all the teachers listed in this book, on behalf of all of your students, we congratulate you for a job well done. You get a big "A+." Now, go back to your classroom and keep on doing what you've done. We all need you.

Paul C. Krouse
Publisher

Selection Criteria and Process

"The Best Teachers in America
Selected by the Best Students™"

The only way a teacher can be included in this publication is to be nominated by one or more of his or her former students. The only students who are invited to select their former teachers are students who are listed in WHO'S WHO AMONG AMERICAN HIGH SCHOOL STUDENTS® or THE NATIONAL DEAN'S LIST®. This universe of the top 5% high school and college students in America represents a unique group of consumers of education, well-qualified to determine which teachers contributed most to their academic success.

Throughout the academic year all students accepted for special honorary award recognition in the two student publications described above are sent a nomination form, and invited to select one teacher from each school they have attended (i.e., one teacher from K-5, one from 6-8, and one from 9-12) who "made a difference" in their education. Student nominators selected an average of 2.5 teachers each although the typical student was taught by approximately 40 to 50 teachers. Many of the teachers were nominated by more than one student.

There is no greater tribute a teacher can receive than to be recognized for teaching excellence by former students, particularly, when the students themselves have been as successful as those included in this process. The selectivity demonstrated by the student nominators further validates the quality of the teachers listed in this book.

Advisory Committee

Educational Communications, Inc. is dedicated to ensuring that the recognition of the teachers in WHO'S WHO AMONG AMERICA'S TEACHERS ™ is one of the most meaningful honors a teacher can receive. We are also committed to helping to ensure that all students have excellent teachers.

Through the development and publication of WHO'S WHO AMONG AMERICA'S TEACHERS ™ a unique and valuable database of exceptional educators has been developed and will continue to expand. We intend to use this resource to produce much-needed research and other information so vital to improving the quality of education in our country. In plain English, we know the teachers listed in this book are effective and we want to find out how and why from them and share this information with others.

Therefore, we have established an Advisory Committee of the following distinguished educators who will provide us with on-going advice and counsel to accomplish our objectives. Our Committee members include:

Kathleen DeFloria
Associate Executive Director
The National Association of
Secondary School Principals

Jeremiah Floyd
Associate Director
National School Boards Association

Darlene Pierce
Director
National Teacher of
the Year Program

Marilyn Rauth
Assistant to the President
American Federation of Teachers

William Saunders
Executive Director
National Alliance of
Black School Educators

Joseph Scherer
Executive Director
National School Public
Relations Association

On the following pages, we are pleased to present editorials written by prominent educators who represent teachers' partners and colleagues in the education community.

Editorials

Principal-Teacher Cooperation

Timothy Dyer
Executive Director
National Association of Secondary School Principals

Teacher-principal cooperative planning has always been of utmost importance in good school management. As educators enter the 21st century much will be discussed on the subjects of school-based management, teacher empowerment and principal-teacher teamwork. The National Association of Secondary School Principals has always held that cooperative planning between teachers and administrators is central to good schools. It is ludicrous to think otherwise.

As a child profits from cooperative parental direction, the student learns best in a setting where teachers and administrators jointly plan the educational program. There has been no time in the history of American education when challenges are so obvious. As teachers and administrators focus on the changing needs of students in an unknown future, even greater teamwork effort will be required. The recent changes in Eastern Europe are visible reminders of how fast our world is changing. Democratic principles have never been revealed with so much spontaneity.

This last decade of the 20th century will be a time when educators are called upon to restructure schools at a rapid pace. The stage was set in September 1989 at the President's Summit at the University of Virginia. The governors, in assessing the needs of our country, established six important national goals. By consensus the governors charged the schools with the responsibility for ensuring that by the year 2000:

- All children in America will start school ready to learn.

- The high school graduation rate will increase to at least 90 percent.

- American students will leave grades 4, 8 and 12 having demonstrated competency over challenging subject matter including English, mathematics, science, history and geography.

- U.S. students will be first in the world in mathematics and science achievement.

- Every adult American will be literate.

- Every school will be drug free.

No one would think of addressing these goals without cooperative planning by teachers and principals. Indeed it will require the maximum efforts of teamwork to ensure success in meeting these goals.

The Underachiever: The Challenge to Teachers

William Saunders
Executive Director
National Alliance of Black School Educators

The present day practice of remediation needs to be re-examined. To minimize student underachieving time, no remediation should take place without a thorough examination of the instructional delivery process. As soon as a student is identified as an underachiever, the critical factors that may have played a role in creating this underachiever should be evaluated. If the critical factors have not been satisfied, it is doubtful that a repeat (remediation) of the same process will work effectively the second time around. What is needed is an examination of why the critical factors were not satisfied for the student. Inclusive in this examination should be an examination of the instructional material used for remediation. In most cases, 95 percent of the instructional materials used for academic skill remediation is the same material used in the first unsuccessful teaching and learning experience. New or modified teaching methodologies and materials must be used when reteaching an underachiever.

Staff development should have priority over other program interventions. There is no question that computer literacy is important to the overall education of a student. The question that should be raised is when should computers be introduced and at what cost to whom. Computer competence is an essential skill for the high school curriculum. Whether or not it is essential for elementary school students is questionable. To think of computer intervention in any terms other than as an enrichment to the existing curriculum or as an instructional tool for trained teachers is a pedagogical error and a lack of attention to the needs of too many children.

School district personnel, who continue to spend tens of thousands of dollars on computers, software, and computer literacy programs, at the expense of those students who are in need of trained teachers in child development theory and practice, mathematics, science, language development, classroom management, teaching methodologies, and computer literacy, are denying these students the opportunity to prepare themselves for a successful high school experience. Such students are at risk of becoming permanent underachievers.

Language development should be considered a basic skill, yet ninety percent of the talking that goes on in the elementary school classroom is done by the teacher. Students must be given numerous opportunities to express and test their understanding of concepts and ideas in other ways than just paper and pencil responses. Many minority students do not have the opportunity for free expression in the home. When these students are also denied access to oral expression in the classroom, it is likely that they will leave elementary school severely underdeveloped in their overall language skills. Since language development is the foundation to all further learning, its absence will make the student an underachiever in other discipline areas as well.

Parent intervention is critical in preventing students from entering the class of permanent underachievers. When financial resources are available for program intervention, parent programs should be given a high priority. The parent must be made to understand that they are the most valuable resource in the education of their children. They must be made to accept the responsibility for their own children's educational development.

The value of a teacher is priceless when she equips herself with the skills, knowledge, and commitment necessary to guarantee her students access to quality teaching and instruction. How successful a teacher is in preventing the underachiever virus from infecting her class defines the value of any teacher.

Teachers and Schools, An Image Alike

Joseph Scherer
Executive Director
National School Public Relations Association

Borrowing a fundamental formula from service oriented companies and applying it to education helps improve our understanding of why the public's image of teachers and their schools is so much alike. Private sector companies develop their image based on the following relationships:

a) 90% of a service organization's image is determined by its people, by its employees. School district employees are in the public eye 365 days a year and 24 hours a day. The public's impression of its schools extends beyond the classroom. What teachers do in the community with action groups and parents has a substantial impact on the school district's image.

b) 7% of a service organization's (in this case a school district's) image is determined by how well it listens to the community.

c) 3% of the formula relates to the information that is given back to the public generally in the form of a newsletter.

The school's image is ultimately determined by its people and the largest and most visible group of school personnel are teachers.

Teachers are the key to making programs and activities visible to the public. The notion of what constitutes the schools' public has expanded well beyond parents and students. The schools' expanded social role includes, according to Matthew Prophet, Superintendent of Schools in Portland, Oregon — "feeding students, checking their hearing, vision and teeth, instructing them in hygiene and nutrition, carrying the main burdens for integrating neighborhoods and providing recreation, teaching safe driving habits, preventing the abuse of drugs and alcohol, counseling the upset, encouraging the listless, searching for the absent, providing for the uninterested, motivating the lazy and challenging the gifted."

Schools that consistently respond to societal changes maintain the public's trust. Teachers, because of their unique role, weave an understanding that leads to trust. Teachers realize the needs that lead to trust. Teachers realize the needs of children, create or encourage adults to view the school as part of their extended family, solicit support from voters, promote open door policies, narrow the gap between the real world and the school, coordinate health and other social services and stop defensive reactions to warranted criticism by improving the learning environment. To many, the teacher's responsibilities are impossible and riddled with pain. Most teachers could have done without the pain but then they would have had to miss the dance and there isn't a good teacher anywhere who would have missed the dance.

A Message to Teachers

Albert Shanker
President
American Federation of Teachers

On behalf of the American Federation of Teachers, I congratulate the outstanding teachers recognized in WHO'S WHO AMONG AMERICA'S TEACHERS. While the intrinsic rewards in teaching are great, it's time that teachers had external recognition, as well. So, I also congratulate Educational Communications, Inc. for launching this long overdue way of honoring great teachers.

Inclusion in WHO's WHO ranks among the most prestigious of professional honors, because you have been singled out by students as the mentors who strongly influenced their lives and contributed to their success. All of the students in the nominating process are high achievers.

They reflect broad diversity in economic backgrounds, race, creed and gender. You found the strength and potential in each student and nurtured it. It is the student who learns, but the teacher who must open the doors to learning.

This book commemorates you as excellent teachers for what you have accomplished, but it does not say how you accomplished it. What you know about teaching and learning is inaccessible to most other teachers. Teachers remain isolated in classrooms, their experiences and discoveries are not available to their colleagues, nor are they published in journals or included as part of the formal preparation of prospective teachers. To the extent that successful teachers can pass on their expertise, it is only through the oral tradition. In fact, one of the ways we'll know that teaching has emerged as a full profession is when, in addition to finding outstanding teachers' names in WHO'S WHO, their methodologies and school and classroom research are a part of education's professional literature and training.

The need for the full professionalization of teaching has become especially acute. For despite the successes of many teachers, many challenges remain. Some of the most serious result from societal problems, such as drug abuse, inadequate health care or the crisis in the family. But we cannot let these external problems be an excuse, no matter how heavily they weigh on the schools; serious deficiencies in our educational system are also implicated in America's shockingly poor record of student achievement, not only among our at-risk youngsters but among most students. Our job as a professional is to find the keys to helping the majority of youngsters achieve at the high levels demonstrated by the students who singled you out for excellence.

To teachers everywhere then, I offer the challenge to reflect upon your teaching and the ways in which students learn and to become leaders in the effort to reform public education. Consider the school system not as it is, but as it should be to foster a high level of achievement among diverse youngsters who learn in different ways and at different rates. How, for example, might we best involve students actively in their own learning, help them construct meaning from their own experience, encourage them to believe in themselves, and show them the paths to previously discovered knowledge, as well as the creation of new knowledge? Should we be using cross-age grouping, peer tutoring, cooperative small groups and coaching? Do we need to throw out the textbooks or use them in new ways? In what ways could education technology improve instruction? Might a group of teachers stay with a group of students over a period of years? Should teachers, rather than bells or arbitrary time limits, determine the timeblocks into which the curriculum fits? What should be the role of the teacher and other personnel in a school in which each staff member's first priority was the success of all students? What assessment strategies will tell us what students know and are able to do?

These questions represent only a few of the important issues facing the professional today. If they are answered through the blinders of school tradition, we will lose a generation of youth and, very likely, public education in the bargain. This is a time of danger, but it is also a time of opportunity. More and more of the public realize that to invest in public education represents the social, political and economic hope of the future. They also realize that in this changing society, more of the same is no longer enough.

As teachers, you are leaders. We must learn together how to create schooling through which all children are equipped with the knowledge and skills necessary to contribute to and thrive in our increasingly complex society. As a profession, we must insist upon change and guide it to accomplish this goal. And in the proccess, we must dare to think new thoughts and devise new strategies for fulfilling the traditional aspirations of public education in a democratic society.

Pedagogy: The Indispensable Dimension in the Making of a Teacher

Thomas A. Shannon
Executive Director
National School Boards Association

"Alternative certification" of teachers is the proposal to waive college of education courses that prepare people to teach. Its theory is that if a person truly knows his or her subject matter well enough — such as mathematicians, chemists or physicists with practical experience in private corporations or agencies of government — that in itself is sufficient to qualify one to teach those subjects in the elementary and secondary schools.

Admittedly, this is a neat way to accommodate desires of people to make midcareer changes and to fill critical shortages of teachers in fields of short supply. But, without training in teaching, is "alternative certification" of subject matter experts as teachers really good for children?

The answer hinges on the importance of pedagogy — the study of how people (especially children) learn and how they may best be taught. Does a teacher have to know more than his or her subject matter to be successful? One of the greatest persons in the history of American education, Horace Mann, would have answered that question with a resounding "Yes!"

A lawyer and politician, Horace Mann became president of the Massachusetts Board of Education in 1837. In a report to the Board in 1840, Horace Mann wrote *On the Art of Teaching* and it has been reprinted in small book form by the Horace Mann League. In today's world, when "alternative certification" advocates downplay the importance of pedagogy, Mann's words deserve a new look. Contrary to the thinking of the "alternative certification" advocates, Mann recognized that there's a whole lot more to it than mastery of subject matter.

Of course, such mastery is indispensable. Mann called it the "first intellectual qualification of a teacher." It consisted (in Mann's words) of " a critical thoroughness, both in rules and principles, in regard to all the branches required by law to be taught in the common schools; and a power of recalling them in any of their parts with a promptitude and a certainty hardly inferior to that which (the teacher) could tell his own name." But Mann identified three other capacities that, together with mastery of subject matter, made up the complete teacher.

"Aptness to teach" was the first of the triumvirate. Wholly different from the ability to acquire knowledge, it "involves the power of perceiving how far a (student) understands the subject matter to be learned, and what, in the natural order, is the next step to take. It involves the power of discovering and solving at the time the exact difficulty by which the learner is embarrassed. The removal of a slight impediment, the drawing aside of the thinnest veil which happens to divert his steps or obscure his vision..."

Aptness to teach, according to Mann, addresses the questions: "How much does the pupil comprehend of the subject? What should his next step be? Is his mind looking toward a truth or an error?" The answers to these questions, Mann said, "must be intuitive in the person who is apt to teach."

What Mann describes as the "the art of managing a classroom" is another vital attribute of the teacher. Branding it another "independent qualification," this attribute is necessary to prevent school from being "temporarily converted into a promiscuous rabble, giving both the temptation and the opportunity (to immature youngsters) for committing every species of indecorum and aggression."

This is only natural, Mann said, when one considers that "with lessons to set; with so many classes to hear; with difficulties to explain; with the studies to be assisted; the idle to be spurred; the transgressors to be admonished or corrected; with all these things to be done, no considerable progress can be made" without order (or what today we pompously call an "optimal learning environment"). Indeed, Mann wrote, "If order (does) not pervade, in the school as a whole, and in all its parts, all is lost."

Finally, Mann said a teacher molds "good behavior" of students. This is conduct that "includes the elements of that equity, benevolence, conscience, which, in their great combinations, the moralist treats of in his books of ethics and the legislator enjoins in his codes of law." This is especially true in our democracy because, Mann says (citing unnamed British visitors of the 19th Century) in a country where virtually everybody "above 21 years of age claims to be a sovereign, he is, therefore, bound to be a (lady or) gentleman."

Pedagogy is a vital dimension to teaching in the elementary and secondary schools. It deserves the respect accorded any other dimension of a learned profession. Any "alternative certification" plan that does not recognize this rubric and make provision for pedagogical training of latecomers to teaching will flop. That's because the wisdom of Horace Mann abides.

Glossary of Abbreviations

To incorporate as much useful information as possible within the available space, abbreviations and acronyms are frequently used. Below is a list of the most frequently used abbreviations and acronyms.

AA Associate in Art

AAPT American Association of Physics Teachers

AASA American Association of School Administrators

AATF American Association of Teachers of French

AATG American Association of Teachers of German

Acad Academy

ACEI Association for Childhood Education International

ACSI Association of Christian Schools International

Act Activities

Addr Address

Admin Administration, Administrator, Administrative

Adv Advisor

AFB Air Force Base

AFSA American Federation of School Administration

AFT American Federation of Teachers

Ag Agriculture

ai: Additional Information

AIFS American Institute for Foreign Study

AK Alaska

AL Alabama

Amer American

AOJT Association of Orthodox Jewish Teachers

AR Arkansas

AS Associate in Science, American Samoa

ASCA American School Council Association

ASCD Association for Supervision & Curriculum Development

Assn Association

Assoc Associate

Asst Assistant

ATE Association of Teacher Educators

AVA American Vocational Association

Ave Avenue

Awd Award

AZ Arizona

b: Place of Birth

BA Bachelor of Arts

BAE Bachelor of Art Education, Arts in Education, Agricultural Engineering, Aeronautics, Aeronautical Engineering, Architectural Engineering

BBA Bachelor of Business Administration

BCE Bachelor of Chemical Engineering, Christian Education, Civil Engineering

BD Bachelor of Divinity, Board

BE Bachelor of Education, Engineering

BEE Bachelor of Electrical Engineering

BES Bachelor of Engineering Sciences, Science of Engineering

BFA Bachelor of Fine Arts

BIE Bachelor of Industrial Engineering

Biling Bilingual

Bio Biology

BLS Bachelor of Liberal Studies

BS Bachelor of Science

BSA Bachelor of Science in Agriculture, Boy Scouts of America

Bsbl Baseball

Bsktbl Basketball

BSC Bachelor of Christian Science

BSE Bachelor of Science in Education

BSEE Bachelor of Science Electrical Engineering, Elementary Education, Engineering & Economics

BSME Bachelor of Science in Mechanical Engineering, Mining, Music Education

BSN Bachelor of Science in Nursing

BT Bachelor of Science in Theology, Teaching

Bus Business

BVA Bachelor of Science in Vocational Agriculture

c: Children

CA California

Cath Catholic

CEC Council for Exceptional Children

Cert Certification

Chem Chemistry

Chldhd Childhood

Chm Chairman

Chrldr Cheerleader

Chrstn Christian

Cmmty Community

Cmptr Computer

Cncl Council

Cnslr Counselor

Cntrl Central

Cntry Country

CO Colorado

Coll College

Comm Committee, Communications, Community

Coord Coordinator

cr: Career Information

CT Connecticut

Cty County

Curr Curriculum

DC District of Columbia

DE Delaware

dec Deceased

Dept Department

Dev Development

Dir Director

Dist District

E East

Ec Economics

ed: Education

Ed Editor, Education

Educl Educational

Elem Elementary

Eng English

Engr Engineer

Exch Exchange

Excl Excellence

Exec Executive

Fed Federation

FFA Future Farmers of America

FHA Future Homemakers of America

FL Florida

Fnd Foundation

Fr French

Frosh Freshman

Ft Fort

Ftbl Football

GA Georgia

Ger German

Grad Graduate

GU Guam

HI Hawaii

His History

Hlth Health

Hrs Hours

HS High School

Hum Humanities

Hwy Highway

IA Iowa

ID Idaho

IL Illinois

IN Indiana

Ind Independent

Inst Institute, Institution

Instr Instructor

Intnl International

ISD Independent School District

ITS International Thespian Society

Jr Junior

Jrnlsm Journalism

JTA Jewish Teachers Association

K/Kndgtn Kindergarten

KS Kansas

KY Kentucky

LA Louisiana

Lang Language

Lib Library
Lit Literature
LLB Bachelor of Laws
Luth Luthern
m: Married
MA Massachusetts, Master of Arts
MADD Mothers Against Drunk Driving
Math Mathematics
MBA Master of Business Administration
MD Maryland
ME Maine, Master of Education, Engineering
Mem Member

Meth Methodist
MFA Master of Fine Arts
Mgr Manager
MI Michigan
Mid Middle
MN Minnesota
MO Missouri
Mrktg Marketing
MS Master of Science, Mississippi
MSW Master of Social Work
MT Montana
MTNA Music Teachers National Association
N North
NAEA National Art Education Association
NABE National Association for Bilingual Education
NAEYS National Association for Education of Young Children

NABT National Association of Biology Teachers
NACST National Association of Catholic School Teachers
NAESP National Association of Elementary School Principals
NASSP National Association of Secondary School Principals
Natl National

NBEA National Business Education Association
NC North Carolina
NCEA National Catholic Education Association
NCBE National Council for Better Education
NCSS National Council for Social Studies
NCTE National Council of Teachers of English
NCTM National Council of Teachers of Mathematics
ND North Dakota
NE Nebraska
NEA National Education Association
NH New Hampshire
NHS National Honor Society
NJ New Jersey
NM New Mexico
Nom Nominated
NRTA National Retired Teachers Association
NSTA National Science Teachers Association
NV Nevada

NY New York
Ofcl Official
OH Ohio
OK Oklahoma
OR Oregon
Orch Orchestra
PA Pennsylvania
Phys Physical
Pkwy Parkway
Pl Place
PR Puerto Rico
Pres President
Presbyn Presbyterian
Presch Preschool
Prin Principal
Prgm Program
Prof Professional
Psych Psychology
PTA Parent Teacher Association
Rd Road
Rdng Reading
Regnl Regional
Rep Representative, Represented
Ret Retired
RI Rhode Island

S South
SADD Students Against Driving Drunk
SC South Carolina
Sch School
Schlsp Scholarship
Sci Science
Scndry Secondary
SD South Dakota
Secy Secretary
Sftbl Softball

Soc Social
Soph Sophomore
Span Spanish
Spec Special
Spon Spontaneous
Sq Square
Sr Senior
St State
Stan Standard
Stu Student
Stud Studies
Supt Superintendent
Supvr Supervisor
Tchr Teacher
Tech Technical, Technology
TN Tennessee
Treas Treasurer
Trng Training
Twp Township
TX Texas
Univ University
USAF United States Air Force
UT Utah
VA Virginia
Var Varsity
VI Virgin Islands
Vlybl Volleyball
Voc Vocational
VP Vice President
VT Vermont
w: Widowed
WA Washington
WI Wisconsin
Wkshp Workshop
WV West Virginia
WY Wyoming
Yr Year
Yrbk Yearbook

Sample Biography Keyed to Data

Biography

❶JOHNSON, ALISON BREWSTER; ❷ Math Dept Chairperson; **❸***b*: Bailey's Harbor, WI; **❹***m*: George M. **❺***c*: Stephen F., Denise J., John J.; **❻***ed*: (BS) Scndry Ed, Univ of WI Madison 1971; **❼***cr*: Math Teacher, Shawnee HS 1971-73, Grissom HS 1973-76; Math Teacher 1976-79, Math Dept Chairperson 1979— Philip Hansen HS; **❽***ai*: Math Marathon Adv; Jr Class Adv; WI Council of Teachers of Mathematics 1973—, Pres 1984-85, Outstanding Achievement Awd 1988; Natl Council of Teachers of Mathematics 1976—; NEA; Women and Child Abuse Shelter Volunteer; Rio Creek Chamber of Commerce Teacher of the Year 1982; Philip Hansen HS Dedicated Teacher Awd 1989; **❾** office: Philip Hansen HS 543 Fairway Green Rio Creek WI 54231

Key

❶ Name
❷ Current Position
❸ Place of Birth
❹ Marital Status (spouse's name)
❺ Children (names)
❻ Education
❼ Career Information
❽ Additional Information (Extracurricular Responsibilities, Professional Memberships, Civic, Service or Other Organization Memberships, Professional Achievements)
❾ Address (at biographee's discretion)

Each biography is presented in a uniform order as shown in the foregoing fictional listing. Biographees are listed in alphabetical order by surname. In those cases where surname is identical, biographees are arranged first by surname, then by first and middle name, and finally by age as denoted by Sr., Jr., or I, II, etc. For alphabetical arrangement, names having a space (Mc, Von, Des, etc.) or punctuation (O'Hara) are properly spelled but treated as though there was no space or punctuation. These surnames are listed under the first character of the surname (i.e., Mc under M). Surnames beginning with Saint (spelled either Saint or St.) will appear following Sains and be listed according to the first character of the second name. Abbreviations and acronyms most frequently used are shown in the glossary.

BIOGRAPHIES

A

AARON, BRENDA COLLEEN, Coach & Phys Ed Teacher; *b:* Edinburg, TX; *ed:* (BS) Phys Ed, Pan Amer Univ 1984; *cr:* Teachers Aide Edinburg CISD 1970-83; Teacher/Coach Edinburg CISD/Brewster Sch 1985-; *ai:* Vlybl Coach Jr HS Girls; Track Coach Jr HS Girls; TCTA 1985-.

AARON, WOODROW V., JR., Middle School Math/Sci Teacher; *b:* Rochester, PA; *m:* Jo Anne Tarquinio; *c:* Meagan E.; *ed:* (BS) Elem Ed/Eng, 1971, (MED) Rdng Specialist, 1973 Westminster Coll; *cr:* 6th Grade Teacher Pleasant View Elem 1971-88; Admin Asst Moon Jr HS 1988-89; Math/Sci Teacher Moon Area Mid Sch 1989-; *ai:* Mid Sch Steering Comm; 6th Grade Class & Stu Cncl Spon; NEA, PSEA; MEA (Treas, Building Rep); *office:* Moon Area Mid Sch 1407 Beers School Rd Coraopolis PA 15108

ABATO, BARBARA, Jr HS Mathematics Teacher; *b:* Brooklyn, NY; *ed:* (BA) Child Study/Math, St Joseph Coll 1984; Brooklyn Coll Grad Level 1987-89; Math/Ed, Various Math Courses, Wkshps offered through Diocese; Prgm for The Dev of Human Potential 1989; Skills for Adolescents Wkshps 1990; *cr:* Bookkeeper/Cashier Trainer King Kullen Supermarket 1978-80, Waldbaums Inc 1982-87; Receptionist Pensley-Abato 1986-87; 6th-8th Grade Math/8th Grade Teacher St Therese of Lisieux Schl 1984-; *ai:* Math Coord; Elem Math Cncl Mem; Coordinate Math League Scholastic Contests; Teach Math IX Course for Advanced Stus; Rap Group Leader; Math Elem Cncl 1987-; St Josephs Coll Medaille Schlsp; Accepted & Completed Prgm Math & Ed Grad Study; Spec Teacher Awd 1986; *home:* 2336 Jerome Ave Brooklyn NY 11235

ABBEY, LINDA LEE, Team Leader; *b:* Atlanta, GA; *m:* Gary R.; *c:* Nichole, Lauren; *ed:* (BS) Phys Ed, W GA Coll 1976; *cr:* Phys Ed Teacher Union Elem 1976-82; Phys Ed/Sci Teacher Paulding Cty Jr HS 1982-86; Sci Dept Head/Math Teacher P B Ritch Mid Sch 1986-; *ai:* PAGE Sch Rep 1987-; *office:* P B Ritch Mid Sch Rt 1 Box 2808B Ridge Rd Hiram GA 30141

ABBOTT, BRIAN RAY, Jr HS Math Teacher; *b:* Lafayette, IN; *m:* Trisha Ann Glaub; *c:* Tyler; *ed:* (BS) Math Ed, Huntington Coll 1983; Math, Ball St Univ; *cr:* Math Teacher Brookville Jr HS 1983-84; Eastbrook Jr HS 1984-; *ai:* Head Bsbl Coach; 7th Grade Boys Bsktbl Mathcounts Adv; *office:* Eastbrook Jr HS 560 S 900 E Marion IN 46953

ABBOTT, JO ANN BECKER, 4th Grade Teacher; *b:* Gary, IN; *m:* John Alexander; *c:* Alane E., Alexis A.; *ed:* (BS) Ed, IN Univ 1965; (MLA) Eng, Valparaiso Univ 1970; *cr:* 4th Grade Teacher Foster Rd Sch 1965-66; 4th/5th Grade Math/Sci Teacher 1966-68, 4th Grade Teacher Lang Arts 1968-69 Pittman Square Sch; 2nd Grade Teacher 1979-87, 4th Grade Teacher 1987-, Prin 1990 Nativity of Our Savior Sch; *ai:* Mentor Teacher Prgm 8th Grade Mentor 1989-; Stu Teaching Prgm Supvr 1987; Young Authors Conference Comm; Intnl Rdng Assn Rep; *office:* Nativity of Our Savior Sch 2929 Willowcreek Rd Portage IN 46368

ABBOTT, LORI J. (ADAMS), Business Education Teacher; *b:* Orlando, FL; *m:* Michael J.; *c:* Nathaniel, Kelsea; *ed:* (BS) Bus Ed, Southern Coll of 7th Day Adv 1983; *cr:* Bus Ed Teacher Mt Vernon Acad 1983-85, Teacher Cecils Jr Coll 1986-87; Treas Greater Dallas Acad 1987-88; Bus Ed Teacher/Asst Treas Jefferson Adventist Acad 1988-; *ai:* Sr Class & Newspaper Spon; *office:* Jefferson Adventist Acad P O Box 528 Jefferson TX 75657

ABBOTT, PATRICIA JOHNSON, Language Arts Teacher; *b:* Piedmont, AL; *m:* Edward Earl; *c:* Elizabeth Chadbourne, David M., Donald R.; *ed:* (BS) Eng, Jacksonville St Univ 1970; Univ of AL; *cr:* Lang Art Teacher Centre Elem Sch 1970-75, Centre Mid Sch 1975-; *ai:* Centre Mid Sch Spelling Bee; Publicity Comm; Yrbk Adv 1985-88; NCTE 1989; Goshen United Meth Church Organist 1955-; Babe Ruth Baseball Team Mother 1985-87; Centre Mid Sch Teacher Hall of Fame 1989 & Teacher of Yr 1989; Cherokee Cty Teacher of Yr 1989; *home:* Rt 3 Box 125 Piedmont AL 36272

ABDEL-AL, FAYEK H., 7th-8th Grade Math Teacher; *b:* Cairo, Egypt; *m:* Samiha; *c:* Amy; *ed:* (BS) Scndry Math Ed, Einshams Univ 58; (MA) Scndry Math Ed, UCF 1973; (MS) Scndry Math Ed. Univ of AZ 1973; Sci Fnd Math Instution Northwestern Univ 1970; High Acturail Institute of Insurance Cairo Univ 1964; *cr:* Math Chairperson Dawawin Scndry Sch 1959-69; Math Teacher Jackson Jr HS 1969-; Part Time Faculty Brevard Comm Coll 1978-; *ai:* Spon Math & Algebra Club; Coach Intramural Tennis; Coach Racquetball; Brevard Fed of Teachers 1987-; NCTM 1988-; Brevard Cncl of Teachers of Math 1988-; FL Assn for Gifted 1988-; La Cita Cty Club 1986-; Natl Sci Fnd Schlsp NorthwesteRn Univ Study His of Math & Cmptr Sci 1970; Natl Sci Fnd Master of Sci Teaching Univ of AZ; *office:* Andrew Jackson Mid Sch 1515 Knox Mc Rae Dr Titusville FL 32780

ABDULAVIC, PETER, 6th Grade Teacher; *b:* Munich, Germany; *m:* Susan J. Graney; *c:* Amy, Katie, Carey; *ed:* (BSED) Elem, Slippery Rock St Coll 1972; (MED) Ed, Univ of Pittsburgh 1977; *cr:* 6th Grade Teacher St Elizabeth Elem Sch 1972-74, South Fayette Township Sch Dist 1974-; *ai:* Asst Elem Chorus Dir; NEA, PSEA 1974-; PA Cncl Teachers of Math 1985-; YMCA Indian Princess Prgm Treas 1987-89; PTA Exec Bd 1980-, Lifetime Mem 1989; Nom Natl PTA Phoebe Apperson Hearst Outstanding Educator Awd 1990; Dept Chairperson Upper Elem; Lead Teacher; Natl Cncl Accreditation of Teachers Ed; Observer Panel for PA; *office:* South Fayette Elem Sch RD 2 Box 206-C Mc Donald PA 15057

ABELLA, JOHN ANTHONY, Industrial Arts Teacher; *b:* Hackensack, NJ; *m:* Barbara Jean Zuzolo; *c:* John Jr.; *ed:* (BA) Industrial Art, Montclair St 1970; *cr:* Teacher Watchung Hills Regional HS 1966-70; *ai:* Curr Comm; Automotive Service Industries Assn 1986-; Policy Bd Somerset Cty Headstart Prgm; *office:* Watchung Hills Regional HS 108 Stirling Rd Warren NJ 07060

ABER, TOMASINE DAWN, Fourth Grade Teacher; *b:* Clovis, NM; *ed:* (BA) Elem Ed, 1958, (MA) Elem Ed, 1963 TX Western; Ed, Univ TX El Paso; *cr:* 4th Grade Teacher Cooley Sch 1958-63; 6th Grade Teacher 1963-64 Ashlawn Elem; Great Falls Elem 1964-66; Coldwell 1966-67; Gadsden Ind Sch Dist 1967-; *ai:* Honors Banquet Comm; NEA, NM Ed Assn (Assn Rep, Secy, Delegate) 1958-; Gadsden Ed Assn Chairperson Local Nomination & Elec Comm; Delta Kappa Gamma (Pres, Delegate); Classroom Elem Teacher; *home:* PO Box 1411 Anthony NM 88021

ABERCROMBIE, WILLIAM I., Science Teacher; *b:* Elizabeth Township, PA; *m:* Charlotte D. York; *ed:* (BA) Music, Alderson Broaddus Coll 1967; Grad Stud Univ of MI, MI St Univ; *cr:* Music Teacher Akron Schls 196769; Music Teacher 1969-81, Sci Teacher 1981 Wyandotte Schls; *ai:* Ski Club & Green Thumb Plant Club Spon; Nom MI Teacher of Yr 1989-; *office:* Wilson Mid Sch 1275 15th Wyandotte MI 48192

ABEREGG, BERNADINE ERB, First Grade Teacher; *b:* Jersey City, NJ; *m:* Robert L.; *c:* Nicholas, Katherine; *ed:* (BS) Elem Ed, Salem Coll 1979; (MA) Elem Ed, WV Univ 1983; *cr:* 5th Grade Teacher Sistersville Elem 1979-81; Math Teacher Hedgesville Mid Sch 1981-82; Kndgtn Teacher Inwood Primary 1982-83; 1st/5th Grade Teacher Back Creek Valley Elem 1983-; *ai:* Cultural Art Chairperson; Staff Dev Person; WVEA 1989-; WV PTA 1979-; *home:* Rt 2 Box 237 Hedgesville WV 25427

ABEREGG, JOAN DULANEY, Gifted-Teacher; *b:* Pine Grove, WV; *m:* Terry H.; *c:* Terry J., Ed, Tammy Morgan; *ed:* (BA) Elem Ed, West Liberty St Coll 1977; (MA) Spec Ed Gifted, WV Univ 1983; Post Masters Studies, Curr; Gifted; Teaching Strategies; Salem Coll; WVU; Duquesne Univ; *cr:* Teacher Short Line/Reader Schl 1966-83; Gifted Teacher New Martinsville Sch 1983-87; Performance Learning Instr Salem Coll 1982-87; Gifted Teacher Shortline Sch 1987-; *ai:* Acad Coach Sls 1982-83; Comm Math Field Day Act; Co-Producer Musical Prod;spon Newspaper Prod; NEA/WVEA 1966-; CEC/TAG 1982-; PTA 1966-; Rdng Cncl 1989; Cub Scout Den Mother 1967-68; Co-Organizer Parents of Gifted 1987; Presenter Rgnl Teachers Conf; Presenter Wkshps Cty/Sch; Spon Video Prod; *home:* Box 220 Reader WV 26167

ABEYTA, RAYMOND LEE, Sixth Grade Teacher; *b:* Trinidad, CO; *m:* Pamela Marlene Zell; *c:* Bradley P., Ryan A.; *ed:* (AA) Journalism, El Paso Comm Coll 1976; (BS) Ed, Univ of CO Colorado Springs 1978; (MA) Creative Art, Lesley Coll 1987; *cr:* 2nd/6th Grade Teacher Rudy Elem 1978-86; 6th Grade Teacher Patrick Henry Elem 1986-; *ai:* 5th-6th Bsktbl Coach 1978-; Cmptr Coord; PTA Teacher Rep 1982-83, T-For-Two 1983; Intovative Teaching Grant; *office:* Patrick Henry Elem Sch 1310 Lehmberg Colorado Springs CO 80915

ABHALTER, PEGGY J., Spanish Teacher/Dept Chair; *b:* Chicago, IL; *m:* David N.; *c:* Elizabeth; *ed:* (BA) Span, N Cntrl Coll 1971; (MSED) Curr/Supervision/Ed Admin, N IL Univ 1975; *cr:* Teacher E Aurora Public Schls 1971-77, Geneva Public Schls 1984-85; Teacher/Dept Chairperson Indian Prairie Sch Dist 204 1985-; *ai:* Amer Field Service; Study Tour Spon; Foreign Lang Curr Leader HS & Mid Sch Prgms; ASCD 1975-78, 1987-; Amer Assn Teachers of Span & Portuguese 1989-; Phi Sigma Iota 1971-; N Wheatland Township Homeowners Assn Bd Mem 1976-79; *office:* Waubonsie Valley HS 2590 Rt 34 Aurora IL 60504

ABOOD, RICHARD MICHAEL, Social Science Teacher; *b:* Akron, OH; *c:* Christopher, Brian; *ed:* (AA) General Ed, Grossmont Coll 1972; (BS) Soc Sci, US Intnl Univ 1975; Grad Teacher Trng; *cr:* Asst Ftbl Coach US Intnl Univ 1976-78; Teacher Grossmont Union HS Dist 1978-81, Imperial HS 1981-85, Mt Empire Jr/Sr HS 1985-; *ai:* Head Ftbl & Jr Var Bsbl Coach; Lettermans, Soc Stud Adv, Hugs Not Drugs Club; Drug Free Schls, Hugs Not DrugS Grant; MEHS Curr Author Accreditation of Western Assn Schls; *office:* Mountain Empire Jr/Sr HS 3305 Buckman Springs Rd Pine Valley CA 92062

ABORNE, MORRIS MICHAEL, History Teacher; *ed:* (BAED) Geography, 1963, (MA) Geography, 1967 AZ St Univ; *cr:* Teacher Dale Jr HS 1963-71, Appolo Jr HS 1971-80, Walker Jr HS 1980-; *ai:* Odyssey of Mind Regional Prgm Dir; NCSS, NEA; BSA Ad Adv 1981-89; Univ of CA Santa Barbara Tech Inst Fellow; Awd of Excl Soc Stud Prgm Presented by NCSS 1989; *office:* Walker Jr HS 8132 Walker St La Palma CA 90623

ABRAHAM, DELORES MADISON, English Teacher; *b:* Franklin, LA; *m:* Millard; *ed:* (BS) Soc Stud, Southern Univ 1962; (MED) Rdng/Psych, Nicholls St Univ 1977; *cr:* Eng Teacher Franklin Jr HS 1962-86, Franklin Sr HS 1986-; *ai:* Eng Remediation Center Weekly; Assist Prin Weekly; LA Ed Assn 1963-; Ladies Auxiliary VFW Secy 1980-; Public Ed 25 Yr Service Plaque; *office:* Franklin Sr HS PO Box 798 Baldwin LA 70514

ABRAHAM, ROBERT PAUL, Assistant Principal; *b:* Harvey, IL; *m:* Laura Mann; *c:* Barrett; *ed:* (BS) Phys Ed, Eastern IL Univ 1976; (MS) Phys Ed, IL St Univ 1978; Type 75 Admin Cert, Northern IL Univ 1986; *cr:* Asst Phys Ed Teacher Motcalf Laboratory Sch IL St Univ 1978-79; Phys Ed 1979-89, Asst Prin 1989- Twin Groves Sch; *ai:* Bsktbl & Track Coach; Asst Prin; Supervise Extra Curr Act; Teachers Union Pres; Park Dist Dir; *office:* Twin Groves Jr H S 1072 Ivy Hall Ln Buffalo Grove IL 60089

ABRAM, MARY KATHRYN, Teacher; *b:* Kilmichael, MS; *m:* Felix; *c:* Sean, Kineshia; *ed:* (BA) Soc Stud, MS Valley St 1967; *cr:* Teacher E Marion HS 1967-70, Columbia Training Sch 1970-74, E Marion Elem 1977-; *ai:* NEA; Women Society 1986-90; *office:* E Marion Elem Sch Rt 5 Box 496 Columbia MS 39429

ABRAMS, BARBARA KROHNER, 4th Grade Teacher; *b:* Chicago, IL; *m:* Peter David; *c:* Lizz, Jason, Darren, Allison; *ed:* (BA) Span/Elem Ed, Northeastern IL 1965; (MSED) Admin, Northern IL Univ 1978; Gifted Training Prgms/Curr; *cr:* Teacher Haskin Sch 1965-69; Prin Migrant Prgm 1975-80; Teacher De Kalbs Schls 1969-; *ai:* Dir Medieval Feast; Pi Lambda Theta Treas 1987-89; AFT Mem 1980-; Northern IL Jewish Cmmty (VP, Pres, Treas 1980-); United Way Building Coord 1985-; Authorized Creative Dramatics: Presented Wkshps; *office:* Lincoln Elem Sch 2nd & Sunset Sts De Kalb IL 60115

ABRON, CHRISTINE BODDIE, Math Department Contact; *b:* Phenix City, AL; *m:* Robert L. Sr.; *c:* Mollita L., Robert L. Jr.; *ed:* (BS) Elem Ed, Morris Brown Coll 1967; (MED) Elem Math, GA St Univ 1973; *cr:* Teacher A D Williams Elem 1967-70, R L Hope Elem 1970-72, O Keefe Mid 1973-79, Inman Mid 1979-; *ai:* Mathcounts Coord; Inservice Comm; Cmptr Contact Person; United Teaching Profession AAE, GAE, NEA (Building Rep, Alternate) 1977-; Delta Sigma Theta Recording Secy 1987-89;

Morris Brown Coll Alumni Assn (VP 1985-86, Corresponding Secy 1988-89), Presidential Citation 1985, Alumnus of Yr 1986; Glenwood Hills Athletic Assn (Team Mother, Coach, Womens Auxillary Statistician 1982-89); Cmmty Enhancement Awd 1987; Spring Valley Civic Assn (Secy, Block Captain) 1975-; Teacher of Yr 1979-80, 1988-89; Ebony Magazine Outstanding Teachers 1988; Academic Achievement Incentive Awd 1985, Area III Atlanta Public Schls 1985; *office:* Inman Mid Sch 774 Virginia Ave Ne Atlanta GA 30306

ABSHAGEN, CHARLES EUGENE, World History Teacher; *b:* Paw Paw, MI; *m:* Sharon Mc Grew; *c:* Doug, Danica, Denise; *ed:* (BS) Poly Sci, W MI Univ 1968; (MA) Scndry Ed/Poly Sci, Cntrl MI Univ 1984; *cr:* World His/US Government Teacher Onaway Area Cmmty Schls 1968-; *ai:* Coach Jr HS Bsktbl, Asst Ftbl, Var Ftbl, Odyssey of Mind; Class Adv; Jr & Sr Play Dir; Onaway City Cncl Commissioner 1979-; *home:* Rt 3 Box 1254 Onaway MI 49765

ABSHER, FAITH SIMPSON, Sixth Grade Soc Stud Teacher; *b:* Hamlin, TX; *m:* Charles Ray; *c:* Lisa Vasquez, Pamela Robison, Bill; *ed:* (BS) Ed, Baylor Univ 1657; Elem Ed, Hardin-Simmons Univ 1965; Grad Stud Hardin-Simmons Univ; *cr:* 1st Grade Teacher Rotan Ind Sch Dist 1965-66; 1st-5th Grade Teacher Hamlin Ind Sch Dist 1966-79; 3rd/4th Grade Teacher Vidar Ind Sch Dist 1979-; *ai:* Delta Kappa Gamma Pres 1986-88; ATPE Pres 1983-84; Hamlin Ind Schls Teacher of Yr 1973; *home:* 685 Maplewood Vidor TX 77662

ABSTON, CAROL RUFFIN, 5th Grade Teacher; *b:* Columbus, MS; *m:* Richard Allan; *c:* Adrienne C. Egger, Allan; *ed:* (BS) Elem Ed, Livingston Univ 1969; (MA) Elem Ed, Univ of AL 1979; *cr:* 4th Grade Sci Teacher Hopewell Elem 1969; 3rd/6th Grade Teacher Opelika City Schls 1969-75; 3rd Grade Teacher Reform Elem 1975-79; 5th Grade Teacher Vernon Elem 1979-; *ai:* Jr HS & Var Chrldrs; Lamar Cty Ed Assn, NEA, AL Ed Assn 1969-; Alpha Delta Kappa (Secy, Treas, VP, Pres); *office:* Vernon Elem Sch P O Box 2060 Vernon AL 35592

ACALEY, PHILIP B., History Teacher; *b:* Sellersville, PA; *m:* Beverly; *c:* Chelsea; *ed:* (BS) Scndry Ed/Soc Stud, Kutztown St Coll 1979; Grad Stud Temple Univ & Wilkes Coll; *cr:* 7th Grade World His Teacher Manheim Cntrl Sch Dist 1979-; *ai:* PA St Ed Assn 1979-; Gift of Time Tribute 1988; Amer Family Inst Valley Forge; *office:* Manheim Cntrl Jr HS 71 N Hazel St Manheim PA 17545

ACERRA, BARBARA THOMAS, 4th Grade Teacher; *b:* Youngstown, OH; *m:* John J.; *c:* John R., Jennifer M., Anthony J.; *ed:* (BSED) Elem Ed, 1971, (MSED) Rdng Specialist, 1974 Youngstown St Univ; Gifted Ed Cert, Kent St Univ; Child Study Leadership Trng, Univ of Dayton; Sci Field Study, Youngstown St; *cr:* Kndgtn Teacher 1971-75, 1st Grade Teacher 1975-83, 4th-6th Grade Teacher 1983-84, Teacher/Coord Gifted Prgms 1984-88, 4th-6th Grade Teacher 1988- Mac Donald Elem; *ai:* Sci Fair Coord; Eng Festival & Spelling Bee Judge, Coach, Building Pronouncer; Math Curr Comm; Lake to River Sci Fair Judge; Wellsville City Teachers Assn (Building Rep 1980-84, 1988-89, VP 1989-); OEA, NEA, OH Assn for Gifted Children; Youngstown Area Chamber of Commerce, Mahoning Valley Management Assn; Ed Fnd Schlsp Fund Secy; Church Cncl Secy; Acerra & Assoc Inc (Secy, Treas); *office:* Mac Donald Elem Sch 305 9th St Wellsville OH 43968

ACETO, CHERYL L., 7th Grade Mathematics Teacher; *b:* Akron, OH; *ed:* (BS) Ed, Bowling Green St Univ 1971; *cr:* 3rd Grade Teacher Caldwell Exempted Schls 1971-73; 3rd Grade Teacher 1973-77, 4th Grade Teacher 1977-83, 5th Grade Teacher 1983-84 West Elem; 7th Grade Math/Pre-Algebra Teacher De Soto Mid Sch 1984-; *ai:* Southern Assn Colls & Schls Comms; After Sch Tutor; Saturday & Summer Sch Teacher; Co-Coach Math Club; De Soto Cty Teachers Assn, FL Ed Assn Mem 1973-; *office:* De Soto Mid Sch 420 E Gibson St Arcadia FL 33821

ACEVEDO, AMELIA, 4th Grade Bilingual Teacher; *b:* Patillas, PR; *m:* Gregorio; *c:* Francis, Gregory Jr.; *ed:* (BS) Elem Ed, D Youville Coll 1979; (MA) Amer Stud, St Univ of NY Buffalo 1988; *cr:* 6th Grade Teacher 1980-81, Pre-K Teacher 1981-84, 4th Grade Teacher 1984-85, 5th Grade Teacher 1985-86, 4th Grade Teacher 1986- Herman Badillo Bi-ling Acad 76.

ACKER, LORA LEE LANGAN, French & Spanish Teacher; *b:* Reading, PA; *m:* Ronald G.; *ed:* (BS) Scndry Ed/Span/Fr, Kutztown St Univ 1977; *cr:* Eng as Second Lang Teacher 1977-78, Span/Fr Teacher 1978-79 Norfolk Public Schls; Span/Fr Teacher Currituck Cty HS 1979-84, Chesapeake Public Schls 1984-; *ai:* Span Club Co-Adv; Prins Advisory Comm; Teacher of Yr Currituck Cty HS 1984; *office:* Great Bridge HS 301 W Hanbury Rd Chesapeake VA 23320

ACKER, NORMA JEAN, English Teacher; *b:* Howell, MI; *m:* Douglas Alan; *c:* Nicholas, Samuel, Elizabeth; *ed:* (BA) Eng Ed, Oakland Univ 1976; Grad Stud Lang Art; *cr:* Substitute Teacher Area Schls 1976-78; Free Lance Newspaper Reporter Grand Rapids Press 1981-85; 7th-12th Grade Eng Teacher Maple Valley Schls 1978-; *ai:* All Sch Musical Dir; Gifted/Talented & Honors Night Comm HS Rep; Chm High Expectations for Success Action Team; Sch Improvement Prgm; Maple Valley Ed Assn Public Relations Chm 1987-; NEA, MEA; Friends of the Lib Bd of Dir 1979-85; Publish Local Newsletter; *office:* Maple Valley Jr/Sr HS 11090 Nashville Hwy Vermontville MI 49096

ACKER, ROGER, 5th & 6th Grade Teacher; *b:* Elizabeth, NJ; *m:* Dale; *c:* Jodi S. Bohr, Roger S.; *ed:* (BS) Elem Ed, East Stroudsburg Univ 1958; *cr:* Elem Teacher Edison NJ 1958-61; Minden-Gardnerville NV 1961-62; Tinton Falls NJ 1962-68; Blairstown NJ 1968-; *ai:* NJEA Treas 1968-; *office:* Blairstown Elem Sch Stillwater Rd Blairstown NJ 07825

ACKERMAN, DAVID, Principal; *b:* New York, NY; *m:* Arlene Antognoli; *c:* Joanna, Jennifer, David M., Anthony Antognoli, Matthew Antognoli; *ed:* (BA) Ed, Harris-Stowe St Coll 1970; (MAT) Ed, Webster Univ 1976; *cr:* Teacher St Louis Public Schls 1970-75, Flynn Park Sch 1975-85; Dir Math/Sci/Cmptr Curr Teacher Univ City Sch Dist 1985-86; Prin Delmar-Harvard Sch 1988-; *ai:* Teaching Methods Course in Teacher Ed Depts WA Univ & Natl Coll of Ed; ASCD, NSTA; Meritorious Teaching Awd Univ City Schls 1982, 1984; Appointed Governors Comm for Career Ladders; Distinguished Alumnus Awd Harris-Stowe St Coll 1987; *office:* Delmar-Harvard Sch 711 Kingsland University City MO 63130

ACKERMAN, DAVID LAWRENCE, 7th-9th Grade Math Teacher; *b:* Pocatello, ID; *m:* Loretta Mardell Woody; *c:* Steven, Bradly; *ed:* (BA) Math, Coll of ID 1960; (MS) Math, Univ of ID 1968; *cr:* Math/Sci Teacher Hailey HS 1960-64, Genesee HS 1964-67; Math Teacher Lakeview HS 1967-68, Prairie HS 1968-75, Lakeland Jr HS 1975-; *ai:* Mathcounts; Faculty Advisory, Dist Hot Lunch Comm; NEA 1965-66, 1974, 1976-; IEA 1965-66, 1976-; OEA 1974; Local Ed Assn (VP, Pres) 1965-66, 1974; Natl Sci Fnd Grant 1964; Honor Schlshp Coll of ID 1956-60; Teacher of Yr Lakeland Sch Dist 1984-85; Whos Who in Coll; *home:* 1470 State St Rathdrum ID 83858

ACKERMAN, LORETTA ANN, HS Soc Stud Teacher/Sr Advisor; *b:* Ellwood City, PA; *m:* John; *c:* Michael, Melisa, Melana; *ed:* (BA) His, Indiana Univ of PA 1959; Curr/Instruction, Ashland Univ 1990; Bicentennial Constitution Wkshp; Mentorship Prgm; Taft Inst; *cr:* Teacher Longfellow Jr HS 1959-60, Olean Schls 1961-63, Fredericktown Schls 1965-; *ai:* Sr Class Adv; Prin Advisory; NCSS; OH Cncl of Soc Stud; ASCD; AAVW; Fredericktown Ed Assn Building Rep; Fredericktown Bd of Ed Recognition.

ACKERMAN, RUTH A., Sixth Grade Teacher; *b:* Fremont, OH; *c:* Chris, Kim Blodgett; *ed:* (BS) Elem Ed, Bowling Green St Univ 1966; *cr:* 6th Grade Teacher St Joseph Elem 1965-66; 5th Grade Teacher Old Fort Local Schls 1967-70; 6th Grade Teacher Fremont City Schls Stamm Elem 1971-; *ai:* Stu Cncl; OH Ed Assn 1966-; NEA 1966-; Fremont Ed Assn 1971-; Northwest OH Ed Assn 1966-; Jennings Scholar; *office:* Stamm Elem Sch 1038 Miller St Fremont OH 43420

ACKMAN, KEITH EDWARD, Counselor; *b:* Monongalela, PA; *m:* Norma Holzapfel; *c:* Edward, Michael; *ed:* Accounting/Bus Admin, Douglas Sch of Bus 1953; (BBA) Bus Admin, 1959, (MED) Cnslr Ed, 1967 Duquesne Univ; *cr:* Court Stenographer First Cavalry Division HQ 1953-55; Cost Accountant Combustion Engineering 1955-56; Dispatchers Asst Norwalk Truck Lines 1958; Bus Teacher Rosthaver Township Schls 1959-67; Cnslr CA Sch Dist 1968-69, Bethlehem Center Jr HS 1969-; *ai:* Sch Improvement & FOCUS Teams; NEA, PSEA 1959-; Mon Valley Radio Control (Secy, Treas) 1967-77; Acad Model Aero (Leader, Mem) 1951-; Private Pilot Single Engine & Sail Planes; *home:* 1st Ave New Eagle PA 15067

ACORD, KATHRYN MACE, Business Department Chair; *b:* Charleston, WV; *m:* Michael F.; *c:* Michael, Lindsey K.; *ed:* (BS) Bus Comprehensive, Concord Coll 1974; (MA) Specific Learning Disability, WV Coll 1979; *cr:* Spec Ed Teacher Independence HS 1974-78; Elem Ed Teacher Crab Orchard Elem 1978-81; Spec Ed Teacher Woodrow Wilson HS 1981-85; Bus Ed Teacher Independence HS 1985-; *ai:* FBLA Spon; Graduation Coord; WV Bus Educators Assn 1985-; Raleigh Cty Bus Educators Assn; Sophia-Soak Creek PTA VP 1989-; *office:* Independence H S Drawer AA Coal City WV 25823

ACOSTA, JESSE J., Principal; *b:* Douglas, AZ; *c:* Cassandra N.; *ed:* (BS) Psych, 1978, (MA) Guidance/Counseling, 1980 N AZ Univ; *cr:* 6th Grade Teacher 1980-85, 7th Grade Teacher 1985-86, Asst Prin 1986-89 Kyrene Sch Dist; Prin Murphy Sch Dist 1989-; *ai:* Bsktbl, Sftbl, Ftbl & Track Team Coach; After Sch Sports Prgm Coord; AASA, ASA Mem 1985-; ASCD Mem 1989-; *office:* A F Garcia Sch 1441 S 27th Ave Phoenix AZ 85009

ACOSTA, MINERVA CORONA, 6th Grade Teacher; *b:* El Paso, TX; *m:* Jorge Fernando; *c:* Jorge Jr.; *ed:* (BA) His, Univ of TX El Paso 1967; (MA) Cmptr Ed, Lesley Coll 1989; Advanced Trng; Grad Work Univ of TX El Paso; *cr:* 3rd Grade Teacher 1967-72, 6th Grade Teacher 1972-89 Thomas Manor Elem; 6th Grade Eng Teacher Pasodale Mid & Elem 1989-; *ai:* Sch Excl, Communication, Campus Action Plan Comm; TX St Teachers Assn, Natl Teachers Assn 1968-; Intnl Rdng Assn 1979-; Greater El Paso Cncl Math Teachers 1985-; El Paso Cncl Teachers of Eng 1988-; City Parks & Recreation (Chm 1988-89, VP Chm 1989-, Advisory Comm); Voc Ed Handicapped Ind Sch Dist (Chm 1980-82, Secy 1989-, Advisory Comm); PTA Life Mem 1986; Teacher of Yr Thomas Manor 1985.

ACTON, APRIL MAYER, English Teacher; *b:* Cedar Rapids, IA; *m:* Stephen Patrick; *c:* Erica, Tara, Brennan; *ed:* (BA) Speech, Univ of N IA 1977; *cr:* Eng/Speech Teacher Gladbrook HS 1977-88; Eng Teacher Gladbrook-Reinbeck Mid Sch 1988-; *ai:* Drama & Speech Dir; NCTE, IA St Ed Assn, NEA; GladBrook Ed Assn Secy 1989-; Pres Bd of Dir Secy 1987-88; *office:* Gladbrook Community Sch 307 Washington Gladbrook IA 50635

ACTON, SARA JANE ADAMS, Fourth Grade Challenge Teacher; *b:* Philadelphia, PA; *m:* Phil Gordon; *c:* Gordon, Dorothy Arlen Harper, Yale; *ed:* (BA) Lang/Elem Ed, Dowling Coll 1968; (MA) Elem Ed, Adelphi Univ 1969; Gifted Ed; *cr:* Teacher Islip Public Schs 1968-69, Urbana Sch Dist 116 1969-74, Valley View Sch Dist 365 U 1974-78; Gifted Teacher Valley Wiew Sch Dist 365 U 1979-; *ai:* Staff Dev Comm; IL Fed of Teachers (Bldg Rep 1980- Senator 1984-); PTA Teacher Rep 1987; Northern IL Rdng Cncl Mem 1989; Homeowners Assoc Bd Mem 1980-882 & 1987-88; Wood View Sch Excl Ed Awd 1988; Open Ed Grant 1971; Gifted Ed Grant 1984-86; *office:* Wood View Elem Sch 197 Winston Dr Bolingbrook IL 60439

ACUFF, KAREN, French/English Teacher; *b:* Washington, IN; *m:* Curt; *c:* Nathan, Celeste; *ed:* (BS) Ed, IN Univ 1986; *cr:* Fr/ Eng Teacher NE Dubois HS 1986-87, 1989-; *ai:* Asst Vlybl Coach; Fr Club & Beta Club Spon; *home:* 401 Clay St Jasper IN 47546

ADAIR, DEBBIE PEARCE, 4th Grade Teacher; *b:* Talladega, AL; *m:* Jerry M.; *c:* Michael, Myles; *ed:* (BS) Elem Ed, 1974; (MS) Elem Ed, 1977 Jacksonville St Univ; Beeson Fellowship Scholar Samford Univ; *cr:* 1st Grade Teacher Graham Elem 1973-74; 4th Grade Teacher Sylvan Elem 1974-75; 2nd Grade Teacher Mountainview Elem 1975-76; 4th Grade Teacher Indian Valley Elem 1976-; *ai:* 4th Yr 4-H Spon; Sch Soc Stud Fair Spon; Alpha Delta Kappa Ed Society; AL Ed Assn; NEA; Syl Teachers Assn; Sylacaugas Nom AL Teacher Yr 1988-89; AL Soc Stud Teacher Yr 1989-; Mem Cncl of Natl Teachers of Soc Stud; Al Cncl of Teachers of Soc Stud; 1st Bapt Church (GA Teacher/ Vacation Bible Sch Teacher/Sunday Sch Teacher); Assn for Retarded Citizens; Syl Little Leag Team Mother; Syl Cncl for Arts & Humanities; Chrstn Womens Club; PTA; Sylacauga Jaycee Outstanding Young Educator 1986; Talladega Cty Outstanding 4-H Leader 1986; Beeson Fellowship Scholar 1989; Sylacaugas Nom for Jacksonville St Hall of Fame 1988-89; *office:* Indian Valley Elem Sch Rt 6 Oldfield Rd Sylacauga AL 35150

ADAIR, JERRY DWAIN, Biology Teacher; *b:* Hohenwald, TN; *m:* Jacqueline Kay Mc Kenzie; *c:* Jerry Jr., Jennifer; *ed:* (BS) Scndry Ed/Bio, TN Tech Univ 1971; (MED) Admin/Supervision, W GA 1986; Grad Stud Sci Ed; *cr:* Teacher Cobb Cty Sch System 1971-; *ai:* Asst Wrestling & Ftbl Coach; Atlanta Area Ftbl Ofcl Assn 1980-88, Back Judge of Yr 1985; *home:* 4196 Irish Highland Powder Springs GA 30073

ADAMCIK, ERWIN F., Mathematics Department Chm; *b:* Smithville, TX; *m:* Ewell M.; *c:* Angela A. Adamcik Carver *ed:* (BS) Ed/Math, Univ of TX Austin 1964; Earlham Coll, SD Sch of Mines, Gettysburg Coll; *cr:* Prof Land Surveyor Continental Oil Co 1945-61; Teacher Austin TX Ind Sch Dist 1964-65, Smithville Tx Ind Sch Dist 1965-; *ai:* UIL Math Competition, Dept Math Chm; TX Surveyors Assn Mem, TX St Teachers Assn; 1st Baptist Church Deacon 1981-; Phi Theta Kappa 1962; Grants to Earlham Coll, SD Sch of Mines, Gettysburg Coll; Summer Teams in Math; *home:* 908 Charleston Blvd Smithville TX 78957

ADAMITZ, RUTH TENNEY, Retired 1st-6th Grade Teacher; *b:* Ithaca, NY; *m:* Harry W.; *ed:* (BA) Eng Lit, Oberlin Coll 1953; Teaching Cert Denver Univ 1960; *cr:* 6th Grade Teacher Denver CO 1960-62, Moses Lake WA 1962, Ft Collins CO 1962-63, 1st-6th Grade Teacher Bellevue & Issaquah WA 1964-88; *ai:* NEA Prin Awd 1987; WEA Supts Awd 1988; IEA; PTA Secy 1968, Golden Acorn Awd 1972.

ADAMOWITCH-LAPORTE, CARYL, 6th Grade Teacher; *b:* Nashua, NH; *m:* Clifton O. Jr.; *c:* Evan, Allison; *ed:* (BS) Elem Ed, Univ of Lowell 1970; (MED) Curr & Instruction, Northeastern Univ 1975; Fitchburg St Coll Fitchburg Area Collaborative for Excl Tchg Sci; Simmons Coll NSF Grant Project for Excl Elem Sch Sci; Mt Wachusett Comm Coll; Phys Sci Institute; *cr:* 5th Grade Teacher Fitzpatrick Sch 1970-77; 7th Grade Teacher Varnum Brook Mid Sch 1977-87; 6th Grade Teacher Ashby Elem Sch 1987-; *ai:* Sci Club Leader; Odyssey of the Mind Coach; Chairperson Dist Sci Curr Com; Mem Dist Math Curr Com; MA Assoc of Sci Teachers 1980-; Natl Sci Teachers Assn 1980-; Delta Kappa Gamma 1989-; Presenter at NSTA Convention 1989; Leader of Numerous Wrkshps Concerning Hands-On Sci & Math 1988-; *office:* Ashby Elem Sch Main St Ashby MA 01431

ADAMS, BARBARA FOLLETTE, Art Teacher; *b:* Atlanta, GA; *m:* Leroy John Jr.; *c:* Kristin, Mark; *ed:* (BFA) Interior Design, La Polytechnic Coll 1970; (MAT) Art, Tulane Univ 1973; *cr:* Art Teacher Thomas A Edison Elem Sch 1970-71, Booker T Washington Sr HS 1971-72, Chalmette Sr HS 1972-73, Br Martin HS 1973-77; Interior Design Teacher Delgado Comm Coll 1981-85; Art Teacher Ketterlinus Mid 1987-; *ai:* Yrbk Art & Art Club Adv; Teacher Ed Center Cncl Rep; Mid Sch Ed Specifications Comm Rep; Progress in Mid Ed Teacher; St Johns Art Teachers Treas 1987-; NAEA 1989-; FL Art Ed Assn 1989-; Cath Formation Prgm Bd Secy 1988-; *office:* Ketterlinus Mid Sch 75 Orange St Saint Augustine FL 32084

ADAMS, BETTY JOHNSON, Fourth Grade Teacher; *b:* Coffee Cty, AL; *m:* Charles Robert; *c:* Angelia Adams Burns, Charles G.; *ed:* Spartanburg Jr Coll 1955; (BS) Elem Ed, Troy St Univ 1958; (MED) Early Chldhd Ed, Brenau Coll 1984; W Carolina Univ & N GA Coll; *cr:* 3rd Grade Teacher City of Brewton 1959-60, Mt View Elem 1960-63; Librarian Towns Cty HS 1964-65; 4th Grade Teacher Paxton Schls 1967-70; Elem Teacher Union Cty Elem 1972-; *ai:* Writing Prgm Coord Union Cty Elem; 4th Grade Stu Support Team Chairperson; Union Cty Writing Comm Mem; Alpha Delta Kappa (Pres 1984-86, Athens Dist Necrology Chairperson 1986-88, Chaplin 1988-); GA Assn of Educators Governing Bd Dist Dir 1983-86; Order of Eastern Star (Worthy Matron 1966-67, Star Point 1990); Union Cty Teacher of Yr 1989;

GAE Uni-Serv Area 2 Outstanding Leadership Awd 1983-86; *home:* PO Box 235 Walker St Young Harris GA 30582

ADAMS, BEVERLY CHISM, Second Grade Teacher; *b:* Kokomo, IN; *m:* Roger; *c:* Adrienne; *ed:* (BS) Elem Ed, 1972, (MS) Elem Ed, 1974 IN Univ 1974; *cr:* 2nd Grade Teacher Western Primary Sch 1973-; *ai:* Accreditation Comm on Curr; *home:* 1015 W Elm Kokomo IN 46901

ADAMS, CAROL HOFFMAN, Eng Teacher/Eng Dept Chair; *b:* Pratt, KS; *m:* David V.; *ed:* (BS) Eng/Speech/Theatre, Fort Hays St Univ 1974; (MS) Cmmty Counseling, KS St Univ 1978; Womens Stud; Rdng; Internship in Leadership; Staff Dev in Cooperative Learning; Learning/Thinking Styles; Collaborative Writing; *cr:* Eng/Speech Teacher Westmoreland HS 1976-78; Eng Teacher 1978-, Eng Dept Chair 1980- Manhattan HS; *ai:* Futures Comm; KS Dept of Ed Standards Bd 1989-; K-12 Lang Art Curr Review 1984-; K-12 Lang Art Curr Writing Comm 1984-; Scndry Coord 1980-; Curr Cncl 1980-89; KS St Univ Grant Review Bd & Hum Planning Comm for KS Commission for Hum 1983-84; KS St Univ Task Force Teacher Ed 1980-81; Action Team 1984-; Future Educators of America Club Spon; Unified Sch Dist 383 Cooperative Pilot Prgm 1984-85; NCTE 1982-; KS Assn of Teachers of Eng (Exec Bd Mem 1984-87) 1982-; NSCD 1988-; Delta Kappa Gamma 1984-; Alpha Delta Kappa 1987-; NEA 1978-; KS Natl Ed Assn 1978-; Manhattan Ed Assn (Public Relations Co-Chm 1984-85) 1978-; St Isidores Cath Church Lector/Ministry 1974-; KS Master Teacher Awd 1985; Outstanding Young Educator Nom 1985; Univ of KS Outstanding Teacher of Gifted Stus 1984; USD 383 Excl in Teaching Awd 1984, 1987; William A Black Master Teacher Endowed Chair 1988; Co-Dir Peer Assistance Cadre Manhattan HS 1989-; USD #383 Leadership Cadre 1988-; Chm North Cntrl Evaluation Steering Comm Manhattan HS; North Cntrl Evaluation Visiting Comm 1984, 1985; Contributing Writer Various Publications; *home:* 1725 Wildcat Creek Rd Manhattan KS 66502

ADAMS, CAROL JEAN, A P European History Teacher; *b:* Menominee, MI; *c:* Todd A. Rice; *ed:* (BA) Eng/His/Soc Stud, Western MI Univ 1963; (MA) His, Univ of MN 1971; Oxford Univ England, Univ of Louvain Belgium; *cr:* Eng Teacher John F Kennedy HS 1964-66; World His Teacher Elmira Free Acad 1967-68; His/Eng Teacher Marshall Jr HS 1968-70, Humdoldt HS 1970-79, Washington Jr HS 1980-81, Como Sr HS 1982-; *ai:* Close Up; St Paul Fed of Teachers Exec Bd Bargaining Chairperson 1987-, Chairperson Awd 1987-; St Paul Teachers Retirement Trustee 1988-; MN Assn of Commerce & Industry MN Teacher of Excl 1986; Ecolab Excl Awd 1986; St Paul Mini Grant 1987; *home:* 1991 Hunter Ln Mendota Heights MN 55118

ADAMS, CARROLL HAYDON, 7th/8th Grade Teacher; *b:* Cadiz, KY; *m:* Faye Litsey; *ed:* (BA) Eng/Soc Stud, W KY Univ 1965; (MA) Religious Ed, S Baptist Theological Seminary 1974; *cr:* Classroom Teacher Howard Elem Sch 1968-69, Howard Mid Sch 1971-72, St Marys Grade Sch 1979-; *ai:* Diocese of Owensboro Cath Educators Building Rep 1989-; Intnl Rdng Assn; Owensboro Area Cncl Pres 1985-87; NCEA 1987-; *home:* 1715 Prince Ave Owensboro KY 42303

ADAMS, CATHY FLOYD, English Teacher/Dept Chair; *b:* Denver, CO; *m:* Philip V.; *c:* Allison, Michael, Jonathan; *ed:* (BA) Comm, 1978, (MA) Guidance, 1987 Morehead St Univ; *cr:* Rdng Teacher Letcher HS 1978-79; Eng/Journalism Teacher Fleming Neon HS 1980-; *ai:* Jr Spon; Yrbk, Newspaper, SADD Adv; Activity Period Planning, Teachers In-Service Comm; NEA, KEA, LCTO 1982-; Delta Phi Secy 1982-; Neon Volunteer Fire Dept Ladies Auxiliary Pres 1978-83; *office:* Fleming Neon HS PO Box 367 Neon KY 41840

ADAMS, CHARLES LESLIE, Principal/English Teacher; *b:* Memphis, TN; *m:* Shirley Sue Scott; *c:* Jamie D., Shawn C.; *ed:* (BA) Phys Ed, OK Baptist Univ 1967; (MS) Admin, E Cntrl St Univ 1987; *cr:* Teacher/Coach Bethel Sch 1968-69; Teacher/Coach/Admin S Rock Creek 1969-; *ai:* OEA, NEA; Shawnee Sftbl Assn Dir 1983-; 5 Alive Teacher Awd; *office:* S Rock Creek Sch Rt 5 Shawnee OK 74801

ADAMS, CINDY L., Reading & Religion Teacher; *b:* Golden Meadow, LA; *ed:* (BS) Speech & French Ed, LSU 1979; Addl Studies Certified By Ardiocese of New Orleans in Religious Ed for Elem & HS; *cr:* Teacher St. Christopher Sch 1980-; *ai:* Yrbk Adv; Moderator of Rainbow Group; 8th Grade Coord; Rdng Coord; *office:* Saint Christopher Sch 3900 Derbigny St Metairie LA 70001

ADAMS, DARRYL RODNEY, Journalism Dept Chair; *b:* Merced, CA; *m:* Angela Marie; *ed:* (BA) Poly Sci/Journalism, Univ of S CA 1984; Working towards Masters in Ed & Counseling; *cr:* Teachers Asst Manual Arts HS 1983-85; Teacher John Glenn HS 1984-; *ai:* Journalism, Peer Counseling, Stus for Other Clubs Adv; Frosh Ftbl Coach; Girls Jr Var Bsktbl, Bsbl Coach & Girls Var Bsktbl Asst Coach; NEA, CA Teachers Assn, Teachers Assn of Norwalk & La Mirada 1985-; Alpha Phi Alpha Dean of Pledges 1983-84; Black Stus Union (Pres 1981-84), Outstanding Mem 1984; Columbia Univs Press Competition 2nd Pl Newspaper; Quoted in Newsweek; *office:* John Glenn HS 13520 Shoemaker Ave Norwalk CA 90650

ADAMS, DEANNA BOLES, Life Science Chairperson; *b:* Abilene, TX; *m:* Joe Mark; *c:* Julie; *ed:* (BS) Bio/His Ed, W TX St Univ 1974; *cr:* Undergraduate Asst W TX St Univ 1973-74; Earth/Life Sci Teacher Goliad Jr HS 1974-77; Bio Teacher 1977-79; Life Sci Chairperson Goliad Mid Sch 1979-; *ai:* Jr HS Tennis & Girls Tennis Coach; Cheerleading Spon; Curr Deav Comm; 1st Baptist Church *home:* 2104 Cecilia St Big Spring TX 79720

ADAMS, DERITH STONER, 4th Grade Teacher; *b:* Indianapolis, IN; *m:* William H.; *c:* Kristina, Mark; *ed:* (BA) Elem Ed, Ball St Univ 1960; Chico St CA; *cr:* Elem Teacher Washington TWP Sch 1960-65, Yuba City Schls 1965-71, St Vrain Valley Schls 1971-; *ai:* NEA; CEA; *office:* Mountain View Elem Sch 1415 14th St Longmont CO 80501

ADAMS, DONNA BOCK, 6th Grade Teacher; *b:* Cape Girardeau, MO; *m:* Terry R.; *c:* Brooke, Danielle; *ed:* (BS) Elem Ed, 1971, (MA) Elem Ed, 1979 SE MO St Univ; *cr:* 2nd Grade Teacher Perry Cty Dist #32 1971-80; Kndgtn Teacher Reynolds Cty R 1980-81; 6th Grade Teacher Lesterville R-4 1981-84, Arcadia Valley R-2 1984-; *ai:* Arcadia Valley CTA, MSTA, ADK; *office:* Arcadia Valley Mid Sch 550 Park Dr Ironton MO 63650

ADAMS, DOROTHY PEOPLES, Government/Economics Teacher; *b:* Atmore, AL; *m:* Clarence Ben; *ed:* (BA) Phys Ed, Stillman Coll 1970; (MED) Phys Ed, Southern Univ 1977; Health Ed Wkshp, Univ of AL Birmingham 1984; *cr:* Teacher/Coach Southside HS; *ai:* Red Cross, Jr & Sr Class Spon; Faculty Cncl Mem; Sr Honor Society; Dallas Cty Prof Assn, NEA 1970-; AL Ed Assn 1970-, Service Awd 1980; Amer Red Cross Bd of Dir 1986-88, Volunteer of Yr 1984; Appointed to Bd of Dir & Head of Phys Ed Dept 1979-84; Humanitarian Awd 1990; *home:* PO Box 55 Orrville AL 36767

ADAMS, EVE, Mathematics Teacher; *b:* Buffalo, NY; *c:* Darlene L., Danica Pylinski, BRuce, Jon Q.; *ed:* (AA) Liberal Arts, Hilbert Coll 1971; (BS) Ed, St Univ of NY Buffalo 1973; (MA) Counseling, N AZ Univ Flagstaff 1980; Gifted Specialist; Effective Schls Trng; *cr:* 5th-6th Grade Teacher Armor Elem 1973-76; 7th-8th Grade Rdng Teacher Wickenburg AZ 1977-81; 4th-8th Grade Rdng/Math Teacher Washington Sch Dist 1983-84; 7th-8th Grade Math Teacher Cottonwood-Oak Creek Sch Dist 1984-; *ai:* Yrbk; Cmptr Lab Word Processing; Newsletter; ASCD, NCTM 1984-; Rebecca Lodge Nobel Grand 1956-65; 5 St Dance Competition 1977-81, 1st Place 1979; Teacher of Yr Hamburg Dist; Outstanding Math Teacher Sigma Xi; Article Published; *home:* 525 Posse Ground Rd Sedona AZ 86336

ADAMS, FORREST EUGENE, Mathematics Teacher; *b:* Lakin, KS; *m:* Romona Jean Thomas; *c:* Jeanine; *ed:* (BS) Math, Panhandle St Univ 1963; (MS) Ed, KS St Univ 1968; Natl Sci Fnd Math Inst; *cr:* Math Teacher Elkhart HS 1963-; *ai:* Jr & Sr Class Spon; Bsktbl Coach; NEA, KS Natl Ed Assn 1963-; Elkhart Ed Assn (Pres, Treas) 1963-, Master Teacher Awd; Phi Delta Kappa 1968-77; Elkhart Jaycees 1968-70; *office:* Elkhart HS Wildcat Ave Elkhart KS 67950

ADAMS, FRANCES DANETTE, Co-op Voc Ed Coordinator; *b:* Americus, GA; *m:* Darryl Turpin; *c:* D. Tionn, Makeisha D.; *ed:* (BS) Bus Ed, Albany St Coll 1972; (BS) Coordinating-Coop Voc Ed, GA Southern 1989; Lib Sci, Albany St Coll; Working Towards Masters Bus Ed; *cr:* Teacher Preparatory Sch of Ed Germany 1973-75, Peachtree HS 1984-87; Coord Mc Nair Sr HS 1987-; *ai:* Voc Opportunities Clubs of America; Philosophy & Goals, Voc Awds, Sch Facilities, Career Dev Comm; GA Voc Assn, Amer Voc Assn, GA Assn of Ed; Delta Sigma Theta Hospitality Comm; Wesley Chapel Church Bd of Trustees; Red Cross; *office:* Mc Nair Sr HS 1804 Bouldercrest Rd Atlanta GA 30316

ADAMS, GERARD EARL, English Teacher; *b:* Detroit, MI; *ed:* (BS) Lit/Eng, 1962, (MA) Lit/Eng, 1967 Eastern MI Univ; (MS) Univ of Birmingham England; *cr:* Eng Teacher Redford Union HS 1962-; *office:* Redford Union HS 17711 Kinloch St Redford MI 48240

ADAMS, GINA WERRICK, Science Teacher; *b:* Toronto On, Canada; *m:* William N.; *ed:* (BA) Elem Ed, Augusta Coll 1979; *cr:* Biological Laboratory Technician Entomological Research Laboratory 1969-72; Classroom Aide Garden City Elem 1972-76; Bio Laboratory Technician Univ of FL 1976-77; Classroom Teacher Floyd Graham Elem 1979-88, Hephzibah Mid Sch 1988-; *ai:* Yrbk Adv; Family Dynamics Teacher in Residence; Curr Comm; Inservice Wkshps; NEA, NSTA, CSRA Soc Stud Assn; Natl Wildlife Assn; Pres Aides Assn 1974; Co-Author Articles on Sandfly Stud; *office:* Hephzibah Mid Sch PO Box 248 Hephzibah GA 30815

ADAMS, IONA L., Kindergarten Teacher; *b:* Detroit, MI; *m:* Raymond I. Norris Jr.; *c:* Laura Norris, Ray III, Adam; *ed:* (BA) Elem Ed, Eastern KY Univ 1975; (MS) Cmmty Dev, Univ of Louisville 1983; *cr:* Kndgtn Teacher Mt Sterling Elem 1976-77, Mt Washington Elem 1977-; *ai:* Various Sch & Sch Dist Comm; NEA, KEA Mem 1977-; BCEA (Mem, Rep) 1977-; *office:* Mt Washington Elem Sch PO Box 39 Hwy 44 Mount Washington KY 40047

ADAMS, JAMES CHARLES, Techonology Coord & Teacher; *b:* Black River Ralls, WI; *m:* Diane; *c:* Donald, Greg, Chrissy; *ed:* (BSAAE) Aeronautical & Astronautical Engrineering, Northrop Univ 1966; Trajectory Analysis; Astronomy; Cmptr Systems; *cr:* Aerospace Engr NASA Johnson Space Center 1966-68; Project Engr Dept of Defense 1968-78; Teacher Chetek Area Schls 1978-; *ai:* Academic Decathlon Adv; Northwestern WI Ed Assn 2nd VP 1987; Northwest United Ed 1978-; WI Math Cncl 1978-; Six Lakes Aero Modelers Pres 1988-; Acad of Moda Aeronautics 1986-; Grant Cray Research Inc to Teach Aeronautics Class; Excl in Engr Grant Sattelite Comm in Classes Completed Cmptr Graphics & Microcomputer Prof; *office:* Chetek H S 1001 Knapp St Chetek WI 54728

ADAMS, JANICE LYNN (THOMPSON), Fourth Grade Teacher; *b:* Thomaston, GA; *m:* William Allen; *ed:* (BA) Sociology/Psych, West GA 1972; (MS) Elem, Mercer Univ 1975; Specialist Early Chldhd Ed, West GA 1985; Data Collector; *cr:* 4th-6th Grade Phys Ed Teacher atwater Sch 1973-74; 4th Grade Teacher Yatesville Sch 1974-88, Upson Elem Sch 1988-; *ai:* Curr Comm; Sponsored Sch Wildflower Project 1989-; GA Assn of Educators (Treas 1982-83, Spelling Bee Coord 1988-89) Plaques 1982 & 89; Master Teacher for 11 Years 1979-; Nom Teacher of Yr 1985; *home:* 259 Bonanza Dr Thomaston GA 30286

ADAMS, JIMMY D., Science Teacher; *b:* Marshall, AR; *m:* Jackye Lee Mc Bride; *ed:* (BS) Phys Sci, 1968, (MS) Scndry Counseling, 1971 Univ Cntrl AR; PET Trng; Assertive Discipline; *cr:* Teacher/Cnslr Leslie Public Sch 1968-; *ai:* Class & Fire Marshall Spon; Personnel Policy Comm; *home:* Rt 1 Box 4C Leslie AR 72645

ADAMS, JOYCE ANN, Kindergarten Teacher; *b:* Newcastle, WY; *ed:* (AA) Mt Vernon Comm Coll 1967; (BS) Elem Ed, Oakland City Coll 1970; Remedial Rdng, E IL Univ Charleston; *cr:* Head Start Teacher WADI Rural Resource Center 1970-72; Remedial Rdng/Kndgtn Teacher New Hope Sch 1970-; *ai:* Sunday Sch Teacher; Delta Kappa Gamma Personal Growth Comm Chm & Communication Comm; Delta Kappa Gamma 1982-; IL Ed Assn, NEA 1983-; Amer Chldhd Ed Grant 1969; *home:* 115 Young Dr Fairfield IL 62837

ADAMS, JOYCE MC CRACKEN, Kindergarten Teacher; *b:* Springfield, MO; *c:* Bryan D.; *ed:* (BS) Elem Ed, 1973, (MA) Elem Ed, 1981 SW MO St Univ; *cr:* Kndgtn Teacher Springfield R-XII Public Schls 1974-; *ai:* Hands on Sci Coord Springfield Public Schls; Prof Dev Comm 1988-; Springfield Ed Assn, Intnl Reading Assn 1985-; Kndgtn Advisory Cncl Chairperson 1986-88; *office:* Alice Pittman Elem Sch 2934 E Bennett Springfield MO 65804

ADAMS, JUDITH MYERS, Social Studies Chairperson; *b:* Dayton, OH; *m:* Keith Guy; *c:* Collin M.; *ed:* (BA) Poly Sci/His - Magna Cum Laude, Franklin Coll of IN 1971; (MED) Scndry Sch Admin, Xavier Univ 1974; Washington Semester Poly Sci, Amer Univ 1970; *cr:* Teacher Rodger O Borror Sch 1971-; *ai:* Adv & Founder Natl Jr Honor Society Myron Halley Chapter 1981- & Friends of Ed 1987-; Incentives Comm 1988-; Peer Tutoring Adv 1985-; NEA 1972-74, 1980-; OH Ed Assn 1971-74, 1980-; Wilmington Ed Assn Secy 1973-74, 1990, Distinguished Service Awd 1985; Natl Assn of Stu Act Advs 1973-; Phi Alpha Theta 1969-; Phi Delta Kappa 1988-; 1st Chrstn Church (Choir 1987-, Ed Comm Mem 1986-, Chrstn Womens Fellowship Secy 1985-, Mem) 1984-; China Lake Conference Center (Cnslr, Dir) 1974-76; Robert F Kennedy for Pres Johnson Cty Coord 1967-68; Order of Eastern Star (Marshal 1976-77, Chaplain 1973-75); Clinton Cty Historical Society 1986-89; Natl Sch Public Relations Assn Golden Achievement Awd 1989; Wilmington Jaycees Outstanding Young Educator 1976; OH Assn of Stu Cncls All-OH Adv 1984-85; OH House of Reps Outstanding Educator Citation 1985; Hopewell Spec Ed Regional Resource Center Exceptional Achievement Awd 1985; Published Work; Ashland Oil Teacher Achievement Finalist Awd 1988; OH Dept of Ed OH Teacher of Yr 4th Place 1986; Wilmington Ed Fnd Positive Living Grant 1989; *home:* 689 Hiatt Ave Wilmington OH 45177

ADAMS, KATHY GOVER, Fifth Grade Teacher; *b:* Somerset, KY; *m:* John M. Jr.; *ed:* (BA) Elem Ed, Univ of KY 1975; Elem Ed, E KY Univ 1979; Career Ed Trng 1976-77; *cr:* 2nd Grade Teacher Ferguson Elem 1975-79; 2nd/4th Grade Teacher Southern Elem 1979-; *ai:* Brownie Troop Leader 1976-81; Career Ed Trng Inservice Pulaski Cty 2nd Grade Teachers 1977; PCEA, KEA, NEA; Beta Sigma Phi (Secy 1984-, VP 1981-82), Girl of Yr 1982, 1985; Staging & Production Local Jr Miss Scholastic Prgm Coord; *office:* Southern Elem Sch 4030 Enterprise Dr Somerset KY 42501

ADAMS, LAURA WISE, Fifth Grade Teacher; *b:* Crestview, FL; *m:* Philip L.; *c:* Allison, Jason; *ed:* (BS) Elem Ed, FL St Univ 1964; *cr:* 1st Grade Teacher Southside Elem 1965-68; 6th Grade Teacher Bob Sikes Elem 1972-73, King Mid Sch 1976-; 5th Grade Teacher Gulf Breeze; *ai:* Natl Teachers Assn, FL Teachers Assn; Teacher of Yr King Mid Sch 1984; Outstanding Math Teacher Holley-Navarre 1990; *office:* King M S 1936 Navarre School Rd Gulf Breeze FL 32566

ADAMS, LEANN COX, Humanities Teacher; *b:* Fort Worth, TX; *m:* Robert Gordon; *c:* Ashley A.; *ed:* (BA) His, 1966, (MA) His, 1969 TX Chrstn Univ; Loyola Univ Rome Italy; London Sch of Ec; *cr:* His Teacher Arlington Heights HS 1966-70, I M Terrell HS 1971-72; His Instr Tarrant Cty Jr Coll 1971-72; His Teacher Trinity Valley Sch 1973-77; Hum Teacher Paschal HS; *ai:* Academic Decathlon Coach; Campus Coordinating Comm Chm; Management Team; Ft Worth Cncl Teachers of Soc Stud VP; Ft Worth Corral of Westerners (Sheriff, Pres); Historic Preservation Cncl Tarrant Cty Pres 1986; Berkeley Place Assn Pres 1988-89; Jr League of Ft Worth VP 1984; TX Boys Choir Bd Mem; Youth Orch of Greater Ft Worth Bd Mem; Published Author 1968; *office:* R L Paschal HS 3001 Forest Park Blvd Fort Worth TX 76110

ADAMS, LOUISE BARTIK, Fifth Grade Teacher; *b:* New York, NY; *m:* Russell Norman; *c:* Rusty; *ed:* (BS) Elem Ed, Trenton St Coll 1961; Grad Work Trenton St Coll, Georgian Court Coll; *cr:* 3rd Grade Teacher R Hunter Sch 1961-65, Schirra Sch 1965-66; 3rd-5th Grade Teacher E Dover Elem 1966-; *ai:* Worked with Young Authors Conferences; Working with Disaffected Stus; Affirmative Action Textbook Selection Comm; Worked with Gifted Children; Ocean Cty Rdng Cncl Corresponding Secy

1985-88; NJEA, NEA 1961-; VFW Auxiliary, PTA; St of NJ Comm-TEPA-Worked on Teacher Cert; *office:* E Dover Elem Sch 725 Vaughn Ave Toms River NJ 08753

ADAMS, LOUISE ORDOYNE, Chapter I Reading Teacher; *b:* Raceland, LA; *m:* Harold Joseph; *c:* Celeste, Andre; *ed:* (BA) Elem Ed, 1968, (MED) Rdng, 1972 Nicholls St Univ; Grad Stud; Prof Improvement Prgm; Master Teacher Trng; LA Teacher Internshp Prgm; LA Teacher Evaluation Prgm; *cr:* 2nd Grade Teacher 1968-84, Chapter I Teacher 1984- Golden Meadow Lower; *ai:* Public Relations Comm & Amer Ed Week Chm; Adopt-A-Sch Comm; Intnl Rdng Assn, LA Rdng Assn, Nicholls Rdng Cncl, Lafource Teacher Incorporated; Alpha Delta Kappa (Recording Office Secy 1977-79, Corresponding Secy 1979-81); Confraternity Chrstn Doctrine Teacher 1977-89; Dixie Youth Bsbl Parent Worker 1983-88; Biddy Bsktbl Parent Volunteer 1984-89; *home:* PO Box 303 Golden Meadow LA 70357

ADAMS, LUCILLE, Retired Kindergarten Teacher; *b:* Chapmanville, WV; *c:* Joyce Moltumyr, Mary A. Hunt, Phyllis Sizemore, Joseph A., Arnold; *cr:* Kndgtn Teacher Pike Cty Bd of Ed 1974-82; *home:* PO Box 48 Phyllis KY 41554

ADAMS, MARK R., Natural/Computer Sci Teacher; *b:* Johnstown, PA; *m:* Pamela Jo; *c:* Teressa, Ryan; *ed:* (BS) Composite Sci Ed, Bob Jones Univ 1979; (MSED) Curr & Instruction, Univ of KS 1988; *cr:* Scndry Sci/Math/Cmptr/Bible/ Speech Teacher Berean Chrstn Sch 1979-; *ai:* Jr Class, Amer Chrstn Honor Society Spon; Elem Bsktbl Prgm Dir; *office:* Berean Chrstn Sch 15020 Black Bob Rd Olathe KS 66062

ADAMS, MARY GILLESPIE, US History/Adv History Teacher; *b:* Tazewell Cty, VA; *m:* William B.; *c:* Mary A. Hemsworth, Flora B., Nicholas F., William B. Jr.; *ed:* (BA) His/ Math, Converse Coll 1951; (MA) Ed, VPI & SU 1977; *cr:* His/ Math/Acctg Teacher Richlands HS 1952-54; His/Math/Eng/Phy Ed Teacher Calverton HS 1954-56; His & Eng Teacher Osborne HS 1956-57; US His/Adv Amer His Richland HS 1970-; *ai:* Model United Nations Spon; Tazewell Cty Academic Competition Coach Soc Stud; Delta Kappa Gamma 1983-; *office:* Richlands H S Richlands VA 24641

ADAMS, MARY HOLLADAY, 5th Grade Teacher; *b:* Dawson, TX; *m:* Don A.; *c:* Debbie Mitchell, Joey; *ed:* (BS) Elem Ed, E NM Univ 1970; Grad Stud CSW Hobbs, NMJC Hobbs, E NM Univ Portales; *cr:* Jr HS Lang Art Teacher Tatum Municipal Schls 1970-78; 3rd-6th Grade Elem Ed/3rd-5th Grade Self Contained Classroom/4th-6th Grade Soc Stud Teacher Tatum Elem Sch 1978-; *ai:* NEA Secy 1970-; NM Cncl for Soc Stud 1985-; PTA; *office:* Tatum Elem Sch Box 685 Tatum NM 88267

ADAMS, MARYON THOMAS, Retired; *b:* Pawnee City, NE; *m:* Ross B.; *c:* Lanette Nies; Patricia Tushla; *ed:* (BS) Elem Ed, 1954, (MS) Admin/Supervision, 1958 Peru St Coll; Remedial Diagnostic Rdng, Omaha Univ; Early Chldhd Study in Europe, Univ of CA; *cr:* Kndgtn Supvr/Coll Professor Elem Ed Peru St Coll 1954-68; Kndgtn Teac Her/Elem Music Supervision/ Librarian Peru Elem Sch 1968-84; *ai:* Volunteer Work Church/ Cmmty; NEA/NSEA/AARP/AART (Lifetime Mem. Pres, Secy, Sch Rep) 1956 Teacher of Yr 1962; OFA WM 1960-84; PEO/Am Legion Auxillary Guard 1982; Delta Kappa Gamma Pres 1970-72; Traveled Studying Early Chldhd Ed England, France, Denmark & Belgium; *home:* 800 Mulberry St Peru NE 68421

ADAMS, MYRA MC GEE, Physical Education Teacher; *b:* Chattanooga, TN; *m:* Virgil Shannon; *c:* Sara E., Leah M.; *ed:* (BS) Phys Ed/Health, W GA Coll 1974; (MED) Phys Ed/Health, 1975, (EDS) Phys Ed/Health, 1983 Univ of GA; RAMP Trng; CPR Trng ARC; Identifying Abused Child Wkshp; *cr:* Grad Teacher Asst Univ of GA 1974-75; Phys Ed/Health Teacher Hart Cty Jr HS 1975-76; Phys Ed Teacher Oconee Cty Intermediate Sch 1977-; *ai:* Phys Ed Curr Planning; Olympic Day in Public Schls 1990; PAGE 1985-; GAE 1975-85; Stu Support Team Mem 1987-89; Compiled, Edited & Submitted GA Sch of Excl Data & Application 1988-89; *office:* Oconee Cty Intermediate Sch Colham Ferry Rd Watkinsville GA 30677

ADAMS, NANCY CANSLER, Mathematics Dept Chairman; *b:* Detroit, MI; *m:* Bob R.; *c:* Mark, Sandra Adams Smith; *ed:* (BA) Bio, 1963, (MA) Math/Ed, 1965 Austin Peay; (Rank I) Supervision/Admin, W KY 1972; *cr:* Math Teacher Christian Cty HS 1963-65, Greenville HS 1965-; *ai:* Math Coach; Jr Spon; KEA; NEA; Chamber of Commerce; *home:* Rt 1 Greenville KY 42345

ADAMS, NANETTE ALICE, 4th Grade Teacher; *b:* Delta, CO; *ed:* (BA) Elem Ed, Univ of Northern CO 1965; (MA) Elem Ed, Adams St Coll 1973; *cr:* 3rd Grade Teacher Los Banos Elem Sch 1965-68; 2nd/3rd/4th Grade Teacher Montrose Cty Sch-RE-1J 1968-; 2nd/3rd Grade Teacher Oak Grove Elem 1968-86; 4th Grade Teacher Olathe Elem Sch 1986-; *ai:* Leadership Team; NEA 1968-; CEA 1968-; UVEA 1968-.

ADAMS, PAIGER PARKIN, Algebra-Geometry Teacher; *b:* Salem, OR; *m:* Paul R.; *ed:* (BS) Phys Ed/Math, Weber St Coll 1985; *cr:* Math Teacher N Ogden Jr HS 1984-85, N Davis HS 1985-87, Farmington Jr HS 1987-, Viewmont HS 1990; *ai:* Intramurals; Ski Club Adv; Girls Vlybl, Fast Pitch Sftbl, Head Var Vlybl Coach; UEA, NEA, DEA 1984-88; *home:* PO Box 238 Farmington UT 84025

ADAMS, PAM L., 1st Grade Teacher; *b:* Macon, MS; *m:* C. Morgan Jr.; *c:* Brooke; *cr:* 1st Grade Teacher Central Acad 1973-; *ai:* Sunday Sch Teacher; MS Private Sch Assn 1973-; Macon Jr Auxiliary (Assoc, Corresponding Secy) 1975-80; Outstanding Young Women of America 1988; *home:* 208 Pleasants St Macon MS 39341

ADAMS, PATRICIA KIEWICZ, Dean of Students; *b:* Chicago, IL; *m:* Gary C.; *c:* Mark A.; *ed:* (BED) Ed/Math, Chicago Teachers Coll 1964; (MA) Sch Admin, St Xavier Coll 1977; Grad Stud Chicago St Univ, Governors St Univ, N IL Univ; *cr:* Math Teacher Lindblom HS 1964-69; Math Teacher 1969-88, Dean of Stus 1988- Tinley Park HS; *ai:* At Risk Comm; IEA, NEA, ASCD, IL Cncl Teachers of Math, Phi Delta Kappa, IL St Deans Assn; *office:* Tinley Park HS 6111 W 175th St Tinley Park IL 60477

ADAMS, PAUL EDWIN, 7th-8th Grade Science Teacher; *b:* Salamanca, NY; *m:* Barbara Ann Jones; *c:* Lucas, Casey; *ed:* (BS) General Sci, Houghton Coll 1974; (MSED) Sci Ed, Buffalo St Coll 1979; *cr:* 6th Grade Sci Teacher Grand Island Mid Sch 1974-76; Admissions Cnslr Houghton Coll 1976-78; 6th-8th Grade Sci Teacher Chrstn Heritage Sch 1978-81; 7th-9th/12th Grade Sci Teacher Chrstn Sch of York 1981-; *ai:* Mid Sch Bsbl Coach; Outdoor Ed & Sch Paper Sports Coord; York Rock & Mineral Club 1988-; York Cty Sci & Engineering Fair VP 1988-; *office:* Christian Sch of York 907 Greenbriar Rd York PA 17404

ADAMS, RALPH EDWARD, Social Studies Teacher; *b:* Cincinnati, OH; *m:* Angela Carol Hull; *c:* Walker M., Briana D.; *ed:* (AA) Soc Stud, Univ of Cincinnati 1975; (BSE) Soc Stud, Emporia St Univ 1986; *cr:* Teacher/Coach El Dorado Springs HS 1988-; *ai:* Head Jr HS Boys Bsktbl & Asst HS Bsbl Coach; Forum Club Spon; MO Assn of Rural Ed Delegate 1990; *home:* 214 W 3rd Ave Garnett KS 66032

ADAMS, RICHARD THOMAS, JR., Teacher; *b:* Port Jefferson, NY; *m:* Julia Belfield; *ed:* (BA) Soc Stud Ed, Niagara Univ 1987; Working Towards MA Stoney Brook Univ; *cr:* Soc Stud Teacher Valley Stream Cntrl HS 1987-; *ai:* Law Club & Debate Team Adv; Sr Awds, Schlsp Awds, NHS Comm; Bsbl Coach; Long Island Cncl of Soc Stud, NCSS 1988-; NY St Cncl of Soc Stud 1986-; ASCD 1989-; Mid Island Fire Dept Captain 1983-, 50 Percent High Point Awd 1988-89; Phi Lamba Theta 1983-; Presenter at NY Cncl of Soc Stud Conference 1988; Stu Teacher of Yr Awd Niagara Univ 1987; His Dept Awd 1987; *office:* Valley Stream Cntrl HS Fletcher Ave Valley Stream NY 11580

ADAMS, ROBERT PATRICK, First Grade Teacher; *b:* St Louis, MO; *m:* Vicky Lynn; *c:* Margaret, Madeline; *ed:* (BS) Art, Cntrl MO St 1970; (MAT) Comm, Webster Coll 1979; *cr:* 1st-8th Grade Art Teacher 1970-73, 1st-3rd Grade Teacher 1973-77, 3rd Grade Teacher 1977-79, 4th Grade Teacher 1979-87, 1st Grade Teacher 1987- Meramec Valley R3; *ai:* MVNEA Salary Negotiations; Teacher Assistance Team; Prof Dev Comm.

ADAMS, ROBERT VINCENT, Fifth Grade Teacher; *b:* Kearney, NJ; *m:* Kathleen Diane Mc Clain; *c:* Jennifer, Katie, Jonathan; *ed:* (BS) Elem Ed, Nyack Coll 1977; Grad Courses Curr, Instruction, Univ WI Milwaukee; *cr:* 5th Grade Teacher 1977-88, 5th Grade/Jr HS Teacher 1988- Oostburg Chrstn Sch; *ai:* Girls Var Bsktbl & Boys Jr HS Soccer Coach; Jr HS Athletic Dir; Ed Comm Teacher Rep; 1st C R Church Deacon 1981-83; *office:* Oostburg Chrstn Sch 610 Superior Ave Oostburg WI 53070

ADAMS, SALLY BROWN, High School English Teacher; *b:* Louisville, KY; *m:* Roy W.; *c:* Michael, Rachel; *ed:* (BA) Eng, Univ of Louisville 1969; (MA) Scndry Guidance/Counseling, E KY Univ 1979; *cr:* Lang Art/Eng Teacher Ballard HS 1969-77; Eng Teacher Shelby Cty HS 1977-81, Western Hills HS 1984-; *ai:* Sr Class & Juniorettes Spon; Membership Faculty Comm; KEA, NEA 1969-; NCTE, KCTE, FCEA 1984-; Band Boosters Cmmty Rep 1990; PTA Secy 1985-89; Article Published 1990; All Academic Faculty Mem 1990; *office:* Western Hills HS 100 Doctors Dr Frankfort KY 40601

ADAMS, SAMUEL DAVID, Mathematics Teacher/Coach; *b:* Ft Worth, TX; *m:* Kristen Aver; *ed:* (BA) Bio - Cum Laude, WA St Univ 1979; *cr:* Math/Phys Ed Teacher Clarkston HS 1982-; *ai:* Ftbl & Bsktbl Coach; Natural Helpers Adv; Phi Betta Kappa 1979; Young Life (Leader, Dir) 1982-; *home:* PO Box 362 Clarkston WA 99403

ADAMS, SHELLEY BROOKS, Third Grade Teacher; *b:* Talladega, AL; *M:* Joseph G.; *c:* Joseph G. II, Emily B.; *ed:* (BS) Elem Ed, 1977; (MA) Elem Ed, 1983 Univ of AL; *cr:* Rdng Teacher 1977-78, Eng Teacher 1978-80 Talladega Mid Sch; 3rd Grade Teacher Graham Elem Sch 1980-; *ai:* Mem of Steering Comm at Graham for Southern Sch Accreditation; Eng Txtbk Comm; Lib Comm; Kappa Kappa Iota 1986-; *office:* Graham Elem Sch 403 Cedar St Talladega AL 35160

ADAMS, SUE PULLEY, 4th Grade Teacher; *b:* San Antonio, TX; *m:* Russell L.; *c:* Scott, David; *ed:* (BS) Scndry Ed, 1962, (MS) Elem Ed, 1963 Southwest TX St Univ; *cr:* 3rd Grade Teacher San Antonio Ind Sch Dist 1963-64; Bus/3rd Grade Teacher San Marcos Baptist Acad 1964-67; 3rd Grade Teacher San Antonio Ind Sch Dist 1967-68; 2nd/4th/5th Grade Teacher Putnam City Sch Dist 1980-; *ai:* Eng Vertical Team Chairperson; Yrbk, Putnam City Plan for Excl Comm Mems; OK Ed Assn, NEA 1980-; OK Rdng Cncl 1983-; Putnam City Assn Classroom Teachers 1980-; Will Rogers PTA 1983-; KWTV Channel 9 My Favorite Teacher Awd 1988; *home:* 1600 Thunderbird Edmond OK 73013

ADAMS, SUSAN MC GLOIN, Sixth Grade Teacher; *b:* Detroit, MI; *m:* Robert Ray; *c:* Andrew R.; *ed:* (BA) Eng, 1967, (MA) Elem Ed, 1974 W KY Univ; *cr:* 7th/8th Grade Lang Art Teacher Warren Cty Jr/Sr HS 1967-68; 5th Grade Teacher Park City Elem Sch 1968-73; 4th-6th Grade Teacher Red Cross Elem Sch 1974-76; 5th/6th Grade Teacher Park City Elem Sch 1976-; *ai:* EIP, Sch Landscaping, Comm & Safety, Sch Cmmty Relations Comm; NEA, KEA, BCEA; *home:* 394 S B Thomas Rd Bowling Green KY 42103

ADAMS, TERRI REED, First Grade Teacher; *b:* Fort Eustis, VA; *m:* Gregory; *c:* Elizabeth A., Sydney M.; *ed:* (BA) Elem Ed, Nicholls St Univ 1977; *cr:* 6th/7th Grade Soc Stud Teacher Grand Caillou Elem 1977-79; 6th Grade Teacher Oakshire Elem 1979-87; 7th Grade Eng/8th Grade Sci Teacher Ellender Memorial 1988; 1st Grade Teacher Oakshire Elem 1988-; *ai:* Gamma Lambda (Pres 1988-) 1984-, Girl of Yr 1989; Beta Sigma Phi City Cncl VP 1989-; *office:* Oakshire Elem Sch 3620 Vicari Dr Houma LA 70364

ADAMS, TIMOTHY CLARK, Gifted Education Teacher; *b:* Elmira, NY; *m:* Virginia Wright Kleber; *c:* Steven, Sarah, Cameron; *ed:* (BA) Poly Sci, St Univ NY Fredonia 1967; (PHD) Organizational Behavior, St Univ NY Buffalo 1978; Scndry Ed Cert 1987; Gifted Ed Cert Wichita St Univ 1988; *cr:* Assoc Dir N Plains Ed Consortium 1976-78; Exec Dir Associated Coll Cntrl KS 1978-80; Quality Control Manville Corporation 1980-87; Gifted Ed Teacher Newton HS 1988-; *ai:* Coll Bowl Coach; Building Team Mem; KS Gifted, Talented, Creative Assn, KNEA 1988-; Mc Pherson Cty Republican Party Precinct Chm 1988-; United Meth Church Sunday Sch Teacher 1980-; *office:* Newton HS 900 W 12th Newton KS 67114

ADAMS, WILLIAM FRANCIS, Business Teacher; *b:* Kansas City, MO; *m:* Sandra Kay Meyer; *c:* Katelyn; *ed:* (BS) Bus Management, 1981, (BS) Scndry Ed, 1983 NW MO St Univ; (MBA) Management, Univ of MO Kansas City 1990; *cr:* Bus Teacher/Coach William Chrisman HS 1983-; *ai:* Bsktbl Coach; NEA 1985-; *office:* William Christman HS 1223 N Noland Rd Independence MO 64050

ADCOCK, PATRICIA W., English/Art Teacher; *m:* Harry; *c:* Josh Gerow, Leslie Gerow; *ed:* (BA) Eng/Lit Art, Univ of TN Knoxville 1966; *cr:* Teacher Halls HS 1975-; *ai:* Drama Coach; Art Club & Sr Class Spon; Creative Writing Class; Dir Weekly Art Exhibits & Sch Play; TN Ed Assn, NEA, LCEA 1975-; NCTE 1987-; WCTE; Laudervale Cty Arts Cncl 1990; DAR; Restoration of WW II Painting; Homecoming Exhibit 1986; Univ of TN Knoxville GOvernors Writing Acad; Vanderbilt Univ TN Art Cncl; *office:* Halls HS Tigrett St Halls TN 38040

ADDINGTON, DUARD GALE, Mathematics Instructor; *b:* Richlands, VA; *m:* Connie Jane Liebsch; *c:* Arthur Emmett; *ed:* (BS) Ed, Concord Coll 1973; (MS) Occupational Safety, Marshall Univ 1980; Mining Engineering Technology; PhD Prgm, VA Polytech Inst; *cr:* Math Instr Bluefield HS; *ai:* Academic Decathlon Coach; Bluefield HS Federal Grant Writing & North Cntrl Evaluation Comm; NEA, CEA 1975-; *office:* Bluefield HS 535 W Cumberland Rd Bluefield WV 24701

ADDISON, CLAIRE K., Social Studies Teacher; *b:* Chicago, IL; *m:* Douglas P.; *c:* Juliet W., Douglas R.; *ed:* (BA) Intnl Relations, Univ of CA Los Angeles 1963; Grad Work at Columbia Univ; *cr:* Teacher St Peters Episcopal Sch 1984-88; Soc Stud Dept Chairperson/Teacher 1988-89, Dean of Stud/Hum Dept Chairperson/Gut/Econ/Advanced Placement US History Teacher Mary Star of the Sea HS 1989-; *ai:* Archdiocesan Curr Comm; NCSS 1988-; San Pedro Assistance League Palos Verdes 1973-; *office:* Mary Star of the Sea HS 810 W 8th St San Pedro CA 90731

ADDY, CAROL P., First Grade Teacher; *b:* Cedar City, UT; *m:* Randy C.; *c:* Casey P.; *ed:* (BS) UT St Univ Logan 1969-; *cr:* Teacher Grantsville Elem; *ai:* Developing Units to Teach; *home:* 27 Deseret Cir Grantsville UT 84029

ADE, DEBORAH MOE, Second Grade Teacher; *b:* Ft Wayne, IN; *m:* James Edward; *c:* Tracie, Chris, Brian; *ed:* (BA) Elem Ed, Purdue Univ 1974; (MS) Elem Ed, IN Univ Southeastern 1981; *cr:* 2nd Grade Teacher Leavenworth Elem 1977-; *office:* Leavenworth Elem Sch Box 37 Leavenworth IN 47137

ADKINS, CHANDRA POWER, English Teacher; *b:* Athens, GA; *m:* H. Bruce; *c:* Alexandra, Jessica; *ed:* (BSED) Eng Ed, 1980, (MED) Eng Ed, 1982 Univ of GA; *cr:* Teacher Hart Cty HS 1980-83, Washington Wilkes HS 1983-86/1988-; Part Time Instr Truett McConnell Coll 1983-; *ai:* Yrbk/Newspaper/Literary Magazine Spon; NCTE 1983-; GA Cncl of Teachers of Eng 1983-; Salem Baptist Church 1983-; *office:* Washington-Wilkes H S 304 Gordon St Washington GA 30673

ADKINS, DONALD TODD, French/World History Teacher; *b:* Huntington, WV; *m:* Charmarie Easton; *c:* Nathaniel E.; *ed:* (BA) Fr/Soc Stud, Marshall Univ 1983; Working Towards Masters Soc Stud, Marshall Univ; *cr:* Teacher Valley Local Schls 1983-; *ai:* Fr Club Spon; OH Foreign Lang Assn 1983-; *home:* 1024 Thornburg St Huntington WV 25701

ADKINS, ELIZABETH A., Fourth Grade Teacher; *b:* Huntington, WV; *ed:* (BA) Elem Ed, Marshall Univ 1971; *cr:* 2nd/ 3rd Grade Teacher Gallaher Elem 1971-75; 1st/3rd Grade Teacher Fellowship Chrstn Sch 1975-77; 3rd/4th Grade Teacher Timberlake Chrstn Sch 1977-82; 4th/5th Grade Teacher Lynchburg Chrstn Acad 1982-; *ai:* Elem Spon ACSi Speech Meet;

Alpha Delta Kappa Intnl Corresponding Secy 1988-; *office:* Lynchburg Chrstn Acad Sch 701 Thomas Rd Lynchburg VA 24514

ADKINS, GWENDOLYN ALICE, Assistant Principal; *b:* Rocky Mount, VA; *c:* Allyson; *ed:* (AA) His, Ferrum Coll 1970; (BS) Spec Ed/Regular Ed, East TN St Univ 1974; (MS) Learning Disabilities, Radford Univ 1983; Educl Admin; *cr:* Teacher Continuing Ed Center 1975-78, Franklin Cty Mid Sch 1978-89; Asst Prin Benjamin Franklin Mid Sch 1989-; *office:* Benjamin Franklin Mid Sch Rt 1 Box 3700 Rocky Mount VA 24151

ADKINS, PAUL MICHAEL, Social Studies Teacher; *b:* Tulsa, OK; *m:* June Melton; *c:* Jason, Brett; *ed:* (BA) Poly Sci, 1972, (MS) Ed/His, 1974 OK St Univ; *cr:* Soc Stud Teacher Central Mid HS 1974-82, Moore HS 1982-88, Westmoore HS 1988-; *ai:* Sr Class, OK Close Up, Citizens Bee Competition Spon; Chm of North Cntrl Evaluation Comm for Soc Stud; Secy of Moore Staff Dev, Chm of Teacher of Yr Comm; NCSS & OK Cncl for Soc Stud 1989-; NEA & OK Ed Assn 1974-; OK St Univ Coll of Ed Alumni Bd Dir 1989-; OK St Jaycees (Secy, Treas) 1980-85, Top 5 Young Educator 1985; OK Heritage Assn 1985-; Daughters of Amer Revolution Amer His Teacher of Yr 1981; Daughters of Colonial Wars; Amer His Teacher of Yr 1989; OK St Teacher of Yr 1988-89; Freedom Fnd at Valley Forge Natl Medal of Excl 1989; Ger Marshal Fund Fellowship 1990; Forum Co-Chm Burger King In Honor of Excl 1989; Inaugural Experience Washington DC 1989; *home:* 710 NW 16th Oklahoma City OK 73103

ADKINS, PEGGY ANN (JOHNSTON), Principal; *b:* Washington, DC; *m:* Larry Z.; *c:* Ronald, Kimberly, Hilary; *ed:* (AB) Elem Ed, 1979, (MA) Educl Admin, 1982, (MA) Mid Sch Endorsement, 1989 Marshall Univ; Early Chldhd Ed, WV Prin Acad; Leaders of Learning; *cr:* Teacher SW Cmmty Action 1976-79, Lincoln Cty Bd of Ed 1979-87; Prin Lincoln Cty Bd of Ed 1987-; *ai:* Atenville Elem PTO; Phi Delta Kappa, Lincoln Cty Ed Assn, NEA; Harts Vol Fire Dept Ladies Auxillary, SW Cmmty Action, Lincoln Cty 4-H Leaders; Lincoln Cty Prin of Yr 1988; Acad of Sch Excl 1988; Lincoln Cty Rep Project EAST; Finalist WV Outstanding Educator Merit Awd; *office:* Atenville Elem Sch Rt 2 Box 28 Harts WV 25524

ADKINS, SANDRA SIZEMORE, Spanish Teacher; *b:* Gary, IN; *m:* John; *c:* Brett, Amy; *ed:* (BS) Elem Ed, Univ WI Oshkosh 1971; Lang Acquisition Univ Whitewater; *cr:* 4th Grade Teacher Cudahy Public Schls 1971-74; Pre-Sch Dir 1981-83, Pre-Sch Teacher 1983-84 Presbyn Church; 8th Grade Span Teacher Mukwonago Area Schls/Parkview Jr HS 1985-; *ai:* Dept Chm Jr HS Foreign Lang; WI & Amer Foreign Lang Teachers; ACTFL; Phi Kappa Phi 1989; Educl Honor Society for Grad Sch; *office:* Parkview Jr H S 930 N Rochester Mukwonago WI 53149

ADKINS, TERESA SIMMONS, Teacher of Gifted & Talented; *b:* Grayson, KY; *m:* Ronnie Gale; *c:* Justin A., Ronica N.; *ed:* (BS) Bus Ed, 1980, (MS) Scndry Ed, 1984 Morehead St Univ; Endorsement Gifted Ed, Univ of KY 1989; *cr:* Homebound Teacher 1980-81, Adult Ed Teacher 1982-83, Teacher of Gifted & Talented 1983- Elliott Cty Schls; *ai:* HS Acad Coach; Coord of Gifted Prgm; Magistrate Elliott Cty Fiscal Court 1981-; *home:* RR 1 Box 1593 Sandy Hook KY 41171

ADKINS, WANDA IONA-BROWN, 5th Grade Teacher; *b:* Elizabeth City, NC; *m:* Wm. Edward; *c:* Letasha, Shakira, Wm. E. Jr.; *ed:* (BS) Intermediate Ed, Elizabeth City St Univ 1978; (MS) Admin Ed, Norfolk St Univ 1989; *cr:* Teacher Southeastern Elem, Great Bridge Intnl; *ai:* MS Read-A-Thon & 5th Grade Level Chairperson; Adopt-A-Sch Co-Chairperson; CEA, NEA Mem 1989-; Sr Ushers Antioch Baptist Church Mem; Teacher of Yr 1987-88; *home:* 916 Baron Ct Chesapeake VA 23323

ADKISSON, BONNIE RAMSEY, Academic Intern Teacher; *b:* Cincinnati, OH; *m:* David Cyrus; *c:* Kendra, Cyrus; *ed:* (BS) Elem Ed, 1975, (MA) Elem Ed, 1976 Georgetown Coll; (Rank I) Ed, W KY Univ 1980; *cr:* Mid Sch Teacher 1976-87, HS Teacher 1987-, Summer Sch Prin 1988 Daviess Cty Schls; *ai:* NEA, KY Ed Assn, Daviess Cty Ed Assn 1976-; Habitat for Hum (Comm Chairperson 1988-, Fundraising Chairperson 1990); Owensboro Womens Coalition 1990; Mini Grant Writing Project; Grant St Dept of Ed; Charter Mem Commonwealth Inst for Teachers.

ADLER, FRANCES M., COE Coord/Business Dept Chair; *b:* Long Branch, NJ; *ed:* (BS) Bus Ed, Monmouth Coll 1966; COE Teacher Coord; *cr:* Teacher/Teacher Coord Matawan Regional HS 1966-; *ai:* FBLA Adv; NJSIAA Track & Field Ofcl; NJCOECA Recording Secy 1988-; NJBEA 1970-; Juvenile Conference Comm Secy 1974-; *office:* Matawan Regional HS Atlantic Ave Amberdeen NJ 07747

ADLER, RANDEE HARTZ, Teacher of Gifted and Talented; *b:* New York, NY; *ed:* (BS) Elem Ed/Early Chldhd Ed, Skidmore Coll 1973; (MS) Educl Comm, St Univ NY 1976; Critical Thinking Trng Prgm NYSUT/AFT; Cert Adjunct Grad Professor Long Island Univ; Several Wkshps; *cr:* 5th Grade Teacher 1973-80, Specialist Teacher of Gifted & Talented 1980- Niskayuna Cntrl Schls; Part-Time Educl/Critical Thinking/Teaching for Thinking/Consultant Niskayuna Cntrl Schls Inservice Prgm 1986-; *ai:* Newsletter, Inservice, Gifted & Talented Selection Building Comm; NY St Assn for Advocates for Gifted & Talented 1980-; ASCD 1987-; Critical Thinking Network 1986-; World Wildlife; Capital Dist Ski Cncl Secy 1990; Upper Hudson Planned Parenthood; Teacher-Scholar Recognition Awd NY St 1989; Co-Author of Curr Niskayunas Elem Gifted & Talented Prgm 1979-; *office:* Niskayuna Cntrl Schls Craig Sch 2566 Balltown Rd Schenectady NY 12309

ADNEY, CAROLYN ROSE, History Teacher; *b:* East Liverpool, OH; *ed:* (BS) Scndry Ed/His, Youngstown St Univ 1982; *cr:* His Teacher East Liverpool Chrstn Sch 1983-; *ai:* Vlybl Asst Coach; Spirit Coord; Guidance Comm; United Brethren in Christ Church 1982-; *home:* 860 Grandview Ave East Liverpool OH 43920

ADONIZIO, ROBERT JOSEPH, 6th Grade Science Teacher; *b:* Pittston, PA; *c:* Allison, Bobby; *ed:* (BS) Elem Ed/Sci/Spec Ed MR, Mansfield 1969; Alfred Univ NY, Penn St; *cr:* Teacher Port Jervis Mid Sch 1969-72, Pittston Area Sch Dist 1972-; *ai:* Mid Sch Adv Ski & Sci Club; Started Wrestling Prgm & Head Coach Pittston Area Sr HS; Luzerne Cty Sci Teachers Assn; Loyal Order of Moose; *office:* Martin L Mattei Mid Sch New St Pittston PA 18640

AELVDET, DENISE SPADAFORE, Biology Teacher; *b:* Doylestown, PA; *m:* Paul; *c:* Rene, Erin; *ed:* (BA) Bio, Incarnate Word Coll 1983; Grad Courses Bio; Cert to Teach Bio & Chem; *cr:* Earth Sci McDowell Mid Sch 1983-84; Life Sci Teacher Devine Mid Sch 1984-86; Bio/Environmental Sci Teacher Hondo HS 1986-; *ai:* Stu Cncl Spon; Dentention Hall Supvr; STAT 1985-; TX Women for Ag (VP 1985-86, Mem) 1983-86; Jr Service League 1986-87; *office:* Hondo H S PO Box 308 Hondo TX 78861

AEPPEL, ROSWITHA MARIA, German Teacher; *b:* Landsberg/Lech, W Germany; *m:* Detlev C.; *ed:* (BA) Ger/Eng, 1976, (MA) Ger Ed, 1984, (PhD) Prgm Ger Lit, Univ of FL 1990; Trainer for Programmed Learning Systems; TEACH, PRIDE, Teaching through Learning Channels; Russias Method of Foreign Lang Teaching; *cr:* Asst Ger Teacher Univ of S FL 1980-81; Ger Instr Gulf HS 1981-, Eng Instr Gulf HS Adult Ed 1985-87; Adjunct Coll Ed Teacher Univ of S FL 1987-; Adjunct Hum Teacher Paseo-Hernando Comm Coll 1989-; *ai:* Ger-Amer Partnership Prgm, Delta Epsilon Phi, Philosophy Club Spon; Literary Magazine Co-Spon; AATG 1981-; Phi Kappa Phi 1980-; Amer Cncl Teachers of Foreign Lang 1989-; Granted Sabbatical Leave from Pasco Cty to Pursue PhD in Ger Lit 1990; Poetry Published; Core Comm Mem for Dev Initial Cert Exam for FL for Ger; *office:* Gulf HS 5355 School Rd New Port Richey FL 34652

AERTS, RITA J., Fifth Grade Teacher; *b:* Green Bay, WI; *c:* Andrea L., Carrie L.; *ed:* (BA) Elem Ed, St Norbert Coll 1964; Courses at Univ of WI Whitewater, Univ of WI Green Bay; *cr:* 5th Grade Teacher Champaign IL 1965-66, 6th Grade Teacher Whitewater Public Schls 1966-68, Appleton Public SchLs 1968-69; 5th Grade Teacher Notre Dame 1976-; *home:* 1605 Ridgeway Blvd De Pere WI 54115

AGEE, CHRISTINE KATHRYN, Business Education Teacher; *b:* Grangeville, ID; *ed:* (BS) Bus Ed, 1975, (MS) Bus Ed, 1988 Univ of ID; *cr:* Bus Teacher Grangeville HS 1975-; *ai:* Grangeville HS NHS, Class of 1992, YMCA Youth Government, Jr Statesman Adv; Delta Kappa Gamma Pres 1990; Cntrl ID Ed Assn 1976-; Grangeville Art Assn 1989-; Idaho Cty Cattlewomen Assn 1975-; Cmmty Concert Assn 1980-; *office:* Grangeville HS PO Box 299 910 South D Grangeville ID 83530

AGENLIAN, MURAD, Teacher; *b:* Chicago, IL; *m:* Rose Bova; *c:* Leticia De Maio, Michele, Angela, Natalie; *ed:* (AA) Liberal Art, N Park Coll 1952; (BA) Lewis Coll 1954; Certificate of Ed, Chicago Teachers Coll 1957; John Marshall Law Sch; *cr:* Teacher Carpenter Elem Sch 1960-72; Truant Dept Attorney Chicago Bd of Ed 1972-78; *ai:* Chicago Bd of Ed Human Relations Dept Law Sch Lecturer; *office:* Hibbard Elem Sch 3244 W Ainslie Chicago IL 60625

AGNEW, PATRICIA ANDREGG, Fifth Grade Teacher; *b:* Hoxie, KS; *m:* David T.; *c:* Jennifer, Elizabeth; *ed:* (BA) Elem Ed, Wichita St Univ 1980; Grad Stud Fort Hays St Univ 1966-70; Grad Sch Wichita St Univ; *cr:* 5th Grade Teacher West Elem 1981-; *ai:* 4th/5th Grade Curr Cncl Coord; KNEA, NEA, VCNEA, ASCD; *office:* West Elem Sch 501 N West St Valley Center KS 67147

AGOSTINO, JOSEPH PATRICK, Religion Teacher/Coord; *b:* Brooklyn, NY; *ed:* (BS) Comm Stud, 1981, (MA) Deafness Ed, 1982 NY Univ; Moral Theology, St Johns Univ; *cr:* 9th Grade HR Contained Classroom Teacher Edward R Murrow HS 1982-83; 7th/8th Grade Religion Sch St Mary by the Sea 1983-85; Teacher/Coord/Moderator Monsignor Farrell HS 1985-; *ai:* Retreat Team Founder, Coord, Moderator; SADD & DARE Moderator; Frosh Bsktbl & Bsbl Dev Co-Dir; Brooklyn Liaison Person; Cncl for Ed of Deaf, Natl Assn for Deaf 1982-; NCEA 1985-; Mid Sts Evaluation Process Sch & Cmmty Chairperson; Article Published; *office:* Monsignor Farrell HS 2900 Amboy Rd Staten Island NY 10306

AGUILAR, LEE, Spanish Teacher; *b:* La Garita, CO; *m:* Isabel Valdez; *c:* Catherine Waugh, Christopher; *ed:* (BA) Span, 1959, (MA) Span, 1965 Adams St Coll; Numerous Univs; *cr:* Teacher/Coach Capulia HS 1957-59; Teacher Powell HS 1959-; *ai:* Class of 1990 & Span Club Spon; Sch Dist Credit Union Credit Comm Chm; WY Foreign Lang Teachers Assn Pres 1985-87, Career Service Awd 1988; Powell Ed Assn Treas 1967-69; WEA, NEA Mem 1959-; NOWCAP Asst Cnslr 1962-65; Powell Police Dept Interpreter 1960-85; Powell Bd of Adjustments Mem 1965-85; Runner Up WY Teacher of Yr 1989; Fullbright Schlsp to Spain 1966; Powell HS FTA Teacher of Yr 1969; Powell Valley Chamber of Commerce Teacher of Yr 1982-83; NEA Journal Contributor 1984; Univ of WY Kappa Delta Pi Teachers Teacher of Yr 1980; *office:* Powell HS 2nd & Evarts Powell WY 82435

AGUILERA, LEOPOLD BENJAMIN, HS English Teacher; *b:* San Jose, CA; *m:* Virginia Olson; *c:* Adam; *ed:* (BA) Eng, Stanislaus St Univ 1975; Addl Studies Ed, Creative Writing; *cr:* US Postal Clerk US Post Office-Turlock Ca 1971-76; Eng Teacher Thomas Downey HS 1976-; *ai:* Club Adv Cinematic Fine Arts Club; Faculty Senate-Sec; Phi Delta Kappa 1977-; Modesto Teachers Assn Sch Site Rep 1976-; NEA 1976-; Lion Club Stu Speech Contest Coord 1988-; United Pentecostal Church Mem 1972-; Scenic Designer Modesto Performing Arts Assn 1982-86 & Townsend Opera Players 1987; Music Dir for Church 1980-89; Church Newsletter Editor 1989-; Church Drama Dir 1974-; *office:* Thomas Downey H S 1000 Coffee Rd Modesto CA 95355

AHBE, DOTTIE REBOKAS, Fifth Grade Teacher; *b:* Chicago, IL; *m:* Richard; *ed:* (BS) Ed, IL St Univ 1967; Grad Stud; *cr:* K/3rd-5th Grade Teacher Berkeley Sch Dist 1967-; *ai:* Sch Dist Fire Safety Coord; St of IL Co-Coord of St Fire Safety Prgm; Staff Dev, Achievement Testing, Promotion & Retention Dist Comms; Berkeley Ed Assn Pres 1970-72; IL Ed Assn, NEA 1967-; Riley Sch PTA Pres 1984-86, Life Mem 1978; Intnl Assn of Fire Educators Regional Dir 1988-; Natl Fire Protection Assn Ed Section Exec Bd 1985-; MTI Coronet Films Peak Performer Awd 1987; IL Fire Inspectors Fire Prevention Achievement Awd 1987; Articles in Instr & Life Magazines; Authored & Published Fire Safety Activity Books; *home:* 430 Cardinal Ave Addison IL 60101

AHERN, JUDITH M., Senior Counselor; *b:* Mc Keesport, PA; *ed:* (BS) Fr, Indiana Univ of PA 1967; (BS) Eng, 1974, (MS) Guidance/Counseling, 1974 Duquesne Univ; Cmptrs Ben Franklin Grant, Carnegie Mellon Univ; Penn St Cert; Drug/Alcohol Cnslr St Francis Hospital; *cr:* Fr Teacher Homeville Jr Hs 1967-72; Fr/Eng Teacher North HS 1972-82; Cnslr South HS 1982, North HS 1983-, Comm Coll Area HS Allegheny Cty Summers; *ai:* Faculty Cncl NHS; Bus Advisory & HS Steering Comm; Mid States Evaluation Negotiating Team; Mon Yough Ed Consortium Liason; AFT (Dist Negotiating Team 1989-, Building Rep 1989); Duquesne Univ Alumni Assn 1974-; IUP Alumni Assn 1967-; Allegheny Cty Cnslrs Assn 1974-; PA Assn of Sch Cnslrs 1982-; Ben Franklin Grant Cmptr Study; Dist Mentor Teacher.

AHERN, ROGER J., Science Teacher; *b:* Staten Island, NY; *ed:* (BBA) Marketing, Pace Coll 1969; (MA) Psychosocial Study of Human Movement, Teachers Coll Columbia Univ 1984; Doctoral Stu in Motor Learning, T C Columbia Univ; *cr:* 7th-8th Grade Sci Teacher Our Lady of Mt Carmel, St Benedicta Sch 1969-70, Sacred Heart Sch 1970-81; 6th-12th Grade Sci Teacher Staten Island Acad 1981-; *ai:* Sia Citizenship Panel Chm; Building, Grounds & Academic Planning Comm Mem; Head Coach Girls Var Bsktbl & Sftbl; Chess Club & Young Astronauts Moderator; Kappa Delta Phi Honor Society 1983-; Natl Coaches Assn, Century Club 1985-; Staten Island Sci Teachers Assn 1981-; Natl Assn Neurolinguistic Programming 1984-; Sacred Heart Youth; Acts Cncl 1970-81, Man of Yr 1975; Fellowship TC Wkshp in Cmptr Enhanced Instruction Scndry Sch Sci & Math; Amer Fed of Teachers Citation for Service; *office:* Staten Island Acad 715 Todt Hill Rd Staten Island NY 10304

AHLBERG, GRANT W., Social Studies Dept Chair; *b:* Chicago, IL; *m:* Gloria Mengarelli; *c:* Gary, Gregory; *ed:* (BA) His, De Pauw Univ 1962; (MA) His, IN Univ 1964; Working Towards PhD Amer Univ 1968-71; *cr:* Teacher Elk Grove HS 1963-68; Instr Amer Univ 1968-71; Teacher Rolling Meadows HS 1971-89; Dept Chm John Hersey HS 1989-; *ai:* Boys & Girls Tennis Coach; Talented & Gifted Coord; NCSS 1968-; IL Cncl Soc Stud 1980-; ASCD 1987-; Dist 214 Ed Assn Pres; Albert J Beveridge Fellowship IN Univ; *office:* John Hersey HS 1900 E Thomas Arlington Heights IL 60004

AHLBORN, PATRICIA LEE (HORN), Mathematics Department Head; *b:* Norristown, PA; *m:* Thomas John; *c:* Karen, Janet, James; *ed:* (BSED) Math, West Chester Univ 1969; (MS) Math, Univ of DE 1972; *cr:* Instr West Chester Univ 1971; Adjunct Professor Univ of DE 1988-; Math Dept Head Wilmington Chrstn Sch 1977-; *ai:* NHS Adv; Dept Heads Comm Chairperson; Math Team Coach; Academic Awds Banquet Coord; Academic Advisory Comm Mem; NCTM 1977-; DE Cncl Teachers of Math 1977-; Math Assn of America 1988-; Evangelical Presbyn Church 1988-; New Covenant Fellowship 1978-88; Natl Sci Fnd Fellowship Univ of DE 1985; DE Presidential Awds for Excl Prgm; St Awd Math 1987-89; Webber Awd for Contributions Math Ed Univ of DE 1989; Teaching Fellow Univ DE Summer Coll 1988-; DE Math Advisory Comm Mem; Co Author of Article Published; Wilmington Chrstn Sch Yrbk Dedication 1986; *office:* Wilmington Christian Sch P O Box 626 Hockessin DE 19707

AHLBRAND, DONNA JEAN, 8th Grade Lang Art Teacher; *b:* Jasper, IN; *c:* Jason, Brad; *ed:* (BS) Elem Ed, 1969; (MS) Elem Ed, 1974 IN St Univ; Eng; *cr:* Teacher Greater Island Paradise Sch 1973-74; Jasper Schls 1975-; *ai:* Academic Coach; Jasper Ftbl Boosters Secy 1989-; Teacher of Yr Awd 1980,88,89; Teacher VUJC Comm Coll Camp 101 for Credit; *office:* Jasper Mid Sch 340 W 6th St Jasper IN 47546

AHLM, DONIVER RAY, 6th Grade Teacher; *b:* Stillwater, MN; *m:* Jean Bernadette Barrett; *c:* Cory, Dana, Molly; *ed:* (BS) Elem Ed, St Cloud St Coll 1972; (MS) Curr/Instruction, St Thomas Univ 1979; Trng in Cmptrs; *cr:* 6th Grade Self Contained Room Teacher N Branch Elem Sch 1972-75; 6th-8th Grade Math/Eng/Art/Music/Soc Stud/Cmptr Literacy Teacher N Branch Mid Sch 1975-; *ai:* 7th-8th Grade Wrestling, Boys & Girls Golf Coach; Staff Dev Comm; Teacher Cert Rep Mid Sch; 6th Grade Team Mem; NEA, MEA 1972-; N Branch Ed Assn Treas 1973-74; Employee of Month N Branch Sch 1987; *office:* North Branch Mid Sch 320 Main North Branch MN 55056

AHNE, JOHN PAUL, English Teacher; *b:* Milwaukee, WI; *c:* Andrea; *ed:* (BA) Eng, Univ of Dallas 1983; *cr:* Mid Sch Teacher St Bernard of Clairvaux Sch 1983-86; Eng Teacher Sunset HS 1986-; *ai:* Project Discovery Theater Experience Spon; Faculty Adv Comm Mem Sunset HS; Fulbright Awd to United Kingdom 1989-; *office:* Sunset H S 2120 W Jefferson Blvd Dallas TX 75208

AHRENS, GERARD JOSEPH, Junior High School Teacher; *b:* Cincinnati, OH; *m:* Lynn Thompson; *c:* John, Andrew, Charlotte; *ed:* (BA) Classics, 1971, (BS) Ed, 1971 Univ of Cincinnati; (JD) Law, N KY Univ 1977; *cr:* Jr HS Teacher Nativity Sch 1972-; *ai:* Stu Cncl Moderator; Dir Canned Food Collection for Poor; Field Day Coord; Religion & Foreign Lang Dept Chm; NCEA 1980-; Phi Beta Kappa 1971 OH Bar Mem 1977-; Bd of Ed 1987-; Parish Cncl 1990; Prison Ministry 1990; Latin Schlsp Horace Prize 1970; Legal Schlsp Torts Awd 1978; Educl Leadership Awd 1987; Natl Exemplary Sch Awd Washington DC 1988; *office:* Nativity Sch 5936 Ridge Ave Cincinnati OH 45213

AIKEN, SANDRA WALLIS, Chairman Science Department; *b:* Gadsden, AL; *m:* Charles H.; *c:* Jennifer, Michael; *ed:* (BS) Bio, Memphis St Univ 1964; (MS) Botany, Univ TN Knoxville 1966; *cr:* Teacher Treadwell HS 1965-67, Truett Mc Connell Jr Coll 1967-73, White Cty HS 1975-; *ai:* Page; *office:* White County H S Old Blairsville Hwy Cleveland GA 30528

AILLAUD, CINDY LOU VIRGINIA (PETETT), 4th/5th Grade Teacher; *b:* Renton, WA; *m:* Whitney Lane; *c:* Jason, Brian; *ed:* (BA) Elem Ed, WA St Univ 1977; Spec Ed Endorsement Cntrl WA Univ 1989; *cr:* 6th Grade Teacher N Auburn Elem 1977-78; K-5th Grade Teacher Arctic Village Sch 1978-79; 5th/6th Grade Teacher Delta Jct Elem 1979-82; 4th/5th Grade Teacher Ft Greely Elem 1989-; *ai:* Enrichment Planning, Teacher of Yr Selection Comm; Delta/Greely Ed Assn 1979-; CEC 1988-; Election Bd Clerk 1983-89; Clearwater Homemakers 1979-; Delta/Greely Arts Cncl Secy 1981-83; Newspaper Photos & Articles Published; *office:* Ft Greely Elem Sch PO Box 647 Delta Junction AK 99737

AIRD, DEBRA WALLS, Social Studies Teacher; *b:* Terre Haute, IN; *m:* Michael G.; *c:* Amanda, Michael G. Jr., Amy L.; *ed:* Soc Sci Ed, 1976, (MS) Soc Sci Ed, 1979 IN St Univ; *cr:* Soc Stud Teacher Terre Haute North HS 1976-; *ai:* Craft Club Spon; After Sch Teachers Exercise Class Teacher; *office:* Terre Haute North HS 3434 Maple Ave Terre Haute IN 47804

AIRHEART, DEBRA REED, English/Spanish/Drama Teacher; *b:* Terrell, TX; *m:* Terry Lee; *c:* Laura D.; *ed:* (BA) Eng/His, 1978, (MA) Eng, 1982 E TX St Univ; Working Towards PhD E TX St Univ; *cr:* Teacher Kemp Ind Sch Dist 1978-80; Asst Instr E TX St Univ 1980-83; Instr Navarro Coll 1984-; Teacher Wortham Ind Sch Dist 1983-; *ai:* Drama & Span Club; One Act Play Dir; Textbook & Gifted & Talented Planning Comm; UIL Literary Coach; NCTE 1976-; TJCTE 1983-; Article Published; *office:* Wortham HS PO Box 247 Wortham TX 76693

AKERS, DENNIS LEE, Dean of Students; *b:* Terre Haute, IN; *m:* Jeanell L.; *c:* Jarod B.; *ed:* (BS) Phys Ed, IN St Univ 1976; (MS) Educl Admin, S IL Univ Edwardsville 1988; Specialists Prgm; *cr:* Teacher/Coach 1979-86, Dean of Stu 1987- Jennings HS; *office:* Jennings Sr HS 8850 Cozens Ave Jennings MO 63136

AKERS, DIXIE GREENE, Music Teacher; *b:* Lexington, KY; *m:* Dennis R.; *c:* Ryan W.; *ed:* (BA) Music, Univ of KY 1969; (BM) Music Ed, Ball St Univ 1975; *cr:* Strings Teacher Woodford Cty 1969-70; Music Teacher Dillsboro Public Sch 1970-77, Jones Jr HS 1978-; *ai:* Asst HS Band Dir; Private Studio Voice/Flute/Piano; Amer Heart Fund Volunteer 1988-; Asst Choir Dir 1st Baptist Church 1978-88; MENC-KMEA Pres 1987-88; NEA/KEA/BCEA 1979-; Sigma Alpha Iota VP 1968-70 Sword of Honor 1970; Church Choir 1974-; Mid Sch Teacher of Yr 1987 & 1989; *home:* 21 Marys Ct Florence KY 41042

AKEY, CRAIG A., English Instructor; *b:* Madison, WI; *m:* Kathleen Radtke; *c:* Torin M., Rian P.; *ed:* (MA) Eng, N AZ Univ 1972; Grad Stud Univ of WI Stevens Point, Univ of WI Oshkosh, Univ of MN, Webster Coll; *cr:* Eng Instr Blue Ridge HS 1968-70, Clintonville HS 1970-; *ai:* Frosh Bsktbl Coach; Honors Rdng Colloquium Dir; Stu Cncl Past Adv; Forensics Past Dir; WI Cncl Teachers of Eng 1970-, Pooley Fnd Awd 1986; NCTE 1986-; CWWP Bd of Dir Chm 1986-; Clintonville Dance Club Pres 1984-, Youth League Pres 1980-84; United Way Pres 1979-83; Lib Bd Pres 1974-; Cntrl WI Writing Project Fellowship; Natl Endowment for Hum Fellowship; 1st Recipient Hillshire Teacher of Yr Awd; Articles Published WI Eng Journal & Others.

AKEY, KENNETH DEE, Sixth Grade Teacher; *b:* Auburn, IN; *m:* Vonda Lynn Myers; *c:* Neah, Kraig; *ed:* (BS) Elem Ed, 1974, (MS) Elem Ed/Phys Ed, 1978 St Francis Coll; Working on Cert Admin/Elem Prin, 1990; *cr:* 2nd-6th Grade Teacher Lima Elem Sch 1974-85; 6th Grade Teacher Lakeland Jr HS 1985-86, Lima Brighton 1986-; *ai:* Lakeland HS Cross Cntry Coach; Lakeland Ed Assn VP 1989-; NEA, ISTA 1974-; Howe Volunteer Firemen (Secy 1986-) 1978; Howe Meth Church Trustee 1988-; Lakeland Sch Corporation Teacher Awd 1990; *home:* 106 Union St Howe IN 46746

AKIN, SUE GARBER, Third Grade Teacher; *b:* Boonville, MO; *m:* Larry; *c:* Suzanne, Landon; *ed:* (BSED) Elem Ed/Bio, Cntrl Meth Coll 1971; *cr:* 4th Grade Teacher 1971-85, 6th Grade Teacher 1985-88, 3rd Grade Teacher 1988- Morgan Cty RII Schls; *ai:* Teacher Action Comm; Yearly Sci Fair Judge; MO St Teachers Assn 1971-; Certified Teachers Assn (Treas 1975-76) 1971-; 4-H Project Leader 1986-; Meth Church (Sunday Sch Teacher 1989-, Youth Choir Dir 1970-); BSA Leader 1989-; Beta Sigma Phi (Pres 1985-86, Secy 1980), Girl of Yr 1985; Nom Sch Dist Teacher of Yr 1986; Nom Presidential Awds Excl in Sci & Math Teaching 1990; *office:* Morgan Cty RII Sch 309 S Monroe Versailles MO 65084

AKINS, CHRISTINE WARRINER, Life Science Teacher; *b:* Chester, PA; *m:* J. Paul Linnan; *c:* Elizabeth A., D. Adam; *ed:* (BS) Scndry Ed/Bio, Clarion Univ 1975; Sci/Cmptr Ed, Clarion Univ; Microbiology, Penn St; Cmmty of Scholars Prgm Univ of Pittsburgh; *cr:* Life Sci Teacher Freeport Jr HS 1982-; *ai:* Sci Club Spon; Sci Olympiad Team Coach; Discipline & Self-Esteem Comm; *home:* RD 2 Box 150 Brookville PA 15825

AKINS, GARY WADE, 7th/8th Grade Teacher; *b:* Williamsburg, KY; *m:* Janie Lou Mc Donald; *c:* Rebecca, Sarah; *ed:* (BS) Recreation/Park Admin, 1979, (BS) Phys Ed, 1980, (MAED) Ed, 1981 E KY Univ; *cr:* Teacher/Coach Burgin Ind Sch Dist 1982-86, Williamsburg Ind Sch Dist 1986-88, Burgin Ind Sch Dist 1982-86; *ai:* Boys Var Bsktbl & Bsbl Head Coach; Girls Jr HS Bsktbl Coach; KY Ed Assn, KY HS Athletic Assn; Burgin Ed Assn VP 1988-; *office:* Burgin Ind Schls Main St Burgin KY 40310

AKINS, STEPHEN MICHAEL, Pre-Algebra/Math Teacher; *b:* Athens, TN; *m:* Sandra Juanita Amburn; *c:* Chadwick, Kelley; *ed:* (AS) Elem Ed, Cleveland St Coll 1970; (BS) Elem Ed, 1972, (MS) Math, 1978 Univ of TN; St Tech Inst; *cr:* Elem Math Teacher E K Baker Elem Sch 1972-85, Algebra Teacher Mc Minn Cty HS 1985-; *ai:* Interact Club Spon; Head Frosh Ftbl Coach; Asst Var Ftbl Coach; TN Ed Assn, Mc Minn Cty Ed Assn, TN Athletic Coaches Assn Mem 1990; Nominee Presidential Awd of Excl in Teaching Math & Sci 1983-85; *office:* Mc Minn County HS Congree Pkwy Athens TN 37303

AKINS, VAL L., Science Teacher; *b:* Los Angeles, CA; *m:* Linda; *ed:* (BS) Geography, Univ of MN Duluth 1964; (MS) Environmental Sci, Univ of Dominguez Hills 1977; *cr:* Teacher Los Angeles Unified Schls 1964-75; Instr Saddleback Comm Coll 1978-84; Teacher Capistrano Unified 1976-; *ai:* CA Teachers Assn 1964-; Capistrano Unified Ed Assn 1976-; Orange Cty Astronomers 1976-; Articles & Pictures in Astronomy Magazine; *office:* Newhart Jr HS 25001 Oso Viejo Mission Viejo CA 92692

AKLONIS, RAYMOND JOHN, History Teacher; *b:* Elizabeth, NJ; *ed:* (BA) His, Upsala Coll 1971; (MA) His, Seton Hall Univ 1978; Amer Stud, Ball St Univ; His, NY Univ; Grad Ed, Seton Hall Univ; *cr:* World His Teacher Grover Cleveland Jr HS 1971-74; US His Teacher Thomas Jefferson HS 1974-77; US His/Mod Eur His Elizabeth HS 1977-; *ai:* NHS Adv; ASCD 1990; Elizabeth Ed Assn Edward Kappy Awd Outstanding Educl Leadership 1983; *office:* Elizabeth H S 600 Pearl St Elizabeth NJ 07202

AKRIDGE, JACQUELINE LOUIS WILSON, English/Journalism Teacher; *b:* Campbellsville, KY; *m:* Paul Edwin; *c:* Mariah M.; *ed:* (BA) Eng, Campbellsville Coll 1977; (MA) Eng, W KY Univ 1988; Grad Hours in Counseling; *cr:* Asst Dir of Admissions Campbellsville Coll 1977-82; Grad Asst/Eng Teacher W KY Univ 1982-83; Eng/Journalism Teacher Taylor Cty Schls 1985-; *ai:* Newspaper & Yrbk Adv; Class Night Slide Show Coord; Taylor Cty Ed Assn, KY Ed Assn, NEA 1985-; KY Journalism Advs Cncl 1988-; United Meth Women (Missions Chm 1988-89) 1985-; United Meth Youth Fellowship Leader 1979-; Bus and Prof Womens Club Young Careerist 1978-79; *office:* Taylor Cty HS Ingram Ave Campbellsville KY 42718

AKUCEWICH, PAULA BERT, Health Occupations Instructor; *b:* Providence, RI; *m:* Edward S. Jr.; *c:* Edward S., Guy D., Lisa H.; *ed:* RN Registered Nurse, RI Hospital Sch of Nursing 1958; (BS) Health & Soc Serv, Roger Williams Coll 1976; (MED) Spec Ed, RI Coll 1987; Red Cross CPR & First Aid Instr; *cr:* Registered Nurse RI Hospital 1962-74, Women & Infants Hospital 1974-76; Teacher Woonsocket Area Voc Tech Facility 1976-; *ai:* VICA Opening & Closing Ceremonies Team Coach; RI Health Assn; *office:* Woonsocket Area Voc Tech 400 Aylsworth Ave Woonsocket RI 02895

AKUNE, JANE ELIZABETH, English Teacher; *b:* Inglewood, CA; *m:* Jerry K.; *c:* Todd, Darren; *ed:* (BA) Soc Sci/Eng, Univ of CA Santa Barbara 1981; Working Towards MA Scndry Ed & Rdng, CA St Univ Northridge 1990; *cr:* Eng Teacher Hueneme HS 1985-; *ai:* Soph Class Adv; Peer Helper; Stu Achievement & Prof Staff Dev Comm; NCTE 1986-; AAUW 1985-; *office:* Hueneme HS 500 Bard Rd Oxnard CA 93030

ALAHA, NANCY SIFFORD, Fourth Grade Teacher; *b:* Lubbock, TX; *m:* Donald H.; *c:* Kelly, John; *ed:* (BS) Elem Ed, E NM Univ 1976; *cr:* 6th-8th Grade Math Teacher Farwell Jr HS 1976-77; 4th Grade Teacher Farwell Elem Sch 1977-79, Granbury Intermediate 1979-82, Acton Elem Sch 1982-; *ai:* Spelling Bee & UIL Number Sense Spon; Faculty Advisory Cncl; ATPE Secy 1980-81.

ALAKZAY, MARGARET KERN, Fifth Grade Teacher; *b:* Akron, OH; *m:* Joseph J.; *c:* Joann, James; *ed:* (BSE) Elem Ed, Univ of Akron 1953; Grad Stud; *cr:* 5th/6th Grade Teacher Akron Public Schls 1952-56; 3rd/6th Grade Teacher Covina Unified Sch Dist 1958-66; 4th/6th Grade Teacher Pomona Unified Sch Dist 1966-72; 5th Grade Teacher Lakeport Unified Sch Dist 1972-; *ai:* CA Teachers Assn (St Cncl, Spec Ed Coordinating Comm) 1986-, WHO 1989; Lake City Coordinating Cncl Chairperson 1986-; Lakeport Teachers Assn Pres 1986-; Delta Kappa Gamma Rural Caucus Secy 1988-; Amer Assn Univ Women (Pres, Comm Chairperson); Lib Advisory Bd Chairperson 1978-85; Lake Cty Democratic Cntrl Comm Secy 1988-; Founder Friends of Lib Lake Cty; *home:* 1030 Boggs Ln Lakeport CA 95453

ALANIZ, ADELINA BAZAN, Mathematics Department Chair; *b:* Mission, TX; *m:* Manuel Jr.; *c:* Gerardo M., Selina A.; *ed:* (BS) Math, 1969, (MED) Scndry Ed, 1984 Pan Amer Univ; St Conference for Advancement of Math Teaching; UIL Stu Act Conference Number Sense; Gifted/Talented Wkshps Region 1 Ed Service Center; TX Assn of Gifted/Talented Annual Conference; *cr:* Teacher Aide/Tutor La Joya Ind Sch Dist/Pan Amer Univ 1967, 1967-69; Math Teacher Blissfield Migrant Sch & Wild Rose Migrant Sch 1973-82; Math Teacher/Dept Chairperson Mission Jr HS 1969-70, 1987, Kenneth White Jr HS 1988-; *ai:* UIL Number Sense, Mathcounts Coach; Math Club Adv; Rio Grande Cncl Teachers of Math, TX Cncl Teachers of Math 1970-; NCTM 1978-, Presider 1986; Assn of TX Prof Educators 1980-, Teacher of Yr Finalist 1990; TX Math & Sci Coaches Assn 1985-; St John Fields Cath Church 1982-; Teacher of Yr Mission Jr HS 1986; Kenneth White Jr HS Teacher of Month 1988-89, Teacher of Yr 1989; *home:* PO Box 741 Mission TX 78572

ALANIZ, NORMA LINDA, Fifth Grade Teacher; *b:* Kingsville, TX; *m:* Emiliano Jr.; *c:* Emiliano III, Adrian D., Andres J.; *ed:* (BA) Elem Ed, TX A&I Univ 1978; (MS) Rdng Specialist, Corpus Christi St Univ 1988; *cr:* 5th Grade Teacher Dave Odem Elem 1979-; *ai:* ATPE 1979-; Taft Womens Club 1989-; Career Ladder; *office:* Dave Odem Elem Sch 800 E Sinton St Sinton TX 78387

ALARID, ELAINE HERRERA, Spanish Teacher/Dept Chair; *b:* Albuquerque, NM; *m:* Nicholas M.; *c:* Jason, Ryan; *ed:* (BA) Span/Tesol/Eng, Univ of NM 1972; Spanish Lit, Universidad De Guadalajara; *cr:* Eng/Tesol Teacher W Mesa HS 1972-74; Eng/Span Teacher Cibola HS 1974-76; Span/Dept Chairperson Del Notre HS 1976-; *ai:* NHS Span Spon; Ballet Folklorico De Del Norte Spon; Amer Assn of Teachers & Portugese Mem 1983-; Ballet Folklorico De Nuevo Mexico Mem 1990; Teacher of Yr Cibola HS 1976; Teacher of Yr Del Norte HS 1980; Best All Around Teacher Del Norte HS 1990; *office:* Del Norte HS 5323 Montgomery Blvd NE Albuquerque NM 87109

ALBANESE, BETH KULLMAN, Social Studies Teacher; *b:* Zanesville, OH; *m:* Paul Joseph; *ed:* (BS) Soc Stud, OH St Univ 1986; *cr:* Teacher New Lexington HS 1987-; *ai:* Var Vlybl & Sftbl Coach; His Day Adv; OCSS 1988-; *office:* New Lexington HS 2549 Panther Dr New Lexington OH 43764

ALBANESE, LINDA BORELLA, Spanish Teacher; *b:* Jersey City, NJ; *m:* Donald R.; *c:* Michael V., Mark D.; *ed:* (BA) Span/Eng, Montclair St Coll 1964; Lit, Montclair St Coll; *cr:* Span/Eng Teacher 1964-70, Basic Skills Instr 1979-86 Belleville Jr HS; Span Teacher Belleville HS 1986-; *ai:* Curr Comm; Amer Fencing Assn 1964-; Grant St of NJ Summer Course Scndry Span Teachers 1989 Rider Coll; Ofcl Assessor SRA in Span St of NJ; *home:* 56 Renner Ave Bloomfield NJ 07003

ALBAUGH, PAULINE HOWARD, Second Grade Teacher; *b:* Shelley, ID; *m:* Ronald C.; *c:* Melissa, Michael; *ed:* Assoc Ed, Ricks Coll 1975; (BS) Early Chldhd Ed, Brigham Young Univ 1978; Project Wild, Stress Management for Teachers, Sci of Teaching, Writing Road to Rdng; *cr:* Kndgtn Teacher 1978-85, 2nd Grade Teacher 1985- Parker-Egin Elem; *ai:* Head Teacher Park-Egin Elem; ID Ed Assn 1978-; Fremont Ed Assn Building Rep 1979-83; Rotary Club Teacher of Month 1989.

ALBERT, CHARLES L., Science Teacher; *b:* Fernandine Bch, FL; *m:* Ernie Tyson; *c:* Reginald, Cheryl, Rashad; *ed:* (BS) Sci, FL A&M Univ 1959; Coll of St Teresa, Tuskegee Inst, Wake Forest Univ; *cr:* Sci Teacher Peck HS 1960-69, Fernandina Mid Sch 1969-; *ai:* Little League Bsbl & Pop Warner Ftbl Coach; FTP, NEA (Teacher 1960-, Pres 1976-80); NAACP 1985; BSA Leader 1960-62; Serve as Mayor City of Fernandina Beach & Presently City Cnclman; *home:* 612 S 11th St Fernandina Bch FL 32034

ALBERT, CHARLES WILLIAM, Teacher; *b:* Jamaica, NY; *m:* Barbara Gural; *c:* Jason, Nicholas, Nadine; *ed:* (BA) Sci/Phys Ed, Wilmington Coll 1964; (MA) Educl Admin, C W Post Coll 1974; Food Mgrs Course, 1983, Camp Dir Course, 1988 Suffolk Cty Health Dept; Elem Ed, Adelphi Coll 1965; *cr:* Chem Teacher Clinton Massie HS 1963-64; 5th Grade Teacher Gatelot Avenue Sch 1964-66; 3rd-5th Grade Teacher Tremont Avenue Sch 1966-73; 1st-6th Grade Math Specialist Patchogue-Medford Sch Dist 1974-75; Asst Prin Barton Avenue Sch 1975-78; 6th Grade Teacher Oregon Avenue Mid Sch 1978-; Camp Dir Episcopal Diocese of Long Island 1984-; *ai:* Bsbl, Soccer, Gymnastics, Math Olympics Coach; Honor Society; Play Productions; Class Adv; Home Teaching; NY St Teachers Assn 1966-; Lions Club St Dist Service Chm 1970-78, Long Island Service 1978; St Pauls Episcopal Church Vestry 1968-75; Christ Episcopal Church (Vestry, Lay Reader) 1975-; Camp De Wolfe Dir 1984-; *office:* Oregon Avenue Mid Sch S Ocean Ave Patchogue NY 11772

ALBERT, ELIZABETH E., Biology Teacher; *b:* Philadelphia, PA; *ed:* (BS) Bio, Ursinus Coll 1959; (MS) Bio, Colby Coll 1970; *cr:* Sci Teacher Pottstown HS 1959-; *ai:* Ecology Club Adv; Montgomery Cty Sci Teacher Assn; Green Valleys Assn; Boyertown Area Historical Society Dir 1990; Historical Society of Cocalico Valley Dir 1989-; Adams Cty Historical Society, Goschen Hoppen Historians; Natl Sci Fnd Grants 1964-65, 1967-69; *office:* Pottstown Sr HS N Washington St Pottstown PA 19464

ALBERT, JACK CONSTANTINE, Biology Teacher; *b:* Cleveland, OH; *m:* Cheryl Lynn Fitz; *c:* Georgia, Anathea, Mary, Jack, Lynn; *ed:* (BS) Zoology, Univ of MI 1969; (MEd) Ed, Univ of Windsor 1989; *cr:* Substitute Teacher Detroit Bd of Ed 1983-84; Sci Teacher Cass Tech 1984-; *ai:* Sci Fair; Detroit Fed of Teachers; *office:* Cass Tech HS 2421 Second Detroit MI 48201

ALBERT, PAMELA JO, 5th Grade Teacher; *b:* Cheyenne, WY; *ed:* (BA) Elem Ed, Univ of Mary 1976; Various Courses Minot St, Dickenson St, Black Hills St, Northern St, SD St, Univ of ND, ND St; *cr:* 3rd-4th Grade Teacher Lehr Public 1976-79; 4th Grade Teacher 1987-88, 5th Grade Teacher 1979- Hettinger Public; *ai:* Bookkeeper Girls & Boys HS Bsktbl, Girls Vlybl; Make-Up Supvr Jr/Sr HS Plays; Chaperon Jr HS Dances; Religion Teacher 1981-85; Substitute 1986-89; Shade Tree Players of Bismarck 1974-76; Asst Dir 1980-85, 1988-; Bus & Prof Women 1985-; NEA, NDEA, HEA, LEA 1976-77; ND Ed Assn; Hettinger Ed Assn (Secy 1983-84, Negotiator 1981-82); Lehr Ed Assn Negotiator 1977-78; GSA (Leader, Consultant) 1987-88; St Annes Secy 1984; Holy Trinity General Alter Society VP Elect 1990; Holy Trinity Cath Church Youth Ministry; Hettinger Booster Club Secy 1981-83; Participant in Study of Growing Up Amer St Scholastica Duluth Grant; Outstanding Cath HS Stu 1972; Outstanding Young Women of America 1980; Jr/Sr Prom Banquet Speaker Lehr HS 1987, Hettinger HS 1990; Univ of Mary Roast of Athletic Dir Speaker 1989; *office:* Hettinger Public Sch Box 1188 Hettinger ND 58639

ALBERTSON, KENNETH A., Sci Teacher/Math Dept Chair; *b:* Fort Dodge, IA; *m:* Ella Jean Shable; *c:* Kevin N., David K.; *ed:* (BA) Math, Union Coll 1966; (MA) Physics, Univ of Northern CO 1975; Classes Taken Various Univ & Colls; *cr:* Math/Eng Teacher Cedarvale Sch 1966-69; Math/Physics Teacher Sunnydale Acad 1969-73; Math/Physics/Cmptr Teacher Tunderbird Adventist Acad 1973-; *ai:* Sr Class Adv; Academic Standards Comm; Chairperson Supervision Team; Scndry Teacher Rep AZ SDA K-12 Educl Bd; Comm Mem Pacific Union Comm Dev & Curr for Talented & Gifted Stus; PA & Sound for Sch; NCTM Mem 1971-; Amer Assn of Physics Teachers Mem; AZ Assn of Teachers of Math Mem 1973-; Orpheus Male Chorus of Phoenix (VP, Secy, Librarian) 1974-; Ambassadors Quartet Mem 1982-; Thunderbird 7th Day Adv Church 1st Elder 1978-89; Research Grant AZ St Univ 1989; AZ Acad, Thunderbird Acad Alumni Awd for Appreciation 1983; Thomas & Violet Zapara Excl in Teacher 1989; *office:* Thunderbird Adventist Acad 7410 E Sutton Dr Scottsdale AZ 85260

ALBRACHT, ROBERT D., Jr High Social Studies Teacher; *b:* Carlinville, IL; *m:* Judith M. Selvo; *c:* Renee M., Kelley A.; *ed:* (BA) Sociology, Blackburn Coll 1971; *cr:* 6th Grade Teacher 1971-86, 7th Grade Soc Stud Teacher 1986- Hillsboro Jr HS; *ai:* Track Coach 1971-88 & 1990; Boys Bsktbl Coach 1975-76 & 1982-86; Girls Bsktbl Coach 1987-; Hillsboro Unit Ed Assn (Pres 1977-78) 1971-; Charter Mem Hillsboro Sertoma Club (Pres 1979-80 & 1987-88) 1973-; Knights of Columbus 1975-; Chm City of Hillsboro Campgrounds Renovation Comm 1986; Hillsboro City Cncl 1987-; *home:* 623 Eccles St Hillsboro IL 62049

ALBRECHT, VERNON L., 7th Grade English Teacher; *b:* Carsonville, MI; *ed:* (BS) Speech/Drama, Cntrl MI Univ 1962; Eng, MI St Univ 1967; *cr:* HS Speech/Soc Stud Teacher Lapeer HS 1962-64; Eng/Drama Teacher St Clair Mid Sch 1964-; *ai:* Benevolent & Protective Order of Elks Exalted Ruler 1976-77, 1980-81; *office:* St Clair Mid Sch 301 N 6th St Saint Clair MI 48079

ALBRIGHT, PATRICK D., Publications Advisor; *b:* Bend, OR; *m:* Ginny Brown; *c:* Margaret; *ed:* (BA) Ed, OR St Univ 1970; Lang Art, E OR St Coll 1978; *cr:* Reporter/Photographer E Oregonian 1971-75; Teacher/Adv S Eugene HS 1975-77, Springfield HS 1977-; *ai:* Newspaper Adv; OJEA; *office:* Springfield HS 875 N 7th St Springfield OR 97477

ALBRIGHT, SYRIE LANCE, 3rd Grade Teacher; *b:* Chico, CA; *m:* Dennis; *c:* Aubin C., Mallory; *ed:* (BA) Eng, CA St Univ Chico 1974; Elem Teacher; *cr:* 2nd-7th Grade Teacher Queensland Dept of Ed 1975-77; 1st Grade Teacher 1977-79, Kndgtn Teacher 1979-80, 3rd Grade Teacher 1980-87 Jackson Heights Elem; 3rd Grade Teacher Metteer Elem 1987-; *ai:* Dist Lang Arts Comm; Tehama Cty Lang Arts Consortium; Tehama Cty Rdng Cncl Treas 1988-; *office:* Metteer Elem Sch 695 Kimball Rd Red Bluff CA 96080

ALCAZAR-CHAVEZ, GLORIA M., 9-12 ESL Reading Teacher; *b:* Denver, CO; *m:* Roberto Partida Chavez; *ed:* (BA) Single Subject Soc Sci, CA St Northridge 1975; Eng as 2nd Lang, CA St Northridge 1975; Advanced Trng in Rdng Improvement; Foster Parent for Emotionally Disturbed Children; Trng in High Risk Students; *cr:* Teacher/Core Brownell Jr HS 1975-79; Teacher/Adv Dist Migrant Ed 1975-; High Risk Teacher 1982, 1986, ESL Rdng Teacher 1980- Andrew Hill HS; *ai:* Migrant Ed Support Teacher Adv; Adv Mesa Math, Engineering, Sci Achievement; Dept Chairperson for ESL Dept; CA Fed of Teachers Mem 1975-; Math, Engineering, Sci Achievement Volunteer 1980-, Appreciation; ESL/Migrant Ed Wrote Prgm 1980-, Appreciation; Dept Chairperson for Eng as 2nd Lang; Outstanding Young Women of America 1986; ESL Curr for East Side Unified Sch Dist; Public Service Awd Mesa; Project Prep & Migrant Ed; Outstanding Staff Mem; Teacher of Yr; *office:* Andrew Hill HS 3200 Senter Rd San Jose CA 95117

ALCE, MARGARET ROSE, Teacher; *b:* Dubuque, IA; *m:* John R.; *c:* Andrew, Mark (dec); *ed:* (BA) Math, Clarke Coll 1963; (MA) Intnl Relations, Univ of S CA 1981; Cmptr Sci, IA St Univ 1983-84; *cr:* Data Clerk Ray Chemical Corporation 1965-67; Programmer Standford Research Inst 1967-69; Teacher Lakenheath Mid Sch 1969-83, Woodbridge HS 1984-; *ai:* Cmptr Coord; NCA Steering Comm; Phi Delta Kappa 1990; Liturgy Comm (Scheduler 1988-, Lector Trainer 1986-88); Sabbatical of Yr IA St Univ 1983-84; *home:* Box 988 APO New York NY 09405

ALCONCHER, CAROLINE BERNADES, Third Grade Teacher; *b:* Cebu City, Philippines; *m:* Rodolfo Flores; *c:* Rudy B., Carol A., Cheryl A., Abigail, Ronald; *ed:* (BS) Elem Ed - Magna Cum Laude, 1958, (MA) Elem Ed, 1959 Philippine Normal Coll; (MA) Elem Ed, Fresno St 1967; Philippine Folk Dances; *cr:* Teacher Holy Ghost Coll 1957, Stratford Sch 1966-; *ai:* Literacy Prgm Volunteer; Philippine Folk Dance Troupe Directress; Sunday Sch Dir; Club Adv; CTA, NEA Mem 1966-; Lang Art Comm 1989-; Curr Comm 1988-89; Filipino Amer Directress 1969-80; Assn of Kings Cty Secy 1968-70; Assn Univ Women Mem 1966-70; Univ Women Grant 1958; Philippine Normal Coll Schlsp 1956-58; *office:* Stratford Sch 19348 Empire St Stratford CA 93266

ALCORN, JOAN T., Elementary Challenge Teacher; *b:* Denver, CO; *ed:* (BA) Eng/Journalism, Marymount Coll 1959; (MA) Elem Ed, Univ of Denver 1965; (MED) Soc Sci Ed, Univ of WA 1968; Numerous Hrs in Soc Sci, Gifteed & Talented, General Elem Ed; *cr:* 1st Grade Teacher Sabin Elem Sch 1961-67; 4th-6th Grade Soc Stud Teacher 1968-88, 3rd-5th Grade Challenge/Resource Teacher 1988- Traylor Elem Sch; *ai:* Stu Newspaper Spon; General Act Coord; NEA, CO Ed Assn, Denver Classroom Teachers Assn; NCSS Exec Bd 1972-74, CO Cncl for Soc Stud Exec Bd 1975; Delta Kappa Gamma World Fellowship Chairperson 1990; NDEA Grant Univ of WA, Soc Sci Ed 1967-68; Denver Distinguished Teacher Awd 1982; Rotary Club Ec Ed Awd 1979-80; Adopt-A-Sch Outstanding Sch Coord 1986-87; Outstanding Young Women of America 1970; Merit Teacher for Natl Cncl Geographic Ed 1973; Notable Amer 1976; Academic Freedom Comm of Natl Cncl for Soc Stud Chm 1977; Served as Evaluator for Natl Cncl for the Acrreditation of Teacher Ed 1975-; *office:* Traylor Elem Sch 2900 S Ivan Way Denver CO 80227

ALDEN, DENNIS J., Teacher; *b:* Freeport, IL; *m:* Linda Brandon; *c:* Julie, Tom, John; *ed:* (AB) Ed, Greenville Coll 1968; *cr:* Teacher Chadwick Schls 1968-83, Grace Cmmty Sch 1983-; *home:* 1528 Crockett Tyler TX 75701

ALDEN, DONNA SCHERRER, Third Grade Teacher; *b:* St Louis, MO; *c:* Carrie, Jonathan; *ed:* (BS) Elem Ed, Southeast MO St Univ 1968; (MA) Educl Processes, Maryville Coll 1987; *cr:* 3rd Grade Teacher Hancock Place Elem 1969-; *ai:* Hancock Place Cmmty Teachers Assn Pres Membership Awd; Eden United Church of Christ Secy 1988-; Youth Fellowship Spon 1985-89; Gamma Sigma Sigma VP 1965-68 Service Awd 1967; *office:* Hancock Place Elem Sch 9101 S Broadway Saint Louis MO 63125

ALDER, VIRGINIA BARGER, 7th Grade English Teacher; *b:* South Pittsburg, TN; *w:* Edgar B. (dec); *c:* Sandra A. Johnson; *ed:* (BS) Elem Ed, Univ of Chattanooga 1953; Elem Ed, 1959-62; *cr:* 4th/5th/6th Grade Teacher Jasper Elem 1946-55; 8th Grade Sci/Health/9th Grade Civics/7th Grade Eng Teacher Maron Cty HS 1955-79; 7th Grade Eng Teacher Jasper Mid Sch 1979-; *ai:* JMS Spelling Bee Chairperson; Marion Cty Ed Assn (Pres 1960-63 VP 1963-64); Delta Kappa Gamma Society (VP 1975-77 Secy 1972-74); NEA 1963; TN Ed Assn; Legislature Delg 1961-62; VFW Aux Pres 1956-58; Cumberland Presbyn Church Womens Sunday Sch Teacher; Honorary Mem TN House of Rep 1980; Honorary Mem TN General Assembly in Recog of Outstanding Service to the St 1981; *home:* 505 Phillips Ave P O Box 246 Jasper TN 37347

ALDERSON, CYRLA JAN, Science Dept Chair; *b:* Kansas City, MO; *m:* Lyle Master; *c:* Aaron, Mary; *ed:* (BS) Bio/Phys Sci, Cntrl St Univ 1969; (MA) Bio, Univ of MO 1974; Numerous Courses & Wkshps at Various Univs; *cr:* Sci Teacher Pittmans Hills Jr HS 1969-81, Raytown S HS 1981-; *ai:* Booster Club, Sci Olympiad Fun Organizer; Sci Club, Pittman Hills Sci & Outing Club, Sch Sci Honor Society Spon; Raytown Classroom Teachers Assn Corresponding Secy 1974; Greater Kansas City Sci Teachers Assn (Mem, VP) 1981-89; BSA Explorer Post of Yr 1984-85, Adv of Yr; Amer Assn of Univ Women (Raytown Branch Pres, St Politics of Food Chairperson, St VP) 1970-81; Cave Springs Assn Prgm Organizer & Presenter 1976-78; Organized Group Line Creek Archeological Museum & Indian Cultural Center 1974-75; Burroughs Audubon Society Conservation Comm Mem 1986-88; Organizer for Lakeside Nature Center (Adv, Coord, Volunteer) 1973; Outstanding Young Educator 1974, Sci Teacher Awd, MO Acad of Sci 1975, Conservation Educator, Conservation Fed of MO 1978; MO Sci Educator Awd, Sci Teachers of MO 1979; Spec Recognition Greater Kansas City Sci Teachers Assn for Initiating & Co-Chairing Sci Knowledge Bowl 1985; St Awardee Presidential Awd Excl in Sci & Math Teaching 1986-88; Public Service Awd, Natl Weather Service 1987; Scientific Research Society Awd 1987; *home:* 1511 S 19th Blue Springs MO 64015

ALDERSON, NIKI ADCOCK, English/Speech Teacher; *b:* Tulsa, OK; *m:* Bob; *c:* Kyle; *ed:* (BA) Speech/Eng, 1981, (MA) Comm, 1985 Northeastern St; *cr:* Teacher KEOTA HS 1982-; *ai:* HS Speech & Drama Team; Academic Team; Yrbk, Sr HS Chrldrs; Haskell Cty Teachers Secy 1982; Eastern Star Assoc Conductress 1989-; New Century United Meth Church Childrens Dir 1990; Articles Published; Outstanding Speech & Drama Stu in Coll; Outstanding Young Woman of America.

ALDOUS, R. GARY, Mathematics Teacher; *b:* Salmon, ID; *m:* Shawna Sager; *c:* Becky, Rochelle, Dustin; *ed:* (BA) Scndry Ed/Math/Phys Ed, 1974, (MPE) 1983 ID St Univ; *cr:* Math Teacher/Coach Salmon HS 1974-77, William Thomas Mid Sch 1977-80 Amer Falls HS 1980-; *ai:* Asst Track; Math Curr Comm; AFEA, IEA, NEA Pres 1974-; NCTM 1990; Amer Falls Ed Assn Pres; Amer Falls HS Teacher of Yr 1980; *home:* 1624 Hillcrest American Falls ID 83211

ALDRIDGE, LAUREN HAM, 7th Grade Teacher; *b:* Franklin, LA; *m:* Craig; *ed:* (BS) Elem Ed, LA St Univ 1977; *cr:* 5th Grade Teacher River Oaks Elem 1978; 4th Grade Teacher Howell Park Elem 1978-81; 7th/8th Grade Teacher Edgar Martin & Milton Elem 1981-82; 8th Grade Teacher Lee Road & Mandeville Jr HS 1982-85; 7th/8th Grade Teacher San Jacinto Jr HS 1985-; *ai:* Chrldr Spon; Jr League of Midland Incorporated; Spec Childrens League; *office:* San Jacinto Jr HS 1400 North N Street Midland TX 79701

ALDRIDGE, LAWRENCE YEWELL, 6th Grade Teacher; *b:* Eudora, MS; *m:* Vernice Ulesta; *c:* Stephen J., Lawrence Y. Jr., Anthony B., Kevin S.; *ed:* (BS) Health/Phys Ed, Jackson St Univ 1959; (MSED) Supervision/Curr, Miami Univ Oxford 1970; Grad Stud Miami Univ Oxford; *cr:* Teacher 1964-68, Asst Prin 1968-72 Taft Elem; Prin Harrison Elem 1972-77; Dir Hamilton Alternative Sch 1977-78; Teacher Mc Kinley & Jefferson & Monroe 1978-; *ai:* ASA HS Umpire; NAACP Exec Comm; PTO (Pres, Mem) 1975; Omega Mem 1957-; Middletown Teacher Assn Building Rep 1986-; Giant Step Incorporated Pres 1978-79; Cncl of Churches Pres 1975-76; Administrative Group Pres 1977-78; BSA Adv; Bethel AME Church (Steward, Cnslr); City of Middletown Outstanding Citizen 1988; Democratic Party Comm Chm 1989; Detroit Schlsp 1955-56; Academic Schlsp 1957-58.

ALDRIGE, ALICE JORDAN, Third Grade Teacher; *b:* St Louis, MO; *ed:* (BA) Sociology/Soc Welfare, 1972, (MS) Ed, 1975 S IL Univ Edwardsville; Rdng Cert S IL Univ Edwardsville 1985; Inservice Trng 1983, 1988, 1989; *cr:* 1st Grade Teacher 1972-78, 2nd Grade Teacher 1978-80, 3rd Grade Teacher 1980- John Robinson Sch; *ai:* Spell Down Building Spon; Staff Inservice Enrichment Prgms Chairperson Lewis & Clark Rdng Cncl Mem 1988-89; Parent-Teachers Cncl Mem 1975-; Alpha Kappa Alpha Recording Secy 1971-, Soror of Yr 1989-; Amer Bus Womens Assn Educl Chairperson 1986-; Amer Cancer Society (Building Chairperson, Dist Public Ed Chairperson) 1983-; United Negro Coll Fund (Building Chairperson, Volunteer Comm) 1988-; Univ of MO St Louis Black Leadership Forum 1988-89; Friendship Missionary Baptist Church UNCF Chairperson 1987; Gemm-Gateway East Metropolitan Ministry Cultural Art & Media Centre 1990; Revise African Amer Stud 1989; Help Develop Dist Developmental Learning Objectives.

ALESKIEWICZ, ISABELLE TWOMEY, Second Grade Teacher; *b:* Norwich, CT; *m:* Matthew; *c:* Michael; *ed:* (BS) Early Ed, Eastern CT St Coll 1973; Eastern CT St Coll; *cr:* 2nd Grade Teacher 1973-74, 1st Grade Teacher 1974-75 Wequonnoc Sch; 2nd Grade Teacher John Moriarty Sch 1975-; *office:* John M. Moriarty Sch 20 Lawler Ln. Norwich CT 06360

ALESSANDRI, THOMAS PAUL, English/Theatre Arts Teacher; *m:* Judith Bury; *c:* Katie, Maren; *ed:* (BA) Eng/Hum, Univ of San Francisco 1973; (MA) Eng, Univ of WA 1975; *cr:* Eng Teacher Bellarmine Coll Preparatory 1975-; *ai:* Theatre Arts Dir; Olmsted Teaching Prize Williams Coll 1984; San Jose St Univ Eng Teaching Prize; *office:* Bellarmine Coll Preparatory 850 Elm St San Jose CA 95126

ALEXANDAR, LINDA FIORITI, Third Grade Teacher; *b:* Jacksonville, NC; *m:* Thomas Edwin; *ed:* (AA) Pre-Elem Ed, Coastal Carolina Comm Coll 1975; (BA) Early Chldhd Ed, Univ of NC Wilmington 1977; Cmptr Competency Basic Skills Level 1; Effective Teacher Trng Course; *cr:* 3rd Grade Teacher 1977-, Conceptually Oriented Math Prgm Contact Person 1982- Morton Elem Sch; *ai:* Conceptually Oriented Math Prgm; Math Comm For SACS Self Study Chairperson; NEA 1977-85; Intnl Rdng Assn 1977-; NC Cncl Of Teachers Of Math 1985-; Jacksonville Womens Civitan Club 1977-80; Served On SACS Comm To Re-Accredit Camp Lejeune Schls 1982; PTO VP 1979; Morton Sch Teacher Of Yr 1982; PTO Historian 1978; Morton Outstanding Young Educator Nominee Onslow Cty 1982; Nom 1987 For NC Awds Prgm for Outstanding Teacher of Math; Whos Who Among Stus in Amer Jr Colls 1974-75; *office:* Morton Elem Sch Rt 2 Jacksonville NC 28540

ALEXANDER, ALICE FAYE, First Grade Teacher; *b:* Asheville, NC; *ed:* (BA) Psych, King Coll 1962; Summer Schls East TN St, Western Carolina; Extension Courses Univ of VA; *cr:* 2nd Grade Teacher Centreville Elem 1962-65; 1st Grade Teacher Collins Elem 1965-66, Bedford Elem 1966-70, Meadowview Elem 1970-; *ai:* VA Ed Assn, Washington Cty Ed Assn, Southwest VA Cncl Teachers of Math, Southwest VA Cncl Intnl Rdng Assn; Honarary Life Mem VA Congress of Parents & Teachers; Mentor Teacher Prgm Emory & Henry Coll; *home:* 122B Oxford St Abingdon VA 24210

ALEXANDER, ANN LORRAINE ROMANCHEK, First Grade Teacher; *b:* Chicago, IL; *m:* Paul; *c:* Patrick, Sharon; *ed:* (BS) Biological Sci/Psych, Northwestern Univ 1953; Philosophy/Ethics, Loyola Univ; Ed, Northeastern Univ; *cr:* Research Asst IL Neuro Psychiatric Inst 1953-57; Kndgtn Teacher Mozart Sch 1969; 1st Grade Teacher Hay Cmmty Acad 1970-; *ai:* Gold Apple Awd.

ALEXANDER, BERNICE C., Second Grade Teacher; *b:* Victoria, TX; *m:* Walter P.; *c:* Patricia, Deborha, Sandra; *ed:* (BS) Elem Ed, TX A&I 1970; *cr:* 3rd Grade Teacher Cresent 1964-65; 2nd Grade Teacher Hutchins Elem 1965-; *ai:* TSTA, NEA, Mid-Coast Rdng; *home:* PO Box 1054 El Campo TX 77437

ALEXANDER, CAROLYN MC CLARY, Business Department Chair; *b:* Oklahoma City, OK; *m:* John; *c:* John M.; *ed:* (BS) Bus Ed, Cntrl St Univ OK 1968; (MED) Occupational Ed, Univ of Houston 1979; *cr:* Bus Teacher Harding Jr HS 1968-72, J Frank Dobie HS 1972-73; Bus Dept Chairperson Alief Hastings HS 1975-84, Langham Creek HS 1984-; *ai:* FBLA Co-Spon; Delta Pi Epsilon, Pi Omega Pi; *office:* Langham Creek HS 17610 F M 529 Houston TX 77095

ALEXANDER, CYBELE JOYETTE, English Teacher; *b:* St Thomas, VI; *ed:* (BS) Ed Bus/Eng/Earth Sci, Baylor Univ 1987; (MA) Liberal Arts, Houston Baptist Univ; NJ Writing Inst; *cr:* Eng Teacher Dulles HS 1987-; *ai:* Jr Var Chrldr Spon; Teams Preparation Tutor; Dulles HS Teacher of Yr Nominee 1989-; *office:* Dulles HS 500 Dulles Ave Sugar Land TX 77487

ALEXANDER, DIMITRY NICHOLAS, Professor; *b:* New York, NY; *c:* Keith, Tamara; *ed:* (AB) Broadcasting, 1954, (JD) Law, 1974 Univ of Miami; *cr:* Faculty Miami-Dade Comm Coll 1967-; *ai:* FL Bar 1974-; DC Bar 1976-; Producer-Dir Numerous Media Productions; Emmy, Columbus Film Festival, Clio, NY Art Dirs Awds; *office:* Miami-Dade Comm Coll 11380 NW 27th Ave Miami FL 33167

ALEXANDER, FRANCES BIZZELL, Second Grade Teacher; *b:* Kinston, NC; *m:* William Douglas; *c:* William D. Jr.; *ed:* (BS) Primary Ed, E Carolina Univ 1951; *cr:* Teacher Tarboro City Schls 1952-59, 1968-; *ai:* NEA 1968-; NC Ed Assn 1990; *home:* 2610 Beechwood Dr Tarboro NC 27886

ALEXANDER, GARY F., 6th Grade Teacher; *b:* Dayton, OH; *m:* Patricia A. Mitchell; *c:* Bryan S.; *ed:* (BS) Elem Ed, Miami Univ 1975; (MS) Educl Admin, Univ of Dayton 1980; Univ of Dayton; *cr:* Teacher Harold Schnell 1975-; Substitute Prin West Carrollton Elem Schls 1989-; *ai:* Safety Patrol Adv; Spelling Bee Co-Coord; Grade Card Dist & Curr Comm; Math Redesign & Textbook Selection; Phi Delta Kappa Mem 1986-; West Carrollton Ed Assn VP 1984, 1986; OH Ed Assn, NEA Mem; Wee Wildcats Bd Mem 1990; Dayton Public Ed Fund for OR Trail Project & Wkshps Grant; West Carrollton Significant Teacher Awd; *office:* Harold Schnell Sch 5995 Sutdent St West Carrollton OH 45449

ALEXANDER, GENE DENNIS, 5th Grade Teacher; *b:* Albany, NY; *m:* Janet Farrell; *ed:* (BS) Elem Ed, 1967, (MS) Elem Ed, Edinboro St; *cr:* Teacher Wright Sch 1967-; *office:* Wright Sch 426 Wright St Corry PA 16407

ALEXANDER, LINDA BIERBOWER, Jr/Sr High English Teacher; *b:* Brownsville, PA; *m:* Charles E.; *c:* Jennifer; *ed:* (BS) Ed, OH Univ 1971; Spec Ed Classes, OH Univ; Project Pride; *cr:* Eng Teacher Piketon HS 1971-73, Huntington HS 1978-; *ai:* Spelling Coach; OH Ed Assn, NEA, Huntington Local Ed Assn; Ross Cty Historical Society Stus Awarded Many Honors for Writing Abilities; Ross Cty Litter Control Prgm Ross Cty Historical Socieyt; OCTELA Writing Awds; Coached Ross Cty Spelling Bee Winners; *office:* Huntington HS 188 Huntsmen Rd Chillicothe OH 45601

ALEXANDER, LUCRETIA ANN, Guidance Counselor; *b:* Booneville, MS; *m:* Jack Bevan; *c:* Karla, Clement, Van; *ed:* (BS) Bus Ed, 1967, (MS) Counseling, 1987 MS St Univ; *cr:* Bus Teacher Vina HS 1968-71; Sci Teacher Tishomingo Elem 1971-73; Librarian 1974-77, Bus Teacher 1977-87, Guidance Cnslr 1987-Belmont HS; *ai:* Yrbk & FBLA Spon; MS Counseling Assn 1986; NE Counseling Assn 1987, Cnslr of Yr 1989; Amer Assn of Counseling & Dev 1988-; *office:* Belmont HS PO Box 250 Belmont MS 38827

ALEXANDER, MARY RANDOLPH, History Teacher; *b:* Brandon, MS; *m:* Tom Sr.; *c:* Tom Jr.; *ed:* (BS) Soc Sci, Jackson St Univ 1970; Working Towards MA; *cr:* Collection Teller Deposit Guaranty Bank 1970-75; *ai:* Jr HS Stu Cncl; Soc Sci Dept Chairwoman 1982-89; In-Service; Soc Stud MS Prof; Annual Staff Dedication 1990; *home:* 140 Mandy Dr Brandon MS 39042

ALEXANDER, MELISSA JUSTIN, 4th-6th Grade Teacher; *b:* Washington, DC; *m:* Samuel Thompson; *c:* Eric M., Ian J., Irene S.; *ed:* (BA) His, Univ of CA Berkeley 1965; (MA) Curr Instruction, Univ of WI Madison 1968; *cr:* Teacher Selma Avenue Sch 1968-71, Los Alamos Schls 1973-80, Chamisa 1980-; *ai:* Sci Fair, Speech Contest, Geography Bee Adv; *office:* Chamisa Elem Sch 301 Meadow Ln Los Alamos NM 87544

ALEXANDER, REBECCA LEA (HOLT), 2nd Grade Teacher; *b:* Springfield, MO; *m:* Craig E.; *c:* Christy L. Alexander Bosserman; *ed:* (BS) Elem Ed, 1972, (MS) Elem Ed, 1981 SW MO St; *cr:* Kndgtn Teacher 1972-77, 5th Grade Teacher 1983-84, 2nd Grade Teacher 1977- Logan Rogersville Schls; *ai:* Logan-Rogersville Cmmty Teachers Assn (Pres 1990, VP 1989-); Logan-Rogersville Athletic Boosters; *home:* Rt 1 Box 357 Rogersville MO 65742

ALEXANDER, RICHARD CLAYTON, Phys Ed Teacher/Coach; *b:* St. Louis, MO; *m:* Mercedes Mitchell; *c:* Bruce R.; *ed:* (BSE) Phys Ed 1973, (MSE) Scndry Admin 1979 AR St Univ; PET,Univ of AR; *cr:* Phys Ed/Coach, Forrest City Jr H S 1973-78; Phys ED/Coach, Ridge Rd Jr H S 1978-89; Phys Ed/Coach, Ole Main H S 1989-; *ai:* Head Bsktbl Coach, Ole Main H S; Forrest City Clsrm Teachers 1973-78; AR Ed Assoc 1973-81; Natl Ed Assoc 1973-81;Alpha Phi Alpha Frat,Dean Pldgs 1979-; AR St Univ Alumni Assoc, VP 1984; PTA 1973-; AR Assoc Hlth,Phys Ed,Rcrtn & Dance; AR HS Coaches Assoc; AR Assoc Prof Educrs; AR Adv Cncl Scndry Ed 1977-80; AR Game & Fish Comm,Hunter Safty Instr 1978; E AR Comm Coll,Summer Tennis Instr 1977-78; Phys Ed Head, Intrml Dir 1978-89, Ridgeroad Jr HS; Vacation Bible Sch Chm, Mens Day Chm, Bible Sch Rcrtn Dir, Celestial Choir Mem, Deacon Board, Van &Trans Ministry Dir, Eighth St Baptist Church; Booster Clb Fund Raising Comm, Phys Ed & Athl Inservice Comm, Interim Board Fclts Study Comm-Tri Dist Cnsldtn, Elem Field Day Adv, N Little Rock Sch Dist; US Lawn Tennis Assoc, Sch Prgm Part; Athl Schlsp Bsktbl, MVP 1969-70, MO Baptist Coll; Athl Schlsp Bsktbl, Kappa Delta Phi, AR St Univ; Teacher Yr Nom 1984, Super Teacher Mth 1987, N Little Rock Sch Dist; AR HS Coaches Assoc Clinic Lectr 1985; Greater Little Rock Chmbr Commrce"Excl Ed" Awrd Nom 1984; AR Assoc Hlth Phys Ed Rcrtn & Dance "Teacher Yr" 1987; Nom "Outstanding Young Men Amer" 1989; *office:* Ole Main H S 22nd & Main ST North Little Rock AR 72114

ALEXANDER, RUSHIA HALL, Teacher; *b:* Dawson, GA; *m:* Landon; *c:* Willyoung M., Michael, Christopher, Joses, Landon; *ed:* (BS) Elem Ed, 1972, (MS) Elem Ed, 1973 Ft Valley St Coll; GA Southwestern Coll Americus; *cr:* Teacher East Laurens Primary; Title I Teacher Lillie Cooper Sch; Teacher Richland Elem Sch; *ai:* Literary Coord; GA His Day Coord; GAE; Grant; *office:* Richland Elem Sch PO Box 399 Richland GA 31825

ALEXANDER, SANDRA (BINGHAM), 4th Grade Teacher; *b:* Longview, TX; *m:* James David; *c:* Millicent L., David G.; *ed:* (BA) Elem Ed, Baylor Univ 1963; Teaching Methods & Information; *cr:* 3rd Grade Teacher Houston Ind Sch Dist 1963-64, Dickinson Ind Sch Dist 1964-66, Clear Creek Ind Sch Dist 1966-68; 4th Grade Teacher Clear Creek Ind Sch Dist 1976-; *ai:* Grade-Level Chairperson; Schedule Planning Comm; NEA, TX St Teachers Assn; Natl Cancer Society Share Group Adv 1988-; Masters Vessels Gospel Quartet Pianist 1982-; *home:* 1907 Rampart St League City TX 77573

ALEXANDER, SHELBY L., Biology Teacher/Science Dept; *b:* Canton, MS; *m:* Gail Gwinette Griswold; *c:* Alicia, William, Rebecca; *ed:* (BA) Bio/His, 1979, (MAT) Bio, 1981 W NM Univ; NSF Summer Inst Univ of NM; Cmptrs in Sci 1986; *cr:* Grad Asst/W NM Univ 1980-81; Sci Teacher Chinle Jr HS 1981-82; Sci Teacher Alamo Navajo Cmmty Sch 1982-84; Bio Teacher Grants HS 1985-; *ai:* NABT 1985-; Conducted NM Jr Acad of Sci Paper Competition at Regional Level 1990; Spon Stu to St Jr Acad of Sci Paper Competitiion, Stu in Sci Fair at Local St Intnl Level;Served on Teacher Review Comm For NASA Pilot Prgm in Space Physiology; Prgm for America 1989-; Field Tested in NM 1990; Regional Jr Sci & Hum Symposium Paper Competition Univ of NM Spon Stus; *office:* Grants High Sch PO Box 8 Grants NM 87020

ALEXANDER, SONNIA MOSCOLIC, Chemistry/Mathematics Teacher; *b:* Butte, MT; *m:* Marty; *c:* Martilyn, Michael; *ed:* (BS) Chem, MT Coll of Mineral Sci & Technology 1979; (BA) Math, Univ of MT 1980; *cr:* Math Teacher Cntrl Jr HS 1980-83; Math/Sci Teacher Butte HS 1984-87; Chem/Math Teacher Anaconda HS 1988-; *ai:* Sr Class Spon; Camp Fire Treas 1985-, 15 Yr Pin 1989; *home:* 2125 Phillips Ave Butte MT 59701

ALEXANDER, STEPHEN PAUL, Math Teacher/Math Dept Supvr; *b:* Philadelphia, PA; *m:* Sally Kay Eppelheimer; *c:* Benjamin P., Scott R.; *ed:* (BA) Math, Wittenberg Univ 1973; (MED) Scndry Ed, Xavier Univ 1976; Grad Stud; *cr:* 7th Grade Sci Teacher 1973-80, 7th Grade Sci/7th-8th Grade Math Teacher 1980-84, 7th-8th Grade Math 1984- Sycamore Jr HS; *ai:* Sycamore HS Jr Var Golf Coach & Sycamore Jr HS Golf Instr 1974-; *office:* Sycamore Jr HS 5757 Cooper Rd Cincinnati OH 45242

ALEXANDER, SUSAN HORTON, Choral Dir/Music Dept Chair; *b:* Rapid City, SD; *c:* Katey, Wade; *ed:* (BS) Music Ed, Radford Coll 1971; George Mason Univ, Univ of VA, Grove City Coll; *cr:* Music Teacher Kilmer Intermediate Sch 1971-74; Choral Dir Woodson HS 1975-76; Music Teacher Dogwood Elem Sch, Herndon ELem Sch, Centreville Elem Sch, Terra-Centre Elem Sch 1976-83; Choral Dir Fairfax HS 1983-; *ai:* Musical; Tri-M Music Honor Society; Amer Choral Dirs Assn 1983-; Music Educators Natl Conference 1975-; VA Music Educators Dist Chairperson 1987-89; Fairfax Cty Choral Dirs VP 1989-; Fairfax Choral Society, MADD; Fairfax Cty Curr Dev for Gifted & Talented 1985; Summer Enrichment 1986; Inst for Art Music Dept Chair 1989; *home:* 10460 Armstrong St Fairfax VA 22030

ALEXANDER, SUSAN KATRIN, English Teacher; *b:* Juneau, AK; *ed:* (AA) Liberal Art, Stephens Coll 1978; (BA) Eng, 1983, Scndry Teaching, 1984 Lewis & Clark; *cr:* Eng Teacher Mat-Su Comm Coll 1984-85, Palmer HS 1984-; *ai:* NCTE; NEA 1987, Vide Bartlett Awd for Contributions to Womens Rights; Articles Published in Eng Journal, AK Magazine 1989, Womens Stud Quarterly 1984; In-Service Facilitator, Cross-Cultural Lit 1987; *home:* 1242 Hillcrest Dr Anchorage AK 99503

ALFARO, AIMEE DE LA CONCEPCION, Spanish/French Teacher; *b:* Havana, Cuba; *m:* Juan Gualberto; *c:* Aimee, Veronica; *ed:* (BA) Fr/Italian, Montclair St 1972; SCATT Teachers Trng Prgm; *cr:* Cnslr Brewster Acad 1981; Instr 1982- Osceola HS; *ai:* Fr & Span Honor Societies, Fr Club, Pep Club Faculty Adv; Dept Chairperson, One for the Children Campaign, Pennies for Pride Campaign; PCFLTA Pres 1989-; AATF, AATSP 1987-; PCTA Sch Rep 1982-87; Jones Intercable Schlsp 1989; Fr Government Schlsp 1989; Triade Paris Teacher of Yr 1988; *office:* Osceola HS 9751 98th St N Seminole FL 34647

ALFORD, BARBARA ANN (SKIPPER), 5th/6th Grade Art Director; *b:* Roswell, NM; *m:* John D. Jr.; *c:* Kimberlee A., Leanette D.; *ed:* (BS) Art, E NM Univ 1969; (MED) Elem Ed, Wayland Baptist Univ 1985; *cr:* Art/Eng Teacher Yucca Jr HS 1969-71; Art/Lang Art Teacher Kiser Elem Sch 1980-; *office:* Kiser Elem Sch 16 S 2nd Ave Clayton NM 88415

ALFORD, CECILE LINTON, Fourth Grade Teacher; *b:* Brookhaven, MS; *m:* Winston Ray; *c:* Patricia, Lin, Cindy, Judy, Jan, Rebekah; *ed:* (BS) Home Ec, Univ of S MS 1949; Grad Stud Univ of SE LA, MS Coll, LA St Univ, Univ S MS; *cr:* 4th/5th Grade Teacher Carters Creek 1947-48; Home Ec Teacher Mt Hermon 1949-52. Dexter 1951-52, Lexie 1954-55; 1st/2nd Grade Teacher Loyd Star; 1st-6th Grade Teacher Spring Creek 1964-; *ai:* 4-H Club, Pep Squad, FHA, Jr HS Bsktbl Spon; NEA, LEA, MEA; United Meth Church Sunday Sch Teacher; Cmmty Gardenetts Charter Mem; *home:* Star Rt Box 93B Kentwood LA 70444

ALFORD, MARGARET MAHOOD, Science Teacher; *b:* Gove City, PA; *m:* Robert William; *c:* Mildred, Roberta; *ed:* (BS) Ed/Bio, Edinboro St Univ 1973; Masters Equivalency St of PA, Clarion Univ 1986; Graduate Courses Clarion Univ; Cmptr Trng ITEC; *cr:* Sci Teacher St Joseph Sch 1973-; *ai:* PA Jr Acad of Sci Spon; Environment Camp Leader; Beta Beta Beta Honorary Biological Society Mem 1972-; Natl Cath Educl Assn Mem 1989-; PA Sci Teachers Assn 1990; *office:* St Josephs Sch 760 E State St Sharon PA 16146

ALFORD, MARTHA EVANS, Special Assignment Teacher; *b:* Rich Square, NC; *m:* Lawrence; *c:* Kjuanji, Jennifer Evans, Harold Evans; *ed:* (BA) Elem Ed, Elizabeth City St Univ 1965; (MA) Early Chldhd Ed, Kean Coll 1975; *cr:* 5th Grade Teacher Sudlersville Elem Sch 1965-66; 3rd Grade Teacher Kentopp Elem Sch 1966-67; Teacher Alexander St Sch 1967-68; 2nd/3rd/5th Grade Teacher Columbian Sch 1968-85; Special Assignment Teacher Kentopp Sch 1985-; *ai:* Coord & Wkshp Facilitator in Parents as Tutor Prgm After Sch; Kentopp PTO; Alpha Kappa Alpha Anti Grammateus 1988-89; NJ Ed Assn, E Orange Ed Assn, NEA; Teacher of Yr E Orange Sch Dist 1985; E Orange Cadet Prgm 1989-; Educl Policy Fellowship Prgm 1989-; *office:* Kentopp Sch 1 Grove Pl East Orange NJ 07017

ALFRED, JUDITH SALTZMAN, Mathematics Teacher; *b:* Findlay, OH; *m:* Norris M.; *c:* Nathan; *ed:* (BS) Math, Univ of Findlay 1980; *cr:* Teacher Arcadia 1980-83, Wynford 1984-85, Fostoria HS 1985-87, Tiffin Calvert 1987-; *home:* 312 S Crawford St Vanlue OH 45890

ALFRED, KENNETH EDWARD, Principal; *b:* Morgan City, LA; *m:* Judy Aucoin; *c:* Michele L., Kenneth J., Jacob M.; *ed:* (BA) Math, 1972, (MED) Ed Admin/Supvr, 1985 Nicholls St Univ; Prof Improvement Prgm 1982; LA Teaching Evaluation Prgm 1990; *cr:* Teacher 1973-74, Teacher/Coach 1974-87, Teacher/Athletic Dir 1987-89, Prin 1989- Morgan City HS; *ai:* Co-Spon Extra Curr Acts in Sci; Schlsp Comm St Mary Parish Prin Assn; Assn of Prof Educators 1973-; LA Assn of Prin 1989-; NASSP 1989-; St Mary Parish Assn of Prins 1989-; St Bernadette Cath Church 1975-; State AAA Coach of Yr 1982; Dist Coach of Yr 1982-85; *office:* Morgan City HS 2400 Hemlock St Morgan City LA 70380

ALHADEFF, BARRY S., 8th Grade Science Teacher; *b:* Atlanta, GA; *c:* Seth, Andy; *ed:* (BS) Sci, GA St Univ 1979; *cr:* Teacher Mimosa Elem 1979-83, Haynes Bridge Mid Sch 1983-; *ai:* Sons Bsbl Coach; Taught Gymnastic; *home:* Rt 3 Old Fincher Tr Canton GA 30114

ALICHNIE, CONNIE SPATZ, First Grade Teacher; *b:* Kingston, PA; *m:* Richard D.; *c:* Amy, Jeffrey; *ed:* (BS) Elem Ed, Bloomsburg Univ 1971; (MED) Ed, Penn St/Liu 1987; *cr:* 4th/5th/6th Grade Teacher Church Street Sch 1971-72; 3rd Grade Teacer Third Avenue Sch 1972-75; 2nd Grade Teacher Washington Avenue Sch 1976-78; 1st Grade Teacher State Street Sch 1978-; *ai:* Scheduling Comm; Staff Dev Comm; Textbook Comm; *home:* 348 State St Larksville PA 18704

ALICO, ROBERT J., 5th Grade Teacher; *b:* Chicago, IL; *m:* Judith M.; *c:* Lauren A.; *ed:* (BS) Phys Ed, W IL Univ 1969; (MED) Curr/Instruction, Natl Coll of Ed 1987; Grad Stud; *cr:* Teacher Brook View Elem 1969-; *ai:* Labor Force 2000; Copyright & Published Act Cards; *office:* Brook View Elem 520 Gary Dr Bolingbrook IL 60439

ALIO, AL, English/Computer Teacher; *b:* Brooklyn, NY; *m:* Josephine Quattrone; *ed:* (AA) Bus, NYC Comm Coll 1969; (BA) Eng - Cum Laude, 1971, (MALS) Liberal Stud, 1973 Suny Stony Brook; Mid-Career Counseling Certificate; *cr:* Instr Suny Stony Brook 1982-84; Cnslr Suny Stony Brook & Mid-Career Counseling Center 1982-86; Teacher Hauppauge Mid Sch 1971-; *ai:* Cmptr Clubs Hauppauge Schls; Alumni Recruiter for SUNY Stony Brook Undergrads; Teacher Trng Cmptr Applications; Continuing Ed Stu Government Pres 1984-88; Chi Epislon Delta Honor Society Induction 1973; Alumni Assn Bd of Dirs Bd Mem 1984-, Distinguished Service 1990; Italian Amer Assn Pres 1967-68, Distinguished Service 1968; *office:* Hauppauge Schls 600 Townline Rd Hauppauge NY 11788

ALISESKY, DAVID JOHN, Instrumental Music Teacher; *b:* Pittsburgh, PA; *m:* Susan Hartley; *c:* Mark, Kevin; *ed:* (BS) Music, 1964; (MS) Ed Cnslng, Duquesne Univ 1969; Madeline Hunter Staff Dev Cadre Trng Prgm 1986-88; *cr:* Instr Music Teacher Mc Kees Rocks HS 1964-66; South Park Sch Dist 1966-70; Bethel Park Sch Dist 1970-; *ai:* Jazz Band Dir; Stage Technician Spon; Amer Band Dir Assn 1972-; PA Music Educators Assn 1966-; Leader - Prof Dance Combo 1960-; *home:* 2108 Hillard Rd Bethel Park PA 15102

ALKIRE, ROSE MARIE, Fourth Grade Teacher; *b:* Parkersburg, WV; *m:* John D.; *c:* John T., Zachary T.; *ed:* (BA) Elem Ed, OH St Univ 1976; (MA) Rdng Supervision, OH Univ 1984; *cr:* 3rd Grade Teacher 1976-80, 5th Grade Teacher 1980-82, 4th Grade Teacher 1982- Little Hocking Elem; *ai:* OH Cncl of Teachers of Math, Heritage Cncl, OH Rdng Assn; *office:* Little Hocking Elem Sch Rt 1 Box 0 Little Hocking OH 45742

ALLAN, MARY ANN (MACKEY), Science/English Teacher; *b:* Avon Park, FL; *m:* Robert Boyd; *c:* Mary C.; *ed:* (BA) Bio Ed, Univ of S FL 1965; (MS) Zoology, Univ of GA 1973; Working Towards PhD Univ of GA; *cr:* Teacher Van Buren Jr HS 1966-70; Instr Clemson Univ 1975-79; Teacher Tuscumbia City Schls 1980-; *ai:* Sci Club Spon; Jr & Sr Prom Asst; AL Acad of Sci, NEA, AL Ed Assn; Amer Legion Auxiliary, Delta Kappa Gamma; Clemson Univ Bio Laboratory Manuel; Univ of GA Outstanding Grad Stu; *office:* Deshler HS N Commons St Tuscumbia AL 35674

ALLCORN, SUNDY, Reading Teacher; *b:* St Petersburg, FL; *ed:* (BS) Elem Ed, 1972, (MS) Rdng, 1973 FL St Univ; Educl Leadership Trng & Cadre Mid Sch Trng, Univ of S FL; *cr:* Rdng Teacher Gretna Elem Sch 1973-74, Oak Grove Mid Sch 1974-76, Bay Point Mid Sch 1978-82; Dept Head/Rdng Teacher Madeira Beach Mid Sch 1982-; *ai:* Lang Art & Rdng Dept Chairperson; Natl Jr Honor Society Spon; Prime Grant Coord; FL Cncl Teachers of Eng, Pinellas Cncl Teachers of Eng 1988-; Pinellas Rdng Cncl Historian 1988-89; Chamber of Commerce Gulf Beaches 1989-; Orion Lung Assn 1989-; Cadre Mid Sch Group; Nom Teacher of Yr & Educator of Yr 1989-; *office:* Madeira Beach Mid Sch 591 Tom Stuart Causeway Madeira Beach FL 33708

ALLEGRE, DARLENE ELAINE, Phys Ed/Health Teacher; *b:* Hood River, OR; *ed:* (BS) Phys Ed/Health, Eastern OR St Coll 1978; Phys Ed, Central WA Univ 1983; Phys Ed for Handicapped Chldrn; *cr:* Phys Ed Teacher Vale Sch Dist 15 1978-; *ai:* Coach 8th Grade Girls Volleyball/Basketball; Athletic Dir Mid Sch Sports; Western ID Conf (VP 1987-88/Pres 1988-89); St Comm for Dvlpng Common Curr Goals Phys; *office:* Vale Elem Sch 403 W E Vale OR 97918

ALLEN, ADA KAY, Business Teacher; *b:* Marshall, TX; *c:* Victoria J. Benkendorfer, Lawerance F., Deborah K. Lennox, Cynthia S. Dillard,; *ed:* (BS) Bus, East TX Baptist Coll 1969; (MS) Bus, East TX St Univ 1971; *cr:* Teacher North Mesquite HS 1969-; *ai:* Stu Cncl Spon; *home:* 4011 Topaz Mesquite TX 75150

ALLEN, BETTY GRAY, Math-Computer Science Teacher; *b:* Hazlehurst, MS; *m:* Harry R.; *c:* Julie Allen Ferriss, Steven J., Leslie L., Steven J. Croll; *ed:* (BS) Math, Millsap Coll 1953; Cmptr Sci, Univ of Southern MS; *cr:* Math Teacher Jackson MS Public Schls 1953-55, Houston TX Public Schls 1955-56, Batesville MS Public Schls 1956-57, Long Beach MS Public Schls 1967-82; Math/Comptr Sci Teacher Hancock Cty Public Schls 1985-; *ai:* Stu Cncl Spon; MS Economic Cncl Star Teacher 1985-88.

ALLEN, BETTY REA, Mathematics Teacher/Dept Chair; *b:* Memphis, TN; *ed:* (BS) Math, Ouachita Baptist Coll 1959; (MA) Eng, George Peabody Coll 1960; (MS) Math, TX Womans Univ 1968; LA St Univ; AR St Univ; Memphis St Univ; Certificate Gifted/Talented Ed; *cr:* Math Teacher Benton HS 1960-61, Charleston HS 1961-64, Hughes HS 1964-; *ai:* Stu Cncl, Mu Alpha Theta, Quiz Bowl Team & Jr Class Spon; Personnel Policies Comm; Math Assn Amer; NCTM; Hughes Ed Assn Pres 1980-81; Hughes PTA Pres 1981-82; Amer Assn of Univ Women; Delta Kappa Gamma Secy 1970; MENSA; PTA Life Membership; Grants Kodak/Southwestern Bell Telephone; Presidential Awd for Excl Math Teaching 1987; AR Outstanding Teacher of Yr 1987; Hughes Blue Devil Yrbk Dedication 1989; Articles in Math Teacher, Arithmetic Teacher; Natl Semi Finalist Outstanding Teacher; Tindy Technology Scholars Prgm; *office:* Hughes HS Box 9 Hughes AR 72348

ALLEN, BRENDA FAYE, Reading Teacher; *b:* Cleveland, TN; *m:* David; *c:* Jennifer, Jason; *ed:* (BS) Elem Ed, Mid TN St Univ 1972; Working Toward Masters Univ of TN 1985; *cr:* CDC Bradley Cty Schls 1978-79; 8th Grade Lang Teacher North Mid Sch 1979-80; 1st Grade Chapter 1 Teacher 1981-82, 5th Grade Rdng/Sci Teacher 1982- Eaton Elem Sch; *ai:* Track Meet Coach; 4-H Club Sponsorship; Level III Career Ladder Teacher of TN; TN Educl Assn; *office:* Eaton Sch Rt 8 Lenoir City TN 37771

ALLEN, CATHERINE FLEMING, Fourth Grade Teacher; *b:* Greenville, SC; *m:* James H.; *c:* Joseph Robinson, Gabriella Robinson, James Jr.; *ed:* (BA) Elem Ed, Johnson C Smith Univ 1959; (MA) Elem Rdng, Furman Univ 1979; SC St Coll; *cr:* 3rd Grade Teacher W Greenville Elem Sch 1959-63; 7th Grade Teacher Bakers Chapel Elem Sch 1963-68; 6th/7th Grade Teacher W Greenville Elem Sch 1968-69; 3rd Grade Teacher Armstrong Elem 1969-71; 4th Grade Teacher Grove Elem 1971-83, Plain Elem 1983-; *ai:* United Teaching Profession 1959-; Sigma Gamma Rho; Nicholtown Presbyn Church Women Pres 1982-83; Grove Elem Teacher of Yr 1977; *office:* Plain Elem Sch 106 Neely Ferry Rd Simpsonville SC 29681

ALLEN, DAVID GENE, Junior HS Band Director; *b:* Hobbs, NM; *m:* Beth Ann Crist; *c:* Stacy L.; *ed:* (BM) Music Ed, 1969, (MA) Music Ed, 1975 E NM Univ; *cr:* Asst Band Dir Clayton Public Schls 1969-70; Band Dir Houston Jr HS 1970-; *ai:* Marching, Concert, Solo & Enseemble, Jazz Band Dir; Phi Beta Mu Mem 1970-; SW Symphony Band (Mem, Conductor) 1985-; Kappa Kappa Psi Mem 1966-69; BSA Eagle; Highland Chrstn Church Deacon; Band Judge; All Region Bands Dir; Clinician; Whos Who in Amer Colls & Univs 1968; *home:* 109 Permian Pl Hobbs NM 88240

ALLEN, DEBORAH JILL, 3rd Grade Teacher; *b:* Mc Minnville, TX; *ed:* (BS) Elem Ed, Mid TN St Univ 1977; (MA) Elem Ed, TN Technological Univ 1984; *cr:* 3rd Grade Teacher William Biles Elem 1977-; Part-Time Adjunct Inst Motlow St Comm Coll 1986-; *ai:* Warren Cty Ed Assn Faculty Rep 1983-84; TN Ed Assn; NEA; Alpha Delta Kappa (Recording Secy 1984-86, Pres 1988-); 1983 Teacher of Quarter & Teacher of Yr Mc Minnville Jaycees; Whos Who Among Amer Prof 1988; *office:* William Biles Elem Sch 201 Locust St Mc Minnville TN 37110

ALLEN, DONNA HALL, Life Science Teacher; *b:* Coxs Creek, KY; *m:* James Edward Jr.; *c:* Brianna Aundrea, Vanessa Lorraine, Maria Bernadette, Adrienne Ragene, Jamie Lydanne; *ed:* (BS) Elem Ed, Nazareth/Spalding 1971; (MA) Elem Ed, 1976, Rank I Principalship/Supervisory, 1982 Univ of Louisville; *cr:* 6th Grade Teacher Coxs Creek Elem 1972-73; 7th-8th Grade Teacher Old KY Home Mid Sch 1973-; *ai:* Beta Club Spon; Curr Comm; Coord Soil Conservation Essays; Sci Fair; Leadership Comm; Phi Delta Kappa; Youth Coord; Vlybl Captain; *home:* 533 N St Gregory Church Rd Coxs Creek KY 40013

ALLEN, DOROTHY BLAKELY, 8th Grade/Algebra/Math Teacher; *b:* Blount Cty, AL; *m:* Jesse B.; *c:* Michael, Patricia; *ed:* (BA) Soc Stud/Eng, Univ of AL 1971; (MED) Scndry Ed/Soc Stud, 1977; (EDS) Scndry Ed/Soc Stud, 1979 AL A&M Univ; Math Cert, Athens St Coll 1985; *cr:* Secy Redstone Arsenal 1955-57; Teacher Madison Cty Bd of Ed 1971-; *ai:* Math Team Coach; Volunteer Math Tutor; Coord Awds Day Ceremony; Madison Cty Ed Assn VP/Pres 1987-89; AL Cncl of Math 1986-; NCTM 1986-; Alpha Delta Kappa Pres-Elect 1988-; Order Eastern Star Worthy Matron 1960- Grand Organist 1976-77; Shindiggers Square Dance Club Pres 1985; 1986 Madison Cty Teacher of Yr Scndry Div; Excl Teacher Awd Toney Historical Cmmty; Whos Who Among Jr Coll 1968; Best Teacher Awd; *home:* 203 Joel Dr Madison AL 35758

ALLEN, DOROTHY JEANNE, 7th Grade Amer His/Civics; *b:* Muskogee, OK; *m:* Tommy Leroy; *c:* Laura C., Allen Staton, Aaron W.; *ed:* (BS) Elem Ed, 1970, (MA) Ed/Soc Stud, 1972 Northeastern St; Ec/Politics, OK Chrstn Coll; Teaching Constitution, Wake Forest Univ; *cr:* 4th Grade Teacher 1970-72, 5th Grade Teacher/Coach 1972-73, 6th Grade Teacher 1973-74 Hilldale Elem; 7th Grade Amer His/Civics Teacher Hilldale Mid Sch 1974-; *ai:* Bsktbl & Academic Team Coach; Soc Stud Dept Chairperson; Textbook Selection Consultant Merrill Publishing Political Action Curr Comm; Building Rep; OK Ed Assn, NEA 1970-; Hilldale Assn Classroom Teachers 1970-; Cncl for Soc Stud 1980-; Teacher of Yr Hilldale Dist 1985, Soc Stud Cncl 1986; George Washington Medal of Honor Valley Forge PA 1974; Motivational Speaker-Staff Dev; Author Book 1985; *home:* Rt 4 Box 96-B Muskogee OK 74401

ALLEN, DREMA RAY, 6-8th Grade Lang Arts Teacher; *b:* Victoria, TX; *m:* Maynard Charles; *c:* Amy, Lori; *ed:* (BS) Eng, Our Lady Holy Cross Coll 1969; Ed 450 Linguistic S I Wkshp 1975; *cr:* 10th/11th Grade Eng Teacher Hanson HS 1969-70; 7th Grade Eng Teacher Immaculate Conception 1970-71; 8th Grade Lang Arts Teacher Christ the King Parish Sch 1972-78 & 1979-80; 6th/8th Grade Lang Arts Teacher Visitation of Our Lady 1981-84; 6th/7th/8th Grade Lang Arts Teacher Christ the King Parish Sch 1984-; *ai:* Drama Club Coach & Moderator; *home:* 5157 Mt Shasta Ln Marrero LA 70072

ALLEN, HAZEL, 4th Grade Teacher; *b:* Hartwell, GA; *c:* Naaman; *ed:* Elem Ed, Savannah St 1979; Lib & Elem Sci; Drug Awareness; *cr:* 4th Grade Teacher Hartwell Elem 1979-; *ai:* Sci Contact Teacher; Drugs Awareness Comm; GA Assn of Ed, Civic Ed, Savannah St Alumni; Achievement Club Pres 1989-, Pres Awd 1990; Just Say No Spon 1986-; Abuse Learning Fnd Pres 1988-; *office:* Hartwell Elem Sch 325 College Ave Hartwell GA 30643

ALLEN, HELEN LOUISE, First Grade Teacher; *b:* Kinder, LA; *ed:* (BA) Elem Ed, Mc Neese St Univ 1967; (MA) Elem Ed, LA St Univ 1976; *cr:* 3rd Grade Teacher Franklin Elem 1967-68; 1st Grade Teacher N Parkerson Elem 1968-69, Elton HS 1969-; *ai:* LTIP & LTEP Master Teacher; Just Say No Club Spon; Children of Alcoholics Support Groups Facilitator; *home:* PO Box 517 Elton LA 70532

ALLEN, I. DIANNA, Mathematics Teacher; *b:* Effingham, IL; *m:* R. Steven; *c:* Scott, Tarne, Misty, Daniel; *ed:* (BSED) Math, E IL Univ 1969; Grad Stud Math, E IL Univ; *cr:* 9th-12th Grade Math Teacher 1974-76, 7th/9th-12th Grade Math Teacher 1976-77 Newman Grade Sch/HS 1976-77; 6th-8th Grade Math Teacher Newman Grade Sch 977-82; 7th-12th Grade Math Teacher Newman Grade Sch & HS 1982-; *ai:* Scholastic Bowl Coach; Advisory Comm & Math Dept for Educl Service Center 13; IL Cncl for Teachers of Math 1978-; Prof Educators of Newman 1983-; Wesley Chapel Dir Vacation Bible Sch 1976-89; SKINS 1988-.

ALLEN, JANICE BLACKBURN, 8th Gr Math/Lang Arts Teacher; *b:* Endicott, KY; *m:* Denzil; *c:* Renee Dauer, David P. II; *ed:* (AB) Elem Ed, 1964; (MA) Elem Ed, 1968; Elem Ed, 1978 Morehead ST Univ; *cr:* 7th/8th Grade Latin Teacher 1964-65; 6th Grade Teacher 1965-73; 5th Grade Teacher 1973-84; 7th/8th Grade Teacher 1984-89; 8th Grade Teacher 1989- Prestonsburg Elem; *ai:* Math Counts Team Spon; Jr Beta Club Spon; Young Authors Project; Academic Improvement Comm; NEA/KEA/FCEA Pres 1980; NMSA/KMSA Featured Teacher 1990; Prestonsburg Jr Womans Club Treas/Pres; Eastern KY Horse Show Assn (Pres 1981-82 Sec Treas); KY Walking Horse Assn Ladies Aux Pres 1988-89; Alternate Roots Grant; Doing Research Value of Learning Logs 8th Grade Classrooms; *home:* 483 S Lake Dr Prestonsburg KY 41653

ALLEN, JANIS M. OYLER, 3rd Grade Teacher; *b:* Norwich, KS; *m:* Jerry L.; *c:* Brian L.; *ed:* (BS) Elem Ed, Emporia St Univ 1961; *cr:* 3rd Grade Teacher Delmer Day Sch Greensburg 1961-63; 3rd Grade Teacher 1963-67, 1973- Unified Sch Dist Coldwater; *office:* Unified Sch Dist #300 301 N Boston Coldwater KS 67029

ALLEN, JOYCE ELAINE, First Grade Teacher; *b:* Gouverneur, NY; *ed:* Phys Ed, St Lawrence Univ 1954-55; Bus/Secretarial, Canton ATC 1955-57; (BS) Elem Ed, SUNY Coll Potsdam 1957-61; *cr:* 2nd Grade Teacher Heuvelton Cntrl Sch 1961-64; 1st-2nd Grade Teacher Wood Park Sch 1964-67; 1st Grade Teacher Heuvelton Cntrl Sch 1967-; *ai:* Curr & Report Card Comm; Commack Sch Dist Arts & Crafts Instr; Summer Sch Prgm; Heuvelton Teachers Assn 1961-64, 1967-; NYSUT AFT 1961-; St Lawrence Athletic Club 1954-55; Canton Youth Comission Playground Instr & Lifeguard 1954-57, 1969-71; Canton ATC Outing Club 1955-57; Alpha Delta Potsdam 1958-61; Lesson Plans Chosen as Model for Stu Teachers 1970; Nom as Outstanding Leader in Elem Ed 1976; *home:* R 4 Box 33425 Canton NY 13617

ALLEN, JOYCE IVY, Second Grade Teacher; *b:* Hot Springs, AR; *m:* James Brent; *c:* Alisa Blanchard, Shelley Kirk; *ed:* (BSE) Elem, (MSE) Rdng, 1976 Henderson Univ; *cr:* 4th Grade Teacher Lake Hamilton Elem 1970-72; 5th Grade Teacher Forest City Area Schls 1973-76; 2nd/3rd Grade Teacher Rhodes Elem 1976-; *ai:* NEA Building Rep 1980-85; FL Teaching Profession Grade Level Chm 1990; Outstanding Teacher of America 1975; *home:* 5774 Truluck Ave Milton FL 32570

ALLEN, JUDITH ANN, History/Humanities/Lit Teacher; *b:* Beardstown, IL; *ed:* (BSED) Eng/His, 1961, (MA) Contemporary European His, 1970 SE MO St Univ; NEH Summer Inst; 17th Century England, N AZ Univ; Multi-Cultural Heritage, Univ of HI; Gifted & Talented Ed, Univ of N CO; *cr:* Eng/His Teacher Richwoods Cmmty HS 1961-64, A T Mahan HS Iceland 1964-65; His Teacher Bitburg HS Bitburg Air Base Germany 1965-66; Eng/His Teacher Bloomington HS 1966-68; Substitute Teacher SE MO Area 1968-69; Asst Instr SE MO St Univ 1969-70; His Teacher Titusville HS 1970-71; Eng/His/Hum Teacher Fruita Monument HS 1971-; *ai:* NHS Co-Spon; Delta Kappa Gamma Pres 1986-88; Phi Alpha Theta 1970-; Harmony Intnl Region 8 (Public Relations 1987-89, Bulletin Editor 1989-); Bus & Prof Womens Club Pres 1967-68; Alpha Delta Pi Secy 1960-61; Natl Endowment for Hum Seminar; Co-Chairperson St Supreme Court Session in the Schls; Nom SPICE II Prgm of CRADLE; *office:* Fruita Monument HS 1815 J Rd Fruita CO 81521

ALLEN, KATHRYN PETERSON, 6th Grade Teacher; *b:* Ashton, ID; *m:* Wm. James; *c:* Derek; *ed:* (AS) Elem Ed/Phys Ed, Ricks Coll 1970; (BS) Elem Ed/Phys Ed, Brigham young Univ 1972; Grad Stud UT St Univ; Gifted & Talented Cert 1986; *cr:* 6th Grade Teacher Washington Elem 1973-78; 5th Grade Teacher Brookwood Elem 1978-81; 7th Grade Soc Stud Teacher West Jordan Jensen Mid Schls 1981-87; 6th Grade Teacher of Gifted & Talented Cottonwood Heights 1987-88, Sunrise Elem 1988-; *ai:* Phys Ed Coach; Future Problem Solving Sch Dir; FPS St Evaluator; Ski Prgm Supvr; Sci Projects Dir; Jordan Ed Assn, UT Ed Assn, NEA Mem 1978-; Latter Day Saints (St Homemaking dir 1968-69, Ward Sports Dir 1972-74, 1988-, Teacher 1989-), Golden Gleaner 1972; Wrote Childrens Stories; Tutor; *home:* 485 E Bridlewalk Ln Salt Lake City UT 84107

ALLEN, KIMBERLY ANN, Middle School Art Teacher; *b:* Cleveland, OH; *m:* Gregory C.; *ed:* Working Towards Masters Ed, Scndry Ed, Art Ed; *cr:* Art Teacher Nordonia Hills HS 1986-89, Nordonia Hills Mid Sch 1989-; *ai:* Soph Class, Art Club, Play Props Adv; OH Art Ed Assn, NAEA, Nordonia Hills Ed Assn 1986-.

ALLEN, LINDA (HONTS), Third Grade Teacher; *b:* Durant, OK; *m:* John Barton; *ed:* (BS) Elem Ed, 1962, (MED) Ed, 1970 SE OK St Univ; Remedial Rdng, Austin Coll; *cr:* Teacher Hamlet Elem 1962-66, US Amer Dependents Sch 1967, Fairview Elem 1968-; *ai:* TX Classroom Teachers, Sherman Classroom Teachers; Cntrl Chrstn Church (Pres Brotherhood Class 1986-87, Song Leader Brotherhood Class 1987-89); NOEA Grant Childrens Lit SE OK St Univ 1968-69; Multi Cultural Teaching Strategies Grant Austin Coll 1977; Rdng Instruction Teacher Schlsp Austin Coll 1980; *home:* 1522 N Woods Sherman TX 75090

ALLEN, MAGNOLIA GALLOWAY, English Teacher; *b:* Bradenton, FL; *m:* Ernest Donald; *c:* Ava, Leah; *ed:* (AA) Sci, Manatee Jr Coll 1969; (BA) Eng, FL St Univ 1972; *cr:* Teacher Cairo HS 1972-73, Turkey Creek Jr HS 1973-79, Brandon HS 1979-84, Armwood HS 1984-; *ai:* Debinettes Club Spon; Stu Affairs Advisory, Stu Act, NHS Advisory, Cty Curr Guide Comms; Hillsborough Cty Teachers of Eng, FL Cncl Teachers of Eng, NCTE, Hillsborough Cty Classroom Teachers; Beginning Teacher Cert Team; *office:* Armwood HS 12000 US Hwy 92 Seffner FL 33584

ALLEN, MAJELLE, Kindergarten Teacher; *b:* Spring Hope, NC; *ed:* Licensed Practical Nurse, 1958, (BS) Home Ec, 1966 NC Cntrl Univ; Endorsements Sociology 1-7, Kndgtn Ed; Grad Courses Univ Va, Va Commonwealth Univ; *cr:* 1st/2nd Grade Teacher Second Union Sch 1966-69; 1st Grade Teacher Goochland Elem Sch 1969-73; Head Teacher Lighthouse Prgm 1973-74, Kdngtn Teacher 1974 Goochland Elem Sch; *ai:* Child Study Comm Mem; Sch Improvement Comm Chm; Dominion Political Action &

Steering Comm Mem 1989; Goochland Ed Assn Sch Rep 1981-; Womens League of Richmond 1990; *office:* Goochland Elem Sch 3150 River Rd W Goochland VA 23063

ALLEN, MARILYN SUE (ABDELLA), Third Grade Teacher; *b:* Nelsonville, OH; *m:* William Wallace; *c:* Whitney M., Courtney R.; *ed:* (BA) Elem Ed, OH Univ 1980; *cr:* 4th Grade Teacher 1980-81, 5th Grade Teacher 1981-87, 3rd Grade Teacher 1987- Chauncey Elem; *ai:* AEA, OEA; *home:* 12 Canterbury Dr Athens OH 45701

ALLEN, MARY THOMPSON, Third Grade Teacher; *b:* Durham, NC; *m:* Schuyler Lee; *ed:* (BA) Elem Ed, Saint Augustines Coll 1955; Hampton Institute; *cr:* 2nd/3rd Grade Teacher Spaulding HS 1955-63; 3rd Grade Teacher Cooper Elem Sch 1963-68, Clayton Elem Sch 1968-70, Clayton Primary Sch 1970-88, Clayton Elem Sch 1988-89; *ai:* PTA Secy/Advisory Bd 1985-86; NCAE Rep 1985-87; Broughton HS Booster Club Secy 1980-81; Teacher of Yr/Plaque 1983; Cmmty Watch Organization Chairperson; *home:* 805 Cotton Pl Raleigh NC 27601

ALLEN, NANCY LEFFINGWELL, 1st Grade Teacher; *b:* Albany, NY; *m:* Robert S.; *ed:* (BS) Elem Ed, St Univ of NY Oneonta 1970; Working Towards Permanent Cert, St Univ Oneonta 1974; *cr:* Kndgtn Teacher 1970-76, 1st Grade Teacher 1976- Ichabod Crane Cntrl Sch; *ai:* Grade Level Chairperson; Sch Improvement Team; Pre-First Selection & Bus Comm; Ichabad Crane Teachers Assn Treas 1975-76; Stuyvesant-on-Hudson Garden Club, Stuyvesant Reformed Church Women; *office:* Ichabod Crane Cntrl Sch State Farm Rd Valatie NY 12184

ALLEN, POLLY HOPE BELL, Substitute Elementary Teacher; *b:* Ethel, MS; *m:* John Samuel; *c:* Michael, Paul; *ed:* (AA) Elem Ed, Holmes Jr Coll 1950-51; (BS) Elem Ed, 1958-61, (MED) Elem Ed, 1975 MS St Univ; MS Coll, MS St Univ; Inservice Wkshps 1986-88; *cr:* 2nd Grade Teacher Le Flore Cty Sch 1951-52; 5th/6th Grade Teacher 1962-68; 6th Grade Teacher Ethel Elem Sch 1962; 5th/6th Grade Teacher French Camp Elem Sch 1967; 1st/2nd Grade Teacher Choctaw Cty Sch 1969-74; 2nd Grade Teacher Magnolia Acad 1974-76; 2nd Grade Teacher Cntrl Hinds Acad 1976-78, Mt Salus Chrstn Sch 1978-87, Hillcrest Acad 1987-88; K-6th Grade Substitute Teacher Jackson, Clinton MS 1989-; *ai:* MS Ed Assn 1960-74; S Assn of Chrstn Schls 1974-88; MS Private Sch Assn 1974-88; *home:* 904 Kent Dr Clinton MS 39056

ALLEN, REBECCA FOSTER, Third Grade Teacher; *b:* Columbia, MO; *m:* Larry Webb; *c:* William, Thaddeus; *ed:* (BS) Elem Ed, Univ of MO Columbia 1964; (MA) Elem Ed, Webster Univ 1981; *cr:* 4th & 5th Grade Teacher Southern Boone Cty 1964-65; 3rd Grade Teacher R III Schls 1968-; *ai:* Beta Sigma Phi (Pres, VP, Treas) 1980-87; *office:* Potosi Elem Sch R III Potosi MO 63664

ALLEN, RODNEY LEE, 9th Grade Health Teacher; *b:* Raleigh, WV; *m:* Pat Lynn Smith; *c:* Gary W., Angie R., Kristy L.; *ed:* (BS) Lib Sci/Health/Phys Ed, Concord Coll 1975; Sports Medicine, WV Univ; Advance Trng CPR & First Aid; Quest Trng; Bus Management, Beckley Coll; *cr:* Mgr Inventory Controy Fairchild Incorporated 1974-80; Coach/Teacher Greater Beckley Chrstn Schls 1980-84; Trainer/Teacher Shady Springs Jr HS 1984-; *ai:* Ftbl Team Trainer; Raleigh Cty Ed Assn Mem 1984-; WV Ed Assn Mem, 1989-; NEA Mem 1989; Open Bible Baptist Pastor 1981-86; Princewick Baptist Pastor 1986-88; Stanaford Baptist Youth Pastor 1988-; Coach of Yr 1983.

ALLEN, SAUNDRA EILEEN (MC GRUDER), Art Instructor; *b:* Jefferson City, MO; *m:* Tyronne Maurel; *c:* Robert P., Rhonda D.; *ed:* (BS) Art Ed, 1970, (MS) Counseling/Guidance, 1976 Lincoln Univ; Grad Stud for Extended Cert in Art & Counseling, Lincoln Univ; *cr:* Bus Office Stu Worker Lincoln Univ 1966-70; Cmptr Printout Analyst MO Dept of Revenue 1970-72; Art Instr Blair Oaks HS 1972-73; Lang Art Teacher St Peter Cath Sch 1973-88; Art Instr East Elem Sch 1988-; *ai:* Nana B Richardsons Girls Club Spon; Jefferson City Transit Comm Mem; Delta Kappa Gamma Music Chm 1987-; NEA 1988-; Amer Legion Auxiliary (Unit Pres, 8th Dist Historian, St Membership Chm SE Division) 1975-; Modern Priscilla Art & Charity Club 2nd VP 1975-; Jefferson City Cmmty Center Assn Secy 1986-; Nom for Jefferson City Outstanding Young Woman; Mayors Transportation Commission Mem; Outstanding Coll Stu of America 1989; *office:* East Elem Sch 1229 E Mc Carty St Jefferson City MO 65101

ALLEN, SHARON KAY (TENNISON), Third Grade Teacher; *b:* Lebanon, MO; *m:* Gary W.; *c:* Jeffrey W., Karen K.; *ed:* (BA) Elem Ed, Southwest Baptist Coll 1973; Working Toward Masters Elem Ed; *cr:* 2nd Grade Teacher 1973-77, 1979-84, 6th Grade Teacher 1984-88, 3rd Grade Teacher 1988- Raymondville R-7; *ai:* Sch Newspaper & Yrbk Co-Ed; Raymondville Teachers Assn (VP 1987-88, Pres 1989-); Bado Bd of Trustees Trustee 1987-; Union Cemetery Bd Secy 1989-; PTO Fund Raising Comm Head; *home:* Rt 2 Box 129 Cabool MO 65689

ALLEN, SUSAN SMITH, Language Art Teacher; *b:* Gastonia, NC; *c:* David M.; *ed:* (BS) Ed/Soc Stud/Phys Ed/Eng, Gardner Webb 1974; Working Towards Masters Mid Sch Ed, Appalachian St Univ 1987; *cr:* 6th Grade Teacher Rutherford Coll Sch 1975-76; 5th Grade Teacher Wake Forest Elem 1976-79; Teacher/Coach W Lincoln Jr HS 1979-84, Fairplains Elem 1984-; *ai:* Var Tennis Coach W Wilkes HS; Bsktbl, Sftbl Coach Fairplains Sch; AAU Jr Olympic Coach Brush Mountain; NC Assn Educators Mem 1975-; NC Intnl Rdng Assn 1977-; NC HS Coaches Assn 1986-; Wilkes Teen Pregnancy Cncl Mem 1988-; NC Sr Games Comm Mem 1987-; Womens Intnl Tennis Assn 1986-; NC 1st Responder EMT Trng 1981-; *office:* Fairplains Elem Sch 14 School St North Wilkesboro NC 28659

ALLEN, VIRGINIA JEANNE (WALTERS), Teacher of Gifted & Talented; *b:* Indianapolis, IN; *m:* L. James; *ed:* (BS) Elem Ed, IN Univ 1972; (MA) Early/Mid Chldhd OH St Univ 1978; Tribes Facilitator; *cr:* 4th-6th Grade Teacher 1972-89, 2nd-6th Grade Teacher of Gifted/Talented 1982-85 Worthington City Schls; 6th Grade Teacher Ind Sch Dist of Plano 1985-86; 5th Grade Teacher of Gifted/Talented Metropolitan Sch Dist of Pike Township 1989-; *ai:* NEA, OEA, Local WEH 1972-89; NEA, ISTA Local PTA 1989-; Gamma Phi Beta (Pres, VP, Alumni Secy) 1972-80; Twigs Volunteer Group 1983-85; Worthington Sch System Honored as Recipient Innovation Awd 1990; *home:* 9199 Cinnebar Dr Indianapolis IN 46268

ALLEN, WANDA WALLER, English/Social Studies Teacher; *b:* Savannah, TN; *m:* Ricky Lee; *ed:* (BA) His/Eng, Univ of TN Martin 1979; Working Towards Masters His; *cr:* Eng/Speech/ Drama Teacher Big Sandy HS 1980-81; US His/Rdng Teacher Briarwood Jr HS 1981-83; Psych/Sociology/Civics/Geography/ World His/Advanced Amer His/Eng/US Government Teacher Camden Cntrl HS 1984-; *ai:* Jr Class, US Govt Club, Advanced Amer His Club Spon; Southern Assn of Schls Accreditation Comm; TN Geographic Alliance 1989-, Educator of Yr 1990; NCSS, TN Ed Assn, NEA 1980-; Camden Lioness Club Secy 1985-, Secy Awd 1989-; Benton Cty Univ of TN Alumni Assn Secy 1987-; BSA Troop Comm; Cumberland Presbyn Women Reporter 1986-; TN Writers Guild Poety Contest Winner; Great Books Cert; Certified Lions Quest Instr; *office:* Camden Cntrl HS Washington Ave Camden TN 38320

ALLGOOD, MARILYN TYNON, Math/Computer Teacher; *b:* Nebraska City, NE; *m:* Clyde E.; *c:* Steven, Teresa, Mark, Bret; *ed:* (BS) Math/Physics, Peru St Coll 1960; Peru St Coll/IA St Univ/Cmptr NWMSU; *cr:* Math/Physics Teacher Bratton Union HS 1960-62, Johnson-Brock HS 1963-64; Math Teacher Lourdes HS 1968-72; Math Cmptr Teacher Fremont-Mills HS 1972-; *ai:* 9th Grade Spon; NEA 1972-; ISEA 1972-; FMEA 1972-; NCMT 1988-; *home:* 1906 1st Ave Nebraska City NE 68410

ALLGOOD, TONY ALLAN, Art Teacher; *b:* Nebraska City, NE; *ed:* (BA) Art/Phys Ed, Midland Luth Coll 1988; *cr:* Art Teacher/Coach North Bend Cntrl HS 1988-; *ai:* Prom, Art Club, Jr Class, Weightlifting Spon; Asst Ftbl, Bsktbl, Track Coach; Legion Bsbl Coach; VFW 1989-, Patriotic Awd 1989, 1990; *office:* North Bend Cntrl HS 15 & Pine North Bend NE 68649

ALLINDER, RICHARD O., Geography Teacher; *b:* Mc Kees Rocks, PA; *m:* Cathleen S. Shawin; *c:* Ryan M.; *ed:* (BS) Elem Ed, 1976, (ME) Elem Ed, 1980 Edinboro Univ PA; *cr:* 4th Grade Teacher Graysville Elem 1976-80; 5th/6th Grade Teacher Aleppo Elem 1980-82; 6th-8th Grade Geography Teacher W Greene Mid Sch 1982-; *ai:* 6th Grade Trip to Washington DC Spon; Kappa Delta Pi 1976-80; W Green Ed Assn (VP 1978-79, Pres 1979-80); Richhill Township Volunteer Fire Dept (Pres 1983-84, VP 1981-83) 1976-86; Elks 1982-; *office:* West Greene Mid Sch RD 5 Box 36-A Waynesburg PA 15370

ALLING, MARK THOMAS, Biology Teacher; *b:* Rochester, NY; *m:* Martye Seay; *ed:* (BA) Soc Stud Ed, Purdue Univ 1971; (BA) Bio, Univ of CA at Santa Cruz 1980; (MAT) Bio, GA St Univ 1985; *cr:* Bio Teacher Jackson HS 1980-; *ai:* Sci Club Adv; Sci Bowl/Olympiad Coach; NEA 1981-; GA Assn of Educators 1981-; *office:* Jackson H S 323 Harkness St Jackson GA 30233

ALLISON, ELEANOR ADELE, Anatomy/Physiology Teacher; *b:* Raleigh, NC; *ed:* (BS) Phys Ed, 1970, (MED) Ed, 1971 Auburn Univ; *cr:* Grad Asst Auburn Univ 1970-71; Teacher Bartow Sr HS 1971-; *ai:* Medical Cmmty Sch Bus Partnership; Bartow HS Teacher Network Chm; Internal Improvement Comm; Sci Dept Chairwoman; FL Assn of Prof Health Educators 1987-; Bartow HS Teacher of Yr 1989-; St FL Performance Measurement System Clinical Educator Trainer; *office:* Bartow Sr HS 1270 S Broadway Ave Bartow FL 33830

ALLISON, JANET MARIE PINGEL, Bus Education Dept Chairperson; *b:* Chippewa Falls, WI; *m:* Clyde; *c:* Martin; *ed:* (BS) Bus Ed/Ec, Univ WI Eau Claire 1965; Grad Courses & Wkshps UW-Whitewater, UW-Stout, CO St Univ, N IL Univ; Courses in Cmptr Technology, Chippewa Valley Tech Coll; *cr:* Bus Ed Teacher Gilman HS 1965-66, Park Sr HS 1966-68, Bloomer HS 1968-; *ai:* Adv Future Bus Leaders of America; Schlsp Comm for Sch; Ed for Employment Comm; Coord of Coop Prgm; WI Bus Ed Assn (Pres, Mem) 1990; Natl Bus Ed Assn; Intnl Bus Ed Assn NC Rep 1983-; United Way (Campaign Chairperson 1980-); Church Sunday Sch Teacher; Articles Published in Intnl Society of Bus Ed; Newsletter WI Bus Ed Assn; Newsletter Voc Educator; *office:* Bloomer HS 1310 17th Ave Bloomer WI 54724

ALLISON, NANCY LEE (MORROW), First Grade Teacher; *b:* Miami, FL; *m:* Maurice L.; *c:* Karen, Donna Machlah, Gail Giangregorio, Maurice Jr.; *ed:* (BS) Early Chldhd Ed, FL S Coll 1954; Masters Equivalency Univ of MD & Trinity Coll; *cr:* Classroom Teacher Mulberry Elem Sch 1954-55, Parkway Elem Sch 1958-60, Langley Park-Mc Cormick Elem Sch 1973-; *ai:* Pantry & Clothing Comm; Mentor; Self Esteem Comm; Delta Kappa Gamma Intnl VP 1988-; Langley Park Coalition 1987; St Senatorial Schlsp Comm; Hospice of Prince Georges Cty; Univ Baptist Church Deacon; *home:* 1700 Langley Way Adelphi MD 20783

ALLMON, STEVEN CHARLES, J H Dept Chair/Soc Stud Chair; *b:* Valparaiso, IN; *m:* Kimberly Sue Hallberg; *c:* Brandon, Christopher; *ed:* (BS) Soc Sci Ed, IN St Univ 1985; Organized Crime & Western Stud, Purdue Calumet; *cr:* Teacher South Haven Chrstn Sch 1985-; *ai:* Athletic Dir; J H Sunday Sch Teacher; *home:* 80 E 1050 N Chesterton IN 46304

ALLRED, KATHRYN REDMON, 6th Grade Math/Science Teacher; *b:* Asheville, NC; *m:* Nick D.; *ed:* (BS) Elem Ed, 1969, (MA) Mid Sch Ed Math & Sci Concentrations, 1983 Appalachian St Univ; *cr:* 6th Grade Teacher Amity Hill Elem Sch 1969-71; 3rd-5th Grade Teacher 1971-83, 6th Grade Math/Sci Teacher 1983- Yadkinville Elem Sch; *ai:* Stu Cncl Spon; Math Counts Team Spon; YCAE/NCAE/NEA 1970-; NC Cncl Teachers of Math 1988- Outstanding Math Teacher Awd 1988; NC Sci Teachers Assn 1988-; *office:* Yadkinville Elem Sch P O Box 518 Yadkinville NC 27055

ALLRED, LAURA GAIL LUKER, 6th Grade Teacher/Art Teacher; *b:* Pensacola, FL; *m:* Bill; *ed:* (AA) Art Ed, Pensacola Jr Coll 1971; (BA) Art Ed, 1973, (BA) Elem Ed, 1978 Univ of W FL; *cr:* Resource Teacher East Milton Elem 1973-74; Art Teacher Chumuckla & Allentown 1974-78; 6th Grade Teacher 1978-, Art Teacher 1984- Chumuckla Elem; *ai:* Sch Yrbk, 6th Grade Graduation, 6th Grade Stock Market Game Spon; Cmmty Fair Exhibit; Santa Rosa Prof Educators Dist II Rep 1986-88, Chumuckles Teacher of Yr 1983-; FL Teaching Prof 1976-; NEA 1973-, Finalist Santa Rosa Teacher of Yr 1988-89; Santa Rosa Democratic Womens Club 2nd VP 1989-; FL Democratic Womens Club Dist 5 Recording Secy 1989-; Santa Rosa Democratic Exec Bd Precinct 19 Comm Women 1988-; Chumuckla PTO Treas 1987, 1988, 1990; Pensacola Jr League Mini-Grant Awd 1988; FL Legislators Discussion Panel Ed Comm; Santa Rosa Mid Grade Curr Cncl.

ALLUMS, BRENDA LEA, Counselor; *b:* Atlanta, GA; *ed:* (BS) Health/Phys Ed, W GA Coll 1972; (MED) Health/Phys Ed, Univ of GA 1973; (MED) Sch Counseling, GA St Univ 1984; (EDS) Sch Counseling, W GA Coll 1989; *cr:* Teacher/Coach Riverdale Jr HS 1973-77, Riverdale Sr HS 1977-79, Pointe South Jr HS 1979-88; Cnslr N Clayton HS 1988-; *ai:* Frosh & Jr Cnslr; Amer Alliance for Health, Phys Ed, Recreation; GA Sch Cnslrs Assn; Kappa Delta Pi; Phi Delta Kappa; Natl Assn for Sports & Phys Ed; Natl Assn for Girls & Women in Sports; St Timothy United Meth Church Mem; Phys Educator of Yr Clayton Cty 1987; Phoebe Apperson Outstanding Educator Awd 1984-85; *home:* 1848 Enid Dr Lithonia GA 30058

ALMANY, AUDREY HELVIE, SIA Teacher/Kindergarten; *b:* Memphis, TN; *m:* Wilbur Keith; *c:* Leslie L.; *ed:* (AA) Early Chldhd, Stephens Coll 1952; (BS) Elem Ed, Henderson St Teachers 1955; Early Chldhd Course, Vasser; *cr:* 3rd Grade Teacher Houston TX Ind Sch Dist 1955-57; 1st Grade Teacher Washington Cty Dept of Ed 1958-64; 2nd Grade Teacher 1964-86, SIA/Kndgtn Teacher 1990 Walker Cty Dept of Ed; *home:* Rt 2 Box 2540 Flintstone GA 30725

ALMAS, ALANA A., Spanish Teacher; *b:* San Francisco, CA; *ed:* (BA) Botany/Span, 1977, (MA) Span, 1979 Univ of CA Davis; Impact Trng 1987; Critical Thinking/Effective Teaching Trng 1986; TESA Trng 1989; *cr:* Teaching Asst Univ of CA Davis 1978-79; ESL Instr Davis Adult Sch 1979-80; Span Instr N Tahoe HS 1980-81; Span/ESL Teacher Oakdale Jr HS 1981-83; Span Instr Elk Grove HS 1983-; *ai:* Chemical Action Team; CA Teachers Assn, CA Foreign Lang Teachers Assn, Foreign Lang Asst Greater Sacramento 1985-; EGUSD Mentor Teacher 1986-89; *office:* Elk Grove HS 9800 Elk Grove-Florin Rd Elk Grove CA 95624

ALMEIDA, RODERICK R., Mathematics Teacher; *b:* Springfield, MA; *m:* Karen M.; *ed:* (BS) Math, Amer Intnl 1967; (ME) Math, PA St 1982; Univ of AL, PA St Univ; *cr:* Teacher Longmeadow HS 1967-69, Escola Graduada Sao Paulo Brazil 1969-70, Collegio Americano Cavacas Venezuela 1970-71, William Tennent 1972-; *ai:* Var Soccer Coach; NCTM; *home:* Ridge Rd New Hope PA 18938

ALMETER, MARSHA LYNN, Sixth Grade Teacher; *b:* Portland, OR; *ed:* (BS) Ed, 1968, Spec Ed, 1972 Univ of OR; Peace Corps San Francisco St, Philippines, Lewis Clark, Oceanography; *cr:* 6th Grade Teacher Mc Kay Elem; 5th-6th Grade Teacher Chehalem Elem; Spec Ed Teacher Eugene Sch Dist; 6th Grade Teacher Raliegh Hills-Beaverton; *ai:* Comm Excl Dist; Health Facilitator Bldg Social Comm; Dist Speakers Bd Bond Levy; Prof Enhancement Comm Bldg; Beaverton Ed Assn (Pres, Secy, VP, Poly Rep), 1983-84; OEA Comm Relations 1984; Beaverton Teachers Assn Pres; Spec Olympics Track Coach; Cascade Aids Project Volunteer; Dist Dr Wild Grant; Challenge Rdng Handicapped Unit Curr; *office:* Mc Kay Elem Sch PO Box 200 Beaverton OR 97075

ALMOND, DONALD E., Guidance Counselor; *b:* Hope, AR; *m:* Roxy; *c:* Brian, Shawn; *ed:* (BSE) Scndry Eng, 1970, (MSE) Scndry Counseling, 1976 Henderson St Univ; *cr:* Scndry Eng Hampton HS 1970-77, Scndry Cnslr Rison HS 1977-; *ai:* AR Schl Cnslrs Assn 1985-; AR Guidance Counseling & Dev Assn 1980-; *office:* Rison Public Sch P O Box 307 Rison AR 71665

ALMOND, JACKIE LOWDER, K/1st Grade Teacher; *b:* Albemarle, NC; *m:* Johnny R.; *c:* Jennifer, Jeremiah; *ed:* (AB) Early Chldhd Ed, Pfeiffer 1975; *cr:* Substitute Teacher Locust Elem Sch 1976; Kndgtn Teacher Stanfield Elem Sch 1976-77; Teacher Aquadale Elem Sch 1977-; *ai:* Sch Cadre, Guidance Comm & Sci Curr Comm Mem; NEA, NC Assn of Educators; United Meth Women (Secy 1988-, Mem); 1st Street United Meth

Church Mem; PTO; Teacher of Yr 1985-86; *home:* PO Box 591 Albemarle NC 28001

ALMQUIST, JON L., Athletic Trainer/Teacher; *b:* New York, NY; *m:* Rebecca O Bryhim; *ed:* (BS) Health/Phys Ed/Industrial Arts Ed, Penn St Univ 1982; *cr:* Voc Teacher S John Davis Center 1983-86; Head Athletic Trainer/Teacher Marshall HS 1983-; *ai:* Marshall Sports Medicine Club Spon; Head Athletic Trainer; N VA Sports Medicine Assn Pres 1987-, Trainer of Yr 1989; Natl Athletic Trainers Assn HS St Rep 1980-; Fairfax Cty Athletic Trainers Chm 1989-; *office:* George C Marshall HS 7731 Leesburg Pike Falls Church VA 22043

ALMS, PAULA J., French/English Teacher; *b:* Columbus, NE; *m:* La Verne; *c:* Laura, Linda; *ed:* (BS) Scndry Ed/Home Ec, Univ oF NE 1959; Fr, Eng Endorsements; *cr:* Teacher Grand Island Public Schls 1971-75, Stromsburg Public Schls 1977-; *ai:* Amer Assn Teachers of Fr, DKG; Grant Sponsored by Quebec Govt Study Fr Univ of Montreal 1987; *office:* Stromburg Sr HS 401 E 4th St Stromsburg NE 68666

ALONGI, CLAUDIA KNIGHT, History Teacher; *b:* Pasco, WA; *m:* Michael L.; *c:* Rachel, Dee A.; *ed:* (BA) Soc Stud/Ed, WA St Univ 1969; E WA Univ; Seminars & Classes Various Insts; *cr:* Teacher Winlock HS 1974-; *ai:* Knowledge Bowl Coach; Jr Statesmen Adv; Ed Assn (Pres 1989-, Negotiator, VP 1982-84); *office:* Winlock HS 241 N Military Rd Winlock WA 98596

ALPHIN, ANN BYRD, Fifth Grade Teacher; *b:* Duplin Cty, NC; *m:* Vance C.; *c:* Laura, Van, John; *ed:* (BA) Elem Ed, East Carolina Univ 1970; *cr:* Teacher Kenansville Elem 1970-89; *ai:* Just Say No Club; Sch Improvement Team; NC Ed Assn 1970-; NEA 1970-; *office:* Kenansville Elem Sch P O Box 98 Kenansville NC 28349

ALSMAN, PHILIP RICHARD, Principal; *b:* Vincennes, IN; *m:* Dorothy June Mayr; *c:* Kristina, Abbi; *ed:* (BS) Chem/Phys Ed, Oakland City Coll 1969; (MS) Admin, 1975, (EDS) Specialist, 1982 E IL Univ; Admin Acad 1990; Cmptr Trng 1988-89; *cr:* Teacher Hutton Sch 1969-72; Coach/Sci Teacher Parkview Jr HS 1972-88; Prin Arlington Sch 1988-; *ai:* 6th Grade Bsktbl Coach; IL Bsktbl Coaches Assn 1972-, Coach of Yr 1974, 1978-79, 1982-83; Speakers Bureau 1985-; Rotary Intnl Secy 1984-; Chamber of Commerce Chamber Bd 1986-89; Pan Am Games Bsktbl Coord 1986-87; Bsktbl Dir Capital Classic in Lawrenceville HS; Book Published 1982; *home:* 1705 Locust Lawrenceville IL 62439

ALSOBROOK, LYNN KNEEDLER, First Grade Teacher; *b:* St Louis, MO; *m:* James Robert; *c:* Curt, Ronald; *ed:* (BA) Elem Ed, Southwest Baptist Coll 1971; (MAT) Comm/Lang Art, Webster Univ 1990; *cr:* 3rd Grade Teacher Pevely Elem 1971-74; 1st Grade Teacher Hillsboro Elem 1979-; *ai:* MO St Teacher Assn, Jefferson Cty Dist Educl Assn 1979-; *home:* 5552 Kellridge Ln Saint Louis MO 63128

ALSTON, BETTY JEAN (BRUNER), Second Grade Teacher; *b:* Concord, NC; *m:* Henry C. Sr.; *c:* Henry C. Jr., Terry V.; *ed:* (BS) Ed, Barber-Scotia Coll 1955; A & T St Univ 1957; Appalachian St Univ 1969; *cr:* Teacher Biarwood Eem Sch 1969; *ai:* NEA; NC Assn of Educators; PTA/Odell Elem Sch Sec 1979; PTSA/Northwest Mid Sch Sec 1980; First United Presby Church Chairperson/Bd of Trustees 1981; Northwest Booster Club Sec 1982 VP 1983; Publication Poem Teachers Invitation to Writing 1983; First United Presby Church Elder 1983; Democratic Womens Organization Sec 1983; Cabarrus Cty Bd of Edu 1983; Democratic Party of Cabarrus Cnty 1st Vice Chairperson 1985; 4H Fnd Inc Sec 1987; Cabarrus Cty Resource Dept of Correction Whos Who Among Black Americans 1985; Optimist Club/Cert for Commty Support 1986; Omega Psi Phi Fraternity Scroll of Honor for Ed/Cmmty Svc; Cabarrus Cty Democrat Party Plaque 1987; Truth Temple Church Outstanding Svc Awd 1988; St of NC Cert of Appreciation 1988; Price Memorial Church Cert of Appreciation for Cmmty Support 1988; *home:* PO Box 1365 Concord NC 28025

ALSTON, RUTHENA ALSTON, 7th Grade Math Teacher; *b:* Georgetown, SC; *c:* Aronette Graham; *ed:* (BS) Elem Ed, SC St Coll 1955; (MS) Ed, A&T St Univ 1971; *cr:* Teacher/Prin Nightengale Sch 1955-56; Math Teacher Howard HS 1958-59; 2nd Grade Teacher J B Beck 1960-63; Math Teacher Jamestown/ Macedonia Schls 1965-75, Choppee Mid Sch 1977-; *ai:* Math Club; Metric Trng for Teachers; Big Mac Mem; NEA Mem 1955-; SC Ed Assn Mem 1955-; Georgetown Ed Assn Mem 1955-; Girl Scout Troop Leader 1958-61; Teacher of Yr 1980 & 1983; *home:* 915 Church St Georgetown SC 29440

ALSUP, LINDA SUE PATTON, English Teacher; *b:* Merkel, TX; *c:* Floyd D., Randall B., Sharon C.; *ed:* (AA) Eng/Fr, Odessa Jr Coll 1961; (BA) Eng/Fr, N TX St Univ 1964; (MLA) Liberal Art, Houston Baptist Univ 1987; Rice Writing Project; *cr:* Eng Teacher North Shore Jr HS 1964-65, Milby Sr HS 1965-; *ai:* Houston Area Cncl Teachers of Eng 1980-, Certificate of Achievement 1985; Delta Kappa Gamma Society Intnl 1985-, Jane Carradine Schlsp 1987; *office:* Milby Sr HS 1601 Broadway Houston TX 77012

ALSUP, SARAH WILLIAMS, Kindergarten Teacher; *b:* Mobile, AL; *c:* J. Christopher; *ed:* (BS) Elem Ed, Auburn Univ 1966; (ME) Early Chldhd Ed, Univ of S AL 1982; *cr:* 2nd Grade Teacher 1974-77, 1st Grade Teacher 1977-78, 3rd Grade Teacher 1979-80, Kndgtn Teacher 1982- Tanner Williams Elem; *ai:* Schls Historian Comm; PTA Historian 1987-89, Co Scrapbook 1988, Outstanding Teacher 1989; Dist I AL Elem Teacher of Yr 1987; *office:* Tanner-Williams Elem Sch Rt 1 Box 78 Wilmer AL 36587

ALT, PATRICIA WORSHAM, Science Teacher; *b:* Waynesville, NC; *m:* Daniel K.; *c:* Roddy, Kevin, Jeffery; *ed:* (BS) Home Ec/Sci, Mars Hill Coll 1971; (MAT) Ed, Winthrop 1974; *cr:* Kndgtn Teacher Lewisville Elem 1971-74; Sci Teacher Trinity Chrstn Sch 1984-; *ai:* Homecoming Comm; 7th Grade & Society Spon; Trinity Chrstn Sch Teacher of Yr 1987; 2nd Runner Up St Teacher of Yr 1987; SC Regional Family of Yr 1989; *office:* Trinity Chrstn Sch 505 University Dr Rock Hill SC 29730

ALTAFFER, GLENDA FAYE, 2nd Grade Teacher; *b:* Wagoner, OK; *m:* Ray P.; *c:* Philip R., Scot A.; *ed:* (BS) Ed, 1966; (MS) Ed, 1979 Northeastern St Univ; *cr:* Classroom Teacher Wagoner Public Schs 1966-; *ai:* Building Rep 1988-89; Negotiator 1985-87 Wagoner Classroom Teachers Assn; Bus and Prof Womens Organization Mem 1978-80; 1st Bapt Church Organist 1988-; *office:* Maple Park Elem Sch 700 N Story Wagoner OK 74467

ALTEMOSE, CONSTANCE S., First Grade Teacher; *b:* Wind Gap, PA; *m:* Richard; *c:* Mark, Jeffrey; *ed:* (BS) Elem Ed, 1964, (MS) Ed, 1969 E Stroudsburg Univ; *cr:* Remedial Rdng Teacher 1967-69, 1st Grade Teacher 1971- Pen Argyl Area Sch Dist; *ai:* Primary Coord; Plainfield Addition Steering Comm; PA St Ed Assn, NEA 1971-; PTA Life Membership 1989; Whos Who in Amer Colls & Univs; *home:* 270 Sycamore Dr Wind Gap PA 18091

ALTENHOFEN, ROSANNE MARTIN, Kindergarten Teacher; *b:* Cedar Rapids, IA; *m:* William James; *c:* Lynn A., Daniel W.; *ed:* (BS) Home Ec/Elem Ed, Mt Mercy 1966; *cr:* 3rd Grade Teacher Clear Creek Cmmty Schls 1960-64; 1st Grade Teacher Benton Cmmty Schls 1966-69; 1st Grade/Kndgtn Teacher Linn-Mar Cmmty Schls 1969-; *home:* 2655 Northview Dr Marion IA 52302

ALTFATHER, MIRIAM GARZA, Elementary Music Teacher; *b:* San Antonio, TX; *m:* Robert; *ed:* (BS) Music Ed, Trinity Univ 1956; *cr:* 3rd-4th Grade Teacher Herff & Hillcrest Elem 1956-65; Music Teacher E Terrell Hills & Camelot Elem 1965-72; 1st/5th Grade Teacher 1980-84, Music Teacher 1984- Southwest Elem; *home:* 255 Latch Dr San Antonio TX 78213

ALTHERR, FRED B., Occupational Work Teacher; *b:* Jackson, OH; *m:* Helen Forshey; *c:* Jeff; *ed:* (BS) Elem Ed, Rio Grande Coll 1958; (MED) Elem Guidance, OH Univ 1968; Occupational Work Adjustment Prgm; Numerous Wkshps; *cr:* 3rd Grade Teacher Cleveland City Schls 1958-59; 5th Grade Teacher Commercial Point Schls 1959-60; 6th/7th Grade Teacher Franklin Valley Sch 1960-70; 9th Grade Teacher Jackson City Schls 1970-; *ai:* Canvas Crew; OWA Adv; ICEA Treas; Jackson City Ed Assn Treas 1970-75; Occupational Work Adjustment Endurance Awd 5 Yr 1975, 10 Yr 1985, 15 Yr 1990; United Commercial Travelers (Secy, Treas 1975-80); *office:* Jackson HS Tropic St Jackson OH 45640

ALTHOUSE, ROBERT LEE, Soc Stud Teacher/Dept Chairman; *b:* Reading, PA; *m:* Linda Haag; *c:* Michael; *ed:* (BSED) Scndry Ed/Comprehensive Soc Stud, 1970, (MED) Scndry Ed/Soc Stud, 1975 Kutztown Univ; Grad Stud Penn St Univ, Wilkes Coll, Carlow Coll; *cr:* His/Government/Ec HS Teacher 1970-, Soc Stud Chm 1989- Hamburg Area Sch Dist; *ai:* Dist Coord Aces Prgm; Mem Faculty Advisory Cncl; Hamburg Area Sch Dist Soc Stud Co-Chm Curr, Instruction Comm 1988-; NCSS 1989-; NEA, PSEA 1970-; HAEA (2nd VP, Chief Negotiator 1973-80, Mem) 1970-; Police Civil Service Commission Chm 1980-88; Dauberville DX Assn (Pres, VP) 1982-88; Amer Radio Relay League 1978-; Red Cross (Emergency Comm Coord, Comm Officer, Diaster Preparedness Plan 1990) 1987-; *office:* Hamburg Area Sch Dist Windsor St Hamburg PA 19526

ALTMAN, LESLIE JOAN, Director Lower Sch/Eng Teacher; *b:* Cambridge, MA; *m:* Michael L.; *c:* Christopher, Timothy; *ed:* (AB) Eng, Smith Coll 1964; (MA) Eng, NY Univ 1967; (PhD) Eng, Boston Coll 1973; (MC) Educl Psych, AZ St 1981; *cr:* Teacher Various Public Schls 1964-71; Asst Professor AZ St Univ 1977-81; Sch Cnslr Tempe AZ 1981-86; Teacher/Admin St Sebastians Cntry Day Sch 1987-; *ai:* Dir Mid Sch Academics St Sebastians; Yrbk Adv; NEATE Comm Chairperson 1989-; ASCA Ed 1983-86; NEH Summer Seminar 1989; CBE Grant 1990; Various Publications On Medieval & 18th Century Lit; *office:* St Sebastians Cntry Day Sch 1191 Greendale Ave Needham MA 02192

ALTMAN, LYNDA SUSAN, English Teacher; *b:* Denver, CO; *m:* Morton I.; *c:* Effie R. Iannacito; *ed:* (BA) Eng, Univ of N CO 1968; (MS) Eng/Scndry Ed, Univ of NM 1985; Grad Stud Eng; *cr:* Eng Teacher Miami Public Sch System 1969-72, Albuquerque Public Sch System 1983-; *ai:* NHS Spon; Sch Improvement Team Chairperson; Phi Delta Kappa 1986-; Kappa Delta Pi 1983-; NCTE 1968-; NM Cncl Teachers of Eng 1983-; *office:* Del Norte HS 5323 Montgomery NE Albuquerque NM 87110

ALTMAN, THOMAS C., Physics Teacher; *b:* Nurenberg, Germany; *m:* Mary Jean Larkin; *c:* Virginia, Benjamin, Jonathan; *ed:* (BS) Sci Ed, 1981, (MS) Physics Ed, 1985 St Univ of NY Oswego; PhD Work Research Techniques, Univ of NM; *cr:* Radio Repairman USAF 1972-78; Sci Tutor St Univ Coll Oswego 1979-81; Physics Teacher Oswego HS 1981-; *ai:* Sci, Chess, Cmptr Club; Frosh Class Adv; Diving & Track Coach; Faculty Schlshp & Elem Sci Comm; Summer Cmptr Camp Dir; NY St United Teachers 1984-, Runner-Up Teacher of Yr 1986, 1987, Teacher of Yr 1988, 1st Runner Up NY St Teacher of Yr 1988; Kappa Delta Pi 1981-; Syracuse Technology Club Outstanding Technology Teacher 1990; Gideons Intnl 1988-; AAPT 1986-; NSTA 1985-; Laser Research Grant; Participant Natl Teacher Research Prgm; Mem Natl Sci/Math Conference; Books & Articles Published; Invented Altman Holography Method; *office:* Oswego HS 2 Buccaneer Blvd Oswego NY 13126

ALTMAYER, ROBERT C., Mathematics/Science Teacher; *b:* Menomonee Falls, WI; *m:* Linda A. Druml; *c:* Michael, Steven, Julie; *ed:* (BS) Elem Ed, 1975, (MS) Ed Psych, 1980 Univ of WI Milwaukee; Doctoral Prgm Urban Ed/Ed Psych, Univ of WI Milwaukee 1990; *cr:* Elem Teacher 1975-80, Mid Sch Teacher 1980- Germantown Public Schls; *ai:* Stu Assistance Prgm Facilitator/Group Leader; Dist Math Comm; Kennedy Mid Sch Earth Week 1990 Project Coord; WI Ed Assn 1975-; Amer Assn for Counseling & Dev 1978-83; Alma Moon Lake Dist Chm 1987-; Germantown Area PTA 1983-85; 84th Div USAR 1965-71, Milwaukee Journal Distinguished Service Awd 1968; *home:* N 80 W 23658 Plainview Sussex WI 53089

ALTVATER, PHYLLIS A., 6th Grade Teacher; *b:* Cambridge, OH; *ed:* (BA) His, Sociology, Malone Coll 1973; (Add Cert) Elem Educ Muskingum Coll 1987; *cr:* 8th Grade Teacher Cambridge City Schls 1890-81; 6th Grade Teacher Buckeye Trail Mid Sch 1984-; *ai:* Funding Task Force; Washington DC Trip Coord - 7th Grade; Ohio Ed Assn/NEA Sec/Treas 1985-; Team Leader-Buckeye Trail Mid Sch; *office:* Buckeye Trail Mid Sch P O Box 128 Old Washington OH 43768

ALVARADO, LUCY ANNA LOPEZ, 8th Grade Counselor Dept Chair; *b:* Montemorelos, Mexico; *m:* Armando Sr.; *c:* Armando Jr., Zita M. Gaytan, Eduardo R., Jaime J., Zelda M.; *ed:* (BA) Elem Ed/Spec Ed, 1961, (MED) Counseling/Guidance, Pan American Univ 1976; Consultant, Coord, Career Ed, Span Minor; *cr:* Spec Ed Teacher Edinburg Consolidated Ind Sch Dist 1961-65; Elem Teacher 1965-70, Career Ed Coord 1970-72, Cnslr/Mig Voc Reg 1972-79 Pharr Ind Sch Dist; Cnslr Edinburg Consolidated Ind Sch Dist 1980-; *ai:* Cnslr Dept Head & Say No to Drugs Spon; Jr HS Natl Honor Society, Gifted, Talented Comm Mem; TX St Teachers Assn; TX Outlook Magazine Article on Rdng 1969; *home:* Rt 1 Box 358 B Edinburg TX 78539

ALVAREZ, MANUEL JUNIOR, Mathematics Department Chair; *b:* Scottsbluff, NE; *m:* Carla Mae Vance; *c:* Scott W., Tracy R.; *ed:* (BS) Math, Chadron St Coll 1972; (MA) Math, Kearney St Coll 1980; Phys Ed, Coaching Endorsement; *cr:* Teacher/Coach Sidney St Patricks HS 1972-74, Gering Jr HS 1974-; *ai:* Jr HS Athletic Dir; Head Frosh Ftbl Coach; Phi Delta Kappa 1984-; NE Ed Assn 1974-; Kappa Mu Epsilon 1971; Western NE All-Star Ftbl Game Asst Coach; Officiated Girls & Boys St Bsktbl Tournaments; Whos Who Among Stu Amer Univs & Colls 1972; *home:* 1485 Bonanza Gering NE 69341

ALVAREZ, MIGDALIA ROMAN, 8th Grade Bilingual Teacher; *b:* Bronx, NY; *m:* George William; *c:* Adam H., Matthew S.; *ed:* (BS) Early Chldhd Ed, Wheelock Coll 1977; (MA) Admin Supervision, Jersey City Coll 1985; NY Bi-ling/Bicultural Teachers Trng Prgm, Spec Emphasis from Puerto Rican Family Inst 1977-78; *cr:* Kndgtn/2nd-4th Grade Teacher Jersey City Public Schls 1978-85; 8th Grade Bi-ling Teacher Nicolaus Copernicus Sch 1985-; *ai:* CCD Teacher St Nicholas Parish; Character Ed Comm; *office:* Nicolaus Copernicus Sch 3385 Kennedy Blvd Jersey City NJ 07307

ALVERSON, GEORGIA HOFFIS, Science Teacher; *b:* Glens Falls, NY; *m:* J. Maynard; *c:* James, David; *ed:* (MS) Ed Psych, Coll of St Rose 1986; (BS) Medical Technology, Russell Sage 1967; *cr:* 7th Grade Sci Teacher Queensburg Jr HS 1985-86; 7th & 8th Grade Sci Teacher Fort Ann Cntrl 1986-; *ai:* 9th Grade Class Adv; Child Study Team; Curr Dev Comm; *office:* Ft Ann Central Sch Elizabeth St Fort Ann NY 12827

ALVIS, DEBRA J., Biology/Science Teacher Chm; *b:* Princeton, WV; *ed:* (BSED) Bio-Gen Sci, Concord Coll 1978; (MSED) Voc Ed Spec Needs, Marshall Univ 1983; Prgm PIE; Basic-Computing; Physics for HS Teachers; Effective Schls Trng; *cr:* Bio Teacher Matoaka HS 1978-79; Gen Sci Teacher Spanishburg HS 1979-83; Operations Mgr Hills Dept Store 1983-84; Bio-Sci Teacher Oakvale HS 1985-; *ai:* Cty Sci Fair Comm; Sci/Math Dept Chm; Effective Schls Comm; Frosh Homeroom Spon; Oakvales Drug-Free Coord; Samara Conservation Testing; Drug-Free Comm; Know Your St Government Day Spon; Mercer Cty Rdng Cncl; NEA; ASCD; WV Ed Assn; Mercer Cty Ed Assn Building Rep 1985-; Textbook Selection Comm; Prin Awd for Outstanding Achievement; Honorary Chapter FFA Delegate WV Ed Assn Convention; *office:* Oakvale Jr Sr HS PO Box 188 Oakvale WV 24739

ALWELL, MARIANA FRANCESCA, 6th Grade Teacher; *b:* Denver, CO; *m:* John Avery Wells; *c:* Dustin D. Wells, Nicholas Sayer Wells; *ed:* (BA) Poly Sci, Grinnell Coll 1968; (MA) Elem Ed, Claremont Grad Sch 1975; Cooperative Learning, Math, Univ of CA Santa Cruz; Trng Technology in Classroom 1987-; *cr:* 4th-6th Grade Spec Ed Teacher Chino Unified Sch Dist 1969-71; Spec Ed Teacher Collins Jr HS 1971-74; 5th Grade Teacher Murdock ELem Sch 1974-77; 5th/6th Grade Teacher Garden Gate Elem Sch 1977-; *ai:* Math Lead Teacher; Model Technology Project Mem; Cupertino Ed Assn 1972-; Camp Fire Leader 1987-; Boulder Creek Elem Sch (Site Cncl 1987-, VP 1989-); Garden Gate Elem Sch Teacher of Yr 1987, 1988, Natl Exemplary Ed Awd 1986; *office:* Garden Gate Elem Sch 10500 Ann Arbor Ave Cupertino CA 95014

ALWINE, JUDITH S. (WEIGLE), Third Grade Teacher; *b:* Johnstown, PA; *m:* Robert Allen; *c:* Camille S., Robert W.; *ed:* (BS) Elem Ed, IN Univ of PA; *cr:* Teacher St Michael Sch 1966-67, 1970-71, Visitation Sch 1967-69, St Patrick Sch 1969-70, St Benedict Sch 1978-; *ai:* A-V Equipment; Private Tutoring; Evaluation Comm; Sci Teaching & LearnIng Prgm; Phi Delta

Kappa Mem; NCEA; PA St Coll of Ag; Cooperative Extension 4-H Teacher 1987-; PA Jr Acad of Sci Judge, Spon; *office:* St Benedict Sch 2306 Bedford St Johnstown PA 15904

AMAN, J'ANN PAYNE, Mentor Teacher/Eng Dept Chm; *b:* Waco, TX; *m:* William Burns; *c:* Micah S. Aman Goode; *ed:* (BA) Ed/Eng/His, Baylor Univ 1957; Grad Stud Ed, Eng, His, Baylor Univ; *cr:* 5th Grade Music Teacher 1957-58, 6th Grade Music Teacher 1958-60, 1st-6th Grade Music Teacher 1960-61 Meadowbrook Elem; 6th Grade Music Teacher Parkdale Elem 1961-72; 6th Grade Math Teacher R L Smith 6th Grade Center 1972-80; 7th/8th Grade Teacher Tennyson Jr HS 1980-89; Career Summary/Writing Lab/Mentor Teacher Lake Air Mid Sch 1989-; *ai:* Eng Dept Chm; Co-Spon Lake Air Yrbk; Campus Action Chm; Univ Interscholastic League Organizer; Assn of TX Prof Educators, NEA, TX St Teachers Assn, Waco Classroom Teachers Assn, NCTE, ASCD; 1st Assembly of God Music Coord 1980-, Honored 1990; Waco Civic Chorus; Daughters of The Amer Revolution; Waco Euterpean Music Pres 1980-82, Honored 1983; Delta Kappa Gamma Society (Pres 1986-88, St Music Chm 1987-89), Achievement 1988; Teacher of Yr Waco Classroom 1987, Tennyson 1988, Waco Ind Sch Dist 1988-89; TX St Teacher of Yr Nom 1989.

AMATO, ANTHONY T., Vice Principal; *b:* Easton, PA; *m:* Lois Guiles; *c:* Christopher, Alicia; *ed:* (BS) Ed, E Stroudsburg St Coll 1967; (MED) Admin, E Stroudsburg Univ 1984; Spec Ed, Environmental Ed; *cr:* Teacher 1967-88, Vice Prin/Coord of Spec Services 1988- White Township Sch; *ai:* NAESP; White Township Environmental Commission; Youth Athletic Assn Pres 1980-85; *office:* White Township Cons Sch RR 03 Box 580 Belvidere NJ 07823

AMBERG, CAROL SCOTT, English Teacher; *b:* Gouverneur, NY; *m:* Frank M.; *c:* Tess; *ed:* (BA) Eng/Comm Stud - Cum Laude, St Univ Coll Oswego 1977; (MSED) Scndry Eng, SUNY Potsdam 1987; *cr:* Eng Teacher Watertown HS 1983-85; Comm/Eng Instr Mater Dei Coll 1986-87; Eng Teacher Gouverneur HS 1987-; *ai:* Stage Plays & Musicals Dir; Instruction Comm; SUNY Potsdam Outstanding Stu Teacher Awd 1983; *office:* Gouverneur HS 133 E Barney St Gouverneur NY 13642

AMBERG, PATRICIA L., Biology Teacher, Science Chair; *b:* Sault Sainte Marie, MI; *ed:* (BS) Bio/Phys Ed, St Mary Coll 1963; Genetics, Univ of MO 1970; Philosophy, Coll of Palo Verde 1971; Dance & Statistics, Univ of N CO 1972; Psych, Regis Coll 1985; Electrocardiogram Technician; *cr:* Speech/Bio/Phys Ed Teacher Billings Cntrl 1963-66; Bio/Phys Ed Teacher Girls Cntrl 1966-69; Chem Teacher Hogan 1969-70; Bio/Health Teacher Immaculata 1970-72; EKG Technician Valleyview Hospital 1972-74; Bio/Math/Phys Ed Teacher Holy Family 1975-83; *ai:* HS Bsktbl, Vlybl, Track & Field, Sftbl & Speech Team Coach; Soph Class Spon; Spirit Club Adv; Tumbling Team Spon; Self Study, Curr & Ethics Comm; NSTA, NEA, CO Assn of Sci Teachers; Regis Coll Liturgical Music Group; Amer Sftbl Assn Umpire; Pros Umpire Assn; Natl Fnd Physics Grant Univ of CO; Bsktbl Coaching Awd; Womens Sftbl Camp St Champs 1977, Runner-Up 1978, League Champs 1983, 1985, 1989; *home:* 4931 Quitman St Denver CO 80212

AMBROSE, JOHN W., Social Studies Teacher; *b:* Mineola, NY; *ed:* (BA) His, Stony Brook Univ 1988; *cr:* Part Time Soc Stud Teacher E Meadow HS 1988-89; Soc Stud Teacher W T Clarke HS 1989-; *ai:* Var Golf Coach E Meadow HS; 7th Grade Bsktbl Coach Clarke HS; Faculty Adv Clarke HS Environment Club; Amnesty Intnl Mem 1986-; *office:* W T Clarke HS Edgewood Dr Westbury NY 11590

AMBROSE, JOSEPH EUGENE, Social Studies Teacher; *b:* Reading, PA; *c:* Joseph E. Jr., Genevieve A.; *ed:* (BSED) Comprehensive Soc Stu, Kutztown St Coll 1968; (MA) Amer His, Villanova Univ 1972; *cr:* Soc Stud Teacher Reading Sr HS 1968-; *ai:* PA Cncl for Soc Stud 1983-; Knights of Columbus 1973-; Rdng Allentown Cursillo Cmmty 1976-; Beginning Experience to aid Widowed & Divorced Individuals 1989-; *office:* Reading Sr HS 13th & Douglas Sts Reading PA 19604

AMBROSE, KIM D., 8th Grade Team Leader; *b:* Conway, SC; *ed:* (BS) Sci Teaching, Clemson Univ 1984; (MED) Natural Sci, Univ of SC 1985; (EDS) Scndry Ed/Sci, Univ of AL 1990; *cr:* Teacher Dade Mid Sch 1985-; *home:* Rt 2 Box 138-G Sunset Dr Rising Fawn GA 30738

AMBROSIO, ANTHONY LOUIS, Principal; *b:* Chicago, IL; *m:* Katherine Panfilo; *c:* John P.; *ed:* (BED) Ed, Chicago Teachers Coll 1954; (MED) Guidance/Counseling/Admin, De Paul Univ 1966; Cultures of Disadvantaged; *cr:* Teacher US Grant Sch 1958-61, Fredrick Funston Sch 1961-65, Avondale Sch 1965-69; Teacher/Cnslr H C Anderson EVGC 1969-72; Teacher/Asst Prin 1972-, Prin 1990 Norwood Park; *ai:* Kappa Delta Pi Life Mem 1967-; Lincolnwood Park & Recreation Bd Mem 1988-; *office:* Norwood Park Elem Sch 5900 N Nina Chicago IL 60631

AMBURN, MAGGIE TAYLOR FRAZIER, English Teacher; *b:* Hillsville, VA; *m:* Arnold Ralph Sr.; *c:* Richard A. Frazier, Arnold R. Jr., Troy C., Alice M., Harriett A. Amburn Bernard; *ed:* (BS) Home Ec/Chem, 1956, Eng Cert, 1959 Radford Univ; Working Toward Masters in Eng; *cr:* Home Ec Teacher Galax HS 1956-57; 11th/12th Grade Eng Teacher Willis HS 1957-62; Frosh Eng Teacher Ferrum Coll 1961; 11th Grade Eng Teacher Independence HS 1962-65; 8th Grade Eng Teacher Independence Mid Sch 1985-; *ai:* Drama Club St Competition 1962, 1968, 1971, Creative Writing 1st Place St Trophy 1983, Newspaper Spon 1st Place St 1982; 8th Grade & Jr Class Head Spon; Grayson Cty Ed Assn (Treas 1964) 1962-; VA Ed Assn, NEA 1956-; Floyd Cty Ed Assn 1957-62; Galax Jr Womans Club Pres 1962; Order of Eastern Star Assoc Matron 1970; VA Dept of Ed Evaluation Comm Lebanon Cty Schls 1976, Comm for Dev of Standards of Learning, Teacher of Experimental Lang Prgm Grayson Cty 1974-76; *home:* 102 Ernie Pyle St Galax VA 24333

AMELING, GLENN ALAN, Foreign Language Teacher; *b:* Houston, TX; *m:* Linda La Fawn Dastrup; *c:* Christina, Robert; *ed:* (BA) His, 1979; (MA) Latin Amer His, 1981 Brigham Young Univ; 2nd Ed Certificate UT 1980; BYU Standard Ed Certificate OR 1989; PSU 2 Yr Mission in Mexico; *cr:* His/Span Teacher Mc Kenzie HS 1986-87, The Dalles 1987-; *ai:* Pep, Span Club Adv; Confederation of Oregon Foreign Lang Teachers Mem 1987-; ADCD Mem 1987-; BSA Scoutmaster 1987-; King Don Carlos Fellowship to Madrid Spain 1990; Admiral & Diplomat William Banks Caperton Agent of US Naval Policy in Latin America 1915-; *office:* The Dulles HS 200 E 10th St The Dalles OR 97058

AMES, JENNIE M., English Teacher; *b:* Memphis, TN; *m:* Gerald; *ed:* (BA) Eng, Le Moyne-Owen Coll 1968; *cr:* Teacher Memphis City Schls 1968-; *ai:* Jr/Sr Prom Coord; Sr Class Adv; Memphis Ed Assn, NEA, NCTE 1968-; Mid America Performing Arts Theatre 1990; Published Childrens Books, Poetry, Article.

AMES, KATHIE NEILL, Kindergarten Teacher; *b:* Springfield, IL; *m:* William C.; *c:* Rebecca, Sara, Matt, Robyne; *ed:* (AA) Sci, Orange Coast Coll 1965; (BS) Ed, E IL Univ 1969; *cr:* Kndgtn Teacher Calvary Acad 1977-; *ai:* Calvary Temple Church 1970-; *office:* Calvary Acad 1730 W Jefferson Springfield IL 62702

AMESBURY, NORINE MARY, English Teacher; *b:* Wilkes-Barre, PA; *ed:* (BA) Eng, Coll Misericordia 1972; (MA) Eng, Univ of Scranton 1977; *cr:* Eng Teacher Dallas Sch Dist 1972-; *ai:* Stu Cncl Adv; Interfaith Resource Center for Peace & Justice Educators Group Mem 1988-; *office:* Dallas Mid Sch PO Box 2000 Dallas PA 18612

AMIOT, CLAIRE P., 5th Grade Teacher; *b:* Fall River, MA; *ed:* (BA) Pre-Med, Univ of MA Amherst 1967; (MED) Rdng, Bridgewater St Coll 1974; *cr:* Sci/Math/Economics Teacher Fall River Girls Vocational Sch 1967-68; Spec Abilities Itinerant/4th-6th Grade Sci-Gifted Teacher 1968-69; 5th Grade Teacher Wiley Elem Sch 1969-71; 6th Grade Math Teacher 1971-72, 5th & 6th Grade Rdng Teacher 1972-78 Talbot Mid Sch; 5th Grade Teacher Coughlin Elem Sch 1978-; *ai:* Adv Sch Store Management & Operation; ADK 1987-; GSA Troop Leader 1974-83 Weetamoe Awd; Service Unit Chairperson; Thanks Badge; Our Lady of Good Cncl Medals; St Ann Medal; *home:* 369 Bullock St Fall River MA 02720

AMIRO, BARBARA DI SANTI, Sixth Grade Teacher; *b:* W Chester, PA; *m:* Joseph A. Jr.; *ed:* (BS) Elem Ed, West Chester St Coll 1973; *cr:* 6th Grade Teacher St Patrick Sch 1973-79, Holy Name Sch 1979-; *ai:* NCEA; *office:* Holy Name Sch 535 W Roxbury Pkwy West Roxbury MA 02132

AMIS, JEROME, Social Studies Chair; *ed:* (BA) His/Poly Sci, Albany St Coll 1978; GA St Univ; *cr:* Teacher Henry Cty HS 1978-; *ai:* Phi Alpha Theta; City of Mc Donough Cncl Mem; Henry Cty Recreation Bd; *home:* 39 Cemetery Street Mc Donough GA 30253

AMMES, PATTY ALDER, Headmaster & 3rd Grade Teacher; *b:* Memphis, TN; *m:* Don E.; *c:* Curt, Staci; *ed:* (BSE) Elem Ed, AR St Univ 1963; In-Service Trng Pensacola Chrstn Coll; *cr:* 4th Grade Teacher Bay Elem 1963-64; 2nd-4th Grade Teacher West & East Elem 1965-70; 7th Grade Lang Art Teacher 1975, Kndgtn Teacher 1976-77 Osceola Public; 1st Grade Teacher 1978, Headmaster 1983- Presbyn Chrstn; *ai:* GFWC Mississippi Cty Women of Achievement 1990.

AMMONS, DAVID FRANKLIN, Fifth Grade Teacher; *b:* Pickens, SC; *m:* Sherilyn Barker; *ed:* (BA) Elem Ed, 1968, (MA) Elem Ed, 1973 Furman Univ; Grad Hrs Above Masters Degree; *cr:* Teacher Greenbrier Elem Sch 1968-70, Morton Elem Sch 1970-71; Acting Prin 1971-72, Teacher 1972- Morton Elem Sch; *ai:* Southern Assn of Coll & Schls Chm; Sch Chm Math, Cmptr, Soc Stud; Kappa Delta Pi 1990; NSTA 1987-; Northgate Baptist Church (Deacon 1978-, Choir 1973-, Sunday Sch Teacher 1978-); Illustrator of 3 Historical Novels; Teacher of Yr 1980-81, 1988-89; *home:* 1108 Brushy Creek Rd Taylors SC 29687

AMMONS, MARLA JEAN (TENNANT), 5th & 6th Grade Teacher; *b:* Fairmont, WV; *m:* Kevin D.; *c:* Erin, Jason; *ed:* (ABED) Elem Ed, Fairmont St Coll 1976; (MA) Elem Ed/Curr/Instruction, WV Univ 1982; Pre-Voc Ed, Marshall Univ; Cmptr Ed, WV Univ; *cr:* Stu Secy Fairmont St Coll 1973-74; Teacher Downs Elem 1976-77; Ind Contractor Consolidation Coal Company 1982-85; Teacher Jakes Run Elem 1977-; *ai:* AIDS Trainer; Math Curr Cncl; Lang Art & Math Textbook Adoption Comm; Alpha Delta Kappa (Recording Secy 1990) 1988-; WVEA 1977-; Jakes Run PTO 1977-, Dedicated Service 1985; Jakes Run Parent Advisory Cncl 1985-; Teacher in Charge; *home:* Rt 1 Box 78 Fairview WV 26570

AMMONS, SHERILYN B., Fourth Grade Teacher; *b:* Greenville, SC; *m:* David F.; *ed:* (BA) Psych/Music/Eng, Carson Newman Coll 1968; (MA) Elem Ed, Furman Univ 1989; Grad Stud; *cr:* Teacher Mountain View Elem 1968-70, Bethel Elem 1970-72, Morton Elem 1972-; *ai:* Sch Chm Rdng, Eng, Natl Earth Week; Kappa Delta Pi 1989-; NSTA 1987-; Northgate Baptist Church (Choir, Sunday Sch Teacher) 1973-; Sci Mini Grant 1987-88; Morton ELem Teacher of Yr 1982-83, 1986-87; *home:* 1108 Brushy Creek Rd Taylors SC 29687

AMOS, HAZEL PEACE, English Teacher; *b:* Waverly, VA; *m:* Marvin O.; *c:* Gena; *ed:* (BA) Eng, VA St Univ 1948; (MLITT) Eng Lit, Univ of Pittsburgh 1954; Post Grad Stud Univ of Pittsburgh; *cr:* Eng Instr Huntington HS 1949-55; Eng/Speech/Journalism Instr NW Jr HS 1955-59, 1960-64; Eng Instr Johnson C Smith Univ 1964-78, E Mecklenburg HS 1978-; *ai:* NEA, NC Assn of Educators, Sigma Tau Delta, Iota Sigma Lambda; *office:* East Mecklenburg HS 6800 Monroe Rd Charlotte NC 28212

AMOS, NANCY STOCKWELL, Kindergarten Teacher; *b:* Findlay, OH; *m:* Charles; *c:* Jill; *ed:* (BSED) Elem Ed, Bowling Green St Univ 1966; *cr:* 2nd Grade Teacher Otsego 1966-69; 2nd Grade Teacher 1975-76, 1st Grade Teacher 1976-80, Kndgtn Teacher 1980- Anthony Wayne Schls; *ai:* Anthony Wayne Dist Curr Comms; NEA, OH Ed Assn, Anthony Wayne Ed Assn Building Rep; Martha Holden Jennings Scholar 1985-86; *home:* 861 Carol Rd Bowling Green OH 43402

AMOS, PATRICIA COOK, Latin/Spanish Teacher; *b:* Miami, FL; *m:* William Joseph; *c:* William J. Jr.; *ed:* (AB) Span/His, Shorter Coll 1959; Univ of Guadalajara, W GA Coll, GA Southern Magill Univ, Univ of SC; *cr:* Teacher Model HS 1959-; *ai:* Sr Class Spon; Admin Leadership Chm; Interim SACS Study Team Media Comm; Chm Foreign Lang; NEA, GA Assn of Educators, Floyd Cty Assn of Educators 1959-; Amer Assn of Teachers of Span & Portuguese, Foreign Lang Assn of GA, Amer Classical League; STAR Teacher; Yrbk Dedication Twice; Teacher of Month; *office:* Model HS 3252 Calhoun Hwy NE Rome GA 30161

AMREIN, ALLAN G., Phys Ed/Amer His Teacher; *b:* Colby, KS; *m:* Susan Kay (Painter); *c:* Donielle, Erin; *ed:* (AA) HPER, Dodge City Comm Coll 1980; (BS) HPER, 1982, (MS) Athletic Admin, 1986 Fort Hays St Univ; *cr:* Teacher/Coach St Marys Sch 1983-84; Coach Thomas More Preporatory HS 1984-86; Teacher/Coach Lewis HS 1986-88, Ness City HS 1988-; *ai:* Ftbl, Track, Field Head; Natl Strength Coaches Assn 1983-; Natl Fed of Interscholastic Coaches 1985-; KS Assn of Health, Phys Ed, Recreation, Dance 1982-; KS 8-Man All-Star Ftbl Game Asst Coach 1988; Ftbl Clinician Various Clinics Around St; *office:* Ness City HS 200 N 5th Ness City KS 67560

AMUNDSON, MAXINE (KILLEANEY), Vocal Music Teacher; *b:* Sioux Falls, SD; *m:* Earl F.; *c:* David, Marin, Daniel; *ed:* (BA) Music, Augustana Coll 1955; (MA) Music Ed, Northwestern Univ 1960; Grad Stud Univ Southern CA; *cr:* Dir of Music United Luth Church 1956-60; Voice/Music Ed/Choral Music Instr Augustana Coll 1960-63; Teacher West Jr HS 1963-66, Sanborn/Lamberton Elem Jr-Sr HS 1981-; *ai:* Dir Triple Trio, Swing Choir, Small Group Ensembles; Adv Sanborn/Lamberton Chapter-Natl Honor Society; Lamberton Ed Assn (Secy 1985-86, Treas 1987-88); MEA, NEA 1981-; MENC 1985-; Lamberton Area Cmmty Choir Dir & Founder 1974-; Lamberton Lib Bd (chm, Treas) 1975-; MN Fed Womens Clubs (Pres, Secy, Treas) 1968-; Lamberton City Cncl Acting Mayor 1982-; Bd Mem Luth Soc Service MN Service Awd; FFA Voc Awd Honorary Chapter Farmer; WCCO Good Neighbor Awd 1984; Nom MN Teacher of Yr 1988; *home:* 400 S Main Lamberton MN 56152

AMUNDSON, NORMA JEAN, Sixth Grade Teacher; *b:* Blooming Prairie, MN; *m:* Marvin J.; *c:* Lisa Farencamp, Steven, Evin; *ed:* (BS) Elem Ed, Mankato ST Univ 1973; *cr:* 5th Grade Teacher Winnebago Elem Sch 1957-59, Great Falls MT 1959-60; Rdng Dir 1974-76, 6th Grade Teacher 1976 Blooming Prairie; *ai:* NEA 1974-; MEA 1974-; Outstndng Educator 1989; *office:* Blooming Prairie Elem Sch 110 1st St NW Blooming Prairie MN 55917

AMUNDSON, SALLY DELONG, Voc Agriculture Teacher; *b:* Elkhorn, WI; *m:* Thomas E.; *ed:* (BS) Ag Ed, UW River Falls 1982; *cr:* Vo Ag Instr Clayton HS 1982; *ai:* FFA Adv; 8th Grade Adv; JV Girls Bsktbl; WAVIAI 1982; *home:* Box 186 A Clayton WI 54004

ANACKER, ROBERT JOHN, Science/Mathematics Teacher; *b:* Menomonie, WI; *m:* Roxanne; *c:* Tracey; *ed:* (BS) Soc Sci/Phys Sci, Carthage Coll 1968; (MS) Geography, NE IL Univ Chicago 1979; Admin, Cntrl WA Univ 1987; *cr:* Teacher/Coach Jack Benny Jr HS & Waukegan West 1968-78, Palatine HS 1983, Kalama HS 1983-; *ai:* Head Ftbl Coach; Weight Lifting Instr; Knowledge Bowl Adv; WA St Coaches Assn 1988-; Natl Cncl Geographic Ed (Past Mem, Mem Awd Comm) 1975-76; Consultant Denoyer Gepport Elem Geography Materials; *office:* Kalama HS 548 China Garden Rd Kalama WA 98625

ANCHORS, BETTY SMITH, Fifth Grade Teacher; *b:* Opp, AL; *m:* Sidney J.; *c:* Elizabeth D. Holland, Sydna Young; *ed:* (BS) Elem Ed, Troy ST 1952; *cr:* 1st-6th Grade Teacher Port St Joe elem 1952-57, 1960-63, 1965-; *ai:* Stu Cncl & Good Morning Show Spon; Publicity Comm Chm; Gulf Cty Classroom Teachers Assn Pres 1984-85; United Meth Women Pres 1982-84, Pin 1984; Church Trustee 1985-86; Mission Group III Chm 1988-; *home:* 619 Garrison Ave Port Saint Joe FL 32456

ANCLADE, BRUCE MICHAEL, Bio/Work Experience Teacher; *b:* Chicago, IL; *m:* Cathleen C. Vogel; *ed:* (BS) Bio, Bradley Univ 1976; (MS) Sci, Nova Univ 1984; Teacher Cert, W IL Univ; *cr:* Bio Teacher/Tennis Coach Peoria Manual HS 1977-81; Bio Teacher/Bsktbl Coach Twin Lakes HS 1981-84; Bio/Work Experience Teacher/Bsktbl Coach Boca Raton HS 1984-86, Palm Beach Lakes HS 1986-; *ai:* Tennis & Bsktbl Coach; Intramural Dir; CTA Mem 1985-; NFICA Mem 1984-; *office:* Palm Beach Lakes HS 3505 Shiloh Dr West Palm Beach FL 33407

ANDAHAZY, MARIUS JOSEPH, K-12th Grade Dept Ballet Dir; *b:* Minneapolis, MN; *m:* Krisztina Gloria Simonffy; *c:* Ferenc, Anna, Chiara, Maria; *ed:* Sch of Amer Ballet; Trained with Bolshoi Ballet of Moscow & Kirov Ballet of Leningrad; *cr:* Dancer Royal Swedish Ballet 1975-79; Dir Andahazy Ballet Company & Sch of Classical Ballet 1986-; Ballet Dept Head Convent of Visitation Sch 1984-; *ai:* Lectures; Choreography; Intnl Ballet Video Series Spon; Amer Guild of Musical Artists Mem 1971-; Royal Swedish Ballet (Dancer, Choreographer) 1975-79; MN Fed of Music Clubs Mem 1983-; Prin Dancer Andahazy Ballet Company; Guest Artist US, Portugal, Madeira, Sweden; Amer Ballet Theatre Sch NY Schlsp; *office:* Convent of the Visitation Sch PO Box 11480 Saint Paul MN 55111

ANDEREGG, TERRI L., English Teacher/Coach; *b:* Crane, TX; *ed:* (BS) Phys Ed, SW TX St Univ 1977; Working Toward Masters Educl Admin, Univ of N TX Denton; *cr:* Eng Teacher/Coach Monahans HS 1977-81, Austin Jr HS 1981-; *ai:* 8th Grade Girls Bsktbl & Track Coach; Fellowship of Chrstn Athletes Co Spon; Assn of TX Prof Educators; *office:* Austin Jr HS 825 E Union Bower Irving TX 75061

ANDERS, BONNIE FAWCETT, Rdng Teacher/Lang Art Chair; *b:* Kokomo, IN; *m:* Richard R.; *c:* Christopher, Mark; *ed:* (BS) Elem Ed, Hanover Coll 1965; Grad Work Univ of TN; *cr:* Teacher Lawrence Elem 1965-66, Boyd Elem 1966-67, Gaithersburg Elem 1967-68, Cedar Bluff Mid Sch 1978-; *ai:* Drama Club Spon; Speech Coach; TN Assn of Mid Schls Secy 1986-88; Phi Delta Kappa, NCTE, Intnl Rdng Assn; Inaugural Class of Leadership Ed Mem 1989-; Career Level III Teacher 1985-; Knox Cty & E TN Dist Teacher of Yr 1991; *office:* Knox Cty Schls 707 N Cedar Bluff Rd Knoxville TN 37923

ANDERS, CAROL PETRILLA, 6th-8th Grade Home Ec Teacher; *b:* Norristown, PA; *m:* P. Frank; *ed:* (BS) Home Ec Ed, Albright Coll 1972; (MS) Home Ec Ed, Drexel Univ 1977; *cr:* Home Ec Teacher Springfield HS 1972-73, Arcola Intermediate Sch 1973-; *ai:* Accompany Sch Choirs; Act Night, Discipline, Heterogeneous Grouping Comms; Amer Home Ec Assn, Kappa Omicron Phi, Amer Guild of Organists; *office:* Arcola Intermediate Sch Eagleville Rd Norristown PA 19403

ANDERS, GLENN KALE, Biology Teacher/Sci Dept Chair; *b:* Knoxville, TN; *m:* Deborah Kay Clark; *c:* Andrew, Amanda; *ed:* (BS) Bio, 1967, (MS) Bio, 1973 E TN St Univ; *cr:* Bio Teacher Cocke Cty HS 1968-; *ai:* NEA, TN Ed Assn, E TN Ed Assn, Cocke Cty Educl Assn 1968-; Cocke Cty Teacher of Yr 1981; Cocke Cty HS Stu Cncl Teacher of Yr 1988-89.

ANDERS, KAY, Business Education Teacher; *b:* Hendrix, OK; *m:* Harold; *ed:* (BS) Bus Ed, 1967, (MS) Bus Ed, 1973 SE OK St Univ; *cr:* Soc Worker Bryan Cty Cmmty Action Agency 1967-71; Teacher Achille Public Schls 1971-; *ai:* NHS Adv; Class Spon; Staff Dev Comm Chairperson; Delta Kappa Gamma (VP, Secy, Parliamentarian) 1979-; NEA, OK Ed Assn, Bryan Cty Ed Assn 1971-; Order of Eastern Star; Bryan Cty Fed of Democratic Women; Outstanding Young Woman of America 1979; FFA Service Awd 1985; FHA Service Awd 1989.

ANDERSEN, BRIAN C., Spanish Teacher; *b:* Logan, UT; *m:* Irene M.; *c:* Kayley; *ed:* (BA) Span, 1977, (MA) Span, 1984 CA St Sacramento; *cr:* Span Teacher El Camino HS 1982-; *ai:* Girls Jr Var Bsktbl Coach; San Juan Teachers Assn, NEA 1989-; Amer Philatelic Society 1978-; Span Main Society 1988-; *office:* El Camino HS 4300 El Camino Ave Sacramento CA 95821

ANDERSEN, DAWN ANDERSON, Fifth Grade Teacher; *b:* St Paul, MN; *m:* Keith Roger; *c:* Paul M., Paige R.; *ed:* (BA) Elem Ed, 1973, (MA) Elem Ed/Lang Art/Childrens Lit, 1980 Univ of IA; Working Toward Cert in Elem Admin Univ of IA; *cr:* Title I Ottumwa Cmmty Sch Dist 1974; Title I/5th Grade Teacher Centerville Cmmty Sch Dist 1974-80; K/5th/6th Grade self Contained Classroom Teacher Benton Cmmty Sch Dist 1981-; *ai:* Mem of Teachers & Supts Advisory Comm; Sch Soc Comm Chm; Pi Lambda Theta 1973-85; NEA, IA St Ed Assn 1974-; IA Rdng Assn 1987-; Amer Heart Assn 1988-89; Nom for Local Golden Apple Awd 1990; *office:* Benton Cmmty Schls 217 4th Ave Atkins IA 52206

ANDERSEN, JOHN WILLY, 6th Grade Teacher; *b:* Salt Lake City, UT; *m:* Peggy Facer; *c:* Kari, Spencer, Tessa, Tyler, Brinton; *ed:* (MS) Speech Pathology/Audiology, Univ of UT 1968; Elem Admin Cert, Univ of AL Anchorage 1980; *cr:* Teacher UT Sch for Deaf 1968-70; Teacher 1970-80, Admin Intern 1980-82, Teacher 1982- Anchorage Sch Dist; *ai:* Chess Sponsorship; Bkstbl Coach; Anchorage Ed Assn (Insurance Comm 1988-, Building Site Comm 1988-); Church of Jesus Christ of Later Day Saints Stake Presidency 1980-; Delta Kappa Gamma Golden Aple Awd 1988-89; *office:* Scenic Park Elem 3933 Patterson Rd Anchorage AK 99504

ANDERSEN, LAURIE, Seminary Teacher; *b:* Hamilton, New Zealand; *m:* Carol Lyn Byrnes; *c:* Shane, Lance, Lisa Phillips, Jared, Cody, Brandon, Darla, Derek, Devron; *ed:* (BS) Geography, 1970, (MED) Scndry Ed/Admin, 1971 Brigham Young Univ; *cr:* Teacher Kamas UT 1970-73; Teacher/Prin Church Coll of New Zealand 1973-76, Morgan UT 1976-80, Roy UT 1980-; *home:* 1985 Deep Creek Rd Morgan UT 84050

ANDERSEN, MARILYN CLAY, Math Teacher-Dept Chm; *b:* Brigham City, UT; *m:* Fred Y.; *c:* Barbara Walpole, Kathryn Bradley, Jane Christenson; *ed:* (BS) Math, 1957; (MED) Math, 1975 Univ of UT; Weber St Coll; *cr:* Math Teacher Bountiful Jr HS 1957-; *ai:* UCTM Bd Mem 1986-87; UEA; DEA; NEA; NCTM; UT Cncl of Teachers of Math Awd 1983; LDS Church Teacher; GSA Asst Leader 1973-74; Recipient of Natl Sci Fnd Grants; *office:* Bountiful Jr HS 30 W 400 N Bountiful UT 84010

ANDERSEN, SHARON RAHNKE, Teacher; *b:* Fresno, CA; *m:* Paul F. Andersen Sr.; *c:* P. Flindt Andersen Jr., Kathleen Andersen Storelli; *ed:* (BA) Geography, CA St Univ Fresno 1974; *cr:* Teacher Fresno Unified Sch Dist 1975-; *ai:* NEA, CTA, Fresno Teachers Assn, CA Rdng Assn; CA St Univ Fresno Alumni Trustee; *office:* John Burroughs Sch 166 N Sierra Vista Fresno CA 93702

ANDERSEN, THERESA NUZZO, 7th/8th Grade Math Teacher; *b:* Brooklyn, NY; *m:* Gene D.; *c:* Jennifer; *ed:* (BA) Eng Lang Arts, 1971, (MS) Early Childhood Ed, 1974 Hunter Coll; Math & Teaching Scndry Math; Brooklyn Coll 1989; In-Service Math Wkshps, Bishop Kearney HS 1990; *cr:* 3rd/4th/7th/8th Grade Lang Arts Teacher St Clare Sch 1971-77; 2nd Grade Teacher 1981-84, 6th Grade Lang Arts Teacher 1984-87, 7th/8th Grade Math Teacher 1987 St Catharine of Alexandria; *ai:* Adv 7th/8th Grade Math League Sponsored By Elem Math Cncl; NY ST Elem 1988- Nom 1989; Math Cncl Math Teacher Yr; ASCD 1987-; Columbiettes of Knights of Columbus Cncl #126 1979-; *home:* 1385 E 58th St Brooklyn NY 11234

ANDERSON, ALICE WEKANDER, Retired Teacher; *b:* Froid, MT; *m:* Wm. J. (dec); *c:* James A.; *ed:* Grad Teaching, E MT Normal Sch 1935; (BA) Ed, E WA Coll of Ed 1956; MT St Univ, W WA Coll of Ed, East Coll of Ed; *cr:* Teacher Roosevelt Cty 1935-38; Grade Sch Teacher/Prin Culbertson Grade Sch 1938-43; Prin/Teacher New Cntrl Grade Sch 1943-51; Teacher Cntrl & Plummer Elem Schls 1960-84; *ai:* Cub Scout Leader Den Mother; Brownie Scout Leader; 4-L Civic Club Pres; Delta Kappa Gamma; Lincoln Cty Ed Assn Pres 1943; Roosevelt Cty Ed Assn 1935; PTA VP; Christ Luth Church (Sunday Sch Supt, Bd, Choir, Circle) 1943-60; Local Winner Teacher Innovative Project Contest 1960; Nominee St Teacher of Yr 1968; Outstanding Elem Teacher of America 1975; *home:* 1022 Utah Libby MT 59923

ANDERSON, ANN MARIE, Band/Chorus Dir/Music Teacher; *b:* Chicago, IL; *ed:* (BM) Music Ed, Roosevelt Univ 1971; (ME) Ed, Natl Coll 1987; Grad Courses Roosevelt Univ, Natl Coll, St Xavier, Governors St Univ; *cr:* 5th Grade Teacher Guggenheim Sch 1971; Music Teacher North & Park Schls 1972, Sch Dist 104 1972-73, Beale Sch 1974, Feehanville Sch 1975, Chippewa Sch 1975-76; Instrumental/General Music Teacher Bannockburn Sch 1976-78; Instrumental/Vocal Music Teacher Union Ridge Sch 1978-; *ai:* Music Curr Comm; MENC 1970-; IMEA Dist Festival Competition Judge; Greenpeace, ACLU; Dir Triton Coll Talent Contest 1988; *home:* 1122 N Dale Arlington Hgts IL 60004

ANDERSON, AVIS MC LAUGHLIN, 7th Grade Science Teacher; *b:* Louisa, VA; *m:* John B.; *c:* Kevin L., April M.; *ed:* (BS) Elem Ed, VA St Univ 1980; (MA) Elem Ed, Univ of VA 1981; Guidance Ed; *cr:* Teacher Louisa Mid Sch 1981-; *ai:* Math/Sci Club Leader; Mem Career & Stu/Teacher Incentives Comm; Skills for Adolescence Adv; Louisa Cty Ed Assn Mid Sch Rep 1981-; Natl Assn for the Advancement of Colored People 1990; Alpha Kappa Alpha; Wayland Baptist Church Pianist 1957-.

ANDERSON, BARBARA BOLING, Language Arts Dept Chair; *b:* Atlanta, GA; *c:* Michael L., Lynnda L. Anderson Sarinske, Robert S.; *ed:* (AB) Lang Art, FL St Univ 1950; (MED) Ed - Summa Cum Laude, Cntrl St Univ 1972; Staff Dev Wkshps; *cr:* Eng Teacher Shawnee Mission Schls 1964-66, Putnam City Schls 1966-; *ai:* Lang Art Chairperson; NHS Spon; N Cntrl Steering & Dist Staff Dev Comms; NEA Delegate 1974-87, Hilda Maehling 1976; OK Ed Assn (Delegate, Public Relations Chairperson, Bd of Dirs) 1975-; Putnam City Assn of Classroom Teachers (Pres, Secy) 1972-; OK Prof Practices Commission Mem 1974-81; OK Prof Standards Bd Mem 1984-88; OK Bicentennial Project Co-Chairperson 1980-; Putnam City Dist Teacher of Yr 1978, 1982; OK Congress of Parents & Teachers Honorable Mention Educator of Yr; *office:* Putnam City HS 5300 N W 50th Oklahoma City OK 73122

ANDERSON, BARBARA MILLS, Guidance Counselor; *b:* Washington, DC; *m:* Samuel Leonard; *c:* Lori, Dawna, Dorrence; *ed:* (BA) Bus Ed, WV St Coll 1957; (MS) Scndry Ed, Amer Univ 1967; (MS) Scndry Counseling, Bowie St Univ 1980; *cr:* Soc Worker Dept of Welfare-Public Assistance 1960-65; Bus Teacher 1965-85, Guidance Cnslr 1985- Spingarn HS; *ai:* FBLA & Distributive Ed Clubs of America Spon; NBEA 1965-85; DC Assn for Counseling Dev, DC Sch Cnslr Assn 1985; Glenwood Park Civic Assn Membership Chairperson 1983-; Kalabards Inc VP 1988-; Jones United Meth Church Ed Chairperson 1988-; *office:* Spingarn HS 26th & Benning Rd NE Washington DC 20002

ANDERSON, BETTY DAVIS, Kindergarten Teacher; *b:* Murphy, NC; *m:* Jerry E.; *c:* Tracy, Travis, Ryan; *ed:* (BS) Elem Ed, 1969, (MA) Early Chldhd Ed, 1986 Western Carolina Univ; Rdng Cert, W Carolina Univ 1986; *cr:* Spec Ed Teacher Cntrl Elem Sch 1968-69; 1st-6th Grade Rdng Teacher Cherokee Elem Sch 1969; 1st/2nd Grade Teacher Ogden Elem 1972-74; Kndgtn Teacher Hayesville Elem 1974-; *ai:* Kappa Delta Pi, NEA, NC Assn of Educators; Clay Cty Historical Art Cncl, Friends of Moss Memorial Lib; *office:* Hayesville Elem Sch 487 Hicks Cir Hayesville NC 28904

ANDERSON, BETTY SMITH, Teacher; *b:* Galveston, TX; *c:* Charles; *ed:* (BA) Phys Ed, Huston-Tillotson Coll 1961; (MED) Phys Ed, N TX St Univ 1968; (EED) Supervision/Bio, E TX St Univ 1981; Earth Sci, KS St Univ; Chem Cert, TX Womens Univ; *cr:* Teacher Dallas Ind Sch Dist 1961-; *ai:* Pupil Assistance Support System; Sci Dept Chairperson; Sch Improvement Plan Comm; TX Sci Teachers Assn, NSTA; St Senate 23rd Dist Outstanding Teacher 1989; Huston-Tillotson Coll Academic Achievement 1985; Meadows Fnd Advanced Placement Study Grant 1990; Historical Black Coll & Univ Secy; Dallas Chapter Huston-Tillotson Alumni Pres; *home:* 2315 Blue Creek Dr Dallas TX 75216

ANDERSON, BRAD SCOTT, American History Teacher/Coach; *b:* Granbury, TX; *ed:* (BA) His/Phys Ed, Abilene Chrstn Univ 1982; *cr:* 8th/10th Grade Teacher/His Teacher/Coach Eastland Ind Sch Dist 1982-85; 8th Grade Amer His Teacher/Coach Granbury Mid Sch 1985-; *ai:* 8th Grade Head Track & Asst Ftbl Coach; TX HS Coaches Assn, TX St Teachers Assn; *office:* Granbury Mid Sch 217 N Jones St Granbury TX 76048

ANDERSON, CAROL J., Fourth Grade Teacher; *b:* Fargo, ND; *ed:* (BS) Elem Ed, Valley City St 1968; Grad Classes Various Univs; *cr:* 4th Grade Teacher Warren Elem Sch 1968-; *ai:* Delta Kappa Gamma Society Intnl (Chapter Pres 1977-81, St Comm 1989-); General Fed of Womens Clubs Dist Pres 1984-86; Godel Memorial Lib Bd 1982-; *office:* Warren Elem Sch 224 E Bridge Warren MN 56762

ANDERSON, CATHERINE WILKINSON, Third Grade Teacher; *b:* Cody, WY; *m:* Merlin Duane; *c:* Milan D., Dallas E., Michael D. (dec); *ed:* (BS) Ed, 1967, (MED) Ed, 1972 Univ of ID; *cr:* 2nd-3rd Grade Teacher Moscow Sch Dist 1967-; *ai:* Lang Art Comm Chairperson; Alpha Delta Kappa 1970-; NEA, ID Ed Assn, Moscow Ed Assn; Amer Cancer Society; *office:* Russell Sch 119 N Adams St Moscow ID 83843

ANDERSON, CHARLEEN, Language Arts Dept Chair; *b:* Ottumwa, IA; *m:* Lee R.; *c:* Geoffrey Gallatin; *ed:* (BA) Eng, Univ of IA 1961; Rdng, Curr Dev & Educl Practices; Cmptr Literacy Prgm Consultants; Cmptr Sales & Customers Service Trng, Televideo Cmptr Systems; *cr:* Rdng/Lang Art Teacher East HS 1966-69, George Washington HS 1969-76, Agat 1976-77, Isaragan Jr HS 1977-78; Sch Prgm Consultant/Inservice Guam Dept of Ed 1978-83; Dir of Trng Equestorial Cmptr Systems 1983-84; Lang Art Dept Chairperson Teacher Sanchez HS 1984-; *ai:* Journalism Club; Steering Comm Accreditation; Intnl Rdng Assn Guam Pres 1984-85; NCTE Guam Pres 1990; Amer Assn of Univ Women Pres 1973-74; NDEA Inst in Rdng Univ of N IA 1967; NEH Inst in Literary Criticism, Auburn Univ 1988; Article Published in Service Book 1989; *home:* PO Box 2908 Agana GU 96910

ANDERSON, CHRISTIAN EDWARD, Social Studies Teacher; *b:* Oakland, CA; *m:* Mary Ruth Lamb; *ed:* (BA) His, Univ of Northern CO 1984; Working Towards Masters His, Univ of Northern CO; *cr:* Soc Stud Teacher Greeley West 1984-; *ai:* Head Tennis Coach Boys & Girls; NHS Faculty Cncl; HUGS Spon; NCSS 1989-; Dist 6 Coaches Assn Building Rep 1989-, Head Coach of Yr 1987-88, Dist Coach of Yr 1988; *home:* 2013 31st St Rd Greeley CO 80631

ANDERSON, CONSTANCE CRAMER, Third Grade Teacher; *b:* Peoria, IL; *m:* Dennis Robert; *c:* Kristin, Meredith, Melissa; *ed:* (BS) Psych, Univ of IL 1974; Ed Classes, Augustana Coll; *cr:* 2nd Grade Teacher Southwest Grade Sch 1975-77; 2nd Grade Teacher 1977-79, 3rd Grade Teacher 1980- Northbrook Elem; *ai:* Sch Halloween Prgm Chm; Earth Day Comm; IL Ed Assn 1975-; Malden Cmmty Club 1985-; IL Pork Women 1983-; Tracys Sch of Dance, Gymnastics Parents Club 1989-; *office:* Northbrook Elem Sch 1804 Guiles Ave Mendota IL 61342

ANDERSON, CRIS MICHELLE (KLING), Secondary Language Art Teacher; *b:* Cando, ND; *m:* Glenn; *ed:* Eng Ed, Univ of ND; (BS) Eng Ed, Moorhead St Univ 1980; *cr:* Jr HS Lang Art Teacher MN Ind Sch Dist 544 1980-; *ai:* 7th Grade Girls Track & Speech Division Coach; MN Educl Effectiveness Prgm Leadership Team; NEA, MN Ed Assn 1980-; Fergus Falls Ed Assn Various Offices 1980-; NCTE 1989-; Delta Kappa Gamma Prgm Co-Chm 1986-; Bus & Prof Women MN St Young Career Woman of Yr 1984; Cmmty Concert Assn Bd of Dirs 1986; Bethlehem Church Forum Host 1988; Conducted Writing Seminars Otter Trail Power Company 1987-89; Fergus Falls Luth Leadership Conference Seminar Presenter 1989; NOW Regional Conference Presenter 1988; NSP Womens Career Dev Day Keynote Speaker 1987.

ANDERSON, CYNTHIA M., Educl Alternatives Teacher; *b:* Ft Lauderdale, FL; *c:* Andrianne Anderson-Coward, Brigitte; *ed:* (BA) Elem Ed, Bethune-Cookman Coll 1969; (MA) Elem Ed, FL Intl Univ 1979; Ed Specialist Admin & Supervision, Nova Univ 1981; *cr:* 4th Grade Teacher Westwood Height Elem 1969-70; 3rd Grade Teacher Village Elem 1970-72; 3rd Grade Teacher 1972-77, 4th/5th Grade Educl Alternatives Teacher 1977- Lloyd Estates Elem; *office:* Lloyd Estates Elem Sch 750 NW 41st St Oakland Park FL 33309

ANDERSON, CYNTHIA R. CARLISLE, Home Economics Teacher; *b:* Vancouver, WA; *m:* Brian Paul; *c:* Jessica M., Jaclyn R.; *ed:* (BS) Home Ec Ed, Viterbo Coll 1979; *cr:* Home Ec Teacher Arkansas HS 1980-81, Boscobel HS 1981-; *ai:* FHA Adv; Southwest Teachers Assn Mem 1981-; WI Home Ec Assn Mem 1980-; Vernon Cty Homemakers Secy 1985; St Marys Womens Auxiliary Mem 1981-; *office:* Boscobel Sch Dist 300 Brindley St Boscobel WI 53805

ANDERSON, CYNTHIA S., Physical Education Teacher; *b:* Latrobe, PA; *m:* Dennis L.; *c:* Lynnette; *ed:* (BS) Health/Phys Ed, Slippery Rock Univ 1968; Grad Stud Various Univs; *cr:* Health/Phys Ed Teacher Francis Mc Clure Jr HS 1968-69, Suitland Elem 1969-74, Lord Baltimore Jr HS 1974-77, Oxon Hill 1977-78, Benjamin Tasker 1978-79 Phys Ed Teacher James Madison Mid Sch 1979-; *ai:* Vlybl, Sftbl, Floor Hockey Coach; Chrldrs, Pep Club

Spon; AFT, Amer Assn of Health, Phys Ed, Recreation; *office:* James Madison Mid Sch 7300 Woodyard Rd Upper Marlboro MD 20772

ANDERSON, DALE MICHAEL, 4th-8th Grade Teacher; *b:* Chicago, IL; *ed:* (BS) Phys Ed, S IL Univ Edwardsville 1971; *cr:* Phys Ed/Speech/Eng/Drivers Ed Teacher/Coach St Henry Preparatory 1971-75; 5th-6th Grade Soc Stud Teacher St Marys Grade Sch 1974-75; Phys Ed Teacher/Coach Princeton HS 1978-80; 6th/8th Grade Spelling/5th Grade Soc Stud Teacher Immaculate Conception 1981-; *ai:* Athletic Dir; A Team Boys Bsktbl Coach; Special Minister of Eucharist for Belleville Diocese; Appoint Lectors for Weekday Mass; NCEA 1980-; Metro-CYO Exec Comm Mem 1987-; Certified Catechist Belleville Diocese; *office:* Immaculate Conception Sch 321 S Metter Columbia IL 62236

ANDERSON, DAVID CARL, Physical Education Teacher; *b:* St Croix Falls, WI; *m:* Susan Maurine Heller; *ed:* (AA) General Stud, Univ of WI Barron Cty 1984; (BA) Phys Ed/Health Coaching, Univ of WI River Falls 1987; *cr:* General Worker Centuria Commercial Laundry 1979-87; Summer Recreation Dir St Croix Falls 1985-; Phys Ed/Health Coach Taylors Falls HS 1987-; *ai:* Head Girls Vlybl & Asst Boys Bsktbl Coach; Head Schls Drug Comm; Booster Club Mem; MAHPERD 1988-; MN Assn of Girls Sports 1987-; Redeemer Evangelical Luth Church Pres Ed Comm 1980-; Conference Coach of the Yr 1988; *office:* Taylors Falls HS 670 West St Taylors Falls MN 55084

ANDERSON, DELLA J., Business/Computer Instructor; *b:* Hardin, MT; *m:* Micheal H.; *ed:* (BA) Bus Ed, MT St Univ 1979; *cr:* Bus Instr Poplar HS 1979-80, Campbell Cty HS 1980-81, Ft Peck Comm Coll 1979-80, Little Big Horn Coll 1986-89, Lodge Grass HS 1985-; *ai:* Bus Prof of America Club, NHS, Sr Class Adv; MT Voc Assn; MT Bus Ed Assn Historian 1978-79; Alpha Delta Kappa VP 1990; NBEA, AVA 1979-; MEA, LGTA Treas; NBEA Journal Article 1988; *office:* Lodge Grass HS 124 N George St Lodge Grass MT 59050

ANDERSON, DENNIS EARL, Teacher/Coach; *b:* Kingsport, TN; *m:* Sandra Kay Cradic; *c:* Rachel N.; *ed:* (BS) Phys Ed/ Health/Eng, 1977, (MED) Elem Ed, 1984 E TN St Univ; *cr:* Teacher/Coach Surgoinsville HS 1978-79, Volunteer HS 1979-; *ai:* Bsktbl, Ftbl, Bsbl, Golf, Cross Cntry Coach; Upper E TN Cncl Teachers of Eng 1985-; NEA, TEA, HCEA 1978-; Grace Missionary Baptist Church (Song Leader, Sunday Sch Teacher) 1966-; Upper Level Career Ladder Teacher St of TN; *office:* Volunteer HS PO Box 247 Church Hill TN 37642

ANDERSON, DONA H., Health Education Teacher; *b:* Susanville, CA; *m:* Melvin P.; *c:* Donald H., Melva; *ed:* (AA) Bus, Lassen Jr Coll 1947; (BS) Phys Ed, 1950, (MS) Recreation/Phys Ed, 1964 Brigham Young Univ; CPR Instr; Mastery Learning; Health Ed Cert; Healthy Lifestyle Trng; *cr:* Phys Ed Teacher/ Dean of Girls Lehi HS 1950-52; Phys Ed Teacher 1960-80, Health Ed Teacher 1980- American Fork Jr HS; *ai:* Cert for Life Guards; UT Assn for Health, Phys Ed, Recreation, Dance (Girls Sports 1976-78, Health VP 1988-), Outstanding Public Sch Teacher 1987; Lehi Civic Improvement Assn Queen Contest Chairperson 1970-80; Alpine Sch Dist Finalist Outstanding Ed Certificate 1975; *home:* 360 S 2 W Lehi UT 84043

ANDERSON, DONALD JOSEPH, Soc Stud/Health Teacher; *b:* Butte, MT; *m:* Harriet J. Finberg; *c:* Chris, Jodi; *ed:* (BA) His/ Poly Sci/Health/Phys Ed, Univ of MT 1967; Driver Ed, Traffic Safety; *cr:* Soc Stud/Phys Ed/Drivers Ed Teacher/BB/Track Coach Garfield Cty HS 19 68-70; Soc Stud/Health/Phys Ed/ Driver Ed Drummond HS 1970-; *ai:* Stu Cncl Adv; Asst Boys Bsktbl & Head Coach Boys & Girls Track; MT Traffic Ed Assn 1968-, 20 Yr Certificate 1988; MT Coaches Assn 1968-, COY Nominee 1980, 1983, 1986; MT Fed Teachers 1989-; St Michaels Church Parish Cncl 1980-; DTO (Secy 1981-86, Pres 1984-86); Ruby Lodge #6 Outstanding Teacher Awd 1978; Scholastic Coach Magazine Natl HS Gold Coaching Awd 1989; *home:* Box 247 960 Old Hwy 10A Drummond MT 59832

ANDERSON, ELINOR C., Third Grade Teacher; *b:* Wendell, ID; *m:* Wayne D.; *c:* Vickie Foiles, Kathy Lauda, David, Patti; *ed:* (BS) Elem Ed, 1971, (MS) Elem Ed, 1976 Univ of ID; *cr:* 3rd Grade Teacher Russell Elem 1971-; *ai:* Selection of Supt, Calendar, Prof Stud, Curr Comms; Screening Comm for New Teachers; Phi Delta Kappa, Alpha Delta Kappa; PEO; *office:* Russell Elem Sch 119 N Adams Moscow ID 83843

ANDERSON, ELLEN MARIE, English Teacher; *b:* Chicago, IL; *ed:* (BA) Eng, IL St Univ 1974; (MA) Eng, Chicago St Univ 1984; Working on Phd in Ed, Univ of Chicago 1987-; *cr:* Eng Teacher Richards HS 1976-78, Andrew HS 1978-; *ai:* Speech Team Coach; NCTE, Conference on Coll Composition & Comm , NCTE Assembly for Research; Resource Recycling Center Bd of Dirs 1983-; Article to be Published in Encyclopedia of Educl Research; *home:* 1359 E 57th St Chicago IL 60637

ANDERSON, GARY LOUIS, 7th/8th Lit Based His Teacher; *b:* San Jose, CA; *m:* Nancy L.; *c:* Christopher, Amanda; *ed:* (BA) Soc Sci, 1969, Teachers Cred Soc Sci, 1970 San Jose St; Admin Cred St of CA 1976; *cr:* 5th Grade Teacher 1970-73, 7th/8th Grade Rdng/Lit Teacher 1973-88, 7th/8th Grade Lit/His Teacher 1988- Twain Harte Elem; *ai:* 8th Grade Girls & Boys Bsktbl Coach; Impact Mentor Teacher; Teacher of Yr 1980, 1988; *office:* Twain Harte Elem Sch Box 339 Twain Harte CA 95383

ANDERSON, GERRY, Social Studies Teacher; *b:* Forest, MS; *ed:* (BS) Soc Stud, MS St Univ 1987; *cr:* Teacher Ackerman HS 1987-; *ai:* 10th Grade Class Spon; Stu Cncl; Staff Dev Trainer; Phi Theta Kappa 1984-87; MAE, NEA 1989-; PTA Teacher Rep; Most Outstanding Stu in Ed for Blacks 1987; *home:* 303-B Glenn St Starkville MS 39759

ANDERSON, GLENNA (TRAMMELL), Second Grade Teacher; *b:* Winfield, TN; *m:* Gary W.; *c:* Kimberly, Gail, Trammell; *ed:* (BS) Elem Ed, Cumberland Coll 1962; *cr:* Teacher Mc Creary Cty Sch System 1960-; *home:* HC 82 Box 506 Pine Knot KY 42635

ANDERSON, GLORIA JACKSON, Elementary Resource Teacher; *b:* Pensacola, FL; *m:* Ernest L. Hollingsworth; *c:* Walter, Charles, Brenda Rees; *ed:* (BS) Elem Ed, 1975, (MED) Ed Leadership, 1982 Univ of W FL; *cr:* Rdng Teacher Richbourg Jr HS 1975-77; 1st Grade Teacher 1977-84, Elem Res Teacher 1984- Freeport Elem; *ai:* Coord PREP & Prime Prgms; Asst Teachers; WCEA 1977-; Teacher of Yr 1987.

ANDERSON, GLORIA VICKERS, First Grade Teacher; *b:* Martinsville, VA; *m:* Curtis C.; *c:* Carla D., Curtis C. Jr., William A., Vicki L.; *ed:* (BS) Elem Ed, VA St Univ 1964 Grad Stud Univ of VA; *cr:* Classroom Teacher Franklin Cty Sch Bd 1967-; *ai:* Teacher Expectation & Stu Achievement, Supervision & Evaluation Model Wkshp Teacher Trainer; Teacher of Gifted& Talented Summer Wkshp; VA Ed Assn, NEA 1968-; Roanoke Valley Rdng Cncl 1972-89; Delta Sigma Theta Historian 1980-; VA Teacher of Yr 1990; Chamber of Commerce Cmmty Service Awd; VA St Univ Distinguished Alumni Awd; *home:* Rt 2 Box 118 Rocky Mount VA 24151

ANDERSON, HELEN GRIFFIN, Fifth Grade Teacher; *b:* St Paul, MN; *m:* Calvin Jr.; *c:* Marcus, Michael, Autumn; *ed:* (BS) Elem Ed, WV St Coll 1969; Masters Equivalency Towson St Univ, Loyola Coll; *cr:* Teacher St Paul Public Schls 1969-70, Pimlico Elem 1970-74, Medfield Heights Elem 1974-; *ai:* Alpha Kappa Alpha; Cross Cntry Elem PTO (VP 1985-86, Pres 1986-88); St James Episcopal Church Guild; Cross Cntry Elem Fnd Secy 1989-; Bishop Claggett Diocesean Center Bd of Trustees; *office:* Medfield Heights Elem Sch 4300 Buchanan Ave Baltimore MD 21211

ANDERSON, HELEN SALATA, 7th & 8th Grade Math Teacher; *b:* La Porte, IN; *m:* Steven Robert; *ed:* (BA) Elem Ed, Univ of IL 1980; *cr:* Math Teacher Mannheim Jr HS 1980-; *ai:* Yrbk Spon; Mannheim Teacher Assn Cncl; *office:* Mannheim Jr H S 2600 Hyde Park Ave Northlake IL 60164

ANDERSON, JACKIE REFOAR, 7th Grade Lang Art Teacher; *b:* Valdese, NC; *m:* William Mackie; *c:* Billy; *ed:* (BA) Sociology/ Health Ed, Appalachian St Univ 1974; (BA) Intermediate Ed, Lenoir Rhyne Coll 1976; (MA) Mid Grade Ed, Appalachian St 1990; *cr:* 5th Grade Classroom Teacher Drexel Elem 1977-78; 7th Grade Lang Art Teacher Hildebran Jr HS 1978-79; 6th Grade Teacher Baton Elem 1979-81; 7th Grade Lang Art Teacher Gamewell Mid Sch 1981-; *ai:* Stu Cncl Adv; Faculty Fund Chairperson Senate Bill 2 & Southern Assn Steering Comm; Past Dept Chairperson; Humanitarian Awd; Outstanding Grad Stu Asu; *office:* Gamewell Mid Sch Rt 6 Box 272 Lenoir NC 28645

ANDERSON, JAMES CARROLL, Instructor; *b:* Dallas, TX; *m:* Priscilla Jack; *c:* Rachel L.; *ed:* (BA) Bio, Bryan Coll 1975; (MED) MS in Educl Admin, Liberty Univ 1990; Grad Work Bio, E Carolina Univ; *cr:* Grad Teaching Fellow E Carolina Univ 1976-79; Instr Lynchburg Chrstn Acad 1980-83, Cntrl VA Governors Sch 1986-; *ai:* VA Acad of Sci 1986-; VA Educl Computing Assn 1986-89; *home:* 577 Brightwells Mill Rd Madison Heights VA 24572

ANDERSON, JAMES EDWARD, Math Dept Chairperson; *b:* Tell City, IN; *m:* Ronda Kay Jeffries; *c:* Jeffrey A., Tracy L., Scott E.; *ed:* (BS) Math/Physics, Oakland City Coll 1966; (MA) Math/ Physics Ed, Univ of Evansville 1972; *cr:* Math/Physics Teacher Pioneer HS 1966-68, N Posey HS 1968-; *ai:* Math Academic Coach; NEA (Assembly Rep 1987-) 1966-; IN St Teachers Assn 1966-; N Posey Ed Assn (Negotiations Chm 1970-75) 1968-; *office:* North Posey HS R R 1 Poseyville IN 47633

ANDERSON, JAMES ENOCH, Geography Teacher; *b:* San Francisco, CA; *m:* Donna Sue Young; *c:* Monica D., James E.; *ed:* (BAED) Soc Sci, 1970, (MAED) Soc Sci, 1972 Northeastern OK; *cr:* Geography/Athletics Teacher Pansy Kidd Mid Sch 1970-; *ai:* Coach 7th-8th Grade Girls Bsktbl & Track; OK Alliance for Geographic Ed, NCSS 1987-; Nom Teacher of Yr 1980; Poteau Teacher of Yr, Excl in Ed Awd 1987; *home:* 116 Marie Poteau OK 74953

ANDERSON, JAMES HOWARD, Math Department Chairman; *b:* Chicago Heights, IL; *m:* Nancy Eriksen Anderson; *c:* Joanna, Michael; *ed:* (BA) Math, Blackburn Coll 1966; (MS) Admin & Sch Bus Mgmt, North IL Univ 1977; Math, IL Institute of Technology; Teaching Methods, Natl Coll of Ed/St Xavier Coll/Elmhurst Coll; *cr:* Math Teacher/Dept Chm Robert FRost Jr HS 1966-; *ai:* Bsktbl Coach; Track Coach; Wrestling Coach; Math Team Adv; Math Comm; Prgm Assessment/Testing Comm; IL Cncl Teacher of Math; Natl Sci Fnd Grant; Natl Coll Corridor Partnership Grant; *office:* Robert Frost Jr H S 320 W Wise Rd Schaumburg IL 60193

ANDERSON, JANE ISRAEL, 6th Grade Teacher; *b:* Santa Maria, CA; *m:* Howard A.; *c:* Steve, Sunny; *ed:* (BS) Elem Ed, Northeastern St Univ 1970; Creative Writing/Elem Sci, OK St Univ; *cr:* 1st Grade Teacher Cntrl Elem 1970; Librarian Vails Gate 1970-; 1st Grade Teacher Cntrl Elem 1971; 6th Grade Teacher 1976-86, 4th Grade Teacher 1986-88, 6th Grade Teacher 1988- Garfield Elem; *ai:* Acad Team Coach; Bsktbl Coach; Sand Springs Schls Outstanding Awd 1986-87; Amer Legion 1985-; *office:* Garfield Elem Sch PO Box 970 Sand Springs OK 74063

ANDERSON, JANICE JORDAN, 6th Gr Math/Soc Stud Teacher; *b:* Coral Gables, FL; *m:* Paul G.; *c:* David P., Jeffrey A.; *ed:* (BA) Elem Ed, Univ of S FL 1967; Ed Leadership, Miami Dade, St Leo Coll; *cr:* Teacher Mt Prospect 1967-69; Substitute Teacher Ft Lauderdale Area 1975-80; Teacher Westwood Chrstn Sch 1981-87; Teacher/Grade Leader Suwannee Mid Sch 1987-; *ai:* 6th Grade Academic Leader, Adv Leader; Brain Bowl & Jr Beta Club Spon; FL Gifted Assn; *office:* Suwannee Mid Sch 617 Ontario Live Oak FL 32060

ANDERSON, JARVIS, 6th Grade Teacher; *b:* Idaho Falls, OH; *m:* Venetta Buttars; *c:* Trina K. Ramirez, Teresa Allen, Thomas J., Travis L., Jalin N., John A.; *ed:* (AS) Sci, Ricks Coll 1969; (BA) Elem Ed, 1975, Elem Ed Curr, 1988 ID St Univ; Wkshps Math, Sci & Rdng; *cr:* Teacher Goodsell Sch 1968-83; Prin/Teacher Taylor Sch 1969-71; Dist Curr Dir/Teacher 1984-88; 6th Grade Teacher 1988-; Migrant Ed Teacher Shelley Dist; *ai:* PTSO Stuart Elem Sch Rep 1989-; Staff Profl Dev Comm 1989-; Curr Dev Comm Health 1990; Math Needs Assessment Comm 1985; NEA Mem 1968-89; NCTM Mem 1988-; Merrill Publishing Advisory Cncl 1888-; LDS Church Bishop 1984-89; Quest for Excl Awd Shelley Sch Dist 1985 Nom & Selected By Parents PTSO Comm & Admin; *office:* Hazel Stuart Sch 475 W Center Shelley ID 83274

ANDERSON, JOAN C., 7th Grade Health Teacher; *b:* St Cloud, MN; *c:* Scott, Steven, Judith Lallier, Karen Kaskinen; *ed:* (BS) Phy Ed/Health, St Cloud St 1963; (MED) Health/Sch/Cmmty Public Health, Univ of MN 1973; Post Grad Stud Various Courses; *cr:* Health Teacher Metropolitan St Comm Coll 1967-69; Anoka Ramsey St Comm Coll 1969-71; Health Teacher Armstrong Sr HS 1973-78, Roosevelt Jr HS 1978-; *ai:* Tennis & Swimming Coach; Set Up Phys Ed Dept; MEA, MFT 1967-; *office:* Roosevelt Jr HS 650 Main St NE Blaine MN 55434

ANDERSON, JOE L., JR., Industrial Arts/Sci Teacher; *b:* Tuscaloosa Cty, AL; *m:* Mary B. Williams; *c:* Beverly D., Synethia J.; *ed:* (BS) Mechanical Arts, 1959, Certificate Printing, AL A&M Univ; Certificate Commercial Illustration, Dekalb Jr Coll 1971; Industrial Arts, Univ of GA 1971; Career Ed, GA St Univ 1972-73; Commerical Illustration, Dekalb Comm Coll & Atlanta Area Tech 1971; *cr:* Part Time Instr Atlanta Area Tech 1972; *ai:* Photographer & Industrial Arts Club; GA Teachers Assn, NEA; Alpha Phi Alpha; F & AM Masonic Lodge; Teacher of Yr 1976; Atlanta Journal Apprenticeship; *home:* 2739 Crescendo Dr NW Atlanta GA 30312

ANDERSON, JOHN WAYNE, Spanish/Science/Phys Ed; *b:* Johnstown, PA; *m:* Cindy Kay Miller; *c:* Greta L.; *ed:* (BA) Bible, Bob Jones Univ 1970; Span Amer Short Stories, Penn Univ; Introduction Bio, Liberty Univ; Biblical Principles Ed, Santa Rosa Chrstn Coll; *cr:* Span/Sci Santa Rosa Chrstn Schls 1971-83; Span/Sci/Phys Ed Emmanuel Baptist Schl 1983-; *ai:* JV Soccer Coach; Athletic Dir; Amer Red Cross Water Safety Instr Trainer; Instr Trainer; Lifeguard Trng; YMCA Progressive Swimming Instr; SC Conference Foreign Lang Teaching Mem 1989-; YMCA Swim Team Coach Coaches Awd 1989; *office:* Emmanuel Baptist Sch Rt 1 Box 80 Hartsville SC 29550

ANDERSON, JUDITH RUTH, French Teacher; *b:* Camden, NJ; *ed:* (BA) Fr/His, Houghton Coll 1965; Med Prgm Univ of Richmond; Various Univs; *cr:* 5th Grade Teacher Upper Penns Neck Sch Dist 1965-67; Jr/Sr HS Fr Teacher West Shore Sch Dist 1967-73; Fr Teacher Fairfax Chrstn Sch 1974-79, Loudoun Cntry Day Sch 1979-86, Cumberland Cty Public Schls 1987-; *ai:* Le Cercle Francais; Academic Competition for Excl Soc Stud Team Coach; NEA, VEA, CEA 1988-; AATF 1980-; Fulbright Alumni Assn 1985-; Intnl Visitors Information Service 1984-87; Fulbright Exch Teacher to France 1983-84; *home:* 11959 Briarpatch Dr W Midlothian VA 23113

ANDERSON, JUDY MC QUEEN, Spanish/English Teacher; *b:* Berea, KY; *m:* Gerald; *c:* Janee; *ed:* (BA) Eng/Poly Sci, 1977, (MA) Rdng, 1980, (Rank I) Supervision, 1983 E KY Univ; *cr:* Scndry Span/Eng Teacher Jackson Cty HS 1977-; *ai:* Span Club Adv; Amer Assn of Teachers of Span & Portuguese; KY Ed Assn, NEA; Jackson Cty HS Teacher of Yr 1980; *office:* Jackson Cty HS Box 427 Mc Kee KY 40447

ANDERSON, JUDY MEHL, Librarian/Cmptr Coord; *b:* Rock Island, IL; *m:* Thomas Edmund; *c:* Jodie Lynn, Beth Marie; *ed:* (BA) His, Clarke Coll 1970; (MA) Lib Sci, Northern IL Univ 1978; *cr:* Librarian 1971-82; Librarian/Gifted Coord 1982-88; Librarian Cmptr Coord 1988- Montmorency Comm Cons Sch Dist; *ai:* NEA/IL Ed Assn 1971-; Montmorency Ed Assn VP 1971-; *office:* Montmorency Comm Cons Sch 9415 Hoover Rd Rock Falls IL 61071

ANDERSON, KAREN (WEST), Kindergarten Teacher; *b:* Spencer, WV; *m:* Kenneth; *c:* Pamela K., Alana J.; *ed:* (AB) Elem Ed/Soc Stud, GlenvilLe St Coll 1971; Grad Stud WV Coll; *cr:* 1st Grade Teacher Walton Elem 1965-67, Reedy Roberts Stewart Elem 1968-70; Kndgtn Teacher Spencer Primary 1971-; *ai:* WV Ed Assn 1965-; *home:* 834 Charleston Rd Spencer WV 25276

ANDERSON, KARLEEN LEISETH, English Teacher; *b:* Buffalo, MN; *m:* Darrell R.; *c:* Ramona Backman, Conrad, Daniel, Nathan; *ed:* (BA) Eng/Ed, Gustavus Adolphus Coll 1957; St Cloud St Univ, St Thomas Coll, Univ of MN, Diploma from Inst of Childrens Lit; *cr:* Eng Teacher Maple Lake HS 1957-; *ai:* Natl Jr Honor Society Adv; Curr Comm; MN Ed Assn 1957-; Maple Lake Ed Assn (Pres, Secy); Luth Church Women (Pres, Secy) Luth Church (Sunday Sch Teacher, Organist, Choir Mem); Nom for MN Teacher of Yr 1976; Stephen Ministry Grad; Bethel Bible Series Grad & Teacher; Publication Author; *home:* Rt 6 Box 108 Buffalo MN 55313

ANDERSON, KEVIN MARK, Educational Consultant; *b:* Willmar, MN; *m:* Cindy Lou Ortgies; *c:* Mark K., Lindsey D.; *ed:* (BA) Elem Ed/His, Luther Coll 1976; (MA) Curr & Inst, Univ of Northern IA 1981; Ed-D Prgm Univ of Northern IA; *cr:* 3rd Grade Teacher/Coach Meservey Thornton Schls 1976-78, Central Elkader Schls 1978-85; 2nd-3rd Grade Teacher/Coach Des Moines Public Schls 1985-87; Ed Consultant Keystone Area Ed Agency 1987-; *ai:* Head HS Bsbl Coach Cntrl Elkader Schls; Liaison to St Mandated Early Chldhd Ed Comm; Phi Delta Kappa 1980- Pres 1990-91; IA Assn of Supervision & Curr Dev 1987-; IA HS Bsbl Coaches Assn 1977-; Head Coach All Star Series 1981; Bethany Luth Church Choir Dir 1988-; Opera House Players 1978-; Elkader Pre-Sch Bd 1988-; *office:* Keystone Area Education Agency RR 2 Box 19 Elkader IA 52043

ANDERSON, KIETH JOHN, Mathematics Department Chair; *b:* Los Angeles Cty, CA; *c:* Karen Pirotto, Julie; *ed:* (BA) Psych, Sterling Coll 1960; (MS) Math Ed, Univ of OR 1975; *cr:* Teacher Arkansas Avenue Sch 1960-61; Math Teacher Audubon Jr HS 1961-62, Sequoia Jr HS 1962-83, Hale Jr HS 198 *ai:* Stu Cncl Adv; Sch Leadership Cncl; NCTM, CMC (Mem, Wkshp Leader) 1965-; LACTMA (Mem, Wkshp Leader) 1965-, Recognition 1978, 1985, 1987; Phi Delta Kappa Mem 1974-; Los Angeles City Sch Outstanding Math Teacher Nom 1987-88 & Teacher of Yr Nom 1989; Co-Author Metric & Math Lab Act Los Angeles City Schls, Math Lab Jr HS Action Math Assocs; Author Dice Games for Basic Skills Action Math Assocs; *office:* George Ellery Hale Jr HS 23830 Califa St Woodland Hills CA 91364

ANDERSON, KRISTIN OSBORN, English/Drama Teacher; *b:* Seattle, WA; *m:* John P.; *ed:* (BS) Elem Ed, Univ of UT 1978; Numerous Courses; *cr:* 1st Grade Teacher Our Lady of Lourdes 1978-79; Kndgtn/1st/2nd/5th Grade Teacher Billup Sch Dist 65 1980-81; Eng/Drama Teacher Cascade HS 1988-89; *ai:* Active in Cmmty Theater; WA Ed Assn 1987-; Artist in Residence Nome AK 1983; *home:* 19920 Sound View Pl Stanwood WA 98292

ANDERSON, LA MAR MARVIN, Chemistry Instr/Lecturer Chem; *b:* Salt Lake City, UT; *ed:* (BS) Scndry Ed, 1956, (MS) Phys Sci, 1965 Univ of Ut; Brigham Young Univ, Toulene Univ, UT St Univ; *cr:* Phys Sci Teacher Salt Lake City Schls 1956-65; Sci Teacher St Josephs Sch 1965-69; Chem Teacher Logan Sr HS 1969-; Chem Lecturer UT St Univ 1985-; *ai:* Sci Club, Commencement Speaker Adv; UT Sci Teacher (Bd of Dir 1956-) Outstanding Sci Teacher Awds 1983 & 1988; UT Ed Assn 1956-UT Teacher of Yr 1981; Logan Ed Assn 1969- Outstanding Logan Teacher; Brigham Young Univ UT Outstanding Phys Sci Teacher 1988; Appeared on Television; Numerous Sci Demonstrations for Scouts, Public, Univ Sci Teachers.

ANDERSON, LARRY E., Science & Mathematics Teacher; *b:* Fillmore, UT; *m:* Patricia Roger; *c:* Jeffery L., Joseph C., Leisa Ward; *ed:* (BS) Animal Husbandry/Voc Ed, UT St Univ 1958; Grad Stud; *cr:* Teacher South Sevier HS 1963-73, Richfield Jr HS 1973-85, Red Hill Mid Sch 1985-; *ai:* Sci Dept Chm; Sci Dept Chair; Sci Fair Bds; UT Ed Assn 1963-; Lions Club All Offices 1963-, 100 Per Cent Membership; UT Cattlemans Assn; Amer Quarter Horse Assn; 1000 Acre Ranch Mgr & Operator; *home:* 310 S 1st West Monroe UT 84754

ANDERSON, LARRY WAYNE, English/Literature Teacher; *b:* St Joseph, MO; *m:* Marcha Lynn Rankin; *ed:* (BS) Eng, 1973, (MA) Eng, 1977 NW MO St Univ; Grad Stud Admin, Eng; *cr:* Teacher Graig R-III Sch Dist 1974-77, Nodaway-Holt R-7 Sch 1977-84, Savannah R-III Sch 1984-; *ai:* Savannah Jr HS Instructional Improvement Comm Chm; Schlsp Comm; MSTA; CTA 1974-; Lions Club Reporter 1990; Nodaway-Holt Jr HS Building Supvr 1979-84; Part Time Eng Instr NW MO St Univ; Poetry Publications; Literary Chm Nodaway Arts Cncl 1981-82; *office:* Savannah R-III Jr HS 701 W Chestnut Savannah MO 64485

ANDERSON, LAVINA KIP, Physical Education Teacher; *b:* Aspermont, TX; *ed:* (BS) Phys Ed, Univ of Houston 1982; Grad Stud Sam Houston St Univ; *cr:* Teacher/Coach Conroe HS 1982-; *ai:* Jr Var Girls Bsktl & Asst Girls Track Coach; *office:* Conroe HS 3200 W Davis Conroe TX 77304

ANDERSON, LINDA MARIA, Science Teacher; *b:* Carteret, NJ; *ed:* (BS) Bio/Chem, Univ of CO Boulder 1984; Working Towards Masters Biochem, Univ of CO Colorado Springs; Wkshps HS Chem Teachers UNC Greeley; Yearly FallCoach Inc Clinics CO St Univ; *cr:* Sci Teacher Rampart HS 1985-87; Cross Cntry Coach 1987-, Track Coach 1988-, Sci Teacher 1988- Liberty HS; *ai:* NCA Comm Mem; Curr Dev, Sci Lancer Alternatives, Drug & Alcohol Abuse Comm; CAST, CBTA, NSTA 1985-; CHSCAA 1987-.

ANDERSON, LINDA SMITH, 4th Grade Soc Stud/Art Teacher; *b:* Linden, TN; *m:* Willie Ray; *c:* Deborah D. Anderson Johnson, Brian C.; *ed:* (BS) Bus Ed, George Peabody Coll for Teachers 1960; *cr:* 6th Grade Teacher Lipscomb Elem Sch 1960-62; Kndgtn Teacher 1969-72, 5th Grade Teacher 1972-82, 4th Grade Teacher 1982- Fairview Elem; *ai:* Grade Level Chairperson; 4-H Adv; NEA, TEA 1960-62, 1972-; WCEA (Human Relations Comm 1978) 1960-62, 1972-; Westview United Meth Church (Secy of Admin Bd 1980-82, 1988, 1990, Ed Chairperson 1983-84, Youth Group Spon 1976-82); *office:* Fairview Elem Sch 1708 Fairview Blvd W Fairview TN 37062

ANDERSON, LISA M., Sixth Grade Teacher; *b:* Idaho Falls, ID; *ed:* (BA) Elem Ed, Boise St Univ 1 982; *cr:* 6th Grade Teacher Ethel Boyes Elem 1982-; *ai:* Stu Cncl Adv; Jump Rope for Heart Coord; Jump Rope Team Coach; Track Coach; IFEA; Lily Rebekah Lodge #33 1983-; *home:* 3008 Westmoreland Cir Idaho Falls ID 83402

ANDERSON, LOREN C., English Teacher; *b:* Westhope, ND; *m:* Pennie Olson; *c:* Lorna Lautenschlager, Brent, Layton, Lance Ceynar, Erin Ceynar; *ed:* (BA) Eng, Minot St Univ 1960; Numerous Courses & Univs; *cr:* Eng Teacher 1960-62, Bus Ed Teacher 1962-63 Kenmare Public Sch; Eng/Driver Trng Teacher Williston HS 1963-; *ai:* NCA Evaluation Philosophy & Objectives Comm; NEA 1960-; ND Ed Assn Dir 1972-78; Williston Ed Assn Pres 1985-86; Benevolent & Protective Order of Elks Exalted Ruler 1979-80; Williston Jaycees 1965-69, Outstanding Young Educator 1966; Natl Defense Ed Act Grant 1966; *home:* 812 W 14th St Williston ND 58801

ANDERSON, LOREN CHARLES, Chem Physics IPS Teacher; *b:* Springfield, IL; *m:* Juanita M. M. Cochran; *c:* Charles, Byron, Cheryl, Valerie Mc Callum; *ed:* (AB) Bio, Olivet Nazarene Univ 1951; (MS) Bio, Univ Of IL 1959; (PHD) Sci Ed, Sussex Coll Of Technology 1970; KS St Univ/NE Wesleyan Univ/Univ of GA/ Univ of MO/Univ Of Chicago, Roosevelt Univ/Millikin Univ/ Western OR St Coll; *cr:* 7th-12th Grade Teacher Mt Auburn Comm Univ 1953-54; Sci Teacher/Dept Chairperson Mt Zion Jr HS 1953-65; IPS/Bio Teacher Glenband East HS 1965-82; Chrstn Center Acad 1984-87; IPS Chem/Physics Teacher Salem Acad 1987-; Bio Teacher Coll of Dupage 1978-82; *ai:* VP Local Assn; Two Times Pres of Local Assn; Curr Comm Several Times; Evalator for North Cntrl Assn of Coll/Scndry Schls; NEA Life Mem; NSTA; GEA 1965-82; Church Of Nazarene Pastor & Assoc Pastor 1951-82, Ordained 1954; Boy Scout Comm Man & Merit Badge Cnslr 1965-82; Grants KS St Univ/NE Wesleyan Univ/ Univ of GA/Univ of Chicago/RooseveIT Univ/Univ Of IL; Nominated for Sci Teacher of Yr; St Judging Chm IL Jr Acad Sci 1966-76; *home:* 4732 Serra Ct NE Salem OR 97305

ANDERSON, LORRAINE LEE, High School Art Teacher; *b:* Harlan, IA; *m:* Joseph Hardy; *c:* Jack Hardy, Elizabeth Hardy; *ed:* (BA) Eng/Art, Univ of N IA 1973; Grad Stud Drake Univ, Des Moines Univ, Marycrest Coll, IA St Univ; *cr:* Jr HS Eng/Art Teacher Lake Mills Cmmty Schls 1973-74; Art Teacher Portage Cntrl HS 1974-76, Adel-De Soto HS 1976-; *ai:* Art Club; Coord of Conference & Local Art Festivals; Adel-De Soto Educl Assn, IA St Educl Assn, NEA, Art Educators of IA; IA St Univ New Art Basics Mem; Volunteer Work at Holy Trinity Church; Teacher of Yr 1986-87; *office:* Adel-De Soto HS 801 S 8th St Adel IA 50003

ANDERSON, MARGARET PAGE, Counselor; *b:* Roanoke Rapids, NC; *m:* Austin A.; *c:* Austin Jr., Judy P. Ritchie; *ed:* (BA) Music Bible, Atlanta Christian Coll 1958; Cert Eng, Wesleyan 1974; Sch Counseling, NC Cntrl Univ; *cr:* HS Eng & Music Teacher Gaston HS 1963-74; HS Eng Teacher Roanoke Rapids HS 1974-80; Prin Roanoke Chrstn Sch 1980-88; Sch Cnslr Northwest Halifax HS 1988-; *ai:* Spokesperson Halifax Cnty Cnslrs; Mem Effective Sch Team; Mem Prin Comm; NCAE Halifax Cty; NCAE; NEA; Church Choir (Dir) 1963-78; Young Peoples Group (Ldr) 1963-89; Secy NC Symphony Society; VP ADK; VP Music Club; Helping Hand Awd; Teachers Service Awd; Young Peoples Appreciation Awd; *office:* Northwest Halifax HS Rt 2 Box 274 Littleton NC 27850

ANDERSON, MARIANNE BIENIEK, Science & Mathematics Teacher; *b:* Milwaukee, WI; *m:* Robert Curtis; *c:* Aran, April; *ed:* (BA) Bio/Ed, Cardinal Stritch Coll 1963; (MS) Plant Morphology, Marquette Univ 1965; (PHD) Plant Bio Chem, Purdue Univ 1970; Summer Sci Teacher Research Appt, ID Natl Engineering Lab 1988; Learning Cycle, UT St Univ 1987-88; Inst of Chemical Ed, Univ of CA Berkeley 1986; *cr:* Part Time Bio Instr ID St Univ 1970-75; Eng Teacher Amer Univ of Cairo 1983-84; Sci/Math Teacher Pocatello HS 1978-; *ai:* Sr Class Adv; Stu Government Co-Adv; NSTA 1978-, Presidential Sci Teacher Awd 1989; NCTM 1985-; Phi Delta Kappa 1987-; *office:* Pocatello HS 325 N Arthur Ave Pocatello ID 83204

ANDERSON, MELODY LYNN (TREAT), English/Science Teacher; *b:* Holdenville, OK; *m:* Arthur Mark; *c:* Zachary, Daniel, Bethany; *ed:* (BS) General Home Ec, East Cntrl Univ 1978; Certified IN Eng Cntrl St Univ; *cr:* Home Ec Teacher Sasakwa Public Schls 1978-80; 7th/8th Grade Sci Teacher 1980-83, 7th/ 8th Grade Eng/Sci Teacher Amber-Pocasset HS 1987-; *office:* Amber-Pocasset HS P O Box 38 Amber OK 73004

ANDERSON, MICHAEL RAY, Math Teacher/Computer Coord; *b:* Grand Rapids, MN; *m:* Lynn A. Cyrus; *c:* Paul M., Shawna M.; *ed:* (BS) Math, 1968, (MS) Math, 1976 St Cloud St Univ; *cr:* 7th-9th Grad Math Teacher Cambridge Jr HS 1968-76; 7th/8th Grad Math Teacher Isanti Mid Sch 1976-; *ai:* Var Asst Hockey; Cmptr Coord; Math Leadership Team; Cambridge Isanti Ed Assn Treas 1980-; MEA Delegate 1990; Ducks Unlimited Dir 1980-; MN Deer Hunters Assn Treas 1987-; MN Firearms Instr 1968-; *office:* Isanti Mid Sch Isanti MN 55040

ANDERSON, PATRICIA A., Second Grade Teacher; *b:* Rosenberg, TX; *ed:* (BS) Elem Ed, SW TX St Univ 1958; (MED) Elem Ed, Sam Houston St Univ 1965; Spec Ed Endorsement 1974; *cr:* 1st Grade Teacher 1958-66, 3rd Grade Teacher 1966-70, 2nd Grade Teacher 1970-71, Resource Teacher 1971-74, 3rd Grade Teacher 1974-78 El Campo Ind Sch Dist; 1st Grade Teacher 1978-79, 2nd Grade Teacher 1979- El Campo Ind Sch Dist; *ai:* TX St Teachers Assn (Secy 1970-71, VP 1971-72, Pres 1972-73); El Campo Jaycees Outstanding Young Educator 1973; TX Cncl of Admin of Spec Ed Regular Educator of Yr 1987-88; *office:* Hutchins Elem Sch 1006 Roberts El Campo TX 77437

ANDERSON, PETER JOHN, English Teacher; *b:* Waltham, MA; *m:* Betty Ginsberg; *ed:* (BA) Eng/Creative Writing, Univ of AZ 1977; (MFA) Eng, Univ of IA Writers Wkshp 1980; *cr:* Instr Pima Comm Coll 1982-86; Teacher Canyon Del Oro HS 1986-; *ai:* Writers Guild; CDO Literary Magazine; Articles Published; *office:* Canyon Del Oro HS 25 W Calle Concordia Tucson AZ 85737

ANDERSON, RAHN E., Language Art Instructor; *b:* Monte Vista, CO; *ed:* (BA) Eng/Scndry Ed/Psych, Adams St Coll 1970; Creative Writing Prgms Dev Univ of CO; Ind Study Consultation Univ of N CO; Dev of At Risk Prgm Univ of Denver; *cr:* Lang Art Instr Arapahoe HS 1970-; *ai:* Dir Arapahoe Pantomime Wkshp 1970-; Adv Perceptions Literary Magazine Arapahoe HS; Crisis Awareness & Rehabilitation in Ed Prgm; NEA 1970-; CO Lang Arts Society 1984-; CO Regional Writers Group 1982-, Poet of Yr 1989; CO Cherries Dir of Public Relations, Hospice Charity 1987; Sovereign Court (VP 1988) 1987-88, Fundraising 1988; Brigham Young Univ Outstanding Teacher Awd 1989; Guest Speaker Strategies for Integrated Ed Conference 1990; Poetry Published Parnassus by Mile High Poetry Society 1990; *office:* Arapahoe HS 2201 E Dry Creek Rd Littleton CO 80122

ANDERSON, ROBERT EDWARD, 8th Grade US History Teacher; *b:* Mainstee, MI; *m:* Nancy Jean Boertman; *c:* Julie, Ricky, Kelly, Jill; *ed:* (BS) Soc Stud, Cntrl MI Univ 1963; Grad Stud, Cntrl MI Univ; *cr:* 5th-8th Grade Teacher Filer City Sch 1961-63; 7th Grade Teacher Jefferson & Washington Schls 1963-65; 8th Grade Teacher Manistee Jr HS 1966-; *ai:* Collective Bargaining Mem; Elem Bsktbl Coach 1961-67; Frosh Ftbl Coach 1965-68; MI Ed Assn, NEA 1961-; Manistee Teacher Assn VP 1977; FOE Eagles (Pres 1974) 1965-; Moose Lodge Inside Guard 1984-; Amer Legion Post 10 Manistee 1986-; Teacher of Yr Awd Manistee Jr HS; *home:* 391 Gloria Ln Manistee MI 49660

ANDERSON, ROBERT LES, Biology Teacher; *b:* New Orleans, LA; *m:* Linda Knight; *ed:* (BA) His, Jacksonville Univ 1974; *cr:* Teacher Mt Dora HS 1985-86, Seabreeze HS 1986-; *ai:* Head Swim Coach Seabreeze HS 1986- & Mt Dora HS 1976-85; FL Swim Mem 1976-; 5 Star Conference Coach of Yr 1986, 1987, 1988, 1989; *home:* 112 Ocean Grove Dr Ormond Beach FL 32176

ANDERSON, RODNEY GENE, Biology-Physiology Teacher; *b:* Lewellen, NE; *m:* Dianna D. Soderlin; *c:* Mike, Marrs; *ed:* (AA) Sci, NE Jr Coll 1969; (BA) Bio, 1972, (MA) Bio, 1982 Western St Coll; Entomology, Univ of Reno; Environmental Stud, Univ of CO; *cr:* Teacher St Petersburg HS 1973-74; Teacher/Coach 1972-80, K-12th Grade Prin 1980-82 Dolores Cty HS; Teacher/Coach Bennett Cty HS 1982-; *ai:* Head Ftbl & Asst Track Coach; Soph Class Spon; SDFCA 1987-, Region 8 Ftbl Coach of Yr 1989; City Councilmen 1989-; Aritcle Published 1982; Environment Work Union Carbide 1979-83; *office:* Bennett Cty HS Box 580 Martin SD 57551

ANDERSON, ROY, JR., Retired Substitute Teacher; *b:* Kuttawa, KY; *m:* Mary Louise Fitts; *c:* Brenda L., Cynthia A.; *ed:* (BS) Elem Ed/Ag, Murray St Coll 1954; Ag Teacher Trng, Univ of KY; *cr:* Teacher Lyon Cty 1943-47, Caldwell Cty 1948-51, Caldwell Cty Schls 1951-78; Teacher/Asst Prin Westside Elem Sch 1979-84; *ai:* Local KY Retired Teachers VP 1989-; Lions Club Mem; Mason Mem 1983-; Baptist Church (Sunday Sch Teacher, Dir Royal Ambassadors, Pres Brotherhood); *home:* R 1 Box 74 Princeton KY 42445

ANDERSON, RUTH FINLEY, Fifth Grade Teacher; *b:* Temple, TX; *m:* Willie James; *c:* Michael, Marchele; *ed:* (BA) Music Ed, 1952, (MA) Music Ed, 1957 Prairie View A&M Univ; Grad Stud E TX St Univ & Univ of TX Tyler; *cr:* Teacher O J Thomas Sch 1952-55, 1956-57, Dunbar HS 1955-56, O L Price Sch 1957-59, Tyler Ind Sch Dist 1961-; *ai:* TX St Teachers 1970-; Tyler Ed Assn VP 1970-; Delta Sigma Theta Financial Secy 1981-85; PTA (Financial Secy 1978-79, Book Custodian 1987-88, Life Mem), Teacher of Yr, Plaque & Pin 1987-88; *office:* T J Austin Elem Sch 1105 W Franklin Tyler TX 75702

ANDERSON, SANDRA KAY, Mathematics Teacher; *b:* Wheeler, TX; *ed:* (BA) Ed, 1965, (MED) Ed, 1972 W TX St Univ; Counseling Certificate; *cr:* Math Teacher James Bowie Jr HS 1965-66, Sanford-Fritch 1966-; *ai:* NHS Spon; UIL Number Sense Coach; *office:* Sanford-Fritch HS Box 1290 Fritch TX 79036

ANDERSON, SANDRA L., Second Grade Teacher; *b:* Lorain, OH; *ed:* (BS) Ed, OH St Univ 1972; (MED) Learning Disabilities, Kent St Univ 1982; *cr:* 3rd Grade Teacher North Elem 1972-73; 2nd/3rd Grade Teacher Tarhe Elem 1973-76; 4th Grade Teacher Muraski Elem 1976-77; 2nd Grade Teacher Zellers Elem 1977-; *office:* Zellers Elem Sch 18199 Cook Rd Strongsville OH 44136

ANDERSON, SARA JONES, English Teacher; *b:* Pensacola, FL; *m:* Samuel Lee Jr.; *c:* Samuel L. III, Ashlyn B., Christopher G.; *ed:* (BA) Ed, Univ of SC 1965; *cr:* Eng Teacher N Augusta HS 1966-; *ai:* Yrbk Bus Adv; NHS Chm; Stu Exch Prgm; NCTE;

office: N Augusta HS 2000 Knobcone Ave North Augusta SC 29841

ANDERSON, SHEILA WADE, Mathematics/Computer Teacher; *b:* Atlanta, GA; *m:* Stephen Leon; *c:* Michelle L. Pittard; *ed:* (BSED) Math Ed, 1969, (MED) Math Ed, 1975 Univ of GA; (SED) Math Ed, GA St Univ 1983; Cmptr Classes; Data Collector; *cr:* Teacher Rockdale Cty HS 1973-; Part-Time Teacher De Kalb Coll 1984-; *ai:* Jr Class & Jr/Sr Prom Spon 1976-1987; NCTM 1985-; Kappa Delta Pi 1983-; GA Cncl of Ec Ed Summer Wkshp Prgm 1980; *office:* Rockdale Cty HS 1174 Bulldog Circle Conyers GA 30207

ANDERSON, SHIRLEY LE ANN (PAUS), Science Teacher; *b:* Superior, NE; *m:* Larry; *c:* Jeffrey, Jeremy; *ed:* (BS) Bio, Dana Coll 1967; (MED) Scndry Ed, Univ of NE 1971; *cr:* Instr Barneston Public Sch 1967-68, Southern Public Sch 1968-69/1979-; *ai:* NSEA, SEA, NEA.

ANDERSON, TAMMY LABORDE, 8th Grade English Teacher; *b:* Baton Rouge, LA; *m:* John Kenny; *c:* Joshua; *ed:* (BA) Journalism, LA St Univ 1981; *cr:* Sales Rep/Commercial Producer WLCS/WQXY Radio Station 1981-84; Teacher Leesville Jr HS 1984-; *ai:* Chrldr Spon; SADD Asst Spon; Stus With Problems Teacher Group Team Mem; *home:* 108 Country Club Ln Leesville LA 71446

ANDERSON, TAYLORIA STROUD, Retired Substitute Teacher; *b:* Charlotte, NC; *m:* Leon Jr.; *c:* Patricia, Leon III; *ed:* (BA) Elem Ed, Johnson C Smith 1956; *cr:* Teacher Billingsville 1956-58; Teacher 1958-89, Enrichment Teacher 1976- Marion Sterling; *ai:* Volunteer Bolton Elem Sch 1989-, Miles Park Elem Sch 1989-91, Miles Reader Sch Amer; Delta Sigma Theta 1956-; Martha Holden Jennings Fnd Scholar 1984-85; *home:* 3579 Beacon Dr Beachwood OH 44122

ANDERSON, TERRI RAE HARRIS, Third Grade Teacher; *b:* San Bernidino, CA; *m:* Stanley Eugene; *c:* Lynnsey, Matthew, Benjamin; *ed:* (BS) Elem Ed/Spec Ed, Univ of ND Grand Forks 1973; *cr:* Supplemental Rdng Instr Melrose MN 1974; EMH Instr Richardton ND 1974-75, Ashley ND 1975-78; 1st Grade Instr Hettinger ND 1978-79; Title I Philip SD 1979-80; 3rd Grade Instr Wall Elem Sch 1980-; *ai:* Church Sch Teacher 1989-; Wall Elem Sch Outstanding Young Educator; *home:* 802 Hustead Wall SD 57790

ANDERSON, THERESA ANNE, Art Teacher; *b:* Lafayette, IN; *m:* Daniel J. Slisz; *ed:* (BA) Art Ed, Ball St Univ 1976; (MS) Art Ed, IN Univ 1982; *cr:* Art Teacher Spencer Elem 1976-78, Owen Valley Mid Sch 1978-87, Owen Valley HS 1988-; *ai:* Frosh Class Spon; NAEA 1980-; IN St Teachers Assn 1976-; Developed Mid Sch Gifted/Talented Art Class & 1st-8th Grade Performing Arts Prgm; *office:* Owen Valley HS RR 4 Box 13 Spencer IN 47460

ANDERSON, THOMAS JEFFERSON, HS Social Studies Teacher; *b:* Braymer, MO; *m:* Marilyn Gene Wallace; *c:* Angela, Amie, Aaron; *ed:* (BSE) Phys Ed, 1970, (MSE) Phys Ed, 1976 Cntrl MO St Univ; Working on Specialist Degree Admin Scndry Schls, Cntrl MO St Univ; *cr:* Soc Stud/Phys Ed Teacher Malta Bend HS 1971-73, Santa Fe HS 1973-79; Soc Stud Teacher Carrollton R-7 HS 1987-; *ai:* Jr HS Boys Ftbl, Bsktbl, Girls Var Track Coach; Soph Class Spon; MO St Teachers Assn 1987-; Carrollton Teachers Assn 1987-89; Carrollton Volunteer Fire Dept VP 1989-; Carroll Cty Little League Sftbl Pres 1986-87; Carrollton Chamer of Commerce Bd Mem 1985; *office:* Carrollton R-7 HS E 9th St Carrollton MO 64633

ANDERSON, VIVIAN NORSWORTHY, Speech Teacher; *b:* Baton Rouge, LA; *m:* Ronald R.; *c:* Erin, Ron; *ed:* (BS) Speech Ed, 1969, (MA) Admin/Supervision, 1980 LA St Univ; Prof Improvement Prgm 1986; *cr:* 7th Grade Speech Teacher Broadmoor Jr HS 1969-70; 6th-8th Grade Speech/Drama Teacher Northwestern Mid Sch 1970-; *ai:* Yrbk Spon; Chm Electives Dept; Mem Sch Advisory Cncl; Awds Day Prgm & NMS Family Happening Coord; Teacher Radio Broadcasting Pilot Prgm; Delta Kappa Gamma Corresponding Secy 1981-83; LA Assn of Educators 1969-; NEA 1972-; LA Farm Bureau (Parish Womens Chm 1972-, St Talk Meet Chm 1977, St Queens Chm 1984); Northwestern Mid Sch Teacher of Yr 1989-; E Baton Rouge Parish Mid Sch Teacher of Yr 1989-; Regional Winner, St Finalist Teacher of Yr 1989-; *home:* Po Box 79 Ethel LA 70730

ANDOLINA, NANCY JEAN, Oral Lang Study Skills Teacher; *b:* Dunkirk, NY; *ed:* (BA) Ed, 1971, (MA) Eng, 1976 SUNY Fredonia; Center for Modern Dance 1974-83; Las Vegas Dance Theatre Studio 1984-; Skills for Adolescence, Lions Quest Intnl 1988; *cr:* Rdng/Eng Teacher Fredonia Cath Sch 1971-72; 1st Grade Teacher Cuba Cntrl Sch 1972-74; 1st/4th Grade Teacher Lois Craig Elem Sch 1974-79; 4th Grade Teacher John S Park Elem Sch 1979-86; Oral Lang Study Skills Dell H Robison Jr HS 1986-; *ai:* Dance & Drama Group Instr 1986-; Optimist Club Speech Contest Coach 1987-89; Speech & Drama Festival Coach 1990; Ronnie Greenblatt Modern Dance Theatre 1980-83; Ecdysis Dance Theatre 1983-84; Juvenile Court Services Tutor 1979-79; Allied Arts Cncl Co-Dance Dir 1984-85; PTA Parenting Conference Speaker 1989; Darwin R Barker Lib Summer Puppet Show Production 1989; Electives Dept Art Festival Grant 1987; Above & Beyond Awd 1988; Las Vegas Search for Talent Contest Judge; *office:* Dell H Robison Jr HS 825 N Marion Dr Las Vegas NV 89110

ANDRADE, CLARA, Physical Education Teacher; *b:* Pawtucket, RI; *ed:* (BA) Phys Ed/Health, Univ of Bridgeport 1966; Grad Stud Providence Coll; *cr:* Phys Ed/Health Teacher Cntrl Falls HS; 9th-12th Grade Teacher 1966-74, 7th-12th Grade Teacher 1975- Cntrl Falls Jr/Sr HS; *ai:* Chrldr Adv; Ski Club; Prins Advisory Comm; AAHPER; *office:* Cntrl Falls Jr-Sr HS 24 Summer St Central Falls RI 02863

ANDRADE, DONNA MARIE, Dir/Stu Support Services; *b:* Bridgeport, CT; *ed:* (BA) Eng, Univ of CT 1977; (MA) Educl Media, Fairfield Univ 1982; (PD) Admin/Supervision, Fordham Univ 1990; Working Towards EdD, Fordham Univ; *cr:* Eng Teacher Bassick HS 1977-80, Upward Bound 1979-85, Fairfield Coll Prep Sch 1980-86; Dir Coll Access Prgm Fairfield Univ 1989; Dir Stu Support Services Fairfield Prep 1986-; *ai:* Natl Coalition of 100 Black Women 1989-; New England/Latin Stu Assn Area Rep; Sisters of Notre Dame Advisory Bd 1988-; African Amer Cmmty Service Awd Muslim Center 1988; Jesuit Scndry Ed Assn Outstanding Ministry Awd 1989; *office:* Fairfield Coll Preparatory Fairfield University Fairfield CT 06430

ANDRADE, JEANETTE MARIE, Fourth Grade Teacher; *b:* Phoenix, AZ; *ed:* (AA) Elem Ed, Phoenix Coll 1967; (BA) Elem Ed, 1969, (MA) Elem Ed, 1972, Rdng Specialist Certificate 1974 AZ St Univ; Grad Stud AZ St Univ 1974-; Learning Disabilities/Spec Ed, Univ of Phoenix 1982; Eng as Second Lang, Chapman Coll 1988-, Univ of Phoenix 1989; *cr:* 4th Grade Teacher Scottsdale Public Sch Dist 1969-72, Palos Verdes Peninsula Unified Sch 1972-73; 5th Grade Teacher Mirror Lake Elem Sch 1973; Spec Rdng Teacher Skiff Elem Sch 1974-76; 4th Grade Teacher Wilson Sch 3rd-8th 1976-; *ai:* Soc Stud Adoption, Eng as a Second Lang, Bi-ling Evaluation Comm; NEA, AZ Ed Assn, Wilson Classroom Teacher Assn 1974-; Experiment in Intnl Living Schlsp; Recipient & Participant Intnl Living Prgm 1967; *office:* Wilson Sch 3rd-8th 2929 E Fillmore Phoenix AZ 85008

ANDREE, ROBERT G., Sixth Grade Math Teacher; *b:* Grand Rapids, MI; *m:* Mary K. Diephuis; *c:* Mark, Katherine, Elizabeth; *ed:* (AB) His, Hope Coll 1958; W MI Univ, Aquinas Coll, Calvin Coll; *cr:* 6th Grade Teacher Rockford Elem Schls 1959-61, Holland Public Schls 1961-; *ai:* Various Comms Local Level Teaching; Private Swim Club Mgr; HS Var Swim Coach; MI Cncl Teachers of Math (Speaker 1980-87, Regional Exec Comm); NEA, MI Ed Assn; Holland Ed Assn Exec Bd 1963-64; Lions Club Speaker 1988; Nom Teacher Excl; Hope Coll Instr; Inserviced Holland Teachers in Metric System; Interviewed by Local Radio Station on Metric System; *home:* 721 Marylane Dr Holland MI 49423

ANDREPONT, CATHERINE GARZOTTO, Chapter I Gifted Specialist; *b:* New Iberia, LA; *m:* Wilbur Charles; *ed:* (BA) Eng/His, Southwestern LA Inst 1957; (MED) Humanities, Univ of Southwestern LA 1958; (MA-Admin) Admin, Univ of Laverne 1985; *cr:* Gifted Teacher Page Manor Sch 1957-58; 2nd-3rd Grade Classroom Teacher Joshua Sch 1968-72; 1st-5th Grade Classroom Teacher 1973-88, 1st-6th Grade Chapter I Specialist 1988- Sunnydale Sch; *ai:* Chm Site Improvement 1985-; Gate Contact 1980-; Cmptr Club Adv 1989-89; Chm Child Study Comm 1989-; CA Assn for the Gifted 1970-; Site Improvement Consortium of 1985-; Antelope Valley Math Inst of CA Southern Section 1980-; Amer Assn of Univ Women 1965-80; Young Mens Chrstn Assn 1965-88; Save the Children Fed 1980-95; Sigma Sigma Sigma 1955-; *home:* 43730 N Lively Ave Lancaster CA 93536

ANDRESEN, SHERRY GUYNN, 7th/8th Grade English Teacher; *b:* Pearisburg, VA; *m:* John; *c:* John, Sara; *ed:* (BS) His/Eng, Radford Univ 1965; *cr:* 8th Grade Eng Teacher Giles HS 1965-66; 9th Grade Eng Teacher Copperas Cove HS 1966-67; World His/Eng Teacher Blacksburg HS 1967-69; 7th/8th Grade Soc Stud/Eng Teacher Virginia Jr HS 1979-; *ai:* NEA, VEA, BVEA 1979-; NCTE, VA Assn of Gifted Educators 1989-; VA Mid Sch Assn; St Columbas Altar Guild; Chairperson Gifted Ed Comm; Chm Eng VA St; Evaluation Comm for Graham Mid Sch; *home:* 203 Cloverdale Pl Bristol TN 37620

ANDREW, DONNA LOMAX, Mathematics Teacher; *b:* Easton, MD; *m:* Richard Lee; *c:* Kari Andrew Farnell, Kory L., Katie L., Kasey S. L.; *ed:* (BS) Ed/Scndry Math, Salisbury St Coll 1973; (MED) Concentration Math, Salisbury St Univ 1990; *cr:* Math Teacher Preston Jr HS 1966; Math/Music Teacher Federalsburg Jr HS 1967-70; Music Teacher Federalsburg Elem 1973-74; Math Teacher Wicomico Jr HS 1975-76, Riverview Mid 1976-77, Lighthouse Acad 1978-81, 1983-85, Colonel Richardson Sr HS 1986-; *ai:* NCTM 1986-; Choir Talbot Bible Church Dir 1988-; *home:* Rt 1 Box 46 Federalsburg MD 21632

ANDREWS, ANNE C., Teacher; *b:* Leominster, MA; *m:* Martin Edwin; *c:* Darcie; *ed:* (BS) Elem Ed, 1970; (MS) Rdng 1974 Fitchburg St Coll; Admin Certified Rdng Supervisor & Prin; Drug Ed; Admin Ed; Courses Pertaining to Personal Growth; *cr:* 1st Grade Teacher Fallbrook Elem Sch; *ai:* NEA 1970-; MA Teachers Assn 1970-; Leominster Ed Assn 1970-; Leominster Charter Commission Elected Mem 1981-84; Religious Ed Bd Pres 1987-; Leominster Concerned Citizens Mem 1978-82; Curr Dev Comm; Competency Testing Comm; K-8 Prgm Comm; Rdng Comm; *office:* Fallbrook Elem De Cicco Dr Leominster MA 01453

ANDREWS, BRENDA GAIL (STEPHENS), Secondary Business Teacher; *b:* Waco, TX; *m:* Kenneth Dale; *c:* Britney, Brennan; *ed:* (BBA) Bus/Eng, Tarleton St Univ 1977; Grad Stud Bus & Ed, Tarleton St; *cr:* Scndry Migrant Teacher 1979-84, Scndry Bus Teacher 1984- Hamilton HS; *ai:* Class Spon; Univ Interscholastic League Coord HS Campus; UIL Accounting & Keyboarding Coach; Textbook & Gifted & Talented Ed Prgm Implementation Comm; TSTA HS Rep 1990; Beta Sigma Phi 1979-85, Girl of Yr 1984; Marian Cummings Schlsp Tarleton St Univ; *office:* Hamilton HS PO Box 392 Hamilton TX 76531

ANDREWS, CARMELLA MARIE, Reading/Math Teacher; *b:* Pitcairn, PA; *m:* Everette C.; *c:* Joseph, John, Andrea M. Coggins; *ed:* (BS) Elem Ed, Columbus Coll 1978; *cr:* Chapter I Rdng Teacher 1978-81, 4th Grade Teacher 1981-88, Chapter I Rdng/Math Teacher 1988- Benning Hills Elem; *ai:* Newspaper Staff; Alpha Delta Kappa Historian 1987; Gold Star Wives Secy 1973-74; *office:* Benning Hills Elem Sch 190 Munson Dr Columbus GA 31903

ANDREWS, JAMES MICHAEL, Assistant Principal; *b:* Mobile, AL; *m:* Jorina Scott; *c:* Letitia; *ed:* (BS) Elem Ed, AL St Coll 1965; (MED) Ed, Univ of MN 1977; Elem Ed & Prof Admin; *cr:* Teacher Field Elem Sch 1970-88; Intern Prin Lyndale Elem 1988-89; Asst Prin Minneapolis Public Sch Acad 1989-; *ai:* Kappa Alpha Psi; Phi Delta Kappa, MN Elem Sch Prins Assn, Minneapolis Public Sch Prins Assn; Minneapolis NAACP; Awarded Teacher of Excl & Among Ten Finalists for Teacher of Yr; Mike Andrews Humanitarian Awd; *office:* Minneapolis Public Sch Acad 919 Emerson Ave N Minneapolis MN 55411

ANDREWS, JAMES ROBERT, Mathematics Teacher; *b:* Mc Alester, OK; *m:* Mary Remondini; *c:* Nicholas J., William E., Joseph B.; *ed:* (BA) Math, 1979, (MAT) Math, 1981 W NM Univ; Electronic Cmptr System Repair USAF; *cr:* Hot Springs HS 1979-80; Artesia HS 1980-86; Math Teacher Mayfield HS 1986-; *ai:* Jr Var Bsktbl Coach; *office:* Mayfield HS 1955 N Valley Dr Las Cruces NM 88005

ANDREWS, JEFFREY JAY, Social Studies Teacher; *b:* Mc Kees Rocks, PA; *m:* Paulette; *ed:* (BA) Soc Stud, Waynesburg Coll 1974; Working Towards Masters His, Univ Pittsburgh 1974-80; *cr:* Teacher/Coach Avonworth Schls 1974-84, Quaker Valley Schls 1985-; *ai:* Stu Government Spon; *office:* Quaker Valley HS Beaver Rd Leetsdale PA 15056

ANDREWS, JERRELL DWAINE, Physical Education Teacher; *b:* Vallejo, CA; *ed:* (BS) Phys Ed, San Jose St Univ 1971; *cr:* Phys Ed/Health Teacher Bret Harte Jr HS 1974-75; Phys Ed Teacher Orville Wright Jr HS 1975-76; Dean Calvin Simmon Jr HS 1982-83; Phys Ed/Wrestling Teacher Skyline HS 1983-; *ai:* Skyline HS Head Wrestling Coach; Omega Psi Phi KRS 1988-89; San Jose St Univ Athletic Schlsp 1966; *home:* 394 Orange St Apt 7 Oakland CA 94610

ANDREWS, JUDY CRADDOCK, Science Dept Chair/Bio Teacher; *b:* Sylacauga, AL; *m:* Thomas Perry; *c:* Amy C.; *ed:* (BS) Bio/Scndry Ed, Jacksonville St Univ 1968; *cr:* Bio Teacher Anniston HS 1968-70; Bio/Music Teacher B B Comer Memorial Sch 1970-; *ai:* Jr Class & Sci Club Spon; Prin Advisory, Chairperson Schlsp, Homecoming, Chairperson Graduation Music Comm; AL Sci Teachers Assn 1989-; NEA, AL Ed Assn 1968-; Talladega Cty Ed Assn (Prgm Chm 1975) 1970-; AL Alpha Delta Kappa (Cntrl Dist Chm 1986-88, St Historian 1988-); Delta Omicron, Periwinkle Garden Club, Sylacauga Cmmty Chorus; *office:* B B Comer Memorial Sch Seminole & 8th St Sylacauga AL 35150

ANDREWS, MARY ROBERTS, Elementary School Principal; *b:* Bertie Cty, NC; *m:* John Mc Kinley Jr.; *c:* Alan A.; *ed:* (BS) Elem Ed, Elizabeth City St Coll 1954; (MA) Sch Admin, E Carolina Univ 1976; *cr:* Teacher Beaufort Cty Schls 1954-60, Dist of Columbia Sch 1960-62, Ayer MA & Washington NC & Edenton NC 1962-69; Teacher/Prin Martin Cty 1969-; *ai:* Martin Cty Assn of Educators Prins Division Pres 1988-, Prin of Yr 1989-; Williamston Bus Prof Womens Club Prgm Chm 1989-; Alpha Kappa Alpha Pres 1986-88, Plaque 1988; Minority Citizen of Yr Martin Cty 1986; *office:* Williamston Primary Sch 400 W Blvd Williamston NC 27892

ANDREWS, MICHAEL R., 5th-6th Grade Teacher; *b:* Dayton, OH; *m:* Lillion Barnes; *ed:* (BS) Elem Ed, Cntrl St Univ 1975; Sci Courses Wright St Univ; Chem Supplements/Field Geology Miami Univ OH; Hands-On Sci; *cr:* Elem Teacher/Jr/Sr HS Coach Jefferson Elem 1975-79; Asst Dir Upward Bound Prgm IN Univ 1979-80; Mid Sch Teacher/Jr HS Coach Jefferson Township Jr HS 1980-81; Elem Teacher/HS Track/Elem Bsktbl Coach Townview Elem 1981-; *ai:* 5th/6th Grade Girls Bsktbl, HS Girls Track, Volunteer Coach; After Sch Manhood/Womanhood 6th Grade Trng Townview; Sci Curr Comm Sch Dist; OH HS Track Coaches Assn 1985-; Dayton Masters Track Coaches Pres 1982-; Teacher Initiative Grant; 3 St Championship Teams Asst Coach; *office:* Townview Elem Sch 5280 Gardendale Ave Dayton OH 45427

ANDREWS, MIRIAM C., Reading Specialist; *b:* Schenectady, NY; *ed:* (BA) Russian/His/Government, 1969, (BS) Elem Ed, 1971, (MS) Mid Sch Ed, 1978 Univ of Dayton; Rdng Specialist; Data Processing; *cr:* 6th Grade Teacher St Albert The Great 1969-70; 7th-9th Grade His/Eng/Rdng Teacher Ankeney Jr HS 1970-; *ai:* Vlybl, Sftbl, Cross Cntry Coach; Animal Lovers Club Spon; Phi Delta Kappa 1978-; *office:* Ankeney Jr HS 4085 Shakertown Rd Dayton OH 45430

ANDREWS, ROBERT L., History Department Chair; *b:* Volga, SD; *ed:* (BA) His, Cntrl WA Univ 1958; Univ of WA 1967, 1968, 1971; *cr:* Teacher Olympic Jr HS 1958-61, Keflavik Iceland Military Dependents Sch 1961-62, Evergreen HS 1962-; *ai:* WA Cncl on Intnl Trade, WA St Cncl for Soc Stud, WA St Cncl of Ec Ed; Pepperdine Univ Fellowship 1979-81; Batelle Inst 1978; Highline Fed of Teachers Pres 1972; *office:* Evergreen HS 830 SW 116th Seattle WA 98146

ANDREWS, SARA NELL, Social Studies Teacher; *b:* Ozark, AL; *ed:* (BSED) Soc Sci, Troy St Univ 1973; (MED) Soc Sci, GA Southwestern 1977; (MED) Mental Retardation, 1980, (MED) Learning Disabilities, 1982 Auburn Univ; *cr:* Soc Stud Teacher Worth Cty HS 1973-77, Loganville HS 1978-79; Learning Disabilities Teacher Alexander City Jr HS 1980-81; EMR Teacher 1981-82, Learning Disabilities Teacher 1982-88, Soc Stud Teacher 1988- Dothan HS; *ai:* Ftbl Chrldr Spon; Scholars Bowl Coach; AL Ed Assn 1980-; NEA 1973-; Dothan Ed Assn 1980-; *office:* Dothan HS 1000 S Oates St Dothan AL 36301

ANDREWS, SUSAN SPIRIDONDES, Third Grade Teacher; *b:* Dover, NH; *m:* Robert L.; *ed:* (BS) Elem Ed, Plymouth St Coll 1972; *cr:* 3rd-4th Grade Teacher Parker Hancock Sch 1972-73; 3rd Grade Teacher Bessie C Rowell 1973-; *ai:* Granite St Rdng Cncl; Weirs Beach Chamber of Commerce 1989; *home:* 61 Elaine Dr Belmont NH 03220

ANDREWS, VALERIE WARNER, Foreign Lang Dept Chair; *b:* New Haven, CT; *m:* Howard K.; *ed:* (BS) Fr/Eng, 1962, Fr, 1971, S CT St Univ; Working Towards Admin Degree; *cr:* Fr Teacher 1962-, Foreign Lang Dept Chairperson 1989- Cheshire HS; *ai:* Yrbk Adv; NHS Comm; AATF VP 1986-; Alliance Francaise of Greater New Haven Bd of Dirs 1988-; *office:* Cheshire HS 525 S Main St Cheshire CT 06410

ANDREYK, ALICE HULLS, Fifth Grade Teacher; *b:* Ruston, LA; *m:* Andrew; *c:* Allison Andreyk Kullenberg; *ed:* (BS) Home Ec, Northwestern St 1957; (MSED) Elem Ed, Mc Neese Univ 1978; *cr:* Home Ec Teacher Wisner HS 1957-59; 6th Grade Teacher Frasch Elem Sch 1959-60, E K Key Elem 1960-62; 5th Grade Teacher Le Blanc Elem 1962-67, E K Key Elem 1967-; *ai:* NEA, LA Educl Assn; Calcasieu Educl Assn, Delta Kappa Gamma VP 1985-87, 1989-; Holy Trinity Episcopal Church (Vestry Mem, Bible Sch Teacher).

ANDRIANO, THERESA, Fifth Grade Teacher; *b:* New York, NY; *ed:* (BA) Elem Ed, Jersey City St 1973; *cr:* Teacher St Anthony Sch 1968-; *ai:* Bsbl Coach; After Sch Prgm; Rdng Coord; Amer Chemical Society Alternate Councilor 1986-, Outstanding Teacher Awd 1988; NE FL Engineers Society 1989, Outstanding Teacher; FL Cross Cntry Coach of Yr 1980; Articles Published; Reader Advanced Placement Chem Exam 1989-; *office:* St Anthonys Sch 700 Central Ave Union City NJ 07087

ANDRIS, DIANE HOBBS, Guidance Counselor; *b:* Neosho, MO; *m:* Jack Jr.; *ed:* (BS) Elem Ed, SW MO St Univ 1968; (MS) Guidance/Counseling, Pittsburgh St Univ 1977; *cr:* Elem Ed Teacher Chanute KS 1968-70, Rogersville MO 1970-72, Neosho MO 1972-77; Cnslr Joplin MO 1977-88, Granby MO 1988-; *ai:* NHS Adv; At-Risk Coord 1990; MO St Teachers Assn, MO Sch Cnslr Assn; *office:* East Newton HS Rt 1 Granby MO 64844

ANDRIST, JOHANNE WRIGHT, 3rd/4th Grade Teacher; *b:* Isabella, OK; *m:* Franklin Delano; *c:* Calvin, Jared, Melissa, Justin; *ed:* (BS) Elem Ed, Minot St Univ 1982; Elem Ed Prin Cert 1984; *cr:* Elem Teacher Grenora Public Sch 1959-63, Chaffee Public Sch 1963-65, Palermo Public Sch 1965-68, Sawyer Public Sch 1970-71; Elem Teacher/Prin Deering Public Sch 1975-; *ai:* Cmmty Club Secy 1988-; *office:* Deering Public Sch Box 39 Deering ND 58731

ANDRITZ, LEAH DALEY, Art Teacher; *b:* Erie, PA; *m:* Stephen J.; *c:* Robert; *ed:* (BS) Art Ed, Univ of Edinboro 1970; Working Towards MS in Art Ed, Cmptr Graphics, Univ of Cntrl FL; *cr:* Art Teacher Beaty Jr HS 1970-80, Astronaut HS 1985-; *ai:* Stu Government Assn, Natl Art Honor Society, Election Bd Adv; Natl Art Assn; Delta Kappa Gamma Society Intnl Pres 1982-84; Alpha Delta Kappa; *office:* Astronaut HS 800 Wareagle Blvd Titusville FL 32796

ANDRUS, MARY PATRICIA HYMEL, Home Economics/ Science Teacher; *b:* Lafayette, LA; *c:* Ray J. Jr.; *ed:* (BS) Home Ec Ed, 1970, (MED) Home Ec Ed, 1988 Univ of SW LA; Supervision of Instruction; *cr:* Home Ec Teacher Acadiana HS 1970-71; Sci Teacher Paul Breaux Mid 1975; Home Ec/Sci Teacher Scott Mid Sch 1976-; *ai:* Faculty Advisory Comm; NEA, LA Ed Assn, Lafayette Parish Voc Ed Teachers, Lafayette Parish Assn of Classroom Teachers, Lafayette Parish Assn of Educators; *home:* 107 Stable Creek Dr Lafayette LA 70506

ANDRUS, SHIRLEY M., 5th Grade Teacher; *b:* Aurora, MO; *ed:* (BS) Elem Ed, 1967; (MS) Elem Ed, Southwest MO St Univ 1971; *cr:* 5th Grade Teacher Fox C-6 Schls 1967-; *ai:* Started Math Club; Grade Level Adv Math Club Spon; Direct after Sch Chorus; NEA; MNEA; Delta Kappa Gamma; Personal Growth/Services Chm; 1st Baptist Church of Arnold Mem 1968; Volunteer Mission Work; Outstndng Young Educator Awd Arnold Jaycees 1972; *office:* Sherwood Elem Fox C-6 Dist 1769 Missouri State Rd Arnold MO 63010

ANDUSS, JANET FLEMING, Mathematics Teacher; *b:* Tulsa, OK; *m:* Larry P.; *c:* Patricia, Mark; *ed:* (BS) Math/Ed, OK St Univ 1962; Grad Courses, Univ of Tulsa, Madison Coll, Church Coll, Sacramento St Coll, Baylor Univ; *cr:* Math Teacher Barnsdall HS 1980-83, Panama Canal Coll 1984-86, Curundu Jr HS 1983-87, Madison Mid Sch 1987-; *ai:* OK St & Madison Mid Sch Mathcounts Team Coach; NCTM, OK Cncl Teachers of Math, US Tennis Assn; Great Dane Club of America, Heart of OH Great Dane Club, Tulsa Area Tennis Assn; Mid Sch Statistics Summer Inst Univ of Tulsa; *home:* PO Box 248 Barnsdall OK 74002

ANGALICH, DANIEL THOMAS, Math Teacher/Chairman; *b:* Jacksonville, NC; *m:* Kimberly Ann Brayec;; *c:* George M.; *ed:* (BS) Industrial Engineering, WV Univ 1986; *cr:* Management Engr OH Valley Medical Center 1986-88; Math Teacher Bishop Donahue HS 1988-; *ai:* Boys Bsktbl Coach & Var Asst Wheeling Cntrl Cath HS; Girls Bsktbl Coach & Var Asst Bishop Donahue; *office:* Bishop Donahue HS 325 Logan St Mc Mechen WV 26040

ANGEL, TRAVIS L., Fine Arts Chairman/Choral Dir; *b:* Snyder, TX; *m:* Charlotte Crowell; *c:* Courtney, Holland; *ed:* (BMED) Vocal Music, 1975, (MMA) Conducting, 1981 W TX St Univ; Grad Stud Choral Music, AZ St Univ; *cr:* Choral Dir Canyon Jr HS 1975-76; Fine Arts Supvr/Choral Dir Spearman Ind Sch Dist 1976-83; Fine Arts Chm/ChoraL Dir A&M Consolidated HS 1983-; *ai:* TX Music Educators Assn (Regional Vocal Chm 1988-, St Choir Section Leader 1989-); TX Choral Dir Assn, Amer Choral Dirs Assn; Choirs Won 300 Awds Univ Interscholastic League Contest; Music Festivals in Various Cities; *office:* A&M Consolidated HS 701 W Loop S College Station TX 77840

ANGELICH, DAVID LAWRENCE, Physical Education Teacher; *b:* Chicago, IL; *ed:* (BA) Phys Ed, Univ of IL 1972; *cr:* Phys Educator Montview Elem 1973-75, Aurora Hills Mid Sch 1975-82, Columbia Mid Sch 1982-; *office:* Columbia Mid Sch 17600 E Columbia Ave Aurora CO 80013

ANGELINA, JAMINE, Jr HS Literature Teacher; *b:* Chicago, IL; *ed:* (BSE) Ed, Alverno Coll 1967; Advanced Courses in Lang Art; Cmptr Ed; Art Wkshps; Advanced Theology Courses; *cr:* Primary Teacher Sacred Heart Sch 1959-64; Primary-Intermediate Teacher St Raphael Sch 1964-71; Jr HS Lit Teacher St Walter Sch 1971-83, St Philip the Apostle 1983-; *ai:* Asst Prin; Stu Patrol Moderator; Adoption of Rdng Series Curr Chairperson; Adoption of Eng Series Curr Mem; NCEA 1959-.

ANGELINE, FRANCIS JOSEPH, Latin/German Teacher; *b:* Endicott, NY; *m:* Patricia A. Hanley; *c:* Christopher, Laurence, Vaun; *ed:* (BA) Latin/Phys Ed, 1956; (MA) Latin/Phys Ed, 1957 Colgate Univ; *cr:* Asst Ftbl Coach/Dir Intramurals Colgate Univ 1956-57; Latin/Health Teacher/Head Ftbl Coach Johnson City HS 1957-60; Latin/Ger Teacher/Head Ftbl/Tennis Coach Union Endicott HS 1960-; *ai:* Head Ftbl Coach; Horky Dove Memorial Ftbl Schlsp Chm; Head Tennis Coach; Fran Angeline Ftbl Schlsp Comm; Frederica Hollister Memorial Latin Schlsp Chm; Endicott Rotary Club 1963-73; NY St United Teachers; NEA 1957-; Johnson City/Endicott Teachers Assn 1957-; Amer Ftbl Coaches Assn/HS Ftbl Coaches Assn 1957-; NY St Sports Writers Assn 1957 Coach of Yr Ftbl (NY St 1979 & 1989; Nation 1979; Several Articles Published; Guest Lecturer at Clinics-Wkshps & SVC Clubs; *office:* Union-Endicott H S 1200 E Main St Endicott NY 13760

ANGELL, ELISSA BECKER, Librarian; *b:* Chicago, IL; *m:* Robert; *ed:* (BA) Eng & Span, Beliot Coll 1957; (MA) Eng, Univ of Chicago 1962; (MA) Librnshp, Univ of Denver 1968; *cr:* Span & Eng Teacher Crystal Lake Cmmty HS 1957-58; Secretary Univ of Chicago 1958-65; Librarian Durham Public Lib 1966-67; Coronado Hills Jr HS 1970-77; Meritt Hutton Jr HS 1977-; *ai:* In Charge of Instr in Appreciation of Fine Arts; Field Trips to Perf in Fine Arts; CEMA; Classic Chorale 197-83; Denver Audubon Society 1975-; Speaking to Prof and Comm Organ on His Fiction for Young Adults; Speaking to Prof Organ on Opera Ed for Young Adults; *home:* 702 S Corona St Denver CO 80209

ANGELO, CLEVIO ALBERT, US History Teacher/Team Leader; *b:* Darby, PA; *m:* Rosemary L. Biggerstaff; *c:* Philip, Alicia, Rebecca; *ed:* (BS) Ed, West Chester Univ 1973; USAF Security Police Sch; USAF Advanced Weapons Trng Sch; *cr:* US His/Eng Teacher Unionville Mid Sch 1973-; *ai:* Girls Bsktbl Coach; Soc Stud Curr Comm; Admin Cncl; Team Leader; PSEA/ NEA 1973-; Avondale Presbyn Church Deacon 1986-; *office:* Unionville Mid Sch Rt 82 Unionville PA 19375

ANGER, SHIRLEY ALDER, 3rd Grade Teacher; *b:* Pima, AZ; *m:* Edgar H.; *c:* Michael E., PauL R.; *ed:* (BA) Elem Ed, AZ St Univ 1962; AZ St Univ; Univ of AZ; *cr:* 4th Grade Teacher Solomon Elem Sch 1962-63; 6th Grade Teacher Tempe Elem Sch 1966-69; 5th Grade Teacher Buckeye Elem Sch 1975-81; 3rd/5th/ 7th-9th Grade Teacher Pima Unified Schls 1981-; *office:* Pima Jr HS 129 S Main Pima AZ 85543

ANGERT, MARY CATHERINE, Mathematics Teacher; *b:* New Castle, PA; *ed:* (BS) Math Ed, Slippery Rock St 1973; (MS) Math Ed, Univ of Pittsburgh 1976; *cr:* 7th Grade Math Teacher Butler Area Jr HS 1973-85; 9th/10th Grade Math Teacher Butler Area Intermediate HS 1985-; *office:* Butler Intermediate HS 167 New Castle Rd Butler PA 16001

ANGILLY, BETH R., 7th & 8th Grade Teacher; *b:* New York City, NY; *m:* Walter; *c:* Allyson, Gregory; *ed:* (BA) Ed, Queens Coll 1965; Grad Work Queens Coll/Montclair St Coll; *cr:* Teacher Jamaica Ave Sch 1965-67, John Hill Sch 1967-71 & 1976-; *ai:* Chrldng Adv; Stu Cncl Adv; Trip Coord; Coop Relations Comm Chaperone; NJ Assn of Stu Cncls Co-Exec Dir; Leadership Trng Conference Co-Dir; Boonton Ed Assn Exec Bd 1967-; NEA; NJ Ed Assn 1967-; NJ Assn Stu Cncl Co-Exec Dir 1979-; Natl Assn of Wrkshp Adv 1979-, Wrkshp Adv of Yr 1989; NJ Teachers Recognition Awd 1987; Lincoln Park Bd of Ed; Lincoln Park Juvenile Justice Comm; Family Life Parenting Course Grant; Adv Spotlight Leadership Magazine NASSP.

ANGLE, LISA DEESE, Eng 10 Teacher/Dept Co Chm; *b:* Wadesboro, NC; *m:* Steven C.; *ed:* (BS) Eng, Mary Washington Coll 1986; *cr:* 9th/12th Grade Eng Teacher 1986-87; 10th Grade Eng Teacher 1987- Franklin Cty HS; *ai:* Stu Cncl Spon; Eng Dept Co-Chm; Sponsored in Past Jr Varsity Chrldrs & Soph Class; NCTE Mem 1989-; Rocky Mount United Meth Church Choir Mem 1989-; *office:* Franklin Cty HS 506 Pell Ave Rocky Mount VA 24151

ANGLE, STEVE CARTER, Business Teacher; *b:* Rocky Mount, VA; *m:* Lisa Michelle Deese; *ed:* (BS) Bus Admin, VA Tech 1975; *cr:* Bus Teacher Franklin Cty HS 1975-; *ai:* Bsktbl Coach; Fbla Spon; Franklin Cty Ed Assn, VA Ed Assn, NEA 1975-; Natl HS Athletic Coaches Assn, VA HS Coaches Assn 1979-; Franklin Cty Hokie Club Bd of Dir 1988-; Rocky Mount United Meth Church Bd of Trustees 1990; Franklin & Patrick Ctys Project Discovery Bd of Dir Chm; New Prin Se arch Comm 1988; *home:* 114 Ann Sink St PO Box 173 Rocky Mount VA 24151

ANGLEMYER, ROMA KATHLEEN (WYMAN), Fourth Grade Teacher; *b:* Wakarusa, IN; *m:* Keith Alois; *c:* Debra Anglemyer Mc Nally, Linda Anglemyer Stolley; *ed:* (BS) Ed, Goshen Coll 1955; (MA) Spec Ed, St Marys Coll 1966; Instructional Asst Coll of the Gifted and Talented, IN Univ Bloomington 1984; *cr:* K-5th Grade Elem Teacher Bremen Cmmty Schls 1955-59; Kids on Campus Enrichment Goshen Coll 1985; K-5th Grade Elem Teacher Wa-nee Cmmty Schls 1960-; *ai:* Lang Art Adoption Comm; Pi Lambda Theta (N IN Chapter Pres 1987-89, Great Lakes Regional Secy 1988-, Biennial Cncl Delegate 1987, 1989); Progessive Homemakers Pres 1984-85; Wakarusa 4-H Club Spon 1874-76; IN Univ Instructional Asst Grant; Dept of Ed Certificate of Merit; Wa-Nee Schls 25 Yrs of Service Recognition 1987; *home:* 28584 CR 38 Wakarusa IN 46573

ANGLEN, DONALD EDGAR, Mathematics Department Chair; *b:* Chicago, IL; *m:* Laura Sue Roller; *c:* Elizabeth D., John J.; *ed:* (BS) Math, 1968, (MS) Math, 1973 E IL Univ; Nuclear Engineering, Univ of IL 1975; Materials Engineering, Univ of IL 1990; *cr:* Math Teacher Cisne HS 1968-69, Chrisman HS 1969-; *ai:* Scholastic Bowl, Mathlete, JETS Team, Ecology Team Coach; Nom 3 Times Natl Math Teacher of Yr; *home:* 197 Western Ave Hume IL 61924

ANGLES, BESS M., Elementary Principal; *ed:* (BA) Elem Ed, (M) Learning Disability, OH Univ; Prin & Supt Cert Xavier Univ; Ashland Coll; *cr:* 2nd Grade Teacher 1966-67, 4th Grade Teacher 1967-69, 1st Grade Teacher 1969-81, Teacher of Learning Disabilities 1981-82, Elem Prin 1982- Union-Sciote Local Schls; *ai:* Martha Holden Jennings Scholar; *office:* Union-Scioto Primary Sch 1432 Egypt Pike Chillicothe OH 45601

ANGLIN, BARBARA GAYLE (HAWTHORNE), Art Teacher; *b:* Jackson, MS; *m:* E. Gary; *c:* Beth, Jonathan; *ed:* (BA) Art, MS Coll 1980; *cr:* Teacher Alta Woods Baptist Kndgtn 1975-77, Florence HS 1984, Magnolia Jr HS 1985-; *ai:* Annual & Paper Staff Adv; Discipline Comm; Adult Sunday Sch Teacher; Interpreter for Deaf; Set Designs; Moss Point Jr Miss Set Designs; *home:* 3707 Crosby Pascagoula MS 39567

ANGLIN, LINDA MC CLUNEY, 5th Grade Teacher; *b:* Turrell, AR; *m:* Joe V.; *c:* Van, Cheryl Vaughn, Dent, George; *ed:* (BA) Sociology, Millsaps Coll 1951; (MED) Elem Ed, MS Coll 1970; (EDSP) Elem Ed, MS St Univ 1974; *cr:* 5th Grade Teacher St Andrews Episcopal Sch 1952-53; Carthage Elem Sch 1956-57; 3rd-6th Grade Teacher Jackson Public Schls 1957-; *ai:* Registered Lobbyist Ed & Childrens Issues in MS Legislature; Public Ed Forum MS Bd Dir; Advisory Bd Assn Learning Disabilities; MS Prof Educators Pres 1979-82; Tau Chapter/Delta KAPPA Gamma Pres 1986-88; Jackson Prof Educators Pres 1988-; Jackson Area Rdng Cncl (Pres 175-76, Outstanding Svc Awd 1988); KAPPA Delta Pi Honor Society Ed 1970-; Phi KAPPA Phi Honor Society for Schlsp 1974-; Founded MS Prof Educators 1979; Distinguished Svc Ed Awd Beta Chapter Delta KAPPA Gamma Society Intl; Whos Who Amer Ed; Book of Golden Deeds Awd Exchange Club of North Jackson; *home:* 785 Cedarhurst Rd Jackson MS 39206

ANGULO, CECILIA PATRICIA, 2nd Grade Teacher; *b:* Nogales Sonora, Mexico; *m:* Alejandro D.; *c:* Alejandro, Marissa; *ed:* (BA) Ed, AZ St 1978; Continuation of Ed, Univ of AZ 1983; *cr:* 3rd Grade Teacher 1981-83, 2nd Grade Teacher 1983- Craycroft Elem; *ai:* Leadership & Minority Affairs Comm; Supt Advisory Cncl; NEA 1981-; AZ Ed Assn Mem; Sunnyside Ed Assn; *office:* Craycroft Elem Sch 5455 E Littletown Rd Tucson AZ 85706

ANIBAS, ROBERT ANTHONY, Sixth Grade Teacher; *b:* Durand, WI; *m:* Carol Jean Mc Mahon; *c:* Heidi, Jason, James; *ed:* (BS) Broad Area Scndry Soc Sci, Univ of WI River Falls 1965; (MST) Elem Sci, Univ of WI Oshkosh 1979; Space Technology, Marine Ecology Technology, Sci Methods Leadership, Glacial & Soil His, Assertive Discipline, Interraltionships of Curr Diversity & technology; *cr:* 11th/12th Grade Soc Sci Teacher West Allis HS 1965-67; Infantry US Army 1967-69; 7th/8th Grade Teacher 1969-79, 6th Grade Sci/Lang Teacher 1979- Weyauwega-Fremont Mid Sch; *ai:* Waupaca Cty Youth Advisory Comm 1989-; Natl Sci Teachers Assn, WI Elem Sci Teachers Assn, WI Aerospace Ed Assn 1988-; WI Society of Sci Teachers, WI Assn for Environmental Ed 1986-; NEA, WI Ed Assn Cncl 1965-; Weyauwega-Fremont Ed Assn 1969-; Weyauwega City Lib Bd 1987; Cub Scout Leader 1986-89; Wkshps & Conventions Presenter; Congressional Internship Awd 1965; 3 Natl Schlshps; NEWEST; Christa Mc Auliffe Inst for Educl Pioneering 1989; St Awds for Innovative Lessons 1982, 1989; *office:*

Weyauwega-Fremont Mid Sch 310 E Main St Weyauwega WI 54983

ANIOL, BETTY SUE TROUTMAN, Assistant Principal; *b:* San Antonio, TX; *m:* William R.; *c:* Robert W., Kimberly L.; *ed:* (BA) Early Chldhd/Elem Ed, Univ of TX San Antonio 1976; (MA) Early Chldhd Ed, Incarnate Word Coll 1984; Trinity Univ; *cr:* 2nd Grade Teacher 1976-78, 1st Grade Teacher 1978-81, K-5th Grade Teacher 1981-89, Asst Prin/Teacher of Gifted & Talented 1990 Castle Hills Elem; *ai:* US Dept of Ed Steering Comm; Castle Hills Elem Recognized as Natl Exemplary Sch 1988; 1st Runner Up NE Ind Sch Dist Teacher of Yr 1987; Castle Hills Teacher of Yr 1979, 1987; *home:* 109 Aspen Ln San Antonio TX 78232

ANKENY, VIRGINIA DALEY, 5th Grade Computer Teacher; *b:* Pittsburgh, PA; *m:* Arthur A.; *c:* Kimberle A. Solnosky, Kevin A.; *ed:* (BA) Elem Ed, CA St Univ of PA 1964; Early Chldhd & Sci; *cr:* Kndgtn Teacher Carlynton Schls 1964-66; Pre-Sch Teacher Henderson Settlement Misson 1967-68, Rdng Specialist Teacher Cntrl Cambira Schls 1970-71; Pre-Sch Teacher Cambria Cty Child Dev Corporation 1973-76; 4th-6th Grade Cmptr Teacher/Asst Prin St Benedict Schls 1979-; *ai:* Alpha Kappa Delta (Chaplain 1988-, Historian 1990-); Published Magazine & Soc Stud Textbooks; PHEA Grants to Study Sci, Cmptrs; *office:* St Benedict Sch S Church St Carrolltown PA 15722

ANKER, BEVERLY ELAINE, 4th Grade Teacher; *b:* Buffalo, NY; *ed:* (EDB) Ed, SUNY 1963; (MS) Ed, NY Coll 1968; *cr:* 1st Grade Teacher Thomas Marks Elem Sch 1962-63; 2nd Grade Teacher 1963-64; 1st Grade Teacher 1964-65; 2nd Grade Teacher 1965-76 Wurlitzer Elem Sch; 3rd Grade Teacher 1976-77; 5th Grade Teacher 1977-85; 4th Grade Teacher 1985- Meadow Elem Sch; *ai:* North Tonawanda United Teachers Elem VP 1986-88; United Teachers Delegate/Ed 3 1987-; Niagara Frontier Rdng Cncl; Delta Kappa Gamma Intnl Soc Treas 1988-92; NY St Historical Assn; *office:* Meadow Elem Sch 455 Meadow Dr North Tonawanda NY 14120

ANKER, MORTEN, Teacher; *b:* Copengagen, Denmark; *ed:* (BA) His/Lang Art, Tonder St Teachers Trng Coll 1965; Hum, Cmmty Dev, Aid To Third World, United Nations Agencies; Peoples Intnl Coll Elsinore Denmark 1967-68, Madison Project Hands-On Math PS 41 New York City Bd of Ed 1974-75; *cr:* 3rd/5th Grade Teacher Blans Sch 1966-67; 5th-7th Grade Teacher Levring Sch 1968-71; 1st/3rd/4th Grade Teacher United Nations Intnl Sch 1971-; K-4th Grade Math Specialist Center For Gifted Teachers Coll Columbia Univ 1983-; *ai:* United Nations Math Lab Specialist After-Sch & Summer Prgms; Columbia Univ Teachers Coll Saturday Enrichment Prgm at Center for Gifted; Chief Organizer of Intnl Math Conference; United Nations Jr Sch Redesign Comm Chm; NCTM Conference Speaker 1988-89; NCSS, ASCD, European Cncl of Intnl Schls; Presenter World Conference on Gifted & Talented Children 1985, Intnl Congress on Math Ed 1988; Sch Project Leave European Stud Tour of Math Centers 1985-86; Teacher Exch Vienna Intnl Sch 1986-87; Math Article & Chapter Published; *office:* United Nations Intnl Sch 24-50 Franklin D Roosevelt Dr New York NY 10010

ANKROM, NILAH WALKER, Social Studies Teacher; *b:* Jewett, OH; *m:* Jay C.; *c:* Karan S. Princic, Terry J.; *ed:* (BS) Scndry Ed/Soc Stud Comprehensive, Coll of Steubenville 1957; (MED) Scndry Ed/His, Kent St Univ 1974; Gifted Ed, Kent St Univ; *cr:* Frosh Eng Teacher 1957-58, Amer His Teacher 1958-71, Teacher of Gifted & Talented 1979-86, Amer His/Amer Government Teacher 1971- Carrollton HS; *ai:* Adv Chrldr 1959-74, Close-Up Club 1981-89, Homecoming 1966-70, Mock Trial Competition 1990, NHS 1976-79, Citizens Bee 1988-; NEA, OH Ed Assn, E Cntrl OH Teacher Assn, Carrollton Ed Assn 1957-; Delta Kappa Gamma Assn 1971-; Martha Holden Jennings Scholar 1981-82.

ANNA, DOROTHY (BEARER), English Teacher; *b:* Cambria Cty, PA; *m:* Dennis F.; *c:* Jude, Susan, Jennifer, Matthew; *ed:* (BA) Lib Sci, Clarion Univ 1968; (BA) Comprehensive Eng, PA St 1976; Power Writing, Impact, SAP Trng; *cr:* Librarian/Teacher Cambria Heights Sch Dist 1969-72, 1976-89; *ai:* Stu Asst Comm; NEA, PSEA; CHEA Recording Secy 1969-71; Hastings Public Lib Bd 1978-82; *home:* Saint Boniface PA 16675

ANNEGAN, SIRI KESSINGER, Secondary English Teacher; *b:* Lock Haven, PA; *m:* Patton R.; *c:* Amy, Matthew, Ryan; *ed:* (BS) Eng Ed, Lock Haven Univ 1972; Shippensburg Univ, Marywood Coll; *cr:* Teacher Carlisle HS 1972-75, Jersey Shore HS 1977-85, Mc Dowell HS 1986-; *ai:* NWPCTE 1987-; British/Amer Exch Prgm Coord; Coord/Teacher for Advanced Placement Prgm Publication Recognition Jersey Shore HS; *home:* 7694 Royann Dr Fairview PA 16415

ANNIS, ANGELA BARNES, Computer Science Teacher; *b:* Burbank, CA; *m:* Harold E.; *c:* Barnard H.; *ed:* (BS) Math, OK Baptist Univ 1968; (MA) Experimental Psych, Univ of TX Arlington 1974; Stu Teaching, TCU: Cmptr Sci, TX Womans Univ; SE IN Univ, Spalding Coll, UTA; AP Wkshps; *cr:* Math Teacher Eastern Hills HS 1975-78, Jeffersonville HS 1978-83; Math/Cmptr Teacher Grapevine HS 1983-; *ai:* Grapevine HS Campus Cmptr Specialist; Prin Advisory, Campus Improvement Comm; AP Cmptr Sci Teacher & Spon; TX St Teachers Assn, TX Cmptr Ed Assn, IN St Teachers Assn; Memorial Baptist Church (Personnel, Pastor Search, Long Range Planning Comm); Nom Presidential Awd Excl in Teaching Math & Sci; Article Published 1976; *office:* Grapevine HS 3223 Mustang Dr Grapevine TX 76051

ANNUNZIATA, ADELAIDE DE LUCIA, Chapter I Teacher; *b:* New Haven, CT; *m:* Edward C.; *ed:* (BA) His/Sociology, Albertus Magnus Coll 1961; (MA) Elem Ed, S CT St Univ 1966; Prof Dev, St Joseph 1988; *cr:* 2nd Grade Teacher Centerville Sch 1961-65, Wintergreen Sch 1965-79; 3rd/4th Grade Teacher Dunbar Hill Sch 1979-83; 2nd-6th Grade Teacher Spring Glen Sch 1983-; *ai:* Remedial Assistance Planning Team Coord; Sch Staff Dev & Staff Dev Advisory Comm Mem; Crisis Intervention, Liaison, PTA Cafeteria/Recess, EERA/Tutorial Implementation, Chapter I Parent Advisory Comm; NEA, CEA, HEA, Phi Delta Kappa; Cath Charity Bd of Dir 1987-88, 1990; Amer Heart Assn; Bonyai Service Awd 1989.

ANSCHUTZ, GERALDINE SUNDELIUS, Mathematics Teacher; *b:* Iron River, MI; *m:* Richard W.; *c:* Janet, Sue, Karen; *ed:* (BA) Bus/Math, Northern MI Univ 1956; (MA) Ed, Univ of MI 1957; Fort Hays St Univ/Univ KS Lawrence/Radio Shack Cmptr Center; *cr:* Instr Southern IL Univ 1957-60, Colby Public Schls 1976-; *ai:* Spon Natl Honor Society; NCTM 1980-; KS Assn of Teachers of Math Pres 1987-88; Phi Delta Kappa Treas 1986-87; Prof Dev Cncl Colby Schls; Western Plains Arts Assn Mem Chm; Colby Presbyn Church Ruling Elder; PEO; Colby Girl Scouts; USD 315 Teacher of Yr 1988-89; Articles Published in KATM Bulletin; Mem KS Math Standards Comm 1989-; *home:* 1125 Brookside Colby KS 67701

ANSEL, STEHANIE WILSON, Physical Education Teacher; *b:* Richmond, TX; *m:* Mark Hinson; *c:* Stephen, Morgan; *ed:* (BAT) Phys Ed, Sam Houston St Univ 1977; Grad Stud TX Womens Univ, Sam Houston St Univ, Univ of Houston; *cr:* Teacher/Coach Alvin Jr HS 1978-; *ai:* Vlybl, Bsktbl, Track, Tennis Coach Alvin Jr HS; Athletic Coord Alvin Jr HS; Climate Comm Chm Alvin Jr HS; Campus Communication Comm Mem Alvin Jr HS; TX HS Girls Coaches Assn 1974-; Alvin Jr HS Teacher of Yr 1988, 1989; *office:* Alvin Jr HS 2301 W South St Alvin TX 77511

ANSELL, JOAN GREEN, Graphic Design Teacher; *b:* Oakland, CA; *m:* William H.; *ed:* (BAED) Art, 1951, (MFA) Fine Art, 1952 CA Coll of Arts & Crafts; Ceramics, Mills Coll; Ceramics, Photography, Graphics, CA Coll of Arts & Crafts; *cr:* Art Instr Claremont Jr HS 1953-74; Graphic Design Instr Skyline HS 1974-; *ai:* Natl Congress of Parents & Teachers Honorary Life Membership 1959; CA Congress of Parents, Teachers & Stu Honorary Service Awd 1986; Pilot Study Work Behavior & Attitudes Ceres Sch Dist 1977-78; Craft Curr Guide Oakland Public Schls 1964-68; Printmaking Demonstrations CA Art Ed Assn 1965.

ANSELL, SAMUEL TILDEN, III, English Department Chair; *b:* Washington, DC; *m:* Sara Green; *c:* Susan, Sara; *ed:* (AB) Philosophy/Span, Washington & Lee Univ 1965; (MED) Eng, Univ of S AL 1979; *cr:* Teacher 1970-85, Teacher/Dept Chm 1985- Fairhope Mid Sch; *ai:* Fairhope Variance Bd Vice Chm 1979-86; 3rd Place AL St Poetry Contest; Published Unit Teaching Logic; Outstanding Graduate Stu Ed Univ of S AL; *office:* Fairhope Mid Sch Fairhope Ave Fairhope AL 36532

ANSELM, DIANE MORAN, 1st Grade Teacher; *b:* Detroit, MI; *m:* Gregory N.; *c:* Todd M.; *ed:* (BA) Ed, 1965; (MA) Guidance Counseling, 1969 Univ of MI; *cr:* 1st/2nd/3rd/5th/6th Grade Teacher Livonis Public Schls 1965-; *ai:* Whole Lang Rdng Comm; Elem Math Comm; Cmptr Ed Steering Comm; Livonia Ed Assn 1965-; NEA 1965-; PTA 1965-; BSA Den Leader/Comm Chairperson 1986-; Favorite Teacher Awd Detroit News 1968; Teacher of Yr Livonia Jaycees; Elem Sch Teacher of Yr Livonia Public Schls 1989-; Golden Apple Awd Wayne Cty Intermediated Sch Dist; *office:* Buchanan Elem Sch 16400 Hubbard Livonia MI 48154

ANSELMO, HAROLD THOMAS, US History/Soc Stud Teacher; *b:* Spokane, WA; *m:* Kathleen M.; *c:* Phil, Paul; *ed:* (AA) Ed, North ID Coll 1968; (BA) Ed, Eastern WA Coll 1970; Law in Admin, Principalship; *cr:* Teacher Newport Jr HS 1972-; *ai:* Stu Body Adv; Boys Bsktbl Coach; Newport Associated Teachers 1972-; NEA 1972-; ASCD 1986-; Elks Club 1974-; Booster Club 1972-; *office:* Newport Jr/Sr HS P O Box 70 Newport WA 99156

ANSLEY, KATHERINE CLARK, Fifth Grade Teacher; *b:* Sarasota, FL; *m:* Mark V.; *c:* Alexis; *ed:* (BA) Elem Ed, FL A&M Univ 1979; Early Chldhd Ed, Nova Univ; *cr:* Teacher Booker Elem 1980-; *ai:* Sarasota Cty Teachers Assn 1985-; Saratoga Ctys Rdng Cncl 1988-; NAACP 1988-; Westcoast Center for Human Dev 1979-; Grade Level Chm 1987-89; Soc Stud Textbook Adoption Comm 1987-88; *home:* 1046 N Jefferson Ave Sarasota FL 34237

ANSON, MARION ANN HIGGINS, History Department Chair; *b:* Longview, TX; *ed:* (BSE) Phys Ed/His, 1975, (MSPE) Phys Ed/Ed, 1976 Midwestern St Unv; *cr:* Gov/Sci Teacher/Phys Ed Coach Notre Dame HS 1976-79; Sci Teacher/Coach Singapore Amer Sch 1979-80; Phys Ed Teacher/Coach Hirschi HS 1980-83; TX-Amer His/Speech Teacher Barwise Jr HS 1983-; *ai:* Academic Pentathlon Coach; Chrldr, Stu Cncl Spon; Sch Photographer; TX St Teacher Assn Building Rep; NEA; Adopt-A-Nursing Home Project Sch Coord; Bsktbl Ofcls Bd Recording Secy; Teacher of Yr 1990; Ofcl of Yr 1990; *office:* Barwise HS 3807 Kemp Wichita Falls TX 76308

ANSTETT, CHERYL ANN (WILLIAMS), Third Grade Teacher; *b:* Celina, OH; *m:* Dee C.; *ed:* (BS) Elem Ed, Tri St Univ 1975; (MS) Elem Ed, IN Purdue Univ 1978; Quest Skills for Growing K-5, Teaching Staff Summer 1989; *cr:* 2nd Grade Teacher 1975/77, 4th Grade Teacher 1988, 3rd Grade Teacher 1976/1978-87/1989- Prairie Heights Comm Sch Corp; *ai:* PTO Rep Local; Elem Curr Rep Local; Young Authors Comm Rep Local; Pokagon Rdng Cncl Pres 1979-80; Alpha XI Chapter Nominations Chairperson 1988-; Pleasant Lake United Meth (Organist/Pianist 1963-, Sunday Sch Teacher 1962-, Worship-Music Comm Chairperson 1970-); Prairie Heights Ed Assn (Pres 1982-84 Treas 1986-); *home:* W Ozark St Po Box 45 Pleasant Lake IN 46779

ANSWINE, ILOA ADAMETZ, English Teacher; *b:* Etna, PA; *m:* Demaree J.; *c:* Todd, Matt; *ed:* (BS) Health/Phys Ed/Composition Eng, 1964, (MED) Health/Phys Ed, 1970 Slippery Rock; Post Grad Stud Univ of Pittsburgh 1980; *cr:* Teacher Gateway Sch Dist 1964-65, Kiski Area Sch Dist 1965-67, Allegheny Valley Sch Dist 1967-68, Kiski Area Sch Dist 1968-; *ai:* PSEA; *home:* 795 Zubal Rd Apollo PA 15613

ANTALE, ANDREW F., Mathematics Teacher; *b:* Philadelphia, PA; *m:* Patricia E. Joie; *c:* Joel, Melanie; *ed:* (BA) Poly Sci, Univ of N FL 1976; (MA) Scndry Ed/Math & Curr Dev Glassboro St Coll 1983; Photographic Arts, Stockton St Coll & Phila Coll of Art 1976-77; Math & Cmptr Sci, Glassboro St Coll 1978-79; *cr:* Radioman US Navy 1972-76; Math Teacher Landis Jr HS 1979-80; Adjunct Prof Cmptr Sci/Math Glassboro St Coll 1979-; Math/Cmptr Sci Vineland HS 1980-; *ai:* Sr Class Adv; Commencement Comm; NJ Minimun Basic Skills, HSPT Comm; Assn of Math Teachers of NJ Glassboro Conference Chairperson 1983; Monroe Twp Little League Bd of Dir Mem 1986-87; S NJ Cmptr Awareness Project, S NJ Regional Teachers Center, Master Sci Teacher Prog Grants; *office:* Vineland HS 2880 Chestnut St Vineland NJ 08360

ANTHONY, BEVERLY BELLAVANCE, Gifted & Talented Prgm Teacher; *b:* Putnam, CT; *m:* Joel F.; *c:* Michele Anthony Mc Carthy, Stephen, Lynwood; *ed:* (BA) Elem Ed, 1962, (MA) Lang Art, 1972 E CT St Univ; *cr:* 1st/2nd Grade Teacher Sprague Elem Sch 1963-65; 3rd/4th Grade Teacher Windham Public Schls 1968-; *ai:* Evaluation & Rdng Textbook Selection Comm Windham Public Schls; Kappa Delta Pi 1962-; Windham Fed Teachers, CT Fed Teachers 1968-; CT Writing Project Honorable Mention Celebration of Excl; *office:* Windham Public Schls High St Willimantic CT 06226

ANTHONY, BILLIE C., Teacher of Gifted & Talented; *b:* Hartford, CT; *m:* Michael.; *ed:* (BA) Eng, Univ of CT 1971; (MED) Urban Ed, Univ of Hartford 1973; *cr:* Intern/Eng Teacher Hartford Public Schls 1971-73; Eng Teacher Weaver HS 1973-74, Moylan Alternative Sch 1974-75; Sci Teacher 1975-77, Honors Eng Teacher 1977-79, Teacher of Gifted & Talented 1979- Fox Mid Sch; *ai:* Mayors Task Force for Quality Ed; Debate Team & Drama Coach; Fox Journal Adv & Ed; Pre Law & Pre Medical Club Adv; Pre Engineering Prgm & Project Friendship Coord; Governing Bd Greater Hartford Acad of Performing Art; RAAP Adv; Responsible Adolescents Advocating Peace; I Have a Dream Prgm Stu Mentor; CT Associated of Gifted, CT Educl Network for Talented & Gifted; CT Historical Sociey, CT Law Related Ed Consortium, Wintonbury Historical Society, Ed Commission, Bloomfield United Meth Church; Written & Produced Plays for Children; Wrote Scripts for Educl Films; Wrote Scrpit for Hartford Symphony Orch Youth Series; *office:* Lewis Fox Mid Sch 305 Greenfield St Hartford CT 06112

ANTHONY, DAVID BERTRAM, Social Studies Dept Chairman; *b:* Newport News, VA; *m:* Lynn Ann Smith; *ed:* (BA) His, Randolph Macon Coll 1976; *cr:* Soc Stud Teacher Brunswick Sr HS 1977-80, Randolph Macon Acad 1980-82, Mathews HS 1982-; *ai:* NHS Faculty Comm; Mathews Cty Bicentennial (Planning Comm, Mem) 1989-; *office:* Mathews HS Box 38 Mathews VA 23109

ANTHONY, DEBRA DIETRICK, Health & Physical Ed Teacher; *b:* Williamsport, PA; *m:* George T.; *ed:* (BS) Health/Phys Ed, West Chester 1974; CPR, First Aid, NDEITA Cert Fitness Instrs; *cr:* Health/Phys Ed Teacher Lower Cape May Regional Sr HS 1975-78, Northampton Sr HS 1979-; *ai:* Var Field Hockey Coach & Asst Var Sftbl Coach; Boys Bsktbl Crowd Control; Wellness Comm; Word Processing Instr for Educators & Adults; Amer Assn of Health, Phys Ed & Recreation; Amer Heart Assn; *office:* Northampton Sr HS 1619 Laubach Ave Northampton PA 18067

ANTHONY, ELIZABETH ANN (GREEN), 6th Grade Reading Teacher; *b:* Des Moines, IA; *m:* Dwayne L.; *c:* Dwayne M., Diamond L., Durell h.; *ed:* (BA) Elem Ed/Sociology, Drake Univ 1972; *cr:* Teacher Lansing Sch Dist 1972-74, Atchison Sch Dist 1974-; *ai:* Pep Club & Cheerleading Spon; Vlybl Coach; *office:* Atchison Jr HS 301 N 5th St Atchison KS 66002

ANTHONY, ELIZABETH MOSBY, French Teacher; *b:* San Augustine, TX; *c:* Willard II *ed:* (BA) His, Lamar Univ 1964; (MA) Ed, United States International Univ 1988; Fr/San Diego St Univ; *cr:* Teacher Samuel F B Morse HS 1976-; Teacher Adult Ed Prgm 1974-76; *ai:* Adv Societe Honoraire De Francais; CFLTA Outstanding Teacher 1986; Amer Cncl Teaching of Foreign Lang; AAT Fr; Assn Black Educators; Phi Delta Kappa Sec 1985-88; Francophone Africa Prgm 1989; Excel Awd Corporation for Excl Public Ed 1985; *office:* Samuel F B Morse H S 6905 Skyline Dr San Diego CA 92114

ANTHONY, SALLIE SHEFFIELD, Third Grade Teacher; *b:* Atlanta, GA; *m:* Samuel L.; *ed:* (BS) Elem Ed, Morris Brown Coll 1955; (MA) Early Chldhd Ed, GA St Univ 1972; Grad Stud Univ of GA, Emory Univ, Atlanta Univ, GA St Univ; *cr:* Teacher Carrollton Bd of Ed 1955-57, Atlanta Bd of Ed 1960-; *ai:* Math Club Spon & Contact Person C W Hill Elem Sch; Chm of Leadership Team & 3rd Grade Team Leader of C W Hill Elem Sch; NEA, AEA, ATA; Teacher of Yr C W Hill Elem Sch 1974-75; Outstanding Elem Teacher of America 1974, 1975, 1981;

Arithmetic Teacher Magazine Adv; Mem of ECD Comm for Math on Primary Level; *office:* C W Hill 386 Pine St Ne Atlanta GA 30308

ANTHONY, WANDA FOSTER, Science Teacher; *b:* Paris, TX; *c:* Chris, Andrea; *ed:* (AS) Elem Ed - Magna Cum Laude, Paris Jr Coll 1983; (BS) Elem Ed, E TX St Univ 1985; Grad Stud Elem Ed, Earth Sci, ETSU; *cr:* Teacher Crockett Mid Sch 1985-; *ai:* Chrldr Spon; UIL Sci Coach; TX Classroom Teachers Assn Secy 1989-; Sci Teachers Assn of TX 1986-; Phi Theta Kappa, Kappa Delta Pi 1984; TX St Ed Assn Pres 1985; Alpha Chi 1984; Paris Jr Coll Pres Honor List 1983; Deans List E TX E TX St Univ 1984.

ANTIL, STEPHEN GILLES, Science/Theology Teacher; *b:* Holyoke, MA; *m:* Susan; *c:* Anthony, Peter, Clare, Andrew; *ed:* (AS) Art/Sci, Holyoke Comm Coll 1972; (BS) Environmental Design/Ed, 1974, (MED) Cmmty Ed, 1976 Univ of MA; Environmental Interpretation Outward Bound Ed Trng; *cr:* Teacher Falmouth HS 1975; Environmental Educator Colombia South America Peace Corps 1976-77; Teacher/Cnslr Berkshire Learning Center 1978-80; Teacher St Joseph Cntrl HS 1980-; *ai:* Cross Cntry Coach; Running Club Adv; NHS Exec Bd Mem; NCEA 1980-; Returned Peace Volunteers of America 1987-; Lee Cmmty Soccer Coach 1987-; MA Dept of Forest & Parks Ed Guides Published; Smithsonian Inst Grant Recipient 1976-77; *office:* St Joseph Cntrl HS 22 Maplewood Ave Pittsfield MA 01201

ANTINORE, DAVID, Math Teacher; *b:* Queens, NY; *m:* Rosalia Maria Polizzi; *c:* Christopher, John; *ed:* (BA) Math, Pace Univ 1970; (MA) Ed, Adelphi Univ 1975; *cr:* Math Teacher Mother Butler Memorial & Sacred Heart HS 1970-78, St Catharine Acad 1978-; *ai:* Jr Ring Day Organizer & Moderator; *office:* St Catharine Acad 2250 Williamsbridge Rd Bronx NY 10469

ANTLE, DAVID KENT, Phys Ed/Social Studies Teacher; *b:* Monett, MO; *m:* Rana; *ed:* (BS) Phys Ed, SW Baptist Univ 1986; *cr:* Teacher/Coach Bronaugh R-7 1988-; *ai:* Head Var Girls Sftbl & Bsktbl, Jr HS Girls Bsktbl, Asst Girls Track Coach; 1st Baptist Church of Exeter Sunday Sch Teacher 1987-88; *office:* Bronaugh R-7 Sch 527 E 6th Bronaugh MO 64728

ANTLE, TRACEY ROY, Advanced English Teacher; *b:* Cincinnati, OH; *m:* Mark D.; *c:* Logan R.; *ed:* (AA) Eng, Lindsey Wilson Jr Coll 1982; (BA) Eng, 1984, (MA) Scndry Sch Counseling, 1987 W KY Univ; *cr:* Creative Writing 1987-88, Gen Eng/Rdng 1988-89, Adv Eng I 1989- Russell Cty Jr HS; *ai:* Jr HS Chrldr Coach; Extension Homemakers (Secy 1987-88, Pres 1989-); *home:* Rt 3 Box 82-C Jamestown KY 42629

ANTONACCI, DENISE CENTRELLA, School Social Worker; *b:* Montclair, NJ; *ed:* (BA) Psych, Montclair St Coll 1973; Grad Stud Montclair St Coll & Georgian Court Coll; *cr:* K-3rd Grade Teacher 1977-83; Sch Social Worker Bricktown Sch System 1983-; *ai:* Eleanora Gruppuso Memorial Schlsp (VP, Treas) 1981-; Natl Multiple Schlerosis Assn 1986-.

ANTONIO, ROBERT JOHN, 7th/8th Grade Math Teacher; *b:* New Haven, CT; *c:* Kimberly, Robert Jr.; *ed:* (BS) Ed, 1969; (MS) Ed Research, 1970; Ed Admin & Suprv, 1973 Southern CT St Univ; *cr:* 7th/8th Grade Math Teacher Simon Lake Sch 1970-72; Teacher/Vice-Prin Lenox Avenue Sch 1972-81; 6th Grade Teacher 1981-83; 7th/8th Grade Math Teacher 1983- John F Kennedy Sch; *ai:* Head Girls Bsktbl Coach Jonathan Law HS 1985; John F Kennedy Sch Yrbk Adv 1983-; Milford Ed Assn (Treas 1970-71 VP 1971-72 Pres 1972-73); CT Ed Assn 1969-; Natl Ed Assn 1969-; Amer Cancer Society Asst Dir Camp Rising Sun 1986-; CT HS Coaches Assn 1983-; Fellowship for Masters Deg Eductl Research 1970; Nom for Outstanding Milford Educator Awd 1978-81 & 1983-86; Nom for CT Teacher of Yr Awd 1988 & 1989; *home:* 5 Whippoorwill Dr Milford CT 06460

ANTONOWICZ, RAYMOND C., Teacher of Gifted & Talented; *b:* Danbury, CT; *m:* Leolyn Geary; *c:* Stefan; *ed:* (BS) Physics, W CT St Univ 1969; (MS) Scndry Ed, Univ of Bridgeport 1972; *cr:* Teacher Cloonan Mid Sch 1970-; *ai:* Mathcounts Team Coach; Teacher Expectation/Stu Achievement Staff Developer; SEA, CEA, NEA 1970-; *office:* Cloonan Mid Sch 11 W North St Stamford CT 06902

ANTUS, ROBERT LAWRENCE, English Teacher; *b:* New York City, NY; *c:* Robby; *ed:* (BA) Eng, Norte Dame Univ 1967; (MA) Eng, Northwestern Univ 1969; (MED) Admin, Loyola Univ 1976; (MST) Scndry Ed, Univ of Chicago 1978; Eductl & Stu Teaching/Basic Counseling, Loyola Univ; Basic Acting, Columbia Coll & Victory Gardens Theatre; *cr:* Stu Teacher Mather HS 1971; Eng Teacher New Trier East HS 1971-74, Morton East Hs 1975-; Part-Time Eng Teacher Mac Cormac Jr Coll 1989-; *ai:* Published Notre Dame & Mothers Manual Magazine; *home:* 329 Kimbell Ave Apt 11 Elmhurst IL 60126

ANZALONE, A. CARMEN (TOWER), Sixth Grade Teacher; *b:* Lyons, WI; *m:* Dominic Charles; *c:* Rick D., Lisa J. Miller-Anzalone; *ed:* (BA) Elem Ed, Dominician Coll 1974; (MS) Classroom Guidance Counseling, Carthage Coll 1988; *cr:* 6th Grade Teacher Janes Elem Sch 1974-83, James F Gilmore Mid Sch 1983-; *ai:* Stu Asst Prgm Mem; *home:* 1100 Prairie Dr Racine WI 53406

APANA, JAMES L., English Department Chair; *b:* Cleveland, OH; *m:* Sandra Lee; *c:* Jeff, Christy, Scott; *ed:* (BA) Eng, Western Reserve Univ 1967; (MA) Ed, John Carroll Univ 1975; Many Wkshps, In-Service Courses; *cr:* Teacher Lincoln Jr/Sr HS 1967-69; Dept Chm Lincoln Jr HS 1969-75, Wilbur Wright Intermediate Sch 1975-; *ai:* Natl Jr Honor Society & Academic Challenge Adv; Many Textbook Adoption Comm; Curr Writing Comm Mem; NCTE; Greater Cleveland Cncl Teachers of Eng; OH Eng/Lang Art Assn; Wilbur Wright PTA Lifetime Membership 1977; Cub Scouts Den Leader 1977-79; Whos Who Amer Ed 1989-; Martha H Jennings Teacher/Leader 1977-78; Martha H Jennings Scholar 1979-80; Articles Published OH Eng/ Lang Art Bulletin; *office:* Wilbur Wright Jr HS 11005 Parkhurst Dr Cleveland OH 44111

APAP, CHUCK ROBERT, Math Teacher/Head Ftbl Coach; *b:* Detroit, MI; *m:* Carrie Ann Wood; *c:* Chris, Chad; *ed:* (BS) Math, MI Tech Univ 1970; (MS) Scndry Ed Math, E MI Univ 1973; ITEP Trng 1988-89; *cr:* Math Teacher/Asst Ftbl Coach Andover HS 1970-71, Northville HS 1971-78; Math Teacher/Head Ftbl & Bsbl Coach Walled Lake Western HS 1978-; *ai:* Head Ftbl Coach; MI HS All Star Coach & Defensive Coord 1990; MI HS Ftbl Coaches Assn (Region Dir in Region 7 1985) 1976-; PTA (Schlrsp Chm 1985-89, Academic All St Chm 1987-); Ofcl Sports Center 14th Annual Excl Awd 1986; MHSFCA Region 7 Dir 1985-89; PTA Teacher Merit Awd 1990; Consumer Math Book 1977; Coaching Awd Gary Championship 1983; St Championship Team Bsbl 1984; Natl Yrbk of Outstanding Teacher 1974-75; *office:* Walled Lake Western HS 600 Beck Rd Walled Lake MI 48088

APEL, CARMIE C., Retired Business Teacher; *b:* Paintsville, KY; *m:* Earl C.; *ed:* (BS) Bus Ed, Morehead St Univ 1960; *cr:* Elem Teacher Van Lear Ind 1951-53, Johnson Cty 1954-55; Bus Teacher Meade Memorial 1955-56, Bath Cty HS 1960-89; *ai:* KEA, NEA 1951-89; Bath Cty Ed Assn 1960-89; KRTA, NRTA, BCRTA 1989-.

APODACA, RICHARD STEPHEN, 6th Grade Life Sci Teacher; *b:* Alburquerque, NM; *ed:* (BS) Elem Ed, Univ of Albuquerque 1976; *cr:* Teacher Los Lunas Consolidated Schls 1976-79, Albuquerque Public Schls 1979-; *ai:* Stu Review Bd Mem; Stu Teacher & Stu Success Tutoring Supvr; Albuquerque Sci Teachers Assn; NM Classroom Teachers Assn; US Chess Fed; Ladera Mens Golf Assn; *home:* 4812 Platinum NE Rio Rancho NM 87124

APOSTOLIDES, CATHERINE ANGELAKIS, 3rd Grade Teacher; *b:* Peabody, MA; *m:* Paul; *c:* Paul J.; *ed:* (BS) Elem Ed, Salem Teachers Coll 1951; *cr:* 2nd Grade Teacher Brown Sch 1951-52; 3rd Grade Teacher Thomas Carroll Sch 1952-; *ai:* North Shore Rdng Cncl 1980-90; Peabody Fed of Teachers; Carroll Sch PTO Vice Pres 1960-64; St Vasilios Church Sch (Asst Supt 1954-90, Educational Comm Sec 1975-85, Parishoner of Yr Youth Group Adv 1960-70, Testimonial Dinner 1984); *office:* Thomas Carroll Sch 60 Northbend St Peabody MA 01960

APPEL, JANIS MARIE, Mathematics Teacher; *b:* Fort Thomas, KY; *ed:* (BS) Math, 1984, (MA) Scndry Ed, 1986 Morehead St Univ; *cr:* Math Teacher Pendleton Cty HS 1985-; *ai:* Girls Bsktbl Head Coach; Stu Act Comm; *office:* Pendleton Cty HS Rt 5 Falmouth KY 41040

APPELHOLM, ROBERT ALLAN, Elementary Principal; *b:* Appleton, MN; *m:* Linda L. Anderson; *c:* Christine, Lisa, Jennifer, Sara; *ed:* (BS) Elem Ed, St Cloud St Univ 1970; (MS) Voc Ed/ Spec Needs, Univ of WI Stout 1987; Eductl Admin, Univ of WI Madison 1988; *cr:* Elem Teacher 1970-71, Teacher Unity Mid Sch 1971-; Elem Prin Prairie Farm Sch Dist 1990; *ai:* Prof Staff Dev Comm Chm; Children At Risk Dist Coord; 2nd Opportunity HS Completion Prgm Dir; NEA, WI Ed Assn 1970-; Lions Club Secy 1988-; Sears Fdn Fellowship; *home:* Rt 3 Box 8 Milltown WI 54858

APPERT, LEO STEPHEN, Sixth Grade Teacher; *b:* Bismarck, ND; *m:* Bertha Neigum; *c:* Laura, Christine, David; *ed:* (BS) Soc Stud/Scndry Ed, 1968, Elem Ed/Phy Ed, 1972 Moorhead St Coll; *cr:* 7th/8th Grade Teacher Regan Public Sch 1968-1970; 6th Grade Teacher North Sargent Pub Sch 1970-73, Mandan Public Sch 1972-; *ai:* Midwest Region Team; Rdng Curr Adv Comm; Gifted & Talented Comm; NEA; Mandan Ed Assn; Knights of Columbus 1973-83; *office:* Mary Stark Elem Sch 405 8th Ave SW Mandan ND 58554

APPLEBAUN, LESLIE JILL, Secondary English Teacher; *b:* Denver, CO; *ed:* (BA) Eng Lit - Cum Laude, Bowdoin Coll 1983; (MA) Eng Lit, Univ of IA 1986; *cr:* Promotion/Author Appearances Globe Corner Bookstore 1983-84; Eng/His Instr Gorham HS 1986-; *ai:* Class of 1991 Adv; Poetry Club; Scheduling & Evaluation Sub Comm; Bd to Awd Sears-Roebuck Teacher Awd at Bowdon Coll; Restricting Team Mem 1988- & Co-Chm 1989-;STaff Dev Chm 1989-; Bowdoin Alumnae in Ed Exec Cncl Mem 1988-; *office:* Gorham HS 41 Morrill Ave Gorham ME 04038

APPLEBEE, TERRI KORMAN, 5th Grade Teacher; *b:* Chicago, IL; *m:* Donald Joseph; *c:* Ashley E.; *ed:* (BS) Elem Ed, N IL Univ 1973; *cr:* 4th-6th Grade Teacher Coronado Elem 1975-; *ai:* Stu Cncl, Sch Spelling Spon; Outdoor Ed Coord; Parent Teacher Cmmty Organization Teacher Rep to Bd 1976-86, 10 Yr Awd 1986; Tucson Area Rdng Cncl Mem 1986-; Great Books Leader Certificate Dist 10 Yr Service Awd; *office:* Coronado Elem Sch 3401 E Wilds Rd Tucson AZ 85738

APPLEFORD, LYNN ALLYSON, Third Grade Teacher; *b:* Port Huron, MI; *ed:* (BA) Eng/Soc Sci, W MI 1973; (MA) Elem Ed, Saginaw Valley 1988; *cr:* 3rd Grade Teacher Gearing Elem 1974-; *ai:* Various Sch Dist Comms; Building Union Rep; Delta Kappa Gamma 1986-; *office:* Gearing Elem Sch 200 N Carney Dr Saint Clair MI 48079

APPLEGATE, TODD EDWARD, Social Studies Teacher; *b:* Houston, TX; *m:* Mary Pavlas; *c:* Sara, Christopher; *ed:* (AA) Ed, Lee Coll 1971; (BA) Elem. Ed, Univ Houston 1973; (MED) Ed, Sam Houston St Univ 1977; TX Future Problem Solving - State Evaluator;Soc Stud, Geography Wkshps; *cr:* Teacher Waller Ind Sch Dist 1973-76; Spring ISD 1976-1979/1983-; *ai:* Team Leader - 6th Grade Interdisciplinary Team; Assn TX Prof Educators 1983-; TX Cncl Soc Stud 1985-; Southbrook Civic Assn VP 1981; *office:* Dueitt Mid Sch 5119 Treschwig Spring TX 77373

APPLETON, JULIA ELIZABETH, Director of Public Relations; *b:* Denver, CO; *ed:* Eng/Archaelogy, Univ Coll Galway Republic of Ireland 1986; (BA) Eng/Archaeology, Tufts Univ 1987; Grad Ed Courses, Fitchburg St Teachers Coll; *cr:* Study Skills Teacher Readak Educl Services 1987-88; Summer Sch Teacher-Eng 1988-, Eng Teacher 1988-89, Dir of Public Relations 1989- St Lukes Sch; *ai:* Environmental Club Faculty Support; Coll Advising Adv; Mid Sch Field Hockey Coach; Mid Sch Newspaper Adv; Natl Assn of Female Execs 1990; *office:* St Lukes Sch 377 N Wilton Rd New Canaan CT 06840

APRILE, V., MPF, Eighth Grade Teacher; *b:* Jersey City, NJ; *ed:* (AA) Elem Ed, Villa Walsh Coll 1961; (BA) Elem Ed, Cath Univ of AmericA 1965; (MS) Bus Ed, Marywood Coll 1972; *cr:* 6th Grade Teacher St Bartholomew Elem Sch 1956-58, St Anthony Elem Sch 1958-59, St Joseph Elem Sch 1959-60; Stu/Secy Cath Univ of America & Apostolic Delegation 1960-65; Bus Ed Chairperson/Bus Teacher St Joseph HS 1965-73; 8th Grade Teacher Holy Rosary Sch 1973-82, St Anthony of Padua Sch 1982-; *ai:* 8th Grade Forensics Coach; NCEA 1989-; *office:* St Anthony of Padua Sch 700 Central Ave Union City NJ 07087

APTER, KATHERINE BARNES, English Teacher; *b:* Ann Arbor, MI; *m:* Robert; *c:* Kim, Dana, Raphael-Allan; *ed:* (AB) British His, Vassar Coll 1961; Ed/Remedial Rdng, Johns Hopkins 1961-62; His Eng Lang, Columbia 1964-65; Black Culture/Rdng/ Literacy/Composition, Wayne St Univ 1969-73; *cr:* Eng Teacher Woodlawn Sr HS 1961-63; Rdng Specialist Prince Edward Free Sch Assn 1963-64; Eng/Remedial Rdng/Adult Literacy Teacher Dodge Vocational Hs 1964-68; Eng Teacher/Rdng Spec Long Fellow Mid Sch 1969-80; Composition Teacher Henry Ford HS 1980-; *ai:* Adv Literary Magazine, Stu to Stu Handbook Henry Ford HS 1986-89; Chairperson Summer Rdng Project Comm Henry Ford 1989; NCTE 1980-; MI Cncl Teachers of Eng 1987-; Ludington MMS Local Sch Cmnty Organization 1981-; Cass Tech HS LSCO 1984-; Designed/Taught Writing Improvement Course 1986-; Awd of Merit Literary Magazine MI Fine Arts Festival 1988; Wrote/Published Lit Materials for Perfection Forms Company-1987; *home:* 14315 Woodmont Detroit MI 48227

APWISCH, MADELINE T., First Grade Teacher; *b:* New Madison, OH; *m:* Louis A.; *c:* Ronald, Michael, Betty K. Kurkowski, Rebecca A. Kohler, Anita C. Sink; *ed:* Cadet Ed, Manchester Coll 1943-46; Miami Univ, Wright Univ, Univ of Dayton; *cr:* 4th Grade Teacher Tri Village 1945-48; 1st Grade Teacher Covington Elem Sch 1965-; *ai:* CEA Secy 1977-78; OEA, NEA; Covington Church of Brethren 1948-; Teacher of Yr 1983-84; *home:* 204 Grant St Covington OH 45318

AQUINO, CARMEN LOPEZ, ESL & Spanish Teacher; *b:* Chicago, IL; *m:* A. L.; *c:* Carmen A. Severino, William L., James J., Mariaelena A. Hudson, Janet A. Hartley; *ed:* (BA) NE IL Univ 1974; *ai:* Bi-ling Coord; Folk Dancing Instr; Drama Coach; Chicago Fed of Cmmty Comms Outstanding Service Merit Awd 1976; Mexican Cmmty Comm of S Chicago Outstanding Educator 1987; Chicago Sun Times Jefferson Awd 1982; *office:* Orville T Bright Sch 10740 S Calhoun Chicago IL 60617

ARAMBURU, MICHAEL JOSEPH, 5th-6th Grade Teacher; *b:* Fresno, CA; *m:* Nora Lynn Janjigian; *c:* Mathew, Jason; *ed:* (BA) Liberal Stud, Fresno St 1978; Working Towards Rdng Specialist Fresno Pacific Coll; *cr:* 4th-6th Grade Teacher Monroe Elem 1979-82; 5th-6th Grade Teacher Slater Elem 1983-; *ai:* Traffic Squad Coord Track; Bsktbl Coach; Fresno Teachers Assn, CA Teachers Assn, NEA 1979-; *home:* 218 N Shirley Fresno CA 93727

ARBOGAST, MICHAEL RONALD, 5th Grade Teacher; *b:* Muskegon, MI; *m:* Vicki Ann; *c:* Matthew, Melinda, Molly, Mark; *ed:* (BS) Ed, 1972, (MA) Ed, 1979 W MI Univ; *cr:* Teacher Hesperia Cmmty Schls 1972-; *ai:* Hesperia Ed Assn Pres 1974; MI Ed Assn, NEA; *home:* 8512 4 Mile Rd Hesperia MI 49421

ARBORE, BEVERLY, Spanish Teacher; *b:* Indiana, PA; *m:* James; *c:* Julie, James, Crystal; *ed:* (BS) Span, Indiana Univ of PA 1973; Cert/Eng, California Univ of PA 1976; Grad Stud; Admin Prgm for Prin, California Univ of PA, Working Towards Masters Scndry Prin; *cr:* Span/Eng Teacher Ft Cherry HS 1974-; *ai:* Cheerleading, Span Club Spon; Foreign Travel Prgm Coord & Spon; Span Dept Chairperson; Instructional Stategies Comm Mem; PA St Ed Assn; Amer Leadership Study Group Spon 1975-76, 1978; *office:* Fort Cherry HS PO Box 145 Mc Donald PA 15057

ARBUTISKI, MARY HARENSKI, English/German Teacher; *b:* Pittsburgh, PA; *m:* Thomas; *c:* Anne M., Thomas B.; *ed:* (BA) Ger, Seton Hill Coll 1962; (MA) Ger, Duquesne Univ 1966; (MLS) Lib Sci, Univ of Pittsburgh 1981; *cr:* Teacher New Kensington Sr HS 1962-64, New Kensington Jr HS 1965, Highlands Sch Dist 1971-; *ai:* Ger Club; AATG, NCTE; Beta Phi Mu Honorary; NEH Fellowship.

ARCEMENT, SYLVIANE BENAIM, Third Grade Teacher; *b:* Casablanca, Morocco; *m:* Richard; *c:* Marc, Michelle; *ed:* (BS) Elem Ed, Nicholls St Univ 1978; Stenotypoist Sch Orleans France 1963; Beauty Sch 1967; *cr:* Stenographer/Translator US Army 1962-64; Hairstylist Hair Acad 1967-78; Teacher Larose Lower Elem 1978-; *ai:* US Constitution Comm Chairperson; Homework Recognition & Textbook Adoption Comm Adv; Creative Writing Assessment Prgm Adv; La Fourche Parish Comm on Excl Adv; Publication to Help Evaluate La Fourcher Parish Sch System; 4th Grade Lang Art Test for St Basic Skills Test.

ARCENEAUX, PATRICIA SHANNON, Social Studies Teacher; *b:* Shreveport, LA; *m:* Robert P. III; *c:* Angie, Lisa; *ed:* (BA) His, Univ of SW LA 1972; Working Toward Masters in Soc Stud Ed, Univ of New Orleans; *cr:* 4th Grade Teacher Downing Elem 1980-82; 7th Grade Teacher St Clement of Rome 1982-84; 7th-8th Grade Soc Stud Teacher Our Lady of Divine Providence 1984-; *ai:* Elem Quiz Bowl; Spelling Bee; Stu Cncl Adv; Drug Awareness Coord; Soc Stud Comm; NCEA 1984-; NCSS 1985-86; Our Lady of Divine Providence Sch Meitler Study of Archdiocese Planning Comm; Local TV Station Commercial About Coastal Erosion; *home:* 1516 N Bengal Rd Metairie LA 70003

ARCHER, GEORGE EDDIE, Fifth Grade Teacher; *b:* Jellico, TN; *m:* Vickie Nayles; *ed:* (BA) Elem Ed, Cumberland Coll 1972; *cr:* Teacher Boston Elem Sch 1972-74; Teacher 1974-77, Prin/Teacher 1977-81 Newcomb Elem Sch; 6th-8th Grade Soc Stud Teacher 1981-89, 5th Grade Teacher 1989- Jellico Elem Sch; *ai:* 4-H Jellico Elem Sch Volunteer Leader 1983-84, Natl 4-H Leadership Awd 1983; *home:* Rt 1 Box 38 Newcomb TN 37819

ARCHER, THOMAS L., 7th Grade Life Science Teacher; *b:* Akron, OH; *m:* Jeanne Fagerstrom; *c:* Joshua, Emily, Sarah; *ed:* (BS) Phys Ed Carson-Newman Coll 1973; (MED) Elem Prin, Westminster Coll 1979; Advanced Trng Various Courses; *cr:* K-7th Grade Phys Ed Teacher 1973-83, 5th-7th Grade Elem Sci/Health Teacher 1983-86, Jr HS Sci Teacher 1986- Girard City Sch Dist; *ai:* Jr HS Ftbl, Prep Bowl Coach; Programming for New Sch Buildings Citizens Comm; Natl Assn for Curr Dev 1985-87; NEA, OH Ed Assn, Girard Ed Assn 1973-; OH HS Athletic Assn 1989-; Parent Teacher & Stu Assn 1973-; Career Grants for Lib 1983-86; *home:* 1660 Squaw Creek Dr Girard OH 44420

ARCHIE, WILDA BOWYER, 4th Grade Teacher; *m:* Melvin; *c:* Steven; *ed:* (BA) Elem Ed/Lang Arts/Soc Stud, Morris Harvey 1969; Coll of Grad Stud; WV Univ; *cr:* Aide Eccles Elem 1965-66; Teacher Brooks Adair 1966-67; Fairdale Elem 1967-68; Mark Twain 1968-71; Eccles Elem 1971-73; Fairdale Elem 1973-; *ai:* Prin Designee; Former 4-H Leader; Parent Advsry Cncl; Fairdale PTO; NEA/WVEA 1969-; Harper Free Meth Church; *office:* Fairdale Elem School Box 10 Fairdale WV 25839

ARCONTI, JOSEPH ALDO, 7th Grade Earth Sci Teacher; *b:* Danbury, CT; *m:* Ilona Amalia Nagy; *c:* Joseph Jr., Erika; *ed:* (BS) Elem Ed, 1973, (MS) Ed, 1978, (MS) Guidance/Counseling, 1989 W CT St Coll; *cr:* 4th Grade Teacher 1973-81, 5th/6th Grade Teacher 1981-84 Shelter Rock Elem Sch; 8th Grade Teacher 1984-86, 7th Grade Teacher 1986- Rogers Park Jr HS; *ai:* Frosh Bsbl & HS Golf Coach; NEA, CEA, DEA, 1973-; *home:* 13 Hunting Rdg Rd Brookfield CT 06804

ARDARY, KELLY VINCENT, English Instructor; *b:* Grove City, PA; *m:* Rick W.; *c:* Miranda, Megan; *ed:* (BSED) Eng/Comm, 1981, (MED) Scndry Eng, 1986 Slippery Rock Univ; Ed Doctoral Prgm, Cmptr Integration, IN Univ of PA; *cr:* 8th-11th Grade Eng Instr Clearfield Area Sch Dist 1982-; *ai:* Adv Socially & Politically Aware Stu; Key Club; Track, Swimming, Vlybl Coach; Clearfield Ed Assn Exec Comm 1989-; Cystic Fibrosis Society Cty Chm 1986-88; Educl Advocates Advocate 1986-; Natl Wildlife Fed 1989-; Nom by Sch Bd for The Christa Mc Auliff Awd 1987; *office:* Clearfield H S PO Box 910 Clearfield PA 16830

ARDOIN, LINDA GARRISON, Elementary Fine Art Teacher; *b:* Houston, TX; *m:* Frank Jr.; *c:* Curtis W., Michelle L.; *ed:* (BS) Elem Ed, 1977, (MED) Admin, 1984 Univ of Houston-Victoria; Early Chldhd Ed; General Psych; *cr:* 5th Grade Teacher Inez Elem 1978-84; Continuing Substitute Teacher Jubail Acad Saudi Arabia 1984-85; Elem/Fine Art Teacher Inez Elem 1985-; *ai:* UIL Music Memory Team Coach; Writer/Dir/Producer Annual Christmas Prgm; Delta Kappa Gamma Society for Women Educators 1988-; TX Music Educators Assn 1985-; Assn of TX Prof Educators 1980-; *office:* Inez Elem Sch Rt 1 Box 1-K Inez TX 77968

ARELLANES, JOANNE ELAINE, 5th/6th Grade Teacher; *b:* East Chicago, IN; *m:* Robert V.; *c:* Paul, Peter, Lisa; *ed:* (BA) Ed, Long Beach St Coll 1959; (MA) Ed, Univ of San Francisco 1976; *cr:* 4th Grade Teacher Mark Twain Elem 1959-60; 4th-6th Grade Teacher Thomas Edison Sch 1960-64; 5th/6th Grade Teacher Cambridge Heights Sch 1970-; *ai:* CA Assessment Prgm Task Force; Mentor Teacher; Writing Specialist; CA Teachers Assn Innovative 1979; SJUSD Dev Prof Excl 1987; St John Vianney Parish Cncl Pres 1980-81; *home:* 2317 Pinturo Way Rancho Cordova CA 95670

ARELLANO, ANDREW MICHAEL, Speech Teacher; *b:* Chicago, IL; *m:* Sandra R Moore; *c:* Angela, Andrea; *ed:* (BA) Speech, Mac Murray Coll 1972; (MA) Speech, NE IL Univ 1989; Grad Stud Skills For Critical Thinking, IL Renewal Ins 1985; *cr:* Speech Teacher 1972-, Speech/Debate/Congress Coach 1972-86, Speech Moderator 1973-, Hum Dept Chairperson 1984- Fenwick HS; Public Speaking/Bus Comm Amer Inst of Banking 1981-86; *ai:* Speech Moderator; Hum Dept Chairpersn; Disciplinary Bd Mem; NHS Selection Comm Mem; Several Stu Donation Campaigns for Charities Spon; Presented Plaque by Art of Living Ins for Fundraising Efforts of Stu; *home:* 7829 W 41st Ct Lyons IL 60534

ARELLANO, ORALIA R., Science Teacher & Dept Chm; *b:* Cotulla, TX; *m:* Rene; *c:* Amy Leah; *ed:* (BA) Bio/Chem, TX a & I Univ 1977; (MS) Scndry Supervision, Pan Amer Univ 1985; Teacher Expectation & Stu Achievement; Teaching Strategies for Sec Sci; *cr:* Sci Teacher Cotulla Jr HS 1978-80; Brown Jr HS 1980-; *ai:* UIL Sci Coach; Sci Dept Chm; Faculty Adv Comm; ATPA 1989-; ASCP; Kappa Kappa Iota Trea 1989-; *office:* Brown Jr H S 2700 S Ware Rd Mc Allen TX 78503

ARENDSEN, RUTH NEUMAN, Third Grade Teacher; *b:* Chicago, IL; *m:* David; *c:* Peter, John; *ed:* (BA) Elem Ed, N Cntrl Coll 1965; (MS) Rdng/Elem Ed, N IL 1969; *cr:* 2nd Grade Teacher Cicero Public Sch 1965-66, De Kalb Public Sch 1966-68, 3rd Grade Teacher Hawthorn Sch 1979-; *ai:* IL Ed Assn, NEA 1979-; 1st Presbyn Church of Libertyville (Deacon, Choir Mem); St of IL Master Teacher Awd 1984; *home:* 431 E Austin Ave Libertyville IL 60048

ARENDT, DONALD M., Social Studies Dept Chair; *b:* York, PA; *m:* Elizabeth A.; *c:* Heather, Paul, Emily; *ed:* (BS) Ed, 1967, (MED) Ed, 1970 Shippensburg St Coll; Supervision of Instruction, Millersville Univ; *cr:* Teacher 1968-, Soc Stud Dept Chm 1982-, Supvr of Soc Stud 1988- Dover Area; *ai:* NEA, PSEA Local Pres 1973-75; Mason Dixon Cncl for Soc Stud Secy 1989-; ASCD; Natl Endowment for Hum Seminar Fellowship 1985, 1988; *office:* Dover Area HS W Canal St Dover PA 17315

ARFT, ELAINE E., 1st Grade Teacher; *b:* Detroit, MI; *m:* Leonard; *c:* Kenneth Fritsch, Kerry Fritsch, Kregg Fritsch; *ed:* (BS) Soc Stud/Fine Arts 1969, (MA) Ed, 1973 E MI Univ; Counseling; *cr:* 6th Grade Teacher Parochial Schls & Newport News Public 1953-58; Teacher New Haven Public Schls 1970-; *ai:* New Haven Cmmty Chorus Dir 1985-; Christ Luth Church Choir Dir 1982-; *home:* 57890 North Ave New Haven MI 48048

ARGADINE, PENNIE LEA, Junior High Reading Teacher; *b:* Bloomington, IL; *ed:* (BSED) Elem Ed, IL St Univ 1984; Peer Counseling, Parkside Resolve Center; Baseline II Prevention Ed; *cr:* Substitute Teacher Peoria Sch Dist 1984-85; Teachers Aide Marquette Heights Sch Dist 1985-86; Teacher Herscher Sch Dist 1986-; *ai:* Cheerleading Spon; Scholastic Bowl & Literary Club Coach; Co-Dir of Peer Support Groups; Teacher Curr Advisory, Lang Art Comms; Baseline II Core Team; Two Rivers Rdng Cncl Mem 1986-88; IL Teen Inst Co-Facilitator 1989-; Operation Snowball Bd Mem 1989-; St John United Church of Christ (Chrstn Ed Comm 1987-, Youth Fellowship Adv 1987-); *office:* Limestone Elem Sch R R 4 Box 242a Kankakee IL 60901

ARGENCOURT, ROGER GEORGE, SC, History Teacher/Dept Chm; *b:* Lewiston, ME; *ed:* (BA) His, St Michaels Coll 1965; (MED) Ed, Wayne St Univ 1972; (MA) His, Scranton Univ 1978; Univ of NH; Hofstra Univ; St Marys Univ; St Louis Univ; St Catherines Coll; Univ of San Francisco; *cr:* Admin/Teacher Mount St Charles Acad 1961-64; Teacher St Francis Sec 1965-67; Teacher/Dept Head Notre Dame HS 1968-72, Bishop Guertin HS 1972-78; Teacher St Francis Sec 1978-81; Admin/Teacher Mount St Charles Acad 1981-86; Techer/Dept Head Bishop Guertin HS 1987-; *ai:* Academic Cncl; Parents Club; Natl Assn of Religious Brothers 1983-; NCEA 1981-; Superior Burlington VT 1986-87; Superior Bishop Guertin 1989-91; Numerous Schl Bds 1969-91; *home:* 194 Lund Rd Nashua NH 03060

ARGENT, BUZZ REED, Mathematics Department Teacher; *b:* Bismarck, ND; *m:* Sandra Lee Wentz; *c:* Stacey, Jim; *ed:* (BA) Math, Concordia 1965; Grad Stud; *cr:* Accelerated Algebra Teacher Moorhead Sr HS 1965-; *ai:* Asst Wrestling; MEA 1965-; NCTM 1970-; Church (Youth Cmt 1981-, Church Cncl 1974-75); *home:* 417 Rensvold Blvd Moorhead MN 56560

ARGENTO, SANTINA J., Fourth Grade Teacher; *b:* Pittston, PA; *ed:* (BS) Elem Ed, Misericondia Coll 1964; (MS) Elem Ed, Univ of Scranton 1971; *cr:* 4th Grade Teacher Lake Hopatcong 1964-69; 4th Grade Teacher 1969-74, Kndgtn Teacher 1974-86, 4th Grade Teacher 1986- Nanticoke Sch; *ai:* Act 178 Staff Dev & Mid Atlantic Sts Steering Comm; Nanticoke Ed Assn & PA Ed Assn 1969; Natl Teachers Assn 1964; *home:* 133 Vine St Pittston PA 18640

ARGEVINE, BETTY GRAY, English Teacher/Yrbk Sponsor; *b:* Providence, KY; *m:* Philip D.; *c:* Geoffrey, Jennifer, Melissa; *ed:* (BA) Eng, Western KY Univ 1966; (MA) Ed, Austin Peay Univ 1983; Eng Vanderbilt Univ; *cr:* Eng Teacher Univ of MD 1970; Univ of KY/Hopkinsville Comm Coll 1971-73; Cheatham Cty Central HS 1978-; *ai:* Yrbk Adv; Quiz Bowl; Curr Cncl; Faculty Adv Comm; Yrbk Produced By DesKtop Publishing; NCTE; NEA; TN Ed Assn; Cheatham Cty Ed Assn; Modern Lang Assn; Delta Phi Alpha 1966; Sigma Tay Delta 1966; Woodrow Wilson Eng Awd 1966; Western KY Univ; Article Published-Research in Teaching of Eng 1983; Graduate Asst Western KY Univ 1966/Austin Peay Univ 1979; *office:* Cheatham County HS 1 Cub Cir Ashland City TN 37015

ARGO, BRETT L., Music Director; *b:* Norman, OK; *m:* Mary; *ed:* (BME) Instrumental Music Ed, E NM Univ 1980; (MA) Instrumental Music Ed, Western St Coll 1984; *cr:* Music Dir West End Schls 1981-83, Cedaredge Schls 1984-87; Band Dir Ruidoso Schls 1987-88; Music Dir Dolores Schls 1988-; *ai:* Boys Bsktbl Coach; Yrbk Faculty Adv; Jazz Band, Pep Band, Choir, Marching, Concert Bands Teacher; Kappa Kappa Psi (Dist Pres 1977-79, Chapter Pres 1978-79); Phi Mu Alpha Warden 1978-79; Mt View Baptist Church Youth Music Leader 1988-.

ARGO, JANET EILEEN, 6th Grade Math/Sci Teacher; *b:* Beatrice, NE; *m:* Douglas Lee; *c:* Jared, Charis; *ed:* (BS) Elem Ed, Univ of NE Lincoln 1979; *cr:* 6th-8th Grade Elem Teacher Liberty Public Sch 1979-80; Jr HS Math/Sci Teacher Summerfield Public 1980-82; 6th Grade Math/K-6th Grade Sci/Phy Ed Teacher Summerfield Elem 1985-; *ai:* Summerfield Annual, Concession, Pep Club, Chrldr, Class Spon; Jump for Heart, Field Day Coord; *home:* Box 11 Liberty NE 68381

ARGYLE, DOROTHY M., 3rd Grade Intern Coordinator; *b:* Los Angeles, CA; *m:* Reed B.; *c:* Edward L. Bearnson, Karen B. Harwood, Joy Jasperson, Shaun R.; *ed:* (BA) Elem Ed, 1956, (MA) Elem Admin, 1966 Brigham Young Univ; Essential Elements of Instruction; Talents Unlimited; Gifted & Talented Instruction; Cmptr, Teacher Ed; *cr:* 1st Grade Teacher Alpine Sch Dist 1956-58; Kndgtn Teacher Cntrl Sch 1958-59; 2nd Grade Teacher Sherman Elem Sch 1961-67; Kndgtn Teacher 1975-84, 3rd Grade Teacher 1984-85, 3rd Grade Intern Coord 1985- Wilson Elem Sch; *ai:* NEA, UEA 1975-; Amer Legion Auxiliary 1969-87; Jr Cultus Club Pres 1980-81; Federated Womens Club Dist Recorder 1990; *office:* Wilson Elem Sch 590 W 500 S Payson UT 84651

ARIANS, H ARTHUR, Biology Teacher; *b:* Sterling, CO; *m:* Terry Smith; *c:* Alison, Benjamin; *ed:* (BA) Bio, 1961; *cr:* Sci Teacher Leadville Jr HS 1963-64; Bio Teacher 1964-, Sci Dept Chairperson 1976 East Anchorage HS; *ai:* Coord HS Cross Cntry Ski Races Anchorage; NEA, AK Ed Assn; Anchorage Ed Assn VP 1964-; Teacher & Sch Employees Credit Union Bd (VP, Pres, Mem) 1977-89; Nordic Ski Club VP 1986-87; NABT AK Outstanding Bio Teacher Awd 1971; *home:* 14101 Golden View Dr Anchorage AK 99516

ARIAS, MARILYN HASBUN, Literature/Lang Art Teacher; *b:* San Salvador, El Salvador; *m:* Gustavo; *c:* Marianna, Jason; *ed:* (BA) Span/Bi-ling/Crosscultural, Univ of CA Los Angeles 1980; (MA) Ed, CA St Univ Dominguez Hills 1990; Parent Trainer Inservice CICC; *cr:* 7th/8th Grade Bi-ling Teacher Felton Sch 1981-87; 6th Bi-ling Teacher Lennox Mid Sch 1987-; *ai:* Arts & Crafts Club Spon; New Teacher Coach; Tutoring Club; Phi Delta Kappa Mem 1989-; Natl Teacher Assn Mem 1981-; *office:* Lennox Mid Sch 11033 Buford Ave Lennox CA 90304

ARKOW, DEBRA MARY, Library Science & Math Teacher; *b:* Evergreen Park, IL; *ed:* (BS) Elem Ed/Eng, St Xavier Coll 1978; St Certified Lib Sci/Media, Rosary Coll 1990; *cr:* 2nd Grade Teacher 1978-82, 5th Grade Teacher 1982-86 Woodgate Elem Sch; 7th Grade Lib Sci Teacher Marya Yates Elem Sch 1986-; *ai:* Curr Comm Dist 159; Stamp Club Adv; Lib Helpers; Audio Visual Stu Services; *office:* Marya Yates Elem Sch 6131 Allemong Matteson IL 60443

ARLOW, BARBARA, Social Studies Teacher; *b:* New York, NY; *ed:* (BA) Ed, Brooklyn Coll 1957; (MS) Ed, City of New York Univ 1961; Counseling, Chapman Coll; *cr:* Elem Teacher Paradise Canyon Sch 1963-79; 6th Grade Teacher Foothill Intermediate Sch 1979-82; Sci Teacher La Canada Elem 1982-88; Math Teacher La Canada HS 1988-89; Soc Sci Teacher Palm Crest Sch 1989-; *ai:* Soc Sci Curr Writing; La Canada Teachers Assn (Bargaining Chairperson, Treas) 1963-, WHO 1986; CA Teachers Assn Steering Comm 1963-, WHO 1981; Assn of Sci Teachers 1981-88; Sci Mentor Teacher 1985-88; Scientific Research Schlsp Tracking Herons France 1986; UCLA Facilitator Project RISE-LA 1983-86; Freedoms Fnd Schlsp Amer His 1988; *office:* Palm Crest Sch 5025 Palm Dr La Canada CA 91011

ARMANDAN, ALAN ANTHONY, Fifth Grade Teacher; *b:* Pomona, CA; *m:* Annelle Hortness; *c:* Scott Anthony; *ed:* (BS) Soc Sci, Cal Poly Pomona 1965; (MS) Ed/Sch Adm, CA St Fullerton 1984; Admin Trainee Bonita Unifed Sch Dist; *cr:* 6th Grade Teacher 1967-70, 4th Grade Teacher 1970-72, 5th Grade Teacher 1972- J Marion Roynon Sch; *ai:* Teacher Adv to Sch Safety Patrol; Mem of Sch Site Cncl; Mem of Soc Stud Task Force; CBEDS Coord Bonita Unified Sch Dist; Bonita Unified Teachers Assn Teacher Rep 1967-; CTA 1967-; NEA 1967-; City of Laverne Cmmty Service Awd 1982; PTA Honorary Life Membership; Spec Service Awd Wood Memorial Hospital 1988; *office:* J Marion Elem Sch 115 W Allen Ave San Dimas CA 91773

ARMBRUSTER, ROBERT EUGENE, Jr High Hist/English Teacher; *b:* Mayfield, KY; *m:* Deborah Pflughaupt; *c:* Jason, Justin; *ed:* (BS) His, 1974, (MACT) Eng 1978, (SCT) Rdng, 1980 Murray St Univ; *cr:* Teacher Fulgham Elem Sch 1975-78, Hickman Cty Jr HS 1978-, Paducah Comm Coll Adjunct Faculty 1990; *ai:* Jr HS Acad Team; Jr Class Spon; KEA 1975-; NEA 1975-; *office:* Hickman County Jr H S Cresap St Clinton KY 42031

ARMELIN, DALE BENJAMIN, 2nd Grade Teacher; *b:* Lafayette, LA; *m:* Clyde R.; *c:* Brandon; *ed:* (BA) Elem Ed, 1973; (MED) Elem Ed, 1978 Southern Univ; *cr:* 1st Grade Teacher M D Shannon Elem 1973-76; 2nd Grade Teacher Baldwin Elem 1977-; *ai:* Textbook Adoption Chairperson; Creative Writing Comm Leader; Bible Sch Teacher; Assoc Prof Ed of LA 1986-89; St Mary Teacher Assn 1982-; Southern Alumni 1973-; Just Us Civic & Social Club 1988-; *home:* 1701 Martin L King Dr Jeanerette LA 70544

ARMELIN, SYLVIA JEAN, 4th Grade Teacher; *b:* Baldwin, LA; *ed:* (BA) Elem Ed, 1972, (MA) Elem Ed, 1982 Southern Univ; *cr:* Teacher Mary Hines Elem Sch 1973, Patterson HS 1973-75, Crowell Elem Sch 1975-85, Willow Street Elem Sch 1985-; *ai:* SMAE, LA Assn of Educators 1973-; Alpha Kappa Alpha Recording Secy 1980-; Nom Elem Teacher of Yr 1988-; *home:* 203 John St Baldwin LA 70514

ARMENDARIZ, GEORGE ANN, 6th Grade Teacher; *b:* Dallas, TX; *m:* Avelardo; *c:* Esteban, Armando; *ed:* (BA) Elem Ed, Southeastern St 1966; *cr:* 6th Grade Teacher Gonzales Elem 1966-72; 4th-6th Grade Teacher Chaparral Elem 1973-; *office:* Chaparral Elem Sch Avenida Chaparral Santa Fe NM 87501

ARMENTROUT, CAROLYN BASS, Fr/Span/Eng/Rdng Teacher; *b:* Richmond, VA; *m:* Albert S.; *c:* Katherine S., Benjamin K.; *ed:* (BA) Span, Mary Baldwin Coll 1970; (MED) Teaching Rdng, Univ of VA 1974; *cr:* Span/Eng Teacher Riverheads HS 1970-71; Eng Teacher A T John Jr HS 1971-72, William Monroe HS 1972-74; Rdng Specialist William Monroe Elem Sch 1974-75; Span/Eng/Rdng Teacher King George Mid Sch 1977-78; Fr/Eng Teacher Powell Valley HS 1984-85; Span/Fr/Eng/Rdng Teacher Powell Valley Mid Sch 1985-; *ai:* Foreign Lang Club Spon; VA Assn Teachers of Eng 1984-; Mt View Extension Homemakers Club Pres 1981-84, Homemaker of Yr 1983.

ARMEZZANI, ANNE MC DONNELL, 7th Grade English Teacher; *b:* Kingston, PA; *m:* John; *c:* Maura, Catherine; *ed:* (BS) Ed/Eng, E Stroudsburg Univ 1971; (MA) Eng, Univ of Scranton 1974; Grad Stud Univ of FL 1979, Penn St, Univ of Scranton Marywood; *cr:* 7th Grade Eng Teacher Abington Heights 1971-; *ai:* Cheerleading, Drama Club, Newspaper Adv; Blakely Bus & Prof Womens 1982-; *office:* Abington Heights Mid Sch Grove St Clarks Summit PA 18411

ARMFIELD, JUDITH MC MANUS, English Department Chairperson; *b:* Charlotte, NC; *m:* Robert M.; *c:* Jeff, Chris; *ed:* (AA) Liberal Arts, Brevard Coll 1960; (BA) Eng, Pfeiffer Coll 1962; Grad Work, Univ of South AL & NC St Univ; *cr:* 9th-12th Grade Eng Teacher Stanly Cty Schls 1962-64; 10th-11th Grade Eng Teacher Charlotte-Mecklenburg Schls 1964-66; 8th-10th Grade Eng Teacher Cntrl Baptist Sch 1976-77; 7th-9th Grade Eng Teacher Raleigh Acad 1978-83; 9th-11th Grade Eng Teacher/Dept Chairperson Wake Cty Public Schls 1983-; *ai:* Legacy Adv; Effective Schls Prgm Comm Chairperson; Crisis Intervention Team Mem; NCTE, NC Eng Teachers Assn 1987-; Parent Teachers Stu Assn 1988-; Nom Wake Cty Teacher of Yr 1989-; Creative Grant Wake Cty Ed Fnd 1988-89; Mentor Teacher Trng Prgm Selection 1988; *office:* Apex H S 1501 Laura Duncan Rd Apex NC 27502

ARMISTEAD, PATRICIA PETTIJOHN, 2nd Grade Teacher; *b:* Abernathy, TX; *m:* Sydney E.; *c:* Jenny R., Julie A.; *ed:* (BS) Elem Ed, W TX St Univ 1968; *cr:* 2nd Grade Teacher Petersburg Ind Sch Dist 1966-69, Peebles Elem Sch 1969-; *ai:* Killeen Assn of TX Prof Educators 1989-; Killeen Classroom Teachers Assn 1980-89; Alpha Delta Kappa (Pres 1986-87, VP 1989-), Bus Woman of Yr 1976; PTA VP 1989-, TX Life Membership 1989; *home:* 2004 Standridge Killeen TX 76543

ARMSTEAD, TRESSA MADDUX, English Teacher; *b:* Pecos, TX; *m:* Karl Frank; *c:* Stephen K., Tiffany J.; *ed:* (BS) Chem/Eng, Sul Ross St Univ 1970; (MA) Eng, E NM Univ 1977; *cr:* Eng Teacher Pleasanton Ind Sch Dist 1971-72; Chem/Eng Teacher Boyd Ind Sch Dist 1972-73; Eng Teacher Pecos-Barstow-Toyah Ind Sch Dist 1973-75; Grad Asst E NM Univ 1975-76; Eng Teacher Pecos-Barstow-Toyah Ind Sch EDist 1976-79, Midland Ind Sch Dist 1981-; *ai:* TX Classroom Teachers Assn 1982-; NCTE 1981-; Delta Kappa Gamma (2nd VP 1988-, 1st VP 1990); 1st Baptist Church; *home:* 1207 E Cty Rd 128 Midland TX 79701

ARMSTRONG, ALICE FAYE, 5th Grade Teacher; *b:* Crosby, TX; *c:* Darryn; *ed:* (BA) Sociology, 1971, (MS) Ed, 1973 CA St Univ Los Angeles; *ai:* United Teachers Los Angeles, NEA 1971-; St Eugene Cath Church Mem 1975-; Knights of Peter Claver Ladies (Grand Lady 1987-88, Finance Secy 1888-) Mem.

ARMSTRONG, AMY LAUREL, First Grade Teacher; *b:* Bridgeport, CT; *m:* James Lee; *c:* Noelle, Glenn; *ed:* (BA) Elem Ed, Occidental Coll 1957; Grad Work Ed; *cr:* 2nd Grade Teacher Happy Valley Sch 1957-60, Golden Hill Sch 1960-62; 1st/2nd Grade Teacher Mc Dowell Elem Sch 1963-64; 2nd Grade Teacher Golden Hill Elem Sch 1965-66; 2nd/3rd Grade Teacher San Juan Capistrano 1966-68; 1st-4th Grade Teacher Moulton Sch 1980-; *ai:* Safety Patrol; Christmas Prgms; Master Teacher Univ of CA Berkeley, Fullerton St Univ, The Natl Schls; *office:* Moulton Elem Sch 29851 Highlands Ave Laguna Niguel CA 92677

ARMSTRONG, DEBRA A., Math Teacher,Dept Chair; *b:* Redding, CA; *m:* David R.; *c:* Stephen, Matthew; *ed:* (AA) Math, Shosta Coll 1974; (BA) Math, CA St Univ Sacramento 1977; CA Math Project CA St Univ Chico; *cr:* Teacher Nova HS 1978-79; Teacher/Math Dept Chairperson Mercy HS 1980-85, Enterprise HS 1985-; *ai:* GATE Comm Mem; Faculty Comm Treas; Shasta Union HS Dist Fiscal Oversight Comm Mem; NCTM 1984-; CA Math Cncl 1986-; Mt Lassen Math Cncl (Treas, Registrar, Scndry Rep) 1982-; CA Teachers Assn, NEA, Shasta Scndry Employees Assn 1985-; *office:* Enterprise HS 3711 Churn Creek Rd Redding CA 96001

ARMSTRONG, DENISE LYNN (PERKINS), Spanish Teacher; *b:* Gallipolis, OH; *m:* Dean Lance; *c:* Carrie L., Lara L.; *ed:* (BSED) Span/Eng, OH Univ 1974; (MSED) Sch Cnslr - Magna Cum Laude, Univ of Dayton 1987; *cr:* 7th-12th Grade Span/Eng Teacher Jackson HS 1974-; *ai:* Span Club Adv 1974-79; JCEA, OEA, NEA, OFLA 1974-; Wesley United Meth Church Secy of Admin Bd 1985-; Scioto PTO Treas 1989-; *office:* Jackson HS Tropic And Vaughn St Jackson OH 45640

ARMSTRONG, ELAINE RISK, Head Teacher; *b:* Richmond, KY; *m:* Joseph B.; *c:* Joanna Watercutter, Steven; *ed:* (BS) Home Ec, Berea Coll 1954; Grad Wrkshp Miami Univ OH, Elem Cert E KY Univ; *cr:* Sci/Home Ec Teacher Evarts HS 1954-58; Elem Teacher Evarts Elem 1958-63, Eli Brown 1967-68; Home Ec Teacher Bardstown Ind 1974-75; Elem Teacher Chaplin Elem 1975-; *ai:* Head Teacher; Serve on Cty Curr & Gifted & Talented Comms; Schls Guidance, Health & Safety, Parenting & Family Life Skills Comm; NEA, KEA, NCEA; WMU; Sch Received Flag of Excl & Flag of Progress St Dept of Ed 1988; *home:* 1903 Stringtown Rd Bardstown KY 40004

ARMSTRONG, FAYE PATRICIA, First Grade Teacher; *b:* Orlando, FL; *ed:* (AA) Valencia Comm Coll 1972; (BA) Elem Ed, Univ of Cntrl FL 1974; Rdng, Early Chldhd & Spec Ed; Wkshps/Seminars, Writing Process, Rdng Process, Whole Lang Concepts & Strategies; *cr:* 5th Grade Teacher 1974-79, 6th Grade Teacher 1979-86 Orlando Chrstn Sch; 4th Grade Teacher 1986-87, Kndgtn Teacher 1987-88, 1st Grade Teacher 1988- Blankner Elem Sch; *ai:* Grade 1 Team Leader; Earth Day Coord; Rdng Comm; PTA Faculty Rep; NEA, Orange Cty Classroom Teachers Assn 1986-; Orange Cty Rdng Cncl, Intnl Rdng Assn 1990; *office:* Blankner Elem Sch 720 E Kaley St Orlando FL 32806

ARMSTRONG, JOHN GRAHAM, Economics Teacher; *b:* New Kensington, PA; *m:* Susan Konnovitch; *c:* Blaze, Bryce, Brandon; *ed:* (BA) Soc Stud, West Liberty St Coll 1972; (MA) C&I, Salem Coll 1982; *cr:* Spec Ed Teacher Tyler Cty HS 1972-83; Soc Stud Teacher Saint Marys HS 1983-; *ai:* Head Girls, Boys Bsktbl Coach; NHS Advisory Comm; Academic Boosters CLub Sch Improvement Comm; North Cntrl Evaluation Comm; AFT 1988-89; WV Athletic Coaches Assn 1983-; WV Bsbl Coach Assn 1989-; Natl Fed Interscholastic Coaches Assn 1985-; Jaycees 1987-; WV Region 2 Coach of Yr Boys 1987, Girls 1989; Little Kanawha Conference Coach of Yr 1982; *office:* St Marys H S 1002 2nd St Saint Marys WV 26170

ARMSTRONG, JUDITH PATRICIA, Kindergarten Teacher; *b:* Miami, OK; *ed:* (AA) Hm Econ, Northeastern A&M 1964; (BS) Elem Ed/Hm Econ, Northeastern St Univ 1966; *cr:* 2nd Grade Teacher 1966-1982; Kndgtn Teacher 1982- Wyandotte Public Schl; *ai:* Staff Dev Comm 1981-; Sch Dist Title V-C Comm 3 Yrs, Secy 2 Yrs, Now VP; NEA; OK Ed Assn; Wyandotte Ed Assn Secy 1985; Teacher of Month 1981; Wyandotte Teacher of Yr 1985; Wyandotte PTO 1966; Fisher Flat Church Song Ldr/Sndy Sch Teacher; Awd Troph Prof Educator 1980-81; *home:* Rt 1 Box 254 Wyandotte OK 74370

ARMSTRONG, LORENE STARK, 2nd Grade Teacher; *b:* Oberlin, OH; *m:* Jerry Robert; *c:* Timothy, Scott; *ed:* (BS) Elem Ed, Ashland Univ 1963; Bowling Green St Univ; *cr:* 2nd Grade Teacher N Ridgeville Sch Dist 1963-64, Perkins Public Schls 1967-; *ai:* Rdng Textbook Adoption Comm; Delta Kappa Gamma Corresponding Secy 1974-; Perkins Teachers Assn 1967-; OH Ed Assn 1967-; NEA 1967-; Congretational Church of Sandusky; YMCA; Natl Tole Society 1986-; Outstanding Elem Teachers of Amer 1973; Jennings Scholar 1976-77; Erie Cty Primary Teacher of Yr 1988-89; *office:* Furry Elem Sch 310 Douglas Dr Sandusky OH 44870

ARMSTRONG, MORTON CHARLES, English Teacher; *b:* Randolph, NY; *m:* Kathryn Mae Anderson; *c:* Thomas, Charles; *ed:* (BA) Eng, Roberts Wesleyan Coll 1957; (MA) Eng, St Univ of NY Fredonia 1969; *cr:* Eng/Soc Stud Teacher N Point Jr HS 1959-60; Eng Teacher Cassadaga Valley Cntrl Sch 1960-; *ai:* A-Plus Selection Comm Rep; Area Wide Creative Arts Prgm Sponsored by Local Newspaper; NYS United Teachers; Cassadaga Area Jaycees Outstanding Educator Awd 1990; Mem Bd of Dir Heritage Village Retirement Center & Gerry Nursing Home Company; *office:* Cassadaga Valley Cntrl Sch Sinclairville NY 14782

ARMSTRONG, VERONICA MAY-LAMB, English Teacher; *b:* Jamaica, West Indies; *m:* Michael; *c:* Mark, Marsha; *ed:* (AA) Elem Ed, West Indies Coll 1960; (BA) Elem Ed, Atlantic Union Coll 1965; (MA) Eng Ed, Lehman Coll; Grad Ed, City Univ Grad Division; *cr:* Teacher Gretna Green Elem Sch 1960-63, R T Hudson Elem Sch 1965-82; Teacher/Asst Prin Westchester Area Sch 1982-; *ai:* Fundraising Chairperson; Church Clerk; Sch Choir Directress; Sr Class Spon; Academic & Discipline Comm Mem; Assn of Adventist Educators; Nom Lehman Coll Grad Division Schlsp; *home:* 3313 Hickham Ave Bronx NY 10469

ARNELL, DALLAS HODGES, 8th Grade Mathematics Teacher; *b:* Montpelier, ID; *m:* Theresa Mae Ellett; *c:* Jennifer, Daryl, Bryan, Tonya, Rick; *ed:* (BA) Elem/Phys Ed, UT St Univ 1973; Grad Stud Math, Coaching; *cr:* 6th Grade Teacher 1973-74, 7th Grade Teacher 1974-75, 4th Grade Teacher 1975-80, 4th/5th Grade Teacher 1980-81 Paris Elem; 6th-8th Grade Teacher B L Mid Sch 1981-; *ai:* Honor Society Adv; 7th Grade Coach; *home:* Box 53 Saint Charles ID 83272

ARNER, MEL GLENN, Band Director; *b:* Oklahoma City, OK; *m:* Linda Sue Sumner; *c:* Jennifer E.; *ed:* (BMED) Music Ed, OK St Univ 1978; *cr:* Band Dir Chelsea Public Schls 1978-85, Ponca City Public Schls 1985-; *ai:* OMEA 1975-; OEA, NEA Building Rep 1989-; ASBDA, OBM 1989-; TMEA 1989-; TBA 1988-; NBA 1989-; OMAA 1985-; NFIMA 1988-; NCDA 1986-; Ponca City Playhouse Pit Orch Mem 1990; 1st Baptist Church Orch Dir 1985-; *home:* 2405 Ames Ponca City OK 74604

ARNETT, GEORGIA LEE (HERRING), Math/Computer Literacy Teacher; *b:* Windsor, CO; *m:* Eugene; *c:* Brian; *ed:* (BA) Math/Chem/Elem Ed, CO St Coll 1959; Archeology, Adams St; Ed, Univ of N CO; CO Univ, Mesa Coll; *cr:* Teacher Carson City Public Schls 1959-61; Teacher Mesa Cty Public Schls 1961-64, 1968-; *ai:* MVEA Treas 1961-; CEA, NEA; Audubon Society; Lambda Sigma Tau 1957; Kappa Mu Epsilon; *home:* 1760 Hwy 3140 Box 181 Fruita CO 81521

ARNETT, JAN MC ALLISTER, 7th Grade Science Teacher; *b:* Birmingham, AL; *m:* Donald Eugene; *c:* Stacy Arnett Hill, Jon A., David C.; *ed:* (BS) Ed, Univ of Montevallo 1976; Sci In-Service Summer Programs Jacksonville St Univ; Sea-Lab Dolphin Island AL; *cr:* Teacher Moody Chrstn Acad 1976-77; 3rd Grade Teacher Coosa Valley Sch 1977-78; 4th Grade Teacher Iola Roberts Elem Sch 1978-81; 4th /6th Grade Teacher Walter M Kennedy Mid Sch 1981-84; 6th/ 7th Grade Sci Teacher O D Duran Jr HS 1984-; *ai:* NEA 1978-; AL Ed Assn 1978-; Pell City Ed Assn 1983-; Americas Clogging Hall of Fame Bd of Dir 1982-86; *office:* O D Duran Jr HS 309 12th St South Pell City AL 35125

ARNETT, SHIRLEY G., Teacher/Asst Principal; *b:* Santa Fe, NM; *m:* James Burton; *c:* Christina, Cari, Cheryl, Caralyn, Cobi; *ed:* (BA) Elem Ed, Weber St Coll 1966; (MED) Educl Admin, Brigham Young Univ 1979; (EDD) Ed Admin, Univ of UT 1988; GESA Facilitator, UT St Bd of Ed 1989; *cr:* K-6th Grade Teacher Davis Dist 1966-; Asst Admin Layton Elem 1988-; *ai:* Conflict Resolution Team; SWAT Sch Discipline; UT Cncl Cmptr Ed 1987-; Phi Delta Kappa 1985-; Davis Ed Assn 1966-; NCTM 1989-; Davis Organization for Handicapped Pres 1979-84; KSL Teacher of Day 1972; Teaching Asst Univ of UT, Cmptrs 1985-87; *office:* Layton Elem Sch 369 W Gentile Layton UT 84041

ARNEY, HELEN TROISI, English Teacher; *b:* Williamsport, PA; *m:* Paul E.; *c:* Catherine, William, Mary M. Martin, Theresa. Michael, Stephen; *ed:* (BA) Eng, 1971, (MA) Eng, 1977 Bradley Univ; Grad Stud Bradley, Eureka Coll, IL St Univ, Northern IL Univ; *cr:* Teacher Dunlap HS 1973-; *ai:* NHS Adv; Phi Delta Kappa 1990; Pi Lambda Theta; Phi Kappa Phi; Mortar Bd; Sigma Tau Delta Charter Mem; 2nd Pl Continental Bank Fnd Awd for Teaching of Economics 1981; Published Writing; Completed a Novel; *home:* 8660 N Picture Ridge Rd Peoria IL 61615

ARNOLD, ALAN D., Mathematics Teacher; *b:* Decatur, IN; *m:* Pamela Isch; *c:* Coley, Courtney, Kimberly; *ed:* (BS) Math, Huntington Coll 1975; (MS) Ed, IN Univ 1979; *cr:* Teacher Culver Cmmty Schls 1975-76, Adams Cntrl Cmmty Schls 1976-; *ai:* HS Stu Cncl Spon; Mid Sch Ftbl Coach; Project Journey Facilitator; Alcohol Drug Awareness Prevention Team; Monroe United Meth Church Trustee 1989-; Cntrl Cmmty Schls Teacher of Yr 1989; *office:* Adams Cntrl Cmmty Schls 222 W Washington Monroe IN 46772

ARNOLD, BARBARA STUDEBAKER, Reading/Communications Teacher; *b:* Troy, OH; *m:* Herbert B. Jr.; *c:* Mark, Micque Arnold Brickson, Matt; *ed:* (BA) Elem Ed, Antioch Univ 1979; (MS) Rdng Supervision, Univ of Dayton 1986; Wittenberg Univ, KS St Univ; *cr:* Teacher Bethel Local Schls 1960-61, New Carlisle Bethel Schls 1961-62; Substitute Teacher 1962-79, Teacher 1979- Mad River Green Schls; *ai:* Indian Valley Sch Stu Cncl; Drama & Journalism Club; Talent Show; Chrldr Adv; Power of Pen Writing Coach; Greenon HS Drama Club; Phi Delta Kappa 1987-; NCTE 1986-; ASCD 1988-; GSA (Trainer, Leader, Neighborhood Chm) 1969-, Thanks Badge 1982; Sundial Garden Club (Pres, Prgm Dir) 1965-; Booklet Published; ABWA, Wright St Univ Prof Speaker; *home:* 162 Green Vista Dr Enon OH 45323

ARNOLD, CATHY ELAINE, 1st Grade Teacher; *b:* El Reno, OK; *ed:* (AA) General, El Reno Jr Coll 1964; (BS) Ed, 1966, (MS) Ed, 1972 Southwestern OK St Univ; *cr:* 1st Grade Teacher Tyrone Public Sch 1966-; *ai:* OK Ed Assn, TX Cty Ed Assn 1966-; NEA 1975-; Tyrone Teacher of Yr 1973; Outstanding Young Women of America 1978; *home:* Box 132 Tyrone OK 73951

ARNOLD, CORNELIUS MATTHEW, Retired; *m:* Pearl Powell Arnold; *c:* C. M. Jr., Carl E.; *ed:* (BA) Soc Stud, TX Coll Tyler 1948; (MED) Adm, Supervision, TX Southern Univ 1955; North TX St Univ; *cr:* Prin Booker T Washington HS 1948-66; Teacher Midlothian Hs 1966-69; Soc Stud Teacher Midlothian Mid Sch 1969-89; *ai:* Assn for TX Prof Ed 1985-89; *home:* 1585 E Kiest Blvd Dallas TX 75216

ARNOLD, DAVID HAMLIN, Math Teacher/Dir of Studies; *b:* Worcester, MA; *m:* Andra Jean Crawford; *c:* David G.; *ed:* (BA) Math, Middlebury Coll 1963; (MA) Math, Rutgers Univ 1967; (PHD) His of Sci/Math/Physics, Univ of Toronto 1978; Integration Theory Mathematical Fnd Univ of WI 1970; *cr:* Math Teacher Hun Sch 1963-66; Math Lecturer Univ of Toronto 1974-76; Math Instr 1967-, Dir of Stud 1988- Phillip Exeter Acad; *ai:* Curr Comm Chm; Acad Advising Comm; Prin Staff; Var Boys Tennis Coach; Math Assn America; Natl Sci Fnd Academic Yr Inst Fellowship; Brown Fund Outstanding Teacher Awd; *office:* Phillips Exeter Acad Exeter NH 03833

ARNOLD, DEBORAH HERSEY, Science Teacher; *b:* Frankfurt, West Germany; *m:* James; *ed:* (BS) Voc Home Ec Ed, Memphis ST 1975; (MS) Scndry Sci Ed, Valdosta St 1990; *cr:* Sci/Home Ec Teacher Lambert Jr HS 1976-77; Chem/Bio Teacher Natchez Trace Acad 1980-81, Southwood Preparatory Sch 1981-82; Sci Teacher Ware Cty Jr HS 1982-; *ai:* Academic Bowl, Sci Olympiad, Geography Bee Coach; Sci Club Spon; Amer Home Ec Assn, NSTA, GA Sci Teachers Assn; GA Assn of Eucators, NEA; Certified Home Economist; Whos Who in Amer Ed 1988-89; *home:* 403 Cherokee Ave Waycross GA 31501

ARNOLD, DON GEORGE, French Teacher/Lang Dept Chair; *b:* High Point, NC; *ed:* (BA) Fr, Univ of NC Chapel Hill 1969; (MED) Fr Ed, 1974, Univ of NC Greensboro 1981; *cr:* Lang Art/Soc Stud Teacher Northeast Jr HS 1969-71; Fr Teacher T W Andrews HS 1971-; *ai:* Stu Cncl, Fr Club, Inter-Club Cncl, Natl Fr Honor Society Adv; NEA 1969-; AATF St VP 1971-; Foreign Lang Assn of NC (St Secy, Treas, Charter Officer) 1971-; Sherrod Park Historic Dist Co-Chairperson 1989-; High Point Teacher of Yr 1976, 1983; NC Regional Teacher of Yr 1976, 1983; Terry Sanford Awd for Creativity in Ed 1976; Ind Scholar Cncl for Basic Ed 1984; Author of Several Articles; *office:* T W Andrews HS 1920 Mc Guinn Dr High Point NC 27265

ARNOLD, GARY PETER, 8th Grade English Teacher; *b:* Dickinson, ND; *m:* Linette Steffan; *c:* Karen, Catherine, James; *ed:* (BS) Eng, Dickinson St Coll 1977; *cr:* Eng/His Teacher Almont HS 1977-78; 8th Grade Eng Teacher Sidney Mid Sch 1978-; *ai:* 7th/8th Grade Ftbl Coach; MT Ed Assn 1978-; Sidney Ed Assn Pres 1982; Teacher of Yr Sidney Mid Sch 1982, 1987; *home:* 1148 Sunflower Ln Sidney MT 59270

ARNOLD, IRMA RUTH, First Grade Teacher; *b:* Evansville, IN; *ed:* (BA) Elem Ed, Marian Coll 1977; (MA) Rdng, Clarke Coll 1983; *cr:* 1st Grade Teacher St Marys Sch 1967-68, Immaculate Conception Sch 1968-74; 3rd Grade Teacher St Joseph Sch 1974-75; 1st Grade Teacher St Wendel Sch 1975-; *ai:* Childrens Church Choir Dir; HS Youth Group Leader; Cath Teacher of Yr Nom 1990; *office:* St Wendel Sch 4725 St Wendel-Cyn Rd Wadesville IN 47638

ARNOLD, JAMES AUSTIN, Band Director; *b:* Ruleville, MS; *m:* Mary H.; *ed:* (BM) Music, 1974, (MME) Music, 1977 Univ of MS; Doctoral Prgm Univ of AL 1986-; Working Towards EDD Music Ed; *cr:* Dir Lamar Cty HS 1974-; *ai:* AL Ed Assn Rep 1990; AL Bandmasters Assn (Vice Chm 1989-, Local Rep); Natl Band Assn Natl Conference; Kappa Delta Pi; Walker Coll Honor Band Pres 1989-; *office:* Lamar Cty HS PO Box 369 Vernon AL 35592

ARNOLD, JAMES CARL, 7th/8th Social Studies Teacher; *b:* Dallas, TX; *m:* Kathleen Galambos; *c:* Robert G.; *ed:* (BS) Ed/Curr Instruction, TX A&M Univ 1975; Grad Stud; *cr:* 7th/8th Grade Soc Stud TeacherW B Atkins Jr HS 1977-; *ai:* Lubbock Ind Sch Dist Schedule Comm 1990-; Lubbock Ed Assn, TX St Teachers Assn, NEA 1989-; Llano Estacado Cncl of Soc Stud 1980-; BSA (Asst Scoutmaster 1978-82, Scoutmaster 1983-), Silver Beaver Awd 1988; PTA 1977, Lifetime Membership 1989; *office:* W B Atkins Jr HS 5401 Avenue U Lubbock TX 79412

ARNOLD, JEANNETTE CUTINO, Teacher; *b:* Monterey, CA; *m:* Richard Ray; *c:* Katherine, John; *ed:* (BA) Psych, San Francisco St 1974; *cr:* Kndgtn Teacher St Francis Day Sch 1974-75; Substitute Teacher Pittsburg Sch 1975-76; 3rd Grade Teacher Soledad Public Schls 1976-80; Substitute Teacher Newport Public Schls 1980-81, Alpine Public Schls 1981-82; *ai:* T-Ball Coach; GSA Brownie Asst; PTA Mem; Cath Church; Homeowners Assn; Navy Wives Club; *home:* 14523 William Carr Ln Centreville VA 22020

ARNOLD, JENNIFER J. (MASON), Biology Teacher; *b:* Youngstown, OH; *m:* James L.; *c:* Amanda K.; *ed:* (BSED) Biological Sci, 1971, (MA) Biological Sci, 1980 Kent St Univ; Numerous Courses; *cr:* Teacher David Anderson HS 1971-; *ai:* Sci Club Adv; NHS Adv; Scholastic Bowl Coach; Bio Olympics Coach; Envirothon Coach; Honors Banquet Spon; Lisbon Schls Retirement Comm Mem; NSTA 1985-; NABT 1987-; NEA 1971-; Lisbon Alumni Assn 1987-; Lisbon Historical Society 1990; Lisbon Music Study Club Publicity Chm 1988-; Nom For Ashland Oil Teacher Achievement Awd 1990; Elder of 1st Presbyn Church; Past VP & Treas Lisbon Ed Assn; *office:* David Anderson H S 260 W Lincoln Way Lisbon OH 44432

ARNOLD, JOHN CHARLES, 5th/6th Grade Science Teacher; *b:* Erie, PA; *m:* Carole Ann Goss; *c:* Jennifer, Christine; *ed:* (BS) Elem Ed, 1966, (MED) Elem Ed, 1970 Edinboro St Coll; *cr:* 5th-6th Grade Sci Teacher Clark Elem Sch 1966-; *ai:* Harborcreek Ed Assn, PA St Ed Assn, NEA 1966-; BSA 1966-; Nom Teacher in Space Prgm & Presidential Excl in Sci; *office:* Clark Elem Sch 3650 Depot Rd Harborcreek PA 16421

ARNOLD, JUNE KING, Sixth Grade Teacher; *b:* Norfolk, VA; *m:* Thomas Withers Sr.; *c:* Pamela D. Arnold Strcula, Thomas W. Jr.; *ed:* (BA) Elem Ed, James Madison Univ 1947; *cr:* 3rd/4th Grade Teacher Norfolk City Schls 1947-53; 6th Grade Teacher Carollton Oaks Sch 1955-57, 1959-61, 1963-65; 10th Grade Teacher Rock Hill Acad 1962-63; 6th Grade Teacher Belpre City Schls 1965-; *ai:* 6th Grade Team Leader; Partners in Ed Comm with Peoples Bank; SE OH Ed Assn Mem 1965-; Belpre Ed Assn Treas 1980-82; OH Ed Assn, NEA; Belpre Womans Club Pres 1971-72; *home:* 2723 Mead St Belpre OH 45714

ARNOLD, KATHARINE BENNETT, Fifth Grade Teacher; *b:* Alexandria, LA; *m:* Darrell Lyn; *c:* Blake, Brent; *ed:* (BA) Elem Ed, NW St Univ Natchitoches 1971; (MA) Elem Ed, LA St Univ Baton Rouge 1978; Grad Courses in Elem Ed; *cr:* 3rd Grade Teacher 1971-74, 1976-77, 2nd Grade Teacher 1975-76, 1977-80, 5th Grade Teacher 1980-88, 1989- England AFB Dependent Sch; *ai:* Sch Choir Accompanist; Hospitality Comm Chm; Grade Level Chairperson 1984-85, 1987; Prin Advisory Comm 1987, 1989; Published Magazine Article; *office:* England AFB Dependent Sch Mssq-Msd E A F B Alexandria LA 71311

ARNOLD, KELLIE BARTON, Teacher; *b:* Pell City, AL; *m:* Teresa T.; *c:* Jared, Justin; *ed:* (BS) Scndry Ed/His, 1980, (MS) Scndry Ed/His, 1989, (EDS) Scndry Ed/His, 1990 Jacksonville St Univ; Admin Cert; *cr:* His Teacher Ragland HS 1980-83, Ashville Mid Sch 1983-; His Instr Gadsden St Comm Coll 1990; *ai:* NEA, AEA; James D Truss Masonic Lodge Historian 1985-; City of Ragland (Cncl 1976-83, Mayor 1983-88), Youngest Ofcl in St; Outstanding Young Men of America 1989; St Clair Cty Mayors Assn Chm 1986; *home:* PO Box 302 Ragland AL 35131

ARNOLD, LEE PUGH, English Department Chairperson; *b:* Asheboro, NC; *m:* Bernard Hines; *c:* David, Jared, Benjamin; *ed:* (BA) Eng, NC St Univ 1972; *cr:* Teacher Plymouth St HS 1973-74, E Wayne Jr HS 1974-79, Pender HS 1979-; *ai:* Eng Dept Chairperson; Media Advisory & Sch Improvement Plan Dev Comm Mem; NCTE, NCETA, NCAE; NC Poetry Society, NC Writers Network.

ARNOLD, MARY ANN BARNETT, Mathematics Dept Chairman; *b:* Batesville, MS; *m:* Charles III; *c:* Michael C., Amy R.; *ed:* Assoc Math, NW MS Jr Coll 1966; (BSE) Math, Delta St Univ 1968; (MST) Math, Memphis St Univ 1973; *cr:* Math Teacher Horn Lake HS 1968-; *ai:* Fellowship of Chrstn Stu Spon; MS Prof Educators; Alpha Delta Kappa (Chaplain, Pres); 1st Baptist Church of Horn Lake Teacher; MS Ec Cncl STAR Teacher; Horn Lake HS Annual Dedication; *home:* 5530 Pravin Rd Horn Lake MS 38637

ARNOLD, MARY VANATER, Fifth Grade Teacher; *b:* South Charleston, WV; *m:* Jimmie D.; *c:* Robert D., Carolyn Briers, Margo Walker, John H., Daniel O. (Dec); *ed:* (BA) Elem Ed Marshall Univ 1966; (MA) Elem Ed, WV Coll of Grad Stud 1974; *cr:* 1st-3rd Grade Teacher Pleasant View Elem Sch 1965-; 5th Grade Teacher Culloden Elem Sch 1966-; *ai:* Cabell Cty Textbook Adoption Comm 1983 & 1990; NEA/WVEA/CCEA 1965-; WV & Cabell Cty Rdng Cncls By-Laws/Nomi Comm; *office:* Culloden Elem Sch 2100 Rt 60 E Culloden WV 25510

ARNOLD, NANCY CREEL, Mathematics Teacher; *b:* Galveston, TX; *m:* Warren Eugene; *c:* Jamie; *ed:* (BS) Math, Sam Houston St Univ 1965; *cr:* Math Teacher La Porte HS 1965-66, Dulles HS 1971-72, Bowie Jr HS 1972-77, Permian HS 1981-87, Kingwood HS 1987-; *ai:* Tutoring; ATPE Building Rep 1987-; *office:* Kingwood HS 2701 Kingwood Dr Kingwood TX 77339

ARNOLD, PATSY R., Second Grade Teacher; *b:* Muskogee, OK; *m:* Carlee J.; *c:* Debby Hamilton, Mike, Carla Carter; *ed:* (BA) Elem Ed, 1968, (MS) Elem Ed, 1971 NE OK St Univ; *cr:* 3rd Grade Teacher Edison Elem 1968-87; 2nd Grade Teacher Creek Elem 1988-; *ai:* St Curr Revision Comm Safety 1990; Muskogee Ed Assn, OK Ed Assn, NEA; Muskogee Classroom Teachers Assn VP 1970-71; Muskogee Ed Assn (Bd of Dir 1980-81, Elections Comm 1983-84); Teacher of Yr Candidate 1979-84; *office:* Creek Elem Sch 200 S Country Club Rd Muskogee OK 74403

ARNORE, JANET (LATERRA), Mathematics Teacher; *b:* Norwich, CT; *m:* Frank A.; *c:* Ashley J.; *ed:* (BA) Math/Ed, E CT St Coll 1973; (MA) Ed, Trinity Coll 1980; *cr:* Teacher Ellington HS 1974-; *ai:* Assn Teachers of Math in CT, NCTM 1978-; Bolton Womens Club 1980-, Arts Chairperson 1989; *office:* Ellington HS Maple St Ellington CT 06226

ARNSON, MARCY M., English Teacher; *b:* Lansing, MI; *m:* Gary Robert; *c:* Christine, Kathryn; *ed:* (BS) Comm/Ed, W MI Univ 1977; Elem Cert; Counseling/Personnel; *cr:* Teacher St Augustine Sch 1979-; *ai:* Faculty Sch Bd Rep; Ski Club & Cheerleading Adv; Enrollment Task Force; Divisional Chairperson; NCEA, Kalamazoo Valley Intermediate Sch Dist 1979-; Chi Omega Alumni 1977-; Kalamazoo Valley Intermediate Sch Dist Prof Dev Awd 1987; *office:* St Augustine Sch 600 W Michigan Ave Kalamazoo MI 49007

ARONOFSKY, SUZANNE, Biology Teacher; *b:* Pueblo, CO; *ed:* (BS) Bio, Univ of S CO 1980; Working Toward Masters Ed, Leslie Coll; *cr:* Substitute Dist #60 1980-81; Bio Teacher Centennial HS 1982-; Medical Technologist Parkview Episcopal Hospital 1982-; *ai:* Stu Government Spon; Policies & Procedures, Act, Math Comm; *office:* Centennial HS 2525 Mt View Rd Pueblo CO 81008

ARQUIETA, JOSEPH, JR., Social Sciences Teacher; *b:* Los Angeles, CA; *m:* Barbara Elizabeth English; *c:* Treasure J.; *ed:* (BA) Soc Sci/Span, CA St Los Angeles 1973; (BTH) Theology, LIFE 1976; (PHD) Philosophy, CA Grad Sch 1977; *cr:* Soc Sci Teacher Ontario HS 1977-; *ai:* Asian Club Adv; Curr Comm Chm; Mentor Teacher Selection Comm; Free Mason Shriner Secy; Order Knight Templar Knighted 1988, Maltese Cross Awd; *office:* Ontario HS 901 W Francis Ontario CA 91762

ARRANTS, DONALD L., 6th-8th Grade Phys Ed Teacher; *b:* Kearney, NE; *m:* Marilyn Arrants Lucas; *ed:* (BA) His/Poly Sci, Phys Ed, Kearney St Coll 1973; Grad Work; *cr:* 9th-12th Grade Eng/His Teacher Overton NE Dist 4 1974-76; 6th-8th Grade Soc Stud Teacher Dist 38 Shoemaker 1976-84; 6th-8th Grade Phys Ed Teacher Westridge Mid Sch Dist 2 1984-; *ai:* 7th & 8th Grade Ftbl Coach; 8th Grade Bsktbl; Grand Island Ed Assn, NEA, NE Ed Assn; *home:* 2320 Gateway Ave Grand Island NE 68803

ARREDONDO, ANNA GLORIA, English Teacher; *b:* Falfurrias, TX; *m:* Amador; *c:* Annette, Annela, Amador Jr.; *ed:* (BS) Span/Eng, 1971; (MS) Sch Admin, 1982 TX A&I Univ; *cr:* 7th Grade Eng Teacher Memorial Mid Sch 1971-77; 8th Grade Eng Teacher Falfurrias Jr HS 1979-; *ai:* UIL Spelling Coach 6th-7th-8th; TSTA 1971-77; NEA 1979-; *home:* 404 S Negri Falfurrias TX 78355

ARRESTOUILH, KIMBERLYN HALSTEAD, 6th Grade Teacher; *b:* Prosser, WA; *m:* Eugene Ray; *c:* Jaimee, Krista; *ed:* (BAED) Psych/Child Dev, E WA Univ 1973; Grad Stud E WA Univ, Portland St Univ, Cntrl WA Univ, Seattle Pacific Univ, Whitworth Coll; *cr:* 6th Grade Teacher 1973-74, 5th Grade Teacher 1974-79 Wellpinit Elem; 4th Grade Teacher 1979-87, 6th Grade Teacher 1987- Artz-Fox Elem; *ai:* Elem Gifted Ed Task Force; Curr Comm; Young Authors Conference; Career Ed Week Coord; Delta Kappa Gamma 1983-85; Kappa Delta Pi 1973; Friendship Baptist Church (Childrens Club, King Kids Asst); Intnl Order Rainbow Mother Adv 1979-81; *office:* Artz-Fox Elem Sch PO Box 40 Mabton WA 98935

ARRIAGA, MARICELA, Span, French, Sci Teacher; *b:* Mexico City, Mexico; *ed:* (BS) Sci, Univ of Mexico City 1979; (MS) Lang, Univ Sorronne Paris 1982; Teaching Ed, Albuquerque NM Univ; *cr:* Teacher Univ of Mexico City 1980-82, Albuquerque NM HS 1985-86, Beth Eden Baptist Sch 1986-; *office:* Beth Eden Baptist Sch 2600 Wadsworth Denver CO 80215

ARRINGTON, DEITRA EATON, Fifth Grade Teacher; *b:* Winston-Salem, NC; *c:* Letia, Kimberly; *ed:* (BS) Elem Ed/Music Ed Winston-Salem St Univ 1969; Heart of Teaching; Lee Canter Assertive Discipline Work; Mentor Trng Cert; *cr:* 6th Grade Teacher Dunbar Elem Sch 1969-70; 3rd Grade Teacher Rich Acres Elem Sch 1970-72; 5th-7th Grade Music Teacher AP Hill & Westview Elem 1972-73; 1st-6th Grade Music Teacher Robert E Lee Elem & Westview Elem 1973-74; 5th Grade Teacher Little River 1978-; *ai:* NCAE, DCAE 1978-; Delta Kappa Gamma, Intnl Teachers Society.

ARRINGTON, GLORIA BURNEY, Teacher; *b:* Griffin, GA; *m:* James H.; *c:* Stanley J., Millicent Arrington Williams, Stephanie C.; *ed:* (BA) Elem Ed, Clark Coll 1959; Albany St Coll, Atlanta Univ, OK St Univ, SC St Coll, Columbia Coll; *cr:* Teacher Palmyra Elem Sch 1968-72; Tutorial Cnslr Miles Coll 1973-75; Librarian Birmingham Public Sch System 1975-77; Teacher Orangeburg Sch Dist 1978-; *ai:* Sch & Natl Jr Honor Society Advisory Comms; SC Ed Assn Sch Rep 1988-; NEA 1960-; Alpha Kappa Alpha 1956-; New Mount Zion Baptist Church Youth Adv 1985-, Mother of Yr 1989; *office:* Bennett Mid Sch 919 Bennett Ave Orangeburg SC 29115

ARRINGTON, HELGA PRZEWOSNY, German & French Teacher; *b:* Beuthen, Germany; *m:* Alton P.; *c:* Christina, Andrew; *ed:* (BA) Ger, AZ St Univ 1971; Eng, Univ of S MS; *cr:* Teacher Harrison Cntrl 1967-69, Pearl River Cntrl 1969-73, Biloxi HS 1973-77, Pascagoula HS 1985-; *ai:* Foreign Lang Club; MEA, NEA, PEA; MS Assn of Lang Teachers, Natl Assn of Lang Teachers; PTA Pres 1980, 1990, 2nd in St 1980-81; *home:* 3800 Kendale Dr Gautier MS 39553

ARROWOOD, GRACE BLASCHKE, Elementary Music Specialist; *b:* Oak Park, IL; *ed:* (BM) Music/Ed, Simpson Coll 1965; (MA) Voice, Univ of IA 1970; Appalachian Culture, Cmptr, WV Univ; *cr:* Elem Music Teacher Jefferson Elem 1965-66, Creston Cmmty Schls 1966-69; Jr HS Music Teacher 1971-75, Elem Music Teacher 1975- Wood Cty Schls; *ai:* Wood Cty Elem Music Festival Comm Mem; Prepare Stus for WV Childrens Chorus; Delta Kappa Gamma Pres 1984-863; Amer Guild of Organists 1986-; NEA 1965-; Music Educators Natls Conference 1964-; Parkersburg Choral Society 1972-; Church (Choir Dir, Bd of Ed); Rockefeller Fnd Grant 1971; Classical Music Seminar Schlsp Eisenstadt Austria 1982; *office:* Mineralwells Elem Sch PO Box 40 Mineralwells WV 26150

ARTHAUD, PATRICIA DIBBLE, Fourth Grade Teacher; *b:* Hazleton, IA; *m:* Robert Joseph; *c:* Dianne Loughren, Denise, Douglas, Donna; *ed:* (BS) Elem Ed/His, Upper IA Univ 1970; Grad Stud Drake Univ, Univ of N IA, Marycrest Coll, Viterbo Coll; *cr:* 4th Grade Teacher Strawberry Point IA 1957-58, Oelwein IA 1967-; *ai:* Mem Lang Curr & Secy Phase III Comms; Oelwein Cmmty Ed Assn Pres 1985; NE IA Rdng Cncl VP 1989-; NE IA Lang Art Cncl; St Marys Parish Cncl Chairperson 1989-; Hazleton City Treas 1989; Buchanan Cty 4-H Volunteer 1960-; Rotary Club Teacher of Month 1990; *office:* Wings Park Sch 111 8th Ave NE Oelwein IA 50662

ARTHUN, THALE MARIE SCOTT, Third Grade Teacher; *b:* Wolf Point, MT; *m:* Donald R.; *c:* Scott W., David R.; *ed:* (BA) Elem Ed, Eastern MT Coll 1970; *cr:* 6th Grade Teacher 1966-67, 3rd Grade Teacher 1967-68 Brockton MT; 3rd Grade Teacher Absarokee Elem Sch 1970-; *ai:* Local Coord for Amer Inst for Foreign Study; Negotiating Team Absarokee Ed Assn; MT Ed Assn 1966-; Absarokee Ed Assn (Secy, Treas) 1989-; 4-H Organizational Leader 1983-87; Luth Youth Group Leader 1985-; Church Cncl Mem 1988-; *office:* Absarokee Elem Sch Box 430 Absarokee MT 59001

ARTHUR, DENISE ASHBY, Fifth Grade Teacher; *b:* Chester, PA; *m:* Lawrence Sr.; *c:* Kelly, Larry, Denise M.; *ed:* (BS) Elem Ed, W Chester St Coll 1974; Elem Math, Elem Sci W Chester St Coll; *cr:* ECIA Sci Teacher Immaculate Heart of Mary Sch 1975-76; 5th Grade Teacher Jeffris Elem Sch 1976-80; Math Teacher Pulaski Mid Sch 1981-82; 5th Grade Teacher Christopher Columbus Elem Sch 1982-; *ai:* AIMS Building Coord; Competency Based Curr; 5th Grade Chairperson; Chester Upland Ed Assn (Treas 1984-87) 1975-; PA St Ed Assn, NEA, NCTM 1975-; *office:* Christopher Columbus Elem Sch 10th & Barclay St Chester PA 19013

ARTHUR, KAREN R., Fourth Grade Teacher; *b:* Adams, MA; *m:* Ronald C.; *c:* Tanya K. Blue, Aileen K.; *ed:* (BS) Elem Ed, Lock Haven Univ 1964; (MS) Elem Ed - Cum Laude, St Univ of NY Cortland 1975; Grad Stud Univ of VT Burlington & Univ of

NH Durham; *cr:* 4th Grade Teacher Molly Stark Sch 1964-66; K-2nd Grade Teacher New Hartford Cntrl Schls 1967-76; 3rd-5th Grade Teacher Memorial Park Elem 1977-; *ai:* Music Dept Theatre Production; Chm Geography Comm & Prize Speaking; Sci & Soc Stud Curr Dev; Project Mind; NYSUT; *office:* Waterville Cntrl Sch E Bacon St Waterville NY 13480

ARTHUR, MOLLIE SUE, Political Science Teacher; *b:* Denver, CO; *m:* Richard C.; *c:* Arianne, Amanda; *ed:* (BA) Poly Sci, 1969, (MS) Curr/Dev, 1976 Univ of N CO; Taft Inst Fellow 1987; *cr:* Teacher Byers Jr HS 1971-80; TV Instr KRMA Channel 6 1973-75; Teacher/Forensics Coach 1980, Stu Cncl Adv 1986- JFK HS; *ai:* Stu Cncl Adv & Act Dir; Advanced Placement Poly Sci Teacher; Freedoms Fnd Spon JFK; Bicentennial Team Coach; NAASP, CAASA 1985-; Natl Ftbl League Coach 1980-; Mayors Cncl Keep Denver Beautiful 1990; Taft Fellow; Bicentennial St Championship Coach 1989-; Natl Forensics Coach 1980-87; City Champion Coach in Interpretive Events 1985-86; *office:* John F Kennedy HS 2855 S Lamar Denver CO 80227

ARTHUR, TERRY MC NABB, Counselor; *b:* Erwin, TN; *m:* Robert (dec); *c:* Tracy Arthur Crockett, Jennifer, Michael; *ed:* (BS) Health/Phys Ed, 1963, (MED) Counseling/Mid Sch Ed, 1982, (EED) Counseling, 1989 Univ of GA; Grad Stud Adult Ed, Rdng, Early Chldhd, Supervision & Admin; *cr:* Phys Ed Teacher/ Bsktbl Coach Jefferson HS 1963-64; Nursery Sch Teacher Green Acres Nursery 1973-76; Rdng Teacher 1976-86, Cnslr 1987- Hilsman Mid Sch; Adult Ed Rdng Teacher Athens Area Tech Sch 1983-; *ai:* Stu Support Team Coord; NEA, GA Ed Assn 1976-; GSCA 1987-; GAEPSE 1985-; Adult Ed Teacher ABE 1982-, Celebrate 1984; Fnd for Excl Nom Clark Cty Literacy Recipient 1985; Presented Paper GSCA St Conference 1989-90; Presented Prgm on Learning Disabilities GAPSE Conference; Presented Rdng Prgm Adult Literacy Rdng; GA St Organization Schlsp Awd; *office:* Hilsman Mid Sch 870 Gaines Sch Athens GA 30605

ARTINGER, JOHN, Social Studies Teacher; *b:* Allentown, PA; *m:* Glennda Anne; *c:* Gretchen, Heidi, Krista; *ed:* (AA) Sociology, Lehigh Cty Comm Coll 1978; (BS) Scndry Ed, Kutztown Univ of PA 1980; Grad Work in Spec Ed; *cr:* Teacher/Coach Swain Sch 1981-84, Elkton HS 1985-; *ai:* Ftbl & Bsktbl Coach; NEA 1985-; Arundel Civic Assn Pres 1986-; Natl His Contest Judge; *office:* Elkton HS 110 James St Elkton MD 21921

ARTIS, ARTHUR, Mathematics Teacher; *b:* Speers, PA; *m:* Mary C. Gladys; *c:* Shelly Cardinale, Scott, Kristi; *ed:* (BS) Math, California Univ of PA 1963; *cr:* 7th Grade Teacher Allapattah 1963-64; 7th-9th Grade Teacher Elizabeth Forward Jr HS 1964-; *ai:* NEA, PA Ed Assn, Elizabeth Forward Ed Assn 1964-; *home:* Box 276 New Eagle PA 15067

ARTZ, SUSAN WHALEY, English Teacher; *b:* Corpus Christi, TX; *m:* Andrew Stephen; *c:* Brian Andrew; *ed:* (BS) Scndry Ed/ Eng/His Summa Clum Laude Univ of TX Austin 1977; *cr:* His/ Eng Teacher Wells Mid Sch 1977-79; Paralegal/Anti-Trust Litigation Butler Binion Rice Cook & Knapp Attonryes-At-Law 1979-83; Eng Teacher Pflugerville HS 1983-; *ai:* Eng I Lead Teacher; Helping Hands Cnslr for At-Risk Stu; Frosh Class Spon; NCTE; TX Joint Cncl Teachers of Eng; U T Ex Stu Assn; Kappa Delta Pi; Phi Kappa Phi; *office:* Pflugerville H S 1301 W Pecan Pflugerville TX 78660

ARUNDELL, JAMES EDWARD, 5th & 6th Grade Teacher; *b:* Oxnard, CA; *m:* Diane Elaine Southwick; *c:* Jamie, Julie; *ed:* (BA) Soc Sci/Phys Ed, CA St Univ-Northridge 1972; *cr:* Teacher Fillmore Jr HS 1972-74, Piru Elem Sch 1974-; *ai:* Adv Piru Sch Farm-Lead Teacher; Budget Comm; Curr Comm; FUSD Coach Girls Jr Varsity Bsktbl 1989-; Boys Bsktbl 1970-78; Boys Bsbl 1972-74; Jr Varsity Ftbl 1973-74; Mentor Teacher Sci; Dev Piru Sch Farm Project; *office:* Piru Elem Sch 3811 E Center St Piru CA 93040

ARVIN, GAIL ANNETTE, Language Arts Teacher; *b:* Evansville, IN; *m:* Thomas; *c:* Michael Hasewinkle; Jared Hasewinkle; *ed:* (BS) Elem Ed, Olney Cntrl Coll 1967; (BS) Elem Ed/Sci/Eng, 1969, (MSED) Rdng, E IL Univ; Gifted Cert S IL Univ; *cr:* 2nd Grade Teacher West Salem 1969-70; 1st Grade Teacher Albion 1970-71; 4th Grade Teacher 1971-72, 5th Grade Teacher 1972-73, 4th Grade Teacher 1973-87 West Salem; Teaching Gifted 1982; 6th-8th Grade Lang Art Teacher 1987-; *ai:* Scholastic Bowl Coach 1983-; IL Ed Assn, Nea 1969-; Edwards Cty Teachers Assn Pres 1989-91; Phi Delta Kappa 1985-; Cncl for Gifted Children 1982-; Zion United Meth Church, PTO; Presenting Local 4 County Inst 1988; Gifted Fellowship 1982; Conducting Wkshps ESC #17 1988, 1990; Presented Cntrl IL Gifted Conf 1990, E IL Rdng Conf 1987; *office:* West Salem/ Edwards Cty Schls 105 E School St Box 367 West Salem IL 62476

ARVISO, RONNIE JOSEPH, 7th/8th Mathematics Dept Chair; *b:* Yuma, AZ; *m:* Laura Anne De Grande; *c:* Ronnie II, Petier, Dominique, Angela; *ed:* (AAS) Ed, AZ W Coll 1972; (BA) Elem Ed, AZ St Univ 1977; Studing for Master In Eng as 2nd Lang, N AZ Univ; *cr:* Kndgtn Teacher Murphy Sch Dist 1978-79; Soc Stud/Civics Teacher Gila Vista Jr HS 1979-80; Quality Control Supvr The Tanney Companies 1980-85; Math Teacher Gila Vista Jr HS 1985-; *ai:* Yuma HS Soccer & Women Slowpitch League Asst Coach; Yuma Youth Soccer Assn Bd Mem & Coach; Soccer Referee; Arviso Karate Sch Instr; Math Curr Comm; NEA, AEA 1986-; Knights of Columbus 1986-; *home:* 118 S 12th Ave Yuma AZ 85364

ARWOOD, BARBARA CROSS, English Teacher; *b:* Rusk, TX; *m:* Charles Frazier; *c:* Robert A. Smith, Barbara C. Smith; *ed:* (BS) Elem Ed/Eng, 1958, (MED) Elem Admin, 1960 Stephen F Austin St Univ; Post Grad Stud E TX St Univ, KS St, Julliard Sch of Music; *cr:* Eng Teacher Robert E Lee Jr HS 1959-60; Phys Ed Teacher Troup Jr/Sr HS 1960-64; 6th Grade Eng Teacher Troup HS 1964-70, Bowie Elem 1970-74; 7th Grade Eng Teacher Greenville Jr HS 1974-81; 7th/8th Grade Eng Teacher Troup Mid Sch 1981-; *ai:* Girls Bsktbl, UIL Oral Rdng, UIL Ready Writing Coach; TX St Teachers Assn Lifetime Mem; NEA; PTA Pres; Stephen F Austin St Univ Alumni Life Mem; Kappa Delta Pi; Order of Eastern Star Deputy Grand Matron 1958; Daughters of Amer Revolution; Assn of Univ Women; Polio Drive Chm; Troup Public Lib Planning Comm.

ARYAIN, PATRICIA DENTON, Kindergarten Teacher; *b:* Durant, OK; *m:* Jameil; *c:* Linda Robins, Amy Carpenter, Dwight; *ed:* (BS) Elem Ed, CSW; (MS) Early Chldhd Ed, TX Tech Univ 1975; *cr:* Kndgtn Teacher Frybarger Private Sch 1950-51, Aryains Private Kndgtn 1954-73, Seminole Public Schls 1973-; *ai:* TX Classroom Teachers Assn 1973-; Seminole Classroom Teachers Assn (Past Pres 1981-82) 1973-; Delta Kappa Gamma 1988-; Seminole Federated Music Club (Past Pres, Charter Mem) 1954-; Amer Assn Univ Women 1954-65; *office:* F J Young Primary Sch Box 900 Seminole TX 79360

ARZBERGER, MARY MC BEE, Fourth Grade Teacher; *b:* Washington, IA; *m:* William H.; *c:* Barry, Jason; *ed:* (BS) Elem Ed, Geneva Coll 1969; *cr:* 4th Grade Teacher East Liverpool Chrstn Sch 1979-; *ai:* Speech Meet Coord; Guidance Comm Mem; Stu Cncl Adv; ACSI 1980-; Reformed Presbyn Church Mem; Wkshp Leader Right-Brained Learning OH Teacher Convention 1988; *home:* 511 Smiths Ferry Rd Midland PA 15059

ASATO, MICHAEL KENEZ TSUGIO, 8th Grade Mathematics Teacher; *b:* Honolulu, HI; *m:* Rebecca Gail; *c:* Bonnie E. Meiko; *ed:* (BA) Math, Univ of HI 1970; *cr:* 8th Grade Math Teacher Aliamanu Intermediate Sch 1971-; *ai:* Bsktbl Coach; Dance Comm Adv; HSTA 1970-; Hickam Air Force Youth Act (Boys Bsktbl Coach 1971-74, Girls Sftbl Coach 1972-73); *office:* Aliamanu Intermediate Sch 3271 Salt Lake Blvd Honolulu HI 96818

ASBERRY, ALMEDA V. JOINER, 5th Grade Teacher; *b:* Palestine, TX; *m:* Lee Andrew; *c:* Ettro L. Smith Monk; *ed:* (BA) Ed, Huston-Tilletson 1952; TX Southern Houston, Univ of TX Austin, E TX St Commerce; *cr:* Teacher Lincoln Elem 1957-67, Reagan Elem 1967-71, Southside Elem 1971-83, Story North Sch 1983-; *ai:* Negro Bus & Prof Womens Pre-Teens Club Spon; TSTA, NEA, Classroom Teachers Assn 1957-; Negro Bus & W C Asst Secy 1987-89; United Meth (Youth Dir, Stewardess, Youth Sunday Teacher) 1987-89; Cancer Society; Cmmty Service Plaque; St Paul United Meth Church Devoted Service Plaque; *home:* 118 Columbia PO Box 41 Palestine TX 75801

ASBURY, BARBARA ANNE SMITH, Mathematics Teacher; *b:* Springfield, MO; *ed:* (BSED) Math, East Cntrl St Univ 1971; (MED) Ed, Univ of OK 1987; (JD) Law, OK City Univ 1990; *cr:* Math Teacher Mid Del Public Schls 1971-73, Norman Public Schls 1974-76, Jefferson Cty Public Schls 1976, Univ of OK 1980, 1986, Norman Public Schls 1977-, Univ of OK Continuing Ed Prgm 1988-; *ai:* Prof Educators of Norman Pres; Stus at Risk Prgm; How to Prepare for Act Wkshp Teacher; PEN Pres 1989-; OEA, NEA 1977-; OK Bar Assn Schlsp.

ASCHER, HOPE SCHNEIDER, Gifted Studies Teacher; *b:* Annapolis, MD; *m:* Larry O.; *c:* Jennifer, James, Seth; *ed:* (BA) Eng, FL Southern Coll 1973; (MA) Hum, Univ of S FL 1975; Cert Admin, Stetson Univ 1978; Cert Gifted, Nova Univ 1988; Cooperative Learning, Micro Cmptrs; *cr:* Grad Research Asst Univ of S Fl 1973-75; Eng/Hum/Teacher of Gifted Melbourne HS 1974-; Adjunct Professor Brevard Comm Coll 1975-; *ai:* Odyssey of Minds; Future Problem Solving; Jr Ambassador Prgm; Cooperative Learning Trainer; SACS Comm Chair: SEARCH Prgm Coord; Phi Delta Kappa 1975-; ASCD 1988-; FL Assn for Gifted 1989-; Quaker Meeting (Sunday Sch Teacher, Correspondent, Clerk) 1973-; FL Inst of Tech (Campus Ministry, Liason, Volunteer) 1985-; Ocean Breeze Advisory Cncl (Secy, Co-Chairperson) 1987-; Dolphin City Playground (Steering Comm, Grant Comm Chairperson) 1987; Melbourne City Cncl & Brevard Cty Sch Bd Recognition; Jaycees Outstanding Educator Awd; Whos Who in Amer Ed; South Brevard Teacher of Yr; Natl Teacher Mini Grant Competition 1st Place Arts & Entertainment; Phi Delta Kappa Jenkins Mini Grant; Cmmty Fnd & Brevard Fnd Grants; *office:* Melbourne HS 74 Bulldog Blvd Melbourne FL 32901

ASCHER, KATHLEEN ANNE, Spanish Teacher; *b:* Minneapolis, MN; *ed:* (BA) Span/Eng, 1985; (MA) Eng, 1987, Creighton Univ; Span, Univ of MN, Ortega Y Gasset Fnd; *cr:* Teaching Fellow Creighton Univ 1985-87; Span/Eng Teacher 1987-88, Span Teacher 1988- Park HS; *ai:* Mock Trial Coach; Friend-to-Friend Adv; Park Partners of Americas Uruguay Coord; Span Club; AFS Visitors; Mexico Spring Break Trip; Amer Assn Teachers of Span & Portuguese, NEA, MCTFL 1987-; King Juan Carlos I Fellowship 1989; Creighton Univ Eng Fellowship 1985-87; *office:* Park HS 8040 S 80th St Cottage Grove MN 55016

ASCHER, MARY ROPS, Fourth Grade Teacher; *b:* Austinville, IA; *m:* August Ed Jr.; *c:* Brent, Pamela; *ed:* (AA) Elem Ed, Ellsworth Jr Coll 1960; (BA) Elem Ed, Univ of N IA 1977; Grad Stud; *cr:* 3rd Grade Teacher 1960-65, 2nd Grade Teacher 1965-66, 4th Grade Teacher 1978- Wellsburg Sch; *ai:* Phase III & Performance Base Pay Comm; Hardy Rdng Cncl, IA Rdng Cncl 1988-; *home:* RR 1 Box 126 Grundy Center IA 50638

ASENDORF, SHEILA GRIFFIN, Art/Chemistry Teacher; *b:* Toledo, OH; *c:* John, Mary; *ed:* (BA) Fine Art/Chem, Mary Manse Coll 1969; *cr:* Freelance Commercial Artist 1969-; Teacher Toledo Public Sch 1978-85; Instr Lourdes Coll 1983-86; Teacher St Ursula Acad 1985-; *ai:* Yrbk Instr; Cmptr Instruction Comm; Delta Kappa Gamma Comm Chm 1986-; Friends of Lib Chairperson 1978-; Mary Manse Alumnae Assn Alumna of Yr 1976; *office:* St Ursula Acad 4025 Indian Rd Toledo OH 43606

ASH, DONNA STILLWELL, Art Teacher; *b:* Camden, NJ; *m:* Patrick C.; *ed:* (BS) Art Ed, Millersville St Coll 1977; *cr:* Art Teacher Williamstown HS 1977-80, Oak Knoll Mid Sch 1980-86, Williamstown HS 1986-; *ai:* Scenery Design Dir; Ftbl Game Chaperone Comm; Stu Art Exhibts, Stu Cmmty Service Project Spon; AFT 1979; Nativity Womens Service Guild 1988-; *office:* Williamstown HS Clayton Rd Williamstown NJ 08094

ASH, STEPHANIE BAIRD, Math Teacher; *b:* Coral Gables, FL; *m:* Nicholas R.; *c:* Christopher; *ed:* (AS) Wallace Comm Coll 1967; (BS) Math Ed, Troy St Univ 1974; (MSED) Math, Troy St Univ Dothan 1988; Advanced Placement Calculus Inst Univ of AL 1984; Grad Math Courses Troy St Univ Dothan; Adjunct Teacher Troy St Univ Dothan/Wallace Comm Coll; *cr:* Teacher Houston Acad 1970-71, Southside Elem 1974-75, Girard Jr HS 1975-78, Honeysuckel Mid 1978-84, Dothan HS 1984-; *ai:* Club Adv Students & Technology a Math and Sci Club; NEA/DEA/AEA Building Rep 1985-86; NCTMF; Published Articles in Media & Methods; Teaching K-8 Covering the Use of Cmptrs in the Math Classroom.

ASHBURN, BARBARA SCHRIMSCHER, Eighth Grade Teacher; *b:* Gadsden, AL; *m:* William Henry; *c:* William H., Michael A., Amanda A. Durden; *ed:* (BS) Elem Ed, GA Coll 1975; *cr:* 8th Grade Teacher Morgan Cty Mid Sch 1975-; *ai:* Media Center Comm; Sci Fair Coord; GAE 1975-80; GA Sci Teachers 1980-; Jaycettes (VP/Pres) 1965-75, Outstanding Young Women 1970; Team or Grade Leader; *office:* Morgan Cty Mid Sch 920 Pearl St Madison GA 30650

ASHBY, KATHLEEN ANN, German/English Teacher; *b:* Dayton, OH; *ed:* (BSE) Ed, 1981, (MA) Linguistics, 1989 Univ of KS; Univ of Erlangen/Nuremberg, West Germany 1987-88; *cr:* Ger/Eng Teacher Newton HS 1981-85, Maize HS 1988-; *ai:* Ger Club Spon; Fellowship Chrstn Athletes Spon; Maize HS Intervention Team Mem; NCTE, KS Foreign Lang Assn; Woodland United Meth Church Choir; Fulbright Travel Grant 1987-88; Pearson Fellowship Grad Study Abroad 1987-88; KS Univ Grad Stu Direct Exch Univ of Erlangen/Nuremberg West Germany 1987-88; *home:* 6747 Par Ln #1701 Wichita KS 67212

ASHFORD, LOMA MORRISON, Fourth Grade Teacher; *b:* Arcadia, FL; *m:* Jesse Jr.; *c:* Odeciea A. Roberts, La Treace, Jesse III; *ed:* (BS) Elem Ed, FL Memorial Coll 1964; (MS) Ed, Boston Univ 1977; *cr:* 6th Grade Teacher Hopewell Elem/Jr HS 1964-68, Hart Elem 1968; 4th Grade Teacher Lockdale Elem 1969; 3rd Grade Teacher Butzbach Amer Sch 1970; 5th Grade Teacher West Elem 1970-71; 2nd Grade Soc Stud/Head Teacher Amer Sch Stuggart Germany 1974-80; 6th Grade Teacher Button Gwinnett 1980-83; 4th/5th Grade Teacher West Elem 1983-88; 4th Grade Teacher Fred Wild 1988-; *ai:* Cth Health Advisory, SACS, Textbook Comm; Helped Develop De Soto Cty Curr Chapter I; Highlands Cty Rap Prgm; FL Rdng Assn, NEA, FEA, HCTA; Elizabeth Baptist Church, NAACP, Cmmty Rap Prgm; Teacher of Yr West Elem 1987; Black Educator Recognition Awd Highlands Cty 1990.

ASHKER, LORETTA QUIMINO, 6th Grade Teacher; *b:* Koloa, HI; *m:* James; *c:* James D., Michael; *ed:* (BED) Elem Ed, Univ of HI 1961; *cr:* 6th Grade Teacher Gardenhill Elem Sch 1961-62; 3rd/6th Grade Teacher Niemes Elem Sch 1963-; *ai:* CA Teachers Assn, NEA 1961-; ABC Teachers Assn 1963-; *office:* John H Niemes Elem Sch 16715 S Jersey Ave Artesia CA 90701

ASHLEY, CHARLOTTE PIGG, English Teacher; *b:* Jackson, MS; *m:* Ronald Frank; *ed:* (AA) Eng, Hinds Comm Coll 1967; (BA) Eng, MS St Coll for Women 1969; MS Coll, MS St Univ; *cr:* Eng Teacher Raymond HS 1969, Edwards Jr HS 1970, Rankin Acad 1970-71, Copiah Acad 1971-; *ai:* Beta Club, Jr Class & Newspaper Spon; MS Private Sch Ed Assn (Dist Chairperson 1978-79, St Eng Chairperson 1979-80); STAR Teacher 1988; Whos Who in MS Membership 1990; *home:* Rt 1 Box 191 A Hazlehurst MS 39083

ASHLEY, CHERYL LYNN (ALLEMAND), Mathematics Department Chair; *b:* Newark, NJ; *m:* Glenn Barry; *c:* Brian, Jennifer; *ed:* (BS) Scndry Ed/Math, Old Dominion Univ 1985; *cr:* Math Teacher Suffolk Chrstn Sch 1978-81, Alliance Chrstn 1981-; *ai:* Sr Class Adv; Accreditation Steering Comm Chm; ACSI; *office:* Alliance Chrstn Sch 5809 Portsmouth Blvd Portsmouth VA 23701

ASHLEY, JANEANE RAESENER, English Teacher; *b:* Llano, TX; *m:* Carlos C. Jr.; *c:* Mandy, Dan; *ed:* (BA) His, TX A&M Univ 1969; *cr:* Remedial Rdng Teacher Llano Jr HS 1970-72; Eng Teacher Llano HS 1981-85; Rdng Improvement Teacher Llano Jr HS 1986-88; Eng Teacher Llano HS 1988-; *ai:* UIL Coach Poetry Interpretation, Ready Writing, Litergy Criticism; Yrbk & Class Spon; TSTA, NEA, NCTE; *office:* Llano HS Hwy 71 E Llano TX 78643

ASHLEY, REGINA BROOME, Math Department Chairperson; *b:* Cornelia, GA; *m:* Roger D.; *c:* Brian, Kristi, Brandon; *ed:* (BA) Math, Winthrop Coll 1970; (MED) Scndry Ed, Clemson Univ 1977; *cr:* Teacher Westside HS/Lakeside Jr HS 1971; Belton Mid Sch 1971-72/1974-76; Teacher 1976-; Dept Chm 1981- Belton Hynea Path HS; *ai:* Spon-Keywanettes; Spon-Beta Club; NCTM; *office:* Belton Honea Path HS Rt 2 Honea Path SC 29654

ASHLOCK, KAREN BROOKS, 1/2/3 Grade Lang Arts Teacher; *b:* Chickasha, OK; *c:* Michele Ashlock Mc Daniel, Gregory, Casey B.; *ed:* (BA) Ed, Stephen F Austin St Univ; (MED) Rdng, Univ of TX Tyler 1990; *cr:* 1st Grade Teacher Brandon Elem; Elem Teacher Trinidad Elem 1969-; *ai:* Delta Kappa Gamma Recording Secy 1988-; *home:* 609 E Dewey Malakoff TX 75148

ASHTON, ROBERT WILLIAM, 7th/8th Grade Science Teacher; *b:* Wilkes Barre, PA; *m:* Mary Ann Siedlecki; *c:* Michael R., Joseph W., Susan, Ann M.; *ed:* (BA) Bio, Wilkes Univ 1969; Bio, Bloomsburg Univ, Wilkes Univ; *cr:* Scndry Teacher Highland Park HS 1969-71, Hanover Area Jr/Sr HS 1971-; *ai:* Stu Cncl Adv; Handbook Comm; Cty Inservice Comm Rep; Jr HS Sci Club; Luzerne Cty Sci Teachers Assn Pres 1986-87, Secy 1985-86) 1987-; Cub Scouts Webelos Asst Scout Master 1984-87; Little League Bsbl Head Coach 1985-87; Hanover Recycling Comm Mem 1988-, Governor Recognition; Hanover Booster Club Mem 1976-80; Teacher of Yr Hanover Dist 1987; Bsbl Coach of Yr Cty Level 1978; *home:* 240 Lyndwood Ave Wilkes-Barre PA 18702

ASHWORTH, DOVIE HARDIN, 5th Grade Mathematics Teacher; *b:* Cartersville, GA; *m:* Roland James; *c:* Melanie; *ed:* (BS) Mid Grades Math, Kennesaw Coll 1982; (MS) Mid Grades Math, Berry Coll 1988; *cr:* 6th Grade Teacher Cass Elem 1982-85, 6th Grade Teacher 1985-89, 5th Grade Teacher 1989- Mission Road; *ai:* Recreational Advisory Comm Mem Bartow Cty; Ladies Tennis Team Mem; Bartow Cty Math Bowl 6th Grade Spon 1985-88, 1st Place Team; Bartow Cty Cmmty Leadership Mem 1988.

ASHWORTH, RICK ALAN, Principal; *b:* Great Falls, MT; *ed:* (BA) Soc Welfare, 1972; Elem Ed, 1975; (MED) Admin, 1986 Univ of MT; *cr:* 5th Grade Teacher Choteau Elem 1975-88; 6th Grade Teacher Colegio Americano 1988-89; Elem Princ Dutton Elem 1989-; *ai:* MT Teen Inst-Teens in Partnership Drug Free Sch; Comm Intervention Initiated and Coord Drug Abuse Classes; Coaching HS-Jr HS Boys & Girls Bsktbl; Stu Comm Adv; Choteau Ed Assn Pres 1980-83; MT Ed Assn 1975-88; MT Assoc Elem/Mid Sch Prin 1989-; Jaycees VP/Pres 1979-81; Lions Club 1989-; 2 Outstanding Educator Awds Jaycees 1976 & 1987; St Runner-Up for MT Assn of Elem Sch Prin Schlsp; Implemented & Dir Elem Sci Fair 1980-87; *office:* Dutton Elem Sch Box 48 Dutton MT 59433

ASHWORTH, THOMAS DAVID, Fifth Grade Teacher; *b:* Dayton, OH; *m:* Barbara Anne Gerkin; *c:* Thomas D. Jr., Stephen M.; *ed:* (BA) Elem Ed, Bryan Coll 1965; *cr:* 3rd-4th Grade Teacher Waldens Ridge Elem Sch 1965; 9th Grade Eng Teacher Rhea Cty HS 1966; 6th Grade Teacher Daisy Elem Sch 1966-68, Sales Creek Sch 1968-70; 6th Grade Teacher 1970-74, 5th Grade Teacher 1974- Brickey Elem Sch; *ai:* Lunch Room Comm; East TN Ed Assn, TN Ed Assn, NEA 1970-89; PTA 1970-, Lifetime Mem 1989; *office:* Brickey Elem Sch Dry Gap Pike Knoxville TN 37918

ASKEW, BARBARA ELLEN (DIXON), Third Grade Teacher; *b:* Carlsbad, NM; *m:* Lloyd Lee; *ed:* (BA) Elem Ed, David Lipscomb Univ 1973; Arts Ed, Trevecca Coll; Cmptrs for Teachers & Advanced Logo, Nashville Tech Sch; *cr:* 1st-4th Grade Teacher Gra-Mar Elem Sch 1973-; *ai:* Faculty Advisory Comm; Pro-Team; Cmptr Chm; Comprehensive Comm & Rdng Prgm Cmptr Coord; Stu Cncl Spon; Nashville Inst of Arts Teacher; Excel Teacher Academically Talented; NEA, TN Ed Assn Mem 1973-; Metro Nashville Ed Assn (Rep 1978-82, Mem 1973-); Mid TN Rdng Assn Mem 1973-; PTA Bd Mem 1982-84; Dalcon Arts in Schls Awd 1988-89; *office:* Gra-Mar Elem 575 Joyce Ln Nashville TN 37216

ASKEW, RITA GERALDINE, 5th Grade Teacher; *b:* Wadena, MN; *m:* James Harry Kraemer; *c:* Desiree, Alexandra, Hannah; *ed:* (BS) Elem Ed, 1975, (MED) Elem Ed, 1982 Univ of MN; Grad Stud; *cr:* 5th Grade Teacher Delano Mid Sch 1975-80; 3rd-5th Grade Sci Teacher New York Mills Elem 1980-; *ai:* Jr HS Building Advisory Comm 1989-; Girls Track Coach 1975-78; All Sch Act Comm 1989-; Gender Fair Multi-Cultural Curr Comm 1989-; Teachers Advisory Team 1986-88; Univ of MN Alumni Club Bd Mem 1985-; MEA, Chairpersonship, Outstanding Women in Leadership Awd 1983; NEA Local Union Chairpersonship; Intnl Rdng Assn 1985-; Univ of MN Alumni 1985-; NW Rdng Cncl; NOW N Cntrl Friends of Lib (VPP 1982, Pres 1983-), MN NOW, Natl NOW; Democratic Party (Delegate to St Convention, Facilities Study Task Force 1989, Affirmative Action Officer, Cntrl Comm Mem); Safe House Volunteer Recognition.

ASKEW, THOMAS MILTON, Principal/Teacher; *b:* Marietta, GA; *m:* Linda Lanere Smith; *c:* Ethan, Michael, Samuel, Timothy; *ed:* (BA) Eng, W GA Coll 1968; (MT) Scndry Ed, Univ of AZ 1988; Post Baccalaureate Elem Ed, Univ of AZ 1976; Grad Stud Teacher Ed, Univ of AZ 1992; *cr:* Eng as a Second Lang Teacher Pui Ching Mid Sch Hong Kong 1968-70; HS Eng Teacher Dallas HS 1970-71; 5th Grade Teacher Grace Chrstn Sch 1976-77; Combined 1st-8th Grade Teacher Faith Chrstn Sch 1977-79; Prin/Teacher Shiloh Chrstn Sch 1979-; *ai:* Stu Leadership Training & Spon; Concert & Handbell Choir Dir; Natl Beta Club Cncl; Gideons Intnl 1978-; *office:* Shiloh Chrstn Sch 200 North Ave Sierra Vista AZ 85635

ASKEW, VIRGINIA D., 5th Grade Retired Teacher; *b:* Kenly, NC; *ed:* (BA) Elem Ed, St Andrews 1947; Grad Stud Univ of VA, George Mason Univ, La Verne Coll, Univ of NC; *cr:* 5th Grade Teacher Wyncoff HS 1947-49, North Elem 1949-63, Washington Mill Elem 1963-72, Kings Glen Elem 1972-77, Little Run Elem 1977-88; *ai:* Eng as Second Lang Prgm Volunteer Teacher-Dir; NEA, NC Ed Assn 1947-63; VA Ed Assn 1963-; Fairfax Ed Assn Local Meetings Rep 1963-; Alpha Delta Kappa (Treas 1972-74, VP 1984-86, Corresponding Secy 1988-); Whos Who Amount Elem Teachers 1975; *home:* 6510 Yadkin Ct Alexandria VA 22310

ASKEY, DAVID MALL, Chemistry Teacher; *b:* Ponca City, OK; *m:* Jamie Wright; *ed:* (BS) Geophysics, 1982, (BA) Sci Ed, 1986 Univ of OK; Sci Ed in Chem; *cr:* Exploration Geophysicist Atlantic Richfield Exploration Company 1982-85; Chem Teacher Norman HS 1986-; *ai:* Active New Life Bible Church; Sci Advisory Bd Mem Norman Schls; Phi Beta Kappa Mem; *office:* Norman HS Main & Berry Rd Norman OK 73069

ASLESEN, TERRY LYNN, Assistant Principal; *b:* Watertown, SD; *m:* Cheryle Ann Johnson; *c:* Anne, Adam; *ed:* (BA) Ed, Univ of SD 1978; (MS) Admin, SD St Univ 1985; Post Grad Stud; Numerous Conferences & Wkshps, Including 3 Natl Conferences; *cr:* Instr Mitchell Public Schls 1979-87; Adjunct Instr Huron Coll 1982-83; Summer Sch Coord Mitchell Schls 1986-88; Asst Prin Mitchell Sr HS 1987-; *ai:* Stu Cncl Adv; Lib Review, Scndry Sch Recognition, Sr HS Homework Policy, Sr HS Grading System, Boys & Girls St Selection Comm Chm; Prom & Baccalaureate Commencement Comm Co-Chm; Inservice Planning & Drug & Alcohol Comm; Pay & Calendar Comm Chm; Academic Letter, 10-12 Grade Math Review Comm;K-12 Grade Sci Curr Review, Health & Phys Ed Curr Review, K-12 Soc Stud Curr Review Comm; Prins Cabinet; 3 Evaluation Policy Comm; Sr HS Honor Roll Comm; Sch Admin of SD; Phi Kappa Phi Honor Society Stu Act Assn; SD Scndry Sch Admin; ASCD; NASSP; Area Principals Assn; Exch Club; First Luth Church; Quarterbacks Club Treas 1986-89; Booster Club; 4 Gubernatorial Appointments; Mitchell Jaycees Outstanding Young Educator 1984-85; SD Jaycees Outstanding Young Educator 1984-85; Outstanding Young Men of Amer 1984; Phi Kappa Phi Honor Society Membership 1984; USD Grad with Honors 1978; SDSU Grad with Honors 1985; NHS Membership 1974; *office:* Mitchell Sr HS 920 N Capital Mitchell SD 57301

ASPENES, MARY FABRICIUS, Fourth Grade Teacher; *b:* Ames, IA; *m:* Donald D.; *c:* Kathryn Aspenes Proeschold, Ann Aspenes Ulring, Karin J., David J.; *ed:* (BS) Ed, Univ of MN 1955; Univ of WI Eau Claire, Univ of WI River Falls, Univ of WI Superior; *cr:* 8th Grade Teacher River Falls Jr HS 1956-60; 4th Grade Teacher Greenwood Elem 1972-87; 2nd Grade Teacher 1987-89, 4th Grade Teacher 1989- Hayward Elem; *ai:* Phi Delta Kappa 1980-; PEO Phitanlhopic (Educl Organization Guard, Corresponding Secy, Treas) 1960-; 1st Luth Church (Church & Society Altar Guild) 1955-; St Croix Valley Teacher Rdng Circle Assn 1972-87; Eau Claire Teachers Convention Presenter; WI Improvement of Stu Teacher/Interns St Bd; Indian Ed St Advisory Comm.

ASSAD, HELLAS M., Spanish Teacher; *ed:* (BA) Span/Elem Ed/Scndry Ed, Boston Coll 1975; *cr:* Span Teacher Norwood Jr HS 1975-; *ai:* Cheerleading Coach 1975-79; Mexico & Spain Stu Trip Chaperone 1986, 1988, 1990; MA Foreign Lang Teachers Assn, Amer Assn of Teachers of Span & Portuguese; St George Orthodox Church Parish Cncl Mem 1983-86; Greater Boston Real Estate Bd Mem 1980-; *office:* Norwood Jr HS Endean Park Norwood MA 02062

ASSAF, ALICE WARR, Spanish Teacher; *b:* Cartagena, Colombia; *m:* Raymond; *c:* Dennis M., Melanie Assaf Orr, Timothy R., Leslie A.; *ed:* Assoc Span/Soc Stud, St Clair Cty Comm Coll 1972; (BA) Span/Soc Stud 1975, Endorsement Bi-ling/Span 1981 Oakland Univ; *cr:* Jefferson Adult Center 1983-85, Chippewa Jr HS 1985-86, Holland Woods Jr HS 1986-88, Port Huron Northern HS 1988-; *ai:* Soc Stud Curr & Bi-ling Prgm Dev Comms; Spon & Organize Foreign Lang Trip to Europe; MITESOL, NEA, MI Ed Assn Mem; Hispanic Cncl Exec Bd; League of Cath Women Pres; Amer Syrian/Lebanese Cedar Club Pres; *office:* Port Huron Northern HS 1799 Krafft Rd Port Huron MI 48060

ASSENMACHER, SUE TOMASZEWSKI, Junior High Teacher; *b:* Detroit, MI; *m:* Jerome Edward; *ed:* (BS) Educl Leadership/Bio, E MI Univ 1978; Grad Work Mid Sch Ed; Religious Ed Cert Archdiocese of Detroit; *cr:* 5th-8th Grade Teacher St Stephen 1980-83; Jr HS Teacher St Mary 1983-; *ai:* Sch Yrbk & Sch Newspaper Adv; Stu Cncl & Liturgy Coord; Phi Kappa Phi Mem 1978-; *office:* St Mary Sch 34565 Sims Wayne MI 48184

ASSETTO, HENRY JOHN, Soc Stud Teacher/Dept Head; *b:* Coatesville, PA; *m:* Angelina Mariniello; *c:* Lena, Anthony, Rita, Philip, Michael; *ed:* (BA) Comprehensive Soc Sci, West Chester Univ 1968; (MA) His, Penn St Univ 1975; Pembroke Coll Oxford Univ England; *cr:* World Geography Teacher Harrisburg Area Sch Dist 1968-69; 8th Grade Amer His Teacher Coatesville Area Sch Dist 1969-; *ai:* Soccer Coach; Soc Stud Dept Head; Graduation Comm; Class Trip Spon; PA St Educators Assn, NEA 1968-; Coatesville Area Ed Assn 1969-; Knights of Columbus Secy 1987; City Government Reorganization Comm 1978; City of Coatesville Civil Service Commissioner 1985-; Author; *office:* Gordon Mid Sch 351 Kersey St Coatesville PA 19320

ASTOURIAN, ROSALIND, History Teacher; *b:* Detroit, MI; *ed:* (BA) His/Sociology/Anthropology, Univ of MI 1982; Scndry Teaching Credential His/Soc Stud, 1984, Working Towards MA Scndry Ed Univ of MI; *cr:* Buyers Asst J L Hudson Company 1982-84; Substitute Teacher Dearborn Public Schls 1985-87; His Teacher Divine Child HS 1987-; *ai:* Model United Nations Club Coach, Valedictorian/Salutatorian Selection Revision & Public Relations Comm Divine Child HS; NCSS, MI Cncl for Soc Stud 1984-; Smithsonian Assocs 1981-; St Johns Armenian Church Choir (Mem 1986-, Corresponding Secy 1988-89); *home:* 7300 Wilderness Pk #201 Westland MI 48185

ATCHISON, BETH TILLOTSON, First Grade Teacher; *b:* Boise, ID; *m:* James Edward; *c:* James, Thomas; *ed:* (BS) Ed, 1951, (MS) Ed, 1960 Univ of ID; Univ of OR, San Francisco St, CA St Univ Hayward, Univ of CA; *cr:* 4th Grade Elem Teacher Potlatch ID 1951; Teacher Payette Jr & Sr HS 1951-52; Elem Teacher West Fir Elem 1952-54; Teacher Willamette City Elem 1957-58; Elem Teacher Pittsburg CA 1960-; *ai:* Pittsburg Educl Assn, NEA; Assn of Univ Women; Teacher of Yr 1982; *home:* 4297 Ridge Dr Pittsburg CA 94565

ATCHLEY, TERESA FINGER, English Teacher; *b:* Lincolnton, NC; *m:* Ronald Gene; *c:* Jordan; *ed:* (AA) Liberal Arts, Central Piedmont Comm Coll 1974, (BA) Eng, 1977; (MA) Scndry Ed, 1989 UNC-Charlotte; *cr:* 6th Grade Teacher Cntrl Elem 1978; Lang Arts Teacher East Lincoln Jr HS 1978-89; Eng Teacher East Lincoln Sr HS 1989-; *ai:* Stu Cncl Adv; NC Assn of Educators 1978-; NEA 1978-; ST Finalist 1989; Terry Sanford Awd Given By NC Assn of Educators; *office:* East Lincoln H S Hwy 73 West Denver NC 28037

ATCHLEY, TINA KAY, English Teacher; *b:* Selma, CA; *m:* Dennis Lee Cauthron; *c:* Matt Cauthron, Ryan Cauthron; *ed:* (BA) Theatre Art, Fresno St Univ 1981; (MA) Ed, CA Poly Pomona 1990; *cr:* Drama Coach Sanger HS 1982-83; Eng Teacher Sierra Vista HS 1983-; Writing Teacher Mt San Antonio Coll 1988-; *office:* Sierra Vista HS 3600 Frazier Baldwin Park CA 91706

ATEN, IRVIN, Fifth Grade Soc Stud Teacher; *b:* Factoryville, PA; *m:* Anna Borove; *c:* James, Jeremy; *ed:* (BS) His/Soc Stud, Mansfield 1965; (MS) Elem Ed, E Stroudsburg 1967; Grad Stud Ed; *cr:* 5th Grade Teacher Blue Ridge Elem 1966-68; 5th Grade Soc Stud Teacher Elk Lake Sch Dist 1968-; *ai:* Bsbl & Sftbl Ofcls Commissioner; Penn Can Refrees Secy; Schlsp Party Fund Raiser & Stu VIP Breakfast Chm; Elk Lake Ed Assn 1968-; PSEA, NEA 1966-; Nicholson Athletic Assn Pres 1979-86; Nicholson Masonic Lodge 438 1988-; Susquehanna Umpires Chapter Secy; *office:* Elk Lake Sch Dist Box 133 Dimock PA 18816

ATENCIO, BERNICE ARCHULETA, 8th Grade Lang Arts Teacher; *b:* Dixon, NM; *m:* Samuel J.; *c:* Angelo D., Audra L., Arlette M.; *ed:* (BA) Elem Ed, Adams St Coll 1973; (MA) Guidance & Counseling, Highlands Univ 1987; *cr:* Stu Intern Teacher Adams St Coll 1971-73; Elem Teacher Alamosa Sch Dist 1974-75; Albuquerque Schs 1975-76; Lang Arts Teacher Espanola Schs 1977-; *ai:* Stu Cncl Spon; Dept Chm-Eng; ASAA Mem Alcohol & Substance Abuse Prgm Mem; AFT Bldg Rep 1988-; Los Caballeros 4-H Club Leader 1986-; *office:* Espanola Jr H S P O Box 249 Espanola NM 87532

ATER, TERRY DAVID, Language Art Teacher; *b:* Clarksburg, OH; *m:* Mary Ellen Cook; *c:* Bret, Brad, Amy, Brian; *ed:* (BA) Eng Ed, Otterbein Coll 1964; (MA) Ec Ed, OH Univ 1978; Various Wkshps; *cr:* 8th Grade Lang Art Teacher Circleville City Schls 1964-67, Chillicothe City Schls 1967-; *ai:* Bsktbl, Bsbl, Ftbl Coach; OH Ed Assn 1964-; NEA 1970-; US Trotting Assn 1965-; OH Harness Horsemans Assn 1970-; Poems Published; *home:* 10020 SR 138 Clarksburg OH 43115

ATILANO, JESSE J., HS Biology Teacher; *b:* Jalisco, Mexico; *m:* Brenda Whittington; *ed:* (BS) Zoology, CA Polytechnic Univ Pomona 1984; *cr:* Bio Teacher Don Antonio Lubo HS 1985-; *ai:* Adv Cycling Club; CA Teachers Assn 1985-.

ATKINS, BETTY GWYN, English Teacher; *b:* Corinth, MS; *m:* Richard; *ed:* (BS) Bus Ed, Blue Mountain Coll 1963; Univ of MS, MS St Univ, MS Coll, Freed Hardaman Coll; *cr:* Teacher Kossuth HS 1963-; *ai:* Jr HS Beta Club Spon; NCTE, Alcorn Cty Teachers Assn; *home:* 1303 Poplar Rd Corinth MS 38834

ATKINS, DAVID W., Mathematics Teacher; *b:* Palmersville, TN; *ed:* (BS) Math, Murray St Univ 1984; (MA) Scndry Ed, W KY Univ 1987; Masters Stud Sch Admin; *cr:* Math Teacher Logan Cty HS 1984-; *ai:* Stu Cncl Co-Spon; LCEA Building Rep 1987-; KEA, NEA; *office:* Logan Cty HS 2200 Bowling Green Rd Russellville KY 42276

ATKINS, FRANKLIN GEORGE, Social Studies Teacher; *b:* Port Huron, MI; *m:* Esther Sharon Ouellette; *ed:* (BS) Phys Ed, Faithway Baptist Coll 1979; *cr:* Teacher/Coach/Athletic Dir Cmmty Baptist Schls 1979-86, Knoxville Baptist Chrstn Sch 1986-; *ai:* Var Soccer, Var Girls Bsktbl, Asst Boys Var Bsktbl, Var Bsbl Coach; Spon of Var Club; SE Chrstn Conference Pres 1984-86; E TN Chrstn Athletic Conference Chaplin 1988-; *office:* Knoxville Baptist Chrstn Sch 2434 E 5th Ave Knoxville TN 37917

ATKINS, GARY LEE, 8th Grade Language Art Teacher; *b:* Marion, IN; *m:* Linda Jo Leckron; *c:* Mark A., Bradley D.; *ed:* (BA) Eng, Taylor Univ 1972; (MA) Scndry Ed, Ball St Univ 1978; *cr:* Jr HS Teacher Charles Beard Memorial Sch Corp 1972-73, Taylor Cmmty Sch Corp 1973-; *ai:* Jr HS Boys Track Coach; 8th Grade Class Spon; Jr HS NHS Faculty Comm; N Cntrl Accreditation Steering Comm Mem; IN St Teachers Assn; NEA 1972-; Taylor Ed Assn 1973-; Center Chrstn Church Bd Pres 1987-; Nom for Howard Cty Young Educator of Yr Awd 1985; *office:* Taylor Jr/Sr HS 3794 E Cty Rd 300 S Kokomo IN 46902

ATKINS, JANET TUTEN, English Teacher; *b:* Allendale, SC; *m:* Michael David; *c:* David A., Elisabeth La Claire; *ed:* (BA) Eng/Speech/Theatre Carson Newman Coll 1978; *cr:* Lang Art Teacher Fairfax Mid Sch 1979-81; Eng Teacher Wade Hampton HS 1983-;

ai: Jr Class Spon; NCTE, ASCD, SC Historical Society; *home:* Rt 1 Box 73B Brunson SC 29911

ATKINS, JOAN BURKHART, 5th Grade Teacher; *b:* Jacksonville, FL; *m:* Ed; *c:* Scott, Kristie Atkins James; *ed:* (BS) Elem, MS Univ for Women 1963; *cr:* 4th Grade Teacher 1963-64, 6th Grade Teacher 1966-69 Barrow Elem; 6th Grade Teacher Stokes-Beard Elem 1969-72, Brandon Elem 1972-76, Hughes Elem 1976-; *ai:* MAE, NEA, MPE; Kappa Kappa Iota, Cumberland Presbyn Women; *home:* 8 Black Creek Rd Columbus MS 39701

ATKINS, MARJORIE ANN, Mathematics Teacher; *b:* E Liverpool, OH; *ed:* (BS) Math, Clarion Univ 1968; *cr:* Math Chairperson Midland HS 1970-86; Math Teacher Lincoln HS 1986-; *ai:* Ushers Club Spon; NCTM Mem; Outstanding Teacher of Yr 1972; Mem Mid St Evaluation of PA; *office:* Lincoln HS 501 Crescent Ave Ellwood City PA 16117

ATKINS, THOMAS WILSON, 6th Grade Lang Art Teacher; *b:* Los Angeles, CA; *m:* Patricia Schlauch; *c:* Thomas, Daniel, Patrick; *ed:* (BA) Eng, 1975, (BA) Religious Stud, 1975 Westmont Coll; *cr:* 3rd/4th Grade Teacher 1975-76, 5th Grade Teacher 1977-80, 7th/8th Grade Teacher 1982-85 Mother Lode Chrstn Sch; 6th Grade Teacher Summerville Elem 1985-; *ai:* 5th/6th Grade Boys Flag Ftbl, 5th-6th Boys Bsktbl, K-2nd Grade T-Ball Coach; Peaceful Valley Church (Deacon 1982-85, Elder 1985-89, Chm of Bd 1989-); *home:* 20853 Sunswept Dr Tuolumne CA 95379

ATKINSON, NANCY JO HARRISON, 7th Grade Science Teacher; *b:* Stanton, KY; *c:* Johanna, Jolie, Jill; *ed:* (BS) Home Ec, 1965, (MA) Scndry Ed, 1968, (Rank I) Lib Sci, 1979 E KY Univ; *cr:* Family Living Teacher Thomas Jefferson HS 1966-70; Home Ec Teacher Powell Cty HS 1970-71, Lynch Ind HS 1971-72; Career Exploration Teacher Trimble Cty HS 1972-74; 7th Grade Sci Teacher Belmont Jr HS 1974-; *ai:* NEA, KY Ed Assn, Cntrl KY Ed Assn 1980-; *home:* 106 Windridge Dr Winchester KY 40391

ATKINSON, PAUL GERALD, Mathematics Dept Teacher; *b:* San Jose, CA; *m:* Ellen Elizabeth Bauer; *c:* Rosalie M., Paul A.; *ed:* (BS) Agriculture DH, CA Polytechnic St Univ 1952; (MA) Educl Admin, Chapman Coll; (EDD) Educl Admin, Univ of the Pacific 1981; JD Law, Humphreys Coll 1989; Grad Stud CA St Univ Fresno, CA St Univ San Francisco, CA St Univ Stanislaus, Stanford Univ; *cr:* 6th Grade Teacher Mitchell K-6 Elem Sch 1957-65; 7th-8th Grade Math Teacher Mitchell Sr Elem Sch 1965-70; Asst Prin/Teacher Dir Data Processing & Research Atwater Sch Dist 1970-80; Supvr of Stu Teachers Univ of the Pacific 1972-73; 7th-8th Grade Math Teacher Mitchell Sr Elem Sch 1980-; *ai:* Calid Jr Schlsp Fed Chapter Founder; Yrbk, Newspaper Supvr & Adv; Stu Cncl, Act Adv; Alpha Zeta 1950-; Phi Delta Kappa 1972-; Delta Theta Phi (Dean, Tribune) 1985-; NEA Dept of Classroom Teachers Washington DC; Atwater Traffic Comm Mem 1974-82; Atwater Castle AFB Recreation Commission Rep 1976-80; Natl Conference Prof Negotiations 1961; *office:* Mitchell Sr Elem Sch 1753 5th St Atwater CA 95301

ATKINSON, PEGGY SCHMITZ, First Grade Teacher; *b:* Montello, WI; *m:* Wayne R.; *c:* Dale, Micheal, Mary Daggett, Catherine Giese; *ed:* (BA) Elem Ed, Stevens Point Coll 1973; *cr:* Secy Attorney 1952-58, Juneau Cty Sch System 1959-61; Bookkeeper Drug Store 1963-69; Teacher Montello Schls 1969-; *ai:* Womans Club Pres 1964-66; St Anns Church Group Pres 1968-70; Salutatorian 1950; *home:* 148 Siesta Dr Montello WI 53949

ATLAS, ARTHURLEAN JOHNSON, Vocal Music Teacher; *b:* Bastrop, LA; *m:* John Wesley; *c:* Mavis J., Candace L., Jamila K., Amina K.; *ed:* (BS) Music Ed, Grambling Coll 1963; (MA) Music Ed, Wayne St Univ 1972; Prof Wkshps in Orff, Choral Techniques; Elem Vocal Music; *cr:* Vocal Music Teacher Morehouse HS 1963-64, Union HS 1964-65, Detroit Public Schls 1965-; *ai:* Directress & Spon Mc Kenny Sch Sr Glee Club; Accompanist for St Johns CME Gospel Ensemble; Coord of Childrens Prgm; Musician for St Johns Vocation Bible Sch; Accompanist & Directress St Johns Angelic Choir; Detroit Fed of Teachers (Building Rep 1985-86, Cert of Excl 1986); Music Educators Natl Conference Mem 1960-86; Essie M Adams Missionary Circle Prgm Coord 1989; St Johns Hostess Bd Hostess 1986-; Detroit Diamond Express Leadership Mem 1984-, Gold Direct 1986; Delta Sigma Theta 1961-, Schlsp 1959; Awd for Outstanding Contribution to the 1st Annual Pontiac Area Black Family Conference 1988; Certificate of Appreciation Inspirational Prayer Comm Chairperson; *home:* 9212 W Outer Dr Detroit MI 48219

ATLWOOD, PAUL ROBERT, Spanish Teacher; *b:* Inglewood, CA; *m:* Janis Elaine Westover; *c:* Amy, Kristina, Eric, Jamie, Heidi, Kyle; *ed:* (BA) His, Brigham Young Univ 1975; *cr:* Eng Second Lang Teacher Inglewood HS 1977-79; His Teacher Roy Martin Jr HS 1979-82, Lowell Scott Jr HS 1982-87; Span Teacher Centennial HS 1987-; *ai:* Soph Girls Bsktbl & Asst Girls Sftbl Coach; Drivers Ed Instr; *office:* Centennial HS 4600 Mc Millan Rd Meridian ID 86342

ATTIG, JOHN CLARE, History Teacher; *b:* Chicago, IL; *m:* Harriet Rinehart; *c:* Laura Clemens, Victoria; *ed:* (BA) Poly Sci, De Pauw Univ 1958; (MA) Poly Sci, Univ of Chicago 1961; Grad Work at Numerous Univs; *cr:* His Teacher Lyons Township HS 1961-65, Palo Alto Schls 1965-72; Stu Teacher Supvr Simon Fraser Univ 1972-73; His Teacher Palo Alto Schls 1973-; *ai:* Millard Fillmore Hunt ChampionShip Team Spon; Gunn HS Faculty Senate; Western His Assn; CA Cncl for Soc Stud Santa Clara Cncl Pres 1971-72; Educl Excl Network Organization of His Teachers; Palo Alto First United Meth Church Admin Bd Secy 1981-83; NDEA Fellowship 1967; NSF Fellowship 1970; Robert A Taft Inst of Government Fellow 1980; NEH Seminars 1983, 1989; NEH Ind Study Fellow 1987; Articles Published; *office:* Henry Gunn Sr HS 780 Arastradero Rd Palo Alto CA 94306

ATTLESON, MIMI BARBOUR, French/English Teacher; *b:* Denver, CO; *ed:* (BA) Fr, Comparative Lit, Univ of NM 1971; (MA) Rdng Disability, NM St Univ 1973; (MA) Literature, Univ NM 1989; Rdng Specialist Cert; *cr:* Teacher Chaparral Jr HS 1978; Teacher Rio Grande HS 1978-; *ai:* Fr Club Spon; AATF 1982-; Albq Lang Teachers Assn 1982-; Awd from Albuquerque Chamber of Commerce 1988;Stu Nom for Most Influential Teacher;Rockefeller Fellowship; Summer Study in France 1989; *office:* Rio Grande HS 2300 Arenal Southwest Albuquerque NM 87105

ATTY, JANICE ELIZABETH, First Grade Teacher; *b:* Altoona, PA; *ed:* (BS) Elem Ed, Indiana Univ of PA 1960; (MED) Elem Ed, PA St Univ 1963; *cr:* 1st Grade Teacher Altoona Sch Dist 1960-65, Pomona Sch Dist 1965-67, Volusia Cty Sch Dist 1967-; *ai:* Grade Level Chm; Volusia Cty Rdng Assn, FL Rdng Assn; Local Sch Teacher of Yr; Soc Stud Teacher of Yr; *office:* South Daytona Elem Sch 600 Elizabeth Pl South Daytona FL 32119

ATWATER, CLEOPHAS, SR., JROTC Instructor; *b:* Barnesville, GA; *m:* Gwendolyn I.; *c:* Stephanie, Cleophas Jr., Cory, Charity; *ed:* (AA) Theology, Carver Bible Coll 1983; Instr Course 1953; Advance Armor Sch Ft Knox KY 1954; 7th Army NCO Acad Ft Knox KY 1955, Germany 1962; Germany Drill Sergeant Acad 1967; *cr:* 1st Sergeant US Army 1951-71; JROTC Instr Atlanta Public Sch System 1971-; *ai:* Sch Drill Team Coach; Color Guard; SE Drill Meet; Prin & Staff Adv; Retired Enlisted Men Assn Chaplain 1978-85; AFT Mem 1971-; Parish Cncl Mem 1979-81; ONAA Little League Coach 1976-82; Alliance Men Organization (Pres, Cmmty Alliance Chm) 1981-84; SGA Carver Bible Coll Pres 1981-83; Baptist Ministry License 1988-; *office:* Daniel M Therrell HS PO Box 309 Yatesville GA 31097

ATWOOD, JUANITA E. (DOWNEY), Seventh & Eighth Grade Teacher; *b:* Xenia, OH; *m:* James William; *ed:* (BS) Elem Ed, 1979, (MA) Ed/Instructional/Design/Technology, 1987 OH St Univ; *cr:* Cmptr Repair & Maintenance Sochor Schls; Apples Teacher Trng Schlsp Prgm; *cr:* Substitute Teacher Licking Cty Schls 1979-80; Tutor/Substitute Teacher Newark City Schls 1979-80; Teacher Northridge Local Schls 1980-; *ai:* 8th Grade Class Adv; Math & Soc Stud Curr Comm; Cmptr Ed Dist Rep Sch Study Cncl of OH; 7th & 8th Grade Girls Bsktbl Coach 1982-84; NEA, OEA, COTA 1980-; NREA Past Bldg Rep 1980-; Cmptr Ed Dist Rep Sch ; OCTM 1983-; Outstanding Young Women of America Awd 1985; Eastern Star 1989-; Hartford Parent Teacher Society 1980-; Columbus Zoo Mem 1988-; Licking Cty Math Study Cncl Mem 1990-91; Pilot Teacher for OH St Univ 7th-8th Grade Approaching Algebra Numerically Project; *office:* Northridge-Hartford Elem Sch 10843 Foundation Rd N W Croton OH 43013

ATWOOD, STEPHEN JAMES, Chemistry/Biology Teacher; *b:* Boone, NC; *m:* Linda Kaye Wilson; *c:* Daniel; *ed:* (BS) Bio/Sci, 1980, (MA) Bio, 1988 Appalachian St Univ; *cr:* Teacher/Coach Mitchell HS 1981-; *ai:* Jr Var Ftbl & Wrestling Head Coach; Fellowship of Chrstn Athletes Spon; NEA 1981-; Spruce Pine First Baptist Church 1983-; Outstanding Young Men of America; NC Wrestling Coach of Yr 1988; NC Fellowship of Chrstn Athletes Coach of Yr 1988.

AUBIN, PATRICIA A., Director of English; *b:* Worcester, MA; *c:* Megan S. O Halloran; *ed:* (BA) Eng, Salve Regina Coll 1968; (MA) Eng, 1969, Cags Rdng, 1976 Boston Coll; (EDD) Eng Ed, Boston Univ 1980; *cr:* Teacher Watertown HS 1972-81; K-12th Grade Dir of Eng Watertown Public Schls 1981-; *ai:* NCTE (All Regional, St Affliates); Phi Delta Kappa; NSCD; Article Published in CT Eng Journal; *office:* Watertown Public Schls 50 Columbia Ave Watertown MA 02172

AUBREY, ANNE WRIGHT, 7th Grade Soc Stud Teacher; *b:* Fort Knox, KY; *m:* L. Brent; *ed:* (BA) His/Scndry Ed, Bellarmine Coll 1974; (MA) Guidance & Counseling, Western KY Univ 1977; *cr:* 7th Grade Soc Stud Teacher Mac Donald Mid Sch 1974-; *ai:* Mac Donald Natl Jr Honor Society, Geography Bee, Jr KY United Nations Assembly Team, Young Astronauts Spons; Ft Knox Peer Coach; Ft Knox Cmmty Schls Strategic Planning Action Team Leader; Textbook Adoption, Curr Writing, Staff Dev Comm; KY Cncl for Soc Stud (Secy 1985-86, Treas 1987-88, Pres 1988-), Outstanding Soc Stud Teacher Awd 1988; KY Mid Sch Assn Sister Sch Coord 1989-; Ft Knox Teachers Assn Secy 1985-; St Christopher Church Service Chairperson 1984-86; Radcliff Womans Club 1990-; Ashland Oil Teacher Achievement Awd 1990; Golden Apple Awd 1989; KY Prgm of Excl Awd 1988; Natl Cncl for Soc Stud Awds Comm; Geography Curr Writing Comm for KY Dept of Ed; Presenter at the KY Cncl for Soc Stud Conference; Presenter at KY Mid Sch Assn; *office:* Mac Donald Mid Sch 7729 Mc Cracken St Fort Knox KY 40121

AUCHENPAUGH, ELLEN HAYES, 4th Grade Teacher; *b:* Atlanta, GA; *m:* Richard; *c:* Daniel, Amanda; *ed:* (BS) Elem Ed, Jackson St Univ 1980; *cr:* 4th Grade Teacher Clarkdale Elem Sch 1980-; *ai:* Comm of 100 Mem; Cty Lang Art Curr Guide Comm; Kappa Delta Epsilon Pres 1979-80; Hollydale United Meth Church (Choir Mem 1985-, Sunday Sch Teacher 1987-89); Jacksonville St Sch of Ed Top Grad Forney Awd 1980; Clarkdale Teacher of Yr 1984, 1988; Articles Published 1985, 1990; *office:* Clarkdale Elem Sch 4455 Wesley Dr Austell GA 30001

AUDILET, DEVEREUX OLDFIELD, Chemistry/Biology Teacher; *b:* Quantico, VA; *m:* Garland Ottis; *c:* Allison Corcoran, Alex, John, Elizabeth; *ed:* (BS) Bio, Mary Washington Coll of Univ VA 1965; (PHD) Bio, Georgetown Univ 1973; Scndry Sch Chem, Woodrow Wilson Natl Fellowship Fnd 1989-; *cr:* Adjunct Professor George Mason Univ 1972-81; Georgetown Univ 1978-79; Montgomery Coll 1981-85; *ai:* Bsktbl Coach; Publicity, Pep, Spirit, Sci Clubs; *home:* 13400 Bonnie Dale North Potomac MD 20878

AUFILL, LA DORA AYRES, Mathematics/Computer Teacher; *b:* Plainview, TX; *m:* Don Peyton; *c:* Robert C., Don P. Jr., Steven C., Jeffrey G.; *ed:* (BS) Math Ed, Univ of Houston 1971; (MA) Math Ed, TX Tech Univ 1990; *cr:* Math Teacher Pasadena Sch Dist 1971, 1975-77; Math/Cmptr Teacher Lockney Sch Dist 1978-; *ai:* Math & Cmptr Team Spon; Lockney Assn of TX Prof Educators Pres 1986-88; Delta Kappa Gamma Treas 1988-; NCTM; TX Cmptr Ed Assn; *home:* Box 129 Lockney TX 79241

AUFRANC, GARY LEE, Ninth Grade Science Teacher; *b:* Hamilton, OH; *m:* Donna Burg; *c:* Brooke L., Griffin J.; *ed:* (BA) Chem, 1967, (MED) Scndry Ed, 1972 Univ of Cincinnati; *cr:* 8th Grade Teacher 1965-67, 9th Grade Sci Teacher 1967- Wilson Jr HS 1967-; *ai:* Yrbk Adv & Photographer; Textbook & Curr Comm; AFT Mem 1966-70; HCTA Exec Comm 1968-72; OH Ed Assn, NEA 1965-75; Published Graded Course of Stud & Curr Guides; *office:* Wilson Jr HS 714 Eaton Ave Hamilton OH 45013

AUGHTRY, MARSHA ANN, First Grade Teacher; *b:* Norfolk, VA; *ed:* (BS) Elem Ed, GA Coll 1958; (MS) Elem Ed/Gifted Ed, Univ of GA 1974; *cr:* 4th Grade Teacher Oak Grove Elem 1958-68, Coralwood Elem 1968-71; 4th-7th Grade Teacher for Gifted Heritage Elem 1971-76; 1st-7th Grade Teacher for Gifted 1976-86, 1st Grade Teacher 1986- Oak Grove Elem; *ai:* Strategic Planning Comm; De Kalb Assn of Educators Building Rep; Ga Assn of Ed, NEA 1958-; Ga Assn of Gifted Ed 1971-86; Freedom Fnd Awd; *office:* Oak Grove Elem Sch 1857 Oak Grove Rd Atlanta GA 30345

AUGUSTE, GABRIEL J., Mathematics Teacher; *b:* Cap Haitien, Haiti; *m:* Evelyne Angrand; *c:* Joanne, Stephane, Tania; *ed:* (BA/MA) Ec, Poitiers Univ France 1970; Math Scndry Schls, Brooklyn Coll; *cr:* Math Teacher Prospect Heights HS 1985-; *ai:* Coach Young Adults for HS Equivalency Examination; New York Assn Teachers of Math; Assn of Cmptr Educators Mem; Haitian Amer Alumni Assn Mem 1986-; Certificate of Recognition for Services to Stus Bureau of Bi-ling Ed NY St 1988; *office:* Prospect Heights HS 883 Classon Ave Brooklyn NY 11225

AUGUSTINE, ANTHONY JAMES, Science Teacher; *b:* Youngstown, OH; *m:* Dolores Maiorana; *c:* Anthony, Debbie, Kerri; *ed:* (BSED) Sci/His/Government, Youngstown St Univ 1969; Grad Stud, Youngstown St; *cr:* Teacher Edison Jr HS 1969-87, Niles Mc Kinley HS 1987-; *ai:* Bsktbl Coach; Audio Visual; Niles Classroom Teachers Assn VP 1976-77; NE OH Teachers Assn, OH Ed Assn 1969-; Trumbull Cty Coaches Assn, OH HS Athletic Assn 1971-89; Trumbull Cty Division 1 Boys Bsktbl Coach of Yr 1987-88; *office:* Niles Mc Kinley HS 616 Dragon Dr Niles OH 44446

AUGUSTINE, CAROLYN, 1st Grade Teacher; *b:* Uniontown, PA; *ed:* (BS) Elem Ed, CA Univ of PA 1970; *cr:* 2nd Grade Teacher South Ward Elem 1970-78; 1st Grade Teacher East Ward Elem 1978-; *ai:* PA St Ed Assn 1970-; NEA 1970-; Central Greene Ed Assn 1970-; Waynesburg Spec Events Treas 1983-88; Parents Anonymous Bd Mem 198-89; Greene Cty Hstrcl Society Bd Mem 1990.

AUGUSTINE, EDWARD S., 3rd Grade Teacher; *b:* Ashland, WI; *m:* Nancy Preu Augustine; *c:* Scott, Chad; *ed:* (BS) Elem Ed, Univ WI 1974; Prof Dev; *cr:* 4th Grade Teacher Birnamwood Elem 1974-78; 4th/5th Grade Teacher Evergreen Elem 1978-79; 5th/6th Grade Teacher 1978-86; 3rd Grade Teacher 1986- Riverside Elem; *ai:* Unit Leader; Cub Scout Advisory Comm; Teacher Rep PTO; WI Ed Assn; NEA; 1989 Elem Teacher of Yr D C Everest Public Sch System; *office:* Riverside Elem Sch R12231 River Rd Ringle Ringle WI 54471

AUGUSTINE, JAMES PHILIP, Essential Skills/Math Teacher; *b:* Geneva, NY; *m:* Barbara A. Hennings; *c:* Donna, Conni, Jimmy; *ed:* (BA) Math, St John Fisher Coll 1972; (MS) Ed Admin, SUC Brockport 1974; Certificate of Advanced Study, SUC Brockport 1976; *cr:* Math Teacher Gates-Chili Cntrl Schls 1972-79; Dean of Stus Wheatland-Chili Cntrl Schls 1979-83; Math Teacher Greece Cntrl 1983-87; Jr/Sr HS Prin Gananda Cntrl 1987-88; Essential Skills/Math Teacher Athena Mid Sch 1988-; *ai:* PTSA Faculty Rep Greece Athena Mid Sch 1988-; St John Fisher Coll Excl in Preparation to Teach Awd 1972; *home:* 329 Northwood Dr Rochester NY 14612

AUGUSTINE, LARRY JOE, 6th Grade Teacher; *b:* Hays, KS; *c:* Casie; *ed:* (BA) Psych, 1980, (BS) Ed, 1981 MO Southern; (MS) Ed, Southwest MO St 1987; *cr:* 6th Grade Teacher Westview C-6 1981-82, Diamond R-4 1982-; *ai:* Spelling Bee Coord; Math Coord; Sci Fair Coord; *office:* Diamond R-4 Elem Sch PO Box 68 Diamond MO 64840

AULT, DEBRA MARIE, Social Studies Teacher; *b:* Atlanta, GA; *ed:* (BSED) Soc Stud/Geography, Univ of GA 1981; (MED) Soc Stud/Ec, 1987, Admin/Supervision 1989 GA St Univ; *cr:* Soc Stud Teacher American Fork HS 1983-84, Cross Keys HS 1984-89, Sequoyah Jr HS 1989-; *ai:* Educl Management Team Chairperson; Graduation Comm; Sr Class & 8th & B Team Chrldng Spon; Flag & Rifle Corp; NCSS 1986-; Joint Cncl on Ec

Ed 1985-; League of Women Voters 1989-; Technology Park Grants; GA HS Ec Teacher of Yr 1989.

AULT, DIANE ANDERSON, Mathematics Teacher; *b:* Bowling Green, OH; *m:* Steven R.; *c:* Jessica, Zachariah; *ed:* (BS) Math, 1973, (MS) Scndry Ed, 1984 Bowling Green St Univ; *cr:* Math Coord Penta Cty Voc HS 1974; Math Teacher Elmwood HS 1974-; *ai:* Math Dept Chairperson, FTA Adv; NCTM; Heart Assn Area Annual Drive Leader 1988-; *office:* Elmwood HS 7650 Jerry City Rd Bloomdale OH 44817

AUMAN, LYNN EVERAGE, Instrumental Music Teacher; *b:* Greensboro, NC; *m:* Barry R.; *c:* Chad; *ed:* (BSME) Music, Univ of NC Greensboro 1973; *cr:* Instrumental Music Teacher Grimsley HS 1974-79, Concertmaster Philharomia of Greensboro 1978-88; Instrumental Music Teacher Page HS 1979-; *ai:* Prof Violinist Greensboro Sumphony Orch & Other Piedmont Cmmty Orch; Section Coach Greensboro Symphony Youth Orch; NC Music Educators Assn 1974-; Greensboro Music Center Volunteer; *office:* Page HS 201 Alma Pinnix Dr Greensboro NC 27405

AUSAMARA, DAVID SWAYDAN, French & Spanish Teacher; *b:* Worcester, MA; *m:* Laurel Elizabeth Rutkaus; *c:* Ilse; *ed:* (BA) Fr, Coll of Holy Cross 1969; (MA) Fr, Middlebury Coll 1970; Harvard Univ; Advanced Placement Course, St Johnsbury Acad; *cr:* Fr Teacher Malden HS 1970-72; Fr/Span Teacher Governor Dummer Acad 1972-; *ai:* Mens & Womens Cross Cntry Head Coach; Mens & Womens Track Distance Coach; Dormitory Master; Prize Comm Secy; Acad Adv; MA Foreign Lang Assn; Newburyport Historical Society; Winners Circle Running Club; *office:* Governor Dummer Acad Byfield MA 01922

AUSBY, DONNA D., Mathematics Teacher; *b:* Evergreen, AL; *ed:* (BS) Applied Math, Univ of CA Los Angeles 1987; *cr:* Math Teacher Washington Preparatory HS 1988-; *ai:* Girls Gymnastics Team Coach; *office:* Washington Preparatory HS 10860 S Denker Ave Los Angeles CA 90044

AUSMOUS, PAULINE, Kindergarten Teacher; *b:* Speedwell, TN; *w:* John F. (dec); *c:* Art, Craig, Clint; *ed:* (BA) Eng/Elem Ed/ Span/Bio, Lincoln Memorial Univ 1953; (MA) Early Chldhd Ed, 1981, Admin/Supervision, 1983 Union Coll; *cr:* 5th/6th Grade Teacher Bolinger Sch 1960-63; Eng Teacher La Follette HS 1963-65; Eng Teacher 1970-71, Kndgtn Teacher 1971- Powell Valley Elem; *home:* Rt 3 Davis Creek Rd Speedwell TN 37870

AUST, BRENDA ROMINGER, Third Grade Teacher; *b:* Bedford, IN; *m:* Allen K.; *c:* Kristina, Winter, Amber; *ed:* (AS) Elem Ed, Vincennes Univ 1972; (BA) Elem Ed, Oakland City Coll 1974; (MS) Elem Ed, IN St Univ 1979; *cr:* 1st Grade Teacher 1976-77, Kndgtn Teacher 1984-85, 3rd Grade Teacher 1974- Winslow Elem Sch; *ai:* Pike Cty Sch Curr Writing Comm; Textbook Comm; Elem Stu Cncl; Elem Chrldr Spon; Girls Sftbl Team Mom; 4-H Leader; Pike Cty Rdng Cncl Pres 1981-82; Pike Cty Teachers Assn, IN St Teachers Assn, NEA 1974-; *office:* Winslow Elem Sch Porter Winslow IN 47598

AUSTEN, MARCY KATHLEEN, Elem Teacher-Remedial Math; *b:* Ellwood City, PA; *m:* Robert J.; *ed:* (BS) Elem Ed, 1970; (MA) Rdng, 1979 Slippery Rock St Coll; *cr:* 5th Grade Teacher Monroe Cty Schls 1970-72; 2nd Grade Teacher Haine Elem 1972-83; Teacher Gifted Prgm 1983-86; Specialist-Math/Gifted Rdng 1987- Seneca Valley Schls; *ai:* SVEA-PSEA-NEA Bldg Rep; PAGE-Sv Page Exec Comm; IRA; Nom Locally PA Teacher of Yr 1981; *home:* 1933 Mt Royal Blvd Glenshaw PA 15116

AUSTERMAN, DONNA LYNNE, Spanish Teacher; *b:* Colorado Springs, CO; *m:* Randy Lynn; *c:* Thomas R. Brown, Michael N.; *ed:* (BSE) Span, 1970, (MS) Ed/Span, 1971 Pittsburgh St Univ; KS Univ; OK Univ; OK St Univ; *cr:* Span/Eng Teacher Liberal HS 1970-72, Jayhawk-Linn HS 1972-74, Nowata HS 1983-86; Span Teacher Bartlesville Mid HS 1986-; *ai:* Span Club Spon; Secy of Foreign Lang Cncl; Vice Chm of Prof Improvement Comm; Chm of Teacher of Yr Comm; Amer Assn of Teachers of Span & Portuguese 1986-; NEA 1983-; OK Ed Assn 1983-; *office:* Barlesville Mid-High 5900 SE Baylor Dr Bartlesville OK 74006

AUSTIN, ALICE BLACKMAN, English Advisor/ Communications; *b:* Cleveland, OH; *m:* Bob R.; *c:* Allan W., Phillip T.; *ed:* (BA) Eng, Union Coll 1962; Various Courses & Wkshps; *cr:* Eng Teacher Akron Garfield HS 1963-68, Manchester HS; *ai:* Speech Club, Literary Magazine; NHS; MEA, OEA, NEA; Eng Dept Chm Garfield HS; Teacher of Yr; Lib Patron of Yr Summit Cty; Nom Educator of Yr Summit Cty; *office:* Manchester HS 437 W Nimsilk Rd Akron OH 44319

AUSTIN, BARBARA WHEELER, Retired K-5th Grade Teacher; *b:* Apperson, OK; *c:* Barbara A. Jones, Grey W. Baker; *ed:* (BA) Eng/Span, W TX St Univ 1946; TX Technological & KS St; *cr:* 2nd/3rd Grade Teacher Amarillo Ind Sch Dist 1952-60; Span/Eng Teacher Lamesa Ind Sch Dist 1961-66, Lefurs Ind Sch Dist 1966-71; Bi-ling Teacher Abernathy Ind Sch Dist 1972-73; K-5th Grade Teacher Kelton Ind Sch Dist 1973-85; *ai:* Delta Kappa Gamma, Amer Assn of Univ Women, TX Prof Educators; Sr Citizen, Amer Assn of Retired Persons, NRTA; KS St Eng Grant; *home:* 2800 Lometa Apt 207 Amarillo TX 79109

AUSTIN, DIANE COOPER, Counselor; *b:* Bogalusa, LA; *c:* Trent P., T. Alayna; *ed:* (BA) Eng/Soc Stud, Centenary Coll 1966; (MS) Guidance Northwestern 1970; Admin, LA Tech Univ 1977; *cr:* Eng Teacher Ridgewood Mid Sch 1966-70; Cnslr J S Clark Mid Sch 1970-81, Broadmoor Mid Laboratory Sch 1981-; *ai:* LA Assn for Counseling & Dev Exec Bd 1986-; LA Sch Cnslrs Assn Pres 1988-89, Mid Sch Cnslr of Yr 1986; Phi Delta Kappa; PTSA Exec Bd 1984-, Distinguished Educator of Yr 1990; *office:* Broadmoor Mid Laboratory Sch 441 Atlantic Ave Shreveport LA 71105

AUSTIN, GLADYS, Science Teacher/Sci Dept Chair; *b:* Laurel, MS; *ed:* (BS) Bio, TN A&I S Univ 1950; (MS) Bio, N AZ Univ 1961; Grad Stud Various Univs; *cr:* Sci Teacher Mc Nair HS 1950-59; Sci Teacher Harris Jr Coll 1959-60; Chairperson/Sci Teacher Oak Park HS 1960-70, R H Watkins HS 1970-80; *ai:* NSTA, NEA, MS Ed Assn, Laurel Ed Assn (Pres, Treas); St Paul United Meth Church Chairperson Admin Bd 1989-; NAACP (Asst Secy, Comm) 1988-; AKA 1949-; YWCA 1978-; Natl Sci Fnd Grants 1957, 1959, 1962, 1966-68; St of MS Dept of Ed Comm on Sch Accreditation 1975-83; Natl Sci Fnd Fellowship For Scndry Sch Teacher 1960; *home:* 811 Woodbury Ave PO Box 2064 Laurel MS 39442

AUSTIN, GWENDOLYN HOLLINSHED, Home Economics Teacher; *b:* Kansas City, KS; *m:* Dwight Austin Sr.; *c:* Dwight Jr., Gerald A.; *ed:* (BSE) Home Ec, Emporia St Univ 1978; Grad Courses, Ottawa St, Avila Coll; *cr:* Teacher Coronado Mid Sch; *ai:* Singing in Church Choir; Sewing, Crocheting, Embroidery; Chrldr & Pep Club Spon; KS Cncl Home Ec Mem 1980-; Mt Carmel Choir Secy 1987-88; KS East St Choir Mem 1987-88.

AUSTIN, JANE S., 6th Grade Teacher; *b:* Hartford, KY; *m:* Franklin D.; *c:* Elizabeth, Ellen; *ed:* (BA) Music Ed, 1957, (MA) Ed, 1971 Western Ky Univ; *cr:* Music/English Teacher Kalamazoo Public Schls 1957-61; Eng Teacher 1967-70, Consultant/Music Teacher 1971-76, Elem Teacher 1976- Rockford Public Schls 1976-; *ai:* Stu Cncl; Patrol Adv; REA Building Comm; Stu Exchange Pgm; Books for South Africa Coord; Delta Kappa Gamma VP/Prgm Chairperson 1984-86; NEA/Rockford Ed Assn; Nom for Teacher of Yr 1985; *home:* 3603 Cardinal Ln Rockford IL 61107

AUSTIN, KENNETH, SR., English Teacher; *b:* Valley Stream, NY; *m:* Wanda Mc Kinney; *c:* Gail Austin Butler, Ken Jr., Susan Austin Wilson, Kay; *ed:* (AB) Eng/His, Univ of Notre Dame 1948; (MA) Eng/His, Univ of TX Austin 1953; GA St Univ; *cr:* Teacher Cntrl Cath HS 1948-51; Instr Univ of Ft Edwards 1951-53; Private Bus Teacher 1953-85; Teacher Peachtree HS 1985-88, Peachtree Jr HS 1988-; *ai:* Yrbk; Newspaper; Concession Stand; Sch Store; Publicity; Honors, Teacher of Yr Comm; GA Assn of Journalism Dir Pres 1989-; Prof Assn of GA Educators Bldg Rep; De Kalb Assn of Educators Bd Mem; GA Mid Sch Assn; Teacher of Yr; *office:* Peachtree Jr HS 4664 N Peachtree Rd Dunwoody GA 30338

AUSTIN, MARTHA ELIZABETH, First Grade Teacher; *b:* Taylorsville, NC; *ed:* (BA) Elem Ed, Berea Coll 1976; (MS) Curr/ Instruction, Trevecca Coll 1986; *cr:* Teacher Whitwell Elem Sch 1976-84, Jasper Elem Sch 1984-; *ai:* NEA, TN Ed Assn 1976-; Marion Cty Ed Assn (Faculty Rep, St Convention Rep, Various Comms) 1976-; *home:* PO Box 5 Jasper TN 37347

AUSTIN, NEVILLE PERRY, Social Studies Teacher; *b:* Flemington, NJ; *m:* Cynthia Tompkins; *c:* Neville, Noah; *ed:* (BA) Soc Stud/Scndry Ed, Eastern Coll 1977; (MA) His, West Chester Univ 1982; (MA) Prin Cert, Penn St Univ 1990; Drug & Alcohol Trng COAD Penn St Univ; Learning Styles Courses, Wilkes Coll; *cr:* Teacher/Coach Downington Sr HS 1977-81, Lionville Jr HS 1981-; *ai:* Asst Soccer, Asst & Head Track Coach; SAP Team Chm; 7th Grade Level Chm; PSEA, NEA 1977-; Coatesville Zoning Appeals Bd Asst Chm 1988-; Coatesville Little League Coach 1988-; Coatesville Weblows Scout Leader 1989-; Nom PA Teacher of Yr 1989; *office:* Lionville Jr HS 50 Devon Dr Downingtown PA 19335

AUSTIN, SALLIE BOYD, Psychology Teacher; *b:* Laurens, SC; *m:* William C.; *c:* Ashelon K.; *ed:* (BS) Psych, SC St Coll Orangeburg 1971; (MED) Spec Ed, Converse Coll 1982; Specialist Certificate Clemson Univ, Univ of SC Spartanburg, Furman Univ; *cr:* Soc Stud Teacher Ford Elem 1971-72; Spec Ed Teacher Laurens Jr HS 1972-82, Hillcrest HS 1982-86; Psych Teacher Greenville HS 1986-; *ai:* Co-Jr Class Spon; Area Steering Comm Rep; Faculty Cncl Mem; Wellness Fitness Coord; Dists Supts Cabinet Comm Mem & Secy; Var Chrldr Coach; Natl, St, Local Ed Assn (Sch Rep, Delegate, Mem) 1971-; Phi Delta Kappa; Alpha Kappa Alpha (Secy, Courtesy Chairperson); NAACP, Urban League Guild, Natl Cncl of Negro Women Charter Mem; Aquarian Service Club; *home:* 1418 Brentwood Way Simpsonville SC 29681

AUSTIN, SALLY ANN (BALDWIN), Kindergarten Teacher; *b:* Newark, NJ; *m:* John Allan; *c:* Kelly A., Mary J. Scarborough; *ed:* (BA) Early Chldhd Elem Ed, Kean Univ 1960; Psych, Kean Univ 1961; Painting I & Comm Health, Okaloosa Walton Jr Coll 1976; Micro Cmptr in Ed, Univ of W FL 1982; *cr:* 2nd Grade Teacher Milton Avenue Sch 1960-61; Kndgtn Teacher USAF Base Kndgtn 1961-62; 2nd Grade Teacher Brooke Elem 1962-64; Kndgtn Teacher Oak Hill Elem 1976-; *ai:* Okaloosa Cty Least Restrictive Environment Task Force, Pre-Kind 2nd Comm Mem; NEA, Okaloosa Cty Ed Assn Mem 1976-; Poly Action Comm Mem 1987-; Oak Hill Elem Teacher of Yr Awd 1988; Okaloosa Cty Kndgtn Comm Mem 1985-88; Presentor of Okaloosa Cty Kndgtn Plan 1987 Convention of FL Admin & Supvrs; *office:* Oak Hill Elem Sch 101 Chinguapin Dr Eglin AFB FL 32542

AUSTIN, TERRI L., Sixth Grade Teacher; *b:* Hilliard, OH; *m:* Kenneth S.; *c:* Rick, Aaron; *ed:* (BED) Elem Ed, 1981, (MED) Lang/Literacy, 1990 Univ of AK Fairbanks; AK St Writing Consortium 1982-84; British Writing Consortium 1984; Inst of Critical Thinking & Writing 1986; Inst of Cooperative Learning 1986; *cr:* 4th-5th Grade Teacher Barnette Elem 1981-82; 6th Grade Teacher Ft WainWright Elem 1982-; Instr of Rdng Univ of AK Fairbanks 1986-; *ai:* Teacher Advisory Cncl; Intnl Rdng Assn, NCTE 1979-; ASCD 1981-; Delta Kappa Gamma Golden Apple Awd 1990; Denali Womens Cncl Chairperson 1988-89; Outstanding Student Awd, Sch of Ed 1981; Educl Grants 1982, 1983, 1987, 1990; *office:* Ft Wainwright Elem Sch 4166 Neely Rd Fort Wainwright AK 99703

AUSTIN-FRESH, GINA S., Drama Teacher; *b:* Carlsbad, NM; *m:* Richard; *ed:* (BSE) Speech/Theatre, 1969, (MS) Speech/ Theatre, 1970 Emporia St Univ; *cr:* Teacher Greenland HS 1971-72, Wichita West 1972-; *ai:* Thespian Club; Stage Play & Musical Dir; Forensics Asst; AFT, Delta Kappa Gamma; Assn of KS Theatre Outstanding HS Drama Teacher 1988; Natl Organization for Women; *office:* Wichita HS West 820 S Osage Wichita KS 67213

AUTHEMENT, NANCY GENNUSO, Third Grade Teacher; *b:* Lake Charles, LA; *m:* Eric John Jr.; *c:* Michael; *ed:* (BA) Elem Ed/Spec Ed of Mentally Retarded, 1981, (MED) Admin/ Supervision, 1986 Mc Neese St Univ; *cr:* 3rd Grade Teacher J I Watson 1981-; *ai:* Delta Kappa Gamma 1988-; Alumni of Alpha Delta Pi Alumni; *office:* J I Watson Sch PO Box 687 Iowa LA 70647

AUTRY, SHIRLEY LANGSTON, 5th Grade Teacher; *b:* Green Cty, NC; *m:* Timothy J.; *ed:* (BS) Elem Ed, Fayetteville St Univ 1960; (MS) Ed, A&T St Univ 1968; E Carolina Univ, SC St Coll; *cr:* 4th/5th Grade Teacher Woodington Sch 1960-69; 6th Grade Math Teacher Bayard Mid Sch 1969-72; 5th Grade Teacher Catherine T Reed Elem 1972-73, Felton Laboratory Sch 1973-; *ai:* Teaching Adult Basic Ed; Kids in Kollege Basic Math Teacher; Culminating Prgm Co-Chairperson; Drama Club Dir & Publicity Chairperson; SC Employees Assn 1986-; Natl Laboratory Assn 1973-; Phi Delta Kappa 1985-; Delta Sigma Theta Journalist 1988-, Service Awd 1986; Felton Laboratory Sch Drama Club Service Awd; *office:* Felton Laboratory Sch SC St Coll Orangeburg SC 29117

AUXER, CATHY WEDO, First Grade Teacher; *b:* Chambersburg, PA; *m:* Jeffery L. Sr.; *c:* Jeffery L. Jr.; *ed:* (BS) Elem/Lib Sci, 1974; (MED) Elem/Early Chldhd, 1978 Shippensburg Univ; *cr:* 1st Grade Teacher Mooreland Elem Sch 1975-; *ai:* PTO Teacher Liaison; Carlisle Area Ed Assn 1975-; NEA 1975-; Beta Sigma 1977-; Phi Sorority (Corres Sec 1979-80, Recrdg Sec 1980-81) Women of Yr Awd 1981; *home:* 9084 Possum Hollow Rd Shippensburg PA 17257

AVALLONE, PATRICIA LIBERATORE, Sixth Grade Teacher; *b:* Norwalk, CT; *m:* Neil Anthony; *c:* Tara Maturo, Scott Maturo, Melissa, Donna; *ed:* (BA) Eng, Univ of New Haven 1969; Elem Ed, S CT St Univ 1985; Working Towards Masters in Counseling, S CT St Univ; Educl Research & Dissemination Comm Amer Fed of Teachers Trends in Ed Albany & Washington DC; *cr:* 2nd Grade Teacher St Aloysius Sch 1968-70; 1st/3rd Grade Teacher 1970-72, 5th-6th Grade Teacher 1977-80 St Lawrence Sch; Dir/Choreographer Patti Maturos Dance Aerobics 1980-85; 6th Grade Teacher Forest Elem 1985-; *ai:* Career Incentive Comm 1989; Staff Dev Comm Organizer & Presenter 1990; West Haven Bd of Ed Retirement Comm Master of Ceremonies 1989-; Schlsp Dance Comm Chairperson 1988-; West Haven Fed of Teachers (Elem VP 1986, Public Relations Co-Chm 1990); Educl Research & Dissemination Comm (Local Site Coord, Natl Comm Mem) 1988-; West Haven PTA 1979-; Cty H Chamber of Commerce Chairperson 1986-87, Recognition Awd, Briefcase Awd; CT St Fed of Teachers Public Relations Comm 1985-; Sch Rep to PTA Cncl; Commercial with Howard Hessman Promoting Proper Public Relations Among Labor Groups; Wrote & Hosted 12 Segments for Educl Programming in CT 1988, 1990; CT Celebration of Excl Winner Honorable Mention 1988-89; St Assessor, Research Comm; CT BEST Prgm; Mentor Teacher 1990; Forest Sch Staff Presenter for CEUS; *home:* 99 Honeypot Rd West Haven CT 06516

AVALOS, IRMA ELDA, Fifth Grade Teacher; *b:* Del Rio, TX; *ed:* (BS) Elem Ed, Sul Ross St Univ 1980; Effective Teaching Practices Conferences 1987; Teams Writing 1989; Whole Lang Approach 1990; At Risk Kids Rdng 1990; *cr:* 3rd Grade Elem Teacher 1980-81, 5th Grade Teacher 1981- East Side Elem; *ai:* Just Say No Club 1988-; Del Rio Boys Club Girls Bsktbl 1983-; *home:* 609 Avenue T Del Rio TX 78840

AVEDISSIAN, JANICE AIKENS, 5th/6th Grade Science Teacher; *b:* Milan, IN; *c:* Mariam; *ed:* (BA) Home Ec, 1955, (MAT) Home Ec, 1967 IN Univ; Grad Stud Sci, Purdue Univ; *cr:* Spec Ed Teacher Homestead Elem 1965; 6th-8th Grade Soc Stud Teacher Jac-Cen-Del 1965-66; Sci Teacher Versailles Elem 1968-; *ai:* Delta Kappa Gamma Pres 1988-; South Ripley Classroom Teachers Assn (Membership Chairperson, Negotiator 1985-); Kappa Kappa Kappa (VP 1972-73, Pres 1973-74); St of IN Project SAVE Winner 1974; Natl Energy Ed Dev Project IN Steering Comm; *office:* Versailles Elem Sch R 1 Versailles IN 47042

AVERY, DONNA WYNN, 4th Grade Teacher; *b:* Daytona Beach, FL; *m:* Michael B.; *c:* Michael S.; *ed:* (AA) Assoc of Arts, Daytona Beach Comm Coll 1968; (BS) Elem Ed, FL St Univ 1970; *cr:* 2nd Grade Teacher Bonner Elem 1970-71; 3rd Grade Teacher Cntrl Chrstn 1973-74; 5th Grade Teacher Lackawana Elem 1975-76; 6th Grade Teacher 1978-79; 4th Grade Teacher 1980-Edgewater Elem; *ai:* Edgewater Elem Sch Soc Stud Chairperson; Volusia Cty Rdng Cncl 1978-79; Volusia Educators Assn 1978-; NEA 1978-; FEA 1978-; 1st Bapt Church New Mem Trng 1978-80; 1st Bapt Church Out Reach Leader 1987-88; Grade

Level Chm-1983-87; Human Relations Chm 1979-80; *home:* 1370 Old Mission Rd New Smyrna Beach FL 32168

AVERY, DOUGLAS ALAN, Music Department Chairman; *b:* Constableville, NY; *m:* Susan Jane Cressman; *ed:* (BM) Music Ed, Eastman Sch of Music 1976; (MM) Music Ed, Ithaca Coll 1982; *cr:* Music Teacher Seneca Falls Intermediate Sch 1977-84, Mynderse Acad 1984-; *ai:* Jazz, Rock Ensemble, Fall Play, Music, Vocal Dir; Drama Club Adv; MENC 1976-; ACDA 1985-; IAJE 1987-; *office:* Mynderse Acad 105 Troy St Seneca Falls NY 13148

AVERY, JAMES B., Kindergarten Teacher; *b:* Huntington, NY; *m:* Carol I. Chadwick; *c:* William, Susan, Nancy Schneider, Julee Aguilar, Kris Nelson, Kim Nelson; *ed:* (BA) Psych/Bio, Amherst Coll 1957; Masters Prgm Lesley Coll; *cr:* Specialist US Army Missle Corps 1957-60; Field Engr Sperry Gyro Company 1960-62; Supvr Elect Boat Company 1962-68; Kndgtn Teacher St Vrain Valley Schls 1971-; *ai:* CEA, NEA 1971-; Assisted in Design & Dev of Erie Nature Trail; *office:* Erie Elem Sch PO Box 700 Erie CO 80516

AVERY, JOYCE CANNON, Third Grade Teacher; *b:* Halls, TN; *m:* Paul C. Jr.; *c:* Carol Averly Wilson, Paula Beth; *ed:* (BA) Elem Ed, Union Univ 1965; Memphis St/Union Univ; *cr:* 1st & 3rd Grade Central 1961-64; Teacher Halls Elem 1964-; *ai:* TEA/NEA/LEA 1961-; Alpha Delta Kappa 1976-; Space Wkshp Memphis St; *home:* 202 Wilson St Halls TN 38040

AVERY, VICKI WEST, Chapter I Rdng & Math Teacher; *b:* Pine Bluff, AR; *m:* Bill Drue; *c:* Carmen L. Avery Parks, Jason D.; *ed:* (BS) Commercial Art, Memphis St Univ 1961; (ME) Admin/Supervision, Trevecca Nazarene Coll 1988; *cr:* 1st/2nd Grade Primary Teacher Winchester Sch 1969-70, Blessed Sacrament 1970; 1st Grade Primary Teacher Model Sch 1971-73; 1st-3rd Grade Primary/Chapter I Teacher Michie Elem 1977-; *ai:* Stu Assistance Prgm Comm Mem; Initiator & Supvr Construction of Outdoor Classroom; Teaching Summer Soc Stud Enrichment Prgm 1989-; NEA, TN Ed Assn; Mc Nairy Cty Ed Assn Faculty Rep 1986-87; Elks Ladies Auxiliary Pres 1986-87; 1st United Meth Church Higher Ed Dir 1987-; Beta Sigma Phi Secy, Girl of Yr 1977; Lawrence KS Newcomers Club Pres 1976-77; Career Level Teacher TN Merit Pay System; SACS Evaluation Comm 1986-87; Michie Sch Teacher of Yr Awd 1987; *home:* 2112 Walnut Dr Corinth MS 38834

AVEY, DIXIE WATSON, Teacher; *b:* Como, MS; *m:* Omer Norris; *c:* Deborah Avey Barksdale; *ed:* (BS) Art/Eng, 1957, (MAT) Art, 1983 Memphis St Univ; *cr:* Teacher Briarcrest Chrstn Sch 1990, Memphis City Schls 1957-; *ai:* Art Club & Stu Cncl Spon; Eng Dept Chm; Advisory Comm Art Dept Memphis St Univ; NEA, TEA, WTEA, MEA; Greentrees Civic Assn VP 1980-83; Bellevue Baptist Church Sunday Sch Teacher 1971-; *home:* 6929 Silver Maple Cv Memphis TN 38119

AVILA, HERLINDA SANDOVAL (LOPEZ), Bilingual Teacher; *b:* Flagstaff, AZ; *m:* Jose Estrada Lopez; *c:* Ruben J., Augustine D. Ambriz, Jose L.; *ed:* (BA) Multiple Subjects/Soc Sci, CA St Univ Stanislaus 1974; Licensed Cosmetologist; *cr:* 6th Grade Teacher 1986-87, 5th Grade Teacher 1987-88, 4th Grade Teacher 1988- Richard Valenzuela M/M Sch; *ai:* St Marys Church Religious Class Helper.

AWTRY, GORDON WILLIAM, Social Studies Teacher; *b:* Big Spring, TX; *m:* Carrol Sue Clee; *c:* Aaron, Andy, Allan, Alex; *ed:* (BSED) Phys Ed/Soc Stud, Abilene Chrstn Univ 1972; *cr:* Teacher/Coach Midland Chrstn Sch 1972-; *ai:* Var Ftbl, Var Girls Bsktbl, Var Track Coach; Spon NHS; TX Chrstn Assn 1972-; TX Assn of Private & Parochial Schls 1984-; Jr Achievement of Midland 1982-; *office:* Midland Chrstn HS 2001 Culver Midland TX 79703

AXSOM, GLENDA YINGLING, Fifth Grade Teacher; *b:* Gettysburgh, PA; *m:* Ronald B.; *c:* Mari L., Emily J.; *ed:* (BS) Elem Ed, Millersville 1974; (MS) Developmental Rdng/Remedial Rdng Penn St 1978; Ed, Spec Ed, Cmptr Sci; *cr:* 2nd Grade Teacher 1974-76, 3rd Grade Teacher 1976-78 Fishing Creek Elem; Rdng Specialist Hillside & Fishing Creek 1978-79, Newberry Elem 1979-81; 3rd Grade Teacher 1981-86, 1st Grade Teacher 1987-88 Fishing Creek Elem; 5th Grade Teacher Hillside Elem 1988-; *ai:* W Shore Ed Assn Building Rep 1977-78.

AXT, JOAN S., Economics/History HS Teacher; *b:* Jersey City, NJ; *m:* Charles Mark; *c:* Don, Veronica, Kim Johnson, Karen, Lloyd, Dehn, Mark; *ed:* (BA) His, Montclaire St Coll 1972; Learning Disabilities Kean Coll; Research & Dev Univ of IL Urbana; Early Prevention of Chldhd Ed, Rdng Prgm, Univ IL; Ec & Stock Market, Univ of S FL; *cr:* Rdng/Soc Stud Teacher Orange Mid Sch 1974-78; Rdng Specialist Teacher Jefferson Annex Charlotte Amalie HS 1978-86; Ec/World His Teacher Dixie Hollins HS 1986-; *ai:* Curr 1989-; Attendance Comm 1988-89; Kaleidoscope Club Co-Spon 1988; Delta Sigma Theta 1969-; Prof Womens Assn 1972-; Prof & Civic League of Women Voters 1979-; NAACP 1966-; 12th Grade Ec & Stock Market Game, 1st/2nd Place Pinellas Cty 1987-88, 1st Place 1989, 2nd Place HS Div 1989; *office:* Dixe Hollins HS 4940 62nd St N Saint Petersburg FL 33709

AXWORTHY, BETTY JEAN, 3rd Grade Teacher; *b:* Detroit, MI; *m:* Dwayne; *c:* Karen Zook, Jan, Laura, Robert; *ed:* (BS) Eng/Soc Stud/Music, Wayne St Univ 1949; (MRE) Religious Ed, E Baptist Theological Seminary 1952; *cr:* 1st Grade Teacher Harding Sch 1949-50; Substitute Teacher Livonia Public Schls 1957-63, Natrona Cty Sch Dist 1970-76; 3rd Grade Teacher Verda James Elem Sch 1976-; *ai:* NEA, WY Ed Assn, Natrona Cty Ed Assn 1976-.

AYALA, RONALD PAUL, Teacher of Gifted & Talented; *b:* Hollister, CA; *m:* Marilyn N. De Rose; *c:* Andrea M., Nathal P.; *ed:* (AA) Liberal Stud, Gavilan Coll 1973; (BA) Liberal Stud, San Jose St Univ 1976; Grad Stud CA South Bay Writing Inst; Prof Growth Courses; *cr:* 6th Grade Teacher Glen View Elem Sch 1976-82; 8th Grade Teacher of Gifted & Talented/7th Grade AVANTE Teacher South Valley Jr HS 1983-; *ai:* Girls 8th Grade Vlybl, 7th Grade Bsktbl & 8th Grade Boys Bsktbl Coach 1983-; CA Teachers Assn 1976-; *office:* South Valley Jr HS 385 Ioof Ave Gilroy CA 95020

AYERS, JOHN E., Social Studies Chairman; *b:* Logansport, IN; *m:* Rovena G. Lucas; *c:* Michael, Brian, Kelly, Janalee Ayers Kovacs; *ed:* (BS) Phys Ed/Soc Stud, IN St Univ 1959; (MS) US His, Ball St Univ 1968; Taft Scholar, E KY Univ 1987; *cr:* HS Phys Ed/Soc Stud Teacher/Bsbl Coach Tipton Twp HS 1959-63; HS Soc Stud Teacher/Bsbl Coach Lewis Cass HS 1963-; *ai:* Soc Stud Chm; Var Bsbl; Bsktl Asst; IN HS Bsbl Coaches Assn Region Rep 1968-77, 200 Wins 1976; Lions Club Pres 100 Per Cnt Awd; Little League Pres; SE Ed Assn Pres; Taft Scholar 1987; Elected Walton Town Bd; *office:* Lewis Cass HS St Rd 218 W Walton IN 46994

AYERS, MARYANNE (SMITH), 4th Grade Teacher; *b:* Flora, IL; *m:* C. Ronald; *c:* Brock E., Bryce A.; *ed:* (BS) Ed K-9th, Southern IL Univ 1965; Diagnosing & Remediating Rdng Problems; Calligraphy; Cert As Great Books Leader; *cr:* Kndgtn Teacher 1965-66, 5th Grade Teacher 1966-75, 6th Grade Lang Arts Teacher 1975-78, 5th Grade Teacher 1978-83, 3rd Grade Teacher 1983-84, 4th Grade Teacher 1984- Carl L Barton Elem; *ai:* Classroom Play Dir; Calligrapher for Certificates; Chm Youth Activities Through Optimists Intnl; IL Ed Assn 1965-; Kappa Delta Pi 1965-; Intnl Rdng Assn 1965-75; NEA 1965-; Jr Womans Club Secy 1968; United Church of Christ Vacation Church Sch Co-Dir 1975; Optimists Bd of Dir 1988-89; Youth Activities Chm 1988-89; 1985 Freeburg Jaycees Outstanding Educator Awd; Co-Dir of Liberty Fair to Raise Money for Statue of Liberty Renovation; Citizens for a Drug Free Amer Supporter/Volunteer; *home:* 412 N Pitts-Renois Freeburg IL 62243

AYERS, TERRANCE L., Social Studies Teacher; *b:* Attleboro, MA; *m:* Carole; *c:* Sarah, Stephen; *ed:* (BS) Soc Stud, W MI Univ 1966; (MA) Ed, Northwestern Univ 1970; *cr:* Teacher/Coach Lowell HS 1966-68, Northwestern Univ 1969-70, Fenton HS 1968-; *ai:* Head Bsbl Coach; Asst Bsbl, Ftbl, Wrestling Coach; NEA Life Mem; IEA 1968-; Fellowship Northwestern Univ; Township Trustee; Du Page Cty Regional Planning Commission; *office:* Fenton HS 1000 W Green St Bensenville IL 60106

AYERS, WILLIAM H., Fifth Grade Teacher; *b:* Ft Payne, AL; *m:* Judith Ann; *ed:* (BA) Elem Ed, Jacksonville St Univ 1975; (MA) Elem Ed, Univ of AL 1980; Cert Admin, Jacksonville St Univ 1984; *cr:* Teacher Williams Ave Sch 1975-80, Plainview Sch 1980-; *ai:* 4-H Club Spon; Bsktbl & Ftbl Times Statistician; NEA, AEA 1975-; DEA 1980-; Rainsville Civic Center (Secy, Bd of Dir) 1990; *office:* Plainview HS P O Box 469 Rainsville AL 35986

AYLOR, SUZANNE MARLEY, Vocal Music Teacher; *b:* Ardmore, OK; *m:* David Lynn; *c:* Brian, Christie; *ed:* (BME) Piano, OK Baptist Univ 1971; Post Scndry Stud Rose St Univ; Working Towards MME Cntrl St Univ 1991; *cr:* Vocal Music Teacher Barnes Elem 1971-80, Carl Albert Jr HS 1980-; *ai:* Dir Performing Choirs Carl Albert Jr HS; MENC, ACDA, OMEA; Epsilon Sigma Alpha 1982-; Carl Albert Jr HS Teacher of Yr 1989-; *office:* Carl Albert Jr HS 2515 S Post Rd Midwest City OK 73130

AYLWARD, WILLIAM P., 8th Grade Soc Stud; *b:* Prairie du Sac, WI; *m:* Joan Davidson; *ed:* (BS) Soc Stud/Poly Sci, Univ WI Steven Point 1966; (MS) C&I Ed, Univ WI Madison 1987; Alcohol & Other Drug Act Group Facilitator; *cr:* Substitute Teacher Madison WI Public Sch 1970-; Soc Stud Teacher Sauk Prairie Sch 1972; *ai:* Referee; Sauk Prairie Teachers; NCSS 1980-; WI Cncl for Soc Stud Presenter at Convention 1989; Lake WI C C Bd Mem 1970; *office:* Sauk Prairie Mid Sch 207 Maple St Sauk City WI 52583

AYRES, AUDREY JOHNSON, Reading Teacher; *b:* New Canton, VA; *m:* William H. Jr.; *c:* William III, Chevonne; *ed:* (BS) Elem Ed, St Pauls Coll 1967; (MS) Learning Disability, S CT St Univ 1975; *cr:* 5th/6th Grade Teacher Prince Street Sch 1967-70; 6th Grade Teacher Baldwin Street Sch 1970-73, East Rock Mid Sch 1974-75; Rdng Teacher Sheridan Mid Sch 1975-; *ai:* TAPS Distinguished Sch Service Awd 1986; *home:* 4 Fountain Terr New Haven CT 06515

AYRES, CHARLES LOUIS, High School English Teacher; *b:* Spencer, IA; *m:* Erica Koshiba; *c:* Omay, Jonathan; *ed:* (BA) Eng, MacAlester Coll 1967; (MAT) Eng, Mankato St Univ 1974; Trng Peace Corps 1967-72; Teaching Eng 2nd Lang Micronesian Culture; *cr:* Teacher U S Peace Corps 1967-70, Micronesian Occupational Center 1970-72, Bellingham Public Schls 1974-76, Waseca HS 1976-; *ai:* Wrestling Coach; Drama Jr/Sr CLass Plays; Problem Solving Coach.

AZEVEDO, CLARA MARGARET, HS Bilingual Counselor; *b:* Ripon, CA; *c:* Alan, Loren, Stephen, Ann Gould, Lynn; *ed:* (AA) Span/Phys Ed, Stockton Jr Coll 1945; (BA) Span/Phys Ed, Univ of Pacific 1947; (MA) Ed/Counseling, CA St Univ Stanis 1972; *cr:* Teacher Davis Joint Union HS 1948-49, Escalon HS 1949-50, Adult Evening HS 1951-58; Elem Span Teacher Ripon & River & Atlanta 1961-66; Teacher 1967-75; Bi-ling Cnslr 1975- Modesto City Schls; *ai:* Vlybl, Swimming & Sftbl Coach; Girls League Eng as 2nd Lang & Foreign Exch Stu Adv; Mod Cnslrs Assn Pres 1975-; Delta Kappa Gamma Pres 1988-; Soroptimist Intnl Pres 1990-; Leadership Modesto 1985-86; Our Lady of Fatima Lector 1981-; PTA 1966-75; Selected for Leadership Modesto Class of 1985 & Alumni Group; *office:* Thomas Downey HS 1000 Coffee Rd Modesto CA 95355

AZHAR, ASIF ALI, Math/Physics/Hum Teacher; *b:* Karachi, Pakistan; *ed:* (BA) Physics/Math, Pomona Coll 1984; (MS) Physics, Brown Univ 1986; *cr:* Math/Physics/Hum Teacher Viewpoint Sch 1986-; *ai:* Chess & Video Club Adv; *office:* Viewpoint Sch 23620 Mulholland Hwy Calabasas CA 91302

B

BAAB, LINDA JEANNE (KIRKBRIDE), 6th Grade Teacher; *b:* Fremont, OH; *m:* Kenneth D.; *c:* Rachel, Ethan; *ed:* (BS) Ed, Bowling Green St Univ 1965; Grad Work Lang Art & Childrens Lit; *cr:* Teacher Cloverdale Cmmty Sch 1965-66, Durant Tuuri Mott 1966-68, Pierce Cmmty Sch 1968-; *ai:* Teacher Rep Parent Advisory Cncl; Ski Club Spon; Hall Guard Spon; Adv Pierce Park & Playground Rennovati On; Delta Kappa Gamma 1984-; Flint Jr League 1978-83; Mem Lang Arts Curr Comm Flint Public Schls; Writing Comm Pierce Creative Arts Curr; *home:* 1126 Woodside Dr Flint MI 48503

BAACKE, TIMOTHY ALLEN, Director of Instrumental Music; *b:* Pittsburgh, PA; *ed:* (BS) Music Ed, Edinboro Univ of PA 1982; Vandercook Coll of Music; West Chester Univ; IN Univ; Univ of Pittsburgh; *cr:* Dir of Instrumental Music Conemaugh Township Area HS 1982-88, Bald Eagle-Nittany HS 1988-89, Penn Cambria HS 1989-; *ai:* Marching & Symphonic Band; Jazz Ensemble; PA Music Ed Assn 1982-; Music Educators Natl Conference 1982-; Cadets of Bergen Cty Drum & Bugle Corps 1989; Natl Deans List 1982; Outstanding Young Men of America 1985; *office:* Penn Cambria Sch Dist Jefferson Heights Gallitzin PA 16641

BAADE, MARY ANN A., Business Education Teacher; *b:* Glen Cove, NY; *ed:* (AAS) Secretarial Sci, Nassau Comm Coll 1981; (BS) Bus Ed, 1983, (MS) Educl Technology, 1986 C W Post Coll; *cr:* Bus Teacher Briarcliffe Secretarial Sch 1983-86, Elmont Memorial HS 1986-; *ai:* FBLA Adv; Nassau Cty Bus Ed Assn 1983-; *office:* Elmont Memorial HS 555 Ridge Rd Elmont NY 11003

BAAREE, GLORIA NAJEEBAH, Asst Prgm Devlpr/Pre-Sch Coord; *b:* Yazoo City, MS; *M:* Amin N.; *c:* Candace, Basim; *ed:* (BS) Elem Ed, 1973, (MS) Spec Ed, 1976, (EDS) Spec Ed, 1986 Jackson St Univ; MS Ed Admin Leadership Inst for Women; *cr:* Spec Ed Teacher Como Elem/Jr HS 1976-79, Spec Ed Teacher Canton HS 1985-89; Asst Spec Ed Pgrm Dev/Pre-Sch Coord Canton Public Schls 1989-; *ai:* Cncl for Excptnl Children 1985-; MS Ed Assn 1985-; *office:* Canton Public Schls 403 E Lincoln St Canton MS 39046

BABATSKY, ANGELINE CARRATO, Kindergarten Teacher; *b:* Shenandoah, PA; *m:* Joseph John Jr.; *c:* Jeffrey, Jenna, Janel, Joelle; *ed:* (BA) Elem Ed, 1971, (MED) Ed, 1976 Bloomsburg Univ; *cr:* Kndgtn Teacher Mahanoy Area Sch Dist 1971-; *ai:* PSEA, MAEA; GSA Asst Leader 1989-.

BABATSKY, JOSEPH JOHN, English Teacher; *b:* Shenandoah, PA; *m:* Angeline Theresa Carrato; *c:* Jeffery, Jenna, Janel, Joelle; *ed:* (BS) Scndry Eng, Bloomsburg 1970; Grad Stud Field of Eng, Bloomsburg; *cr:* Eng Teacher Shenandoah Valley Jr/Sr HS 1970-; *ai:* Spelling Bee Coord; NEA; PSEA Treas 1981; Knights of Columbus Friendship Fire Cty; St George Church (Lector, Lay Minister); *home:* 524 W Laurel Frackville PA 17931

BABB, JUDY INGRAM, Mathematics Teacher; *b:* Norfolk, VA; *c:* Christine L., T. Austin; *ed:* (BS) Scndry Math, E Carolina Univ 1972; (MAED) Scndry Math, Pembroke St Univ 1990; *cr:* Math Teacher W Craven HS 1972-73, Hoke HS 1973-77, Anne Chesnutt Jr HS 1977-; *ai:* Spon Algebra I, Geometry, Technology Teams; NC Assn of Educators 1987-; NCTM, NC Cncl Teachers of Math 1986-; Anne Chesnutts Teacher of Yr 1985-86; Finalist Cumberland Cty Outstanding Educator 1985-86; Participant NC Center for Advaancement of Teachers; *home:* 5711 Loch Ness Ct Fayetteville NC 28304

BABB, MARY FINLEY, Math Teacher/Curr Asst; *b:* Easley, SC; *m:* Richard L.; *c:* Amy, Rick; *ed:* (BA) Elem Ed, Furman Univ 1965; (MA) Math Ed, Clemson Univ 1970; Grad Studies Math, Calculator & Cmptr Pre-Calculas Project; Advanced Placement Calculus Trng, OH St; *cr:* 6th/7th Grade Teacher Flat Creek Elem Sch 1965-67; 8th/9th Grade Teacher Monaview Jr HS 1967-70; Math Teacher Berea HS 1973-84, Liberty HS 1984-; *ai:* Mu Alpha Theta, Math, Jets Spon; Girls Track Coach; CBE Evaluator; St Algebra Competency Comm; OH St Math Project Teacher; SC Assoc of Advanced Placement Math Teachers Pres 1987-88; SC Presidential Awd in Math 1988; Alpha Delta Kappa Teachers

(Pres/VP), 1978-79; SC Acad of Sci Awd for Excl in Sci/Math Teaching 1988; NCTM 1974-; SC Assn of Math Teachers Presenter 1974-; Math Assn of America 1987-; Natl Cncl of Supervisors of Math 1988-; Cncl of Presidential Awardees in Math 1988; SC Target 2000 Grant for Technology in Math & Sci Classes; Presidential Grant Math; Univ of Chicago Algebra I Pilot Teacher; Berea HS Teacher of Yr 1979; Liberty HS Teacher of Yr 1988; *office:* Liberty HS 319 Summit Dr Liberty SC 29657

BABBITT, GERALD ALLEN, Band/Music Director; *b:* San Antonio, TX; *m:* Cheryl Anne Hansen; *c:* Ryan, James, Karen; *ed:* (BM) Music Ed, 1964, (MS) Admin/Music Ed, 1966 TX A&I Univ; Post Grad Courses Music Ed & Admin; *cr:* Band Dir Memorial Jr HS 1964-67, Pearsall HS 1967-73; Dir of Bands/Music Round Rock Ind Sch Dist 1973-79, WestLake HS 1980-85, Hays HS 1985-; *ai:* Hays HS Symphonic Band, Marching Band, Hays CISD Band, Music Ed Hays CISD Dir; Hays HS Academic Affairs Comm Mem; Phi Beta Mu St Bd of Dirs 1990; TX Music Educators Assn (St Bd of Dirs 1969-71, St Music Advisory Comm 1986-), Leadership & Achievement Awd 1982; Natl Bandmasters Assn 1981-, Citation of Excl 1982; TX Music Adjudicators Assn St Bd of Dirs 1988-; TX Bandmasters Assn 1964-; TX Univ Interscholastic Exec Secy 1975-; Great Hills Baptist Church Orch Dir 1980-; TX A&I Univ Distinguished Alumni Recognition 1984; Commendations from TX Governor Bill Clements; TX House of Rep; TX Governor Mark White, US Rep Jake Pickle, Mayor of Austin; First US HS Band to Tour Republic of China 1984; Honored in Washington DC by Rep Pickle; UIL Sweepstakes Awd for 23 Yrs; Selected Outstanding HS Band in TX 1981; 1st Runner Up for St Marching Championship 1984, 1986-87; Won Many Band Festivals throughout Southern US; *home:* 222 Maple Dr Buda TX 78610

BABCOCK, MARY ELIZABETH (STEINER), Retired Primary Teacher; *b:* French Township, IN; *m:* Harold G.; *ed:* Curr Primary Grades, 1939, (BS) Elem Ed, 1947, (MA) Elem Ed, 1957 Ball St Teachers Coll; *cr:* 1st-3rd Grade Teacher One Room Sch French Township 1939-41; 2nd Grade Teacher Petroleum IN 1941-48, Portland City Schls 1948-66; 3rd Grade Teacher Bluffton-Harrison MSD 1966-82; *ai:* Delta Kappa Gamma Recording Secy 1976-78; Wells Cty Retired Teachers Assn Secy 1985-89; IN Retired Teachers Assn; First United Meth Church; Natl Society Daughters of Amer Revolution (Registrar 1976-86, Vice Regent 1986-88, Regent 1988-); *home:* 1320 Old Creek Trl Bluffton IN 46714

BABCOCK, MARY SHEPARD, Elem Teacher/Asst Principal; *b:* Worcester, MA; *m:* Luther; *ed:* (BS) Ed, UVM 1962; *cr:* Rural Teacher S Walden VT 1937-39, Joes Brook 1940-41; 2 Room Rural Teacher Stamford VT 1941-42; Walden Heights 1955-57; Swanton VT 1957-; *ai:* Local, St, NEA 1957-; Lib Trustee 1980-; Historical Trustee 1985-; Congregational Church 1957-; Teacher of Yr Awd Franklin Cty 1988; *home:* 9 Furman Pl Swanton VT 05488

BABCZAK, NANCY ELIZABETH, English Teacher; *b:* Sondra, CA; *ed:* (BA) Eng, Univ of CA Davis 1969; *cr:* Eng Teacher Washington Jr HS 1971-83, Salinas HS 1983-; *ai:* Newspaper, Yrbk, Jr Class Adv; Dir Stu Body Act; Curr Revision Comm; CATE 1984-; GATE 1982-85; *office:* Salinas HS 726 S Main St Salinas CA 93901

BABICH, IVAN PAUL, Mathematics Dept Chairman; *b:* Aliquippa, PA; *m:* Margaret Jean Mc Elhaney; *c:* Robert, Kathy, Paul; *ed:* (BE) Ed, Duquesne Univ 1957; *cr:* Teacher Hopewell Area Sch Dist 1957-60, Center Area Sch Dist 1960-; *ai:* Stu Cncl, Yrbk, Newspaper Spon; Jr HS to Mid Sch Transition Coord; Center Ed Assn, PA St Ed Assn, NEA, Natl Mid Sch Assn; Valovi Tamburitzans Music Dir 1970-; Beaver Valley Jr Tamburitzans Music Dir 1980-; Distinguished Teacher Awd 1989; *office:* Center Area Jr HS Baker Rd Ext Monaca PA 15061

BABLES, MARY HILL, Teacher; *b:* Jackson, MS; *m:* Edward E.; *c:* Davida L. Moore, Winston; *ed:* (BS) Lang Art, (MA) Eng, Jackson St Univ; Linguistics Wkshp MS St Univ; Foreign Lang Inst Emory Univ; Certificate Drug Abuse Wkshp CA St San Bernardino; Wkshp Teaching Eng Second Lang; *cr:* Teacher Biloxi Public Schls; Adjunct Instr Jackson St Univ; Tutor Tougoloo Coll Learning Center; Teacher Hesperia Jr HS; *ai:* Former Dir Organizer of Hesperia Tutorial Prgm; Substitute Teacher Hesperia Jr HS Tutorial Prgm; Mem Hesperia Soc Club; NEA, Hesperia Ed Assn 1981-; NCTE 1989-; CA Teachers Assn 1979-; Natl Cncl of Negro Women Secy 1988-89; Emmanuel Temple AME Church Mem; Mountain High Rdng Assn; Poem Published New Amer Poetry 1989; Active Participant of Annual Gradiating Sr; Employee of Month 1988; Former Mem of Sigma Tau Delta; *office:* Hesperia Jr HS 10275 Cypress St Hesperia CA 92345

BABY, BRIAN CHRISTOPHER, Art Teacher; *b:* Cleveland, OH; *m:* Lois Jean Martin; *c:* Justin, Erin; *ed:* (BFA) Sculpture, 1968, (MFA) Photography, 1972, (BA) Art Ed, 1977 OH St Univ; *cr:* Art Teacher Mt Vernon HS 1977-; Assoc of Instruction Kenyon Coll 1983-; *ai:* In The Know Adv; OH Art Ed Assn 1977-; Society for Photographic Ed 1973-; Inter-Society Color Cncl 1988-; *home:* 433 Walnut View Dr Sunbury OH 43074

BACA, GEORGE, JR., Biology/Science Teacher; *b:* Sewickley, PA; *m:* Linda K. Sroka; *c:* Andrew; *ed:* (BS) Bio, 1975, (MED) Guidance/Counseling, 1977 Duquesne Univ; Cmptr Stud Cores I, II, III, Univ of Pittsburgh & Prof Enrichment Prgm Duquesne Univ; *cr:* Bio/Life/Phys Sci Teacher Montour Sch Dist 1975-; Supplemental Part Time Adjunct Professor Duquesne Univ 1990; *ai:* Jr HS Club Adv; NSTA, PA Sci Teachers, PA St Ed Assn; *office:* Montour Sch Dist Porters Hollow Rd Coraopolis PA 15108

BACCILE, LAWRENCE, Latin Teacher; *b:* Philadelphia, PA; *ed:* (BA) Fr, La Salle Coll 1952; (MA) Fr - Cum Laude, Univ Laval Quebec 1962; Univ de Valencia Espana Diploma 1963; Estudio Intntl Sampere Madrid Diploma 1973; *cr:* Fr/Latin Teacher Millville HS 1952-55, Wantagh HS 1955-59; Eng/Span Teacher Coll Moderene de Garcons Bourges France 1959-61; Fr/Span Teacher St Josephs Univ 1963-69; *ai:* Latin Club; Greenhouse Asst; Millville HS Bowling Club Most Valuable Player 1986; NJEA, NEA 1980-; Fullbright Travel Grant & US Dept of St Fr Government Teaching Awd Bourges France 1959-61; Rockefeller Fellow Amer Acad in Rome 1988; *home:* RD 4 Box 749 Franklinville NJ 08322

BACCUS, AMELIA DIANE DUNHAM, Third Grade Teacher; *b:* Toledo, OH; *m:* Lennon; *c:* Lennon A. I; *ed:* (BASC) Speech Comm/Eng, Bowling Green St Univ 1978; (MDPAD) Human Resource Dev/Public Admin, Bowie Univ 1991; Numerous Ed & Trng Cert in Areas of Abuse, Counseling, Crisis Intervention, Family Dynamics; *cr:* Youth/Teen Dir Young Womens Chrstn Assn 1978-81; Youth Life Educator/Caseworker Lucas Cty Childrens Services Bd 1981-84; Elem/Jr HS Teacher St Margaret Sch 1984-; *ai:* Playwright, Song Writer & Performer; St Margaret Sch Spec Prgms Coord 1984-; Childrens Dance & Singing Groups Dir; Tutorial Peer Tutoring Coord; Foster Parent Drug Awareness Prgm OH & MD; Bowling Green Alumni Assn Mem 1978-; FCC Awd Bowling Green Univ 1975; NECA Awds Service, Cath Sch Involvement; Civic Achievement Awd; Young Republican Club; *office:* St Margarets Catholic Schl 410 Addison Rd S Seat Pleasant MD 20743

BACHAND, WAYNE RENE, 7th Grade Mathematics Teacher; *b:* New Bedford, MA; *m:* Patricia Rossi; *c:* Joshua; *ed:* (BA) Spec Ed, Bridgewater St 1973; *cr:* Spec Ed/Resource Teacher 1973-82, 7th Grade Math Teacher 1982- Mastricola Mid Sch; *ai:* Coord Environmental Ed Prgm; Comm to Re-Organize Current Resource Room & Spec Stud Schedule; Merrimack HS Bsktbl Asst Coach 1986-88; Mastricola Mid Sch Bsktbl Coach 1980-85; NEA, NH Ed Assn 1986-; Merrimack Teachers Assn 1986-, Teacher of Yr 1979; S Little League Coach 1988-; S Soccer League Asst Coach 1989-; *office:* Mastricola Mid Sch Baboosic Lake Rd Merrimack NH 03054

BACHMAN, CONNIE ELIZABETH, Mathematics Teacher; *b:* Richmond, VA; *c:* Sherri E., Wendi L.; *ed:* (BS) Bus Management/Ec/Math, Frederick Coll 1968; Grad Stud William & Mary, Univ of VA, VCU; *cr:* Teacher Liberty Jr HS 1969-72, J Sargeant Reynolds Comm Coll 1978-86, Harry F Byrd Mid Sch 1972-; *ai:* Activity Period Prgm Coord; Stu Decorating Specialists Spon; Local, St, Natl Math Conference Speaker; GRCTM 1975-; VCTM Co-Ed 1986-87; NCTM 1986-; Henrico Cty Gilman Awd Winner 1989; Byrd Mid Sch Teacher of Yr 1988-89; Article Published; Whos Who in Amer Ed 1989; *office:* Harry F Byrd Mid Sch 9400 Quioccasin Rd Richmond VA 23233

BACHMAN, WEN, Electronics Instructor; *b:* Bainbridge, NY; *m:* Beverly Jean Mc Kerracher; *c:* Mark, Rob; *ed:* (AAS) Chem/Chemical Technology, Broome Technical Coll 1962; (BS) Physics/Earth Sci/Scndry Ed, SUCO 1968; (MS) Media Comm Technology, SUNY 1974; Engineering Courses CO St Univ; Electronics Courses Front Range Comm Coll-Larimer Cty Center; *cr:* Sci Dept Chm/Teacher S Kortright Cntrl Sch 1972-78; Sci Teacher Thompson Sch Dist 1978-79; Research & Dev Engineering Technician NCR Microelectronics 1981-85; Scndry Electronics Instr Front Range Comm Coll-Larimer Cty Center 1985-; *ai:* Voc Industrial Clubs of America Adv 1985-; Front Range Comm Coll-Larimer Cty Center Faculty Senate Exec, Facilities, Safety Comms; CO Teachers Assn 1989; CO Industrial Assn, Technology Ed Assn 1990; Teacher Visitation Awd; *office:* Front Range Comm Coll 4616 S Shields PO Box 2397 Fort Collins CO 80522

BACHMANN, DON, Mathematics Teacher; *b:* Hammond, IN; *ed:* (BS) Math, Valparaiso Univ 1970; (MS) Math, Purdue Univ 1978; *cr:* Teacher Morton Mid Sch 1970-71, Spohn Mid Sch 1971-72, Hammond Voc-Tech 1972-76, Hammond HS 1976-77, Hammond Clark 1978-; *ai:* Boys & Girls Tennis Coach; IN Lake Shore Conference Coach of Yr 1985-89; *office:* George Rogers Clark HS 1921 Davis Ave Whiting IN 46394

BACHRODT, MICHAEL P., Chemistry Teacher; *b:* Rockford, IL; *m:* Esther; *c:* Kira, Stefan, Gretchen; *ed:* (BS) Biochem, 1979, (MSED) Scndry Ed, 1982 N IL Univ; Working towards CAS Degree Cmptr Ed, Natl Coll of Ed; *cr:* Chem Teacher William Fremd HS 1980-; *ai:* Frosh Gymnastics Coach; Scholastic Bowl Asst Spon; IL Assn of Chem Teachers 1980-; Fremdchem Newsletter Publisher; Demonstrations Presenter; *office:* William Fremd HS 1000 S Quentin Rd Palatine IL 60067

BACICA, CRISTINA GARCIA, Mathematics/Chemistry Teacher; *b:* Freeport, TX; *m:* David L.; *c:* Nicholas; *ed:* (BA) Chem, Univ of Houston Clear Lake 1984; Grad Work in Math; *cr:* Chem/Math Teacher Brazosport HS 1984-; *ai:* NCTM, Gulf Coast Cncl Teachers of Math; *office:* Brazosport HS P O Drawer Z Freeport TX 77541

BACK, JAMES MICHAEL, Assistant Band Director; *b:* Ft Thomas, KY; *m:* Andrea Marie; *ed:* (BME) Music, Morehead St Univ 1981; *cr:* Band Dir Sequoyah HS 1984-85; Asst Band Dir Walton HS 1985-; *ai:* Marching, Symphonic, Concert, Jazz Band; Percussion Ensemble; Phi Mu Alpha; Percussion Instr & Arranger Spirit Atlanta Drum Bugle Corps; *home:* 2308 River Station Terr Woodstock GA 30188

BACK, SANDRA ANN, Fourth Grade Teacher; *b:* Jeremiah, KY; *ed:* (BA) Elem Ed, Berea Coll 1962; Art Classes; Weaving Classes; *cr:* Elem Teacher Blackey Sch 1962-65, Charleston Sch 1965-66, Blackey Sch 1965-71, Letcher Elem 1971-; *ai:* Letcher Cty Teachers Organization 1962-; KY Ed Assoc 1962-; NEA 1962-; *office:* Letcher Grade Sch Letcher School Rd Letcher KY 41832

BACKMAN, CAROL ANN, 7th Grade Math Teacher; *b:* New York, NY; *ed:* (BS) Ed, SUNY Plattsburgh 1969; (MA) Ed, Hofstra Univ 1974; Coop Learning; *cr:* Math Teacher Islip Public Schls 1969-; *ai:* 7th Grade Math League Adv; Co Chairperson Dist Observation-Evaluation Comm; NCTM; Suffolk Cty Math Teachers Assn; Islip Teachers Assn Vp; *office:* Islip Mid Sch 215 Main St Islip NY 11751

BACON, GEORGE SEWELL, Science/Health Teacher; *b:* Bangor, ME; *c:* Mary E.; *ed:* (BS) Family Life/Health Ed, Univ of ME Orono 1975; Emergency Medical Technician, CPR & Advanced First Aid Instr, Dropout Prevention; Stu Assistance Prgm, Charter Springs Hospital; *cr:* Kndgtn Teacher Bangor Childrens Home 1975-79; Sci Teacher Crystal River HS 1979-; *ai:* Co Spon Ecology Club; Teacher Rep Stu Assistance Prgm; Teachers as Advs Prgm Steering Comm; Textbook Selection Comm; Teachers Assn Pres 1985-88; FL Assn Sci Teachers; Volunteer Firefighter Line Officer 1979-89; *office:* Crystal River HS 1205 NE 8th Ave Crystal River FL 32629

BACON, MARYLAN K., Fourth Grade Teacher; *b:* Houston, TX; *ed:* (BS) Elem Ed, 1967, (MA) Eng, 1972 Hardin-Simmons Univ; *cr:* 4th Grade Teacher Memorial Elem 1967-69; 3rd Grade Teacher Hopkins Elem 1969-70; 4th/5th Grade Teacher Jane Long Elem 1971-; *ai:* Campus Action Plan, Rdng Fundamental Comm; Abilene Educators Assn, PTA, Tx St Teachers Assn Life Mem; *home:* 3826 Wilshire Abilene TX 79603

BACON, MICHAEL C., English Teacher; *b:* Newark, OH; *m:* Beverly Jean Yonker; *c:* Lissa, Michael Jr., Katie; *ed:* (BA) Eng, Univ of Dubuque 1965; (MAT) Calvin Coll 1978; Teaching of Writing, Instructional Theory into Practice; *cr:* Eng Teacher E Kentwood HS 1978-; Frosh Comp Teacher Grand Valley St Univ 1987-; Assoc Mem of Grad Faculty W MI Univ 1989-; *ai:* Co-Spon Teen Inst; Yrbk Adv; Lang Arts Curr Comm Co-Chairperson; Co-Dir of Writing Process; Peninsula Writers Founding Pres 1984-87; MI Writing Project Asst Dir 1986-88; Kentwood Ed Assn Public Relations Chairperson 1980-86; Lions Club Pres 1984-85; Cmmty Acts Comm Chm 1984-85; Several Articles & Poems Published; *office:* E Kentwood HS 6178 Campus Park Ave SE Kentwood MI 49508

BACON, RON, Mathematics Teacher/Dept Chair; *b:* Newport Beach, CA; *m:* Cathlene; *c:* Cory; *ed:* (BA) Phys Ed, San Diego St Univ 1980; Teaching Credenital Phys Ed, 1981, Add-On Credential Math, 1983 Long Beach St Univ; *cr:* Teacher Stanford Mid Sch 1981-; *ai:* Bsktbl Coach; Long Beach Teachers Assn; *office:* Stanford Mid Sch 5871 Los Arcas Long Beach CA 90815

BACOTE, EUGENE CHARLIE, JR., Mathematics Teacher; *b:* Society Hill, SC; *m:* Mary Geiger; *c:* Tanisha, Lanola; *ed:* (BS) Math, SC St Coll 1970; (MED) Math Ed, Univ of SC 1980; Math Specialist Cert, Advanced Placement AB Calculus Cert, Francis Marion Coll 1989; *cr:* Math Teacher Rosenwald HS 1970-72, Brunson Dargan Jr HS 1972-; *ai:* Darlington Cty Night Learning Lab Adult Ed Instr; NEA, SC Ed Assn, Darlington Cty Ed Assn 1970-; Brunson Dargan Jr HS Teacher of Yr 1988; Nom Presidential Awd Academic Excl 1988, 1989; *home:* Rt 3 Box 411 Effingham SC 29541

BADA, NANCY L. (MOENCH), 5th Grade Teacher; *b:* Metuchen, NJ; *m:* Daniel A.; *ed:* (BA) Elem Ed/Early Chldhd/Art Ed, Trenton St Coll 1977; Sch Counseling, Glassboro St Coll; Numerous Courses at Learning Inst; CPR Cert; Drug & Alcohol Heres Looking at You 2000 Cert; *cr:* Teacher Runnemede Bd of Ed 1977-; *ai:* Adopt a Grandparent Prgm; Homework & Cmptr Clubs; Teacher of Yr Governors Awd 1986-87; *office:* Bingham Sch 1st Ave Runnemede NJ 08078

BADEAUX, MARGARET MARY, History Dept Chairperson; *b:* Houston, TX; *ed:* (BA) His, 1971, (MA) His 1979 Sam Houston St; Cmptr Technology & Archaelogy; *cr:* Teacher Attucks Jr HS 1972-73, Smith Mid Sch 1974; *ai:* Natl Jr Honor Society; Sch Store; Comm Club; Ho Co Soc St Parlimentarian 1983 -; TX COS S 1983-; NCSS 1983-; TX Archaelogy 1988-; Mary Rose Society 1981-; Smithsonian 1975-; Executive Bd HCSS 1983-; Wrote Advanced Placement Test 8th His; Dist & Regional His Fair Judge; *office:* E O Smith Mid Sch 1701 Bringhurst Houston TX 77020

BADER, CONRAD F., Jr HS Soc Stud/Math Teacher; *b:* Rockville Center, NY; *m:* Carol Fedyk; *c:* Julie, Janice, Lynette; *ed:* (BA) Ec, Union Coll 1959; (MA) Ed, St Univ of NY Albany 1963; *cr:* 7th Grade Teacher Bell Cty Schls 1960-61; Jr HS Soc Stud Teacher Sharon Springs Cntrl 1961-; *ai:* Extracurricular Act Treas; NEA Local Pres 1980-; Dorloo Meth Church Trustee 1980-; *office:* Sharon Springs Cntrl Sch P O Box 218 Sharon Springs NY 13459

BADGER, CHRISTINE STEDING, 6th-8th Grade Grammar Teacher; *b:* Galveston, TX; *m:* George Jr.; *c:* Jessica E., Joseph C.; *ed:* (BA) Ger/Eng, TX Luth Coll 1973; (MAT) Ger/Linguistics, SW TX St Univ 1975; Studied at Goethe Univ Freiburgam Breisgau West Germany; *cr:* Teaching Asst SW TX St Univ 1973-75; Eng Teacher Hitchcock HS 1975-76; Teacher Trinity Episcopal Sch 1981-; Eng/Ger Instr Galveston Coll 1982-; *ai:* Yrbk

Adv; Literary Magazine Ed; 1st Luth Church (Choir 1979-, Vestry 1982-85, Sunday Sch Music Coord 1989-); Academic Excl Booster Club Top 50 Teachers 1985, 1987-88, 1990; *office:* Trinity Episcopal Sch 720 Tremont Galveston TX 77550

BADGLEY, JUDETH BIRDWELL, Learning Consultant; *b:* Cheyenne, WY; *m:* Michael; *c:* Sara P., Brian J.; *ed:* (MA) Ed Admin, N AZ Univ 1987; Assertive Discipline, Lee Canter; Essential Elements & Clinical Supervision, Madeline Hunter; Goal Setting/See You at the Top, Zig Ziggler; *cr:* Teacher 1979-87, Admin 1987-88 Crane Elem Dist; Part-Time Professor N AZ Univ 1989-; Learning Consultant Sucess Express 1988-; *ai:* Vlybl, Bsktbl & Sftbl Coach; Stu Cncl & Cheerleading Adv; Merit Pay, Curr, Staff Dev Comms; New Teacher Coord; Crane Ed Assn, AZ Ed Assn Secy; Assn for Supervision & Curr; Phi Delta Kappa; Yuma Planning Task Force; GSA; Beta Sigma Phi; AZ Finalist Teacher in Space; Whos Who in Amer Colls & Among Amer Educators; *home:* 1239 40th Dr Yuma AZ 85364

BADINA, VALERIE W., Computer Department Chair; *b:* Jacksonville, FL; *c:* Chet I.; *ed:* (AA) Liberal Art, Dayton Beach Comm Coll 1969; (BS) Elem Ed, FL St Univ 1971; (MS) Elem Ed, Stetson Univ 1977; Inservice Stud Cmptr Sci Ed; Sci Ed, FIT; Problem Solving & Cmptr, Univ of OR; *cr:* Teacher Woodward Avenue Elem 1971-73; Enrichment Resource Teacher De Land Enrichment Center 1973-77; Teacher Long-Lake Helen Elem Sch 1977-85; Cmptr Dept Chairperson Silver Sands Jr HS 1985-89; Cmptr Teacher Deltona Mid Sch 1989-; *ai:* Drama Club, Performing Arts Club, Sch Talent Show Spon; Dept Chm Deltona Mid Sch 1989-; Curr & Cmptr Courses Guidelines Comms; Textbook Reviewer; Developed Silver Sands Cmptr Curr; Phi Delta Kappa, FL Assn Instructional Computing, Intnl Cncl for Cmptrs in Ed, ASCD, Volusia Cty Assn of Sci; FL Educl Technology Conference (Prgm Comm 1988-, Volusia Cty Liaison 1989-, St Dept of Ed Liaison 1989-); Christa Mc Auliffe Fellowship 1988-89; Whos Who in Amer Ed 1988, 1989; Whos Who of Amer Women 1989-; Teacher of Yr 1989; TOPS Grant Writer & Recipient 1988; Wkshp Conductor; *office:* Deltona Mid Sch 250 Enterprise Rd Deltona FL 32725

BADINGER, TAMI JO-VIGUE, Spanish Teacher; *b:* Spokane, WA; *m:* Bruce Allan; *c:* Brooke L.; *ed:* (BA) Eng/Span, WA St Univ 1980; Grad Stud; *cr:* Teacher Central Valley Sch Dist 1981, East Valley Sch Dist 1982-83, Spokane Public Schls 1986-; *ai:* Var Chrldr & Jr Var Chrldr Adv; Foreign Lang Club Adv; WEA 1981-; Iris & Supvr Club 1984-; Kappa Kappa Gamma 1976-; *office:* Joel E Ferris HS E 3020 37th Spokane WA 99223

BADOLATO, NICHOLAS FRANCIS, Art Teacher; *b:* New Britain, CT; *m:* Patricia Czellecz; *c:* Nicholas J., Marcus C., Trisha L.; *ed:* (BA) Elem Ed, 1969; (MS) Art Ed, 1976 Central CT St Univ; *cr:* 3rd Grade Teacher 1969-79; 2nd Grade Teacher 1979-88; Art Teacher 1988- Memorial Elem Sch; *ai:* Career Incentive Comm; Strategic Planning Comm-Building Project; CT Ed Assn; NEA; Good Apple Awd 1989; *office:* Memorial Elem Sch Smith St East Hampton CT 06424

BAEDER, ALBERT PHILIP, Science Department Chairman; *b:* Philadelphia, PA; *m:* Nancy; *c:* Dorothy, Jason, Nyla; *ed:* (BA) Biological Sci/Phys Sci, Seattle Pacific Univ 1968; (MA) Counseling & Guidance, 1977, (MA) Admin, 1979, Pt Loma Coll; *cr:* Teacher Maranatha HS 1968-79; Prin Seattle Chrstn HS 1979-82, W Chrstn Sch 1982-85; Dept Chm Whittier Chrstn HS 1985-; *ai:* Sr Class & CA Schlsp Fed Spon; Faculty Soc Chairperson; NSTA; Music Published; *office:* Whittier Chrstn HS 2300 W Worth Ave La Habra CA 90631

BAER, JENNIFER K. (HUGHES), Fourth Grade Teacher; *b:* Lafayette, IN; *m:* Philip O.; *c:* Jay, Jared, John P.; *ed:* (BA) Elem Ed, 1975, (MS) Elem Ed, 1989 Purdue Univ; *cr:* 1st Grade Teacher 1975-79, 4th Grade Teacher 1984- Tri Cty Schls; *home:* R 2 Box 132 Wolcott IN 47995

BAERG, ELIZABETH SLOCUM, Mathematics Teacher; *b:* Glendale, CA; *m:* Robert De Wayne; *c:* Marlene A., Donna J.; *ed:* (BA) Physics, 1962, (MA) Physics, 1964 La Sierra Coll; *cr:* Math Teacher/Guidance Cnslr Indiana Acad 1964-66; Math Teacher Monterey Bay Acad 1966-; *ai:* NCTM 1964-; CMC 1966-; Alumnus of Yr La Sierra Alumni Assn 1985; LLU, Sch of Ed Zapara Excl in Teaching Awd 1989; Cntrl CA Conference of SDA; *office:* Monterey Bay Acad 783 San Andreas Rd La Selva Beach CA 95076

BAETHGE, SAM J., Mathematics Teacher; *b:* Tulsa, OK; *m:* Edwina J. Rockman; *c:* Kathryn, Barbara; *ed:* (BS) Math, TX Luth Coll 1962; *cr:* Math Dept Chm Southwest HS 1976-83; Teacher Clark HS 1983-85; Math Dept Chm Southwest HS 1985-88; Teacher Sci Acad of Austin 1988-; *ai:* Sci Acad of Austin Math Teams Coach; TX Math League Dir; Amer Regions Math League Meet TX Teams Coach & SW Regional Rep; NCTM 1967-; Math Assn of America 1986-; Outstanding HS Teacher Awd Rose-Hulman Inst of Technology 1989; Published Math Problem Solutions; *home:* 1504-A Braes Ridge Austin TX 78723

BAGGARLY, BRUCE DAVID, Social Studies Teacher; *b:* New Bedford, MA; *m:* Patricia Ann Kaczorowski; *c:* David, Steven, Kathryn; *ed:* (BA) His, Univ of MA 1959; (MED) Ed, Bridgewater St Coll 1962; Grad Stud Brown Univ, Gettysburg Coll, Univ of MA; *cr:* Soc Stud Teacher Keith Jr HS 1959-62; Dept Chm 1968-71, Soc Stud Teacher 1962- Dartmouth HS; *ai:* Human Services Volunteer Prgm Coord; Schlsp & Awds Comm Chm; DEA, MTA, NEA, Cncl for Soc Stud; PTO Bd Mem 1970-72; Little League Coach 1972-80; Democratic Town Comm Mem 1974-76; Horace Mann Grant; Exemplary Prgm Honoree; *office:* Dartmouth HS 366 Slocum Rd North Dartmouth MA 02747

BAGGELAAR, LINDA MILLER, 7th Grade Teacher; *b:* Los Angeles, CA; *m:* William C.; *c:* David; *ed:* (AA) General, El Camino 1972; (BS) General Ed, 1974, (MS) Ed, 1975 Univ of S CA; Admin Credential; Quest Intnl Trng; *cr:* 6th Grade Teacher 1976-85, 7th/8th Grade Teacher 1986- Hawthorne Sch Dist; *ai:* Positive Incentive Comm 1989-; *office:* Yukon Intermediate Sch 13838 S Yukon Ave Hawthorne CA 90250

BAGGETT, ALLEN, Soc Stud/Amer His Teacher; *b:* Castleberry, AL; *m:* Karen Liebeknecht; *c:* Julie, Matthew, Sarah; *ed:* (AA) Bus Management, Tarrant Cty Jr Coll 1980; (BA) Scndry Ed/Soc Sci Composite, 1983, (MS) Scndry Ed/Soc Sci Composite, 1987 Univ of S AL; *cr:* Teacher Citronelle HS 1984-88, Mattie T Blount HS 1988-; *ai:* His Club Spon; Ftbl & Golf Coach; NCSS 1989-; Mobile Cty Ed Assn; Seminar Grants 1987; *home:* RR 1 Box 328H Beverly Jeffries Hwy Citronelle AL 36522

BAGGETT, CONNIE EDLIN, Business Education Teacher; *b:* Clarksville, TN; *m:* Kenneth Lawrence; *c:* Kara, Kyle; *ed:* (BBA) General Bus, Austin Peay St Univ 1981; *cr:* Secy Woodlawn Elem 1985-86; Teacher Stewart Cty HS 1986-; *ai:* Cmptr Club Spon; Adult Ed Teacher; Stewart Cty Teacher Assn (Secy, Treas) 1990; Natl Teachers Assn, TN Teacher Assn 1990; *home:* 104 Lilac Ct Clarksville TN 37042

BAGGETT, GLORIA WIX, US History Teacher; *b:* Kilgore, TX; *m:* Frank; *c:* Frank B. Jr.; *ed:* (AS) His, Government, Kilgore Jr Coll 1968; (BS) His, Government, Stephen F Austin St Univ 1970; Prof Growth Hrs; *cr:* Teachers Aide 1970-75; Teacher 1975- Kilgore Jr HS (Renamed Maude Laird Mid Sch); *ai:* TSTA Rep 1975-76; Awarded PTA-Terrific Teachers Local & State Level TX 1984; *office:* Maude Laird Mid Sch 2500 Shasta Way Kilgore TX 75662

BAGGETT, KAY BRYAN, Biology/Life Science Teacher; *b:* Greenwood, MS; *m:* Gregory Davis; *ed:* (BS) Scndry Eng Ed MS St Univ 1969; Scndry Sci Ed/Bio & General Cert Univ of S MS 1983; *cr:* 2nd-4th Grade Eng Teacher W Jefferson HS 1969; 8th Grade Eng Teacher Center Jr HS 1970-71; Bio/Life Sci/Amer His/Earth Sci Teacher Ocean Springs Jr HS 1983-; *ai:* Sci Club, SADD Spon; Under 19 Girls Soccer Coach; Audubon Society; Greenpeace; Guest Speaker Gulf Islands Natl Seashore; MTAI Evaluator; Teacher of Yr 1990; Star Teacher 1986; Participant Energy Wkshp MS Power Company 1988; *office:* Ocean Springs Jr HS Government St Ocean Springs MS 39654

BAGGETT, KERRY J., Mathematics Teacher; *b:* Springfield, TN; *ed:* (BS) Bus Ed, W KY Univ 1980; (MAED) Curr/Instruction, Austin Peay Univ 1985; *cr:* Teacher Lecento Mid Sch 1981-82, White House Mid Sch 1980-81, 1982-84; Math Teacher Northwest HS 1985-; *ai:* Frosh Boys Bsktbl Coach 1989-; Sr Prom Coord 1989-; Sr Class Coord 1988-; NCTM 1988-; NEA 1980-; White House Mid Sch PTO 1980-84, Teacher of Yr 1983-84; White House Sch Beta Club 1983-84, Teacher of Yr 1983-84; TN Beta Club Quiz Bowl Coord 1988-89; Northwest HS Beta Club Founding Spon 1986; *home:* 3119 Caribou Dr Clarksville TN 37043

BAGGS, CHERYL A., German Teacher; *b:* Philadelphia, PA; *m:* Robert E. Jr.; *ed:* (BA) Ger, Ursinus Coll 1965; (MA) Ger, Middlebury Coll 1969; Clark Univ 1976; Goethe Inst Courses Boston 1981-82, Berlin 1986; Harvard Univ 1986-87; *cr:* Ger/Latin Teacher Cinnaminson HS 1965-66; Eng Teacher Sabeischule Munich Germany 1966-67; Ger Teacher Cherry Hill HS 1968-71, Shrewsbury HS 1972-79, Natick HS 1980-; *ai:* German Club Adv; Ger Amer Partnership & Exch Prgms Teacher & Coord; Amer Assn Teachers of Ger (Treas 1976-80, Natl Testing Commission Mem 1981-84) 1972-, Certificate of Merit 1989; MA Foreign Lang Assn 1980; Horace Mann Grant 1987; Natick Public Schls Distinguished Educator 1986; Amer Assn of Teachers of Ger Chaperone Natl Awd Winners to Germany 1975-82, 1988; *office:* Natick HS 15 West St Natick MA 01760

BAGILEO, GERALD JAMES, Teacher/Admin Assistant; *b:* Montclair, NJ; *m:* Marie Hammond; *c:* Anthony, Michael, Dina; *ed:* (BA) His, Rutgers Univ 1966; (MA) Admin/Supervision, Kean Coll 1981; *cr:* 7th/8th Grade Teacher St Josephs R C Sch 1966-68; 5th/6th Grade Teacher 1968-83, 7th/8th Grade Teacher/Admin Asst 1983- Union Avenue Mid Sch; *ai:* Bsbl, Soccer; Gifted & Talented, Affirmative Action, Eng Curr Comm; NJEA; Learning Disabilities Assn Monmouth Cty (Dir Summer Camp Prgm, CAMP REAP, Exec BD Mem) 1973-; *office:* Union Avenue Mid Sch 1639 Union Ave Hazlet NJ 07730

BAGNARDI, KATHYANNA MARSHALL, 4th Grade Teacher; *b:* Margaretville, NY; *m:* Carl; *c:* Vito, Stefano; *ed:* (BA) Educl Psych, SUCO 1972; *cr:* Kndgtn Teacher 1972-83, 1st Grade Teacher 1983-89, 4th Grade Teacher 1989- Gilboa Conesville; *ai:* Faculty Assn Secy; Growing Healthy Certificate; Essentials of Teaching Trng & Certificate; CIMS Trng; *home:* 1 Cold Spring Ln Stamford NY 12167

BAHEN, DENNIS M., 7th-8th Grade Soc Stud Teacher; *b:* Steubenville, OH; *m:* Linda Archer; *ed:* (AA) Liberal Art, OH Valley Coll 1972; (BA) Soc Stud, W Liberty St 1974; (MA) Educl Admin, Univ of Dayton 1984; *cr:* 11th/12th Grade His/Government Teacher Strasburg HS 1974-78; 7th/11th Grade His Teacher Stanton HS 1978-82; 9th Grade Civics Teacher Crescent City HS 1982-83; 7th/8th Grade His Teacher Ft Frye HS 1983-; *ai:* Stanton Head Bsktbl, Bsbl Coach 1980-82, Ftbl Coach 1978-82; Ft Frye Head Bsktbl Coach 1984-86, Head Gents Sftbl Coach 1988-; Sftbl Coaches Assn 1988; Beverly Village Cncl 1988-; Knights of Columbus 1988; *home:* P O Box 713 Beverly OH 45715

BAHNER, PAUL DAVID, Science Teacher; *b:* Hamilton, OH; *m:* Debra R. Zians; *c:* Stephaine, Nathan, Daniel, Matthew; *ed:* (BS) Sci Ed, OH St Univ 1972; Elem Ed, 1984, (MA) Elem/scndry Admin, 1985 Xavier Univ; Sci Alliance, Natl His Museum 990; *cr:* 8th Grade Sci Teacher Greenhills Mid 1973-89; Summer Sch Dir GHFP Sch Dist 1983-85; 8th Grade Sci Teacher Greenhills Forest Park Mid 1989-; *ai:* Mid Sch Sci Fair Dir; GFP Sch Dist Mentor Prgm; NEA, OEA Mem 1973-; NSTA Mem 1985-; Outstanding Teacher Dist Awd 1986 & 1990; SW OH Region Teacher of Yr Runner-Up Miami Univ Awd; *office:* Greenhills-Forest Park Mid Sch 825 Waycross 825 Waycross Rd Forest Park OH 45240

BAHNER, RICHARD JOHN, Math Department Chair; *b:* Sedalia, MO; *m:* Janice Baker; *c:* Katherine, Ann, Christina; *ed:* (BS) Math, Rockhurst Coll 1974; (MA) Math, SW MO St Univ 1978; *cr:* Teacher Sacred Heart HS 1975-; *ai:* Var Soccer & Ftbl Coach; Asst Athletic Dir; Math Team Spon; Cmptr Coord; NCTM 1985-; MO Cncl of Teachers of Math; NCEA 1975-; Cath Educator of Yr 1988; Instr for Jeff City Diocesan Summer Honors Prgm; *office:* Sacred Heart HS 416 W 3rd Sedalia MO 65301

BAHR, SANDRA, Science Teacher/Dept Chair; *b:* Washington, MO; *m:* David Paul; *c:* Justin; *ed:* (BS) Botany, 1980, (MA) Sci Ed, 1984 NE MO St Univ; *cr:* Asst Instr NE MO St Univ 1982-84; Teacher 1983-, Teacher/Dept Chairperson 1987- Kirksville R-III Sr HS; *ai:* Sci Club & Quiz Bowl Spon; Prof Dev & Prins Faculty Advisory Comm; Sci Teachers of MO, NSTA, NABT; *office:* Kirksville R-III Sr HS 1300 S Cottage Grove Kirksville MO 63501

BAILEY, ALICE W., Mathematics Teacher; *b:* Nelsonville, OH; *m:* Rand E.; *ed:* (BS) Elem Ed, Edinboro St Coll 1974; Various Subjects; *cr:* 5th-8th Grade Teacher Richwood Grade Sch 1975-78; Math Teacher Richwood Jr HS 1978-; *ai:* Awds/Certificate Comm; WVEA, NEA; Presbyn Church Elder 1989-; Beta Sigma Phi Pres 1980-81; 1st WV Teachers Forum Cty Rep; *office:* Richwood Jr HS 1 Valley Ave Richwood WV 26261

BAILEY, ANN, Home Economics Teacher; *b:* Baileysville, WV; *c:* Jeanne, Marie, McGill; *ed:* (BA) Home Econ, 1961; (BA) Eng, 1961 Concord Coll; (MS) Clothing & Textiles, 1965; (Special Degree) Supervision of Voc Teachers, 1976 Kent St Univ; *cr:* Teacher Baileyville Elem Sch 1961-62; Lincoln H S 1962-75; McKinley Sr H S 1976-86; Lehman Jr H S 1987-; *ai:* Adv Future Homemakers of America; Amer Home Econ Assn 1961-; NEA 1962-; OH Educators Assn 1962-; Canton Prof Educators Assn 1962-; Canton Board of Realtors 1973-77; *office:* Lehamn Jr H S 1120 15th St N W Canton OH 44703

BAILEY, ARNOLD B., Computer Coordinator; *b:* Plainfield, NJ; *ed:* (AB) Math, Bowdoin Coll 1969; (MS) Cmptr Applications, Dartmouth Coll 1983; Digital Equipment Corp; *cr:* Math Teacher 1970-80, Cmptr Dept Chm 1980-, Cmptr Coord 1986- Milford Sch Dist; *ai:* Math Team Adv St, Regional Championships; Cmptr Team Adv Natl, Regional Awds; NH Assn Cmptr Educators Founding Exec Bd Educator of Yr 1983; NH Assn Computer Coord Exec Bd; NCTM ATMNE; Summer Grad Sch Faculty Dartmouth Coll 1984-; NSF Grant Integration of Comptr Technology; NH Technology Grant Project Coord; Articles in Cmptr Teacher Local, Regional Publications; *office:* Milford Area Hs West St Milford NH 03055

BAILEY, BERNICE MITCHELL, Chapter I Reading Teacher; *b:* Lincoln Cty, TN; *m:* Roy Lee; *c:* Johnny, Carol, Tommy, Donna; *ed:* (BA) Elem Ed, Athens St Coll 1975; (MA) Elem Ed, Univ of N AL 1980; *cr:* Chapter I Rdng Teacher E Limestone 1987-; *ai:* Chapter I Rdng Wkshps; St Jude Mathathon; 3rd & 4th Grade Rdng Coord; AEA, NEA; PTO; Baptist Church Sunday Sch Teacher.

BAILEY, BEVERLY SUDOL, Fifth Grade Teacher; *b:* Nashua, IA; *m:* Donald Henry; *c:* Terry P, Anita M. Sullivan, Kirk D.; *ed:* (BA) Elem Ed, Wartburg Coll 1972; UNT 1977-79, 1982, 1986-87; Coll of St Thomas 1980; Mary Crest 1987; Drake Univ 1988; Viberto 1989; *cr:* Elem Teacher Rural Sch 1952-55, 1957-58; 5th Grade Teacher Fredericksburg Cmmty Sch 1967-; *ai:* Sci Curr, Peer Coaching, Thinking Skills Comm; ISEA, NEA; FEA (Secy 1985-86, Building Rep, Elem Building Rep); Little Brown Church Supt Cradle Roll 1987-; *home:* RR 1 Box 227 Nashua IA 50658

BAILEY, CAROL ALBRIGHT, 7th Grade English Teacher; *b:* Athens, TX; *m:* Jack Thomas; *c:* Ginger Gross, Brandon B.; *ed:* (BS) His/Eng, E TX St Univ 1971; (MS) Ed/Rdng, Univ of TX Tyler 1977; Comparative Ed/Studying Ed in UK 1985; Admin Cert; *cr:* Eng/His Teacher Malakoff Ind Sch Dist 1972-74, Athens Ind Sch Dist 1974-77; Athens Ind Sch Dist 1978-; *ai:* Co-Spon Natl Jr Honor Society; UIL Oral Rdng Coach; TX Classroom Teachers Assn, Athens Classroom Teachers Assn.

BAILEY, CYNTHIA BOND, French Teacher; *b:* Norfolk, VA; *m:* Harold Robert; *c:* Jillian G.; *ed:* (BA) Eng/Fr, Randolph-Macon Womans Coll 1984; *cr:* Fr Teacher Gretna HS 1984-; *ai:* Cheerleading Spon; Fr Club Adv; *office:* Gretna HS P O Box 398 Gretna VA 24557

BAILEY, DEBORAH M., Science Teacher; *b:* Rolla, MO; *m:* David Charles; *c:* Tanya J., Sabrina R.; *ed:* (BS) Bio, Sul Ross St Univ 1978; *cr:* Research Technician FMC Corporation 1978; Cty Reference Librarian Val Verde Cty Lib 1978-83; Sci Teacher Del

Rio HS 1983-; *ai:* Sci Fair Coord; ATPE 1988-; STAT 1986-; *office:* Del Rio HS 100 Memorial Dr Del Rio TX 78840

BAILEY, DOUGLAS VINCENT, American Government Chair; *b:* Cheyenne, WY; *m:* Lauri Jean Adams; *c:* Nicole, Ryan, Katelyn; *ed:* (BS) Soc Stud/Gen Sci, Boise St Univ 1977; *cr:* Earth Sci Teacher Melba HS 1977-79; US His Teacher Jefferson Jr HS 1979-81; Bio/Phys Sci Teacher Oakley HS 1981-83; Bio/US His Teacher Minico HS 1983-86; Amer Government Teacher Burley HS 1986-; *ai:* Asst Var Ftbl, Head Var Bsbl, Stu Cncl Adv; ID Coaches Assn 1981-, Coach of Yr 1982; Optimists 1981-83; Burley HS Teacher of Yr 1988; *office:* Burley HS #1 Bobcat Blvd Burley ID 83318

BAILEY, ELAINE MOORE, 6th-8th Grade English Teacher; *b:* Chester, GA; *m:* Charles A.; *c:* Charles A. II, Lea A.; *ed.* (BA) Mid Grades Ed, 1979, (MS) Mid Grades Ed, 1982, Specialist Mid Grades Ed, 1985 GA Southwestern; *cr:* Teacher Chester Elem Sch 1979-; *ai:* Cty Consolidation Comm; Dodge Cty Prof Educators (Reporter 1989-, Local Pres 1986-88); Chester Garden Club; Chester Baptist Church; *home:* PO Box 207 Chester GA 31012

BAILEY, EMILY KATTNER, Math/Computer Teacher; *b:* Waco, TX; *m:* Dana M.; *c:* Chris, Brenda, Lou Ann; *ed:* (BS) Math, 1959, (MA) Math, 1964 Baylor Univ; Summer Sci Inst, Randolph Macon Coll, Advanced Academic Trng; *cr:* Math Teacher Carter Jr HS 1959-61, Lutcher Stark HS 1961-62; Physics Teacher Richfield HS 1962-70; Math Teacher Valley Mills HS 1970-; *ai:* Future Teachers of America & Class Spon; 4-H Leader; Technology Comm Chm; Assn of TX Prof Educators (Treas, Pres) 1980-; TX Cmptr Ed Assn 1989-; Nom for TX Cmptr Teacher of Yr 1990; *office:* Valley Mills HS PO Box 518 Valley Mills TX 76689

BAILEY, EVELYN RIDER, Fifth Grade Teacher; *b:* Terre Haute, IN; *m:* William O.; *c:* Ryan C., Laurel J., Darren M.; *ed:* (BS) Early Chldhd, 1973, (MS) Early Chldhd, 1977 S IL Univ; *cr:* Kndgtn Teacher 1973-85, 5th Grade Teacher 1985- Jonesboro Elem; *office:* Jonesboro Elem Sch Cook Ave Jonesboro IL 62952

BAILEY, GARY D., Mathematics Department Teacher; *b:* Portsmouth, OH; *ed:* (BS) Industrial Art/Math, E KY Univ 1983; *cr:* Teacher Minford HS 1983-; *ai:* Ftbl & Bsktbl Coach 1983-; Bsbl Coach 1983-87; OEA 1984-; Eagles 1990; *home:* 7210 Gallia Sciotoville OH 45662

BAILEY, JAMES W., Vocational Agriculture Teacher; *b:* Holt, MO; *m:* Helen Hartell; *c:* Becky Bailey Findley, Cathy Wolkenhauer, Susan Silgailis, J. William; *ed:* (BS) Crop Sci, CA Polytechnic Univ Pomona 1956; (MA) Ed, CA Polytechnic Univ San Luis Obispo 1963; *cr:* Teacher Hanford HS 1958; Voc Agriculture Teacher Fullerton Union HS Dist 1958-; *ai:* FFA Adv; Jr Livestock Adv Orange Cty Fair; CA Agriculture Teachers Assn 1958-; Disciples of Christ Church Chm of Bd; CA Teacher of Excl; Honorary Amer Farmer; Orange Cty Teacher of Yr; *home:* 314 W Whiting Fullerton CA 92632

BAILEY, JANE, English Teacher; *b:* Dyersburg, TN; *m:* Perry; *c:* Casey Essary, Troy; *ed:* (BS) Ed, Univ TN Martin 1977; (MS) Eng, Memphis St Univ 1985; Several Wkshps on Teaching Writing; *cr:* Teacher Crockett Cty HS 1978-, Dyersburg St Comm Coll 1988-; *ai:* Literary Magazine Adv; Beta Club Past Spon; Speech Coach; Helped Write Eng Curr.

BAILEY, JOE KENNETH, Mathematics/Art Teacher; *b:* Greenville, KY; *m:* Ann Shelton; *c:* Dena, Laura, Ryan; *ed:* (BA) Art, 1968, (MA) Cnslr Ed, 1976 W KY Univ; *cr:* Teacher Lewisburg Elem & HS 1968-; *ai:* 8th Grade & Jr HS His Club Spon; NEA, KEA, LCEA; *office:* Lewisburg Elem Sch Stacker St Lewisburg KY 42256

BAILEY, JOHN WALLACE, JR., Social Studies Teacher; *b:* Strawberry Plains, TN; *m:* Cynthia Gale Matthews; *c:* Holly Hicks, Amanda, Kevin Hicks; *ed:* (BS) Phys Ed, Carson Newman Coll 1975; Elem Certificate Elem Ed, 1975, (MS) Educl Admin/ Supervision, 1983 Univ of TN; TN Instructional Model 1988; *cr:* 1st-5th Grade Phys Ed Teacher Rush Strong Elem 1975-83; 6th Grade Math/Soc Stud Teacher 1983-88, 7th/8th Grade Soc Stud Teacher 1988- Rush Strong Mid Sch; *ai:* Ftbl & Track Coach; Offensive Coord; TSSAA Bsktbl Ofcl; TN Ed Assn 1975-; Jefferson Cty Ed Assn 1975-87; TN Scndry Schls Athletic Assn 1987-; PTO 1975-; Rush Strong Booster Club (Pres 1986-88) 1980-; Jr Pro Bsktbl Dir 1981-; Strawberry Plains Optimist Club 1987-89; TN Homecoming Awd 1986; *office:* Rush Strong Mid Sch Rt 3 Box 128 Strawberry Plains TN 37871

BAILEY, JULIA TUNSTILL, Lang Art/Soc Stud Teacher; *b:* Athens, AL; *m:* James Douglas; *c:* Melissa A. Looney, Angela D. Barnes, Anita J., Jamie L.; *ed:* (BS) Elem Ed, Athens Coll 1974; (MA) Elem Ed, AL A&M 1985; Working on AA Certificate; *cr:* 4th Grade Teacher 1974-87, 5th/6th Grade Teacher 1987 Johnson Jr HS; *ai:* Recycling & Drug Awareness Comm; NEA, AL Ed Assn, Limestone Cty Ed Assn 1974-; *home:* Rt 14 Box 96 Athens AL 35611

BAILEY, KAREN CAMPBELL, 5th Grade Teacher; *b:* Clifton Forge, VA; *m:* William A.; *c:* Julie A., Amy L.; *ed:* (BED) Elem Ed, Concord Coll 1969; WV Coll of Grad Stud; *cr:* Peterstown Elem 1968-72, 1974-; *ai:* WV Ed Assn 1967-; Peterstown Meth Church (Trustee 1988-, Pastor Parish Comm 1990).

BAILEY, KATHY CARVALHO, Third Grade Teacher; *b:* Fayetteville, NC; *m:* William Franklin; *c:* William N.; *ed:* (BS) Early Chldhd, 1979, (MED) Early Chldhd, 1986 Campbell Univ; Mentor Teaching; Math Lead Teacher; *cr:* 3rd Grade Teacher S Harnett Primary 1979-; *ai:* PTA Exec Cncl; Media Comm; Math Lead Teacher; NC Assn of Educators Building Rep 1979-; NC Cncl Teachers of Math 1989-; Intnl Rdng Assn 1984-; Friends of Lib 1989-; Teacher of Yr 1989-; *office:* S Harnett Primary Sch Rt 1 Box 222 Bunnlevel NC 28323

BAILEY, LILLIE C., Chapter I Resource Teacher; *b:* Sparkman, AR; *m:* Everett; *c:* James E.; *ed:* (BA) Elem Ed, Bishop Coll & AM&N Coll 1958; (MS) Elem Ed, IN St Univ 1967; *cr:* Elem Teacher Sparkman Trng Sch 1957-59, Gary Cmmty Schls 1959-86; Rdng Resource Teacher/Chapter I Supvr Gary Schls 1986-; *ai:* In-Service Wkshp; Stu & Elem Cncl; Gary Rdng Cncl Membership 1984-87, Attendance 1984-87; Assn Supervision Curr Soc Stud; Phi Delta Kappa Public Relations 1984-88, Excl 1986; Natl Assn Black Educators 1986-; Ec/Government St Grant 1965; *office:* Gary Cmmty Sch Tolleston Sch 2700 W 19th Ave Gary IN 46404

BAILEY, MARY LOU, Social Studies Teacher; *b:* Klamath Falls, OR; *ed:* (BS) Ec/Geography, Univ of OR 1983; Grad Work in Ed, Univ of OR; Working Toward Masters S OR St; *cr:* Rural Womens Extension Agent US Peace Corps Kenya 1983-85; Stenographer Puget Sound Natl Bank 1985-86; Soc Stud Teacher Mazama HS 1988-; *ai:* Stus for Stu Asst Adv; 20/20 Grant Comm; NCSS 1988-; OR Stu Public Interest Group 1979-80, 1987-88; MA Stu Public Interest Group Project Coord 1980-81; Oregonians for Frohnmayer Election Comm 1989-; OR St Schlp to Recruit Teachers; Teacher of Month 1989 Presented by Mazama Stu Cncl; *office:* Mazama HS 3009 Summers Ln Klamath Falls OR 97601

BAILEY, MARY ROSE (HALL), Sixth Grade Teacher; *b:* Wheelwright, KY; *w:* Wallace R. (dec); *ed:* (BS) Elem Ed, W KY Univ 1968; (MA) Elem Ed, E KY Univ 1971; Multi-Media & Cooperative Learing Wkshp; Cmptr Trng Class; *cr:* 4th Grade Teacher 1968-69, 6th Grade Teacher 1969- Paintsville City Sch; *ai:* NEA, KEA; Paintsville Ed Assn Treas 1969-72; *office:* Paintsville Elem Sch 2nd St Paintsville KY 41240

BAILEY, PATRICIA HENSLEY, Mathematics Teacher; *b:* Shreveport, LA; *w:* James Albert (dec); *c:* Larry Abshire, Daryle Abshire, Donna Cookson; *ed:* (BA) Elem Ed, 1965, (MED) Ed, 1969, (MED) Educl Technology, 1978 Mc Neese St Univ; *cr:* Teacher 1965-, Math Dept Chairperson 1987- W W Lewis Mid Sch; Supervising Teacher Mc Neese St Univ 1983-86, 1989-; *ai:* Coach Mathcounts; Math Chairperson; Substance Abuse Coord; Calcasieu Ed Assn, NCTM, LA Teachers Assn, NEA 1965-; LA Assn Teachers of Math Parish Rep 1965-; Nom Teacher of Yr 1987, 1988; Teacher of Yr 1988; Personalities of South 1971; Dist Math Coach of Yr 1987; *office:* W W Lewis Mid Sch 1752 Cypress St Sulphur LA 70663

BAILEY, PATTI A., Science Lab Instructor; *b:* Atlanta, GA; *ed:* (BS) Ed, Univ of TN Knoxville 1977; Memphis St Univ; *cr:* Sci/ Phys Ed Teacher Frayser Baptist HS 1978-81; Health/Phys Ed Teacher Auburndale Sch 1981-82; Sci Teacher Crump Elem Sch 1982-87; Sci Lab Instr Kirby Mid Sch 1987-; *ai:* Sci Dept Chairperson; Sci Fair Judge; TN Dept Ed Curr Comm 7th-8th Grade Sci Ed; Shelby Cty Sci Teacher Assn 1989-; NSTA 1988-; Shelby Cty Ed Assn 1982- Schlsp Awd 88; *office:* Kirby Middle School 6670 E Raines Rd Memphis TN 38115

BAILEY, PEGGY ANN PRESLEY, Fourth Grade Teacher; *b:* Welch, WV; *m:* Donny L.; *c:* Jennifer; *ed:* (AA) Beckley Jr Coll 1965; (BS) Scndry Ed, Bluefield St Coll 1971; Grad Studies WV Coll; *cr:* Phys Ed Teacher Anawalt Elem 1968-69; 1st Grade Teacher Iaeger Elem 1969-70; 5th Grade Teacher 1971-88; 4th Grade Teacher Anawalt Elem 1988-; *ai:* Sch Advsry Cncl; WV Ed Assn; *home:* PO Box 13 Skygusty WV 24883

BAILEY, PHYLLIS ROMANS, US History Teacher; *b:* Hensley, WV; *m:* Carl A.; *c:* Patricia A. Warren, Carl A. II, J. Thomas, Rebecca J. M.; *ed:* (BA) His, Mary Washington Coll 1975; (MED) Guidance & Counseling, Univ VA 1985; *cr:* Teacher Fauquier HS 1975-; *ai:* Drug Awareness Seminars 1982-83; *office:* Fauquier HS 705 Waterloo Rd Warrenton VA 22186

BAILEY, RICHARD LEE, English Teacher; *b:* Clearfield, PA; *m:* Sharon Marlene Dutton; *c:* Kirk; *ed:* (BA) Scndry Ed, Southeastern Coll 1976; (MED) Rdng Specialization, Kent St Univ 1980; *cr:* Eng Teacher Warren Chrstn 1976-; Media/ABE Teacher Trumbull Cty Joint Voc 1985-; *ai:* Jr-Sr Adv; Testing Coord; *office:* Warren Christian Sch 2640 Parkman Rd NW Warren OH 44485

BAILEY, SHIRLEE STORM FREEMAN, Vocal Music Specialist; *b:* Elk City, OK; *m:* Benjamin N.; *c:* Jeanne A. F. King, Margaret E. F. Copley; *ed:* (BME) Vocal Music Ed, OK St Univ 1952; (ME) Music Ed, SW OK St Univ 1975; Kodaly Methodology Cert, Silver Lake Coll 1987; Early Chldhd Ed, Silver Lake Coll, Univ of OK; *cr:* 1st-12th Grade Vocal Music/7th/8th Grade Eng Teacher Navajoe Sch 1964-66; 1st-6th Vocal Music Teacher Rivers Elem Sch 1967-; *ai:* Navajoe Sch Jr Class Spon; Altus Supt Advisory Comm; Altus Music Teachers Chm; Music Educators Natl Congress; Organization Kodaly Educators; OK Music Educators Assn; OK Kodaly Educators (Treas, SW Dist Rep 1989-; Amer Guild Eng Handbell Ringers 1980-84; Amer Choral Dirs Assn St Elem St 1982-85; United Meth Women Honorary Life Membership 1986; Altus Assoc Chrstn Ministries Outstanding Churchman Awd 1983; 1st United Meth Church Handbell Choir Dir 1978-88; Masonic Teacher of Today Awd 1988; Rivers Teacher of Yr Awd 1987-88, 1988-89, 1989-; Pres Advisory Cncl; Pres Advisory Bd; Childrens Choirs St Chairperson; Natl Kodaly Conference Chairperson 1987; OMEA Hall of Fame Comm 1989-; Altus Cmmty Chorus; *office:* Rivers Elem Sch Altus A F B Altus OK 73521

BAILEY, TAMALA GRAHAM, Eighth Grade Teacher; *b:* Murphy, NC; *m:* Jimmy; *c:* Tessa; *ed:* (BA) Mid Grade Ed, 1983, (MS) Mid Grade Math, 1990 W Carolina Univ; *cr:* 6th-8th Grade Teacher Ranger Elem 1983-; *ai:* Annual Spon; NCAE; *office:* Ranger Elem Sch Rt 6 Box 93 Murphy NC 28906

BAILEY, VICTORIA SEIRSDALE, Fourth Grade Teacher; *b:* Tallahassee, FL; *m:* Glen A.; *c:* Adam, Kyle; *ed:* (BS) Elem Ed, 1979, (MED) Elem Ed, 1986 Univ of S MS; MS Teacher Assessment Instrument Evaluator; *cr:* 4th Grade Teacher E Marion Elem 1979-; *ai:* Elem Stu Cncl Spon 1987-89; Kappa Delta Pi 1978-79; NCTM 1983; MS Prof Educators 1987-; Beta Sigma Phi 1990; Hattiesburg Historical Neighborhood Assn 1986-; *home:* 509 Ronie St Hattiesburg MS 39401

BAILEY, WILLIAM O., Physics/Chemistry Teacher; *b:* Terre Haute, IN; *m:* Evelyn J. Rider; *c:* Ryan C., Laurel J., Darren M.; *ed:* (BS) Chem, 1968, (MS) Chem, 1972 E IL Univ; *cr:* Physics/ Chem/Math Teacher Sullivan IL HS 1968-69, Westfield IL HS 1969-71; Phsics/Chem/Calculus Teacher Anna-Jonesboro HS 1972-; *home:* Box 689 Jonesboro IL 62952

BAILIE, ANN (NESEMANN), United States History Teacher; *b:* Algoma, WI; *m:* Keith; *c:* Matthew, Sara A.; *ed:* (BA) His, Marquette Univ 1964; Bradley Univ; *cr:* Eng/His Teacher Dodson Jr HS 1964-65, Kubasaki Jr HS 1967-68, Morton JR HS 1968-69; His Teacher Sholes Mid Sch 1965-67, 1969-; *ai:* WI Cncl for Soc Stud; St Marks Luth Church; *office:* Sholes Mid Sch 4965 S 20th St Milwaukee WI 53221

BAILY, BETH FILGO, Home Economics Teacher; *b:* Dallas, TX; *m:* Mel D.; *c:* Brendan; *ed:* (BS) Home Ec, 1984, (MS) Home Ec, 1986 TX Tech Univ; Lift Impact Trng for Crisis Intervention Team; *cr:* Teacher Berkner HS 1986-; *ai:* FHA & Teen Drug Addicts Support Group Spon; Crisis Intervention Team Lift Leader; Chrldr Coach & Spon; Richardson Ed Assn 1986-; Voc Home Ec Teachers Assn of TX 1987-89; Assn of TX Prof Educators 1986-88; *office:* Berkner HS 1600 E Spring Valley Richardson TX 75081

BAIN, ANGELA CHARLENE (WESTON), Fifth Grade Teacher; *b:* Knoxville, TN; *m:* Steve C.; *c:* Steven B., Stephanie B.; *ed:* (AS) Elem Ed, Walters St 1979; (BS) Elem Ed, Carson-Newman 1981; (MS) Curr & Instruction, Univ of TN Knoxville 1986; *cr:* 5th Grade Teacher West Elem 1982-; *ai:* Patrol Supvr; Inservice Comm; Perfect Attendance Comm 1989-; Lakeway Rdng Cncl 1982-; Cherokee Hills Baptist Church Pianist; PTO Treas 1987-88; Teacher of Yr 5th-8th Grade 1987-88; *office:* West Elem Sch 235 W Converse St Morristown TN 37814

BAIN, PATRICA GILLEY, High School Teacher; *b:* Madison, TN; *m:* R. Douglas; *c:* Diana; *ed:* (BA) Eng, Belmont Coll 1974; Graduate Study, Mid TN St Univ, Trevecca Coll; *cr:* Teacher Pioneer Acad 1974-80, Donelson Acad 1980-83, Davidson Acad 1983-; *ai:* 8th Grade Class Spon; Yrbk & Newspaper Adv; *office:* Davidson Academy 1414 Old Hickory Blvd Nashville TN 37207

BAINBRIDGE, ANNE LUKING, 5th Grade Teacher; *b:* Louisville, KY; *M:* Carl Jr.; *c:* Michael W.; *ed:* (BA) Ger, 1975; (MED) Rdng Specialist, 1984 Univ of Louisville; Mid Sch Soc Stud; *cr:* Sub Teacher Jefferson Cnty Public Schls 1975-76; 8th Grade Teacher St Ignatius 1976-82; 5th Grade Teacher St Athanasius 1982-; *ai:* Coord-Intermediate Level; Writing Coach - KY Academic Assn Governors Cup Competition; NCEA 1976-; Greater Louisville Cncl-Intnl Rdng Assn 1976-86; *office:* St Athanasius Sch 5915 Outer Loop Dr Louisville KY 40219

BAIONE, JAMES ANTHONY, Band Director; *b:* Philadelphia, PA; *m:* Barbara Slaski; *c:* Jimmy, Thomas, Joseph; *ed:* (BA) Applied Music, 1961, (BA) Music Ed, 1962 Combs Coll of Music; (MA) Music Ed, Glassboro St Coll 1972; *cr:* Music/Orch/Band Teacher Florence HS 1963-64; Music Dir/Band Teacher Gateway Regional HS 1964-72; Music Dir Delmar HS 1973-; *ai:* Sr Band, Choir, Jazz Ensemble; Natl Music Ed Assn, DE St Assn; St Francis de Sales Church Band Instr 1988-89; *office:* Delmar HS 8th & Jewel Sts Delmar DE 19940

BAIR, JAMES F., English Teacher; *b:* Pittsburgh, PA; *m:* Janet Machalowski; *c:* Joanna, Emily; *ed:* (BA) Eng, Harvard Univ 1972; (MS) Eng, S Ct St Univ 1987; *cr:* HS Eng/Math/Fr Teacher Grace Heritage Chrstn Sch 1980-83; HS Eng Teacher Chrstn Heritage Sch 1984-; *ai:* NHS; Class Spon; Quiz Team; Christianity Lit Conference; Full Gospel Businessmens Fellowship Chapter Secy 1979-84; The Gideons; CT Ornithological Assn; Articles Published; *office:* Christian Heritage Sch 575 White Plains Rd Trumbull CT 06611

BAISDEN, GENEVA C. HAGER, Retired Teacher; *b:* Ramage, WV; *m:* Harold A.; *c:* Ellen C. Mezerski; *ed:* (BA) Sci Ed, Marshall Univ, Morris Harvey Univ, Charleston Univ 1960; Lang Art Inservice; *cr:* Jr HS Teacher Logan Cty, Boone Cty Schls 1950-89; Substitute Teacher Boone Cty Schls; *ai:* Vlybl, Chrldr, Newspaper Coach; Luting Aspirations of Children 1961; Delta Kappa Gamma Publicity Chm; United Meth Church (Teacher, Youth Leader), Many Minute Awds; Ladies Society Pres; PTA Life Honorary 1974, Teacher of Yr; Local Newspaper Teacher of Yr 1989; *home:* Rt 1 Box 284 Danville WV 25053

BAITY, JANE TRIMNAL, 8th Grade Lang Arts Teacher; *b:* Thomasville, NC; *m:* Robert Glenn Jr.; *ed:* (BA) Intermediate Ed, High Point Coll 1973; (MA) Intermediate Ed, NC A&T St Univ 1982; Effective Teacher Trng; Teacher Performance Appraisal System Trng; Mentor Support Trng; *cr:* 7th Grade Lang Arts/Soc Stud Teacher Fair Grove Elem 1973-75; 7th-8th Grade Lang Arts/Dept Chairperson 1975-79, 8th Grade Lang Arts/Dept Chairperson 1979-88, 8th Grade Lang Arts/Ag/Soc Stud/Dept Chairperson 1988- Brown Mid Sch; *ai:* Mentor Teacher; Summer Sch Lead Teacher; Spon Sch Spelling Bee; Spon Cmmty Related Act/Contests; Past Adv Sch Yrbk 1975-88; NC Assn of Academically Gifted Teachers 1988-; NC Assn of Educators 1973-78; Davidson Co NCAE Educator of Month 1976; Bus/Prof Womens Organ 1973-77; Thomasville Career Girl 1974; Fair Grove United Meth Church; Pastor Parish Comm Mem; Admin Bd Mem; Cncl of Ministries Mem; Race Relations Comm Chairperson; 1987 Outstanding Young Educator of Yr Thomasville Jaycees; Davidson Co Nominee Governors Bus Awd Prgm for Excl in Teaching Lang Arts 1987-88; Instr Effective Teacher Trng; *office:* E. Lawson Brown Middle School 1140 Kendall Mill Rd Thomasville NC 27360

BAKER, A;EME INGRAM, Mathematics Teacher; *b:* Tennessee Colony, TX; *:* Keith L. Ingram; *ed:* Grad Stud Math; Scndry Math Wkshps; *cr:* Math Teacher I M Terrell HS 1964-69, L G Pinkston HS 1969-72, H Grady Spruce HS 1972-76, Bus Management Magnet HS 1976-; *ai:* Sr Class & Teams Jeopardy Spon; Math Dept Lead Teacher; Classroom Teachers of Dallas, TX St Teachers Assn, NEA; Zeta Phi Beta Historian 1986-87; Antioch Fellowship Missionary Baptist Church Sch Teacher 1988-; Bus Management Center Teacher of Yr 1985; Meadows Fnd Grant; *office:* Business Management Center 2218 Bryan St Dallas TX 75201

BAKER, ALICE J., Third Grade Teacher; *b:* Lake Charles, LA; *m:* Don Russell; *c:* Leah A. Baker Clark; *ed:* (BA) Elem/Scndry, Univ of SW LA 1961; *cr:* Speech Therapist Iberia Parish 1960-61; 2nd Grade Teacher Weeks Island 1960-62; 2nd Grade Teacher 1970-71, 3rd Grade Teacher 1971- Nelson Wilks Elem; *ai:* Finance Comm Mountain Home Public Schls; *office:* Nelson Wilks Elem Sch 618 N College Mountain Home AR 72653

BAKER, ARLENE TAYLOR, English Teacher; *b:* Pittsburgh, PA; *m:* Clayton W.; *ed:* (BS) Eng 1973; (ME) Scndry Schl Admin, 1988 Edinboro Univ; *cr:* Eng Conneaut Lake HS 1973-83; Conneaut Valley HS 1983-; *ai:* Natl Honor Society Adv; Conneaut Ed Assn Pres 1983-85; *office:* Conneaut Valley H S Rd 3 Conneautville PA 16406

BAKER, BARBARA ALLEN, 6th Grade Science Teacher; *b:* Hornell, NY; *m:* Robert Lewis; *c:* Cindi Baker Norton, John R., William M.; *ed:* Assoc Dental Hygiene, Eastman Sch for Dental Hygienist 1957; (BS) Bio/Health, Brockport 1970; Alfred Univ, Buffalo St; *cr:* Dental Hygiene Teacher Cuba & Fillmore 1959-61; Substitute Dental Hygiene Teacher Andover Angelica 1962-64; Dental Hygiene Teacher Hornell Sch Dist 1964-69; Substitute HS Teacher Wellsville Alfred-Almond Hornell 1969-70; 6th Grade Sci Teacher Hornell Intermediate SchDist 1971-; *ai:* Staff Dev; Teacher Expectation Stu Achievement 1989-; Effective Schls, Rentention, High Expectations Comm; Church Pianist & Organist; Hornell Teachers Assn (Back to Sch Comm, Co-Chairperson) 1985; NEA, Dental Hygiene Teacher Assn; Amer Cancer Society Bd 1983-89, Residental Chairperson Awd 1987; Crisis Pregnancy Hotline Cnslr Honored for Over 200 Hours on Hotline 1989; *office:* Hornell Intermediate Sch 21 Park St Hornell NY 14843

BAKER, BARBARA JEAN (MONTGOMERY), 3rd Grade Teacher; *b:* Marion, IL; *m:* Robert Lee; *c:* Michelle, Tricia, Janette; *ed:* (BS) Elem Ed, Southern IL Univ 1969; Assoc Chrstn Ed, Cahokia Bible Inst 1990; Bill Gothard Youth Conflicts Seminars; *cr:* 3rd Grade Teacher 1974-76, 5th Grade Teacher Chenot Elem Sch; 4th Grade Teacher Penniman & Elizabeth Morris; 3rd Grade Teacher H Huffman Elem 1989-; *ai:* Wellness Comm; Parklane Baptist Church Pianist, Vocalist, Teacher; Work with Underpriviledged; Parklane Baptist Acad Advisory Cncl Mem 1984-; *home:* 1323 Morningstar Cahokia IL 62206

BAKER, BARBARA SIMPSON, Spanish Teacher; *b:* Sioux City, IA; *m:* Ross J.; *c:* Jennifer, Philip, Carolyn; *ed:* (BA) His/Span, 1968, (MS) Elem Ed, 1985 Univ of TN; Trip to Costa Rica with Missionary Group from United Meth Church 1987; *cr:* Span/General Sci Teacher East HS 1986-; *ai:* Span Club Spon; Project Graduation Comm; Hamblen Cty Ed Assn, TN Ed Assn, NEA, TN Foreign Lang Teaching Assn, Amer Assn Teachers of Span & Portuguese, Pi Lambda Theta 1986-; Jr Rdng Circle VP; Ladies Rdng Circle Secy 1976-; Morristown Dental Wives (Pres, Secy, Treas) 1975-; Amer Red Cross Clinic Worker 1982-86; First United Meth Church Finance Comm 1973-; TN Governors Acad for Foreign Lang Teachers 1988 & 1989.

BAKER, BETTY THOMAS, Sixth Grade Teacher; *b:* Mulberry, FL; *m:* Clifforol; *c:* Bertha Baker-Lopez, Yvonne Vass-Hartzog; *ed:* (BS) Phys Ed/Health, 1956, (MED) Rdng, 1970 FL A&M Univ; Working Toward EDS Rdng, Univ of S FL; Admin Supervision, SCATT Clinical Teacher, Writing Specialist; *cr:* Teacher Greenville HS 1956-57, Eustis Voc 1957-60; Phys Ed Teacher Carver Elem 1960-69; Rdng Teacher Robles Elem 1969-; *ai:* Music Comm; Schlsp & Budget Spon; Youth Group; Alpha Kappa Alpha Basileus 1990-; Allen Temple Church Trustee 1970-, Outstanding Service Plaque 1989; Eastern Stars Point 1969-, Certificate of Excl; Shriners Daughters of Isis Secy 1970-, Plaque 1988; Golden Circle Secy 1970-, Certificate Awd 1989; Hills Cty Schls Lit & Shriners Bookkeeping Wkshps; Train Beginning Teachers; Sings Choir; *home:* 3914 Pine St Tampa FL 33607

BAKER, BOB LOUIS, Social Studies Teacher; *b:* Fort Wayne, IN; *m:* Diane; *c:* Jillian, Shayna; *ed:* (BA) Soc Stud/Health/Phys Ed, 1972, (MA) Soc Stud/Health/Phys Ed, 1975 Ball St Univ; *cr:* Teacher Portland HS 1972-75, Red Bud HS 1975-78, Austin HS 1978-80, Arthur HS 1980-82, Tri Cty HS 1982-84, Kankakee Valley HS 1984-86, Gateway HS 1986-; *ai:* Var Bsktbl Coach; Fellowship Chrstn Athletes Spon; NEA 1972-; FL Coaches Assn 1986-; Teacher of Yr Gateway HS 1989; Nom St Teacher of Yr 1989-; *office:* Kissimmee Gateway HS 801 Osceola Blvd Kissimmee FL 32744

BAKER, BONNIE HUOT, 4th Grade Teacher; *b:* Jefferson City, MO; *m:* Ronald; *c:* Lorie S., Kurt, Mark; *ed:* (BS) Elem Ed, Lincoln Univ; Grad Classes Elem Ed; *cr:* Kndgtn Teacher 1979-80, 4th Grade Teacher 1980- Linn R-2 Sch; *ai:* Sci Fair Spon; Linn Teachers Assn Treas 1985-86, 1988-89; Linn PTO; Incentive Grant 1987; *home:* Rt 2 Box 70 Linn MO 65051

BAKER, CAROLYN HALL, Second Grade Teacher; *b:* Gary, IN; *m:* William F.; *c:* William T., R. Scott; *ed:* (BS) Elem Ed, 1970, (MS) Elem Ed, 1973 IN Univ; *cr:* 2nd Grade Teacher Portage Township Schls 1970-; *ai:* Cmptr Comm; NEA, IN St Teacher Assn; Portage Assn of Teachers (Building Rep, Negotiation Team); St of IN Dept of Instruction Prime Time Awd.

BAKER, CYNTHIA, English Teacher; *b:* St Petersburg, FL; *ed:* (BS) Psych, TX Tech Univ 1984; Educl Cert Univ of Houston; *cr:* 7th Grade Eng Teacher Dickinson TX Ind Sch Dist 1988; 9th Grade Premium/Average Eng Teacher 1988-89, 9th Grade Premium/Gifted & Talented Eng Teacher 1989- Alvin Ind Sch Dist; *ai:* Frosh Class Spon; Stu Assistance Prgm Core Team; Drug Awareness Week Core Team & Comm; Chairperson Sch Effectiveness Core Team; Assn of TX Prof Educators, NCTE 1988-; TX Assn for Gifted/Talented 1989-; *office:* Alvin HS 605 House St Alvin TX 77511

BAKER, D. JOYCE BAINE, Math Teacher/Cmptr Dept Head; *b:* Dillion, SC; *m:* Gary L.; *ed:* (BA) Math, Univ of WA 1972; (MA) Cmptrs in Ed, Lesley Coll 1990; *cr:* Math Teacher/Math Dept Head/Coach Illahee Jr HS 1973-76, Kilo Jr HS 1976-77; Math/Cmptr Teacher/Coach Bellarmine Preparatory 1977-79, Decatur HS 1979-; *ai:* Cmptr Dept Head; Sr Class Adv; Dist Technology & Dist Cmptr Advisory Comm; NWCCE, WCCE, NMC, WEA; FWEA Building Rep; Amer Heart Assn, Amer Cancer Society Volunteer; *office:* Decatur HS 2800 S W 320th Federal Way WA 98003

BAKER, DEE, Algebra Teacher/Coach; *b:* Memphis, TN; *m:* Becky Ralph; *c:* Christy, Brad; *ed:* (BBA) Bus Management, 1971, (EDAS) Admin/Supervision, 1982 Memphis St Univ; *cr:* Teacher/Coach Frayser HS 1976-80, Evangelical Chrstn Sch 1980-; *ai:* Girls/Boys Var Cross Cntry & Frosh Boys Bsktbl Coach; Sports Information Dir; Memphis Area Cncl of Teachers of Math, NCTM 1976-; TN Athletic Coaches Assn 1987-; Jaycees Outstanding Young Men of America 1976; St Tech Inst of Memphis Distinguished Teachers Awd 1985; *office:* Evangelical Chrstn Sch 7600 Macon Rd Cordova TN 38018

BAKER, DONNA CHALOVICH, English Teacher; *b:* Pittsburgh, PA; *m:* Gary L.; *ed:* (BS) Ed, Edinboro Univ 1971; (MA) Ed, Allegheny Coll 1974; Media Specialist Cert Edinboro Univ; *cr:* Eng Teacher Conneaut Valley HS 1973-; *ai:* Sch Newspaper Adv; NWCTE 1990; *office:* Conneaut Valley HS Rt 18 Conneautville PA 16406

BAKER, DONNA MALED, 5th Grade Teacher; *b:* Indpls, IN; *m:* Max Grant; *c:* Jessica M., Mary J.; *cr:* 6th Grade Teacher St Boniface Sch 1968-69; 5th/6th Grade Teacher Immaculate Heart of Mary Sch 1970-72; Substitute Teacher Indianapolis Public Schls 1977-79; 1st/3rd/5th Grade Teacher St Michael Sch 1980-; *ai:* Textbook Adoption Comm; Extra Curr Groups; Midwest Amputee Assn Dir 1975-; Alpha Chi Phi Mem 1984; *office:* St Michael Sch 3352 W 30th St Indianapolis IN 46222

BAKER, DOROTHY MOORE, 7th-8th Grade Reading Teacher; *b:* Shreveport, LA; *c:* Lakisha; *ed:* (BA) Eng, Grambling St Univ 1975; (MA) Scndry Ed/Eng, LA Tech Univ 1981; *cr:* Span/Eng Teacher Beufort Hs 1975-76; Eng/Rdng Teacher Youree Drive Mid Sch 1976-; *ai:* LEA, NEA.

BAKER, FRED C., Retired Teacher; *b:* Boonville, IN; *m:* Joyce Clark; *c:* Jed, Jon, Jay; *ed:* (BA) His, 1948, (MS) Ed, 1959 IN Univ; *cr:* Teacher Rockport HS 1948-50, Lynnville HS 1956-59; Prin Tennyson Sch 1959-77; Teacher Boonville Jr HS 1977-86; *home:* 508 Hwy 261 Boonville IN 47601

BAKER, GARY NEIL, Art Instructor; *b:* Portsmouth, OH; *ed:* (BSED) Elem/Art Ed, 1974, (MA) Economic Ed, 1981 OH Univ; Gifted Ed OH Univ/Miami Univ; Biblical Stud Univ of Biblical Stud; *cr:* 5th Grade Teacher Northwest Union & McDermott Elem 1975-84; 3rd-8th Grade Gifted Teacher Northwest Dist-Wide 1984-87; 9th-12th Grade Art Instr Northwest HS 1987-; *ai:* Stu Venture Spon; Arts Comm; Natl Assn of Chrstn Educators 1986-; OH Arts/Craft Guild 1989-; Stu Venture Vital-Linc 1990-91; Cmptr Grant-Benjamin Aaron Fried Fund; *office:* Northwest HS Rt 1 Box 114 Mc Dermott OH 45652

BAKER, JAMES L., 7th Grade Teacher/Asst Prin; *b:* Dover, OH; *m:* Donna Marie Kaczorowski; *c:* Pamela Suenkens, James G., Luke G.; *ed:* (BA) His/Psych/Math, Marquette Univ 1965; Masters of Ed Work, Loyola Univ; *cr:* Supervisor Marquette Univ 1963-65; Peace Corps Volunteer Urban Cmmty Dev 1965-67; Teacher St Turibius Sch 1967-; *ai:* Asst Prin St Turibius Sch; Sci Dept Head; Dir Patrol; Dir Confirmation; Leadership Comm; Head Cmptr Lab; NCEA 1967-; Mc Graw Hill Publishing Company 1989; Excl & Outstanding Leadership Qualities Awd 1989; Extra-Ordinary Minister of Communion 1974-; *office:* St Turbius Sch 4120 W 57th St Chicago IL 60629

BAKER, JANE CLARK, 4th Grade Teacher; *b:* Macon, GA; *m:* Harold E.; *c:* Mark E., David A., Phillip C.; *ed:* (BS) Elem Ed, Tift Coll 1972; (MED) Elem Ed, Mercer Univ 1984; *cr:* 2nd Grade Teacher 1972-84; 4th Grade Teacher 1984-; Elem Supv 1980; Central Fellowship Chrstn Acad; *office:* Cntrl Fellowshp Chrstn Acad 8460 Hawkinsville Rd Macon GA 31206

BAKER, JANE EILEEN, 7th Grade Life Science Teacher; *b:* Kenton, OH; *m:* Bruce Charles; *ed:* (BA) Bio/Comprehensive Sci, OH St Univ 1974; (MS) Curr/Supervision, Wright St Univ 1989; *cr:* Teacher Kenton Mid Sch 1974-; *ai:* Help with Sch Play; Co-Chairperson Sci Fair; Kenton Ed Assn VP 1989-; Delta Kappa Gamma Secy 1987-88; Cmmty Concert Assn Pres 1986-89; Amer Cancer Society Local Unit Pres 1984; *office:* Kenton Mid Sch 300 Oriental St Kenton OH 43326

BAKER, JANET TEAGUE, Sixth Grade Teacher; *b:* Monroe, NC; *m:* Wesley Lee; *c:* Tonya M., Travis B.; *ed:* (BA) Eng, 1973, (MS) Ed, 1976 Univ of NC Charlotte; *cr:* 8th Grade Lang Art Teacher Levi White Elem Sch 1973-74; 5th Grade Lang Art Teacher Waxhaw Elem 1974-75; 6th Grade Lang Art Teacher Parkwood Mid Sch 1975-; *ai:* Jr Civitan Club Spon; Exceptional Childrens Comm Mem; Parkwood Mid Sch Teacher of Yr 1987; Jr Civitan Club 1985-, Intnl Cmmty Project Awd 1989, 1st Runner Up Internation Spon of Yr Awd 1989; Just Completed Book Manuscript; A J Fletcher Fnd Grant 1989; *office:* Parkwood Mid Sch 3219 Parkwood Schl Rd Monroe NC 28110

BAKER, JEFFREY L., Fifth Grade Teacher; *b:* Massillon, OH; *m:* Paula Fox; *c:* Janelle, Keara; *ed:* (BS) Ed, Malone Coll 1975; (MS) Admin, Univ of Dayton 1982; *cr:* 4th-6th Grade Teacher Louisville City Schls 1975-; *ai:* After Sch Act Dir 1977-; OH Ed Assn, Louisville Ed Assn, NEA 1975-; *office:* Louisville City Schls 418 E Main St Louisville OH 44641

BAKER, JOHANNA E., 2nd Grade Teacher; *b:* Newport, RI; *m:* Gary E.; *c:* Erin, David; *ed:* (BS) Elem Ed 1974, (MA) Elem Ed 1983 Ball St Univ; Cmptr Literacy, Ball St Univ 1984; *cr:* Kndgtn Teacher Jackson Elem 1983-84, Lapel Elem 1984-85; 1st Grade Teacher 1985-86/1988-, 2nd Grade Teacher 1986-87 Lapel Elem; *ai:* West Cntrl Ed Assn; Nea; *office:* Lapel Elem sch P O Box 518 Lapel IN 46051

BAKER, JOHN LESLIE, Choral Director; *b:* Montgomery, AL; *m:* Kimberley C.; *c:* Brad, Chris, Mitchell; *ed:* (BS) Music Ed, Auburn Univ 1982; *cr:* Choral Dir Americus HS 1982-85, Enterprise HS 1985-; *ai:* Dir of Theater; Enterprise HS Encores; Amer Choral Dir Assn 1979-; Music Educators Natl Conference 1979-; NEA 1985-; Coffee Cty Arts Alliance Bd Mem 1988-; St Luke Meth Church Choir Dir; Choirs Have Sung for St Music Educators; Won Numerous Choral Contests; European Concert Tour 1985; *office:* Enterprise HS 500 Watts Ave Enterprise AL 36330

BAKER, KAREN CLINE, Chapter 1 Reading Teacher; *b:* Muskogee, OK; *m:* Jerry Wayne; *c:* Rebecca, Bradley; *ed:* (BS) Elem Ed, 1974, (MS) Rdng, 1979 E TX St Univ Commerce; *cr:* Elem Teacher Bland Elem Sch 1975-85, Caddo Mills Elem Sch 1988, Bland Elem Sch 1989-; *office:* Bland Elem Sch Rt 3 Greenville TX 75401

BAKER, KATHERINE JUNE (SHERRILL), 4th Grade Teacher; *b:* Dallas, TX; *m:* George William; *c:* Kirk G., Kathleen K. Baker Kozak; *ed:* (BS) & (BA) Art, 1953, (MED) Educl Supervision, 1979 TX Womans Univ; (DD) Honorary Amer Fellowship Church 1981; Religious Ed Certificate Meadville Theological, Univ of Chicago; Doctoral Degree Study, Univ of N TX 1994; *cr:* Dir Extended Day Prgm 1975-78, 3rd Grade Teacher 1978-79 Hamilton Park Elem; 4th Grade Teacher Dover Elem 1979-80, Jess Harben Elem 1980-; *ai:* Harben Site Based Management, Soc, PTA Nominating Comm; 4th Grade Cmptr Assisted Instruction; ASCD, NCSS, TX Soc Stud Cncl, Phi Delta Kappa, NEA, TX St Teacher Assn, ASCD, TX Rdng Assn Sch Rep; YWCA (Camp Treas Rios, Camp Dir) 1975-76; Unitarian Univ Womens Fed Day Care Advocate 1975-76; Dallas Moslom Assn; Sokol Athletic Assn (Treas 1965) 1975-; Flame Fellowship Intnl Field Rep 1989-; Whos Who in Amer Ed 1988-; Whos Who in Amer Women 1989-; Sch View Column Dallas Unitarian Newsletter; Hamilton Park Magnet Sch Richardson Ind Sch Dist Newsletter; *office:* Jess Harben Elem Sch 600 S Glenville Richardson TX 75081

BAKER, KATHY MC FADDEN, First Grade Teacher; *b:* Terre Haute, IN; *m:* Bill D.; *c:* Wyatt, Levi, Darby; *ed:* (BS) Elem Ed-Early Chldhd, 19 73, (MS) Elem Ed, 1976 IN St Univ *cr:* Kndgtn Teacher 1973-86, 1st Grade Teacher 1987- Graysville Elem; *ai:* Turman Township 4-H Leader; Pi Lambda Theta 1976-; 4-H Cncl 1986-; Sullivan Cty Fairboard Sec 1986-; *home:* R 2 Box 137 Sullivan IN 47882

BAKER, KAY, Mathematics Teacher; *b:* Vernal, UT; *ed:* (BS) Math/Cmptr Sci/Applied Statistics, UT St Univ 1983; *cr:* Teacher Uintah HS 1983-; *ai:* Sterling Scholar Adv; Sch Improvement Leader; Inservice Leader; NCTM Mem 1983-; NVEA/UEA Mem 1983-; Uintah Sch Dist Scndry Teacher of Yr 1990; *office:* Uintah HS 1880 W 500 N Vernal UT 84078

BAKER, KEVIN D., 8th Grade US History Teacher; *b:* Indianapolis, IN; *ed:* (BA) His, 1983, Cert Scndry Soc Stud 1984 IN Univ; MS Guidance/Counseling SW MO St 1992; *cr:* Dept Chm/8th Grade US His/Soc Stud Teacher Pershing Jr HS 1984-; *ai:* Pershing Intramurals & Ec Dir; Quiz Team; 7th Grade Boys Bsktbl Coach; Organizer & Leader Annual Washington DC Trip; *office:* Pershing Jr HS 2120 Ventura Springfield MO 65804

BAKER, KURT MICHEAL, History Teacher; *b:* Reed City, MI; *m:* Cynthia Ann Haynes; *ed:* (BAA) Broadcasting/His, Cntrl MI Univ 1983; Scndry Cert Cntrl MI 1985; Ftbl Grad Asst S IL Univ; Post Grad Stud Athletic Admin, S IL & Cntrl MI Univ 1985-88; *cr:* Soc Stud Teacher W Frederick Mid Sch 1985-86; Grad Asst S IL Univ Carbondale 1986; His Teacher Lake City Area Sch 1987-; *ai:* Jr Var Ftbl & 7th Grade Bsktbl Coach; Class of 1992 Spon; MI HS Ftbl Coaches Assn 1988-; *office:* Lake City Area Sch Russell St Lake City MI 49651

BAKER, LA NEIL POWELL, Fourth Grade Teacher; *b:* Friendship, TN; *m:* Karl Keith; *c:* Karla N. Walker, Elizabeth C. Puryear, John R.; *ed:* (BS) Elem Ed, Murray St Univ 1955; *cr:* 1st Grade Teacher Lawrenceville IL 1955-56, Jefferson Cty KY 1956-57, Fayette Cty KY 1957-58; 1st/2nd/4th-6th Grade Teacher Elizabethtown Ind Schls 1960-62, 1968-73, 1975-; *ai:* NEA; Elizabethtown Ed Assn (Pres 1984-85, Secy 1986-88); KY Assn For Gifted Ed Mem 1988-; *office:* Morningside Elem Sch Morningside Dr Elizabethtown KY 42701

BAKER, LAREEN SKOGI, Kindergarten Teacher; *b:* Sacramento, CA; *m:* Larry Farnsworth; *ed:* (BA) Eng Lit, CA Luth Univ 1966; Working Towards St Credential; Partial MA Ed Psych, Learning & Rdng Disorders, CA Univ Northridge; Ed Trng Classes; *cr:* 4th-6th Grade Art Teacher El Toro Marine Sch 1967-68; 1st/3rd Grade Teacher Manzanita Sch 1968-72; K-2nd Grade Teacher 1972-79, Kndgtn Teacher 1979- Aspen Elem; *ai:* Sch Site Cncl Alternate 1979-80; Soc Comm Chm 1976-80; Stu Cncl Asst Adv 1989-; Delta Kappa Gamma (Music Chm 1987-, Prof Growth & Dev Chm 1985-87); PTA Faculty Rep 1980-, Honorary Service Awd 1988-89; CA Teachers Assn, NEA Mem 1967-; Society of Childrens Bookwriters Mem 1989-; GSA (Troop Leader 1980-82, Freelance Entertainer 1982-), Tres Condados Cncl Awd, Appreciation Pin 1988; Open Court Publishing Company 1st Grade Field Study Critical Reader 1981; Certificated Employee of Month Conejo Valley Unified Sch Dist 1988; Course of Study Writer Kndgtn Soc Stud 1984, Lang Arts 1989 Conejo Valley Unified Sch Dist; *home:* 1225 Los Amigos Ave Simi Valley CA 93065

BAKER, LINDA K. (MC NIEL), English, Civics & Geo Teacher; *b:* Tahlequah, OK; *m:* Tommy Dale; *c:* Casey, Cassy; *ed:* (BS) Ed, Northeastern 1973; *cr:* Teacher Hulbert HS 1973-; *ai:* Sr Spon; Elem BB & Track, Jr HS BB & Track, Sr HS Track Coach; Negotiations Comm; OK Ed Assn Mem 1973-; NEA Mem; *home:* Rt 1 Box 348 Tahlequah OK 74464

BAKER, MARIE RAYMOND, Piano Teacher; *b:* Muskegon, MI; *ed:* (BM) Piano 1952, (MM) Piano, 1960, (MM) Music Theory, 1962 American Conservatory of Music; Several Univ; *cr:* Piano Teacher/Liturgist St Joseph Parish 1937-42, 1966-68, St Mary Magdalene Parish 1942-43, St Jospeph Parish 1943-44, 1951-52, 1953-55; Piano Teacher Marywood Acad 1944-48; Teacher/Liturgist S S Peter & Paul; 1948-51, St Josephs Parish 1952-53, St Mary Cathedral 1956-66, Holy Rosary Acad 1968-79; Piano Teacher Greater Muskegon Cath Schls 1979-; *ai:* Church Related Act, Lector, Commentator, Eucharistic Minister St Joseph Parish; Natl Cath Music Educators Assn Treas 1966-76; Diocese of Saginaw MI Liturgy Commission 1966-79; Pius XII Inst of Fine Art Florence Italy 1955-56; *office:* Greater Muskegon Cath Schls 1145 W Laketon Muskegon MI 49441

BAKER, MARLENE PALLOTTA, Core Department Chair; *b:* Crockett, CA; *m:* Robert G.; *c:* Kurt, Elaine; *ed:* (BA) US His, Univ CA Berkeley 1953; Grad Stud; *cr:* Eng Teacher Garretson Elem 1954-56; Eng/Soc Stud Teacher Loma Vista 1956-58, El Dorado 1958-64, Oak Grove 1964-68, Sequoia 1975-78, Riverview 1978-; *ai:* Lit Comm Mentor Teacher; Lang Art & Soc Stud Dept Chm; Mt Diablo Ed Assn & Mt Diablo Unified Sch Dist Excl Ed Awd 1987; Mentor Teacher 1985-87, 1988-; *office:* Riverview Mid Sch 205 Pacifica Ave West Pittsburg CA 94565

BAKER, MARY HICKMAN, Business Teacher; *b:* Houma, LA; *m:* Robert Erwin Jr.; *c:* Robert III., John T.; *ed:* (BS) Bus Ed, Univ of SW LA 1973; (MS) Admin/Supervision, Mc Neese St Univ 1979; *cr:* Bus Teacher, South Cameron HS 1973-74, Hackberry HS 1974-; *ai:* FBLA Spon; Hackberry Sch Evaluating Steering & Cameron Parish Testing Comm; NBEA, LA Voc Assn; *office:* Hackberry HS 1390 School St Hackberry LA 70645

BAKER, MARY KAY, Business Educator; *b:* Monroe, WI; *ed:* (BSE) Bus Ed, Univ of WI Whitewater 1982; *cr:* Bus Educator Campbellsport HS & Jr HS 1982-; *ai:* Sch Newspaper Adv; Stu Assistance Prgm Group Facilitator; Kettle Moraine Bus Teachers 1985-; *office:* Campbellsport HS 114 W Sheboygan St Campbellsport WI 53010

BAKER, NOELLE DORA (STRANG), English & Mathematics Teacher; *b:* Calgary AB, Canada; *m:* Brett R.; *ed:* (BS) Eng/Math, Chadron St Coll 1986; Grad Stud Developmental Counseling; *cr:* 11th/12th Grade His Teacher 1986-88, 9th/11th Grade Eng Teacher 1986-, 9th Grade Math Teacher 1988- Rushville Jr/Sr HS; *ai:* Lincoln-Douglas Debate Coach; Jr Class, Jr HS Pep Club, Chrldr Spon; Boys & Girls St & Jr Law Cadet Asst; Jaycees Bd of Dir 1990; Master Teacher Math & Sci Learning Center Chadron St Coll; *home:* 527 Chapin St Chadron NE 69337

BAKER, PATRICIA, CDP, Director of Liturgy; *b:* Pittsburgh, PA; *ed:* (BSM) Music Ed, 1973, (MM) Music Ed, 1979 Duquesne Univ; *cr:* 5th-6th Grade Intermediate Teacher St Basils Sch 1971-72; 9th-12th Grade Music Dir Divine Providence Acad 1973-77; K-8th Grade Music Dir Queen of Peace Sch 1977-82; 6th Grade Intermediate Teacher St Basils Sch 1982-83; K-8th Grade Music Dir and 4th-8th Grade Intermediate Teacher St John the Baptist Sch 1983-89; Dir of Music & Liturgy Nativity Church 1989-; *ai:* Sisters Alumnae Duquesne Univ 1973-; Natl Catholic Educators of America 1973-89.

BAKER, PATRICIA ANN, 2nd Grade Teacher; *b:* San Antonio, TX; *m:* Robert; *c:* Amy, Charlie; *ed:* (BS) Elem Ed, SW TX St Univ 1967; *cr:* 1st Grade Teacher Randolph Elem 1967-69, Lone Star Elem 1976-81; 2nd Grade Teacher Lone Star Elem 1986-.

BAKER, PATRICIA VOTAW, English Teacher; *b:* Harrodsburg, KY; *m:* David Lee; *c:* Davette, Jared; *ed:* (BA) Eng, 1968, (MA) Eng, 1972 Eastern KY Univ; *cr:* Rdng/Eng Teacher Boyle Cty HS 1968-71; Rdng Teacher Danville Youth Dev Center 1980-83; Eng Teacher Boyle Cty HS 1985-; *ai:* Teens Who Care Club; Sr Class Spon; NEA/KEA/BCEA/NCTE/KCTE; 4-H Cncl Pres 1985-86; *home:* 1375 Bohon Rd Harrodsburg KY 40330

BAKER, RUBY REEDER, Business Education Teacher; *b:* Carlisle, PA; *m:* Galen; *ed:* (BS) Bus Ed 1971;)MED) Office Admin, 1977 Shippensburg Univ; *cr:* Bus Ed Teacher Daniel Boone HS 1972-73; Bus Ed Teacher Boiling Springs HS 73-81; Bus Ed Teacher Big Spring HS 1981-; *ai:* Bus Yrbk Club Ad; Big Spring CMmnty Advisory Cncl; Delta Pi Epsilon; Phi Delta Kappa; Pa Bus Ed Assn; Big Spring Ed Assn; PA ST Ed Assn; NEA; *office:* Big Spring H S 45 Mount Rock Rd Newville PA 17241

BAKER, SANDRA ACKER, English Teacher; *b:* Utica, NY; *m:* John W.; *c:* Joshua K.; *ed:* (BA) Eng Ed, 1971, (MS) Ed, 1984 St Univ of NY Oswego; Lib Sci, Syracuse Univ; *cr:* Eng Teacher N Syracuse HS 1971-; *ai:* Dist Planning Team Writing Process Chairperson; Eng Coach-Academic Decathalon Team; Annual Stu Awds Ceremony Comm Mem; *office:* Cicero-North Syracuse HS Rt 31 Cicero NY 13039

BAKER, SARAH JANE, Social Studies Teacher; *b:* Westfield, MA; *m:* John C.; *c:* Leslie A., Emily Clark, Elizabeth Hansen; *ed:* (BA) Scndry Soc Stud, St Univ of NY Cortland 1965; (MS) Scndry Soc Stud, St Univ of NY Oswego 1984; *cr:* 7th Grade Soc Stud Teacher Durgee Jr HS & Ray Mid Sch 1978-88; 11th/12th Grade Soc Stud Teacher C W Baker HS 1988-; *ai:* Cntrl NY Cncl for Soc Stud, NY St Cncl for Soc Stud, NCSS; Mc Harris Legacy; *office:* C W Baker HS E Onieda St Complex Baldwinsville NY 13027

BAKER, SHELBY MOSLEY, Second Grade Teacher; *b:* Toxey, AL; *m:* Edgar H.; *ed:* (BS) Elem Ed, Livingston Univ 1960; U.S. Space Acad NASA; *cr:* 1st Grade Teacher Huffman Sch 1960-62; 2nd Grade Teacher William J Christian Sch 1963-; *ai:* Sci Txtbk Revw Comm; Rdng Revw Comm City; Birmingham Area Rdng Cncl 1980-; Delta Kappa Gamma Socty Intnl 1979-; PTA 1960-; ACE (Birmingham City Pres 1978-79, St of AL Pres 1980-81); WBRC TV Teacher of Wk 1989; Favorite Teacher Awd 1962; *office:* W J Christian Sch 725 Mountain Dr Birmingham AL 35206

BAKER, SHERRY M., Curriculum Coordinator; *b:* Jackson, MS; *c:* William E., Douglas E., Deborah; *ed:* (BS) Elem Ed, Jackson St Univ 1976; (MA) Elem Ed/Rdng, OH St Univ 1976; *cr:* Teacher Holy Family Cath Sch 1979-81; Rdng Teacher Brinkley Jr HS 1982-85; Soc Stud Teacher 1985-89, Curr Coord 1990- Bailey Magnet Sch; *ai:* Chrldr Spon; Black His Challenge Bowl Coach; Staff Dev Trng & Responsibility Trng Comm; Cooperative Learning, Multicultural Ed/Curr Trainer; Supt Advisory Comm; ASCD, NCSS, NASSP; PTA Pres 1987-88, Life Membership Awd 1988; Good Apple Awd; *office:* Bailey Magnet Sch 1900 N State St Jackson MS 39206

BAKER, SUSAN LEIGH (GILLIAT), Dance Teacher; *b:* Salt Lake City, UT; *m:* Aron Bruce; *ed:* (BA) Dance Specialization, Brigham Young Univ 1988; Heatlh Ed, Brigham Young Univ 1988; *cr:* Dance Instr Payson Childrens Sch of the Arts Playmakers 1988; Dance/Aerobics Teacher Provo HS 1988-; *ai:* Dance Company Adv; Sch Musical Choreographer; *office:* Provo HS 1125 N University Ave Provo UT 84604

BAKER, SUZANNE MARKVART, Mathematics Teacher; *b:* Chicago, IL; *m:* Edward Brice; *ed:* (BS) Math/Ed, Univ of IL 1970; (MS) Math, Purdue 1974; Ed/Math/Cmptr Courses Various Universities; *cr:* Math Teacher Thornridge HS 1970-75; *ai:* Mathlettes Asst; Discipline & Teacher Safety Comm Mem; NCTM, ICTM, PTA; *office:* Thornridge HS Sibley & Cottage Grove Dolton IL 60419

BAKER, TERESA MOORE, Music Teacher; *b:* Detroit, MI; *m:* John E.; *ed:* (BS) Music Ed, TN Technological Univ 1974; (MM) Music Ed, West Chester St Univ 1981; *cr:* Music/Band/Chorus Dir Calvert & Cecilton Elem 1976-80, Rising Sun Elem 1980-; *ai:* Host Conductor All-Cty Mid Sch Band; Talent Show Coord; Renovation Comm; Delta Kappa Gamma VP 1988-; Music Educators Natl Conference; MD Music Educators; Hopewell Meth Church (Pastor Parish Relation 1984-87, Worship Comm 1987-); PTA (Exec Comm 1987-88) 1976-, Lifetime Membership Awd 1984; Nom Teacher of Yr 1990; Published in Magazine; *office:* Rising Sun Elem Sch Wilson Ave Rising Sun MD 21911

BAKER, WYLIE JAMES, JR., Chemistry Teacher; *b:* Meridian, MS; *m:* Sara Margaret Stodard; *c:* Celia A., James P.; *ed:* (BS) Chem, Meth Coll 1969; (MAT) Chem/Ed, Duke Univ 1973; USAF Electronics Trng 1961-63; *cr:* Chem/Phys Ed Teacher J F Webb Sr HS 1971-78; Sci Teacher Governors Honors Prgm GA 1984-85; Chem Teacher Morrow HS 1978-; *ai:* Sci Club, GA Jr Acad of Sci Adv; After Sch Tutorial Prgm Dir; NSTA 1985-; GSTA 1979-; NEA, GAE, CCEA 1978-; GA Acad of SC 1986-; PTSA (Chm of Committees 1985-88, Pres 1988-89), Life Membership 1985-86; Sch Teacher of Yr 1983, 1990; STAR Teacher 1984; Cty Nom Presidential Excl in Sci & Math Teaching 1983; Cty Nom Outstanding Scndry Sci Teacher 1983; *office:* Morrow HS 2299 Old Rex Morrow Rd Morrow GA 30260

BAKKE, JEAN BLACK, Language Art Department Chair; *b:* San Marcos, TX; *m:* Richard H.; *c:* Randi L., Katie; *ed:* (BA) Eng/Home Ec, Sam Houston St Univ 1972; (MED) Ed, Stephen F Austin 1985; *cr:* 8th Grade Lang Art Teacher Friendswood Ind Sch Dist 1972-76; 6th Grade Lang Art Teacher Pasadena Ind Sch Dist 1978-85, Conroe Ind Sch Dist 1976-77; 8th Grade Lang Art Teacher Humble Ind Sch Dist 1985-; *ai:* Stu Cncl & Drug Awareness Day Spon; ATPE 1985-; 8th Grade Curr Drug Prgm Baylor Coll; Teacher of Yr Humble Mid Sch 1988-89; Presenter TX Mid Sch Assn Conf 1988-89.

BAKKO, BARBARA ALLEN, English Teacher; *b:* Breckenridge, MN; *ed:* (BS) Eng, Moorhead St Univ 1971; Grad Work Eng, Rdng, Sped Ed; *cr:* 10th-12th Grade Eng Teacher Sauk Centre Sr HS 1971-; *ai:* Jr/Sr HS Faculty & Youth Advisory Cncl; Mentorship & Mentor Advisory & PER Comm; Sauk Centre Ed Assn, MN Ed Assn, NEA; *office:* Sauk Centre Sr HS 9th And State Rd Sauk Centre MN 56378

BALAS, CAROL BUDRY, First Grade Teacher; *b:* Reese, MI; *m:* Lawrence C.; *c:* Wendy S. (dec), Christopher L.; *ed:* (BSED) Elem Ed/Eng, Cntrl MI Univ 1963; Grad Stud Permanent Cert, MI St Univ 1964-65; *cr:* 3rd Grade Teacher Fairview Sch 1963-67; 2nd-3rd Grade Teacher N Oakview Sch 1975-82; 2nd Grade Rdng Teacher St Jude Cath Sch 1982-84; 1st-3rd Grade Teacher W Oakview Sch 1984-; *ai:* MI Ed Assn, NEA, Northview Ed Assn; *home:* 3516 Olderidge Dr NE Grand Rapids MI 49505

BALASCHI, KIMBERLY HEALY, Spanish Teacher; *b:* Brockton, MA; *m:* William F.; *ed:* (BA) Spanish, Providence Coll 1983; Addl Studies Advanced Placement Lang Seminar Taft Educl Ctr; *cr:* Span Teacher Xaverian Brothers HS 1983-; *ai:* Moderator Span Club, Jr Prom Comm; Faculty Rep Soph Appeals Bd; MAFLA Mem 1983-; *office:* Xaverian Brothers H S 800 Clapboardtree St Westwood MA 02090

BALCEROVICH, MARJORIE ANN, 3rd Grade Elementary Teacher; *b:* Ramah, CO; *m:* Bernard; *c:* Steven; *ed:* (BA) Elem Ed, Univ of N Co; Guidance & Soc Stud, Intnl Stud; *cr:* 1st-5th Grade Teacher Agate CO 1947-48; 1st-8th Grade Teacher Kiowa CO 1948-50; 1st/2nd Grade Teacher Elizabeth CO 1950-51; 3rd/4th Grade Teacher 1951-60, 5th/6th Grade Teacher 1960-72 Kiowa CO; HS Cnslr 1972-78; 5th/6th Grade Teacher 1979-82; HS Cnslr 1979-88; 3rd Grade Teacher 1989-; *ai:* Sch Cnslr; US Academic Dec, NHS, Natl Jr Society Spon; CO Health Agency Appointed Bd of Dirs 1972-78; Region V Comprehension Health Mem; *office:* Elbert Cty Consolidated Sch Comanche St Kiowa CO 80117

BALCERSKI, FRANK JAMES, 7th & 8th Grade Teacher; *b:* New Brunswick, NJ; *c:* David, William; *ed:* (BS) Sci Ed, Seton Hall Univ 1964; (MA) Environmental Sci, Montclair St Coll 1978; Biotech, Wm Paterson Coll; Marine Bio, Amer Inst for Creative Ed St Thomas; Radiological Officer Trng Dept of Civil Defense Univ of Lowell MA; *cr:* Sci Teacher Madison Twp HS 1964-65, Roosevelt Intermediate Sch 1965-; *ai:* Crisis Mgmt Team Mem; Saturday Suspension Adv; NJSTA 1988-; Westfield Ed Assn Liason Comm Mem Delegate 1964-; NJEA 1964-; Smithsonian Assn 1988-; Amer Littoral Society 1988-; Natl Sci Fnd Grant Chem Inst St Peters Coll; *office:* Roosevelt Intermediate Sch 301 Clark St Westfield NJ 07090

BALDELLI, LARRY ALBERT, Science Teacher; *b:* New Haven, CT; *ed:* (AA) Liberal Arts, Quinnipiac 1960; (BA) His, MI St Univ 1962; Working Towards Masters S CT St Coll; Admin, Bridgeport Univ; *cr:* Sci Teacher Moran Mid Sch 1963-; *ai:* Stu Citizenship Comm Adv; NEA, CT Ed Assn; Wallingford Ed Assn Negotiation Team 1980-; Branford Fire Dept Treas 1963-, Man of Yr 1982; Marchegian Sportsmens Club Pres 1973-, Man of Yr 1986; Marchegian Society Pres 1988-; Natl Sci Fnd Grant 1969.

BALDOCK, JUDY LEE, 7th & 9th Grade Sci Teacher; *b:* Russell Cnty, KY; *m:* Lynn; *ed:* (AA) Bio, Lindsey Wilson Jr Coll 1970; (BS) Bio, Campbellsville Coll 1972; (Rank II) Scndry Ed/Bio/Chem, W KY Univ 1978; *cr:* 7th Grade Teacher Russell Springs Elem 1972-73, Union Chapel Elem 1973-75, Salem Elem 1975-88; 7th & 9th Grade Teacher Russell Cty Jr HS 1988-; *office:* Russell Cty Jr HS RR 7 Box 230 Russell Springs KY 42642

BALDWIN, ALLISON COMSTOCK, Sixth Grade Teacher; *b:* La Junta, CO; *m:* Dr. John B.; *c:* Shannon Chelson, Shawn; *ed:* (BME) Music ED, 1961; (ME) Elem Ed, Wichita ST Univ 1964; *cr:* Strings/Vocal Music Wichita Public Sch 1961-65; Vocal Music Lansing Public Sch 1965-67; String Teacher Central MI Univ 1967-68; Vocal Music 1969-70; Fifth & Sixth Grade 1970-71 Oshkosh WI Public Sch; Second, Third, Fifth and Sixth Grade Teacher Boise Public Sch 1971-89; *ai:* Boise Philharmonic Mem 1st Violin Sectron, Personnel Mgr; Private Studio Violin Teacher; Assoc Prin 2nd Violin Bear Valley Music Festival; Music Educators Natl Convention; NEA; ID Ed Assn; Boise Ed Assn; DAR; Served on Soc Stud Curr Dev Comm & Wrote 6th Grade Soc Stud Curr; Mem Instructional & Prof Dev Comm; Selected As

Lecturer/Clinician on Classroom Mgt for Northwest Regional MENC; *office:* Mc Kinley Sch/Boise Public Sch 6400 Overland Rd Boise ID 83709

BALDWIN, EDEA PITRE, English Teacher; *b:* New Orleans, LA; *m:* Robert B.; *c:* Edea, Bobby, Emma; *ed:* (BA) Eng/Liberal Arts, Nicholls St Univ 1975; Rdng; Educl Research; *cr:* Eng/His Teacher South Lafourche HS 1980-87; Eng Teacher 1987- Galliano, Quitman HS, Quitman Mid Sch; *ai:* Beta Club Spon; Drop-By Center Volunteer Tutor 1989-; *office:* Quitman HS 210 S Jackson Quitman MS 39355

BALDWIN, JACQUELYN ALBRECHT, 5th Grade Teacher; *b:* Vero Beach, FL; *m:* Russell T. Jr.; *c:* Brett, Brandon; *ed:* (BA) Elem Ed, SE Coll of Assemblies of God 1976; (MED) Rdng Specialist, Rollins Coll 1978; *cr:* 5th Grade Teacher 1976-78, Teacher of Gifted Prgm 1980-84 Wauchula Elem; Teacher of Gifted Prgm 1984-89, 5th Grade Teacher 1989- Crystal Lake Elem; *ai:* Chm Faculty & Staff Soc Comm; *office:* Crystal Lake Elem Sch 700 Galvin Dr Lakeland FL 33801

BALDWIN, JOHN KELLY, Vocational Agriculture Teacher; *b:* Abbottsburg, NC; *m:* Jo Ann Dove; *c:* John A., Timothy I.; *ed:* (BS) Ag Ed, 1961, (MED) Ag Ed, 1972 NC St Univ; *cr:* Voc Ag Teacher Midway HS 1961-63, Bladenboro HS 1963-; *ai:* Bladenboro HS & Bladenboro Fed Adv; FFA; NC Voc Ag Teachers Assn VP; NC Voc Assn, AVA, Natl Voc Ag Teachers Assn 1961-; Bladenboro Rotary Club Pres 1983-86; Bladneboro Jaycees Pres 1963-70; Article Published; Honorary St FFA Degree Awd; Honorary Amer FFA Degree Awd; Bladen Cty Teacher of Yr 1989; *office:* Bladenboro HS P O Box 459 Bladenboro NC 28320

BALDWIN, JON ROGER ERIC, Elementary Band; *b:* Memphis, TN; *m:* Claudia Wood; *c:* Vanessa; *ed:* (BS) Music Ed, 1969, (MA) Music Ed, 1974 Crane Sch of Music; *cr:* Band Instr Canajoharie Cntrl Sch 1969-70; Elem Band Instr Penn Yan Elem Sch 1970-; *ai:* Elem Running Club Adv; *office:* Penn Yan Elem Sch Maple Ave Penn Yan NY 14527

BALDWIN, KAREN SUE, Third Grade Teacher; *b:* Charleston, WV; *m:* Edward R.; *c:* Criag, Kimberly; *ed:* (BS) Elem Ed, 1969, (MS) Elem Ed, 1973 WV Univ; *cr:* 3rd Grade Teacher Big Chimney Elem Sch; *ai:* KTA, WVEA; Karawta Teachers Assn Faculty Rep; *home:* PO Box 486 Big Chimney WV 25302

BALDWIN, MARY JOYCE SHAW, Third Grade Teacher; *b:* Tell City, IN; *c:* Jeffery S, Steven E.; *ed:* (BA) Ed, Univ of Evansville 1969; (MS) Ed/Counseling, IN Univ 1972; Grad Stud Several Univs; *cr:* 3rd/4th Grade Teacher Wheeler Elem Sch 1968-72; 6th-8th Grade Lang Art Teacher Scott Elem Sch 1972-75; 5th-7th Grade Lang Art Teacher Dexter Elem Sch 1975-76; 3rd/4th Grade Teacher Lodge Elem Sch 1976-; Adult Basic Ed Evansville Sch Corp 1975-77; *ai:* Young Authors Sandcastles; Spelling Comm; Co Chm Rdng Cncl Intnl, Natl, St; Local Rdng Book Adoption Comm 1989; Input Eng Book Adoption Comm 1990; Parent Advisory; NEA (Delegate Washington DC 1989) 1968-; ISTA, ICTA, ACE, IRA, AAUW, ABWA; Pi Lambda Theta 1989-; MEA, ETA, In st Teachers Assn 1968-; Amer Red Cross; BSA; Nursing Homes, Evansville Leadership Trng Muscular Dystrophy Volunteer Candidate 1973; Civitan Club, St Benedicts Church, IN Univ Booster Club; *office:* Lodge Elem Sch 2000 Lodge Ave Evansville IN 47714

BALDWIN, PATRICIA ANN, Vocational Home Ec Teacher; *b:* Wheelwright, KY; *m:* Raymond Luther; *c:* Keith, Kerri; *ed:* (BS) Home Ec, Bio Union Coll 1964; (BS) Voc, Miami Univ 1975; *cr:* Home Economics Teacher Betsy Lane HS 1965-; Bio Teacher Prestonburg HS 1966-69: Home Economics Teacher Mc Kinley Mid Sch 1972-78; Voc Home Economics Teacher Verity Mid Sch 1978-; *ai:* FHA Club; Core Team Dealing with at Risk Kids; Middletown Teachers Assn Apple Awd 1989; Jennings Awd 1978; *office:* George M Verity Mid Sch 1900 Johns Rd Middletown OH 45044

BALENTINE, ORA MAE RAY, Third Grade Teacher; *b:* Weir, MS; *m:* William B.; *c:* William R., Roy A.; *ed:* (AA) Northwest Jr Coll 1956; (BS) Elem Ed, MS St Univ 1962; *cr:* Jr HS Eng Teacher Eudora Sch 1957-59; 3rd Grade Teacher Ethel Sch 1962-67; Weir Attendance Ctr 1967-; *ai:* MS Prof Ed; Weir Bapt Church; Governors General Conf Ed 1981; *home:* PO Box 17 Weir MS 39772

BALES, H. G., Health/Phys Ed Teacher; *b:* Somerset, KY; *m:* Alice Neeley; *c:* Jace, Zach; *ed:* (BS) Phys Ed, 1978, (MA) Sch Health, 1980 E KY Univ; *cr:* Teacher Burnside Sch 1978-81, Burnside Jr HS 1981-87, Southern Jr HS 1987-; *ai:* 8th & 9th Grade Girls Bsktbl Coach; Jump Rope for Heart Sch Coord; Sch Guidance Comm Mem; KEA, NEA, PCEA 1978-; *home:* 366 Oakhill Rd Somerset KY 42501

BALES, MARYLEE, Social Studies Teacher; *b:* Belleville, IL; *m:* Richard R.; *ed:* (BS) Poly Sci Ed, S Il Univ 1964; *cr:* Teacher Cahokia HS 1964-66, Richwoods HS 1966-; *ai:* Jr Class Spon; Bus Mgr Excalibur Yrbk; Chm Steering Comm; *office:* Richwoods HS 6301 N University Peoria IL 61614

BALES, WANDA FORD, 6th Grade Teacher; *b:* Fremond, MO; *d:* Wayne O.; *c:* Penny L. Bales Mathes; *ed:* (BA) Bus, SW Baptist-Bolivar 1959; (BS) Elem Ed, Univ MO St Louis 1978; *cr:* Accounts Receivable/Reception MO Baptist Hospital 1959-61, 1967-73; Teacher S Reynolds R-II 1979-; *ai:* Bd Policy, Textbook Adoption For Math, Rdng, Soc Stud, Sci Comm; Cheerleading Spon; MO Natl Teachers Assn (Pres, Secy) 1987-88; Three Rivers Area Rdng Cncl 1987-; St Louis Metropolitan Sewer Dist Schlsp Awd; *home:* PO Box 497 Van Buren MO 63965

BALFOUR, LINDA GRACIA, English/Journalism Teacher; *b:* Santa Maria, CA; *m:* Warren Harlow; *ed:* (BA) Eng, CA Polytechnic St Univ 1983; *cr:* Teacher Atascadero Jr HS 1983-88, San Luis Obispo HS 1988-; *ai:* HS Newspaper Adv; CATE 1984-; NCTE 1982-; JEA 1988-; *office:* San Luis Obispo HS 1350 California Blvd San Luis Obispo CA 93403

BALL, AMANDA LORRETTA, 9th-12th Grade Math Teacher; *b:* Supulpa, OK; *m:* Monte W.; *c:* Andrew M.; *ed:* (BS) Math/Ed, Sterling Coll 1987; *cr:* Math Teacher Dighton HS 1987-; *ai:* Head Girls Bsktbl & Vlybl Coach; KNEA, Dighton Teacher Assn 1989-; *office:* Dighton HS 200 S Wichita Dighton KS 67839

BALL, BONNIE MC DONALD, French Teacher/Dept Chair; *b:* Baltimore, MD; *m:* Ronald E.; *c:* Wendy E., Brian A.; *ed:* (BA) Span/Fr, Mary Baldwin Coll 1977; *cr:* Span/Fr Teacher Natural Bridge HS 1977-81, Fort Defiance HS & Stewart Mid Sch 1981-84; Fr Teacher Ft Defiance HS 1984-; *ai:* Ft Defiance HS Jr Class; Fr, Travel Club; Vlybl, Track, Sftbl, Cheerleading Coach; Alpha Delta Kappa 1982-; NEA, VEA, ACEA 1981-; GSA (Day Camp Dir 1986-, Area Registrar 1989-); *home:* 129 Valley View Ave Mount Sidney VA 24467

BALL, CONNIE, Principal; *b:* Del Rio, TN; *m:* Marsha Hurley Ball; *c:* Amy J., Connie Jr.; *ed:* (BS) Phys Ed/Health/Recreation/ Elem Edu; Carson-Newman 1973; (MED) Supervision/Admin, ETSU 1988; *cr:* Teacher Edgemont Elem Sch 1973-79; Teacher/ Prin Del Rio Elem Sch 1979-82; Supv Stokely Van Camp 1982, Electro-Voice 1983; Prin Del Rio Elem Sch 1984-; *ai:* TEA/NEA 1973-; ETEA/CCEA 1973-; Del Rio Ruritan Club 1989-; Cocke Cty Sportsman Club 1982-88; Outstanding Service 1988; Teacher of Yr at Del Rio Schl; *office:* Del Rio Elem Sch Rt 2 Box 188 Del Rio TN 37727

BALL, JACKIE GAINES, Reading/Keyboarding Teacher; *b:* Clarksburg, WV; *m:* Jack D.; *c:* Mike Westfall; *ed:* (BA) Fr/ Secretarial, Fairmont St Coll 1972; (MS) Rdng, WV Univ 1982; *cr:* Fr/Rdng 7th Grade Teacher Grafton Mid Sch 1972-82; Rdng 7th Grade Teacher South Harrison HS 1982-86; 7th-9th Grade Teacher Rdng/Typing Bridgeport Jr HS 1986-; *ai:* NEA 1982-; Art Center Drama Comm 1985-87; *home:* 234 Jefferson St Bridgeport WV 26330

BALL, LINDA ANN, Art Teacher; *b:* La Plata, MD; *ed:* (BA) Phys Ed/Health/Art, Glenville St 1970; *cr:* Teacher Logan Cntrl Jr HS 1970-; *ai:* Logan Cntrl Girls Bsktbl Team; Art Club Spon; AFT; Logan Cty Schls Elem Phys Ed Illustration; *office:* Logan Cntrl Jr HS 300 Kanada St Logan WV 25601

BALL, PATRICIA MARYLYN, English Teacher & Curr Coord; *b:* Manchester, NH; *ed:* (BA) Eng/Soc Stud, Notre Dame Coll 1966; Grad Work, Univ of Va; *cr:* Eng Teacher George Mason Jr Sr HS 1967-76; Assoc Dir of Admissions NH Coll 1976-79; Eng Teacher Hillside Jr HS 197-; *ai:* Building Level Instructional Coord; Fall Church Ed Assn Secy 1972-73; Manchester Ed Assn 1979-; Article Published the Creative Teacher Natl Magazine 1971; *office:* Hillside Jr H S 112 Reservoir Ave Manchester NH 03104

BALL, PATRICIA SIX, 5th & 6th Grade Teacher; *b:* Princeton, WV; *M:* Ronald G.; *ed:* (BS) Elem Ed, Soc Stud, Bluefield St Coll 1979; (MA) Speech, Comm, WV Univ 1982; *cr:* Teacher Oakvale Elem 1979-; *ai:* Cty Spelling Bee Spon; Cty Soc Stud Fair Cty Spon; Mercer Cty Rdng Cncl; WV Mini-Grant; St Vs Gold E Locks; *home:* 604 Ritchie St Princeton WV 24740

BALL, RICHARD JOSEPH, 7th/8th Grade Soc Stud Teacher; *b:* Iowa City, IA; *m:* Deborah Loewenberg; *c:* Joshua, Sarah; *ed:* (BS) His/Phys Ed, 1977, (MA) Classroom Teaching, 1982 MI St Univ; *cr:* 8th Grade Teacher Jackson Cath Mid Sch 1977-80; 7th/ 8th Grade Teacher St Thomas Aquinas Sch 1980-; *ai:* Stu Cncl Adv; MI St Univ Mentor Teacher; Ingham Cty Bar Assn Teacher of Yr 1987; *office:* St Thomas Aquinas Sch 915 Alton Rd East Lansing MI 48823

BALL, SHEILA KAY, Sixth Grade Teacher; *b:* Charleston, WV; *m:* Lawrence D.; *ed:* (BA) Soc Stud, Glenville St Coll 1971; (MA) Elem Ed, WV Coll of Grad Stud 1976; Great Book, Assertive Discipline Trng, APL Trng, Effective Schls Trng; *cr:* 6th Grade Teacher Elizabeth Elem 1971-; *ai:* 6th Grade Spon; Textbook Comm; WV Ed Assn, Wirt Cty Ed Assn; Delta Kappa Gamma; Wirt Cty Emergency Squad; Womens Auxiliary Pres 1976-78, 1983-85; WV Ed Fund Mini Grants 1987, 1989, 1990; *office:* Elizabeth Elem Sch PO Box 220 Elizabeth WV 26143

BALL, SHIRLEY MARIE (GALINSKI), 6th Grade Teacher; *b:* Cleveland, OH; *m:* Owen Keith Jr.; *ed:* (BS) Elem Ed, Univ of KS 1978; Grad Stud, Univ of KS; *cr:* 5th Grade Teacher 1978-81, 4th/ 5th Grade Teacher 1981-82, 5th Grade Teacher 1982-83, 6th Grade Teacher 1983- Schwegler Elem; *ai:* Adjunct Clinical Instr Univ of KS Sch of Ed; Lawrence Rdng Assn, Phi Delta Kappa; *office:* Schwegler Elem Sch 2201 Ousdahl Lawrence KS 66046

BALLANCE, SYLVIA MARIE, English Teacher; *b:* Wilson, NC; *ed:* (BA) Eng/His, Atlantic Chrstn Coll 1978; *cr:* Eng Teacher E Wayne HS 1978-83, E Wayne Jr HS 1983-; *ai:* Yrbk & Newspaper Adv; 9th Grade Graduation Comm; NC Assn of Educators; E Wayne Jr HS Teacher of Yr 1990; *home:* Rt 1 Box 394 Fremont NC 27830

BALLANGER, ALBERT O., Mathematics/Computer Teacher; *b:* Austin, MN; *m:* Margaret Atwood; *c:* Michelle, David; *ed:* (AA) Pre Eng, Austin Jr Coll 1961; (BS) Math/Phys Sci, Winona St Univ 1963; (MS) General Sci, Syracuse Univ 1968; Grad Stud Industrial Tech, Univ WI Platteville 1979; *cr:* Math/Cmptr Sci Teacher Ceylon Public Sch 1981-; *ai:* Voluntary Timer HS Athletic Events; Ceylon Ed Assn, MN Ed Assn, NEA (Treas, Mem) 1981-; Gideons Intnl 1975-; Natl Sci Fnd Academic Yr Syracuse Univ 1967-68; *office:* Ceylon Public Sch 301 West Grant St Ceylon MN 56121

BALLARD, BETTY PEEK, 3rd Grade Teacher; *b:* Mars Hill, NC; *m:* Bobby L.; *c:* Tamara L., Terry D.; *ed:* Elem Ed, Mars Hill Coll 1961; (BS) Elem Ed, East TN St Univ 1963; *cr:* 4th Grade Teacher Ebbs Chapel Elem 1963-64; 3rd Grade Teacher Charles C Bell Elem 1964-65, Mars Hill Elem 1965-; *ai:* NC Ed Assn; NEA Teacher of Yr 1987-88; Laurel Branch Baptist Church; *office:* Mars Hill Elem Sch Bailey St Mars Hill NC 28754

BALLARD, BEVERLY SULLIVAN, Social Studies/French Teacher; *b:* Ackerman, MS; *m:* Richard P.; *c:* Will, Dane, Luke; *ed:* (BAE) Soc Stud/Eng, Univ of MS 1979; *cr:* Eng Teacher W Panola Acad 1979-81; Soc Stud/Fr Teacher Winston Acad 1985-; *ai:* Yrbk & Sr Spon; Schlsp, Homecoming Comm; MS Private 1979-81; Sch Ed Assn 1985-; First Baptist Church Sunday Sch Teacher 1988-; Star Teacher 1989; *home:* Rt 4 Box 224B Louisville MS 39339

BALLARD, BRUCE BOLLING, Physical Education Teacher; *b:* Great Falls, MT; *m:* Carol Lynn Mc Cutchan; *ed:* (BS) Phys Ed/ Health, Univ of ME 1973; (MA) Curr/Instruction, MI St Univ 1980; Adaptive Phys Ed Credential Brockport St Univ; Adaptive Phys Ed Guide-Contributin Ed Univ of S FL; TESA Los Angeles St Univ; Ed Theory into Pacific Seattle Pacific Univ; *cr:* Phys Ed Teacher Athens Elem Sch 1973-75, Croughton Mid Sch 1975-; *ai:* Var Ftbl, Wrestling, Track & Jr Var Soccer, Bsktbl Coach; Mid Sch Bicycle Club Spon; AAHPERD 1982-; Overseas Ed Assn 1978-; Sch Advisory Comm (Mem, Chairperson 1986-87); Excl in Teaching Superior Awds 1974-75, 1986-87.

BALLARD, CECIL MERLE, Fifth Grade Teacher; *b:* Detroit Lakes, MN; *m:* Jane Svedberg; *c:* Katie, Anne; *ed:* (BS) Elem Ed, Bemidji St Univ 1973; Working Towards Masters Moorhead St Univ; *cr:* 3rd Grade Teacher 1973-82, 5th Grade Teacher 1982-86, Title I Teacher 1986-88, 5th Grade Teacher/Building Prin 1988- Ogema Elem; *ai:* Sci & Stu Cncl Adv; Waubun Ed Assn Pres 1978-79; PTA Pres 1976-77; Jaycees Local Pres 1979; *home:* 320 E Willow Detroit Lakes MN 56501

BALLARD, DANA JEAN, Mathematics Teacher/Coach; *b:* Houston, TX; *ed:* (BS) Phys Ed, TX A&M Univ 1985; Post Grad Stud E TX St; *cr:* Teacher Irving Ind Sch Dist 1986; Teacher/ Coach Lake Highlands HS 1986-; *ai:* Jr Var Vlybl & Bsktbl Coach; Stu Cncl & Girls Service League Spon; Young Life Cnslr; Assn TX Prof Teachers 1985-; Richardson Ed Assn 1986-; Phi Epsilon Kappa VP 1984-85; Dallas Assoc Soc Chm 1989-; Chi Omega Alumnae 1985-; TX A&M Univ Century Club 1985-; Lake Highlands Teacher of Yr 1988-89; TX A&M Coll Ed Outstanding Grad 1985; *office:* Lake Highlands HS 9449 Church Rd Dallas TX 75243

BALLARD, ELAINE ROBERTSON, Fifth Grade Teacher; *b:* Logansport, IN; *m:* Thomas O.; *c:* Andrea J., Benjamin T.; *ed:* (BS) Elem Ed, Taylor Univ 1972; (MS) Elem Ed, Purdue Univ 1975; *cr:* 3rd Grade Teacher Fowler Elem Sch 1972-78; 3rd/4th Grade Teacher Boswell Elem Sch 1979-80; 5th Grade Teacher Fowler Elem Sch 1980-; *ai:* Delta Kappa Gamma 1988-; *office:* Fowler Elem Sch 301 E 2nd St Fowler IN 47944

BALLARD, ELIZABETH LYONS, Eng/Debate/Acting Teacher; *b:* Purcell, OK; *ed:* (BAED) Eng/Speech/Theatre, E Cntrl St Univ 1973; (MA) Eng, 1975, (PHD) Eng, 1989 Univ of OK; *cr:* Grad Teaching Asst Univ of OK 1973-76; Teacher Norman HS 1976-; *ai:* Competitive Acting & Debate Squad Coach; Norman HS Natl Forensic League Spon; OK Speech & Theatre Cmmty Assn Teacher of Yr; Prof Ed of Norman Teacher of Yr; OK Ed Assn, NEA; Stone Soup Theatre (Founding Bd Mem, Pres); OK Scndry Schls Act Assn Advisory Bd; Western Dist Natl Forensic League Comm Mem; OSTCA Speech Teacher of Yr 1983; Norman Public Schls Teacher of Yr 1985; Poetry Published; *office:* Norman HS 911 W Main Norman OK 73069

BALLARD, FRANCES PORTER, Kindergarten Teacher; *b:* Knox City, MO; *m:* Harold S.; *c:* Tom, Jim, Bill, Doug, Greg, Rhonda, Jill; *ed:* Overseas Prgm Univ of MD, Miami-Dade Comm Coll; *cr:* K-5th Grade Teacher Lyonsdown Sch 1963-73, Princeton Chrstn Sch 1973-; *ai:* Elem Sch Cnslr; United Meth Women Pres 1973-77; PTA Secy; Brownies, Cub Scout Leader 1958-67; Runner Up Amer Mother of Yr Overseas 1958; *office:* Princeton Chrstn Sch 24795 SW 134th Ave Princeton FL 33032

BALLARD, JOYCE DAVIS, English Teacher; *b:* Louisburg, NC; *m:* Maurice Leon; *ed:* (BA) Eng, St Augustines Coll 1963; Working Towards Masters NC St Univ, Old Dominion Univ; *cr:* Eng Teacher J W Ligon HS 1963-66, Carnage Jr HS 1967-72, Ferguson HS 1973-; *ai:* Forensics Coach & Spon; Drama Coach; Newport News Ed Assn 1975-; VA Assn of Teachers Eng 1978-; BATE; Alpha Kappa Alpha; Outstanding Coach Awd 1970-71.

BALLARD, MARCIA DORAN, Fifth Grade Teacher; *b:* Macomb, IL; *m:* Roger Alan; *c:* Roger A. Jr. (dec); *ed:* (BS) Elem Ed, 1963, (MS) Rdng Specialist, 1973 Western IL Univ; Grad Stud Various Univs; *cr:* 4th Grade Teacher Avon Elem Sch 1963-64; 3rd-5th Grade Teacher E Peoria Elem Dist 86 1964-; *ai:*

Soc Stud Comm; NEA, IL Ed Assn; E Peoria Elem Ed Assn Secy of Local 1986-88; E Peoria Youth Cncl 1986-; E Peoria Centennial Comm; Writing & Preparing Book for Drama.

BALLARD, RUTH ROBINSON, Teacher/Dept Chair; *b:* Newton, TX; *m:* Eddie; *c:* Mark, Julie; *ed:* (BS) Music/Eng, Stephen F Austin St Univ 1964; TX Womens Univ; TX Wesylan Coll; *cr:* Music/Eng Teacher Carrol Thompson Jr HS 1965; Eng Teacher Levelland Ind Sch Dist 1965-68, Waxahachie HS 1969-; *ai:* Curr Comm; TX St Teachers Assn 1965-; TX Joint Cncl Teachers of Eng 1975-; Teacher of Yr 1987; *home:* 201 Cumberland Waxahachie TX 75165

BALLESTY, PETER JOSEPH, Soc Stud/Cmptr Teacher; *b:* New York, NY; *m:* Dianne Lynn Watson; *c:* Taryn, Peter K.; *ed:* (BA) Amer His, Cath Univ 1965; (MA) Scndry Ed, NY Univ 1970; Math, Fairfield Univ & City Coll of NY; Cmptr Sci, City Coll of NY & Iona Coll; *cr:* 7th-8th Grade Teacher Holy Name Sch 1965-70; 7th-10th Grade Math Teacher 1970-80, Soc Stud/Cmptr Teacher 1980- Valhalla Public Schls; *ai:* NY St Assn for Cmptrs & Technologies in Ed, NY St Cncl on Soc Stud, Westchester Cncl on Soc Stud; *office:* Valhalla Public Schls 300 Columbus Ave Valhalla NY 10595

BALLEW, PATRICIA ANN, Jr HS Language Arts Teacher; *b:* Ft Worth, TX; *m:* William Lee; *c:* Bret L.; *ed:* (BA) Eng, TX Wesleyan Coll 1978; (MA) Ed/Rdng Specialist, Angelo St Univ 1989; *cr:* Soph Eng Teacher Springtown HS 1979-82; Jr HS Lang Art Teacher Robert Lee Jr HS 1983-; *ai:* UIL Literary Events Spelling, Oral Rdng, Ready Writing; Chrldr, Pep Squad, 8th Grade Class Spon; NCTE, TX Joint Cncl of Teachers of Eng; Co-Conducting Summer Teacher In-Service Rdng Wkshps; *office:* Robert Lee Jr HS HC 61 Box 303 Robert Lee TX 76945

BALOG, SHARON LEWIN, Mathematics Teacher; *b:* New York, NY; *m:* Gilbert E.; *c:* Joshua, Aliza; *ed:* (BA) Hum, St Univ of NY Binghampton 1969; (MS) Guidance/Counseling, Lehman Coll 1976; *cr:* Math Teacher Evander Childs HS 1971-73, Theodore Roosevelt HS 1973-; *office:* Theodore Roosevelt HS 500 E Fordham Rd New York NY 10458

BALOUN, CHARLENE MARY, Kindergarten Teacher; *b:* Chicago, IL; *ed:* (BA) Math, Mundelein Coll 1964; (MED) Early Chldhd Ed, Univ of IL 1967; Natl Coll of Ed/Lewis Univ/Northeastern IL Univ/Elmhurst Coll/George Williams Coll; *cr:* K-1st Grade Teacher Argo Summit Dist #104 Schls 1964-69; Kndgtn Teacher Hawthorne Sch 1969-76; K-1st Grade Teacher Holmes Sch 1976-; Resource Instr to Grad Stu Natl Coll of Ed 1989-; *ai:* Oak Park Kndgtn Comm; Holmes Sch Building Plan Comm; NEA 1964-; IL Ed Assn 1964-; Delta Kappa Gamma Chair Several Comms 1976-; St Cyprian Cath Church Lay Minister of Communion 1985-; Honorable Mention Awd-Those Who Excel in Ed 1985; Golden Apple Awd Nominee 1990; Lesson Plan Published In 4 Mat in Action 1983; *office:* Oliver Wendel Holmes Elem Sch 500 N Kenilworth Ave Oak Park IL 60302

BALSAM, BARBARA CAROL, Latin/English Teacher; *b:* Boston, MA; *c:* Danial L., Katherine A.; *ed:* (BA) Classics, Tufts Univ 1966; (MA) Lit, Wesleyan Univ 1970; Grad Work CT St Coll, Amer Acad in Rome, Rutgers Univ, Drew Univ; *cr:* Latin/Eng Teacher Durham HS 1966-69, Governor Livingston Regional HS 1980-; Latin New Providence HS 1989-; *ai:* Latin Club Adv; Amer Classical League, NJ Classical Assn 1980-, Schlsp 1985; Classical Society of Amer Acad of Rome 1985-; NCTE 1990; PTA Faculty Rep; Union Cty Regional Adult Sch Bd Mem 1987-; Tufts Univ Interviewer 1981-; *home:* 14 Dorset Rd Berkeley Heights NJ 07922

BALSTER, BARBARA MAY, 3rd Grade Teacher; *b:* Ames, IA; *m:* David; *c:* Brian, Kevin; *ed:* (BSS) Sociology/Elem Ed, Cornell Coll 1972; (MA) Elem Ed, Univ of N CO 1977; *cr:* 3rd Grade Teacher Monticello Schls 1978-; *ai:* Wellness, Various Curr, Climate Control & Phase III Performance Based Pay Comms; NEA, IA St Ed Assn 1977-; Beta Club 1985-; *office:* Shannon Elem Sch 321 W South St Monticello IA 52310

BALTES, SANDRA VILLELLI, Resource Teacher/SID Coord; *b:* St Paul, MN; *c:* Michelle, Lisa B. Lewis, Stacey, Craig; *ed:* (BA) Eng, Univ of CA Riverside 1974; (MA) Educl Admin, USIU 1989; *cr:* Elem Teacher Midland Sch 1977-81; Mid Sch Teacher Washington Mid Sch 1984-86; Resource Teacher/SID CHI Coord Walnut Sch 1986-; *ai:* CA New Teacher Project Mem Rep; Gifted & Talented Coord/Teacher; Chapter I Coord/Teacher; Summer Sch Prin; Lead Teacher Mentor; La Habra Educators Assn (Treas, Secy 1985) 1984-; Southern Ctys Women in Educl Management 1989-; CA PTA (VP, Secy) 1971- Honorary Service Awd 1976; Moreno Valley C of C Citizen of Yr 1977; *office:* Walnut Sch 635 N Walnut La Habra CA 90631

BALTHAZOR, ROBERTA I., 3rd Grade Teacher; *b:* Phoenix, AZ; *m:* Leo R.; *c:* Steven, Krista, Scott; *ed:* (BS) Elem Ed, Northern AZ Univ 1967; AZ St Univ; *cr:* 2nd Grade Teacher John Adams Sch 1967-68, Catalina Sch 1968-71; 3rd Grade Teacher Barcelona Sch 1973-; *ai:* Meet & Confer Team; Ladies Oriental Shrine of N Amer Unit Pres 1989-; Daughters of the Ni E 1985-; NEA 1973-; *office:* Barcelona Elem Schl 4432 W Maryland Ave Glendale AZ 85301

BALTON, SHEILA VADEN, Fourth Grade Teacher; *b:* Pontiac, MI; *m:* Mark Christopher; *c:* Patrick; *ed:* (BS) Ed, Univ of TN 1979; *cr:* 4th Grade Teacher Holy Rosary Sch 1979-; *ai:* NCEA; *home:* 5946 Baird Dr Memphis TN 38119

BALTUTAT, SALLI POAT, Second Grade Teacher; *b:* Battle Creek, MI; *m:* Fritz; *c:* Brett M.; *ed:* (BA) Elem Ed, Univ of MI 1978; (MA) Elem Ed, W MI Univ 1982; Physically Impaired Spec Ed Endorsement; MI Model in Sci Trng; Math-Their-Way Trng; Essential Elements for Effective Instruction Trng; *cr:* 1st/2nd Grade Teacher Battle Creek Public Sch 1978-; *ai:* 5th/6th Grade After Sch Sports Prgm; Grade Level Comm; Grading System Revision; Battle Creek Ed Assn 1978-; Jr League of Battle Creek 1982-; Amer Assn of Univ Women 1980-; Delta Gamma Treas 1980-; *office:* Urbandale Elem Sch 123 N Bedford Rd Battle Creek MI 49017

BALTZ, JANET LUCILLE, Third Grade Teacher; *b:* Rhinelander, WI; *m:* Donald E.; *c:* Melanie; *ed:* (BS) Elem Ed, Univ of WI Stevens Point 1963; *cr:* 4th Grade Teacher Rhinelander 1961-62, D C Everest Sch 1963-64, Germany 1964-65; 3rd Grade Teacher D C Everest Sch 1965-69; 5th Grade Teacher Mosinee Elem Sch 1969-70; 3rd Grade Teacher Stoddard Elem Sch 1970-72; 4th Grade Teacher 1972-73, 3rd Grade Teacher 1976-89 Mosinee Elem Sch; *ai:* Cheerleading Coach; Mosinee Ed Assn Soc Comm 1976-89; NEA 1976-89; WI Ed Assn (Delegate 1971-72) 1976-89; Lions Quest Trainee; Cmmty Service Projects; *home:* 850 Naugart Dr Merrill WI 54452

BALTZ, VIRGINIA RUTH, First Grade Teacher; *b:* Elmhurst, IL; *m:* John L.; *c:* Margaret, Michael, Thomas, Brian, William; *ed:* (BS) Elem Ed, N IL Univ 1966; *cr:* 2nd Grade Teacher Parkview Elem Sch 1966-68; 4th/5th Grade Teacher 1978-79, 3rd Grade Teacher 1979-87, 1st Grade Teacher 1987- Cathedral of St Raymond Sch; *ai:* Primary Dept Chairperson; Liturgy, Discipline, Sch Handbook Comms; NCEA Mem 1978-; St Raymonds Parish Cncl VP 1986-89; *home:* 407 N William Joliet IL 60435

BALUSEK, MELISSA JANE, Fifth Grade Teacher; *b:* Houston, TX; *m:* Emil Louis; *c:* Laurel Jane Cooper; *ed:* (BS) Elem Ed, Texas Wesleyan 1978; *cr:* 4th Grade Teacher B H Carroll Elem 1979-82; 5th Grade Teacher Brentwood Chrstn Sch 1982-89; *ai:* Elem Service Project Dir; Wrote & Developed the Bible Curr for Elem Grades; *office:* Brentwood Chrstn Sch 11908 N Lamar Austin TX 78753

BALZANO, JOHN G., Mathematics Teacher; *b:* Gloversville, NY; *m:* Barbara Anne Gilman; *c:* Kristine, Joseph, Julie; *ed:* (BA) Math, Le Moyne Coll 1971; (MAT) Math, Univ of VT 1973; Educl Admin, SUC Brockport; *cr:* Teaching Intern Burling HS 1971-73; Math Dept Leader Martha Brown Jr HS 1975-86; Adjunct Ed Teacher St John Fisher Coll 1978-83; Math Teacher Martha Brown Jr/Sr HS 1973-; *ai:* Math Team Coach; Homebase Guidance Comm; NCTM 1973-; AMTNYS (Vice Pres, Cty Choir) 1973-; Phi Delta Kappa 1989-; Parish Church (Parish Cncl, Trustee, Organist, Choir, Minister, Teacher) 1971-; Macedon Zoning Appeals Bd 1978-83; Pal-Moc Youth Soccer Dir 1982-89; Grad Teaching Fellow 1971-73; Fairport Teacher of Yr 1986; Author/Teacher Consultant Unified Math; *office:* Martha Brown Mid Sch 665 Ayrault Rd Fairport NY 14450

BALZUM, MARY JEAN PROCHNOW, Fourth Grade Teacher; *b:* Springfield, MO; *m:* Keith; *c:* Nathan; *ed:* (BA) Elem Ed, Concordia Coll 1974; *cr:* 3rd Grade Teacher Christ Luth Sch 1974-76; 4th Grade Teacher St Johns Luth Sch 1976-; *ai:* MN Rdng, Luth Ed Assn; *office:* St Johns Luth Sch 109 W Main St Young America MN 55397

BAMBARGER, BETTYE STONE, Mathematics Teacher; *b:* Selma, AL; *m:* John Thomas; *c:* Anne Raynie; *ed:* (BS) Math/Music, Livingston Univ 1969; Gifted Ed, Concentration Space Sci; *cr:* Teacher Private Sch 1969-70, Northport Jr HS 1970-; *ai:* Math, Stock Market Team; Young Astronauts; Adopt-A-Sch Rep; Steering Comm; Self Study Southern Assn Accreditation; Sch Wide Attendance Report; AEA, NEA 1970-; NCTM, NSTA 1985-, Newmast 1987; Delta Kappa Gamma (VP, Secy, Comm Chairperson) 1980-; Children Hands on Museum 1987-89; Summer Enrichment 1986-; Delta Kappa Gamma Grants; Piloted Space Ed Teacher I & II; Nom Teacher of Yr; *home:* 1265 Northwood Lake Northport AL 35476

BAMBAS, STEVE W., 7th/8th Grade Science Teacher; *b:* Tyndall, SD; *ed:* (BA) Bio, Mt Marty 1983; *cr:* Jr HS Sci Teacher Tri-Valley Sch Dist 1983-; *ai:* HS Wrestling Head, 7th/8th Grade Ftbl, Asst HS Track Coach; SD Jaycees; *office:* Tri-Valley Sch Dist Box 8 Lyons SD 57041

BAMFORD, TERRIE (MAURER), Mathematics Teacher; *b:* Shamokin, PA; *m:* Daniel G.; *c:* Brooke; *ed:* (BS) Math, Shippensburg Univ 1970; Grad Stud Millersville Univ; *cr:* Math Teacher Lancaster City Sch Dist 1970-72, Shamokin Area Sch Dist 1972-; *ai:* NEA, PA Ed Assn, Shamokin Ed Assn 1972-; PA Cncl of Teachers of Math 1990; *office:* Shamokin Area HS 2000 W State St Shamokin PA 17872

BANASIK, CARMELA MUGNANO, Junior High Teacher; *b:* Cleveland, OH; *w:* Leonard (dec); *c:* Victoria J., John M.; *ed:* (BS) Elem Ed, Western Reserve Univ 1964; Art Therapy; Creative Writing; Music Ed; *cr:* Teacher St Aloysius Sch 1955-60; St Clare Sch 1960-64; Washington Sch 1964-66; Sub Teacher South Euclid Lyndhurst System 1966-70; Teacher St Clare Sch 1970-; *ai:* Sch Musical Dir; Grade Level Coord; Musical Dir for Comm Theaters; Pianist Jazz/Swing Band Nostalgia; Natl Catholic Ed Assn Mem 1976-; OH Choral Dir Assn Mem 1989-; Isabella Guild Pres 1968-70; Wrote Chapter Ohio History Book Published By Diocese of Cleveland; *home:* 1263 W Miner Rd Mayfield Hts OH 44124

BANCO, JOHN HAROLD, Language Art/English Teacher; *b:* Wheeling, WV; *m:* Mary Katherine; *c:* Jonathan; *ed:* (BA) Speech/Drama/Eng, W Liberty St Coll 1964; (MA) Comm, WV Univ 1990; Grad Stud; *cr:* Teacher Chester Jr HS 1963-64, Shadyside HS 1964-76, Wheeling Park HS 1976-; *ai:* Wheeling Park HS Stu Cncl, Jr Town Meeting of Air, Shadyside HS Thespian Club Adv; SAch Dances Decorator, Designer, Consultant; Ohio Cty Ed Assn 1976-; OH Ed Assn (Cty Rep 1967-69, Mem 1965-76); Shadyside Ed Assn (Pres 1966-67, Mem 1965-76); Belmont Cty Ed Assn (Pres 1967-68, Mem 1965-76); NEA 1964-; YMCA Indian Guides 1987-89; Little League Bsbl Coach 1988-; Stu Folk Singers Dir 1970; Summer Day Camp Prgm Dir; Wrote & Dir HS Musical; Jennings Scholar Awd for Outstanding Teachers in OH 1967-68; Organizer & Singer with Prof Folk Singing Group.

BANCROFT, CONNIE MELINDA, Third Grade Teacher; *b:* Cleveland, TN; *ed:* (AS) Elem Ed, Cleveland St Comm Coll 1977; (BS) Elem Ed, Lee Coll 1979; (MS) Admin/Supervision, Trevecca Coll 1989; Working Towards Masters Admin & Supervision; *cr:* 2nd/3rd Grade Teacher 1979-80, 3rd Grade Teacher 1980- Prospect Sch; *ai:* Faculty Rep of Teachers Study Cncl & Rdng Assn; Bradley Cty Ed Assn, Tn Ed Assn, NEA 1979-; TN Teachers Study Cncl (System Chair, Dist Secy); Cleveland & Bradley Rdng Assn VP-Elect 1990; Bancroft Church of God Missions Coord 1987, Outstanding Leadership 1987; Delta Kappa Gamma 1987-; Bancroft Church of God (Sunday Sch Teacher 1982-, Childrens Church Dir 1979-); System Level Teacher of Yr 1987; Jaycees Distinguished Service Awd Nom 1988-89; *office:* Prospect Sch 2450 Prospect School Rd Cleveland TN 37311

BANDARRA, GILBERT, Biology/Physiology Teacher; *b:* New Bedford, MA; *m:* Jovita Correia; *c:* Diane Aberle, Linda, Paul, Amy, Kim; *ed:* (BS) Bio/Chem, Stonehill Coll 1953; (MED) Ed, Bridgewater St Coll 1957; Attended Boston Coll, Brown Univ, Simmons Coll, Woods Hole Marine Biological Lab, Natl Sci Fnd, MIT Nuclear Tech Seminars; *cr:* Bio Teacher 1954-63, Dir of Sci 1960-63 Dartmouth HS; Dir of Sec Summer Sch 1968-70, General Sci/Bio Teacher 1963- Braintree HS; *ai:* Ecology & Audio-Visual Club; NABT, NEA, MA Braintree Ed Assn; Dartmouth Teacher Assn VP 1960-61; MA Mohawk Winner Winnebabgo (VP 1987-88, Pres 1988-89); Square Dance Club Exec Comm 1983-85; Natl Sci Fnd & Horace Mann Grants; Newspaper Articles on Sci Teaching & Intnl Sci Fair; *home:* 45 Washington Park Dr Norwell MA 02061

BANDELIN, LILLIAN SALMELA, 5th Grade Teacher; *b:* Chicago, IL; *c:* Wayne, Lori; Sherry; *ed:* (BSE) Elem Ed, 1965; (MSE) Rdng, Northern IL Univ 1972; *cr:* 5th Grade Teacher Lake in the Hills Elem 1966-; *ai:* Young Authors Coord; Impact Comm for Better Schls; NEA 1966-; IL Ed Assn 1966-; *home:* 1103 Pine St Lake In The Hills IL 60102

BANDISH, ELIZABETH CERJANEC, 1st Grade Teacher; *b:* Waynesburg, PA; *m:* James H.; *c:* Shannon R., Megan E.; *ed:* (BS) Elem Ed, CA St Coll 1971; (MA) Early Chldhd Ed, WV Univ 1975; *cr:* 2nd Grade Teacher West Greene Schl Dist 1971-74; 3rd Grade Teacher 1974-75; 1st Grade Teacher 1975- Carmichaels Area Schl Dist; *ai:* Comm Mem Curr Dev Rdng & Math; Stud Teacher/Supv Teacher; Staff Person Comm Whole Lang Dev in Ed; PSEA; NEA; CAEA; AAUW 1985-; St Hugh R C Church CCD Teacher 1989-; *office:* Nemacolin Elem Sch PO Box 157 Nemacolin PA 15351

BANDLOW, RICHARD FRANK, Eng Dept Chair/Cmptr Coord; *b:* Detroit, MI; *m:* Diane C. Yehl; *c:* Jason, Jennifer, David, Laurel; *ed:* (BA) Eng, Alma Coll 1969; (MA) Eng, 1974, Cmptr Sci, 1987 Cntrl MI Univ; *cr:* Teacher/Coach/Cmptr Coord/Adult Ed Teacher Evart Public Schls 1969-; *ai:* Track, Ftbl, Bsktbl Coach; Jr Class, Sr Class, NHS Spon; Cmptr Coord; Eng Dept Chairperson; EEA (Pres, Secy, Building Rep) 1980-88; MACUL, MEA, NEA, NCTE, MCTE; Co-Author Book; Outstanding Person in Ed Evart Public Schls 1989-; *office:* Evart Jr-Sr HS 321 N Hemlock Evart MI 49631

BANE, RICKY L., Science Teacher; *b:* Ackerman, MS; *m:* Darlene Fryery; *c:* E. J., Patrick; *ed:* (BS) Phys Ed, 1979, (MS) Educl Admin, 1989 MS St Univ; *cr:* Coach 1979-81, Sci Teacher Eiland Mid Sch 1981-; *ai:* MS Prof Educataors 1983-; Nom MS Sci Teacher of Yr; *office:* Eiland Mid Sch 508 Camile Ave Louisville MS 39339

BANEY, TODD MICHAEL, Sixth Grade Teacher; *b:* Sayre, PA; *ed:* (BS) Elem Ed, 1972, (MED) Elem Ed, 1976 Bloomsburg Univ; *cr:* 5th Grade Teacher 1972-84, 6th Grade Teacher 1985- Millville Elem Sch; *ai:* Elem Lang Arts Dept Head; Dir of Safety Patrol; Asst Dir of Elem Intramurals; Coach Elem Boys/Girls Bsktbl & Little League Sftbl Minor League; NCTE 1987-; ASCD 1986-; NEA 1972-; PA St Ed Assn Millville Ed Assn 1972-; Millville Ed Assn Pres 1974-76; Pine Street Luth Church Congregational Cncl Lay Pres 1988-; Selection for Whos Who Among Young Amer Prof 1988; *office:* Millville Elem Schl P O Box 300 Millville PA 17846

BANG, TIMOTHY DONALD, English Teacher/Dept Chair; *b:* Red Wing, MN; *m:* Anne Elizabeth Schmidt; *ed:* (BS) Broad Area Eng, Univ of WI River Falls 1986; *cr:* Eng Dept Chm Foley HS 1986-; *ai:* Asst Speech Coach; One Act Play Dir; SADD Adv; Literary Journal; Meep & Positive Stu Comm; NCTE, Sigma Tau Delta, AFT; Maywood Covenant Church; E F Prucha Schlsp Excl in Writing; Bloom Schlsp Literary Scholar Promise; *office:* Foley HS 520 Dewey St Foley MN 56329

BANIECKI, PATRICIA KRAJNAK, Language Art Teacher; *b:* Masontown, PA; *c:* John, Laura, Mary L.; *ed:* (BS) Home Ec, IN Univ of PA 1962; (MA) Rdng Specialist, WV Univ 1975; St Cert Elem, CA Univ of PA; Grad Stud; Several Wkshps; *cr:* Home Ec Teacher Center Township HS 1962-63, Kawamhee Jr HS 1963-65; Elem Teacher Tucson Cath Schls 1965-68; Rdng Specialist 1975-77, Lang Art Teacher 1977- Cntrl Greene Sch Dist; Upward Bound Eng Teacher Waynesburg Coll 1980-; *ai:* Dept Chairperson 1979-88; Dist Curr Cncl Mem 1979-88; Phi Delta Kappa, PA St Ed Assn, Cntrl Greene Teachers Assn 1990; Cntrl Green PTA; PA Assn for Supervision & Curr Dev Presenter; PA Cncl Teachers of Eng; PA Mid Sch Conference; Curr Art Resources & Ed Services; Upward Bound Parent Presentations; *home:* 311 S Vine St Carmichaels PA 15320

BANION, SUZANNE WILT, 7th & 8th Grade Lit Teacher; *b:* Springfield, OH; *ed:* (BS) Ed, 1975, (MS) Ed, 1982 Wright St Univ; Cmptr Programming; *cr:* 3rd Grade Teacher 1975-82, 7th/8th Grade Lit Teacher 1983 Miami View Sch; *ai:* 8th Grade Vlybl & Jr HS Track Coach; Peer Tutor Coord; Hall of Fame Comm Mem; NEA, OH Ed Assn, Southeastern Local Ed Assn 1975-; *office:* Miami View Sch 230 Clifton Rd South Charleston OH 45368

BANISZEWSKI, DAVID EDMUND, 1st-12th Grade Lead Teacher; *b:* Erie, PA; *m:* Heidi Tofel; *c:* Carrie, Casey; *ed:* (BA) Eng, Gannon Univ 1978; Scndry PA Teaching Certificate, Edinboro Univ of PA 1986; Grad Work Edinboro Univ of PA, Pensacola Chrstn Coll; Candidate MRE Grand Rapids Baptist Seminary; *cr:* Prin/Teacher Erie Chrstn Acad 1979-82; Sr HS Teacher/Academic Prin Heritage Chrstn Acad 1983-84; Prin/Lead Teacher NE Chrstn Acad 1984-; *ai:* Drama Club, Soccer & Sftbl Coach; Church of God Ed Assn 1985-; *office:* North East Chrstn Acad 5335 Station Rd North East PA 16428

BANKS, ALICE HALL, 4th Grade Teacher; *b:* Burnsville, MS; *m:* Huel D.; *c:* Alan, Carl, Benita K.; *ed:* (BA) Eng, St Bernard 1960; (BA) Elem Ed, Univ of MS 1974; *cr:* 4th Grade Teacher Belmont Elem 1969-; *ai:* 4-H Club 1978-; Sunday Sch Teacher; *home:* PO Box 75 Belmont MS 38827

BANKS, DAVID WAYNE, Coord/Teacher of Gifted Ed; *b:* Whitesburg, KY; *m:* Jan Jones; *c:* Boyd, Andrew; *ed:* (BM) Music Ed, Union Coll 1970; (MA) Elem Ed, 1980, (Rank I) Elem Ed, 1980 Eastern KY Univ; *cr:* Music Teacher Evarts Elem & Evarts HS 1970-71, Stanford Elem 1975-76; Elem Classroom Teacher 1978-83, Teacher of Gifted Ed 1983- Casey Cty Schls; *ai:* KY Assn for Gifted Ed 1983-; KY Ed Assn, NEA 1975-; Liberty 1st Chrstn Church (Treas, Minister of Music) 1988-; Cub Scout Pack 47 Cubmaster 1984-87; Casey Cty 4-H Cncl 1982-85; *home:* PO Box 354 Liberty KY 42539

BANKS, JAN SUE (ROGERS), Remedial Reading Teacher; *b:* Mc Alester, OK; *m:* John Robert; *c:* Eddie, Steve; *ed:* (AA) Elem Ed, E OK St Coll 1974; (BA) Elem Ed, 1976, (MS) Rdng Specialist, 1982 E Cntrl OK St Univ; Bible Survey, Hillsdale Freewill Baptist Bible Coll 1974; *cr:* 4th Grade Teacher 1976-88, Remedial Rdng Teacher 1988- Crowder Sch; *ai:* Crowder Ed Assn (Pres 1986-88, Rep); Jr 4-H Club Leader 1977-86; *home:* Box 268 Crowder OK 74430

BANKS, JANETH CASPER, Soc Stud/Language Arts Teacher; *b:* Monett, MO; *ed:* (BSED) Soc Sci, MO Southern ST Coll 1975; Addl Studies Pittsburg ST Univ; Southwest MO ST Univ, Univ of MO; *cr:* Teacher Southwest Barry R-5 Sch 1976-; *ai:* Sr Class Spon, Jr Class Spon; 7th Grade Class Spon, 8th Grade Class Spon, Chrldr Spon, Stu Cncl Spon, Bsktbl Scorekeeper, Sftbl Scorekeeper, Prof Dev Curr Comm; NCSS 1979,89,90; MSTA 1976-; CTA Sec 1982-84; PTO 1988-; *home:* 1505 Townsend Cassville MO 65625

BANKS, JOAN E., English Teacher; *b:* Manchester, NH; *c:* Jennifer, Jodi, John; *ed:* (BA) Eng, Notre Dame 1965; *cr:* Teacher Cntrl HS 1978-; *ai:* Peer Outreach Facilitator; Manchester Ed Assn, NEA; *office:* Central HS 207 Lowell St Manchester NH 03104

BANKS, JON M., Science Department Chairman; *b:* Henderson, TX; *m:* Jennie Hawkins; *ed:* (BS) Bio, Stephen F Austin 1967; (MED) Guidance/Counseling, Lamar Univ 1977; *cr:* Teacher/Coach Nederland HS 1967-80, Gregory-Portland HS 1980-81, W Mesquite HS 1981-; *ai:* Boys Var Bsktbl Coach; Sr Class Spon; HS At-Risk Coord; Sat Preparation Presenter; Bsbl Announcer; Mesquite Ed Assn 1981-; TX St Teachers Assn 1967-; TX HS Coaches Assn 1968-; TX Assn of Bsktbl Coaches 1975-; Teacher Of Yr 1990; Published Article 1990; Presenter St At-Risk Conference 1990; *office:* West Mesquite HS 405 E Davis Mesquite TX 75149

BANKS, LORRAINE MILES, Third Grade Teacher; *b:* Catskill, NY; *m:* Emil; *c:* Todd, Toby, Shawn; *ed:* (BS) Elem Ed, Oneonta St Univ 1972; *cr:* 3rd Grade Teacher Gilboa-Conesville Cntrl Sch 1972-; *ai:* Drama Club Co Dir; NY St Teachers Union (Secy, VP) 1976-78; PTA VP 1985-86.

BANKS, MARYELLEN CLINE, 7th Grade Unified Stud Teacher; *b:* Kansas City, KS; *m:* Jerry R.; *c:* Adison; *ed:* (AA) Soc Stud, KS City Comm Coll 1974; (BA) Psych, 1976, (BSE) Eng/Soc Stud, 1978 Univ of KS; (MA) Soc Stud/Scndry Ed, Univ of MO 1986; *cr:* 7th Grade Eng/World His/11th Grade Amer His Teacher Piper Jr/Sr HS 1979-81; 7th Grade Unified Stud Teacher Indian Trail Jr HS 1981-; *ai:* Cheerleading Spon 1979-81; Pep Club Spon 1982-83; Kayettes Spon 1983-86; Sch Spelling Bee Coord 1984-; NEA 1989-; Nom Excl in Teaching Awd 1987; Article Published 1977; *office:* Indian Trail Jr HS 1440 E 151st St Olathe KS 66062

BANKS, PATRICIA ANN, Jr HS English Teacher; *b:* Brooklyn, NY; *ed:* (BS) Eng, St Peter Coll 1971; (MED) Rdng, William Paterson Coll 1987; Certificate NJ Rdng Specialist; *cr:* Eng Teacher Morris Hills Regional HS 1971-72, Bayley-Ellard HS 1972-73; 5th-8th Grade Teacher St Anthony Sch 1973-; *ai:* 8th Grade Adv; Faculty Rep Home Sch; NCEA, NCTE; Petrienne Alumna Society, Honorary Thespian Society; Master Thesis Published as Research in Text; *office:* St Anthony Sch 270 Diamond Bridge Ave Hawthorne NJ 07506

BANKS, RITA CARVER, 7th Grade Mathematics Teacher; *b:* Elizabeth, NC; *m:* Wilbert L.; *c:* Heith Carver, Shanae, Jeremy; *ed:* (BS) Intermediate Ed, Elizabeth City St Univ 1974; *cr:* Teacher 1974-75, All Subjects Teacher 1975-80 D F Walker Sch; Sci Teacher Chowan Jr HS 1980-85; Math Teacher Elizabeth City Jr HS 1985-; *ai:* NCAE 1970-; Math Sci Educl Network; *office:* Elizabeth City Jr HS 306 N Road St Elizabeth City NC 27909

BANKS, ROSALIND MOYD, Mathematics & Science Teacher; *b:* Jersey City, NJ; *m:* Jerry Louis; *c:* Ashley N., Alicia Y.; *ed:* (BA) Elem Ed, Benedict Coll 1981; (ME) Elem Ed, SC St Coll 1985; *cr:* Math/Sci Teacher Cross Elem 1981-; *ai:* 5th Grade Math & Sci Chairperson; NEA; Teacher of Yr 1988; *office:* Cross Elem Sch Rt 1 Box 2 Cross SC 29436

BANKS, SANDRA C. (PEAVIE), Teacher; *b:* Carthage, MO; *m:* George Jr.; *c:* Jermaine, Erin; *ed:* (BA) Elem Ed, Jackson St Univ 1974; Various Wkshps; *cr:* Asst Teacher St Louis Public Schls 1976-77; Teacher Normandy Public Schls 1977-; *ai:* MNEA, Normandy Teachers Assn Mem 1977-; Alumni JSU (Active Mem, Asst Secy) 1980-; *office:* Bel-Ridge Elem Sch 8930 Boston Ave Saint Louis MO 63121

BANKS, STELLA PERRY, Typing Teacher; *b:* Jersey City, NJ; *c:* Fred, Martin; *ed:* (BS) Bus Admin, Jersey City St Coll 1987; Mgrs & Supvrs Dev, Opportunities Acad of Management Trng; *cr:* Operating Statistical Unit Specialist Opportunities Industrialization 1972-79; Voc Instr Center of Hudson Cty 1979-80; Typing Instr Essex Cty Coll of Bus 1983-84; Bus Instr Jersey City Bd of Ed 1980-83, 1984-; *ai:* Jersey City Ed Assn, NJ Ed Assn, NEA; Intnl Free & Accepted Modern Masons & Order of E Star (Worthy Matron 1972-88, Most Worthy Vice 1987-, Most Ancient Matron 1988-), Trophy/Plaque 1984, 1988; Zion Baptist Church Co-Adv Jr Usher Bd; Olivetti Awd of Merit; *home:* 55 Clerk St Jersey City NJ 07305

BANKS, TOMMIE FOSTER, English & French Teacher; *b:* Tuscaloosa, AL; *m:* Erskine; *c:* Eric Eldridge; *ed:* (BA) Eng, Stillman Coll 1966; MS St Univ; *cr:* Eng/Fr Teacher Davidson HS 1966-70, Bib Cty HS 1970-; Bus/Eng Natl Career Coll 1970; *ai:* Fr Club Spon; Steering Comm For Southern Assn Scndry Schls Evaluation; AL Ed Assn 1966-; NEA 1966-; AATF 1989-; AATF 1989-; Stillman Coll Alumni Assn Miss Alumni Awd 1988-; Dir of Vacation BibleSch 1984-89; St Paul United Meth Church Trustee Bd Secy 1984-89; Eng Textbook Comm Rep; *office:* Bibb County H S 214 Birmingham Rd Centreville AL 35042

BANKSTON, DAVID BRUCE, 8th Grade US History Teacher; *b:* Holdenville, OK; *m:* Regina Lynn Daughtery; *c:* Cameron D.; *ed:* (BA) His/Phys Ed, Univ of TX Arlington 1983; Working Towards Masters in His; *cr:* US His Teacher Alvarado Mid Sch 1984-87; World His/Govt/Ec Teacher Midlothian HS 1987-88; US His/Civil War His Alvarado Mid Sch 1988-; *ai:* UIL Impromptu Speaking Coach; HOPE Spon; Assn of TX Prof Educators 1985-; *home:* 3512 Socorro Rd Fort Worth TX 76116

BANNAR, DOROTHY KEMBLE, Mathematics Teacher; *b:* Philadelphia, PA; *m:* Thomas Joseph; *c:* Thomas M.; *ed:* (BS) Math, Ursinus Coll 1965; (MA) Teaching of Math, Villanova Univ 1979; *cr:* Teacher Marple Newtown Sr HS 1965-66, Boyertown Area Sr HS 1966-68, Boyertown Area Jr HS 1969, Penncrest Sr HS 1969-72, Marple Newtown Sr HS 1978-; *ai:* SADD Spon; Chm Math Dept; Mid St Self Evaluation; Coord April is Math Month Celebration; Marple Newtown Ed Assn; PA St Ed Assn; NEA; NCTM; Assn Teacher of Math Phila; Lynnewood Elem PTO Recording Secy 1983-85; 1st Class Townships PA St Convention Comm Chm Ladies Prgm 1986; Haverford HS Band & Orch Parents Trip Chm 1989-; Fellow in Teaching Lehigh Univ 1968; *office:* Marple Newtown H S 120 Media Line Rd Newtown Square PA 19073

BANNECKER, SUSAN LYNN, Primary Teacher; *b:* St Louis, MO; *m:* Richard Scott; *c:* Mark R., Kathryn L.; *ed:* (BS) Ed, SE MO St Univ 1978; *cr:* Primary Grades Teacher Fox C-6 Sch Dist 1978-83; *ai:* MO St Teachers Assn 1978-83.

BANNERMAN, WILLIE MC KOY, Fifth Grade Teacher; *b:* Maple Hill, NC; *m:* Bradford; *c:* Bradford, Brandon; *ed:* (BA) Intermediate Ed, 1981, (MS) Elem Ed, 1989 Fayetteville St Univ; *cr:* Teacher Pender HS 1982-83, Burgaw Elem 1983-; *ai:* Grade Chairperson; NCAE 1983-; Pender Cty Math Teacher 1988-89; Math-Sci Grant 1987-89; Cmptr Grant Summer 1989; *home:* Rt 1 Box 73-A Maple Hill NC 28454

BANNINGER, LOREN LYNN, 6th Grade Teacher; *b:* Salina, KS; *m:* Susan Mc Auliffe; *c:* Christopher, Laura; *ed:* (BA) Ed, KS Weslyan Salina 1974; (MS) Ed, KS St Univ 1986; *cr:* Elem Teacher Unified Sch Dist 305 1980-; *ai:* Elks BPOE 718; Saline Cty Teacher Credit Union Past Pres; Unified Sch Dist 305 Employee Excl Awd; *office:* Sunset Elem Sch 1510 W Republic Salina KS 67401

BANNISTER, KATHLEEN BEARDSLEY, Mathematics Teacher; *b:* Warsaw, NY; *m:* Lewis R.; *c:* Lance, Christopher; *ed:* (BS) Math Ed, SUNY Geneseo 1971; Grad Stud SUNY Geneseo; *cr:* Sr HS Math Teacher Letchworth Cntrl Sch 1971-; *ai:* Math League Adv; NY Assn of Math Teachers; NY Ed Assn Delegate 1978-; Letchworth Honor Society Teacher of Yr 1989; *office:* Letchworth Cntrl Sch School Rd Gainesville NY 14066

BANNON, MICHAEL, Science Teacher; *b:* New York City, NY; *m:* Sara Manion; *c:* Patrick, Carolyn; *ed:* (BA) Chem, Cath Univ 1960; (MS) Chem, Notre Dame 1969; Numerous Univs; *cr:* Teacher St Xavier HS 1960-61; Teacher/Dept Chm Xaverian HS 1961-70, Brentwood HS 1970-; *ai:* Sci Olympiad Coach; Suffolk Cty Sci Teachers VP 1970-, Teacher of Yr 1987; NY St Sci Teachers Dir for Chem 1970-; Amer Chemical Society Local & Regional Teaching Awds 1989; St Philip & James Sch Sch Bd 1982-85; St Patricks Soccer League Coach; Chem-4 Dreyfus Woodrow Wilson Chem Team Mem; Conduct Wkshps on Methods of Teaching Chem; *office:* Brentwood HS Ross Center Brentwood NY 11717

BANSCHBACH, THOMAS B., Mathematics Department Chair; *b:* Batesville, IN; *m:* Amanda M., Timothy J.;; *ed:* (BS) Math/His, E TX St Univ 1977; Grad Work; *cr:* Teacher Callisburg Ind Sch Dist 1978-79; Teacher 1979-83, Math Dept Chm 1983- Princeton HS; *ai:* UIL Literary Dir; Number Sense Spon; *office:* Princeton HS 321 Panther Pkwy Princeton TX 75004

BANTA, ROBERT ORA, Mathematics Teacher; *b:* Oquawka, IL; *m:* Sharon; *c:* Debra Pompe, Robert R.; *ed:* (BS) Math, W IL Univ 1966; (MA) Math, Univ of IL 1970; *cr:* Math Teacher Avon HS 1966-; *ai:* Jr Class Spon; Educl TV Classroom Calculus Facilitator; NEA, IL Ed Assn 1975-; Natl Sci Fnd Fellowship Univ of IL; *home:* RR 1 Box 301 Oquawka IL 61469

BANTZ, JOHN PETER, Guidance Cnslr/Math Teacher; *b:* Bronx, NY; *ed:* (BA) Math, Marist Coll 1963; (MS) Math, Yeshiva Univ 1969; A P Calculus, Hope Coll; *cr:* Math Teacher St Josephs HS 1963-64, Cardinal Hayes HS 1964-71, Luke M Powers HS 1971-77; Math Instr/Acad Dean Christopher Columbus HS 1978-83; Math Instr/Prin Mount St Michaels Jr HS 1984-89; Math Instr/Guidance Cnslr Mount St Michael Acad 1989-; *ai:* Track Coaching; Bd of Trustees; Natl Sci Fnd Grant; Hospital Ministry Volunteer; *office:* Mt St Michael Acad 4300 Murdock Ave Bronx NY 10466

BARAJAS, ANTHONY THOMAS, Third Grade Teacher; *b:* Sterling, IL; *m:* Barbara Anderson; *c:* Nicholas, Nathan; *ed:* (BS) Ed, N IL Univ 1975; *cr:* 3rd Grade Teacher Grace M Nicholson Elem Sch 1975-; *ai:* Rdng, Cmptr Comms; Elem Sports Coach; *office:* Grace M Nicholson Elem Sch 649 N Main St Montgomery IL 60538

BARAJAS, MARIA LOURDES, 6th Grade Teacher & Coord; *b:* Nogales, Mexico; *ed:* (BA) Elem Ed, 1974, (MED) Bi-ling Ed, 1976, (MED) Early Chldhd Ed, 1980 Univ of AZ; Teacher Residency Prgm; Lions Quest Skills for Adolescence; *cr:* K-1st Grade Teacher Elm Street Sch 1974-81; Kndgtn Teacher Elm Kndgtn Sch 1981-82; 1st/3rd Grade Teacher Pierson Elem Sch 1982-86; Cmmty Liaison 1986, 6th-8th Grade Teacher 1987- Pierson Mid Sch; *ai:* Girls Vlybl, Boys Asst Track, Girls & Boys Bsktbl Coach; 6th Grade Curr Coord; Equipment Mgr; Track Dir; Prin Advisory Cncl; Prof Educators of Nogales (Pres 1977-78, VP 1976-77, Public Relations Chairperson 1974-75, Building Rep 1974-77, Soc Chairperson 1975-76); Andale Nogales Chairperson Corporate Spon 1989; Prof Relations Cncl Secy 1975-77; AZ Ed Assn Local Delegate 1975-77; Pierson Teacher of Yr Awd; Chamber Commerce Outstanding Achievenemt in Ed 1985; Brave Awd 1986-87; *home:* 1137 Live Oak Dr Nogales AZ 85621

BARANEC, DIANA PATERNOSTER, Mathematics Teacher; *b:* Brooklyn, NY; *m:* Gregory; *c:* Andrew, David; *ed:* (BA) Math, 1969, (MA) Math, 1971 St Johns Univ; *cr:* Teacher Islip HS 1970-; *ai:* Mathlete, Peer Leadership Adv; BSA Den Leader 1983-88; St Marys RC Church Religion Teacher 1980-89; St Marys RAP Leader 1988-; Islip HS Grant for Math Dev; *office:* Islip HS 2508 Union Blvd Islip NY 11751

BARANOWSKI, CRYSTAL MEYER, Spanish/Language Art Teacher; *b:* Wheeling, WV; *m:* Robert; *c:* Yvonne Jacobs; *ed:* (BA) Span, W Liberty St Coll 1971; Grad Stud WV Univ; *cr:* Teacher Woodsdale Jr HS 1971-75, Triadelphia Jr HS 1976-; *ai:* Forensic Chairperson; OH Valley Lang Art Cncl; NEA, WV Ed Assn, OH Cty Ed Assn 1971-; Alpha Delta Kappa (Corresponding Secy 1984-86, VP 1987-88); *office:* Triadelphia Jr HS 1636 National Rd Wheeling WV 26003

BARASSI, LOUIS W., History Teacher; *b:* New York, MA; *ed:* (AB) His, Boston Coll; (MA) His, Columbia Univ; *cr:* His Teacher St Vincent Ferrer Sch 1985-; *ai:* USSR Stu Travel & Study Coord; NEH Summer Seminar 1989; NEH Summer Inst 1990.

BARBANTINI, ROBERT LOUIS, Middle School Teacher; *b:* Detroit, MI; *m:* Sally M. Gale; *c:* Michele, Melissa, Sarah; *ed:* (BA) Elem Ed, 1969, (MA) Elem Ed, 1975, Ed Specialist Spec Ed/Gifted & Talented, 1986 Wayne St Univ; Cmptr Repair; *cr:* Math/Soc Stud/Lang Art/Rdng Teacher Slocum Truax & Monguagon Mid Schls 1971-79; 6th Grade Teacher Taylor Elem Sch 1980-81; Media Center Specialist Owen & Hedke Elem Schls 1984-87; Math/Soc Stud/Lang Art/Rdng Teacher Slocum Truax & Monguagon Mid Sch 1987-; Cmptr Specialist Monguagon Mid Sch 1988-; *ai:* Sftbl Coach; Stu Cncl Adv; Gifted & Talented Planning Comm; Cmptr Task Force Mem; Project Challenge;

Summer Sch Remedial Teacher; *home:* 20186 HCL Jackson Grosse Ile MI 48138

BARBARA, FORTUNATA J., Social Studies Teacher; *b:* Englewood, NJ; *ed:* (BS) Elem Ed, Seton Hall Univ 1962; *cr:* Teacher St Leo 1958-62, St Rita 1961-67, St Anthony 1967-70; Teacher/VP Madonna 1970-; *ai:* Sch Newspaper; Yrbk; Natl Jr Honor Society Adv & Curr Coord; Mrktg Acitivity Comm; Home-Sch Exec Bd; Ft Lee Alcohol & Drug Abuse Cncl; NCEA; Cedar Court Condominium Assn Exec Bd VP; Parish Rosary Society Pres; Acad of Holy Angels Alumni Comm; Archdiocese of Newark Awd of Merit 1981 & Golden Apple 1987; Madonna Sch Outstanding Teacher 1985; Certificate of Personal Dev 1978; CYO Appreciation Awd; Cath Ed Golden Apple Service Awd.

BARBE, SUSAN MOLEY, Mathematics Teacher; *b:* New Orleans, LA; *m:* Victor Joseph; *c:* Jacques, Renee; *ed:* (BS) Math Ed, Univ of New Orleans 1971; *cr:* Teacher L W Higgins HS 1971-73, 1979-; *ai:* Moving Up Comm; Jefferson Parish Rdng Comm; Visitation of Our Lady Church CYO volunteer; *office:* L W Higgins HS 7201 Lapalco Blvd Marrero LA 70072

BARBER, BETTY R., Third Grade Teacher; *b:* Ashford, AL; *m:* Walton Timothy Sr.; *c:* Timothy II, Jeffrey E.; *ed:* (AA) Elem Ed, Chipola Jr Coll 1971; (BA) Elem, Univ of W FL 1973; *cr:* Teacher Kate M Smith Elem 1974-; *home:* Rt 2 Chipley FL 32428

BARBER, DEAN NEWTON, First Grade Teacher; *b:* Yukon, OK; *m:* Murray Frank; *c:* Keith, Phil, Randy, Steven; *ed:* (BS) Elem Ed, Bethel Coll 1958; Austin Peay St Coll, W GA Coll; *cr:* 1st Grade Teacher Leroy Pope Elem Sch 1958-59; 1st/3rd Grade Teacher Mc Eachern 1959-65; 1st Grade Teacher Hollydale Elem 1971-72; 1st-3rd Grade Teacher Compton Elem 1972-; *ai:* Teacher of Yr 1986; *home:* 4430 Gaydon Rd Powder Springs GA 30073

BARBER, FRANCES NOEL, Eng Dept Chair/Teacher; *b:* Middletown, OH; *m:* John Kenneth; *c:* Matthew, Luke; *ed:* (BS) Ed, Miami Univ 1974; (MS) Admin, Univ of Dayton 1988; *cr:* Head Start Teacher Pike Cty 1974; Eng Teacher Valley View HS 1974-79, Cedarville HS 1979-; *ai:* Valley View Chairperson; Eng Goals & Objectives Curr Comm; Future Teachers of America, Stu in Action for Ed, NHS Club Adv; Cedarville Eng Curr Comm Chairperson;Cedarville Writing Minimum Competency Prgm K-12th Chairperson; Cedarville Rdng Minimum Competency Prgm K-12th Mem; Phi Delta Kappa Mem; NCTE; Dayton Childrens Hosptial (Christmas Bazaar Chairperson, Secy of Club); Miami Univ Alumni Schl Review Comm; Top 10 Finalist St Teacher of Yr 1982; Teacher of Yr 1982, 1987; Valedictorian Spec Teacher Awd 1987; *office:* Cedarville HS Box 45 Cedarville OH 45325

BARBER, JANIS SHAPIRO, Resource Room Teacher; *b:* New York, NY; *m:* Stan; *ed:* (BA) Sociology/Elem Ed, 1973, (MS) Elem Ed, 1976 Lehman Coll; (MS) Spec Ed, Coll of New Rochelle 1980; *cr:* Health Conservation Teacher Public Sch 96 Bronx 1978-79, Public Sch 150 Bronx 1979-80; Resource Room Teacher Public Sch 68 Bronx 1980-; *ai:* Teacher of Rdng & Math Through the Culinary Art; Mainstream Comm Mem; Pupil Personnel Comm Mem; Bronx Rdng Cncl; NY St Rdng Assn; Jewish Teachers Assn; *office:* Public Sch 68 Bronx 4011 Monticello Ave Bronx NY 10466

BARBER, KITTY SUE, 10th Grade English Teacher; *b:* Baytown, TX; *ed:* (BA) Eng/Scndry Ed, Brigham Young Univ 1953; Grad Stud Brigham Young Univ, Univ of Houston; *cr:* Teacher/Eng Dept Chm David Crockett Jr HS 1953-55, 1958-74; Missionary Church of Jesus Christ Latter Day Saints 1955-57; Teacher Channelview HS 1975-; *ai:* Jr HS Eng Dept Chm; Stu Cncl, HS Class, 8th Grade Spon; TX St Teachers Assn, Channelview Teachers Assn, Assn of TX Prof Educators, Channelview Assn of Prof Educators; Church of Jesus Christ Latter Day Saints (Pres, Teacher); Ywmia Ward, St Level; *home:* 3319 Wisconsin St Baytown TX 77520

BARBER, SANDRA WALKER, Mathematics Teacher; *b:* Chester, SC; *m:* Jesse; *c:* Kevin, Patrick, Brian; *ed:* (BA) Math, Winthrop Coll 1974; (ME) Ed, Francis Marion Coll 1988; *cr:* Math Teacher Chester Sr HS 1974-77, S Florence HS 1979-; *ai:* Jr Class Spon; Schlsp Comm Co-Chm; NCTM, SCCTM 1986-89; Zeta Phi Beta (Anti-Basileus 1985-89, Basileus 1989-); Teacher Incentive Awd 1986-89; Supt Meritorious Service Awd 1986; *home:* 139 Holly Cir Darlington SC 29532

BARBER, SHARON NOBLE, Fifth Grade Teacher; *b:* Muskegon, MI; *m:* Neal J.; *c:* Deborah, Heather; *ed:* (BS) Group Soc Sci/Group Sci, 1968, (MA) Rdng, 1972 W MI Univ; *cr:* 5th Grade Teacher Orchard View Elem; *ai:* Coach Odyssey of Mind 1990; Educator Achievement Awd 1987, 1989; *office:* Orchard View Elem Sch 1074 Shonat Muskegon MI 49442

BARBER, WANDA JUNE, History Teacher; *b:* Carrollton, GA; *ed:* (BA) His/Scndry Ed, Tift Coll 1983; Grad Work, W GA Coll 1989; *cr:* Personnel Mgr Daniel Radiator Corporation 1984-87; Teacher Heard Cty HS 1988-; *ai:* Jr Co-Ed Y Club Adv; Band Flag Corps Coord; Heard Assn of Educators Secy 1989-; *home:* Rt 3 Box 294 Franklin GA 30217

BARBERICH, LINDA KAY (KOVACIC), 7th Grade Lang Arts Teacher; *b:* Pittsburg, KS; *m:* George Matthew; *c:* George M. Jr.; *ed:* (BS) Eng, 1978, (MA) Eng, 1980 Pittsburg St Univ; *cr:* 9th Grade Eng Teacher Roosevelt Jr HS 1979-80; 7th Grade Lang Arts Teacher Pittsburg Mid Sch 1980-; *ai:* Mid Sch Curr Cncl Mem; NEA, KNEA, PEA 1979-; NCTE 197; KS Assn of Teachers of Eng 1987-; Phi Kappa Phi 1978-; Kappa Kappa Iota 1984-; Peo Chapter CJ Guard 1984-; Sigma Tau Delta 1976-; McPherson Grad Fellowship; Stu KS Natl Educl Assn; Outstanding Scndry Stu Teacher; Whos Who Among Stu in Amer Univ & Coll; Whos Who in Amer Ed 1990; Nom for Clyde U Phillips Outstanding Educator Awd 1985; Charles Guardian Scholar; *office:* Pittsburg Middle School 14th & Broadway Pittsburg KS 66762

BARBETTI, ROBERT R., Sixth Grade Teacher; *b:* Vineland, NJ; *m:* Donna Miller; *ed:* (BA) Elem Ed, 1968, (MA) Advanced Elem Ed, 1974 Glassboro St Coll; Cert Stu Personnel Services, Guidance Counseling; *cr:* Teacher D Ippolito Intermediate Sch 1968-; *ai:* Safety Patrol Adv; Vineland Ed Assn (Assn Rep 1969-73, Legislative Chm 1970-72); NJ Ed Assn, NEA; YMCA Y Men Assn 1968-69; Chamber of Commerce; Vineland Public Sch System Outstanding Safety Patrol Adv Awd; *office:* D Ippolito Intermediate Sch 1578 N Valley Ave Vineland NJ 08360

BARBIN, GERALDINE MARIE, Science Teacher; *b:* Mansura, LA; *m:* Furgus P.; *c:* Bryan, Ava, Myra; *ed:* (BS) Bio, Grambling St 1963; Prof Improvement Prgm Higher Learning; Stud Sci, Dillard Univ 1968, LSUA 1969-70, Southern Univ 1971-72; *cr:* Teacher Carver HS 1963-65, Queens Public Sch 75 1965-68, Marksville HS 1969-; *ai:* Spon Jr Sr Prom 1987-, Taxidermy Stud Group; Comm of AIDS Ed; Co-Spon Little League Bsktbl; Natl Teachers, LEA, AEA, Sci Teachers 1969-; VFW Auxiliary Pres 1988-, Honorary Mem 1989; Selective Service Mem 1988-; Humana Hospital Bd of Dir; Dillard Natl Sci Fnd Summer Inst Fellowship; Selective Service Bd Mem; Humana Hospital Marksville Bd of Dir; *office:* Marksville HS 316 W Bontemp St Marksville LA 71351

BARCLAY, DONALD L., JR., Social Studies Dept Chairman; *b:* St James, MN; *m:* Annette M.; *c:* Robert, Michael; *ed:* (BS) Elem Ed, Univ of NV Las Vegas 1972; (MS) Ed Systems, Nova Univ 1981; *cr:* 6th Grade Teacher CVT Gilbert Sixth Grade Center 1972-77, Kit Carson Sixth Grade Center 1977-83; 7th Grade Teacher 1983-84, 8th Grade Teacher 1984- Dell Robison Jr HS; *ai:* Speech, Stu Assistance Prgm, Dept Chm; NV Cncl for Soc Stud 1985-; Clark Cty Sch Dist Excl in Ed Awd 1983; NEA Natl Resolutions Comm Mem 1990; *office:* Del H Robison Jr H S 825 Marion Las Vegas NV 89110

BARCLAY, KAREN MC KINLEY, Kindergarten Teacher; *b:* Raleigh, NC; *m:* Tom Keith; *c:* Christa, Lisa; *ed:* (BS) Elem Ed, 1974, (MS) Curr/Instruction/Early Chldhd Ed 1985 OK St Univ; *cr:* Kndgtn Teacher Tulsa Public Schls 1974-81, Bartlesville Public Schls 1981-; *ai:* Mid Sch Sunday Sch Teacher & Youth Spon; NEA, OEA, BEA; OK Early Chldhd Teachers Assn Secy 1989-; Friends of Day Care Wkshp Presentor 1975-; SACUS, OACUS 1978-; Alpha Delta Kappa Secy; *home:* 5927 Martin Ln Bartlesville OK 74006

BARCLAY, THOMAS ADISON, Mathematics Department Chair; *b:* Brady, TX; *m:* Betty Lee Anderson; *c:* Jeannie L., Kelly N.; *ed:* (BA) Scndry Ed, Howard Payne Coll 1970; *cr:* Math Teacher/Coach Richland Springs HS 1964-65; Math Teacher Cuero HS 1965-68, Brookesmith HS 1969-70; Math Teacher/ Coach Bangs HS 1970-72, Sonora HS 1972-73; Math Teacher Cross Plains HS 1975-; *ai:* NHS & Frosh Class Spon; *office:* Cross Plains HS P O Box 669 Cross Plains TX 76443

BARDEN, LILLIE CHASE, Third Grade Teacher; *b:* Hazlehurst, MS; *c:* Carlo L.; *ed:* (BS) Elem Ed, Jackson St Univ 1967; *cr:* Headstart Teacher Sophia Sutton 1967-68; K-3rd Grade Teacher Hazlehurst Elem 1969-; *ai:* Bsktbl Coach 1969-70; MAE Membership; 4-H Club, Cub Scouts of America, Order of Eastern Star, Home Mission; Church (Choir, Sunday Sch Teacher, Pulpit Comm); *home:* 113 Wilson St Hazlehurst MS 39083

BARDWELL, ROSEMARY ANN (WINGATE), 5th-8th Grade English Teacher; *b:* California, MO; *m:* Mark S.; *ed:* (BS) Ed/Eng, Lincoln Univ 1981; Quest Intnl Trng 1989; *cr:* 6th Grade Teacher St Francis Xavier 1981-82; 5th-7th Grade Teacher Annunciation Sch 1982-83; 5th-8th Grade Eng Teacher St Martins Sch 1983-; *ai:* 8th Grade Homeroom Teacher; Dir 8th Grade Spring Play; Several Poems Published; *office:* St Martins Cath Sch 7148 Business 50 W Jefferson City MO 65109

BARDWELL, SUZANNE BROWN, Social Studies Teacher; *b:* Corsicana, TX; *m:* Jim; *c:* Joshua; *ed:* (AS) General Ed, Navarro Coll 1975; (BS) Bd/Fd/Soc Sci, 1978, (MS) Amer His, 1981 E TX St Univ; *cr:* Grad Teacher Asst E TX St Univ 1978-80; Teacher Windamere Sch for Learning Disabilities 1981, Spring Hill Jr HS 1981-84; Part-Time Instr Kilgore Coll 1981-; Teacher Spring Hill HS 1984-; *ai:* Campus Plan & Self-Responsibility Comms; Assn TX Prof Ed (Past Pres, Regional Secy) 1981-; Delta Kappa Gamma Intnl 1985-; E TX Cncl Soc Stud 1981-; TX Assn Future Educators Spon Outstanding St Chapter 1986; Upshur Cty Child Protective Services Bd (Treas 1990) 1989-; Chrstn Women Fellowship Prgm Leader 1989-; E TX Oil Petroleum Inst Schlsp; Outstanding Young Woman in America 1989; E TX St Univ Coll of Liberal & Fine Art Grad Teaching Asst 1980; TX Acad of Sci Art; *home:* Rt 1 Box 595 Gilmer TX 75644

BARE, DAVID J., Director of Instrumental Music; *b:* Ironton, OH; *m:* Betty Christine Mc Intyre; *c:* Ellen; *ed:* (BA) Music Ed, Marshall Univ 1976; Marshall Univ; *cr:* Dir of Inst Music South Point Schls 1977-78, Rock Hill Schls 1978-; *ai:* All Music Act Mid & HS; OH Music Ed Mem 1979-, OH Ed Assn Mem 1979-; Music Ed Natl Conference Mem 1979-; River Cities Cultural Cncl Chm HS Night of Arts 1990; Pres of Lawrence Cty Music Teachers Assn; VP Rock Hill Ed Assn; Chm Dist 17 Honors Band; *office:* Rock Hill H S Rt 3 Box 234 Ironton OH 45638

BARE, DIANA ABSHER, Second Grade Teacher; *b:* Jefferson, NC; *m:* Dennis D.; *ed:* (BS) Early Chldhd, Appalachian St Univ 1976; *cr:* Teacher Nathans Creek Elem 1976-; *ai:* Mentor Teacher; Taught Effective Teacher Trng Classes; NC Assn of Educators, NEA 1976-; NC Assn of Teacher Assts Wkshp Presentor; Delta Kappa Gamma Mem; Southern Assn of Colls Visiting Comm; Selected Mem of Model Clinical Teachers Team for Appalachian St Univ; 3 Time Teacher of Yr; Article Published; *home:* Rt 1 Box 182-A Crumpler NC 28617

BARE, MARY DANCY, Fourth Grade Teacher; *b:* Jefferson, NC; *m:* Jimmy Dale; *c:* Jamie; *ed:* (BA) Elem Ed, Warren Wilson Coll 1971; *cr:* 4th Grade Teacher Sparta Elem 1971-; *ai:* Grade Chm; NCAE, NEA; *office:* Sparta Elem Sch Rt 3 Box 789 Sparta NC 28675

BAREFOOT, FARLEY, Physics Chemistry II Teacher; *b:* Hallsboro, NC; *m:* Joe Blake; *c:* Jo Anne Barefoot Biser, Frederick A.; *ed:* (BS) Sci, 1956, (MS) Sci, 1960 E Carolina Univ 1960; Sci, Univ of SC 1982; Grad Stud Numerous Coll; *cr:* Teacher Columbus Cty 1955-64, Whiteville City 1964-; *ai:* Dept Chairperson; Mentor Teacher; Presidental Awd Pres 1983; NC Region IV Bus Awd 1983-87; NSTA Dist IV Dir; Alpha Delta Kappa Pres 1986-88, E Carolina Univ Alumni Outstanding Educator 1986, Sigma XI Awd 1986; Co-Authored 2 Textbooks; Growth Initiative for Teachers Awd 1984; IA Honors Wkshp 1984; Austin Bond Awd for Distinguished Service to Sci Ed 1984; *office:* Whiteville HS N Lee St Whiteville NC 28472

BAREFOOT, PAMELA BLACKWELDER, 8th Grade Soc Stud Teacher; *b:* Concord, NC; *m:* Rowen C.; *c:* Evan R.; *ed:* (BA) Intermediate Ed/Soc Stud, Lenoir-Rhyne Coll 1980; *cr:* 5th Grade Teacher Davenport Elem 1980-84; 4th Grade Teacher Trinity Luth Day Sch 1984-85; 8th Grade Soc Stud Teacher Hillcrest Mid Sch 1985-; *ai:* Soc Stud Club & Natural Helpers Spon; Simpsonville United Meth Womens Circle Soc Chairperson 1988-; Teacher of Yr 1982-83; Co-Authored Cty 8th Grad Curr Guide 1987; *office:* Hillcrest Mid Sch 510 Garrison Rd Simpsonville SC 29681

BAREFOOT, SALLIE HOLLEY, Third Grade Teacher; *b:* Four Oaks, NC; *m:* Eldrige R. Sr.; *c:* Eldridge R. Jr.; *cr:* 4th Grade Teacher 1965-80, 3rd/4th Grade Teacher 1980-85, 3rd Grade Teacher 1986- Manchester Elem Sch; *ai:* Grade Group Chairperson; Testing Comm Cty; Sci Chairperson; Chairperson Brotherhodd Act; Chairperson Sch Prgm/Var Comm; Mentor Teacher Beginning Teachers; NEA/NCEA/ACT Del NCAE Convention 1982; ASCD; Cross Creek RdNg Cncl; Cty Comms Sr Citizens/Church/Teachers; Home Demo Club; 1st Place Awd/ Teaching Economics Elem Sch/Cumberland Cty; Mentor Teacher Dist 1; *home:* Rt 1 Box 431 Spring Lake NC 28390

BARFIELD, JAN GREENE, Spanish Teacher; *b:* Lynchburg, VA; *m:* Jiles Mc Natt; *c:* Michael, Rebecca, Anna L.; *ed:* (BSED) Span/Eng, GA Southern 1975; Working Towards Masters Span; Data Collection; *cr:* Span Teacher Vidalia Comprehensive HS 1975-77; Eng Teacher Mt de Sales HS 1977-80; Span Teacher Vidalia Comprehensive HS 1980-; *ai:* Span Club Spon; Stu Appeals Comm Chm; PAGE; *home:* 503 Durden St Vidalia GA 30474

BARFIELD, KENNY DALE, Principal/Academic Dean; *b:* Florence, AL; *m:* Nancy Ann Cordray; *c:* Amber E., Lora A.; *ed:* (BA) Speech Comm, David Lipscomb Univ 1969; (MA) Speech Comm, Univ of AL 1972; (EDS) Educl Admin, Univ of N AL 1986; (EDD) Educl Admin, Univ of AL 1989; *cr:* Dir of Forensics 1969-, Bible/Eng Instr 1969-, Academic Dean 1986-, Prin 1990 Mars Hill Bible Sch; *ai:* Amer Forensic Assn (Educl Practices Comm, HS Affairs Comm) 1969-; Natl Forensic League Deep South Dist Chm 1970, Distinguished Service Awd 1981, 1986; AL Forensic Educators Assn Pres; AL Speech Comm Assn 1970-, AL Speech Teacher of Yr 1977; ASCD 1988-; NASSP 1987-; Published Book 1981; Published Articles; *office:* Mars Hill Bible Sch 698 Cox Creek Pkwy Florence AL 35630

BARFIELD, NANCY CORDRAY, Counselor/Home Ec Teacher; *b:* Waynesboro, AL; *m:* Kenny Dale; *c:* Amber E., Lora A.; *ed:* (BS) Home Ec Ed, David Lipscomb Coll 1970; (MA) Counseling/Guidance, Univ of North AL 1976; *cr:* Sci Teacher 1970-75, Cnslr/Home Ec Teacher 1976- Mars Hill Bible Sch; *ai:* Spon Girls 4-H Club; AL Assn Mem 1987-; North AL Home Economist Assn Mem 1985-; Lauderdale Cty 4-H Club Outstanding Spon 1986; *office:* Mars Hill Bible Sch 698 Cox Creek Pkwy Florence AL 35630

BARGANIER, GRADY LYNN, English Teacher/Coach; *b:* Temple, TX; *m:* Linda Marie; *c:* Caitlin, Luke; *ed:* (BS) Phys Ed/ Eng, SW TX St Univ 1970-74; Drivers Ed; *cr:* Eng Teacher/Coach Academy Mid Sch 1974-; *ai:* Ftbl, Bsktbl, Track, Tennis Coach; TX HS Coaches Assn, Assn of TX Prof Educators Mem 1974-; St Lukes Cath Church Organist 1978-; *office:* Academy Mid Sch Rt 2 Temple TX 76501

BARGANIER, SUSAN CUMBIE, English Lit/Amer His Teacher; *b:* Greenville, AL; *m:* Brooks; *c:* Matt, Mary C., Joy, Anne; *ed:* (BA) His/Eng, Univ of AL 1974; Working Toward Masters in Ed-Scndry-Eng, Auburn Univ; *cr:* 6th-9th Grade Eng Teacher Fort Deposit Acad 1983-86; 8th-11th Grade His/Eng Teacher Ft Dale-S Butler Acad 1987-; *ai:* Newspaper Spon; Mass Media Teacher; Delta Kappa Gamma 1989-; Kappa Delta Pi, Phi Alpha Theta, Chi Delta Phi; Bethel Baptist Church Sunday Sch Teacher; *office:* Fort Dale-S Butler Acad PO Drawer 777 Greenville AL 36037

BARGATZE, STEPHEN RAY, 8th Grade Teacher; *b:* Louisville, KY; *m:* Carol Hartung Bargatze; *c:* Nathanael, Derek, Abigail; *ed:* (BS) Elem Ed, Trevecca Nazarene Coll 1984; *ai:* Coach Jr HS Boys Bsktbl.

BARHAM, JEAN H., Middle School Teacher; *b:* Norfolk, VA; *w:* Samuel E. (dec); *ed:* (BA) Health/Phys Ed, Old Dominion Univ 1971; Family Life; *cr:* Teacher Arrowood Acad & Rosemont Jr HS 1971-80, Azalea Mid Sch 1980-; *ai:* Officiate Vlybl Games After Sch; Organizer of Double Dutch Rope Group; NEA, VEA, EAN 1971-; Teacher of Yr Rosemont & Arrowood Acad; Teacher of Month Azalea; *home:* 1342 Riva Ridge Run Virginia Beach VA 23454

BARHORST, SANDRA ELIZABETH, 6th Grade Teacher; *b:* Cincinnati, OH; *m:* Floyd E. Jones; *c:* Micah, Caley; *ed:* (BA) Elem Ed, Coll of Mt St Joseph 1971; (MS) Spec Ed, Univ of AZ Tucson 1975; *cr:* 2nd-3rd Grade Teacher St Michael Sch 1971-73; Spec Ed Teacher Cincinnati Public Schls 1975-76; Elem Teacher Union Sch Corp 1976-; *ai:* Little Hoosier Historians Spon; Comm Prgm Improvement Plan Chapter 1; Textbook Adoption; NEA, ISTA 1976-; Delta Kappa Gamma Soc Chairperson 1988-; Muncie Area Rdng Cncl; GSA Daisy Leader 1989-; *office:* Union Elem Sch R R 1 Modoc IN 47358

BARI, FLAVIA, Fourth Grade Teacher; *b:* Anzano/Puglia, Italy; *m:* Sebastiano J.; *c:* Maria, Carmelo; *ed:* (BS) Elem Ed, Boston St Coll 1970; (MED) Ed, Cambridge Coll 1989; *cr:* 3rd Grade Teacher 1970-73, 2nd Grade Teacher 1973-76 Belmont Sch Malden; 5th Grade Teacher 1977-82, 4th Grade Teacher 1983- Lincoln Elem Sch; *ai:* Malden Teachers Assn Union Crisis, Prof Dev, Sch Fund Raiser Comms; Great Books Leader; *office:* Lincoln Elem Sch 33 Cross St Malden MA 02148

BARICH, MICHAEL PETER, Mathematics Teacher; *b:* Spokane, WA; *m:* Jill Stephanie Amos; *ed:* (AA) Math, Edmonds Comm Coll 1977; (BA) Math, W WA Univ 1979; *cr:* Math Teacher Newport HS 1980-82, Highland Jr HS 1982-83, Tolt HS 1984-; *ai:* Head Boys Bsktbl Coach; Tolt Booster Club 1984-; Scndry Teacher Awd Riverview 1985; *office:* Tolt HS 3740 Tolt Ave Carnation WA 98014

BARINGER, DEBORAH ANN SHREVE, Health & L D Teacher; *b:* Defiance, OH; *m:* Bill M.; *c:* Anissa L.; *ed:* (BS) K-12 Phys Ed, 1973, (BS) 7-12 Health, 1974 Defiance Coll; Working on Masters; Finishing Elem 1st-8th 1990; Taking L D Classes; *cr:* Teacher Ayersville Schls 1973-74, Hicksville Schls 1976-; *ai:* 7th-12th Grade Girls Track & Field Coach; Working on Winning Group Adv; Hicksville Ed Assn Secy 1983-85; HPER; Church Session Mem 1988-; Youth Adv 1980-84; Coach of Yr Awd Defiance Coll 1985-86; *office:* Hicksville Schls Smith St Hicksville OH 43526

BARKA, ANGELA (HONG), Learning Disabilities Teacher; *b:* Eau Claire, WI; *m:* Randy John; *ed:* (BS) Spec Ed/Elem Ed, 1983, (MSE) Spec Ed/Learning Disabilities, 1987 Univ of WI Eau Claire; Several Wkshps; *cr:* K-8th Grade Teacher of Learning Disabilities Blair-Taylor Sch Dist 1984-; *ai:* Coach Jr HS Girls Bsktbl 1988-, Jr Var Sftbl 1986-88, Var Sftbl 1988-; EEN Coord 1985-88; Stu Asst Prgm, At Risk Prgm Mem 1989-; Taylor Ed Assn Treas 1988-89; Blair-Taylor United Ed Assn Faculty Building Rep 1989-; Consolidation Comm Dept Chairperson for Spec Ed 1988-89; Osseo Evangelical Luth Church (Sunday Sch Teacher 1987-88, Supt 1988-); Blooms Slowpitch Sftbl Team (3rd Basemen 1982-, Treas 1987-); Cooperative Ed Services Agency Mem; Prgm Evaluation Task Force 1985; *home:* 747 E Thomas St Osseo WI 54758

BARKER, BETTY LANE JARVIS, Kindergarten Teacher; *b:* Baltimore, MD; *w:* John E. (dec); *c:* John D.; *ed:* (BS) Ed, Towson St Univ 1950; Loyola Coll; Johns Hopkins Univ; *cr:* 1st Grade Teacher John Eager Howard Sch 1950-57; Pupil Personnel Baltimore Cty MD 1957; Kndgtn Teacher Everett Elem Sch 1980-; *ai:* Everett Area Ed Assn 1981-; NEA 1981-; PA Ed Assn 1981-; Order of Eastern Star (Worthy Matron 1965-66/Dist Deputy 1968-69/Grand Matron of Grand Chapter of PA); Nom Teacher of Yr PA 1990; *office:* Everett Elem Sch E 1st Ave Everett PA 15537

BARKER, DURLAND B., Accounting Instructor; *b:* Norway, ME; *m:* Cheryl A. Senior; *c:* Karen, Kevin, Kyle, Stephen; *ed:* (BS) Accounting, Husson Coll 1970; *cr:* Instr S Portland HS 1986-87, Fryeburg Acad 1987-; *ai:* Sr Class Adv; Bsbl Coach; BEAM 1986-; Stoneham Fire Dept Secy 1970-; Town of Stoneham Selectman 1980-; Knights of Pythias Chancellor 1972-; *office:* Fryeburg Acad 152 Main St Fryeburg ME 04037

BARKER, GARY KEITH, Mathematics/Sci Dept Teacher; *b:* Middletown, OH; *m:* Jean B. Roettig; *c:* Molly, Corrie; *ed:* (BSED) Biological Sci, 1964, (MAT) Biological Sci, 1968 Miami Univ of OH; *cr:* Teacher Carmen Sch Dist 1964-65, Hilliard Sch Dist 1966-69, Arthur Hill HS 1969-81, Center for Art & Sci 1981-; *ai:* Sci Fair Adv; MI Sci Teachers Assn 1982, Certificate of Recognition 1985; Finalist MI Sci Teacher of Yr 1989; Natl Aeronautics & Space Admin Honors Teacher Awd; Natl Sci Fnd Teacher Awd 1985; Search for Excl Sci Certificate of Recognition MI Dept of Ed 1982; Certificate of Commendation MI Environmental Youth Awds, Society of Exploration Geophysicists 1988; Amer Society of Microbiology Certificat of Recognition 1985; Saginaw Public Schls Bd of Ed 1984; *office:* Center for Art & Sci 115 W Genesee St 115 E Gennessee Saginaw MI 48602

BARKER, JACQUELYN ANN, Mathematics Teacher; *b:* Sterling, CO; *m:* Terrance G.; *ed:* (BA) Psych/Math, UCSB 1970; *cr:* Teacher Carlsbad HS 1984-; *ai:* CA Math Cncl 1984-; Cardiff Town Cncl VP 1977-83; *office:* Carlsbad HS 3557 Monroe St Carlsbad CA 92008

BARKER, JAMES RICHARD, 7th Grade Soc Stud Teacher; *b:* Lincoln, NE; *m:* Pamela Sue Mihane; *c:* Caleigh, Carling; *ed:* (BS) His, NE Wesleyan Univ 1973; (MED) Educl Admin, Univ of NE Lincoln 1983; *cr:* Teacher Wheatland Public Schls 1975-80, North Platte Public Schls 1980-81, Scottsbluff Public Schls 1981-; *ai:* Coach Head Boys Var Cross Cntry, Boys & Girls Var Track; Scottsbluff Educl Assn 1981-; Phi Delta Kappa 1984-; *home:* 2415 Avenue B Scottsbluff NE 69361

BARKER, JIMMIE DEAN, 6th Grade Teacher; *b:* Joplin, MO; *m:* Neva Davee; *c:* Deana A., James D.; *ed:* (BA) Elem Ed, 1969, (MA) Elem Ed, 1969 AZ St Univ; (EDS) Educl Admin, Univ of NM 1976; Rdng Specialist, Pittsburg St Univ 1987; *cr:* Elem Teacher Albuquerque Public Schls 1969-81, Miami Public Schls 1981-; *ai:* Textbook Selection Comm; Curr Comm Mem; Miami Assn of Classroom Teachers, Rdng Cncl, OK Ed Assn, Green Cntry Rdng Assn, NEA, Intnl Rdng Assn; Church of Christ Mem; *office:* Wilson Sch 308 G NW Miami OK 74354

BARKER, JUDITH STEVENS, Mathematics Teacher; *b:* Rocky Mount, NC; *m:* Moses Closs Jr.; *c:* Brett; *ed:* (BS) Math Ed, East Carolina Univ 1970; Mentor Trng, NCSU 1989; *cr:* Teacher Northern HS 1970-71, Needham Broughton HS 1971-; *ai:* Jr Var & Var Chrldr Adv; NHS Selection, Media Advisory Comm; Service Club; Class Adv 1985-87, 1990; NCTM, NCCTM 1970-; NEA, NCAE 1970-80; Delta Kappa Gamma (Secy, Membership, Awareness Comm Head) 1980-; Wake Cty Educl Fnd Mini-Grant; Jenrette Chair of Teaching Excl; *office:* Needham B Broughton HS 723 St Marys St Raleigh NC 27605

BARKER, MARTHA CAROL, Mathematics Dept Chairman; *m:* Richard Michael; *c:* John R., Carol A.; *ed:* (BS) Math/Sci, 1962, (MS) Curr/Instruction, 1985 Univ of TN Martin; Elem Certificate Ed, 1965; Natl Sci Fnd Inst George Peabody Coll 1964; *cr:* Math Teacher Peabody HS 1962-67, Gadsden HS 1974-77, 1978-83, Crockett Cty HS 1983-; *ai:* Future Teachers Spon; Delta Kappa Gamma 1984-; Exchangette Club (Pres, Secy) 1966-; United Meth Women 1961-; Pilot Project for Math & Sci Mem Univ TN Martin; Outstanding Teacher UT Martin Frosh Prgm 1989-; *home:* 1402 Bradford Dr Humboldt TN 38343

BARKER, MAYSEL ROYCE (SCHWARTZ), 2nd Grade Teacher of Gifted; *b:* Brownstown, IN; *m:* William E.; *c:* Rebecca D. Barker Morrison, William E. Jr.; *ed:* (BA) Elem Ed, Franklin Coll 1970; (MS) Elem Ed, IN Univ 1974; Gifted Talented Classes; *cr:* 2nd Grade Teacher of Gifted & Talented East Side Elem 1970-; *ai:* Edinburgh Amer Legion Teacher of Yr 1989-; *office:* East Side Elem Sch 810 E Main Cross Edinburgh IN 46124

BARKER, MICHAEL RAY, Spanish/English Teacher; *b:* Wichita Falls, TX; *ed:* (AA) Lib Art, GGJC 1976; (BA) Eng, SOSU 1978; (MS) Span, E TX St Univ 1983; *cr:* Teacher Wynona Ind Sch Dist 1978-79, Mt Vearon Ind Sch Dist 1979-81, Prosper Ind Sch Dist 1981-; *ai:* Stu Cncl Spon; TSTA; *home:* 521 E Windsor #10 Denton TX 76201

BARKER, PATRICIA ANN, US His/7th Gr Religion Teacher; *b:* Chicago, IL; *m:* James W.; *c:* James, Janet, John; *ed:* (BS) Ed, Loyola Univ 1957; Admin; *cr:* Kndgtn Teacher Chicago Public Schls 1957-67; 4th & 5th Grade Teacher 1973-82, Jr HS Teacher 1982-84, 5th Grade Teacher 1984-85, Jr HS Teacher 1985- St Damian Sch; *ai:* Soc Stud, Religion & Soc Comm; NCEA 1973-; South Suburban Rdng Cncl 1987-; Heart Assn South Cook Cty 1988-; *office:* St Damian Sch 5300 West 155th St Oak Forest IL 60452

BARKER, PATRICIA YVONNE, First Grade Teacher; *b:* Denton, TX; *m:* Steven Ray; *c:* Brad A., Stephanie R., Steven K.; *ed:* (BA) Elem Ed, Cntrl St Univ 1973; (MED) Elem Sch Guidance/Counseling, 1990; *cr:* 2nd Grade Teacher Justus Elem 1973-76, South Coffeville Elem 1976-77; 1st Grade Teacher Traub Elem 1977-; *ai:* Girls Bsktbl & Vlybl Coach; Sch Yrbk; Faculty Office Treas; Soc, Book Selection, Math Curr Comm Mem; NEA, OK Ed Assn, ASCD; Midwest City Assn of Classroom Teachers (Sch Rep, Dist Grievenance Comm 1988-); *office:* Traub Elem Sch 6500 SE 15th Midwest City OK 73110

BARKER, PAULINE PACK, Second Grade Teacher; *b:* South Shore, KY; *m:* Lonnie; *ed:* (BA) Elem Ed, Morehead St Univ 1962; (MA) Curr/Rdng, Miami Univ of OH 1968; Prin Cert SW MO St Univ 1975; *cr:* 4th Grade Teacher Greeup Cty Schls 1958-60; 2nd Grade Teacher Fairview Ind Schls 1960-63, Clermont NE Schls 1964-71, Greenwood Lab Sch 1972-; *ai:* Curr, Merit Pay, Search, Young Authors Comms; Intnl Rdng Assn Pres 1984-85; ASCD 1980-; Delta Kappa Gamma Pres 1987-89; Delta St World Fellowships Comm St Chm 1984-; Greenwood Teacher of Yr 1984; *home:* 2652 Wildwood Rd Springfield MO 65804

BARKER, SHIRLEY MONROE, Third Grade Teacher; *b:* Port Arthur, TX; *m:* Robert W.; *c:* Jane B. Hankins, Donald, Anne B. Matthews; *ed:* (BS) Ed/Sci, KS St Univ Pittsburg 1952; Grad Work at Various Univ; *cr:* 6th Grade Teacher Avondale Sch Dist 1962-65; Primary Grade Teacher La Mesa-Spring Valley Sch Dist 1966-76; 3rd Grade Teacher Priest River Elem Sch 1977-; *ai:* ID Centennial Building Rep; Dist Alternate Sch Schedule & Curr Dev, Artist in Residence Comm; Textbook Selection; Alpha Delta Kappa (Corresponding Secy, Chapter Historian) 1978-; IEA, BCEA, NEA 1977-; LMSVEA, CEA, NEA 1966- 6; Womens Aglow Prayer Cnslr 1977-87; PTA 1985-; Luth Church Cmmty Child Dev Chm 1973-76; Team-Teaching Pilot Project; Master Teacher; Fuller Theological Seminary Dist Rep for Cty Wide Racial Awareness Project; *home:* Star Rt Box 362 Spirit Lake ID 83869

BARKER, WILEY RICHARD, Social Science Teacher; *b:* Albany, GA; *ed:* (BA) His/Ed, GA Southwestern Coll Americus 1978; GA Stud Inst Univ of GA; *cr:* Teacher Martin Luther King Jr Mid 1978-; *ai:* Dougherty Cty Assn of Educators (Elections & Credentials Comm Chm, Treas); GA Cncl for Soc Sci Dist Dir Area 8; Teacher of Yr 1988-89; *office:* Martin Luther King Jr Mid Sch 2235 M L King Jr Blvd Albany GA 31701

BARKLEY, MARY PIEPKOW, First Grade Teacher; *b:* Charlotte, MI; *m:* Joey; *c:* Jay, Jeffrey; *ed:* (BA) Elem Ed, MI St Univ 1978; ITIP, Co-operative Grouping, Math Their Way, Cognitive Coaching; *cr:* 1st Grade Teacher Olivet Cmmty Schls 1978-79; 1st/3rd/4th Grade Teacher Potterville Public Schls 1979-85; 1st/2nd Grade Teacher Olivet Cmmty Schls 1985-; *ai:* Dir K-3rd Grade Musical Production; Sch Improvement Comm; Lee Center Church (Bd Secy 1979-, Dir Vacation Bible Sch 1979-89); Teacher Exch Dominican RepubliC 1989; Write to Read Team Mem.

BARKLEY, PHYLLIS M. GIFFORD, 5th Grade Teacher; *b:* Chillicothe, OH; *m:* John Richard; *c:* Cynthia, Bryant, Brent; *ed:* (BS) Elem Ed, 1972; (MS) Elem Ed, 1978 OH Univ; *cr:* 4th Grade Teacher 1972-73; 4th Grade Teacher 1973- Atwater Elem; 5th Grade & Head Teacher High St 1979-81; *ai:* Drug Prevention Prgm "IMPACT"; AAUW; OH Realtor Saleswoman 1989-; Pickaway Cty Reality Assn 1989-; *home:* 331 Tariton Road Circleville OH 43113

BARKOVITZ, ROBERT WALTER, Physics Teacher; *b:* Jersey City, NJ; *m:* Jean Lavelle; *c:* Robert, Brian; *ed:* (BA) Physics, St Peters Coll 1973; (MS) Religion, Fordham Univ 1979; Grad Stud Various Colls & Univ; *cr:* Physics/Math Teacher St Aloysius HS 1972-75; Physics/Earth Sci Teacher Secaucus HS 1975-84; Math Teacher Passaic Cty Comm Coll 1979-81; Exec Dir Contact Hotline 1981-; Physics Teacher Millburn HS 1984-; *ai:* Bsktbl Coach 1975-79; Involvement with Peer Counseling Group 1986-; AAPT 1973-75, 1987-; Public Service Electric & Gas Company Educl Adv 1982-; St Marys Sch Bd Mem 1980-83; Contact USA (mem, Natl Bd of Dir) 1988-; Wrote, Edited, Compiled Contact Hotline Trng Manual; *office:* Millburn HS 462 Millburn Ave Millburn NJ 07041

BARKS, SHIRLEY LOU (HOXWORTH), Third Grade Teacher; *b:* Risco, MO; *m:* Marion E.; *ed:* (BSED) Eng/Spec Ed, 1961, (MA) Elem Ed/Elem Admin, 1971 SE MO St Univ; Grad Stud; *cr:* Pre-Sch Teacher Trng Center for Handicapped Children 1960-61; Spec Ed Teacher 1961-66, 3rd Grade Teacher 1966- Woodland R-IV; *ai:* Mentor to New Teacher, Cooperating Teacher SE Mo St Univ; Instructional Management System; NHS; MO St Teachers Assn 1961-; Bollinger Cty Teachers Assn Rep Exec Comm 1961-; Woodland Cmmty Teachers Assn Secy 1961-; Woodland PTO (Various Comm, Membership Drive) 1961-; Alpha Delta Kappa (Pres, VP, Recording Secy, Corresponding Secy, Treas, Historian, Dist Historian 1961); Brownies (Former Leader, Former Day Camp Leader); Marble Hill Lutesville Jr Womens Club of MO Former Mem; Federated Womens Club (Secy, Treas, VP, Pres, Historian Scrapbook Chairperson of 9th Dist); Cmmty Act Centennial Pellegrino Park Dedication; Red Cross Bloodmobile; Cerebral Palsy Telethon; Heart Fund; Publicity Chairperson for Cancer; Regents Schlsp to SE MO St Univ; Cerebral Palsy Schlsp; Outstanding Young Women of America; Outstanding Elem Teachers of America; *home:* Rt 1 Box 633 Marble Hill MO 63764

BARKUS, DAVID WILLIAM, Choral Director; *b:* Ft Benton, MT; *m:* Lucy Ellen Sather; *c:* Chasity J., Nicole R., Chelsea M.; *ed:* (BA) Music Ed, Jamestown Coll 1978; *cr:* Music Dir Hoffman-Kersington Schls 1978-80, Jameston HS 1980-81; Choral Dir Lakes HS 1982; Music Dir Sturgis HS 1982-89; Choral Dir Brookings HS 1989-; *ai:* Jazz Choir; Boys & Girls Ensemble; SD ACDA West Region Chm 1982-; *office:* Brookings HS 530 Elm Ave Brookings SD 57006

BARLAU, BESS L., 8th/9th Grade Teacher; *b:* Gorman, TX; *m:* Danny P.; *ed:* (BSED) Eng/Bus, N TX Univ 1968; Lib Art & Talented Gifted Ed; *cr:* Teacher Nimitz Jr HS 1968-78; Secy Gibsons Mrktg 1978; Teacher Nimitz Jr HS 1979-; *ai:* Ector Cty Ind Sch Dist Comm Cncl for Instructional Staff, Nimitz Jr HS Advisory Comm Mem; Nimitz Jr HS Decathlon Coach; TX St Teachers Assn 1968-; TX Classroom Teachers Assn 1975-; TX Joint Cncl of Eng Teachers 1985-; Luth Womens Missionary League VP 1984-85; *office:* Nimitz Jr HS 4900 Maple Odessa TX 79762

BARLEY, GEORGE M., Mathematics/Computer Instr; *b:* Mexico, MO; *m:* Patricia A. Saak; *c:* Stacey Lansche, Bryan G.; *ed:* (BAED) Math, 1962, (MA) Math, 1968 Northeast MO St Univ; *cr:* Math Isntr Milwaukee Public Schls 1962-64; Math/Cmptr Instr Montgomery Cty R-2 Schls 1964-; *ai:* Math Team Adv; Golf Coach; MNEA; NEA; MEA Pres 1980-82; CTM; NCTM; Montgomery City Bd of Aldermen; Natl Sci Fnd Grant; Nom MO Outstanding Math Teacher.

BARLOW, BARBARA ANN, Sixth Grade Teacher; *b:* Winston-Salem, NC; *ed:* (BS) Elem Ed, Appalachian St Univ 1959; Post Grad Stud Univ of VA, Univ of NC, George Mason Univ, Coll of Notre Dame; *cr:* 7th/8th Grade Eng/Soc Stud Teacher Winston-Salem NC 1959-63; 6th Grade Teacher Washington Mill 1963-72, Kings Glen 1972-77, Little Run 1977-;

ai: Stu Cncl Assn Spon; NCEA 1959-63; Fairfax Ed Assn 1963-; NEA 1959-; Alpha Delta Kappa 1966-.

BARLOW, EVELYN FAULCON, Guidance Counselor; *b:* Dewitt, VA; *m:* Cornell A.; *c:* Colette D.; *ed:* (BS) Elem Ed, 1975, (MED) Guidance/Counseling, 1979 VA St Univ; Math Cert; *cr:* Teacher Westview Elem 1975-85; Math Instr Peabody Jr HS 1985-88; Admin Asst 1988-89, Guidance Cnslr 1989- Peabody Mid; *ai:* Math Club Adv; Jr Var Sftbl Coach; Chairperson Various Comms; VA Math League, NEA, VA Ed Assn, Petersburg Ed Assn, Southside Cncl of Rdng Ed; Walk America March of Dimes; Walk for the Hungry; Teacher of Month; Team Leader; *home:* 2953 Rollingwood Rd Petersburg VA 23805

BARLOW-GILLIS, JODY, Special Consultant to Gifted; *b:* El Paso, TX; *m:* Lawrence Edward Gillis; *c:* Pamela S. Homenick; *ed:* (BA) Elem Ed, San Diego St Univ 1960; Gifted Teachers Cert Prgm; *cr:* 4th/5th Grade Teacher Northmont Elem 1960-68; Dir/Teacher Something More Cooking Sch 1972-79; Drama Teacher Actors Cmmty Theatre Sch 1974-84; Consultant of Gifted Rolando Elem 1980-88; Consultant of K-6th Grade Gifted Murray Manor Elem 1978-; *ai:* Arts Comm La Mesa Sch Dist 1988-89; CA Teachers Assn, NEA 1960-68; Intnl Assn of Cooking Schls; San Diego Civic Light Opera Assn; Amer Assn of Univ Women 1968-; Cmmty Theatre Sch 1974-84; Food Ed Culinary Publications; Guest Contributor Various Publications; *home:* 10345 Woodpark Dr Santee CA 92071

BARNABY, ANNE MARIE FAYAN, Mathematics Dept Teacher; *b:* Fall River, MA; *m:* James P.; *c:* Marisa A.; *ed:* (BA) Math, Salve Regina Coll 1977; *cr:* Math Dept Teacher St Xavier Acad 1977-81, Bishop Connolly HS 1981-; *office:* Bishop Connolly HS 373 Elsbree St Fall River MA 02721

BARNARD, CAROLE CAMP, Math Teacher; *b:* Oil City, PA; *m:* Patrick W.; *ed:* (BA) Math, Rosary Hill Coll 1969; (MS) Ed, Canisius Coll 1974; *cr:* Math Teacher Tonawanda Jr Sr HS 1969-; Asst Treas Tonawanda Sch Employees Fed CU 1983-; *ai:* Adv for THS Help-A-Neighbor Org; Adv for THS Musical Dinner Theater; NCTM 1979-; Assn Math Teachers of NY St 1980-; NYS United Teachers/AFT 1969-; Tonawanda Ed Assn 1969-; Distinguished Service Awd 1982-; Tonawanda City Schls Teacher of Yr 1982; *office:* Tonawanda Jr Sr H S Fletcher & Hinds St Tonawanda NY 14150

BARNARD, GAYLA PFEIFFER, Counselor; *b:* Hardin Cty, KY; *m:* Kenneth L.; *c:* Allison, Jonathan; *ed:* (BA) Elem Ed, Campbellsville Coll 1971; (MA) Elem Counseling, W KY Univ 1980; Rank I Elem Counseling, W KY Univ 1990; Working Towards Cert Eng as a Second Lang; *cr:* Math/Sci Teacher 1971-75, Eng Teacher 1976-77 T K Stone Jr HS; 3rd Grade Teacher Helmwood Heights Elem 1977-87; 7th/8th Grade Cnslr T K Stone Jr HS 1987-; *ai:* Beta Club & Bookstore Spon; Sch Based Planning, Curr Advisory, K-3rd Grade Curr, Calendar In-Service, Guidance Comm; NEA, KY Ed Assn, Elizabethtown Ed Assn 1971-; KY Assn of Counseling & Dev, FDCA Fourth Dist Cnslrs Assn 1987-; OH Valley Assn of Sch Admin 1987-; Delta Kappa Gamma 1980-; Helmwood Heights ELem Sch Teacher of Yr 1983-84; *office:* T K Stone Jr HS Morningside Dr Elizabethtown KY 42701

BARNARD, JANICE M., Kindergarten/Chapter I Teacher; *b:* Blair, NE; *m:* Richard G.; *c:* Deanna, Bruce, Mark; *ed:* (BA) Elem Ed, Dana Coll 1976; Grad Stud; *cr:* 3rd Grade Teacher Plattsmouth 1959-61, Tacoma 1961-62, Omaha Public Schls 1963-66; Kndgtn/Chapter I Rdng/Math Teacher Tekamah-Herman Schls 1976-.

BARNARD, KATHRYN ANN, Dance/Business Teacher; *b:* Phoenix, AZ; *ed:* (BA) Phys Ed/Dance, 1971, (MBA) Personnel Management, 1983 AZ St Univ; *cr:* Phys Ed Instr Washington Elem Sch 1971-72, Glendale HS 1972-80; Dance Instr/Bus Teacher Moon Valley HS 1980-; *ai:* Spon Moon Valley Dance Club; Choreographer & Dir Moon Valley Dance Productions; Choreographer Moon Valley Theatre; Acad Awds Judge Moon Valley Thespians; Classroom Teachers Assn, AZ Educl Assn; Natl Educl Assn; Amer Alliance for Health, Phys Ed, Recreation & Dance; *office:* Moon Valley HS 3625 W Cactus Rd Phoenix AZ 85029

BARNER, LILLIE PETTY, Mathematics Teacher; *b:* Sunflower, MS; *m:* James Earl; *c:* Reginald, Ronald; *ed:* (BS) Math, MS Valley St Univ 1964; Delta St Univ; *cr:* Teacher Gentry HS 1963-; *ai:* Yrbk Adv; Indianola Teacher Assn Building Rep 1988-; MAE; NEA; Willing Workers Society Secy 1987-; Selected Star Teacher 1973, 1984, 1985; *home:* 504 Slim St Indianola MS 38751

BARNES, CALLIE BOND, 1st Grade Teacher; *b:* Jackson, TN; *c:* Christopher, Jennifer; *ed:* Elem Ed, Lane Coll 1974; (MA) Elem Ed, Memphis St Univ 1976; *cr:* 5th Grade Teacher Haywood Cty 1974-75; Beech Bluff Elem 1975-77; 1st Grade Teacher 1977-79; 5th Grade Teacher 1979-86, 1st Grade Teacher 1986- Lincoln Elem; *ai:* Jackson Ed Assn 1977-; TN Ed Assn 1974-; NEA 1974-; *office:* Lincoln Elem Sch 425 Berry St Jackson TN 38301

BARNES, CATHERINE E., Lang Arts/Reading Teacher; *b:* Dodge City, KS; *m:* Perry L.; *c:* Jenna, Matt; *ed:* (BA) Speech/Drama, St Mary of Plains Coll 1971; (MED) Educl Therapy, Natl Coll of Ed 1982; *cr:* Teachers Aide, Behavior Disabilities Teacher 1980-82, Learning Disabilities Teacher 1982-83 Mac Arthur Mid Schl; Lang Art/Rdng Teacher Northlake Mid Sch 1983-; *ai:* Creative Theatres Club, Newspaper Spon; West Suburban Rdng Cncl; NCTE; Awarded Honary Life Membership IL Congress of Parents & Teachers; *office:* Northlake Mid Sch 202 S Lakewood Northlake IL 60104

BARNES, CHARLES, Teacher/Basketball Coach; *b:* Kings Mountain, NC; *ed:* (BS) Health/Phys Ed, 1974; (MA) Health/Phys Ed, 1982 Appalachian St Univ; *cr:* Phys Ed Teacher Kings Mountain Schls 1973-74; Teacher/Coach Holbrook Jr HS 1978-81, Richmond Sr HS 1982-87, Westside HS 1987-; *ai:* Var Head Bsbl, Asst Ftbl, Jr Var Track Coach; NEA, GEA Mem 1986-; St Coaches Assn Mem 1982-; *office:* Westside HS 1002 Stelling Rd Augusta GA 30907

BARNES, CHRISTOPHER RAYMOND, Sci Teacher/Ftbl & Bsbl Coach; *b:* Phoenix, AZ; *m:* Terrie Ann Jamsa; *c:* Michelle, Courtney; *ed:* (BS) Bio, AZ St Univ 1979; (MA) Voc Ed, N AZ Univ 1986; Grad Stud; *cr:* Teacher/Coach Greenway HS 1979-80, Deer Valley HS 1980-; *ai:* Frosh Bsbl & Jr Var Ftbl Coach; Dist Course Instr Sci Curr for Dist Teachers; NEA, AEA 1979-89; AFT 1989-; Published Geology/Astronomy Lab Manual.

BARNES, CLARA THRASHER, Fifth Grade Teacher; *b:* Glasgow, KY; *m:* Roger F.; *c:* Suzanne, Brian; *ed:* (BS) Elem Ed, Campbellsville Coll 1970; (MS) Elem Ed, 1975, (Rank I) Elem Ed, 1980 E KY Univ; *cr:* Spec Ed Teacher Jamestown Elem 1970-72; 5th Grade Teacher Union Chapel Elem 1972-; *ai:* Guidance Comm; *office:* Union Chapel Elem Sch Rt 3 Jamestown KY 42629

BARNES, DOROTHY MADEN, Kindergarten Teacher; *b:* Jonesborough, TN; *m:* Robert L.; *c:* Donna, Diane Mc Kinny, Robert; *ed:* (BS) Ed, E TN St Univ 1971; Grad Stud E TN St Univ; *cr:* Kndgtn Teacher Sulphur Springs Sch, Jonesborough Elem; *ai:* Washington Cty Ed Assn Faculty Rep; Jonesborough Elem Sch Human Relations & Math Curr Comm; Washington Cty Ed Assn, NEA, Gilbreath Rdng Cncl Assn 1971-91; Womens Missionary Union Prgm Chairperson 1971-85; Childrens Choir Dir 1980-85; Young Republicans Club 1971-85; Career Ladder Level III Awd 1985; Teacher of Yr 1988; Excel Teacher Awd Washington Cty 1988; *office:* Jonesboro Elem Sch 306 Forest Dr Jonesboro TN 37659

BARNES, EVELYN WRIGLEY, Third Grade Teacher; *b:* Malta, ID; *m:* Paul Dean; *c:* Ronda, Del Ray, Paul, Trina; *ed:* (BA) Ed, ID St Univ 1976; Working Towards Masters Psych & Ed; *cr:* 3rd Grade Teacher Paul Elem Sch 1976-79; 2nd Grade Teacher 1979-86, 3rd Grade Teacher 1986- Malta Elem Sch; *ai:* Delta Kappa Gamma Society Intnl Mem 1985-; Amer Cancer Assn Cancer Drive Chm 1986-88; Amer Farm Bureau Malta Area Mem 1970-; PTA Mem 1985-; Ladder Day Saints Church Active Mem; Natl Freedoms Fnd Public Speaking Awd; *office:* Raft River Elem Sch 427 W Center St Malta ID 83342

BARNES, GENEVA MC GHEE, US History Teacher; *b:* Montgomery, AL; *m:* Willie W. Sr.; *c:* Sheryl L., Willie W. Jr., Edward A.; *ed:* (BS) Soc Stud, 1964, (MED) Ed, 1974 AL St Univ; *cr:* His/Eng Teacher Center HS 1964-65, Carver HS 1965-66; His Teacher Jefferson Davis HS 1974-; *ai:* Curr & Instruction Comm Mem; Montgomery Cty Soc Stud Textbook & Media Selection Comm; Citizen Bee Contest Judge; Montgomery Cty Ed Assn, AL Ed Assn, NEA 1974-; Zeta Phi Beta, Sigma Rho Sigma Honor Society 1963-; *office:* Jefferson Davis HS 3420 Carter Hill Rd Montgomery AL 36111

BARNES, GEORGE JOHN, Science Teacher; *b:* Pittsburgh, PA; *m:* Katherine M. Sotnyk; *ed:* (BS) Bio, Edinboro Univ 1970; *cr:* Sci Teacher Homestead Mid Sch 1971-79; Woodlawn Mid Sch 1979-; *ai:* Sci Fair Spon; Mid Sch Budget Comm; PA Sci Teachers Assn; *office:* Woodlawn Mid Sch Woodlawn Ave Munhall PA 15120

BARNES, JANA SHEPHERD, Vocational Homemaking Teacher; *b:* Cooper, TX; *m:* Bobby; *c:* Mickey; *ed:* (BS) Home Ec, E TX St Univ 1966; *cr:* Substitute Teacher Bisbee AZ 1966-75; Resource Teacher Delmar Ind Sch Dist 1975-76; Homemaking Teacher Roxton HS 1976-; *ai:* FHA Adv & Alumni Adv; Sr Class Spon; Voc Home Ec Teachers Assn of TX; Lamar Cty Home Ec Assn Secy 1980-81.

BARNES, JANICE TAYLOR, Second Grade Teacher; *b:* Kenly, NC; *m:* Thomas Scott; *c:* Katrina, Sean; *ed:* (BS) Ed, 1963, (MA) Ed, 1965 E Carolina; Teaching Profession Classes; *cr:* 6th/7th Grade Teacher Glendale Sch 1963-65; 3rd/4th Grade Teacher Micro Sch 1965-67; 3rd/7th/8th Grade Teacher Rosewood Sch 1967-74; 1st-5th Grade Teacher Lee Woodard Sch 1974-; *ai:* Accreditation Steering Comm; Lib Advisory Bd; Sch Base Team; PTO Secy; Sch Assistance Team; Co-Spon Lee Woodward Rhythm Band; NEA, NC Assn for Educators, PACE Mem 1963-; Teacher of Yr; Officers for Beddingfield Music Boosters & Sunday Sch Class Officer; *home:* Rt 1 Box 388 Lucama NC 27851

BARNES, KAY CARROLL, Mathematics Department Chair; *b:* Atlanta, GA; *m:* William Mc Kenzie; *c:* Kara E., Walter H.; *ed:* (BA) Math - Magna Cum Laude, Wesleyan Coll 1960; *cr:* Math Teacher Oconee Cty HS 1960-61, Miller Sr HS 1961-62, Meriwether HS 1964, Flint River Acad 1969-; *ai:* Sr Class & Math Team Spon; Phi Delta Phi, Sigma Alpha Iota, Phi Kappa Phi; Woodbury Baptist Church Organist 1963-; Woodbury Garden Club 1963-66; Sch & Cty STAR Teacher; *home:* PO Box 305 Woodbury GA 30293

BARNES, KEITH E., Science Instructor; *b:* Topeka, KS; *ed:* (BSED) Biological Sci, 1961, (MSED) Scndry Sch Admin, 1965 Pittsburg St Univ; (MAT) Sci, Univ of NC Chapel Hill 1966; Numerous Univs; *cr:* Sci Instr Webb City Jr HS 1961-69, MO S Univ 1968, Olathe HS 1969-80, Olathe S HS 1981-; *ai:* KSTA, NABT, NSTA, NEA; NSF Academic Yr Inst; *home:* 911 Cathy Cir Olathe KS 66062

BARNES, KEN LEE, Mathematics Dept Chair; *b:* Ft Oglethorpe, GA; *ed:* (BS) Math/Phys Sci, Eureka Coll 1986; Sangamon St Univ; *cr:* Math Dept Chm Williamsville HS 1986-; *ai:* Track & Frosh Ftbl Coach; NCTM, Amer Math Society, Math Assn of America; Williamsville Chrstn Church Deacon 1988-; *home:* PO Box 2 Williamsville IL 62693

BARNES, LORENE TAYLOR, English Teacher; *b:* Jackson, MS; *c:* Michael; *ed:* (BA) Eng, Jackson St Univ 1966; (MS) Black Literature, Governors St Univ 1978; *cr:* Eng Teacher Coleman HS 1966-68; 5th Grade Teacher Henson Elem 1969-71; 6th Grade Teacher Hay Upper Grade Center 1971-72; Eng Teacher Taft HS 1972-86, Corliss HS 1986-; *ai:* Eng Coach Academic Olympics; Parent Teacher Stu Assn Parliamentarian 1989-; ASCD 1990; Academic Olympics 1989, Plaque, Cert; Outstanding Teacher Awd Univ of Chicago 1985; *office:* Corliss HS 821 E 103rd St Chicago IL 60628

BARNES, MARGIE RIGSBY, English Teacher; *b:* Cumberland County, KY; *m:* Wilbur K.; *c:* B. B. II, Bradley K.; *ed:* (BS) Elem Ed, W KY Univ 1963; *cr:* 2nd Grade Teacher Jamestown Elem 1964-74; Kndgtn Teacher 1974-75, 1st Grade Teacher 1975-79, 5th-8th Grade Lang Art Teacher 1979-87 Union Chapel Elem; 8th Grade Eng Teacher Russell Cty Jr HS 1987-; *ai:* Russell Cty Jr HS Academic Team Coach; *home:* Rt 3 Box 157 A Jamestown KY 42629

BARNES, MARIE MATERN, Social Studies Dept Chairman; *b:* Newburgh, NY; *m:* George H. Jr.; *c:* Marie R., Erika L.; *ed:* (BAE) Scndry Soc Stud, 1968, (MED) Scndry Soc Stud, 1977 Univ of FL; *cr:* Teacher Bell Sch 1968-69, Chiefland HS 1969-80; Teacher/Dept Head Bronson HS 1980-84, Chiefland HS 1984-; *ai:* Academic Competing Team & 10th Grade Spon; Levy Cty Ed Assn Collective Bargaining 1980-89; Chiefland HS Teacher of Yr 1989; *office:* Chiefland HS P O Box 39 Chiefland FL 32626

BARNES, MARY FRALEY, First Grade Teacher; *b:* Ronceverte, WV; *c:* Maurine, Milton; *ed:* (BS) Elem Ed, Kent St Univ 1972; *cr:* 1st Grade Teacher N Kingsville Elem Sch 1973-; *ai:* N Kingsville Book Factory Publishing Center Spon & Comm Mem; ACEI; Nature Conservancy Arbor Day Fnd; Outstanding Conservation Teacher 1987.

BARNES, MICHAEL L., Social Studies Chair; *b:* Sault Ste Marie, MI; *c:* Kathryn L., Elizabeth J.; *ed:* (BA) His, Alma Coll 1971; MA Prgm, Cntrl MI Univ; *cr:* Teacher Sault Ste Marie Area Schls 1972, Vestaburg Cmmty Schls 1972-.

BARNES, PATRICIA QUINN, French Teacher; *b:* Hartford, CT; *m:* Brian A.; *c:* Brad, Todd; *ed:* (BA) Fr, Coll of New Rochelle 1965; (MAT) Fr/Ed, Boston Coll 1967; Cert Universite Laval 1965, Universite De Paris 1964, Universite D Avignon 1987; *cr:* Fr Teacher Glastonbury HS 1966-67, Naugatuck HS 1967-71; Asst Professor Fr Post Coll 1971-73; Fr/Span Teacher Holy Cross HS 1981-; *ai:* Spon La Societe Honoraire De Francais; Mem Holy Cross Academic Bd; Adv Advanced Placement Fr Lang; AATF, CT Organization of Lang Teachers, Delta Kappa Gamma Intnl 1981-; Womens League of Waterbury Symphony Pres 1967-71; Gilbert & Sullivan Troupe of Greater Waterbury 1978-88; Jr League of Greater Waterbury Pres 1970-; Distinguished Service Awd Jaycees 1978; AATF Fellowship to Study Fr Universite D Avignon 1987; Univ of CT Cooperative Teacher 1988-; *office:* Holy Cross HS 587 Oronoke Rd Waterbury CT 06708

BARNES, REBECCA ANN, Fourth Grade Teacher; *b:* Dothan, AL; *m:* Gene; *c:* Bart, Matt; *ed:* (BS) Bus Ed, 1962, (MS) Bus Ed, 1963 Univ of S MS; Elem Ed, Univ of S MS; *cr:* Bus Instr Nicholls St Univ 1962-63, Univ of MD 1963-64; Bus Teacher Baton Rouge HS 1966-67; Elem Ed Teacher Hattiesburg Public Schls 1978-; *ai:* Spirit Comm Chm; Prof Affairs Rep; Delta Kappa Gamma, Kappa Kappa Iota, AFT; Jr Auxiliary; Racquet Club Bd Mem; Thousand Lines of Poetry Published & Copyrighted 1988-89; Grad Teaching Fellowship; *home:* 119 Wildwood Trace Hattiesburg MS 39402

BARNES, SHARON KRAUS, Spanish Teacher; *b:* Tulsa, OK; *ed:* (BA) Span, 1969, (MA) Span, 1973 Wichita St Univ; Working on Phd; *cr:* Span Teacher El Dorado Jr HS 1969-74, Argentine Mid Sch 1974-81, J C Harmon HS 1981-; *ai:* Span Club & Jr Class Spon; Homebound & Advanced Placements Instr; Effective Schls Team, Writing Across the Curr Comm; KS Foreign Lang Assn; KS City Cmmty Opera Company 1985-; Johnson Cty Cmmty Chorus 1978-86; Presenter at Cntrl Sts Foreign Lang Conference 1979; Natl Endowment for Hum Grant Recipient 1984; Co-Presenter at KS Foreign Lang Assn Fall Seminars 1989; *home:* 525 N Walnut Olathe KS 66061

BARNES, STEPHEN JAMES, Sixth Grade Teacher; *b:* Spokane, WA; *m:* Peggy Louise Barnes Stretch; *c:* Brandon J., Brittney N.; *ed:* (BA) Rdng, 1982, (MA) Curr, 1987 E WA Univ; *cr:* 6th Grade Teacher Nine Mile Falls Elem 1983-87, Browne Elem 1987-; *ai:* Coaching Soccer, Bsbl, Bsktbl, Wrestling, Track, Vlybl, Ftbl & Sftbl; Clubs & Comm; Sci Coord & Spelling Bee Leader; *office:* Browne Elem Sch N5134 Driscoll Blvd Spokane WA 99205

BARNES, TAMMY KAYE, 8th Grade English Teacher; *b:* Tulsa, OK; *m:* Johnny Wayne; *c:* Valerie, Chris, Brittany, Johnson; *ed:* (BA) Speech/Drama, Northeastern St 1981; Madeline Hunter Effective Trng Prgm; *cr:* Teacher Mannford Public Schls 1981-82, Hominy Public Schls 1982-86, Glenpool Mid Sch 1986-; *ai:*

6th-12th Grade Coord of Gifted & Talented; OK Stus Offer Solutions Chairperson; Glenpool Homecoming Comm 1990; Glenpool Ed Assn Rep 1989-; OK Ed Assn, NEA 1981-; Jenks United Meth Church 1965-; Glenpool Homecoming Video Production 1989-; Educator of Month; Recipient Intl Grant Authors of Tomorrow; *office:* Glenpool Mid Sch 146th & Elm Glenpool OK 74033

BARNES, WANDA FAYE, Elementary Math Teacher; *b:* Licking, MO; *m:* David; *c:* Kent, Kurt; *ed:* (BA) Elem Ed 1980; (ME) Elem Ed, 1988 Drury Coll; *cr:* Rem Lang Arts Teacher Licking Public Schls 1979-80; Rem Math Teacher 1980-81; 4th/6th Grade Math Teacher 1981-Licking Elem; *ai:* League Math Contest Coord; Tutoring Prgm; MSTA 1981-; Kappa Delta Pi 1981-; NCTM 1987-88; *office:* Licking Elem Sch P.O. Box 179 Licking MO 65542

BARNES, YVETTE, Mathematics Teacher; *b:* Edgefield, SC; *ed:* (BS) Sci Teaching/Math, Clemson Univ 1984; (MAE) Math, The Citadel 1987; *cr:* Teacher Alston Mid 1985, Du Bose Mid 1985-; *ai:* Stu Cncl Adv; NEA, SC Ed Assn, Summerville Ed Assn 1985-; Delta Sigma Theta 1990; *office:* Du Bose Mid Sch 1000 Du Bose Dr Summerville SC 29483

BARNETT, BARBARA WILLIAMS, Teacher; *b:* Philadelphia, PA; *m:* Leon Arthur; *c:* Frank A., Lee A.; *ed:* (BS) Ed, West Chester St Univ 1955; (MS) Ed/Rdng Specialist, St Josephs Univ; Univ of Pa, Temple Univ, Univ of West Indies; *cr:* Teacher Shaw Jr HS 1955, 1964-76, Sulzberger Jr HS 1957-64; Dist Coord Sch Dist Of Philadelphia 1976-82; Teacher HS For Creative & Performing Art 1982-; *ai:* Sr Class Advisory Comm; NHS Adv; Friends of Free Lib Secy 1985-86; Amer Assn of Univ Women; NCTE; Women in Ed 1989-; Zeta Phi Beta Treas 1980-82, Service Awd 1990; *office:* Creative & Performing Arts HS 11th & Catharine Sts Philadelphia PA 19147

BARNETT, CHERYL ANNE, Jr High Choral Director; *b:* Watertown, NY; *m:* Charles B; *c:* Charla, Chad, Cherylyn; *ed:* (AA) Music, Tacoma Cmmty Coll 1971; (BM) Music, Univ Puget Sound 1973; Guidance & Counseling, Univ of Puget Sound; *cr:* Music Lib Univ of Puget Sound 1974-75; Music Teacher McIlvaigh Jr HS 1975-78; Hudtloff Jr HS 1978-; *ai:* Drill Team Coach; Girls Jr Varsity Track Coach; Natural Helper Teacher; Dir of Main Event Vocal Ensemble; Co-Trainer for Parent Classes-The Drug Free Years; NEA 1975-; PTSA Music Teacher 1988- Golden Acorn 1988; McIlvaigh Jr HS Music Teacher 1975-78 Teacher of Yr 1977; Tacoma Chrstn Ctr (Choir Dir 1989- Music Minister 1987-); Dightmans Bible Book Store 1st Pl Vocal Contest 1987-88; *office:* Hudtloff Jr H Schl 7702 Phillips Rd SW Tacoma WA 98498

BARNETT, DANA, English Teacher/Dept Chair; *b:* Santa Maria, CA; *m:* Peter; *c:* Michael, Kevin; *ed:* (BA) Eng, 1976, (MA) Eng, 1979 CA St Univ Hayward; CA Scndry Life Credential, CA St Univ Hayward 1980; *cr:* Instr CA St Univ Hayward 1977-82; Teacher St Joseph Notre Dame HS 1980-84; Summer Sch Prin 1986-88, Teacher 1984-, Eng Dept Chairperson 1986- Holy Names HS; *ai:* AP Eng Coord; NCTE 1985-; NCEA 1980-; Alpha Delta Kappa (Corresponding Secy 1990-92) 1989-; Oakland Youth Lacrosse Parent Bd Secy 1984-87; Natl Endowment Hum Summer Seminars for Sch Teachers Fellowship Summer 1990; Nathaniel Hawthorne in Theory & Context SUNY Buffalo; *office:* Holy Names HS 4660 Harbord Dr Oakland CA 94618

BARNETT, DE ANNA DAWM, 6th Grade Teacher; *b:* Atlanta, GA; *m:* Stephen James; *c:* Bryan D., James R., Terry A.; *ed:* (BA) Eng, Milligan Coll 1972; (MS) Elem Ed, IN Univ 1978; *cr:* 4th Grade Teacher Stinesville Elem 1972-73, Paragon Elem 1973-75; Pre-Sch Teacher Town & Cntry Pre-Sch 1979-82; 6th Grade Teacher Mt Mission Sch 1983; *ai:* Dormitory Supvr; Pianist for Singing Groups; Sunday Sch Teacher; *office:* Mt Mission Sch 1 Hurley St Grundy VA 24614

BARNETT, DONNA VOYLES, Sixth Grade Teacher; *b:* Carnegie, OK; *m:* Jackie W.; *c:* Winston, Monica; *ed:* (BA) Bus Admin 1981, (BA) Elem Ed 1984 Univ Sci & Arts of OK; (MS) Scndry Admin, Central St Univ 1989; *cr:* 5th-8th Grade Teacher Verden Mid Sch 1982-89, 6th Grade Teacher Verden Elem 1989-; *ai:* Staff Dev Comm 1982-86; Phi Beta Lambda; Pi Gamma MU; Kappa Delta Pi; NBEA Merit Awd 1982; *home:* PO Box 683 Anadarko OK 73005

BARNETT, LAURA HARBISON, First Grade Teacher; *b:* Athens, TN; *m:* Rick; *c:* Sara, Robert; *ed:* (BS) Ed, Univ of TN 1979; *cr:* 1st Grade Teacher Benton Elem Sch 1979-; *office:* Benton Elem Sch School Dr Benton TN 37307

BARNETT, PAMELA JOYCE, Eng/Typing/Accounting Teacher; *b:* Cullman, AL; *ed:* (BS) Music Ed, 1980, (MS) Scndry Ed/Eng, 1988 Jacksonville St Univ; *cr:* 7th-12th Grade Choral Music Teacher 1980-83, Business Math Teacher 1984-86, Accounting I Teacher 1983-, 8th Grade Eng Teacher 1980-88, 9th/11th/12th Grade Eng Dept Head 1980-, Guidance Cnslr 1989- Trinity Chrstn Acad; *ai:* Sr Class Spon; Fine Arts Competition & Academic Competition Coord; Delta Omicron (Chaplain 1979-80) 1978-80; *office:* Trinity Christian Acad 1500 Airport Rd Oxford AL 36203

BARNETT, RUSSELL CLYDE, Social Studies Teacher; *b:* New York, NY; *m:* Janet Frances; *c:* Tyler, Jessica; *ed:* (BA) Ec, Fairleigh Dickinson Univ 1968; (MA) Philosophy, City Coll City Univ 1972; *cr:* 7th/8th Grade Teacher Paterson NJ 1968-69; 5th Grade Teacher Minisink Valley Elem 1969-73; Adjunct Instr/Philosophy Teacher Ladycliff Coll 198-81, Rockland Comm Coll 1981-83; *ai:* Dev of Crisis Intervention, Admin Hiring, Dropout Prevention Comms; Adv Class, Fine Arts, Adventure Clubs, Youth Against Hunger; Meeting the Needs of Gifted; The Open Classroom; Ed for Democracy 10th Honors Curr; Deep Coord 12th Ec Curr; *office:* Minisink Valley HS Rt 6 Slate Hill NY 10973

BARNETT, VELDA NICKERSON, Public Speaking Teacher; *b:* Dallas, TX; *m:* Donald Alexander Sr; *c:* Donald A. II, Vae B.; *ed:* (BA) Speech Comm Univ of N TX 1979; *cr:* Scndry Teacher Wilmer-Hutchins HS 1979-; *ai:* Class Spon; Univ Interscholastic League Poetry Coach 1980-85; Alpha Kappa Alpha Incorporated (Hostess, Treas); Hs Teacher of Yr Wilmer-Hutchins 1987-88; Nom Dist Teacher of Yr 1987-88; Outstanding Teacher Excl Awd TX Univ of TX Austin 1988; *office:* Wilmer-Hutchins HS 5520 Langdon Rd Dallas TX 75241

BARNETTE, BEVERLEY BONER, Sr HS English Teacher; *b:* Tuscaloosa, AL; *m:* William Mack; *c:* William K., Eva K.; *ed:* (BS) Bus Ed, Troy St Univ 1973; (BA) Eng, Judson Coll; (MA) Eng, Troy St Univ Montgomery 1988; *cr:* Bus Teacher Woodbury HS 1973-74, 1975-79; Teller/Bookkeeper Bank of Abbeville 1974-75; Eng Teacher Elmore Cty HS 1979-; *ai:* Academic Team Coach; Advanced Placement Literary Magazine, Stu Cncl, Jr Class Spon; WMU Church (Dir 1986-, Associational Missions Dir 1989-, Youth Comm 1988-); STAR Teacher Achievement Recognition Woodbury GA 1978; Teacher of Yr Elmore Cty 1987; Outstanding Young Women of America 1988; *office:* Elmore Cty HS PO Box 690 Eclectic AL 36024

BARNFIELD, ROSE RENE, US His/Elem Phys Ed Teacher; *b:* Dallas, TX; *ed:* (BA) Health/Phys Ed, Univ of TX Arlington 1977; Phys Ed; *cr:* Teacher/Coach Kennedale Jr HS 1977-81, 1977 Kennedale HS; *ai:* Var Vlybl; Frosh Bsktbl; Jr Var & Var Tennis; Asst Track; *office:* Kennedale HS 930 Bowman Springs Kennedale TX 76060

BARNHARD, JOANN R., Business Teacher; *b:* San Bernardino, CA; *m:* Richard; *c:* David, Dawniel; *ed:* (BS) Bus Ed, ID St Univ 1987; *cr:* Teacher Mackay HS 1987-; *ai:* Bus Prof America; Frosh Class Adv; Mackay Ed Assn, IBEA, NEA 1989-; Outstanding Coll Stu of America; Natl Deans List; Outstanding Young Women of America; *office:* Mackay HS PO Box 390 Mackay ID 83251

BARNSHAW, ROBERT GARY, History Teacher; *b:* Philadelphia, PA; *m:* Gloria M. Luck; *ed:* (BA) His, Penn St Univ & Glassboro St Coll 1979; (MA) Amer His, Villanova Univ 1988; *cr:* Substitute Teacher Black Horse Pike Regional Schls 1980-81; Teacher Washington Township HS 1981-; *ai:* Model United Nation Assn; Dist Affirmative Action Comm; Mem Hands Across Water Prgm; Teaching in USSR; NEA 1981-; Phi Alpha Theta Society 1978-; Civil War Society 1990; Chews Meth Church (Sunday Sch Teacher 1978-, Pastor-Parish Relations Comm 1979-); Teacher of Yr Washington Township HS 1988-89; YMCA Model United Nations & Government Participation Awd 1981; *office:* Washington Township HS Hurfville Cross Keys Rd Sewell NJ 08080

BARNUM, DEBRA LOUISE, Drama Teacher/Dept Chair; *b:* Brooklyn, NY; *ed:* (BA) Theatre Ed, Adelphi Univ 1973; Grad Cr Theatre Ed, Univ of S FL; Vocal Trng, Jerome Walman & Bill Cusick; Credits for Spec Ed; *cr:* Substitute Teacher/Various Jobs Pinellas Cty Sch Bd 1973-77; Public Relations Teacher Jewish Cmmty Center & Fed 1977-79 C D Clerk/Bookkeeper Palm St Bank 1979-81; Drama Teacher Pinellas Cty Sch Bd 1982-; *ai:* FL St Thespian Dir; Thespian Club at Dixie Hollins; Back to Sch & Assembly Comm; Intnl Thespian Society St Dir 1988-, Best Conf 1989; FL Assn for Theatre Ed (Bd of Dir 1988-, Secy) 1987-88; Footlight Theatre (VP 1981-82, Stage Mgr 1981), Favorite Stage Mgr 1981; Grant for Drug Abuse Presentation, Article in Fall Issue, 1989; Southern Theatre, Wrote & Produced Full Length Play; Organized & Master of Ceremonies for Muscular Dystrophy Pre-Telethon on Stage & Radio; Ed for Local Paper; *office:* Dixie Hollins HS 4940-62nd St N Saint Petersburg FL 33709

BARNWELL, ANNE CARTER, Mathematics Teacher; *b:* Paris Island, SC; *m:* Jon M.; *c:* Elizabeth, Jon Jr., Hayne; *ed:* (BA) Math/Fr, MSCW 1966; *ai:* NHS Spon; Mathcounts Coach; *office:* Pillow Acad Po Box 1880 Greenwood MS 38930

BARNWELL, BETTY ATKINS, Social Studies Teacher; *b:* Tryon, NC; *m:* Robert Burton; *c:* Barney, Betsy Ellington, Byron, Beth French; *ed:* (AS) Sci, Spartanburg Jr Coll 1951; (BA) Soc Stud, Limestone Coll 1973; Working Towards Masters; *cr:* Soc Stud Teacher Campobello-Grambling 1974-; *ai:* PTA Lifetime Membership 1983; BPW VP 1976-; *home:* 200 Dickson Rd PO Box 52 Gramling SC 29348

BARO, ELIZABETH MAC GREGOR, 5th Grade Teacher; *b:* Oakland, CA; *m:* Joseph; *c:* Toni E., Christopher Mac Gregor; *ed:* (BS) Elem Ed, Univ of NV 1965; Math & Sci Wkshps; *cr:* 2nd Grade Teacher Lemmon Valley Elem 1965-66, Harker Heights Elem 1966-67; 4th-6th Grade Teacher Mamie Towles Elem 1967-70; 5th Grade Teacher Lemmon Valley Elem 1980-; *ai:* Sci Fair Coord; HS Rodeo Club; Washoe Cty Teachers Assn Mem 1965-70, 1979-; *office:* Lemmon Valley Elem Sch 255 W Patrician Way Reno NV 89506

BARON, DONALD C., Mathematics Teacher/Curr Coord; *b:* Skowhegan, ME; *m:* Diane Jarzabek; *c:* Adam; *ed:* (BS) Math/Eng, 1970, (MS) Admin/Supervision/Curr, 1976 Cntrl CT St Coll; Cooperating Teacher; Mentor Trng; *cr:* 7th/8th Grade Math Teacher Cromwell Mid Sch 1971-; *ai:* Intramural Golf; Staff Dev; Admin Cncl; Math Coord; Negotiations Comm; Cromwell Ed Assn (Treas 1986-, VP 1980-84); ATOMIC; Polish Amer Natl Home 1985-; *office:* Cromwell Mid Sch Mann Memorial Dr Cromwell CT 06416

BARONE, ANTHONY JOHN, 7th/8th Grade History Teacher; *b:* Long Island City, NY; *m:* Helen; *c:* Matthew; *ed:* (BA) His, St Univ of NY Geneseo 1970; Working Towards Masters; *cr:* 7th Grade Teacher Precious Blood Sch 1970-; *ai:* Knights of Columbus 1970-75; *office:* Most Precious Blood Sch 32-52 37th St Long Island City NY 11106

BARR, BILL RAY, Sci/Health/Phys Ed Teacher; *b:* Johnday, OR; *m:* Melanie; *c:* Micaela, Chelsea; *ed:* (BA) Phys Ed, NW Nazarene Coll 1983; *cr:* Life Sci/Health/Phys Ed Teacher West Jr HS 1985-89; Phys Sci/Health/Phys Ed Teacher Marsing Mid HS 1989-; *ai:* Head Ftbl, Wrestling, Track Coach; Okinawan Karate Kobudo Fed 1982-, Shodan 1986; World Kenpo Karate Assn 1986-, Shodan 1987; Marsing Chamber of Commerce Distinguished Citizen Awd 1990; *office:* Marsing Mid HS PO Box 340 Marsing ID 83639

BARR, DAVID B., Third Grade Teacher; *b:* Kane, PA; *m:* Carol J. Hain; *c:* William R.; *ed:* (BS) Elem/Spec Ed, Lock Haven St Coll 1978; (MS) Elem Ed, Shippensburg Univ 1982; *cr:* 3rd Grade Teacher Portico Elem Sch; *ai:* Chambersburg Area Ed Assn VP 1987-88; PA St Ed Assn, NEA 1978-; Coast Guard Auxiliary, Masonic Lodge; *office:* Portico Elem Sch 5222 Ft Mc Cord Rd Chambersburg PA 17201

BARR, KAREN BRYANT, Resource/Bus/Phys Ed Teacher; *b:* Gorman, TX; *m:* Jody Lynn; *ed:* (BS) Phys Ed, Tarleton St Univ 1988; *cr:* Bus/Resource/Jr HS Phys Ed Teacher Priddy Ind Sch Dist 1988-; *ai:* Jr HS Girls Cross Cntry, Bsktbl, Track & Jr HS Boys Track Coach; Jr HS Chrldrs & Soph Class 1990 Spon; *home:* Box 487 Comanche TX 76442

BARR, PATRICIA ANN, English/Journalism Teacher; *b:* Seattle, WA; *m:* Robert Charles; *ed:* (BA) Eng/Scndry Ed, Portland St Univ 1987; Working Toward Masters OR Writing Project, Lewis & Clark Coll; *cr:* Teacher Sandy Union HS 1987-; *ai:* Sch Newspaper Adv; Co-Instr WAC Class; Stu Writing Group Adv; Organized & Implemented Week Long Writing Festival; OR Journalists Educators Assn, OR Eng Assn, NCTE; Teacher who Makes a Difference; Produce Newsletter for Exch Club Center for Prevention of Child Abuse; Produce Young Woman of Yr Prgm; *office:* Sandy Union HS 17100 Bluff Rd Sandy OR 97055

BARRACLOUGH, JEAN CAMPBELL, Principal; *b:* Los Angeles, CA; *w:* Robert P. (dec); *c:* Amy L., Douglas Campbell; *ed:* (BA) His, Univ of CO 1953; UCLA; Univ of San Francisco; *cr:* Fr Teacher 1964-65; 6th Grade Teacher 1965-74; 2nd Grade Teacher 1974-76; Prin 1976- Prince of Peace Luth Sch; *ai:* Coach-Girls Vlybl; ACSI 1989-; CA Assn of Private Schls; Amer Luth Ed Assn; Kappa Alpha Theta Alumni Assn; Orange Cty Rdng Assn; Kiwanis Awd; *office:* Prince Of Peace Lutheran Sch 2987 Mesa Verde Dr Costa Mesa CA 92626

BARRAGAN, JEAN KELLAR, Social Studies Teacher; *b:* Havre, MT; *m:* Michael R.; *c:* Jason K. Sutton *ed:* (BS) Soc Stud/His, 1970 (PC) Eng/His, 1980 N MT Coll; *cr:* Hum Teacher Whitehill Tech HS Bendigo Australia 1985; Soc Stud/Eng Lit Teacher Evergreen Jr HS 1974-84, 1986-, Soc Stud Teacher Kalispell Jr HS 1988-; *ai:* Tennis Coach; Annual Staff & Stu Cncl Adv; Care Facilitator; Photographer; Evergreen Ed Assn Pres 1987-88; Expanding Your Horizons Bd 1984-88;l Phi Delta Kappa Historian 1989-; Republican Women Treas 1988-; MT Aerobics Instrs 1981-; Natl Assn of Stu Cncls 1984-; Intnl Teaching Fellowship Australia 1985; Nom Gonzaga Teacher of Yr 1988; Spunk Parent Teacher Dedication Awd; *home:* Box 60 Lakeside MT 59922

BARRERA, SYLVIA LAURA, Phys Ed/Psychology Teacher; *b:* Laredo, TX; *ed:* (BS) Phys Ed, TX Womans Univ 1981; (MS) Phys Ed, TX A&I Univ 1990; *cr:* Teacher/Coach L J Christen Jr HS 1981-83, Dr Leo G Cigarroa HS 1983-; *ai:* Jr Var Vlybl, Var Bsktbl Coach; Intramural Prgm Dir; TX Girls Coaches Assn; *office:* Dr Leo G Cigarroa HS 2600 Zacatecas Ave Laredo TX 78041

BARRETT, FRANCES PATRICIA (RODMAN), Lang Arts/Soc Stud Teacher; *b:* Yakima, WA; *m:* John W.; *c:* Deed C., Thea, Holly Kerfoot; *ed:* (BS) Ed, Mary Hurst Coll 1956; 5th Yr Scndry Ed, Univ of WA 1972; Univ of HI, W WA, Cntrl WA; *cr:* 5th/6th Grade Teacher Kern Elem 1956; 8th Grade Teacher Leuellyn Elem 1966, Edmond Sch Dist 15 1968-; HS Teacher Edmonds Comm Coll 1975-78; *ai:* Dept Chm; WEA, EEA 1968-; *office:* Alderwood Mid Sch 20000 28th Ave W Lynnwood WA 98036

BARRETT, JAMES JOSEPH, French Teacher; *b:* Jersey City, NJ; *ed:* (BA) Fr/Span, St Peters Coll 1973; Italian, Rutgers Univ 1990; Latin & Continuing Fr/Italian 1990; *cr:* Fr/Span Teacher Ferris HS 1979-85, Dickinson HS 1985-; *ai:* Fr Club Adv; Fr Inst/Alliance Francaise 1975-; *office:* William L Dickinson HS 2 Palisades Ave Jersey City NJ 07306

BARRETT, JANET ANNE, Driver Education Teacher; *b:* Decatur, IL; *ed:* (BSED) Phys Ed, E IL Univ 1971; (MSED) Health/Safety, S IL Univ 1978; Health & Drives Ed Courses & Wkshps; *cr:* Coach 1971-80, Teacher 1971- Du Quoin HS; *ai:* Vlybl, Bsktbl, Sftbl, Track & Field Coach 1980; IAHPER 1971-89; IHSCDEA 1975-; *office:* Du Quoin HS 500 E South St Du Quoin IL 62832

BARRETT, JANET LANE, English Teacher; *b:* Port Huron, MI; *m:* Thomas Cawood; *ed:* (BA) Eng, Cntrl MI Univ 1972; (MA) Eng, Oakland Univ 1980; *cr:* Eng Teacher Port Huron Northern HS 1973-79, Port Huron HS 1979-; *ai:* K-12th Lang Art & Soc Comms; NCTE, MEA, NEA; Quota Intnl; *home:* 4440 Gratiot Ave Port Huron MI 48060

BARRETT, JUSTIN JAMES, Fourth Grade Teacher; *b:* Valley City, ND; *m:* Ann Rosell Nevins; *c:* Elizabeth, Paul; *ed:* (BA) Ed, Valley City St Univ 1970; Psych, Id St Univ; *cr:* 4th/5th Grade Teacher MT 1970-80; 5th Grade Teacher 1980-88, 4th Grade Teacher 1988- Holy Rosary Sch; *ai:* Id Cncl Intnl Rdng Assn; Natl Geographic Society; *office:* Holy Rosary Sch 161 9th St Idaho Falls ID 83404

BARRETT, KATHLEEN ANNE, 4th Grade Teacher; *b:* Jersey City, NJ; *ed:* (BA) Elem Ed/Spec Ed - Cum Laude, IA Wesleyan Coll 1976; *cr:* Kndgtn/2nd/6th/7th Grade Opportunity Class/ 2nd/4th Grade Teacher Jersey City Bd of Ed 1976-; *ai:* NEA, NJEA; JCEA Dir 1979-80; Zeta Tau Alpha Rush Chm 1974; *office:* Martin Luther King Jr HS 886 Bergen Ave Jersey City NJ 07306

BARRETT, MARGARET MINICHAN, Teacher of Gifted Eng; *b:* Charleston, WV; *m:* Robert Dennis; *c:* Bo, Beth; *ed:* (BA) Voc/ Home Ec, 1958, (MA) Guidance/Counseling, 1960, (MA) Gifted Ed, 1982 Marshall Univ; Advanced Placement Eng; Rdng Scndry Level; *cr:* Teacher Barboursville Jr HS 1958-68, Barboursville HS 1980-81, Milton HS 1981-; *ai:* Stu Cncl Adv; Steering Comm for North Cntrl Evaluation; WVEA, CCEA 1958-68, 1980-; Christ the King Luth Church Cncl 1987-; Amer Red Cross 1958-, Volunteer of Month 1985; GSA (Area Chm 1982-86, 1989; *office:* Milton HS 1302 W Main St Milton WV 25541

BARRETT, MARY JUNE, First Grade Teacher; *b:* Cambridge, MA; *ed:* (BSED) Ed, Regis Coll 1956; (BSED) Ed, 1961, (MAED) Ed, 1976 St Coll of Boston; *cr:* 1st Grade Teacher St Agatha Sch 1953-56, Martin Luther King Jr Sch 1957-; *ai:* Involved With K-3 Model-Whole Lang with Don Holdaway; NCTE 1980-; Intnl Rdng Assn 1981-; Cambridge Teacher Assn Corresponding Secy 1970-76; NCA, MTA 1960-; Affiliated with Suffolk Univ & Lesley Coll in Trng of Stu Teachers & Core Stus; *office:* Dr Martin Luther King Jr Sch 120 Putnam Ave Cambridge MA 02139

BARRETT, PATRICIA LOUISE, Mathematics Teacher; *b:* Pittsburgh, PA; *m:* Telford H. Jr.; *c:* Joseph K., Telford L.; *ed:* (BS) Math Ed, 1969, (MED) Math Ed, 1970 Valdosta St Coll; (EDS) Math Ed, GA Southern Coll 1985; *cr:* Classroom Teacher Lowndes HS 1970-83; Math Coord Lowndes Cty Schls 1984-86; Part-Time Math Instr Valdosta St Coll 1975-; Classroom Teacher Lowndes HS 1986-; *ai:* Math Team; NCTM 1968-; GA Cncl Teachers of Math (Mem 1970-, Dist Chairperson 1981-83), Gladys M Thompson Awd 1986; NEA, GA Assn of Educators, Lowndes Assn of Educators (Local Pres 1981-82, Local Treas 1979-80); 1st Baptist Church Children III Sunday Sch Dir 1972-; Amer Assn of Univ Women 1982-; STAR Teacher Twice; Teacher of Yr 3 Times; GA Math Conference Chairperson; Congressionl Dist Math Sci Roundtable Mem; *office:* Lowndes HS 1112 St Augustine Rd Valdosta GA 31602

BARRETT, REBECCA ANN, Spanish Teacher/Dept Chair; *b:* Akron, OH; *ed:* (BA) Modern Languages, 1968, (MA) Span, 1975 Univ of Akron; Grad Stud Span, Comm, Educl Admin; *cr:* Span Teacher/Dept Head Copley HS 1968-; *ai:* Speech Coach; Curr Dev Comm; Contract Negotiator; North Cntrl Evaluation Chairperson; Assn Rep; Copley Teachers Assn Rep 1983-89; NE OH Teachers Assn, NEA 1968-; Montrose Zion Meth Church (Parish Comm Staff 1988-, Choir 1990); Weathervane Theatre Womens Bd 1977-; Lambda Pi Local Lang Honorary 1968; Sigma Delta Pi 1988; *office:* Copley HS 3807 Ridgewood Rd Copley OH 44321

BARRETT, SCOTT RAY, Physical Education Teacher; *b:* Glasgow, MT; *m:* Lisa A. Johnston; *c:* Jennifer, Heather, Brandon; *ed:* (BS) Phys Ed, Boise St Univ 1984; *cr:* Phys Ed Teacher Elko HS 1985-; *ai:* Head Wrestling & Asst Ftbl Coach; Natl HS Athletic Coach Assn 1989-; Natl Fed of St HS Assn 1988-; The Amer Alliance for Health, Phys Ed, Recreation & Dance 1990; Police Athletic League, USA Freestyle Wrestling Coach 1986-; Babe Ruth Umpire 1988-; Inducted to Boise St Hall of Fame 1989; *office:* Elko HS 987 College Elko NV 89801

BARRETT, SUSAN MANNING, 4th Grade Teacher; *b:* Freeport, NY; *m:* Scott; *c:* Laurie, Marie; *ed:* (BA) Elem Ed, Long Island Univ 1976; (MA) Spec Ed, WV Coll of Graduate Stud 1985; *cr:* 2nd Grade Teacher 1978-84; 4th Grade Teacher 1984- Cherry River Elem Sch; *ai:* Lib Comm; Sch Environment Team; WVEA 1978-; Coord Schoolwide Prgms Math Field Day Sci Fair and Olympic Celebration; *office:* Cherry River Elem Sch Riverside Dr Richwood WV 26261

BARRETT, THERESIA ANN, 4th Grade Teacher; *b:* Mannhiem, Germany; *m:* Randall Joe; *c:* Ian; *ed:* (AS) Elem Ed, Vincennes Univ 1972; (BS) Elem Ed/Early Chldhd, 1973, (MS) Elem Ed/Early Chldhd, 1976 IN St Univ; *ai:* IN St Teachers Assn, NEA, SW Sullivan Ed Assn; *office:* Cntrl Elem Sch 215 N Court St Sullivan IN 47882

BARRETT, VIRGINIA G., Teacher of Gifted Program; *b:* Kansas City, MO; *m:* John S. Sr.; *c:* John S. Jr., Amy G.; *ed:* (BA) Elem Ed, Univ of MO Kansas City 1972; Grad Stud in Ed; Working Toward Masters Degree in Elem Admin; *cr:* 5th Grade Teacher Thomas B Chian Elem 1972-79; Owner/Teacher Lathrop Pre-Sch 1981-84; K-8th Grade Gifted Prgm Teacher Lathrop R-II Sch Dist 1985-; *ai:* Dist Prof Dev Comm Chairperson; Stus That Oppose Pollution Club Spon; Sci Olympiad Team Coach; Partners in Ed Comm Mem; Gifted Assn of MO, MO St Teachers Assn 1985-; MO Excl in Ed Grant 1986-89; Prgm Project Think; *office:* Lathrop R-II Sch Dist 700 Center St Lathrop MO 64465

BARRGANIER, GRADY LYNN, English Teacher/Coach; *b:* Temple, TX; *m:* Linda Marie; *c:* Caitlin, Luke; *ed:* (BS) Phys Ed/ Eng, SW TX St Univ 1970-74; Drivers Ed; *cr:* Eng Teacher/Coach Academy Mid Sch 1974-; *ai:* Ftbl, Bsktbl, Track, Tennis Coach; TX HS Coaches Assn, Assn of TX Prof Ed Mem 1974-; St Lukes Cath Church Organist 1978-; *home:* Rt 3 Box 280A Temple TX 76501

BARRICK, MINETTA FLINT, Fifth Grade Teacher; *b:* Warren, OH; *m:* Wm. M.; *c:* M. Michelle, Michael M., April R. Ball; *ed:* (BA) Elem Ed, Fairmont St 1973; (MA) Rdng Specialist/ Supvr, WV Univ 1976; Writing Across Curr, Coll of Grad Stud; Advanced Courses Rdng; Teaching Cert 1951, 1965; *cr:* 2nd/3rd Grade Teacher Harford Cty Schls 1951-53; 1st/4th/5th Grade Teacher Harrison Cty Schls 1954-56; 3rd/4th Grade Teacher St James Cath Sch 1965-70; Rdng Specialist Harrison Cty 1971-79; 5th Grade Teacher Johnson Sch 1979-; *ai:* Remedial & Acceleration Comm; Sch of Excl Group; Jr Women VP 1955-62; Jaycettes 1957-62; Writing Across Curr Grant; Conduct Rdng & Math Clinic at Home; *office:* Johnson Elem Sch 531 Johnson Ave Bridgeport WV 26330

BARRINGER, CHARLENE DAY, Kindergarten Teacher; *b:* Erie, PA; *m:* John P.; *c:* Lynne R. Quirk, William S.; *ed:* (BA) Elem Ed, Villa Maria Coll 1970; (MS) Elem Ed, Gannon Behrend Edinboro 1973; *cr:* Teacher Robison Elem Sch 1967-; *ai:* PA St Ed Assn, NEA, Ft Le Boeuf Ed Assn, Villa Maria Alumni Assn 1967-; PTA (Auditor 1968-, Teacher Rep 1975-) 1968-; Chester Heights Assn Secy 1985-86; *home:* 324 Stuart Way Erie PA 16509

BARRINGTON, VIVIAN HANSEN HANCOCK, 5th Grade Teacher; *b:* Bay City, TX; *m:* Joe C.; *c:* Brooke, Brandy, Ben R.; *ed:* (BA) Elem Ed, Sam Houston St Univ 1970; (MED) Elem Ed, Stephen F Austin St Univ 1985; Task Force for Writing Region V 1979-80; *cr:* 4th Grade Teacher Roark Elem 1970-71; 3rd Grade Teacher Parnell Elem 1971-85, 3rd Grade Teacher 1985-88, 5th Grade Teacher 1988- Rowe Elem; *ai:* Creative Writing United Interscholastic League Coach 1989-; TX St Teachers Assn, NEA 1970-; 1st United Meth (Admin Bd 1988-89, Altar Guild 1988-, Family Life Comm 1989); Career Ladder 1985; Career Ladder Level 3 1988-; Inclusion in Notable Women of TX 1984-85; *home:* 2110 Pinecrest Jasper TX 75951

BARRON, DEBORAH STOKES, 6th Grade Teacher; *b:* Clearwater, FL; *m:* Gerald O.; *c:* Alex; *ed:* (BS) Elem Ed, Lee Coll 1974; *cr:* Teacher White Elem 1975-78, Harvest Temple Chrstn Acad 1978-81, Beasley Mid Sch 1981-84, Baycrest Elem 1984-87, Beasley Mid Sch 1987-; *ai:* Beasleys Show Choir Dir; Teacher of Yr Beasley Mid Sch 1984; *office:* Beasley Mid Sch 1100 S 18th Ave Palatka FL 32177

BARRON, DEBRA BULGER, English Teacher/Debate Coach; *b:* Ft Benning, GA; *m:* Brian Raymond; *c:* Phillip T., Matthew S., Andrew N.; *ed:* (BA) Eng Ed, Univ of S FL 1975; *cr:* Eng Teacher Brandon HS 1974-75, Turkey Creek Jr HS 1975-77; Eng Teacher/ Debate Coach Mauldin HS 1987-; *ai:* Mauldin HS Debate Team Coach; NFL & SC Forensics; Sr Powderpuff Spon; YMCA Model Legislature; VFW Speech Contest; SC Forensic Coaches Assn 1988-; NCTE 1987-; Presbyn Church USA Elder 1984-; *office:* Mauldin HS 701 E Butler Rd Mauldin SC 29662

BARRON, MARY LEA MC AFEE, Fifth Grade Teacher; *b:* Maud, OK; *m:* Ronald F.; *c:* Sid Ingram; *ed:* (BS) Elem Ed, E NM Univ 1965; Advanced Ed Courses; *cr:* 1st Grade Teacher Floyd Elem 1965-66, Farwell Elem 1966-67, Petersburg Public Schls 1968-79, Yucca Elem 1980-; *ai:* VA Ed Assn Building Rep 1968-79; NM Ed Assn Building Rep 1980-; Delta Kappa Gamma 1985-; *office:* Yucca Elem Sch 906 Quay Artesia NM 88210

BARRY, IRENE MURRAY, Foreign Language Teacher; *b:* Johnstone, Scotland; *s:* John J.; *c:* (BA) Fr, Univ of Me 1979; (MA) Fr, Boston Coll 1988; *cr:* Foreign Lang Teacher Shrewsbury Jr HS 1979-80, Ashland HS 1980-81, King Philip Jr HS 1981-82, Tahanto Regional HS 1982-; *ai:* Jr Class Adv; Exam Evaluation Comm; Jr Class Adv; Phi Beta Kappa, Phi Kappa Phi, Phi Sigma Iota 1979; *office:* Tahanto Regional HS Main St Boylston MA 01505

BARRY, JEFFREY ANTHONY, English Teacher; *b:* Pisgah, IA; *m:* Donna Jo Gell; *c:* Carley Jo; *ed:* (BA) Scndry Eng, Univ of Northern IA 1981; *cr:* Eng Teacher & Coach Yutan HS 1981-87, Harlan Mid Sch 1987-; *ai:* 8th Grade Boys Bsktbl Coach; Boys & Girls Varsity Tennis Coach; Asst Varsity Bsbl Coach; Ftbl/Cross Cntry & Track Coach; Optimist Club 1988-; *home:* 1217 College Blvd Harlan IA 51537

BARRY, JOHN MATTHEW, 4th Grade Teacher; *b:* Evanston, IL; *m:* Margaret Mechan; *c:* Erin, Kevin; *ed:* (BA) Ed, N IL Univ 1972; (MA) Admin, Pacific Luth Univ 1983; *cr:* 5th Grade Teacher Sugar Grove Elem 1972-73; 2nd-5th Grade Teacher Pioneer Elem 1973-89; 4th Grade Teacher Centennial Elem 1989-; *ai:* Asst Girls Soccer Coach; Dir After Sch Sports Prgm; Co-Chm & Staff Dev Comm; Centennial El; Olympia Ed Assn (Uniserv Rep 1977-79, Teacher Rep 1976-79); *office:* Centennial Elem Sch 1655 Carlyon AveSE Olympia WA 98501

BARRY, PEGGY STEINBECK, 11th Grade English Teacher; *b:* Ola, AR; *m:* David Hale; *c:* Michael, Russell; *ed:* (BSE) Eng/ Speech, Univ of Cntrl AR 1958; Rdng, Memphis St Univ; Creative Writing, Univ of Cntrl AR; Cmptr Programming, E AR Comm Coll; AR Writing Project, Ouachita Baptist Univ; *cr:* 7th-12th Grade Speech/Eng Teacher Crawfordsville Public Sch 1958-59; 11th Grade Eng Teacher Forrest City HS 1960-63; 7th Grade Eng Teacher Forrest City Jr HS 1968-81; 10th Grade Eng TeachEr 1981-83, 11th Grade Eng Teacher 1983- Forrest City HS; *ai:* Delta Kappa Gamma Intnl Recording Secy 1988-; Forrest City Ed Assn Recording Secy 1985-86; AEA, NEA; Natl Endowment For Hum; Readers Digest Teacher/Scholar; AR Recipient 1990-91, Ind Study of 20th Century Southern Lit; *office:* Forrest City HS 476 Victoria Forrest City AR 72335

BARSKI, MARGARET BITTNER, 7th & 8th Grade Teacher; *b:* Berwick, PA; *m:* Walter M.; *c:* Kris A.; *ed:* (BS) Elem, Bloomsburg St Coll 1962; *cr:* 2nd Grade Teacher Canaseraga Sch 1962-63; 4th Grade Teacher Lake Lehman Sch 1963-70; 4th Grade/Head Teacher Northwest Sch 1970-71; 5th-8th Grade Teacher Holy Family Consolidated Sch 1972-; *ai:* Sch Newspaper Adv; NCEA 1972-; First United Church of Christ (Pres, Consistory Elder); *home:* 605 Butternut St Berwick PA 18603

BARTA, MARILYN LERUM, First Grade Teacher; *b:* Shelby, MT; *m:* Alan Joseph; *c:* Daniel, Eric; *ed:* (BA) Elem Ed, Univ of MT 1977; Gessell Inst Child Dev Sch Readiness Testing; Learning Styles Courses; *cr:* 1st/3rd Grade Teacher Kevin Sch 1977-80; 2nd/3rd Grade Teacher 1980-81, 1st/2nd Grade Teacher 1981-82, 1st Grade Teacher 1982- Moore Sch; *ai:* Moore Sch 1st Grade Bear Club Spon; NEA, MT Ed Assn 1980-; MT Rdng Cncl 1985-88; Cntrl MT Rdng Cncl Pres 1986-; Intnl Rdng Assn 1986-88; Moore Ed Assn Exec Comm; Parents & Teachers Together 1988-; Sunburst Luth Church Cncl Secy 1978-80, Sunday Sch Teacher 1977-); Big Brothers & Sisters 1977-80; Cntrl MT Jaycees; Toys for Tots; Cystic Fibrosis Bowl for Breath; St Jude Math-A-Thon; Whos Who Among Americas Women; MT Rdng Prgm Office of Public Instruction; *home:* RR 2 Box 2260 Lewistown MT 59457

BARTEK, AVA LYNNE (PONCIK), 6th Grade General Sci Teacher; *b:* Austin, TX; *m:* Eugene John; *c:* Gena W.; *ed:* (BS) Elem Ed/Bi-ling Bicultural Endorsement, Saint Edwards Univ 1977; *cr:* 6th-8th Grade Teacher of Migrant 1977-78, 6th Grade Rdng/Eng/Phys Ed Teacher 1978-79 Belton Jr HS; 5th Grade Sci Teacher Belton Mid Sch 1979-82; 6th Grade Sci Teacher Belton Jr HS 1982-; *ai:* Belton Jr HS UIL Asst Coord, Spon, Coach; Sci Club Spon; TX St Teachers Assn Local Secy 1989-; Cntrl Elem Belton Ind Sch Dist PTA Assn VP 1986-88; *office:* Belton Jr HS 400 N Wall Belton TX 76513

BARTELS, MICHAEL STANLEY, Jr HS Soc Stud Chairperson; *b:* Nelsonville, OH; *m:* Janet Lee Kennedy; *c:* Jacqueline J., Michael W.; *ed:* (BS) Elem Ed, OH Univ 1978; (MS) Admin/Supervision, Univ of Dayton 1984; *cr:* 1st/3rd-5th Grade Teacher Bethesda Elem 1978-83; 6th-8th Grade Teacher Belmont Jr HS 1983-; *ai:* 8th Grade Class Adv; OH Ed Assn, NEA 1978-; Union Local Assn of Classroom Teachers Building Rep 1978-, Full Membership 1986; Lions Intnl 1988-; *home:* 73255 Mercer Rd St Clairsville OH 43950

BARTH, DEBRA JAYNE, English Teacher; *b:* Toledo, OH; *ed:* (BSE) Comprehensive Comm/Eng/Speech/Journalism/Rdng, Ashland Coll 1980; OH Ed Assn Collective Bargaining Sch; Level II Cert Coaching Vlybl, US Vlybl Assn; *cr:* 7th-12th Grade Eng Teacher Bettsville HS 1980-; *ai:* Lang Arts Curr Comm; Head Vlybl Coach 1980-; Girls Jr HS Bsktbl Coach; New Teachers at Bettsville HS Adv; US Vlybl Assn 1984-; OH Ed Assn, NEA 1980-; *office:* Bettsville HS 118 Washington St Bettsville OH 44815

BARTHOLOMEW, DIXIE ANN (STOVALL), Sixth Grade Teacher; *b:* Roseburg, OR; *m:* Milton L. Jr.; *c:* Mike; *ed:* (BS) Ed, OR St Univ 1971; Various Courses; *cr:* 6th Grade Teacher Winchester Elem Sch 1971-; *ai:* Grade Level Leader; Soc Stud Comm Mem; Roseburg Ed Assn 1971-; Alpha Delta Kappa (Secy, Treas) 1980-; Onward to Excl (Site Comm Mem, Secy); Rotary 1981, Distinguished Teacher Awd for Roseburg 1981; Altrusa Club of Roseburg 1980-84; Beta Sigma Phi Service Club 1974-84; Jaycees Nom by Faculty for Citizen Awd for Cmmty Runner Up; *office:* Winchester Elem Sch PO Box 778 Winchester OR 97495

BARTHOLOMEW, ROBIN LANE, HS Physical Education Teacher; *b:* Penn Yan, NY; *m:* Gary; *c:* Albert J., Audrey M., Ronald G.; *ed:* (AAS) Liberal Arts, Comm Coll of Finger Lakes 1973; (BA) Phys Ed, SUNY Cortland 1975; Cert Oswego; *cr:* Corning Cntrl Sch 1975-76; Cato-Meridian Cntrl Sch 1976-; *ai:* Var Field Hockey Coach; Modified Vlybl & Bsktbl; Girls Var Club Adv; OHSL Field Hockey Chairperson; C-M Teachers Assn Secy 1981-83; NYSUT; 4-H Leader; 2 Mini-Grants Through BOCES; *office:* Cato-Meridian Cntrl Sch Rt 370 Cato NY 13033

BARTHOLOMEW, TIMOTHY ALAN, 5th Grade Teacher; *b:* Harrisburg, PA; *m:* Linda Auch; *c:* Amanda, Amy; *ed:* (BS) Elem Ed, PA St Univ 1980; Grad Stud Various PA St Colls: *cr:* 5th Grade Teacher Hummelstown Nye Building Sch 1980-; *ai:* Flag Ftbl Coach; Helping Hands, Model Club, Rocket Club Adv; Sch Pit Band Guitar Player Mem; Research & Dev Comm Mem; NEA, PA St Educators Assn, Educators of Lower Dauphin 1987-; St Peters Luth Church Sunday Sch Teacher 1980-; Tee-Ball (Coach, Asst Coach) 1980-84; Frank T Miller Outstanding 1st Yr Teacher Awd 1980-81; Elem Classroom Teacher Awd 1982; *office:* Hummelstown Nye Building Sch Short & John Sts Hummelstown PA 17036

BARTIK, THOMAS FRANK, Sci Teacher/Dir of Sports Med; *b:* Elizabeth, NJ; *m:* Beverly Anne Garrity; *ed:* (BA) Sci Ed, 1969; (MA) Sch Admin & Supt, 1971 Newark St; E Carolina Sch of Medicine; EMT Intermed 1986; EMT Adv Inter 1988; Sci Ed E Carolina Univ; *cr:* Teacher Burnet Jr HS 1969-82, Southern Nash HS 1984-85; Teacher/Dept Chm/Dir of Sprots Medicine Chocowinity HS 1985-; *ai:* Dir of Sports Medicine; NEA; E Pines Rescue 1987-; Recieved 2 NC St Grants to Begin 2nd Masters in Sci Ed; *office:* Chocowinity HS P O Box 100 Chocowinity NC 27817

BARTKOWSKI, HENRY S., English Coordinator; *b:* New Castle, PA; *m:* Pamela; *ed:* (BA) Eng/His Ed, Westminster Coll 1951; (MED) Eng, St Lawrence Univ 1956; Eng Courses, Composition, Linguistics, Educl Technologies; *cr:* Teacher New Castle HS 1951, Cochranton Cntrl Sch 1951-54, Beaver River Cntrl Sch 1954-56; Coord/Eng Teacher Springville Griffth Inst 1956-; *ai:* AP Publications Co, Yr Video Productions, Contest Speaking Adv; NCTE 1962-; NYSEC 1962-, Teacher of Excl 1984; WNY Natl Writers (Fellow, Mem) 1986-; Kiwanis Pres 1980-85; Amer Legion 1989-, Cmmty Service 1988; Developed Young Writers Conference for Stus; *office:* Springville Griffith Inst 290 N Buffalo St Springville NY 14141

BARTLET, WILLIAM HENRY, Mathematics/Science Teacher; *b:* Spokane, WA; *ed:* (BS) Biochemistry, WA St Univ 1972; Ed, WA St Univ 1975; Grad Stud Univ of MT 1978; Working Towards Masters Admin, Whitworth Coll 1980-; *cr:* Peace Corps Volunteer Kaula Lumpur Malaysia 1973-74; Teacher/Coach Aquinas Coll 1974-75, St Iquatius HS 1975-77, Charlo HS 1977-78; Tanana HS 1978-79, *ai:* Dept Chm 1980-81, Vice Prin 1981-82 Amer Coll Mexico; Coach/Teacher Ashgrove Coll 1982-87; Mary Walker HS 1987-; Head Ftbl Coach; Teacher Union Pres; WA Water Power Good Stream Rehabilitation Grant; *office:* Mary Walker HS Gen Del Springdale WA 99173

BARTLETT, ALAN PAUL, Science Teacher; *b:* Hibbing, MN; *m:* Joyce A. Doshane; *c:* Emma; *ed:* (BA) Anthropology, Univ of CO 1969; (MS) Sci for Teachers, Union Coll 1982; *cr:* 8th Grade Sci Teacher 1970-78, Spec Sci Teacher 1978-83, 8th Grade Sci Teacher 1983- Shaker Jr HS; *ai:* Shaker HS Var Girls Swimming & Modified Swimming Coach; Suburban Cncl Girls Swimming Rep 1981-; Saratoga Chapter Red Cross Swimming Instr 1978-88; *office:* Shaker Jr HS 475 Watervliet Shaker Rd Latham NY 12110

BARTLETT, GEORGIA PASTERCHICK, Language Arts Teacher; *b:* San Antonio, TX; *m:* Eric L.; *c:* Armanda, Marisa; *ed:* (BS) Ed, SW TX St Univ 1977; *cr:* Track Coach/Phys Ed/Eng Teacher James Madison HS 1977-80; Phys Ed Teacher Oaks Elem 1983-84; 7th/8th Grade Girls Coach/Lang Art/Phys Ed/Health Teacher Humble Mid Sch 1980-; *ai:* 7th-8th Grade Chrldr & HS Drill Team Spon; Assn of TX Prof Educators; TX Assn of Phys Ed, Health, Recreation; Humble Ind Sch Dist Commendation Awd; Humble Mid Sch Outstanding Achievement Organization & Presentation of Teams Pep Rally.

BARTLETT, PATRICIA SHY, First Grade Teacher; *b:* Fort Valley, GA; *m:* Ernest W. Jr.; *c:* Brian, Lillian, Steven, Johnathan; *ed:* (BS) Elem Ed, GA Coll 1973; (MED) Elem Ed, GA Coll 1977; Gifted Cert West GA Coll 1979; Cmptr Trng Ed Tech Trng Ctr 1988; *cr:* Elem Teacher Wheeler Cty Sch 1970-75; Pike Cty Sch 1975-; *ai:* Grade Chm; Teacher Welfare Comm; Teacher Yr Comm Chm; Teacher Xmas; Hospitality Chm; Curr Comm; VP 1986-87; Pres 1987-88; Secy 1989- Pike Cty Assn of Ed; NEA/GAE Mem 1970-; Flint River Cncl of Intl Rdng Assn Secy 1977-78 Apprctn Awd 1977; GAE 1979-81; PTA (VP 1987-89 & Secy 1989-); Pike Cty 1st Responders Med Tech 1982-85; Fincher Untd Meth Church Sunday Sch Supt 1983-85; Boy Scouts Den Leader 1978-81; Girl Scouts Den Leader 1986-88; Pike Primary Teacher Yr 1984; Pike Elem Teacher Yr 1990; Pike Cty Teacher Yr 1990; 4-H Svc Awds 1972-74; *home:* P O Box 344 Meansville GA 30256

BARTLETT, SUSAN D., Instrumental Music Teacher; *b:* Hobart, IN; *m:* Raymond Jerold; *c:* Elizabeth F., Rebecca A.; *ed:* (BME) Music Ed, IN Univ 1974; (MA) Music Ed, Univ of S FL 1980; Grad Assistantship Univ of S Fl; Schlastic Schlsp IN Univ; *cr:* Vocal/General Instrumental Teacher Banyan Elem Sch 1974-77; Instrumental Teacher N Miami HS 1977-79; Choral/Instrumental Music Teacher Marshall Jr HS 1980-81; Instrumental Music Teacher Nicholas Orem Mid Sch 1981-89, Martin Luther King Mid Sch 1989-; *ai:* Music Educators Natl Conference 1974-; Alpha Lambda Delta Frosh Womens Honorary Scholastic Society; Phi Kappa Phi Collegiate Honor Society.

BARTO, DONNA MARIE RIGONI, Fourth Grade Teacher; *b:* Ironwood, MI; *m:* David S.; *ed:* (BS) Elem Ed, Univ of WI 1960; (MA) Ed, Northern MI 1981; *cr:* 3rd Grade Teacher Wakefield Sch Dist; 3rd Grade Teacher 1961-89, 4th Grade Teacher 1989- Gwinn Area Cmmty Schls; *ai:* Gifted & Talented Instr & Dist Wide Planning Comm Mem; Young Authors Participant & Planning Comm; MI Rdng Assn 1980-; Marquette/Alger Rdng Assn 1975-; MI Assn of Gifted & Talented Educators; MI Ed Assn/NEA & Gwinn Ed Assn; Delta Kappa Gamma (Corresponding Secy) 1976-; MI Gifted/Talented Grant for Gwinn Area Cmmty Schls.

BARTON, BETTE SMITH, Sixth Grade Teacher; *b:* Pleasant Hill, IL; *c:* William E., Candace Barton Reis, Cynthia Barton Brame, Robert J.; *ed:* (BS) Elem Ed, S IL Univ 1967; Grad Stud; *cr:* 6th Grade Teacher Roxana Unit Dist #1 1967-; *ai:* Rdng & Young Authors Comm; Chairperson Elem Curr Comm; Delta Kappa Gamma; Roxana Ed Assn Past Pres; *office:* S Roxana Elem Sch 410 Chaffer Roxana IL 62084

BARTON, BETTIE, Reading Lab Teacher; *b:* Kosciusko, MS; *ed:* (BS) Elem Ed, Cntrl St Univ 1969; (MA) Rdng/Learning Disabilities, Univ of Detroit 1976; *cr:* 4th Grade Teacher George E Parker Elem Sch 1969-76; Lang Art Teacher 1976-85, Rdng Lab Teacher 1985- Clark D Brooks Mid Sch; *ai:* Sch Improvement Team; Article III Advisory, Rdng Comms; Academic Games & Drama Club Spon; Earth Day Organizer; Phi Delta Kappa (Historian 1986-87, Pres 1987-88), Service Awd 1986, Certificate of Recognition 1987, Teacher of Yr 1988; Detroit Unity Temple (Schlsp Comm 1987-88, Lay Minister for Spec Events & Health 1987-89, Choir Historian 1988-, Sunday Sch Consultant 1990); The Jim Davis Outstanding Academic Games Coord Awd 1981; Natl Lang Art Chairperson Natl Academic Games Project 1982-88; Detroit Teacher of Yr 1984-85; St Finalist MI Teacher of Yr Prgm 1985; Inclusion Detroit Historical Museums Exhibit; Black Women in MI; City of Detroit Distinguished Service Awd Presented by City Cncl 1985; John Dalida Awd Outstanding Spon; Newsweek-WDIV Outstanding Teacher Awd 1987; *office:* Brooks Mid Sch 16101 W Chicago Detroit MI 48228

BARTON, BRUCE ANDREW, World History Teacher; *b:* Mount Vernon, NY; *m:* Kathryn Allen Polley; *c:* Bruce A., John D., Andrew M.; *ed:* (BA) Soc Stud, San Diego St Coll 1955; Los Angeles St Coll, Whittier Coll, Univ of HI, San Francisco St Coll; Sonoma St Coll, San Diego St Coll, Univ of CA Berkeley; *cr:* Instruction Supvr Dept of Ed 1967-71; Asst Prin Middletown Jr-Sr HS 1971-76, Twenty Nine Palms HS 1977-84; Teacher Yucca Valley HS 1985-; *ai:* ACDA 1977-84; MUSMA Pres 1982-83; CTA, NEA, MTA 1985-; Rotary Intnl (Pres 1973-74, Dist Speech Contest 1980-84, Founder 1985); *home:* 57831 Bandera Rd Yucca Valley CA 92284

BARTON, CAROLYN SANDERS, Sixth Grade Teacher; *b:* Lawrence, KS; *m:* Garland G.; *c:* Matthew, Michael; *ed:* (BS) Ed, 1977, (MS) Ed, 1986 Southwest MO St 1986; *cr:* Remedial Lang Arts Teacher 1977-78, 5th Grade Teacher 1978-79, 6th Grade Teacher 1979- Alton Elem; *ai:* Young Authors Coord; Alton Free Will Baptist Youth Dir 1978-; *home:* Rt 2 Box 2077 Alton MO 65606

BARTON, GAYLYN WILLIAMS, Chapter II Mathematics Teacher; *b:* Baton Rouge, LA; *c:* Genetha, Dorian, Doresa; *ed:* (BA) Sociology, Southern Univ 1973; (MED) Ed, Southern Univ 1973; Ed, S LA St Univ 1988; *cr:* Teacher Westdale Mid Sch 1973-74, Walnut Hills Elem Sch 1974-87; Math Basic Skills Teacher Walnut Hills Elem Sch 1987-; *ai:* NEA, Natl Math Assn, LA Ed Assn; Zeta Phi Beta; 4-H (Advisory Bd, Club Leader); Baptist Youth Leader; PTA Treas; *home:* 12523 Langer Ave Baton Rouge LA 70814

BARTON, JON ROBERT, 5th Grade Teacher; *b:* Charleston, WV; *m:* Charlene Taylor; *c:* Gary W. Hess, La Shawna G. Hess; *ed:* (BA) Elem Ed, Morris Harvey Coll 1973; (MA) Educl Admin, WV Coll of Grad Stud 1979; Grad Stud; *cr:* Teacher Mary Ingles Elem 1973-84, Cedar Grove Cmmty Sch 1984-; *ai:* Just Say No Club Spon; WV Ed Assn Mem; Kanawha Teachers Exec Comm (Du Pont Area Rep, Mem).

BARTON, KIRK E., Sixth Grade Teacher; *b:* San Antonio, TX; *m:* Lana Sue Dickman; *c:* Kriss, Rachel, Rebeca; *ed:* (BS) Elem Ed, IL St 1975; *cr:* 5th Grade Teacher Woodland 1975-76, Auburn 1976-89; 6th Grade Teacher Auburn 1989-; *ai:* Sr Class Co-Spon; HS Club-Kids that Care; Jr HS Bsbl; Jr HS Bsktbl; Auburn Ed Assn VP 1978-79; *office:* Auburn Elem Sch 5th St Auburn IL 62615

BARTON, MARY BETH, History Dept Chairman; *b:* Larado, TX; *m:* Terry D.; *c:* Andrea; *ed:* (BA) Soc Sci, William Carey Coll 1981; *cr:* Teacher Baker Sch 1986-; *ai:* Stu Cncl Spon; Schlsp Comm; Club Act Comm; Alpha Delta Kappa; Okaloosa News Journals Educator of Yr; *home:* 546 Nassau Dr Niceville FL 32578

BARTON, NANCY NIEMI, First Grade Teacher; *b:* Newport, NH; *m:* Douglas Robert Jr.; *c:* Kathleen; *ed:* (BED) Elem Ed, Keene St Coll 1971; *cr:* 3rd Grade Teacher 1971-74, 2nd-3rd Grade Teacher 1975, 2nd Grade Teacher 1976-79, 1st Grade Teacher 1980-86, Transitional Teacher 1987-88, 1st Grade Teacher 1989- Richards Elem Sch; *ai:* EPSF Coord; NEA, NH Ed Assn, Newport Teachers Assn, Granite St Rdng Cncl; Newport Opera House Assn (Secy 1976-80, Treas 1980-84); *office:* Richards Elem Sch School St Newport NH 03773

BARTON, THOMAS WITHERINGTON, Physical Science Teacher; *b:* Ripley, TN; *m:* Tiny Rose; *c:* Kit, Mary Collin; *ed:* (BS) Natural Sci, Univ of TN Martin 1976; *cr:* Teacher Sunny Hill Elem Sch 1976; Teacher/Coach Covington HS 1976-; *ai:* Asst Var Ftbl Coach; Fellowship of Chrstn Athletes Spon; NEA, TEA, WTEA, TCEA 1980-; 1st Presbyn Church (Chm Diaconate 1989, Secy 1988); *office:* Covington HS 803 S College St Covington TN 38019

BARTOS, JOANNA OSIF, Russian Teacher; *b:* Binghamton, NY; *m:* Lewis J.; *c:* Carrie, Stephen; *ed:* (BA) Russian Lang/Lit, Harpur Coll 1967; (MA) Comparative Lit Russian/Eng, SUNY Binghamton 1974; Middlebury Coll 1969; Several Wkshps, Seminars; *cr:* Russian/Eng Teacher 1967-69, Eng Teacher 1969-83, Chm Eng 11 1974-85, Eng/Russian Teacher 1983- Vestal Sr HS; *ai:* Russian Club Adv; Coord of US & USSR Academic HS Partnership Prgm; Stu Exch with Borovichi USSR; NEA, NY Ed Assn, Amer Cncl of Teachers of Russian, Amer Assn of Teachers of Slavic & East European Langs; Binghamton Borovichi Sister City Society Bd of Dir Mem 1988, Life Membership Awd 1988; Broome Tioga Teachers Center Bd Mem 1987-; NCTE Awd for Outstanding Teaching 1982; *office:* Vestal Sr HS Woodlawn Dr Vestal NY 13850

BARTRAM, ANNE LAUX, Science Teacher; *b:* Allentown, PA; *m:* Bert W.; *c:* Bryan, Katherine; *ed:* (BSED) Scndry Ed, 1972, (MED) Health, 1976 TX Tech Univ; *cr:* Sci/Health Teacher Smylie C Wilson Jr HS 1973-81; Sci Teacher Vista Del Sol Elem 1985-; *ai:* Stu Cncl, Sci Club Spon; Awds Comm Chm; TX St Teachers Assn, NEA; *home:* 2012 Greenlee El Paso TX 79936

BARTZ, LAURIE GUNLIKSON, Business/Phys Ed Teacher; *b:* Williston, ND; *m:* Ronald; *ed:* (AA) Univ of ND Williston 1972; (BS) Bus Ed/Phys Ed, Dickinson St Coll 1976; *cr:* Bus/Phys Ed Teacher Harvey HS 1976-; *ai:* Vlybl Coach; ND Ed Assn, NEA, Harvey Ed Assn, ND Alliance of Health, Phys Ed, Recreation, Dance; *office:* Harvey HS North St Harvey ND 58341

BARZILLA, SANDRA GOOD, 3rd Grade Teacher; *b:* El Campo, TX; *m:* Frank L.; *c:* Nicole, Scott; *ed:* (BS) Elem Ed, Sam Houston Univ 1966; *cr:* 3rd Grade Teacher Aldine Ind Sch Dist 1966-67, Conroe Ind Sch Dist 1977-68, Pasadena Ind Sch Dist 1968-73; 2nd Grade Teacher Hitchcock Ind Sch Dist 1976-78; 3rd Grade Teacher Clear Creek Ind Sch Dist 1978-; *ai:* TX St Teachers Assn 1968-; NEA 1968-.

BASARA, JUDITH S., Kindergarten Teacher; *b:* Chester, PA; *m:* Edward; *c:* Beth, Dennis; *ed:* (BS) Elem Ed, West Chester Univ 1963; (MED) Ed Admin, Wilmington Coll 1990; *cr:* 2nd Grade Teacher Ridley Township Sch Dist 1963-64; 3rd Grade Teacher Millsboro Sch Dist 1964-66; Kndgtn Teacher Indian River Sch Dist 1969-; *ai:* NEA, DSEA, IREA 1964-; Schls Teacher of Yr 1986-87; *office:* E Millsboro Elem Sch 500 E State St Millsboro DE 19966

BASARA, JUDY BELCAK, Mathematics Department Chair; *b:* Philadelphia, PA; *m:* Thaddeus S.; *ed:* (BS) Scndry Ed/Math, St Joseph Univ 1970; (MA) Guidance/Counseling, 1971, (MS) Scndry Sch Sci, 1978 Villanova Univ; Germantown Hospital Sch of Medical Technology 1968; Lay Ministry, Youth Ministry, St Charles Seminary 1983; *cr:* Math Lecturer Manor Jr Coll 1973-83, Harcum Jr Coll 1975-78, Gwynedd-Mercy Coll 1977-87; Math Chm St Hubert HS 1970-; *ai:* Math Curr Chm; Joint Elem/Scndry Math Curr Comm Archdiocese of Philadelphia; NCTM, NCSM; ATMOPAV Exec Bd 1976-78; Youth Ministry 1983-; Church Lecturer 1973-82; Pres Math Chm Archdiocese of Philadelphia 1980-84; Nominee Presidential Awd for Excl Teaching Math 1989; *office:* St Hubert HS 7320 Torresdale Ave Philadelphia PA 19136

BASCH, RONALD ARTHUR, 5th Grade Elementary Teacher; *b:* Council Bluffs, IA; *ed:* (BA) Elem Ed, Parsons Coll 1970; *cr:* 5th Grade Rdng/Sci/Health Teacher Lewis Cntrl Schls 1970-; *ai:* Elem Cadre; Health Comm; Stu Cncl & Bus Patrol Spon; NEA 1990; IA St Ed Assn; Operation Pride of Cncl Bluffs 1985-89; *home:* 229 Wendy Hts Council Bluffs IA 51503

BASFORD, PHILIP, Classroom Teacher; *b:* Ft Lauderdale, FL; *ed:* (AA) Ed, Broward Comm Coll 1976; (BA) Ed, FL Atlantic Univ 1978; Wkshp Trng Gifted Ed, Sci, Rdng, Whole Lang Ed, Soc Stud; *cr:* 5th Grade Classroom Teacher 1980-83, 1st-5th Grade Gifted Ed Classroom Teacher 1983-85, K-5th Grade Cmptr Ed Classroom Teacher 1985-86 Banyan Elem; 5th Grade Classroom Teacher Sandpiper Elem 1986-; *ai:* Drama Club Adv; *office:* Sandpiper Elem Sch 3700 NW Hiatus Rd Sunrise FL 33351

BASHAM, AUSTIN E., English Teacher; *b:* Dublin, MD; *m:* Rebecca Chapman; *c:* George, Pamela A. Austin; *ed:* (AA) NM St Univ Alamogordo 1978; (BS) Eng/His, 1979, MAT Composition/Rhetoric Ed, 1981 NM St Univ Las Cruces; NM St Writing Project, NM St Univ Las Cruces 1979; *cr:* Eng Instr NM St Univ Las Cruces 1981-83; Teacher Cmmty Chrstn Sch 1983-84; Honors Eng Teacher Tularosa HS 1984-; Eng Instr NM St Univ Alamogordo 1984-; *ai:* Advanced Placement & Honors Prgm Chm; NEA 1987-; Charter Mem NM St Writing Project; Nom Teacher of Yr; *office:* Tularosa HS 504 1st St Tularosa NM 88352

BASHAM, BETTY ROBERTSON, Third Grade Teacher; *b:* Princeton, WV; *w:* Ralph Newman (dec); *c:* Judy B. Bush, David, Kathy, Kenneth; *ed:* (BS) Bus Ed, Radford Coll 1956; Elem Ed Cert Classes, 1970-73; *cr:* 3rd Grade Teacher Weller Baker Sch 1970-73, Christiansburg Primary Sch 1973-74, Christianburg Elem Sch 1974-; *ai:* NEA, VEA, MCEA 1970-; New River Valley Rdng Assn 1989-; Rotary Awd 1986-87; *home:* 200 Evans St Christiansburg VA 24073

BASHAW, CRAIG LEE, English Teacher; *b:* El Paso, TX; *c:* Jennifer, Derek; *ed:* (BS) Eng/Bio, Univ of Montevallo 1986; Working Towards Masters in Admin; *cr:* Eng Teacher Kecoughtan HS 1986-; *ai:* Sr Class Literary Magazine; Teenage Republicans Suicide Crisis Prevention Team; SAT Improvement Comm Facilitator; *home:* 102 Shenandoah Rd Hampton VA 23661

BASHOR, MICHAEL E., 6th-7th Grade History Teacher; *b:* Willmar, MN; *m:* Sharon Kay; *c:* Shelby, Libby, Troy; *ed:* (BS) Scndry Ed/His, W MT Coll 1968; (MS) Counseling, N MT Coll 1978; Admin Endorsement; Elem Ed Endorsement; *cr:* 5th Grade Teacher Lincoln Elem Sch 1969-73; Substitute Teacher Great Falls MT 1974-75; His Teacher Part Gibson East Jr HS 1975-77; Cnslr Power/Dutton Schls 1978-80; Elem/Jr HS Teacher Meadowlark & Shelby Mid Sch 1981-; *ai:* Ftbl & Bsktbl Coach; MEA (VP, Pres) 1985-87; MT Soc Stud 1989-; Elks Secy 1985-88; Jaycees 1970-72; *home:* 835 N Granite Shelby MT 59474

BASHORE, FRANK M., Mathematics Teacher; *b:* Lancaster, PA; *m:* Carla Maas; *c:* Frank M., Henry W., George T., Carrie Bashore Donovan, Amy M.; *ed:* (BS) Military Engineering, US Military Acad West Point NY 1951; Mandated Educl Courses

Univ of TX El Paso 1978-79; Grad Stud Univ of NM 1982-89; *cr:* Eng Teacher Guillen Mid Sch 1979-80; Math Teacher Bowie HS 1980-81, Santo Domingo Jr HS 1981-82, Bernalillo HS 1982-; *ai:* Sch Improvement & Management Team Mem; Sr Class Co-Spon; NM Cncl Teachers of Math HS VP 1987-89; *office:* Bernalillo HS P O Box 640 Bernalillo NM 87004

BASKIND, BRUCE PHILLIP, HS Social Studies Teacher; *b:* Brooklyn, NY; *ed:* (BS) Scndry Ed/His, SUNY New Paltz 1977; (MA) US His, SUNY Stony Brook 1978; ABD at SUNY Stonybrook; SUNY Inter Campus Fellowship 1980; *cr:* Teaching Asst SUNY Stonybrook 1977-81; Soc Stud Teacher Seward Park HS NYC Bd of Ed 1983-; *ai:* UFT Chapter Chm 1989-; SUNY Inter Campus Fellowship 1981; Teaching Assistantship SUNY Stony Brook His Dept 1977-81; *office:* Seward Park HS 350 Grand St New York NY 10002

BASLER, LAWRENCE EDWARD, Principal; *b:* Altoona, PA; *m:* Linda J. Gerber; *c:* Elizabeth A., Anne M.; *ed:* (BS) Elem Ed, 1964; (MED) Elem Ed, 1969 Shippensburg Univ; Addl Studies Penn St Univ; Western MD Coll; *cr:* Teacher 1964-86; Prin 1986 Shippensburg Area Sch Dist; *ai:* NAESP 1986-; PAESP 1986-; Phi Delta Kappa 1972-; Lions Club Tailtwister/Bd of Dir 1964-; Meml Luth Church Lay Pres 1984; *office:* Nancy Grayson Elem Sch Lurgan Ave Shippensburg PA 17257

BASNIGHT, STEPHEN G., III, Amer His Teacher/Ftbl Coach; *b:* Elizabeth City, NC; *m:* Sharon Marie Frazelle; *c:* Joshua S. IV; *ed:* (BS) Soc Stud, E Carolina Univ 1985; Effective Teacher Trng; *cr:* Teacher/Coach Manteo HS 1985-; *ai:* Head Coach JV Ftbl & JV Bsktbl; Asst Coach Offensive Coord Var Ftbl; Problems in Democracy & Class Adv; Screening Comm; NCHSAA 1985-; NC Cncl for Soc Stud 1986-88; NEA, Dare Cty Ed Assn 1985-86; Bethany United Meth Church 1975-; Dare Cty Recreational League Bsktbl, Vlybl, Sftbl 1985-; Assisted in Book Publication; *home:* Box 1032 Steve Basnight Rd Manteo NC 27954

BASS, CAROLYN JUNE, Kindergarten Teacher; *b:* Searcy, AR; *m:* Carroll Wayne; *c:* Michael S.; *ed:* (BSE) Elem Ed, Univ of Cntrl AR 1973; (MED) Elem Ed, Harding Univ 1988; *cr:* Kndgtn Teacher Pangburn Public Schls 1973-74, Searcy Public Schls 1974-; *ai:* Math Curr Guide Comm; Substitute 2nd Grade Teacher; NEA, AEA, SEA, AR Assn for Children Under 6; White Cty Assn for Children Under 6 Treas 1986-; Phi Delta Kappa Ed Society; 1st Assembly of God Church (Youth Teen Spon, Childrens Church Worker); *home:* 206 Aztec Dr Searcy AR 72143

BASS, DEBBIE HUNT, Fifth Grade Teacher; *b:* Shaw, MS; *m:* Charles Edward; *ed:* (AA) Elem Ed, MS Delta Jr Coll 1979; (BS) Elem Ed, Delta St Univ 1981; *cr:* 5th Grade Teacher Cypress Park Elem Sch 1982-; *ai:* Staff Dev Comm Mem; NEA, MAE, CAE 1986-; MRA 1990; *home:* PO Box 754 Cleveland MS 38732

BASS, GLORIA BAILEY, Mathematics Department Chair; *b:* Macon, GA; *m:* Jerry Wayne; *c:* Dwayne Carlton; *ed:* (BA) Math, Mercer Univ 1969; (MA) Math/Ed, GA Coll 1974; Cmptr Programming, Macon Coll 1982; Radio Shack Cmptr Center Introduction to Basics 1982 & Advanced Basics 1983; Atlanta NCTM Seminar 1983; Mercer SAT Seminar 1988; *cr:* Math Teacher Jones Cty HS 1969-73, Northeast HS 1973-78; Math Teacher/Dept Chm First Presbyn Day Sch 1978-; *ai:* Sr Class Spon; GA Cncl Teachers of Math (Regional Chm 1979-81) 1968-; NCTM 1968-; Delta Kappa Gamma (Budget Comm Chm 1986-88, Finance Comm Chm 1984-86) 1983-; Macon Jr Womens Club 1974-, Family of Yr 1983; First Baptist Church Nominating Comm Chm 1986-89; Mu Alpha Theta Spon; Jones Cty 1972, Northeast HS 1978, First Presbyn Day Sch 1983, Bibb Cty STAR Teacher; Nom Presidential Awds Excl in Sci & Math Teaching 1986; Tandy Technology Scholars Prgm Nom Outstanding Teacher 1989; *office:* First Presbyn Day Sch 5671 Calvin Dr Macon GA 31210

BASS, MARJORIE LONG, English Teacher; *b:* Kingstree, SC; *m:* Benjamin J.; *c:* Mary; *ed:* (AA) Brevard Coll 1957; (BA) Religion, Columbia Coll 1959; (MED) Ed, Francis Marion Coll 1976 *cr:* Eng/World His Teacher Saluda HS 1965-66; Eng Teacher Johnsonville HS 1966-72; Eng/Choral/Music Teacher Southside HS 1972-80; Lang Arts/Soc Stud Teacher Westover Jr HS 1980-86; Eng Teacher Dillon HS 1986-; *ai:* Supt Liaison Comm Dillon Dist 2; Palmetto St Teachers Assn; NCTE; Delta Kappa Gamma Pres Elect 1990-92; Intnl Rdng Assn; Latta Presbyn Church; Florence Masterworks Choir; Teacher of Yr Southside Jr HS 1978; Yrbk Dedication Johnsonville HS 1971; *office:* Dillon H S Hwy 301 N Dillon SC 29536

BASS, MARY CUNNINGHAM, Kindergarten Teacher; *b:* Fayetteville, TN; *m:* Larry Thomas; *c:* Melinda, Larry Jr., William, Jennifer; *ed:* (BS) Home Ec, Mid TN St Univ 1972; (MED) ECE, Mercer Univ 1978; *cr:* Home Ec Teacher Elder Jr HS 1972-74; Kndgtn Teacher Ingram Elem 1974-76, Hartley Elem 1976-81, Union Elem 1983; *ai:* Discipline & Materials Acquisition Comm; Kappa Omicron Phi 1972-; Phi Delta Kappa 1978-; Hartley PTA Teacher of Yr 1978; Union Elem Spirit Awd 1990; *office:* Union Elem Sch 4831 Mamie Carter Dr Macon GA 31204

BASS, ROBERT CARL, Mathematics/Phys Ed Teacher; *b:* Northridge, CA; *ed:* (BA) Phys Ed, San Diego St 19 8; *cr:* Teacher Virgil Jr HS 1979-; *ai:* Store Reps Comm; *office:* Virgil Jr HS 152 N Vermont Ave Los Angeles CA 90004

BASS, SUSAN FEDELE, English Teacher; *b:* New Haven, CT; *m:* David Whitney; *ed:* (MS) Eng Ed, S CT St Univ 1989; (BA) Eng, Univ of CT Storis 1983; Univ of Londons Bedford Coll, London U K; *cr:* Eng Teacher Sacred Heart Acad 1988-; *ai:* Moderator for Sacred Heart Acads Prism Awd Winning Literary Journal; Head Coach Vlybl 1988; NCTE 1988-; *home:* 409 Ellsworth Ave New Haven CT 06511

BASSETT, ARLENE ROLLINS, 4th Grade Teacher; *b:* Portis, KS; *m:* Don W.; *c:* Marcus, Bradley J.; *ed:* (BA) General Sci/Elem Ed, MaryMount Coll 1965; (MS) Curr/Instruction, KS St Univ 1975; Grad Stud in Gifted Ed; *cr:* Teacher Unified Dist 305 1965-68; Social Worker Title III Area Center 1968-70; Adult Ed Teacher Area Vocational Tech Sch 1970-72; Elem Teacher Unified Dist 305 1972-; *ai:* Dist Wide Sch Improvement Project Team Leader; NEA Delegate 1977-80; KS Ed Assn (Delegate, IPD Comm) 1975-80; Salina Ed Assn (Treas, Comm Chm) 1974-80;Delta Kappa Gamma Pres 1979-81; Phi Kappa Phi 1982-; KS Assn of Teacher of Sci; Salina Youth Care Home (Dir, Treas) 1975-89; Television Awareness Licensed St Trainer; Local in Service & Natl Sci Grants; *office:* Heusner Sch Unified Dist 305 425 E Jewell Salina KS 67401

BASSETT, F. CHARLES, Jr HS Social Studies Teacher; *b:* Great Falls, MT; *m:* Alice Ann Carter; *c:* Lance, Laura; *ed:* (BS) Eng, MT St Univ 1965; *cr:* Jr HS Eng Teacher Lambert Public Sch 1965-67; Jr HS His Teacher Big Timber Grade Sch 1967-; *ai:* Jr HS Girls Bsktbl Coach; Big Timber Ed Assn Pres 1971-72; Masonic Lodge Master 1979, 1984; Big Timber Cmmty Needs Bd Mem 1989-; Church Finance Bd Mem 1990; *home:* Box 1194 Big Timber MT 59011

BASSETT, JUDITH ANN, Early Childhood Director; *b:* Midland, MI; *m:* William; *c:* Bennett, Leslie; *ed:* (BA) Elem Ed, MI St Univ 1964; Math Wkshp Gesell Inst; Working on Masters in Child Dev MSU; Early Chldhd, St of MI; *cr:* Kndgtn Teacher Livonia Public Schls 1965-68; 1st Grade Teacher Adrian Public Schls 1968-70; Kndgtn Teacher Faith Chrstn Sch 1974-76, Jackson Baptist Sch 1976-78; 1st Grade/Kndgtn Teacher Lansing Chrstn Sch 1978-; *ai:* Early Chldhd Dir; *office:* Lansing Chrstn Sch 1028 W Barnes Ave Lansing MI 48910

BASSETT, MARY JANE, Science Teacher-Dept Chair; *b:* Enid, OK; *m:* Milton Earl; *c:* Candyce, Carma; *ed:* (BS) Natural Sci, NW OK St Univ 1968; Advanced Placement Bio; *ai:* Pep Club; Head of Dept; NEA, WEA, OEA; St Peters Cath Church; Teacher of Yr Candidate.

BATCHELOR, CATHIE DIECKMANN, Fifth Grade Lang Arts Teacher; *b:* Camp Lejeune, NC; *m:* Danny Rudolph; *c:* Kristina A., Steven D.; *ed:* (AA) Coll Transfer, Coastal Carolina Comm Coll 1979; (BA) Intermediate Ed, Univ NC Wilmington 1981; (MAED) Intermediate Ed, E Carolina Univ 1988; Licensed Ventriloquist; *cr:* Intermediate Lang Art Teacher Blue Creek Elem Sch 1981-; *ai:* Lang Art Curr Coord; Cty Elem Rep Senate Bill II Impact Comm; Mem Southern Accreditation Steering, Media Advisory Comms; NC Assn Educators, Intnl Rdng Assn Mem 1981-; Tarheel Horsemans Assn Mem 1985-; Amer Quarter Horse Assn Mem 1989-; Outstanding Teacher Awd 1985; Jaycees Outstanding Young Educator 1989; Outstanding Young Educator Awd Territorial Finalist; *home:* 713 Christopher Ct Jacksonville NC 28540

BATEMAN, ANGELIA MORGAN, Media Coordinator; *b:* Asheville, NC; *m:* Morris; *ed:* (BA) Early Chldhd Ed, Mars Hill Coll 1979; (MA) Mid Grades Ed/Intermediate Grades Ed, W Carolina Univ 1984; *cr:* Media Supvr/Teacher Nantahala Sch 1979-; *ai:* Sr Class & Jr Beta Club Spon; Southern Assn of Coll & Schls Accreditation Comm Chm; NEA, NCAE 1979-; NCLA, NCASL 1988-; Order of Eastern Star 1972-; Mt View Baptist Church Pianist 1985-; *office:* Nantahala Sch Star Rt Topton NC 28781

BATEMAN, JOAN KUSHNIR, Accounting & Typing Teacher; *b:* Duquesne, PA; *m:* Robert; *c:* Sandy, Bill; *ed:* (BSED) Bus Ed, 1962, (MED) Bus/Accounting, 1967 IN Univ of PA; *cr:* Bus Teacher W Mifflin Sch Dist 1962-67, Norwin Sch Dist 1967-70, Yough Sch Dist 1984-; *ai:* PA St Ed Assn 1962-; Yough Ed Assn, PA Bus Ed Assn 1984-; NEA 1962-; *office:* Yough Sr HS 99 Lowber Rd Herminie PA 15637

BATEMAN, JOSEPH G., Physical Education Teacher; *b:* Shenandoah, IA; *m:* Sherrie Sue Clark; *c:* Kristi, Jeff; *ed:* (BS) Industrial Technology/Health/Phys Ed, 1965, (MS) Industrial Technology/Phys Ed, 1969 NW MO St Univ; Quest Intnl Skills Adolescence Instr; Teacher/Trainer Prevention Research Inst; Prof in Residence Trng Beatty Ford Center; *cr:* Teacher Westside Cmmty Schls 1965-; *ai:* Phys Ed Health Dept Chm; Asst Athletic Dir; Wrestling Head Coach; AAHPERD 1984-; NEA 1965-; *office:* Arbor Heights Jr HS 8601 Arbor St Omaha NE 68124

BATEMAN, LINDA DUMBAULD, Fifth Grade Teacher; *b:* Allison Park, PA; *m:* David Charles; *c:* Dylan, Dana; *ed:* (AS) Ed, Alleghany Comm Coll 1971; (BS) Elem Ed, CA St Coll PA 1973; Grad Stud WV Coll, WV Univ; *cr:* 5th Grade Teacher Hemphill Elem Sch 1973-89, Welch Elem Sch 1989-; *ai:* Girls Bsktbl Coach 1977-78; NEA 1973-; WV Ed Assn St Delegate 1987-; Beta Sigma Phi (VP 1989) 1984-, Pledge of Yr 1985, Girl of Yr 1987; Hemphill PTO Treas 1975-86.

BATEMAN, ROSANNE CUNNINGHAM, Curriculum Specialist; *b:* Wilmington, DE; *m:* Henry William; *ed:* (ABT) Elem Ed, High Point Coll 1971; (MED) Elem Ed, Winthrop Coll 1985; Working Towards Eds Curr & Admin, Winthrop Coll; *cr:* 2nd Grade Teacher Forest City Elem 1972-73; Kndgtn Teacher Tinicum Elem 1975-76; 3rd Grade Teacher Marshville Elem 1976-87; Elem Curr Specialist Union Cty Schls 1987-; *ai:* Phi Kappa Phi 1985-; ASCD 1986-; United States Power Squadrons 1986-; Marshville Elem Teacher of Yr; Union Cty Schls Teacher of Yr; *office:* Union Cty Schls 500 N Main St Monroe NC 28110

BATES, BRUCE MONROE, 6th Grade Lang Art Teacher; *b:* Iowa City, IA; *m:* Roseanne Petersen; *c:* Nicholas, Nathan, Nelson; *ed:* (BS) Elem Ed, Dana Coll 1975; Working Towards Masters in Elem Ed, Marycrest Coll; *cr:* 6th Grade Lang Art Teacher Garfield Elem Sch 1975-; *ai:* Safety Patrol Supvr; Davenport Ed Assn (Rep 1976-85, Exec Bd 1985-87); *office:* Garfield Elem Sch 902 E 29th St Davenport IA 52803

BATES, DAWNA RICHARDS, Health/Physical Ed Teacher; *b:* Latrobe, PA; *m:* Craig Robert; *c:* Jody L.; *ed:* (BA) Health/Phys Ed/Recreation, 1970, (MS) Individual Prescripted Instr, 1976 Slippery Rock Univ; *cr:* 9th-12th Grade Health/Phys Ed Teacher Ringold Sch Dist 1970-71; Health/Phys Ed Teacher Greater Latrobe Sch Dist 1971; *ai:* Girls Bsktbl & Jump Rope Demonstration Team Coach; NEA, PSEA, AAHPERD, PSHPERD 1970-; Amer Red Cross (Instr, CPR & First Aid Trainer, Aids Facilitator) 1970-; *office:* Greater Latrobe Jr HS Country Club Rd Latrobe PA 15650

BATES, MELVIN DEAN, Biology/History Teacher/Coach; *b:* Hearne, TX; *m:* Judy Ellen Wilson; *c:* Emily, Scott, Brian; *ed:* (BA) Phys Ed, Univ of Mary Hardin-Baylor 1982; *cr:* Stu Asst Coach Univ of Mary Hardin-Baylor 1981-82; His Teacher/Coach Belton HS 1983-85; Bio/His Teacher/Coach Salado HS 1985-; *ai:* Soph Class Spon; Ftbl & Jr HS Bsktbl Asst; Bsbl Head; TX St Teachers Organization 1989-; TX HS Coaches Assn, TX HS Bsbl Assn 1983-; Career Ladder Level 2; Dist 17A Coach of Yr 1986; *home:* Rt 4 Box 436E Belton TX 76513

BATES, NANCY H., Teacher of Gifted Math Courses; *b:* Miami, FL; *m:* Thomas L.; *c:* Cathy B. La Hayne; *ed:* (BS) Math/Eng, FL St Univ 1950; (MED) Math Ed, 1967, Ed Specialist Math Ed, 1969 Univ of GA; Various Courses Gifted Ed, Supervision of Stu Teachers, Teacher Assessment; *cr:* Math Teacher St Lucie Cty Jr HS 1962-63, S Habersham HS 1964-66, N Habersham HS 1967-70, Habersham Cntrl HS 1970-; *ai:* Stu Cncl & Literary Magazine Adv; Math Dept Chm; Debate Coach; NCTM 1965-; GA Cncl Teachers of Math (Secy, Pres-Elect) 1970-, Life Mem NEA, GAE 1964-; Habersham Chrstn Learning Center Bd of Trustees 1982-; Natl Sci Fnd Academic Yr Inst Univ of GA 1966-67; Habersham Cty STAR Teacher 1965, 1971, 1974, 1977, 1983, 1985, 1988-89; Teacher of Yr 1976; Governors Honors Prgm Selection Comm; *home:* 100 Grandview Cir Cornelia GA 30531

BATES, PAMELA H., Math Teacher; *b:* South Boston, VA; *m:* Kennard R.; *ed:* (BS) His, Longwood Coll 1973; Math Endorcement 1987; *cr:* Teacher Charlotte Elem 1973-80, Cntrl Mid 1980-; *ai:* Girls Sftbl Coach; Piedmont Math Assn 1987-; *office:* Central Mid Sch PO Box 748 Charlotte Crt Hse VA 23923

BATES, SHARON BYRAM, Teacher of Gifted & Talented; *b:* Almira, WA; *c:* Michael, Rick; *ed:* (BA) Elem Ed, 1967, (MED) Elem Ed, 1972 E WA Univ; Lib Sci, Gifted Ed; *cr:* 4th-6th Grade Teacher Medical Lake Elem 1967-71; Librarian Medical LakE Elem 1971-73, E WA Univ 1973-75; Jr HS Librarian Medical Lake Mid 1974-; *ai:* Curr Cncl Coord; Self-Study Comm; Knowledge Master Open Coach; NEA, WA Ed Assn 1986-87; Medical Lake Ed Assn Rep 1986-87; WA Lib Media Assn Mid Levels Chairperson 1984-87, Region 7 WA Lib Med Assn Pres 1987-88; E WA Univ Lib Sci Class Teacher.

BATES, SUSAN ELIZABETH, Social Studies Teacher; *b:* Springfield, MA; *m:* Gary W. Michaels; *c:* Nicholas W. Michaels; *ed:* (BS) Poly Sci, Northeastern Univ 1983; (MA) Scndry Ed, Univ of PA 1986; *cr:* 8th Grade Soc Stud Teacher Upper Perkiomen Mid Sch; *ai:* NCSS 1986-; *office:* Upper Perkiomen Mid Sch Jefferson St East Greenville PA 18041

BATES, WILLA CHARLENE, Third Grade Teacher; *b:* Richmond, MO; *w:* Smith A. (dec); *c:* Willa A. Williamson, Jerry S.; *ed:* (BS) Elem, Cntrl MO St Warrensburg 1964; Grad Stud; *cr:* Rural 1st-8th Grade Cntry Teacher Ray Cty; Kndgtn Teacher Private; Elem Teacher Excelsior Springs MO; *ai:* MO Ed Assn; *home:* RR Box 335 Richmond MO 64085

BATES, WINFREY PHELPS, Librarian/Reading Teacher; *b:* Louisville, KY; *m:* R. Brooks; *c:* Amy Walker, Anne, Charles Brooks; *ed:* (BS) Elem Ed, Campbellsville Coll 1973, (MA) Elem Ed, 1979, (Rank I) 1981 W KY Univ; Working on Educl Specialist Degree; Mellon Seminar on Foxfire Berea Coll 1987; Writing Project IV W KY Univ 1989; Teachor Mentor Trng; *cr:* 3rd Grade Teacher 1975-82, 1st Grade Teacher 1982-83 Taylor Cty Elem; Librarian/Rdng Teacher Mannsville Elem 1984-; *ai:* Co-Spon Mannsville Young Historians; Photography 4-H Leader; KY Lib Assn Mem 1985-; E KY Teachers Network Exec Comm 1987-; KY Cncl Teachers of Eng 1989-; Taylor Cty 4-H Cncl Mem 1988-; Taylor Cty Young Woman of Yr (Bd of Dir, Chairperson Selection Comm); Taylor Cty Boosters Club 1988-; Campbellsville Jr Womans Club Outstanding Young Woman 1975; KY Educl Televisions Media Specialist Awd 1986; Campbellsville Bus & Prof Womens Club Woman of Achievement 1986; Co-Authored Educl Innovative Incentive Grant; KY Book Fair, KY Educl Fnd, Foxfire Grants *home:* 1441 Old Lebanon Rd Campbellsville KY 42718

BATEY, ANDREA COBOS, Reading Specialist; *b:* Laredo, TX; *m:* Robert Jeffery; *c:* Karol A., Robert F.; *ed:* (BS) Guidance Stud/Eng, North TX St Univ 1977; (MS) Rdng, Laredo St Univ 1984; *cr:* Teacher Austin Ind Sch Dist 1978; Laredo Ind Sch Dist 1978-; *ai:* Coach UIL Poetry/Prose; Spon Project RAIL (Readers Against Illiteracy in Laredo); Attendance Appeal Comm; TX St Rdng 1989-; UNT Alumni Ed Adv 1988-; Laredo Little Theatre Secretary 1986; All Star Cast 1985; Runner-Up Teacher of the Yr; Most Popular Teacher; Pres Faculty Club; *office:* Martin H S 2002 San Bernardo Laredo TX 78040

BATH, MARSHA PATTERSON, 7th Grade Geography Teacher; *b:* Tulsa, OK; *m:* Ron Lee; *c:* Forrest K.; *ed:* (BA) Poly Sci, 1972, (MED) Soc Stud, 1976 Cntrl St Univ; *cr:* 6th Grade Eng Teacher 1981-85, 7th Grade Eng/Geography Teacher 1986-Cimarron Mid Sch; *ai:* Geography Textbook Edmond, Curr for Soc Stud Planning Comms; OK Ed Assn, Edmond Assn Classroom Teachers 1981-; OK Cncl of Soc Stud, OK Assn of Geography Ed 1988-; OK Shakespeare in Park, Edmond Cmmty Theatre Guild Mem 1982-89; Book Dedication; *office:* Cimarron Mid Sch 3701 South Bryant Edmond OK 73013

BATISTE, WENDALL HARDY, Second Grade Teacher; *b:* Rockford, AL; *m:* Alexis Jr.; *c:* Lisa; *ed:* (BS) Elem Ed, AL St Univ 1972; *cr:* 4th Grade Teacher Milwaukee Public Schls 1973-76; 2nd Grade Teacher Atlanta Public Schls 1977-; *ai:* Amer Assn of Educators 1977-; Amer Bus Women Assn Treas 1988-; *office:* Venetian Hills Elem Sch 1910 Venetian Dr Atlanta GA 30311

BATISTICH, EVALEE M., 4th Grade Teacher; *b:* Hoboken, NJ; *ed:* (BA) Soc Stud Teacher, 1974, Elem Sch Teacher, 1975, (MA) Prin/Supvr, 1989 Jersey City St Coll; Acad for Advancement of Teaching & Management NJSDE; Instructional Theory in Practice; Bureau of Ed & Research; Teaching Writing with Power; *cr:* K-12th Grade Substitute Teacher 1974-76; Remedial Rdng Teacher Connors Sch 1976-77; 3rd Grade Calabro Sch 1977-80; Evening Eng as 2nd Lang Teacher Hoboken HS 1980-86; 4th Grade Teacher Calabro Sch 1990; *ai:* On Site Management Cncl Chairperson; Curr Dev, Lang Art Book, Report Card Comm; Affirmative Action Rep; NJ Ed Assn, Hoboken Teachers Assn; *office:* Calabro Sch 524 Park Ave Hoboken NJ 07030

BATLLE, MARY CATHERINE BUSH, 8th Grade English Teacher; *b:* Ft Worth, TX; *m:* Daniel E.; *c:* Aaron, Logan; *ed:* (BS) Psych/Eng, TX Wesleyan Univ 1980; Grad Stud Occupational Therapy; Working Towards Masters Univ of TX Arlington; *cr:* Occupational Therapy Asst Millwood Hospital 1980-83; Classroom/Eng Teacher Workman Jr HS 1983-; *ai:* Yrbk Staff, Care Team, Honors Assembly Spon; Tutor; Assn TX Prof Educators; *office:* Workman Jr HS 701 Arbrook Bld E Arlington TX 76014

BATON, NANCY LEIGH, Director of Gifted & Talented; *b:* Plainfield, NJ; *m:* William C.; *c:* Kim Dickey, Michael Dickey; *ed:* (BA) Span/Scndry Ed, St Francis Coll 1970; (MA) Admin/Supervision/Curr, Kean Coll 1988; *cr:* Teacher 1976-, Gifted & Talented Dir 1984- David Brearley Regional HS; *ai:* Natl Span Honor Society Adv; Teacher & Bd of Ed Relations Comm; Phi Kappa Phi, Kappa Delta Pi Mem 1988-; Amer Assn of Teachers of Span & Portuguese Mem 1980-; St Helens Church (Pres, Pastoral Cncl) 1990; Governor Kean Teacher Recognition Awd for Outstanding Teaching Awd 1986; *office:* David Brearley HS Monroe Ave Kenilworth NJ 07033

BATTAGLER, JO ANN, Math/Reading Teacher; *b:* Orrick, MO; *m:* Louis L.; *c:* Tracie Twyman, Kerri Hartwick; *ed:* (BS) Elem Ed, Cntrl MO St Univ 1981; Grad Stud; *cr:* 3rd Grade Teacher Orrick Elem 1983-88; 7th-9th Grade Math/7th-8th Grade Lang Art Teacher Orrick HS 1988-; *ai:* Pom Pon & Sr Class Spon; PDC & Drug Comm; Orrick Teacher Assn, MO Math Teachers, Mid Sch Assn; Orrick Fire Dept Ladies Auxiliary Secy 1985-87; *home:* Rt 1 Box 316 Orrick MO 64077

BATTAGLIA, FRANK LOUIS, Social Studies Teacher; *b:* Buffalo, NY; *ed:* (BS) Soc Stud, 1964, (MS) Soc Stud, 1969 St Univ of NY Coll Buffalo; Post Grade Stud Numerous Univs; *cr:* Teacher Troy HS 1964-65, Starpoint Cntrl HS 1965-; *ai:* Sr HS Stu Cncl Adv 1971; Stu At Risk Consultation Comm; NY St United Teachers; NASSP Stu Affairs; Toy Train Operations Society Dir At Large 1990; Cystic Fibrosis Research Fnd Awd 1978-79; NY St Grant 1970; Taft Seminar Grant CCNY 1977; *office:* Starpoint Cntrl Jr/Sr HS 4363 Mapleton Rd Lockport NY 14094

BATTEN, JENNY LOU, Lang Art/Soc Stud Teacher; *b:* Smithfield, NC; *ed:* (BS) Ed, E Carolina Univ 1975; *cr:* Teacher Smithfield Jr HS 1975-87, Smithfield-Selma Mid Sch 1987-; *ai:* Natl Jr Honor Society Adv; Soc Stud Dept Chm; Senate Bill 2 Sch Comm; Natl Mid Sch Assn 1990; Smithfield Jr Womans Club (Secy 1986-87, Pres 1987-88, Dept Chm 1989-), Club Woman of Quarter 1986, Distinguished Club Woman of Yr 1988; *office:* Smithfield-Selma Mid Sch PO Box 2270 Buffalo Rd Smithfield NC 27577

BATTERBERRY, SHAWN NORMAN, Social Studies Teacher; *b:* Jamestown, ND; *m:* Linda Kolbo; *ed:* (AA) Liberal Arts, Bismarck Jr Coll 1980; (BS) Soc Stud, Moorhead St Univ 1982; Working Towards MS Educl Admin, ND St Univ 1990; *cr:* Soc Stud Teacher Roosevelt Public Sch Dist 1982-83, Mandan Sr HS 1983-; *ai:* Dir Summer Driver Ed Prgm; Jr HS Ftbl Coach; Boys Intramurals; Mandan Ed Assn Pres 1989-; ND Ed Assn, NEA 1983-; Elks 1982-; ND Driver Traffic Safety Ed Assn Teacher of Yr 1988; *home:* 1509 Shannons Dr #1 Mandan ND 58554

BATTERSHELL, BARBARA L., First Grade Teacher; *b:* Sherman, NY; *m:* Jim; *c:* Ty, Jana; *ed:* (BA) Elem Ed, 1967, (MED) Curr/Instruction, 1989 Univ of WY; *cr:* 5th Grade Teacher Glenrock Elem 1967; 3rd Grade Teacher North Grade 1967-69; 4th Grade Teacher South Grade 1971-74; 1st Grade Teacher Westside Elem 1976-; *ai:* Delta Kappa Gamma Recording Secy 1986-; 1st Baptist Church (Vocal Music Ed, Chrstn Ed) 1975; *office:* Westside Elem Sch 160 N Evarts Powell WY 82435

BATTLE, BEVERLY CHERYL, Second Grade Teacher; *b:* Goldsboro, NC; *ed:* (BS) Elem Ed, DC Teachers Coll 1972; Grad Stud Home Sch Inst Trinity Coll; *cr:* Coll Aide 1967-72, Cmmty Sch Teacher 1972-77 Harrison Cmmty Sch; Classroom Teacher Harriet Tubman Elem Sch 1972-; *ai:* Safety Patrol, Stu Government Spon; Union Building Rep; Fundraising, Spelling Bee, Safety & Security Comms; DCABSE, DCASCD, Intnl Rdng Assn 1988-; Delta Sigma Theta Pres 1971-72; Washington Teachers Union Building Rep 1985-; Favorite Teacher Awd Region V; Ward I Cncl Teacher of Yr Awds; AAA Distinguished Service Awds; *office:* Harriet Tubman Elem Sch 13th & Kenyon Sts NW Washington DC 20010

BATTLE, GENEVA POLITE, JR., Retired-Fifth Grade Teacher; *b:* Ray City, GA; *m:* Albert Jr.; *c:* Albert III, Ellamease O. Jones, Theresa L. Harris; *ed:* (BS) Ed, 1949, Cert Elem Ed, 1953 Fort Valley St; Data Collection, GA Southwestern Coll 1980; *cr:* Soc Sci Teacher Lakeland HS 1949-50; 2nd/3rd Grade Teacher Nunn Industrial Sch 1951-57; 6th-8th Grade Soc Sci/4th-6th Grade Rdng/Eng Teacher Northeast Elem Sch 1957-85; *ai:* Lakeland HS Girls Bsktbl Coach; Sr Class, Tri-Hi-Y Club Adv; Northeast Elem Interpretive Dancer Teacher; Co-Chairperson Assembly Prgms; Drama Chairperson; Sumter Assn of Ed, GAE, NEA; Americus Retired Teachers #2 Prgm Comm Co-Chairperson 1985-; GA Retired Teachers Assn 1985-; Cathedral Choir (VP 1981-82 Pres 1983-88); Les Femmes Joyouses Soc Comm 1986-; Amer Legion Auxilary; Excelsior Club; Willing Workers Club; Northeast Elem Teacher of Yr 1972-73; *home:* 203 Rucker St PO Box 251 Americus GA 31709

BATTLE, ISAAC L., 4th Grade Teacher; *b:* Cuthbert, GA; *m:* Minnie Green; *ed:* (BA) Bus Admin/Ed, Stillman Coll 1967; (MA) Guidance Counseling, Heed Univ 1977, Ed Admin Supervision, Chicago St Univ 1980; Educl Admin/Supervision Heed Univ 1980; *cr:* Teacher 1970-79, Cnslr 1979-80, Teacher 1980-82 Robert Emmet Elem Sch; Teacher Marconi Cmmty Acad 1982-86, Ralph J Bunche Elem Sch 1986-; *ai:* Phi Delta Kappa 1983; *home:* 9252 S Union Ave Chicago IL 60620

BATTLE, PATRICIA ANN, Art Teacher; *b:* Bay City, TX; *ed:* (BS) Ed, Prairie View A&M Univ 1979; *cr:* Art Instr 1980-85, 4th Grade Teacher 1985-87, Art Instr 1987- Linnie Roberts Elem; *ai:* Campus Comm Cncl; Parents Teachers Comm; TX Classroom Teachers Assn 1985-88; NAEA 1990; Young Womens Assn Matron 1986-88; Olive Leaf Chapter 219 1987-.

BATTLE, SAUNDRA SNYDER, 6th Grade Teacher; *b:* Emporia, VA; *m:* Robert James; *c:* Lisa; *ed:* (BA) General Ed, Kean Coll 1971; *cr:* 6th Grade Teacher Quitman Street Sch; *ai:* Grade Level Chairperson; NTU; Church Admin Cncl Chairperson 1989-; Delta Sigma Theta, Gamma Sigma Sigma.

BATTLES, BETTY J. MC GEHEE, Language Arts Teacher; *b:* Oak Grove, LA; *w:* Bennie M. (dec); *c:* Benita J. Battles Weaver, Bernard; *ed:* (BS) Elem, Chicago St Univ; (MS) Ed/Rdng, Natl Coll of Ed 1981; Office Machines, Peters Bus Coll; *cr:* Cmptr Processor Dept of Public Aid 1969-71; Teacher Chicago Archdiocese 1971-72, Chicago Bd of Ed 1972-; *ai:* Lang Art, Essay Writing, Spelling Bee Comms; Midwest Bridge Unit Mem; Trinity United Church Stewardship Cncl; Teacher of Yr 1985-86; *home:* 9525 S Dobson Chicago IL 60628

BATTLES, MARION ISHMAEL, Social Studies Teacher; *b:* Petersburg, IN; *m:* Lavada Joan; *c:* Kreg, Dale; *ed:* (BS) Elem Ed - Magna Cum Laude, Oakland City Coll 1957-57; (MS) Elem Admin, IN St Univ 1958-59; *cr:* 6th Grade Teacher North Sch 1958-59; 5th/6th Grade Teacher Clark Sch 1959-61; 7th/8th Grade Teacher Clark Jr HS 1962-87; 8th Grade Teacher Clark Mid Sch 1988-; *ai:* Natl Geographic Contest & Educl Game Club Spon; NEA, IN St Teachers Assn Mem 1958-; First Church of God (Bd of Trustees & Ed 1970-80, Sunday Sch Teacher 1965-70); *office:* Clark Mid Sch 500 Buntin Vincennes IN 47591

BATTON, ANN BURNEY, 2nd Grade Elem Head Teacher; *b:* Jackson, MS; *m:* Price; *c:* Dianne Ham, Richard; *ed:* (BS) Elementary Ed, MS Coll 1967; Univ Southern MS; MS St Univ; MS Coll; *cr:* 1st Grade Teacher Crystal Springs Attend 1967-70; 2nd Grade Teacher 1981-; Elem Head Teacher/Prin 1986 Copiah Acad; *ai:* Issues Comm; MPSEA Dir 1981-83; NPSEA Dist 4 Lower Elem Chairperson 1986-87; Public Lib Trustee 1980-; Teacher of Yr 1986-87 Copial Acad; *home:* Rt 2 Box 462 Crystal Springs MS 39059

BATTS, JAMES CLARK, English Teacher; *b:* Melrose Park, IL; *m:* Karen Uhlhorn; *c:* Allyson, Erik, Christopher; *ed:* (BFA) Drama/Speech Drake Univ 1963; (MA) Drama, Northwestern Univ 1965; *cr:* Eng Teacher Rich East HS 1965-67, Niles West HS 1967-; *ai:* Dir Spring Play; NHS Comm; Ivy Lynn Chaplik Humanitarian Awd Comm; NCTE 1990; NEH Grant to Study Pascals Pensees Notre Dame Univ 1988; *home:* 1002 Westgate Mount Prospect IL 60056

BATTUELLO, ROSALIE ANN, 3rd Grade Teacher; *b:* Litchfield, IL; *ed:* (BS) Elem Ed, Southern IL Univ 1968; *cr:* 3rd Grade Teacher Mt Olive Grade Schl 1968-; *office:* Mt Olive Grade Sch 804 W Main Mount Olive IL 62069

BATTY, LINDA L., Gifted/Talented Teacher; *b:* Oklahoma City, OK; *ed:* (BA) Eng Ed, Cntrl St Univ 1966; (MED) Eng, GA St Univ 1974; Counseling Gifted OK St Univ 1989; *cr:* Eng Teacher Washington Jr HS 1966-68, Lovenberg Jr HS 1968-69, Stewart Mid Sch 1969-74, Cave Springs Jr HS 1974-76; Teacher of Gifted & Talented/Eng/Psych Teacher Claremore HS 1977-; *ai:* HS Academic, Jr Hs Academic Coach; St Problem Captain for Classics Div of Odyssey of the Mind; Teach ACT Prep Classes; Conduct Coaching, Judging Wkshps for Odyssey of the Mind; Chm of the Weighted Grading Comm; Claremore Classroom Teachers Assn 1977-; NEA 1981; NEA, Nut Teacher Exch 1982; Natl Claremore Teacher of Yr 1982; Claremore Cmmty Concerts Bd Mem; Regional Awd 1989; Citizen Bee Competition Coach; OK St Univ 6th Annual Texaco Star Academic Challenge Semi Finalist Coach; *office:* Claremore Public Schls 100 W 4th St Claremore OK 74017

BAUCH, GLORIA JEAN (MEYER), Third Grade Teacher; *b:* La Crosse, WI; *m:* Richard C.; *ed:* (BS) Elem Ed, WI St Coll La Crosse 1963; (MED) Lang Art, NE IL Univ 1974; *cr:* 2nd Grade Teacher Pitsch Sch 1963-64; 3rd Grade Teacher Summit Sch 1964-68, Merrill Sch 1968-73, Franklin Sch 1973-; *ai:* WI Ed Assn 1963-68; PREA, IEA, NEA 1968-; *office:* Franklin Sch 2401 Manor Ln Park Ridge IL 60068

BAUCHE, KURT DOUGLAS, Director of Bands; *b:* Washington, MO; *m:* Susann Lynn Mehler; *c:* Kathryn; *ed:* (BME) Instrumental/Vocal Music, SE MO St Univ 1980; (MME) Instrumental Music, Univ of Louisville 1982; Teacher Effectiveness, Stu Achievement 1989; *cr:* Teaching Asst Univ of Louisville 1980-82; Dir of Bands Farmington HS 1982-; *ai:* Coord Stu Participation All Dist & St Band Act; Dist Music Solo & Ensemble Festival; Marching Bands & Their Respective Auxiliary Units; Music Educators Natl Conference; MO Music Educators Assn Band VP Dist 7 1988-; MO Bandmasters Assn, MO St Teachers Assn, Phi Beta Mu, Phi Mu Alpha; Benevolent & Protective Order of Elks 1765 Chaplain 1985-86; *office:* Farmington HS #1 Black Knight Dr Farmington MO 63640

BAUCK, MELVIN ROBERT, Business Teacher; *b:* Vassar, KS; *m:* Carol Lorraine Helmke; *c:* Aaron, Lyle; *ed:* (BS) Bus Ed/Eng, 1962, (MS) Ed, 1966 Emporia St Univ; Continuing Ed; *cr:* Bus/Eng Teacher Welda HS 1962-67; Bus Teacher/Dept Chm Garnett HS 1967-; *ai:* Octagon Club Head Spon; Optimist Model Legislature Adv; NHS Selection Comm; Delta Pi Epsilon 1966-; KS Ed Assn; NEA (Convention Delegate 1967, 1969) 1962-; Anderson Cty Teachers Assn (Pres 1965-66) 1962-66; Garnett City Teachers Assn VP 1966-67; N Anderson Cty Teachers Assn (Secy 1984-85) 1967-; Trinity Luth Church (Elder 1979-82, Substitute Organist 1977-, St Convention Delegate 1988); *home:* Rt 3 Garnett KS 66032

BAUCOM, GREGORY LEE, US History Teacher; *b:* Brownwood, TX; *m:* Kimberly Doern; *ed:* Working Towards Masters Ed, TX A&M Univ; *cr:* US His Teacher Odessa HS 1986-; *ai:* Ftbl, Jr Var Bsktbl, Head Cross Cntry, Asst Track Coach; TX Classroom Teachers Assn 1986-; *office:* Odessa HS 1301 Dotsy Odessa TX 79763

BAUCUM, BEVERLY GUTELIUS, 10th Grade World His Teacher; *b:* Houston, TX; *c:* Constance, Rebecca; *ed:* (BA) Eng/His/Span, 1964, (MA) Eng, 1972 Baylor; (MS) Counseling, Amer Technological Univ 1979; *cr:* Teacher Bay City Jr HS 1964-66, Victoria HS 1966-67; Admin/Teacher Cntrl TX Coll 1974-80; Teacher Clark HS 1984-; *ai:* Textbook Comm; TX Cncl for Soc Stud; *office:* Clark HS 51150 Dezavala San Antonio TX 78231

BAUER, ANN MARIE (STREIFEL), Sixth Grade Teacher; *b:* Hillsview, SD; *m:* John; *c:* David; *ed:* (BS) Elem Ed - Cum Laude Northern St Univ Aberdeen 1970; Renewal Credits; Wkshps; *cr:* Rural Sch Teacher Mc Pherson Cty 1944-46, 1951-52, 1955-67; 6th Grade Teacher Eureka Elem Sch 1967-; *ai:* City Lib (Trustee 1960-, Secy 1961-78); *home:* 702 11th St Eureka SD 57437

BAUER, CONSTANCE JOAN, English Teacher; *b:* Philadelphia, PA; *ed:* (BSED) Eng, West Chester Univ 1987; Working Towards Masters Admin; *cr:* Eng Teacher Bridgeton HS 1987-; *ai:* Adv Sr Class of 1989, NHS 1988-, Sch Newspaper, Yrbk; Commencement Comm Mem 1988-; NCTE 1989-; NASSP 1988-; NEA 1987-; *office:* Bridgeton HS West Ave Bridgeton NJ 08302

BAUER, DEBORAH NEWMAN, Elementary Librarian; *b:* Greenville, KY; *m:* Lewis; *c:* Robert L., Will S., Sarah K.; *ed:* (BS) Elem Ed, 1977, (MS) Elem Ed/Kndgtn Endorsement, 1980, (Rank I) Sch Media Librarian, 1983 W KY Univ; *cr:* 3rd Grade Teacher Longest Elem 1977-79; Dormitory Dir Western KY Univ 1979-80; 4th-6th Grade Lang Art Teacher 1980-88, Elem Librarian 1988- Hiseville Elem; *ai:* Lib Club Spon; KY Ed Assn 1977-; KY Lib Assn 1988-; *home:* 244 W Hiseville Main St Cave City KY 42127

BAUER, DOUGLAS GEORGE, Science Department Chair; *b:* Englewood, NJ; *m:* Joanne Mc Ginley; *c:* Jennifer, Jody, Ryan, Jaime; *ed:* (BA) Bio, Susquehanna Univ 1968; (MED) Ed, Temple Univ 1970; *cr:* 7th-9th Grade Teacher Neshaminy Jr HS 1968-; *ai:* Var Soccer, Var Girls Bsktbl, Jr Var Boys Bsktbl Coach; Hughes Intern Research Experience Grant Lehigh Univ 1990; *office:*

Neshaminy Jr HS 1200 Langhorne-Newtown Rd Langhorne PA 19047

BAUER, EILEEN M. DOYLE, English/History Teacher; *b:* Bethlehem, PA; *m:* Thomas S. Jr.; *c:* Kristen, Mark; *ed:* (BS) Soc Stud/Scndry Ed, Moravian Coll 1968; Grad Stud Soc Stud; *cr:* His Teacher 1968-76, His/Eng Teacher 1984- Freedom HS; *ai:* Scholastic Scrimmage Club; His Day, Citizen Bee, Model United Nations Adv; PSEA, Bethlehem Ed Assn; Amer Field Service 1968-74; Articles Published; *office:* Freedom HS 3149 Chester Ave Bethlehem PA 18017

BAUER, ELAINE BOYAN, Teacher; *b:* Teaneck, NJ; *m:* Richard G.; *c:* Matthew, Jennifer; *ed:* (BA) Elem Ed/Early Chldhd Ed, Seton Hall Univ 1980; *cr:* 4th Grade Teacher Holy Rosary Sch 1980; 5th Grade Teacher 1980-82, 4th Grade Teacher 1982-85 Our Lady of Mt Carmel Sch; *ai:* Tutoring 8th Grade Stu all Subjects, Tutoring Algebra & Span Frosh HS Stu; NHS 1974-76; Phi Beta Kappa Honor Society 1979-80; Amer Heart Assn 1990; *home:* 29 Notchwood Rd Butler NJ 07405

BAUER, FRIEDERIKE BARBARA, German Teacher; *b:* Hamburg, West Germany; *m:* Geffrey P.; *ed:* (BA) Ger Lang/Lit, Univ of Kiel West Germany 1984; (MA) Ger Lang/Lit, Univ of Pittsburgh 1987; Cert Stud Elem Ed, Lycoming Coll 1990; *cr:* Stu Teacher Univ of Pittsburgh 1985-87; Ger Teacher Montoursville Area HS 1987-; *ai:* Ger Club & Ger Honor Society Club Adv; AATG; Phi Sigma Iota.

BAUER, JAMES FRANCIS, Teacher; *b:* Durand, WI; *m:* Joretta; *c:* Patricia Dela Cruz, Pamela Jensen, James F. Jr., Susan Thompson, Jeffery A.; *ed:* (BS) Ed, Univ of Mary-Hardin Baylor 1984; *cr:* Teacher Florence Jr HS 1984-; *ai:* Spon Calculator Applications & Life/Earth Sci; Univ Interscholastic League Competition; TCTA 1984-; TESTA 1988-; NESTA 1988-; *home:* 2404 Custer Cir Killeen TX 76543

BAUER, JOYCE MARIE, 1st Grade Teacher; *b:* Des Moines, IA; *m:* Lowell D.; *c:* Zachary, Whitney; *ed:* (BA) Elem Ed, Central Coll 1971; *cr:* 1st Grade Teacher Monroe Elem Sch 1971-; *ai:* Bldg Comm; NEA; ISEA; Monroe Ed Assn; *office:* Monroe Elem Sch 400 N Jasper Monroe IA 50170

BAUER, KARLENE HUMPHREY, Biology Teacher; *b:* Salt Lake City, UT; *m:* Joel P.; *c:* Brad L., Keldon J., Barry T.; *ed:* (BS) Composite Biological Sci, SUSC 1973; Grad Stu Univ of UT; *cr:* General Sci Teacher Butler Jr HS/Mid Sch 1973-79; Bio Teacher Jordan HS 1979-; *ai:* Sci Bowl & Asst Gymnastics Coach; Sr Class Comm; Sci Fair Adv; UT Sci Teachers Assn Scndry Rep 1986-89; Alpha Delta Kappa 1986-; JEA, UEA, NEA 1973-; Latter Day Saints Church Lifetime; BSA Merit Badge Cnslr 1973-; Helped Write Sch, Dist, St Level Curr; Sch & Dist Teacher of Yr; *office:* Jordan HS 9351 S State St Sandy UT 84070

BAUER, LAURIE KOENIG, Science Educator; *b:* Mohall, ND; *m:* Cary Mc Ateer; *c:* J. D., Matthew; *ed:* (BS) Zoology, TX A&M Univ 1975; (MS) Sci Ed, Univ of S MS 1989; Doctoral Stu Sci Ed, Univ of S MS; *cr:* Educator C E Ellison HS 1978-80, Crosby HS 1982-84; Dept Head Stroman HS 1984-88; Educator Oak Grove HS 1988-; *ai:* Region I Sci Fair Cty Dir; Regional & St Sci Fair SRC Comm; ISEF Advisory Bd; Public Relations Chairperson; Drill Team, Sci Club, Chrldr Spon; Dept Head; Soc Comm Chm; Local Sci Fair Coord; NSTA Mem 1975-; MS Teacher Assn, SE Regional Chem Teachers Assn Pres 1990; Golden Cresent Society Engineering Society Exec Comm 1984, Star Teacher 1984; AAPT Reg Dir 1985; Amer ACA Adv Sci Mem 1975-; MS Assn Educators Pres 1988-; Presidential Awd Excl in Sci Teaching 1988; Teacher of Yr 1988; Gifted & Talented Ed Grant 1988; Apple-Time Share Finalist 1988; Sci Teacher Article 1990; Int Sci & Engineering Fair Advisory Bd 1989-; USM Fellowship 1990; Outstanding Young Women of America Awds 1979, 1981; *office:* Oak Grove HS Rt 4 Box 1121 Hattiesburg MS 39402

BAUGH, RICHARD ALLEN, Mathematics/Reading Teacher; *b:* Jeannette, PA; *m:* Vanessa Solomon; *c:* Maria E., Timothy A.; *ed:* (BS) Elem Ed, Edinboro St Coll 1975; Millersvale St, Penn St, Univ of Dayton Tactics for Critical Thinking; *cr:* 3rd Grade Teacher 1976-78, 7th/8th Grade Rdng Teacher 1979-81, 6th Grade Math Teacher 1982-88, 6th Grade Rdng/Math Teacher 1989- Penn-Trafford Sch Dist; *ai:* Coaching Bsktbl, Asst Var Girls HS Sftbl, Boys & Girls Jr HS Bsktbl Coach; Penn-Trafford Ed Assn Treas 1988-; PSEA, NEA 1985-; Penn Borough Cncl (Councilman, Recreation Prgm); Iota Sigma Kappa 1973-; Penn-Trafford Sch Dist Pride Teaching Excl Awd; *office:* Penn Mid Sch Claridge PA 15623

BAUGHMAN, HARRY HILL, Air Force Junior ROTC Instr; *b:* Stanford, KY; *m:* Karen Ann O Callaghan; *c:* Harry Hill Jr., Dale M. Baughman Roberts; *ed:* (BS) Bus Admin, Univ KY 1956; (MS) Personnel Management, Troy St Univ 1980; Air Force Squadron Officers Sch; Air Force Personnel Officer Course; Air Force Command & Staff Coll; Air Force Personnel Staff Officers Course; *cr:* Pilot Trainee/Radar Control/Personnel Officer Air Force 1957-68; Asst Prof Air Sci MS St Univ 1968-71; Personnel Dir Air Force 1971-74; Ed Services Officer Air Force Air Univ 1974-78; Air Force JROTC Instr Ballard HS 1980-; *ai:* Faculty Advisory Comm; Air Force Assn 1980-; Retired Officers Assn 1978-; Air Force ROTC Outstanding Instr 1981-82; *office:* Ballard HS 6000 Brownsboro Rd Louisville KY 40222

BAUGUS, SHARON PHARIS, 5th Grade Teacher; *b:* Alexandria, LA; *m:* William Arthur; *c:* Will, Valerie; *ed:* (BA) Elem Ed, Mc Neese St Univ 1974; *cr:* 5th-7th Grade Teacher Cameron Elem 1975-78; 4th-6th Grade Teacher Corteret Cty Bd of Ed 1980-; *ai:* Asst Girls Vlybl Coach; Grade Team Leader; Teacher Asst Team; Systems Leadership Team Sub-Comm; NEA, NCAE 1980-89; NC Cncl Teachers of Math 1988-; Little League Secy 1989-; Cert Cty Gifted and Talented Teacher Prgm.

BAUM, SUSAN DIANE, Guidance Coordinator; *b:* Baltimore, MD; *c:* Allison, Meredith; *ed:* (BA) Psych, 1970, (MED) Guidance/Counseling, 1971 Amer Univ; (PHD) Measurement/ Statistics, Univ of MD 1982; *cr:* Math/Algebra Teacher Prince Georges Cty 1971-77; Math/Algebra/Cmptr Teacher 1983-87, Guidance Cnslr 1987- Palm Beach Cty; *ai:* Book Store Spon; MENSA 1990.

BAUMAN, ALBERT O., Math Teacher/Department Chm; *b:* Reeder, ND; *m:* Susan A.; *c:* Michael, Thomas; *ed:* (BS) Math/ Phy Ed/Soc, Dickinson St Coll 1959; Math Grad Stud; *cr:* Teacher Hettinger HS 1959-60, Washburn HS 1960-66, Bottineau HS 1967-71, Little Falls HS 1972-; *ai:* Math Team Coach; Math Club Supvr; Asst Ftbl; MEA, NCTM, MCTM Dist Dir; Lions Bd Mem; MN Coaches Assn; *office:* Little Falls Cmmty HS 1001 5th Ave SE Little Falls MN 56345

BAUMAN, JOAN LOU CLYMER, 3rd Grade Teacher; *b:* Bluffton, OH; *c:* Michael, Maureen Noe, Calvin; *ed:* (BS) Ed, Bluffton Coll 1954; (MA) Counseling, Univ of Dayton 1990; *cr:* Teacher Cleveland Public Schls 1954-58, Cory-Rawson Public Sch 1973-; *ai:* Bluffton Coll Womans Cncl Pres/VP; First Mennonite Church Bd; First Mennonite Church Choir; Amer Womans Club 1970-73; Bluffton Cmmty Hosp Trustee 1980-86; AFS (Cory-Rawson Chapter Pres 1983-84/Northwest OH Dist Rep 1986-87); *office:* Cory-Rawson Elem Sch 220 S Main Rawson OH 45881

BAUMAN, RONALD E., Art Teacher; *b:* Hamilton, OH; *m:* Judy E. Monsey; *ed:* (BA) Art Ed, 1973, (MS) Admin, 1980 Miami; US Army NCO Trng Ft Knox, Officer Trng Sch; Teacher Hamilton Elem Schls 1973-74, Harding Jr HS 1974-80, Hamilton HS 1980-; *ai:* Harding Jr HS Head Coach Ftbl 1974-80, Track 1974-80; HCTA, NEA, OH Ed Assn; *office:* Hamilton HS 1165 Eaton Ave Hamilton OH 45013

BAUMANN, MAROLYN DOROTHY (COLNESS), Second Grade Teacher; *b:* Minneapolis, MN; *m:* Philip H.; *c:* Robert, Alan; *ed:* (BS) Kndgtn/Primary/Elem, Winona St Univ 1957; Apple Cmptr; Behavior Disorder Trng Bloomington Sch Dist; *cr:* 1st Grade Teacher St Louis Park 1957-59; Kndgtn Teacher Valley Kndgtn 1961-66 2nd Grade Teacher Cedar Elem 1972-; Behavior Disorder Consultant Bloomington MN 1966-67; *ai:* Soc Stud DSC Elem Rep K-3; (MFT) 1972-; Lions 1972- Pres 1975/1985/1990; Cub Scouts Den Mother/Den Mother Coach 1966-72; Lions Intnl Youth Camp Cnslr/Co-Founder 1982-89 Intnl Pres Awd 1990; Curr Rep; *office:* Cedar Elem Sch Cedar Dr Cedar MN 55011

BAUMBACH, DAVID E., Humanities Teacher; *b:* Parkersburg, WV; *ed:* (BS) Elem Ed, 1967, (MED) Elem Ed, 1972 Indiana Univ of PA; Aeneid Inst Miami Univ 1986; PA Writing Inst Univ of Pittsburgh 1987; *cr:* 5th/6th Grade Teacher Sheraden Elem 1967-74; 1st/5th Grade Teacher of Gifted Carmalt Elem 1974-86; Part Time Professor Miami Univ 1989; 4th/5th Grade Teacher of Gifted Woolslair Elem Gifted Center 1986-; *ai:* Instructional Cabinet; Elem Teachers of Classics Pres 1986-88; PA Assn for Gifted Ed 1974-, Teacher of Yr Finalist 1986; AFT 1969-; Amer Classical League, Vergilian Society 1986-; Natl Endowment for Hum Fellowship 1986; Natl Sci Fnd Fellowship; Pittsburgh Fund for Arts Ed Grants 1988-89; Articles Published; *office:* Woolslair Elem Gifted Center 501 40th at Liberty Pittsburgh PA 15224

BAUMEL, ABRAHAM, Principal; *b:* Zloczow, Poland; *m:* Betty Fogel; *c:* Judith Baumel Ghitelman, Ellis, Sara Baumel Markowitz; *ed:* (BS) Physics, CCNY 1949; (MS) Guidance, City Univ 1954; (MS) Physics, Manhattan 1959; Grad Work Physics Columbia Univ, Fordham, NY Univ, Hunter Coll; Undergrad Work NC St Univ Raleigh; *cr:* Teacher Morris HS 1950-53, Jr HS 52 1953-57, Bronx HS of Sci 1957-67; Phys Sci Chm Stuyvesant HS 1967-77; Prin New Dorp HS 1977-83; Prin Stuyvesant HS 1983; *ai:* AAPT, Chem Society, Physics Society; Assn of Phys Sci (Chm, Pres) 1977-79; NAASP, ASCD, NY City HS Prin Assn; Bnai Brith; Citizens Union; Natl Geographic Museum of Natural History; Articles Published; NSF Grants Fellowship Philosophy NEH; *office:* Stuyvesant HS 345 E 15th St New York NY 10003

BAUMER, PATRICK A., 5th/6th Grade Science Teacher; *b:* St Marys, OH; *m:* Sharon Kruse; *c:* Benjamin, Janel; *ed:* (BS) Elem Ed, Miami Univ Oxford 1980; (MS) Educl Admin, Univ of Dayton 1983; *cr:* 3rd/4th Grade Teacher Russia Local Schls 1980-85; 5th/ 6th Grade Teacher Minster Local Schls 1985-; *ai:* Jr HS Girls Bsktbl Coach; 5th Grade Five-Alive Adv; NEA, OH Ed Assn 1980-; *home:* 5230 Wuebker Rd Minster OH 45865

BAUMGARTNER, BRENDA B. HURD, Kindergarten Teacher; *b:* Warsaw, IN; *m:* Joe A.; *c:* Blair, Myra, Jeffrey; *ed:* (BS) Elem Ed Early Chldhd, Ball St 1974; (MS) Elem Ed, IN Univ 1981; *cr:* 4th Grade Teacher Union Cmmty Sch Corp 1974-75; Kndgtn Teacher Noblesville Cmmty Schls 1975-79; 2nd Grade Teacher 1979-81; Kndgtn Teacher 1981- Wa-Nee Cmmty Schls; *ai:* Kappa Kappa Kappa (Sec 1980/Treas 1985) *home:* 300 N Hartman Nappanee IN 46550

BAUMNER, ELEANOR DEININGER, 6th Grade Teacher; *b:* Abington, PA; *m:* William L. III; *c:* William I. IV, Drew; *ed:* (BS) Elem Ed, Gordon Coll 1962; Spec Ed, Temple Univ 1963-64; *cr:* Teacher East Kingston NH 1967-69; Spec Ed Teacher/Summer Camp Dir for Handicapped Owls Head 1975-78; Cooking/Craft Instr Channel 22 TV 1978-80; Elem Ed Teacher Keswick Chrstn Sch 1982-; *ai:* Newtown Garden Club Pres 1972-75; E Kingston Lib Bd Mem 1970-75; Cmnty Concerts Bd Mem 1975-78; Cub-Scout Leader 1970-75; Pen-Bay Hospital Auxilary Dir 1975-78; Fair/Blind Assn Fair Dir 1972-75; Cntry Dilettantes Dir, Fund Raiser 1972-75; Outstanding Educator Teacher of Yr 1986; *office:* Keswick Chrstn Sch 10101 54th Ave N Saint Petersburg FL 33708

BAUR, JAMES CHRISTOPHER, Theology Teacher; *b:* Saint Louis, MO; *ed:* (BA) Theology, Coll of St Thomas 1979; Pontifical Univ of St Thomas; St Louis Univ; *cr:* Theology Teacher St Elizabeth Acad 1983-; *ai:* Moderator Mission Club St Elizabeth; Moderator Spirit Club St Elizabeth; Rosary Group St Elizabeth; Soccer Coach; Mem Philosophy Comm, Study Skills Tutor; Knights of Columbus; Catholic Forum of St Louis; Book Published-Morality-A Study of Chrstn Joy & Happiness; *office:* Saint Elizabeth Acad Schl 3401 Arsenal Saint Louis MO 63118

BAUSTIAN, BRADLEY KEVIN, 4th Grade Homeroom/1-5 Phys Ed; *b:* Staples, MN; *M:* Debra R. Jameson; *c:* Katie R., Meagan L.; *ed:* (BS) Elem Ed, Univ of MN 1981; *cr:* Elem Teacher Finlayson Elem 1981-; *ai:* JV Bsktbl; Kappa Delta Phi Mem 1980-81; MN Fed of Teachers Mem 1981-; Sandstone Volunteer Fire Dept Mem 1983-; United Church of Christ Comm Chm 1989-.

BAUTISTA, ADA LACANGLACANG, Sixth Grade Math Teacher; *b:* Makati, Philippines; *m:* Christopher Canonigo; *c:* Alden, Monzell, Leslie, Lawrence; *ed:* (BSED) Elem Ed, Natl Teachers Coll 1970; Grad Stud Univ of GU 1978-81; Part-Time Nursing Stu, Univ of GU 1986; *cr:* Teacher Harmon Loop Elem Sch 1976-81, Andersen Elem Sch 1981-82, Dededo Mid Sch 1982-; *ai:* Promotion & Retention Comm Mem Dededo Mid Sch; GU Fed of Teachers Mem 1976-; Society of Filipino Amer Teachers Mem 1987-88; Saturday Scholar Prgm Teacher Volunteer 1990; *home:* 60 Dona Ln Dededo GU 96912

BAUTZ, WILLIAM F., Fifth Grade Teacher; *b:* Buffalo, NY; *m:* Judy; *ed:* (BA) Religion, Houghton Coll 1967; (MA) Liberal Stud, St Univ of NY Stony Brook 1972; Grad Stud; *cr:* Teacher Mt Sinai 1971-; *ai:* Sci Mentor; Grants-mid East Suffolk Teachers Center; *office:* Mount Sinai Elem Sch Rt 25A Mount Sinai NY 11766

BAVERY, WILLIAM FLOYD, Math and Science Teacher; *b:* Basco, IL; *m:* Kathryn J. Brackensick; *c:* Floyd, Suerrette; *ed:* (BS) Math, Eastern IL Univ 1965; (MCS) Math, Chem, 1969, (MS) Ed Admin, 1971 Univ of MS; Western IL Univ; Eastern IL Univ; MS Coll; *cr:* Teacher Rova Schls 1965-66; Stronghurst Schls 1966-; Coach Burlington HS 1989-; *ai:* Coached Boys Track Bsktbl Ftbl & Girls Bsktbl & Stu Cncl Adv; Varsity Club Spon; IL Ftbl Coaches Assn; IA Ftbl Coaches Assn; NCTM; IEA/NEA; A J Fort Recreation Co Dir/Treas 1980-; Natl Sci Fndtn Fellowship 1967-69; IL HS Ftbl Coaches Hall of Fame 1989; *home:* RR 1 Stronghurst IL 61480

BAXA, BARBARA CRUMRINE, Third Grade Teacher; *b:* Buckhannon, WV; *m:* David L.; *c:* Caraline, Timmy J.; *ed:* (MS) Elem Ed, WV Weselyan 1988; *cr:* 5th-6th Teacher Greenbrier Elem 1975-77; 1st-3rd Grade Teacher Century Elem 1978-79; Kndgtn Teacher Valley Head/Pickens 1980-81, Pickens 1982-83; 6th Grade Teacher Pickens 1983-84; 3rd/6th Grade Teacher Coalton 1985-; *ai:* WVEA 1990:

BAXTER, HELMA CORIECE, 2nd Grade Teacher; *b:* Greeneville, TN; *ed:* (BS) Elem Ed, Tusculum Coll 1964; East TN St; *cr:* Teacher/Prin New Bethel 1954-56; Primary Teacher Brookside 1956-57; Mosheim Elem 1957-77; De Busk Elem 1977-88; Sunnyside Elem 1988-89; Doak Elem 1989-; *ai:* Secy Cty-Wide 2nd Grade Level; NEA 1955-; TEA 1955-; Greene Cty Ed Assn 1955-; Upper East TN Ed Coop 1980-; Order of Eastern Star 223 1951-; Young Farmers/Homemakers (Alumni 1970-, Pres 1988); New Bethel Cumberland Presbyn Church Elder, Treas 1985-; Greene Cty Primary Teacher of Yr; Awd Nom 1985 Cert; *office:* Doak Elem Sch Tusculum Station Greeneville TN 37743

BAXTER, LINDA L., English Teacher; *b:* Terre Haute, IN; *c:* Rebecca S.; *ed:* (BS) US His/Sociology, 1971, (MS) Scndry Ed, 1975 IN St Univ; Rdng Certificate; *cr:* Teacher Honey Creek Jr HS 1971-; *ai:* Coach Eng Hoosier Academic Team; Team Leader 8th Grade; Lioness Secy 1989-; *office:* Honey Creek Jr HS 6215 Honey Creek Rd Terre Haute IN 47802

BAXTER, RICHARD KEITH, Science Teacher/Sci Dept Chm; *b:* Klamath Falls, OR; *c:* Michele, Michael; *ed:* (BS) Phys Ed, 1965, (MED) Ed, 1969 OR St Univ; CA St Univ Hayward, San Diego St Univ, Univ MD; *cr:* Elem Sch/Phys Ed Teacher Fremont Unified Sch Dist 1969-71; 7th/8th Grade Sci/Phys Ed Teacher Heilbronn Elem & Mid Sch 1971-73; 9th-12th Grade Sci Teacher Heidelberg HS 1973-; *ai:* Sci Dept Chm; Tennis Coach; NEA, Overseas Ed Assn 1971-; NSTA 1980-; European Sci Teachers Assn Phys Sci Coord 1986-89; US Prof Tennis Assn 1985-; Walldorf Astoria Tennis Club Head Tennis Prof 1981-; European Sci Teachers Assn Founding Mem; Nominee Presidential Awd Excl Sci Teaching; *office:* Heidelberg Amer HS Mark Twain Strasse 1 APO New York NY 09102

BAXTER, RICHARD LLEWELLYN, English Teacher; *b:* Milwaukee, WI; *m:* Jeanne Connor; *c:* Brian C., Ned L.; *ed:* (BS) Bus/Ec, Univ of Miami 1956; (MA) Eng/Admin, Northwestern Univ 1966; Grad Work Northwestern Univ; *cr:* Eng/Soc Stud Teacher Howard Jr HS 1962-65; Eng Teacher Deerfield HS 1965-; *ai:* Spon Stu Cncl; Swimming Coach; Curr & Writing Comm; Comm for Interdistrict Communications; NCTE, ASCD; *home:* 1335 Pinehurst Dr Glenview IL 60025

BAXTER, ROBERT MARTI, Director of Choral Activities; *b:* Williston Park, NY; *m:* Eva M.; *c:* Melinda Sparacio, Robert M., Richard M., Russell M., Roger M.; *ed:* (BM) Trumpet, Oberlin Conservatory 1952; (MA) Music Ed, NY Univ 1959; (PHD) Musicology, Cath Univ 1970; *cr:* Choral Dir Marathon Cntrl Sch 1956-59, Washington-Lee HS 1960-78; Dir of Choral Act Yorktown HS 1978-, Williamsburg Intermediate 1978-; *ai:* Chorus Master Yorktown HS Musicals; Music Honor Society Tri-M Spon; VA Choral Dir Assn Pres 1988-; Amer Choral Dir Assn Pres 1982-84; Scndry Teachers Cncl on Instruction Chm 1971-72; St Advisory Cncl for Gifted Mem 1985-88; Nom Phoebe Apperson Hearst Outstanding Educator 1986; Mem Robert Shaw Chamber Chorale 1989; *home:* 7712 Fisher Dr Falls Church VA 22043

BAY, DAVID L., Fifth Grade Teacher; *b:* Norton, VA; *m:* Carol F. Rooker; *c:* Kristi, Patrick; *ed:* (BA) Elem Ed, Glenville St Coll 1975; WV Coll of Grad Studs; *cr:* 3rd Grade Teacher Glade Elem 1975-78; 3rd Grade Teacher 1978-83, 5th Grade Teacher 1983- Cherry River Elem; *ai:* WV Ed Assn; *home:* PO Box 696 Craigsville WV 26205

BAYLESS, BEVERLY BLUE, Fourth Grade Teacher; *b:* Peoria, IL; *m:* Larry; *c:* Christopher, Curt; *ed:* (BS) Elem Ed, IL St Univ Normal 1958; *cr:* 4th Grade Teacher Harrison Sch 1958-60; Head Start Teacher Burbank IL 1966-68; 3rd Grade Teacher Nottingham Sch 1969-80; 4th Grade Teacher Maddock Sch 1980-; *ai:* NEA, IEA (Treas 1975-83) 1969-83; AFT 1983-; *office:* Maddock Sch 8258 S Sayre Ave Burbank IL 60459

BAYLESS, CHRISTINE PEZOLDT, 7th/8th English Teacher; *b:* Allentown, PA; *m:* Richard L.; *c:* Susan Robertson, Karen Pennington, Shana Roush, Jennifer Mutter, Jonathon Mutter; *ed:* (BA) Ed, Wittenberg Univ 1963; Grad Stud OH St Univ; *cr:* 4th Grade Teacher Irving Sch 1963-64; 6th Grade Teacher George Washington Sch 1965-66; 7th-8th Grade Teacher Ridgedale 1967-; *ai:* Eng Curr Study Comm; Ridgedale Teachers Assn Pres 1968-69; Cntrl OH Teach Assn; NEA; OH Teachers of Eng & Lang Art; Parents Without Partners Pres 1972-73; Emanuel Luth Church; *office:* Ridgedale Mid Sch 3105 Hillman Ford Rd Morral OH 43337

BAYLOR, NANCY H., Developmental Teacher; *b:* Albany, NY; *m:* Wayne E.; *c:* Stephen, Holly, Susan, Kristen; *ed:* (BA) Elem Ed, Cntrl Coll 1974; *cr:* 5th Grade Teacher 1977-89; Developmental 1st Grade Teacher 1989- Lincoln Elem; *ai:* NEA, KNEA; OEA Rep 1985-88; OHS Booster Club Treas 1989-; Presbyn Westminster Church Elder 1989-; Beta Sigma Phi Pres, Girl of Yr; Spec Friend of Unified Sch Dist #290 1987; *office:* Lincoln Elem Sch 728 N Cedar Ottawa KS 66067

BAYSINGER, RONALD ANTHONY, 6th Grade Teacher; *b:* Tell City, IN; *ed:* (BS) Elem Ed, Univ of Southern IN 1974; (MS) Elem Ed, IN St Univ 1977; Cmptr Trng, Univ of Southern IN 1983-84; *cr:* 6th Grade Teacher MSD of North Posey 1974-; Cmptr Instr Univ of Southern IN 1984-86; *ai:* Dir 6th Grade Musical; Kappa Delta Pi VP 1977-; NEA 1974-; PTA Treas 1974-; Kiwanis VP 1974-84; *home:* 1116 Regency Ct Evansville IN 47710

BAYZA, SAMUEL PAUL, 6th Grade Teacher; *b:* Charleroi, PA; *m:* Rosemarie K. Mazurek; *c:* Crista L., Carrie B., Erin C.; *ed:* (BS) Elem Sci, California Univ of PA 1971; (MA) Elem Ed, WV Univ 1978; *cr:* Classroom Teacher Cameron Elem Sch 1971-; *ai:* WV Ed Assn Building Rep 1971-.

BAZELI, MARILYN WEERTS, 4th Grade Teacher; *b:* Peoria, IL; *m:* Frank P.; *c:* Sara Greene, Susan Greene, Carolyn Greene, Peter; *ed:* (BS) Elem Ed 1971, (MS) Elem Ed, 1979 N IL Univ; (EDD) Instructional Technology N IL Univ 1990; *cr:* Teacher Mundelein Sch Dist 1959-63, Sycamore Sch Dist 1971-; Cmptr Coord North Elem 1985-86; *ai:* Adv Afternoon Sci Scholars Prgm Adv; Sycamore Sch Dist Long Range Technology Planning Comm Mem; Sycamore Interconnections 90 Team Mem; Kappa Delta Pi 1985- Nom Outstanding Ed Awd 1987; Intnl Visual Literacy Assn 1989-; Assn for Ed Comm & Technology 1989-; Sycamore Ed Assn (Public Relations 1981-83, Welfare Comm 1983-86), Grants 1986-89; IVLA Intnl Conference Presenter 1990; *home:* 110 Ilehamwood De Kalb IL 60115

BAZYN, RICHARD W., Physics/Mathematics Teacher; *b:* Belle Plaine, IA; *m:* Elgene Ann Garrels; *c:* Matt, Tim, Laura; *ed:* (BS) Physics, IA St Univ 1973; Grad Stud; *cr:* Physics Teacher Mac Robertson Girls HS 1973-76; Physics/Sci Teacher Olin Schls 1976-78; Physics/Math Teacher Henry Senachwine HS 1978-; *ai:* Stu Cncl & Photo Club Spon; Administrative Bd of Henry United Meth Church Vice Chm 1989-; Nom Presidential Awd of Excl 1984; *home:* RR 1 Box 116 Henry IL 61537

BAZZIE, BEVERLY MC CLUNG, 5th/6th Grade Lang Art Teacher; *b:* Harvey, WV; *m:* Donald Ray; *ed:* (BS) Elem Ed, Concord Coll 1958; Grad Work WV Univ; *cr:* 8th Grade Music Teacher 1958-65, 6th Grade Teacher 1965-89, 5th/6th Grade Lang Art Teacher 1989- Bradley Elem; *ai:* Helping Teacher to Assist Prin; Civic Oration Contest Spon; Concord Coll Alumni 1987-89; Bradley Sch Advisory Cncl 1974-86; Bradley Sch PTO 1958-; Cotton Hill Baptist Church Pianist 1977-; Biography in Outstanding Leaders Elem & Scndry Ed 1976; Notable Amer 1976; Raleigh Cty Teacher of Yr 1981; Finalist WV Teacher of Yr; WV Ed Fund 7 Minigrants Awds 1983-89; Outstanding Elem Educator Merit Awd Finalist 1987, Winner 1988; Raleigh Cty Sch System Excl in Teaching Awd 1988; Excl in Teaching Awd Raleigh Cty Sch System 1988; *home:* PO Box 252 Bradley WV 25818

BEACH, CAROL A. BAKER, Fifth Grade Teacher; *b:* Shelby Cty, OH; *m:* Morton Kennedy; *ed:* (BS) Elem Ed, Bowling Green St Univ 1955; Grad Courses Univ of AZ; *cr:* 4th Grade Teacher Findlay Public Schls 1955-67, Montgomery Cty Schls 1967-70; Substitute Teacher Tucson & Sunnyside Schls 1970-72; 5th Grade Teacher Marana Unified Schls 1972-; *ai:* Spelling Bee Coord; Bear Essentials News Adv; Crisis Response Team; Mentor Teacher; NEA, OH Ed Assn Life 1955-; AZ Ed Assn 1972-; PTO 1955-; Volunteer Worker for Amer Cancer Society, Easter Seals, March of Dimes, Univ of AZ Health Sci Center Cancer Research Prgm Volunteer Prgm; Order of Eastern Stars Eureka Chapter 136 1961-; Master Teacher 1985; Marana Sch Dist Teacher of Yr Ambassador of Excl 1987-88; Stu Teacher Trng Prgms Bowling Green St Univ & Findlay Coll & Wright St Univ & Miami Univ & Univ of AZ; *home:* 6780 E 4th St Tucson AZ 85710

BEACH, MICHELE RAYMONDE, English Department Chair; *b:* Watford Herts, United Kingdom; *ed:* (BA) Eng, Columbia Union Coll 1981; (BA) Eng Ed, 1983, (MA) Eng, 1987 Univ of MD; Diploma Earned Univ of Paris; *cr:* Eng Teacher Osbourn HS 1983-84, Takoma Acad 1984-89; Chairperson Takoma Acad 1989-; *ai:* Sch Newspaper Adv; NCTE, Journalism Ed Assn, Sigma Tau Delta, MD Scholastic Press Advs Assn, ACSD; Natl Museum of Women in Arts Charter Mem; Folger Theatre Volunteer Group; Natl Endowment for Hum Fellowship for Summer Seminar Scndry Teachers Princeton Univ 1990; *home:* 1750 Wilcox Ln Silver Spring MD 20906

BEACHLY, MEREDITH JAN, Life Science Department Head; *b:* Denver, CO; *ed:* (BSE) Elem Ed, Emporia St Univ 1982; *cr:* Sci Teacher Central Mid Sch 1982-; *ai:* 8th Grade Spon 1986; 7th Grade Spon 1990; Yrbk Co-Adv 1987 & 1989-; Track Coach 1983; Swimming Coach Washington HS 1984; *office:* Central Mid Sch 925 Ivandale Kansas City KS 66101

BEAGLE, TERRY ANN (GARRISON), Social Studies Teacher; *b:* Layafette, IN; *m:* Thomas C.; *c:* Debra S. Oslund, Marcia Grandstaff; *ed:* (BA) Soc Stud, Depauw Univ 1962; (MA) Teaching, IN Univ 1975; *cr:* 4th Grade Teacher KS City KS Schls 1962-63; 8th Grade Soc Stud Teacher Greenfield Jr HS-Greenfield Cntrl 1966-67; 5th Grade Soc Stud Teacher Harris Elem-Greenfield Cntrl 1970-73; 6th & 8th Grade Soc Stud Teacher Maxwell Mid Greenfield Cntrl Schls 1973-; *ai:* Natl Geographic Historical Pictorial Map Contest, 8th Grade Party Spon; NCSS; In Cncl Soc Stud; Greenfield CTA; NEA; Amer Red Cross Summer Learn to Swim Prgm Organizer 1980-; Whos Who in Amer Teaching 1990; *office:* Maxwell Mid Sch 102 N Main St Maxwell IN 46154

BEAL, JO ANN, 2nd Grade Teacher; *b:* Lexington, TN; *ed:* (BS) Elem Ed, Univ of TN Martin 1973; (MED) Admin & Supervision, Trevecca Nazarene Coll 1989; Career Ladder Level III, St of TN 1985; *cr:* 2nd Grade Teacher Paul G Caywood Sch 1973-; *ai:* Caywood Inservice Comm 1986-; Lexington Ed Assn (Secy 1979-80, Mem 1973-); NEA 1973-; TN Teachers Study Cncl Rep 1985-86; *office:* Paul G Caywood Sch 162 Monroe St Lexington TN 38351

BEAL, LINDA EASTRIDGE, Mathematics/Computer Teacher; *b:* Campbellsville, KY; *m:* James F.; *c:* Hannah L.; *ed:* (BS) Math, Campbellsville Coll 1969; (MA) Math, W KY Univ 1972; Math Ed, Univ of KY, Univ of Louisville; Cmptr Ed, W KY Univ; Several Wkshps; *cr:* Cmptr Teacher Campbellsville Coll 1986; Math/Cmptr Teacher Taylor Cty HS 1969-; Lindsey Wilson Coll 1985-; *ai:* Cmptr Team Coach; Jr & Sr Class Spon; Stu Cncl; Intnl Society for Technology Ed, NEA, KY Ed Assn, Taylor Cty Ed Assn; Taylor Cty Parent/Teacher/Stu Organization, Taylor Cty Academic Boosters Club; Dir Taylor Cty Sci Fair; Minigrant to Setup Desktop Publishing Sch; Math Lessons Published K-8th Math Textbook Series Merrill; *office:* Taylor Cty HS 300 Ingram Ave Campbellsville KY 42718

BEAL, PAMELA LOUISE, Fifth Grade Teacher; *b:* Waterville, ME; *ed:* (BS) Eng, 1969, (MS) Counseling, 1974 Univ of ME Portland; Grad Stud Univ of Pau-Pau France 1973; *cr:* Teacher Seymour HS 1969-71, Gray-New Gloucester HS 1971-74, Mahoney Mid Sch 1974-88, Howard C Reiche Cmmty Sch 1989-; *ai:* Homework Helpers Comm Mem; Informational Newsletter Staff; NEA 1969-; ME Teachers Assn 1971-; Portland Teachers Assn 1989-; Univ of ME (Bd of Dir 1985-) Block M 1984; Portland Club Univ of ME Alumnae Pres 1982-84; Alliance Francaise Correspondence Secy 1987-89; Recipient of Grant for Ec Ed, Ec Ed Advanced Class; *office:* Howard C. Reiche Cmmty Sch 166 Brackett St Portland ME 04102

BEAL, WILLIE ROY, 9th-12th Grade US His Teacher; *b:* Dallas, TX; *m:* Charolette Lynn Brown; *c:* Stefani L., Cheri L.; *ed:* (BS) His/Phys Ed, Bishop Coll 1976; (MS) Admin Ed, Prairie View A&M Univ 1984; *cr:* Teacher/Coach Waxahachie Ind Sch Dist 1976-83, Dallas Ind Sch Dist 1983-; *ai:* Head Girls Bsktbl Coach & Teacher; Advisory Comm; TX HS Coaches Assn 1976-; TX Assn Bsktbl Coaches 1984-; Dallas Coaches Assn 1984-, Coach of Yr 1988; *office:* Franklin D Roosevelt Sch 525 Bonnie View Rd Dallas TX 75203

BEALER, JONATHAN MILES, Science Department Chair; *b:* San Jose, CA; *m:* Virginia Anderson Caretto; *c:* Ian, Glynis; *ed:* (BA) Zoology, Univ of CA Santa Barbara 1969; (MNS) Natural Sci, AZ St Univ 1979; NSF Honors Wkshp Bioethics & Human Genetics; *cr:* Teacher Sierra Vista Jr HS 1971-73, Buena HS 1973-; *ai:* HS Cmptr Coord; MED-START Club Spon; NABT 1969-; NEA, AEA, SVCTA (Spokesperson 1971-) 1980; NSTA 1982-; Natl Audubon (Prof Naturalist 1973-) 1983; Huachucha Audubon Soc Pres 1973-, 1978; AZ Teacher of Yr Ambassador of Excl; Outstanding Bio Teacher; Golden Bell Awd AZ Sch Bd Assn; Article Published; Journal of Research in Sci & Math Teaching; *office:* Buena HS 3555 Fry Blvd Sierra Vista AZ 85635

BEALL, REBECCA BROWN, Special Education Teacher; *b:* Poplar Bluff, MO; *m:* Phillip Anderson; *c:* James A.; *ed:* (BSE) Elem Ed, 1981, (MSE) Spec Ed/Learning Disabilities, 1982 Univ of Cntrl AR; *cr:* Spec Ed Teacher Osceola HS 1982-83, Sallie Humble Elem 1983-84; 4th Grade Teacher 1984-89, Spec Ed Teacher 1989- Osceola W Elem; *ai:* Delta Kappa Gamma 1989-; Jr Auxilary 1988-; Amer Red Cross Instr 1982-; *home:* 1515 W Semmes Osceola AR 72370

BEALLES, MARY JO WOLFGONG, Fourth Grade Teacher; *b:* Butler, PA; *c:* Alexander; *cr:* 6th Grade Teacher Butler Area Sch Dist 1962; 5th Grade Teacher Elderton Area Sch Dist 1962-63; 6th Grade Teacher Baden-Economy Schls 1963-65; 4th Grade Teacher Butler Area Schls 1969-; *ai:* Long Range Sch Planning Comm; PSEA, NEA, BEA 1969-; Butler Cty Symphony Bd Mem 1984-86; Daughters of Amer Revolution 1969-; AAUW 1970-88; *office:* Center Township Sch 950 Mercer Rd Butler PA 16001

BEALS, DALLAS LAYNE, Art Teacher/Counselor; *b:* Silesia, MT; *m:* Shirley M. Sielinsky; *c:* Valerie Neuschwander, Steve; *ed:* (BS) Industrial Art/Art, MT St Univ 1967; (MS) Guidance/Counseling, N MT Coll 1979; *cr:* Industrial Art/Art Teacher Browning HS 1967-70; Industrial Art/Auto Mechanic Teacher Broadview HS 1970-79; Cnslr/Art Teacher Plains HS 1979; *ai:* Sr Adv; MT Assn Counseling & Dev; Plains Lions Pres 1986-87; Ponemah Masonic Lodge #63 Master 1984-85; Algeria Shrine; Eastern Star Ideal Worthy Patron 1985-86; *home:* PO Box 290 Plains MT 59859

BEAM, GAY OSBURN, English Teacher; *b:* El Dorado, AR; *ed:* (BSE) Eng/Speech, Univ of AR 1970; (MLA) Liberal Arts, S Meth Univ 1989; *cr:* Eng Teacher Springdale HS 1971-77, North Garland HS 1977-; *ai:* Literary Club Spon; Phi Delta Kappa; *office:* North Garland HS 2109 Buckingham Garland TX 75042

BEAMAN, SUSAN MARIE, 8th Grade Math/Soc St Teacher; *b:* Kinston, NC; *ed:* (BS) Elem Ed, 1970, (MA) Mid Grades Ed, 1986 East Carolina Univ; *cr:* 4th Grade Teacher 1970-84, 6th Grade Teacher 1984-85 West Greene Sch; 7th-8th Grade Teacher Greene Cntrl Jr HS 1985-; *ai:* Team Leader 1988-89; Dist Leadership Cncl 1989-; Math Counts Coach 1985-; NCAE (Secy, Treas); Delta Kappa Gamma Song Leader; Friendship FWB Church (organist 1970-, Choir Leader 1980-, Treas 1985-); Outstanding Elem Math Teacher of Yr 1984-85; Teacher of Yr GCJH 1986-87; *home:* Rt 1 Box 322A Farmville NC 27828

BEAMISH, SHARON K., Yearbook Advisor; *b:* Midland, MI; *m:* Neil; *c:* Cory, Chris, Jennifer; *cr:* Lib Aide 1983-85; Placement Coord 1985-89; *ai:* Yrbk, SADD, Newspaper, Jr Class Adv; *office:* Coleman HS PO Box W Coleman MI 48618

BEAMON, CLAUDIA GRANTHAM, Third Grade Teacher; *b:* Wilson, NC; *c:* C. Michelle, Sharon N.; *ed:* (BS) Early Chldhd, Atlantic Chrstn Coll 1975; *cr:* 3rd Grade Teacher Snow Hill Primary 1976-; *ai:* Chairperson; Sch Leadership Comm; NCEA; Alpha Delta Kappa; *office:* Snow Hill Primary Sch 502 SE 2nd St Snow Hill NC 28580

BEAMS, BOBBY GENE, Social Studies Teacher; *b:* Louisville, KY; *m:* Barbara Ann Wright; *c:* Crystal J., Baptista A.; *ed:* (BS) Soc Sci Area, Campbellsville Coll & W KY Univ 1969-74; *cr:* Teacher Memorial Elem Sch 1969-87, Hart Cty HS 1988-; *ai:* Jr HS Beta Club Spon; Jr HS Girls Bsktbl Coach; Teacher Assn Pres 1973-74; Brotherhood Pres 1990-; Mason Sr Warder 1990-; Cmmty Ed Comm Mem 1987; *office:* Hart County HS Hwy 31-E Munfordville KY 42746

BEAN, ATHENA HAFNER, Counselor; *b:* Belleville, IL; *m:* Fred; *c:* Chris, Jackson; *ed:* (BS) Latin, Baylor Univ 1970; (MED) Counseling, Tarleton St Univ 1990; *cr:* Teacher United HS 1978-80; Brownwood HS 1980-89; Cnslr Cooperative Alternative Prgm HS 1989-; *ai:* ATPE 1985-; TX Assn of Counseling & Dev 1988-; Coleman Cty Literacy Cncl Secy 1989-; Whos Who Among Amer Coll Stus; *home:* 3508 Arrowhead Brownwood TX 76801

BEAN, BONNIE L., 5th Grade Teacher; *b:* Sayre, PA; *ed:* (BS) Elem Ed, Bloomsburg St Coll 1975; *cr:* 1st Grade Teacher 1975-76, Kndgtn Teacher 1976, 3rd Grade Teacher 1977, 6th Grade Teacher 1977-79, 5th Grade Teacher 1979- Athens Area Sch; *ai:* YAD Cheerleading Adv; Head Teacher Lynch Elem Sch; NEA, PA St Ed Assn, Athens Area Ed Assn, PA Sci Teachers Assn; *office:* Athens Area Sch Dist 204 Willow Athens PA 18810

BEAN, DIETRA SEARS, 2nd Grade Teacher; *b:* Bedford, IN; *m:* Tony E.; *c:* Andrew, Alexander; *ed:* (BS) Elem Ed, Western KY Univ 1979; (MS) Elem Ed, IN Univ 1984; *cr:* Elem Teacher M R Brown Elem Sch 1979-; *ai:* Mem Prgm Improvement Process Chapter 1 Brown Elem; Seymour Ed Assn; Church of Christ Mem; *office:* Margaret R Brown Sch 550 Miller Ln Seymour IN 47274

BEAN, EDNA ELIZABETH, English Teacher; *b:* Petersburg, WV; *m:* William H.; *ed:* (BA) Eng/Lib Sci, Fairmont St Coll 1975; (MA) Rdng, WV Univ 1978; *cr:* Librarian/Rdng Teacher Valley Jr HS 1975-; Rdng Teacher Petersburg HS 1980-82; Eng Teacher Shepherd Coll 1985-89, Petersburg HS 1982-; *ai:* Grant Cty Ed Assn Faculty Rep 1985-; Delta Kappa Gamma Legislative Chairperson 1984-; WV Ed Assn Mem 1976-; Article Published; Ed Travel Grant; WV Teachers Acad Grant; *office:* Petersburg HS Jefferson St Petersburg WV 26847

BEAN, LINDA DACUS, Fifth Grade Teacher; *b:* Augusta, GA; *m:* Earlston E. Sr.; *c:* Shemeicka, Earlston E. Jr.; *ed:* (BA) Elem Ed, Benedict Coll 1971; (MA) Elem Ed, S Caroline St 1977; Data Collector Richmond Cty Sch System; *cr:* 4th Grade Teacher Barton Chapel Elem; 2nd Grade Teacher Cntrl Elem; 6th Grade Teacher Blythe Elem; 5th Grade Teacher Bayvale Elem; *ai:* 5th Grade Dept Chairperson; GA Assn of Ed, NEA, Richmond Cty Assn of Educators; Delta Sigma Theta; Richmond Ctt Teachers Credit Union Bd of Dir 1987-; Young Women Club VP 1989-; Teacher of Yr 1987-88; *home:* 2720 Wicklow Dr Augusta GA 30909

BEAN, PAMELA OWENS, Asst Phys Ed Dept Chair; *b:* Chicago, IL; *c:* Toni L., Cara Stockton; *ed:* (BA) Ed/Phys Ed, Chicago St Univ 1972; (MA) Urban Stud, Roosevelt Univ 1984; Drug Free Sch Prgm; Impact Drug Intervention Prgm St Elizabeth Hospital; Admin Trng in Ed; *cr:* Phys Ed/Instr Senn Metropolitan Acad 1976-; Phys Ed/Libarian John Hay Elem Sch 1974-76; *ai:* Coach of Boys Gymnastics Team, Spon of African Amer Dancer 1987-, Prom Comm 1985, 1988, Afro Amer Club 1983-88; Inst for Ed & Athletics 1987-; Drug Free Sch Team Leader 1989-; Asst Dept Chm Prin Selection 1986-; Mem of Prof Problems Comm 1986-88; Mem of Principals Prof Advisory Comm 1989-; Stu Body Woman of Yr 1989; *office:* Senn Metropolitan Acad 5900 N Glenwood Chicago IL 60660

BEAN, SUSAN MONTGOMERY, English Teacher; *b:* Knoxville, TN; *ed:* (BS) Eng, E TN St Univ 1971; (MED) Eng, 1980, (EDS) Eng, 1987 GA St Univ; *cr:* 7th Grade Eng Teacher Fountain Jr HS 1972-76; 8th Grade Eng Teacher Babb Jr HS 1976-77; 10th-12th Grade Eng Teacher N Clayton HS 1977-79, Riverdale HS 1979-; *ai:* AFT 1979-81; NEA 1982-; GA Assn of Educators (St Convention Delegate 1989-) 1982-, Make it Happen Awd 1988, Outstanding Contribution to Ed Process Awd 1989; Clayton Cty Ed Assn (Exec Bd, Poly Lobbyist 1989-, Secy 1989, Mem) 1982-, Outstanding Leadership Awd 1987-88; Natl Organization for Women 1979-; GA Womens Poly Caucus, Cobb Cty Womens Poly Caucus 1980-; Kappa Delta Pi Mem 1987-; *home:* 4247 Laurel Brook Dr Smyrna GA 30082

BEAR, JANICE GILSON, English IV Teacher; *b:* Crockett, TX; *m:* John Roland; *c:* Elizabeth S., John R.; *ed:* (BAT) Speech/Radio/TV, Sam Houston St Univ 1973; Counseling, Sam Houston St Univ 1990; *cr:* Soc Worker Dept Human Services 1973-80; Teacher Latexo Ind Sch Dist 1980-81, Crockett Ind Sch Dist 1981-; *ai:* Sr Class & Yrbk Spon; HS Gifted/Talented Prgms Coord; Academic Screening Comm; Eng Dept Chm; TCTA 1985-; Eastern Star, Pythian Sisters, Beta Sigma Phi; Teacher of Yr 1989-; *office:* Crockett HS PO Box 481 Loop 304 W Crockett TX 75835

BEARD, DAVID C., Civics Teacher; *b:* Mt Savage, MD; *m:* Beverly Cuffley; *c:* Michael, Kelley G. Smith; *ed:* (BS) Soc Stud/His Frostburg St Univ 1965; APC MD Dept of Ed; *cr:* Supvr Boys Forestry Camp 1965-69; Teacher S Garrett Sr HS 1969-; *ai:* Soph Class Adv; Garrett Cty Fed of Teachers (VP 1978, Pres 1979); Demorcatic St Cntrl Comm (Chm 1986-, Treas 1974-78); Oakland Optimist Club Past Pres Friend of the Boy Awd 1973, Leadership Awd 1972; Amer Legion Proctor Kildow Post 71; Mt Lake Park Lions Club Bd of Dir; W MD Labor Cncl Mem; Mt Top Civic Center (Bd of Dir, Mem); S Garrett Athletic Assn Mem Citizen of Yr 1986; Garrett Cty Democrat Club Mem; Garrett Cty Bd of Election Supvrs 1982, 1985; Oakland-Mt Lake Park Merit Awd 1984; *home:* Rt 1 Box 136 Swanton MD 21561

BEARD, GAYLE SPRADLING, 8th&11th Grade Engish Teacher; *b:* Bruce, MS; *m:* Byron Dean;; *c:* Caleb, Sarah; *ed:* (BAE) Eng, Univ of MS 1974; Grad Work MS St Univ; *cr:* Eng Teacher Calhoun City Mid Sch 1975-76; 2nd Grade Eng Teacher Charleston MS Schls 1976-79; Eng Teacher West Point MS Municipal Schls 1979-87, Water Valley HS 1987-; *ai:* Jr HS Beta Club Spon; Spelling Bee Coord; MAE, NEA; 1st Meth Church Sunday Sch Teacher; N MS Emmaus Cmmty; Natl Assn Jr Auxilliary; Schlsp MS Heritage Inst 1985 UM; *home:* Rt 3 Box 87B Water Valley MS 38965

BEARD, GWENDOLYN MARX, 6th Grade Teacher; *b:* Moss Point, MS; *m:* Henry Leo; *c:* April, Henry Jr., Daryl, Ashleigh; *ed:* (BS) Elem Ed, Alcorn St Univ 1968; (MS) Elem Ed, Univ of S AL 1978; Prgm for Effective Teaching; MS Teacher Assessment Instruments Trainer; Newspaper in Ed; *cr:* Rdng Teacher Fair Elem 1968-69; Soc Stud Teacher Arlington Elem 1969-70; 6th Grade Sci Teacher Eastlawn Elem 1971-; *ai:* Eastlawn Elem Sci Fair Co-Coord; Univ of S MS Stu Teaching Advisory Comm Chairperson; MS Gulf Coast Comm Coll Bus & Office Technology Advisory Comm Mem; NEA, Pascagoula Assn of Educators; NAN Bus & Prof Women Secy; Zeta Phi Beta Financial Secy; Pascagoula Sch Employees Credit Union Bd of Dir; Singing River Hospital Cholesterol Count Down Teacher Rep; *home:* 4018 Karen St Moss Point MS 39563

BEARD, IRENE LANDWEHR, 4th Grade Teacher; *b:* Orange, NJ; *m:* Richard D.; *c:* Gregory, Donna; *ed:* (BS) General Elem Ed, Glassboro St Coll 1959; *cr:* Teacher a P Morris Sch 1959-61; Teacher Shark River Hills Sch 1968-; *ai:* Neptune Twp Ed Assn Bldg Rep 1978-; NJ Ed Assn 1968-; *office:* Shark River Hills Sch Brighton Ave Neptune NJ 07753

BEARD, JANIS MILLER, Second Grade Teacher; *b:* Waco, TX; *m:* David O.; *c:* Colleen, Lilliard Travis, Brady Lilliard; *ed:* (BS) Ed/Eng, Univ of N TX 1972; Advanced Academic Trng Ed; Grad Course Supervising Stu Teachers, Baylor Univ; *cr:* 2nd Grade Teacher 1972-73, 3rd Grade Teacher 1973-74, 2nd Grade Teacher 1974- Bruceville-Eddy; *ai:* Eng as Second Lang Textbook Comm Chm; UIL Co-Dir; Co-Dir & Co-Producer PTA Prgms; Cntrl Chrstn Church Deaconess 1990-; Cntrl Chrstn Church Outreach Comm; Midway Little League Team Mem; Toornburg Sch of Dance Backstage Mom; *home:* 1005 Tillamook Hewitt TX 76643

BEARD, JO ANN, Business Teacher; *b:* Grapevine, TX; *ed:* (BS) Bus Admin, Union Univ 1974; (MS) Elem Ed, Univ of TN Martin 1978; *cr:* 4th Grade Teacher Briarwood 1974; HS Teacher Holladay HS 1974-76; 5th Grade Teacher Briarwood 1976-78; Jr/Sr HS Teacher Knoxville Baptist Chrstn Sch 1978-; *ai:* Honor Society Adv; TN Assn of Chrstn Schls 1978-; Knoxville Baptist Chrstn Sch Dedicated Service Awd 1978-88; *office:* Knoxville Baptist Chrstn Sch 2434 E 5th Ave Knoxville TN 37917

BEARD, JOAN THOMPSON, Vocal Music Teacher; *b:* Lake Forest, IL; *c:* Michael J.; *ed:* (BA) Eng, Univ of AR 1968; (MAT) Music, SE MO St Univ 1973; *cr:* 7th-12th Grade Vocal Music Teacher Richland Public Schls 1967-69, Perryville Public Schls 1970-74; Substitute Aide Richland Public Schls 1974-76; Vocal Music Teacher Twin Rivers Public Schls 1976-86, Dexter Public Schls 1986-; *ai:* Musicals, Concerts, Cmmty Entertainment, Advisory, Legislative, Ways & Means Comm; Cmmty Teacher Assn Advisory Comm Chairperson 1989-, Leader of Yr 1990; SE Dist Teachers Assn (Pres, 1st & 2nd VP) 1986-89; MO St Teacher Assn Resolutions Comm 1989-92; Music Educators Natl Conference, MO Music Educators Assn, Alpha Delta Kappa; 1st Baptist Church (Secy, Music Ministry) 1987-, Altrusan of Yr 1978, 1985; Altrusa Club (Pres, 1st & 2nd VP) 1980-83; Amer Cancer Society (Secy, Bd Mem) 1989-; Dexter Literacy Project Coord; Beta Sigma Phi Pres 1984-85; Bell Telephone/Dexter Chamber of Commerce Volunteer of Yr Awd Nom 1987, 1989; *home:* 703 Park Ln Dexter MO 63841

BEARD, KENNETH FRANKLIN, Band Director; *b:* Atlanta, GA; *m:* Cynthia Elaine Priester; *c:* Kenneth Jr., Jonathan; *ed:* (BM) Music Ed, GA St Univ 1976; (MM) Performance/Lit in Clarinet, Eastman Sch of Music 1978; Post Grad Study GSU; *cr:* Band Dir Forest Park HS 1977-80, Newton Cty HS 1980-81, Fayette Cty Jr HS 1981-89, Fayetteville Elem 1989-90, Fayette Cty HS 1990; *ai:* Band; GA Music Educators Assn Dist Chm 1977-; Natl Bandmasters Assn Awd of Excl 1986; Omicron Delta Kappa 1976-; Gideons Secy 1987-; GA Teacher Preparation Assessment Instrument Data Collector; GA Teacher Cert Test Revision Comm; *office:* Fayette Cty HS 440 Hood Ave Fayetteville GA 30214

BEARD, ROBERT JOSEPH, JR., English Teacher/Administrator; *b:* Hagerstown, MD; *m:* Susan Snyder; *c:* David; *ed:* (BS) Eng/Scndry Ed, Shippensburg Univ 1969; (MA) Scndry Ed/Eng, Univ oF MD College Park 1979; Admin/Supervision Certificate, Western MD Coll; *cr:* 9th/10th Grade Eng Teacher 1969-, Eng Dept Chm 1982-89 N Hagerstown HS; Admin Washington Cty Evening HS 1988-; *ai:* Asst Bsktbl Coach 1972-78; Head Boys Bsktbl Coach 1978-82; Yrbk Co-Adv 1969-72; Interim Stu Government Adv 1982; Washington Cty Teachers Assn, MD St Teachers Assn, NEA 1969-87; NCTE 1969-87; NCTE 1982-84, 1986-88; *home:* 34 Red Oak Dr Hagerstown MD 21740

BEARD, RUTH COX, Second Grade Teacher; *b:* Berryville, AR; *m:* Jim; *c:* Kerry, Kenton; *ed:* (AA) Music, SW Baptist Coll 1957; (BSHE) Home Ec, Univ of AR Fayetteville 1960; Teaching Cert Elem Ed, Sch of Ozarks; *cr:* Headstart Kndgtn 1965, 2nd Grade Teacher 1960-64 Blue Eye Sch; *ai:* Elem Honor Choir Accompanist; Delta Kappa Gamma Recording Secy; Baptist Church Organist & Pianist; *home:* PO Box 56 Blue Eye MO 65611

BEARD, SHELIA JONES, Mathematics Teacher; *b:* Camden, AR; *m:* Beau; *c:* Tashia Cole, Becky; *ed:* (BSE) Math, Henderson St Univ 1963; Houston Baptist Univ; *cr:* Sci Teacher Malvern Jr HS 1963-64; Math Teacher Sugarland Jr HS 1980-85, Fairview Mid Sch 1985-; *ai:* Future Problem Solving Coach; Academic Excl Comm Chm Rewards Prgm; Fairview Ed Assn, AR Ed Assn, NEA, AR Cncl Teachers of Math, NCTM, Delta Kappa Gamma; *home:* 905 S Hills Rd Camden AR 71701

BEARD, WANDA CARTER, Academically Gifted Teacher; *b:* Fayetteville, NC; *w:* Edwin L. (dec); *c:* Jennifer, Lamar; *ed:* (BA) Elem Ed/Eng - Cum Laude, Meth Coll 1967; Cnslr Ed, E Carolina Univ; Nutrition; *cr:* 5th Grade Teacher W H Owen Elem Sch 1967-68; 4th/5th Grade Teacher Montclair Elem Sch 1969-71; 3rd Grade Teacher Haynie Sch 1976-77; 5th/6th Grade Cumberland Rd Elem 1977-88; Classroom Teacher Academically Gifted Ed Morganton Rd Elem 1988-; *ai:* Writing Process & Proper Nutrition Wkshp Teacher; Speech Contest, Volunteer Coord; CEC, NCAGT 1988-; NCAE 1977-; Published Article; *home:* PO Box 218 Fayetteville NC 28301

BEARDEN, SUSAN (ROULSTON), Mid Sch Eng/Speech Teacher; *b:* Dallas, TX; *m:* William V. Jr.; *c:* Michelle, Lori, Jennifer; *ed:* (BA) Speech/Hearing Path, 1975; (BA) Elem Ed, 1977 Northeastern St Univ; *cr:* 1st Grade Teacher Washington Elem 1975-78; 2nd Grade Teacher Wayside Elem 1978-81; 1st/2nd Grade Teacher Wilson Sch 1981-83; 8th Grade Eng/Speech Teacher Morris Mid Sch 1985-; *ai:* Mid Sch Chrldr Coach; Acad Team Coach; NEA; OEA; NCTE; Beta Sigma Phi (Pres VP & Secy) Woman of Yr; *office:* Morris Public Sch PO Box 1 Morris OK 74445

BEARDLSEY, JUDY MAE, Math/Sci Teacher/Math Chair; *b:* Lanesboro, MN; *m:* Donald Bennett; *c:* Barbara Beardsley Costales, Robert D.; *ed:* (BS) Child Dev, UT St 1980; Ed, Univ of CA Northridge; Working Towards Masters Counseling, Univ of La Verne; *cr:* Home Art Teacher 1980-82, 7th/8th Grade Teacher 1982-83, Math/Sci Teacher 1983- Almondale Mid Sch; *ai:* Math Dept Chm; Helping Hands Prgm Asst; Sch Improvememt Planning & Child Study Team Mem; CA Teacher Assn, NEA, Kepple Teachers Assn, CA Math League; *office:* Almondale Mid Sch 9330 East Avenue U Littlerock CA 93543

BEARDMORE, NELLIE HESS, Biology/Mathematics Teacher; *b:* Marietta, OH; *c:* Janet Mincks, Thomas, Kathryn Jenks; *ed:* (BS) Bio, Marietta Coll 1961; *cr:* Jr HS Math Teacher Marietta City Schls 1964-67; Jr HS Math/Sci Teacher 1967-, HS Bio/Math Teacher 1990 Wolf Creek Local Schls; *ai:* Chrldr & Stu Cncl Adv; NEA, OEA; Wolf Creek Ed Assn (Secy 1980-81, Building Rep 1985-); Appointed WA Cnty Sci Curr Course of Study Comm; WA Cnty Math Curr Course of Study Comm; Alternative Methods Math Comm OH Bd of Ed; New Dimensions in Sci Comm OH Bd of Ed; *office:* Waterford HS Star Route 339 Waterford OH 45786

BEASLEY, ELMA M., Second Grade Teacher; *b:* Petersburg, TN; *m:* Farris; *c:* Daniel, Glenn, Bill; *ed:* (BA) Elem Ed, Mid TN St Univ 1959; (MA) Admin Supervision, Trevecca 1986; *cr:* 2nd Grade Teacher Caldwell Elem 1956-58; 1st Grade Teacher Opelika 1958-59; 2nd Grade Tacher Lincoln Schls 1966-69; 2nd/7th-9th Grade Teacher Fayetteville Jr HS & Ralph Askins 1969-.

BEASLEY, HANNAH NELSON, 8th Grade Mathematics Teacher; *b:* Harkers Island, NC; *m:* Joseph Thomas; *c:* Joseph Jr., David; *ed:* (BS) Home Ec, E Carolina Coll 1959; (MA) Rdng, E Carolina Univ 1984; Intermediate Ed 1984; *cr:* Teacher Smyrna HS 1960-62, Morehead Elem 1964-65, Lower Cape May Regional HS 1965-69, Harkers Island Elem 1971-89; *ai:* Chrldr Coach; FHA Adv; Negotiation Comm; PTO Treas; System Leadership Team & SAC Comm Chairperson; FIscal Management & Budget Prep; NEA, NCEA Building Rep; NJEA; Delta Kappa Gamma 1985-; Family His Center Dir 1988-; Stake Young Womens Prgm 2nd Cnslr 1971-73; Harkers Island Rescue Squad 1978-85; *home:* Cape Lookout Dr Harkers Island NC 28531

BEASLEY, TROY DANIEL, English Department Chairman; *b:* Whitestone, GA; *m:* Debbie Louise Jones; *c:* Flannery, Annalise, Ammelia; *ed:* Grad Stud Ed, W GA Coll; *cr:* Eng Dept Chm Murray Cty HS 1975-; *ai:* Drama Club & Beta Club Spon; Murray Cty HS Players Dir; Literary Coord; Honors & Advanced Placement Coord; NEA, NCTE, GA Assn of Educators, Murray Cty Assn of Educators 1973-; STAR Teacher 1976-78, 1980, 1984; *office:* Murray Cty HS Green Rd Chatsworth GA 30705

BEASON, KARL CASON, JR., AP Eng/Latin Teacher; *b:* Greer, SC; *ed:* (BA) Eng/Comparative Lit/Religion - Cum Laude, Univ of SC 1965; (MAT) Eng - Magna Cum Laude, Converse Coll 1968; (AA) Latin - Summa Cum Laude, Univ of GA 1987; *cr:* Advanced Composition/World Lit Teacher Greer HS 1967-84; Advanced Placement Lit/Composition Trng Course Master Teacher Univ of SC 1988-89; 11th Grade Honors Teacher 1966-, Journalism/Yrbk Teacher 1967-, Advanced Placement Eng Teacher 1973-, Latin Teacher 1985- Greer HS; *ai:* Le Flambeau Adv 1967-; Scholastic Scoreboard Lang Art Judge 1990; Greer HS Chm Eng Dept 1989-, Faculty Cncl 1988-89; Advanced Placement Consultant Greenville Sch Dist 1980-, Coord Greer HS 1973-; Reader Advanced Placement Test ETS 1985-, Coll Bd Eng Composition Test ETS 1989; Arts in Ed Grant Selection Comm; Natl Endowment Hum & Latin Inst 1986-87; Teacher of Yr 1979; Star Teacher 1971; Jaycees Outstanding Educator 1969; Greenville Cty Sch Dist Outstanding Achievement Awd 1985, 1990; *home:* Box 688 Hogback Mountain Rd Tryon NC 28782

BEASY, WILLIAM BRYAN, III, Science Teacher; *b:* Louisville, KY; *m:* Suzanne Frazier Bell; *c:* Suzie, Tina, Missy; *ed:* (BS) Elem Ed, 1976, (MS) Elem Ed, 1977 Univ of Louisville; *cr:* Classroom Teacher Centerfield Elem Sch 1977-79; Sci Teacher Oldham Cty Mid Sch 1979-; *ai:* Astronomy, Earth Sci, Ham Radio Club Spon; Governors Cup & Vlybl Coach; KY Sci Teachers Assn 1987-; KY Mid Sch Assn 1984-; NSTA 1989-; Cntrl St Hospital Human Rights Comm Chm 1979-; Alpha Kappa Delta Sociological Honor Society Charter Mem 1976; Univ of Louisville Joe E Wilkes Awd Outstanding Achievement in Ed 1976; KY Congress Parents & Teachers Certificate of Appreciation 1987; KY Educl Fnd Grant 1988; S Cntrl Bell Grant 1989; Visiting Lecturer Univ of Louisville 1977; *home:* 9415 La Grange Rd Louisville KY 40242

BEATON, RICHARD JOSEPH, Latin Teacher; *b:* Boston, MA; *m:* Mary Ellen Foye; *c:* Meghan, Siobahn; *ed:* (BA) Classics, Cath Univ of America 1971; (MA) Latin, 1972, (PHD) Latin, 1984 St Univ of NY Albany; *cr:* Latin Teacher Griffin HS 1976-; *ai:* Jr Class Adv; Stu of Week & Faculty Hospitality Comm Chm; GA Foreign Lang Assn (Secy, 2nd VP, Pres, Past Pres) 1982-, Teacher of Yr 1984; Classical Assn of Mid West & South Comm Chm 1987-, Good Teaching Awd 1987; GA Classical Assn Teacher of Yr; Griffin HS & Spalding Cty Teacher of Yr; WTBS Teacher of Yr; Atlanta Journal/Constitution Honor Teacher of Yr; *home:* 648 Mc Laurin Griffin GA 30223

BEATTY, HELEN GAIL, Mathematics Dept Chairperson; *b:* Dayton, OH; *ed:* (BS) Math, Maryville Coll 1968; *cr:* Math Teacher Southern Local HS 1968-; *ai:* NHS Adv; Mem of Sch & Dist CORE Team & ON-TASC; SLTA, OEA, NEA; Bethel Presbyterian Church (Elder 1990-93, Church Choir Dir); Intnl, St & Local Chrstn Endeavor; *office:* Southern Local HS 38095 State Rt 39 Salineville OH 43945

BEATTY, JAMES JOSEPH, III, Spanish Teacher; *b:* St Louis, MO; *m:* Judie Ann Jakle; *c:* Janice Y., Carolyn R.; *ed:* (MA) Span Lit, St Louis Univ 1986; (BA) Span/Ed, Rockhurst Coll 1982; *cr:* Span Instr St Louis Preparatory Seminary 1982-89, Lindbergh HS 1989-; *ai:* MO Foreign Lang Assn; *office:* Lindbergh HS 4900 S Lindbergh Saint Louis MO 63126

BEATTY, KRISTIN LOGHRY, Band Director; *b:* Iowa City, IA; *m:* Cary; *ed:* (BMSU) Music Ed, Lawrence Univ 1977; (MA) Music Ed, Univ of IA 1979; *cr:* Band Dir 1979-83, Band/General Music Teacher 1983-88 Regina Elem Sch; 5th-12th Grade Band Regina Schls 1988-; *ai:* Soph Class Adv; Asst Dir Sch Musical; IBA, SEIBA 1988-; *office:* Regina HS 2150 Rochester Ave Iowa City IA 52245

BEATY, GLORIA KING, Third Grade Teacher; *b:* Milwaukee, WI; *c:* Joanthan, Kimberly; *ed:* (BS) Elem Ed, TX Womans Univ 1962; (MA) Ed, AZ St Univ 1970; Spec Ed, Learning Disabilities, EMH; *cr:* 3rd Grade Teacher Roosevelt Sch Dist 1962-65; 1st/4th/6th Grade Teacher Dept Defense Schls 1965-68; Migrant Dir/Title 1 Teacher Seguin Sch Dist 1971-72; Spec Ed Teacher 1973-79, 3rd Grade Elem Teacher 1979- Tombstone Sch Dist; *home:* HC Box 3112 Tombstone AZ 85638

BEATY, MARY R., Third Grade Teacher; *b:* Sturgis, MI; *c:* Rebecca Beaty Davis, Terry A., Laurie Beaty Storm, Robert E., Elaine A.; *ed:* (BS) Elem Ed, 1960, (MS) Elem Ed, 1975 Anderson Univ; *cr:* Elem Teacher Anderson Public Schls 1960-61, Indianapolis Public Schls 1967-; *ai:* IN Ed Assn 1967-; Alpha Delta Kappa 1980-; *home:* 8249 Stone Ring Cir Indianapolis IN 46268

BEATY, MARY S. BELEW, Librarian; *b:* Winters, TX; *m:* Rodney O.; *c:* Kevin D., Karen S., Chris L.; *ed:* (BA) Eng Ed, Abilene Chrstn Univ 1961; (MS) Lib Sci, East TX St Univ 1989; Eng/Cmptrs, Univ TX Tyler; *cr:* Eng Teacher Austin Ind Sch Dist 1961-63; Span Teacher Sabin Ind Sch Dist 1970-71; Eng Teacher Kilgore Ind Sch Dist 1979-88; Librarian LeTourneau Univ 1989-; *ai:* Visiting Comm Mem/Eng Dept; TX Classroom Teachers Assn; Kilgore Classroom TA Pres 1984-85; NCTE; Pphi Delta Kappa; PTA Pres 1972-73; Chamber of Commerce; Founding Insurance Advisory Comm Teachers Retirement Systems of TX; *home:* 1202 Hillvale Kilgore TX 75662

BEATY, MONTY QUADE, Technology Education Teacher; *b:* Clovis, CA; *m:* Vanalyn Sue Carinder; *c:* Kelsey, Tyler; *ed:* (BS) Industrial Art, Cntrl St Univ 1976; *cr:* Teacher Wellston Schls 1676-78, Luther Schls 1978-81, Cashion Schls 1981-; *ai:* TSA Adv; Asst Ftbl & Tennis Coach; OTEA Bd Mem 1983-; Lions Club Mem 1987; Elks Club Mem 1988; *office:* Cashion Schls 3rd & Guthrie Cashion OK 73016

BEATY, TRACY GLEN, Mathematics, Phys Ed Teacher; *b:* Dallas, TX; *m:* Becky Jolene Welch; *c:* Trevor J.; *ed:* (BS) Phys Ed, N TX St Univ 1979; *cr:* Math Teacher/Coach 1979-82, Math Teacher/AD/Prin 1982-84 Benjamin Ind Sch Dist; Math Teacher/Coach Howe Ind Sch Dist 1984-; *ai:* Jr HS Boys Coach; 8th Grade Spon; *office:* Howe Ind Sch Dist 301 N Denney St Howe TX 75059

BEAUCHAMP, LUCIE, French Teacher; *b:* Paris, France; *w:* Joseph K Mc Lawhorn (dec); *c:* Sophie Hunt; *ed:* (MA) Fr, Univ of Richmond 1976; *cr:* Teacher Ecole De Gargons/Rue Du General Lasalle 1957-59, Richmond Public Sch 1960-62, Goochland HS 1963-; *ai:* Dept Head; Fr Club Spon; Fr Exchange Coord; Fullbright Schlsp 1960; Endowment for Hum Schlsp; *office:* Goochland HS 1868 Sandy Hook Rd Goochland VA 23063

BEAUCHEMIN, MARY WAIDE, Art Teacher; *b:* Portales, NM; *m:* Charles Joseph; *ed:* (BA) Art, 1969, (MA) Art Ed/Counseling, 1971, (EDS) Admin/Supervision, 1975 E NM Univ; Rdng; *cr:* Trust Dept Security Natl Bank 1976-77; Art Teacher Roswell Ind Schls 1973-76; Arts/Crafts Teacher Hagerman Municipal Schls 1977-80; Art/Lang Art Teacher Roswell Ind Sch Dist 1982-; *ai:* Just Say No Spon; Wkshps for Roswell Museum; Art & Roswell Adult Centers; Amer Bus Womens Assn Woman of Yr 1981; Pi Kappa Pi 1975-; NEA Exec Bd; Roswell Cmmty Little Theater, Roswell Fine Arts League; Artists of Month Roswell Public Lib 1987; Outstanding Rdng Ed Stu 1983; Artists of Month Golden Lib E NM Univ 1985; Art Talent Schlsp 1964; *home:* 1108 W 4th Roswell NM 88201

BEAUDIN, CHRISTOPHER, English Teacher; *b:* North Woodstock, NH; *m:* Deborah Ann Charboneau; *c:* Jason, David; *ed:* (BA) Math/Eng, SUNY Potsdam 1978; (MS) Ed, SUNY Plattsburgh 1983; *cr:* 7th-9th Grade Math/Eng Teacher Crown Point Cntrl Sch 1978-79; 9th-12th Grade Eng Teacher Plattsburgh Sr HS 1979-; *ai:* Frosh Class, Stu Cncl, Intramural Vlybl Adv; *office:* Plattsburgh HS Rugar St Plattsburgh NY 12901

BEAUDRIE, CATHARINE D., Teacher of Gifted; *b:* Philadelphia, PA; *m:* Kenneth Raymond Jr.; *c:* Elisabeth A., Jonathan D.; *ed:* (BS) Spec Ed, Univ of S AL 1979; (MA) Scndry Ed, Univ of AL Birmingham 1984; Space Orientation for Prof Educators Huntsville Prgm 1987 & Capital Area Prgm 1989; Writers Conference Samford Univ 1990; *cr:* Tutor Hillsdale 1977-78; Teacher Bottenfield Jr HS 1979-; *ai:* Math Counts, Math Team, Future Problem Solving Coach; Sch Review Team; AL Future Problem Solving Evaluator 1988-; Gardendale 1st Baptist Church Childrens Choir Worker 1989-; ESEA Grants Space Orientation Prgms Univ of AL Huntsville; *office:* Bottenfield Jr HS 400 Hillcrest Rd Adamsville AL 35005

BEAUVAIS, HERBERT LEE, JR., Mathematics Instructor; *b:* Kadoka, SD; *m:* Gail Lavon Fleeger; *c:* Lee, Hal, Lane; *ed:* (BS) Math, Northern St Coll 1966; Math Related Stud, St Cloud St Univ; *cr:* Math Instr Hazel Ind Sch Dist 1966-68, Willmar Jr HS 1968-; *ai:* Sr HS Appeals Comm; WEA Treas; WCTM 1973-; MCTM 1978-; NCTM; Church Bd of Ed 1987-89; Willmar Sportsmans Club (Pres, Secy) 1970-; Ducks Unlimited 1976-; *office:* Willmar Sr HS 824 SW 7th St Willmar MN 56201

BEAVER, DONALD W., Mathematics Teacher; *b:* San Antonio, TX; *m:* Gayla Ann Parks; *c:* Alyssa, Cara; *ed:* (BA) Math, 1972, (MS) Math, Univ of TX Austin; Working Toward MS in Math, Univ of TX Austin; *cr:* Instr Univ of TX Austin 1972-74; Teacher Lago Vista HS 1977-80, O Henry Jr HS 1980-86, Austin Comm Coll 1980-, Anderson HS 1986-; *ai:* Growth Initiatives for Teachers Grant; *office:* O Henry Jr H S 8403 Mesa Austin TX 78759

BEAVERS, DEBORAH WARD, Mathematics Teacher; *b:* Louisville, KY; *m:* Dennis R.; *c:* Michael; *ed:* (BS) Math Ed, 1978, (MAED) Math, 1979 E KY Univ; *cr:* Instr Watterson Coll 1982-83; Lecturer Univ of Louisville 1982-83; Math Teacher Meadowbrook Jr HS 1985-86, Loch Lowe Preparatory Sch 1986-; *ai:* Mu Alpha Theta Spon; Yrbk & Cheerleading Adv; NCTM 1980-; FL Cncl Teachers of Math 1985-; Alpha Gamma Delta; *office:* Loch Lowe Preparatory Sch PO Box 950670 Lake Mary FL 32746

BEAVERS, JOYCE JENKINS, 7th Grade Social Stud Teacher; *b:* Chattanooga, TN; *m:* James M.; *c:* Jodi, Joshua; *ed:* (BS) Elem Ed, Univ of TN Chattanooga 1984; Working Toward Masters in Scndry Admin; *cr:* 7th Grade Soc Stud Teacher Soddy Daisy Mid Sch 1984-89; *ai:* Pep Club Spon; Team Leader; Soc Comm; Outstanding & Most Influential Mid Sch Teacher Soddy Daisy HS; *office:* Soddy-Daisy Mid Sch 200 Turner Rd Soddy-Daisy TN 37319

BEAZLEY, THOMAS R., Social Studies Chair; *b:* Chicago, IL; *m:* Mary A. Fuller; *c:* Jennifer, Michael, Andrew, Eileen, Stephanie; *ed:* (BA) His, Duquesne Univ 1973; (MA) Amer His, Millersville Univ 1982; Theology, Mary Immaculate Seminary 1973-75; *cr:* Bio/Earth Sci/Rdng/Religion Teacher St Marys Regional Sch 1977-83; Soc Stud/Religion Teacher Lebanon Cath Jr Sr HS 1983-; *ai:* YMCA Youth Government, NHS, Presidential Classroom Moderator, Ftbl Asst Coach; Sftbl Head Coach; Amer Historical Assn, Organization of Amer Historians, Acad of Poly Sci; Knights of Columbus 3rd Degree 1988-; Elected Annville Township Commissioner 1985, 1989; VP Bd of Commissioners; Responsible for Highways Dept; *office:* Lebanon Cath Jr Sr HS 1400 Chestnut St Lebanon PA 17042

BE BEAU, STANLEY BERNARD, Jr HS Teacher; *b:* Glidden, WI; *m:* Veronica Marie; *c:* Michael, Christine Hulmer, Derral, Gregory, Kathleen, David; *ed:* (BA) Elem Ed, Northland Coll 1973; Admin; *cr:* Jr HS Teacher Ondossagon 1973-; *ai:* Little League Coach/Mgr/Pres 1971-81; Weblos Scouts Scout Master 1971-73; City Cncl Councilman 1983-86; Alternate Japanese Amer Stud; *home:* 501 20th Ave W Ashland WI 54806

BECHARD, REBECCA JEAN, 9th Grade Mathematics Teacher; *b:* Rouses Point, NY; *ed:* (BS) Scndry Ed/Math, SUNY Oswego 1986; Grad Prgm SUNY Cortland; *cr:* 8th Grade Math Teacher 1987-88, 9th Grade Math Teacher 1988- Durgee Jr HS; *ai:* Ski Club Chaperone; Awds Assembly Comm; NYS Math Teachers Assn 1989-; Kappa Delta Pi 1987-; Empire St Fellowship for Teachers; *office:* Durgee Jr HS E Oneida St Baldwinsville NY 13027

BECHMAN, MICHAEL DEAN, Mathematics/Science Teacher; *b:* Ann Arbor, MI; *m:* Sandra Jo Ann Hawkins; *c:* Michael T., Tammy J., Jonathan W.; *ed:* (BS) Bio, Bob Jones Univ 1968; (MA) Bio Ed, Univ of IN 1976; *cr:* HS Teacher Indianapolis Baptist Sch 1972-81, Faith Chrstn Sch 1981-; *ai:* HS Guidance Dir; Bio Test Author 1981; *office:* Faith Christian Sch PO Box 1230 Williams Bay WI 53191

BECK, DOLORES MARIE, 5th & 6th Grade Math Teacher; *b:* Guthrie Center, IA; *ed:* Elem Certifcate Ed, IA St Teachers Coll 1953; (BS) Ed, Drake Univ 1964; *cr:* 5th Grade Teacher Scranton Consolidated Sch 1953-59; 5th Grade Teacher 1959-75, 5th/6th Grade Math Teacher 1975- Guthrie Center Cmmty Sch; *ai:* Chaperone & Scorekeeper HS Girls Bsktbl; Scorekeeper HS Boys Bsktbl; Guthrie Center Ed Assn, IA St Ed Assn, NEA; Women of Arts Charter Mem; *office:* Guthrie Center Cmmty Sch N 4th St Guthrie Center IA 50115

BECK, ELLEN RUTH BAKER, Phys Ed Teacher/Coach; *b:* Minden, LA; *m:* Rodger Ray; *c:* Steven, Douglas; *ed:* (BS) Health & Phys Ed, Northwestern St Univ 1962; Educl & Coaching Coursees, Univ of Houston, Lamar Univ, Stephen F Austin Univ; *cr:* Phys Ed Teacher Katy Jr HS 1962-67; Health/Phys Ed Teacher Katy Jr/Sr HS 1971-75; 7th Grade Sci Teacher Katy Jr HS 1975-76; Phys Ed Teacher Katy HS 1976-; *ai:* Var Vlybl & Track Coach; TX Girls Coaches Assn 1971-, All-Star Coach 1989-; Beta Sigma Phi 1968-74; Natl Vlybl Coaches Assn 1988-; Assn of TX Prof Educators 1980-; TX All-Star Coach 1990; *office:* Katy HS 6331 Highway Blvd Katy TX 77450

BECK, JAMES WALTER, Mathematics Teacher; *b:* Doylestown, PA; *m:* Dorothy M. Mahoney; *c:* Kathleen, Elizabeth, David, Peter; *ed:* (AB) Philosophy, Villanova Univ 1969; *cr:* Math Teacher Cntrl Montgomery Cty Voc Tech 1969-76, Upland Cntry Day Sch 1976-; *ai:* Math & Woodshop Club; Natl Sci Fnd Grant; *office:* Upland Cntry Day Sch 420 W Street Rd Kennett Square PA 19348

BECK, JEANNE ANN, Sixth Grade Teacher; *b:* Columbus, OH; *ed:* (BA) Elem Ed, Otterbein Coll 1971; (MALL) Marietta Coll 1981; *cr:* 6th Grade Teacher Lowell Elem 1971-89; *ai:* Intnl Rdng Assn, OH Ed Assn, NEA; OH Cncl Intnl Rdng Assn Treas 1988-; Ft Frye Local Schls Teachers Assn (Treas, Secy); Delta Kappa Gamma Finance Chairperson 1988-; Pythian Sisters, Evergreen Bible Church.

BECK, JOHN BERNARD, 4th Grade Teacher; *b:* Anderson, IN; *m:* Neva Ann Mc Cord; *c:* Reanna L.; *ed:* (BS) Elem Ed, 1964, (MA) Elem Ed, 1968 Ball St Univ; Admin License; *cr:* 4th-6th Grade Teacher Killbuck Elem Sch 1974-; *ai:* Enrichment Team; Phi Delta Kappa 1986-; Mt Moriah Lodge 77 F&AM Chaplain 1989-; *home:* 5001 Woodrose Ln Anderson IN 46011

BECK, KENNETH LEE, 3rd Grade Teacher; *b:* Winchester, IN; *m:* Judith Marie Foster; *c:* Kourtney L., Joshua M.; *ed:* (BA) Elem Ed, Purdue Univ 1975; (MA) Elem Ed, Ball St Univ 1978; *cr:* 5th Grade Teacher Randolph Southern Elem 1975-78, Washington Center Sch 1978-83; 3rd Grade Teacher Washington Center Sch 1983-; *ai:* Intnl Rdng Assn 1987-; Jaycees St Dir 1976-77; *office:* Washington Center Sch 7961 S Washington Rd Columbia City IN 46725

BECK, LILLIAN MAE (MATTINGLY), Second Grade Teacher; *b:* Leonardtown, MD; *m:* Charles W.; *c:* Charleen; *ed:* (BS) Elem Ed, Catherine Spalding 1968; Kndgtn Cert Franciscan Univ 1972; Teach, In-Service, Child Abuse Wkshps; Early Chldhd Ed; *cr:* 1st Grade Teacher St Marys 1969-72; Kndgtn Teacher North Sch 1972-74; 3rd Grade Teacher Hilltop Sch 1974-82; 2nd Grade Teacher Elm Elem 1982-; *ai:* Elm Talent Show Coord; Elem Spelling Curr & OH Univ Stu Teacher Adv; NEA, OEA, MFEA 1972-; *office:* Elm Elem Sch Euclid Ave Martins Ferry OH 43935

BECK, MARILYN LARSON, 4th Grade Teacher; *b:* Rake, IA; *w:* Floyd (dec); *c:* Ann Green, Michael, Patrick; *ed:* (CE) Elem Ed, Luther Coll 1952; (BA) Elem Ed, Mankato St 1972; Addl Studies Mankato St; Hamlin Univ; St Thomas; *cr:* 1st Grade Teacher 1952-53; Private Tutor 1953-54; 2nd Grade Teacher 1954-56; 1st-4th Grade Teacher Kiester-Walters 1967-87; 2nd-4th Grade Teacher South Centrl Elem 1987-; *ai:* MEA; NEA; KEA; Luth Church Deacon 1988-; *home:* 101 S 1st St Box 126 Kiester MN 56051

BECK, MAUREEN VINCENT, Social Services Prgms Director; *b:* Pittsfield, MA; *w:* James Tossey (dec); *c:* Stephen V., Andrew D. (dec), James T. Jr.; *ed:* (AB) His, Wellesley Coll 1954; (MA) His, Rutgers Univ 1960; Certificate Classics, Amer Acad of Classical Stud Rome 1978; *cr:* Teacher Madeira Sch, Hightstown HS, Rutgers Univ, Stuart Sch, Groton Sch 1954-; Dean of Stu/Soc Service Prgms Dir Groton Sch 1984-; *ai:* Soccer; Debate; Soc Service; New Faculty Orientation; CANE 1978-; ACL, AAR; NICA Rome Scholar Awd 1978; Papers on Roman His & Teaching of Classics; Local Service Awds; Classics Awds; *office:* Groton Sch P O Box 991 Groton MA 01450

BECK, NANCY ANN, 5th Grade Teacher; *b:* Columbus, OH; *m:* Thomas F.; *c:* Thomas R., Timothy E., Linda J.; *ed:* (BS) Elem Ed, OH St Univ 196 *cr:* Teacher Columbus Bd of Ed 1969-; *ai:* Adv Sch Newspaper; Sch Chairperson Multicultural Comm; Sch Advisory Bd Comm Pres; Twigs of Childrens Hospital (Bd Indv Events 1964-66 Gen Treas 1966-68); Teacher of Yr PTA 1985, Jennings Scholar 1984; *office:* Columbus Bd of Ed 40 E Stewart Ave Columbus OH 43206

BECK, SANDY NEIMAN, Spanish Teacher; *b:* Reading, PA; *m:* Keith; *ed:* (BS) Span/Scndry Ed, Millersville Univ 1981; (MED) Ed/Eng, Kutztown Univ 1985; EEI Trng Prgm Through Intermediate Unit; *cr:* Span Teacher Boyertown Jr HS East/West 1981-82; Boyertown Sr HS 1982-; *ai:* Key Club Adv; PSEA/NEA 1982-; *office:* Boyertown Sr HS 4th & Monroe Sts Boyertown PA 19512

BECK, SUE RAWLINGS, Mathematics Teacher; *b:* Owingsville, KY; *m:* Douglas John; *ed:* (BA) Math, 1970, (MA) Ed, 1975 Morehead St Univ; (Rank I) Ed/Math; *cr:* Math Teacher Bath Cty HS 1970-; *ai:* KY Cncl of Teachers of Math, NEA, KY Ed Assn, Delta Kappa Gamma; Kiwanis Service Organization; KY Innovative Incentive Grant on Teacher Problem Solving in Classroom Daily; *home:* RR 1 Ridgeway Ests Owingsville KY 40360

BECKER, ANN STANTON, Science Teacher; *b:* Wilkes-Barre, PA; *m:* Charles N.; *c:* W. Scott, Craig Tuchfarber; *ed:* (BA) Liberal Stud, 1982, (MA) Ed, 1986 CA Poly; Supplementary Authorization Eng, Soc Sci, General Sci; *cr:* Teacher Kenmore Elem 1982-85, Jones Jr HS 1985-; *ai:* Sci Dept, SIP, Sci Curr Adv; E Hills Homeowners Assn Treas 1985-; *office:* Jones JR HS 14250 East Merced Baldwin Park CA 91706

BECKER, DAVID ERNEST, Fourth Grade Teacher; *b:* Reading, PA; *m:* Donna Jean (Rothermel); *c:* Michael, Erin; *ed:* (BS) Elem Ed, Cntrl MO St Univ 1970; *cr:* 4th Grade Teacher Womelsdorf Elem Sch 1970-; *ai:* Stamp Club Adv; Dist Cmptr Comm; NEA; PA Ed Assn; Conrad Weiser Ed Assn; Lions Club Past Pres 1970-; Robesonia Boy Scouts Comm Mem 1987-; Church Cncl 1990; *home:* 220 W Ruth Ave Robesonia PA 19551

BECKER, GEORGE L., English Teacher; *b:* Kenosha, WI; *c:* David, Daniel, Darren, James; *ed:* (BA) Scndry Eng, Univ of WI Parkside 1970; (MA) Eng, Univ of WI Milwaukee 1972; *cr:* Teacher Kenosha Unified Sch Dist 1970-; *ai:* Golf Coach.

BECKER, JAMES J., Mathematics/Computer Teacher; *b:* Hazen, ND; *m:* Ellen Bavkol; *c:* Elizabeth, Sarah; *ed:* (BA) Scndry Math, Dickinson St 1974; Working Towards Masters Math; *cr:* Phys Ed Teacher Dickinson HS 1974; 7th-12th Grade Math/Phys Ed Teacher Goloa HS 1974-75; 7th-12th Grade Math/Phys Ed/Ger/Drama/Cmptr Teacher Zap HS 1975-; *ai:* Coach & Dir HS Drama; Jr HS Bsbl Coach; NDMTA 1988-; NDDEA 1974-80, ND Teacher of Yr 1977; Zap City Cncl (Alderman 1977-82, City Auditor 1982-); St Luke Church (Secy, Treas) 1976-88; ND

Driver Ed Teacher of Yr 1977; Dwight D Eisenhower Grant 1988-; *office:* Zap HS Box 67 4th Ave E Zap ND 58580

BECKER, JERRY K., History Teacher; *b:* Le Mars, IA; *m:* Gloria Jean Stellmatch; *c:* Brenda, Greg; *ed:* (BA) Soc Stud, Westmar Coll 1959; (MA) His, Univ of N CO 1963; *cr:* Teacher/Coach Colo Cmmty Schls 1959-63, Sutherland Cmmty Sch 1963-73, Eagle Grove Cmmty Schls 1973-; *ai:* Boys Track & Cross Cntry Head Coach; Jr Class Spon; IA St Ed Assn, NEA 1959-; IA Cncl Soc Stud 1987-; IA Assn Track CoacheS 1975-, St Coach of Yr 1984-87; Eagle Grove Meth Church 1973-; Educator of Yr Eagle Grove Chamber Commerce 1990; Series Newspaper Articles 1988; *office:* Eagle Grove Cmmty Schls N Iowa St Eagle Grove IA 50533

BECKER, JOHNNIE COLE, 4th & 5th Grade Eng Teacher; *b:* Carlsbad, NM; *m:* Anthony James; *c:* Blair; *ed:* (BS) Elem Ed/Eng, Hardin Simmons Univ 1961; (MA) Eng/Ed, Western NM Univ 1971; Directed Study, NM St Univ; His Field Study, Western NM Univ; Cmptr Trng Prgm; Intermediate Phys Ed; *cr:* 3rd Grade Teacher Edison Elem 1961-64; Peace Corps Volunteer Brazil 1964-66; Asst Prin Monterrey Elem 1970-; 4Th/5th Grade Eng Teacher Monterrey 1970-; *ai:* Boys 5th/6th Grade Bsbl Team Coach; Security Guard Var Soccer; Inlow Youth Camp Dir; NEA, NEA of NM 1966-; Amer Assn of Univ Women 1973; *office:* Monterrey Elem Sch 1001 N 9th Carlsbad NM 88220

BECKER, MARY FOXWORTH, Fourth Grade Teacher; *b:* Norfolk, VA; *m:* Bryan Rall; *c:* Kristin M.; *ed:* (BA) Span Ed, Norfolk St Univ 1975; *cr:* 4th-6th Grade Teacher 1975-76, Math Specialist 1977-76, 4th Grade Teacher 1978- Norfolk Public Schls; *ai:* Cmptr Club Spon; Soc Stud Curr Comm; Ed Assn of Norfolk, VA Ed Assn, NEA 1975-; Classroom Teacher Assn; New Mt Zion Organist 1966-; AME Church Trustee 1987-; Norfolk Public Schls Bell Awd; Certificate of Appreciation-NSAS-Name the Orbiter; *office:* Larchmont Elem Sch 5210 Hampton Blvd Norfolk VA 23508

BECKER, PHYLLIS JEANNE, 2nd Grade Teacher; *b:* Oklahoma City, OK; *m:* Robert; *c:* Stephanie, Stacie; *ed:* (BS) Elem Ed, 1981, (MS) Ed, 1984 CSU; *cr:* Teacher Wellston Public Schls 1981-; *home:* Rt 1 Box 108 Wellston OK 74881

BECKER, WALTER SIEGFRIED, History Teacher; *b:* Bronx, NY; *m:* Mary M. Steigerwald; *c:* Lori A. Lanson, Erik J.; *ed:* (BA) Soc Sci, 1961, (MA) European His, 1966 SUNY Albany; *cr:* Teacher Coxsackie-Athens Cntrl 1961-; *ai:* Sr HS Stu Cncl Adv; Coxsackie-Athens Teachers Assn Pres 1978-80; Capital Dist Soc Stud Cncl 1975-; Dutch Reformed Church Deacon 1962-64; *office:* Coxsackie-Athens Cntrl HS 104 Sunset Blvd Coxsackie NY 12051

BECKETT, MONA CARPENTER, Third Grade Teacher; *b:* Wallingford, KY; *m:* Bill R.; *ed:* (BA) Elem Ed, 1970, (MA) Elem Ed, 1975, (Rank I) Ed, 1988 Morehead St Univ; Cmptr Wkshps, Writing Process Wkshps; IBM Writing Process Approach Trng; *cr:* 6th Grade Teacher 1970-71, 5th/6th Grade Teacher 1971-72 Mt Carmel Elem; 2nd Grade Teacher Mt Carmel & Flemingsburg Elem 1972-88; 3rd Grade Teacher Flemingsburg Elem 1988-; *ai:* Promoting & Retention, Curr Comm; Fleming Cty Ed Assn, KY Ed Assn, NEA; Pleasant Valley Church of Christ Nursery Class Teacher; Fleming Cty Homemakers, Farm Bureau, Flemingsburg PTO; *office:* Flemingsburg Elem Sch W Water St Flemingsburg KY 41041

BECKETT, ROBIN LEWIS, Earth Science/Biology Teacher; *b:* Saltville, VA; *m:* Thomas Allen; *c:* Malcolm T. J., Steven; *ed:* (BS) Animal Sci, VA Polytechnic Inst 1981; Ed, Emory & Henry Coll 1982; Recertification Radford Univ, Univ of VA 1983-; *cr:* Phys Sci Teacher Marion Jr HS 1983-85; Earth Sci/Bio Teacher Marion Sr HS 1986-; *ai:* Marion Sr HS Sci Fair Asst Dir; Smyth Cty Bio Curr Revision Comm; Smyth Cty Ed Assn, NEA; *office:* Marion Sr HS 848 Stage St Marion VA 24354

BECKHAM, LILLIAN ANN LAWSON, Chemistry Teacher; *b:* Lebanon, KY; *w:* Harold Ronald (dec); *c:* Robin, Regyna, Ruston; *ed:* (BS) Chem, 1960, (MA) Chem, 1967, (Rank I) Ed, Western KY; *cr:* 3rd Grade Teacher Lincoln Trail Elem 1958-59; Sci/Math Teacher Lebanon HS 1960-61, Harrodsburg HS 1961-62; Chem Teacher Warren Cty HS 1962-63; Chem/Math Teacher Bowling Green HS 1963-65; Chem Teacher Russellville HS 1966-70, Washington Cty HS 1970-; *ai:* Beta Spon; Local, St, Voc Ed Assn; KY Assn for Progress in Sci; Order of Eastern Star Star Point 1961-62, 25 Yr Pin 1985; *office:* Washington Cty HS Lincoln Park Rd Springfield KY 40069

BECKHAM, OPAL CARR, Fifth Grade Teacher; *b:* Kilgore, TX; *m:* Othello Jr.; *c:* Cicely, Courtney; *ed:* (BS) Elem, E TX St Univ 1977; *cr:* Spec Ed Teacher Crockett Elem 1978-79, Thomas Jefferson HS 1979-81; 5th Grade Teacher Dowling Elem 1981-; *ai:* Stu Cncl Spon; Grade Level Chm; Assn of TX Prof Educators 1987-; *home:* 1082 Meadowvale Dr Beaumont TX 77760

BECKMANN, NANCY BOURKE, Second Grade Teacher; *b:* St Louis, MO; *m:* Vernal; *c:* James, Janet; *ed:* (MA) Soc Sci, Webster Univ 1981; *cr:* 1st Grade Teacher Buder Sch 1962-64, Tillman Sch 1964-67; 2nd Grade Teacher Barretts Sch 1975-; *ai:* Parkway Dist Lang Art Curr Cncl; Barretts Sch Effectiveness & Care Teams; Maryville Coll Cooperating Teacher for Stu Teachers; Friends of Gifted Awd 1981; Pillar of Parkway Nom 1982; *office:* Barretts Parkway Dist Sch 1780 Carmen Rd Manchester MO 63021

BECKMON, TIM A., Chemistry Instructor; *b:* Greeley, CO; *ed:* (BS) Bio, CO St Univ 1971; (MA) Sci Ed, 1981, (EDS) Chem/Statistics, 1986 Univ of NM 1986; *cr:* Bio Teacher Shashe River Sch; Bio/Chem Instr Santa Fe Indian Sch; Math Instr Santa Fe HS; Chem Instr Capital HS, Santa Fe Comm Coll; *ai:* Sr Class Spon; 9th Grade Wrestling; Rodeo Club; Kappa Delta Phi 1986-; Natl Sci Fnd Grant Univ of AZ Advanced Chem Wkshp 1990; *office:* Capital HS 4851 Pasco Del Sol Santa Fe NM 87505

BECKWITH, MAXINE HUBER, Secondary Prin/Bus Teacher; *b:* Hazen, ND; *m:* Gary D.; *c:* Jason; *ed:* Secretarial Certificate 1959, (BS) Bus Admin, 1961 Jamestown Coll; (MA) Curr/Instruction, Univ of N CO 1972; *cr:* Secy Sweetheart Bakeries 1959-60; Bus Teacher Great Falls HS 1961-65, Charles Russell HS 1965-66, Golden HS 1966-67; Secy Stanford Univ 1967-68; Bus Teacher Awalt HS 1968-69; Secy Southwest Gas 1969; Bus Teacher Denver Womans Coll 1969-70, Westminster HS 1970-72, Zap HS 1974-76; Prin/Teacher Golden Valley-Dodge HS 1982-; *ai:* Stu Cncl Adv; ND Assn of Scndry Sch Prin (Regional Dir 1986-88, Secy 1989-); NASSP 1987-; Concert Series (Pres 1988, Membership Chm 1990); Bison Boosters 1985-; Knife River Chorale 1974-; *office:* Golden Valley-Dodge HS P O Box 158 Golden Valley ND 58541

BECKWITH, ROBERT E., Biology Teacher; *ed:* (BS) Bio, 1972, (MED) Scndry Admin, 1989 Coll of ID; Math, Ed, Sci Curr, Instruction Model, Boise St Univ; Bio, Energy, Curr Dev, Coll of ID; *cr:* Bio/Comprehensive Bio/Advanced Bio/Ecology Teacher Nampa Sr HS 1972-80; Dept Chm CBSO 1978-80, Dist Sci Curr Coord 1979-80 Nampa Sch Dist; 7th Grade Life Sci/8th Grade Earth Sci/9th Grade Phys Sci/Bio/Advanced Bio Teacher 1980-84, Title IV-C Grant Dir 1980-82 Cambridge Sch Dist; 8th Grade Phys Sci/9th Grade Earth Sci/Advanced Earth Sci/Electronics Teacher 1984-87, Sci Dept Chm Meridian 1985-87 Meridian Jr HS; Bio Teacher Centennial HS 1987-; *ai:* Sci Club 1972-80; NASA Space Sci Stu Involvement Project 1982-; ID Sci Day Chm; ID Local Ed Assn, NEA, ID Sci Teachers Assn 1972-; Cambridge Ed Assn Past Pres; Energy & Mans Environment 1981-85; ID Sci Day Chm 1986-; ID Sci Teachers Assn (Pres Elect, Pres, Past Pres) 1986-89.

BECKWITH, ROBERT NICHOLAS, Phys Sci Teacher/Sci Dept Head; *b:* Morristown, NJ; *m:* Margaret A. Kerr; *c:* Betth A., Tracy L.; *ed:* (BS) Bio, Davis & Elkins Coll 1967; (Ma) Teaching, WV Wesleyan 1978; *cr:* Teacher Coalton HS 1967-68; Bio Teacher Parons HS 1968-69; Bio Teacher/Coach Middletown Twp HS 1969-74; Teacher/Coach/Sci Dept Head Elkins Jr HS 1974-; Part-Time Instr Davis & Elkins Coll 1979-80; *ai:* Stu Natural Assistance Prgm Snap Adv; Top Teacher Search Comm; Randolph Cty Ed Assn 1974-; WV Ed Assn 1974-; NEA 1974-; Davis & Elkins Coll Alumni Assn (Pres 1985-86); D & E Natl Alumni Cncl 1985-; 1st Runner-Up Cnty Teacher of Yr 1989; NASA Sky Sch Top Gun Teacher/Instr 1989; Natl Sci Fnd Teacher of Yr WV Nom 1987; Ashland Oil Teacher Achvmt Awd Nom 1990; *office:* Elkins Jr H S Robert E Lee Ave Elkins WV 26241

BECWAR, MARY MEYER, Title I Teacher; *b:* Chicago, IL; *m:* Jerome Albert; *ed:* (BA) Elem Ed, 1953, (MA) Ed, 1966 Roosevelt Univ; *cr:* Kndgtn/4th/5th Grade Teacher Costello Elem Sch 1953-59; 4th Grade Teacher 1959-69, 3rd-4th Grade Teacher 1970-74, Learning Center Coord/K-4th Grade Teacher 1974-75 Winnetka Public Sch; 4th Grade/Title I Teacher Kelliher Public Sch 1980-; *ai:* Kelliher Public Lang Art Comm; NEA 1959-75, 1980-; MN Ed Assn 1980; Kelliher Ed Assn (Treas, Grievance Comm) 1985; Green Sr Center Chicago Volunteer of Yr Awd; *office:* Kelliher Public Sch Kelliher MN 56650

BEDENBAUGH, CYNTHIA BROWN, Soc Stud Teacher/Dept Chair; *b:* York, SC; *m:* Michael L.; *c:* R. Hance; *ed:* (BA) His/Ed, Clemson Univ 1974; (MED) Ed, Francis Marion Coll 1982; *cr:* Teacher Adamsville Mid Sch 1978-79, Bennettsville Intermediate Sch 1979-80, Bennettsville Mid Sch 1981-; *ai:* Jr Beta Club Spon; *office:* Bennettsville Mid Sch Cheraw St Bennettsville SC 29512

BEDFORD, THERESA LOUISE, HS Science Teacher; *b:* Lancaster, OH; *m:* Kelly Paul; *ed:* (BS) Geology, TX A&M Univ 1985; *cr:* HS Sci Teacher Snook Sch 1988-; *ai:* Tennis Coach; Sci Teachers Assn of TX 1985-; *office:* Snook Sch Box 87 Snook TX 77878

BEDWELL, RALPH K., Hum/Performing Arts Dir; *b:* Indianapolis, IN; *m:* Elizabeth Bodkin; *c:* Katherine E., Emily E.; *ed:* (BS) Soc Stud, 1962, (MS) Guidance/Soc Stud, 1967 IN St Univ; (MAT) Soc Stud, IN Univ 1971; *cr:* Soc Stud Teacher Hamilton Heights Schls 1962-67, MSD Lawrence Township 1967-68; Deputy Dir GED Ft Harrison 1968-69; Soc Stud Dept Chm Indianapolis Public Schls 1969-79; Dir Magnet Prgms/Hum Performing Arts Broad Ripple HS 1979-; *ai:* Phi Delta Kappa 1982-; NCSS 1967-; IN Cncl Soc Stud 1966-, Outstanding Soc Stud HS Teacher Awd 1977; ACSD 1980-; Ronald Mc Donald House Volunteer 1985; IN Univ, USEO, Ford Fnd Grant 1970; *office:* Indianapolis Public Schls 1115 Broad Ripple Ave Indianapolis IN 46220

BEEBE, SANDRA E., English Teacher; *b:* March AFB, CA; *ed:* (AB) Eng/Speech, UCLA 1956; (MA) Ed, CSULB 1957; Advanced Trng in Scndry Admin & Credential; *cr:* Eng Teacher Garden Grove HS 1957; Attendance Supvr, GGHS 1976-83; *ai:* Honors Eng III; Block US His Specialist; Consultant on Eng Studies, Honors; Valedictorian/Salutatorian Coach; Tradition Chairperson at GGHS; GGEA/CTE/NEA 1957; Jr League of Long Beach Kappa Kappa Gamma Alumnae; Famous Watercolorist, Cover Artist of Exploring Painting By Gerald F Brommer; Author of Chapter on Symbolism in NCTE Text They Really Taught Us How to Right; Author 5 Articles in Eng Journal & CA Eng Journal; Invitational Memberships Including the Natl Watercolor Society & the Rocky Mountain Noted Lecturer and Exhibitor Natl; *office:* Garden Grove H S 11271 Stanford Ave Garden Grove CA 92640

BEEBY, DONALD MC CALLEN, Social Studies Teacher; *b:* Philadelphia, PA; *ed:* (BS) Geography, James Madison Univ 1983; Univ London England; Univ IL Chicago Teaching Cert; *cr:* Teacher West Potomac HS 1985-; *ai:* Dist St Championships Cross Cntry, Track & Field Coach; Soph Class Rep 1988-; Fairfax Journal 1989 Coach of Yr 1989; The Wire 1989 Coach of Yr 1988-89; Va Track & Field/Cross Cntry News 1989 Coach of Yr 1989; Honored by Fairfax Cty Public Schls Annual Teacher Recognition Ceremony 1990; *office:* West Potomac H S 6500 Quander Rd Alexandria VA 22307

BEECHER, RHONDA, 5th Grade Teacher; *b:* Baxley, GA; *ed:* (BS) Bio, GA Southern Coll 1980; GA Drug Awareness for Mid Grade Courses; *cr:* 5th/6th Grade Remedial Teacher 1980-81, 5th Grade Teacher 1981- Jeff Davis Mid Sch; *ai:* Lib, Staff Dev, Stu Support Team, Textbook Evaluation Comms; GA Know to Say No Coord Jeff David Cty; GA Assn of Educators Building Rep 1980-89; Prof Assn of Ga Educators 1989-; Order of Eastern Star Worthy Matron 1990-; Church 1st/2nd Teacher 1990-; Whos Who for Coll Stus; *office:* Jefferson Davis Mid Sch Coffee St PO Box 625 Hazlehurst GA 31539

BEELER, PATRICIA S BROOKS, 6th Grade Teacher; *b:* Oak Hill, WV; *w:* George H. Jr. (dec); *ed:* (BA) Psych, Berea Coll 1949; Elem Ed, Western CT St Univ 1966; *cr:* Ungraded Class Slater Road Sch 1955-56; 3rd Grade Teacher Thos Jefferson Sch 1956-59; 6th Grade Teacher Consolidated Sch 1959-61; 6th/7th/8th Grade La/Rdng Teacher 1961-73; 6th Grade La/Rdng Teacher 1973- Meeting House Hill Sch; *ai:* New Fairfield Ed Assn Secy/Treas/Pres; Ladies Aux VFW St Pres 1979-80; Outstanding Teacher Awd 1980; CT Celebration of Excl Awd 1987; *home:* 1 Goldmine Rd New Milford CT 06776

BEELER, RICHARD WILLIAM, 5th Grade Elementary Teacher; *b:* Chambersburg, PA; *ed:* (BS) Elem Ed 1970, (MED) Rdng Specialist, 1972 Shippensburg Univ; *cr:* 5th Grade Teacher St Thomas Elem Sch 1970-; *ai:* Tuscarora Amer Field Service Chapter Family Coord; Tuscarora Ed Assn Building Rep, PA St Ed Assn, NEA; PTA VP; Tuscarora Area Cmmty Theater Pres 1986, 1988; *office:* St Thomas Elem Sch 70 Schoolhouse Rd Saint Thomas PA 17252

BEELER, SUSAN LYNNE, English Department Chair; *b:* Knoxville, TN; *m:* Steven Louis; *c:* Stephen J.; *ed:* (BS) Ed/Eng/Speech/Theatre, Univ of TN Knoxville 1983; *cr:* Teacher Knoxville Cath HS 1983-; *ai:* Adv Y-Teens; Stu Cncl; Eng Dept Head; NCEA 1987-; YWCA 1986-, Adv of Yr 1989; Natl Right to Life 1988-; Knoxville Zoological Society 1989-; Teacher of Yr Knoxville Cath HS 1987-88; *office:* Knoxville Cath HS 1610 Magnolia Ave Knoxville TN 37917

BEEM, LAURA ROBINSON, English Teacher; *b:* Nashville, TN; *m:* Edwin L.; *c:* Joshua S., Misti D.; *ed:* (BA) Eng, Belmont Coll 1968; (MA) Curr/Instruction, Univ of N CO 1980; Grad Work Trevecca Coll, TN St Univ; *cr:* Eng Teacher Cumberland Jr/Sr HS 1968-78, Joelton HS 1978-80, Whites Creek Comprehensive HS 1980-; *ai:* Frosh Vlybl Coach; Bsktbl Scorekeeper; Soph Adv; White Creek HS Lang Art, Philosophy & Objectives, Lang Art In-Service & Sports Comms; Eng Tutor; Nashville Cncl Teachers of Eng Secy 1986-87; Mid TN Rdng Assn; TACA, MNEA, NEA, TEA; TN Cncl Teachers of Eng; Cofers Chapel Womans Auxiliary Missions Action Chairperson 1989-; Metropolitan Nashville Writers Wkshp; *office:* Whites Creek Comprehensive HS 7277 Old Hickory Blvd Whites Creek TN 37189

BEENE, RICHARD GLEN, HS Social Studies Teacher; *b:* Lindsay, OK; *m:* Dana Evelyn Dempsey; *c:* Nicholas, Alexander; *ed:* (BA) Soc Stud, SW OK St 1981; (MS) Scndry Admin, Fort Hays St 1990; Cntrl St 1988-89; *cr:* Soc Stud Teacher Alex HS 1981-88, OK City Mc Guinness HS 1988-89, Garden City HS 1989-; *ai:* Head Boys Bsktbl & Asst Cross Cntry Coach; Intramural Dir; Stu Cncl Adv; Rep of Constitution Bicentennial Stud Dallas, Rep 1987; OK Coaches Assn, Coach of Yr 1989; SW KS Coach of Yr 1990; *office:* Garden City HS 1412 Main St Garden City KS 67846

BEENE, SHERRON BRADKE, Fifth Grade Teacher; *b:* Conway, AR; *m:* Larry S.; *c:* Brad; *ed:* (BSE) Early Chldhd/Elem Ed, St Coll of AR 1973; (MSE) Rdng, Univ of Cntrl AR 1980; *cr:* Kndgtn Teacher 1974-80, 5th Grade Teacher 1980-83, 4th Grade Teacher 1983-84, 5th Grade Teacher 1984- Quitman Elem Sch; *home:* Rt 2 Box 8 Enola AR 72047

BEENE, VIRGIL DAVID, Director of Instrumental Music; *b:* Kilgore, TX; *m:* Vicki Utsey; *c:* Corey Bobbitt, Kyle Bobbitt, Jordan; *ed:* (BA) His, 1972, (BME) Music Ed, 1974 TX Chrstn Univ; (MA) Music, Univ of Tx 1983; *cr:* Asst Band Dir De Kalb Ind Sch Dist 1974-75; Jr HS Band Dir Van Ind Sch Dist 1975-79; Band Dir Overton Ind Sch Dist 1979-86; Dir Inst Music Palestine Ind Sch Dist 1986-; *ai:* TMEA, TBA, NAMMB; *office:* Palestine Ind Sch Dist Loop 256 E Palestine TX 75801

BEER, ESTHER RAE, Sixth Grade Teacher; *b:* Chicago, IL; *ed:* (BSED) Elem Ed, 1971, (MSED) Curr/Supervision, 1975 Northern IL Univ; Gifted Ed, Critical & Creative Thinking, Problem Solving, Lang Art, Interpersonal Relationships, Admin; *cr:* 3rd/4th Grade Teacher/Unit Leader 1971-78, 5th/6th Grade Teacher/Unit Leader 1978- Fierke Ed Center; Ed Teacher Lewis

Univ 1988; Gifted Coord Fierke Ed Center 1989-; *ai:* Gifted, Curr Coordinating, Lang Art, Sci, Math, Rdng & Writing Comm; Sch Enrichment Team; IL Cncl for Gifted Mem 1989-; Fnd for Excl in Teaching Acad Comm 1988-89; IL Fed of Teachers Local 604 Treas 1974-75; Golden Apple Winner Fnd for Excl in Teaching 1988; *office:* Fierke Ed Center 6535 W Victoria Dr Oak Forest IL 60452

BEERLY, SANDRA KAY GRENINGER, Elementary Aide; *b:* Webb City, MO; *m:* John Ervin Sr.; *c:* John E. Jr., Donald R.; *cr:* Aide Cntrl Chrstn Acad 1977-88, Baldwin Elem 1990.

BEERS, PETER K., Music Department Chair; *b:* Los Angeles, CA; *m:* Robin Jo Sipots; *c:* Bradford, Jonathon; *ed:* (BA) Music/Eng, Occidental Coll 1974; Grad Stud Music, CA St Fullerton; Sch Counseling, CA St Northridge; *cr:* Teacher Wilson Jr HS 1975-; *ai:* Pop Ensemble; Sch Improvement Act; Sch Site Cncl; Technology Advisory Comm; Southern CA Vocal Assn (Secy 1978-80, Mem) 1977-; CTA, NEA 1975-; Church Choir Dir; Masonic Awd for Outstanding Teaching; Glendale Chamber of Commerce Outstanding Teacher Awd 1990; Awarded Music Grant for Cmptr & Synthesizer Equipment; Intnl Chorus Dir 4th Place Awd 1985; Farwestern Dist Barbershop Quartet Champion 1977, 1985; *office:* Wilson Jr HS 1221 Monterey Rd Glendale CA 91206

BEESLEY, JUDY K., English Teacher; *b:* Ogden, UT; *m:* Richard; *c:* Marc, Deborah, Mathew; *ed:* (BA) Eng, UT St Univ 1969; Additional Work in Ed, Eng, & Rdng; *cr:* Teacher Rigby HS 1970-71, Madison Jr HS 1981-88, Madison HS 1989-; *ai:* Chrldr Adv; Eng Chairperson; NCTE, NEA; Rexburg Ed Assn Secy 1985-86; ESA Pres 1972-85; *home:* PO Box 154 Rexburg ID 83440

BEESON, JANICE THORWALDSEN, Teacher; *b:* Fargo, ND; *m:* Robert Dale; *c:* Brittany, Braden; *ed:* (BS) Eng, Moorhead St Univ 1979; Working Toward Masters Scndry Admin; *cr:* Scndry Eng Instr Detroit Lakes Sr HS 1979-80, Barnesville Sr HS 1980-84, Moorhead Sr HS 1985-86; *ai:* Tennis, Speech & Debate Coach; Barnesville Jr Class Adv; GSA Leader 1989-; *home:* 1813 Keller Lake Dr Burnsville MN 55337

BEEZLEY, SALLY RISSER, Vocational Education Coord; *b:* Sheridan, MO; *m:* Paul Fern; *c:* Alisha K. Beezley Biasella, Darin P.; *ed:* (BS) Bus/Eng, 1961, (MS) Voc Bus/Management, 1971 NW MO Univ; NE MO Univ, Drake Univ, Univ of Northern IA, IL St Univ, Univ of WI Whitewater, Marycrest Coll; *cr:* Bus/Eng Teacher Sheridan RII 1961-64; Bus Educator NE Nodaway RV 1967-70; Voc Ed Coord Bedford HS 1970-85, Washington HS 1985-; *ai:* Stu Organization, Bus Prof of America, Soph Class Spon; Delta Kappa Gamma Recording Secy 1989-; WEA, ISEA, NEA 1985-; BEA, ISEA, NEA Secy; Order of Eastern Star Secy, Bus & Prof Women Secy, MO Fed of Womens Clubs Past Pres; *office:* Washington HS 313 S 4th Ave Washington IA 52353

BEGGERLY, HARRY D., Science Teacher; *b:* Parsons, KS; *m:* Janet K. Barnard; *c:* Abigail L., Stephanie A.; *ed:* (BS) Bio, 1970, (MS) Comm Coll Teaching, 1978, (EDS) Higher Ed, 1986 Pittsburg St Univ; Biotechnology Wkshp, Tulsa Univ 1989; *cr:* Sci Teacher B & B HS 1973-78, Miami HS 1978-; *ai:* Sr Class Spon; Sci Club; Bldg Rep; Negotiations Team; Pres & Treas of Teachers Local; PRR Chm; NEA 1973-; OK Ed Assn, Miami Assn of Classroom Teachers 1978-; Co-Author Article in Journal of Abnormal Psych; *office:* Miami HS 2000 E Central Miami OK 74354

BEGGS, BETTY CRONEY, Third Grade Teacher; *b:* Elkton, TN; *m:* Albert Truman; *c:* Joy A. Harbin, Randall T., Larry D.; *ed:* (BS) Elem Ed, Athens St Coll 1972; (MA) Elem Ed, A&M Univ 1990; *cr:* Elem Teacher Clements HS 1972-; *ai:* AL Ed Assn, NEA, LCEA; PTA; *home:* Rt 5 Box 361 Athens AL 35611

BEGGS, WILLIAM THOMAS, Math & Cmptr Science Teacher; *b:* Chicago Heights, IL; *m:* Jean Rieger; *c:* William, Amy; *ed:* (BS) Math, 1975, (MS) Math, 1980 Western IL Univ; Summer Inst for Math 1987; Teachers at Fermi Natl Accelerator Laboratory in Batavia IL; *cr:* 7th-8th Grade Math Teacher Geneseo Jr HS 1975-79; 7th Grade Math Teacher Hadley Jr HS 1979-80; Math/Cmptr Sci Teacher Glenbard North HS 1980-; *ai:* Math Team Coach at Glenbard North 1982-; Mem Chm for Glenbard North Ed Assn; IL Cncl of Teachers of Math Regional Mem Chm 1986-; NCTM Mem 1975-; St Thomas Hospice Volunteer 1989-; Ministry of Care St Marks Parish Volunteer 1983-85; Friends of Ferri Laboratory Mem 1987-; 1988-89 Received Those Who Excel Awd of Merit from IL St Bd of Ed; Awd of Excl from the IL Math/Sci Acad 1988; 3 Nationally Published Articles on Math Problem Solving; *office:* Glenbard North H S 990 Kuhn Rd Carol Stream IL 60188

BEGLEY, JAMES WALTER, III, Social Studies Teacher; *b:* Brooklyn, NY; *m:* Susan Elizabeth Jensen; *c:* Elizabeth, Thomas; *ed:* (BA) Ed, 1966, (MS) Ed His, 1969 SUNY Brockport; SUNY Stoneybrook; C W Post NY; *cr:* 4th Grade Teacher 1966-68, 5th Grade Teacher 1960-69 Pulaski Road Elem Sch; Soc Stud Teacher Middleville Jr HS 1969-88, Middleville Road Mid Sch 1988-; *ai:* After Sch Supervision; United Teachers of Northport 1966-; NY St United Teachers 1966-; Amer Fed of Teachers 1980-; Bd of Cooperative Educl Services Spec Ed Division Awd 1989; United Teachers of Northport NY Membership Services Rep 1983-86; *home:* 8 Richmond Blvd Centereach NY 11720

BEHLERS, GERALDINE HAVEKOST, Mathematics Teacher; *b:* Bancroft, NE; *m:* Merlin M.; *c:* Deb Angerman, Steve, Bob, Jim; *ed:* (BA) Bus, Wayne St Coll 1957; Grad Stud Unified Sch Dist, Morningside Coll: *cr:* Bus/Math Classroom Teacher Ponca Public Sch 1957-59; Math Classroom Teacher Sioux City Public Sch 1966-; *ai:* NEA, IA St Ed Assn, Sioux City Ed Assn 1966-; Delta Kappa Gamma 1983-; Alpha Delta Kappa Treas 1982-; *office:* East Mid Sch 1720 Morningside Ave Sioux City IA 51106

BEHNKE, KARL K., Government Teacher; *b:* Battle Creek, MI; *m:* Joan Brown; *c:* Greg, Andy, Brad; *ed:* (BS) His, Kellogg Comm Coll 1967; (BA) Poly Sci/His, W MI Univ 1969; Grad Work W MI Univ; *cr:* Teacher Battle Creek Public Schls, Springfield HS 1969-; *ai:* Sr Class, Project Close-Up, Model United Nations Adv; Effective Schls Comm; MI Ed Assn, NEA 1969-; Pennfield Lions VP 1989-; St Paul Luth Church Trustee; Teacher of Yr Springfield HS 1986; Excl In Ed Awd 1984, 1986, 1987; *home:* 485 Sylvan Dr Battle Creek MI 49017

BEHNKEN, DONNA D., Second Grade Teacher; *b:* Sheboygan, WI; *ed:* (BA) Elem Ed, Concordia Teachers Coll 1969; Assorted Classes & Wkshps; *cr:* Dir of Chrstn Ed/Kndgtn Teacher Luth Church of Epiphany 1969-71; 2nd Grade Teacher Grace Luth Sch 1971-; *ai:* Cheerleading Coach; Math Curr Comm; Luth Ed Assn Secy 1981-83; Huntsville Cmmty Chorus (Personnel Chm, Ticket Chm, Singer) 1972-; S Dist of Luth Church MO Synod (Bd of Dir 1986-88, Parish Ed Comm 1988-, Schls Comm 1988-); *office:* Grace Luth Sch 3321 S Memorial Pkwy Huntsville AL 35801

BEHREND, ELISABETH KUGEL, 7th/8th Grade Soc Stud Teacher; *b:* Brenham, TX; *m:* Don R.; *c:* Scott; *ed:* (BS) Elem Ed/Eng Lit, Concordia Teachers Coll 1963; (MS) OK St Univ 1967; *cr:* 3rd Grade Teacher 1st Luth Sch 1963-68; Kndgtn Teacher Zion Luth Sch 1969-70; 1st-3rd Grade Teacher Our Redeemer Luth Sch 1973-74; 6th Grade Teacher S Hutchinson Grade Sch 1974-75; K-4th Grade Teacher 1975-78, 6th/Dep 7th-8th Grade Teacher 1978- Zion Luth Sch; *ai:* Accreditation Chm; Chrldr Coach; Jr NHS Comm Spon; Luth Ed Assn 1976-; NASSP, NCSS 1988-; Dallas Luth Teachers Assn Chm; TX Dist Pastor Teachers Conference Region B Co-Chm; Dallas Historical Society Volunteer 1985-; Natural His Museum Volunteer 1989-; Wrote Ed Materials for Dallas Historical Society; *office:* Zion Luth Sch 6121 E Lovers Ln Dallas TX 75214

BEHREND, LOUIE DANIEL, 6th Grade Teacher; *b:* Maquoketa, IA; *m:* Carla Muhlhausen; *c:* Angela, Kimberly; *ed:* (BA) Elem Ed, Univ of N IA 1972; Teacher As Researcher, Mary Crest Coll 1990; *cr:* 4th Grade Teacher Ar-We-Va 1972-75; 6th Grade Teacher St Marys 1975-76, Northeast Sch 1976-77; 4th Grade Teacher Clinton Schls 1977-78; 6th Grade Teacher Preston Schls 1978-; *ai:* Soccer Coach; Phase III Writing Comm; Preston Cmmty Ed Assn Treas 1986-; River Valley Rdng Mem 1989-; IA Conservation Mem 1988-; PTA Carnival 1988-; Creative Learning Center Day Care Bd Pres; *office:* Preston Cmmty Schls Box 10 Preston IA 52069

BEHRENDT, BARBRA JANE, Second Grade Teacher; *b:* Zanesville, OH; *m:* Marc Edward; *ed:* (BA) Elem Ed, Wittenberg Univ 1977; (MA) Elem Ed/Rdng, OH Univ 1980; Learning Disabilities, Behavior Disorders, Muskingum Coll 1981; *cr:* 2nd Grade Teacher Crooksville K-8th Sch 1977-; *ai:* Rdng, Math, Lang Art, Educl Excl Curr Committees; Delta Kappa Gamma 1987-; GSA Brownie Leader 1977-81; Martha Holden Jennings Fnd Grant 1989; *office:* Crooksville K-8 Sch 12400 Tunnel Hill Rd NE Crooksville OH 43731

BEHRENS, JERRY LEIGH, Mathematics Instructor; *b:* Harvard, IL; *m:* Muriel Ann Mc Farland; *c:* Sarah, Carrie; *ed:* (BS) Math, 1969, (MSED) Educl Admin, 1975 IL St Univ; Ed, Univ of WY; Accounting & Ed Admin, Bradley Univ; *cr:* Math Teacher Trewyn Jr HS 1969-74, Peoria Cntrl HS 1974-84; Accounting Instr IL Cntrl Coll 1982-84; Math Teacher Cody HS 1984-; *ai:* Head Spon Soph & Jr Class; Bus Yrbk Adv; NEA 1969-74; NCTM 1988-89; *office:* Cody HS 1225 10th St Cody WY 82414

BEHRENS, VIRGINA S., English Department Chairperson; *b:* Wilmington, NC; *m:* Harry Johannes Albert; *c:* Harry Jr., Katie, Karl; *ed:* (BA) Eng, 1968, (MAT) Eng Ed, 1977 Winthrop Coll; Pre-Doctoral Stud, Somerset Univ, Columbia Pacific Univ; *cr:* Instr Winthrop Coll; Teacher Charlotte-Mecklenburg Sch System, Truett-Mc Connell Coll, Mc Duffie Cty Sch System; *ai:* Beta Club Spon; 9th-12th Grade Lang Art Curr Comm Chairperson; Phi Delta Kappa 1988-; NCTE 1986-; Fiction Awd Winthrop Coll, Penn St; Asst Field Research/Writing; Miscellaneous Short Stories & Romantic Fiction Novels.

BEHRMAN, MICHAEL WILLIAM, Physical Education Teacher; *b:* Washington, DC; *m:* Barbara H. Holley; *c:* Sarah E.; *ed:* (BS) Bus/Phys Ed, VA Tech 1970; (MS) Admin/Supervision, Radford 1974; (EDD) Educl Leadership Vanderbilt Univ 1985; Doctoral Cert Health/Phys Ed, W GA Coll 1987; *cr:* Health/Phys Ed Teacher Robert E Lee Jr HS 1972-73; Phys Ed Teacher Edwin A Gibson Mid Sch 1973-79, Bill Arp Elem Sch 1979-; Part Time Instr Mercer Univ 1988-; *ai:* Coord Phys Ed Club, Patriot Pride Club; Co-Coord Just Say No Club; GAHPERD 1987-; DEA, VEA 1972-79; DCEA, GAE 1979-; NEA 1972-; Atlanta Journal/Constitution K-4 Honor Teacher of Yr 1988; *home:* 4050 Lakeland Hills Dr Douglasville GA 30134

BEHRNS, GARY M., French/Spanish Teacher; *b:* N Tonawanda, NY; *m:* Nancy L. Lombardi; *c:* Eric, Maria, Steven; *ed:* (BA) Fr/Span, SUNY Albany 1969; (MA) Fr Lit, Univ of WI 1972; Grad Courses SUNY Buffalo, Univ Avignon France, Univ of Rochester; *cr:* Fr Teacher Niagara Falls HS 1969-70; Fr/Span Teacher Amherst Cntrl HS 1970-74; Fr Teacher Maryvale Sr HS 1974-76, West Seneca Cntrl Schls 1976-; *ai:* Var Bowling & Intramural Bowling Coach; Fr Club; Spon Trips to Quebec & Europe; AATF Chm of Fr Contest 1970-75, Schlsp Study France 1977; NY St Assn of Foreign Lang Teachers Comm Chm; Western NY Foreign Lang Educators Cncl Conference Planning Comm; Wheatfield Neighborhood Church (Organist, Choir Dir, Teacher of Adults) 1969-; Schlsp Natl Endowment of Hum 1985, Fr Government 1977; *home:* 342 Elmwood Ave North Tonawanda NY 14120

BEHROOZ, JUDY GRAHAM, Kindergarten Teacher; *b:* Salisbury, NC; *m:* Ghulam Seddiq; *c:* Jonathan O., Susan E.; *ed:* (AA) Pre-Sch Ed, Wingate Coll 1973; (BA) Early Chldhd Ed, Pfeiffer Coll 1978; *cr:* Teacher Wonderworld Day Care Center 1973-76; Asst Teacher Rowan/Salisbury Schls 1978-80; 3rd Grade Teacher 1980-82, Kndgtn Teacher 1982- China Grove Elem; *ai:* PENC 1986-; NCAE 1978-85; Intnl Womens Club 1983-; *office:* China Grove Elem Sch 514 S Franklin St China Grove NC 28023

BEICHNER, LINDA GRAHAM, Second Grade Teacher; *b:* Oil City, PA; *m:* Gerald Leo; *ed:* (BA) Elem Ed, Indiana Univ of PA 1970; *ai:* PSEA 1970-.

BEIER, ALAN M., Chemistry Teacher; *b:* New York, NY; *m:* Anita; *c:* Amy, Adam; *ed:* (BS) Chem/Ed, Univ of MD 1976; Working Towards Masters Equivalent; Courses Adolescent Behavior, Cmptrs, Sci; *cr:* Chem Teacher Northwestern HS 1976-77, High Point HS 1977-; *ai:* Sr Class & NHS Spon; Sci Fair & Awds Comms; Talent Show Faculty Act; NSTA 1977-; PTSA, NEA, MSTA, PGCEA 1976-; Outstanding Sci Educator 1987; Stu Newspaper Poll Voted Coolest, Most Helpful, Most Sch Spirited; Author Academic Center Magurt Sch Chem Curr; St of MD Safety Manual Chem Section Contributor; *office:* High Point HS 5601 Powder Mill Rd Beltsville MD 20705

BEILHARZ, CATHY L., Mathematics/Chemistry Teacher; *b:* Kansas City, MO; *ed:* (BA) Chem, St Olaf Coll 1986; *cr:* Math/Chem Teacher Perryville HS; *ai:* Sr Class & NHS Spon; Iota Sigma Pi, NSTA, ADK Teachers Organization; *home:* Rt 1 Perryville MO 63775

BEISER, JULIE SUE, French Teacher; *b:* Los Angeles, CA; *ed:* (BA) Fr, CA St Univ Northridge 1979; *cr:* Teacher Lincoln Jr HS 1981-82, Bel-Air Preparatory Sch 1982-86, Canyon HS 1986-; *ai:* Fr Club; Drill Team Adv; AATF 1989-; Foreign Lang Grant Senate Bill 513; *office:* Canyon HS 19300 Nadal St Canyon Country CA 91351

BEITO, HOWARD DEAN, Social Studies/Phys Ed Teacher; *b:* Hallock, MN; *m:* Michelle R. La Doucer; *c:* Kara, Toni; *ed:* (AA) General, Northland Comm Coll 1981; (BS) Soc Stud/Phys Ed, Mankato St Univ 1985; Working towards Masters Phys Ed, Admin; *cr:* Soc Stud/Phys Ed Teacher/Head Hockey Coach Delta Greely Sch Dist 1985-; *ai:* Jr Class Spon; Head Hockey Coach; *office:* Delta Junction HS Pouch #1 Delta Junction AK 99737

BEJARANO, MICHAEL ANTHONY, Social Studies Teacher; *b:* Tucson, AZ; *m:* Carrie Broughton; *ed:* (BA) Poly Sci, Univ of AZ 1988; *cr:* World Geography Teacher Santa Rita HS 1988-; *ai:* AZ Model United Nations Club Spon; Project SOAR Mentor; Asst Var Bsbl Coach; NEA, NCSS, Amer Bsbl Coaches Assn 1988-; *home:* 1347-B E Ft Lowell Tucson AZ 85719

BEJEC, LILIA SANTIAGO, Elementary Teacher; *b:* Bascaran Solano, Philippines; *m:* Eulogio V.; *c:* Dwight; *ed:* (BSE) Elem Ed, Arellano Univ 1968; (MA) Sci Ed, Philippine Normal Coll 1975; Ed Leadership, Natl Coll of Ed 1990; CAS Sci Ed, Natl Coll of Ed: *cr:* 6th Grade Teacher 1975-76, 3rd Grade Teacher 1976-79, Sci Teacher 1979-87 Bible Baptist Chrstn; 5th Grade Teacher Dieterich Elem 1987-; *ai:* Sci Curr Cncl Mem; Sci Club Adv; Sunday Sch Teacher; Cesi Mem 1989- Presidential Awd for Excl; IACS Mem 1975-87; Phil Ed of Amer Mem Nom 1987-; Amberwood Homeowners Mem 1989-; Village Baptist Assn Church Secy 1990; PTA Cncl Rep 1989-; Teachers Service Awd 1987; *office:* Dieterich Elem Sch 1141 Jackson St Aurora IL 60505

BEJIN, ROZANNA MARIE HANSON, English Teacher; *b:* Eau Claire, WI; *m:* Gary W.; *c:* Rachael; *ed:* (BA) Eng, 1975, (ME) Prof Dev, 1988 Univ of WI Eau Claire; *cr:* Eng Teacher North HS 1979-80, Memorial HS 1980-81, Delong Jr HS 1981-; *ai:* Co Adv Excalibur Yrbk; Played Edith Frank Chippewa Valley Theatre Guilds 1989 Production the Diary of Anne Frank; West Cntrl WI Writing Project Assn with Natl Writing Project 1981; Classroom Research 1990; *office:* Homer Delong Jr H S 2000 Vine St Eau Claire WI 54703

BELAK, THEODORE ALLAN, Math/Soc Stud Teacher; *b:* Warren, OH; *m:* Cynthia Yuson; *c:* Andrew, Jennifer; *ed:* (BS) Math, St Bonaventure Univ 1966; *cr:* 5th-6th Grade Teacher Erwin Elem 1971-78; 6th-8th Grade Teacher Edgewood Mid Sch 1978-; *ai:* Math Club; Ftbl, Bsktbl, Track Sftbl Coach 1978-86; Yrbk Adv 1982-85; NCTM 1985-; Books Published; *office:* Edgewood Mid Sch 14135 Fairgrove La Puente CA 91746

BELAND, JANE MARIE, Fifth Grade Teacher; *b:* Tecumseh, MI; *m:* Franz B. Koch; *c:* Sydney, Jack; *ed:* (BA) Elem Ed, Univ of MI 1979; (MA) Elem Ed, Univ of Toledo 1987; LETS; *cr:* 5th-8th Grade Teacher Deerfield Public Schls 1979-; *ai:* Equations Coach; 9th Grade Class Adv; Prin Advisory Comm; Chm for Grandparents Day & Spelling Bee; Equations Admin for Cty Varsity Track Coach; Lenawee Rdng Cty 1979-; Deerfield Fire Dept Aux Pres 1990; Outstanding Young Women of Amer Awd 1988; *home:* 381 E River St Deerfield MI 49238

BELANGER, ALBERT EDWARD, 7th Grade English Teacher; *b:* Salem, MA; *m:* Sandra Louise Blanchard; *c:* Stephen, Dianne Plante, Aaron, Daniel; *ed:* (BSED) Jr HS Eng, 1961, (MAT) Linguistics, 1974 Salem St Coll; Grad Stud NH Voc Tech Coll, Leslie Coll, Univ of NH; *cr:* Eng/Fr Teacher Hampton Acad Jr HS 1961-66; Jr HS Eng Dept Chm 1967-82, Eng Teacher 1966-Pentucket Regional Jr HS; *ai:* Coll Bowl Coach; Prin Advisory Cncl; Pentucket Assn of Teachers Building Rep, MA Cncl of Teachers of Eng, NCTE; Town of Brentwood Trustee of Trust Funds 1982-; Brentwood Newsletter Editorial Comm 1990; Published Articles in Historical & Geneological Journals; Co-Authored Book of Poetry; *office:* Pentucket Regional Jr HS Main St West Newbury MA 01985

BELCHER, CLADENE LANDERS, Second Grade Teacher; *b:* Collinsville, TX; *m:* Danny G.; *ed:* (BS) Ed, 1970, (MED) Elem Ed/Supervision, 1973 N TX St Univ; *cr:* Teacher Whitesboro Ind Sch Dist 1970-; *ai:* TX Classroom Teachers Assn 1988-; Delta Kappa Gamma Secy 1988-; PTO Treas 1987-88; Contemporary Womans Club Secy 1988-; Whitesboro Golf Assn Secy 1988-; *home:* 725 White St Whitesboro TX 76273

BELCHER, CLARK, World History Teacher; *b:* Belcher, KY; *m:* Carolea Pechacek; *c:* Gregory C., Dorothy R., Darryl W.; *ed:* (BS) His Pikeville Coll 1970; (ME) Admin/Supervision Univ of North FL 1980; Med Instr US Army Reserve Forces; *cr:* Art Instr Clay Jr/Sr HS 70-71; Soc Stud Green Cove Springs Mid Sch 72-83; World His Orange Park HS 83-; *ai:* Past Class Spon; NCSS; Green Cove Spring Athletic Assn VP 86-88; Boy Scouts 76-81; Coached Little Leaque 1973-88; Teacher of Month; Army Achvt; Army Commendation; FL Meritiorious Svc Awd.; *office:* Orange Park HS 2300 Kingsley Ave Orange Park FL 32073

BELCHER, JACQUELINE ANN, Kindergarten Teacher; *b:* Mexico, MO; *ed:* (BS) Elem Ed, TX Tech Univ 1973; (MA) Early Chldhd Ed, Univ of TX San Antonio; NE Math Inst; NE Rdng Wkshp TX St; Math Module Trng; Numerous Inservices; *cr:* Teacher Kelly Elem 1973-77, Clear Spring Elem 1977-88, Woodstone Elem 1988-; *ai:* Mem NE Math Comm; NE Math Inst; Woodstone Elem Grade Level Chm 1990-; Delta Kappa Gamma 1989; ATPE; NE Teachers Assn Faculty Rep 1982-83, Human Relations Awd 1982; San Antonio Conservation Society; Alpha Phi (Secy, VP, Philanthroply); San Antonio Museum Assn; Sierra Club; *office:* Woodstone Elem Sch 5602 Fountainwood San Antonio TX 78233

BELCHER, JEANETTE, First Grade Teacher; *b:* Pikeville, KY; *m:* Franklin D.; *c:* Christopher; *ed:* (BS) Elem Ed, Pikeville Coll 1966; *ai:* DCEA, NEA; *home:* 276 Dry Branch Rd Pikeville KY 41501

BELCHER, JULIE ADAMS, Mathematics Teacher; *b:* Honolulu, HI; *m:* Robert W.; *ed:* (BS) Scndry Ed, Old Dominion Univ 1982; *cr:* Math Teacher Indian River Jr HS 1983-; *ai:* Courtesy Comm Chm; Child Study Team Math Rep; VEA, NEA, CEA Mem 1983-; NCTM, VCTM, TCTM Mem 1988-; Teacher of Yr 1988-89; *office:* Indian River Jr HS 2300 Greenbrier Rd Chesapeake VA 23325

BELCHER, SHERRI RICHMOND, Science/Mathematics Teacher; *b:* London, KY; *m:* Stephen R.; *c:* Shon S.; *ed:* (BS) Elem Ed, 1974, (MS) Elem Ed, 1976 IN Univ; Gifted Ed; Sci, Math, Lang Art, Soc Stud Jr HS; *cr:* Kndgtn Teacher 1974-77, 3rd Grade Teacher 1977-79, 6th Grade Teacher 1979-83 Indian Heights Elem; 6th Grade Teacher 1983-86, 3rd Grade/Gifted Ed Teacher 1986-89, 5th Grade/Sci/Math/Health/Soc Stud Teacher 1989-Taylor Elem; *ai:* Writing Gifted & Talented Grant; ISTA, NEA, 1974-; TEA Secy 1974-; HASTI 1989-; Kakomo Jaycees Outstanding Young Teacher of Yr 1985; *office:* Taylor Cmmty Sch 3700 E 300 S Kokomo IN 46902

BELCHER, WILLIAM JOSEPH, Mathematics Department Chair; *b:* St Louis, MO; *m:* Linda K.; *c:* Christopher, Carrie; *ed:* (BS) Math, 1970, (MS) Cnslr Ed, 1974 S IL Univ Edwardsville; *cr:* Math Teacher Chrstn Brothers Coll HS 1970-; *ai:* Asst Var Soccer & Jr Var Golf Coach; *office:* Christian Brothers Coll HS 6501 Clayton Rd Saint Louis MO 63117

BELDEN, STANLEY L., 6th Grade Teacher; *b:* Beloit, KS; *m:* Connie; *c:* Terry, Matthew; *ed:* (BA) Phys Ed, Bethany Coll 1971; (MED) Elem Ed, AZ St Univ 1980; *cr:* 4th Grade Teacher Constitution Elem Sch 1977-79, Desert Winds Elem Sch 1979-89; 6th Grade Teacher Desert Winds Elem Sch 1989-; *ai:* Stu Cncl Adv; Math Comm; Yrbk Editor; Stars Coord; Deer Valley Ed Assn 1987-; Pres AZ Natl Soccer Club; *home:* 5804 W Harmont Glendale AZ 85302

BELEGAL, PORFIRIA BRUCAL, Second Grade Teacher; *b:* Dolores Quezon, Philippines; *m:* Pete Magbuhat; *c:* Phil, Portia, Priscilla; *ed:* (BSED) Elem Ed, Luzonian Univ 1963; (MS) Elem Ed, Valparaiso Univ 1978; *cr:* 4th Grade Teacher Dolores Elem Sch 1963-67, Canaan Elem Sch 1967-69; 2nd/3rd Grade Teacher Boone Grove Elem Sch 1969-; *ai:* Performance Based Accreditation, Parent Involvement, Rdng Textbook Adoption Comms; Porter Cty Rdng Assn, Alpha Delta Kappa; *office:* Boone Grove Elem Sch 325 W 550 S Boone Grove IN 46302

BELFER, CLAIRE JEAN, History, English Teacher; *b:* Deadwood, SD; *m:* Harvey Alan; *c:* Arthur, Robert, Daniel; *ed:* (BA) His, Aquinas Coll 1969; MI St Univ, Univ of MI, Western MI; *cr:* Teacher E Grand Rapids Mid Sch 1970-; *ai:* E Grand Rapids Sch Dist Instructional Policies, Soc Stud Comm Mem; Dist Spon Natl His Day Competition; NCSS, MI Cncl for Teaching of Soc Stud, MI Assn of Mid Sch Educators; E Grand Rapids Jr HS Teacher of Yr 1976; Project Bus Teacher of Month; MI St Univ Law Ed Fellowship 1986.

BELFI, MARY GRACE, Art Teacher; *b:* Brooklyn, NY; *m:* William; *ed:* (BA) Art, St Johns Univ 1969; (MA) Art Ed, Queens Coll 1971; Art & Ed Courses at Various Colls; *cr:* Art Teacher Jr HS 117 Bronx/Nathaniel Hawthorne Ind Sch Dist 74; *ai:* Yrbk Art Adv; Sr Affairs Coord; *office:* Nathaniel Hawthorne Ind Sch 74 61-15 Oceania St Bayside NY 11364

BELK, AUDREY, 7th Grade Teacher; *b:* Albany, GA; *m:* Ralf B.; *c:* Chad B., Kimberly M.; *ed:* Elem Ed, Sociology, West Georgia 1973; Ga St Univ; *cr:* 1-6 Grade Rdng Teacher Union Elem 1973-76; 6th & 7th Grade Lang Arts Teacher Snellville Mid Sch 1976-78; 7th Grade Teacher E T Booth Mid Sch 1984-; *ai:* Team Mgr E T Booth Mid Sch; NEA; 7th Grade Chrldng Spon E T Booth Mid Sch; Soc Stud Coord E T Booth Mid Sch; *office:* E T Booth Mid Sch Putnam Mill Rd Woodstock GA 30188

BELK, LINDA MOORE, Third Grade Teacher; *b:* Holly Springs, MS; *m:* Fred M. Jr.; *c:* Tish, Fred III, Fielding, Jonathan; *ed:* (BA) Elem Ed, Univ of MS 1963; *cr:* 4th Grade Teacher Holly Spgs Primary Sch 1964-69; 3rd Grade Teacher Marshall Acad 1980-; *ai:* SAC Curr Overview Chm; MPSEA 1980-; MPSEA Dist Chm Lower Elem 1986-87; *home:* 490 Salem Ave Holly Springs MS 38635

BELL, ALLISON TYLER, Spanish Teacher; *b:* Tucson, AZ; *ed:* (BA) Span, Georgetown Coll 1987; *cr:* Span Teacher Trimble Cty HS 1987-; *ai:* Mid Sch Girls Bsktbl Coach; Span Club Spon; KCTFL, ACTFL; *office:* Trimble Cty HS Rt 2 Bedford KY 40006

BELL, AMY MASSEY, French & English Teacher; *b:* Parris Island, SC; *m:* Curtis J.; *c:* Lydia, Kathryn, Clint; *ed:* (AB) Eng, 1967, (MEd) Eng, 1986 Univ of GA; Courses to Update Certificate; *cr:* 8th Grade Eng Teacher Morgan Cty Mid Sch 1976-83; Sr Eng/Advanced Placement Eng/Fr I & II Teacher Morgan Cty HS 1986-; *ai:* Y-Club Adv; Eng Dept Chairperssn; Graduation Coord; Phi Beta Kappa 1967-; Phi Kappa Phi 1986; Delta Kappa Gamma 1989; Teacher of Yr Morgan Cty HS & Morgan Cty System 1986; *home:* 1941 Seven Islands Rd Buckhead GA 30625

BELL, ANNE BROWN, French Teacher; *b:* Fountain Head, TN; *m:* Harold L.; *c:* Jeffrey L.; *ed:* (BA) Fr/Span, W Carolina Univ 1962; Grad Stud MI St Univ, W Carolina Univ, OH St Univ, Univ in Lyon France; *cr:* Teaching Asst MI St Univ 1962-63; Fr/Span Teacher Danville Sr HS 1963-65, Fr Instr Danville Jr HS 1963-65; Teacher Moline Sr HS 1965-; *ai:* Natl Fr Honor Society Curr Cncl Adv; Moline IL Natl Ed; IL Foreign Lang Teachers, NE Foreign Lang Teachers, Amer Cncl of Foreign Lang; Teaching Assistantship MI St Univ; *office:* Moline Sr HS 3600 23rd Ave Moline IL 61265

BELL, BETTY E., History Teacher; *ed:* (BS) Sociology, Fayetteville St Univ 1976; (MA) Adult Ed, Univ of DC 1989; *cr:* Supvr Woodward & Lothrop 1976-87; Teacher DC Public Schls 1987-; *ai:* Close Up & Presidential Club Coord; Co-Spon Jr Class; Phi Delta Kappa Mem 1988; Church New Members Club Mem 1984; Fayetteville St Alumni Mem 1989; Perfect Attendance; Teacher of Month; *office:* Eastern HS 17th & E Capital St NE Washington DC 20003

BELL, CAROLYN ROBERTSON, Mathematics Teacher/Dept Chair; *b:* Winston-Salem, NC; *m:* John B.; *c:* William T.; *ed:* (BS) Math, 1971, (MED) Math, 1974 Univ of NC Greensboro; Teach the Academically Gifted; *cr:* Teacher/Dept Chm Ledford Sr HS 1971-; *ai:* Sr Class Spon; Attendance Waiver & Schlsp Comm; NEA; NCAE (Secy 1984-86, Schlshp Chm 1985-89) 1971-; NCTM 1974-; Alpha Delta Kappa (Secy 1988-, VP 1990) 1987-; *office:* Ledford Sr HS Rt 4 Box 773 Thomasville NC 27360

BELL, CATHERINE ANN, 7th/8th Grade Reading Teacher; *b:* Long Island, NY; *ed:* (BA) Ed/Eng, Mt Saint Mary Coll 1967; Masters Candidate, Loyola Univ 1968-70; *cr:* 7th Grade Teacher St Christophers Sch 1966-67; Cmmty Worker Graham Avenue Cmmty Center 1967-69; 7th/8th Grade Teacher St Alphonsus Sch 1970-73, St John Vianney Sch 1973-; *ai:* Stu Cncl Moderator; NCEA 1973-; El Salvador Labor Comm in Solidarity 1988-; St Bruno Refugee Project 1985-88; Connections Peace Justice Project 1983-86; CA St Fellowship 1968-70; *office:* Saint John Vianney Sch 4601 Hyland Ave San Jose CA 95127

BELL, CONNIE S., Teacher; *b:* Louisville, KY; *c:* Laura M.; *ed:* (BS) Health/Phys Ed, Campbellsville Coll 1970; (MA) Scndry Ed, W KY Univ 1983; *cr:* Teacher J T Alton Mid Sch 1971-75, E Hardin HS 1984-; *ai:* Cheerleading Coach; *office:* E Hardin HS 129 College St Glendale KY 42740

BELL, DIANNE GARDINER, Reading Specialist; *b:* Washington, DC; *c:* Matthew, Nathan; *ed:* (BS) Elem Ed/Spec Ed, Towson St Univ 1974; (MS) Rdng Ed, Bowie St Univ 1978; *cr:* Classroom Teacher Oakcrest Elem 1974-77, Oxon Hill Elem 1977-82, William Beanes Elem 1984; Rdng Specialist Oxon Hill Elem & J Frank Dent 1984-85, Oxon Hill Elem 1985-; *ai:* Test Coord; Sch Management Team Mem; Curr Comm Chairperson; Prince Georges Cty Rdng Cncl, Intnl Rdng Assn, St of MD Intnl Rdng Assn Cncl 1986-; Southern MD Youth Organization Team Mother 1985-; *office:* Oxon Hill Elem Sch 7701 Livingston Rd Oxon Hill MD 20745

BELL, DONNA CANTWELL, Resource Teacher of Gifted Ed; *b:* Poughkeepsie, NY; *c:* Paul D., Kristen L.; *ed:* (BA) Elem Ed/Psych, Potsdam Coll 1968; Grad Courses, Univ of VA Charlottesville, George Mason Univ; Courses Towards Masters in Gifted Ed, George Mason Univ; *cr:* Classroom Teacher Owego-Appalachin Cntrl Schls 1968-69, Prince William Cty Schls 1974-86; Resource Teacher of Gifted Prgm Prince William Cty Schls 1986-; *ai:* NEA, VA Ed Assn, Prince William Ed Assn, VA Assn for Ed of Gifted 1974-; N VA Cncl for Gifted & Talented Ed Outstanding Teacher of Gifted 1989-; *office:* Prince William Cty Schls Box 389 Manassas VA 22110

BELL, DOROTHY ANN, Span/Amer Government Teacher; *b:* Parkville, MO; *m:* Frank; *c:* Jeffrey, Jennifer, Joshua, Joseph; *ed:* (BA) Soc Sci, 1986, (MAED) 1987 Harding Univ; Grad Stud Univ of San Diego, Mexico; *cr:* Cabot Sr HS 1986-; *ai:* Natl Span Honor Society Spon; Mock Trial Team; Stock Market Game; Teachers of Span 1987-; Natl Organization of Women 1987-; AR Womens Political Caucas 1990; *office:* Cabot Sr HS 504 E Locust Cabot AR 72023

BELL, DOTSIE M. (ST. JULIAN), English Department Chairperson; *b:* Alexandria, LA; *m:* Frank N. III; *c:* Frank N. IV, Dhanna M.; *ed:* (BA) Eng, Prairie View A&M Coll 1966; (MA) Eng, TX Southern Univ 1974; Gifted & Talented Ed Cert Univ CA Riverside; *cr:* Eng Teacher Lincoln HS 1966-70, Sharpstown Jr HS 1970-72, Bellaire HS 1972-74, Kolb Jr HS 1974-; *ai:* Dist Eng Curr Comm; Dist Competency Test Grading Team; Site Writing Celebration Organizer; Jr HS Writing Team Coach; NEA, CTA, Rialto Ed Assn, CA Assn Teachers of Eng, Southland Cncl Teachers of Eng; Delta Sigma Theta, Alpha Delta Kappa, The Links Inc; Fellow Inland Area Writing Project; Mentor Teacher Rialto Unified Sch Dist; Teach Univ CA Riverside Early Outreach Writing Wkshp; *office:* Kolb Jr H 2351 N Spruce Rialto CA 92376

BELL, GREGORY E., Advanced Placement Bio Teacher; *b:* Los Angeles, CA; *m:* Anita W. Wyne; *c:* Michael L., Steven G., Rebecca A.; *ed:* (BA) Bio/Phys Ed, 1969, (MA) Ed, 1972 Whittier Coll; (MA) Counseling, Chapman Coll 1976; Biotechnology, Univ of CA Davis; Advanced Placement Bio, Stanford & Univ of VA; *cr:* Sci Teacher Atwater HS 1972-; *ai:* Fellowship of Chrstn Athletes Adv; Ftbl & Var Tennis Coach; Mentor Teacher Bio; NEA, CA Teachers Assn 1972-; NABT, CA Sci Teachers Assn 1980-; *office:* Atwater HS PO Box 835 Atwater CA 95301

BELL, GWENAVE, Sixth Grade Teacher; *b:* Monticello, KY; *m:* Marion L.; *ed:* (BS) Elem Ed, Cumberland Coll 1963; Elem Ed, 1980/1982 Western KY Univ;N KY Univ; *cr:* Teacher One Room Sch 1957-63; 1st/2nd Grade Teacher Old Glory 1963-65; 4th-7th Grade Teacher Meadow Creek 1965-66; 6th Grade Teacher Wayne Cty Elem #3 1966-; *ai:* Spokesperson Accreditation; Book Comm; 4-H Leader; Nazarene Church Sunday Sch Secry 1958-88; Nazarene Church Bd Mem 1975; Nazarene Church Churchwomen of Yr 1975; *home:* Rt 5 Box 335Q Monticello KY 42633

BELL, JAMES GARY, Science Teacher/Dept Chair; *b:* Saginaw, MI; *ed:* (BA) Bio/His, Adrian Coll 1971; (MED) Curr/Instruction, 1977, Ed Specialist Admin/Supervision 1979 Univ of Toledo; Grad Stud Cetacean Bio, Coll of Atlantic; *cr:* Teacher Bedford Public Schls 1971-; *ai:* Sch Improvement Comm; Sci Curr Cncl; NSTA 1977-; MI Sci Teachers Assn 1980-; MI Earth Sci Teachers Assn 1989-; Amer Cetacean Society, Society of Marine Mammology 1987-; Cousteau Society 1989-; *office:* Bedford Jr HS 8405 Jackman Rd Temperance MI 48182

BELL, JANICE DOLIN, Fifth Grade Teacher; *b:* Ironton, OH; *c:* Amanda Bell Crabtree; *cr:* 5th Grade Teacher West Ironton Elem 1975-; *ai:* Safety Patrol Adv; IEA; OEA; NEA; *office:* West Ironton Elem Sch 1207 N 3rd St Ironton OH 45638

BELL, JUDI WILLIAMS, Career Ladder Evaluator; *b:* Lewisburg, TN; *m:* William C. Jr.; *c:* Jarratt; *ed:* (BS) Eng, 1968, (MED) Eng/Curr/Instruction, 1985 Mid TN St Univ; Career Ladder Evaluator Trng; *cr:* Eng Teacher Neelys Bend Jr HS 1969-82, Madison HS 1982-85, Hunters Lane Comprehensive HS 1986-89; Career Ladder Evaluator St of TN 1989-; *ai:* Stu Cncl Spon; Faculty Advisory Comm Chm; Alpha Delta Kappa Recording Secy 1986-; Nashville Cncl Teachers of Eng; Mid TN Cncl Teachers of Eng; Sabbatical Leave Grant 1984-85; Prof Travel Grant London England 1988; Hospital Corporation of America Writing Grant in Critical Thinking 1987; *home:* 506 Menees Ln Madison TN 37115

BELL, KATHRYN TAMBLYN, English/Journalism Teacher; *b:* Bad Axe, MI; *m:* Stephen Peter; *c:* Jordan J., Stephanie C.; *ed:* (BA) Eng/Sociology, 1972, (MA) Journalism, 1978 Cntrl MI Univ; Writing, MI St Univ; Lang/Cmptrs, E MI Univ; Journalism, U of MI; *cr:* Teacher Caro HS 1972-80, Hillsdale HS 1980-; *ai:* NHS, Literary Magazine & Stu Newspaper Adv; Scndry Lang Art Curr Chairperson; Chief Negotiator Hillsdale Ed Assn; Sch Dist Communications Comm Co-Chairperson; NCTE 1972-; MI Cncl of Teacher of Eng 1972-; Journalism Ed Assn 1972-; MI Interscholastic Press Assn (Regional Dir, Treas) 1982-88; Domestic Harmony (Chairperson, Bd of Dir) 1986-89; 1st Presbyn Church Elder 1990; Amer Assn of Univ Women 1980-83; Dow Jones Newspaper Fund Fellow 1975; Session Presenter; Annual Fall & Spring Conferences MI Interscholastic Press Assn; Instr Summer Journalism Wkshp MI St Univ; Cover Story Leadership Magazine; *office:* Hillsdale HS 30 S Norwood St Hillsdale MI 49242

BELL, MARGARET SHEARIN, Assistant Principal; *b:* High Point, NC; *m:* Alonzo Randolph Sr.; *c:* Alonzo, Steven; *ed:* (BS) Speech/Drama/Eng, 1960, (MA) Ed/Eng, 1971 Hampton Inst; Urban Service, Admin, Management, Old Dominion Univ 1990; *cr:* Eng Teacher Newport News Public Schls 1961-88; Dir Newport News Dropout Prevention/Rehabilitation Prgm 1988; Asst Prin Newport News Public Schls 1988-; *ai:* NEA 1961-88; NASSP, ASCD 1988-; Amer Assn of Univ Women 1990; Newport News Ed Assn (Treas, Bd of Dirs); VA Ed Assn Bd of Dirs; Kappa Delta Pi Pres; *office:* Denbigh HS 259 Denbigh Blvd Newport News VA 23602

BELL, MARY STINSON, English Teacher; *b:* Evergreen, AL; *m:* Jimmy Leon; *c:* William L., Shelley E.; *ed:* (BS) Eng/Health/Phys Ed, Univ of AL 1975; (MED) Eng, Livingston Univ 1987; Advanced Placement Eng, Univ of AL 1989; *cr:* 5th/8th Grade Eng/His Teacher Glen Oaks Elem 1975; 7th-9th Grade Phys Ed Teacher Forest Hills Mid Sch 1975-76; Career Ed Teacher Conecuh Cty Schls 1976-79; 7th-12th Grade Eng Teacher Sparta Acad 1982-84; 11th-12th Grade Eng Teacher Evergreen HS 1985-89, Hillcrest HS 1989-; Eng Composition I Teacher Jefferson Davis Jr Coll 1990; *ai:* Lang Arts Team; Sr Class Spon; NHS Faculty Adv; Delta Kappa Gamma Secy 1990; NCTE 1984-; AL Educl Assn, NEA, Conecuh Cty Teachers Assn; *home:* 200 Bruner Ave Evergreen AL 36401

BELL, OSCAR LARKIN, Social Studies Teacher; *b:* Charlotte, NC; *m:* Karen Markle; *c:* Kathryn, Mary; *ed:* (AB) Poly Sci, Univ of NC Chapel Hill 1975; Cert Scndry Soc Stud, Univ NC Charlotte 1979; (MED) Admin, Univ of NC Chapel Hill 1984; Admin & Supervision Grad Stud; *cr:* Teacher Glade Valley HS 1979-81; Teacher/Coach The Orme Sch 1981-82; Teacher Culbreth Jr HS 1982-83, Chapel Hill HS 1983-; *ai:* Outdoor Club; NC Cncl of Soc Stud 1984-; Project EQ Grant; Visions of the Future Curr Planning; *home:* 28 Red Pine Rd Chapel Hill NC 27516

BELL, PAMELA KAY (WEIRICH), Business Teacher; *b:* Mansfield, OH; *m:* Michael Alan; *ed:* (BS) Bus Ed, Ashland Univ 1983; *cr:* Adult Bus Ed Teacher 1983-85, Bus Ed Teacher 1985- Pioneer Joint Voc Sch; *ai:* Bus Prof of Amer & OH Vocationally Talented Youth Conference Adv; Pioneer Joint Voc Sch Teacher of Yr Nominating & Crawford Cty In-Service Planning Comm; North Cntrl OH Bus Teachers Assn (Secy 1990) 1986-; OH Bus Teachers Assn 1986-; OH Voc Assn, AVA, Delta Kappa Gamma 1987-; Crestview Academic Boosters Awd; *home:* 160 Vennum Ave Mansfield OH 44903

BELL, PATRICIA BANKS, English Department Chair; *b:* Greenville, MS; *c:* Rodney Bell Jr.; *ed:* (BA) Amer Stud, Wheaton Coll 1974; (MA) Adult Ed/Admin/Supervision, Univ of DC 1979; Problem Solving, Rapid Mastery Learning, Higher Level Thinking Advanced Academic Trng Honors Wkshps; *cr:* Substitute Teacher DC Public Schls 1976-77; Eng Teacher Jefferson Jr HS 1977-81, Pearce Jr HS 1981-86; 7th Grade Eng Teacher/Dept Chairperson Kealing Magnet 1986-; *ai:* Natl Jr Honor Society & Career Fair Spon; Univ of DC Alumna 1979-; Wheaton Alumna 1974-; St Marys PTA 1989-; Kealings PTA 1986-; Pearce Jr HS Teacher of Yr 1984-86; Tracor Scholar 1985-86; Kealing Jr HS Magnet Sch Teacher of Yr 1987-88; *office:* Kealing Jr HS 1607 Pennsylvania Ave Austin TX 78702

BELL, ROBERT LAVERNE, Industrial Technology Teacher; *b:* Grinnell, IA; *m:* Agnes Schuelka; *c:* Tim, Pat, Peggy; *ed:* (AA) Marshalltown Jr Coll 1952; (BA) Phys Ed, IA Wesleyan Coll 1954; (MA) Industrial Art, N CO 1960; IA St Univ, N IA, Univ of IA, Drake Univ; *cr:* Teacher/Coach Albion HS 1956-58, Anson Jr HS 1958-; *ai:* Ftbl, Bsktbl, Track Coach; Officated Ftbl, Bsktbl, Track; Sr Class Spon; Local Sch Comms; Marshalltown Ed Assn Building Rep 1960-66, 1973, 1983, 1989; IA Industrial Arts Assn 1970-89; NEA Life Mem 1956-; IA Boys & Girls Officate St Assn (Local Pres 1972) 1959-; Teachers Awd for St Top Stu Project Awd 1982; *home:* 2671 260th St Marshalltown IA 50158

BELL, SANDY MORTON, English Teacher; *b:* Charleston, WV; *c:* Kendra, Stacy; *ed:* (BS) Elem Ed, SW TX St Univ 1970; (MS) Mid Management, TX A&M & TX A&T 1990; Creative Writing, Teams Writing Wkshps; *cr:* Eng Teacher Harlandale Mid Sch 1970-79, Krueger Mid Sch 1979-82, Bradley Mid Sch 1982-; *ai:* Scores & Curr Writing Team 1987; San Antonio Teacher Ed Advisory Center Outstanding Supervising Teacher 1987; Favorite Teacher by Stu; Presented at Natl Mid Sch Conference Toronto Canada 1989; *office:* Bradley Mid Sch 14819 Heimer Rd San Antonio TX 78232

BELL, SHARON ROCHELLE HICKS, Mathematics Teacher; *b:* St Louis, MO; *m:* William Simpson Jr.; *c:* Jeannie M., Wm. S. III; *ed:* (BS) Math, SE MO St Univ 1971; (MED) Scndry Ed/Math, Univ of St Louis 1974; NE MO St Univ; *cr:* Math Teacher/Dir of Title IVC Prgm Hazelwood Sch Dist 1971-81; Math Teacher Francis Howell Sch Dist 1984-; *ai:* NHS Spon; Vlybl & Bsktbl Coach; Math Club Greater St Louis, NCTM 1971-; Francis Howell Sch Dist 1984-, Nom Teacher of Yr 1989; Kappa Delta Pi 1971-82; Article Published; *office:* Francis Howell Sch Dist 7001 Hwy 94 S Saint Charles MO 63303

BELL, TERESA N., 7th Grade English/Lit Teacher; *b:* Sylva, NC; *m:* Alex C.; *c:* Lindsay, Luke; *ed:* (BS) Sci Ed/Earth Sci, 1975, (MA) Lang Art, 1977 W Carolina Univ; *cr:* 8th Grade Teacher 1975-76, 4th/5th Grade Teacher 1976-79, 5th/6th Grade Teacher 1979-83, 6th Grade Teacher 1983-85, 7th Grade Teacher 1985- Fairview Elem; *ai:* Sch Paper Spon; Sci Fair & Parent Action Team Comm; NC Assn of Educators Treas 1988-; NCTE; Alpha Delta Kappa Mem 1989-; Sylva Jaycees, Sylva Recreational Dept; Bus & Prof Women Newsletter Chm 1989-; *office:* Fairview Elem Sch 507 E Main St Sylva NC 28779

BELL, WILZETTA MABLE BURNS, Counselor; *b:* Wewoka, OK; *c:* Jared, Jenone; *ed:* (BA) Elem Ed, Harris Teachers Coll 1962; (MA) Cnslr Ed, St Louis Univ 1973; Cert in Eng, Educl Admin; *cr:* Elem Teacher St Louis City Schls; Jr HS Cnslr Normandy Jr HS; Eng TeacHer/Jr HS & Sr HS Cnslr Hazel Wood West HS; Honors Eng Teacher Palomares Jr HS; Cnslr Pomona HS; *ai:* Peer Cnslrs Supvr; Coll Outreach, Schlsps, Awds Comm; 9th-12th Grade Curr Rep; NEA, CA Assn of Counseling & Dev, Delta Sigma Theta; Nom Most Outstanding Young Woman of St Louis; *home:* 10273 Heather Rancho Cucamonga CA 91701

BELLAFIORE, JOHN ALBERT, Mathematics/Civics Teacher; *b:* Chicago, IL; *m:* Kristena Ann; *c:* Amber; *ed:* (BA) Soc Stud, 1971, (MED) Scndry Ed, 1976 Univ of AZ; *cr:* Teacher/Coach Toltec Sch Dist 1972-; *ai:* Ftbl, Bsktbl, Sftbl, Soccer Coach; Field Trip Prgm Coord; Graduation Dir; *office:* Toltec Elem Sch Rt 1 Box 390 Eloy AZ 85231

BELLAK, SHARON LEE, Mathematics Teacher; *b:* Cleveland, OH; *m:* Ernest Martin; *ed:* (BA) Math/Ger, Capital Univ 1968; Supervision Practicum for Gifted, Project Teach, Elem Probability, Pre-Calculus, Real Analysis, Univ of S FL; *cr:* Math Teacher Horace Mann Jr HS/Mid Sch 1968-73; Math/Teacher of Gifted Gulf Jr HS/Mid Sch 1973-; *ai:* Mathcounts Coach Regional, St & Natl Levels; Supervising Teacher for Interns; Prof Peer Reviewer for Dept of Ed; Math Contest Coord; Math Team Coach; Peer, Clinical Teacher; Dept Head; Team Leader; Organizer of St Jude Mathathon; Sch Recognition Prgm & Cty Summer Inst Steering Comm; Cty Math Rep; Task Force for Standardized Test Questions; Cty Curr; Textbook Adoption Contest, Dev, Gifted Curr Standards of Excl & Laser Disc Technology Comm; NCTM 1980-; FL Cncl of Teachers of Math 1987-; Pasco Cncl of Teachers of Math Treas 1989; Pasco Cncl of Teachers of Math VP 1990; Assoc Master Teacher; Mathcounts Coach for St of FL; Presidential Awd for Excl in Teaching Math & Sci Regional Runner Up 1985; Presidential Awd for Excl in Teaching Math & Sci Nom 1990; Supts Recognition Pin; Outstanding Personal Achievement Awd; Recognition by the Univ of S FL Center of Excl; Letter of Commendation from Supt; Teacher of Yr; Yrbk Dedication; Nom for Women in Admin.

BELLAMY, AGNES MARIA, Eng/Communications/Jrnlsm; *b:* Ary, KY; *ed:* (BA) Journalism/Broadcasting, 1978, (BA) Eng, 1986, (MA) Eng, 1986 Eastern KY Univ; Morehead St Univ; *cr:* Eng Teacher Dilce Combs HS 1982-84; Grad Asst/Instr Eastern KY Univ 1984-85; Comm/Eng Teacher Breathitt HS 1985-; *ai:* Furture Problem Solving Team Coach; Weekly Sch Newspaper Adv; Peerleader Adv; Cty Sch System Drug Adv Cncl; Sigma Tau Delta VP 1980 -82; Champions Against Drugs Treasurer 1988-; Coalition Against Teen Pregnancy 1989; Outstanding Young Woman of America 1980 & 1986; Recognition 99 Percentile Scores NTE; *office:* Breathitt H S 402 Court St Jackson KY 41339

BELLAMY, CLARENCE, Social Studies Teacher; *b:* Quincey, FL; *m:* Patricia A. Ferrell; *c:* J. Christopher; *ed:* (BA) Soc Stud Ed, FL St Univ 1976; *cr:* Soc Stud Teacher Graceville HS 1978-79, Malone HS 1979-; *ai:* Girls Var Bsktbl, Var Bsbl Coach.

BELLAMY, JON P., English Teacher; *b:* Pittsburgh, PA; *m:* Sharom M. Pandrock; *c:* Nicholas J., Neil G.; *ed:* (BA) Eng Ed/psych, Alliance Coll 1975; Scndry Sch Admin; *cr:* Teacher Carroll Mid Sch Ringgold Sch Dist 1977-; *ai:* Asst Track Coach 1980-81; Boys/Girls Intramurals Spon 1984-87; Newspaper Staff Spon 1977-; 1st Slovak Wreath & The Free Eagle Secy 1985-; Donora Bsbl Assn Secy 1987-88; Carroll Mid Sch PTA VP 1990; Selected Scndry Level Dist Coord Writing Prgm; *office:* Carroll Mid Sch 120 Alexander Ave Monongahela PA 15063

BELLER, ELAINE COHEN, Third Grade Teacher; *b:* New York, NY; *m:* Irv; *c:* Greg, Julie, Beth; *ed:* (BA) Elem Ed, George Washington Univ 1960; Grad Work George Mason Univ, Univ of VA; *cr:* 3rd Grade Teacher Montgomery Cty Schls 1960-63; 4th Grade Teacher Arlington Cty Schls 1963-64; 2nd Grade Teacher 1979-80, 3rd Grade Teacher 1980-83, 5th Grade Teacher 1983-85, 3rd Grade Teacher 1985- Fairfax Cty Schls; *ai:* Patrol Spon; Faculty Rep to PTA; Elem Writing Project; Human Relations, Faculty Advisory, GT Screening, Hospitality Comm; ILA Team; Cooperating Teacher; Mentorship Prgm; Phi Delta Kappa 1989-; NEA, Fairfax Ed Assn 1980-; Delta Gamma; Parents Club Pres 1989-; Clinical Faculty George Mason Univ; Peer Observer; *home:* 9920 Corsica St Vienna VA 22181

BELLESEN, DAVID ANTHONY, Science Teacher/Tennis Coach; *b:* Seguin, TX; *m:* Eliza Jane Adams; *c:* David Jr., Dana; *ed:* (BS) Bio, SW TX St 1975; Supervision of Instruction for Cooperating Teachers, SW TX St Univ; *cr:* Life Sci Teacher/Tennis Coach Dobie Mid Sch 1979-84; Bio/Phys Sci Teacher Samuel Clemens HS 1984-85; Earth Sci Teacher/Tennis Coach 1985-86, Life Sci Teacher/Tennis Coach 1986- Corbett Jr HS; *ai:* 7th/8th Grade Boys & Girls Tennis Coach; Sci Teachers Assn of TX 1986-; Corbett Jr HS Teacher of Yr 1989-; Sigma Xi Sci Educator of Yr Nom 1989-; *office:* Ray D Corbett Jr HS 301 N Main Schertz TX 78154

BELLI, JOSEPHINE, 5th Grade Teacher; *b:* Fitchburg, MA; *ed:* (BS) Elem, Fitchburg St Coll 1965; (MED) Soc Stud, Framingham St Coll 1968; Post Masters Studies Lesley Coll; Worcester St Coll; North Adams St Coll; Fitchburg St Coll; *cr:* 2nd/3rd Grade Teacher Markham Sch 1965; 5th Grade Teacher Lincoln Elem Sch 1965-66; 1966-69; 4th Grade Teacher 1969-70 Potter Rd Sch; 4th Grade Teacher West Fitchburg Elem Sch 1970-74; Reingold Elem 1974-78; 5th/6th Grade Teacher Reingold Elem 1978-81; 5th Grade Teacher Reingold Sch 1981-; *ai:* Supervising Teacher for Stu Teachers from Local Coll; Woodworking after Sch Weekly for 5th Graders; Social Comm Reingold Sch; Phi Beta Kappa 1987-; Bus & Prof Women-World Affairs Civic Comm 1985; MA Teachers; NEA; Fitchburg Teachers Assn; Osage WV Volunteer Poverty Area 1970; Camp Xavier Ctr Volunteer Cook/Svc 1968-79; Bishops Fund Volunteer 1969-; Eucharistic Minister to Homebound 1988-; Input for MA Teacher Competency Testing Prgm 1986; Ginn & Co Rdng Wkshp 1986; Letter of Commendation from Fitchburg Art Museum; Cross-Cultural Curr Wkshp St Dept Ed; Wkshp Gifted & Talented Students 1980; Rating Writing Wkshp 1979; Elem Music Study Comm 1979; Integrated Arts Prgm 1977-80; Classroom Teacher Curr Planner; Conf Fusion of Lang Arts & Rdng 1977; Master Teacher 1977-81; *office:* Reingold Elem Sch 70 Reingold Ave Fitchburg MA 01420

BELLI, PETER S., Guidance Counselor; *b:* Queens, NY; *m:* Mary R. Alleva; *c:* Michelle, Jennifer; *ed:* (BA) Philosophy, Cathedral Coll 1969; (MS) Cnslr/Ed, St Johns Univ 1973; *cr:* Teacher Mary Louis Acad 1971-73; Cnslr Bishop Ford HS 1973-76, Holy Trinity HS 1976-78, Smithtown Sch Dist 1978-79, Sachem HS 1979-; *ai:* 12th Grade Lead Cnslr; W Suffolk Cnslr Assn 1986-; *office:* Sachem HS 212 Smith Rd Lake Ronkonkoma NY 11779

BELLICINI, ELIZABETH R. (ADAMS), Fifth Grade Teacher; *b:* Charlerio, PA; *m:* Paul; *c:* Shawn, Christopher; *ed:* (BS) Elem, CA St Coll 1971; *cr:* 5th Grade Teacher 1st Street Elem 1971-74, Wylandville Elem 1975-76, Cecil Elem 1976-77, South Cntrl Elem 1978-; *ai:* Bentleyville Youth Bsbl Secy 1985-; *office:* South Cntrl Elem 230 S Central Ave Canonsburg PA 15317

BELLINA, LORETTA, Principal; *b:* Shamokin, PA; *m:* Anthony; *c:* Andrew, Nicole; *ed:* (BA) Elem Ed, Fairleigh Dickinson 1975; (MS) Admin/Supervision, Fordham 1987; Prin Center at Harvard; *cr:* 3rd Grade Teacher 1978-83, 7th/8th Grade Teacher 1983-87, Rdng Coord 1983-87 Norwood Public Sch; Vice Prin 1987-89; Prin 1989-; *ai:* Stu Cncl, Ski Club, Yrbk Adv; Cheerleading Coach; BCEMSAA Corresponding Secy 1988-; NJ PSA Comm 1988-; Intnl Rdng Assn 1983-; Norwood Teachers Assn Pres 1985-87.

BELLINGER, LAURA JEAN, Secondary Bus Ed Teacher; *b:* Amsterdam, NY; *ed:* (AAS) Secretarial Sci, Suny Cobleskill 1984; (BS) Bus Ed, 1986, (MS) Bus Ed, 1987 Suny Albany; *cr:* Bus Ed Teacher Fonda-Fultonville Cntrl HS 1987-; *ai:* SADD Adv & Coord of All Night After Prom Party; Cap Dist Assn of Bus Ed & Mrktg Teachers; Cooperative Extension Secy 1988-; Camp Bd of Dir Treas 1988-; *home:* 11 E Montgomery St Johnstown NY 12095

BELLITO, MICHAEL JOHN, English/Speech Teacher; *b:* Evanston, IL; *m:* Joan Sandberg; *c:* Matthew, Joy; *ed:* (BA) Eng/Speech, Cornell Coll 1972; (MA) Speech Comm, 1973, (MED) Sch Admin, 1984 Univ of IL; *cr:* Teacher Univ of IL 1972-73, John Hersey HS 1974-; *ai:* Head Individual Events Speech Coach; IL Speech & Theatre Assn 1974-; Sparks Awana Church Youth Organization (Leader, Co-Dir) 1985-; John Hersey HS Teacher of Yr Runner-Up 1986; HS Dist 214 Excl in Ed Awd 1989; Article Published 1989; *office:* John Hersey HS 1900 E Thomas St Arlington Heights IL 60004

BELLONE, HARRIET ANN, Science-Mathematics Teacher; *b:* New Orleans, LA; *ed:* (BS) Dietetics, Dominican Coll 1967; NSF Courses in Sci; Grad Level Math Courses, Univ of S MS; *cr:* 7th-8th Grade Math/Sci Teacher Mater Dolorosa 1965-68; 7th-8th Grade Sci Teacher St Clare 1968-71, 1974-75; 7th-9th Grade Sci Teacher Our Lady Acad 1971-74; 7th-8th Grade Sci Teacher Divine Redeemer 1975-77; 7th-8th Grade Sci/Math Teacher St Clare 1977-; *ai:* Stu Cncl; Drama; Drug Ed Coord; NCEA 1965-; St Clare Parish Cncl Secy 1988-89; Bay-Waveland Lib Bd 1983-84; Cmmty Service Awd Waveland MS 1989; Rotary Teacher of Month Bay St Louis-Waveland 1990; *office:* St Clare Sch 234 S Beach Blvd Waveland MS 39576

BELLOR, SUSAN J., Spanish Teacher; *b:* Massena, NY; *m:* Kenneth P.; *c:* Jennifer, Katherine; *ed:* (BA) Span, 1973, (MS) Rdng, 1978 SUNY Potsdam; Univ of Madrid Spain 1971-72; *cr:* Span Teacher H W Smith Jr HS 1973-77, T J Corcoran HS 1977-80; Span Instr St Lawrence Univ 1981-83; Span Teacher Massena HS 1986-; *ai:* Span Club Adv; Building Management Team; AATSP 1989-; Massena Womens Coll Club Pres 1986-87; Bus & Prof Women 1st VP 1978-79; Sacred Heart Church Usher 1990-; Wrote Curr for Sch Credit Span 1988; Translated Election Ballot for Comm of Elections to Span Syracuse as Public Service 1974; Public & Private Inst Grant to Teacher Extra Class of Below Average, Emotionally Handicapped Rdng Stus 1976-77; *home:* 19 Churchill Ave Massena NY 13662

BELMAS, BRUCE J., Elementary Principal; *b:* Ashland, WI; *m:* Jenny Lynn Willing; *c:* Bruce Jr., Boyd, Byron; *ed:* (AGS) General Stud, Gogebic Comm Coll 1963; (BS) Inter-Upper Grades Ed, Univ of WI Superior 1966; (MS) Elem Admin N MI Univ Marquette 1975; 5th Grade Teacher White Pine Sch Dist 1966-69; 3rd Grade Teacher 1969-70, 4th-7th Grade Teacher 1970-84, Rdng Teacher/Prin 1984- Ironwood Area Schls; *ai:* Jr HS Ftbl Coach; Sch Dist Rep Prof Dev; Dist Cmptr Comm & Cmptr Curr Chm; MI Elem & Mid Sch Prin Assn Mem 1984-; Ironwood MI Ed Assn, NEA 1966-84; PTO Admin Rep 1984-; Ironwood Little League Pres 1988-; Bd of Parish Ed Chm 1988-; Gamma Delta Pres 1964-66; Church (Bd of Elders, Sunday Sch Teacher, Teacher Trng Instr, Choir, Youth Spon, Teen Club Adv, Summer Camp Waterfront Dir); Intnl Ski-Flying Copper Peak Distance Marker; *office:* A L Norrie Elem Sch Alfred Wright Blvd Ironwood MI 49938

BELOBRAJDIC, PATRICE M., English Teacher; *b:* Trenton, MO; *m:* William M.; *c:* Dawson J., Matthew H.; *ed:* (BA) Span, Univ of MO Columbia 1975; (BSED) Scndry Ed, Univ of Mary Hardin-Baylor 1987; *cr:* Eng Teacher Moody HS 1987-; *ai:* Yrbk Spon; Faculty Advisory Comm; UIL Literary Events Coach; Assn of TX Prof Educators 1987-; TX Joint Cncl of Teachers of Eng 1989-; *office:* Moody HS PO Box 448 Moody TX 76557

BELTER, JAMES EDWARD, Fourth Grade Teacher; *b:* St Louis, MO; *m:* Elizabeth Burmeister; *c:* Shari Jones, Carla Vandenburgh, Joshua, Daryl Falkenhein, Heidi; *ed:* (BA) Speech, 1970, (BS) Cnslr Ed, 1977 S IL Univ; US Army; *cr:* 4th Grade Teacher St Peter & Paul Sch 1970-71; 7th Grade Teacher St Henry Grape Sch 1973-74; 5th Grade Teacher Columbia Grade Sch 1974-75; 4th Grade Teacher Red Bud Elem Sch 1976-; *home:* 1325 Salem Dr Belleville IL 62221

BELTRAME, IRVIN FRANCIS, History-Economics Teacher; *b:* Visalia, CA; *m:* Kathleen Valentine; *c:* Valentine, Perry, Anne; *ed:* (BA) His, 1953, (MA) His, 1959 Univ of Redlands; San Francisco St Univ, Univ of NV, San Jose St Univ; *cr:* Teacher/Coach Esparto Union HS 1956-59, Hillsdale HS 1959-; *ai:* Track Ofcl; Stu Help Team; Career Increment & Staff Dev Comm; CTA; San Mateo Cty Rdng Assn Exec Bd 1983, 1986, Celebrate Literacy Awd 1986; Cystic Fibrosis Research Inc 1969-; NDEA Grant 1964; Teacher of Yr Nom 1976-77; PTSA Outstanding Teacher Awd 1980; Rotary Club Outstanding Teacher Awd 1982; Chi Omega Golden Owl Awd 1987; KABL Radio Outstanding Citizen Awd 1986; Bd of Ed San Mateo Union HS Dist Certificate Outstanding Teaching 1982; Initiated Cty Rdng Day; Co-Authored Article 1969.

BELUE, MICHAEL ALLEN, Chorus Teacher/Bsktbl Coach; *b:* Gaffney, SC; *m:* Patricia Gragg; *ed:* (BM) Music Ed, Carson Newman Coll 1976; Music; *cr:* Choral Teacher Mc Intosh HS 1979-82, Azalea Mid Sch 1982-; *ai:* Boys Bsktbl Coach; Mobile Honor Choir Comm; MENC 1982-; AEA & NEA 1986-; St Pauls Choral Society 1990; Lions Club 1st Yr Most Outstanding Mem; *office:* Azalea Mid Sch 3800 Pleasant Valley Rd Mobile AL 36609

BELVEL, RICHARD, Teacher; *b:* Ottumwa, IA; *m:* Virginia Lois Graves; *c:* Robin L., Steven L., William B.; *ed:* (MED) Scndry Ed/Soc Stud, Univ of S MS 1980; Basic & Advanced Electronics; *cr:* Technician USAF 1954-74; Teacher Biloxi Schls 1977-89, St Martin HS & Jackson Cty Schls 1989-; *ai:* Sportfishing & Spirit Clubs; SADD; ROTC Teacher of Yr 1984; Yrbk Dedication 1984; Biloxi HS STAR Teacher 1987-89; *office:* St Martin HS 10300 Yellow Jacket Dr Ocean Springs MS 39564

BEMUS, ALICE KOEPSELL, Kindergarten Teacher; *b:* West Bend, WI; *m:* Arthur W.; *c:* Scott W., Brian J., Rachel Brown; *ed:* (BA) Elem Ed, Oshkosh ST Univ 1965; *cr:* 1st-8th Grade Teacher Rural Sch Dodge Cty WI 1948-50; 1st/2nd Grade Teacher State Graded Sch Merton WI 1950-51; Kndgtn Teacher Horicon Public Sch 1964-; *ai:* Horicon Garden Club 1975- Secy & Pres; *home:* 408 N Clark St Horicon WI 53032

BENASH, KATHLEEN SERAFINELLI, Physical Sci/Reading Teacher; *b:* Woodbury, NJ; *m:* Chet; *c:* Randi L., Stephanie; *ed:* (BA) Ed, Glassboro St Coll 1972; *cr:* Sci Teacher Monongehela Mid Sch 1972-74, 1975-76, C W Lewis Mid Sch 1983-; *ai:* Cheerleading Coach; Yr of the Younger Reader After Sch Rdng Club Adv; Spirit Week, Grievance Liason Comm Mem; NJAMLE Mem 1988-; Pitman Sch Bd Pres 1986-; Franklin Inst (Teacher, Adv) 1988-; NJ Inst of Bus & Sci Grant Winner; Pitman Sch Bd Mem 1983-; NJ Sch Bd Voc Sch Comm Mem 1987; *office:* C W Lewis Mid Sch 875 Erial Rd Blackwood NJ 08012

BENAVIDEZ, ANNETTE ARAGON, Mathematics Teacher; *b:* Belen, NM; *m:* Carlos R.; *c:* Melissa, Celeste, Tawnya; *ed:* (BA) Elem Ed/Math, W NM Univ 1978; *cr:* Math Teacher Belen HS 1978-80; Elem Teacher Cntrl Elem 1980-85; Math Teacher Belen Jr HS 1985-87; Belen HS 1987-; *ai:* Class Spon; FFA Greenhand Chaperone; NM Cncl Teachers of Math 1978-80.

BENDA, RUSSELL BRUCE, Science Teacher; *b:* Tacoma, WA; *m:* Donna Koeppen; *c:* Michael, Suzanne, Robert; *ed:* (BSED) Broad Field Sci, Univ of ID 1967; Grad Stud; *cr:* 6th Grade Teacher Asa Wood Jr HS 1967-69; 7th/8th Grade Sci Teacher Libby Jr HS 1969-85; Bio/General Sci/Phys Sci Teacher Libby HS 1985-; *ai:* Sr Class Adv; MT Sci Teachers Assn, NEA, MT Ed Assn, Libby Ed Assn; *office:* Libby HS 150 Education Way Libby MT 59923

BENDER, GERALDINE SMITH, French/German Teacher; *b:* Port Gibson, MS; *m:* Melvin; *c:* Meverta, Melvin II, Samuel; *ed:* (BS) Foreign Lang/Fr/Ger, MS Valley St Univ 1966; Bus Management, Jackson St Univ; Advanced Ger, Univ of S MS Hattiesburg; *cr:* Teacher Jones Cty Schls 1967-72, Jackson Public Schls 1986-; *ai:* Foreign Lang Club; Concerned Teens (Teen Pregnancy & Suicide); SADD, Making it Work (Faculty Organization); AATG, Modern Foreign Lang Assn 1989-; Jackson Cncl PTA (3rd VP 1988-) Service 1988-89; Callaway PTA Pres 1989-; Natl Cncl of Negro Women (Pres 1979-81), MS Woman of Yr 1980; Fellowship Jackson St Univ Summer Writing Inst; *home:* 150 Wimbledon Ct Jackson MS 39206

BENDER, HILDEGARD (GROSECLOSE), Eng Teacher/ Writing Lab Co-Dir; *b:* New York, NY; *m:* C. Earl; *c:* William S., Clifford E., Jennifer Smiley, Amy L. Bender Vincent; *ed:* (BA) Eng, 1973, (MA) Eng, 1984 Univ of Akron; *cr:* Eng Teacher/ Writing Lab Co-Dir Highland HS 1973-; Eng Instr Univ of Akron & Wayne Coll 1989-; *ai:* Numerous Dist Wide Teacher & Admin Comm; Highland Ed Assn 1973-; Delta Kappa Gamma Chapter Pres 1988-; Amer Cancer Society (Ed Comm Chm 1988-, Bd of Dir 1990); Editorials Published; Writing Project Wkshp Instr Ashland Univ 1987-88; *office:* Highland HS 3880 Ridge Rd Medina OH 44256

BENDER, KENNETH E., Contemporary World Cultures; *b:* Chambersburg, PA; *m:* Doris J.; *c:* Michael, Mark; *ed:* (BA) Scndry His, 1966, (MA) Scndry His, 1969 Shippensburg Univ; Scndry Supervision Certificate Western MD Coll 1976; Classroom Management/Learning Theory, Villanova Univ; Near East Stud, Princeton; Classroom Ethnic Stud; *cr:* Amer His/Geography Teacher 1966-86; Dept Chm Greencastle-Antrim Mid Sch 1966-86; Contemporary World Cultures Teacher 1986-; *ai:* Spon Field Experiences to Soviet Union, China, German Republic; Long Range Planning Comm; NEA; PA St Assn, ASCD; Shippensburg Historical Society; Christa Mc Auliffe Fellowship for Innovative Teaching 1989-; *office:* Greencastle-Antrim HS 300 S Ridge Ave Greencastle PA 17225

BENDER, KIMBERLY PENSINGER, Fifth Grade Teacher; *b:* Chambersburg, PA; *m:* Ron; *ed:* (BA) Elem Ed, Shepherd Coll 1978; (MS) Ed, Shippensburg Univ 1985; *cr:* 3rd Grade Teacher 1979-80, 4th Grade Teacher 1980-81, 5th Grade Teacher 1981- St Thomas Elem; *ai:* TEA, PTA; *office:* St Thomas Elem Sch 70 School House Rd Saint Thomas PA 17225

BENDER, LESLIE SUE, Counselor; *b:* Columbus, OH; *m:* James R.; *ed:* (BA) Eng/Speech, Capital Univ 1975; (MS) Ed/ Counseling, Univ of Dayton 1986; *cr:* Teacher/Drama Dir Bishop Ready HS 1977-86; Teacher Duncanville HS 1986-87; Counseling Duncanville 9th Grade Sch 1987-; *ai:* At Risk Comm; Teams, Gifted & Talented Ed Testing Coord; Frosh Class Spon; *office:* Duncanville 9th Grade Sch 7101 W Wheatland Dallas TX 75249

BENDER, SUSAN ARLYCE, A P Bio/Adv Bio/Chem Teacher; *b:* Seattle, WA; *ed:* (BS) Bio/Chem, Jackson St Univ 1984; (MS) Sci/Admin, MS Coll 1991; Sci, AP Bio Summer Inst/Howard Hughes Medical Inst Fellow; *cr:* AP Bio/Adv Bio/General/Chem Teacher Northwest Rankin Attn Center 1984-; *ai:* Stu Cncl Spon; Jr Class Spon; MS Sci Teachers Assn St Legislative Rep 1989-; NSTA 1984-; MS Acad of Sci Published 1990; *home:* PO Box 855 Brandon MS 39043

BENDER, YVONNE NEVADA, English Teacher; *b:* Youngstown, OH; *c:* Jennifer, Carrie; *ed:* (BA) His/Eng, Youngstown St Univ 1969; (MSED) Guidance/Counseling, Univ of Dayton 1981; Grad Stud; *cr:* Service Rep Ohio Bell Telephone Company 1961-69; Teacher Boardman HS 1969-; *ai:* NCTE, NEA, OEA, BEA; Canfield Swim Club Pres 1989-; *office:* Boardman HS 7777 Glenwood Ave Boardman OH 44512

BENEDETTO, SHEILA HORNE, Fifth Grade Teacher; *b:* Erwin, TN; *m:* Tony; *ed:* (BS) Music, 1972, (MA) Elem Ed, 1979 ETSU; Storytelling, Advanced Storytelling, Basic Cmptr Programming, Methods of Rdng, Aerospace Wkshp, Natl Sci Fnd Wkshp; *cr:* 3rd/4th Grade Teacher Flag Pond Elem 1974-80; 4th/ 5th Grade Teacher Love Chapel Elem 1980-85; 5th Grade Teacher Unicoi Elem 1985-; *ai:* Keep Record Book Elem Bsktbl Games; Sch Yrbk; Teach Piano; Tutor Stus Math & Rdng; Served on Unicoi Cty Negotiating Team; Attended Leadership Sch for Negotiations; NEA; TN Ed Assn Rep Legislative Assembly; Unicoi Cty Ed Assn Treas 1980; First Freewill Baptist Organist; ETSU Trng Sci Ed 1989; Natl Sci Fnd & Aerospace Wkshps 1990; *home:* Rt 2 Box 81-A Unicoi TN 37692

BENEDICK, MARGIE SUE HOLLAND, Third Grade Teacher; *b:* Idaho Falls, ID; *m:* Lou D.; *c:* Bruce A.; *ed:* (BS) Elem Ed High Honors, Brigham Young Univ 1966; Grad Courses Numerous Colleges; *cr:* 2nd Grade Teacher Sch Dist 91 Dora Erickson Elem 1966-67; 3rd Grade Teacher Sch Dist 91 Linden Park Elem 1968-; *ai:* Idaho Falls Ed Assn ; NEA; Natl Rdng Teachers; Amer Assn of Univ Women; *home:* 910 Safstrom Dr Idaho Falls ID 83401

BENEDICT, DEBORAH ANKLAM, English Teacher; *b:* Ventura, CA; *m:* Jeffrey Scott; *c:* Katie, J. P., Jason, Rowan; *ed:* (BA) Eng, Univ of AZ 1979; *cr:* Dept Chairperson/Eng Teacher Providence HS 1981-83; 8th/9th Grade Eng Teacher Kitty Hawk Jr HS 1983-84; 10th Grade Eng Teacher Judson HS 1984-85; 9th-12th Grade Eng Teacher Oscar Smith HS 1985-87; 9th/11th Grade Eng Teacher Tempe HS 1988-; *ai:* Contest Coord; Interact Spon; Altamira Spon 1990-; Care Support Team; Stress & Concern Facilitator; Newspaper Adv Providence HS 1981-83, Oscar Smith HS 1985-87; Alpha Delta Kappa Treas 1986-87; NCTE; Kyrene de Los Lagos PTA Treas 1988-89; Pointe Tennis League, AZ Tennis League 1988-, Doubles Championship; Ahwataukee Swim Team Parents Bd 1989; Dow Jones Fellowship; Educl Bd Advanced Placement Stipend; *office:* Tempe HS 1730 S Mill Ave Tempe AZ 85281

BENEDICT, JOYCE ARENDOSH, Third Grade Teacher; *b:* Uniontown, PA; *m:* John A.; *c:* Matthew, Leah; *ed:* (BS) Elem/ Kndgtn Ed, PA St Univ 1974; Resident Supervisory Support For Teachers; *cr:* Permanent Substitute Teacher Laurel Highlands Schls 1974-75; 3rd Grade Teacher West Elem 1975-; *ai:* Sunday Sch Teacher & Coord Parents Organization; Delta Kappa Gamma 1985-; OH Ed Assn, NEA, Napoleon Faculty Assn 1975-; PA St Ed Assn 1974-75; Child Conservation League 1985-; *office:* West Elem Schl 700 Clairmont Ave Napoleon OH 43545

BENEDICT, KAREN ROBEY, Teacher; *b:* Washington, DC; *m:* George W.; *c:* Scott, Michael, David; *ed:* (BS) Zoology, Clemson 1969; Cmmty Intervention I & II; Teachers in Industry & Technology; *cr:* TAG Coord Farragut Intermediate 1984-85; Bio/ Physiology/Chem Teacher Bearden HS 1985-; *ai:* Core Team Coord; Cheerleading Coach; Adopt-A-Sch Comm; Parent to Parent Coord; Co-Facilitator of Drug Counseling Groups Support Insight Children of Alcoholics; Parent to Parent Teacher 1989; *office:* Bearden HS 8352 Kingston Pike Knoxville TN 37919

BENEDUSI, LESLEY ANN, English Department Chairperson; *b:* Mount Kisco, NY; *ed:* (BS) Eng/Ed, St Univ of NY Brockport 1968; (MS) Eng/Scndry Ed, Univ of Bridgeport 1972; *cr:* Teacher Lakeland Mid Sch 1968-70; Eng Teacher 1970-, Engl/Dept Chairperson 1988- Fauquier HS; *ai:* Adv Comm; NHS Adv Bd; VA Assn of Teachers of Eng 1985-; VEA, NEA 1970-; *office:* Fauquier H S 705 Waterloo Rd Warrenton VA 22186

BENEFIELD, MARILYN COOTS, Eighth Grade English Teacher; *b:* Fort Payne, AL; *m:* Dorrell R.; *c:* Brian; *ed:* (BA) Eng, Univ of AL Huntsville 1974; *cr:* Eng/His Teacher Fyffe HS 1965-67; Eng Teacher Davis Hills Mid Sch 1974-; *ai:* Newspaper Spon; Spelling Bee Coord; Huntsville Ed Assn 1974-; AL Ed Assn, NEA 1965-67, 1974-; Davis Hills PTA Outstanding Teacher 1986; *office:* Davis Hills Mid Sch 3221 Mastin Lake Rd Huntsville AL 35810

BENEFIELD, MARY AMBERLY (WHISNANT), 6th Grade Teacher; *b:* Columbus, GA; *m:* James David Jr.; *c:* Justin; *ed:* (BS) Elem Ed, Tift Coll 1969; (MA) Elem Ed, Oglethorpe Univ 1974; *cr:* Classroom Teacher Tara Elem 1969-79, Mt Zion Elem 1979-89, Adamson Mid Sch 1989-; *ai:* Prin Advisory Comm Mem; Grade Level Chairperson; Youth to Youth Club Spon; Sch Fund Raising Comm; Soc Stud Contact Person; Task Force Comm to Develop Philosophy for Lang Art; Clayton Cty Intnl Rdng Assn Pres 1985-86 Rdng Teacher of Yr 1986; GA Assn of Educators 1969-; Alpha Delta Keppa Pres-Elect 1988-; Atlanta Zoo Mem 1986-; Clayton Cty Arts Mem 1990; Mt Zion Elem Teacher of Yr 1989; Clayton Cty Finalist Teacher of Yr 1989; Top Ten Finalist Thanks to Teacher Awd 1990; *office:* Adamson Mid Sch 3187 Rex Rd Rex GA 30273

BENFIELD, KENNETH WILLIAM, Sixth Grade Teacher; *b:* Manitowoc, WI; *m:* Debora H. Volz; *c:* Ranada Hassemer, Julie A. Melini, Elizabeth Waniger, Paul; *ed:* Teaching License Elem Ed, Manitowoc Teachers Coll 1952; (BS) Elem Ed, Univ of WI Oshkosh 1961; (MS) Educl Psych, Univ of WI Milwaukee 1971; Post Grad Work Univ of WI Milwaukee; *cr:* 1st-8th Grade Teacher Maple Corner Sch 1954-56; 8th Grade Teacher Kiel Public Schls 1956-61; 5th/6th Grade Teacher Manitowoc Public Schls 1961-; *ai:* Manitowoc Ed Assn Exec Bd 1985-86; Kettle Moraine Uni-Serv Cncl Delegate 1980-88; WI Ed Assn Delegate 1976; NEA; *home:* 2302 S 11th St Manitowoc WI 54220

BENFORD, GLORIA TRUE, 8th Grade English Teacher; *b:* Montgomery, AL; *c:* Carl Jr.; *ed:* (AA) Ed, Kennedy King Coll; (BA) Ed, Chicago St Univ 1973; (MA) Ed, Concordia Coll 1986; *cr:* Teacher Horace Mann Elem Sch 1973-79, John Hay Sch 1979-80, Langston Hughes 1980-81, Mozart Sch 1981-83, John Hay Acad 1983-; *ai:* Church Youth Leader; Coord for Drug Abuse Prgm; Spon for Childlife Network Prgm Spon; Outstanding Service Awd.

BENGIER, JOSEPH PETER, 7th-8th Grade Math Teacher; *b:* Steubenville, OH; *m:* Andrea Lesho; *c:* Jessica Reagan, Andrew J.; *ed:* (BA) Bus Management/Finance, WV Univ 1974; Ed Cert Classes, Math Ed, George Mason Univ; Metropolitan Insurance Sch Licensed Insurance Agent; Real Estate Advanced Course Long/Foster Real Estate; *cr:* Area Supvr/Troubleshooter Allied Chemical & Detroit Coke 1978-82; Metropolitan Life Insurance & Long/Foster Real Estate 1982-83; Substitute Math Teacher Woodbridge Mid Sch 1984; Math Teacher Potomac HS 1984-85; Math Teacher/Admin Asst Rippon Mid Sch 1985-; *ai:* Natl Steel Corp Management 1974-78; Prime-Time Exploratory Activity Period Developer & Admin; Boys Track, Asst Ftbl Coach; Sch Planning Cncl; Cooperative Learning Specialist; At-Risk Students in Math Consultant; Kappa Sigma Soc Chm 1970-74; Nom Teacher of Yr Washington Post 1989-; Articles Submitted for Publication; Co-Author of Articles; *home:* 15629 Golf Club Dumfries VA 22026

BENISH, RONALD EUGENE, Mathematics/Science Teacher; *b:* Richland Center, WI; *m:* Mary K. Schmitz; *c:* Jackie, Jean, Mary Jo, Pat; *ed:* (BA) Ed, 1969, (MS) Ed, 1979 Univ of WI Platteville; Sci, Math, Cmptr Sci; *cr:* 6th Grade Teacher Cassville Public Sch 1964-65; Math/Sci Teacher Highland Jr HS 1965-; *ai:* 8th Grade Class Adv; Jr HS Bsktbl Coach; WI Math Cncl 1975-; WI Sci Assn 1980-; Highland Ed Assn Pres 1980-81; Lions Club Pres 1979-80; Highland Village Bd 1979-; *office:* Highland Jr HS 526 Isabell St Highland WI 53543

BENJAMIN, LEE J., Physics/Meteorology Teacher; *b:* Newton, NJ; *m:* Margaret J. Stephens; *c:* Julia Holdren, Jennifer Holdren, Chris; *ed:* (BS) Physics/Scndry Ed, Mansfield St Coll 1970; (MS) General Sci/Ed, Univ of Scranton 1980; Grad Stud Cmptr Courses, Wkshps, Laboratory Interfacing; *cr:* Physics Teacher Plains Twp Consolodated HS 1970-71, N Pocono HS 1971-; *ai:* HS Local Area Network & Dist Grants Admin; ITEC Grant 1987; *office:* N Pocono HS Church St Moscow PA 18444

BENJAMIN, MARGARET HUTTON, Biology Teacher/ Chairperson; *b:* Eutaw, AL; *m:* Earl; *c:* Shannon T.; *ed:* (BS) Bio, AL St Univ 1973; (MS) Ed, LA St Univ Shreveport 1989; *cr:* Teacher Hernando HS 1973-79, Cntrl HS 1979-85, Woodlawn HS 1985-; *ai:* Stu Cncl Adv; Jr Class & Peer Facilitators Spon; Prin Advisory Comm Mem; Leadership Shreveport & Bossier 1989-, Diploma 1990; NEA 1973-85; ASCD 1989; GSA Leader 1973-75; Sunday Sch Teacher 1981-85; Natl Sci Fnd Grant Auburn Univ

1985; Notary Public; *office:* Woodlawn HS 7340 Wyngate Dr Shreveport LA 71106

BENJAMINSON, CONNIE ANDERSON, Third Grade Teacher; *b:* Minot, ND; *m:* James A.; *c:* Heidi, Kelli, Jennifer; *ed:* (BS) Soc Stud, 1972, (BS) Elem Ed, 1973 Minot St Univ; Post Grad Courses Univ of ND; *cr:* 6th Grade Teacher 1974-79; 4th Grade Teacher 1979-80; 3rd Grade Teacher 1980-; *ai:* Amer Assn of Univ Women (Schlsp Chm 1987-) 1975-; Walhalla Cntry Club Womens Pres 1988-89; Walhalla Ridge Riders Riding Club Secy 1987-88; *home:* Box 345 Walhalla ND 58282

BENKE, ROBERT JOHN, Youth/Evangelism Pastor; *b:* Milwaukee, WI; *m:* Mary Elizabeth Schuelke; *c:* Jacob, Katherine; *ed:* (AA) Concordia Univ of WI 1973; (BSAED) Ed/Speech/Drama Concordia Coll 1975; (MDiv) Theology, Concordia Seminary 1985; Theology, Ed, Concordia Univ River Forest; *cr:* 3rd Grade Teacher Zion Luth Sch 1975-81; Pastor Our Saviour & Good Shepherd 1985-88; Youth/Evangelism Pastor St John Luth Church 1988-; *ai:* Jr & Sr HS Church Youth Cnslr; Meridian RSVP Bd Mem 1986-88; Butler Ministerial Assn VP 1987-88; Article Published 1990; *home:* 1128 N 8th Ave Maywood IL 60130

BENNER, ELOUISE WRIGHT, 5th Grade Teacher; *b:* Chicago, IL; *m:* Larry Edward; *ed:* (BA) Elem Ed, Univ of WI Whitewater 1970; *cr:* 4th/5th Grade Teacher Quarry Sch 1970-72; 5th Grade Teacher Meadowbrook 1972-; *ai:* Sci Fair Adv; Citizenship, Lang, Health Comms; Cty Town Meeting Chairperson; Sci Presenter; Girls Vlybl & Sftbl Coach; *office:* Meadowbrook Sch 3130 Rolling Ridge Dr Waukesha WI 53188

BENNER, PATRICIA LEE, Eng & Amer Lit/Spanish Teacher; *b:* Shenandoah, IA; *m:* Glenn Dee; *c:* Stacey, Shannon; *ed:* (BS) Eng, NW MO St Univ 1970; (MA) Eng, Univ of MO Kansas City 1986-; *cr:* Eng/Span Teacher West Platte RII 1970-73, Platte Cty RIII 1973-75, West Platte RII 1977-; *ai:* NHS & Jr Class Spon; Faculty Adv Comm Mem; Cmmty Teachers Assn (Treas 1985, VP 1986, Secy 1989, Chm Public Relations 1989); Weston Chrstn Church Elder 1989; Weston Dev Comm Kids Day Comm 1988-89; Number 1 Club Faculty Awd; HS Teacher Recognition Awd Univ of KS.

BENNER, SCOTT MICHAEL, Social Studies Teacher; *b:* Spokane, WA; *m:* Michelle Ann Blovin; *c:* Marcus A., Thomas S.; *ed:* (BA) His, Seattle Pacific Univ 1982; Grad Stud Numerous WA St Univs 1988-89; *cr:* Soc Stud Teacher/Debate Coach Wenatchee HS 1982-; *ai:* NEA, WA Ed Assn, Wenatchee Ed Assn Mem 1982-; ASCD Mem 1989-; WA St Cncl for Soc Stud Mem 1983-84; Natl Forensic League Mem 1983-, Outstanding Distinction 1989; Young Life Comm Person 1982-; Christa Mc Auliffe WA St Excl in Ed Awd 1990; Cntrl WA Univ Most Outstanding Teacher Awd 1989; *office:* Wenatchee HS 1101 Millerdale Wenatchee WA 98801

BENNETT, BARNEY LEA, Music Teacher; *b:* Youngstown, OH; *ed:* (BM) Music Theory, Kent St 1977; Teaching Certificate Music, Youngstown St 1981; Grad Work Kent & Youngstown; *cr:* 5th-12th Grade Band/Choir/General Teacher Southern Local 1985-87; 1st-12th Grade Band/Choir/General Teacher Adams Cty Chrstn 1987-88; K-8th Grade Band/Choir/General Teacher Holy Trinity 1988-; *ai:* OMEA, MENC 1985-87; AFM 1973-; *home:* 483 Valley Rd Salem OH 44460

BENNETT, BILLIE ANN, English Teacher; *b:* Cadillac, MI; *ed:* (AB) Eng, 1972, (MED) Eng Ed, 1980 GA St Univ; *cr:* Eng Teacher Morrow Jr HS 1973-89, Morrow HS 1989-; *ai:* Yrbk & Literary Magazine Adv; Clayton Cty Eng Lang Art 1975-; Cobb Cty Bd of Realtors 1989-; Music Schlsp Awd; Annual Dedication; *home:* 3204 Lakeridge Dr Marietta GA 30067

BENNETT, BONNIE CLOWSER, Fourth Grade Teacher; *b:* Glenville, WV; *m:* Danny Lee; *c:* John R. Clowser, Justin S. Clowser; *ed:* (BA) Elem Ed/Soc Stud, Glenville St Coll 1972; Working Towards Masters in Ed, WV Univ; *cr:* 5th-7th Grade Teacher Sand Fork Sch 1972-73; 2nd-4th Grade Teacher Normantown Sch 1973-74; Home Sch Coord 1977-80, 4th Grade Teacher 1980- Barbour Cty Schls; *office:* Junior Grade Sch Gen Del Junior WV 26275

BENNETT, CAROLYN J. RICHART, Fifth Grade Teacher; *b:* Robinson, IL; *m:* Sam R.; *c:* Kevin, Barry, Brett Bennett, C. R., Cassi Simpson; *ed:* (BS) Sociology/Psych, Eastern IL Univ 1969; *cr:* 5th Grade Teacher Robinson Cmmty Dist 2 1972-; *ai:* 1st Chtstn Church; *office:* Lincoln Elem Sch East Poplar St Robinson IL 62454

BENNETT, DELORES ANN, 7th/8th Grade Lang Art Teacher; *b:* Stonega, VA; *m:* Eugene; *c:* Stephen; *ed:* (AB) Eng, Union Coll 1961; *cr:* Teacher Cumberland HS 1961-62, King Elem 1962-63, Boone Elem 1964-; *ai:* Academic Team Coach; Journalism Club Spon; Boone Sch Curr & Guidance Comms; UCEA, KEA, NEA; *office:* Boone Elem Sch HC 81 Box 532 Barbourville KY 40906

BENNETT, DOROTHY HARRAWAY, 7th-Math/Sci/Health-Teacher; *b:* Blairs, VA; *m:* Percy D. Jr.; *c:* Pat B. Tony, Jan B. Hamilton, Fred R., David R.; *ed:* (BA) Ed/Mid Sch, Averett Coll 1980; Rdng Endorsement K-12th; *cr:* Teacher Aide/Asst 1974-78, Teaher 1980- Cntrl Mid Sch; *ai:* Delta Kappa Gamma Society Schlsp Comm 1988-; Intnl Beta Chi Chapt Er; Chatham Presbyn Church (Elder 1989-91, Treas 1973-); *home:* PO Box 687 65 Holt St Chatham VA 24531

BENNETT, EULA DAMEWOOD, 4th Grade Elementary Teacher; *b:* New Market, IA; *m:* Philip E.; *cr:* 3rd Grade Teacher Manilla Cmmty 1960-62; 1st/3rd-4th Grade Teacher Cncl Bluffs Sch System 1962-66; 4th Grade Teacher 1966-, Chapter 1 Teacher 1968-70 South Page Cmmty; *ai:* Bsktbl Chaperone for Girls 1960-62; NEA, TSEA, Local (Pres/Secy) 1977; *home:* Box 336 Clarinda IA 51632

BENNETT, FERN ARTHUR, 2nd Grade Teacher; *b:* Crystal, NM; *m:* Ralph Bennett Jr.; *c:* Arthur; *ed:* (BS) Elem Ed, UNM 1975; *ai:* Cub Scout Leader; BSA Silver Fawn 1973; *home:* Box 1276 Navajo NM 87328

BENNETT, FRANCES TROHA, English Teacher; *b:* Winnsboro, LA; *m:* Charles E.; *c:* Tracie D., Christopher C.; *ed:* (BA) Eng, Sam Houston St Teachers Coll 1960; (MA) Eng, Sam Houston Univ 1969; Grad Stud NCTE Inst, A&M Univ; Rdng, Univ of Houston Clear Lake; *cr:* 7th Grade Teacher Travis Jr HS 1960-61; 9th-11th Grade Eng Teacher Columbus HS 1961-63; 11th/12th Grade Eng Teacher Dickinson HS 1963-65; 9th-12th Grade Eng Teacher Spring HS 1965-67; 9th Grade Eng Teacher Texas City HS 1967-68; 10th/11th Grade Eng Teacher Dickinson HS 1968-81; 11th Grade Eng Teacher Clear Lake HS 1981-; *ai:* Univ Interscholastic League Lit Criticism Coach; TX St Teachers Assn, NEA Sch Rep 1960-; Columbus Coll Prep Sch Team Teaching Project 1962; S MO Univ Teacher Who Influenced Stus Most 1988; NCTE Eng Fellowship A&M Univ 1966; Article Published; *office:* Clearlake HS 2929 Bay Area Blvd Houston TX 77058

BENNETT, GARY A., Chemistry-Biology Teacher; *b:* Elmira, NY; *m:* Janice M.; *ed:* (BS) Bio, Univ of Rochester 1966; (MS) Ed, Elmira Coll 1972; *cr:* Sci Teacher Ernie Davis Jr HS 1967-84, Elmira Free Acad 1984-; *ai:* Jr Var Bsbl Coach 1971-75; Jr HS Sci Club Adv 1968-72; NYSUT 1967-; NEA; AFT; BPO Elks 1973-; Natl Sci Fnd Study Grant 1971; *office:* Elmire Free Acad 933 Hoffman St Elmira NY 14905

BENNETT, GEORGENA FENTRESS, 4th Grade Teacher; *b:* Leitchfield, KY; *m:* David C.; *c:* Christi; *ed:* (BA) Elem Ed, 1974; (MA) Elem Ed, 1975 Western KY Univ; Rank I Elem Ed, Western KY Univ 1977; *cr:* 4th Grade Teacher H W Wilkey Elem 1978-; *ai:* Yrbk Adv 1978-; Studio B Sftbl Spon; Studio B Dance Instr; Guidance Comm; Extra Curr Act Comm; Southern Sch Assn Self-Study Comm; KEA/NEA 1978-; Grayson Cty Fair Bd Beauty Contest Coord 1987-; Fiddlin Festival Beauty Contest Coord 1985-; Leitchfield Recreation Appreciation Awd Softball; Studio B Dance-1st Place Regency Talent; 2nd Place Star Power Talent; *home:* Rt 1 Box 43 Falls Of Rough KY 40119

BENNETT, GERALDINE DELORES (WARD), 4th Grade Teacher; *b:* Staples, MN; *m:* Edward A.; *c:* Jonathan, Chad; *ed:* (BS) Elem Ed, St Cloud St Univ 1966; *cr:* 1st Grade Teacher; 3rd Grade Teacher; 2nd Grade Teacher; 4th Grade Teacher 1966- Rocori Dist 750; *ai:* Curr Comm; Meet & Confer Chairperson; Tech Comm; Govt Relations Uniserv Chm; Secy; VP Rocori Ed Assn; Teacher of Yr Nom 1982; *home:* Box 51 Rockville MN 56369

BENNETT, JAMES PIERCE, Youth Pastor; *b:* Atlanta, GA; *m:* Deborah Leigh Bobo; *c:* John, Joey, Tiffani; *ed:* (BA) Biblical Ed, FL Bible Coll 1976; (MA) Biblical Stud/Chrstn Ed, Dallas Theological Seminary 1986; Doctorate Ministry Degree Specializing Teaching Teenagers; *cr:* Elem Teacher Clayton Chrstn Sch 1976-81; Scndry Teacher Old Natl ChrstN Acad 1981-82; Scndry Teacher 1982-83, nlem/Scndry Teacher 1986-88 Clayton Chrstn Sch; *ai:* Clayton Cmmty Church Youth Pastor; *office:* Clayton Chrstn Sch 5900 Reynolds Rd Morrow GA 30260

BENNETT, JANE ELLEN, English Teacher; *b:* St Louis, MO; *m:* Richard H.; *c:* Cynthia Bennett Maddox, David R., Thomas M.; *ed:* (BA) Eng, Washington Univ St Louis 1965; (MA) Eng, Univ of MO 1981; Rdng Specialty Scndry Level; *cr:* Eng Teacher Mc Cluer HS 1965-68; Writing Instr Univ of MO St Louis 1978-82; Eng/Writing Instr Mid TN St Univ 1982-83; Eng Teacher De Kalb Cty HS 1983-; *ai:* Upward Bound Club Spon; Title II Grant Writer & Admin; Eng Lab Dev; NCTE 1982-; TN Eng Teachers 1983-; Meth Church Worship Chairperson 1984-87; Meth Pre-Sch Bd (Charter Writer, Publicity) 1986-89; *office:* DeKalb Cty HS 1130 W Broad St Smithville TN 37166

BENNETT, JOSEPHINE ADAMS, Advanced Placement/Bio Teacher; *b:* Knoxville, TN; *m:* Arthur T.; *ed:* (BS) Bio/Chem, VA St Univ 1960; (MST) Earth/Chem, Memphis St Univ 1972; Numerous Courses & Schls; *cr:* General Sci/Bio Teacher Booker T Washington HS 1960-66, Mitchell HS 1966-67; General Sci/Earth Sci/Bio Teacher 1967-74, Advanced Placement Bio/Advanced Bio Teacher 1974- Whitehaven HS; *ai:* Princeton NJ Table Leader Ed Testing Service Bio; Spon Natl Conference Chrstns & Jews Club 1974-; Teenage Improvement Club; Dr R Q Venson Schlsp Awds Comm Chm; Memphis City Sch Speakers Bureau Mem; Memphis St Univ Project 30 Advisory Cncl; Inservice Sci Comm Chm; NSTA Charter Mem, Presidential Awd 1983; NABT Nominating Comm 1979, Outstanding Bio Teacher Awd; TN Ed Assn Distinguished Classroom Teacher Awd 1987; Center for Civic Ed Salute to Amer Teachers 1990; Alpha Kappa Alpha Pres 1982, Outstanding Service & Leadership Awd 1982, Cmmty Service Awd 1983; Memphis City Schls Rotary Club 1967-, Teacher Excl Awd 1983; Natl Conference Chrstns & Jews HS Spon 1974-, Cmmty Service Awd 1990; Natl Sci Fnd Grants 1962-86; Biological Sci Curr Stud Writer 1971 & St Dept of TN 1980; Howard Hughes Medical Grant; Prominent Black Woman 1981; Whitehaven HS Dedication of Yrbk by Faculty & Stu Body 1974; TN Acad of Sci Distinguished Teacher Awd 1975; Key Club Intnl Salute to Teachers Day Awd 1975; Mallory Knights Charitable Organization Certificate of Honor; Monumental Church Certificate of Recognition Awd 1984; *office:* Whitehaven HS 4851 Elvis Presley Blvd Memphis TN 38116

BENNETT, JUANITA ALEXANDER, Sixth Grade Teacher; *b:* Dallas, TX; *m:* James Edward; *c:* Joffree L., Akilah D.; *ed:* (BS) Spec Ed/Elem, Univ of NV Las Vegas 1979; Early Chldhd, Nova Univ 1988; *cr:* 2nd/3rd/6th Grade/Spec Ed Teacher Lincoln Elem Sch; *ai:* 6th Grade Drill Team Adv; *office:* Lincoln Elem Sch 3010 Berg St North Las Vegas NV 89030

BENNETT, KATHLEEN D., Second Grade Teacher; *b:* Odum, GA; *m:* John B.; *c:* James E.; *ed:* (BS) Elem Ed, Univ of GA 1954; *cr:* 2nd Grade Teacher Dodge Cty 1954-55; 6th Grade Teacher 1962-64, 2nd Grade Teacher 1970-71, 1989- Sylvania Elem; *home:* Rt 5 Box 1 Sylvania GA 30467

BENNETT, KATHY THOMPSON, Sixth Grade Teacher; *b:* New Albany, MS; *m:* Mitchell Ames; *c:* Jeremy, Chelsea; *ed:* (BS) Elem Ed, Blue Mountain Coll 1980; *cr:* 2nd Grade Teacher Ashland Elem 1980-82; 6th Grade Teacher Hickory Flat Elem 1982-; *ai:* 4-H Volunteer; MS Assn of Educators 1980-89; MS Prof Educators 1989-; *home:* Hwy 78 PO Box 264 Hickory Flat MS 38633

BENNETT, LARRY JAMES, Fourth Grade Teacher; *b:* Cambridge, NY; *m:* Margaret Peterson; *c:* James, Lauren; *ed:* (BED) Scndry Soc Stud, Keene St Coll 1972; (MED) Sci Ed, Fitchburg St; Fitchburg Area Collaborative for Excl in Teaching Sci 1985-87; *cr:* 5th Grade Teacher Cambridge Cntrl Sch 1972-73; Visiting Lecturer Fitchburg St Coll 1987; 3rd-5th Grade Teacher T C Passios Elem 1973-; *ai:* Sci Curr Comm; Lunenburg Ed Assn, NEA, MTA 1973-; MA Assn Sci Teachers, NSTA 1986-; ASCD 1989; Lions 1989-; Horace Mann Grant 1986; Commonwealth Inservice Grant 1986; Elem Sci Inservice Coord 1986-87; NEASC Cert Team 1988; *office:* T C Passios Elem Sch 1025 Massachusetts Ave Lunenburg MA 01462

BENNETT, LYNN C., 1st Grade Teacher; *b:* Athens, GA; *ed:* (BS) Elem Ed, 1970, (MED) Elem Ed, 1974 Univ of GA; *cr:* 2nd Grade Teacher Colbert Elem 1970-74; 1st Grade Teacher Rehoboth Elem 1974-76; 1st Grade Teacher Smoke Rise Elem 1976-90; *ai:* Cmptr Rep for Faculty; DAE; Sheffield Manors Homeowners Assn Treas 1987- ; Teacher of Yr 1988-89; Grade Level Chairperson; *home:* 6130 Queen Anne Ct Norcross GA 30093

BENNETT, MARIE, First Grade Teacher; *b:* Gainesville, GA; *m:* Leland; *c:* Connie; *ed:* (BS) Elem Ed, N GA Coll 1956; (MED) Early Chldhd, Brenau Coll 1984; Certified in Gifted Ed, Brenau Coll; *cr:* 2nd Grade Teacher Riverbend Sch 1956-59; 1st Grade Teacher Main Street Sch 1959-60, Enota Elem Sch 1960-72; 1st Grade Teacher/Extended Learning Prgm Dir Lakeview Acad 1972-; *ai:* Lower Sch Newspaper Spon; Super Summer Prgm for Gifted Children & Extended Learning Prgm Dir; Lakeviews Admin Staff Mem; Delta Kappa Gamma, GA Supporters for Gifted Ed, N GA Assn of Young Child; Teacher of Yr Riverbend Sch; Teacher of Month Lakeview Acad; *office:* Lakeview Acad 796 Lakeview Dr Gainesville GA 30505

BENNETT, MARY ELLEN METZGER, 1st Grade Teacher; *b:* Carthage, NY; *m:* Charles; *ed:* (BA) Elem Ed, SUC Potsdam NY 1972; St Univs, Potsdam, Jefferson CCC, St Lawrence Univ; *cr:* 1st/3rd/4th Grade Teacher Carthage Cntrl Sch Dist 1972-76; 4th Grade Teacher Adirondack Cntrl Sch Dist 1976-80; 1st/2nd Grade Teacher Adirondack Cntrl Sch Dist Boonville 1980-; *ai:* Effective Schls Planning Team; NYSUT 1972-; AAUW Prgm Chairperson 1977-82; Boonville Historical Club Prgm Chairperson 1987-; Set Up & Organized the Oneida Cty Spelling Bee 1982-87; *home:* 105 East Rd Boonville NY 13309

BENNETT, MARY TOBIN, History & English Teacher; *b:* Alexandria, IN; *m:* Thomas Walter; *c:* Brian J., Dorothy A.; *ed:* (BS) Amer His/World His/Eng, 1972, (MS) Amer His/World His/Eng, 1973 Ball St Univ; Grad Stud; *cr:* Teacher Oak Hill Jr HS 1973-; *ai:* Phi Alpha Theta 1970-; *office:* Oak Hill Jr HS 7760 W Delphi Pike Converse IN 46919

BENNETT, NAOMI ANN (HOBBS), Business Education Teacher; *b:* Anaconda, MT; *m:* Melvin Ray; *c:* Nancy E. Sedlacek, Ronald W., Philip A.; *ed:* (BS) Eng, Lewis-Clark St Coll 1968; Various Univ in WA; Univ of MT; *cr:* Eng Teacher 1968-71, Bus Ed Teacher 1971- Quilcene Jr-Sr HS; *ai:* Quilcene Voc Ed Club Adv; QEA Schlsp Comm; NBEA, WBEA, WWBEA, NEA, WEA; QEA (Secy-Treas 1980-81); *office:* Quilcene HS P O Box 40 Quilcene WA 98376

BENNETT, PAMELA JANE, 2nd Grade Teacher; *b:* Seattle, WA; *m:* Rodney L. King; *ed:* (BA) Elem Ed, WA St Univ 1966; Addl Studies Dev Rdng Univ of WA 1991; *cr:* 1st/8th Grade Teacher US Peace Corps 1966-68; 3rd Grade Teacher Cascade Elem Sch 1969-78; 2nd/3rd Grade Teacher Roosevelt Elem Sch 1978-; *ai:* Early Chldhd Ed Comm Yakima Sch Dist; Intnl Rdng Assn 1988-; WA Orgnzn for Rdng Dev 1988-; Renton Ed Assn Pres 1976-78; Yakima Ed Assn Sec 1986-; WA Ed Assn 1969-; NEA 1969-; *office:* Roosevelt Elem Sch 120 N 16th Ave Yakima WA 98902

BENNETT, PATRICIA ANGLIN, English Teacher; *b:* Bogalusa, LA; *m:* Thomas Pepo; *c:* Mecy K., Thomas P.; *ed:* (BA) Eng Ed, SE LA Univ 1988; *cr:* Eng Teacher Pine HS 1989-; *ai:* Sr Class Spon; NEA 1988-; Phi Kappa Phi 1987-, Outstanding Jr 1986, Outstanding Honors Stu 1987; Articles Published 1988; Skit & Poem Published; *home:* PO Box 205 Bogalusa LA 70429

BENNETT, SOLOMON FREDERICK, 7th-8th Grade Teacher/Gifted; *b:* Mobile, AL; *m:* Yvonne Sibley; *c:* Monique, Kierre, Solomon III, Janvier; *ed:* (BA) Fr, Talladega Coll 1969; Vocal-Instrumental Music, Chicago St Univ 1972; Gifted Prgm Trng, Chicago Bd of Ed; Phys Sci 1973; Philosophy of Gifted Ed 1974; Creative Writing 1976; Advanced Math 1978; Biological Sci 1981; *cr:* 7th Grade Teacher 1969-73, 8th Grade Teacher 1973-75, Fr Instr 1975-76, 7th-8th Gifted Prgm Teacher 1976- Bryn Mawr Elem; *ai:* Band Dir 1986-; Chicago South Cntrl Cmmty Services Inc; Distinguished Service Awd in Ed 1985; City of Chicago Superior Public Service Awd for Outstanding Prof Employee 1987; *office:* Bryn Mawr Elem Schl 7355 S Jeffery Blvd Chicago IL 60649

BENNETT, THOMAS LEE, Social Studies Teacher; *b:* Austin, PA; *m:* Irene Fay Hamilton; *c:* Phyllis A., Thomas A., Timothy L., Tamara L.; *ed:* (BSED) Eng/Soc Stud, Mansfield St Coll 1959; (MSED) Eng, Shippensburg St Coll 1965; Wesley Theological Seminary Washington DC; Theological Seminary Delaware OH; *cr:* Eng Teacher Newport HS 1959-62, Pt Allegany Jr/Sr HS 1962-69; Minister Meth Church 1964-72; Soc Stud Teacher Pt Allegany Jr/Sr HS 1969-; *ai:* Newspaper, Dramatics, Wrestling, Track, Ftbl, Bsbl Coach; Class & Chess Club Adv; Ec Club; Pt Allegany Ed Assn Pres 1971-73; PSEA, NEA 1959-; United Way 1971-73; COE Fnd Schlsp; Natl Sci Fnd Ggant; BSA Service Awd; *home:* Main St Roulette PA 16746

BENNETT, TOM REGAN, Mathematics Teacher; *b:* Kittery, ME; *m:* Christine Anne Buechler; *ed:* (AA) General Stud, Southwestern Jr Coll 1984; (BA) Math, San Diego St Univ 1987; (MA) Ed, US Intnl Univ 1989; *cr:* Adjunct Math Professor Cuyamaca Comm Coll 1987-; Math Teacher El Cajon Valley HS 1987-; *ai:* Future Teachers Club, Class of 1993, Braves Against Drugs Adv; Math A Comm; El Cajon Valley HS Sch Improvement Comm; NCTM 1986-; CA Math Cncl 1989-; Greater San Diego Math Cncl, NEA, CA Teachers Assn 1987; San Diego St Univ Outstanding Stu Teacher Awd 1987; GTE GIFT Fellowship Awd 1990; *office:* El Cajon Valley HS 1035 E Madison Ave El Cajon CA 92020

BENNETT, VALERIE WILLIAMS, English Teacher; *b:* Walterboro, SC; *m:* William Gregory; *c:* Channing; *ed:* (BA) Drama Ed, SC St Coll 1985; Grad Eng; *cr:* Eng Teacher Clover HS 1986-; *ai:* SADD Adv; SCEA 1988-; SCIRA 1990; Alpha Psi Omega 1984-; Theta Alpha Phi 1985-; *office:* Clover H S 1625 Hwy 55 Clover SC 29710

BENNICK, BRENDA CORL, 6th Grade Teacher; *b:* Reading, PA; *m:* David Duane; *c:* Sarah, Julie; *ed:* (BS) Elem Ed, E Stroudsburg Univ 1972; (MED) Elem Ed, Temple Univ 1976; *cr:* 6th Grade Teacher S Heidelberg Elem 1972-73; 4th Grade Teacher 1973-80, 5th Grade Teacher 1980-82, 6th Grade Teacher 1982- Womelsdorf Elem; *ai:* NEA, PSEA, CWEA; *office:* Conrad Weiser Area Womelsdorf School South Third Street Womelsdorf PA 19576

BENNIN, JEANELLE LENZ, Second Grade Teacher; *b:* Sheboygan, WI; *m:* Neil W.; *ed:* (BS) Elem Ed, Univ of WI Platteville 1967; Elem Ed; *cr:* 2nd Grade Teacher Wilson Elem 1967-71; 1st/2nd Grade Teacher Riverview Elem 1971-; *ai:* Building Coord; *office:* Riverview Elem Sch 437 N Wisconsin Ave Howards Grove WI 53083

BENNING, JANE MACK-ADAMSON, Fifth Grade Teacher; *b:* Easton, PA; *m:* Michael A.; *c:* Brooke, Christopher; *ed:* (BA) Elem, E Stroudsburg Univ 1965; (MS) Elem, Kutztown Univ 1972; Inservice Unit Wkshps; *cr:* 4th Grade Teacher Frelinghuysen NJ 1965-66, Hooper Avenue Elem Sch 1966-67, Foglesville Elem 1967-82; 5th Grade Teacher Parkway Manor Elem 1982-; *ai:* S Mountain Preservation Assn Secy 1970-72; Lehigh Cty Humane Society Secy 1971-72; Apple for Outstanding Teacher Awd; *office:* Parkway Manor Elem Sch N Parkway Rd Allentown PA 18104

BENNING, KAREN ANN, Teacher of Gifted & Talented; *b:* Buffalo, NY; *ed:* (AA) Liberal Arts/Ed, Genesee Comm Coll 1974; (BA) Elem Ed/His, 1976, (MS) Early Chldhd Ed, 1981 St Univ Coll Geneseo; Curr Compacting Turn-Key Trainer; *cr:* Kndgtn/4th/Pre-1st Grade Teacher Alexander Cntrl Sch Dist 1977-81; 4th Grade Teacher 1981-84, Teacher of Gifted & Talented 1984- Springville-Griffith Inst; *ai:* Cmptr Curr Comm; In-Service Cmptr Instr for Dist Staff Dev; *office:* Springville-Griffith Inst 307 Newman St Springville NY 14141

BENOIT, CINDY PERRODIN, Fourth Grade Teacher; *b:* Crowley, LA; *m:* Gordon J.; *ed:* (BA) Elem Ed, Mc Neese St Univ 1973; *cr:* 4th Grade Teacher S Crowley Elem 1981-; *ai:* 4th Grade Chairperson; *home:* 326 W 14th St Crowley LA 70526

BENSEN, PAT WILSON, Teacher of Gifted & Talented; *b:* Saratoga, WY; *m:* Len; *c:* Kathy Mc Creary, Brian; *ed:* (BA) Elem Ed, Univ of WY 1960; Working Towards Masters; *cr:* 2nd Grade Teacher Encampment Elem 1960-61; Jr HS Girls Phys Ed/Gifted & Talented/Kndgtn-8th Grade Teacher Saratoga Schls 1962-; *ai:* Rdng is Fundamental Co-Chairperson 1980-81; Accompaniest for Music Groups; N Cntrl Evaluation Team; Gifted & Talented Comm; Delta Kappa Gamma 1967-; Carbon Cty 2 Ed Assn Pres 1988-89; WY Ed Assn 1960-; NEA; Saratoga Planning Commission Mem 1981-84; Jobs Daughters Guardian 1970-79; Presbyn Church (Organist, Elder) 1970-89; Outstanding Young Woman of America 1968; WY Teacher of Yr Nom 1986; Amer Legion Dist 6 Techer of YR 1986; WY Teacher of Yr Scottish Rite Fnd 1986; Carbon Cty Sch Dist #2 Outstanding Educator 1985; *office:* Saratoga Elem & Mid Schls Box 1710 122 W Elm Saratoga WY 82331

BENSKO, DIANE GRAHAM, 4th-6th Grade Gifted Teacher; *b:* Springfield, IL; *m:* Raymond A. Jr.; *c:* Dustin; *ed:* (BS) Ed, IL St Univ 1976; St of IL Gifted Cert; *cr:* 6th Grade/4th-6th Grade Gifted Teacher Pleasant Plains Elem 1976-; *ai:* Teacher Evaluation, Gifted, Learner Assessment, Textbook Selection Comms; Cheerleading Spon; Prin Advisory Team; *home:* 527 E Rte 125 Pleasant Plains IL 62677

BENSLEY, HEIDI LEHTO, Spanish Teacher; *b:* Berkeley, CA; *m:* William S.; *c:* William B.; *ed:* (BA) Span/Linguistics, UCLA 1977; Ed, San Francisco St Univ; *cr:* Span/Fr Teacher Stone Valley Sch 1980-85; Dept Chairperson 1986-88, Span Teacher 1985-, Mentor Teacher 1989- CA HS; *ai:* Span, Ski Club Adv; Teacher of Yr CA HS 1988-89; *office:* California HS 9870 Broadmoor Dr San Ramon CA 94583

BENSON, ANN ELIZABETH, Fifth Grade Teacher; *b:* Joliet, IL; *ed:* (BS) Elem Ed, Northern IL Univ 1973; Addl Studies Madeline Hunter Conferences; Effective Sch Conference; *cr:* 2nd Grade Teacher 1973-79; 5th Grade Teacher 1979- Crystal Lawns Sch; *ai:* Outdoor Ed; NEA/IEA/Assn of Plainfield Teachers 1973; Delta Kappa Gamma 1980; Intnl-Rho Chapter; Negotiations/ Building Rep/By-Laws Chm; Crystal Lawns PTA 1973; King's Daughters (Mabel Fox Circle) 1983; IL PTA Distinguished Service Scroll Crystal Lawns PTA; *office:* Crystal Lawns Elem Sch 2544 Crystal Dr Joliet IL 60435

BENSON, BARBARA PETERSON, English Teacher; *b:* Wilmington, NC; *m:* Stephen Bruce; *c:* Erik S., Lincoln A.; *ed:* (AB) Eng, High Point Coll 1969; (MA) Eng, NC St Univ 1977; Cert Teaching Gifted & Talented Stu; *cr:* Eng Teacher Jamestown Jr HS 1969, Wareham Mid Sch 1969-70, Boone Trail HS 1970-71, Watauga HS 1978-; *ai:* Watauga HS Stu Assistance Team Mem; Region SAT Task Force; NCTE, NC Eng Teachers Assn 1979-; NC Assn of Educators Building Rep 1979-; Fellowship in Appalachian Writing Project & Southern Highlands Inst of Educators; Consultant to Globe Publishing 1990; Articles Published 1989; *office:* Watauga HS Rt 6 Box 30 Boone NC 28607

BENSON, BEVERLY NORRIS, 7th Grade Lang Art Teacher; *b:* Erwin, NC; *m:* Tony Rolon; *c:* Tony K.; *ed:* (BA) Elem Ed, Campbell Univ 1980; *cr:* Teacher W Harnett HS 1983-84, Harnett Mid Sch 1984-85, Dunn Mid Sch 1985-; *ai:* Girls Bsktbl Coach; NEA; *office:* Dunn Mid Sch 401 N Orange Ave Dunn NC 28334

BENSON, DONALD EUGENE, JR., English Teacher; *b:* New Castle, PA; *m:* Barbara Jean Chapin; *c:* Michael, David, James; *ed:* (BS) Ed, Slippery Rock St Coll 1967; (MED) Eng, Westminster Coll 1970; *cr:* Eng Teacher Mohawk Area Schls 1967-; *ai:* Jr Class Adv; Sch Musical Dir; Mohawk Area Ed Assn, NEA 1967-; Neshannock Township Volunteer Fire Company 1970-, Chiefs Awd 1985; *home:* 3008 Spring Garden Ave New Castle PA 16105

BENSON, EMILY R., Fourth Grade Teacher; *b:* Columbus, GA; *m:* Lanny C.; *c:* Lanny C., Edward K.; *ed:* (BS) Elem Ed, W GA Coll 1963; (MS) Elem Ed, Berry Coll 1977; Data Collector GTAI Teacher Cert Prgm; *cr:* 6th Grade Classroom Teacher Pleasant Grove Elem 1963; 3rd Grade Classroom Teacher Winder Elem 1964; 1st Grade Classroom Teacher Armuchee Valley Elem 1964-65, Naomi Elem 1965-73; 1st-3rd Grade Classroom Teacher Fortune Elem 1973-87; 4th Grade Classroom Teacher N Lafayette Elem 1987-; *ai:* Prof Assn of GA Educators 1986-; Natl Assn of Educators 1963-86; Walker Cty Assn of Educators 1963-86; Stu Teacher Achievement Recognition 1989; *office:* N Lafayette Elem Sch 610 N Duke St La Fayette GA 30728

BENSON, MARIE GUIDICE, Jr & Sr HS Mathematics Teacher; *b:* Chicago, IL; *m:* Robert L.; *c:* James, Paul; *ed:* (BSED) His, N IL Univ 1974; *cr:* Jr/Sr HS Math Teacher Hiawatha 1980-; *ai:* Jr Var & Var Vlybl Coach; Soph Class Adv 1989-; 8th Grade Adv; Curr & Discipline Comm; Hiawatha Classroom Teachers Assn (Pres 1989-, Secy 1988-89); NCTM; Dekalb Sport Boosters 1989-; *home:* 110 River Dr De Kalb IL 60115

BENSON, MARY ELMORE, 5th Grade Teacher; *b:* Hillsboro, OH; *c:* Josie Bevin; *ed:* (BA) Ed, 1971, (MA) Rdng, 1977 OH St Univ; Cmptr; *cr:* 3rd/4th Grade Teacher Washington 1969-74; 6th Grade Accelerated Teacher 1974-76, 6th Grade Lang Teacher 1977-80 Marshall; Career Ed Coord 1980-89, 5th Grade Teacher 1980- Washington; *ai:* Phi Delta Kappa 1986-; NEA, OEA, HEA 1971-; EFC Church Chrstn Ed Comm 1987-; Jennings Scholar; *office:* Washington Elem Sch 200 N East St Hillsboro OH 45133

BENSON, MAX EUGENE, Principal; *b:* Palestine, IL; *m:* Marilyn Jean Pratt; *c:* Doris, Delores, Deborah, Lucas, Mukakami; *ed:* (BS) Bus Admin, Manchester Coll 1964; M Div Pastoral/Chr Ed, Green Theological Seminary 1970; *cr:* Pastor Servir United Church of Christ 1960-64, Wolf Lake Baptist Church 1965-71, Calvary Ind Church 1971-81; Prin/HS Teacher Mercer Chrstn Acad 1981-; *ai:* Athletic Dir Jr/Sr HS; WV Chrstn Sch Athletic Conference Dir 1988-; Mercer Chrstn Acad Sch Bd Ex Officio 1984-; *office:* Mercer Chrstn Acad 314-A Oakvale Rd Princeton WV 24740

BENSON, PATRICIA ANN BARNHILL, 1st Grade Teacher; *b:* Greenwood, MS; *m:* Bobby; *c:* Newt, Elizabeth; *ed:* (AA) Ed, Northwest Jr Coll 1975; (BA) Ed, Univ of MS 1976; Univ of Ms; *cr:* 1st Grade Teacher Batesville Elem Sch; *ai:* Adv Comm Mem; Trained CPR Group; Rdng Curr Comm; Kappa Delta Pi 1975-77; MAE/NEA 1976-; Jr Womens League (Publicity Chm/Chm Little Ms Batesville) 1976-80; Natl Assn Jr Auxiliaries (Placement Chm Harvest Movie Chm Charity Ball Chm Needy Sch Chldrn Chm Chm Safety Town) 1979-85; *office:* Batesville Elem Sch 209 College St Batesville MS 38606

BENSON, PATRICIA CAMERON, 6th Grade Elementary Teacher; *b:* Seattle, WA; *m:* George L.; *ed:* (AA) Behavioral Sci, Anchorage Comm Coll 1973; (BED) Elem Ed/His, 1975, (MED) Counseling, 1977 Univ of AK Anchorage; Credit Hrs Beyond Bachelors Degree; *cr:* 1st Grade Teacher Oceanview Elem 1975-77; 4th Grade Teacher Oceanview & Birchwood Elem 1977-80; 5th Grade Teacher Birchwood 1980-81; 6th Grade Teacher Baxter Elem 1981-; *ai:* Track & Field; Sci Fair; Stu Cncl; Acting Prin; Soc Stud Curr, Sci & Math Curr Comms; Amer Lib Assn AK Mem 1981-83; NEA Mem 1975-88; Chrstn Educators Assn Intnl 1980-; Phi Delta Kappa 1988-; NCSS Mem 1986-; Anchorage Area Cncl for Soc Stud Secy 1987-88; PTA Mem (Faculty Rep 1980-81, Volunteer 1988-89) 1975-; Chrstn Womens Bus & Prof Organization.

BENSON, REBA EMERSON, Mid Sch Lang Arts Teacher; *b:* Evansville, IN; *m:* William J.; *c:* Rebecca R. Harris; *ed:* (BS) Ed - Cum Laude, Oakland City Coll 1959; (MS) Ed, IN St Univ 1963; *cr:* Phys Ed/Eng Teacher North Posey Jr HS 1959-62; Elem Music/Phys Ed/Eng Teacher Owensville Sch 1962-65, 1972-; *ai:* Lang Arts Book Adoption Comm; Chairperson Sch Spelling Bee; Mentor Teacher; Delta Kappa Gamma Treas; Bethlehem General Baptist Church 1952-; *home:* RR 3 Box 196 Owensville IN 47665

BENSON, WILLIAM EDWARD, Sixth Grade Teacher; *b:* Shelbyville, IN; *m:* Linda L. Copple; *c:* Christopher T., Brenda A. Benson Pavnica; *ed:* (BS) Elem Ed, IN Cntrl Univ 1967; (MS) Elem Ed, IN Univ 1972; *cr:* 6th Grade Teacher Northwestern Consolidated Schls 1967-68, Shelbyville Cntrl Schls 1968-; *ai:* PBA Comm Mem; NEA Life Membership, HASTI.

BENSON, WILLIAM FARNUM, Social Studies Teacher; *b:* Brockton, MA; *m:* Katherine; *ed:* (BA) His, Amer Intnl Coll 1971; (MED) Admin, Suffolk Univ 1983; (ALM) Government, Harvard Univ 1987; Fellowship to Amer Constitutional His Inst 1987; *cr:* Teacher Bourne HS 1975-76, Memorial HS 1976-88, Pen Lee Sch England 1988-89, Memorial HS 1989-; *ai:* Debate & Granite St Challenge Team; Fulbright Alumni Assn 1989-; Fulbright Scholar Teaching England 1988-89; Fellowship Amer Constitutional His Inst 1987; Delegate Leader Initiative for Understanding Soviet Union 1990; Selected by N H Bicentenial Commission to Speak on Constitution; *office:* Memorial HS S Porter St Manchester NH 03103

BENTLEY, ANNIE BOND, Lang Art/Soc Stud Teacher; *b:* Plymouth, NC; *ed:* (BS) Elem Ed, Winston-Salem St Univ 1959; Grad Work Univ of CT; *cr:* 8th Grade Teacher Robersonville Jr HS 1959-; *ai:* 8th Grade Spon; NEA, NCAE, MCAE; Delta; *office:* Robersonville Jr HS Academy St Robersonville NC 27871

BENTLEY, LINDA (CAVINS), 8th Grade Lang Art Teacher; *b:* Milltown, IN; *m:* Russell I. Jr.; *c:* Alexander T., Angelica R.; *ed:* (BA) Ed, Univ of Evansville 1968; (MS) Ed, IN Univ 1972; Grad Stud Gifted & Talented, Cmptr Ed, Ec, Purdue Univ 1986; *cr:* 2nd Grade Teacher Marrs Elem 1968-70; 2nd/3rd Grade Teacher Eastlawn Elem 1970-75; 3rd-5th Grade Advanced Teacher Rose Hill Elem 1976-85; 8th Grade Lang Art Teacher River Valley Mid Sch 1985-; *ai:* Academic Spelling Bowl Team; Phi Delta Kappa Mem 1982-; Alpha Delta Kappa (VP 1982-84, Pres 1984-86); Natl Paper Company Honorable Mention for Exemplary Teaching Ec 1985; Greater Clark Schls Recognition Cert 1986, 1990; Olin W. Davis 1st Pl Scndry Div 1989; *office:* River Valley Mid Sch 2220 New Albany Charlestown Rd Jeffersonville IN 47130

BENTON, JENNA SHAVERS, 2nd Grade Teacher; *b:* De Kalb, TX; *m:* Barmas; *c:* Robert C., Glenn; *ed:* (BA) Home Ec, Prairie View Univ 1948; Mural Painting; Bay Writing; Eng Strategies in Comp; Child Psych; Methods of Drawing-Geneology; *cr:* 3rd Grade Teacher New Boston Elem 1949-50; H E Teacher New Boston HS 1950-64; 3rd Grade Teacher 1977-86; 2nd Grade Teacher 1986- De Kalb Elem; *ai:* YAC Club Adv; Honesty Club Spon; TX St Teachers Mem 1949-; NEA Mem 1977-; Garland Museum Schlsps (Pres 1980- Adv 1987-); Teacher Svc Awd; *office:* De Kalb Elem Sch 417 S W Fannin St De Kalb TX 75559

BENTON, JO ANN HALL, Language Art Teacher; *b:* Mc Comb, MS; *m:* Robert Howard; *c:* Tracy A. Raybourn, Tamara L. Chapman, Frances P. Drouin, Robert H. Jr.; *ed:* (BS) Elem Ed, LA Coll 1979; *cr:* Teacher Bunkie Mid Sch 1979-82, Alexandria Jr HS 1982-83, Bunkie Elem Sch 1983-84, Bunkie Mid Sch 1984-; *ai:* Chrldr & Yrbk Spon; ADK 1984-86; *office:* Bunkie Mid Sch PO Box 470 Bunkie LA 71322

BENTON, RICHARD HAZE, Fourth Grade Teacher; *b:* N Wilkesboro, NC; *ed:* (AA) Wilkes Comm Coll 1967-69; (BS) Scndry Soc Stud, 1971, Cert Elem, 1971-72 Appalachian St Univ; *cr:* 7th/8th Grade Teacher Moravian Falls Elem 1971-72; 3rd-6th Grade Teacher Union Township Sch 1972-80; 4th Grade Teacher Millers Creek Intermediate 1980-; *ai:* Millers Creek Stu Cncl, Chief Chrldrs Spon; Wilkes Cty Youth Soccer Coach, Cty Champions; Wilkes YMCA Church Bsktbl Coach; NC Assn of Educators Mem 1971-; Assn of Classroom Teachers Pres 1979-80; Intnl Rdng Assn Mem 1971-; Wilkes Cty Teacher of Yr 1978-79; Terry Sanford Awd for Creativity & Innovation in Teaching 1978-79, 1985-86; Wilkes Jaycees Young Man of Yr Nominee 1978-79; WKBC Citizen of Week 1978; *home:* PO Box 88 Roaring River NC 28669

BENTON, ROSE MARY, Mid Sch Teacher/Counselor; *b:* Batavia, OH; *m:* Max M. Sr.; *c:* Max M. Jr., Douglas W., James A.; *ed:* (BA) Phys Ed/Health, Morehead St Univ 1962; (MS) Sch Counseling, Univ of Dayton 1986; Grad Stud Drug Ed; *cr:* Teacher Clermont Northeastern Sch Dist 1962-63, W Clermont Sch Dist 1963-64; Teacher 1964-, Cnslr 1986-, Drug Prgm Dir 1986- Valley View Sch Dist; *ai:* Drug Prgm Dir; Part Time Intramural Prgm

Vlybl Dir; NEA, OH Ed Assn, Valley View Teachers Assn 1962-; Washington Heights Baptist Church 1980-; Dayton Philharmonic Chorus 1984-; Valley View Citizens Against Substance Abuse Secy 1986-; *home:* 52 Apple Dr Farmersville OH 45325

BENTS, THEODORE FREDICK, Mathematics/Science Teacher; *b:* Cumberland, WI; *m:* Janice Ilene Knudson; *c:* Roxane Evans, Theodor, Daniel; *ed:* (BS) Elem Ed, Univ of WI Superior 1965; Additional Stud Univ of WI Platteville, Univ of WI River Falls, Univ of Superior; *cr:* 6th Grade Teacher Osceola Elem 1965-67; Math/Sci Teacher Osceola Mid Sch 1967-; *ai:* Sci & Math Curr Comm Mem; NUE, WEA 1965-; Lions Club Dir 1983-88; City Cncl (Trustee, Mem) 1986-; Airport Commission Chm 1987-; Lib Bd Mem 1986-; NSF Grants 1970-72; *home:* 612 Summit St Osceola WI 54020

BENTZ, KATHRYN DE BORD, 4th Grade Teacher; *b:* Johnson City, TN; *m:* Reece C.; *c:* Adriane, Ross, Chad; *ed:* (AA) Elem Ed, Gulf Park Jr Coll 1968; (BS) Elem Ed, Univ of S MS 1974; (ME) Elem Ed, William Carey Coll 1978; *cr:* Teacher Harper Mc Caughan Elem 1974-; *ai:* AFT Mem 1974-84; Childrens Intnl Summer Village Mem 1989-; St Thomas Parish Cncl Area Rep 1987-89; *office:* Mc Caughan Elem Sch Jeff Davis Ave Long Beach MS 39560

BENZ, BETH ANN, Mathematics Teacher; *b:* Milwaukee, WI; *ed:* (BS) Math, Univ of WI Stevens Point 1987; Cray Acad 1989; WI Math Cncl Wkshps; *cr:* Long Term Substitute Math Teacher Stratford HS 1988; Substitute Teacher Various Schls 1988; Math Teacher Loyal HS 1988-; *ai:* Frosh Class & Cheerleading Adv; Work Release & Cmptr Comm; Athletic Ticket Seller & Chaparone; Loyal HS Silver Wrestling Anniversary Comm; WI Math Cncl 1988-; Jaycees Local Dir 1990, Outstanding New Jaycee 1990; *office:* Loyal HS 514 W Central Loyal WI 54446

BEOUGHER, BARBARA A., Language Arts Instructor; *b:* Bird City, KS; *m:* Kenneth L.; *c:* Beverly Schottler, Timothy, Kathryn, Amy Andrews; *ed:* (BA) Eng, 1986, (MS) Scndry Ed, 1986, K-12th Grade Admin, 1990 Ft Hays St Univ; *cr:* Lang Art Teacher Morland HS 1985-89, Cheylin HS 1989-; *ai:* Jr Class & Spelling Team Spon; Yrbk Adv; NCTE, NEA, AAUW; *home:* RR 2 Box 7A Bird City KS 67731

BERARD, JOSEPH ALTON, Math Teacher; *b:* Parks, LA; *m:* Rita Jeanne Faulk; *c:* Clyde, Renette Howard; *ed:* (BA) Math/Ed, Southern Univ 1942; (MA) Admin, Columbia Univ 1953; Math, Univ of IL 1964; Math & Educl Wkshps; *cr:* Teacher Fontana HS; *ai:* Help Stus Before & After Sch; Natl Teachers Assn; Fontana Teachers; Featured Teacher of Week Math Demonstration on Television; *home:* 2384 Via Fresa San Dimas CA 91773

BERARD, ULRIC CLAIBORNE, Social Studies Teacher; *b:* Washington, DC; *m:* Diana Lillian Sorgen; *c:* Erica C., Christian Southwell; *ed:* (BA) Sociology/Anthropology, Washington & Lee Univ 1968; (MA) Asian Stud/Ed NY Univ 1974; Real Estate Licensed Agent Commonwealth of VA 1976-; *cr:* Volunteer Peace Corps 1969-70; Soc Stud Teacher George C Marshall HS 1971-; *ai:* Idylwood Knolls Civic Assn Pres 1980-82; Cub Scout Pack 1537 Packmaste 1984-86; Joyce Kilmer Intermediate Sch PTA Pres 1989-; NY Univ Grant 1972; Sabbatical Leave 1975-76; SE Asian & E Asian Ed; WA Gas Company Grant 1984; Home Energy Consumption Survey & Article; Groups to USSR, Finland, Canada & West Berlin; *home:* 7734 Virginia Ln Falls Church VA 22043

BERDINE, CEDRIC, Vocal Music Teacher; *b:* Hebron, IN; *m:* Barbara Jean Neuman; *c:* Aline E., John C., Scott A.; *ed:* Cert Piano, Sherwood Music Sch 1951; (AB) Music Ed, Valparaiso Univ 1955; (MMED) Music Ed, Butler Univ 1964; *cr:* Music Teacher Fulton Sch 1955-59, Caston Educl Center 1959-; *ai:* Drama Club & Swing Choir Spon; ISTA, NEA, CCTA Pres 1962-64; F & AM Master 1979-80; OES Patron 1985-86; Scottish Rite; *home:* RR 1 Box 86 Rochester IN 46975

BERENS, EDWARD STEVEN, Educational Evaluator; *b:* Monticello, NY; *ed:* (BS) Art Ed, St Univ Coll Buffalo 1974; (MS) Spec Ed, St Univ Coll New Paltz 1979; *cr:* Teacher PS 48 Joseph Rodman Drake Sch 1980-87; Educl Evaluator CSE-8 New York City Bd of Ed 1987-; *ai:* Pupil Personnel & Mainstreaming Comm.

BERENTZ, WILLIAM C., Social Studies/Science Teacher; *b:* New Matamoras, OH; *m:* Jerrie L. Oyster Berentz; *c:* Christine; *ed:* (BS) His Govt, 1961; (MED) Ed, 1967 OH Univ; *cr:* Soc Stud/ Bio Teacher Barnesville HS 1961-63; Marietta HS 1963-; *ai:* Soc Stud Course of Study Comm; Natl Honor Society Adv Comm; Marietta Ed Assn 1963-; OH Ed Assn 1961-; NEA 1961-; Masonic Lodge Master 1967; Un Meth Church Parish/Pastor Comm; Martha Holden Jennings Scholar; Honor Ed 1987-89; North Central Evaluator 1985/89; *home:* Rt 8 Box 425 Dayton Rd Marietta OH 45750

BERES, BETTY ROSE, Fourth Grade Teacher; *b:* East Chicago, IN; *ed:* (BS) Elem Ed, St Joseph Coll 1970; (MS) Elem Ed, IN Univ 1973; *cr:* 3rd Grade Teacher 1970-79, Math Teacher 1980-86, 4th Grade Teacher 1987- Carrie Gosch Sch; *ai:* Head Teacher 1976-; Cmptr Lab Coord 1988-; Stu Cncl Spon 1989-; AFT 1971-; PTA 1971-, Service Awd 1986, 1990; Fatima Pres 1956, 1974, 1978; Holy Trinity Church Parish Cncl (Pres, VP) 1984-; Strategic Task Force Service Awd 1985; Hoosier Heritage Prgm & Service Awd 1987; *home:* 4809 Kennedy Ave East Chicago IN 46312

BERGBOM, JOANNE PICCARELLA, Teacher/Director of Stu Act; *b:* Brooklyn, NY; *m:* Bruce; *c:* Kristin, Nancy, Bart, Brad; *ed:* (BA) Eng, Cornell Hofstra Univ 1965; (MS) Scndry Ed, Hofstra Univ 1985; Lincoln Center Summer Inst for Aesthetic Ed; Grad & In Service Work; *cr:* Eng Teacher Floral Park Memorial HS 1983, H Frank Carey HS 1983-; Dir of Stu Act H F Carey HS 1989-; *ai:* Sr Class Adv; Faculty Schlsp Comm; Mid St Self Evaluation; Sch Cmmty Comm Chairperson; NCTE 1983-; PTSA (GCP Pres 1974-76, NHPHS Pres 1982-84, Sewanhaka Cncl Pres 1980-82), Honorary Life 1976, Distinguished Service 1984, Natl Life 1982; *office:* H Frank Carey HS 230 Poppy Ave Franklin Square NY 11010

BERGEL, STEVEN PETER, Earth Science Teacher; *b:* Manhattan, NY; *m:* Patricia Ann Hucke; *c:* Afton P.; *ed:* (BS) Scndry Ed, 1967, (MED) Earth Sci, 1970, (PHD) Academic Curr/Instruction, 1976 Penn St Univ; *cr:* Sci Teacher 1967-89, Sci Dept Chm 1984-87 Bellport Mid Sch; Earth Sci Teacher Bellport HS 1989-; *ai:* Phi Delta Kappa, Phi Kappa Phi 1976; NY Sci Teachers Assn Mem 1990; Rocky Point Concerned Citizens Pres 1983; North Shore Little League Coach 1990; *office:* Bellport HS Beaverdam Rd Brookhaven NY 11719

BERGEN, MICHAEL WILLIAM, Commercial Arts Teacher; *b:* Fond Du Lac, WI; *ed:* (BA) Philosophy, St Joseph Rennslaer 1965; (MA) Theology, Capuchin Seminary 1967; (MA) Hum, CO Coll Colorado Springs 1977; Media MI St 1971; Writing process 1982; Assertive Discipline 1988; Learning Styles, Study Skills 1989-; *cr:* Speech/Religion Teacher St Mary Springs HS 1967-69; Media/Religion Teacher Xavier HS 1969-74; Eng Teacher Roosevelt Jr HS 1973-74; Media/Forensics Teacher Appleton HS East 1975-; *ai:* Theatre, Forensics, Academic Teams Union Rep; NCTE Center of Excl 1985-89; WCTE, SCS, WCA Creativity 1982; Natl Forensics League 1975-89, Diamond Coach; WI Comm Assn VP 1990; NBC Network News Classroom 1988; CBS Television Worth Teaching 1989; *office:* Appleton HS East 2121 S Emmers Dr Appleton WI 54915

BERGENSKE, M. DIANE, 3rd/4th Grade Teacher; *b:* Bear Creek Twp, WI; *m:* Myron D.; *c:* M. Daniel II, Nikolas; *ed:* (BS) Elem Ed, Univ of WI Madison 1963; (MEPD) Ed/Gifted & Talented/Rdng, Univ of WI Platteville; Post Masters Stud Univ of WI Madison 1965-70; *cr:* 2nd Grade Teacher Knapp Elem Sch 1963-64; 1st Grade Teacher Elgin IL 1964-65; 2nd Grade Teacher Oregon Sch System 1965-70; 3rd/4th Grade Teacher Mineral Point Elem Sch 1979-; *ai:* Stu Teacher Cooperating & Supervising Teacher; Gifted & Talented, At-Risk, Sci Health Comm; SW Ed Assn Bd Rep 1989-; Music Boosters Secy 1987-; Church Sunday Sch Teacher; Articles Published; WI St Journal Who Made a Difference 1987; *office:* Mineral Point Elem Sch Cothern St Mineral Point WI 53565

BERGER, LEE HOLLINGSWORTH, HS English Teacher; *b:* Rocky Mount, NC; *m:* Frederick A.; *c:* Jennifer, Amy, Stephanie; *ed:* (BA) Elem Ed, UNC Chapel Hill 1971; (MA) Early Chldhd, Western Carolina Univ 1985; *cr:* 6th Grade Teacher 1971-72; Gifted/Cmptr Teacher 1985-86 St Louis Cty Sch; HS Teacher Macon Cty Sch 1987; *ai:* Swim Team Asst Coach; Kappa Delta Phi; Beta Sigma Phi 1975-; Girl Scouts 1973-; *office:* Franklin HS 23 School St Franklin NC 28734

BERGER, MYRA SUE, 2nd Grade Teacher; *b:* Kenton, OH; *ed:* (BS) Elem, OH Northern Univ 1972; Counseling, Univ of Dayton; *cr:* 6th Grade Teacher Allen East Local 1972-73; Learning Disabilities Teacher 1975-78, 1st Grade Teacher 1978-83, Transitional 1st Grade Teacher 1983-85, 2nd Grade Teacher 1985- Ada Exempted Village; *ai:* Pres Teacher Assn; Athletic & Music Supporter; Mem Chemical Abuse Prevention Team; Ada Ed Assn Pres 1985-87; OH Ed Assn; NEA; *office:* Ada Elem Sch 500 Grand Ave Ada OH 45810

BERGER, RONALD VINCENT, Eighth Grade Teacher; *b:* Chicago, IL; *ed:* (BS) Sociology, Loyola Univ 1967; Grad Courses in Ed, Loyola Univ 1970-71; *cr:* 6th Grade Teacher 1967-73, 7th Grade Teacher 1973-80, 8th Grade Teacher 1980- St Martha Sch; *ai:* Athletic Dir; NCEA; *office:* St Martha Sch 8535 Georgiana Ave Morton Grove IL 60053

BERGER, STEVEN, Director of Mathematics; *b:* Brooklyn, NY; *m:* Virginia Greser; *c:* Jamie, Adam; *ed:* (BA) Math, 1974, (MA) Scndry Ed, 1979 NY Univ; (SAS/SDA) Admin, C W Post & Long Island Univ 1985; *cr:* 8th/9th Grade Math Teacher Kings Park Jr HS 1975-76; 7th-11th Grade Math Teacher Wyandanch HS 1976-78; 7th-9th Grade Math Teacher Milton L Olive Mid Sch 1978-88; *ai:* NCTM, NY St Assn of Math Supvrs 1988-; NY St Assn Supervision & Curr Dev 1990; Milton L Olive Mid Sch Outstanding Teacher 1981; *office:* Wyandanch Unified Sch Dist Straight Path Wyandanch NY 11798

BERGER, SUE ANNE, Chemistry Teacher; *b:* Wichita, KS; *ed:* (BA) Chem/Math, KS St Teacher Coll 1963; (MS) Combined Sci, Univ of MS 1968; (MS) Mineral Ec, CO Sch of Mines 1982; Honor Wkshp Advanced Placement Chem; Woodrow Wilson Summer Dreyfus Chem Inst; Dow Industry Honors Wkshp in Chem; Chem Comm Resource Teacher Wkshp; *cr:* Phys Sci Davy Crockett Jr HS 1963-67; NSF Academic Yr Inst Univ of MS 1967-68; Chem Teacher Bear Creek HS 1968-; *ai:* Sci Olympiad Team Coach; Amer Chemical Society Chem Olympiad; Jr Sci & Hum Symposium Coach; CO Assn Sci Teachers Pres 1990; Amer Chemical Society 1963-, Outstanding Chem Teacher 1987; CO Sch of Mines Sigma Xi, Outstanding HS Sci Teacher 1990; Phi Delta Kappa 1986-; Parent-Teacher Stu Assn 1968-; NSTA 1985-; Jefferson Fnd Venture Grant; Published Articles Journal Chemical Ed, Sci Teacher; Book Element of Week Flinn Scientifics Inc; *office:* Bear Creek HS 3490 S Kipling St Lakewood CO 80227

BERGERON, THOMAS ERNEST, Teacher of Hearing Impaired; *b:* Bridgeport, CT; *ed:* (BA) His/Amer Stud, Sacred Heart Univ 1976; (MA) Deaf Ed, NY Univ 1983; *cr:* 1st-3rd Grade Primary Teacher Blessed Sacrament/St Mary Sch 1978-86; Teacher of the Hearing Impaired Blackham Sch 1987-; *ai:* Stu Cncl Adv Blessed Sacrament & St Mary 1983-86; Jump Rope for Heart Organizer 1983-86; Parent Adv; Parent Child Counseling Prgm SKI-HS; General Electric Fnd Grant 1984-; Bridgeport Area Fnd Mini Grant 1988-89.

BERGGREN, CAROL HUMPHREY, Sixth Grade Teacher; *b:* Philadelphia, PA; *m:* John W.; *c:* John A., Peter C.; *ed:* (BSED) Elem Ed, SUNY Oswego 1962; Grad Stud; *cr:* 3rd Grade Teacher Webster Cntrl Schls 1962-63; 4th Grade Teacher 1963-65, Kndgtn Teacher 1973-76, 3rd Grade Teacher 1976-78, Kndgtn Teacher 1978-80, 4th Grade Teacher 1980-82, 6th Grade Teacher 1982- N Colonie Cntrl Schls; *ai:* NY St Outdoor Ed Assn Annual Conference Registrar 1973-, Service Awd 1980; NY St United Teachers, AFT, N Colonie Teachers Assn 1973-; Ballston Spa Cmmty Blood Bank Chm 1969-73; WMHT-TV Utilization of Instructional Television Prof Staff In-Service Wkshp Leader; *office:* Southgate Elem Sch Southgate Rd Loudonville NY 12211

BERGLES, MATTHEW PAUL, Social Studies Teacher; *b:* Pueblo, CO; *ed:* (BS) Soc Sci, Univ S CO 1979; Working Towards Masters US His, Univ of CO 1990; *cr:* Teacher/Coach Walsh HS 1980-82, Rangeview HS 1983-; *ai:* Var Ftbl Coach; Aurora Ed Assn (Dir, Bd of Dir 1989-91); CEA, NEA; Natl Wildlife Ed, Green Peace, Nature Conservancy, Natl Geographic So ciety; *office:* Rangeview HS 17599 E Iliff Ave Aurora CO 80013

BERGLIN, BRIAN KELLY, Mathematics Department Teacher; *b:* Harvey, ND; *m:* Jeanette F.; *c:* Michelle, Kathryn; *ed:* (BS) Psych, Univ of SD 1974; (ME) Educl Admin, SD St Univ 1987; *cr:* Math Teacher Beresford Mid Sch 1976; Dist Sales Mgr Ralston Purina Company 1976-79; Realtor Hegg Realtors 1979-82; Math Teacher Axtell Park Jr HS 1982-; *ai:* Gymnastics, Vlybl, Track Coach; NEA, SDEA (Negotiator, Rep) 1982-86; NCTM 1982-; Phi Kappa Phi 1986-; SD St Univ Deans Advisory Cncl; Univ of SD Deans list; *office:* Axtell Park Jr HS 201 N West Sioux Falls SD 57104

BERIAU, DAVID L., English Teacher; *b:* Worcester, MA; *m:* Helen Paradis; *c:* Clea; *ed:* (BA) Eng, Coll of the Holy Cross 1972; Grad Stud; *cr:* Hum Prgm Teacher/Dept Chm Holy Spirit HS 1972-78; Eng Teacher Mt Anthony Union HS 1979-; *ai:* SAT Prep Course; Vermont Ed Assn, NEA; Big Brothers of America 1970-; *office:* Mt Anthony Union HS Park St Ext Bennington VT 05201

BERKMAN, MARTIN LEWIS, Social Studies Teacher; *b:* Bridgeport, CT; *ed:* (BS) Scndry Ed, 1969; (MS) Scndry Ed, 1970 Univ of Bridgeport; *cr:* Teacher Hillcrest Mid Sch 1971-; *ai:* Newspaper Adv; Cmptr Club Adv; Lafayette Lodge 141 1972- Master 1977; Jerusalem Cncl #16 1973- Thrice Illustrious Master 1973 Ish Sodi 1988; Baldwin Chapt 13 1973- High Priest 1981; *office:* Hillcrest Mid Sch 530 Daniels Farm Rd Trumbull CT 06611

BERLINER, NANCY KANE, Art Instructor; *b:* Wyndotte, MI; *c:* Ryan, Kate; *ed:* (BS) Art Ed, Western Carolina Univ 1972; *cr:* Art Instr Asheboro JR HS 1972-86, Westlee JR HS 1986-; *ai:* Art Coord Central Office Art Displays; Chairperson Amer Ed Week; Co-Spon Westwinds Annual Staff; Spon 9th Grade Prom; NAA 1972-73 & 1984-86; Randolph Art Guild 1982-88; Temple Theatre 1988-; Grant Funding Art Spec Stu 1984 & 1985; Grant Christa McCaula-Guest Artists 1987; Teacher Yr Nom Asheboro JR HS 1985; *office:* West Lee Jr HS 3301 Wicker St Sanford NC 27330

BERMAN, CHRISTINE MORIN, English Teacher; *b:* Haverhill, MA; *m:* Joel R.; *c:* Adam; *ed:* (BA) Poly Sci/Eng, Amer Intnl Coll 1973; (MA) Eng, Univ of MA Boston 1989; Lucretia Crocker Critical Thinking Wkshp; Basic Alcohol Safety Ed Teacher Trng Project; *cr:* Eng Teacher Scituate HS 1973-; *ai:* Sch Newspaper Adv; NHS, Stu Handbook, Curr Dev Comm; Cmmty Service Exec Bd; Sch Improvement Cncl; NCTE 1988-; NEA 1973-; ASCD 1989-; MA Teachers Assn 1973-; Scituate Teachers Assn Rep; Hingham PTA 1987-; Clean Water Assn Way & Means; BSA Den Leader Pack 27 1988-89; Teacher of Month; *home:* 504 Tuckers Ln Hingham MA 02043

BERMUDEZ, FLORINDA LEONOR, Principal; *b:* Havana, Cuba; *ed:* (PHD) Literature, St Thomas De Villanueva 1960; (BA) Sch Admin & Supervision, Univ of PR 1966; (MA) Religion, Barry Univ 1978; *cr:* Teacher Perpetuo Socorro 1958-70; Prin-Teacher St Matthew Sch 1967-70; Teacher St Monica Sch 1973-81; Teacher 1981-89; Prin 1989- St Michael the Archangel Schl; *ai:* Home & Sch Bd Advisor; St Michael Festival Comm; *office:* St Michael The Archangel Sch 300 Nw 28 Ave Miami FL 33125

BERNABEI, ALAN J., Principal; *b:* Indiana, PA; *m:* Rita J. Przyuski; *c:* Alan, Timothy, Raymond; *ed:* (BS) Elem Ed, Millersville St 1973; (MA) Sch Admin & Supervision, RideR Coll 1982; Essential Elements of Instruction-Trnr; *cr:* 4th & 5th Grade 1973-86, Princ 1986- Valley Elem; *ai:* Audio-Visual Coord; after Sch Recreation Supv; PA Assn of Elem Sch Principals; Outstanding Young Educator-North Southampton Jaycees 1989; *home:* 2 Easthill Dr Doylestown PA 18901

BERNACHE, CAROLYN, Resource Specialist - ESOL; *b:* Washington, DC; *m:* Normand Albert; *c:* Joyce, Janice; *ed:* (BA) Span, Univ of MD 1968; Grad Stud Univ of MD Baltimore Campus; *cr:* Span Teacher Thomas Johnson Jr HS 1968-76, Charles Carroll Mid Sch 1977-78; Adult Ed Teacher Prince

Georges Cty 1980-83; ESOL Teacher Greenbelt Mid Sch 1983-86,Bladensburg Sr HS 1986-89; Resource Specialist Bladensburg Sr HS 1989-; *ai:* Intnl Bazaar & Fashion Show; NEA, PGCEA; Coll Park Evening Homemakers Pres 1990; PTA Templeton Pres 1982-84; Adult Ed Curr, 7th Grade Sci Units P G Cty; *office:* Bladensburg Sr HS 5610 Tilden Rd Bladensburg MD 20710

BERNAL, HENRY PAUL, Spanish Teacher; *b:* Bakersfield, CA; *m:* Lydia Vega Velazquez; *c:* Timothy J., Amanda P.; *ed:* (BA) His, Fresno St Univ 1969; (BA) Span, 1974, (MA) Admin, 1976 CA St Univ Bakersfield; Summer Sessions Univ of San Francisco Guada La Jara Mexico 1971; Univ of San Francisco Valencia Spain 1972; Univ of Guanajuato Mexico 1974; *cr:* 4th-6th Grade Teacher Myrtle Avenue Sch 1969-74; 9th-12th Grade Teacher South HS 1974-; *ai:* Span Club Intnl Travel; NEA, CA Teachers Assn 1969-; South HS Faculty Club VP 1984-86; *office:* South HS 1101 Planz Rd Bakersfield CA 93304

BERNARDINE, KILIAN, FSC, Mathematics Teacher; *b:* St Joseph, MO; *ed:* (BS) Math, St Marys Coll 1940; (MA) Ed, De Paul Univ 1946; Sabbatical Stanford Univ 1975-77; *cr:* Teacher St Mel HS 1940-46, Christian Brothers HS 1946-47; Prin/Teacher La Salle Inst 1947-59; Teacher St Mel HS 1959-60; Admin/Teacher 1960-75, Teacher 1977- Bishop Kelley HS; *ai:* Assist Academic Counseling; St Gregorys Coll Bd of Trustees 1978-89; Shell Merit Fellow 1962; Mapco Teacher Achievement Awd 1987; Outstanding Teacher Awd Univ of Chicago 1987; Stu Infuencial Teacher Awd MA Inst of Tech 1987; NSF Grants Stanford, Rtgers, Boston Coll; *office:* Bishop Kelly H S 3905 S Hudson Tulsa OK 74135

BERNARDO, ALICE, Teacher; *b:* Bronx, NY; *m:* Richard; *c:* Richard, David, Lori Ann; *ed:* (BS) Ed, Empire St Coll 1983; *cr:* CCD Teacher St Francis 1972-79; Teacher-Aide Blessed Sacrament Sch of Spec Ed 1975-83; Teacher St Joan of Arc Sch 1983-; *ai:* Prgm for the Dev of Human Potential; Rap Group Cnslr.

BERNARDO, CAROLAN PENKUL, Math Teacher; *b:* Lynn, MA; *c:* Andrea, Alexander; *ed:* (BS) Elem Ed/Math, Salem St Coll 1972; *cr:* Math/Rdng Teacher St Michael Sch 1972-76; K-8th Grade Math Coord/7th-8th Grade Math Teacher Our Lady of the Assumption; Math Teacher St Mary Jr/Sr Regional HS 1984-; *ai:* Class & Academic Trivia Adv; Assn for Women in Math, NCTM 1988-; NCEA 1984-; Lynn Youth Soccer Registrar 1989-; *office:* St Mary Jr/Sr Regional HS 35 Tremont St Lynn MA 01902

BERNARDUCCI, MATTHEW DANIEL, 7th Grade Language Art Teacher; *b:* Jersey City, NJ; *m:* Robin Eirmann; *c:* Matthew Jr., Lauren; *ed:* (BS) Bus, IN St Univ 1974; (MED) Lang Art, William Paterson Coll 1981; Elem Cert; *cr:* 1st Grade Teacher 1976-78, 2nd Grade Teacher 1978-80, 5th Grade Teacher 1980-87, 6th/7th Grade Teacher 1987- Maywood Avenue Sch; *ai:* NJ Governors Teacher Recognition Awd 1987; *office:* Maywood Avenue Sch 452 Maywood Ave Maywood NJ 07607

BERNBACH, CAROLYN ANN, Cultural Enrichment Teacher; *b:* New York, NY; *ed:* (BS) Ed, 1969, (MS) Ed, 1972 Fordham Univ; Work Beyond Masters at Various Insts; Prof Diploma Prgm Admin Supervision, Fordham Univ; *cr:* 2nd Grade Classroom Teacher 1969-76, 1st Grade Classroom Teacher 1976-78, 4th Grade Classroom Teacher 1978-80, Pre-K Classroom Teacher 1980-85, K-2nd Early Chldhd Lang Art Teacher 1986-88, 3rd-6th Grade Remedial Rdng Teacher 1987-88, 2nd-6th Grade Cultural Enrichment Teacher Public Sch 17 1988-; *ai:* Child Abuse, Family Living, Sex Ed Comm; Gifted, Talented, Cultural Arts Coord.

BERNER, KAREN V., Library-Media Coordinator; *b:* Prince George BC, Canada; *m:* Eugene E.; *c:* Jeffry, Beth A., Jonathan, Rebecca; *ed:* (BS) Elem Ed, Concordia Teachers Coll 1962; (MLS) Lib/Information Sci; Brigham Young Univ 1977; Grad Stud UT St Univ; *cr:* K-8th Grade Teacher Lutheran Parochial Schls 1962-75; Lib Media Coord Jordan Sch Dist 1977-81, Provo Sch Dist 1981-; *ai:* Career Ladder Leadership; Soc Media & Lib Automation Networking Project for Six Schls & Public Lib; Dist Technology Comm; UT Educl Lib Media Pres 1986, Distingushed Service 1990; UEA, NEA, AASL, ALA, ULA; UT Lib Assn Schlsp 1976; Beta Phi Mu; Leadership for Implementation of Grant, Co-Authored Grant; Co-Chairperson Local Arrangements AASL Natl Convention 1989; *home:* 1978 Falcon Hill Cir Sandy UT 84092

BERNER, MARCIA, Spanish/English Teacher; *b:* Indianapolis, IN; *ed:* (BS) Span/Ed, Univ of Tulsa 1966; (MA) Ed, Butler Univ; *cr:* Span/Eng Teacher Southwestern HS 1966-; *ai:* Stu Cncl Spon; After Sch Tutoring Prgm Coord; NCTE, Amer Assn Teachers of Span & Portuguese; SW Consolidated Classroom Teachers Assn Pres 1989; St Georges Luth Church; *office:* Southwestern HS RR 4 Box 245-A Shelbyville IN 46176

BERNER, TOM E., Middle School Guidance Cnslr; *b:* Minneapolis, MN; *m:* Cheryl L.; *c:* Alan, Jamie, Aaron; *ed:* (BA) Soc Stud/Sociology, Macalester Coll 1982; (MSE) Guidance Counseling, Univ of WI River Falls 1989; *cr:* Soc Stud/Phys Ed Teacher Sky Ranch for Boys 1983-84; Soc Stud Teacher Unity Mid Sch 1984-87; Guidance Cnslr Hayward Sch 1987-; *ai:* Asst Var Ftbl Coach; Free of Chemical Use Stus Club; *office:* Hayward Mid Sch PO Box 860 Hayward WI 54843

BERNHARD, DAVID C., SR., Mathematics Teacher; *b:* Chicago Heights, IL; *m:* Patti Pfingsten; *c:* Dave, Carri; *ed:* (BS) Math, Bradley Univ 1975; (MA) Comm Sci, Governors St Univ 1981; *cr:* Math Teacher Peoria Sch Dist 1975-76, Lincoln-Way HS Dist 1976-; *ai:* Lincoln-Way HS Head Bsbl Coach; Lights Comm Mem; Coaches Salary Comm; Bsbl Clinic Speaker; IL Cncl Techers of Math 1989-; IL HS Bsbl Coaches Assn 1976-; Amer Bsbl Coaches Assn 1985-; NEA, IL Ed Assn, Lincoln Way Ed Assn 1986-; Franklin Circle of Coaches Awd; *home:* 13323 W 184th St Mokena IL 60448

BERNHARD, PAULA JORDAN, Teacher of Gifted & Talented; *b:* Monahans, TX; *m:* Bill R.; *c:* Wes, Hollie; *ed:* (BS) Ed Music, Howard Payne Univ 1968; (ME) Ed, Sul Ross Univ 1975; *cr:* 3rd Grade Teacher La Mesa Ind Sch Dist 1968-69; Music Teacher 1969-75, Kndgtn Teacher 1975-81, 5th Grade Teacher 1981-89, 6th Grade Teacher 1989- Ector Cty Ind Sch Dist; *ai:* Odessa Amer Spelling Bee Coach; UIL Oral Rdng Coach; TSTA Life Mem; *office:* Milam Elem Magnet Sch Box 3912 Odessa TX 79760

BERNHEIM, DAVID MAYER, Theatre Arts Director/Teacher; *b:* Memphis, TN; *m:* Mary Josephine Wickerson; *ed:* Heather; (BA) Intermediate Ed, Univ of NC Charlotte 1983; Skills for Living Certified; Qualified US Army Ranger & Paratrooper; *cr:* Infantry Officer US Army 1983-86; Eng/Civics Teacher Anacoco HS 1986; Eng/His/Drama Teacher R J Reynolds HS 1987-; *ai:* Drama Club, Thespian Honor Society, Video Yrbk Spon; Videographer for Var Ftbl; Plays Dir; Serving on Stu Improvement Comm; Forsyth Assn of Eng Teachers 1987-; Theatre Ed Assn 1989-; Alpha Sigma Phi Regional Pres 1980-83; Appointed Chm of Curr Revision Comm Forsyth Cty; Teachers of Theatre HS 1989-; *office:* R J Reynolds HS 301 N Hawthorne Rd Winston-Salem NC 27104

BERNING, LARRY DEAN, Third Grade Teacher; *b:* Scott City, KS; *ed:* (BS) Elem Ed - Summa Cum Laude, St Mary of the Plains Coll 1975; (MS) Spec Ed - Summa Cum Laude, 1987, Learning Disabilities Specialist, 1987 Pittsburg St Univ;Curr Dev, Master Teacher Acad 1989; Advanced Trng Teacher Effectiveness, Master Teacher Acad 1989; *cr:* 3rd Grade Teacher Tipton Elem Sch 1975-77, Lakin Grade Sch 1977-; *ai:* Spec Ed Pre-Assessment 1984-86; Stu at Risk 1988-89; Dist Goals & Curr Dev 1984-85; Supt Advisory Comm 1985-86; NEA, KS Ed Assn 1977-88; Lakin Teachers Assn 1977-88, Teacher of Yr 1980, 1986; Knights of Columbus 1987-; Natl Deans List 1987; *home:* 405 Albert St Box 571 Lakin KS 67860

BERNINI, LINDA J., Second Grade Teacher; *b:* Salt Lake City, UT; *m:* David L.; *c:* Gregory; *ed:* (BS) Elem Ed/Early Chldhd Endorsement 1970, (MED) Ed, 1985 UT St Univ; Univ UT/Brigham Young Univ/UT Univ/Granite Dist Inservice Classes; *cr:* 3rd Grade Teacher Riley Elem 1970-71, Substitute Teacher Matsac Elem 1973-74, Kndgtn Teacher 1974-88, 2nd Grade Teacher 1988- Plymouth Elem; *ai:* Sci Facilitator for Wild Goose Sci Lab Granite Dist 1988-; Teacher Chairperson-Spec Persons Day 1989-; Performance Bonus Teacher 1987-; Teacher VP Plymouth PTA-1987-89; PTA Nominating Comm 1987-89; Grade Level Chairperson 1987-88; Granite Ed Assn Faculty Rep 1981-84; UT Ed Assn Delegate House of Delagates 1981-84; NEA Delegate-Natl Convention 1981; PTA Teacher VP 1987-89; Outstanding Educator Awd Runner Up 1990; Granite Ed Assn Public Relations Comm 1984; Presentor-Intnl Rdng Assn Conference; Presentor-USU Rdng/Lang Workshop for Teachers; Presentor IGE St Conference; Instr Class for Teachers-UT St Univ Granite Sch Dist; Career Ladder Teacher 1985-; Presentor Educator in Action-Granite Dist Bd of Ed 1989; *office:* Plymouth Elem Sch 5220 S 1470 West Salt Lake City UT 84123

BERNSTEIN, BEVERLY CHUCHIAN, 6th Grade Teacher/Chairman; *b:* Los Angeles, CA; *m:* Robert Paul; *c:* Brenda L. Ridley, Brigette L.; *ed:* (AA) Lang Art, Bakersfield Coll 1951; (BA) Journalism/Eng, 1954, (MS) Ed, Univ of S CA 1958; Counseling Courses; *cr:* Eng Teacher/Newspaper Adv Ventura Sr HS 1955-56; Eng Teacher/Literary Book Adv East Bakersfield HS 1956-58; Eng Teacher/Newspaper Adv John Adams Jr HS 1958-62; 2nd-6th Grade/GATE Teacher Bakersfield City Schls 1971-83; 6th Grade Teacher Noble Elem Sch 1984-; *ai:* Stu Store Adv; Soc & Effective Schls Comm Mem; Theta Sigma Phi Pres 1953-54; Bakersfield Elem Teachers Assn Teacher of Yr 1978; CA Teachers Assn, NEA; Toastmistress VP 1956; Outstanding Woman Journalist Grad USC 1954; Feature Writing Awd 1951; Wrote Special Articles from USSR 1956; *office:* Noble Elem Sch 1015 Noble Ave Bakersfield CA 93305

BERNZEN, JOHN F., Band Director; *b:* Quincy, IL; *m:* Beverly J. Behrman; *c:* Theresa; *ed:* (BS) Music Ed, Quincy Coll 1972; (MS) Music Ed, Univ of IL 1978; Mrchg Band Wkshps, Univ of WI 1980-81; Condctg Wkshps, Sam Houston St Univ 1983-86; Instrmntl Music Wkshp, Univ of Houston 1985; *cr:* Dand Dir, Nokomis Publ Schls 1972-73; Ft Madison Cath Sch System 1973-80; La Salle Peru Twnshp HS 80-82; Freeport Intermed Sch 1982-; *ai:* Natl Jr Honor Socty-Faclty Advisor; Parent Invlvmnt Comm-Chm; Stu Need a Pat & Push-Faclty Partcpnt; TX Bandmasters Assn 1982-; TX Music Educators Assn 1982-; Natl Band Assn 1976-; Knights of Columbus; Quincy IL Musicians Union 265; Natl Eagle Scout Assn; Brazosport Symph Orch; Phi Delta Kappa-HP Chptr 1979; Brazosport Symph Orch Cncl-Dir 1986-89; Brazosport Symph Orch Cncl-Pres 1986-88; Organizer TX All-St Band 1987; Eagle Scout-Boy Scts of Amer 1966; *home:* 527 Oleander Lake Jackson TX 77566

BERRI, KENNETH JAMES, Mathematics Teacher; *b:* San Francisco, CA; *c:* Angela, Christopher, Jaime; *ed:* (AA) Math, Coll of San Mateo 1967; (BA) Math, San Francisco St 1969; (MA) Ed, Chico St; *cr:* Math Teacher Yuba City HS 1970-; Part Time Math Teacher Yuba Coll 1982-; *ai:* Frosh Class Adv; CA Math Cncl 1973-; Yuba City Unified Ed Assn VP 1974-; *home:* 842 Bunce Rd Yuba City CA 95991

BERRIAN, JAMES EDWIN, Biology Teacher; *b:* Pasadena, CA; *m:* Robyn M. Garcia; *c:* Nathaniel; *ed:* (AA) Zoology, Southwestern Comm Coll 1976; (BS) Zoology, San Diego St Univ 1978; *cr:* Collections Mgr San Diego Museum of Natural His 1981-84; Sci Teacher Montgomery Mid Sch 1984-85; Bio/Theory of Knowledge Teacher Bonita Vista HS 1985-; *ai:* Stus for Environmental Awareness & Philosophical Discussion Group Club Spon; Society of Vertebrate Paleontology Mem 1985-; Nature Conservancy Mem 1987-; San Diego Zoological Society Mem 1974-; Museum of N AZ Mem 1989-; Articles Published Zoological Journals; *office:* Bonita Vista HS 751 Otay Lakes Rd Chula Vista CA 92013

BERRIER, HARRIET LOUISE, Second Grade Teacher; *b:* Clarksville, TN; *ed:* (BA) Elem Ed, Emory & Henry Coll 1977; (MED) Admin/Supervision, Lincoln Memorial Univ 1990; *cr:* Teacher Sevierville Primary 1977-; *ai:* Sch Based Support Team Mem; TN Ed Assn, NEA 1977-; Sevier Cty Ed Assn (Pres 1982, Treas 1989); Teacher of Yr Sevierville Primary Sch 1989; *office:* Sevierville Primary Sch 300 Cedar Sevierville TN 37862

BERRODIN, ROBERT L., Science/Health Teacher; *b:* Canton, OH; *ed:* (BS) Bio, Mt Union Coll 1962; (MED) Health Ed, Kent St Univ 1966; (MTS) Bio, Coll of William & Mary 1970; First Aid, Ornithology, Malone Coll; Supervision Stu Teaching, Akron Univ; Ecology, Theil Coll; Radiation Bio, St Lawrence Univ; *cr:* Bio Teacher Massillon Washington HS 1962-67, N Canton Hoover HS 1967-78; Life Sci/Health Teacher N Canton Mid Sch 1978-; *ai:* 7th Grade Girls Bsktbl Coach; NCEA Teacher of Month 1982; OEA, NEA; Fellowship of Chrstn Athletes 1968-78; 5 Natl Sci Fnd Summer Inst; *office:* N Canton Mid Sch 200 Charlotte St NW North Canton OH 44720

BERROTH, RHONDALYN HELEN, 8th Grade English Teacher; *b:* Lincoln, KS; *m:* Bradford; *ed:* (BS) Theatre Ed, KS St Univ 1979; *cr:* Teacher Newton HS 1979-81, Concordia HS 1981-85, Hocker Grove Mid Sch 1985-; *home:* 1114 E Charlotte Town Rd Olathe KS 66061

BERRY, AGNES STEVENS, Kindergarten Teacher; *b:* Clifton Forge, VA; *m:* Lonzia J.; *c:* Lonzia M., Stephanie Berry Collier, Candace, Allyson; *ed:* (BS) Home Ec, Stover Coll 1946; Hampton Inst; Stetson Univ; Univ of Cntrl FL; St Leo Coll; Lake Sumter Comm Coll; *cr:* Elem Teacher Jefferson Sch 1946-55; Pre-Sch Dir Joyland Kndgtn 1955-67; Elem Teacher Rimes Elem 1967-69; Early Chldhd Skeen Elem 1969-; *ai:* Grade Level Chm; Lake Cty Teachers Assn; Leesburg Day Care Chairperson 1986-; St Paul AME Church Organist 1956-; Early Chldhd Ed Evening Classes Instr Lake Cty Area Voc Tech Center; *home:* 900 Mc Cormack St Leesburg FL 34748

BERRY, CHRISTOPHR EDWARD, Social Studies Dept Chair; *b:* Columbus, MS; *m:* Joan Monks; *c:* Lauren N., Miranda P.; *ed:* (BA) Soc Stud/Ed, David Lipscomb Univ 1981; Working Toward Masters Counseling Psych, AL A&M Univ; *cr:* Teacher/Coach Pacific Chrstn Acad 1981-82, Solano Chrstn Acad 1982-84; Soc Stud Chm/Coach Madison Acad 1984-; *ai:* Athletic Trainer; Ftbl & Bsbl Asst Coach; Stu Government Assn Scholars Bowl Team Spon; Jr Var Bsbl Coach; Jr Class Spon; Outstanding Young Men of America 1989; *office:* Madison Acad 301 Max Luther Dr Huntsville AL 35810

BERRY, DONNA ALSPAUGH, 4th Grade Teacher; *b:* Franklin, KY; *m:* Robert Eugene; *c:* Jennifer; *ed:* (BS) Elem Ed, 1968, (MA) Elem Ed, 1970 Western Ky Univ; *cr:* 6th Grade Teacher Lincoln Elem 1968-69; Round Pond Elem 1970-75; 3rd Grade Teacher Franklin Elem 1975-80; 4th Grade Teacher Simpson Elem 1980-; *ai:* NEA, KEA, SCEA 1968-; *office:* Simpson Elem Sch Box 409 Witt Rd Franklin KY 42134

BERRY, DORIA NEAL, 8th Grade English Teacher; *b:* El Dorado, AR; *m:* Mike; *c:* Scott, Michael; *ed:* (BA) Eng, Univ of AR Monticello 1976; *cr:* 7th Grade Rdng Teacher Forrest City Jr HS 1976-77; 8th Grade Eng Teacher Dermott Jr HS 1978-; *ai:* Stu Cncl Spon Dermott Jr HS; Dermott Ed Assn, AR Ed Assn, NEA 1987-89; *office:* Dermott Jr HS Hwy 35 E Dermott AR 71638

BERRY, GLENN PATRICIA, Soc Stud Teacher/Dept Chair; *b:* Lawton, OK; *ed:* (BA) His, KY Wesleyan Coll 1974; (MA) Educl Psych, 1980, (Rank I) Ed, 1982 Western KY Univ; Grad Stud Ec, Univ of DE 1985; *cr:* Soc Stud Instr Davies Cty HS 1976-; Psych Instr Univ of KY Owensboro 1985; Ec Consultant Audubon Center for Ec Bresara Coll 1985-; Ec Instr KY Wesleyan Coll 1989; Soc Stud Teacher/Dept Chairperson Davies Cty HS 1988-; *ai:* Co-Ed Y & Mock Trial Competition Adv & Spon; APA, KCSS, NCSS, KCEE, JCEE, APA, SHA, AFT; March of Dimes 1985-; Green River Comprehensive Care Center 1984-87; Kazanjian Schlsp 1985; Outstanding Young Soc Stud Teacher 1985; Outstanding Soc Stud Educator Awd KY Cncl for Soc Stud; *office:* Daviess Cty HS 4255 New Hartford Rd Owensboro KY 42301

BERRY, GREGORY WAYNE, English/Drama Instructor; *b:* La Grande, OR; *ed:* (BA) Scndry Ed/Eng, 1986, (MS) Eng Ed, 1990 Eastern OR St Coll; *cr:* Eng Teacher Ontario Jr HS 1986-89; Eng Instr Treasure Valley Comm Coll Adjunct; Eng/Drama Instr Ontario HS 1989-; *ai:* Drama Club Adv & Coach; NCTE 1984-; NEA 1986-; Local Music & Theatre Groups; 2 Academic Awds; 2 Stu Service Awds; Sigma Tau Delta Natl Eng Honor Society; *office:* Ontario H S 1115 W Idaho Ave Ontario OR 97914

BERRY, JACK G. W., II, Elementary Phys Ed Teacher; *b:* Sulphur, LA; *m:* Donna Pelt-Berry; *ed:* (BS) Health/Phys Ed, 1983, (MED) Admin/Supervision, 1987 Mc Neese St; Working Toward Certificate in Counseling; *cr:* Sci/Math Teacher Leesville

Jr HS 1984; Phys Ed Teacher Rosepine HS 1984-86, Rosepine Elem 1987-; *ai:* 5th/6th Grade Boys & Girls Bsktbl, Jr HS Var Ftbl Coach.

BERRY, MARILYN BLAKE, English Teacher; *b:* Portland, ME; *m:* Robert; *c:* Linda Berry Ashworth. Greg; *ed:* (BSED) Eng, Univ of ME 1958; Post Grad Stud Washington & Jefferson Coll, Univ of ME, California Univ of PA; *cr:* Eng Teacher Brewer HS 1958-59, Greely Inst 1959-60, Old Town Public Schls 1960-63, Mc Guffey HS 1967-; *ai:* Parental & Cmmty Involvement Task Force Chairperson; NEA, PA Ed Assn, Mc Guffey Ed Assn, NCTE 1967-; W PA Cncl Teachers of Eng 1983-; AMI (Pres, VP, Finance Chm, Personnel Chm) 1982-; Mental Health Assn Washington Cty Prof of Yr 1983; Natl Writing Project Fellowship 1982; *office:* Mc Guffey HS RD 1 Box 219 Claysville PA 15323

BERRY, PATRICIA REED, Choral Department Chair; *b:* Louisville, KY; *m:* Kenneth; *c:* Megan, Matthew; *ed:* (BME) Choral Music, E KY Univ 1976; MME, E KY Univ; *cr:* Music Teacher Bloomfield Jr HS 1978-79; New Haven Elem & Jr HS 1980-86; Dept Chairperson Nelson Cty HS 1986-; *ai:* Pep Club; Renaissance Guild; Prom & Sports Prgm Comm; Stu Act Chairperson; MENC, KMEA, NEA; *office:* Nelson Cty HS 1070 Bloomfield Rd Bardstown KY 40004

BERRY, RAYMOND HARVEY, 8th Grade Soc Stud Teacher; *b:* La Grande, OR; *m:* Mertice Johnson; *c:* Holly A. Smith, Tamilyn, Eldon R., Elwin J., Darrell R., Tracie M. Goggia; *ed:* (BA) Scndry Ed, 1959, (MS) Scndry Ed, 1969 E OR St Coll; Extern Prgm Leadership Trng, OR St Univ 1973-74; Career Ed Trng, E OR St Coll 1974; Assertive Discipline, Univof La Vern, Law Related Ed, E OR St Coll 1986; *cr:* Industrial Arts Teacher 1959-63, Sci Teacher 1963-66, Vice-Prin 1966-69 La Grande Jr HS; Soc Stud Teacher La Grande Mid Sch 1977-; *ai:* Soc Stud Club Adv; Spon 8th Grade Soc Stud Field Trip; Judge for Citizenship Bee E OR St Coll; Dist Curr Cncl; St Advisory Comm Mem 1972-74; La Grande Sch Bd Chm 1976-77; La Grande Ed Assn (Pres 1970-71, VP 1969-70); St Dept of Ed; BSA (Dist Cncl 1964-66, Institutional Rep 1964-66, Merit Badge Cnslr 1973-77); E OR Alcohol & Drug Cncl 1973-77; NW OR Law Enforcement Cncl 1970-77; Natl Sci Fnd Grant UT St Univ 1964; Grant Natl Security Seminar Valley Forge 1987; Grant Wkshp Amer Revolution Boston to Philadelphia; Freedoms Fnd Valley Forge 1987.

BERRY, RENEE REDONIA, Chemistry Teacher; *b:* Washington, DC; *ed:* (BS) Chem, Howard Univ 1986; (MA) Educl Admin, Univ of DC 1990; *cr:* Chemist Natl Inst of Health 1986-87; Chem Teacher H D Woodson Sr HS 1987-; *ai:* Sci Fair Coord; Amer Chem Society 1989-; NOBCCHE; Teacher/ Counselor GW Univ Sci & Engr Apprentice; Chem Instr Howard Univ Upward Bound Prgm; *office:* H D Woodson Sr HS 55th & Eads Sts NE Washington DC 20019

BERRY, RUTH SMITH, 3rd Grade Teacher; *b:* Lock Haven, PA; *M:* C. R.; *c:* Christina M.; *ed:* (MA) Ed, Bloomsburg Univ 1971; (Bs) Sci, Lock Haven Univ 1967; *ai:* PSEA; ACCE; NEA; Sugar Valley Lions; Mackeyville United Meth Women; Pumpkin Pole Article in Instr 1975; Grant-Writing An Ongoing Process 1984; *home:* RR 2 Box 159 Loganton PA 17747

BERRY, VIOLA KAY, HS Language Arts Teacher; *b:* Tulsa, OK; *ed:* (BS) Lang Arts/Ed, OK St Univ 1980; *cr:* Eng/Speech/ Yrbk Teacher Wynona HS 1980-; *ai:* Yrbk Adv; Jr Class Spon; Staff Dev Comm; Eng Dept Head; Testing & Curr Comm Chairperson; Consultant Teacher For Intern Teacher; Osage Cty Ed Assn, NEA, OK Ed Assn 1980-; Wynona Teacher of Yr 1987; WhoS Who Among Young Amer Women 1984; *home:* Rt 2 Box 437 Cleveland OK 74020

BERRYHILL, ROY H., Band/Choir/Theatre Art Teacher; *b:* Freeport, TX; *m:* Margaret Suzanne; *c:* Debbie L., Mark R.; *ed:* (BME) Music, Sam Houston St Univ 1970; Various Stud at Various Univ & Colls; *cr:* Band Teacher Huntsville Jr HS 1970-77, Katy Jr HS 1977-83, Burnet Jr HS 1983-; *ai:* TX Music Educators, TX Band Master 1970-90; TX Choral Dir 1983-; Minister of Music Church; Honorary Chapter Mem; Phi Mu Alpha; Speak & Entertain Numerous Band Banquets; *office:* Burnet Jr HS 308 E Brier St Burnet TX 78611

BERRYMAN, AUDREY SIMMS, 6th Grade Rdng/Math Teacher; *b:* Burkeville, VA; *m:* Curtis Winston; *ed:* (BS) Elem Ed, 1978, (MS) Rdng, 1987 Longwood Coll; Math Endorsement & Developmental Rdng; Working on Endorsement; *cr:* 4th Grade Teacher 1978-83, 6th Grade Teacher 1983-87, Chapter I Coord/ 6th Grade Teacher 1987- Appomattox Cty Schls; *ai:* Child Study, Chapter I Advisory, St Chapter I Comm; SACCS (Mem, Visiting Comm); Delta Kappa Gamma Pres 1986-88; AFT, ASCD; Phi Delta Kappa Nominee; *home:* Rt 2 Box 905 Farmville VA 23901

BERSOLA, GERTRUDES APILADO, ESL/Lang Arts/Math Teacher; *b:* Caba La Union, Philippines; *m:* Florentino C.; *c:* Florentino Jr., Michael, Martin, Theodora J., Irene D.; *ed:* (BSED) Eng, Natl Univ 1953; (MA) Foreign Lang/ESL Teacher, Columbia Univ Teachers Coll 1956; Teachers Certificate CA St Univ Sacramento 1986; Asian-Amer Educators Seminar, Boston Univ 1982; Inst of Asian Lang & Culture, Tokyo Univ Japan 1975; Working Towards PHD in Anthropology & Linguistics, Univ of Philippines 1973-76; *cr:* Assoc Professor Technological Univ of Philippines 1953-79; ESL Teacher Napa Coll 1981-83; Teacher Head Start 1983-84; Voc Eng Instr CA Human Dev Corporation Skills Center 1984-86; Teacher Grant HS 1986-; *ai:* Assn of Oriental Stus Spon 1988-; Mem Task Force for Dev of Multicultural Ed 1989-; CA Assn of Bi-ling Teachers Mem 1986-; CA Teachers of Eng to Speakers of Other Langs 1987-; St Joseph Church Eucharistic Minister 1989-; Philippine Assn of Univ Women 1986-; Fulbright Smith Mundt NY, Regional Eng Lang Center Singapore, Philippine Assn of St Colls & Univs, Univ of Philippines, Japan Fnd Tokyo Japan Grantee.

BERTACCINI, JO PISTARINO, 8th Grade Teacher; *b:* San Jose, CA; *m:* Edward A.; *c:* Edward J., Lisa Bertaccini Ward; *ed:* (BA) Eng, Coll of Notre Dame 1954; *cr:* 6th Grade Teacher Berryessa Dist 1954-56; 7th-8th Grade Teacher Santa Clara Dist Wm A Wilson 1956-57, Campbell Dist Monroe Sch 1957-62; Western Nursery Sch 1967-69; 4th/6th-8th Grade Teacher Sacred Heart Sch 1969-; *ai:* Santa Clara Cty Soc Studs (Corresponding Secy 1982-83; Rdng Cncl Rep); *home:* 1704 Fabian Dr San Jose CA 95124

BERTAGNA, RITA ANNETTE, Science Teacher; *b:* Long Branch, NJ; *c:* Lisa Velte, David, Gregory; *ed:* (BA) Art Ed, 1974, (BS) Elem Ed, 1976 Kean Coll; Elem Admin, Kean Coll; *cr:* Real Estate Sales 1957-60; Restaurant Management 1965-80; Sci Teacher St James Sch 1974-; *ai:* Art Teacher; Stu Cncl; Girls Bsktbl Coach; NCEA 1975-; Natl Assn Teachers of Rdng 1975-85; Kean Coll Alumni Assn; NSTA 1982-; St James PTA VP 1978-80; *office:* St James Sch Amboy Ave Woodbridge NJ 07095

BERTAIN, KARL PETER, Bio & Advanced Bio Teacher; *b:* Berlin, Germany; *m:* Lynne Bolz; *c:* Tristan, Patrick, Joeseph; *ed:* (BS) Bio/Geography, Univ of WI Eau Claire 1983; UCI Summer Sci Inst; *cr:* Sci Teacher La Quinta HS 1984-85, Pacifica HS 1985-; *ai:* Jr Class & Bio Club Adv; Academic Decathalon Sci Coach; Grant 1984-85; Academic Decathalon Recognition; *office:* Pacifica HS 6851 Lampson Ave Garden Grove CA 92645

BERTELLI, PATRICIA CORTEZ, Educational Consultant; *b:* Starkville, MS; *m:* Noel J.; *c:* Stacy Fields, Sandee Levan, Susan Shumate, Sara Shumate; *ed:* (BA) Elem Ed, CA St Univ Long Beach 1956; Grad Studies Univ of Houston Clear Lake 1977-85; *cr:* Elem Teacher Long Beach Schls 1956-65; Clear Creek Ind Sch Dist 1971-85; Educl Consultant Silver Burdett & Ginn 1985-; *ai:* Conduct Prof Inservice & Wkshps Throughout Southern States for K-8th Grade Sch Dist; Gifted-Talented Curr Author; Sch Newspaper Faculty Spon; NEA 1972-85; NSTA 1990; Classroom Teachers Assn 1972-85; Alpha Delta Kappa; League of Womens Voters; Bus & Prof Womens Assn; *home:* 15707 Springcourt Dr Houston TX 77062

BERTELSEN, TERRI LYNN, Elementary Music Teacher; *b:* Madison, WI; *m:* David Bruce; *c:* Jinna; *ed:* (BS) Music Ed, 1978, (MS) Music Ed, 1987 Univ of WI Madison; AODA Facilitation Class; *cr:* Kndgtn-6th Grade Music Teacher Random Lake Elem Sch 1978-; *ai:* Coreographer of HS Swing Choir/HS Musicals; 6th Grade Musical Dir; Dir of Elem Choirs; Church Choir Dir; MENC 1988-; ACDA 1987-; Random Lake Area Theatre Fund Pres 1986-; Teacher of Yr for Random Lake Schls 1985; *office:* Random Lake Elem School 605 Random Lake Rd Random Lake WI 53075

BERTGES, MARILYN ANN, Sixth Grade Teacher; *b:* Erie, PA; *m:* Gerald T.; *ed:* (BA) Ed, Mercyhurst Coll 1973; (MS) Rdng, SUNY Fredonia 1976; *cr:* 6th Grade Teacher Westfield Acad & Cntrl Sch 1973-; *ai:* Chairperson Parents as Rdng Partners Prgm; NEA, NY St Ed Assn, Chautauqua Cty Rdng Assn 1973-; Teacher of Yr Westfield Acad & Cntrl Sch 1984; Parents as Rdng Partners Prgm St Awds 1987-88; *office:* Westfield Acad & Cntrl Sch E Main St Westfield NY 14787

BERTHOLD, SANDRA JEAN (BUSH), Soc Stud Teacher/ Dept Chair; *b:* Albany, NY; *m:* Robert R.; *c:* Sean; *ed:* (BA) Soc Stud, 1967, (MA) Soc Stud Ed, 1968 St Univ of NY Albany; His, St Univ of NY Albany; Guidance & Counseling, SD St Univ; *cr:* Soc Stud Teacher Clarence HS 1969-72, Chelmsford Jr HS 1972-74, Francis Howell HS 1978-80, Barnwell Jr HS 1980-86; Soc Stud Teacher/Dept Chairperson Francis Howell North HS 1986-; *ai:* Francis Howell Writing Project Co-Dir; Soc Stud Curr Revision Steering Comm; Francis Howell North Cntrl Evaluation Comm Co-Chm; NCSS, Phi Delta Kappa; Barnwell Jr HS Teacher of Yr 1980; Howell of Fame Nom 1990; *office:* Francis Howell N HS 2549 Hackmann Rd Saint Charles MO 63303

BERTINO, ANTHONY J., A P Biology Instructor; *b:* Geneva, NY; *m:* Nancy Helen Marsh; *c:* Karen, Victoria, David; *ed:* (BS) Bio, Hobart Coll 1967; (MS) Ecology, St Univ of NY Geneseo; Wkshp Univ of Rochester; *cr:* Teacher 1967-, Coord/Teacher of Gifted Ed 1988- Canandaigua Acad; *ai:* Coord Odyssey of Mind; Supvr Sch & City of Canandaigua Ski Prgm 1970-; Canandaigua Teachers Assn 1967-, Teacher of Yr 1979; Sci Teachers of NY St 1967-; NSTA 1989-; Red Cross CPR Instr 1980-; Natl Sci Fnd Grants 1967-68, 1975, 1986-; Supvr Stu Teachers 1971-; Presenter Sessions St Sci Teachers Conference 1981; Dist Teacher of Yr 1979; Nom Presidential Excl in Teaching Awd 1990; *office:* Canandaigua Acad Granger St Canandaigua NY 14424

BERTRAM, JANICE KING, First Grade Teacher; *b:* Bracken Cty, KY; *m:* Henry W.; *c:* Jeffrey A. Page; *ed:* (BA) Elem Ed, 1967, Elem Ed, 1976 Morehead St Univ; *cr:* 5th Grade Teacher Camargo Sch 1967-68; 1st Grade Teacher Lake Orion Schls 1968-70; 3rd Grade Teacher Springs Valley Schls 1971-72; 6th Grade Teacher 1972-82, 1st Grade Teacher 1982- Pendleton Cty Schls; *ai:* NEA 1967-; KY Ed Assn 1972-; *home:* Rt 4 Box 291 Falmouth KY 41040

BERTRAND, HAROLD ROBERT, 6th Grade Math/Sci Teacher; *b:* Menominee, MI; *m:* Lynda Kay Yost; *ed:* (BS) Elem Ed, Univ of WI Oshkosh 1968; Grad Work Towards Masters Elem; Certificate Drug & Alcohol Facilitator; *cr:* 5th/6th Grade Math/Sci Teacher/Building Prin Brillion Public Schls; *ai:* Sch Calendar, Child-At-Risk, NASA Tomato Seed Project, Cmptr Lab, Sci/Math, Drug & Alcohol Facilitator, Campbell Soup Labels, Ugly Person Contest Comms; Brillion Ed Assn VP 1969-70; AFT Mem 1968-; Fox Valley Humane Society (Bd Mem 1989- Volunteer 1980-); Natl Hum Convention; Slide Project; *office:* Brillon Public Schls 315 S Main St Brillion WI 54110

BERTSCHE, NANCY L., Spanish Teacher; *b:* Petaluma, CA; *c:* Christopher; *ed:* (BA) Span, S St Univ 1969; General Scndry Teaching Credential; *cr:* Span Teacher Analy HS 1970-; *ai:* Sr Class Adv; Analy Dist Teachers (Pres 1974, Secy 1970, 1973, Treas 1982, 1984); CA Teachers Assn, NEA 1970-; Assn of Amer Teachers of Span & Portuguese, Foreign Lang Teachers Assn of CA, Foreign Lang Teachers Assn of N CA 1970-; Sonoma-Marin Cty Foreign Lang Teachers Assn 1980-; 4-H Leader 1964-74; Grange Mem 1969-; Order of Eastern Star 1964-; Sch-Prins & Supt Advisory Comms; *office:* Analy H S 6950 Analy Ave Sebastopol CA 95472

BERTULEIT, NANCY LIUDAHL, Teacher/Counselor; *b:* Euclid, OH; *m:* Michael John; *c:* Julie, Lindsay; *ed:* (BS) Elem Ed, 1976, (MA) Counseling Ed, 1982 W KY Univ; Children Cognitive Behavior Therapy; Future Problem Solving Prgm Evaluator & Coach; Certified Quick Recall Ofcl; KY Internship Prgm Resource Teacher; *cr:* Teacher St Joseph Interparochial 1985-; *ai:* Yrbk Spon; Math Coach; NCTM, NCEA 1983-; St Josephs Outstanding Young Educator 1988-89.

BERTUN, MARY CROFF, First Grade Teacher; *b:* Lima, OH; *m:* Knut Michael Rustung; *c:* Anna K. Bertun Loving, Mary E.; *ed:* (BA) Elem Ed, 1966, (MED) General Stud, 1976 OR St Univ; *cr:* 7th-8th Grade Teacher Gregory Heights Sch 1968-69; 4th Grade Teacher Riverside Sch 1969-70; 1st Grade Teacher Yaquina View Elem Sch 1971-; *ai:* Lincoln Cty Sch Dist Curr Coordinating Cncl; Building Curr Cncl Chairperson; Site Team Comm Mem; Fine Arts Day Chm; OR Rdng Assn 1985-; *office:* Yaquina View Elem Sch 351 SE Harney Newport OR 97365

BERTY, MARY ANN (YOSKEY), Scndry English/Speech Teacher; *b:* Waynesburg, PA; *m:* Gerard Henry; *ed:* (BS) Ed/ General Speech/Eng, 1971, (MS) Ed/Socially & Emotionally Maladjusted, 1974 Univ of CA PA; Grad Stud Univ of Pittsburgh, Univ of UT, Washington & Jefferson Coll; *cr:* Scndry Eng/Speech Teacher Trinity Area Sch Dist 1973-; *ai:* Forensics Coach; Voice of Democracy Spon; Usherette, Sr Class, Speech for Academic Decathalon Team Adv; Amer Legion Oratory, Essay Coord; Trinity HS Blood Drive Co-Spon; PA, Dist, Natl Forensic League Comm; Alpha Delta Kappa Secy; Phi Kappa Delta; Alpha XI Delta Corporation Alumni Bd; Pittsburg Public Theatre Volumteer; PA HS Speech League Dist 4 Chairperson; Natl Forensic League Double Diamond Recipient; *office:* Trinity Schls Park Ave Washington PA 15301

BERUBE, JANICE LEE (WOOD), Senior English/Speech Teacher; *b:* Warren, OH; *m:* Richard; *c:* Michael, Paul; *ed:* (BS) Scndry Ed/Eng/Speech, 1973, (MA) Rhetoric/Comm, 1980 Kent St Univ; Newspaper & Writing Wkshps; *cr:* Speech/Dramatics Coach Plain Local Schls 1973-76; Eng/Speech Teacher/Comm Instr Culver-Stockton Coll 1977-79; Eng Teacher/Speech Coach North Canton Sr HS 1979-;Eng Teacher North Canton Jr HS 1983-87; Teacher/Speech Coach/Newspaper Adv Marlington HS 1988-; *ai:* Speech Team Coach; OHSSL Speech 1973-; OH HS Speech League; NEA 1973-; OH Ed Assn (Building Rep 1984-86) 1973-; Christ Prebyn Church Cradle Guild Comm 1989-; Nom Speech Teacher of Yr 1981; *office:* Marlington HS 10450 Moulin Ave NE Alliance OH 44601

BERVE, LESLIE JO JENKINSON, English/Theatre/Speech Teacher; *b:* Bismarck, ND; *m:* Doyle A.; *c:* Meg, Jenny; *ed:* (BS) Scndry Eng - Suma Cum Laude, Dickinson St Coll 1975; Grad Stud Eng; *cr:* Eng Teacher Williston HS 1975-81, Central Campus 1989-; *ai:* Asst Dir Central Campus Playmakers; NEA, NDEA, PACE 1981-85, 1989-; Symphony Women 1988-; *office:* Minot HS Central Campus 110 2nd Ave SE Minot ND 58701

BESCH, DOROTHY RUTH, 3rd Grade Teacher; *b:* Beaumont, TX; *m:* Al; *c:* Michael, Jeri, Bobby; *ed:* (BS) Phys Ed, Lamar Univ 1959; (MED) Elem Ed, Univ of AK Anchorage 1983; *cr:* Phys Ed Teacher Kenedy HS 1960-67; Elem Teacher Bristol Basy Borough Schls 1967-70, Kena Peninsula Borough Sch Dist 1970-; *office:* Mount View Elem Sch 315 Swires Rd Kenai AK 99611

BESCHTA, PATRICIA, English Teacher; *b:* Oconto, WI; *ed:* (BA) Eng, Univ Of WI Oshkosh 1974; Univ of WI Green Bay, Univ of WI Oshkosh; *cr:* Eng Teacher Suring Hs 1974-; *ai:* Sr Class & Sr Class Play Adv; Forensics Coach; Schlsp & Early Graduation Comm; Vlybl Referee; Bsktbl Score Keeper; Dist Teacher of Yr 1982; *office:* Suring HS Algoma St Suring WI 54174

BESCO, JANIS FENNELL, Calculus Teacher; *b:* Allerton, IA; *c:* Gretchen; *ed:* (BA) Math, Drake Univ 1967; (MA) Math, Univ of TX Arlington 1978; *cr:* Teacher Lancaster HS 1967-79, Athens HS 1979-84, L V Berkner HS 1984-; *ai:* Assoc Academic Decathlon Coach; NCTM, Assn of TX Prof Educators; N TX Area Assn of Advanced Placement Math Teachers Pres 1989-; PTA Outstanding Service 1987; Berkner Honor Society Honorary Mem 1988; Univ of TX Ex-Stu Assn Excl in Scndry Teaching Awd 1989; *office:* L V Berkner HS 1600 E Spring Valley Rd Richardson TX 75081

BESS, BARBARA KENNEDY, English Teacher; *b:* Muskegon, MI; *c:* Robert S., Emily M., Lindsay E.; *ed:* (BA) Eng, Univ of CO 1972; (MA) Hum, CO Coll 1988; *cr:* K-2nd Grade Teacher Polton Elem Sch 1972-73; Eng Professor Univ of Guadalajara Mexico 1973-76; K-2nd Grade Teacher Polton Elem Sch 1976-83; Eng Teacher Smoky Hill HS 1983-; *ai:* Womens Gymnastic Coach; Cherry Creek Teachers Assn 1984-; NEA 1972-; Phi Beta Kappa; Jr League of Denver 1976-; At-Risk, Bus Network Grants; CO Coll Honor Grad 1988; *office:* Smoky Hill HS 16100 E Smoky Hill Rd Aurora CO 80015

BESS, SYLVIA RENEE, Spanish/French Teacher; *b:* Philadelphia, PA; *ed:* (BA) Span, 1971, (MEd) Foreign Lang Ed, 1973 Temple Univ; Grad Stud; *cr:* Teacher William Penn HS 1971-; *ai:* William Penn Rep Sch Dist Foreign Lang K-12 Comm Meetings; AATF 1986-; Modern Lang Assn of Philadelphia & Vicinity 1980-; Women in Ed 1988-; *office:* William Penn HS Broad & Masters Sts Philadelphia PA 19122

BEST, CAROLYN JEANETTE, 6th-8th Grade Soc Stud Teacher; *b:* Sweetwater, TN; *ed:* (AA) Hiwassee Jr Coll 1970; (BS) Soclgy, East TN St Univ 1973; Cert Renewed Univ of TN; Cert Compltn Staff Dev Trng Tims; *cr:* Teacher Tellico Plains Jr HS 1974-; *ai:* Yrbk Edtr 1989-; Txtbk Selctn Comm 1989-; Phi Theta Kappa Mem 1969; Pi Gamma Mu Mem 1971; TN Geogrphc Alliance Mem 1986-; Cane Creek Baptist Church Mem; Career Ladder; Nom Teacher of Yr Awd 1988; *home:* Rt 5 Box 586 Madisonville TN 37354

BEST, PHYLLIS JEAN CRAVALHO, Third Grade Teacher; *b:* Paia Maui, HI; *m:* Gary J.; *c:* Mary E., David M.; *ed:* (BAED) Eng, Fort Wright Coll of the Holy Names 1968; Additional Credits for BA; *cr:* 1st Grade Teacher Woodmont Elem 1968-69, Brigadoon Elem 1969-75; 1st-4th Grade Teacher Twin Lakes Elem 1975-; *ai:* Project TEACH Instr; FWEA, WEA, NEA; Ec Ed for Elem Schls Especially Book Company & Marketplace; *office:* Twin Lake Elem Sch 4400 S W 320th St Federal Way WA 98023

BESTEN, JOHN JOSEPH, Instrumental Music Teacher; *b:* Springfield, MA; *m:* Susan Marie O'Connor; *c:* Richard, Karen; *ed:* (AAS) Music Ed, Onondaga Comm Coll 1973; (BM) Music Ed, Syracuse Univ 1975; Grad Stud Music Ed, Potsdam St Univ & Syracuse Univ; *cr:* Music Teacher La Fayette Cntrl Schls 1975-76, Syracuse Parochial Schls 1976-78, La Fayette Cntrl Schls 1978-; *ai:* Auditorium & Music Coord; Dixieland Combo Dir; Sch Improvement Team Mem 1988-; NY St Sch Music Assn Active Mem 1978-; Onondaga Cty Music Educators Assn (VP, Mem 1988-) 1978-; Music Educators Natl Conference Mem 1978-; Onondaga Cty Music Educators Assn Festivals Guest Conductor 1983, 1984, 1988; Cortland, Tioga Cty Music Festival Guest Conductor 1988, WY Cty Music Festival Cuest Conductor.

BESTIC, BARBARA NELSON, Fifth Grade Teacher; *b:* Youngstown, OH; *m:* Mark M.; *c:* Mark N., Matthew, Michael; *ed:* (BS) Elem Ed, Youngstown St Univ 1975; *cr:* 6th Grade Math Teacher 1975-78, 5th Grade Rdng Teacher 1978- Springfield Intermediate; *ai:* OEA, NEA, Springfield Local Classroom Teachers Assn 1975-; Intnl Rdng Assn 1984-; Honor Society of Phi Kappa Phi 1975, 1989-; Youngstown Mothers of Twins Club Membership Co-Chairperson 1988-.

BESTUL, SUSAN KAY SEMLING, Special Education Teacher; *b:* Winona, MN; *m:* Robert Lee; *c:* Katherine, Amy, David; *ed:* (BS) Spec Ed, St Cloud St Univ 1978; *cr:* ESL Teacher 1980-84, Spec Ed Teacher 1984- Anoka Henn Sch Dist #11; *office:* Washington Elem 2171 6th Ave Anoka MN 55303

BETANCOURT, CELINA, Spanish Teacher; *b:* Barichara, Colombia; *m:* Robert W.; *c:* Angela B., Deborah C.; *ed:* (BS) Psych/Ed, Natl Univ Bogota 1965; Validation Span, Univ of KY 1975; (MS) Ed, Union Coll 1982; *cr:* Teacher South America, Berea Cmmty Sch 1976-78, Knox Cntrl HS 1980-; *ai:* Spon Sociedad Honoraria Hispanica, Span Club; Amer Assn Teachers of Span & Portuguese; KY Cncl for Teaching of Foreign Langs; Working on Short Stories; *home:* 333 Sycamore Dr Barbourville KY 40906

BETHEL, MICHAEL BRAD, Administrative Assistant; *b:* Peoria, IL; *m:* Karen T. Santangelo; *c:* Stephen, Sarah; *ed:* (BA) Elem Ed, Western IL Univ 1980; (MS) Educational Admin, IL St Univ 1987; Trng in Transportation Dept of Sch Dist; *cr:* 5th Grade Teacher Dunlap Grade Sch 1980-81; 8th Grade Sci Teacher Pioneer Jr HS 1981-89; Admin Asst Dunlap HS 1989-; *ai:* Stu Cncl Adv; Dir of Stu Act; IL St Deans Assn 1989-; IL Ed Assn 1984-89; Dunlap Ed Assn 1984-89; Awd of Excl By IL Math/Sci Acad; *office:* Dunlap HS Shaw Rd Dunlap IL 61525

BETTENBERG-POHL, MARIA (VAN ERP), Computers/Mathematics Teacher; *b:* Geffen, Netherlands; *m:* Fred P.; *c:* Peter, Lisa; *ed:* (BA) Elem Ed, Mount Marty Coll 1969; Grad Courses Cmptr Sci, Elem Ed; *cr:* 6th Grade Teacher St Marys Sch 1966-67, Corpus Christi Sch 1967-73; Jr HS Soc Stud Teacher 1981-85, Cmptr Teacher 1985-, Cmptr/Jr HS Math Teacher 1990 St Peter Sch; *ai:* Part-Time Librarian; Resource Coord; Diocesan Cmptr Curr Comm; St Peter Sch Bd of Ed 1978-81; GSA (Leader 1986-88, SME Dist Chairperson 1989); Maplewood N St Paul Task Force Partnership (Chairperson 1987-88) 1987-; *office:* St Peters Sch 2620 N Margaret St North Saint Paul MN 55109

BETTENDORF, VICTORIA, English/Math/Reading Teacher; *b:* Cleveland, OH; *c:* Linda; *ed:* (BA) Elem Ed, 1966, (MA) Elem Ed, 1968, (MED) Media, 1978 Kent St Univ; Working of PhD Akron Univ 1978-; *cr:* Teacher Berea City Sch Dist 1966-67, Cuyahoga Falls Schls 1967-68, Berea City Schls 1968-; *ai:* Girls HS Swim Coach; Stu Cncl; Book Store Mgr; Recreational Swim Co-Dir; Berea City Schls Curr Writing; Berea Ed Assn Mem 1968-71; NE OH Ed Assn Mem; Juvenile Diabetes Swimathon 1985-; Instructional Advisory Cncl; Grad Asst Kent St; Pamphlet Published; Outstanding Young Educator Awd 1972; Gifted Educl Packets Published 1978-80; Young Authors Conference Dir; IRA Convention Speaker; *office:* Roehm Mid Sch 7220 Pleasant St Berea OH 44017

BETTERTON, BONNIE HARRIS, Second Grade Teacher; *b:* Farmville, VA; *m:* John Thomas Jr.; *c:* Nicole, Bradley; *ed:* (BS) Early Chldhd, Radford Coll 1970; *cr:* 1st Grade Teacher Washington-Coleman Elem 1970-71; Kndgtn Teacher C H Friend Elem 1971-74, North Elem 1974-75; Kndgtn Teacher 1977-81, 2nd Grade Teacher 1982- Roxboro Chrstn Acad; *ai:* Spelling Bee & Field Day Chm; Roxboro Jr Service League 1973-79; Roxboro Baptist Church 1985-; *home:* 139 Richland Rd Roxboro NC 27573

BETTON, IRA BREWER, Reading Specialist; *b:* Plumerville, AR; *c:* Kim, Sherri; *ed:* (BS) Elem Ed, Univ of AR Pine Bluff 1961; (MS) Elem Ed, Ouachita Baptist Univ 1975; Univ of IN, Univ of Cntrl AR, Univ of AR Little Rock; *cr:* 3rd Grade Teacher Columbia Elem Sch 1961-64; 2nd Grade Teacher J C Cook Elem Sch 1964-70; 3rd Grade Teacher 1970-89, Rdng Specialist 1989- Cloverdale Elem; *ai:* Partners in Ed Comm Chairperson; Stu Advisory Bd Mem; AR Ed Assn, Little Rock Classroom Teacher Assn, NEA; Univ of AR Pine Bluff Alumni Assn 1987-88, MS Alumni Awd 1987; Alpha Kappa Alpha Mem; Mt Zion (Sr Usher, Bd Mem); Headstart Prgm Grant Summer 1967; *office:* Cloverdale Elem Sch 6500 Hinkson Rd Little Rock AR 72209

BEVELANDER, NANCY WEEKS, 5th Grade Teacher; *b:* Bayshore, NY; *m:* Donald C.; *c:* Jeffrey, Caroline; *ed:* (BS) Ed, SUNY Cortland 1967; (MA) Ed, Adelphi Univ 1970; Grad Courses SUNY Stony Brook, Coll of St Rose, Long Island Univ; *cr:* Teacher Sachem Cntrl Schls 1967-; *ai:* Sci Fair Comm; PTA, PTO 1967-; *office:* Tecumseh Sch 179 Granny Rd Farmingville NY 11738

BEVERLY, DIANA CHUBB, Physical Education Instructor; *b:* Seminole, TX; *m:* Barry Carroll; *c:* Taysha S., Toyah R., Tyanna L.; *ed:* (BA) All-Level Phys Ed/Eng, Mc Murray & E TX St 1980; UTPB Trng, Counseling, Discipline; *cr:* Eng/Phys Ed Teacher Cisco Ind Sch Dist 1980-81; Phys Ed Teacher Merkel Ind Sch Dist 1981-82; Phys Ed/Health Teacher Crane Ind Sch Dist 1982-; *ai:* Brazilian Intnl Fellowship Stu Spon 1988-89; Head Phys Ed Dept; In Charge of Elem Track Meet; Boys & Girls BB Tournaments; Jr HS Girls Sports Coach 1980-83, 1985-89; CTA 1984-85; Crane Chrstn Church 2/3 Yr Old Teacher 1987-89; In Charge of Jumprope-A-Thon; *office:* Crane Ind Sch Dist 511 W 8th Crane TX 79731

BEVERLY, SHARON WOOD, Fourth Grade Teacher; *b:* Grundy, VA; *m:* Kendall R.; *c:* Justin; *ed:* (BA) Elem Ed, Clinch Valley Coll 1978; (MA) Elem Ed, WV Coll 1983; *cr:* 4th Grade Teacher Coeburn Mid Sch 1979-; *ai:* Boys Var Tennis Coach; WCEA, NEA, NCTM, VSRA; *home:* PO Box 52 Wise VA 24293

BEYER, BETTY J. (MC LAUGHLIN), Reading/English/Art Teacher; *b:* Aberdeen, SD; *m:* Maurice E.; *c:* Gayle Bortnem, Karen Sween, David Mc Laughlin; *ed:* (BS) Elem Ed, Northern St Coll 1969; Wkshps Sioux Falls Coll, Augustana Coll, Northern St Coll, Dakota St Coll; *cr:* 6th Grade Teacher Dell Rapids Schls 1969-75; 7th-9th Grade Teacher Garretson Schls 1975-76; 6th Grade Teacher Bridgewater Schls 1976-78; Title I-Art/Eng/Rdng/Art Teacher Chester Area Schls 1978-; *ai:* Jr/Sr HS Oral Interp & Jr/Sr One Act Plays Coach; BPW 1971-76; United Meth Church Educl Responsibilities 1963-74; His Conference Paper 1988.

BEYER, JUDITH ANN, Fifth Grade Teacher; *b:* Waukegan, IL; *ed:* (BS) Ed, N IL Univ 1974; Working Towards Masters Natl-Louis Univ; *cr:* 5th Grade Teacher Holy Family Sch 1974-77, Fox Lake Dist 114 1977-; *ai:* Mem Math Curr Comm 1977-, Implementing Gifted Prgm Organization Comm; Fox Lake Ed Assn (VP 1984-85, Pres 1985-); Altar & Rosary Womens Society Secy 1985-89; Governors Master Teacher Prgm Semi-Finalist 1984; *office:* Fox Lake Dist 114 101 S Hawthorne Lane Fox Lake IL 60020

BEYER, PATRICIA S., English Teacher; *b:* Passaic, NJ; *m:* James P.; *c:* Joseph, Jamie; *ed:* (BA) Eng, Montclair St Coll 1962; *cr:* Eng Teacher Passaic Valley HS 1962-; *ai:* Passaic Valley Ed Assn VP 1989-; NJEA, NEA; *office:* Passaic Valley HS E Main St Little Falls NJ 07424

BEYER, RITA BERARDI, 2nd Grade Teacher; *b:* Fort Spring, San Marino Rep; *m:* Thomas E.; *ed:* (BS) Art Ed, Hofstra Univ 1971; Addl Studies Fine Arts/Ed C W Post Coll 1975; *cr:* Art Teacher 1971-75; 2nd Grade Teacher 1975- West Hempstead Sch Dist; *office:* Cornwell Ave Sch 250 Cornwell Ave West Hempstead NY 11552

BEYER, SARA LA SETTA (SCHUTZ), Spanish & English Teacher; *b:* Elgin, ND; *m:* Dennis R.; *c:* Amy, Andrea, Corey; *ed:* (BA/BS) Eng, 1964, (BA/BS) Span, 1988 Dickinson St Univ; Grad Courses Taken at UND, NDSU, Univ of Mary; Study in Cuernavaca Mexico, UNAM Mexico City, Granada Spain; *cr:* Span Teacher/Librarian Bowman HS 1964-68; Eng Teacher Rhame HS 1969-70; Eng/Span Teacher Bowman HS 1981-; *ai:* Span Club; Soph Class Adv; Building Level Support Team; Amer Assn of Teachers of Span & Portuguese Pres 1986-87; Foreign Lang Assn of ND (Secy, Treas, Advisory Cncl) 1987-; Cntrl States Conference on Teaching of Foreign Languages; ND Cncl of Teachers of Eng 1988-; Bowman Luth Church Women Pres 1975; Bowman Cty 4-H Cncl Asst Leader 1984-86, 1989-; Cntry Crafts Hobby Club Pres 1977; Bowman Luth Sunday Sch Staff 7th Grade Teacher 1977-89; ND Bd of Higher Ed Grant to Study in Mexico 1987, Spain 1988; Articles Published Alleluia News 1988, 1989; *office:* Bowman HS 8th Ave SW Bowman ND 58623

BEZANSON, CHARLES A., Science Teacher; *b:* Cambridge, MA; *ed:* (BS) Phys Ed, Northeastern Univ 1969; (MED) Guidance/Counseling, Bridgewater St Coll 1975; W WA St Coll, MA Inst of Technology, Antioch Coll, E Nazarene Coll; *cr:* Sci Teacher Taunton HS 1970-; *ai:* Brockton Chrstn Regional HS Bd Chm; NEA, MTA, TEA Mem; 1st Baptist Church of Duxbury Choir, Teacher; Multiple Natl Sci Fnd Schlsp Grants; *office:* Taunton HS 50 Williams St Taunton MA 02780

BEZONI, PEGGIE THOMASSON, Third Grade Teacher; *b:* Farmers Branch, TX; *m:* John Paul; *c:* Paula, Preston; *ed:* (BS) Elem Ed, TX A&I 1954; *cr:* 2nd Grade Teacher Flato Elem 1954-55; 5th Grade Teacher Cntrl Ward 1955-59, 1963-69; 4th Grade Teacher Pleasanton Elem 1969-78; 5th/6th Grade Teacher D Odem 1978-80; 3rd Grade Teacher Lamar 1980-; *office:* Lamar Elem Sch 800 San Patricio Sinton TX 78387

BIANCHI, DARLENE ANDERSON, Third Grade Teacher; *b:* Ironwood, MI; *m:* Ronald L.; *ed:* Assoc Elem Ed, Gogebic Comm Coll 1970; (BS) Elem Ed/Scndry Ed, N MI Univ 1972; Elem Ed; *cr:* 1st Grade Teacher White Pine Elem Sch 1972-73; 1st Grade Teacher 1973-85, 3rd Grade Teacher 1985- Ironwood Area Schls; *ai:* Norrie PTO; Ironwood Schls Schlsp Fnd Bd of Dir; Ironwood Ed Assn Treas 1983; *office:* Norrie Elem Sch Alfred Wright Blvd Ironwood MI 49938

BIBBEE, LORA W., Sixth Grade Teacher; *b:* South Charleston, WV; *m:* Mac; *c:* Ann, John; *ed:* (BA) Elem Ed, Morris Harvey Coll 1976; Grad Stud WV Coll; *cr:* Teacher High Lawn Elem 1976-89; *ai:* 6th Grade Patrol Washington DC Trip Spon; High Lawn Elem Soc Stud Fair Coord; *office:* High Lawn Elem Sch 2400 Kanawha Terr Saint Albans WV 25177

BICHER, STEPHANIE ANN (KEENEY), Third Grade Teacher; *b:* Lebanon, PA; *m:* Dane William; *c:* Matthew D., Allison N.; *ed:* (BS) Elem Ed, Shippensburg Univ 1979; Grad Courses Millersville Univ; Great Books Leader Trng Course; *cr:* 2nd Grade Teacher Womelsdorf Elem Sch 1981-82; 3rd Grade Teacher Schaefferstown Elem Sch 1982-83; 5th Grade Teacher Myerstown Elem Sch 1983-89; *ai:* ELCO Math Comm; NEA, PSEA.

BICKEL, DAVID W., English Teacher; *b:* Minneapolis, MN; *ed:* (BS) Eng Lit, Concordia Teachers Coll 1972; (MAT) Hum, Univ TX Dallas 1981; Scndry Eng, MI St Univ; E Asia Writing Project, UC Berkeley; Advanced Inst on Writing, NE Boston; Thinking & Writing, NW IL; *cr:* 2nd Grade Teacher Immanuel Luth Sch 1972-78; Eng Dept Chm/7th-12th Grade Eng Teacher Luth HS of Dallas 1978-81; Eng Dept Chm/10th-12th Grade Eng Teacher Hong Kong Intnl Sch 1981-86; 9th-12th Grade Eng Teacher Milwaukee Luth HS 1986-; *ai:* Ftbl Coach; NCTE, ASCD; E Asia Writing Project (Teacher, Consultant) 1984-; Milwaukee Area Eng Academic Alliance; Univ of Chicago Outstanding Teacher Awd 1985.

BICKEL, KENNETH LEE, World Geography Teacher; *b:* Saginaw, MI; *m:* Janice Carol Ivey; *c:* Brent, Jennifer, Lance; *ed:* (BS) Soc Stud, 1965, (MA) Scndry Admin, 1968 Cntrl MI Univ; *cr:* Teacher Farwell HS 1965-68, Rudyard HS 1968-; *ai:* Ftbl Coach; Regional Coach of Yr Awds; *office:* Rudyard Area Schls 2nd & Williams St Rudyard MI 49780

BICKEL, TED, JR., Teacher; *b:* Danville, KY; *m:* Nancy Ernst; *c:* Ted, Tim; *ed:* (BS) Chem, Univ of Louisville 1971; (MBA) Bus, Bellarmine Coll 1981; *cr:* Teacher Old Hamcty HS 1984-; *ai:* Asst Head Ftbl Coach; Jr Var & Var Bsktbl Games Timer; Spirited Sr Dist Testing Comm Spon; Sci Dept Co-Chm; Kappa Delta Pi, Phi Delta Kappa, NSTA; Church (6th-8th Grade Sunday Sch Teacher, Choir); Article Published 1989; *home:* 6817 Holly Lake Dr Fern Creek KY 40291

BICKERSTAFF, ELLEN RAMBO, Second Grade Teacher; *b:* Columbus, GA; *m:* Howard Jefferson; *c:* H. Jefferson Jr., Charles D.; *ed:* (BS) Elem Ed, Univ of GA 1963; Conference Wkshps; *cr:* 2nd Grade Teacher Ft Clayton Sch 1964-65, Brookstone Sch 1974-; *ai:* Lower Sch Math Curr Comm; Intnl Rdng Assn; Goodwill Auxiliary (Pres 1970-71) 1968-72, Outstanding Volunteer of Yr 1971; Jr League of Columbus (House Chm 1973-74) 1969-; Historic Columbus Fnd, Columbus Museum 1989-; Brookstone Lower Sch Teacher of Yr 1972; *office:* Brookstone Sch Incorporated 440 Bradley Park Dr Columbus GA 31995

BICKETT, AGNES IRENE, Part-Time School Librarian; *b:* Morganfield, KY; *ed:* (BA) Ed, Brescia Coll 1969; (MA) Ed, Murray St Univ 1975; *cr:* 4th Grade Teacher St Brigid Sch 1970-89.

BICKFORD, LAWRENCE ALAN, Computer Coordinator; *b:* Bridgeport, CT; *m:* Helene Laliberte; *ed:* (BA) Math, Dartmouth Coll 1972; *cr:* Math Teacher Berlin Jr HS 1972-77, Math Teacher 1981-87, Cmptr Coord 1987- Hopkinton HS; *ai:* Advisor to Literary Magazine; Mem Math/Eng Curr Comm; Supts Cmptr Comm; NCTM Pres 1972-77; NH Assn Cmptr Coord 1987-, Exec Bd, Membership Chm 1989-; Author A Schedulers Notebook 1990; *office:* Hopkinton HS RFD 1 Box 1 Contoocook NH 03229

BICKFORD, MARTHA MCLAURINE, Fifth Grade Teacher; *b:* Birmingham, AL; *ed:* (BA) Elem Ed, Belhaven Coll 1967; Addl Studies Courses Psych/Cnslng Birmingham Theological Seminary; Courses Teaching Methods Covenant Coll; *cr:* 2nd Grade Teacher Irondale Jr High 1967-69; 2nd Grade Teacher Irondale Elem 1969-70; Kndgtn/2nd Grade Teacher 1970-71; 5th Grade Teacher 1971- Briarwood Christian Sch; *ai:* Washington DC Travel Coord 1976-; Textbook Evaluation Local/State; Neighborhood Bible Club Coordin; Written/Produced Plays; Soloist-Briarwood Choir; Performed Avery Fischer Hall-Mid-Amer Spring 86 Choir Ensemble Performed Amer Choral Dir Assn Regional 1990; Southern Assn Christian Sch 1972-; DARE; Operation New Pace-Inner City Outreach-Adv Comm 1969-74; Nom Teacher of Yr 1970, 1977; Illustrated Book of Poetry-"The Dreaming Heart"; Dev Cty Wide Soc Stud Curr; Dev 5th Grade Soc Stud Curr; Stu Teacher Adv; *office:* Briarwood Chrstn Sch 2204 Briarwood Way Birmingham AL 35243

BICKFORD, VICKY LEA, Kindergarten Teacher; *b:* Oak Hill, WV; *ed:* (BA) Elem Ed/Early Chldhd, 1974, (MA) Early Chldhd Ed, 1979 Marshall Univ; *cr:* Kndgtn Teacher Kingston/Pax Elem 1974-80, Ansted Elem 1980-; *ai:* Yrbk Ed; WV Ed Assn (Co-Pres of Local 1989-, Secy of Local 1990, Faculty Rep); Delta Kappa Gamma Comm Chm 1990; Oak Hill Jr Womans Club (Pres 1980-84, Secy 1978-80), Jr of Yr 1980-81, Outstanding New Mem 1976; Oak Hill Civic League, Oak Hill Baptist Church Mem; Outstanding Young Woman of America 1982; Ansted Elem Sch Teacher of Yr 1989; *home:* 547 Terry Ave Oak Hill WV 25901

BICKLE, DENISE SMITH, Fifth Grade Teacher; *b:* Laredo, TX; *m:* David Alan; *c:* Lindsey, Andrew; *ed:* (BAT) Elem Ed, 1979, (MED) Elem Supervision, 1983 Sam Houston St Univ; *cr:* Teacher Wilkerson Intermediate 1979-81; Teacher of Gifted Creighton Intermediate 1981-82; Teacher/Team Leader Meadow Point Elem 1982-83; Teacher Saigling Elem 1983-86/ 1989-; *ai:* Odyssey of the Mind Spontaneous Coach; Sci & Clean Campus Comm; Textbook Adoption Comm; TSTA/NEA Local Treas 1980-81; Phi Delta Kappa 1982-; ATPE 1989-; TAGT 1983-; Wilkerson Intermediate Teacher of Yr 1980; Saigling Elem Teacher of Yr 1985; *office:* Saigling Elem Sch 3600 Matterhorn Plano TX 75075

BICKLE, JULIE RAE CHAMBERLAIN, Scndry Art Education Teacher; *b:* Medford, OR; *m:* Lowell Maddison; *c:* Ben J.; *ed:* (BS) Scndry Art Ed, SOSC 1980; (MS) Scndry Art Ed, Lewis & Clark 1986; Personal Growth Art Areas Oil Paint, Airbrush, Calligraphy, Art His; *cr:* Scndry Art Teacher Hidden Valley HS 1981-; *ai:* Overnight Trips Mountains & Pacific Ocean, Compete Many Art Shows & Contests; Art Club; JCEA, NEA; Church Sunday Sch Supvr for Lower Grade Levels; Teacher of Month; *office:* Hidden Valley HS 651 Murphy Creek Rd Grants Pass OR 97527

BICKLEIN, RONALD ROY, Geography/Soviet Stud Teacher; *b:* Belleville, IL; *m:* Alice B. Mueller; *c:* Tavia, Royce; *ed:* (BA) Soc Stud/His/Geography, S IL Univ 1967; Grad Stud Geography, Urban Planning, His; Summer Inst Geographical Ed; *cr:* Soc Stud/ World Geography/His/Soviet Stud/Classroom Teacher Judson HS 1986-; *ai:* Judson HS Naturalist Club Spon; Natl Cncl for Geographic Ed, NCSS; Presented Paper at Natl Cncl For Geographic Ed 1988; *office:* Judson HS 9695 Schaefer Converse TX 78109

BIDAL, MARING GACUSANA, Language Arts Teacher; *b:* Olaa, HI; *m:* Clarion; *c:* Tanya M. Kuulei Mc Calla-Lee, Alison I. Mc Calla, Conrad C., Pearla D.; *ed:* (BS) Elem Ed, Atlantic Union Coll 1962, Soc Sci, San Jose St Univ 1972; Admin Credential, Univ of San Francisco 1983; Admin Credential, Univ of HI 1990; *cr:* 3rd Grade Teacher Northshore Sch 1962-63; 4th Grade Teacher Ravenswood Sch Dist 1965-68; 3rd-8th Grade Teacher Milpitas Unified 1968-88; 9th-12th Grade Teacher Pahoa HS 1988-; *ai:* Host Teacher Univ of HI Dept of Ed; Sr Class & Future Teachers of America Adv; SLEP Prgm; Lang Art Curr Comm; Onward Towards Excl; NEA, CTA 1966-88; Natl Assn for Women in Careers 1984-86; HI St Teachers Assn 1988-; Outstanding Contribution to Ed Awd 1986; Whitney Fnd 1985; Outstanding Teacher Alexandor Rose Sch 1983; Teacher of Yr Russell Jr HS 1976; Outstanding Leaders in Elem & Scndry Ed 1972; Outstanding Elem Teachers of America 1970; Outstanding Teacher Milpitas Jr Chamber of Commerce 1970; *home:* PO Box 974 Keaau HI 96749

BIDDULPH, JEAN KOCH, Mathematics Teacher; *b:* Chicago, IL; *m:* Robert L.; *ed:* (BS) Math, 1959, (MA) Music, 1961 Univ of Chicago; NSF, Northwestern Univ; Grad Math Courses, Univ of IL Chicago; Cmptr Courses, De Paul & Chicago City Colls; *cr:* Curr Writer Chicago Bd of Ed 1986-87; Project Mgr Gifted Summer Scholars 1988-89; Teacher Lane Tech HS 1961-; *ai:* Math Club Adv; Math Team Head Coach; Chicago Citywide Math League Site Coord; NCTM; Alpha Delta Kappa Pres 1982-84; Univ of IL Ed Advisory Comm 1987-; Prof Personnel Advisory Comm Chm; Teacher of Yr 1989; Lakeview Citizens Cncl Teacher of Yr 1988; Nom Kate Maremont Fnd Dedicated Teacher Awd 1988; *office:* Lane Tech HS 2501 W Addison Chicago IL 60618

BIDNEY, KATHLEEN MARY, Art Teacher; *b:* Fairfield, CT; *ed:* (BS) Art Ed, 1969, (MS) Art Ed, 1976 S CT St Coll; Cooperating Teacher Prgm 1988-; Art, S CT St Coll 1989; *cr:* Art Teacher W Haven HS 1969-; Travel Agent Carr Travel Limited 1985-; *ai:* Awds Comm; Co-Chairperson Teacher-to-Teacher Networking; Constorium Cooperating Teachers Bd; Cooperating Teacher; CT Art Ed Assn 1980-; W Haven Teacher Center Dir 1983-87; CT Teacher Center Network 1982-85; New England Assn of Schls & Colls Visiting Comm 1983-84; W Haven Fed of Teachers (Exec Cncl Mem 1972-, Steward 1972-79, 1984-, Soc Chairperson 1974-79, VP of Cmmty & Soc Services 1981-83, Negotiating Team 1978); Intnl Order of Runeburg Secy 1987-; Big Brother/Big Sister E Dist 1981-82; Young Democrats 1980-83; *office:* West Haven HS 1 Circle St West Haven CT 06516

BIEDENHARN, JANE A., English Teacher; *b:* Springfield, TN; *m:* John U.; *c:* John, Joseph; *ed:* (BA) Latin, Rhodes Coll 1959; W KY St Univ; FL St Univ; FL Atlantic Univ; Univ of WI; *cr:* Latin/ Eng Teacher Johnstown-Monroe HS 1959-62; Eng Teacher St Lucie Cty Jr HS 1965-66; Eng/Latin Teacher Ft Pierce Cntrl HS 1971-79; Eng Teacher Ft Pierce Westwood HS 1982-83, Lincoln Park Acad 1989-; *ai:* Newspaper Adv; CTA, NEA, 1971-79; NCTE 1990; TAG, FLAG 1975-77; AAUW 1959-75; PEO 1977-; Eta Sigma Phi Pres 1958-59; Amer Clasical League 1971-; FL Dist STAR Teacher 1974; *home:* 1206 S 10th St Fort Pierce FL 34950

BIELIZNA, JUDY FOLEY, Math Teacher/Team Leader; *b:* Naugatuck, CT; *w:* (dec); *c:* Raymond, Tama; *ed:* (BS) Ed/Math, 1973, (MS) Ed/Psych, 1973, Supervision & Curr, 1976 W CT St Univ; 1976; Admin Certificate S CT St Univ 1978; Best Prgm Mentor Teacher/Cooperating Teacher; Hunter Prgm Coach; *cr:* 5th Grade Teacher Meeting House Hill Sch 1965-68; 3rd Grade Teacher Consolidated Sch 1968-81; 8th Grade Teacher New Fairfield HS/Mid Sch 1981-; *ai:* Mathcounts Coach & Coord; Pi Lambda Theta, Delta Kappa Gamma, Phi Delta Kappa, Atomic, NFEA, CEA, NEA; *home:* 13 Barnum Rd New Fairfield CT 06812

BIELKE, MARIANN JEANETTE OHNHEISER, Homemaking Teacher; *b:* Schulenburg, TX; *m:* Charles; *c:* Garth, Patti; *ed:* (BS) Home Ec, SW TX Univ 1962; *cr:* Homemaking Teacher Marion Ind Sch Dist 1962-; *ai:* Frosh Class Spon; Guad Cty Youth Show; FHA Adv & Regional Officer; Voc Home Ec Teachers Assn TX 1988; TX St Teachers Assn Life Mem; Beta Xi Natl Homemaking 1972-; TX FHA Regional V & St Honorary Mem; *home:* PO Box 8 Marion TX 78124

BIERBRODT, PATSY MILFORD, Spanish Teacher; *b:* Memphis, TN; *m:* Jerry Wilson; *c:* Wilson, Cassie; *ed:* (BS) Ed, Univ of TN Martin 1981; *cr:* Math Teacher Elliston Baptist Acad 1982-83; Span Teacher Evangelical Chrstn Sch 1983-; *ai:* Chrldr, Span Spon; Faculty Salaries & Benefits Task Force; SACS Evaluation Stu Act Comm Chairperson; Stu Government Adv; TN Foreign Lang Teachers Assn 1986-; Amer Assn of Teacher Span & Portugese 1986-; Colonial Baptist Church (Outreach Officer 1988-, Ordinance Comm 1989-); Medical Mission Trip Guatemala City 1990; Stus Placed in Natl Span Exam 1987, 1990; *office:* Evangelical Christian Sch 7600 Macon Rd Cordova TN 38018

BIERSACK, LESLIE SKUMATZ, Junior High School Teacher; *b:* Menominee, MI; *m:* Steven Richard; *c:* Ashlie, Gregory; *ed:* (BS) Elem Ed, Univ of WI Madison 1978; *cr:* Jr HS Teacher St Kilian Sch 1979-; *ai:* Soc Stud & Jr HS Chairperson; WI Math Cncl 1989; *office:* St Kilian Sch 245 High St Hartford WI 53027

BIESEMEYER, JOHN H., English Teacher; *b:* New Franklin, MO; *m:* Elizabeth Lambert; *c:* Joshua, Leigh, Cole; *ed:* (BA) Eng, Univ of MO-Columbia 1971; *ai:* Academic Bowl; *office:* Fayette HS Herndon St Fayette MO 65248

BIFFLE, RONALD EDWIN, Band Director; *b:* Atlanta, GA; *m:* Donna Bartlett; *c:* R. Kreg, Kendra L.; *ed:* (BMUS) Music Ed, GA St Coll 1970; (MMUS) Music Ed, GA St Univ 1975; *cr:* Band Dir Jonesboro Sr HS 1970-74, Forest Park Jr HS 1974-79, Morrow Jr HS & Mid Sch 1979-; *ai:* Phi Beta Mu Mem; Music Educators Natl Conference; GA Music Educators (St VP, Various Offices); Riverdale 1st Baptist Deacon 1981-; Band Performances Numerous Clinics.

BIGALKE, GREG EUGENE, Economics Teacher; *b:* Little Falls, MN; *m:* Diane Marie Knutson; *c:* Troy, Ryan, Brett; *ed:* (BS) Bio & Soc Sci, 1974, (MS) Ec Ed, 1979 St Cloud St Univ; *cr:* 9th Grade Economics Teacher Osseo Jr HS 1975-; *ai:* Gifted & Talented Performance Teacher; Ftbl & Bsktbl Coach; Ossco Fed of Teachers 1975-; *office:* Osseo Jr HS 10223 93rd Ave N Osseo MN 55369

BIGGAR, PAULA KAY, 7-12th Grade Eng/Span Teacher; *b:* Montebello, CA; *ed:* (BA) Eng, Foreign Lang, Lit-Span, WA St Univ 1984; Trng Process Writing/Writing Curr, TESA; Latin Amer Stud, Univ KS 1991; *cr:* Eng/Span Teacher Kaycee US 1984-89; *ai:* Forensics Coach 1984-89; Span Club Adv 1984-89; Mexico Trip Spon; Class Adv 1984-89; Dist Writing Comm 85-88; Technology Comm 88-89; NEA/WEA 1984-89; Johnson Cty Ed Assn Bldg Rep 1986-87; *home:* 9338 Stamps Ave Downey CA 90240

BIGGS, BAILEY ELWOOD, Physical Education Teacher; *b:* Roanoke Rapids, NC; *m:* Martha Clair Boyer; *c:* Scott, Bonnie, Brian, Karen; *ed:* (BS) Health/Phys Ed, E Carolina Univ 1977; Grad Courses at E Carolina Univ, Univ of SC; *cr:* Teacher/Coach A G Cox Grammar 1977-84, Plymouth HS 1984-85, Wando HS 1985-; *ai:* Jr Var Ftbl, Jr Var Girls Bsktbl, Var Girls Sftbl Coach; *office:* Wando HS 1560 Mathis Ferry Rd Mount Pleasant SC 29464

BIGGS, CYNTHIA GARDNER, 8th Grade Soc Stud Teacher; *b:* Jacksonville, FL; *m:* Alan Keith; *ed:* (BS) Psych, 1976, (MED) Soc Stud, 1978 GA Coll; Various In-Service; *cr:* Soc Stud Teacher Jones Cty HS 1976-80, Hawthorne Jr/Sr HS 1982-83, A L Mebane Mid Sch 1983-; *ai:* Soc Stud Dept Chm; Cooperative Learning Peer Teacher Coach; Performance Learning Systems Instr; 8th Grade Team Leader; FL Close Up Spon; NCSS 1987-; Alachua Cty Mid Sch Assn 1988-; Trinity United Meth Church; Grant from Natl Endowment for Hum; Summer Inst on Civil War/Reconstruction CA St Univ 1990; *office:* A L Mebane Mid Sch Rt 1 Box 4 Alachua FL 32615

BIGGS, KAREN SUE, Third Grade Teacher; *b:* Valparaiso, IN; *ed:* (BS) Elem Ed, 1965; (MA) Elem Ed, 1968 Ball St Univ; *cr:* 3rd Grade Teacher East Side Elem 1965-; *ai:* Mentor for 1st Yr Teacher; Stu Teacher Critic; IN St Teachers Assn 1965-; NEA 1965-; Intl Rdng Assn 1970-; Delta Kappa Gamma (Chm of Nom Comm) 1984-.

BIGHAM, LAMAR BRAGG, Teacher; *b:* Raleigh, NC; *ed:* (BS) Elem Ed, Campbell Univ 1972; Foundation Approaches Sci Teaching II & III, Univ of HI; *cr:* Teacher Apex Elem 1972-76, Apex Mid Sch 1976-; *ai:* Bsktbl Coach 1972-73 & Ftbl Coach 1978-82; Teacher Athletic Trainer 1977-82; Concessions Mgr 1983-; NC Assn of Ed Building Rep 1972-74; *office:* Apex Mid Sch 400 E Moore St Apex NC 27502

BIGHAM, MARSHA ELLIS, Social Studies Teacher; *b:* Bristow, OK; *m:* Jerry; *c:* Matthew, William; *ed:* (BS) Soc Stud Comp, W TX St Univ 1980; Model for Effective Teaching Supervision Trng; Panhandle Energy Inst Educators; Amer Citizenship Inst; OK Chrstn Coll; *cr:* 6th Grade Soc Stud/7th Grade TX His Teacher Borger Mid Sch 1981-84; Ec/Amer His Teacher Palo Duro HS 1984-85; Ec/Ec Honors/Government/ Government Honors/World His/World His Honors Teacher Canyon HS 1985-; *ai:* Dist Wide Instruction Comm; Canyon Ind Sch Dist Instructional Advisory Comm; Canyon HS Prin Advisory Comm; TX St World His Textbook Comm; TX Classroom Teachers Assn (Local Pres 1982) 1980-90; Delta Kappa Gamma 1990; Key Club Teacher Month 1988; Sunday Sch Teacher/Dept Head 1974-; Navigators Leader Bible Study 1984-; Borger Family of Yr Finalist Family 1980; Poly Rally & Parade Organizer 1988.

BIGHAM, ROBERT JOHN, 5th Grade Teacher; *b:* Danbury, CT; *ed:* (BS) Elem Ed, Western CT St Univ 1973; *cr:* Teacher John Pettibone Sch 1973-; *ai:* Boys & Girls Intramural Instr; Coach New Milford Jr Var Girls Bsktbl; Sci Curr Mem; Prin Advisory Comm; Ct Ed Assn Mem 1973-; NEA Mem 1973-; New Milford Ed Assn (Building Rep 1973- /1975-77, Secy 1977-78, VP 1978-79, Pres 1979-81, Building Rep 1981-83); Danbury Little League Coach 1973-79; New Milford Parks & Recreation, Bsktbl Coach 1976; New Milford Youth Bsktbl Coach, Mem Bd 1981-83; New Milford Hoopsters Founder, Pres, Coach Bsktbl League 1983-85; New Milford Youth Bsbl, Sftbl Umpire 1982; NMYSB/ SB (Head Umpire, Mem Exec Bd 1983- , Coach 1984-87, Pres, Coach 1988-); 1982 New Milford Jaycees Outstanding Young Educator; 1986-87 New Milfords 1st Teacher of Yr; 1986 New Milford Bd of Ed Volunteer Service Awd; 1983 Outstanding Young Men of America; *office:* John Pettibone Sch 2 Pickett District Rd New Milford CT 06776

BIGLER, VIRGINIA GRAHAM, Theatre Art/Speech Teacher; *b:* Uvalde, TX; *m:* Robert L.; *ed:* (BS) Ed/Eng/Drama, Howard Payne Univ 1983; Grad Stud Eng, Univ of TX San Antonio; *cr:* 7th Grade Regular/Advanced Eng Teacher Southside Jr HS 1984-85; Regular/Honors/Theatre Eng I Teacher 1985-87, Regular/ Honors Eng/Theatre Art Teacher 1987-89, Theatre Art/Speech Teacher 1989- Southside HS; *ai:* Drama Club & UIL Coord & One-Act Play Dir; TX Educl Theatre Assn, ITS 1988-; UIL One-Act Play Dist Champions 1988, 1990, Dist & Area Champions 1989; *office:* Southside HS 1610 Martinez-Losoya Rd San Antonio TX 78221

BIGOSKI, FRANK PAUL, III, Music Instructor; *b:* Norfolk, VA; *m:* Teri L.; *c:* Shiloh, Sabrina, Ryan, Frankie IV; *ed:* (BA) Music, Sonoma St Univ 1972; Music, Dominican Coll 1974; *cr:* Music Teacher Vallejo Sr HS; Jazz/Bands Instr Solano Coll; Head of Rec Bands Greater Vallejo Rec Dist; *ai:* Dir Marching, Jazz, Concert, Adult Cmmty Jazz & Concert Bands; AF of M Mem 1962-, Tester 1976-86; CMEA Mem 1974-; NAJE Mem 1987-; Kajukenbo Assn Publicity Chm 1969-, Black Belt 3rd 1989; CMEA Adjudicators 1980-; Vallejo HS Teacher of Yr; *office:* Vallejo Sr HS 840 Nebraska St Vallejo CA 94590

BIHL, LEONE MEREDITH, Spanish I & II/Latin I & II; *b:* Buford, OH; *m:* J. C.; *c:* Amy; *ed:* (BA) Eng, Morehead St Univ 1966; Univ of Dayton; Wilmington Coll; Rio Grande; *cr:* Teacher Pendleton Cty HS 1966; Bradford HS 1966-70; Russia HS 1972-73; Bradford HS 1975-77; Whiteoak HS 1978-81; Hillsboro HS 1981-; *ai:* Lang Club Adv; Ambrosia Literary Magazine Adv; NEA Treas; OEA; HEA; OFLA; *office:* Hillsboro H S 358 W Main St Hillsboro OH 45133

BIHR, SHIRLEY ANN, Lang Arts & Religion Teacher; *b:* Hamilton, OH; *ed:* (BS) Span/Typing, 1975, (BS) Elem Ed, 1987 Miami Univ; Religious Ed Cert Archdiocese of Cincinnati; *cr:* Substitute Teacher SW Local Schls & NW Local Schls 1975-77; Jr HS Teacher St John the Baptist Sch 1977-; *ai:* Graduation & Confirmation Coord; Newspaper Adv; Scheduling Comm; Co-Dir Jr HS Play; Kappa Delta Pi, Sigma Delta Pi 1974-79; Nom Ashland Oil Teacher Achievement Awd; *office:* St John the Baptist 110 Hill St Harrison OH 45030

BIKSON, BRUCE E., Drama/Public Speaking Teacher; *b:* Minneapolis, MN; *m:* Faith Burmister; *c:* Terijo Nason, Paula Hawkins; *ed:* (AB) Speech, 1957, (MS) Speech, 1980 San Diego St Univ; *cr:* Speech Therapist Cajon Vly Union Sch Dist 1958-74; Eng/Drama/Public Speaking Montgomery Mid Sch 1974-; *ai:* Plays Presented Yrly; Cajon Vly Ed Assn Rep 1958-; NEA 1958-; PTA Life Awds; Mentor Teacher Oral Comm; *office:* Montgomery Mid. Sch. 1570 Melody Ln El Cajon CA 92021

BILBOW, IDA TAMARGO, Biling Rdng/Lang Art Teacher; *b:* Habana, Cuba; *m:* William Dalton Jr.; *c:* Alexander III; *ed:* (BA) General Elem, Kean 1972, (MA) Bi-ling Bicultural Ed, 1978 Kean Coll of NJ; *cr:* Self Contained Bi-ling 1st Grade Teacher Sch #10 Perth Amboy 1972-77; 5th-8th Grade Lang Art/Soc Stud/Rndg in Eng & Span Teacher 1982, 5th-8th Grade Rdng in Eng & Span Teacher 1983- Wm C Mc Ginnis Sch; *ai:* Founder/Coord Stu of Month Prgm; Bilingual Stu Recognition Awd; Inservice 2 Yrs 1st Grade Teasting Revision; Rdng & Textbook Selection; Bi-ling Promotion Policy; Parking Resolution Chairlady; Muscular Dystrophy Spelling Bee; Distruptive Stu Comm; Bi-ling Ed Advisory Bd Mem 1988-89, Co-Chairperson 1989-; Class Play Wardrobe Mistress; Spelling Bee; Initiator of Stu Recognition Awds Prgm; 5th-8th Grade Bi-ling Prgm Wm C Mc Ginnis Sch 1983; NJ St Advisory Co-Chairlady 1987-; Comm on Bi-ling Ed; Governors Outstanding Teacher, Teachers Recognition 1987; PTO; NJTESOL; BSA; Presenter TESOL Convention May 1988; Beti Swap Shop 1987; Projected Presenter; Georgetown Univ Bi-ling Ed Service Annual Regional Conference September 1988; Wkshp Presenter; Georgetown Univ 2nd Annual Regional Confrerence Bi-ling Ed; Videotaping Perth Amboy Sch System 1987; Critical Thinking Skills 1988; Finalist Teacher of Yr 1989; Outstanding Teacher Awd Wm C McGinnis Sch 1987; Governors Teacher Recoognition Prgm; Team Mem Wm C Mc Ginnis Bi-ling Prgms; *office:* Wm C Mc Ginnis Sch 271 State St Perth Amboy NJ 08861

BILBRUCK, ANN R. (HAMILTON), K/1st Benchmarks Teacher; *b:* New Deal, TX; *m:* William J.; *c:* Leslie Limbocker, Raeann Limbocker; *ed:* (BA) Music Ed, Wayland Baptist Coll 1966; (ME) Rdng, West TX St Univ 1985: Grad Stud TX Tech; *cr:* 3rd Grade Teacher Petersburg Elem 1966-67; Eng Readiness/1st Grade Teacher Frisco Elem 1967-69; Kndgtn Teacher Ash Elem 1970-72, Thunderbird Elem 1972-88; K-1st Benchmarks Teacher Thunderbird Elem 1988-; *ai:* PTA Life Membership, Schlsp Chm; Extension Homakers Club; PTA Pres 1985-87 Life Mem 1986; TASCD 1989-; TAG 1990; TCTA; *home:* 400 S Date Plainview TX 79072

BILETA, GRACE ELENA, Italian Teacher; *b:* Brooklyn, NY; *ed:* (BA) Italian Scndry Ed, 1984; (MS) Bi-Ling, Elem Ed, 1989 Brooklyn Coll; *cr:* HS Italian South Shore HS 1985-; *ai:* Our World Foreign Language Magazine Editor 1986-87; *office:* South Shore H S 6565 Flatlands Ave Brooklyn NY 11236

BILIDES, LINDA WHEELER, 6th Grade Language Art Teacher; *b:* New Haven, CT; *m:* John; *c:* Joshua, Justin; *ed:* (BS) Elem Ed, Univ of CT 1978; (MED) Counseling, Univ of N TX 1984; *cr:* Teacher Mineral Wells Ind Sch Dist 1978-; *ai:* Odyssey of Mind, Soccer, T-Ball Coach; Supt Advisory Comm; TX Classroom Teachers Assn 1978-; Team Mem Effective Schls Projects Tarleton St Univ; Wkshp Presentor TX Elem Prin & Supvrs Assn; *office:* Lee Intermediate Sch 1200 SE 14th Ave Mineral Wells TX 76067

BILKO, A. DANIEL, Chemistry Teacher; *b:* Spangler, PA; *m:* Ann L. Sherry; *c:* Daniel, Matthew, Julie, Robert, Mary, Benjamin, Stephen; *ed:* (BS) Chem, Indiana Univ of PA 1966; Project IMPACT; *cr:* Teacher Penn Cambria HS 1966-67, Cambria Heights HS 1967-; *ai:* Jr Class Spon; NEA, PSEA 1966-; Cambria Heights Ed Assn Pres 1972-73; *home:* 614 Magee Ave Patton PA 16668

BILL, KENNETH GEORGE, English Teacher/Dean; *b:* Chicago, IL; *m:* Marie Bill Bohn; *c:* Justin, Clayton, Thaddeus, Christina; *ed:* (BA) Eng, Rockford Coll 1961; (AMA) Art/Art His, NM Highlands Univ 1963; Amer Stud, Univ of KS; Ed Prgm, Coll Admin Curr, Instruction, IL St Univ; *cr:* Teacher/Dean Reavis HS 1965-; *ai:* Var Boys Tennis Coach 1969-; Yrbk, Newspaper, Literary Magazine, Sr Class Spon; Speech Team Individual Events; NCTE, IL Deans Assn, IL HS Tennis Coaches Assn; Tennis Coach Bronze Awd 1988; Natl HS Coaching Awd; IL HS Tennis Coaches Assn Century Club Awd 1988; Univ of Chicago Teacher Awd 1988-89; *office:* Reavis HS 77th & Austin Burbank IL 60459

BILLEDEAUX, RUTH SANNER, First Grade Teacher; *b:* Lake Charles, LA; *m:* Ronald James; *c:* Corey, Elise, Leah, Clay; *ed:* (BA) Early Chldhd Ed, Mc Neese St Univ 1973; *cr:* Kndgtn/2nd Grade Teacher Johnson Bayou HS 1973-76; 1st Grade Teacher Hackberry HS 1976-; *ai:* Cameron Parish Educators Assn, LA Assn of Ed, NEA; *office:* Hackberry HS 1390 School St Hackberry LA 70645

BILLETT, LYNDA LAUDIG, Kindergarten Teacher; *b:* Williamsport, PA; *m:* Marc L.; *c:* Suzanne, Jennifer; *ed:* (BS) Elem, Lock Haven Univ 1973; *cr:* Kndgtn Teacher Greater Latrobe Sch Dist 1974-; *ai:* Midget Ftbl Cheerleading Adv; PA Ed Assn, Greater Latrobe Ed Assn; *office:* Latrobe Elem Sch 1501 Ligonier St Latrobe PA 15650

BILLETT, MARC LINDSEY, Health/Physical Ed Teacher; *b:* Sharon, PA; *m:* Lynda Lee Laudig; *c:* Suzanne, Jennifer; *ed:* (BA) Health and Phys Ed, Lock Haven Univ 1972; PA St, Duquesne Univ; *cr:* Health & Phys Ed Teacher Greater Latrobe 1972-; *ai:* Jr HS Wrestling Coach 1972-; Greater Latrobe Ed Assn Faculty Recognition 1987-88; Jr WPIAL Coach of Yr 1979-80; 1982-83; Westmoreland Cty Chapter PA Sports Hall of Fame; Distinguished Coaching Awd 1983; *office:* Greater Latrobe JR HS Country Club Rd Latrobe PA 15650

BILLINGS, JILL MANON, Biology Teacher/Sci Dept Head; *b:* Louisville, KY; *m:* James B.; *ed:* (BS) Wildlife Resources, 1978, (MA) Scndry Ed, 1985 WV Univ; Emergency Medical Technician 1983-88; *cr:* Wildlife Biologist WV Dept of Natural Resources 1979-81; White Water Raft Guide/Trip Leader Appalachian Wildwaters Incorporated 1980-88; Substitute Teacher Fayette Cty Sch System 1984-86; Bio Teacher Mt Hope HS 1986-; *ai:* Jr Class Spon; NEA 1985-; SW PA GSA Nature Sanctuary Tech Consultant 1976-; Co-Author & Co-Ed 1982; *office:* Mt Hope HS 10 High School Dr Mount Hope WV 25880

BILLINGS, KAY M. (SANDERS), Spanish Teacher; *b:* Winona, MN; *m:* Michael B.; *c:* Alexa, Blair; *ed:* (BA) Elem Ed/Span, Luther Coll 1983; Grad Stud Span, Summer Inst Foreign Lang Teachers, Univ of N IA; *cr:* 3rd/4th Grade Elem Teacher North Fayette Cmmty Schls 1983-87; 9th-12th Grade Span Teacher Cntrl Cmmty Schls 1987-; *ai:* Span Club Spon; IA Assn Teachers of Span & Portuguese 1987-; *office:* Cntrl Cmmty HS 400 1st St NW PO Box 70 Elkader IA 52043

BILLINGS, ROBERT A., Music Teacher; *b:* Portage, PA; *ed:* (BME) Music Ed, Nyack Coll 1970; Post Grad Work Duquesne Univ & Univ of Pittsburgh Johnstown; *cr:* Instr General/Instrumental Music Forest Hills Elem Sch 1970-; *ai:* Asst HS Band Dir; Forest Hills Ed Assn Mem 1970-; Music Educators Natl Conference Mem 1970-; PA Music Educators Assn Mem 1970-; *office:* Forest Hills Sch Dist F H Elem Sidman PA 15955

BILLINGSLEY, BARBARA ANN, English/Drama Teacher; *b:* Birmingham, AL; *ed:* (BA) Poly Sci, 1975, (MAT) Eng, 1977, (MED) Educl Leadership, 1986 Univ of W FL; *cr:* Eng Teacher Pensacola Jr Coll 1975-78, Escambia HS 1978-89; Eng/Drama Teacher Pine Forest HS 1989-; *ai:* Drama, Scholars Bowl, Escambia Cty Academic All Stars Equestrian Club; Prin & Admin Pool Trng; Escambia Cty Cncl Teachers of Eng (VP 1985-86, Pres 1986-87); FL Cncl Teachers of Eng; Escambia Ed Assn; Amer Horse Show Assn, LA Amer Saddlebred Assn, Amer Saddlebred Assn, Amer Saddle Horse Breeders Assn; ECCTE VP & Pres; Fnd for Excl & Escambia Sch Dist Grant; *office:* Pine Forest HS 2500 Longleaf Dr Pensacola FL 32526

BILLMAN, DIANE PENDREY, Kindergarten Teacher; *b:* Tiffin, OH; *m:* Roger; *ed:* (BS) Early Chldhd Ed, Kent St Univ 1973; (MED) Early Chldhd Ed, Wright St Univ 1983; Miami Univ Oxford OH/Ashland/Otterbein OH/Wright St Univ OH; *cr:* Kndgtn Teacher Favorite Hill Elem 1973-74, Shade Elem 1974-78, Nicholas Elem 1978-; *ai:* Dayton Assn for Young Children (VP 1986-88, Bd Mem 1985-88, Wkshp Chairperson for St Conference 1990-91); People For The Ethical Treatment Of Animals 1987-; Greenpeace 1985-89; Recipient of Excl in Teaching Awd 1990; Nine Creative Teaching Grants; Martha Holden Jennings Scholar; Frequent Presenter At St & Local Conferences; Instr Univ Of Dayton/Sinclair Coll; *office:* Frank Nicholas Sch 3846 Vance Rd Moraine OH 45439

BILLOTTE, DONALD DUANE, II, Social Studies Teacher; *b:* Clearfield, PA; *ed:* (BS) Scndry Ed/Soc Stud, Clarion Univ of PA 1987; Beginning Instructional II Course Work, PA St Univ; *cr:* Soc Stud Teach Clearfield Area Sch Dist 1988-; *ai:* Girls Bsktbl, Asst Jr Var & Var 8th Grade Girls Bsktbl Coach; Key Club Adv; Clearfield Ed Assn, PA St Ed Assn, NEA; United Emanuel Meth Church; *office:* Clearfield Area Sch Dist PO Box 710 Clearfield PA 16830

BILLOTTO, ROBERT JOHN, Ger/Social Studies Teacher; *b:* Staten Island, NY; *m:* Barbara Ann Hansen; *c:* Stacy D., Michael R.; *ed:* (BS) Scndry Ed/Ger/Soc Stud, Univ of Dayton 1974; Various Courses at Numerous Colls; *cr:* Teacher/Coach Henry HS 1978-80, Waverly HS 1980-83, Canova HS 1983-84, Bridgewater HS 1984-88, Eureka HS 1988-; *ai:* Asst Girls Bsktbl, Head Boys Bsktbl & Asst Track Coach; Sch Improvement Comm; SD Ed Assn 1980-83 1989-; SD HS Coaches Assn 1980-; SD Bsktbl Coaches Assn 1986-, Region Asst Coach of Yr 1989; St Josephs Cath Church Parish Cncl 1989-; Negotiator at Henry, Waverly, Bridgewater & Eureka; *home:* Box 101 Eureka SD 57437

BILLUPS, DELORES RICHARDSON, 7th Grade Teacher; *b:* Savannah, GA; *m:* Woodrow Alexander; *c:* Natasha Z., Woodrow A. III; *ed:* (BS) Elem Ed, Savannah St Coll 1966; (MS) Elem Ed, Savannah St Coll & Armstrong 1975; *cr:* 3rd Grade Teacher Annie E Daniels 1966-69; 7th Grade Teacher Swainsboro Elem Sch 1969-88, Swainsboro Mid Sch 1988-; *ai:* NEA 1966-; Eastern Star Olive Leaf 295 1975-.

BILLUPS, JOANNE ELIZABETH, Reading Laboratory Director; *b:* Bloomsburg, PA; *m:* James Randolph; *c:* Adam L.; *ed:* (BS) Elem Ed, Kutztown Univ 1973; (MS) Rdng/Eng, Millersville Univ 1977; Pre-Doctoral Prgm Admin, Supervision, Univ of PA 1977-78; *cr:* Supvr/Custodial Teacher of Educable Mentally Retarded Keifer Trng Center 1973; K-1st Grade Teacher Caleb Bucher Elem Sch 1973-76; Prgm Initiator/Coord for Pre-Kndgtn Transitional Class John Henry Neff Elem Sch 1976-78; 3rd/4th Grade Teacher Garden Elem Sch 1978-83; 6th/8th Grade/Eng Teacher 1983-87, 6th/7th Grade Teacher/Rdng Lab Dir 1987- Venice Area Mid Sch; *ai:* Sch Wide Goal Comm; Long Range 5 Yr Sch Based Management; Sarasota Cncl of Eng 1988-; Intnl Scndry Rdng Cncl, FL Scndry Rdng Cncl, Sarasota Cty Scndry Rdng Cncl 1983-; Amer Assn of Univ Women 1984-; Venice Friends of Lib 1987-; Venice Area Womens League 1974; Nom Sarasota Cty Advisory Cncl; Mary Sergeant Stu Achevement Awd for Outstanding Scholastic Achievement; Panhellenic Awd for Most Outstanding Improvement in Schlsp & Service; *office:* Venice Area Mid Sch 1900 Center Rd Venice FL 34292

BILYEU, DEBRA CALHOUN, Chem/Earth Sci Teacher; *b:* Muskogee, OK; *m:* Larry E.; *c:* Jonathan, Charity; *ed:* (BSMT) Medical Technology, AR Tech Univ 1975; *cr:* Teacher Greenwood Jr/Sr HS 1975-; *ai:* Greenwood Schls Sci Fair Dir; NEA, AR Ed Assn, Greenwood Ed Assn 1978-; NSTA, AR Sci Teachers Assn 1986-; Baptist Church Various Offices 1975-; Greenwood Jr HS Outstanding Teacher 1983-85; *office:* Greenwood HS 460 E Gary St Greenwood AR 72936

BINAGHI, GIULIO PAUL, Spanish Teacher; *b:* Stoneham, MA; *ed:* (BA) Span/Ed - Summa Cum Laude, E Nazarene Coll 1982; Grad Work Univ of MA, Summer Inst Salamanca Spain; *cr:* Span Teacher Timberlane Regional HS 1982-; *ai:* Founder & Adv Sociedad Honoraria Hispanica Garcilaso de la Vega Chapter Timberlane Regional HS; Frosh Class Adv; Eligibility & Peace Day Comm Mem; Amer Assn Teachers of Spanish & Portuguese Mem 1982-; MA Foreign Lang Assn Mem 1988-; New England Assn Scndry Schls & Colls Evaluation Team Mem; Recipient Certificate Excl in Lang Study NE Conference Teaching Foreign Lang; *office:* Timberlane Regional HS 36 Greenough Rd Plaistow NH 03865

BINGAMAN, ROSE A., Kindergarten Teacher; *b:* Wheatland, MO; *m:* Daniel C.; *c:* Gregory T., Timothy D.; *ed:* (BS) Elem Ed, SW MO St 1960; (MAT) Early Chldhd Ed, Webster Univ St Louis 1982; Numerous Univs; *cr:* Kndgtn Teacher Long Elem 1960-66, Kennerly Elem 1977-86, Truman Kndgtn Center 1986-; *ai:* MO St Teachers Pres 1983-84; Lindbergh Leader Awd Lindbergh Sch Dist 1987; Dandforth Fnd Funded & Spons by Network, First St Louis Teaching Acad 1989-; *office:* Truman Kndgtn Center 1222 S Eddie & Park Rd Saint Louis MO 63127

BINGHAM, GLENDA FREEMAN, Lang Art & Soc Stud Teacher; *b:* High Point, NC; *m:* Steven Thomas; *ed:* (BS) Ed, W Carolina Univ 1968; *cr:* 5th Grade Teacher Gaston Cty Schls 1968-69; 3rd-8th Grade Teacher Ramseur Sch 1969-88; 7th/8th Grade Teacher Farmer Sch 1988-; *ai:* Jr Beta Club Co-Spon; NCAE, NEA, Natl Assn for the Preservation & Perpetuation of Storytelling; ABWA 1980-82; Ramseur Sch Teacher of Yr 1981-82; *office:* Farmer Sch Farmer Rural Sta Asheboro NC 27203

BINGHAM, JUDE BOYLL, Science Department Chairperson; *b:* Terre Haute, IN; *c:* Barton E., Michael B.; *ed:* (BS) Life Sci, 1973, (MS) Life Sci, 1974 IN St Univ; Lilly DNA Wkshp 1987; IN Wildlife Fed Wkshps 1983; Sam Rhine Genetics Update Conference 1983-85, 1990; *cr:* Instr IN St Univ 1973-74; Sci Teacher 1975-80, Bio Teacher/Sci Dept Chairperson 1980- Otter Creek Jr HS; *ai:* Vigo Cty Sci Curr Comm; North Cntrl Assn Sci Comm Chairperson; Hoosier Assn of Sci Teachers Incorporated (Membership Chairperson 1977-80, Publications Chairperson 1981-) 1972-, Outstanding & Dedicated Service Awd 1987; IN Acad of Sci 1985-86; Vigo Cty Teachers Assn (Building Rep 1978-81) 1973-; IN St Teachers Assn, NEA 1973-; Pi Lambda Theta (VP 1974-76, 1977-78, Pres 1976-77, Secy 1978-81, Delegate Natl Bi-Annual Conference 1977) 1972-; Nature Conservancy 1978-; World Wildlife Fund 1988-; North Shores Animal League 1989-; Hoosier Sci Teacher Assoc Editor 1972-; IN Acad Sci Dev Fellowship for Scndry Sci Teachers 1985-86; IN Regional Sci Textbook Adoption Comm Chairperson 1980-81; Various Publications 1972-, 1973, 1984, 1985; *office:* Otter Creek Jr HS 3055 Lafayette Ave Terre Haute IN 47805

BINGHAM, MARY ANN CORNETT, Social Studies Teacher; *b:* London, KY; *m:* Donald R.; *c:* Lisa A. Weldon, Donna L,; *ed:* (BS) Phys Ed/Health/His, 1965, (MA) Health, 1970, Phys Ed, 1980 Union Coll; *cr:* Teacher Knox Cntrl HS 1965-; *ai:* Co-Spon Soph Class; Knox Cty Nutrition Comm Chairperson; Knox Cty Ed Assn Pres 1970-71; KY Ed Assn Delegate 1970; NEA; Barbourville Garden Club VP 1988-89; East Barbourville Baptist Church Teacher 1975-; North Concord WMU Assn (Dir 1987-, Book Study Chm 1978-); E KY Univ Nutritional Grant 1979; *home:* HC 66 Box 1716 Barbourville KY 40906

BINGLE, CARL A., German/French Teacher; *b:* W Carthage, NY; *m:* Janna Greene; *c:* Kathryn, Peter; *ed:* (BA) Fr/Ger, St Univ Coll 1973; Grad Stud SUNY Potsdam, SUNY Oswego, St Lawrence Univ; *cr:* HS Teacher Carthage Cntrl Sch 1974-75; 9th-12th Grade Ger/Fr Teacher Belleville Henderson Cntrl Sch 1975-; *ai:* NHS Adv; Quiz Team Coach; Effective Schls Chairperson; NY St Assn of Foreign Lang Teachers; NY St Regents Ger Examination Comm.

BINNETTE, URSULA, Latin Teacher; *b:* Old Town, ME; *ed:* (BA) Latin/Eng, Coll of New Rochelle; (MA) Eng, Boston Coll 1962; (MA) Theology, 1975; Latin, Tufts Coll, Boston Coll; Art, Boston Univ, MA Coll of Art; *cr:* Teacher ME Elem Schls 1951-56, Ursuline Acad 1956-62, New Rochelle Elem Sch 1963-64, Dedham HS 1965-66, Springfield HS 1966-69, Dedham HS 1969-; *ai:* Hum Club Adv 1969-; Latin Club Adv 1988-; Dedham Choral Society Bd of Dirs 1969-; NEH Bowdoin Coll Inst for Greek Stud 1986-87; NEH Fellowship Tufts Univ 1990; *home:* 65 Lowder St Dedham MA 02026

BINNINGER, PATRICIA BAKER, English Teacher; *b:* Fostoria, OH; *m:* Robert W.; *c:* Annette Ohl, Teresa Kessler, Julia Bauer, Bobbi Dayton; *ed:* (BS) Span/Eng, Bowling Green St Univ 1955; Elem Ed Trng, Spec Rdng Ed; *cr:* Span/Eng Teacher New Washington HS 1956-59, Attica HS 1959-62; Eng Teacher Seneca East HS 1972-; *ai:* Prom Adv; Negotiations Comm; Eastern Stars Star Point 1989-.

BINNS, DONALD VICTOR, Amer History & English Teacher; *b:* Champagne, IL; *m:* Carolyn Jo; *c:* Donna, Alex, Brook; *ed:* (BS) Ed, 1970, (MA) Curr/Instruction, 1984 KS Univ; *cr:* Teacher Cntrl Jr HS 1972-; *ai:* Head Girls Bsktbl & Asst Ftbl Coach; Sch Improvement Cntrl Comm; NEA Mem.

BINNS, GERALDINE HORTON, 2nd Grade Teacher; *b:* Tillar, AR; *m:* J. C. Sr.; *c:* Marshalla D., Kimberly R., JeffF J.; *ed:* (AA) Bus Ed, Seward Cty Cmmty Jr Coll 1973; (BS) Bus Ed, Panhandle St Univ 1978; *cr:* Clerk Typist Panhandle E Pipeline Company; Teacher Washington Sch 1980-; *ai:* Natl Assn for Advancement of Colored People Mem 1978-; Black His Awareness Mem Special Certificate, Certificate of Appreciation 1988; Cmmty Baptist Prayer Band Dir; Washington Sch PTA Treas.

BINZ, MARIAN CUCCARO, 8th Grade Teacher; *b:* Midland, PA; *c:* Cary, Michele Craig, Eric; *ed:* (BS) Elem Ed, Duquesne Univ 1959; Grad Stud Duquesne Univ, Carlow Coll, Allegheny Intermediate Unit; *cr:* 1st Grade Teacher Pittsburgh Public Schls 1959-61; K-8th Grade Substitute Teacher Diocesan Schls 1972-78; 8th Grade Teacher St Francis Xavier Sch 1978-; *ai:* Upper Elem & Lang Arts Chairperson; NCEA 1979-; St Athanasius PTG Exec Bd 1982-83; St Athanasius Parish Cncl Ed Comm Chairperson 1981-83.

BIRCHEM, MAUREEN GOGGIN, Teacher; *b:* Park Rapids, MN; *m:* Ron; *c:* Stay, Nicole, Natalie, Michelle; *ed:* (BS) Elem Ed, Moorhead St Univ 1969; Grad Stud; *cr:* Kndgtn Teacher Valley City Public Schls 1970-; *ai:* Sch Evaluation Team; VCEA (Comm Mem, Building Rep); NDEA Mem; Delta Kappa Gamma Secy 1983-84, 1985-86; Barnes Cty Lib Bd; Jaycee Women 1977-79; Cath Church (CCD Teacher, Bible Sch Teacher).

BIRCHEM, RONALD NICHOLAS, History Teacher; *b:* Rosholt, SD; *M:* Maureen L. Goggin Birchem; *c:* Stacy, Nicole, Natalie, Michelle; *ed:* (BS) Soc Sci/Phys Ed, Northern St Univ 1967; Univ of ND/ND St Univ; *cr:* Teacher & Coach Clinton MN Public Schls 1967-70, Valley City Public Schls 1970-; *ai:* Retired from Coaching Duties; Valley City Ed Assn Pres 1987-88; NEA 1967-; Benevolent & Protective Order of Elks (Exalted Ruler 1984-85/State Trustee 1985-); Bd Mem Hi-Liner Booster Club; Bd Mem St Catherines Religious Ed; Knights of Columbus; Renegade Riflemen Muzzleloaders Club; *office:* Valley City Public Sch 493 N Central Ave Valley City ND 58072

BIRCHFIELD, GARY H., Biology Teacher; *b:* Elizabethton, TN; *m:* Phyllis Ann Morrell; *c:* David A. C., John S. T., Raychel L. R.; *ed:* (AA) Bio, Hiwassee Coll 1964; (BS) Bio, E TN St Univ 1970; (MA) Scndry Ed, Union Coll 1981; *cr:* Bio Teacher Church Hill HS 1970-80, Volunteer HS 1980-; *ai:* Bio Club Adv; Sci Fair Team, Taxidermy Club Spon; Lib Media Selection, Steering Comm Mem for Accreditation by SACS; Hiwassee Coll Alumni Assn Local Chapter Pres 1970-, Alumni of Yr 1981; Carter Cty Naturalist Advisary Bd Mem 1984-; Elizabeth Mock Schshp Fund Chmn of Bd 1990; H B Stamps Memorial Lib Bd Mem 1988-; *home:* 134 Lane St Church Hill TN 37642

BIRCHFIELD, JENNIFER GODDARD, Chemistry Teacher; *b:* Elizabethton, TN; *m:* Randall; *c:* Ashley B., Alexandria L.; *ed:* (BS) Medical Technology/Health Sci, E TN St Univ 1973; Teachers Cert Milligan Coll 1973-74; Working Towards Masters E TN St Univ; *cr:* 8th Grade Phys Sci Teacher T A Dugger Jr HS 1974-79; Mid Sch Teacher Bethel Chrstn Acad 1985-86; Chem/Bio Teacher Elizabethton HS 1986-; *ai:* Civinette Co-Spon; Jr Var Chrldr; T A Dugger Jr HS Var Chrldrs; Sch Newspaper; Explorer Club; Pep Club; Inservice Comm; Alpha Delta Kappa 1975-79, 1989-; TN Ed Assn, NEA 1975-; Womens Civic Club (Prgms Chm, Secy) 1979-85; United Meth Church (Family Life Pres, Cncl on Ministry Chm) 1981-83; Nom Teacher of Yr; Teacher of Month; Teachers Industry & Environment Convention Chem Teachers Nashville; *home:* 2204 Edgewood Dr Elizabethton TN 37643

BIRCHFIELD, VIVIAN FORD, Jr High English Teacher; *b:* Pikeville, KY; *m:* Fred; *c:* Barry, Valerie; *ed:* (BS) His, Pikeville Coll 1967; (MA) His, Morehead St 1975; *cr:* 2nd Grade Teacher Freeburn; Jr HS Eng Teacher Kimper & Johns Creek; *ai:* Teacher United for Fairness Comm Mem; Pike Cty Ed Assn Ad Hoc Comm; Pike Cty Ed Assn Building Rep 1989-; E KY Ed Assn Delegate 1989-; *home:* 398 Zebulon Hwy Pikeville KY 41501

BIRD, LINDA BURDETTE, Fourth Grade Teacher; *b:* Procious, WV; *m:* Von Richard; *c:* Richard E., Donna S.; *ed:* (BA) Elem Ed/Soc Stud, Morris Harvey 1971; (MA) Elem Admin, WV Coll of Grad Stud 1975; WV Real Estate License; *cr:* Teacher Sandy Knob 1965-69, Bridge Elem 1969-76, Elkview Elem 1976-; *ai:* Soc Stud Fair, Conservation Club Coord; WV Ed Assn Area Rep 1972-76; Elk Valley Womans Club 1976-80; Kansas Cty Conservation Teacher of Yr; Conservation Grant Dept of Natural Resources; *office:* Elkview Elem Sch 902 Main St Elkview WV 25071

BIRD, MICHELLE FRANK, Language Arts Teacher; *b:* Des Moines, IA; *m:* Gregory Paul; *c:* Michael, Megan; *ed:* (BS) Comm, NW MO St Univ 1974; Eng, Drake Univ; Madeline Hunter Trng; Teacher Expectation Stu Achievement; *cr:* HS Lang Art Teacher NE Hamilton Consolidated Sch Dist 1975-78; Lang Art Teacher Prairie City Cmmty Sch Dist 1985-; *ai:* Mid Sch Musical Drama Dir; NCTE 1989-; IA St Ed Assn 1989-; Sch Bd Advisory Comm Chairperson 1987-89; *office:* Monroe-Prairie City Mid Sch 405 Plainsmen Rd Prairie City IA 50228

BIRD, TERRY WOODS, Fr Teacher/Foreign Lang Chair; *b:* Williamsburg, KY; *m:* Kenneth W.; *ed:* (BA) Eng, Cumberland Coll 1968; (MED) Ed, Wright St Univ 1983; *cr:* Eng/Fr Teacher Little Miami HS 1968-; *ai:* Foreign Lang Chairperson; Fr Club Spon; Faculty Advisory Comm; NEA, OH Educl Assn 1969-; Little Miami Teachers Assn Secy 1977-78; OH Modern Lang Assn 1975-; Nom Teacher of Yr 1988, 1989; *office:* Little Miami HS 605 Welch Rd Morrow OH 45152

BIRDSALL, GINA YVONNE, 9th Grade English Teacher; *b:* Abilene, TX; *m:* Clark Eugene; *ed:* (BA) Phys Ed/Eng, Univ of TX Arlington 1986; Masters Stud Eng UTA; Various Wkshps; *cr:* Eng Teacher/Track Coach Nimitz HS 1986-; *ai:* Coach Girls & Boys Cross Cntry& Girls Track; Fellowship of Chrstn Athletes; Spon Frosh Class, Stus Working All Together; Assn of TX Prof Educators 1986-; NCTE 1986-; Plymouth Park United Meth Church Mem 1978-; *office:* Nimitz H S 100 W Oakdale Rd Irving TX 75060

BIRKENHOLZ, JEANNE MARIE, Elementary Guidance Counseler; *b:* Ottumwa, IA; *m:* Doug; *ed:* (BA) Elem Ed, 1977, (MA) Guidance Cnslr, 1989 IA St Univ; Matthew, Tony; *cr:* 6th Grade Teacher Lincoln Elem 1978-89; Guidance Cnslr Lincoln Elem, Aurora Heights Elem, Kellogg Elem 1989-; *ai:* Stu Cncl; NEA, IA St Ed Assn 1978-; Amer Assn for Counseling & Dev, IA Assn for Counseling & Dev, Amer Sch Cnslr Assn, IA Sch Cnslr Assn 1988-; Questers (VP 1987-88, Treas 1988-); Alumni Bd VP 1987-; *office:* Newton Cmmty Schls 310 E 23rd St S Newton IA 50208

BIRKES, DARLENE PROUSE, Journalism/English Teacher; *b:* Topeka, KS; *m:* Wallace B.; *c:* Cheryl R. Birkes Smith, Dean W.; *ed:* (BJ) Journalism, 1954, (BA) Eng, 1955, (MA) His, 1957 Univ of TX Austin; Grad Work W TX St Univ 1975-76; *cr:* Journalism/Eng Teacher Blinn Coll 1955-56; Elem/Jr HS Teacher Pampa Ind Sch Dist 1973-79; Journalism/Eng Teacher White Deer HS 1985-; *ai:* Sr, UIL in Ready Writing, Journalism, SADD, Yrbk, Newspaper Spon; Theta Sigma Phi; TX Classroom Teachers Assn; Gray Cty Historical Commission Pres 1986-; Pampa Fine Arts Assn Past Pres; United Meth Women; AFS Exch Prgm; Pampa Garden Club; Cty Sesquicentennial Chm 1986; Quivira GSA Cncl Past Pres; United Way Drive Chm; Pampa Beautification Fnd; Co-Ed His Book; Ed Cookbook; Free Lance Writer; *home:* 2356 Aspen Pampa TX 79065

BIRKHEAD, RETA BURNETT, Third Grade Teacher; *b:* Hobbs, TX; *m:* E. P. Jr.; *c:* James E.; *ed:* (BA) Elem Ed, Sul Ross St Univ 1962-; Grad Stud in Gifted & Talented, Univ of TX Tyler 1982; *cr:* 1st Grade Teacher Ector Cty Ind Sch Dist 1962-63, San Antonio Ind Sch Dist 1963-65; 2nd/3rd/6th Grade Teacher of Gifted Ector Cty Ind Sch Dist 1965-; *ai:* Just Say No Building Adv; 4th-6th Grade Oral Poetry Rdng Univ Interscholastic League Coach; Support Teacher Univ of TX Permian Basin Stu Teacher; TX St Teachers Assn Building Rep 1962-; TX Gifted & Talented Assn 1980-84; Coll for Kids Odessa Jr Coll Advisory Bd & Planning Comm 1982-83, 1984; Elem Magnet Sch at Blackshear Teacher of Yr 1989; *home:* 6408 S Cty Rd 1210 Midland TX 79763

BIRKHOFER, DONALD DEAN, Math Teacher & Dept Chair; *b:* Musactine, IA; *m:* Jean M. Buysse; *c:* Jeff, Tony, Melissa; *ed:* (BA) Math Ed, 1973; (MA) Math Ed, 1980 Univ of IA; *cr:* Math Teacher Regina HS 1973-78; North Scott JR HS 1978-82; Aspen HS 1982-83; North Scott HS 1983-; *ai:* Coaching Asst Varsity Ftbl JR HS Track & Bsktbl; ICTM; NCTM; Amer Legion; *office:* N Scott Sr HS 200 S 1st St Eldridge IA 52748

BIRKHOLD, LINDA HORNER, Second Grade Teacher; *b:* Paoli, IN; *m:* Richard A.; *c:* Richard A. Jr. *ed:* (BS) Ed, 1963, (MS) Ed, 1970 IN Univ; *cr:* Kndgtn Teacher Northcrest Sch 1964-69; Kndgtn Teacher 1970-73, 2nd Grade Teacher 1973-Merle J Abbett; *ai:* IRA, NEA; Psi Iota Xi (2nd VP 1980-81, Prgm Chm); *home:* 10026 Circlewood Dr Fort Wayne IN 46804

BIRKLAND, LESLIE OKADA, Japanese Teacher; *b:* Osaka, Japan; *m:* Dale Lewis; *c:* Jeffrey, Douglas, Michael; *ed:* (BA) Eng Lit/Fr, Univ of La Verne 1970; Cert Japanese/Eng, Univ of WA 1985; Japanese Teaching Methods Wkshp, Univ of IL; Continuing Ed Courses, Univ of WA, Seattle Pacific Univ; TPR Methods, Western WA Univ; *cr:* Elem Teacher Amer Sch in Japan 1972-77; Japanese Teacher Rabaul Adult Ed Papua New Guinea 1973-74; Personnel Admin Vivitar Cmptr Products 1983-85; Japanese Teacher Lake Washington HS 1985-; *ai:* Multi-Cultural Club Adv; Japanese Lang Camp Teacher 1990; Organized Exch Trips to Japan; Foreign Lang Curr Comm; WA Assn Foreign Lang Teachers Bd Mem 1989-; Amer Assn Teachers of Japanese Pres 1989-; PTA Membership Chm 1983-84; PTSA Liaison 1985-86; Univ of Chicago Outstanding Teacher Awd 1986; Japanese Teachers Networking Organization Regional Rep 1988; Articles Published; *office:* Lake Washington HS 12033 NE 80th Kirkland WA 98033

BIRKMEYER, STEPHANIE, Chemistry Teacher; *b:* North Braddock, PA; *m:* William; *c:* Mark, Diane, Karen; *ed:* (BS) Chem, Univ of Pittsburgh 1960; Teaching Cert Chatham Coll 1987; *cr:* Chemist PPG Industries 1960-67; Domestic Eng 1967-89; Teacher New Kensington-Arnold Schls 1987-; *ai:* Sci Club Adv; PSTA 1987-; ACS 1988-; Natl Sci Fdn Chem Grant Hope Coll 1989; *office:* Valley HS Stevenson Blvd New Kensington PA 15068

BIRKMIRE, JOANNE, 7th Grade English Teacher; *b:* Brooklyn, NY; *m:* Phillip; *c:* Jayme; *ed:* (BA) Scndry Ed-Eng, Rider Coll 1974; *cr:* 7th Grade Eng Teacher, Northern Burlington Cnty Reg Jr/Sr H S 1975-; *ai:* NEA 1987-90; NJ Ed Assoc; NJ Govenors Teachers Recog Awd; *office:* N Burlington Cnty Reg Jr/Sr HS Georgetown-Mansfield Rd Columbus NJ 08022

BIRLEY, DOROTHY WALLENSTIEN, Kindergarten Teacher; *b:* Pensacola, FL; *m:* Thomas L.; *c:* Michael S., Krista K.; *ed:* (BA) Soc Sci, E WA St 1966; *cr:* 4th Grade Teacher West Valley Elem 1967-70; 4th Grade/Kngtn Teacher Calabazas 1970-74; Kndgtn/2nd Grade Teacher Stocklmeir 1974-; *ai:* CEA, NEA; Primary Phys Ed Grant 1984; Technology Grant 1986; Math Their Way Follow-Up Instr 1989-; *office:* Stocklmeir Sch 572 Dunholme Way Sunnyvale CA 94087

BIRNEY, BARB VIRGINIA, 1st Grade Teacher; *b:* New Athens, OH; *m:* James Carl; *c:* Tammy, Kimberly Birney Tooms; *ed:* (BS) Elem Ed, OH Univ 1965; Grad Stud OH Univ 1986; *cr:* Teacher Buckeye Local 1963-64, Trenton Avenue 1964-65, Scioto-Darby 1965-67, Freeport Elem 1970-71, Madison Elem 1974-; *ai:* Report Card, Soc Stud, Health Advisory Comms; OEA, NEA 1963-; E Guernsey Local 1974-; Home & Sch Presbyn Church (Fund Raiser, Sunday Sch Teacher); *office:* Madison Elem Sch 19153 Cadiz Rd Lore City OH 43755

BISAGNO, EUGENE, JR., Biology Teacher; *b:* Stockton, CA; *m:* Virginia Acosta; *c:* Julie L., Anne M.; *ed:* (BA) Biol, CA St 1966; (MS) Bio, Univ of Pacific 1987; *cr:* Teacher Stockton Unified Sch Dist 1968-; *ai:* Asst Coach-Sci Olympiad-3 Yrs; SUSD Curr Revision Comm-1982-85; CTA/NEA 1968-; Valley Assn of Sci Teachers 1989-; Sabbatical Leave-1980-81; *office:* Edison Sr H S 1425 S Center Stockton CA 95206

BISCHEL, LEONARD F., Science Teacher; *b:* Rapid City, SD; *m:* Arlin Edith Drake; *c:* Dianne, Leolyn, Justin, Kevin; *ed:* (BA) Psych, Univ of Denver 1955; (MED) Sci Ed, Sam Houston St Univ 1965; Sci, AZ St Univ; Univ of AZ, Univ of UT, Univ of CA San Jose; *cr:* 4th Grade Teacher Aptos Union Elem 1960-63; 6th Grade Teacher Montvue Elem 1964-66; 7th-9th Grade Sci Teacher Center Jr HS 1967-73; 6th-8th Grade Sci/Math Teacher Camelback Desert Private Sch 1978-79; 7th-9th Grade Sci Teacher Rhodes Jr HS 1980-; *ai:* Poetry Club Spon; Sci Club Co-Spon; CA Elem Sch Sci Assn Regional VP 1971-72; CA Sci Teachers Assn St Secy 1972-73; NEA, AZ Ed Assn, Mesa Ed Assn; Mensa Gifted Childrens Prgm Coord 1987-; United Poets Laureate Intnl SW USA Dir 1985-, Poet Laureate Man of Letters 1985, Century Poets Awd 1986, Distinguished Service Awd 1986, Grand Medal of World Culture 1988; AZ St Poetry Society Treas 1989-; Tri City Poetry Society Pres 1989-; Greater Phoenix Mensa Gifted Children Prgm Coord 1987-; Experienced Teacher Fellowship Sci Ed; Natl Sci Fnd Physics, Astronomy, Geology Grants; Author Poetry Books; *home:* 36 W Del Rio Cir Tempe AZ 85282

BISCHOFF, JANET BUCKNER, 4th Grade Teacher; *b:* Waco, TX; *c:* Misty, Jared; *cr:* 4th Grade Teacher Lorena Elem 1975-; *home:* 234 Thompson Cir Lorena TX 76655

BISCHOFF, MABLE ANN, Second Grade Teacher; *b:* Lovell, WY; *ed:* (BS) Elem Ed, Univ of WY 1962; *cr:* Kndgtn Teacher Black Eagle Elem/Meadowlark Elem 1962-65; 1st Grade Teacher North Park Elem 1965-79; 2nd Grade Teacher Lovell Elem; *ai:* Curr Comm; Kappa Delta Gamma 1980-82; Lovell Ed Assn Secy 1982-83; WY Ed Assn 1979-; NEA 1962-; MT Ed Assn 1962-79; *home:* 333 W 7th St Lovell WY 82431

BISHARD, LOIS BURD, 5th Grade Teacher; *b:* Doylestown, PA; *m:* Bradford L.; *c:* Elizabeth, Suzanne, Brett; *ed:* (BS) Elem Ed, Elizabethtown Coll 1972; *cr:* 2nd/3rd/5th Grade Teacher Dover Sch Dist 1972-.

BISHOP, BETTY F., 4th Grade Teacher; *b:* Brownsville, TX; *m:* James H.; *c:* Jennifer C.; *ed:* (BS) Elem Ed, Univ of Tn 1968; (MED) Elem Ed, Memphis St Univ 1981; *cr:* 8th Grade Teacher 1967-68, 4th Grade Teacher 1968-73, 1st Grade Teacher 1974-76, 5th & 6th Grade Eng/Rdng Teacher 1976-82, 4th Grade Teacher 1982- Dyer Cty Bd of Ed; *ai:* Young Astronauts Spon; NEA, TN Ed Assn, Dyer Cty Ed Assn, NCTM, TN Aerospace Ed Assn, Air & Space Smithsonian; Civil Air Patrol, Southside Baptist Church; Aerospace Presentations for Children & Educl Wkshp; *office:* Holice Powell Sch P O Box 98 Fowlkes TN 38033

BISHOP, CHARLES, 5th Grade Teacher; *b:* Jackson, TN; *c:* Susan, Gina B. Hayes; *ed:* (BA) His/Art/Lit, Univ of IL 1971; (MS) Ed/Media, Univ of IN 1976; *cr:* 7th Grade Cath Teacher St George 1962-65; Curator Audio-Tutorial Bio Labortory Univ of IL 1966-71; Frosh Eng Teacher Malcolm X Coll 1971-74; Eng Teacher Purdue Univ 1975; Teacher Chicago Bd of Ed 1976-; 5th Grade Teacher C E Hughes 1990; *ai:* CORE Planning Team Project Canal; African Amer His Club; Black His Pageant Scenery Coord; Beta Sigma Tau; Service Awd 1987; United Negro Coll Fund 1986-89.

BISHOP, DORIS BASS, Language Art Teacher; *b:* Madison, FL; *m:* Donald Wayne; *c:* Teresa, Don Jr.; *ed:* (AA) N FL Jr Coll 1964; (BS) Eng Ed, FL St Univ Tallahassee 1966; *cr:* Eng Teacher Madison HS 1966-67, Lee Jr HS 1969-71, Pinetta Jr HS 1976-; *ai:* Newspaper Adv; Madison Cty Ed Assn 1976-; Delta Kappa Gamma Secy 1986-88; Teacher Ed Cncl Secy 1984-87; Pinetta Teacher of Yr 1988; Madison Cty Dist Teacher of Yr 1990; *home:* Rt 2 Box 54 Madison FL 32340

BISHOP, HILDA HOLCOMB, 10th/12th Grade Eng Teacher; *b:* Fulton, MS; *m:* Victor; *c:* Chris, Merrie Bishop Wright, Ann M.; *ed:* (BMED) Music Ed, MUW 1960; (BA) Eng, Univ of MS 1985; *cr:* Music Teacher W P Daniel HS 1961-64, Fulton Jr HS 1966-68, 1974-; Eng Teacher Itawamba HS 1985-; *ai:* Music Educators Natl Conference, MS Assn of Educators; Fulton Civic Club; First Baptist Church Music Dir; *home:* PO Box 563 Fulton MS 38843

BISHOP, JANE DODSON, Home Economics Teacher; *b:* Washington, DC; *m:* James William; *c:* James D.; *ed:* (BS) Home Ec, Howard Univ 1946; (MA) Home Ec Ed, NY Univ 1950; Univ of MA, Univ of DC; *cr:* Home Ec Teacher Spingarn Sr HS 1952-; *ai:* FHA Co-Spon Womens League Steering Comm; Attendance

Improvement Comm; Amer Home Ec Assn, DC Home Ec Assn; Delta Sigma Theta.

BISHOP, KATHRYN, Second Grade Teacher; *b:* Dublin, GA; *m:* Thomas Franklin; *c:* Tom, Frank; *ed:* (AA) General Ed, Mid GA Coll 1974; (BS) Elem Ed, GA Coll 1976; *cr:* 2nd Grade Teacher NW Laurens Primary 1976-; *ai:* Textbook Adoption Comm; Data Collector; Alpha Delta Kappa Pres Elect 1988-; PTA; Prof Assn of GA Educators; Beta Sigma Phi (Pres 1982-83, 1st VP 1981-82, 2nd VP 1977-78, Treas 1979-80, 1985-86); Woman of Yr 1981; Valentine Queen 1982; Daughters of Amer Revolution; *office:* NW Laurens Primary Sch PO Box 97 Dudley GA 31022

BISHOP, LEROY JAMES, 5th Grade Teacher; *b:* Libby, MT; *M:* Kim M.; *c:* Bryce, Blake; *ed:* (BA) Ed, Eastern WA Univ 1973; *cr:* 5th Grade Teacher Sadie Halstead Elem 1974-; *ai:* WA Ed Assn; Newport Teachers Assn; *home:* Box 918 Newport WA 99156

BISHOP, MIKE, Mathematics Teacher; *b:* Fayetteville, TN; *m:* Betsy Johns; *ed:* (BS) Health/Phys Ed, Univ of AL 1977; (MED) Admin, 1978, (EDS) Admin 1980 Mid TN St; *cr:* Phys Ed Teacher Jones Elem Sch 1977-79; Math Teacher Connelly Mid Sch 1980-; *ai:* Head Ftbl Coach; Jr Var Bsktbl Coach; Marshall Cty Ed Assn Pres 1985-86; Lions Club; Lewisburg Jaycees; *home:* 509 Berkley Cir Lewisburg TN 37091

BISHOP, PAMELA A., Social Studies Teacher; *b:* Nashville, TN; *ed:* (BS) His/Scndry Ed, Univ of TN 1969; (MED) Public Sch Curr, Mid TN St Univ 1974; Cmptr Instruction, Nashville Tech Inst; *cr:* Asst Librarian Franklin HS 1969-70; Teacher/Librarian College Grove HS 1970-76; Soc Stud Teacher Page HS 1976-81, Page Mid Sch 1981-; *ai:* Team Leader; Stu Staying Straight Club Core Team Mem; UTP 1969-; Williamson Cty Ed Assn (Secy 1988-89, Newsletter Ed), 1st Place Newsletter 1987, Teacher of Yr 1984, Competition TEA 1988; First United Church UCC Deacon 1988; Williamson Cty Bd of Ed Sick Leave Bank Trustee 1988-; Selected Williamson Cty Teacher of Yr 1984; Evaluated & Achieved Career Ladder III Status 1985; *office:* Page Mid Sch 6262 Arno Rd Franklin TN 37064

BISKUP, SUSAN LYNN, Chemistry Teacher; *b:* Beaver Falls, PA; *m:* Rodney G. Sr.; *c:* Rodney Jr.; *ed:* (BS) Chem, Univ of Pittsburgh 1983; Cert Instructional I Ed, 1984, Cert Instructional II Ed, 1987 Geneva Coll; *cr:* Chem Teacher Quigley Cath HS 1984-; *ai:* NHS Spon; *office:* Quigley Cath HS Franklin Ave Ext Baden PA 15005

BISSELL, HAROLD PRESTON, Social Studies Chair; *b:* Provo, UT; *m:* Mary Kay Brummel; *ed:* (BS) Geography, Brigham Young Univ 1963; (MA) Geography, Univ of HI 1965; (PHD) Georgraphy, Univ of OK 1971; *cr:* Instr Bemidji St Coll 1965-68; Asst Professor Univ of WI Eau Claire 1971-73; Dir Chippewa Valley Museum 1974-78; Teacher Mc Dowell Cntrl HS 1978-; *ai:* NHS Adv; Chippewa Area Cath Schls Cmptr Comm; East-West Cntrl Grantee 1963-65; Outstanding Educator Chippewa Falls 1989; *office:* Mc Donell Cntrl HS Bel Aire Blvd Chippewa Falls WI 54729

BISSONNETTE, VEVA KARLENE, Speech Teacher/Dir Of Forensic; *b:* San Francisco, CA; *m:* Charles Jenkins; *ed:* (BA) Speech Comm, Brigham Young Univ 1979; (MA) Ed/Learning DisabilitiEs, Santa Clara Univ 1983; *cr:* Spec Ed Teacher 1980-82, Speech Coach 1980-83 Cupertino HS; Spec Ed Teacher Homestead HS 1982-83; Speech/Eng Teacher Saratoga HS 1983-; *ai:* Coach Speech & Debate Team-Head Coach; Natl Forensic League 1973-; Diamond Coach 1986; CA Speech Comm Assn 1988-; CA Coast NFL Exec Comm Mem 1985-; Amnesty Intl 1986-; Greenplace 1986; Pres Coast Forensic League 198283; Outstanding Service Awd-pTSAC 1988; Dir of Debate Coast Forensic League 1987; Published Article CA HS Speech Assn Bulletin 1989; *office:* Saratoga H S 20300 Herriman Ave Saratoga CA 95070

BISTANY, SONIA M., Teacher; *b:* Brooklyn, NY; *ed:* (BBA) Bus Admin, City Coll of the City Univ of NY 1962; (MA) Ed, Fairleigh Dickinson Univ 1976; *cr:* Teacher Lincoln Elem Sch 1968-; *ai:* NEA 1968-; NJ Ed Assn 1968-; Pompton Lakes Ed Assn 1968-; Governors Teacher Recognition Awd 1986; Commissioners Symposium for Outstanding Teachers; *office:* Lincoln Elem Sch Mill St Pompton Lakes NJ 07442

BITER, MIRIAM RITA, Business Teacher; *b:* New Brunswick, PA; *ed:* (AS) Bus, Mt Alorpurs Jr Coll; (BS) Bus Ed, Misericordia Coll; (MA) US His/Church His, Villanova Univ; Numerous Wkshp; *cr:* Religion/Bus Teacher Williamstown Cath HS; Bus/His/Religion Teacher Bishop Carroll HS; *ai:* St Michael Parish LOretto Religious Ed Dir; NCEA; *office:* Bishop Carroll HS Ebensburg PA 15931

BITLEY, CHARLES WARREN, 8th Grade Math Teacher; *b:* Troy, NY; *m:* Maureen Dolores Houck; *c:* Matthew E. Thomas, Sarah A.; *ed:* (BA) Math/Sociology, 1974, (MA) Math Ed, 1976 SUNY Albany; *cr:* 7th/8th Grade Math Teacher W K Doyle Mid Sch 1977-; *ai:* Doyle Mid Sch Shared Decision Making Comm Mem; Memorial United Meth Church Supt of Sunday Schls 1975; Cntry Knolls West Civic Assn Treas 1986-88; CROP Hunger Walk Co-Coord 1975; Bertha Brimmer Medal 1988; Greater Capital Region Teacher Center Grant; Troy City Sch Dist Mini-Grant; *home:* 4 Merion Ave Clifton Park NY 12065

BITTERS, CONRAD L., Biology/Zoology Teacher; *b:* Waco, TX; *m:* Karen Kay; *c:* Rebecca K., Brian C.; *ed:* (BA) Biological Sci, CA St Univ Fresno 1969; Post Grad Stud Bio, Ed, Health, Geology; *cr:* Dept Chm 1973-80, Bio/Zoology Teacher 1970-, Bio Coord 1980- Clovis HS; *ai:* Vertebrate Advisory Comm; Jr Division Judge & Sr Division Coach Cntrl Valley Sci Fair; Dist Rep Jr Sci & Hum Symposium Univ of CA Berkeley; Spon Ecology & Foreign Stud Club; Cast Univ Fresno Tri-Beta Sci Honor Society 1968-74; NSTA 1978; Faculty Awd Eastman Kodak Company 1980; Faculty Commendations Intnl Sci & Engineering Fair 1982, Natl Jr Sci & Hum Symposium, Army Research Office 1985, Lawrence Hall of Sci 1985, 1987, John D Isaacs Schlsp Comm 1985, CA St Sci Fair 1988; Merit Awds Fresno Rotary 1985, 1988; Outstanding Sci Teacher Awd Fresno Cty Dow Chemical Company 1986; Presidential Awd Sci Teaching CA St Dept of Ed 1986; CA Educl Initiative Fund Grant; *office:* Clovis HS 1055 N Fowler Clovis CA 93612

BITTINGER, JOHN MATTHEW, Science Teacher; *b:* Ft Wayne, IN; *m:* Gayle A. Fritschle; *ed:* (AA) Gr River Comm Coll 1981; (BS) Bio Chem, 1983, (MSE) Sci Ed, 1988 Western WA Univ; *cr:* Lab Instr Western WA Univ 1984; Sci Instr Everett HS 1985-; *ai:* Natl Energy Fnd Comm; Soph Class Adv; WA Ed Assn, NEA; *office:* Everett HS 2416 Colby Ave Everett WA 98201

BITZES, JOHN G., Teacher; *b:* Omaha, NE; *m:* Helen E. Loras; *c:* James G., Mark J.; *ed:* (BA) His/Poly Sci, Univ of NE 1954; (MA) His, Univ of Omaha 1964; (PHD) Modern European, Univ of NE Lincoln 1976; 3rd World Conference Omaha, Duquesne Univ PA, US Naval Acad, Amer Military Inst MO Valley Conference; *cr:* Teacher Creston HS 1959-61, Omaha Public Schls 1961-; Part Time Lecturer Univ of NE 1966-; *ai:* Academic Decathlon Coach; Red Cross Youth Cncl Bryan Spon; Honor Banquet & Red Cross Bloodmobile Comm; In-Sch Suspension Room Comm Chm; Omaha Ed Assn (Building Rep 1977-79, VP 1990); NE Ed Assn; Phi Beta Kappa; Red Cross Volunteer 1975-; NE Historical Society Best Article Awd 1970; James L Sellers Awd 1971; NE Assn for Gifted Grant 1983; Book Published 1989; *home:* 13575 Walnut St Omaha NE 68144

BIVINS, BARBARA JONES, Teacher; *b:* Roberta, GA; *m:* Bert III; *c:* Belinda, Bert IV; *ed:* (BS) Soc Stud, 1971, (BS) Elem Ed, Ft Valley St Coll; Working Towards Masters Degree; *cr:* Teacher St Peter Claver Cath Sch 1974-75, Winship Elem 1975-; *ai:* Grade Level Chairperson; NAACP; GA Assn of Ed, NEA, Bibb Assn of Ed; Teacher of Yr; *home:* 733 Key Ct Macon GA 31204

BIZAR, DOREEN SHARON, Chapter I Reading Specialist; *b:* Chicago, IL; *m:* Lawrence; *c:* Jeff, Dawn; *ed:* (BA) Speech Ed, Northwestern Univ 1965; (MA) Rdng, NE IL Univ 1987; *cr:* 3rd/4th Grade Teacher Orrington Sch 1965-67; 3rd Grade Teacher Devonshire Sch 1967-69; 6th Grade Teacher Mark Twain Sch 1983-84; 7th/8th Grade Rdng Teacher Gemini Jr HS 1981-83, 1985-87; 2nd-6th Grade Chapter 1 Rdng Specialist Stevenson Sch 1987-; *ai:* Drama Club; Federal Government Honor Outstanding Chapter 1 Prgm in Cntry.

BIZZELL, NANCY ROBNETT, 5th Grade Teacher; *b:* Big Spring, TX; *m:* Gary; *c:* Skylar, Pipar; *ed:* (BS) Home Ec/Child Dev, TX Tech Univ 1967; Grad Stud Teaching Cert; *cr:* 3rd Grade Teacher 1967-68, 5th Grade Teacher 1968-69 Ralls Elem; 8th-12th Grade Eng Teacher Spade Elem 1969-70; 5th Grade Teacher Hale Center Mid Sch 1976-; *ai:* UIL Oral Rdng Coach; Stu/Cooperating Teacher; Gifted & Talented Comm; ESL Bi-ling, Goals, Actions, Textbook Comm; Southern Assn of Colls & Schls Evaluation Team; ATPE (Pres 1984-85, Secy 1988-89); TX Career Ladder II & III 1984-85, 1988-89; *office:* Hale Center Mid Sch 1208 Avenue G Hale Center TX 79041

BJERKE, MARIE BOT, English Instructor/Dept Chair; *b:* Great Falls, MT; *m:* C. G.; *c:* David D. Bot, Jayne M. Bot Schlicht; *ed:* (BS) Eng/Elem, Mayville SC 1963; Accepted into Counseling Prgm 1973; *cr:* Teacher One Room Rural Sch & Elem Jr HS Ransom Cty 1947-63; Eng Instr Lisbon HS 1964-; *ai:* Stu Cncl, Prospective Teachers Club, Frosh & Sr Class Adv; Chairperson Eng Dept; NEA, NDEA; Lisbon Ed Assn Pres 1956-; Delta Kappa Gamma (VP, Recording Secy, Parlimentarian, Charter Mem) 1983-; St Maternal & Child Care Mem, Lisbon Cmmty Memorial Hospital, Long Range Planning Comm Pres; AAUW Sheyenne Branch (VP, Charter Mem); Mem N Cntrl Evaluation Team; NDEA Lobbying St Legislature; *home:* 607 2nd Ave W Lisbon ND 58054

BLAAUBOER, PETER R., Teacher & Dept Head; *b:* Albany, NY; *m:* Joanne Convery; *c:* Mark, Kelley, Scott, Michael, Shylo, Jacob, Laura; *ed:* (BS) Bio, Fordham Univ 1963; (MA) Bio, Wesleyan Univ 1969; (SAS) Admin/Curr, St Univ Albany 1975; Conf NY St Scndry Sci Supvrs 1981-89; *cr:* Teacher Mt Carmel Sch 1958-64; Dean Of Men/Teacher Cardinal Mooney HS 1964-67; Teacher Shaker Jr/Sr HS 1967-70; Dept Head/Teacher Saratoga Springs Jr HS 1970-; *ai:* Parent-Teacher Meetings, Awds Night & Orientation Presenter; NY St Scndry Sci Supvrs 1981-; NSF Grant Wesleyan Univ 1964-69; Harvard Project Physics Grant 1969; Rennsaelear Polytechnic Inst; NYS Mentor-Presenter to Train All Cty Elem Teachers for New Sci Syllabus 1987; *office:* Saratoga Springs Jr H S W Circular St Saratoga Springs NY 12866

BLACK, ALMA JEAN, Fourth Grade Teacher; *b:* Mound City, IL; *m:* Holston E.; *c:* Stephanie L., Anthony E. Petty; *ed:* (BS) Elem Ed, S IL Univ Carbondale 1959; (MS) Lang Art, Webster Univ 1972; *ai:* Kratz Sch Sci Fair Coord; NEA Pres 1986-88, Gavel 1988; Alpha Kappa Alpha Mem; Teachers Study Guide 1989; *office:* Kratz Elem Sch 4301 S Edmundson Rd Saint Louis MO 63134

BLACK, CHARLES REED, American History Teacher; *b:* Oklahoma City, OK; *m:* Marysia Nowosad; *c:* Erik; *ed:* (BA) Psych/Sociology, Baker Univ 1965; (MLA) Liberal Art, Southern Meth Univ 1976; Natl Geographic Society Summer Inst 1987; *cr:* Soc Stud Teacher Eastgate Jr HS 1969-80; Amer His Teacher Oak Park HS 1980-; *ai:* NCSS, Natl Cncl Geographic Ed, NEA; MO Cncl for Soc Stud Bd of Dir 1989-; MO Geographical Alliance Steering Comm 1987-; *office:* Oak Park HS 825 NE 79th Terr Kansas City MO 64118

BLACK, CONNIE BUTLER, Business Teacher; *b:* Chicago, IL; *m:* Herbert Sterling; *c:* Stephen, Shaun; *ed:* (BS) Bus, 1964, (MS) Bus, 1965 S IL Univ; IBM Educators Trng; *cr:* Bus Teacher E J King Sch 1966-67, Roosevelt HS 1967-68, Cass Tech HS 1968-; *ai:* NHS Adv; MI Bus Ed Assn Mem; Metro-Bus Teachers Club Mem 1988-89; AFT, Detroit Fed of Teachers Mem 1968-; Oak Grove AME Church, Amer Cancer Assn Volunteer 1989; E MI Univ Honors Prgm Certificate of Merit, Outstanding Achievement as NHS Adv 1987-89; Detroit Bd of Ed Perfect Attendance Awd 1987-; *office:* Cass Tech HS 2421 Second Detroit MI 48201

BLACK, DAVID ALBERT, Ag/Horticulture Instructor; *b:* Union City, TN; *m:* Gail Lee Forsythe; *c:* Lauren E., Adrienne N.; *ed:* (BS) Ag/Horticulture, 1981, (MS) Ag Ed, 1985 Murray St Univ; *cr:* Ag/Horticulture Instr Bartlett HS 1981-82, Fulton Cty HS 1982-; *ai:* Jr Class Spon; FFA & Reg FFA Adv; FCEA Sch Rep; Ag Advisory Bd & Sick Leave Bd; Ag Dept Chm; Fulton Cty Ed Assn Rep 1982-; KY Ed Assn, KY Ag Teachers Assn, Natl Voc Ag Teachers Assn 1982-; Optimist Club 1987-; Horticulture Society 1982-; Alpha Gamma Rho 1981-; KY Outstanding Young Teacher; Outstanding Young Man of Yr; *office:* Fulton Cty HS Rt 4 Hwy 94 Hickman KY 42050

BLACK, ELEANORA LOUISE SCHMIDT, Fourth Grade Teacher; *b:* New Castle, PA; *m:* Robert Charles; *ed:* (BS) Ed, The Youngstown Univ 1961; (MS) Ed, Westminster Coll 1967; *cr:* Teacher Neshannock Township Sch Dist 1961-; *ai:* NEA, PSEA, NTEA 1961-; *home:* RD 5 Box 610 Neshannock Hills New Castle PA 16105

BLACK, EVELEYN IRENE (KLAMM), Business Education Teacher; *b:* Hospers, IA; *m:* Albert; *c:* Dennis, James, Vern; *ed:* (BA) Bus Ed, NW Nazarene Coll 1970; Wkshps, Extended Stud, Voc Conferences; *cr:* Bus Ed Teacher Sch Dist 25 1969-; *ai:* Riverton Ed Secy 1969-; WY Ed, NEA 1969-; *home:* HC 36 Box 2066 Riverton WY 82501

BLACK, GRETCHEN ZIMMER, Fifth Grade Teacher; *b:* Poughkeepsie, NY; *m:* Charles Eugene; *c:* Stephan R., Karl B., Lori L. Laufenburger; *ed:* (BA) His, Douglass Coll/RutgerS 1956; (MED) Ed, Cornell Univ 1957; *cr:* 2nd Grade Teacher 1957-58, 5th Grade Teacher 1958-59 Yates Elem; 5th GRade Teacher Stonewall Elem; *ai:* Soc Stud Building Rep; Academic Coach; Assembly Chrstn Sch, Sch Bd 1987-91; Ford Fnd Fellowship Research for Chrstn Author Article Published; *office:* Stonewall Elem Sch Cornwall Dr Lexington KY 40503

BLACK, HARRIET MARTIN, Director-Instructor; *b:* Millard, NE; *m:* Oscar Hall; *c:* Walter P., Janice B. Vaughn, Lucy B. Wykoff, Cyndy B. Moon; *ed:* Voc Home Ec, Univ of NE 1937; Early Chldhd Ed, NM St Univ; Early Chldhd Ed, Univ of CO; *cr:* Voc Home Ec Teacher Holmesville NE Sch 1937-38, Carson IA 1938-39, Arnold NE 1939-40; Home Demonstration Agent Alma NE Cty Agents Office 1940-43; Founder/Owner/Admin Coll Heights Kndgtn 1954-; Founder Mesilla Valley Chrstn Sch 1974-; *ai:* Omicron Nu 1936-37; Amer Mothers Comm, NM Mother of Yr Awd 1977; Natl Mother of Yr Assembly Spec Awd Ed; *office:* Coll Heights Kndgtn Sch 1210 Wofford Las Cruces NM 88001

BLACK, JOY LOWMAN, 8th Grade Earth Sci Teacher; *b:* Vidalia, GA; *c:* Angela Markwell, Chris; *ed:* (BA) Elem Ed, Augusta Coll 1974; *cr:* Teacher S W Laurens 1974-76, Ursula Collins 1976-77; Instr Ed Branch 1977-78; Teacher N Columbia & S Harlem & Harlem Mid 1978-; *ai:* Harlem Mid Sch Sci Fair Coord; NEA, GAE 1987-; GA Jaycettes (Secy 1978-79, Pres 1979-81), Project Chm of Yr 1979; CSRA Sci & Engineering Fair Incorporated Scientific Review Comm 1988-; *office:* Harlem Mid Sch W Forest St Harlem GA 30814

BLACK, KEITH DONALD, Fifth Grade Teacher; *b:* Waynesboro, PA; *m:* Carol Louise Nogle; *c:* Andrew K.; *ed:* (BS) Elem Ed, Shippensburg St 1970; *cr:* 4th-5th Grade Teacher Greencastle-Antrim Elem 1970-; *ai:* NEA; PSEA; GAEA; BSA Den Leader; *office:* Greencastle-Antrim Elem Sch 500 E Leitersburg St Greencastle PA 17225

BLACK, LARRY A., 7th/8th Grade Soc Stud Teacher; *b:* Newark, NJ; *m:* Barbara Ann Stoughton; *ed:* (BA) Soc Stud, Jersey City St 1960; (MA) Elem Ed, CO Coll 1974; Grad Work UCCS, Adams St, Newark St; *cr:* Substitute Teacher Wall Township Schls 1960-65; 6th Grade Teacher Garfield Sch 1966-67; 6th Grade Rdng/Soc Stud Teacher Woodland Park Sch 1967-; *ai:* Stu Cncl 1972-82; Project Bus 1980-84; N Cntrl & Soc Stud Comm; Woodland Park Ed Assn (Pres 1975-76, 1969-71); NEA 1966-; NCCS 1976-; Ute Pass Historical Society Exec Bd 1990; *office:* Woodland Park Mid Sch PO Box 6790 211 N Baldwin Woodland Park CO 80866

BLACK, LYNNE HARTMAN, 7th Grade Mathematics Teacher; *b:* Camden, NJ; *m:* Billy Lee; *c:* Lance, Rebecca; *ed:* (BA) Elem Ed, Austin Coll 1963; Grad Stud E TX St Univ, Univ of TX Tyler, N TX St Univ; *cr:* 3rd-5th/7th Grade Math Teacher Mt Auburn; 7th Grade Math Teacher Moore Jr HS; 6th Grade Math Teacher Orr Elem; 7th/8th Grade Math Teacher Hogg Jr

HS 1979-81; 7th Grade Teacher Lindale Jr HS 1981-; *ai:* Stu Cncl Spon; CTA (VP 1987, Membership Chairpeson 1988); ATPE; *home:* 302 Lakeview Lindale TX 75771

BLACK, NEIL JAMES, Health/Phys Ed Teacher; *b:* Toledo, OH; *m:* Leslie Ann Mc Creery; *ed:* (BS) Health/Phys Ed, Cedarville Coll 1988; *cr:* Health/Phys Ed Teacher Emmanuel Baptist HS 1987-89; *ai:* Girls Var Bsktbl Coach & Boys Var Bsbl Asst Coach; *office:* Emmanuel Baptist HS 4207 Laskey Rd Toledo OH 43623

BLACK, SANDRA LEDBETTER, VOE Data Processing Teacher; *b:* Nashville, TN; *m:* Ronald J.; *c:* Shelley, Jamie; *ed:* (BS) Bus Ed, Mid TN St Univ 1976; (MAED) Bus Ed, TN St Univ 1980; Grad Stud Cmptr Sci; *cr:* Teacher Falls Bus Coll 1975-76; Bus Teacher Hume-Fogg HS 1976-77, Antioch HS 1977-81; VOE Data Processing Teacher Maplewood HS 1981-83; Bus Teacher Madison HS 1983-85; VOE Data Processing Teacher Hunters Lane HS 1985-; *ai:* Faculty Advisory Comm Mem; NBEA, Metro Nashville Ed Assn 1976-; Bus Prof of Amer Spon 1981-; TN Cmptr Conference Speaker; Career Ladder III; Articles Published; *office:* Hunters Lane HS 1150 Hunters Ln Nashville TN 37207

BLACK, SUE BANNISTER, First Grade Teacher; *b:* Anderson, SC; *c:* Jennifer; *ed:* (BS) Elem Ed, 1969, (MAED) Elem Ed, 1973 Univ of GA; *cr:* 1st Grade Teacher Nevitt Forest Elem 1969-70, Hartwell Elem 1970-; *home:* 506 E Franklin St PO Box 51 Hartwell GA 30643

BLACK, VALERIE BENDIX, Fifth Grade Teacher; *b:* New Orleans, LA; *m:* Elmo Kenneth; *c:* Kathleen Black Nash, Colleen, Eileen Black Kienzle; *ed:* (BS) Ed/Phys Ed, NW Univ of LA 1947; Elem Ed Cert; *cr:* 2nd-5th Grade Teacher St Leonard Cath Sch 1961-66; 4th/5th Grade Teacher Maple Grove Sch 1966-; *ai:* Greenfield Ed Assn Building Rep 1970-76; WI Ed Assn Delegate-At-Large 1976-78; NEA Pres Elect 1978; Greenfield Teacher of Yr 1976.

BLACKARD, LARRY PAUL, Mathematics Department Chair; *b:* Clarksville, AR; *m:* Carol Acord; *c:* Jeff, Eric, Nick; *ed:* (BS) Comp/Natural Sci, Univ of O 1965; (MS) Math, Univ of AR 1968; PET AR St Dept of Ed; Grad Work AR Tech Univ; *cr:* Teacher Clarksville HS 1965-; *ai:* Math Club; Soph & Weighted Class, Salary Comms; *office:* Clarksville HS 1701 Clark Rd Clarksville AR 72830

BLACKBURN, BETTY LOU (MARTIN), Voc Home Economics Teacher; *b:* Checotah, OK; *m:* Jack Jay; *c:* Krista Mc Knight, Derek; *ed:* (BS) Voc Home Ec, OK St Univ 1965; Staff Dev; *cr:* Voc Home Ec Teacher Konowa HS 1965-67; Life Sci Teacher 1967-69, Voc Home Ec Teacher 1969-76 Central Jr HS; Voc Home Ec Teacher South Intermediate HS 1976-88, Broken Arrow Sr HS 1988-; *ai:* FHA; St Adoption Textbook Comm; BAEA Treas 1970-71; OEA, NEA, OVA; Beta Sigma Phi (Treas, Secy); Field Test Materials for Mc Knight Publishing Company; Work on Curr Materials; *office:* Broken Arrow Sr HS 1901 E Albany Broken Arrow OK 74012

BLACKBURN, DONNA TRENT, English Teacher; *b:* South Wiliamson, KY; *m:* Tennyson R.; *c:* Barry W., Arlan A., Marcella L.; *ed:* (BA) Speech/Comm/Drama, Purdue Univ 1983; (MS) Ed, IN Univ 1987; Various Trng; *cr:* Sub Eng Teacher Northrop HS 1984-87; Speech/Eng Teacher South Side HS 1987-88; Eng Teacher West-Oak HS 1989-; *ai:* Sr Adv; Drama Dir; Natl Speech Assn 1987-88; Best Supporting Actress 1984; Chosen Teacher Who Most Influenced Their Lives Sr Class; Certificate of Excl Teacher Ed Prgm IN Univ Ed Dept; Short Story Published 1989; *office:* West-Oak HS 130 Warrior Ln Westminster SC 29693

BLACKBURN, KRISTA DAVIS, Science/Math Teacher; *b:* Huntland, TN; *m:* Bruce Everett; *ed:* (BS) Scndry Ed, Hyles-Anderson Coll 1986; *cr:* Math/Sci Teacher Rosehill Chrstn Sch 1987-; *ai:* Sci Act; *office:* Rose Hill Christian Sch 1001 Winslow Rd Ashland KY 41101

BLACKBURN, MARGARET YOUNG, Teacher & Supervisor; *b:* Brownwood, TX; *m:* Thomas R.; *c:* Kimberly, Kelly; *ed:* (BS) Phys Ed/Health, Howard Payne Univ 1968; (MS) Phys Ed/Health, Tarleton St 1979; *cr:* Teacher Brownwood Jr HS 1968-73, Brownwood HS 1973-78, Howard Payne Univ 1978-83; Supvr Brownwood Ind Sch Dist 1989-; *ai:* NHS; Class, Drill Team Dir; Annual Staff Spon; TX St Teachers Assn Key Club Officer; NEA; TX Assn of Health, Phys Ed, Dance & Aerobic Fitness TX Style; Amer Heart Assn Bd of Dir, Amer Cancer Society; Teacher of Yr 1988; Teacher of Month; *office:* Brownwood HS 10th & Slayden Brownwood TX 76801

BLACKLEY, MARY SUE SUMMERS, 1st Grade Teacher; *b:* Martin, TN; *m:* Billy Wilson; *c:* James S., Daryl W.; *ed:* (BS) Early Chldhd Ed, 1976, (MS) Curr/Instruction, 1978, (MS) Supervision/Admin, 1980 Univ TN Martin; *cr:* 1st Grade Teacher Obion Elem 1976-86; Teacher Hillcrest Elem 1986-; *ai:* Cmptr Classes; Obion Cty Ed Assn Pres 1980-81; TN Ed Assn Delegate 1978-89; NEA Delegate 1980, 1983; IRA 1980-; TN Teacher St Cncl Local Pres; Univ of TN Martin Teacher of Yr 1989; *office:* Hillcrest Elem Sch Rt 2 Box 13 Troy TN 38260

BLACKMAN, ELISE PAUL, 5th Grade Teacher; *b:* New York, NY; *ed:* (BA) Academic/Regents Sch, St Gabriels HS 1953; (BA) His, Our Lady of Good Cncl Coll 1957; (MS) Ed, Hunter Coll 1977; Grad Studies; *cr:* Teacher St Pauls Sch & Resurrection & Sacred Heart & Grims Sch & Traphagen Sch 1966-; *ai:* NYSUT, NEA; MVFT Building Rep 1983-84, 1989-; NSTA, NCSS 1990; NRTA; Sacred Heart Church Mass Lector; Schlsp to Our Lady of Good Cncl Coll; Cath Natl Schlsp for Negroes Incorporated; *office:* Traphagen Sch 165 N Columbus Ave Mount Vernon NY 10551

BLACKMAN, KENT, Agriculture Education Teacher; *b:* Campbell, MO; *ed:* (BS) Ag Ed, Univ of MO 1978; *cr:* Ag Teacher Holcomb HS 1978-; *ai:* FFA Adv;Jr Class, Stand Spon; MSTA 1978-88; AVA Mem 1988-89;MVA Mem, MVATA Mem 1978-82, 1988-; CTA Pres 1978-82, 1988-; Kiwanis Mem 1978-79; Holcomb Farmers & Merchants VP 1980-; MVATA Awd; *office:* Holcomb HS R3 102 Cherry St Holcomb MO 63852

BLACKMER, SALLY, Global Studies Teacher; *b:* Canandaigua, NY; *c:* Cynthia, Mark; *ed:* (BS) Ed- Cum Laude, SUNY Geneseo 1964; (MED) Ed, Univ of Rochester 1970; Numerous Courses Soc Stud & Instruction; *cr:* 5th Grade Teacher Honeoye Cntrl 1964-66; 4th Grade Teacher Canandaigua Sch System 1966-67; 6th Grade Teacher 1967-69, Scndry Soc Stud Teacher 1969- Honeoye Cntrl; *ai:* His & Natural His Club; Wider Horizons; Project Intervention; Dist Sch Improvement Comm; Natl Womens His Month Steering Comm; Honeoye Teachers Assn (VP, Treas, Secy, Negotiations Comm & Grievance Chairperson) Teacher of Yr; NY St United Teachers 1964-; Finger Lakes Soc Stud Cncl 1988-; Natl Organization of Women 1980-; Natl Audubon 1987-; Honeoye Area Historical Society 1985-; Ontario Cntry Historical Comm 1990; Public Television WXXI Rochester NY Utilization of Television in Ed Awd 1988 Regional 2 & St Awd 1986; Joint Cncl on Ec Ed 1978; St & Natl Awds; Univ of Rochester Awd for Excl in Scndry Sch Teaching 1988; Yrbk Dedication 1989; *office:* Honeoye Cntrl Sch Rt 20-A Honeoye NY 14471

BLACKMON, LOLA BELL, Fourth Grade Teacher; *b:* Henderson, TX; *m:* Melvin; *c:* Robert; *ed:* (BA) Elem Ed, TX Coll 1953; (MED) Elem Ed, TX Southern Univ 1969; (EDD) Elem Ed, Univ of Houston 1975.

BLACKWELDER, JOEL DAVID, JR., 6th Grade Teacher; *b:* Shelby, NC; *ed:* (BS) Elem Ed/Soc Stud/Art, Appalachian St Univ 1981; *cr:* 5th Grade Teacher 1984-89, 6th Grade Teacher 1989- Gardner Park Elem Sch; *ai:* Self Study, Art, Music, Soc Stud, Sci Comms; Asst Coach Odyssey of Mind Team 1984-85; NC Assn of Educators, NEA 1984-; *office:* Gardner Park Elem Sch 820 Sandy Ln Gastonia NC 28054

BLACKWELL, SAMAUEL M., Amer History/Pol Sci Teacher; *b:* Memphis, TN; *ed:* (BA) Ed, Parsons Coll 1970; (MA) His, 1977, (CAS) His Northern IL Univ 1986; PHD Candidate in His, Northern IL Univ 1990; *cr:* Teacher/coach Oakview Jr HS 1971-73; Teacher/Dept Chm Sandwich HS 1973-; Parttime Instr Waubonsee Comm Coll 1978-; *ai:* Soc Stud Dept Chm; His Club & Jr Class Adv; NHS, Curr, Sick Bank & Gifted Ed Comm; Organization Amer Historians 1980-; IL St Historical Society 1986-; Civil War Round Table Chicago 1987-; IL Ed Assn Local VP 1971-; IL Army Natl Guard 1967-73 Awd of Merit-Those Who Excel in Ed IL St Bd of Ed 1988; 4 Articles Published in IL Magazine 1981-84; Presenter Womens His Conference NIU 1985; Contributor to Centennial His of Hometown; Several Newspaper Articles Published; Wrote His of 66th Infantry Brigade for Recruiting Brochure; *office:* Sandwich HS 515 E Lions Rd Sandwich IL 60548

BLACKWOOD, SHIELA KAY, Mathematics Department Chair; *b:* Herrin, IL; *m:* James; *c:* James M.; *ed:* (BA) Math, S IL Univ Carbondale 1969; (MS) Math, Notre Dame Univ 1974; Grad Stud S IL Univ Carbondale; *cr:* Math/Sci Teacher Belle Valley Sch 1969-70; Math Teacher Frankfort Cmmty HS 1970-; *ai:* Future Teachers of America; Curr & Steering Comms; S IL Alumnae Assn, Univ of Notre Dame Alumnae Assn; Pi Mu Epsilon, Alpha Lamba Delta, Kappa Delta Pi, Phi Kappa Phi; Outstanding Young Woman of America; Teacher of Yr 1977, 1984, 1986, 1989; Favorite Teacher 1987, 1988; IL Math & Sci Acad Awd of Excl 1989; Natl Sci Fnd Presidential Awds 1988-89; *office:* Frankfort Cmmty HS 601 E Main St West Frankfort IL 62896

BLAD, PHIL, Science/Math/Phys Ed Teacher; *b:* Payson, UT; *m:* Sharon Mae Simmons; *c:* Chris, Shanette, David, Michael, Stacia; *ed:* (BS) Phys Ed, S UT St Coll 1977; *cr:* Sci Teacher Millard HS 1980-82; Algebra/Sci/Phys Ed Teacher Fillmore Mid Sch 1983-; *ai:* HS Ftbl, Bsbl, Mid Sch Bsktbl Coach; Dist ODDM Team Mem; Dist Sci Fair Chm; UEA, NEA Mem 1980-; Natl Math Teachers Assn Mem 1989-; BSA Scoutmaster Troop 207 1986-; Pres Awd of Merit, Dist Awd of Honor 1989; *home:* Box 64 Kanosh UT 84637

BLAINE, JOHN MICHAEL, Instructor-Culinary Food Trade; *b:* Cornwall, NY; *m:* Geraldine Bushnell; *ed:* (AOS) Culinary Arts, Culinary Inst of America 1978; VTE, SUNY; NY St Home Ec Curr Writing Team Mem; *cr:* Pastry Chef Bluebeards Castle Hotel 1978-82; Owner Cookie Factory 1982-84; Instr Cullinary Food Trades 1985-; Owner an Affair to Remember 1990-; Instr Cont Ed OCCC 1990; *ai:* Highland Engine Co No 1 Mem; Head Umpire Maybrook Little League; Food Service Exec Assn (Pres, Jr Branch CIA) 1974-78 Spec Service Citation 1978; NY Bsbl Umpires Assn Inc 1990; Bethleham Rod & Gun Club 1990-; Culinary Inst of America Mentor Prgm 1990; NYSUT Mem, AFT 1985-; *office:* Orange-Ulster B O C E S Sch RD 2 Gibson Rd Goshen NY 10924

BLAINE, SUSAN SCOTT, Mathematics Teacher; *b:* Lexington, VA; *m:* James C.; *ed:* (BSE) Math Ed, 1968, (MED) Math Ed, 1977 Delta St Univ; *cr:* Math Teacher Solomon Jr HS 1968-70, Washington Sch 1970-; *ai:* Jr Beta Club & Chi Alpha Mu Spon; MCTM, NCTM 1968-; MPSEA 1970-; Delta Kappa Gamma 2nd VP 1980-; *office:* Washington Sch 1605 E Reed Rd Greenville MS 38703

BLAIR, ANNA BRUMFIELD, Sixth Grade Teacher; *b:* Wayne, WV; *w:* Kyle (dec); *c:* Steve, Shawn; *ed:* (AB) Elem Ed, 1972, (MA) Ed Admin, 1984 Marshall Univ; Prof Dev; *cr:* Teacher Atenville Elem 1965-; *ai:* Spon 6th Grade Graduation & Prom; Sch Improvement Comm; Phi Delta Kappa; WV Mini Grant 1989; Lincoln Cty Teacher of Month 2 Times; *home:* Rt 1 Box 6 Harts WV 25524

BLAIR, BARBARA ELAINE (BAHL), Second Grade Teacher; *b:* Mansfield, OH; *m:* Thomas L.; *c:* Andrea, Christin; *ed:* (BS) Elem Ed, Miami Univ 1964; Grad Stud; *cr:* 5th Grade Teacher Ashland City Schls 1964-66, Madison Local Schls 1966-67; Kndgtn Teacher 1977-84, 2nd Grade Teacher 1984- Hamilton City Schls; *ai:* Amer Assn of Univ Women 1964-78; Zion Luth Church Mem; *home:* 510 Sanders Dr Hamilton OH 45013

BLAIR, CINDA J., Sixth Grade Teacher; *b:* Kenton, OH; *m:* Charles Evan; *c:* Emily, Jeffrey; *ed:* (BS) Elem Ed, OH St Univ 1980; (MA) Admin Leadership, Wright St Univ 1989; *cr:* 4th Grade Teacher 1968-69, Teacher of Learning Disabilities 1970-72 Indian Lake Schls; 6th Grade Teacher Rivewrside Schls 1980-; *ai:* Safety Patrol Adv; Warm Clothes for Kids Comm; REA (Secy, Treas) 1987-; OEA, NEA; Logan Cty Easter Seals Secy 1974-79; Consumer Ed Grant Awd 1989; *office:* Riverside Schls 101 South St Quincy OH 43343

BLAIR, DORIS STARR, English Teacher; *b:* Williamson, WV; *m:* Michael Emerson; *c:* Michael, Katheranne, Heather, Brian; *ed:* (BA) Scndry Ed/Area Eng, Univ of KY 1974; (AME) Scndry Ed/Eng, Morehead St Univ 1984; *cr:* Substitute Teacher Greenup Cty Schls 1982-84, Russell Ind Schls 1984-85; Eng Dept Chairperson St Joseph HS 1985-; *ai:* Sr Class Adv, Homecoming Ceremonies & Dance, Sr Caps, Gowns, Invitations, Baccalaureate, Commencement, Exercise, Prgms, Sr Dinner, Fund Raising; *home:* 1231 Terry St Raceland KY 41169

BLAIR, JAMES BILLY, Science, Physical Ed Teacher; *b:* Jennings, FL; *m:* Carol Buchanan; *c:* Marsha B. Dukes, James B. Jr., Suzanne, Stephen; *ed:* (BS) Ag/Sci, Berry Coll 1958; (MED) Phys Ed, 1973, (EDS) Phys Ed, 1977 Univ of GA; Teachers Cert, Valdosta St Coll, Summer Sci & Math Inst; *cr:* 7th-10th Grade Sci Teacher Jennings HS 1958-59; US Army 1960-62; 7th-11th Grade Sci/Soc Stud Teacher Jennings HS 1962-65; 3rd-8th Grade Phys Ed Teacher/6th-8th Grade Sci Teacher N Hamilton Elem 1966-; *ai:* Ftbl, Bsktbl, Bsbl & Track Coach; Athletic Dir; FL Ed Assn, Hamilton Cty Ed Assn, FL HS Act Coaching Assn 1962-; PTO; Chamber of Commerce; Advisory Comm Hamilton Cty 4-H 1970-87; FL Sheriffs Assn 1985-; Jennings Meth Church (Sunday Sch Supt 1975-, Chm Bd of Trustees 1982-); *office:* N Hamilton Elem Sch Rt 1 Box 6 Jennings FL 32053

BLAIR, JUDY WILLIS, 1st-6th Grade Music Specialist; *b:* Tucson, AZ; *m:* Donald C. Jr.; *c:* Benjamin, Jonathan, Joshua; *ed:* (BA) Elem Ed/Fine Art, Brigham Young Univ 1971; *cr:* 5th Grade Teacher Litchfield Elem 1971-72, Arrowhead Sch 1972-73; 5th/6th Grade Teacher Ulatis Sch 1973-76; Music Specialist Eugene Padan Elem Sch 1976-; *ai:* Early Bird Chorus Dir; City Wkshp Instr; Private Piano Instr; Eugene Padan PTA Teacher of Yr 1980; *office:* Eugene Padan Elem Sch 200 Padan School Rd Vacaville CA 95687

BLAIR, MARY HELEN PICKERING, Retired Teacher; *b:* Paris, TX; *m:* Richard H.; *c:* Stan; *ed:* (BS) Elem Ed, Baylor Univ 1944; *cr:* 3rd Grade Teacher Mission TX 1944-48; 1st Grade Teacher Waco TX 1948-52; 2nd Grade Teacher Mc Allen TX 1956-82; *ai:* Volunteer at Rio Grande Radiation Center & Mc Allen Public Schls; TX St Teachers Assn, Classroom Teachers Assn, Natl Teachers Assn; Calvary Baptist Church (Sunday Sch Teacher, Prayer Chm); *home:* 1121 Ash Mission TX 78572

BLAIR, ODEMA GAIL, Reading/English Teacher; *b:* Beggs, OK; *m:* Larry Edward; *c:* Melody G.; *ed:* (BSED) Elem Ed/Lang Art/Soc Stud, NE St Univ Tahlequah 1980; *cr:* Rdng/Eng Teacher Wagoner Jr HS 1980-; *ai:* Jr HS Cheerleading Spon; OK Rdng Cncl Mem 1980-; *office:* Wagoner Jr HS 202 N Casaver Ave Wagoner OK 74467

BLAIR, OMIE TIDWELL, Counselor; *b:* Camden, AR; *m:* George Henry; *c:* George K.; *ed:* (BA) Eng, 1973, (MED) Counseling, 1982 Southern AR Univ; Advanced Sch Cnslr Cert; *cr:* Teacher Eng/Span Stephens HS 1973-82; Cnslr Grades 9-12 Fairview HS 1982-; *ai:* Sr Class Spon; Stu Cncl Spon; Chairperson Guidance Dept; Southwest AR Sch Cnslr Assn Pres 1983-84; AR Sch Counselor Assoc Treas 1986; AR Assn of Counseling Treas Guidance & Dev 1987-89; Governors Volunteer Excl Awd 1989; Epsilon Omega Sorority Pres 1980; *home:* Rt 3 Box 40 Stephens AR 71764

BLAIR, RUTH HEDGES, Teacher; *b:* Mason, KY; *m:* William Keith; *c:* Brian K., Betsy A.; *ed:* (BA) Ed, Georgetown Coll 1969; (MS) Ed, N KY Univ 1980; *cr:* Teacher Grant Cty Bd of Ed 1960-73, Campbell Cty Bd of Ed 1977-; *ai:* Campbell Cty Ed Assn, KY Ed Assn, NEA 1977-; First Twelve Mile Baptist Church (Teach Youth Sunday Sch, Dir of Vacation Bible Sch); Alexandria Elem Sch PTA Lifetime Membership; *home:* Rt 1 Box 131 California KY 41007

BLAIR, THOMAS CLARK, Health Education Teacher; *b:* Auburn, NY; *m:* Bonny Jo Williams; *ed:* Korynne, Ryan; (AAS) Liberal Arts, Auburn Comm Coll 1971; (BS) Phys Ed, 1974, (MS) Health Ed, 1981, SUNY Cortland; *cr:* 8th Grade Health Teacher

Auburn Enlarged City Sch Dist 1975-; 12th Grade Health Teacher BOCES 1980-; *ai:* Asst Var Ftbl Coach; Mid Sch SADD; *office:* East Mid Sch 159 Franklin St Auburn NY 13021

BLAIR, WAYNE, Science Teacher; *b:* Jeremiah, KY; *m:* Lettie Jane Wagner; *c:* Teresa L. Kirkman, Tina L., Michael W.; *ed:* (BA) Bio/His/Scndry Ed, Univ of KY 1961; (MS) Sci/Scndry Ed, Ball St Univ 1973; *cr:* Teacher Whitesburg HS 1961-62, Springfield Township Sch 1962-67, Connersville Jr HS 1967-; *ai:* Sch Improvement Comm; AFT; *home:* RR 3 Box 334 Connersville IN 47331

BLAIS, ARMAND, Third Grade Teacher; *b:* Lewiston, ME; *m:* Linda Moore; *c:* Angela; *ed:* (BS) Elem Ed, Univ of ME Farmington 1980; *cr:* Bsbl/Soccer Coach 1983-, Drama Coach/ 3rd Grade Teacher 1980- Wales Cntrl Sch.

BLAIS, DEBORA LYNNE, Teacher; *b:* Los Angeles, CA; *m:* Bradford A.; *c:* Heather; *ed:* (BA) Math, Univ of CA Los Angeles 1977; Credential CA St Univ 1978; (MA) Admin, Azusa Pacific Univ 1990; Accounting, CA St Univ 1978-82; *cr:* Teacher Paul Revere Jr HS 1978-80; Math Teacher Alhambra HS 1980-; *ai:* Boys Fed Adv; CA Schlsp Fed Co-Adv; Ftbl Prgm Faculty Tutor; Math Dept Act Chairperson; CA Model Technology Sch Prgm Mem; CA Math Cncl 1979-89; NCTM 1979-83; *office:* Alhambra HS 101 S 2nd St Alhambra CA 91801

BLAKE, BEVERLY A., Teacher-Librarian; *b:* Blue Island, IL; *m:* Ronald L.; *ed:* (BA) Eng/Ed, Wartburg Coll 1962; (MA) Ed/Lib, Southern IL Univ Edwardsville 1979; *cr:* 10th/11th Grade Eng Teacher Waverly Shell Rock HS 1962-63; 10th/12th Grade Teacher Nokomis HS 1963-73; 9th/11th Grade Eng Teacher Metro-East Luth HS 1978-80; 11th-12th Grade Eng Teacher/ Librarian Maypearl HS 1986-; *ai:* NHS Adv; Frosh Class Spon; UIL Dir; Quality Circle Chm; ATPE Building Rep 1989-; Kappa Delta Pi 1979-; *home:* 1125 Maree Dr Waxahachie TX 75165

BLAKE, DEBRAH F., Social Studies Teacher; *b:* Hattiesburg, MS; *ed:* (BS) Soc Sci, Alcorn St Univ 1974; Elem Ed/Rdng, USM; Spec Ed; *cr:* Commissioned Salesperson Sears Roebuck Co 1975-78; Project Dir SEMCA 1978-79; Teacher Alternative Ed 1980-87; Soc Stud Teacher Earl Trallion Jr HS 1982-; *ai:* Spon Earl Travillion Stu Cncl Past Coord 5-Year Plan for Accreditation; Staff Dev Rep; Peer; Evaluator for MTAL; MAE 1982-; Zeta Phi Beta Pres 1984-; Hattiesburg Boys Club Volunteer Tutorial Prgm; Sweet Pilgrim Baptist Church; Mission Circle 2 Secy 1985-; NAACP Spec Olympics Spon; *home:* 3300 W 7th St #32 Hattiesburg MS 39401

BLAKE, ELLA JANE, 1st Grade Teacher; *b:* Clearfield, PA; *ed:* (BA) Elem Ed, Lock Haven Univ 1971; (MS) Elem Ed, Clarion Univ 1975; *cr:* 2nd/4th Teacher 4th Grade Teacher Glen Richey Sch; 5th Grade Teacher Centre Sch; 1st Grade Teacher Third War D Sch; *ai:* Cmptr Club for 5th Graders Centre Sch; AAUW 1987-; *office:* Clearfield Area Schls PO Box 710 Clearfield PA 16830

BLAKE, TOMI MC CAMPBELL, English Teacher; *b:* America Cty, AL; *m:* Paul Edward; *ed:* (BA) Eng Ed, 1972, (MS) Rdng/ Writing Scndry Level, 1975 Wayne St; *cr:* Eng Teacher Cass Tech HS 1972-; *ai:* Yrbk Spon 1980-84; Outstanding Teacher Awd 1987-89; *office:* Cass Tech HS 2421 Second Ave Detroit MI 48201

BLAKELY, ANNE PRICE, French Teacher/Dept Chair; *b:* Seneca, SC; *m:* Ray Melton; *c:* Keith, Tim, Gretchen; *ed:* (BA) Fr, Furman Univ 1954; Ed, Foreign Lang; *cr:* Fr/Eng Teacher Westminster HS 1954-55, 1957; 8th Grade Teacher USAF Sch Nurnberg Germany 1956; Fr/His Teacher Greer HS 1974-; *ai:* Foreign Lang Dept Chairperson; AATF, SCOL 1985-; *office:* Greer HS 505 N Main St Greer SC 29651

BLAKELY, PAUL EDWARD, Social Studies Dept Chairman; *b:* Selmer, TN; *m:* Betty L. Martin; *c:* Tammy, Ricky, Michael, Thomas, Wendy; *ed:* (BS) His, Union Univ 1979; Ed, Memphis St Univ; *cr:* Medical Technology US Navy 1960-68; Teacher Ramer Elem 1979-80, Mc Nairy Cntrl HS 1980-; *ai:* NHS & Stu Government Assn Adv; *office:* Mc Nairy Cntrl HS Mc Nairy Central Rd Selmer TN 38375

BLAKELY, ROBERT THOMAS, Physics Teacher; *b:* Detroit, MI; *m:* Linda Lee Benke; *c:* Robert L.; *ed:* (BS) Physics, 1972, (MED) Guidance/Counseling, 1981 Wayne St Univ; Grad Stud Physics, Ed; *cr:* Physics Teacher Cntrl HS 1972-75, Osborne HS 1975-80, Martin Luther King HS 1980-; *ai:* JETS Club & GAPP Co-Spon; Star Schls & Labnet Participant; Telecommunications Spon Sci Fair & Sci Olympiad; AAPT Mem 1981-; NSTA Mem 1980-; Woodrow Wilson Fellowship 1989; Dept of Energy Research Grant 1990; Honors Physics Wkshp VA Military Inst 1982; *office:* Martin Luther King HS 3200 E Lafayette Detroit MI 48207

BLAKEMAN, BEVERLY KURTZ, Kindergarten Teacher; *b:* Toledo, OH; *m:* Gary George; *c:* Brian, Kristen; *ed:* (BS) Early Chldhd, Kent St Univ 1973; Working Towards Masters Early Chldhd; *cr:* Substitute Teacher 1973-74, Rdng Specialist 1974-75, 3rd Grade Teacher 1975-82, Kndgtn Teacher 1982- Sylvania Schls; *ai:* Dist Soc Stud Comm Mem; NEA, Sylvania Ed Assn, OH Ed Assn; Olivet Luth Church Chrstn Ed; Childrens Conservation League Past VP 1988; Nom For Sylvania Educator of Yr 1989; *home:* 7630 Grenlock Sylvania OH 43560

BLAKEMORE, E. JANE RUSH, Fourth Grade Teacher; *b:* Springfield, MO; *m:* Ralph W.; *ed:* (BA) Elem Ed, Univ of N CO 1969; Grad Stud Univ of N CO, CO Univ, CSU; *cr:* 4th Grade Teacher Washington Elem 1969-71, Kohl Elem 1972-; *ai:* Odyssey of Mind Judge; Talented & Gifted Stus Identification & Sch Wide Publishing Center Planning Comm; BVEA 1978-; *office:* Kohl Elem Sch 1000 W 10th Broomfield CO 80020

BLAKENEY, DIANA (SCHRODER), Health/Phys Ed Teacher; *b:* Wichita, KS; *m:* James Clifford; *c:* T. J. Clevenger; *ed:* (BS) Health/Phys Ed, SMSU 1982; Health Ed; *cr:* Teacher/Asst Vlbybl Coach Logan-Rogersville HS 1983-; *ai:* Girls Weight Club Spon; Asst Girls Vlybl Coach; Dir of Blood Drive; MSTA 1988-; Amer Alliance for Health/Phys Ed/Recreation/Dance 1989-; MO Assn for Health/Phys Ed/Recreation/Dance 1990; Natl Fed Interschlstc Coaches Assn 1989-; Care Team Pres 1989-; Schl/ Comm Drug Abuse Prevention & Health Advisory Comm 1989-; Dist Scndry Phys Ed Teacher of Yr 1989; *office:* Logan Rogersville H S Rt 4 Box 75 Rogersville MO 65742

BLAKENEY, DOUG B., Gifted/Talented Instructor; *b:* Yazoo City, MS; *m:* Pamela Lee Woodcock; *c:* B. B., Amy; *ed:* (BS) Ed, MS St Univ 1972; (MS) Ed, William Carey Coll 1977; Gifted/ Talented, Univ of S MS; *cr:* Teacher/Coach St John HS 1973-74, Gautier Jr HS 1974-78, Magnolia Jr HS 1978-81, Ocean Springs Schls 1981-; *ai:* Var & Jr Var Cross Cntry, Track & Field, Ftbl Coach; SADD & Athletic ClUb Spon; Sch Bd Faculty Rep; MS Assn Gifted/Talented 1982-, MS Assn Coaches 1973-, Natl Fed Coaches 1981-; Drug Advisory Schls Comms 1987-, Little League 1980-88; MS Economic Cncl STAR Teacher Ocean Springs HS 1988; St Championship Awd Girls Cross Cntry 1986, 1988, 1989; Spec Achievement Awd Dept of Interior 1984; *office:* Ocean Springs Jr HS Government St Ocean Springs MS 39564

BLAKENEY, JO ANNE SELLERS, First Grade Teacher; *b:* Waynesboro, MS; *m:* Cecil; *c:* Alan, Cecilia; *ed:* (AA) Home Ec, Jones Jr Coll 1960; (BS) Home Ec, USM 1962; (MS) Elem Ed, William Cary Coll 1979; Trng Towards Specialist Degree; *cr:* Teacher Beat Four Elem; *ai:* Staff Dev for Teachers; St Jude Research for Children Coord of Math-A-Thon; MS Teacher Assessment Instruments Evaluator.

BLALOCK, DENNIS WARREN, Science Department Chairman; *b:* Danville, VA; *m:* Kathy Lynn Gray; *ed:* (BS) Bio, Averett Coll 1973; (MED) Sci Ed, Univ of VA 1977; *cr:* Teacher Climax Elem 1973-80, Brosville Elem 1980-83, Tunstall HS 1983-, Instr Danville Comm Coll 1988-; *ai:* Pittsylvania Cty Schls Sci Curr Comm Chm; Tunstall HS Sci Club Spon; Tunstall HS Jr Sci Club Co-Spon; Phi Delta Kappa 1990-; VA Regional Governors Sch for Gifted Instr; *office:* Tunstall HS Rt 1 Box 265 Dry Fork VA 24549

BLALOCK, MARJORIE GILLIAM, Mathematics Teacher/ Dept Chm; *b:* Kingport, TN; *m:* C James; *c:* Patrick; *ed:* (BS) Math, Radford Coll 1971; *cr:* Teacher Gate City HS 1971-; *ai:* Sr Class Spon; Academic Bowl Team Spon & Coach; Gifted Coord; Awds Comm Co-Chm; NEA, VA Ed Assn, Scott Cty Ed Assn 1988-; Ruritan 1988-; Teacher of Yr 1985; Teacher of Month 1988; Cty Math Dept Chm; *home:* Rt 1 Box 375 Gate City VA 24251

BLANCATO, PATRICIA CIARLONE, Spanish Teacher; *b:* Waterbury, CT; *m:* Joseph; *c:* Joseph, Jeffrey; *ed:* (BA) Span/ Scndry Ed, 1971, (MS) Bilingual Ed, 1981, Admin/Supervision, 1988 SCSU; *cr:* Span Teacher 1971-, Foreign Lang Chairperson 1980- Sacred Heart HS; *ai:* Stu Cncl Co-Adv; Teaching Learning Comm Chairperson; Faculty Cncl Mem; CT Organization of Lang Teachers; CT Organization Lang Teachers Public Relations Comm; Coord of Foreign Lang CT; Natl Assn Stu Act Adv; Admins & Supvrs Assn of SCSU, NCEA; *office:* Sacred Heart HS 142 S Elm St Waterbury CT 06722

BLANCHARD, BARBARA CHAPLIN, 5th Grade Teacher; *b:* St Louis, MO; *m:* Carl R.; *ed:* (BS) Ed, 1961, (MA) Ed SuperviSion/Admn 1972, Southeast MO St Univ; Teaching Acad; Additional CourSes Beyond MA; Various Wkshps & seminars: *cr:* 5th Grade Teacher Festus Elem 1961-62; 4th Grade Teacher Cape GirardeaU Public Sch 1962-64, Duschesne Elem 1964-66; 1st Grade Teacher Festus Elem 1966-68; 5th Grade Teacher Cape Girardeau Pub Sch 1968-; *ai:* Courtesy Comm; Mentor Teacher; CTA; MSTA; Ramblewood Garden Club Pres 1986-88; Have Submitted Grant for Washington Sch Destination Self Esteem; *home:* Rt 2 Twin Lakes Box A533 Cape Girardeau MO 63701

BLANCHARD, GLENN A., World History Teacher; *b:* Chicago, IL; *m:* Patricia Hamilton; *c:* Richard; *ed:* (AA) His, Brevard Comm Coll 1980; (BS) His, Rollins Coll 1981; *cr:* Teacher De Laura 1982-; *ai:* Stu Cncl; Youth for Christ; Guitar Club; Brain Bowl Team; De Laura Teacher of Yr 1985; *office:* De Laura Jr HS 300 Jackson Ave Satellite Beach FL 32937

BLANCHARD, GREGORY ALLEN, Health Teacher/Coach; *b:* Odessa, TX; *m:* Beverly Anne Bradley; *c:* Brad, Kelli; *ed:* (AA) Mc Lennan Comm Coll 1978; (BS) Ed/Phys Ed, 1980, His, 1985 Baylor Univ; *cr:* His Teacher/Coach Lorena Jr HS 1980-81; His Teacher/Coach 1981-86, Health Teacher/Coach Lorena HS 1986-; *ai:* Ftbl Offense 1st Asst Coach; Head Bsbl; THSBCA 1986-; THSCA 1980-; Career Ladder III Teacher; Dist Bsbl Coach Yr 1984-86; Nom Super Centex Coach 1985-89; *office:* Lorena HS 1 Leopard Ln Lorena TX 76655

BLANCHARD, JANIE MONDAY, 7 Grade Math/Sci/Rdng Teacher; *b:* Richmond, VA; *m:* Norman H.; *c:* Donald, Earl; *ed:* (BS) Elem Ed, Radford Univ 1969; (MED) Elem Ed, Univ of VA 1972; *cr:* 2nd Grade Teacher 1969-70, Nongraded Primary Teacher 1970-71 Valley Elem; 3rd Grade Teacher Brownsville Elem 1971-72; Rdng Asst Lib Henley Hr HS/Murry Elem 1972-73; 7th Grade Teacher Botetourt Intermediate 1990-; *ai:* Math Dept Chairperson Botetourt Intermediate Sch 1983-86; Vice-Chm S Tud Services Comm 1989-; Bath Educl Assn Reporter 1969-71; Botetourt Educl Assn Mem 1980-; VA Educl Assn Mem 1980-; NEA Mem 1980-; Roanoke Valley Rdng Assn Mem 1985-; Blue Ridge Cncl Teachers of Math Mem 1983-; Alpha Delta Kappa Mem 1989-; Buchanan Presbyn Church Mem 1975-; Bd of Dir Fincastle Pre Sch 1976-79; *office:* Botetourt Intermediate Sch Rt 2 Box 41 Fincastle VA 24066

BLANCHARD, M. JOAN, Home Economics Teacher; *b:* Seneca Falls, NY; *m:* James G.; *c:* Gregory; *ed:* (AS) Merchandising, Maria Regina Coll 1978; (BS) Home Ec Ed, Oneonta St Coll 1979; (MSED) Rdng Ed, St Bonaventure Univ 1985; *cr:* Home Ec Teacher Hinsdale Cntrl Sch 1979-82, Romulus Cntrl Sch 1982-87, Mynderse Acad & Seneca Falls Mid Sch 1987-; *ai:* Seneca Falls Mid Sch Stu Cncl Adv; Big Brother/Big Sister Prgm Adv; HETA 1989-; Delta Kappa Gamma Recording Secy 1990; *office:* Mynderse Acad 105 Troy St Seneca Falls NY 13148

BLANCHARD, SANDRA MALETTE, Fourth Grade Teacher; *b:* Nashua, NH; *m:* Glenn R.; *c:* Amy; *ed:* (BA) Elem Ed, Notre Dame Coll 1970; Co-Operative Learning; Hanson-Silver-Strong Teaching Strategies; *cr:* 4th Grade Teacher Memorial Sch 1970-74, Library Street Sch 1974-78; 6th Grade Eng Teacher Memorial Sch 1981-86; 4th Grade Teacher Library Street Sch 1986-89; Dr H O Smith Sch 1989-; *ai:* Research Survey Public Ed Issues St of NH The Becker Inst Inc 1989; Phi Delta Kappa 1987-; ASCD 1988-; AFT Building Rep 1986-88; St John the Evangelist Parrish Cncl 1987-; Memorial Sch PTA 1989-; Outstanding Young Woman of America 1974; Hudson NH Elem Teach of Yr 1974; *office:* Dr H O Smith Sch 33 School St Hudson NH 03051

BLANCHARD, WALTER JOSEPH, English Teacher; *b:* Wakefield, RI; *c:* Jeanne B. Hebert, Norman; *ed:* (AB) Soc Stud, Univ of RI 1955; (MED) Scndry Admin, RI Coll 1964; (PHD) Curr/Supervision, Univ of CT 1974; Cooperative, Economic Ed; Guidance & Counseling; *cr:* Soc Stud/Eng Teacher Warwick Sch Dept 1955-63; Professor RI Coll 1963-86, MST Univ Bangkok Thailand 1986-88; Teacher Providence Public Schls 1988-; *ai:* Sch Newspaper Adv; Ethnic Tensions Comm; RICTE 1988-; PDK 1974-; *home:* 119 Metropolitan Rd Providence RI 02908

BLANCHE, SCOTT ADAM, Mathematics Teacher; *b:* Bradenton, FL; *ed:* (AA) Math Ed, Manatee Jr Coll 1983; (BS) Math Ed, FL St Univ 1985; *cr:* Math Teacher Lincoln HS 1985-; *office:* Lincoln HS 3838 Trojan Trail Tallahassee FL 32301

BLANCHE, TONYA LEWIS, 5th/6th Grade Teacher; *b:* Port Arthur, TX; *m:* Richard Steven; *c:* Cole L.; *ed:* (BA) Elem Ed, NE LA Univ 1977; *cr:* 5th Grade Teacher Tensas Acad 1978-; *ai:* Cosmopolitan Club (Treas 1981-83) 1979-; Tensas Jaycees 1990; *home:* Rt 1 Box 124 C3 Saint Joseph LA 71366

BLANCHETTE, DONALD JAMES, Fourth Grade Teacher; *b:* Houlton, ME; *ed:* (BS) Elem Ed, Univ of Southern ME 1973; *cr:* 4th Grade Teacher Bowdoin St Sch 1974-78; Houlton Elem 1978-; *ai:* Cmptr Comm; Progress Report Comm; *home:* 25 South St Houlton ME 04730

BLANCHETTE, MICHELLE MARIE, Mathematics Teacher; *b:* Kankakee, IL; *ed:* (BS) Phys Ed, CO St Univ 1983; Grad Stud Fr, Math, Sci, CO St Univ; *cr:* Math Teacher/Gymnastic/Vlybl/ Sftbl Coach Bradley-Bourbonnais Cmmty HS 1983-; *ai:* Vlybl Coach 1983-; Sftbl Coach 1984-88; Gymnastic Coach 1983-84; Stu Cncl Spon 1990; NCTM 1990-; Amer Alliance of Health, Phys Ed, Recreation & Dance 1978-88; *office:* Bradley-Bourbonnais Cmmty HS 700 W North St Bradley IL 60915

BLANCO, LINDA SUE, Second Grade Teacher; *b:* Fort Stockton, TX; *m:* Luis; *c:* Adrian, Erinn; *ed:* (BS) Elem Ed, Sul Ross Univ 1977; Addl Studies, Rdng Spec Cert; *cr:* 2nd Grade Teacher Apache Elem 1978-; *ai:* Classroom Teachers Assn 1988-.

BLAND, BESSIE CARR, 8th/9th Grade English Teacher; *b:* Halifax, VA; *m:* Eddie Harold; *c:* Jamala M., Eddie J.; *ed:* (BS) Eng, Elizabeth City St Coll 1966; (MA) Amer Lit, VA St Univ 1981; *cr:* Eng Teacher Queen Anne Cty HS 1966-67, Maxwell Voc HS 1967-68, Southside Comm Coll 1976, Russell Jr HS 1968-; *ai:* Drama Coach; NCTE 1989-; VATE 1988-; NEA, VEA 1968-; NAACP 1968-; Delta Sigma Theta; Jack & Jill of America Inc Ed 1988-; *office:* James Solomon Russell Jr HS Rt 1 Box 239 Lawrenceville VA 23868

BLAND, SARAH BELL, Fifth Grade Teacher; *b:* Gaffney, SC; *m:* Charles; *c:* Barry, Wayne, Helen Bland Gardner, Barbara B. West, Angela; *ed:* (BA) Elem Ed, Columbia Coll 1955; Grad Stud; *cr:* 4th Grade Teacher West End 1955-56; 2nd/3rd Grade Teacher Volusia Cty 1958-78; 6th Grade Teacher 1979-84, 5th Grade Teacher 1985- Cowpens Elem; *ai:* Broome HS Cheerleading Spon; SCEA 1979-; Spartanburg Cty Ed Assn; Volusia Cty Ed Assn 1958-78; NEA; Cowpens Garden Club VP 1985; United Meth Women Secy 1986-.

BLANDFORD, MARK ALAN, Science Department Chairman; *b:* Owensboro, KY; *m:* Tina Jacob; *c:* Megan Renee, Marcia Marie; *ed:* (BS) Elem Ed, Brescia Coll 1982; Elem Ed, Western KY Univ; *cr:* Sci Teacher St Joseph Sch 1982-85, Mary Carrico Meml Sch 1985-; *ai:* Diocese of Owensboro Cath Educators Rep 1984-87; *office:* Mary Carrico Mem Sch 9515 Ky 144 Philpot KY 42366

BLANEY, JAMES MARTIN, JR., Agriculture Teacher; *b:* Beaumont, TX; *m:* Mary Estelle Franklin; *c:* Whitney, Steve; *ed:* (BS) Ag Ed, LA Tech Univ 1978; MS Admin/Supervision, NE LA Univ 1990; *cr:* Ag Teacher Cntrl HS 1979-84, Enterprise HS

1984-; *ai:* FFA Adv; LA Voc Ag Teachers Assn, LA Voc Assn 1985-; Enterprise Booster Club Parliamentarian 1984-89; Enterprise HS Teacher of Yr 1985; *office:* Enterprise HS P O Box 100 Enterprise LA 71425

BLANEY, VIRGINIA BRIGGS, Mathematics Teacher; *b:* Warren, OH; *m:* Clifford Dean; *c:* Lynnette, Bridget; *ed:* (BSED) Math, Kent St Univ 1966; (MSED) Master Teacher Math, Youngstown St Univ; Wrkshp Math/Drug Ed; *cr:* Math Teacher 1966-72, 1976- Mineral Ridge HS; *ai:* Ski Club Spon; Chairperson of Crisis Intervention Team Sch Dist; Mem of Substance Abuse Prevention Comm; Weathersfield Teachers Assn Past Treas & Past Pres; OEA; E OH Cncl of Teachers of Math; Braceville United Meth Church Past Treas; La Brae Bd of Ed VP 1984-; Trumbull Mobile Meals Volunteer; Past Mem of Braceville Mother of CCL; Past Coach of Summer Sftbl; *office:* Mineral Ridge HS 1337 Seaborn St Mineral Ridge OH 44440

BLANK, GAIL L., Fifth Grade Teacher; *b:* Mt Pleasant, PA; *ed:* (BS) Elem Ed, IN Univ of PA 1976; Elem Ed, Spec Ed, IN Univ of PA; *cr:* 5th Grade Teacher 1976-80, 4th Grade Teacher 1980-81 Norvelt Elem Sch; Elem Teacher of Gifted Prgm Mt Pleasant Area Sch Dist 1981-85; 2nd Grade Teacher Donegal Elem Sch 1985-86; 5th Grade Teacher Norvelt Elem Sch 1985-; *ai:* Elem Chorus Pianist; After Sch Cmptr Prgm Instr; Dist Long Range Planning Comm Staff Mem; PSEA, NEA 1976-; Amer Red Cross Volunteer 1983-; *office:* Norvelt Elem Sch RD 1 Mount Pleasant PA 15666

BLANK, RAYMOND HENRY, Mathematics/Computer Teacher; *b:* Englewood, NJ; *m:* Carol Dumas; *c:* Lauren (dec), Alex; *ed:* (BA) His, Boston Coll 1972; (MST) Math, Fitchburg St 1980; *cr:* Math Teacher CAPS Collaborating 1976-77, 1977-79, Narragansett Regional; Math/Cmptr Teacher Merrimack HS 1979-; *ai:* Cmptr Team Adv; Stu Act Comm Chm; NHATM 1988-; *office:* Merrimack HS 38 Mc Elwain St Merrimack NH 03054

BLANKENSHIP, GERALDINE VICKERS, Soc Stud/Lang Art Elem Teacher; *b:* Morrisvale, WV; *m:* W. Lansing (dec); *c:* Anna G. Heinzerling, Jackson L., Joel K.; *ed:* (BA) Elem & Scndry Ed/Soc Sci, Charleston Univ 1958; Advanced Trng Courses; *cr:* 2nd Grade/Jr HS Teacher Wharton Elem & Jr HS 1950-56; 3rd Grade Teacher Van Elem 1956-58; 5th Grade Teacher Riverview Elem 1958-62, Mims Elem 1962-1965; 5th/6th Grade Teacher S Lake Elem 1965-; *ai:* Art for All 6th Grade; Comms for Restructuring S Lakes Curricular & Discipline Plan; NRTA 1983-; NEA, FEA CTA 1958-83; SACS (Soc Stud Comm 1981, Chm 1987-); Soc Stud Teacher of Yr 1988-89; Teacher of Yr 1989-; *home:* 3478 South St Titusville FL 32780

BLANKENSHIP, JOYCE, Second Grade Teacher; *b:* Hazard, KY; *m:* Alex Jr.; *cr:* Teacher Livingston Grade Sch 1962-63, Pinnell Grade Sch 1965-74, Granville Wells Elem 1975-; *ai:* Communications Research, Chrldr; ISTA, NEA Mem 1965-; Delta Kappa Gamma; Outstanding Elem Teacher of America 1974; *home:* 1302 Ashley Dr Lebanon IN 46052

BLANKENSHIP, ROBERT ROY, Eighth Grade Science Teacher; *b:* Cristobal, Panama; *m:* Lori Leigh Mc Clinton; *c:* Bobby, Kristen, Drew, Wesley; *ed:* (BS) Health, Trevecca Nazarene Coll 1976; *cr:* Teacher Donelson Chrstn Acad 1979-83; Cnslr Family Educl Advisory Assn 1983-84; Teacher Cameron Mid Sch 1984-; *ai:* Sci, Lib Comm; Public Broadcasting Service Person; NEA Natl Awd For Advancement of Learning Through Broadcasting; *office:* Cameron Mid Sch 1034 1st Ave S Nashville TN 37210

BLANKS, JOANNE WADE, Social Studies Dept Chairman; *b:* Durham, NC; *m:* James E. Sr.; *ed:* (BA) Liberal Arts/His, NC St Univ 1971; (MAT) Soc Stud, Duke Univ 1976 Teacher Trng; *cr:* Librarian Northern Jr HS 1972-73; 11th & 12th US His Teacher Person SrHS 1973-74; 8th & 9th Social Studies Teacher Northern Jr HS 1974-; *ai:* Stu Cncl Adv; Dept Chairperson Soc Stud; Media Comm; Daughters of Amer Revlution; Amer His Teacher of Yr 1985; Northern Jr HS Young Ed of Yr Nom 1983 & 1985; *office:* Northern Jr H S PO Box 3130 Roxboro NC 27573

BLANNER, DEBORAH ELLEN, Foreign Lang Dept Chair; *b:* Coral Gables, FL; *m:* Robert R.; *c:* Gregory T.; *ed:* (BA) Ger, Univ of S FL Coll of Lang & Lit 1973; *cr:* Ger Teacher Titusville HS 1973-, St Lukes Luth 1989-; *ai:* Ger Club, Ger Honor Society, Homestay Exch Prgm with Germany Spon; St Ger Convention Exec Bd; AATG 1974-, FL Ger Teacher of Yr 1985; FL Assn Teachers of Ger 1974-; Delta Kappa Gamma 1989-; Tri Delta Rush Chm 1971-, Best Pledge 1972; Titusville HS & FL Teacher of Yr; Kathe Wilson Awd; Brevard Cty Outstanding Accomplishments Awds; *home:* 5424 Albert Dr Winter Park FL 32790

BLANTON, ANNALENE SPENCER, Social Studies Teacher; *b:* Stanton, KY; *m:* Jimmie R.; *ed:* (BS) Elem Ed, 1964, (Rank II) Elem Ed, 1975 Eastern KY Univ; (Rank I) 1981; *cr:* Elem Teacher Stanton Elem 1955-57, Prater-Borders Elem 1957-67, Bowden Elem 1968-76; Family Horizon Prgm Dir Alice Lloyd Coll 1965-66; Mid Sch Teacher Powell Cty Mid Sch 1976-; *ai:* Powell Cty Mid Sch Building Rep; Academic Coach; Soc Stud Curr, Powell Cty Mid Sch Educl Fnd Advisory Comms; Powell Cty Ed Assn; KY Ed Assn; NEA; ASCD 1988-; KY Colonel; Whos Who in Amer Ed; *office:* Powell Cty Mid Sch 770 W College Ave PO Box 400 Stanton KY 40380

BLANTON, MARY BROWN, Kindergarten Teacher; *b:* Demoplis, AL; *m:* Henry J. Sr.; *c:* Patricia Mc Curdy, Henry Jr., Kenneth, Adrian; *ed:* Bus Admin Lawson St; *cr:* Teacher & Dir Macedonia 17th St No; Teacher Harriman Park; Teacher & Dir Establish My Own Bus; *ai:* United Usher Bd Sec 1989; Choir VP 1990; Deaconess Bd 1986.

BLANTON, SALLY STROUD, Kindergarten Teacher; *b:* Rutherford County, NC; *m:* Weldon Percell; *c:* Michael, Christopher; *ed:* (BS) Early Chldhd Ed, 1988, (MS) Early Chlhd Ed, Gardner Webb Coll; *cr:* 7th & 8th Grade Asst Teacher New Hope Sch 1983-88; Kndgtn Teacher Forest City Elem Sch 1988-; *ai:* Early Chlhd Schlsp Phi Theta Kappa; *office:* Forest City Elem Sch Caroleen Rd Forest City NC 28043

BLASCH, BARBARA RENK, Learning Disabilities Teacher; *b:* Winona, MN; *m:* Bruce B.; *c:* Erik, Ian, Kyle; *ed:* (BS) Elem Ed, 1962, (MS) Ed/Rdng, 1964 N IL Univ; (MA) Elem Ed, W MI Univ 1967; (MA) Spec Ed, Univ of WI 1979; Cooperative Learning & Mentor Wkshp; *cr:* 1st/2nd Grade Teacher Elk Grove Village Public Schls 1962-64; 1st Grade Teacher Granite Public Schls 1964-66; 2nd/3rd Grade Teacher Kalamazoo City Schls 1966-67; 1st-3rd Grade Teacher Lansing City Schls 1967-69; 2nd/3rd Grade Teacher Irwin Public Schls 1969-70; Dir On We Go Nursery Sch 1973-76; Elem Teacher of Learning Disabilities Beloit City Schls 1979-86; Teacher of Learning Disabilities Gwinnett Cty Public Schls 1986-; *ai:* Future Problem Solving St Evaluator; Odyssey of Mind Coach; NEA, CEC; Gwinnette Cty Assn of Ed Secy 1989-; Evangelical Luth Church Peacemaking Network; All Saints Luth Church Cncl Mem; Assistantship to Pursue Grad Work N IL Univ; *home:* 456 Angie Way Lilburn GA 30247

BLASCO, JOHN S., Teacher; *b:* Detroit, MI; *m:* Patricia S.; *c:* John M., Vicky A., Andrew J.; *ed:* (BA) His, Detroit Ins Tech 1967; (MA) Scndry Curr, 1969, Cert Scndry Curr, 1969 Eastern MI Univ; *cr:* Teacher Highland Park Schls 1969-89; *ai:* Phi Delta Kappa 1982-89; *office:* Ferris Schl 60 Cortland Highland Park MI 48203

BLASINGAME, ROSEMARY CHRISTELLO, Earth Science Teacher; *b:* Ft Smith, AR; *m:* Billy E.; *c:* Angela, Larry, Francie; *ed:* (AA) Phys Ed, Westark Comm Coll 1964; (BSE) Phys Ed/Bio, Univ of Cntrl AR 1966; *cr:* Sci/Phys Ed Teacher Stuttgart Jr HS 1966-70; Sci Teacher Lonoke Jr HS 1971-73, Annie Camp Jr HS & Jonesboro Jr HS 1973; Earth Sci/Phys Ed Teacher Van Buren Jr HS 1974-83; Earth Sci Teacher Alma Mid Sch & HS 1983-; *ai:* Sci Fair Comm; Chrldr Spon; AR Mid Sch Assn 1989-; Kappa Kappa Iota (Treas 1986-88) 1985-; AR St Sci Assn 1988-; *office:* Alma Mid Sch PO Box 2229 Alma AR 72921

BLASKO, CAROL ANN, 6th Grade Teacher; *b:* Brooklyn, NY; *m:* John; *c:* Dana, Christopher; *ed:* (BS) Elem Ed, St Univ of NY Cortland 1972; (MS) Ed, Adelphi Univ 1975; Grad Stud; *cr:* 4th Grade Teacher 1972-74, 5th Grade Teacher 1976-80 Cayuga Sch; 6th Grade Teacher Waverly Avenue Sch 1981-; *ai:* St Jude Childrens Research Hospital Project Sch Coord; AFT AFL-CIO, NY St United Teachers, Sachem Cntrl Teachers Assn 1972-; PTA 1972-; *office:* Waverly Avenue Sch 1111 Waverly Ave Holtsville NY 11742

BLASTENBREI, SHERRY LYNN (EARLY), Spanish/English Teacher; *b:* Litchfield, IL; *m:* Robert H. Jr.; *c:* Jeremy, Robert III, Todd; *ed:* (BA) Span Ed, Greenville Coll 1976; *cr:* Span/Eng Teacher Livingston HS 1976-77; Jr HS Eng Teacher Granite City Jr HS 1977-78; Span/Eng Teacher Witt HS 1978-79, Steeleville HS 1979-80; Office/Accounts Receivable Mgr Gelco Truck Leasing 1980-87; Span/Eng Teacher Livingston HS 1987-; *ai:* Newspaper & Class Spon; NCTE, Foreign Lang Teachers of America 1988-; AFT 1987-; Evangelical Luth Church Women Local Nominating Comm 1990; *office:* Livingston H S SAR 3 Box 400 Livingston IL 62058

BLASTICK, PHYLLIS JANE, 2nd Grade Teacher; *b:* Gary, IN; *m:* Wade Martin; *c:* Robin Clements, Kimberly Opasinski, Brad; *ed:* (BS) Ed, 1972, (MS) Ed, 1975 IN Univ; Grad Stud; *cr:* Rdng Teacher Valparaiso Cmmty Schls 1969-71; 3rd Grade Teacher 1972-80, 2nd Grade Teacher 1980- Thomas Jefferson Elem; *ai:* Facilitator Building Based Team; Valparaiso Teachers Assn Negotiation & Steering Comm; IN St Teacher Assn, Valparaiso Teacher Assn Rep at Large, Intnl Rdng Assn Bd Mem; Kappa Kappa Kappa Cor Secy 1979-; Church Cncl; Delta Kappa Gamma 1986-; Ed Honorary; *office:* Thomas Jefferson Elem Sch 1700 Roosevelt Rd Valparaiso IN 46383

BLATHERWICK, CHARLES A., 9th Grade Science Teacher; *b:* Pratt, KS; *m:* Carol L. Meline; *c:* Chad, Adam, Luke, Joy; *ed:* (BA) Bio, Monmouth Coll 1967; (MA) Population Genetics, Wesleyan Univ 1969; Teaching Cert, Glassboro St Coll 1972-73; Working Towards PHD in Molecular Genetics, Rutgers St Univ 1969-71; *cr:* 9th Grade Sci Teacher Edgewood Regional Jr HS 1972-; *ai:* Wood Carving Club Adv; Jr HS Wrestling Team Coach; Winslow Township Park Commission 1990; Ward Fnd 1987-; *office:* Edgewood Regional Jr HS 200 Coopers Folly Rd Atco NJ 08004

BLATT, HILLA GUZDER, Dept Chair/English Teacher; *b:* Bombay, India; *m:* George Marcle; *c:* Brian; *ed:* (BA) Eng, SUNY 1971; (MSED) Ed, Univ of S CA 1974; Critical Thinking & Strategies; *cr:* Teacher Noble Sch 1971-72; Teacher 1977-, Dept Coord 1985- Francis Howell HS; *ai:* Undergrad Work Full Schlsp; Excl in Ed 1986; Outstanding Teacher 1985; Outstanding Dept Coord 1987; *office:* Francis Howell HS 7001 Hwy 94 S Saint Charles MO 63303

BLAU, ARTHUR DAVID, Guidance Counselor/Coll Adv; *b:* Brooklyn, NY; *m:* Beth Virginia Garretson; *c:* Matthew, Jennifer; *ed:* (BA) Music, 1968, (MA) Music, 1970 Brooklyn Coll; (MA) Ed Admin, NY Univ 1974; (MS) Counseling, St Johns Univ 1986; Mannes Coll of Music, Manhattan Sch of Music, Queens Coll; *cr:* Music Teacher Mark Twain Jr HS 1968-69, James Madison HS 1969-75; Music Dir Chelsea HS 1975-86; Cnslr Prospect Heights HS 1986-; *ai:* Coll Office; Natl Assn Coll Admissions Cnslrs 1989-; NY Assn for Counseling & Dev 1986-; Temple Emmanuel 1978-; *office:* Prospect Heights HS 883 Classon Avenue Brooklyn NY 11225

BLAU, BEATRICE BRAININ, Retired 8th Grade Teacher; *b:* New York City, NY; *m:* Sidney; *c:* Eric M., Cathy E. Blau Betts; *ed:* (BA) Ed/Liberal Art, Brooklyn Coll 1942; (MA) Pupil Personnel Services, CA St Univ Sacramento 1978; *cr:* Cnslr 1986, Teacher 1966- Winston Churchill Intermediate; *ai:* Sacramento Area Cncl for Soc Stud Mem 1976-86, Outstanding Contribution to Soc Stud 1979; NEA, SJTA, CTA Mem 1966-86; Assembly of Bahais Awd-Outstanding Humanitarian Contributions in Ed; *home:* 1421 El Tejon Way Sacramento CA 95864

BLAUT, CONNIE MARLENE (COPE), Second Grade Teacher; *b:* Amarillo, TX; *m:* Dale Arthur; *c:* Cassie D., Brandon S.; *ed:* (BS) Elem Ed, W TX St Univ 1972; *cr:* Music Teacher Green Acres Elem 1972-73; 4th Grade Teacher Sunray Elem 1974-77; 2nd Grade Teacher Channing Elem 1977-; *ai:* Channing Sch Improvement Plannig Comm; 1st Baptist Church (Nominating Comm 1988-89, Organist 1982-89); *home:* Box 102 Channing TX 79018

BLAXTON, DARYL LEE, Mathematics Teacher; *b:* Harrisburg, AR; *m:* Patricia Evelyn Bell; *c:* Tyler L.; *ed:* (BSE) Math, AR St Univ 1983; Coaching Endorsement, AR St Univ; *cr:* Math Teacher/Coach Highland HS 1983-; *ai:* Girls Bsktbl Head Coach; Natl Fed Coaches Assn, AR HS Coaches Assn; Coach of Yr 1986, 1987; All St AR Coach Nom 1988, 1989; *office:* Highland HS PO Box 419 Hardy AR 72542

BLAZ, STAN L., Principal Intern; *b:* Anaconda, MT; *ed:* (BA) Elem Ed, 1972, (MA) Ed, 1979 Western MT Coll; Elem Rdng Endorsement; *cr:* Elem Teacher Dwyer Elem 1972-73, West Elem 1973-85, Lincoln 1985-89; Prin Intern Dwyer Elem 1989-; *ai:* HS Swim Coach 1981-82; HS GAA Spon 1982-; NAESP 1990; MFT, AFT All Offices 1978-88; Croatian Fraternal Union (Treas 1972-, Natl Office 1979-); Head Start Policy Bd (Pres, VP) 1982-; City/Cty Commissioner Dist 3 1982-; Outstanding Young Man Awd 1979; Ellected Advisory Cncl Dist 3 1979-82; *office:* Dwyer Elem Sch 1510 W Parl St Anaconda MT 59711

BLAZER, DOLORES H., Kindergarten Teacher; *b:* Ft Benning, GA; *m:* Bill; *c:* April, Laura, Clay; *ed:* (BS) Elem Ed, 1977, (MS) Supervision/Admin, 1985 E TN St Univ; *cr:* Kndgtn Teacher Parrottsville Elem Sch 1977-; *ai:* Boys Bsktbl Asst Coach; TN Ed Assn, NEA; *home:* Rt 2 Box 130 Parrottsville TN 37843

BLEDSOC, ROBERT TROY, Math Teacher; *b:* Warren, AR; *ed:* (BA) Phys Ed, 1975, (MA) Ed, 1981 Western St Coll; *cr:* Math Teacher Arriba HS 1975-79, Castle Rock Jr HS 1979-83, Rampart HS 1983-84, Northeast Jr HS 1984-87, Erie HS 1987-; *ai:* Girls Bsktbl & Track Head, Asst Ftbl; *office:* Erie Jr Sr H S 650 Main St Erie CO 80516

BLEDSOE, D. COLEEN MURRAY, Fifth Grade Teacher; *b:* Mancos, CO; *m:* Bert E.; *c:* Debbie Purton, Melanie Lawson; *ed:* (BS) Elem Ed, 1972, (ME) Elem Ed, East Cntrl Univ 1975; Staff Dev; *cr:* 3rd Grade Teacher Irving Elem 1971-72; 5th Grade Teacher Willard Elem 1972-; *ai:* Principals Adv Bd; Ada Ed Assn; Exec Comm; Asst Prin; Co-Spon Spelling Bee; Teacher Ed Advisory Cncl of ECU; OEA 1972-; NEA 1972-; AEA (VP 1980-82/Sec 1979-80); Kappa Kappa Iota Pres 1986-87; Grant Unit on Space 1988; Teacher of Yr Nom; Nom By Prin for Elem Math Teacher in OK 1984; Natl Sci Fnd G Rant-Earth Sci; *office:* Willard Elem Sch 817 E 9th Ada OK 74820

BLEDSOE, IONE ALLGOOD, Fifth Grade Teacher; *b:* Indian Creek, TX; *w:* Milton Lewis (dec); *c:* Ray, Gary; *ed:* (BS) Elem Ed, 1959, (MA) Elem Ed, 1970 Howard Payne; Preservation of Amer Freedoms St Francis Coll; Spec Ed, Angelo St, A&M Univ, Sul Ross; Poly & Phys Geography, Univ of TX; *cr:* 5th/6th Grade Teacher Early Elem Sch 1959-; *ai:* Jr HS Bsktbl Coach 1960-75; TSTA (Local Secy, Pres); ATPE; Valley Forge Classroom Teachers Medal 1963; Teacher of Yr 1989.

BLEDSOE, JUDY ROWLAND, Vocational Guidance Counselor; *b:* Bruceton, TN; *m:* Jackie R.; *c:* Christopher B.; *ed:* (BS) Eng/Sociology, 1976, (MS) Guidance/Counseling, 1989 Austin Peay St Univ; *cr:* Eng Teacher Charlotte Jr HS 1976-89; Voc Guidance Cnslr Dickson Cty Sr HS 1989-; *ai:* TN Comprehensive Career Dev Prgm, Dickson Sr HS Stu Asst Team Mem; Dickson Cty Ed Assn, TN Ed Assn, NEA 1976-; Kappa Delta Schlsp Chm 1975-76, Schlsp Awd 1976; Phi Kappa Phi 1988-; Eastside Baptist Church 1984-; Dickson Bus & Prof Womens Club Outstanding Teacher of Day 1977; Journal Article Published 1990; *home:* 1077 Hickman Rd Bon Aqua TN 37025

BLEDSOE, MARILYN WEAVER, Math Dept Chairperson/Teacher; *b:* Jefferson, NC; *m:* William Carlyle; *c:* Mark, Danny, Betty Meikle; *ed:* (BS) Home Ec, Berea Coll 1954; (BS) Elem Ed, Appalachian St Univ 1971; *cr:* 6th Grade Teacher Jefferson Elem Sch 1967-68; Sci Teacher Haw Creek Sch 1968-71; 6th/7th/8th Grade Math Teacher East Yancey Mid Sch 1971-89; *ai:* Stu Cncl Adv; NCAE Rep; Math Counts, Sci Fair Coach; NC Assn

Educators Secy 1976-77; NC Cncl Teachers of Math 1975-89; *office:* East Yancey M S Burnsville NC 28714

BLEDSOE, MARY JO, English Teacher; *b:* Moultrie, GA; *m:* James Moten; *c:* Rock N., Meri R.; *ed:* (BS) Ed, 1959, (MS) Ed, 1989 Valdosta St Coll; *cr:* Eng Teacher Norman Park HS 1959-61; 6th Grade Teacher Okapilco 1961-64; 8th Grade Teacher Moultrie Jr HS 1965-71; 4th-6th Grade Teacher Pineland Sch 1971-83; 8th Grade Eng Teacher Colquitt Cty Jr HS 1983-; *ai:* SGA Spon; 4-H Club Adv; NEA, GAE 1959-71; PAGE 1983-; SEALS 1971-83; Delta Kappa Gamma Secy 1971-; 4-H Volunteer 15 Yr Awd; *home:* 1335 4th St SW Moultrie GA 31768

BLEHM, SHIRLEY R. (SETTLES), English Teacher; *b:* Scotts Bluff, NE; *m:* E. Larry; *c:* E. Scot, Kristen; *ed:* (BS) Eng, Univ of NE Lincoln 1973; PEER-Character Ed Spec Trng; SAT Trng; Grad Work Ed; *cr:* Eng/Publications/Rdng Teacher 1974-, Stu Cncl Adv 1978- Mitchell HS; *ai:* Yrbk; Stu Cncl; SAT Team; N Cntrl Steering Comm Co-Chm; Dist 31 Leadership Team for OBE; After Prom Act Comm; MEA Public Relations, NSEA, NEA; United Meth Church (Church Cncl, Youth Dir, Lifetime Mem) 1980-; Mitchell HS Band Parents Pres 1978-; Public Lib (Bd Mem, Officer); Area Cncl Help for Teens; Sch Correspondent Local Paper; Cmmty Volunteer Work; *office:* Mitchell HS 1819 19th Ave Mitchell NE 69357

BLEIBTREY, KAREN ANN PRONOVOST, Summer Program Director; *b:* Billings, MT; *m:* James Edmond; *c:* Chase, Vanessa, Sunni; *ed:* (BA) His, Univ of MT 1977; Grad Stud, Univ of MT, MT St, & W MT Coll; *cr:* Chapter I Teacher 1978-79, 5th Grade Teacher 1979-86, Gifted/Talented Prgm Dir/Teacher 1986-87 Corvallis Elem; Summer Prgm Dir Evergreen Kids Corner 1988-; *ai:* Fund Raising Comm, New Prgm Dev Comm, Hiring Teacher Comm Evergreen Kids Corner; Evergreen Kids Corner (Pres 1988-89, Secy 1987-88); *home:* 2813 White Ln Victor MT 59875

BLENDERMAN, JOSEPH E., Drawing/Painting Teacher; *b:* Sioux City, IA; *m:* Elizabeth K.; *c:* Jennie R., Rod M.; *ed:* (BA) Fine Arts, Wayne St Teachers Coll 1960; (MA) Art Ed, CA St Univ Long Beach 1979; Watercolor Painting Wkshps; *cr:* Art Teacher Horace Mann Jr HS 1961-63, Lindbergh Jr HS 1963-71, Marshall Jr HS 1971-73, Millikan HS 1973-77, Hoover Jr HS 1977-86, Millikan HS 1986-; *ai:* Art Dept Head; Art Society Stu Club Spon; Teachers Assn Long Back; CA Teachers Assn; NEA; Art-A-Fair Festival Laguna Beach Bd of Dir 1983-88.

BLENNER, PEGGY DEWANE, Jr H S Language Arts Teacher; *b:* Harvard, IL; *m:* Tom; *ed:* (BS) Elem Ed, IL St Univ 1978; (MS) Rdng, Northern IL Univ 1983; *cr:* Lang Art Teacher, Simmons Jr H S 1978-79; 5th Grade Teacher, Christ The King Sch1979-80; Lang Art Teacher, Keller Jr H S, Dist 54 1980-85; Lang Art Teacher, Addanis Jr H S 1985-; *ai:* Intnl Rdng Assoc; *office:* Jane Addams Jr H S 700 Springinsguth Rd Schaumburg IL 60193

BLESSING, DELORES ELAINE, Secondary English Teacher; *b:* Mc Alester, OK; *w:* David W. (dec); *c:* Greg, Shana Blessing Olinger, Shelly; *ed:* (BA) Lang Art/Lib Sci, E Cntrl Univ 1984; *cr:* Librarian/12th Grade Eng Teacher Haileyville 1984-85; 7th-10th Eng Teacher Indianola 1986-; *ai:* Soph Class Spon; *office:* Indianola Sch P O Box G Indianola OK 74442

BLESSING, LEWIS HAROLD, Mathematics Teacher; *b:* Forrest City, AR; *m:* Marian Colette Letourneau; *c:* Lewis K., Collette M.; *ed:* (MS) Sch Admin, FL Intnl Univ 1975; *cr:* Teacher Village Green Elem Sch 1970-74; Area Support Teacher SW Area Dade Cty Schls 1974-75; Teacher Kendale Lakes Elem Sch 1975-; *ai:* Dept & Faculty Cncl Chairperson; W Kendall Optomist Bsktbl Coach; United Teachers of Dade Faculty Rep 1982-, Frosh Steward Awd 1982; *office:* Kendale Lakes Elem Sch 8000 SW 142nd Ave Miami FL 33183

BLESSING, STEPHEN WAYNE, Mathematics Department Chair; *b:* Shelbyville, TN; *ed:* (BS) Math, 1984, (MS) Math, 1987 Mid TN St Univ; *cr:* Grad Teaching Asst 1984-85, Adjunct Teacher 1988-89 Mid TN St Univ; Teacher Cntrl HS 1985-; *ai:* Asst Band Dir; NCTM 1990; Mid TN Math Teachers 1985-89; Mid TN St Band & Orch Assn 1985-; *office:* Central HS 2001 Mc Arthur Dr Manchester TN 37355

BLESSINGER, TIMOTHY L., Language Art Teacher; *ed:* (BS) Scndry Ed, St Bernard Coll 1975; (MS) Eng/Phys Ed/Health, IN St Univ 1980; Grad Stud Univ of S IN & IN Univ; *cr:* Lang Art Teacher Heritage Hills HS 1975-; *ai:* Yrbk Adv; NEA 1975-; NCTE 1985-; IN Cncl Teachers of Eng 1980-; N Spencer Rdng Cncl Pres 1975-; *office:* Heritage Hills HS Box 317 Lincoln City IN 47552

BLEVINS, ANDREA ELIZABETH, Social Studies/English Teacher; *b:* Colorado Springs, CO; *m:* Bobby Eldon; *ed:* (BA) Poly Sci, 1966, (MA) Poly Sci, 1969 WA St Univ; Ed, West GA Coll; *cr:* Teacher Pointe South Jr HS 1982-; *ai:* Yrbk Adv; Swim Team Coach; Sch Publications Newsletter; NCTE, NCSS, Prof Assn of GA Educators, Pi Sigma Alpha; Educator of Month 1990; *office:* Pointe South Mid Sch 626 Flint River Rd Jonesboro GA 30236

BLEVINS, BETTY HENLEY, 6th Grade Teacher; *b:* Montrose, AR; *d:* Ray; *c:* Tambra J. Blevins Phillips, Karen A. Blevins Ford; *ed:* (BA) Elem Ed, Univ of AR Monticello 1981; Grad Work Univ of AR Little Rock; *cr:* 7th/8th/9th Grade Developmental Rdng Teacher Delta Spec HS 1981-84; 4tH/5th/6th Grade Health/Sci Teacher 1984-87, 6th Grade Self-Contained Teacher 1987- Delta Spec Elem; *ai:* AEA; Kelso Baptist Church (Sunday Sch Adult Teacher 1976-78, 4 & 5 Yr Old Teacher 1963-76).

BLEVINS, BETTY JENNINGS, Chapter I Mathematics Teacher; *b:* North Tazewell, VA; *c:* Elizabeth, Keith; *ed:* (BS) Elem Ed, Radford Univ 1973; *cr:* Chapter I Math Teacher Graham Intermediate 1974-80; 4th Grade Teacher Rivermont Elem 1980-85; Chapter I Math Teacher N Tazewell Elem 1985-; *home:* Rt 4 Box 123 A North Tazewell VA 24630

BLEVINS, BRENDA SHELTON, English & Reading Teacher; *b:* West Hamlin, WV; *m:* Donald Floyd; *c:* Stephanie, Michael; *ed:* (AA) Elem Ed, Ashland Comm Coll 1969; (BA) Elem Ed, 1971, (MA) Remedial Rdng, 1974 Morehead St Univ; Elem Prin; Creative Writing, 1st KY Writing Institute; *cr:* Elem Teacher 1971-, 4th Grade Teacher 1971-82, Split Levels Teacher 1982-84, 3rd Grade Teacher 1984-88, 5th Grade Teacher 1988- Fairview Ind Schls; *ai:* Lang Arts Fair Coord/Chm Philosophy Comm; Academic Coach Governors Cu P; Chm Spelling Bee; Ladies Fellowship Group; Substitute Coach Girls Sftbl Team; Score Keeper Little League Bsbl; Lineman Cty Soccer League; Sci Fair Coord; Fairview Ed Assn (Secy 1975-77 Pres 1982-84 Building Rep 1984-87); Raceland Boosters Club Historian 1986-88; Racelands Womans Club 1989-; Prgm Dir PTA; Spon Elem Sch Newspaper; Ashland Jaycees Outstanding Young Educator; Grant Economic Cncl Better Ed; KY Colonel Commonwealth Institute Teachers; *office:* Fairview Ind Schls 2100 Main St Ashland KY 41101

BLEVINS, CYNTHIA ANN SMITH, Social Studies Teacher; *b:* Charleston, WV; *m:* William Aaron; *ed:* (BS) Poly Sci, 1972, (BS) His, 1972 Radford Univ; Grad Work WV Coll; *cr:* Teacher Rhodell Elem 1972-74, Bradley Elem 1974-86; Attendance Dir/ Teacher Beckley Jr HS 1986-; *ai:* Secy Beckley Jr HS; SPTO; Academic Awds Chm; Faculty Advisory Cncl Mem; Delta Kappa Gamma 1987-; WV Ed Assn Building Rep 1986-; Presbyn Church Supper Circle 1986-; Raleigh Cty Teacher of Yr Finalist 1988; Raleigh Cty Delegate WV Teachers Forum 1988; Raleigh Cty Rep Hum Fnd Wkshp Constitution 1987; *office:* Beckley Jr HS 320 S Kanawha St Beckley WV 25801

BLEVINS, FRANCES MUSOLIN, Mathematics Teacher; *b:* Bluefield, WV; *m:* James Robert; *c:* Mary F., Sarah E.; *ed:* (BSED) Math, Concord Coll 1974; (MA) Math, WV Univ 1977; Math Ed, WV Univ & Marshall Univ; *cr:* Fr Teacher 1974-75, Math Teacher 1975-78 Welch HS; Math Teacher Bluefield HS 1978-; *ai:* Various Clubs Spon; Math Field Day Helper; Faculty Advisroy Comm; Math Tutor; Cooperating Teacher; WVEA, NEA Mem 1974-; Certificate of Merit for Teaching 1987; *office:* Bluefield HS Cumberland Rd Bluefield WV 24701

BLEVINS, JAMES RAYMOND, Business Education Teacher; *b:* Athens, TN; *m:* Sheila Guess; *c:* James R. Jr.; *ed:* (BS) Bus Ed Ec, Auburn Univ 1967; *cr:* Teacher/Coach Madison Cty AL System 1968-71, Jackson Cty AL System 1979-; *ai:* 10th Grade Class Spon; NEA, AL Ed Assn; Jackson Cty Ed Assn Faculty Rep 1989-; *home:* 200 Grove St Stevenson AL 35772

BLEVINS, MAXINE WEAVER, Sixth Grade Teacher; *b:* Grassy Creek, NC; *m:* Garner; *c:* John; *ed:* (BS) Elem Ed, Appalachian St Univ 1960; *cr:* 5th Grade Teacher Jesse Wharton Elem 1960-62; 4th Grade Teacher 1966-80, 6th Grade Teacher 1980- Jefferson Elem; *ai:* NCAE Building Rep; NEA Building Rep 1960-; Fletcher Memorial Baptist Church; Fnd Grant Awarded by Ashe Cty Ed Fnd Incorporated 1989; Ashe Cty Teacher of Yr 1989-; *home:* 107 Cherry Hill Ridge Jefferson NC 28640

BLEVINS, RHONDA HESS, Health & Physical Ed Teacher; *b:* Richlands, VA; *m:* Rickie Lee; *ed:* (AA) Ed, SVCC 1978; (BS) Health/Phys Ed, ETSU 1980; CPR Instr; *cr:* 8th Grade Health/ Phys Ed Teacher Richlands Mid Sch 1980-; *ai:* Intramurals; *home:* Rt 2 Box 414 Cedar Bluff VA 24609

BLEVINS, RICHARD LINDLE, Health Teacher/Bsktbl Coach; *b:* Batesville, AR; *m:* Carolyn Trivitt; *c:* Brooks, Kermit; *ed:* (BSE) Phys Ed, Univ of the Ozarks 1971; *cr:* Coach Violet Hill HS 1971-84, Mt Pleasant HS 1984-; *ai:* Coaching Girls Bsktbl, HS & Elem; AR Coachs Assn; Fairview Baptist Church; Class B Boys Bsktbl St Champions Coach 1983; 2-B Cntrl Dist Coach of Yr 1983, 1985, 1988-1989; *office:* Mt Pleasant HS Bluebird Ave Mount Pleasant AR 72561

BLEVINS, RICKIE LEE, Biology Teacher; *b:* Marion, VA; *m:* Rhonda Hess; *ed:* (BA) Bio, Emory & Henry Coll 1980; *cr:* Bio/ Human Anatomy Teacher Richlands HS 1980-; *ai:* Jr Class Co-Spon; Fellowship of Chrstn Athletes; Calvary Baptist Church Youth Dir 1980-88; Ratliff Chapel Baptist Church Pastor 1988-; Natl Fed of St HS Assn Outstanding Coach; VA HS Coaches Assn Victory Milestone of 50 & 100; *office:* Richlands HS Rt 460 Richlands VA 24641

BLEVINS, SHAUNE DALLETT, Director/Owner; *b:* West Point, NY; *m:* Dennis Edward; *c:* Anna E.; *ed:* (BA) Eng, 1973, (MS) Elem Ed, 1978 Univ of TN; *cr:* 7th Grade Eng Teacher Sweetwater Jr HS 1973-75; 3rd Grade Teacher Ridgeview Elem Sch 1975-78; 5th Grade Teacher Kingston Elem Sch 1978-87; Pres Educl Services Inc 1984-; Dir/Owner The Primer Sch 1988-; *ai:* Sweetwater Ed Assn Publicity Chm 1975; Roane Cty Textbook Comm Chm 1977-78; Roane Cty 3rd Grade Curr Comm Chm 1977; NEA, TN Ed Assn Mem 1974-81; Natl Assn for Ed of Young Child Mem 1988-; Chamber of Commerce Mem 1988-; Jaycee Primary Teacher of Yr Awd 1983; TN Republican Teachers St Chm 1985-87; Pizza Hut Appreciation Awd 1986; Delta Kappa Gamma 1980-83; *office:* The Primer Sch 310 N Kentucky St Kingston TN 37763

BLEVINS, SUSAN LOWE, Math Teacher; *b:* Norfolk, VA; *m:* Carl Thomas; *c:* Jonathan, Eric; *ed:* (BA) Math Ed, VPI & SU 1974; Curr & Dev; *cr:* Math Teacher Webber Township HS 1985-; Math Instructor Rend Lake Comm Coll 1978-79; Math/Sci Lynch HS 1975-76; *ai:* Spon Jr Class; Tutor Stud after School-Math; PTO Secy 1988-89; Pewee Bsbl 1987-89; Bluford Planning Secy Bd 1979-80; *office:* Webber Township H S S Elm Bluford IL 62814

BLICKENSTAFF, NANCY (GREENLEE), Language Art Teacher; *b:* Scott City, KS; *m:* Steven J.; *c:* Julie, Lisa; *ed:* (BA) Eng, St Mary of Plains Coll 1987; *cr:* Teacher Garden City Sr HS 1988-; *ai:* NHS Spon; NCTE 1987-; *office:* Garden City HS 1412 N Main Garden City KS 67846

BLIELER, STEVEN MARK, Mathematics Department Chair; *b:* Fremont, MI; *m:* Mary Lynn Fowler; *c:* Mark R., Melanie J., Mindy J., Matthew W.; *ed:* (BS) Math, Ferris St Univ 1970; (MA) Math Ed, Cntrl MI Univ 1977; *cr:* Teacher Walkerville Rural Cmmty Schls 1971-85, Hesperia Cmmty Schls 1985-; *ai:* Jr Var Ftbl, 8th Grade Vlybl, Var Bsbl; Math Dept Head; Math Curr Comm; MCTM, NCTM 1986-; White Cloud Sch Bd 1982-86; Newaygo Cty Ind Sch Dist Outstanding Citizen 1989; *office:* Hesperia HS 96 S Division Hesperia MI 49421

BLIGEN, ALVIN EARL, Chapter I Math Teacher; *b:* Charleston, SC; *m:* Cassandra Ann; *c:* Morgan B.; *ed:* (BS) Math, TX Coll 1975; *cr:* Math Teacher Burke HS 1975-76; 8th Grade Math Teacher James Island Mid 1976-77; Chapter I Math Teacher Bd Schroder Mid 1977-; *ai:* Good Morning Schroder, Math Bowl Adv; SC Cncl Teachers of Math; Omega Psi Phi; Edisto Island Cmmty Center Bd Mem 1984-87; Charleston Cty Human Services Commission 1985-88; Edisto Island Presbyn Church; BSA Scoutmaster; Teacher of Yr 1983-86; *home:* 1860 Mary Seabrook Rd Edisto Island SC 29438

BLIGHTON, MARGIE A., 7th Grade Mathematics Teacher; *b:* Emmetsburg, IA; *m:* Richard; *c:* Scott, Lisa; *ed:* (BS) Elem Ed, Univ of Dubuque 1973; (MS) Elem Ed, Clemson Univ 1977; Grad Stud Math; Supervision, Clemson Univ; *cr:* Math Teacher Wren Mid Sch 1973-; *ai:* Mathcounts & Knowledge Masters Team Coach; Math Dept Chairperson; NEA, SCEA, ACEA (Treas, Pres) 1973-; SCCTM, NCTM 1983-; Alpha Delta Kappa 1988-; SC Teachers Grant 1985; *office:* Wren Mid Sch Rt 1 Piedmont SC 29673

BLIGHTON, RICHARD DEAN, Teacher of Gifted/Talented/ Sci; *b:* Estherville, IA; *m:* Margie Ann Anderson; *c:* Scott, Lisa; *ed:* (AA) Bio, Estherville Jr Coll 1962; (BS) Bio/Ed, Mankato St 1965; (MAT) Bio/Ed, Univ of NC Chapel Hill 1971; Specialists Admin Clemson 1978; Gifted/Talented, Converse Coll, Citadel; *cr:* 7th/8th Grade Sci Teacher/Coach IA Public Schls 1965-73; *ai:* Odyssey of Mind, Future Problem Solving for Teams, Academic Bowl Coach; Sci Fair Coord; Advisory Bd Mem Future Problem Solving; Local Ed Assn Pres 1978; St Ed Assn, NEA; Academic Yr Inst Univ of NC; Conservation Teacher of Yr Anderson Cty 1977, 1978; Teacher of Yr Bryson Mid Sch 1982; *office:* Bryson Mid Sch Bryson Dr Fountain Inn SC 29644

BLIN, JACKIE KAY (CARYL), Third Grade Teacher; *b:* Cedar Rapids, IA; *m:* Keith R.; *c:* Deidra K, Derek Dixon; *ed:* (BA) Elem Ed, Mount Mercy 1973; *cr:* 3rd/5th Grade Teacher North Linn 1973-; *ai:* IA Rdng Assn; ICTE; North Linn Ed Assn; IA St Ed Assn; NEA; IA Chapter; Cystic Fibrosis Fnd Spec Recognition Awd; *office:* North Linn Elem Sch 408 E Linn St Coggon IA 52218

BLINN, JON MARK, Phys Ed-Math Teacher; *b:* Exeter, NH; *m:* Lola Carlene; *c:* Julie D., Marcia J.; *ed:* (BS) Soc Sci, NW Nazarene Coll 1970; CO St Univ, CA St Univ; *cr:* Academic Teacher NV Youth Trng Center 1972-81; Teacher/Coach Carlin Combined Sch 1981-; *ai:* Head Ftbl Coach; Asst Girls Bsktbl; Elko Cty Classroom Teacher Assn 1982-; Natl HS Athletic Coaches Assn 1986-; *home:* 220 Pine Elko NV 89801

BLISS, JOYCE MOWRY, 2nd Grade Teacher; *b:* Syracuse, NY; *m:* Stephen D.; *c:* Matthew, David; *ed:* (BA) Elem Ed, 1972; (MS) Elem Ed, 1976 St Univ Coll Cortland; *cr:* 2nd Grade Teacher 1975-80; 1st Grade Teacher 1980-81; 3rd Grade Teacher 1981-84; 2nd Grade Teacher 1984- South New Berlin Central; *ai:* Mem Morning Prgm Team; Faculty Drug & Alcohol Awareness Team; Mem Arts Comm; So New Berlin Faculty Assn Treas 1978-80; Delta Kappa Gamma (Chm Personal Growth & Svc 1986-88, Chm Music Comm 1988-); Developer South New Berling Morning Prgm 1983; *office:* S New Berlin Central Sch Main St South New Berlin NY 13843

BLISS, KENNETH O., History/Global Issues Teacher; *b:* Osman, IL; *m:* Norma J. Stuhr; *ed:* (BS) Industrial Arts, Univ of NE 1959; (MED) His, Univ of OR 1962; Soc Sci, Univ of OR 1963, 1973, 1980-81, Suzhoc PRC 1983; *cr:* Teacher Eugene Sch Dist 4-J 1959-; *ai:* Phi Delta Kappa 1959-61; NCSS 1972-73; Better World Society 1986-; Published Article; Natl Endowment for Hum Seminar Participant 1984; Panelist Natl Cncl of Geographers Convention Houston 1970; *home:* 3220 Fillmore St Eugene OR 97405

BLISS, SALLY M., Third Grade Teacher; *b:* Grove City, PA; *m:* Paul W.; *c:* Bill; *ed:* (BA) Elem Ed, 1968, (MS) Elem Ed, 1973 Clarion Univ; *cr:* 6th Grade Teacher Valley Grove Sch Dist 1968-69; Head Start Prgm 1969-71; 6th Grade Teacher 1971-81, 3rd Grade Teacher 1981- Valley Grove Sch Dist; *ai:* NEA, PSEA, VGEA; *home:* RD 2 Stoneboro PA 16153

BLISS, SHARON CUSWORTH, Health Occupations Teacher; *b:* New Hartford, NY; *c:* Catherine A.; *ed:* (MS) Ed, 1979, (BS) Voc Tech Ed, 1978 SUNY Utica Rome; Dental Hygiene License Grad Eastman Sch of Dental Hygiene; Private Pilot; *cr:* Instr Onodaga Comm Coll 1978-80; Asst Professor Broome Comm Coll 1980-82; Instr MVCC Utica 1986-89; Health Occupational Teacher Oneida Cty BOCES Sch 1986-; *ai:* Phi Delta Kappa 1984-88; Ninety Nine Pres 1976-78; Cty 4-H Volunteer; 4-H Coach St Competition Teams; Intnl Organization of Women Pilots; NY St Dept of Ed Consultant for St Competency Exams 1987-; SUNY Oswego Consultant for Health Exams 1987-; *home:* 6355 Trenton Rd Utica NY 13502

BLIXT, ELIZABETH HAINES, Teacher/Administrator; *b:* Tulsa, OK; *m:* Clarence H.; *ed:* Bus Admin/Music Ed, Tulsa Univ; (BE) Elem Ed, San Francisco St Univ 1960; (MA) Elem Sch Admin, Univ of Pacific 1966; CA Life Sci; *cr:* Teacher Dent Elem Sch 1957-67; Prin Van Allen Elem Sch 1967-73; Teacher/Vice Prin Dent Elem Sch 1973-; *ai:* Sch Improvement Prgm Comm; Master Teacher Univ of CA Stanislaus; CA Teachers Assn (Chairperson 1965-66, Child Welfare Comm, St Cncl); Assn of CA Sch Administrators 1966-; Phi Delta Kappa 1978-; Modesto Symphony Orch Musician 1970-; Modesto Chtstn Sch Trustee 1977-87; Modesto Neighborhood Church Choir Dir 1962-72; Dental Health Ed Grant Univ of CA; *home:* 1618 Fisk Ave Escalon CA 95320

BLIZZARD, NANCY SNYDER, Gifted Ed Resource Teacher; *b:* Philadelphia, PA; *m:* Michael R.; *c:* Robert, Jessica; *ed:* (BA) Eng, St Marys Coll of MD 1974; (MED) Rdng, Univ of MD 1979; Trng of Trainers & Additional Specialized Advanced Trng; *cr:* Lang Art/Rdng Teacher John Hanson Mid Sch 1974-78; Part Time Instr Loyola Univ 1982; Eng Dept Chairperson Benjamin Stoddert Mid Sch 1978-86; Gifted Ed Resource Teacher Charles Cty Bd of Ed 1986-; *ai:* Spon Benjamin Stoddert Mid Sch Odyssey of Mind; Coach Arthur Middleton Elem Sch Odyssey of Mind Structure Team; Co-Spon Benjamin Stoddert Natl Jr Honor Society; NCTE; People Against Child Abuse 1989-; Good Shepherd Chancel Choir; Exemplary Lang Art Teacher Charles Cty; Agnes Meyer Awd Nom; *office:* Benjamin Stoddert Mid Sch 2040 St Thomas Dr Waldorf MD 20602

BLOCK, BETTY L. TREFFRY, 2nd Grade Teacher; *b:* Hastings, NE; *m:* Victor F. Jr.; *c:* Kristin, Justin; *ed:* (BS) Elem Ed, Northern St Univ 1970; Improving Instr; Basic Cmptr; Effective Classroom Management; Music; Creative Teaching; Problems in Ed Drugs/Alcohol; Crafts; Lang Arts; *cr:* Instrumental Music Teacher White Lake SD 1971-72; K/12th Grade Vocal Music/ Fresh Eng Teacher Selby SD 1973-75; 2nd Grade Teacher Westside Elem Sch 1975-; *ai:* Cub Scout Webelos Leader; CCD Teacher; Asst Varsity Coach Mid Sch/Jr HS Coach; Elem Sch Coach; SDEA 1975-89; NEA; *home:* 511 East Spruce Sisseton SD 57262

BLOCK, BONNEY GEORGIA (RUDD), Algebra Teacher; *b:* Moose Lake, MN; *m:* James Russell; *c:* Jared W.; *ed:* (BS) Elem Ed, Bob Jones Univ 1976; *cr:* Math Teacher Bob Jones Jr HS 1976-88; Algebra Teacher Bob Jones Acad 1988-; *ai:* Teachers Manual Author; *home:* 710 Crestwood Dr Greenville SC 29609

BLOCK, JULIETTE ARLINE, Dept Chairperson-Sci Teacher; *b:* Long Beach, NY; *c:* Bernard, Adriana; *ed:* (BS) Bio Sci Ed, 1971, (MS) Bio Sci Ed, 1972 SUNY Coll Buffalo; Sci Ed, Effective Teaching. Mid Sch Strageties; *cr:* Sci Teacher 1971-, Dept Chairperson 1977- Longmont Jr HS; *ai:* Chrldr Pom Pom Dir Spon; Sci Curr Cncl for Dist; Drama Club Stage Design Dir; Lib & Media Advisory Cncl; *office:* Longmont Jr H S 1300 S Sunset St Longmont CO 80501

BLOCKER, JANIS KINSEY, AP/Honors/CP English Teacher; *b:* Round O, SC; *m:* David Ladson; *c:* David Z., Teresa M., Derral W.; *ed:* (BA) Eng, Baptist Coll at Charleston 1974; (MAT) Eng, The Citadel 1981; Univ of SC Journalism Inst; *cr:* Eng Teacher John C Calhoun Acad 1974-84; Adjunct Prof Univ of SC Salkehatchie 1985-87; Eng Teacher Walterboro HS 1984-; *ai:* Academic Team Coach; Philosophy Club Adv; Co Adv Sch Newspaper & Yrbk; Delta Kappa Gamma Chapter Pres 1984-86; Colleton Cty Ed Assn Pres 1989-; Colleton Cty Lib Bd 1989-; Aphrodite Fine Arts Club Pres 1988-89; Charleston Atlantic Presbyn Recording Clerk 1988-; Outstanding Teacher in Colleton Cty; First Lady Service Awd Beta Sigma Phi; Chamber of Commerce Outstanding Educator; *home:* Rt 1 Hwy 61 Round O SC 29474

BLOM, TENA (VANDER WAAL), Former Third Grade Teacher; *b:* Sommerville, NJ; *m:* William Lee; *c:* Gary, Arie, Elizabeth, Clazina; *cr:* 3rd Grade Teacher Netherlands Reformed Chrstn 1981-83; *home:* RR 2 Box 58 Doon IA 51235

BLOMQUIST, JEAN CARLSON, Mathematics Teacher; *b:* Houston, TX; *m:* Herbert Lionel; *c:* Laura Blomquist Murph, Carla Blomquist Murray; *ed:* (BA) Math, Univ of TX Austin 1957; (MED) Supervision Gifted, TX Womans Univ 1978; N TX St Univ 1979; Southern Meth Univ 1981; Univ of TX Dallas 1984, 1986; *cr:* Math Teacher Allen Jr HS 1957-59, Bryan Adams HS 1960-61, 1663-64; Math Teacher/Dept Head Comstock Mid Sch 1975-78, Alex W Spence Talented & Gifted 1978-89; Math Teacher Hillcrest HS 1989-; *ai:* Math Coach; Math Club Spon; SAT Preparation Comm; Hillcrest Athletic Booster Club; Phi Delta Kappa Treas 1975-; TX Assn of Prof Educators Dallas Secy 1980-, Region X Scndry Teacher of Yr 1989; NCTM; Highland Park United Meth Church Admin Bd 1986-88; Delta Zeta Pres 1957-; Hillcrest PTA; Finalist Dallas Teacher of Yr 1986; St PTA Life Membership Alex W Spence Mid Sch 1990; *office:* Hillcrest HS 9924 Hillcrest Rd Dallas TX 75230

BLOMSTROM, LARS, Third Grade Teacher; *b:* Manhasset, NY; *ed:* (BA) Phys Ed/Health Ed, Univ of WI Lacrosse 1981; (MS) Elem Curr, Univ of NV Las Vegas 1987; Teacher Expecations Stu Achievement Coord; *cr:* Elem Phys Ed Teacher Mabel Hoggard Elem Schls 1981; 3rd/4th Grade Teacher Robert E Lake Elem Sch 1982-; *ai:* Intramural Sports; CCTA 1985-; *home:* 4750 Illustrious St Las Vegas NV 89117

BLOOD, MARIE ALISA, Exceptional Stu Educ Teacher; *b:* Mount Pleasant, IA; *m:* John F.; *c:* Dylan M., John A.; *ed:* (AA) Liberal Arts/Ed, Daytona Beach Comm Coll 1973; (BA) Exceptional Stu Ed, Univ of South FL 1975; (MA) Admin & Supv, Nova Univ 1987; *cr:* Exceptional Ed Teacher Okeechobee Jr HS 1975-78; Graham Mid Sch 1978-83; Owner Mgr Childrens Village Dev Pre-Sch 1983-85; Exceptional Ed Teacher Spruce Creek Elem 1985-87; Ormond Beach Jr HS 1978-88; Seabreeze HS 1988-; *ai:* Exceptional Stu Dept Chairman; Stu Study Team Chairman; Varsity Chrldng Coach; Asst Sftbll Coach; Phi Kappa Phi 1975-; Cncl for Exceptional Children 1974-78; NEA 1976-; Univ of South FL Honor Stu Awd; Deans Honor List; Phi Kappa Phi Honor Soc; ESE Teacher of Yr Nom 1987; *office:* Seabreeze SR H S 2700 N Oleander Ave Daytona Beach FL 32118

BLOOM, BARBARA KYLE, Fifth Grade Teacher/Dept Head; *b:* Greene, IA; *m:* Ronald D.; *c:* Jeffrey, Karen Bloom Green; *ed:* (BA) Elem Ed, Buena Vista 1971; Grad Work in Elem Supervision ; *cr:* 4th Grade Teacher 1956-59, 3rd Grade Teacher 1966-67, 4th Grade Teacher 1967-78, 5th Grade Teacher 1978- Odebolt Arthur Sch; *ai:* Dept Head; IA Rdng Assn Zone Dir 1987-; Intnl Rdng Assn; Quint Cty Rdng (Pres, Treas, Membership) Rdng Teacher 1983; ICTE; *home:* 48 R Wall Lake IA 51466

BLOOM, DOLORES SHIFLER, Second Grade Teacher; *b:* Union Bridge, MD; *m:* Robert C. Sr.; *c:* Robert C. Jr. *ed:* (BS) Early Chldhd Ed, Towson St Univ 1976; Grad Stud W MD Coll, Hood Coll; *cr:* 2nd Grade Teacher New Windsor Elem 1963-70, Elmer A Wolfe Elem 1970-; *ai:* 2nd Grade Team Leader; Carroll Cty Ed Assn, MD St Teachers Assn, NEA 1963-; GSA Asst Leader 1954-60; *home:* 401 Thomas St P O Box 282 Union Bridge MD 21791

BLOOM, FRACIS A., Mathematics Teacher; *b:* Clearfield, PA; *m:* Paulette Ruth Irwin; *c:* Jamie F.; *ed:* (BS) Math/Ed, Clarion St Coll 1971; Grad Stud Math, PA St Univ, US Army Command & General Staff Coll; *cr:* Math Teacher Tyrone Area HS 1972-; *ai:* Math Competitions Coord; Mathcounts Coach; Tyrone Area Ed Assn, PA Ed Assn, NEA, Rifle Assn, Natl Guard Assn; Amer Legion; Tyrone Sch Dist Outstanding Employee Recognition Awd 1985; *office:* Tyrone Area Sch Dist Clay Ave Ext Tyrone PA 16686

BLOOM, FRANCES RAY, Third Grade Teacher; *b:* Centralia, KS; *m:* Earl Jr.; *c:* Danny, Jolene, Marsha Bloom Walters; *ed:* (BS) Elem/Jr HS, Emporia St Univ 1957; KS St Univ Manhattan; KS Univ Lawrence; Washburn Topeka; *cr:* Teacher Goff, Onaga, Marysville KS 1936-48; 3rd Grade Teacher Frankfort KS & Westmoreland KS 1955-62, Centralia Dist 380 1962-; *ai:* Onaga B B Spon; Univ of KS Sch of Ed Cert Appreciation Awd 1988; Nom Teacher of Yr & Master Teacher.

BLOOM, GISELLDA DILL, Third Grade Teacher; *b:* New Orleans, LA; *c:* Gigi, Jeff, George; *ed:* (BS) Elem Ed, Loyola Univ 1962; (MED) Elem Ed, Univ of New Orleans 1971; Grad Stud 1988; *cr:* 1st Grade Teacher Vic A Pitre Sch 1962-66, Bissonet Plaza Sch 1966-67; 2nd Grade Teacher St Andrew the Apostle Sch 1976-86; 3rd Grade Teacher Isidore Newman 1986-; *ai:* Newman Sch Soc Comm Chm; Newman Sch Archaueological Stud Grant Crow Canyon Cortez CO; Speaker New Orleans ISAS Conference 1989; Gulf Port Staff Dev Presenter 1990; *office:* Isidore Newman Sch 1903 Jefferson Ave New Orleans LA 70115

BLOOMER, DIANE BUNCH, Second Grade Teacher; *b:* Petros, TN; *m:* Benny A.; *c:* Matthew, Timothy; *ed:* (BS) Elem Ed, E TN St Univ 1967; Rdng Specialist, Univ of VA; *cr:* Spec Ed Teacher Norton Elem 1967-69; 2nd Grade Teacher Powell Valley Primary 1975-; *ai:* Various Textbook Adoption & Cty Discipline Comms; *office:* Powell Valley Primary Sch Rt 1 Box 520 Big Stone Gap VA 24219

BLOOMFIELD, STANLEY, English Teacher; *b:* Brooklyn, NY; *m:* Susan Merle Perkins; *c:* Melissa, Jill; *ed:* (BA) Eng, 1960, (AA) Eng Ed, 1966 Brooklyn Coll; *cr:* Teacher Sands Jr HS 1960-61, Seth Low Jr HS 1961-66, Midwood HS 1966-71, John Dewey HS 1971-, Kingsborough Comm Coll 1987-; *ai:* Literary-Art Magazine & Sch Newspaper Faculty Adv; Vanguard Publicity & Promoting Sch Coord; Interdisciplinary Teacher Wksps Coord & Lecturer; Alliance for Art NY Advisory Commission for Cultural Affairs, Teacher of Yr Awd 1988; United Fnd of Teachers Scholars Consortium Scholar 1989; NY Library Assn St Conference Lecturer 1985; NY St Art Teachers Conference Lecturer 1979; Natl Endowment for Hum Seminar 1990; NEH Seminar 1985; NEH Inst Individualism 1988; NEH Inst Western Literat ure 1986; NEH Inst Shakespeare 1989; *office:* John Dewey HS 50 Ave Brooklyn NY 11223

BLOOR, RUTH DAVISON, Mathematics Teacher; *b:* Tekeman, NE; *m:* Sidney Russell; *c:* Elizabeth Edminster, Lynn, Dan; *ed:* (BS) Math, Geneva-Beaver Falls 1955; Univ of Pittsburgh; *cr:* Math Teacher Westinghouse Atomic Power 1955-57; Teacher Toronto HS 1957-58, Deshler HS 1966-68, Patrick Henry HS 1971-; *ai:* Patrick Henry Schls Rotating Adv & Cty Math Curr Chm; Phi Delta Kappa 1971-74, OEA, NEA, PHEA Exec Rep 1989-; 1st United Presbyn Church Choir (Deacon 1983-89, Choir 1963-); Outstanding Scndry Educators of America 1975; Jennings Scholar 1982-83; *home:* 217 W Main St Deshler OH 43516

BLOSE, PATRICK ALLEN, Biology Teacher; *b:* Richard, IN; *m:* Margaret Anne Rademaker; *c:* Annette, Catherine, David; *ed:* (BA) Bio, IN Univ 1974; (MS) Bio, St Francis Coll 1977; Grad Studs Sch Admin, IN Univ; *cr:* Sub-Teacher Fort Wayne Comm Schls 1974-75; Bio/General Sci Teacher Geyer Jr HS 1975-79, Blackhawk Mid Sch 1979-84; Bio Teacher R Nelson Snider HS 1984-; *ai:* Head Boys Track Coach; NAS Get Away Prgm Spon; NEA 1975-; ISTA 1975-; FWEA Rep 1975; St Charles Cath Church (VP 1988-89, Pres 1989-); *office:* R Nelson Snider HS 4600 Fairlawn Pass Fort Wayne IN 46815

BLOSSER, LYDIA HOLLY, 9th Grade Teacher; *b:* Mobile, AL; *m:* Donald M.; *ed:* (BA) Lang Arts, Mobile Coll 1986; (AS) OFC Admin; *cr:* Eng Teacher Baldwin Cty HS 1986-; *ai:* Frosh Class Spon; JV Chrldng Spon; 1st Bapt Church Fairhope Sunday Sch (Outreach Ldr/ Secy 1988-); Mobile Coll Aux Awd 1986; Hum Fine Arts Awd 1986; Ed Div Awd 1986; *office:* Baldwin County H S 600 Blackburn Ave Bay Minette AL 36507

BLOUGH, DORIS BROWDER, English Teacher; *b:* Andrews, SC; *m:* William J.; *c:* Eric B., David R.; *ed:* (BA) Eng, Carson-Newman Coll; (MA) Eng, Univ of NC Chapel Hill 1963; Winthrop Coll; the Bread Loaf Sch of Eng; *cr:* 5th Grade Teacher Chattanooga Public Schls; Eng Instr Atlantic Chrstn Coll; Eng Teacher Catawba Sch; York Sch Dist 1 1981-; *ai:* Adv the Write Group; NEA, NCTE, SC Cncl Teachers of Eng; 2 Grants the Bread Loaf Sch of Eng 1984-86; Presentations 2 Spring Conferences 1987 & 1989; Article Published in Carolina Eng Teacher 1982; Article Accepted By Learning Magazine; *home:* 1974 Huntington Pl Rock Hill SC 29732

BLOXOM, GAYLA COFFEY, 3rd Grade Teacher; *b:* Amarillo, TX; *m:* Benny A.; *c:* Melissa; *ed:* (BS) Elem Ed, W TX St Univ 1973; Academic Trng Lubbock Ind Sch Dist; *cr:* Teacher of Learning Disabilities/4th-6th Grade Lang Teacher 1973-76, 6th Grade Teacher 1976-78 Posey Elem; 6th Grade Teacher 1983-89, 3rd Grade Teacher 1989- Martin Elem; *ai:* Safety Patrol Adv; Martin Spelling Bee Dir & Sci Fair Coord; TX Classroom Teachers Assn 1983-; Trinity Baptist Church 1982-; Chi Omega 1971-73; Chi Omega Alumni Assn 1977-78.

BLOYCE, EZEKIEL ALPHONSO, 8th Grade Science Teacher; *b:* Christiansted, VI; *m:* Alex; *c:* Shameka, Chevon; *ed:* (BS) Bio, Univ of Virgin Islands 1975; Grad Work George Washington Univ, MD Univ, Trinity Coll; *cr:* Chem/Bio/Sci Teacher Dunbar Sr HS 1979-85; Sci Teacher Madison Mid Sch 1985-86, G Gardner Mid Sch 1986-; *ai:* Sci Club & Young Astronaut Club Spon; Academic Team Leader; Effective Sch Comm Mem; Conduct Wkshps Physics Teaching for Colleagues; Outstanding Sci Teacher Awd 1989; Outstanding Educator Awd 1990; NSTA, MD Sci Teachers Assn Membership; Service Awd Howard Univ 1983; Certificate of Recognition Prince Georges Cty Public Schls; Recognition Awd Georgetown Univ Medical Sch; *office:* G Gardner Shugart Mid Sch 2000 Callaway St Hillcrest Heights MD 20748

BLUBAUGH, DEBORAH SUE, Mathematics Teacher; *b:* Frankfort, IN; *ed:* (BA) Math/Ed, Ball St Univ 1987; Masters Math/Scndry Ed, Butler Univ; *cr:* Math Teacher Mooresville HS 1987, Knox HS 1987-; *ai:* Jr Class Spon; Peer Tutoring Prgm Mentor; NEA, IN St Teachers Assn 1987-; Knox Classroom Teachers Assn Negotiating Team 1987-; Kappa Kappa Kappa 1990; *home:* 5615 N 150 W Lebanon IN 46052

BLUE, MARK LA MONT, Supervising Principal; *b:* Los Angeles, CA; *m:* Christy Lynn Johnson; *c:* Mark C., Noelle A.; *ed:* (BA) His, CA St Univ Northridge 1973; (MA) Admin/ Leadership, 1987, (EDS) Admin/Leadership, 1989 Loma Linda Univ; *cr:* Jr HS Teacher Los Angeles Union SDA Sch 1973-81; Teacher/Prin Madera SDA Sch 1981-87; Supervising Prin Fresno Adv Acad 1987-; *ai:* Cntrl CA Confrence of 7th Day Adv Exec Comm; *office:* Fresno Adv Acad 5397 E Olive Ave Fresno CA 93727

BLUESTONE, FRAN SCHWARTZ, Social Studies Teacher; *b:* New York City, NY; *m:* Stewart J.; *c:* Sarah; *ed:* (BA) Scndry Ed/ His, 1970, (MA) Scndry Ed/His, 1973 Queens Coll; *cr:* Soc Stud Teacher Russell Sage Jr HS 1970-76 & 1979, Halsey Jr HS 1979-82, Russell Sage Jr HS 1982-; *ai:* Teacher of Gifted Prgm; Assn of Soc Stud Teachers; *office:* Russell Sage Jr HS 68-17 Austin St Forest Hills NY 11375

BLUHM, JOHN M., Chemistry Teacher; *b:* South Bend, IN; *m:* Anne Nichols; *ed:* (BS) Scndry Ed, WV Univ Morgantown 1966; (MST) Scndry Sci, Colby Coll 1975; *cr:* Teacher Norwin Sr HS 1966-; *ai:* Woodrow Wilson Master Teacher Inst 1988; PA Acad of Sci Judge Awd 1975; *office:* Norwin Sr HS 251 Mc Mahon Rd North Huntingdon PA 15642

BLUMENSTOCK, BETH MARIE, Choir Director; *b:* Springfield, MO; *ed:* (BA) Vocal Ed & Performance, Sch of Ozarks 1983; (MM) Vocal Performance, NE LA St Univ 1985; *cr:* Choral Music Teacher Summersville R-II Schls 1985-; *ai:* Jr/Sr HS Honors Choir; S MO StUniv Invitational Choir; Music & St Music Festival; Private Voice & Piano Lessons; Amer Choral Dir Assn; Music Educators Natl Conference; MO Music Educators Assn; Sorosis; Plaque from Raymondville Sch Outstanding Service; *home:* HCR 5 Box 779 Houston MO 65483

BLUNT, BESS, Eighth Grade English Teacher; *b:* Presque Isle, ME; *ed:* (BS) Eng Ed, Northeastern Univ 1973; (MA) Systems Dev & Analysis/admin/Ed, Boston Univ 1981; *cr:* Teacher Leominster HS 1973-81, Notre Dame Preparatory Sch 1982-83, Hawthorne Brook Mid Sch 1983-; *ai:* Faculty Advisory Comm; Sch Improvement Cncl; Facilities Chairperson of Sch Accreditation;

Rdng Curr Comm; Stu Cncl Adv; Cable Comm Advisory; Public Relations Liason Between Sch & Local Newspapers Through Stu Generated Articles; Phi Delta Kappa 1988-; Natl Mid Sch Assn 1990; *home:* 126 Shore Dr Peabody MA 01960

BLUSH, RUTH ANN (TERRELL), First Grade Teacher; *b:* Archbold, OH; *m:* Lawrence Dayne; *ed:* (AA) Elem Ed, Goshen Coll 1956; (BSED) Elem Ed, Defiance Coll 1965; *cr:* 2nd Grade Teacher Swanton Schls 1956-57; 1st Grade Teacher Archbold Schls 1957-63, Bridgeport Exempted Village Schls 1963-; *ai:* NEA, OH Ed Assn, Bridgeport Ed Assn, PTO 1963-; Intnl Rdng Assn 1987-; Early Childhood Ed Intnl 1990; Thomson Meth Church (Treas, Bd of Trustees) 1990; *home:* 228 Bennett St PO Box 8 Bridgeport OH 43912

BLY, CLIFFORD L., Mathematics Teacher; *b:* Fairview, PA; *m:* Barbara Klemencic; *c:* Sharon, Daniel, Kenneth; *ed:* (BS) Math, 1962, (MS) Guidance/Counseling, 1968 Indiana Univ of PA; *cr:* Math Teacher Freeport Jr HS 1962-67; Guidance Cnslr Freeport Sr HS 1968-78; Math Teacher Freeport Jr HS 1979-; *home:* 222 Cole Rd Sarver PA 16055

BOAL, MARILYN RAE, Sixth Grade Teacher; *b:* Mt Pleasant, IA; *m:* Robert D.; *c:* Pam Fosdick, Steven R., Kim Granback; *ed:* (BA) Elem Ed, IA Wesleyan Coll 1971; *cr:* 4th/5th Grade Teacher Crawfordsville Consolidated 1951-53; Teachers Aide Waco Cmmty Sch 1969-71; 6th Grade Teacher Mediapolis Cmmty Sch 1971-; *ai:* Performance Based Pay Comm; Mediapolis Cmmty Ed Assn Treas 1988-; Delta Kappa Gamma Corresponding Secy 1985-; Intnl Rdng Assn 1987-89; Amer Legion Auxiliary Pres 1954-; TTT Society Corresponding Secy 1988-.

BOATRIGHT, MARSENA WHEELER, English Teacher/Dept Head; *b:* Atlanta, GA; *m:* Darrell Jr.; *ed:* (BSED) Eng, 1979, (MED) Mid Grades, 1983 GA Southern Coll; *cr:* 5th Grade Teacher Bacon Cty Elem 1979-84; K-12th Grade Teacher of Gifted Bacon Cty Systemwide 1984-86; Eng/Teacher of Gifted Bacon Cty HS 1986-; *ai:* Soph Class & Soph Stu Support Team Chairperson; Literary Coord; GAE Membership Chairperson 1985; Delta Kappa Gamma 1989; STAR Teacher 1988; *office:* Bacon Cty HS 901 N Pierce St Alma GA 31510

BOBB, KATHERINE JEAN RUDNICKI, First Grade Teacher; *b:* Detroit, MI; *m:* Paul D.; *ed:* (BA) Elem Ed/Spec Ed/Deaf & Hard of Hearing, MI St Univ 1967; *cr:* 1st-3rd Grade Teacher Montlieu Avenue Elem 1967-; *ai:* 1st Grade Level Chairperson; Senate Bill-2 Co-Chairperson; Media, Writing, Sci Lab, Lang Arts, Textbook Selection Comm; Mentor Teacher; NEA, NCAE 1967-; Delta Kappa Gamma (Pres 1978-80, VP 1976-78) 1973-; ACEI High Point Pres; Intnl Rdng Assn 1980-; Hospice Volunteer 1986-; First Presbyn Church (Deacon 1987-89) 1968-; High Point Outstanding Elem Math Teacher 1990; Rotary Club Excl in Teaching Awd 1972-73; *home:* 603 Havershire Dr Jamestown NC 27282

BOBBEY, E. JEAN, Learning Center Monitor; *b:* Warsaw, NY; *m:* David M.; *c:* Jonathan, Steven, Mary; *ed:* Elem Ed, Marion Coll; ACE Trng; Inst in Basic Youth Conflicts; *cr:* Monitor Northeast Chrstn Acad 1979-81, 1985-; *ai:* Sr Spon/Adv; Choir Dir-Sch; Organist.

BOBBINS, STEPHEN GERALD, 6th Grade Mathematics Teacher; *b:* Atlantic City, NJ; *ed:* (BA) Jr HS Teaching, 1964, (MA) Elem Admin & Supervision, 1971 Glassboro St Coll; *cr:* Teacher Eugene A Tighe Sch 1964-; *ai:* Senator Bill Bradleys Geography Recognition Awd St of NJ 1989; *office:* Eugene A Tighe Sch Amherst & Essex Aves Margate City NJ 08402

BOBBY, ROSALIE SKERTICH, English/Literature Teacher; *b:* East Chicago, IN; *m:* Richard M.; *ed:* (BA) Eng, St Josephs Calumet 1977; (MS) Ed, Eng Endorsement, Purdue Univ Coll 1980; *cr:* Jr HS Eng Teacher St John the Baptist Cath Sch 1977-; Lang Art Tutor Academic Counseling Services 1981-84; *ai:* Jr HS Coord; Yrbk Spon; Teach Er Soc Dir; Spelling Bee Co-Organizer; NCEA 1977-; *office:* St John The Baptist Sch 1844 Lincoln Ave Whiting IN 46394

BOBLITT, EDMOND RAY, Assistant Principal Curriculum; *b:* Bellefontaine, OH; *m:* Debra G. Fortunato; *c:* Shelly R., Brett A.; *ed:* (BS) Eng, Anderson Coll 1961; (MED) Guidance & Counseling, Univ of Toledo 1969; Grad Stud Admin & Higher Ed; *cr:* Teacher Lima & Toledo Public Schls 1961-68; Cnslr Univ Toledo & Toledo Public Schls 1968-71; Asst Prin Bowsher HS 1970-; *ai:* Stu Body Government Exchange Prgms; PDK VP 1971-77; TAAP Mem.

BOBO, DAWN SWING, 4th Grade Teacher; *b:* Shelbyville, TN; *m:* James David; *c:* Amy, Matthew, Rachel; *ed:* (BA) Elem Ed, Mid TN St Univ 1976; Grad Courses Sch Law & Educl Admin; *cr:* 4th-6th Grade Teacher Cmmty Sch 1976-77; 2nd Grade Teacher 1977-79, 4th Grade Teacher 1979-89 Deery Eakin Elem; 4th Grade Teacher Thomas Intermediate Sch 1989-; *ai:* Adapted Aquatics Instr Red Cross 1989-91; BCEA, TEA 1976-; NEA 1990; Southside Baptist Church (Sunday Sch Teacher, Choir Mem); Amer Red Cross (Water Safety Instr, Adult CPR, First Aid) 1977-; Career Ladder Level II 1985-86; Extended Contract Level II 1989-; *home:* 394 New Center Church Rd Shelbyville TN 37160

BOCCHETTI, RICHARD WILLIAM, 2nd Grade Teacher; *b:* Lakewood, NJ; *m:* Sandra Justus; *c:* Vincent, Brooke; *ed:* (BA) Elem Ed 1970; (MED) Elem Ed 1975, Trenton St Coll; Prin/Supv Certificate 1978; *cr:* 2nd Thru 6th Grade Teacher Drum Point Road Sch 1970-; *ai:* NEA 1970-; NJ Ed Assn 1970-; Ocean Cty Ed Assn 1970-; Bricktwp Ed Assn Rep Cncl; Jackson Twp Little Leag Coach 1987-; Ocean Cty Bd Realtors Assoc 1976-85; 50th Armored Div Tank Commander Instr 1967-73; T & E Basic Skills Mgmt Comm; Lang Arts Curr Comm Elem Schls; Drum Point Road Sch Sci Coord; *office:* Drum Point Road Sch 41 Drum Point Rd Brick Town NJ 08723

BOCK, JUDITH KATHERINE, Teacher of Gifted & Talented; *b:* Chicago, IL; *ed:* (BA) Elem Ed, 1971, (MA) Geography/ Environmental Stud, 1982 NE IL Univ; Spec Seminars, Insts; *cr:* 6th Grade Teacher 1972-82, Teacher of Gifted/Talented 1982- Intermediate Sch; Part-Time Instr NE IL Univ 1987-; Wkshp Inst Facilitator Natl Geographic Society & IL Geographic Alliance 1988-; *ai:* Soc Stud Advisory & Articulation; Natl Cncl for Geographic Ed Comm Work 1970-; Environmental Ed Assn IL 1980-; NCSS 1970-; Exemplary Teacher Awd 1989; Published Soc Stud for Young Learner; Reviewer for Geography 7th-12th Grades; *office:* Intermediate Sch 133 Mc Kinley Ave Lake Villa IL 60046

BOCKENSTEDT, DIANE LINN (ROTH), Upper Elem Mathematics Teacher; *b:* Guttenberg, IA; *m:* Gene Francis; *c:* Derrick, Jennifer; *ed:* (BA) Elem Ed, Univ of N IA Cedar Falls 1977; Working Towards Master, Clarke Coll; *cr:* 4th Grade Teacher St Josephs Sch 1977-78; 6th Grade Teacher 1978-80, Math Teacher 1980- Guttenberg Cmmty Sch; *ai:* Safety Patrol Supvr; Jr HS Girls Bsktbl Coach; Majorette Spon; Performance Based Pay Comm Mem; 6th Grade Math Bee Coach; IA Cncl of Teachers of Math, Natl Cncl of Teachers of Math, ISEA, NEA; Sunday Sch Accompianist; St Judes Math-A-Thon Coord; *office:* Guttenberg Cmmty Sch 131 S River Park Dr Guttenberg IA 52052

BODDIE, SHIRLEY LYONS, Math Teacher/Dept Chair; *b:* Carbon Hill, AL; *m:* Willie Thomas; *c:* Willie Jr., Stephanie F.; *ed:* (BS) Eng, AL St Univ 1963; (MA) Scndry Ed, Univ of N AL 1976; *cr:* Teacher Boteler Jr HS 1963-68, Dunbar Sch 1970-71, Beaumont Jr HS 1971-75, Carver Sr HS 1975-76, Houston Hill Jr HS 1976-; *ai:* Natl Jr Honor Society Adv; Jr HS Curr Inservice Comm Mem; Montgomery Public Schls Faculty Rep; Montgomery Cty Ed Assn; NEA, Montgomery Cty Ed Assn 1976-; Houston Hill PTA 1976-, Teacher of Yr 1989-; *office:* Houston Hill Jr HS 215 Hall St Montgomery AL 36104

BODE, GERTRUDE BETH, Fifth Grade Teacher; *b:* Porto Rico, WV; *ed:* (BA) Art, Salem Coll 1972; Grad Hrs WV Univ; *cr:* 5th Grade Teacher Lost Creek Elem 1973-76, Ziesing Elem 1976-77, Adamston Elem 1977-; *ai:* Soc Stud Fair Coord Adamston Sch; Ed Fair Window Display Co-Coord Adamston Sch; NEA 1972-; WV Ed Assn 1972-; Harrison Cty Ed Assn 1972-; Harrison Cty Watercolor Society Treas 1979-; Alpha Delta Kappa Historian 1985-86; Adamston PTA; Harrison Cty Cmcl Intnl Rdng Assn; *office:* Adamston Elem Sch 1636 W Pike St Clarksburg WV 26301

BODE, HAROLD, Science Teacher; *b:* Jacinto City, TX; *m:* Linda Ann Hurry; *c:* Brandi, Bradley, Brent; *ed:* (BS) Wildlife & Fisheries Sci, 1977, (MAGR) Wildlife & Fisheries Sci, 1981 TX A&M Univ; *cr:* Elem Sci Teacher Allen Acad 1977-79; Dir Brazos Valley Museum of Natural Sci 1980-82; Sci Teacher Waller HS 1983-; *ai:* Ftbl, Bsktbl, Bsbl Coach; Beta Club Spon; Sci Dept Chm; TX HS Coaches Assn Mem 1987-; Waller Sports Assn Mem 1987-; St Johns Luth Church Cncl Mem 1987-89; *office:* Waller HS 2402 Waller St Waller TX 77484

BODIN, WESLEY JAMES, Social Studies Teacher; *b:* Minneapolis, MN; *m:* Marja-Leena Onermaa; *c:* Jon, Lisa; *ed:* (BA) His/Phys Ed, Augsburg Coll 1955; Numerous Univs; *cr:* Soc Stud/Phys Ed Teacher/Coach Biwabik Jr & Sr HS 1957-60; Soc Stud Teacher Edina HS 1960-61, Mound HS 1961-62; Soc Stud Teacher/Coach St Louis Park HS 1962-; *ai:* Congress on Intnl Priorities Atu Group Adv; Natl Cncl on Religion & Public Ed Pres 1984-87; NCSS Comm Chairperson 1983-85; MN Cncl for Soc Stud (Comm Chairperson, Membership); MN Dept of Ed (Comm Chairperson, Various Comm Memberships, Data Bank Test Items Contributor); St Louis Park Cncl for Soc Stud (Founder, Pres, Bd of Dir); St Louis Park HS Faculty Senate (Founder, Pres, Mem); Amer Assn of Scndry Sch Admin, NASSP, MN St Sch Bds Assn, ASCD; United Nations in Geneva Switzerland; Intnl Cncl on Islam in Jerusalem Israel; Natl Cncl for Religion in Public Ed; Amer Acad of Religion; Foreign Policy Assn; Public Ed Religions Stud Center; Soc Stud Curr Center; Religious Ed Assn; MN Cncl of Churches; MN Dept of Planning & Dev; Natl Fellow for Ind Study in Hum Sponsored by Natl Endowment for Hum 1990; Ashland Oil Teacher Achievement Awd; Materials & Articles Published; *office:* St Louis Park HS 6425 W 33rd St Saint Louis Park MN 55426

BODISON, VERA M., English Teacher; *b:* Walterboro, SC; *m:* Bernard Charles; *c:* Vernisa, Bernard Jr., Robert; *ed:* (BA) Eng - Cum Laude, Claflin Coll 1970; (MED) Ed, SC St Coll 1975; Univ of SC, Columbia Coll, Clemson Univ; Ed Specialist Candidate Prgm The Citadel; *cr:* Eng Teacher Colleton HS 1970-82, Walterboro HS 1982-; *ai:* Walterboro HS Drama Club Dir, Crisis Intervention Team Chairperson, NHS Advisory Cncl Mem; Colleton Cty Ed Assn (Pres 1986-87, Membership Chairperson 1987-88); Zeta Phi Beta Reporter 1987-; United Meth Church Commission on Religion & Race Chairperson 1983-89; Wesley United Meth Church (Financial Secy 1988-, Part-Time Musician 1972-); Writing Wkshp Local Staff Dev Leader 1986; Walterboro HS Crisis Intervention Team Inservice Leader 1990; *home:* PO Box 181 Walterboro SC 29488

BODNAR, HELEN, Honors Biology Teacher; *b:* Perth Amboy, NJ; *ed:* (BA) Pre-Med/Bio, Douglass Coll 1958; (MA) Bio, Hunter Coll 1967; (MS) Environmental Health Sci, Hunter Coll/ Bellevue Medical Center 1981; Studio Art, Human Anatomy, NJ Inst Visual Art 1988; *cr:* Bio Teacher Edison HS 1958-66, Lakenheath Air Base 1966-67, Edison HS 1967-; *ai:* Extensive Mural Painting Classroom Walls & Walls of Hallways on Evolution & Endangered Species done by Honors Bio Stu Volunteers 1988-; Coach & Tutor Honors Bio Stu Bio Achievement Exam; Prep Stu for Summer Prgm Sci; NEA, NJEA, MCEA, ETEA 1958-; Phi Beta Kappa 1958-; Tri Beta 1957-; Phi Sigma 1964-; Deborah Fnd (Secy 1987-) Mem 1978-; PETA, ISAR Membership 1978-; Phi Beta Kappa, Tri Beta Douglass Coll; Phi Sigma Alpha Kappa Chapt Hunter Coll; *office:* John P Stevens H S Grove Ave Edison NJ 08820

BOEDER, CURTIS IVER, JR., Principal/6th Grade Teacher; *b:* Glencoe, MN; *m:* Victoria Birch; *c:* James, John; *ed:* (BS) Elem Ed, Concordia-Seward NE 1977; (MED) Elem Sch Admin Coll of ID 1984; *cr:* 6th Grade Teacher/Athletic Dir St Pauls Luth 1977-79; 7th-8th Grade Teacher/Prin St Marks Luth 1979-81; 6th Grade Teacher/Prin Zion Luth 1981-; *ai:* Soccer & Track Coach; 4th-6th Phys Ed; Lunch Coord; ASCD 1989-; ID Fed of Ind Sch Pres 1986-87; NAMPA Chamber of Commerce 1988-; Serving on Elem Sch Approval Comm for St of ID; *office:* Zion Lutheran Sch 1012 12th Ave Rd Nampa ID 83686

BOEH, PATRICK JOHN, Physical Education Teacher; *b:* White City, KS; *ed:* (BA) Phys Ed, Ottawa Univ 1988; *cr:* Teacher/ Coach Ottawa HS 1988-; *ai:* Asst Ftbl Coach; Head Girls Bsktbl; NEA, KS Ed Assn 1989-.

BOEHM, GLORIA SCHAFFER, Elementary Physical Ed Teacher; *b:* Navasota, TX; *m:* Bill; *c:* Shelly; *ed:* (BS) Phys Ed, Sam Houston St Univ 1968; Grad Courses Ed; *cr:* Phys Ed Teacher Navasota Ind HS 1968-74, Navasota Mid Sch 1974-77, Anderson-Shiro Elem 1980-; *ai:* Bike-A-Thon; Career Ladder Selection & Attendance Comm; Little Shooters Bsktbl Prgm; Vlybl Coach; PTA Local Secy 1980-81; ALpha Delta Kappa Teacher 1988-; Masonic Chalkboard Awd for Outstanding Teacher 1987; *home:* Rt 1 Box 1540 Anderson TX 77830

BOEHM, STANLEY ERIC, Science Teacher; *b:* Whittier, CA; *m:* Elizabeth Carol Salvador; *c:* Stanley, Branden; *ed:* (BS) Health Sci, Long Beach St 1982; *cr:* Teacher Northview Mid Sch 1983-; *ai:* CETA Summer Prgm Remediation Teacher; Ftbl & Bsktbl Coach; NEA Mem 1983-; *home:* 1330 Cogswell South El Monte CA 91733

BOENDER, KAREN HELLENGA, Math Teacher; *b:* Kalamazoo, MI; *m:* Thomas; *c:* Ryan; *ed:* (BS) Math, 1978, (MAT) Teaching of Math, 1981 Western MI Univ; *cr:* Math Teacher Delton-Kellogg Mid Sch 1979-81, Constantine HS 1982, Martin HS 1982-; *ai:* 9th Grade Class Adv; NCTM 1989-; MCTM 1979-; Robert Seber Awd WMU 1981; *office:* Martin H S 1556 Chalmers St Martin MI 49070

BOENISCH, CYNTHIA BREHM, First Grade Teacher; *b:* Wharton, TX; *m:* Mark Russell; *c:* Brett R., Shelley J., Kaylyn E.; *ed:* Assoc Wharton Cty Jr Coll 1976; (BA) Elem Ed, SW TX St Univ 1978; Advanced Trng Classes; *cr:* 1st-2nd Grade Teacher 1978-80, 1st Grade Teacher 1980- Rice Consolidated Ind Sch Dist; *ai:* Campus Improvement Plan Comm; Past Cheerleading Spon Jr HS; Textbook Comm; TCTA (VP 1987-88, Class Rep 1983-, Mem 1978-); Garwood Comm Assn 1988-; St Marys Cath Church; *office:* Garwood Sch Box 368 Hwy 71 Garwood TX 77442

BOERNER, RONALD R., Chemistry Teacher; *b:* Nebraska City, NE; *m:* Sheila Fahey; *c:* James W., Kevin A., Brian P., Sharleen A., Anne M., Cynthia L.; *ed:* (BS) Chem, 1969, (MED) Sci Ed, 1975 Univ of NE; NSF Chem & Physics Course, Kearney St Coll 1978-79; Advanced Placement Chem Inst, Univ of AL 1989; *cr:* Chem Teacher North Platte HS 1969, Mid Plains Comm Coll 1986-; *ai:* North Platte Ed Assn Pres 1979-80; NSTA; North Platte Amateur Radio Operators VP 1988-89; NE Section Amer Chemical Society Chem Teaching Awd 1974; Distributive Ed Teacher of Yr Awd 1975; Univ of KS HS Teacher Recognition Awd 1989; Univ of Chicago Outstanding Teacher Awd 1989; *home:* 1802 Birchwood Rd North Platte NE 69101

BOERST, WILLIAM JAMES, English Teacher; *b:* Jamestown, NY; *m:* Rachel Molin; *c:* Robin, Julie; *ed:* (BSED) Eng Ed, St Univ Coll Fredonia 1962; Grad Courses St Univ Coll, Fredonia, Potsdam, Syracuse Univ, Coll of St Rose; *cr:* 7th Grade Eng Teacher Indian River Cntrl 1962-63; 2nd-6th Grade Teacher Peace Corps Liberia W Africa 1963-65; 11th Grade Eng Teacher Watertown HS 1965-67; 7th-9th Grade Eng Teacher Lincoln Jr HS 1967-78; 10th-12th Grade Eng Teacher Jamestown HS 1978-; *ai:* NEA (Instr, Prof Dev Comm Mem) 1977-78; Chautaugua Area Writers Bd of Dir 1989-; Chautaugua Cty Rdng & Writing Process Teachers Bd of Dir 1989-; Judson Fellowship Pres of Cncl 1988-; NCTE Jr HS & Mid Sch Assembly Newsletter Ed 1976-78; Proposal Writer Local Teacher Center Policy Bd 1977-78; Mem Jamestown Public Schls Curr Cncl 1977-78; Wkshp Leader NY St Speech Assn Convention 1978; Published Articles & Poetry 1982-; Awarded Mini Grant Chautaugua Cty Teachers Center Research & Generate Act for Lang Processes 1988; *office:* Jamestown HS 350 E 2nd St Jamestown NY 14701

BOESCHENSTEIN, SALLY (PENZOTTI), English Teacher; *b:* Monroe, MI; *m:* Charles E.; *c:* Beth, Ralph, Michael, David, John; *ed:* (BA) Eng - Magna Cum Laude 1960, (MA) Ed, 1974 W MI Univ; *cr:* Eng Teacher Kalamazoo Loy Norrix HS 1961-62, Mendon Cmmty Schls 1973-74, Three Rivers Cmmty Schls 1974-77, Centreville HS 1978-84, Constantine HS 1985-; *ai:* NHS

Spon; Reach Gifted/Talented Comm; N Cntrl Evaluation Chairperson; St Joseph Cty EEDP 1988, Career Educator of Yr; Co-Author of Book; Co-Presenter at Career Ed Conference MOEA; *office:* Constantine Public Schls 260 W 6th St Constantine MI 49042

BOESLING, SUE ANN SILER, Third Grade Teacher; *b:* Defiance, OH; *m:* Thomas Allen; *ed:* (BS) Elem Ed, Bowling Green St Univ 1973; (MA) Ed, Coll of Mt St Joseph 1988; Grad Level Courses Bowling Green St Univ; Univ of Indianapolis; IN Univ Fort Wayne; Coll of Mt St Joseph; *cr:* 1st Grade Teacher 1973-80, 3rd Grade Teacher 1980- Paulding Elem; *ai:* NEA, OEA, Paulding Ed Assn 1973-; *office:* Paulding Exempted Village Sch 405 N Water St Paulding OH 45879

BOETTCHER, BLASE WARD, English Department Chair; *b:* Vernal, UT; *m:* Kathleen A. Hesse; *c:* Marisa, Jerome, Adrienne; *ed:* (BA) Philosophy, St Louis Univ 1973; Eng, St Louis Univ Grad Sch; Journalism, E IL Univ; *cr:* Teacher Guardian Angel Day Care 1973-74, Beaumont HS 1974-81; Teacher/Chm Cardinal Ritter Prep Sch 1981-; *ai:* Cross Cntry Coach; Newspaper Moderator; NCTE 1974-; MO Track & Cross Cntry Coaches Assn 1977-, Coach of Yr 1985, 1989; St Louis Archdiocesan Teacher Assn 1981-; BSA Scoutmaster 1970-, Silver Beaver 1986, Dist Awd of Merit 1981; Dow Jones Fellowship 1984; *office:* Cardinal Ritter Prep Sch 5421 Thekla Saint Louis MO 63120

BOGAN, CYNDIE, Counselor-Dept Chairperson; *b:* Inglewood, CA; *m:* Robert Alter; *c:* Jennifer L. Jones, Jason A. Alter; *ed:* (AA) General Ed, Cypress Coll 1981; (BS) Child Dev, CA St Univ 1983; (MS) Counseling, Fullerton 1986; *cr:* EOP Counselor CA St Univ 1985-87; Counselor Whittier Union HS Dist 1988, Canyon Springs HS 1989-; *ai:* Chairperson Schlsp Comm; Celebration of Achievemeent Coord; CA Assn Ed Young Children 1983-90 Grad Stu Awd 1985; NAEYC 1983-90; C A Assn for Counseling Dev 1984-88; La Habra Womans Club Schlsp 1986 Service Prgm Awd; CSUF Dept of Counseling, Alumni Outstanding Grad 1985; CA Assn of Young Children Grad Awd 1984; Theta Sigma Phi Schlsp Spec Ed 1984; CA St Univ Fullerton Outstanding Sr Child Dev 1983; CSUF Pres Sch Human Dev & Cmmty Service Alumni Cncl 1986-87, Mem Exec Cncl Alumni 1986-87, Pres Grad Counseling Stu Assn 1984-85, Pres Child Dev Stu Assn 1982-83; *office:* Canyon Springs H S 23100 Manzanita Ave Moreno Valley CA 92388

BOGARD, MARGO WILSON, 5th Grade Teacher; *b:* Union, MS; *m:* Larry Eugene; *c:* Matthew, Brett; *ed:* (BA) Elem Ed, Univ of S MS 1976; (MS) Elem Ed, William Carey Coll 1982; Admin, USM; *cr:* Remedial Math Teacher 1977-78, 5th Grade Teacher 1978-79 Brandon Mid Sch; ESL Teacher Gorenflo & Howard II Elem 1980-82; 5th Grade Teacher Howard II Elem 1982-; *ai:* Sch Store Coord; Safety Patrol Co-Spon; Alpha Delta Kappa Chaplain 1982-; Howard II PTA Treas; Howard II PTA & Prin Awd of Appreciation in Dedication & Service 1987-88; *office:* Howard II Elem Sch 260 Howard Ave Biloxi MS 39530

BOGDAN, BARRY LOUIS, Mathematics Teacher; *b:* Bethlehem, PA; *m:* Eileen Ann Yuhasz; *ed:* (BS) Math, Wake Forest Univ 1972; *cr:* Teacher Easton Area HS 1974-; *ai:* Math Club Adv; *office:* Easton Area HS 25th St And Wm Penn Hwy Easton PA 18042

BOGDANOFF, STEWART, Head Teacher; *b:* London, England; *m:* Eileen Dolan; *c:* Suelyn, Jennifer, Andrew; *ed:* (BS) Health/Phys Ed, The Kings Coll; (MA) Health/Phys Ed, NY Univ 1965; Ed/Sch Admin, NYU; Sch Admin/Supervision, SUNY New Paltz; Multicultural Ed/Promoting Interpersonal Dev in Sch Age Children, Harvard Univ; *cr:* Phys Ed Teacher 1965-83, Head Teacher 1984- Thomas Jefferson Elem Sch; *ai:* Intramural Dir; Coach Cross-Cntry, Bsktbl, Gymnastics; Coach Disabled Athletes; Dev of Syllabi for NY St Ed Dept; Phi Delta Kappa-Rho Chapter NYU 1965- Service Awd 1989; Natl St Teachers of Yr 1983; Amer Alliance for Health, Phys Ed, Recreation & Dance 1965- Merit Awd 1976; Muscular Dystrophy Exec Bd 1983-85 Distinguished Cmnty Service Awd 1983; Amer Heart Assn 1980- Outstanding Volunteer Awd 1989; Shrub Oak Athletic Club 1965- Distinguished Cmnty Service 1983; NY St Teacher of Yr 1983; York Town Jaycees Outstanding Achievement in Ed Awd; Empire St Medal for Service to Youth; Yorktown Jaycees Distinguished Cmnty Service Awd; *office:* Thomas Jefferson Elem Sch 3636 Gomer St Yorktown Heights NY 10598

BOGGESS, JAMES FRANK, General Supervisor; *b:* Huntington, WV; *m:* Sandra Feese; *c:* Matt; *ed:* (AB) Biological/General Sci, 1970, (MS) Bio, 1974 Marshall Univ; Grad Stud Educl Admin; *cr:* Teacher Beverly Hills Jr HS 1972-74, Barboursville HS 1974-89; General Supvr/HS & Mid Sch Sci/Math Teacher Cabell Cty Bd of Ed 1989-; *ai:* Barboursville HS Stu Cncl Spon; Cty Curr Cncl Secy & Pres; Cty Sci & Media Comm Past Chm; Cty & St Math Cncl; WV Sci Teachers Assn; Assn of Supervision & Curr Dev; Phi Delta Kappa; Steele Memorial United Meth Church 1990; BSA Troop 790 Comm Chm 1990; Barboursville Park & Recreation Bd 1985-88; Cabell Cty Teacher of Yr 1984; *office:* Cabell Cty Bd of Ed 620 20th St Huntington WV 25701

BOGGS, JENNALEE SUE, Language Art Teacher; *b:* Mc Pherson, KS; *m:* Dennis L.; *c:* Derek L.; *ed:* (BA) Elem Ed, KS St Univ 1971; Grad Stud Teaching, Wichita St, Ft Hays Univ, Emporia St Univ; *cr:* 5th-8th Grade Lang/Soc Stud Teacher Selden Elem 1971-74; 7th/8th Grade Lang Art Teacher Hesston Mid Sch 1974-80, Prairie Hills Mid Sch 1980-; *ai:* Teacher Adv & Facilitator Coord 1982-; Hesston Mid Sch Girls Bsktbl Coach 1974-80; KS Assn for Mid Level Ed (Cncl Rep 1978-83, Pres 1983-84); Natl Mid Sch Assn; Delta Kappa Gamma Treas 1987-88; Kappa Kappa Iota (Treas 1984-85, VP 1985-86, Pres 1986-87), St Necrology Chairperson 1987-88; KS Assn for Mid Level Ed Symposium Presentor; *office:* Prairie Hills Mid Sch 3200 Lucille Dr Hutchinson KS 67502

BOGGS, LYNNE ALISON, Science Teacher; *b:* San Antonio, TX; *ed:* (BSED) Bio, Abilene Chrstn Univ 1985; (MA) Guidance/Counseling, Adams St CO 1990; Level 1 Track Coach, The Athletic Coll; *cr:* Teacher Emerson Jr HS 1985-; *ai:* Track & Vlybl Coach; Health Cnslr; NEA, CSEA 1985-; *office:* Emerson Jr HS 4220 E Pikes Peak Ave Colorado Springs CO 80909

BOGGS, TERESA JUNE, English/Journalism Teacher; *b:* New Martinsville, WV; *ed:* (AB) Ed, 1985, (BA) Journalism/Eng, 1985 Fairmont St; Grad Stud Public Relations & Journalism, WV Univ; *cr:* 12th Grade Eng/Journalism Teacher Washington Irving HS 1985-; *ai:* Publications Adv; Stu Cncl Spon; Partnership Comm Faculty Rep; WV Scholastic Press Assn VP 1989-; Columbia Scholastic Press Assn 1985-, 1st Place 1990; Various Publications Teacher; Herff Jones Yrbk Wkshps; *home:* 214 Charleston Ave Clarksburg WV 26301

BOGUE, EVA MARIE, Assistant Head Teacher; *b:* Minot, ND; *m:* John; *c:* Bonnibelle, Endi, Farris, Ginger, Emerald; *ed:* (BS) Ed, OR St Univ 1963; (MA) Ed, Stanford Univ 1965; *cr:* Cnslr Ackerman Lab Sch & Island City Sch 1983-84; 3rd Grade Teacher Greenwood Sch 1984-86; 4th Grade Teacher 1986-88, Teacher/Staff Developer 1988-89, Asst Head Teacher 1989- HI Preparatory Acad; *ai:* Long Range Plan Comm; Cnslr; Staff Dev.

BOGUE, JAN CRAWFORD, English Teacher; *b:* Houston, TX; *m:* Jeff; *c:* John, Jemma; *ed:* (BS) Eng/His, TX A&M Univ 1987; Working Toward Masters Univ of TX Tyler; Teach Gifted & Talented Stus of Eng Trng; *cr:* Eng Teacher Chapel Hill Ind Sch Dist 1987-; *ai:* TX Classroom Teachers Assn (Treas 1990, Campus Rep 1987-); *office:* Chapel Hill HS Rt 7 Box 34 Tyler TX 75707

BOHACEK, CHEO M., Spanish Teacher; *b:* Sheboygan, WI; *m:* Jerry; *c:* Dann, Holly; *ed:* (BA) Span, Univ of MN 1972; Grad Courses in Ed, 1987-89; *cr:* Teacher Sprayberry HS 1985-; *ai:* Span Club Spon; Jr Class Adv/Spon; AATSP Mem 1985-; *office:* Sprayberry HS 2525 Sandy Plains Rd Marietta GA 30066

BOHALL, WILLIAM DAVID, Eng/Teacher of Gifted/Talented; *b:* Phoenix, AZ; *c:* Weston; *ed:* (BS) Eng/Journalism Ed, Univ of Evansville 1972; Grad Work Spec Ed, Gifted & Talented Ed, N IL Univ, IN Univ; *cr:* Teacher Glenbrook North HS 1972-77, Columbus East HS 1977-79; Information Specialist Dept of Mental Health 1980-85; Teacher/Coach South Decatur HS 1985-; *ai:* Jr HS Ftbl & HS Var Track Coach; HS & St Odyssey of Mind St Champions Coach; Teacher Expectations & Stu Achievement Participant; IN St Teachers Assn 1985-; Fellowship of Chrstn Athletes Spon 1986-; Bible Study Fellowship 1987-89; Contributor to Textbook; Writer & Ed of Films for Dept of Mental Health Ed Staff Dev; *office:* South Decatur HS RR 5 Box 277 Greensburg IN 47240

BOHANAN, RITA DIANE, Fifth Grade Teacher; *b:* Benton, IL; *m:* James Dale; *c:* Dana L. Smith; *ed:* (BA) Elem, 1969, (MS) Elem, 1969 Ball St Univ; *cr:* 2nd Grade Teacher New Castle IN 1969-71; 1st Grade Teacher Mt Summit IN 1977-80, Fowler IN 1981-82; 5th Grade Teacher Kentland IN 1982-; *office:* Kentland Elem Sch 410 N 4 Kentland IN 47951

BOHANNON, ANNIE GLADIS, English Teacher; *b:* Dekalb, MS; *ed:* (BA) Eng, Wiley Coll 1951; (MA) Eng, TN St Univ 1959; Bible as Lit, IN Univ; Black Lit, Meredith Coll; Writing Wkshp MS St Univ Meridian; *ai:* NCTE, MS Assn of Eng Teachers, NEA; *home:* 1923 10th Ave Meridian MS 39301

BOHLEN, MARVIN F., Teacher; *b:* Charles City, IA; *ed:* (BA) Math Ed, Univ N IA 1973; (MS) Cmptr Sci Ed, E WA Univ 1985; *cr:* Math Teacher Savanna Cmmty Schls 1973-82, Mead Cmmty Schls 1982-; *home:* N 6908 Jefferson Spokane WA 99208

BOHLENDER, BRAD ALAN, Middle School Science Teacher; *b:* Colorado Springs, CO; *m:* Courtney Campbell; *c:* Tiffanny, Mandy, Brett; *ed:* (AA) Liberal Art, Otero Sr Coll 1972; (BA) Ed, Univ of Northern CO 1978; *cr:* Teacher Rawlins Mid Sch 1978-; *ai:* HS Tennis & Mid Sch Wrestling Coach; US Prof Tennis Assn 1987-; WY Tennis Coach of Yr 1987; *office:* Rawlins Mid Sch Brooks & Harshman St Rawlins WY 82301

BOHME, VIRGNIA ANN, Mathematics Teacher; *b:* Detroit, MI; *m:* Craig R.; *c:* Amy, Clare, Andrew, Daniel; *ed:* (BA) Math/Ed, MI St Univ 1974; Marilyn Burns Math Solution Course; Cooperative Learning Trng; *cr:* Math Teacher Univ of AZ 1983, Tucson HS 1977-; *ai:* Mem Greater Univ Partnership; NCTM (Regional Math Lab Presentation 1986) 1983-; AZ Assn of Math (Alternative General Math Presentation 1990) 1985-; PTA 1985-; Teacher of Yr Tucson HS 1989; *office:* Tucson Magnet HS 400 N 2nd Ave Tucson AZ 85705

BOHUSLAV, DIANA AWTREY, English/Sociology Teacher; *b:* Fairfax, OK; *m:* Frank Jr.; *ed:* (BA) Eng - Summa Cum Laude, Midwestern St Univ 1978; Several Wrkshps; *cr:* Eng/Soc Teacher Burkburnett HS 1980-; *ai:* NHS Spon 1984-87; TX Joint Cncl Teachers of Eng Secy 1988-89; Burkburnett HS Teacher of Yr 1985; *office:* Burkburnett HS 109 Kramer Rd Burkburnett TX 76354

BOIKE, DOROTHY ROBERTS, Teacher; *b:* Hillsboro, OH; *m:* Stephen Daniel; *c:* Jeffrey S., Constance Cole, Sandra St Clair, Robert D.; *ed:* (BS) Math Ed/Sci Ed, OH St Univ 1952; Cmptr Programming, Univ of Dayton & Sinclair Comm Coll; *cr:* Teacher Fairfield HS 1952-53; 7th/8th Grade Teacher Hilliard Elem Sch 1953-54, 1964; Substitute Teacher Scioto-Derby System 1962-64; Teacher Sudlow Jr HS 1965-67, South-Western City Sch 1967-78; Substitute Teacher Lynchburg Clay Schls 1978-80, Beavercreek Schls 1981-83; Teacher Trotwood-Madison HS 1983-; *ai:* Schlsp & Honor Society Comm; Trotwood-Madison Teacher Assn, OEA, NEA; *home:* 1350 Fudge Dr Beavercreek OH 45385

BOISVERT, JANET CLAIRE, 4th Grade Teacher; *b:* Keene, NH; *ed:* (BA) Sci/Elem Ed, Catholic Teachers Coll 1956; (MA) Guidance/Counseling Ed, Cath Univ 1970; Doctoral Work Behavioral Sci, MD Univ 1971; Travel Courses in Milan Bavaria/London/Norway & Switzerland 1984-; *cr:* HS Sci Teacher St Claires Acad 1957-59; Thevenet Hall Acad 1960-62; H S Eng Teacher Regina HS 1963-65; Jr HS/Art Teacher Francis Scott Key Jr HS 1967-69; Resource Hlth Ed Teacher Prince Georges Cty 1970-71; Plymouth Elem Sch Teacher Grades 4th/5th/6th 1971-; *ai:* Sci Fair; Sketching Mini-Course; Young Authors Day Coord; Jr Golf Prgm in Comm; Friends Arts Spon; NHEA 1971-; NEA 1956-; PEA 1971-; New England Rdng Assn; Natl Sci Fnd Grants to Study Chem; Teacher of Yr 1971-72; Gresham Conf Partcpnt.

BOITNOTT, LINDA A., 4th Grade Teacher; *b:* Roanoke, VA; *m:* Basil G.; *c:* Dale, Andrea; *ed:* (BS) Elem Ed, Radford 1963; *cr:* 2nd/3rd Grade Teacher Rocky Mount Elem 1963-65; 4th Grade Teacher Boones Mill Elem 1966-; *ai:* Young Homemakers; Upsilon Alpha Delta Kappa Pres; Fr Cty Cmmty Action; *home:* Rt 3 Box 262 Boones Mill VA 24065

BOKESCH, DANIEL J., Principal; *b:* Canton, OH; *m:* Dena Maria; *c:* Cara M., Danny A.; *ed:* (BSED) Sociology/Sci, Youngstown St 1970; (MSED) Guidance/Counseling, Westminster Coll 1976; Sch Admin, Westminster Coll 1984; Project Leadership Ashland Coll 1988-89; *cr:* Teacher 1970-87, Prin 1987- Austintown Mid Sch; *ai:* Steel Valleo Conference Mid Sch Div Pres 1989-; Mahoning Cty Prin Assn; Austintown Prin Assn 1987-; Austintown PTA Treas 1989-; *office:* Austintown Mid Sch 5800 Mahoning Ave Youngstown OH 44515

BOKHART, ELAINE ANN (HOOPINGARNER), Phys Ed/Health Teacher; *b:* Goshen, IN; *m:* Donald August; *c:* Janice, Brent; *ed:* (BA) Phys Ed/Health/Elem Ed, 1975, (MS) Phys Ed/Health/Elem Ed, 1979 Ball St Univ; *cr:* Phys Ed/Health Teacher Warsaw Cmmty Schls 1975-76; Mid Sch Teacher Wawasee Cmmty Schls 1977-; *ai:* 7th/8th Grade Trach Coach; HS Vlybl & Gymnastics Ofcl; St Performance Based Accreditation Chm; IN Coaches of Girls Sports Assn 1990; IN Mid Sch Assn, IN Assn Health, Phys Ed & Recreation 1989-; NATL Fed St HS Assn, IN HS Athletic Assn Ofcl 1975-; St Martin DePorres Cath Church 1989-; *home:* RR 6 Box 221 Syracuse IN 46567

BOKUM, CHARLIE W., 4th Grade Teacher; *b:* Chicago, IL; *m:* Carol Gay; *ed:* (BS) W IL Univ 1974; Cert Elem Ed, MT St Univ 1978; *cr:* 2nd Grade Teacher 1978-86, 3rd Grade 1980-86, 4th Grade Teacher 1986- Bitterroot Elem Sch; *ai:* NEA, MEA 1978-; *office:* Bitterroot Sch 1801 Bench Blvd Billings MT 59105

BOLAN, LINDA GRINNELL, 6th Grade Teacher; *b:* Rochester, NY; *m:* James A.; *c:* Kimberly, Theodore, Nicole; *ed:* (BS) Elem Ed, SUNY Oswego 1966; (MA) Elem Ed, Univ of Rochester 196 9; *cr:* K-4th Grade Teacher 1969-70, Substitute Teacher 1970-81 Newark Public Schls; 5th-9th Grade Math/Soc Stud Teacher St Michaels Sch 1981-85; Math Resource/6th Grade Teacher Phelps-Clifton Springs Sch Dist 1985-; *ai:* St Dominics Church Curr Coord 1976-87; *office:* Midlakes Mid Sch Main St Phelps NY 14532

BOLDEN, CHARLES C., 9th Grade Physical Sci Teacher; *b:* Greenville, MS; *m:* Alma Jackson; *c:* Angel, Charsette; *ed:* (BS) Chem, MS Valley St 1964; (MS) Sci Ed, Memphis St Univ 1974; *cr:* Teacher Memphis City Sch 1968-; Part Time Teacher Memphis St Tech Inst 1985-; *ai:* Sci, Jazz, Astronauts Club Spon; Sci Grade Chm; Discipline Comm; Memphis Ed Assn Faculty Rep 1977-78; TN Ed Assn, NEA; Natl Sci Fnd Grant 1968; 3rd Place Winner 9th Grade Class Women Auxilary Medical Contest 1973; Olympiad Contest 1989; *office:* Wooddale Jr HS 3467 Castleman St Memphis TN 38118

BOLDEN, GAIL COX, 4-8th Writing Resource Teacher; *b:* Burlington, NC; *ed:* (BS) Primary Ed, East Carolina Univ 1959; *cr:* 3rd Grade Teacher Grove Park Schl 1959-61; 3rd Grade Teacher Archer Elem Scl 1961-62; 4th Grade Teacher Grove Park/Smith Elem 1962-81; 4th-8th Grade Writing Resource Teacher Grove Park/Hillcrest/Smith Elem-Turrentin Mid Sch 1981-; *ai:* NC Assn of Educators; Burlington City Assn of Educators; Co-Author & Co-Editor when Shoeshines Were a Nickel-An Oral History of Alamance County NC; *home:* 1819 Meadowview Dr Graham NC 27253

BOLDEN, NAOMI JONES, Business Ed Teacher/Dept Chm; *b:* Newport News, VA; *m:* Timothy; *c:* Katina D., Kelle D.; *ed:* (BS) Bus Ed, Norfolk St Univ 1968; (MS) Bus Ed, Old Dominion Univ 1976; Curr Dev Stress in Classroom, Classroom Management; Cmptr Introduction Word Perfect; Desktop, Inventory Control; *cr:* Bus Teacher Woodrow Wilson HS 1968-72, Cradock HS 1973-; Bus Ed Dept Chm Cradock HS 1982-; *ai:* FBLA Co-Adv; Cradock HS Advisory Comm Mem; Voc Ed Week Activity Chm; Study Comm Mem; Portsmouth Ed Assn, VA Ed Assn 1968-; Parent Teacher Stu Assn 1989-, Nom Teacher of Yr Awd 1989; Sunbeams Spon 1987-, Outstanding Adv 1988-89;

Concerned for Youth Comm (Co Chm 1988-, Adv); Bd of Chrstn Ed BdMem 1987-; Several Letters Appreciation Chairmanship Comms; Self Study Voc Ed Chm; Prof Service City of Portsmouth 20 Yr Pen; *home:* 222 Watkins Dr Hampton VA 23669

BOLDEN, WILLIE FRANK, Fourth Grade Teacher; *b:* Thomasville, GA; *ed:* (BS) Elem Ed, Bethune-Cookman Coll 1959; Stetson Univ; *cr:* Teacher Bonner Elem 1959-69, Highlands Elem 1969-; *ai:* Intermediate Dept, Testing, Budget Chairperson; SACS Steering Comm Mem; VEA, FTP, NEA Mem 1959-; Mt Lion AME Church Organist 1953-; Teacher of Yr Nom 1983; *home:* 630 Whitehall St Dayton Beach FL 32114

BOLDERMAN, MARY FOX, Fifth Grade Teacher; *b:* Newark, NJ; *m:* George F.; *c:* Susan M. Spinola, Thomas A. Spinola, James A. Spinola, Carolyn Renner, William A. Spinola, Matthew J. Spinola; *ed:* (BS) Elem Ed, Seton Hall Univ 1961; Mont Clair St Coll/Fairleigh Dickenson Univ/Georgian Court/Brookdale Comm Coll; *cr:* 2nd/4th Grade Teacher Lake Parsippany 1967-70; 3rd Grade Teacher Clark Mills 1970-71; Basic Skills Teacher Brielle 1976; Various Grades Teacher Manas Uan 1976-; *ai:* Gifted/Talented Comm Mem; Sci Fair Comm; Soc Stud Fair Comm; NSTA 1988-; *home:* 903 Clairidge Dr Spring Lake Hgts. NJ 07762

BOLDING, MELANIE HAGERDON, First Grade Teacher; *b:* Claremore, OK; *m:* Marion; *c:* Matthew, Michael; *ed:* (BS) Elem Ed, NSU 1975; Trained & Wrote Act for Cooperative Learning 1st Grade Level Math; *cr:* 1st Grade Teacher Grant Foreman Elem 1975-; *ai:* Staff Dev Comm; NEA, OK Ed Assn, Muskogee Ed Assn; Kappa Kappa Iota Pres 1987-88; Delta Kappa Gamma; Sign Lang.

BOLDON, EILEEN J., First Grade Teacher; *b:* Burlington, IA; *m:* Michael D.; *c:* Margo, Blake, Marissa; *ed:* (AA) Southeast IA Area Comm Coll 1968; (BA) Elem Ed, Univ of Northern IA 1970; *cr:* Teacher Webster City Cmmty Schls 1970-71; Private Pre-Sch Teacher 1971-72; Kndgtn Teacher 1972-73, 1st Grade Teacher 1973- Clarke Cmmty Sch; *ai:* Mem Dist Effective Schls Team; Co-Author PACE Prgm 1st Grade; Kappa Delta Pi 1970; Rdng Cncl 1972-; CCEA 1972-; TTT VP 1970-80; Clarke Cty Historical Society 1972-; Nom US West Direct Outstanding Teacher Prgm; Grade Chm Career Ed 1973-80; Resource Person Implementation of Integrated Lang in Curr; *home:* 321 E Mc Lane Osceola IA 50213

BOLDREGHINI, MIKE, Health Teacher; *b:* Collierville, TN; *m:* Sandra Janice Bartholomew; *c:* Matthew; *ed:* (BSED) Phys Ed/Health, Univ of TN Martin 1976; *cr:* Teacher Richland Jr HS 1976-78, Treadwell HS 1979-85, Westside HS 1986-; *ai:* Fellowship of Chrstn Athletes; Bsktbl, Vllybl, Sftbl Coach; NEA 1976-; TN Interscholastic Coaches Assn 1986-; *office:* Westside HS 3389 Dawn Dr Memphis TN 38127

BOLE, LISA M., Eighth Grade Teacher; *b:* Canton, OH; *ed:* (BA) Elem Ed, Mount Union Coll 1981; Several Grad Wkshp in Ed Walsh Coll; Religion Ed Trng; Sports Medicine Wkshps; *cr:* 6th Grade Teacher 1981-82, 8th Grade Teacher 1982- St Louis Sch; *ai:* Chrldr & Sch Newspaper Adv; Asst Track Coach; Statistician; Spelling Bee Comm; Athletic Dir; NCTE 1980-; NCEA 1981-; Mt Union Alumni Assn 1982-.

BOLEK, SHEILA BORN, Eighth Grade Teacher/Asst Prin; *b:* Cleveland Heights, OH; *ed:* (BA) Home Ec, Ursuline Coll 1963; Elem Teaching Cert Cleveland St Univ 1974; Cmptr Sci, Educl Admin, Ursuline Coll; *cr:* 3rd/5th Grade Teacher St Jerome Sch 1964-67; 5th Grade Teacher St Timothy Sch 1967-71, Hebrew Acad 1971-72; 2nd-8th Grade Teacher St Henry Sch 1972-79; Teacher/Asst Prin Our Lady of Peace Sch 1979-; *ai:* Safety Patrol Adv; Cantor for Liturgies; Cmptr Coord; Our Lady of Peace Sch Sci Fair Coord; St Clare & St Ann Schls Sci Fair Judge; Diocesan Soc Stud Teachers Assn Treas 1982-; Our Lady of Peace Church Dir of Confirmation Prgm 1985-; *office:* Our Lady of Peace Sch 12406 Buckingham Ave Cleveland OH 44120

BOLER, BARRY KEMP, Biology Teacher/Coach; *b:* Meridian, MS; *m:* Janet Anderson; *c:* Jeremy, Jared; *ed:* (AA) General Sci, Clarke Coll 1981; (BS) Athletic Admin/General Sci/Bio, Univ of S MS 1984; MTAI Approved; *cr:* Teacher/Coach Jefferson Davis Acad 1984-85, Stringer Attendance Center 1985-86, Petal HS 1986-; *ai:* Girls Bsktbl & Track Coach; Asst Bsbl Coach; MS Coaches Assn 1984-; Jeff Davis Acad STAR Teacher 1984; *home:* 410 Ford Dr Petal MS 39465

BOLER, TRAN CHARLTON, Health Educator; *b:* Gadsden, AL; *m:* R. Clark Sr.; *c:* Rod II, Leslie; *ed:* (AS) Health/Phys Ed, Gadsden St Coll 1969; (BS) Health/Phys Ed, 1972, (MA) Ed, 1973 Bloomsburg St Coll; Grad Stud Univ of AL, George St Univ, PA St Univ; *cr:* Phys Ed Teacher Cntrl Columbia HS, Cntrl Columbia Mid Sch, Fair Oaks Elem; Health Educator Oakwood Kenwood HS, De Kalb Comm Coll; *ai:* Choral & Teen Peer Helper Spon; Red Cross Blood Drive, Battle of Bands Coord; Crisis Intervention Team; GA Assn for Health, Phys Ed, Dance; AFT; Cntry Music Assn Mem 1978-; Mt Paran Church of God Mem 1982-; Marietta Daily Journal Cntry Music Journalist 1983-; Helped Develop Pilot Course Connections; *office:* Oakwood HS 1650 Joyner Ave Marietta GA 30060

BOLIAN, IDA MAY, Fourth Grade Teacher; *b:* Natchez, MS; *m:* Dan; *c:* Shellie Bolian Mahaffey, Danny, Jody Bolian Hester; *ed:* (BS) Ed, MS St Univ 1949; Post Bac Elem Ed, MS Coll 1987; Grad Work Elem Ed, MS Coll 1982-83; Rdng Conference, Univ of S MS 1978; Rdng for Children, Jackson St Univ 1977; Cmptr Programming Lang Course 1987; *cr:* 6th Grade Teacher Mc Clure Sch 1971-75; 2nd Grade Teacher Brandon Acad 1975-80; 5th Grade Teacher 1980-86, 4th Grade Teacher 1986- Hillcrest Chrstn Sch; *ai:* Hillcrest Spelling Bee Chairperson; 4th Grade Head Teacher; Tour Guide for Hillcrest Sch Tour to Washington DC 1990; MPSA Dist Spelling Bee Chm 1984; Cntrl Presbyn Church (Circle Chm 1980, WOC Bd 1985-, Joy Gift Chm 1989-); Poetry Published in Religious Materials; *office:* Hillcrest Chrstn Sch 3565 Wheatley Dr Jackson MS 39212

BOLICH, MARGARET VANDERKARR, 4th-6th Grade Math Teacher; *b:* Woodstock, IL; *m:* Gene Marco; *c:* Amy M., Jason S.; *ed:* (BSED) Elem Ed, Alverno Coll 1963; (MSED) Elem Ed, W IL Univ 1985; Elem Math, Counseling, Rdng; Midwest Regional Drug Free Sch Trng 1989; Dept of Ed St Trng ABC Math 1987; *cr:* 5th/6th Grade Homeroom Teacher Milwaukee Public Schls 1963-68; 4th-6th Grade Math Teacher Davenport Cmmty Schls 1981-; *ai:* Math Bee Coach; Champs Have and Model Positive Peer Skills Adv; Sch Improvement Comm Mem; Designated Math Leader; NCTM; IA Cncl Teachers of Math Elem Math Teaching Finalist 1986; Golden Apple Awd 1989; ICTM Journal 1990; UNI Speaker Math Conference 1989; ICTM Speaker Math Conference St 1987, 1989, 1990; Chapter II Grant 1988; ABC Math Wkshp Leader 1988-; Area Math Bee 6th Grade 1st Place 1990, St 4th 1987; *office:* Davenport Cmmty Schls 1716 Kenwood Ave Davenport IA 52803

BOLINGER, JOHN ALLEN, Science Department Chair; *b:* Albuquerque, NM; *m:* Rada B. Carl; *c:* James, Mathew; *ed:* (BA) Speech Comm, Univ of NM 1970; Teacher Cert; *cr:* Chem/Physics Teacher 1987-88, Drama/Bio Teacher 1988-89, Sci Chm 1989- Bernalillo HS; *ai:* Sandia Summer Prgm; Drama Club; Speech Team; NSTA 1987-; *office:* Bernalillo HS P O Box 640 Bernalillo NM 87004

BOLLENBACK, DIRK, Soc Stud Teacher/Dept Chm; *b:* Evanston, IL; *m:* Beverly Jane Colvin; *c:* Ann E. Jamison, Sarah J. (dec); *ed:* (BA) Government, Wesleyan Univ 1953; (MS) Intnl, Johns Hopkins Sch of Advanced Intnl Stud 1955; Cert Ed, Wesleyan Univ 1958; John Hay Fellow Univ of Chicago 1963-64; Ed, His, W CT St Univ; *cr:* Research Analyst/Instr US Army Psychological Warfare Sch for Officers 1955-57; Soc Stud Teacher 1958-, Dept Chm 1964- Ridgefield HS; *ai:* Ridgefield HS Curr Cncl Prgm; Steering Comm NEASC Evaluation of Ridgefield HS; Stu Selection Comm; NEA, Ct Ed Assn 1958-; Ridgefield Teachers Assn Past Pres; Cmmty Resources Comm Chm 1968-70; Republican Town Comm 1964-68; Vestry Saint Stephens Episcopal Church 1973-79; Baird Memorial Assn Exec Comm 1981-; St Stpehens Episcopal Church (Archivist, Historian) 1990; Union Carbide Teacher of Yr Awd 1987; *home:* 67 Grandview Dr Ridgefield CT 06877

BOLLING, IMANI, School Social Worker; *b:* White Plains, NY; *ed:* (BA) Urban Stud, Cornell Univ 1973; (MS) Soc Work/Bus Admin Columbia Univ 1980; *cr:* Mrktg Researcher Natl Black Network 1973-75, The Gillette Company 1975-77; Sch Admin The Henry Buckner Sch 1977-78; Sch Soc Worker White Plains Public Schls 1980-; *ai:* Chairperson of the White Plains Public Schls Soc Work Dept; Instr of Peer Leadership Trng Prgm; Parent Wkshp Coord of Minority Cncl; Assn of Black Social Workers 1979-; NY St Sch Soc Workers Assn 1980-; NY St Assn of Cnslrs 1988-; NY St United Teachers 1980-; White Plains Comm to Combat Drugs 1987-88; Fairview Greenburgh Cmmty Action Prgm Bd of Dirs 1986-89; Greater Cmmty Cncl of White Plains 1990; White Plains PTA Jenkins Awd 1989; Outstanding Young Women of America 1985; *office:* White Plains HS 550 North St White Plains NY 10605

BOLLINGER, DARREL LANE, Industrial Arts Instructor; *b:* Portales, NM; *m:* Brenda; *c:* Justin, Jalaina; *ed:* (BA) Industrial Ed, 1974, (MS) Industrial Ed, 1979 E NM Univ; *cr:* Draftsman E NM Univ 1974-76; Teacher Portales Jr HS 1976; *ai:* Discipline Review, Voc Curr Comm; NM Industrial Technology Assn Quadrant Rep 1988-; Curry Cty 4-H Leader 1985-, Leadership Awd 1988; 4-H Parent/Leader Assn 1987-; NM Hunter Safety Instr 1980-; *home:* Rt 4 Box 258 Clovis NM 88101

BOLLINGER, GAIL EICK, Third Grade Teacher; *b:* Lewistown, PA; *m:* J. Michael; *c:* Jeremy Houghtaling; *ed:* (BA) Elem Ed, Mansfield Univ 1967; Grad Stud; *cr:* Teacher N Tioga Sch Dist 1967-; *ai:* Psea; N Tioga Ed Assn Exec Cncl; Westfield Boro Cncl (Mem, Pres, Vp) 1986-; Mt Pleasant Cem Assn 1986-; Tioga Cty Assn of Boroughs (Pres 1989) 1986-; *home:* 212 Maple St Westfield PA 16950

BOLLINI, CONNIE O'CONNOR, Kindergarten Teacher; *b:* Alton, IL; *m:* William T.; *c:* Steven, Linon; *ed:* (BS) Elem Ed, Southern IL Univ 1990; *cr:* 5th Grade Teacher St Peter & Paul 1964-66; 1st-3rd Grade Teacher 1974-88, Kndgtn Teacher 1988- St Marys; *ai:* NAEYC 1989-; NCEA 1974-89; 4-H Jr Leader St Outstanding 1959; Home Extension 4-H Key Club; NAEYC; NCEA; *office:* St Marys Sch 536 E 3rd St Alton IL 62002

BOLLMANN, DAVID J., Social Studies Teacher; *b:* Muskegon, MI; *m:* Darla O Bryan; *c:* Christina, Rachel, Brandt, Sarah; *ed:* (BA) His, E IL Univ 1983; Grad Work His; *cr:* Teacher Mc Lean Cty Unit 5 Parkside Jr HS 1984-; *ai:* Frosh Bsktbl & Bsbl; Spirit, Athletic Club; Soc Stud Curr Revision Comm; NEA, IL Ed Assn 1986-; Phi Alpha Theta, Kappa Delta Pi 1982-83; E IL Univ Soc Sci Writing Awd 1983; Charles & Dorthee Coleman Schlsp 1983; Annie L Weller, & Distinguished Stu Teacher Awds 1983; *office:* Parkside Jr HS 101 N Parkside Rd Normal IL 61761

BOLLMEYER, DEBORAH KAY SINGLETON, Third Grade Teacher; *b:* Kansas City, MO; *m:* Larry E.; *c:* Jonathan M., Tiffany M.; *ed:* (BS) Elem Ed, Cntrl MO St Univ 1974; Working Toward Masters in Guidance & Counseling; *cr:* 3rd Grade Teacher 1974-77, 1st Grade Teacher 1977-78, 3rd Grade Teacher 1978- Leslie Bell; *ai:* Dist Sci Curr Chairperson; Cntrl Teachers Assn (Secy, Legislative Chairperson, Rights & Responsibilities); MSTA; Welcome Wagon Pres; GSA Leader; *office:* Leslie Bell Elem Sch 400 S 20th St Lexington MO 64067

BOLTON, CARL HARPER, Social Studies Teacher; *b:* Kansas City, MO; *m:* Sue Alter; *c:* Megan S.; *ed:* (BS) His, 1967, (MS) Counseling/Psych, 1969 Univ of MO; *cr:* Teacher Hillcrest Jr HS 1970-86, Shawnee Mission NW 1986-; *ai:* Spon Intnl & SADD Club; *office:* Shawnee Mission NW HS 12701 W 67th St Shawnee Mission KS 66216

BOLTON, DOROTHY ROBERTS, Guidance Counselor; *b:* Crestview, FL; *m:* Curtis Raymond; *c:* Stephen, Rodney, Alicia; *ed:* (MA) Elem Ed, Univ of W FL 1984; Working Towards Masters Admin & Counseling; *cr:* 6th Grade Teacher Bob Sikes Elem Sch 1976-77; 2nd Grade Teacher 1977-83, 1st Grade Teacher 1983-84, Primary Specialist 1984-89 Northwood Elem Sch; Guidance Cnslr Richbourg Mid Sch 1989-; *ai:* Cty Health Nutrition Comm; Sci Fair Coord; *home:* 3138 Forrest Ave Crestview FL 32536

BOLTON, GARY L., Jr HS Principal; *b:* Stromsburg, NE; *m:* Denise Best; *c:* Lindsey; *ed:* (BS) Soc Stud, 1971; (MA) Counseling, 1977; (EDS) Admin, 1986 Univ NE; *cr:* His Teacher 1971-83; Dean of Students 1983-87; Prin 1987- Fremont Jr HS; *ai:* NASSP 1987-; NCSA 1987-; Phi Delta Kappa 1980-; Rotary 1989-; NE Outstanding Young Educator 1978; Demolay Teacher of Yr 1981; *office:* Fremont Jr H S 130 E 9th St Fremont NE 68025

BOLTON, LOIS STRANGE, 8th Grade Math Teacher/Chm; *b:* Parrotsville, TN; *w:* William E. (dec); *ed:* (BS) Elem Ed/Curr Adm/Super, Lincoln Memorial Univ 1952; (MS) Elem Ed/Curr Adm/Super Univ of TN 1962; Variety of Institutions/Wkshps; *cr:* 1st Grade East TN 1948-59; 8thGrade Math Teacher Morristown Jr HS/Meadowville Mid 1959-; *ai:* Hamblen Cty Ed Assn (Pres 1984-85/1988-89, Negotiation Chief Spokesperson 1985-); TN Ed Assn Comm Mem 1984-; NEA; Natl Rep Assn Rep 1982-; Morristowns Girls Club of America Exec Bd of Dir 1983-89; North Hamblen Cty Property Owners Assn Exec Comm; *office:* Meadowview Middle School 1623 Meadowview Ln Morristown TN 37814

BOLTON, SHIRLEY WOODS, 4th Grade Teacher; *b:* Hays, KS; *m:* Frederick A.; *c:* Janine, Jacob; *ed:* (BSE) Elem Ed, KS St Teachers Coll 1969; *cr:* Elem Teacher Bryant Elem Sch 1969-79, Munson Primary & Mulvane Grade Sch 1979-; *ai:* MADD; *office:* Mulvane Grade Sch 411 SE Louis Blvd Mulvane KS 67110

BOLTON, THOMAS WALTER, Athletic Director/HS Teacher; *b:* Johnstown, PA; *m:* Judith Lynne Bretz; *c:* Derrick Q., Heather D., Craig T.; *ed:* (BS) Missions, Toccoa Falls Coll 1976; (MS) Scndry Ed, Pensacola Chrstn Coll; Bible, Columbia Bible Coll; *cr:* Asst Prin 1979-84, Coach/Teacher/Athletic Dir 1976- Gadsden Chrstn Acad; *ai:* Coaching Var Bsktbl & Golf; Tallahassee Democrat Sftbl Coach of Yr 1987.

BOLTZ, FRANCES SPELL, Gifted & Talented Teacher; *b:* Hazelhurst, GA; *m:* Daniel Robert; *c:* Matthew, Adam, Jason; *ed:* (BS) Elem Ed, FL St Univ 1960; Masters Prgm Rdng Ed, GA St Univ; Gifted Ed; *cr:* 1st Grade Teacher Palm Springs Elem 1960-61; 4th-6th Grade Teacher Cntry Day 1961-64; 3rd Grade Teacher Mt Brook Elem 1964-65; Pre-Sch Teacher Shallowford Learning Center 1965-69; 3rd Grade Gifted Teacher St Thomas Elem 1969-72; 1st/4th-8th Grade Teacher Coleman & Lounsberry 1972-; *ai:* Peace Club; Variety Show; Readers Theatre; Literary Magazine; Knowledge Master Open; Acad Bowls; Leadership Trng; Symposium of Arts & Learning Carnival; Environmental Ed Outdoor Camp; Prin Comm Senator 1989-; NJEA 1972-; NJ Educators Gifted & Talented 1981-; NEA 1960-; Natl Assn Gifted Ed 1981-; Democratic Club Secy 1980-81; Historical Society 1980-89; DE Raptor Center 1989-; Peace Messenger Awd Secy General United Nations 1990; Warren Cummings Awd Service to Ed SCEA 1989; WWOR TV Grant 1989; Teacher of Yr Vernon Schls & Sussex Cty 1981; *office:* Lounsberry Hollow Mid Sch PO Box 219 Sammis Rd Vernon NJ 07462

BOLTZ, GERALD MICHAEL, Sixth Grade Teacher; *b:* Lebanon, PA; *m:* Jeanne L. Geesey; *ed:* (BS) Elem Ed, Mansfield Univ 1967; (MED) Elem Ed, Millersville Univ 1972; *cr:* 6th Grade Teacher Palmyra Area Sch Dist 1967-; *ai:* Assembly Comm; Sr HS Track Coach; PAEA Treas 1968-70; PA St Ed Assn, NEA; Quittapahilla Audubon Society Pres 1987-; PA Design & Craftsman 1982-; Lancaster Designer Craftsman 1982-; *home:* 25 Woodbine Dr Hershey PA 17033

BOLYARD, MATTIE AVICE JAMES, Retired Teacher; *b:* Augusta, GA; *c:* James O.; *ed:* (BA) Soc/Drama, Shorter Coll 1938; Numerous Univs; *cr:* Soc Worker Dept of Public Welfare 1938-43; Teacher/Kndgtn Dir W Minster Chrstn Sch 1944; Teacher Miami FL 1967-89; *ai:* Amer Assn of Univ Women (Pres, VP, Treas, Prgm Chm), Melanie Rosborough Awd 1988; 1st Baptist Church S Miami; *home:* 8086 Camino Ct Miami FL 33143

BOLYARD, PAUL DAVID, JR., 7th/8th Grade US His Teacher; *b:* Morgantown, WV; *ed:* (BS) Elem Ed, Frostburg St Univ 1975; (MS) Guidance/Counseling, Bowie St Coll 1982; *cr:* Teacher Stevensville Mid Sch 1975-; *ai:* Soc Stud & Stu Assistance Prgm Chm; Girls Bsktbl; Cath Univ Constitutional Stud;

Bicentennial Commission 1986; Facing His & Ourselves Grant 1989; *office:* Stevensville Mid Sch Stevensville MD 21666

BOMAN, JAMES PAUL, Theatre Arts Teacher; *b:* Edenville, MI; *m:* Mary Helen Cooley; *c:* Stephen, Timothy J.; *ed:* (BS) Speech, 1962, (MA) Speech Arts, 1971 Cntrl MI Univ; Sam Houston St Univ; *cr:* Teacher Hillman Cmmty Schls 1962-63, Gladstone Public Schls 1963-67, Sandusky Cmmty Schls 1967-82, B F Terry HS 1982-; *ai:* Dir of Theatre; Dir of UIL One-Act; TSCA Past Drama Chm 1987-89; TETA Mem 1986-; TSSCA Mem 1986-; LCTA Teacher Relations Chm 1989-; Fort Bend Cmmty Players Bd of Dir 1984-86; First United Meth Church Mem 1982-; Terry Scndry Teacher of Yr 1988; NHS Teacher of Month 1989; Outstanding Coach 1987-89; Published in Creative Teacher 1971; *office:* B F Terry H S 5500 Avenue N Rosenberg TX 77471

BOMAR, ROBERT LINTON, Assistant Principal; *b:* Americus, GA; *m:* Laura Beth Elliott; *ed:* (AA) Pre-Forestry, Clayton Jr Coll 1979; (BA) Poly Sci, Univ of GA 1981; (MED) Soc Stud Ed, GA St Univ 1983; Finished Coursework for PhD in Educl Admin, GA St Univ; *cr:* Soc Stud Teacher Henry Cty HS 1983-1990; Asst Prin Locust Grove Elem Sch 1990-; *ai:* 4-H Club & Model United Nation Spon; Advanced Placement & Literary Coord; Dept Co-Chairperson; Phi Delta Kappa 1990; Kappa Delta Pi, Prof Assn of GA Educators 1983-; ASCD 1987-; Salem Baptist Church (Deacon, Sunday Sch Teacher 1988-); Habitat for Humanity (Mem, Partner) 1985-; Henry Cty HS Teacher of Yr 1986-88 & Star Teacher 1989, 1990; RESA Griffin Outstanding Literary Coord 1988.

BOMBERGER, BRENDA WHITE, Business Education Teacher; *b:* Flintville, PA; *m:* A. James; *ed:* (BA) Bus Ed, Newberry Coll 1970; (MED) Bus Ed, Shippensburg Univ 1982; *cr:* Bus Ed Teacher Frederick HS 1970-76, Lebanon HS 1977-83, East Lebanon Cty HS 1983-; *ai:* Co-Adv FBLA Club; Stu of Month Selection, Bus Advisory Comm; Delta Kappa Gamma; Delta Pi Epsilon; East Lebanon Cty Ed Assn Secy 1987-; NEA; *office:* Eastern Lebanon Cty HS 180 Elco Dr Myerstown PA 17067

BONACCI, JEAN LEONARD, Music Teacher; *b:* Scranton, PA; *m:* Ronald P.; *c:* Ronald Jr., Jennifer, Maria; *ed:* (BM) Music Ed/Voice/Piano, Marywood Coll 1970; Cert in Elem Ed 1972; *cr:* 4th-6th Grade Math/Soc Stud Teacher Fell Elem Sch 1970-75; 5th-6th Grade Teacher Lakeland Elem Sch 1976-83; 7th-8th Grade Music/9th-12th Grade Chorus Teacher Lakeland Jr/Sr HS 1983-; *ai:* HS Chorus & Stage Management Club; NEA, PMEA, MENC; *home:* RD 1 Box 372 Olyphant PA 18447

BONACQUISTA, JOSEPH MARTIN, Social Studies Teacher; *b:* Trinidad, CO; *m:* G. J. Lewinson; *c:* Jeffrey J., Janelle J.; *ed:* (BA) Soc Sci, 1964; (MA) Admin, 1966 Univ Northern CO; *cr:* SS Teacher/Coach Weld Central Jr-Sr HS 1964-65; Roncalli HS 1966-67; SS Teacher Corwin Jr HS 1967-70; SS Teacher/Coach East HS 1970-; *ai:* HS Bsbl Coach 10 Yrs; 17 Championships Including Summer and HS Leagues; East HS Lettermans Club Spon 5 Yrs; Sponsored Citizenship Club Corin Jr HS; Pueblo Ed Assn 1967-; CO Ed Assn 1964-; NEA 1964-; Runyon Field Bd of Dir Pres 1977-79; Bsbl Corp Sec 1969-74; Prgm Coord 1980-; 3 Time South-Central Leag Coach of Yr; Inducted Greater Pueblo Sports Assn Hall of Fame-1977; Civic Awd for Coaching 4 Yrs YMCA Bsktbl; Civic Awd for Coaching 3 Yrs of Jr HS Bsktbl; *office:* East H S 9 Mac Neil Rd Pueblo CO 81001

BONAR, JUDY ANN (RATAICZAK), Third Grade Teacher; *b:* Bellaire, OH; *m:* Joseph E.; *c:* Jeffrey J., Jon D., Jason J.; *ed:* (BS) Elem Ed, Muskingum Coll 1974; Kndgtn Theories & Methods, OH Univ; Comm, WV Univ; Early Chldhd, Univ of Cntrl FL; Eng, Brevard Comm Coll; *cr:* 4th Grade Teacher Jefferson Avenue Elem 1982-84; Eng Leona Avenue Mid Sch 1984-86; Eng Hoover Jr HS 1986-87; 3rd-5th Grade Teacher Christa Mc Auliffe Elem 1987-; *ai:* FL Ed Assn; Amer Assn of Univ Women; Grace Luth Church; Meritorious Sch Awds Hoover Jr HS 1986-87, Christa Mc Auliffe Elem 1989-; *home:* 300 Shannon Ave Melbourne Beach FL 32951

BOND, DOROTHY JEAN MANN, 5th Grade Teacher; *b:* Brownsville, TN; *m:* Joe Thomas; *c:* Jessica M.; *ed:* (BA) His/ Sociology Lane Coll 1973; Elem Cert, Univ TN Martin; Working Toward Elem Counseling (MA) MemphisSt Univ; *cr:* 11th Grade His Teacher Haywood Co HS 1973-74; 7th & 8th Grade Teacher 1973-74, 5th Grade Teacher 1974- , Anderson Grammar Sch; *ai:* Natl Jr Beta Club Adv; *home:* 2560 Hwy 19 Brownsville TN 38012

BOND, FOREST ELWIN, Retired Teacher; *b:* Nortonville, KS; *m:* Evelyn Doris Rogers; *ed:* (BA) His/Poly Sci, Ottawall 1950; (ME) Guidance/Admin, KS Univ 1957; WY Univ, Pittsburg St, Emporia St; *cr:* Teacher/Prin Rantoul Grade Sch 1950-53; Teacher/Prin/Coach Williamsburg Grade Sch 1953-88; *ai:* Franklin Cty Pres 1956-57; KS St Teachers Assn 1950-85; NEA 1950-85; Lions Club Lion Tamer 1956-; Mason (Master, Secy 1959-); Eastern Star Worthy Patron 1959; KS Teacher Hall of Fame Dodge City; *home:* 128 N Robey Williamsburg KS 66095

BOND, JAMES JOSEPH, Fifth Grade Teacher; *b:* Fond Du Lac, WI; *ed:* (BA) Math/Sci, MI St Univ 1974; (MS) Guidance/ Counseling, Univ of WI Oshkosh 1982; Cmmty Intervention Incorporated Minneapolis Substance Abuse Seminar 1984; *cr:* 5th Grade Teacher Evans Elem Sch 1974-; Head Jr Var Ftbl Coach 1974-81, Asst Wrestling Coach 1978-81, Head Ftbl Coach 1982- L P Goodrich HS; *ai:* Head Ftbl & Strength Coach Goodrich HS; Just Say No & Invention Convention Sci Prgms Evans Elem; WI HS Ftbl Coaches Assn; St & Natl Counseling Assn; Kiwanis Youth Services 1988-89; Cardinal Quarterback Club; Gifted & Talented Teacher of Yr 1986; WI St Ftbl Champions 1987; *office:* Evans Elem Sch 140 S Peters Ave Fond Du Lac WI 54935

BOND, JOAN, First Grade Classroom Teacher; *b:* Americus, GA; *ed:* (BSE) Early Chldhd, 1975, (MED) 1979, Specialist in Ed, 1982 Univ of GA; *cr:* Secy Research Asst Univ of GA 1966-73; Classroom Teacher Danielsville Elem 1975-; *ai:* Madison Cty Assn of Educators (Mem 1975-83, VP, Pres); Prof Assn of GA Educators 1983-; Hull Baptist Church (Sunday Sch, Pre-Sch Dir, Teacher 1968-87, Adult Women SS Asst 1987-); *home:* Rt 2 Box 48 Glenn Carrie Rd Hull GA 30646

BOND, MARY KATHRYN, Fourth 4th Grade Teacher; *b:* Wytheville, VA; *ed:* (BS) Elem Ed, James Madison Univ 1974; *cr:* 6th Grade Teacher, Amelia Cty Elem Sch 1974-77; 4th Grade Teacher, Woodlawn Elem Sch 1977-; *ai:* Sci Comm Chm; Woodlawn Elem Sci Fair Spon; Sch Census Enumerator; Cooperating Teacher VA Commonwealth Univ; Hopewell Ed Assn Faculty Rep 1974-; VA Ed Assn, NEA 1974-; Woodlawn PTO; Jr Womans Club of Hopewell Ed Chm 1985-86, 1989-, First Place Dist 198-; Woodlawn Teacher of Yr 1990; VFW Teacher of Yr Nom; *office:* Woodlawn Elem Sch 1100 Dinwiddie Ave Hopewell VA 23860

BOND, VIRGINIA FRANCES, Sixth Grade Soc Stud Teacher; *b:* Madison, WV; *ed:* (BS) Elem Ed, Salem Coll 1977; (MA) Elem Ed, Marshall Univ 1982; *cr:* Art/Music/Rdng Teacher Van Grade Sch 1977-80; 5th Grade Teacher Danville Grade Sch 1980-86; 6th Grade Soc Stud Teacher Madison Mid Sch 1986-; *ai:* Exemplary Sch 1988-89 & Continuing Ed Comm 1989-; Parent/Teacher Advisory Cncl 1987-; Madison/Danville Jaycees Individual Dev VP 1989-90, Speak-Up & Write-Up 1989; Madison Baptist Church Dir of Bible Sch 1986, 1989; Appalachian Cmmty Theatre Bd of Dirs 1980-88; *office:* Madison Mid Sch 404 Riverside Dr Madison WV 25130

BONDARCHUK, LOIS ASH, Mid Sch Mathematics Teacher; *b:* Philadelphia, PA; *m:* Kenneth; *ed:* (BS) Elem Ed, Temple Univ 1971; (ME) Ed, Penn St Villanova 1980; *cr:* Teacher Tinicum Elem 1972-80; Math Teacher Tinicum Sch 1981-; *ai:* Math Curr Comm; Drama Club Coach; Sch Store, Stu Cncl Adv; Sch Trip, Yrbk Spon; Publicity Coord; Sch Dances Chm; *office:* Tinicum Sch 1st & Seneca Sts Essington PA 19029

BONDE, ROWENA M., Fifth Grade Teacher; *b:* Hamlin, WV; *c:* Melinda Pauly, Timothy Mc Callister, Leslie Mc Callister; *ed:* (BA) Elem Ed, Elmhurst Coll 1972; (MA) Personalized Ed, Concordia Coll 1980; Grad Stud; *cr:* Teacher Lincoln Cty 1951-58, Lombard 1972-; *ai:* Sci & Health Comm; Health Curr Writer; Lombard Ed Assn VP 1985-; IL Ed Assn 1972-; NEA 1972-; Pioneer Girls America Chm 1965-69; First Baptist Church Sunday Sch Teacher 1968-75; Lombard Ed Assn Negotiator.

BONDS, JONAS L., English Teacher; *b:* Jackson, MS; *ed:* (BS) Eng/Soc Stud, 1973, (MS) Early Chldhd, 1976, (EDS) Elem Ed/ Admin Supervision, 1981 Jackson St Univ; (PHD) Mid Chldhd Ed, MO Univ 1990; MS St Univ; AFT Wkshp; *cr:* Teacher Canton Elem Sch 1974-79, Nichols Mid Sch 1979-; *ai:* Former Mem Textbook Comm; Nichols Homer Society Spon; 7th Grade Pres Adv; AFT Building Rep 1974-, Cert 1989; MFT Building Rep 1974-, Cert 1989; Natl Assn for Young Children 1986-; Valley North Area Reporter 1988-; AFT Wkshp; *home:* 5120 Sun Valley Rd Jackson MS 39206

BONDS, LELLA GANTT, Laboratory School Instructor; *b:* Beaufort, SC; *m:* Charles W.; *c:* Charles W. III; *ed:* (BA) Elem Ed, Benedict Coll 1966; (MED) Elem Ed, Southern Univ 1972; (EDS) Early Chldhd Ed, GA Southern Coll 1976; (EDD) Early Chldhd Ed, Univ of SC 1987; Grad Stud Valdosta St Coll, Univ of FL; *cr:* Teacher Aiken Cty SC Public Schls 1966, Wrens Elem Sch 1967-70, W Gordon Elem Sch 1970-72; Instr P K Yonge Lab Sch Univ of FL 1976-77, GA Southern Univ Laboratory Sch 1974-; *ai:* Kappa Delta Pi, NEA, GA Assn of Ed Mem; Phi Delta Kappa, Bulloch Assn of Educators, Sigma Gamma Rho, GA Cncl of Intnl Rdng Assn, Natl Assn Laboratory Schls; Southeastern Assn Laboratory Schls; Black Women of Profession Pres; Amer Cancer Society; Stabucette Civic Organization; Natl Assn for Advancement of Colored People; Articles Published; *office:* GA Southern Univ Box 8 Statesboro GA 30460

BONDS, RONETTA JONES, Fifth Grade Teacher; *b:* Memphis, TN; *c:* Toni D., Roslyn E. Bonds Phillips; *ed:* (BS) Elem Ed, Le Moyne Coll 1963; (MS) Elem Ed, Memphis St Univ 1972; *cr:* Teacher E A Harrold Elem, Millington E Elem; *ai:* Sci Fair Coord; Grade Chairperson; NEA; SCEA 25 Yr Pen Awd; *home:* 4052 University Memphis TN 38127

BONDS, SHIRLEY ATKINSON, Fourth Grade Teacher; *b:* Kansas City, MO; *m:* Larry Odom Sr.; *c:* Teresa Newcomer, Larry Jr., Susan; *ed:* (BAE) Elem Ed, Univ of MS 1956; *cr:* 3rd Grade Teacher 1956-60; 5th Grade Teacher 1962-64; 4th Grade Teacher 1970-Houston Elem Sch; *ai:* Delta Kappa Gamma; Cosmopolitian Club; *home:* Rt 2 Box 80 Houston MS 38851

BONE, DONNA PRYOR, Science & 5th Grade Teacher; *b:* Nurnberg, Germany; *m:* Richard D.; *c:* Joshua, Sarabeth; *ed:* (BS) Soc Stud, 1981, (BS) Earth Sci, 1981 Northern MI Univ; (MS) Sci Ed, TX Womens Univ 1984; *cr:* 8th/12th Grade SS/Math/Sci Teacher Crete Monee Altern HS 1981-82; 8th Grade Earth Sci Teacher Forest Oak Mid Schl IW ISD 1982-86; 7th/12th Grade Sci Teacher Chrstn Temple Sch 1986-89; 5th Grade & Sci Bethesda Chrstn Sch 1989-; *ai:* Sci Fair Adv/Coord; TX St Teachers Assn Lobbist 1985-86; Cast 1982-; TX St TA Mem 1982-; *office:* Bethesda Chrst Sch 4700 N Beach Fort Worth TX 76147

BONELLO, ROBERT L., Secondary Gifted Ed Teacher; *b:* Leechburg, PA; *m:* Virginia L. Baird; *c:* Lisa, Eli; *ed:* (BA) Geography/Soc Stud, Edinboro Univ 1966; (MS) Gifted Ed/ Psych, Univ of Pittsburgh 1985; Numerous Wkshps & Conferences; *cr:* Teacher Kiski Area Sch Dist 1966-72, Apollo-Ridge Sch Dist 1972-; *ai:* Math League & Quiz Bowl Team Spon; Future Problem Solving & Super Bowl of Problem Solving Spon & Teacher; PA Assn for Gifted Ed 1975-; PA St Ed Assn, NEA 1966-; Little League Coach Head Coach 1980-83; Creative Teacher of Yr, Superbowl of Problem Solving 1989; Creator of Skull Games a 5 Sch Academic Competition; Three Grants from our Intermediate Unit; *office:* Apollo-Ridge HS Star Rt Box 46a Spring Church PA 15686

BONEY, MARTHA MARLENE OGLE, Fourth Grade Teacher; *b:* Maryville, TN; *m:* J. Wayne; *c:* Lisa, Edana; *ed:* (BS) Elem Ed, Carson Newman 1965; Univ of TN, Johnson Bible Coll; *cr:* 3rd Grade Teacher Phi Beta Phi Elem 1965-66, South Elem 1966-68; 4th Grade Teacher New Center Elem 1968-69, Ritta Elem 1969-71; 4th-6th Grade Teacher Bonny Kate Elem 1971-; *ai:* Staffing Team Mem; Cmmty Care Leader; Heart Fund Rep; Local Booster Club Volunteer; Teacher of Gifted & Talented; Sch Advisory Comm; Cmptr Inservice Presenter; NEA Mem, TN Ed Assn Mem 1965-; KY Cty Ed Assn (Sch Rep 1988-) 1971-; Knoxville Rdng Prgm Assn Chm 1989-; E TN Ed Assn Presenter 1988-; TN Instructional Model Ed Assn 1985, Certificate 1985; Elected Mem Task Force St of TN Writing Cmptr Curr; *home:* 704 Ala Dr Knoxville TN 37920

BONHAM, CAROL E., Science/Mathematics Teacher; *b:* Shawnee, KS; *m:* Mike; *c:* Kirsten, Nathan; *ed:* (BS) Sci Ed, KS St Univ 1978; Natl Sci Fnd Grant Prgm, KS St Univ; Chem, WSU; *cr:* Sci/Math Teacher Attica HS 1979-; Adjunct Faculty Pratt Comm Coll 1988-; *ai:* Scholars Bowl Coaching; Harper Meth Church Ed Comm Mem 1988-; *home:* 1804 Oak Harper KS 67058

BONHAM, LANE E., Teacher of Gifted/Talented Sci; *b:* San Antonio, TX; *m:* Laura Thomson; *c:* Linda Rickson Martin; *ed:* (EDD) Scndry Ed, Univ S MS 1972; (AM) Zoology, Univ MO 1962; (BA) Bio, Univ TX 1960; Academically Gifted Univ New Orleans 1988; *cr:* Sci Teacher Terrell Wells Jr HS 1962-63; Instr/ Bio Teacher 1963-66, Audio-Visual Dir 1966-83 Univ of New Orleans; Sci Teacher 1983-87, Sci Teacher Gifted 1987- John Ehret HS; *ai:* Consultant/Chairperson for Visiting Comms for Southern Assn of Coll & Schls, LA Comm; Jefferson Parish Cncl Pres 1977-79; Intnl Rdng Assn; LA Rdng Assn (Pres 1978-79, Intnl by Laws Comm 1982); LA Sci Teachers Assn 1983-; Natl Assn for Gifted 1987-; NSTA 1983-; *home:* 5905 Boutall St Metairie LA 70003

BONI, MARY HELTERLINE, 5th Grade Teacher; *b:* St Cloud, MN; *m:* David Roger; *c:* Roger; *ed:* (BS) Elem, St Cloud St 1958; (ME) Elem, Lehigh; *cr:* Teacher Hoyt Lakes MN 1958-61, Bethlehem PA 1961-66, Bel Air MD 1978-; *ai:* Patriot Awd; Harford Cty Ed Assn/MD Ed/NEA; St Margarets Sch Bd 1986-; DAR Outstanding Teacher of His Harford Co; DAR Outstanding Teacher of His MD; Teacher Historian Harford Co WA Historical Society; *office:* Prospect Mill Elementary 101 Prospect Mill Rd Bel Air MD 21014

BONICA, DIANE MC NICHOLAS, Pre-School/Lead Teacher; *b:* S Weymouth, MA; *m:* Joseph Jr.; *c:* Ashely E., Adam J., Andrew L.; *ed:* (BA) Child Dev, Stonehill Coll 1974; (MED) Early Chldhd Ed, Westminster Coll 1982; Lang Arts in Early Chldhd; *cr:* 5th Grade Teacher North Easton Mid Sch 1975-76; Kndgtn Teacher Granite Sch Dist 1974-81; Curr Consultant Freelance 1981-; Lead Teacher Living Savior Pre-Sch 1988-; *ai:* PTA Exec Comm; Talent Show Chairperson; Church Lay Minister; Pre-Sch Advisory Comm; OAECE 1988-; Outstanding Young Woman in America 1977; Tualatin Soccer Team Mother 1990; Published Educl Books; *office:* Living Savior Pre-Sch 8470 Sagert Rd Tualatin OR 97062

BONN, TERRY WALTER, Math Teacher; *b:* Fredericksburg, TX; *m:* Joan Michelle Schmidt; *c:* Garret; *ed:* (BA) Math, TX a & M 1973; *cr:* Coach Fredericksburg HS 1973-80, 8th Grade Math Teacher Fredericksburg Mid Sch 1973-89; *ai:* UIL Number Sense Coach; ATPE 1984-89; TSTA 1973-84; Church Cncl Pres 1980-84; Dist Cncl Mem 1985; *office:* Fredericksburg Mid Sch 202 W Travis Fredericksburg TX 78624

BONNAU, RUTH SNYDER, Fourth Grade Teacher; *b:* Reading, MI; *m:* Stephen Michael; *c:* Mona Gary, April Gary; *ed:* (BA) Ed, Hillsdale Coll 1972; (MA) Ed, Siena Heights Coll 1982; *cr:* 5th Grade Teacher 1972-73, 2nd Grade Teacher 1973-83, 3rd Grade Teacher 1983-84, 4th Grade Teacher 1984- Camden Frontier Sch; Coord/Project Self Reliance Brandywine Comm Ed Niles MI 1987-88; Ed Instr Hillsdale Coll 1989; *ai:* Prof Dev Comm; Delta Kappa Gamma (Pres, Secy, Prgm Chm) 1977-; NEA 1972-; Phi Delta Kappa 1984-; MI Rdng Assn 1982-; MI Ed Assn Pres 1972-; Domestic Harmony Bd Mem; Delta Kappa Gamma Mini-Grant; *office:* Camden Frontier Sch 4971 Montgomer Rd Camden MI 49232

BONNAVIAT, BARBARA ANN, French/Soc St/Lang Art Teacher; *b:* Jersey City, NJ; *ed:* (BA) Fr, Middlebury Coll 1962; (MA) Fr, The Sorbonne Middlebury Grad Sch of Fr 1965; Post MA Credits Numerous Colls; *cr:* Fr Teacher Roosevelt Jr HS 1962-64; Fr/Soc Stud/Lang Arts Teacher & Dormitory Adv Dept of Defense Overseas Schls 1965-78/1985; Fr Teacher Millburn HS 1983-85, Cranford HS 1983; *ai:* Federal Womens Prgm Rep; Enrichment Course Comm; NEA 1962-; Overseas Ed Assn Le

Club Francais De Harrogate 1989-; Parent-Teacher-Stu Organization 1989-; Dept of Defense Outstanding Rating & Sustained Superior Performance Ankara Turkey 1967-68, Keflavik Iceland 1986-88.

BONNELL, SANDRA GAYE (HORTON), 8th/9th Grade Soc Stud Teacher; *b:* Belmont, NC; *m:* William Gerald; *c:* Charles W.; *ed:* (ABA) Sociology, Sacred Heart Coll 1957; (BA) Sociology, Univ of NC Greensboro 1960; Gifted & Talented Cert; Effective Teacher Trng; *cr:* 8th Grade Teacher Wm H Owens Elem Sch 1965-66; 6th Grade Teacher Seoul Amer Mid Sch S Korea 1970-72; 6th/7th Grade Teacher Elizabeth Carswell Elem Sch 1974-75; 7th/9th Grade Teacher Lewis Chapel Jr HS 1975-77; 7th-9th Grade Teacher Stanley Jr HS 1978-; *ai:* Jr Beta Club Adv; Chairperson Soc Stud Dept; SACS Chairperson for Stu Act Prgm & Soc Stud; NC Assn of Educators 1974-89; Prof Educators of NC 1989-; United Meth Women (Pres 1974-76) 1961-, Life Membership 1975; Park St United Meth Church (Historian 1990, Choir Mem, Sunday Sch Teacher, Admin Bd Mem); *office:* Stanley Jr HS 317 Hovis Rd Stanley NC 28164

BONNER, GRADY CLARK, Enrichment Teacher; *b:* La Grange, GA; *m:* Martha Elizabeth Rushing; *c:* Elizabeth D., David C., Daniel C.; *ed:* (BA) Eng, 1963, (MED) Mid Grades, 1988 La Grange Coll; Teacher of Gifted Certificate W GA Coll; *cr:* Teacher Hill Street Jr HS 1967-70; Teacher/Coach La Grange Boys Jr HS 1970-72, Troup Jr HS 1980-86, Whitesville Road Mid 1986-; *ai:* Asst Ftbl Coach & Head Defensive Coord Region Champions 1988-89, St Champions 1988; Track Coach; Head Boys Bsktbl; Region Chm; St Championship Track 1985; Prof Assn of GA Educators System Rep 1985-; Covenant Presbyn Church (Secy, Treas 1988-, Bd of Trustees 1987-;)

BONNER, IDA MAY (SPENCER), Fourth Grade Teacher; *b:* Gilmer, TX; *m:* Bobby Jack; *c:* Robert, Russell; *ed:* (BS) Bus Ed, 1956, (MED) Elem Ed, 1960 E TX St Univ; *cr:* Teacher Spurger Ind Sch Dist 1957-62, Ennis Ind Sch Dist 1962-63, Forreston Ind Sch Dist 1963-66, Palmer Ind Sch Dist 1966-; *ai:* Assn TX Prof Educators.

BONNER, PATSY STONE, 4th Grade Teacher; *b:* Brownwood, TX; *c:* Teresa L., Alicia L.; *ed:* (BS) Elem Ed, 1970, (MED) Rdng Specialist, 1985 W TX St Univ; Grad Stud Math & Sci; *cr:* Kndgtn Teacher Claude Elem 1978; Kndtgn/1st Grade Teacher Groom Elem 1979-80; 4th Grade Teacher Panhandle Elem 1980-; *ai:* Delta Kappa Gamma 1989-; Panhandle Classroom Teachers Assn Pres Elect 1989-; TX Cncl Teachers of Math 1989-; *office:* Panhandle Elem Sch 106 W 9th PO Box 1030 Panhandle TX 79068

BONOMO, DONALD E., Mathematics Teacher; *b:* Clinton, IN; *m:* Antoinette Ferro; *c:* Donna, Debbie, Donald J.; *ed:* (BS) Bus Ed, IN St 1962; *cr:* Teacher South View Mid Sch 1966-; *ai:* DEA 1966-; IEA, NEA; Lions Club; Danville Public Schls Outstanding Teacher 1989; *office:* South View Mid Sch 133 E 9th Danville IL 61832

BONSEY, NANCY K., Sixth Grade Teacher; *b:* Watertown, SD; *ed:* (MS) Counseling & Guidance, CA Luth Univ 1986; (BA) Sociology, CSULB 1975; (AA) Soc Sci, Cerritos Jr Coll 1972; Marriage & Family Therapy, Univ of La Verne; Instructional Media & Technology, CA Poly Pomona; *cr:* ESL Teacher Payne Elem Sch 1980-83; Teacher Parkview Elem 1983-; *ai:* Gate Teacher; Stu Cncl; Newspaper Production Staff; Coached Team of Stu for Appearance on Kidquiz TV Show; CA Assn of Marriage & Family Therapists; CTA; NEA; Kappa Delta Pi; *office:* Parkview Elem School 12044 Elliot Ave El Monte CA 91732

BONSTROM, G. DANA, Mathematics Dept Chairman; *b:* Spokane, WA; *m:* Janet E. Johnson; *c:* Logan C.; *ed:* (BA) Math, Univ of WA 1970; Cmptr Sci, Ed, E WA Univ; *cr:* Math Teacher West Jr HS 1972-77; Math/Cmptr Ed Teacher Kettle Falls HS 1978-; *ai:* Kettle Falls HS Math & Knowledge Bowl Team Adv; Kettle Falls Ed Assn Treas 1980-89; WA St Math Cncl 1978-; Intnl Cncl for Cmptrs in Ed 1981-; BSA Troop 965 Committeeman 1978-; Kettle Falls Sch Dist Awd of Merit 1981; Kettle Falls HS Faculty Mem of Month 1986-88; *office:* Kettle Falls HS 1275 Juniper Kettle Falls WA 99141

BONSTROM, JANET JOHNSON, Resource Room Teacher; *b:* Whittier, CA; *m:* G. Dana; *c:* Logan; *ed:* (BA) Elem Ed, NW Nazarene Coll 1973; E WA Univ; *cr:* Math Teacher West Jr HS 1973-74, Russell Jr HS 1975; Learning Center Teacher West Jr HS 1976-77; Math/Spec Ed Teacher Kettle Falls HS 1977-; *ai:* Natural Helpers; Impact Core Team; Kettle Falls HS Ed Assn Staff Mem of Month 1988; K F Ed Assn; *office:* Kettle Falls HS PO Box 300 Kettle Falls WA 99141

BONURA, LUKE JOSEPH, English Teacher & Chairman; *b:* New Orleans, LA; *m:* Maria E.; *c:* Luke Jr., Joseph; *ed:* (BA) Philosophy, Creighton Univ 1970, (MA) Theology-Grad Stud; St Marys Univ 1979; *cr:* Biblical Stud/Philosophy Coll Professor Pan Amer Univ 1973-79; 12th Grade Eng Teacher Edinburg HS 1981-; *ai:* NHS Faculty Adv; Ready Writing Coach-UIL 1983-89; Spelling Coach-UIL 1987-89; Literary Criticism Coach-UIL 1988-89; Cntrl Elem Gifted & Talented PTA Pres 1987-88; Published Book 1973; *office:* Edinburg HS 801 E Canton Rd Edinburg TX 78539

BONVILLAIN, SHIRLEY K., Business Teacher; *b:* Thibodaux, LA; *m:* Larry Paul; *c:* Christopher, Eric; *ed:* (BS) Bus Ed, Nicholls St Univ 1973; *cr:* Teacher Thibodaux HS 1974-; *ai:* FBLA Spon; NEA, LA Ed Assn 1987-; St Genevieve Parent Teacher Club 1983-; *office:* Thibodaux HS 1355 Tiger Dr Thibodaux LA 70301

BONYHADY, ELIZABETH M., Teacher; *b:* Szekesfehervar, Hungary; *ed:* (BA) Eng, San Fernando Valley St Coll 1967; Specialization Elem Teaching & Child Psych; *cr:* Librarian Coldwell Banker Real Estate Co 1967-69; Teacher Hubbard St Sch 1970-71, Chandler Sch 1971-; *ai:* Faculty Rep; UCLA Stus Observing & Participating in Class; Coord & Teacher of Gifted Children; Master Teacher; United Teachers of Los Angeles (Chapter Chairperson, Faculty Rep) 1989-; Chandler Sch (Gifted Coord, Grade Level Chairperson) 1971-.

BOOGAARD, DOROTHY JANE, Second Grade Teacher; *b:* Appleton, WI; *m:* Bernard; *c:* Tom, Michael, Mark, Marti A.; *ed:* (BA) Ed, Mt Mary Coll 1955; *cr:* Kndgtn Teacher Ben Franklin 1955-56, Edison 1956-57; Substitute Teacher Kimberly Sch 1969-76; 1st/2nd Grade Teacher Little Chute Elem 1976-.

BOOGNL, MARY HOAR, Teacher; *b:* Butte, MT; *m:* Albert E.; *c:* Scott, Albert, Adam; *ed:* (BA) Math, Univ of MT 1974; Working Toward Masters UNM, NMSU, MSU, & Univ of MI; *cr:* Teacher 1974-76, Heights Teacher 1978- West Jr Hs; *ai:* Quality Circle; NHS Advisory Bd; NCTM, FCTM, Delta Kappa Gamma 1988-89; Coord CCD At Church; NSF Grant 1989; Farmington Fnd Excl Ed; *home:* 1117 E Cooper Farmington NM 87401

BOOHER, REBECCA JEANNE REA, English Teacher; *b:* Washington, PA; *m:* Donald William Jr.; *c:* Donald W. III; *ed:* (BA) Eng, Washington & Jefferson Coll 1979; *cr:* Eng Teacher Trinity Area HS 1985-; *ai:* SADD & Debate Team Adv; Theater Makeup; NEA, PA St Ed Assn, Trinity Ed Assn 1985-; Federal Order of Police Auxiliary (Charter Mem, Trustee) 1989-; *office:* Trinity Area HS Park Ave Washington PA 15301

BOOK, STEPHEN MARK, 8th Grade Science Teacher; *b:* Clarksburg, WV; *m:* Judith Byrd; *c:* Brittany M., Brett L.; *ed:* (BA) Ed, Fairmont St Coll 1977; *cr:* 4th-8th Grade Sci/Soc Stud/Phys Ed Teacher Northview Elem 1977-81; 8th Grade Sci Teacher Sevierville Mid Sch 1981-; *ai:* Stu Cncl & Sci Olympiad Adv; Family Life Ed Coord; NEA, TEA 1977-; Sevier Cty Ed Assn Faculty Rep 1984-87; TN Hunter Safety Ed Teacher of Yr 1986; Sevierville Mid Sch Teacher of Yr 1987; *home:* 321 Mount Rd W Kodak TN 37764

BOOKER, GWENDOLYN STROUD, Biology Teacher; *b:* Macon, GA; *m:* William D.; *c:* Elbert, Adrain; *ed:* (BS) Sci, Fort Valley St Coll 1966; Univ of GA; GA Coll; Mercer Univ; *cr:* Sci/Math Teacher Ballard Hudson Jr HS 1966-67; Bio Teacher Northeast HS 1968-; *ai:* Adv Northeast Sci Club; Asst Girls Track Coach; Scorekeeper Varsity Bsktbl; GA Athletic Coaches Assn Asst Coach of Yr 1986; Natl Sci Teacher; GA Sci Teacher; NABT; Cncl of Cath Women Pres/Sec Women of Yr 1986; *office:* Northeast H S 1654 Upper River Rd Macon GA 31211

BOOKER, MAE JULIA, Sixth Grade Math/Sci Teacher; *b:* Langdale, AL; *ed:* (BS) Elem Ed, AL St Univ 1955; (MED) Elem Ed, La Grange Coll 1975; IN Univ Bloomington; *cr:* 3rd Grade Teacher Rehoboth HS 1955-67; Phys Ed Teacher Valley Jr HS 1967-75; 6th Grade Teacher Fairfax Elem 1975-; *ai:* Spon Chrldr 1967-71, Majorette 1967-71, Sci Fair 1982-87, Spelling Bee 1975-87; CCTA, AEA 1955-; NEA; Fairfax Elem Teacher of Yr 1985-86, 1989-; *home:* 5002 31st Ave Valley AL 36854

BOOKER, WILMA TIBBS, Teacher; *b:* Toney, AL; *m:* Arthur Douglas Jr.; *c:* Reginald D., Wendy J., Regina L., Cynthia B.; *ed:* (BS) Math, 1968, (MS) Math/Scndry Ed, 1972, (AA) Math/Scndry Ed, 1976, (EDS) Math/Scndry Ed, 1981 AL A&M Univ; Several Wkshps; *cr:* Math Teacher Davis Hills Mid Sch 1968-; *ai:* Math Club & Team Spon; Huntsville Ed Assn, AL Ed Assn, NEA; Mt Zion M B Church (Youth Dir, Sunday Sch Teacher, Choir Mem, Bible Class Teacher, Sr Citizens Worker, Missionary Teacher), Sr Citizen Recognition; Teacher of Yr 1989-; *office:* Davis Hills Mid Sch 3221 Mastin Lake Rd Huntsville AL 35810

BOON, SUSAN BARTOW, Science Teacher; *b:* Lancaster, PA; *m:* Wyndham H.; *c:* David, Jennifer; *ed:* (BS) Chem/General Sci, Allegheny Coll 1967; Grad Stud; *cr:* Sci Teacher Lynch Jr HS 1973-76, Louisville Jr HS 1976-; *ai:* Louisville Educators Against Drugs; Dist Sci Comm; Sci Day Coord; Phi Beta Kappa 1965-; OH Acad of Sci 1984-; NEA, OH Ed Assn, Louisville Ed Assn 1976-; Martha Holden Jennings Fellowship; Natl Sci Fnd Fellowhip; *office:* Lousville Jr HS 300 E Gorgas St Louisville OH 44641

BOONE, JAMES RAYMOND, Biology 1 & 2 Teacher; *b:* Picayne, MS; *m:* Diane Stephens; *c:* Scott, Cody; *ed:* (BS) Bio/Chem, Delta St Univ 1964; (MED) Bio, Univ of S MS 1980; Masters in Biological Sci; *cr:* Teacher/Coach Pearl River Cntrl HS 1964-70, Pearl River HS 1970; *ai:* Athletic Dir & Asst Ftbl Coach; Sch Building Level & Discipline Comm; MS Acad of Sci 1964-; AFT 1976-; Natl Fed of Interscholastic Coaches 1980-; City of Picayne Park & Recreation Commission 1990; *office:* Pearl River HS P O Box 1210 Pearl River LA 70452

BOONE, LIBBY SUE, Sixth Grade Teacher; *b:* Deming, NM; *c:* Leslie; *ed:* (BA) Elem Ed, Univ of AZ 1972; Theatre Dance Trng; *cr:* Teacher Saguaro Elem Sch 1972-; *ai:* Cntrl AZ Comm Coll Fine Art & Casa Grande Union HS Consultant; Owner & Operator of Dance Bus; NEA, AZ Ed Assn, Casa Grande Elem Assn of Classroom Teachers Building Rep 1972-87; Casa Grande Town Hall (Mem, Bd of Dirs) 1983-85; Outstanding Young Woman in America 1982; Casa Grande Partners in Ed Finalist Teacher of Yr 1989; Casa Grande Elem Sch Dist Teacher of Yr 1989; *office:* Saguaro Elem Sch 1501 N Center Casa Grande AZ 85222

BOONE, MARIE CROSS, 5th Grade Teacher; *b:* Asheboro, NC; *m:* Harvey Claxton Jr.; *c:* Nichole, Camille; *ed:* (BS) Intermediate Ed, Winston Salem St Univ 1978; *cr:* 5th Grade Teacher Lindley Park Sch 1978-; *ai:* Cowboy Cheerleading Squad Adv; Daisy Scout Troop Co-Adv; NC Assn of Ed Mem 1978-; Winston Salem St Alumni Assn 1986-; Teacher of Yr 1987-88; *home:* 607 Parkview St Asheboro NC 27203

BOONE, RUTH LAMB, Home Economics Teacher; *b:* Roper, NC; *m:* Melvin R.; *ed:* (BS) Voc Home Ec, Shaw Univ Raleigh NC 1959; Hampton Univ, VA St Univ Petersburg; *cr:* Rdng Teacher Seaboard Elem 1963-67, John Randolph & Booker T Washington 1967-68; Voc Home Ec Suffolk HS 1968-69, Booker T Washington 1969-; *ai:* FHA Spon; Suffolk FHA City-Wide Spon; Suffolk Home Ec Teachers Comm Past Chairperson; Amer Voc Assn, Suffolk Ed Assn, VA Ed Assn, NEA; VA Baptist Conv (Women) Pres 1988-; Lott Carey Baptist Foreign Mission Conv USA Pres 1989-; VA Seminary & Coll Bd of Mgrs 1986-; Co-Founder Metropolitan Baptist Church Home for Elderly; *home:* 605 E Washington St Suffolk VA 23434

BOONER, ANNA LOUISE CARR, American History Teacher; *b:* Bryn Mawr, PA; *m:* Ralph Garnett Jr.; *c:* Ralph G. III, Nicholas Whitley; *ed:* (BS) Soc Sci, E TN St Univ 1971; (MS) Ed, Union Coll 1980; TN Ed Assn Leadership Dev Sch; *cr:* Teacher VA Intermont Coll 1969-73; Geography Teacher 1973-75, Alternate Sch Teacher/Coord 1975-78, Honors Teacher 1975-85 Vance Jr HS; Alternate Sch Teacher 1986-87, Amer His/World His/Civics Teacher 1987- TN HS; *ai:* Big Brothers/Big Sisters Club Adv; Citizen Bee Team Coach; System Wide Policy Comm; Eng as Second Lang Afterschool Prgm; NEA, TN Ed Assn 1973-; Bristol TN Ed Assn (Treas 1989-, Pres Elect 1988-89); Alpha Delta Kappa, VA Alpha Psi Pres/VP 1988-; Bristol TN City Schls Teacher of Yr 1986, 1990; TN Dept Ed Test Specification Developer; Item Writer/ED for Area Test Cert in Geography; Milligan Coll Teacher Advisory Comm; *office:* Tennessee HS 1112 Edgemont Ave Bristol TN 37620

BOORD, JAMES EDWARD, II, Music Teacher/Fine Arts Chair; *b:* Charleroi, PA; *m:* Deborah Isael; *c:* James E. III; *ed:* (BS) Music Ed, 1981, (MED) Admin/Supervision, 1987 Frostburg St Univ; *cr:* Band/Chorus/General Music/Music His Teacher N Garrett Sr HS 1981-; *ai:* Marching Band; Guard Adv; Faculty Advisory; Garrett Cty Scndry Music Teachers Lead Teacher; MD Music Educators Assn 1989-; Phi Delta Kappa 1986-; Lions Club Intnl Rawlings 1st VP 1987-; MD Music Credit Count Comm Mem; *home:* 505 Woodlawn Dr Rt 3 Rawlings MD 21557

BOOS, ERIN LEE, 5th Grade Teacher; *b:* Alhambra, CA; *m:* Bryan Lynn; *c:* Jonathon, Joanna; *ed:* (BA) Liberal Stud, CA St Univ Long Beach 1976; *cr:* Teller Citizens Savings & Loan 1973-79; Teacher Long Beach Unified Sch Dist 1977-; *ai:* Stu Cncl Adv; Master Teacher; *office:* Burcham Elem Sch 5610 Moncaco Rd Long Beach CA 90808

BOOTH, BERTHA E. ANDURAY, 4th Grade Teacher; *b:* Tegucigalpa, Honduras; *m:* John W.; *c:* John W. II; *ed:* (BA) Ed, 1960, (MS) Ed, 1964 Fordham Univ; Admin, Univ of WI Madison; Rdng Disabilities, Dominican Coll; *cr:* 2nd/3rd Grade Teacher Commander Shea Sch 1952-84; 7th/8th Grade Teacher St Clares Sch 1954-64; 7th/8th Grade Teacher/Prin St Maria Goretti Sch 1964-69; 5th Grade/Master Teacher Mazommanie Grade Sch 1970-71; 6th-8th Grade Teacher Salem Grade Sch 1972-76; 3rd/4th/6th Grade Teacher Bristol Consolidated Sch 1976-; *ai:* Bristol Ed Assn Treas; Sisters Oblate to Divine Love (Sister 1949-69, Teacher 1949-69, Superior & Prin 1964-69); *home:* 8424 198th Ave Bristol WI 53104

BOOTH, LOLA A., English Teacher; *b:* Payette, ID; *m:* James C.; *c:* Scott F., Jeremy J.; *ed:* (BA) Eng Ed, E OR St Coll 1967; (MA) Eng Ed, Boise St Univ 1987; Various Writing Courses Area Schls 1980, 1984, 1988; *cr:* Eng Teacher Taft Jr HS 1967-68; Eng/Journalism/Drama Teacher Griswold HS 1968-70; Eng Teacher West Jr HS 1978-82, Nampa Sr HS 1982-; *ai:* Jr & Soph Class Adv; Literary Magazine Adv; Characters in Costume; Dramatic Production of Stu Writing; ID Cncl Teachers of Eng (Liason 1983-84) 1979-; NCTE 1985-; Nampa Ed Assn (Rep 1979, 1985) 1978-; Snake River Young Writers Conference Alternate 1980-; Poetry Published; Writing Projects Fellowships; Essay Contest Awd ID Press Tribune; Sch Teacher of Yr 1981, Dist 1987; Honorable Mention St Teacher of Yr 1987-88; Teacher Fnd Awds 1982-; *office:* Nampa HS 203 Lake Lowell Ave Nampa ID 83651

BOOTH, MAY Y., Reading/Language Arts Teacher; *b:* Thomaston, AL; *m:* James R.; *c:* Khalfani, Kefentse, Jayson; *ed:* (BS) Elem Ed/Lib Sci, AL St Univ 1973; N IL Univ 1978; Wayne St Univ; *cr:* 6th Grade Teacher Hutchins Mid Sch 1978-79, Nolan Mid Sch 1979-80; 7th Grade Teacher Von Steuben Mid Sch 1980-82; 7th-8th Grade Teacher Jackson Mid Sch 1984; *ai:* Amer Bus Woman Assn 1975-77; *home:* 18975 Alcoy Detroit MI 48215

BOOTH, NANCY KNOWLTON, English Department Chair; *b:* Willimantic, CT; *m:* Daniel E.; *c:* Nathaniel, Otis; *ed:* (BA) Eng, Barrington Coll 1964; (MALS) Eng/Psych, Wesleyan Univ 1981; Grad Stud Wesleyan; *cr:* Psych Teacher Emma Willard 1974-76; 10th/11th Grade Eng Teacher Marin Acad 1977-79; 10th/12th Grade Eng Teacher Choate 1980-83; Jr Dean/Chm of Eng Dept/11th/12th Grade Eng Teacher Campbell Hall 1984-; *ai:* 11th Grade Dean; Chm Eng Dept, Curr Comm; Sr Seminar Comm; NATE, CATE, NAIS; NEH Grant Wesleyan Univ; Most Valuable Teacher Marin Acad; *office:* Campbell Hall Sch 4533 Laurel Canyon Blvd North Hollywood CA 91607

BOOTHE, CLARISSA BUSSE, Second Grade Teacher; *b:* Omaha, NE; *m:* William Mayo; *c:* Frederic, Terry, *ed:* (BA) Elem Ed, Austin Peay 1977; *cr:* 2nd Grade Teacher 1977-88, 3rd Grade Teacher 1988-89; 2nd Grade Teacher 1989- Woodlawn Elem; *home:* 1260 Dotsonville Rd Clarksville TN 37042

BOOTHE, JUDI ANN, World History Teacher; *b:* Boonville, MO; *m:* Michael L.; *c:* Amy, Brendon; *ed:* (BSED) Soc Stud, 1966, (MA) His, 1968 Cntrl MO St Univ; *cr:* Teacher Ervin Jr HS 1967-74, Hickman Mills HS 1977-; *ai:* Peer Coaching Team Mem; Frosh Class Spon; NEA, MNEA, UTA 1967-; Greater Kansas City Assn for Supervision & Dev; Building Rep PAC Comm; UTA Exec Bd; *office:* Hickman Mills HS 9010 Old Santa Fe Rd Kansas City MO 64138

BORAH, WILLIAM BRYAN, English Teacher; *b:* Dallas, TX; *m:* Janice Loraine Guy; *ed:* Comm; *cr:* Teacher Ross S Sterling HS 1979-; *ai:* Academic Decathelon Spon; NCTE, NFL, TFL, AFA, BCTA, TCTA; *office:* Ross S Sterling HS 300 W Baker Rd Baytown TX 77521

BORCHARDT, CINDY JEAN (ROEHL), English Teacher; *b:* Thief River Falls, MN; *m:* Jeffrey A.; *c:* Jeffrey A. II, John C.; *ed:* (BS) Scndry Ed/Bible/Phys Ed, Maranatha Baptist Bible Coll 1979; *cr:* Teacher/Coach Faith Baptist Sch 1979-81, Brentwood Baptist Chrstn Acad 1985-; *ai:* Vlybl & Cheerleading Coach; Brentwood Baptist Church Womens Comm Head Chairperson 1984-86; Brentwood Baptist Nursery Coord 1983-; *office:* Brentwood Baptist Chrstn Acad 588 Dara James Des Plaines IL 60016

BORCHARDT, KATHLEEN MARIE, Reading Department Chairperson; *b:* Oak Park, IL; *ed:* (BA) Eng, Mundelein Coll 1972; (MED) Rdng, Univ of IL 1984; Grad Work Rdng, Cooperative Learning, TESA; *cr:* 3rd Grade Teacher Immaculate Conception 1972-73; 3rd-8th Grade Teacher St Pancratius 1973-83; Rdng Teacher Cooper Jr HS 1983-85; Rdng Dept Chairperson Addison Trail HS 1985-; *ai:* Key Club Faculty Adv; Learning to Learn Comm Co-Chairperson; Cmmty Ed Adult Literacy; Intnl Rdng Assn, IL Rdng Cncl, Scndry Rdng League, ASCD; Kiwanis-Addison; Initiative Prgm Secy; Exemplary Scndry Chapter I Prgm 1989; Rdng Research Quarterly 1984; Journal of Educl Research 1985; *office:* Addison Trail HS 213 N Lombard Rd Addison IL 60101

BORCHERT, CHERYL, Visual Arts Instructor; *b:* Muskegon, MI; *m:* John C.; *c:* John, Jennifer; *ed:* (BS) Art Ed, W MI Univ 1971; Grad Courses in Ed & Art; *cr:* Visual Art Instr Ravenna Public Schls 1971-73, N Muskegon Public Schls 1974-76, Adult Ed 1978-87, Muskegon Museum of Art 1971-87, Orchard View Public Schls 1978-; *ai:* Jr Class Adv; Orchard View HS New Attendance Policy Draft Comm; N Muskegon Art Fair Chm 1977-87; MI Ed Assn 1971-73, 1986-; MI Art Ed Assn 1989-, Annual Purchase Awd 1989, 1990; Orchard View Ed Assn 1986-; NAEA; Gallery Upstairs 1982-; Wren Gallery Treas 1984-; Muskegon Fine Arts Guild Treas 1982-83, Annual Show 1987; N Muskegon Public Service Awd 1978; Best of Show, 1st, 2nd, 3rd Place Awds in Painting Coca Cola Art Show 1974; N Muskegon Art Show 1989; Muskegon Art Festival 1986; Art Consultant 1980-89; *office:* Orchard View HS 2310 Marquette Muskegon MI 49442

BORCI, PRISCILLA MAC DONALD, Fourth Grade Teacher; *b:* Boston, MA; *m:* Guy Peter; *c:* Guy J., Michael P.; *ed:* (BS) Ed, 1970, (MS) Ed, 1973 Worcester St Coll; Grad Stud Spec Needs, Worcester St Coll; *cr:* Teacher Grafton Elem Sch 1970-81, South Grafton Elem Sch 1981-; *ai:* Teacher Rep for Parent Teacher Group; S Grafton Elem Sch Improvement Cncl Mem; Cooperaing Teacher for Stu Teachers-in-Trng from Worcester St Coll; NEA, MA Teachers Assn, Grafton Teachers Assn 1970-; New England Assn of Schls & Colls Visiting Comm Mem 1989; Grafton Sports Booster Club Co-Chairperson Fundraising Comm 1990; Worcester St Coll Teacher Advisory Cncl 1989; *office:* S Grafton Elem Sch 90 Main St South Grafton MA 01560

BORDEN, FRANCES ELBERTA, English Teacher; *b:* Wasco, CA; *ed:* (AA) Eng, Lubbock Christian Coll 1964; (BSED) Speech/ Eng, 1967; (MED) Speech, 1973 Texas Tech Univ; *cr:* Eng/ Speech Teacher Mason Ind Sch Dist 1967-69; Gruver Ind Sch Dist 1969-71; Sublette Unified Sch Dist 1971-75; Eng Teacher Midland Chrstn Sch 1975-76; Milford Cntrl 1982-84; South New Berlin Cntrl 1984-; *ai:* Odyssey of the Mind Coach; Class of 1995 Spon; Spirit Comm Mem; NEA; Poetry Published in CSP World News & in Thirteen; Assc Editor of Thirteen 1981; *home:* RD 3 Box 102 Oneonta NY 13820

BORDENKIRCHER, DAVE, Director of Music; *b:* Denver, CO; *m:* Patty Bordenkircher; *c:* Kayleigh; *ed:* (BS) Music Ed, William Paterson St Coll of NJ 1985; *cr:* Chorus Dir Hugo Jr HS & SR HS 1985-86; Media Specialist Fruitland Park Elem 1987; Music Dir Tavares HS 1987-; *ai:* FL Bandmasters Assn, FL Music Educators Assn, Music Educators Natl Conference 1987-; Tavares HS Teacher of Month; *office:* Tavares HS 603 N New Hampshire Ave Tavares FL 32778

BORELLI, VINCENT J., Speech/Theater Teacher; *b:* Jersey City, NJ; *m:* Angela Mangione; *c:* Annamaria, Antonia F.; *ed:* (BA) Speech/Theater, Montclair St 1972; MA Speech/Theater, Hunter Coll 1991; *cr:* Teacher Long Branch Jr HS 1972-79, Long Branch HS 1979-; *ai:* Drama, Forensic, Announcement Club; Speech & Theatre Assn VP 1979-, Teacher of Yr 1988, Distinguished Service Awd 1990; NJ Forensic League VP 1985-; Alliance for Arts in Ed 1988-; Long Branch HS Teacher of Yr 1988; Long Branch Schls Teacher of Yr 1988; Speech/Theater Teacher of Yr 1988; Distinguished Service to Arts 1990; Public Issues Service Teaching Grant 1990.

BOREMAN, E. DANIEL, Sixth Grade Math Teacher; *b:* Lewistown, PA; *m:* Salinda D. Mc Clellan; *c:* Daniel W., Kimberly; *ed:* (BA) His/Soc Stud, Messiah Coll 1966, (MED) Elem Ed, Shippensburg Univ 1970; *cr:* 6th Grade Classroom Teacher New Oxford Elem Sch 1966-67; 6th Grade Teacher Wellsville Elem Sch 1967-72, Northern Mid Sch 1972-; *ai:* Math Dept Chairperson; Frosh Ftbl Coach; Mid Sch Bsktbl Coach; Gifford Pinchot Ed Assn (Pres, Pres-Elect) 1974-80; PA St Ed Assn, NEA Life Mem 1966-; Immanuel Church Elder 1983-89; Dillsburg Jaycess Outstanding Young Educator Awd 1979; N York Cty Sch Dist Teaching Excl Awd 1986-87.

BORENS, BETTY T., Jr HS Math Teacher; *b:* Golden Pond, KY; *m:* James L.; *c:* Melody, Wendy; *ed:* (BS) Bus Ed, Murray St Univ 1964; Elem Ed, Mid TN St Univ 1975; Elem Ed, Columbia St Comm Coll 1975; (MA) Bus Ed, Murray St Univ 1983; Post Masters Studies Ed Elem Ed Murray St Univ; Cmptr Skills Trng St of TN; *cr:* Bus Ed Teacher Ferguson Ind Schls 1963-65; 3rd/4th Grade Teacher Bumpus Mills Sch 1965-67; Title I Dir Stewart Cty Schls 1968-70; Sec Stewart Cty Schl Supt 1972-73; 3rd/4th Grade Teacher W T Thomas 1977-79; Jr HS Math Teacher North Stewart Elem 1979-87; 5th Grade Teacher 1987-89; Jr HS Math Teacher 1989- Dover Elem; *ai:* Beta Club Co-Spon; Stewart Cty Ed Assn Sec; TN Ed Assn 1965; NEA 1965; Mid TN Ed Assn 1965; TN Math Teachers Assn 1987; (DPE Chapter President 1986-88/Recording Secreta Y 1988-); Delta Pi Epsilon-Rep to Natl Cncl 1989-; Delta Kappa Gamma-1987-; Teacgers Study Cncl-Bldg Rep 1986; Freed-Hardeman Coll Associates 1980; Adjunct Faculty Mem-Office Systems-Murray St Univ 1987; K-6 St Cmptr Skills Task Force-Nashville; Piloted Cmptr Skills Prgm for 7th & 8th Grade St of TN; TN Career Ladder III Cert 1989; 5th & 6th Grade Cmptr Skills Presentation TASCD 1985; *office:* Dover Elem Sch P O Box 130 Dover TN 37058

BORERI, ROBERT JOHN, History Teacher; *b:* Taunton, MA; *m:* Janice Claire; *c:* Kurt, Alicia; *ed:* (BA) His, Stoneyhill Coll 1955; (MA) His, Bridgewater St Coll 1975; *cr:* Teacher Coyle HS 1955-71, Coyle-Cassidy HS 1971-73, Martin Mid Sch 1974-79, Mulcahey Mid Sch 1979-; *ai:* Head Teacher Soc Stud Dept Mulcahey Mid Sch.

BORG, ANDREA JEAN (BILLY), English/Speech/Drama Teacher; *b:* Cleveland, OH; *m:* Donald O.; *c:* Shane D., Heather A.; *ed:* (MED) Drama/Scndry Curr, Univ of HI 1971; (BSE) Speech, OH St Univ 1967; *cr:* Eng/Speech Teacher Greenwich HS 1967-72, Holmdel HS 1972-75; Eng Teacher Brookings HS 1975-84; Substitute Teacher Grand Island Public Schls 1984-85; Eng/Speech Instr Cntrl Comm Coll 1986; Eng/Speech/Drama Teacher St Johns HS 1986-; *ai:* Natl Forensic League Spon; Speech Team & Drama Coach; Sr Class Adv; Alpha Delta Kappa 1978-; Pi Lambda Theta 1978-; Natl Collegiate Players 1966-; Natl Forensic League 1988-, Degree of Honor; Cub Scouts of America Webelos Leader 1988-; CCD Instr 1984-; *office:* St Johns HS P O Box 429 Saint Johns AZ 85936

BORGREEN, JAMES CARL, High School Art Teacher; *b:* Great Falls, MT; *m:* Patricia Ann Mausenund; *c:* Molly A., Michael J.; *ed:* (BA) Art Ed, MT St Univ 1972; Scndry Ed, Coll of Great Falls 1982; *cr:* Sculptor 1972-74; Wildlife Artist 1972-; Educator Lewistown Public Schls 1974-; *ai:* Faculty Cncl Rep; Parents for Performing & Fine Arts Group Secy; Art Clubs; MT Ed Assn Mem 1972-; Ducks Unlimited 1972-; Natl Rifle Assn, Nature Conservancy 1990; PTA; C M Russell Art Auction Selections; Audubon Wildlife Art Exhibit Winner; Many Varied Art Shows & Exhibits; *home:* 415 2nd Ave N Lewistown MT 59457

BORKOWSKI, BARBARA A., Mathematics Dept Chairperson; *b:* Amsterdam, NY; *m:* Robert; *c:* Stephen, Thomas; *ed:* (BS) Math, Pace Univ 1969; (MS) Math Ed, NY St Albany 1973; Madeline Hunter & Effective Teaching; *cr:* Math Teacher Estee Mid Sch 1969-; *ai:* Dist Math & Long Range Planning Comms.

BORLAND, CYNTHIA KECK, Second Grade Teacher; *b:* Kansas City, MO; *m:* Keith Paul; *c:* Trent, Amanda; *ed:* (BS) Elem Ed, SW MO St Univ 1978; (MS) Curr/Instruction, Cntrl MO St Univ 1987; *cr:* 2nd Grade Teacher Odessa R-7 1978-; *office:* Odessa R-7 607 S 3rd St Odessa MO 64076

BORMAN, BARRY J., Science Dept Chairman; *b:* Cincinnati, OH; *m:* Patricia Ann E. Borman Rundo; *c:* Jonathan, Matthew, David, Jill, Tracy, Christopher; *ed:* (BA) Microbiology, 1968, (MED) Scndry Admin, 1972 Univ of Cincinnati; *cr:* Teacher Cinti Public Schls 1968-69; Teacher/Sci Dept Chm Moeller HS 1969-; *ai:* Alumni Affairs Dir; Jr Var Bsbl Coach; Academic & Sch Cncl Mem; Advisory to Prin; All Saints Parish Bd of Ed Pres 1979-82; Distinguished Alumni Awd Moeller HS; Cincinnati Track Coach of Yr 1975; *office:* Moeller HS 9001 Montgomery Rd Cincinnati OH 45242

BORN, FRANCES HOLLICK, Art/Reading Teacher; *b:* Bridgeport, Philippine Isl; *m:* Philip L.; *c:* Frank E.; *ed:* (BS) Art, Northern St Coll 1970; (MED) Curr/Instruction, Univ of TX El Paso 1982; *cr:* Art Teacher Grand Junction HS 1970-82; Art/Lang Arts/ Rdng Teacher East Mid Sch 1982-; *ai:* Art Curr Comm; Art Inservices Teacher 1988-89; Mesa Valley Ed Assn, CO Ed Assn, NEA Building Rep 1978-; CO Art Ed Assn, NAEA 1978-; NCTE 1984-86; Delta Kappa Gamma Society Intnl (2nd VP, 1st VP, Pres) 1978-84; First United Meth Choir 1974-; Classmates Magazine Craft Idea 1989; Delta Kappa Gamma St Schlhps; Local Bus Volunteer Artwork; Curr Guide Artwork; *office:* East Mid Sch 830 Gunnison Ave Grand Junction CO 81501

BORNARTH, NORMA L., English Teacher; *b:* Creston, IA; *m:* Robert L.; *c:* Bruce M., Daniel R., Craig A., Stacey C.; *ed:* (BA) Eng, Univ of IL 1956; (MA) Rdng, VA Polytechnic & St Univ 1976; Univ of VA, George Mason Univ, Marymount Coll, High Point Coll; *cr:* Teaching Asst Univ of IL 1959-60; Teacher White Oak Day Sch 1962-63, Sterling Elem Sch 1966-71, Sterling Mid Sch 1971-73, Broad Run HS 1973-; *ai:* Superior Learner Prgm, Trivia Club, Peer Coaching Coord; Spon Lang Art Prgm for Loudain Cty Chm; Numerous Wkshps Presenter; NCTE; VA Assn Teachers of Eng Nom Outstanding Teacher 1986; NEA Nom Outstanding Teacher 1987; Loudoun Ed Assn; Loudoun Assn of Retarded Citizens Co-Founder 1963; Loudoun Cty Cmmty Services Bd Chm 1981-87; Loudoun Cty Task Force on Affordable Housing; Fellowship NEH Chaucer Inst at Marymount Coll, Shakespeare Inst High Point Coll; Co-Author Loudoun Cty Prgm for Effective Teaching; *office:* Broad Run HS PO Box 200 Ashburn VA 22011

BORNHORST, CAROL ANN, Science Teacher/Dept Chair; *b:* Wichita Falls, TX; *m:* Dale Ronald; *c:* Heather A., Erika L.; *ed:* (AA) E Los Angeles Jr Coll 1964; (BA) Zoology/Chem, Univ of CA Santa Barbara 1966; Courses Offered Through Dist that Enhance Stu Progress & Success; *cr:* Chem/Bio/Life Sci Teacher Mar Vista HS 1967-70; Sci Teacher Bonita Vista Jr HS 1985-; *ai:* Thematic Inquiry Federal Grant; 100 Schls CA Grant; ASDEG, San Diego Sci Teachers; Amer Youth Soccer Assn; Tiffany Sch PTA (Treas, VP, Bd Mem) 1980-86, Service Awd 1982, Continuing Service Awd 1986; Faculty Advisory Comm Mem 1989-; *office:* Bonita Vista Jr HS 650 Otay Lakes Rd Chula Vista CA 92010

BOROSKI, NAOMI L., Sixth Grade Teacher; *b:* Mt Pleasant, OH; *m:* Richard J.; *c:* Adam, Elena L., Jason E.; *ed:* (BS) Elem Ed, OH Univ 1965; (MS) Admin, Univ of Dayton 1978; *cr:* 5th/6th Grade Teacher Harrisville Elem 1960-64; 6th/7th Grade Teacher Martins Ferry 1965-66; 4th-6th Grade Teacher Buckeye Local 1966-; *ai:* Dir of Outdoor Ed; Comm for Textbooks & Course of Studies Eng, Sci, Soc Stud; Comm to Help Formulate Discipline Code; NEA, OH Ed Assn 1960-; Buckeye Local Classroom Teachers Contract Negotiation Bd 1965-; Mt Pleasant Historical Society; Jennings Scholar 1987-88; Nominee Teacher of Yr Dillonvale Elem 1980; Jefferson Cty Mini Grant Study Skills Dev; *home:* West St Mount Pleasant OH 43939

BORRELLI, JERRY F., Science Teacher; *b:* New Rochelle, NY; *m:* Elaine C.; *c:* Elizabeth, Michael, Victoria, Deborah; *ed:* (BS) Sci Ed, Iona Coll 1959; (MA) Sci Ed, NY Univ 1962; *cr:* Sci Teacher Isaac E Young Jr HS 1959-65; Chm Sci Dept 1970-75, Sci Teacher 1965- Taylor Finley Jr HS; *office:* J Taylor Finley Jr H S Greenlawn Rd Huntington NY 11743

BORRUANO, SUSIE P., Business Teacher; *b:* Plaquemine, LA; *m:* Angelo Jr.; *ed:* (BS) Bus Ed, Nicholls St Univ 1978; *cr:* Teacher St John HS 1978-80, Delta Coll 1980-87, St John HS 1987-; *ai:* Stu Cncl, Natl Bus Honor Society, Jr Class Homeroom Records Spon; NCEA, NBEA; St John Cath Church, Nicholls St Univ Alumni; Teacher of Month.

BORTNER, MARGARET MIKESELL, Second Grade Teacher; *b:* Greenville, OH; *m:* Eric L., Michael S.;; *ed:* (BA) Elem Ed, 1969, (MA) Elem Ed, 1973 Ball St Univ; *cr:* Kndgtn Teacher Brookville Local Schls 1969-70; 1st Grade Teacher 1970-76, 2nd Grade Teacher 1976- North Side Elem; *ai:* Public Relations, Chapter I Improvement, Four Star Awds Comm; Math Curr St Contact Person; ISTA, NEA, RECTA Treas 1983-; *office:* North Side Elem Sch 907 N Plum St Union City IN 47390

BORZYKOWSKI, JANIS THONE, Math/English Teacher; *b:* Milwaukee, WI; *w:* Anthony (dec); *c:* Jody Borzykowski Medinger, Kristin Brozyskowski Burditt; *ed:* (BS) Eng/Recreation Ed, Univ of WI Milwaukee 1959; Continuing Ed on Bachelors Degree; *cr:* Recreation Dir Milwaukee Recreation Dept 1955-59; Phys Ed/ End Teacher Messmer HS 1959-60; 3rd Grade Teacher Meadow Elem 1960-62; Math/Eng Teacher St Charles Elem 1967-; *ai:* Civic Oration Contest & Sch Spelling Bee Dir; Dist Eng Curr Steering Comm; Dist Environmental Ed Site Planning & Developing Comm; WI & US Tennis Assn (Political Party, Local Bd); Acting Prin; *office:* St Charles Elem Sch 526 Renson Rd Hartland WI 53029

BOSCH, GERDA M. GROSS, Chemistry/Physics Teacher; *b:* Bucharest, Rumania; *m:* Emil G.; *c:* Walter R., Eric M., Susan C.; *ed:* (AB) Ed/Chem, WA Univ St Louis 1957; (MAT) Webster Univ St Louis 1990; Chem, Physics Woodrow Wilson Wkshps 1987; Various Wkshps & Seminars; *cr:* Physics Teacher Normandy HS 1957-58; Ger Scientific Papers Translator Monsanto Chemical Company 1960-67; Substitue Teacher St Louis Cty Sch Dists 1967-75; Sci Teacher Oakville HS 1975-; *ai:* Oakville HS Local & St level Sci Olympiad Team Spon & Coach; Amer Chem Society Ed Group, AAPT Mem; *office:* Oakville HS 5557 Milburn Rd Saint Louis MO 63129

BOSCH, JEANINE THATCHER, 5th Grade Teacher; *b:* Salt Lake City, UT; *m:* Donald Ray; *c:* Michael R., Rebecca Blaine, Lori A. Wilcox; *ed:* (BS) Elem Ed, Univ of Ut 1970; Davis Sch Dist Advanced Trng Prgm; *cr:* 5th-6th Grade Teacher Oakhills Elem 1970-83, Columbia Elem 1983-; *ai:* Joint Staff Study Comm; Drug Alcohol Facilitator for Davis Cty Schls; Trouble Shooting Team; UT Prof Practices Commission (Vice Chairperson 1988, Chairperson 1989) 1986-89; Amer Assn of Univ Women Ed of Monthly News Letter; League of Women Voters Ed Stud; Level Five in Career Ladder Performance; UPPAC Appointed by St Supt of Public Instruction 1986-89; Sci Comm to Correlate Primary & Scndry Schls; *home:* 1455 Madera Hills Dr Bountiful UT 84010

BOSCH, LINDA WEBER, Mathematics Department Chair; *b:* New Orleans, LA; *m:* Lloyd G.; *c:* Laura, Christopher; *ed:* (BS) Math, 1973, (MED) Scndry Ed, 1975 SE LA Univ; Natl Sci Teachers NASA Wkshp; Cmptr Sci; Woodrow Wilson ALgebra & Geometry Wkshps; NCTM Regional Conference; *cr:* Sci/Math Teacher Tangipahoa Parish Sch Bd 1973-75; Math Teacher E Baton Rouge Sch Bd 1975-; *ai:* Jr Class Spon; Pantherette Spon; Math Dept Chairperson; Curr Dev Comm; Supervision of LA St Univ Stu Teachers; NCTM, Baton Rouge Area Cncl of Teachers of Math, LA Assn Teachers of Math; River City Symphonic Band; Woodlawn Advisory Cncl Secy; Natl Sci Teachers Newmast Recipient; Woodlawns Advisory Cncl Secy; *office:* Tuttle Schls 14939 Tiger Bend Rd Baton Rouge LA 70817

BOSCHERT, CAROL LEROY, Second Grade Teacher; *b:* St Louis, MO; *m:* Roy W.; *c:* Douglas, Kirk, Neal; *ed:* (BA) Elem Ed, Principia Coll 1963; (MED) Early Chldhd Ed, Univ of MO 1984; Post Masters Studies Cooperating Teacher for Stu Teachers Lindenwood Coll; *cr:* 1st Grade Teacher Ville Maria Sch 1963-64; 3rd Grade Teacher 1966-68; 2nd Grade Teacher 1970-73; 2nd Grade Teacher 1977- Central Elem Sch; *ai:* Mem/Sec Prof Dev Comm for Francis Howell Sch Dist; Former Grade Level Coordin Grades 1 & 2 Central Elem Sch; Finance Chm 1982-84; Mem 1982- Delta Kappa Gamma; St Charles Jaycees Outstanding Young Educator Awd 1967; Outstanding Teacher Central Sch 1985; *office:* Central Elem Sch 4525 Central School Rd Saint Charles MO 63303

BOSDOSH, STEPHANIE SUZANNE, Third Grade Teacher; *b:* Greensburg, PA; *ed:* (BA) Ed, Edinboro Univ 1972; *cr:* Remedial Rdng Teacher Mt Pleasant Area Sch Dist 1972-78; 3rd Grade Teacher Rumbaugh Elem Sch 1978-; *ai:* Math Comm; *office:* Rumbaugh ELem Sch Box 1200 School St Mount Pleasant PA 15666

BOSESKI, MARTHA ANNE, Latin Teacher; *b:* Charleston, SC; *ed:* (BA) Fr, 1975, (MAT) Fr, 1977 Univ of SC; Univ of GA, Universite de Laual, Coll of Charleston; *cr:* Fr/Latin Teacher East Cooper Sch 1977-85; West Oak HS 1985-89; Latin Teacher Wando HS 1989-; *ai:* Latin Club Adv; Prom Comm; AATF 1978-89 Laval Summer Schlsp 1981; Phi Beta Kappa; NEH Amer Classical League Latin Inst Univ of GA 1987; NEH Summer Seminar Harvard Univ 1988; *office:* Wando HS Mathis Ferry Rd Mount Pleasant SC 29464

BOSICA, ANNA MARIE, Religion Teacher; *b:* Baltimore, MD; *ed:* (BA) Soc Stud/Scndry Ed, Loyola Coll 1970; (MLA) Liberal Art/His, Johns Hopkins Univ 1978; Continuing Ed Rdng, Spec Ed, Scndry Level Intro to Spec Ed; Data General CPU Operations & Maintenance; *cr:* Teacher Mercy HS 1970-75, St Vincent Pallotti HS 1975-81; Admin One Call Concepts Incorporated 1981-86; Teacher Archbishop Spalding HS 1986-; *ai:* Cmptr Operations Dir; Sch Admin; Jr Var Girls Field Hockey Coach; Youth Ministries Retreat Prgm; NCEA 1985-; AIMES 1989-; APWA 1983-85; *office:* Archbishop Spalding HS 8080 New Cut Rd Severn MD 21144

BOSIGER, GAIL WITCHER, Physics Teacher; *b:* Lynchburg, VA; *m:* John F. Jr.; *c:* Wesley J., Scott T., Melissa A.; *ed:* (BS) Chem, Radford Univ 1967; (MED) Educl Admin, Univ of VA 1981; *cr:* Teacher Gretna HS 1967-69, Halifax Cty Sr HS 1969-73, 1980-; *ai:* Peer Helpers Chairperson; ACE Coach; NEA, VA Ed Assn 1969-; Delta Kappa Gamma Pres 1988-; Hand Bell Choir Dir 1985-; Project Piedmont Participant Univ of NC Greensboro 1989-; *home:* Rt 2 Box 658 Halifax VA 24558

BOSL, THOMAS MICHAEL, Sixth Grade Teacher; *b:* Cleveland, OH; *m:* Debra A Khulman; *ed:* (BS) Elem Ed, 1974, (MED) Admin/Supervision, 1977 Bowling Green St Univ; Grad Stud Ed Related Courses, Bowling Green St Univ; *cr:* Teacher Lake Elem Sch 1974-; *ai:* Grade Level Coord; Lang Art Course Study Comm; Jr HS Girls Bsktbl 1979-84 & Intramural Bsktbl Coach 1974-86; NEA, OEA, LEA 1974-; *office:* Lake Elem Sch 28150 Lemoyne Rd Millbury OH 43447

BOSS, CHET W., Mathematics Teacher; *b:* Grand Rapids, MI; *m:* Diane Joy Berry; *c:* Kelli L., Jason M.; *ed:* (BS) Math, 1970, (MA) Admin, 1974 MI St Univ; *cr:* Teacher Pontiac Area Schls 1970-72, Utica Cmmty Schls 1972-; *ai:* Golf Team Coach; Natl Sci Fnd Grant Hamilton Coll 1973, MI St Univ 1974; *home:* 15822 Lorway Dr Mount Clemens MI 48044

BOST, JANIE P., Fourth Grade Teacher; *b:* Salisbury, NC; *ed:* (BS) Elem Ed, Appalachian St Univ 1970; *cr:* 6th Grade Teacher 1970-71, 4th-6th Grade Teacher 1971-73, 4th Grade Teacher 1973-74 Lakeview Elem; 4th Grade Teacher Merrick-Moore Elem 1974-89, Easley Elem 1989-; *ai:* Grade Chairperson; Prof Dev System Intermediate Grade Co-Chairperson; Soc Stud Dept Leader; Textbook Selection Comm; Cty 4th Grade Soc Stud Curr Guide; Intermediate Grade Coord; Cty Report Card Comm; Teacher Cncl Rep; ACT (Sch Rep 1971-72) 1970-; NCAE 1970-; Merrick Moore Teacher of Yr 1981-82.

BOSTICK, JOHN HENRY, Eighth Grade Math Teacher; *b:* Ashland, MS; *m:* Theresa Smith; *c:* Cornelius, Julius, Justin; *ed:* (BS) Math, Rust Coll 1974; (MED) Scndry Ed/Math, 1979, Specialist Scndry Ed/Math, 1986 Univ of MS; *cr:* Testing Cnslr Benton Cty Schls 1974-76; Math Teacher Ashland Mid Sch 1976-; *ai:* Chm Funding Raising Comm; Benton Cty Teachers Assn Pres 1982-83; PTO Teacher of Yr 1979; Benton Cty Writing/Thinking Classes; *home:* Rt 1 Box 323 1/2 A Lamar MS 38642

BOSTON, BEVERLY DANIELLE, Mathematics Department Head; *b:* Baltimore, MD; *m:* Frank D. Jr.; *c:* Carmen, Frank III; *ed:* (BS) Math, Morgan St Univ 1962; (MED) Supervision/Admin, Loyola Coll 1975; Grad Stud; *cr:* Teacher Lombard Jr HS 1964-70, Walbrook HS 1970-78; Curr Coord Diggs Johnson Jr HS 1978-82; Math Dept Head Forest Park HS 1982-; *ai:* NHS Adv; Testing Coord; NCTM 1989-; MD Cncl Teachers of Math 1964-; United Meth Women Dist Pres 1970-, Service 1981; Delta Sigma Theta Nom Chm 1962-, Service 1982; BSA Den Leader 1967-81, Service 1970; NAACP 1965-; Presenter & Presider at Numerous St & City Math Meetings; Co-Writer Geometry Curr Guide Baltimore; Writer Math Curr Guides; Reviewed Items for Content Bias for CTB/MC Graw Hill; Finalist in Teacher of Yr Competition; *office:* Forest Park HS 3701 Eldorado Ave Baltimore MD 21207

BOSTON, FLORENCE ANN (WILKINS), 9th/10th Grade English Teacher; *b:* Lake City, AR; *m:* Dudley Kelly; *c:* Laurie Jackson, Susan, Cratin; *ed:* (BSE) Eng, Memphis St Univ 1960; Ed, Journalism; *cr:* 7th/8th Grade Teacher Snowden Jr HS 1960-62; 8th/9th Grade Eng Teacher Kingsbury Jr-Sr HS 1964-66; Teacher Les Passes Rehabilitation Center 1976; 9th/10th Grade Teacher Briarcrest Christian HS 1977-85, Collierville HS 1986-; *ai:* Chrldr Spon; Quill & Scroll, Yrbk Adv; NEA, TN Ed Assn, Shelby Cty Ed Assn, Shelby Cty Teachers of Eng Assn; Maternal Welfare League of Memphis Comm Chm 1974-75; *home:* 8404 Wicklow Way E Germantown TN 38138

BOSWELL, JOY M., Sixth Grade Teacher; *b:* Peru, IN; *m:* Ronnie L.; *c:* Jeffrey, James, Jason; *ed:* (BS) Ed, Manchester Coll 1962; (MA) Ed, Ball St Univ 1967; *cr:* Elem Teacher Maconaquah Sch Corporation 1963-68, Peru Cmmty Schls 1969-73, 1975-; *ai:* Head Teacher & Spelling Bee Coord Lincoln Elem; Peru Cmmty Ed Assn 1969-; IN St Teachers Assn, NEA 1962-; Mexico Church of Bretheren Chrstn Ed Commission; *office:* Peru Cmmty Schls 25 S Benton St Peru IN 46970

BOTIELHO, CHARLOTTE ABREU, Language Arts Teacher; *b:* Puunene, HI; *m:* Alfred M.; *c:* Eric A., Janis M.; *ed:* (BA) Speech/Ed, Chapman Coll 1972; *cr:* Lang Arts Teacher St Joseph Sch 1972-82; Lang Arts/Forensics Teacher H P Baldwin HS 1982-; *ai:* Adv Speech, Debate Team, SCHWA Society, HS Chapter of Natl Forensic League; HI Speech League Dist Rep 1982-; NCTE; Natl Fed for Speech/Debate Teachers; *office:* H P Baldwin H S 1650 Kaahumanu Ave Wailuku HI 96793

BOTTA, KENNETH MARIE, Fourth Grade Teacher; *b:* Baltimore, MD; *ed:* (BA) Elem Ed, Notre Dame of MD 1978; *cr:* Teacher St Pius X 1968-71, Our Lady of Perpetual Help 1971-; *ai:* Parish Athletic Dir 1975-83; Midget Girls Bsktbl Coach 1971-83; NCEA Speaker Phys Ed in Elem Grades; *office:* Our Lady of Perpetual Help Sch 1409 V Street SE Washington DC 20020

BOTTS, SUSAN TIBBEN, Second Grade Teacher; *b:* Atlantic, IA; *m:* Randall Lee; *c:* Aaron, Keila; *ed:* (BS) Elem Ed, NW MO St Univ 1973; Grad Stud; *cr:* 2nd Grade Teacher Fremont-Mills Elem Sch 1973-; *ai:* Area 13 Math & Health Curr Comm; Sr Trip & Jr HS Athletic Spon; *home:* 903 Park Tabor IA 51653

BOUCH, CECILY HOPKINS, Math Teacher; *b:* Orlando, FL; *m:* David Michael; *c:* Gabriel, Ashley; *ed:* (BS) Math Ed, FL St Univ 1975; (MSED) Scndry Math, Univ of Cntrl FL 1986; *cr:* Math Teacher Lake Howell HS 1978-79, Lyman HS 1979-80, Seminole Comm Coll 1980-81, Lake Howell HS 1981-89; *ai:* Math Club; Fellowship of Chrstn Athletes; Seminole Cty Cncl Teachers of Math, FL Cncl Teachers of Math, Seminole Ed Assn, FL Teaching Prof, NEA; *office:* Lake Howell HS 4200 Dike Rd Winter Park FL 32792

BOUCHER, CHARLOTTE CHAKAN, Inter Resource Instructor; *b:* Takoma Park, MD; *m:* Douglas H.; *c:* John M., Ellen R.; *ed:* (BA) Eng/Fr, Vanderbilt Univ 1971; (MAT) Fr Lit/Ed, Wesleyan Univ 1973; *cr:* Fr/Eng Teacher Broome Jr HS 1972-73, Grass Lake Jr/Sr HS 1975-79, Earle B Wood Mid Level Sch 1985-; *ai:* 6th Grade Team Leader; Sch Leadership Team Mem; Mentoring Prgm Liason Comm; Montgomery Cty Ed Assn, MD St Teachers Assn, NEA 1985-; Delta Kappa Gamma 1987-; Gamma Phi Beta; *office:* Earle B Wood Mid Level Sch 14615 Bauer Dr Rockville MD 20853

BOUCHER, JUDY ELAINE, Reading Specialist; *b:* Albuquerque, NM; *m:* Robert B.; *c:* Colleen, Dianne Brown; *ed:* (BS) Elem Ed, Univ of NM 1971; (MA) Elem Ed, Univ of NM 1973; (EDS) EdAdmin, Univ of NM 1981; *cr:* 2nd-6th Grade Teacher Albuquerque Public Schls 1971-80; 5th Grade 1981-85, Remedical Rdng 1985 Teacher Clark Cty Schls 1985-; *ai:* NV Rdng Week Act; Natl Literacy Day Act; Intnl Rdng Assn 1989-; Rdng Improvement Cncl Pres 1985-; Rdng Rep Mtn View Sch; Cmptr Resource Person Mtn View Sch; Grade-Level Chairperson 1985-; *office:* Mountain View Elem Sch 5436 E Kell Ln Las Vegas NV 89115

BOUCHER, RONALD H., Business Teacher; *b:* Northridge, CA; *m:* Sara Lynn Harding; *c:* Janae J.; *ed:* (BS) Ag Ec, CA St Univ Fresno 1981; Bus Admin, MBA; *cr:* Shipping Mgr Ballantine Produce Company Incorporated 1979-81; Branch Mgr Production Credit Assn Ag Finance 1981-86; Teacher/Coach Mt Whitney HS 1987-; *ai:* Jr Var Ftbl, Boys & Girls Var Tennis Head Coach; FBLA & Distributive Clubs of America Asst; Ag One 1981-86; CA Teachers Assn 1986-; Reedley First Baptist Church Youth 1988-; *office:* Mount Whitney HS 900 S Conyer Visalia CA 93277

BOUDREAU, CECELIA MARY, 3rd Grade Teacher; *b:* Lyons, NY; *m:* Edward Mark; *c:* Deborah J. Di Lorenzo, Mark J., Joan E. Lincoln, Edward L.; *ed:* (AA) Liberal Arts, Auburn Comm Coll 1974; (BS) Eng/Elem, Oswego St Teacher 1976; *cr:* 4th Grade Teacher Waterloo Cntrl Schls 1977-84; 1st Grade Teacher Waterloo Skoi-Yase Sch 1984-85; 3rd Grade Teacher Waterloo Cntrl Schls 1985-; *ai:* 3rd & 4th Grade Level Chairperson 1980-; Mentor Intern Prgm 1989-; Lafayette Building Cncl; Waterloo Yorker Club Supvr; Phi Beta Bi 1980-; Waterloo Hospital Guild 1955-70; St Marys Rosary Society; Favorite Teacher 1990 Essay Writing Contest Waterloo Cntrl Sch Dist; 1St Place Winner Favorite Teacher Contest Deans List Auburn Comm Coll 1974-76; *home:* 56 Taylor Ave Waterloo NY 13165

BOUDREAU, ROBERT RICHARD, Elementary Music Teacher; *b:* Downs, IL; *m:* Margaret Ann Robertson; *c:* Aimee, Adrienne; *ed:* (BS) Music Ed, Quincy Coll 1965; Grad Classes & Wkshps, W IL Univ; *cr:* Music Teacher Barry Cmmty Unit Schls 1964-65, Triopia Cmmty Unit Schls 1965-73; Elem Band Teacher Sch Dist #117 1976-; *ai:* 6th Grade Honor Band Dir; HS Girls Tennis Coach; NEA, IEA 1965-; MENC, IMEC 1965-73; Jacksonville Sym Bd 1985-88; Jacksonville Big Band 1984-; Elks 1975-; Play for Passavant Hospital Musical Fund Raisers; *office:* Sch Dist #117 516 Jordan Jacksonville IL 62650

BOUDREAUX, DARNELL NOONAN, Soc Stud Dept Chm/Teacher; *b:* New Orleans, LA; *m:* Gerald P.; *ed:* (BA) Soc Stud Ed, LA St Univ New Orleans 1971; (MED) Scndry Sch Prin, S LA Univ 1984; *cr:* 8th Grade Teacher A J Bell Jr HS 1971-75, St Ann Sch 1976-80; 7th/8th Grade Teacher/Dept Chm Soc Stud Clearwood Jr HS 1980-; *ai:* Stu Cncl & 8th Grade Spon; LA Cncl Soc Stud Treas 1989-; NCSS Mem 1984-; Krewe of Iris Mem 1986-; AFT Mem 1980-; Magnolia Forest Home Owners Assn Mem 1988-; Project Bus Awd for Teacher Coord; *office:* Clearwood Jr HS 130 Clearwood Dr Slidell LA 70458

BOUDREAUX, KATHLEEN DUPLECHAIN, Second Grade Teacher; *b:* Ville Platte, LA; *m:* John Rixby; *c:* Marcy H., Joseph R.; *ed:* (BA) Elem Ed, Mc Neese St Univ 1976; *cr:* 5th Grade Teacher 1979-80, 2nd Grade Teacher 1980- Sacred Heart Elem; *ai:* Spon Stu Cncl; Grandparents Day & Sch Building Level Comm; NCEA, Evangeline Parish Rdng Assn, Intnl Rdng Assn, NCTM 1980-; Church Summer Bible Sch Teacher; Master Catechist in Religion Classes 1987; *home:* Rt 4 Box 81C Ville Platte LA 70586

BOUDREAUX, PEGGY ESTAY, Second Grade Teacher; *b:* Cut Off, LA; *m:* Ted A.; *c:* Jason J.; *ed:* (BA) Elem Ed, Francis T Nicholls St Univ 1965; *cr:* 2nd Grade Teacher Golden Meadow Lower Elem 1965-; *office:* Golden Meadow Lower Elem Sch 2617 Alcide St Golden Meadow LA 70357

BOUDREAUX, WILBERT, Accounting Teacher; *b:* New Orleans, LA; *m:* Linda Ann Frye; *c:* Jonathan, Jessica; *ed:* (BS) Accounting, 1977, (MBA) Bus Ed, 1980 Nicholls St Univ; Tax Issues & Cmptr Applications, LA Society of CPAs; *cr:* Math Teacher Patterson Jr HS 1985-88; Bus Teacher Morgan City HS 1988-; *ai:* Jr Beta Club Spon; Mathcounts; NHS Co-Spon; Amer Inst of CPAs, LA Society of CPAs 1982-; Alpha Phi Alpha Pres 1976, Schlsp 1977; Article Published; Homemakers Tax Checklist; *home:* PO Box 395 Schriever LA 70395

BOUKNIGHT, GAIL ANDERSON, Second Grade Teacher; *b:* Greenville, SC; *m:* Charles Raymond Jr.; *c:* Travis A., Allison G.; *ed:* (BS) Elem Ed/Early Chldhd Ed, Lander Coll 1976; *cr:* 4th Grade Teacher Mc Cormick Schls 1976-77; 1st Grade Teacher 1977-88, 2nd Grade Teacher 1988- Ware Shoals Primary Sch; *ai:* NEA, SC Ed Assn; W Side Baptist Church; *home:* 107 Lynn St Greenwood SC 29649

BOULANGER, SHIRLEY J., Mid Sch Language Arts Teacher; *b:* Sedan, KS; *c:* Andrea Novak, Darby Cole, Stacy Hicks, Kirk; *ed:* (BS) Phys Ed/Home Ec, Emporia St Univ 1949; Grad Work Pittsburg St Univ, Emporia St Univ, Laverne Coll; *cr:* HS Home Ec/His Teacher Admire Rural HS 1949-50; Phys Ed Instr Wichita HS 1950-52; 1st-8th Grade Elem Teacher Osage Cty 1956-57; Lang Art/Phys Ed Teacher Sedan Mid Sch 1961-; *ai:* Pep Club Spon; Jr HS Track Coach; Numerous Advisory & Curr Comms; Baptist Church Choir Dir 1974-; *home:* RR 2 Box 15A Sedan KS 67361

BOULDEN, GEORGE ROBERT, III, Band Director; *b:* Chattanooga, TN; *m:* Kim Brierley; *ed:* (BME) Music Ed, Univ KY 1983; (MME) Music Ed, Univ Sc 1986; *cr:* Band Dir Blue Ridge Mid Sch 1986-87, Eustis HS 1987-; *ai:* Instrumental Music Act Dir;dept Chm Music Dept; FMEA/FBA Dist Chm 1990; Intl Assn Jazz Educators, FBA Executive Bd, Phi Mu Alphia Sinfonia, Menc, P Kappa Lamboa Music Society, Kappa Kappa Psi Band Mem; Natl Band Assn; Published Results Study Article; Natl Band Assn Journal 1987; *office:* Eutis HS 1300 Washington Ave Eustis FL 32726

BOUMANS, RANDALL JOSEPH, Industrial Arts Teacher; *b:* Conrad, MT; *m:* Ila Kay Cushing; *c:* Amanda Maia; *ed:* (BA) Industrial Arts, MT St Univ 1976; Summer Quarter MT St Univ 1976; Cert Classes E MT Coll; *cr:* Teacher/Adv Valier HS 1976-; *ai:* Frosh Class Adv; Valier Ed Assn 1976-85; Valier Fed of Teachers, AFT 1985-; VICA Valier Adv 1976-, Outstanding Adv 1984, 1990, Outstanding St Chapter; *office:* Valier HS 322 Choteau Ave Valier MT 59486

BOUNDS, DAVID ALAN, History/Geography Teacher; *b:* Oklahoma City, OK; *ed:* (BS) Scndry Ed/Soc Stud, Univ of OK 1980; Working on Masters Degree in His, Univ of OK; *cr:* Substitute/Summer US His Teacher Putnam City Public Schls 1981-83; Soc Stud Teacher Little Axe Public Schls 1983-; *ai:* HS Stu Cncl Spon; Little Axe HS Teacher of Yr 1989-; *office:* Little Axe HS Rt 2 Box 266 Norman OK 73071

BOUNDS, ELIZABETH RANDLE, Kindergarten Teacher; *b:* West Point, MS; *m:* Robert Walter; *c:* Andrew R., Walter B.; *ed:* (BA) Elem Ed, MS Univ for Women 1969; (MS) Elem Ed, MS St Univ 1972; *cr:* 3rd Grade Teacher Keystone Heights Sch 1969-70, West Point Sch 1970-78; Teacher 1st Baptist Kndgtn 1979-84, Oak Hill Acad 1984-; *ai:* Delta Kappa Gamma; West Point Jr Auxiliary; *home:* Rt 3 Box 466-A West Point MS 39773

BOURBEAU, CAROL ANN, Mathematics Teacher; *b:* Burlington, VT; *m:* Raymond M.; *ed:* (BS) Ed, Univ of VT 1984; *cr:* Math Teacher Rice Memorial HS 1984-; *ai:* Yrbk Co-Adv; Master Scheduler; VT Cncl of Teachers of Math 1984-; NCEA 1985-; *office:* Rice Memorial HS 99 Proctor Ave South Burlington VT 05403

BOURDESS, PETER LESUE, History/Art Teacher; *b:* Kansas City, MO; *m:* Anna Heesh; *c:* Micah L.; *ed:* (BS) ScnEry Ed, Bob Jones Univ 1984; *cr:* His Art HS Moncie Chrstn 1985-86; 5th/10th Grade Teacher Faith Acad 1986-87; His Art HS Shawnee Mission Chrst 1987-; *ai:* Head Coach Girls Vlybl/Bsktbl; Yrbk Adv.

BOURESSA, KEN D., Vocal Music Teacher; *b:* Appleton, WI; *m:* Sharon L.; *c:* Kari, Tyler, Nicholas; *ed:* (BME) Vocal Music Ed, Univ of WI Oskhosh 1982; Stu Assistance Counseling Chemically Dependant Children; Grad Stud Continuing Ed; *cr:* Teacher Little Chute Public Schls 1982-; *ai:* HS & Mid Sch Musical Theatre, Swing Choirs, Music Festivals; HS Ski Club; WMENC Mem; Fox Valley Symphony Choir Mem 1984-; Kaukauna Cmmty Players Mem 1986-; Winnegamie Dog Club Mem 1990; St Vocal Music Festival Judge 1989-; *office:* Little Chute Public Schls 1402 N Freedom Rd Little Chute WI 54140

BOURG, HELEN OTT, English Teacher; *b:* Starkville, MS; *m:* Roger Court; *c:* Laura W.; *ed:* (BS) Elem Ed, MS St Univ 1961; (MED) Elem Ed, GA St Univ 1980; Staff Dev Classes; Creative Writing, Writing Across Curr, Whole Lang Eng & Rdng Teaching Approach Seminars; *cr:* 4th-6th Grade Teacher Richard B Russell Elem 1961-70; 6th/8th Grade Teacher Daniell Mid Sch 1977-81; 7th/8th Grade Teacher E Cobb Mid Sch 1981-; *ai:* Writing Fair Comm; Stu Forum Adv; St Sch of Excl & SACS Comm; CCAE Building Rep 1967-68; GAE, NEA 1961-; Holy Family Church Lay Teacher 1976-82; St Recognition for Stu Work Published; *office:* E Cobb Mid Sch 380 Holt Rd Marietta GA 30068

BOURGEOIS, CATHERINE WAGUESPACK, Fourth Grade Teacher; *b:* New Orleans, LA; *m:* Danny P.; *c:* Jared P., Vicki L., Brittany L.; *ed:* (BA) Elem Ed, 1976, (MED) Curr/Instruction, 1984 Nicholls St Univ; 5 Yr Prof Improvement Plan Participant; *cr:* 4th Grade Teacher Paulina Elem 1976-; *ai:* 4-H Club Organizational Leader; St James Parish Sci Fair Spec Awds Dir; Safety Week Dir; SACS & SPUR Comms; Delta Kappa Gamma Parliamentarian 1988-; LAE, NEA; LAE for Gifted & Talented Stus Teacher Book Club; St Judes Math a Thon Spon; St James Parish Trash Bash Comm; St James Parish Teacher of Yr 1982-83; Received 4-H Silver & Gold Clover Awds; Lutcher Gramercy Jaycees Outstanding Young Educator 1986; Selected as Outstanding Young Woman of America 1983; *home:* 1570 Cabanose Ave Lutcher LA 70071

BOURKE, KEVIN MICHAEL, 6th Grade Teacher/Asst Prin; *b:* Columbus, OH; *m:* Janet Lynn; *c:* Theodore P.; *ed:* (BA) Elem Ed, Purdue Univ 1980; (MS) Elem Ed, IN Univ 1987; Cert Elem Admin, IN Univ 1989; *cr:* 4th-6th Grade Teacher Monrovia Elem 1980-84; 5th/6th Grade Teacher Allison Elem 1984-87; 6th Grade Teacher/Asst Prin Fisher Elem 1987-; *ai:* HS Wrestling Coach; Lang Art Textbook Adoption Comm; *office:* Fisher Elem Sch 5151 W 14th St Speedway IN 46224

BOURLAND, MARGARET JEAN, English & Journalism Teacher; *b:* Kansas City, MO; *m:* Eric Brettschneider; *c:* Karen L. Jacobs, Kathy L. Cole; *ed:* (BA) Eng, 1965, (MA) Eng, 1969 Univ of CA Fullerton; Boston Univ Overseas Campus, Univ of MD, RI Coll; *cr:* 4th/5th Grade Teacher Sunnyside Elem 1965-74; 5th Grade Teacher Bamberg Elem 1974-81; 11th/12th Grade Teacher Stuttgart HS 1981-; *ai:* Sch Newspaper Adv; Stu Ski Club Spon; Overseas Educators Assn; PTA Pres 1962-63, Life Time Membership 1963; Article Published; *office:* Stuttgart Amer HS Stuttgart Germany APO New York NY 09176

BOURNER, OLETA CARLYLE, Retired; *b:* Kaskaskia Island, IL; *m:* Robert Earl; *c:* Robert Jr., Anne, William; *ed:* (BA) Elem Ed, Mc Kendree Coll 1962; S IL Univ E; *cr:* Elem Sch Teacher Menard Sch 1941-42; Phys Ed Teacher Sparta Lincoln 1942-45; 1st Grade Teacher Sparta Lincoln 1955-78, Sparta Primary 1978-85; *ai:* Delta Kappa Gamma Pres 1976-78; Garden Club VP 1988-; Museum Bd Delta Theta Tau 1986-; Choir Church Cmmty Chorus Patron of Yr 1986; PTA Phoebe Hearit Nominee; *home:* 400 S Vine St Sparta IL 62286

BOURQUE, MARY JO, Third Grade Teacher; *b:* Detroit, MI; *c:* Douglas, Kathleen Bourque Bushe; *ed:* (BA) Eng Lit, Univ of Detroit 1963; (ME) Elem Ed, TX Chrstn Univ 1985; Cnslr Ed, TX Womans Univ; *cr:* 5th/6th Grade Teacher 1977-78, 3rd Grade Teacher 1978- Arlington TX; *ai:* Math Textbook Comm Arlington Ind Sch Dist; Sci Region XI Consultant; Team Leader; Metropley Assn Teachers of Elem, Sci Treas 1989-; PTA (Treas, Life Mem) 1975; Teacher of Yr Rankin Elem 1975.

BOUTERIE, KAREN HEBERT, 5th Grade Lang Arts Teacher; *b:* Thibodaux, LA; *m:* Paul F.; *c:* Lauren, Alison; *ed:* (BA) Kndgtn Elem Ed, Nicholls St Univ 1973; *cr:* 3rd Grade Teacher Thibodaux Elem 1973-74; Prytania Private Sch 1974-75; Kndgtn Teacher St Joseph Elem 1975-77; Our Lady of Promt Succor Sch 1977-78; St Joseph Elem 1978-80; 5th Grade Teacher St Joseph Elem 1981-; *ai:* NCEA; LA Rdng Assn; Nicholls St Univ Rdng Cncl; PTA; Teacher Rep Bd 1983-85; Femmes Natales Pres 82-83; Enthusiasm 1983; Krewe of Cleophas; *office:* St Joseph Elem Sch 501 Cardinal Dr Thibodaux LA 70301

BOUTON, PAULA VELAZQUEZ, Remedial English Teacher; *b:* Lackawanna, NY; *m:* Michael L.; *c:* James, Jennifer; *ed:* (BS) Elem Ed/Rdng Ed, Medaille Coll 1975; (MS) Rdng Ed, Canisius Coll 1980; *cr:* Corrective Rdng Teacher Buffalo Public Schls 1977-83; Remedial Eng Teacher Emerson Voc HS 1984-; *ai:* Sr Class & Drill Team Adv; Leadership Club; SADD; RCT Coord; BTF, NEA 1977-; *office:* Emerson Voc HS 1405 Sycamore St Buffalo NY 14211

BOUTWELL, JANICE COOPER, Second Grade Teacher; *b:* Baldwyn, MS; *m:* Ernest Edward; *c:* Amy, Christy; *ed:* (AA) Itawamba Comm Coll 1971; (BA) Elem Ed, 1974, (MS) Elem Ed, 1983 Univ of MS; *cr:* 1st Grade Teacher 1974-85, 2nd Grade Teacher 1985- Saltillo Elem; *office:* Saltillo Elem Sch P O Box 460 Saltillo MS 38866

BOUVET, STEVEN BERNARD, Vocational Agriculture Teacher; *b:* Garfield, NM; *m:* Nellie A.; *c:* Melissa Russell, Steven Jr., Leslie; *ed:* (BS) Ag/Extension Ed, NM St Univ 1973; *cr:* Voc Ag Teacher Raton HS 1973-74, Hatch Valley HS 1985-; *ai:* FFA Adv; NVATA, NMVATA, NMVA 1985-; *office:* Hatch Valley HS PO Box 790 Hatch NM 87937

BOUVIER, FUMIE (NAKAGUKI), Teacher; *b:* Tsuchiura-Shi, Japan; *c:* Marie, James; *ed:* Assoc Liberal Arts, Springfield Jr Coll 1963; (BS) Eng, Brescia Coll 1966; (MA) Ed, W KY Univ 1976; Rank I Rdng W KY Univ; *cr:* Teacher Shiragiku Gakuen HS 1965-67, Mc Lain Cty HS 1976-77, Daviess Cty HS 1977-, Owensboro Comm Coll 1985-; *ai:* EMT Instr; KY EMT Prgm Region III Coord; NEA 1976-; KY Cncl of Teachers of Eng 1986-; KY EMT Instrs Assn Regional Coord 1979-; Amer Heart Assn; CPR Instrs Assn (Instr, Trainer, Affiliate Faculty) 1983-87, St Outstanding CPR Instr 1986; Attended Writing Inst at W KY Univ 1986; Japanese Lang Instr KY Governors Scholars Prgm 1989, 1990; *office:* Daviess Cty HS 4255 New Harford Rd Owensboro KY 42301

BOW, AMEN YVON, English/Drama Teacher; *b:* Ann Arbor, MI; *m:* Diane Hall; *c:* Ryan; *ed:* (BA) Comm, MI St Univ 1975; Grad Work MI St Univ; *cr:* 11th Grade Eng Teacher Ottawa Hills HS 1975-77; Eng/Journalism/Drama Teacher Iroquois Mid Sch 1977-; *ai:* Sch Newspaper Ed-In-Chief; Learning Fair Chairperson; Grand Rapids Ed Assn, MI Ed Assn 1975-; Excl Ed Awd Fnd Grant 1989; Recognition Outstanding Educl Excl 1987-89; *office:* Iroquois Mid Sch 1055 Iroquois St Grand Rapids MI 49506

BOWARD, HENRIETTA KRUSE, Retired Fourth Grade Teacher; *b:* Petersburg, IL; *m:* Kenneth J.; *c:* David G., Glenn D.; *ed:* (BS) Elem, IL St Univ Normal 1961; Working Towards Masters; *cr:* 4th Grade Elem Teacher Middletown Elem & New Holland Mid Sch 1952-87; *ai:* IEA, NEA; *home:* 107 S Anson Box 48 Middletown IL 62666

BOWDEN, DENNY RUSS, Process Writing Specialist; *b:* Norfolk, VA; *m:* Barbara Ash; *c:* Heather M., Jessica L., Laura E., Robert R.; *ed:* (BA) Eng Ed, Univ of S FL 1970; (MA) Eng, Stetson Univ 1985; *cr:* Eng Teacher Mainland HS 1971-75, Spruce Creek HS 1975-77, 1980-82, Mainland HS 1982-89; Scndry Process Writing Specialist Volusia Cty Schls 1989-; *ai:* NCTE, ASCD, S Atlantic Modern Lang Assn, FL Assn for Cmptr Ed; Halifax Historical Society; Natl Endowment for Hum Fellowship to Study Thoreau & Emerson 1986, Emerson & William James 1989; Volusia Cty Teacher of Yr Finalist 1989; *office:* Educl Dev Center Box 1910 Daytona Beach FL 32115

BOWDEN, GLENDA EDWARDS, Mathematics/Science Teacher; *b:* Mineral Wells, TX; *m:* James Bruce; *c:* Alyssa, Serena; *ed:* (BS) Math, Tarleton St Univ 1971; (MS) Chem, Baylor Univ 1973; Cmptr Programming, Abilene Chrstn Univ; *cr:* Teacher Wylie Ind Sch Dist 1974-; *ai:* Stu Cncl Spon; UIL Calculator & Sci Coach; Assn of TX Prof Educators Treas 1982-; Amer Bus Womens Assn 1987-88; Nom Outstanding TX Teacher; *home:* 6426 Inverrary Dr Abilene TX 79606

BOWDEN, JAMES E., Fifth Grade Teacher; *b:* St Louis, MO; *m:* Patricia Benedict; *c:* Theodore J. P., Jared S.; *ed:* (BA) Ed, 1971, (BA) His, 1972 Cntrl WA St Coll; (MED) Curr/Instruction, Univ of OR 1980; Grad Stud & Admin Certificate; *cr:* 7th/8th Grade Eng/Math Teacher 1972-73, 6th Grade Teacher 1973-74, 5th Grade Teacher 1974-75 Michigan Avenue Sch; 5th Grade Teacher Bunker Hill Elem Sch 1975-; *ai:* Cmptr Coord; Coos Bay Sch Dist Micro Cmptr Advisory Comm; Onward to Excl Leadership Team; Coos Bay Ed Assn, OR Ed Assn, NEA 1972-; SW OR Youth Act (Mem, Bd of Dirs) 1985-88; *office:* Bunker Hill Elem Sch PO Box 509 Hwy 101 S Coos Bay OR 97420

BOWDEN, VIRGINIA GALLOP, 5th & 6th Grade Teacher; *b:* Harbinger, NC; *m:* Clyde M.; *c:* Ann S., Lori A.; *ed:* (BS) Elem Ed, Old Dominion Univ 1971; (MA) Intermediate Ed, E Carolina Univ 1986; *cr:* Prof Educator Trantwood Elem 1972-75, Cntrl Elem 1975-80, Griggs Elem 1980-; *ai:* Drama Coach & Just Say No Spon; Lang Art & Media Center Comm; Writing Coord; NC Assn of Educators 1976-; Powells Pt Chrstn Church (Dir Youth Church 1980-84, Ladies Aid 1976-); *office:* Griggs Elem Sch PO Box 37 Poplar Branch NC 27965

BOWELL, GERALD CARR, Biology Teacher; *b:* La Porte, IN; *m:* Lucy Ann Guard; *c:* Tyrone, Douglas; *ed:* (BSED) Phys Ed/Bio, 1966, (MAED) Phys Ed/Bio, 1989 Ball St Univ; Numerous Seminars; Quest Skills for Living; *cr:* Teacher/Coach Aiken HS 1966-68, Lawrenceburg Cmmty Schls 1968-74; VP Denbo Guard Corporation 1974-84; Teacher/Coach Lawrenceburg Cmmty Schls 1984-; *ai:* Head Wrestling & Asst Ftbl Coach; Var Lettermans Club; Co-Chm Assertive Discipline Comm; Faculty Advisory, PBA, N Cntrl Evaluation Comm; HASTI 1984-; Lawrenceburg Fed of Teachers Pres 1972-74; Natl Arbor 1986-; IN Curr Dev Grant 1985; GTE Sci Gift Grant 1986; Teacher of Yr 1987-88; Outstanding Teacher 1984, 1985, 1986, 1988; *office:* Lawrenceburg HS 100 Tiger Blvd Lawrenceburg IN 47025

BOWEN, HAZEL ANNA, Chemistry Instructor; *b:* Huntington, WV; *m:* Clinton R.; *c:* Dennie Annett, Clinton Jr., C. Bradley Paul B.; *ed:* (AB) Ed, 1976, (MS) Ed, 1986 Marshall Univ; *cr:* Math Instr Milton Jr-Sr HS 1976-77; Math Instr 1977-81, Chem Teacher 1981-Barboursville HS; *ai:* Improvement Comm Chairperson; Dept Co Chairperson; Phi Delta Kappa 1984; WV Sci Math Outstanding Teacher Awd 1988; Amer Chemical Society Outstanding Chem Instr 1988-89; *office:* Barboursville HS 1400 Central Ave Barboursville WV 25504

BOWEN, JACQUELINE LEE, Music & Art Teacher; *b:* Winthrop, MA; *c:* Jennifer L. Blackwell, Jonathan, Jeremy, Joshua, Jolene, Justin, Jeffrey, Jason; *ed:* (BSED) Elem Ed, Fitchburg St Col 1962; (MSED) Elem Ed, IN Univ Southeast 1988; *cr:* 2nd Grade Teacher 1962-64, Rdng Teacher 1964-68 Rowley Elem; Spec Ed Teacher Camden HS 1969-71; Music Teacher New Washington Elem 1980-; Music/Art Teacher New Wasington Elem Sch & Utica Elem Sch 1986-; *ai:* New Washington Elem Sch & Utica Elem Sch Cultural Arts Chm; IN Elem Music Educators Assn 1987-; Kappa Delta Pi 1987-88; PTA Bd 1983-; New Washington PTA St Life 1990; Fitchburg St Coll Whos Who in Amer Colls 1962; *home:* RR 1 Gill Rd Nabb IN 47147

BOWEN, JAMES DENNIS, Science Teacher; *b:* Alpena, MI; *m:* Johanna S. Fallas; *c:* Mary A. De Caire, James, Betsy; *ed:* (BS) Sci/Health & Phys Ed, Northern MI Univ 1964; (MA) Ed, MI St Univ 1967; Driver Ed Certified; *cr:* Teacher-Coach Athletic Dir Kinde N Huron HS 1967-68, Saginaw St Stephen HS 1968-69; Teacher-Coach Bridgeport HS 1969-72; Teacher-Coach-Athletic Dir Freeland HS 1972-; *ai:* Drivers Ed Instr; Class Spon; MEA, NEA; MI HS Athletic Assn 1964 20 Yr Awd 1984; Knights of Columbus 1959-; *home:* 5603 Adrian Saginaw MI 48603

BOWEN, JAMES WILLIAM, Chemistry Teacher; *b:* Bloomsburg, PA; *m:* Lynette Kay; *c:* Jamie, Matthew, Kelly; *ed:* (BA) Sci, Houghton Coll 1961; Chem, Physics, Math Bucknell Univ; Astronomy, Dickinson Coll; Earth Sci, Geology, Ed, Bloomsburg Univ of PA; Grace Theological Seminary; *cr:* General Sci Teacher Fillmore HS 1961-62; 5th Grade Teacher Seven Valleys Elem 1962-63; Earth/Space/General Sci Teacher Spring Grove HS 1965-70; Chem/Life Sci Teacher Millville HS 1970-; *ai:* Adult Womens Sftbl Coach; GED Teacher; Baptist Church (Sunday Sch Teacher 1975-, Pulpit Comm 1990, Supvr Adult Classes 1979-); *office:* Millville Area Sch P O Box 260 Millville PA 17846

BOWEN, JUNE GUDMANSON, Retired English Teacher; *b:* Mc Allen, TX; *w:* James Nathaniel Sr. (dec); *ed:* (BA) Span/Ed, Baylor Univ 1946; (MA) Elem Ed, George Peabody Coll for Teachers 1954; Spec Ed, George Peabody Coll for Teachers; *cr:* 1st Grade Teacher White Cty Schls 1946; 4th Grade Teacher Lee Cty Sch System 1951-52; 1st/6th-8th Grade Teacher 1952-63, Prin 1960-62, Supvr of Spec Ed 1962-63 Davidson Cty Sch System; 7th Grade Eng/7th-8th Grade Word Wealth Montgomery Bell Acad 1963-87; *ai:* Volunteer Literacy Prgm 1988-; Tutoring Iranian Woman in Eng; Delta Kappa Gamma Society 1960-; The Cum Laude Society 1982-; TN Congress of Parents & Teachers Life Mem 1962; Article Published 1967; *office:* Montgomery Bell Acad 4001 Harding Rd Nashville TN 37205

BOWEN, KENNETH RAY, Language Arts Teacher; *b:* Washington, NC; *ed:* (BA) Eng/Span, Atlantic Chrstn Coll 1968; (MA) Ed, East Carolina Univ 1971; Univ of NC-Advanced Trng in Creative Writing & Lit for Children; NC Writing Project; *cr:* Eng Teacher Oscar Smith HS 1968-69; Elem Teacher Pinetown Elem Sch 1969-82; Lang Arts Teacher Aulander Elem Sch 1984-; *ai:* Lang Arts Dept Chairperson; Lang & Writing Comm Chairperson; Southern Assn of Coll & Schls; Steering Comm Co-Chm; NEA/NCAE 1969-; NCTE; Bertie Art Cncl; ACC Alumni Chapter Pres 1980; Teacher of Yr Aulander Elem Sch 1988; *home:* 109 Beech St Rosedale Washington NC 27889

BOWEN, LEWELLYN MURPHY, English/Gifted Teacher; *b:* Snow Hill, NC; *m:* Travis Lee; *ed:* (BS) Elem Ed, George Peabody Coll for Teachers 1955; (MA) Elem Ed, Univ of NC Greenville 1960; Grad Stud Temple Univ, Univ of DE; Ventriloquism, Maher Studios; *cr:* 6th Grade Teacher 1955-56; 4th Grade Teacher Snow Hill HS 1956-57; 6th Grade Teacher Teachers Memorial 1957-61; 6th-7th Grade Teacher George Read Jr HS 1961-66;6th-8th Grade Teacher Ogletown Jr HS 1966-78; 7th-8th Grade Gifted Teacher Christiana Sch Dist 1979-; *ai:* Debate Clue, Odyssey of Mind Coach; New Sch Planning Comm; Perform Ventriloquism, Magic, Classic Drama for Children; NEA, DE Ed Assn; Alpha Delta

Kappa; Article on Gifted Ed Published by Univ DE Ec Dept; *home:* 722 Art Ln Newark DE 19713

BOWEN, MELANY HAGAN, English & French Teacher; *b:* Swainsboro, GA; *m:* Stuart Bland; *c:* Justin, Mary Mc Leod; *ed:* (BA) Eng - Magna Cum Laude, GA Southern Coll 1987; *cr:* Fr/Eng Teacher Emanuel Cty Inst 1987-; *ai:* Literary Competition Essay & Extemporaneous Speaking; GA Southern Coll Foreign Lang Oratorical Competition; Young GA Writers Exposition; NCTE 1986-; NEA 1987-; Phi Kappa Phi 1987-; Pi Delta Phi 1987-; *office:* Emanuel Cty Inst P O Box 218 Twin City GA 30471

BOWEN, WOODY, Mathematics & Science Teacher; *b:* Allock, KY; *m:* Judith Carolyn Reed; *c:* Kimberly Bowen Spatola, John, Michael, Mindi; *ed:* (BA) Elem Ed, Morehead St Univ 1965; *cr:* Math/Sci Teacher Flat Gap Elem Sch 1965-; *ai:* KEA, NEA; Masonic Lodge Master 1972; *home:* HC 85 Box 390 Flatgap

BOWENS, GEORGE AUSTIN, Mathematics Teacher; *b:* Sonoro, TX; *m:* Barbara Peterson; *c:* Lenecia D., Karessa H.; *ed:* (BS) Math, Angelo St 1976; *cr:* Math Teacher Franklin Jr HS 1977, Mann Jr HS 1977-86, Abilene HS 1986-; *ai:* Mentoring Teachers Comm; Mini Bsktbl & Soccer Coach; Campus Action Plan Curr Comm; TSTA, NEA 1977-; *office:* Abilene HS 2800 N 6th Abilene TX 79601

BOWER, JACK R., Instrumental Music Teacher; *b:* Berwick, PA; *m:* Pamela J. Carey; *c:* Jon, Scott; *ed:* (BS) Music Ed, Wilkes Univ 1974; Grad Stud Ithaca Coll; *cr:* Instrumental Music Teacher NW Area Sch Dist 1974-76, Danville Area Sch Dist 1976-; *ai:* Stand Tall Adv; NEA, Music Educators Natl Conference 1974-; Intnl Trumpet Guild 1986-; *office:* Danville Mid Sch Rt 11 Danville PA 17821

BOWER, WILLIAM RICHARD, Math Teacher/Swimming Coach; *b:* Jamestown, NY; *c:* Ashley, William, Matthew, Sarah; *ed:* (BA) Ed, Tulane Univ 1977; (MS) Math, Loyola Univ 1988; *cr:* Math Teacher/Swimming Coach Kiski Sch 1977-86, St Martins Episcopal Sch 1986-88, Tuloso Midway HS 1988-, Kiski Sch 1990; *ai:* Var Swimming Coach; Championship Swim Teams; Coach of Yr; *office:* Kiski Sch 1888 Brett Ln Saltsburg PA 15681

BOWERS, AMY LLOYD, Social Studies Dept Teacher; *b:* Altoona, PA; *m:* Bazel R.; *ed:* (BS) Scndry Ed, Bob Jones Univ 1972; Old Dominion Univ; *cr:* Soc Stud Teacher Portsmouth Chrstn Schls 1972-; *ai:* Gideons Auxiliary Chaplain 1988-89; *office:* Portsmouth Chrstn Schls 3214 Elliott Ave Portsmouth VA 23702

BOWERS, BARBARA JEANNE, 3rd-4th Grade Teacher; *b:* San Diego, CA; *m:* Mitchell R. Woodbury; *ed:* (BA) Ed, San Diego St Univ 1965; US Intnl Univ; *cr:* 2nd/5th Grade Teacher Florence Elem Sch 1965-; *ai:* Sch Chorus Dir 1970-80; Race Human Relations Comm Chairperson; San Diego Teachers Assn Rep 1976-82; NEA; CTA; Young Friends of SD Symphony Ed Comm 1980-82; Selected By Peers & Admin As Mentor Teacher 1986-89; *office:* Florence Elem Sch 3914 1st Ave San Diego CA 92103

BOWERS, GLORIA MILLS, Art Teacher; *b:* Brookville, PA; *m:* Ralph Gordon; *c:* Amy L.; *ed:* (BS) Art Ed, Penn St Univ 1973; *cr:* Elem Art Teacher Jersey Shore Elem 1973-76; Scndry Art Teacher Lock Haven HS 1982-; *ai:* Giving Assn for Progress & Service Adv; Sr Breakfast; Assn of Clinton Cty Educators, PA St Ed Assn; Pi Lambda Theta NHS for Women in Ed 1970- Penn St Univ; Beta Sigma Phi (Pres 1983, VP 1982) 1980, Woman of Yr 1984, 1985; *office:* Lock Haven HS West Church St Lock Haven PA 17745

BOWERS, JOHN ARTHUR, Computer Instructor; *b:* Chicago, IL; *m:* Anne Hiss; *ed:* (BAE) Ed, Univ of FL 1976; *cr:* Programmer Analyst Amer Cmptr 1976-80; Algebra Instr Gables Atlantis Acad 1981-84; Systems Engr NCR Corporation 1985-88; Cmptr Instr Pine Castle Chrstn Acad 1989-; *ai:* Sunday Sch Instr; *office:* Pine Castle Chrstn Acad 731 E Fairlane Ave Orlando FL 32809

BOWERS, SARA WILLIAMS, Retired Third Grade Teacher; *b:* Jefferson Cty, AL; *m:* William M.; *c:* Ralph W.; *ed:* (BS) Elem Ed, Samford Univ 1972; *cr:* Prin/Teacher Sulphur Springs Elem 1956-66; Teacher Hayden Elem 1966-88; *ai:* Delta Kappa Gamma VP 1975-76; *home:* Box 224 Hwy 160 Hayden AL 35079

BOWERSOX, DAVID F. A., Health/Physical Ed Teacher; *b:* Findlay, OH; *m:* Lisa Rothgerber; *c:* Timothy, Danielle; *ed:* (BS) Health/Phys Ed, West Chester Univ 1976; Post Grad Stud; *cr:* Health/Phys Ed Teacher/Athletic Dir Woodbridge Mid Sch 1976-78; Health/Phys Ed Teacher Osbourn HS 1978-80; 6th Grade Sci Teacher Manassas Park Intermediate Sch 1980-82; Heatlh/Phys Ed Teacher Littlestown HS 1983-; *ai:* Jr HS Ftbl & Head Wrestling Coach; HS Stu Cncl, Peer Support, Jr Class Adv; Littlestown Hershey Track & Field Youth Fitness Prgm Dir; Littlestown Youth Wrestling Club Dir 1988-89.

BOWIE, GERALDINE R. BASLEY, Principal; *b:* Chicago, IL; *m:* Walter Jr.; *c:* Kimberly, Walter III, Pamela D. Williams; *ed:* (BS) Elem Ed, Knox Coll 1968; (MS) Early Chldhd, 1976, (PHD) Ed, 1978 S IL Univ; *cr:* Asst Professor S IL Univ; Teacher Bailey Magnet Sch 1984-87; Prin Poindexter Elem Sch 1987-; *ai:* Phi Delta Kappa, Phi Kappa Phi, Pi Lamda Theta 1974-; Alpha Kappa Alpha Basileus 1980-84, Soror of Yr 1982; Gamma Kappa; Dissertation Research Awd SIU 1976-77; Governors Appointee White House Conference on Children & Families 1976; *office:* Poindexter Elem Sch 1017 Robinson Jackson MS 39203

BOWIE, LEEANNE L., English/Mathematics Teacher; *b:* Centralia, WA; *m:* Eddie Lock; *c:* Jordan, Elizabeth; *ed:* (BA) Eng, 1970, (MAT) Eng, 1979 Univ of WA; Teaching of Writing, Univ of WA; *cr:* Eng Teacher Sharples Jr HS 1971-76, Ballard HS 1976-81, Mercer Mid 1981-82, Eckstein Mid 1982-83; Eng/Math Teacher 1984-, Eng Dept Head 1988-89 Ballard HS; *ai:* Dance Group & Games Club Adv; NCTE 1975-; *office:* Ballard HS 1418 Nw 65th St Seattle WA 98117

BOWKER, LINDA W., Head English Dept; *b:* Memphis, TN; *m:* William H; *c:* Daniel, Andrew; *ed:* (BA) Eng, Centenary Coll of LA 1966; (MA) Eng Ed, Univ of KY 1976; *cr:* Eng Teacher Lafayette HS 1966-69; Danville HS 1970-72; Franklin Cty HS 1973-79; Eng Teacher Dept Head Western Hills HS 1980-; *ai:* Moderator Academic Team; Co-Chm Honors Day; Project Graduation Comm Mem; KY Cncl of Teachers of Eng; First Presbyn Church Mem 1976-; Franklin Cty All-Academic Faculty; Western Hills Teacher of Yr 1989; Natl Honor Soc; *office:* Western Hills HS 100 Doctors Dr Frankfort KY 40601

BOWLER, TERRY WAYNE, Spanish/History Teacher; *b:* St George, UT; *m:* Melanie F. Potter; *c:* Adam, Jason, Amy, Joy, Nathan, Joel T.; *ed:* Assoc General, Dixie Coll 1971; (BA) Sociology, St Univ Ut 1973; (ED) Scndry Ed, Univ St UT 1977; *cr:* Teacher Enterprise HS 1973-; *ai:* Span Club Adv; Bsbl & Wrestling Coach; St Winners Bsbl; NEA, UEA, WCEA 1973-; Enterprise City Cncl 1974-; Supts Awd for Excl 1989.

BOWLES, DEBORAH BEUTH, Chemistry Teacher; *b:* Charleston, WV; *m:* David E.; *c:* Nathaniel, Aaron; *ed:* (BS) Chem, 1978, (MS) Chem, 1979 VA Tech; *cr:* Analytical Chemist 1980-82, Analytical Supvr 1982-84 Hoechst-Celanese; Chem Teacher Forest Glen & John Yeates HS 1986-88, Forest Glen & Suffolk HS 1988-; *ai:* Amer Chemical Society 1979-85; Homeowners Assn Treas 1988-; Published Article; *office:* Forest Glen HS 200 Forest Glen Dr Suffolk VA 23437

BOWLES, GAYLE EILEEN LONG, 6th Grade Mathematics Teacher; *b:* Dallas, TX; *m:* Michael Ray; *c:* Michelle, Melissa; *ed:* (BA) Ed/Math, TX Tech Univ 1974; (MA) Ed, E TX St Univ 1977; *cr:* Math Teacher R L Thornton DISD 1974-; *ai:* Math Contest Spon; Team Leader, 4th-6th Grade Coord; Operation Involvement Rep; Math Curr Writer; Math Conference Wkshps Presenter; TX Classroon Teachers Assn, Natl Classroom Math Teachers; R L Thornton Teacher of Yr; Nom Cabell Awd 1985; Nom Jack Lowe Awd 1981; *office:* Robert L Thornton Sch 6011 Old Ox Rd Dallas TX 75241

BOWLES, LARRY CLARK, Soc Sci Teacher & Dept Chair; *b:* Kansas City, KS; *m:* Betty Jean Lukas; *c:* Stacy, Letitia; *ed:* (BA) Soc Sci, 1974, (MA) Ed, 1981 CA St Univ San Bernardino; Technology in Curr Coord Univ of CA Irvine 1987; *cr:* Soc Stud Teacher Rialto Jr HS 1975-76; Eng Teacher 1976-81, Dist Rdng Specialist 1981-83, Soc Stud Teacher 1983-89 Hemet Jr HS; Soc Stud Teacher W Valley HS 1989-; *ai:* Soc Sci Curr Comm; CTA, NEA 1975-; Hemet Teachers Assn Cncl Rep 1983; Hemet Public Lib Bd Mem 1981-85; San Jacinto-Hemet Genealogical Society 1986-; Hemet Jr HS Teacher of Yr 1982; *office:* Hemet Jr HS 831 E Devonshire Hemet CA 92343

BOWLIN, ANNA SHELLEY, Sixth Grade Teacher; *b:* Williamsburg, KY; *m:* Wesley; *c:* Laurel, Patrick; *ed:* (BA) Elem Ed, Cumberland Coll 1963; (MA) Elem Ed, Union Coll 1974; *cr:* 2nd Grade Teacher Fairlawn Elem Sch 1963-64; 5th Grade Teacher Ansonia Elem Sch 1964-67; 4th/5th Grade Teacher Revelo Elem Sch 1967-71; 1st/2nd Grade Teacher Jellico Creek Elem 1973-75; 1st/4th/6th Grade Teacher Liberty Elem 1978-89; 6th Grade Teacher Whitley Cty Cntrl Elem; *ai:* NEA; KEA Delegate; WCEA; *home:* Rt 3 Box 57A Williamsburg KY 40769

BOWLIN, MARY PATRICK, Second Grade Teacher; *b:* Sumner, KY; *m:* Will T.; *c:* Deborah Owens, Pamela Yarborough; *ed:* Elem Ed, Cumberland Coll 1945; (BS) Sci/Bio, E KY St Univ 1951; Early Chldhd Ed, LMU Taswell 1974; (MA) Union Coll 1980; *cr:* 1st Grade Teacher Mason Elem 1957-62; 1st/3rd Grade Teacher Hodgenville & Radcliff 1962-71; K/1st/6th Grade Teacher Bell Cty 1971-75; 1st/2nd/4th Grade Teacher Bracken Cty & Whitley Cty 1975-89; *ai:* Curr & Phys Ed Comm; Sci Club 1946-51; *home:* Rt 4 Box 923 Williamsburg KY 40769

BOWLING, ALICE MARIE (DANIELS), First Grade Teacher; *b:* Wapakoneta, OH; *m:* Raleigh David; *c:* Brian D., Brett T., Belinda J. High; *ed:* (BS) Ed, Wright St Univ 1973; *cr:* Primary Teacher W Elkton Elem 1957-58, Mendon Union Sch 1958-; *ai:* Girls Athletic Assn 1958-59; MUEA, OEA, NEA Pres 1982-86; *home:* 204 Mill St Mendon OH 45862

BOWMAN, AMY HARRIS, Math Teacher; *b:* Cleveland, NC; *m:* Terry D.; *ed:* (BA) Math, UNC-Charlotte 1986; *cr:* Teacher a L Brown HS 1986-; Instr Math/Sci/Ed Center UNCC Summer Ventures Prgm 1986-; *ai:* Natl Honor Society Adv; Math Contest Adv; NEA, NCAE 1986-; NCCTM 1986-; *office:* Ah Brown H S 415 E 1st St Kannapolis NC 28081

BOWMAN, BARBARA STOVALL, Third Grade Teacher; *b:* Dodson, LA; *m:* Joe Larry Sr.; *c:* Joe L. Jr., Susan C. Hanson; *ed:* (BA) Elem Ed, LA Tech Univ 1960; (ME) Ed, Univ of S MS 1977; *cr:* 3rd Grade Teacher Lincoln Parish Schls 1960-61; 2nd Grade Teacher Natchez Public Schls 1961-63; 1st Grade Teacher Trinity Episcopal Schls 1971-74; 3rd Grade Teacher Natchez Public Schls 1974-; *home:* 2 Alta Rd Natchez MS 39120

BOWMAN, BEAULAH TURNER, Elementary Teacher; *b:* Searcy, AR; *c:* Teyra E., Tondra; *ed:* (BA) Eng/Soc Stud, Saginaw Valley St Coll 1975; (MA) Guidance/Counseling, Cntrl MI Univ 1977; *cr:* Classroom Teacher Saginaw Sch Dist 1975-; *ai:* Math Olympics & Spelling Bee Coach; Safety Patrol Supvr; Young Writers Coord; Saginaw Area Rdng Cncl, Delta Kappa Gamma Recording Secy 1987-88; NAACP, NEA, MEA, SEA; Outstanding Young Women of America 1983; *home:* 4142 Nancy Dr Saginaw MI 48601

BOWMAN, BEVERLY HATFIELD, English Teacher; *b:* Kenova, WV; *m:* Max N.; *c:* Kimberli, Bryce; *ed:* (BA) Eng, Houghton Coll 1968; (MS) Ed, Univ of Bridgeport 1979; Credits Toward Doctoral Prgm In Eng Ed, NM St Univ; Post Grad Stu S IL Univ Edwardsville; *cr:* Eng Teacher NY Schls 1968-74; Instr Lees M Rol Coll 1979-80; Lecturer Boston Coll 1980-81, Kent St Univ & Akron Univ 1985-86; Public Relations Consultant El Paso Comm Coll 1982; Lecturer Univ of TX El Paso 1983-86; Gifted & Talented Conference Chm El Paso TX 1985-86; Eng Teacher Greenville HS 1986-; *ai:* Presenter Cooperative Learning at Inservice for Teachers; Bd Mem El Paso Assn for Gifted & Talented; Musician & Music Comm Mem for Church; Musical Teen Team Mem 1967; NCTE 1987-; NEA 1986-; Greenville Ed Assn (HS Rep 1988-89) 1986-; Gifted & Talented Fellowship 1987-88; Author of Cooperative Learning; Articles Published; *home:* 409 S 4th St Greenville IL 62246

BOWMAN, CINDY LYNN, Home Economics Teacher; *b:* Fullerton, CA; *m:* Earl Glenn; *c:* Bradley, Matthew, Kyle; *ed:* (BA) Home Ec, Fresno St Univ 1979; *cr:* Teacher Mc Farland HS 1980-; *ai:* FHA Adv; Self Esteem Mentor Teacher; *office:* Mc Farland HS 259 Sherwood Ave Mc Farland CA 93250

BOWMAN, CONNIE JO (HOWARD), Math Teacher/Math Dept Chair; *b:* Huntington, IN; *m:* John Ezra; *c:* Audrea L. Hess; *ed:* (BS) Scndry Ed/Math, Manchester Coll 1971; (MAT) Math, Purdue Univ 1977; *cr:* Math Teacher Wabash Jr HS 1971-72, Whitko HS 1973-78; Part Time Instr Manchester Coll 1979-80; Math Teacher Jr Sr HS 1980-; *ai:* Math Dept Chm; ISTA, NEA, ICTM, NCTM; Leo United Meth Chruch Choir Dir 1985-; *office:* Eastside Jr Sr HS 603 E Green St Butler IN 46721

BOWMAN, JAN ALBRIGHT, English Teacher; *b:* Lancaster, PA; *m:* Timothy Lee; *c:* Erin Delfert, Ray W. II; *ed:* (BS) Comm/Scndry Ed - Summa Cum Laude, Lock Haven St Univ 1976; *cr:* 7th/8th Grade Eng Teacher Marticville Mid Sch 1976-77; 9th-12th Grade Eng Teacher Shade HS 1977-84; 12th Grade Eng/Advanced Placement Eng Teacher Conemaugh Township HS 1984-; *ai:* Forensics & Scholastic Quiz Coach; NCTE 1975-; PA St Ed Assn 1976-; Geraldine Dodge Fnd Grant for Celebration of Teaching Project 1990; *office:* Conemaugh Township Area HS W Campus Ave Davidsville PA 15928

BOWMAN, JANICE PAULINE, English Teacher; *b:* Tulsa, OK; *ed:* (MS) Ed, 1975, (BA) Eng, 1966 OK St Univ; CO Univ/Univ Tulsa/OK St Univ; *cr:* Teacher Thomas Gilereas Jr HS 1966-69, Highlands Mid Sch 1969-70, Thomas Gilereas Jr HS 1970-74, Charles Mason HS 1974-79, Memorial HS 1979-81, Chester Nimitz Jr HS 1981-83, Memorial HS 1983-; *ai:* Natl Honor Society Memorial Chapter Spon; Tulsa Classroom Teachers Assn 1966-; OK Ed Assn 1966-; NEA 1966-; Tulsa Teacher of Yr 1982; Outstanding Young Women of America 1981; *office:* Memorial H S 5820 S Hudson Tulsa OK 74136

BOWMAN, JEANNE KRAEMER, Third Grade Teacher; *b:* Buffalo, NY; *m:* Raymond P.; *c:* Mary B.; *ed:* (BSED) Elem Ed, 1970, (MSED) Early Chldhd Ed, 1974 St Univ Coll Buffalo; *cr:* Kndgtn Teacher 1970-80, 3rd Grade Teacher 1980- North Tonawanda Public Schls; *ai:* Cooperating Teacher W NY Inst Arts in Ed, 3rd Grade Push-In Prgm; Mem Sch Improvement Planning Team; North Tonawanda United Teachers PAC Mem 1988-89, Outstanding Teachers Awd 1984; Alpha Delta Kappa 1990; NY St United Teachers, AFT 1970-; Buffalo Philharmonic Society, Buffalo Zoological Society, Society for Prevention of Cruelty to Animals; Collaborated in Writing of Publication; *office:* Meadow Elem Sch 455 Meadow Dr North Tonawanda NY 14120

BOWMAN, JED R., Science/Mathematics Teacher; *b:* Colorado Springs, CO; *ed:* (BS) Geology, CO St Univ 1986; *cr:* Teacher Asst CO St Univ 1985-86; Math/Sci Teacher Air Acad HS 1986-87, Liberty HS 1987-; *ai:* Sr Class Spon; Head Boys Golf, Asst Boys Hockey, Head Girls Soccer Coach; North Cntrl TAG, North Cntrl Math, Trash Busters Comm Mem; NCTM 1987; CO Cncl Teachers of Math 1987-; Girls Soccer Coach of Yr 1988-89; *office:* Liberty HS 8720 Scarborough Dr Colorado Springs CO 80920

BOWMAN, MARY EVELYN, Second Grade Teacher; *b:* Pecos, TX; *m:* Fletcher C. Jr.; *c:* Janet L. Koesters, Charlene L., Kathryn; *ed:* (BA) Elem Ed, Mc Murry Coll 1958; *cr:* 1st Grade Teacher Bell Smith & Memorial Elem 1959-71; 2nd Grade Teacher Chaparral Elem 1980-; *ai:* NEA; PEO 1973-; *office:* Chaparral Elem Sch 1400 E Holly Deming NM 88030

BOWMAN, PHYLLIS DUFF, English Teacher; *b:* Ricetown, KY; *m:* James R.; *c:* Amelia A.; *ed:* (BA) Eng 1967, (MA) Ed/Eng, E KY Univ; *cr:* Eng Teacher E KY Univ 1967-; Part-Time Instr Lees Jr Coll 1988-; *ai:* Band Boosters Pres; Beta Club Spon; JTPA Work Prgm Cnslr & Bookkeeper; KEA 1988-; *home:* Box 612 Booneville KY 41314

BOWMAN, RODGER LEE, Mathematics Teacher; *b:* Levenworth, KS; *m:* Catherine R.; *c:* Reggan A. Ruppenthal, Ryan M. Ruppenthal; *ed:* (AA) Scndry Ed, Garrett Comm Coll 1980; (BS) Math/Phy Ed Teacher, WV Univ 1982; Addl Stud Frostburg

St Univ; *cr:* Math Teacher W Preston HS 1982-83: Math/Physics Teacher E Preston HS 1983; *ai:* Var Girls Bsktbl Coach; Garrett Comm Coll Asst Coach; *office:* E Preston HS 1 Eagle Way Terra Alta WV 26764

BOWMAN, SUELLEN WHITSON, Kindergarten Teacher; *b:* Detroit, MI; *m:* Gordon; *ed:* (BA) Ed, 1965, (MA) Rdng, 1967 MI St Univ; Madeline Hunter Wkshps Univ of CA Los Angenes 1972-76; Educl Therapy Trng Marianne Frostig Center 1977; *cr:* 1st Grade Teacher Adams 1965-66; 2nd Grade Teacher Cadillac 1968-70; 1st Grade Teacher 1970-84, Kndgtn Teacher 1984-Burbank; *ai:* Sch Improvement Comm 1986-87; Dist Curr Dev Math 1974 & Soc Stud 1976; Intnl Rdng Assn; Pasadena Partners in Ed Treas 1988-; *office:* Luther Burbank Elem Sch 2046 N Allen Ave Altadena CA 91001

BOWNS, JANE ANN, Mathematics Coordinator; *b:* Grayling, MI; *ed:* (BA) Soc Stud, Univ of MI 1968; (MA) Ed Admin, Cntrl MI Univ 1975; *cr:* 6th Grade Teacher Birch Run Cmmty Schls 1968-69; Jr HS Math Teacher 1969-76, 6th Grade Teacher 1976-85, 5th Grade Teacher 1985-89, Math Coord 1989-Brigeport-Spaulding Cmmty Schls; *ai:* Soc Stud, Sci, Math Curr Comm; Textbook Adoption, Nation at Risk, Mid Sch Reorganization Task Force, Lang Art, Restoration of Red Sch House Comm; MI Ed Assn, NEA, NCTM; Bridgeport Ed Assn Pres 1971-73; Bridgeport Historical Society, Thursday Night Quilt Society; *office:* Bridgeport-Spaulding Cmmty Sch 3878 Sherman Bridgeport MI 48722

BOWSER, ANITA QUINLISK, 6th-8th Grade Science Teacher; *b:* Punxsutawney, PA; *m:* James P.; *c:* Timothy, Stephen, Dee Anne, Julie; *ed:* (BA) Ed, Chapman Coll 1970; (MS) Guidance/Counseling, Univ of NE 1977; *cr:* Dir Little Big Sch 1975-78; Prin Franciscan Sch 1978-80; 6th/7th/8th Grade Sci Teacher Saints Cosmas & Damian 1981-; *ai:* Yrbk Adv; Church Youth Group Coord; NSTA, PA Sci Teachers Assn, NCEA; Amer Cancer Society Bd of Dir.

BOWSER, KAREN WILSON, English Teacher; *b:* Johnstown, PA; *m:* Lee H.; *c:* Jason L., Kari J.; *ed:* (BS) Scndry Engl Ed, IN Univ of PA 1972; (MED) Teaching/Cur Penn St 1986; *cr:* Drama Dir/Eng Teacher Lower Dauphin HS 1972-74; Engl/Comtpr Literacy West Shore Dist 1981-84; Cmptr Specialist/Eng Abrams Hebrew Acad 1985-86; Eng Mechanicsburg Intermediate Sch 1986-87;Eng/Dir of Musical Mechanicsburg HS 1987-; *ai:* Adv Sch Newspaper the Torch; Dir of Fall Play; Dir of Writing Ctr; NCTE 1987-90 Civic Club of New Cumberland (Pres 1980-81, Vice Pres 1979-80; Who's Who in Amer Ed 1988-90; Service to Pupils Awd for Exceptional or Innovative Teaching, Extraordinary Ldrshp in Extracurricluar Activites; *office:* Mechanicsburg H S 500 S Broad St Mechanicsburg PA 17055

BOWSER, NANCY EVERHART, First Grade Teacher; *b:* Thomasville, NC; *m:* William Frederick; *c:* Jane Croyle, Robert F.; *ed:* (BA) Primary Ed, Univ of NC Greensboro 1952; *cr:* 1st Grade Teacher Fair Grove Sch 1952-57, Centreville VA 1957-58; 3rd Grade Teacher Memphis TN 1958-59; 4th Grade Teacher Baltimore MD 1959-60; 1st Grade Teacher Oak Hill 1960-63, Fair Grove NC 1973-; *ai:* Cultural Arts & Arts-Crafts Chm; NEA, NCEA, Davidson Cty Ed Assn 1952-; Thomasville Womans Club VP; Meth Church Womans Society Pres; Beta Sigma; *home:* 132 Maplewood Ave Thomasville NC 27360

BOWYER, KATHY MC PHEE, 7th Grade Teacher; *b:* St Louis, MO; *m:* Earl A.; *c:* Greg, J. T.; *ed:* (BA) Ed/Geography, WA St Univ 1969; (MS) Math Ed, Portland St Univ 1984; Math Endorsement Portland St Univ 1990; *cr:* 5th Grade Teacher Archdiocese of Spokane 1969-70; Substitute Teacher Yakima Valley Schls 1979-80; 7th Grade Teacher St Joseph Sch 1980-; *office:* St Joseph Sch 6500 Highland Dr Vancouver WA 98661

BOYAR, THREASA Z., Mathematics Teacher; *b:* Hamilton, TX; *c:* Jonathan, Laura Mayberry; *ed:* (BA) Math, N TX St Univ 1966; *cr:* Math/Sci/Typing Teacher Pottsville Ind Sch Dist 1973-74; Math Teacher Gatesville HS 1976-78, Wharton HS 1978-; *ai:* Chrldr Spon; TCTA 1976-; *office:* Wharton HS 1 Tiger Ave Wharton TX 77488

BOYATT, LOUIS, Health/Phys Ed Teacher/Coach; *b:* Oneida, TN; *ed:* (BA) Health/Phys Ed, Cumberland Coll 1972; (MA) Health/Phys Ed, N GA Coll 1980; *cr:* Teacher/Coach Varnell Sch 1972-75, N Whitfield Mid Sch 1975-; *ai:* Ftbl, Bsbl, Track Coach; GAHPERD, WEA, GAE, NEA; *home:* 152 Beaverdale Rd NE Dalton GA 30721

BOYD, ANDREA PADGETT, English Teacher; *b:* Philadelphia, PA; *ed:* (BS) Scndry Eng, Millersville St 1968; (MS) Ed, Temple Univ 1974; Grad Stud Penn St; *cr:* Teacher Benjamin Franklin Jr HS 1968-74, Armstrong Jr HS 1974-75, Delhaas HS 1974-78, Truman HS 1978-81, Armstrong Jr HS 1981-; *ai:* Writing Across Curr, Essential Elements of Instruction, Dist Eng Comm; NEA, PA St Ed Assn, Bristol Township Ed Assn 1968-; *office:* Bristol Township Schls 800 Coates Ave Bristol PA 19007

BOYD, BARBARA LINER, Second Grade Teacher; *b:* Ruston, LA; *m:* Gary Jack; *c:* Gary S., Karen E.; *ed:* (BA) Elem Ed/Lib Sci, 1971, (MA) Elem Ed, 1975 LA Tech Univ; Elem Ed, LA Tech Univ 1990; *cr:* 1st Grade Teacher 1972-77, 2nd Grade Teacher 1979- Ruston Elem Sch; *ai:* Faculty Senate 1986, 1990; Lincoln Parish Advisory Cncl 1987; Kappa Kappa Iota Eta St (Treas 1975) 1975-; Ruston Church of Christ Mem; Young Teacher of Yr 1973; Ruston Elem Sch Teacher of Yr 1990; *office:* Ruston Elem Sch Bernard St Ruston LA 71270

BOYD, BETTYE SMITH, Science Teacher; *b:* Gadsden, AL; *c:* William J.; *ed:* (BS) Ed/Sci, 1972, (MA) Ed, 1975 Univ of AL Birmingham; Advanced Trng in Physics, Univ of AL Huntsville; *cr:* 5th Grade Sci Teacher John S Jones Elem Sch 1972-; *ai:* Sci Club; Hands on Field Trips; Etowah Ed Assn (VP, Pres Elect) 1980-81; *home:* Rt 4 Box 627 Gadsden AL 35904

BOYD, BRUCE GREGORY, 5th Grade Teacher; *b:* Reno, NV; *c:* Michael, Max; *ed:* (BA) Speech/Public Address, Pasadena Coll 1969; 5th Yr Elem Ed, Univ of CA Los Angeles 1972; Early Chldhd, Univ of CA Los Angeles & CA St Los Angeles 1970-74; Learning Styles, NW Nazarene Coll 1986-; *cr:* 3rd-4th Grade Soc Sci Teacher 1970-74, Kndgtn Teacher 1974-76 Emperor Sch; 7th-8th Grade Soc Stud/9th Grade Eng Teacher South Jr HS 1976-77; Prof Speech/Comm Teacher NW Nazarene Coll 1977-79; 4th Grade Teacher Lincoln Elem 1980-81, Mtn View Elem 1981-82; 2nd Grade Teacher 1982-89, 5th Grade Teacher 1989- Centennial Elem; *ai:* Debate, Youth Bsktbl Coach; Cmptr Coord; Summer Cmptr Camp; Drama Society; Comm of Twelve; Career Recognition Comm Chm; GMS NNC Spon; Valley Rdng 1985-89; NEA, ID Ed Assn 1981-; Nampa Ed Assn (Pres, VP) 1989-; Teacher Fnd Grants; Nom Christa Mc Auliffe Fellowship Awd; Co-Author Cmptr Ed ID St Dept of Ed; Nom US West Direct Teacher Recognition Prgm; Nom Teacher of Yr Prgm; IBM/Classroom Comp Learn Magazine; Nampa Sch Dist 131 Teacher of Yr Nom; *office:* Centennial Elem Sch 522 Mason Ln Nampa ID 83686

BOYD, CATHERINE GARRETT, Fourth Grade Teacher; *b:* Caldwell County, KY; *m:* Joe Lee; *c:* Lynn B. Werner, Patti J.; *ed:* Provisional Elem, Paducah Jr Coll 1942; (BA) Elem Ed, Murray St Univ 1969; Various Courses to Update Teaching; *cr:* 4th Grade Teacher Lone Oak Elem 1955-; *ai:* 4-H Club Adv; Easter Seals Telethon for Crippled Children Spon; NEA, KEA, FDEA; Mc Cracken Cty Ed Assn Rep 1976-77 Perfect Attendance Awd 1979; Intnl Rdng Assn; Lone Oak Church of Christ Dept Head; Delta Kappa Gamma; Mc Cracken Cty Teachers Supervisory; Federal Credit Union Cmmty-supervisory 1970-; Lone Oak Womens Club; Chamber of Commerce Extra Mile Awd; Yrbk Dedication; Sch of Excl Rep; *home:* 420 Charleston Ave Paducah KY 42001

BOYD, CINDY HUSKIN, Math Teacher; *b:* Abilene, TX; *c:* Tisha; *ed:* (BSED) Math Ed, 1973, (MSED) Mid-Management, 1990 Abilene Christian U niv; TX Ed Agency Staff Dev Teacher Trainer In Geometry/Algebra/Calculators/Cmptr/Numeration/Computation & Error Diagnosis; Challenge of The Unknown; *cr:* Math Teacher Moran Ind Sch Dist 1973-79, Abilene Ind Sch Dist 1979-; *ai:* Campus Technology Comm; Math Fair Coord; UIL Math Coach; Class Spon; Tutor for Math Tutorials-Lunch; Official Textbook Adoption Comm Mem; Cooperating Teacher for Stu Teachers; Accreditation Comm Mem; Review Team; Homework Hotline Staff; NCTM 1988-; TX Cncl of Teacher of Math 1988-; ASCD 1989; Big Cntry Cncl of Teachers of Math 1989-; TX St Teachers Assn 1973-; Comm that Wrote Essential Elements for Pre-Algebra & Informal Geometry/Proclamation 67 For TEA; Speaker TX St Math Convention 1988; Inservice/Wkshp Presenter; TX Ed Agency Math Staff Dev Teacher Trainer in Geometry/Algebra/Calulators/Cmptr/Numeration Computation & Error Diagnosis; Super Trainer in Calculators/Cmptrs; Author Skit-So-Phrenia & We Fear-em No Theorem; *office:* Abilene H S 2800 N 6th St Abilene TX 79603

BOYD, DAISY WHITE, 3rd Grade Teacher; *b:* Morton, MS; *m:* Newtie J.; *c:* Noland J.; *ed:* (BS) Elem Ed, Alcorn St Univ 1972; Metric Spec; *ai:* Co-Chairperson Staff Dev; MAE; NEA; NPTA; Eastern Star; NCNW; 1979 Yrbk Dedication; *office:* Morton Attendance Center PO Drawer L Morton MS 39117

BOYD, DORIS GODWIN, English Teacher; *b:* Gatesville, TX; *m:* Donald Alvin; *c:* Bradley D., Kelley D. Boyd Palmer; *ed:* (BS) Eng, 1964, (MED) Guidance & Personnel Services, 1973 Memphis St Univ; Rdng; *cr:* Teacher Gragg Jr HS 1964-66, Knight Road Sch 1966-67, Wooddale HS 1967-69, Wooddale Jr HS 1970-; *ai:* Spon Wordsmith Club; Mem Discipline Comm; Chmn Steering Comm Self Study; Rotary Awd for Teacher Excl Mem 1988-; Memphis-Shelby Cncl of Teachers Eng (Mem 1970-, Parliamentarian 1979-80); NCTE Mem 1988-; Germantown Cmmty Theater Mem Bd of Dir 1985-88; Rotary Awd for Teacher Excll 1988; Local Cmmty Theater 1985-88; *office:* Wooddale Jr HS 3467 Castleman Memphis TN 38118

BOYD, EDITH J. MAJOR, 8th Grade Soc Stud Teacher; *b:* Newark, NJ; *m:* Jeffrey E.; *ed:* (BA) His/Scndry Ed, Hofstra Univ 1972; *cr:* 7th-9th Grade Soc Stud Teacher Mc Manus HS 1972-; *ai:* Project Bus Adv 1984-; Book Fair Coord 1978-; Peer Leadership Adv 1984-85; Amer Ed Coord 1979, 1981, 1985-86; Linden Educl Fnd 1988-; Continental Societies Incorporated 1989-; NJ Governors Teacher Recognition Awd 1987; Jr Achievement Distinguished Service Awd 1988; *home:* 60 Fleetwood Dr Hazlet NJ 07730

BOYD, ERNEST ALPHONSO, Band Director; *b:* Greenville, FL; *m:* Mary Frances Everette; *c:* Franchon A., Felecia A.; *ed:* (BA) Music Ed, Bethune Cookman 1959; Certified Elem Ed, Florida a & M Univ 1961; (MA) Music Ed, Vander Cook Coll 1976; *cr:* Band Dir Charles R Drew HS 1959-61; 7th Army Orch 1962-64; Hungerford HS 1964-81; Carver Mid Sch 1982-; *ai:* FL Bandmaster Assn; FL Music Educators Assn; Kappa Alpha Psi Treas 1978; Man of Yr 1979; St Johns Episcopal Church Sr Warden 1968-; Jaycees Outstanding Young Man of Amer 1974; Southern Assn Evaluation Visiting Comm Mem; Orange Cty Teacher of Yr 1987; Adjunct Instr of Music Univ of Central FL 1970-76; Concert Clinician AL St Univ Summer Band Camp 1983-84; *home:* 2242 Pipestone Ct Orlando FL 32818

BOYD, GEORGINA MARIE (MELLO), 4th Grade Teacher; *b:* Fall River, MA; *m:* George F.; *c:* Jean M., Christopher, Amy L., John P.; *ed:* (AA) His, Solano Cmty Coll 1964; (BA) His, Holy Names Coll 1966; His, CA St 1968; Ed Courses Ottawa Univ; *cr:* Soc Worker Solano Cty Welfare Dept 1966-67; City Census Taker Vallejo 67; 5th Grade Teacher Suisun Unified Sch Dist 68; 3rd Grade Teacher Fairfield-Suisun Unified Sch Dist 1968-; *ai:* Dist Soc Stud Comm; Amy Blanc Soc Comm; Mem Year-Round Calandar Comm; Rdng Assn 78; Latin Amer Parents Assn Trustee 1988-90; Solano Cty Adoption Support Group 1989-90; Our Lady of Mount Carmel Church 1985-90; *office:* Amy Blan Elem Sch 230 Atlantic Ave Fairfield CA 94533

BOYD, GLENDA LORNEY (RINEY), Vocational Home Ec Teacher; *b:* Evansville, IN; *m:* Gerald David; *ed:* (BA) Home Ec, 1971, (MA) Home Ec, 1975 Univ of Evansville; Vocational Cert; *cr:* Home Ec Teacher Lincoln Elem 1971-76, Central HS 1976-; *ai:* Mascot Spon; Amer Home Economists, IN Home Economists, Evansville Home Economists 1971-; Natl Teachers Assn St/Local 1971-; *office:* Central HS 5400 1st Ave Evansville IN 47710

BOYD, GORMAN FRANKLIN, 7th/8th Grade Science Teacher; *b:* Oliver Springs, TN; *ed:* (BA) Ed, Cumberland Coll 1973; (MA) Ed, TN Technological Univ 1988; *cr:* Teacher Oliver Springs Elem 1973-; *ai:* Sci Outdoor Chm; Team Leader; Head Sci Dept; TEA, NEA, RCEA 1973-; *office:* Oliver Springs Elem Sch Drawer A Oliver Springs TN 37840

BOYD, IONA VICK, 6th Grade Teacher; *b:* Franklin Co, NC; *m:* Elvas G.; *c:* Kimberly Jon; *ed:* (BS) Elem Ed, Elizabeth City State Univ 1959; Writing, William & Mary; Lang Arts Univ of VA; *cr:* 7th Grade Teacher Perrys HS 1959-67; 4th/5th Grade Teacher Epsom HS 1967-68; 7th Grade Teacher Alanton Elem 1968-69; 6th/7th Grade Teacher Windsor Woods Elem 1969-; *ai:* Drama Club Spon/Adv; VA Beach Rdng Cncl 1984-; Les Gemme VP 1980-; *home:* 5104 Kittery Lndg Virginia Beach VA 23464

BOYD, JOSEPH LEE, Art Teacher; *b:* Welch, WV; *ed:* (BS) Art Ed, Concord Coll 1980; Working Toward Masters Rdng; *cr:* Art Teacher Welch Jr HS 1980-84, Big Creek HS 1985-; *ai:* Sr Class, NHS, Miss Hoot & Miss Owl Pageants Spon; Prom Decorating Comm; WV Ed Assn, NEA 1980-; Gamma Beta Phi Pres 1980; War Pentacostal Church Teen Teacher 1988-; Project Graduation Chm 1990; *office:* Big Creek HS Main St War WV 24892

BOYD, NAOMI C. CRAFT, Fourth Grade Teacher; *b:* Sciotoville, OH; *m:* Raymond D.; *c:* Bethany R., Julie E. Johnson; *ed:* (BS) Ed 1969, (MS) Elem Ed 1983 OH Univ; *cr:* 4th Grade Teacher 1969-73/1978-, 2nd Grade Teacher 1973-78 Harding Elem; *ai:* Portsmouth City Teachers Assn (Mem 1983-87/1st VP 1987-88/Pres 1989-); *home:* Rt 4 Box 463-A Portsmouth OH 45662

BOYD, NIKIE JOHNSON, Science Teacher; *b:* Baltimore, MD; *ed:* (BS) Bio, Morgan St 1969; Environmental Stud, Johns Hopkins, Baltimore City; Methods of Ed, Cappin St; Teaching Sci Towson St; Cmptr Basics, Baltimore City & Johns Hopkins Univ; *cr:* Life Sci Teacher Roland Park Jr HS 1969-70; Phys Sci Teacher Woodburne Jr HS 1970-71, Harlem Park Jr HS 1971-73; Earth/Phys & Life Sci Teacher Robert Poole Mid Sch 1973-; *ai:* Treas Robert Poole Mid Sch; Sci Olympiad Spon Robert Poole Mid Sch 1989-; Team Leader 7th Grade Teachers; Thinking Skills Club Spon; Instr Upward Bound Prgm; City Wide Aids Instr Staff Dev; Teach Adult in GED Prgm; Delicados Inc Treas 1989-91; *office:* Robert Poole Mid Sch 1300 W 36th St Baltimore MD 21211

BOYD, NORMA SCHULTZ, Second Grade Teacher; *b:* Deposit, NY; *m:* Earl; *c:* Sharon Lehr, Janet Walker, Linda; *ed:* (BS) Elem Ed, 1956, (MS) Elem Ed, 1973 St Univ Coll Oneonta; Grad Stud Elem Ed; *cr:* 2nd Grade Teacher Morris Cntrl Sch 1963-; *ai:* NY St Rdng Assn, NYSUT; *home:* Box 70A RD 1 Morris NY 13808

BOYD, PATRICIA QUARELS, Science Department Chair; *b:* New Orleans, LA; *m:* Thomas Jr.; *c:* Valencia, Varonna, Thomas V.; *ed:* (BA) Elem Ed, Southern Univ 1975; *office:* Lawless HS 5300 Law St New Orleans LA 70117

BOYD, SHIRLEY LOCK, 8th Grade Science Teacher; *b:* Waverly, MO; *m:* Paul Clifton Jr.; *c:* Celeste, Jeffrey; *ed:* (BS) Ed, Univ of MO Kansas City 1972; (MA) Ed, Univ of MO Columbia 1976; *cr:* 2nd Grade Teacher Warren Cty R-II Sch Dist 1972-73, N Kansas City Sch Dist 1973-78; 1st/3rd/4th Grade Teacher Mc Gowen Stephens 1978-80; 5th Grade Teacher Meridith Elem 1980-81; Sci Teacher Lamar Mid Sch 1981-; *ai:* Stu Cncl, Sci Fair Spon & Dir, UIL Sci Coach, Temple ISD Peer Assisted Leadership & Support; Sci Teachers Assn of TX, NEA, TX St Teachers Assn; Alpha Delta Kappa Past Pres; Scott & White Auxillary; Rotary Club Educator of Yr 1988; Jaycees Educator of Yr 1990; *office:* Lamar Mid Sch 2120 N 1st Temple TX 76501

BOYER, JOAN GRAFFIS, Social Studies Department Head; *b:* Winamac, IN; *m:* R. David; *c:* Katherine, Dave, Beth, Tom; *ed:* (BA) Soc Stud, Taylor Univ 1961; (MED) Ed Guidance, IN Univ 1968; *cr:* Teacher Pulaski IN, Cherry Hill NJ, New Haven IN, Ft Wayne Chrstn; *ai:* Yrbk, Stu Cncl, NHS Adv; Class Spon; NEA; Cedar Creek Womens Club Secy 1976-78; *office:* Ft Wayne Chrstn Sch Box 11120 Fort Wayne IN 46805

BOYER, MARGARET ZANOR KENNY, 4th Grade Teacher; *b:* Jersey City, NJ; *m:* Joseph Boyer; *c:* Mary L., Robert; *ed:* (BA) Teacher of Handicapped/Elem Sch, Jersey City St Coll 1977; *cr:* 4th Grade Teacher St Pauls Sch; *ai:* Jersey City Womens Club

Corresponding Secy 1975-77; *office:* St Pauls Sch 193 Old Bergen Rd Jersey City NJ 07305

BOYER, REBECCA TURNER, English Teacher; *b:* Provo, UT; *m:* Jorgen Jarrett; *c:* Kenneth Jorgen, Brent Turner, Kirsten, Shaunalei, Michelle, Jenae; *ed:* (BA) Eng Composite Teaching, Brigham Young Univ 1984; Masters Prgm, Brigham Young Univ; *cr:* Eng Teacher Spanish Fork Jr HS 1985-86, Springville Jr HS 1986-; *ai:* Sch Gifted & Talented Comm; Assn of Eng Teachers 1985-87; Springville Lib Bd Mem 1989-; Phi Kappa Phi Mem 1988-.

BOYKIN, REGINA TAYLOR, English/Literature Teacher; *b:* Mobile, AL; *c:* Vaniti E.; *ed:* (BA) Eng, 1980, (MA) Counseling, 1990 AL St Univ; *cr:* Eng/Rdng Teacher Alba HS 1982-83, Baker HS 1983-89; Eng/Lit Teacher Le Flore HS 1990; *ai:* Frosh Chrldr Spon; Baker HS Speech Class Interviewer for Ms Sherry Mullins United Fund Rep; Spelling Bee Coord Baker HS; NCTE Active Mem 1989-; Alpha Kappa Alpha 1976-; *office:* Le Flore HS 700 Donald St Mobile AL 36617

BOYKINS, KATHY LYNETTE, Assistant Principal; *b:* Augusta, GA; *c:* Rance I. Kizer II; *ed:* (BS) Elem Ed, FL Memorial Coll 1977; (MS) Admin/Supervision, Nova Univ 1987; Certified Mid Sch Ed, Lang Art; *cr:* Teacher New River Mid 1977-88; Intern/Asst Prin Ramblewood Mid & Crystal Lake Mid 1988-89; Asst Prin Pioneer Mid 1989-; *ai:* All Extra Curr Act & Clubs Admin; Discipline Comm Admin; FL Assn of Sch Admin, Broward Prin & Asst Prin Assn; Zeta Phi Beta; Outstanding Accomplishments with Stu Cncl & Honor Society Awd 1985-87; Dedication & Service to Stu & Faculty 1977-88.

BOYKINS, ROSEMARYE D., Second Grade Teacher; *b:* Covington, GA; *m:* Samuel L.; *c:* Sabrina B. Everett, Susanne V., S. Kendall; *ed:* (AA) Elem Ed, Thomas Birdwood Coll 1969; (BS) Elem Ed, 1971, (MED) Early Chldhd Ed, 1983 Valdosta St Coll; Staff Dev Courses Continuing Ed 1984-89; *cr:* 6th Grade Teacher S H Dunlap Elem 1971-72; 2nd Grade Teacher J K Harper Elem 1972-; *ai:* System Wide Curr Comm; Writer of Guide-Plans for System Wide 2nd Grade Lang Art; Annual Sch Evaluation Steering Comm; Writer Schls Philosophy & Objectives Sch Design of Learning; Thomasville Assn of Educators, GA Assn of Educators, NEA Building Rep 1971-; Natl Cncl of Negro Women Secy 1987-; Thomasville Cultural Center Bd of Trustees 1987-, Service Awd 1988; J K Harper Teacher of Yr 1982; Kappa Alpha Psi Outstanding Local Educator 1988; *home:* 323 Augusta Ave Thomasville GA 31792

BOYKO, THOMAS M., 3rd Grade Teacher; *b:* Hazleton, PA; *m:* Terri M. Novarnik; *c:* Zachary; *ed:* (BA) Elem Ed, Bloomsburg Univ 1974; Coll of Grad Stud WV Inst; *cr:* 3rd Grade Teacher Wharton Elem 1979-; *ai:* Jr HS Bsktbl Coach; Sci Fair Coord; WVEA Building Rep 1987-; WVEA, NEA Mem 1979-; Rdng Cncl 1979-; *home:* PO Box 228 #1119 Barrett WV 25013

BOYLAN, BURTON LYLE, Gifted Eng/US His Teacher; *b:* Kelso, WA; *ed:* (BA) Hum, Stanford 1949; Ed, Stanford; Ed Admin & Counseling, San Francisco St; *cr:* Teacher Walla Walla HS 1954-55; Pioneer Jr HS 1955-57; Pleasant Hill Intermediate & Sequoia Mid Sch 1957-; *ai:* Sequoia Schlsp Societies; Yrbk, Newspaper, Stu Govt Adv; Stu Act; Gifted Prgms Chm; Dist Gifted Comm Sch Rep; NEA 1954-; CA Teachers Assn, MT Math Ed Assn 1957-; PTA Life Mem; Teacher Grant Mentor; Yrbk Dedication; *home:* 514 O Hara Ave Oakley CA 94561

BOYLE, ALICE T., English Teacher; *b:* Bayonne, NJ; *ed:* (AB) Eng, Chestnut Hill 1971; (MA) Eng, Seton Hall Univ 1976; Admin, Villanova Univ; *cr:* Primary Teacher St Annes 1957-59, Holy Rosary 1959-62, St Kevins 1962-65, St Pius X 1965-70; Primary/Jr HS Teacher Our Lady of Valley 1970-75; HS Eng Teacher Archbishop Kennedy 1975-79; Admin St John the Baptist 1979-83; HS Eng Teacher Queen of Peace HS 1983-; *ai:* Moderator Yrbk; NCTE; *office:* Queen of Peace HS 191 Rutherford Pl North Arlington NJ 07032

BOYLE, BETTY HARVEY, Seventh Grade Teacher; *b:* Richmond, CA; *m:* Richard Daniel; *c:* Susan Boyle-Fakhrai, Jeanne Rice, John; *ed:* (BA) His, Holy Names Coll 1952; Gifted & Talented Endorsement, Kearney St; Grad Stud Kearney St, Wayne St, Univ of NE Lincoln; *cr:* 1st Grade Teacher Hilaan Sch 1952-53; Substitute Teacher Martinez 1969-71; 7th Grade Teacher St Catherine 1971-72; 7th Grade Teacher, 8th Grade His/Eng Teacher 1973- Dist 10; *ai:* Dist 10 Vlybl Coach 1974-77; CA Jr Schlsp Fed 1971-72; NE St Ed Assn Local Pres 1975-76; *home:* Rt 3 Box 219D Columbus NE 68601

BOYLE, MARY ANN, Eighth Grade Teacher; *b:* Jersey City, NJ; *ed:* (BA) Eng, Coll of St Elizabeth 1960; *cr:* Teacher Our Lady of Mt Carmel Sch 1956-60, St Francis of Assisi Sch 1960-; *ai:* Yrbk Adv; NCEA 1956-; Educl Ministry Bd of Adv 1988-; Sisters of Charity St Elizabeth 1953-; *office:* St Francis of Assisi Sch 110 Mount Vernon St Ridgefield Park NJ 07660

BOYLE, MICHAEL WARNER, English Teacher; *b:* Amityville, NY; *m:* Judith Marie Cesaro; *c:* Caitlin; *ed:* (BA) Eng, Long Island Univ 1972; Grad Stud; *cr:* Teacher/Cnslr VISTA 1969-71; Teacher St Hugh of Lincoln Jr HS 1972-73, Deer Park HS 1973-82, Sachem HS 1982-; *ai:* Sci Fiction Club; Summer Enrichment Sci Fiction; *office:* Sachem HS 51 School St Ronkonkoma NY 11779

BOYLE, ROBERT JOSEPH, Social Science Scndry Teacher; *b:* Dodgeville, WI; *m:* Jeanne Reichling; *c:* Joseph, Kristina; *ed:* (BS) Broadfield Soc Sci/Phys Ed, Univ WI La Crosse 1971; Grad Work Univ of WI La Crosse & Univ of WI Platteville; *cr:* Soc Sci Teacher/Athletic Dir Shullsburg HS 1972-; *ai:* Alcohol & Drug Abuse Coord; Voice of Democracy & Oratorial Contest; Schlshp Comm; Stu Assistance Prgm Drug Abuse & Alcohol; Core Mem; NEA 1972-; Shamrock Club 1986-, Irishman of Yr 1986; Democratic Party of Lafayette Cty VP 1987-; WEAC Legislative Comm 1986-87; Alcohol & Drug Abuse Fellowship 1989; Mondale 2nd Congressional Dist WI Delegate 1984; *home:* 440 Horizon St Darlington WI 53530

BOYLE, STEVEN LEONARD, Instrumental Music Teacher; *b:* Yakima, WA; *ed:* (BAED) Music, Cntrl WA Univ 1979; Working on Masters in Admin; *cr:* Substitute Teacher Yakima Sch System 1979; 6th-8th Music Teacher Housel Mid Sch 1979-88; 6th-12th Grade Teacher Prosser Schls 1988-; *ai:* Mustang Band; Natural Helpers; Music Educators, Natl Conference, WA Ed Assn, NEA 1979-; Prosser Ed Assn Pres 1988-89; BSA Asst Scout Master 1980-; St of WA Honorable Mention Teacher of Yr; *office:* Prosser Sch Dist 2001 Highland Dr Prosser WA 99350

BOYLE, SUSAN, English Teacher; *b:* Jersey City, NJ; *ed:* (BA) Eng Ed, Montclair St Coll 1982; *cr:* Teacher Point Pleasant Beach HS 1982-84, Brick Township Memorial HS 1984-; *ai:* Class Adv; Cheerleading & Girls Spring Track Coach; *office:* Brick Memorial HS 2001 Lanes Mill Rd Brick NJ 08724

BOYLES, CAROLYN SUE, Cmptr Science/Soc Stud Teacher; *b:* Elkin, NC; *ed:* (BA) Elem Ed, High Point Coll 1969; (MA) Early Chldhd & Mid Grades 1975, (EDS) Admin & Curr Instruction 1989 Appalachian St Univ; *cr:* 1st Grade/5th Grade Teacher Shoals Elem Sch 1971-87; 6th-8th Grade Soc Stud Teacher/Cmptr Sci Pilot Mountain Elem Sch 1987-; *ai:* Surry Cty Mid Grades Task Force; Pilot Mountain Elem Sch Mid Sch Comm; Cmptr Materials Coord; Curr Dev Comm; Chairperson SAC Personnel Comm; NC Assn Educators/NEA (Mem 19 71-Local VP 1977-78); ASCD 1990; PACE Mem 1976-84; Pilot Mtn Democratic Precinct Comm 1st VP 1988-; Surry Cty Young Democrats Mem 1971-77; Teacher of Yr Schoals Elem Sch 1978-79; *home:* 135 Lynchburd Rd PO Box 655 Pilot Mountain NC 27041

BOYLES, CYNTHIA KING, Social Studies/Science Teacher; *b:* Mt Airy, NC; *M:* Jimmy D.; *ed:* (BS) His, 1982, (MA) Ed Sci, 1986 Appalachian St Univ; *cr:* Soc Stud Teacher 1984-, Sci Teacher 1986- Chestnut Grove Jr HS; *ai:* Former Stu Cncl Spon; Phi Alpha Theta Sec/Treas 1981-82; Alpha Chi 1981-82; NEA-NCAE 1984-86; Mid Sch Assn 1986-; ASU Readmission Bd Stu Adv 1982; Girl Scout Spon 1982; *office:* Chesnut Grove Jr H S Rt 4 King NC 27021

BOYNTON, MADGE BOUCHER, History Teacher; *b:* Timpson, TX; *c:* Rebecca Boynton Burke, Nancy Boynton Hightower; *ed:* (BS) Piano/Voice, TSCW 1948; (MA) Amer His, TWU 1970; *cr:* 1st Grade Teacher R L Turner 1949; His Teacher/Stu Cncl Adv/Congress/Calhoun Jr HS 1970-84; His Teacher Denton Sr HS 1984-; *ai:* Status Comm 1971-75; NEA, TSTA, DEA; Delta Kappa Gamma (Membership, Schlsp Chairperson); Phi Delta Kappa; TEA Univ Evaluation Team; United Way Denton HS Chairperson 1988; TCC Pres 1986-87; Stu Tours to Washington DC; UNT, TWU TED Cncl; Teacher of Month 1989; Teacher Spirit Awd 1987-89; Recipient TWU Recent Amer His Stud Grant 1968-70; *office:* Denton Sr HS 1007 Fulton St Denton TX 76201

BOYNTON, PHILIP HENRY, Social Science Dept Chairman; *b:* Pasadena, CA; *m:* Thelma Elizabeth Burston; *c:* Bronwen A., Megan R.; *ed:* (BA) His, San Diego St Univ 1964; (MA) Curr/Instruction, Univ of San Francisco 1984; Overseas Ed, Columbia Univ 1964; *cr:* Territorial Ed Officer Mbale Sr Scndry Sch 1964-66; Soc Sci Teacher Orangeglen HS 1967-69; Soc Sci Dept Head Yap HS 1969-72; Eng/Soc Sci Teacher Ukiah HS 1972-79; Soc Sci Teacher Singapore Amer Sch 1979-81, Ukiah HS 1981-; *ai:* Curr Writing & Editing; Coll Selection & Financing Cnslr; *office:* Ukiah HS 1000 Low Gap Rd Ukiah CA 95482

BOYNTON, THOMAS EDWIN, Sixth Grade Teacher; *b:* Aurora, IL; *m:* Sally F.; *c:* Alex J., Thomas J.; *ed:* (BS) Poly Sci, Univ of WI Whitewater 1973; Polygraph Examiner, Holistic Scoring Trainer; *cr:* 7th/8th Grade Soc Stud Teacher Franklin Mid Sch 1973-81; 6th Grade Teacher Nicholson Elem 1981-; *ai:* 7th Grade Bsktbl & Ftbl Head Coach; HS Golf Coach; Mid Sch Athletic Dir; Stu Cncl Adv; IEA, NEA; Aurora Moose 400; *office:* Nicholson Elem Sch 649 N Main St Montgomery IL 60538

BOYSON, STEVE R., Eng Teacher; *b:* Provo, UT; *m:* Linda Henderson; *c:* Jeffrey, Jill, Mark, Molly, Scott, Susan, Sarah; *ed:* (BA) Eng, Brigham Young 1970; (MED) Ed, UT St 1976; *cr:* Eng Teacher Roy HS 1970-; *ai:* Public Address Announcer for Ftbl, Bsktbl, Bsbl; Soph Class Adv; Night Sch Coord; *office:* Roy HS 2150 W 4800 S Roy UT 84067

BOYTE, CHERYL JAMES, English/French Teacher; *b:* Nashville, TN; *m:* Richard H.; *c:* Lane, Leigh; *ed:* (BA) Eng, Univ of TN 1969; *cr:* Teacher Weakley Cty 1969-; *ai:* Eng Dept Chairperson; Anchor & Fr Club Adv; Advanced Placement Coord; Univ of TN Outstanding Teacher 1988, 1990; Pilot Club Outstanding Teacher 1981, 1986; Delta Kappa Gamma Secy 1986-88; Pilot Club Pres 1974-75; TN St Dept of Ed Project EQ Rep; Valley Forge Freedom Fnd Honorable Mention Essay, St Winner TN Essay; *office:* Martin Westview HS Stella Ruth Rd Martin TN 38237

BOZARTH, KATHY DYE, 1st Grade Teacher; *b:* Kansas City, MO; *m:* Terry; *c:* James L., Sean B.; *ed:* (BS) Elem Ed, 1976, (MS) Curr/Instruction, 1987 Cntrl MO St Univ; *cr:* 2nd Grade Teacher 1976-84, Kndgtn Teacher 1985, 1st Grade Teacher Oak Grove Elem 1986-89; *ai:* Cmmty Teachers Assn (VP 1988-89, Treas 1985-86); MO St Teachers Assn 1976-; Teacher, Admin, Bd Rep Elem, Drug Comm Rep Elem, 1st Grade Level Coord 1989-; Outstanding Young Woman Sponsored by Oak Grove Jaycees; *office:* Oak Grove Elem Sch 1200 S Salem Oak Grove MO 64075

BOZARTH, PAUL GENE, JR., United States History Teacher; *b:* Dallas, TX; *ed:* (BA) Scndry Ed/Soc Stud, Univ of Dallas 1977; *cr:* Western Civ Teacher Jesuit Coll Prep 1978-79; TX His Teacher R T Hill 1976-86; US His Teacher Woodrow Wilson 1986-; *ai:* Var Ftbl & Golf; TX HS Coaches Assn Mem 1979-; Bsbl Coach of Yr; *office:* Woodrow Wilson HS 100 S Glasgow Dallas TX 75214

BRAATEN, GLENN ORLEN, Science Teacher; *b:* Rolette, ND; *m:* Bonita Bartholomay; *c:* Christi, Laurie; *ed:* (BA) Bio, Concordia Coll 1960; (MA) Ed, CA Luth Univ 1976; Various Natl Sci Fnd Insts; *cr:* Sci Teacher Barnesville HS 1960-63, Oak Grove HS 1963-64, Hughes Jr HS 1964-73; Sci Adv Los Angeles Unified Sch Dist 1973-78; Sci Teacher Columbus Jr HS 1978-82, Cleveland HS 1982-; *ai:* 9th Grade Adv; Mentor Teacher Los Angeles Unified Sch Dist 1986-; NSTA, CA Sci Teacher Assn, United Teachers Los Angeles; PTA Honorary Service Awd 1978; Earthwatch Fellowship 1989; *home:* 239 E Ave De Los Arboles Thousand Oaks CA 91360

BRABY, JACK ROLLIN, Elementary Principal; *b:* Mt Ayr, IA; *m:* Lois Taylor; *c:* Vicki L. Beebe, Jacquie Braby Bethel, Michael S.; *ed:* (BA) Soc Sci/Elem Ed, Drake Univ 1966; (MA) Elem Ed, 1970; (MA) Scndry Admin 1974 NE MO St Univ; Project Empathy & Personal Dynamics Cert; *cr:* 6th Grade Selt Contained Teacher Dexfield Cmmty Sch 1959-62, Johnston Cmmty Sch 1962-69; 7th-10th Grade Soc Stud Teacher 1969-70, Elem Prin 1970-76 Lamoni Cmmty Sch; Elem Prin Creston Cmmty Schls & Jefferson Elem 1974-76; Scndry Prin Lamoni Cmmty Schls 1978-83; Dir Youth Acts RLDS Church 1983-84; Elem Prin Strasburg C-III ELem Sch 1984-86, Eagleville R-3 Elem Sch 1986-88, Strasburg C-III Elem Sch 1988-; *ai:* Jr HS Girls & Boys Bsktbl; Blue Grass Conference Scndry Sch Prin Pres 1980-81; Area XIV Assn Scndry Sch Prin Secy 1979-80; NASSP 1978-83; Cntrl MO Sch Admin Assn 1984-86, 1988-; MO Sch Admin Assn, MO Elem Prin Assn 1984-; Lions Club; Lamoni Planning & Zoning 1980-83; Lamoni Parks & Recreation Comm 1978-80; NEA Lifetime Mem 1960-; Lamoni Cmmty Involvement Talented & Gifted Prgm; Lamoni Cmmty Voc Ed Pilot Prgm; Lamoni Sch Mini-Course Prgm; Lamoni Sch Drug Ed Wkshp; Strasburg Sch Bond for New Gymnasium.

BRACE, MYRA BOOTH, Sixth Grade Teacher; *b:* Blossburg, PA; *m:* Frederick L.; *c:* Gregory S.; *ed:* (BS) Elem Ed, Mansfield Univ 1958; (MS) Admin, St Bonaventure Univ 1964; Guidance & Counseling, St Bonaventure 1965-88; *cr:* 6th Grade Teacher Washington W & Eastview Elem Sch 1958-89; *ai:* Olean Teachers Assn (Past Officer 1975, Sch Rep 1988-); NY Ed Assn, NEA; Ran Jr Olympics Track Team; Team Leader Developing Educl Prgm Eastview Elem; *office:* Olean City Sch Dist Washington St Olean NY 14760

BRACEWELL, MARK ANDREW, Vocational Agriculture Teacher; *b:* Montgomery, AL; *m:* Peggy; *c:* Kyle; *ed:* (AA) Ag, Chipola Jr Coll 1979; (BS) Ag, Univ of FL 1981; (MED) Ed Admin/Supervision, Univ of N FL 1987; *cr:* Teacher Union Cty HS 1981-83, Lake Butler Mid Sch 1983-; *ai:* Lake Butler Jr FFA Natl Bronze Emblem Chapter Adv 1984-89; FL Voc Ag Teachers Assn (Pres, Young Mem 1985), Outstanding Young FL Mem 1985; AVA, Natl Voc-Ag Teacher Assn 1987-; Bradford-Union Cattlemans Assn Cty Dir 1985-; Union Soil & Water Conservation Dist Dist Dir 1984-89; Lake Butler FFA Alumni 1984-, Honorary St FFA Degree 1987; Lake Butler Mid Sch Teacher of Yr 1989, 1990; Union Cty Teacher of Yr 1990; FL Outstanding Young Ag Teacher 1985; *office:* Lake Butler Mid Sch 150 SW 6th St Lake Butler FL 32054

BRACEY, JERRY ALEXANDER, Director of Bands; *b:* Jackson, MS; *m:* Elois Pitchford; *c:* Fitima, Lois, Jerri; *ed:* (BME) Music Ed, 1974, (MME) Music Ed, 1982 Jackson St Univ; Certificate De Stage Nice Academic Intnl D ete France; NE LA Univ Monroe; *cr:* Dir of Bands Tensas Parish Schls 1975-81; Teaching Assistantship Jackson St Univ 1981-82; Dir of Bands Tensas prish Schls 1982-84, Jackson Public Schls 1984; *ai:* Dir of Bands, Instr of Instrumental Music; MS Bandmasters Assn, Kappa Kappa Psi, AFT, AFL, CIO; Anderson United Meth Church; TC Almore Lodge No 242 FLAM; Jackson Consistory No 117 United Supreme Cncl; Good Apple Awd Jackson Public Schls; NAJE Schlsp Hartt Sch Music, Univ of Hartford; Finalist Karl Bohm Fellowship in Conducting.

BRACKEEN, JOAN BRYER, Fifth Grade Teacher; *b:* Marshall, TX; *m:* William Anderson; *c:* Leslie Brackeen Gullo, Glenn; *ed:* (BA) Ed, E TX St Univ 1960; George Washington Univ, TX Womens Univ, N TX Univ; *cr:* 5th Grade Teacher Garland Ind Sch Dist 1960-66, Irving Ind Sch Dist 1966-71; 4th Grade Teacher Anne Arundel Cty 1971-74; 5th/6th Grade Teacher Garland Ind Sch Dist 1974-; *ai:* Team Leader; Garland Assn TX Prof Educators; *office:* Hickman Elem Sch 3114 Pinewood Garland TX 75044

BRACKIN, EVA LEE RUSSELL, Fifth Grade Teacher; *b:* Maryville, TN; *m:* John B.; *c:* Vickie Jackson; *ed:* (BS) Elem Ed, Univ of TN 1959; *cr:* Teacher Blount Cty Schls 1955-56, 1957-58, Morristown City Schls 1959-65, Clayton Cty Schls 1965-66,

Fulton Cty Schls 1966-74, Fayette Cty Schls 1977-; *ai:* GA Assn of Educators; New Hope Baptist Church; *home:* 635 New Hope Rd Fayetteville GA 30214

BRADBURY, C.JOYCE ROGERSON, Pre-First Grade Teacher; *b:* Richford, VT; *m:* Lorne; *c:* Linda Schultheis, Betsy Pond, Sally Zito; *ed:* (BS) Elem Ed, Univ of VT 1950; (MS) Elem Ed, SUNY 1975; *cr:* 5th Grade Teacher Thayer Sch 1950-52; 1st Grade Teacher Thayer & Flynn Schls 1952-54; Private Kndgtn Teacher 1959-67; 1st Grade Teacher Deforest Hill Elem Sch 1969-; *ai:* PTO Playground Comm; PARP Comm; Building Adv Comm Mem 1988-; NYSUT Secy 1984-86; Republican Party Comm Person 1980-; Cath Church Volunteer Work 1980-; Skenandoa Ladies Golf Chm 1973-74; Tennis Chm 1988-89; Kirkland Art Center Volunteer Prgms Asst; *office:* De Forest Hill Elem Sch Rt 233 Westmoreland NY 13490

BRADDOCK, CHARLENE KNAPIK, First Grade Teacher; *b:* Waynesburg, PA; *m:* Phillip C.; *c:* Matthew, Patrick, Jamie; *ed:* (BA) Elem Ed, Waynesburg Coll 1974; Masters Equivalency WV Univ; *cr:* 1st Grade Teacher East Franklin Elem 1974-; *ai:* Cntrl Greene Ed Assn Secy 1981-83; Soc Service League 1975-79; *office:* East Franklin Elem Sch 300 North St Waynesburg PA 15370

BRADDOCK, RITA CLEMMER, Fifth Grade Eng/Rdng Teacher; *b:* Ripley, MS; *m:* Philip A.; *c:* Chad, Adam; *ed:* (BS) Elem Ed, 1972, (MAED) Elem Ed, 1975 Univ of MS; *cr:* 5th Grade Teacher Ripley Mid Sch 1972-; *ai:* Kappa Kappa Iota Secy 1988-; *home:* Rt 4 Box 153 Ripley MS 38663

BRADDY, ESQURIDO BRADSHER, English Teacher; *b:* Burlington, NC; *m:* James H.; *c:* Jeffrey, Timothy, Kevin; *ed:* (BA) Ed, 1980, (MED) Ed, 1988 UNC Chapel Hill; Mentor Teacher, Effective Teacher Trng; *cr:* 7th Grade Teacher A L Stamback 1980-87, C W Stamford Mid Sch 1987-88; 9th Grade Teacher Orange HS 1988-; *ai:* Homecoming Court Advisory Comm; NCAE, NCTE; 3rd Place Winner Purina Writing Contest; Nom Thanks to Teachers; *office:* Orange HS 222 Orange High School Rd Hillsborough NC 27278

BRADFORD, CHERYL RENE, Var Sftbl/Soccer Coach/Teacher; *b:* Pasadena, TX; *ed:* (BAT) Phys Ed, Sam Houston St Univ 1984; Scndry Ed, Sam Houston St Univ; *cr:* Teacher/Coach Liberty Ind Sch Dist 1984-86, Cypress-Fairbanks Ind Sch Dist 1986-; *ai:* Var Sftbl & Soccer Head Coach; Fellowship of Chrstn Athletes Spon; At Risk Teacher & Adv; TX Girls Coaches Assn, TX Assn of Soccer Coaches 1986-; Assn of TX Prof Educators 1984-; US Federal Soccer Assn 1984-; Amateur Sftbl Assn 1974-; US Sftbl Assn 1979-; Natl Sftbl Assn 1981-; Teacher of Month 1988; *office:* Langham Creek HS 17610 FM 529 Houston TX 77095

BRADFORD, PAMELA EYLER, Second Grade Teacher; *b:* Hershey, PA; *m:* Douglas E.; *c:* Douglas, Ryan; *ed:* (BS) Child Dev, Univ Ma 1976; (MSED) Curr/Instruction, N IL Univ 1979; Water Safety Instr Amer Red Cross; *cr:* 4th Grade Teacher Town & Cntry Day Sch 1977-78; 2nd/3rd Grade Teacher Enosburg Elem Sch 1979-; *office:* Enosburg Elem Sch Dickinson Ave Enosburg Falls VT 05450

BRADHAM, CHARLES HUGH, 8th Grade Soc Stud Teacher; *b:* Dunn, NC; *m:* Lisa Goodman; *ed:* (BS) Health/Phys Ed, E Carolina Univ 1984; Working on Admin Degree; *cr:* Teacher/Coach Anderson Creek Mid Sch 1984-85, Dunn Mid Sch 1985-; *ai:* Ftbl & Bsbl Coach; Athletic Dir; 1st Presbyn Church Deacon; Yrbk Dedication by Stu Body 1987; *home:* 1106 Merry St Dunn NC 28334

BRADLEY, BETTY ALOHA, Vice Principal; *b:* Hawthorne, CA; *ed:* (AA) His/Art, El Camino Coll 1971; (BA) His/Art, 1977, (MA) Ed/Curr, 1985 CA St Univ Dominguez; Creative Writing Courses, Seminard, CSUDH, ECC; *cr:* 1st Grade Teacher 1970-74, 7th Grade Teacher 1974-78/1984-86, 8th GradE Teacher 1978-81/1985-87, Vice Prin 1981- Hawthorne Chrstn Sch; *ai:* Teacher Inservices; Curr Dev Comms; Dev Testing Instrument Comms; Womens Missionary Society (Secy 1972-74 Pres 1974-75; Church Lifetime; PTA 1970; Poetry Published Sch Newspaper; Taught Art Teachers Coll; *home:* 1592 Andrea Cir Simi Valley CA 93065

BRADLEY, CHRISTINE OWEN, English Teacher; *b:* Indianapolis, IN; *m:* Glenn Harvey; *c:* Colin J., Owen P.; *ed:* (BS) Eng, Univ of VA 1980; Hum Prgm, Penn St Univ; *cr:* Eng Teacher VA Beach Bayside Jr HS 1980-82, Palmyra Jr HS 1983-84, Elizabethtown Area HS 1986-; *ai:* Yrbk & Jr Class Adv; NCTE 1989-; PSEA, NEA 1986-; Fellowship Capitol Area Writing Project 500 Grant; *office:* Elizabethtown Area HS 600 E High St Elizabethtown PA 17022

BRADLEY, DENNIS LEE, Teacher; *b:* Washington, IN; *m:* Mary Frances Gates; *c:* Robert, Philip, Joseph, Rachel, Sarah, Frances, Rose; *ed:* (AS) Math, Vincennes Univ 1968; (BS) Math/Scndry Ed, 1970, (MS) Math/Scndry Ed, 1976 IN St Univ; *cr:* Prin/Teacher Washington Cath Mid Sch 1970-79; Physics Teacher Washington HS 1980-81; Bus Math Teacher Vincennes Univ 1986-88; Teacher Washington Cath Mid Sch 1980-; *ai:* Sch Study Curr Comm; PTO Faculty Rep; Math for Moms & Dads; Liturgy Music Practice Dir; IN Math League, Continental Math League; Amer Assn of Jr HS Math; Holy Name Society Secy 1989-; WCHS Band Boosters; WC PTO; St Peters Choir; Cath Ed Dev Prgm Certificte of Merit 1974; Key Club Distinguished Servce Awd 1976; Washington Cath Schls Appreciation Awd 1982, 1985; *home:* Box 621 Montgomery IN 47558

BRADLEY, DOLORES JORDAN, English Teacher; *b:* Memphis, TN; *c:* Deborah Boyce; *ed:* (BA) Hum, Le Moyne Coll 1968; (MA) Urban Ed, NY Univ 1969; Ec/Admin/Supervision, Memphis St Univ, Trevecca, Coll of Nazarene; *cr:* Teacher Craigmont HS; *ai:* Shelby Memphis Cncl Teacher of Eng Corresponding Secy 1988-89; NCTE; Black Alliance for Soc Equity Educl Dir 1989-; Mission Possible; Chrstn Outreach Service Mission Youthinar Dir 1990; *office:* Craigmont HS 3333 Covington Pike Memphis TN 38128

BRADLEY, JACQUELINE DIANE, English Teacher; *b:* Dallas, TX; *ed:* (BA) Literary Stud, Univ of TX Dallas 1988; Computerized Writing Lab Trng; *cr:* Eng Teacher R L Turner HS 1988-; *ai:* Quality Team Comm; NCTE; *home:* 9928 Bowman Blvd Dallas TX 75220

BRADLEY, JANICE ROBINSON, 2nd Grade Teacher; *b:* Cincinnati, OH; *m:* Larry Phillip; *c:* Megan; *ed:* (BA) Early Chldhd, Univ of SC 1978; *cr:* 3rd Grade Teacher 1979-80, 2nd Grade Teacher 1980- Heath Springs Elem; *ai:* Sch Improvement Cncl; Selected Teacher of Yr Lancaster Dist 1987-88; Served on NASTEC Evaluation Team for St Dept of Ed 1989-; *home:* Rt 2 Box 134A Kershaw SC 29067

BRADLEY, JESSIE ANN, Fourth Grade Teacher; *b:* Hardtner, KS; *m:* Jim Paul; *c:* Ashlee; *ed:* (BA) Elem Ed, Southwestern Coll 1971; (MS) Curr & Dev, Emporia St Univ 1977; *cr:* 4th Grade Teacher Dexter Elem Sch 1971-; *ai:* NEA, KS Ed Assn 1971-87; Dexter Ed Assn (Pres 1982, Treas 1987); KS Sci Teachers Assn Mem 1977-79; Southwestern Coll Alumni Bd (Pres, VP, Secy, Mem) 1985-; Dexter 4-H Adult Leader 1988-; Grouse Valley Manor Auxiliary (Pres, Secy, Treas, Mem) 1976-; Natl Sci Fnd Grant for Masters Prgm; *home:* Box 124 Dexter KS 67038

BRADLEY, JUDY E., Mathematics Dept Chair/Teacher; *b:* Berlin, Germany; *m:* Gerald S.; *c:* Keith, Steven; *ed:* (BA) Soc Sci, Univ of CA 1960; Advanced Coursework Math; *cr:* 6th Grade Teacher Stockton Unified Schls 1962-63, Los Angeles Schls 1963-64, Livermore Schls 1966-79; Math Teacher/Chairperson Junction Avenue Sch 1979-; *ai:* Honor Society Adv; Math Contest Master; Academic Olympics; Livermore Schls Math Curr Rep; *office:* Junction Avenue Mid Sch 298 Juntiton Ave Livermore CA 94550

BRADLEY, LARRY ROY, Social Studies Teacher; *b:* Bluefield, WV; *m:* Elizabeth Bowen; *c:* Bradford A.; *ed:* (BS) Soc Stud, Bluefield St Coll 1971; *cr:* Teacher/Coach Sullivan East HS 1971-74, George Wythe HS 1974-77, Grundy HS 1977-81, Lexington HS 1981-83, Andrew Lewis Mid Sch 1982-; *ai:* Mid Sch Ftbl & Wrestling Head Coach; Salem HS Track Head Coach; VA St Coaches Assn Coached St Wrestling Champs 1978; *office:* Andrew Lewis Mid Sch 616 College Ave Salem VA 24153

BRADLEY, LUCINDA ROSTOLLAN, English Teacher; *b:* Ironwood, MI; *m:* Dale C.; *c:* Sarah E.; *ed:* (BA) Eng, Bethel Coll 1971; (MA) Ed, North Adams St Coll 1984; *cr:* Eng Teacher Pardeeville Area Schls 1973-77, Pine Cobble Sch 1978-84, Mt Greylock Regional HS 1984-; *ai:* Yrbk Adv 1987-; Sch Climate Comm 1989; Mt Greylock Faculty Assn VP 1988-; NEA 1985-; NCTE 1988-; *office:* Mt Greylock Regional HS 1581 Cold Spring Rd Williamstown MA 01267

BRADLEY, MARY JACKSON, Teacher; *b:* Evergreen, LA; *c:* Charlotte G., Mc Coy Jr.; *ed:* (BA) Upper Elem Ed, Northwestern St Univ 1974; Grad Work Northwestern St Univ, LA St Univ, Southern Univ, Univ of Southwestern Univ; *cr:* Teacher Mansura Elem 1975, Marksville Mid Sch 1975-80, Bunkie Mid Sch 1980-; *ai:* Booster Leader; Awds Day Comm Co-Chm; Energy & Sch Dress Code Comm; LAE, NEA 1975-; Salem Missionary Baptist Church Treas 1984-; *home:* 414 E Oak Bunkie LA 71322

BRADLEY, MILTON, Theatre Instructor; *b:* Lake City, FL; *m:* Verdya Pratt; *c:* Miche, Quintin; *ed:* (BS) Theatre, FL A&M Univ 1973; (MS) Theatre, Bowling Green St Univ 1980; *ai:* Drama Guild Spon; *office:* Sarasota HS 1001 S Tamami Tr Sarasota FL 34232

BRADLEY, NICHOLAS HOLT, English Teacher/Eng Dept Chair; *b:* New Haven, CT; *m:* Rhonda Cindrich; *c:* Amber, Augustine A.; *ed:* (BA) Eng, MI St Univ 1965; (MA) Eng, CA St Univ Northridge 1987; Berklee Coll of Music 1969-71; *cr:* Teacher 1984-, Eng Dept Chm 1986-, Mentor Teacher 1988- Sun Valley Jr HS; *ai:* Creative Writing Teacher; Inklings Ed; 8th/12th Grade Rdngs Table Leader CA Assessment Prgm; *office:* Sun Valley Jr HS 7330 Bakman Ave Sun Valley CA 91352

BRADLEY, RENEVA SPARKMAN, Lang Arts/Math Teacher; *b:* Gordon, KY; *m:* Merlin; *c:* Charles S., Kimberly S.; *ed:* (BS) Commerce, Cumberland Coll 1968; (MA) Ed, Union Coll 1972; *cr:* Typing/Shorthand Teacher Whitesburg HS 1964-65; 1st-3rd Grade Teacher Hurricane Gap Elem 1965-68; Bus Ed Teacher 1968-72, 7th/8th Grade Lang Arts Teacher 1972- Kingdom Come HS; *ai:* Moderator of Academic Team; 8th Grade Spon; *home:* HCR 77 Box 650 Gordon KY 41819

BRADLEY, TERESA WILLIS, Computer Teacher; *b:* Selmer, TN; *m:* David Allen; *c:* David A. Jr.; *ed:* (BS) Scndry Ed, Univ of TN Martin 1978; *cr:* Teacher Glenmore Acad 1979-83, Mc Nairy Cntrl HS 1983-; *ai:* NEA, TEA, MCEA; Selmer Jr Civic League Way & Means 1989-; YMCA Prgm Comm 1990; 1st Baptist Church Childrens Dir 1989-; *office:* Mc Nairy Cntrl HS Hwy 64 E Selmer TN 38375

BRADNEY, HELEN H., Fourth Grade Teacher; *b:* Salem, NE; *m:* William S.; *c:* Bonnie Murch, Debra Callaghan; *ed:* (BS) Elem Ed, Glassboro St Coll 1968; *cr:* 2nd Grade Teacher 1968-84, 3rd Grade Teacher 1984-87, 4th Grade Teacher 1987-89 Thomas Paine Sch; *ai:* Governors Teacher Recognition Prgm St of NJ 1986-87; *office:* Thomas Paine Sch 4001 Church Rd Cherry Hill NJ 08002

BRADOVICH, CONSTANCE J., Media Director/Admin Asst; *b:* Chisholm, MN; *ed:* (AA) Hibbing Comm Coll 1970; (BS) Eng - Magna Cum Laude, Bemidji St Univ 1972; (MS) Information Media, St Cloud St Univ 1975; Experiental Ed, Mankato St Univ; Media Technology, Mankato St Univ; Bay Area Writing Prgm Univ of CA Berkley; *cr:* Media Generalist John F Kennedy Sr HS 1975-81; Eng Teacher Bloomington Public Schls 1981-85; Media Specialist Dept of Defense Dependents Schls 1985-87; Eng Teacher 1987-, Media Dir/Admin Asst 1990 Thomas Jefferson Sr HS; *ai:* Jefferson HS SADD & Frosh Jeffleaders Adv; Jefferson HS Fall Wkshp Planning Comm; MN Coalition vs Censorship VP 1984-85; MN Ed Assn Task Force on Academic Freedom Wkshp Presenter 1982-84; Bloomington Ed Assn Secy 1977-78; MN Fed of Teachers; Minneapolis Inst of Art Lib Cncl 1990; BSA Explorer Leader 1989-; Sierra Club, MN Public Interest Research Group, Humane Society, Clean Water Action, MN Educl Media Organization, Center for Intnl Folk Art; Dept of Defense Dependents Schls Performance Awd 1987; Article Published 1978; *office:* Thomas Jefferson Sr HS 4001 W 102nd St Bloomington MN 55437

BRADSHAW, CAROLYN TANNEHILL, Mathematics Teacher; *b:* Mc Alester, OK; *m:* Ronald A.; *c:* Amy B.; *ed:* (BA) Art/Math, Northeastern St Univ 1969; (MA) Art/His, Univ of Tulsa 1977; *cr:* Teacher Barnard Elem 1969-72; Art Curator Gilcrease Museum Tulsa 1972-75; Teacher Tulsa Jr Coll 1977-78, Edison Mid Sch 1982-; *ai:* Tulsa Classroom Teachers of Math, Tulsa Classroom Teachers Assn, NEA; Bank of OK Grant Univ of Tulsa 1971; *office:* Edison Mid Sch 2800 E 41st St Tulsa OK 74105

BRADSHAW, JEAN RAYFORD, 3rd Grade Teacher; *b:* Tyler, TX; *m:* Bruce D.; *c:* Bitsy Jeffers, Julie Watson, Jamie; *ed:* (BSED) Elem Ed, 1964; (MED) Elem Ed, 1972 Stephen F Austin St Univ; *cr:* 1st Grade Teacher Eastside Elem 1964-65; Pinewood Park Elem 1965-66; 3rd Grade Teacher E E Sims Elem 1966-67; London Elem 1967-; *ai:* Delta Kappa Gamma; TX St Teachers Assn.

BRADSHAW, JUDY FANN, Kindergarten Teacher; *b:* Nashville, TN; *m:* Daryl Glenn; *c:* Harold R., Denise L., Darla G. (dec); *ed:* (BS) Elem Ed, David Lipscomb Univ 1969; (MED) Rdng, Mid TN St Univ 1972; Early Chldhd/Elem Ed, W KY Univ 1978; FL Plan for Performance Measurement 1986; KY Performance Measurement Plan 1989; Supervision of Stu Teachers 1987; *cr:* Elem Teacher Knifley Grade Center 1969-77; Elem Teacher 1977-85, Kndgtn Teacher 1985- Colonel Wm Casey Elem Sch; *ai:* Kndgtn Spokesperson 5 Yr Accreditation; Intern Supvr for KY Performance Plan; Teach Ed Course at Local Coll; Kndgtn Registration & Head Start Stu Comm; Adair Cty Ed Assn, KEA, NEA 1969-77, 1979-; CIT 1988-; Colonel Wm Casey Faculty Assn Secy 1984-86; Homemaker Club Secy 1987-; Teacher of Yr Awd Jaycees 1982; Grant from Forward in the Fifth 1988-89; Mini-Grant from KY Arts Cncl 1989; Selected to Give Presentation at CIT 1989; *office:* Colonel Wm Casey Elem Sch Greensburg St Columbia KY 42728

BRADSHAW, MARY CATHERINE, AP Amer His/Amer Lit Teacher; *b:* Nashville, TN; *ed:* (BA) Philosophy, Vanderbilt Univ 1978; (MA) Eng, Bread Loaf Sch of Eng Middlebury Coll 1985; Freedoms Fnd & NEH Seminars; NAPPS Storytelling Inst; *cr:* Teacher/Coach Franklin Road Acad 1978-81, The Lovett Sch 1981-83, Amer Cmmty Sch Athen Greece 1983-84, Hillsboro HS 1984-; *ai:* Global Affairs & Government Stud Club, Stu Cncl, People to People Spon; Asst Sftbl & Bsktbl Coach; NCTE, NCSS, MNEA, TEA, NEA; United Nations Assn Bd 1989-; Hillsboro Teacher of Yr 1988-; Metro Public Schls Runner Up Teacher of Yr 1988-; NCCJ Brotherhood Sisterhood Awd 1988; NEH Seminar Eskine Grant Global Affairs; Problem Solving Instr Gau Sch Intnl Stud; *office:* Hillsboro Comprehensive HS 3812 Hillsboro Rd Nashville TN 37215

BRADSHAW, MARY KAY ALLSBROOK, 4th-8th Grade Ag Teacher; *b:* Scotland Neck, NC; *m:* Scott Michael; *c:* Justin, Meredith; *ed:* (BA) Psych, 1977, Cert K-3 Early Chldhd, 1977 Meredith Coll; K-12th Academically Gifted, 4th-8th Lang Art Cert; *cr:* AG Teacher Wake Cty Schls 1977-78; 2nd Grade Teacher 1978-79, 3rd Grade Teacher 1979-80, 4th Grade Teacher 1980-81, 4th-8th Grade Teacher 1981- Washington Cty Schls; *ai:* Adv Academic Quiz Bowl Team; NCAE 1978-; Alumni of Kappa Nu Sigma; Alumni of Silver Shield Meredith Coll Leadership; Psi Chi Psych Honor Society at Meredith Coll; First Baptist Church Handbell (Choir Dir, Soloist, Choir Mem, Youth Sunday Sch Teacher, Worker); Outstanding Young Woman of Washington Cty Nom; *office:* Washington Cty Union PO Box 309 Roper NC 27970

BRADSHAW, SANDRA CUMMINGS, Third Grade Teacher; *b:* Miles City, MT; *m:* Steve; *c:* Tyler, Travis; *ed:* (BS) Elem/Spec Ed, Eastern MT Coll 1974; Talents Unlimited/Project Succss Writing Prgm/Right-Left Brain Ed Approaches; *cr:* 1st Grade/Spec Ed Teacher Huntley Project Sch 1974-78; 1st/2nd Grade Teacher Hardin Primary Sch 1978-82; 1st Grade Teacher Annette Island Schools 1982-84; 3rd Grade Teacher Mount View Elem 1989-; *ai:* MT Ed Assn 1989-; Beta Sigma Phi VP 1989; *office:* Mountain View Elem Sch 311 S Oaks Red Lodge MT 59068

BRADSHAW, SERENA MOODY, Social Studies Teacher; *b:* Princeton, KS; *m:* Fredrick L.; *c:* Paul M.; *ed:* (BA) His, CO St Univ 1963; (PHD) Amer Colonial/Revolutionary His, OH St Univ 1977; NEH Fellow CO Univ 1986; *cr:* Lib Asst CO St Univ 1963-64; Lib Asst/Rare Books 1965-68, Assoc Teaching Asst 1968-72 OH St Univ; Asst Dir Hillel Fnd 1972-73; Teacher Whitehall City Schls 1973-; *ai:* EACH Gifted Stu, Soc Stud Curr, Ec Ed Comm; Pi Gamma Ma, Phi Kappa Phi, Phi Delta Kappa, Phi Alpha Theta, Amer His Assn, OH Assn for Gifted Stu, NEA; Whitehall Academic Boosters, OH St Univ Friends of Lib, CO St Univ Friends of Lib; Presidential Fellowship OH St Univ; Martha Holden Jennings Schlsp for Outstanding Teachers; Natl Endowment for Hum Fellowship 1986; *office:* Whitehall-Yearling HS 675 S Yearling Rd Whitehall OH 43213

BRADT, CHARLENE SUSAN, Teacher; *b:* Buffalo, OK; *m:* Myron J.; *c:* Jerad L., Nicholas J., Lisa D.; *ed:* (BA) Speech Ed, 1978, (MS) Ed, 1982 NW OK St Univ; Debate Inst, Baylor 1979-81; Free Standing Wkshp, OK St Univ 1984; Acting Wkshp, Central St Univ 1979; *cr:* GED Cadet Teacher NW OK St UniV 1976-77; Night Teacher NW OK St Univ 1985; Teacher Alva Public Schls 1978-; *ai:* Drama Club; Debate Coach; Natl Forensic League; Drama Dir; Speech Coach; Stu Cncl Spon; Positive Attitude About Rdng Set Up Comm Mem; OK Speech Theatre Comm Assn Forensic Chm 1984-, Outstanding Young Speech Teacher 1985; Delta Kappa Gamma 1986-; Meth Church (Youth Advisory Bd 1988-, Jr HS Youth Spon 1978-80); Delta Zeta Dir 1979-80; OK Scndry Schls Act Assn Speech Advisory Comm 1982-; State of the State Report 1988, 1989; *office:* Alva HS 14th & Barnes Alva OK 73717

BRADWAY, JIMMY L., 8th Grade Mathematics Teacher; *b:* Warsaw, IN; *m:* Janet Marie Clemons; *c:* Kenneth, Michelle, Christina; *ed:* (BA) Phys Ed/Math, IN St Univ 1971; (MS) Ed, IN Univ 1979; *cr:* Teacher Greenfield Jr HS 1972-; *ai:* Academic Team Math; Boys & Girls Swim Coach 1972-; Golf Coach 1985-; Teacher of Yr Rep 1987, 1988; *home:* 309 N Noble Greenfield IN 46140

BRADWELL, SYLVIA WYNETTE (CLARY), Social Studies Teacher; *b:* Quincy, FL; *m:* James Edward; *c:* Joi S.; *ed:* (BS) Sociology, FL A&M Univ 1966; (MA) Soc Sci, S A&M Univ 1973; Spec Ed Cert Stud; *cr:* Teacher Rochester City Sch Dist 1967, DC Public Schls 1967-71, 1973-75; Educl Consultant III Dept of Ed 1975-77; Assoc Professor FL A&M Dev Research Sch 1977-; *ai:* Co-Spon Natl Beta Club; NEA, Natl Assn Laboratory Schls, NCSS; Jack & Jill of America Inc Secy; Delta Sigma Theta, NAACP; 10 Yr Meritorious Service Certificate Awd; Book Published; *home:* 1701 Lake Bradford Rd Tallahassee FL 32310

BRADY, ERIN, Third Grade Teacher; *b:* New Orleans, LA; *c:* Kathleen B. Fullilove, Rebecca P. Fullilove; *ed:* (BS) Elem Ed, LA St Univ 1961; Gifted & Talented, LA St Univ Baton Rouge; *cr:* 5th Grade Elem Teacher E Baton Rouge Parish Sch Bd 1961-62; 3rd Grade Teacher Southfield Sch 1965-72, E Baton Rouge Parish Sch Bd 1972-74; St Martins Episcopal Sch 1974-; *ai:* Dir St Martins after Sch Prgm 1988-; Faculty Adv to Bd of Dir St Martins Sch; St Martins Episcopal Sch Swim Coach; ISAS, NAIS; *office:* St Martins Episcopal Sch 5309 Airline Hwy Metairie LA 70003

BRADY, KATHLEEN MARY, Mathematics Teacher; *b:* New York, NY; *m:* Brian T.; *c:* Kristopher, Katherine, Kelley J.; *ed:* (BA) Math Ed, Univ of FL 1986; *cr:* Math Teacher Boyd Anderson HS 1986-; *ai:* Club Adv; Cath Church CCD Teacher 1987-89; *office:* Boyd Anderson HS 3050 NW 41st St Lauderdale Lakes FL 33310

BRADY, NANCY ANN (CARL), 6th Grade Teacher; *b:* Detroit, MI; *m:* Kenneth L.; *c:* Adam, Matthew; *ed:* (BA) Soc Stud, Univ of MI 1966; Addl Studies Ed; *cr:* 2nd Grade Teacher Polk Elem Sch 1966-67; 6th Grade Teacher Evans City Elem Sch 1973-; *ai:* PA St Ed Assn 1973-; MI Ed Assn 1966-67; Cherry Hill United Presbyn Coop Nursery Sch Pres 1971-72; Parents Coop Pre Sch Bd Mem 1973-75; Ellwood City Area Historical Society Sec 1989-; Ellwood City Coll Club Pres 1985; *office:* Evans City Elem Sch W Main St Evans City PA 16033

BRAGG, CHRISTOPHER LAMAR, Social Studies Teacher; *b:* Rome, GA; *m:* Cynthia Ann Dean; *c:* Zachary; *ed:* (BS) Soc Sci, Shorter Coll 1985; *cr:* Teacher/Coach Pepperell HS 1985-86, Coosa HS 1987-; *ai:* Ftbl & Track Coach; *home:* 125 Pinebower Dr Rome GA 30161

BRAGG, JUDITH HARRISON, Mathematics/Science Teacher; *b:* Plymouth, NC; *c:* Kathryn L.; *ed:* (BS) Home Ec, 1962, (MS) Home Ec Ed, 1971 E Carolina Univ; *cr:* Home Ec Teacher Randleman HS 1963-64, Grainger HS 1964-65; Math/Sci Teacher Washington Cty Schls 1966-; *ai:* Natl Jr Honor Society Co-Adv; Textbook Comm; NEA, NC Assn of Ed, Washington Cty Assn of Ed; Roper Baptist Church Asst Sunday Sch Teacher 1988-; Teacher of Yr 1984-85, 1989-; *home:* 302 Pettigrew Dr Plymouth NC 27962

BRAGG, KATHLEEN KAE (HALL), K-12th Grade Music Teacher; *b:* Forest City, IA; *m:* R. Dennis; *c:* Kimberly K. Bragg Young, Tyler D.; *ed:* (BM) Music Ed, Northwestern Coll 1965; Music, Univ of N IA 1966, 1976; Grad Stud Univ of MN 1963; *cr:* Organ/Piano/Psych Teacher Maranatha Baptist Bible Coll 1968-70; K-12th Grade Music Teacher Walnut Ridge Baptist Acad 1973-78, Calvary Chrstn Acad 1979-88, Emmanuel Baptist Chrstn Sch 1988-; *ai:* Select Choir, Spec Ensembles, Childrens Musicale Dir; MENA 1965-67; Ladies Mission Society Pres 1968-70; Walnut Ridge Baptist Church Interim Music Dir 1975-76; *office:* Emmanuel Baptist Sch 4207 Laskey Toledo OH 43623

BRAGG, MARCY PAULINE NIXON, Marketing Teacher/DECA Advisor; *b:* Pendleton, OR; *m:* Robert T.; *c:* Lynn E., Julie A. Bebee, Steven T.; *ed:* (BS) Bus Ed, OR St Univ 1953; Seattle Pacific Univ, Cntrl WA Univ, W WA Univ; *cr:* Teacher Corvallis HS 1953-54, Clover Park 1955-56, Mercer Island HS 1983-; *ai:* Distributive Ed Clubs of America Class Adv 1985; Kappa Delta Pi 1952-; Phi Kappa Phi 1953-; Mortar Bd 1952-; Kappa Kappa Gamma 1950-; PEO 1958-; Theta Sigma Phi 1950-; Matrix Table Woman of Achievement.

BRAGOZ, LLOYD THOMAS, English & Humanities Teacher; *b:* Rockville Center, NY; *ed:* (BA) Eng, FL St Univ 1962; (MAT) Eng/Ed, Jacksonville Univ 1973; *cr:* Teacher Forrest Sr HS 1963-68, St Johns Cntry Day Day Sch 1968-69, Wolfson Sr HS 1969-77, Andrews Sr HS 1977-; *ai:* Adv Jr Jaycees 1980-; Interact 1970-77; Conducted Hum Tours of NY City1970-85; Swimming Coach 1975; Annual Amer Red Cross Blood Drive Spon 1980-; Phi Delta Kappa 1973-77; NC Assn of Ed 1977-; Greensboro Choral Society; St Grant UNC Chapel Hill 1989; Local Grant Hum Seminar 1986; Chm Character & Values Building Comm 1985; Nom Governors Awd Excl in Teaching 1989; *office:* T Wingate Andrews Sch 1920 Mc Guinn Dr High Point NC 27265

BRAID, SARA ROBERTS, Biology Teacher; *b:* Augusta, GA; *c:* Trey, Leah; *ed:* (BSA) Botany, Univ of GA 1965; Grad Stud Augusta Coll, Univ of SC Aiken, Various Wkshps; *cr:* Bio Teacher 1966-68, Bio Teacher/Dept Head 1976-82 Aquinas HS; Product Sales Rep Texas Instruments 1983; Bio Teacher Evans HS 1982-; *ai:* Pep Club Spon; Homebound Teacher; Prof Assn GA Educators 1984-; Right to Life Pres; Columbia Cty Humane Society Medical Coord 1989; Earth Sci Inst Univ SC Aiken 1989; *office:* Evans HS Cox Rd Evans GA 30809

BRAIN, PATRICIA ANNE, English Teacher; *b:* Minneapolis, MN; *m:* Thomas Philip; *c:* Cyrissa; *ed:* (BS) Eng, St Cloud St Univ 1972; (MA) Curr & Instruction, St Thomas Coll 1979; Grad Courses in Gifted Ed; *cr:* Eng Teacher North Branch Mid Sch 1972-87, North Branch HS 1987-; *ai:* Jr Class Adv; Co-Adv Stus Taking New Approach to Respect; Prin Advisory Cncl; North Branch Ed Assn 1972- Teacher of Yr 1989; MN Mid Sch Assn 1986; Integrating Technology into Eng Classes North Branch Mid Sch; Addressed MN Mid Sch Assn Conference 1986; *office:* North Branch Sr H S 320 Main St North Branch MN 55056

BRALICK, ANTHONY J., US History Teacher; *b:* Waukesha, WI; *m:* Nancy Blomquist; *c:* Emily; *ed:* (BA) His, Carroll Coll 1972; (MA) His, Univ of WI Milwaukee 1978; Univ of WI Whitewater, Univ of WI Milwaukee, Univ of WI Madison; *cr:* Teacher Waukesha South HS 1972-74, Waukesha North HS 1974-; Instr Carroll Coll 1981-; *ai:* WI St Stu Caucus; Head Boys Cross Cntry; NHS Review & Prin Advisory Comm; Close-Up Fnd Teacher Coord; Organization of Amer Historians 1974-; Phi Alpha Theta 1971-; Waukesha Cty Historical Society Dir 1984-86; Taft Fellow 1982; DAR WI His Teacher of Yr 1983; *office:* Waukesha North HS 2222 Michigan Ave Waukesha WI 53188

BRALY, SUZANNE, American His/Health Teacher; *b:* Tyler, TX; *ed:* (BSED) Health/Phys Ed, Stephen F Austin St 1983; *cr:* Sci Teacher Wills Point Ind Sch Dist 1984-88; Amer His/Health Teacher Bullard Ind Sch Dist 1988-; *ai:* Frosh Class Spon; Head Bsktbl & Track, Asst Vlybl Coach; ATPE, TGCA 1984-; TAHPER, AAHPERD 1984-88; *office:* Bullard HS P O Box 250 Bullard TX 75757

BRAMMER, GRANVIL R., Vice Principal; *b:* Huntington, WV; *ed:* (BA) Elem Ed, OH Univ 1972; (MA) Educl Admin, Marshall Univ 1974; *cr:* Teacher 1972-81, Vice Prin 1982- Chesapeake Mid Sch; *ai:* 7th/8th Grade Boys Track & 7th Grade Bsktbl Coach; 7th/8th Grade Athletic Dir; *home:* Rt 2 Box 283 South Point OH 45680

BRAMONTE, PATRICIA P., 5th Grade Teacher; *b:* Hopewell, VA; *m:* Sebastian N.; *c:* Patti, Michael, John; *ed:* (AA) Ocean Cmmty Coll 1971; (BA) Elem Ed, Fl Atlantic Univ 1978-79; *cr:* 5th Grade Teacher Rosewood Elem 1979-; *ai:* Grade Level Chairperson; Kappa Kappa Iota 1982-87; Alpha Delta Kappa 1983-85; 1st United Meth Church Youth Dir 1976-80; Church Sch Teacher 1958-83; *office:* Rosewood Elem Sch 3850 16th St Vero Beach FL 32960

BRANCH, BARBARA JUNE, 8th Grade Language Art Teacher; *b:* Mars Hill, NC; *m:* Robert Michael; *c:* Jonathan M. Bacon; *ed:* (BA) Fr/Eng, Mars Hill Coll 1968; Grad Stud Ed Counseling, W Carolina Univ; *cr:* 4th Grade Teacher Palo Alto Elem Sch 1969; Employment Interviewer Inc Employment Security Comm 1971-74; Remedial Rdng Teacher Mountain Heritage HS 1979-80; 6th-8th Grade Eng Teacher E Yancey Mid Sch 1980-; *ai:* Sch Newspaper; NCAE, NEA 1979-; Yancey Baptist Assn Church Trng Dir 1982-89; *home:* Rt 6 Box 233 Burnsville NC 28714

BRANCH, DIANA L., Business Ed Teacher/Dept Chair; *b:* Pensacola, FL; *ed:* (BS) Bus Ed, FL Intnl Univ 1981; (MS) Cmptr Ed, Nove Univ 1990; *cr:* Bus Teacher South Dade Sr HS 1981-82, Charles R Drew Jr HS 1982-83; Bus Teacher/Dept Chair W R Thomas Jr HS 1983-; *ai:* Adv FBLA; Dade Cty Bus Ed Assn Mem 1984-; FL Bus Ed Assn Mem 1985-; FBLA Mem 1984-; Teacher of Yr W R Thomas Jr HS 1987-88; Certificate of Appreciation Jackson Memorial Burn Center 1984, Neva King Cooper Educl Center 1984-87, Project Bus Jr Achievement 1989; *office:* W R Thomas Jr H S 13001SW 26th St Miami FL 33175

BRANCH, KIRBY TODD, Teacher; *b:* Quincy, IL; *ed:* (BA) Art, Grace Coll 1985; Word of Life Bible Inst Schroon Lake NY; Moody Bible Inst Chicago IL; *cr:* Teacher Indianapolis Baptist Schls 1986-89; *home:* 14940 Senator Way Carmel IN 46032

BRANCH, TANA NEWMAN, Art Teacher; *b:* La Fayette, AL; *m:* Charles E.; *c:* Virginia, Ben, Catherine; *ed:* (BFA) Visual Design, Auburn Univ 1965; Cert Art Ed, Auburn Univ 1977; (MS) Art Ed, Troy St Univ 1982; Working on Masters Cert in Sch Counseling; *cr:* Art Teacher Auburn City Schls; *ai:* Yrbk Spon; NJHS Founder of Chapter at Jr HS; Co-Founder Auburn Jr Arts Assn; Delta Kappa Gamma Historian; AEA, NEA, ACTA, AL Art Ed Assn, NAEA; Auburn-Opelika Alumnae Panhellenic Assn Pres 1989-; Phi Mu Alumnae Assn Phallenic Delegate 1987-; Episcopal Church Women & Choir Mem; Auburn Arts Assn Bd Mem 1983-85; Auburn Jr HS PTA Teacher of Yr Awd 1988, 1990; Hosted US-USSR Cmmty Wide Youth Art Exch 1990; Chairperson Cartoonist Morrie Turners Visit for Martin Luther Kings Birthday; *office:* Auburn Jr HS 332 E Samford Auburn AL 36830

BRANCH, VICKI HALL, Second Grade Teacher; *b:* Carlsbad, NM; *m:* Bobby G.; *c:* Summer L., McKenzie N.; *ed:* (BA) Elem Ed/Early Chldhd Ed, NM St 1980; (MS) Elem Ed/Admin, 1985; *cr:* 3rd Grade Teacher Hermosa Elem 1980-84; Kndgtn Teacher Grand Heights Early Chldhd Center 1984-86; 4th Grade Teacher 1986-88, 2nd Grade Teacher 1988- Hermosa Elem; *ai:* Sunday Sch Teacher Presbyn Church; HS Cheerleading Coach; Dir of Presbyn Church Childrens Choir; Chairperson Supervisory Comm For Artesia Public Schls Credit Union; Artesia Educl Assn (Secy 1983-84) 1980-; Presbyn Church (Deacon, Elder) 1986-88; *home:* 2107 Centre Ave Artesia NM 88210

BRANCICH, MARY HODGSON, Fourth Grade Teacher; *b:* Oklahoma City, OK; *m:* Jasper David; *c:* Mindy Brown, Mike, Tony; *ed:* (BS) Elem Ed, Cameron Univ 1979; *cr:* 4th Grade Teacher Empire Elem Sch 1979-; *ai:* 4-H Leader; Curr Alignment Comm; Stephens Cty Rdng Cncl (Secy 1987-89, Mem 1981-); Stephens Cty Media Center Pres 1985-89; Intnl Rdng Cncl Mem 1987-; OK Rdng Cncl Mem 1981-; Empire Ed Assn VP Elect; Duncan Literacy Cncl (Treas 1989-, Tutor 1985-); OK Ed Assn Delegate 1988-; Empire Teacher of Yr 1989; *office:* Empire Elem Sch Rt 1 Box 155 Duncan OK 73533

BRAND, CAROL MARIE, English Instructor; *b:* Parkers Prairie, MN; *m:* William A.; *c:* Lisa, Jason, Erik, Alison, Dave; *ed:* (BS) Eng/Bio, St Cloud St Univ 1964; *cr:* 11th-12th Grade Eng Teacher Holdingford Public HS 1965; 11th-12th Grade Eng Teacher 1967-68, 9th-10th Grade Eng Teacher 1968-69, 7th-8th Grade Eng Teacher 1978- Foley Public HS; *ai:* Salary & Honors Breakfast Comm; Faculty Senate; Comm Dept & Negotiating Team Mem; MEA, NEA 1965-; FEA Secy 1981-83; MFT 1987-; GSA; Cub Scouts Blue & Gold Banquet Chm 1989; *office:* Foley Public Sch Dist 51 Dewey St Foley MN 56329

BRANDENBURG, SHERYL WHITAKER, Fourth Grade Teacher; *b:* Mattoon, IL; *m:* Victor; *c:* Neil, Teri; *cr:* 2nd Grade Teacher Streamwood Sch 1964-65; Remedial Rdng Teacher 1966, 4th Grade Teacher 1966-68 Mattoon Schls; Substitute Teacher Cumberland Cty 1968-75; 4th Grade Teacher Neoga Schls 1975-; *ai:* Neoga Teachers (VP 1989-, Pres 1990); United Meth Women VP 1990; *office:* Neoga Elem Sch W 6th St Neoga IL 62447

BRANDON, GENUA O'NEAL, 6th Grade Soc Stud/Eng Teacher; *b:* Johnston County, NC; *m:* Ivery C.; *c:* Bettye J. Wilkerson, Tresavon D., Inga C. Pinnix; *ed:* (BS) Soc Stu, Elem Ed, Miles Coll 1970; *cr:* Librarian Birmingham Public Lib 1969-72; Teacher Craven Elem Sch 1974-82; Morehead Elem Sch 1982-86; Jackson Mid Sch 1986-; *ai:* Builders Club Jackson Mid Sch; Voluntary Tutor Cmmnty Fund Raising Activities-Cmmnty & Church; Den Mother Boy Scouts of Amer; Sunday Sch Teacher; Choir Mem; Ordained Deaconess; Voluntary Hosp Worker; Sewing Instr for Preteens; NCAE (REP 1974-82, MEM 1974-); NEA Mem 1974-; Alpha Phi Alpha Wives (Vp 1971-72, Outstanding Attendance 1971-72, Asst Secy 1973-74); Delta Sigma Theta Inc Mem; *home:* 4302 Belfield Dr Greensboro NC 27405

BRANDSTED, JANICE TORKELSON, Mathematics/Computer Teacher; *b:* Grafton, ND; *m:* Ronald J.; *c:* Gregory, Kent; *ed:* (BAE) Math/Phys Ed, Mayville St 1966; (ME) Cmmty Ed, CO St Univ 1985; Scndry Admin, CO St Univ 1989; Cmptr Programming; *cr:* Phys Ed/Health Teacher Morgan Public Schls 1967-69; Math Teacher Ft Dodge Public Schls 1970-71; Learning Center Coord IA Cntrl Cmmty Coll 1973-82; Math/Cmptr Teacher Caliche Jr/Sr HS/Re-1 Valley Sch Dist 1982-; *ai:* Frosh Class Spon; NEA, CEA, SPEA Building Rep 1985-87; NCTM, CCTM; Delta Kappa Gamma Treas 1988-; NCTM, CO Council Teachers of Math; Logan Cty Chamber of Commerce STAR Teacher Awd 1984, 1988; Caliche NHS Honorary Mem; *office:* Caliche Jr/Sr HS RR 1 Iliff CO 80736

BRANDT, B. SHIRLEY, English Teacher; *b:* Lehr, ND; *m:* James O.; *c:* Dana, Marie, Brandt; *ed:* (BS) Speech, Eng, Phy Ed Valley City St Univ 1963; Addl Studies, UNR-Reno 1966-88; *cr:* Phys Ed/Eng Teacher Park River HS 1963-64; Douglas HS 1964-68; Carson Valley Mid Sch 1968-87; Eng Teacher Douglas HS 1987-; *ai:* NV St Teachers Assn 1965-; NEA 1965-; NCTE 1986-; Douglas Ctys Teacher of Yr 1979; NV Teacher of Yr Runner-Up 1979; Whos Who in Amer Ed 1989-; *office:* Douglas County Sch Dist P O Box 1888 Minden NV 89423

BRANDT, CAROL VOELKER, English Teacher; *b:* Kansas City, MO; *m:* Randolph C.; *c:* Christine, Evan; *ed:* (BA) Scndry Ed/Eng, Univ of MO Kansas City 1976; *cr:* Eng Teacher Spring Hill HS 1976-84, Richmond HS 1984-85, Adrian HS 1986-88,

Raymore-Peculiar HS 1988-; *ai:* Stu Cncl, Literary Magazine Spon; NEA 1988-; NCTE; Fellow in Greater KS City Writing Project; *office:* Raymore-Peculiar HS Peculiar MO 64078

BRANDT, GLORIA JEAN, 7th-9th Grade Choral Music; *b:* Watertown, SD; *c:* Jon, David; *ed:* (BA) Music, Dakota Wesleyaan Univ 1969; Black Hills St Univ; SD St Univ; Gifted Ed, Univ of SD 1988; *cr:* K-6th Grade Vocal Music Teacher Meadowbrook Elem 1969-70; 7th-9th Grade Vocal Music Teacher West Jr HS 1970-74; 7th-9th Grade Vocal Music Teacher/Eng Dakota Jr HS 1980-; *ai:* Dakota Jr HS Concerts/Aud Show/Jass Choir; Rapid City Childrens Chorus; Amer Sings in Washington DC; Curr Comm; Amer Choral Dir Assn; RCEA; SDEA; NEA; Alpha Delta Kappa; Guest Choral Dir; Clinician Sch & Music Conf; Rapid City Teacher of Yr 1988-89; Candidate for SD Teacher of Yr 1988-89; Choral Dir for SD Ambassadors of Excellence; Performed 8th World Conf for Talented & Gifted Australia; *office:* Dakota Sr HS 615 Columbus St Rapid City SD 57701

BRANDT, JUNE KATHLEEN (BIELER), 5th & 6th Grade Math Teacher; *b:* Cincinnati, OH; *m:* Robert S.; *ed:* (BED) Elem Ed, 1965, (MED) Ed, 1969 Univ of Cincinnati; Paideia, MIET; *cr:* 5th-6th Grade Math/Sci Teacher Whittier Elem 1965-88; 5th-6th Grade Math Teacher/4th Grade Math Coach 1988-89, 5th-6th Grade Math Teacher/4th Grade Problem Solving Lab Coach 1989-, 5th-8th Grade Math Coach 1990 Robert Paideia Acad; *ai:* Delta Kappa Gamma Auditor; Kappa Delta Pi; NEA, OH Ed Assn, Cincinnati Teachers Assn; Westwood United Meth Church Sunday Sch Supt 1988-; Delhi Hills Baptist Church Librarian 1970-79; Trianon (Natl Pres, VP, Treas, Local Pres, VP, Secy); *home:* 5475 Sidney Rd Cincinnati OH 45238

BRANDT, ORPAH JEAN, 8th Grade Mathematics Teacher; *b:* Gardners, PA; *ed:* (BS) Elem Ed, Lee Coll 1973; (MS) Mid Sch, Univ of TN Chattanooga 1979; *cr:* 6th Grade Teacher North Whitfield Mid Sch; 4th/5th Grade Pleasant Grove Elem Sch; 8th Grade Whitfield Mid Sch; *ai:* 8th Grade Team Leader; Prof Assn for GA Educators; Pleasant Grove Elem Teacher of Yr 1980-81; Whitfield Cty Sch System Teacher of Yr Runner-Up 1980-81; *home:* 5021 Village Dr Cohutta GA 30710

BRANDT, PAUL CHARLES, Religion Teacher; *b:* Norristown, PA; *ed:* (BS) Philosophy, 1979, (MDIV) Theology, 1984, (MA) Religious Stud, 1989 St Charles Borromeo Seminary; *cr:* Religion Faculty Roman Cath HS 1987-; *ai:* Sch Ministry; Stu Cncl & Bsktbl Moderator; *office:* Roman Cath HS Broad & Vine St Philadelphia PA 19107

BRANDT, TIM JAMES, Director of Bands; *b:* Alva, OK; *m:* Cynthia Jean Lamb; *c:* James, John; *ed:* (BME) Music, SW OK St Univ 1979; Grad Work Music Ed, Wichita St Univ & SW OK St; *cr:* Dir of Bands Boise City Public Schls 1979-80, Wichita Cty Schls 1980-84, Blackwell HS 1984-; *ai:* Marching & Concert Band; Jazz Ensemble; Intnl Assn of Jazz Educators OK Pres 1990; OK Music Educators Assn All-St Jazz Chm 1989-; OK Bandmasters Assn; Phi Beta Mu, Kappa Delta Pi; 1st Baptist Church Deacon 1988-; Leoti Jaycees Outstanding Young Educators Awd; Outstanding Young Men of America; *home:* 208 Stevens Blackwell OK 74631

BRANHAM, ANNE KINNEY, Creative Writing/Eng Teacher; *b:* Louisville, KY; *m:* Leslie B. Jr.; *c:* Erin, Kristin, Bronwyn, Ryan, Megan; *ed:* (BA) Creative Writing, S IL Univ 1973; (MED) Eng Ed, Shippensburg Univ 1980; *cr:* Creative Writing/Eng Teacher Chambersburg Area Sr HS 1983-; *ai:* Adv & Ed LIterary Magazine Collections; Assistance Judging FOrensics Tournaments; Philosophy & Objectives Comm 1988-89; NCTE Superior Ranking Chambersburg Area Sr HS Collections 1989-; *office:* Chambersburg Area Sr HS 511 S 6th St Chambersburg PA 17201

BRANIGHAN, WENDIE, Sixth Grade Teacher; *b:* Buffalo, NY; *ed:* (BA) Elem Ed, Old Dominion Univ; (MS) Admin, George Washington Univ; *cr:* 2nd/4th/6th Grade Teacher Trantwood Elem; 5th/6th Grade Teacher White Oaks Elem; 6th Grade Teacher Parkway Elem; *ai:* Friends of Norfolk Juvenile Court Volunteer Tutor; Virginia Beach Republican City Comm Mem.

BRANN, CAROL PENTECOST, Home Economics Teacher; *b:* Murray, KY; *m:* Hugh E.; *c:* Julie Brann Ragan, Jeffery E.; *ed:* (BS) Home Ec, Univ TN Knoxville 1957; (MS) Home Ec/Family Rel, Murray St Univ 1969; *cr:* Teacher Weakley Cty 1959, 1963-; *ai:* FHA Adv, Jr Class Spon, Partner in Ed Coord, St Curr Dev; Carrier Ladder Comm; NEA, TN Ed Assn, TN Home Ec Assn, AVA; Delta Gamma Kappa Pres; Southern Assn Steering Comm; Auxilary of Reciaton; Auxilary of Natl Pestwester League; Auxilary of Amer Legion; Church Pianist; Outstanding Young Women of America.

BRANNAN, REITHA FRANCES, Second Grade Teacher; *b:* Austwell, TX; *m:* Roy William Jr.; *c:* Bill, Gary P., Cynthia A.; *ed:* (BS) Elem Ed/Eng, Howard Payne Univ 1949; Howard Payne Univ; *cr:* 5th Grade Teacher Pyote Army Air Base Public Sch 1949-50; 4th Grade Teacher 1950-51, Spec Ed Teacher 1961-62, 2nd Grade Teacher 1962- Comanche Elem; *ai:* First Baptist Church Sunday Sch Teacher; Classroom Teachers of Comanche, TX St Teacher Assn 1961-; Heritage Study Club Pres 1984-86; Dist & St Fed of Womens Club (Dist Treas) 1988-92.

BRANNMAN, WARD SCOTT, Director of Bands; *b:* Seattle, WA; *m:* Barbara Jean Coates; *c:* Andrea; *ed:* (BA) Music Ed, 1985, (BM) Music, 1985 Univ of WA; *cr:* Band Dir Northshore Jr HS 1985-86, Kamiakin Jr HS 1986-; *ai:* Music Educators Natl Conference 1985-; Mountlake Terrace Firefighters Assn 1987-, Firefighter Awd; *office:* Kamiakin Jr HS 14111 132nd NE Kirkland WA 98034

BRANNON, PATRICIA ANN, Language Art Teacher; *b:* Washington, DC; *ed:* (BA) Phys Ed/Lang Art, Glenville St Coll 1971; *cr:* Phys Ed Teacher Justice Grade Sch 1971-76; USMC 1976-82; Phys Ed Teacher Christian Grade Sch 1982-83; Lang Art Teacher Logan Jr HS 1983-; *ai:* Drama Club Spon; Head Bsktbl Coach; WV Competitive Grant 1990; Published Curr Guide for Elem Phys Ed Teachers 1973; *office:* Logan Jr HS 500 University Ave Logan WV 25601

BRANNON, RANDALL LANIER, Band Director; *b:* Parkersburg, WY; *m:* Tina Ann Wilcoxen; *ed:* (BMUS) Music Ed, WV Univ 1974; (MMUS) Clarinet Performance, OH Univ 1976; *cr:* Band Dir Petersburg HS 1976-82, Edison Jr HS 1982-; *ai:* All Band Act Edison Jr HS & Elem Schls; NEA, Music Educators Natl Conference, WV Bandmasters Assn 1976-; *office:* Edison Jr HS 1201 Hillcrest St Parkersburg WV 26101

BRANON, JACK KENT, Social Studies Teacher; *b:* Huntington, WV; *m:* Sharon Marie Smith; *c:* Beth, Michael; *ed:* (BS) Health/Phys Ed, Cedarville Coll 1966; Teacher Cert His/Government, OH Univ 1967; (MA) His/Poly Sci, Marshall Univ 1974; *cr:* Soc Stud Teacher Clay HS 1967-69, Green HS 1969-74, Wheelersburg Jr HS & HS 1974-; *ai:* Head Cross Cntry, Asst Bsktbl, Head Bsbl Coach; Phi Alpha Theta His Honor Society 1967-; OH HS Bsbl Coaches Assn 1982-; OH HS Bsktbl Coaches Assn 1988-; Wheelersburg Baptist Church Deacon 1985-; KYOVA Generlogical Society; *office:* Wheelersburg HS Pirate Dr Wheelersburg OH 45694

BRANSTETTER, CARMEN E., Reading Teacher; *b:* Ironton, MO; *m:* Michael R.; *c:* Amy, Ryan; *ed:* (BS) Scndry Ed/Eng, SE MO St Univ 1970; (MAT) Comm, Webster Univ 1982; *cr:* Lang/Rdng Teacher 1970-88, Rdng/Lit Teacher 1988- Evans Mid Sch; *ai:* Instructional Management Comm; Cty Teachers Assn; MO St Teachers Assn; NCTE; MO Federated Womens Clubs 1977-79; Beta Sigma Phi 1980-89; *office:* Evans Mid Sch 305 S Lead St Potosi MO 63664

BRANSTETTER, MELINDA KAYE (MILLER), Third Grade Teacher; *b:* Laramie, WY; *m:* Joseph Wayne; *c:* Anna-Marie, Dustin; *ed:* (BS) Elem Ed, SE MO St 1982; Grad Stud; *cr:* 5th Grade Teacher 1982-85, 3rd Grade Teacher 1985- Arcadia Valley Elem; *ai:* Talent Show, Yrbk, Academic Olympic Comm; ADK Secy 1990; *office:* Arcadia Valley Elem Sch 700 Park Ironton MO 63650

BRANTLEY, GLORIA ALEXANDER, 5th Grade Teacher; *b:* Madison, FL; *m:* Samuel D.; *ed:* (BS) Elem Ed, Edward Waters Coll 1976; (MS) Elem Ed, FL A&M Univ 1987; Cashier Sales Certificate Jacksonville Industralization Center 1971; *cr:* Teacher/Aide Duval Cty Sch Bd 1975-76; Driver/Teacher Aide Madison Assn for Retarded Citizens 1977-78; *ai:* Grade Chairperson; Data Collector; GTOI Coord; Textbook Adoption Comm; Alpha Sigma Tau Pres 1975-76; Kappa Delta Pi Honor Society 1987; Dormitory Citizenship Awd 1976; Mid Sch Teacher of Yr 1987-88; Outstanding Woman of Yr 1987; Cum Laude Grad Edward Waters Coll 1976; Natl Deans List 1987-88; *home:* PO Box 2721 Valdosta GA 31604

BRANTLEY, JOHN FLAKE, Agriculture Teacher; *b:* Mooresville, NC; *ed:* (BS) Ag Ed, NC St Univ 1984; *cr:* Research Asst NC St Univ 1981-84; Teacher Clyde A Erwin HS 1984-87, North Buncombe HS 1987-; *ai:* FFF Landscape Design/Maintenance; AVA, NCVA, NCVATA 1984-; Optimist (Pres, Lt Governor) 1985-, President Awd 1989; *office:* North Buncombe HS 890 Clarks Chapel Rd Weaverville NC 28787

BRANTON, CONSTANCE C., Junior High Choir Teacher; *b:* Marquette, MI; *m:* Donald C.; *c:* Anna, Sarah; *ed:* (BMUS) Music, Westminster Choir Coll 1973; (MED) Music, Boise St Univ 1986; Further Stud, Germany, Austria; Numerous Summer Wkshps; *cr:* Music Teacher Vieja Valley Elem 1976-79; Choir Teacher Boise HS 1981- 84, North Jr HS 1981-89; Music Teacher Cole Elem 1984-87; Choir Teacher South Jr HS 1987-; *ai:* All Choral Groups Spon; Natl Music Educators Convention St Jr HS Chairperson 1981-; Amer Choral Dirs Assn Northwest Womens Rep 1979-; Amer Guild Organists Dean St Coord 1979-; NEA, ID Ed Assn, BEA 1981-; Whitney Meth Church Choir Dir 1981-; Turkish Childrens Choir Festival USA Rep 1988; *home:* 1012 S Latah Boise ID 83705

BRANUM, JACQUELYN MURRAY, 8th Grade Science Teacher; *b:* Oklahoma City, OK; *c:* Mary Worland, Debi Garvin, Judy Brown, Claudia; *ed:* (BS) Elem Ed, Univ of TX El Paso; (MA) Elem Ed, Univ of NM; Marine Ecology, Barry Univ; Rdng, NM St & E NM Univ; Oral Lang Prgm, SW Cooperative Educl Laboratory; *cr:* Pre-1st/1st Grade Teacher Ysleta Sch Dist 1960-70; 1st Grade Teacher 1970-73, 6th Grade Teacher 1973-75, Oral Lang Prgm Coord 1975-77 Albuquerque Public Schls; Sci Teacher Capitan Municipal Sch 1977-79, El Paso Public Schls 1979-80, Ruidoso Mid Sch 1980-; *ai:* Sci Bowl Team Spon; All Knowledge Bowl Team; Sci Fair Dir; Knowledge Masters & Sci Club Spon; Advisory Cncl, Sci Curr Comm; Official Scorekeeper Vlybl & Bsktbl; NEA 1960-; NSTA; Village of Ruidoso Downs (Trustee 1984-88, (Elected Official), Mayor-Pro-Tem 1985-88, 1990-94); Alpha Delta Kappa 1989-; Co-Authored Complete Hands-On Sci Curr K-2nd Grade; Summer Sci Fellowship Rimate Research Laboratory; Holloman AFB NM 1986-88; Woman of Yr in Sci Ruidoso Womans Club 1986; Schlsp to Marine Resources Wkshp 1989; *home:* Box 746 Ruidoso Downs NM 88346

BRANYAN, CAROLE L., Honors English 12 Teacher; *b:* Memphis, TN; *ed:* (BA) Eng, Rhodes Coll 1967; (MED) Guidance, Memphis St Univ 1970; Sch Admin Scndry; *cr:* Eng Teacher Trezevant HS 1967-83; Eng Teacher White Station 1983-; *ai:* Stu Cncl Adv; Memphis Ed Assn, TN Ed Assn, NEA 1967-; Alpha Delta Kappa (Herald 1988-89) 1985-; Idlewild Presbyn (Secy 1988, Deacon Elder 1990-93); Nomination for Teacher of Excl Awd 1989-; Judge for Bnai Brith Youth Organization Regional Convention 1988-; Awd for Contribution to Hearing Impaired Stu Services Memphis City Schls 1986; *office:* White Station HS 514 S Perkins Memphis TN 38117

BRASHEAR, BEATRICE BANKS, Retired Elementary Teacher; *b:* Napfor, KY; *m:* Keith; *c:* Barbara A., James K., Stephen S.; *ed:* Certificate Elem Ed, Lees Jr Coll 1955; (BS) Elem Ed, Cumberland Coll 1965; *cr:* 1st-3rd Grade Teacher Rogers Branch Elem 1955-64; 2nd Grade Teacher Viper Elem 1964-88; *ai:* KEA, NEA, PCEA 1964-88; *home:* Rt 1 Box 75A Viper KY 41774

BRASHEAR, SANDRA COMBS, Language Arts Teacher; *b:* Hazard, KY; *m:* Richard A.; *c:* Jason L., Waukesha L.; *ed:* (BS) His, 1976, (MA) Ed, Union Coll 1978; *cr:* His Teacher Mc Napier HS 1977-78; Lang Art Teacher Viper Elem 1978-; *ai:* Governors Cup Spon; Sch Academic Team Coach; Teacher of Gifted & Talented; Lang Art Comm; *home:* PO Box 562 Cornettsville KY 41731

BRASHER, SHARON DAVIS, US History/Civics/Span Teacher; *b:* San Fernando, CA; *m:* Jeff; *c:* Shelly, Grant; *ed:* (BA) Scndry Ed/Soc Stud, Purdue Univ 1983; Cmmty Intervention Inc; *cr:* Teacher Benton Hall HS 1986-; *ai:* Yrbk Adv; Bowling Club Co-Spon; Drug/Alcohol Awareness Faculty Core Team Mem; Benton Hall Headmaster Search Comm; Drug/Alcohol Insight Group Cnslr; *office:* Benton Hall HS 4800 Franklin Rd Nashville TN 37220

BRASSEA, NANCY CRAMER, Fifth Grade Teacher; *b:* Chicago Heights, IL; *m:* Donald C.; *c:* Donna Ransdell, William H.; *ed:* (BS) Phys Ed, Culver-Stockton Coll 1952; (MED) Elem Ed, Univ of AZ 1976; *cr:* 6th Grade Teacher Crete & Monee Cmmty Unit 1952-53; 5th/Jr HS Phys Ed Teacher Polo Elem Sch 1953-55; Elem Phys Ed Teacher Peotone Cmmty Unit 1955-57; Jr HS Phys Ed Teacher Steger Elem Schls 1960-61; Elem Phys Ed Teacher Park Forest Sch Dist 1966-68, Matteson Sch Dist 1968-70; 5th Grade Teacher Eloy Elem Sch Dist 11 1970-; *ai:* Chairperson Lang Art Book Selection Comm; Mem Rdng Revision Comm; 5th Grade Chairperson; Eloy Fed Teachers Pres 1987-; AZ Cncl Ec Ed Fellowship For Studying 2-Party System of Government; *office:* Eloy Intermediate Sch 1005 N Santa Cruz Eloy AZ 85231

BRASURE, WENDY RAVEN, 5th Grade Teacher; *b:* White Plains, NY; *m:* Stephen C.; *c:* Jason, Alex; *ed:* (BA) Elem Ed Cum Laude, SUNY Redonia 1973; Ed Niagara Univ; Tactics Trng; Project Write; *cr:* 5th Grade Teacher 1976, 6th Grade Teacher 1976-77, Corrective Rdng 1977-78, 3rd Grade Teacher 1978-79, 5th Grade Teacher 1979-80 & 1982-84 Wilson Cntrl Sch; *ai:* Odyssey of Mind Coach; Insect Club-Stud of Etomology; Reading-Math Comn; Written Curr for Lit Based Rdng; Kappa Delta Phi 1973; Thomas Marks PTA (Teacher Rep 1987-88/VP 1989-).

BRATER, KATHIE ROLFES, 2nd-6th Substitute Teacher; *b:* Hamilton, OH; *m:* John C.; *c:* Jeffrey A., Scot D.; *ed:* (BS) Elem Ed, Coll of MT St Joseph; Apprentice Prgm Funeral Dir License, St of OH; *cr:* 3rd Grade Teacher St John the Baptist 1966-68, St Peter Sch 1968-69; 6th Grade Teacher Southwest Local Schls 1977-79; 5th/6th Grade Teacher 1979-80, 3rd Grade Teacher 1980-85, 4th Grade Teacher 1984-87 St John the Baptist; Substitute Teacher St John the Baptist & Southwest Local 1987-; *ai:* Village Historical Society Incorporated (VP 1982-86, Pres 1986-); *home:* 215 S Vine St Harrison OH 45030

BRATTON, PATRICIA ANN (SEIBERT), Science Teacher; *b:* Kansas City, MO; *m:* Terry Lee; *c:* Shawn, Peyton; *ed:* (BSE) Bio, Cntrl MO St Univ 1980; Grad Stud Cntrl MO St Univ, Univ of MO Kansas City, Univ of MO Columbia; *cr:* Sci Teacher Wellington-Napoleon HS 1981-; *ai:* Sci Knowledge Bowl Team, Academic Team, 8th Grade Class Spon; Career Ladder Comm Secy; MO St Teachers Assn 1981-; NSTA, Sci Teachers of MO 1987-; Cmmty Teachers Assn VP; Excl Ed St Grant; Nom Outstanding Math/Sci/Cmptr Sci Teacher Awd.

BRATTSTROM, MARTHA ANN, Science Department Teacher; *b:* New London, CT; *m:* Bayard H.; *c:* Robert; *ed:* (BS) Life Sci, San Diego St Univ 1952; Wkshp, Advanced Courses Bio, Univ of CA Berkley & Irvine, CA St Univ Fullerton, Pepperdine Univ, Chapman Coll; *cr:* Teacher San Lorenzo CA Sch 1953-64, Garden Grove Unified Sch Dist 1964-; *ai:* Sci Club & Sch Newspaper Adv; Sci Curr, Sex Ed, Sci Textbook Adoption, Faculty Rep to Union, Sch Dist Reorganization Comms Mem; NABT, NSTA; Sch Dist Sex Ed Pilot Prgm; *office:* Hilton D Bell Intermediate Sch 12345 Springdale Ave Garden Grove CA 92645

BRAUDAWAY, GARY WAYNE, English Teacher; *b:* Ft Worth, TX; *ed:* (BA) Eng/Bible, Hardin-Simmons Univ 1982; His/Ed, Univ of North TX; Eng as a Second Lang, TX Wesleyan Univ; Numerous Courses; *cr:* Eng/His Teacher Diamond Hill-Jarvis HS 1983-86; Eng Teacher Trimble Teach HS 1986-; *ai:* After Sch Tutoring; NHS & Campus Coord Comm; Management Team; Uil Literary & Academic Decathalon Coach; Spon Literary Magazine; Chaperon on Band Trips; PSAT & SAT Coach; Sr Prgm Dir; Class Spon Pac Comm; Ft Worth Area Cncl Teachers of Eng 1986-87; Nom Eng Teacher of Yr by Ft Worth Area Cncl

Teachers of Eng 1984-85; Published Articles & Radio Interview; *office:* G B Trimble Tech H S 1003 W Cannon Fort Worth TX 76104

BRAUN, ALBERT CARL, World History Teacher; *b:* Dorchester, WI; *m:* Connie Marvelle Swender; *c:* Scott P., Stanton T.; *ed:* (BS) His/Geography, 1955, (MST) Broadfield Soc Stud/Ed, 1971 Univ of WI Stevens Point; Sophia Univ, Oxford Univ, Univ of Milwaukee, Univ of WI Eau Claire, Ball St; *cr:* Teacher Antigo HS 1955-57, Brookfield East HS 1957-58, Dept of Defense Schls 1958-73, Tokyo Japan & Wicsbaden Germany 1973-; *ai:* NHS Spon; NEA, WEA, CEA Past Pres 1973-; WI Cncl of Soc Stud 1985-; Lions Intnl (Past Pres 1984-, Pres 1989); Dorchester Park Bd Treas of PR 1985-; Natl Sci Fnd; World Travel; Started Current Affairs & Street Law Electives at HS; *office:* Colby HS N 2nd St Colby WI 54421

BRAUN, CYNDY, Latin & French Teacher; *b:* Plainfield, NJ; *ed:* (BA) Liberal Arts, PA St Univ 1970; (MA) Classics, Univ of MT 1979; *cr:* Teaching Asst 1978-79, Instr 1979-80 Univ of MT; Teacher Missoula Cty HS 1981-; *ai:* Adv NHS; Amer Classical League, AATF, Alliance Francaise, Pacific NW Cncl on Foreign Lang, MT Assn of Lang Teachers, MT Ed Assn, NEA; Missoula Humane Society; Missoula Bicycle Club Pres; Missoula Road & Track Club; *office:* Missoula Cty HS 3100 South Ave W Missoula MT 59801

BRAUN, WESLEY, Secondary Counselor; *b:* Henderson, NE; *m:* Mary Elois; *c:* Steven D., James S., Robert L.; *ed:* (BA) Eng/Bio, Tabor Coll 1957; (MS) Guidance/Psych, Emporia St Univ 1960; (MA) Eng, Univ of KS 1969; Hum, Williams Coll Williamston MA 1964; Ed, The Univ of Amsterdam 1976; *cr:* Recreational Therapist Child Care Menninger Fnd 1958-60; Eng Instr Silver Lake HS 1960-62, Washburn Rural HS 1962-69, Amer Sch of Hague 1969-78; Univ of MD 1976-77; Scndry Cnslr Washburn Rural HS 1978-; *ai:* Class Adv; Amer Sch of Hague Teachers Assn (Chief Negotiator, Pres) 1974-76; Auburn-Washburn Assn Mem 1988-; NCTE 1960-69; Dutch Anglo Amer Literary Society; Univ of Leiden 1975-76; Outstanding Teacher Awd Amer Sch of Hague 1976-78; Classroom in England Founder/Coord 1973-78; John Hay Hum Fellowship Williams Coll 1964; *home:* 3327 Friar Rd Topeka KS 66614

BRAWLEY, DENNIS M., 7th-8th Grade Soc Stud Teacher; *b:* Akron, OH; *m:* Carol Ann Furey; *c:* Kevin; *ed:* (BAED) Soc Stud Comp, Univ of Akron 1964; *cr:* Soc Stud Teacher Mogadore HS 1964-82, O H Somers Sch 1982-; *ai:* 8th Grade Class Adv, Faculty Advisory Comm; Mogadore Ed Assn, OH Ed Assn, OH Cncl for Soc Stud 1964-; NEA 1978-; Tallmadge Fire Dept Captain 1975-, Cmmty Service Awd 1985; Dist Candidate OH Teacher of Yr 1987; PTA Educator of Yr 1990; *office:* O H Somers Sch 3600 Herbert St Mogadore OH 44260

BRAWLEY, JOAN P., 6th Grade Teacher; *b:* Fulton, KY; *c:* Stacey, Scott; *ed:* (BS) Elem Ed & Eng, 1967, (MA) Elem Ed, 1975 Murray St Univ; Gifted Ed; *cr:* 2nd Grade Teacher Owensboro Ind Schls 1967-68; 2nd Grade Teacher 1968-71, 6th Grade Teacher 1973 Hickman Cty Elem; *ai:* Elem Acad Coach Hickman Cty; Hickman Cty Spelling Bee Coord; Delta Kappa Gamma (Recording Sec 1978-80 Corresponding Sec 1984-86); PTO; Bykota Homemakers Pres 1989; Hickman Cty 4-H Cncl Pres 1986-87 Pres Awd 1987; *home:* Rt 1 Box 46 Clinton KY 42031

BRAWLEY, PAM A., English Teacher; *b:* Natchez, MS; *m:* Dennis G.; *c:* Erin, Erica; *ed:* (BA) Eng, 1976, (MHDL) Eng Ed, 1982 Univ of NC Charlotte; Effective Teacher Trng, Thinking Skills, Assertive Discipline, Madeline Hunter Wkshps; *cr:* Rdng Instr South Rowan Sr HS 1976-77; Eng Instr Rowan Cabarrus Comm Coll 1976-79; Eng Teacher Cntrl Cabarrys HS 1977-79, Northwest Cabarrus HS 1979-; *ai:* Teacher Recruiter NC Dept of Public Instruction; Future Teachers of America Spon; Schlsp Comm; Sr Class Adv; NEA/NCAE 1977-; Intnl Rdng Assn 1980-; Cabarrus Cty Eng Teacher of Yr 1988-89; *home:* 6825 Plyler Rd Kannapolis NC 28081

BRAWLEY, PATRICIA LYNNE, English Teacher/Dept Head; *b:* Birmingham, AL; *m:* Michael L.; *c:* Donald, Marjalana, John; *ed:* (BS) Eng/Ed, Univ of WI River Falls 1967; TX Weslyan Ft Worth; Univ of WI River Falls; Univ of NV Las Vegas; Univ of NV Reno; Clark Cty Comm Coll; *cr:* Teacher Tonopah Jr HS 1967-73, Tonopah HS 1975-, Clark Cty Comm Coll; *ai:* Sr Class Spon; Yrbk Adv; Lions Club Speech Coach; Hum Curr Comm; NSEA; PEO Pres; Delta Kappa Gamma Pres; Commencement Speaker 1983, 1985; Nye Cty Teacher of Yr 1985.

BRAWLEY, VICKI DAVIS, 1st Grade Teacher; *b:* Mooresville, NC; *m:* Robert T.; *c:* Leslie, Adam, Kari; *ed:* (BA) His/Soc Stud, Univ of NC Charlotte 1977; *cr:* Kndgtn Teacher Ida Rankin Elem 1977; 1st Grade Teacher 1977-83, 1985-88, Kndgtn Teacher 1984-85, 1988-89, 1st Grade Teacher 1989- Park View Elem; *ai:* Media & NC Heritage Comm; Publicity Chm; NC Assn of Educators 1977-; Mooresville Jr Civic League 1977-79; *office:* Park View Elem Sch 217 W Mcneely Ave Mooresville NC 28115

BRAWNER, LYNNELL (FOUTS), First Grade Teacher; *b:* Rule, TX; *m:* John H.; *c:* Brett, Brian, Bowen; *ed:* (BS) Home Ec, TX Tech Univ 1961; (MED) Elem Ed, N TX St Univ 1970; Advanced Academic Trng Certified by St of TX; *cr:* Home Ec Teacher Stamford HS 1961-62, Brewer Jr HS 1962-63; Primary Teacher Cresson Elem 1966-67; Primary Teacher Cresson Elem 1966-67; 1st Grade Teacher Granbury Ind Sch Dist 1972-; *ai:* Granbury Ed Assn Pres 1988-89; TX St Teachers Assn, Nea 1970-; Delta Kappa Gamma 1980-; Granbury Womens Club Teacher of Yr 1985; *home:* 29 Holmes Dr Granbury TX 76048

BRAXTON, GWENDOLYN C. JACKSON, 2nd Grade Teacher; *b:* Sumter, SC; *c:* Chanel D. Braxton Jones, Daly N. IV; *ed:* (BS) Ed, Edward Waters Coll 1976; Cert Elem Cmptr Ed & Early Chldhd; *cr:* 2nd Grade Teacher Bryceville Elem Sch 1976-; *ai:* Bryceville Elem Sch Teacher of Yr 1982; Phys Ed Contimuum Comm, Health Coord 1982-83; *office:* Bryceville Elem Sch Church Ave P O Box 3 Bryceville FL 32009

BRAXTON, LINDA SHERER, Third Grade Teacher; *b:* Birmingham, AL; *c:* Erica; *ed:* (BS) Elem Ed, Miles Coll 1973; (MED) Elem Ed, AL St Univ 1976; Univ of AL 1980-81; *cr:* 1st Grade Teacher 1973-86, 1st-2nd Grade Teacher 1986-89, 3rd Grade Teacher 1989- West Blocton Elem; *ai:* Delta Sigma Theta, NEA, AL Ed Assn.

BRAXTON, SHEILA MELINDA, English Teacher; *b:* Washington, DC; *ed:* (BA) Eng, 1972, (MA) Eng, 1977 The American Univ; Staff Dev, Univ of MD; *cr:* Eng Teacher High Point HS 1972-; Professor/Eng Teacher Prince Georges Comm Coll 1989-; *ai:* Future Teachers of MD Adv; Black His & Awd Comm; Contest Comm Chairperson; Schlsp Comm; Girls & Boys St Comm; Faculty Advisory Cncl; Prince Georges Cty Ed Assn Rep 1989-; NCTE Mem 1988-; NEA Mem 1972-; MD St Teachers Assn Mem 1972-; MD Cncl Teachers of Eng Mem 1988-; MADD 1986-; NAACP 1990; Writing Curr Academic Center; Writing Course Arts Hum; Teacher of Yr 1990; Letter from Cty Exec Parris Glendening for Sponorship FTM Club; Letter MS St Senate Outstanding Teaching; *office:* High Point Sr H S 3601 Powder Mill Rd Beltsville MD 20705

BRAY, ELOUISE KAYE, 7th Grade Eng Teacher/Chair; *b:* Lexington, KY; *c:* Edward T.; *ed:* (BS) Ed, 1973, (ME) Diagnostic/Remedial Ed, 1979 Miami Univ Oxford; *cr:* 5th Grade Teacher Middletown Chrstn Sch 1974-80; 6th-8th Grade Diagnostic/Remedial Rdng Specialist/Lab Teacher/Consultant 1980-86, 7th/8th Grade Eng Teacher 1986-, 7th Grade Eng Chairperson 1987- Carlisle Jr HS; *ai:* Rdng & Eng Curr Comm; Building Leadership Team; NEA 1980-; OH Ed Assn; Carlisle Teachers Assns 1981-; Unity in Christ Church Bd Mem 1988-; *office:* Carlisle Jr HS 720 Fairview Dr Carlisle OH 45005

BRAZIL, HUGHLENE HALL, Mathematics Teacher; *b:* Jackson, MS; *m:* Robert Edward Lucas; *c:* Hugh E. Jr.; *ed:* (BA) Math, Univ of MS 1963; (MAT) Math, Winthrop Coll 1982; *cr:* Math Teacher Greenville HS 1963-64, Solomon Jr HS 1968-70, Clarke Cntrl & Cedar Shoals HS 1970-79, Willis HS 1979-80, The Catawba Sch 1980-83, South Mecklenburg HS 1983-; Applied Statistics Lecturer Winthrop Coll 1983-; *ai:* Comprehensive Competition Math Team Coach; Academic Excl, Media Center Steering, Schlsp & Awds Comm; Sch Assistance team; NCTM 1972-; NC Cncl Teachers of Math, SC Assn for Advanced Placement Math Teachers 1983-; Amer Assn for Univ Women 1980-; Natl Sci Fnd Grant 1970; STAR Teacher Clarke Cty GA 1978; *office:* South Mecklenburg HS 8900 Park Rd Charlotte NC 28210

BRAZZLE, JANICE MARLENE, Teacher; *b:* Detroit, MI; *ed:* (BS) Elem Ed, David Lipscomb Univ 1973; (MS) Elem Ed, Austin Peay St Univ 1976; Rdng Specialist & Admin Supervision Austin Peay 1987; *cr:* Kndgtn Teacher Waverly Elem 1973-; *ai:* Kids Involved Doing Challenging Objectives Chairperson 1988-89; Delta Kappa Gamma Treas 1985-; Warioto Rdng Cncl Treas; NCTM; United Daughters of Conf (secy 1980-84, Pres 1984-86); Daughters of Amer Revolution; Outstanding Young Woman of America 1980; *home:* Rt 1 Box 202 Mc Ewen TN 37101

BREAKEY, CURTIS EMERY, Social Studies Teacher; *b:* Ridgway, PA; *m:* Jacqueline Mahoney; *c:* Ian, Donny; *ed:* (BS) Scndry Ed/Soc Stud, Clarion Univ of PA 1983; Cert in Drivers Ed 1985; *cr:* HS Soc Stud/Drivers Ed Teacher Ridgway Area HS 1984-88, Johnsonburg Area HS 1988-; *ai:* Ftbl, Track & Field Asst Coach; Intramural Dir; Soph Class Adv.

BREAULT, LOIS BRELSFORD, Fifth Grade Teacher; *b:* Oakland, CA; *m:* Ronald F.; *c:* Adrienne Breault Palmer, Ronald C., Matthew K.; *ed:* (BA) Letters/Sci, Univ of CA Berkeley 1956; *cr:* 5th Grade Teacher Oliver Hartzell Sch 1957-61, Albany Unified Schls 1972-; *ai:* CA Math Cncl, CA Cncl for Soc Stud 1989-; AFS Intnl Treas 1978-; PTA 1972-, Lifetime Mem Awd 1980; Albany Mentor Math Teacher; Soc Stud Teachers Wkshps; *office:* Marin Elem Sch 1001 Santa Fe Ave Albany CA 94706

BREBNER, NANCY ATTEBERRY, English Teacher; *b:* Mercedes, TX; *c:* Debbie Demrow, Lynne Morton, Rick, Judy Mc Daniel; *ed:* (BS) Scndry Ed/Eng, TX A&I Univ Kingsville 1955; Grad Stud Bi-ling Ed, Working Towards Masters in Ed, Guidance & Counseling; *cr:* Eng Teacher Weslaco HS 1960-61; 5th Grade Eng Teacher Sam Houston Elem 1963-66, Louise Black Elem 1968-73; Mid Sch Eng Teacher Progreso Ind Sch Dist 1978-80; 8th Grade Eng Teacher Mary Hoge Jr HS 1980-; *ai:* Co-Facilitator Life Management Skills Retreats for At Risk Stus; Stu Cnslr for Childrens CHALLENGE Gifted Prgm Univ of TX Pan Amer; Assn of TX Prof Educators 1980-; NCTE 1980-88; Delta Kappa Gamma 1988-; *office:* Mary Hoge Jr HS 506 E 6th St Weslaco TX 78596

BRECHT, KENNETH A., Social Studies Head/Teacher; *b:* Holy Cross, IA; *m:* Evelyn C. Alt; *c:* Christine, Brian, Carrie; *ed:* (BA) His, 1959, (MA) His, 1971 Loras Coll; *cr:* Teacher Riverside Military Acad 1960-63, Ryan 1963-67, Marquette Hs 1967-; *ai:* Magazine Subscriptions Comm; NHS Spon; NCEA; VFW; *home:* 2594 Dove Dubuque IA 52001

BRECK, BARBARA ASKEW, 7th Grade Teacher; *b:* Mitchell, SD; *m:* James E.; *c:* James Jr., Mark; *ed:* (BA) Eng, Mt Marty Coll 1964; Grad Courses, Univ of SD, Univ of AZ; *cr:* Eng Teacher Pipestone HS 1964-66, Emery HS 1968-69; 7th Grade Teacher St Francis of Assisi Sch 1976-; *ai:* Mathcounts Coach; CO Teachers of Rdng Membership Chairperson 1987-.

BRECKEL, JILL, Social Studies Teacher; *b:* Utica, NY; *ed:* (BA) His/Scndry Ed, Elmira Coll 1969; (MAT) Soc Stud, Colgate Univ 1974; *cr:* Soc Stud Teacher Whitesboro Cntrl Sch 1969-; *ai:* Whitesboro Teachers Assn Schlsp Comm; Whitesboro Jr HS Flower & Gift Chair; Whitesboro Teachers Assn, NY St Unified Teachers 1969-; Morajian Church Adult Teacher, Altar Comm, Womens Fellowship, Stewardship, Evangelism for Shut Ins; Success of the Morajian Missions in Nicaragua & Honduras-Book Published by Church; Natl Sci Fnd Grant; Freedoms Fnd Grant; 1985 Outstanding Educator Rotary; Grant His Teacher Inst NY Cncl for Hum; *office:* Whitesboro Cntrl Sch 67 Whitesboro St Yorkville NY 13495

BREDAHL, ROGER D., 6th Grade Teacher/Asst Prin; *b:* Stanley, ND; *m:* Judy; *c:* Jeff, Jodi Bredahl Shorma; *ed:* Elem Stan Diploma, 1962, (BS) Elem Ed, 1970 Minot St Univ; (MS) Elem Ed, Univ of ND 1971; (MS) Rdng, E TX St Univ 1984; Doctorial Prgm E TX St Univ 1983-84; *cr:* 5th/6th Grade Teacher Roosevelt Sch 1962-64; 6th Grade Teacher N Hill Sch 1964-66; 6th Grade Teacher/Asst Prin Roosevelt Sch 1984-; *ai:* Bill Martin Jr Literacy Conference, Intnl Inst of Literacy Learning, Innovative NW Teachers Educl Consultant; Minot Ed Assn Pres 1964-65; Intnl Rdng Assn, Phi Delta Kappa, ND Ed Assn, NEA; Minot Jaycees Pres 1966-67, Outstanding Young Man 1967; PTA VP 1977-78, Life Membership 1978; E TX St Univ Doctorial Grad Teaching Asst 1983-84; Intnl Grad Research Fellowship 1970-71; Whos Who in Amer Ed 1989.

BREECE, CAROLYN MILLER, Mathematics Teacher; *b:* Waynesville, NC; *c:* Sara; *ed:* (BS) Ed, 1971, (MA) Ed, 1974 W Carolina Univ; *cr:* Math Teacher Bethel Jr HS 1971-; *ai:* Stu Cncl Adv; NEA, NCAE 1971-; *home:* 326 Howell St Waynesville NC 28786

BREED, FREDA ANNETTE, Director of Choral Music; *b:* Fort Worth, TX; *ed:* (BME) Vocal Music Ed, TX Chrstn Univ 1979; Grad Stud Choral Conducting, Westminster Choir Coll 1988-89; *cr:* Choral Dir/Gen Music Educator Handley Mid Sch 1982-87; Grapevine Mid Sch 1987-88; Choral Dir Grapevine HS 1988-; *ai:* Fine Arts Consultant Acad Decathlon Team; Curr Guide Dev; Textbook Comm; Choral Performances P corrd Sncdry Choral Act Grapevine-Colleyville Ind Sch Dist; TX Music Educators Assn 1987-; Assn of TX Prof Educators 1987-; TX Choral Dir Assn 1987-; Amer Choral Dir Assn 1987-; Church Music Assn of Amer 1987-; Dallas Symphony Chorus Mem 1989-; St Lukes Cath Cmmty Choir Mem 1989-; Holy Family Cath Church Choir Dir 1987-89; Choral Clinican/Adjudicator for Various Cmmty & Sch Organizations 1987-; *office:* Grapevine H S 3223 Mustang Dr Grapevine TX 76051

BREEDING, CAROLL KENNEDY, Sixth Grade Teacher; *b:* Welch, WV; *m:* Sam Leon; *ed:* (BS) Elem Ed, Bluefield St 1976; *cr:* Teachers Aide 1968-76, Teacher 1976-77 Bradshaw Elem; Teacher Jolo Elem 1977-; *ai:* Sch Newspaper & Spelling Bee Spon; Sch Advisory Comm Pres; NEA 1976-; WVEA 1968-; PTA (Treas 1989-) 1977-; Outstanding Young Women of Amer 1983; Nom Teacher of Yr; *home:* Box 146 Jolo WV 24850

BREEDLOVE, JANE MARTIN, 7th/8th Grade Lang Art Teacher; *b:* Coshocton, OH; *m:* Roger D.; *c:* Nicole E.; *ed:* (BA) Engl - Summa Cum Laude, IN Wesleyan Univ 1968; (MA) Eng, Ball St Univ 1971; *cr:* 7th Grade Teacher Eng East Sch 1968-69; Eng Teacher Mississinewa HS 1970; Literature Teachers East Sch 1971-77; 8th Grade Lang Arts Teacher Jr Basket T Mid Sch 1978-; *ai:* Coaching Stu for Spelling Bee; Spons RJB Spelling Bee; Grant Cty Spelling Bee Winners 1986 & 1988; Mississinewa Teachers Assn 1972-76; Natl Ed Assn 1968-; in St Teachers Assn 1968-; Feature Article in Local Newspaper.

BREEDLOVE, PAMELA S. (GILBERT), 4th Grade Teacher; *b:* Springfield, MO; *c:* Lisa, Christy, Darren; *ed:* (BS) Elem Ed, S MO St Univ Springfield 1967; Grad Stud S MO St Univ & Drury; *cr:* 2nd Grad Teacher Hartville Elem 1967-70; Teacher Strafford Elem 1971-; *ai:* Young Authors Spon; Strafford NEA Pres 1988-; IRA; *office:* Strafford R-6 Schls Box 97 Strafford MO 65757

BREEN, GARY R., Seventh Grade Teacher; *b:* Canton, OH; *c:* David R., Danielle L.; *ed:* (BS) Elem Ed, Malone Coll 1969; (MS) Elem Ed, Univ of Akron 1973; *cr:* 6th Grade Teacher Warstler Elem 1969-75, Edgefield Elem 1975-77, Day Elem 1977-79; 7th-8th Grade Teacher Taft Mid Sch 1979-; *ai:* Martha Holden Jennings Scholar 1984; *office:* Taft Mid Sch 3829 Guilford NW Canton OH 44718

BREGE, KAREN ELIZABETH, Fifth Grade Teacher; *b:* Geneva, NY; *ed:* (BS) Elem Ed, St Univ Coll Geneseo 1965; (MS) Ed, St Univ Coll Buffalo 1967; Supvr Courses, St Univ Coll Buffalo; *cr:* 5th Grade Teacher Kenmore Public Schls & Alexander Hamilton Sch 1965-; *ai:* Poetry-Prose Chm; Delta Kappa Gamma 1979-; Albright-Knox Art Gallery 1975-; PTA Rep; First Place W NY United Against Drug Abuse; *office:* Kenmore Public Schls 1500 Colvin Blvd Kenmore NY 14217

BREHMER, STEVEN LESTER, Physics Teacher; *m:* Linda M. Yeager; *c:* Sarah, David; *ed:* (BS) Physics, Mankato St Univ 1974; Working Towards Masters; NASA Trng; *cr:* Chem/Physics Teacher Wanamingo Public Sch 1976-88; Physics Teacher

Rochester Public Sch 1988-; *ai:* Sci Challenge Team; MSTA, NSTA; MEA, NEA Local Pres; City of Wanamingo City Cncl 1984-; Democrates St Delegate 1988, 1990; MN Energy Mini Grants; Honeywell Soviet Exch; People to People Space Camp Chaperone; Teacher in Space MN Rep; Congressional Intern; *office:* Mayo HS 1420 SE 11th Rochester MN 55904

BREIDERT, DENNIS DEAN, Teacher, Athletic Dir; *b:* Lake City, IA; *m:* Kathleen Gail Sohn; *c:* Jason, Angela; *ed:* (BS) Ed/Sci, Concordia Teachers Coll 1970; (MS) Ed, Univ of CO Boulder 1975; Grad Stud for Re-Cert; *cr:* Teacher/Athletic Dir 1970-, Asst Prin 1985- Bethlehem Luth Schl; *ai:* Boys Soccer & Bsktbl, Boys & Girls Track Coach; Head of Sci Dept; Fellowship Chrstn Athletes 1985-; Rocky Mountain Teachers Conference VP 1981-82; Denver Luth HS Sch Bd 1980-83; Bethlehem Luth Church Secy 1977-79; *office:* Bethlehem Luth Sch 7470 W 22nd Ave Lakewood CO 80215

BREITHAUPT, KEITH ALTON, Mathematics Dept Chairman; *b:* Oneida, NY; *m:* Wendy T.; *ed:* (BA) Bus Admin, 1964, (MBA) Bus Admin, 1966, (MAT) Math Ed, 1966 Rollins Coll; *cr:* Math Teacher 1966-, Dept Chm 1968- De Laura Jr HS; *ai:* Golf Coach; Math Dept & Site Comm Chm De Laura Jr HS; Co-Chm Cty Math Tournaments; FCTM Bd of Dirs 1966-; BCTM (Pres, VP) 1966-; NCTM 1966-; FL Presidential Awd Finalist 1988; FL Assoc Master Teacher Awd 1984; Brevard Cty & FL Finalist Teacher of Yr 1981; *office:* De Laura Jr HS 300 Jackson Ave Satellite Beach FL 32937

BRELAND, EARLENE MC CULLUM, English/French Teacher; *b:* Hinds, MS; *m:* Charles Edward; *c:* Kenneth A., Alphonso B.; *ed:* (BS) Lang Art, 1967, (MET) Eng, 1975 Jackson St Univ; Cmptr Literacy, Darkroom Dev, Fr; *cr:* Teacher Tougaloa Coll Upward Bound 1977-78, Pelahatchie HS 1967-, Brandon HS 1979-; *ai:* Yrbk Adv; Sr Class, Fr Club, Former Pep Club Spon; Head of Fr Dept; MS Assn of Ed, NEA 1967-90; Whos Who Among Outstanding Young Women of America; *office:* Pelahatchie HS P O Box 569 Pelahatchie MS 39145

BRELAND, JOHN O., History Teacher; *b:* Montpelier, MS; *m:* Jane Morgan; *c:* John Jr., Lisa, Stephen; *ed:* (BSE) Soc Sci, Delta St Univ 1959; (MED) Phys Ed, MS St Univ 1970; His, Ole MS; *cr:* Teacher/Coach Mantachie HS 1966-70, Pine Grove HS 1970-72, Ripley Mid Sch 1972-; *ai:* Ftbl Coach Ripley Mid Sch.

BRELAND, LARRY EUGENE, 5th Grade Teacher; *m:* Brenda; *c:* Larry E. II, Larenda E., Lorenzo E.; *ed:* (BA) Geography/His, 1966-70, (MS) Elem Ed/Early Chldhd Ed, 1970-72, Specialist Elem Ed/Admin/Supervision, 1972-76 Jackson St Univ; *cr:* 5th Grade Teacher 1972-77, 5th Grade Teacher/Asst Prin 1977-84, 5th Grade Teacher 1984-87 Nicholson Elem Sch; 5th Grade Teacher East Side Main 1987-88, Nicholson Elem Sch 1988-; *ai:* MS Educl Television Instructional TV Advisory Comm, Rep; MS Assn of Educators (Delegate, Bd of Dir) Mem of Yr 1985; Picayne Assn of Educators (Pres 1985-86, 1988-89, Faculty Rep); Jackson St Univ Alumni Assn; NEA Delegate 1986-88; Phi Beta Sigma; Pleasant Valley Baptist Church (Sunday Sch Teacher, Trustee, Comm Mem, Secy), Outstanding Cmmty Service 1982; BSA Troop #480; Nicholson Elem PTA Life Membership 1990, Outstanding Mem 1982; Natl Assn Advancement of Colored People; Teacher of Term Certificate of Awd 1988; Staff Dev Certificate of Awd 1985-86; Horace Mann Awd 1985; Inst in Cmmty Leadership Certificate 1979; Inst Dev of Cmmty Leadership Certificate of Recognition 1978; Certificate of Recognition Outstanding Service Building Rep 1978; Classroom Teachers Certificate of Service 1976.

BRELJE, SANDRA G., 3rd Grade Teacher; *b:* Springfield, MN; *m:* Allen; *c:* Travis, Timothy; *ed:* (BS) Elem Ed, MN St Univ 1969; Grad Stud; *cr:* Elem Teacher Winthrop Sch Dist 735 1969-; *ai:* Sci Comm; NEA, MEA, Winthrop Ed Assn (Secy, Treas); VFW Ladies Auxiliary; *home:* RR 1 Box 72 Glencoe MN 55336

BREMER, CHERYL BOWERS, 4th Grade Teacher; *b:* Great Falls, MT; *m:* Harvey L.; *c:* Kristin, Kimberly; *ed:* (BA) Elem Ed, Fr, Rocky Mountain Coll 1966; Elem Ed; *cr:* 4th Grade Teacher Englewood Sch 1966-67; Meadowlark 1967-72; 2nd/3rd Grade Teacher 1973-; 4th Grade Teacher 1990 Fairfield Elem; *ai:* Fairfield HS Pep Club Adv; Chrldg Coach/Adv; MT HS Assn; Chrldr Adv Comm; Delta Kappa Gamma Socty 1985-; Alpha Mu St 1985-; Alpha Gamma Chapter Chm Prof Affairs Comm 1985-; *home:* PO Box 181 Fairfield MT 59436

BREMER, JANIS KNIPMEYER, English Teacher; *b:* Coffeeville, KS; *m:* Marc Lynn; *c:* Marcilyn, Jelaine; *ed:* (BSE) Eng, Ouachita Baptist Univ 1980; PET Trng Inst in Basic Youth Conflicts; TESA Trng Intensive Instructional Supervision; *cr:* Teacher Little Rock Chrstn Schls 1982-83, Abundant Life Schls 1983-86, AR Baptist Sch System 1986-87, Northwood Jr HS 1987-88, Jessieville HS 1988-; *ai:* Beta Club Spon; Expression Ministries (Bd of Dirs, Secy) 1980-; Permanent Casting Incorporated Bd of Dirs 1984-; Rebuilders Incorporated Bd of Dirs 1990; *home:* 113 Parkview Dr Hot Springs AR 71901

BRENNAN, DAVID W., Dir of Dev/Alumni; *b:* Philadelphia, PA; *m:* Deborah Ann Reardon; *c:* David, Ryan, Caitlin; *ed:* (BA) Eng, St Josephs Univ 1975; Level I Trng Project Impact, Cath Sch Management Dev Prgm; Working Towards Masters in Ed, St Josephs Univ; *cr:* Eng Teacher Bishop Kenrick HS 1978-82; Eng Teacher 1982-87, Eng Dept Chm 1987-88, Dir of Dev 1988- Cardinal Dougherty HS; *ai:* Alumni Act & Dramatics Dir Bishop Conwell HS; CASE Mem 1988-; NCEA Mem 1976-; ASCD Mem 1987-; *office:* Cardinal Dougherty HS 2nd St Above Godfrey Ave Philadelphia PA 19120

BRENNAN, DEBORAH ANN, Phys Ed & Health Teacher; *b:* Farmington, MN; *ed:* (BS) Health/Phys Ed, Winona St Univ 1980; Develop Mental Adaptive Phys Ed; Drivers Ed; Coaching Cert; *cr:* K-10th Grade Phys Ed/Health Teacher Ogilvie Public Sch 1981-; *ai:* Vlybl, Boys & Girls Track Head Coach; Jr HS Girls Bsktbl Coach; Ogilvie Ed Assn Treas 1989-; MN Ed Assn, MN Girls Coaching Assn 1981-; City Zoning Commission Mem 1989-; St Kathyrns Womens Guild 1987-; *office:* Ogilvie Public Sch Box 160 Ogilvie MN 56358

BRENNAN, KATHRYN ALTIZER, Science/Social Studies Teacher; *b:* Riner, VA; *m:* Gerald F. Sr.;; *c:* Shannon B. Sheffield, Gerald F. Jr., Kelly S.; Brien B.; *ed:* (AB) Sociology, Univ NC ChapelHill 1950; (MA) Teaching Soc Stud, Teachers Coll Columbia 1953; *cr:* 4th Grade Teacher Christiansburg Primary 1950-52, Boulder Creek Elem 1953-54, Narimasu Elem 1954-55, Harmon USAF 1955-57; 2nd Grade Teacher Belview Elem 1957-58; 5th Grade Teacher Yigo Elem 1970-72; 6th-7th Grade Teacher Sci/Soc Stud Auburn Mid 1972-; *ai:* Pep Club; Mid Sch Chlrdr; Archeology Ecology Club; Soc Stud Academic Coach; Report Card Comm; Sci Curr; Montgomery Cty Ed Assn, VA Ed Assn, NEA 1972-; NSTA 1980-; Auburn Boosters Memership Chm 1978-; Sandlut Ftbl Chrldr Spon 1979-; Trophy 1987; Montgomery Cty Improvement Cncl 1986-; Mental Health Awd 1988; Channel 7 TV Hometown Hero 1990; Cty Nomination Teacher of Yr 1987; VA Ecology Awd 1986; *home:* Rt 3 Box 16 Riner VA 24149

BRENNAN, NEIL, Computer Science/Math Teacher; *b:* Queens, NY; *m:* Margaret Delaney; *ed:* (BA) Math, St Johns Univ 1969; (MA) Liberal Stud, St Univ of NY Stonybrook 1973; (AAS) Cmptr Sci, Suffolk Comm Coll 1984; *cr:* Cmptr Sci Teacher Suffolk Comm Coll 1986-87; Cmptr Sci/Math Teacher 1969-, Cmptr Assisted Instruction Coord 1987- Kings Park HS; *ai:* Cmptr Club Adv; Developed & Taught Teachers Inservice Trng; Dist Cmptr Organization Comm; Suffolk Cty Math Teachers Assn 1983-; Parent Faculty Organization 1969-; *office:* Kings Park HS Rt 25A Kings Park NY 11754

BRENNAN, THOMAS G., Science Teacher; *b:* Boston, MA; *m:* Patricia A. Sayce; *ed:* (BA) Eng, St Anselm Coll 1967; Sci, Bridgewater St Coll; *cr:* Teacher/Coach Randolph HS 1967-; *ai:* Ftbl Coach Randolph HS; Intramural Bsktbl Prgm Dir; NEA, MA Teachers Assn, Randolph Teachers Assn, Sci Teachers Assn; St Anselm Coll Pres 1985-86; Natl Sci Fnd Grants; *office:* Randolph HS Memorial Dr Randolph MA 02368

BRENNER, GWEN APPLEGATE, English Teacher; *b:* Murphysboro, IL; *m:* John H.; *c:* Daniel, Philip; *ed:* (BA) Journalism, S IL Univ 1954; (MA) Linguistics, NE IL Univ 1972; *cr:* Eng Teacher Chicago Public Schls 1975-84, Ft Pierce Cntrl HS 1984-; *ai:* NHS Spon; Academic Team & Linguistics Team Coach; Spelling Bee Spon; Congressional Awd Comm; Articles Published in Newspaper Recipient of Excellency in Teaching Awd by MAPCO Corp; *office:* Ft Pierce Cntrl HS 1101 Edwards Rd Fort Pierce FL 34982

BRENNER, JOEL H., Physics Teacher; *b:* New York, NY; *ed:* (BS) Mechanical Engineering, Cooper Union 1967; (MS) Aero Engineering Princeton Univ 1969; (MS) Ed Admin & Supervision, St Johns Univ 1977; *cr:* Physics Teacher South Shore HS 1972-; *ai:* Woodrow Wilson Physics Wkshps 1987-89; *office:* South Shore HS 6565 Flatlands Ave Brooklyn NY 11236

BRENT, DENNIS MICHAEL, English Teacher; *b:* Youngstown, OH; *m:* Denise Marovich; *c:* Emily A.; *ed:* (BA) Eng, San Jose St Coll 1969; (MS) Spec Ed, CA Luth Coll 1980; *cr:* Eng Teacher Duarte HS 1972-74, Jordan HS 1974-75, Long Beach Sch for Adults 1975-77; Ward Instr Univ of S CA Medical Center 1975-76; Elem Teacher Pacific Boulevard Sch 1976-77; Spec Ed Teacher Columbus Tustin Jr HS 1977-78, Faye Ross Jr HS 1978-84; Eng Teacher Whitney HS 1984-; *ai:* Sch Newspaper, NHS, Builders Club Adv; Sch Success Team Coord; Pi Kappa Alpha Chapter Adv 1987-; Distinguished Faculty Awd; Article Published; *office:* Whitney HS 16800 Shoemaker Ave Cerritos CA 90701

BRENTZEL, MARYLNN HOPKIN, 5th Grade Teacher; *b:* Columbus, NE; *m:* Richard E.; *c:* Pamela J., Vicki L. Beene; *ed:* (BS) Ed, Univ of Omaha NE 1980; Ed, Wayne St Coll 1981-83; *cr:* K-8th Grade Teacher Dist 23 Platte Cty 1956-57; Handicapped Teacher Arc Columbus Opportunity Center 1962-63; 3rd/4th Grade Teacher Dist 93 Dodge Cty 1980-85; 5th Grade Teacher Liberty Chrstn Sch 1987-88; *ai:* Epsilon Sigma Alpha Treas 1969-75, The 1st Pearl 1970, 1st Deg Palbs Athene 1972; Mental Health Assn Chairperson 1974, Successful Campaign 1974; 1st Congregational Church Bd Trustee 1975-77; Parents Dist 93 Cert of Appreciation Providing Sense Personal Pride & Accomplishment Each Stu for Work Well Done 1982.

BREON, TISANA MARIA, 6th Grade English Teacher; *b:* Lock Haven, PA; *ed:* (BA) Eng, Penn St Univ 1968; (MLS) Lib Sci, Univ of Pittsburgh 1972; *cr:* Eng Teacher Shrub Oak Mid Sch 1968-69; Librarian Clairton Jr HS 1969-70; Eng Teacher Canonsburg Mid Sch 1970-; *ai:* Newspaper Spon; Beta Phi Mu Lib Honors Society; *office:* Canonsburg Mid Sch 25 E College St Canonsburg PA 15317

BRERETON, GERARD A., Spanish Teacher; *b:* Manhattan, NY; *ed:* (BA) Span, Marist Coll 1963; (MA) Span Lit, Loyola Univ 1970; Religious Stud Rome Italy, Fribourg Switzerland 1973; *cr:* Span Teacher Marist HS 1963-72, 1974-83; Eng Teacher Marist Bros Intnl Sch 1983-86; Span Teacher Marist HS 1986-; *ai:* Marist HS Alumni Assn; Amer Assn Teachers of Span & Portuguese 1960-79, 1987-, Schlsp Univ of Madrid 1966; Eng Instr Escuela Normal Superior 1971-72; ESL Teacher Marist Brothers Canidates Seoul 1985-88; *home:* 4200 W 115th St Chicago IL 60655

BRESHEARS, JOAN REED, English Teacher; *b:* Mt Pleasant, MI; *m:* Kenneth Argene; *c:* Jean A. Breshears-Fisher; *ed:* (BS) Scndy Ed/Eng/Soc Stud, 1978, (MS) Curr/Instruction, 1981 OK St Univ; *cr:* Classroom/Eng/Soc Stud Teacher Perry HS 1978-; Eng Instr N OK Coll 1988-; *ai:* Chm Steering Comm N Cntrl Evaluation; NHS Adv; Jr Class Spon; OK Ed Assn, NEA 1979-; Christ Luth Church (Mem, Schlsp Comm); Perry Golf & Cntry Club; Chm Amer Red Cross Bloodmobile; Perry Ed Fnd Grant; *office:* Perry HS 900 Fir St Perry OK 73077

BRESLIN, PAMELA CONROY, Spanish Teacher; *b:* Scranton, PA; *m:* Andrew Jesse; *c:* Luke, Sam; *ed:* (BA) Eng, Wheaton Coll 1972; (MA) Span, Middlebury Coll 1990; *cr:* Faculty Teacher Windsor Mountain Sch 1972-74, Berkshire Chrstn Coll 1975-82, Miss Halls Sch 1982-; *ai:* Intnl Stus Adv; Teachers of Eng as Second Lang Academic Alliance; *office:* Riss Halls Sch Holmes Rd Pittsfield MA 01201

BRESSAN, ANTHONY MARK, History Teacher; *b:* Renton, WA; *m:* Linda Sue Klein; *cr:* Teacher St Anthonys Sch 1974-75, Evergreen HS 1975-76, Kalama Jr/Sr HS 1976-77, North Kitsap Mid & HS 1977-; *ai:* Jr HS Bsktbl Coach; Sr Homecoming, ASB, Jr Class Adv; NEA Rep 1978-79; Associated Stu Pres 1969-70; Ex-Official Mem Green River Comm Coll Bd of Trustees; Cntrl WA Univ Coll Faculty Senate Mem; *office:* North Kitsap HS 1780 NE Hostmark St Poulsbo WA 98370

BRESSERT, ROBERT T., 5th Grade Teacher; *b:* Lawrenceburg, IN; *m:* Amy Lynn; *ed:* (BS) Elem Ed, E KY Univ 1982; Working Toward Masters Elem Ed, Mt St Joseph; *cr:* 5th Grade Teacher Manchester Sch 1984-; *ai:* 7th Grade Boys & 8th Grade Girls Bsktbl Coach; *office:* Manchester Sch RR 2 Aurora IN 47001

BRETSCHNEIDER, FREDERICK EDWARD, Science Instructor; *b:* Chicago, IL; *m:* Maggie Irene Miller; *c:* Frederick, Elizabeth Fisher, Mary Head, Antoinette Parker, Marcus, Catherine Taylor; *ed:* (BA) Biological/Phys Sci - Cum Laude, 1950, (MA) Sch Admin, 1954 OH St Univ; Muskingum Coll, Juniata Coll, Kent St Univ, Adelphi Univ, Wittenburg Univ, Case Inst of Technology, OH St Univ, OH Univ, Rutgers; *cr:* Elem Teacher Sch Sixteen 1950-51; Bio Teacher Carrollton HS 1951-52, Cambridge HS 1952-65; Sci Teacher Chardon HS 1965-; *ai:* OH Acad of Sci Outstanding Teacher Awd 1961; OH Sch of Alcohol Stud Dean 1961; US Government Federal Parole Adv 1958-64; General Electric 1958, Atomic Energy Commission & Natl Sci Teachers 1959, PA Sch of Alcohol Studs 1960 Fellowships; *home:* 129 Chardon Ave Chardon OH 44024

BRETT, JUDITH HOUSEKEEPER, High School English Teacher; *b:* Louisville, KY; *m:* James Walter; *c:* Ruch Deemer, Tammy Deemer; *ed:* (BA) Eng, Univ of Mi 1966; (MAT) Eng Ed, 1967, (ABD) Eng Ed, 1972 Northwestern Univ; Worked on Northwestern Univ Project Eng Prgm Wrote Curr for Teaching Writing; *cr:* Eng Teacher Niles Township West HS 1967-76, Dulles HS 1979-82, Clements HS 1982-88, I H Kempner HS 1988-; *ai:* Academic Decathlon Coach; UIL Ready Writing Coach; Curr Writer Soph Honors Eng; Writer Advanced Placement Eng II Exam; NCTE; Soccer Team Mother 1982-88; NCTE Article Published; Teacher of Yr Houston Comm Coll 1979; Teacher of Month Kempner HS 1990; Wkshp Presenter NCTE Convention, Composition Convention 1975; *home:* 6006 Valkeith Houston TX 77096

BRETZ, ROSEMARY SPARKS, Second Grade Teacher; *b:* Chillicothe, MO; *m:* James Russel; *c:* Gretchen E.; *ed:* (BSE) Elem, 1970, (MSE) Learning Disabilities, 1977 Cntrl MO St Univ; Grad Stud Univ of MO Kansas City, CMSU, AVILA, Learning Exch; *cr:* Teacher Tots-A-Time Day Nursery & Kndgtn 1967-68; 1st/2nd/4th Grade Teacher Ft Osage Schls 1968-73; Teacher of Learning Disabilities/1st/2nd Grade Teacher James Lewis Elem 1973-; *ai:* Just Say No Co-Spon; Peer-Coaching With Teachers; Grade Level Membership Comm; MO St Teachers Assn (Delegate, Membership Comm) 1970-; Cmmty Ed Assn Membership Comm 1970-; Phi Delta Kappa, Delta Kappa Gamma 1985-; PEO Chapter KN (1st VP 1990, Mem 1973); PTA James Lewis 2nd VP 1989-; Blue Springs R-IV & St of MO Outstanding Young Educator 1977; Blue Springs Outstanding Citizen Nominee 1988; *office:* James Lewis Elem Sch 717 Park Rd Blue Springs MO 64015

BRETZ, WILLIAM FRANKLIN, Social Science Dept Chairman; *b:* Urbana, IL; *ed:* (AA) His/Government, Springfield Coll IL 1957; (BA) His/Government, IL Coll 1959; (MA) His, Georgetown Univ 1972; Project Top IL St Bd of Ed Title IV C-ESEA/Teacher; Laval Univ-Quebec City Summer Inst-Fr Culture; Georgetown Univ Grad Study/Research; *cr:* His Teacher Lanphier HS 1964-77; Soc Sci Teacher Feitshans Grade Center Project Top 1978-79; His Teacher/Chm Franklin Mid Sch 1979-; *ai:* Center for Fr Colonial Stud in IL Charter Mem; IL Assn for the Advancement of His Mem; NEA; IL Ed Assn; SpringField Ed Assn Mem; IL Historic Preservation Agency-Site Interpreter-Lincolns Tomb 1988-; Chief Senate Page IL General Assembly 1957-63; Univ Scholar Georgetown Univ-Dept of His 1959-60; Lyndon B Johnson Teacher-Intern U S Congress 1975; *office:* Benjamin Franklin Mid Sch 1200 Outer Park Dr Springfield IL 62704

BRETZ, WILLIAM THOMAS, 6th Grade Soc Stud/Team Leader; *b:* Cincinnati, OH; *m:* Karen Brandenburg; *ed:* (AA) Elem Ed, Univ of Cincinnati 1970; (BA) Geography, Morehead St Univ 1972; Working Towards Masters Comm Arts, Xavier Univ; *cr:*

World Geography/His Teacher Franklin HS 1972-73; 8th Grade His Teacher 1974, 7th Grade Soc Stud Teacher 1977-88 Norwood Jr HS; 6th Grade Soc Stud Teacher Norwood Mid Sch 1988-; *ai:* Team Leader 6 Blue Cluster; Track & Field & Cross Cntry Jr HS Level 1976-84, Var Girls Track 1985-89, Reserve Cross Cntry Coach 1985; Norwood Teachers Assn, OH Ed Assn, NEA 1974-; Video Tapes for Sch Purposes Over the Last Few Yrs; HS Sports Events & Shows for Cable Television & Produce Cable News Show Done by 6th Grade Stus; *office:* Norwood Mid Sch 2060 Sherman Ave Norwood OH 45212

BRETZEL, MILTON JAMES, Mathematics/Computer Teacher; *b:* Milwaukee, WI; *m:* Janis Mary Kaminski; *c:* Nicholas, Kate, Michelle, Kristin; *ed:* (BSE) Math, Univ of WI Whitewater 1972; (MSE) Curr/Instruction, Univ of WI Milwaukee 1987; *cr:* Teacher St Francis HS 1972-; *ai:* Yrbk Adv; NEA, WEA 1972-; WI Math Cncl 1988-; WI Assn Prof Engr Teacher of Yr 1989; *office:* Saint Francis HS 4225 S Lake Dr Saint Francis WI 53207

BREWBAKER, MINNIE HENDERSON, Third Grade Teacher; *b:* Roanoke, VA; *m:* Sidney E.; *c:* Jacob, Nathan; *ed:* (BS) Spec Ed/Elem Ed, James Madison Univ 1972; *cr:* 5th Grade Teacher Chuckatuck Elem 1972-73; 2nd Grade Teacher Belview Elem 1975-79; 3rd/4th Grade Teacher Gilbert Linkous Elem 1980-; *ai:* Steering Comm for Selt Study Mem; Cty Wide Sch Calender Comm; Montgomery Cty Ed Assn (Pres 1988-89, Sch Rep) 1975-; *office:* Gilbert Linkous Elem Sch Toms Creek Rd Blacksburg VA 24060

BREWER, ANN BUSH, Teacher; *b:* Macon, MS; *m:* John Samuel; *c:* Terrence; *ed:* (BS) Bus Ed, Rust Coll; (MA) Ed, Natl Coll; *cr:* Teacher Washington Sch 1970-; *ai:* Chrldr Coach; *office:* Washington Elem Sch 1111 Washington Blvd Maywood IL 60153

BREWER, CAROLYN GROOVER, Third Grade Teacher; *b:* Chattanooga, TN; *m:* Donald L.; *c:* Brian, Beth; *ed:* (BS) Home Ec, Univ of TN 1961; *cr:* 3rd Grade Teacher Briarlake Elem 1961-62; 1st Grade Teacher Winder Elem Sch 1963-65, Gainesville Elem Sch 1966-67; 3rd Grade Teacher Atkinson Sch 1975-; *office:* Atkinson Sch 2510 Old Kanuga Rd Hendersonville NC 28739

BREWER, FERN SMALLWOOD, Fourth Grade Teacher; *b:* Stanton, KY; *m:* John Breckenridge; *c:* Charlotte F. Estes, John C., Arnetia J. Jolly; *ed:* (BS) Elem Ed, 1974, (Rank II) Elem Ed, 1979, (Rank I) Elem Ed, 1980 E KY Univ; Kndgtn Cert 1974; Basic Skills 1979; Contemporary Art; Project Write 1987-88; St Dept of Ed TESA Wkshp 1989-; *cr:* Teacher Headstart 1966-74; 4th Grade Teacher Stanton Elem 1974-; Teacher Adult Basic Ed 1974-; *ai:* 4-H Leader; St Advisory for Exceptional Children 1985-89; Powell Cty Teachers Assn & KEA Mem 1974-; Order of KY Colonels St of KY Mem; Stanton Baptist Church Sunday Sch Teacher; Order of Eastern Star Pilot Knob Chapter 359; PTA Mem; *office:* Stanton Elem Sch PO Box 367 Breckinridge St Stanton KY 40380

BREWER, GILBERT LEE, JR., Math/Science/Cmptr Sci Teacher; *b:* Corry, PA; *m:* Tammy Sue Smith; *c:* Samuel L.; *ed:* (BA) Hum, Bob Jones Univ 1986; *cr:* Math/Sci/Cmptr Sci Teacher Grace Acad 1986-; *ai:* Cmptr Programming Teacher; *office:* Grace Acad 530 N Locust St Hagerstown MD 21740

BREWER, JOHN WILLIAM, 7th Grade Science Teacher; *b:* Chicago, IL; *m:* Mary L. Stevens; *c:* John, Erique, Jacquie Walbridge, Michelle Paradis, Elizabeth Slain; *ed:* (BS) Geology, Northwestern Univ 1950; (MS) Elem Ed, IN Univ 1970; Coop Learning; US EPA Ground Water Protection; *cr:* Sales Dodge Mfg Co 1950-62; Sci Teacher Warren Sch 1962-75; Jackson Mid Sch 1975-; *ai:* Bldg Comm; Stu Adv Team Spon; NEA 1984-; AFT; Syracuse Lions Club (VP 1974-75 Pres 1975-76 Lion Tamer 1987-); In Env Mgmt Bd; Adv Comm; Turkey Creek Twp Bd Zoning Appeals; Adv Comm Turkey Creek Twp Regional Sewer Bd; *office:* Andrew Jackson Mid Sch 5001 S Miami St South Bend IN 46614

BREWER, MARILYN JUANICE, Language Arts Teacher; *b:* Overland Park, KS; *m:* Ronald G.; *ed:* (BA) Ed, Univ of MO Kansas City 1969; (MS) Ed, Emporia St Univ 1985; Advanced Trng & Wkshp Beyond Masters; *cr:* Eng/Soc Stud Teacher 1969-85, HS Teacher 1986- Shawnee Mission West; *ai:* NEA, KNEA, NCTE; Local PTA Teacher of Yr 1984; *office:* Shawnee Mission West HS 8800 W 85th Overland Park KS 66212

BREWER, MARK RICHARD, Social Studies Teacher; *b:* Worcester, MA; *m:* Laurie Facciarossa; *c:* Nicholas; *ed:* (BA) Scndry Ed, Glassboro St Coll 1984; US His, Temple Univ; *cr:* Teacher Oak Knoll Mid Sch 1984-; *ai:* Boys Bsktbl Coach Oak Knoll Mid Sch; Drama Dir Oak Knoll Mid Sch; Governors Teacher Recognition Prgm Teacher of Yr 1988; 4th TX Cty B Civil War Reenactment (Private, Company Clerk) 1983-; Articles Published; *office:* Oak Knoll Mid Sch 23 Bodine Ave Williamstown NJ 08094

BREWERTON, ELIZABETH WELLS, English & Spanish Teacher; *b:* Greenwood, MS; *ed:* (BA) Eng, MS Univ for Women 1972; (MA) Eng, E KY Univ 1977; Master of Art, Degree in Eng, E KY Univ 1977; *cr:* Eng Teacher Amory HS 1972-76; Grad Asst E KY Univ 1976-77; Eng/Span Teacher Monticello HS 1977-; Eng Instr Univ of KY 1979-; *ai:* Jr & Sr Class, Span Club, NHS Spon; Monticello Ed Assn, KY Ed Assn, NEA 1977-; Outstanding Service Awd Campbellsville Coll 1987; *office:* Monticello HS 135 Cave St Monticello KY 42633

BREWKA, NATTALIE LAKOS, Junior High Teacher; *b:* Cleveland, OH; *m:* Myron L.; *c:* Nicholas, Michael; *ed:* (BA) Elem Ed, AZ St Univ 1979; Elem Ed, St John Coll; *cr:* 4th-8th Grade Teacher St Josaphats Sch 1957-63; 4th-5th Grade Teacher Most Holy Trinity 1975-77; 4th Grade Teacher 1979-82, Jr HS Teacher 1984- Our Lady of Perpetual Help; *ai:* Speech Coach; Spelling Bee Coord; Yrbk Adv; Sch Newspaper; ASCD, NCEA; Kappa Delta Pi; Masters Catechists Religion Awd; AZ St Univ Coll of Ed Scholastic Excl Awd 1978-79; *office:* Our Lady of Perpetual Help Sch 7521 N 57th Ave Glendale AZ 85301

BREWSTER, DIANE LAYLAND, 5th Grade Teacher; *b:* Warsaw, NY; *m:* Gary L.; *c:* Linda Brewster Docking, Tammy L.; *ed:* (BA) Elem Ed, St Univ Geneseo 1964; *cr:* 5th Grade Teacher Canandaigua Schls 1964-65, Heim Mid Sch 1965-66, Caledonia-Mumford Cntrl Sch 1966-; *ai:* Genesee Cty Girls Church Sftbl League Team Coach; Caledonia-Mumford Teachers Assn 1966-; *office:* Caledonia-Mumford Cntrl Sch 99 North St Caledonia NY 14423

BREWSTER, JERRY HILTON, 8th Grade Amer His Teacher; *b:* Brookeland, TX; *m:* Maggie Ellen Shepherd; *c:* Azalee J. Brewster Moore, Lynda M. Brewster Laird, Patricia L. Brewster Greer, Michael L.; *ed:* (BS) Scndry Ed, Lamar Univ 1964; *cr:* Jr/Sr HS Teacher Chester Jr HS 1964; Coach/Teacher 1964-66, 8th Grade His Teacher 1966- Martin Jr HS; *ai:* Jr HS UIL Dir & Coach; 7th/8thGrade Poetry UIL Coach; 7th/8th Grade Calculator; Yrbk Adv; Coord Washington DC trip; Chm Sch Climate Comm for Campus Improvement;Stu Cncl Adv 1979-81; 1 Act Play Dir 1987; Honor Society Adv 1981-83; Prose Spon 1982-84; Natl Assn of Stu Activity Adv 1987-; TX Classroom Teachers Assn 1985-; TX St Teachers Assn 1965-85; Kirbyville Little League (Bd of Dir, Secy 1966-69, VP 1971-73, Girls Sftbl VP); Sr League 1981; S Rural Water Secy 1988-; Call Junction Baptist Church (Sunday Sch Dir 1972-73, Royal Ambassador Dir 1966-76); Kirbyville 1st Baptist Church (Youth Dir 1970-80, Royal Ambassador Dir 1976-81); TX Math & Sci Coaches Assn St Contest Dir 1988-89; Royal Ambassador Assn (Sabine Valley Secy 1977-80, Regional Secy 1978); *office:* Kirbyville Jr HS 2200 S Margaret St Kirbyville TX 75956

BREWSTER, LILLIE GRENWELGE, Fourth/Fifth Grade Teacher; *b:* Winters, TX; *m:* John E.; *c:* Carol, Matthew; *ed:* (BS) Math, Univ Cntrl AR 1969; Math, Eng & Elem Cert, Univ of AR/West AR Jr Coll/Univ of Ozarks/ AR Tech Univ; *cr:* 7th Grade Teacher Miller Jr HS 1969-76; Various Assignments Elem/ Mid Sch/HS 1977-87; 4th/5th Grade Teacher Scranton Upper Elem 1987-; *ai:* AEA 1969-72; Extension Homemakers Reporter 1986-; *office:* Scranton Upper Elem Sch PO Box 86 Scranton AR 72863

BREY, EILEEN, 1st Grade Teacher; *b:* Callicoon, NY; *m:* Warren A.; *c:* Stephanie, Jill; *ed:* (BA) Ger, Houghton Coll 1963; Cert at Oneonta SUNY; Orange Cty Comm Coll Span I & II; *cr:* 5th Grade Teacher Iroquois Cntrl Sch 1963-64, Eldred Cntrl Sch 1964-66; 4th Grade Teacher 1966-67, 5th Grade Teacher Jeffersonville-Youngsville Cntrl 1968-72; 1st/3rd-5th Grade Teacher 1973-; *ai:* Alpha Delta Kappa (Pres 1974-76, VP, Corresponding Secy, Recording Secy 1976-); Meth Church (Organist 1982-, Sunday Sch Teacher 1964-82, Treas of Parsonage Fund 1982-); *office:* Jeffersonville-Youngsville Cen Box 308 Schoolhouse Rd Jeffersonville NY 12748

BRICE, SALLY GOODRIDGE, Fourth Grade Teacher; *b:* Robstown, TX; *c:* Brande Brice Lowry, Blake; *ed:* (BS) Elem Ed, TX A&I Univ 1965; *cr:* 1st Grade Teacher Calallen Ind Sch Dist 1965-66; 2nd Grade Teacher Freeport/Brazosport Ind Sch Dist 1966-68; 3rd Grade Teacher Tuloso Midway Ind Sch Dist 1970-79; 4th Grade Teacher North East Ind Sch Dist 1979-; *ai:* Grade Level Chm; NETA & Faculty Rep; TX St Teachers Assn 1965-; North East Teachers Assn 1979-; NEA 1965-; PTA (Newsletter Ed 1987-88) 1965-; *home:* 2650 Thousand Oaks #701 San Antonio TX 78232

BRICKER, PATSY SMITH, English Teacher; *b:* Bright Star, AR; *m:* Billy G.; *c:* Chip; *ed:* (BS) Elem Ed, 1955, (MED) Elem Ed/Eng, 1959 E TX St Univ; Advanced Academic Trng; *cr:* Elem Eng Teacher Bright Star Ind Sch Dist 1954-57; Elem Teacher Campbell Ind Sch Dist 1957-59, Odessa Ind Sch Dist 1959-61; Eng Teacher Atlanta HS 1961-66; Elem Eng Teacher Bloomburg Ind Sch Dist 1966-; *ai:* Atlanta Stu Cncl Spon; Atlanta & Bloomburg Sr Class Plays Dir; Bloomburg Prom Dir; Interscholastic League Contests Sports Banquet & Homecoming Act; TX St Teachers Assn, NEA 1962-; Amer Assn of Univ Women 1954-; TX Joint Cncl Eng Teachers 1988-; Bloomburg Cntry Fair Comm, PTA; *home:* PO Box 162 Bloomburg TX 75556

BRICKHAUS, PATRICIA KAY, 7th Grade Math Teacher; *b:* Perryville, MO; *ed:* (BS) Math, 1976, (MAT) Math, 1986 SE MO St Univ; *cr:* Corrective Math Teacher 1977-78, 7th Grade Math Teacher 1978- Dexter Public Schls; *ai:* NCTM, MO Cncl Teachers of Math, SE MO Cncl Teachers of Math Wkshp Presenter; Cmmty Teachers Assn Building Rep; *office:* T S Hill Mid Sch Brown Pilot Ln Dexter MO 63841

BRIDDELL, DEBORAH AMBROSIA, Teacher of Visually Impaired; *b:* Dover, DE; *c:* Larry S. Jr.; *ed:* (BA) Spec Ed, Marywood Coll 1974; Human Resource Management; *cr:* Teacher of Visually Impaired Milford Sch Dist & Seaford Sch Dist; *ai:* Natl Fed of the Blind (St, Chapter Pres); Phi Delta Kappa; Order of Eastern Star Outstanding Achievement Awd 1984; *home:* 244 Greenblade Dr Dover DE 19901

BRIDGEMAN, JANE RAY, Fifth Grade Teacher; *b:* Clinton, SC; *c:* Brian, Darin; *ed:* (BS) Elem Ed, Winthrop Coll 1959; Working Towards Spec Ed Cert; *cr:* 1st Grade Teacher Leesville Elem Sch 1959-61; 7th/8th Grade Eng Teacher Clinton Jr HS 1963-66; Teacher of Phys Handicapped 1968-70, Lib/Media Services Teacher 1974-79 Whitten Center for Mentally Handicapped; 5th Grade Teacher M S Bailey ELem Sch 1979-; *office:* M S Bailey ELem Sch Elizabeth St Clinton SC 29325

BRIDGERS, LINDA BROTHERS, Advanced Placement Eng Teacher; *b:* Florence, SC; *m:* Emery Lee; *c:* Traci S.; *ed:* (BA) Eng, Furman Univ 1963; (MED) Admin/Scndry Ed, Clemson Univ 1976; Prgm for Effective Teaching; *cr:* Teacher R B Stall HS 1963-73, Edgewood Mid Sch 1973-75, Ninety Six HS 1975-; *ai:* Sr Class Adv; Sch & Dist Improvement Comm; Dist PREEM & Southern Assn Visiting Comm 1966, 1987; Delta Kappa Gamma VP 1988-89; Palmetto Teachers Assn; Greenwood Little Theater 1983-84; Teacher of Yr 1968-69; Star Teacher 1970, 1979, 1988; J C Boozer Teacher Awd 1977, 1979, 1987-89; *office:* Ninety Six HS Johnson Rd Ninety Six SC 29666

BRIDGES, DEBORAH JANE, 7th Grade Mathematics Teacher; *b:* Gary, IN; *m:* Stan; *c:* Natalie, Emilyjane; *ed:* (BS) Elem Ed, 1972, (MA) Ed, 1974, (MA) Admin/Supervision, Murray St Univ 1980; *cr:* 4th-5th Grade Teacher Arlington Elem Sch 1971; 6th-8th Grade Teacher Trigg Cty Mid Sch 1972-; *ai:* Mid Sch Stu Cncl Spon; KY Ed Assn 1971-; PTA; NEA; KY Sub-Comm Cmptr Cert 1985; *home:* 211 Indian Hill Trace Cadiz KY 42211

BRIDGES, JON PATRICK, Mathematics Dept Chair; *b:* Portland, OR; *ed:* (AM) Poly Sci, 1985, (AB) Ed, 1986 Stanford Univ; *cr:* Math Teacher W Linn HS 1986-88; Math Dept Chm Dayton Jr/Sr HS 1988-; *ai:* Hi-Q Team Coach; Citizen Bee, Model UN, Youth & Government, Jr Class, Prom Adv; Academic Testing Coord; OR Cncl of Teachers of Math 1986-; Phi Sigma Epsilon 1985-86; *office:* Dayton Jr-Sr HS 801 Ferry St Dayton OR 97114

BRIDGES, KAREN FORD, 5th Grade Teacher; *b:* Glasgow, KY; *ed:* (BS) Elem Ed, David Lipscomb Univ 1979; *cr:* 5th Grade Teacher Hickmann Cty Mid Sch 1979-; *ai:* Chairperson Easter Seal Spell-A-Thon; Directing Plays & Writing a Prgm Presented By 5th Graders; NEA 1979-; TEA 1979-; HCEA 1979-; *office:* Hickman County Mid Sch 1639 Bulldog Blvd Centerville TN 37033

BRIDGES, KAREN SUE PACKER, 8th Grade Teacher; *b:* Detroit, MI; *m:* John Lorin; *c:* Kyle, Courtney; *ed:* (BSED) HPER/Soc Sci, 1981, (MED) Ed, 1984 SW OK St Univ; *cr:* Teacher Mustang Mid Sch 1982-; *ai:* Head Vlybl & Sftbl Coach; Scholastic Team, Pep Club, 8th Grade Class & OM Spon; *office:* Mustang Mid Sch 906 S Heights Dr Mustang OK 73064

BRIDGES, RHONDA REYNOLDS, Mathematics Teacher; *b:* Longview, TX; *c:* Brandy, Cody, Clay; *ed:* (BS) Math, 1979, (ME) Elem Ed, 1981 Stephen F Austin; *cr:* Math Teacher Pine Tree Mid Sch 1979-81, Union Grove HS 1987-; *ai:* Sr Class, Stu Cncl, UIL Number Sense Spon; *office:* Union Grove HS P O Box 1447 Gladewater TX 75647

BRIDGEWATER, MICHAEL K., Director of Performing Arts; *b:* Indianapolis, IN; *m:* Judith A.; *c:* Hayley, Jason, Justin; *ed:* (BS) Music Ed, Univ of Indianapolis 1973; (MM) Music Ed, Butler Univ; *cr:* Vocal Music Dir Lebanon Mid Sch 1974-79, Lebanon HS 1979-82; Vocal Music Dir 1982-, Performing Art/Vocal Music Dir 1988- Lawrence Cntrl HS; *ai:* Performing Art & Vocal Music Ensembles Dir; Lawrence Cntrl Technology Comm Mem; IN St Sch Music Assn Exec Bd Mem 1977, 1990; Lebanon Ed Assn Pres 1980-81; Actors Equity Assn 1981-; Lilly Endowment Teacher Creativity Grant Recipient 1989; *office:* Lawrence Cntrl HS 7300 E S 6th St Indianapolis IN 46226

BRIDWELL, BOBBIE CLARK, Social Studies Teacher; *b:* Lindale, TX; *m:* Richard C.; *c:* William R., Allan D., Melissa B. Bolton; *ed:* (AB) Music, Tyler Jr Coll 1950; (BS) Elem Ed/Eng, N TX St Univ 1952; (MED) Valdosta St Coll 1981; Ed Specialist Mid Sch Ed, Valdosta St Coll 1985; *cr:* 1st/3rd Grade Teacher Swan Elem Sch 1951-53; 3rd/4th Grade Teacher Mt Clemens MI 1953-55; 4th/7th Grade Teacher Owensboro KY 1955-58; 4th Grade Teacher Tyler TX 1958-59; 3rd/4th Grade Teacher Cheyenne WY 1959-62; 3rd Grade Teacher Tyler TX & Ft Worth TX 1962-1969; 4th-7th Grade Colquitt Cty GA 1970-; *ai:* Delta Kappa Gamma Pres; NCSS; NEA, GA Ed Assn, Doeran Ed Assn 1952-, Teacher of Yr Runner Up 1989; 1st Baptist Church Pianist; Air Force Sergeants Auxiliary Kentucky Colonels; AARP; *home:* PO Box 353 Doerun GA 31744

BRIETBACH, PAUL STEPHEN, K-8th Grade Phys Ed Teacher; *b:* Des Moines, IA; *ed:* (BA) Phys Ed, Loras Coll 1983; Working Towards Masters Counseling; *cr:* K-8th Grade Physical Ed Teacher St Jude Grade Sch 1983-; Coach La Salle HS 1984-; *ai:* Bsktbl, Ftbl, Sftbl Coach; AAHPERD 1983-; Big Brothers Big Sisters 1985-; *office:* St Judes Sch 50 Edgewood Rd NW Cedar Rapids IA 52405

BRIGGS, CAROLE A., Elementary Enrichment Teacher; *b:* Appleton, WI; *m:* Keith Darr; *c:* Andrew H., John A., Gretchen Briggs Dinger; *ed:* (BS) Elem Ed, Clarion Univ of PA 1972; (MED) Ed, Indiana Univ of PA 1977; 6th Yr Certificate Gifted Ed, Univ of CT 1986; Mansfield Univ of PA, OH St Univ, Kent St Univ, Chatham Coll; Several Wkshps; *cr:* 2nd/3rd Grade Teacher Pars Intnl Sch Abadan Iran 1967-71; 3rd Grade Teacher Dubois Area Sch Dist 1972-76; 3rd Grade Teacher 1976-81, Elem ENR Teacher 1981- Brookville Area Sch Dist; *ai:* Natl His Day Coach

& St Judge; NEA, PSEA 1972-; Brookville Area Ed Assn Pres 1988-; Phi Delta Kappa Secy & Treas 1990; Amer Assn Univ Women PA VP 1984-86; PA Assn & Natl Assn for Gifted Children 1981-; Jefferson Cty Lib Bd Pres 1980-83; Jefferson Cty His & Gen Soc Curator 1989-; Published in Papers & Magazines; Poetry in Anthology; Awarded PA His & Museum Commission Grant for Local Preservation 1990; *office:* Brookville Area Sch Dist Janks St Brookville PA 15825

BRIGGS, ETHEL LOUISE, Fifth Grade Teacher; *b:* Willard, OH; *m:* Charles John;; *c:* Christopher, Michael; *ed:* (BS) Elem Ed, Ashland Coll 1968; (MS) Educl Admin, Bowling Green ST U 1980; Quest Trng; Sci is Fun Trng for Lab Sci Elem Classrooms; *cr:* 1st Grade Teacher Shiloh Elem 1965-69; 4th Grade Teacher Plymouth Elem 1972-76; 5th Grade/Head Teacher Shiloh Elem 1976-; *ai:* Head Teacher Shiloh Elem Sch; Dist Communications Comm; D/A Awareness Comm; Aids Policy Comm; Intervention Team Comm; Negotiations Chairperson PlymoutH Ed Assn; Plymouth Ed Assn Treas/Pres 1985-87; OH Ed Assn; NEA; Order of Eastern Stars Worthy Matron 1970-82; 1st Luth Church Cncl Mem 1986-; *office:* Plymouth Local Sch Dist 26 Mechanic St Shiloh OH 44878

BRIGGS, EVA MAE, Kindergarten Teacher; *b:* Burgaw, NC; *m:* Hollis; *c:* Daniel, Termonja; *ed:* (BA) Early Chldhd Ed, Univ of NC Wilmington 1977; Bus Machine Sch; *cr:* Kndgtn Teacher 1977-80, 1st Grade Teacher 1981-87 Willard Elem; Kndgtn Teacher Penderlea Elem 1988-; *ai:* Media Comm Mem; Sch Base Comm Mem 1982-85; NCAE, NEA 1978-; PTA; Salem Lodge Asst Secy; Union Chapel Baptist Church Reporter; Willard Sch Excl in Teaching Certificate; Certified Volunteer Teacher Cape Fear Literacy Cncl; Teacher of Yr Candidate 1982-83; *home:* Rt 1 Box 178 Currie NC 28435

BRIGGS, JAMIE REDMON, Kindergarten Teacher; *b:* Marshall, NC; *m:* Hubert B.; *c:* Deborah (dec), Gregory, Tammy (dec); *ed:* (BA) Early Chldhd Ed, Mars Hill Coll 1973; *cr:* Kndgtn Teacher Mars Hill Elem Sch 1973-76, Marshall Elem 1976-77, Mars Hill Elem 1977-; *ai:* NEA, NCEA; Auxiliary Veterans Foreign Wars (Youth Chm 1985-89, Voice of Democracy Chairperson 1985-89); Mars Hill Baptist Church Youth Groups; *office:* Mars Hill Elem Sch 176 Bailey St Mars Hill NC 28754

BRIGGS, JANE ELLEN, Business Teacher; *b:* Dayton, OH; *m:* Bradley F.; *ed:* (BS) Bus Ed, 1984, (MS) Ed, 1987 Bowling Green St Univ; *cr:* Teacher Wapakoneta City Schls 1984-86; Grad Asst Bowling Green St Univ 1986-87; Teacher Eastland Career Center 1987-; *ai:* Bus Prof of America Chapter Adv 1984-86, 1987-; AVA Mem 1984-; OH Voc Assn Membership Chairperson 1989-; OH Bus Teachers Assn Mem 1984-; Prof Secys Intnl Mem 1987-; Published Effective Advisory Comm Booklet; New Prof Awd AVA 1987; *office:* Fairfield Career Center 4000 Columbus-Lancaster Rd Carroll OH 43112

BRIGGS, REMBERT, English Teacher; *b:* New York City, NY; *m:* Taylor Morrison; *c:* Reeves, Emily, Nathan, Lydia, Avery; *ed:* (BA) Eng, St Thomas Coll 1969; (MA) Eng, SUNY Albany 1972; *cr:* Teacher Vinland Integrated Schls 1970-71; Eng Teacher Montesorri Volkschule Germany 1971-72, Hyde Park Cntrl Schls 1973-; *ai:* Documentary Filmmakers Club; NCTE, ASCD; NY Cncl of Art & Arts in Ed Grants 1987-; *home:* White Schoolhouse Rd Rhinebeck NY 12572

BRIGGS, ROGER PAUL, Physics Teacher; *b:* Boulder, CO; *m:* Mary Ann; *c:* Travis, Justin; *ed:* (BA) Physics, 1973, (MA) Sci Ed, 1990 Univ of CO; *cr:* Math/Sci Teacher Southern Hills Jr HS 1973-76; Cross Cntry/Track Coach 1976-85, Physics Teacher 1976- Fairview HS; *ai:* Boulder Area Coord Cmmty Partnerships in Sci; AAPT; *home:* 498 Canyonside Dr Boulder CO 80302

BRIGHT, DOROTHY BROWN, 7th Teacher/Co Chm Eng Dept; *b:* Shreveport, LA; *m:* George G.; *c:* Gary C.; *ed:* (BA) Sociology, Wiley Coll 1971; (MS) Elem Ed, Univ of KY 1974; Rank I Univ of KY; Admin Univ of Louisville; *cr:* Teacher Carmichael Wilt Blue Lick Elem 1972-84; Lassite Mid Sch 1984-85; Jeff Cty Traditional Mid Sch 1985-; *ai:* Stu Cncl; Young Authors; Eng Dept Co-Chm; Gamma Sigma Sigma 1968-; Delta Sigma Theta 1969-; *office:* Jefferson Co Trad Mid Sch 1418 Morton Ave Louisville KY 40204

BRIGHT, MOLLYE HUNT, French Teacher; *b:* Pine Bluff, AR; *c:* George III, Kyle; *ed:* (BS) Soc Stud, Philander Smith 1963; (MA) Fr, IL St Univ 1971; TX Southern Univ 1964; Fr, NDEA Inst; Univ d Avignon 1977; Univ de Grenoble 1971; Univ de Paris La Sorbonne 1988; *cr:* Teacher Lincoln HS 1963-65, Merrill HS 1965-68, Washington Gifted Sch 1969-; *ai:* Red Cross Adv; Pep & Walking Club; Gifted Sch Selection & Sch Improvement Comms; AATF Contest Dir 1979-88, Service; IL Foreign Lang Assn 1969-; 1691 Fnd Tricennial; Bethel Cncl on Ministries Chairperson 1979-88, Service; Peoria Historical Society; Amer Assn of Univ Women; Rockefellow Fellowship; AATF Grant.

BRIGHT, THERESA J., 2nd Grade Teacher; *b:* Brooklyn, NY; *c:* Christopher, Timothy; *ed:* (BA) Eng/Soc Stud, St Johns Univ 1954; (MS) Elem Ed, Brooklyn Coll 1962; Grad Stud; *cr:* Elem Teacher Carroll St Sch 142 1954-62; Learning Disabilities Teacher 1965-68, Elem Teacher 1968- Smithtown Sch System; *ai:* Soc Stud & Report Card Comm; Smithtown Teachers Assn Rep 1982-; *office:* Tackan Elem Sch Midwood Ave Nesconset NY 11767

BRIGHTON, KENNETH LYLE, 6th Grade Teacher/Dept Chair; *b:* Bloomington, IN; *m:* Maryanne Newsom; *ed:* (AB) Zoology, IN Univ 1971; (MAT) Ed, E TN St Univ 1973; Gifted & Talented Trng, IN Univ, IN St Univ; *cr:* Teacher Intern Cntrl Elem 1971-73; Teacher/Dept Chm Owen Valley Mid Sch 1973-; Teacher in Residence IN St Univ 1989-; *ai:* Textbook Adoption, Faculty Search, North Cntrl Evaluation Comm; Natl Mid Sch Assn, IN Assn for Gifted; Spencer Chrstn Church (Elder, Bd Chm, Sunday Sch Teacher); Teacher in Residence IN St Univ to Teach Mid Sch Methods Classes & Supervise Field Experience Stu & Stu Teachers; *home:* RR 4 Box 504 Spencer IN 47460

BRIJALBA, JESSE V., Freshman Band Director; *b:* Pecos, TX; *m:* Nora Sanchez; *c:* Adrian; *ed:* (BA) Music, Sul Ross St Univ 1978; *cr:* Band Dir Presidio HS 1978-79; Asst Band Dir Del Rio HS 1980-81; Band Dir Del Rio 8th Grade 1981-85, Del Rio Frosh Sch 1985-; *ai:* Asst HS Band & All Level Band; Del Rio Frosh Marching & Concert Bands; Won Numerous Trophies; Superior Ratings in UIL Contest; Sweepstakes Winner UIL Contest; *office:* Del Rio Frosh Sch 90 Memorial Dr Del Rio TX 78840

BRILL, FRED S., English Teacher; *b:* Chicago, IL; *m:* Cynthia; *c:* Naya, Spencer; *ed:* (BA) Eng, Univ of MI 1984; (MA) Ed, San Francisco St 1990; *cr:* Dir Outdoor Adventure Prgm 1982-86; Teacher Seneca Center 1985-86, Albany HS 1986-; *ai:* Cross Cntry Coach; Peer Counseling Adv; Bicycling Club; Natl Endowment Hum Awd; Cranbrook Writers Conference Awd; *office:* Albany HS 603 Key Rt Blvd Albany CA 94706

BRILL, KIRK L., Biology & Study Skills Teacher; *b:* Des Moines, IA; *m:* Monica A. Ryan; *ed:* (BA) Bio, 1963, (MA) Bio, 1969 Drake Univ; Drake; Univ of IA; IA St Univ; Univ of N IA; WY Univ; *cr:* Bio SE Polk HS 1963-; *ai:* Ecology Club Spon; IA Acad of Sci Bio Teacher of Yr 1974; Soil Conservation Regional Teacher of Yr 1974; IA Conservation Teacher of Yr 1975; Study Skills & Environmental Ed Wkshp Presenter; *office:* SE Polk HS 8325 NE University Runnells IA 50237

BRILL, MARTHA CARTER, English Teacher; *b:* Burlington, NC; *w:* Richard B. (dec); *c:* Stephenie Brill Self, Korte M.; *ed:* (BA) Eng/Bio, Catawba Coll 1963; Grad Stud William & Mary Coll, Univ of VA, Old Dominion Univ, Mary Washington Coll; *cr:* Teacher Middlesex HS 1963-66, Chesapeake Acad 1977-78, Ware Acad 1978-81, York Acad 1981-; *ai:* Forensic Spon; Assn of Private Acads; *office:* York Acad Rts 14 & 33 Shacklefords VA 23156

BRIM, RUTH BRIGHT, Second Grade Teacher; *b:* New Castle, IN; *m:* Robert O.; *c:* Deborah B. Tucker, Cynthia B. Nichols, Teresa L.; *ed:* (BA) Ed, Trevecca Nazarene Coll 1963; (MED) Rdng, Mid TN St Univ 1976; *cr:* 1st/2nd Grade Teacher Gladeville Elem Sch 1963-64; 1st-3rd Grade Teacher Wilder Elem Sch 1964-66; 5th/6th Grade Teacher York Elem 1966-67; 1st/2nd/5th/6th Grade Teacher Pine Haven Elem 1967-69; 2nd Grade Teacher Huntland Sch 1970-; *ai:* Franklin Cty Ed Assn, NEA 1970-; TN Ed Assn 1963-70; *home:* Rt 2 Box 2757 WI Winchester TN 37398

BRIMM, WARDELL C., French/English Teacher; *b:* St Louis, MO; *m:* Rosalind Phillips; *c:* Marlin, Myron, Mylin; *ed:* (BA) Eng, 1971, (MA) Eng, S IL Univ Edwardsville 1978; Doctoral Stud Eng, St Louis Univ 1981-84; Working Towards Educl Admin Certificate S IL Univ Edwardsville; *cr:* Eng Teacher Sumner HS 1972-79; Eng Teacher 1979-88, Fr Teacher 1988- East St Louis Sr HS; *ai:* Eng Dept Chm; *office:* East St Louis Sr HS 4901 State East Saint Louis IL 62205

BRINER, KAY JEANNINE, Fifth Grade Teacher; *b:* Findlay, OH; *m:* Paul A.; *c:* Sean E., Joel C.; *ed:* (BSED) Elem Ed, OH Univ 1964; (MAED) Elem Ed, MI St Univ 1971; *cr:* 6th Grade Teacher North Cntrl Sch 1964-67, Montpelier Schls 1971-74; 5th Grade Teacher Camden-Frontier Sch 1978-; *ai:* Co-Chm Math Curr & Revision Comm; Co-Coord Campbells Labels for Ed Prgm; MEA, NEA; CFEA (Assn Rep 1988-; Treas 1985-88, Pres); Alpha Delta Kappa (Treas 1984-, Pres 1980-82); *home:* Rt 2 Box 84 Montpelier OH 43543

BRINK, BEVERLY ANN, Fourth Grade Teacher; *b:* Midland, MI; *ed:* (BA) Eng, Cntrl MI Univ 1971; (MA) Admin, Saginaw Valley St Univ 1985; *cr:* 5th Grade Teacher 1973-77, 6th Grade Teacher 1977-81, 7th-8th Grade Teacher 1981-82, 6th Grade Teacher 1982-85Freeland Mid Sch; 7th-12th Grade Teacher Freeland Jr/Sr HS 1985-89; 4th Grade Teacher Freeland Elem Sch 1989-; *ai:* MEA, NEA, FEA; Midland Jaycees 1981-85; St Johns Luth Church 1972-; *office:* Freeland Elem Sch 710 Powley Dr Freeland MI 48623

BRINK, DAVID ERNEST, Physics Teacher; *b:* Ft Worth, TX; *m:* Mary Jane Williams; *c:* Kyle D., Richard K.; *ed:* (BS) Physics/Math, TX Chrstn Univ 1972; (MED) Ed Physics/Math, W TX St Univ 1979; *cr:* Physics Teacher Frank Phillips Coll 1980-83, Borger HS 1973-; *ai:* Sr Class, UIL Sci Team Spon; Odyssey of Mind Sch Coord & Coach; AAPT, NSTA, TCTA, TMSCA; TX AAPT Excl Physics Teaching Awd 1988; NASA Ed Wkshp for Math & Sci Teachers; NEWMAST Honors Teacher 1989; Woodrow Wilson Master Teacher 1988; *office:* Borger HS W 1st St Borger TX 79007

BRINKLEY, CANDACE LEA, Spanish Teacher; *b:* Washington, DC; *m:* Paige S. Jr.; *c:* Matthew; (BA) Span, 1974, (MA) Span, 1976 George Mason Univ; *ed:* Grad Work Eng Linguistics; *cr:* Lecturer George Mason Univ 1980-86; Teacher Broad Run HS 1986-; *ai:* Span Club Spon; Literary Magazine Adv; Amer Assn of Teachers Span & Portuguese 1985-; Amer Assn of Univ Proessors 1985-86; Sigma Delta Pi 1980-; *office:* Broad Run HS Box 200 Ashburn VA 22011

BRINKLEY, MARTHA JOHNSON, English/Speech/Drama Teacher; *b:* Chillicothe, MO; *m:* Dwight H.; *c:* Nicholas, Jacob; *ed:* (BS) Eng, CMSU 1973; *cr:* Eng/Speech/Drama Teacher Meadville MO 1974-76, Northwestern of Mendon 1976-77; Eng Teacher Brookfield Mid Sch 1977-82; Eng/Speech/Drama Teacher Braymer C-4 1984-; *ai:* Yrbk & Stu Cncl Adv; Sch Play; Beta Zeta Pres 1989-.

BRINTON, VICTORIA RUTH, AP European/World His Teacher; *b:* Provo, UT; *ed:* (BA) His, Brigham Young Univ 1973; (MED) Cult Fnds of Ed, Univ of UT 1981; Grad Stud Teaching Certificate 1974; *cr:* Teacher Millard Jr/Sr HS 1974-76, Cyprus HS 1977, Hillcrest HS 1977-; Adjunct Prof Salt Lake Comm Coll 1989-; *ai:* Sterling Scholars Awds Prgm Top Scholars; Model United Nations; St & Natl Close-up Washington Dc; Career Ladder Comm; Jordan UT NEA 1973-; UT Endoweent of Hum 1988-; UT Cncl of Soc Stud 1985-; Fulbright Summer Scholar Taiwan; UT St Bd Curr Dev Egypt; UT Textbook Selection Comm Soc Stud; *office:* Hillcrest HS 7350 S 900 E Midvale UT 84047

BRIONES, MAX, JR., Sixth Grade Teacher; *b:* Oakland, CA; *m:* Margaret A. Bolich; *c:* Joii P., Peter M.; *ed:* (BA) Soc Sci, San Jose St 1970; *cr:* 5th-6th Grade Teacher Christopher/Santa Teresa Elem 1972-79; 6th Grade Teacher Park Avenue 1981-89, A Kaperos 1989-; *ai:* Mentor Teacher; Teacher Assn Rep; Controversial Issues, Meet & Consult Comm; *office:* Andros Karperos Sch 700 Palora Ave Yuba City CA 95991

BRIONES, PAUL OLIVAS, Biology Teacher; *b:* Ojinaga, MX; *m:* Dee Ann Picon; *ed:* (CC) Bio, Odessa Coll 1976; (BS) Bio, Univ of TX Permian Basin 1976; Univ of TX Permian Basin 1976 Post Grad Work; *cr:* Sci Teacher Pecos HS 1979-81; Bio Teacher Permian HS 1982-; *ai:* Stu Assistance Services & CORE Team Mem; Sci Club Spon; Regional Sci Fair Co-Spon; TX St Teachers Assn 1988-; Sci Teachers Assn of TX 1983-; Assn of TX Bio Teachers 1990; St Marys Cath Church Parish Cncl Mem at Large 1989-; Youth Minister Search Chrstn Maturity 1986-; Learning Grant ECISD Bd of Trustees 1990; Co-Author Permian HS Botanical Garden Brochure 1990; *home:* 4210 E 53rd #1326 Odessa TX 79762

BRISBANE, GENE DENNIS, Sixth Grade Teacher; *b:* Greensburg, PA; *m:* Carol L. Backus; *c:* Kelli, Mindy, Shawn; *ed:* (BS) Elem Ed, 1974, (MED) Elem Ed, 1979 Univ of Pittsburgh; *cr:* 4th Grade Teacher 1974-75, 6th Grade Teacher 1975-85, 5th Grade Teacher 1985-86, 6th Grade Teacher 1986- Maxwell Elem; *ai:* HS Bsktbl Coach; Outdoor Ed Prgm; NASA Seeds Project; NEA, PA St Ed Assn, Hempfield Area Ed Assn; Westmoreland Cty Coaches Assn; Maxwell PTO (Pres, VP, Treas); Elks Club; Amer Family Inst Positive Teaching Awd; *home:* RD 6 Box 41-A Greensburg PA 15601

BRISCHETTO, BARBARA PALMIERI, Mathematics Teacher; *b:* San Antonio, TX; *m:* Robert R.; *c:* Christina, Brenda; *ed:* (BA) Math/Chem, St Mary Univ 1967; (MED) Rehabilitation Counseling, Our Lady of the Lake Univ 1975; Univ of TX Austin, Univ of TX San Antonio; *cr:* Math Teacher Manor HS 1967-68, St Marys Univ 1987-, Marshall HS 1975-; *ai:* NHS Spon; Dist Faculty Forum Rep; NCTM, Alamo Dist Teachers of Math; St Marys Univ Alumni Bd of Dirs VP 1985-88; TX Ed Agency Meritorious Service Awd ; Natl Sci Fnd Advanced Placement Stipend; *office:* John Marshall HS 8000 Lobo Ln San Antonio TX 78240

BRISCOE, ALLENE VICKERS, English/Speech Teacher; *b:* Taft, TX; *m:* Horace Blake; *c:* Vicki L. Burnell, Ben R., Deborah B. Burnell; *ed:* (BA) Government/Eng, TX A&I Univ 1956; *cr:* Teacher Sinton Jr HS 1947-48, 1960-63, Taft Jr HS 1953-57, 1959, Eureka HS 1958, Odem HS 1964-68, Robstown HS 1976-77, Mathis HS 1978-; *ai:* Coach Literary Events Univ Interscholastic League; Order of Eastern Star, Soc Order of Beauceant, Daughters of Nile, Pioneer Womens Club.

BRISCOE, MICHELE LOEFFEL, French Teacher; *b:* Paris, France; *m:* Jack; *c:* Danielle Loeffel, Eric Loeffel; *ed:* (BA) FR, Seton Hill 1972; Univ of Pittsburgh; LASU; USD; *cr:* Fr Teacher Banning HS 1986; Franklin HS 1983-86; Amer His Teacher St Elizabeth 1980-83; Fr Teacher Hempfield Sch 1973-77; *ai:* Fr Club; Amer Army (Translator/Secy to Cardinal 1961-62); *home:* 150 Ximeno Long Beach CA 90803

BRISCOE, RONALD MALCOLM, English Department Chair; *b:* Nitro, WV; *m:* Susan Mac Kenzie; *c:* Kristen, Nicole, Joshua, Malcolm; *ed:* (BA) Speech, Anderson Univ 1971; (MA) Theater, W IL Univ 1976; (MED) Admin, Nicholls St Univ 1984; *cr:* Speech/Eng Teacher Larose - Cut Off Jr HS 1978; *ai:* Frosh Asst Ftbl & Head Bsktbl Coach; Lafourch Parish Eng Guide Comm Chm; Quiz Bowl & Thespian Club Spon; Alpha Psi Omega, Lambda Theta Cast, Phi Kappa Phi; Lafourche Parish Teacher of Yr 1988-89; *office:* Larose - Cut Off Jr HS 806 W Main PO Box 1390 Larose LA 70373

BRISENDINE, LINDA JOHNSON, Amer History/Phys Ed Teacher; *b:* Fort Payne, AL; *m:* David E.; *c:* Tad, Nathan; *ed:* (BA) Phys Ed, Jacksonville St Univ 1974; (MS) Phys Ed, Univ of AL Birmingham 1977; *cr:* Teacher Glencoe Elem 1975; Teacher/Coach Fyffe Elem 1975-83, Fyffe HS 1983-; *ai:* B Team, Var, Jr HS Vlybl Coach; SADD Spon; De Kalb Ed Assn, AL Ed Assn 1975-; NEA (Delegate Convention 1982) 1975-; *office:* Fyffe HS PO Box 7 Church St Fyffe AL 35971

BRISKER, PAUL OWEN, Science Teacher; *b:* Gallipolis, OH; *m:* Mary Elizabeth Mullen; *c:* Matthew O., Benjamin L.; *ed:* (BA) Soc Stud Comp, Rio Grande Coll 1980; *cr:* Soc Stud Teacher Frontier HS 1980-81, Oak Hill HS 1981-84; Sci Teacher Green HS 1984-85, Everts Mid Sch 1985-; *ai:* Var Asst Ftbl & 8th Grade Bsktbl Coach; Head Coach Girls Var Track; OH Mid Sch Assn, United Ed Profession 1985-; Dist 10 Bsktbl Coaches Assn 1987-, Dist 10 Coaches Awd 1988-90; Cntrl OH Track & Cross Cntry Coaches Assn 1989-; *home:* 134 Park St Circleville OH 43113

BRISSEY, RONALD CROEL, NJROTC Teacher/Instructor; *b:* Gainesville, GA; *m:* Linda J. Freeman; *c:* Dena Brissey Fafard, RoniLynn Brissey Ramos; *ed:* Psych & Speed Rdng, Commercial Pilots License, Prof Parachutist, Electricity & Air Conditioning, Emergency Hydraulic Sprinkler Systems; Management Schls & Leadership Acads in Military; *cr:* Platoon Leader US Marine Corps 1957-70; Production Coord US Steel 1971-77; Rangemaster/Drill Instr US Navy 1977-88; Teacher/Instr Evans HS 1988-; *ai:* Teach Tandem Parachuting; Lecturer to Inmates & Church Organizations; US Parachutist Mem 1960-, Gold Wings 1971, Diamond Wings 1975, Double Wings 1990; Aircraft Owners & Pilots Assn Mem 1989-; First Baptist Church Mem 1984-; *office:* Maynard Evans HS 4949 Silver Star Rd Orlando FL 32808

BRISSON, DONALD PAUL, English Teacher; *b:* New York, NY; *m:* Margaret Fody; *c:* Christine, Michael, Daniel, Nancy; *ed:* (BA) Eng, Le Moyne Coll 1966; (MA) Liberal Stud, SUNY Stony Brook 1971; Mass Media/Film Stud; *cr:* Jr HS Eng Teacher Dawnwood Jr HS 1966-70; Sr HS Eng Teacher Centereach HS 1970-; Adjunct Lecturer/Eng Teacher Adelphi Univ 1980-; *ai:* Public Relations Coord Centereach HS; NYSUT 1969-; AFT Delegate 1971-75; Charismatic Renewal Service of Long Island Coord 1987-; *office:* Centereach HS 14 43rd St Centereach NY 11720

BRISTER, BONNIE ARENDALE, Fifth Grade Teacher; *b:* Crowder, MS; *c:* Victoria Brister Markley, Anthony R.; *ed:* (BA) Bus Ed/Bible, Blue Mountain Coll 1955; (ME) Elem Ed, Univ of Toledo 1980; *cr:* Substitute Teacher 1961-64, 6th Grade Teacher 1964-66 Toledo Public Schls; 6th Grade Teacher Memphis Public Schls 1966-67; 5th Grade Teacher Toledo Public Schls 1967-; *ai:* Writing Across Curr & Toledo Public Schls 5th Grade Sci Seminary Leader; Intnl Rdng Assn 1970-; OR Bus & Prof Women 1987-88; E Toledo Baptist Church Clerk 1978-; Womans Missionary Union Past Pres 1955-60; Girls Auxilary Dir 1960-65; Writer/Dir Church & Sch Plays; *home:* 2707 Pickle Rd Apt 60 Oregon OH 43616

BRISTER, RAMONA BUTLER, Kindergarten Teacher; *b:* Jackson, MS; *m:* David; *c:* Ryan; *ed:* (BS) Ed, MS St Univ 1980; *cr:* 1st Grade Teacher Brandon Acad 1980-83; Kndgtn Teacher St Judes Kndgtn 1983-87, Brandon Acad 1988-; *ai:* MPSEA; *home:* 2750 Sycamore Cove Pearl MS 39208

BRISTOL, SUSAN ELLEN, Gifted/Talented Coord/Teacher; *b:* Lansing, MI; *ed:* (BS) Elem Ed, Summit Chrstn Coll 1973; Grad Work MI St Univ; *cr:* Teacher Capital City Chrstn Sch 1973-76, Lansing Chrstn Sch 1976-86, Shepherds Home & Sch 1987-88; Gifted & Talented Coord Heritage Chrstn Sch 1986-; *ai:* Curr Academic Prin 5th/6th Grade Teaching Staff; WI Cncl of Gifted Teachers 1990; FOCUS Singles Fellowship VP 1978-79; *office:* Heritage Chrstn Sch 1300 S 109th St Milwaukee WI 53214

BRISTOW, ELWANA PEARL, Mathematics Teacher; *b:* Vivian, LA; *ed:* (BS) Math, Northwestern St 1966; (MED) Scndry Ed, LA St Univ 1975; Pips Prof Improvement Plan; *cr:* Math/Phys Ed Teacher Opelousas HS 1966-69; Math Teacher Iota HS 1969-; *ai:* Curr Improvement Comm; Frosh Spon; APEL 1988-; *office:* Iota HS PO Box 780 Iota LA 70543

BRITAIN, MAYNARD DRYDEN, 7th & 8th Grade Teacher; *b:* Hot Springs, SD; *m:* Le May Parduhn De Lapp; *c:* Van E. Britain Miller, Kari K. Britain Jastorff; *ed:* (BA) Soc Sci, Dakota Wesleyan Univ 1958; (MA) Elem Admin, Chadron St Coll 1982; Black Hills St Univ 1962-63, 1968, 1973; SD St Univ 1968, 1971, 1989; Univ of SD 1976, 1977; Chadron St Coll 1989-; *cr:* Jr HS Teacher 1961-63, Sr HS Teacher 1963-64, Jr HS Teacher 1964- Oelrichs Sch Dist 23-3; *ai:* Curr Comm; Oelrichs Sch Bsktbl Scorekeeper Girls 1973-87 & Boys 1965-87, Ftbl Line Crew 1962-87; Oelrichs Centennial Comm 1989-; SD Ed Assn, NEA; Oelrichs Ed Assn (Pres 1982-83, VP 1988-); SD Farm Bureau 1959-; Chadron NE Elks Lodge #1399 1961-; Oelrichs United Meth Church 1959-; Amer Legion (Commander 1989-) 1969-; Oelrichs Historical Society (VP 1985-) 1982-; KOTA TV Teacher of Week 1990; *home:* PO Box 17 Oelrichs SD 57763

BRITNELL, DON FRANKLIN, Agribusiness Teacher; *b:* Russellville, AL; *m:* Linda Jo Rich; *c:* Jamie, Jason; *ed:* (BS) Agri-Bus Ed, 1972, (MED) Agri-Bus Ed, 1977 Auburn Univ; (AA) Agri-Bus, A&M Univ 1986; *cr:* Teacher Burell-Slatter AVS 1972-74, Lawrence Cty Voc Sch 1974-79, Mt Hope HS 1979-; *ai:* FFA Adv; AEA, NEA 1972-; NVATA; Lawrence Cty Teacher of Yr, Voc Teacher of Yr 1987; Amer FFA Degree 1989; *office:* Mt Hope HS 8455 County Rd 23 Mount Hope AL 35651

BRITSCHGI, DORIS WALKER, Fifth Grade Teacher; *b:* Palo Alto, CA; *m:* Russell W.; *ed:* (BA) Elem Ed, Univ of Pacific 1965; San Francisco St Coll, San Jose St Univ, Hayward St Coll; Continuing Ed, Santa Clara Cty Office of Ed; *cr:* 5th/6th Grade Teacher Los Padres Sch 1965-66; 6th Grade Teacher Scott Lane Sch 1966-69; 4th/5th Grade Teacher C W Haman Sch 1969-; *ai:* Sch Cmptr Comm; Delta Kappa Gamma (VP 1986-88, Treas 1988-); United Teachers of Santa Clara (Sch Rep, Mem) 1965; NEA 1965-; Willow Glen United Meth Church (Ed Commission, Monte Toyon Dev Comm Secy) 1979-; Stu Teaching Assignment Durango Mexico; *office:* C W Haman Sch 865 Los Padres Blvd Santa Clara CA 95050

BRITT, JANE Y. WIEMER, 6th Grade Teacher; *b:* Independence, WI; *m:* Kenneth D.; *c:* Kenneth, Wendy Facinger, Ross, Douglas; *ed:* (BS) Sociology, Carroll Coll 1952; Teaching Certified Marion Coll 1969; *cr:* 4th Grade Teacher 1970, 6th Grade Teacher 1970-, 5th/6th Grade Teacher 1989- Pier Elem; *ai:* Gifted & Talented Comm; FEA, WEA, NEA; Teacher of Yr Awd; *home:* 852 Kings Ct Fond Du Lac WI 54935

BRITT, KATHERINE SAVAGE, Teacher/Math Dept Chair; *b:* Elizabethtown, NC; *m:* Arthur Rudolph Jr.; *c:* Julie, Clark; *ed:* (BS) Math, Pembroke St Univ 1980; *cr:* Teacher E Bladen HS 1980-; *ai:* Jr Class Spon; Health Careers Club; Homecoming Parade Chairperson, Effective Schls & Schlsp Comm; NCCTM, NCAE; *office:* E Bladen HS PO Box 578 Elizabethtown NC 28337

BRITT, NANCY CAROLYN BURNS, First Grade Teacher; *b:* Greensboro, NC; *m:* Lenox; *c:* Lenox G., Emily L Patterson; *ed:* (BA) Elem Ed, Duke Univ 1957; Addl Studies East Carolina; Pembroke St Univ; UNC; Meredith; *cr:* Wiley Sch 3rd Grade 1957; Teacher 1st Grade Tanglewood Sch 1957-88; Summer Headstart Hargrove Sch, Knuckles Elem; Interim Prin 1987-88; Teacher 1st Tanglewood Sch 1989-; *ai:* NCAE President 1971; NEA; SACS Team Chm; First Baptist Church Choir; Lady Lions; Jr Services League; Phi Beat Kappa, Duke Univ; Kappa Delta Pi; Delta Kappa Gamma Past President; Zeta Tau Alpha Outstanding Pledge; Lumberton Jaycees Outstanding Young Educator 1966; Teacher of the Year; Terry Sanford Award 1982-83; *home:* 301 West 34th Street Lumberton NC 28358

BRITT, PATRICIA SMITH, Third Grade Teacher; *b:* Roanoke Rapids, NC; *m:* James Albert Jr.; *c:* James A. III, Clifton W.; *ed:* (BS) Elem Ed, Atlantic Chrstn 1966; *cr:* 6th Grade Teacher Battle 1966-67; 4th Grade Teacher Winstead 1967-68, Woodard 1968-69; 6th Grade Teacher Pasquotank 1972-73; 3rd Grade Teacher Cntrl 1978-; *ai:* Staff Club Pres; Accreditation Comm Chm; Team Leader; Alpha Delta Kappa (Corresponding Secy 1988-, Pres Elect 1990-92); NEA, NCAE; Jr Womens Club Corresponding Secy 1987-88, Outstanding New Mem 1986; Church Circle Leader 1988-; *home:* 226 Small Dr Elizabeth City NC 27909

BRITT, RUTHIE JUANITA, Third Grade Teacher; *b:* Brookhaven, MS; *ed:* (BS) Elem Ed, 1970, (MS) Elem Ed, 1977 Univ of S MS Hattiesburg 1977; MTAI Evaluator of Teachers 1987-; *cr:* Math Teacher Loyd Star Sch 1970-71; 6th Grade Teacher Hall Cty Sch 1971-72; 3rd Grade Teacher Loyd Star Sch 1972-; *ai:* Kappa Kappa Iota Mem; USM Alumni 1st VP 1989-; *home:* Rt 1 Box 205 Wesson MS 39191

BRITT, SADIE S., Fourth Grade Teacher; *b:* Talladega, AL; *c:* David C.; *ed:* (BS) Elem Ed, AL A&M Univ 1960; (MS) Elem Ed, Univ of AL Birmingham 1977; Elem Ed, Univ of AL Birmingham; *cr:* Teacher 1960-61, Librarian 1961-66 Talladega Coll; Teacher Talladega Cty Bd of Ed 1966-; *ai:* Talladega Cty Selection Comm for Teacher Hall of Fame 1989-; Talladega Cty Calendar Comm 1990; 4-H Club Leader; Talladega Cty Textbook Selection Comm Mem; NEA, AL Ed Assn, Talladega Cty Ed Assn 1966-; PTA (Pres 1979) 1966-; Lincoln Lib Bd Chairperson 1989-; Pine Grove Baptist Church Clerk 1985-; Lincoln Medical Bd Secy; Nom Talladega Cty Teacher Hall of Fame 1986; *home:* 485 Drew Ave Lincoln AL 35096

BRITT, THOMAS MILTON, Mathematics Teacher/Ftbl Coach; *b:* Springhill, LA; *m:* Barbara Jean Nichols; *c:* Thomas J.; *ed:* (BS) Math, LA Tech Univ 1971; (MS) Math, LA St Univ 1972; (MED) Ed Leadership, Univ of West FL 1974; *cr:* Teacher/ Coach Benton HS 1972-73, Meigs Jr HS 1973-78; Dir Choctawhatchee Adult Ed 1974-82; Teacher/Coach Ft Walton Bch HS 1978-; *ai:* Ftbl Coach; NCTM, FCTM 1978-; OCTM 1986-; Masonic F AM 1971-; Shriner Hadji Temple 1986-; Komedian Dir 1989-; *office:* Fort Walton Beach HS 400 Hollywood Blvd Fort Walton Beach FL 32548

BRITTAIN, NORMA JEAN, Fifth Grade Teacher; *b:* Gordo, AL; *m:* James R. Jr.; *c:* James R. III., Terry L., CheryL D. Peters; *ed:* Elem, Penascola Jr Coll 1975; (BA) Elem, Univ of W FL 1977; Working Towards Masters in Elem Ed, Univ of W FL; *cr:* 5th Grade Teacher Sherwood Elem 1977-; *ai:* Escambia HS & Myrtle Grove Cmmty Club Sftbl Coach; Escambia Ed Assn 1977-; NEA 1977-; Alpha Delta Kappa 1988-; Myrtle Grove Ladies Club 1964-84; *office:* Sherwood Elem Sch 501 Cherokee Tr Pensacola FL 32506

BRITTEN, PATRICK JAMES, 5th Grade Mathematics Teacher; *b:* Alma, MI; *m:* Dixie Lee Hock; *c:* Aimee, Nikki, Allison, Peter J.; *ed:* (AA) Soc Work, Ferris St Univ 1973; (BS) Elem Ed, Cntrl MI Univ 1976; Post Grad Stud Cntrl MI Univ & W MI Univ; *cr:* 3rd Grade Classroom Teacher 1977-82, 4th Grade Classroom Teacher 1982-83 Reed City Elem Sch; 5th Grade Classroom Teacher Philips Elem Sch 1983-87; 5th Grade Math Teacher Reed City Mid Sch 1987-; *ai:* Organize & Implement 5th Grade Reproductive Health Unit; Amer Legion Post 98 Commander 1982-83; *office:* Reed City Mid Sch W Lincoln St Reed City MI 49677

BRITTON, CATHY DILLMAN, Fourth Grade Teacher; *b:* Marion, VA; *m:* David Lee; *c:* Jennifer; *ed:* (BA) Elem Ed, Emory & Henry Coll 1974; *cr:* 6th Grade Teacher Scott Memorial Elem 1974-76; Rdng Aide Johnson City Schls 1976-78; Lang Art Teacher Churchville Elem 1978-80; 4th Grade Teacher Springville Elem Sch 1980-81; 4th-5th Grade Teacher Tazewell Elem Schls 1981-; *ai:* NEA 1981-; VA Ed Assn, Tazewell Ed Assn; Brownie Troup 2295 (Asst Leader 1987-, Treas); Sarah Dunsmore Circle Treas 1985-; *home:* 135 Harman St North Tazewell VA 24630

BRITTON, JENNALEE STEWART, Fourth Grade Teacher; *b:* Robinson, IL; *m:* James; *c:* Mike, Becky, Amie; *ed:* (BS) Elem Ed, OH St Univ 1975; Gifted Coord; Shakespeare Study of Literature England; *cr:* Kndgtn Teacher 1979-81, 2nd-8th Grade Gifted Teacher 1981-83, 4th Grade Teacher 1983- Oblong Elem; *ai:* Gifted Comm; IL Ed Assn/NEA 1983-; Oblong Ed Assn; Ladies Elks Club 1988-; *office:* Oblong Elem Sch 600 W Main Oblong IL 62449

BRITTON, JILL, French Teacher; *b:* Columbus, OH; *ed:* (BA) Fr/Eng/Ed, Otterbein Coll 1980; (MA) Foreign Lang Ed, OH St Univ 1988; Oral Proficiency Testers Trng 1987; Summer Wkshps in France 1982-; *cr:* Fr/Eng Teacher West HS Columbus 1980-81; Fr Teacher South HS Columbus 1981-88, Fort Hayes Arts & Academics HS 1988-; *ai:* Dept of Cultural Stud/Foreign Lang Chairperson; Foreign Lang Olympics Comm; Columbus Public Schls Coord, Group Leader Fr Exch Prgm; Prof Dev & Steering Comms; Cntrl OH Foreign Lang Alliance; OH Foreign Lang Assn 1982-; AATF 1985-; Amer Cncl on Teaching Foreign Lang 1986-89; Alternate-Fulbright Awd 1980 & Rockefeller Fnd Fellowship 1986; Winner Best of OH Foreign Lang Assn 1986, Best of Cntrl St 1987, OH Foreign Lang Assn Schlsp Oral Proficiency 1987; Presented Wkshps at Local, Regional & Natl Level 1985-; *office:* Fort Hayes Arts & Academics HS 546 Jack Gibbs Blvd Columbus OH 43215

BRIX, WAYNE A., English Teacher; *b:* Richmond, MN; *ed:* (BA) Philosophy, St Johns Univ 1959; (BS) Eng/Speech, 1962, (MS) Eng, 1967 St Cloud St Univ; Various Courses Numerous Univs; *cr:* Eng Litchfield Jr HS 1962-; *ai:* Speech Debate Tournaments Judge; MN Cncl Teachers of Eng, NCTE; Univ of WY Amer Fellowship 1965; Andrew Mellon Fellowship Augustana Coll 1986; Natl Endowment for Hum Schlsps Northwestern Univ 1987, Vanderbilt Univ 1988, W Ky Univ 1989; *office:* Litchfield Jr HS 114 N Holcombe Litchfield MN 55355

BRIZENDINE, WILMA H., Second Grade Teacher; *b:* Sugar City, ID; *m:* Luther James; *c:* Kaylene, Christine, Joanne; *ed:* (BA) Basic Ed/Lang Art, Cntrl WA 1971; *cr:* Teacher Longview Elem 1972-81, Larson Heights Elem 1988-.

BRIZZI, MADALYN FROST, Retired Elementary Teacher; *b:* Clarksville, MI; *m:* Carl A.; *c:* Steve, Kenneth, Keith, Carlene Brizzi Berg; *ed:* (BA) Chrstn Ed, Bob Jones Univ 1949; (MA) Elem Ed, San Jose St Univ 1960; Grad Work Univ of CA Los Angeles, San Francisco St Univ, AR St Univ; *cr:* Elem Teacher Corcoran Union Elem 1948-50, Hanford Public Schls 1950-55; Elem Teacher 1955-59, Elem Prin 1959-70 San Jose Unified Sch Dist; Elem Ed Instr AR St Univ 1972-78; Elem Teacher Saddleback Unified Sch Dist 1979-85; *ai:* CA Teachers Assn Mem; NEA, NAESP; AR Ed Assn Treas 1977-78; AR Assn Children Under Six (Prgm Comm 1975, Leg Comm 1974, Spec Events 1976-77); Quota Club of San Jose; Alpha Delta Kappa Chaplain 1975-77; Phi Delta Kappa; *home:* 7677 Helmsdale Dr San Jose CA 95135

BROAD, SHARON MERSEREAU, Fifth Grade Teacher; *b:* Mars Hill, ME; *m:* Stephen D.; *c:* Heidi Broad Smith, Stephen M.; *ed:* (BA) Elem Ed, Univ of ME Presque Isle 1969; (MA) Elem Ed, Univ of Southern ME 1987; *cr:* 2nd Grade Teacher Bridgewater Grammar 1968-70; 5th Grade Teacher Fort Street Sch 1970-; *ai:* Steering Comm; Support Team Coach; ME Teachers Assn, Natl Teachers Assn 1969-; Cntrl Aroostook Teachers Assn 1968-; *office:* Fort Street Sch Fort St Mars Hill ME 04758

BROADBENT, LORENE (RILEY), High School Counselor; *b:* Rocky Ford, CO; *m:* William; *c:* Michael G. Wise, Gregory T. Wise; *ed:* (BA) Elem Ed, 1961, (MA) Psych/Guidance, 1968 Adams St Coll; Additional Classes Counseling & Guidance Various CO Coll; *cr:* 2nd Grade Teacher Crowley Elem Sch 1957-60; 4th Grade Teacher Sugar City Elem Sch 1960-62; 1st Grade Teacher Crowley Cty Elem Sch 1963-66; Cnslr Crowley Cty Elem/Jr HS 1966-74; Cnslr Crowley Cty HS 1974-; *ai:* NHS Spon; Guidance Curr Dir; CO Sch Cnslrs Assn 1975-, Honorable Mention Cnslr of Yr 1984; St Peter Cath Church; Selected Lady of Yr by Beta Sigma Phi 1985; *home:* 721 Main St Ordway CO 81063

BROADBENT, PEGGY SUE (MC CREERY), First/Second Grade Teacher; *b:* Brockton, MA; *m:* Frank William; *c:* F. William Jr., Susan A.; *ed:* (BS) Early Chldhd Ed, Wheelock Coll 1956; (MS) Early Chldhd Ed, Syracuse Univ 1975; *cr:* Nursery/Kndgtn Sch 1956-66, 1st Grade Teacher Rochester NY 1970-73; 1st/2nd Grade Teacher Fayetteville-Manlius Sch Dist 1979-; *ai:* AFT 1970-; Article Published 1973; *office:* Fayetteville Elem Sch Fayetteville-Manlius Rd Fayetteville NY 13066

BROCCOLO, PATRICIA ANN, Kindergarten Teacher; *b:* Pasadena, CA; *m:* Frank A.; *c:* Frank J., Ryan; *ed:* (BA) Sociology, CA St Los Angeles 1969; (MS) Early Chldhd Ed, Pepperdine 1975; *cr:* Kndgtn Teacher 1970-76, Kndgtn/1st Grade Teacher 1976-81, Kndgtn Teacher 1981- Eader Elem; *ai:* Sip Comm & Grade Level Rep; Grant Received to Improve Kndgtn Listening Skills; Huntington Beach City Sch Dist Bd Recognition Awd; *home:* PO Box 6021 Huntington Bch CA 92646

BROCK, BETTY POPE, Mathematics Department Chair; *b:* Magnolia, MS; *m:* Jep S.; *c:* Marsha Grava, Rebecca Davis, Susan Clark, Bae; *ed:* (BS) Elem Ed, Univ of S MS 1963; (MED) Elem Ed, MS Coll 1972; Math, Univ of S MS; Rdng, Jackson St & MS St Univ; *cr:* 5th Grade Teacher Rolling Fork Elem 1963-64; 6th

Grade Teacher 1966-70, 5th Grade Teacher 1970-81 Mc Comb Public Schls; 8th Grade Math Teacher Denman Jr HS 1981-; *ai:* Mathcounts Team Coach; MCTM Math Contest Spon; Summer Math Camp Cnslr; MS Cncl Teachers of Math; NCTM; MS Prof Educators Sch Rep; Delta Kappa Gamma; PTA Pres 1957-58; 1st Baptist Church Sunday Sch Teacher 1972-; Outstanding Teacher of Yr Mc Comb Public Schls 1975-76; Mc Combs Mother of Yr 1958; *office:* Denman Jr HS 1211 Louisiana Ave Mc Comb MS 39648

BROCK, BILL, Social Science Teacher; *b:* Toccoa, GA; *m:* Leigh; *ed:* (BSED) Soc Sci, GA Southwestern Coll 1981; Soc Sci, GA Southwestern Coll; *cr:* Phys Ed Teacher GA Southwestern Coll 1980-81; Soc Sci Teacher Franklin Cty HS 1981-82, Jefferson City HS 1983-84, Franklin Cty HS 1984-86, Long Cty HS 1986-; *ai:* Help Clubs, Sports Teams & Band; Stu of Month Comm Chm; GA Assn of Educators (Uniserve Secy 1989-, Exec Cncl Chm 1989-, Local Unit Pres 1988-89); Long Cty Star Teacher 1990; Long Cty Yrbk Dedication 1989; Nom Young Man of Yr 1984; *home:* Rt 2 Box 20 Ludowici GA 31316

BROCK, KAREN WHITEHEAD, English Teacher; *b:* Union, SC; *m:* Anthony Wayne; *c:* Raymond, Kip, Ginny, Beth; *ed:* (AA) Eng, Univ of SC Union 1977; (BA) Eng, Univ of SC 1979; (ME) Elem Ed, Converse Coll 1986; *cr:* Eng Teacher Sims Jr HS 1979-82, Union HS 1982-; *ai:* Beta Club Spon; NCTE; *home:* Meadowwoods Rd Buffalo SC 29321

BROCK, LINDA M., English/Journalism Teacher; *m:* Christopher L.; *ed:* (BSE) Eng, Cntrl MO St Univ 1986; Scndry Admin, Cntrl MO St Univ 1988; *cr:* Teacher/Adv Blue Springs HS 1986-; *ai:* 9th-12th Grade Yrbk Adv; NCTE 1985-; Journalism Educators of Metropolitan Kansas City 1987-; MO St Teachers Assn 1987-; *office:* Blue Springs HS 2000 W Ashton Blue Springs MO 64015

BROCK, LUCY BRANNEN, Head Science Dept; *b:* Atlanta, GA; *m:* Michael L.; *c:* Eric, Jason; *ed:* (BS) Animal Sci, Univ of GA 1972; (MS) Reproductive Physiology, 1975, (PHD) Reproductive Phys, 1981 NC St Univ; *cr:* Lab Dir/Research Assoc Center for Reproductive Research & Testing 1981-85; Teacher 1985-86, Teacher/Sci Dept Head 1986- Wake Chrstn Acad; *ai:* Coord Annual Sci Fair; Spon Sci Club; Amer Assn for Advancement of Sci 1989-; Sigma Xi 1977-; Amer Fertility Society 1985-88; Intnl Platform Assn 1989-; NY Acad of Sci 1988-; World Wildlife Fund 1987-89; Natl Wildlife Fed 1987-; Natl Audubon Society 1988-; Articles Published Scientific Journals; Given Lectures, Seminars Local, St Level; Presented Research Natl Meetings; Whos Who Amer Women 1988; Whos Who Women Execs 1989; *office:* Wake Chrstn Acad 5500 Academy Dr Raleigh NC 27603

BROCK, MARILYN F. (MORRIS), 7th/8th Grade English Teacher; *b:* Oklahoma City, OK; *m:* Doyle P.; *c:* Robert D., Jeannie Castor, Peggy Morgan, Molly; *cr:* 6th Grade Teacher Tulakes Elem 1968-71, Overholser Elem 1971-82; 7th Grade Teacher 1982-88, 8th Grade Teacher 1988- Cntrl Jr HS; *ai:* NEA, OEA; Putnam City ACT Rep 1989-; *office:* Putnam City Cntrl Jr HS 4020 N Grove Oklahoma City OK 73122

BROCK, PHYLLIS WOOTEN, Business Education Teacher; *b:* Edgecombe Cty, NC; *m:* Jimmy L.; *c:* John, Kathryn; *ed:* (AA) Liberal Arts, Mount Olive Coll 1962; (BS) Bus Ed, E Carolina Univ 1964; (MS) Bus Ed, UNC Greensboro 1971; Effective Teaching Trng, Mentor Trng, Various Inservice Act; *cr:* Bus Teacher Randolph Cty Schls 1964-66, Winston-Salem 1966-70, Pinecrest 1973-; *ai:* Chief Adv FBLA; Teacher Advisory Cncl; Schlsp Comm; FBLA St NC Adv of Yr 1988; AVA; NC Voc Assn Bd of Dir 1980-; B E DIO Secy; NBEA, NCBEA 1968-; Alpha Delta Kappa (Pres, VP, Secy, Treas, Historian) 1978, Honorary Teacher 1978; GSA Lead Comm Mem 1980-85; Red Cross Volunteer 1978-; BSA Comm Mem 1982-85; Oustanding Young Educator 1974; Teacher of Yr 1979; *office:* Pinecrest HS P O Box 1259 Southern Pines NC 28388

BROCK, RICHARD DONALD, 8th Grade Soc Stud Teacher; *b:* Columbus, NE; *m:* Mary Sheriff; *c:* Charles, Chris Servias, Carrie, Brian; *ed:* (BA) Liberal Art/General, Marquette Univ 1958; (MS) Educl Admin, UW Superior 1984; Elem Credits Cert St Norbert Coll 1969; *cr:* 6th Grade Teacher Southern Door Jr HS 1969-71; 8th Grade Teacher Bay View Mid Sch 1971-; *ai:* 7th Grade Ftbl Coach; Girls & Boys Athletic Dir; Soc Stud Curr Comm Mem; Natl Soc Stud Assn; Nom Mid Sch Teacher of Yr; *home:* 829 Lark St Green Bay WI 54303

BROCK, SAMMY JOE, Teacher; *b:* Wheaton, MO; *m:* Mary Frances Walker; *c:* Kay, Sandy; *ed:* (BA) Scndry Ed, 1973, (MA) Scndry Ed, 1980 Univ of MO Kansas City; 7th-12th Grade Math MO; *cr:* Teacher Cabool Schls 1973-76, Bridger Jr HS 1976-; *ai:* Math Club & Natl Jr Honor Society Spon; Asst Frosh Girls Bsktbl Coach; Independence Cmmty Teachers Assn; MO St Teachers Assn (Pres, VP, Treas) 1973-, Outstanding CTA Leader 1985; KS City Area Teachers of Math 1988-; Outstanding Young Educator Finalist 1986; Independence Teacher of Yr Finalist 1988-89; *office:* Bridger Jr HS 2110 Speck Rd Independence MO 64057

BROCKDORF, JEANETTE GURSKE, Fourth Grade Teacher; *b:* River Hills, WI; *m:* Robert; *c:* Vernette, Vicki, Valerie Hayes, Vincent, Vernon; *ed:* (BS) Eng Ed, Concordia Teachers Coll 1952; *cr:* 2nd/3rd Grade Teacher Trinity Luth 1952-53; 6th Grade Teacher 1963-69, 4th-8th Grade Departmental Teacher 1975- St Johns Luth; *ai:* Hot Lunch Prgm Admin; Confirmation Class Instr; Human Care Comm of S WI Dist Bd Mem 1985-; Greater Milwaukee Fed of Luth Churches Arts Commission Chm 1985-; Luth Counseling & Family Services Bd Mem 1989-; Task Force for Luth Spec Sch Chm 1984-85; Greentree Convalescent Nursing Home Volunteer Devotional Leader; *office:* St Johns Luth Grade Sch 7877 N Port Washington Rd Glendale WI 53217

BROCKMAN, FRANK WILLIAM, III, Mathematics Teacher/Dept Chair; *b:* Pasco, WA; *m:* Zenaida Rifareal; *c:* Melissa; *ed:* (BA) Ed, Univ of WA 1972; *cr:* Teacher Seattle Public Schls 1973-; *ai:* Math Club; Team Leader; Registar; Dept Head; *office:* Hamilton Mid Sch 1610 N 41st St Seattle WA 98103

BROCKMEYER, DALE L., Science Teacher; *b:* Burlington, CO; *m:* Helen Behrends; *c:* Brent, Gary, Glen; *ed:* (BA) Bio, Buena Vista Coll 1960; (MNS) Botany, Univ of SD 1964; IA St Univ, Drake Univ, SD St Univ; *cr:* Sci Teacher Klemme Cmmty Schls 1960-64; Botany/Bio Instr SD St Univ 1964-68; Asst Bio Prof Cottey Coll 1968-77; Sci Teacher Bronaugh R-7 Sch 1980-; *ai:* NABT 1964-77; IA Acad of Sci 1960-66; SD Acad of Sci 1964-68; BSA Scout Master 1966-68; Outstanding Bio Teacher Awd Prgm 1965-68, Dir 1966-68.

BRODERICK, ELEANOR A. SCOTT, Fourth Grade Teacher; *b:* Smithville, MO; *m:* Dennis B.; *ed:* (AB) Elem Ed, William Jewell Coll 1962; (MS) Curr/Instruction, KS St Univ 1986; Grad Stud; *cr:* 1st Grade Teacher Kearney Consolidated 1962-63; 1st-3rd Grade Teacher 1963-79, 4th Grade Teacher 1979- Cntrl Elem; *ai:* Effective Teachers Team; NEA Faculty Rep 1962-; NSTA 1981-88; *office:* Central Elem Schl 8th & Barnett Kansas City KS 66101

BRODEUR, HELEN SANCHEZ, Third Grade Teacher; *b:* Albuquerque, NM; *m:* Alphonse Maurice Sr.; *c:* Alphonse M. Jr., Maria E.; *ed:* (BS) Elem Ed, Sacred Heart Coll 1964; (MS) Elem Ed, Univ of NM Albuquerque 1977; *cr:* 3rd Grade Teacher St Francis of Assisi Sch 1962-63; 2nd/3rd Grade Teacher St Edwards Cath Sch 1963-64; 7th/8th Grade Teacher St Joseph Sch 1964-65; 6th Grade Teacher Heights Cath Sch 1965-66, 1968-69; 5th Grade Teacher Our Lady of the Assumption 1966-68; Migrant Prgm Teacher 1981, 3rd-5th Grade Teacher 1969- Albuquerque Public Schls; *ai:* Nom Distinguished Teacher Awd 1984; Certificate of Appreciation 1989; *office:* Emerson Elem Sch 620 Georgia S E Albuquerque NM 87108

BRODEUR, LORAINE ANN (CANDELET), 1st-5th Grade Music Teacher; *b:* Fitchburg, MA; *ed:* (BS) Elem Ed, 1968, (MS) Elem Ed, 1982 Fitchburg St Coll; Orff Music Trng; *cr:* 7th/8th Grade Rdng/Math Teacher Peace Corps Ethiopia Africa 1968-70; 2nd Grade Teacher Reingold Elem Sch 1970-88; 1st-5th Grade Music Teacher South St Elem 1988-; *ai:* Music Lip Sync Show Putting on the Hits 1989-; Performing Arts Comm 1989-; Fitchburg Teachers Assn Rep 1978-82; MA Teachers Assn; NEA; Horace Mann Grant 1986; Lang & Math Skills Achievement Monitoring Comm 1977-78; *office:* South St Elem Complex 366 South St Fitchburg MA 01420

BRODNAX, SARAH FRANCES, 8th Grade Mathematics Teacher; *b:* Centerville, GA; *ed:* (BS) Elem Ed, 1968, (MED) Elem/Mid Ed, 1974 GA Coll; *cr:* 5th Grade Teacher W C Britt Elem 1968-73; Librarian Centerville Elem 1973-75; 7th-8th Grade Math Teacher 1975-76, 6th Grade Teacher 1976-82, 8th Grade Math/Algebra Teacher 1982- Snellville Mid; *ai:* Math Club Spon & Coach; Mid Sch Messenger Newspaper Staff; Algebra Inservice Instr; GA Assn of Educators 1968-; *office:* Snellville Mid Sch 3155 E Pate Rd Snellville GA 30278

BRODSKY, NORMA, Retired Teacher; *b:* New York, NY; *m:* Seymour; *c:* Neal H., Paul D.; *ed:* (BA) Sociology, Hunter Coll 1965; (MA) Ed, Bank Street Coll 1975; *cr:* 1st-3rd Grade Teacher 1966-85, Resource Teacher 1985-88 Public Sch 84; *ai:* Phi Beta Kappa 1966; *home:* 80 La Salle St New York NY 10027

BRODZINSKI, ANDREA THARP, Home Economics Teacher; *b:* Granite City, IL; *m:* Kenneth P.; *c:* Jeffrey, Mark; *ed:* (BS) Ed, W IL Univ 1968; *cr:* Home Ec Teacher Granite City Sr HS 1968-, Grigsby Jr HS 1989-; *ai:* IL Voc Assn; Amer Fed of Teachers; *office:* Granite City Sr HS 3801 Old Cargill Rd Granite City IL 62040

BROEDER, IOLA IRENE, Math Teacher; *b:* North Platte, NE; *ed:* (BA) Elem, Univ of Northern CO 1950; (MA) Elem, Univ of Northern CO 1964; 60 Grad Hrs Math; Mid Sch Ed; *cr:* Teacher O'Fallon Sch 1943-47; Hazelton Sch 1950-54; Highland Sch 1954-; *ai:* Ed Assn Treas; Master Agreement Comm Mem; Sec 1964-65; VP 1965-66; Pres, CO Classroom Teachers; Local NEA/CEA; 4-H Clubs Leader/Cty Cncl 1950-60 10 Yr Pin 1960; Delta Environmental Protection Assn Sec 1975-80; Evangelical Free Church (Sunday Sch Supt 1986-, Bronze Plaque 1990, Chrstn Ed Comm 1986-); Local Ed Assn Pres; Speaker Mid-Yr Conference at UNC; CO Ed Assn Exec Cncl Mem; Delegate CO Delegate Assembly.

BROERING, DONALD LAWRENCE, Agricultural Education Teacher; *b:* Cranberry, OH; *m:* Janice K Woeste; *c:* Dan, Dale, Julie, Doug, Jennifer; *ed:* (BS) Ag Ed, 1964, (MS) Ag Ed, 1971 OH St Univ; *cr:* Ag Teacher St Henry Consolidated Local 1964-; *ai:* FFA Adv; NVATA, OVATA, AVA 1965-; Mercer Cty Pork Producers Pres 1985-86; *office:* St Henry HS 181 S Walnut St Saint Henry OH 45883

BROGAN, CAROL JENKE, Administrative Intern; *b:* San Antonio, TX; *m:* Tim; *ed:* (BSE) Soc Stud/Eng/Ed, OK Chrstn Coll 1975; (MED) Spec Ed/Learning Disabilities, Cntrl St Univ 1985; Scndry Admin, Univ of OK; Grad Stud Scndry Admin, Danforth Prin Preparation Prgm, Univ of OK 1988; *cr:* Teacher Jackson Mid Sch 1980-82, Roosevelt Mid Sch 1983-88; Admin Intern Capitol Hill HS 1989-, Office of Intensive Sch Improvement 1990; *ai:* NOLPE 1990; OK Cncl for Soc Stud 1987; OASCD 1990; OK Citizens for Animals 1984-; Candidate for Danforth Prin Preparation Prgm by OKCPS, OK Dept of Ed & Univ of OK Coll of Ed.

BROGDEN, ZENA P. RICKMAN, 5th Grade Teacher; *b:* Franklin, NC; *m:* C. E.; *c:* Rickey, Mack; *ed:* (BS) Ed, Music, Brevard Jr Coll 1947; (BS) Elem Ed, Western Carolina Univ 1958; Effective Teacher Trng/Mgmt of Classroom; Comp Prgm Innovative Sci/Math Concepts; Sequential Prgm of US; Rythmical Dev/Music Technique; *cr:* 4th Grade Teacher Dublin Elem Sch 1947-48; 1st Grade Teacher Otto Elem Sch 1955-56; 5th Grade Teacher 1958-67; 5th-8th Grade Lang Arts/Music Teacher 1967-77; 5th Grade Teacher 1977- Cowee Elem Sch; *ai:* NCAE Rep Cowee Sch; Previous Sac Chairperson; Senate Bill II Rep; Parent-Teacher Liason Rep PTA Cncl; NCEA VP 1970-; PTA (Pres VP 1960; PTA Soc Finance Chm 1978-84; Cmmty Dev Prgm Chairperson Pres; Cowee Bapt Church Pianist Music Dir 1952-66 Youth Dir 1961-72 S S Dir 1983-90; this is Your Life 1958; Teacher of Yr Nom 1970; *home:* 8 Cowee School Rd Franklin NC 28734

BROHAMMER, MARTHA S., Art/Spanish Teacher; *b:* Lawrence, KS; *ed:* (BAE) Art Ed, Univ of KS 1984; *cr:* K-12th Grade Art Teacher 1985-86, 8th-12th Grade Art/His/Span Teacher 1986-88 Richland R-IV Schls; 7th-12th Grade Art/His/Span Teacher Cheney Unified Sch Dist 268 1988-; *ai:* Jr Class Spon; KS Foreign Lang Assn 1989-; KS Art Educators Assn 1988-; *office:* Cheney Unified Sch Dist 268 100 W 6th Cheney KS 67025

BROM, JOYCE A., English Teacher; *b:* West Bend, IA; *m:* Steven G.; *c:* Michael, Kim, Ruth, Matthew, Mark, Sarah, Lin, David; *cr:* Lang Art Teacher Huron Jr HS 1969-70, Center Point Cmmty Sch 1970-72; Eng Teacher Riceville Cmmty Sch 1980-87; Eng III Teacher Ulysses HS 1987-; *ai:* Study Skills Coord; Unified Sch Dist 214 Dream Team, Drug Intervention Team Mem; KS Ed Assn 1987-; *home:* 126 N Hickok Ulysses KS 67880

BROMLEY, LINDA ANN, English Teacher; *b:* New Castle, PA; *ed:* (BS) Eng/Ed, Youngstown St Univ 1976; IBM Cmptr Trng Schl; Psych, Westminster Coll; *cr:* Eng Teacher New Castle HS 1976-80, Dade Cty Schls 1987-88, St Lucie Cty Schls 1988-; *ai:* Grant Writing & Steering Comm Mem; Curr Fair Adv; Classified Teacher Assn Bldg Rep 1989-; *office:* Port St Lucie HS Lennard Rd Port Saint Lucie FL 34952

BROMMER, WANDA MARSHALL, Dept Chair/French Teacher; *b:* Easton, PA; *m:* George Kenneth Jr.; *c:* George K. III, Lucas M.; *ed:* (BA) Fr, Montclair St Coll 1970; Grad Stud Rdng, Kutztown Univ; *cr:* Fr Teacher 1970-, Dept Chairperson 1985- Salisbury Township Sch Dist; *ai:* NEA, PSEA; Neidig PAL Pres 1986-87; *office:* Salisbury Mid Schl & HS 3301 Devonshire Rd Allentown PA 18103

BRONAUGH, KAREN DALTON, Latin Teacher; *b:* Gretna, VA; *m:* John L.; *ed:* (BS) Eng/Latin, Radford Coll 1973; *cr:* Eng/Latin Teacher Roanoke Cty Schls 1973-82; Latin Teacher Prince William Cty Schls 1983-84; Latin/Vocabulary Teacher Christiansburg Mid Sch/HS & Auburn Mid Sch/HS 1984-; *ai:* Latin Club Spon; NEA, VEA, MCEA 1973-82, 1984-; Amer Classical League; *office:* Christiansburg HS 1200 Independence Blvd Christiansburg VA 24073

BRONNY, CHRISTOPHER MICHAEL, 7-8th Grade Science Teacher; *b:* Galesburg, IL; *m:* Mary Kay; *c:* Krystiana; *ed:* (BA) Elem Ed, Elmhurst Coll 1981; (MS) Biological Sci, Western IL Univ 1990; *cr:* 5th Grade Teacher 1981-84, 7th-8th Grade Sci Teacher 1984- Galva Mid Sch; Naturalist Teacher Byron Forest Preserve Dist 1990; *ai:* WAITT; In-Sch/Cmmty Recycling Prgm; Society for Ecological Restoration 1988-; the Nature Conservancy 1982-; Natural Resources Defense Cncl 1985-; Natural Areas Assn 1988-; Conservation Teacher Yr Henry Cty 1983-84; Voice of the Prairie Western IL Think-Tank 1990; the Nature Conservancy Volunteer Steward 1990; Article on Oak Savannas in Restoration and Management Notes; *office:* Galva Mid Sch Morgan Rd Galva IL 61434

BROOKE, ANNA J., Science/Biology Teacher; *b:* Hayesville, NC; *ed:* (BS) Bio, W Carolina Univ 1965; (MS) Bio, W GA Coll 1971; Grad Work Oglethorpe Univ, Emory Univ, GA St Univ, Kennesaw Coll; *cr:* Teacher Atlanta Public Schls 1965-70, Douglas Cty Public Schls 1970-79, Cobb Cty Public Schls 1979-; *ai:* Jr Advisement Coord, Faculty Awds Day & Assembly Chairperson; Class Spon; Stu Cncl; NHS; Sci, Step Ecology Club, Interclub Cncl; Alpha Delta Kappa (Pres, VP, Secy) 1972-; GA Sci Teachers Assn; GA Assn of Ed; Mt Paran Chrstn Sch Admin Bd Mem 1985-; GA Conservancy; Habitat for Humanity; Atlanta Historical Society; Atlanta Landmarks Assn; Wheeler HS Teacher of Yr; Teacher Hall of Fame; STAR Teacher Yrbk Dedication George HS; *office:* Joseph Wheeler HS 375 Holt Rd Marietta GA 30068

BROOKMAN, GENEVA KILGORE, Second Grade Teacher; *b:* Tracy City, TN; *m:* Marshall E.; *c:* Mary E. Brookman Layne; *ed:* (BS) Elem Ed, 1962, (MS) Rdng, 1972, (MS) Curr/Instruction, 1982 Mid TN St Univ; *cr:* Teacher Nunley Sch 1954-55, Monteagle Elem 1955-; *ai:* Delta Kappa Gamma 1960-; TN Ed Assn, NEA 1954-; Phi Delta Kappa 1989-; Order of Eastern Star Worthy Matron 1975, 1981, 1988; Monteagle PTA (Pres 1968, 1972, Secy 1969); TN Teacher Study Cncl (Dist Secy 1988-) 1985-; *home:* PO Box 3 Tracy City TN 37387

BROOKS, ANGELA CAMARDO, Head Math Dept; *b:* Utica, NY; *m:* James A.; *ed:* (BA) Math, Utica Coll of Syracuse Univ 1965; Syracuse Univ; *cr:* Math Teacher 1965-87; Math Dept Head/Teacher 1987- Thomas R Proctor Jr HS; *ai:* Co-Adv Thomas R Proctor Natl Jr Hnr Society; NEA; Assn Teachers NY St; Oneida Cty Assn Math Teachers; Utica Sch Bd Excl in Ed Awd 1989; *office:* Thomas R Proctor Jr HS 1203 Hilton Ave Utica NY 13501

BROOKS, ANGELINE NELSON, History/Social Studies Chair; *b:* Roxboro, NC; *c:* Chris, Nelson; *ed:* (BS) His, NC A&T St Univ 1966; *cr:* Eng/Soc Stud Teacher Northern Jr HS 1966-71; 7th-9th Grade His/Civics/Ec/Law Teacher Southern Jr HS 1971-; *ai:* Tar Heel Historian Club, 9th Grade, SADD Adv; NEA, NC Assn of Ed, Person Cty Assn of Ed Building Rep 1966-; Alpha Kappa Alpha, Democratic Party Precinct Chairperson, Blue Ribbon Ed Comm 1989-; Dept of Corrections Governors Advisory Cncl Secy 1982-; Person Cty Teacher of Yr 1989-; Region V Teacher of Yr 1990; St Teacher of Yr Finalist 1990.

BROOKS, ANNA LOIS STATON, Eng/Accounting/Typing Teacher; *b:* Calhoun, TN; *m:* David N.; *c:* David N. Jr., Harriet Brooks Mc Kay; *ed:* (BS) Bus/Accounting, Athens Coll 1945; *cr:* Bus Teacher Franklin Cty HS 1945-46; Bus/Eng Teacher Athens Bible Sch 1959-; *ai:* Past Beta Club Spon; Past Prins Advisory & Disciplinary Comm Mem; *office:* Athens Bible Sch 507 S Hoffman St Athens AL 35611

BROOKS, BARBARA WALKER, English Teacher; *b:* Longview, TX; *m:* Calvin Doyle; *c:* Robert O., Ronald D.; *ed:* (BA) Scndry Ed, Baylor Univ 1952; (MSLS) Lib Sci, E TX St Univ 1968; *cr:* Eng Teacher Buena Vista Ind Sch Dist 1953-54, Tom S Lubbock 1955-57, Rusk Ind Sch Dist 1964-65; Librarian Rusk HS 1965-80; Eng Teacher Woodrow Wilson Jr HS 1980-82, Gentry Jr HS 1982-83; Librarian Robert E Lee HS 1983-85; Eng Teacher Rusk Jr HS 1985-; *ai:* Theatre Arts; Gifted & Talented; NCTE; *office:* Rusk Jr HS Salem Rd Rusk TX 75785

BROOKS, BESSIE BURRUS, Sci Dept Chair/Bio Teacher; *b:* Orange Cty, VA; *m:* John Edward; *c:* John E. Jr., Richard Moore; *ed:* (BS) Bio, Westhampton Coll 1962; (MED) Sci Teaching, Univ of VA 1974; *cr:* Bio/General Sci Teacher Orange Cty HS 1962-72; Bio Teacher Culpeper Cty HS 1973-; *ai:* 4-H Club Spon; HS Steering Comm; Southern Assn Evaluation; NABT, NEA, VA Ed Assn, VA Assn of Sci Teachers; Culpeper Cty Ed Assn Schlsp Chm 1989-; Culpeper Memorial Hospital Auxiliary; Orange Jr Womens Club (Secy, Pres) 1968-70; Amer Assn of Univ Women Recording Secy 1988-; Culpeper HS Teacher of Yr 1970; Outstanding Young Women of Yr 1970; *office:* Culpeper Cty HS 475 Achivement Dr Culpeper VA 22701

BROOKS, BONNIE G., Mathematics Teacher; *ed:* (BA) Physics, 1978, (MS) Applied Math, 1986 Rutgers Univ; *cr:* Research Associate Exxon Research 1978-86; Math Teacher Watchung Hills Regional HS 1986-; *ai:* Amnesty Intnl Adv; Fresh Air Fund Host; SIAM, APS; 15 Publications Sci Journals; *office:* Watchung Hills Regional HS 108 Stirling Rd Warren NJ 07060

BROOKS, CAROL R., Spanish Teacher; *b:* Malden, MA; *m:* Robert I.; *ed:* (BA) Span, 1983, Certificate Comm/Public Relations, Regis Coll 1983; Working Towards MAT Foreign Lang, Sch of Intnl Trng; *cr:* Span Teacher Matignon HS 1984-; *ai:* Foreign Lang Club; *office:* Matignon HS 1 Matignon Rd Cambridge MA 02140

BROOKS, CATHERINE CABANISS, 8th Grade Math Teacher; *b:* Lumberton, NC; *m:* Robert E. Jr.; *c:* Chris, Kelly; *ed:* (BA) Intermediate Ed, E Carolina Univ 1973; Math Leadership Inst Dept of Public Instruction Phase I 1988, Phase II 1989; *cr:* 6th Grade Teacher Carver Elem 1973-76; 8th Grade Teacher Southport Elem 1976-80; 8th Grade Teacher S Brunswick Mid 1981-; *ai:* Spon for Stu Involvement Rep Stu Government; 8th Grade Team Leader; Math Chairperson Southern Assn Accreditation; Cty Math Curr Comm Mem; NC Assn of Educators (Secy 1974) 1973-; NC Cncl Teachers of Math 1985-; Cmmty Tutorial Prgm 1988-; *office:* S Brunswick Mid Sch Cougar Dr Southport NC 28461

BROOKS, CHARLES WILLIAM, High School English Teacher; *b:* Beaver Dam, WI; *ed:* (BS) Ed/Eng/Speech, Univ of WI Eau Claire 1982; *cr:* Eng Teacher Rosemount HS 1982-; *ai:* Direct Plays; Write Scripts for Shows; Announce Events for Athletics-MC at Pep Festivals/Assemblies; Publicity Liason; Ski Club, Sr Breakfast, Video Yrbk Adv; Performing Arts Leadership Team; NCTE Mem; Faculty Speaker Graduation 1987; *office:* Rosemount HS 3335 142nd St W Rosemount MN 55068

BROOKS, CHERYL CHRISTINE, Science Teacher; *b:* Miami, FL; *m:* Gary F.; *c:* John, Eric, Molly; *ed:* (BS) General Sci Composite, E NM Univ 1985; Operation Physics Trng, San Diego 1989; *cr:* 5th/6th Grade Teacher Sacred Heart Sch 1985-87; Sci Teacher Clovis HS 1987-; *ai:* Sci Club Spon; NEA 1987-; NSTA, Kappa Delta Pi 1985-; Sertoma Club Citizen of Yr 1988; Sacred Heart Church Youth Group Leader 1985-; Summer Food Service Prgm Admin 1987-; Operation Physics Wkshp Presenter 1989; NSF Grant; *office:* Clovis HS 1900 Thornton St Clovis NM 88101

BROOKS, CURTIS, Science Teacher/Coach; *b:* Lexington, MS; *m:* Erma Sly; *c:* Curtis Jr., Jimmy, Barbara Smith; *ed:* (BA) Health/Phys Ed, MS Valley St 1958; Grad Stud Univ of MS & MS St Univ; *cr:* Teacher/Coach Walnut HS 1958-61, Line HS 1963-69; Sci Teacher/Coach Ripley Mid Sch 1969-; *ai:* 7th Grade Boys Ftbl Coach; Ripley Mid Sch Sci Dept Rotating Chairperson; Tippoli Cty Teachers Assn Pres 1965-66; NEA, MS Ed Assn, MS Assn of Sch Curr Dev; N MS Athletic Assn (Secy, Treas) 1966-69; *home:* PO Box 31 Ripley MS 38663

BROOKS, DAVID GENE, 6th-8th Grade Eng/His Teacher; *b:* Madisonville, KY; *m:* Menny Goodrich; *c:* Grant; *ed:* (BS) Eng/His, 1965, (MS) Ed, 1973, Admin, 1978 Murray St Univ; Assoc Bus Madisonville Comm Coll 1982; Commonwealth Inst for Teachers E KY Univ 1988; *cr:* Eng Teacher 1965-69/1973-78, Prin 1978-80 North Clay HS; Eng Teacher Nortonville Mid Sch 1980-; *ai:* Chess Club Adv; Curr Eng Comm; KY Ed Assn, NEA 1980-; US Chess Fed 1985-; Hopkins Cty Food Bank 1985-; Meth Church Sunday Sch Teacher 1985-; Hopkins Cty Mid Sch Teacher of Yr 1988; Chess Article Visions of Teaching & Learning; Exemplary Mid Level Projects; *office:* Nortonville Mid Sch PO Box 1610 Nortonville KY 42442

BROOKS, DONALD JAMES, Middle School Band Director; *b:* Ft Benning, GA; *m:* Rebecca Hill; *c:* Melody, Shan; *ed:* (BME) Music, 1975, (MS) Music, 1985 Troy St Univ; Self Improvement Seminars; *cr:* Band Dir Crossville HS 1975-78, A S Clark Mid Sch 1978-; Asst Band Dir Crisp Cty HS 1978-; *ai:* Asst Stu Cncl Spon; Asst Fellowship Chrstn Athletes; Mgr Sr League Cordele Little League Organization; MENC 1978-; GMEA (Dist 2 Asst Vice Chm 1990) 1978-; Cordele/Crisp Concert Assn Vice Chm 1988; Cordele Evening Lions (Tail Twister, 1st VP 1986); Cordele Heart Assn Bd of Dirs 1987-89; *home:* 103 Cedar Lake Cir Cordele GA 31015

BROOKS, EVANNE SINCLAIR, Fourth Grade Teacher; *b:* Bridgeport, CT; *m:* James Joseph; *c:* David; *ed:* (BA) Art, Emmanuel Coll 1968; (MS) Ed, Univ of Bridgeport 1976; Ed Stud St Josephs Coll; *cr:* 1st-6th Grade Teacher John Winthrop Sch 1969-; *ai:* Cooperating/Mentor Teacher Beginning Ed Support, Early Intervention Stu Support Team Trng Prgms; Dist Lang Arts Trade Book Guide Comm; Sch Improvement Action Plan Mem; BEA, CEA, NEA 1969-; ASCD 1988-; Intnl Rdng Assn 1989-; NCTE 1990; CT Audubon Society 1985-; Cncl of Cath Women 1980-; St Andrew Church Catechist 1988-, 1st Level 1990; 1st Place New Newspaper Dist Awd Adv 1990; *office:* John Winthrop Sch 85 Eckart St Bridgeport CT 06606

BROOKS, GEOFFRY NEIL, Social Studies Teacher; *b:* Portland, OR; *m:* Donna R. Smith; *c:* Chelsea; *ed:* (BS) Soc Sci/Ed, OR St Univ 1973; Cmptr Sci; Computing Bus; Portland St Univ 1976-81; Standard Teaching Certificate & Grad Stud Soc Sci; *cr:* Amer Government/Global Stud/Soc Stud Teacher Jefferson HS 1972-; *ai:* World Arts Fnd Inc Tech St Consultant 1980-; Natl Assn of Black Sch Educators 1987-; Portland Teachers Assn, OR Ed Assn, NEA Mem 1974-; Oregon Black Teacher Mem 1973-74; Portland Assn Teachers Secy 1976-77; Outdoor Sch Experience 1975-76; OR St Univ Cmptr Operator 1970-72; Fernwood Mid Sch Planning Task Force 1976; Black Stu Union Chairperson 1970-72; Diversified Educl Services Consultant 1979-80; United Way Agency Bd Mem 1976-80; OMSI Project Outreach Adv Bd Mem 1983-86; *office:* Jefferson HS 5210 N Kerby St Portland OR 97217

BROOKS, GLENDA A., English Teacher; *b:* Roanoke, AL; *ed:* (BA) Eng, Univ of Montevallo 1973; (MED) Eng Ed, La Grange Coll 1977; *cr:* Supply Teacher Roanoke City Schls 1974; 9th/11th Grade Eng Teacher Lafayette HS 1974-; *ai:* Jr & Sr Yrbk Adv; Beta Club & Frosh Class Spon; Chambers Cty Ed Assn, NCTE, NEA, AL Ed Assn 1974-; Lafayette PTO Chaplain 1988-; Pilot Intnl (AL Governor Elect 1990) 1975-, Roanoke Pilot of Yr 1981; 1985 Outstanding Young Women in America.

BROOKS, JAMES ANTHONY, Eng/Latin/Journalism Teacher; *b:* Jefferson, NC; *ed:* (BS) Eng/Ed, Appalachian St Univ 1985; Grad Stud Eng, Latin, Appalachian St Univ Inst; Natl Endowment for Hum Fulbright Teacher Exch; *cr:* Teacher West Wilkes HS 1985-; *ai:* Stu Cncl, Yrbk, Latin Club, Drama Club, Fellowship of Chrstn Athletes; NCAE 1985-; Wilkesboro United Meth Church Music Dir 1989-; Fulbright Fellows 1989-; Mellon Fnd Grant; Local Ed Grant C B Eller Teaching Awd; Wilkes Ed Fnd Grant; *office:* West Wilkes HS PO Box 469 Millers Creek NC 28651

BROOKS, JAMIE CARVER, History Teacher; *b:* Lebanon, TN; *m:* Larry V.; *ed:* (BS) His, TN St Univ 1974; Belmont Coll & Trevecca Nazarene Coll; *cr:* Teacher Mt Juliet Jr HS 1974-; *ai:* Co-Spon Mt Juliet Jr HS Beta Club; NEA, TN Ed Assn 1974-; Wilson Cty Ed Assn Minority Affairs Comm Chm 1974-; St Andrews CME Church; *office:* Mt Juliet Jr HS 480 S Mt Juliet Rd Mount Juliet TN 37122

BROOKS, JOYCE HOLDER, Fourth Grade Teacher; *b:* Eastman, GA; *m:* Robert Otis; *c:* Robert M., Aaron B.; *ed:* (BS) Early Chldhd Ed, GA Coll 1969; (MS) Early Chldhd Ed, 1981; *cr:* Teacher Hawkinsville GA 1955-56, Houston Cty 1957-; *ai:* Perry Lead Teacher; Prof Assn of GA; 1st Baptist Adult Choir Soloist; Akikta Club Past Pres.

BROOKS, MARY ANN W., Span Teacher/Fine Art Dept; *b:* Calhoun, GA; *m:* Terry W.; *c:* Robbin, Curtis; *ed:* (AB) Journalism/Span, 1976, (MED) Foreign Lang Ed, 1980 Univ of GA; Working Towards Masters Univ of Valencia Spain 1977; Eng, Univ of TN Chattanooga, W GA Coll 1982-84; *cr:* Span/Eng/Newspaper Teacher 1976-85, Fine Art Dept Chairperson 1981-85 Clahoun HS; Span Teacher/Fine Art Chairperson Gordon Cntrl HS 1985-; *ai:* Lead Sr Adv; Span NHS Spon; Foreign Lang Assn of GA Secy 1986-88, Mem 1978-88); Amer Assn of Teachers Mem 1978-88, Nom Teacher of Yr 1990; Amer Cncl Teaching of Foreign Langs Mem 1978-88; 1st Baptist Choir Soprano Section Leader 1989-; Article Published; Nom Teacher of Yr.

BROOKS, MARY EARLINE ALSTON, Kindergarten Teacher; *b:* Sanford, NC; *c:* Tonda L. Glover, Donna M., Zackary A.; *ed:* (BS) Early Chldhd Ed, 1974, (MS) Early Chldhd Ed, 1977, (MED) Educl Admin/Supervision, 1980, (MS) Soc Stud/Intermediate, 1982, (MS) Curr Instructional Specialist I, 1982 NC A&T St Univ; Various Trng Seminars; *cr:* 4th Grade Teacher Nathanael Greene Elem 1973; 2nd Grade Teacher Alamance Elem Sch 1973-74; K-2nd Grade Teacher Nathanael Greene Elem 1974-; Summer Sch Site Supv Sedalia Elem 1989-; *ai:* At Risk Stus Improvement Prgm Dir; Prof Rights & Responsibilities Comm 1979; Staff Dev 1980; NC Assn of Educators (Faculty Rep 1980) 1973; NC Assn of Classroom Teachers 1973-; NC A&T St Univ Alumni Assn 1959-; Eta Phi Beta 1977-; Guilford Cty (Bd of Elections, Registrar Commissioner, Registered Voter); GSA (Brownie Troop Leader, Jr Scout Troop Leader); Heart Fund Drive Block Chairperson; NC Testing Commissioner St Dept of Public Instruction Raleigh 1987; NC Task Force to Study 1st & 2nd Grade Testing 1988; *office:* Nathanael Greene Sch 2717 NC 62 E Liberty NC 27298

BROOKS, MARY KATHLEEN, US History Teacher; *b:* Reno, NV; *ed:* (BA) His/Eng, Univ of Tx Arlington 1984; UTA in Amer His; *cr:* Rdng Improvement/Arts Teacher 1984-85, US His Teacher 1985- TW Browne Mid Sch; *ai:* PSAT Seminar Leader; Mentoring Prgm; Project Early Options; Pupil Assistance Support System; Spec Olympics Coach; Sch Safety Comm; Univ Outreach Coord; Dallas Cncl of Soc Stud 1985-; Kappa Delta Pi 1984; Phi Alpha Theta 1983; Favorite Teacher of Yr; Natl Alliance of Black Sch Educators Awd of Appreciation; *office:* T W Browne Mid Sch 3333 Sprague Dallas TX 75233

BROOKS, RALPH GORDON, English as Second Lang Teacher; *b:* Arlington, MA; *ed:* (BA) Eng Lit, 1970, (MA) Applied Linguistics, 1986 Univ of MA Boston; Advanced Grad Courses Northeastern Univ, CA St Univ Northridge, CA St Univ Los Angeles; *cr:* Jr HS Eng Teacher Arlington Public Sch 1971-75; Eng as Second Lang Teacher Roosevelt Jr HS 1979-84; Eng as Second Lang Instr Glendale Comm Coll 1981-84, Roxbury Comm Coll 1985-; Eng as Second Lang Teacher Lawrence HS 1986-; *ai:* Faculty Senate Dept Rep; MA Assn Teachers of Eng to Speakers of Other Lang Mem 1985-; MATSOL Conference Presenter 1987; *office:* Lawrence HS 58 Lawrence St Lawrence MA 01840

BROOKS, ROBERT SAMUEL, JR., Teacher; *b:* Dallas, TX; *m:* Patricia Lybrand; *c:* Adam, Eric; *ed:* (BBA) Banking & Finance, SMU 1968; *cr:* Owner Brooks Bldg Supply 1975-85; Teacher Wills Point HS 1986-; *ai:* Stu Cncl Spon; UIL Calculator Applications Coach; Natl Honor Society Comm; ATPE; Teacher Yr Wills Point HS 1988; *office:* Wills Point HS Wills Point TX 75169

BROOKS, STEPHEN MARION, Speech/English Dept Chair; *b:* Wichita Falls, TX; *m:* Rebecca Lynn Means; *c:* Fallin N.; *ed:* (BS) Ed/Comm, Univ of TX Austin 1978; Working Toward Masters; *cr:* Teacher W TX Childrens Home 1979-81; Teacher/Coach Grandfalls Royalty Ind Sch Dist 1981-; *ai:* Athletic Coach Ftbl, Bsktbl, Track, Golf; Academic Coach Team Debate, Lincoln Douglas Debate, Persuasive Speaking, Informative Speaking; Speech Club, Sr Class Spon; Natl Fed Speech & Debate Assn 1986-; TX HS Coaches Assn 1981-87, 1988-; Lions Club (Pres 1984-86, 1987-88, Zone Chm 1985-87, Deputy Dist Governor 1987-88), 100 Percent Attendance Awd 1981-88; Natl Debate Topic Selection Comm Meeting Delegate; Region 18 Ed Service Center Consultant; TX Univ Interscholastic League; Poetry Published; *office:* Grandfalls-Royalty HS PO Box 10 Grandfalls TX 79742

BROOKS, VANESSA PAYNE, 7th Grade Teacher; *b:* Asheboro, NC; *m:* Jimmy Boyce; *c:* Spencer, Ashley; *ed:* (BS) Intermediate Ed, Winston-Salem St 1978; *cr:* 7th Grade Teacher Randleman Mid Sch 1978-; *ai:* Chrldng Spon; Stu Cncl Spon; Rdng Textbook Adoption Comm; Lang Art Comm Southern Assn Accredidation; Mentor Teacher; NC Assn of Educators Rep 1986-89; NCAE Distinguished Service Awd 1989; NC Conference of Soc Stud Teachers 1988-; Winston-Salem St Univ Alumni Assn Mem 1978-; *office:* Randleman Mid Sch Box 625 Randleman NC 27317

BROOKS, WANDA JEAN, English Teacher; *b:* Madison, KS; *c:* Charles, Rhonda Hoedl; *ed:* (BS) Eng, 1957, (MS) Eng, 1966 Emporia St Teachers Coll; *cr:* Eng Teacher Haysville Jr HS 1958-60, Conway Springs Jr HS 1961-69, Hiawatha HS 1969-; *office:* Hiawatha H S Redskin Dr Hiawatha KS 66434

BROOKS, WILLIAM ROBERT, Sixth Grade Teacher; *b:* Whittier, CA; *m:* Linda; *c:* Taylor; *ed:* (BA) Child Dev, Whittier Coll 1977; (MA) Ed, Azusa Pacific Univ 1982; *cr:* 7th-8th Grade Sci Teacher Gidley Sch 1977-79; 6th Grade Teacher Bonita Canyon Sch 1979-85, Eastshore Sch 1985-; *office:* Eastshore Elem Sch 155 Eastshore Dr Irvine CA 92714

BROOKS, WILMA BREWER, Math Teacher/Dept Chair; *b:* Pennington Gap, VA; *m:* Sherley F.; *c:* Sherry Gilliam, Elaine; *ed:* (BS) Math, Lincoln Memorial Univ 1949; Several Classes Univ of VA; *cr:* Math/Physics Teacher Big Stone Gap HS 1949-59, Powell Valley HS 1959-63; Math/Eng Teacher Powell Valley HS 1964-66; Math Teacher Appalachia HS 1967-; *ai:* Beta & Jr Class Spon; Dir Prom Grand March; Prom, Faculty Soc, Faculty Flower, Biennial Plan Comm; Supvr Intern Teacher; Jr Class Day Act; NEA, VEA; Wise Cty Educl Assn Faculty Rep 1989-; Delta Kappa Gamma; Intermont Garden Club Secy 1983-87, Life Membership 1988; 1st Baptist Church; *office:* Appalachia HS 205 Lee St Appalachia VA 24216

BROOKSHIRE, DON WAYNE, Teacher/Coach; *b:* Waco, TX; *m:* Elisabeth Krauskopf; *c:* Casey, Ann; *ed:* (BS) Health & Phys Ed, TX A&M Univ 1975; Educl Management; *cr:* Phys Ed Teacher Starkey Elem 1975-77; Sci Teacher/Coach Fredericksburg Mid Sch 1977-82; Health & Phys Ed Teacher/ Coach Fredericksburg HS 1982-; *ai:* Head Coach Girls Varsity Bsktbl; Asst Track Coach; Spon Fellowship of Chrstn Athletes; TX Assn of Bsktbl Coaches 1982-; TX Girls Coaches Assn All St Selection Comm 1982-; TX St Teachers Assn 1975-; First Baptist Church Deacon; All Cen-TX Coaches Honor Roll 1983-84; All Cen-TX Coach of Yr 1985; Select Circle Coaching Awd 1987; *office:* Fredericksburg H S 202 W Travis Fredericksburg TX 78624

BROOKSHIRE, KATHY LANGFORD, Teacher of Gifted & Talented; *b:* Meridian, MS; *m:* Brian N.; *c:* Brian Jr., Cooper; *ed:* (BS) Elem Ed, MS St Univ 1973; *cr:* 1st Grade Teacher Northeast Elem Sch 1973-77; 1st/2nd Grade Teacher Lamar Elem Sch 1979-85; Teacher of Gifted & Talented Poplar Springs Elem 1987-; *ai:* Alpha Delta Kappa 1988-; Matag 1987-; *office:* Poplar Springs Elem Sch 4101 27th Ave Meridian MS 39305

BROOME, RONALD ALLEN, 5th Grade Teacher; *b:* Chicago Heights, IL; *m:* Linda Patricia Karr; *c:* Robert, Julie; *ed:* (BS) Bus/Accounting, Andrews Univ 1965; Grad Work Cmptr Ed, Univ Cntrl FL; *cr:* Accountant IL Inst of Technology 1965-66; 6th/7th Grade Math Teacher Brookwood Jr HS 1967-76; 9th/10th Grade Sci/Math Teacher Ft Myers Jr Acad 1976; 5th Grade Teacher/ Network Admin Forest Lake Elem Educl Center 1977-; *ai:* Cmptr Lab Admin; Cmptr Aid Spon; Faculty Administrative Cncl; NEA 1967-76; Glenwood Ed Assn Treas 1968-69; 7th Day Adv Church (Primary & Jr Division Leader 1980-, Church Elder 1978-); Young Republicans 1988-89; Kiwanis Schlsp, 7th Day Adv FL Conference Service Awds; *home:* 1225 Yvonne St Apopka FL 32712

BROOME, TOMMIE FOUNTAIN, English Teacher; *b:* Carnesville, GA; *m:* John Marshall; *c:* Terri, John K.; *ed:* (BA) Eng/Sociology, Piedmont Coll 1963; (MED) Eng, Clemson Univ 1977; *cr:* Eng Teacher Truett Mc Connell Coll 1977-82, Stephens Cty HS 1966-; *ai:* Chrldng Spon; Y Club Adv; Eng Dept Chm; Sr Spon; NCTE 1982-; NEA, GA Educators Assn 1972-; Parents Against Drugs 1988-; Optimist Club Teacher of Yr 1989 & Teacher of Month 1990; *home:* 306 Willowdale Dr Toccoa GA 30577

BROSTAD, JOHN CHARLES, 8th Grade Math Teacher; *b:* Cherokee, IA; *m:* Roxie Click; *c:* Jared, Matthew, Michael; *ed:* (BS) Math, Buena Vista Coll 1973; (MA) Guidance & Counseling, Univ of SD 1977; *cr:* 8th Grade Teacher Storm Lake Jr HS 1974-79; Applied Math/General Math Teacher Storm Lake HS 1979-80; 8th Grade Math Teacher Storm Lake Jr HS 1980-; *ai:* Head Boys & Girls HS Cross Cntry Coach; Head Varsity Girls Track Coach; Asst Varsity Girls Sftbl Coach; Asst 7th-8th Grade Girls Bsktbl Coach; IA Cncl Teachers of Math; IA Girls Athletic Assn Track & Field Advisory Comm 1987-; IA Athletic Coaches Assn Dist Bd of Dir 1987-; Storm Lake Jaycees Outstanding Young Educator 1977 & 1982; Girls Class 2-A Dist Cross Cntry Coach of Yr 1981 & 1984-86; Boys Class 2-A Dist Cross Cntry Coach of Yr 1987; Buena Vista Coll Coach of Yr Cross Cntry 1986; *office:* Storm Lake Cmmty Schls 310 Cayuga Storm Lake IA 50588

BROTHERS, CHERYL PATRICIA, Mathematics Teacher; *b:* Norfolk, VA; *ed:* (BS) Math, Howard Univ 1970; Numerous Univs; *cr:* Teacher Blair Jr HS 1970-83, Lake Taylor HS 1983-; Adjunct Faculty Staff Instr Univ of IL 1989-; Adjunct Faculty Tidewater Comm Coll 1989-; *ai:* Co-Spon Cooperating Hampton Roads Organizations Minorities in Engineering, Pep Club; Spon Dance Club; NEA, VA Ed Assn, Ed Assn of Norfolk; Tidewater Cncl Teachers of Math, VA Cncl Teachers of Math, NCTM; VA Comm Coll Assn; Iota Phi Lambda; Amer Bus Womens Assn; Greenbrier Property Owners Assn; Teacher of Yr Lake Taylor HS 1989-; Apple for Teacher Awd Outstanding Teachers 1988; Staff Mem IL Inst for Statistics Ed; *home:* 1919 Devonwood Common Chesapeake VA 23320

BROTHERS, JANA PORTER, 5th/6th Grade Teacher; *b:* Los Angeles, CA; *m:* William; *c:* Landon, Cameron; *ed:* (BA) Elem Ed, Ball St Univ 1976; (MA) Elem Ed, DePauw Univ 1979; Maintaining Teacher Effectiviness IU; *cr:* 4th Grade Teacher Russellville Elem 1976-781 5th/6th Grade Soc Stud Teacher 1978-79, 5th/6th Grade Lang Art Teacher 1979-86, 3rd Grade Teacher 1986-88, 4th Grade Teacher 1988-89, 5th/6th Grade Lang Art Teacher 1989- Roachdale Elem; *ai:* Mid Sch Dev; Lang Art Curr; Lib Comm; Delta Theta Tau (Pres 1980-82, VP 1987-88, Pres 1988-); *office:* Roachdale Elem Sch PO Box 309 Roachdale IN 46172

BROTHERS, MARY ANN, Sixth Grade Teacher; *b:* Johnstown, PA; *ed:* (BS) Elem Ed/Early Chldhd Ed, 1981, (MED) Rdng, 1982 Edinboro Univ; *cr:* Rdng Specialist NW Tri-Cty Intermediate Unit 1983; 3rd Grade Teacher 1983-84, 6th Grade Teacher 1984- Holy Rosary Sch; *ai:* Altar Boys Coord; Edinboro Univ Rdng Clinic Grad Assistantship; *office:* Holy Rosary Sch 1012 E 28th St Erie PA 16504

BROTHERS, MARY BETH BETH (KEIL), Fourth Grade Teacher; *b:* Toledo, OH; *m:* Robert; *ed:* (BA) Elem Ed, Capital Univ 1973; Univ of Toledo; *cr:* Kndgtn Teacher Delta Elem Sch 1975-87; 5th Grade Teacher 1987-89, 4th Grade Teacher 1989- York Elem Sch; *ai:* York Intervention Team; Alpha Delta Kappa 1983-; Pike Delta York Ed Assn Building Rep 1978-85;5; *office:* York Elem Sch 4-4945-10 Wauseon OH 43567

BROTT, BARBARA BERRY, Gifted Language Art Teacher; *b:* Chicago, IL; *m:* T. Michael; *ed:* (BA) Ed, Univ of IL 1968; (MA) Vocational/Tech Ed, Univ of IL 1981; Northern IL Univ; Governors StUniv; Curr Trng Natl St Leadership Training; *cr:* Jr HS Sch Dist 135; Soc Stud/Eng Teacher Orland Jr HS 1969-; *ai:* Curr Dev for Gifted Education; Cmptrs; South Suburban Rdng Cncl; Andrew Fnd Schlsp Comm; Co-Author Career Ed Act Used at Northern IL Univ for Teacher Trng; *office:* Jerling Jr HS 8851 W 151st St Orland Park IL 60462

BROUGHAM, JOSEPH HARRY, 5th Grade Teacher; *b:* Johnson City, NY; *m:* Cynthia Henson; *c:* Melody, Michael, Michelle; *ed:* (BS) Elem Ed, 1968, (MS) Elem Ed, 1972 NY St Univ-Cortland; *cr:* 6th Grade Teacher Apalachin Mid Sch 1968-79; 4th-6th Grade Teacher Apalachin Elem Sch 1979-; *ai:* Adv Apalachin Elem Sch Store; OATA Exec Bd 1981-83; *office:* Apalachin Elem Sch Pennsylvania Ave Apalachin NY 13732

BROUSSARD, EVELYN BAUDOIN, Bus/Fr/Cmptr Literacy Teacher; *b:* Jennings, LA; *c:* Evette R., Lonnie D.; *ed:* (BS) Bus Ed, 1967, 2nd Lang Specialist Fr, 1972, (MED) Supervision of Instruction, 1982, (MS) General, 1983 Mc Neese St Univ; *cr:* 8th Grade Teacher 1971-72, Bus/Fr Teacher 1972- Lake Arthur HS; *ai:* Sr & Fr Club Spon; Honor Banquet Comm Chairperson; Delta Kappa Gamma VP 1983-85; HS Religion Prgm Coord 1983-.

BROUSSARD, IDA L., 7th/8th Grade Lang/Sci Teacher; *b:* Lake Arthur, LA; *m:* Wilbert O.; *c:* Rhonda, Mark; *ed:* (BA) Elem Ed, Mc Neese St Univ 1977; *cr:* 7th Grade Teacher Northside Jr HS 1977-79; 7th/8th Grade Teacher Lake Arthur HS 1979-; *ai:* 8th Grade Class Spon; Jr HS 4-H Leader; Easter Seals Contact Person; NEA, LAE 1977-87; *office:* Lake Arthur HS PO Box AP Lake Arthur LA 70549

BROWER, BARBARA JEAN (REID), First Grade Teacher; *b:* New Paris, OH; *m:* Donald E.; *c:* C. Christopher; *ed:* (BA) Bus, 1949, (MED) Elem Ed, 1965 Miami Univ; *cr:* 1st Grade Teacher C R Coblentz Elem 1963-; *ai:* Delta Theta Tau (Pres, Chm 1959-60, Gamma Province 1960-61); *home:* 205 E Cherry St New Paris OH 45347

BROWER, CHARLENE BARNUM, Third Grade Teacher; *b:* Glendale, CA; *m:* Melvin D.; *c:* Charmel Pavlich, Craig, Colleen Lindsay; *ed:* (BA) Ed, Pasadena Coll Renamed Point Loma Nazarene Coll 1958; (MA) Ed, Univ of Redlands 1980; *cr:* Kndgtn Teacher 1958-59, 1st Grade Teacher 1959-63 Center Sch; Valleydale Sch 1963-71; Teacher Educationally Handicapped Valleydale Azusa CA 1971-74; 1st Grade Teacher Valleydale Sch Azusa CA 1974-80; Director Discovery Center Valleydale Sch Azusa CA 198 0-86; Primary Teacher Valleydale Schazusa CA 1986-; *ai:* Superintendents Advisory Comm Azusa Unified Sch Dist; Azusa Unified Scl Dist Curr Comm; Azusa Educators Assn Building Rep 1958-; CA Teachers Assn 1958-; NEA 1958; Valleydale Teacher of Ur 1987-88; Mentor Teacher Azusa Unified Dist 1985-87; *office:* Valleydale Elem Sch 700 S Lark Ellen Ave Azusa CA 91702

BROWER, MARY SWEENEY, Spanish/French Teacher; *b:* Sweetgrass, MT; *c:* Martin A., Clay S.; *ed:* (BA) Modern Lang, 1951, (MA) Fr, 1952 Univ of MT; Universide de Poitiers Poitiers France, Universidad De Mexico Mexico DF, Univ of WA, E MT Coll Billings, MT St Univ Bozeman, Rocky Mountain Coll; *cr:* Span/Fr/Eng Teacher Havre HS 1953-60; Span/Fr Teacher Missoula Cty HS 1960-65, Roundup HS 1975-; *ai:* Yrbk & Jr HS Stu Cncl Adv; Onward to Excl Faculty Comm; Roundup Ed Assn VP 1988-89; MT Ed Assn, NEA 1953-; St Benedicts Cath Church 1965-; Pine Echo Extension Society (Pres, VP) 1971-; Fulbright Research Scholar France 1952-53; Natl Defense Ed Schlsp 1959; *home:* Box 853 Roundup MT 59072

BROWER, PAT HOWARD, Kindergarten Teacher; *b:* Jacksonville, NC; *c:* Amy M., Kathryn L.; *ed:* (BS) Early Chldhd/ Elem Ed, Atlantic Chrstn Coll 1977; Teacher Effective, Performance Appraisal & Mentor Trng; *cr:* 1st Grade Teacher 1977-78, 2nd Grade Teacher 1978-86, Kndgtn Teacher 1986- Spring Hope Primary; *ai:* NC Super Smiles Comm Chairperson; Sci Olympiad & SACS Steering Comm; NCAE Rep 1978; Beta Sigma Phi (Pres 1986-87, Corresponding Secy 1984) Prgm of Yr 1987; *home:* 506 E Elm St Nashville NC 27856

BROWN, ALBERTA CONCHO, 2nd Grade Teacher; *b:* Albuquerque, NM; *m:* Angus L.; *c:* Leanna Fernando, Arlis, Bernard, Alden; *ed:* (AA) Early Chldhd Ed, 1974-; (BS) Elem Ed, 1976 Univ of NM; Math and Sci Inst; Health and Space Inst; *cr:* Educ Aide Laguna Elem Sch 76; Kndgtn Classroom Teacher 1976-82; 3rd Grade Classroom Teacher 1983-86; 2nd Grade Classroom Teacher 1987 Laguna Elem Sch; *ai:* Amer Indian Sci and Engineering Society Mem 1985-; Math and Sci Assn Mem 1985; Teachers of Whole Lang Assn Mem 1988; Comm Mem to Achieve Accrediation Through North Central Accrediation of Elem Schls; Certificate of Appreciation from Supt; *office:* Laguna Elem Sch P O Box 191 Laguna NM 87026

BROWN, ALEENE, History Teacher; *b:* Prestonsburg, KY; *ed:* (BA) Soc Stud, Univ of KY 1969; (MA) Ed, Univ 1978; *cr:* HS Teacher Prestonsburg HS 1970-; *ai:* KY Ed Assn; NEA Honorable Order KY Colonels KY Colonel 1984; *office:* Prestonsburg H S North Lake Dr Prestonsburg KY 41653

BROWN, ALICE BENNETT, Second Grade Teacher; *b:* Victoria, TX; *m:* L.b.; *c:* Robbi Gant Carter; *ed:* (BS) Music Ed, Bishop Coll 1966; (MS) Elem Ed, Prairie View A&M Univ 1975; *cr:* Primary Music Teacher Robert L Thorton 1966-72; Primary Music/2nd Grade Teacher Leslie a Stemmons 1972-; *ai:* Asst Spon Sch Prgms; Mem Prin Adv Comm; Tutorial Prgm; Natl Teachers Assn 1966-; TX St Teachers Assn 1966-; Classroom Teachers of Dallas 1966-; Zeta Phi Beta 1978-; *office:* Leslie A Stemmons Sch 2727 Knoxville Dallas TX 75211

BROWN, ALICIA REAVES, Media Director; *b:* Mayfield, KY; *m:* Ronald B.; *c:* Matt; *ed:* (BS) His/Eng, 1969, (MS) Comm, 1972, (Rank I) Admin, 1976 Murray St Univ; Various Seminars Related to the Comm Field; *cr:* Teacher Graves Cty Sch System 1969-; *ai:* Adv to WGCE HS Educl Access TV Channel; Graves Co Ed Assn, KY Ed Assn, NEA 1969-; Graves Cty PTA Teacher of Yr 1988; KY Teens Who Care Adv of Yr 1984; *home:* 305 Canterbury Mayfield KY 42066

BROWN, AMANDA R., Mathematics Department Chair; *b:* Midville, GA; *m:* Ralph E.; *c:* R. Bernard, Connie, Garrett, LaShonda; *ed:* (BS) Math Ed, Ft Valley St Coll 1968; (MED) Math Ed, Univ of GA 1969; (EDS) Math, GA Southern Univ 1983; *cr:* Teacher Swainsboro HS 1970-; *ai:* Math Dept Chairperson; System Math Coord; Data Collector; GA Cncl Teachers of Math 1970-; Emanuel Assn of Ed Pres 1989-; GA Assn of Ed, NEA 1970-; Amer Cancer Society Volunteer 1987-; NAACP 1989-; Sunday Sch Adult Teacher 1982-; Swainsboro HS Teacher of Yr 1988-89, STAR Teacher 1988-; *office:* Swainsboro HS Hwy 1 S Swainsboro GA 30401

BROWN, ANITA LONG, Spanish Teacher; *b:* Marion, NC; *m:* Buddy T.; *c:* David C.; *ed:* (BA) Span, Univ of NC Greensboro 1959; NDEA Lang Inst; *cr:* Classroom Teacher Shelby HS 1959-; *ai:* Foreign Lang Dept Head; Annual Co-Adv; Span Club Spon; Schlsp, Curr & Parent Involvement Comms; NCAE, AATSP, FLANC; Awarded Exemplary Teacher Levels I & II 1986-; STAR Teacher Awds; Shelby HS Teacher of Yr 1984; *office:* Shelby HS East Dixon Blvd Shelby NC 28150

BROWN, ANN BUTLER, 6th Grade Teacher; *b:* Canton, MS; *c:* Erick, Christopher; *ed:* (BA) Elem Ed, Chicago St Univ 1968; (MS) Cultural Stud, Governors St Univ 1975; Jr Great Books Certificate, Chicago Bd of Ed; *cr:* 8th Grade Teacher Cullen Sch 1968-72, Garrett A Morgan Sch 1972-83; 6th Grade Teacher Ft Dearborn Sch 1983-; *ai:* Speech Contestant 1987, 1988, 1989; After Sch Rdng.

BROWN, ANN MARIE, 4th Grade Teacher; *b:* Ft Belvoir, VA; *m:* Stephen John; *c:* Eric, Jeff; *ed:* (BA) Elem, Moorhead St Univ 1980; *cr:* 4th Grade Teacher Sebeka Elem 1980-; *ai:* Effective Schls Exec Team Leader 1986-88; *office:* Sebeka Elem Sch Dist 820 Sebeka MN 56477

BROWN, ANN WILSON, 6th Grade Math & Sci Teacher; *b:* Greensboro, NC; *M:* Wallace E. Jr.; *c:* Chris, Scott, Chad; *ed:* (BS) Prim Ed, Appalachian St 1974; (MED) Mid Grade Math/Sci, Western Carolina 1983; *cr:* Kndgtn Teacher 1974-80, 3rd Grade Teacher 1980-81, 2nd Grade Teacher 1982-83, 5th Grade Teacher 1983-, 4th/5th Grade Teacher 1989 Leicester Elem; 6th Grade Teacher Erwin Mid 189-; *ai:* NCAE 1990; *home:* Rt 2 Box 267-A Leicester NC 28748

BROWN, ANNABELLE, Retired Teacher; *b:* Rotan, TX; *ed:* (BS) Elem Ed, Mary Hardin-Baylor Coll 1941; *cr:* 5th/6th Grade Teacher Longworth TX 1941-42; 3rd/4th Grade Teacher Seymour Elem Sch 1946-82; *ai:* TX St Teachers Assn Life Mem; Amer Heart Assn, 1st Baptist Church; *home:* 604 N Stratton Seymour TX 76380

BROWN, ARLAN K., Science Teacher/Department Chm; *b:* Beaconsfield, IA; *m:* Linda E. Heft; *c:* Heather, Allison, Lindsay; *ed:* (BA) Bio/Ed, Simpson Coll 1957; (MBA) Basic Sci, Univ of CO 1964; Grad Stud Drake Univ, IA St Univ, Univ of IA, Univ of N IA; *cr:* Sci Teacher Mt Ayr Cmmty HS 1957-62; Volunteer Peace Corps 1964-66; Consultant Teacher Corps Nepal 1971; Sci Teacher 1962-63, Dept Chm 1966- IndianolaCmmty HS; *ai:* ISEA, NEA, NSTA, NABT, IA Acad Sci, IA Sci Teachers; Y Men Intnl; Natl Balloon Champion (Pres, Event Dir); Natl Balloon Museum Secy 1989-; Natl Sci Fnd Acad Yr Instr 1963-64; Cmmty Service Governors Leadership Awd 1983; *home:* 1101 North C Street Indianola IA 50125

BROWN, BARBARA BOWLER, Third Grade Teacher; *b:* Miami, FL; *m:* Jimmie Lanier; *c:* Jennifer, Gregory; *ed:* (BS) Elem Ed, FL St Univ 1968; *cr:* 1st Grade Teacher Davy Crockett Elem 1968-70, Martin Luther King Elem 1970-71; 2nd-3rd Grade Teacher Miami Cntry Day 1979-; *ai:* Rdng Curr Coord; FL Rdng Assn 1989-; *office:* Miami Cntry Day Sch 601 NE 107th St Miami FL 33161

BROWN, BARBARA HAMMETT, 7th Grade Mathematics Teacher; *b:* Columbia, SC; *m:* Nathan Joseph; *c:* Brenden, Charisse, Marshall; *ed:* (BA) Elem Ed, Univ of SC 1972; (MED) Elem Counseling, Univ of Louisville 1976; *cr:* Teacher E L Wright Mid Sch 1972-74, Lassiter Mid/Conway Mid 1974-77, Deer Park Sch 1977-83, College Park Mid 1983-88, Hopkins Mid Sch 1988-; *ai:* Lib Selection Comm, String Art Club, SACS Steering Comm; Teacher of Yr 1982; *home:* 2705 Pleasant Ridge Dr Columbia SC 29209

BROWN, BETTY LOU WILLIAMS, Kindergarten Teacher; *b:* Belhaven, NC; *m:* Elbert W.; *c:* Cynthia B. Howard, Roderick W., Debra B. Glisson; *ed:* Bus, Louisburg Coll 1953; (BS) Primary Ed, E Carolina Univ 1958; Early Chldhd, E Carolina Univ 1975; *cr:* 1st/2nd Grade Teacher Rocky Mount NC 1958-64; Kndgtn Teacher 1969-73, 1st Grade Teacher 1973-75, Kndgtn Teacher 1975- Kinston City NC; *ai:* NCAE, NEA 1958-; E Carolina Univ

Sci & Psych Grant 1962; *office:* Teachers Memorial Sch 500 Marcella Dr Kinston NC 28501

BROWN, BETTY LOUISE, 7th Grade Math Teacher Chair; *b:* Sanford, FL; *ed:* (BS) Elem Ed, FL Memorial 1969; (MS) Ed/Math, Univ of Cntrl FL 1975; *cr:* Teacher Nargani Elem 1970-71; Math Teacher S Seminole Mid Sch 1972-74, Sanford Mid Sch 1975-; *ai:* Math Club Coach; Sec ME Spon; Seminole Ed Assn, NCTM, NEA; Zeta Phi Beta; *office:* Sanford Mid Sch 1700 S French Ave Sanford FL 32771

BROWN, BEVERLY SNELL, Choral Director; *b:* Eunice, NM; *m:* Gilford Lee; *c:* L. Kyle, Tricia L. Brown; *ed:* (BME) Music, W TX St Univ 1957; Grad Stud Permian Basic, Univ of TX; *cr:* Choral Dir San Jacinto Jr HS 1958-59; Asst Dir Odessa HS 1961-63; Private Voice/Piano Choral Dir Bowie Jr HS 1984-89; *ai:* TX Choral Dirs Assn, TX Music Educators Assn 1961-; Judging of TX Univ Interscholastic League Contest Concert & Sightreading; Choirs Rated I UIL Contests & Outstanding Choir Lubbock Festival; Solo & Esemble, St Choral Concert Judging; *office:* Bowie Jr HS 500 W 21st Odessa TX 79762

BROWN, BILLIE CARMICHAEL, Retired Teacher; *b:* Bluefield, WV; *m:* Stanley Gerod; *c:* Pattie Ford, Stanette; *ed:* (BA) Elem Ed, WV St Coll 1956; (MED) Rdng, John Carroll Univ 1978; *cr:* Teacher Miles Standish Elem Sch 1956-66; Major Work Teacher Adlai Stevenson Elem Sch 1966-87; *ai:* Academic Challenge Spon 1982-86; Stu Cncl Spon 1983-85; Cleveland Teachers Union Asst Building Chm 1985-87; WV St Coll Alumni Secy 1983-, 110 Percent for Services 1988; Alpha Kappa Alpha Pecunious Grammateus 1987-; Jennings Scholar 1984-85; Master Teacher 1984-85, 1986-87; *home:* 19205 Lanbury Ave Warrensville Hts OH 44122

BROWN, BRUCE BAILEY, Mathematics Department Chair; *b:* Manchester, NH; *ed:* (BA) Geography, St Anselm Coll 1979; Math, Univ of NH 1983-87 & Rivier Coll; *cr:* 7th-8th Grade Sci/Math/Soc Stud Teacher Hood Memorial Jr HS 1980-84; 7th-12th Grade Math Teacher Nute Jr/Sr HS 1984-; *ai:* Jr Class Adv; Stu Cncl Co-Adv; Jr Var Bsktbl Coach; *office:* Nute Jr/Sr HS Elm St Milton NH 03851

BROWN, C. DWIGHT, Choral Director; *b:* Birmingham, AL; *ed:* (BME) Music Ed, 1979, (MME) Music Ed, 1986 Univ of Montevallo; Handbell Techniques; Choral Conducting; *cr:* Choral Dir Ensley HS 1981-89, Gardendale HS 1989-, Bragg Jr HS 1989-; *ai:* 4th-6th Grade Teacher AL St Music Camp; Baptist Music Dept 1981-; AL Vocal Assn Dist Chm 1990; Amer Choral Dir Assn, Music Educators Natl Conference 1981-; AL Vocal Assn Chm Dist III 1990; 1st Baptist Church (Assoc Minister of Music, Dir Youth Choir, Handbell Choirs, Ensemble); Pi Kappa Lambda 1987; Enley HS Teacher of Yr 1986; *office:* Gardendale HS 850 Mt Olive Rd Gardendale AL 35071

BROWN, CAROL BRUTON, 5th/6th Grade Teacher; *b:* Kerrville, TX; *m:* Frederic; *c:* Tracy Terrell, John Duthie; *ed:* (BS) Elem Ed, TX Womans Univ 1970; (MED) Ed Curr/Instruction, TX A&M Univ 1976; *cr:* 2nd/3rd Grade Teacher Austin Ind Sch Dist 1970-73; Grad Asst Teacher TX A&M Univ 1974-76; 4th Grade Teacher Houston Ind Sch Dist 1977-78; 2nd Grade Teacher Nome Public Schls 1978-83; 4th-6th Grade Teacher Mat-Su Borough Sch Dist 1983-; *ai:* 4th-6th Grade Speech Coach; Dist-Wide Math Curr Comm; NEA, NCTE, Intnl Rdng Assn; LADV 1985-; AK St Teacher Incentive Grant Awd 1985; *home:* PO Box 123 Sutton AK 99674

BROWN, CAROL CARMEL, Business Education Teacher; *b:* Carrollton, GA; *ed:* (BS) Bus Ed, 1986, (MED) Bus Ed, 1988 W GA Coll; Working Towards Specialist Bus Ed 1990; *cr:* Admissions Rep W GA Coll 1986-87; Bus Ed Teacher Lindley Mid Sch 1987-88, Bus Ed Teacher/CBE Harris Cty HS 1988-; *ai:* FBLA; Harris Cty Soc Comm Chairperson; MBNA, AVA, GVA 1987-: Columbus Jaycees Mem 1989-; Stu League Chm 1986-87; Prof Bus Womens Schlsp 1982; 2nd Place Impromtu Speaking PBL Natl Competition 1986; Whos Who in Amer Colls & Univs 1986; Whos Who in PBL 1986; *office:* Harris Cty HS PO Box 448 Hamilton GA 31811

BROWN, CAROL JANE, 6th Grade Mathematics Teacher; *b:* Decorah, IA; *m:* Robert D.; *c:* Lance Cheever, Laine Cheever, Lyle Cheever; *ed:* (BS) Elem Ed, 1970, (MS) Elem Ed, 1974 IN Univ; *cr:* Kndgtn Teacher De Motte United Meth Church 1968-70; 4th/6th Grade Teacher De Motte Elem 1970-79; 6th Grade Math Teacher Kankakee Valley Mid Sch 1979-; *ai:* Math Dept Chairperson; Math Club Spon; Pod Leader; 6th Grade Academic Coach; Mentor Teacher; Stu Teacher Supvr; NEA, IN Teachers Assn 1970-; Kankakee Valley Teachers Assn (Building Rep, 1st VP, Rec Secy, Discussion Team, Negotiating Team) 1970-, Good Apple 1984-89; NCTM 1975-; Natl Mid Sch Assn 1980-; De Motte Jr Womens Club (VP, Secy, Ed Chairperson) 1976-, Volunteer of Yr 1986; N Newton Chamber of Commerce Bd of Dir 1980-; IN Semifinalist Presidential Awd for Excl Sci & Math Teaching 1986, Nom 1990; Kankakee Valley Teacher of Yr 1988-89; *home:* Box 129 Roselawn IN 46372

BROWN, CHARLES EDWARD, 8th Grade Math Teacher; *b:* Starkville, MS; *m:* Annie Gibson; *c:* Taryn, Samuel, Monique Jordan, Torris; *ed:* (AA) Ed, Mary Holmes Coll 59; (BS) Elem Ed, Alcorn St Univ 1961; MS St Univ; Jackson St Univ; MS Valley St Univ; *cr:* Teacher/Coach Starkville City Sch System 1961-70; Holmes Cty Schl System 1970-; *ai:* Jr HS Boys Bsktbl Coach; HS Asst Ftbl Coach; Chairman Meth Men Epworth United Meth Church; Chairman Admin Bd Epworth United Meth Church; Holmes Cty Teacher Assn 1970-; MS Assn Coaches 1968-; NEA; MA Teachers Assn; Natl Fed Interscholastic Coaches Assn 25 Yr Pin 1985; Alcorn St Natl; Alumni Assn; Holmes Cty Alcorn Club VP 1984-85; Rocc Awd Outstanding Svc 1988; *office:* Jacob J Mc Clain H S P O Box 270 Lexington MS 39095

BROWN, CHARLOTTE PAZANT, English Department Chair; *b:* Beaufort, SC; *m:* David Allen; *c:* Rena, Patricia Bailey, William Bailey; *ed:* (BS) Eng, A&T St Univ 1971; (MED) Ed, Pepperdine Univ 1975; Effective Teaching Prgm; Eng Advanced Placement Instruction; Individualized Learning Art; Assessment for Prof Teachers; *cr:* Teacher Beaufort HS 1971-73; Teacher 1973-77, Dept Chairperson 1977- Battery Creek HS; *ai:* Beauty Pageant; Gospel Choir; SC Exit Exam/Basic Skills Comm; BCEA, SCCTE 1971-; Delta Sigma Theta Corresponding Secy 1987-; Gospel Choir; Gullas Fest Comm Bd of Dir 1984-; Small Grants US Bd of Ed Comm; Teacher of Yr 1989; Adult Ed Admin; *office:* Battery Creek HS 2900 Mink Pt Blvd Burton SC 29902

BROWN, CHAROLETTE ANN (GUNSELMAN), 5th & 6th Grade Band Teacher; *b:* Savannah, MO; *m:* Dale E.; *c:* Stephen E., Mary A., James; *ed:* (BA) Music Ed, 1956, (MA) Music Ed, 1957 Northeast MO St Univ; Ed; *cr:* Vocal Music Teacher Hurdland Schl 1956-57; HS Band Teacher Newtown Harris Schls 1958-60; Music Classroom Teacher North Harrison R-III 1960-62; Music Classroom Teacher Shawnee Mission Sch Dist #512 1962-; *ai:* Shawnee Mission North Area Elem Honor Band Dir; MENC/KMEA 1962-; NEA/NEASM 1962-; Mu Phi Epsilon VP 1980-; Alpha Delta Kappa Past Pres 1965-; Shawnee Mission North Area Elem Honor Band Performed KS Music Educators Convention 1984 & 1987; *office:* Comanche Sch 8200 Grant St Overland Park KS 66212

BROWN, CHERYL BESHKE, English Teacher; *b:* Palo Alto, CA; *m:* Randall W.; *ed:* (BA) Eng, Univ of MI 1981; (MA) Eng, Boston Coll 1986; *cr:* Eng Teacher St Anne HS 1982-84, Sharon HS 1986-; *ai:* Sr Class Adv; METCO after Sch Tutor; NCTE 1985-; NEA 1986-; Horace Mann Grant Recipient 1989; *office:* Sharon HS 180 Pond St Sharon MA 02067

BROWN, CHRISTINE HUSBAND, Teacher; *b:* Maxie, MS; *m:* Charles Jerome; *c:* Kevin, Jerome, Jermaine; *ed:* (BA) Soc Sci, 1975, (MA) Eng, 1979 William Carey Coll; *cr:* Receptionist Dr J R Todd 1975; Teacher Earl Travillion 1976-; *ai:* Cheerleading Spon; Forrest Cty Assn of Educators (Secy 1984-85, Treas 1989-); MS Assn of Educators, NCTE; True Light Baptist Church Jr Womens Auxiliary Pres 1980-89; S MS Writing Project Summer Fellowship 1987; Outstanding Young Women of Yr 1988; *home:* 609 Dabbs St Hattiesburg MS 39401

BROWN, CHRISTY HAWES, English/Speech Teacher; *b:* Athens, GA; *m:* Thomas W.; *c:* Jane, Emily; *ed:* (BSED) Speech, Univ of GA 1972; (MED) Eng, 1979 GA Coll; Gifted Added to Certificate at GA Coll 1977; *cr:* Teacher Bel Air Elem 1972-73, Norris Mid Sch 1973-74, Thomson HS 1974-78, 1982-; *ai:* Key Club, Academic Quiz Bowl, One-Act Play, Oral Interpretation & Extemporaneous Speaking Spon; Prof Assn of GA Educators, GA Cncl Teachers of Eng 1985-; 1st Meth Church Admin Bd Mem at Large 1988-; Thomson HS Teacher of Yr 1987; Thomson & Mc Duffie Cty Star Teacher 1988-89; GA Speech Teacher of Yr 1975; *office:* Thomson HS PO Box 1077 Thomson GA 30824

BROWN, CLARENCE HAROLD, Band Director; *b:* Meridian, MS; *m:* Daisy Washington; *c:* Reginald R., O. Muminah; *ed:* (BME) Music Ed, Jackson St Univ 1971; Grad Courses Univ of Dayton; *cr:* Teacher Jefferson Township Schls 1971-; *ai:* Trotwood-Madison Lions Club Bd of Dir 1987-, Pin Plaque 1988; Sinclair Coll Concert Band 1st Clarinetist 1977-80; Trotwood Concert Band 1st Clarinet Section 1989-; *home:* 412 Stuckhardt Rd Dayton OH 45426

BROWN, CLAUDIA ANNE, Mathematics/Journalism Teacher; *b:* Santa Monica, CA; *ed:* (BA) Ed/Norwegian, Pacific Luth Univ 1975; (MA) Ed, CA St Univ Northridge 1979; Credential Ed Admin, Azusa Pacific Univ 1988; Southwestern Univ Sch of Law 1989-; *cr:* Math Teacher Laurel Hall Chrstn Day Sch 1975-80; Math/His Teacher Village Chrstn HS 1980-82; Math/Journalism Teacher Huntington Jr HS 1982-; *ai:* Yrbk, Newspaper, Math Teams Adv; San Marino Unified Sch Dist Math Curr Comm; CA Assn for Gifted, CA Math Cncl, NCTM, Amer Bar Assn Law Stu Division; 1st Presbyn Church of Hollywood; Glendale YMCA; CA Teachers Instructional Improvement Prgm Grant Recipient 1987; Johns Hopkins Univ CA Teacher Recognition Awd 1989; *office:* Huntington Jr HS 1700 Huntington Dr San Marino CA 91108

BROWN, D. ROBIN LINSENMANN, 1st/5-8th Grades Rdng Speclst; *b:* Cleveland, OH; *m:* Ross H.; *ed:* (BA) Elem Ed-Cum Laude, WV Wesleyan Coll 1971; (MA) Ed, Ashland Univ 1988; Rdng Recovery OH St; Post Masters Studies Ashland Univ; *cr:* 6th/Gen Teacher Lost Creek Elem Sch 1972-72; 6th/7th Math/Sci Teacher Leesburg Mid Sch 1972-75; 6th/Gen Teacher Northmoor Elem 1975-79; 1st Grade Teacher Jonathan Alder Local Schls 1979-; *ai:* Pat Teacher Mentor Prgm; Kappa Delta Pi; Ira; Pi Gamma Mu; Exxon Sci Awd 1974; Sigma Eta Sigma; Tri-Beta; *home:* 825 Highview Dr Worthington OH 43235

BROWN, DANA FRANCIS, Teacher/Peer Leader Advisor; *b:* Malden, MA; *m:* Marie L. De Candia; *c:* Dana-Marie, Jacqueline; *ed:* (BA) His/Scndry Ed, Boston Coll 1981; (MED) Ed Admin, Univ of MA Boston 1988; *cr:* Teacher Williams Jr HS 1982-87; Bsktbl Coach MA Bay Comm Coll 1982-; Teacher Malden HS 1987-; *ai:* Peer Leader & SADD Adv; Drug/Alcohol & Health Advisory Comms; Natl Assn of Bsktbl Coaches, MA Assn of Bsktbl Coaches, MA Teacher Assn 1990; Boston Coll Alumni Interviewer 1987-; Malden Sftbl League Pres 1986-89; *office:* Malden HS 77 Salem St Malden MA 02148

BROWN, DAVID EDWARD, German & English Teacher; *b:* Tucson, AZ; *ed:* (BS) Ger/Eng Ed, IN Univ 1983; *cr:* Teacher Shenandoah HS 1986-; *ai:* Ger Club Spon; AATG 1989-; IN Assn Teachers of Ger 1987-; Shenandoah Ed Assn Treas; *office:* Shenandoah HS RR 1 Middletown IN 47356

BROWN, DAVID STUART, 5th/6th Grade Math Teacher; *b:* Cleveland, OH; *m:* Sandra Kay Griffith; *c:* Seth, Joshua, Lucas, Justin; *ed:* (BA) Eng, Lake Forest Coll 1968; (MA) Spec Ed, Northeastern IL 1972; Cmptr Sci, Jamestown Comm Coll; Univ of WI Racine, John Carroll Univ; *cr:* 3rd/6th Grade Teacher Gavin Sch Dist 1968-71; 6th Grade Teacher Allendale Sch for Boys 1971-73; 4th-6th Grade Math Teacher Sherman Cntrl Sch 1973-; *ai:* Lunchroom Monitor; IMPACT CORE Comm; PDK 1988-; NEA Life Mem 1968-; Farm Bureau 1973-; Stanley Hase Cty VFD Pres 1990; Hurlbut Memorial Church Finance Chm 1987-; Sherman Teachers Assn Pres 1982-; Highlights for Children Bd of Dirs 1990; Chautauqua Cty Teacher Center Bd of Dir Steering Comm; Chautauqua Cty Cmptr Comm 1980-88; *home:* RD 1 Box 263 Sherman NY 14781

BROWN, DEANNA F. (LA FEVERS), 6th Grade Teacher; *b:* Hillsboro, TX; *m:* Thomas Stephen; *c:* Abigail E.; *ed:* (BS) Elem Ed, MO Southern St Coll 1970; (MS) Elem Sch Admin/Supvr, Pittsburg St Univ 1973; Chem Demonstrations Wkshp Univ of N CO 1987; KSAM Project & Aide Teachers in Geology, Drury Coll 1989; *cr:* 4th Grade Teacher 1970-78, 5th Grade Teacher 1978-85 Eugene Field Elem Sch; 4th-6th Grade Teacher of Gifted Mark Twain Elem Sch 1985-86; 6th Grade Teacher Eugene Field Elem Sch 1986-; Kndgtn/6th Grade Sci & Math Teacher Drury Coll 1990; *ai:* Southern Plus & MO Southern St Coll Prgm for Children; Prof Dev Comm; After Sch Hands on Sci Prgm Coord; MO St Teachers Assn 1970-; WC Cmmty Teachers Assn Pres 1970-74; NSTA 1987-; Incentive Grant from MO 1987; Webb City Teacher of Yr 1989; KODE TV Excl in Ed Awd for Hands on Sci; *home:* Rt 2 Box 99A Jasper MO 64755

BROWN, DEBORAH BYRD, 7th Grade Math/Science Teacher; *b:* Erwin, NC; *m:* Thomas Eugene; *c:* Jason E., Casey A.; *ed:* (BS) Elem Ed, Campbell Coll 1974; (MED) Mid Grade Math, Campbell Univ 1990; *cr:* Teacher Coats Elem Sch 1974-; *ai:* Media Comm; Sci Fair Coord; 7th & 8th Grade Lead Teacher; NCCTM 1990; Nom Presidential Awds Excl in Sci & Math Teaching; *home:* Rt 2 Fuquay Varina NC 27526

BROWN, DEBORAH MC ALLISTER, Second Grade Teacher; *b:* Washington, DC; *m:* Richard C.; *c:* Katie, Kristie; *ed:* (BS) Elem Ed, 1976, (ME) Elem Ed, 1982 Univ of MD; *cr:* 2nd Grade Teacher 1977-80, 3rd-4th Grade Teacher 1981-84, 2nd Grade Teacher 1985- A Middleton; *ai:* Teacher Assistance Team Chairperson; Clinical Classroom Teacher Univ MD; Teacher in Charge; Soc Stud Curr Comm; Cooperating Teacher; Sci Fair Coord; NEA, MSTA, & EACC Membership Chairperson 1976-; MD Assn Teacher Educators 1984-; Multicultural Coalition of MD 1984-; Nom WJLA TV Excl Ed Awd; Adjunct Faculty Mem Univ MD; *home:* 3465C Marigold Pl Waldorf MD 20602

BROWN, DENICE JOHNSTON, English Teacher; *b:* Brownwood, TX; *m:* Aubrey W. III; *c:* Brittany N.; *ed:* (BBA) Mrktg, Angelo St Univ 1984; Teacher Cert Region 20 Alternative Cert Prgm Eng; *cr:* Bus Teacher 1986-87, Eng II Teacher 1987-88, Eng II/Honors Eng II Teacher 1988- Pleasanton HS; *ai:* Asst Prose & Poetry Coach; UIL Act; Dance Team Dir 1986-89; Pleasanton HS Pacesetters Dir; NCTE 1989-; Dance Team Dirs of America 1986-89; *office:* Pleasanton HS 831 Stadium Dr Pleasanton TX 78064

BROWN, DENNIS JAY, Mathematics Teacher; *b:* Harrisburg, PA; *m:* Kathy J. Smiffer; *c:* D. Timothy; *ed:* (BS) Math, 1973, (MA) Ed, 1977 Millersville Univ; *cr:* Math Teacher Elizabethtown HS 1973-; *ai:* Girls Sftbl Coach; Supts Advisory Cncl; EAEA (Pres 1989-) Mem 1973; NCTM Mem 1977; *office:* Elizabethtown HS 600 E High St Elizabethtown PA 17022

BROWN, DIANN ELLEN, Social Studies & Eng Teacher; *b:* Napoleon, OH; *m:* William Dana; *c:* William L. Geiser, Jayson J. A. Geiser, Stacy J. E. Geiser; *ed:* (BS) Music, OH Northern Univ 1970; (ME) Elem Ed, Bowling Green St Univ 1975; Grad Stud; *cr:* 5th/12th Grade Vocal Music Teacher Patrick Henry HS 1970-74; Elem Ed Teacher 1974-82, 7th/8th Grade Soc Stud/Eng Teacher 1982- Patrick Henry Schls; *ai:* Luther League, Stu Cncl Adv; Asst Dir Musical; Guidance & Building Steering Comm; Patrick Henry Ed Assn Pres 1984-86; NW OH Ed Assn Distinguished Service Awd 1985-86; OH Ed Assn, NEA; Amer Legion Auxiliary Americanism Chm; St Stephen Luth Church (Asst Organist, Dir Bible Sch Music, Elder); Taft Seminar 1988; Ashland Oil Golden Apple Achiever Awd 1988; *office:* Patrick Henry Schls St Rt 109 Hamler OH 43524

BROWN, DONNA, Drama Coach; *b:* Altus, OK; *ed:* (BA) Span, 1970, (MS) Theater, 1978 Southwestern; *cr:* Teacher Jet-Nash 1970-71, Tipto Public Schls 1971-78, Navajo Public Schls 1978-86, Putnam City HS 1986-; *ai:* Competitive Drama Coach; Directing Plays; OEA, NEA; OK Speech & Drama Teacher of Yr; Tipton & Navajo Teacher of Yr; *home:* 6060d NW Expressions Oklahoma City OK 73132

BROWN, DONNA MAXWELL, Career Investigation Educator; *b:* Jacksonville, TX; *m:* Cecil Dewayne; *c:* Angela R., Heath W.; *ed:* (AA) Home Ec, Tyler Jr Coll 1969; (BS) Home Ec, 1971, (BSHE) Home Ec/Ed, 1977 Stephen F Austin St Univ; Peer Trainer/Adv Region VII Ed Service Center 1988; At-Risk Stu Trng 1988-89; *cr:* Home Ec Teacher Tyler Ind Sch Dist 1977-80; HECE Teacher/Coord 1980-85, Career Investigation Educator 1985- Chapel Hill Ind Sch Dist; *ai:* 7th Grade At-Risk Teacher;

At-Risk Campus Curr Coord Mid Sch; Peer Helper Adv/Teacher; Voc Home Ec TAT Area VII Pres 1977-85; TX Voc Guidance Assn (Coord, Secy 1985-, Area Pres 1977-85); Outstanding CI Teacher 1986; Bus & Prof Women Pres, Woman of Yr 1989; Delta Kappa Gamma Society Secy 1978-; Teacher of Yr Awd Chapel Hill Ind Sch Dist 1988; *office:* Chapel Hill Ind Sch Dist Rt 7 Box 34A Tyler TX 75707

BROWN, DOROTHY FRANCES, First Grade Teacher; *b:* Tucson, AZ; *ed:* (BS) Elem Ed, Southwestern St Coll 1966; (MA) Elem Ed, N AZ Univ 1973; *cr:* 2nd Grade Teacher Sunray Elem 1966-68; 1st Grade Teacher Cntrl Elem 1968-; *ai:* Drug & Alcohol Core Team; NEA 1966-; NMEA, BEA 1968-; NCTM 1978-80; ABWA 1985-; PTA 1986-; GSA 1969-; *office:* Cntrl Elem Sch 310 W Sycamore Bloomfield NM 87413

BROWN, EDWARD J., Science Teacher; *b:* Washington, DC; *m:* Judith Taylor; *c:* Kirstin, Elisabeth; *ed:* (BS) Zoology, 1964, (MA) Curr, 1970 MI St Univ; Medical Sch Univ of MI 1964; *cr:* Sci Teacher Whittier Jr HS 1966-67, Kinawa Mid Sch 1967-; *ai:* Habitat for Humanity 1987-; Cmmty Mental Health Bd 1979-; Teacher Trng MI St Univ 1985; *office:* Kinawa Mid Sch 4006 Okemos Rd Okemos MI 48864

BROWN, EDWARD JAMES, JR., English/Mentor Teacher; *b:* Tampa, Guam; *m:* Amy E.; *ed:* (BA) Eng, San Diego St Univ 1985; (MA) Educl Admin, US Intnl Univ 1989; *cr:* Eng Teacher Lake Elsinore Jr HS 1985-86; Eng Teacher/Mentor/Act Dir Terra Cotta Jr HS 1986-; *ai:* Act Dir; Mentor Teacher; Nothing Club Adv; *office:* Terra Cotta Jr HS 29291 Robb Rd Lake Elsinore CA 92330

BROWN, ELIZABETH ANN, Mathematics Dept Chm; *b:* Gaffney, SC; *m:* Robert Earl Sr.; *c:* Richard E., Robert E. Jr., Larry W.; *ed:* (BA) Elem Ed, Limestone Coll 1973; (MED) Math, Converse Coll 1978; AP Cmptr Sci Inst Winthrop Coll; *cr:* 8th Grade Math Teacher Pacolet Mid Sch 1973-76; Math/Cmptr Sci Teacher Broome HS 1976-; *ai:* Stu Government Assn Adv; Boys & Girls Track Scorekeeper; Girls Track Coach Asst; NCTE, SC Ed Assn, NEA; Eastside Baptist Church (Organist 1982-, Sunday Sch Teacher 1982-); *office:* Broome HS 381 Cherry Hill Rd Spartanburg SC 29302

BROWN, ELIZABETH FEREBEE, Third Grade Teacher; *b:* Clinton, NC; *m:* Robert Alan Sr.; *c:* R. Alan, Richard C., Corydon R., Cynthia L.; *ed:* (BA) Eng, Coll of William & Mary 1952; Grad Stud Univ of AL Huntsville; *cr:* 1st Grade Teacher 1969-79, 3rd Grade Teacher 1979- Randolph Sch; *ai:* Historic Huntsville Fnd, Huntsville Botanical Garden 1987-; Alliance for Mentally Ill 1986-.

BROWN, EMMA CAROL, Social Stud Teacher-Hist Instr; *b:* Covington, KY; *ed:* (BA) His, 1969, (MA) His, 1974 Morehead St Univ; *cr:* Teacher Simon Kenton HS 1969-74; Merchandiser J C Penney Company 1974-82; Store Mgr Fashion Bug Stores 1982-83; Teacher/Instr St Thomas Sch 1983-, St Catharine Coll 1989-; *ai:* St Thomas Jr Beta Club Spon; NCEA 1983-; Kenton Cty Faculty Assn Treas 1981; His Article for Bicent His of KY Publ 1992; *home:* 189A Old Sutherland Ln Bardstown KY 40004

BROWN, ETHELE HARVIN, Business Dept Chairperson; *b:* Sumter, SC; *m:* Elmo R.; *c:* Elaine, Erica; *ed:* (BS) Bus Ed, Wilberforce Univ 1949; MA Prgm, Montclair St Coll; Real Estate, Bergen Comm Coll; *cr:* Bus Dept Chairperson St Mary HS 1978-; *ai:* Veritas Yrbk Bus Mgr 1982-; Prom Comm Adv 1985-; Sunshine Fund 1980-; Modeling Club Co-Chairperson 1989-; NBEA, NJ Bus Ed Assn 1979-; Natl Realtor Assn, E Bergen Cty Bd of Realtors 1985-; Womens Assn Presbyn Church of Teaneck Treas 1986-; Spring Glen Woods Inc Secy 1980-; Quettes, Omega Psi Phi, Nu Beta Beta Treas 1990; Headstart Prgm Bd Mem; Bergen Cty Child Care Coordinating Cncl Proposal Comm Mem; PTA (Mem, Officer); Afro Amer Educl Center (Chairperson, Saturday Volunteer); YWCA Bd Mem; *office:* St Mary HS 64 Chestnut St Rutherford NJ 07070

BROWN, EVELYN ERELENE, Fifth Grade Teacher; *b:* Taswell, IN; *m:* Lester Lewis; *c:* Beth Brown Rominger, Bradley C.; *ed:* (BS) Ed, Oakland City Coll 1954; (MS) Ed, IN Univ 1960; Grad Stud Ed, IN Univ, Butler Univ; *cr:* 3rd Grade Teacher Paoli Cmmty Schls 1954-63; 5th Grade Teacher MSD Warren Township 1974-; *ai:* Delta Kappa Gamma 1958-63; Alpha Delta Kappa Pres 1978-80, 1990; Phi Beta Psi Treas 1955-63; Glen Oaks Garden Club 1990; *office:* MSD Warren Township 1850 N Franklin Rd Indianapolis IN 46219

BROWN, FLOYD ERNEST, Mathematics Teacher; *b:* Knoxville, TN; *m:* Deidre Lynn Wilkes; *ed:* (BA) Math Ed, Warren Wilson Coll 1982; *cr:* Math Teacher West Mecklenburg HS 1982-83, Unaka HS 1983-; *ai:* Stu Cncl Adv; Faculty Advisory, Parents Advisory, Test-Improvement Comm; Math Dept Chm; NCTM, NEA, TN Ed Assn; Carter Cty Ed Assn Scndry Level Teacher of Yr 1989; Math Ed Grant Upper E TN Cncl Teachers of Math 1989; Math Consortium Participant 1988-89; *home:* Rt 3 Box 1990 Butler TN 37640

BROWN, FLOYD IVAN, History Teacher/Dept Chair; *b:* Plainview, NE; *m:* Judith Marie Rautenberg; *c:* David L., Darin G.; *ed:* (BAE) His/Phys Ed, Wayne St 1966; Values Ed; *cr:* His/ Phys Ed Teacher Girls Trng Sch 1966-68; His/Coach Niobrara HS 1968-70, Republican Valley HS 1970-71, Lyons & Lyons-Decatur NE 1971-; *ai:* His Dept Chairperson; Sr HS Head Boys Track; Letterman Spon; Jr HS Ftbl Coach; Lyons Ed Assn Pres 1980-81; Meth Church; Lyons-Decatur Northeast Teacher of Yr 1984-85; *home:* 625 Lincoln Lyons NE 68038

BROWN, FRANCES COOLEY, Assistant Principal; *b:* Ronoke Rapids, NC; *m:* Ralph Nayland; *c:* Carla Shows, Connie Hilbun, Ben, Karen, Roland, Glenda Wright, Sandra Zumbro; *ed:* (A) Bus Ed, 1959, Elem Ed, 1969 USM; (AA) Elem Ed, William Carey 1 979, Adm, Univ Southern MS 1988; *cr:* Bus Mgr George Cty Schls 1960-68; 4th Grade Teacher Rocky Creek Attendance Center 1968-88; Asst Prin Lucedale Elem Sch 1988-; *ai:* Asst Test Coord George Cty Schls; Staff Dev Comm; George Cty Grant Comm; George Cty Ed Assn-VP 1985; *home:* Rt 8 Box 2 Lucedale MS 39452

BROWN, GERALD DAVID, 5th Grade Teacher; *b:* Riverhead, NY; *m:* Marilyn Elliott; *c:* Mary, David, Paul, Donna, Steven; *ed:* (BS) Elem Ed, SUNY Oswego 1964; *cr:* 6th Grade Teacher Mattituck Sch Dist 1964-68; 6th Grade Teacher 1968-85, 5th Grade Teacher 1985- Riverhead Sch Dist; *ai:* NY St United Teachers 1964-; RHD Faculty Assn Pres 1979-82; *office:* Pulaski Street Sch 300 Pulaski St Riverhead NY 11901

BROWN, GERRY EUGENE, General Science Teacher; *b:* Plymouth, IN; *m:* Deborah Sullivan; *c:* Jameson; *ed:* (BS) Earth Sci, 1974, (MS) Earth Sci, 1981 Ball St Univ; *cr:* Drivers Ed Teacher John Glenn HS 1976-89; Sci Teacher Urey Mid Sch 1974-; Athletic Dir Urey Mid Sch, N Liberty, Walkerton Elem Schls 1981-; *ai:* Athletic Dir Urey Mid Sch, N Liberty, Walkerton Elem Schls; Var Asst Ftbl Coach John Glenn HS; IN Interscholastic Athletic Admin Assn 1982-; *office:* Urey Mid Sch 406 Adams St Walkerton IN 46574

BROWN, GLENDA ALLEN, 5th and 6th Grade Teacher; *b:* Callao, MO; *m:* Jerry K.; *c:* Dynea, Les; *ed:* (BSED) Elem Ed, Northeast MO St Univ 1963; (MED) Elem Ed, Univ of Southern MO 1968; Univ of VA; *cr:* 3rd Grade Teacher Quincy Public Schls 1963-67; 1st Grade Teacher St James Sch Dist 1967-68; 4th Grade Teacher Crawford Cty R-II Sch Dist 1968-69; 3rd Grade Teacher Charlottesville City Sch System 1970-77; 5th-6th Grade Teacher Callao C-8 Sch 1981-; *ai:* Grade Level Chm; Callao Teachers Assn Pres 1989; PTO Pres; Callao Meth Church; Annual Teacher Evaluation Assessments; Master Teacher of Stu Teachers from Univ of VA; *home:* Rt 1 Box 7 Callao MO 63534

BROWN, HARRY ROSS, Math Teacher; *b:* Williston, ND; *ed:* (BA) Math/His, Concordia Coll 1967; (MA) Curr/Instruction, Coll of St Thomas 1981; *cr:* Math Teacher Forest Lake Jr HS 1969-77; Math/His Teacher Schweinfurt Amer Jr HS 1977-79; Math Teacher Incirlik HS 1979-80, Southwest Jr HS 1980-82, A T Mahan HS 1982-85, Schweinfurt Amer Sch 1985-86; Math/Sci Teacher Darmstadt Mid Sch 1986-87; Math Teacher David Glasgow Farragut HS 1987-; *ai:* Natl Jr Honor Society, NHS Spon; Co-Spon Stu Cncl; Girls Var Bsktbl Team Coach; NCTM, Overseas Educl Assn; Local Ed Assn Pres 1984-85; NEA; Amer Indian Ed Coord 1975-76; *office:* David Glasgow Farragut HS Box 63 FPO New York NY 09540

BROWN, HARRY THOMAS, JR., Social Science Teacher; *b:* New York, NY; *m:* Sheila Tooley; *ed:* (BA) Psych/Scndry Ed/Soc Stud, St Univ of NY New Platz 1983; Masters Degree Work Educl Leadership, Nova Univ 1988-; *cr:* Teacher Northeast Sr HS 1984-87; Intnl Baccalaureate Prgm Teacher St Petersburg Sr HS 1987-; *ai:* Inter-Club Cncl Spon; Ten Yr Self Study Steering Comm Chm; Pinellas Cty Soc Stud Curr Cncl; FL Cncl for Soc Stud, Pinellas Classroom Teachers Assn, NCSS; Big Brothers & Big Sisters; St Petersburg HS Teacher of Yr 1989; Rotary Intnl Service Awd; Northeast HS Teacher of YR 1986; *home:* 3034 15th St N Saint Petersburg FL 33704

BROWN, HELEN OTTINGER, Teacher/Counselor of LD; *b:* Hinton, OK; *w:* W. L. (dec); *c:* Sharalee Brown Savage; *ed:* (BS) Child Dev, OK St Univ 1953; (ME) Elem Ed, E NM Univ 1967; Learning Disability; *cr:* Teacher of Multihandicap 1953-55, Teacher of Visual Handicap 1955-56 Ft Worth Public Schls; 1st Grade Teacher Clovis Public Schls 1964-76; Teacher of Learning Disabilities/Cnslr Hydro Public Schls 1977-; *ai:* NHS Spon; System St Testing Admin; CEC (VP 1975-76) 1989-; Assn for Children with Learning Disabilities; Farm Bureau 1976-; Meth Church (Teacher, Church Bd Mem 1976-); St of NM Behavior Disorder Design Prgm Grant Comm Mem; *office:* Hydro HS 529 E 6th St Hydro OK 73048

BROWN, HELGA SEINSOTH, Foreign Language Teacher; *b:* Prum/eifel, West Germany; *m:* Thomas Gwynn; *ed:* (BA) Fr/Ger, 1973, (MA) Ger, 1974 Univ of N Las Vegas; Grad Stud Univ of Avignon France 1983, Univ of WA Seattle 1984; *cr:* Foreign Lang Teacher Hyde Park Jr HS 1973-80, Basic HS 1980-; *ai:* Deutschklub; European Club; AATG Mem 1968-; AATF Mem 1970-; NV Foreign Lang Teachers Assn (Mem, VP, Pres 1979-80) 1980-81; Clark Cty Foreign Lang Teachers Assn 1973-; Foreign Lang Assn of NV Mem 1990; Amer Bus Womens Assn (VP 1982-83, Pres 1983-84), Woman of Yr 1975; CCFLTA (Treas, VP, Pres); *office:* Basic HS 400 S Palo Verde Henderson NV 89015

BROWN, IONA BURKE, Mathematics Teacher/Dept Chair; *b:* Richmond, VA; *m:* Cornelius E. III; *c:* Iona R.; *ed:* (BS) Math, VA Union Univ 1953; (MTS) Math, Catholic Univ 1969; Numerous Univs; *cr:* Teacher Maggie L Walker HS 1954-63, Douglass Jr HS 1963-66, Paul Jr HS 1967-; *ai:* Natl Jr Honor Society & Math Club Spon; NCTM, DC Cncl Teachers of Math, Mathematical Assn of America; Montgomery Cty Swim League Secy 1988-; St Stephen & Incarnation Episcopal Church; TV Tutoring Host; Module Writer NITV/DCPS Math Series 1988; Mid Sch Math Project Advisory Bd Mem 1985; *office:* Paul Jr HS 8th & Oglethorpe Sts NW Washington DC 20011

BROWN, IRMA KING, 5th Grade Teacher of Gifted; *b:* St Louis, MO; *m:* Andrew J.; *c:* Bernadette, Andrew Jr., Angela Meadors, Madonna, Monica, Maureen; *ed:* (BA) Elem Ed, Stowe Teachers Coll 1945; (MA) Elem Ed, Univ of IL 1948; Washington Univ, Webster Univ, St Louis Univ, Univ of MO St Louis; *cr:* Demonstration Teacher Simmons Elem Sch 1946-52; 5th Grade Teacher Columbia Elem Sch 1956-74; Teacher Wade Gifted Center 1974-76, Kennard Gifted Center 1976-80; Teacher of Gifted Classical Jr Acad 1980-; *ai:* Urban Archaeology; Urban Anthropology; Consumer Ed; Law in Ed; Stock Market Game; Writing Wkshps; Newspaper in Ed; Gifted Assn of MO 1974-, Excl in Teaching Awd 1987; Intnl Rdng Assn, Greater Cncl Teachers of Eng 1946-; Iota Phi Lambda Apple for Teacher Awd 1989; Local 420 AFLCIO Building Rep 1956-88; AFT, MO Fed of Teachers 1956-; MO Dept Elem & Scndry Ed Advisory Bd 1989-; Teacher of Yr St Louis Public Sch 1988-89; Excl in Teaching Awd Emerson Electric Company 1989; Excl in Teaching VP Fair Fnd 1989; Univ of MO St Louis Excl in Stock Market Project Grand Prize Winner 1986; St Louis Post Dispatch Educl Advisory Bd; Area IV Writing Awd; *office:* Classical Jr Acad 5351 Enright Ave Saint Louis MO 63112

BROWN, JAMES ALTON, 4th Grade Teacher; *b:* Ft Campbell, KY; *ed:* (AA) Valencia Comm Coll 1978; (BA) Elem Ed, 1980, (MED) Elem Ed, 1986 Univ of Cntrl FL; *cr:* 5th Grade Teacher Englewood Elem 1980-87, Ventura Elem 1987-88; 4th Grade Teacher Ventura Elem 1988-; *ai:* After Sch Prgm Dir & Coord; Latch Key Kids; Cmptr Instr for Parents; Engelwood Elem Teacher of Yr; Featured in Magazines; Innovative Classroom Practices Awd; *office:* Ventura Elem Sch 4400 Wooodgate Blvd Orlando FL 32802

BROWN, JANET CORINNE, Second Grade Teacher; *b:* Fruitport, MI; *c:* Corinne D. Benoit, Lisa D. Graham, Dennis H., Natalie R. Cates, Allyson E. Miller; *ed:* (BS) Elem Ed/Eng/His, FL S Coll 1955; (MA) Guidance/Rdng, Stetson Univ 1972; Grad Stud; Real Estate License; *cr:* Teacher Henry St Sch 1953-54, Lee Elem 1955-56; Practice Teachers Supvr Auburn Univ 1956; Teacher Mary Bryan Elem 1957-59, St Cloud Elem 1957-; Substitute/Teacher Beverly Shores Elem 1960-; *ai:* FL Barrel Racers Assn Mem; Natl Womens Prof Barrel Racer; FL Womens Prof Barrel Racers 1987-88, St Champion Super Srs 1989; FL Barrel Racers Top 15 in St 1986; FL Cowboy Assn Top 15 in St 1986; 1st Baptist Church (Mem, Womens Care Center Cnslr); Owned a Restaurant & Land Dev Corporation.

BROWN, JANICE WATSON, Mathematics Teacher; *b:* Columbia, SC; *m:* Harry Roscoe; *ed:* (BA) Math, 1972, (MAT) Math/Ed, 1975 Univ of SC; *cr:* Math Teacher Spring Valley HS 1972-78, Richland NE HS 1978-; *ai:* Sr Class & NHS Spon; NCTM 1979-; SC Cncl Teachers of Math (Pres, VP, Scndry) 1980-, Outstanding Contributions Math Ed SC 1988; SC Assn of Advanced Placement Math Teachers (Secy, Treas) 1985-; Delta Kappa Gamma 1986-; Leading Math into 21st Century SC Comm 1990; Presidential Awd Excl in Sci & Math Teacher; Richland Northeast HS Teacher of Yr; SC Mathematical Sci Coalition Co-Dir; Tandy Technology Schlolar Outstanding Math Teacher; *office:* Richland Northeast HS 7500 Brookfield Rd Columbia SC 29223

BROWN, JEAN VANDER LINDEN, Home Economics Teacher; *b:* Oskaloosa, IA; *m:* Ronald E.; *c:* Brian, Scott; *ed:* (AS) Home Ec Ed, Ottumwa Heights Jr Coll 1969; (BS) Home Ec Ed, IA St Univ 1971; *cr:* HS Home Ec Teacher Albia Cmmty Schls 1971-72; Jr HS Home Ec Teacher Moline Schls 1972-74; Adult Microwave Instr Quasar Company 1983-84; HS Home Ec Teacher Rockridge Schls 1984-; *ai:* Head Frosh Class, Rocket Spirit Club, Home Ec Club Spon; Jr Achievement & Applied Ec Teacher; Quad City Area Home Economists Secy 1977-79; Jr Womans Club of Rock Island Project Chm 1977-84, Club Woman of Yr 1982; Meth Church (Sunday Sch Supt 1978-87, Youth Dir 1989-); Developed First Food for Athlete Course in the Area; Led Seminars Among Prof Groups; Nom Omicron Nu Honary Home Ec Sorority Mem; *office:* Rockridge HS 14110 134th Ave W Taylor Ridge IL 61284

BROWN, JEANETTE ADERHOLD, Teacher; *b:* Durham, NC; *m:* Frank W.; *c:* Constance B. Squires, Jeanne B. Miller, Deborah L.; *ed:* Literary, Averett Coll 1949; (BA) Religious Ed, Westhampton Coll 1951; Remedial Rdng, 1968-69, Gifted Ed, 1980-83, Mid Sch Curr 1986-87 Univ of VA; *cr:* Elem Teacher Patrick Henry Elem 1953-54, Chatham Elem 1967-69, Woodlawn Acad 1969-71; 7th Grade Teacher Cntrl Elem 1971-76; 7th/8th Grade Gifted Teacher Fluvanna Mid Sch 1976-; *ai:* 7th Grade Team Leader; Leadership Team Mem & Coord; Stu Government Spon 1971-85; VA Ed Assn & Fluvanna Ed Assn 1971-76; NCTE 1989-; Natl Soc Stud Assn 1979-80; PTA Pres 1967; Daughters of Amer Revolution 1989-; Chatham Baptist Church Youth Dir 1965-71; Garden Club (Pres 1966, Show Chairperson 1967); *home:* PO Box 81 Rt 15 Fork Union VA 23055

BROWN, JEFFREY STEVEN, 5th Grade G.A.T.E.; *b:* Sacramento, CA; *ed:* (BA) His, CSU Stanislaus 1972 Elem Ed, CSU Fresno 1974; Completing Masters Math & Sci,Fresno Pacific Coll; *cr:* Rdng Specialist Tuolumne Elem 1975-76; 6th Grade Bi-Ling/GATE Teacher 1976-80; 4th-6th GATE Teacher Modesto City Schls 1980-; *ai:* Math Olympiad Steering Comm; GATE Elem Teacher; CA Rdng Assn 1977-79; CA Bi-Ling Assn 1978-79; CA Assn of Gifted 1981-89; 1st Baptist Church Teacher 1982-86; Co-Writer Metric Ed for Modesto City Schls; Review Comm Sci Ed, Bi-Ling Ed Modesto City Schls; *office:* Sonoma Elem Sch 1325 Sonoma Ave Modesto CA 95355

BROWN, JOHN, English & Poetry Teacher; *b:* Longmeadow, MA; *ed:* Lit/Philosophy, St Pauls Coll; (BA) Lit, Villanova Univ 1964; Eastern Stud, Univ of PA; Jungian Psych, Eranos Switzerland 1972; Hermetic Tradition, Hawkwood Coll England 1973; Poetics/Oriental Lit, Naropa Inst 1974-80; Wkshps at Glassboro St Coll, Immaculata Coll, Coll of Art, York Univ, Naropa Inst; *cr:* Eng Teacher Cardinal O Hara HS 1965-; Poetry Teacher Wallingford Art Center 1980-; Dir Jungian Study Center 1985-; Writing Prgm/Poetry Teacher W Chester Univ 1988-; *ai:* Stu Literary Magazine Moderator; Green Environment Club; Sch & Cmmty Comm Mem; Round Table Assn Dir 1985-; W Chester Poetry Assn Planner 1984-88; CODA; NY Nalanda Fnd 1974-; Rose Tree Park Full Moon Poetry Rdng (Judge 1988) 1984-; De Valley Writers Mem 1984-; Shambhala Staff 1980-, Great Eastern Sun 1985; Chapbooks of Poetry; NJ Cncl for Art Visiting Poet Stockton St Coll Grant 1988; *office:* Cardinal O Hara HS 1701 Sroul Rd Springfield PA 19063

BROWN, JOHNNIE RUTH JOHNSON, 6th Grade Math/ Science Teacher; *b:* Port Gibson, MS; *m:* James Wesly Jr.; *c:* James W. III; *ed:* (bs) Elem Ed. 1967, (ms) Elem Ed, 1976 Alcorn St Univ; *cr:* Elem Teacher Mixon Elem 1967-; *ai:* 6th Grade Chairperson 1990; Hinds Assn of Educators Pres 1976-77 Plaque; NEA Delegate 1977-78 Certificate; Sigma Gamma Pres 1974-78 Trophy; Eastern Star Court Mem 1990; Herions of Jerioch Mem 1990; Mercy Seat M B Church (Bd of Trustees, Mem) 1990; Delegate NCTM Conference 1990, Natl Assn of Educators 1978; Outstanding Teacher Awd Hinds Cty Schls 1978; *home:* Rt 1 Box 193 Port Gibson MS 39150

BROWN, JOY MC LELLAND, Social Studies/Fr I Teacher; *b:* Meridian, MS; *m:* William Barney; *c:* Mary Ellen; *ed:* (BA) His, MS Univ for Women 1973; Additional Stud Early Chldhd Ed; Working Towards Masters in Scndry Ed, His, MS St Univ; *cr:* Kndgtn Teacher 1975-80, Soc Stud Teacher 1978-, Fr I Teacher 1986- Kemper Acad; *ai:* Annual Staff Adv; Sr Class Spon; MS Economic Cncls STAR Teacher 1979, 1986, 1987, 1988, 1990.

BROWN, JUANITA CURTIS, Sixth Grade Teacher; *b:* Jeffersonville, GA; *m:* Joseph Harrison; *c:* Jona L., Joseph C.; *ed:* (BS) Elem Ed, Ft Valley St Coll 1968; Grad Stud Ft Valley St Coll; *cr:* 3rd Grade Teacher Mt Olive Elem Sch 1968-70; 1st Grade Teacher Jeffersonville Elem Sch 1970-74; 5th Grade Teacher Elberta Elem Sch 1974-76; 6th Grade Teacher Bonaire Elem Sch 1976-82, Elberta Elem Sch 1982-; *ai:* GA Assn of Educators; NEA; *home:* 608 Forest Lake Dr Warner Robins GA 31093

BROWN, JUDY ANN, Math Teacher; *b:* Phillipsburg, NJ; *m:* Jay S.; *c:* Jennifer; *ed:* (BS) Math Ed, Coll Misericordia 1975; (MS) Educl Technology, Lehigh Univ 1985; *cr:* 8th Grade Math Teacher Stelson Jr HS 1975-77; Math Teacher Bradford Area HS 1978-79; 9th Grade Math Teacher School St Jr HS 1979-81; 8th Grade Math Teacher Pleasant Valley Mid Sch 1981-; *ai:* Bear Times Newspaper Staff Adv; Math Counts Coach; Rdng Fair Comm Mem ; Planning Comm Mem; NCTM 1973-; PA Cncl of Teachers of Math 1985-; Eastern PA Cncl of Teachers of Math 1985-; NASA Educl Wkshp Math/Sci; Teachers Honors Wkshp 1987; Contributing Author for K-8 Math Workbook Series; *office:* Pleasant Valley Mid Sch Rt 115 Brodheadsville PA 18322

BROWN, JUDY FRIEDRICK, German & Mathematics Teacher; *b:* Cullman, AL; *m:* Robert Doyle; *c:* Sarah, Laura; *ed:* (BA) Math, St Bernard Coll 1974; (MA) Eng, Univ of AL Birmingham 1978; *cr:* Teacher Dowling Sch 1975-85, Good Hope Sch 1985-; *ai:* NHS Spon; March of Dimes Walk-A-Thon Youth Groups; Delta Kappa Gamma 1988-; *office:* Good Hope Sch Rt 6 Box 490 Cullman AL 35055

BROWN, JULIA STIMSON, Sixth Grade Teacher; *b:* St Louis, MO; *m:* Andrew G.; *c:* Amy E. Chew, Matthew A.; *ed:* (BA) His, Tulsa Univ 1963; *cr:* 6th Grade Teacher Robert Fulton Elem 1963-68, Ray Bjork Elem 1968-69, Jane Addams Elem 1969-70, C E Gray Elem 1970-; *ai:* Prin Advisory Comm; Bixby Ed Assn (VP 1984-85, Secy 1986-87).

BROWN, JUNE PILCHER, Business Teacher; *b:* Buena Vista, GA; *m:* Asa Richard; *c:* Adaire Brown Spaulding; *ed:* (BSED) Bus, GA Southern 1957; Working Towards Masters Univ of GA; Cmptr Classes, Brunswick Coll; *cr:* Bus Teacher Glynn Mid Sch 1957-69, Glynn Academy 1970-71, Frederica Acad 1972-76, Glynn Academy 1976-; *ai:* FBLA Accounting Contests Stu Coach; GA Bus Ed Assn; *office:* Glynn Academy HS PO Box 1678 Brunswick GA 31521

BROWN, KATHLEEN ROSE, Third Grade Teacher; *b:* Lorain, OH; *m:* Gregory C.; *c:* Jonathan; *ed:* (BSED) Elem Ed/Spec Ed, Bowling Green St Univ 1973; (MED) Elem Ed, Unin of Toledo 1979; Several Wkshps & Seminars; *cr:* Learning Disabilities Specialist 1974-76, 2nd Grade Teacher 1976-78, 3rd Grade Teacher 1978 Glenwood Elem Rossford Sch Dist; *ai:* Delta Kappa Gamma Recording Secy 1968- Jennings Scholar 1979; OH Ed Assn 1976-; Rossford Assn of Classroom Teachers 1976-; NEA 1976-; Outstanding Young Women of Amem 1986; Penta Cnty Voc Schls Career Dev Grant 1987; Sunday Sch Teacher 1984-8 7; *office:* Glenwood Elem Sch 8950 Avenue Rd Perrysburg OH 43551

BROWN, KATHY JO, Driver Ed/Phys Ed Teacher; *b:* Wytheville, VA; *ed:* (BS) Phys Ed/Health, Radford Coll 1977; Pre Teacher, Wytheville Comm Coll 1975; *cr:* Teacher Tazewell HS 1984-; *ai:* Girls Vlybl & Tennis Coach; Intramural Dir; VEA, TEA Mem 1984-; *office:* Tazewell H S Fincastle Tpk Tazewell VA 24651

BROWN, KENT D., Speech/Drama Teacher; *b:* Decatur, IL; *ed:* (BA) Speech/Comm, E IL Univ 1978; *cr:* Teacher Effingham HS 1978-; *ai:* Tennis Coach; IEA, NEA, Effingham Classroom Teachers Assn; Cty of Effingham Fine Art; Elks Lodge #1016; *office:* Effingham HS 600 S Henrietta Effingham IL 62401

BROWN, LARRY JEROME, 8th Grade Teacher; *b:* Chicago, IL; *c:* Jeffery; *ed:* (BS) Elem Ed, Chicago St Univ 1973; (MA) Guidance & Counseling, Northeastern IL Univ 1978; *cr:* Teacher Julius Hess Upper Grade Center 1973-76, John T Blaine Elem 1976-78, R Nathaniel Dett Elem 1978-87, Charles E Hughes Elem 1987-; *ai:* Teacher Facilitator-curr Coord; Sch Newspaper, Stu Cncl Spon; Cultural Coord Schl Act; IL Fed of Teachers; *office:* Charles E Hughes Sch 4247 W 15th Chicago IL 60623

BROWN, LAURA KLINNER, English Teacher/Academic Coach; *b:* Clanton, AL; *m:* James Nathan; *c:* Brandon P., Natalie A.; *ed:* (BS) Ed/Eng, Aurburn Univ 1972; (MA) Ed/Eng, Univ of AL Birmingham 1976; *cr:* 8th Grade Eng Teacher E Highland Mid Sch 1972-76; 10th Grade Eng Teacher Sylacauga HS 1976-; Jr Coll Eng Instr Cntrl AL Comm Coll 1985-; *ai:* Academic Coach; Red Cross Club & Class Spon; Delta Kappa Gamma Pres 1977-; Whos Who in Amer Ed; *office:* Sylacauga HS P O Drawer 88 Sylacauga AL 35150

BROWN, LEONETTE TAYLOR, Fifth Grade Teacher; *b:* Tallulah, LA; *m:* Fred; *c:* Monifa, Ashley; *ed:* (BA) Elem Ed/Eng, Univ of NV Las Vegas 1971; (MS) Ed, Hunter Coll 1975; Advanced Ed Courses Coll of New Rochelle, Univ of NV Las Vegas; *cr:* Teacher Mayflower Elem 1971-80, Jefferson Elem 1980-; *ai:* Bowling Club Team Captain; Delta Sigma Theta Corresponding Secy 1972-73; Natl Cncl of Negro Women Inc; GSA; *office:* Jefferson Elem Sch 505 North Ave New Rochelle NY 10801

BROWN, LINDA LAWRENCE, Resource/Special Ed Teacher; *b:* Madison, WI; *m:* Scott W.; *ed:* (BS) Teaching Mentally Handicapped, Ball St Univ 1974; (MS) Teaching Learning Disabled, IN Univ 1978; *cr:* Spec Ed/Resource Teacher Indianapolis Public Schls 1975-; Resource Teacher J K Lilly Sch 1975-81, T C Steele Jr HS 1981-86, John Marshall Jr HS 1986-; *ai:* Cheerleading Coach; Stu Cncl Adv; Stu Offering Service Spon; Admin Cncl; Mid Grades Improvement, Stu Act, At Risk Stu Comm; Phi Delta Kapp, CEC; Beta Sigma Phi VP 1989-; Teacher of Yr 1987-89; Above & Beyond Call of Duty Awd 1987, 1989; *office:* John Marshall Jr HS 10101 E 38th St Indianapolis IN 46236

BROWN, LUCY GOODPASTER, Mathematics Teacher; *b:* Bethel, KY; *m:* Roy Arlin; *c:* Razetta L., Dava J., Royce A.; *ed:* (BA) Math, 1969, (MAED) Ed/Math, 1974 Morehead St Univ; *cr:* Teacher Montgomery Cty HS 1969-; *ai:* Star Teacher; Educator of Yr 1986-87; Nom Ashland Oil Teacher Achievement Awds 1989; Certificate for Outstanding Teaching Univ of KY 1988; *home:* 721 Woodford Dr Mount Sterling KY 40353

BROWN, MARILYN J., 8th Grade Soc Stud Teacher; *b:* Natrona Heights, PA; *m:* Harry H.; *c:* Mary E., Ann E., Alice E.; *ed:* (BA) Elem, Thiel Coll 1961; (BA) Scndry Soc Stud, York Coll 1985; Many & Varied Undergrad Credits; *cr:* 4th Grade Teacher Fox Chapel Sch Dist 1961-62; 5th Grade Teacher Red Lion Area 1962-64; 7th/8th Grade Soc Stud Teacher Red Lion Jr HS 1973-; *ai:* Dual Spon Young Astronauts Club; Negotiations Comm; Delta Kappa Gamma Treas 1985-89; Church Choir (Past Pres, Comms, Admin Bd); *home:* 101 S Franklin St Red Lion PA 17356

BROWN, MARION LOUISE SHAMBLEE, 9th-12th Grade Math Teacher; *b:* Kosciusko, MS; *m:* Harry; *c:* Harry II, Rufus; *ed:* (BA) Math, Alcorn A&M Coll 1967; (MS) Math, Delta St 1984; *cr:* Math Teacher Sadie V Thompson 1967-69; Humphrey Cty Sch Syst 1969-; *ai:* Jr Class Spon; Math Club Spon; NCTM; MCTM; MAE; HCAE; Natl Cncl of Negro Women; Black Progressive Women; Star Teacher 8 Years; Teacher of Yr 1976; M-Reach Participant 1986; *office:* Humphreys Cnty H Sch 700 Cohn St Belzoni MS 39038

BROWN, NADINE KOLLMANN, Sixth Grade Teacher; *b:* Mankato, MN; *c:* Darleen Brown Burr, Robert J., Janine Brown Schulte; *ed:* (BS) Scndry Ed, MSU 1945; (BS) Elem Ed, 1962, (MS) Elem Ed, 1969 Mankato St Univ; Elem Ed Specialist; Elem Counseling; *cr:* Jr HS Teacher El Paso Public Schls 1945-46; 6th Grade Teacher Gaylord Public Sch 1958-60, Jefferson Elem 1960-; *ai:* Sci Fair & Stu Cncl Adv; Numerous Curr & Drug Abuse Comms; Amer Assn of Univ Women Treas 1985-87; Delta Kappa Gamma Several Offices 1969-; NEA, MEA, Mankato Teachers Assn Membership 1980-85; *home:* 1327 Warren Mankato MN 56001

BROWN, NATHANIEL N., Social Studies Teacher; *b:* Laurinburg, NC; *ed:* (BS) Soc Stud, DC Teachers Coll 1969; (MA) His, Howard Univ 1972; *cr:* Teacher H D Woodson Sr HS 1987-89; *ai:* NCSS, Amer Historical Assn 1987-89; *office:* H D Woodson Sr HS 55th & Eads Streets NE Washington DC 20019

BROWN, NORMA JANE (BRAY), English Teacher; *b:* Bloomington, IL; *m:* Ronald Dale; *c:* Ronda S., Anthony C., Ryan W.; *ed:* (AA) Liberal Arts, Lee Coll 1967; (BA) Eng/His, N IL Univ 1970; (MSED) Admin, IL St Univ 1980; Post Grad Work FL St Univ, IL Wesleyan Univ, Sangamon St Univ; *cr:* Eng Teacher Parkside Jr HS 1974-; *ai:* Soc Sci Club Spon; Geography Bee Spon; Steering Comm for Fall Regional Teachers Inst; NCTE, ASCD 1989-; Phi Delta Kappa 1981-; Staff Dev Cncl Presenter 1986-; Northpoint Sch PTA (Pres 1989-, VP 1988-89); Brokaw Hospital Service League Mem 1984-; Author/Ed 1982-85; T-UFEA NewsLetter 1983-84; Short Story Anthology Resource 1976; Feature Article Magazine 1972; Published Newspaper Articles 1968-; *home:* 2218 Woodfield Rd Bloomington IL 61704

BROWN, NORMAN ALLEN, Mathematics Teacher; *b:* Evansville, IN; *m:* Deanna Mae Martin; *c:* Tamara Jones, Bret; *ed:* (BS) Elem Ed, Evansville Coll 1961; (MS) Elem Ed, IN Univ 1963; *cr:* Teacher Evansville Vanderburgh Sch Corporation 1961-; *ai:* Math Team Coach; Stu Cncl Spon; NEA, IN St Teachers Assn; Evansville Teachers Assn Bd Dirs 1976-78; *office:* Washington Mid Sch 1801 Washington Ave Evansville IN 47714

BROWN, PATRICIA, Social Studies Teacher; *b:* Prentiss, MS; *m:* James A.; *c:* Frances E., Etheredge, James A., Janice P.; *ed:* (BS) Elem, Alcorn St Univ 1963; (MS) Elem, TX Southern Univ 1971; (EDD) Elem, Jackson St Univ 1989; Cmptr Ed; MS Educl Admin Leadership Inst Women; *cr:* 2nd Grade Teacher Oakley Elem Sch 1963-65; 1st Grade Teacher Hazelhurst Elem Sch 1965-67; 3rd/4th Grade Teacher Eugene Separate Sch Dist 1968-69; 1st/5th Grade Teacher Mixon Elem Sch 1967-68; 6th Grade Teacher Jackson Public Sch 1974-; *ai:* Attend Jackson Teachers Appreciation Day 1989; Trainer-Best Prgm Jackson Public Schls 1988; Jackson Assn of Ed 1989-90; MS Assn of Ed Delegate 1970-71; Natl Ed Assn 1989-90; Zeta Phi Beta Sorority Inc 1963-; CME Church Mem Merit/Appreciation 1987; Steward Bd Mem 1989- Merit/Appreciation 1989; Recorded Ministry Chairperson 1981-82 Merit/Appreciation 1982; Preps Inc Comm 1986 Appreciation Cert; Fellowship TX Southern Univ Summer Sch; Crossover Inst Jackson St Univ; Rutgers Univ Acad Yrs 1974-75; Cmptr Sci Jackson St Univ 1984-85; *home:* 3345 Albermarle Rd Jackson MS 39213

BROWN, PATRICIA LAWRENCE, Art Teacher; *b:* Scranton, PA; *c:* John, Timothy, Kenneth, David; *ed:* (BA) Art/Art Ed, Marywood Coll 1963; *cr:* 9th-12th Grade Art Teacher Dunmore HS 1974-79; 7th-8th Grade Art Teacher Dunmore Mid Sch 1980-82; K-8th Grade Art Teacher Dunmore Elem 1982-84; Art Teacher Dunmore HS 1984-; *ai:* Yrbk Adv 1974-; Stu/Faculty Advisory Comm 1984-; Dir Stu Act, Sr Class Adv 1985-87; PA Coalition for Arts 1989-; *office:* Dunmore HS Quincy & Warren St Dunmore PA 18509

BROWN, PATRICIA S., HS Language Arts Teacher; *b:* Le Mars, IA; *m:* Andrew Porter; *ed:* (BA) Scndry Ed/Eng, Morningside Coll 1973; Grad Courses Wichita St Univ; *cr:* 7th Grade Eng Teacher 1975, 8th Grade Eng Teacher/ Inter-Disciplinary Team Leader 1976-78 Truesdell Jr HS; 9th Grade Eng/Honors Eng Teacher North HS 1979; 9th Grade Eng/ Jr Honors Prgm Teacher Wichita North 1990; *ai:* Ticket Mgr; Athletic Events Announcer; PA All Athletic Events & Sch Act; Unified Sch Dist 259 Good Apple Awd 1988; Supt Round Table; *office:* Wichita HS North 1437 Rochester Wichita KS 67203

BROWN, PAULA HALFAST, French/Spanish Teacher; *b:* Muskogee, OK; *m:* James C.; *ed:* (BA) Fr/Span, Northeastern St Univ 1971; Grad Stud; *cr:* Fr/Span Teacher Coweta HS 1971-85; Fr Teacher Wheaton North HS 1985; Fr/Span Teacher Columbine HS 1985-88, Glenpool HS 1988-; *ai:* Coweta HS Chrldr Spon; AATSP (St Secy, Treas); AATF, OEA, NEA, GEA; Alpha Sigma Alpha (Natl Schlsp Chm, Province Dir) 1974-84; Alpha Sigma Alpha Tulsa Aulmnae Pres 1989-; OK St Comm to Review Objectives for Fr Teacher Cert Exam St of OK; *home:* 6904 E 78th St Tulsa OK 74133

BROWN, PEGGY MILDRED, Social Studies Teacher; *b:* Detroit, MI; *ed:* (BA) Sociology/Unified Sci/Secndry Soc Stud 1980; (MA) Secndry Soc Stud Pending ; *cr:* Sci Teacher Pelham Mid Sch 1985-86; His Teacher Chadsey HS 1986-; *ai:* Head Girls Bsktbl Coach; Close-Up Govt Spon; Gifted & Talented Comm Mem; OES; MHSCA; *office:* Chadsey H S 5335 Martin Ave Detroit MI 48210

BROWN, PENELOPE WEEKS, Secondary Sch English Teacher; *b:* Orangeburg, SC; *m:* Lawton Rutledge; *c:* Andrew, David, Whitney; *ed:* (BA) Eng, Baptist Coll Charleston 1979; *cr:* Eng Teacher Mims Acad 1978-81, Holly Hill Acad 1983-; *ai:* SABRE Yrbk Adv; Outstanding Young Readers Coord & Spon; Potpourri Garden Club Recording Secy 1988-; Corinth Baptist Church Organist 1990; *office:* Holly Hill Acad P O Box 757 Holly Hill SC 29059

BROWN, PHILIP EUGENE, Phys Ed/Science Teacher; *b:* Cincinnati, OH; *m:* Katherine Marie Ferris; *c:* Aaron P., Katherine C., Jacob C., Nathan L.; *ed:* (BS) Phys Ed/Health, Univ of Cincinnati 1975; Elem Ed; *cr:* Teacher Mc Kinley Elem 1975-; Youth-Teen Prgm Dir Columbia Parkway YMCA 1986-; *ai:* Extended Phys Ed; Safety Patrol Spon; Discipline Comm Coord; Sci Fair; Sports Awd; Halloween Parade & 6th Grade Recognition Comm; Incentive Prgm Coord; Phi Epsilon Kappa (Corresponding Secy, Pres 1982-83, Pres 1983-84), Service 1984; OH Assn of Health, Phys Ed, Recreation, Dance, Natl Alliance; Columbia Parkway YMCA Volunteer Youth 1978-85, Service Awd 1979-84; Cincinnati Public Schls Outstanding Teacher Awd 1980; Presenter at St, Regional, Natl Phys Ed Conventions; Career Ed & Content Rdng Prgm; Apple Teacher Grant 1984; *office:* Mc Kinley Elem Sch 3905 Eastern Ave Cincinnati OH 45226

BROWN, PHYLLIS ANN (STITT), Scndry Business Ed Teacher; *b:* Marion, IN; *m:* Morris E.; *c:* Philip E., Rodney M.; *ed:* (BS) Bus Ed, Ball St Univ 1986; Minors in US His, Government & World His; Endorsement in Voc Bus; *cr:* Bus Ed Teacher Eastbrook HS 1986-88, Tucker Voc Sch 1986-89, Madison Grant HS 1988-89, Western HS 1989-; *ai:* Stu Cncl Spon 1988; Madison-Grant HS Speech Team Coach 1988-89; *home:* RR 2 Box 56 Summitville IN 46070

BROWN, RAYMOND EUGENE, Assistant Principal; *b:* Jennings, LA; *m:* Laura Ann Trahan; *c:* Raymond T., Erica N., Aaron A.; *ed:* (BA) Upper Elem Ed, 1969, (MA) Admin/Supervision, 1976 Mc Neese St; Grad Stud; *cr:* Teacher Ward Elem 1967-70; Teacher/Coach 1970-89, Asst Prin 1989- Welsh-Roanoke Jr HS; *ai:* LA Assn of Educators 1969-; NEA 1968-; LA Assn Teachers of Math 1988-; LA Assn of Prins 1989-; LA Assn of Sch Execs 1989-; Lions Club 1975-; *office:* Welsh Roanoke Jr HS P O Box 9 Roanoke LA 70581

BROWN, REBECCA ANN (SCHULTE), French Teacher; *b:* Springfield, OH; *m:* Keith Daniel; *c:* Michael J.; *ed:* (BA) Fr/Eng, OH Dominican Coll 1975; (MA) Ed, Coll of Mt St Joseph 1988; *cr:* Eng Teacher 1975-80, Fr Teacher 1975- Pleasant HS; *ai:* Adv/Chaperone for Trip to France; Adv for Summer Prgm Hosting Fr Stus In Sch Dist; OH Ed Assn Mem of St Membership Comm 1982-84; Pleasant Assn of Teachers (Pres 1980-81, Secy 1987-88) 1989-; OH Foreign Lang Assn Mem 1975-; Amer Assn of Univ Women Mem 1988-; *office:* Pleasant HS 1101 Owens Rd W Marion OH 43302

BROWN, REBECCA ANNE, 1st Grade Teacher; *b:* Grand Rapids, MI; *m:* David M.; *c:* Meredith, Derek; *ed:* (Bs) Elem Music Ed/Elem Ed, W MI Univ 1978; *cr:* Pre-Sch Teacher S Kent Cmmty Ed 1978-81; 1st/5th Grade Teacher Kentwood Public Schls 1978-; *ai:* Piano Instr S Kent Cmmty Ed 1980-81; Private Music Instr 1980-85; MI Ed Assn, NEA, MI Rdng Assn 1978-; Create & Open Area Pre-Sch Readiness Prgm Bd Head; *office:* Glenwood/Kentwood 912 Silver Leaf SE Kentwood MI 49508

BROWN, REBECCA RECTOR, Teacher of Gifted & Talented; *b:* Wichita, KS; *m:* David Randal; *c:* Kellan Davidson, Casen Brereton; *ed:* (BSED) His/Poly Sci, 1979, (MSED) Admin, 1980 Baylor Univ; *cr:* His/Eng/Drama/Government Teacher Moody HS 1980-81; Gifted & Talented/His/Cheerleading Teacher Vines HS 1981-; *ai:* Adv/Coach Vines Frosh & Soph Chrldrs; Spon Vines Acad Octathlon Team; TX St Teachers Assn, Plano Ed Assn 1981-89; Dallas Shakespeare Festival Bd 1989-; City of Plano Proclamation Vines Chrldr Day 1990; Teacher of Yr 1984-85; *office:* Vines HS 1401 Highedge Plano TX 75075

BROWN, RITA RACHEL, English/Social Studies Teacher; *b:* Russellville, AR; *m:* Dale G.; *c:* Tami, Marshall; *ed:* (BA) Elem Ed, 1965, (MA) Elem Ed, 1969 Harding Coll; *cr:* 4th Grade Teacher Rose City Elem 1965-66; 6th Grade Teacher Harding Acad 1966-69, Shreve Chrstn 1978-80, Metro Chrstn 1980-; *ai:* Speech Coord; One-a-Chord Singing Group; *office:* Metro Chrstn Sch Waldron & Grand Fort Smith AR 72903

BROWN, ROBERT GRADY, 7th-8th Grade Science Teacher; *b:* Dayton, KY; *m:* Julie Ann Frendenberg; *c:* Maggie, Jane; *ed:* (AA) Elem Ed/Phys Ed, Brewton Parker Jr Coll 1972; (BA) Elem Ed/Phys Ed, N KY Univ 1975; (MA) Phys Ed, Xavier Univ 1979; *cr:* 6th Grade Teacher Dora Cummings Elem 1975-77; 8th Grade Teacher Newport Jr HS 1977-; *ai:* Var Boys Bsktbl & Bsbl Asst Coach; Jr HS Girls Vlybl Coach; St of KY Geology Grant; US Government Marine Sci Grant; *office:* Newport Jr HS 8th & Columbia Newport KY 41071

BROWN, RONALD JOSEPH, Third Grade Teacher; *b:* Albany, CA; *m:* Nancy J. Fritzell; *c:* Kelley N.; *ed:* (BA) Soc Sci, CA St Univ Chico 1972; *cr:* 3rd Grade Teacher Orland Public Schls 1976-79; 4th Grade Teacher 1979-81, 3rd Grade Teacher 1981- Evergreen Sch; *ai:* Coaching; Guitar Instr; AFT Treas 1983-84; Written, Produced & Published Songs for Teaching Childrens Lit; *office:* Evergreen Sch 19415 Hooker Creek Rd Cottonwood CA 96022

BROWN, RONALD LEE, HS Mathematics Teacher; *b:* Anamosa, IA; *m:* Debbie Leigh Dirks; *c:* Damian; *ed:* (BS) Math, Western IL Univ 1975; Certificate Coaching, Univ of IA 1976; Grad Stud Admin, W IL Univ, Ed, N IL Univ; *cr:* Math Teacher/Coach Morning Sun Sch 1975-77, North Scott HS 1977-; *ai:* 10th Grade Ftbl, Girls Shot & Discus Coach; NSEA/ISEA/NEA, MBUU, ICTM 1977-; Jaycees 1971-74; *office:* North Scott HS 200 S 1st St Eldridge IA 52748

BROWN, S. ANN DODSON, Fourth Grade Teacher; *b:* Lubbock, TX; *m:* E. Don; *c:* Tad, Amy; *ed:* (BS) Elem Ed, N TX St Univ 1962; TX Wesleyan, N TX Univ; *cr:* 4th Grade Teacher Shady Oaks Elem 1962-66, Midway Park Elem 1967-70; Pre Sch/Kndgtn Teacher First Baptist of Euless 1972-77; 4th Grade Teacher Bedford Heights 1978-79, Hurst Hills 1979-; *ai:* ATPE; Delta Kappa Gamma 1967-; *home:* 1760 Renee Hurst TX 76054

BROWN, SADIE THOMPSON, English Teacher; *b:* Durham, NC; *m:* Herbert Drayton II; *c:* Herbert III, Julian, Camilla; *ed:* (AA) Speech, 1976, (BA) Eng, 1977 Univ of Tampa; Charleston Area Writing Project; *cr:* Eng Teacher Millwood HS 1977-78; Ed Coord/Teacher Mabel Bassett Correctional Ctr 1978-81; Soc Stud Teacher Moore HS 1981-82; Eng Teacher James Island HS 1982-; *ai:* Alpha Chi Natl Schlsp Honor Society 1976-; Kappa Delta Phi Natl Ed Society 1976-; AF Officers Wives Club Pres Germany 1971-72; Canadian Officers Wives Club Pres Canada 1974-75; Univ of Tampa Cum Laude; Danforth Fellowship Nom; CAWP; *office:* James Island H S 1000 Fort Johnson Rd Charleston SC 29412

BROWN, SALLY JANE, Language Arts Teacher; *b:* Milwaukee, WI; *m:* Robert S.; *ed:* Eng/Lang Art, La Crosse St Univ 1972; Ed, CO St Univ 1984-; Training Carol Cummings Advanced Elements of Instruction 1987-88; *cr:* Eng Teacher Oak Creek Jr HS 1972-75; Speech Teacher Loveland HS 1975-76, Thompson Valley HS 1976-80; Lang Art Teacher Blevins Jr HS 1984-; *ai:* Yrbk Teacher & Spon; NEA 1984-; Math/Engineering/Sci Achievement Honor Teacher 1985/89; Honor Teacher of Quarter Blevins Jr HS 1989; *office:* Blevins Jr HS 2101 S Taft Hill Rd Fort Collins CO 80526

BROWN, SANDRA J., 8th Grade Teacher; *b:* Denver, CO; *m:* Frank; *c:* Thaddeus, Alicia; *ed:* (BS) Biological Sci, CO St Univ 1970; Various Stud; *cr:* Substitute Teacher Littleton Public Schls 1970-72; Teacher Grant Jr HS 1972-81, Goddard Mid Sch 1981-; *ai:* Sci Chairperson; Instructional Improvement Cncl; Dissection Club; Parent Ed Nights; NEA Faculty Rep 1985-89; Family Life Educators 1983-; Natl Organization for Women 1981-; Nominee CO Awds 1983; Teacher of Month 1988, 1990; Littleton Public Schls Dist Sci Chairperson 1980-81, 1988-89; CO St Dept of Health Trainer AIDS Project; Curr Writer All Sci & Health LPS 1972-; *office:* Goddard Mid Sch 3800 W Berry Littleton CO 80123

BROWN, SANDRA LEE, Seventh Grade Reading Teacher; *b:* Washington, DC; *m:* Daniel D.; *c:* Andrew, Amanda, Luis; *ed:* (BS) Elem Ed, Millersville Univ 1976; Stu Assistance Team Trng; *cr:* 6th Grade Teacher Hambright Elem 1979-81; 7th Grade Rdng Teacher Marticville Mid Sch 1981-; *ai:* Stu Assistance Team-Chm; Peer Helpers-Adv; Study Skills Comm-Chm; PSEA/NEA; PA Peer Helpers Assn 1987-; Millersville Women of Today Pres 1978 & 1981 Outstanding Mem 1982 & 1983; PA Jaycettes Childrens Programming & Energy Chm; Suicide/Depression Task Force Mem 1988-; Penn Manor Outstanding Teacher of Yr 1988; *home:* 2628 Pike Ln Lancaster PA 17603

BROWN, SHANNON D., Industrial Technology Teacher; *b:* Safford, AZ; *m:* Wendy Coray; *c:* Natasha, Shannon L., Tashina, Leah D., Shaleece; *ed:* General Ed, Ricks Coll 1983; (BS) Industrial Arts, Brigham Young Univ 1985; *cr:* Industrial Arts Teacher W Minico Jr HS 1985-; *ai:* Industrial Technology Stu Assn Club Adv; BSA Scout Master 1986-, Silver Tomahawk 1989; *office:* West Minico Jr HS Hwy 27 S Paul ID 83347

BROWN, SHARON CARY, US History Teacher/Dept Chair; *b:* Elkins, WV; *m:* Harold E.; *c:* Jenna F.; *ed:* (BS) His, Lee Coll 1970; Elem Cert Rdng Specialist, Cleveland St Comm Coll 1973; Teaching Gifted Students, UTC Chattanooga; Classroom Management, Trevecca Coll; *cr:* 1st Grade Teacher Meadowview Elem Sch 1970-75; 6th-8th Grade Teacher Ooltewah Mid Sch 1978-; *ai:* His Academic Olympics Team Coach; Hamilton Cty Academic Champions Spon & Coach; Mid Sch Task Force Mem; Hamilton Cty Mid Schls Staff Dev; Public Ed Fnd Steering Comm; TN Ed Assn Univ Wkshps Presenter; Soc Stud Dept Chairperson; Hamilton Cty Soc Stud Task Force; Hamilton Cty Ed Assn Membership Chair 1982-; TN Ed Assn, PTO, NEA 1970-; TN Assn of Mid Schls Presenter 1989-; Natl Mid Sch Assn 1989-; Greater Chattanooga Soc Stud Cncl 1988-; TN Soc Stud Cncl 1990; Hamilton Cty Ed Assn Bd of Dir 1990, Bd of Dirs Awd 1984-85, 1988; Hamilton Cty Assn for Children with Learning Disabilities Advisory Bd 1985-86; Project 2000 Delegate 1988; Hamilton Cty Fund for Excl Sch Spon 1988-; Westmore Church of God Eng Instr for 8 Russian Refugees 1989; Public Ed Fnd Staff Dev Steering Comm 1989-; Multiple Sclerosis Assn Volunteer 1986-; Amer Heart Assn Volunteer 1987-; Co-Recipient Jr League Grant; Hamilton Cty Mid Sch Teacher of Yr 1990; Nom 9 Spec People Chammel 9 TV; Ooltewah HS Sr Class & Mid Sch Teacher Who Most Influenced Their Lives 1988, 1990; Ooltewah Mid Schls Soc Stud Teacher of Yr 1987-89; SE TN Dist Mid Sch Teacher of Yr 1990; Reader Consultant TN His Textbook; *home:* 2909 Linda Cir Cleveland TN 37311

BROWN, SHARON WEBB, Art Teacher; *b:* Whitesburg, KY; *m:* Bob; *c:* Alyn, Ashley; *ed:* (BA) Art/Fr, Georgetown Coll 1964; Art Ed, Georgetown Coll; Mid Sch Cert; Murray St Univ; *cr:* Art Teacher Pleasure Ridge Park HS 1964-72; Art Curr Coord Louisville City Schls 1972-73; Lang Arts Teacher Gilbertsville Elem 1973-74; Fr/Art Teacher Marshall Cty HS 1974-75; Art Teacher North Marshall Mid Sch 1978-; *ai:* Yrbk Adv; Chrldr Coach; Jefferson Cty Ed Assn, Jefferson Cty Art Ed Assn 1965-70; Marshall Cty Ed Assn, KY Ed Assn, NEA 1978-; Speed Museum Childrens Gallery Dir Bd 1972-73; 1st Presbyn Church Session Elder 1985-88; KY Assn Pep Organization Spons (St Pres 1981-82, Bd Mem, Sectional VP 1973-81); *home:* 1720 Laurel Dr Calvert City KY 42029

BROWN, SHIRLEY JEAN, US History Teacher; *b:* Greencastle, IN; *ed:* (BA) His/Poly Sci, Bridgewater Coll 1986; *cr:* Teacher/Coach Fauquier HS 1986-; *ai:* Vlybl & Bsktbl Asst Coach; Var Club Co-Spon; Sr Class Spon; VA HS Coaches Assn, Natl HS Athletic Coaches Assn 1986-; *home:* 225 Hillandale Harrisonburg VA 22801

BROWN, SHIRLEY URTSO, 6th Grade Teacher; *b:* Clarksburg, WV; *m:* Robert Carl; *c:* Shannon Mazzie, Shelley Mazzie; *ed:* (BA) Elem Ed, Fairmont St Coll 1970; (MA) Elem Ed, Salem Coll 1983; *cr:* 4th/6th Grade Teacher Fort Hunt Elem 1970-71; 5th/6th Grade Teacher Wolf Trap Elem 1971-73; Rdng Teacher Johnson Elem 1973-74; 4th/6th Grade Teacher Broadway Sch 1975-83; 6th Grade Teacher Norwoo D Elem 1983-; *ai:* Soc Stud Fair Coord; Harrison Cty Staff Dev Cncl; Harrison Cty Ed Assn Secy 1979-82; Grant from Union Carbide Parental Involvement; *home:* 25 Conifer Dr Bridgeport WV 26330

BROWN, SUSAN HORTON, Home Economics Educator; *b:* Elizabeth City, NC; *m:* Timothy K.; *c:* Kevin, Christopher, Lauren; *ed:* (BA) Home Ec, E Carolina Univ 1978; Pre-Vocation Assoc Degree; *cr:* Home Ec Teacher Pasquotank Cty Schls 1979-; *ai:* FHA & HERO Co-Adv; Southern Assn Steering & Faculty Adv Cncl Comm Mem; NCAE 1986-; Elizabeth City Jr Womans Club 1988-; Elizabeth City Jr HS Teacher of Yr 1985; Northeastern HS Teacher of Yr 1988-89; *office:* Northeastern HS 923 Oak Stump Rd Elizabeth City NC 27909

BROWN, SUSAN MARIE, Mathematics & Science Teacher; *b:* Addison, MI; *ed:* (BS) Math, MI St Univ 1977; (MA) Scndry Ed, Siena Heights Coll 1986; *cr:* Math/Sci Teacher Grandville HS 1977-84, Addison HS 1984-; *ai:* Soph Class Adv; Siena Heights Coll Grad Stu Awd; Developed & Taught Unit on Tessellations to Math Stu Teacher & Gifted & Talented Children; *office:* Addison HS 219 Comstock St Addison MI 49220

BROWN, SUSAN MIRACLE, 7th/8th Grade English Teacher; *b:* Danville, KY; *m:* Michael Albert; *c:* Mari Beth; *ed:* (AA) Eng/Math, Lindsey Wilson Jr Coll 1971; (BA) Elem Ed, Morehead St Univ 1973; (MA) Elem Counseling, 1978, (Rank I) Elem Counseling, 1983 Eastern St Univ; *cr:* 2nd Grade Chapter I Teacher Crab Orchard Elem 1973-74; 6-10 Yr Old Trainables Teacher Graysbranch Elem 1974-75; 5th-8th Grade Chapter I Teacher 1976-83, 7th-8th Grade Eng Dept Teacher 1983- Crab Orchard Elem; *ai:* KEA, NEA 1976-; Eastern Star Worthy Matron 1986-87; Ashland Campus Oil Day; Sch Attendance Grant 1989-; *home:* Meadowlark Dr Crab Orchard KY 40419

BROWN, SUSAN STEPHENS, Elementary Music Teacher; *b:* Indianapolis, IN; *m:* Steven Nicholas; *c:* Kelley, Christina; *ed:* (BME) Music Ed, IN Univ 1970; (MA) Ed, Univ of Indianapolis 1977; *cr:* Elem Music Teacher West Grove Elem 1970-; *ai:* Advanced Recorders Performing Group; Private Piano Studio; Mu Phi Epsilon Natl Archives Chm 1980-83; Music Educators Natl Conference, ISTA 1970-; Kappa Kappa Sigma (VP 1982-83, Pres 1983-85); Eastern Star 1988-; *home:* 8810 Rocky Ridge Rd Indianapolis IN 46217

BROWN, THOMAS ALLEN, Math Teacher; *b:* Cottonwood, AZ; *m:* Darnel Hatch; *c:* Lena, Lance, Janae, Benjamin; *ed:* (BA) Ed, Northern AZ Univ 1972; (MA) Elem Ed, Northern AZ Univ 1977; Admin Cert Stud 1980-81; *cr:* 5th/6th Grade Teacher Thomas Weitzel Elem Sch 1973-83; Admin Asst W F Killip Elem Sch 1983-85; 5th Grade Teacher Marshall Elem Sch 1985-86; 8th Grade Math Teacher East Flagstaff Jr HS 1986-; *ai:* Jr Var Girls Bsktbl Coach Coconino HS; Prof Growth & Dev Comm; Elem Preparation Time Comm Chm; NEA/AEA/Flagstaff Ed Assn Pres 1989-; Phi Delta Kappa; Flagstaff Officials Assn Pres 1983; BSA Scoutmaster 1984-89; East Flagstaff Jr Chess Club Coach 1975-83 St Championships 1976 & 1982; Flagstaff Ed Assn Negotiating Team Spokesperson 1981-83; Flagstaff Town Hall Ed Restructuring Delegate 1990; *home:* 2608 Elder Dr Flagstaff AZ 86004

BROWN, THOMAS LORING, Physical Education Teacher; *b:* Sunrise, WY; *m:* Andrea Alberta Hoagland; *c:* Deborah L. Quintard, Loring I.; *ed:* (BA) Phys Ed, Univ of WY 1971; *cr:* Teacher/Coach Sublette Cty Sch Dist 9 1971-; *ai:* Boys & Girls Swimming Coach; Lettermen Club Spon; NISCA 1989-; WY Coaches Assn 1974-, Coach of Yr 1980; *home:* Box 446 Big Piney WY 83113

BROWN, TIMOTHY STEPHEN, Science Teacher/Coach; *b:* Amory, MS; *m:* Donna Gale Moorman; *ed:* (BS) Ed/Phys Ed, Delta St Univ 1983; *cr:* 7th Grade Teacher/Coach North Pontotoc Attendance Center 1983-; *ai:* Jr/Sr HS Head Ftbl & HS Head Track Coach; MS Prof Educators; Ecru Park Commissioner Dir; *office:* North Pontotoc Attendance Ctr Rt 1 Box 252 D Ecru MS 38841

BROWN, V. K., Physics Teacher; *b:* Chicago, IL; *m:* Elizabeth A. Mc Carthy; *c:* V. K. III, Steven M.; *ed:* (BS) Psych, IL Inst Technology 1952; (MST) Physics, Roosevelt Univ 1971; Lake Forest Coll, IIT, Univ of WI, Univ of AR, Univ of Chiago, Roosevelt; *cr:* Physics Teacher Parker HS 1959-61, Bogan HS 1961-64, South Shore HS 1964-75, Univ of Chicago 1967, Lindblom Tech HS 1975-; *ai:* Chicago HS Physics Teachers Assn (Pres, Secy, Treas) 1959-72; Amer Assn Advanced Sci 1960-72; AAPT 1960-82; NSTA 1960-78; Chicago Teachers Union (Chm, Poly Action, Chm Prof Problems, Exec Bd) 1969-75; Articles & Letters Published Am Physics, Physics Teacher, Sci Teachers, Sci & Children; *home:* 4800 S Chicago Beach Dr Apt 2516N Chicago IL 60615

BROWN, VICKI C., Health & Physical Ed Teacher; *b:* Butte, MT; *ed:* (BS) Health/Phys Ed, 1974, (MS) Health/Phys Ed, 1987 Univ of MT; *cr:* Health & Phys Ed Hellgate HS 1974-; *ai:* Head Vlybl coach; Asst Sftbl Coach 1984-; MT HS Assn Athletic Comm 1986-; Amer Vlybl Coaches Assn 1989-; MT Coaches Assn 1974-; MT Ed Assn 1974-; MT Coaches Assn 1974-89, 15 Yr Athletics Service Awd 1989; Amateur Sftbl Assn Umpire in Chief 1985-88; MT Coaches Assn Coach of Yr 1987; Natl HS Vlybl Comm Region 7 Natl Vice Chairperson; MT TAC Cultural Exch to China Head Vlybl Coach 1987-88.

BROWN, VICTORIA COLSTON, First Grade Teacher; *b:* York, PA; *d:* Thomas H.; *c:* Jason, Tamara; *ed:* (BS) Elem Ed, Shippensburg St Univ 1955; Course Work Newark St Coll, Montclair St Coll, Monmouth Coll; *cr:* Teacher Bangs Avenue Sch 1955-; *ai:* Soloist Chancel Choir; NJ Ed Assn, NEA, Asbury Park Ed Assn; Twinks Civic & Soc Clubs Inc (Secy 1980-81, Parlimentarian 1984-87, Historian 1988); St Stephen AME Zion Church Bd of Trustees; Westside Cmmty Center Club Adv; Published Poet; *office:* Bangs Avenue Sch 1300 Bangs Ave Asbury Park NJ 07712

BROWN, VIRGINIA POTTER, 5th Grade Teacher; *b:* Ironwood, MI; *c:* Dawn Price; *ed:* (BA) Eng Lit, Wayne St Univ 1965; (MA) Educl Admin, Cntrl MI Univ 1990; Teacher Trng, Univ of CA Santa Barbara 1970-71; Continuing Teacher Cert/Mid Sch Endorsement, Cntrl MI Univ 1974-75; *cr:* Teacher St Helen Elem Sch 1971-73, Roscommon Mid Sch 1973-85, Roscommon HS 1985-86, Roscommon Mid Sch 1986-88, St Helen

Elem Sch 1988-; *ai:* Odyssey of Mind Judge; Lang Art Curr Advisory & Bay City Times Editing Selection Comm; Roscommon Ed Assn (VP, Negotiator); *office:* Saint Helen Elem Sch 1350 St Helen Saint Helen MI 48656

BROWN, VONTELLA, Transition Teacher; *b:* Blackfoot, ID; *m:* Alma T.; *c:* Alma T. Jr., Emma Brown Christoffersen; *ed:* (AS) Elem Ed, 1943, (BA) Elem Ed, 1956 Ricks Coll; Grad Stud Early Ed, Spec Ed; *cr:* 1st/2nd Grade Teacher Wilson 1943-47, Sugar Salem 1947-53, Edmunds Sch 1953-63; 1st/2nd/4th Grade Teacher 1963-85, Transition Teacher 1982-88 Lovell Elem; *ai:* NEA (Primary Dept Chm, Mem) 1951-52; ID Educl Assn 1943-63; Local Ed Assn 1943-; WY Ed Assn 1963-; PTA; Church of Jesus Christ of Latterday Saints Youth Group Leadership Roles; *home:* 812 Lane 14 1/2 Lovell WY 82431

BROWN, WANDA STAMEY, Phys Ed & Health Teacher; *b:* Clayton, GA; *m:* Charles T.; *c:* Amanda, Monica, Megan, Charlie; *ed:* (BS) Phys Ed, W Carolina 1986; Elem Ed, WCU; *cr:* Phys Ed/Health Teacher Nantahala HS 1988-; *ai:* Vlybl Head Coach; Senate Bill 2 Differentiated Pay Plan Comm; NC Assn of Educators, NEA, NC Alliance for Health, Phys Ed, Recreation, Dance; Little League.

BROWN, WAYNE RUSSELL, Science Teacher; *b:* Grants Pass, OR; *m:* Sandra L. Axelson; *c:* Jamie, Stefanie; *ed:* (BA) Scndry Ed, 1979, (MA) Scndry Ed/Bio, 1985 S OR St; Natl Oceanic & Atmospheric Admin; Foreign Observer Prgm; OR Dept Fish & Wildlife Salmon Trout Enhancement Prgm; *cr:* Sci Teacher Hidden Valley HS 1980-; *ai:* Voc Scholar & Academics; HS Wrestling Coach; OR Sci Teacher Assn 1986-; OR Dept Fish & Wildlife Volunteer 1986, Salmon Trout Enhance Prgm 1989; NW Steelheaders 1986, Top Volunteer 1989; OR Dept Ed Semi-Finalist Kyotarutrust 1989; Izaak Walton League of America Inc Golden Beaver Awd 1990; Tandy Technology Scholars Semi-Finalist 1990; *office:* Hidden Valley HS 651 Murphy Creek Rd Grants Pass OR 97527

BROWN, WILLIAM LEE, JR., Social Studies Teacher; *b:* Valley Park, MO; *c:* Stacy L.; *ed:* (BS) Scndry Ed/Soc Stud/Phys Ed, Southeast MO St Univ 1973; Univ of MO St Louis; *cr:* Soc Stud Teacher/Coach Bernie HS 1973-76, Campbell HS 1976-79, Bloomfield HS 1979-85, Eureka Sr HS; *ai:* Var Bsbl Coach; Curr Advisory Cncl Pres 1990-; NCSS Mem 1988-; Lions Club Intnl; *home:* 1115 Shadowoak Ballwin MO 63021

BROWN, WILLIAM MORGAN, 4th Grade Teacher; *b:* Fall River, MA; *m:* Pamela M. Tamburo; *c:* Erin M., Patrick M.; *ed:* (BS) Elem Ed, Amer Intnl Coll 1970; (MAED) Spec Ed, Westfield St Coll 1978; Continuing Ed Courses, Amer Intnl Coll/Westfield St Coll; *cr:* 4th Grade Teacher Edgar H Parkman Sch 1970-74; Form 3 Teacher Broadway Jr Boys Sch 1974-75; 5th Grade Teacher 1975-82, 4th Grade Teacher 1982- Edgar H Parkman Sch; *ai:* Intramural Sports 1971- E H PArkman Sch; NEASC Accreditation Comm; Philosophy Chm 1988-; Phys Ed 1988-; Pupil Performance/Ed Results 1988-; Enfield Teachers Assn 1970 El VP 1978; CT Ed Assn 1970-; NEA 1970-; New England Outdoor Writers Assn 1985-; RI Party & Charter Boat Assn 1983- RI St Record Blue Shark 1989/3 Tournaments Won 1989; Amer Prof Captains Assn 1988-; RI Marine Sportfishing Alliance 1987-; Fulbright Hayes Exchange Teacher Coventry GB England 1974-75; Salt Water Ed Northest Woods & Waters Feature Writer/Speaker/The Edge Regional Corrspondent/ Big Game Annual Feature Writer/Free Lance Writer for Other Saltwater Publications; US Coast Guard License Master of Near Coastal Waters; *office:* Edgar H. Parkman School 165 Weymouth Rd Enfield CT 06082

BROWN, WILLIE ALBERT, JR., Language Art Teacher; *b:* Birmingham, AL; *ed:* (BS) Ed, Univ of AL Birmingham 1980; *cr:* Teacher Powell Elem Sch 1984-; *ai:* Creative Learning Rep; AEA 1984-; STAR Teacher Space Technology Prgm; Birmingham Service Guild Schlsp 1977-81; Natl Endowment for Art Schlsp 1989; *home:* 1670 18th Way SW Birmingham AL 35211

BROWN, WILLIE OLA, Social Studies Teacher; *b:* Duck Hill, MS; *ed:* (BS) Home Ec/His, Alcorn Univ 1964; Grad Stud MS St Univ, Univ of MS; *cr:* Home Ec Ed Teacher Patton Lane HS 1965-70; Elem Ed Teacher Lizzie Horn Elem 1970-73; Soc Sci Ed Teacher Grenada Jr HS 1973-; *ai:* Jr Historical Society & PTA Scrapbook Adv; NEA 1970-; MTA 1965-; Alcorn Alumni Assn Asst Secy 1988-; Natl Assn of Colored Womens Club 1986-89; Duck Hill Federated Club (Secy, Adv) 1985-, Outstanding Mem of Yr 1989; NAACP 1985-; *home:* 211 Martin Luther King Jr Dr Duck Hill MS 38925

BROWNFIELD, NANCY REEVES, English/Language Arts Teacher; *b:* Breckenridge, TX; *c:* A. D., Kelley M.; *ed:* (BS) Elem Ed, TX Tech Univ 1969; (MED) Admin, Eastern NM Univ 1990; *cr:* Teacher Dallas Ind Schls 1969-70, NM Military Institute 1981, Roswell Ind Schls 1981-; *ai:* Newspaper/Annual Spon; Stu Cncl Spon; Honor Society Spon; Delta Kappa Gamma Mem 1987-; Roswell Girls Club VP Bd of Dir 1980-84; Published-Amer Poetry Assn; *office:* Mesa Mid Sch 1601 E Bland Roswell NM 88201

BROWNFIELD, ROBERT BEAUMONT, JR., Fourth Grade Teacher; *b:* Akron, OH; *m:* Joan Bazelides; *c:* Robert III; *ed:* (BS) Ed/Soc Stud, 1970, (BS) Elem Ed, 1974 Univ of Akron; Wkshp Way BGSU 1981; Martin Holden Jennings Writing Project 1987; Classroom of Future 1988; *cr:* 5th Grade Teacher Samuel Bissell Elem 1970-73; 4th Grade Open Teacher Twinsburg Elem Sch 1973-; *ai:* Math Curr Comm Building Rep to TEA; Spon Continental Math Contest; Adv Geography Club; Sunshine Comm; Twinsburg Ed Assn VP 1984-86, 1988; OH Ed Assn Rep 1984-86; NE OH Teachers Assn Delegate 1984-86; *office:* Twinsburg Elem Sch 8897 Darrow Rd Twinsburg OH 44087

BROWNING, BENNIE PERRY, Fifth Grade Teacher; *b:* Ackerman, MS; *w:* James (dec); *c:* James Jr., Michael, Kim B. Hutchins; *ed:* (BS) Home Ec, MS Univ for Women 1955; (MS) Guidance/Counseling, 1976, Spec Elem Ed, 1980 MS Coll; *cr:* Home Economist MS Extension Service 1955-56; 5th Grade Teacher Indianola 1958-60, Clinton Public Schs 1964-; *ai:* MS Coll Stu Teacher Supvr; NEA, MAE; CAE (Pres, VP, Treas) 1970, 1986-; ABWA (Pres, Secy) 1986-; Jaycees Teacher of Yr 1968; *office:* Eastside Elem Sch 201 Easthaven Blvd Clinton MS 39056

BROWNING, CATHERINE SCHWARTZMILLER, Fifth Grade Teacher; *b:* Lebanon, KY; *m:* James Kenneth; *c:* Elizabeth C., Stacey L., James K. Jr.; *ed:* (BS) Elem Ed, Campbellsville Coll 1981; (MAE) Ed, W Ky Univ 1986; *cr:* 5th Grade Teacher Campbellsville Mid Sch 1982-84, Campbellsville Elem Sch 1984-89, Campbellsville Mid Sch 1989-; *ai:* NEA, KY Ed Assn, Campbellsville Ed Assn 1982-; Jr Miss Prgm (Mem at Large Exec Bd 1988, Secy Exec Comm 1989); Young Woman of Yr Bd Mem 1990; *office:* Campbellsville Mid Sch Roberts Rd Campbellsville KY 42718

BROWNING, DAVID ROBERT, Science Teacher; *b:* Decatur, IL; *m:* Stephanie; *c:* Sarah; *ed:* (BS) Bio, Millikin Univ 1982; (MS) Admin, E IL Univ 1984; Grad Stud Cmptr Sci; *cr:* Track, X-Cntry Coach 1982-87; Vllybl Coach 1987-88, Bio/Phys Sci Teacher 1982- Mt Zion Jr HS; *ai:* Track, Vlybl, Cross Country Coach; Presbyn Church Elder 1980-84; *office:* Mt Zion Jr HS 305 S Henderson Mount Zion IL 62549

BROWNING, JOANNA JACOBSEN, Language Art/Soc Stud Teacher; *b:* Merced, CA; *c:* Corbett, Jennifer Browning Euker; *ed:* (BA) Soc Sci/His - Magna Cum Laude, CA St Univ Long Beach 1967; *cr:* 7th Grade Teacher Imperial Jr HS 1969-70; 8th Grade Teacher Mitchell Sr Elem 1970-; *ai:* Academic Pentathlon Team Coach; CA Jr Scholastic Fed, Sch Yrbk & Newspaper Adv; Phi Kappa Phi Honor Society 1967-; Atwater Teachers Assn, CA Teachers Assn, NEA, NCTE; Amer Assn of Univ Women; *office:* Mitchell Sr Elem Sch 1753 5th St Atwater CA 95301

BROWNING, LYNNE SCHNEIDER, Teacher of 3 Yr Olds; *b:* Chicago, IL; *m:* David L.; *c:* Greg, Amanda; *ed:* (BA) Ed, Concordia Univ 1977; *cr:* 2nd Grade Teacher 1977-83, Teacher of 3 Yr Olds 1989- Luth Sch; *ai:* Luth Ed Assn Mem 1989-; *office:* Luth Sch 800 Belvoir Ave Chattanooga TN 37412

BROWNING, SANDRA WILLIAMS, Sixth Grade Teacher; *b:* Springtown, TX; *c:* Marc, Sara; *ed:* (AA) Elem Ed, Weatherford Jr Coll 1961; (BA) Elem Ed, TX Wesleyan Coll 1975; *cr:* 5th Grade Teacher White Lake Sch 1975-77; 5th/6th Grade Teacher Overcoming Faith Chrstn Sch 1981-82; 6th Grade Teacher Calvary Acad 1983-; *ai:* Steppingstone Church Bd of Dir 1987-; *office:* Calvary Acad 1600 W 5th St Fort Worth TX 76102

BROWNSON, WAYNE DARREL, Vocal Music Director; *b:* Baker, MT; *m:* Judy; *c:* Jane, Scott; *ed:* (BS) Vocal Music, Eastern MT Coll 1969; (MA) Admin, MT St Univ 1979; *cr:* Vocal Music Teacher Greybul Public Schls 1969-70, Billings Public Schls 1970-; *ai:* Student Store; NEA 1970-; MT Ed Assn 1970-; Billings Ed Assn 1970-; *home:* 519 Avenue D Billings MT 59102

BROWSE, CAROLYN (CONFORTI), English Teacher; *b:* Birmingham, AL; *m:* R. Latta; *ed:* (BA) Eng, Colgate Univ 1983; Mals Hum, Wesleyan Univ; *cr:* Eng Teacher/Cnslr Blair Acad 1984-; *ai:* Var Sftbl Coach; NACAC; *office:* Blair Acad 16476 Main St Blairstown NJ 07825

BROYLES, ELIZABETH ANN, Counselor; *b:* Trenton, MO; *c:* Emily E. Dombek, Steven R. Dombek; *ed:* (BS) Home Ec Ed, NE MO St 1968; (MED) Ed, Univ of MO Columbia 1979; (MA) Counseling, Univ of MO St Louis 1984; Natl Certified Cnslr; *cr:* Sci/Home Ec Teacher N Biloxi Jr-Sr HS 1968-69; Home Ec Teacher 1972-86, Instr 1975-76 Parkway Sch Dist; Instr Continuing Grad Ed Webster Univ 1984-86; Cnslr Progressive Youth Center 1985-86; Case Worker Life Crisis Services 1986-87; Cnslr Parkway Sch Dist 1986-; *ai:* Peer Counseling; Peer & Cadet Teaching; Planning & Assessment Team, Health Advisory, Wellness Bd Curr Dev Comm; Assn Humanistic Ed; Amer Assn Counseling & Dev; 4-H Club Leader St Louis Cty 1986-; MO Consumer Newsletter Author & Writer; *office:* Parkway Sch Dist 801 Hanna Rd Manchester MO 63021

BROZICK, JAMES R., English Teacher; *b:* Blairsville, PA; *ed:* (MED) Rdng/Lang Art, 1971, (PHD) Lang Comm, 1976, Certificate Ed Admin, 1989 Univ of Pittsburgh; *cr:* Teacher N Hills Schls 1965-; Instr Univ of Pittsburgh 1976-78; *ai:* PSEA, NEA Mem; NCTE; Natl Conference on Research in Eng Mem; NCTE Promisining Researcher 1976; Articles Published; *office:* N Hills Schls 53 Rochester Rd Pittsburgh PA 15229

BROZIK, DONNA JEAN (ROEDL), Rural Elm Grades 3-5 Teacher; *b:* Janesville, WI; *m:* Michael L.; *c:* Michael D., Ryan J., Wade J.; *ed:* (BA) Elem Ed, Sioux Falls Coll 1973; *cr:* Teacher Winner Sch Dist 59-2 1973-; *ai:* MO Valley Rdng Cncl (Pres 1979-80, Mem 1979-); SDEA/NEA 1973-; Local Teacher of Yr 1988; *home:* RR 1 Box 24 Winner SD 57580

BRUBECK, JUDITH ANN, Physical Education Teacher; *b:* Frederiksted, VI; *ed:* (BA) Phys Ed, AZ St Univ 1969; *cr:* Phys Ed Teacher Manzanita Elem Sch 1969-71, Shaw Butte Elem Schl 1971-77, Ironwood Elem Sch 1977-79, Desert Foothills Elem Sch 1979-80, Sunset Elem Sch 1981-; *ai:* AEA; *office:* Sunset Elem Sch 4626 W Mountain View Rd Glendale AZ 85302

BRUCE, BARBARA CARGILE, Fourth Grade Teacher; *b:* Marshall, NC; *m:* Hall R.; *c:* Beverly B Ramsey; *ed:* (AA) Elem Ed, Mars Hill Coll 1956; (BS) Primary/Elem Ed, ASU 1959; *cr:* Teacher Madison Cty Schls 1957-60; Soc Worker Madison Cty DSS 1960-6 1; Madison Cty Schls 1966-67; Teacher Flat Creek Sch 1967-; *ai:* Diciplinary Bd Mem North Buncombe HS; Sch Improvement Comm; Landscape Comm Co Chairperson; NCAE/NEA; Democrat Women Precinct Judge; *office:* North Buncombe Elem Sch 251 Flat Creek Church Rd Weaverville NC 28787

BRUCE, BARRY ANTHONY, Social Studies Teacher; *b:* Schenectady, NY; *m:* Sharon O'Hara; *c:* Rebecca; *ed:* (BA) Intnl Stud/Poly Sci/Russian, 1963, (MA) Poly Sci/His, Univ of Louisville; Cert E MI Univ; Law Ed, Univ of Detroit; *cr:* Grad Asst Univ of Louisville 1964-65; Soc Stud Teacher Clawson Jr HS 1966-70; Teacher Clewson HS 1970-; *ai:* Chess Club & Quiz Bowl Coach; Stu Court & Stu Senate Adv; NHS Comm; Clawson Ed Assn (St Rep, Assembly Delegate) 1971-, Teacher of Month; NEA 1972-73; MI Ed Assn St Rep 1972-; Democratic Party (Precinct Delegate, St Convention Delegate); *office:* Clawson HS 101 John M St Clawson MI 48917

BRUCE, BEVERLY, Social Studies Chair; *b:* Chicago, IL; *m:* Ednamay; *c:* Nancy, David, Thomas; *ed:* (BS) Ed/Geography, W IL 1951; (MED) His/Geography, Univ of IL 1959; Various Insts; *cr:* 7th/8th Grade Soc Stud Teacher Niantic-Harristown 1953-55; 6th Grade Teacher/Prin Deland Welden 1956-57; 7th/8th Grade Soc Stud Teacher Pekin 1957-59; 7th/8th Grade HS Soc Stud Teacher Virden Public Schls 1959-; *ai:* Jr HS Stu Cncl; Virden Lib Bd Pres; BSA Cncl; *office:* Virden Public Schls 231 W Fortune Virden IL 62690

BRUCE, RICKIE, English/Fine Art Teacher; *b:* Houma, LA; *ed:* (BA) Eng/Liberal Art, Nicholls St Univ 1974; (MA) Eng/Creative Writing, Univ of SW LA 1980; Gifted/Talented Nicholls St 1985; LSU Writing Project Summer Inst 1988; Gifted/Talented, Nicholls St 1985; *cr:* Eng Grad Teaching Asst Nicholls St 1977; Eng/Math Teacher S Lafourche HS 1977-80; Writer-in-Schls St Charles Parish Public Schls 1980-83; Eng/Fine Art Teacher Destrehan HS 1983-; *ai:* NHS & Lit Magazine Spon; Chm Schlsp Comm; Teacher Rep Crisis Intervention Comm; NCTE, LA Cncl Teacher of Eng, LA Rdng Assn, St Charles Parish Rdng Cncl; LA St Univ Writing Project Summer Inst Co-Dir; Natl Writing Project; LA Artist Residency Roster 1986-; Natl Fellow for Ind Study Hum 1987; LSU/Natl Writing Project Fellow 1988; Destrehan HS Teacher of Yr; St Charles Parish HS Teacher of Yr 1988-89; Published Articles in Creative Writing, Poetry, Prose 1979-; *office:* Desterhan HS P O Drawer A Destrehan LA 70047

BRUCE, ROBERT ALAN, Band Director; *b:* Memphis, TN; *ed:* (BBA) Banking/Finance, 1982, (BME) Instrumental Music, 1985 Univ of MS; *cr:* Asst Band Dir Philadelphia HS 1985-86; Band Dir Iuka HS 1986-; *ai:* Sr Class Spon; Stu Handbook, Promotion & Retention, Guidance, Stu Act Comms; NE MS Jr HS Band Dir Assn (Secy, Treas) 1989-; MS Band Dir Assn, Natl Fed of Coaches Mem; *office:* Iuka HS 507 W Quitman Iuka MS 38852

BRUCE, SUE A., Teacher/Administrator; *b:* Beaumont, TX; *m:* James E.; *c:* Jennifer Bruce Touchett; *ed:* (BA) Elem Ed, 1963, (MA) Elem Ed/Rdng, 1984, (MA) Mid-Management, 1986, (MA) Counseling, 1988 Lamar Univ; Eng as 2nd Lang Cert Lamar Univ 1990; *cr:* Teacher Beaumont Ind Sch Dist 1963-65; Teacher 1965-85, Admin 1985-, Cnslr 1988- Hardin-Jefferson Ind Sch Dist; *home:* 6795 Linkwood Beaumont TX 77706

BRUCIE, KAREN ANN (GABIC), Third Grade Teacher; *b:* Rochester, NY; *m:* Joseph; *c:* Joseph, Sherry; *ed:* (BS) Ed, SUNY Brockport 1968; (MS) Ed, Elmira Coll 1974; Steuben-Allegany BOCES Prof Dev Prgm; *cr:* 3rd Grade Teacher Addison Sch Dist 1969-70; 7th Grade Teacher Rochester Sch Dist 1970-71; 2nd/3rd/5th/6th Grade Teacher 1971-89, 3rd Grade Teacher 1989- Addison Sch Dist; *ai:* Tuscarora Elem Sch Communications Comm Mem; NEA 1989-; *office:* Tuscarora Elem Sch 1 Cleveland Dr Addison NY 14801

BRUEGGEMANN, DENNIS W., Business Manager; *b:* Alton, IL; *m:* Peggy F. Imboden; *c:* Sarah; *ed:* (BS) Math/Government, 1973, (MS) Math Ed, 1977 S IL Univ Edwardsville; Admin Cert 1983; *cr:* Jr HS Amer His Teacher 1973-77, Jr HS Math Teacher 1977-84, Asst Prin/Math Teacher 1984-85, Bus Mgr/Math Teacher 1985- Highland Cmmty Sch Dist; *ai:* Jr HS Mathcounts Coach; IL Cncl Teachers of Math 1973-85; NCTM 1973-; IL Assn of Sch Bus Ofcls 1986-; Alhambra Baptist Church (Deacon, Chm 1982-, Sunday Sch Teacher 1981-); IL Master Teacher Awd 1984; Early Adolescent Ed Assn of IL St Bd of Dirs; *office:* Highland Cmmty Unit Sch Dist 1800 Lindenthal Ave Highland IL 62249

BRUGGEMAN, GERALDINE REINTS, 6th Grade Teacher; *b:* Clarksville, IA; *w:* Melbourne (dec); *c:* Debra, Douglas; *ed:* Elem Ed, IA St Teachers Coll 1948; (BA) Elem Ed, Univ of N IA 1972; *cr:* K-8th Grade Teacher Butler Cty Rural Sch 1944-45; 3rd/4th Grade Teacher Marble Rock Consolidated 1945-48, Waverly Public Schls 1948-49; 3rd-9th Grade Teacher Marble Rock Elem 1949-; *ai:* ISEA, NEA 1944-; *home:* 219 S Main St Marble Rock IA 50653

BRUGMAN, CAROL LEE, Sixth Grade Teacher; *b:* Louisville, KY; *m:* Eugene V.; *c:* Karl, Barbara, Becky, Bernie; *ed:* (BS) Psych/Elem Ed, Univ of MD 1960; Univ of VA; *cr:* 5th Grade Teacher St Columba Sch 1961-63; 2nd/4th/5th Grade Teacher St

Johns Sch 1967-74, 1976-78; Substitute Teacher Amer Dependent Schls Germany 1974-76; 6th Grade Teacher Westside Elem 1978-; *ai:* Math Scope & Sequence Comm; Teacher Expectations & Stu Achievement; NEA, EAR 1978-; ACE Rep 1978-; Delta Kappa Gamma 1980-; Bonnie Grimes Schlsp; *home:* 1010 S 19th St Rogers AR 72756

BRUHN, JULIA ANN (POAD), Science Teacher; *b:* Lone Rock, WI; *m:* Frank John (dec); *ed:* (BS) Elem Ed, Univ of WW Platteville 1962; (BS) Univ of WI Richland Center; Sci & Classroom Management; *cr:* 1st-8th Grade Teacher Rural School Pine Bluff 1955-58; Rural Sch Mill Creek 1958-61; Grades for Sci 1968-; *ai:* Jr HS Sci Olypiad Team Coach; Sci Dept Head for Dist 7th-12th Grade; Co-Chairperson Sch Evaluation Consortium; Sex Equity Comm for Dist; Mem & FFFilitator Stu Assistance Prgm; NEA, WI Ed Assn Cncl, CAUS South River Valley Ed Assn, NSTA, NABT, WI Society of Sci Teachers, WI Assn Mid Level Ed; Univ of WI Platteville Alumni Assn, Univ of WI Richland Center Alumni Assn Exec Bd; Sci World 1989; Dist Teacher of Yr 1988-89; *office:* River Valley Jr H S 660 W Daley St Spring Green WI 53588

BRUINS, OLIVE (UPTON), English Teacher; *b:* Freeport, ME; *m:* Robert H.; *c:* Jeffrey R., Debra J.; *ed:* (BA) Eng, Univ of ME Orono 1945; Grad Stud Univ of ME, Syracuse Univ, Long Beach St, Univ of S CA, CA St Univ Northridge; *cr:* Eng Teacher North Yarmouth Acad 1944-47, Boothbay Harbor HS 1948-50; Brockport HS 1950-54, Bellflower HS 1954-57, Norwalk HS 1959-60, Saugus HS 1969-; *ai:* CA Teachers Assn, NEA, Hart Dist Teachers Assn; Amer Assn of Univ Women (Treas, Educl Fellowship Chm, Membership VP).

BRUMBELOE, JEAN JACKSON, Second Grade Teacher; *b:* Rome, GA; *m:* Andrew Neal; *c:* Jeffrey N.; *ed:* (BS) Music Ed, Jacksonville St Univ 1970; (MED) Music Ed, Auburn Univ 1974; Auburn Univ 1975; Early Chldhd Cert, Berry Coll 1980; Jacksonville St Univ 1980-81; *cr:* Band Dir Cedartown Jr HS 1970-71, La Grange Jr HS 1971-73; Title I Remedial Teacher Robinson Springs Elem Sch 1973-78; Band Dir Lanett Jr HS 1978-79; 2nd Grade Teacher North Heights Elem Sch 1979-; *ai:* NEA 1970-; GA Music Educators Assn 1970-73; Natl Bandmasters Assn; Rome Symphony Orch 1979-82; 1st Baptist Church 1960-; North Heights Elem Teacher of Yr 1983; *office:* North Heights Elem Sch 26 Atteiram Dr Rome GA 30161

BRUMELS, DORIS TAYLOR, Fifth Grade Teacher; *b:* Mc Bain, MI; *m:* Bruce C.; *c:* Blaine, Kirk, Joy; *ed:* (BA) Eng/Span, Hope Coll 1962; Cntrl MI Univ; MI St Univ; *cr:* 4th-5th Grade Teacher Marion Public Sch 1962; 5th Grade Teacher Cadillac Public Sch 1962-63; Part Time/Sub Teacher Mc Bain/Cadillac/Marion/Falmouth Schls 1963-76; 4th-6th Grade Teacher Marion Public Sch 1976-; *ai:* Safety Patrol Adv; Marion Schls Ed Assn Treas 1980-82/1986-; Teacher of Yr Awd 1989; Wrote & Received Grant Form MI Cncl for Hum; *home:* 7978 S Lucas Mc Bain MI 49657

BRUMFIELD, HERBERT, Biology Teacher; *b:* Independence, LA; *m:* Melva J. Dillon; *c:* Kendra, Beonka, Jermaine, Trishelle; *ed:* (BS) Bio, 1964, (MED) Admin/Supervision, 1974 Southern Univ; Bio, Univ of MO Kansas City, Dillard Univ, Jackson St Univ; *cr:* Bio/Gen Sci Teacher Washington Parish HS 1964-69; Bio Teacher Franklinton HS 1969-80; Upward Bound Bio Teachers SE LA Univ 1983-84; Bio Teacher Amite HS 1980-; *ai:* 4-H Club Spon; Amite HS Substance Abuse Prevention Ed Club Adv & Co-Spon; LAE, NEA Sch Rep 1980-; *home:* 505 S Richardson St Amite LA 70422

BRUMLEY, CONNIE SUE, Resource Teacher; *b:* Sherman, TX; *m:* Conrad Scott; *c:* Campbell S.; *ed:* (BA) Eng/Psych, Sam Houston St Univ 1969; (MED) Ed Psych, TX Tech Univ 1988; Grad Courses Psych, TX Tech; *cr:* Eng/Rdng Teacher Donna Migrant Sch 1969-72; Teacher All Saints Episcopal Sch 1975-80; Sci/Math/Rdng Teacher St Joseph Cath Sch 1981-85; Ed Diagnostician SE Lubbock Cty Organization 1990; Resource Teacher Lubbock Cooper Jr HS 1985-; *ai:* Resource Teacher & Spec Ed Cnslr/Diagnostician; TX Classroom Teachers Assn 1985-; TX Educl Diagnostics Assn 1989-; TX Assn of Episcopal Schls 1975-80; Stu Amer Psychological Assn 1972-75; Unit Neighborhood Assn 1977-; Presented Paper Rocky Mountain Psychological Assn 1974; *office:* Lubbock-Cooper Jr HS Rt 6 Box 400 Lubbock TX 79412

BRUMLEY, LEANN LOUISE, 2nd Grade Teacher; *b:* El Dorado, KS; *m:* Victor Ray; *ed:* (BA) Elem Ed, 1983, (MS) Elem Ed, 1985 East Cntrl Univ; *cr:* 5th/6th Grade Teacher Graham Public Schls 1983-85; 2nd Grade Teacher Ardmore City Schls 1985-; *ai:* Lang Art Curr Review Comm; Sci Fair Chairperson 1986-87; Ardmore Ed Assn Building Rep 1988-; OK Ed Assn, NEA 1983-; Beta Sigma Phi VP 1989-; *office:* Jefferson Elem Sch PO Box 1709 Ardmore OK 73401

BRUNDAGE, PATSY O'REAR, Cosmetology Teacher; *b:* Dallas, TX; *m:* Edwin Earl; *c:* Michael, Darrell; *ed:* (BA) Sci, TX A&M 1978; Hair Design; *cr:* Teacher TX Beauty Coll 1972-76; Lancaster HS 1976-; *ai:* VICA Adv; TX Industrial Voc Assn Dir 1984-; Cosmetology Inst of Public Schls Parliamentarian 1986-88; *office:* Lancaster H S 822 W Pleasant Run Lancaster TX 75134

BRUNE, DAVID JOSEPH, Science Teacher; *b:* Fort Madison, IA; *m:* Linda Steffensmeier; *c:* Kevin, Ryan, Eric, Todd; *ed:* (BA) Sci/Phys Ed, IA Wesleyan Coll 1971; Grad Stud Sci; *cr:* Sci Teacher/Coach Harmony Cmmty Schls; *ai:* Jr HS Ftbl, Bsktbl, Track, Sci Fair; IAS; *home:* 615 N 5th St West Point IA 52656

BRUNELLE, CHARLES DAVID, Soc Studies Teacher/Chairman; *b:* Price, UT; *m:* Lilo Koss; *c:* Douglas, Anthony; *ed:* (BA) Soc Stud, Univ of UT 1973; Boston Univ, S CA; *cr:* Teacher Beatty HS 1973-80, Bamberg HS Germany; *ai:* Voice of Democracy; NHS; OEA Rep 1986-88; *office:* Bamberg Amer HS Box 23668 APO New York NY 09139

BRUNELLE, EDWARD JAY, Science Teacher; *b:* Marquette, MI; *m:* Sandra Lee Brady; *c:* Laura A., Jeffrey A.; *ed:* (BS) Bio Ed, 1971, (MA) Bio Ed, 1983 N MI Univ; Sci Ed in Mid Sch Cadre Trng; Project Act Integrating Math & Sci Trng; Wkshp Presentation Trng for MI Dept of Ed; Educl Research NSF Wkshp Cntrl MI Univ; *cr:* Negotiator MI Ed Assn 1980-; Grad Level Wkshp Presenter N MI Univ 1988-; *ai:* Grading & Standards, Spec Ed Mainstreaming, Curr Comms; Project SEMS & St Advisory Bd Mem; Phi Kappa Phi NHS 1983-; MI Ed Assn 1971-; Upper Peninsula Ed Assn Pres 1984-; Blue Lodge #269 (Sr Warden, Menominee Commandery) 1987-; Educator of Yr Menominee Jaycees 1983 & Chamber of Commerce 1989; Educl Research NSF Cntrl MI Univ 1986; *office:* Menominee Mid Sch 1230 13th St Menominee MI 49858

BRUNER, JUDITH VENTURELLA, Kindergarten Teacher; *b:* Oil City, PA; *m:* Daniel P.; *c:* Daniel, Jayna, Jeffrey; *ed:* (BS) Elem Ed, 1970, (MED) Elem Ed, 1985 Clarion Univ of PA; *cr:* 6th Grade Teacher Hasson Heights Elem Sch 1970-71; 3rd Grade Teacher Dakota Elem Sch 1971-74; Nursery Sch Teacher Lullaby Day Nursery Sch 1975-76; Immaculate Conception Sch 1977-84; Kndgtn Teacher Clarion Area Elem 1985-; *ai:* Elem Sch Stage Plays; Introduction of Cmptrs-Primary; Elem Comm Chairperson; Seneca Rdng Cncl Bd Mem 1986-89; PTO Treas 1983; Kappa Delta Pi 1985-; Nom for Jaycees Outstanding Young Educator of Yr Awd 1983-84; *home:* 109 Crestmont Dr Marianne PA 16254

BRUNER, REBECCA BEARD, Basic Skills Teacher; *b:* Hardinsburg, KY; *ed:* (BA) Elem Ed, 1967, (MS) Elem Ed, 1972 W KY Univ; Rdng Recovery Prgm; *cr:* 2nd Grade Teacher Greenwood Elem 1967-79; 4th Grade Teacher 1979-87, Basics Skill Remediation Teacher 1987- Price Elem; *ai:* NEA, KY Ed Assn, Jefferson Cty Teachers Assn 1967-; Jefferson Cty Teachers Assn Rep 1980-81; *office:* Price Elem Sch 5001 Garden Green Way Louisville KY 40218

BRUNER, VIRGINIA JANE (DUNLAP), HS English Teacher; *b:* Oklahoma City, OK; *m:* Larry D.; *c:* Julie K.; *ed:* (BA) Eng, E Cntrl Univ 1980; *cr:* Kndgtn/5th/6th Grade Lang Art Teacher 1980-81, 1st Grade Teacher 1981-84 Fox Public Sch; 7th-10th Grade Eng Teacher 1984-85, 7th/9th-11th Grade Eng Teacher 1985-86, 7th/9th-11th Grade Rdng/Spelling/Eng Teacher 1986-87, 7th/10th-12th Grade Rdng/Spelling/Eng Teacher 1987-88, 10th-12th Grade Teacher 1988-89, 9th-12th Grade Eng Teacher 1989- Fox HS; *ai:* Sr Class Spon; Prin Advisory & Staff Dev Comm; Supts Project Head; OK Ed Assn, NEA 1980-; Fox Assn of Classroom Teachers (Pres 1981-82, Mem 1980-); First Baptist Church, OK Eastern Star Mem; Del City Assembly Order of Rainbow for Girls Majority Mem; Fox Public Schls Teacher of Yr 1984-85; *office:* Fox HS Box 248 Fox OK 73435

BRUNING, HAROLD, Jr HS Teacher; *b:* Solen, ND; *ed:* (BS) Elem Ed/Phys Ed, Mayville St Univ 1962; *cr:* Rural Teacher Ambulance Butte 1953-57, Ft Rice 1957-59; Jr HS Teacher Zeeland Public Sch 1962-89; *home:* Box 55 Zeeland ND 58581

BRUNK, LON RUSSELL, Teacher/Computer Coordinator; *b:* Wilmington, DE; *m:* Trudy Quinalty; *c:* Tim, Scott; *ed:* (BA) His, Long Beach St 1974; (MSEC) Computing, Pepperdine Univ 1987; Minor Math, Comm; *cr:* Teacher Faye Ross Jr HS 1974-887, Fullerton Coll 1984-87, Tetzlaff Jr HS 1987-; *ai:* Cmptr Coord; ABC Fed of Teachers 1974-, CA Press Awd 1977, 1978; Union Press Editorials, AFT, PTA Teacher of Yr; *office:* Tetzlaff Jr HS 12351 E De Lamo Blvd Cerritos CA 90701

BRUNKEN, LAUREL KING, School Counselor; *b:* Concordia, KS; *m:* Delane; *c:* Erin, Jessica; *ed:* (BM) Applied Music, 1973, (BME) Music Ed, 1973 Wichita St Univ; (MM) Music Ed, KS St Univ 1983; K-12th Sch Cnslr Cert 1985; Cnslr Ed, Emporia St Univ; *cr:* Music Teacher Kaw Valley 1973-79; GTA Music Teacher for Elem Teachers KS St Univ 1979-81; GTA Supvr for Stu Teachers Univ of KS 1982-83; K-8th Grade Sch Cnslr Royal Valley 1985-; *ai:* Sch Improvement, Child Study Team; Inservice Cncl; Curr Comm; Impact Aid Summer Sch Dir; AACD, KACD 1985-; KSCA (Mid Level VP 1986-87) 1985-; KAMLE 1985-; KS St Dept of Ed Human Sexuality Trainer; KSU Human Sexuality & AIDS Ed Task Force Mem; Wkshp Presenter; *home:* 2413 SW Pepperwood Cir Topeka KS 66509

BRUNKER, JERRY, Assistant Principal; *b:* Cynthiana, KY; *m:* Ann McCauley; *c:* Angela, Alicia, Marilou; *ed:* (BA) Soc Sci, Morehead St Univ 1969; (MA) Guidance/Counseling, Eastern KY Univ 1977; Ed Admin, Eastern KY Univ 1979; *cr:* Sci Teacher Twenhofel Jr HS 1969; Soc Stud Teacher 1969-86; Asst Prin 1987 Harrison Cty Mid Sch; *ai:* Mid Sch Bsktbl Coach; Boys & Girls Organized Trips Washington DC & NY Mid Sch Stu; Han Cty Ed Assn Pres 1971-72; KY Ed Assn/NEA 1969-; KY Assn of Sch Admin 1987-; Teacher of Yr 1971-72; *office:* Harrison County Mid Sch Box 149 Education Dr Cynthiana KY 41031

BRUNN, HERMAN PHILIP, 6th Grade Elementary Teacher; *b:* Nanticoke, PA; *m:* Frances Edna Krasnansky; *c:* James, Frances, Mary; *ed:* (BA) Elem, Kings Coll 1953; Rutgers Univ; *cr:* 6th Grade Teacher Alexander Batcho Intermediate Sch 1954-; *ai:* Yrbk Adv; Intramural Sports; NJEA; *office:* Alexander Batcho Sch N 13th Ave N 13th Ave Manville NJ 08835

BRUNNER, LEO ROBERT, 7th Grade Geography Teacher; *b:* Moline, IL; *ed:* (BA) His, Augustana Coll 1970; Mid Sch Convention, Eau Claire WI 1988; Prevention Inst, Champaign IL 1989; Mid Sch Convention, Lombard IL 1989; *cr:* Substitute Teacher Sch Dist #40 1974-83; Teacher Wilson Jr HS 1984, John Deere Jr HS 1986-; *ai:* 8th Grade Ftbl, Bsktbl, Pitching Coach; Trendsetter Just Say No Spon; Mem Self Esteem, Positive Motivation, Soc Stud Testing Comm; Rdng CADRE Group Mem; PTO Life Membership 1983-, Honor Scroll 1990; Natl Cncl for Geographic Ed, Natl Geographic Society, Natl Trust for Historic Preservation 1989-; ASCD 1988-; Society of Bsbl Research 1987-; Amer Legion Teacher of Yr Finalist 1989; *home:* 2613 6th Ave Moline IL 61265

BRUNNER, PATRICIA HAIN, English Teacher; *b:* Dayton, OH; *m:* John Howard; *c:* William C., Mark D., Paul H.; *ed:* (BA) Eng, Univ of Co 1960; *cr:* Eng Teacher Smiley Jr HS 1960-62;Rdng Teacher Denver Elem Schls; Voc Ed Tutor Thomas Jefferson HS 1976-78; Eng Teacher NE Jr HS 1979-; *ai:* Stu Cncl Spon 1979-81; Co-Spon Jr JHS; NCTE Mem, Co Lang Art Assn Mem, NEA, St Vrain Valley Ed Assn 1979-; Calvary Baptist Church; St Vrain Valley Sch Dist Nominee Governors Awd Excl Ed 1988-89; Nominee for 1st Salute to Amer Teacher Spon Walt Disney Company & Center for Civic Ed 1989; *home:* 7437 N 95th St Longmont CO 80503

BRUNO, MARY E. KELSO, Teacher; *b:* Fairfield, ID; *m:* Owen J.; *c:* Calvin, Lynn J.; *ed:* (BA) Ed, OR St Univ 1973; Sci Ed 1978; *cr:* Teacher Challis ID 1961-68, Lakeview Elem 1968-71, Seven Oak 1971-; *ai:* Sftbl Coach; 8th Grade Adv; Chamber of Commerce 1984-89, Outstanding Teacher in Forestry 1984; *home:* 34612 Ranchero Ave Albany OR 97321

BRUNS, GAYLE ANDERSON, Business Ed/Library Instr; *b:* Fairmont, MN; *m:* George L.; *c:* George D.; *ed:* (BA) Bus Ed/Lib/Media, Mankato St 1962; *cr:* Librarian Estherville HS & Jr Coll 1962-64; Jr HS Typing Teacher Cherry Jr HS 1964-65; O E Coord Estherville HS & Jr Coll 1965-66; Librarian/Bus Ed Ellsworth HS & Elem Sch 1966-; *ai:* Yrbk Adv; Delta Pi Epsilon; MN Bus Educators Inc; MEMO; *home:* RR 1 Box 120 Rock Rapids IA 51246

BRUNS, PATRICIA MORSE, Physical Education Instructor; *b:* Newton, MA; *c:* John G., Robert G., James A., Laura Bruns White, Thomas L., Jacquelyn A., Katherine M.; *ed:* (BS) Phys Ed, Boston Univ & Sargent Coll 1956; *cr:* Phys Ed Instr Antioch Coll 1956-57, Univ of OH Cincinnati 1957-58, St Lawrence Sch 1972-; *ai:* Jr HS Vlybl, Bsktbl, Track, Tennis Coach; Girls Youth Sports League Pres; NCEA 1972-; FL Allied Health, Phys Ed, Recreation & Dance 1978-88; *home:* 5603 Forest Haven Cir #103 Tampa FL 33615

BRUNSON, BARBARA CROFTON, 6th Grade Hmrm Rdng Teacher; *b:* Mineral Springs, AR; *m:* Glen E.; *c:* Tina Skahill, Geoffrey; *ed:* (BS) Ed, Chicago St 1969; *cr:* 6th Grade Rdng Teacher St Thaddeus 1973-; *ai:* Asst Prin; Rdng Coord; *office:* St Thaddeus Sch 9538 S Harvard Chicago IL 60628

BRUNSON, ETHEL D., Teacher; *b:* Conway, SC; *ed:* (BA) Eng, Livingstone Coll 1965; (MA) Eng, Hampton Univ 1976; Effective Teaching Prgm; Teacher Effectiveness Trng; HS Assertive Discipline; *cr:* 10th Grade Eng Teacher Upchurch HS 1965-67; 6th Grade Teacher Booker T Washington Elem 1967-69; 8th Grade Teacher Newport News HS 1969-71; 9th Grade Teacher Newport News Intermediate 1971-81; 10th Grade Teacher Warwick HS 1981-; *ai:* Homebound Instr Newport News Sch System; AFT Mem 1987-89; VA Assn of Eng Teachers 1981-; Greater Walters AME Zion Church (Chm Chrstn Ed Bd, Dir, Womans Day Speaker) 1971-, Service Rendered Certificate; Greater Walters Tutorial Service Dir 1977-, Service Rendered Certificate; *home:* 815 18th St Newport News VA 23607

BRUNSON, JOSEPHINE GADSDEN, 7/8th Grade Lang Arts Teacher; *b:* Saint Stephen, SC; *m:* Lawrence; *c:* Jamie; *ed:* (BS) Elem Ed, Claflin Univ 1967; (MS) Ed/Minor Guidance, SC St Coll 1978; *cr:* Teacher Allen Elem Sch 1967-69, Brunson Elem Sch 1969-73, Elloree Elem Sch 1973-89, Elloree HS 1989-; *ai:* Grade Level Chairperson; Elloree Ed Assn (Pres, VP) 1973; SC Ed Assn 1967- Membership 1989; NEA 1967; PTA Pres 1987-89; St Paul Episcopal Church Mem; Uniserve Guidelines Comm; APT Observer; P R Chairperson; *home:* Rt 2 Box 350 Cameron SC 29030

BRUNSON, NANCY ANN (COMSTOCK), Home Economics Teacher; *b:* Longview, WA; *m:* Ronald Roy; *c:* Randal C., Kevin L.; *ed:* (BA) Home Ec, Humboldt St Univ 1970; *cr:* Aide/Teacher N Humboldt Union HS Dist 1971-80; Home Ec Teacher Arcata HS 1980-, Mc Kinleyville HS 1981-; *ai:* FHA Home Ec Related Occupations Adv & Region Coord; Voc Tech Dept Head; Curr Advisory Comm; NHUHSD Staff Dev Comm; CTA; Faculty Salary Comm; Teaching Through Learning Channels Teacher & Trainer; AHEA, CAHEA 1968-; HETAC (Treas 1989-) 1982-; CAVE 1989-; NAVET 1987-; Blue Lake Chamber of Commerce (Pres 1978) 1975-88; Beta Zigma Phi (Pres, VP, Secy, Treas) 1964-, Girl of Yr Awd 1976, 1984; Blue Lake Museum Society 1984-; Amer Assn Univ Women (VP, Membership) 1973-79; Coll of Redwoods Mc Kinleyville Branch Advisory Comm 1978-; *office:* Mc Kinleyville HS 1300 Murray Rd Mc Kinleyville CA 95521

BRUNSWICK, LORI ANN, Social Studies/Health Teacher; *b:* Coldwater, OH; *m:* Jay; *c:* Nathan, Jordan; *ed:* (BS) Elem Ed, Wright St Univ 1984; Courses in Ec Ed & AIDS Ed; *cr:* 8th Grade Amer His Teacher 1984-86, 6th Grade Soc Stud/Health Teacher 1984- Arcanum Butler Mid Sch; *ai:* 6th Grade & Geography Bee Adv; Building Advisory & Earth Day Comms; Jennings Scholar

1986-87; *office:* Arcanum Butler Mid Sch St Rt 127 S Arcanum OH 45304

BRUNT, KAY L., Kindergarten Teacher; *b:* Monroe, MI; *m:* Dale; *c:* Erika, Jessica; *ed:* (BS) Soc Sci/Creative Drama/Planned Prgm, E MI Univ 1972; Post Grad Stud; *cr:* Kndgtn Teacher 1972-74, 1st Grade Teacher 1975-76, Kndgtn Teacher 1977- Ida Public Sch; *ai:* Schlsp Comm; Teacher of Summer Safety Prgm; MI Ed Assn; *office:* Ida Public Schls Ida St Ida MI 48140

BRUSH, LEA, Mathematics Teacher; *b:* San Francisco, CA; *ed:* (BS) Bible/Mission Ed, Maranatha Baptist Bible Coll 1973; (MS) Math Ed, Univ of SC 1988; *cr:* 4th Grade Teacher Gold Coast Chrstn Sch 1973-77; Elem/Jr HS Teacher Temple Chrstn Sch 1977-80; HS Math Teacher Sumter Chrstn Sch 1980-; *ai:* Vlybl & Sftbl Coach; Yrbk & Class Adv; Sch Athletic Trainer All Sports; GSA Neighborhood Chm 1982-87, Recognition 1987; *office:* Sumter Chrstn Sch 420 S Pike W Sumter SC 29150

BRYAN, DIANE (KLEPFER), 5th Grade Lang Art Teacher; *b:* Kokomo, IN; *m:* Richard A.; *ed:* (BS) Elem Ed, Ball St Univ 1965; (MS) Elem Ed, IN Univ 1972; Gifted/Talented, Learning Disabled, Writing Process & Math Instruction; *cr:* 6th Grade Teacher Griffith Schls 1965-66; 4th Grade Teacher Taylor Sch Corp 1966-67; 3rd/5th Grade Teacher Eastern Howard Sch Corp 1967-; *ai:* Stu Teaching Supvr; Advisory Cncl Ed IN Wesleyan Univ; St Task Force Dept of Ed Restructuring; Lang Art Rep; Book Adoption Comm; Comm for Natl Recognition; ISTA/NEA Local Bargaining Team 1968-; IN Retired Teachers Assn (Rep 1984-86) 1985-; Eastern Howard Sch Corp Classroom Teachers Assn; IN Rdgn Assn 1985-; Church Mission Society Secy 1988-; Mother-Daughter Banquests Speaker; Teacher Quality Grant Peter Review State Speaker; St Finalist Teacher of Yr 1982; Articles Published; *office:* Eastern-Howard Elem Sch 301 S Meridian Greentown IN 46936

BRYAN, HENRY COLLIER, Math Teacher; *b:* Atlanta, GA; *ed:* (BS) Math, Cheyney Univ 1962; (MDIV) Theology, Eastern Baptist Theological Seminary 1968; Numerous Colleges; *cr:* Math Teacher Masterman Demonstration Sch 1968-71, Philadelphia HS for Girls 1971; *ai:* Chm of Human Relations Comm; Phi Delta Kappa Life Mem 1985; NCTM Life Mem 1989; Assn of Teachers of Math Philadelphia & Vicinity Life Mem 1985; Alpha Phi Alpha Life Mem 1970; Amer Baptist Churches Ministers Cncl Life Mem 1969; Natl Assn for Advancement of Colored People Life Mem 1988; Philadelphia Heath Users Group Cmptr Charter Mem 1980; YMCA Charter Mem North Branch Y Men Assn 1972; Pres Awd Cheyney Univ 1962; Ordained Chrstn Ministry Zion Baptist Church Phila Amer Baptist 1968; Outstanding Young Men of Amer 1971; *home:* 17 West Brook Dr Cherry Hill NJ 08003

BRYAN, JANET SMITH, Mathematics Dept Chm/Teacher; *b:* Pennsville, NJ; *m:* Ronnie Lenier; *c:* Steven, Daryl; *ed:* (AA) Math, Okaloosa-Walton Jr Coll 1968; (BA) Math, 1970, (MED) Ed Leadership, Univ of W FL 1981; *cr:* Teacher Richbourg Jr HS 1970-71, Baker Sch 1973-75; Teacher/Dept Chm Baker Sch 1975-; *ai:* Jr Class Spon; OCTM Treas 1987-; FCTM Bd of Dir 1988-89; NCTM, OCEA, FTP, NEA 1973-; Delta Kappa Gamma 1987-; Mu Alpha Theta Spon; Dist STAR Teacher 1977; *office:* Baker Sch Rt 2 Box 231 Baker FL 32531

BRYAN, JEAN YOUNG, Chemistry Teacher; *b:* Banner Springs, TN; *m:* Harry E. Jr.; *c:* Mary N., Harriet; *ed:* (BS) Chem, George Peabody Coll 1962; (MED) Ed, Mid TN St Univ 1972; Grad Stud Ed, Univ of TN 1989; *cr:* Sci Teacher Bridgeforth Mid Sch 1972-87; Chem Teacher Giles Cty HS 1987-; *ai:* Sci Dept Chm; Mid Sch Beta Club Spon; Giles Cty Ed Assn Pres 1988-89, Certificate 1989, Distinguished Teacher of Yr 1986, Teacher of Yr 1987; Delta Kappa Gamma 1982-; Church Supt 1980-89; Sci Teachers Research Involvement for Vital Ed 1986, 1987; Stokely Fellows Seminar 1989; *office:* Giles Cty HS Magazine Rd Pulaski TN 38478

BRYAN, JOSEPH W., English Teacher; *b:* Atlanta, GA; *m:* Lorri Griggs; *ed:* (AB) General Liberal Arts, De Kalb Comm Coll 1979; (BSE) Eng, Jacksonville St Univ 1981; (MED) Scndry Eng, GA St Univ 1987; *cr:* Eng Teacher Columbia HS 1981-88, Heritage HS 1988-; *ai:* Ftbl Offensive Coord; Track; General Mgr WHHS; Parent Teacher Stu Assn 1981-; NEA 1986-; Natl Fed Interscholstic Coaches Assn 1988-; Sigma Nu Alumni Assn 1980-; Honorary Lt Colonel GA St Militia 1989; *office:* Heritage HS 2400 Granade Rd Conyers GA 30208

BRYAN, MIKE A., Spanish/English Teacher; *b:* Snyder, TX; *m:* Louise Raymond; *c:* Joshua, Jacob, Samuel, Matthew, Lucas; *ed:* (BA) Span, Brigham Young Univ 1976; *cr:* Migrant Teacher Home-Sch Coord Parma Sch Dist 1976-77; Teacher Clair E Gale Jr HS 1977-; *ai:* NEA, IEA Building Rep 1977-; Selected Ancient World Inst Participant; *office:* Clair E Gale Jr HS 955 Garfield Idaho Falls ID 83401

BRYANT, ANNA SUE, 1st Grade Teacher; *b:* Harrison, AR; *m:* Leonard Ray; *c:* Kimberly A. Shearer, Kerrin L.; *ed:* (AS) Elem Ed, NACC 1976; (BS) Elem Ed, S of O 1978; (MS) Elem Ed, SMSU 1990; Elem Ed, Southwest MO St Univ 1991; *cr:* 1st Grade Teacher Omaha Sch; *ai:* Teacher Asst Team 1989-; AEA, NEA 1987-89; *home:* Rt 1 Box 216A Omaha AR 72662

BRYANT, CARLA A., Reading Teacher; *b:* Philadelphia, PA; *c:* Myeshia Moore, Demetrius; *ed:* (BS) Elem Ed, Cheyney St 1974; *cr:* Teacher St Francis of Assisi 1974-76, Camden NJ Pyne Poyat 1978-81, Turner Job Corps 1984-86, Southside Mid Sch 1986-89; *ai:* Sunshine Club; Drill Team; Media Comm Mem; Probe Hospital Volunteer; *home:* 1815 Lincoln Ave Albany GA 31707

BRYANT, DEBBIE L., 2nd Grade Teacher; *b:* Port Arthur, TX; *m:* Greg Bryant; *ed:* (BA) Elem Ed, Lamar Univ 1977; Supervision; *cr:* 2nd Grade Teacher 1978-81; Spec Ed Teacher 1981-82; 2nd Grade Teacher 1982-Ridgewood Elem; *ai:* Selected to Serve on Textbook Comm; Curriculum Comm; TAAS Field Test Review Comm; *office:* Ridgewood Elem Sch 2820 Merriman Port Neches TX 77651

BRYANT, DEBORAH PALMER, Spanish Teacher; *b:* Middletown, OH; *m:* Jerry; *c:* Jaime L., Jacob R.; *cr:* Span Teacher Glen Este HS 1981, Lakota HS 1981-83, Lebanon HS 1988-; *ai:* OFLA, Lebanon Ed Assn 1988-; *office:* Lebanon HS 160 Miller Rd Lebanon OH 45036

BRYANT, DOREEN MARIE, Mathematics Teacher; *b:* Oak Harbor, WA; *m:* James Andrew; *c:* Jaime C.; *ed:* (AA) Math/Sci, Amer River Coll 1982; (BA) Math, CA St Univ Sacramento 1985; Working Toward Masters; *cr:* Math Teacher Casa Roble Fundamental HS 1985-86, El Camino Fundamental HS 1986-; *ai:* Mathletes Adv; CTA, NEA 1985-; Nom Presidential Awd; Mentor Teacher San Juan Unified Sch Dist 1990; *office:* El Camino Fundamental HS 4300 El Camino Ave Sacramento CA 95821

BRYANT, DORIS JACKSON, 5th Grade Math Teacher; *b:* Roper, NC; *m:* Harry Lee; *c:* Brandon J.; *ed:* (BS) Intermediate Ed/Math/Sci, Elizabeth City St Univ 1974; Teacher Trng Prgm; *cr:* 6th Grade Teacher Washington Cty Union 1974-77; 5th/6th Grade Teacher Gregory Elem Sch 1977-; *ai:* Math Chairperson, Responsible for Math Fair; Math Week, Math Thinkathon; NC Cncl of Teachers of Math Mem 1986-; 1st Runner Up Outstanding Elem Math Teachers Awd 1987; *office:* Gregory Elem Sch 319 S 10th St Wilmington NC 28401

BRYANT, GAIL, 6th Grade Teacher; *b:* Hobbs, NM; *ed:* (BA) Elem Ed, TX Tech 1975; (MS) Elem Ed, Univ of NM 1976; *cr:* Substitute Teacher Ruidosa Public Schls 1977; Teacher Gallup-Mc Kinley Public Schls 1977-78, Hobbs Public Schls 1978-; *ai:* Book Adoption, Cmptr Curr, Budget Comm; HTA, NMRA 1979-; HWTA Night Coord 1989-; Whos Who in Amer Women 1979; *office:* Taylor Elem Sch 1520 N Breckon Hobbs NM 88240

BRYANT, JAN JOHNSON, 5th-8th Grade Teacher; *b:* Glendale, CA; *m:* Ed; *c:* Joshua, Heidi, Sarah; *ed:* (BA) Eng/Fr, Univ of CA Santa Barbara 1976; CSULB; CSUDH; *cr:* 5th-8th Grade Teacher Peninsula Chrstn Sch 1977-; *ai:* Christmas & Spring Musical Dir; Curr Writing; Faith Presbyn Church Music & Childrens Ministries; Published Books; *office:* Peninsula Chrstn Sch 22507 S Figueroa St Carson CA 90745

BRYANT, JANICE L., 7th & 8th English Teacher; *b:* Mt Clemens, MI; *ed:* (BA) Ed, Concordia Univ 1966; (MA) Lit, Sangamon St Univ 1982; *cr:* 2nd Grade Teacher Bethany-Trinity Luth Sch 1966-68; 7th/8th Grade Teacher Luther Sch Assn 1968-; *ai:* Coaching; Publicity & Eng Comm; Winterim-Co-Chairperson; Bd of Ed; Luth Ed Assn, Delta Kappa Gamma 1987-; Amer Field Service Act Dir 1989-; *home:* 222 N 16th St Decatur IL 62521

BRYANT, JEFF A., Director of Bands; *b:* Roanoke, VA; *m:* Teresa D.; *c:* Nathaniel A., Carrington D.; *ed:* (BA) Music Performance, Berklee Coll of Music 1978; (MS) Music Ed, Radford Univ 1980; Educl Admin, WV Coll; *cr:* Dir of Jazz Stud Radford Univ 1978-80; Dir of Bands Greenbrier East HS 1980-; *ai:* Marching Band, Concert Band, Wind Ensemble, Jazz Ensemble, Indoor Guard, Indoor Percussion; Cope Team Chm; Effective Schls Comm Mem; Music Educators Natl Comm, Intnl Jazz Educators Assn, NEA; Berklee Coll of Music Art Farmer Jazz Masters Awd; *office:* Greenbrier East HS Fairlea Rt 2 Lewisburg WV 24901

BRYANT, JOSEPH BARTON, American History Teacher; *b:* Seneca, SC; *m:* Susan Elaine Carroll; *c:* Jonathan, Mark; *ed:* (BA) His, Furman Univ 1971; Grad Courses Clemson Univ, Univ of SC; *cr:* Teacher Oakway HS 1972-83, West Oak HS 1983-; *ai:* Sports Video Club; Church (Deacon, Sunday Sch Teacher, Musician, Direct Vacation Bible Sch, Grounds Maintenance); US Army Reserve Drill Instr; St Dar & West Oak Teacher of Yr 1987; *home:* Rt 1 Townville SC 29689

BRYANT, LYNN ANN, Special Education Coordinator; *b:* Las Vegas, NM; *m:* Lannie Zane; *c:* Erin, Cole; *ed:* (BA) Elem Ed/Spec Ed, Highlands Univ 1972; (MA) Spec Ed, Univ of NM 1976; Educl Diagnostics, Educl Admin, Mediation Techniques Cert; *cr:* 1st Grade Teacher Albuquerque Public Schls 1973-74; Spec Ed Teacher Tularosa Public Schls 1974-76, Alamogordo Public Schls 1976-79; Advanced Ed Prgm Facilitator 1981-89, Educl Diagnostician 1979-, Spec Ed Coord 1990 Las Cruces Public Schls; *ai:* Spec Ed Advisory Comm NM; Delta Kappa Gamma Comm; Phi Kappa Pi 1984-; Delta Kappa Gamma 1986-; CEC 1988-; Las Cruces Symphony Guild 1988-; Suzuki Music Assn 1988-; Daughters of Amer Revolution Awd & Schlsp; *office:* Las Cruces Public Schls 301 W Amador Las Cruces NM 88005

BRYANT, PAMELA POWELL, Kindergarten Teacher; *b:* Idabel, OK; *m:* Paul E.; *c:* Jamie; *ed:* (BA) Elem Ed, 1976, (MED) Elem Ed, 1978 E TX St Univ; Cmptrs, Gifted & Talented; *cr:* 6th Grade Math Teacher 1976-78, 2nd Grade Teacher 1978-82, Kndgtn Teacher 1982- Clarksville Ind Sch Dist; *ai:* Delta Kappa Gamma 1982-; Assn of TX Prof Educators Building Rep 1984-; Kndgtn Teachers of TX 1985-; GSA (Bd Mem 1990, Day Camp Bus Mgr 1988-, Asst Leader 1989-), Volunteer of Yr 1989; In-Service Speaker Dist Meetings.

BRYANT, PAULINE PRIOLEAU, Math & Science Teacher; *b:* Russellville, SC; *m:* Robert L.; *c:* Robert P., Leah P.; *ed:* (BS) Chem, Morris Coll 1967; (MED) Ed, Univ of SC 1982; Duke Univ, Citadel, Coll of Charleston, SC St Coll Orangeburg; *cr:* Math/Sci Teacher Cross HS 1967-; *ai:* NHS Adv; SACS, Steering, Amer Ed Week Comm Mem; Sch Improvement Cncl Mem; NSTA Mem 1970-; SCEA Mem, NEA Mem, BCEA Mem 1968-; Concerned Citizens Mem 1988-; St James Baptist Church (Deaconess Bd, Secy) 1980-; NAACP Mem 1981-; Salutatorian Russellville HS; Graduated 1st Morris Coll; Teacher of Yr Cross HS 1985; *home:* PO Box 247 Eutawville SC 29048

BRYANT, PEARLEEN WILLIAMS, Third Grade Teacher; *b:* Rhine, GA; *ed:* (BS) Early Chldhd Ed, Fort Valley St Coll 1975; (MA) Early Chldhd Ed, GA Southwestern Coll 1981; (EDS) Sch Counseling, Univ of GA 1990; GA ST Certification T-5 Early Chldhd Ed; Sch Guidance Cnsling; *cr:* Kndgtn Teacher Pearl Stephens Elem 1975-79; 3rd Grade Teacher Centerville Elem 1979-; *ai:* Sch Soc Comm Mem; Houston Assn of Educators Building Rep; Active Classroom Teachers Pres 1978-79; Houston Assn of Educators Treas 1979-80; Amer Sch Cnslr Assn 1989-; GA Sch Cnslr Assn; Selected Candidate/Mem 1987-89.

BRYANT, ROBERT JOHN, HS Social Studies Teacher; *b:* Allentown, PA; *m:* Laurie Jo Wagner; *ed:* (BS) Scndry Ed/Soc Stud/His, Kutztown St Coll 1980; (MA) Scndry Ed, Kutztown Univ 1986; *cr:* Soc Stud Teacher Northampton Area Sr HS 1980-; *ai:* SADD Adv; Track, Ftbl, Wrestling Coach; NEA, PSEA Union Mem 1980-; PA St Coaches Assn 1980-82; *office:* Northampton Area Sr HS 1619 Laubach Ave Northampton PA 18067

BRYANT, RUBY HUIETT, Math Teacher; *b:* Twincity, GA; *m:* Johnny A.; *c:* Renee L., Runee L.; *ed:* (BS) Math, Savannah St Coll 1961; *cr:* Math Teacher Jeff Davis Cty HS 1961-62; Seringer Elem Sch 1962-64; Oconee HS 1964-68; Thomas Jefferson HS 1968-85; Washington Cty HS 1985-; *ai:* Sr Class Comm; GAE; NEA; Springfield Baptist Church Asst Sunday Sch Teacher; Springfield Baptist Sr Choir Secy; Springfield Youth Fellowship Dir 1985-; Teacher of Yr 1984-85; Fellowship to Study Math Montclair St Coll 1966; *office:* Washington County H S 420 Riddleville Rd Sandersville GA 31082

BRYANT, YVONNE, Assistant Principal; *b:* Hattieburg, MS; *ed:* (BA) Ed, USM 1970; (MA) Ed/Admin/Principalship, 1979, Specialist Ed, 1982 William Carey; *cr:* Math Teacher Hattiesburg Public Schls 1970-87; Asst Prin Hawkins Jr HS 1987-; *ai:* Discipline Comm Chairperson; Screening Comm Hattiesburg Public Schls Mem; People United to Save Our Youths Chairperson; NASSP; Natl Assn of Black Educators; ASCD; *office:* Hawkins Jr HS 526 Forrest St Hattiesburg MS 39401

BRYCE, HELEN REPKO, English Teacher; *b:* Trenton, NJ; *m:* Joseph A.; *c:* Michael J., Joseph C., Kevin J.; *ed:* (BA) Eng, Trenton St 1964; (MA) Supervision/Curr Dev, Georgian Court Coll 1980; *cr:* Eng Teacher Lakewood HS 1964-65; SAT/GED/Eng 2nd Lang Teacher Lakewood Cmmty Sch 1968-78; Eng Teacher Lakewood HS 1974-; *ai:* Eng Club Adv; HS Sunshine Fund; NCTE Natl Convention Wkshp Presenter 1983, 1974-; NJCTE Bd of Dir 1982-84; NJ Rdng Assn Outstanding Research Project 1981; Deborah Hospital Fnd VP 1974-80, Queens Pin 1975; Lakewood Schls Teacher of Yr 1986; *office:* Lakewood HS E 7th St & Somerset Ave Lakewood NJ 08701

BRYMESSER, CONNIE CLEVENGER, Third Grade Teacher; *b:* Newville, PA; *m:* Steve F.; *ed:* (BS) Elem Ed, 1970; (MED) Elem Ed, 1972 Shippensburg St Coll; *cr:* 3rd Grade Teacher Plainfield Elem Sch 1969-; *ai:* BSEA 1970-; PSEA 1970-; NEA 1970-; *office:* Plainfield Elem School 7 Springview Rd Carlisle PA 17013

BRYNGELSON, SHIRLEY JOHNSON, Fourth Grade Teacher; *b:* Warren, MN; *w:* Donald (dec); *ed:* (AA) Jr Coll, N Park Coll 1955; (BS) Elem Ed, Univ of MN 1957; *cr:* Teacher San Diego City Schls 1957-58, Minneapolis Public Schls 1958-63, Lake Forest Public Schls 1963-; *ai:* Stu Service Spon; Cmptr Comm; Pres Literacy Prgm; *office:* Deerpath Mid Sch 300 S Waukegan Rd Lake Forest IL 60045

BRYSON, BRENDA SMITH, 6th Grade Soc Stud Teacher; *b:* Lyons, GA; *m:* Terry; *c:* Peyton, Stephanie; *ed:* (BSE) Elem, GA Southern Coll 1970; *cr:* Teacher Screven Cty Mid Sch 1970-71, Julia P Bryant Mid Sch 1972-75, Lyons Elem 1975-76, Lyons Jr HS 1977-; *ai:* GA Assn of Educators; NEA; *office:* Lyons Jr H S 306 N State St Lyons GA 30436

BRYSON, MARGARET VINSON, Language Arts Teacher; *b:* Clayton, GA; *m:* Walter Neville Jr.; *c:* Joshua A.; *ed:* (AA) Montreat-Anderson Jr Coll 1968; (BS) Ed, Western Carolina Univ 1970; Grad Work Western Carolina Univ; *cr:* HS Phys Ed/Soc Stud Teacher Highlands Sch 1970-71; 7th Grade Teacher Rabun Cty Elem Sch 1971-72; Teacher/Mentor Highlands Sch 1972-; Mentor Instr Southwestern Comm Coll 1989-; *ai:* Mentor; Jr Beta Club Co-Spon; Schlsp Comm; Media Comm; Adv Comm Co Sch Bd; Mem Steering Comm STEPE; PTO; Cty Senate Bill 2 Steering Comm; NCAE (Cty Treas 1972-73, Building Rep); ASCD; Highlands Playhouse VP 1988-89; Alliance for Arts 1987-89; Highlands First Baptist Church Sunday Sch Teacher; Teacher of Yr 1978; Local Jaycee Awd; NCAE Teacher Appreciation Awd Macon Cty 1985/1987-88; *office:* Highlands Schl Pierson Dr Highlands NC 28741

BRYSON, PATRICIA GRAGG, Russian/German/Spanish Teacher; *b:* Kingsport, TN; *d:* Joseph C.; *c:* Clay, Lisa, Holly; *ed:* (BA) Russian, Univ of TN Knoxville 1970; Certificate Russian, Lenin Inst Moscow 1970; (MED) Admin, GA Southern 1975; *cr:* Teacher Lenoir City HS 1977-80; Eng as Second Lang Coord Knox Cty Schls 1981-83; Teacher Walland Acad 1983-84, South Mid Sch 1984-; *ai:* Red Cross & Foreign Lang Club Spon; AATG, TN Assn of Mid Schls 1988-; Amer Red Cross (Water Safety Instr, Lifeguard Instr, Standard/Advanced 1st Aid Instr, Soviet Friendship Comm Mem 1989-) 1965-, Lifesaving Awd of Merit 1979, Service to Humanity 1978, Certificate of Service & Appreciation 1989, 25 Yr Service Pin 1990; Governors Acad Ger Foreign Lang 1988; Governors Certificate of Appreciation 1982; Career Level II Teacher 1988-; *office:* South Mid Sch 801 Tipton St Knoxville TN 37920

BUBB, GEORGANNE H., English Teacher; *b:* Bloomington, IN; *m:* John Hays II; *c:* Amy, Catherine, John III; *ed:* (BA) Eng, 1982, (MA) Rdng, 1990 Glassboro St Coll; *cr:* Teacher St Mary of the Lakes 1981-83, Edgewood Regional Sr HS 1984-; *ai:* Interact Adv; NHS, Literary Magazine Co Adv; Shakespeare Festival Comm Chairperson; ADK Teaching 1987-; Grant for Shakespeare Festival; *office:* Edgewood Regional Sr HS 250 Cooper Folly Rd Atco NJ 08004

BUBB, TERRY LEE, Spanish Teacher; *b:* Covington, KY; *ed:* (BA) Span - Magna Cum Laude, Furman Univ 1984; Working Towards Masters; *cr:* Teaching Asst Duke Univ 1984; Span Teacher Middleton HS 1985-86; Teaching Asst Vanderbilt Univ 1986-87; Span Teacher Gallatin HS 1987-; *ai:* Beta Club, Span Club, Intnl Club Spon; Sr Honors Night, Homecoming Reception, Cabaret Comm; Foreign Lang Rural Educators Alliance of Tn Bd Mem 1989-; Kappa Delta Pi; Phi Sigma Iota 1983-; Phi Beta Kappa 1984; Hendersonville Tennis Assn VP 1989-; US Tennis Assn 1989-; Lloyd HS Valedictorian Class 1980; Furman Univ Span Awd 1984; *home:* 228 Sanders Ferry Rd M-173 Hendersonville TN 37075

BUBONOVICH, CAROL HINES, Sixth Grade Teacher; *b:* Uniontown, PA; *c:* Gerald, Nicholas; *ed:* (BA) Elem Ed, 1969, (MS) Elem Ed, 1974 California Univ of PA; Elem Admin; *cr:* 6th Grade Math/Music Teacher South Laurel Jr HS 1969-72; 6th Grade Self Contained Teacher R W Clark Elem Sch 1972-; *ai:* Sch Yrbk & 6th Grade Act Spon; LHEA, PSEA, NEA; BSA Den Mother 1977-81; *office:* R W Clark Elem Sch 200 Water St Uniontown PA 15401

BUCCHIONI, LARRY PAUL, 7th Grade Soc Stud Teacher; *b:* Boston, MA; *m:* Maria Hendrickson; *c:* Joshua; *ed:* (BS) Scndry Soc Stud, Cortland St Univ 1973; 32 Grad Credits, St Univ NY 1977; *cr:* Classroom Teacher Non Graded-All Subjects Sus Valley Home Binghamton City Schls 1973-79; 7th Grade Soc Stud Sus Valley Jr HS 1979-; *ai:* Varsity Ftbl & Track Coach; Stu Cncl & Weight Club Adv; NEA 1973; Society for Promotion & Ed of Animal Kindness 1973-85; Intnl Powerlifting Alliance (St Chm 1989- Natl Masters Chm 1989-); NYS Powerlifting Champion 1989; PA St Champion 1990; IPA Natl Powerlifting Champion 1989; Nom for NYS Amer His Teacher of Yr 1988; *office:* Susquehanna Valley Jr H S 1040 Conklin Rd Conklin NY 13748

BUCHANAN, BONNIE M., English Teacher; *b:* Roxboro, NC; *m:* Merritt; *c:* Karen, Kathy, Kevin; *ed:* (BA) Elem/Eng, Elon Coll 1983; *cr:* Eng Teacher Williams HS 1983-84, Broadview Mid Sch 1984-85, Gulf Coast Chrstn Acad 1985-; *ai:* Jr Class & Drama Team Spon; *home:* 4996 Prieto Dr Pensacola FL 32506

BUCHANAN, JOYCE CAMPBELL, Mathematics Department Teacher; *b:* Artemus, KY; *m:* Lloyd Eugene; *c:* Kevin T., Stacy M.; *ed:* (AB) Elem Ed/Eng, 1961, (MA) Ed, 1980 Union Coll; 1st-8th Grade Artemus Elem; 9th Grade Artemus HS; 10th-12th Knox Cntrl HS Barbourville; *cr:* 1st-8th Grade Teacher Knox Cty 1961-64; Jr HS/4th/6th Grade Teacher Barbourville City Sch 1964-; *ai:* Asst for Academic Team Jr HS 1989-; Jr HS Cheerleading Spon; Parenting, Family Life Comm, Teacher Evaluation Comm; Barbourville City Ed Assn Pres 1988-89; Teacher of Excl Awds 1988-89; NEA, KY Ed Assn 1961-; First Baptist Church Choir 1987-; *home:* HC 83 Box 1084 Barbourville KY 40906

BUCHANAN, MELFIN LEE, Mathematics Teacher; *b:* Carthage, MO; *m:* Bill; *c:* Jeremy, Amy, Sarah; *ed:* (BSE) Math, S MO St Coll 1985; *cr:* Math Teacher Carthage HS 1985-; *ai:* Math Club & Pep Club Spon; Teams Coach; NCTM, MO Cncl Teachers of Math, MO-KAN Cncl Teachers of Math; Center Point Chrstn Church; PTA; Teachers Teaching Teachers Participant N AZ Univ 1989.

BUCHANAN, ROBERT BRUCE, Sixth Grade Teacher; *b:* Kitchener ON, Canada; *ed:* (BA) Music, San Jose St 1968; *cr:* Vocal Music Specialist Oak Grove Sch Dist 1969-80; 6th Grade Teacher Sakamoto Sch 1980-; *ai:* Stu Cncl Adv; Teacher in Charge; Drama Dir; MENC 1969-80; NEA, CTA 1969-; Aloha Roller Skating Club 1981-, Regional Champion 1987, 1989; *office:* Sakamoto Elem 6280 Shadelands Dr San Jose CA 95123

BUCHANAN, RUTH ETTA, Vocational Home Ec Teacher; *b:* Madisonville, KY; *m:* William Dean; *c:* Ginger Rogers; *ed:* (BS) Voc Home Ec, 1974, (MS) Voc Home Ec, 1979 Murray St Univ; Voc Home Ec, Murray St Univ 1987; *cr:* Voc Home Ec Teacher Lyon Cty HS 1974-; *ai:* FHA Adv; Voc Dept Chm; Long Range Planning; KAVHET (Pres, VP) 1974-; KVA 2nd Region Pres 1976-; KEA Local Pres 1974-; KNEA; Womens Club VP 1978-; Eddyville United Meth Church Sunday Sch Supt 1990; Jaycees Outstanding Young Educator 1983; *home:* Box 224 Eddyville KY 42038

BUCHANAN, WILLIAM GEORGE, SR., Social Studies Dept Chairman; *b:* Home, PA; *m:* Roberta Jean Mc Lachlan; *c:* William G., Lana J. Marcoline, Robert Meade; *ed:* (BSED) Soc Stud, Indiana Univ of PA 1942; (MS) US His, Univ of Pittsburgh 1949; US His, Univ of Pittsburgh, PA St Univ, Bloomsburg Univ of PA; *cr:* Rep St House of Reps; Chm/Mem St Bd of Private Academic Schls; K-12th Grade Soc Stud Dept Chm/Instr Purchase Line Sch Dist; *ai:* Jr Class Spon; NEA, Phi Delta Kappa, PA Historical Assn; Grange Masonic Bodies; Alumni Awd for Outstanding Service Univ of PA; Phi Delta Kappa Exemplary Service Awd; United Private Academic Sch Assn Awd; Cmmty Leader of America Awd; St Young Republican Hall of Fame; *home:* 380 Poplar Ave Indiana PA 15701

BUCHER, MICHAEL KERMIT, Math Dept Chairman; *b:* Gettysburg, PA; *m:* Gail Charles; *c:* Michael S., John D.; *ed:* (BA) Math/Soc Stud, Shippensburg St Coll 1962; Univ of DE; Shippensburg Univ; *cr:* Teacher New Castle-Gunning Bedford Sch Dist 1962-75, Upper Adams Sch Dist 1975-; *ai:* Coaching Ftbl, Wrestling, Track; Dept Chm; Dist III Wrestling Coach of Yr 1987-88; *home:* 770 Schoolhouse Rd Aspers PA 17304

BUCHHEIT, VELDA F., Eighth Grade Educator; *b:* Perryville, MO; *ed:* (BS) Elem Ed, SE MO St Univ 1972; (MED) Elem Ed, Univ of MO St Louis 1981; *cr:* 6th Grade Educator 1972-84, 8th Grade Educator 1984- Senn-Thomas Mid Sch; *ai:* MNEA; St Louis Jaycees (Secy 1987-88, Dir 1988-); *office:* Dunklin R-5 Sch Dist 204 Main St Herculaneum MO 63048

BUCHHOLZ, CLAYTON GRANT, English-Literature Teacher; *b:* Tacoma, WA; *m:* Sharon G.; *c:* Natasha, Daric; *ed:* (BA) Poly Sci, Univ of Puget Sound 1971; Puget Sound Writers Wkshps, Several Grad Courses; *cr:* Eng/Lit/His Teacher 1971-, Vice Prin 1976- St Patrick Sch; *ai:* Archdiocese of Seattle, Eng Curr Comm; Stu Cncl Adv; Instructional Leadership Curr & Dramatic Arts Dir; NCSS; St Patrick Cath Church; *office:* St Patrick Sch 1112 North G Street Tacoma WA 98403

BUCHNER, BETTY A., English Teacher/Drill Team Dir; *b:* Lincoln, MI; *ed:* (BS) Phys Ed, Cntrl MI Univ 1971; Grad Stud; *cr:* Phys Ed/Eng Teacher Alpena HS 1971-82; Eng Teacher Washington Jr HS 1982-85, Conroe HS 1985-; *ai:* MI Cheerleading Coach; TX Drill Team & Chrldrs Coach; MCCA Pres 1979, 1981, Lifetime 1982; TJCTE, NJCTE, TDDTDA, DDTDA; Articles Published; Washington Jr HS Teacher of Yr 1985; *office:* Conroe HS 3200 W Davis Conroe TX 77304

BUCK, CAROLYN JANETTE, 5th Grade Eng/Lang Art Teacher; *b:* Elizabethton, TN; *m:* Robert K.; *c:* Lisa Reavis, Robert T.; *ed:* (BS) Elem Ed/Spec Ed, 1976, (MA) Rdng, 1984 E TN St Univ; *cr:* Secy Univac 1957-66; Teacher North Side Sch 1976-; *ai:* Curr Cncl Comm Mem; Annual 5th Grade Field Trip Coord; Southern Assn Philosophy & Objectives Comm Mem; Kappa Delta Pi 1984-; NEA, TEA 1977-; Immanuel Baptist (Dir, Teacher of 5th Grade Sunday Sch) 1969-; Excel Teacher 1989-; *home:* 1999 Eagle Dr Elizabethton TN 37643

BUCK, CONNIE SEIFFERT, 2nd Grade Teacher; *b:* Westhope, ND; *m:* Wayne J.; *c:* Michael W.; *ed:* 2 Yr Standard Minot State Univ 1959; (BS) Elem Sch, Univ of ND 1971; *cr:* 2nd Grade Teacher Divide Cty Elem Sch 1959-; *ai:* NEA Treas; ND Ed Assn; St Patricks Church Altar Guild 1966-; Cancer Society Youth Dir 1987-; District Bsktbl Tourney Evaluator for Chrldrs 1989-; Meals on Wheels 1986-; Nom Natl Teachers Forum 1986; Rep Divide Cty Elem Washington DC Excl in Ed Awd; Initiated Spalding Phonics Prgm; *home:* 607 1st St SW Crosby ND 58730

BUCK, JANA OSTROM, Latin Teacher; *b:* Seattle, WA; *m:* Gary; *c:* Christy, Gretchen, Jonathan, Justin; *ed:* (BA) Latin, 1964, (MA) Latin, 1967 Univ of WA; Natural Helper Guidance Cert, IOTA Trng; *cr:* Latin Teacher Jefferson HS 1964-66; Substitute Teacher Ogallala NE 1977-79; Latin/Fr Teacher Snohomish HS 1979-87; Latin Teacher Liberty HS 1987-88, Air Academy HS 1988-; *ai:* Operated Home Pre-Sch 1975-79; Air Academy HS JCL Spon; Amer Classical League 1979-; Amer Assn of Univ Women 1971-75; Kappa Kappa Gamma Treas 1963-64; Book Published; *home:* 675 Blackhawk Dr Colorado Spgs CO 80919

BUCK, JEANNINE STRANGE, English Department Chair; *b:* Lexington, KY; *m:* G. Wayne; *c:* Elizabeth Erhardt, Clay; *ed:* (BA) Eng, GA St Univ 1962; Univ of GA, Hebrew Univ; Clincical Pastoral Ed, GA Baptist Medical Center; *cr:* Caseworker Dept Family & Children Services 1962-64; Teacher Rome City Schls 1966-69, Floyd Cty Schls 1969-70, Mt Paran Schls 1985-; *ai:* Mt Paran Schls Literary Club Spon; Floyd Cty STAR Teacher; *home:* 2700 Powers Ferry Dr Marietta GA 30067

BUCK, JUDITH KENNEMORE, Instructor/Dept Chairperson; *b:* Blytheville, AR; *m:* James C.; *c:* Keith, Kimberly; *ed:* (BS) Bus Ed, AR St Univ 1967; (MAT) Bus Ed, SE MO St Univ 1978; Grad Stud Bus Ed, Voc Ed; *cr:* Instr Richland HS 1967-68, Bloomfield HS 1968-70, Sikeston HS & AVTS 1971-; *ai:* FBLA Adv; MO St Teachers Assn 1967-; Sikeston Cmmty Teachers Assn, AVA, MO Voc Assn 1971-; MO Bus Ed Teachers Assn 1971-, SE Dist Most Outstanding Bus Educator 1980; SE MO Dist Teachers Assn (Pres 1976-77, VP 1975-76, Secy 1974-75, Treas 1974-75) 1971-; Phi Delta Kappa 1983-; *home:* 913 Stanford Sikeston MO 63801

BUCK, NANCY SLAGLE, Science Teacher; *b:* Bluefield, WV; *m:* Jack A.; *c:* Jack S., Michael D.; *ed:* (BS) Bio, E TN St Univ 1951; Grad Stud; *cr:* 1st-6th Grade Teacher/Prin Green Pine Elem 1950-51; 5th/6th Grade Teacher South Side Elem 1951-52; Sci Dept Teacher Elizabethton HS 1952-; *ai:* Civinettes Club & Y-Teens Club Adv; Spon Charge of Graduation; EEA, ETEA, TEA, NEA 1950-80; Alpha Delta Cappa (Chaplin 1982-84, Pres-Elect 1990); Bus & Prof Women 1975-84; Teacher of Yr City of Elizabethton 1988-89; Sci Teacher of Yr TN Acad of Sci 1975; *office:* Elizabethton HS West E Street & Rogosin Dr Elizabethton TN 37643

BUCKHART, MARGARET GRAVES, Third Grade Teacher; *b:* Hopkinsville, KY; *m:* Billy F.; *c:* Nancy Smith, Donna De Priest, Jennifer L; *ed:* Home Economics, Bethel Coll 1952; (BS) Elem Ed, Austin Peay St Univ 1958; (MA) Admin Supervision, Trevecca Nazarene Coll 1989; *cr:* 5th Grade Teacher Lafayette Elem Sch 1952-53; Crofton Elem Sch 1954-56; 1st Grade Teacher 1956-58; 5th Grade Teacher 1958-59 Morning Side Elem Sch; 3rd Grade Teacher 1962; 6th Grade Teacher 1962-63 Sinking Fork Elem Sch; 5th Grade Teacher Millbrooke Elem Sch 1963-64; 1st/2nd Grade Teacher Sinking Fork Elem Sch 1964; 3rd Grade Teacher Byrns Darden Elem Sch 1965-72; Ringgold Elem Sch 1973-74; 4th Grade Teacher Ringgold Elem 1974-76; 5th Grade Teacher 1979-88; 3rd Grade Teacher 1988-90 Woodlawn Elem Sch; *ai:* Taught Summer Sch 1985-90; Rep Woodlawn Sch Teachers Stud; Cncl Comm 1987-90; after Sch Tutoring 1987-90; Clarksville-Montgomery Cty Ed Assn 1965-90; TN Ed Assn 1965-90; NEA 1965-90; 1st Grade Teacher Sunday Sch 1978-85; Career Ladder I 1985; Career Ladder II 1985-95 TN Dept of Ed; *home:* 528 Aurelia Lynn Dr Clarksville TN 37042

BUCKHAULTER, BARBARA HARPER, Social Studies Teacher; *b:* Vicksburg, MS; *m:* Dilly Dean; *c:* Rico J., Karan J., Craig T.; *ed:* (BA) Soc Sci, Alcorn Univ 1970; Elem Ed K-8, Adult Ed, Career Ed; *cr:* Librarian Finch Elem 1970-71; 6th Grade Teacher Rosa Fort 1971-76; 7th Grade Teacher Brandon Mid Sch 1977-81; 5th Grade Teacher Mc Laurin 1981-82; 7th Grade Teacher Brandon Mid Sch 1982-; *ai:* Tutor; United for Global Awareness 1988-; MS Geographic Alliance Steering Comm 1988-89; Jerusalem Church Librarian; Cub Scouts Leader 1981-82; Friends of Children Volunteer 1980-81/1986-88; Grant to Study Africa; Grant to Study MS Culture 1985; *home:* Rt 1 Box 302-A Braxton MS 39044

BUCKLE, CHARLES STEWART, History Teacher; *b:* Richmond, VA; *m:* Deborah Cornett; *c:* Anne E.; *ed:* (BS) His, 1977, (MA) His, 1978 Appalachian St Univ; *cr:* His Teacher Booth Jr HS 1978-81, Mc Intosh HS 1981-; *ai:* Head Mens & Womens Cross Cntry Teams, Track Asst Coach; Phi Alpha Theta 1975; Pi Gamma Mu 1976; Sigma Phi Epsilon 1975; *office:* Mc Intosh HS 201 Waltbanks Rd Peachtree GA 30269

BUCKLEN, JO LYNN BURRESS-HENDERSON, Fourth Grade Teacher; *b:* Mc Pherson, KS; *c:* Shari Henderson, Kathi Lowry; *ed:* (AA) Gen, Bakersfield Jr Coll 1958; (BA) Elem Ed, Fresno St Coll 1960; Mc Pherson Coll; Fresno Pacific; CA Lutheran; Fresno St; San Diego; *cr:* 2nd Grade Teacher Beardsley Sch 1960-63; 2nd Grade Teacher Fowler Elem 1963-65; 2nd/3rd Grade Teacher Cottage Lake 1967; 2nd/4th Grade Teacher Standard Sch Dist 1968-; *ai:* Lang Arts Curr Comm; Delta Kappa Gamma Prof Growth 1988-; NEA 1960-; CTA Various Comm 1960-; Standard Sch Teachers Sch Rep/Comm 1968-; Curr Comm Work; *office:* Wingland Sch Standard Dist 2000 Diane Dr Bakersfield CA 93308

BUCKLES, BENITA HIGHBAUGH, Reading Coordinator; *b:* Bonnieville, KY; *m:* James Terry; *c:* Kasey S., Kelly E.; *ed:* (BA) Elem Ed, 1976, (MS) Elem Ed, 1978, (Rank I) Elem Ed, 1982 W KY Univ; Rdng Specialist Cert, W KY Univ 1989; *cr:* 2nd Grade Classroom Teacher 1976-87, Collaborating Teacher 1987-88, Rdng Coord 1988- G C Burkhead Elem; *ai:* Hardin Cty Natl Young Readers Acts Coord; Sch Contact Person; Newspaper in Ed; Journal Young Authors; Cty Master Inservice Comm; Intnl Rdng Assn (Awds Chairperson 1988-89, Membership Chairperson 1989-); PTA (Publicity Chairperson 1986-87, Nom Comm Chairperson 1988-89); Rdng Article; Natl Recognition Awd Chairperson; *office:* G C Burkhead Elem Sch 521 Charlemagne Blvd Elizabethtown KY 42701

BUCKLES, GUY, Computer Literacy Teacher; *b:* Cheyenne, WY; *m:* Janie R. Mc Cain; *c:* Guy, Karrie, Amy; *ed:* (BA) Government/Poly Sci, San Antonio Univ 1983; (MS) Sch Admin, TX A&I Kingsville 1986; Cert of Ed Southwest TX St Unin San Marcos 1983; *cr:* Soc Stud Teacher 1984-85, Comptr Literacy Teacher 1985- Devine Mid Sch; *ai:* Univ Interscholastic League Coord; Voc Dept Chm; Dist Comptr Technology Coord; US Army Retired 1951-71 Honoralbe Awd 1971; Appointed Jusitce of The Peace Medina Cty.

BUCKLES, HUGH FREDERICK, Social Studies Teacher; *b:* Elizabethton, TN; *ed:* (EDS) Educl Admin/Supervision, Univ of MS 1988; (BS) Poly Sci/His, 1976, (MA) Educl Admin/Supervision, 1980 TN St Univ; *cr:* Soc Stud Teacher Unaka HS 1978-83, Unaka Elem Sch 1984-87, 1988-; *office:* Unaka Elem Sch R R 5 Elizabethton TN 37643

BUCKLEW, MARY KATHRYN, Kindergarten Teacher; *b:* Vernon, TX; *m:* J. W.; *c:* John, Jerry; *ed:* (BS) Scndry Educ, North TX St Coll 1958; (ME) Early Chldhd Educ, TX Womans Univ 1972; (ED) Doctorial Work in Educ; *cr:* 2nd Grade Teacher Sanger Elem 1958-59; Kndgtn Teacher 1964-71; Sanger Elem 1971-; *ai:* ATPE Pres 1985-87; United Meth Church Pres 1974-76; Outstanding Teacher of Sanger Elem 1988-89; *office:* Chisholm Trail Elem Sch P O Box 188 Sanger TX 76266

BUCKLEY, GAIL GUTHRIE, 6th Grade Teacher; *b:* Cleveland, TN; *m:* William A.; *c:* Bill, Mike, Rachel, Taryn; *ed:* (BS) Elem Ed, Carson Newman Coll 1980; (MS) Curr & Instruction, Univ TN 1982; *home:* Rt 2 Box 336 Englewood TN 37329

BUCKLEY, KENNETH WELCH, Math Dept Teacher/ Chairman; *b:* Columbia, MS; *m:* Mary Margaret Brumfield; *c:* Kent, Joan M. Whitley; *ed:* (BS) Math, 1951, (MS) Math, 1958 Univ of Southern MS; Math, USM 1959; *cr:* Math Teacher Univ of Southern MS 1951-52; Squadron Adjutant USAF 1952-53; Math Teacher Gulfport HS 1953-54, Yazoo City HS 1955-; *ai:* Math Dept Chm; Stu Cncl Adv; MS Cncl Teachers of Math, NCTM; Star Teacher 1977/1979/1980/1987; Yrbk Dedication 1963/1972; *home:* 2031 Wildwood Terr Yazoo City MS 39194

BUCKLEY, LENORA GREEN, Retired Jr HS English Teacher; *b:* Birmingham, AL; *m:* H. Frank; *c:* Nancy Buckley Wilson, Mary Buckley Sutton, Mark; *ed:* (AB) His, Univ of Montevallo 1942; Extension Courses Univ of AL; Courses at MS St Coll for Women; *cr:* Jr HS His/Eng Teacher Sulligent HS 1942-45, 1957-85; *ai:* Spec Ed Volunteer; Lamar Cty Teachers Assn (Treas 1959-61) 1942-45, 1957-85; AL Ed Assn 1942-45, 1957-85; NEA 1957-85; Sulligent Study Club Secy 1957-67; Secy Lamar Cty Teachers Assn 1965-67; *home:* PO Box 426 Sulligent AL 35586

BUCKLEY, WILLIAM F., Social Studies Teacher; *b:* Scranton, PA; *ed:* (BS) Scndry Ed/His, Univ of Scranton 1969; (MS) His, Marywood Coll 1974; *cr:* 5th-8th Grade Soc Stud Teacher St Frances Cabrini Sch 1969-70; 6th-8th Grade Soc Stud Teacher Wm Prescott Sch 1970-73; 8th Grade Soc Stud Teacher East Scranton Jr HS 1973-74; 7th/8th Grade Soc Stud Teacher West Scranton Intermediate 1974-; *ai:* Sch Treas; Scranton Fed of Teachers (VP 1985, Mem) 1970-; Phi Delta Kappa Treas, Kappan of Yr 1974; St Lucys Choir; St Lucys Confraternity of Chrstn Doctrine Teacher.

BUCKNER, DANNY KEITH, Sixth Grade Teacher; *b:* Princeton, WV; *m:* Karen Sue Comer; *c:* Jonathan Noah; *ed:* (BS) Elem Ed, Concord Coll 1982; (MA) Ed Admin, Univ of WV Coll of Grad Stud 1987; Assertive Discipline; Prgm Instructional Effectiveness; Effective Schls; *cr:* 5th/6th Grade Teacher Oakvale Elem 1982-; *ai:* Supervisor of Soc Stud Fair; Supervisor of Sch Safety Patrol Pgm; Asst Coach of Phys Ed Field Day Team; Parent Adv Comm/Mem; Mercer Cty Rdng Cncl Mem 1989-; WV Ed Assn Mem 1982-; Mercer Cty Ed Assn Mem 1982-; NEA Mem 1982-; Fairview Christian Cmmty Church (Bd Mem 1987- Teenage Sunday Sch Teacher 1980-89- Sunday Sch Supt); Christian Yth Ambassadors Secy 1985; Teacher of Yr 1988-89; *office:* Oakvale Elem Sch Oakvale WV 24739

BUCKNER, DEBRA K., Drama Director; *b:* Lubbock, TX; *ed:* (BA) Eng/Sociology, 1976, (MFA) Acting/Directing Theatre Arts, 1983 TX Tech Univ; *cr:* Eng Teacher Lubbock Public Schls 1978-81, 1983; Acting Teacher TX Tech Univ 1982-83; Drama Dir Albuquerque HS 1985-88, Sandia HS 1988-; *ai:* Thespian Drama Club Spon; Restructuring Comm; NM Drama Educators Assn (Mem, VP) 1987-88; NM Alliance for Arts Ed Bd Mem 1989-; Amer Alliance for Theatre in Ed Mem; Albuquerque Arts Alliance Mem; Vortex Theatre Bd Mem 1984-85; Natl Arts Ed Research Team of Scndry Drama Teachers; *office:* Sandia HS 7801 Candelaria NE Albuquerque NM 87111

BUCY, LIZABETH LEIGH, 4th-6th Grade Curriculum Coord; *b:* Morgantown, WV; *ed:* (BS) Ec, 1969, (MA) Curr & Instruction, 1978 WV Univ; *cr:* Math Teacher Towers Elem 1975-78; 1st Grade Teacher 1978-81, 4th Grade Teacher 1981-87 Alta Vista Elem; 4th-6th Grade Curr Coord Harrison Cty Schls 1988-; *ai:* Intnl Rdng Cncl 1975, 1988-; ASCD 1988-; Harrison Cty Rdng Cncl VP 1990-92; *office:* Harrison Cty Schls PO Box 1370 Clarksburg WV 26301

BUDA, KAREN LECKEY, Fourth Grade Teacher; *b:* Philadelphia, PA; *m:* Anthony J.; *ed:* (BS) Elem Ed, E Stroudsburg Univ 1982; *cr:* 5th Grade Teacher 1984-88, 4th Grade Teacher 1988- Montague Township Elem; *ai:* Stu Cncl Adv; MEA (VP 1988-89, Secy-Treas 1986-87); *office:* Montague Township Elem Sch RD 5 Box 573 Montague NJ 07827

BUDD, RICHARD DOUGLAS, Technology Chair; *b:* Middletown, NY; *m:* Mary Jo Flynn; *c:* Richard Jr., Jason R.; *ed:* (BA) Industrial Art, 1977, (MS) Technology Ed, 1982 SUNY Oswego; *cr:* Technology Instr Minisink Valley Mid Sch 1978-; *ai:* Kiwanis Builders Club & Yrbk Adv; Sch Improvement Team Comm; Technology Chairperson; NY St Technology Ed Assn; RockLand Orange Sullivan Technology Ed Assn; Epsilon Pi Tau; *office:* Minisink Valley Cntrl Sch PO Box 217 Rt 6 Slate Hill NY 10973

BUDD, SHARON LEIGHTON, ASSIST Teacher; *b:* Seattle, WA; *m:* Charles J. Jr.; *ed:* (BA) Elem Ed, 1962, (MS) Elem Admin, 1988 W WA Univ; *cr:* 5th Grade Teacher Gregory Heights Highline Sch Dist 1962-63; 3rd-5th Grade Teacher New S Wales Dept Ed 1963-64; 4th Grade Spec Ed Teacher Olympic View Edmonds Sch Dist 1966-69; 5th Grade Teacher Pearson Elem 1969-88; ASSIST Teacher/Vice Prin Suquamish Elem 1988-; *ai:* Co-Pres N Kitsap Cncl; WA Organization Rdng Dev; Spon Family Math; Teacher Assisting Teacher Comm; Delta Kappa Gamma (Pres, Schlsp Chairperson) 1975-; ASCD, WEA, NEA 1988-; Intnl Rdng Assn WORD Co-Pres 1988-; PTSA 1969-; Kiwanis 1988-; Sons of Norway 1972-; St Grant Native Amer Soc Stud Unit 4th-5th Grades; N Kitsap Leadership Team; *office:* Suquamish Elem Sch 18950 Park Ave NE Suquamish WA 98392

BUDGE, SUSETTE FLETCHER, Third Grade Teacher; *b:* Logan, UT; *m:* Rex R. (dec); *c:* R. Seth, Marilyn B. Anthony, Lynn F., Rodney C., James R.; *ed:* (BS) Elem Ed, UT St Univ 1947; Various Wkshps BYU, USU, ISU, BSU, BYU HI; *cr:* 3rd Grade Teacher Hillview Elem Sch; *ai:* Sch Planning Comm EBEA, IRA, Music; Spec Centennial Prgm; Act Comm; East Bonneville Ed Assn; ID Rdng Assn Historian; Phi Kappa Phi, Piano Teacher, Cub Scout Leader, Latter Day Saints Church Mem; *office:* Hillview Elem Sch 3075 Teton Idaho Falls ID 83406

BUDNICK, THOMAS, Business Department Teacher; *b:* York, NE; *ed:* (BS) Bus Ed, Peru St Coll 1977; *cr:* Bus Teacher Guide Rock HS 1977-83; Bus/Cmptr Teacher Keya Paha Cty HS 1986-; *ai:* Coached Ftbl, Boys & Girls Bsktbl, Boys & Girls Track; Athletic Dir; NE Coaches Assn 1980-; Eight Man Coaches Assn 1982-; NEA 1977-; Hampton Public Sch Bd of Ed Bd Secy 1984; *office:* Keya Paha Cty HS Box 218 Springview NE 68778

BUDY, BETTY ANNE (SHORT), Second/Third Grade Teacher; *b:* Denver, CO; *m:* Donald F.; *c:* Stacey D., Kyle G.; *ed:* (BA) Elem Ed, Westminster Coll 1963; (MS) Spec Ed, S CT St Coll 1973; Grad Stud; *cr:* 2nd Grade Teacher Lincoln-Jefferson 1963-65; 3rd Grade Teacher Marvin-Ludlow 1965-67; 1st Grade Teacher Kings Highway 1967-73; 2nd/3rd Grade Teacher Sagebrush 1978-; *ai:* Sagebrush Elem Sch Advisory Comm Mem 1987-; Cherry Creek Teachers Assn, NEA 1978-; Amer Assn of Univ Women (Branch VP 1977-78, Branch Educl Rep 1990), Educl Fnd Named Gift; Parker United Meth Church (Cncl of Ministries Vice-Chm 1990, Mission Chm 1989-); *office:* Sagebrush Elem Sch 14700 E Temple Pl Aurora CO 80015

BUEGE, DEBORAH A., Mathematics Teacher; *b:* La Crosse, WI; *m:* Kenneth S.; *c:* Beth, Andy; *ed:* (BS) Ed, Univ of WI La Crosse 1972; *cr:* Math Teacher St Pius X 1973-76, Onalaska Mid Sch 1976-; *ai:* Cmptr & Math Curr Comms; Team Leader; NEA 1976-; WAMLE 1988-89; PTO 1988-; *office:* Onalaska Mid Sch 711 Quincy St Onalaska WI 54650

BUEHNER, RICHARD ANDRE, 8th Grade US History Teacher; *b:* Cleveland, OH; *m:* Brenda Dorenkott; *c:* Rick, Lisa, Brett, Eric; *ed:* (BS) His/Poly Sci, Bowling Green St Univ 1970; Grad Stud Mt St Joseph, Cleveland St, Ashland Univ, Bowling Green St Univ; *cr:* US His Teacher Firelands Local & S Amherst Jr HS 1970-; *ai:* Chess Club; Bsbl & Soccer Coach; Lorain Cty Textbook & Curr Comm; Local Cath Sch Bd Mem; NEA, OH Ed Assn 1970-; Firelands Teacher Assn VP 1970-; Company of Military Historians 1987-; Assn of Amer Military Uniform Collectors 1977-; Tau Kappa Epsilon Act Chm 1965-70, 25 Silver Awd 1990; BSA Comm Chm; Awarded Army Commendation, Achievement Medals; *office:* South Amherst Jr HS South Amherst OH 44074

BUELOW, JUDITH SALISBURY, English Department Chairperson; *b:* Ft Wayne, IN; *m:* Gary A.; *c:* Sven, Sean; *ed:* (BS) Eng, IN Univ 1971; Lake Cty Mastery Rdng Prgm, Correspondce Course, Sam Houston St Univ; Advanced Academic Trng Classes; *cr:* Eng/His Teacher Avon Center Sch 1978-79; Eng Teacher Highland Jr HS 1984-85, Houston Ind Sch Dist 1985-; *ai:* NHS Spon; Curr Comm Mem; Houston Area Cncl Teachers of Eng, NASSP 1987-; PEO 1984-; Building Rep Teacher of Yr 1987-88; Twice Teacher of Month; *office:* HS of Law Enforcement 4701 Dickson St Houston TX 77007

BUERGLER, BETTY HESS, Teacher; *b:* Wynne, AR; *m:* Ben R.; *c:* Benjamin R.; *ed:* (BA) Eng, Avila Coll 1965; (MA) Eng, St Mary Coll 1971; Grad Stud AR St Univ & E TN St Univ; *cr:* 9th-12th Grade Teacher Sacred Heart HS 1961-70; 3rd Grade Teacher Manley Elem 1971; 5th-8th Grade Eng Teacher Witt Elem 1971-72; 8th Grade Eng Teacher West View Mid Sch 1972-; *ai:* Scholastic Bowl Coach; St Patrick Church Organist 1971-; *home:* 484 Shaver Dr Talbott TN 37877

BUFF, ANITA S., Fifth Grade Teacher; *b:* Atlantic City, NJ; *m:* Walter W.; *c:* Cheryl, Tammy; *ed:* (BS) Elem Ed, Glassboro St Coll 1963; *cr:* 4th Grade Teacher Oak Valley & Pine Acres Schls 1963-67; 6th Grade Teacher Whitman Sch 1978-84; 5th Grade Teacher Thomas Jefferson 1984-; *ai:* Safety Patrol Adv; Talent Show Coord; NEA, NJ Educl Assn, Washington Township Ed Assn 1978-91; *office:* Thomas Jefferson Sch Altair & Aldeberan Drs Turnersville NJ 08012

BUFF, JUDY M., Third Grade Teacher; *b:* Bellaire, OH; *m:* Don; *c:* Donnie; *ed:* (BS) Elem Ed, OH Univ 1969; *cr:* 1st Grade Teacher St Clairsville Richland Sch Dist 1966-68; Remedial Rdng Teacher 1968-70, 1979-81, 3rd Grade Teacher 1981- Powhatan Elem; *office:* Powhatan Elem Sch 2nd St Powhatan Point OH 43942

BUFFALOE, ANN ELIZABETH, Third Grade Teacher; *b:* Long Beach, CA; *m:* Lee E.; *c:* Cynthia A. Buffaloe Meredith; Lisa M.; *ed:* (BE) Elem Ed, 1973, (MA) Elem Ed, 1976, (AA) Elem Ed/Rdng, 1983 AL A&M Univ; *cr:* 3rd & 4th Grade Teacher Rolling Hills Elem 1973-88; 3rd Grade Teacher Blossomwood Elem 1988-; *ai:* Soc Stud Fair Chm Blossomwood; Sci Club Asst; Alpha Delta Kappa (Sargent-At-Arms Mem) 1988-; Teacher Prof Organization; Huntsville Exec Bd 1986-88; Cmmty Ballet; *office:* Blossomwood Elem Sch 1321 Woodmont Ave Huntsville AL 35801

BUFFIN, BRENDA (BUNCH), Business Teacher & Dept Chair; *b:* Glasgow, KY; *m:* James M.; *c:* Jessee, Sarah; *ed:* (BS) General Bus/Secretarial Sci, W KY Univ 1974; (MED) Scndry Ed/Voc, Univ of Louisville 1980; Cmptr Programming, Univ of Louisville; Cmptr Wkshps KY Dept of Ed; *cr:* Bus Ed Teacher Bullitt Cntrl HS 1977; Part Time Secretarial Instr Sullivan Jr Coll of Bus 1982-83; Bus Ed Teacher Bardstown HS 1978-; *ai:* FBLA Adv; Care Team Stu Assistance Prgm Mem; Delta Pi Epsilon, Phi Kappa Phi 1980-; KY Bus Ed Assn, NEA, KEA, BEA 1990; Bardstown HS Key Club Teacher of Yr 1987; KY Dept of Ed Curr Comm Mem 1988; *office:* Bardstown HS 400 N 5th St Bardstown KY 40004

BUFORD, PHYLLIS GWENN (BROWNING), Social Studies Teacher; *b:* Toledo, OH; *m:* C. H. Jr.; *c:* Marty; *ed:* (BS) Scndry Ed/Soc Stud, 1970, (MA) Curr Instruction, 1975 TN Technological Univ; *cr:* Soc Stud Teacher Hermitage HS 1970-82, Celina HS 1982-; *ai:* Jr Beta Club 1970-82; Class Spon 1970-; Nom Outstanding Teacher of Yr 1976.

BUFORD, RONETTA COURSEY, Fine Arts Chairperson; *b:* Kansas City, MO; *m:* Jimmie Lawrence; *c:* Frederrick K.; *ed:* (BS) Music Ed, Lincoln Univ of MO 1968; (MLA) Liberal Art, Baker Univ 1978; *cr:* Vocal Music Chairperson King Jr HS 1968-71; Music Dept Chairperson Southeast Jr HS 1971-75; Fine Art Chairperson Paseo HS 1975-; Minister of Music NW MO Conference AME Church 1985-; *ai:* BSA Asst Scout Master Troop 194; Coach Midland True Value Hardware Little League Bsbl Team, Girls Bsktbl Paseo HS; Mentor for New Teacher; Stus at Risk; Tri M Music Honor Society Spon 1985-; MENC 1964-; Sigma Alpha Iota Pres 1967-68; Phi Delta Kappa 1968-; Alpha Kappa Alpha Grad Adv 1970-78; Order of Eastern Star Martha 1989-; Royal Order Court of Cyrines 1990; Visiting Professor NE MO St Univ, Lincoln Univ of MO; Developer of Jr HS Vocal Music Tasks Kansas City MO Sch Dist; Adjudicator Dist Vocal Music Contest; *home:* 9807 Smalley Dr Kansas City MO 64134

BUGDEN, JOSEPH EDWARD, Science Department Chair; *b:* Shenandoah, PA; *m:* Julie Farling; *c:* Dylan; *ed:* (BS) Scndry Ed/ Bio, Millersville Univ 1974; Grad Work Earth Sci/Environmental Sci, Franklin & Marshall Coll; *cr:* Sci Teacher Annville Mid Sch 1974-76; Earth Sci Teacher 1976-79, Bio I & II/Applied Sci Teacher 1979-88, General Bio/Advanced Placement Bio Teacher 1988- Annville HS; *ai:* Sci Dept Chm; Stu Assistance Team; NHS & Coord Curr Comm; Lancaster-Lebanon Sci Teachers Assn 1986-; Annville-Cleona Ed Assn Building Rep 1974-, Rookie of Yr 1988; NEA, PA St Ed Assn 1974-; PA Interscholastic Athletic Assn Ftbl Ofcl 1984-, Section Coach of Yr 1983, 1986; Lancaster-Lebanon Ftbl Coaches Assn; Franklin & Marshall Coll Natl Sci Fnd Grant 1976; *office:* Annville-Cleona HS South White Oak St Annville PA 17003

BUGENSE, NANCY (MILLER), Art Teacher/Yearbook Advisor; *b:* Walker Cty, MI; *m:* John G.; *c:* Michael J., Paul A., Patricia L. Knapp, Joan M.; *ed:* (BS) Art/Phys Ed, W MI Univ 1957; (BA) Eng, BCC 1984; *cr:* Art Supvr/Adv Fremont Public Sch 1957; Phys Ed Instr Holy Name Elem 1970-75; Drama/Phys Ed/Yrbk/Art Teacher 1981-82, Yrbk/Art/Eng Teacher 1984- Hoover Jr HS; *ai:* Athletic Contest Worker; Dance Chaperone; Jr Beta; Drama; Yrbk; Track Coach; BFT; SPRA (Secy 1966, Worker 1978-); *office:* Hoover Jr HS #1 Hawk Haven Dr Indialantic FL 32903

BUGG, CATHEY CLARKE, 6th Grade Teacher; *b:* Tulsa, OK; *m:* Steven W.; *c:* Katie, Carrie; *ed:* (BA) Recreation, 1979, (MS) Elem Admin, 1986 Univ of OK; Stan Cert Elem Teacher 1979, Elem Admin, 1988 Univ of OK; *cr:* Asst Prin 1988-89, Elem Teacher 1980- Noble Public Schls; *ai:* Dist for Yr Plan, Curr, Textbook Selection Comm; Pioneer Arts Festival & Odyssey of Mind Coord; Yrbk Spon: OK Ed Fair; Grade Level Chm; NEA, OK Ed Assn 1980-; NAESP, OK Assn Elem Sch Prin 1988-; OK Women in Educl Admin 1989-; Phi Beta Kappa 1978-; PTA Outstanding Educator Awd; Teacher of Yr.

BUGG, PATSY WOOLEY, Fifth Grade Teacher; *b:* Lebanon, KY; *m:* Earl L.; *c:* Larry; *ed:* (BA) Elem Ed, Campbellsville Coll 1961; *cr:* Classroom Teacher Marion Cty 1961-; *home:* Rt 1 Lebanon KY 40033

BUGLOVSKY, BONNIE MC CLAIN, Third-Fourth Grade Teacher; *b:* Marshall, MO; *m:* Frank; *c:* Frank, Karen; *ed:* (BS) Elem Ed, MO Valley 1968; Several Wkshps; Basic Programming MO Valley Coll; *cr:* 1st Grade Teacher Miami Sch Dist 1968-70; 4th Grade Teacher Perth Amboy Sch 7 1970-71; 3rd/4th Grade Teacher Orearville R-4 1977-; *ai:* Phys Ed & Art Classes; Cmptr & Sci Coord; MSTA, CTA; Chapter II Prgm Grants; Mentor Prgm Co-Writer; *office:* Orearville R-4 Sch Rt 2 Slater MO 65349

BUHL, HENRY FRANKLIN, Chm/Soc Studies Teacher; *b:* New Market, VA; *m:* Catherine Summers; *ed:* (BA) His/Soc Stud, 1964, (MA) Ed, 1974 James Madison Univ; *cr:* Teacher 1968-, Chm 1974- Harrisonburg HS; *ai:* Youth in Government Club Spon; Citizen Bee Close Up Natl Fnd, Valley Academic Competition for Excl Coach; NEA, VEA, HEA 1969-; PDK 1978-; VA Cncl of Soc Stud 1980-; Manor Memorial United Meth Church Chm of Bd 1984-; One of Two Top Soc Stud Teachers VA Close Up Fnd 1989; Educator of Yr by VFW 1989; Blue Streak Awd 1985; *home:* PO Box 111 New Market VA 22844

BUHL, MARY JO KADAVY, K-6th Grade Elementary Teacher; *b:* Lincoln, NE; *m:* Dale A.; *c:* Jessica, Crystal, Ginger; *ed:* (BS) Elem Ed, Univ of NE Lincoln 1974; *cr:* 4th-8th Grade Teacher Platte Cty Dist 83 1974-78; K-8th Grade Teacher 1978-84, 4th-8th Grade Teacher 1984-89, K-6th Grade Teacher 1989- Platte Cty Dist 40; *ai:* Platte Cty Rural Teachers (Mem 1974-88, Pres 1978-79); Platte Cty Educators Assn (Secy, Treas, Mem) 1988-; *home:* Box 46 Lindsay NE 68644

BUICE, JANIE, Mathematics Teacher; *b:* Dallas, TX; *ed:* (BS) Elem Ed, 1977, (MED) Elem Ed, 1981 Tarleton St Univ; *cr:* 1st-5th Grade Remedial Math Teacher Weatherford Ind Sch Dist 1978; Self-Contained 7th/8th Grade Teacher Morgan Mill Ind Sch Dist 1978-87; 7th/8th Grade Math Teacher Stephenville Ind Sch Dist 1987-; *ai:* 7th-8th Grade UIL Calculator Math.

BUIKEMA, SHIRLEY ANN, English Teacher; *b:* Muskegon, MI; *ed:* (BA) Eng, Western MI Univ 1970; Ed, Western MI Univ; Rdng Cert, Univ of MI; *cr:* Teacher Muskegon Heights Sr HS 1970-; *ai:* ACT/SAT Preparation; SPT/MHHS Bus Partnership Comm; Muskegan Heights Ed Assn Secy 1972-76; Hackley & Hume Historic Site Guild Secy 1986-88; Alpha Delta Kappa Pi Pres 1984-86; *office:* Muskegon Heights Sr HS 2427 Jefferson St Muskegon Heights MI 49444

BUIS, DIANNA LOVINS, 5th Grade Teacher; *b:* Blanchester, OH; *m:* Douglas E.; *c:* Shaun, Christopher; *ed:* (BA) Elem Ed, Univ of KY 1983; Writing Project 1989; *cr:* 4th/5th/6th Grade Teacher Waynesburg Elem Sch 1984-; *ai:* Currently Obtaining Masters Degree in Counseling; TN Viticultural & Denological Society 1986-; 1989 Energy Grant; Published Article on Child Abduction; Past Asst Coach for Acad Team; Past Coach for Olympics of the Mind; *home:* 11395 Hwy 1247 NE Eubank KY 42567

BUJAKOWSKI, JANE SHARP, Fourth Grade Teacher; *b:* Hopewell, VA; *m:* Michael C.; *c:* Lee J.; *ed:* (BS) Elem Ed, VA Commonwealth Univ 1978; VIP, SU 1974-75; *cr:* 4th Grade Teacher Woodlawn Elem Sch 1972-; *ai:* Sch Spirit Chm; Incentives & Awds Comm; Sch Census Enumerator; Cooperating Teacher VA Commonwealth Univ; Hopewell Ed Assn Faculty Rep 1978-; VA Ed Assn, NEA, Woodlawn PTO 1978-; Jr Womans Club of Hopewell 2nd VP 1980-; James River Ball Assn Patron 1987-; Woodlawn Teacher of Yr 1988; Nom VFW Teacher of Yr; Nom Presidential Awd Excl Math Teaching 1990; *office:* Woodlawn Elem Sch 1100 Dinwiddie Ave Hopewell VA 23860

BUKOVSKY, DIANE HERBOLD, Teacher of Gifted; *b:* Chicago, IL; *m:* Gary; *c:* Jenny, Joanna; *ed:* (BS) Ed, Edgewood Coll 1972; (MA) Ed/Rdng, N IL Univ 1978; *cr:* 7th/8th Grade Lang Art Teacher Dist 111 1972-81; Teacher of Gifted/7th-8th Grade/Lang Art Teacher Dist 159 1982-; *ai:* IL Ed Assn; *office:* Neil Armstrong Sch 5030 Imperial Dr Richton Park IL 60471

BUKTA, MARY P., 5th Grade Teacher; *b:* Greenville, PA; *m:* Michael; *c:* Paul, Aaron; *ed:* (BA) Elem Ed, Mercyhurst Coll 1962; *cr:* 5th Grade Teacher Jefferson Elem 1967-69, Whittier Elem 1971-77, Jefferson Elem 1977-; *ai:* Building Improvement Team 1989-; ISEA Exec Bd 1967-; CEA, NEA 1967-; *home:* 604 S 32nd St Clinton IA 52732

BULEN, STEVE, 4th Grade Teacher; *b:* Salem, OR; *m:* Julie; *c:* Megan, Carlie; *ed:* (BS) Elem Ed, OR Coll of Ed 1979; PSU; WOSC; *cr:* Teacher Salem Heights Elem Sch 1979-80, Cummings Elem Sch 1980-84, Myers Elem Sch 1984-; *ai:* 3rd-4th Grade Team Leader; Salem Bsktbl Ofcls Assn (VP 1990, Pres 1975-, Mem 1987-88); *office:* Myers Elem Sch 2160 Jewel St NW Salem OR 97304

BULL, RUBY JANE, Mathematics Teacher; *b:* Modesto, CA; *c:* Machelle Ritchey Greer, Michael; *ed:* (AS) Ed, W OK St Jr Coll 1976; (BS) Spec Ed Scndry/Scndry Math, - Summa Cum Laude, SW OK St Univ 1978; Act-Prep Trng; *cr:* Spec Ed Learning Disabilities/Math Teacher Erick HS 1978-83; 9th-12th Grade Math Teacher Mangum HS 1983-; *ai:* Teens Against Drugs, Lifeguard on Duty, 1990 Frosh Class, Sr Class Spon 1990; ABE/GED Teacher; At-Risk Coord; ACLD 1978-; MEA, OEA, NEA 1987-; Adult Basic Ed Mem 1989-; Mangum Ed Assn Schlsp Comm; 1978 Scholar-Leadership Prgm at OK Univ Representing SW OK Univ; Honor Grad WOSC 1976; *office:* Mangum HS 300 N Oklahoma St Mangum OK 73554

BULLARD, BEVERLY LOEB, Third Grade Teacher; *b:* Huntsville, AL; *c:* Robin M.; *ed:* (BS) Elem Ed, Univ of AL 1970; (MA) Elem Ed, 1980, (MS) Elem Admin, 1987 AL A&M; Week Internship Bank Street Coll 1974; Exec Dev Prgm 1986-88; *cr:* 1st Grade Teacher Terry Heights Elem Sch 1970-76; 3rd Grade Teacher Weatherly Heights Elem Sch 1976-; *ai:* Present Insurance Rep Huntsville City Schls; Steering, Staff Dev Mini Grant Comms; PTA Faculty Rep; Alpha Delta Kappa Treas 1985; NEA, AEA, HEA Rep 1980-84; Outstanding Elem Teacher of America 1975; PTA 1970-; Kappa Alpha Theta Pres 1990-; Employee of Quarter 1989; Selected for Exec Dev Prgm Peabody Coll of Vanderbilt Univ, Huntsville City Schls 1986-87, Univ of AL 1987-88; Huntsville City Schls Insurance Bd Chm 1988-89; City Wide Policy Comm mem; Textbook Comm Chm 1983-84; *office:* Weatherly Heights Elem Sch 1307 Canstatt Dr Huntsville AL 35803

BULLARD, CARL EDWARD, Special Ed Teacher/Coach; *b:* Anderson, AL; *m:* Cheryl Lynn; *c:* Joshua R.; *ed:* (BS) His, 1975, (MA) Scndry Ed, 1978, (MA) Spec Ed 1982 Univ N AL; *cr:* Army Intelligence US Army 1966-70; Teacher Adult Basic Ed of AL 1972-74; Coach/Spec Ed Teacher Wilson HS 1979-; *ai:* Girls Bsktbl & Sftbl Coach; Fellowship Chrstn Athletes & Beta Club Spon; NEA, AL Ed Assn; St of AL Class 4A Coach of Yr 1989; Coach of Yr Area 16 Coach of Yr 1988, 1989, 1990; *home:* 1105 Lorraine Pkwy Florence AL 35630

BULLARD, SUSAN LEE, TV Production Teacher; *b:* Santa Barbara, CA; *m:* Robert Wigton; *c:* Kirby Wigton; *ed:* (BA) Radio Tv & Film, 1979, (BA) Journalism, 1979 CA St Univ-Northridge; *cr:* News Dir KDAR-FM CA St Univ Northridge 1979; News Producer/Reporter/Anchor/ 1979-88, Assignment Editor 1979-88 KTHI-TV; *ai:* YWCA Bd Mem 1989-; YWCA Woman of Yr Comm Chm 1987-; Woman of the Yr Prof 1987; Hotline Volunteer 1982-84; *office:* Fargo South HS 1840 15th Ave S Fargo ND 58103

BULLINGTON, JOYCE ENOCHS, Social Studies Teacher; *b:* Mc Ewen, TN; *m:* Ernest Ray; *c:* Patricia B. Davis, Rebecca B. Davis; *ed:* (BS) Elem Ed/Scndry His, Austin Peay St Coll 1951; (MA) His/Admin Austin Peay St Univ 1973; *cr:* 1st-8th Grade Teacher Liberty Sch 1946-52; 1st-3rd Grade Teacher Central View 1952-54; Soc Stud Teacher Mc Ewen HS 1954-81; 8th Grade Soc Stud Teacher Waverly Jr HS 1981-; *ai:* Wavelry Jr HS Future Teachers Spon; Mc Ewen HS Jr Class Spon 1954-81; HCEA Secy 1965-; Daughters of Amer Revolution Publicity Chairperson 1988; United Daughters of Confederacy 1990; Judson Assn of Baptist Churches Vacation Bible Sch Dir 1985-86; Liberty Baptist Church (Clerk 1981-, WMV Pres 1985-, Intermediate Sunday Sch Teacher 1940-); Cmmty News Writer 1980-82; *home:* Rt 1 Box 227 Mc Ewen TN 37101

BULLOCK, ANNIE POWELL, Science Department Chairperson; *b:* Oxford, NC; *m:* Edd A.; *c:* Edd Jr., Shelly A.; *ed:* (BS) Elem Ed, Fayetteville St Univ 1963; (MED) Elem Ed, Duke Univ 1973; *cr:* Teacher Carver Elem, Aycock Sch, Eaton Johnson Mid; *ai:* Sci Dept Chairperson; 8th Grade Mid Sch Team Leader; NEA Mem 1963-; NCSTA Mem 1980-; 4-H Group Leader 1970-, Dist Leader of Yr 1990; PTA VP; Semiconductor Research Company Fnd Fellow 1989, 1990; *home:* 1312 Alpha St Henderson NC 27536

BULLOCK, BARBARA STAFFORD, Mid Sch Language Art Teacher; *b:* Franklinton, LA; *m:* Arthur; *c:* Alisa, Scott; *ed:* (BA) Elem Ed, LA St Univ 1968; Rdng Endorsement Boise St Univ; *cr:* Elem Teacher North Bend 1968-70, Nyssa 1970-78; Mid Sch Teacher Nyssa 1978-; Part Time Instr Treasure Valley Cmmty Coll 1988-; *ai:* Parent Advisory & Onward Excl Comms 1990; Co-Author Instructional Theory into Practice; OR Ed Assn Building Rep 1984-; NEA Negotiator 1987-86; *home:* 705 Park Ave Nyssa OR 97913

BULLOCK, BARBARA WEATHERLY, Third Grade Teacher; *b:* Memphis, TN; *m:* Hugh V. Jr.; *c:* Jeremy M., Justin W.; *ed:* (BS) Elem Ed, Blue Mountain Coll 1971; Grad Work Univ of MS; *cr:* 1st-3rd Grade Teacher Cntrl Elem 1971-72, Dawnville Elem 1972-74; 3rd Grade Teacher Walls Elem 1974-; *ai:* Faculty Club Pres 1980-84; 3rd Grade 4-H Spon 1985-; MS Assn of Educators 1988-; Alpha Delta Kappa 1978-85; Delta Kappa Gamma 1989-; *home:* Box 681 Byhalia MS 38611

BULLOCK, JUNE ODOM, Counselor; *b:* Philadelphia, PA; *ed:* (BS) Elem Ed, West Chester Univ 1961; (MS) Counseling, Temple Univ 1973; Cert Elem Ed U of PA 1962-63; *cr:* Grade Teacher 1961-72; Cnslr 1973- Martha Washington Schl; *ai:* PA Cnslrs Assn 1987-90; Alpha Kappa Alpha Sorority 1959-90; Boy Scouts of America Phila Cncl Corporate Mem at Large 1985-90; Natl Cncl of Negro Women 1990; *office:* Martha Washington Elem Sch 44th And Aspen St Philadelphia PA 19104

BULLOCK, KAREN FAYE, Assistant Principal; *b:* Atlanta, GA; *ed:* (BA) Elem Ed, 1975, (MED) Elem Ed, 1977 La Grange Coll; W GA Coll 1988; *cr:* 4th Grade Teacher Hollis Hand Elem 1975-78; 5th Grade Teacher Fayetteville Elem 1978-89; Asst Prin Peachtree City Elem 1989-; *ai:* Phi Delta Kappa 1989-; GA Assn of Educators, Fayette Cty Assn of Educators Pres 1985-86; GA Assn of Educl Leaders 1989-; Poll Mgr Fayette Cty Bd of Elections Absentee Poll; *office:* Peachtree City Elem Sch 201 Wisdom Rd Peachtree City GA 30269

BULLOCK, NANCY CATO, English Teacher; *b:* Jacksonville, TX; *c:* Michael; *ed:* (BBA) Bus Ed, Univ of N TX 1958; (MED) Scndry Ed, USIU San Diego 1974; *cr:* Bus Teacher S Oak Cliff HS 1959-62, Granger Jr HS 1962-63; Eng/Geography Teacher Castle Park Mid Sch 1964-; *ai:* Adv East Coast Travel Group.

BULLOCK, PATSY PESNELL, 7th/8th Grade Math Teacher; *b:* Ruston, LA; *m:* John Kemp; *c:* Kimberly K. Bullock Kircus; Johnelle K., John P.; *ed:* (BA) Elem Ed, 1963, (MA) Counseling, 1977 LA Tech Univ; Grad Stud Admin, LA Tech Univ 1979; Additional Stud Elem Grades, Principalship, Cnlsr Elem Grades, Supvr Stu Teaching, Supvr of Instruction; *cr:* Elem Grades Teacher Terrebonne Parish, Jefferson Parish, Lafayette Parish, Bossier Parish, St Marys 1964-74; 7th/8th Grade Math Teacher Ruston Jr HS 1974-; *ai:* VP Boys Bsktbl; Ruston HS Booster Club; JTPA Summer Project Voc Dir 1986-89; LA Tech Univ Project Mata Asst Dir; Ruston Jr HS Teacher of Yr 1988-89; *home:* Rt 3 Box 952 Ruston LA 71270

BULLOCK, SHELBY VANN, Kindergarten Teacher; *b:* Roanoke Rapids, NC; *m:* Nathan Wayne; *c:* Andy, Brandy; *ed:* (BS) Early Chldhd, 1972, (MAED) Elem Ed, 1985 ECU; *cr:* Teacher Grifton Sch 1972-; *ai:* Cooperating Teacher for Stu Teachers; ECU Mentor Adv; *office:* Grifton Sch PO Box 219 Grifton NC 28530

BULLOCK-BARNHILL, KATHY JO, Performing Art Teacher; *b:* Des Moines, IA; *m:* Steven A.; *ed:* (BA) Music, San Jose St Univ 1970; Masters Prgm Music, San Jose St Univ; *cr:* Eng/Music Teacher James Lick HS 1971-74; Eng Teacher Piedmont Hills HS 1974-76; Performing Art Teacher Independence HS 1976-; *ai:* Sch Dramas Assoc Dir; Sch Musicals Vocal Dir & Costumer; Musical Comedy Production Dist Curr Co-Author; Dist Piano Curr Guide Author; *office:* Independence HS 1776 Educational Park Dr San Jose CA 95133

BULTEMA, HARLAN G., Fifth Grade Teacher; *b:* Valley City, ND; *m:* Peggy Paosch; *c:* Travis, Rochelle, Brent, Mindy J.; *ed:* (BS) Elem Ed/Bus Ed, Valley City St Univ 1972; (MS) Elem Ed, Moorhead St Univ 1988; Environmental & Conservation Ed; *cr:* 5th Grade Teacher Valley City Public Sch 1972-; *ai:* ND Ed Assn, NEA; Valley City Ed Assn, Elks, Farmers Union, Epworth Meth Church, ND Wildlife Fed; Conservation Educator of Yr Awd 1989-; Developed Outdoor Sci Ed Resource Guide; *home:* 1050 Riverview Dr Valley City ND 58072

BUMBALES, CHARLES J., Dean of Students; *b:* Gary, IN; *m:* Cynthia; *c:* Melissa, Kelsey; *ed:* (BA) Eng, E IL Univ 1983; (MA) Curr/Instruction, Concordia Univ 1987; *cr:* Eng Teacher Streamwood HS 1983-85; Eng Teacher 1985-89, Dean of Students 1989- Jacobs HS; *ai:* Ftbl & Bsktbl Coach; NHS; Sch Climate Comm; All Sch Awd Assembly; Little City Collection & UNICEF Collection Chairperson; *office:* Jacobs HS 11111 Randall Rd Algonquin IL 60102

BUNCH, ALAN BRET, Vocal Music Director; *b:* Baytown, TX; *m:* Leslie Lynn; *c:* Daniel; *ed:* (BS) Music Ed, NW MO St Univ 1985; *cr:* Vocal Music Dir Lewis Mid Sch 1985-88, Ft Osage HS 1988-; *ai:* All Vocal Music Act; All Sch Musical; Amer Choral Dir Assn, MO Music Educators Assn 1985-; Nom BSA Leadership Awd; *office:* Fort Osage HS 2101 Twyman Independence MO 64058

BUNDRICK, ELIZABETH ANN HENTHORN, Second Grade Teacher; *b:* Shidler, OK; *m:* Doyle Dwain; *c:* Robert; *ed:* (BA) Elem Ed, Univ of OK 1968; Piano & Voice; *cr:* 2nd Grade Teacher Dungee Elem 1968-70, Ida Freeman Elem 1970-; *ai:* Ida Freeman Elem Arts Coord; KWTV 9 My Favorite Teacher Awd; Roman Nose Arts Inst Speaker; *office:* Ida Freeman Elem Sch 501 W Hurd Edmond OK 73034

BUNN, BETTY TAYLOR, English Teacher; *b:* Roanoke, AL; *m:* Roy H.; *c:* Stephanie, Jonathan; *ed:* (BS) Eng, Auburn Univ 1970; (MS) Eng, Jacksonville St Univ 1985; Working on Ed Specialist Degree; *cr:* Teacher Handley Mid Sch 1972-79, Randolph Cty HS 1985-; *ai:* Jr Class Spon; Kappa Delta Pi, NCTE, NEA; *office:* Randolph Cty HS P O Box 696 Wedowee AL 36278

BUNN, RUTH BROWN, Teacher of Gifted & Talented; *b:* Burkes Garden, VA; *m:* Joe H.; *c:* Kimberly Bunn Robinson, Brian, Brett, Joel; *ed:* (BA) Latin, Emory & Henry Coll 1963; NK-3 Ed Cert Radford Univ 1975; *cr:* 3rd/4th Grade Teacher Burkes Garden Elem Sch 1961-62; 5th Grade Teacher Cedar Bluff Elem Sch 1964-65; 5th-7th Grade Teacher Oakland Elem 1965-66; 3rd Grade Teacher Fancy Gap Elem 1967-69; Latin Teacher Carroll Cty HS 1969-73; K-1st Grade Teacher Fancy Gap Elem 1977-86; Teacher of Gifted & Talented/Latin Teacher Carroll Cty HS 1986-; *ai:* Latin Club & Newspaper Spon; Coord of Gifted & Talented; Carroll Ed Assn, VA Ed Assn, NEA 1965-; BSA (Den Mother 1983-85, Comm Mem 1986-); Hillsville Jaycees Outstanding Young Educator 1973; Univ of Richmond Governors Sch for Hum Presidential Citation 1989; *home:* Rt 1 Box 15 Fancy Gap VA 24328

BUNNELL, KATHRYN COLLINS, 5th Grade Teacher; *b:* Allen Park, MI; *m:* John; *c:* Steven, Debbie; *ed:* (MA) Elem Ed, Alma Coll 1972; Gen Sci & Music; *cr:* Math/Sci Teacher Florence Jr HS 1972-73; 4th Grade Teacher Florence Elem 1973-74; 5th Grade Teacher Kenwood Elem 1975-79; 3rd Grade Teacher Lincoln Elem 1979-80; 4th/5th Grade Teacher 1980-84, 5th Grade Teacher 1985- Mc Kinley Elem; *ai:* Dist Sci Comm 1985 Co-Leader 1985-88; Sch Improvement Plan Comm; SPIN Teacher Gifted & Talented; CEA (Building Rep, Exec Bd) 1975-; MI Ed Assn 1975-; NEA 1972-; Cadillac Child Study Club I (Pres 1987-88, Mem 1986-); Asst Brownie Leader 1988-; Nom for the 1990 Presidential Awds for Excl in Elem Sch Sci Teaching; Teacher Trainer for Sci Act Resource Person for Herpetology Unit 1990; *office:* Mckinley Elem Sch 601 E North St Cadillac MI 49601

BUNTING, SUZANNE M., Instrumental Music Teacher; *b:* Denison, IA; *m:* Michael R.; *ed:* (BS) Instrumental Music Ed, Mankato St Univ 1985; *cr:* Dir of Bands Sheffield-Chapin & Meservey-Thornton Sch 1985-; *ai:* IA Bandmasters Assn 1985-; N Cntrl IA Bandmasters Assn Cty Chairperson 1988; N IA Symphony Orch (Flutist, Personnel Mgr) 1985-; N IA Concert Band 1988-; *office:* Sheffield-Chapin HS Box 617 5th & Park Sts Sheffield IA 50475

BUOB, PATRICIA ANDERSEN, 2nd Grade Teacher; *b:* Wisconsin Dells, WI; *m:* Frederick J.; *c:* Laurie, Michael; *ed:* (BE) Ed, Univ of WI Whitewater 1960; Cooperative Learning; TESA; *cr:* 1st-2nd Grade Teacher Roosevelt Sch 1960-62; 1st Grade Teacher Winaequah Sch 1962-64, Euclid Sch 1964-65; 2nd Grade Teacher Plum Grove Sch 1965-66; 2nd-3rd Grade Teacher Cntrl Road Sch 1976-; *ai:* Natl PTA Contest Rdng Incentive Comm Co-Chm; Staff Dev Team Sch; Book Adoptions Soc Stud; AFT; Employee of Month CCSD 15 1989; Article Published 1989; *office:* Palatine Cntrl Road Sch 3800 Central Rd Rolling Meadows IL 60008

BUONO, LAWRENCE J., Social Studies Teacher; *b:* Hornell, NY; *m:* Blanche M. Mc Lean; *c:* John, Margaret; *ed:* (BA) His, Alfred Univ 1962; (MA) His, St Univ of Buffalo 1970; Robert Taft Fellowship in Poly Sci, Pace Univ 1974; *cr:* Teacher Holland Cntrl Sch 1962-; *ai:* NHS Faculty Comm; Holland Teachers Assn Pres 1969-70; NY St Ed Assn, NEA; *office:* Holland Cntrl Sch Pearl St Holland NY 14080

BUONOCORE, ANNA ODOARDI, Mathematics Teacher; *b:* Pescara, Italy; *m:* Salvatore B.; *c:* Loren, Marco; *ed:* (BA) Math, 1974, (MA) Math, 1980 Herbert H Lehman Coll; Gifted & Talented Trng, Columbia Univ; Human Relations Trng & Sequential Math Revisions, Yonkers Bd of Ed; *cr:* Math Teacher Mark Twain Mid Sch 1974-76, Gorton HS 1976-77, Mark Twain

Mid Sch 1977-81, Emerson/Mark Twain Gifted Prgm 1985-86, Hawthorne Jr HS for Gifted & Talented Stus 1986-; *ai:* Continental Math League Coach; Yrbk Adv; Yonkers PTA Mem; *office:* Hawthorne Jr HS for Gifted Stu 350 Hawthorne Ave Yonkers NY 10705

BUQUO, DAVID SCOTT, Bio/Anatomy/Physiology Teacher; *b:* Cincinnati, OH; *ed:* Sci Curr Re-Write, Miami Univ; *cr:* Bio/Anatomy/Physiology Instr Spencerville HS 1985-86, Lockland HS 1986-; *ai:* Stu Cncl Adv; Faculty Advisory Comm; Boys Reserve Bsktbl Coach; Academic Intervention Instr; OEA, NEA, LEA 1989-; *office:* Lockland HS 249 W Forrer Cincinnati OH 45215

BURCH, BOBBY JOE, Physics/Biology HS Teacher; *b:* Monticello, AR; *m:* Diane Joan Brewer; *c:* Morgan A.; *ed:* (BS) Earth Sci Comp, Univ of AR Monticello 1972; (MS) Sci Ed, Univ of S MS 1973; *cr:* 9th/10th Grade Phys Sci Teacher Pass Chrstn HS 1973-74; Instr Univ of AR Monticello 1974-75; Teacher/Prin Selma Sch 1975-79; Sci Teacher Drew Cntrl HS 1979-83; Physics/Bio Teacher Lake Hamilton HS 1983-; *ai:* Governors Quiz Bowl & Knowledge Master Spon & Coach; NEA Mem 1983-; AEA (VP 1987-88, Mem) 1983-; Natl Sci Fnd Curr Coord 1973; ESCP Gulf Coast Region; *home:* 412 Woodlawn Hot Spg Natl Pk AR 71913

BURCH, DANIEL SCOTT, Cmptr Coord/Math Chair; *b:* Winston Salem, GA; *m:* Judy Diane Pierce; *c:* Justin, Jenee; *ed:* (AS) Sci, Young Harris 1975; (BSED) Math Ed 1977, (MED) Math Ed, 1985 Univ of GA; *cr:* Math Teacher 1977-, Cmptr Coord 1984-, Math Chm 1985- Rabun Cty HS; Math Teacher Truett Mc Connel Jr Coll 1986-; *ai:* NCTM 1985-; GAE 1978-; STAR Teacher 1989; Rabun Cty HS Teacher of Yr 1990; *office:* Rabun Cty HS Rt 1 Box 1335 Tiger GA 30576

BURCH, JENISE K., Voc Home Economics Teacher; *b:* Nevada, MO; *m:* Jerry W.; *c:* Jered, Laura; *ed:* (BSED) Voc Home Ec, SW MO St Univ 1969; *cr:* Voc Home Ec/Soc Stud Teacher Walker R-4 HS 1978-; *ai:* FHA Adv; Sr Class Spon; MO St Teachers Assn Local Pres; MO Home Ec Teachers Assn; Vernon Cty Democrat Women Pres 1987-; Walker 4-H Club Cmmty Leader 1988-; Carl Perkins Grant; *office:* Walker R-4 HS Walker MO 64790

BURCH, SHIRLEY ANNE, 5th Grade Teacher; *b:* Albuquerque, NM; *m:* Clinton M.; *c:* Robert M., Gary A.; *ed:* (BA) Elem Ed, Eastern NM Univ 1957; Addl Studies Univ of NM; *cr:* 4th Grade Teacher 1957-60; Sub Teacher 1966-70; Educ Aide 1971-74; 5th Grade Teacher 1975-Albuquerque Public Schls; *ai:* Youth Leadership Prgm Spon 1986-90; Elem Sci Advisory Comm 1981-83; Sch Cmptr Rep 1983-; Sci Text Selection Comm 1986; Math Text Selection Comm 1987; Grade Level Rep 1985-89; NEA 1983-; NM Sci Teachers Assn 1988-; Church (Financial Sec 1986- Youth Dir 1989-).

BURCHEL, PAT, 7th-8th Grade English Teacher; *b:* Broken Arrow, OK; *m:* Doy E.; *c:* Dan, Darin; *ed:* (BSE) Ed, OK Chrstn Univ of Sci & Art 1964; Grad Stud in Gifted Ed; *cr:* 6th Grade Teacher Prairie Queen/Oklahoma City Public Schls 1964-66, Newcastle Public Schls 1977-78; 3rd Grade Teacher 1978-80, High Challenge Teacher of Gifted 1981-86, 7th/8th Grade Eng Teacher 1987- Newcastle Public Schls; *home:* 5024 SW 174th Newcastle OK 73065

BURCHETTE, FATHA LEE (ROBERTS), 6th Grade Soc Stud Teacher; *b:* Carthage, TX; *m:* Roy Lee; *c:* Kiesha; *ed:* (BA) Broadfield Soc Sci, Culver-Stockton Coll 1974; (MS) Scndry Ed, Stephen F Austin St Univ 1989; *cr:* Teacher Carthage Ind Sch Dist 1979-; *ai:* Baker-Koonce Campus Planning Comm Mem; Positive Action Comm Mem; TX St Teachers Assn (Secy, Membership Chm) 1979-; TX Classroom Teachers Campus Rep 1979-; E TX Cncl of Soc Stud; Carthage Ind Sch Dist Service Awds 1984, 1989.

BURCHETTE, SANDRA WHITE, Kindergarten Teacher; *b:* Greeneville, TN; *m:* Joseph W.; *c:* Chad, Darrin; *ed:* (BS) Elem Ed, East TN St Univ 1974; (MS) Elem Ed, Univ of TN 1979; *cr:* Kndgtn Teacher Parrottsville Elem 1974-77; Newport Grammar Sch 1977-; *ai:* Chairperson of Transitional Class Comm; Alpha Delta Kappa; *office:* Newport Grammar Schl 202 College St Newport TN 37821

BURCHFIELD, CURTIS DEAN, Amer His Teacher/Soc Stud Chm; *b:* Pontotoc, MS; *ed:* (BS) Soc Stud Ed, MS St Univ 1982; (MED) Scndry Ed, Univ of MS 1989; *cr:* 8th Grade Amer His/9th Grade Civics/MS His Teacher 1982-84, 8th Grade Amer His/MS His/9th Grade Civics/9th-12th Grade Geography Teacher 1984-85, 8th Grade Amer His/Amer Government/12th Grade Sociology Teacher 1985-87 Pontotoc HS; 8th Grade Amer His Teacher Pontotoc Jr HS 1988-; *ai:* 8th Grade Class Spon; Video Cameraman Pontotoc Warrior Ftbl Team 1988-; Chm Soc Stud Comm; Civil War Re-enactor Cleburns Brigade CSA 60th NY USA; ASCD 1989-; Pontotoc Historical Society Chm Historic Site Comm 1989-; Sons of Confederate Veterans 1988-; Military Order of the Stars & Bars 1989-; Stipen Study of Economics Univ of MS 1989; *home:* Rt 1 Box 154 Hurricane Rd Thaxton MS 38871

BURCKHARD, RHONDA BRITSCH, English Teacher/Librarian; *b:* Rugby, ND; *m:* Rodger L.; *ed:* (BS) Eng/Speech.Theatre Art, Dickinson St Univ 1986; *cr:* 7th-9th Grade Eng Teacher/K-12th Grade Librarian 1986-88, 7th-12th Grade Eng Teacher/Librarian 1988- Anamoose Public Sch; *ai:* Drama Club Adv; Speech Team Coach; Frosh Class Adv; NCTE 1985-; NDEA, NEA, ND Speech & Theatre Assn 1988-; Anamoose Ed Assn Pres 1986-.

BURDEN, JACK WILLIAM, English/History Teacher; *b:* Mitchell, NE; *m:* Cindy White-Burden; *ed:* (BS) Soc Sci, 1983, (BA) Scndry Ed/Soc Sci, 1985 Univ of WY; *cr:* Teacher Kingman HS 1986-; *ai:* Sch Newspaper Spon; Chess Team Coach; US Chess Fed 1984-.

BURDETT, BEVERLY JEAN (CORNETT), Spanish/World History Teacher; *b:* Muskogee, OK; *m:* Kevin M.; *ed:* (BA) His/Span, 1976, (MA) His/Ed, 1983 Brigham Young Univ; Participating in Russian Cross-Trng Prgm; *cr:* Soc Stud Teacher Liberty HS 1976-79; Teaching Asst Brigham Young Univ Dept of Scndry Ed 1980-81; Soc Stud/Span Teacher 1981-, Foreign Lang Dept Chairperson 1985- Springville HS; *ai:* Span Club Adv; Liberty HS AFS Club Adv; Teacher/Cnslr 10 Day Seminar in Mexico; *office:* Springville HS 1205 E 900 S Springville UT 84663

BURDETTE, OTHEL DAVIS, Retired; *b:* Elkhurst, WV; *w:* Chester (dec); *c:* Betty Burdette Robinson, Doris Burdette Mc Kown, Chester A. Jr., Charles R.; *ed:* (BS) Eng/Soc Sci, Morris Harvey 1964; *cr:* 1st-8th Elem Teacher Valley View Elem Sch 1955-56; Elem Teacher Harners Fork Elem Sch 1956-59; Class Room Teacher Dulls Creek Elem Sch 1957-64, Bridge Elem 1964-86; *ai:* NEA, WVEA 1955-86; PTA 1964-86; *home:* Rt 3 Box 1 Procious WV 25164

BURDICK, KATHY BULLARD, 7th/8th Grade English Teacher; *b:* Greenville, MI; : Loren; *c:* Ross, Adam; *ed:* (BS) Eng/Music, Cntrl MI Univ 1969; *cr:* Elem/Jr HS Music Teacher Cmmty Schls 1969-70; 8th Grade Eng Teacher 197073, 7th Grade Eng Teacher/8th Grade Eng/Music Teacher 1975- Montabella Cmmty Schls; *ai:* Blanchard Womens Club Pres 1977-78; Blanchard Lib Club Treas 1987-; Blanchard Church of God Choir Dir 1975-78; *office:* Montabella Mid Sch 300 W Main St Edmore MI 48829

BUREL, BONITA PASS, Teacher/Math Dept Chair; *b:* Buford, GA; *m:* Ronnie D.; *c:* Steve, Julie; *ed:* (AS) Math, Gainesville Jr Coll 1971; (BS) Elem Ed/Math/Sci, 1972, (MED) Elem Ed/Math/Sci, 1973 W GA Coll; Data Collector Peer Teacher Evaluator; *cr:* Classroom/Math/Sci/Soc Stud Teacher Buford Mid Sch 1973-; *ai:* 7th Grade Level Chairperson; Beta Club Spon; GA Assn of Educators, NEA 1973-; Teacher of Yr Buford Mid Sch 1987; *home:* 2301 Buford Dam Rd Buford GA 30518

BURGAN, DIANE (FUELLING), Home Economics Teacher; *b:* Decatur, IN; *m:* David N.; *c:* David A., Dana E.; *ed:* (BS) Voc Home Ec, Purdue Univ 1975; (MA) Home Ec Ed, Ball St Univ 1978; *cr:* Home Ec Teacher S Wells Cmmty Schls 1975-83, Concordia Luth HS 1986-; *ai:* Chrldr Coach; *office:* Concordia Lutheran HS 1601 St Joe River Rd Fort Wayne IN 46805

BURGATTI, JOSEPH C., Social Studies Teacher; *b:* Malden, MA; *ed:* (BA) His, St Anselms Coll 1968; (MA) His, Univ of NH 1975; (MED) Admin/Supervision, Plymouth St Coll 1979; Extensive Travel in Europe & Overseas; *cr:* 8th Grade Amer His Teacher 1970, 7th Grade World Stud Teacher 1970- Southside Jr HS; *ai:* Prin Advisory, Grading, Tracking Comms; NEA, NH Ed Assn Life Mem 1970-; Manchester Ed Assn Building Rep 1987-; *office:* Southside Jr HS 140 S Jewett St Manchester NH 03103

BURGDOLF, MARILYN TIMMONS, Business Chairperson; *b:* Princeton, KY; *c:* Adam W.; *ed:* (BS) Bus Ed, 1976, (MA) Bus Ed, 1980; Rank I Voc Ed, 1981 Murray St Univ; *cr:* Secy/Bookkeeper Sigler Ford 1976-77; Deputy Clerk Lyon Cty Courthouse 1977-78; Bus Teacher Lyon Cty HS 1978-; *ai:* FBLA Adv; Hopewell Baptist Church Sunday Sch Teacher; KVA Secy 1985-86; Lyon Cty Teachers Organization Secy 1978-; KEA, SBEA 1978-; *office:* Lyon Cty HS P O Box 400 Eddyville KY 42038

BURGESS, BRENDA KAY (TOPE), Fifth Grade Teacher; *b:* Blackfork, OH; *m:* Donald E.; *c:* Sharon, Todd E. Mayes, Theresa Addis, Chad M.; *ed:* (BS) Elem Ed, Rio Grande Coll 1971; *cr:* 2nd Grade Teacher 1961-64, 3rd Grade Teacher 1964-68 Fairborn City Schls; 4th-5th Grade Teacher Tecumseh Local Schls 1969-; *ai:* Modern Woodman of America Speech & Creativity Writing Contest Teacher Adv; NEA, OH Ed Assn, Cntrl OH Ed Assn, Tecumseh Local Assn; Eastern Star-Dayton Division Mem 1989; Winner of Wone & Ashland Oil Educator Awd 1988-89; *home:* 3035 Old Dayton Yellow Springs Fairborn OH 45324

BURGESS, KELLY VINTON, Seventh Grade Teacher; *b:* Smith Center, KS; *m:* Becky Joy Hendrich; *c:* Vinton Hendrich, Caleb J., Emily J.; *ed:* (BS) His, Ft Hays Univ 1980; *cr:* 7th Grade Teacher Randall Mid Sch 1981-; *ai:* Coach Jr HS Girls Vlbl, Boys & Girls Bsktbl & Track, HS Asst Boys Bsktbl; Act Spon; *office:* Randall Mid Sch Randall KS 66963

BURGESS, LYLE D., Bus/Phys Ed Teacher Admin Asst; *b:* Casper, WY; *m:* Laura M. Bermes; *c:* Nicholas R.; *ed:* (AA) Phys Ed, Northwest Comm Coll 1977; (BA) Phys Ed, E MT Coll 1980; Bus, E MT Coll 1980; *cr:* Construction Labor Jeffrey City 1980-81; Teacher/Coach Jeffrey City Public Sch 1981-83, Ryegate Public Sch 1983-; *ai:* Sr Class & Lettermen Club Adv; Admin Asst; Girls Bsktbl & Boys, Girls Track Coach; MT Coaches Assn 1984-; Ryegate Teachers Assn Negotiations Rep; Ryegate Volunteer Fire Dept Secy 1989-; Golden Valley 1st Responders Ryegates Rep 1990; Franklin Select Circle Natl HS Athletic Coaching Awd 1989; *office:* Ryegate Public Schls 207 2nd Ave W Ryegate MT 59074

BURGETT, DAVID ROBERT, Science Teacher; *b:* Columbus, OH; *m:* Miriam A. Waite; *c:* Malea R., Robert T.; *ed:* (AA) Ed, Miami Dade Jr Coll 1969; (BS) Ed, MS Coll 1972; Clear Choices Drug Ed Conf; NASA Ed Wrkshp; Southern Assn of Schls Trng Session; *cr:* Eng Teacher Kendall Elem Sch 1972; 5th Grade Teacher North Lakeland Elem Sch 1972-76, Morningside Elem Sch 1976-81; Sci Teacher Azalea Mid Sch 1981-; *ai:* Head of Comm Southern Assn of Schls/Coll; Safety Patrol Spon; Stu Cncl Spon; *office:* Azalea Road Mid Sch 3800 Pleasant Valley Rd Mobile AL 36609

BURGHDORF, HARRY PAUL, English Teacher; *b:* South Gate, CA; *m:* Marilyn Pierce; *c:* Kristin, Andrew, Kimberley; *ed:* (BA) Eng, 1962, (MA) Guidance/Counseling, 1967 Pasadena Coll; (MA) Eng Stud, Univ of Edinburgh 1969-; *cr:* Coach 1961-62, Eng Teacher 1962-63 Pasadena Acad; Eng Teacher/Coach Peace Corps 1963-65; Eng Teacher Pasadena Acad 1965-66; Cnslr First Avenue Jr HS 1966-67; Eng Teacher Hoover HS 1967-69, Glendale HS 1970-80, Rift Valley Acad 1980-81, Glendale HS 1981-85, Rift Valley Acad 1985-71, Glendale HS 1987-; *ai:* Speech Adv; CTA 1989-; Most Outstanding Teacher Glendale HS 1988-89; Dist Service Awd Glendale Unified 1989; *home:* 2525 Teasley St La Crescenta CA 91214

BURHOE, GLORIA T., English Teacher; *b:* Boston, MA; *m:* Richard L.; *c:* Shane, Melissa, Jared; *ed:* (BA) Eng, Bridgewater St Coll 1967; *cr:* Eng Teacher Provincetown HS 1967-; *ai:* Provincetown Jr HS Comm; MA Teachers Assn 1967-; Lower Cape Ed Assn 1967-; NEA 1967-; Parent Teacher Stu Assn 1987-; *home:* Knowles Hts Rd North Truro MA 02652

BURISE, BARBARA LANCASTER, Elementary Teacher; *b:* Memphis, TN; *m:* James; *c:* Tamal, Jamal; *ed:* (BA) Elem Ed, Lane Coll 1968; (MS) Rdng, W MI Univ 1975; *cr:* Teacher Washington Elm Sch 1968-; *ai:* Dist Sch Improvement Team; MI Ed Assn, NEA, Battle Creek Ed Assn 1989-; Urban League Guild (Pres 1986-87, Treas 1989-); Delta Sigma Theta Pres 1990; Admin Intern Prgm 1987-88; *home:* 126 Bonney Battle Creek MI 49017

BURK, PAULA DICKENS, Mathematics Department Chair; *b:* Coronado, CA; *c:* Laura, Samuel; *ed:* (BAT) Math, Sam Houston St Univ 1977; (MA) Math, Sam Houston St Univ 1987; *cr:* Teacher Klein Strack intermediate Sch 1977-78, C E King HS 1978-80, Livingston Jr HS 1982-83; Teacher/Dept Chairperson Livingston HS 1983-; *ai:* Schlsp & NHS Comm; Assn TX Prop Educators, TX Math Teachers Assn, NCTM 1986-; TX Cmptr Educators Assn 1988-; Pilot Club (VP, Pres) 1988-89; Area Math Teachers Cncl Bd Mem 1986-87; Brewton Math Schlsp Sam Houston St Univ 1985, 1986; Whos Who Among Amer Young Women 1989; *office:* Livingston HS 1500 E Church Livingston TX 77351

BURK, SANDRA WALLEN, English Chairperson; *b:* Del Rio, TX, *m:* Victor E., *c:* Gregory Meyer, Jeffrey Meyer, Daryl G. Meyer; *ed:* (BS) Elem Ed, TX A&I Univ 1972; Eng, Gifted & Talented Cert; *cr:* 7th Grade Sci/Eng Teacher St James Episcopal Sch 1972; 5th Grade Teacher Mathis Elem 1973; 7th Grade Eng Teacher Calallen Mid Sch 1973-77; 7th/8th Grade Eng Teacher Tuloso-Midway Mid Sch 1977-; *ai:* Stu Cncl Spon; UIL Literary; TX St Teachers Assn Treas 1979; Coastal Bend Cncl of Eng 1980-; NCTE 1982-; Optimist Club 1988-; Amer Assn of Coll Women 1987-; Outstanding Conservation Teacher 1989; *office:* Tuloso-Midway Mid Sch 9760 La Branch Corpus Christi TX 78410

BURKE, CAROL CONNOLLY, 4th Grade Teacher; *b:* Scranton, PA; *m:* William V.; *ed:* (BA) Elem Ed, Marywood Coll 1961; (MS) Elem Ed, Univ of Scranton 1965; *cr:* Elem Teacher Garfield Sch 1961-65, John F Kennedy 1965-; *ai:* PSEA, NEA, Scranton Ed Assn, Scranton Women Teachers Club; Marywood Coll Alumnae Natl Pres 1976-78; Delta Kappa Gamma; St Josephs Center Auxiliary Handicapped Children; *office:* John F Kennedy Elem Sch Prospect Ave & Saginaw St Scranton PA 18505

BURKE, DEBORAH EDMUNDSON, Sixth Grade Teacher; *b:* Richmond, VA; *m:* Robah Kerner Sr.; *c:* R. K. Jr., Charles E.; *ed:* (BSB) Elem Ed/Intermediate Ed, Appalachian St Univ 1973; Grad Courses Appalachian St Univ 1973-74; Sci, Univ HI; *cr:* 6th Grade Teacher Gamewell Elem 1973-77, Bethel Hill Elem 1977-78, South Elem Sch 1978-; *ai:* Co-Chm Hospitality Comm; Plan & Organize Promotion Ceremony & Reception for Stu; Delta Kappa Gamma Recording Secy 1988-; NC Cncl Math Teachers; PTA (Bd of Dirs, Secy); Roxboro Bus & Prof Womens Club (Pres 1982-83, Recording Secy 1989-), Woman of Yr 1982; South Elem Teacher of Yr 1982; *office:* South Elem Sch 1040 S Main St Roxboro NC 27573

BURKE, JACQUELINE T., Chem/Earth Sci Teacher; *b:* Tamaqua, PA; *m:* James; *c:* Patrick, Jacqueline; *ed:* Assoc Medical Technology, Penn St Center 1960; (BS) Biological Sci, E Stroudsburg Univ 1963; *cr:* Fr Teacher Tamaqua HS 1963-64; Bio Teacher S Brunswick HS 1968-70; 6th-8th Grade Teacher St Joseph Sch & Cathedral Grammar Schls 1980-88; Chem/Earth Sci Teacher Mc Corristin HS 1988-; *ai:* Teach Piano Lessons; Hightstown HS Adult Ed Evening Prgm Art Teacher; Tri Cty Art Assn (Show Dir 1972-80, Teacher); Earthwatch; Dodge Fnd Fellowship to Study the Rain Forests; Prof Artist Awds; *home:* 16 Washington Dr Cranbury NJ 08512

BURKE, JANEY POLLAN, English Teacher; *b:* Ennis, TX; *m:* Jimmie D.; *c:* Dale, Cody, Joni, Stoney; *ed:* (BS) Ed, TX Tech 1968; Gifted & Talented Ed; *cr:* Teacher Dallas Ind Sch Dist 1968-71, Highland Ind Sch Dist 1985-; *ai:* Class Spon; Jr HS UIL

Academic Coach; Natl Assn of Eng Teachers, TX Assn of Gifted & Talented; *home:* Rt 1 Box 65A Roscoe TX 79545

BURKE, JOYCE HENDERSON, 5th Grade Teacher; *b:* Ft Worth, TX; *m:* David A.; *ed:* (BA) Elem Ed, Houston-Tillotson Coll 1968; (NED) Elem Ed, VA St Univ 1976; TX Wesleyan Univ; *cr:* 4th Grade Teacher Jackson Elem Sch 1969-70; 2nd Grade Teacher Kaiserslautern Elem 1972-73; 5th/6th Grade Blandford Elem 1973-79; 6th Grade Teacher Virginia Ave Elem 1979-80; 5th Grade Teacher J W Bishop Elem 1980-; *ai:* Instructional Advisory Comm; Dost Ins Comm; Campus Level Attendance Comm; Assn of TX Prof Educators; *office:* J W Bishop Elem Sch 501 Vaughn St Fort Worth TX 76140

BURKE, MARIA T. MIROCKE, Reading Specialist; *b:* Shenandoah, PA; *m:* James J.; *c:* Christopher, Marisa, Timothy; *ed:* (BA) Biological Sci, Immaculata Coll 1951; Cert in Elem Ed & Rdng Specialist Bloomsburg Univ; *cr:* Microbiologist Merck & Company 1951-57; Adult Ed Teacher Danville St Hospital 1975-76; Rdng Specialist Danville Jr HS 1976-88, Danville Mid Sch 1988-; *ai:* Prof Dev Comm; Susquehanna Valley Rdng Cncl, Keystone St Rdng Assn 1974-; Delta Kappa Gamma 1987-; PSEA, NEA 1976-; Alpha Psi Omega 1950-; *home:* 1011 Avenue F Box 174 Riverside PA 17868

BURKE, MARY E., Physical Education Teacher; *b:* Sciotoville, OH; *ed:* (BSED) Ed/Phys Ed/Health, 1969, (MSED) Guidance/Counseling, 1980 OH St Univ; *cr:* Phys Ed Teacher Everts Mid Sch 1969-; *ai:* 9th Grade Bsktbl & Vlybl Coach 1977-79; GAA Adv 1969-76; Reserve Bsktbl Coach 1980-81; Cheerleading Adv 1969-76; Varsity Sftbl Coach 1977-83; Intramural Dir 1969-; Reserve Vlybl Coach 1980-88; Phi Delta Kappa 1980-89; Circleville Ed Assn, OH Ed Assn, NEA 1970-; *office:* Everts Mid Sch 520 S Court St Circleville OH 43113

BURKE, MICHAEL J., Mathematics Teacher; *b:* Bronx, NY; *m:* Sharon Palmer; *c:* Jeff, Michele; *ed:* (AS) Math, OCCC 1972; (BA) Math, 1976, (MS) Math, 1977 SUNY New Paltz; *cr:* Math Teacher Susquehanna Valley Jr HS 1977-; *ai:* Ski & Cmptr Clubs; Boys Var & Girls Jr Var Tennis; Teachers Assn Exec Cncl; *office:* Susquehanna Valley Jr HS 1040 Conklin Rd Conklin NY 13748

BURKE, MYRTIS EDGECOMBE, 6th Grade English Teacher; *b:* W Palm Beach, FL; *m:* Gerald Clayton; *c:* Gerunda Burke Hughes, Michael A., Patricia Burke Lewis, Marcus G., Tanya Y.; *ed:* (BS) Eng, Ag & Tech Univ 1948; (MED) Curr/Instruction, FL Atlantic Univ 1969; Cert Elem Ed, FAMU Tallahassee 1962; Grad Stud Guidance/Counseling, FL Atlantic Univ 1972; *cr:* Critic/Eng Teacher Lucy Moton HS 1948-49; Lake Shore Elem 1949-51; 8th Grade Teacher Everglades Camp Sch 1951-58; 1st Grade Teacher Rosenwald Elem 1958-59; 4th Grade Teacher Everglades Elem 1960-62; 6th Grade Eng Teacher Lincoln Elem 1962-; *ai:* Tutoring AOIP; Math Olympiad Club Spon; Classroom Teachers Assn 1949-; NEA; Alpha Kappa Mu NHS Honor Record 1944-48; Alpha Kappa Alpha (Ivy Leaf Reporter, Charter Mem) 1985; Assault on Illiteracy Prgm Service to Youth 1987-89; Episcopal Church Women Secy Chairperson of Womens Day Awd; St Patricks Episcopal Church Mem Dedication & Service 1982; Excl in Ed Awd 1989; Links Awd 1985; Speech Writer; William Dwyer Excl in Ed Awd 1989.

BURKETT, CAROLE BONE, 1st Grade Teacher; *b:* Newport, AR; *m:* Mike; *c:* Brad, Fran; *ed:* (BSE) Early Chldhd/Elem, 1973; (MSE) Early Chldhd, 1979 AR St Univ; *cr:* Remedial Rdng Beedeville Elem 1973; 5th Grade Teacher 73-74; Kndgtn Teacher 74-79; 1st Grade Teacher 1980- Mc Crory Elem Sch; *ai:* Delta Kappa Gamma; Faith Missionary Baptist Church Pianist 1975-; SS Secy 1988-; North Central Steering Personnel Policy Comm; *office:* Mc Crory Elem Sch Mc Crory AR 72101

BURKETT, GAIL ZETTLER, Resource Teacher for Gifted; *b:* Savannah, GA; *c:* Ryan; *ed:* (BS) Early Childhood Ed, 1973, (MA) Early Childhood, 1981 GA Southern Coll; *cr:* 4th Grade Teacher 1974-82, Resource Teacher of Gifted 1982- Saul Chatham; *office:* Pooler Elem Sch 308 Holly Ave Pooler GA 31322

BURKETT, JUDITH MAIDES, Sixth Grade Teacher; *b:* New Bern, NC; *m:* Thomas Eugene; *c:* Brian, Adam, Amy; *ed:* (AS) Radio/TV Broadcasting, Lenoir Comm Coll 1974; (BA) Intermediate Ed, E Carolina Univ 1978; *cr:* 4th Grade Teacher Trenton Elem Sch 1980-81; Rdng Teacher 1982-83, 6th Grade Teacher 1983- W Craven Mid Sch; *office:* W Craven Mid Sch 515 N West Craven Middle Sc Rd New Bern NC 28565

BURKEY, THOMAS LYNN, Social Studies Dept Chair; *b:* Greeneville, TN; *m:* Janet Hudson; *ed:* (BS) Scndry Ed, Univ of TN 1974; *cr:* Substitute Teacher Oak Ridge Schls 1975; Instr Aide Robertsville Jr HS 1975-76; Teacher Jefferson Jr HS 1976-77, Robertsville Jr HS 1978-; *ai:* Robertsville Jr HS Vlybl Coach & Team Leader; Oak Ridge HS Asst Girls Bsktbl Coach; NCSS 1987-; Amateur Athletic Union Volunteer Coach Girls Bsktbl 1977-, Natl Championships 1985, 1989; Freedom Fnd George Washington Medal of Honor Civics Curr; *home:* 11001 Roane Dr Knoxville TN 37922

BURKHARDT, BEVERLY ADAMS, 3rd & 4th Grade Teacher; *b:* Sugarcreek, PA; *ed:* (BS) Elem Ed, 1956, (MED) Ed Admin, 1958, Certificate Rdng Specialist, 1971- PA St Univ; Rdng Specialist, PA St Univ 1971; Grad Courses, IN Univ of PA; Additional Courses & Wkshps at St Coll Area Sch Dist & Intermediate Unit #10 1989; *cr:* Elem Teacher Altoona Area Sch Dist 1955-60; Field Dir/Camp Dir Blair Cty GSA Cncl 1960-63; Parks/Recreation Leader Altoona City Bd of Parks & Recreation 1963-64; Elem Teacher St Coll Area Sch Dist 1964-; *ai:* Sch Newsletter Publication, Sch Dist Soc Stud Prgm Structure Revision, Lang Arts/Soc Stud Units Revisions Ed; Building Rep Prof Dev, Lang Arts, Soc Stud, Report Card Comm; NEA Life Mem; PA St Ed Assn Life Mem; St Coll Area Ed Assn 1964-; Quarter Century Club 1989-; St Coll Arts Festival (Cmmty Volunteer, Classical Music Comm) 1988; The Eng Speaking Union 1988-; Amer Assn of Retired Persons Teacher Division 1987-; 25 Yrs Continuous Service Dist Logo Pin 1989; *home:* 133 S Buckhout St State College PA 16801

BURKHART, MARY MELINDA, First Grade Teacher; *b:* Zanesville, OH; *ed:* (BS) Ed, OH Dominican Coll 1965; (MS) Ed, Marygrove Coll 1973; Wkshps & Seminars in Elem Ed, Religious Ed, Alcohol & Drug Abuse, Alternatives to Violence; *cr:* 1st Grade Teacher St Clare Sch 1961-63, St Mary Sch 1963-64, Blessed Sacrament Sch 1964-65, Our Lady of Peace Sch 1965-68, Sacred Heart Sch 1968-70, St Anthony Sch 1970-71, Our Lady of Peace Sch 1971-73, St Thomas Sch 1973-77, Holy Trinity Sch 1977-; *ai:* Holy Trinity Liturgy Comm Mem 1983-; Chairwoman Offertory Comm 1977-; NCEA 1982-; OH Cath Ed Assn 1971-; Congregation of St Mary of Springs 1959-; Extraordinary Minister of Eucharist 1985-.

BURKHART, WILLIAM FRANKLIN, JR., Chapter I Math Teacher; *b:* Berkeley Springs, WV; *m:* Gloria French; *ed:* (BS) Phys Ed, 1961; (BA) Elem Ed, 1971 Shepherd Coll; *cr:* Prin-Teacher Mt Garfield 1961-64; Teacher-Coach Berkeley Springs Jr HS 1964-65; Math Teacher 1965-86; Chapter I Math Teacher 1986 Widmyer Elem; *ai:* WVEA/NEA 1961-88; AFT 1988-; Outstanding Elem Teachers Amer 1972; *office:* Widmyer Elem Sch Rt 522 S Berkeley Springs WV 25411

BURKHOLTZ, MARYANN KORCH, Performing Arts Dept Chair; *b:* Perth Amboy, NJ; *m:* Gust J.; *ed:* (BA) Drama, Trenton St Coll 1964; Post Grad Work; *cr:* Teacher Bridgeton Jr HS 1964-65, Perth Amboy HS 1966-69; Teacher 1970-, Dept Chairperson 1979- Park Jr HS; *ai:* Drama Club; SIP Rep Elective Depts; Discipline, Sch Leadership, Awds Comms; Chm Faculty Comm; ASCD 1989; NCTE 1987; Coast Guard Auxiliary Publications Officer 1984-; CTA Innovative Teaching Practice Merit Awd; Teacher of Month Park Jr HS.

BURKS, CARRIE STOUT, Sixth Grade Teacher; *b:* Fairfield, CA; *m:* Donald; *ed:* (BS) Elem Ed, Pensacola Chrstn Coll 1984; *cr:* 6th Grade Teacher Garland Chrstn Acad 1984-; *office:* Garland Chrstn Acad 1522 Lavon Dr Garland TX 75040

BURKS, JUDY HALL, 5th Grade Math Teacher; *b:* Nashville, TN; *m:* John Tigrett; *c:* Lisa Burks Escue, John T.; *ed:* (BA) Elem Ed, MS St Univ 1967; Univ of TN, Memphis St Univ; *cr:* Classroom Teacher Dyersburg Intermediate Sch 1967-; *ai:* Southern Assn of Schls Steering Comm; Legislation Comm Dyersburg Ed Assn; NEA, TN Ed Assn, Dyersburg Ed Assn 1967-; TN Math Teachers Assn 1989-; Amer Field Service Treas 1979-; Young Life Comm 1986-; Cotillon Club Pres 1970-71; Lay Reader Episcopal Church 1980-; *office:* Dyersburg Intermediate Sch Tibbs St Dyersburg TN 38024

BURKS, LINDA S., Fourth Grade Teacher; *b:* Corinth, MS; *m:* Joseph A. Sr.; *c:* Joseph A. Jr., Laura L.; *ed:* (BS) Elem Ed, 1967, (MA) Elem Ed, 1975 W KY Univ; Voc Ed Basic Cmptrs, Art Techniques for Sch Classroom; *cr:* Head Start Teacher 1969-71, Teacher 1957- Hart Memorial Elem; *ai:* Chrldr Spon; Project Hart, PTA, PTO; Hart Cty Teachers Organization; Delta Kappa Gamma 1979-; PTA 1957-; Womans Club 1957-75; *office:* Memorial Elem Sch 1400 N Jackson Hwy Hardyville KY 42746

BURKUS, JEAN CASALE, Biology Teacher/Sci Dept Chair; *b:* New York City, NY; *m:* John; *c:* Anne G. Burkus Chasson, J. Kenneth, Gregory J.; *ed:* (BA) Bio, Hunter Coll 1948; (MA) Zoology, Duke Univ 1951; Ed, Hartford Univ 1978; Sci, Technology, Society, Genetics, Bio Ethics Natl Sci Fnd Honors Wkshps; *cr:* Teaching Asst Duke Univ 1949-51; Substitute Teacher Amity Regional 5 1965-68; Bio Teacher 1968-, Sci Dept Chairperson 1982- Amity Regional Jr HS; *ai:* Mentor & Cooperating Teacher CT St Dept Ed; Marine Sci Bermuda Biological Station Ind Stud Spon; NABT 1977-, Outstanding Bio Teacher 1982; Natl St Dept Ed Presidential Awd Sci Teacher 1984; CT Dept Ed & Milken Family Fnd Awd for Excl 1989; Hunter Coll Alumni Assn Hall of Fame 1990; March of Dimes Grant 1976; CT Sci Supvrs Assn Treas 1982-, Celebration of Excl 1986; Amity Awd Excl Teaching 1977; Nom Teacher of Yr Amity Dist; Present Wkshps at NSTA, NABT, Conventions; *office:* Amity Regional Jr HS Ohman Ave Orange CT 06477

BURLESON, JEANIE BALL, Fifth Grade Teacher; *b:* Jacksonville, FL; *m:* James L. Jr.; *c:* Glenn D., James H.; *ed:* (AA) Chipola Jr Coll 1964; (BS) Elem Ed, Troy St Univ 1967; Grad Stud; *cr:* 3rd Grade Teacher Dream Lake Elem 1967-68, Rolling Hills Elem 1968; Phys Ed Teacher Forest HS 1972-73; Remedial Math Teacher Marianna HS 1977-79; 1st/5th Grade Teacher Riverside Elem 1979-; *ai:* 5th Grade Chairperson; Ladies of the Elks Pres 1979-80.

BURLESON, JOY CONCANNON, Physical Education Teacher; *b:* Michigan City, IN; *m:* Joseph Henry Jr.; *c:* Joni, Jana, Jami; *ed:* (BS) Phys Ed, San Jose St Univ 1977; (MA) Phys Ed, Univ NV Las Vegas 1980; Health Sci; *cr:* Phys Ed Teacher J D Smith Jr HS 1978-84, Kenny C Guinn Jr HS 1984-; *ai:* Current Mem Curr And Instruction Comm; Past Cheerleading Adv, Vlybl, Swimming & Sftbl Coach & Intramural Dir; NV Alliance Phys Health Ed & Recreation 1988-; NV Gaming Mini Grant 1987; Excl Clark Cty Ed Awd 1987-89; *office:* Kenny C Guinn Jr HS 4150 S Torrey Pines Dr Las Vegas NV 89103

BURLEY, SANDEE CHILTON, Computer Coord/Math Teacher; *b:* Beardstown, IL; *m:* Robert D. Jr.; *c:* Trey; *ed:* (BS) Math, W IL Univ 1970; (MAT) Math, Emory Univ 1972; Cmptr Programming; *cr:* Teacher Henderson HS 1971-; *ai:* Beta Club; Graduation; Outstanding Achievement Cmptr Technology 1989; Star Teacher 1979, 1988; Teacher of Yr 1986-87, 1987-88, 1989-; *office:* Henderson HS 2830 Henderson Mill Rd Chamblee GA 30341

BURLEY, THERESE KATHERINE, Social Studies Teacher; *b:* Bethesda, MD; *m:* Ronald C. Anderson; *ed:* (BA) Elem Ed, Univ of FL 1981; *cr:* 5th-6th Grade Teacher Spring Hill Mid Sch 1981-84; 6th Grade Teacher Wertheim Elem Sch 1984-86; 6th/7th Grade Teacher Spring Hill Mid Sch 1986-; *ai:* Stu Cncl Dir; Outward Bound Alumni; GSA Cadette-Sr Leader; *office:* Spring Hill Mid Sch P O Box 907 High Springs FL 32643

BURLINGAME, VIRGINIA JONES, Mathematics Teacher; *b:* Canton, OH; *c:* Jennifer, Janice; *ed:* (BSED) Span/Math, Bowling Green St Univ 1962; Saltillo St Teachers Coll, Malone Coll, Walsh Coll; *cr:* Teacher Herbert Slater Jr HS 1963-65; Substitute Teacher Canton City Schls 1966-76; Teacher Mc Kinley Sr HS 1976-; *ai:* Teen Bd Adv; Trinity UCC Deacon 1990-92; Intnl Order of Jobs Daughters (Guardian 1973-76, Grand Chaplain 1974-75) 1980-83; *office:* Mc Kinley Sr HS 2323 17th St NW Canton OH 44708

BURMEISTER, RICHARD, Science Department Chair; *b:* Ridgway, PA; *ed:* (BS) Chem Engineering, 1959, (MED) Phys Sci, 1963 Penn St; Med Sch, Univ of PA; *cr:* Chem/Physics Teacher Glendale Jr/Sr HS 1959-; *ai:* Sr Class, Yrbk, Soph Class Adv; Glendale Ed Assn, PSEA, NEA 1959-; Coalport Lions Club 1959-; *office:* Glendale Jr/Sr HS Flinton Rd Flinton PA 16640

BURNELL, GERALD WILLIAM, Asst Prin/Soc Studies Teacher; *b:* Portland, ME; *m:* Tricia May Wilson; *c:* Kyle, Craig; *ed:* (BS) Ed, Univ of ME Orono 1979; (MS) Educl Admin, Univ of ME Gorham 1986; *cr:* Soc Stud Teacher 1979-86, Teacher/Asst Prin 1986-88, Acting Prin 1988-89, Teacher/Asst Prin 1989- Marshwood Jr HS; *ai:* Athletic Dir; Assessment Center Chm; Yrbk Adv; Intramural; NAESP 1988-89; Little League Coach 1986-; *office:* Marshwood Jr HS Academy St South Berwick ME 03908

BURNETT, BARBARA BEARD, Science Teacher; *b:* Pine Bluff, AR; *m:* Ronnie Carol; *c:* Angela; *ed:* (BS) Bio, Univ of AR Monticello 1968; Working Towards Masters; *cr:* Teacher Woodlawn HS 1968-70, Lincoln HS 1970-72, Chapel Acad 1972-74, Joel E Barber Sch 1974-; *ai:* Yrbk Spon, Discipline, Salary, Career Ladder Committees; MO St Teachers Assn; *home:* 30 Whispering Oaks Lebanon MO 65536

BURNETT, BARRY CLINTON, Scndry Social Studies Teacher; *b:* Buffalo, NY; *ed:* (BS) Scndry Soc Stud, 1965, (MS) Scndry Soc Stud/Poly Sci, 1969 NYS Coll of Ed Buffalo; *cr:* Scndry Soc Stud Teacher La Salle Jr HS 1965-83, Gaskill Jr HS 1983-87; Assoc Professor Medaille Coll 1984-; Scndry Soc Stud Teacher La Salle Sr HS 1988-; *ai:* NYSTA, Niagara Falls Teachers Local 801 1965-; Grand Island Historical Society Pres 1964-66; Co-Author Article to Save Summer Retreat of Grover Cleveland; Local His Consultant & Journalist; *office:* La Salle Sr HS 1500 Military Rd Niagara Falls NY 14304

BURNETT, CASSIE WAGNON, Sixth Grade Teacher; *b:* Atlanta, GA; *m:* Irvin D.; *c:* Bryan, Brittany; *ed:* (BA) Elem Ed, Oglethorpe Univ 1971; (MS) Elem Ed, GA St Univ 1975; *cr:* 2nd/6th Grade Teacher DeKalb Sch System 1971-82; 6th Grade Teacher Greater Atlanta Chrstn 1982-; *ai:* Jr HS Joy Club Co-Spon; Greater Atlanta Chrstn Sch Teacher of Yr 1984; *office:* Greater Atlanta Chrstn Sch Indian Trl Rd Norcross GA 30071

BURNETT, DIANNE CREED, Math Teacher/Dept Chairperson; *b:* Winston-Salem, NC; *m:* Donald G.; *c:* Bradley A.; *ed:* (BS) Math, Longwood Coll 1969; *cr:* Teacher Woodrow Wilson Jr HS 1969-70, O T Bonner Jr HS 1971-; *ai:* Honor Society-Natl Jr; Yrbk; Personel Policies Comm; Prin Adv Comm; Staff Dev Comm; Math Dept Chairperson; NCTM 1972-; ABWA 1989-; *office:* O T Bonner Jr H S Apollo Ave Danville VA 24541

BURNETT, NANCY HANKS, Speech/English Teacher; *b:* Wilmington, NC; *m:* Gilbert H.; *ed:* (AA) Liberal Arts, Mt Aloysius Jr Coll 1966; (BA) Speech Comm, Carlow Coll 1968; Television/Radio Broadcasting Course; *cr:* Speech Teacher Slippery Rock Area HS 1969-70; Eng/Drama Teacher E Lyme HS 1970-71; Eng/Speech/Drama Teacher New Hanover HS 1972-; *ai:* Speech & Thespian Coach; Drama Adv; Dinner Theatre Dir; NC Teenage Princess Pageant; Miss New Hanover Pageant Coord; Delta Kappa Gamma 1985-; NC Speech Assn 1985-87; NHMH Volunteer 1985-; New Hanover Cty Bar Auxiliary 1975-87; VFW Awd of Service Annual Voice of Democracy Speech Contest 1986, 1987, 1989; *office:* New Hanover HS 1307 Market St Wilmington NC 28401

BURNETTE, ELLA BRADLEY, Third Grade Teacher; *b:* Kingstree, SC; *m:* Isaac Jr.; *c:* Etinnie O., Ethan O.; *ed:* (BS) Elem Ed, Morris Coll 1972; (MS) Elem Ed, IN Univ Northwest 1979; Rdng Endorsement K-12; *cr:* Teacher Holy Trinity Sch 1973-84, Ivy Tech Sch, Wagoner Elem Sch 1984-85, Gary Cmmty Schls 1985-; *ai:* Sunday Sch Teacher; Asst Supt Youth Division; Gary Educators for Christ; Rdng Cncl; *office:* Duncan Elem Sch 1110 W 21st Ave Gary IN 46404

BURNETTE, GAY E., Spanish Teacher; *b:* Americus, GA; *m:* Johnny M.; *c:* Lindsey, Chelsea; *ed:* (BA) Eng/Span, Univ of GA 1977; T4 GA Southwestern Univ 1977; Working Towards Masters; *cr:* Span Teacher Southland Acad; *ai:* Jr Class & Span Club Spon; AATSP 1988-; 1st United Meth Church Bible Sch Teacher; ZTA Alumna; Traveled to Spain 3 Times; ALFS & EF Cnslr; Civitan Essay Awd 2nd in Intnl Competition; *office:* Southland Acad PO Box 1127 Americus GA 31709

BURNETTE, JANICE BARNES, Fifth Grade Teacher; *b:* Franklin, NC; *m:* Roy Warren; *c:* Melvin, Anita, Karen; *ed:* (BSED) Mid Grades, 1973, (MAED) Mid Grades, 1974 W Carolina Univ; *cr:* Title I Rdng/Math Teacher E Franklin Elem 1973-74, Scotts Creek Elem 1974-82; 5th Grade Teacher Scotts Creek Elem 1982-; *ai:* Mid Grade Chorus; NCAE, NEA; Little Savannah Baptist Church (Teacher, Music Dir) 1981-; Tuckasegee Baptist Assn WMU Dir 1990; *office:* Scotts Creek Elem Sch Rt 1 Box 407 Sylva NC 28779

BURNETTE, LINDA ANDERSON, 7th Grade Lang Arts Teacher; *b:* Ellijay, GA; *m:* Tommy; *c:* Ty; *ed:* (AA) Reinhardt Coll 1975; (BS) Bus Ed, Univ of GA 1977; (MS) Mid Grad S Ed, North GA Coll 1984; *cr:* Teacher East Ellijay Elem 1979-87, Ellijay Mid Sch 1987-; Remedial Teacher Rdng/Study Skills 1988-89; *ai:* Steering Comm; GAE Secy 1979-90; Teacher of Yr Nom 1988 & 1989;Watkins Meth Church Childrens Comm; Bible Sch Teacher in Formal Support of Writing; Began Sch Mag for Gilmer Cty; *home:* Rt 2 Box 532 Talking Rock GA 30175

BURNETTE, TREASA ANN, Music Teacher; *b:* Joplin, MO; *m:* Gerald L.; *ed:* (BS) Elem Ed, MO SOuthern St Coll 1972; SouthWestern MO St Univ; *cr:* Teacher Geo Washington Carver Nursery Sch 1973-74; Migrant Tutor Exeter Sch 1974-75; Remedial Teacher 1975-78; Music Teacher 1978- SouthWest R-5 Sch; *ai:* MO St Teachers Assn 1974-; Southwest Cmmty Teachers Assn Building Rep 1988-; Music Educators 1989-; Natl Conference 1989-; *office:* Southwest R-5 Sch Highway 90 Washburn MO 65772

BURNHAM, BARBARA M., Math Teacher/Math Curr Dir; *b:* Philadelphia, PA; *m:* Lem; *c:* Shannon, Lewis, Kara; *ed:* (BS) Elem Ed, Temple Univ 1978; Elem Math Ed, Glassboro St Coll 89-; Working on MA in Ed Math; Participant Mc Sijp Elem Math Fellows Proj Glassboro St Coll 1989-; *cr:* Substitute Teacher Philadelphia Sch Dist 1978-80; Archdiocese of Philadelphia 78-80; Coord of Staffing Teacher Arthur Andersen & Co 1980-84; Teacher 1984-; Math Curr Dir 1985- Most Holy Reedemer Sch; *ai:* Math Counts Prgm St of NJ; Moderator Assn of Cath Stu Cncls 1985-; ASCD 1988-; NCTM 1987-; Assn of Cath Stu Cncls Mem 1987-; NCEA 1985-; Natl Ftbl Leag Wives Assn 1980-90; Natl Ftbl Leag Alumni Assn Better Half 1982-; St John Vianney Womens Club 1982-; *home:* 340 S Almonesson Rd Deptford NJ 08096

BURNHAM, BONNIE LEE MAYO, Latin Teacher; *b:* Richmond, VA; *m:* G. Andrew; *ed:* (BA) Latin, 1966, (MA) Classics, 1978 Coll of William & Mary; Univ of Richmond Summer Study Abroad 1967; Fr, George Mason Univ 1971; Span, VA Commonwealth Univ 1980-81, FL Atlantic Univ & Palm Beach Jr Coll 1982-84; *cr:* Latin Teacher Colonial Heights HS 1966-67; Latin/Eng Teacher Thorpe Jr HS 1967-68; Eng Teacher George Washington HS 1968-70, Osborn HS 1970-73; Eng/Latin Teacher/Foreign Lang Dept Head Varina HS 1973-81; Latin Professor Coll of William & Mary 1981; Latin/Eng Teacher St Josephs Sch 1982-83; Span Teacher Unity Sch 1983-84; Span/Latin Teacher Spanish River Cmmty HS 1984-86; Latin Teacher Stafford HS 1987-88, Fauquier HS 1988-; *ai:* Spon Jr Classical League Latin Club; VA Classical League, Amer Classical League, Eta Sigma Phi, Kappa Delta Pi 1966-; Beta Sigma Phi (Secy 1982-83) 1981-; Kappa Alpha Theta (Chaplain 1965-66) 1966-; Presbyn Church Asst Organist 1986-87; Pilot Eng/Latin Prgm Eastern Henrico Cty VA 1977-79; Selected to Teach Grad Course on Latin Teaching Method Coll of William & MARY; *office:* Fauquier HS 705 Waterloo Rd Warrenton VA 22186

BURNHAM, ELLEN EDWARDS, Retired Teacher; *b:* Burnsville, NC; *w:* Robert Adams (dec); *c:* Mary A. Mc Makin, Robert A. Jr., Elizabeth E. Lightbody, Frieda O. Younts; *ed:* (BS) Home Ec/Sci, Appalachian St Teachers Coll 1949; (MSED) Ed/Geology, Furman Univ 1973; Voc Ed Home Ec, Womens Coll Univ of NC; Earth Sci Inst; City Hospital, Winston Salem Dietetics; *cr:* Home Ec/Sci Teacher Oak Hill HS 1949-50; Dietetics Teacher Winston-Salem City Hospital 1950-51; Home Ec Teacher Glenn Alpine HS 1951-53; Home Ec/Sci Teacher Lake View HS 1953-57; Sci/Dept Chairperson Latla HS 1957-58; Sci Teacher Mc Normia Elem 1965-68; Earth Sci Teacher Hillcrest Jr & Mid HS 1968-89; *ai:* Retired Teachers of SC; *home:* 101 Poinsettia Dr Simpsonville SC 29681

BURNHAM, LYDA ALICE, English Teacher; *b:* Polkville, MS; *w:* Ralph R. Jr. (dec); *c:* Ralph III, Bruce; *ed:* (AA) Eng, Jones Jr Coll 1949; (BS) Eng, MS Southern 1952; *cr:* 4th Grade Teacher Martinville Elem Sch 1950-51; HS Eng Teacher Burns HS 1951-52, Morton HS 1952-58, Puckett HS 1959-; *ai:* Yrbk Adv; Sr Class Spon; Alpha Delta Kappa; Yrbk Dedication 1962, 1967, 1980; Yrbk Appreciation 1975, 1977; STAR Teacher 1982, 1984, 1986; *home:* PO Box 100 Puckett MS 39151

BURNISKI, THOMAS WILLIAM, JR., Social Studies Teacher; *b:* St Louis, MO; *c:* Teri, Tomi; *ed:* (BS) Scndry Ed, SE MO St Univ 1971; (MA) Admin, NE MO St Univ 1979; *cr:* Soc Stu/Span Instr Marion Cty R-II Sch 1974-80; Soc Stud Instr Hannibal HS 1980-81; Asst Prin/Span Instr Highland HS 1981-86; Soc Stud Instr Van-Far R-I HS 1986-; *ai:* Var Girls Bsktbl & Jr HS Track Coach; Mentor Teacher; Frosh Class & Government Club Spon; Honor Society; Select Comm Mem; *home:* 61 Sherwood Apt 57 Hannibal MO 63401

BURNS, BARBARA ANN, Mathematics Department Chair; *b:* Providence, RI; *ed:* (BS) Math Ed, RI Coll; (MED) Math Ed, Boston Univ; Math, Boston Coll 1959-60; Shell Merit Fellow Math, Cornell Univ 1962; Cmptrs Natl Sci Fnd, PA St 1972; *cr:* Math Teacher Hugh B Bain Jr HS 1960-62; Teacher/Coll Supvr 1962-65, Adjunct Instr RI Coll & Henry Barnard Laboratory Sch; Math Dept Chairperson Cranston HS E 1966-; Adjunct Math Instr Bryant Coll 1978-; *ai:* Task Force Curr Writing in Cranston; Math Team Coach 1967-71, 1979-84; RIMTA New England Math Assn, NCTM, MAA; *home:* 68 Briarbrook Dr Seekonk MA 02771

BURNS, BIRDIE BOYD, 4th Grade Teacher; *b:* Knoxville, TN; *c:* Natalie R.; *ed:* (BA) Eng/Ger, Knoxville Coll; Grad Work Univ of PA Philadelphia, Wayne St Univ, Univ of TN Knoxville; *cr:* Teacher Carver HS 1956-59; 4th Grade Substitute Teacher Highland Park Schls 1968-; *office:* Cortland Elem Sch 138 Cortland Highland Park MI 48203

BURNS, ELEANOR M., Third Grade Teacher; *b:* Philadelphia, PA; *ed:* Elem Ed, Philadelphia Normal Sch 1935; (BSED) Elem Ed, Temple Univ 1945; (MSED) Elem Ed, Univ of PA 1952; Courses Taken at Philadelphia Bd of Ed; *cr:* 1st-6th Grade Substitute Teacher Philadelphia Bd of Ed 1935-43; 2nd/4th Grade Teacher Mary C Wister Sch 1943-45; 4th Grade Teacher Potter-Thomas Sch 1945; 5th-6th Grade Teacher Sheridan Sch 1945-51; 2nd-3rd Grade Teacher Franklin Sch 1951-63; 2nd-4th Grade Teacher Fox Chase Sch 1963-87; *ai:* PTA, PSEA, NEA 1943-67; Rose Lindenbaum Awd 1980.

BURNS, ELIZABETH JAYNE, Communicative Skills Teacher; *b:* Dallas, TX; *ed:* (BS) Journalism, 1978, (MS) Curr/Supervision, 1986 OK St Univ; Working Towards EdD Curr & Supervision, OK St Univ; *cr:* Communicative Skills Teacher Haskell Mid Sch 1978-80; Missionary/Teacher Southern Baptist Foreign Mission Bd Taiwan 1980-82; Communicative Skills Teacher Haskell Mid Sch 1982-; *ai:* Natl Jr Honor Soc Adv; Teacher Assistance Team & Young Authors Conference Organizational Comm Chairperson; Effective Schls Trng Teacher & Presenter; Phi Delta Kappa, ASCD 1987-; NCTE 1983-; NEA, OK Ed Assn, Broken Arrow Educators Assn 1978-80, 1982-85; PTO 1978-; Broken Arrow Teacher of Yr Finalist 1990 & Educator of Month Awd 1986; OK Outstanding Educator Phoebe Apperson Hearst Awd 1986; Nom OK Gold Medal Excl in Teaching; *office:* Haskell Mid Sch 412 S 9th St Broken Arrow OK 74012

BURNS, HERMAN GENE, English Teacher; *b:* Alexandria, LA; *ed:* (BS) Eng Ed, Grambling Univ 1975; (MA) Eng Ed, IN Univ 1978; *cr:* Writing Clinic Dir TX Southern Univ 1978 81; Coord of 12th Grade Eng Sterling Sr HS 1983-; *ai:* Facilitator/Seminar Teaching the Reluctant Learner; NCTE 1982-; Alpha Phi Alpha 1974-, Plaque 1975; Certificate of Appreciation 1989.

BURNS, JO ANNE SMITH, Basic Skills Teacher; *b:* Spring Lake, NJ; *m:* Martin J. III; *c:* John M.; *ed:* (BS) Ed, Cabrini Coll 1969; *cr:* 2nd Grade Teacher 1969-80, 6th-8th Grade Lit/Writing/Composition Teacher 1980-86, 1st Grade Teacher 1986-89, K-8th Grade Basic Skills Teacher 1989- Belmar Elem; *ai:* NJ Ed Assn, NEA 1969-; Monmouth Cty Teacher of Yr 1986-87; Poetry Published; *office:* Belmar Elem Sch 1101 Main St Belmar NJ 07719

BURNS, JOANNA CRISP, Fourth Grade Teacher; *b:* Muskogee, OK; *c:* David H., Lisa A.; *ed:* (BS) Ed, OK Coll for Women 1957; Diploma in Piano Performance OK Coll for Women; Numerous Seminars & Wkshps; *cr:* 1st-6th Music/6th Grade Teacher Maysville Public Schls 1957-58; 4th-6th Grade Music/5th Grade Teacher Chickasha Public Schls 1958-59; 2nd/6th Grade/Music Teacher Norman Public Schls 1959-61; 3rd/5th Grade Teacher Midwest City Public Schls 1961-66; 4th Grade Teacher Norman Public Schls 1977-; *ai:* Drug Site Coord; OK Arts Inst Spon; Phi Delta Kappa 1988-89; PTA 1957-87; OEA, NEA 1957-87; Norman Music Club 1975-89; Norman Instrumental Music Parents Assn 1982-88; OK Youth Orch Parents Group 1982-88; Nominee OK Gold Medal Excl Teaching 1987-88; Provided Numerous Wkshps for Norman Teacher Center & Inservice Wkshps for Coopertive Learning; Mc Kinley Teacher of Yr 1984, 1988; Norman Transcript Survey 1987; Favorite Teacher; AIDS Advisory Cncl Mem; Cmmty-Wide Ad-Hoc Drug Commission Mem; *office:* Mc Kinley Elem Sch 728 S Flood Norman OK 73069

BURNS, LUCILLE MINNIFIELD, First Grade Teacher; *b:* Wedowee, AL; *m:* Virgil Lee; *c:* Nikki, Courdera; *ed:* (BS) Elem Ed, AL A&M Univ 1973; (MS) Elem Ed, 1976, (EDS) Elem Ed, 1985 Jacksonville St Univ; Counseling Trng; *cr:* Title I Math Teacher Wedowee Mid 1973-74; 1st Grade Teacher Woodland HS 1975-; *ai:* PR&R Commission AEA; NEA, AL Ed Assn 1973-; Randolph Cty Ed Pres 1990-; Randolph Ed Assn (Pres 1980-81, Secy 1987-88, Treas 1988-89); *home:* Rt 2 Box 47-A Wedowee AL 36278

BURNS, MARIE PARATORE, 8th Grade Language Art Teacher; *b:* Los Angeles, CA; *c:* Jeanne Burns-Haindel, Kathleen Burns Dombrowski; *ed:* (AA) Ed, Pasadena City Coll 1950; (BSED) Ed, Univ S CA 1952; (MA) Elem Teaching, CA St Univ Los Angeles; *cr:* Teacher El Monte Sch Dist 1952-57, Alhambra Sch Dist 1960-; *ai:* Stu Government & Yrbk Adv; Alhambra Teachers Assn (Elem Segment Dir 1972-75, Secy 1986-88); Amer Assn of Univ Women VP 1988-, Named Gift; Delta Kappa Gamma Corresponding Secy 1988-; Holy Angels Church Arcadia Parish Cncl 1989-; Garfield Sch Honorary Service Awd; *office:* Garfield Elem Sch 110 W Mc Lean St Alhambra CA 91801

BURNS, MARTIN BREADEN, 6th Grade Teacher; *b:* Englewood, NJ; *c:* Kelly, Jesse; *ed:* (AA) General, Ceicester Jr Coll 1966; (BA) His, Belnap Coll 1968; Teacher Cert Univ of NH; *cr:* 7th Grade Teacher St Johns Sch 1970-71; 6th Grade Teacher New Franklin 1971-; *office:* New Franklin Sch Dennet St Portsmouth NH 03801

BURNS, MARY CATHERINE, Mathematics/Physics Teacher; *b:* Bridgeport, CT; *ed:* (BA) Math, Hunter Coll 1966; (MALS) Math, Wesleyan Univ 1975; *cr:* Math/Physics Teacher Coyle & Cassidy HS 1965-; Math Dept Head 1979-; Cmptr Lab Dir 1983-; *ai:* Academic Bd Mem; Math Club & Mothers Club Moderator; Physics Olympics at C-C Organizer; NCEA; NSF Grants Physics at Univ of VT, Cmptrs & Related Math Univ of OK; *office:* Coyle & Cassidy HS Adams & Hamilton Sts Taunton MA 02780

BURNS, RICHARD P., Band/Choral Dir/Fine Art Chair; *b:* Cincinnati, OH; *ed:* (BME) Music Ed, Univ of KY 1985; (MME) Music Ed, Cumberland Coll 1990; *cr:* Instr KY Mountain Baptist Coll 1985-86; Band/Choral Dir Oneida Baptist Inst 1985-; *ai:* Fine Arts Chairperson; Sr Class Spon; Phi Mu Alpha Sinfonia Pres 1984-85; KY Music Educators Assn, Music Educators Natl Conference; Clay Cty Cmmty Chorus Dir 1987-; *office:* Oneida Baptist Inst PO Box 67 Oneida KY 40972

BURNS, ROBERT D., Physical Education Instructor; *b:* Clearfield, PA; *m:* Lisa M. Kizer; *ed:* (BS) Phys Ed/Health/Coaching, Penn St Univ 1979; Recertification Barry Univ; *cr:* Teacher/Coach Clearfield Area Mid Sch 1980-82, Glades Cntrl HS 1982-83, Pope John Paul HS 1983-89, Deerfield Beach HS 1989-; *ai:* Head Wrestling; Steering Comm & Host for FL St Wrestling Championships 1989-90, 1990-91, 1991-92; USA Wrestling (Mem, Coach) 1990; FL HS Activity Assn (Mem, Coach) 1982-; Palm Beach Cty Wrestling Coach of Yr 1982-83; *office:* Deerfield Beach HS 910 SW 15th St Deerfield Beach FL 33441

BURNS, ROBERT D., Mathematics Teacher; *b:* Mountain Home, AR; *m:* Carol J. Pittman; *ed:* (BA) Math, Oral Roberts Univ 1970; *cr:* Teacher Charles Page HS 1970-72, Ozark HS 1972-; *ai:* Cross Cntry Coach; *home:* Rt 1 Box 196-A Sparta MO 65753

BURNS, ROBERT WILLIAM, Biology Teacher; *b:* Frankfort, IN; *m:* Barbara Elaine Satlerwhite; *c:* Sean L., Stephen J.; *ed:* (BS) Bio, 1972, (MS) Marine Bio, 1974 Univ of SC; Coll of Fisheries, Univ of WA Seattle 1974-75; *cr:* Teacher E Wake HS 1975-; *ai:* Mentor Teacher; Dept Chm; Wake Cty Ed Fnd Teacher of Excl 1986; E Wake HS Teacher of Yr 1986; *office:* E Wake HS Rt 4 Box 254 Wendell NC 27591

BURNS, SARA ELAINE, Science & Government Teacher; *b:* Dublin, GA; *m:* James Mark; *c:* Anthony, Christopher; *ed:* (BA) Elem Ed, Tift Coll 1985; Grad Stud Mid Grades Ed, GA Southern Univ; *cr:* 8th Grade Teacher Montgomery Cty Jr HS 1985-; *ai:* Media & Curr Comm; Soc Stud & GA His Festival Chairperson; GA Sci Teachers 1985-; Page 1986-; Tarrytown Baptist Church (WMU-Prgm Chairperson, Pianist, Youth Dir); Daniel Baptist Associational Youth Leader; Teacher of Yr Awd 1987; *home:* Rt 2 Tarrytown GA 30470

BURNS, VICKI BARTLETT, 4th Grade Teacher; *b:* Indianapolis, IN; *c:* Casey, Andrea; *ed:* (BA) Sociology, Taylor Univ 1969; (MS) Ed, Butler Univ 1973; Marital Family Therapy Prgm, Butler Univ; *cr:* Elem Teacher Brownsburg Schls 1969-73, Avon Schls 1977-; *ai:* Assn of Grad Cnslr of Butler Univ Pres 1990-; Intnl Myomassethics Fed 1988-89; *home:* 6041 Winged Foot Ct Indianapolis IN 46254

BURNS, VIRGINIA ZIMMERMAN, Teacher; *b:* Hartford, CT; *c:* Howard Bidwell, Marybeth Bender, Susan Williams, Tracy Bidwell; *ed:* (BA) Psych, William Jewell Coll 1955; (MA) Early Chldhd Ed, E CT St Univ 1969; Courses at Trinity Coll, Colby Coll, Brown Univ; *cr:* Teacher Moosup Elem Sch 1967-; *ai:* Moosup News Compiler; Drop-Out Comm; Jump Rope for Heart; NEA, CEA, PEA (Treas 1986-87, Building Rep 1987-88); Early Chldhd Assn 1980-89; PTO; Baptist Fellowship (Choir Mem, Vacation Bible Sch Teacher, Jr Church Teacher) 1980-; EANE 1987-; *home:* Gates Rd Lebanon CT 06249

BURNSIDE, ANNE OWENS, Social Studies/English Teacher; *b:* Star City, AR; *m:* Robert; *ed:* (BA) Eng/His, Univ of AR Monticello 1959; Spec Ed, Global Stud, Rdng; *cr:* Teacher Gillette Schls 1959-61, Carlisle Schls 1961-72, Crownsville Hospital 1972-77, Kingsland Schls 1978-; *ai:* Stu Cncl; Sch Drama Dir; Stu Publications & Yrbk; Sr Class Adv; Chrldr Spon; AEA, NEA, CTA Pres 1979-80, 1989-; *home:* R 2 Box 296A Bearden AR 71720

BURNSIDE, MINNIE P., Mathematics Teacher; *b:* Stockdale, TX; *m:* William H.; *c:* Jeannine, Bill, Cheryl, Jonathan; *ed:* (AA) Long Beach City Coll 1969; (BSSE), John Brown Univ 1971; (MED), Univ of AR 1988; Summer Inst Cmptrs & Math, Univ of NH; *cr:* Math Teacher Decatur Public Schls 1971-72, Elmwood Jr HS 1972-80; Coll Algebra Teacher NW AR Comm Coll Ext 1981-82; Math Teacher Gentry HS 1980-; *ai:* NHS Spon; Hi-Q Team Tutor; Gifted & Talented Stus Faculty Adv; AR Cncl Math Teachers Exec Comm, NCTM 1972-; NW AR Cncl Teachers of Math Pres 1988-; Covenant Presbyn Church Pres Womens Organization 1986-; Concerned Women of America 1985-; Natl

Sci Fnd & AR Dept of Ed Grants; *office:* Gentry HS P O Box 159 Gentry AR 72734

BURPO, JOYCE SWARTZ, Business Education Dept Chair; *b:* Garden City, OK; *m:* Wes; *c:* Mark V., Dana; *ed:* (BS) Bus Ed, Northwestern St 1966; Voc Trng Certificate OK St Univ Stillwater; *cr:* Teacher 1967-82, COE Coord 1977-82 Sooner HS; Teacher/Dept Chairperson Bartlesville HS 1982-; *ai:* FBLA Adv; Positive Action Team; Jr Achievement Bd Mem; Academic Cncl; NBEA, OK Bus Ed Assn Mem 1967-; First Wesleyan Church 1980-; Teacher of Yr 1976-77; *office:* Bartlesville Public Schls 5900 SE Baylor Dr Bartlesville OK 74006

BURR, DAVID JACK, Chemistry/Physics Teacher; *b:* Monticello, UT; *m:* Cheri Lorraine Snow; *ed:* (BS) Phys Sci, S UT Univ 1985; (MED) Ed, UT St Univ 1989; *cr:* Chem/Physics Teacher Dixie HS 1985-; *ai:* Cross Cntry Track Head Coach; Elections & Eligibilities Comm Adv; Sci Club; Sci Fair Faculty Rep 1990; Washington Cty Ed Assn, UEA, NEA, NSTA, NAPT 1985-; Outstanding Chem Teacher of Yr Cntrl UT Chapter Amer Chemical Society 1988-89; *office:* Dixie HS 350 E 700 S Saint George UT 84770

BURR, ESTHER SAUNDERS, English Teacher; *b:* West Blocton, AL; *m:* Joe Kenneth; *c:* Kenneth Lamar; *ed:* (BS) Home Ec, AL a & M UNIV 1968, (MED) Scndry Ed, Univ of Montevallo 1976; *cr:* Teacher Bibb Cty Jr HS 1968-70, West Blocton HS 1970-; *ai:* Sr Class Spon; Annual Co-Spon; AL Ed Assn 1968-; Bibb Cty Ed Assn 1968-; NEA 1968-; *home:* Rt 2 Box 66-D West Blocton AL 35184

BURR, MARTHA ANN MORRIS, Teacher/Dean of Students; *b:* Detroit, MI; *m:* Ronald Stephen; *ed:* (BS) Eng, CA St Coll 1969; Ed Courses, Summer Wkshps; *cr:* Teacher 1969-89, Dean 1989- Canon-Mc Millan Mid Sch; *ai:* Spelling Bee, Lip-Sync Talent Show Spon; Attendance Discipline Dist, Negotiations Comm; CM Ed Assn (Secy 1972-84, Instructional Profession Duties Chairperson 1984-, Parliamentarian); Teacher of Yr 1988; Teacher in Focus 1986.

BURRELL, MICHAEL P., Social Studies Teacher; *b:* Pasadena, CA; *m:* Shel Ann Robinson; *c:* Lindsey, Kacia; *ed:* (AA) Soc Sci, Coll of Marin 1967; (BS) Soc Sci/His, CA Polytechnic St Univ 1969; Teaching Credential Phys Ed & Music Cal Poly Slo; *cr:* Eng Teacher Pacific Eng Lang Inst 1978-79; Basic Ed CA Mens Colony 1984; 7th/8th Grade Soc Stud Teacher Atascadero Jr HS 1972-; *ai:* Jr HS Bsktbl Coach 1988-89; HS Frosh/Soph Bsbl Coach 1979-81; Table Tennis Club Adv; Constitutional Rights Fnd His Day Coord; ADTA, CTE, NEA Building Rep; Natl & St Cncls for Soc Sci; San Luis Obispo Vocal Arts Ensemble (Performer, Singer) 1978-86; Cuesta Master Chorale (Performer, Singer) 1985-; S Poverty Law Center & Klanwatch Project Fr Horn Player 1972-; Mentor Teacher for Atas Unified Sch Dist Soc Stud 1986-88; Applied for the NASA Teacher in Space Prgm; *home:* 320 Indian Knob Rd San Luis Obispo CA 93401

BURRELL, REGINA HOLBROOK, 1st Grade Teacher; *b:* Atlanta, GA; *c:* Beth B. Begs, Leigh; *ed:* (BA) Psych La Grange Coll 1958; (MED) Early Chldhd West GA Coll 1981; *cr:* 1st Grade Teacher River Road Muscogee Cty 1958-61; Buchanan Haralson Cty 1961-62; Kndgtn 1st United Meth Church 1968-79; 1st Grade Teacher Buchanan Primary 1979-81; H a Jones Elem 1981-; *ai:* Literary Magazine Spon; 4-H Adult Adv; NEA 1958-61/1979-; NCTE 1984-; Intnl Rdng Assn 1985-; GA Cncl Teachers of Math 1985-; NEA Building Rep 1981-; NCTE 1983-; Cncl Teachers of Math 1985-; IRA 1987-; Alpha Delta Kappa 1988-90; Bremen City Sys Teacher of Yr 1985; *home:* PO Box 86 Bremen GA 30110

BURRELL, SARAH CURRY, Mathematics Teacher/Dept Chair; *b:* Clover, SC; *m:* Max Eugene; *c:* Jenny; *ed:* (BA) Math, Winthrop Coll 1975; Grad Work Winthrop Coll; *cr:* Math Teacher Clover HS 1975-; *ai:* Math Dept Chairperson; York City NCTM Task Force Comm; SAT Math Coord; Mu Alpha Theta Co-Adv; Catawba Region Math Cncl Secy 1989-; SCCTM, SCCSM.

BURRICHTER, LORENE E., 5th Grade Teacher; *b:* Bluffton, OH; *ed:* (BA) Elem Ed, Elmhurst Coll 1962; (MSED) Supervision of Rdng, N IL Univ 1969; *cr:* 4th Grade Teacher Bensenville IL 1962-66; Elem Teacher St Nicholas Sch 1966-67; 1st/2nd/4th Grade Teacher Aurora IL 1967-72; Rdng Specialist Carol Morgan Sch 1972-78; Rdng Specialist/5th Grade Teacher Oskaloosa IA 1978-; *office:* Garfield Elem Sch 227 South M Street Oskaloosa IA 52577

BURRILL, GAIL FRANCES, Mathematics Department Chair; *b:* Grand Forks, ND; *m:* John; *c:* John, Matthew; *ed:* (BS) Math, Marquette 1960; (MS) Math, Loyola 1963; Marquette Univ 1976-79; Carleton Coll 1981; Women in Engineering, MI Tech 1982; Woodrow Wilson Inst on Statistics 1984; *cr:* Math/Eng Teacher Pius XI HS 1960-62; Coll Algebra Teacher Loyola Univ 1963; Math Teacher/Dept Chair Whitnall HS 1964-; *ai:* Editorial Panel 1988-; Prin Investigator ASA/NCTM Joint Project on Statistics 1987-; Prof Teaching Standards Natl Bd Chairperson 1990; WI Math Cncl Coord; Amer Statistical Assn; NCTM Milwaukee Area Math Cncl; NCSM Task Force on Effecting Change Chairperson 1988-; Quantitive Literacy Project Grant 1987-; Rose-Hulman Inst of Technology Outstanding HS Teacher Awd 1987; Whos Who in Amer Algebra Essentials & Geometry 1984-87; *office:* Whitnall HS 5000 S 116th St Greenfield WI 53228

BURRIS, BETTY THOMPSON, 4th Grade Teacher; *b:* Snow Shoe, PA; *m:* Earl C.; *c:* Deborah Corio, Stephen E., Robert B.; *ed:* (BS) Elem Ed, Lock Haven St Teachers Coll 1943; Addl Studies PA St Univ Cert Scndry Eng; *cr:* 2nd Grade Teacher Bishop St Sch 1941; 1st-8th Grade Teacher Clark Sch 1943-44; 2nd Grade Teacher Bellefonte Elem 1947; Sub Teacher Bald Eagle Area 1950-65; S S/Eng Teacher Millersburg Union Sch Dist 1967-68; 4th Grade Teacher Lenkerville Elem 1968-; *ai:* PTO Bd; Chairperson Grandparents Day 1986; Alpha Sigma Tau Natl Sorority Lifetime Mem 1941-; 1st U M Church Trustee/Comms 1985-; *home:* 603 Lentz Ave Millersburg PA 17061

BURRIS, HOPE AINLEY, Kindergarten Teacher; *b:* Los Angeles, CA; *m:* John Warren; *c:* Melodee Burris Chapman, Carolyn Burris Hughes; *ed:* (BS) Home Ec, Whitworth Coll 1951; San Jose St 1952-53, SW Baptist Coll 1968, Fresno St Univ 1974; *cr:* 3rd Grade Teacher 1951-52, Kndgtn Teacher 1953-56 Orosi CA; Kndgtn Teacher Santa Maria CA 1956-57; 2nd Grade Teacher 1967, Kndgtn Teacher 1967-73 Stockton MO; Resource Teacher 1973-74, Teacher Learning Disability Class 1974-76, Kndgtn Teacher 1976- Woodlake CA; *ai:* PTA Teacher of Yr 1986; Staff F J White Learning Center Teacher of Yr 1988; Woodlake Teachers Assn (2nd VP, Treas, Negoiating Team, Mentor Selection Comm); Developed Kndgtn Prgm & 1st Kndgtn Teacher in Stockton MO Elem Sch Dist; *office:* F J White Learning Center 700 N Cypress Woodlake CA 93286

BURRIS, SUSAN MARY, 1st Grade Teacher; *b:* Sioux City, IA; *m:* Marvin A.; *c:* Rick, Dawn, Eric, Jill; *ed:* (BA) Elem Ed, 1966, (MS) Elem Admin, 1981 Washburn Univ; *cr:* 3rd Grade Teacher Gage Elem 1966-70; 1st/2nd Grade Teacher Linn Elem 1975-; *ai:* NEA, Delta Kappa Gamma, Topeka Whole Lang Assn; *office:* Linn Elem 200 E 40th Topeka KS 66609

BURROUGHS, JON PAUL, 8th Grade English Teacher; *b:* Indianapolis, IN; *m:* Ronda David; *ed:* (BA) Eng, 1972, (MA) Eng, 1976 Univ of Indianapolis; *cr:* Teacher Sch 44 1973-81, Edison Jr HS 1981-; *ai:* MGIP; Public Relations Club; Edison Day Team; IEA 1985-; IMSAC; Runner Up for Indianapolis Teacher of Yr 1988-89; Natl Starch Grant Winner 1989; Edison Jr HS Teacher of Yr 1988-89; 2 Textbooks Have Been PublisheD by IPS 1988-89; *office:* Edison Jr HS 777 S White River Pkwy W Dr Indianapolis IN 46221

BURROW, DAVID MICHAEL, Head Dept of Mathematics; *b:* Moline, IL; *ed:* (BA) Math/Span, Univ N IA 1983; Grad Stud in Ed/Cmptr Sci, Univ of IA & Univ of N IA; *cr:* Span Teacher 1983-86, Math Teacher 1984- Garrigan HS; Tutor IA Lakes Comm Coll 1989-; *ai:* Dir Individual Speech; Stu Adv; NCTM, IA Cncl Teachers of Math, Mathematical Assn of America, IA HS Speech Assn 1983-; 1st Congregational Church Comm Chm 1987-; Countryside Cmmty Playhouse 1989-; IA Democratic Party 1980-; Presentations at Prof Conferences; Evaluator N Cntrl Assn; Articles & Educl Software Published; *home:* 316 W North #1 Algona IA 50511

BURROW, JOHN RANDOLPH, English Dept Head Teacher; *b:* Victorville, CA; *m:* Janet Kay Norton; *ed:* (BS) Eng/Theater, IA Wesleyan Coll 1971; *cr:* Eng Teacher Ft Madison Cmmty Sr HS 1975-77; Eng/Speech/Drama Teacher Andrew Cmmty Sr HS 1977-; *ai:* Drama Dept Fall & Spring Plays Dir; Speech Coach; Thespian Adv; Radio Show Adv & Dir; Stus-At-Risk Comm Chm; ISEA, NEA, Local Asst Teachers Rights Comm 1977-; NCTE 1976-; Modern Lang Assn 1984-; Archaeological Inst of Amer 1973-; Peace Pipe Players Dir 1977-, Man of Yr 1982, 1984-85; Poetry Published 1976; All St Large Group Speech Events 1980, 1987-88, 1990; All St Individual Events Speech 1977-78, 1980-; *office:* Andrew Cmmty Sr HS PO Box 130 Calhoun St Andrew IA 52030

BURT, LOWELL RICHARD, Art Teacher and Art Dept Chair; *b:* Black River Falls, WI; *ed:* (BS) Art Ed, Univ WI Milwaukee 1965; Graduate Work, Univ of WI Milwaukee; *cr:* Art Teacher Mukwonago Area Sch Dist 1965-, Park View Jr HS/Mid Sch 1972-; *ai:* Scheduling Comm for Mid Level Sch Concept; Mid Level Ed Fair & Dist Art Displays & Shows Comm; WI Ed Assn 1965-; NEA 1965-; Natl/WI Art Ed Assn 1990; Mukwonago Ed Assn United Lakewood East 1990; Scndry Teacher Yr; Mukwonago Area Schls 1981-82; *office:* Parkview Mid Sch 930 N Rochester Mukwonago WI 53149

BURTON, DONNA WALKER, Social Studies Teacher; *b:* Dugway, UT; *m:* Larry Michael; *c:* Zachary, Bridgette, Benjamin; *ed:* (BS) His, 1980, (MS) His/Eng, 1985 Jacksonville St Univ; *cr:* Teacher Mellow Valley HS 1980-; *ai:* Sr Spon; NEA, AL Ed Assn 1980-; Blacks Chapel Womens Club Pres 1989-.

BURTON, DRENNA LEE (O'REILLY), Kindergarten Teacher; *b:* Advance, MO; *m:* Donald G.; *c:* Jennifer O'Reilly, Heather O'Reilly; *ed:* (BA) Elem Ed, Lambuth Coll 1970; (MA) Elem Ed, SEMO Univ 1984; *cr:* Med/Dental Asst Inst St Louis Bus Coll 1970; 1st Grade/Kndgtn Teacher Bell City R-2 Elem Sch 1971-74; 1st Grade Teacher 1974-81, Kndgtn Teacher 1981- Delta R-5 Elem Sch; *ai:* MO ST Teachers Assn 1971-; ACSO 1989; MO Assn of Rural Ed 1989-; Adjunct Faculty Coll of Ed Southeast MO ST Univ 1989-; Parents As First Teachers Adv Bd 1984-; PTO 1971-; Cmmty Teachers Assn 1971- Secy & VP; Whos Who in Amer Ed; *office:* Delta R-5 Elem Sch PO Box 219 Hwy N Delta MO 63744

BURTON, GREGORY ROBERT, Band Director; *b:* Camden, AR; *m:* Helen Jean Pope; *ed:* (BME) Music, Henderson St Univ 1981; *cr:* Band Dir Ashdown Jr HS 1981-82, Watson Chapel Jr HS 1982-84, Watson Chapel Sr HS 1982-; *ai:* Marching Band Dir; Concert Band Dir; AR Bandmasters Assn 1981-; Phi Beta Mu 1989-; Sch Band & Orch Assn (Region Chm 1986-87, Treas 1986-87), Sweepstakes Awd 1986-89; Volunteers in Public Schls Service Awd 1986-87; *office:* Watson Chapel Jr H S Rt 7 Box 500 Pine Bluff AR 71603

BURTON, LILLIAN STEPHENSON, Teacher; *b:* Holly Springs, MS; *m:* Grafton Jr.; *c:* Lamarcus, Kathedra; *ed:* (BS) Bio - Cum Laude, MS Ind Coll 1974; (MED) Sci Ed, 1978, Spec Ed ED Admin/Sup, 1989 Univ of MS; *cr:* Teacher Holly Springs Public Sch 1974-; *ai:* Emergency Medical Technician Marshall Cty Hospital 1982-84; NEA, MEA 1974-89; MS Prof Ed 1989-; *home:* PO Box 24 Holly Springs MS 38635

BURTON, SHARON SMITH, Fifth Grade Teacher; *b:* Alpine, TX; *m:* Frank W.; *c:* Justin M., Ryan N.; *ed:* (BS) Ed, 1972, (MED) Ed, 1974 Sul Ross Univ; Educl Mid Management & Admin Cert; *cr:* 5th Grade Teacher East Point Elem 1972-; *ai:* UIL Coach Spelling & Plain Writing; Grade Level Chairperson; Asst Cub Scout Den Leader; TX St Teachers Assn Faculty Rep 1972-; Ysleta Teachers Assn 1972-; Intnl Rdng Assn 1972-; Eastern Star 1975-; PTA 1972-; *office:* East Point Elem Sch 2400 Zanzibar Dr El Paso TX 79925

BURTON, SUSAN SCHOLLENBERGER, Social Studies Teacher; *b:* Columbus, GA; *m:* William S.; *c:* Rad, Megan, Whitney, Beau, Carson, Taylor; *ed:* (BA) Soc Stud, 1972, (MED) Ed, 1975 W GA Coll; *cr:* Teacher Red Bud Sch 1972-74, Ashworth Mid Sch 1974-85, Gordon Cntrl Complex 1985-; *ai:* Cheerleading Coord; Prof Assn of GA Educators; Calhoun-Gordon Cty Swim Team Pres 1986-89; Calhoun-Gordon Cty Wrestling Club Pres 1990; Teacher of Yr 1989; *office:* Gordon Cntrl Complex Sch 335 Warrior Path Calhoun GA 30701

BURTON, WILGUS, JR., Mathematics/Physics Dept Chm; *b:* Dayton, OH; *m:* Janet Louise Bickel; *ed:* (BS) Astronomy, OH St Univ 1979; E TX St Univ; *cr:* Teacher/Dept Head The Alexander Sch 1984-; Planetarium Educator The Sci Place 1985-; *ai:* Sci Club & Rocketry Club Spon; Amer Astronomical Society 1977-; NCTM, NSTA 1989-; TX Astronomical Society (Bd Mem 1983-84, Secy 1984-88); *office:* The Alexander Sch 409 International Pkwy Richardson TX 75081

BURTON, WILLIAM SPEIGHT, Social Studies Department Head; *b:* Marion, AL; *m:* Susan Schollenberger; *c:* Rad, Megan, Whitney, Beau, Carson, Taylor; *ed:* (AB) His/Ed, GA St Univ 1972; (MED) Ed/Soc Stud, West GA Coll 1975; Data Collector-GTEP Evaluator; *cr:* 6th and 7th Grade Soc Stud Teacher Red Bud Sch 1972-; 8th Grade Soc Stud Teacher Ashworth Mid Sch 1974-84; Gordon Cntrl 1984-; *ai:* PAGE Academic Bowl Coach 1989-; GAE 1972-75; PAGE 1983-; *office:* Gordon Central Complex 335 Warrior Path Calhoun GA 30701

BURTT, JAMES, Humanities Teacher; *b:* Freehold, NJ; *m:* Anne Dampman; *ed:* (BSED) Soc Stud, 1971; (MSED) Ed, 1974 Duquesne Univ; (Cert) Latin, 1986; Eng, 1987 La Salle Univ; Post Master Studies Univ of Pgh Ed; Wilkes-Barre Coll; Temple Univ; *cr:* Soc Stud Teacher Columbus Mid Sch 1976-77; Dynamic Springs Prep 1977-79; Springfield Sch Dist 1979-84; Humanities Teacher Bensalem Sch Dist 1984-; *ai:* Coaching Boys Bsktbl & Girls Sftbl; Future Problem Solving Team; PAGE 1984-; Finalist Teacher of the Yr 1987; Cncl for Exceptional Children 1985-; Democratic Party Committeemen 1978-87; Published Articles: Total Growth Dev; Dynamic Springs (A Wholeistic Approach to Ed); Wholeistic Ed; Split Brain Theory & Its Implictions in Teaching; Gov Fellowship in African Stud; *home:* 131 Maple Ave. Willow Grove PA 19090

BURZYNSKI, LOUKATTIE KROLL, Fifth Grade Classroom Teacher; *b:* Richards, TX; *m:* Eugene P.; *c:* Gerard, Leo, Alan, Brian, Anita; *ed:* (BAT) Elem Ed, Sam Houston St Univ 1971; *cr:* 5th Grade Teacher Anderson-Shiro Elem 1971-; *ai:* Career Ladder II; *home:* PO Box 323 Richards TX 77873

BUSALACCHI, PATRICE TAAFFE, Kndgtn Teacher/Grade Level Chm; *b:* St Louis, MO; *m:* Anthony; *c:* Tracy; *ed:* (BS) Elem Ed, 1974, (MA) Guidance/Counseling, 1977 Univ of MO St Louis; Elem Ed, SE MO St, Lincoln UnIv, NE MO St; *cr:* K/1st/4th-6th Grade Teacher Archdioces of St Louis 1964-74; K/2nd Grade Teacher Francis Howell Sch Dist 1974-; *ai:* Schls Hop-A-Thon Chm; Grade Level Chm; *office:* Fairmount Sch 1725 Thoele Rd Saint Peters MO 63376

BUSBEE, MARTHA MURPHY, English Teacher; *b:* Seymour, IN; *m:* Jerry D.; *c:* A. Loren, John D.; *ed:* (AA) Tyler Jr Coll 1973; (BS) Ed/Bio, 1982, (MA) Eng, 1987 Univ of TX Tyler; *cr:* ESL/GED Teacher Tyler Adult Ed Cooperative 1979-82; Eng Teacher Chapel Hill Jr HS 1982-84, Chapel Hill HS 1984-; Part Time Jr Coll Instr Tyler Jr Coll 1988-; Ed Consultant Region VII Ed Service Center 1990; *ai:* Jr HS Stu Cncl & TX Assn of Future Educators Past Spon; UIL Ready Writing Coach; Chapel Hill HS Eng Dept Head 1987-; Amer Assn of Univ Women 1982-, Grant for Innovation in Ed 1985; Delta Kappa Gamma (VP 1988-) 1986-; E TX Cncl Teachers of Eng (VP 1990) 1983-; ASCD 1983, 1989-; *home:* Rt 25 Box 950 Tyler TX 75707

BUSBY, GARY LLOYD, Asst Athletic Dir/Sci Teacher; *b:* Des Moines, IA; *m:* Janice Ann Carlson; *c:* Travis, Nicole; *ed:* (BS) Scndry Ed, 1971, (BS) Fisheries Wildlife Conservation, 1971, (MS) Guidance/Counseling Elem & Scndry, 1975 IA St Univ; Admin Cert Elem & Scndry Principalship Drake Univ 1987; *cr:* Rdng/Sci Teacher 1976-87, Sci Teacher 1972-, Quest/Sci Teacher/Asst Athletic Dir 1988-89, Asst Athletic Dir & Sci Teacher 1989- Johnston Sch Dist; *ai:* Sci Dept Chairperson; 8th Grade Team Leader; Concession Chairperson, Booster Club; PTO;

Busby City Youth & Young Adult Cnslr; Teacher Mentor Prgm; Sci & Health Camp Directorships, Stu at Risk & Intervention Team Prgms; Cheerleading Selection Comm; Asst Athletic Dir; Tour Dir for Washington DC Trip; Natl & Local Olympiads, Sci Fairs & Special Wkshps Comm; Teacher in Charge in Prin Absence; Discipline Review Bd; HS & Mid Schl Wrestling Coach; Track Coach; NEA Rep 1972-82/87/89-; IA St Ed Assn Delegate 1982; Johnston Ed Assn (Pres, VP, Negotiations, Building Rep, Membership Government Comm) 1972-82; IA Acad of Sci 1988-; NSTA 1988-89; Prof Educators of IA 1988; Fellowship of Christian Athletes Spon 1973-76/1989; Youth & Young Adult Cncl; Dallas Center-Grimes Booster Club; Sunday Sch Teacher; BSA Qualifer Nature Badge; Cub Scout Leader; Des Moines Area Church Deacon; Excl Sci Teaching Awd Nom 1990; Natl Alternate Dept Energy Summer Teacher Research Pgrm 1989; Finalist Presidential Awd of Excl in Sci & Math Teaching 1988-89; Drake Univ Stu Bd 1987; NASA Cert of Contribution 1986; Numerous Wrestling Trophies & Awds 1978-81; Nom IA Outstanding Sci Teacher 1980-89; IA Merit Employment Exam 1972; Dormitory VP, Intramural Sports Dir, Secy, Religious Chairperson 1969-71; IA St Univ Fisheries & Wildlife Club 1967-71; *office:* Johnston Mid Sch 6207 Nw 62nd Ave Johnston IA 50131

BUSCH, KAREN LEE (SCHMIDT), Mathematics Teacher; *b:* Greensburg, IN; *m:* Gregory Allen; *c:* Andrew, Michelle; *ed:* (BS) Math Ed, 1983; (MS) Scndry Ed, 1987 IN Univ; *cr:* Math Teacher Emmerich Manual HS 1983-; *ai:* Var Vlybl Coach; Sr Class Spon; Math Club Spon; Climate Comm for Effective Schls; Holiday Schlsp Comm; Alternative Options for Ed Comm; NEA/ISTA/IEA/IN Cncl of Teachers of Math 1988-; VFW Ladies Auxillary 1983-; St Marks Cath Church 1985-; Emmerich Manual HS Teacher of Yr 1989; Finalist for IPS Teacher of Yr 1989; Nom for Presidential Awd for Math 1980; Nom for Above and Beyond the Call of Duty 1989; *office:* Emmerich Manual H S 2405 Madison Ave Indianapolis IN 46225

BUSCH, PHOEBE WOOD, European His/German Teacher; *b:* Rochester, MN; *ed:* (BA) His, Macalester Coll 1964; (MA) European His, Univ of CO 1968; PhD Work in European His at Numerous Univs; *cr:* Teacher Edina-Morningside HS 1965-, Cherry Creek E Jr HS 1969-71, Cherry Creek HS 1971-74, Smoky Hill HS 1975-; *ai:* Model United Nations; Sch Accountability Comm; Cherry Creek Fed of Teachers Pres 1983-88; CO Teacher Awd 1985; Honorable Mention Governors Awd Of Excl 1985, CO Teacher Of Yr 1986; Developed, Promoted Educl Prgms In Commtys; *office:* Smoky Hill HS 16100 E Smoky Hill Rd Aurora CO 80015

BUSCHMANN, JUDITH D'AMICO, Eng Teacher/Writing Lab Dir; *b:* St Louis, MO; *m:* Robert E.; *c:* Robert N.; *ed:* (BS) Ed/Eng, Univ of MO St Louis; (MA) Media Comm, Webster Univ 1980; Gateway Writing Project Fellow; *cr:* Teacher Lafayette HS 1977-; *ai:* Honor Society Spon; Sr Academic Coach Project; NCTE, Learning Initiatives; *office:* Lafayette HS 17050 Clayton Rd Ballwin MO 63011

BUSH, ARALESSA DAVIS, 3rd Grade Teacher; *b:* Mc Keesport, PA; *m:* Joseph J.; *ed:* (BA) Elem Ed, Wilberforce Univ 1964; *cr:* 3rd Grade Teacher John F Kennedy Elem Sch 1964-84; Duquesne Elem Sch 1985-; *ai:* Duquesne Ed Assn Bldg Rep 1964-65.

BUSH, CAROLE SCOTT, English/Humanities Teacher; *b:* Harrisburg, PA; *m:* Jerry O.; *c:* Alexander; *ed:* (BA) Eng/Scndry Ed, Seton Hill Coll 1975; Capital Area Writing Project PA St Univ 1981; Process Writing & Writing Across the Curr; *cr:* Eng Teacher York Cath HS 1975-76; Lang Art Teacher SS Simon & Jude Sch 1977-78, Holy Name of Jesus Sch 1979-81; Eng/Hum Teacher Bishop Mc Devitt HS 19985-; *ai:* NHS Chairperson; Christian Service Club Asst Chairperson; Mid-Semester & Finals Exam Comm; NCTE, PA Cncl Teachers of Eng, NCEA; Latshmere Manor Civic Assn Secy 1987-88; WITF Public Television 1979-; Teacher of Yr 1989; Bishop Mc Devitt Prin Awd; Published K-8th Grades Annotated Bibliography of Childrens Lit 1982; *office:* Bishop Mc Devitt HS 2200 King Blvd Harrisburg PA 17103

BUSH, GWYN FLEMING, Teacher/Science Dept Chair; *b:* San Francisco, CA; *c:* Lori, John; *ed:* (BA) Zoology, 1965, (MED) Sci Ed, 1978 Univ of Cincinnati; Family Life Ed; Drug Alcohol Ed & Intervention; *cr:* Sci/Health Jr HS Teacher Guardian Angels Sch 1979-85; Sci Teacher Mc Nicholas HS 1985-; *ai:* Stu Cncl & SADD Moderator; PTA Faculty Rep; Care Team Coord; Advisory Cncl; NABT, NSTA, PHI BETA KAPPA 1979- OH Acad of Sci; Delta Delta Delta; PTA Faculty Rep; Governors Awd for Outstanding Sci Ed 1989; *office:* Mc Nicholas HS 6536 Beechmont Ave Cincinnati OH 45230

BUSH, HELEN M., Elementary Montessori Teacher; *b:* Hoboken, NJ; *w:* Edward S. (dec); *c:* Ned, Marilyn Bush Huevel, Betty B. Brown, Peter; *ed:* (BS) Ed, Butler Univ 1959; Certificate Montclair St Normal Sch; Orton Slingerland Gillingham Method for Lang Disability Children Dyslexia; *cr:* 1st-6th Grade Teacher 1933; Teacher of Mentally Retarded 1959-68; Teacher of Perceptually Handicapped/Brain Injured Taylor Fnd 1969-73; Directress Montessori Sch 1974-; *ai:* Character Research Project 1959; *office:* Countryside Learning Center P O Box 3030 Anderson IN 46012

BUSH, JUDY BANKS, English Teacher; *b:* Tullahoma, TN; *m:* Dennie E.; *c:* Kent E.; *ed:* (BS) Sociology/Eng, 1970, (MED) Admin/Supervision, 1980 Mid TN St Univ; *cr:* Eng Teacher 1970-73, Librarian 1974-75, Eng Teacher 1975-83 Coffee Cty Jr HS; Librarian E Coffee & N Coffee & New Union Elem Schls 1983-84, N Coffee & New Union & Jones Elem Schls 1984-85; Eng Teacher Cntrl HS 1985-; *ai:* Yrbk Adv; NCTE 1985-; Coffee Cty Ed Assn Secy 1971-72; TN Ed Assn, NEA 1970-; Delta Kappa Gamma 1989-; *office:* Central HS 2001 Mc Arthur Dr Manchester TN 37355

BUSHART, DEBRA WYATT, English Teacher; *b:* Lexington, KY; *m:* William Maxwell; *c:* Whitney, Blaire; *ed:* (BA) Eng/Bus Ed; (MA) Guidance/Counseling; Bus Voc Cert; Writing Wkshp; *cr:* Eng Teacher 1982-83, Sci/Math Teacher 1983-86 N Marshall Mid Sch; Eng Teacher Marshall Cty HS 1986-; *ai:* Chrldr Coach; NCTE, KY Ed Assn, Marshall Cty Ed Assn; St of KY Inservice Teacher; Article Published; *home:* Rt 1 Box 347-A Gilbertsville KY 42044

BUSHER, JANICE J., English Teacher/Dept Chair; *b:* Ravenna, OH; *ed:* (BS) Sociology, 1969, (BA) Scndry Ed/Eng, 1973, (MA) Eng, 1979 Kent St Univ; Numerous Conferences; *cr:* Eng Teacher Immaculate Conception 1970-73; Rdng Teacher 1973-76, Eng Teacher 1976-83 Brown Mid Sch; Eng Teacher 1983-, Eng Dept Chairperson 1987- Ravenna HS; *ai:* Curr & Admin Evaluation Comm; OCTELA, NCTE 1980-; CSSEDC 1987-; REA, OEA, NEA; PPIC Incorporated 1980-89, Valuable Service Awd 1984; Martha Holden Jennings Scholar 1988-; Grantwriter JTPA Summer Sch Remedial Prgm 1980- & Career Ed Prgm 1985-; Nom Teacher of Yr 1988-89, 1989-; *office:* Ravenna HS 345 E Main St Ravenna OH 44266

BUSHEY, LINDA K., 6th Grade Teacher; *b:* Gettysburg, PA; *m:* Joseph F. X.; *c:* Benjamin Pitzer, Rebecca Pitzer; *ed:* (BS) Ed, Cntrl Meth Coll 1968; (MS) Ed, Shippensburg St Coll 1971; *cr:* 1st Grade Teacher 1968-72, 5th Grade Teacher 1980-82 Biglerville Elem Sch; 5th Grade Teacher 1982-83, 6th Grade Teacher 1983- Arendtsville Elem Sch; *ai:* Cmptr Ed, Sci Curr, Study Skills, Amer Ed Week Comms; Peer Coaching Seminar; PSEA 1983-; Band Booster Club 1989-; Church Cncl Missionary Chm 1989-; Old Sch Preservation Comm Chm 1987-; *home:* PO Box 597 Arendtsville PA 17303

BUSHING, ARTHUR BROWN, 5th-8th Grade History Teacher; *b:* Kenosha, WI; *ed:* (BA) His, Univ WI Parkside 1975; *cr:* Teacher Brighton Elem Sch 1970-; *ai:* His Club; 4-H Project Leader 1948-68; *home:* 25000 103rd St Salem WI 53168

BUSHMAN, CONSTANCE BAUER, Bus Education Teacher/Chair; *b:* Eau Claire, WI; *m:* Steven; *c:* Brett, Matthew; *ed:* (BS) Comp Bus Ed, Univ of WI Eau Claire 1976; Numerous Grad Courses & Wkshps in Bus Ed, Classroom Management, Univ of WI; *cr:* Bus Ed Instr/Dept Chairperson Greenwood HS 1976-; Adult Ed Instr Chippewa Valley Tech Coll 1978-; *ai:* Adv FBLA, Sch Newspaper, Frosh Class; Bus World Coord; Mem of NHS Faculty Advisory Cncl; Mem Voc Curr, Cmptr Ed Curr Comm; NBEA, North Cntrl Bus Ed Assn, WI Bus Ed Assn Mem 1975-; FBLA, Phi Beta Lambda Prof, WI FBLA Alumni Mem 1976-; WI FBLA St Exec Bd 1983-84, 1988-89; NEA, WI Ed Assn Mem 1976; Greenwood Ed Assn (Secy 1980-81, Treas 1983--84, Public Relations Comm Mem 1985-, Chairperson 1986-87, 1989-, Mem 1976-) Greenwood Chamber of Commerce Exec Bd (Mem, Treas 1988) 1985-88; Greenwood Area Economic Dev Assn (Mem, Secy 1985, 1986) 1985-; St Anns Society Treas 1986, 1987; St Marys Pastoral Cncl 1986, 1987; St Marys Family Life Comm Mem 1986-; *office:* Greenwood HS 209 S Hendren St Greenwood WI 54437

BUSKER, JEAN A., Choral Music Director; *b:* Sac City, IA; *m:* James; *ed:* (BME) Music Ed, Morningside Coll 1981; Grad Stud; *cr:* Music Teacher Le Mars Cmmty Sch 1981-82; Asst Band Dir 1983-86, Choral Dir 1986- Sioux City E Mid Sch; *ai:* 6th-8th Grade Choruses & Swing Choirs; Talent Show & Spring Musical Dir; NW IA Choral Dir Jr HS Rep 1989-; IA Choral Dir Co-Chm, Opus Jr HS Honor Choir 1990; Music Ed Natl Conference 1978-; NEA 1983-; First Chrstn Church Organist & Choral Dir; Guest Dir Jr HS Choral Festivals; *office:* Sioux City East Mid Sch 1720 Morningside Ave Sioux City IA 51106

BUSKO, SARAH WATSON, Second Grade Teacher; *b:* Dillon, SC; *m:* Robert Wayne; *c:* Sallie, Robyn; *ed:* (AA) Peace Coll 1968; (BA) Ed, St Andrews 1970; (MA) Primary Ed, Appalachian 1975; *cr:* 4th Grade Teacher Newport Elem 1970-71; 2nd/3rd Grade Teacher Ashpole Center 1971-73; 1st-3rd Grade Teacher E Harper 1974-76; 3rd Grade Teacher Edneyville Primary 1977-78; 1st-4th Grade Teacher Washington Park Sch 1978-; *ai:* Lang Art Lead Teacher; Lib Comm; NCAE 1970-89; NCAE Head of Budget Comm 1988-89; Terry Sandford Awd Nom Washington Park 1989-; *home:* 12581 Blue Dr Laurinburg NC 28352

BUSS, EILEEN CHAPMAN, 5th-6th Teacher; *b:* Hanover, IL; *m:* Herbert E.; *c:* Mark D. *ed:* (BS) Elem Ed, Univ of Wi Platteville 1956; (MED) Elem Ed, Univ of NE Lincoln 1968; *cr:* 5th Grade Teacher Barnesville MN 1958-59; 5th-6th Grade Teacher Pershing Elem 1960-; *ai:* Lincoln Ed Assn (Treas 1970-71, Membership 1960-); NE Teachers of Math Treas 1973-74; Team Leader; *home:* 3045 N 60th Lincoln NE 68507

BUSS, ROBERT ALLEN, Mathematics Teacher; *b:* Kalamazoo, MI; *m:* Katherine Myrna Wedge; *c:* Robert, Rebecca; *ed:* (AB) Philosophy, Kalamazoo Coll 1963; (MDIV) Divinity, Seabury-Western 1966; (BED) Math, Dickinson St Coll 1985; *cr:* Priest St Andrews Episcopal Church 1966-74, St Johns Episcopal Church 1974-86; Teacher Austin HS 1986-; *ai:* Published Articles; *office:* Austin HS 3500 Memphis St El Paso TX 79930

BUSSELL, MERRI L., Special Education Teacher; *b:* Bremerton, WA; *m:* Arthur; *c:* Jakob, Breayn; *ed:* (BAED) Child Psych/Early Chldhd Ed, W WA Univ 1974; Post Grad Work E WA Univ; *cr:* Dir/Teacher URRD Prgm Touchet Schls 1974-76; Kndgtn Teacher 1976-78, Spec Ed/Basic Ed Teacher 1978- Touchet Sch; *ai:* Class Adv; Jr HS Vlybl Coach; Dist Test Coord; CEC VP 1986; Intnl Rdng Assn 1985-; *office:* Touchet Sch PO Box 1135 Touchet WA 99360

BUSTEED, PATRICK LEE, Geography/Psych/Cmptr Teacher; *b:* Craig, CO; *m:* Robin Kathryn Pino; *c:* Shawn M., Christopher L.; *ed:* (BA) Soc Stud, 1980, (MS) Ed, 1988 CO St Univ; *cr:* Cmptr Technician CO St Univ 1977-79; Teacher Holly HS 1980-85, Sterling HS 1985-; *ai:* Head Ftbl & Track Coach; CO HS Coaches Assn 1981-; *office:* Sterling HS W Broadway Sterling CO 80751

BUTCHER, FRANCES MC KEE, First Grade Teacher; *b:* Raleigh, NC; *ed:* (BA) Elem Ed, St Augustines Coll 1957; (MS) Elem Ed, IN St Univ 1968; Gifted & Talented Endorsement K-12, Purdue Univ; *cr:* Teacher Banneker Achievement Center 1957-; *ai:* United Negro Coll Fund, Building Rep; ACEI (Building Rep, Sci Comm); AFT Building Comm 1957-; Natl Alliance Black Sch Educators 1990; NEA Building Rep 1977-; IN St Teachers Assn Building Rep 1977-; Gary Rdng Cncl; Banneker PTA VP 1977; St Augustines Alumni Assn; Behavioral Merit Awd 1971; Master Teacher Selected by Research Laboratories; Natl Registration Center Study Abroad Quernavoca Mexico; Supvr Summer Rdng Prgm Parent Awd; *home:* 1584 Hendricks St Gary IN 46404

BUTCHER, LINDA HODNETT, 9th Grade English Teacher; *b:* New Bern, NC; *c:* Krisann, Ryan; *ed:* (BS) Eng, E Carolina Univ 1972; *cr:* 8th/9th Grade Eng Teacher Elizabeth City Jr HS 1986-87; 9th Grade Eng Teacher Northeastern HS 1987-; *office:* Northeastern HS Oak Stump Rd Elizabeth City NC 27909

BUTCHER, MARIAN VIVIAN, Business Education Teacher; *b:* Linton, IN; *m:* Marc Wayne; *ed:* (BA) Bus Ed, Drake Univ 1975; *cr:* Bus Ed ACL Cmmty Sch 1976-79, Martensdale-St Marys Cmmty Sch 1979-; *ai:* NEA, ISEA 1978-; IBEA 1989; *office:* Martensdale-St Marys HS 390 Burlington Martensdale IA 50160

BUTCHER, PAMELA SUE (BUSH), 4th Grade Teacher; *b:* Weston, WV; *m:* Larry; *c:* Shannon B., Juliea E.; *ed:* (BA) Elem Ed/Mental Retardation, Glenville St 1976; *cr:* Spec Ed Teacher 1976-77, Resource Room Teacher 1977-78 Normantown Elem; Elem Teacher Troy Elem 1978-; *office:* Troy Elem Schl Troy Elem Sch Troy WV 26443

BUTEYN, MAUREEN CHERYL, Fourth Grade Teacher; *b:* Waupun, WI; *ed:* Elem Ed, Dodge Cty Teachers 1962; (BA) Elem Ed, Univ of WI Oshkosh 1967; *cr:* 4th Grade Teacher Somers Elem 1962-63; 3rd Grade Teacher Theresa Elem 1963-65; 4th & 5th Grade Teacher Alto Elem 1965-; *ai:* Elem Vlybl & Bsktbl Coach; Dev Rdng Comm; Rdng Intent Comm; WI Ed Assn 1962-; Waupun Ed Assn Exec Comm 1986-; WI St Rdng Assn 1984-; Womens Intnl Bowling Congress 1987-; 1st Reformed Church 1958-; Outstanding Young Women of America Awd 1969; *office:* Alto Elem Sch N3516 Cty Tk Ee Waupun WI 53963

BUTH, WILLIAM DONALD (DEX), Physical Education Instructor; *b:* Shawano, WI; *m:* Susan Lynne Maresch; *c:* Debbie Daneils, Kathy Backes, Besty, Isobel; *ed:* (BS) Bio/Phys Ed, St Norbert Coll 1961; (MEPD) Health/Phys Ed, Univ of WI Whitewater 1990; US Navy Hospital Corpsman; 1st Aid & CPR Instr; *cr:* Teacher/Coach Francis Jordan HS 1961-69, W Allis Cntrl HS 1969-; *ai:* Head Girls Bsktbl; Jr Var Boys Vlybl; Photo Adv; WAMAGO II Adv; WAHPERS; WI Heart Assn; Jaycees; *office:* W Allis Cntrl HS 8516 W Lincoln Ave West Allis WI 53227

BUTKOVICH, JEAN LANIGAN, 5th-6th Grade Teacher; *b:* Cle Elum, WA; *m:* John M.; *c:* Ben, Lisa Browitt, Marty; *ed:* (BA) Lang Art Ed, 1979, (MA) Rdng/Ed, 1982 Cntrl WA Univ; Grad Work for Masters Gifted Ed; *cr:* 5th/6th Grade/Enrichment Teacher Thorp Schls 1979-; *ai:* His Day Coach; WA St Bd Natl His Day Contest Chm; NEA, WEA; WA Cncl for Soc Stud 1985-; Local Union of Teachers Secy; Immaculate Conception Church Organist 1979-; PEO Womens Club; Young Ladies Inst 1988-; *office:* Thorp Schls Box 155 Thorp WA 98946

BUTLAND, BELINDA BUCHLI, Teacher Learning Disabilities; *b:* Rockford, IL; *m:* Albert Wayne; *c:* Becky, Ronny; *ed:* (BS) Ed/Ec, Auburn Univ 1974; (MED) Learning Disabilities, Auburn Univ 1982; (MED) Guidance/Counseling, Troy St Univ 1990; *cr:* Teacher of Learning Disabilities Robert E Lee HS 1982-; *ai:* People Helping People Club Spon 1982-89; CEC 1988-; Assn for Children With Learning Disabilities 1982-; Lee HS Spec Ed Teacher of Yr Awd 1987-88, 1988-89; *office:* Lee HS 225 Ann St Montgomery AL 36107

BUTLER, ANN POLLARD, Pre-School Teacher; *m:* William J. Sr.; *c:* Deborah Butler Clemons, William J. Jr.; *ed:* Early Chldhd, Univ of MD; Child Dev Assoc Pre-Sch 1982, Toddlers 1990; *cr:* Homebase Teacher 1973-79, Asst Teacher 1979-80, Teacher 1980- St Veronicas Head Start; *ai:* PTA Secy 1975-80; *office:* St Veronicas Head Start 2920 Joseph Ave Baltimore MD 21225

BUTLER, BRAD WILLIAM, Science Department Chairperson; *b:* Kansas City, KS; *m:* Nancy Click; *ed:* (AA) General Stud, Cisco Jr Coll 1984; (BED) Composite Sci-Bio Empha Sis, Hardin-Simmons Univ 1987; *cr:* Phys Sci Teacher Watauga Jr HS 1987-88; Life/Earth Sci Teacher 1989-, Sci Dept Chm 1988- Watauga Mid Sch; *ai:* Campus at Risk Comm; Stu Cncl Spon;

Assn of TX Prof Educators 1987-; *office:* Watauga Mid Sch 6300 Maurie Dr Watauga TX 76148

BUTLER, CAROLYN KELLY, 4th/5th Alternative Ed Teacher; *b:* Tallahassee, FL; *c:* Charlene, Michael; *ed:* (BS) Elem Ed, FAMU 1974; Cert Rdng & Early Chldhd Ed; *cr:* Kndgtn-5th Grade Teacher Apalachee & Wesson Elem 1974-85; Rdng/4th-5th Grade Alternative Ed Teacher Apalachee Elem 1985-; *ai:* Sci Coord & Mentor; *office:* Apalachee Elem Sch 650 Trojan Trl Tallahassee FL 32301

BUTLER, CATHY LOUISE BROWN, Honors Science Teacher; *b:* Ashland, KY; *m:* Larry; *c:* Ginny, Jon, Brittany, Bradley; *ed:* (BS) Broad Field Sci, E TX St Univ 1974; Admin Ed, N TX St Univ; *cr:* Phys Sci Teacher Comstock Jr HS 1974-75; Life Sci Teacher Yukon Jr HS 1975, Yukon Mid Sch 1976-84; Chem/Phys Sci Teacher Mansfield HS 1986-; *ai:* Natural Helpers Active Mem; Cheerleading & Stu Cncl Spon; ATPE; Yukon Mid Sch Teacher of Yr; Favorite Teacher of Yr; *office:* Mansfield HS 1520 N Walnut Creek Dr Mansfield TX 76063

BUTLER, CHARLOTTE C., 8th Grade Soc Stud Teacher; *b:* Gloversville, NY; *m:* George Francis III; *ed:* (BA) His, Skidmore Coll 1967; Working Towards Masters in Ed Boston Univ; *cr:* 9th/11th Grade His Teacher Northville Cntrl Sch 1967-69; 10th-11th Grade His Teacher Tenney HS 1969-70; Soc Stud Teacher Woodbury Sch 1970-; *ai:* Stu Cncl Adv; Report & Progress Report Revision Comm Mem; Magazine Fund Drive, Sch Dist Strategic Planning, Elem Sch Recognition Prgm Comms; Nom for Excl in Teaching 1990; NH Cncl for Soc Stud Dept of Ed 1990; *office:* Woodbury Sch Main St Salem NH 03079

BUTLER, DEBORAH DOLMOVICH, Counselor; *b:* Kittanning, PA; *m:* Robert Harold; *ed:* (BS) Health/Phys Ed, Indiana Univ of PA 1972; (MA) Guidance/Counseling, Tulsa Univ 1976; Developing Capable Young People; Chemical Dependency Trng; *cr:* Phys Ed Teacher Westside Jr HS 1972, Northview Elem 1973-74; Cnslr Verdigris Public Sch 1976-; *ai:* Peer Asst Leaders, Just Say No Club Spon; OK Assn of Counseling & Dev 1976-, OK Elem Cnslr of Yr 1990; Amer Assn of Counseling Dev 1978-; Natl Peer Helpers Assn 1988-; OK Ed Assn, NEA 1976-82, 1989-; Verdigris Teacher of Yr 1981-82 1986-87; *office:* Verdigris Public Sch 6101 SW Verdigris Rd Claremore OK 74017

BUTLER, DEBORAH FOX, Teacher of Gifted/Talented; *b:* Corpus Christi, TX; *m:* Jim R.; *c:* Lorette, Joseph R.; *ed:* (BS) Elem Ed, TX A&I Univ 1973; Grad Work; *cr:* 4th Grade Teacher Harlingen Ind Sch Dist 1973-77; 2nd-5th Grade Teacher Taft Ind Sch Dist 1977-78, Odem Ind Sch Dist 1978-; *ai:* NEA Pres 1988-89; TX St Teachers Assn Membership 1973-.

BUTLER, DEBORAH LONG, Kindergarten Teacher; *b:* Russellville, AL; *m:* Stephen Thomas; *c:* Scott, Amy; *ed:* (BS) Early Chldhd Ed, 1975, (BS) Elem Ed, 1975 Univ N AL; *cr:* 1st Grade Teacher Mt Hope Sch 1975-77; Kndgtn Teacher Rockwood Elem 1977-78, Mt Hope Sch 1978-81; 4th Grade Teacher Mt Hope Sch 1981-85; 5th Grade Teacher Bear Elem 1985-86; Kndgtn Teacher Mt Hope Sch 1989-; *ai:* AL Ed Assn, NEA, Lawrence Cty Ed Assn; PTO; *home:* 201 Laurel Oak Dr Muscle Shoals AL 35661

BUTLER, GLORIA FAY, Fourth Grade Teacher; *b:* Alexandria, VA; *ed:* (BS) Ed, James Madison Univ 1970; (MED) Admin & Supervision, Univ of VA 1977; *cr:* 1st-5th Grade Teacher Dale City Elem 1970-; *ai:* 4th Grade Level Chairperson; Phi Delta Kappa Mem 1984-; Prince William Ed Assn, VA Ed Assn, NEA Mem 1970-; PTO Teacher Rep; *office:* Dale City Elem Sch 14450 N Brook Dr Woodbridge VA 22193

BUTLER, JANE KING, 8th-12th Grade English Teacher; *b:* Portsmouth, VA; *m:* Alfred Rawls IV; *c:* Alfred R. V, Charles A.; *ed:* (BA) Eng, Old Dominion Univ 1984; *cr:* 8th Grade Rdng/Lang Art Teacher Southwestern Intermediate 1985-; 10th/12th Grade Eng Teacher Lakeland HS 1990; *ai:* Newspaper Club & Soph Class Spon; Newsletter; Writing Across the Curr Chm; VA Mid Sch Assn, Suffolk Rdng Cncl 1985-; *home:* Rt 1 Box 5 Carrsville VA 23315

BUTLER, JOANN MC CORMIC, Fourth Grade Teacher; *b:* Saint Pauls, NC; *m:* Julian David Sr.; *c:* Julian D. Jr., Larinda J.; *ed:* (BS) Elem Ed, E Carolina Univ 1958; *cr:* 4th/5th Grade Teacher Saint Pauls City Schls 1958-65; 5th Grade Teacher Seventy First Elem 1965-67; 4th/6th Grade Teacher Robeson Cntry Day Sch 1972-77; 4th Grade Teacher Scurlock Elem 1977-; *ai:* NCAE 1958-67, 1977-; Natl Rdng Teachers Assn 1980-83; BSA Den Mother 1976-79; Raeford Presbyn Church 1990; *office:* Scurlock Sch/Hoke Cty Rt 2 Box 505 Raeford NC 28376

BUTLER, JOE L., English Teacher; *b:* Mart, TX; *ed:* (BME) Music Ed, Baylor Univ 1959; Post Grad Stud Eng, Baylor Univ 1973-75; *cr:* Band Dir Bartlett HS 1959-69, Weimar HS 1970-71; Band Dir 1971-75, Eng Teacher 1976- Bartlett HS; *ai:* Bartlett HS Frosh Class, NHS, Spelling Spon; Univ Interscholastic League; Bell Cty Educators Assn Pres 1975-89, Pres Plaque 1975-89; Killeen Local Spec Awd 1980; Bartlett Businessmens Luncheon Club Pres 1971; Bartlett Area Chamber of Commerce (VP, Master of Ceremonies) 1972; Bartlett PTA Pres 1967-69; Bartlett Annual Stag Party Toastmaster 1982; First Baptist Church (Deacon, Minister of Music 1988, Vice Chm of Deacons 1990); *home:* PO Drawer 10 Bartlett TX 76511

BUTLER, JOHNNIE HUEL, Principal; *b:* Gilmer, TX; *m:* Jeanne Hackney; *c:* John D., Wendy C., Jennifer Parker, Ryan A.; *ed:* (BS) His/Eng, 1966, (MED) Ed Admin, 1977 E TX St Univ; Grad Stud E TX St Univ, Univ of TX Tyler; *cr:* Teacher New Boston Jr HS 1966-71; Sports Dir KNBO Radio 1971-76; Teacher New Boston HS 1976-82; Teacher 1982-83, Prin 1983- Ore City HS; *ai:* Extra Curr Act; Coordinate All Coaches & Spon; TX Assn of Scndry Sch Prin 1983-; Lions Club Pres 1966-82; Boston Lodge AF&AM 1970-; Statewide TX Ed Agency Comm 9th Grade Minimum Rdng Skills Test; *office:* Ore City HS P O Box 100 Ore City TX 75683

BUTLER, JULIA BROWN, Sixth Grade Teacher; *b:* Hope, AR; *m:* Richard H.; *c:* Beth; *ed:* (BA) Elem Ed, S AR Univ 1979; (MSE) Elem Ed, TX Womens Univ 1989; *cr:* 6th Grade Teacher Jackson Elem 1980-; *ai:* Asst Coach Girls Sftbl Team; APTE 1987-; 1st Baptist Church 1987-; Teacher of Yr 1988-89; *office:* Jackson Elem Sch 1101 Jackson Dr Plano TX 75075

BUTLER, LINDA CHARLENE (EDGAR), Fifth Grade Teacher; *b:* San Jose, CA; *w:* Gary Scott (dec); *c:* Cheryl, Paul; *ed:* (BA) Ed, Long Beach St Coll 1959; *cr:* 5th Grade Teacher Hamilton Sch 1959, 1962, 1963-64; Spec Ed Teacher Washington Sch 1963; 3rd-5th Grade Teacher Glen Edwards Sch 1975-; *ai:* NEA, CA Teachers Assn; Citizens Against Substance Abuse Trustee 1984-; Lincoln Area Cmmty Center Trustee 1978-86; Loomis Basin Congregational Church (Moderator 1980-81, Bd Mem 1986-88); Outstanding Young Women of America 1968; *office:* Glen Edwards Elem Sch 204 L St Lincoln CA 95648

BUTLER, MARSHALL E., JR., Choral Music Teacher; *b:* Raleigh, NC; *m:* Karen Denise Blocker; *c:* Knachelle, Melody; *ed:* (BS) Music Ed, Winston-Salem St Univ 1980; *cr:* Choral Dir Rocky Mount Sr HS 1984-; *ai:* Choral Dir Edwards Jr HS Thunderbird Chorus; Rocky Mount Sr HS Gospel Choir Dir; NCMENC Exec Bd 1988-; Phi Mu Alpha Sinfonia 1979; NEA 1984-; Omega Psi Phi 1987; Riley Hill Baptist Church Choirs Dir; *office:* Rocky Mount Sr HS 308 S Tillery St Rocky Mount NC 27804

BUTLER, MARY ALICE (BLACKWELL), English Teacher; *b:* Quitman, TX; *m:* Cary; *c:* Paul, David; *ed:* (BA) Eng/Speech, E TX St Univ 1960; (MED) Rdng/Lang/Learning Disabilities, Univ of TX Tyler 1978; Grad Stud Various Univs; *cr:* Eng Teacher Bellville HS 1960-61; Insurance Agent Quitman TX 1961-66; Spec Ed Teacher 1976-78, Eng Teacher 1978-80 Mineola Jr HS; Spec Ed Teacher Bossier Parish 1980-86; Eng Teacher Quitman Jr HS 1986-; *ai:* Class Spon; Debate Coach; Teacher Advisory Comm; Quitman Classroom Teachers Pres 1989-; Delta Kappa Gamma, TX Classroom Teachers Assn Mem 1989-; 1st Baptist Church 1958-89; *office:* Quitman Jr HS Box 488 Quitman TX 75783

BUTLER, PAUL L., Social Science Instructor; *b:* Bisbee, AZ; *m:* Virginia L. Hunt; *c:* Heather L., Holly L.; *ed:* (BS) Soc Sci Ed, 1965, (MA) General Stud His/Sociology, 1965 OR St Univ; Univ of Redlands/Univ of CA Riverside/Chapman Coll; Grad San Bernardino Reserve Sheriffs Acad; *cr:* Instr Boulder City HS 1965-67, Redlands HS 1967- , Univ of CA Riverside Extension 1984-; *ai:* Disaster Preparedness Consultant; His Curr Revision; NEA 1967-; CTA 1967-; RTA Past Sch Rep, Past Election Comm Chm 1967-; San Gorgonio Search & Rescue Team Incorp San Bernardino Sheriffs Office Past Commander, Current Chm of Bd 1978-, Distinguished Service Awd 1936; CA Real Estate Broker; Licensed Rep Natl Assn of Securities Dealers; Finalist Teacher of Yr; Redlands Educl Partnership Fnd; Letter of Commendation CA Assembly; Distinquished Service Awd San Bernardino Cty Sherriff Dept Cncl; Cert of Recognition Industry of San Bernardino; Awd Outstanding Achievement Inland Cncl of the Soc Stud; Certificate of Appreciation Summer Youth Employment Trng Prgm; *office:* Redlands Sr H S 840 E Citrus Ave Redlands CA 92373

BUTLER, RAYBON, History/Drama/Spec Ed Teacher; *b:* Rural Hart Cty, KY; *m:* Quint Cox; *c:* J. Shane, Amy E., Caleb R.; *ed:* (BA) Speech Comm, 1978, (MS) Scndry Ed/Psych, 1986 W KY Univ; Spec Ed Cert; *cr:* Teacher Hart Cty HS 1982-; *ai:* Speech & Drama Coach; NEA, KY Ed Assn 1982-; Hart Cty Ed Assn (Pres 1987-88, Mem) 1982-; *home:* 8997 Priceville Rd Munfordville KY 42765

BUTLER, SAMUEL D. DE LYRA, Spanish Teacher; *b:* Alice, TN; *m:* Marilyn Simons; *c:* James, David, Claudia, Courtney; *ed:* (BA) Span/Fr, TX A&I Univ 1970; (MA) Span, Univ of Houston 1975; Grad Fellow of Rotary Fnd Univ Federal Do Rio De Janeiro 1971; *cr:* Span Teacher Aldine Jr HS 1973-75; Span/Fr Teacher Eisenhower Sr HS 1975-76; Park View Intermediate 1976-79; Milby HS 1986-87; Span Teacher Conroe HS 1987-; *ai:* Span Club Spon, Prins Teacher Advisory Cncl; Amer Assn of Span/Portuguese Teachers, TX Foreign Lang Assn, Society for Accelerative Learning & Teaching; Houston Interamerican Chamber of Commerce; *office:* Conroe HS 3200 W Davis Conroe TX 77304

BUTLER, SANDRA HUDSON, 3rd & 4th Grade Teacher; *b:* Memphis, TN; *m:* James Herman; *c:* Ronald (dec), Karen; *ed:* (BS) Elem Ed/Gen Sci, Andrews Univ 1973; (MED) Elem Supervision, AL A&M Univ 1980; Educl Specialist Degree at AL A&M Univ; *cr:* Teacher Gary Mizpah Parochial 1969-70, Morton Elem 1973-76, Oakwood Coll Acad 1976-; *ai:* Elem Art Coord Oakwood Acad; *office:* Oakwood Acad Oakwood Rd Huntsville AL 35896

BUTLER, SONJA DARBY, Fourth Grade Teacher; *b:* Camden, AR; *m:* Raymond E.; *c:* Michael, Lance; *ed:* (BSE) Elem Ed, S AR Univ 1964; (MSE) Elem Ed, Ouachita Baptist Univ 1983; *cr:* Classroom Teacher Fairview Elem Sch; *ai:* Sunday Sch Teacher; Aerobics; PTA Lifetime Membership Awd; Cullendale 1st Baptist Church (Sunday Sch Teacher, Childrens Church Teacher); *office:* Fairview Elem Sch 2708 Mt Holly Rd Camden AR 71701

BUTORAC, MARYLIN MARIE, Director of Bands & Chorus; *b:* Des Moines, IA; *ed:* (BME) Music Ed, Univ of OK 1984; (MME) Music Ed, TX Tech Univ 1986; *cr:* Grad Asst TX Tech Univ 1985-86; Band Dir Abilene HS 1986-89; Bands/Chorus Dir Piedmont Public Schls 1989-; *ai:* Jazz Band; Chrldr Spon; MENC, OMEA, CODA, OEA, NEA, PAE 1989-; TBA 1986-; EAI, TBE 1982-; OK Univ Alumni Band 1984-; TX Tech Ex-Stu Assn 1986-; *office:* Piedmont HS 917 Piedmont Rd N Piedmont OK 73078

BUTSON, RANDY LEE, 6th Grade Teacher; *b:* Mankato, MN; *m:* Lisa L. Bleyenburg; *c:* Megan; *ed:* (BA) Elem Ed, Mankato St Univ 1977; *cr:* 6th Grade Teacher Edgerton Public Sch; *ai:* Head Vlybl Coach; Jr HS Bsbl Coach; *home:* R R 2 Box 44 Edgerton MN 56128

BUTTERWORTH, DIANE D., English Teacher; *b:* Atlanta, GA; *m:* Michael A.; *c:* Ashley, Amanda; *ed:* (BS) Eng/Ed, Kennesaw St Coll 1984; West GA Coll; *cr:* Teacher Cherokee HS 1984-; *ai:* Stu Cncl Spon; PTSA Publicity Officer 1985-86; NTCE 1984-89; Assn of Educators 1984-; *office:* Cherokee H S 651 Marietta Hwy Canton GA 30114

BUTTREY, DARLENE BROWN, English Teacher/Dept Chair; *b:* Burns, TN; *m:* Gilbert Eugene; *c:* Daryl E., Melissa D., Cheryl E.; *ed:* (BS) Eng/His, Austin Peay St Univ 1968; Cert in Math, TN St Univ 1987; *cr:* Teacher William James HS 1968-72, William James Jr HS 1972-; *ai:* After-Sch Tutoring Prgm Teacher; TN Career Ladder Level III 1985; Dickson Cty 9th-12th Grade Teacher of Yr 1985-86; *office:* William James Jr HS PO Box 169 Trace Creek Rd White Bluff TN 37187

BUTTREY, SUSANNE FORT, Fifth Grade Teacher; *b:* Springfield, TN; *m:* Stacey E.; *c:* Stephanie Baltz, Samuel Baltz; *ed:* (BS) Elem Ed, Austin Peay St Univ 1972; (MED) Elem Ed, TN St Univ 1978; *cr:* 3rd/8th Grade Teacher Pleasantview Elem 1971-; *ai:* Faclty Adv Comm Grades 4th/5th Pves; Cheatham Cty Mem 1971-; Pres 1986-87; Wrote 6th and Part of 5th Grade Math Wkbks St Basic Skills 1985; *office:* Pleasant View Elem School Church St Pleasant View TN 37146

BUTTRUM, HARLAN RAY, Principal; *b:* Hot Springs, AR; *m:* Linda Jeanell Hatmaker; *c:* Lance, Schelly; *ed:* (BSE) Math, 1974, (MSE) Phys Sci, 1987 Henderson St Univ; Ed Specialist, Univ of AR Little Rock; *cr:* Process Tech Pirelli Cable Co 1980-81; Math Teacher Altus-Denning 1981-82; Math/Sci Instr 1984-87, Prin 1987- Magnet Cove HS; *ai:* Quiz Bowl, Little League Bsktbl Coach; Beta Club Adv; AASP 1987-; NSTA 1985-89; NCTM 1985-89; Mountain Pine Assembly of God Deacon 1986-; First Assembly of God Sundy Sch Supt 1988-; Teacher of Yr 1979; Chem Hnr Wkshp USM; Contributing Author Handbook for Chem Teachers; Nom Twice Presidential Awd Excl Sci Teaching; Whos Who Among Coll Stu; *office:* Magnet Cove Hs Harver Hills Box 1 Malvern AR 72104

BUTTS, BRENDA (HORNER), Fourth Grade Teacher; *b:* Portsmouth, OH; *m:* Keith; *c:* Bryan K.; *ed:* (BS) Elem Ed, Rio Grande Coll 1980; Skills for Adolescence 6th-8th Grades, The Quest Natl Center; *cr:* Teacher Aide 1977-79, Teacher 1980- Bloom-Vernon Sch Dist; *ai:* Quest Prgm Sch Carnival; Firebrick United Meth Church Mem 1967-; *home:* Rt 2 Box 249 South Webster OH 45682

BUTTS, ROBBIE HARRISON, Fifth Grade Teacher; *b:* Cockrum, MS; *m:* Jack; *c:* Michael; *ed:* (BS) Elem Ed, Delta St Univ 1952; Memphis St Univ; Univ of MS; *cr:* Teacher Dublin Elem Sch 1952-57; Teacher Crawfordsville Elem Sch 1957-61; Teacher Batesville Elem Sch 1961-71; Teacher West Panola Acad 1971-88; Teacher North Delta Sch 1988-90; *ai:* Art; Phys Ed; Chrldr Spon; Local Spelling Bee Chm; Classroom Teacher; MS Ed Assn; MS Private Sch Ed Assn; Indep Womans Club Pres; Batesville Jr Aux Secy; Garden Club; Teacher of Yr Awd; *home:* 269 Pollard Batesville MS 38606

BUTTZ, JEAN HAHER, English Teacher & Dept Chair; *b:* Decatur, IL; *m:* Barry A.; *c:* Jennifer, Jason; *ed:* (BA) Eng/Soc Stud, Millikin Univ 1966; (MED) Admin, Univ of IL 1976; *cr:* Eng/Soc Stud Teacher Thomas Jefferson Mid Sch 1966-74; Admin Intern Dist #61 1974-75; Dean of Stus Mound Mid Sch 1975-81; Eng Teacher Thomas Jefferson Mid Sch 1981-; *ai:* Mid Sch Action Group; Lang Art Steering, Dist #61 Gifted, Adv & Advisee Steering Comm; Phi Delta Kappa, Phi Kappa Phi; St Marys Hospital Auxiliary; Delta Delta Delta Alumnae; Dist #61 Those Who Excel 1989; Prgm Presenter Decatur Educl Conference 1988; *home:* 2030 Friel Ct Decatur IL 62521

BUXTON, ALICE I., Junior High English Teacher; *b:* Villa Grove, IL; *m:* Donald L.; *c:* David L., Robert W.; *ed:* (BS) Elem Ed, Calumet Coll 1967; (MS) Ed, Purdue-Calumet Campus 1972; *cr:* 4th Grade Teacher Hammond Public Sch System 1967-71; 8th Grade Teacher 1971-72, 6th Grade Teacher 1972-75, 7th-8th Grade Teacher 1975- Gary Diocese; *ai:* Advocate Teacher-Prepared Assignments & Tests; Foreign Travel; NCTE 1980-; US Eng 1984-; Purdue Alumni Assn 1972-; Covenant Presbyn Womens Assn 1967-; *office:* Our Lady Of Grace Sch 3025 Highway Ave Highland IN 46322

BUYDEN, JUANITA EASLEY, 8th Grade Advanced Eng Teacher; *b:* Talladega, AL; *m:* Theo R.; *c:* Monica, Renette, Grant; *ed:* (BS) Eng, AL St Univ 1955; (MS) Public Sch Admin, Prairie View A&M Univ 1980; *cr:* Eng Teacher O S Hill HS 1955-58,

James Guinn Jr HS 1960-67, Ernest Parker Jr HS 1967-70, Mc Lean Mid Sch 1970-; *ai:* Spon Sch Annual, Honor Society, Tops Management Team; Campus Coord Comm Mem; AFT Building Rep 1980-; Eng Cncl 1970-; NAACP Life Mem 1960-; PTA Life Mem; H T Mitchellaires Fed Club Pres 1966-72; Daughters of Baker Mem 1988-; Outstanding Teacher Nom 1975; Outstanding Eng Teacher 1980; Mc Leans Outstanding Teacher 1989-; *home:* 4265 Balboa Dr Fort Worth TX 76133

BUYSSE, BRUCE LEE, Biology Teacher/Sci Chairman; *b:* Lansing, MI; *m:* Ellen R. Cook; *c:* April, Sarah, Joshua, Emily; *ed:* (BSED) Bio, Cntrl MI Univ 1972; Grad Stud; *cr:* Sci Dept Portland St Patricks HS 1972-75; Sci Teacher Corunna HS 1975-; *ai:* Girls Jr Var & Frosh Bsktbl Coach; Girls Var Sftbl Quiz Bowl Coach; Yrbk Adv; Shiawassee Cty Sci Comm; Stu Cncl Adv; Class Spon; NHS Cncl; MI Sci Teachers Assn 1972-; Bio Teachers Assn 1972-75; MI Teachers Assn 1975-; World Wide Marriage Encounter 1972-, 1981-89 Bio Teachers Assn 1972-75; MI Teachers Assn 1975-; St Pauls Pastoral Cncl 1988-; Corunna Teacher of Yr 1984; Article Published; Natl Sci Fnd MI St Univ Wkshp Grant; *office:* Corunna HS 417 E King St Corunna MI 48817

BUZEK, VETA WILLIAMS, Office Educ Teacher/Coord; *b:* Rosenberg, TX; *m:* Michael R.; *c:* Taryn Wilkinson, Brittany; *ed:* (BS) Bus Ed, Univ Houston 1973; *cr:* Teacher Wyndham Ind Sch Dist 1975-76; Teacher/Coord Lamar Cons Ind Sch Dist 1976-; *ai:* Adv Bus Prof Amer; Co-Spon Natl Honor Society; TCTA 1988-; LCTA 1988-; TCEA 1990; Beta Sigma Phi Pres 1979; Outstanding Young Women Amer 1976; Harris Cty Optometric Wives Assn Pres 1971; TX Classroom Teachers Assn; Lamar Classroom Teachers Assn; TX Cmptr Educators Assn; *office:* Lamar Cons HS 4606 Mustang Ave Rosenberg TX 77471

BUZITUS, BETTY JEAN, Challenge Teacher; *b:* Englewood, OH; *m:* Leon William; *c:* Dale E., Janice M. Jacobson, Cynthia K. Wick, Jon L., Kevin L.; *ed:* (BA) Eng/Ed, Bethel Coll 1955; Curr/Instruction, Cntrl WA 1966; (MA) Physics/Gifted, Univ of WA 1976; Numerous Wkshps & Conferences; *cr:* Teacher Mishawaka IN 1955-57, Moxee Sch Dist 1962-66, Edmonds Sch Dist 1966-67, 1969-; *ai:* Higher Level Thinking Skills Teacher In-Service; MEA Pres 1965-66; EEA, WEA, NEA; Lynwood FM Church CE Dir 1972-, Trip to Africa 1976; Bethel Coll Teacher of Yr 1972; WMI VP of Global Missions; Natl Sci Fnd Fellowship; Gifted Fellowship; Books Published; OMEGA Curr; Recipe for Blooms; *office:* Edmonds Sch Dist 15 5409 228th St SW Mountlake Terrace WA 98043

BYARS, DENA GIBSON, Science Teacher; *b:* Troy, AL; *m:* Jack Madison Jr.; *ed:* (BS) Mrktg, 1982, (BS) Comprehensive Sci Ed, 1987 Troy St Univ; Space Camp, Sea Lab for Teachers 1988; *cr:* Sci Teacher D A Smith Mid Sch 1987-; *ai:* Sci Team Spon; *office:* D A Smith Mid Sch 159 Enterprise Rd Ozark AL 36360

BYARS, KATHRYN LUANNE, Kindergarten Teacher; *b:* Cotulla, TX; *m:* Bobby Lon; *c:* Robyn, Sarah; *ed:* (BS) Elem Ed, TX A&M Univ 1975; Span; *cr:* Kndgtn Teacher Vernon Ind Sch Dist 1976-; *ai:* Kndgtn Cmptr Supvr; Chm Campus Improvement Comm; TX St Teachers Assn 1976-; Kndgtn Teachers of TX 1984-; 1st United Meth Church Cncl on Ministries 1989-; Vernon Jr Service League 1979-84; *office:* Mc Cord Elem Sch 2915 Sand Rd Vernon TX 76384

BYERLY, LARRY A., Science Teacher; *b:* Eugene, OR; *m:* Connie E. Evens; *c:* Leslie; *ed:* (BS) Bio, 1975, (MAT) Sci Ed, 1983 Lewis & Clark Coll; *cr:* Sci/Math Teacher Lake Oswego Jr HS 1978-; *ai:* Sch Climate & Soc Comm; Cross Cntry, Track & Field Coach; NEA, OR Ed Assn 1978-; *office:* Lake Oswego Jr HS 2500 SW Country Club Rd Lake Oswego OR 97034

BYERS, JANIE BEATY, Fourth Grade Teacher; *b:* Livingston, TN; *m:* Bobby H.; *c:* Bo W., Ben J.; *ed:* (BS) Elem Ed, 1980, (MA) Elem Ed, 1982, (EDS) Elem Ed, 1989 TN Tech Univ; *cr:* 4th Grade Teacher Allons Elem 1980-81; 4th-6th Grade Teacher Alpine Elem 1981-87; 4th Grade Teacher A H Roberts 1987-; *ai:* TN Rdng Assn, Intnl Rdng Assn, NEA, TN Ed Assn, OCEA; *office:* A H Roberts K-4 Sch 112 Bussell St Livingston TN 38570

BYERS, SARAH ELLENA, Fifth Grade Teacher; *b:* Fulton, KY; *ed:* (BS) Elem Ed, 1971, (MA) Elem Ed, 1979 Murray St Univ; *cr:* 4th Grade Teacher 1972-74, 5th Grade Teacher 1974- Hickman Cty Elem; Basic Adult Ed Teacher, Intern Teachers Resource Teacher 1987- Hickman Cty; *ai:* Natl Jr Beta Club Spon; NEA, KY Ed Assn, Hickman Cty Assn 1972-; Outstanding Young Women of America.

BYINGTON, MARY FRANCES, 5th Grade Teacher; *b:* Pedlar Mills, VA; *m:* Sidney E.; *c:* Noel J., Sandra Cremeens, Jean Edinger, Peggy Lefholz; *ed:* (BS) Elem, Lindenwood Coll 1969; Grad Work MO Northeast St Univ; *cr:* Jr HS Teacher 1969-85; Mid Sch Teacher 1986; Elem Teacher 1990; *ai:* Prof Dev Comm 1988-; MO St Teachers, Cmmty Teachers 1969-; City Government (Mayor 1989, Alderman 1990); *office:* Lincoln Cty R-4 Sch 6th & Elm Sts * Winfield MO 63389

BYMAN, LARRY D., Science Teacher; *b:* Longview, WA; *m:* Barbara J. Juntunen; *c:* Angela, Phillip, Kenneth, Kevin, Travis, Joshua, Joanna; *ed:* (BS) Microbiology, Univ of WA 1977; *cr:* Teacher Mark Morris HS 1978-; *ai:* Sci Club Adv; Technology Team Mem; Credit, Tuition Review, Dist Curr Comms; Cmptr Lab Admin; Phododendron Club Pres 1984-86; *office:* Mark Morris HS 1602 Mark Morris Ct Longview WA 98632

BYRD, BILL, Teacher; *b:* Fort Pierce, FL; *m:* Alma Perdue-Byrd; *c:* Eric D., Tina D., Anthony D., Tarra Perdue; *ed:* (BA) Bus, Univ of NE 1966; (MAE) Guidance/Counseling, Inter Amer Univ PR 1973; (MA) Soc Stud, GA St Univ 1985; *cr:* Teacher/Head Boys Bsktbl Coach Redan HS 1983-; *office:* Redan HS 5249 Redan Rd Stone Mountain GA 30088

BYRD, CONNIE JOHNSON, Second Grade Teacher; *b:* Lynchburg, VA; *m:* Thomas L. Jr.; *ed:* (BS) Elem Ed, Shaw Univ 1966; Grad Work Lynchburg Coll, Cntrl St Univ Edmond; *cr:* 3rd Grade Teacher Branch Elem 1966-67; 2nd-6th Grade Rdng Teacher Armstrong Elem 1967-68; 7th/8th Grade Rdng Teacher Dunbar Jr HS 1968-70; 7th/8th Grade Comm Skills Linkhorne Jr HS 1970-72; 3rd Grade Teacher Intnl Sch Bangkok Thailand 1972-74, Hickam Elem 1979-81; 3rd Grade Teacher 1975-79, 2nd Grade Teacher 1981- Tinker Elem; *ai:* NEA 1967-; OK Ed Assn, Mid-Del Teachers Assn 1975-; Lioness Club, Oklahoma City Fed of Colored Women 1989-; Urban League 1988-; Phi Delta Kappa 1990; 5th Street Missionary Baptist Church (Vacation Bible Sch Arts & Crafts Dir, Youth Spon, Deaconess, Choir Mem, Chairperson Decorating Comm); *office:* Tinker Elem Sch 4409 Mc Narney St Tinker AFB OK 73145

BYRD, ELOISE WASHINGTON, Special Education Teacher; *b:* Dawson, GA; *m:* Warnell; *c:* Bernice Watson Mungin, Karen, James, Michael, Lessie; *ed:* (BS) Elem Ed, Albany St Coll 1952; (MED) Elem Ed, Tuskegee Inst 1959; (EDS) Cnslr Ed, Univ of GA 1971; Fort Valley St Coll, Univ of MD, SC St Coll, GA Southern Univ; *cr:* 6th Grade Teacher Carver HS 1952-59; 5th Grade Teacher Raymond Sch 1959; 6th Grade Teacher Lincoln Heights 1959-64; Cnslr Lillian St Sch 1964-78; Spec Ed Teacher Glascock Cty Primary 1978-80, Metter HS 1980-87, Treutlen Cty Schls 1988-; *ai:* CEC 1976-87; GAE, NEA 1952-87; CETA Spec Summer Sch 1976-80; Cmmty Action Volunteer of Yr 1976; *home:* PO Box 804 Metter GA 30439

BYRD, GERALD LEE, Eng/Advanced Placement Teacher; *b:* Murfreesboro, NC; *m:* Carolyn Sandra Kenney; *c:* Sandra, David; *ed:* (AA) Liberal Art, Chowan Coll 1961; (BS) Soc Stud, E Carolina Univ 1964; (MA) Eng, VA Polytechnic Inst & St Univ 1979; NDEA Eng Inst; *cr:* Soc Stud/Eng Teacher Bassett HS 1964-; *home:* PO Box 362 Bassett VA 24055

BYRD, LISA ALFORD, Mathematics Teacher; *b:* Jackson, MS; *m:* Earl; *ed:* (BS) Math Ed, MS St Univ 1984; *cr:* Math Teacher Mendenhall HS 1984-87, Florence HS 1987-; *ai:* Var Chrldrs Spon; MS Prof Educators; *office:* Florence HS 232 Hwy 469 N Florence MS 39073

BYRD, LISA OHLEMACHER, Earth Science Teacher; *b:* Harlingen, TX; *w:* Carey L. (dec); *c:* Dustan; *ed:* (BS) Scndry Ed - Cum Laude, TX A&I Univ 1980; Grad Stud Sci, Univ of S FL; Project TEACH; *cr:* Geology Lab Instr TX A&I Univ 1978-79; Life/Earth Sci Chairperson Memorial Mid Sch 1980-82; Life/Earth Sci Teachers Bayonet Point Mid Sch 1984-85; Earth Sci Teacher Hudson Mid Sch 1985-; *ai:* Yrbk Co-Spon; Save Our Springs & Sci Club Spon; FACT Canoe Trip; Sea for Me Oceanography Instr; League of Environmental Educators, FL Assn of Sci Teachers 1986-; FL League of Mid Schls 1988-; N Amer Assn for Environmental Ed 1987-; Co-Author; Quality Prgm Awd FL Dept; Nom Presidential Awd Excl in Sci & Math; Pasco Cty Sch Bd Certificate of Appreciation; Alice Ind Sch Dist Certificate of Recognition; *office:* Hudson Mid Sch 14540 Cobra Way Hudson FL 34669

BYRD, LYNDA BERRYHILL, Mathematics Teacher; *b:* Gladewater, TX; *m:* Billy Leon; *c:* Terry L., Joy G. Byrd Collins; *ed:* (BS) Math, 1958, (MS) Math, 1964 E TX Univ; *cr:* Math Teacher TX City Ind Sch Dist 1958-; *ai:* Kappa Delta Pi 1964-89; TX Classroom Teachers Assn; NCTM 1966-; Alpha Delta Kappa (Treas 1980-84, Mem 1971-); *office:* Texas City HS 1800 9th Ave N Texas City TX 77590

BYRD, PHYLLIS DENISE (WALLER), 5th Grade Teacher; *b:* Little Rock, AR; *m:* Cedric W.; *c:* Chelsa, Chandler; *ed:* (BSE) Elem Ed, Harding Univ 1979; (MSe) Rdng, Univ of Cntrl AR 1990; Multicultural Rdng & Thinking Project; Prgrm for Effective Teaching; Classroom Management; Cooperative Learning; *cr:* 5th Grade Teacher Lonoke Elem Sch 1979-; *ai:* Personnel Policy, Sch Climate, Textbook Adoption, Sunshine Comm; at Risk Stu Adv; PTA 1989-; NEA, AR Ed Assn 1979-83; Profiled in AR Educl Television Network Prgm; *office:* Lonoke Elem Sch 501 W Academy Lonoke AR 72086

BYRD, RONALD PAUL, Agriculture Teacher; *b:* Roanoke, VA; *m:* Alexis Stamper; *c:* Ronald P. II, Alex P.; *ed:* (BA) Ag Educ, VA Polytechnic Inst & St Univ 1972; *cr:* Ag. Tcher Flatwoods HS 1972-76; Rocky Gap HS 1976-80; Grayson Co. Voc Sch 1980-; *ai:* FFA Adv; St FFA Advisory Cncl; Adult Ag Educ; Faculty Rep GCEA; VEA; NEA; Mason; VPI & SU Teacher Educ Advisory Cncl- Ag Educ; Honorary State Farmer Degree.

BYRD, TANYE CARROLL, 8th Grade Math Teacher; *b:* Sulphur Springs, TX; *m:* Ronald Wright; *c:* Jordan L., Joshua R.; *ed:* (BS) Math/Ec, E TX St Univ 1981; *cr:* Geometry Teacher Sulphur Springs HS 1981-82; Jr HS Math Teacher Briarcrest Baptist Schls 1982-86; 8th Grade Math/Algebra Teacher Gladewater Mid Sch 1986-; *ai:* UIL Coach, Coord; Media Liasion; NCTM 1981-; ETCTM 1987-; Chrstn Womens Fellowship (Secy 1987-88, VP 1988-).

BYRD, TERI J. CARTER, English Teacher; *b:* Wood River, IL; *m:* Terry A.; *ed:* (BS) Scndry Ed/Eng, TN Temple Coll 1977; (MED) Scndry Ed/Eng, Univ of TN Chattanooga 1982; Ed Specialist Degree, W GA Coll 1990-; Licensed Cosmetologist, St of TN 1973, 1977; *cr:* Eng Teacher Cross Keys Chrstn Acad 1977-78, Richard Cty Sch 1978-79, Rossville Jr HS 1979-80, Lafayette HS 1980-81, Lafayette Jr HS 1981-88, Ridgeland HS 1988-; *ai:* NEA, GAE Mem 1989; NCT Eng, GA Cncl Teachers of Eng Mem 1990; 7th Grade Stu Selected Teacher of Yr Lafayette Jr HS 1985-86; *office:* Ridgeland HS Rt 1 Happy Valley Rd Rossville GA 30741

BYRNE, EILEEN, Language Arts Chairperson; *b:* Sewickley, PA; *ed:* (BED) Eng, Slippery Rock Univ 1967; (MED) Rdng/Lang Arts, Univ of Pittsburgh 1970; *cr:* Teacher Chm 1967-; Public Relations 1987- Hopewell Area Schls; *ai:* HS Newspaper Spon; GATES Gifted Ed Cultural Prgm Spon; High Q Academic Games Team Spon; Weighted Grades Comm/Lang Arts/Cmptr Grant Comm; Hopewell Ed Assn Rec Secy; Journalism Ed Assn 1980-; PA St Ed Assn; NEA; NCTE; Gift of Time Tribute Stu/Cmmty Nom; *office:* Hopewell Sr HS 1215 Longvue Ave Aliquippa PA 15001

BYRNE, JOHN JAMES, Curriculum Coordinator; *b:* New York, NY; *m:* Marilyn; *c:* Lisa, John; *ed:* (BA) Fr, Manhattan Coll 1962; (MA) Linguistics, 1963, (PHD) Linguistics, 1971 Fordham Univ; Allied Fields William Paterson Coll, Lehman Coll, St Francis Coll; *cr:* Teacher/Chm DuBois HS 1963-74; Teacher/Advanced Placement Guidance Alfred E Smith HS 1975-81; Exec Asst Supt New York City Bd of Ed 1981-82; Curr Coord John Dewey HS 1982-; *ai:* MENSA Mem 1974-; CUNY Awd of Excl 1989; Robert F Kennedy Gold Medal Awd 1962; *office:* John Dewey HS 50 Avenue X Brooklyn NY 11223

BYRNE, JUDY SUSANNE, English/French Teacher; *b:* Great Falls, MT; *ed:* (BA) Fr, 1972, (MED) Scndry Ed 1982 MT St Univ Bozeman; MT Writing Project 1987; 5-12 Sch Admin Endorsement 1984, Gifted Ed 1979, Trng Metrics Leaders for MT 1977; *cr:* Eng/Fr Teacher Lewistown Jr HS 1972-74; Fr Teacher Concordia Coll Lang Camp MN 1974; Substitute Teacher Great Falls Public Schls 1974-75; Fr Teacher Coll of Great Falls 1978-79; Drama Teacher Lewistown Jr HS 1975-; *ai:* Stu Cncl, Ski Club Spon; Lang Art Curr Comm Chairperson; Lewistown Writing Assessment Co-Dir; Textbook Selection Comm; Certified Writing Consultant; MT Ed Assn Bd of Dir 1982-, Outstanding Mem Lewistown 1987; MT Assn of Lang Teachers 1975-; MT Assn of Teachers of Eng & Lang Art 1987-; Phi Delta Kappa 1985-; Amer Field Service Stu Selection Chairperson 1979-89; Cntrl MT Democrats Secy 1985-86; Cath Church Catechism Teacher 1979-81; MEA Region 3 Silver Apple Awd 1980; Lewistown Ed Assn (Pres 1978-80, Secy 1987-); MT Assn of Gifted & Talented Ed Charter Mem 1980-84; Phi Kappa Phi 1972-; Amer Assn of Univ Women 1980-87; Title III Grant 1976; Presenter of Fr Childrens Lit MT Assn of Teachers of Fr 1977; *office:* Lewiston Jr HS 914 W Main Lewistown MT 59457

BYRNE, RICHARD PORTER, Teacher, Science Dept Chairman; *b:* Huntsville, AL; *m:* Terry S.; *c:* Rick; *ed:* (BS) General Sci, Auburn Univ 1978; (MA) Sci Ed, Univ of AL 1987; NASA Aerospace Ed Specialist; *cr:* Teacher/Coach Eau Gallie HS 1978-79; Teacher Botelar Jr HS 1980-81, Holt HS 1981-83; Aerospace Specialist Natl Aeronautics & Space Admin 1983-85; Teacher Holt HS 1985-; *ai:* Jr & Sr Honor Society Comm Adv; Jr Sci & Aerospace Clubs Spon; AL Sci Teachers Assn Dist Dir 1988-; Tuscaloosa Sci Teachers Assn (VP 1988-89, Pres 1989-); BSA (Spon, Adv) 1990; Aerospace Sci Curr Guide; NASA Landsat Act for Educators; Sci Dept Chm Holt HS; *office:* Holt HS 3801 Alabama Ave Tuscaloosa AL 35404

BYRNE, VERONICA F., Social Studies Chair; *b:* Richmond Hill, NY; *ed:* (BA) His, 1957, (MA) 20th Century His, 1962 St Johns Univ; (MS) Theology, Fordham Univ 1972; St Grant, SE Asia Stud, Cornell Univ; *cr:* Elem Teacher St Mary Gate of Heaven Sch 1948-57; Scndry His/Eng Teacher St Agatha HS 1957-66; Soc Stud Teacher/Chairperson Christ The King Regional HS 1966-; *ai:* Hall of Fame Comm Mem; NCSS, NY St Soc Stud Cncl; Christ The King HS Outstanding Teacher Awd 1980; Inducted in Hall of Fame 1988; *office:* Christ The King Regional HS 68-02 Metropolitan Ave Middle Village NY 11379

BYRNES, ROSE MARIE, Rural Mail Carrier; *b:* Bardstown, KY; *ed:* (BS) Health/Phys Ed, 1975, Cert Sci, 1977, (MS) Athletic Admin/Coaching 1981 Univ of S MS; TX St Teacher Cert, N TX St Univ; *cr:* Teacher/Coach Richton HS 1975-78, Clark HS 1978-80, Lumberton HS 1980-86; Rural Mail Carrier US Postal Service 1986-; *ai:* NEA 1975-86; MS Assn of Educators 1975-78, 1980-86; TX St Teachers Assn 1977-80; Amer Red Cross CPR Teacher 1974-82; Hattiesburg Recreation Dept Sftbl Ofcl 1974-77; Dist VIII BB Coach of Yr 1984; Outstanding Young Women of America 1981; Presidents List 1974-75; *home:* 408 Dixie Ave Hattiesburg MS 39401

BYRUM, GEORGE DANIEL, Middle School Humanities; *b:* Madisonville, KY; *ed:* (BA) Journalism, Univ of KY 1972; (MS) Scndry Ed, (Rank I) Elem Ed, Murray St Univ; *cr:* Teacher White Plains; *ai:* Academic Team; Yrbk Spon; KEA, NEA; *home:* 2624 Wesco Dr Madisonville KY 42431

BYRUM, KAYE M., 7th/8th Grade Teacher; *b:* Windsor, NC; *m:* Jerry R.; *c:* Holley, Justin; *ed:* (BS) Elem Ed, 1976, (MA) Elem Ed, 1979 E Carolina Univ; Effective Teaching Trng, Teacher Performance Appraisal Trng, Mentor Teacher Trng; *cr:* Title I Rdng Teacher 1976-79, Classroom Teacher 1980- Bertie Cty Elem Schls; *ai:* Sch Newspaper, 8th Grade Dance Spon; Mentor for Beginning Teachers; *office:* Askewville Elem Sch Rt 3 Box 226-A Windsor NC 27983

BYRUM, PHYLLIS COLLIER, Social Studies Teacher; *b:* Franklin, VA; *m:* Jarvis Randall; *ed:* (BA) Soc Stud, Atlantic Chrstn Coll 1973; Advanced Work Grad Level, Old Dominion Univ; Robert Taft Inst, Old Dominion Univ; Grad Stud Univ of VA; *cr:* Soc Stud Teacher/Dept Chairperson John Yeates HS 1973-; *ai:* Sr Class Spon; Soc Stud Coord & Chairperson; Stu Cncl Adv & Spon; Delta Kappa Gamma (Mem 1987-, Secy 1988-89); His Teacher of VA; Outstanding Teacher Under The Sun Awd Suffolk 1989; *home:* 1632 Great Fork Rd Suffolk VA 23438

BYRUM, RITA (CANTRELL), Language Arts Teacher; *b:* Flora, IL; *m:* Charles Larry; *ed:* (BS) Eng, Oakland City Coll 1979; (MED) Scndry Ed, IN St Univ 1985; Several Gifted/Talented Ed Wkshps; Mentor Teacher; *cr:* Teacher Clark Jr HS 1979-84, Fort Branch Cmmty Sch 1984-; *ai:* 7th Grade Vlybl Coach; Newspaper & Hoosier Academic Super Bowl Spon; South Gibson Teachers Assn 1984-; IN St Teachers Assn, NEA 1979-; 1st General Baptist Church Youth Spon 1986-; St Handwriting Book Evaluation Comm 1983; *office:* Fort Branch Cmmty Sch 800 S Hillcrest Fort Branch IN 47648

BYTHEWAY, CHARLOTTE ANN (BRAGG), English Teacher/Dept Chairman; *b:* Holly Grove, AR; *m:* James Edward; *ed:* (BS) Eng Ed, 1964, (MA) Scndry Ed, 1972 TN Technological Univ; *cr:* Eng Teacher Dunedin HS 1964-; *ai:* Dept Chm; Sch Based Comms; Peer & Beginning Teacher Prgm; Pinellas Cncl Teachers of Eng (Pres 1983-84, 1st VP 1984-85, 2nd VP 1982-83, Recording Secy 1981-82); Phi Delta Kappa; FL Cncl Teachers of Eng; Eastern Star; *office:* Dunedin HS 1651 Pinehurst Rd Dunedin FL 34698

C

CABADA, SHIRLEY A., Eng Teacher/Jr HS Dept Chair; *b:* San Antonio, TX; *m:* George M.; *c:* Carol Kothmann, Karen Kolinek, Jeff Moravits, Will Moravits; *ed:* (AA) Elem Ed/Eng, SW TX Jr Coll 1968; (BS) Elem Ed/Eng, TX A&I Univ 1970; (MED) Ed/Rdng, Sul Ross Univ 1981; Grad Stud Sul Ross Univ; *cr:* Teacher Kingsville Ind Sch Dist 1970, Dept of Defense 1971-73, Gregory Portland Ind Sch Dist 1974, Round Rock Ind Sch Dist 1975-78, Uvalde CISD 1978; *ai:* Eng/Lang Art Dept Chairperson; *office:* Uvalde Jr HS 1000 N Getty PO Box 1909 Uvalde TX 78801

CABE, JOSEPHINE ROPER, 4th Grade Teacher; *b:* Franklin, NC; *m:* Charles L.; *c:* Joseph Kenyon; *ed:* (AS) Ed, Gardner Webb Coll 1960; (BS) Ed, Western Carolina Univ 1962; *cr:* 3rd Grade Teacher Forsyth Cty Schls 1962-63; 3rd-5th/7th Grade Teach Er Macon Cty Schls 1963-; *ai:* NEA 1963-; NC Assn of Educators 1963-; *home:* 324 Harrison Ave Franklin NC 28734

CABOOT, BLAIR EDWARD, Mathematics Teacher; *b:* Scranton, PA; *m:* Betty Lou Reitz; *c:* Jason B., Jody L.; *ed:* (BS) Math, E Stroudsburg Univ 1967; (MS) Math/Scndry Ed, Univ of Scranton 1969; Numerous Natl Sci Grants; Scndry Sch Admin; Supvr of Math; *cr:* Math Dept Chm 1968-74, 9th-12th Grade Math Teacher 1966- Abington Heights HS; K-12th Grade Math Coord Abington Heights Sch Dist 1975-; *ai:* Mem Dist Administrative Comms; NE PA Cncl Teachers of Math 1988-; PA Cncl Teachers of Math 1967-, Outstanding Service Awd 1989; PA Cncl Supvrs of Math, NCTM, Natl Cncl Supvrs of Math 1967-; Sigma Zeta Tau 1966-; Phi Delta Kappa 1969-; Civil Service Commission VP 1989-; E Stroudsburg Univ Acad Excl Awd 1966; Commencement Speaker 1981, 1987; Whos Who Among Amer Colls & Univs 1966; *office:* Abington Heights HS North Noble Rd Clarks Summit PA 18411

CABOTT, SANDRA MILLER, 6th Grade Mid Sch Teacher; *b:* West Chester, PA; *m:* Harry Jerome; *c:* Courtney, Jayme; *ed:* (BS) Elem Ed, York Coll of PA 1973; (MS) Outdoor Ed, Penn St Univ 1987; Marine Bio, Environmental Ed, Penn St; *cr:* 5th Grade Teacher Orendorf Elem Sch 1973-88; 6th Grade/Sci Teacher Northeastern Mid Sch 1988-; *ai:* Stu Assist; Chairperson Sci Fair; Curr Coord; Supts Advisory Cncl; Various Textbook Choosing, Negotiations, Building Advisory Comms, Curr Writing; Northeastern Ed Assn Chairperson Various Comms 1973-; PA St Sci Teachers Assn Presentor 1988-89; York Hospital Fete Comm Chairperson 1984-86; Leukemia Society Comm Mem 1984-; *office:* Northeastern Mid Sch Hartman St Manchester PA 17345

CACAL, JUNE MARY, Business Teacher; *b:* Munich, West Germany; *m:* Thoams Byrd; *ed:* (BS) Bus Ed, 1978, (MA) Admin & Supervision, 1980 Austin Peay St Univ; *cr:* Teacher Ft Campbell Jr HS 1979-, Ft Campbell HS 1984-; *ai:* Stu Cncl Spon; Ft Campbell Ed Assn 1979-; KY Assn for Gifted Ed 1990.

CACIBAUDA, JOSEPH ANTHONY, JR., Music Department Chairman; *b:* New Orleans, LA; *m:* Delores Rose Van Acker; *c:* Joseph III; *ed:* (BMED) Instrumental Music, 1971, (MMED) Instrumental Music, 1973 SE LA Univ; *cr:* Band Dir Southwood Acad 1971-72; Supvr/Music Teacher Bay-Waveland Sch Dist 1972-77; Dir of Bands St Martin HS 1977-79; Supvr/Music Instr Biloxi Public Sch Dist 1979-84; Dept Chair/Music Teacher Ocean Springs Public Sch Dist 1984-; *ai:* Band Officers Cncl Spon; Band Parents Auxiliary Adv; Phi Delta Kappa, Gulf Coast Band Dirs Assn, Natl Band Assn, MS Bandmasters Assn; Phi Mu Alpha Sinfonia VP 1970-71; Personalities of South; Personalities of America; Men & Women of Distinction; *office:* Ocean Springs Sch Dist PO Box 7002 Ocean Springs MS 39564

CAESAR, JEANNENE FARROW, Third Grade Teacher; *b:* Winston-Salem, NC; *m:* I. Bruce; *c:* Eric, Kevin; *ed:* (BS) Early Chldhd Ed, Winston-Salem St Univ 1970; *cr:* Teacher Bolton Elem Sch 1971-; *ai:* Mem Sch Improvement Team; Chairperson Thinking Skills Comm & Mentor Support Team; Math Rep; Forsyth Assn of Classroom Teachers Mem; WSSU Alumni Assn Mem; Twice Nom Teacher of Yr & Terry Sanford Awd; Team Mem Evaluator in Teacher Incentive Project; Leader Wkshp for Mentor Support Team Trng; *office:* Bolton Elem Sch 1250 Bolton St Winston-Salem NC 27103

CAETANO, DAVID FRANK, Agricultural Instructor; *b:* Hanford, CA; *m:* Krim Michaud; *ed:* (BS) Ag, CA St Univ Fresno 1979; Grad Stud Ag; *cr:* Instr Tulare Union HS 1979-; *ai:* FFA Adv; CA Ag Teachers Assn 1979-; CA Teachers Assn 1979-; *office:* Tulare Union HS 755 E Tulare Ave Tulare CA 93274

CAFFAS, MARY ELLEN GOLDEN, 7th/8th Grade Eng Teacher; *b:* Wilkes-Barre, PA; *m:* John Louis Jr.; *c:* Joseph, Matthew, John, Edward, Kenneth, James, Michael, David, Jason, Mark, Rick, (adopted); Shane, Patrick (dec), Patricia (dec), Scott (dec); *ed:* (BS) Comm, Bloomsburg Univ 1972; Grad Studs in Ed, Family Living, Counseling; *cr:* Teacher Upper Dauphin Area Mid Sch 1972-; *ai:* Act Coord; Stu Cncl, Newspaper, Literary Magazine Adv; Newspaper in Ed Week Dist Liaison; Patriot News Newspaper in Ed & Pottsville Republican Ed Advisory Comm; Dauphin Cty Dist 8 Adult Rep; PA Assn of Stu Cncls; NEA, PA St Ed Assn 1972-; Upper Dauphin Area Ed Assn (Grievance Chm 1987-) 1972-; Upper Dauphin Area Athletic Assn Secy 1978-83; Upper Dauphin Area Bsbl Boosters Secy 1983-85; Upper Dauphin Cty Goodwill Advisory Bd 1980-84; Tressler Luth Service Assn Parents of Adopted Children Organization Advisory Panel 1974-84; Queen of Peace Roman Cath Church Parish Cncl 1980-82, 1986-88; *office:* Upper Dauphin Area Mid Sch RR 1 Lykens PA 17048

CAFFEY, DEBORAH HEMPERLY, Third Grade Teacher; *b:* Philadelphia, PA; *m:* Edward Russell; *c:* Christine, Diane, Courtney; *ed:* (BS) Ed, SW TX St Univ 1976; Advanced Academic Trng; *cr:* 3rd Grade Teacher 1976-77, 4th Grade Teacher 1977-78 Travis Elem; 3rd Grade Teacher Bowie Elem 1978-83; 4th Grade Teacher 1985-86, 3rd Grade Teacher 1986- Travis Elem; *ai:* Unit Leader; Rdng Curr Comm; TX Classroom Teachers Assn; Beta Sigma Phi Extension Officer 1988; Assn for Retarded Citizens (Bd Mem, Chm Ed Comm) 1987-; TX Parent-Prof Information Network Coord; Mental Retardation Articles; Heroism for Life Saving Act; *office:* Travis Elem Sch PO Box 2340 San Marcos TX 78666

CAFFO, JOHN A., Math/Physics Teacher/Chair; *b:* Washington, DC; *m:* Margaret I. Reed; *c:* Keith; *ed:* (BEE) Electrical Engineering, George Washington Univ 1965; (MS) Space Physics, Air Force Inst of Technology 1969; Ed Courses, Univ of NM 1987-88; *cr:* Retired Lt Colonel Air Force 1965-85; Math Dept Chm/Math/Physics Teacher Hope Chrstn Sch 1989-; *ai:* Natl Jr Honor Society; 8th Grade Class Asst; Tau Beta Pi 1965-; USAF Systems Command Awd for Scientific Achievement 1971; Defense Meritorious Service Medal; Joint Service Achievement Medal; Meritorious Service Medal One Oak Leaf Cluster; Joint Service Commendation Medal; Natl Defense Service Medal; Honor List George Washington Univ 1965; USAF Comms & Electronics Assn Honor Awd 1964-65; *home:* 12915 Punta de Vista Pl NE Albuquerque NM 87112

CAGE, CANDACE ANNE, Social Studies Teacher; *b:* Washington, DC; *ed:* (BA) His, 1986, (MED) Scndry Ed, 1988 Winthrop Coll; *cr:* Grad Asst Winthrop Coll 1986-87; Teacher/Coach Catawba Sch 1987-88, Northern HS 1988-; *ai:* Var Girls Bsktbl Coach; Environmental Club Spon; NEA, NCSS 1988-; Coach of Yr SC 1987-88, MD 1989-; *office:* Northern HS 2950 Chaneyville Rd Owings MD 20736

CAGLE, WALTER NEAL (BUCK), Teacher/Coach; *b:* Clarksville, TX; *m:* Doris Kelsoe; *c:* Denise Cagle Williamson, Charles Reed; *ed:* (BS) Phys Ed, Baylor 1960; *cr:* Teacher/Coach Mesquite Ind Sch Dist 1961-62; Teacher/Coach Clarksville Ind Sch Dist 1982-; *office:* Clarksville Ind Sch Dist PO Box 1016 Clarksville TX 75426

CAGLE, WARNER REDMOND, 4th Grade Teacher; *b:* Nashville, TN; *m:* Billy F.; *c:* Linda, Pickett; *ed:* (BS) Elem Ed TN Tech Univ 1968; *cr:* 5th-8th Grade Teacher/Prin NewHarmony Elem Sch 1957-58; 7th-8th Grade Teacher/Prin 1958-60; 5th-6th Grade Teacher 1960-63, Dill Elem Sch; 5th Grade Teacher Rigsby Elem Sch 1964-74; 5th-6th Grade Teacher Sci Pikeville Elem Sch 1975-87; 4th Grade Teaacher 1988-; *ai:* Bledsoe Co Ed Assn Secy 1960, Teacher of Yr 1978; Sequatchie Valley Church of Christ Mem; *home:* Rt 2 Box 335 Pikeville TN 37367

CAHILL, JEAN SHATTO, Reading Teacher; *b:* Hagerstown, MD; *m:* J. Thomas; *c:* Josh, Ryan; *ed:* (BS) Elem Ed, E Stroudsburg Univ 1971; (MA) Guidance/Counseling, E KY Univ 1972; Rdng Specialist, Univ of PA 1984; *cr:* Guidance Cnslr N A Armstrong Jr HS 1972-76; Elem Teacher Bristol Township Schls 1976-84; Rdng Specialist N A Armstrong Jr HS 1984-; *ai:* Dist Wide Rdng & Guidance Comm; NEA, PA Sch Ed Assn 1971-; Intnl Rdng Assn 1984-; Alpha Sigma Alpha Ed 1967-; PTO 1976-; *office:* Neil A Armstrong Jr HS 475 Wistar Rd Fairless Hills PA 19030

CAHILL, JOAN, Principal; *b:* Newcastle West, Ireland; *ed:* (BA) Elem Ed, Univ of Notre Dame 1967; (MA) Religious Ed, Loyola Univ 1988; SLD Stetson Univ; *cr:* Teacher Limerick Ireland 1952-60; 1st Grade Teacher 1960-79; Prin 1979- St Marys; *ai:* Mem Parish Cncl; Parish Bd of Ed; Home & School Assn; Rainbow Facilitator; Dir of Parent Outreach Prgm; NCEA; Brevard Rdng Cncl; Brevard Cty Schools; Dist Chapter I Needs Assessment Comm Mem; Crises Intervention Team Mem; Teacher of Yr Awd 1969; Jr Womens League; *office:* St Marys Cath Sch 1152 Seminole Dr Rockledge FL 32955

CAHILL, MARY ANN, Mathematics Teacher; *b:* St Paul, MN; *ed:* (BA) Math, Wheaton Coll 1966; (MST) Math, Rutgers Univ 1970; *cr:* Teacher Redmont HS 1966-69, Rose Hill Jr HS 1970-72, Juanita HS 1973-, St Thomas More 1976-77; Math Dept Chairperson Juanita HS 1985-88; *ai:* NCTM 1980-; WA St Mutl Cncl 1983-; Fulbright Exch Teacher London 1976-77; WA St Master Teacher Team Applied Math Mem 1989-; *office:* Juanita HS 10601 NE 132nd St Kirkland WA 98034

CAHILL, THOMAS M., 5th Grade Teacher; *b:* Binghamton, NY; *m:* Barbara Anne Plante; *c:* Mathew T., Brianne; *ed:* (AA) Liberal Arts, Broome Comm Coll Binghamton 1974; (BA) His, SUNY Potsdam 1976; Grad Work Cert SUNY Oswego, Coll of William & Mary; *cr:* 5th Grade Teacher Williamsburg, James City Schls, Burton Heights Elem, Norge Elem 1980-; *ai:* 5th Grade Team Leader; Soc Stud Curr Leader; Math Curr Writer; *office:* Norge Elem Sch 734 Richmond Rd Williamsburg VA 23185

CAHOON, EDNA MAE, 1st & 2nd Grade Teacher; *b:* Conner Creek, ID; *m:* Arley O.; *c:* Ronnie, Karen Jones, Sharon Kimber, Arley Jr.; *ed:* (BA) Media Specialist Elem Ed, ID St 1976; *cr:* 1st/3rd Grade Teacher Malta Elem 1976-85; K-2nd Grade Teacher Almo Elem 1985-; *ai:* Music Dir; Head Librarian; ID Rdng Assn (Rdng Teacher, Rep); Cassia Cty Historical Society Bd of Dirs 1989-; *office:* Almo Elem Sch 150 Main St Almo ID 83312

CAHOON, SANDRA GIESINGER, 4th/5th Grade Math Teacher; *b:* Navasota, TX; *m:* David; *c:* Robin Harris Schultz, Holly Deann Harris, Wendy Charlene Harris; *ed:* (BA) Elem Ed, Sam Houston St Univ 1977; *cr:* 4th Grade Teacher Montgomery Elem 1977-86; Gifted/Talented 4th/5th Grade Math Teacher Montgomery Inter Med 1986-; *ai:* Univ Interschlstc Leag Number Sense Spon; TSTA Campus Rep 1987-88; NEA; Montgomery Ed Assn;TX Assn Gifted & Talented; Bonnie Belle Booster Club (VP 1986-87 Secy 1988-89); NEA Today Nswpr; 2 Articles in Idea Exchange; *office:* Montgomery Intermediate Sch P O Box 1475 Montgomery TX 77356

CAIAZZO, ROBERT JAMES, 6th Grade Science Teacher; *b:* Philadelphia, PA; *m:* Maryellen Reinholt; *c:* Michael J., Kristen M.; *ed:* (BS) Elem, 1973, (MS) Ed, 1978 Trenton St Coll; Scndry Certificate Life Sci; *cr:* 4th Grade Classroom Teacher 1973-74, 6th Grade Classroom Teacher 1974-82, 6th/7th Grade Sci Teacher 1982-89, 6th Grade Sci/Math/Rdng Teacher 1989- Hawthorne Sch; *ai:* Sci Comm & Club; Bsbl & Soccer Coach; Willingboro Ed Assn (Attending Rep 1973-, Rep 1986-); NJ Ed Assn 1973-; NSTA 1988-; Edgewater Park Historical Society; Articles Published in Book & Learning Magazine; *office:* Hawthorne Park Sch Hampshire Ln Willingboro NJ 08046

CAIN, BETTY ROBERTSON, Fourth Grade Teacher; *b:* Birmingham, AL; *m:* James Edgar Jr.; *c:* Sandra Cain Lively, Blair Cain Guynn, James E. III; *ed:* (BS) Home Ec, Univ of AL 1952; Elem Ed Cert Work, Univ of AR Monticello; *cr:* 5th Grade Teacher Eudora Elem Sch 1963-75; 3rd Grade Teacher Montrose Acad 1975-81; 4th-6th Grade Rdng/Math Teacher Ross Van Ness 1981-86; 4th Grade Rdng/Math Teacher Cntrl Upper Elem 1986-; *home:* PO Box 541 Eudora AR 71640

CAIN, CATHIE JEAN, Band Director; *b:* Longview, TX; *ed:* (BFA) Music Ed, Stephen F Austin St Univ 1979; Post Grad Stud Stephen F Austin St Univ; *cr:* Band Camp Instr 1976-, Applied Instr 1980 Stephen F Austin St Univ; Band Dir Nacogdoches Ind Sch Dist 1980-85, Hughes Springs Ind Sch Dist 1985-; *ai:* Ham Radio Operator; NHS Mem; TX Music Educators Assn 1976-; TX Bandmasters Assn, Four States Band Masters Assn, Stephen F Austin St Univ (Lumberjack Band Alumni, Treas) 1981-85, Life Mem; Percussive Arts Society; Natl Assn of Rudimental Drummers; Numerous Awards and Medals from Contests and Competitions; US Natl Individual Band Awds; Various Schlsps; All Amer Scholar Awds; Amer Legion TX Boys St Band Mem; UIL Sweepstakes Awd 1988-89; 1st Division UIL Contests 1988-89; St Honor Band Finalist; Smokey Mountain Music Festivals Awds; Various UIL Divison Contests 1988-; Various Parades 1987-89; TX St UIL Solo & Ensemble Contests Awds & Medals; All Dist & Region Band; E TX Jr/Sr Honor Band Mem; All Amer Hall of Fame Musicians; *office:* Hughes Springs HS P O Box 399 Hughes Springs TX 75656

CAIN, DONALD WAYNE, Soc Stud/Public Spkng Teacher; *b:* Houston, TX; *ed:* (BA) His, Public Speaking, Stephen F Austin St Univ 1969; Ed; *cr:* Teacher Ryan Mid Sch 1970-77; Reagan HS 1984-; *ai:* Faislafe Comm; Jr Class Spon; Teacher of Yr 1984 Regan HS; *office:* John H Reagan Sch 13th & Arlington Houston TX 77008

CAIN, EMMA GRACE, Fifth Grade Teacher; *b:* San Antonio, TX; *m:* Jack M.; *c:* Russell, Robert, Ruth, Rich; *ed:* (BS) Elem Ed, Grand Canyon Coll 1964; Grad Courses; *cr:* 1st Grade Teacher Naturita Sch 1957-63, Riverside Elem 1963-67; 5th Grade Teacher Truth or Consequences Elem 1976-; *ai:* St Ag Chairperson; Sierra Cty Ed Assn VP 1985-86; NEA 1957-67, 1976-; Chamiza Cowbelles; NM Farm & Livestock Bus Ag 1983-;

Soil Conservation Teacher of Yr 1988-89; *home:* Engle Star Rt Truth or Conseq NM 87901

CAIN, GERRE M., Sixth Grade Teacher; *b:* Payette, ID; *c:* Debra M. King; *ed:* (BA) Elem Ed, Coll of ID 1965; Ed Classes Coll of ID, Boise St Univ, Univ of ID; *cr:* 3rd Grade Teacher Eastside 1965-75; 4th Grade Teacher Eastside & Westside 1975-85; 6th Grade Teacher Westside Mc Cain Mid 1985-; *ai:* Delta Kappa Gamma (Pres, Intnl Corresponding Secy 1986-88); Bus & Prof Women Secy 1989-; 1st Baptist Church Treas 1988-; *office:* Mc Cain Mid Sch 1215 Center Ave Payette ID 83661

CAIN, JACQUELINE MALONE, French/Spanish Teacher; *b:* Chicago, IL; *m:* Rodney S.; *c:* John, Rodney, David; *ed:* (BA) Span, Univ of KY 1966; Grad Study Fr, Guidance, Learning Disabilities; *cr:* Teacher Simon Kenton HS 1964-65, Walton-Verona HS 1966; Beech Grove Elem 1977-78; Twenhofel Jr HS 1978, Simon Kenton HS 1979-; *ai:* Foreign Lang Club Spon; CORE Team Mem; Ed Expo Comm Mem; Academic Letter/Recognition Comm; N KY Ed Assn, KY Ed Assn; Jr Bd for Crippled Children (Treas, Pres) 1970-83; Sr Bd for Crippled Children; *office:* Simon Kenton HS 5545 Madison Pike Independence KY 41051

CAIN, JULIA O., English Teacher; *b:* New Orleans, LA; *ed:* (BA) Speech/Eng, NW St Univ Natchitoches 1950; (MAIS) Speech/Eng/Journalism, Univ of TX Tyler 1984; Law S Meth Univ; Real Estate El Centro Coll; Accounting Dallas Coll; *cr:* Scndry Eng Eustace HS 1976-; *ai:* Sr Class & Stu Cncl Spon; UIL Spelling Coach; TSTA, NEA, NCTE, ETCTE; Chamber of Commerce Sch Bell Awd 1988; *office:* Eustace HS P O Box 188 Eustace TX 75124

CAIN, MARY L., Religion Teacher; *b:* Crowley, LA; *m:* Larry E.; *c:* Angelle Kolbe; *cr:* 4th Grade Teacher St Michael Elem 1965-66, St Anthonys 1965-67, Queen of All Saints 1967-68, St Michael Elem 1968-76; 5th-8th Grade Religious Ed/Cmptr Ed Teacher St Michael Elem 1982; *ai:* 8th Grade Spon; Cmptr Lab Instr; NCEA 1987-; *office:* St Michael Elem Sch 805 E Northern Ave Crowley LA 70526

CAIN, NANCY WEST, First Grade Teacher; *b:* Jasper, AL; *m:* Charles David; *c:* Brandon; *ed:* (AS) Ed, Walker Coll 1977; (BS) Elem Ed, 1979, (MA) Elem Ed, 1981 Univ of AL Birmingham; *cr:* Kndgtn Teacher Redmill Jr HS 1979-81; 5th Grade Teacher Eldridge Jr HS 1981-82; 1st Grade Teacher Lupton Jr HS 1982-; *ai:* Yrbk Spon; Walker Cty Ed Assn, AL Ed Assn, NEA 1979-; United Meth Women 1985-; *home:* Rt 2 Box 187-A Jasper AL 35501

CAIN, ROBERT B., Teacher; *b:* Lynch, KY; *m:* Bryna; *c:* Cassie, Jennifer, Jeremy; *ed:* (BA) Eng, Univ of KY 1962; (MED) Admin, FL Atlantic Univ 1966; (EDD) Curr/Eng, Univ of Miami 1972; *cr:* Asst Prof FL Atlantic Univ 1965-84; Teacher Coral Springs HS 1984-; *ai:* Broward Arts Cncl Chairperson 1983-84; *office:* Coral Springs HS 7201 W Sample Rd Coral Springs FL 33065

CAIN, SUSAN K., Third Grade Teacher; *b:* Jackson, MS; *m:* Joseph R. Jr.; *c:* Remy, Corey, Molly; *ed:* Associate Ed MS Gulf Coast Jr Coll 1973; (BS) Elem Ed, Univ Southern MS 1975; William Carey Coll Graduate Level Courses; *cr:* 3rd Grade Teacher GPT City Schls 1975-76; 3rd Grade Teacher Harrison Cty Schls 1976-; *ai:* MEA; MS Talented & Gifted Assn; *office:* Bel-Aire Elem Sch Box 1 Klein Rd Gulfport MS 39503

CAIN, VERGIE WILLIAMS, 2nd Grade Teacher; *b:* Jayess, MS; *m:* Albert; *c:* Monique; *ed:* (BA) Elem Ed, Natchez Coll 1969; (BS) Elem Ed, Alcorn St Univ 1971; *cr:* Teacher Franklin Elem Sch 1971-; *ai:* MS Assn of Ed (Secy 1982-84, Building Rep 1987-); *home:* 78 Pineview Dr Natchez MS 39120

CAINE, BRENDA CLINKINGBEARD, Social Studies Chairman; *b:* Springfield, MO; *m:* John Joseph III; *c:* Natalie, Adam; *ed:* (BED) Comprehensive Soc Stud, SMSU 1976; Grad Work, SMSU, CMSU, MU; *cr:* Teacher Morgan Cntry R-2 1976-77, Eldon R-1 1977-; Soc Stud Chm Eldon R-1; *ai:* Mentor Teacher; Dist Curr Comm; MSTA (Pres, VP) 1976-; NCSS, MCSS 1989-; Eldon Lib Bd (Pres, VP, Secy) 1979-88; Amer Cancer Society 1988-; Red Cross WSI; Congruence Review Team MMAT; *home:* 501 N Aurora Eldon MO 65026

CALABRESE, DONNA CARLISE, English Teacher/Dept Chair; *b:* Canton, OH; *m:* Albert R.; *c:* Anne, Amy; *ed:* (BS) Eng, Malone Coll 1969, (MS) Ed, Akron Univ 1981; *cr:* Eng Teacher Meigs Jr HS 1966-68, Longfellow Jr HS 1968-; *ai:* Citywide Eng Chm Massillon City Schls; Massillon Ed Assn Secy 1988-; OH Ed Assn, NEA; Martha Holden Jennings Scholar 1981; *office:* Longfellow Jr HS 514 North Ave NE Massillon OH 44646

CALABRESE, MARIO, Fifth Grade Teacher; *b:* Greenwich, CT; *m:* Karen Perkins; *c:* Vincent, Avery; *ed:* (MA) Sociology, 1972, (MA) His, 1976 Bridgeport Univ; Admin, S CT St Univ 1983; *cr:* 5th Grade Teacher Elias Howe Sch 1968-71, Prendergast Sch 1972-82; 1st Grade Teacher Lincoln-Hayes Sch 1982-88; 5th Grade Teacher Prendergast Sch 1989-; *office:* Prendergast Sch 59 Finney St Ansonia CT 06401

CALABRESE, MARYLYN JONES, English Department Chairperson; *b:* Scranton, PA; *c:* David; *ed:* (AB) Eng, Bryn Mawr 1957; (MAT) Teaching, Wesleyan 1959; (MA) Eng, 1965, (PHD) Ed/Teaching of Writing, 1987 Univ of PA; *cr:* Eng Teacher Haverford Sr HS 1959-65, Conestoga Sr HS 1969-76, 1980-; Project Dir Tredyffrin/Easttown Sch Dist 1976-80; Dept Chairperson Conestoga Sr HS 1982-; *ai:* Debate Club Adv; NCTE, NEA, Phi Delta Kappa 1976-; Decade of Equity Awd Mid Atlantic Center for Sex Equity 1982; *office:* Conestoga Sr HS Irish Rd Berwyn PA 19312

CALABRIA, ROSARITA MARY, Fifth Grade Teacher; *b:* Reading, PA; *ed:* (BA) Ed, Misericordian 1960; (MA) His, Aquinas 1966; Grad Stud Guidance, Admin; *cr:* Ed Consultant Diocese of Dallas 1962-68; Prin Our Lady of Mt Carmel 1968-74; Teacher St Catherine 1990; *office:* St Catharine of Siena Sch 2330 Perkiomen Ave Reading PA 19606

CALABRO, PATRICIA ANN WINDERLIN, 2nd Grade Teacher; *b:* Scott City, KS; *m:* Gregory J.; *c:* Mary K., Angela R.; *ed:* (BS) Elem Ed, Sacred Heart Coll 1970; Working Towards Masters Ed, Curr, Instruction; *cr:* 1st Grade Teacher St Rose Elem Sch 1969-71; 4th Grade Teacher 1971-77, 5th Grade Teacher 1978-87, 2nd Grade Teacher 1987- Lead Elem; *ai:* ACEI VP 1989-; LDEA (Building Rep, Delegate to Representative Assembly) 1988-; Lead-Deadwood Ed Assn, SD Ed Assn, NEA 1971-; St Patricks Altar Society 1977-; St Patricks Church Cncl 1980-; Lead-Deadwood PTA 1989-; *home:* 113 Grand PO Box 286 Lead SD 57754

CALAIS, ALMA MOREAU, Third Grade Teacher; *b:* Arnaudville, LA; *m:* James M.; *ed:* (BA) Lower Elem, Univ of Southwestern LA 1979; *cr:* Teachers Aide 1975-78, Teacher 1979 Cecilia Primary; *ai:* LEA 1979-; *home:* Rt 4 Box 410 Breoux Bridge LA 70517

CALAMARAS, JAMI JANICE, 4th Grade Teacher; *b:* Aurora, IL; *ed:* (BA) Elem Ed/General Sci, Aurora Univ; Northern IL Univ; *cr:* 4th Grade Teacher Nicholson Sch 1981-; *ai:* Outdoor Ed Spon; Past Mem PTA Bd; CAC; Rdng is Fundamental Comm; Building Leadership Team; Golden Apple Awd 1988; ACSD Mem; *office:* Nicholson Elem Sch W Aurora Dist #129 Aurora IL 60506

CALAMERA, FRAN FICHERA, Biology Teacher; *b:* Brooklyn, NY; *m:* John; *c:* Christopher; *ed:* (BA) Bio, Brooklyn Coll 1969; (MS) Scndry Ed/Sci, Richmond Coll 1972; *cr:* Bio/General Sci Teacher Fort Hamilton HS 1969-70, Curtis HS 1970-; *ai:* Bio Honor Society Adv; Bio Honor Society Digest Publication Adv; *office:* Curtis HS 105 Hamilton Ave Staten Island NY 10314

CALAWAY, NORMAN HARDY, History Teacher; *b:* El Dorado, AR; *c:* Shawn P., Pat R.; *ed:* (BA) European His, OK Coll of Liberal Art 1973; (MED) Adult Ed, Univ of OK 1974; Working towards PHD His & Philosophy of Ed, Univ of OK; *cr:* Teaching Asst Univ of OK 1974-76; His Teacher Heritage Hall Upper Sch 1976-77, Del City HS 1977-; *ai:* Sci Fiction & Fantasy Club; Living His Re-enactments; OK Historical Society, Western His Assn, OK Acad of Sci, NCSS; Democratic Party (Precinct Chm, Delegate) 1984-88; PTO VP 1982-88; Schlsp Leadership Enrichment Prgm Univ of OK; *home:* Rt 1 Box 41 T T Cement OK 73017

CALCAGNO, FRANK W., US History/Geography Teacher; *b:* San Francisco, CA; *m:* Sandra Kay Fisher; *c:* Kevin, Keith, Kyle; *ed:* (BA) US His, Sacramento St Univ 1962; (MA) Ed, OR St Univ 1971; *cr:* Teacher/Coach Grant HS 1967-74; El Camino Fundamental HS 1974-; *ai:* Var Bsbl Coach; Class Spon; Curr Comm; US His Book Selection; NEA, CTA 1967-; N CA Ofcls Assn (Secy 1985) 1974-; Geography Awareness Wkshp; *office:* El Camino Fundamental HS 4300 El Camino Ave Sacramento CA 95821

CALCIANO, MARIE FRANCES, 8th Grade Teacher/Sci Coord; *b:* Bronx, NY; *ed:* (BS) Ed, Fordham Univ 1971; Admin Course; *cr:* 2nd Grade Teacher St Clares Sch 1962-64; 1st Grade Teacher 1964-72, Prin/1st Grade Teacher 1970-72 St Anthonys Sch; 7th/8th Grade Teacher Christ The King 1972-; *ai:* Sci & 7th/8th Grade Cmptr Coord; Summer Sch Admin; Talent Show Dir; Natl Assn for Religious Women Treas 1968-71; Teacher of Yr Awd Archdiocese of Philadelphia 1988; *office:* Christ The King Sch 3205 Chesterfield Rd Philadelphia PA 19114

CALDARO, MARIE DORIO, History Teacher; *b:* New York, NY; *m:* J. Robert; *c:* Christian; *ed:* (BA) Soc Sci, Pace Univ 1973; (MS) Urban Research, Fordham Univ 1976; Supvr & Prin Cert Kean Coll 1987; *cr:* Teacher Jr HS 54 1973-75, Middletown HS South 1980-; *ai:* Prejudice Awareness Coord; Wythicombe Grant 1985; *office:* Middletown HS South 501 Nutswamp Rd Middletown NJ 07748

CALDERONE, JODI A., Kindergarten Teacher; *b:* N Babylon, NY; *ed:* (BS) Behavorial Sci, NY Inst of Technology 1987; (MSE) Ed, Dowling Coll 1989; *cr:* Teacher William E De Luca Elem1989-; *ai:* Var Cheerleading Coach; Kappa Delta Pi 1989-, Honor Society 1989-; N Babylon Athletic Club (Cheerleading Coach 1978-89, Co-Coord Cheerleading 1989-).

CALDERONE, NANCY RICHARDSON, Second Grade Teacher; *b:* Grove Hill, AL; *c:* Lauren E., Samuel A., John D.; *ed:* (BS) Elem Ed, 1975, (MED) Elem Ed, 1981 Univ of S AL; *cr:* 2nd Grade Teacher Boykin Elem 1975; 4th-5th Grade Teacher Glendale Elem 1975; 2nd Grade Teacher Wilmer Elem 1975-; *ai:* Leader SAT Testing, Assemblies, Pride Week Comm; Alpha Delta Kappa (Historian 1988-, Corresponding Secy 1990); NEA, AL Ed Assn 1975-; *home:* 7911 Granato Dr Semmes AL 36575

CALDERWOOD, JOHN CARVER, Social Science Dept Chairman; *b:* Jacksonville, FL; *ed:* (BA) His, Univ of CA Berkeley 1966; (MA) His, 1968, Cert of Russian Inst 1968 Columbia Univ; *cr:* Teacher Lakeside HS 1972-83, Chabot Coll 1975-, Bishop O Dowd HS 1985-; *ai:* NCSS 1989-; Sierra Club 1971-; Articles Published Oakland Tribune; Monterey Penninsula Herold; San Francisco Chronicle Examiner 1981-; *office:* Bishop O'Dowd H S 9500 Stearns Ave Oakland CA 94605

CALDWELL, BARBARA NOEL, Fourth Grade Unit Leader; *b:* Chicago, IL; *m:* Keith A.; *c:* Lori A., Keith L.; *ed:* (BE) Ed, Chicago Teachers Coll 1959; (MA) Inner City Stud, NE IL Univ 1975; *cr:* Teacher Lawson Sch 1959-68; Television Teacher 1968-74, Teacher 1974-77 Dumas Sch; Teacher Bartleme Sch 1977-80, Cook Cty House of Correction 1986-88, Natl Coll of Ed 1987-88; Unit Leader Walt Disney Magnet Sch 1980-; *ai:* Rdng, PPAC, Soc Comm; Public Sch Teachers Pension & Retirement Fund Recording Secy 1989-; Chicago Teachers Union 1959-; Delta Sigma Theta 1959-, Membership 1989; Dusable Museum Publicity Chm1959-; Provident Hospital Womens Auxiliary Womens Bd Secy 1959-; *office:* Walt Disney Magnet Sch 4140 N Marin Dr Chicago IL 60613

CALDWELL, CAROLYN R., Teacher; *b:* Denver, CO; *m:* Carl H.; *c:* Christopher L., Craig B.; *ed:* (BS) Bus Admin, Anderson Univ 1964; (MS) Bus Ed, IN Univ 1974; Cmptr Programming; *cr:* Scndry Ed Hillcrest Girls Home 1965-66; Bus Teacher Martinsville HS 1968-71; Adult Ed Teacher Upper Wabash Voc Sch 1971-76; Bus Teacher Wabash HS 1976-89; Bus Lecturer Manchester Coll 1979-81; *ai:* Sr Class & FBLA Spon; IN Bus Educators Assn 1976-89; Bus & Prof Women of America (VP, Pres) 1980-83; Kiwanis 1990; Manchester Symphony Orch Bd Mem 1987-89; Manchester Child Care Assn Ways & Means Chm 1971-73; Mem North Cntrl Assn Accreditation Teams 1982, 1988; *home:* 101 Tiffany Dr Bridgewater VA 22812

CALDWELL, EARLINE GILLAND, Reading Teacher; *b:* Mount Pleasant, MS; *ed:* (BS) Elem Ed, Rust Coll 1965; (BBS) Bus, Henderson Bus Coll 1959; (MS) Rdng Specialist, AR St Univ 1970; Rdng Memphis St TN Instructional Model Teaching & Trng Personnel; *cr:* Rdng Specialist U S Federal Government Right to Read 1978-82; Basic Audult Ed Teacher Shelby Cty Sch 1980-82; 5th Grade Teacher Barrets Chapel Sch; 8th Grade Rdng Teacher Kirby Mid Sch 1987-; *ai:* Drill Team & Honor Roll Spon; Chairperson Rdng Dept; Youth to Young People Adv; Shelby Cty Ed Assn Faculty Rep; TN Ed Assn; NEA; Just Say No Drug Chairperson 1984-87; Career Awareness Comm; Jr Achievement Awd; Distinguished Teacher of Yr 1985-86; City of Memphis Mayors Cmmty Awd 1988-89; *office:* Kirby Mid Sch 6670 Raines Rd Memphis TN 38115

CALDWELL, EMMA LOUISE, 1st-4th Grade Math Teacher; *b:* Orangeburg, SC; *ed:* (BA) Child Dev/Elem Ed, Spelman Coll 1977; (MS) Spec Ed/EH/LD, Univ MI Ann Arbor 1980; Educl Admin, Univ of SC; Assessment of Performance of Teachers Observer 1982-; Prgm Effective Teachers 1988; Curr Dev, Univ of SC; *cr:* Teacher of Orthopedically Handicapped Bennettsville Elem 1979-80; 5th Grade Teacher 1980-84, 4th Grade Teacher 1984-86, 1st-4th Grade Math Teacher 1986- Sheridan Elem; *ai:* Dist Math Comm; Placement Comm for Gifted & Talented; Sch Intervention Team Chairperson; Team Leader; SC Cncl for Teachers of Math, NCTM 1986-; Phi Delta Kappa 1988, Service Awd 1990; PTA 1989-; Delta Sigma Theta 1985-; Sheridan Elem & Orangeburg Sch Dist Teacher of Yr 1989-; Sch of Ed Fellow Univ of MI; *office:* Sheridan Elem Sch 139 Hillsboro Rd Orangeburg SC 29115

CALDWELL, JO MEREDITH, First Grade Teacher; *b:* Columbia, LA; *m:* Michael Ross; *c:* Chris, Devin; *ed:* (BS) Elem Ed, 1967, (MED) Elem Ed, 1978 NE LA Univ; Grad Stud Elem, Admin & Supervision; *cr:* 1st Grade Teacher Wisner Elem Sch 1975-; *home:* PO Box 128 Wisner LA 71378

CALDWELL, JOAN C., Biology/Chemistry Teacher; *b:* Martin, KY; *c:* Stephen, Todd, Ben, Matthew; *ed:* (BS) Bio, Pikeville Coll 1967; (MA) Ed, Morehead St Univ 1973; *cr:* Bio Teacher Garrett HS 1967-68, Prestonsburg HS 1970-71, Turkey Foot Jr HS 1974-75, Prestonsburg Comm Coll 1987-88, Mc Dowell HS 1971-72, 1975-; *ai:* Beta Club & Sr Spon; Appointed Sci Subject Advisory Chairperson 1989-; Dupont Sponsored Teacher NSTA Natl Meeting 1990; *office:* Mc Dowell HS General Delivery Mc Dowell KY 41647

CALDWELL, MARY PITTARD, Fourth Grade Teacher; *b:* Orangeburg, SC; *m:* Leslie Earl; *c:* Joseph M., Diane Lambert, Fred C.; *ed:* (AA) DeKalb Coll 1968; (BSED) Elem Ed, Univ of GA 1970; (MED) Mid Grade Ed, GA Coll 1984; GA St Univ 1971; Cert Renewal Courses GA Coll 1988-89; *cr:* 7th Grade Teacher Northwoods Elem 1970-71; 4th Grade Teacher Piedmont Acad 1982-; *ai:* DeKalb Ed Assn, GA Ed Assn 1970-71; Gamma Beta Phi 1983-84; Monticello Baptist Church Church Cncl 1971-; Natl Society Magna Charta Dames 1988-; *office:* Piedmont Acad P O Box 231 Monticello GA 31064

CALDWELL, ROSE HILL, Mathematics Teacher; *b:* Lebanon, KY; *m:* Joseph M.; *c:* Mark C., Jeff C.; *ed:* (BA) Math, 1972, (MA) Math, 1974 Univ of KY; Math Ed; *cr:* Math Teacher Lafayette 1974-; Math Chm Paul Laurence Dunbar HS 1990; *ai:* LCTM 9th Grade Math Contest & LCTM Wkshp Chm; LCTM Pres 1987-89; Faculty Governors Scholars Prgm 1987; Grad Teaching Asst 1972-74.

CALDWELL, STEVEN DE WITT, Learning Opportunity Instr; *b:* Sacramento, CA; *m:* Christie Lou; *c:* Michael, Brian, Matthew, Joshua, Thomas; *ed:* (AA) His, Amer River Coll 1967; (BS) Bio/Phys Ed, CA Poly Univ 1971; (MA) Ed Management, Fresno Pacific Coll 1983; Admin Services Credential; Elem Multi-Subject Credential; *cr:* Math/Phys Ed/Sci/Soc Stud/Vice-Prin Wilson Jr HS; 6th Grade Teacher Wilson Elem; Learning Opportunity/Ind Stud Wilson Sch; *ai:* Mid Sch & Elem Sch Act Dir; HS Ftbl, Bsktbl, Bsbl, Golf, Tennis Coach; Negotiating Comm; Prin

Summer Sch Prgm; Exeter Elem Teacher Assn Pres 1973-75, Yrbk Dedication 1985; Exeter Youth Prgm Coach 1975-81, 1985-, Outstanding Coaches Awd 1987; *office:* Wilson Sch 265 Albert St Exeter CA 93221

CALDWELL, WILLIAM M., Choir Director; *b:* Lucedale, MS; *m:* Jane M. Morehead; *c:* Julie, Mandee; *ed:* (BM) Music, AL Coll 1966; (MM) Music Ed, GA St Univ 1973; (PHD) Choral Music Ed, FL St Univ 1980; *cr:* Choral Dir Enterprise HS 1966-67, Fitzgerald Jr/Sr HS 1967-68, Waycross Jr/Sr HS 1968-69, Moultrie Jr/Sr HS 1969-80; Music Coord Colquitt Cty Schls 1973-80; Choral Act Dir SW Baptist Univ 1980-81; Choral Dir Jefferson Cty Schls 1981-84, Colquitt Cty HS 1984-; *ai:* St Louis Symphony, Atlanta Symphony, Tallahassee Symphony, Interlochen Choirs Preparer; GA All St Choir 1973, AL All St Choir Conductor 1989; Music Educators Natl Conference, Amer Choral Dir Assn, Colquitt Cty Art Assn; GA Music Educators Assn Choral Cncl 1976-80, 1987-; ACDA (GA Chapter Pres 1989-, Bd of Dir 1986-); Colquitt Cty STAR Teacher 1977; Jefferson Cty Schls Letter of Commendation 1984; Colquitt Cty Man of Yr 1977; GA Dist 11 Family of Yr 1976; *office:* Colquitt Cty HS 1800 Park Ave Moultrie GA 31768

CALHOUN, DEBY CHAPMAN, SLD Teacher; *b:* Williamson, WV; *m:* Peter Robert; *c:* Jason Workman; *ed:* (BS) Phys Ed/ Health, 1975, (MA) Elem Ed, 1978 Marshall Univ; (MA) Specific Learning Disabilities WV Univ 19 87; *cr:* Teacher of Specific Learning Disabilities Fairland Local 1975-79; 6th Grade Teacher Crab Orchard Elem 1979-80; Teacher of Specific Learning Disabilities Symmes Valley Local 1980-82; 5th Grade Teacher Harman Elem 1982-89; Teacher of Specific Learning Disabilities Tucker Cty HS 1989-; *ai:* 9th Grade Class Spon; Cncl for Exceptional Children 1990; Canaan Valley Volunteer Fire Dept Treas 1982-; Canaan Valley Womans Club 1986-; Canaan Valley Jr Ski Race Team Treas 1984-; Tucker Cty Horse Cncl 1989-; *home:* Rt 1 Box 14 F Canaan Valley Davis WV 26260

CALHOUN, ESTHER BRYAN, English Department Chairperson; *b:* Point Pleasant, NJ; *m:* John Noah; *c:* Bryan T., Sean E.; *ed:* (BA) Eng, Milligan Coll 1965; (MSED) Scndry Admin, Youngstown St 1981; *cr:* Eng I Teacher Wellsville HS 1965-68; Eng III/IV Teacher Southern Local HS 1969-70; Eng III/IV Teacher 1973-, Eng Dept Chairperson 1975- Wellsville HS; Lang Art Coord City Schls 1983-; *ai:* Y Teen Sponsorship; Thespian, Jr/Sr Class Spon; Coll Bowl Coach; Delta Kappa Gamma (1st, 2nd VP) 1984-88; Order of Eastern Star Worthy Matron 1970; Arts Club Pres 1972; Wellsville City Teachers Assn Pres 1982; Jennings Scholar 1980; OH Wesleyan Conference on Writing 1988; *office:* Wellsville HS 929 Center St Wellsville OH 43968

CALHOUN, JOHN C., 5th Grade Teacher; *b:* North Bend, OR; *m:* Sharon O.; *c:* Jason, Janene; *ed:* (BS) Elem Ed, S OR Coll 1971; ITIP 1983-84; Assertive Discipline 1986-; Open Classroom 1974; *cr:* 5th Grade Teacher Hillcrest Elem Sch 1971-; *ai:* Admin Asst; North Bend Ed Assn (Pres 1987-88, Exec Bd 1986-, Pres Elect 1986-87), Pres Citation 1988; PTA 1971-; *home:* 918 Noble Coos Bay OR 97420

CALHOUN, NANCY S., Fourth Grade Teacher; *b:* Gastonia, NC; *c:* Chris; *ed:* (BS) Grammar, Pembroke St Univ 1968; *cr:* Teacher Warlick Elem 1968-72, Myrtle Elem Sch 1973-77, Forest Heights Elem 1977-; *ai:* NCAE, NEA; *home:* 2208 Glenraven Ave Gastonia NC 28052

CALHOUN, PEGGY DARLENE, English/Phys Ed/Teacher/ Coach; *b:* Big Spring, TX; *ed:* (BA) Phys Education's Health, 1983; (BA) Bio, 1983; (BA) Eng, 1985 Angelo ST Univ; (AA) Phys Ed, Howard Coll 1981; *cr:* Teacher/Coach Runnels Jr HS 1983-; *ai:* Coaching, Vlybl, Bsktbl, Track; ATPE; *home:* 2609 Wasson Road Apt #65 Big Spring TX 79720

CALHOUN, RONNIE FORD, Teacher; *b:* Cadiz, KY; *ed:* (BS) Soc Stud, 1964, (MA) Admin, 1970 Murray St Univ; *cr:* Head Teacher Tiline Sch 1964-67; Soc Stud Teacher Livingston Cntrl HS 1967-; *ai:* W KY His Assn 1987-; KY Ed Assn Bd of Trustees 1984-; 1st Dist Ed Assn Secy 1990; Church Clerk 1968-.

CALHOUN, VICKI PHILLIPS, Mathematics Teacher; *b:* Seneca, SC; *m:* Robert Anderson; *c:* Robert, Meghan; *ed:* (BA) Math, Winthrop Coll 1969; (MED) Math Ed, 1972, Specialists Math Ed, 1987 Clemson Univ; *cr:* Teacher Walhalla Jr HS 1969-70, Pine St Elem 1971, Westminster HS 1971-74, Walhalla Mid; *ai:* Beta Club; Mathcounts; Sch & Cmmty SACS Comm Chairperson; PDR, NEA, OCEA, SCEA, NCTM; Paul Hayne Circle Pres 1990; Blue Hills Garden Club Secy 1989-; Womans Club Treas 1990; *office:* Walhalla Mid Sch Razorback Ln Walhalla SC 29691

CALKIN, MARY JANE, Special Education Dept Chair; *b:* New York City, NY; *m:* James F.; *c:* Deborah A., Jacqueline M.; *ed:* (BA) Eng, Hunter Coll 1962; Advanced Trng for Specialist Credentials, Univ of CA Irvine, CA St Univ Fullerton; *cr:* Elem Teacher Placentia Unified Sch Dist 1978-80; Spec Day Class Teacher Chino Unified Sch Dist 1980-; *ai:* Spec Ed Dept Chairperson; Chino Teachers Assn, CA Teachers Assn, NEA; *office:* Magnolia Jr HS 13150 Mountain Ave Chino CA 91710

CALL, DELORA JEAN, Third Grade Teacher; *b:* Barboursville, WV; *m:* Roger D.; *c:* Mark D., Elizabeth; *ed:* (BA) Elem Ed, 1965, (MA) Elem Ed, 1972 Marshall Univ; Grad Stud; *cr:* Headstart Teacher 1965-68; 1st Grade Teacher Barboursville Elem 1965-70, Cox Landing Elem 1974-75; 1st-5th Grade Teacher Nichols Elem 1975-; *ai:* WVEA; Cabell Cty Rdng Cncl Rep; Steele Memorial United Meth Church (Sunday Schl Supt 1986-89, Commission on Ed 1980-); *home:* 113 Brady Dr Barboursville WV 25504

CALL, THOMAS ROBERT, JR., His/Ged Soc Stud/Sci Teacher; *b:* Saginaw, MI; *m:* Susan Frances Brogan; *c:* Kellie Compo, Shannon; *ed:* (BA) His/Sociology, Saginaw Valley St Univ 1974; Continuing Certificate Saginaw Valley St Univ; CPR & First Aid Trng, Red Cross; Child Abuse & Neglect Trng, St of MI; *cr:* Teacher Saginaw Schls 1975-; Teacher/Coach Bay City Schls 1976; Childrens Protective Services Worker St of MI 1978-; *ai:* MI Ed Assn 1976-77, 1988-; NEA 1976-77, 1989-; MI Assn of Soc Workers 1978-; Veterans of Foreign Wars 1984-; Alpha Gamma Sigma 1972-; Saginaw Valley St Univ Fellowship 1975; Red Cross Certificate of Appreciation; St of MI Numerous Certificates of Merit & Acad Awds; Ed & Writer AM River Coll; *home:* PO Box 6631 Saginaw MI 48708

CALLAGHAN, RICHARD MICHAEL, 8th Grade Humanities Teacher; *b:* West Point, NY; *m:* Cindy Jean; *c:* Meghan, Caitlin; *ed:* (BA) Liberal Stud, CA St Univ Hayward 1983; *cr:* 5th Grade Teacher 1983-85, 7th-8th Grade Teacher 1985-88, 8th Grade Teacher 1988- Caruthers Union Elem; *ai:* Sports & Chess Clubs; Ftbl, Vlybl, Bsktbl, Bsbl, Sftbl Coach; Athletic Dir; Mentor Teacher.

CALLAGHER, RITA DAVIS, Substitute Teacher; *b:* Columbus, OH; *m:* Nicholas D. Jr.; *c:* Joseph S., Julia M. Galbreath, Theresa A. Thompson, Margaret M. White, Michael V., Nora E. Fisher, Nicholas D. IV; *ed:* (BS) Ed - Magna Cum Laude, Wright St Univ 1973; *cr:* Substitute Teacher St Patrick Sch & Troy City Schls 1973-74; 1st Grade Teacher 1974-75, 5th Grade Teacher 1975-89, Substitute Teacher 1989- St Patrick Sch; *home:* 701 Gateshead Rd Troy OH 45373

CALLAHAN, CATHLEEN ANNE, Phys Ed Teacher/Coach; *b:* Burbank, CA; *ed:* (BS) Phys Ed/Health, Co St Univ 1975; (MS) Ed Specialty Cmptrs, Lesley Coll 1988; *cr:* Phys Ed Teacher/ Bsktbl Coach Rampart HS 1985-; Asst Bsktbl Coach Univ of CO Colorado Springs 1990; *ai:* Jr Var Bsktbl 1984-87; Frosh Vlybl 1984-88; Jr Var Soccer 1984-86; Var Bsktbl 1987-; Jr Var Sftbl 1989; Asst Univ of CO Colorado Springs 1990; Women Bsktbl Coaches Assn 1987-; CO Coaches of Girls Sports (All St Chairperson 1987-) 1988; CO HS Coaches Assn 1987-89; Coaches Cncl (Secy 1987-) 1987; Covenant Presbyn Church 1987-; Outstanding Young Women America 1988; Volunteer-World Cycling Championships 1986; Natl Sports Festival-Team Handball Mem 1979; Volunteer-Hoopfest Amer Cancer Society 1990; *office:* Rampart HS 8250 Lexington Dr Colorado Springs CO 80920

CALLAHAN, DANIEL F., Science Teacher; *b:* Alma, MI; *m:* Cynthia Lynn; *c:* Megan L.; *ed:* (BS) Bio, Alma Coll 1980; *cr:* Sci Teacher West Cntrl HS 1981-83, Clinton Cntrl HS 1983-87, Marcus HS 1987-; *ai:* Var Wrestling Coach; Asst Frosh Ftbl; TX HS Coaches 1987-; TX Wrestling Coaches 1987-; Quest for Gold Corporation TX Dir 1988-; USA Wrestling N TX Regional Dir 1989-; USA Wrestling Bronze Level & TX St Freestyle Coach 1988-; *office:* Marcus HS 5707 Morress Rd Flower Mound TX 75067

CALLAHAN, DIANE CLEPPER, Fourth Grade Teacher; *b:* Carlisle, PA; *ed:* (MA) Rdng Specialist, Univ of WI Platteville 1982; Gifted Ed; *cr:* 5th Grade Teacher 1978-84, 6th Grade Teacher 1984-87, 4th Grade Teacher 1987- Shady Hills Elem; *ai:* Sci Rep; Sci Fair Dir; Project WILD Facilitator; Teacher of Yr Selected by Peers; *office:* Shady Hills Elem Sch 1900 Shady Hills Rd Spring Hill FL 34610

CALLAHAN, JAMES FRANCIS, Science Teacher; *b:* Lowell, MA; *m:* Irene M. Walsh; *c:* James, Jill; *ed:* (BS) Ed, Lowell St 1969; *cr:* 6th Grade Teacher Pollard Sch 1969-71; 6th Grade Sci Teacher 1971-73, 8th Grade Sci Teacher 1974-89, 7th Grade Sci Teacher 1989- Marshall Mid Sch; *home:* 196 Salem Rd Billerica MA 01821

CALLAHAN, JOY PURTEE, English Teacher; *b:* Portsmouth, OH; *m:* Marion R.; *c:* Jonathan D., Daniel A.; *ed:* (BA) Eng, Tennessee Temple Univ 1974; *cr:* Rdng/Math/Sci Teacher Pennville Elem 1974-75; Speech/Family Living/Eng Teacher Lake City Chrstn 1979-86; Eng Teacher Tennessee Temple HS 1987-; *ai:* Sr Class & Jr HS Chrldrs Spon; *office:* Tennesse N Temple HS 1815 Union Ave Chattanooga TN 37404

CALLAHAN, MARJORIE FLOYD, Second Grade Teacher; *b:* Woodbury, NJ; *m:* Charles W.; *c:* Marjorie Ritchie, Charles W., James P., Michael J.; *ed:* (BS) Elem Ed, Glassboro St Coll 1949; *cr:* 5th-6th Grade Sci/Soc Stud Teacher 1949-54, 5th-6th Grade Classroom Teacher 1954-58 Gloucester City Public Sch; Substitute Teacher Cinnaminson Public Schls 1965-72; 2nd Grade Teacher Westfield Friends Sch 1972-; *ai:* Cooperating Teacher Univ of PA 1988-; *office:* Westfield Friends Sch Moorestown Riverton Rd Cinnaminson NJ 08077

CALLAHAN, REGINA MARIE, RSM, Religion Teacher; *b:* Atlantic City, NJ; *ed:* (BA) Ed, Georgian Court Coll 1972; (MA) Theology, St Charles Seminary 1989; Teacher-Adv Trng; *cr:* 2nd Grade Teacher Holy Spirit Sch 1972-73; 3rd Grade Teacher St Nicholas Sch 1973-76; 4th Grade Teacher St Marys Sch 1976-77; 7th/8th Grade Teacher St Annes Sch 1979-81, 7th/8th Grade Math Teacher St James Sch 1981-83; 10th Grade Religion Teacher Red Bank Cath HS 1983-; *ai:* Life Club Adv; Frosh Teacher/Adv; NCEA 1972-; St Nicholas PTA Outstanding Service Awd 1973-76; Red Bank Soup Kitchen Certificate Appreciation for Outstanding Service 1984; Monmouth Cty Bd of Soc Service Certificate of Appreciation Volunteer Service 1988-89; *home:* 25 Drummond PL St James Convent Red Bank NJ 07701

CALLAHAN, REVA PHELPS, Fifth Grade Teacher; *b:* Labascus, KY; *m:* Ronald Thomas; *c:* Michael T.; *ed:* (AB) Health/Phys Ed/His, Morehead St Univ 1965; (MAED) Elem Ed, GA St Univ 1977; *cr:* Health/Phys Ed/His Teacher Pulaski Cty HS 1965-67; Phys Ed Teacher Eubank Elem & Woodstock Elem 1968-69; 6th Grade Teacher Dawnville Elem 1969-74; 5th Grade Teacher Dug Gap Elem 1974-; *ai:* Stu Support Team; Lib, Sci, Stu Services Comm; PEA, KEA 1965-67; NEA 1965-; GAE 1968-, Teacher of Yr 1984; WEA Building Rep; Intnl Rdng Assn 1980-; Alpha Delta Kappa (Corresponding Secy 1986-88, Mem 1982-); *home:* 1913 Courtland Ln Dalton GA 30720

CALLENDER, EVELYN MAE (WINDOWS), Music Teacher/ Choral Director; *b:* Rochester, PA; *m:* Gail Cortland; *c:* Matthew H.; *ed:* (BA) Music, Westminster Coll 1965; (MM) Music Theory, Duquesne Univ; (MED) Admin/Scndry Elem, Westminster Coll 1986-87; Admin/Dir Elem & Scndry Choral Music, Chatauqua Inst 1970-75; Small Bus Admin Classes, PA St Univ 1978-81; *cr:* Teacher S Butler Cty Sch Dist 1965-, Pittsburgh Public Schls Center for Musically Talented 1970-79; Musical Dir Cty Symphony Choir 1968-70, Butler Musical Theatre Guild 1970-79, 1987-89, Butler Cty Jr Miss 1986-, Trinity United Meth Church 1990; *ai:* Rainbow Girls Adv; Tuesday Musical Club; Madrigal Dinners; Jr & Sr Choral Concerts; Cmmty Entertainment Socials, Churches, Sr Citizens, Amer Legion, VFW, Barbershoppers; PMEA, MENC, AFM 1965-; Phi Delta Kappa 1986-; AFT, PAFT 1980-; BSA Musical Adv; Trinity United Meth Church Choir (Music Dir, Organist) 1970-; Bus Mens Assn 1979-89; Choral & Harpsichord Musical Arrangements; *home:* 122 Crescent Hill Dr Sarver PA 16055

CALLEY, THOMAS PETER, Social Studies Teacher; *b:* Goshen, NY; *m:* Anne Marie; *c:* Daniel P.; *ed:* (BS) Ed, St Univ of NY Oneonta 1964; (MS) Ed, St Univ of NY New Paltz 1974; *cr:* 3rd/5th Grade Teacher E Coldenham Elem & Valley Cntrl 1964-67; 6th Grade Teacher Kerhonkson Elem 1967; 8th/9th Grade Amer His/Global Stud Teacher South Jr HS 1967-; *ai:* NYSTU (Rep 1980-81, Retirement Alternate Rep 1987-); Natl New Windsor Historical Assn (Fund Raising Chm 1980-82, Peace Bell Comm Chm 1980-82); *home:* 14 Ridgefield Ln Newburgh NY 12550

CALLICOAT, ELIZABETH ANN, Biology Teacher; *b:* Oxford, MS; *ed:* (BA) Phys Ed/Bio 1978, (ME) Phys Ed, 1980 Univ of MS; Spec Ed; *cr:* Teacher Barley Jr HS 1980-81; Coach/Teacher Elliston Baptist Acad 1983-84, South Side HS 1984-; *ai:* Coach Var Vlybl & Jr Bsktbl; *office:* South Side HS 1880 Prospect Memphis TN 38106

CALLIGHAN, DAVID EUGENE, Social Studies Teacher; *b:* Kalamazoo, MI; *m:* Ruth Ann Holland; *c:* Jane E. Shively, Mark D.; *ed:* (BS) His, Western MI Univ 1965; (MDIV) Pastoral Stud, Grade Theo Seminary 1972; *cr:* Prin Lake Wales Chrstn Sch 1975-77; Teacher Triton Sch Corp 1986-87, Lakeland Chrstn Acad 1987-; *ai:* 8th Grade Spon; Kiwanis Pres 1986-87; *home:* Rt 2 Box 356 Pierceton IN 46562

CALLISON, DIRK F., Teacher/Vocational Coordinator; *b:* Homestead, FL; *m:* Janet L. Hoover; *c:* Bryan R.; *ed:* (BS) Ag Ed, 1984, (MS) Ag Ed, 1985 TX A&M; *cr:* Grad Asst TX A&M 1985; Teacher Bullard Ind Sch Dist 1985-; *ai:* TX A&M Grad Fellowship 1985; Honorary St Farmer 1989; *office:* Bullard Ind Sch Dist Box 250 Bullard TX 75757

CALLOWAY, CHRISTINE, English Teacher; *b:* Opelika, AL; *ed:* (BS) Eng, AL St Univ 1980; (MED) Eng, W GA Coll 1986; *cr:* Eng Teacher Spalding Jr HS Unit III 1981-87, Taylor Street Mid Sch 1987-; *ai:* Builders Club Adv; Stu Recognition & Amer Ed Week Comm; Honors Day Comm Chairperson; NEA, GA Assn of Educators Assn Rep 1981-; NCTE 1988-; Spalding Cty Assn of Teachers of Eng 1989-; Alpha Kappa Alpha Reporter 1989-; *office:* Taylor Street Mid Sch 234 E Taylor St Griffin GA 30223

CALLOWAY, ETHEL WARREN, US His/Soc Stud Teacher; *b:* Tyler, TX; *m:* Marvin A.; *ed:* (BA) Poly Sci, Prairie View A&M Coll 1961; (MS) His, E TX St Univ 1972; Advanced Stud Anthropology, Ethnic Stud, Free Enterprise, Rdng, Scndry Ed; *cr:* Teacher Emmett Scott HS 1961-63, Stewart Jr HS 1963-68; Teacher 1968-76, Teacher/Coord 1976-77 John Tyler HS; Teacher Stephen F Austin Univ 1977; Teacher/Soc Stud Dept Head John Tyler HS 1977-; *ai:* John Tyler HS Historians Consultant; STEP Black Culture Bowl Question Writer; Amer His Gifted Stu His Exhibition Spon; TX St Teachers Assn, NEA, TX Assn of Gifted Teachers; Phi Delta Kappa Service Awd 1978; TX St Textbook Comm Mem 1978, Service 1978; EXCET Comm Mem 1988, 1990; Natl Assessment Ed Project Comm Mem 1980; His of Tyler P Smith Cty Co-Author 1976; Book Reviewer; John Tyler Teacher of Yr 1988; St Career Ladder Level III; *office:* John Tyler HS 1120 N Northwest Loop 323 Tyler TX 75702

CALLOWAY, STELLA R. (WHITTLER), Typing/Quest Teacher; *b:* Detroit, MI; *m:* James; *c:* Joy D., James L.; *ed:* (BA) Bus Ed, Wayne St Univ 1968; Trained Assertive Discipline Consultant & Quest Teacher; Trained & Certified Marriage Enrichment Leader; *cr:* Intern Teacher Northwestern HS 1968; Bus Teacher Coffey Mid Sch 1968-; *ai:* Blood Drive Coord; DFT Election Comm; Self Esteem & Assertive Discipline Contact; Detroit Fed of Teachers; Marriage Enrichment Inc Natl Bd Mem 1988-; Marriage & Family Life Comm Former MI Coord 1975-; Marital Adventure Through Enrichment Sessions Facilitator 1984-; Success Research Captivators (Founder, Dir) 1988-; *office:* Coffey Mid Sch 17210 Cambridge Detroit MI 48235

CALSOYOS, JUDITH ANN, Language Art/Lit Teacher; *b:* Hammond, IN; *m:* Kyril Alexander; *c:* Leal, Nike R., Isis M., Israel S., Maitreya; *ed:* (BS) Fr/Lit, Univ of CA 1967; (MA) ESL, Pahlaui Univ 1977; Fr, Eng, Lit, ESL Rdng Teaching Cert; *cr:* Fr/Eng Teacher Armijo HS 1971-74; Eng Teacher Pohlaui Univ 1974-78, Hefei Polytech Univ 1979-80; Eng/NAL Teacher Many Farms HS 1980-82; Fr/NAL Teacher Tuba City HS 1982-89; Lang Art/Native Amer Lit Teacher Greyhills HS 1989-; *ai:* Lang Art Curr Advisory Comm; Advisory Comm for Hum Courses; AZ Teachers of Eng Scndry Lang 1982-85; Teachers of Eng Scndry Lang 1980-84; NCTE 1984; Television Article; *home:* PO Box 2978 Tuba City AZ 86045

CALTAGIRONE, JANET MARTIN, Second Grade Teacher; *b:* Texas City, TX; *m:* Don; *c:* Courtney, Thad, Andrew; *ed:* (BSED) Phys Ed, 1980, Elem Ed, 1982 Univ of Houston; *cr:* 6th Grade Teacher Santa Fe Intermediate Sch 1982-86; 1st Grade Teacher 1986-89, 2nd Grade Teacher 1989- Roy J Wollam Elem.

CALVANI, JOSEPHINE ECKERT, Fifth Grade Teacher; *b:* Albuquerque, NM; *m:* Michael; *c:* Andrea J.; *ed:* (BUS) Elem Ed, Univ of NM 1977; *cr:* 5th Grade Teacher Sunset Elem 1980-; *ai:* NEA; Assistance League of Carlsbad; Pi Beta Phi Alumna; Univ of NM Bd of Dirs; *home:* 1101 N Shore Dr Carlsbad NM 88220

CALVERT, RENNA BIGGERS, Science Teacher; *b:* Bremen, GA; *w:* Ralph (dec); *c:* Jennifer T.; *ed:* (BS) Sci Ed, GA S Coll 1969; (MS) Bio, GA Southwestern 1975; Working on Specialist Degree; *cr:* Teacher Crisp Acad 1970-71, Crisp Cty HS 1972-76, Crisp Acad 1977-78, Crisp Cty HS 1978-; *ai:* Girls Sftbl Coach; Beta Club Sci Club Spon; Sci Team Coach; NSTA, GA Sci Teachers Assn, Prof Assn of GA Educators; Advanced Placement Teacher; STAR Teacher; HS Teacher of Yr; *home:* 380 Penia Rd Cordele GA 31015

CAMACHO, ROBERTA AGNES, Head Science Teacher; *b:* Boston, MA; *m:* David; *c:* Christina, Daniel, Alicia; *ed:* (BS) Bio, Coll of St Elizabeth 1964; (MED) Guidance/Counseling, Bridgewater St Coll 1974; (PHD) Curr/Instruction, Boston Coll 1987; *cr:* Sci Teacher NY Public Schls 1965-67, Stoughton Jr HS 1967-; *ai:* Stoughton Comm Substance Abuse Prevention & Ed; Stoughton Teachers Assn, MA Teachers Assn 1967-; ASCD 1989-; MA Assn of Sci Teachers; Save Our Stoughton (Schlsp Comm, Pres, Treas) 1986-; Stoughton Historical Society 1987-; Stoughton Town Meeting Rep 1981-; Stoughton Re-Dev Authority (Elected Office 1985-, Chm 1988-, Secy 1986-88, Treas 1986-88); Stoughton Town Hall Building Comm Past Chm 1986-; Stoughton Strategic Planning Grant Comm Mem 1986-87; Doctoral Comprehensive Examinations Boston Coll 1985; Distinction Assistanship Boston Coll 1976; *home:* 212 Seaver St Stoughton MA 02072

CAMBPELL, FRANK DE GUERRE, Administrative Dean, *b:* Hudson, NY; *m:* E. Jean Wallenthin; *c:* Amy E., Timothy D.; *ed:* (BSE) Math/Sci Ed, Univ of FL 1965; (MED) Admin/Supervision, Stetson Univ 1970; (EDS) Curr/Instruction, Univ of FL 1982; Univ of Cntrl FL, Rollins Coll, Inst for Chrstn Stud; *cr:* Sci Teacher/Asst Headmaster Sanford Naval Acad 1965-68; Bio Teacher/Dean of Stu Trinity Preparatory Sch 1968-78; Math Teacher Memorial Mid Sch 1978-89; Admin Dean Lockhart Mid Sch 1989-; *ai:* Grade Level Coord; Natl Mid Sch Assn (Conference Presenter 1986-89) 1978-; NASSP Presenter 1986; FL League of Mid Schls 1980-, Achievement 1989; Orange Cty League of Mid Schls (Pres 1988-) 1979-, Educator of Yr 1987; Seminole Soccer Club Coach 1982-86; St Christophers Episcopal Church Vestry Treas 1989-; Memorial Mid Sch Teacher of Yr 1988; *office:* Lockhart Mid Sch 3411 Dr Love Rd Orlando FL 32810

CAMEON, BRIAN KEITH, Sixth Grade Teacher; *b:* Clarksburg, WV; *ed:* (BS) Elem Ed, 1981, (MS) Ed Admin, 1984 Bob Jones Univ; *cr:* 6th Grade Teacher Cross Lanes Chrstn 1981-; *ai:* Elem Coord.

CAMERON, BONNIE ROSE, 6th Grade Teacher; *b:* Bottineau, ND; *ed:* (BS) Elem Ed, 1963, (MED) Elem Ed, 1973 Univ of ND; *cr:* 5th Grade Teacher Sheboygan Public Schls 1963-66; 3rd-4th Grade Teacher Minot Public Schls 1966-68; 6th Grade Teacher Northampton Public Schls 1968-69; 4th-6th Grade/Gifted Prgm Teacher Grand Forks Public Schls 1969-; *ai:* Phi Delta Kappa (VP, Secy) 1982-; Pi Lambda Theta Nominating 1986; NEA, NDEA, GFEA; Great Plain Storytelling Guild 1988-; Grand Forks Historical Society 1979-; Outstanding Educator Awd 1988; Published in Insights; *home:* 1627 Library Cir Grand Forks ND 58201

CAMERON, PAMELA MC ADOO, Mathematics Teacher; *b:* Greensboro, NC; *m:* Jasper Thomas; *ed:* (BS) Math, 1975, (BA) Ed, 1977 NC Cntrl Univ; *cr:* Math Teacher Carrington Jr HS 1977-; *ai:* Mathcounts Coach; Mentor; Class Adv for Team; Homebase & Senate Bill 2 Comm; Girls Bsktbl Asst Coach 1977-79; NC Assn of Educators, NEA 1977-; NC Teachers of Math 1988-89; St Josephs AME Church Inspirational Singers (VP, Choir) 1986-87; Tau Beta Sigma Natl Life Mem 1973-; Outstanding Young Women of America 1988; *office:* Carrington Jr HS 227 Milton Rd Durham NC 27712

CAMILLERI, BRUCE THOMAS, Physical Education Teacher; *b:* Bay Shore, NY; *m:* Breta Belinda Wooton; *c:* Bradley, Brent, Bobby; *ed:* (BS) Phys Ed, Kings Coll 1979; (MS) Health Ed, Russell Sage Coll 1987; Amer Red Cross CPR; *cr:* Athletic Dir/Teacher Loudonville Chrstn Sch 1979-; *ai:* 6th-8th Grade Girls Soccer, Boys & Girls Track Coach; Athletic Dir; Amer Alliance of Health, Phys Ed, Recreation & Dance Mem 1981-; Natl Assn of Sports & Phys Ed Mem 1984-; Heritage Baptist Church Deacon 1990; *office:* Loudonville Chrstn Sch 374 Loudon Rd Loudonville NY 12211

CAMMACK, ROENE BURGHARDT, 7th Grade Teacher; *b:* Mc Gregor, IA; *m:* George Wm.; *c:* John M., Thomas H.; *ed:* Elem Ed, IA Wesleyan Coll 1955; (BA) Elem Ed, Univ of IA 1958; (MA) Writing, Marycrest Coll 1989; *cr:* 1st Grade Teacher Newton Public Schls 1955-58; 5th Grade Teacher Denver Public Schls 1959-61, Cedar Rapids Cmmty Sch Dist 1961-65; 7th Grade Teacher Cedar Rapids Cmmty Sch Dist 1973-; *ai:* Multi-Cultural & Teacher Recognition Comm; Curr Dev Ad Hoc; Stu Teacher Mentor; IA Teen Awd Book Cooperating Teacher; Delta Kappa Gamma Pres 1987-89, Jesse M Parker 1988; NEA, IA St Ed Assn, Cedar Rapids Ed Assn, Pi Lambda Theta; St Stephen Church Pres 1986-89; Marion Ind Sch Bd of Ed (Mem 1978-85, Pres 1983-84); PEO, Pi Beta Phi; Natl Mid Sch Convention Dept Chairperson 1983-87; Curr, Dev, Inservice & Seminar Leader; Master Teacher; Pilot Skills For Adolescents 1986-87; Gifted/Talented Teacher 1983-87; Johns Hopkins Univ Study; Assn Teacher Magazine Interview; 19th C Salon Music 1990; *home:* 945 Parkview Dr Marion IA 52302

CAMP, ANGELA H., Algebra Teacher; *b:* Crailsheim, Germany; *c:* Andrew, Jennifer; *ed:* (BA) His/Scndry Ed, La Grange Coll 1973; GA Southern Univ 1978; *cr:* Teacher Lee Grant Acad 1973-74; 6th Grade Teacher Mountville Elem 1975-76; 5th/6th Grade Teacher Rock Hill Emem 1976-78; 4th/5th Grade Math/Sci Teacher Louisville Acad 1978-82; 7th/8th Grade Math Teacher 1982-87, 9th-12th Grade Math Teacher 1987- Louisville HS; *ai:* Math Team Co Adv; Cmptr Club Adv; Louisville HS Curr Comm; NCTM 1987-; GCTM 1987-; Outstanding Young Educator of Yr 1976; PTA, Lousiville United Meth Church 1980-; Jefferson Cty Honor Teacher 1986-88; *office:* Louisville HS Rt 3 Box 432 Louisville GA 30434

CAMP, ELIZABETH A., Physical Ed Teacher/Coach; *b:* Montgomery, AL; *m:* Billy; *ed:* (BS) Phys Ed, Faulkner Univ 1984; Masters Prgm, Auburn Univ; *cr:* Teacher/Coach Holtville HS 1984-; *ai:* Substance Abuse Coord; Vlybl & Sftbl Coach; Soph Class Spon; AL St Assn for Health, Phys Ed, Recreation & Dance, AL Ed Assn, NEA 1984-; *office:* Holtville HS Rt 2 Box 52 Deatsville AL 36022

CAMP, KIM STEWART, Teacher; *b:* Manila, Phillipines; *m:* Richard Leslie; *c:* Lauren, Chelsea, Claire; *ed:* (BS) Poly Sci, James Madison Univ 1982; (MS) Admin of Justice, VA Commonwealth Univ 1984; *cr:* 7th/8th Grade Teacher Holy Ghost Ukrainian Cath Sch 1985-86; *ai:* Org of Crim Just Prof 1983-84; Poly Sci Honor Society 1980-82; Americans for Freedom 1982; Recipient VA Commonwealth Univ Fellowship Admin of Justice 1983.

CAMP, RACHEL SCRUGGS, Mathematics Teacher/Dept Chair; *b:* Macon, GA; *m:* Gerald E.; *c:* Dianne Camp Ellis, Debbie Camp Liles; *ed:* (BA) Math, Mercer Univ 1946; (MAT) Math, Jacksonville Univ 1972; *cr:* 3rd Grade Teacher Virgil Powers Elem 1948-49, Port St Joe Elem Sch 1950-52; Dir/Kndgtn Teacher Highlands Baptist Church 1959-61; 3rd Grade Teacher Sherwood Forest Elem 1961-62; Advanced Math Teacher/Dept Chair Jackson Sr HS 1962-; *ai:* Spon & Coach of Math Field Day; Duval Cty Classroom Teachers of Math; FL Classroom Teachers of Math; Baptist Church (Teacher of Youth/Adult Classes, Drama Coach, Vacation Bible Sch Teacher, Primary Choir Dir); Curr Writing Teams for Cty Math; Consultant in Math UNF CLEP Prgm; Cty Textbook Evaluation Comm; St Standards of Excl Comm; SACS Evaluation Team for Winter Haven HS; Jacksons Yrbk Dedication & Teacher of Yr; Teacher-Stu Humanitarian Awd from Bnai Brith; Natl Math Contest Ind Study Stu 5th Place in St; *office:* Andrew Jackson Sr HS 3816 Main St Jacksonville FL 32206

CAMPAGNOLI, KATHY J., English Teacher; *b:* Baltimore, MD; *ed:* (BA) Eng, W MD Coll 1982; (MA) Sch Admin, Hood Coll 1987; *cr:* Eng Teacher S Carroll HS 1982-83, Governor Thomas Johnson HS 1983-; *ai:* Admin Dir of Attendance 1989-; Academic Team Adv 1987-89; Tennis Coach 1983-86; Newspaper Adv 1983-85; NCTE Mem 1982-; *office:* Governor Thomas Johnson HS 1501 N Market St Frederick MD 21701

CAMPANIZZI, LOUIS DOMONIC, Social Studies Chairman; *b:* Wheeling, WV; *m:* Jana Kasprowski; *ed:* (BS) Scndry Ed, OH Univ 1971; (MS) Ed Admin, Univ of Dayton 1985; *cr:* Teacher Cadiz HS 1971-; *ai:* 7th & 8th Grade Adv; Soc Stud Chrm; NEA; OEA; Harrison Hills Teachers Organization; *home:* 67205 S Almar Ln St Clairsville OH 43950

CAMPASINO, ELLEN MARIE, Third Grade Teacher; *b:* Titusville, PA; *ed:* (BS) Elem/Early Chldhd, Edinboro Univ 1972; Permanent Cert St of PA Elem Ed/Early Chldhd Edinboro Univ; *cr:* 1st Grade Teacher 1975-76, 4th Grade Teacher 1976-77, 3rd Grade Teacher 1977- St Titus Sch; *ai:* Coaching Teacher/Teacher Induction Prgm; Service Awd Diocese of Erie 1988; *office:* St Titus Sch 528 W Main St Titusville PA 16354

CAMPBELL, ANDEAN BOOTH, Third Grade Teacher; *b:* Conway, SC; *m:* Lucius Jr.; *c:* Valerie, Paul; *ed:* (BS) Elem Ed, SC St Coll 1969; (MED) Elem Ed, Coastal Carolina Campus 1976; *cr:* Teacher Waccamaw Elem Sch 1969-; *ai:* Soc Stud of Self Study Comm Chairperson; Directress of Tutorial Prgm True Vine Missionary Baptist Church; NEA, SC Ed Assn, Harry Cty Ed Assn 1969-; Delta Sigma Theta 1976-; Harry Cty Sch Dist 1st Runner-Up Teacher of Yr 1984; Waccamaw Elem Sch Teacher of Yr 1981, 1989-; *office:* Waccamaw Elem Sch Rt 6 Box 20E Conway SC 29526

CAMPBELL, BARBARA FRANCES, Sixth Grade Teacher; *b:* Emmetsburg, IA; *m:* Carey Van; *c:* Van F; *ed:* (BS) Elem Ed, 1982; (BS) Spec ED 1982 Northern AZ Univ; *cr:* Spec Ed Teacher East Flagstaff Jr HS 1984-87; Sixth Grade Teacher Christensen Elem Sch 1988-; *ai:* Rdng Textbook Selection Comm; Sch Teams Offer Prevention; Writing Across the Curr (Inservice Team); NEA; Alpha Delta Kappa; *office:* Christensen Elem Sch 4000 N Cummings St Flagstaff AZ 86004

CAMPBELL, CAROLYN MARCEAUX, English Teacher; *b:* Abbeville, LA; *m:* Charles; *c:* Dustin G. Faulk; *ed:* (BA) Eng/Speech, 1968, (MED) Scndry Ed/Eng, 1973, (EDS) Scndry Ed/Eng, 1979 Univ of SW LA; *cr:* Eng Teacher Abbeville HS 1968-84; Teacher of 7th-12th Grade Gifted & Talented Vermilion Parish 1985-86; Eng Teacher Abbeville HS 1987-89, North Vermilion HS 1989-; *ai:* Yrbk Spon; Academic Rally Co-Adv; Eng Dept Chm; Acadia Cncl Teachers of Eng, LA Cncl Teachers of Eng, Acadiana Rdng Cncl, LA Ed Assn, NEA, Vermilion Assn of Ed Poly Action Comm; Acadiana Young Authors Contest Chm 1989-; LA Lang Art Curr Guide Comm 1979-81; LA Cattle Festival Bd of Dir & Essay Chm 1985-86; Abbeville Bicentennial Comm 1976; *office:* North Vermilion HS Hwy 699 W Rt 1 Box 55 Maurice LA 70555

CAMPBELL, DONNA WOOD, English Teacher; *b:* Ft Payne, AL; *m:* Gary Lynn; *c:* Joe D., Jon P., Laura D.; *ed:* (BA) Eng, Univ of TN Chattanoga 1972; (MED) Admin/Supervision, Trevecca Nazarene 1989; *cr:* Teacher Birchwood Sch 1972-75, Redbank Jr HS 1975-76, Soddy Daisy Mid Sch 1982-; *ai:* IRA Sch Chairperson; Eng Dept Head; Sch Paper Adv; Red Cross; Mindbenders Club; NCTE, HCEA, TEA, NEA, IRA 1972-76, 1982-; N Chattanoga Church (Secy, Treas 1968-69, Sunday Sch Teacher 1966-84) 1968-; ASCD 1989-; PTA 1982-; *office:* Soddy-Daisy Mid Sch 200 Turner Rd Soddy-Daisy TN 37379

CAMPBELL, ELLEN L. (EARHART), Fifth Grade Teacher; *b:* Hamilton, OH; *m:* Robert L.; *c:* Terry Gadd, Michael Gadd; *ed:* (BS) Elem Ed, 1963, (MED) Elem Counseling, 1973 Miami Univ; *cr:* 1st Grade Teacher Morrow Elem Sch 1961-62; 2nd Grade Teacher Wilmington Schls 1962-65; Rdng Teacher Waynesville Jr HS 1966-68; 5th Grade Teacher Waynesville Elem Sch 1968-; *ai:* Faculty Advisory Cncl; OH Cncl Teachers of Math, OEA, NEA; Mary L Cook Public Lib (Secy, VP, Pres, Bd of Trustees) 1979-; SW OH Regional Lib Systems Bd of Trustees 1990; Excl in Teaching Awd 1988; *office:* Waynesville Elem Sch 659 Dayton Rd Waynesville OH 45068

CAMPBELL, EULA FAYE (SKIDMORE), Science Teacher; *b:* Harlan, KY; *m:* Ronald Edward; *c:* Kevin E., Melissa A.; *ed:* (BS) Bio, Cumberland Coll 1965; (MS) Curr/Instruction, Lincoln Memorial Univ 1988; *cr:* Teacher Fairview Elem 1972-; *ai:* 8th Grade Spon; Sci Club & Fair; NSTA 1980-; NEA, TEA 1972-; Blount Cty Ed Assn 1976-; Teachers Study Cncl 1986-88.

CAMPBELL, FRANCES M., Second Grade Teacher; *b:* Las Cruces, NM; *c:* Vicki Campbell-Gull, Rick, Lauri Campbell-Gibson, Debbie Campbell-Forman, Randy, Robert; *ed:* (BS) Elem Ed, NM St Univ 1968; *cr:* 3rd-5th Grade Teacher Cntrl Elem 1969-76; 3rd Grade Teacher Fair Acres Elem 1977-84; 2nd/3rd Grade Teacher Valley View Elem 1985-; *ai:* Children Are People; Trainer Classroom Management Prgm; Sch Cmptr Coord; Alpha Delta Kappa Chaplain 1989-; Delta Kappa Gamma Mem 1978-; Phi Delta Kappa Mem 1983-; LA Union Soil & Water Conservation Dist Supvr 1987-; *home:* Box 667 Mesilla Park NM 88047

CAMPBELL, GERALD, Computer Coordinator; *b:* Ossining, NY; *m:* Irene Marlis; *c:* Tom, Laura, Carolynn, Susan; *ed:* (BS) Ed, 1959, (MS) Admin, 1963 St Univ NY New Paltz; *cr:* 5th Grade Teacher Putnam Valley Elem 1959-83; Cmptr Coord Putnam Valley Cntrl 1983-; *ai:* Effective Sch Improvement Team Chm; Teachers Union Building Rep; NY St Teachers Retirement System Delegate; NY Cmptr & Technology Educators 1983-; NCTM, ASCD; Church of Holy Spirit Clearwater Parish Cncl 1973-75; *home:* 185 Frederick St Peekskill NY 10566

CAMPBELL, GORDON DEE, 5th Grade Teacher; *b:* Oak Ridge, TN; *m:* Rozalind Smith; *c:* Meghan S.; *ed:* (BA) Elem Ed, East TN St Univ 1969; (MS) Elem Ed, Univ of TN 1983; *cr:* Teacher Willow Brook Elem Sch 1969-; *ai:* Bus Monitor Adv/Spon; Invent America Spon; Safety Patrol Adv/Spon; Sch Store Spon; Oak Ridge Ed Assn 1969-; TN Teacher Ed Assn 1969-; NEA 1969-; Inventor; *office:* Oakridge City Schls 298 Robertsville Rd Oak Ridge TN 37830

CAMPBELL, HARRIET LAVERNE, 8th Grade Math Teacher; *b:* Uxbridge, MA; *c:* Eric, Kim; *ed:* (BS) Math/Scndry Ed, Worcester St Coll 1969; Post Grad Courses Worcester St Coll; *cr:* Teacher Lakeside Lodge Sch for Boys 1970-72; Math Teacher Milford Mid Sch 1972-; *ai:* Math Tutoring Center Adv; Supt Search, Advocates Ed Comm; Milford Teachers Assn Pres 1984-; NCTM 1987-; MA Teachers Assn, NEA 1972-; Teacher of Yr Nom 1989; *home:* 14 Talbot Terr Uxbridge MA 01569

CAMPBELL, HUGH, Economics Teacher; *b:* Bridgeport, CT; *m:* Amy Burgess; *c:* Kyle, Eric; *ed:* (BA) His, Springfield Coll 1974; (MA) Ed, Univ of CT 1979; Educl Leadership, Univ of CT; BEST Cert 1988-; Teacher Assessor Trng 1990; *cr:* Soc Stud Teacher Tri-Valley Cntrl Sch 1974-76; Soc Stud Teacher 1976-89, Ec Teacher/Admin Intern 1989- Norwich Free Acad; *ai:* Ftbl, Bsktbl, Bsbl Coach; Comm At-Risk Stu & Health Day Comm Chm; Ger Amer Exch Prgm Coord; CT Ed Assn; Park Congregational Church Sch Chm 1985-87; Bozrah Weylanos Comm Mem 1987-88; People to People Stu Ambassador Prgm CT Delegation

1989; *office:* Norwich Free Acad 305 Broadway Norwich CT 06360

CAMPBELL, JANET ERNST, 2nd Grade Team Teacher; *b:* Lake City, FL; *m:* Charles William; *c:* Mark, Christine, Stephen; *ed:* (BA) Elem Ed, Univ of FL 1967; In Service Wkshps; Course Work Renewing Teaching Certificate; *cr:* 2nd Grade Teacher Stephen Foster Elem 1967-69; 2nd Grade Team Teacher Alachua Elem 1974-; *ai:* Kappa Delta Pi; Amer Paint Horse Assn 1980-; FL Paint Horse Assn 1980-; Dixie Paint Horse Club 1978-; 1st Presbyn Church of Gainesville 1944-; *home:* Rt 3 Box 33 Alachua FL 32615

CAMPBELL, JANICE ELEANOR (DUNFORD), Kindergarten Teacher; *b:* Sullivan Cty, IN; *m:* James C.; *c:* James C. II, Jena E.; *ed:* (BS) Elem Ed, 1959, (MS) Elem Ed, 1962 IN St Teachers Coll; *cr:* 3rd Grade Teacher Elm Park Sch 1959-60, L & M Sch 1960-62; 1st-3rd Grade Substitute Teacher Tecumseh, Harrison, Washington 1963-64; Kndgtn Teacher Franklin 1964-; *ai:* Sch Improvement Planning Comm; Vincennes Ed Assn 1964-; IN St Teachers Assn 1959-; NEA Life Membership 1959-; Knox Cty Rdng Cncl 1985-; 1st United Meth Church (Various Bds & Commissions); Order of Eastern Star Star Point 1961-; Natl Wildlife Fed 1989; Natl Audubon Society 1990; *home:* 3031 Sievers Rd Vincennes IN 47591

CAMPBELL, JEAN MARIE, English Teacher; *b:* Canton, OH; *ed:* (BA) Eng, Malone Coll 1974; Grad Stud Rdng Cert Walsh Coll; *cr:* Eng Teacher Jackson Local Schls 1975-76, Alliance City Schls 1973; *ai:* Newspaper, Academic Challenge, Yrbk Adv; Drug Prgm Cnslr; Lang Art Dept Chairperson; Drama Dept Coach; Curr Comm; Alliance Ed Assn, OH Ed Assn, NEA 1976-; Malone Coll Alumnus of Yr 1983-84; Published 2 Books; *office:* Alliance City Schls 1155 Crescent Dr Alliance OH 44601

CAMPBELL, JOAN L., Fourth Grade Teacher; *b:* Wheeling, WV; *m:* Clyde D.; *c:* Leslie A. Delbrugge; *ed:* (BA) Ed, W Liberty St Coll 1962; (MS) Elem Ed, W VA Univ 1978; TESA; WV Teachers Acad; Cooperative Learning, Johns Hopkins; Grad Stud Beyond Masters W VA Univ, Univ of Detroit; *cr:* 4th Grade Teacher Warwood Grade Sch 1968-; *ai:* First Lady W Liberty St Coll Serve as Adv to Coll Groups & Stu Government; Delta Kappa Gamma; Alpha Delta Kappa (Secy, Treas) 1978-84, OH Cty Teacher of Yr 1985; WVEA, OCEA Exec Comm 1980-84; NEA, PTA Advisory Cncl; Prof Educators Organization Chair Schlsp 1988-; Wheeling Symphony Auxiliary; Alpha Xi Delta 1984-; Mem of Chorus Wheeling Symphony 1989-; *office:* Warwood Grade Sch 1200 Richland Ave Wheeling WV 26003

CAMPBELL, JOSEPH PAUL, Sixth Grade Teacher; *b:* Moosic, PA; *m:* Judith Ann Brown; *c:* Joseph, Jeffrey, Alexandra Hanson, Melissa; *ed:* (BA) Philosophy, Colgate Univ 1951; (MS) Elem Ed, ST Univ Coll at Oneonta 1956; *cr:* 5th & 6th Grade Teacher Walton Central 1953-57; 6th Grade Teacher Oneonta Plains Sch & Greater Plains Sch 1957-; *ai:* Former Asst Varsity Ftbl Coach at Oneonta HS; Citizen of Yr 1979-80, Oneonta Jaycees; *office:* Greater Plains Elem Schl West End Ave Oneonta NY 13820

CAMPBELL, KRISTY ANN, Speech/English Teacher; *b:* Sandusky, MI; *m:* Jerry L; *c:* Troy D, Traci D Sale, Jerry L. II, Nicol M.; *ed:* (BA) Speech, Cntrl MI Univ 1970; (MS) Eng, St Francis Coll 1978; *cr:* Speech/Eng Prairie Heights HS 1971-; *ai:* Speech Club Spon 1987-88; In Future Educators in Action Spon 1983-; Drama Club Spon 1971-72, 1975; Spell Bowl Coach 1989-; Academic Super Bowl Eng Team Coach 1989, 1990; Steering Comm N Cntrl 1988-89; Supt Building Comm 1987, 1990; Prairie Heights Ed Assn Secy 1989-; Kendallville Fire Dept Auxilliary Pres 1984-85; *office:* Prairie Heights HS R R 2 Box 600 Lagrange IN 46761

CAMPBELL, LINDA RUDOLPH, English Teacher; *b:* Dayton, OH; *m:* Ralph R.; *c:* Angela Hill, Stuart, Amy; *ed:* (AA) Ed, Okaloosa-Walton Jr Coll 1968; (BA) Eng, Univ of W FL 1972; Gifted & Talented Wkshp 1989; Issues in Scndry Ed, Univ of Houston Clear Lake 1985; Teaching Rdng, Univ of W FL 1976; Greater Houston Writing Project 1988; *cr:* Spec Ed Teacher 1972-76, Eng Teacher 1976-81 Lewis Jr HS; Dev Writing Teacher San Jacinto Jr Coll 1986; Eng Teacher Clear Creek HS 1981-; *ai:* Stu Assistance Prgm Core Team & Faculty Play Mem; UIL Literary Criticism Coach; Faculty Schlsp Chm; TX Classroom Teachers Assn 1986-; TX St Teachers Assn 1981-86; Beta Sigma Phi Recording Secy 1982-, Sweetheart Awd 1989; Seabrook United Meth Church 1982-; Easy Rdng Romeo & Juliet Published for Clear Creek Ind Sch Dist; Teacher of Yr Lewis Jr HS 1975, 1979; Spec Ed Summer Fellowship Univ of FL 1974; *office:* Clear Creek HS 2305 E Main League City TX 77573

CAMPBELL, LOUISE CABLE, 6th Grade Mathematics Teacher; *b:* Winchester, KY; *m:* James Truman; *c:* Stacie A., Joshua T.; *ed:* (BS) Elem/Soc Stud, MO Western St 1975; (MS) Elem Admin, NW MO St Univ 1980; *cr:* 4th Grade Teacher 1979-84, 5th/6th Grade Math Teacher 1984- Mid-Buchanan Elem; *ai:* Career Ladder Comm; Classroom Teachers Assn Pres 1988-; Daughters of Amer Revolution Vice Regent 1982-84; *home:* Box 100 Faucett MO 64448

CAMPBELL, MARILYN DEAN, Band Director; *b:* Marlette, MI; *c:* Jaime, Carla; *ed:* (BMED) Instrumental Music, 1974; (MA) Curr Dev, 1988 Cntrl Mi Univ; *cr:* Band Dir 1974-; Drama Teacher 1976-79 Mayville Comm Schls; *ai:* Dir Pep Band; Dir Jazz Band; Dir Alumni Band; MSBOA 1974-; Mayville Sch Bd Appreciation Awd 1982; Mayville Schl Bd Svc Awd 1984; Music Published; *office:* Mayville Comm Sch 6210 Fulton Mayville MI 48744

CAMPBELL, MARY ANN, Phys Ed/Health Teacher; *b:* Baraboo, WI; *ed:* (BS) Phys Ed, Univ of WI La Crosse 1969; (MED) Prof Dev, Cardinal Stritch Coll 1987; *cr:* Phys Ed/Health Teacher Thomas Jefferson Mid Sch 1969-; *ai:* Faculty Advisory, Cmptr, Behavior & Discipline Comm; Port Washington-Saukville Schls Awd for Meritorious Service; *office:* Thomas Jefferson Mid Sch 1403 N Holden Port Washington WI 53074

CAMPBELL, MIKE, High School Counselor; *b:* Gunnison, CO; *m:* Jacqui Mader; *ed:* (AA) General Ed, York Coll 1981; (BA) Fine Art, 1983, (MA) Guidance/Counseling, 1988 Western St Coll of CO; *cr:* Art Teacher/Yrbk Adv Soroco HS 1986-88; Cnslr Steamboat Springs HS 1988-; *ai:* Stu Cncl Co-Adv; 8th Grade Boys Bsktbl Coach; CO Cncl on HS/Coll Relations 1988-; *office:* Steamboat Springs HS 45 Maple PO Box 774368 Steamboat Springs CO 80477

CAMPBELL, MONA A. (VAN STEENBERGER), Mid Sch Mathematics Teacher; *b:* Prairie City, IA; *m:* Robert Lewis; *c:* Margaret E., Robert J.; *ed:* (BA) Jr HS Ed, IA St Teachers Coll 1954; Drake Univ, IA St Univ Ames, IA St Teachers Coll Cedar Falls, Marycrest Coll; *cr:* 7th-8th Grade Lang Art Teacher Toledo IA 1954-55; 6th-7th Grade Self-Contained Teacher Beamon IA 1955-56; Spec Educl Teacher Waukon IA 1957; Guidance/Eng Teacher Saginaw MI 1957-58; 6th-8th Grade Lang Art/Math Teacher Postville IA 1966-; *ai:* Grandparent Prgm; 6th Grade Spon; Time Audit Comm; NCA Accredation Philosophy Goals & Course Descriptor Comms; Postville Ed Assn Pres (1985-86) 1987-88; NEA Secy 1989-; PEO 1951-; *office:* Darling Elem Mid Sch Ogden & Post PO Box 717 Postville IA 52162

CAMPBELL, NANCY KYLE, Math Teacher; *b:* Bluefield, WV; *ed:* (BA) Eng/Math 1969; (BS) Ed, 1970; Concord Coll; (MA) Educl Admin WV Coll of Grad Stud 1986; *cr:* Realtor/Broker Century 21 Sheffield 1978-82; Teacher Pocahontas HS 1982-; *office:* Pocahontas HS Pocahontas VA 24635

CAMPBELL, NELLIE QUAN, Mathematics Teacher; *b:* Lowell, MA; *m:* Roy R.; *c:* Daniel R., Michael L.; *ed:* (BA) Elem Ed, Stonehill Coll 1973; (MED) Elem Ed, Bridgewater St Coll 1983; *cr:* Elem Teacher Ellis Brett Sch 1973-80; Math Teacher West Jr HS 1980-; *ai:* Sch Improvement Cncl 1986-; *office:* West Jr HS 271 West St Brockton MA 02401

CAMPBELL, PAMELA SUE, 2nd Grade Teacher; *b:* Broken Bow, NE; *m:* Kenton L.; *c:* Britta; *ed:* (BA) Elem Ed, Kearney St Coll 1971; *cr:* 3rd/5th Grade Teacher Lodgepole Elem 1971-73; 1st-6th Grade Teacher Georgetown Elem 1974-79; 2nd Grade Teacher Midwest Elem 1979-82; 3rd/6th Grade Teacher Georgetown Elem 1982-88; 2nd Grade Teacher Bradley Elem 1988-; *ai:* NEA 1971-89; NE St Ed Assn 1971-73; Lodgepole Ed Assn 1971-73; CO Ed Assn 1974-79; Clear Creek Ed Assn 1974-79; WY Ed Assn 1979-82; Natrona Cty Classroom Teachers Assn 1979-82; Co-Ed Assn 1982-89; Clear Creek Ed Assn 1982-88; KS Rdng Assn 1988-; Intnl Rdng Assn 1989-; *office:* Bradley Elem Sch 7th Cavalry Rd Fort Leavenworth KS 66027

CAMPBELL, PATRICIA TIERNEY, Eighth Grade English Teacher; *b:* Pittsfield, MA; *m:* Ralph E.; *c:* Mary J., John, James, Christopher, Andrew, Anthony; *ed:* (BA) Eng, Our Lady of the Elms 1950; Univ of MA & N IL Univ; *cr:* Teacher Pittsfield Sch Dept 1950-53; Swim Coach Morrison Swim Club 1974-86, Morrison HS 1988-89; Teacher Morrison Jr HS 1976-; *ai:* Assn of Eng Teachers, US Swimming.

CAMPBELL, PAUL D., JR, French/Biology Teacher; *b:* Yadkinville, NC; *ed:* (BA) Fr, Univ NC Charlotte 1984; Summer Study Inst Catholique Paris 1984; *cr:* Teacher Randolph Jr HS 1984-86, Garinger HS 1986-; *ai:* Fr Club, Fr Honor Society, Yrbk Adv; NC Assn of Educators 1984-88; AATF 1986-; Garinger HS Teacher of Yr 1987-88; *office:* Garinger H S 1100 Eastway Dr Charlotte NC 28205

CAMPBELL, PAULETTE BARNWELL, English Teacher; *b:* Birmingham, AL; *m:* Byron Lee; *c:* Bryn E.; *ed:* (BS) Scndry Ed/Eng, Auburn Univ 1975; *cr:* Eng Teacher Mortimer Jordan HS 1975-; *ai:* Kappa Delta Pi 1974-; *office:* Mortimer Jordan HS 8601 Old Hwy 31 Morris AL 35116

CAMPBELL, ROBERT HENRY, Band Director; *b:* Provo, UT; *m:* Gloria June Dotson; *c:* Jeffrey, Gregory, Todd, Patrick, Erik; *ed:* (BS) Music Ed, Brigham Young Univ 1961; *cr:* Musician Percussionist UT Symphony Orch 1959-69; Music Teacher Horace Mann Jr HS 1961-63; Music Instr Brigham Young Univ 1963-71; Music Teacher South Davis Jr HS 1971-; *ai:* Music Educators Natl Conference 1961-; UT Music Ed Assn (VP, Bus Mgr) 1961-; Percussive Arts Society St Pres 1963-; Outstanding Music Educator Davis Cty Schls 1981; *home:* 2860 S 450 E Bountiful UT 84010

CAMPBELL, ROBERT J., Elementary Physical Ed Teacher; *b:* Chatham ON, Canada; *m:* Christine Williams; *ed:* (BS) Phys Ed, Miami Univ of OH 1976; Working Towards Masters Phys Ed, Wright St Univ; *cr:* 5th Grade Classroom Teacher 1977-78, K-6th Grade Phys Ed Teacher 1978- Concord Elem Sch; *ai:* Jr HS & HS Boys/Girls Cross Cntry Coach; NEA, OH Ed Assn, Troy City Ed Assn Negotiations Comm; *office:* Concord Elem Sch 3145 W St Rt 718 Troy OH 45373

CAMPBELL, ROGER ALLEN, Social Studies/PE H S Teacher; *b:* Mount Pleasant, IA; *m:* Patricia Lynn Burk; *c:* Chad E., Jayon A.; *ed:* (BA) His, Luther Coll 1970; (MA) His, Northwest MO St Univ 1972; Teacher Expectations & Stu Achievement; *cr:* Soc Stud Teacher Red Oak Cmmty Schls 1970-76, Centerville Cmmty Schls 1976-; *ai:* Assn Varsity Ftbl Coach; Assn Varsity Track Coach; Scorekeeper; Varsity & JV Bsktbl Adv; Fellowship of Chrstn Athletes; NEA 1970-; IA St Ed Assn 1970-; Centerville Ed Assn Pres 1976-; IA Ftbl Coaches Assn 1970- Dist Coach of Yr 1972; IA Track Coaches Assn 1970-; IA Bsktbl Coaches Assn 1986-; Univ of IA I Club 1976-; Elks 1970-76; Speaker Athletic Banquets-Civil Organizations; Speaker Ftbl Clinics; *office:* Centerville H S 10th & Liberty Centerville IA 52544

CAMPBELL, RUSSELL LEE, Physics/Math/Cmptr Teacher; *b:* Oakland City, IN; *m:* Rosann Scott; *c:* Kelly, Robin White; *ed:* (BS) Physics/Math, Oakland City Coll 1965; (MS) Physics, Ball St 1970; Grad Stud IN St, Rose-Hulman; *cr:* Engr Honeywell 1969-70; Physics/Math Teacher Greencastle HS 1970-73, Paoli HS 1973-74, Rockville HS 1974-; *ai:* Var Bsktbl, Var Tennis, Var Golf Coach; TSTA, NEA; RTA Pres 1988-; Mason 1985-; Scottish Rite, York Rite, Shiner; Oakland City Coll Bsbl Schlsp; *office:* Rockville Jr Sr HS 506 N Beadle Rockville IN 47872

CAMPBELL, SANDRA THRASHER, Language Art Dept Chair; *b:* Pelzer, SC; *m:* William Mimms; *c:* Julia A.; *ed:* (BA) Eng, Winthrop Coll 1967; (MED) Eng, Converse Coll 1980; *cr:* Eng Teacher Woodmont HS 1967-68; Lang Art Teacher Mc Cants Jr HS 1968-71; Teacher/Dept Chairperson Wren HS 1972-81; Teacher of Gifted & Talented/Dept Chair Woodmont Mid Sch 1982-; *ai:* Academic Recognition & Achievement Comm; Delta Kappa Gamma Intnl Chapter Pres 1988-; South Greenville Fire Dept Ladies Auxiliary 1988-; *office:* Woodmont Mid Sch 325 Flat Rock Rd Piedmont SC 29673

CAMPBELL, SHARON K. (MINER), Phys Ed Dept Head/Teacher; *b:* Omaha, NE; *m:* Dennis R.; *c:* Roger, Robb, Shane; *ed:* (BS) Phys Ed, Univ of NE 1965; *cr:* Phys Ed/Sci Teacher Burwell Public Schls 1965-67; Elem & Jr HS Phys Ed Teacher Bellevue Public Schls 1967-71; Teacher Glenwood St Hosp Sch 1979-80; Dept Head/Mid Sch Phys Ed Teacher Plattsmouth Cmmty Schls 1985-; *ai:* 8th Grade Vlybl; Health Curr Comm; NEA, NSEA, PEA 1985-; NAHPER 1985-; Eagles Auxiliary 1980-; VFW Auxiliary 1983-; UNL Alumni Assn 1979-; Nom NE Teachers Recognition Day 1990; Eagles Schlshp Comm Head 1986-88; *home:* 1639 Thayer St Plattsmouth NE 68048

CAMPBELL, STEVE, English & Journalism Teacher; *b:* Los Angeles, CA; *ed:* (BA) Eng, CA St Univ Los Angeles 1965; Additional Classes in Career Expansion; *cr:* Teacher Jordan Jr HS 1965-; *ai:* Adv of Yrbk & Newspaper; Elections, ASB Presidential Gallery Coord; Teacher of 9th Grade Honors Prgm; PTA Service Awd 1973; Dist BRAVA Awd 1984; Yrbk Dedication 1976; Nom Teacher of Yr 1989; Jr HS Top-Rated Newspaper in Nation; Columbia Scholastic Press Assn Medalist; Quill & Scroll Gallup Awd; Named Top Journalism by Pepperdine Univ; Nom for Kiwanis Teacher of Yr; *office:* Jordan Jr HS 420 S Mariposa St Burbank CA 91506

CAMPBELL, STEVEN V., Instrumental Music Director; *b:* Oklahoma City, OK; *m:* Phyllis Anne Lawrence; *c:* Jillian A.; *ed:* (BA) Music Ed, Cntrl St Univ 1981; *cr:* Band Dir Putnam City West HS 1981-82; Western Oaks Jr HS 1982-88; Band & Orch Dir Putnam City HS 1988-; *ai:* Jazz Ensemble, Symphony Orch, Marching Band, Symphonic Winds; Cntrl OK Dir Assn Pres 1986-87; OK Music Educators Assn; OK Band Masters Assn; Straight Superior Ratings with Performing Organizations at St Level Contests; *office:* Putnam City HS 5300 NW 50th Oklahoma City OK 73122

CAMPBELL, SUE RAINES, H S Business Education Teacher; *b:* Stidham, OK; *m:* Charles R. J.; *c:* Charles K., Charles J., Shelley D.; *ed:* (AA) General Ed, Connors St Coll 1962; (BS) Bus Ed, 1964; Bus Ed, 1972 Northeastern St Univ; Addl Studies Staff Dev In-Serv & Ed; *cr:* Teacher Bowring HS 1964-68; Ketchum HS 1968-; *ai:* Homeroom Parent; Private Tutor; Political Action Mem; NEA 1964-; OK Ed Assn 1964-; Prof Educators Assn of Ketchum Treas 1985-87; Ketchum Teacher of Yr; Staff Dev Mem; Negotiating Team Mem; Title IV Mem; Leader of Amer Scndry Ed 1972; Grievance Comm Mem; Peak Exec Bd; *office:* Ketchum H S P O Box 720 Ketchum OK 74349

CAMPBELL, SYLVIA SMITH, Social Studies Teacher; *b:* Union City, NJ; *ed:* (BA) Poly Sci, Mt Holyoke Coll 1952; *cr:* Teacher Cntrl Jr HS 1953-65; Teacher 1965-66, Dept Chairperson 1966-69, Teacher Brooklawn Mid Sch 1969-; *ai:* Drama Club Coach; Parsippany Troy Hills Ed Assn Secy; Morris Cty Cncl of Ed Assn, NJ Ed Assn, NEA, NCSS; Parsipanny Jaycees Outstanding Educator 1983; Natl Audubon Society Envoronmental Defense Fund; World Wildlife Fund; Natl WildLife Fed; Sierra Club; E Africa Wildlife Organization; NJ Conservation Fnd; Center for Marine Conservation Common Cause; NJ Governors Awd 1989; *office:* Brooklawn Mid Sch 250 Beachwood Rd Parsippany NJ 07054

CAMPBELL, TOM, 4th Grade Teacher; *b:* Pawtucket, RI; *m:* Jeanette; *c:* Michele, Michael, Matthew; *ed:* (BA) Soc Stud, Sacramento St Coll 1971; *cr:* Comm Technician USAF 1955-59; Shipping/Receiving/Sales Sears 1959-62; Aircraft Elec/Scheduler US Government 1962-69; Teacher Penryn Sch 1971-; *ai:* CA Teachers Assn 1971-; Lions Club 1980-86; *home:* 5885 King Rd Loomis CA 95650

CAMPBELL, WILDA JEAN, Fourth Grade Teacher; *b:* Saltville, VA; *ed:* (BA) Eng, Emory & Henry Coll 1960; (MED) Curr/Elem Inst, Univ of VA 1982; *cr:* 6th Grade Teacher Bristol Elem Schls 1961-64, 1966-79; Spec Ed Teacher Bristol Jr HS 1964-65; 8th/9th/11th/12th Grade Teacher Bristol HS 1968, 1985, 1988, 1989;5th Grade Teacher Bristol Elem Schls 1979-89;

Adult Basic Ed Bristol HS 1985; 4th Grade Teacher Bristol Elem Sch 1989-; *ai:* BVEA, VEA, NEA; Alpha Delta Kappa (Chaplain 1986-88, Historian 1990); S Bristol United Meth Church (Mem At Large, Admin Bd); United Meth Women Prgm Resource; *office:* Stonewall Jackson Elem Sch 2045 Euclid Ave Bristol VA 24201

CAMPBELL, WILLIAM EDWARD, JR., Life Science Teacher; *b:* Mason, MI; *m:* Judith Ann Leonard; *c:* Scott, Susan Campbell Lawson, Ronald; *ed:* (BA) Bio, Cntrl MI Univ 1962; (MA) Ed Sci, MI St Univ 1968; Curr Dev & Drivres Ed, MI St Univ; *cr:* Teacher Huron Valley Schls 1962-64; Teacher 1964-, Sci Dept Chairperson 1985- Mason Public Schls; *ai:* Jr/Sr Class Spon 1983-84; Stu Activity Spon 1985-86; Contest Mgr Boys Soccer, Girls Gymnastics, Boys Swimming 1985-; MI Ed Assn Mason Dist (VP 1985-86, Rep 1987-88); *office:* Mason Sr HS 1001 S Barnes Mason MI 48854

CAMPBELL-FURTICK, CRISTY LYNN, English Teacher; *b:* Wichita Falls, TX; *m:* Roger; *c:* Dylan, Mackenzie; *ed:* (BA) His, Univ of TX Arlington 1979; Working Towards MA Eng, Tarleton St Univ; *cr:* Eng Teacher Mansfield HS 1979-86, Stephenville HS 1986-; *ai:* UIL Feature Writing Coach; Campus Improvement, Communicable Disease Ed, Gifted & Talented Comm; NCTE; Stephenville Educators Assn (VP 1988-89) 1986-; Mansfield Educators Assn (Pres, VP) 1979-86; TX St Teachers Assn, NEA 1979-; Amnesty Intnl, Natl Arbor Day Fnd; Coll Teachers of Eng Conference Presenter 1990; *home:* Rt 2 Box 43A Bluff Dale TX 76433

CAMPEAU, JANET MARIE, Guidance Department Chair; *b:* Flint, MI; *m:* William Morgan; *c:* Bethany Wallace, Julie A.; *ed:* (BS) Health/Phys Ed, Cntrl MI Univ 1964; (MS) Guidance/ Counseling, Univ of MI Ann Arbor 1968; Grad Stud Guidance, Counseling, Admin; *cr:* Teacher Flint Northern 1964-65; Cnslr Kearsley Schls 1965-; *ai:* Scndry Curr Cncl; Kearsley Ed Assn Membership Chairperson 1984-88; MI Assn for Counseling & Dev 1965-; MI Schl Cnslrs Scndry VP 1987; Genesee Area Assn for Counseling & Dev Pres 1966-; *office:* Kearsley HS 4302 Underhill Dr Flint MI 48506

CAMPISI, PHYLLIS PERRETTA, Coordinator of Gifted/ Talented; *b:* Brooklyn, NY; *m:* Joseph; *c:* Marirose, Christine, Natalie-Lynn; *ed:* (BA) Ed, Queens Coll 1957; Post Grad Work Adelphi Univ & C W Post Coll; *cr:* 2nd-6th Grade Elem Teacher 1957-78; Teacher/Coord of Gifted & Talented 1978-; *ai:* Cmptr Club Adv; Delta Kappa Gamma; NYSUT Delegate; Teachers Union Executive Bd Mem; *office:* Syosset Sch Dist Convent Rd Syosset NY 11791

CAMPOS, CELINA ESTRADA, Assistant Principal; *b:* Brownsville, TX; *c:* Jayme R., Marco A., Amanda C.; *ed:* (BS) Phys Ed/Bio, 1982, (MA) Educl Admin, 1986 PAU-B; *cr:* K-6th Grade Phys Ed Teacher Cromack Elem 1982-85; Bio/Marine Sci Teacher James Pace HS 1985-88; Asst Prin Gladys Porter HS 1988-; *home:* 25 Fruitdale Terr Brownsville TX 78520

CAMPOS, JELICA ZIROJIN PETKOVIC, Science Teacher; *b:* Belgrade, Yugoslavia; *m:* Jose Maria; *c:* Margarita, Tomas, Danica; *ed:* Medical Technology Trng, Huron Road Hospital 1972; (BS) Comprehensive Bio/Chem, Notre Dame Coll 1972; Teachers Credential Scndry, Long Beach St 1977; Deuxieme Degree Fr Lang, Aliance Francaise Paris France 1969; *cr:* Sci Teacher Notre Dame Acad 1972-74; Sci Dept Head St Matthias HS 1974-81; Med Tech Asst Los Alamitos Medical Center 1979-88; Sci Teacher/Dept Head St Bonaventure Sch 1986-; *ai:* Bd Mem Orange Cty Sci & Engineering Fair; Head Sci Olympiad Sch Team; Sch Sci Fair Originator, Organizer, Participator; NEA Mem; Orange Cty Sci & Engineering Fair (Spec Awds, Bd Mem) 1987-, 2nd Pl Engineering Awd 1989; Los Alamitos Medical Center 1979-88, Ruby Achievement Pin 1987; CA St Sci Fair Microbiology Judge Sr Division 1989-; WASC Accreditation Comm Rated Sci Curr & Handbook Excl 1976; Gave Sci Fair Wkshp; *office:* St Bonaventure Sch 16377 Bradbury Ln Huntington Beach CA 92647

CAMPSEN, THERESA ESTRADA, Counselor; *b:* Stockton, CA; *m:* Raymond F.; *c:* Christina, Jessica, Victoria; *ed:* (BA) Bi-ling Ed, SE OK St Univ 1977; (MED) Counseling/Guidance, Univ of AZ 1982; Univ of San Francisco; Fr, Univ de Montreal; *cr:* Span/Fr Teacher 1977-85, Cnslr 1986- Salpointe Cath HS; *ai:* Substance Abuse Prgm; Amer Personnel & Guidance Assn; Leukemia Society; *office:* Salpointe Cath HS 1545 E Copper Tucson AZ 85719

CANADY, JOYCE LOCKLEAR, Jr HS Language Arts Teacher; *b:* Lumberton, NC; *m:* Gregory; *c:* Craig; *ed:* (BS) Intermediate Grades/Mid Grades Phys Ed/Mid Grades Lang Art, 1979; (MS) Intermediate Grades 1989 Pembroke St Univ; *cr:* Jr HS Lang Art Teacher Orrum Jr/Sr HS 1979-; *ai:* Just Say No Club Spon; Shl Base Comm; Books & Beyond Rdng Prgm Chairperson; Sunday Sch Teacher; NC Congress Parents & Teachers Incorporated Certificate of Appreciation 1987; Sch Annual Dedication 1988; *office:* Orrum Jr/Sr HS P O Box 129 Orrum NC 28369

CANADY, SHIRLEY MELISSA, Mathematics Teacher; *b:* Montgomery, AL; *ed:* (BS) Math, 1973, (MSED) Math, 1980, (EDS) Math, 1983 GA Southern; *cr:* Math Teacher Glynn Acad HS 1973-; *ai:* Glynn Acad Coed Y Club Spon; GA Cncl Teachers of Math, NCTM 1982-; STAR Teacher; Glynn Acad Teacher of Yr; GA Cncl of Math Roundtable for Math Teachers; Nom Presidential Awd & Wiley Maurelle Shuttles Awd; *office:* Glynn Acad HS Mansfield St Brunswick GA 31520

CANALES, JUDITH MARTIN, 5th Grade Reading Teacher; *b:* Pittsburgh, PA; *c:* Julie L.; *ed:* (BS) Elem Ed, Univ Mary Hardin Baylor 1982; (MED) Admin Ed, Tarleton St Univ 1986; Post Grad Stud Eng; *cr:* 6th Grade Eng Teacher 1982-87, 5th Grade Rdng Teacher 1987- Avenue E Elem; Developmental Writing Instr Cntrl TX Univ 1989-; *ai:* Alpha Chi Pres 1980-82, Highest GPA 1982; Sigma Tau Delta VP 1980-82; Alamo Writing Project Grant Trinity Univ 1986.

CANCEL, LUZ NEIDA, Emeritus Teacher; *b:* Jayuya, PR; *m:* Ramon Cordero Gonzalez; *c:* Jose R. Cordero, Gloria Cordero, Olga Cordero, Rene Y Luz N. Cordero; *ed:* (BA) Elem Sch Teacher, Univ of PR 1960; World Univ 1970; *cr:* Teacher Dept of Inst PR; *ai:* Contest of Poetry, Rdng & Writing; Stus Leaders Club; Tutorial Classes; Assn De Maestros, NEA; Catechist.

CANCEL, MYRIAM MARTINEZ, Science Professor; *b:* Mayaguez, PR; *c:* Efrain M., Annette; *ed:* (BS) Chem, 1957, (MA) Sch Supervision/Admin, 1983 Univ of PR; Chem Com Resource Teacher Wkshp 1989; Forum 1986; Sci Curr; 1st Arson Symposium PR; Drinking & Waste Water Analytical Course; *cr:* Research Asst Chemist Ag Exp Station 1957-61; Chem Teacher Pilar Coll 1974-77; Project Leader Energy Center Environmental Studs 1983-84; Chem Professor Univ HS 1977-; *ai:* Stu Cncl Moderator; Chem Olympiads & Sci Bowl Coach; Resource, Chem, Physics Wkshp for Scndry Teachers; Resource Center for Sci & Eng; NSTA San Juan Area Convention Comm 1990; PR Sci Teacher Assn 1980; Coll of Chemist PR; Amer Chem Society; Amer Assn for Advance of Sci; Delta Kappa Gamma; Nom Presidential Awds for Excl 1990.

CANDELARIA, DALE DEAN, Sr Govt & A P History Teacher; *b:* Oakland, CA; *m:* Lori Thornton Candelaria; *c:* Troi, Gina, Jenny, Jared; *ed:* (BS) Amer His, 1975; Eng, 1975 CA St Univ; *cr:* Teacher Winton Sch Dist 1978-85; Teacher Atwater Hs 1985-; *ai:* Sr Adv; *office:* Atwater H S P O Box 835 Atwater CA 95301

CANDELARIA, MYRNA, English Teacher; *b:* New York, NY; *ed:* (AS) Nursing, 1979, (BS) Eng, 1981 Atlantic Union Coll; (MA) Eng, NY Univ 1990; *cr:* Nurse Personal Touch Nursing Agency 1979-82; Eng Teacher Greater NY Acad 1982-; *ai:* Honor Societies & Jr Class Spon; Curr Comm Mem Greater NY Acad; NCTE Mem 1988-; ASCD 1989-; Greater NY Conference 7th Day Adventists Exec Bd Trustees Mem 1985-88; Greater NY Acad Sch Bd Mem 1985-88; Atlantic Union Conference Curr Comm Mem 1985-.

CANDIA, ANNE KATHERINE, Fifth Grade Teacher; *b:* Oakland, CA; *d:* Joseph M.; *c:* Michele J. Candia Leonard; *ed:* (BA) His/Sci - Cum Laude, Coll of Holy Names 1946; Span/ Mexican, Cabrillo Jr Coll 1969-72; Child Psych, Univ of CA Los Angeles 1956; Math, Univ of CA Berkeley 1953-54; Impact Trng Drug Strategies 1986-87; *cr:* 5th/6th Grade Teacher El Morris Cox Sch 1947-53; 6th Grade Teacher Rockridge Elem 1954-56, Manzanita Elem 1957-64; 5th/6th Grade Teacher San Lorenzo Valley Elem 1965-; *ai:* Stu Cncl Adv; Noonday Sports Supvr; Great Books Grade Level Leader; Math & Spelling Contests Coord/Preparer; Grade Level Chm; CA Teachers Assn (Local Pres 1970-71, St Cncl Rep 1972-), Ted Buss Poly Awd 1981, Local Who We Honor Ours St WITO 1982; Cntrl Coast Service Center Chm 1980-82; San Lorenzo Valley Teachers Assn (Poly Chm 1980-, Membership Chm 1986-, Grievance Comm Chm 1990); Delta Kappa Gamma 1986-; Kappa Gamma Pi 1946-76; NEA Elected Delegate to 7 Conventions, Congressional Contact Leon Panetta 1977-81; *home:* 7 Rincon Ct Santa Cruz CA 95060

CANDIA-BONNER, VERONICA, Sixth Grade Teacher; *b:* Chicago, IL; *c:* Antoinette; *ed:* (BS) Ed, S IL Univ Carbondale 1969; (MS) Ed, De Paul 1985; *cr:* Teacher Prairie Hills Elem Dist 1969-; *office:* Highlands Jr HS 3420 Laurel Ln Hazel Crest IL 60429

CANDLE, GLADYS M., English Teacher; *b:* Leetonia, OH; *m:* Richard; *c:* Chris, Jeffrey; *ed:* (BS) Elem Ed, Youngstown St Univ 1972; *cr:* Elem Teacher 1968-76, Jr HS Eng Teacher 1976- Leetonia Exempted Village Schls; *ai:* Stu Cncl Adv; OEA, NEA 1968-; Leetonia Alumni Assn Secy 1986-; *office:* Leetonia Exempted Village Sch 450 Walnut St Leetonia OH 44431

CANEDA, FRANCES RICHARDSON, Social Studies Teacher; *b:* Columbia, SC; *m:* Jonathan W.; *c:* Jonathan, Leslie; *ed:* (BA) His/Ed, Lander Coll 1980; *cr:* Soc Stud/Lang Art Teacher Wright Mid Sch 1981-85; Soc Stud/Lang Art/Sci/Rdng Teacher E Augusta Mid Sch 1985-89; Soc Stud Teacher Spirit Creek Mid Sch 1989-; *ai:* 8th Grade Team Leader; Yrbk Spon; New Sch Dedication Comm Chm; Stu Teacher Supvr; Current Events Rally Spon; Richmond Cty Assn of Educators, GA Assn of Educators, NEA 1985-; Martinez United Meth Church 1989-.

CANFIELD, PATTI LEE, Eng Teacher/Choral Conductor; *b:* Kalamazoo, MI; *ed:* (BA) Music/Eng, Nazareth Coll 1943; (MM) Piano, Roosevelt Univ 1955; De Paul Univ; Univ of MI; *cr:* Music/ Eng Dept Head St Benedict Sch 1945-; *ai:* HS Preparatory Eng; Choral Conductor; Accompanist; Favorite Teacher St Benedict, St Rita Detroit News 1968; AMA Awd for Conducting Nurses Choirs 1967; Detroit Archdiocese Awd 1985; Subject of Film on New Ideas in Teaching; Conducted Wkshp at Coba Hall; Directed Teenagers Shows, Musicals for Schls; Teenagers & Adults Speakers for Optimist Club; *office:* St Benedict Sch 53 Candler Highland Park MI 48203

CANG, PAUL, French Teacher; *b:* Saigon, Vietnam; *m:* Margaret Tabor; *c:* Mary Lottermoser, Peter, Michelle, Maureen Caballero; *ed:* Baccalaureate Diploma Fr/Gen Stud, Coll of St Francis Xavier 1953; (BS) Math, Marquette Univ 1963; (MA) Ed/Fr/ Linguistics, Monterey Inst of Intnl Stud 1971; *cr:* Vietnamese Prof Defense Lang Inst 1963-76; Teacher Salinas Unified Sch Dist 1976-78, East Side Union HS Dist 1978-; *ai:* Fr Club; Foreign Lang Assn, Vietnamese Stu Assn; Tough Love Apartment Assn; Various Commendations; *office:* Andrew Hill HS 3200 Senter Rd San Jose CA 95111

CANGEMI, RICHARD ANTHONY, HS Instrumental Teacher; *b:* Syracuse, NY; *m:* Linda J.; *ed:* (BME) Music Ed, Murray St Univ 1968; Permanent Cert Music Ed, NY St & KY Univ 1968; Oswego St Univ, Syracuse Univ, Ithaca Coll; *cr:* Band Dir Hannibal Cntrl Sch 1968-71, Minoa HS 1971-76; Part-Time Consultant/Instr Syracuse Univ 1976-79; Band Dir Skaneateles Cntrl Sch 1976-; *ai:* Skaneateles Cntrl Sch Soph Class Adv 1980-; HS Stage Band Dir; Drug & Alcohol Prevention Comm; NY St Sch Music Assn, Music Educators Natl Conference 1968-; NY St Band Dir Assn 1985-; Skaneateles Teachers Assn (Greivance Chm 1990) 1989-; Phi Mu Alpha Life Mem; St Stevens Church Bingo Worker 1989-; Pro Musica 1980-; Loyal Order of Moose 625 1988-; Skaneateles Cntrl Sch Teacher of Yr 1987; Oswego All-Cty Band Festival Guest Conductor; Skaneateles Dist Music Dept Music Coord; *home:* 725 Hillside St Syracuse NY 13208

CANN, CLAUDIA, Jr HS Gifted Teacher; *b:* Clarksburg, WV; *ed:* (BA) Elem Ed, 1981, (MS) Gifted Ed, 1985 WV Univ; *cr:* 6th Grade Teacher Wallace Elem 1982-87; Jr HS Gifted Teacher Cntrl & Salem Jr HS 1987-; Elem Gifted Teacher Hartman Magnet Center 1990; *ai:* Newspaper Adv; Cheerleading Coach; Clarksburg League for Service 1985-; Beta Sigma Pi 1983-.

CANNAVA, MARIE CRUZ, English Teacher; *b:* San Juan, PR; *m:* Peter Philip; *c:* Peter, Richard; *ed:* (BA) Eng, Hunter Coll 1968; (MS) Eng Ed, Queens Coll 1974; Doctoral Prgm, St Johns Univ; Course Work, Queens Coll Adelphi; *cr:* Eng Teacher Cntrl Commercial HS 1968-69, Carey HS 1969-; *ai:* Faculty Schlsp Comm Mem; HS Yrbk & Class of 1989, Jr Honor Society, Frosh Chrldrs Adv; NCTE, Long Island Lang Art Cncl; Amer Assn of Univ Women Publicity Chairperson 1986-; Smithtown Township Art Cncl 1987-; PTA Branch Brook Elem Sch Comm Chairperson 1984-; Cub Pack 373 (Comm Chairperson, Den Mother 1986-); Yrbk Dedication 1989; *office:* H Frank Carey HS 230 Poppy Ave Franklin Square NY 11010

CANNELLA, MARGARET (KREFFT), Kindergarten Teacher; *b:* Evanston, IL; *m:* Frank; *c:* Donna, Michelle, Jennifer; *ed:* (BSED) Elem Ed - Summa Cum Laude, 1972, (MSED) Outdoor Teacher Ed, 1975 Northern IL Univ; Contemporary Native Amer Ed, Univ of AK Fairbanks; Early Chldhd Ed, Natl Coll of Ed, Northern IL Univ; Educl Admin NM St Univ Las Cruces; *cr:* Teacher Trainer Teachers Trng Coll/US Peace Corps Western Samoa 1972-74; Intern Environmental Ed Dept 1975; 2nd/4th Grade Teacher Bent-Mescalero Elem Sch 1975-78; Kndgtn Teacher Nob Hill Elem Sch 1978-; *ai:* Supts Advisory Cncl Chairperson 1988-89; Cmptr & Sci Comm Mem 1983-; Tularosa Ed Assn Delegate 1976-77; Ruidoso Ed Assn Secy 1979-80; *office:* Nob Hill Elem Sch 100 Sutton Dr Ruidoso NM 88345

CANNON, DONALD EDWARD, English Department Head; *b:* Boston, MA; *m:* Laura Weeden; *c:* Courtney, Amy; *ed:* (BA) Government, Harvard 1968; (MA) Eng, Northeastern 1976; Grad Stud at Various Coll; *cr:* Eng Teacher Walpole E Jr HS 1968-70, Dover Sherborn HS 1970-; *ai:* Runes Henry Magazine & Sch Newspaper Adv; Girls Soccer Coach; NCTE; Teacher of Yr Dove Sherborn HS 1990; Coach of Yr Globe Eastern MA 1990; *office:* Dover Sherborn HS Junction St Dover MA 02030

CANNON, GLORIA ROBERTS, English Teacher; *b:* Seminole Cty, GA; *c:* Stefanie, Marie, Christi K.; *ed:* (BA) Eng, Univ of GA 1959; (MED) Eng, Troy St Univ 1979; *cr:* Teacher Bainbridge Jr HS 1959-60, Tubman Jr HS 1960-61, Seminole Cty HS 1976-; *office:* Seminole Cty HS Marianna Hwy Donalsonville GA 31745

CANNON, JEROME EDWARD, Social Studies Teacher; *b:* Concord, NC; *m:* Kimberly Annette Shouse; *c:* Zachary A.; *ed:* (BA) Ec, Univ of NC Charlotte 1985; (MA) Ed, Wingate Coll 1989; *cr:* Teacher Forest Hills HS 1986-; *ai:* Asst Var Ftbl, Girls Var BsktbL, Jr Var Bsbl Coach; NCHSAA 1986-; Wingate Baptist Church 1988-; *office:* Forest Hills HS PO Box 648 Marshville NC 28103

CANNON, JOY FRY, Retired; *b:* Salem, AR; *m:* George L.; *c:* Diana Cannon Havey, Janice Cannon Witt; *ed:* (BA) Home Ec, S IL Univ 1951; Additional Courses to Develop Elem Classroom Expertise; Adult Ed Degree; *cr:* 4th-6th Grade Elem Classroom Teacher Creve Coeur Sch Dist 76 1957-87; *ai:* PTA Life Membership 1975; IEA, NEA Var Offices Held, Outstanding Service to Teaching Profession Awds 1983, 1987; Substitute Sunday Sch Teacher; Honor Teacher of Excl Awd 1984-85; *home:* 503 Allyn St Creve Coeur IL 61611

CANNON, THERESA, Language Arts Teacher; *b:* Tulsa, OK; *ed:* (BA) Ed/Philosophy, Webster Coll 1956; (MA) Eng, Notre Dame Univ 1963; Hum Prgms, Univ of London & Cambridge Univ; Washington Univ St Louis; *cr:* 1st Grade Teacher Loretto Acad 1956-57; 1st/2nd Grade Teacher St Vincent 1957-59; 8th Grade Teacher St James 1959-62, Blessed Sacrament 1962-63; 10th-12th Grade Teacher St Marys Acad 1963-65, Horton Watkins 1965-; *ai:* Cty Children Saturday Camp; PALS Peer Help for Stu; Stu Recovering from Drug & Alcohol Support Group; Prof Dev Comm Chairperson 1988-; Merit Pay Evaluation Comm Mem 1974-77; Salary Comm Mem & Chairperson 1975-79; NEA 1966-;

NCTE 1970-; Church Food Bank Chairperson 1985-89; Faculty Cncl (Chairperson, Advisory Mem); Innovation Prgm Curr Design 1970-; Peer Coaching Prgm Trainer; Intnl Baccalaureate Grader; Implemented Hunter Model in Dist; Danforth Fnd Comm Mem; *office:* Horton Watkins HS 1201 S Warson Rd Saint Louis MO 63124

CANOY, LISA SCOTTON, 7th Grade Soc Stud Teacher; *b:* Staley, NC; *m:* Mark D.; *ed:* (BS) Ed, Univ of NC Greensboro 1982; *cr:* 7th Grade Teacher Archdale Trinity Mid Sch 1983-; *ai:* Beta Club Spon; NC Assn of Educators 1984-; Intnl Rdng Assn Rep 1987-; *home:* Rt 1 Box 30 Staley NC 27355

CANTERBURY, JUDITH BROWN, 4th Grade Teacher; *b:* Naoma, WV; *m:* Johnnie L.; *ed:* (BS) Scndry Ed, WV St Coll 1972; (MS) Comm, WV Univ 1982; *ai:* WV Ed Assn; Natl Arbor Day Society, Delbert Freewill Baptist Church, Keep Litter Out Group, Laubach Literacy Volunteer; *home:* Box 146 Naoma WV 25140

CANTISANO, RICHARD J., 9th-12th Grade History Teacher; *b:* Paterson, NJ; *ed:* (BA) Urban Ed/Scndry Cert, 1978, (MA) Soc Sci, 1989 William Paterson Coll of NJ; Grad Courses; *cr:* His Teacher Roselle Cath HS 1978-80; His Teacher 1981-, Bsbl Coach 1983-, Soccer Coach 1986- Ramsey Public HS; *ai:* Bsbl & Soccer Coach; NJ Cncl Soc Stud, NEA Mem 1982-; William Paterson Coll Alumni Mem 1978-; Rock Music & Teacher Role Playing Used in Soc Stud Classroom; *office:* Ramsey HS Main St Ramsey NJ 07446

CANTLON, DELORA SUE, First Grade Teacher; *b:* Phoenix, AZ; *m:* Brett; *c:* Kurt, Craig; *ed:* (BA) Elem Ed, Purdue Univ 1977; (MS) Elem Ed, IN Univ, Purdue Univ 1980; *cr:* 1st-3rd Grade Teacher Durbin Elem 1978-; *ai:* Stu at Risk Building Coord; IN Rdng Assn 1988-; *office:* Durbin Elem Sch 18000 Durbin Rd Noblesville IN 46060

CANTRELL, CHERYL L., Science Teacher; *b:* Philadelphia, PA; *ed:* (BA) Biological Sci, Glassboro 1971; (MA) Phys Sci, West Chester 1974; Grad Stud; *cr:* Sci Teacher Academy Park HS 1971-; *ai:* Head Bsktbl Coach; Asst Vlybl & La Crosse; SDEA Recording Secy 1974-75; PSEA, NEA; *office:* Academy Park HS 300 Calcon Hook Sharon Hill PA 19079

CANTRELL, KATHLEEN PEIRONNET, American History Teacher; *b:* Munchen, West Germany; *ed:* (BA) His, Schiller Coll London England 1975; (MED) Soc Stud Ed, Univ of FL 1981; *cr:* 5th/6th Grade Teacher Christ the King Sch 1976-79; Geography Teacher N Marion Mid Sch 1981-85; Geography/His Teacher Ft King Mid Sch 1985-; *ai:* FL Cncl for Soc Stud Mem 1981-, Teacher of Yr 1987; North Marion Mid Teacher of Yr 1984; Marion Cty Soc Stud Teacher of Yr 1987; Marion Cty Amer His Grant 1990; *home:* 106 SE 34th St Ocala FL 32674

CANTRELL, SYLVIA JEAN, 5th/6th Grade Math Teacher; *b:* Franklin, GA; *m:* Monty Dwain; *c:* Andrew; *ed:* (BS) Elem Ed, 1977, (MS) Elem Ed, 1978 Jacksonville Univ; (AA) Elem Ed, Auburn Univ 1980; *cr:* 3rd/4th Grade Teacher 1977-78, 5th/6th Grade Math Teacher 1978- Woodland HS; *ai:* 5th Grade 4-H Leader; Textbook & PTO Budget Comms; Randolph Ed Assn Secy; Outstanding 4-H Leader 1979; *home:* Rt 2 Box 81-D Woodland AL 36280

CANTU, ANNA MARIA, Middle School Lang Arts Supvr; *b:* Raymondville, TX; *ed:* (BA) Eng/Philosophy, Sacred Heart Dominican Coll 1966; (MA) Eng, Lamar Univ 1968; *cr:* Eng Teacher Lamar Univ 1966-68; Eng Teacher 1968-88, Eng Dept Head 1983-88 Edison Mid Sch; Mid Sch Lang Art Supvr Port Arthur Ind Sch Dist 1988-; *ai:* TX St Teachers Assn, NEA, NCTE, TX Joint Cncl Teachers of Eng, Assn of TX Lang Art Supvrs, ASCD, Delta Kappa Gamma Pres 1980-82; TX PTA Life Member; *office:* Port Arthur Ind Sch Dist PO Box 1388 Port Acres TX 77640

CAPARELLI, FRANK PETER, Mathematics Coordinator; *b:* Mt Vernon, NY; *m:* Barbara; *c:* James, Andrew; *ed:* (BS) Physics/Math - Summa Cum Laude, Iona Coll 1955; (MA) Math Ed, 1958, Prof diploma Math Ed, 1960 Columbia Univ; Grad Studs Math, Admin, Supervision; *cr:* 7th-12th Grade Math Teacher Copiague Public Schls 1956-62, Ardsley Public Schls 1960-; Adjunct Professor Math Iona Coll 1965-; Math Coord Valhalla Schls 1962-; *ai:* Treas Extra Classroom Accounts; Coord Math, Sci, Bus & Fine Arts 1990; NCTM; NY St Teachers of Math; Valhalla Teachers Assn; Westchester Cty Math Supvrs; Knights of Columbus; Italian Civic Assn; Parish Cncl Local Parish; Grad Schlsp Fordham Univ, Brown Univ; Fellowship NYU Courant Inst, Univ of NC; Yrbk Dedication Valhalla HS 1966; Outstanding Educator in America 1970; *home:* 20 Edgewood Rd Ossining NY 10562

CAPELLI, MARY GRELL, Language Arts Teacher; *b:* Glens Falls, NY; *m:* Richard Peter; *c:* Peter R., Daniel I.; *ed:* (BS) Scndry Ed Eng, 1973, (MS) Scndry Ed Eng, 1978 SUC Oswego; Writing Project CNY; Essential Elements of Instruction; Various Wkshps; *cr:* 7th/8th Grade Eng Teacher 1973-74, 7th/8th Grade Accelerated Eng Teacher 1974-81, Skaneateles Mid Sch; 7th/8th Grade Advanced Eng Teacher 1982-84, 7th-9th Grade Eng Teacher 1986-89, Skaneateles HS; 7th Grade Lang Art Teacher Skaneateles Mid Sch 1989-; *ai:* Homebase Adv; Team Liaison Comm Mem; Helping Teaching Enrichment Prgm; AFT, NYSUT; Skaneateles Teachers Assn (Secy 1978-79, Newsletter 1989-); Onodaga Park Assn (Exec Bd 1979-85, Secy 1980-81, VP 1981-82, Mem 1979-); Plymouth Congregational Church Choir; Friends of Burnett Park Zoo, Friends of Mundy Branch Lib, IFAW; High Honors SUCO Grad Prgm; Grant Integrate Cmptr into Writers Wkshp 1989; Contact Comm Skills Wrkshps OCETA Workers; *office:* Skaneateles Mid Sch 49 E Elizabeth St Skaneateles NY 13152

CAPES, JAY FRANKLIN, 4th Grade Teacher; *b:* Cleveland, OH; *m:* Kristina Lynn Kiehne; *c:* Kevin A., Kelly L.; *ed:* (BS) Ed, Miami Univ 1967; (MA) Ed Admin, Cleveland St Univ 1978; Post Grad Stud; *cr:* 5th Grade Teacher Orange Sch System 1969-72; Asst Mgr CIT Finance Co 1973; 4th Grade Teacher Warrensville Heights Sch System 1974-; *ai:* Head of Elem Math Curr Comm & Noon Lunch Prgm; Chm of Elem Soc Stud Comm; Warrensville Ed Assn Staff Rep 1977-78; NE OH Teachers Assn, OH Ed Assn 1975-; *office:* Eastwood Elem Sch 4050 Eastwood Ln Warrensville Hts OH 44128

CAPIZOLA, GRACE SYLVESTER, Language Art Teacher; *b:* Iona, NJ; *m:* Joseph Anthony; *ed:* (BA) Jr HS Ed, Glassboro St Coll 1967; *cr:* Teacher Delsea Mid Sch 1967-; *ai:* After Sch Act Chaperone; Curr Comm Mem; Delsea Ed Assn (Treas 1982-86, VP 1988-); NEA; Our Lady of Pompeii Choir Mem 1980-; *home:* 2089 Quail St Vineland NJ 08360

CAPLINGER, JEFFREY LYNN, Director of Bands; *b:* Elkins, WV; *m:* Thelma Kay Hawks; *ed:* (BA) Music Ed, Fairmont St Coll 1988; WV Univ, Davis & Elkins Coll; *cr:* Dir of Bands E Preston HS 1988-89, Philip Barbour HS 1989-; *ai:* Jazz Ensemble, Brass Quintet; Pep, Marching, Concert, Symphonic Band; Key Club Adv; Music Educators N Conference 1986-; WV Bandmasters 1988-; Kappa Kappa Psi Pres 1984-; Kiwanis Intnl 1989-; WV Ed Assn, NEA 1988-; WV Mountain St Forrest Festival Band Dir Comm 1990; *office:* Philip Barbour HS Rt 2 Philippi WV 26416

CAPOROSO, NANCY KOGAN, 1st Grade Teacher; *b:* Passaic, NJ; *m:* Robert; *ed:* (BA) Elem Ed/Math, Glassboro St 1978; (MA) Elem Ed/Math, William Paterson Coll 1988; *cr:* Grade Level Chairperson 1983-86, Teacher 1978-, Early Chldhd Coord 1986- Rolling Hills Primary Sch; *ai:* Dist Sci Curr Comm; NJ Assn for Curr & Supervision, NJ Ed Assn; NJ Governors Teacher Recognition Awd 1987; Prins Awd Distinguished Service 1988; Vernon Township Teacher Scholar in Residence 1989 & Mini Grant Awd 1990; *office:* Rolling Hills Primary Sch Box 769 Sammis Rd Vernon NJ 07462

CAPP, KAREN COSSEY, Chapter I Teacher; *b:* Wallace, ID; *m:* Thomas; *c:* Logan J., Adam T.; *ed:* (BA) Elem Ed, E WA Univ 1981; *cr:* 4th Grade Teacher Wibaux Elem Sch 1981-87; Chapter I Teacher Wibaux Cty HS 1987-; *ai:* MEA, WEA Pres 1986-87; PTA Treas 1983-86; Womans Club 1988-; CCD Teacher 1988-89; Natl Forum for Excl Wibauxs Outstanding Teachers Awd 1987; *office:* Wibaux Elem Sch 400 W Nolan Wibaux MT 59353

CAPPEL, THOMAS JOSEPH, Social Studies Teacher; *b:* Chicago, IL; *m:* Jo Ellen Mc Clure; *c:* Eric, Craig, Keith; *ed:* (BA) Soc Stud/Ed, De Paul Univ 1970; (MA) Cultural Stud, Governors St Univ 1976; *cr:* Teacher St Martin Grade Sch 1970, St Rita HS 1970-73; Teacher/Coach Oak Forest HS 1973-85, Hillcrest HS 1985-; *ai:* Var Bsktbl Coach; Girls Cross Cntry Head; NCSS, IHSA Coaches Assn; Teacher of Month 1988, 1989; *office:* Hillcrest HS 175th Pulaski Country Club Hills IL 60478

CAPPS, CINDY COHEN, Assistant Principal; *b:* Chicago, IL; *ed:* (BA) Elem Ed, 1974, (MED) Rdng, 1976, (CAS) Admin, 1980 Natl Coll of Ed; *cr:* 6th-8th Grade Rdng Teacher Perry Mid Sch 1976-80; 9th-10th Grade Eng Teacher Kenston HS 1980-81; 6th-8th Grade Lang Arts Teacher Central Jr HS 1982-88; Asst Prin Carpentersville Mid Sch 1988-; *ai:* Beta Club Spon; 7th Grade Adv; Intnl Rdng Assn, IL Rdng Assn; KY Colonels; *office:* Carpentersville Mid Sch 100 Cleveland Ave Carpentersville IL 60110

CAPPS, DEBBIE PENICK, Kindergarten Teacher; *b:* Union City, TN; *m:* Don M.; *c:* Christopher, Clinten, Caroline; *ed:* (BS) Ed, 1973, (MS) Curr & Instruction, 1976 Univ of TN Martin; *cr:* Spec Ed/Kndgtn-1st Grade Teacher Sharon Elem; *ai:* Chrldr Spon 1981-82; Sharon Faculty Rep 1986-88; NEA, TEA, WCEA; Sharon PTO 1973-; Sharon Ruritan 1988-; Mt Vernon Meth Church Childrens Ministries Dir; *home:* RR 1 Box 51A Penick Rd Sharon TN 38255

CAPPS, JAMES PRESTON, Mathematics Teacher; *b:* Glasgow, MT; *m:* Carol Ann Denning; *ed:* (BA) His, MT St Univ 1985; *cr:* Math Teacher North Bonneville Jr HS 1985-88, Rocky Boy Elem 1988-; *ai:* 8th Grade Class Adv; NCTM 1987-89; MCTM 1988-; *home:* Box 619 Rocky Boy Rt Box Elder MT 59521

CAPPUCCI, MARIE CIRCO, Mathematics Teacher; *b:* Staten Island, NY; *m:* Salvatore; *ed:* (BS) Math, Wagner Coll 1971; (MS) Math Ed, Richmond Coll 1973; *cr:* Math Teacher St Clares Sch 1971-72; Substitute Teacher New York Bd of Ed 1972-73; Math Teacher New York Bd of Ed Ind Sch 51 1973-; *ai:* NCTM 1973-85; *office:* Markham Ind Sch 51 20 Houston St Staten Island NY 10302

CAPUTI, J. GARY, Science & Economics Teacher; *b:* Flushing, NY; *m:* Jill Christine Steben; *ed:* (BA) Bio, Lafayette Coll 1975; (MS) Bio, NY Univ 1980; (MBA) Mrktg, Univ of CT 1985; *cr:* Teacher/Dean of Stus King Sch 1976-84; Mrktg Analyst Emery Air Freight Corporation 1984-85; Teacher/Dir of Summer Prgm Greens Farms Acad 1985-; *ai:* HS Bowl Team & Amnesty Intnl Chapter Faculty Adv; Girls Jr Var Bsktbl Coach; Admissions Comm Upper Sch Faculty Rep; NSTA 1988-; Lafayette Coll Alumni Admissions Rep 1976-; Greens Farms Acad Chapter of Cum Laude Society Pres 1987-; *office:* Greens Farms Acad 35 Beachside Ave Green Farms CT 06436

CARBARY, ELEANOR S., Art/Social Studies Teacher; *b:* Pikeville, KY; *m:* Charles M.; *c:* Jeannine White, Andrea; *ed:* (BS) Elem Ed, Pikeville Coll 1966; Ed, Coll of Mount St Joseph; *cr:* Teacher Pike Cty Schls 1966-67, Hamilton City Sch Dist 1967-69, New Miami Local Dist 1970-; *ai:* Career Ed & Ed Assn Reps; Care Team & Curr Comm Mem; Sr Class & Stu Cncl Adv; NEA; OEA; New Miami Local Bldg Rep 1984-; Golden Apple Awd Ashland Oil Teacher Awds; *office:* New Miami Jr H S 606 Seven Mile Ave Hamilton OH 45011

CARBERRY, H. ROBERT, Science Department Chairman; *b:* Freeport, PA; *m:* Sandra Chapman; *c:* David, Lisa Suranofsky, Susan, Cynthia, Heather; *ed:* (BS) Bio, Clarion Univ 1965; (MED) Bio, Edinboro Univ 1970; Modern Genetics & Evolution, Clarin Univ; Modern Concepts in Bio, IN Univ; Cmptr Modeling, Univ of Pitt; *cr:* Teacher Eisenhower HS 1965-; *ai:* Sci Club Adv; Sci Curr Dev Comm; Warren Cty Ed Assn Faculty Rep 1985; PA Ed Assn, NEA 1965; Starbrick Volunteer Fire Dept Chief 1984-86; *office:* Eisenhower HS RD 2 Russell PA 16345

CARBONE, BARBARA J., Instrumental Music Teacher; *b:* Youngstown, OH; *ed:* (BMED) Music Ed, Youngstown St Univ 1970; Grad Work Music Performance; Undergrade Work Elem Ed; *cr:* Band Dir Liberty Sch System 1970-71, Steubenville Cath Cntrl 1971-73, Lowellville Local Schls 1974-75, Hubbard Exempted Schls 1976-; *ai:* Music Educator Natl Conference 1970-; Delta Kappa Gamma 1987-; Youngstown Symphony 1969-78; Youngstown St Univ Music Schlsp.

CARBONETTI, LAURENCE S., Teacher of English; *b:* Brooklyn, NY; *m:* Jeanne Leone; *ed:* (BA) Eng, Juniata Coll 1971; (MED) Scndry Ed, Antioch Univ 1989; *cr:* Teacher Bernards HS 1972-82, Springfield HS 1983-; *ai:* Mentor Teacher; VT Outstanding Teacher Awd 1988; *office:* Springfield HS 303 South St Springfield VT 05156

CARD, GERALDINE LOUISE, Gifted & Talented Coordinator; *b:* Lincoln, NE; *m:* Frank E.; *c:* Jennifer Traughber; *ed:* (BS) Elem Ed, Univ of NE 1968; (MS) Spec Ed, ID St Univ 1979; Cert Supvr of Spec Ed, Gifted & Talented, Elem Prin; *cr:* Elem Teacher Ruth Public Schls 1967-69; Elem/Spec Ed Teacher Jerome Public Schls 1970-79; Spec Ed/Gifted & Talented Teacher/Admin Booneville Public Schls 1980-; *ai:* Judge Odyssey of Mind Competitions & Regional Invention Contest; AGATE, NAGC 1986-; Delta Kappa Gamma Treas 1975-; Presenter AR Gifted Talented Ed St Convention & Natl Assn Gifted Children; *office:* Booneville Public Schls 401 W 5th St Booneville AR 72927

CARD, JOSEPH ROBERT, Social Studies Teacher; *b:* Port Jervis, NY; *m:* Sandra Bendas; *c:* Jeb, Matthew; *ed:* (AA) Liberal Art/His, Orange Cty Cmmty Coll 1967; (BS) Ed, St Univ Coll Oneonta 1969; (MS) Ed, St Univ Coll Cortland 1974; *cr:* 4th Grade Teacher A J Smith Elem 1969-70; 5th/6th Grade Teacher Columbus Sch 1970-79; 6th Grade Teacher Woodrow Wilson Sch 1979-82; 6th Grade Soc Stud Teacher West Mid Sch 1982-; *ai:* Yorkers Club Civil War His Club; West Mid Stu Government; *office:* West Mid Sch W Middle Ave Binghamton NY 13905

CARD, TODD THOMAS, Business Teacher; *b:* Wells, MN; *ed:* (BA) Information Management, Gustavus Adolphus Coll 1988; Staff Dev Course Elements in Review; *cr:* Bus Teacher Cosmos HS 1988-; *ai:* Bsbl & Wrestling Head Coach; Jr HS & Elem Ftbl & Wrestling Coach; Jr Class & Cosmos Athletic Club Adv; NBEA 1987-; MN Bus Ed Incorporated 1987-; NEA, MN Ed Assn 1988-; MN St HS Coaches Assn 1988-; MN Wrestling Coaches Assn 1989-; Natl Bus Assn Awd 1988; Nom Region 4A Wrestling Coach of Yr 1989-; *office:* Cosmos HS 320 Saturn St Cosmos MN 56228

CARDANO, REGINA MARIE, 6th Grade Teacher; *b:* Philadelphia, PA; *ed:* (BS) Elem Ed, 1969, (MS) Elem Ed, 1976 St Joseph Univ; Villanova Univ; *cr:* 3rd/4th Grade Teacher St Philip 1960-65; 6th Grade Teacher St Jerome 1965-66; 6th/7th Grade Teacher Epiphany of Our Lord 1966-76; 8th Grade Teacher Holy Spirit 1976-80; 6th-8th Grade Teacher Holy Family 1980-; *ai:* Soc Stud Coord; *office:* Holy Family Sch 242 Hermitage St Philadelphia PA 19127

CARDARELLI, PAULA MIHALKO, Fifth Grade Teacher; *b:* Mc Keesport, PA; *m:* Clyde J.; *ed:* (BS) Elem Ed, 1970; (MED) Elem Guildance, 1974 California St Coll of PA; *cr:* Kndgtn Teacher Lincoln & Port Vue Elem 1970; 4th Grade Teacher Port Vue & Myer Avenue Elem 1970-79; 5th Grade Teacher Lincoln Elem 1979-82, Port Vue Elem 1982-; *ai:* Child Study Team Chairperson; Mem Prof Improvement & Supt Search Comm; Building Coord Natl Historical Map Contest; PSEA (Social Chm, Building Rep 1989-) 1970-; PTA, NEA 1970-; Teacher of Yr 1985-86; *office:* Port Vue Elem Sch 1201 Romine Ave Port Vue PA 15133

CARDEN, NANCY THELMA (ROBERTS), Fourth Grade Teacher; *b:* Warrior, AL; *m:* Wayne; *c:* Nancy Cummings, Greg; *ed:* (BS) Elem Ed, 1963, (MA) Elem Ed, 1968 Univ of AL; *cr:* 4th Grade Teacher Bagley Jr HS 1963-; *home:* 7846 Bagley Rd Dora AL 35062

CARDEN, TERRY LEE, Electronics Instructor; *b:* Atlanta, GA; *m:* Sharon West; *ed:* (AS) Pre-Med, Mid GA Coll 1971; (BS) Bio/Chem, GA St Univ 1975; (MED) Chem, GA Southwestern Coll 1976; (EDS) T&I/Admin, GA St Univ 1988; *cr:* Teacher Crisp Cty HS 1976-78, Forest Park Jr HS 1978-80; Instr Morrow Sr HS

1981-; *ai:* NEA, GAE 1985-; Kappa Delta Pi 1988-; GA Principles of Technology Assn Pres 1990, Teacher of Yr 1990; Conducted Teacher Wkshps in Prin of Technology GA & FL; Mem GA Electronics Revision Comm; *home:* 310 Victoria Dr Ellenwood GA 30049

CARDIERI, ALEXANDER MARIO, Music Teacher; *b:* Brooklyn, NY; *m:* Filis De Rodio; *c:* George, Alexis; *ed:* (MM) Music Theory, 1980, (BM) Piano, 1976 Manhattan Sch of Music; Academic Diploma Major in Music, HS of Performing Arts NY 1971; *cr:* Music Teacher St Anthony Sch 1979-81; Dir of Music St Agatha Church 1981-84; Music Teacher St Joseph HS 1981-84, Patagonia Union HS 1985-; *ai:* Spon for Class of 1992; Music Adv/Band Dir; NEA/AEA Pres Local Sch Dist 1982-, Local Assn of the Month 1989; MENC/AMEA Mem 1985-; St Rita Church Organist/Cantor 1986-, Appreciation for Service in Gods Work 1989; Awarded Plaque Worlds Greatest Band Dir from Patagoula Band Students 1989; *home:* 12770 E Wentworth Ct Vail AZ 85641

CARDILLE, KEVIN SCOTT, Science Teacher; *b:* Nashwauk, MN; *ed:* (BAS) Sci, Univ of MN 1988; Coaching; Math & Cmptr Sci; *cr:* Bsktbl/Track Coach Duluth Public Schls 1986-88; Sci Teacher Ceylon Public Schls 451 1988-; *ai:* Girls Head Bsktbl Coach; 7th Grade Class Adv; Audio-Visual & Cmptr Coord; MN Educl Effectiveness Prgm; Nashwauk July 4th Comm Talent Show Dir 1987-88; Cmmnty Ed Cmptr Teacher 1989; *office:* Ceylon Public Sch 301 West Grant St Ceylon MN 56121

CARDONA, LOIS BYLLESBY, K-2nd Grade Substitute Teacher; *b:* Sioux Falls, SD; *m:* Antonio; *c:* Harold, Carol; *ed:* (BA) Early Chldhd, Univ CA Santa Barbara 1952; (MA) Home Ec/Child Dev, CA St Univ Fresno 1972; Math & Writing Process for Children; *cr:* 2nd Grade Teacher Dept of Ed Amer Samoa 1969-71; K-2nd Grade Teacher Desert Sands Unified Schls 1971-77; K-4th Grade Teacher Saudi Arabian Intnl Schls 1977-87; 4th Grade Teacher Asociacion Escuelas Lincoln 1987-88; Substitute Teacher Desert Sands Unified Schls 1990; *ai:* Substitute Teaching; Volunteer Teaching Literacy/Spec Ed; NEA; CA Teachers Assn; Delta Phi Upsilon; Teacher of Yr Desert Sands Unified Sch Dist 1975; *home:* 45-901 Toro Peak Rd Palm Desert CA 92260

CARDONE, PATRICIA BRENNAN, Religious Studies Teacher; *b:* Kew Gardens, NY; *m:* Michael V.; *c:* Elizabeth; *ed:* (MA) Theology, Providence Coll 1966; (BSED) Ed, Brentwood Coll 1968; (CAS) Ed Admin, Hofstra Univ 1982; Gifted & Talented Ed, Columbia Univ; Symposium Marriage & Family, Dayton Univ; *cr:* Religious Stud Chairperson/Teacher Holy Family Diocesan HS 1966-73, Xaverian HS 1975-80, St Agnes HS 1981-87; Religious Stud Teacher St Agnes Academic Sch 1987-; *ai:* Stu Cncl Moderator; Phi Delta Kappa 1980-; ASCD Pres 1980; Natl Assn Scndry Prins Pres 1988-; Fellowship Hofstra Univ Ed Admin; Author of Morality Made Simple, Teachers Guide-Argus Press; *office:* St Agnes Academic HS 13-20 124th St College Point NY 11356

CARDONI, AGNES A., English Teacher; *b:* Wilkes-Barre, PA; *m:* John Jr.; *c:* Christopher A. Swantek; *ed:* (BA) Eng, Coll Misericordia 1969; (MS) Ed/Eng, Wilkes Coll 1974; Various Wkshps, Seminars & Colls; *cr:* 10th/11th Grade Eng Instr GAR Memorial HS 1969-70; 11th/12th Grade Eng Instr J M Coughlin HS 1971-78; 7th-8th Grade Eng/8th-9th Grade Fr Instr Wilkes-Barre Township Jr HS 1978-79; 7th/8th Grade Eng Instr GAR Memorial HS 1979-80; Composition Instr Wilkes Coll 1981-85, Kings Coll 1986; World Lit Instr Wilkes Coll 1987; 10th/12th Grade Eng Instr J M Coughlin HS 1981-; Lit/Composition Instr Coll Misericordia 1983-; Instr Composition Kings Coll 1988-; *ai:* Poets-in-the-Schls Prgm Coord; Fine Art Celebrations; Class Adv; Fund Raising, Social, Sch, Cmmty Act; Stu Teacher Supvr & Several Teacher Trainees; Phi Delta Kappa, Delta Kappa Gamma, Lambda Iota Tau; NE PA Writing Cncl Exec Bd; NEA, NCTE, PA St Ed Assn, Wilkes-Barre Area Ed Assn; Coll Misericordia Alumni Assn-Fund Raising; St Nicholas Church (Lector, Mem Liturgical Comm, Mem Church Cncl, Reader Parish Outreach Prgm); March of Dimes Birth Defects Fnd Fund Raising; *office:* J M Coughlin HS 80 N Washington St Wilkes-Barre PA 18701

CARDWELL, DAVID EMMANUEL, Earth Science Teacher; *b:* Del Rio, TX; *m:* Consuelo Sandoval; *ed:* (BS) Geology, Univ of WI Oshkosh 1969; *cr:* Sci Teacher San Felipe Del Rio Ind Sch Dist 1971-73; Earth Sci Teacher Cordova Sr HS 1973-; Assoc Professor Geology Summer Field Camp Univ WI Oshkosh 989-89; Assoc Instr Sci Credential Prgm Univ of CA Davis 1989; *ai:* Mentor Teacher for Folsom-Cordova Unified Sch Dist; Mem Steering, Improving & Enhancing Sci Ed, Exec Comms for Sacramento Sci Teachers Assn; Natl Assn of Geology Teachers 1984-; Natl Earth Sci Teachers Assn, CA Sci Teachers Assn 1985-; NEA 1984-; Natl Research Society Sigma Xi Outstanding Geology Sci Teacher 1987; Cordova Sr HS Teacher of Yr 1988; Sacramento Ed Cable Consortium Grant Recipient 1987-88; *office:* Cordova Sr HS 2239 Chase Dr Rancho Cordova CA 95670

CARDWELL, DEBRA JEANNE (HOLLOWAY), Fourth Grade Teacher; *b:* Baltimore, MD; *m:* Michael Robert; *c:* Kate E., Michael D.; *ed:* (BA) Psych, 1974, (BS) Elem Ed, 1976, (MED) Spec Ed/Learning Disabilities, 1984 Kent St Univ; *cr:* 5th-8th Grade Educl Aide Randallwood Mid Sch & Warrensville Heights Jr HS 1974-76; 7th-8th Grade Remedial Teacher Warrensville Heights Jr HS 1976-78; 2nd Grade Teacher 1978-79, 3rd Grade Teacher 1979-80, 4th Grade Teacher 1980- Westwood Elem Sch; *ai:* Cmptr Lab, Environmental Awareness, Safety Patrol, Westwood Wire, Young Authors Conference Adv; Discipline & Writing Comm Mem; Warrensville Heights Ed Assn, OH Ed Assn, NEA, Westwood PTA 1978-; Warrensville Heights City Schls 15 Yr Service Awd 1989; Amer Red Cross Swim Instr 1972-84; Case Study Linguistic Competency 1984; *office:* Westwood Elem Sch 19000 Garden Blvd Warrensville Hts OH 44128

CARDWELL, DOUGLAS WILLIAM, Computer Mentor Teacher; *b:* Weisboton, Germany; *m:* Marian Rachel Lipton; *c:* Ashley, Bryant; *ed:* (AA) Liberal Stud, Fresno City 1977; (BA) Liberal Stud, Fresno St 1979; (MA) Ed/Cmptrs, Pacific Coll 1990; Natl Math Inservice & Cmptr Competency Inservice Trng; *cr:* Calculus/Bio Tutor Fresno City Coll 1974-76; Multi-Grade Teacher Mickey Cox Elem 1980-85; Honors Math/Cmptr Lab Teacher Kastner Intermediate 1985-; *ai:* Mentor Teacher; Staff Inservice; Cmptr Club Coach; Technology Rep; Stud Skill Comm; *home:* 1049 W Pico Fresno CA 93705

CARDWELL, VIRGINIA LANGEL, 5th Grade Teacher; *b:* Lawton, MI; *m:* John P.; *c:* Janet C. Lawson, David, Charles; *ed:* (BS) Elem Ed, James Madison Univ 1958; *cr:* 4th Grade Teacher Lynchburg Public Schls 1958-63; 5th Grade Teacher Timberlake Christian Schls 1973-; *ai:* ACSI 1988-; Gideons Auxiliary Pres/VP/Sec 1971-; *office:* Timberlake Chrstn Sch 300 Horizon Dr Forest VA 24551

CAREY, CAROLYN DEANN (SHANKSTER), 4th Grade Teacher; *b:* Bryan, OH; *m:* David N.; *c:* Angela A.; *ed:* (BS) Elem Ed, Bowling Green St Univ 1970; Bowling Green St Univ; Toledo Univ; *cr:* 4th Grade Teacher Benton Carroll Salem Sch Dist 1970-72; 4th Grade Teacher 1972-73; 5th Grade Teacher 1973-74; 4th Grade Teacher 1974- Stryker Elem; *ai:* Part-Time Instr of Non-Credit Courses-Northwest Tech Coll; NEA; OEA Benton Carroll Salem Ed Assn 1970-72; OEA Life Mem 1972-; Pres 1982-83; Sec 1974-75 Stryker Ed Assn; Building Rep; OH Assn Elem Kndgtn Nursery Educators 1970-76; Psi Iota Xi (VP Treas Corresponding Sec Conductress) 1972-; Fountain City Corvete Club Secy Soc Direct 1972-; Pulaski United Meth Church Mem 1956-; Choir Accompanist 1985-; Sr Choir Mem 1985-; United Meth Women Faith Cir Secy 1989; *home:* Rt 2 Box 257 Bryan OH 43506

CAREY, DOROTHY J., Mathematics Teacher; *b:* Beech Grove, IN; *ed:* (BS) Math, Purdue Univ 1981; (MS) Scndry Ed, IN Univ 1989; *cr:* Teacher Center Grove Schls 1981-82, Indianapolis Public Schls 1982-; *ai:* IEA; ISTA; Shining Star Awd from WTHR Channel 13; *home:* 5704 S Kealing Ave Indianapolis IN 46227

CAREY, ELOISE, Third Grade Teacher; *b:* Boligee, AL; *ed:* (BS) Ed, Stillman Coll 1965; (MS) Counseling/Guidance, IN Univ 1966; Grad Stud, IN Univ Bloomington & Univ of OH Toledo; *cr:* Teacher Lincoln Sch 1966-; *ai:* Team Leader Dial-A-Teacher Prgm; Numerous Curr Comms; Career Specialist; Toledo Fed of Teachers Bd of Dir 1982-; Amer Fed of Teachers; Grace Presbyn Church Ruling Elder 1987-; Toledo Fed of Teachers Building Rep & Comm; Teacher in Charge Lincoln Sch; Grade Level Contributor Silver Burdett & Ginn Soc Stud our Countrys Cmmtys 1988; *office:* Lincoln Elem Sch 1801 N Detroit Ave Toledo OH 43606

CAREY, MARTY E., English Department Chair; *b:* Cheyenne, WY; *ed:* (BS) Elem Ed, NW MO St Univ 1975; (MA) Spec Ed/Talented/Gifted, Univ of N CO 1982; Grad Stud Various Univs; *cr:* 1st Grade Teacher Roosevelt Elem 1975-79; 5th/6th Grade Teacher North Mor Elem 1979-80; 1st Grade Teacher Leroy Drive Elem 1980-81; 4th/5th Grade Teacher North Star Elem 1981-84; 7th-9th Grade Eng Teacher Meritt Hutton Jr HS 1984-; *ai:* Leadership Club Spon; Tutoring Prgm; Forensics Team Coach; Thornton HS Pom Pon Asst; Green River Ed Assn Parliamentarian 1975-79; Dist 12 Ed Assn 1979-; CO Lang Art Assn 1980-; Boomtown Players Cmmty Theatre 1977-79; Northglenn Cmmty Choir Alto Section Leader 1984-85; MENSA 1982-86; Published Wkshp Teacher Handbook; Roosevelt Elem Teacher of Yr 1978; *office:* Meritt Hutton Jr HS 9266 N Washington St Denver CO 80229

CAREY, PEGGY MARIE, English Teacher; *b:* Laurel, DE; *m:* William Michael; *c:* Lindsay M.; *ed:* (BA) Eng, Salisbury St Coll 1976; *cr:* Eng Teacher Indian River HS 1976-77; Eng/Public Speaking Teacher Woodbridge Jr/Sr HS 1977-; *ai:* Public Speaking Coach; DSEA, WEA; *office:* Woodbridge Jr/Sr HS 307 Laws St Bridgeville DE 19933

CAREY, THOMAS KENNY, Social Studies Teacher; *b:* Baltimore, MD; *m:* Mary Esther Carroll; *c:* Thomas K., Timothy J., Patricia Carey Everett, Page Carey Fisher; *ed:* (BS) Ec/His, Loyola Coll 1951; (MSS) Amer His, Morgan St Univ 1973; Course Work on Grad Level Loyola, Towson St, Johns Hopkins; *cr:* Teacher Baltimore Polytechnic Inst 1953-68, Dulaney HS 1969-83, Worcester Cntry Sch 1983-; *ai:* Coaching Ice Hockey, Rifle, Boys & Girls La Crosse, Vlybl; *home:* 3127 Ocean Pines Berlin MD 21811

CAREY, WILLIAM PATRICK, English Department Chair; *b:* Brooklyn, NY; *m:* Shannon Mc Garry; *c:* Erin, Brenna, Patrick, Kieran; *ed:* (BA) Eng, Siena Coll 1967; (MA) Eng, 1969, (MSED) Eng Ed, 1970 Univ of Dayton; *cr:* Teacher Roger Bacon HS 1970-; *ai:* Track Coach; Mem Academic Bd; NCTE 1980-; NCEA 1975-; YMCA Comm of Management 1987-; *office:* Roger Bacon HS 4320 Vine St Cincinnati OH 45217

CARGAL, ERIC MICHAEL, Sr Programmer/Analyst; *b:* Lawton, OK; *m:* VerDel Marie Hill; *c:* Jennifer, David; *ed:* (BA) Pre-Seminary, Southeastern Coll 1983; *cr:* Teacher Harvest Time Memorial 1983-84, Briarcrest Sch 1984-85; Cmptr Programmer Total System Services 1985-89, Blue Cross/Blue Shield of GA 1989-; *ai:* Several Articles Published; *home:* 7857 Crescent Dr Columbus GA 31909

CARGILL, CAROL LOHMANN, Voc Home Economics Teacher; *b:* Paterson, NJ; *c:* Thomas, Brett, Cargill; *ed:* (BS) Home Ec, Mansfield St Coll 1973; *cr:* Secy Codesco 1974-78; Production Control Analyst Pacific Scientific 1983-87; Home Ec Teacher Spruce Creek HS 1987-; *ai:* FHA, HERO Adv; Jr Class Spon; Jr-Sr Prom Comm Chairperson; FHVEA 1988-; VCHETA Secy 1988-; VEA; Teacher of Month 1989; *office:* Spruce Creek HS 801 Taylor Rd Port Orange FL 32127

CARGILL, RODNEY EUGENE, Mathematics Dept Teacher; *b:* Grand Island, NE; *m:* Rebecca C. Donnelley; *ed:* (BS) Math, Univ of NE Lincoln 1982; Head Coaching Endorsement, Univ of NE Lincoln, Univ of NE Omaha, Baker Univ; *cr:* Math Teacher Bellevue East HS 1983-87, Olathe North HS 1987-; *ai:* Asst Wrestling Coach; AFT 1986-; NCTM 1988-; Sigma Alpha Epsilon 1979-; De Molay (Pres 1978) 1976-; *office:* Olathe North HS 600 E Prairie Olathe KS 66061

CARHART, CAROL A., 6th Grade Mathematics Teacher; *b:* New Brunswick, NJ; *ed:* (BA) Elem Ed, Trenton St 1961; (MS) Supervision Prin, Monmouth 1982; *cr:* 5th/6th Grade Teacher Mechanic St Sch & River St Sch 1961-68; 5th/6th Grade Math Teacher Atlantic Elem Sch & Cedar Dr Sch 1968-; *ai:* Math Club; NEA, NJEA, Monmounty Cty Ed Assn; NJ Schoolwomen (Recording Secy, 2nd VP, Pres Elect) 1986-; Alpha Delta Kappa (Treas 1982-86, Pres Elect 1986-88, Pres 1988-); Colts Neck Township Ed Assn Prof Rights & Responsibilities 1980-; 1st Baptist Church (Organist, Choir Dir, Daily Vacation Bible Sch Music Dir); Governors Teacher Recognition Awd 1988; *office:* Cedar Drive Sch Cedar Dr Colts Neck NJ 07722

CARICATO, JOSEPHINE AMANDA (GEMMA), 7th/8th Grade English Teacher; *b:* Pueblo, CO; *m:* Bill Dwain; *c:* Gregory, Kathryn, Glenn; *ed:* (BA) Eng/Speech, Univ of S CO 1981; CO Writing Assessment Wkshp; 4-Mat System Trng in Learning, Teaching; BS with Spec Distinction; *cr:* Eng Teacher/Permanent Substitute Teacher Pleasantview Mid Sch & South HS 1982; Eng Teacher Fremont Mid Sch 1983-; *ai:* Writing Facilitator, Writing Comm; Strategic Options Team; Alpha Delta Kappa (Chaplain 1988-, Corresponding Secy) 1990; Published in Buffalo Sun 1981; Loyde Terry Oratory 1979; Pres Achievement Schlsp 1979-81; Delta Kappa Gamma Schlshp 1981; Natl Deans List 1981-82; Whos Who Amoung Stus in Amer Colls & Univs 1981-82; *office:* Eastern Fremont Mid Sch 500 W 5th Florence CO 81226

CARINO, RICHARD S., Migrant Teacher/Fed Coord; *b:* Casa Grande, AZ; *c:* Alejandro; *ed:* (AS) Liberal Arts, Cntrl AZ Coll 1974; (BA) Ed, AZ St Univ Tempe 1977; (MA) Educl Admin, Northern AZ Univ 1988; Admin Cert Prin 1990; *cr:* 4th Grade Teacher 1977-84, 3rd/4th Grade Teacher 1984-85, 3rd Grade Teacher 1985-87, Coord/Teacher Migrant Summer Sch 1986-87/89 Picacho Elem Sch; Teacher Migrant Class Resource Room 1987-; *ai:* AZ Hispanic Admin; Northern AZ Hispanic; AZ St Alumni Assn; NEA, AEA; Picacho Ed Group; Az Schl Bds Assn; Pinal Cty Hispanic Cncl Juventud-Big Brothers/Big Sisters; Volunteer Group Leader Drug Awareness Prgm; Governing Bd Mem; *office:* Picacho Elem Sch P O Box 8 Picacho AZ 85241

CARL, RICHARD DAVID, JR., Mathematics Teacher; *b:* Baltimore, MD; *m:* Sharon Bytella; *ed:* (AA) General Stud, Essex Comm Coll 1980; (BS) Elem Ed, Towson St Univ 1983; Masters Equivalency Baltimore Cty Bd of Ed; Modern Stud, Loyola Coll; *cr:* Teacher St Josephs Sch 1983-84, Holabird Mid Sch 1984-; *ai:* Stage Crew 1986; Collectors Club 1988-89; Girls Var Bsktbl Dundack HS 1987-; NEA, MD St Teachers Assn 1983-; Teachers Assn of Baltimore Cty 1984-; NE YMCA Sftbl League Coach 1989-; *office:* Holabird Mid Sch 1701 Delvale Ave Dundalk MD 21222

CARLEY, ROSE NIGRI, 5th Grade Teacher; *b:* Waterbury, CT; *m:* Marvin E.; *ed:* (BA) Piano, Julius Hartt Sch of Music 1958; (MS) Elem Ed, Cntrl CT St Coll 1970; Admin/Supervision, Univ of Bridgeport 1980; CT Sch of Broadcasting; *cr:* 5th/6th Grade Teacher Hanover Sch 1959-; *ai:* Work with Talented & Gifted Stus in Field of Performing Arts; Meriden Teachers Assn 1959-; CT Ed Assn, NEA; Amer Diabetes Assn (VP 1976) 1976-77; Delta Kappa Gamma (Membership Chm 1976-78) 1975-88; Meriden Teacher of Yr 1989; Whos Who in Amer Colls & Univs 1958; *office:* Hanover Sch Main St South Meriden CT 06450

CARLILE, JERRY DON, Counselor/Coach; *b:* Webb City, AR; *m:* Arlene; *c:* Jarrod, Brooke; *ed:* (BA) Phys Ed, Univ of the Ozarks 1966; (MA) Ed/Phys Ed, Univ of Cntrl AR 1974; (MA) Guidance Counseling/Admin, 1989 Western St Coll; *cr:* Jr HS Coach/Soc Stud Teacher Fleming Jr/Sr HS 1966-69; Government Teacher/Boys Bsktbl/Asst Ftbl Prairie HS 1969-81; Head Girls Bsktbl/Phys Ed Ozark HS1981-84; Head Ftbl/Boys Bsktbl Coach/Counseling Peetz Sch Dist 1985-; *ai:* Head Ftbl, Boys Bsktbl; CEA, NEA; CO Sch Cnslrs; CO Coaches Assn; Teacher of Yr, Coach of Yr; Advisory Comm Mem for CO Bsktbl; *office:* Peetz Plateau RE-5 HS Box B 311 Coleman Peetz CO 80747

CARLISLE, KATHY A., English Teacher; *b:* Canyon, TX; *m:* Buttons; *c:* Amie, Amanda, Anna K.; *ed:* (BS) Eng Ed/Poly Sci, West TX St Univ Canyon 1974; *cr:* Teacher Tulia Ind Sch Dist 1985-; *ai:* Co-Spon Stud Cncl; Coach UIL Rdng Writing Team, Textbook Comm, Effective Sch Leadership Trng Team & Cmptr Awareness Comm 1989-; *office:* Tulia Jr H S 421 NE 3rd Tulia TX 79088

CARLISLE, M. AVERILL, 7th Grade Teacher; *b:* Christchurch, New Zealand; *ed:* (BA) Biblical Ed, Columbia Bible Coll 1966; (MSED) Sci Ed, Old Dominion Univ 1979; Capernwray Bible Sch Canforth England; *cr:* Teacher Norfolk Chrstn Schls 1968-; *ai:* Environmental Camping Trip Dir; Norfolk Chrstn Schls Academic

Comm; *office:* Norfolk Christian Schls 255 Thole St Norfolk VA 23505

CARLON, BETH NORDIN, 5th Grade Lead Teacher; *b:* Jefferson, IA; *m:* Peter David; *ed:* (BA) Fr/Elem Ed, Univ of TX Arlington 1979; (MED) Supervision, TX Chrstn Univ 1984; Admin Cert; *cr:* 5th Grade Teacher Johns Elem 1980; 4th Grade Teacher Kennard Ind Sch Dist 1980-81; 1st/6th Grade Teacher Johns Elem 1981-88; 5th Grade Teacher Roark Elem 1988-; *ai:* Chm Sunshine Comm, SERVA, Effective Schls Comm; Coord Honor Roll & Before Sch Prgm; TX St Teachers Assn 1988-; Phi Delta Kappa Pres 1988-89; Kappa Delta Pi, Phi Sigma Iota 1980-; Shepherd of Life Luth Church 1983-; Jr Womans Club 1986-; PTA Officer; Roark Elem & Arlington Kiwanis Teacher of Yr 1989-; Arlington Ind Sch Dist Bravo Awd; 1st Grade Sci Curr Project; *office:* Maude Roark Elem Sch 2401 Roberts Cir Arlington TX 76010

CARLS, MICHAEL A., American Government Teacher; *b:* Minneapolis, MN; *m:* Margaret; *c:* Lara, Ariel, Megan; *ed:* (BS) Soc Stud Ed, Univ of MN 1971; Grad Stud Numerous Courses; *cr:* Soc Stud Teacher Glencoe Public Schls 1971-74, Litchfield Public Schls 1974-76; Teacher Hutchinson Public Schls 1976-; *ai:* Head Coach Girls Swimming; Coached Bicentennial Competition Team; Hutchinson Ed Assn 1976-; MN Ed Assn, NEA 1971-; City Cncl (Alderman 1981-89, VP 1984-89); Hospital Bd (Trustee 1984-89, Pres 1987-88); Teacher of Yr Hutchinson Public Schls 1988; *office:* Hutchinson HS Roberts Rd Hutchinson MN 55350

CARLSEN, KENNETH L., Jr High School Science Teacher; *b:* Stanley, WI; *m:* Carole Ellen Blazer; *c:* Mark, Michael, Kevin; *ed:* (BS) Elem Ed, Univ of WI Eau Claire 1969; Elem Admin, Univ of WI Superior; *cr:* 5th/6th Grade Teacher 1962-64, 6th Grade Teacher 1964-66, 7th/8th Grade Teacher/Jr HS Building Prin 1966-87, 7th/8th Grade Teacher 1987- Flambeau Schls; *ai:* Sheldon Fire Protection Dist Fire Inspector; WI Hunter Safety Instr 20 Yr Awd 1987; Amer Red Cross CPR & First Aid Instr; WI Dept of Natural Resources Snowmobile & Recreational Vehicle Instr; *office:* Flambeau Jr HS P O Box 86 Tony WI 54563

CARLSON, BRADLEY PAUL, Math/Geography Teacher; *b:* Grand Rapids, MN; *m:* Debbie A. Watercott; *c:* Connie, Andy, Evan; *ed:* (BS) Math/Soc Stud, Bemidji St Coll 1975; Math/His/Ed; *cr:* 7th/8th Grade Math/His/Civics /Geography Teacher Sebeka; *ai:* Homecoming & Prom Adv; MN 4-H Fnd Trustee 1983-89; Northland Governing Bd MEA; Local MEA Pres; *home:* R 3 Box B12 Sebeka MN 56477

CARLSON, DALE LOUIS, 6th Grade Teacher; *b:* Randolph, NE; *m:* Mary Lou Weber; *c:* Gregory D., Douglas L.; *ed:* (BA) Poly Sci, Univ of NE 1964; (MA) Elem Ed, Wayne St Coll 1973; US Army Officer Candidate Sch, Infantry Officer Career Course, Command & General Staff Coll; *cr:* 6th Grade Teacher Pierce Elem Sch 1973-; *ai:* Pierce Ed Assn VP 1978-79; Amer Legion Post 148 Commander 1981-82; Pierce Cty Red Cross Vice-Chm 1975-; Plainview City Cncl Mem 1983-; Pierce Cty Republicans Chm 1984-89; *home:* 301 Elm Plainview NE 68769

CARLSON, DARRYL RODNEY, Drivers Education Teacher; *b:* Ft Hauchuca, AZ; *m:* Joanna Louise Schmidt; *c:* Lindsay, Tyler, Jared, Kourtni; *ed:* (BS) Phys Ed, N IL Univ 1982; (MA) Ed, Georgetown Coll 1989; Drivers Ed, N IL Univ 1989; *cr:* Phys Ed/Health Teacher Canterbury Sch 1982-86; Phys Ed Teacher Georgetown Coll 1986-87; K-10th Grade Phys Ed/Health Teacher Ninth & O Baptist Acad 1987-88; Drivers Ed Teacher Kaneland HS 1988-; *ai:* Head Bsktbl Coach; Asst Ftbl & Sftbl Coach; NEA; Athletic Conference Pres 1985-86; Head of Fellowship of Chrstn Athletes Georgetown Coll; *home:* 112 Read St Elburn IL 60119

CARLSON, DAVID CHARLES, Mathematics Department Teacher; *b:* Grand Rapids, MN; *c:* Kristine, Mindy, Jacky; *ed:* (AS) Math, Itasca Cmmty 1962; (BS) Math, 1964, (MS) Math, 1974 Bemidji St; *cr:* Math/Sci Teacher Walker HS 1964-65, Mansfield HS 1965-67; 7th/8th Grade Math/Algebra Teacher Bigfork HS 1967-; *ai:* Sr Class Adv; Vlybl Ofcl; Range Area Vlybl Ofcls Pres 1987-89; Grand Rapids Engr Foreman Survey Crew 1979-; Sunday Sch Teacher 1981-; *office:* Bigfork HS Huskie Blvd Bigfork MN 55628

CARLSON, DAVID E., Retired Teacher; *b:* Jefferson, OH; *m:* Barbara J.; *c:* Timothy A.; *ed:* (BS) Ed, Kent St Univ 1964; (MS) Ed/Admin, Westminister Coll 1969; Post Grad Stud, Akron Univ, Univ of CA, Youngstown St, Kent St Univ; *cr:* Teacher 1960-72, Prin 1972-75, Teacher 1976-85 Jefferson Elem Sch; *ai:* Stu Cncl in Elem Schls; Phi Delta Kappa Life Mem; Rotary Jefferson Club Pres 1970-; Chamber of Commerce Bd of Control 1988-; Outstanding Conservation Teacher 1980-81; Martha Golden Jennings Scholar 1969-70; *home:* 45 Linda Ln Jefferson OH 44047

CARLSON, DEA JOHNSON, High School English Teacher; *b:* Miami Beach, FL; *m:* Elwood John; *c:* Bret J., Megan L.; *ed:* (BA) Eng, Whitworth Coll 1977; (MA) Theology, San Francisco Theological Seminary 1981; Ed, Pacific Luth Univ, Antioch Coll, City Univ; *cr:* Eng Teacher Waupun HS 1981-84, Tolt HS 1985-; *ai:* Yrbk & Soph Class Adv; *office:* Tolt HS 3740 Tolt Ave Garn Rd. N.E. Carnation WA 98014

CARLSON, JOHN CURTIS, Math/Computer Specialist; *b:* Minneapolis, MN; *m:* Wendy J. Graese; *c:* Christina M., Kelly Graese; *ed:* (BA) Math, St Olaf Coll 1980; Athletic Trng/Coaching Bemidji St Univ; Cmptr Tech; *cr:* Math Teacher Maynard Public Sch 1980-81; Kelliher Public Sch 1981-; *ai:* Cmptr Coord; Per Comm Mem; Talented & Gifted Comm Mem; Math Counts Adv; Kelliher Math & Sci Girls Adv; Kelligher HS Math League Adv; Jr HS Ftbl Coach; Kelliher Cmmty Ed Instr; Blackduck Cmmty Ed Instr; MN Ed Assn 1978-; Kelliher Ed Assn Chief Negotiator 1981- Teacher of Yr 1989; MN Cncl Teachers of Math 1990-; *office:* Kelliher Public Sch Box 147 Kelliher MN 56650

CARLSON, KAREN JANE, Fourth Grade Teacher; *b:* Minneapolis, MN; *m:* Harlow C.; *ed:* (BA) Elem Ed, 1966, (MA) Elem Ed, 1978 Univ of MN; *cr:* 4th Grade Teacher Hastings Ind Sch Dist #200; *ai:* Author Day Prgm & Poets in Residence Christa Mc Auliffe Sch; Hastings Ed Assn Pres 1987-89; Dist 37B Legislative Ed Advisory Bd Mem 1986-; Dist 200 Mentor Governing Bd Mem 1987-; Univ of MN Kerlan Friends Pres Elect 1989-; Hastings Teacher of Yr 1985; MN Teacher of Excl 1985; Ashland Oil Teacher Achievement Awd 1989; Dist 200 Rep MN Educators Acad 1989; *office:* Christa Mc Auliffe Elem Sch 1601 W 12th St Hastings MN 55033

CARLSON, KATHERINE LEIGH, Fifth Grade Teacher; *b:* Tulsa, OK; *ed:* (BA) Bio, St Mary Coll 1973; (MA) Elem Ed, Tulsa Univ 1990; *cr:* Teacher Sts Peter & Paul 1974-89, Monte Cassino 1989-, Tulsa Jr Coll 1985-; *ai:* NCTM 1985-; Kappa Delta Pi 1988-; Teacher of Yr Sts Peter & Paul 1988-89.

CARLSON, KEVIN SCOTT, Mathematics Instructor; *b:* Heron Lake, MN; *ed:* (BA) Math, 1974, (MAT) Math, 1984 Augustana Coll; Math Ed, Univ of MN 1989; *cr:* 7th-9th Grade Teacher Axtell Park Jr HS 1974-78; 10th-12th Grade Teacher Washington Sr HS 1978-; *ai:* Homecoming Adv; NCTM Mem 1979-; SD Cncl Teachers of Math Mem; Young Mens Chrstn Assn Youth Leader; Sioux Falls Jaycees Outstanding Young Educator Awd 1984; Woodrow Wilson Fellowship Math Inst 1988; *office:* Washington Sr HS 315 S Main Ave Sioux Falls SD 57102

CARLSON, MARGE REIQUAM, Retired K & 1st Grade Teacher; *b:* Conrad, MT; *m:* Raymond F.; *c:* Raymond F. II, Debra S. Carlson Saylor; *ed:* Kndgtn/Primary, Miss Woods 1948; (BA) Elem Ed, Coll of Great Falls 1969; *cr:* 1st Grade Teacher 1948-51, Kndgtn Teacher 1958-75, 1st Grade Teacher 1975-85 Fairfield Elem; *ai:* Local MEA (Secy 1970-71, Pres 1972-73); Delta Kappa Gamma 1962-; Order of Eastern Star Worthy Matron 1961, Grand Page 1961; Jr Womans Club (Secy 1956, Pres 1957); Comm to Re-Write Kndgtn Curr Guide for St of MT 1963; *home:* 309 2nd Ave N Fairfield MT 59436

CARLSON, PAULA GERALDINE, Art Coordinator; *b:* Moline, IL; *m:* David Ward Hardy; *ed:* (BA) Art, 1966, (MA) Art, 1970 N IL Univ; *cr:* Art Teacher Barstow Sch, Sewanhaka HS; Art Chairperson/Dist Art Coord Floral Park Memorial HS 1990; *ai:* Club Adv; Natl Art Honor Society; Advanced Placement Art His Teacher; Dist Lincoln Center Inst Coord; Technology Chairperson; NAEA, NYSATA, LIATA; RI Sch of Design Honors Seminary Summer 1983; *office:* Floral Park Memorial HS 210 Locust St Floral Park NY 11001

CARLSON, RANDOLPH JAY, Social Studies Teacher; *b:* Queens, NY; *m:* Ann Stephens; *c:* Katharine, Jay; *ed:* (BA) His, Clemson Univ 1975; (MED) Scndry Ed, SC Univ 1981; Grad Stud Admin; *cr:* 5th-9th Grade Teacher Columbia Christn Sch 1977-80; Soc Stud Teacher Dillon HS 1980-; *ai:* 1st Baptist Church Deacon 1987-; Clemson & Furman Dist Evaluation Teams of Ed Prgms 1985; Advanced Placement Government Teacher 1986-87; *home:* 107 Ellen Ln Dillon SC 29536

CARLSTROM, CLAUDIA JEAN, 2nd Grade Teacher; *b:* Spearfish, SD; *m:* Larry L.; *c:* Trixie L., Brady W.; *ed:* (BA) Elem Ed, Univ of Northern CO 1969; *cr:* 2nd Grade Teacher 1969-73, 3rd Grade Teacher 1973-75, 5th Grade Teacher 1984-85, 6th Grade Teacher 1985-86, 1st Grade Teacher 1986-87, 2nd Grade Teacher 1987- North Park Sch Dist; *ai:* Curr Comm 1987-89; Girl Scouts Asst Leader 1983-84; Cub Scouts Asst Leader 1986-87; Grant Western St Coll 1989; *home:* 83 Coyote Dr Walden CO 80480

CARLTON, BETTY BLAIR, Teacher; *b:* Lamesa, TX; *m:* Rogers; *c:* Craig; Tracy Kutas; *ed:* (BS) Elem Ed Kndgtn, 1973, (ME) Chldhd Ed, 1983 TX Womans Univ 1983; *cr:* Kndgtn Teacher Stonewall Jackson Denton ISD 1973-79; 1st Grade Teacher Stonewall-Sam Houston Denton ISD 1979-; 6th Grade Teacher 1985, 1st Grade Teacher 1986 Evers Park Denton ISD; *ai:* Teachers Communication Comm; Denton Classroom Teachers 1973-87; NEA 1973-87; *office:* San Houston Elem Sch 3300 Teasly Ln Denton TX 76205

CARLTON, LANA CARTWRIGHT, Math Dept Chair/Teacher; *b:* Shelbyville, TN; *m:* Stephen Douglas; *c:* Stephanie J., Jeremy L.; *ed:* (AA) Math, Martin Meth 1970; (BS) Math, Mid TN St Univ 1972; (MED) Supervision & Admin, TSU 1984; *cr:* Math Teacher Cmnty Sch 1978-; *ai:* Spon of Natl Honor Society; Chairperson of Academic Banquet; Dir of Graduation Exercises; NCTM; *office:* Community H S 3470 Hwy 41A N Unionville TN 37180

CARLYON, MARY ANN, First Grade Teacher; *b:* Sikeston, MO; *m:* Gerald; *c:* James, Ronald, David; *ed:* (BA) Soc Stud, Univ of MO St Louis 1967; (MA) Elem Ed, SE MO St Univ 1987; *cr:* Teacher West Cty R IV Elem; *home:* 105 3rd St Flat River MO 63601

CARMACK, DEBBIE EVERHART, Sixth Grade Teacher; *b:* Wilmington, NC; *m:* James Richard; *c:* Jennifer A., Jon M.; *ed:* (BA) Intermediate Ed, Lenoir-Rhyne Coll 1974; Currently Working on Masters Degree in Mid Sch Ed, Lenoir-Rhyne Coll; *cr:* 4th-6th Grade Teacher Rhodhiss Elem Sch 1974-77; 6th Grade Teacher Startown Elem Sch 1978-79, Blackburn Mid Sch 1980-; *ai:* Purchasing Comm; Asst Team SWARM; NCAE 1974-; NCCTM 1990; Served on S Assn Visiting Team for East Jr HS.

CARMACK, STEPHEN S., Math Teacher; *b:* Halls, TN; *m:* Ann Fisher; *c:* Jennifer, Fisher, Bethany; *ed:* (BS) Sec Ed, Univ of TN Martin 1970; *cr:* Math Teacher Ripley Jr HS 1970-87, Lauderdale Mid Sch 1987-; *ai:* NEA; TEA; *office:* Lauderdale Mid Sch 230 Griggs Ave Ripley TN 38063

CARMAN, LINA T., Science Teacher; *b:* Brooklyn, NY; *m:* Gregory Wright Jr.; *ed:* (AS) Liberal Arts, SUNY Farmingdale 1982; (BSE) G Bio/Ed, AZ Univ 1985; (MA) Elem Ed, Hofstra Univ 1989; *cr:* Teacher Walt Whitman HS 1985-; *ai:* Adv Awd Winning Sci Project Lilco Energy Contest 1989; NABT 1988-; NY Sci Teachers Assn 1985-; *office:* Walt Whitman H S West Hills Ct Huntington Stn NY 11746

CARMEL, CAROL FEELEY, Third Grade Teacher; *b:* Johnstown, PA; *m:* Edward Guy; *c:* Rebekah L.; *ed:* (BSE) Elem, Shippensburg Univ 1975; (MED) Elem, MSDE/Shippensburg 1980; Grad Study W MD Coll, MSDE; *cr:* 3rd Grade Teacher Fountaindale Elem 1975-; *ai:* Cmptr Comm; Sch Improvement Team; Fountaindale Flower & Gift Fund Treas; NEA, MSTA, WCTA Mem 1975-; Zion Evangelical Luth Church; Halfway Fire Auxiliary; *office:* Fountaindale Elem Sch 901 Northern Ave Hagerstown MD 21740

CARMICHAEL, ARGIE ADONDAKIS, English Teacher; *b:* Bingham Canyon, UT; *m:* Mike; *c:* Georgette Kaloudis, Michael Macris, Greg Macris; *ed:* (BS) Elem Ed, 1956, Scndry Certificate Eng, 1966, (MED) Linguistics Composition 1976 Univ of UT; *cr:* Lang Art Teacher/Debate Coach Hillcrest HS 1966-69, Brighton HS 1970-76; Teaching Asst Univ of UT 1977; Lang Arts Teacher Bingham HS 1978-; *ai:* Jr Prom Adv; Soph Team Leader; St Accreditation Team; NEA, UEA, TEA; Teacher of Yr UT in Eng & Lang Arts by UCTE/UWP 1990; Published Text.

CARMICHAEL, KELLY DANIEL, Science Department Chairman; *b:* Dearborn, MI; *m:* Kristi Carole Bloom; *c:* Stacey; *ed:* (BS) Bio, 1984, Teaching Certificate Ed, 1985 Grand Valley St Coll; (MS) Bio, Univ of TX Pan Amer 1989; *cr:* Intro Bio/Bio I & II Teacher 1985-86, Bio I & II/Honors Bio Teacher 1986-88, Physics/Physics Honors/Bio I Teacher 1988-89, Chem I/Bio I Teacher 1989- Raymondville HS; *ai:* Sci CLub Spon; Academic UIL Sci Coach; Campus Action Plan Correlate Leader; Phi Kappa Phi 1985-; Rio Grande Valley Sci Assn 1989-; Univ of TX Outstanding HS Teacher Awd; Nom Tandy Outstanding Sci Teacher Awd & TX Medical Assn Outstanding Sci Teacher Awd; United Blood Service Outstanding Blood Donor Recruitment Awd; *office:* Raymondville HS 1 Bearkat Blvd Raymondville TX 78580

CARMICHAEL, MARILYN ZUPPAN, 8th Grade Teacher; *b:* Oakland, CA; *c:* Celia Carmichael Harshman, Benjamin, Matthew; *ed:* (BA) Elem Ed, Holy Names Coll 1952; Teacher Trng, Holy Names Coll; *cr:* 2nd Grade Teacher Mills Sch 1953-55; 5th Grade Teacher 1955-56, 4th Grade Teacher 1956-60 Carquinez Sch; 3rd/6th-8th Grade Teacher St Basils Sch 1971-; *ai:* Stu Cncl & 8th Grade Fund Raisers Moderator St Basils Sch; NCTE Mem; Teacher of Yr Elks Club 1985; *office:* St Basils Sch 1230 Nebraska St Vallejo CA 94590

CARMON, DONNA MC ARTHUR, Fourth Grade Teacher; *b:* Blakely, GA; *m:* David W.; *c:* Katherine A.; *ed:* (BS) Elem Ed, Auburn Univ 1973; *cr:* Classroom Teacher Early Cty Elem Sch 1974-; *ai:* 4th Grade Team Leader; ECAE, GAE, NEA; PTA; *office:* Early Cty Elem Sch 649 Howell Ave Blakely GA 31723

CARMONY, JAMES WALTER, JR., Teacher/Sr Class Advisor; *b:* Royal Oak, MI; *m:* Mary Elizabeth; *c:* Heather J., Ashlee L.; *ed:* (BA) Ed, Bob Jones Univ 1969; (MA) Scndry Ed, Univ of Toledo; Doctoral Candidate at Univ of Toledo; *cr:* Teacher 1971-89, Prin 1972-73, Teacher/Adv 1973-84, Teacher/Sr Class Adv 1984-89 Emmanuel Baptist Chrstn Schls; *ai:* Boys Jr Var Soccer & Bsktbl; Girls Var Bsktbl & Sftbl; NCTE 1980-89; *home:* 5905 Rambo Ln Toledo OH 43623

CARNAGEY, RUSSELL DEAN, Instructor-Vice President; *b:* Hammond, IN; *m:* Joanne Lucile Kuhn; *c:* Cheryl L. Lowen, Michael T., Richard D.; *ed:* (BRE) Religious Ed, NY Univ 1955; Bible Biblical Stud/Theology, Baptist Bible Seminary 1957; (MRE) Ed, Columbia 1962; Spec Ed, Seminar Trng; *cr:* Teacher Noble Sch for Retarded 1958-62; Dir SE Branch of Noble Sch 1959-62; Teacher/Instr 1964-69, VP 1966-69, Regular Baptist Acad; Teacher/Prin 1970-78, Admin 1978-85, Instr/Pastor 1985- Faith Chrstn Acad; *ai:* Sftbl Coach 1980-84; Bsktbl Coach 1978-80; Future Teacher of America Adv 1974-80; Chm Ed Comm; Dir Teen Age Youth Family Camp 1964-87; Family Camp Week 1988-; Natl Society His Teachers 1975-; ASCD; N Athletic League Pres 1958-62; NHS Adv 1970-, 15 Yr Awd 1985; MO Assn of Chrstn Schls Athletic Assn Pres 1976-82; St Louis Chrstn Sch Society VP 1972-; YMCA Asst 1953-57; Amer Cncl of Chrstn Churches St Louis (Pres 1965-, Exec Comm); Camp Manitoumi GARBC Churches Exec Bd 1964-; Magazine Articles Published; Research Historical Publications; *office:* Faith Chrstn Schls 2300 Parker Rd Florissant MO 63033

CARNAHAN, TERRY L., Second Grade Teacher; *b:* Chicago Heights, IL; *m:* Ramona Marie; *c:* Tamara, Zachary; *ed:* (BS) Ed, 1974, (MS) Ed, 1979 IN Univ NW; *cr:* 4th Grade Teacher Peifer Elem Sch 1975-77; 2nd Grade Teacher Crisman Elem Sch 1977-; *ai:* Established Media Club; Intnl Rdng Assn 1977-88, Outstanding Educator 1980; Knights of Columbus 1990; Outstanding Young Men of America 1970.

CARNELL, MICHAEL ORDRAINE, English Teacher; *b:* Humboldt, TN; *m:* Mary Dianne Johnson; *c:* Sarah, Gabriel, Peter; *ed:* (BSED) Eng, Univ of ID 1988; *cr:* Jr/Sr Eng/Learning Disabilities At Risk Sr Eng Teacher Moscow HS 1988-; *ai:* Jr Adv; Arts Comm Mem; Phi Kappa Phi, NCTE 1988-; Inland NW Cncl Teachers of Eng 1988; Alumni Awd for Excl Univ of ID 1987; Moscow HS Stu Cncl Teacher of Yr 1989; *office:* Moscow HS 401 E Third Moscow ID 83843

CARNES, DARIS TAYLOR, Kindergarten Teacher; *b:* Hendersonville, NC; *m:* David Andrew; *c:* Jason, Adam; *ed:* (BA) Art/Elem Ed, Univ of NC Asheville 1975; *cr:* 1st-3rd Grade Teacher Nebo Elem 1975-77; K-2nd Grade Teacher Etowah Elem 1977-; *home:* 1610 N Main St Hendersonville NC 28792

CARNES, LOIS H ASHER, Social Studies Teacher; *b:* Pineville, KY; *m:* Carl; *c:* Helena, Elizabeth Gilley; *ed:* (BS) Elem Ed, Cumberland Col L 1972; (MA) Elem Ed Rdng, Union Coll 1977; Grad Childrens Literature; *cr:* 1st/3rd Grade Teacher Arjay Elem 1972-83; 5th/6th Grade Teacher Harmony Elem 1984-89; 8th Grade Amer His Teacher Bell Cty Mid Sch 1989-; *ai:* 4-H Leader Bel City Mid Sch; Chldr Comm; Mem Bell Cty Ed Assn; KEA 1972-; Pineville 4-H Cncl 1989-; *office:* Bell County Mid Sch Log Mt Pineville Pineville KY 40977

CARNES, MARCIA LYNN, Second Grade Teacher; *b:* Lawrenceville, GA; *m:* Derrell R.; *c:* Rod; *ed:* (BS) Elem Ed, W GA Coll 1965; *cr:* Teacher Fulton Cty 1965-66, Washington Cty 1966, Rockdale Cty 1967-73, Newton Cty 1974-; *ai:* Prof Assn of GA Educators 1986-; Alpha Delta Kappa 1990; *office:* Ficquett Elem Sch 2207 Williams St Covington GA 30209

CARNEVALE, DIANE D., Eighth Grade Math Teacher; *b:* Staten Island, NY; *m:* Anthony; *c:* Lynn, Jill, Susan; *ed:* (BS) Elem Ed, Wagner Coll 1967; (MS) Ed, Richmond Coll 1970; Supervision, Georgian Court Coll; NJ St Ed Dept Algebra Project 1990; SMURF Sci Prgm, Brookdale Comm Coll 1985; *cr:* 3rd Grade Teacher St Adalbert 1964-67, PS 26 1967-69; Teacher of Ungraded Emotionally Disturbed PS 126 1969-70; 7th Grade Sci/6th-8th Grade Math Teacher St Ambrose 1984-88; 7th/8th Grade Math Teacher St Benedict 1988-; *ai:* Stu Cncl Adv; Career Day Comm; NCEA 1984-; NJSTA 1985-89; Piloted Math Book for Ginn 1966; *office:* St Benedict Sch 165 Bethany Rd Holmdel NJ 07733

CARNEY, MAUREEN, Fourth Grade Teacher; *b:* Troy, NY; *ed:* (AA) Liberal Art, Hudson Valley Comm Coll 1974; (BS) Elem Ed, 1976, (MS) Rdng Specialist, 1980 Coll of St Rose; *cr:* Elem Teacher Stillwater Cntrl Sch 1977-; *ai:* NY St United Teachers, Stillwater Teachers Assn Mem 1977-; Stillwater Historical Society Charter Mem 1971-; Stillwater Bicentennial Comm Mem 1987-; Stillwater Cmmty Schlsp Comm Mem 1987-; St Petes Church Life Mem; Wrote 4th Grade Local His Curr 1986-; Local Bicentennial Celebration Sch Wide Coordinated Flag Contest 1988; *office:* Stillwater Cntrl Sch N Hudson Ave Stillwater NY 12170

CARNEY, PATRICIA LEEDS, Soc Stud/Enrichment Teacher; *b:* Long Branch, NJ; *m:* George Herbert III; *c:* Christine, Erin; *ed:* (BA) His, Douglass Coll 1965; Rutgers Grad Sch of Ed; *cr:* Soc Stud Teacher N Brunswick HS 1980-81; Soc Stud Teacher 1965-, Teacher of Gifted & Talented/Enrichment Prgm 1983- South River HS; *ai:* Law Society Adv; Mock Trial Competition & Future Problem Solving Prgm Coach; NEA 1965-; NJ Ed Assn, S River Ed Assn; NJ St Bar Fnd Mock Trial Subcommittee Mem 1984-, Mock Trial Medal of Honor 1986; Nom Teacher of Yr 1986-87; *office:* South River HS Montgomery St South River NJ 08882

CARNEY, RODGER DALE, Supervisor Humanities Dept; *b:* Springfield, OH; *m:* Lynda Bari Pogach; *c:* Stacey, Gregory, Jodi, Jason; *ed:* (BAE) Soc Stud, Univ of MD 1967; (ME) His/Poly Sci, Trenton St Coll 1973; (MA) Sch Admin/Supervision, Glassboro St Coll 1975; Taft Inst of Government Summer Seminar Trenton St Coll 1972; *cr:* US His Teacher 1967-88, Hum Supvr 1989- Lenape HS; *ai:* Co-Adv Stu Cncl; Boys Tennis Head Coach; Natl Assn Scndry Sch Prins, ASCD, NCSS, Natl Assn Sch Activity Adv; St & Field Coord Presidential Classroom Young Amer St of NJ; *office:* Lenape HS Church & Hartford Rds Medford NJ 08055

CARO, FRANK, Mathematics/Business Teacher; *b:* Kalamazoo, MI; *m:* Nancy Kathleen Crookston; *c:* Anna; *ed:* (BBA) Bus Admin, 1953; (MA) Bus Ed, 1965 W MI Univ; *cr:* Naval Officer US Navy 1956-59; Self-Employed Retail Grocery 1959-62; Math Teacher Dowagiac Jr HS 1962-64; Math Bus Teacher Hackett Cath Cntrl 1964-; *ai:* Bus Dept Chm; NHS Faculty Cncl; *office:* Hackett Cath Cntrl Sch 1000 W Kilgore Rd Kalamazoo MI 49008

CAROLINE, PHYLLIS ELAINE, 2nd Grade Teacher; *b:* Grand Forks, ND; *m:* David James; *ed:* (BS) Elem Ed, Mayville St Coll 1973; Continuing Ed; Rdng Credential 1980; *cr:* 2nd Grade Teacher Bottineau Public Schls 1973-; *ai:* Bottineau Ed Assn Secy 1975-76; Bottineau Jaycees Outstanding Young Educator 1980; *home:* 606 Vera St Bottineau ND 58318

CARON, STEVEN EDWARD, Mathematics Teacher; *b:* Brookings, SD; *m:* Katheen A. Skovlund; *c:* Erin, Abby, Amanda, Christopher, Jonathan; *ed:* (BS) Math/Industrial Art, 1986, (BS) Industrial Arts, Northern St Univ; Grad Stud KS St Univ; *cr:* Grad Asst KS St Univ 1981-82; Math Edgemont Public Schls 1982-83, Aberdeen Cntrl 1983-; *ai:* Tech Dir; NCTM 1984-; Property Comm Chm 1990; Outstanding Young Men of America Awd; *home:* 907 S 16th St Aberdeen SD 57401

CARPENTER, BARBARA Y., English Teacher; *b:* Greenfield, MA; *m:* Cullen S.; *c:* Sara, Michael; *ed:* (BA) Eng, Clark Univ 1965; *cr:* Teacher Lakewood Jr HS 1966-68, Kennett HS 1968-69, SAD 72 1974-; *ai:* NCTE 1980-; Brownfield Public Lib Pres 1980-; Brownfield Budget Comm 1988-; *office:* Molly Ockett Mid Sch Bridgton Rd Fryeburg ME 04037

CARPENTER, ELIZABETH MEGGS, English Teacher; *b:* Lincolnton, NC; *m:* Sidney Richardson; *c:* Margaret Shelton, Susan E.; *ed:* (BA) Fr, Radford Univ 1966; (MA) Eng, VA Tech 1971; *cr:* Title I Teacher Ironto Elem Sch 1966-67; Eng/Drama Teacher Floyd Cty HS 1967-69; Eng Instr VA Tech 1969-71; Eng/Fr Teacher Blacksburg HS 1971-76; Eng Teacher Wallace O Neal Day Sch 1979-80; Eng/Fr Teacher Bishop Mc Guinness HS 1980-85; Eng Teacher Robert B Glenn HS 1985-; *ai:* Sr Class & Graduation Adv; Sch Liaison AT7T Adopt-A-Sch Bus Partnership; Sch Improvement, Cty Grading Policy, Cty Calender Comm; Cty Curr Comm Co-Chm; NC Eng Teachers Assn 1985-; Forsyth Assn Teachers of Eng (Treas 1986-88, Pres 1988-); NC Assn of Educators Sch Rep 1985-, Terry Sanford Awd 1987-88, 1988-89; Delta Kappa Gamma 1988-; Peace Haven Civic Assn (Treas 1981-83, Pres 1983-84); Attend NC Center for Advancement of Teaching 1989; Presenter at Local & St Conferences for Eng Teachers Assn; *office:* Robert B Glenn HS 1600 Union Cross Rd Kernersville OH 27284

CARPENTER, MILDRED CLARK, 1st Grade Teacher; *b:* Cope, SC; *m:* William Brunson; *c:* Cameron C. DeLoach, Graham C., Nancy C. Satcher, William B. Jr.; *ed:* (BA) Elem Ed, Limestone Coll 1945; Grad Work at Augusta Coll, Columbia Coll; *cr:* 4th Grade Teacher Summerville Elem 1945-46; 1st-3rd Grade Teacher Curtis Baptist Sch 1969-; *ai:* Daughters of Amer Revolution; Master Teacher of Yr 1989-89; Data Collector Cntrl Savannah River Area Regional Assessment Center 1980-85; *home:* 802 Hickman Rd Augusta GA 30904

CARPENTER, NANCY ROBBINS, Supervisor; *b:* Portland, OR; *m:* Warren; *ed:* (BS) Elem Ed, Portland St Univ 1975; (MAT) Elem Ed, Lewis & Clark Coll 1978; Admin Cert Prgm; *cr:* 6th Grade Teacher 1978-89, Supvr 1989- Gordon Russell Mid Sch; *ai:* Track/Vllybl Coach; Stu Cncl, Newspaper Adv; Lang Art Dept Chairperson; 6th Grade Advocate; Dist Lang Art Comm; COSA; Gresham Grade Teachers Assn Pres; *office:* Gordon Russell Mid Sch 3625 E Powell Blvd Gresham OR 97080

CARPENTER, PATRICIA CARVER, Jr High Math & Science Teacher; *b:* Maryville, TN; *m:* George Herbert; *c:* Anne, Aimee; *ed:* (BS) Elem Ed, Univ of TN 1974; Elem Ed; *cr:* Teacher Mc Donald Elem 1974-; *ai:* Math Counts Coach; Sci Club Spon; Jr Beta Club Co-Spon; NEA; TN Ed Assn; Greene Cty Ed Assn; Sci Assn of TN; United Meth Church; TN Valley Authority Grant to Write Energy Source Book; Sci Club 2nd Place ST Awd for Natl Energy Ed Dev Project 1988-89; *office:* Mc Donald Elem Sch R R 2 Mohawk TN 37810

CARPENTER, SANDRA KAY (PETTY), Language Art/Reading Teacher; *b:* Amory, MS; *m:* E. C.; *c:* Eric, Matthew, Emily; *ed:* (BS) Elem Ed, 1970, (MS) Elem Ed, 1976 MS St Univ; *cr:* 2nd/3rd Grade Teacher Kilmichael Elem Sch 1970-71; 5th/6th Grade Teacher Hatley Elem Sch 1971-73; 7th Grade Teacher 1973-83, 6th Grade Teacher 1983- Amory Mid Sch; *ai:* Stu Cncl Spon Amory Mid Sch; MS Prof Educators 1989-; Amory Primitive Baptist Church Treas 1980-; Cystic Fibrosis Fnd Fund Raiser 1989-; *home:* Rt 2 Box 334C Amory MS 38821

CARPENTER, VERNA VASSLER, 8th Grade Science Teacher; *b:* Eureka, SD; *m:* Rod; *ed:* (BA) Phys Ed, ND St Univ 1965; *cr:* 7th-12th Grade Phys Ed Instr Steele Public Schls 1965-66, Wolf Point Public Schls 1966-69; 8th Grade Sci Teacher Glendive Public Schls 1972-; *ai:* Girls Bsktbl Coach; Odessey of Mind Coach; St Problem Captain; Natl Jr Honor Society Selection Comm; MT Ed Assn, NEA, Glendive Ed Assn, GEA Schlsp Comm Chairperson 1986-; NSTA; Zion Luth Church Women Pres 1976-77; Zion Church (Cncl, Deacon); Expanding Your Horizons Presentor; Washington Sch Admired Teacher 1983; Nom Presidential Awd Excl Sci Math Teaching 1987-89; Teacher of Yr Washington Sch 1989; Washington Sch Candidate MT Teacher of Yr 1989; Runner Up MT Teacher of Yr 1990; *office:* Washington Sch 505 N Meade Ave Glendive MT 59330

CARPENTER, WILLIAM HENRY, Piano Instructor; *b:* Missoula, MT; *ed:* (BM) Piano Performance, Eastman Sch of Music 1979; (MM) Piano Performance/Lit, Univ of Notre Dame 1981; Trained in Teaching the Suzuki Piano Sch by SAA Certified Teacher Trainers; *cr:* Piano Instr Univ of Notre Dame 1979-81; Staff Accompanist/Piano Instr Univ of New Orleans 1981-83; Ind Suzuki Piano Teacher/Performer 1983-; Piano Instr Univ of NE Lincoln 1989-; *ai:* Chamber Music Coaching; Math & Sci Mentoring; Concert Appearances; Summer Music Camp Instruction; Bright Lights Summer Enrichment Courses; Lincoln Music Teachers VP 1987-; NE Music Teachers IMTF Forum Chm 1987-89; Music Teachers Natl Assn 1984-; *office:* Univ of NE Lincoln UN-L Sch of Music 239 Westbrook & Independent Lincoln NE 68588

CARPER, ANNE WEBB, Retired; *b:* Utica, NY; *m:* Robert F.; *c:* Joyce Burgener, Nancy, Robert M.; *ed:* (BA) Eng, Miami Univ 1945; (MA) Elem Sch Teacher Western MI Univ 1966; *cr:* 5th Grade Teacher Vicksburg Cmmty Sch 1962-85; *home:* 8302 Greensfield Shores Scotts MI 49088

CARPINO, CLYDE PHILLIPS, Student Activities Director; *b:* Butte, MT; *m:* Robin Sue Schrader; *c:* Cody, Todd; *ed:* (BA) Scndry Ed/Ger/Phys Ed/Math, 1968, (MA) Scndry Ed/Phys Ed/Scndry Admin, 1970 MT St Univ; *cr:* Grad Asst Intra Dir Western MT Coll 1968-69; Grad Asst Phy Ed MT St Univ 1969-70; Teacher/Coach 1970-89, Stu Act Dir 1979-89 Fairfield HS; *ai:* Head Track Coach 1971-86; Head Cross Cntry Coach 1971-82; Pep Squad Adv 1980-85; Stu Act Dir 1977-; CADA; Teacher of Yr Fairfield HS 1988-89; *office:* Fairfield H S 205 E Atlantic Ave Fairfield CA 94533

CARR, ELIZABETH MALMO, Spanish/English Teacher; *b:* Memphis, TN; *m:* Victor Jr.; *ed:* (BA) Eng, Univ of MS 1976; Cert in Span & Eng, Memphis St Univ; *cr:* Teacher Horn Lake HS 1982-85; Teacher 1985-, Dept Chairperson/Eng Teacher 1989- Hamilton Jr HS; *ai:* Honor Society & Span Club Spon; NCTE, AFLSP, NEA; Le Bonheur Club; Tri Delta Alumni; Teacher of Yr 1988, Runner Up 1987; Summer Span Inst Memphis St Univ, Wkshps to TN Eng Teachers.

CARR, JANE WINCHESTER, English Teacher; *b:* Breckenridge, KY; *m:* Scott B.; *c:* Beth C. Oliver, Ronald S.; *ed:* (AB) Eng, Western KY Univ 1956; (MA) Ed Curr/Inst VA Polytechnic Inst & ST Univ 1976; Post Masters Studies Recertification & Professional Enrichment Courses at Radford Univ, Univ of VA, & Univ of KY; *cr:* English Teacher Lafayette HS 1962-67; English Teacher Blacksburg HS 1967-; *ai:* Adv to NHS; Spon Forensics, Future Teachers of Amer & Jr Class; Delta Kappa Gamma Pres, VP, 1973-; Phi Kappa Phi 1975; NCTE 1965-; VATE Service Awd 1983; MCEA; VEA; NEA; VCEE 1987-; VA Extension Homemakers Club Pres, VP, Sec, Treas, 1980-; Blacksburg Intermediate Woman's Club Chms 1969-79; Longshop-McCoy Ruritan Club 1990; Blacksburg Chrstn Church Elder/Chm of Bd; Consultant CEE/NCTE Commission on Supervision & Curr Dev 1982-85 & 1985-88; Chm BHS Evaluation (Southern Assn of Scndry Sch),1979-81, Chm Eng Dept 1970-82; Mem ST Evaluation Teams (Southern Assn of Scndry Sch) 1971-80; State Judge NCTE 4 Lit Mag Awds 1986-89, Writing Awds 1974,75,76,77; Who's Who in Amer Coll & Univ 1956; *office:* Blacksburg H S Patrick Henry Dr Blacksburg VA 24060

CARR, KAREN LANG, Kindergarten Teacher; *b:* Ashland, OH; *m:* Richard L.; *c:* Joseph, Howard; *ed:* (BS) Ed, Bowling Green St Univ 1965; *cr:* Kndgtn Teacher Sandusky Public Schls 1965-70, Port Clinton City Schls 1971-; *ai:* Consulting Teacher for Intern/Intervention Prgm; *office:* Bataan Elem Sch W 6th St Port Clinton OH 43452

CARR, KATHERINE N., Fourth Grade Teacher; *b:* Braddock, PA; *m:* Michael V.; *ed:* (BS) Elem Ed, Geneva Coll 1970; (MED) Elem Ed, Univ of Pittsburgh 1974; Intermediate Unit Univ of Pittsburgh; *cr:* Teacher Huntington Sch Dist 1970-73, Hampton Twp Sch Dist 1973-; *ai:* Planned Course Comm; Teacher Induction Prgm; Grade Level Chairperson; Hampton Twp Ed Assn 1973-; *office:* Hampton Twp Sch Dist 4482 Mount Royal Blvd Allison Park PA 15101

CARR, LORRAINE GRANDYS, Third Grade Teacher; *b:* Chicago, IL; *m:* Mel; *c:* Anne, John, Kristen; *ed:* (BSE) Ed, Loyola Univ 1957; *cr:* 2nd/3rd Grade Teacher St Mary Star of Sea 1957-59; 3rd Grade Teacher Tobin Dist 111 1959-63, Visitation 1975-.

CARR, MARCELLINE CARTHAN, Algebra II/Geometry Teacher; *b:* Grady, AR; *m:* David; *c:* David, Michelle D., Ojinga K.; *ed:* (BA) Math, UAPB A M & N Pine Bluff 1968; Math, Univ AR at Fayettville, Univ AR Little Rock; *cr:* Math Teacher Dial Jr HS 1968-69, Sindey Lanier HS 1969-70, Southwest Jr HS 1970-78, Parkview Magnet HS 1978-; *ai:* Sr Class, Beta Club Spon; Track Coach; Henderson Jr HS PTA Co-Pres; St John Baptist Church Family Social Comm Co-Chairperson; Twin Lakes Homeowners Assn Comm Co-Chairperson; Classroom Teachers Assn, Educl Assn, NEA, Building Coordinating Comm Chm; St John Baptist Church Family Soc Comm Chairperson 1986-; Stephens Awd Recipient 1990; Outstanding HS Teacher; Presenter of Speaker at Regional Math Convention; *office:* Parkview Arts/Sci Magnet Sch 2501 John Barrow Rd Little Rock AR 72205

CARR, SANISH LA RAY, Mathematics Teacher; *b:* Joliet, IL; *m:* Karla Jean Anderson; *ed:* (AS) Physics, Olney Cntrl Coll 1983; (BS) Math, Univ of IL 1985; IL St Univ; *cr:* Math Teacher Delavan HS 1985-; *ai:* Bsktbl Asst Coach; Bsbl, Chess, JETS Coach; Post Prom & Class Spon; Optimpt 1986-; Delavan Meth Youth Leader 1987-; W IL Univ Outstanding Teacher Awd; *office:* Delavan HS 907 Locust Delevan IL 61734

CARR, THOMAS BRYAN, Industrial Technology Teacher; *b:* Corpus Christi, TX; *m:* Kristi La Nell Dosher; *c:* Kendra L., Jerrod W.; *ed:* (BA) Industrial Arts, Panhandle St Univ 1981; *cr:* Industrial Arts Teacher Friona HS 1981-; *ai:* Industrial Technology Club & Sr Class Spon; Panhandle Industrial Arts Assn 1981-; *home:* HCR 1 Box 54 Friona TX 79035

CARRATO, RAYMOND JOSEPH, 8th Grade Science Teacher; *b:* Elizabeth, NJ; *m:* Janet Mitrione; *c:* Daniel, Stephanie; *ed:* (BA) Bio, Glassboro St 1971; (MS) Aquatic Bio, Edinboro St Univ 1973; Working Towards Masters Supervision/Admin, Kean Coll; *cr:* 7th/8th Grade Sci Teacher Oak Knoll Jr HS 1971, Joyce Kilmer Sch 1974-; *ai:* Sci Curr Comm Head Milltown Public Schls 1990; NJ Sci Teachers Assn 1989- NJBISEC Intern Awd 1989; NJEA Mem 1974-; Milltown Ed Assn (Faculty Rep 1977-78, Negotiator 1989-); Received Internship Summer Grant NJ Bus & Industrial Consortium; *home:* 187 Burlington Ave Spotswood NJ 08884

CARRAWAY, LAURA D., 1st & 2nd Grade Teacher; *b:* Ville Platte, LA; *m:* Carl R.; *c:* Cynthia Odom, Gary, Cody, Chuncey; *ed:* (BA) Ed, Mc Neese St 1982; *cr:* 5th Grade Teacher Bayou Chicot HS 1983-85; 1st/2nd Grade Teacher Oakdale Elem 1986-; *ai:* Amer Legion Auxiliary (VP 1989, Pres 1990); *home:* PO Box 413 Pine Prairie LA 70576

CARRAWAY, LINDA SHELL, Business Education Teacher; *b:* Bude, MS; *m:* Michael Allen Sr.; *c:* Michael Allen Jr., Milinda Allene; *ed:* (BSED) Bus Ed, MS Coll 1972; *cr:* Bus Ed Teacher Franklin Chrstn Acad 1973-75, Franklin Cty HS 1986-; *ai:* Assist Spon of Sch Newspaper; Prom Spon; Staff Dev; STAR Teacher 1989-; *home:* Rt 1 Box 209B Roxie MS 39661

CARREKER, VICKI LYNN, 10th-12th Grade Bio Teacher; *b:* Macon, GA; *c:* (BS) Environmental Sci, 1981, (MS) Fnds Of Ed, 1982 Troy St Univ; (bs) General Sci Ed, 1985, (MED) General Sci Ed, 1986 Auburn Univ; *cr:* Teacher/Coach Northside Jr HS 1985-86, Northside HS 1986-; *ai:* Sftbl Coach, Girls Bsktbl Asst Coach; Girls Track Spon Fellowship of Chrstn Athletes; Prof Assn Of GA Educators 1985-; GA Sci Teachers Assn 1989-; *office:* Northside HS 926 Green St Warner Robins GA 31093

CARRELL, DONNA M. (NELSON), Retired; *b:* Sargent, NE; *m:* Lloyd Harold; *c:* John, Cynthia Stovall, Kim Juliana; *ed:* (BA) Elem Ed, NE St 1965; *cr:* 1st Grade Teacher Sargent Public Schls 1957-59; 3rd Grade Teacher Ord Public Schls 1960-61; 3rd/6th Grade Teacher Alamogordo Public Schls 1966-70; 2nd Grade Teacher Istanbul Turkey 1970-71; Kndgtn Teacher Thoreau Elem 1971-74; 2nd Grade Teacher Valley View Elem 1974-89; *ai:* NEA; Alpha Delta Kappa 1973-87; Epsilon Sigma Alpha (Local 1967- St Pres 1990-91).

CARRICO, ANN ZULICK, 4th/5th Grade Teacher; *b:* Cardonbale, PA; *m:* Paul; *c:* Gregory; *ed:* (BA) Elem Ed, E MI Univ 1975; Human Reproduction Ed; *cr:* 6th Grade Teacher 1969-75, 5th Grade Teacher 1975-82, 4th/5th Grade Teacher Curr 1982- Lakeview Public Schls; *ai:* Amer Stu Cncl Assn Spon; Wayne St Univ Staff Dev Project Team; Mem of Writing Team for Math St Assessment; MI Cncl of Teachers of Math 1989-90 *office:* Ardmore Elem Sch 27001 Greater Mack Saint Clair Shores MI 48081

CARRIER, BARBARA AUSTIN, Fifth Grade Teacher; *b:* Greeley, CO; *ed:* (BA) Elem Ed/US His, 1969, (MA) Elem Rdng, 1979 Univ of N CO; *cr:* 4th-6th Grade Teacher Aurora Public Schls 1969-; *ai:* Quadrant Coord of Drug Free Schls Federal Grant; Stud At-Risk, Cmptr Instruction Comms; CARE Team; AEA, CEA, NEA 1969-76, 1988-; Phi Delta Kappa 1990; Chapter II Grant for Integrated Curr in Heterogeneous Classroom; *office:* Jewell Elem Sch 14601 E Jewell Ave Aurora CO 80012

CARRIER, CHARLOTTE WRIGHT, Teacher; *b:* Houston, TX; *c:* Louis A. Jr.; *ed:* (MS) Bio/Chem, 1968, (MED) Guidance/Counseling, 1973 TX Southern Univ; Univ of Houston, Rice Univ, Univ of St Thomas; *cr:* Teacher Yates Sr HS 1968, Houston Tech Inst 1969-79; Area 1 1970, Hamilton Mid Sch 1972-; *ai:* Booster Club Spon; Dept Chairperson 1987-88, 1989-; Courtesy & Faculty Advisory Comm; Cath Church Religious Instructions CCD Teacher; Natl Teacher of Yr; *office:* Hamilton Mid Sch 139 E 20th St Houston TX 77008

CARRIGAN, MICHELLE REED, Mathematics Teacher; *b:* Lexington, KY; *m:* Sean B.; *ed:* (BS) Ed, IN Univ 1986; *cr:* Math Teacher Nova HS 1986-; *office:* Nova HS 3600 College Ave Davie FL 33314

CARRIGER, BILLY JOE, 6th Grade Team Coordinator; *b:* Wardville, OK; *m:* Patsy Wyllene; *c:* Robin, Staci; *ed:* (BS) Elem Ed, 1962, (MS) Elem Ed, 1967 SE OK St Univ; *cr:* Teacher Hurst-Euless-Bedford Ind Sch Dist; *ai:* 6th Grade Team Coord; TX Classroom Teachers Assn, Assn of TX Prof Educators; *home:* 865 Russell Ln Bedford TX 76022

CARRILLO, RENE L., French Teacher; *b:* Corpus Christi, TX; *m:* Alicia A. Gonzalez; *c:* Rudy M., Michael A., John E.; *ed:* (BS) Fr/Sociology, TX A&I Univ 1977; *cr:* Spec Ed Teacher San Diego HS 1977-79, Freer HS 1980-81; Fr Teacher United HS 1981-; *ai:* Sr Class, Fr Club & Stu Taking Natl Fr Exam Spon; TX A&I Univ Fr Seminar Schlsp 1988; *office:* United HS 8800 Mc Pherson Laredo TX 78041

CARROL, VERMA L., 6th Grade Soc Stud Teacher; *b:* Sequin, TX; *m:* William L.; *c:* William J., Keith L.; *ed:* (BS) Elem Ed, Prairie View A&M Univ 1950; Grad Stud Elem Ed, Shippensburg Univ; *cr:* 4th Grade Teacher Ball Elem 1951-58; 4th/5th Grade Teacher Mooreland 1960-84; 6th Grade Teacher Lamberton Mid Sch 1985-; *ai:* Interacial Advisory His Comm; NEA, PSEA; ABWA Secy, Woman of Yr 1976, 1984; Shiloh Baptist Church Schlsp Chairperson; *office:* Lamberton Mid Sch 777 S Hanover St Carlisle Barracks PA 17013

CARROLL, AILEENE CAVINESS, Mathematics Teacher; *b:* Asheboro, NC; *m:* Jay Allen; *c:* Jay A. II; *ed:* (BS) Math, Univ of NC Greensboro 1974; *cr:* Math Teacher SE Guilford Jr HS 1974-75, Trinity HS 1975-76, Asheboro Jr HS 1976-87, Asheboro HS 1987-; *ai:* Jr Class Spon 1987-; Homecoming Comm 1989; Ed-Specs Comm 1990; NCAE 1974-; NCCTM; Beta Sigma Phi 1977-79; Asheboro Jr Womans Club 1986-87; Terry Sanford Nom Asheboro Jr HS 1982-83; Teacher of Yr 1989-; *office:* Asheboro HS 1221 S Park St Asheboro NC 27203

CARROLL, CARLA TAYLOR, Choral Director; *b:* Anniston, AL; *m:* Tony Lynn; *c:* Leah R., Leslie D.; *ed:* (BS) Music Ed, 1975, (MM) Music/Vocal Performance, 1986 Univ of TN; Kodaly Music Inst & Univ of TN Chattanooga 1981; TN Arts Acad 1989; *cr:* Elem Music Teacher Spring Creek Elem Sch 1978-81; Choral Dir Heritage HS 1984-86; Music Teacher Brainerd Baptist Sch 1986-87; Elem Music Teacher Lookout Mtn Sch 1987-89; Choral Dir Ridgeland HS 1989-; *ai:* Tri-Hi-Y Club Spon; Ridgeland Singers, Show Choir Dir; Music Educators Natl Conference, GA Music Educators Assn 1989-.

CARROLL, ELEANOR MOSLEY, Fifth Grade Elementary Teacher; *b:* Corsicana, TX; *w:* Ezra L. II (dec); *c:* Ezra L. III, Calvin M., Beverly V.; *ed:* (BA) Music Ed, Jarvis Chrstn Coll 1952; (MAED) Elem Ed, TX Southern Univ 1961; *cr:* Teacher Ballinger Elem 1952-54, Corsicana Ind Schls 1954-; *ai:* Career Ladder & Textbook Comm, UIL Spon; TSTA & NEA Mem 1952-; 6th Avenue Baptist Musician 1955-; Cancer Drive (Eastside Chm 1985-89, Worker 1970-84); *home:* 1012 E Collin St Corsicana TX 75110

CARROLL, ERRIN, Math Teacher; *b:* Manchester, KY; *m:* Sue E.; *c:* Beth Ann; *ed:* (BS) Math, Eastern Ky Univ 1963; (MAT) Math, Univ of the South 1972; Univ TN East TN St Union Coll TN Tech; *cr:* Math Teacher Boone Cty HS 1963-71, Morristown Jr HS 1971-83, Morristown West HS 1983-; *ai:* Students Staying Straight Spon; TN Ed Assn 1971-; East TN Ed Assn 1971-; Hamblen Cty Ed Assn 1971-; Danforth Fellowship; Natl Sci Fnd Awd; Career Level III; *home:* 5861 Timbercreek Ln Morristown TN 37814

CARROLL, FRANCES MARIE, French Teacher; *b:* Philadelphia, PA; *ed:* (BA) Fr/Scndry Ed, Beaver Coll 1964; (MA) Fr Lang/Fr Lit, Ecole Francaise 1976; *cr:* Fr Teacher Kennett Square Consolidated Sch 1965-68; Fr Teacher/Foreign Lang Coord Coucil Rock HS 1968-; *ai:* Fr Club La Bance Francaise; Mid St Comms; Foreign Lang Coord; PA St Ed Assn, NEA, AATF; *office:* Council Rock HS Swamp Rd Newtown PA 18940

CARROLL, GALE (LAPHAM), Mathematics/Computer Teacher; *b:* Plattsburgh, NY; *m:* James D.; *c:* Kelley; *ed:* (BS) Math Ed, 1971, (MS) Math Ed, 1983 SUNY Plattsburgh; Educl Counseling, Univ of ME Orono, Univ of VT; Cmptr Ed, SUNY Plattsburgh; *cr:* Math Teacher Bangor City Schls 1971-72, Orleans Cntrl Schls 1973-80, Mount Assumption Inst 1980-85; Math/Cmptr Teacher Plattsburgh Mid Sch 1986-; Dept of Math Lecturer SUNY Plattsburgh 1988-; *ai:* Sch Improvement Comm; Math League Adv; Faculty Liaison Family Sch Organization; Faculty Rep Dist Gifted And Talented Comm; Phi Delta Kappa Treas 1988-; Plattsburgh Teachers Assn; NY St United Teachers; N Cntry Tennis Assn Coord of Jr Tennis Prgm; Neighborhood Collector of Cancer, Heart, M S Societies; *home:* 57 Cogan Ave Plattsburgh NY 12901

CARROLL, GRETCHEN REIMANN, Assistant Principal; *b:* Bad Axe, MI; *m:* Michael; *c:* Aaron, Adam; *ed:* (BA) Ed, Saginaw Valley St Univ 1980; (MA) Admin, 1985, (EDS) Admin, 1988 Cntrl MI Univ; *cr:* Teacher Birch Run HS 1981-82, South Intermediate Sch 1983-; Asst Prin Lakeville Memorial HS 1990; *ai:* Journalism Adv; 9th Grade Spon; Academic Track Chairperson; Phi Delta Kappa Membership Research 1985-, Research Awd 1989; NEA, MI Educl Assn 1981-; Amer Assn of Univ Women Membership 1984-; Article Published; *office:* Lakeville Memorial HS 12455 Wilson Rd Otisville MI 48463

CARROLL, JANNUTH GATLIN, 3rd Grade Teacher; *b:* Chattanooga, TN; *m:* Stephen Preston; *c:* Lauren K., Sarah E.; *ed:* (BS) Elem Ed, Lee Coll 1975; (MED) Elem Admin, Univ of TN Chattanooga 1980; *cr:* 1st Grade Teacher 1975-80, 3rd Grade Teacher 1980- Stuart; *ai:* Media-Technology Comm; Alpha Delta Kappa; Amer Bus Womens Assn VP 1984-85; *home:* 785 Ashland Terr NE Cleveland TN 37311

CARROLL, JOY YVONNE, 5th Grade Teacher; *b:* Kansas City, KS; *ed:* (BS) Elem Ed, 1972; (MS) Elem Ed, 1973 Emporia St Univ; *cr:* 5th Grade Teacher John Fiske Elem Sch 1973-; *ai:* Effective Sch Team Mem; NEA; Concerned Citizens of Kansas City Incorporated Secy; *office:* John Fiske Elem Sch 625 S Valley Kansas City KS 66105

CARROLL, KENNETH L., Sci Dept Chair/Chem Teacher; *b:* Corona, CA; *m:* Mary Jo Simpson; *c:* Wendi, Thomas, Andrew; *ed:* (BS) Ag Chem, CA Poly 1961; Credential Sci Ed, Univ of CA Davis 1968; (MA) Ed Admin, Univ of San Francisco 1987; *cr:* Lecturer CA St Polytechnic Coll 1963-65; Research Fellow Univ of CA Davis 1965-68; Chem Teacher Ignacio Valley HS 1968-74, Northgate HS 1974-75; Athletic Dir CA HS 1978-83; Instr St Marys Coll 1984-87; Sci Dept Chm/Chem Teacher CA HS 1975-; Research Chemist Lawrence Livermore Natl Lab 1988-; *ai:* Tennis, Wrestling, Swimming, Little League Bsbl, Cmmty Youth Soccer Coach; Wizards, Sr Service, Rodeo Clubs Adv; Chairperson of San Ramon Valley Unified Sch Dist Mentor Staff Dev Comm 1983-85 & Curr Cncl 1987-89; Steering Comm Mem William & Flora Hewlett Fnd 1984-86; CA Teachers Assn, NEA, CA Sci Teachers Assn, CA Chem Assn; Natl Eagle Scout Assn; Westinghouse Fnd Excl in Sci Ed 1981; Outstanding Chem Teacher of Yr Chemical Industries Cncl of CA 1982; CA HS Parents & Stus Excl in Teaching 1986; Guidance & Encouragement in Sci Amer Chemical Assn 1986; Mentor Teacher San Ramon Valley Unified Sch Dist 1983-86; Sci Curr Consultant CA Dept of Ed 1987; Developed Chem & Automobiles Curr San Ramon Valley Ed Assn 1984-85; Conducting Heterocyclicamines Research 1988-; *office:* California HS 9870 Broadmoor Dr San Ramon CA 94583

CARROLL, MARGARET WILKINSON, Third Grade Teacher; *b:* Brady, TX; *m:* Arthur Lee; *c:* Lee W., Richard F., Nancy A. Carroll Bean; *ed:* (BS) Home Ec, Univ of TX Austin 1949; (MS) Spec Ed, Univ of Tx San Antonio 1984; *cr:* Teacher Pecos Ind Sch Dist 1949-51, Schulder Cty Ind Sch Dist 1951-52, Corpus Christi Ind Sch Dist 1967-71, Spring Branch 1974-79, San Antonio Ind Sch Dist 1979-; *ai:* AFT; Alpha Gamma Delta Pres 1989-.

CARROLL, RUTH A., 7th/8th Grade Language Teacher; *b:* Austin, MN; *ed:* (BS) Elem Ed, Mankato St Univ 1972; Working Towards Masters in Educl Admin, CA St Univ Bakersfield; *cr:* 6th-8th Grade Teacher/Coach St Francis Sch 1968-70; 5th/7th Grade Teacher/Coach Visitation Sch 1972-75; 7th/8th Grade Teacher/1st-6th Grade Phys Ed Teacher/Coach Sacred Heart Sch 1976-79; 6th Grade Teacher/Coach Nativity of Mary Sch 1979-85; 6th-8th Grade Teacher/Coach South Fork Sch 1985-; *ai:* Girls Bsktbl Coach; Stu Cncl Co-Adv; Young Authors Adv; Kern Rdng Assn Mem 1990; CA Teachers Assn Mem 1976-; Kern Eastern Sierra Writing Project Invitational 1988-; *office:* South Fork Sch PO Box 1239 Weldon CA 93283

CARROLL, TERI COWIN, First Grade Teacher; *b:* Augusta, GA; *m:* Jerry Lee; *c:* Angela, David, Ashlie; *ed:* (BS) Elem Ed, 1971, (MED) Early Chldhd, 1978 Berry Coll; *cr:* 2nd Grade Teacher Red Bud Elem 1971-73; 1st Grade Teacher Eastside Elem 1974-; *ai:* HS Cheerleading Spon 1971-73; Alpha Delta Kappa Treas 1987-; *home:* 204 Crestmont Dr Calhoun GA 30701

CARRUTH, ANN DELANEY, English Teacher; *b:* Fall River, MA; *m:* J. Vance; *c:* Brian, Nancy; *ed:* (BA) Human Geography, Hunter Coll 1968; (MA) Educl Admin, Cath Univ of America 1973; *cr:* 6th Grade Teacher Sacred Heart Sch 1962-64; 7th Grade Soc Stud Teacher Immaculate Conception 1964-68; Prin St William of York 1968-71; Prgm Assoc New England Prgm in Teacher Ed 1971-72; 9th Grade Teacher St Stephens Indian Sch 1976-78; Government Teacher Jackson Hole HS 1978-79; Head Teacher/Admin Intermediate Sch 1979-81; Eng Teacher Jackson Hole Jr HS 1981-; *ai:* Newspaper; Saturday Sch; Delta Kappa Gamma; Cath Church Organist; *office:* Jackson Hole Jr HS Box 568 Jackson WY 83001

CARSON, ARDEN C., Band Director; *b:* Asheville, NC; *ed:* (BMED) Instrumental Music, Appalachian St Univ 1973; *cr:* Band Dir Lenoir Jr HS 1973-78, Hudson Mid Sch 1978-84, S Caldwell HS 1984-; *ai:* Music Educators Natl Conference; Amer Sch Band Dir Assn; NC Music Educators Assn State Secy 1988- , NW Dist Awd of Excl; Stanbury Awd; Teacher of Yr Hudson Mid Sch 1983; *office:* S Caldwell HS Rt 3 Box 600 Hudson NC 28638

CARSON, CHARLOTTE ANN AGEE, 8th Grade Lang Art Teacher; *b:* Birmingham, AL; *m:* Johnny Jr.; *c:* Cervantes; *ed:* (BA) Eng, Miles Coll 1962; (MA) Sec Ed/Psych, E MI Univ 1972; Mental Health; *cr:* 7th/8th Grade Eng Teacher Bessie Hoffman Jr HS 1966-68; 8th Grade Eng Teacher Ferris Elem 1968-; Asst Admin Carsons Adult Foster Care Incorporated 1974-, Char Di John Homes Incorporated 1981-; *ai:* Phi Delta Kappa 1982-; Wayne Cty Rdng Cncl 1980-; NAACP 1989-; *home:* 157 W Hickory Grove Rd Bloomfield Hlls MI 48013

CARSON, DAVID EMERSON, Science Teacher; *b:* California, PA; *m:* Linda Raytek; *c:* Lynn, Wendy; *ed:* (BS) Earth/Space Sci/Geography, CA St Coll 1963; (MST) Sci Teaching, Antioch Coll 1970; *cr:* Teacher Burgettstown Jr-Sr HS 1963-; *ai:* Asst Girls Var Bsktbl Coach; AFT; Natl Sci Fnd Grant Antioch Coll; *office:* Burgettstown Jr/Sr HS Bavington Rd Burgettstown PA 15021

CARSON, KATHRYN LEWIS, Soc Stud/Lang Art Teacher; *b:* Bethel, NC; *m:* Don Columbus III; *c:* Bo IV, Mark C.; *ed:* (BA) Fr, Meredith Coll 1972; *cr:* Fr/Journalism Teacher Hobgood Acad 1972-73; 9th-12th Grade Fr Teacher Tarboro Edgecombe Acad 1973-75; 6th-8th Grade Lang Art/Soc Stud Teacher Bethel Elem Sch 1979-; *ai:* His Day Chairperson; Quiz Bowl & Stu Cncl Assn Adv; NC Assn of Educators 1979; Bethel Elem Teacher of Yr 1989; *home:* 411 N Main St Box 363 Bethel NC 27812

CARSON, SHARON FARLEY, Spanish Teacher; *b:* Baltimore, MD; *m:* Scott; *c:* Laura; *ed:* (BA) Scndry Ed, 1976; (MED) Scndry Ed, 1982 Towson St Univ; *cr:* Span Teacher Marley Jr HS 1977-89; Span Teacher Marley Mid Sch 1989-; *ai:* Span Club Spon; Mem of Sch Finance Comm; *office:* Marley Mid Sch Baltimore Annapolis Blvd Glen Burnie MD 21061

CARSWELL, DEBORAH BELL, Teacher of Gifted; *b:* Rochester, PA; *m:* Leonard S. Jr.; *c:* Christopher, Timothy; *ed:* (AA) Ed, Brevard Comm Coll 1973; (BA) Scndry Ed/Soc Stud, Univ of Cntrl FL 1975; *cr:* Prgm Consultant Seminole Cty Extension Prgm 1975-76; US His Teacher 1976-77, World His Teacher 1977-78, US His/Geography Teacher 1978-79 Apopka HS; Civics Teacher 1979-85, US His Teacher 1986-89, Gifted Resource Teacher 1989- Apopka Memorial Mid Sch; *ai:* Var Cheerleading; Sftbl Coach, Dist Champions 1977; Washington DC Trip Spon, Team Leader; Orange Cty Classroom Teachers Assn Bd of Dir 1982-85; Orange Cty Mid Sch Organization 1985; Casselberry PTA VP 1984-86; Seminole Cty League of Women Voters Bd of Dir 1981-86; Redeemer Luth Church Pres 1990; FL Teaching Profession Lobbiest; Project Bus Consultant 1987-89; Seminole Cty Commission on Status of Women; Republican FL Teacher Advisory Comm; Outstanding Young Women in America 1986, 1988; Innovative Teaching Awd 1988, 1990; *office:* Apopka Memorial Mid Sch 425 N Park Ave Apopka FL 32712

CART, ELIZABETH MARTIN, 5th Grade Teacher; *b:* Crowley, LA; *m:* Gregory E.; *c:* Cody M., Stefan B., Kori L.; *ed:* (BS) Elem Ed, 1974, (MA) Rdng, 1977 Bethany Nazarene Coll; *cr:* 4th Grade Teacher Church Point Elem 1974-75; 5th Grade Teacher Iota Elem 1975-; *ai:* Supvr of Stu Teachers 1987-; *office:* Iota Elem Sch PO Box 910 Iota LA 70543

CARTAYA, PEDRO PABLO, Spanish Teacher/Counselor; *b:* Havana, Cuba; *ed:* Licenciate Philosophy, Coll of Philosophy Barcelona 1959; Licenciate Theology, 1968, (MA) Arts, 1969, (PHD) Span Lit, 1979 St Louis Univ; *cr:* Span Instr St Louis Univ 1973-76; Sci Moderator Belen Jesuit Prep 1978-82; Span Teacher/Cnslr Loyola HS 1982-87; Span Teacher Belen Jesuit Prep 1987-; *ai:* Loyola Sch & Belen Jesuit Preparatory Sch Astronomy Club Moderator; Loyola Scientific Cmmty Founder; Belen Acad for Sci of Earth & Space Founder; Radio Club Dominicano 1983-87; Fellowship St Louis Univ 1973-76; *office:* Belen Jesuit Preparatory Sch 500 SW 127th Ave Miami FL 33182

CARTER, CINDY NANETTE, 4th Grade Teacher; *b:* Greeneville, TN; *ed:* (BS) Elem and Early Chldhd, Carson-Newman Coll 1974; (MED) Supervision & Admin, East TN St 1986; *cr:* Teacher Mc Donald Elem 1978-; *ai:* Asst Bsktbl Coach; Secy PTO; Mem of Greene Cty Soc Stud Text Book Comm; NEA 1978-; TEA 1978-; GCEA 1978-; *office:* Mc Donald Elem Sch Rt 2 Mohawk TN 37810

CARTER, CONNIE J., Third Grade Teacher; *b:* Bentonville, AR; *m:* Rodney Grant; *c:* Ronda K., Robert G.; *ed:* (BSE) Elem Ed, Univ of AR 1968; (MS) Ed, Sul Ross Univ 1975; Spec Ed Cert, West TX Univ; *cr:* 3rd Grade Teacher Rogers Ind Sch Dist 1968-69; Spec Ed/3rd Grade Teacher Amarillo Ind Sch Dist 1969-73; Spec Ed/2nd Grade Teacher Big Spring Ind Sch Dist 1973-76; Spec Ed/3rd Grade Teacher Denison Ind Sch Dist 1976-80; 4th Grade Teacher Midway Ind Sch Dist 1980-81; 3rd-6th Grade Teacher Bruceville-Eddy Ind Sch Dist 1983-; *ai:* TX St Teachers Assn, NEA; *office:* Bruceville-Eddy Elem Sch P O Box 99 Eddy TX 76524

CARTER, DEBORAH SAVAGE, Business Teacher/Dept Chair; *b:* Nassawadox, VA; *c:* Kris R., Brian E.; *ed:* (BS) Bus Ed, Univ of MD 1970; Grad Stud Bus Ed, George Mason Univ, Univ of VA, James Madison Univ, VPI & St Univ; Fairfax Cty Public Schls Staff Dev Trng Courses; *cr:* Federal Youth Employment Cnslr/Coord US Dept of Navy Naval Facilities Engineering Command 1971-72, 1974-76, US Dept of the Interior Natl Hdgtrs 1980-82; Bus Dept Chairperson 1977-, Bus Teacher 1970- Herndon HS; *ai:* Dept Chairperson; Sch/Bus Advisory, Cty Bus Teachers Advisory, Minority Achievement, Human Relations, Awds, Prins Advisory Comms; FBLA Club Co Spon; Fairfax Ed Assn 1970-81, 1990; Fairfax Cty Fed of Teachers 1981-; Herndon Bus & Prof Womens Assn 1986-88; US Dept of the Navy Superior Achievement Cnslr Awd 1975; Jr Achievement Bus Teachers Awd 1979-80; *home:* PO Box 125 Herndon VA 22070

CARTER, DEBRA LOU PARMAN, First Grade Teacher; *b:* Albuquerque, NM; *m:* Donald E.; *c:* Glenn, Steven; *ed:* (BME) Elem Ed/Music Ed, 1976, (ME) Elem/Early Chldhd, 1979 E NM Univ; *cr:* Kndgtn Teacher 1976-89, Elem Music Teacher 1983-89, 1st Grade Teacher 1989- Logan Sch; *ai:* Chrldr Spon 1976-82; NEA 1976-; *home:* Rt 1 Box 130 San Jon NM 88434

CARTER, DENNIS R., Athletic Dir/Phys Ed Teacher; *b:* Colorado Springs, CO; *m:* Cheryl Jean Glover; *c:* Shannon, Ryan, Devin; *ed:* (BA) Phys Ed/Scndry Ed, Adams St Coll 1970; *cr:* Teacher/Coach Ellicott HS 1970-; *ai:* Athletic & Act Dir; Head Boys Bsktbl & Bsbl Coach; CO Coaches Assn 1971-; CO Athletic Dir Assn 1986-; *office:* Ellicott HS RR 2 Calhan CO 80808

CARTER, DIANTHA THOMAS, 6th Grade Teacher; *b:* Raleigh, NC; *ed:* (BA) Span/His/Ed, Salem Coll 1955; *cr:* 7th Grade Teacher Daniels Jr HS 1955-65; 6th-7th Grade Teacher Carroll Jr HS Mid Sch 1965-; *ai:* Service Club Adv; Media Advisory & Hospitality Comm; Eng Dept Chm 1971-79; Delta Kappa Gamma 1958-; Wake Cty Historical Society, NC Musuem of Natural Sci; Homes Barton Baptist Church Building & Grounds Comm; *home:* 2021 St Marys St Raleigh NC 27608

CARTER, DONNA GRAHAM, Mathematics Teacher; *b:* Leitchfield, KY; *m:* Erdie L.; *c:* Erdie Jr., Lee, Angela; *ed:* (BA) Math, 1974, (MA) Scndry Ed, 1979, (Rank I) Supervision, 1988 W KY Univ; *cr:* Math Teacher North Hardin HS 1974-77, James T Alton Mid Sch 1977-85, North Hardin HS 1985-; *ai:* Collaborative Teaching Team; Math Lab Asst; North Hardin HS Parent Advisory Cncl; KY Ed Assn; Rineyville Baptist Church (WMU Dir 1985-, Choir 1974-); Hardin Cty Schls Teacher of Quarter; *office:* North Hardin HS 801 S Logsdon Pkwy Radcliff KY 40160

CARTER, EDNA MELVIN, Fifth Grade Teacher; *b:* White Oak, NC; *w:* Johnny Allen (dec); *c:* Tisa, Dana; *ed:* (BS) Elem Ed, Fayetteville St Univ 1964; (MA) Elem Ed, NC Cntrl Univ 1978; *cr:* Teacher Bladen Cntrl Elem Sch 1964-70, Beaver Dam Elem Sch 1970-74, Legion Road Elem Sch 1974-; *ai:* NC Assn of Educators, NEA 1964-; Alpha Kappa Alpha; Legion Road Sch Teacher of Yr 1987; *office:* Legion Road Elem Sch Legion Rd Hope Mills NC 28348

CARTER, GEORGE ANN, Social Studies Teacher; *b:* Hornell, NY; *m:* James A.; *c:* Jeffrey, Todd, Heather; *ed:* (BS) Scndry Soc Stud, 1969, (MA) His, 1972 SUNY Geneseo; SUNY Geneseo, St Johns Univ; *cr:* Teacher Perry Cntrl HS 1969-; *ai:* NHS Adv; Awds Comm Chairperson; Perry Teachers Assn, Genesee Valley Teachers Assn, NYSUT, AFT 1969-; Delta Kappa Gamma 1978-; United Church of Warsaw Sunday Sch Co-Supt 1982-89; Soccer Boosters Treas 1989-; Warsaw Summer Soccer; *office:* Perry Cntrl HS 33 Watkins Ave Perry NY 14530

CARTER, GLORIA STRATTON, Fifth Grade Teacher; *b:* Mansfield, LA; *m:* James Jr.; *c:* Roosevelt Smith Jr., Kimberly D. Smith; *ed:* (BS) Home Ec, Grambling St Univ 1966; (MED) Elem Grades, Northwestern St Univ 1985; Numerous Educl Wkshps; *cr:* Classroom Teacher Caddo Parish Sch Bd 1968-; *ai:* 5th Grade Chairperson & Sch Chm; Rdng Club & Speech & Drama Spon; Nursing Homes Volunteer; Cmmty Act; Deaconess; Choir Mem & Treas; LA Assn of Educators, NEA 1968-; Northwestern Rdng Cncl 1986-; Nominee Educator of Yr 1986, 1990; Essay Contest Winner 1989; *home:* 304 Fox Trot Dr Mansfield LA 71052

CARTER, IVY RICHARDSON, Kindergarten Teacher; *b:* Cleveland, MS; *m:* Simon Jr.; *c:* Candrace, Torrey, Danielle, Shandra; *ed:* (BS) Elem Ed, 1979, (ME) Elem Ed, 1988 Delta St Univ; *ai:* MS Ed Assn, MS Assn Children Under 6; *home:* PO Box 331 Cleveland MS 38732

CARTER, JANET FULLER, Health & Physical Ed Teacher; *b:* Mecklengburg Cty, VA; *m:* Jerry Thomas; *c:* Janna, Jill; *ed:* Health/Phys Ed, Mary Washington; (BS) Health/Phys Ed, Atlantic Chrstn 1965; *cr:* Teacher W Branch HS 1965-71, Halifax Cty HS 1978-79; Teacher of Talented & Gifted Laurel Park HS 1979-81; Teacher John Rolfe Mid Sch 1981-; *ai:* Intramurals; Henrico Coaches Assn Sch Rep 1985-, Distinguished Service Awd 1989; PTA Nominating Comm 1988-; *office:* John Rolfe Mid Sch 6901 Messer Rd Richmond VA 23231

CARTER, JEANETTE WALKER, Assistant Principal; *b:* Rock Hill, SC; *m:* James Warlington; *c:* James W. II; *ed:* (BS) Home Ec Ed, NC Cntrl St Univ 1953; (MA) Guidance/Counseling, Cath Univ 1975; PA St Univ 1958; Trinity Coll 1976; Admin & Supervision, George Washington Univ 1977; *cr:* Teacher Thomasville City Schls 1953-65; Tutorial Supvr Neighborhood Youth Corp 1965-66; Teacher Francis Jr HS 1966-67; Teacher 1967-73, Acting Asst Prin 1973-78, Acting Prin 1978-79, Teacher 1979-80 Kelly Miller Jr HS; Teacher 1980-87, Acting Asst Prin 1987-89, Prin 1988, Asst Prin 1990 Fletcher-Johnson Educl Center; *ai:* Coord 9th Grade Act; Sch Based Management, Attendance, Assembly, Staff Dev, Testing, Scheduling Comm; Soc Amenities Adv; Values/Character Ed Delivery System; Parent Club; Cncl of Sch Officers Mem 1973-80, 1987-; Jr HS Admin Assn, Natl Assn for Sch Admin, ASCD Mem 1987-; AFT Mem 1966-73, 1980-87; Delta Sigma Theta Mem 1953-; Milwood-Waterford Civic Assn Mem 1970-; Natl Assn for Advancement of Colored People Mem 1987-; Gethsemane United Meth Church Mem 1967-; Comm for Election Brenda Hughes Prince Georges Bd of Ed Mem 1988-89; Thomasville Chapter NC Teachers Assn Pres 1960-62;Dist VII Home Ec Teachers of NC Pres 1958-60; Davidson Cty Unit NC Teachers Assn Pres 1958-60; PTA; J Walter Lambeth Teacher of Yr Awd 1965; Creative Leadership & Inspiration in Teaching Awd Research Club of Washington DC 1973; Masonic Lodge Schlsp Awd 1949; Numerous Citations for Outstanding & Dedicated Service Awds; *office:* Fletcher-Johnson Ed Center Benning Rd & C Street SE Washington DC 20019

CARTER, JEANETTE YVONNE (ROPP), Business Teacher; *b:* Columbus, MT; *m:* Robert Glenn; *c:* Cassandra J. Y.; *ed:* (BA) Bus Ed, Mt St Univ 1984; Bus, Math, Athletic Coaching/Trng MT St Univ, E MT Coll, E OR St Coll; *cr:* Bus Teacher Augusta Public Sch 1984-; *ai:* Sch Annual, Sch Newspaper, Cheerleading, Pep Club, Concession Stand, Prom Adv; Grade Sch Girls Bsktbl Coach; Asst Drama Dir; Pep Club, Chrldrs, Concession Stand Adv; Augusta Ed Assn (Secy, Treas) 1985-87; MBEA, MVA 1984-89; MEA 1985-88; Augusta Youth Center 1986-89; Pi Beta Phi, Office Ed Assn Club Mem 1982-84; Augusta HS Yrbk Dedication 1989 *office:* Augusta HS 322 N Broadway Box 307 Augusta MT 59410

CARTER, JESSIE ANITA, Mathematics Teacher; *b:* Ft Worth, TX; *ed:* (BA) Math N TX St Univ 1970; (MA) Ed, TCU 1976; *cr:* Instructional Aide 1972-73, Teacher 1973- Ft Worth Ind Sch Dist; *ai:* Future Problem Solving Coach; Sister Cities Youth Intnl Spon; Summer Sch Curr Dev; FWCTA, TSTA, NEA, NCTM 1972-; ASCD, ICCE 1985-; Sid Richardson Cmptrs in Math & Curr Dev for Gifted Grant; Article Published; Notable Woman of TX 1984-85; Whos Who Amer Women 1989-; Whos Who Amer Educators 1988-89; Notable Women of World 1989-; Morningside Mid Sch Outstanding Magnet Teacher 1986-87; TAME Outstanding Math Teacher 1990; Ft Worth Ind Sch Dist Outstanding Math Teacher 1973-74; *home:* 7101 Willis Ave Fort Worth TX 76116

CARTER, JOHNNIE PETTY, Third Grade Teacher; *b:* Wheelock, TX; *m:* Ollie; *ed:* (BS) Home Ec 1955, (MA) Elem Ed, 1961 Prairie View A&M; *ai:* Career Ladder.

CARTER, JOYCE SCOTT, Eng/Drama/Fine Arts Teacher; *b:* Charles City Cty, VA; *m:* Rev. Maurice C. Sr.; *c:* Kevin V. Spencer, Jeffrey R. Spencer, Don, Maurice, Esther, Ann Gilliam; *ed:* (BA) Drama/English, Howard Univ 1959; (MA) English & Ed, Hampton Univ 1966; Post Master Studies VA ST Univ 1959; Northwestern Univ 1960; Coll of William & Mary 1983; Old Dominion Univ 1988; *cr:* Found/Spon Troupe 2757 Intnl Thespian Society; Eng, Speech & Drama Teacher Carver HS; Dir of Drama, Co-Spon Stu Cncl, Spon Newspaper 1959-71; Editor Newport News Teachers' Quarterly 1960-65; Teacher of Drama & Eng; Founder /Spon Troupe 2615 Intnl Thespian Society 1972; Textbook Evaluator - VA 1968-78 Head of Fine & Performing Arts Dept; Dir of Drama Menchville HS 1971-; *ai:* Curr Comm; Philosophy Comm; Graduation Comm; Chairperson Fine & Performing Arts Dept; NN Summer Institute for Arts Comm; Intnl Thespian Society 1963-; Newport News Ed Assn 1959-85; VA ED Assn 1959-85; NEA 1959-85; NCTE 1959-89; VA Theatre Assn 1961-85; Amer Theatre Assn Peninsula League of Women, Inc Pres 1967-71 Sec 1959-65; Outstanding Officer 1986; Zeta Phi Beta 1958-; "Regional Zeta Awd" Outstanding Service in Creative Arts 1984; "Black Achievers Awd" Outstanding Achievement in Arts 1981; Creative Arts 1989; Speech, Drama & Journalism Evaluator ST of VA Textbook Adoption 1968 & 1978; Rep Newport News Public Sch System at ST Fine Arts Convention; Convention Recorder 1980; VA Theatre Conference at Theatre VA in Richmond 1988; 1st Place Ratings in Dist & State One Act Play Festivals for VIA 1961-71 & VHSL 1972; Directed 1 TV Play 1972; Speech, Drama & Journalism Curr Comm ST of VA 1983; *office:* Menchville H S 275 Menchville Rd Newport News VA 23602

CARTER, JUDITH HOWARD, 7th-8th Grade Teacher; *b:* Emma, KY; *c:* James III, Susan R., Rebecca A.; *ed:* (BA) Soc Stud, E KY Univ 1964; Soc Stud, 1980, Soc Stud, 1985 Morehead Univ; Mid Sch Soc Stud Trng 1989; *cr:* Teacher Clark Elem 1964-66, Prestonsburg Elem 1966-68, Clark Elem 1975-; *ai:* 4-H Leader; Academic Team Ofcl; Subject Advisory Comm Soc Stud; Sch Cmmty Partnership Participant; KY Academic Assn Governors Cup Ofcl; KY Ed Assn Delegate; NEA; Floyd Cty Ed Assn (VP, Pres, Bd of Dir) 1980-; ASCD 1990, Excl in Teaching Awd 1988-89; Delta Kappa Gamma (Secy, 1st VP) 1980-, Schlsp 1983; Hospice of Big Sandy Bd of Dir 1980-84; Mc Dowell Cancer Network Bd of Dir 1983-85; Calico Corner Bd of Dir 1970-73; 1st United Meth Church (Mem, Supt Bible Sch, Sunday Sch Teacher); Clark Elem PTA Mem; Meals on Wheels Volunteer; Jenny Wiley Academic Conference 1989; Jenny Wiley Rdng Cncl Pilot Prgm; *home:* 47 Arnold Ave Prestonsburg KY 41653

CARTER, KAREN DIANE, Physical Education Dept Chair; *b:* Bellefontaine, OH; *ed:* (MS) Phy Ed, 1982, (BS) Phys Ed, 1978 Mid TN St Univ; (AS) Ed, Motlow St Comm Coll 1976; *cr:* Phys Ed Teacher Tyner HS 1978-81; Womens Bsktbl Coach Castleton St Coll 1983-85; Recreation Center Dir Lexington Cty Recreation 1985-86; Phys Ed Teacher/Dept Chair South Aiken HS 1986-; *ai:* Head Vlybl & Girls Bsktbl Coach; Aiken Cty Phys Ed Curr Comm; SC Coaches Assn for Womens Sport VP 1987-; SC Coaches Assn 1987-, Girls Bsktbl Coach of Yr 1988; Amer Alliance for Health, Phys Ed, Recreation & Dance 1987-; Bsktbl SC Coach of Yr, AAA Coach of Yr, Region Coach of Yr, Area Coach of Yr; Vlybl Region Coach of Yr, Area Coach of Yr; *office:* South Aiken HS 232 E Pine Log Rd Aiken SC 29801

CARTER, KAY STEPHENS, Kindergarten Teacher; *b:* Florence, SC; *m:* Bobby R.; *c:* John D.; *ed:* (BS) Elem Ed, Francis Marion Coll 1972; Working Towards Masters; *cr:* Kndgtn Teacher Florence Dist #1 1972-; *office:* Mc Laurin Elem Sch 100 Mc Millan Ln Florence SC 29501

CARTER, KENNETH A., English/Soc Stud Teacher; *b:* Mc Keesport, PA; *c:* Stephanie, Grace; *ed:* (BA) Soc Stud, Univ of MD 1955; EDAA Equivalent, 1977; Grad Work, Univ of Pittsburgh Law Sch, Buffalo St, Univ of Buffalo Canisius, Niagara Univ; *cr:* Eng/His Teacher Prince Frederick MD 1958-60; 9th Grade Rdng/Advanced Eng Teacher North Jr 1960-70; Eng/Soc Stud/Human Relations Teacher 1970-; *ai:* Stu Cncl Adv; Cmmty Drug Intervention; Peers Offering Behavior Modification to Peers Adv; Faculty Advisory Cncl 1986-; Building Leadership Comm Chm 1989-; AEA PAC Mem 1982-; Natl Mid Schls Assn Wkshp Adv; Teacher of Yr 1989; Federal Project Teaching Teachers to be More Humane 1969.

CARTER, LANA READ, Sixth Grade Teacher; *b:* Mart, TX; *m:* Doyle Gene; *c:* Lance Holcomb; *ed:* (BS) Elem Ed, Univ of N TX 1972; (MS) Spec Ed, TX Womans Univ 1976; *cr:* Math/Sci Teacher Amelia Earhart Elem 1972-76; 6th Grade Teacher Sudie L Williams Elem 1976-; *ai:* Test Coord; Advisory Comm; Operation Involvement Rep; Phi Delta Kappa 1985-; NEA, Classroom Teachers of Dallas 1972-; *office:* Sudie L Williams Elem Sch 4518 Pomona Dallas TX 75209

CARTER, LILLIAN ISHEE, 4th-7th Grade Math Teacher; *b:* Hattiesburg, MS; *m:* Hugh Jr.; *c:* Donna M. Freeman, Tracy W., Hugh L. Hession, Travis V. Hession, Gregory K., David O., Brian D.; *ed:* (BS) Bus Ed, 1966, (BS) Elem Ed, 1976, (MS) Elem Ed, 1977 Univ of S MS; *cr:* Bus Ed Teacher Beaumont HS 1969-71; Elem Ed Teacher Runnelstown Elem Sch 1972-; *ai:* MS Assn Teachers of Math 1988-; MAE, NEA, PCAE 1966-82; Perry Cty Assn of Educators (Pres, VP); Teacher of Yr 1988-89; *home:* 4798 Hwy 29 Petal MS 39465

CARTER, LOUIS LEE, Math & History Teacher; *b:* Tompkinsville, KY; *m:* Betty J. Monday; *c:* Samuel, Sarah; *ed:* (BA) His, 1971, (MA) Ed/Geography, 1980, Sch Admin, 1984 Western Ky Univ; *ai:* Monroe Cty Ed Assn Pres 1988-; Monroe Cty Sportsmans Club (Pres 1986-88 Treas 1989-;) *home:* 2291 Old Temple Hill Rd Tompkinsville KY 42167

CARTER, LYNN DAVIS, English Teacher; *b:* Waynesville, NC; *m:* Robert Vann Jr.; *c:* Katie, Caroline; *ed:* (BA) Span, Wake Forest Univ 1972; (MA) Mid Grade Ed, Gardner Webb Coll 1988; Working Towards Cert Eng, Univ of NC Chapel Hill; Mentor Trng; Mentor Teacher Cert Trng; *cr:* Span/Eng Teacher Garner HS 1973-74; 8th Grade Teacher Whittier Elem 1974-79; 8th Grade Lang Art/Soc Stud Teacher Rugby Jr HS 1979-; *ai:* Stu Cncl Adv; A-B Honor Roll Comm Chm; NC Eng Teachers Assn, Phi Delta Kappa, NCTE; Mills River United Meth Church (Comm, Circles); *office:* Rugby Jr HS 3555 Haywood Rd Hendersonville NC 28739

CARTER, MAC T., Mathematics Department Chair; *b:* Port Arthur, TX; *m:* Mavis Elizabeth Hughes; *c:* Candace; *ed:* (BSED) Math, 1975, (MSED) Admin, 1984 Stephen F Austin St Univ; *cr:* Teacher Nacogdoches Ind Sch Dist 1975-77, Shelbyville Ind Sch Dist 1977-; *ai:* UIL Math Spon; *office:* Shelbyville Ind Sch Dist P O Box 325 Shelbyville TX 75973

CARTER, MARY KILPATRICK, 2nd Grade Teacher; *b:* Asheville, NC; *m:* Robert C. Sr.; *c:* Robert C. Jr.; *ed:* (BS) Elem Ed, Appalachian St Teachers Coll 1954; (MA) Rdng, W Carolina Univ 1982; Early Chldhd, Univ of NC Asheville; *cr:* 3rd Grade Teacher Aycock Elem 1954-55; 1st Grade Teacher Stephen Knight Elem 1955-58; 2nd Grade Teacher W Buncombe Elem 1975-; *ai:* NEA 1975-; *office:* W Buncombe Elem Sch 175 Erwin Hills Rd Asheville NC 28806

CARTER, MARY WARD, Fourth Grade Teacher; *b:* Gates County, NC; *m:* Delmar Yates; *c:* Mary Kristen; *ed:* (BS) Psych & Ed, Frederick Coll 1965; *cr:* 3rd Grade Teacher Churchland Elem 1965-67, Holland Elem 1967-69, William J Jones Elem 1969-78; 4th Grade Teacher Kilby Shores Elem 1978-; *ai:* EAS 1978-; VEA 1978-; NEA 1978-; Suffolk Rdng C Great Fork Baptist Church (Pres 1978-89/Teacher Lifetime/GA Leader 1989-); *office:* Kilby Shores Elem Sch 111 Kilby Shores Dr Suffolk VA 23434

CARTER, MAVIS ELIZABETH, Kindergarten Teacher; *b:* Center, TX; *m:* Mac T.; *c:* Candace; *ed:* (BS) Elem Ed, 1976, (MED) Elem, 1978 Stephen F Austin St Univ; *cr:* Kndgtn Teacher SW Carter Elem 1977-; *ai:* Assn of TX Prof Educators 1980-; Kndgtn Teachers TX 1983-; Intnl Rdng Assn 1980-; *home:* PO Box 329 Shelbyville TX 75973

CARTER, MELODY BAKER, Mathematics Teacher/Dept Chair; *b:* Ft Hood, TX; *m:* Benjamin P.; *c:* Courtney, Casey; *ed:* (BS) Math Ed, 1977, (MED) Math Ed, 1979 MS St Univ; Work on Cert Admin; Evaluator Trng Course MS Teacher Assessment Instrument; *cr:* Math Teacher Shivers Jr HS 1977-85, Aberdeen HS 1985-; *ai:* Stu Cncl Adv; Beauty Review & Assembly Prgm Coord; Delta Kappa Gamma (VP 1989) 1983-; MS Assn of Educators Building Rep 1977-88; NCTM 1978-; Aberdeen Jr Auxiliary (Pres, Mem) 1983, Outstanding Citizen 1989; Jr Womens League (Pres, Mem) 1982; Riverview Garden Club (Projects Chm, Mem) 1989; Staff Dev Achievement Awd 1987, 1989; Past Pres NE MS Assn Math Teachers; MS Outstanding Young Woman 1983; Outstanding Young Women of America 1983, 1985; *office:* Aberdeen HS PO Drawer 607 Aberdeen MS 39730

CARTER, NELDA ALDERMAN, Science Teacher; *b:* Corsicana, TX; *w:* George O. (dec); *c:* Thomas; *ed:* (BS) Bus, 1958, (MED) Elem Ed, 1966 E TX St Univ; TX Womens Univ; *cr:* Teacher Norris Elem Sch 1966-71; Prin A L Day Elem Sch 1971-80; Asst Prin 1980-83, Teacher 1983- Commerce Mid Sch; *ai:* TX St Teachers Assn Treas 1966-75; TX Classroom Teachers Assn 1966-73, 1983-; NSTA 1985-; Assn TX Prof Educators 1983-; Amer Assn Univ Women VP 1964-70; Delta Kappa Gamma (Pres, VP) 1973-; Administrator of Yr 1982; *office:* Commerce Mid Sch PO Box 1251 Commerce TX 75428

CARTER, PATRICIA WORRELL, First Grade Teacher; *b:* San Francisco, CA; *m:* Darrell Gene; *c:* Jackie, Vickie Struble; *ed:* (BS) Elem Ed, OK St Univ 1972; Elem Counseling, Elem Music, Rdng Instruction; *cr:* 1st Grade/1st-3rd Grade Elem Music Teacher Billings Elem Sch 1972-; *ai:* Jr HS Pep Club & Summer Lib Spon; Private Piano Lesson Teacher; OEA, NEA Mem 1972-; Billings ACT Pres 1979-80, Teacher of Yr 1978; Cimarron Rdng Cncl Mem 1984-; Delta Kappa Gamma Mem 1982-; *office:* Billings Elem Sch PO Box 39 Billings OK 74630

CARTER, PEGGY LEWIS, Third Grade Teacher; *b:* Amherst, TX; *m:* Warren E.; *c:* Dennis W., Brenda M.; *ed:* (BS) Elem Ed, 1971, (MED) Elem Ed, 1980 E NM Univ Portales; *cr:* 3rd Grade Teacher Mt View Elem 1980-; *ai:* Prin Advisory Comm; NEA, Tucumcari Ed Assn 1980-; *office:* Mt View Elem Sch 1608 S Rock Island Tucumcari NM 88401

CARTER, ROCKY K., Social Studies Teacher; *b:* El Reno, OK; *m:* Karen M. Davis; *c:* Ryan, Camilla, Ross; *ed:* (BA) Soc Stud, Cntrl St Univ 1978; *cr:* Teacher/Coach Waurika HS 1978-79, El Reno HS 1979-83, Hinton HS 1983-85, El Reno HS 1985-; *ai:* HS Ftbl Coach; Fellowship of Chrstn Athletes Spon; El Reno Ed Assn, OK Ed Assn, NEA.

CARTER, SANDRA MC INTYRE, Educational Director; *b:* New York, NY; *m:* Anderson Jr.; *c:* Shivonne D. Rush, Jenee L.; *ed:* (BA) His, Hunter Coll 1974; *cr:* Teacher The Modern Sch 1974-85; Asst Camp/Girls Dir/Registrar Minisink 1982-89; Supvr/Teacher 1985-89, Educl Dir 1989- The Modern Sch; *ai:* Career Cnslr; Leadership Trng Class; Minisink Town House; Omicron Epsilon Society 1984-; Medina Court 11 Daughters of Isis 1985-; Tapawingo Honor Society 1962-; *home:* 3333 Broadway Tower D18C New York NY 10031

CARTER, SHARON ANN (SIMMONS), Third Grade Teacher; *b:* Cinn, OH; *m:* Thomas R.; *c:* Thomas David, Charles Timothy; *ed:* (BS) Elem Ed, OH Univ 1971; (MS) Elem Ed, Coll of Mt St Joseph 1989; *cr:* 3rd Grade Teacher Seaman Elem; *ai:* Seaman United Presbyn Church Trustee; Eastern Star.

CARTER, TOM F., Administrator; *b:* Greenville, MI; *m:* Nancy L. Reed; *c:* Joy L., Gary M.; *ed:* (BS) Scndry Ed, Cntrl MI Univ 1967; Certified Athletic Trainer; *cr:* Teacher/Coach Flint Northwestern HS 1968-69; Teacher/Coaching Staff Univ of WI Madison 1969-76; Admin Middleton Chrstn Sch 1976-79; Teacher/Coach 1979-78, Admin 1987- Oakfield Baptist Acad; *ai:* Var Boys & Girls Bsktbl Coach; ASCI 1988-; *office:* Oakfield Baptist Acad 11128 14 Mile Rd Rockford MI 49341

CARTER, TRAVIS LEE, JR., Mathematics/Computer Teacher; *b:* Humbolt, TN; *m:* Margaret Mimion; *c:* Keri A., Travis L. III; *ed:* (AS) Math, Jackson St Comm Coll 1972; (BS) Math, Bethel Coll 1974; (ME) Ed, Memphis St Univ 1984; *cr:* Math Teacher Atwood HS 1974-82, W Carroll HS 1982-83; Math/Cmptr Teacher W Carroll Mid Sch 1983-; *ai:* Asst Ftbl Coach W Carroll HS; Girls Bsktbl Head Coach W Carroll Mid Sch; *home:* PO Box 431 Atwood TN 38220

CARTER, VIRGINIA WOOD, Mathematics Teacher; *b:* Statesville, NC; *c:* Amy; *ed:* (BS) Math, Appalachian St Univ 1967; (MA) Math, Univ of NC Charlotte 1987; *cr:* Teacher South Iredell HS 1967-69, Grimsley Sr HS 1969-73, South Iredell HS 1973-74, West Iredell HS 1974-; *ai:* Stu Cncl Adv; NC Cncl Teachers Math, NCTM 1967-; NC Assn Advancement of Gifted 1986-; Amer Bus Women Scrapbook Chm 1984-, Woman of Yr 1990; Natl Sci Fnd Wkshp Grants; NC Center for Advancement of Teaching; *home:* 937 Armstrong St Statesville NC 28677

CARTER, VUDGER MC GILVERY, 4th-7th Science Teacher; *b:* Hattiesburg, MS; *w:* Benjamin Don Sr. (dec); *c:* Benjamin D. II; *ed:* (BS) Elem Ed, William Carey Coll 1970; *cr:* 4th-7th Grade Sci Teacher Runnelstown Elem & Jr HS 1970-; *ai:* Sci Dept Head Runnelstown Elem Jr HS; Sci Fair Coord Runnelstown Elem & Jr HS; Perry Cty Schls Insurance Comm; MS Assn of Ed, NEA, MS Sci Teachers Assn, Perry Cty Assn of Educators; *home:* 121 Cal Bonner Dr Petal MS 39465

CARTER, WILLIE CHARLES, Sixth Grade Teacher; *b:* Esserville, VA; *m:* Debra Lynn; *c:* Matthew, Charles; *ed:* (BA) Elem Ed, Clinch Valley Coll 1983; *cr:* 7th Grade Teacher 1984-85, 1st Grade Teacher 1985-86, Extension Resource Teacher 1986-89, 6th Grade Teacher 1989- L F Addington Mid Sch; *ai:* Comm Club Co-Spon; Ecology Club Spon; Bsktbl Coach; Wise Cty Ed Assn, NEA 1984-; Wise Lions Club (3rd, 1st VP) 1984-89; PTA; *office:* L F Addington Mid Sch PO Box 977 Wise VA 24293

CARTLIDGE, HELEN KING, Kindergarten Teacher; *b:* Greenville, MS; *c:* Arthur Jr., Byron, Kirsten; *ed:* (BS) Elem Ed, Rust Coll 1966; (MS) Elem Ed, MS Valley St Univ 1976; *cr:* 5th Grade Teacher Melissa Manning 1966-68; 2nd Grade Teacher Lincoln Attendance Center 1968-69; Rdng Teacher 1970-78, Kndgtn Teacher 1978- Leland Elem Sch; *ai:* MEA, NEA, MACUS; St Matthew Church Youth Choir Dir 1970-88; Magnolia Federated Civics Club Secy 1988-; *home:* 244 Wiley St Greenville MS 38701

CARTMELL, DAVID DWAYNE, Mathematics-Science Teacher; *b:* El Dorado, KS; *m:* Judy Ann Frick; *c:* David D. II, Angela M., Douglas D.; *ed:* (BS) Math, 1970, (MS) Scndry Ed, 1976 OK St Univ; *cr:* Teacher Pawhuska HS 1970-80, Morrison Public Schls 1980-; *ai:* Frosh Class Spon; Ftbl Bus Driver; Ftbl Stat Keeper; Bsktbl Scoreboard Keeper; Route Bus Driver; NEA, OEA 1970-80; PEA 1970-80; MEA 1980-; Pawnee Cty Farm Bureau VP 1982-, Washington DC Trip Winner 1989; Pawnee Cty Stockshow Bd 1989-; Pawnee Fair Bd Secy 1990; Pawnee 4-H & FFA Booster Club (Pres 1984, Treas 1985) 1990; OK Academic All-Starter Teacher Nominee 1989; OK Academic All-Starter Best Teacher Rep 1987, 1988; Morrison Teacher of Yr 1986-87; *office:* Morrison Public Schls Box 176 Morrison OK 73061

CARTON, JAMES M., 6th Grade Teacher; *b:* Massena, NY; *m:* Joan M.; *c:* Lisa, Susan Lopez, Jennifer; *ed:* (BS) Ed, 1966, (MS) Ed, 1967 SUNY Plattsburgh; *cr:* 6th Grade Teacher Warwick Valley Cntrl Schls 1967-; *ai:* Warwick Valley Teachers Assn Negotiations Team; Educl Testing Comm; NY St United Teachers; Warwick Valley Teachers Assn (VP 1975-77, Building Rep 1972-73); Outstanding Sci Teacher in Elem Sci Southeastern Section of Sci Teachers Assn of NY St 1984; *office:* Warwick Valley Mid Sch West St Ext Warwick NY 10990

CARTRETTE, MARY COLEMAN, 6th Grade Lang Art Teacher; *b:* Orangeburg, SC; *m:* Jacoby Gordon; *c:* Mary J., Jobi M., Coby G.; *ed:* (BA) Elem Ed, Columbia Coll 1966; (MED) General Ed, Francis Marion Coll 1976; Rdng; *cr:* 2nd Grade Teacher Scranton Elem Sch 1966; 5th Grade Teacher Forest Acres Elem Sch 1966-67; 7th Grade Teacher Hemingway Mid Sch 1967-68; 6th Grade Teacher Marion Elem 1972-; *ai:* Curr, Textbook, Content Area, Enterprise, Southern Assn, Marion Elem Newspaper, Incentive Prgm, Teachers Merit Pay, Prin Apprenticeship Comm; SACS Evaluation Team; Winthrop, FMC Stu Teacher Prgm; Homebound Instr; Inservices Conducted, Rdng, Writing, BSAP, Teacher Merit Day, Lang Art Chairperson Wkshp; Intnl Rdng Assn Building Rep; Parent, Stu, Teacher Assn; Delta Kappa Gamma Intnl; Alpha Etan St Exec Bd 1986-; Alpha Zeta Pres 1986-; Marion Baptist Church (Comm Chm on Comms, Outreach Leader, Choir, Family Ministry, Deacons Wife); York Rite Masonic Charities, Rara, Arteriosclerosis, Eye Fnd; Cancer, March of Dimes, Heart Fund Benefits; Outstanding Elem Teacher of America 1974; Marion Jaycee Outstanding Ed Awd 1979; Marion Elem Teacher of Yr 1989; FMC Grad Schlshp 1988-; *office:* Marion Elem Sch Dist 1 719 N Main St Marion SC 29571

CARTWRIGHT, MARY LOU SANTISO, 5th Grade Teacher; *b:* Ridgway, PA; *m:* Allen C.; *c:* Angela G., Matthew A.; *ed:* (BS) Elem Ed, Villa Maria Coll 1975; (MED) Elem Ed, Edinboro Univ 1978; *cr:* 5th Grade Teacher Our Lady of Mt Carmel 1975-78; 6th Grade Teacher Sacred Heart Sch 1978-80; 5th Grade Teacher Queen of World Sch 1980-; *office:* Queen of World Sch Queens Rd Saint Marys PA 15857

CARTY, LORENDA WONG, Computer Teacher; *b:* San Francisco, CA; *m:* George G.; *c:* Renee; *ed:* (BS) Bus Ed, 1973, (MA) Bus Ed, 1979 San Jose St Univ; *cr:* Teacher Sawyer Bus Sch 1974-75, San Jose HS 1976-79; Part Time Teacher Evergreen Valley Coll 1975-86; Teacher Rancho-Milpitas Mid Sch 1980-; *ai:* Delta Pi Epsilon (Treas, Historian) 1979-; CA Bus Ed Assn, NBEA 1973-; Beta Gamma Sigma 1973.

CARUANA, ANTHONY FRANCIS, English Teacher; *b:* Buffalo, NY; *m:* Diane E. Gilcrist; *c:* Jennifer, Brian; *ed:* (BA) Eng/Philosophy, 1969, (MS) Ed, 1974 Niagara Univ; Educl Admin, Supervision, Niagara Univ, St Univ of NY Buffalo, St Univ Coll of NY Buffalo; US Army Inst of Admin; US Army Command & General Staff Coll; *cr:* Eng Teacher Depew Mid Sch 1969-70; Officer US Army 1970-71; Officer US Army Reserve 1971-; Eng Teacher Depew Mid Sch 1972-; *ai:* Depew Mid Sch Acting Eng Dept Chm; Essay & Speech Adv Sertoma Essay, Chemical & Substance Abuse Comms; NCTE Promising Young Writers Evaluator for NY St; NCTE, AFT, NY St United Teachers; US Army Reserve Commanding Officer; Reserve Officers Assn; Depew Sch Dist Educator of Yr 1981-82; Nom NY St Teacher of Yr 1982; Whos Who in Amer Ed 1989-; *office:* Depew Mid Sch 5201 S Transit Rd Depew NY 14043

CARUSI, MARIA PIA, History Department Chair; *b:* Philadelphia, PA; *ed:* (BA) His, Cabrini Coll 1979; (MA) His, Villanova Univ 1981; *cr:* Summer Sch Instr Archdiocese of Phila Summer Sch WC/Roman Cath Center 1981-; 8th Grade Teacher St Donato Elem Sch 1982-87; His Teacher West Cath Girls HS 1987-88; His Dept Chair Gwynedd Mercy Acad 1988-; *ai:* Forensics Club Moderator Coach; Frosh Sr Class Picnic Faculty Spon; Sr Class Homeroom Moderator; NCSS 1987-; PA Cncl of Soc Stud 1988-; Phila Cncl of Soc Stud 1987-; PA Speech & Debate Assn 1987-; Phila Cath Forensics Leag (Pres 1986-88, IMM Past Pres 1988-); PA HS Speech Lg Dist 11 Chairperson 1990; PA HS Speech Lg Dist 10 Treas 1982-88; PA High Ed AA Grant Regional Cmptr Center; Temple Univ Cmptr for Elem Sch Teachers Course; Mathnet Course ArchDiocese of Phila & Chestnut Hill Coll; *office:* Gwynedd Mercy Acad Sumneytown Pike Gwynedd Valley PA 19437

CARUSO, CAROLYN THIBAULT, Religious Education Director; *b:* St Louis, MO; *m:* Joseph A.; *c:* Daniel, Anthony; *ed:* (BA) Comm Art, Univ of Dayton 1971; (BS) Elem Ed, Carroll Coll 1983; Grad Stud WI St Extension Whitewater, WI Eau Claire, Viterbo Coll; *cr:* 2nd Grade Teacher 1972-74, 1st-3rd Grade Lang Art Teacher 1974-76 Our Lady of Sorrows; 2nd/5th Grade Teacher St Mathias 1976-78; 5th/6th Grade Teacher St Anthonys on the Lake 1984-88; 7th Grade Teacher 1988-89, Dir of Religious Ed 1989- St John Vianney; *ai:* St Josephs Womans Auxiliary, Pewaukee Parents for Soccer; *office:* St John Vianney Elem Sch 17500 Gebhardt Brookfield WI 53005

CARUSO, PENNY M., Kindergarten Teacher; *b:* Jersey City, NJ; *m:* Emileo T.; *c:* Laura, Margo Murphy, Debra; *ed:* (BA) Early Chldhd Ed, Hunter Coll; (MA) Elem Ed, Adelphi Univ; Advanced Courses, Teaching Gifted & Talented; *cr:* K-1st Grade Teacher West Hempstead Public Schls; Nursery Sch Teacher Cmmty Church Nursery Sch; K-4th Grade Teacher Garden City Public Schls; *ai:* Early Chldhd Ed Cncl; Amer Assn Univ Women; Teachers Applying Whole Lang; Kappa Delta Pi Ed Honor Society; Mini Grant Whole Lang Philosophy, Teaching Through Cooking, Teaching Art & the Masters; *office:* Locust Street Sch Boylston & Locust Sts Garden City NY 11530

CARVER, ALAN CLARK, Government/Economics Teacher; *b:* Ft Sill, OK; *m:* Debra Sharon Marlowe; *ed:* (AA) Liberal Arts, Isothermal Comm Coll 1970-72; (BS) Poly Sci, 1972-74, (MA) Amer His, 1976-80 Appalachian St Univ; US Constitution Wkshps, UNC Asheville; Cmptr Classes, Appalachian St Univ; *cr:* Teacher/Coach/Adv East Rutherford HS 1975-; *ai:* Jr Civitan Adv; Girls & Boys Tennis Coach; East Rutherford Sch & Robert M Mc Nair Schlsp Comm; NC Soc Stud Cncl 1987-; NC Assn of Ed, NEA 1976-; Jr Civitan Adv 1976-, Adv of Yr 1982-83, 1985-87; East Rutherfords Most Popular Male Teacher 1977-88; Lancer Annual Dedication Recipient 1990; *office:* E Rutherford HS E High Dr Forest City NC 28043

CARVER, GARY LEE, 9th Grade Eng/Speech Teacher; *b:* Ft Benton, MT; *m:* Shirley Ann Stevenson; *c:* Brett A., Debra Carver O'Neil; *ed:* (BA) Eng/Span, Univ of MT 1963; Coe Coll, Carroll Coll, N MT Coll Havre, W MT Coll Dillon; *cr:* Eng/Span Teacher Power HS 196369; Eng/Span/Speech Teacher Kalispell Jr HS 1969-; *ai:* Stu Cncl Adv; Jr HS Ftbl & HS Asst Wrestling Coach; Curr & Composition Comm; MEA Pres 1963-66; NDEA Ed Grants 1966, 1968; Prof Magazine Articles; Sch Dist 5 Teacher of Yr 1984; Sch Bd Chm 1974-81; *home:* 2729 Foothill Rd Kalispell MT 59901

CARY, DEBRA MARIE (GRAMAN), Fifth Grade Teacher; *b:* Jasper, IN; *m:* William L.; *c:* Jessica M., Jacob W.; *ed:* (BS) Elem Ed, 1973, (MS) Elem Ed, 1978 IN St Univ; *cr:* 5th Grade Teacher S Knox Elem 1974-; *ai:* 5th Grade Chrldr Spon; Sch Advisory Comm; IN St Teachers Assn, NEA; Kappa Delta Pi 1973-; *home:* 1517 Bayou Vincennes IN 47591

CARY, THOMAS DAVID, Mathematics Department Chair; *b:* North Adams, MA; *m:* Diane; *c:* Christina M. Cary Cummings; *ed:* (BA) Math, 1970, (MS) Scndry Admin, 1975 N Adams Coll; *cr:* Math Ed Teacher Berlin Cntrl Schls 1970-; *ai:* Dept Chm; *office:* Berlin Cntrl Jr/Sr HS Rt 22 Cherry Plain NY 12040

CASABAL, MELECIA LUNA, Fourth Grade Teacher; *b:* Talisay, Philippines; *ed:* (BA) Elem Ed, 1952; (BA) Span, 1959; Natl Teachers Coll Manila, Philippines; (MA) Rdng, Clarke Coll 1979; Post Masters Studies Special Trng in Teaching Writing Through ST of IA Writing Project; *cr:* 2nd Grade Teacher Tondo Elem Manila, Philippines 1962-68; 6th Grade Teacher Calamus Comm Sch 1968-69; 4th Grade Teacher Cardinal Elem Sch 1969-82; 4th Grade Teacher Briggs Elem Sch 1982-; *ai:* Editor; Kid's Press (Elem Sch Newspaper); Maquoketa Ed Assn 1969-; IA ST Ed Assn 1969-; Natl Ed Assn 1969-; IA Cncl of Teachers of Eng 1980-; 9 Poems Published 1981-87; Silver Poet Awd 1986; Golden Poet Awd 1987; *home:* 609 South Fifth St Maquoketa IA 52060

CASADA, BETTY TUCKER, Math Teacher; *b:* Monticello, KY; *m:* Paul; *c:* Pamela, Edward; *ed:* (BS) Elem Ed, Cumberland Coll 1964; Elem Ed, 1984-85 Union Coll; *cr:* Teacher Pulaski and Wayne Cty 1957-66; 5th Grade Teacher 1967-89; Math Teacher 1989- Wayne Cty Elem; *ai:* 5th Grade Chairperson; Book Comm; Meadow Creek Baptist (Secy 1955-62 Clerk 1965); *home:* 516 Zion Rd Delta KY 42613

CASAGRANDE, JOHN E., Band Director/Music Dept Chm; *b:* Pen Argyl, PA; *m:* Jo Buckley; *c:* Scott, Tina; *ed:* (BS) Music Ed, 1963, (MS) Music Ed, 1967 Ithaca Coll; Hartt Coll of Music, Temple Univ, W Chester St Univ, Univ of VA, George Mason Univ; *cr:* Band Dir Ambler Jr HS 1963-68, E Stroudsburg HS 1968-78, Mt Vernon HS 1978-82, W T Woodson HS 1982-; *ai:* Marching & Pep Bands; Jazz Ensemble; Symphonic & Concert Band; Fairfax Cty Band Dir Assn Pres 1983-85; First Chair of America MAC Awd 1977; Amer Sch Band Dir Assn 1983-; St Chm for Adjudication PA; PMEA Notes; Citation for Teaching Excl Fairfax Cty Public Schls; Teacher of Yr 1989 W T Woodson HS; Outstanding Music Educator of PA 1978; *office:* W T Woodson HS 9525 Main St Fairfax VA 22031

CASANOVA, DAVID RALPH, Chemistry Teacher; *b:* San Antonio, TX; *ed:* (BS) Chem, St Marys Univ 1981; (MED) Supervision/Ed, Our Lady of Lake Univ 1987; Perspective Cath Admin Prgm; *cr:* 6th Grade Teacher St Pauls Cath Sch 1981-82; Chem Teacher Cntrl Cath Marianist HS 1982-; *ai:* Parents & Racquetball Club Moderator; Amer Chemical Society 1978-; *office:* Cntrl Cath Marianist HS 1403 N Saint Marys St San Antonio TX 78215

CASAS, JOHN THOMAS, Social Studies/History Teacher; *b:* Monterey, CA; *m:* Karen A.; *c:* Nicol; *ed:* (BA) Psych, CSU 1976; Cmptr Ed, Counseling, Electronics; *cr:* Soc Studies Teacher Salinas HS 1979-80; Pacific Grove HS 1980-81; Pacific Grove Continuation HS 1981-85; Soc Stud/His Teacher Pacific Grove Mid Sch 1985-; *ai:* Vlybll Coach; Knowledge Master Adv; Winter Wilderness Adv; Stage Crew Adv; PGTA (Treas 1987-88 Negotiator 1985-86); Monterey Bay Triathlon Club Secy 1986-87; Teachers Awd Pacific Grove Mid Sch 1989; *office:* Pacific Grove Mid Sch 835 Forest Ave Pacific Grove CA 93950

CASE, JEAN HAGANS, 4th Grade Teacher; *b:* Augusta, KS; *m:* Alex; *c:* Deborra Case Darrow, Diana Case Costello, Alex H.; *ed:* (BS) Human Ecology, KS St Univ 1951; Elem Ed, Tabor 1968; Pittsburg St, Wichita Univ, Emporia St Univ, Mc Pherson Coll, Butler Comm Jr Coll, KS St Univ, Fort Hays St Univ; *cr:* Kndgtn Teacher Hiawatha Elem 1951-52; 5th Grade Teacher 1969-88, 4th Grade Teacher 1988- Marion Elem; *ai:* Sci Curr & Prof Dev Comm; PEO Sisterhood Pres 1960-61; 20th Century Pres 1967-68; Amer Legion Auxiliary Pres 1961-62; Presbyn Church Ordained Elder; Delta Delta Delta; *home:* 110 N Lincoln St Marion KS 66861

CASE, MARY LYNN STEPHENS, English Teacher; *b:* Electra, TX; *m:* Donald Wayne; *c:* Mark S., Marian B.; *ed:* (BA) Psych/Eng, Univ of N TX 1959; *cr:* Eng Teacher J T Hutchinson Jr HS 1959-60; Eng/Rdng Teacher Handley Jr HS 1960-63; Eng Teacher Wedgwood Jr HS & Southwest HS 1967-70; Eng/Rdng/Psych Teacher Pampa HS 1970-; *ai:* Spon Red Cross Youth 1975-85; Delta Kappa Gamma Music Chm 1988-89; Panhandle Cncl Teachers of Eng (Secy 1987-88, Pres Elect 1988-89, Pres 1989-); Briarwood Full Gospel Church; Red Cross Cncl 1975-85; Concerned Women of America; Key Club & Keywanette Teacher of Yr 1980; *home:* 1921 Evergreen Pampa TX 79065

CASE, RHEA PARSONS, 8th Grade Eng Teacher/Dept Hd; *b:* Bethlehem, PA; *m:* Glenn L.; *ed:* (BS) Eng/Scdry Ed, Kutztown St Coll 1968; Addl Studies, PA St Univ; *cr:* Eng Teacher Wilson Area HS 1968-74; Philip F Lauer Mid Sch 1974-; *ai:* Teacher Adv Comm; Crisis Intervention Cncl; PA St Ed Assn 1968-; NEA 1968- Wilson Area Ed Assn (VP 1983-85 Building Rep 1982-); *home:* 808 E Mountain Ave Pen Argyl PA 18072

CASE, SUE SANDERS, Speech-Language Pathologist; *b:* Indianapolis, IN; *m:* Monte; *ed:* (BS) Speech Pathology/Audiology, Ball St Univ 1976; (MS) Speech Pathology, Univ of KY 1984; Post Grad Work Univ of KY; *cr:* Speech Pathologist Bracken Cty Schls 1976-89, Pendleton Cty Schls 1989-; *ai:* Pre-Sch Speech Lang Prgm; Curr Comm Responsible for Writing Speech Lang Curr; Amer Speech Lang Hearing Assn 1986-, Certificate of Clinical Competence 1986; KY Speech-Lang Hearing Assn Spch Sch Chm 1976-; Phi Delta Kappa 1988-; PTA 1989-; *home:* PO Box 263 Brooksville KY 41004

CASEY, BARBARA ANN (PEREA), Spanish Teacher; *b:* Las Vegas, NM; *m:* Frank J.; *ed:* (BA) Liberal Arts, 1972, (MA) Span, 1973 NM Highlands Univ; *cr:* Instr NM Highlands Univ 1972-74, NM Military Inst 1975-82; Teacher Robert H Goddard HS 1974-; *ai:* Span Club, Jr Class, Span Natl Honor Society Spon; Delta Kappa Gamma 1988-; Phi Kappa Phi 1971-; NM Endowment Hum (Bd Mem 1986-9), Service to Hum 1989; Amer Bus Women Secy 1982-; NEA Mem 1974-, Advocate of Yr 1986; Elected NM House of Rep 1984; Whos Who Among Hispanic Women Legislators 1989; *office:* Goddard HS PO Box 2667 Roswell NM 88202

CASEY, BETH BALDWIN, Director of Choirs; *b:* Houston, MS; *m:* Brian Dooley; *c:* Sean B.; *ed:* (BME) Music Ed, 1982, (MM) Choral Conducting, 1984 Sam Houston St Univ; TX Music Educators Conference Clinics; TX Choral Music Directors Clinic; *cr:* Private Voice Teacher Tomball Ind Sch Dist 1978-89; Dir of Choirs Spring Branch HS 1984-85, Brazosport HS 1985-; *ai:* Jr Class Spon; Cmmty Chours; Concert Chorale of Houston; Adjudicator; Voice Teacher 1978-; Vocal Clinician; Amer Choral Dir Assn, TX Music Educators Assn, TX Choral Dir Assn 1984-; Sigma Alpha Iota 1977-; Pi Kappa Lambda 1984-; Teacher of Month 1990; Whos Who Among Women in US; TCDA Chorus, Choral of Houston, SHSU Bands Soloist; *office:* Brazosport HS Drawer Z Freeport TX 77541

CASEY, BRENDA VAUGHN, Elementary Counselor; *b:* Ardmore, OK; *m:* Gerald; *c:* Breanna, Michael; *ed:* (BA) Elem Ed, OK St Univ 1969; (MS) Guidance & Counseling Northeastern St Univ 1976; Standard Certificate Admin; Northeastern St Univ; Trng of Trainers-Developing Capable Young People; *cr:* Teacher OK City Public Schls 1969-70; Great Falls Public Schls 1970-73; 1973-76; Cnslr 1976-; Owasso Public Schls; *ai:* Dir of Testing; Retention Comm; Career Comm; Red Ribbon Week Comm; OACD Pres NE Region 1980-82; Cnslr of Yr 1982-83; OSCA Pres 1983-84 Elem Schl of Yr 1984-85; PDK; *office:* Owasso Public Schls 12223 E 91st St Owasso OK 74055

CASEY, JOHN PATRICK, JR., Mathematics Teacher; *b:* Noblesville, IN; *c:* Susan L., Jane Casey Philbrook, Shawn Casey Morrison; *ed:* (BS) His/Math, Univ of S MS 1961; (MS) Intnl Affairs, George Washington Univ 1969; Natl War Coll 1969; Command & General Staff Coll 1965; *cr:* Brigadier General US Army 1951-79; Math Teacher Sara Scott Harllee Mid Sch 1980-; *ai:* PDK Mem 1984-; *office:* Harllee Mid Sch 6423 9th St E Bradenton FL 34208

CASEY, MARGARET AUSTINA, 8th Grade Teacher; *b:* Boston, MA; *ed:* (BS) Ed, St Elizabeth Coll 1953; (MA) Ed/Theology Teacher, Providence 1979.

CASEY, ROBIN BAHR, English/Journalism Teacher; *b:* Trenton, NJ; *m:* John R.; *c:* Lara R. Robbins; *ed:* (BA) Eng, Smith Coll 1964; (MAT) Eng/Ed, Fairleigh Dickinson Univ 1965; Grad Courses Rdng, Rdng Supervision, Dance Pedagogy, His; *cr:* Teacher Summit Jr HS 1964-67, Shrewwbury Sr HS 1976-78; Teacher/Dept Chairperson Bais Chana HS of Yeshiva Acad 1978-85; Teacher Holy Name Cntrl Cath HS 1986-; *ai:* Adv to Napoleon Sch Newspaper; NHS Faculty Cncl Mem; JEA, NCTE; NESPA Bd of Dir 1989-; Assn of MA Dance Ensemble (Bd of Dir 1979-84, Pres 1980-81); Ford Fnd Fellowship for Grad Degree; Dow Jones Fellowship for Summer Journalism Study; *office:* Holy Name Cntrl Cath HS 144 Granite St Worcester MA 01604

CASEY, TERRI LYNN, Mathematics Teacher; *b:* Tucson, AZ; *ed:* (BA) Math, Univ of VA 1985; *cr:* Math Teacher W Potomac HS 1985-; *ai:* Cheerleading Coach; NCTM 1984-85; Chi Omega Alumni Herald, Univ of VA Alumni 1985-; VSAF 1989-; *office:* W Potomac HS 6500 Quander Rd Alexandria VA 22307

CASH, ANNE PETERSON, Kindergarten Teacher; *b:* Clifton, KS; *m:* Robert J.; *c:* Sara; *ed:* (BS) Elem Ed, 1963-; (MS) Ed Admin, 1978 Univ of KS; *cr:* Elem Teacher Horton Elem Sch 1975-; *ai:* Delta Kappa Gamma 1980-.

CASH, DON M., Social Studies Teacher; *b:* Denver, CO; *m:* Ferryl I. Rush; *c:* Jared, Jesse, Janna; *ed:* (BA) Phys Ed, Graceland Coll 1970; (MSED) Scndry Admin, NW MO St Univ 1990; Certified Skills Adolescence Instr; *cr:* K-6th Grade Phys Ed Teacher Troy Grade Sch 1974-78; Soc Stud Teacher Troy Mid Sch 1982-; *ai:* Head HS Ftbl & Track Coach; Troy Ed Assn Head Negotiator 1986-; *office:* Troy Mid Sch 319 S Park Troy KS 66087

CASH, KATREKA FOWLER, 4th Grade Teacher; *b:* Berea, KY; *m:* Ronnie Dean; *c:* Lura; *ed:* (BS) Elem, 1977, (MA) Elem, 1979, Elem, 1981 Eastern KY Univ; *cr:* 1st Grade Teacher 1977-84, 4th Grade Teacher 1985 Livingston Elem Sch; *ai:* 4-H Adv; Guidance Comm; Handbook Comm; KY Assn; NEA; *home:* 65 Willow Ave Brodhead KY 40409

CASHWELL, JANICE ROGERS, Science Department Chair; *b:* Frankfort, Germany; *m:* Barry; *c:* Tara L., Jennifer L., Travis L.; *ed:* (BA) Ed, Meth Coll 1984; Certified 4th-9th Grade Area Sci & Math; Oceanograph Seminars Wkshps; *cr:* Teachers Asst 1977-80; Media Asst 1980-83 Lewis Chapel Jr HS; Teacher Spring Lake Jr HS 1984-; *ai:* Dept Chairperson; Legislators Sch Bd; Sch Base, Media Advisory Comm; Sch Chrldrs, Natl Sci & Technology Week Spon; NSTA; NC Sci Teachers Assn; 4-H Club Spon 1985-87, Cty Achievement Outstanding Club Project Awd 1987; Fayetteville Jr Womens League Grant; *office:* Spring Lake Jr HS 612 Spring Ave Spring Lake NC 28309

CASINI, LOUIS A., Band Director; *b:* Steubenville, OH; *ed:* (BFA) Applied Music, 1972; (MFA) Music Ed, 1974 Carnegie-Mellon Univ; Carnegie-Mellon Univ/WV Univ; *cr:* Band Dir Chester Jr HS 1972-; Instr West Liberty St Coll 1974; *ai:* Band; Jazz Band; St Graded Music Chm; St Jazz Ensemble Festival Chm; Regional Jazz Festival Chm; Phi Mu Alpha Sinfonia Pres 1970-72; B Reist Memorial Awd 1972; Phi Beta Mu Phi Kappa Phi St Chapter Pres 1987 Outstanding Band Dir of WV 1983; VP of WV Bandmasters Assn 1985-; WV Scndry Schls Act Commission Band Comm 1986-; Bands Selected As St Honor Groups 1981/1984/1986 & 1988; *home:* 1001 Neville St Follansbee WV 26037

CASLER, DEANNA VINCENT, Chapter I Supervising Teacher; *b:* Chariton, IA; *w:* Gene R. (dec); *c:* Kevin, Melissa; *ed:* (BS) Elem Ed/Eng, TX A&I Univ 1971; (MS) Elem Ed/Curr, Corpus Christi St Univ 1977; Prof Cert; Process Writing Wkshp; Teacher Expectation Stu Achievement Trng; *cr:* Elem Teacher 1960-61, Kndgtn Teacher, Elem Teacher 1962-83 Flour Bluff Ind Sch; Chapter I Supervising Teacher Flour Bluff Intermediate Sch 1984-; *ai:* At Risk Stu Supervising Teacher; Planning & Organizing Summer Sch; Essay & Oratory Judge Lugana Optimist Club; TX St Teachers Assn (Natl Rep 1975) 1971-; TX St Teachers Performing Outstanding Jobs General Dev of Stud 1974-75; PTA Treas 1972-75; Women of Moose (Treas 1984-85, Acad of Friendship Chm 1986-87); Outstanding Elem Teachers of Amer 1975; *home:* 205 Caribbean Corpus Christi TX 78418

CASNER, SHARON ADE, Math Instructor; *b:* Pana, IL; *m:* Larry R.; *c:* Tracy R., Melinda K.; *ed:* (BA) Scndry Math, Univ of IL 1964; (MS) Gifted Ed, Sangamon St Univ 1981; Certified Aerobics Instr; *cr:* Elem Teacher 1964-66, Math Instr 1966-, Coord of Gifted 1980- Pana CmmTy Schls; *ai:* Stu Cncl Adv; Delta Kappa Gamma St Comm; Intnl Society (Pres, Treas) 1982-; NEA, IL Ed Assn, Pana Ed Assn 1964-; Pana Music Boosters Club 1985-; Pana Sports Booster Club 1987-; Univ of IL Calculus Fellowship 1990; Lambda St Schlsp 1981; S IL Univ Mc Donnell Douglas Awd for Sci & Math Excl 1984; US Achievement Acad Advisory Bd for Math Excl; *office:* Pana Sr HS 201 W 8th Pana IL 62557

CASON, KIMBERLY, English/Drama/Debate Teacher; *b:* Columbus, GA; *m:* Phillip S.; *ed:* (BA) Eng/Lang Art, Auburn Univ 1987; (MS) Eng, Columbus Coll 1990; *cr:* Eng/Drama/Debate Teacher Jordan HS 1987-; *ai:* Jr Class & Prom Spon; Debate Team & Drama Club Coach; Kappa Delta Pi, GA Cncl Teachers of Eng, NCTE; *office:* Jordan HS 3200 Howard Ave Columbus GA 31995

CASON, MARIE MOORE, 2nd Grade Teacher; *b:* Decatur, AL; *c:* Ricky D., Deborah C. Cunningham, Connie C. Allen; *ed:* (BS) Elem Ed, St Bernard 1974; Addl Studies Early Chldhd A&M Univ; Spec Ed; UAB; Personal Dev WSCC; *cr:* Head Start Maid 1966; Head Start Aide 1967-69; Head Start Teacher 1969-75 Cullman Cty Head Start/Hanceville Sch; 2nd Grade Teacher Hanceville Elem Sch 1975-; *ai:* Ofcl Gate Keeper Varsity Ftbl; Varsity Bsktbl; Jr HS Ftbl; Jr HS Bsktbl; Vlybl; NEA 1968-; AL Ed Assn 1968-; Cullman Cty Ed Assn Faculty Rep 1987-88; Girl Scout Volunteer 1984-88; Hanceville Church of Christ Bible Class Teacher 1977-; Garden City Bsktbl Assn Reporter 1989- Plaque 1990; PTA VP 1977-78; PTA Pres 1978-79; PTA Treas 1979-80; Sch Improvement Comm 1988-89; *home:* 306 Linda Warren Cir Hanceville AL 35077

CASPER, ANNABELLE DE VRIES, Substitute Teacher; *b:* Green City, MO; *w:* Vincent F. (dec); *c:* William T.; *ed:* (BS) Elem Ed, 1969, (MS) Rdng Teacher, 1972 NE MO St Univ; Manitoba Teachers Coll 1963-64; *cr:* 4th Grade Teacher Wheeling Elem 1965-66; 2nd Grade Teacher Brashear Elem 1967-72; 3rd Grade Teacher 1972-88, K-6th Grade Substitute Teacher 1988- Lewis Cty C-1 Schls; *ai:* MO St Teachers Assn, MO Retired Teachers Assn, NTCM; PTO.

CASPER, CAROL STAATS, Language Art Classroom Teacher; *b:* Wilmington, DE; *c:* Aleksandra, Mary P.; *ed:* (BA) Art His, Univ of DE 1971; MD Writing Project, Washington Coll 1984; *cr:* Classroom Teacher Bohemia Manor HS 1978-; *ai:* Stu Helping Other People Adv; Washington Coll Stu Teacher Prgm Cooperating Teacher; NEA, MD St Teachers Assn, Cecil Cty Classroom Teachers Assn 1978-; Boosters Club 1986-; Chesapeake City Civic Assn 1973-; GSA Cncl 200 Troop 999 1989-; Chesapeake City PTA 1981-; MD Hum Cncl G651L 1989-; Young Cecil Cty Scholars Prgm; *office:* Bohemia Manor Jr/Sr HS 2755 Augustine Herman Hwy Chesapeake City MD 21915

CASPER, LYNN DEE (HULLINGER), Womens Phys Ed Teacher; *b:* Columbus, OH; *c:* Derek, Darci; *ed:* (BS) Phys Ed, Univ of Indianapolis 1975; (MS) Phys Ed, Ball St Univ 1981; Cpmtr Programming, Ivy Tech Kokomo 1985; Nursing Sch, IN Univ Kokomo; *cr:* Womens Phys Ed Instr 1975-, Soph Health Instr 1976- Peru HS; *ai:* Drama Asst; Tigerettes Spon; Concessions Mgr; NEA, IN St Teachers Assn 1976-; Peru Cmmty Ed Assn Secy 1988-; Sigma Delta Phi Secy 1980-81; *office:* Peru HS 401 N Broadway Ave Peru IN 46970

CASSADY, BARBARA HUTCHINSON, First Grade Teacher; *b:* Savannah, GA; *c:* Linc, Courtney; *ed:* (BS) Elem Ed, Troy St Univ 1971; *cr:* 1st Grade Teacher Mixon Elem 1971-72; Chapter I Rdng Teacher Sanford Elem 1972-73; 1st/2nd Grade Combination Teacher Blue Springs Elem 1973-74; 1st Grade Teacher East Tallassee Primary 1974-; *ai:* Prof Dev & Faculty Advisory Comm; Tallassee Ed Assn 1974-; AL Ed Assn, NEA 1971-; Athene Womens Club 1974-77; Talisi Womens Club 1986-; *office:* East Tallassee Primary Sch 3 Freeman Ave East Tallassee AL 36078

CASSADY, DARLEEN HAIL, Third Grade Teacher; *b:* Buckeye, AZ; *m:* Don R.; *c:* Bob C., Dee C., Christie Cassady Ramsey; *ed:* (BS) Elem Ed, NE OK St Univ 1972; *cr:* 3rd Grade Teacher Muldrow Elem Sch 1972-; *ai:* OEA Building Rep; OK Ed Assn, NEA 1972-; *home:* PO Box 390 Muldrow OK 74948

CASSADY, LINDA E., Social Studies Teacher; *b:* Philadelphia, PA; *m:* Charles D.; *ed:* (BS) His/Government, E Stroudsburg Univ 1970; (MA) Ed/His, Beaver Coll 1982; PA St, Bloomsburg, Beaver; *cr:* HS Teacher Upper Moreland Jr HS 1970-; *ai:* Girls Hockey, Tennis, Bsktbl Coach; Core Team Mem Stu Asst Team; NCSS; Upper Moreland Ed Assn Secy 1986-; *office:* Upper Moreland HS 150 Terwood Rd Willow Grove PA 19090

CASSARA, CRICKET F., 4th/5th Grade Science Teacher; *b:* Miami, FL; *:* Samuel J.; *c:* Regina, Nicholas; *ed:* (AA) Ed, Miami-Dade Jr Coll 1971; (BA) Ed, FL Atlantic Univ 1973; Numerous Courses; *cr:* 6th Grade Teacher Gifford Mid Sch 1973-79; 5th Grade Teacher Osceola Elem 1979-82; Sci Teacher Cartersville Mid Sch 1982-86; 4th/5th Grade Sci Teacher Citrus Elem Sch 1986-; *ai:* Sci, Sci Fair, Earth Day Activity Coord; Sci Summer Inst Trainer; Indian River Cty Rdng Cncl Publicity 1986-, Nominee Rdng Teacher of Yr 1990; FL Assn of Sci Teachers 1987-; Elk Auxiliary, Audubon Society, Save the Manatee Club; Finalist Teacher of Yr 1990; Nominee Presidential Awd of Excl 1990; Wrote Elem Sci Curr Guide Indian River Cty 1990; *home:* 485 36th Ave Vero Beach FL 32968

CASSART, IRENE CHAMBERLAIN, 6th Grade Teacher; *b:* Niagara Falls, NY; *m:* Leonard L.; *c:* Lawrence, Leonard, David, James, Leslie; *ed:* (BS) Exceptional Ed, SUNY 1971; (MS) Ed, SUNY 1976; Post Masters Studies Ed; *cr:* 6th Grade Teacher Starpoint Central Sch 1971-; *ai:* Instructional Cncl; NY St United Teachers; AFT; Starpoint Teachers Assn Schlsp Chairperson; Starpoint PTA; Starpoint Teachers Federal Credit Union Treas 1974-; Soc Sci Awd Niagara Cty Comm Coll; Whos Who Among Stud Amer Jr Coll 1968-69; Conservation Educator Awd - 1977 Niagara Cty Fed Conservation Clubs; *office:* Starpoint Central Sch 4363 Mapleton Rd Lockport NY 14094

CASSETTARI, NANETTE, Science Teacher; *b:* Oak Park, IL; *m:* Thomas; *ed:* (BA) Phys Ed, Northeastern Univ Chicago 1972; *cr:* Sci Teacher, James Giles School 1973-; *ai:* Dance Club; NSTA; Nom Golden Apple; Pres Nom, Sci; *home:* 453 Harvest Lane Roselle IL 60172

CASSIDY, JOHN FRANCIS, Math Teacher; *b:* Tarrytown, NY; *ed:* (BSED) Math, West Chester Univ 1987; SUNY-NEW PALTZ; *cr:* Permanent Sub Math Teacher Peekskill HS 1987-88; Math Teacher Franciscan HS 1988-; *ai:* Jr Class Adv; Ftbl Coach; Bsktbl Coach; Lacross Coach; Model Building Club Adv; *office:* Franciscan H S Lexington Ave Mohegan Lake NY 10547

CASSIDY, JUDITH WARD, English Teacher; *b:* Blytheville, AR; *m:* Jeff L.; *ed:* (BSE) Eng, AR St Univ 1985-89; *cr:* 10th-12th Grade Eng/Journalism Teacher Weiner HS 1989-; *ai:* Jr Class, Journalism, Newspaper Spon; Lambda Iota Tau 1985-87; *office:* Weiner HS P O Drawer 408 Weiner AR 72479

CASSIDY, ROBERT MARK, History/Phys Ed Teacher; *b:* Las Vegas, NM; *m:* Geri Geoffrion; *c:* Jason, Craig; *ed:* (BA) Phys Ed/Health/Soc Sci, NM Highlands Univ 1981; Phys Ed/His, NM Inst of Mining & Technology; His/Phys Ed/Spec Ed, NM Highlands Univ; *cr:* Teacher Magdalena Municipal Schls 1982-85, Mora Ind Sch Dist 1985-; *ai:* Sr Class Spon; Head Bsktbl & Bsbl Coach; Soc Stud Chm; NM Cncl for Soc Stud, NM HS Coaches Assn Mem 1985-; Natl Fed of Coaches Mem 1989-; Selected 1 of 20 Amer to Participate Australian-Amer Amateur Bsktbl League 1980-; *office:* Mora HS PO Box 179 Mora NM 87732

CASSIDY-SMITH, MARY ELIZABETH, Second Grade Teacher; *b:* Boston, MA; *ed:* (BS) Elem Ed, Univ of MA 1967; (MS) Spec Ed, Southern CT St Univ 1972; Diploma 1978; Inst of Childrens Literature; Masters Diploma 1979 6th Year Degree Prgm; *cr:* 1st Grade Teacher 1967-80; 1st/2nd Grade Teacher Rollover Prgm 1980-86; 2nd Grade Teacher 1986-Guilford Lakes Sch; *ai:* Delta Kappa Gamma 1974-; VP 1980-81; Pres 1981-83; Negotiator 1979, 1981-83; 1989 Guilford Ed Assn; *office:* Guilford Lakes Elem Sch Maupas Rd Guilford CT 06437

CASTANEDA, ARMANDO, Fifth Grade Teacher/Chair; *b:* Laredo, TX; *m:* Guadalupe Ortega; *c:* Erica A., Migual A., Laura F.; *ed:* (AA) Liberal Art, Laredo Jr Coll 1972; (BS) Elem Ed, TX A&I Univ 1974; *cr:* Teacher Zapata Ind Sch Dist 1975, Dallas Ind Sch Dist 1975-77, Laredo Ind Sch Dist 1977-; *ai:* Sci Fair Sch Coord; UIL Rdng Coach; *office:* C M Mac Donell Elem Sch 1606 Benavides Laredo TX 78040

CASTEEL, NANCY KAY (HENDRIX), Fourth Grade Teacher; *b:* Grand Island, NE; *m:* Paul Arthur; *ed:* (BA) Ed, 1980, (MS) Ed, 1987 Kearney St; *cr:* 5th Grade Teacher 1980-85, 4th Grade Teacher 1985- Seedling Mile; *ai:* After Sch Vlybl & Track Coach; Sch Improvement Team Facilitator; Phi Delta Kappa; NEA, NE St Ed Assn, Grand Island Ed Assn; Alpha Delta Kappa (Chaplain 1986-88, Secy 1988-, Historian 1990-); *office:* Seedling Mile Elem Sch 3208 E Seedling Mile Grand Island NE 68801

CASTELLANO, JOSEPH PHILIP, English Teacher; *b:* Brooklyn, NY; *m:* Mary C. Mc Hale; *ed:* (BA) Eng, Univ of VA 1978; (MA) Eng, Columbia Univ 1983; Working Toward PhD Eng, City Univ of NY; *cr:* Eng Teacher St Marys HS 1980-81, Arch Molloy HS 1981-82, St Francis Preparatory 1983-; *ai:* Sch Moderator Amensty Intnl; Cartooning Club; Chrstn Awakening Retreat Prgm; NHS Selection Comm 1989; NCTE 1985-; MLA 1987-; Whos Who in Amer Ed 1990; *office:* St Francis Preparatory Sch 6100 Francis Lewis Blvd Fresh Meadows NY 11365

CASTELLUCCI, JOSEPH ALEXANDER, Social Studies Teacher; *b:* Philadelphia, PA; *m:* Diane Rykaczewski; *ed:* (BS) Scndry Ed, Penn St Univ 1985; *cr:* Soc Stud Teacher Marlboro HS 1985-; *ai:* Boys & Girls Winter & Girls Spring Track Coach; Life Discussion Peer Counseling Group Leader; US His, Anthropology, Ec Geography Curr Dev Comm; NJ Ed Assn 1985-; Cape May Beach Patrol Benevolent Assn Trustee 1979-; *office:* Marlboro HS Rt 79 Marlboro NJ 07746

CASTER, JUNE A JONES, Third Grade Teacher; *b:* Las Cruces, NM; *c:* Paul R. Jr., Valinda Moore, Tawnya; *ed:* (BS) Ed, Univ Albuquerque 1964; NMSU 1966; ENMU 186-89; Southwest TX St 1976; *cr:* 3rd Grade Teacher Lavaland Sch 1964, Mesilla Park 1964-74, Espanola 1974-75; 3rd/4th Grade Teacher Prin Hunt ISD 1975-77; 3rd Grade Teacher Carrizozo 1978-; *ai:* NEA; NMEA; Alpha Delta Kappa 1985-89; *office:* Carrizozo Schls P O Box 99 Carrizozo NM 88301

CASTILLO, BEATRICE, Third Grade Bilingual Teacher; *b:* Harlingen, TX; *ed:* (BA) Elem Ed, Pan Amer Coll 1973; Working Toward Masters Bi-ling Ed; *cr:* Teacher Harlingen Sch Dist 1975-76, Mission Sch Dist 1976-78, Dallas Ind Sch Dist 1979-; *ai:* NEA; Teacher of Yr; *home:* PO Box 190983 Dallas TX 75219

CASTILLO, GEORGE S., 5th Grade Math/Sci Teacher; *b:* Los Angeles, CA; *m:* Teresa Cerda; *c:* Melissa, Yliana; *ed:* (AA) Ed, S W TX Jr Coll 1977; (BS) Sci Elem Ed, Laredo St Univ 1980; *cr:* 6th-8th Grade Math Teacher Sterling Fly Jr HS 1980-81; 4th/5th Grade Math/Sci Teacher Benito Juarez Elem 1981-; *ai:* Ftbl, Bsktbl, Track Coach HS Division; UIL Dir Elem, Spon for Number Sense; Crystal City Ind Sch Dist Math Comm; Math/Sci Dept Chm; NEA, TX St Teacher Assn; Crystal City Outdoor Sportsman Club, Little League Assn; *office:* Benito Juarez Elem Sch 805 E Crockett St Crystal City TX 78839

CASTILLO, GERMAN, Assistant Principal; *b:* Brownsville, TX; *m:* Lydia Molina; *c:* German Jr., Javier, Luis; *ed:* (MED) Admin, 1988, (BBA) Management, 1980 UT PAUB; *cr:* Asst Mgr K-Mart Corporation 1980; Math Teacher 1982-89, Asst Prin 1989- Faulk Intermediate Sch; *ai:* NASSP Mem 1989-; ATPE Mem 1987-; *office:* Faulk Intermediate Sch 2200 Roosevelt St Brownsville TX 78520

CASTILLO, ISRAEL, Health & PE Teacher; *b:* Harlingen, TX; *m:* Barbara Joyce Taylor; *c:* Jennifer K., Jeremy I.; *ed:* (BA) Health/Phys Ed/Span, 1979, (MS) Health/Phys Ed/Span, 1981 East TX St Univ; Driver Instr Supvr; USTA Umpire, Linesman, Referee; AAT in Tennis Coaching John Newcombes Tennis Camp 1985-; *cr:* Asst Tennis Coach Men Team 1979-81, Health/Phys Ed Teacher/Tennis Coach 1981-83 East TX St Univ; Health/Phys Ed Teacher/Tennis Coach Mc Allen HS 1983-; *ai:* Mc Allen Parks & Recreation Tennis Instr/Supvr 1983-; Mc Allen HS Tennis Coach 1983-; TTA Schlsp Comm Mem 1987-89; Tennis Coaches Assn Region /IV VP 1987-89; Tn Tennis Coaches Assn Secy & Treas 1989-91; TTA E & R Comm Mem 1987-; South TX Tennis Coaches Assn Tres 1984-86; Coach of Yr 1984-85; GSTTCA; Calvary Baptist Mc Allen Mem 1984-; Los Vecnios Baptist Chapel Mem 1972-75; Youth Group Pres 1972-75; Span Interpreter Youth Baptist Ministry in Mexico; South TX Tennis Coaches Assn; Coach of Yr 1984-85; TX Level Two Teach R 1985-; *office:* Mc Allen H S 2021 La Vista Mc Allen TX 78501

CASTILLO, SHARLENE URAKAWA, English Teacher; *b:* Lihue, HI; *m:* Alfred; *c:* Marc, Christine, Bradley; *ed:* (BA) Ed/Eng, Univ of HI 1967; Prof Teaching Cert, San Francisco St Univ 1968; *cr:* Eng Teacher Radford HS 1968-; *ai:* Former Adv of Future Teachers of America, Youth for Christ; HI St Teachers Assn 1970-; *office:* Radford HS 4361 Salt Lake Blvd Honolulu HI 96818

CASTLE, JAMES LANGLEY, Biology Teacher; *b:* Winchester, KY; *m:* Ann Hunter; *ed:* (BS) Bio, 1975, (MS) Ed/Bio 1985 E KY Univ; *cr:* Bio Teacher Owensboro 9/10 Center 1975-76, George Rogers Clark HS 1976-; *ai:* Faculty Spon & Adv; Martial Arts Club; Sci Curr Comm; 2nd Place Teacher of Yr 1976-77; *office:* George Rogers Clark HS 611 Boone Ave Winchester KY 40391

CASTLEBERRY, JIM A., Sixth Grade Teacher; *b:* Albuquerque, NM; *m:* Pam Shine; *c:* Jimmie, Jeanette, Polly; *ed:* (BA) Phys Ed, Pacific Luth Univ 1963; *cr:* 7th/8th General Sci Teacher Raymond HS 1964; US/WA St His Teacher Montesano HS 1965-67; 6th Grade Teacher Jason Lee Elem 1968-; *ai:* Richland HS Asst Bsktbl Coach; Richland Ed Assn.

CASTO, DIANE WILLIAMSON, Eighth Grade Reading Teacher; *b:* La Porte, IN; *m:* Edward; *c:* Anthony, Dana, Andrew, Denee; *ed:* (BA) Elem Ed, 1972, (MS) Ed, 1973 Purdue Univ; Liberaton Psych Trng; *cr:* 3rd Grade Teacher 1973-77, 6th Grade Teacher 1977-83 Crichfield Elem; 7th Grade Teacher Boston Jr HS 1983-84; 8th Grade Teacher Boston Mid Sch 1984-; *ai:* Pom Pon & Chrldr Spon; Girls Bsktbl Coach; *office:* Boston Mid Sch 1000 Harrison St La Porte IN 46350

CASTRO, LUIS ALFONSO, Spanish Teacher; *b:* Cartago V, Colombia; *m:* M. Eucaris; *c:* Sebastian, Victoria; *ed:* (BA) Spanish, Notre Dame Coll 1982; *cr:* Spanish Teacher Stevens HS 1982-85; Milford Area HS 1985-; *ai:* Eng 2nd Lang Dist Comm Mem; *home:* 59 Gem Dr Manchester NH 03103

CASTRO, ROBERTO GARCIDUENAS, Vice Principal; *b:* Pomona, CA; *m:* Cherri L.; *c:* Linda, Roberto; *ed:* (BA) His - Summa Cum Laude, Bethany Bible Coll 1981; Assertive Discipline, Coll of Notre Dame 1987; Various Cmptr Courses, Sonoma St Univ 1983-84; *cr:* Vice Prin/Jr HS Teacher Marin Chrstn Life Sch 1981-; *ai:* Stu Body Adv; Girls Bsktbl Coach; Delta Epsilon Chi; City of Novato Youth Service Awd 1981-; *home:* 31 George St Cotati CA 94931

CASTRO, SUSAN L., Teacher; *b:* Columbus, OH; *m:* Paul F.; *c:* Jeffrey S.; *ed:* (BA) Eng, 1968, (MA) Ed/Lang Art, 1987 Marycrest Coll; Eng Cert, St of IA; Permanent Prof Certificate; *cr:* Teacher J B Young Jr HS 1968-69, Cedar Grove Jr HS, Bettendorf Mid Sch 1971-; *ai:* Mid Sch Assessment, Senator Maggie Tinsmans Educl Advisory, Bettendorf Sch Dist Goals & Dev Comm; Bettendorf Teachers Assn (Rep Various Yrs, Learson Comm Mem 1988-89) 1989-; Senator Maggie Tinsmans Educl Advisory Comm Mem 1989-; Scott Cty Human Society Mem 1988-; Connie Belin Fellowship Univ of IA 1989; Natl Gifted & Talented Prgm; Scott Cty Teacher of Yr 1990; *office:* Bettendord Mid Sch 2030 Middle Rd Bettendorf IA 52722

CASTRO, VICTOR S., Industrial Arts Teacher; *b:* San Juan, PR; *m:* Zoraida Emmanuelli; *c:* Ricardo S., Yamayra; *ed:* (BA) Industrial Ed, Trenton St 1978; AAS Electronics Technician, Burlington Cty 1973; *cr:* Industrial Art Teacher Eisenhower Mid Sch 1978-79, Bordentown Reg HS 1979-80, Antilles Consolidated Sch System 1980-; *ai:* Sr Class Spon; Dept Chm; Bsktbl Coach; ASCD; AVA; Little League (Spokesperson 1988-89, Coach 1987-) Certificate Champs 1987; *office:* Antilles HS Ft Buchanan San Juan PR 00934

CASWELL, JOSEPHINE LAUTERIA, Reading Teacher; *b:* Wellington, England; *m:* Bruce B.; *ed:* (BA) Eng, 1971, (MED) Rdng, 1975 Univ of Cntrl FL; *cr:* Eng Teacher Colonial HS 1971-72; Eng/Rdng Teacher Ocoee Jr/Sr HS 1972-84; Rdng Teacher Liberty Mid Sch 1984-; *office:* Liberty Mid Sch 3405 S Chickasaw Trl Orlando FL 32829

CASWELL, TED C., Science Department Chairman; *b:* Atlanta, GA; *m:* Carolyn Robinson; *c:* Lauren, Toby, Jennifer; *ed:* (BS) Bio, Emory 1968; (MAT) Chem Ed, 1973, (EDS) Sci Ed, 1975 GA St Univ; Cmptr Programming, West GA Coll 1982; NSF Project Physics, Emory 1978; *cr:* Chem Teacher College Park HS 1969-74; Sci Dept Chm/Chem/Physics Teacher Milton HS 1974-; *ai:* Instr Fulton Cty Staff Dev Cmptr Courses 1980-, Adult Cmmty Ed Cmptr Courses 1985-; NSTA, GSTA, Prof Assn of GA Educators, League of Fulton Cty Ind Educators; Star Teacher 1987, 1990; *office:* Milton HS 86 School Dr Alpharetta GA 30201

CATALINICH, JAMES MARK, History Teacher; *b:* Seattle, WA; *ed:* (BA) Poly Sci, Univ of Puget Sound 1974; (JD) Univ of Puget Sound Sch of Law 1982; Univ of Puget Sound, Pacific Luth Univ; *cr:* Teacher Tacoma Sch Dist 1975-78, Kent Sch Dist 1978-79; Law Firm of Manza Moceri P S 1988-89; Teacher Tacoma Sch Dist 1980-; *ai:* Ftbl, Track, Jr Achievement, Discipline Comm; WA St Bar Assn, ASCD, NCEA, NEA, WA Ed Assn, Tacoma Ed Assn, Tacoma Coaches Assn; Pierce Cty Assn of Cath Educators; PACE Salary & Curr Commissions; St Patrick Sch (Endowment Steering Comm, Parent Club Pres); Tacoma Cmmty Dev & Natural Systems Comms; Amer His Wkshp Freedoms Fnd; *office:* Mason Mid Sch 2812 N Madison Tacoma WA 98406

CATANESO, JAMES J., Social Studies Teacher; *b:* Los Angeles, CA; *m:* Pamela D.; *c:* Kristen, Kena, Cataneso; *ed:* (AA) Liberal Art, Victor Valley Coll 1975; (BA) Soc Sci, CA St Univ San Bernardino 1977; (MA) Ed/Admin, Azus a Pacific Univ 1990; CA Teaching Credential; Scndry Single Subject Soc Sci 1984; CA St Univ San Bernardino; *cr:* Teacher Our Lady of the Desert Sch 1981-84, Hesperia Jr HS 1985-86, Apple Valley HS 1987-; *ai:* Academic Decathlon Coach Apple Valley HS; Selected Teacher of Yr Awd Presentation Hesperia Jr HS 1986; *office:* Apple Valley HS 11837 Navajo Rd Apple Valley CA 92307

CATANIA, ROGER, History/Government Teacher; *b:* Scarsdale, NY; *ed:* (BA) His, St Univ NY at Binghamton 1984; (MA) Teaching, Manhattanville Coll 1986; *cr:* Teacher The Ascension Sch 1986, Gilchrist HS 1986-; *ai:* Bsktbl Coach; NEH Fellowship Combined Study His, Literature.

CATCHINGS, SHIRLEY ANDERSON, English Teacher; *b:* Goodman, MS; *m:* Troy; *c:* Alisa Catchings Carson; *ed:* (BS) Eng, 1964, (MAT) Eng, 1973 Jackson St Univ; *cr:* Eng Teacher North Vaiden HS 1964-66, Coahoma Ag HS 1966-; *ai:* Tiger Star Newspaper Spon; Chairperson 5 Yr Study for SACS; NEA, MS Educators Assn 1964-; Coahoma Cty Educators Assn 1966-; Zeta Phi Beta (Treas, Cotillion Chairperson) 1975-, Service Awd 1982, 1984; Teacher of Yr 1974-75, 1988-89; Teacher of Month 1989, 1990; *office:* Coahoma Ag HS Rt 1 Box 616 Clarksdale MS 38614

CATE, ALFRED B., JR., American History Teacher/Coach; *b:* Athens, TN; *m:* Mary Kathelene Francis; *c:* Al III, Anne E., Janet K.; *ed:* His/Poly Sci, Vanderbilt Univ 1957-61; (BS) His/Poly Sci, 1964, (MA) Latin Amer His, 1971 Memphis St Univ; Infantry Officer Candidate Sch Fort Benning GA 1966; Fort Benning Airborne Sch 1966; *cr:* Teacher/Coach 1968-, Athletic Dir 1973- Cntrl HS; *ai:* Spon Letter Club, Honor Society, Stu Cncl; Head Coach Ftbl 1971-, Bsbl 1973-, Bsktbl 1971-73, Tennis 1968-73; Athletic Dir 1973-; Amer Legion Bsbl Coach 1973-; TN Athletic Coaches Assn Bd of Dir 1985-, Dist Coach of Yr 1983, 1986; Memphis Ed Assn, TN Ed Assn, NEA 1968-; Natl Ftbl Hall of Fame Ftbl Coaches Awd 1986-, Rex Coach Awd 1986; Freedom Fnd Valley Forge, George Washington Natl Teaching Awd 1977; Ben Franklin Ins Natl Coaching Awd 1987; Facing His 1989; *home:* 4733 Gloria Memphis TN 38116

CATES, GRACE WILLIAMS, Fifth Grade Teacher; *b:* Edgewood, TX; *m:* Stewart L.; *c:* Mark, Paul; *ed:* (BA) Elem Ed, 1966, (MS) Lib Sci, 1969 E TX St Univ; *cr:* 1st-5th Grade Teacher Edgewood Ind Sch Dist 1966-; *ai:* Picture Memory & Story Telling Univ Interscholastic League Coach; Delta Kappa Gamma Research Chm 1971-; *home:* PO Box 209 Edgewood TX 75117

CATES, NANCY BARTHOLOMEW, Teacher; *b:* Warrensburg, MO; *m:* Hosea Carl; *c:* Regina Barton, Jeffrey; *ed:* (BSE) Elem Ed, SW MO St Univ 1980; (MSE) Elem Ed, AR St Univ 1986; *cr:* Eng Teacher Alton R-4 1981-; *ai:* Jr HS Chrldr Spon; Spelling Bee Coord; Jr HS Quiz Bowl Spon; Prof Dev Comm; Mentor Teacher; Cmmty Teachers Assn (Secy, Treas) 1988-; *home:* PO Box 127 Alton MO 65606

CATES, PATRICK, English Department Chair; *b:* Crowell, TX; *m:* Deb; *c:* Christopher; *ed:* (BA) Theatre, 1975, (BSED) Drama/Eng Ed, 1976, (MED) Eng Ed, 1982 TX Tech; Natl Leadership Trng Inst for Gifted & Talented Ed 1988; *cr:* Drama Dir 1976-82, Eng Teacher 1979-87, Eng Dept Chm 1987- Lubbock HS; *ai:* NHS Spon; Lubbock Cty & Regional Spelling Bee Pronouncer 1979-; Lit Text, Composition Text, Curr Guide Dist Wide Comm; NCTE 1978-; Lubbock Classroom Teachers Assn Public Relations Chm 1983-84; NEH Summer Seminars for Sch Teachers 1989; Bowdoin Coll Text & Performance; *office:* Lubbock HS 2004 19th Lubbock TX 79401

CATES, TERESA JILL, Biology/Chemistry Teacher; *b:* Johnson City, TN; *m:* Rick; *ed:* (BS) Bio, 1974, (MS) Bio, 1978 E TN St Univ; (AS) Chem Technology, Tri-Cities St Tech 1988; Gas Chromatograph Certified Operator; *cr:* Job Placement Coord Carter Cty Schls 1978-81; Teacher Valley Forge Elem 1981-82; Sci/Bio/Chem Teacher 1982-86, Bio/Chem Teacher 1986- Unaka HS; *ai:* NHS Co-Spon; Sr Class Spon; Prom Comm; NEA, TN Ed Assn, Carter Cty Ed Assn Mem 1983-; *office:* Unaka HS Rt 10 Box 3075 Elizabethton TN 37643

CATHEY, JACQUELINE WATSON, Physical Education Teacher; *b:* Birmingham, AL; *m:* Marvin Dennis Sr.; *c:* Marvin D. Jr.; *ed:* (BS) Health/Phys Ed, TN St Univ 1970; Guidance & Counseling, TN St Univ; Elem Ed, Belmont Coll 1984; *cr:* Phys Ed Teacher Dunham Elem ScH 1970-71; Health Teacher Kennard Jr HS 1972-73; Substitute Teacher/Homemaker Nashville 1973-76; 6th Grade/Phys Ed Teacher Roy Waldron Jr HS 1977-; *ai:* Chrldr Spon; Sch Dance Troupe; NEA; TN Ed Assn; Rutherford Cty Ed Assn; Delta Sigma Theta 1980-; *home:* 385 Strasser Dr Nashville TN 37211

CATLETT, MARCELINE ROLLINS, Admin Asst/6th Grade Teacher; *b:* Fredericksburg, VA; *m:* Victor M.; *ed:* (BS) Elem Ed, VA St Univ 1981; (ME) Elem Ed, Univ of VA 1986; Madeline Hunter; Operation Aware; *cr:* 6th Grade Teacher 1981-; Admin Asst 1989- Walker Grant Mid Sch; *ai:* James Farmer Scholar Spon; Stu CO-OP Assn Spon; Parent Adv Comm; Phi Delta Kappa 1989-; Delta Kappa Gamma 1986-; Fredericksburg Ed Assn Treas 1981-; Delta Sigma Theta Pres 1979; Miss Delta Sigma Theta 1980; Rappahannock Rdng Cncl 1988-; Fredericksburg Host Lioness Club Dir 1988-; Fredericksburg Teacher of Month Sept 1985; Outstanding Young Educator Fredericksburg Jaycees 1988; Fredericksburg Incentive Teaching Awd 1989; *home:* 316 Wolfe St Fredericksburg VA 22401

CATON, JOAN HINRICHS, English Teacher; *b:* Harvey, IL; *m:* Douglas R.; *c:* Matthew, Ross; *ed:* (BA) Eng Ed, Capital Univ 1971; (MA) Lang/Lit, Governor St Univ 1976; General Admin Cert Educl Admin, N IL Univ 1990; Post Grad Stud City of London Polytechnic London England; *cr:* Stu Teacher Eastmoor Sr HS 1971; Eng Instr Coll of Du Page 1978-88; Eng Teacher Reavis HS 1971-; Admin Internship Naperville Cntrl HS 1990; *ai:* Directed All-Sch Musical; Speech Tournament Judge; Originated Designed & Planned 6 Sr Medieval Banquets; NCTE Curr Review, ASCD Mem, IL Assn of Teachers of Eng Mem 1988-; Amer Assn of Univ Women Mem 1978-87; Cncl for Basic Ed/Natl Endowment Ind Study Fellow 1988; Teacher for IL St Univ Natl Endowment Hum Inst 1988; Published Article from NEH Inst 1989; *home:* 322 Oak St Elmhurst IL 60126

CATT, RICHARD K., 6th Grade Teacher/Gr Level Chm; *b:* La Crosse, WI; *m:* Sheila Malone; *c:* Sarah, Rachel; *ed:* (BS) Health/Recreation 1974, (MA) Ed Admin 1982 Central MI Univ; *cr:* Teacher Ludington Area Schls 1975-; *ai:* MHSAA Registered Bsktbl Ofcl; *office:* Ludington Area Schls Anderson Ludington MI 49431

CAUDLE, CORNELIA GADDY, 1st Grade Teacher; *b:* Wadesboro, NC; *m:* William Nelson; *c:* Jeff, Lisa Mitchell, Marty; *ed:* (AA) Assoc of Arts, Wingate Coll 1961; (BA) Elem Ed, Pfeiffer 1964; (MA) Rdng, Appalachian St Univ 1977; *cr:* 2nd Grade Teacher Marshville Elem 1964-70; 3rd Grade Teacher Polkton Elem 1970-86; Teacher Morven Elem 1986-; *ai:* NCAE; Intnl Rdng Assn; Teacher of Yr Polkton Elem 1986; Ed of Month Morven Elem 1989; Rdng Grant 1988-89; *home:* Rt 1 Box 69 Peachland NC 28133

CAUDRON, CORDELL ROBERT, English Teacher; *b:* Los Angeles, CA; *c:* Justin R.; *ed:* (AA) Eng, Ventura Coll 1962; (BA) Eng, Univ of OR 1964; San Jose St Univ, Univ of CO, Portland St Univ; *cr:* Asst Mgr 1st Security Bank of ID 1973-81; Eng Teacher Loveland HS 1983-86, Lewiston HS 1986-; *ai:* Spon Lewiston HS Literary Club; NEA 1983-86; ID Ed Assn 1986-; Smithsonian, World Wildlife Fund, Nature, Humane Society; NEH Stipend Grant Univ of CO, Kutztown Univ; Poems & Story Published; *office:* Lewiston HS 1114 9th Ave Lewiston ID 83501

CAUFF, DEBORAH LEE, Mathematics Teacher; *b:* Reading, PA; *ed:* (BA) Scndry Ed, PA St Univ 1973; Summer Courses, Kutztown Coll; *cr:* Math Teacher Dover HS 1973-; *ai:* NEA, DSEA, CEA 1973-; NCTM; Notary Public 1987; *office:* Dover HS 625 Walker Rd Dover DE 19901

CAULEY, MARY LOU GRIFFIN, Sixth Grade Teacher; *b:* Holyoke, MA; *m:* George Michael; *c:* Judy, Mary, George; *ed:* (BA) Eng/Ed, Our Lady of Elms Coll 1962; (MED) Admin/Ed, Westfield St Coll 1965; Remedial Rdng; *cr:* 4th Grade Teacher Highland Sch 1962-67; 5th Grade Teacher Joseph Metcalf Sch 1967; 6th/8th Grade Teacher Powder Mill Sch 1980-82; 6th Grade Teacher Smith Avenue Sch 1982-; *ai:* MA Teachers Assn, NEA, Westfield Ed Assn; St Marys Parish; Martin de Porres Circle; Elms Coll Alumni Assn; *office:* Smith Avenue Sch Smith Ave Westfield MA 01085

CAULFIELD, JOHN F., Fifth Grade Teacher; *b:* Schenectady, NY; *ed:* (BA) Eng, Siena Coll 1960; (MA) Elem Ed, Coll of St Rose 1975; *cr:* Employee US Post Office Dept 1967-73; Teacher Argyle Cntrl Sch 1974-; *ai:* Argyle Cntrl Family Life, Ed, Staff Dev Comm; *office:* Argyle Cntrl Sch Sheridan St Argyle NY 12809

CAUSEY, NINA C., English Department Chairman; *b:* Chicago, IL; *m:* Jerry; *c:* Ali Early; *ed:* (BS) Ed, Roosevelt Univ 1968; (MA) Music Theory, Univ of IL 1969; Supplementary Authorization Eng, CA St Univ Hayward; *cr:* Music Teacher Cole Jr HS 1974, Beverly Hills 1979-80, Adams Jr HS 1981-82; Eng Teacher Pinole Jr HS 1982-; *ai:* Drama Club Spon; Directed, Choreographed, Produced Broadway Show at Adams Jr HS & Richmond Unified Sch Dist; United Teachers of Richmond 1981-.

CAUSEY, RICHARD T., Math Teacher/Chairman; *b:* Floral Park, NY; *m:* Marilyn Leach; *c:* Elizabeth, Christopher, Matthew, Richard F.; *ed:* (BS) Math, SUNY Albany 1958; Courses at SUNY Albany 1959-61, Boston Coll 1963-65; *cr:* Teacher Scotia-Glenville HS 1958-; *ai:* Var Bsktbl 1959-69 & Frosh Bsktbl 1972-78; Jr Var Ftbl 1972-87; SGTA, NYSUT, NEA, New York St Math Teachers; *office:* Scotia-Glenville HS Sacandaga Rd Schenectady NY 12302

CAUTHEN, GENNELL MINGO, Guidance Counselor; *b:* Lancaster, SC; *m:* Hazle; *c:* Shana K., Milburn C. II; *ed:* (BS) Home Ec, SC St Coll 1972; (MAT) Scndry Ed, 1975, (MAT) Guidance & Counseling, 1990 Winthrop Coll; Certified in Bio, Eng, Mid Sch; Taught Adult Ed; *cr:* Life Sci Teacher South Jr HS 1972-88; Guidance Counselor Lancaster Sr HS 1988-; *ai:* Teen Inst Co-Adv; Volunteers Stu Comm; Teacher Incentive Prgm; Natl & SC Counselors Assns; Delta Sigma Theta Secy, Golden Lifetime Mem 1988; New Hope Baptist Ed Coord; NAACP; *office:* Lancaster Sr HS 655 N Catawba St Lancaster SC 29720

CAUTHEN, KATHY (VARGO), Art Teacher; *b:* Indiana, PA; *m:* David Leonard; *c:* Michelle, Brian; *ed:* (BS) Art Ed, Indiana Univ of PA 1979; Grad Courses Clemson Univ; *cr:* Art Teacher Westside HS 1979-83, Mc Cants Mid Sch 1979-; *ai:* Sch Intervention Prgm Teacher In-Charge; Mc Cants Art Dept Fine Art Fesitval & Gifted & Talented Art Class Spon; NAEA Mem 1986-; Anderson Cty Arts Cncl Mem 1982-; Mc Cants PTA Cultural Art Chm 1987-; Sigma Sigma Sigma Key Alumna 1984-; St Joseph Cath Church Mem 1979-; Starlite Dance Company Mem 1986-; *office:* Mc Cants Mid Sch 105 S Fant St Anderson SC 29621

CAUTHEN, MELBA MOSELEY, Math Teacher; *b:* Forrest City, AR; *m:* Ronnie; *c:* Brian, Kevin, Shane; *ed:* (AA) Math, Phillips Cty Comm Coll 1973; (BSE) Math 1975, (MSE) Math, 1983 Univ Cntrl AR; Grad Courses Math Ed, Univ Cntrl AR; *cr:* Math Teacher Vilonia HS 1975-; *ai:* Class Spon; Math Counts Coach; Gifted and Talented Comm; Vilonia Ed Assn Pres 1979 & 1987; AR Ed Assn 1975-; NCTM & AR Cncl Teachers Math; New Hope Baptist Church; St Public Relations Comm; AEA General Assembly Delegate; Vilonia Ed Assn Salary Comm; Vilonia North Cntrl Steering Comm; *office:* Vilonia HS P O Box 160 Vilonia AR 72173

CAVAGNARO, SUSAN VAN HOOK, History Teacher; *b:* Newfield, NJ; *m:* Raymond; *c:* Jeannine, Raymond, Mark; *ed:* (BS) Eng/His, Villanova Univ 1971; Classes Glassboro, Camden Cty Coll, Rutgers Univ, Misericordia Coll; *cr:* His/Eng Teacher Our Lady of Mercy 1975-; *ai:* Yrbk, Sr Homeroom, Drive for Poor Moderators; Help with Sch Musical Productions.

CAVALEA, JOSEPH ANTHONY, Director of Orchestras; *b:* Astoria, NY; *m:* Barbara Ann Simon; *c:* Dana B., Jonathan J.; *ed:* (BS) Music Ed, Hofstra Univ 1972; (MA) Music Ed, Stony Brook Univ 1975; *cr:* 9th/10th Grade Orch Dir 1972-, Jazz Ensemble Dir 1985- Sachem HS S Campus; *ai:* Chamber Orch Conductor; Music Cncl Adv; NY St Sch Music Assn All St Audition Comm 1985-; Music Educators Natl Conference Mem; Long Island String Festival Assn (Mem, Chairperson) 1973-; Suffolk Cty Music Ed Assn (Mem, Orch Chairperson 1982-88) 1973-; Commendation From United States Congress; Suffolk Cty Proclamation; *home:* 8 Hyanis Ct Mount Sinai NY 11766

CAVALLARO, DONNA ZELESNIKAR, Teacher; *b:* Johnson City, NY; *m:* William A.; *ed:* (BA) Soc Stud/His, 1973, (MA) Eng, 1977 St Univ NY Albany; *cr:* Teacher Iroquois Mid Sch 1973-; *ai:* Team/Teacher Leader; Niskayuna Staff Dev, Schlsp, Mid Sch Liaison, Prof Growth Comm; NY St Staff Dev Task Force; ASCD, Natl Staff Dev Cncl, NY St Staff Dev Cncl, NCTE, NYS Mid Sch Assn, NCSS; Capital Region Center for Arts in Ed; ASCD Natl Mid Sch Consortium Mem 1986-88; Co-Author Manual; St & Natl Trainer Niskayuna Mid Sch Nationally Validated Title IVC Project 1970-; Whos Who in Amer Ed 1987-88.

CAVANAH, DELAIN SIMMONS, First Grade Teacher; *b:* St Louis, MO; *m:* Randall; *c:* Sarah, Amy, Matthew; *ed:* (BS) Ed, Univ of MO; Grad Stud; *cr:* 1st Grade Teacher S Boone Cty 1973-74, Marceline R-V 1974-80, 1982-; *ai:* MSTA 1974-78, 1987-; Eastern Star 1970-; Mothers Study Club 1989-; *office:* Walt Disney Elem Sch 314 E Santa Fe Marceline MO 64658

CAVANAUGH, PATRICK SEAN, Teacher-Learning Disabilities; *b:* Vincennes, IN; *ed:* (BS) His, IN Univ Indianapolis 1988; *cr:* Teacher/Coach Plainfield Jr/Sr HS 1988-; *ai:* 8th Grade Boys Bsktbl Coach;Boys Varsity Tennis Coach; *office:* Plainfield Jr/Sr HS 709 Stafford Rd Plainfield IN 46168

CAVAZOS, CHRISTINA DORIA, Journalism Advisor/Eng Teacher; *b:* Brownsville, TX; *m:* Humberto V.; *c:* Margarita; *ed:* (BS) Journalism, TX A&I Univ 1976; *cr:* Eng Teacher Cummings Jr HS 1976-78, Porter HS 1978-; *ai:* UIL Coord 1988-; UIL Journalism Coach; Newspaper & Yrbk Adv; TX Assn of Journalism Teachers 1985-86; *office:* Gladys Porter HS 3500 International Blvd Brownsville TX 78521

CAVAZOS, VELIA RODRIGUEZ, Counselor; *b:* San Marcos, TX; *m:* Robert L.; *c:* Robert Jr., Cynthia, Sandra, Karen; *ed:* (BA) Bus 1950, (MED) Counseling 1954 Southwest TX St; Fort Kent St Coll; *cr:* 7th Grade Teacher 1963-64, 6th Grade Teacher 1964-65 Damon Elem Sch; Cnslr Intnl Sch of Bangkok 1966-68, Lamar Intermediate 1968-74, Goodnight Jr HS 1974-; *ai:* TX St Teachers Assn Life Mem; NEA Life Mem; TX Assn for Counseling & Dev; Delta Kappa Gamma 12974-85; Archcon 1958-; *home:* 1028 Houston Rd San Marcos TX 78666

CAVE, JO ANN HATZER, 8th Grade Teacher; *b:* Streatór, IL; *m:* George; *c:* Joseph G., Jorge L., Daniel G., Dennis G.; *ed:* (BS) Elem Ed, IL St Univ 1975; *cr:* 3rd Grade Teacher 1975-77, 3rd-4th Grade Teacher 1977-78, 7th Grade Teacher 1980-81, 6th-7th Grade Teacher 1981-82, 8th Grade Teacher 1982- St Stephens Sch; *ai:* Supervised Patrol Prgm; Dir St Stephens Childrens Choir; Girls Vlybl, Scholastic Team, Math Team & Sci Coach; Organized Annual Mission Day & Gym Dandy Day Fund Raising Projects for Sch; Streator Area Achiever Presented by Times Press Outstanding Performance in Teaching Field; *home:* 65 Circle Dr Streator IL 61364

CAVEZZA, CATHERINE SPERRY, Mathematics Teacher; *b:* Clarksburg, WV; *m:* James D.; *c:* Christen V., James D. II, Charles J.; *ed.* (BA) Eng, Salem Coll 1969; *cr:* Math Teacher Washington Irving HS 1971-74, Greensburg Inst of Technology 1977-78; Eng Teacher Yough Sr HS 1978-79; Eng Teacher 1980-81, Math Teacher 1984- Sistersville HS; *ai:* Cheerleading Adv; Math Club Spon; Math Field Day Coach; NEA 1971-; NVEA, TCEA Sch Rep; *home:* Rt 1 Box 74 Sistersville WV 26175

CAVITT, ROGER NELSON, Guidance Dept Chairperson; *b:* Watseka, IL; *m:* Barbara A.; *c:* Ross N., Cheryl A., Alan W.; *ed:* (BA) His, IL Wesleyan Univ 1959; (MS) Guidance, S IL Univ 1960; IL St Univ, Natl Coll of Ed; *cr:* Admin Asst Greenview Public Schls #200 1960-65; Cnslr Bloomington Public Schls #87 1965-; *ai:* Advisory Comm, Sch Name & Colors Chairperson; IL Sch Cnslrs (Pres 1973-74, Secy); NEA Delegate 1964; IL Ed Assn; Bloomington Ed Assn Treas; Mc Lean Cty Retarded Citizens VP 1988; Mc Lean Cty Mental Health Center, Mc Lean Cty Youth Services Pres; IL Sch Cnslrs Assn Service Awd; IL Guidance & Personnel Assn Outstanding Service Awd; *office:* Bloomington Jr HS N Colton Ave Bloomington IL 61701

CAWOOD, KENNETH E., Mathematics Teacher/Dept Chair; *b:* Shelbyville, IN; *m:* Linda D. Baker; *c:* Christina, Teresa; *ed:* (BA) Soc Stud/Math, Purdue Univ 1966; (MA) Math, Ball St Univ 1971; *cr:* Math Teacher Clay Elem 1966-67, Peru Jr HS 1967-; *ai:* IN St Teachers Assn 1966-; Circus City Festival VP 1989-; Peru Maennerchor VP 1990; *office:* Peru Jr HS 30 E Daniel St Peru IN 46970

CAYCE, VELMA SNOW, English/Reading Teacher; *b:* Port Gibson, MS; *c:* Robert, Pamela; *ed:* (BS) Elem Ed, Grambling St Univ 1963; (MS) Rdng, Wayne St Univ 1971; *cr:* 1st Grade Teacher Robinson Elem 1963-64; 3rd Grade Teacher A L Holmes 1964-76; Eng Tutor 1988-, Eng Teacher 1989- Horizons Upward Bound; Eng/Rdng Teacher Cleveland Mid Sch 1990; 7th/8th Grade Teacher Talented & Gifted Stu 1990; *ai:* Charm Club Spon; Natl Cncl of Rdng Teachers; Delta Sigma; *office:* Cleveland Mid Sch 13322 Conant Detroit MI 48212

CAYME, VICTORIO MARTINEZ, Science/Mathematics Teacher; *b:* San Isidro, Philippines; *m:* Grata Cuajunco; *c:* Brenda, Vivian, Vic Jr.; *ed:* (BA) Electronics, 1959, (BSIE) Ind Ed, 1961 Philippines Coll of Art & Trade; (MA) Ed, Arellano Univ 1967; ROTC 1956-58; Quality Reviewer 1989-; *cr:* Shop/Sci/Math Teacher 1970-86, Resource/Project Dir 1986, Sci/Math Teacher 1986-, Athletic Dir 1989- Cantua Elem Sch; *ai:* ASB Adv; All Sports Coach; Field Trips; Filipino/Amer Educators VP 1989-91; CTA (Pres 1980-81, Negotiator 1989-); Instr of Outstanding Awds CA St Fair 1975, 1979-80, Fresno Dist Fair 1975-76, 1979-80.

CAYTON, NANCY M., Journalism Teacher; *b:* Clarksburg, WV; *ed:* (BA) Journalism/Lib Sci, Fairmont St Coll 1979; (MA) Curr/Instruction, WV Univ 1989; Grad Stud WV Univ; *cr:* Journalism Teacher E Fairmont HS 1980-82, Fairmont Sr HS 1982-; *ai:* Publications Yrbk, Video Yrbk, Newspaper, Sch Publicity; Quill & Scroll Journalism Honary Spon; WV Scholastic Press Assn (Pres,

Secy 1989) 1981-; NEA, WV Ed Assn, Marion Cty Ed Assn; Asst Dir Gettysburg Yrbk Experience; Instr Yrbk Wkshps 7 Sts; WV Univ Sch of Journalism Teachers Hall of Fame; 6 Natl Yrbk Awds & 4 St Awds; Finalist Ashland Oil Excl in Teaching Awd 1989; *office:* Fairmont Sr HS Loop Pk Fairmont WV 26554

CAYWOOD, KATHLEEN R., Reading Coordinator; *b:* Constantine, MI; *m:* Ned; *c:* Mary Bogart, Tim, Lynn Brand, Janet A.; *ed:* (BS) Rural Life/Ed, 1967, (MA) Elem Ed, 1978 W MI Univ; *cr:* 2nd/3rd Grade Teacher Fawn River Elem 1964-67; 4th Grade Teacher 1967-89, Rdng Coord 1989- Sturgis Public Schls; *ai:* Curr, Negotiating Comms; Delta Kappa Gamma Society 1980-; 1st Presbyn Church (Deacon 1977-80, Elder 1981-84, Womens Exec Bd 1987-); *home:* 26045 Fawn River Sturgis MI 49091

CAZIER, PATRICIA ALLEN, Third Grade Teacher; *b:* Pasadena, CA; *c:* Nicholas; *ed:* (BA) Elem Ed, Univ CA Santa Barbara 1963; Ed Classes to Acquire OR Credential, Portland St Univ; *cr:* 2nd Grade Teacher C C Lambert Sch 1965-69; 3rd Grade Teacher Tarawa Terrace II Sch 1976-78; 2nd Grade Teacher James John Sch 1978-80; 3rd/5th Grade Teacher Willard Sch 1982-; *ai:* Stu Study & Leadership Team; NEA, CA Teachers Assn, Garvey Ed Assn 1982-; *office:* Willard Sch 3152 N Willard Ave Rosemead CA 91770

CAZIN, JULIA A., Teacher; *b:* Roswell, NM; *m:* Robert; *ed:* (BA) Math, Emory & Henry Coll 1970; (MA) Scndry Ed/ Supervision, Morehead St Univ; *cr:* 7th Grade Math Teacher Linkhorne Jr HS 1970-71; 6th Grade Math Teacher Howe Hall Mid 1971-72; 7th/8th Grade Math Teacher Farquahr Mid 1972-74; 7th Grade Math Teacher Russell Mid Sch 1974-83; 8th/ 9th Grade Math Teacher Bayside Jr HS 1983-85; 8th Grade Math Teacher Daniels Mid 1985-; *ai:* Natl Jr Honor Society Adv 1986-; Honors Night & Attendance Comm; NCTM, NEA 1976-; NC Cncl of Teachers of Math, NC Assn of Educators 1985-; Kappa Delta Gamma 1987-; Teacher of Yr Daniels Mid Sch 1989-; Speaker at Natl Symposium for Cooperative Learning & Sch Change Oakland CA 1990; Nom Governors Awd Excl in Teaching Wake Cty; *office:* Daniels Mid Sch 2816 Oberlin Rd Raleigh NC 27608

CECCONI, RICHARD ALAN, Science Teacher; *b:* Little Falls, NY; *m:* Christine M. Perry Cecconi; *c:* Andrea, Nicholas; *ed:* (BS) Elem/Early Sec Ed, NY St Univ 1974; (MS) Early Sec Sci, SUNY Cortland 1986; *cr:* Sci Teacher Homer Cntrl Sch 1974-90; Recreation Dir Village of Homer 1982-86; Young Conservation Corps Cortland Cty 1974-80; *ai:* Prof Staff Dev Comm; Proj 2000 Comm Jr HS Sci Club Adv; Jr HS Lacrosse Coach; Stanys 1974-; Homer Teachers Assn Negotiatior 1988-; Arbor Day Fnd 1980-; NYSUT 1988-; Bd of Dir 1989-90; Delta Kappa; Beta; Natl Sci Fnd Grant-Energy Ed 1986; Homer Mini-Grant 1987; Conservation Educator of Yr 1976; *home:* 4806 Butler Dr Cortland NY 13045

CECHNICKI, DOREEN L. BROWN, Home Economics Teacher; *b:* Cobleskill, NY; *m:* Gene Raymond; *c:* Brian S., Kimberly B.; *ed:* (BS) Home Ec Ed, St Univ of NY Oneonta 1978; (MS) General Prof Stud, St Univ of NY Albany 1984; *cr:* Home Ec Teacher Sharon Springs Cntrl Sch 1979-; *ai:* FHA & Class Adv; Home Ec Teachers Assn 1980-; St Marys Parish Cncl Pres 1988-; Cub Scout Pack 17 Cubmaster 1989-; NY St Home Ec Inservice Team Region 6 1985-89, FHA St Officer Trainer 1990; Home Ec Core Curr Trainer 1984-86, Action Ed Curr 1990; Proficiency Exam Review Team 1987-; *office:* Sharon Springs Cntrl Sch Box 218 Sharon Springs NY 13459

CECILE, MARCIA BUNN, 8th Lang Art/Reading Teacher; *b:* Winston-Salem, NC; *m:* Larry C.; *c:* Larry Jr., Jennie; *ed:* (BS) Soc Sci, Appalachian St Univ 1969; (MED) Scndry Ed, Univ of SC 1976; Cert Scndry Admin, Mid Sch Lang Art, Rdng; *cr:* Teacher N Myrtle Beach HS 1971-77, Conway HS 1977-78, E Mc Dowell Jr HS 1978-80, Socastee Mid Sch 1980-85, Conway Mid Sch 1985-; *ai:* SACS Steering Comm; Fellowship of Chrstn Athletes Spon; SC Mid Sch Assn 1989-; SC Palmettos Finest Sch Awd 1989-; SC Exemplary Writing Sch Awd 1989-; *home:* Rt 4 Box 61 Conway SC 29526

CEFALO, RONALD GENE, Physics Instructor; *b:* Melrose, MA; *m:* Louise M.; *c:* Trevor, Kristie, Rose, Laurie, Gregg, Grant, Mary A.; *ed:* (BA) Biological Sci Comp, 1967, (MED) Sci, 1968 UT St Univ; PTRA & Physics Teaching Resource Agent; Drivers Ed Cert, Math Cert; *cr:* Grad Asst Brigham Young Univ; Bio Teacher Granite HS; Earth/Physics Teacher North Ogden Jr HS; Physics Teacher Box Elder HS; *ai:* Center for the Sci Adv; Ftbl, Track, Academic Olympiad Team Coach; Sci Fair Judge 1969-; Sci Fair Dir; Sci Club Adv; NSTA 1990; BSA (Chm 1983-89, Scoutmaster), Eagle Scout; Jaycees Comm Chm 1970-73, Jaycee of Month 1971, 1974; Natl Eagle Scout Assn; Order of Arrow; Scholastic Schlsp Kiwanis 1964; Sci Fair Schlsp UT St Univ 1962; 2nd Place UT St Sci Fair 1962; Eagle Scout Scouters Key; Religious Awds; Report to Nation Scout Western Region 1963; Nathan Hale Essay Freedoms Fnd Awd 1964; UT St Univ Sci Ed Stu of Yr 1968; UT St Univ Cum Laude Grad; Intercollegiate Knights Phi Kappa Phi; Brigham Young Univ Grad Assistantship 1968; Granite HS Teacher of Month; *office:* Box Elder HS 380 S 600 W Brigham City UT 84302

CELER, MARY BETH, Fifth Grade Teacher; *b:* Berwyn, IL; *ed:* (BA) Child Dev, Marygrove Coll 1972; Grad Trng in Teaching Rdng, Oakland Univ 1975-78; *cr:* 1st Grade Teacher St Mary of Czestochowa Sch 1972-74, Guardian Angel Sch 1974-78; 1st/4th/ 5th Grade Teacher St Scholastica Sch 1978-; *ai:* Teacher Rep St Scholastica Parent Teacher Guild; Wayne Cty Rdng Cncl 1990; Pax Christi USA 1982-; *office:* St Scholastica Sch 17351 Southfield Rd Detroit MI 48235

CELI, JANET LYN, Spanish Teacher; *b:* Tampa, FL; *m:* Peter; *ed:* (BA) Span/Eng/Scndry Ed, Univ of S FL 1968; (MED) Bi-ling/Multicultural Ed, Univ of MA 1977; Post Grad Stud; *cr:* Eng/Speech Teacher Marlboro HS 1969; Span Teacher Acton-Boxboro Regional HS 1970-73, Woburn HS 1973-; *ai:* Span Exch Prgm & Span Natl Honor Society Coord; Woburn Teachers Assn, MA Teachers Assn, NEA; MA Foreign Lang Assn, Teacher of Yr Finalist 1981; Developed Curr 3 New Courses; Recipient Horace Mann Grants to Develop Curr 1987, 1988.

CELKO, ANNA MARIE SLAIGHT, K-5th Grade Writing Teacher; *b:* Newark, NJ; *m:* Robert Paul; *c:* Amanda, Ryan; *ed:* (BA) Elem Ed, 1968, (MA) Spec Ed; 1976 Trenton St; *cr:* 2nd-4th Grade Teacher Cntrl Sch 1968-80; 1st-5th Grade Rdng Teacher 1980-81, K-5th Grade Resource Room Teacher 1981-84, K-5th Grade Lang Art Teacher Cntrl & Van Derveer Schls 1984-; *home:* 209 2nd St Middlesex NJ 08846

CENCICH, DAVID JOSEPH, Mathematics Instructor; *b:* Detroit, MI; *ed:* (MS) Math, Wayne St Univ 1971; *cr:* Math Teacher Warren HS 1968-; *ai:* Math Contest Coord.

CEPURNIEK, JOY PRICE, Fifth Grade Teacher; *b:* Sidney, TX; *m:* Andris; *c:* Perri A. Cepurniek-Craven, Laura S.; *ed:* (BA) Elem Ed/Bus, Wayland Baptist Univ 1957; Univ of TX, OK St Univ, Tulsa Univ; *cr:* 4th Grade Classroom Teacher Seminole Public Schls 1957-61, Midland Public Schls 1961-62; Classroom Teacher Jenks Public Sch 1970-; *ai:* Staff Dev, Dist Evaluation, Dist Health Insurance, Meet & Confer Comms Jenks Public Schls; Soc Elem Curr Chairperson; Jenks Classroom Teachers Assn Pres 1980-87, Teacher of Yr 1983; OK Ed Assn (Bd of Dir 1987-, Convention Comm 1983-) 1970-; NEA 1970-; OK Soc Stud Cncl 1980-; S Tulsa Homeowners Pres 1970-75; Alpha Delta Kappa Trea 1974-76; Republican Party St Delegate 1989; Camp Fire Cncl Leader 1968-79; OK Republican Educators Caucus Dist II 1987-; Governors Ed Advisory Comm 1988; *office:* Jenks Public Schls 1st & B Streets Jenks OK 74037

CERCLE, DEAN FRANK, Science Teacher; *b:* Friend, NE; *m:* Deborah Davis; *c:* Jay, Jamie; *ed:* (BS) Bio/General Sci, 1968, (MS) Scndry Ed, 1972 Univ of NE; Natl Sci Fnd Seminar Physics, Chem; *cr:* Sci Teacher Roseland Public Schls 1968-86; Silver Lake Public Schls 1986-; *ai:* Jr Class Spon; NE St Ed Assn 1968-; SENSE 1985-; Lions Secy 1983-; Church Bd Secy 1988-; Cub Scouts Den Leader 1986-88; Natl Sci Fnd Grants; *home:* Box 71 Roseland NE 68973

CERLIANO, REBECCA ANN, Spanish Teacher; *b:* Longview, TX; *ed:* (BA) Eng, 1973, (MA) Span, 1975 Stephen F Austin St Univ; *cr:* Span Teacher Jefferson HS 1975-; *ai:* Stu Cncl Spon; Jefferson Ed Assn Consultation Comm; JEA, TSTA, NEA (Pres 1983-85, Secy 1986-); AATSP 1973-; *office:* Jefferson HS PO Box 645 Jefferson TX 75657

CERVANTES, GLORIA VARELA, Eighth Grade Teacher; *b:* El Paso, TX; *m:* Juan; *ed:* (BS) Span/Sociology, Univ of TX El Paso 1980; *cr:* 7th/8th Grade Teacher Crockett Intermediate 1981-; *ai:* Univ Interscholastic League & Spelling Bee Coach; Intnl Rdng Assn 1987-; TX Classroom Teachers Assn 1986-; Juvenile Court Conference Comm Secy 1990; El Paso Cncl Soc Stud 1988-.

CERVENKA, BARBARA ELLEN, Music Teacher; *b:* Schenectady, NY; *ed:* (BS) Music Ed, 1961, (MS) Music Ed, 1965 Crane Sch of Music; Traditional Music Public Sch, Choral Practicum, Saratoga Perf Arts Center; Dulcimer in Classroom, Advanced Conducting Technique; *cr:* K-6th Grade Music Teacher Gloversville Public Sch 1961-62, Scotia-Glenville Centrl Sch 1962-65; K-12th Grade Music Teacher 1965-67, 7-12th Grade Music Teacher 1967- Calway Cntrl Sch; *ai:* Sch Musical Dir; Select HS Choir-Chansonettes & Chair Sch Improvement Team Dir; Galway Teachers Assn Bd of Dir; Saratoga-Warren Music Ed Assn Pres 1983-85; NY St Sch Music Assn 1961-; Delta Kappa Gamma Intnl Mem 1978-; Beta Omega Chapter Pres 1990; Pi State Music Comm 1988-; Music Educators Natl Conference 1961-; Galway Teachers Assn 1961-; Amer Choral Dirs Assn; West Charlton United Presbyn Church Elder 1989-; Galway Womens Club Pres; Galway Players Musical Dir 1971-80; Galway Cntrl Sch Teacher of Yr 1983; 2 Yrbk Dedications 1973/1984; Louise H Blood Schlsp Delta Kappa Gamma 1989; *office:* Galway Central Sch 5317 Sacandaga Rd Galway NY 12074

CESA, GLENN JAMES, Social Studies Teacher; *b:* Paterson, NJ; *m:* Karen L Koehler; *ed:* (BA) His, Montclair St Coll 1983; Fullbright Schlsp to Study in Jamaica 1985; Grad Stud in Ed; *cr:* Soc Stud Teacher Midland Park HS 1983-85, Hanover Park HS 1985-86, Lakeland Regional HS 1986-; *ai:* Ftbl Coach; Var Asst Offensive Line Spec Teams; Boys Track Head Coach; Fellowship of Chrstn Athletes Mem & Adv; NJEA Mem 1983-; San Diego Zoological Society Mem 1984-86; Sussex Cty Republicans 1980-; Wanaque Family Life Center Advisory Comm 1989-; Bethany Church (Mem, Jr HS Teacher) 1986-; Fullbright Scholar Jamaica 1985; Hanover Park Ftbl Clinic Speaker 1986; *office:* Lakeland Regional HS Conklintown Rd Wanaque NJ 07465

CESARONI, ELLEN K., Spanish Teacher; *b:* Derby, CT; *m:* Frank J.; *c:* John, Mark; *ed:* (BS) Scndry Ed/Span/Eng, S CT St Coll 1971; (MA) Ed/Supervision/Admin, 1976; (CAS) Ed/ Supervision/Admin, 1979; *cr:* Span/Eng Teacher Great Oak Mid Sch 1971-; *ai:* Changing Roles in Ed & Span Curr Comm; COLT; Lincoln Sch PTA Membership Chairperson 1988-; *office:* Great Oak Mid Sch 222 Governors Hill Rd Oxford CT 06483

CESTRONE, DIANNE TURNER, Home Economics Teacher; *b:* Philadelphia, PA; *m:* Eugene G.; *ed:* (BS) Bible/Chrstn Ed, Philadelphia Coll of Bible 1973; (MA) Chrstn Ed, Wheaton Coll 1974; Cert Home Ec, Immaculata Coll 1984; Child Dev, Cmptr, Penn St Univ; Culinary Arts, Performance Leaning Systems, Johnson & Wales Univ; *cr:* Dir Chrstn Ed 1st Presbyn Church & 1st Baptist Church 1974-77; Mgr Jo-Anne Fabrics 1977-81; Home Ec Teacher Perkiomen Valley HS 1984-; *ai:* Class Spon; Mem Prins Cabinet, Class Size Comm, Stu Assistance Team; Secy Staff Dev Comm; Track Ofcl; Cty Home Ec 1984-; AHEA 1988-; Various Church Comm Mem; Speaker Youth Retreats, Home Extension Groups; Accomplished Seamstress; Successful Preschool Prgm within HS; *office:* Perkiomen Valley HS Rt 29 Graterford PA 19426

CHADEY, HELEN PUTZ, Sixth Grade Teacher; *b:* Rock Springs, WY; *m:* Henry F.; *c:* Michael F., Katherine A., Mary J., Jeanne M.; *ed:* (BA) Elem Ed, Univ of WY 1953; *cr:* 6th Grade Teacher Washington Sch 1949-50; 4th Grade Teacher Lincoln Sch 1950-52; 6th Grade Teacher Union Lake Sch 1953-55; 7th Grade Teacher Rock Springs Jr HS 1955-58; 4th Grade Teacher Rock Springs Parochial Sch 1967-74; 6th Grade Teacher Yellowstone Sch 1974-75; Walnut Sch 1975-; *ai:* Alpha Delta Kappa; Sweetwater Cty His Society; Kappa Delta; AAUW; WY St His Society; *home:* 413 Fremont Ave Rock Springs WY 82901

CHADWELL, DEBORAH DARLENE, Math Dept Chair & Teacher; *b:* Welch, WV; *m:* Donald Lee Jr.; *c:* Martin, Justin; *ed:* (BA) Math, Bluefield St Coll 1982; *cr:* Classroom Teacher Bradshaw Jr HS 1982-; *ai:* 9th Grade Class Spon; Math Field Day, Mathcounts Coach; NEA, WVEA, CEA 1982-; Mc Dowell Cty Teachers of Math Secy 1988-; *home:* PO Box 189 Rt 80 Avondale WV 24811

CHADWICK, ALDEN CARPENTER, Science Teacher; *b:* Honolulu, HI; *m:* Robin Camus; *c:* Meaghan; *ed:* (BA) Health/ Phys Ed, Baldwin-Wallace Coll 1982; *cr:* Phys Ed Teacher Salem NH 1982-84; Sci Teacher Groton Dunstable Mid Sch 1984-; *ai:* Girls Var Bsktbl; Boys Jr Var Soccer; Natl Wildlife 1980-; Womens Bsktbl Coaches Assn 1990; *office:* Groton-Dunstable Mid Sch N Main St Groton MA 01450

CHADWICK, VICKI ELIZABETH, Early Childhood Education; *b:* Houston, TX; *m:* Robert M.; *c:* Shelley, Robert Jr.; *ed:* Assoc Child Dev, CDA Credential Prgm; Pursuing BS 1990, MS Early Chldhd, Univ of Houston; *cr:* Teacher 1980-89, Dir/ Pre-Sch Teacher 1988-89 Our Lady of Lourdes Sch; *ai:* Chldhd Advocate & Promote Quality Childcare; Spon Week of Young Child Santa Fe & Hitchcock TX 1987-89; Gulf Coast Assn for Ed of Young Child Secy 1990; Cncl for Early Chldhd (CDA Rep, Ofcl Agent); Invited & Attended Natl Conference on Early Chldhd Issues in Washington DC 1988.

CHADWICK, WILLIAM ROBERT, II, Mathematics/Science Teacher; *b:* Mt Pleasant, MI; *m:* Karen G. Pake; *c:* Jaclynn, Chip, Sarah; *ed:* (BSED) Phys Ed, Cntrl MI Univ 1982; *cr:* Substitute Teacher Clare Cty Schls 1982-88; Teacher Harrison Cmmty Schls 1988-; *ai:* Stu Cncl Adv; *office:* Harrison Mid Sch 224 W Main Harrison MI 48625

CHAFIN, HALLIE HENDERSON, Language Arts Teacher; *b:* Saltville, VA; *m:* Abraham L.; *c:* Ricky, Dwayne; *ed:* (BA) Elem Ed, VA Intermont 1973; (MED) Elem Ed, Univ of VA 1975; Gifted Ed; *cr:* Elem Teacher High Point, E B Stanley, Wallace; *ai:* WCEA, VEA, NEA 1973-; VSRA; *office:* Wallace Elem Sch 1376 Wallace Pike Bristol VA 24201

CHAFIN, LYDIA ESTEPP, Dean of Students; *b:* Williamson, WV; *m:* Claude S.; *ed:* (AB) Speech Comm, 1976, (MA) Elem Ed, 1980 Marshall Univ; *cr:* Spec Ed Teacher Lenore Elem Sch 1976-77; 3rd/6th Grade Teacher Red Jacket Grade Sch 1977-80; Soc Stud Teacher 1980-89, Dean of Stu 1989- Matewan Jr HS; *ai:* Natl Jr Honor Society Spon; Lady of Golden Horseshoe 1988, Golden Horseshoe Awd 1988; Matewan Womans Club 1975-; *office:* Matewan Jr HS Box 535 Matewan WV 25678

CHAKEMIAN, K. KENNETH, Foreign Language Instructor; *b:* Fitchburg, MA; *ed:* (AB) Classics and Fr, Tufts Univ 1967; (AM) Classical Philology, 1969; (PHD) Classical Philology, 1974 Harvard Univ; *cr:* Teaching Fellow in the Classics Harvard Univ 1969-71; Latin and Greek Instr Winsor Sch 1974-75; Foreign Lang Instr Memorial Jr HS 1975-81; Fitchburg HS 1981-; *ai:* Chairperson of Foreign Lang Dept Fitchburg HS 1987-89; Head Teacher of Foreign Lang Dept at Memorial Jr HS 1980-81; Mem General Excl Comm and Schlsp Comm; & Natl Honor Society Comm 1981-; Comm Fitchburg HS 1981-; The Classical Assn of New Engl 1965-; the Amer Classical League 1965-; Amer Assn of Teachers of French 1975 -; Fitchburg Teachers Assn/MA Teachers Assn/NEA 1976-; Harvard Univ Graduate Prize Fellow 1967-72; Harvard Univ Fellowships 1972-74; Tufts Univ Summa Cum Laude 1967; Phi Beta Kappa 1966; Deans List 8 Semesters 1963-67; Boston Greek Prize 1965; Honorable Mention Woodrow Wilson Natl Fellowship 1967; Fitchburg Public Sch Curr Grant 1987; Curr Grant 1980; *office:* Fitchburg HS 98 Academy St Fitchburg MA 01420

CHAMBERLAIN, DIXIE R., Sixth Grade Teacher; *b:* Burlington, CO; *m:* Ron; *c:* Mason, Tyler, Angela, Ashley; *ed:* Clerk Typist Bus, Northeastern Jr Coll 1971; (BA) Elem Ed/ Geography, Univ of N CO Greeley 1975; *cr:* 5th-8th Grade Math/ 6th Grade Rdng Teacher 1975-78, 5th-8th Grade Math/6th Grade Rdng/5th-6th Grade Soc Stud Teacher 1981- Idalia Sch; *ai:* HS Stu Cncl Spon; Pi Lambda Theta UNC 1974; Natl Honorary for Women in Ed; *office:* Idalia Sch P O Box 40 Idalia CO 80735

CHAMBERLAIN, ELVA DURAN, English Teacher; *b:* Harlingen, TX; *c:* Isys C., Dax C., Ron C.; *ed:* (BA) Eng, Pan Amer Univ 1970; Working Towards Masters in Educl Guidance & Counseling; *cr:* 7th-8th Grade Eng Teacher Gay Memorial Jr HS 1971-73, Coackley Jr HS 1975-80; 9th-11th Grade Eng Teacher Aldine Sr HS 1980-84; 8th-9th Grade Eng Teacher Coakley Jr HS 1984-85; 10th-11th Grade Eng Teacher Harlingen HS 1985-; *ai:* Stu Cncl Spon 1976-80; 10th Grade Class Spon 1985-88; 9th Grade Class Spon 1982-83; *office:* Harlingen HS/Alamo Campus 1701 Dixieland Rd Harlingen TX 78551

CHAMBERLAIN, GARY, Second Grade Teacher; *b:* Mankato, MN; *m:* Mary E. Leech; *c:* Renetta, Rebecca; *ed:* (BA) Elem Ed, 1978, (MA) Gifted/Talented, 1983 Mankato St Univ; Sci Fair, Inventors Fair Trng; *cr:* Elem Teacher 1978-, Gifted & Talented Coord 1983-, Sci Fair Coord 1984-, Inventors Fair Coord 1987- Waseca Schls #829; *ai:* Sci Fair; Inventors Fair; MEEP Adv; Grade Level Chm; North Cntrl Evaluation Team Mem; North Cntrl Assn Validating Team 1987-89, Service 1989; MN Ed Assn Building Rep 1980-84, Service 1928-84; MN Gifted & Talented Chm 1985-; Cath Order of Foresters Trustee 1986-, Citizenship 1988; St Johns Church CCD Teacher 1988-, Service 1989-; S MN Inventors Fair Chm; *office:* Hartley Elem Sch 605 7th Ave NE Waseca MN 56093

CHAMBERLAIN, HORACE, Social Studies Teacher; *b:* Paterson, NJ; *m:* Joan Colardeau; *ed:* (BS) Elem Ed, Glassboro St Coll 1954; (MA) Soc Stud Ed, NY Univ 1959; Montclair St Coll, Univ of Md; *cr:* 5th Grade Teacher Lenox Sch 1954-56; Instr US Army 1956-58; 6th Grade Teacher Lincoln Sch 1958-60; 7th/8th Grade Teacher Pompton Lakes HS 1960-68; Vice Prin Pompton Lakes Summer Sch 1987-89; 7th/8th Grade Teacher Pompton Lakes Mid Sch 1968-; *ai:* Safety Patrol; Stu Cncl; Dept Comm Chm 1989-; NJ Ed Assn, NEA; Jefferson Township (Cncl Person 1965-74, Mayor 1975-86); Morris Cty DeMocratic Organization Chm 1985-87; NJ Conference of Mayors Vice Chm 1985-86; NJ Reformation for Males Bd of Trustees 1968-75; Greystone St Hospital Bd of Trustees 1980-82; *office:* Lakeside Mid Sch Lakeside Ave Pompton Lakes NJ 07442

CHAMBERLAIN, JUDITH LYNN, Fifth Grade Teacher; *b:* Pittsburgh, PA; *c:* John Mikanik, Janis Mikanik; *ed:* (BS) Elem Ed, Kent St Univ 1975; (MS) Guidance/Counseling, Univ of Dayton 1978; Certified Gifted & Talented Instr; *cr:* Service Rep AT&T Telephone Company 1960-64; Primary Teacher 1976-80, Teacher of Gifted & Talented 1981-84, Elem Teacher 1985- Wellsville City Schls; *ai:* Right to Read Coord; CCICC Rep; Sci Fair & Spelling Bee Judge; Adult Basic Ed Instr; WCTA Building Rep 1989-; OEA, NEA; *office:* Mac Donald Elem 305 9th St Wellsville OH 43968

CHAMBERLAIN, SUSAN REDERUS, English Teacher; *b:* Dubuque, IA; *c:* Austin; *ed:* (BA) Eng, Univ of IA 1968; (MFA) Eng, Univ of IA 1970; *cr:* Instr of Eng Univ of Northern IA 1969-70; Creative Writing Instr Cypress Coll 1971-; Eng Teacher Huntington Beach Union HS Dist 1971-; Eng Teacher Fountain Valley HS 1981-; *ai:* Dist Educators Assn 1972-; Music Schlsp Univ of Dubuque; Tuition Schlsp Writers Wkshp Univ IA; Poetry Published Numerous Literary Magazines; Violist Garden Grove Symphony; *office:* Fountain Valley H S 17816 Bushard St Fountain Valley CA 92708

CHAMBERLIN, JOAN CREWS, World History Honors Teacher; *b:* Lake City, FL; *m:* Steven A.; *c:* Georgia A., Vernon R.; *ed:* (BS) Soc Stud Ed, Univ of GA 1970; (MS) Educl Leadership, Nova Univ 1990; *cr:* Teacher Polk Cty Schls 1971-78; Columbia Cty Schls 1978-; *ai:* Hist Club Spon; Staff Journalist Prof Staff Newsletter; Delta Tau Delta Pol Comm 1986-; Appointed Governors Study Consolidation Lake City Columbia Cty; Teacher of Yr LCJH-E 1987; Soc Stud Teacher of Columbia Cty 1988 FL Cncl of Soc Stud; *office:* Lake City Jr HS E P O Box 1178 Pa Ave Lake City FL 32055

CHAMBERLIN, ROY A., Math/Science/Computer Teacher; *b:* Libertyville, IL; *m:* Rhonda Kocinski; *c:* Dana; *ed:* (BA) Ed, N IL Univ 1981; *cr:* Math/Sci/Cmptr Mc Henry Jr HS 1981-; *ai:* Boys 8th Grade Bsktbl; Girls 8th Grade Vlybl; Soc Comm; Mc Henry Area Jaycees VP; *office:* Mc Henry Jr HS 3711 Kane Ave Mc Henry IL 60050

CHAMBERS, DENNIS EARNEST, 8th Grade Soc Stud Teacher; *b:* Knoxville, TN; *m:* Rebecca Susan Wolfe; *c:* Reanon, Harrison, Joel; *ed:* (BA) Liberal Arts/His, 1983, (MS) Ed & Curr, 1989 Univ of TN; *cr:* 8th Grade Teacher Sevierville Mid Sch 1983-; *ai:* 8th Grade Team Leader; Stu Cncl Spon; Sevier Cty Ed Assn Faculty Rep 1984-86; TN Assn of Mid Schls 1988-; NEA, TEA 1983-; Gideons Intnl Sevier Cty Pres 1987-; Eden Meth Church Sunday Sch Teacher 1978-; Amnesty Intnl 1988-; Parish Relations Bd of Fairgarden Circuit of Holston Charge Chairperson 1987-89; Sevierville Mid Sch Teacher of Yr 1988-89; Sevier Cty Mid Sch Teacher of Yr 1989; *home:* Rt 4 Box 330 Sevierville TN 37862

CHAMBERS, DOROTHY J., Second Grade Teacher; *b:* Dallas, TX; *m:* Jack; *c:* Tommy, Jimmy, Janet Baker; *ed:* (BS) Elem Ed, East TX 1949; *cr:* Teacher Grand Saline ISD 1949-54, Spring Branch ISD 1955-56, Pasadena Isd 1958-59, Hurst-Euless Bedford 1963-65, Martins Mill ISD 1965-; *ai:* TX Classroom Teachers Assn-Mem; PTA.

CHAMBERS, JOYCE EILEEN (MC CAY), Fourth Grade Teacher; *b:* Kokomo, IN; *m:* James M. Jr.; *c:* Brian, Alicia; *ed:* (BS) Elem Ed, Bethel Coll 1968; (MS) Elem Ed, IN Univ South Bend 1974; *cr:* 3rd Grade Teacher 1968-76, 4th Grade Teacher 1976- John F Nuner Sch; *ai:* Spon Nuner Little Hoosier Historians Club; Mem of Soc Sci Curr Team; NEA, ISTA 1968-; IN Jr Historical Society 1981-; Northern IN Historical Society; IN Historical Society 1982-; Sch Mens Wives Club (Recording Secy, 1st & 2nd VP, Pres) 1980-84; S Bend Area Genealogical Society 1985-; Natl Audubon Society 1987-; Outstanding Local Historical Achievement Awd by Northern IN Historical Society 1982; Teacher of Yr 1984; *home:* 18120 Chipstead Dr South Bend IN 46637

CHAMBERS, MARK EDWARD, Reading/Language Art Teacher; *b:* Murphysboro, IL; *m:* Tina Marie Yarber; *ed:* (BS) Elem Ed, S IL Univ 1977; (MA) Ed/Rdng, SE MO St Univ 1984; *cr:* 5th Grade Teacher Mid-Cty Cmmty Dist 4 1977-78; 4th-6th Grade Rdng Lab Teacher 1978-80, 6th Grade Teacher 1980-85, 6th-8th Grade Rdng/Lang Art Teacher 1985- Cairo Unit Sch Dist 1; *ai:* Intnl Rdng Assn, NCTE, IL Ed Assn, NEA; Cairo Assn of Teachers Pres 1983; *office:* Cairo Unit Schl Dist 1 Ciaro IL 62914

CHAMBERS, MARTHA LOMINAC, High School Guidance Teacher; *b:* Somerset, KY; *m:* Oliver E.; *c:* Michael J., Michelle L.; *ed:* (BA) Bio, Cumberland Coll 1975; (MS) Counseling, E Ky Univ 1980; Univ of TN Stu Modification; *cr:* Jr HS Teacher Whitley City Mid Sch 1977-78, Morton Jr HS 1978-79; Teacher 1979-80, 6th-12th Grade Cnslr 1980- Oneida HS; *ai:* Stu Cncl Spon; Sch Improvement Comm Chairperson; TN Teachers Assn 1979-; Smoky Mountain Assn of Counselors 1982-; Homemakers Jetsetters 2nd VP 1983-; Outstanding Admin Selected by Stu Body; *office:* Oneida HS P O Box 439 Oneida TN 37841

CHAMBERS, MARY LUCILLE, Commercial Art Teacher; *b:* Tuckerman, AR; *m:* Ronnie L.; *c:* Beth Gibson, Cheryl L.; *ed:* (BSE) Art, AR St Univ 1965; Scndry Counseling; *cr:* Art/Eng Teacher Gosnell HS 1965-66; Art Teacher Jonesboro HS 1971-78; Commercial Art Teacher Area Voc Tech HS 1978-; *ai:* Voc Industrial Clubs of America Club Adv; Delta Kappa Gamma Society Intnl 1985-89; AR Ed Assn, Classroom Teachers Assn 1971-89; Jonesboro Teachers Assn 1989-; *office:* Area Vo-Tech HS 1727 S Main Jonesboro AR 72401

CHAMBERS, PAMELA SUE, Fifth Grade Teacher; *b:* Muncie, IN; *m:* Thomas J.; *c:* Natalie; *ed:* (BA) Elem Ed, 1970, (MS) Elem Ed, 1973 Ball St Univ; *cr:* Elem Teacher St Marys Elem Sch 1970-73, Middletown Elem Sch 1977-; *ai:* ISTA Building Rep Assorted Comm; Delta Kappa Gamma Prgm Chairperson 1979-.

CHAMBERS, TANIS KNIGHT, 2nd/3rd Grade Teacher/ Coord; *b:* Winston-Salem, NC; *m:* David E.; *c:* Jeremy D., Joshua D.; *ed:* (BRE) Religious Ed, Piedmont Bible Coll 1973; Elem Ed, Elon Coll; *cr:* 1st Grade Teacher Edgewood Chrstn Sch 1973-74; 2nd Grade Teacher Gospel Light Chrstn Sch 1975-76; 2nd-4th Grade Teacher Maranatha Chrstn Acad 1980-83, 2nd-5th Grade Teacher Stone-Eden Chrstn Sch 1985-; *ai:* Sch Coord.

CHAMBERS, VIRGINIA MARIE (SALMON), Retired Remedial Rdng Teacher; *b:* Girard, KS; *m:* J. J.; *ed:* (BA) Elem Ed, 1957, (MA) Elem Admin, 1963 Pittsburg St Univ; Rdng Spec Cert 1973; *cr:* Elem Teacher Bourbon Cty Schls 1944-51; 1st-8th Grade Music/5th/6th Grade Teacher Helper Elem 1953-59; 1st-4th Grade Music/2nd Grade Teacher Uniontown Elem 1959-64; 2nd Grade Teacher Eugene Ware Sch 1964-67; Chapter 1 Remedial Rdng Teacher Uniontown Unified Sch Dist 235 1967-85; *ai:* Bourbon Cty Teachers Assn VP 1960; SE KS Rdng Assn Membership Chairperson 1983; United Meth Women Pres 1986-89; Nom Master Teacher of KS by Bourbon Cty Teachers Assn; *home:* RR 4 Box 104 Fort Scott KS 66707

CHAMPAN, LOUISE HABLE, Science Teacher; *b:* Cleveland, OH; *m:* Cordy; *ed:* (BS) Elem Ed, Univ of WI Madison 1973; (MS) Educl Leadership, Cardinal Stritch Coll; Stu Assistance Prgm Core & Facilitator Trng; *cr:* Teacher Kennedy Mid Sch 1973-; *ai:* Stu Assistance Prgm Facilitator, Dist Inservice & Teacher Prof Improvement Comm; Sci Club Adv; Odessey of Mind Coach; Jump Rope for Heart Coord; NSTA, NEA, Cedar Lake United Educators, WI Society of Sci Teachers, WI Ed Assn Cncl.

CHAMPION, CELINA, Health/Quest Teacher; *b:* Brownsville, TX; *ed:* (BS) Health/Phys Ed, TX Womans Univ 1962; Quest Skills for Living Cert Santa Barbara CA; *cr:* Phys Ed Teacher/ Track/Vlybl Coach Faulk Jr HS 1962-67; Phys Ed/Health Teacher Brownsville HS 1967-74; Health/Girls Bsktbl Coach 1974-80, Health Teacher 1980-88, Skills for Living Quest 1988- Hanna HS; *ai:* Quest Skills for Living Parent Seminars Brownsville Ind Sch Dist; Univ of TX Excl Awd for Outstanding HS Teachers 1989; Excl in Teaching Awd Brownsville Ind Sch Dist 1989; Anacleto Cuellar Asst Supt; Joy Jones Quest Facilitator; *office:* Homer Hanna HS 2615 Price Rd Brownsville TX 78520

CHAMPION, JAMES EDWARD, Band Director; *b:* Florence, AL; *m:* Madeline Malone; *c:* Tracie, Brooke; *ed:* (BS) Music Ed, 1968, (MA) Music Ed, 1978 Univ of N AL; *cr:* Band Dir Landon Jr HS 1968-75, Deshler HS 1975-82, Bradshaw HS 1982-; *ai:* All Band Related Act; AL Bandmasters Dist Chm 1978-81; MEMC, AMEA, NEA, AEA, FEA, Natl Band Assn; Teacher/Stu Humanitarian Awd Landon Jr HS 1973; Teacher of Yr Scndry Level 1987; Teacher of Yr System Wide Florence City Schls 1987; *office:* Bradshaw HS 1201 Bradshaw Dr Florence AL 35630

CHAMPION, LOTTIE M., First Grade Teacher; *b:* Griffin, GA; *ed:* (BS) Elem Ed, Morris Brown Coll 1963; (MED) Rdng Specialist, Atlanta Univ 1976; (EDS) Early Chldhd Ed, W GA Coll 1987; *cr:* 5th Grade Teacher 1963-64, 2nd Grade Teacher 1964-65 Shoal Creek Elem; 1st Grade Teacher Atkinson Elem 1965-; *ai:* Fine Art Comm Leader; Flint River Rdng Assn (Treas, Secy) 1980-88; NEA, Griffin Spalding Ed Assn; Adelphian Club Treas 1978-80; Alpha Kappa Secy 1990; Brownie Troop Leader; Rdng Teacher of Yr 1980, 1982; GA Rdng Teacher of Yr 1983; *office:* Susan B Atkinson Elem Sch 307 Atkinson Dr Griffin GA 30223

CHAN, EVA SIM, Biology Teacher; *b:* Swatow, China; *m:* Franklin K.; *c:* Christopher, Carolyn; *ed:* (BS) Bio, 1971, (MS) Bio, 1973 Univ of Houston; TX Ed Agency Teacher Cert 1978; *cr:* Teacher M B Lamar HS 1978-80, J F Dulles HS 1980-83, W P Clements HS 1984-88, J H Kempner HS 1988-; *ai:* Jr Engineering Tech Society Comm Mem Spon; I H Kempner Campus Action Team Asst Coach; UIL Sci; I H Kempner HS Teacher of Yr 1990; Ft Bend Ind Sch Dist Teacher of Yr Finalist; *office:* I H Kempner HS 14777 Voss Rd Sugar Land TX 77478

CHANCE, KAY WILSON, 9th Grade English Teacher; *b:* Winterville, NC; *w:* Ronald L. (dec); *c:* Shawna L., Ronald L. Jr.; *ed:* (BS) Eng, E Carolina Univ 1974; *cr:* 7th Grade Lang Art/ Math Teacher Beaufort Cty Schls 1974-75; Eng Instr Pitt Comm Coll 1974-75; 9th Grade Eng Teacher Washington City Schls 1976-; *office:* P S Jones Jr HS 820 Bridge St Washington NC 27889

CHAND, NISAR, Composite Science Teacher; *b:* Sialkot, Pakistan; *m:* Nina Deborah Mallard; *c:* Michelle, Nicholas, Zachary; *ed:* (BSC) Botany/Chem, 1969, (BED) Ed, 1971 Univ of Punjab; (BS) Composite Sci, Panhandle St Univ 1978; Cmptr Courses, Amarillo Coll 1985, 1989; Religion, Univ of Dubuque 1974; *cr:* Sci Teacher Ashland HS 1979-80, Dimmitt HS 1980-82, Hartley HS 1983-85; Hereford Jr HS 1985-88; Life Sci Teacher Hereford Jr HS 1988-; *ai:* Prepare UIL Stus; TX Classroom Teachers Assn 1985-; Kiwanis 1986-; *office:* Hereford Jr HS 704 La Plata Dr Hereford TX 79045

CHANDLER, BARBARA HOUSTON, Mathematics Teacher/ Dept Chair; *b:* Bluefield, WV; *m:* Calvin B.; *c:* Calvin Jr.; *ed:* (BS) Math, Bluefield St 1957; (MS) Ed, IN Univ 1962; Kent St Univ, Purdue Univ; *cr:* Math/Cmptr Teacher Tolleston Mid Sch 1959-; *ai:* Class Spon; *office:* Tolleston Mid Sch 2700 W 19th Ave Gary IN 46404

CHANDLER, CYNTHIA SUE (COX), Theater/English Teacher; *b:* Houston, TX; *m:* Richard Daniel; *c:* Kate, Jenny; *ed:* (BS) Speech, Lamar Univ 1974; (MA) Theater, Univ of Houston Clear Lake 1978; *cr:* Theater/Speech Teacher Forest Brook HS 1974-77; Eng/Theater Teacher Clear Lake HS 1977-78; Eng Teacher Lincoln HS 1979; Theater/Speech Teacher Edison Mid Sch 1979-82; Eng/Theater Teacher Hamshire-Fannett HS 1985-87, Liberty HS 1987-; *ai:* One Act & Musical Play; Intnl Thespian Society; Rhetoric & Drama Club; Lincoln & Douglas Debate; *home:* 2395 Pecos Beaumont TX 77702

CHANDLER, DIANE F., Third Grade Teacher; *b:* Bennettsville, SC; *m:* Steve; *ed:* (BA) Eng, Univ of SC 1965; (MS) Eng/Ed, St Univ of NY 1971; *cr:* 3rd Grade Teacher Raeford Elem Sch 1966-67; 4th Grade Teacher 71st Elem Sch 1967-68; 3rd-5th Grade Teacher Eastside Elem 1968-72; 3rd Grade Teacher Union Primary Sch 1972-; *ai:* NYSTA; NCAE, NEA Sch Rep 1974-75; Art, Beach Sci, Coastal His Summer Prgm 1986-89; Union Primary Teacher of Yr; *home:* Rt 6 Box 989 River Rd Shallotte NC 28459

CHANDLER, DORIS ANN (HOLBROOK), 8th Grade Math Teacher; *b:* Seco, KY; *m:* Robert M.; *c:* Robert J.; *ed:* (BA) Soc, 1976; Elem Ed, 1980 Morehead St Univ; *cr:* Teacher Meade Mem Elem Sch 1980-83; Cntrl Elem Sch 1982-83; *home:* HC 83 Box 21 Tutor Key KY 41263

CHANDLER, JUDY STEVENS, Fourth Grade Teacher; *b:* Oscar, KY; *m:* Elbert Wayne; *c:* Mitchell W., Rodney L., Brandon; *ed:* (BS) Elem Ed/His, 1970, (MA) Elem Ed, 1976-77 Murray St Univ; *cr:* 8th Grade Eng Teacher Ballard Cty Mid Sch 1970-71; 3rd Grade Teacher Kevil Elem Sch 1971-74; 11th Grade Amer His Teacher Ballard Memorial HS 1974-75; 4th Grade Teacher Bandana Elem Sch 1975-; *ai:* Textbook Adoption & Sch Calendar Comms; Elem Chrldr Spon; KY Tourism; KY Ed Assn, NEA 1970-; 4-H Leader 1988-89; Bandana Baptist Nursery Chm 1985-; *home:* Rt 1 La Center KY 42056

CHANDLER, KATHERINE MONE, First Grade Teacher; *b:* Santa Cruz, Spain; *m:* Robert Hal; *ed:* (BA) Ed, Wheaton Coll 1967; (MA) Rdng/Lit, 1975, (PHD) Curr/Instruction, 1985 Univ of MN; *cr:* 2nd Grade Teacher Evanston Public Schls 1967-73; 1st Grade Teacher Richfield Public Schls 1974-75, Rosemount Public Schls 1975-; *ai:* Dist Faculty Curr Comm Chm; Univ MN Coll of Ed Adjunct Professor; NCTE; *office:* Northview Elem Sch 14445 Diamond Path Rd Rosemount MN 55068

CHANDLER, LARRY FLOYD, 8th Grade Math-Algebra Teacher; *b:* Frankfort, IN; *c:* Lora L., Lona; *ed:* (MS) Ed Math, IN Univ 1983; (BS) Math, Purdue Univ 1977; *cr:* Math Teacher Noblesville Jr HS 1977-; *ai:* Honor Society Admin Adv Cncl; Jr HS Teacher of Yr 1988-89; *office:* Noblesville Jr H S 1625 Field Dr Noblesville IN 46060

CHANDLER, MARTHA EMMOTT, 5TH Grade Teacher; *b:* Houston, TX; *m:* Chuck O.; *c:* Chip; *ed:* (BA) Elem Ed, Baylor Univ 1969; Rdng Specialist Trinty Univ 1980; Elem Math St Marys Univ 1987; *cr:* 1st Grade Teacher Houston ISD 1969-70; Spec Ed Teacher Waco ISD 1970-71; 2nd Grade Teacher San Antonio ISD 1971-73; 3rd Grade Teacher 1975-85; 5th Grade Teacher 1985 North East ISD; *ai:* Rdng Coord; Rdng Basal Textbook Study; Dyslexia Coord; TTAS Observation Field Practice; Soc Stud Curr Comm; Instructional Teams Writing

Inservice Presenter; North East Teachers Assn 1975-87; Natl Ed Agency 1975-87; Ben Milam PTA Assn Treas 1972-; Wilshire Elem PTA Parliamentarian Hollywood Park Homeowners Assn 1983-; Mothers Against Drunk Driving 1987-; Chrstn Marriage Encounter 1977-85; Teacher of Yr North East ISD Nom; Grade Level Chm 3rd Grade 1976-84; 5th Grade 1987-88; Chamber of Commerce Teacher of Yr Nom.

CHANDLER, RENAE HAVARD, Third Grade Teacher; *b:* Ringgold, LA; *m:* J. Harman; *c:* Rebecca Jackson, Melissa, Walter; *ed:* (BS) Elem Ed, 1972, (MS) Elem Ed, 1978 LA St Univ Baton Rouge; Elem Ed, LA St Univ Shreveport 1982; *cr:* Kndgtn Teacher Northside Elem 1973-75; 1st Grade Teacher 1975-83, 3rd Grade Teacher 1983- South Highlands Magnet; *ai:* 3rd Grade Level Chairperson; NEA, LEA, CAE, Northwestern Rdng Cncl; Delta Kappa Gamma (VP, Historian); Caddo Parish Sch Systems Partners in Ed Prgm; Nom Teacher of Yr Caddo Parish Schls; Attended Summer Courses Queens Coll Oxford England; *office:* South Highlands Magnet Sch 831 Erie Shreveport LA 71106

CHANEY, BETTY A. (REEDER), English Teacher; *b:* Indianapolis, IN; *m:* James; *c:* Ona M., Asha R., Marcus L.; *ed:* (BA) Elem Ed - Cum Laude, Saginaw Valley St Univ 1981; Continuing Cert Scndry Ed, Eng, Soc Sci; Working Towards MA in Scndry; *cr:* Asst Church Secy Mt Olive Baptist Church 1974-88; Substitute Teacher Saginaw Township Schls 1981-83, Buena Vista Township Schls 1981-83; Scndry Eng Teacher Buena Vista HS 1984-; *ai:* Sch Improvement Team Chm; Class Adv; MI Rdng Assn; Teacher Primary Sunday Sch & Mission Classes; Baptist Trng Union Pianist; *office:* Buena Vista Preparatory HS 3945 Holland Rd Saginaw MI 48601

CHANEY, MARGET LEE SOLLENBERGER, Third Grade Teacher; *b:* Longmont, CO; *m:* Jerry Wayne; *c:* Maureen, Wayne; *ed:* (BA) Elem Ed, Univ of Northern CO 1974; Grad Work Univ of Northern CO & Univ of WY; *cr:* 3rd Grade Teacher 1976-79, 6th Grade Teacher 1979-86, 4th Grade Teacher 1986-88, K-12th Grade Rdng Facilitator 1985-, 3rd Grade Teacher 1988- Campbell Cty Sch Dist; *ai:* Rdng Comm, Sunflower BEST Correlate Chairperson; Curr Coordinating Cncl Mem; Intl Rdng Assn 1985-; WY Rdng Assn 1980-; Campbell Cty Rdng Assn (Pres 1985-86) 1980-, Natl Honor Cncl 1986; WY ASCD 1989-; BSA Den Mother 1988-89; Teacher of Yr 1990; Outstanding Young Woman of America 1984, 1985; Jaycees Outstanding Young Educator Nom 1985; *office:* Sunflower Elem Sch 2500 S Dogwood Ave Gillette WY 82716

CHANEY, WILLIE MOORE, Mathematics Teacher; *b:* Leroy, AL; *m:* James Edward; *ed:* (BS) Math, AL St 1958; (MA) Math, Univ of Detroit 1974; Leadership Trng Prgm; *cr:* Teacher Harper HS 1958-61; Mobile Cty Trng Sch 1961-68; Knudsen Jr HS 1968-; *ai:* Sci Fair Adv; Gemmettes Soc Club Adv; Equations Club Spon; Leadership Grant Detroit Bd of Ed; *home:* 14343 Penrod Detroit MI 48223

CHANG, ATHENA S., Kindergarten Teacher; *b:* Kuei-Yang, China; *m:* Chia C.; *c:* Sabrina; *ed:* (BA) Eng Lit/Foreign Lang, Natl Tawian Univ 1966; (MA) Early Chldhd Ed, Lesley Coll 1967; *cr:* Kndgtn Teacher Laboratory Sch 1967; 3 Yr Olds Class Teacher Pineland Sch 1968; 5 Yr Olds Class Teacher Lanely Sch 1969; Kndgtn Teacher Ashlawn Sch 1970; *office:* Ashlawn Elem Sch 5950 N 8th Rd North Arlington VA 22205

CHANGNON, DIANNE LYNN, Health Educator; *b:* Marysville, CA; *m:* Tom; *c:* Garrett, Gabrielle; *ed:* (AA) General Stud, Yuba Coll 1972; (BA) Phys Ed/biological Sci, CSU Chico 1974; Counseling Theory & Practices, San Francisco St Univ; *cr:* Phys Educator 1974-86, Family Life Educator 1980-85, Math Educator 1984-, Health Educator 1986- Somerset Mid Sch; *ai:* Mentor Teacher Health, Wellness & Self Esteem; Ca Assn Health, Phys Ed, Recreation, Dance; St Conference 1988- Cty Nutrition Seminar 1990; US Naval Sea Cadets 1989; CA Assn for Health, phys Ed, recreation, dance 1974-; Delta Kappa Gamma-Beta Sigma 1985-; Omega Nu Charity Organization 1989-; Sherwood Sch PTC Treas 1989-; Bravo Ballet Dance Company 1989; Metropolitan Life Fnd Healthy Me Exemplary Sch Prgm Awd 1987; CA Sch Bd Assn Golden Bell Awd 2nd Place 1990; PTA Founders Day Honorary Service Awd 1986; CTIIP Grant Cmptr & Software Prgm Awd 1985; *office:* Somerset Mid Sch 1037 Floyd Ave Modesto CA 95350

CHAPIN, DONNA WILLIAMS, 4th Grade Teacher; *b:* Waterbury, CT; *c:* Corrie, Christopher; *ed:* Sociology/Elem Ed, Monmouth Coll; (BS) Elem Ed, 1972, (MS) Elem Ed, 1975 Western CT St Univ; *cr:* 5th Grade Teacher 1972-75, 3rd Grade Teacher 1975-87, 4th Grade Teacher 1987- Sherman Sch; *ai:* Soccer Coach; Bsktbl Coach; Dist Facilitator St of CT Best Prgm; Mem Teacher Forum Western CT St Univ; Cooperating Teacher Stu Teaching Prgm; NEA/CT Ed Assn Bd of Dir 1984-85; Pi Lambda Theta 1972-; Kappa Delta Pi; Bd of Ed Shepaug Valley Regional Dist 12 1983-86; Union Carbide Outstanding Teacher 1987-89; Dist Facilitator Sherman Sch System 1988-; *office:* Sherman Sch Rt 37 Sherman CT 06784

CHAPIN, JEAN HUNT, 5th Grade Teacher; *b:* Durham, NC; *m:* John A.; *c:* Lorrie E., Timothy C.; *ed:* (BS) Ed, W Carolina Univ 1970; *cr:* 6th Grade Teacher 1973-, 5th Grade Teacher 1978- Oak Grove; *ai:* Mentor; Personnel Dev Work Group Leader; Technology Advisory, Durham Cty Schls Philosophy, Enrichement Comm; Emergency Response Team; Cmptr Coord; NC Assn of Educators 1973-; Alpha Delta Kappa; Oak Grove Elem Sch Teacher of Yr Awd 1989-; *office:* Oak Grove Elem Sch 3810 Wake Forest Rd Durham NC 27703

CHAPLEAU, ELIZABETH ANN, English/French Teacher; *b:* Memphis, TN; *ed:* (BA) Eng, Univ of the South 1985; (MAT) Curr/Instr, Memphis St Univ 1990; *cr:* Eng Teacher Sky View Acad 1985-; *ai:* Yrbk Adv; Cross Cntry Coach; Awds Comm; NCTE 1989-; Daughters of Amer Revolution 1985-; Teacher of Yr & Yrbk Dedication 1988; Whos Who Amoung Outstanding Young Women of America 1989; *office:* Sky View Acad 3000 University Memphis TN 38127

CHAPLICK, VIRGINIA (GOODHUE), English Teacher; *b:* Buffalo, NY; *m:* Daniel A.; *c:* Gail, Daniel; *ed:* (BA) Eng, Emmanuel Coll 1962; *cr:* Eng Teacher Hart Jr HS 1962-64, Warren Jr HS 1964-66, Whittier Sch 1966-67, Girls Cath HS 1983-; *ai:* Drama; Speech; Publicity; NCEA 1983-; Essay Published 1981; *office:* Girls Cath HS 366 Charles St Malden MA 02148

CHAPLIN, PATRICIA SMITH, 1st Grade Teacher; *b:* Ithaca, NY; *m:* Henry D. Jr.; *c:* James C., Cynthia Chaplin Cronin; *ed:* (BA) Eng, NY St Coll for Teachers 1958; (MS) Ed, St Univ NY Cortland 1977; *cr:* 5th Grade Teacher Marathon Cntrl Sch 1973-74; 3rd Grade Teacher 1974-75, 1st Grade Teacher 1975- DeRuyter Cntrl Sch; *ai:* Parents as Rdng Partners Prgm 1982; Math Curr & Art Comms; Seven Valley Rdng Cncl (Pres 1986-88, VP, Recording Secy); Learn for Adult Literacy (Mem of Bd 1988-, Secy, Tutor, Trng Comm 1988-); Presenter NY St Rdng Assn Conference 1989; Article Published; *office:* Deruyter Central Sch 711 Railroad St De Ruyter NY 13052

CHAPMAN, BARBARA WILLIAMS, Fifth Grade Teacher; *b:* Chicago, IL; *m:* Richard D.; *c:* Casey, Cole; *ed:* (AA) St Petersburg Jr Coll 1972; (BA) Ed, Univ of FL 1974; *cr:* 4th/5th Grade Teacher Walsingham Elem Sch 1974-87; 5th Grade Teacher S Oak Elem Sch 1987-; *ai:* Safety Patrol Spon; Rdng Monitoring Rep; Intnl Rdng Assn 1974-; FL Assn of Sci Teachers 1988-89; NEA 1974-; *office:* S Oak Elem Sch 9101 Walsingham Rd Largo FL 34643

CHAPMAN, CAROL JEAN (MICHEL), Mathematics Teacher; *b:* Sterling, IL; *m:* William E.; *c:* Teri J. Chapman Valentine, Mindi R., William E. Jr., Rebecca L.; *ed:* (BS) Elem Ed/Emphasis in Math & Rdng, N IL Univ 1972; Grad Stud; *cr:* 4th Grade Phys Ed/Art Teacher E Coloma Sch Dist 12 1958-67; Rdng/Remedial Rdng Teacher Galt Sch 1973-79; Remedial Math/Rdng Teacher Sterling Unit #5 1979-85; Remedial Rdng/ Math Teacher Challand Jr HS Sterling Unit 5 1985-; *ai:* CORE; Sterling Ed Assn Head Rep 1988-; NEA, IL Ed Assn; *office:* Challand Jr HS Sterling IL 61081

CHAPMAN, DAVID L., English Teacher; *b:* San Diego, CA; *ed:* (BA) Eng, Whittier Coll 1970; Grad Sch AZ St Univ; Teaching Credential CA St Univ Los Angeles; Amer Film Inst Film & Video for HS Teachers; *cr:* Eng Teacher Don Bosco Tech Inst 1975-84, Belmont Cmmty Adult Sch 1983-89, J H Francis Polytech HS 1984-; *ai:* Moderator Ladies & Squires Service & Cinema Club 1986-87; North Amer Society of Sport His; Aids Project Los Angeles; Articles on His of Bodybuilding, Weight Training; Entry in Dict of Lit Biography; Victorian Prose Writers After 1867; *office:* Francis Polytechnic HS 12431 Roscoe Blvd Sun Valley CA 91352

CHAPMAN, DENNIS EARL, Administrator; *b:* Louisville, KY; *m:* Patricia Irene Harris; *c:* Andrew, Anna, Benjamin, Crishelle; *ed:* (BS) Scndry Ed, TN Temple 1976; *cr:* Admin Asst Tri City Chrstn Sch 1976-85; Admin Morningside Chrstn Sch 1985-; *ai:* Amer Assn Chrstn Sch; *office:* Morningside Chrstn Sch 6100 Morningside Ave Sioux City IA 51106

CHAPMAN, DONNA JEAN, English Teacher; *b:* Wichita, KS; *c:* Marlin, Cynthia, Crystal; *ed:* (BA) Eng Ed, Wichita St Univ 1983; *cr:* Eng Teacher Hadley Jr HS 1983-85, Heights HS 1985-; *ai:* NHS, Multi Cultural Club Spon; NCTE 1985-; Alpha Kappa Alpha Secy 1986-87; Top Ladies of Distinction 1990; HS Teacher Awd Univ of KS 1988; *home:* 1818 N Lorraine Wichita KS 67214

CHAPMAN, DORIS KATHLEENE, 5th/6th Grade Teacher; *b:* Lincoln, NE; *m:* Earl Ray; *c:* Doris A. De Bruyn, Lola E.; *ed:* (BA) Elem Ed/Geography, Los Angeles St Coll 1959; Grad Work His, Geography, Lit, Bio, Univ of NE, Wichita Univ, Genesee Coll, Cornell Univ; *cr:* K-8th Grade Teacher Lancaster Cty Public Schls 1948-55; 2nd/4th Grade Teacher Wichita Public Schls 1950-52; 3rD Grade Teacher Arvada Public Schls 1964; 2nd/6th Grade Teacher Centralia Sch Dist 1958-; *ai:* Civil War Roundtable; Audubon Society & Pen/Quill Handwriting Spon; Safety Patrol Spon/Adv; Soc Sci/Rdng Adoption, Checking Writing Proficiency Tests Comm; Teacher Teaming Coord; Teacher of Gifted & Talented; Chorus Dir; Centralia Sch Assn (Sch Rep 1975, Prof Relations Comm 1972); NEA, NE St Assn, KS St Assn, CA St Assn 1947-; Sch Site Cncl Mem, PTA Prgm Chm, SIP Plan Writing; Master Teacher 1969, 1971; Wildlife Project Grant; Centralia Sch Dist Teacher of Yr 1975; *office:* Walter Knott Sch 7300 La Palma Ave Buena Park CA 90620

CHAPMAN, G. DIANE TROTTER, Substitute Teacher; *b:* La Junta, CO; *m:* Michael D.; *c:* Joseph L., Jonathan M.; *ed:* (BA) Voc Home Ec, NW Nazarene Coll 1979; Prof & Dev Courses & Seminars Home Ec, Cmptrs, Multicultural Ed, Journalism; *cr:* Music Teacher/Librarian Arriba Public Sch 1979-80; Substitute Teacher Weld Cty Dist 1983-85; Home Ec/Journalism Teacher Elbert Cty Sch Dist 1986-88; Substitute Teacher Klawock City Sch & Craig Sch Dist 1988-; *ai:* T-Ball Coach; Curr Dev Comm Klawock City Sch; Church (Sunday Sch Teacher, Musice Dir); *office:* Klawock Sch Dist PO Box 9 Klawock AK 99925

CHAPMAN, GERTRUDE WELSH, Social Studies Teacher; *b:* Philadelphia, PA; *m:* Dennis S.; *c:* James; *ed:* (BS) Scndry Ed/His, West Chester 1972; Grad Stud Temple Univ, La Salle Univ, PA St; *cr:* Teacher Cncl Rock HS 1972-; *ai:* Long-Range Planning Dist, Soc Stud Evaluation, Presidential Classroom Selection Comms; Aid for Friends 1987-; Natl Arbor Day Fnd 1989-; Cncl Roch HS Advanced Placement US His Prgm; Piloted Soc Stud Prgm on TV; *office:* Council Rock HS 62 Swamp Rd Newtown PA 18940

CHAPMAN, JANE BLAIR, Elementary Instructional Supv; *b:* Crawfordville, GA; *ed:* (BS) Elem Ed, 1960; (MED) Elem Ed, 1975; (EDS) Elem Ed, 1976 GA Coll; Supervision Univ of GA 1985-86; *cr:* Teacher Fulton Cty Bd of Ed 1960-72; Taliaferro Cty Bd of Ed 1973-75; Richmond Cty Bd of Ed 1976-77; Fulton Cty Bd of Ed 1977-82; Warren Cty Bd of Ed 1982-86; Instrl Supv Warren Cty Bd of Ed 1986-; *ai:* Delta Kappa Gamma (VP 1984-86 Prgm Chm 1986-88 Research Chm 1988-); *office:* Mildred E Freeman Sch 111 Hopgood St Warrenton GA 30828

CHAPMAN, JANIE COPELAND, English Teacher; *b:* Ripley, MS; *m:* W. M.; *c:* Gregory, Vicky, Amy Shaw; *ed:* (BS) Eng, Soc Stud, Elem, 1953; *cr:* Elem Teacher Pine Grove HS 19550-53; Prin Chapman Elem 1954-56; Eng T Eacher Dumas HS 1956-57; Pine Grove HS 1958-; *ai:* Bsktbl Coach Chapman; 4-H Leader; Cmmty Club Leader; Jr Sr Banquet Spon; Sunday Sch Teacher; Tippah Cty Ed 1960-; MS Assn of Ed 1960-; NEA 1970-; Chapman Cmmty Club-1970-80; Pine Grove PTO-1958-; *home:* Rt 2 Ripley MS 38663

CHAPMAN, JUDITH (LOGAN), Mathematics Teacher; *b:* Galion, OH; *m:* Max K.; *c:* Carol Barford, Ronald; *ed:* (BS) Home Ec Ed, OH St Univ 1965; (MS) Home Ec/Food & Nutrition, Univ of IL 1978; (BS) Math, E IL Univ 1987; *cr:* Cty Extension Agent OH St Univ 1965-66; 1st Grade Teacher Highland Schls 1966; Home Ec Instr E IL Univ 1973-85; Math Teacher Charleston HS 1985-; *ai:* Scholastic Bowl Team Coach; IL Cncl Teachers of Math 1989-; Grassroots Peace Initiative Spokesperson 1979-87; *office:* Charleston HS 1615 Lincoln Ave Charleston IL 61920

CHAPMAN, KAREN RUSSELL, 4th Grade Teacher; *b:* Athens, OH; *c:* Joshua; *ed:* (BA) Elem Ed, OH Univ 1967; *cr:* 4th Grade Teacher The Plains Elem 1967-; *ai:* NEA, OEA, AEA 1967-; United Meth Women (Pres 1985-86, VP 1984-85); Federal Hocking Band Boosters VP 1989-; Martha Holden Jennings Scholar OH Univ 1985-86; *office:* The Plains Elem Sch Plains Rd The Plains OH 45780

CHAPMAN, LA VADA JOAN, Texas History Teacher; *b:* Brownfield, TX; *m:* Jackie Lynn; *c:* Julie, James; *ed:* (BA) Integrated Soc Stud, N TX St Univ 1984; His, Univ of N TX; *cr:* Teacher Clark Mid Sch 1984-; *ai:* His Club; His Trip Coord; Chrldr Spon; *home:* 3211 Lemmontree Plano TX 75074

CHAPMAN, LYNDEN RAY, Social Studies Teacher; *b:* Walla Walla, WA; *m:* Linda Christensen; *c:* Linette, Lyndel; *ed:* (BA) His, Walla Walla Coll 1972; (MA) Ed, Pacific Union Coll 1980; *cr:* Jr HS Teacher Bellflower SDA Sch 1974-76, Lodi Elem 1976-79, Virgil Hauselt Memorial Jr Acad 1979-81;sr HS Teacher Lodi Adventist Acad 1981-83; Resident Dean Monterey Bay Acad 1983-88; Sr HS Teacher Rio Lindo Adventist Acad 1988-; *ai:* Golf Club & Jr Class Spon; Var Bsktbl Coach; Stu Life Comm Mem; Volunteer Fireman; Sabbath Sch Teacher; Adventist Stu Personnel Assn 1984-88; *office:* Rio Lindo Adventist Acad 3200 Rio Lindo Ave Healdsburg CA 95448

CHAPMAN, MARGARET ANN, Reading Teacher; *b:* Gary, TX; *m:* John P.; *c:* John P. Jr.; *ed:* (BS) Home Ec, Stephen F Austin Univ 1961; (BS) Elem Ed, Univ of Houston 1970; *cr:* Kndgtn/6th Grade Teacher Houston Ind Sch Dist 1961-62, 1967-71; Home Ec Teacher Dulles HS 1962-66; Prin Trafton Acad 1972-77; 7th/8th Grade Eng/Soc Stud Teacher St Francis Episcopal 1978-81; Lang Art Teacher Memorial Parkway Jr HS 1981-; *ai:* TX St Teachers Assn, Katy Educl Assn, Greater Houston Area Rdng Cncl; Little League Asst Coach 1976-79; Houston Contemporary Woman Awd 1966; Church Youth Choir Dir 1964-68; *home:* 14006 Chevy Chase Houston TX 77077

CHAPMAN, PATRICIA J., 7th Grade Soc Stud Teacher; *b:* Manhattan, NY; *m:* Thomas J.; *c:* Heather L.; *ed:* (BA) Sociology/ Psych, Furman Univ 1983; Vallencia Comm Coll 1988; Natl Curr Dev 1984; Univ of Cntrl FL 1983-84; Sci Cert Summer Inst 1986-87; Mid Sch Cert; *cr:* 7th Grade Geography Teacher 1983-84, 7th Grade Geography/9th Grade Civics Teacher 1984-87, 6th Grade World Cultures/Sci Teacher 1987-88, 7th Grade Geography/Health Teacher 1988-89, 7th Grade Geography Teacher 1989-, Union Park Mid Sch; *ai:* Stu Cncl Spon; Coach Girls Vlybl; Team Leader; Faculty Advisory & Steering Comm; Stu Assistance Team; Intern Prgm Jr/Sr Block; Parent, Teacher, Stu Assn, Classroom Teachers Assn Orange Cty League Mid Schls; Tuskawilla Presbyn Church; *office:* Union Park Mid Sch 1844 Westfall Dr Orlando FL 32816

CHAPMAN, PAUL EUGENE, At-Risk Programs Coordinator; *b:* Fort Dix, NJ; *m:* Donna Jean Delores Brendle; *c:* Emily R.; *ed:* (BA) Elem Ed, 1978, (MA) Ed Admin, 1988 VPI & SU; Numerous Seminars Mid Level Ed & At-Risk Stus; *cr:* Teacher Bandy Elem 1978-83, Richlands Mid Sch 1983-87; At-Risk Prgms Coord Richland Mid Sch 1987-; *ai:* Life Skills for Adolescents Quest 1986-87; *home:* Rt 2 Box 360-A Cedar Bluff VA 24609

CHAPMAN, PAULINE MC WILLIAMS, English/Psychology Teacher; *b:* Logan, OH; *m:* Robert E.; *c:* Charles, Martha Chapman Plummer; *ed:* (BS) Eng/Psych, Univ of Rio Grande 1972; *cr:* Finance Officer Peoples Finance 1944-55; Homemaker 1955-72; Teacher Jackson HS 1972-; *ai:* OH Ed Assn, NEA 1972-; #1 Club; *home:* 220 High Pl Jackson OH 45640

CHAPMAN, SUE MANTHER, Spanish Teacher; *b:* Owatonna, MN; *m:* Wayne; *c:* Scott, Christopher; *ed:* Fr/Span, MacAlester Coll 1965-67; (BS) Fr/Span, Univ of MN 1969; Credits Beyond BS; *cr:* Fr/Span Teacher South Jr HS 1970-77, Lindbergh HS 1974-80; Span Teacher Hopkins HS 1981-; *ai:* Chairperson of Lindbergh HS Foreign Lang Dept 1978-81; Jr Class Adv 1982-86; MN Cncl of Teachers of Foreign Lang 1975-; *office:* Hopkins H S 2400 Lindberg Dr Minnetonka MN 55343

CHAPPELL, BARBARA HARMON, Guidance Counselor; *b:* Hillsville, VA; *m:* Dale M.; *c:* Kelley L.; *ed:* (BS) Upper Elem Ed, Radford Coll 1964; (MS) Human Services/Guidance, Radford Univ 1988; Quest Skills for Adolescence Leadership Trng Cert; Grad Stud Curr Dev, Guidance & Counseling, Self-Study, Admin Review, Cmptr Trng; *cr:* 6th/7th Grade Teacher Fairview Elem Sch 1964-65; 5th Grade Teacher Galax Elem Sch 1965-66; 7th Grade Math Teacher Galax Elem & Mid Schls 1967-89; Guidance Cnslr Galax Mid Sch 1989-; *ai:* Grade Chairperson 1972-89; Mid Sch SCA Spon 1985-89; K-7th Grade Curr Dev Comm Chairperson 1982-85; Galax Ed Assn (Chairperson for Several Comms, Supt Advisory Comm Rep, Bldg Rep, VP) 1966-; Delta Kappa Gamma (1st VP, 2nd VP, Corresponding Secy) 1970-; VA Teachers of Math VP 1970-72; Phi Kappa Phi Mem 1988-; Bus & Prof Womens Club (Recording 1st VP, Secy, 2nd VP) 1970-80; Women of the Moose (Membership Comm, His Remembrance Comm) 1978-; 1st United Meth Church (Sunday Sch Teacher 1970-82, Circle Chairperson 1974-76); Outstanding Young Women in America 1972; Teacher of Yr 1984; Exec Educator & Natl Sch Bd Assn Outstanding Achievement Awd 1988; *office:* Galax Mid Sch Clark Ave Galax VA 24333

CHAPPELL, KATIE JONES, 4th Grade Teacher; *b:* Tuskegee, AL; *m:* Charlie; *ed:* (BS) His, AL St Univ 1970; (MED) Elem Ed, Univ of GA 1973; *cr:* Teacher Morgan Cty Mid Sch 1970-80, Oglethorpe Ave Elem Sch 1980-; *ai:* GA Assn of Educators Building Rep 1988-; Teacher of Yr 1986.

CHAPPELL, ROGER BERNT, 7th/8th Grade Science Teacher; *b:* Placerville, Ca; *s:* Janice Elaine Peterson; *ed:* (BA) Ed, Sacramento St Coll 1960; *cr:* Phys Ed Teacher Hyde Jr HS 1960-62; 6th Grade Teacher Pinewood Elem 1962-64; 7th/8th Grade Sci/Phys Ed Teacher Pinewood Elem 1964-88; 7th/8th Grade Sci Teacher Sierra Ridge Mid Sch 1988-; *ai:* Wrestling Coach; Winter Venture Club; Cross Cntry Skiing Spon; NEA, CA Teachers Assn 1960-; El Dorado Cty Teachers Assn Pres 1968-70; Natl Ski Patrol 1964-79; El Dorado Nordic Ski Patrol 1980-; El Dorado SECPA Teacher Recogition 1986-87; Pollock Pines Dist Teacher of Yr 1987-88; US Forest Service Certificate of Merit & Cash Awd 1986; El Dorado Cty Sheriff Dept Awd of Appreciation 1986; CA Sci Trng Acad Fellowship 1984-86; Class of 1990 Appreciation Awd 1990; *office:* Sierra Ridge Mid Sch 2700 Amber Trail Pollock Pines CA 95726

CHAPPELLE, BARBARA WOOTEN, 10th & 12th Grade Eng Teacher; *b:* Miami, FL; *m:* Richard A.; *c:* Richard Jr., Beverly J., Kristen N.; *ed:* (BA) Eng, Morris Brown Coll 1961; Univ of FL; Stetson Univ; UMSL; *cr:* Teacher Miami Northwestern Sr HS 1961-68; Teacher/Yrbk Spon Miami Norland Sr HS 1968-77; Teacher Riverview Gardens Sr HS 1979-; *ai:* Spon Pep Club; Mem of Natl Honor Society; Mem Comm Schl & Comm Cmmty Comm for Schls Evaluation; Curr Comm Chm for Eng 2; Chm of Comm for New Courses Eng Skills 9; Mem Tutorial Comm; NEA MO Assn Teachers of Eng 1979-; NCTE 1979-; Greater St Louis Eng Teachers Assn 1979-; Alpha Kappa Alpha; AAUW (Pres 1987-89 Vice Pres 1985-87); Educl Fnd 1989; Sunday Sch (Teacher 1977-88 Supt 1988-89); *home:* 6753 Ryan Crest Dr Florissant MO 63033

CHAPPELLE, GALEN RODNEY, Eighth Grade Teacher; *b:* Birmingham, AL; *ed:* (BS) Bio/Sociology, San Jose St Univ 1977; (MA) Sci Ed, Univ of Southern CA 1980; Math Certificate Loyola-Marymount Univ; *ai:* Academic Coord of Competitions; Vlybl, Bsktbl, Ftbl Coach; CA Jr Schlsp Fed & Stu Cncl Moderator; Western Assn of Schls & Coll Adv; Math Coord; Kappa Alpha Psi (Historian, Bd of Dir) 1977-85, Undergrad Achievement 1977; Alpha Kappa Delta Treas 1980-81, Scholastic Achievement 1979; Black Educators Assn General Mem 1978-, Outstanding Teaching Awd 1986; NAACP 1980-; Black Agenda 1982-; Men of Achievement; Young Men in America; 3000 Top Personalities of World; Whos Who in CA & Black America; *office:* St Agnes Sch 1428 W Adams Blvd Los Angeles CA 90007

CHAPPELLE, KAREN LORRAINE (RANDALL), 5th Grade Teacher; *b:* Conway, SC; *m:* Herman Sr.; *c:* Herman II, Kendall; *ed:* (BA) Elem Ed, SC St Coll 1976; Staff Dev Courses; Data Collector; Several Wkshps; *cr:* Tax Clerk Harry Cty Courthouse 1976; Teacher Fulton Cty Bd of Ed 1978-; *ai:* Lib, Cultural Arts, Awds Comm; Cmmty Scout Work; ASCD Mem; Hillside Intnl Truth Center Inc, Alpha Kappa Alpha Mem; Teacher of Yr Kathleen Mitchell Elem 1983-84; *office:* Harriet Tubman Elem Sch 2861 Lakeshore Dr College Park GA 30337

CHAREST, LORRAINE BEAULIEU, French Teacher; *b:* New Bedford, MA; *m:* Gerard Jr.; *c:* Gerard, Michael, Danielle; *ed:* (BA) Fr, Bridgewater St 1967; Summer Study, Luniversite D Avingnon France; *cr:* Fr/Eng Teacher Bishop Stang HS 1984-; *ai:* NHS & Awds Adv; Teacher & Cnslr for Stu European Trips; Amer Assn Teachers of Fr Mem 1985-; Cath Teachers Assn 1985-; JH Plumb Lib Chm 1981-85; Rochester Arts Cncl Chm 1983-87; Eucharistic Minister St Rose of Lima 1988-; Recipient of Amer Assn Teachers of Fr Schlsp for Study in Avignon France 1987; Developed Fr Cmptr Prgm; Planning Bd for Assn Canado Americaine Summer Camp.

CHARLEFOUR, PEGGY LYNN, Fifth Grade Teacher; *b:* Detroit, MI; *m:* Dick; *c:* Michael, Jennie; *ed:* (BA) Elem Ed/Eng Major Adrian Coll 1968; Eastern Mi/Mi St; Writers Project Summer Institute; *cr:* Title II Teacher Rdng for Disadvantaged Summers 1968 & 1969, Third Grade Teacher 1968-84, Fifth Grade Teacher 1985-Blissfield Elem; *ai:* Served As Grade Level Chairperson 3 Yrs; Direct Outdoor Ed Prgm; Teach An Enrichment Class Challenge U Prgm; MI Rdng Assn 84-; Southwest MI Writers Project 89-; *office:* Blissfield Elem Sch 630 S Lane St Blissfield MI 49228

CHARLES, RALEIGH GLENN, Biology/Computer Instructor; *b:* Murfreesboro, TN; *m:* Michelle M. Meldrum; *c:* Chelsea, Ashleigh, Arianne; *ed:* (BA) Bio/Ed, Oakland Univ 1972; (MS) Bio, E MI Univ 1977; (EDD) Curr Dev, Wayne St Univ 1985; IBM Networking; *cr:* Instr Eppler Jr HS 1972-; *ai:* Eppler Jr HS Cmptr Coord; Toastmasters 573 Pres 1981, Leadership 1982; NSTA 1980-82; ASCD 1990; Utica Ed Assn Building Rep; St Johns TLC Volunteer 1989-; *office:* Eppler Jr HS 45461 Brownell Utica MI 48087

CHARLESTON, DEBORAH JOAN, Fourth Grade Teacher; *b:* Cambridge, OH; *ed:* (BA) Elem Ed, W Liberty St Coll 1971; (MA) Ed, Akron Univ 1980; *cr:* Teacher Beech Grove Elem 1971-80; *ai:* Stu Cncl, Elem Chrldr, TAG Adv; Math Comm Chairperson; Competency, Cmptr Curr, Inservice Comm; Phi Delta Kappa; Delta Kappa Gamma Schlsp Chm; Rolling Hills Ed Assn Secy; AAUW Mem; Chancel & Handbell Choir; Teacher of Yr; Jennings Scholar; *office:* Beech Grove Elem 8900 White Acre Rd Cambridge OH 43725

CHARLTON, SANDRA MANNING, 1st Grade Teacher; *b:* Miami, FL; *m:* Stephen L.; *c:* Chris Edgeworth, Barrett Edgeworth; *ed:* (AA) Elem Ed, E MS Jr Coll 1968; (BS) Elem Ed, MS Univ for Women 1971; *cr:* 1st/2nd Grade Teacher Wilkerson Gardens 1971-74; 1st Grade Teacher Calloway Elem 1974-; *ai:* Birmingham Ed Assn, AL Ed Assn, NEA.

CHARNEY, WILLIAM JAMES, Language Arts Teacher; *b:* Kittanning, PA; *ed:* (BA) Eng, Penn St Univ 1978; *cr:* Lang Art Teacher Stanhope Sch 1979-; *ai:* Lang Art Curr Comm Chm; Newspaper Adv 1982; Asst Vlybl Coach; SEA (Secy 1985, Negotiations Chm 1983-87); SCEA Bargaining Coord 1987-89; NHEA Uniserv Comm 1989; *office:* Stanhope Sch Valley Rd Stanhope NJ 07874

CHARTIER, TOM D., Health/Phys Ed/Drvr Ed Teacher; *b:* Sergeant Bluff, IA; *m:* Ruth A. Rippke; *c:* Megan B., Jill R.; *ed:* (BAE) Phys Ed, Wayne St Coll 1971; Health Counseling Skills for Living Classes; Comm Coll Voc Emergency Medical Technician & Defibrillation; *cr:* Scndry Teacher Woodbury Cntrl Sch 1971-; *ai:* Jr HS Ftbl/Bsktbl/Track Coach; Jr HS Play; AAHPER 1988-; Moville Ambulance Squad Trng Supervisor 1988-; *office:* Woodbury Central H S So 4th St Moville IA 51039

CHASE, ALONZO O., 5th Grade Teacher; *b:* Salamanca, NY; *m:* Jo Ann Scheffer; *c:* Lon, Karen, Paula; *ed:* (BS) Elem Ed, Geneseo St 1972; Electronics; *cr:* Laboratory Technician Consolidated Vacuum Corporation 1964-67; Technician Mallory Corporation 1967-68; Wire Technician Eastman Kodak 1968-70; Teacher Canisteo Cntrl 1973-; *ai:* Elem Sci Comm; Kiwanis Pres 1985-; Sparta Fire Company Pres 1973-; Sparta Town Councilman 1982-86; *office:* Canisteo Cntrl Sch 84 Greenwood St Canisteo NY 14823

CHASE, CHRISTOPHER LOCKWOOD, English Teacher; *b:* Loredo, TX; *ed:* (BA) Eng, 1987, (BA) Fr, 1987 E NM Univ; *cr:* Lit Teacher Van Buren Mid Sch 1987; Eng Teacher Highland HS 1987-; *ai:* Sch Improvement Team & At-Risk Comm Mem; ATF 1987-; Spec Olympics Coach 1988-; Teacher of Week; *office:* Highland HS 4700 Coal Ave SE Albuquerque NM 87108

CHASE, JERALD L., Mathematics Department Chair; *b:* Cincinnati, OH; *m:* Betty Redding; *c:* Timothy, Brad, Will; *ed:* (BS) Math, 1966, (MAED) Music Ed, 1972 E KY Univ; (MRE) Religious Ed, Southern Baptist Theological Seminary 1978; KY Rank I Georgetown Coll 1982; *cr:* Choral Music/Math Teacher Shelby Cty HS 1966-76; Math Teacher Bondurant Jr HS 1979-80; Teacher/Math Dept Chm Western Hills HS 1980-; *ai:* Beta & Math Clubs Spon; Sch Dist In-Service Comm; NCTM, KY Cncl Teachers of Math 1982-; Amer Choral Dirs Assn 1966-82; Music Educators Natl Conference 1966-76; Bridgeport Ruritan Club (Secy 1977-) 1975-, Ruritan of Yr 1987.

CHASE, LA VETA YOUNG, Teacher; *b:* Stillwater, OK; *m:* Daniel L.; *c:* Steven, Rebecca, James; *ed:* (BA) Elem Ed, 1978, (MS) Rdng Specialist, 1982 SE OK St Univ; Adult Ed; *cr:* Classroom Teacher Healdton Mid Sch 1978-; GED Teacher Ardmore Public Schls 1988-; *ai:* Staff Dev Comm; Negotiations Team; Textbook Comm Mem; Drug-Awareness Comm; 4 Yr Plan Comm; Chrldr Coach Healton HS 1978-88, Healton Mid Sch & Jr HS 1980-88; Healdton Assn Classroom Teacher (Pres 1980-81, VP 1979-80, 1988-); OEA, NEA; ESA (Pres, VP) 1971-76; KKAJ Favorite Teacher Healdton Schls 1989.

CHASE, MICHAEL JOHN, Physical Education Teacher; *b:* Bremerton, WA; *m:* Cheryl Anne Schmitz; *c:* John M.; *ed:* (BA) Phys Ed, W WA Univ 1983; His, Univ of WA; *cr:* Phys Ed/Health Teacher 1984-85, Sci Teacher 1985-86, Phys Ed Teacher 1986-Bremerton Mid Sch; *ai:* 8th Grade Boys Bsktbl & Bsbl Coach; PTO Teacher of Month 1989; *office:* Bremerton Mid Sch 1300 E 30th St Bremerton WA 98310

CHASE, PEGGY ANN, 8th Grade Science Teacher; *b:* Boston, MA; *ed:* (BA) Geography, Clark Univ 1975; (MED) Curr & Instruction Scndry Sci Ed, Northeastern Univ 1978; *cr:* 8th Grade Teacher Silver Lake Regional Jr HS 1978 80, Stoneham Mid Sch 1983-; *ai:* Intramural Instr; Kappa Delat Pi 1989; Salem St Collaborative 1987 Outstanding Mid Sch Sci Teacher; Stoneham Teachers Assn Pres 1988-89; Negotiation Chair 1989-90; *office:* Stoneham Mid Sch 101 Central St Stoneham MA 02180

CHASE, SHARON LYNNE (HARRIS), 5th Grade Teacher; *b:* Yakima, WA; *m:* Jerry (dec); *c:* Joseph, Susan; *ed:* (BA) Elem Ed/Scndry Home Ec, Cntrl WA St 1959; Elem Ed, Univ of MT 1975; Grad & Correspondence Work, Cntrl WA St Coll, WA St Univ, Univ of MT, NMC, FVCC, Salish Coll; *cr:* 5th Grade Teacher St John Elem Sch 1959-61, Quincy Elem/Pioneer Sch 1961-64; 7th Grade Teacher Kalispell Jr HS 1964-65; 5th Grade Teacher Evergreen Elem 1965-; *ai:* Onward to Excl, CRISS, Curr Comm; Alateen & Alanon Spon; NEA, MEA, WEA; EEA (Pres, VP, Secy, Treas); Alanon (Secy, Treas 1984-89), 5 Yr Medallion 1989; Chancel Choir 1984-; Received a Leadership Schlsp in Coll; *home:* 348 Jaquette Rd Kalispell MT 59901

CHASEY, VIRGINIA WILBANKS, Science Teacher; *b:* Gadsden, AL; *m:* August Anthony; *c:* Susan, Allen, Sally; *ed:* (BA) Elem Ed, Univ of Fl 1966; (MA) Elem Ed, Univ of W Fl 1975; *cr:* Teacher Orange Park Elem 1966-68; Research Asst Univ of W FL 1975-76; Teacher Lakeside Jr HS 1983-86, Orange Park HS 1986-87, Lakeside Jr HS 1987-; *ai:* 7th Grade Chairperson; Teacher Rep Cty Citizens Advisory Comm; FL Assn of Sci Teachers 1984-; *office:* Lakeside Jr HS 2750 Moody Rd Orange Park FL 32073

CHASTAIN, MARGARET STOKES, Third Grade Teacher; *b:* Greer, SC; *m:* Roger Neil; *c:* Barry M., Glenda Whetstone, Jerry S.; *ed:* (BS) Phys Ed, Winthrop Coll 1957; Grad Stud Rdng, Univ SC Columbia; *cr:* Phys Ed Instr Hill Crest HS 1957-58; 2nd Grade Teacher St Matthews Elem 1959-60; Phys Ed Teacher St Matthews HS 1963-65; 3rd Grade Teacher Wade Hampton Acad 1970-72, Calhoun Acad 1973-; *ai:* Jr Var Bsktbl Coach; Private Swim Instr; Mental Health Chm 1973; *home:* 303 Rucker Dr Saint Matthews SC 29135

CHASTEEN, SYDNEY W., English/Spanish Teacher; *b:* Selma, AL; *m:* Richard Allen; *c:* Richard A. Jr., Jonathan Brooks; *ed:* (BA) Eng, Judson Coll 1975; *cr:* Eng/Span/Speech Teacher Southern Acad 1975-; *ai:* Jr Class & Prom Spon; Play Dir; Beauty Pageant Coord; *office:* Southern Acad 407 College St Greensboro AL 36744

CHATHAM, EDWARD ALLEN, History Teacher; *b:* Burkgurnett, TX; *m:* Erma Gail Arnold; *c:* Roger A., Kyle R., Jaci R., Joshua M.; *ed:* (AS) Phys Ed/Health, Murray St Coll 1963; (BS) Phys Ed/Eng, Southeastern St Univ 1967; (MS) Guidance/Counseling, Northwestern St Univ 1973; Scndry Admin, Cntrl St Univ 1987; *cr:* Soc Stud Teacher/Coach Fox HS 1967-68, Freedom HS 1968-70, Beaver HS 1970-76, Kingfisher HS 1976-84, Healdton HS 1984-86, Wilson HS 1986-; *ai:* All Classes Spon; Plains Indian Club Spon; Girls Track, Bsktbl, Cross Cntry Coach; Boys Track, Ftbl, Bsktbl Coach; OK Ed Assn, NEA 1967-; OK Coaches Assn 1967-, All-St Cnslr; *home:* 628 NW 4th Wilson OK 73463

CHAVEZ, AVELARDO ANTONIO, Health & Physical Ed Teacher; *b:* Alamogordo, NM; *m:* Susie Antonio Avalos; *c:* Steven, Anthony, Chavez; *ed:* (BS) Phys Ed, Univ of TX El Paso 1979; *cr:* Health/Phys Ed Teacher Glen Cove Elem 1979-80, Tierra Del Sol 1980-; *ai:* HS Bsktbl & Boys Var Ofcl; *office:* Tierra Del Sol Sch 1832 Tommy Aaron Dr El Paso TX 79936

CHAVEZ, DEBORAH LEE, Second Grade Teacher; *b:* Albuquerque, NM; *ed:* (AA) Art, Leeward Comm Coll & Univ of HI 1974; (BS) Art Ed, Mid TN St Univ 1976; Working on Cert in Elem Ed & Masters, Mid TN St Univ; *cr:* Pottery Instr Mid TX St Univ 1976-77; 2nd Grade Teacher John Colemon Elem 1978-88, Smyrna Elem 1988-; *ai:* Secret Pals Organizer & Supvr; Art Supply Chairperson; Sch Level & Publicity Campaign Mem; Building Level Rep; Mission Trips; Singles & Adult Choirs; Lib Comm Chairperson; Missions Comm Secy; Art Club; Headed Building Level Attendance Comm; Grievance, Publicity, Title IX, Fair Ethics, Textbook Adoption Comm; NEA 1978-; Rutherford Ed Assn (Building Rep 1979-81) 1978-; TN Ed Assn 1978-; Distinguished Classroom Teacher Awd 1987; Mid TN St Univ Cmmty Chorus; Murfreesboro Chrstn Womens Club; Lifeline (Historian, Music Librarian); Belle Aire Baptist Church (Mem, Librarian, Sunday Sch Teacher); GSA; PTA, PTO Historian; Vacation Bible Sch Backyard Bible Club (Teacher, Trainer, Dir, Song Leader); Sunday Sch (Class Secy, Group/Act Leader); Univ of KS BOEG Schlsp to Art Division Midwestern Music & Art Camp; Art Wkshps; TN Instructional Model Method of Teaching Wkshp; Developed Sch-Wide Tile-Mosaic Art Project; Nom Outstanding Young Educator; Teacher of Yr 1985-86; Belmont Coll Most Creative & Super Calligrapher Awd 1982; Poems Published 1983; *home:* 1614-B Elrod St Murfreesboro TN 37130

CHAVEZ, LORRAINE VERONICA, 3rd Grade Teacher; *b:* Albuquerque, NM; *m:* Ken E.; *c:* Veronica; *ed:* (BA) Elem Ed, 1979, (MS) Elem Ed/Guidance/Counseling, 1986 Univ of NM; *cr:* Teacher Univ of NM 1980-; *ai:* Soc Stud, Sci Fair, Literacy Comm Rep; NEA 1980-; *office:* Atrisco Elem 1201 Atrisco SW Albuquerque NM 87105

CHAVEZ, MILDRED HERNANDEZ, Lang Arts/Speech/Drama Teacher; *b:* Albuquerque, NM; *m:* Ambrose R.; *c:* Jennifer L., Kimberly A., Amanda M.; *ed:* (BS) Elem Ed, Univ of Albuquerque 1980; (MS) Mid Sch Ed, Univ of NM 1990; *cr:* Teacher Los Lunas Mid Sch 1980-; *ai:* Annual Adv; Speech & Drama Spon; Teacher Assisted Prgm Adv; Delta Kappa Gamma 1985-; NM Cncl of Cmptr Users in Ed 1988-89; Civil Air Patrol 1990; Teacher Enhancement Prgm on Internship Univ of NM; Finalist Distinguished Teacher of Yr Los Lunas 1988-; *office:* Los Lunas Mid Sch PO Drawer 1300 Los Lunas NM 87031

CHEATHAM, MARTHA LEE (SMITH), Fifth/Sixth Grade Teacher; *b:* Magnolia, AR; *m:* Dewey; *c:* Michael; *ed:* (BA) Elem Ed, Univ of AR Monticello 1983; Working Towards Masters; *cr:* LD Resource Aide Hastings/Anderson Elem 1975-81; Substitute Teacher Magnolia Public Schls 1983-84; 5th/6th Grade Teacher Waldo Elem 1984-; *ai:* AEA, NEA, Alpha Chi 1982-; *home:* 214 Troy Magnolia AR 71753

CHEATHAM, VAL R., Teacher of Gifted; *b:* Ulysses, KS; *m:* Patricia C. Becker; *c:* Mark, Valerhy Cheatham Harmon; *ed:* (BA) Ed, Mc Pherson Coll 1958; (MA) Ed Admin, Wichita St Univ 1963; Spec Ed, Emporia Coll 1965; NDEA Grant Soc Stud, DC Teachers Coll 1966; *cr:* Teacher Bryant Sch 1958-64, Martin Sch 1964-65; Teacher of Gifted Mc Lean Sch 1965-78, OK Sch 1978-; *ai:* NEA, KNEA, WNEA 1958-; Phi Delta Kappa 1969-; BSA Merit Badge Cnslr; Author, Composer, Cartoonist; *home:* 3915 Bella Vista Wichita KS 67203

CHEEK, DEBORAH LYNN, Mathematics Teacher; *b:* Oregon, IL; *ed:* (BS) Math, Univ of Dubuque 1973; (MS) Scndry Ed, N IL Univ 1983; *cr:* Math Teacher Aplington Sch 1974-; *ai:* Aplington Academic Team Spon; Mathcounts Coach; Gifted & Talented & Cmptr Comm Mem; Polo Ed Assn, IL Ed Assn, NEA 1974-; IL Cncl Teachers of Math 1976-; NCTM 1982-; Kappa Delta Pi 1972; St of IL Scientific Literacy Pilot Prgm Grant Co-Awd; *office:* Aplington Sch 610 E Mason Polo IL 61064

CHEEK, DONNA MATTHEWS, Vocational Home Ec Teacher; *b:* Mt Vernon, MO; *c:* Cary C.; *ed:* (BS) Home Economics, SMSU 1961; (MED) ED, Drury 1973; Univ of AR; *cr:* Hm Ec Teacher Walker HS 1961-66; Substitute Hillcrest HS 1966-67; Hm Ec Teacher Walker HS 1967-71; Southwest HS 1971-; *ai:* FHA; SWAT; Curr Comm St Level; MO St Teachers Assn 1961 Distinguished Service Awd; Southwest MO H E Teachers Secy 1978-80; FHA/HERO 1990; MO Vocational Assn 1973-; FHA/HERO Alumni 1989-; *home:* Rt 2 Box 227-A Cassville MO 65625

CHEEK, GAYLE GULOTTA, Counselor; *b:* New Orleans, LA; *m:* Ronald G.; *c:* Courtney, Meredith; *ed:* (BS) Scndry Ed, 1972, (MED) Guidance/Counseling, 1975 Loyola Univ; *cr:* Teacher 1972-, Cnslr 1985- Adams Mid Sch; *ai:* Stu Cncl Spon; Sch Building Level Comm; Parent Teacher Group Bd Mem; Licensed Prof Cnslr St of LA; *office:* Adams Mid Sch 5525 Heniean Pl Metairie LA 70003

CHEEK, JANA HALEY, Biology/Physical Sci Teacher; *b:* Marietta, GA; *m:* Benjamin Franklin IV; *c:* Rebecca; *ed:* (BS) Bio, Presbyn Coll 1983; (MED) Bio, N GA Coll 1990; *cr:* Sci Teacher Lithia Springs HS 1984-85, Griffin Mid Sch 1985-86, Stephens Cty HS 1986-; *ai:* Sci Olympiad Team Coach; Curr Comm; PAGE Mem 1984-; Jr Womens Club Mem 1986-, Spice of Yr Awd 1989; Toccoa Cotillion Club Mem 1990; *office:* Stephens Cty HS Rt 5 White Pine Rd Toccoa GA 30577

CHEEK, JUDITH ANNE, Third Grade Teacher; *b:* Baltimore, MD; *ed:* (BA) Psych, Univ of MD 1968; Teaching Certificate Elem Ed, Univ of MD Baltimore Cty 1971; (MS) Counseling, Johns Hopkins Univ 1979; Numerous Inservice Courses Ed; *cr:* 4th Grade Teacher Riderwood Elem Sch 1972-75; 5th Grade Teacher Padonia Elem Sch 1975-80; 3rd Grade Teacher Relay Elem Sch 1980-; *ai:* Relays Annual Sci Fair Chairperson; Relays Recycling Prgm Spon; 1st Yr Teachers Demonstration Teacher; Baltimore Cty Soc Stud Cadre; MD St Teachers Assn, NEA, Teachers Assn of Baltimore Cty 1972-; Howard Cty Amer Red Cross Secy 1986-; Calonsville Presbyn Church Elder 1980-82; Awds Excl in Ed Nom; Co-Author Published Psych Articles; *office:* Relay Elem Sch 5885 Selford Rd Arbutus MD 21227

CHEELY, JULIA ELAINE, Middle School English Teacher; *b:* Warrenton, GA; *ed:* (BS) Eng/Bus Ed, Savannah St Coll 1963; Columbia Univ & GA Coll Milledgeville; *cr:* Teacher Taliaferro Cty, Hancock Cntrl Sch; *ai:* Stu Cncl; Dept Chairperson; Team Chairperson & Recorder; Prof Assn of GA Educators; Local Teachers Assn Reporter; SSC Alumni Assn Secy; Fellowship Church; *home:* 801 Dyer Dr Sparta GA 31087

CHEGWIDDEN, DOROTHY C., Honors English IV Teacher; *b:* Great Bend, KS; *m:* Dennis; *c:* Lincoln, Stephanie; *ed:* (AA) Eng, Hutchinson Comm Coll; (BA) Eng, 1974, (MSED) Ed/Curr, 1987 Wichita St Univ; Eng, Corpus Christi St Univ; *cr:* 9th-12th Grade Scndry Eng Teacher 1977-84; Scndry Eng/Honors Eng Teacher Buhler HS 1984-87, Tuloso-Midway Ind Sch Dist 1987-; *ai:* NHS Faculty Comm Rand Morgan HS 1989-; UIL Ready Writing Coach Morgan HS 1989-; Effective Sch TX St Accreditation Preperation, Campus Goals, Schlsp Comms Rand Morgan HS 1988-89; Scndry Eng Curr Writing Co-Chairperson Rand Morgan HS 1988-89; Wrote 12th Grade Honors Curr Rand Morgan HS 1988-89; UIL Literary Criticism Dist Contest Dir Rand Morgan HS 1988-89; Textbook Adoption Comm 1988-89; Curr Revision & Stu Handbook Comms Buhler HS 1984-87; TX Joint Cncl of Eng 1987-; NCTE 1983-86; Teachers Organization of KS; KS Teachers of Eng 1974-84; TX Eng Teachers Cncl; NEA; Teachers Assn Unified Sch Dist #313 Building Rep 1986-87; Most influential Teacher S Methodist Univ.

CHELSTROM, STEPHEN DEAN, Sixth Grade Science Teacher; *b:* Moline, IL; *m:* Rita Jane Sievert; *c:* Kristian, Abby, Nels; *ed:* (BS) Elem Ed, IL St Univ 1974; (MS) Elem Sci Ed, Western Il Univ 1988; *cr:* Title I Math Teacher 1975-76, 5th Grade Teacher 1976-77, 6th Grade Sci Teacher 1977-, Dir of Environmental 1979 Orion Mid Sch Unit Dist 223 & CR Hanna; *ai:* Mem Academic Excl Comm; The Honor Society of Phi Kappa Phi 1988-; NEA/IL Ed Assn/Orion Ed Assn 1975-; IL Sci Teachers Assn 1979-; Ind Order of Vikings Thor Lodge #9 1980-; *office:* Orion Mid Sch 802 12th Ave Orion IL 61273

CHENEY, JONATHAN EDWIN, Mathematics Teacher; *b:* Albuquerque, NM; *ed:* (AS) Engineering, Cntrl WY Coll 1982; (BS) Math, Adams St Coll 1984; *cr:* Teacher Burges HS 1986-; *ai:* Asst Coach Boys Var Bsktbl; *office:* Burges HS 7800 Edgemere El Paso TX 79925

CHENEY, LONNIE E., Computer Mathematics Teacher; *b:* Farrell, PA; *m:* Chryse Croushore; *ed:* (BS) Math/Scndry Ed, 1988, (BA) Psych, 1988 Grove City Coll; *cr:* Cmptr Teacher Hampton HS 1988-; *ai:* Cmptr Club Spon; Jr Var Bsbl Coach; Hampton Ed Assn 1989-; Peninsula Cncl of Math 1988-; VA HS Coaches Assn 1989-; *office:* Hampton HS 1491 W Queen St Hampton VA 23669

CHENIER, EVA PICOU, Science & Physical Ed Teacher; *b:* Lafayette, LA; *m:* Kenneth Wayne; *c:* Brandon; *ed:* (BS) Health/Phys Ed/Safety Ed, 1974, (MED) Scndry Ed/Health/Phys Ed/Safety, 1976 Southern Univ; General Sci, Southern Univ; *cr:* Teacher St Landry Parish Sch Bd 1974-; *ai:* 4-H, Math, Sci Club Adv; LA Ed Assn U974-, Service Awd; St Landry Parish Ed Assn Corresponding Secy 1989-; St Landry Parish Classroom Teachers Assn 1974-; Southern Univ Alumni Assn Treas 1985-89; *home:* PO Box 510 1000 E Leo St Opelousas LA 70571

CHENOWETH, MARGARET LOUISE QUICK, GED-ABE Teacher; *b:* Hugo, CO; *m:* Marion E.; *c:* Charles, Mary A. Chenoweth Alton; *ed:* (BA) Ed, CO Coll 1959; (MA) Ed, Adams St 1976; *cr:* Rural Teacher Big Rock Dist 1948-52; Elem Teacher Springfield RE4 Dist 1953-82; GED-ABE Teacher Baca Cty BOCES 1982-; *ai:* Catechism Teacher Elem Level; Church Cncl, Hospital Auxiliary, VFW auxiliary Mem; Accountability Comm Pres Mem 1980-85; *home:* 700 Fountain PO Box 424 Springfield CO 81073

CHERBAS, CHRISTY ANDREW, Soc Stud Teacher/Dept Chm; *b:* Tacoma, WA; *m:* Wendy C. Wigen; *c:* Andrew, Anthony, Nicholas; *ed:* (BA) Soc Stud, Univ of Puget Sound 1964; (MA) Ed, OR St Univ 1968; Cmptrs/Indstrl Arts/Classroom Mgmt; *cr:* Teacher Montesano HS 1964-65; Hudtloff Jr HS 1965-67; Lochburn Jr HS 1967-; *ai:* Dept Chm Soc Stud; Varsity Bsbl Coach; Self Study Chm; Asst Bsktbl & Ftbl; Yrbk Co-Adv; Prin Adv Chm; Staff Retreat Chm; Dist Soc Stud Cir Dev; Sch for 21st Century Comm; NEA 1965-; WEA 1965-; CPEA 1965-; PTA 1965 Golden Acorn 1968; Lakewood JC Distinguished Svc Awd Prin Awd 1987; Nom Gonzaga Outstanding Teacher Awd; Nom Dist Outstanding Teacher; St Teacher Awd; Nom DAR Teacher Awd; *home:* 8717 92nd St NW Gig Harbor WA 98335

CHERNETSKY, MARILYN ANN, 9th Grade Speech Teacher; *b:* Kingston, PA; *ed:* (BA) Speech/Drama, 1971, (MA) Ed, 1980 Marycrest Coll; *cr:* Teacher Frank L Smart Jr HS 1972-; *ai:* Stu Cncl Adv; Strive Comm Chm Stu Morale; Variety Show Dir; NCA Co Chm Stu Act; Davenport Ed Assn 1972-; NEA 1972-; IA St Ed Assn 1972-; Outstanding Scott Cty Teacher Nom 1988; *office:* F L Smart Jr H S 1934 W 5th St Davenport IA 52802

CHERRIE, LOLITA V., Third Grade Teacher; *b:* New Orleans, LA; *m:* Edward E. Jr.; *c:* Sean, Bradley; *ed:* (BA) Elem Ed, 1968, (MA) Curr/Instructions, 1983 Xavier Univ; *cr:* 4th Grade Teacher Thomas Jefferson 1968-75; 3rd/5th Grade Teacher McDonogh #39 1975-84; 1st/3rd Grade Teacher Little Woods 1985-88; 2nd/3rd Grade Teacher McDonogh #39 1988-; *ai:* Lang Art Chairperson; Discipline & Field Day Comm; Mini Fair Volunteer; Phi Delta Kappa, Intnl Rdng Assn, AFT Mem; *office:* McDonogh #39 Elem Sch 5800 St Roch Ave New Orleans LA 70122

CHERRY, ALICE HIERS, Geography/Related Art Teacher; *b:* Manchester, NH; *m:* James William; *c:* LuAnn, J me, Joelle; *ed:* (BS) Kndgtn/Primary Elem, Glassboro St Coll 1965; Teacher Acad 1988; Advanced Rdng Glassboro St 1983; Pre Sch Glassboro St 1974; *cr:* Kndgtn Teacher New York Ave Sch 1965-66; 2nd Grade Teacher 1966-67, 1st Grade Teacher 1968-69 Dennisville Elem Sch; Interium Teacher Lower Township Elem Sch 1978-80; 7th/8th Grade Rdng/Math/Soc Stud/Related Art Teacher Lower Cape May Regional 1980-; *ai:* Mentor-At-Risk & Club Adv; Voc Sch Trustee Adv; NJEA 1980; Kiwanis Adv Builders Club 1987-; Conferternity of Chrstn Doctrine Adv 1986-; *office:* Richard M Teitelman Jr HS Rt 9 Erma NJ 08204

CHERRY, FAYE HARBER, History & Government Teacher; *b:* Centerville, TN; *m:* Bob; *c:* Leah, Robin; *ed:* (BS) Soc Stud, TN Tech Univ 1962; (MED) Admin/Supervision, TN St Univ 1985; *cr:* Teacher Hickman Cty Jr HS 1962-64, Hickman Cty HS 1980-; *ai:* Co-Spon Sch Wide Fund Raiser; NEA, TEA, HCEA; *office:* Hickman Cty HS 1645 Bulldog Blvd Centerville TN 37033

CHERRY, JEFFREY ALLEN, Earth Science Teacher; *b:* Indianapolis, IN; *m:* Lorrie Bell; *c:* Courtney, Corbin; *ed:* (BS) Phys Ed/Health, IN St Univ 1981; *cr:* Health Teacher S Houston HS 1981-84; Geography Teacher Ellison HS 1984-85; Phys Ed Teacher Webster Intermediate 1985-87; Earth Sci Teacher Eau Claire HS 1987-89, Cloverdale HS 1989-; *ai:* Boys Bsktbl Head Coach; IN Bsktbl Coaches Assn, IN St Teachers Assn; Honorable Mention MI Coach of Yr 1989; *office:* Cloverdale HS RR 3 Box 1 A Cloverdale IN 46120

CHERRY, SHARON HALLMARK, 6th Grade Lang Art Teacher; *b:* Houston, TX; *m:* Craig L.; *ed:* (BS) Ed, Univ of Houston 1975; Working Towards Masters Univ of St Thomas; *cr:* 6th Grade Teacher Corpus Christi Ind Sch Dist 1975-77, Deer Park Ind Sch Dist 1977-; *ai:* NEA, TX St Teachers Assn 1977-; Deer Park Teachers Assn Building Rep 1977-; NCTE 1988-; Deepwater Jr HS, Deer Park Ind Sch Dist Teacher of Yr 1989-; TX St Master Teacher Level III 1989-; *home:* 12706 Old Pine Ln Houston TX 77015

CHERUBINI, PHYLLIS FOY, Secondary English Teacher; *b:* Newport News, VA; *m:* Corkin F.; *c:* Anna J.; *ed:* (BA) Eng, High Point Coll 1966; (MA) Eng, Wake Forest Univ 1974; (EDD) Eng Ed, Auburn Univ 1990; Natl Endowment for Hum Inst Literary Criticism, Auburn Univ 1985; *cr:* Teacher Halifax Cty HS 1966-68, Rowan Cty Schls 1969-72, Calhoun Cty Schls 1972-; *ai:* Yrbk & Sch Newspaper Adv; Literary Team Coord; NCTE 1980-; GA Cncl Teachers of Eng 1984-; GA Assn of Educators (Local Newsletter Chm 1988-) 1972-, Sch Bell Awd 1988-89; Calhoun Cty Historical Society Charter Mem 1990; STAR Teacher 1982; *home:* PO Box 281 Edison GA 31746

CHERUBINI, ROBERT MATTHEW, Computer Specialist; *b:* Ridgway, PA; *m:* Peggy Ann Brubaker; *c:* Candace, Christie, Matthew; *ed:* (BS) Elem Ed, Penn St Univ 1972; (MS) Elem Ed, Clarion St Univ 1989; Grad Credit Work Penn St Univ, Univ of VT, Lesley Coll, Temple Univ; *cr:* 4th Grade Teacher Ridgway Sch Dist 1972-73; 6th Grade Teacher 1973-78, 1978-82, 1982-86, Cmptr Specialist 1986- Brockway Sch Dist; *ai:* Lead Teacher Consortium; Prof Dev Comm, HS Var Golf Coach, Negotiating Comm; NEA, PSEA; Brockway Area Ed Assn (VP, Pres) 1981-82, Prof Leadership Awd 1989; Horton Township Municipal Authority Dir 1988-; CASE VP 1988-; PHEAA ITEC Grant 1985, 1989; Brockway Inc Grant 1985, 1986, 1988, 1989; *office:* Brockway Sch Dist 95 North St Brockway PA 15824

CHESBRO, DAVID C., Social Studies/English Teacher; *b:* Osterville, MA; *m:* Priscilla J. Martin; *c:* David J., Rebecca J., Andrew J., Sarah A.; *ed:* (BA) Bible/Theology/His, Barrington Coll 1958; Bridgewater St Coll, Boston Univ, Boston St Coll; *cr:* Teacher Robert G Shaw Mid Sch 1959-60, Joseph H Barnes Mid Sch 1960-61, Clarence R Edwards Mid Sch 1961-; *ai:* Gideons Intnl Local & St 1976-; Golden Apple Awd 1987; *office:* Clarence R Edwards Mid Sch 28 Walker St Boston MA 02129

CHESHIER, CAROLYN HANCOCK, English Department Chair; *b:* Teague, TX; *m:* W. Pat; *c:* Ryan C., Casey L.; *ed:* (BA) Eng/Bus Ed, SW TX St Univ 1971; Grad Stud Ed; *cr:* Part-Time Instr Cedar Valley Comm Coll 1978-80; Eng Dept Chairperson Red Oak HS 1980-; *ai:* NHS Advisory Bd; Class Spon; Jr Sr Prom Comm Adv; Ellis Cty Rdng Prgm Building Rep; Assn TX Prof Educators; Red Oak HS Teacher of Yr 1983.

CHESHIRE, JANICE ADAIR, Science Teacher; *b:* Marietta, GA; *m:* Harold Terry; *c:* Joshua, Joshua Sacca, Jacob, Julie Sacca; *ed:* (BSED) Elem Ed, GA Southern 1973; Working Towards MED, Kennesaw Coll 1991; *cr:* 6th/7th Grade Math/Sci Teacher DeKalb Cty Schls 1973-75; 5th Grade Teacher DeKalb Chrstn Acad 1976; HS Math/Sci Teacher Mt Carmal 1982-84, DeKalb Chrstn Acad 1985-86; Mid Sch Sci Teacher Mt Paran Chrstn 1986-; *ai:* Natl Jr Honor Society Adv; 8th Grade Washington DC Trip Coord; Sch Fund Raising Comm; Nom Teacher of Yr 1990; *office:* Mt Paran Chrstn Sch 1700 Allgood Rd Marietta GA 30062

CHESKO, RICHARD LEE, History Teacher; *b:* Ellwood City, PA; *m:* Judy; *c:* Beth A., Stephen R.; *ed:* (BS) Scndry His, Slippery Rock Univ 1969; *cr:* His Teacher Linesville HS 1969-; *ai:* Girls Bsktbl & Sftbl, Intamural Bsktbl, Jr HS Girls Bsktbl Coach; NEA, PA Ed Assn; Conneaut Ed Assn 1969-; Little League Umpire 1965-; Teacher of Yr 1985; *office:* Linesville HS Erie St Linesville PA 16424

CHESLER, KAREN L. (RADY), Social Studies Teacher; *b:* Roberts, ID; *m:* Leon F.; *c:* Kellie A., Laurie S. Chesler Lewis, Jeffery M., Kenneth L.; *ed:* (BA) Soc Stud Ed, ID St Univ 1961; (MLA) Liberal Arts, SMU & APU; *cr:* Soc Stud Teacher Dimond-Mears Jr-Sr HS 1969-70, Service-Hanshew Jr-Sr HS 1970-84, Hanshew Jr HS 1984-; *ai:* Cheerleading Spon 1971-76; Class Spon; Service HS Stu Cncl Adv 1979-83; Hanshew Jr HS Stu Cncl Adv 1986-89; AEA 1961-83; Active in Latter Day Saints Church; *office:* Hanshew Jr HS 10121 Lake Otis Pkwy Anchorage AK 99507

CHESLEY, MERRILL L., Kindergarten Teacher; *b:* Chattanooga, TN; *ed:* (BS) Sci, Bennett Coll 1951; Boston Univ, Kean Coll; *cr:* Teacher Laurinburg Inst, Peshine Avenue Sch; *ai:* NJ Governors Teachers Recognition Awd Excl Teaching 1989; *office:* Peshine Avenue Sch 433 Peshine Ave Newark NJ 07112

CHESNUT, ALICE SMITH, Fourth Grade Teacher; *b:* Wilmington, IL; *m:* John L.; *c:* John, Gail; *ed:* (BA) Elem Ed, Andrews Univ 1972; (MAT) Art Teaching, MI St Univ 1980; *cr:* Elem Teacher Three Oaks Elem Sch 1973-; *ai:* Curr Cncl; 4th Grade Chairperson; K-5th Soc Stud Chm; Soc Comm Mem; Bejamin Franklin Stamp Club Spon; Teacher Chm; Ag in Classroom; Wizards of Ed Altruistic; Ways & Means Secy; *office:* Three Oaks Elem Sch 100 Oak St Three Oaks MI 49128

CHESNUT, GAIL A., Agriculture Teacher; *b:* Joliet, IL; *ed:* (BS) W MI Univ 1977; (MA) Ag Ed, Univ of FL 1983; *cr:* 4-H Extension Agent Sarasota Cty Cooperative Extension Service 1977-78; Ag Teacher Sarasota HS 1978-80, Williston HS 1983-84, Leto HS 1984-; *ai:* FFA Adv; FL Voc Assn; Hillsborough Cty Voc Ag Teachers Assn; Jaycees; *office:* Leto HS 4409 W Sligh Ave Tampa FL 33614

CHESSER, JOHN W., Science Teacher; *b:* Shelbyville, Indiana; *m:* Linda R. Read; *c:* Nick; *ed:* (BS) Elem Ed, IN St Univ 1972, (MS) Ed 1975, Mid Sch Sci, 1980 IN Univ; Sci; *cr:* 4th/5th/6th Grade Teacher Lora B Pearson Elem 1972-75; 5th/6th Grade Teacher Thomas a Hendricks Elem 1975-78; 7th Grade Sci Teacher Shelbyville Jr HS 1978-; *ai:* 7th Grade Bsktbl Coach; Chairperson on St Improvement Comm; IN St Teachers Assn VP 1977; IN Bsktbl Coaches Assn 1984-; 100 Wins 1989; IN St Sci Teachers Assn 1979-83; Sertoma Club 1973-84; Old Timers Club of Indianapolis 1975-; Nom Twice for Teacher of Yr; St Book Adoptions Selection Comm; *office:* Shelbyville Jr H S 315 2nd St Shelbyville IN 46176

CHESSON, KAY MYLENE, Spanish/French Teacher; *b:* Lake Charles, LA; *ed:* (BA) Fr Ed, Mc Neese St Univ 1986; *cr:* Fr/Eng Teacher LA Grange HS 1987; Fr/Span/Eng Teacher Tarkington HS 1987-; *ai:* Var Chrldr, Soph Class, Intnl Club Spon; Assn of TX Prof Educators 1987-; Lambda Delta 1983-; Phi Kappa Phi 1986-; Sigma Delta Pi 1989-.

CHESSON, NAN GARDNER, Mathematics Teacher; *b:* Plymouth, NC; *m:* Thomas Bradford; *c:* Greg, Brent; *ed:* (BA) Math, Meredith Coll 1973; *cr:* Math Teacher Chesterfield Cty Schls 1973-74, Washington Cty Schls 1974-76, New Bern-Craven Cty Schls 1984-; *ai:* NHS & Sr Class Adv; Sch & Cmmty SACS Comm Mem; NCAE, NEA (Treas 1975-76, Mem) Broad St Chrstn Church Bd Chm Ed Division 1985-86; *office:* New Bern HS 2000 Clarendon Blvd New Bern NC 28560

CHESTNUT, SANDRA EGGLESTON, Physics Teacher; *b:* Canton, NC; *m:* Mallory L.; *c:* April; *ed:* (BS) Bio, NC Cntrl Univ 1977; (MED) Ed, Cambridge Coll 1987; *cr:* Medical Technologist Harvard Cmmty Health Plan 1980-83, Health Resources Corporation 1983-84, Dana Farber Cancer Inst 1984-; Teacher Boston Public Schls 1985-; *ai:* MA Pre-Engineering Prgm Team Mem & Sci Adv; *office:* Boston Tech HS 55 New Dudley St Boston MA 02119

CHEVIRON, DENISE LYNNE, Counselor; *b:* Canton, OH; *ed:* (BS) Ed/Art/Phys Ed/Health, Malone Coll 1971; (MS) Ed Counseling, Univ of Dayton 1984; Sexual Abuse of Children; Art Therapy; Chemical Dependency; Learning Styles; *cr:* K-8th Grade Phys Ed Teacher Cnaton City Elem 1971-73; Art Teacher Carrollton Exempted Village Schls 1975-78, Residential Treatment Center 1978-86; Sch Cnslr Timken HS 1986-; *ai:* Peer Listening Adv; Teen Help Groups & Chemical Intervention Groups Facilitator; City Wide Crisis Team Mem; Values Ed, City-Wide Testing, Grads Advisory Comms; Phi Delta Kappa 1989-; OH Sch Cnslrs Assn 1985-; Stark Cty Guidance Assn 1986-; Peace Luth Church (Deacon, Church Cncl) 1971-; Cath Cmmty League Primary Prevention Wkshp & Communicate Inst Staff Mem; *office:* Timken HS 521 Tuscarawas St W Canton OH 44702

CHIANG, SUEHING WOO YEE, Math/Sci/Soc Stud Teacher; *b:* Houston, TX; *m:* John Wen Hi; *c:* Christina C. M., Jennifer C. Y.; *ed:* (BS) Elem Ed, Univ of Houston 1966-70; Rdng, Sci, Assentive Discipline, Univ of St Thomas; Career Ed, Univ of Houston; *cr:* 5th Grade Teacher Burris Elem 1970-76; K-6th Grade ESL Teacher Anson Jones 1976-77; 3rd-5th Grade Soc Stud Teacher Meadow 1977-81; 4th Grade Teacher Colony Bend Elem 1981-; *ai:* Natl Geographic Society, Panda Club, Stu Cncl Spon; Sci Fair Chm; TX Classroom Teacher 1985-87; TX St Teacher Assn 1970-72; Houston Teachers Assn Human Relationships Cncl 1970-72; Fund America Inc Dir 1990; Randalls First Consumer Advisory Bd 1988; Chinese Amer Citizen Alliance VP 1975; CACA Ed Schlshp Mem 1986-; Ft Bend Cntry Election Judge & Clerk 1984-; Chinese Prof Club Mem 1970-; Chinese Baptist Church (Vacation Bible Sch Teacher, Sunday Sch, Children Librarian, Youth & Youth Choir) 1970-; Chinese Amer Voter League (Spec Asst to Pres, Spon) 1988-89; *office:* Colony Bend Elem Sch PO Box 1004 Sugar Land TX 77479

CHICK, GREGORY DEAN, Language Arts Teacher; *b:* Danville, IL; *m:* Deborah Ann Hanley; *c:* James S., Matthew D.; *ed:* (AA) General Stud, Lindsey Wilson Jr Coll 1977; (BS) Soc Stud, Campbellsville Coll 1980; (MED) Scndry Ed, Univ of Louisville 1986; Guidance/Admin, W KY Univ; Working Toward Rank I Admin; *cr:* Production Supvr Gulf Oil 1978-84; Asst Plant Mgr Vacuum Depositing Incorporated 1984-85; Teacher Ninth & O Baptist 1985-86; Teacher/Coach Hardin Cty Public Schls 1986-; *ai:* Asst Ftbl Coach Cntrl Hardin HS; Resource Teacher KY Intern Teachers Prgm; KEA, NEA 1985-; Amer Legion 1977-; World of Poetry Golden Poet Awd 1987; *office:* E Hardin Mid Sch 129 College St Glendale KY 42740

CHICK, TINA M., Science Dept Chairperson; *b:* Paw Paw, MI; *m:* Harry; *c:* Suzanne, Lynda, Philip; *ed:* (BS) Elem Ed, Calumet Coll 1979; Atmospheric Sci Ed Prgm, Purdue Univ; *cr:* Jr HS Sci Teacher Our Lady of Grace Sch 1984-; *ai:* Jr HS Sci Fair Coord; Career Day Comm; Natl Sci Fnd Grant; *office:* Our Lady of Grace Sch 3025 Highway Ave Highland IN 46322

CHIDGEY, TERRI WASSMUND, Assistant Principal; *b:* Toledo, OH; *m:* Joseph James; *c:* Kristi M., W. Scott; *ed:* (BA) Ed/Span, SW TX St 1976; (MA) Admin, Trinity Univ 1983; *cr:* 3rd Grade Teacher Wilshire Elem 1976-78, Woodstone Elem 1978-79; 1st Grade Teacher 1981-83, 3rd Grade Teacher 1985-86, 1st Grade Teacher 1986-89 Woodstone Elem; *ai:* Patrols; Math Chairperson; 1st Grade Report Card Comm; TEPSA, NE Elem Prin Assn; Olympia Home Owners Assn Recording Secy 1989; PTA (Recording Secy 1982-83), Life Membership Awd 1986; *office:* Woodstone Elem Sch 5602 Fountainwood San Antonio TX 78233

CHIGHIZOLA, JUNE FEY, Computer Science/Math Teacher; *b:* New Orleans, LA; *m:* Gibson C.; *c:* Jeffrey, Ryan; *ed:* (BS) Scndry Ed, 1968, (MED) Admin/Supervision, 1980 Loyola Univ; Math, Cmptr Sci, Ed, Univ of New Orleans; *cr:* Teacher J F Kennedy HS 1968-70, O P Walker HS 1970-71, Mc Donogh 35 HS 1972-; *ai:* Cmptr Sci Club Adv; Stu Cncl Asst; UTNO 1972-; GNOMT, NCTM 1968-; Cmptr Sci Class Grant 1980; Wrote Various Software for Sch use; *office:* Mc Donogh 35 HS 1331 Kerlerec St New Orleans LA 70116

CHILCOTT, RUTH SWILLEY, Fourth Grade Teacher; *b:* Toronto, KS; *m:* John William; *c:* Beth, Brenda Raven, Patsy Arnold; *ed:* Assoc Elem Ed, Iola Jr Coll 1954; (BS) Elem Ed, Ft Hays St Univ 1984; Continuing Certificate; *cr:* Elem Teacher Rural Schls 1954-59, Barton Cty Schls 1960-64, Great Bend Unified Sch Dist #428 1965-; *ai:* Great Bend KNEA Building Rep; KS Teachers Assn 25 Yr Certificate; NEA; Eastern Star 1955-; Amer Legion Auxiliary Pres 1954-; *office:* Eisenhower Elem Sch 1212 Garfield Great Bend KS 67530

CHILDERS, CINDY MARIE (MONROE), 5th Grade Teacher; *b:* Kansas City, MO; *c:* Johnny, Jason; *ed:* (BA) Elem Ed, 1971, (MS) Elem Ed, 1981 UMKC; Cmptr/Methods/Psych; *cr:* 5th Grade Teacher Ott Elem Sch 1971-75; Substitute Teacher Ind & Raytown Public Schls 1976-78; 4th & 5th Grade Teacher Thomas Hart Benton Elem Sch 1978-; *ai:* Staff Dev Level 3-Presented Workshops for Teachers on Effective Instruction; NEA; ASCD; IRA; Nom Ind Teacher of the Yr & Outstanding Teacher in K C; Excl in Teaching; Rep Sch Dist in Teacher Exch Prgm to England; *office:* Thomas Hart Benton Elem Sch 429 S Leslie Independence MO 64050

CHILDERS, DIANE GLEI, Jr High Teacher; *b:* Hamilton, OH; *m:* Barry L.; *ed:* (BS) Elem Ed, Edgecliff/Xavier Univ 1972-76; *cr:* 3rd Grade Teacher Corpus Christi Sch 1976-78; 2nd Grade Teacher St Bartholomew Sch 1978-79; 7-8 Grade Sci Teacher John XXIII Sch 1979-; *ai:* Co-Adv 8th Grade Civics Club; Mem Cath Schls Week Comm 1986-; Mem John XXIII Capital Fund Drive 1989-; NSTA; St Johns Church Choir; Sigma Phi Gamma (Pres 1985-86 Recording Ser 1989-); *office:* John X X I I 24 Baltimore Middletown OH 45044

CHILDERS, HAROLD DEAN, Principal/Science Teacher; *b:* Edmonton, KY; *m:* Mandane Ennis; *c:* Bradley, Scott; *ed:* (BS) Bio/Ag, 1963, (MA) Ed/Bio, 1965, Ed, 1967 Western Ky Univ; Elem Certificate; *cr:* Head Teacher Northtown Elem 1963-66; Prin Carter Dowling Elem 1966-67; Title I Coord Hart Cty 1967-68; Prin Cab Run Elem 1968-71, Munsfordville Elem 1971-72, Hart Memorial Elem 1972-75, Custer Elem 1975-; *ai:* Spon of Yrbk; Textbook Comm; Academic Team Adv; KEA, NEA, BCEA; Custer Volunteer Fire Dept Mem 1978- Charter Mem; Mem of Masonic Lodge 1973-; Amaranth Royal Patron Life Mem 1976-; *office:* Custer Elem Custer KY 40115

CHILDERS, HAROLD VAN, Fifth Grade Teacher; *b:* Blacksburg, SC; *m:* Julia Earley; *c:* Russell S., Cynthia M., Timothy W.; *ed:* (BA) Soc Stud, Limestone Coll 1970; (MED) Elem Ed, USCS 1979; *cr:* 5th Grade Teacher Limestone Elem 1970-75, Draytonville Elem 1975-; *office:* Draytonville Elem Sch Rt 8 Box 468 Gaffney SC 29340

CHILDERS, MARGARET ANNE, Biology Teacher/Sci Dept Chair; *b:* Boise, ID; *m:* Phillip; *c:* Aaron, Scott; *ed:* (BS) Bio, Boise St Univ 1978; Drug & Alcohol Counseling; Sci, Technology & Society; Drop Out Prevention; Natl Diffusion Network; Grad Level Bio Courses; *cr:* Sci Teacher Hillside Jr HS 1978-79; Bio Teacher Nampa Sr HS 1979-; *ai:* CARE Team; Basic Subjects Review Comm; Faculty Cncl; NABT 1987-; Natl Audubon Society Secy 1979-80; Inservices for Educators; Drug & Alcohol Curr & Prevention Strategies; Aids/HIV Information; STS Instructional Strategies; Outstanding Young Women of America 1985; Dist Scndry Teacher of Yr 1985; St Alternate Christa Mc Auliffe Fellowship 1989; *office:* Nampa Sr HS 203 Lake Lowell Nampa ID 83686

CHILDERS, RITA (WILSON), 4th Grade Teacher; *b:* Birmingham, AL; *m:* Freddy Lee; *c:* Juniata, Alexis; *ed:* (BS) Elem Ed, Ft Valley St Coll 1974; (MA) Early Chldhd, Univ of WY 1975; Mercer Univ; *cr:* Teacher Jos B Riley Sch 1975-76, Univ of WY Prep Sch 1976-79, Rosa Taylor Sch 1979-80, Union Elem Sch 1980-; *ai:* Young Adult Choir; Page; Delta Sigma Theta; *home:* 1757 Anthony Rd Macon GA 31204

CHILDERS, SANDRA KAY, Third Grade Teacher; *b:* Lebanon, IN; *ed:* (BA) Elem Ed, IN St Univ 1968; (MS) Elem Ed, Butler Univ 1973; *cr:* 3rd Grade Teacher Marion Elem 1968-75; 3rd-6th Grade Teacher Adams Elem 1975-85, Marion Elem 1986-; *ai:* Asst Coach Sftbl; IN Rdng Assn 1986-; Cntrl IN Spinal Cord Organization 1986-; Handicapped Organization of Women Treas 1989-; *home:* R R 1 Box 309 Sheridan IN 46069

CHILDRESS, CHRISTINE TANKERSLEY, Biology Teacher; *b:* Ocala, FL; *m:* Edward Bradley Jr.; *c:* Rebecca, Edward III; *ed:* (BA) Bio, Agnes Scott Coll 1973; *cr:* Bio Teacher/Cnslr/Dir of Admissions Mount Vernon Chrstn Acad 1979-; *ai:* Academic Comm; *office:* Mount Vernon Chrstn Acad 4449 Northside Dr NW Atlanta GA 30327

CHILDRESS, HOWARD B., Social Studies Teacher; *b:* Coleman, TX; *m:* Nina Joyce Richardson; *c:* Reginald, Michael; *ed:* (BS) Phys Ed, Prairie View A&M Univ 1957; *cr:* Teacher/Coach Coleman Ind Sch Dist 1957-; *ai:* 7th & 8th Grade Bsktbl & Girls Track Coach; TX HS Coaches Assn 1965-; TX St Teacher Assn 1964-; NEA 1975-; Commissioner Coleman Housing Authority 1984-; Athletic Schlsp Comm Mem 1989-; Coleman Jr Chamber of Commerce Look Up Awd 1983-84; Topcat Awd 1989; *office:* Coleman Jr HS 301 W 15th Coleman TX 76834

CHILDRESS, LINDA S., Fifth Grade Teacher; *b:* Greenville, TX; *ed:* (BS) Elem Ed, E TX St Univ 1968; Advanced, Gifted & Talented Trng; *cr:* 3rd Grade Teacher Melissa Ind Sch Dist 1967-73; Girls Coach/Teacher 1973-79, 5th Grade Teacher 1979- Anna Ind Sch Dist; *ai:* UIL Coord; Girls Sftbl Coach; *office:* Anna Ind Sch Dist Box 128 Anna TX 75003

CHILDS, ELAINE COMPTON, English Teacher; *b:* Manielsville, GA; *m:* Hershel L.; *ed:* (AA) Emmanuel Coll 1964; (BS) Eng/Ed, Univ of GA 1966; *cr:* Teacher Hart Cty HS 1966-70, Anderson Jr Coll 1970-71, Forest Park Sr HS 1971-72, Henry Cty Jr HS 1972-; *ai:* Prof Assn GA Ed; NCTE; Assembly of God (Sectional Secy 1977-88/90-Womens Ministries Pres 1980-84); *office:* Henry County Jr H S 166 Holly Smith Dr Mc Donough GA 30253

CHILES, JEROLD DEE, Earth Sci/Amer His Teacher; *b:* Kingsville, TX; *m:* Ann Prior Dayton; *c:* Jonathan G., Courtney P. Chiles Bird, Carrie D. Chiles Holbrook, Holly E.; *ed:* (BA) Ec, 1959, (MA) His, 1965 TX A&I Univ; Amer His Univ of TX Austin; Earth Sci A&M Univ & TX A&I Univ; *cr:* 8th-9th Grade Teacher Corpus Christi Ind Sch Dist 1963-68; 8th Grade Teacher Tom Browne Jr HS 1968-75; 9th-12th Grade Teacher Ray HS 1975-77; 8th Grade Teacher Burnet Jr HS 1977-; Part-Time Amer His Teacher Cntrl TX Coll 1990; *ai:* Stu Cncl Adv 1975-89; UIL Act & Coaching; TX St Teachers Assn Life Mem 1963-; NEA Mem 1963-; Cassie VFD/EMS (Bd Mem 1988-, Charter Mem 1989); Buena Vista Property Owners Assn (Pres 1984-86, VP 1980-84); Rep to Corpus Christi Classroom Teacher Assn Representive Assembly 1970-77; *office:* Burnet Jr HS Burnet TX 78611

CHIMENTO, DEBORAH ANN, Third Grade Teacher; *b:* Canonsburg, PA; *ed:* (BS) Elem Ed, Edinboro Univ 1977; Cmptr Programming; Technology for Elem Grades; *cr:* 3rd Grade Teacher 1978-82, 6th Grade Teacher 1982-83, 3rd Grade Teacher 1983 Wylandville Elem Sch; *ai:* Tech Supvr IBM Network Cmptr Lab; Talent Show Coord & Dir; Kids in Natures Defense Sch Coord Club 1989-; Mental Health Assn of WA Cty 1984-; Humane Society, World Wildlife 1986-; Natl Wildlife People for the Ethical Treatment of Animals 1990-; Public Services Mental Health Assn; Volunteer Coord of Parent/Stu Awareness; Projects on Environmental Concerns, World Hunger & Humane Act; *office:* Canon-Mc Millan Wylandville Rt 519 Eighty Four Eighty Four PA 15330

CHIN, BETTY LEE, Secondary Mathematics Teacher; *b:* Yonkers, NY; *ed:* (BA) Math, St Univ of NY New Paltz 1970; Grad Stud in Ed & In-Service Credits in Cmptr; *cr:* Scndry Math Teacher J Watson Bailey 1970-89, Kingston HS 1989-; *ai:* Mid Sch & HS Ski Club Adv; *office:* Kingston HS 403 Broadway Kingston NY 12401

CHIPMAN, DEBORAH (GRAY), Kindergarten Teacher; *b:* Topeka, KS; *m:* Scott; *c:* Trevor, Blake; *ed:* (BA) Elem Ed, Fort Hays St Univ 1974; *cr:* 3rd Grade Teacher 1974-78, 2nd-3rd Grade Teacher 1987-79;3rd Grade Teacher 1979-81 Lincoln Sch; Kndgtn Teacher Central Sch 1985-; *ai:* Lang Art Curr Dev Comm 1989-; *office:* Central Sch 1100 Central Ave Dodge City KS 67801

CHISHOLM, CLAIRE LANG, Gifted & Talented Teacher; *b:* Santa Barbara, CA; *m:* Willie James; *c:* Cheryl, Renee; *ed:* (BS) Phys Ed/Health Ed, Loma Linda Univ 1958; (MA) Urban Ed, Pepperdine Univ 1975; *cr:* 2nd Grade Teacher 1960-62, 1st Grade Teacher 1962-69 Grape Street Elem; 2nd Grade Teacher 1971-88, 1st/2nd Grade Teacher Screening Gifted & Talented 1988- Angeles Mesa Elem; *ai:* Gifted/Talented Coord; Black His Month Comm; Homecoming Career Day Chairperson; Shared Decision Making Cncl Alternate; CA Teachers Assn, NEA; Questionettes Soc & Service Organization (Secy 1962-64, Historian 1975-77, Treas 1984-86); *home:* 5322 Deane Ave Los Angeles CA 90043

CHITWOOD, BOBBIE JOAN (STONE), Soc Stud/Remedial Teacher; *b:* Perryville, AR; *m:* Howard Leon; *c:* Jason D.; *ed:* (BSE) Elem Ed, 1980, (MSE) Rdng Specialist, 1982 Univ of Cntrl AR; Productive & Effective Teaching, Learning Strategies Trng; *cr:* Secy/Service Rep/Office Mgr AR Soc Services 1970-77; 5th/6th Grade Teacher Casa Elem Sch 1980-81; Spec Ed/Resource Teacher East End Elem Sch 1981-84; 7th/8th Grade Soc Stud/

Remedial Rdng/Math Teacher Perryville Jr-Sr HS 1984-; *ai:* Faculty Rep; Policy Comm Mem; 9th Grade Spon; AR Historical Assn 1990; Perryville Youth Assn 1987-; Conway Gymnastics Parents Club 1989-; *home:* P0 Box 603 Perryville AR 72126

CHMELKA, ROSALYN M., Retired Teacher; *b:* Bee, NE; *ed:* (BA) Soc Stud, 1959, (MS) Ed, 1971 Concordia Teachers Coll; Admin Courses 1973; *cr:* Rural Teacher Seward Cty Rural Schls 1948-52; Primary Teacher Bee Public Sch 1952-62; Elem Teacher/Prin E Butler Public Schls 1962-88; *ai:* Stamp & Room Club Spon; Labels for Ed Prgm Spon; E Butler Ed Assn (Secy 1971) 1971-88; NE St Assn of Ed Active Mem 1948-; NEA Mem 1980-; Seward Cty Historical Society Secy 1989-; Seward Cty Genealogical Society Secy 1988-; Dwight Altar Society Secy 1990; Delta Kappa Gamma (Corresponding Secy 1989-, Pres, VP); *home:* Box 67 Dwight NE 68635

CHMIELEWSKI, PATRICIA CAVANAUGH, Fifth Grade Teacher; *b:* Chicago, IL; *m:* Vernon Lloyd; *c:* Vernon P., Edward C., Bridget A., Timothy F.; *ed:* (BA) Elem Ed/Phys Ed, Chicago Teachers Coll 1954; Bus Ed Microcomputers; Black Child in Suburban Schs; Advanced Methods of Teaching Readiness; Beyond Textbook Sci; Teaching of Writing to Culturally Diverse Stu Population; *cr:* Phys Ed Teacher Chicago Park Dist 1954-58, Perry & Schmid Schls 1958-59; Remedial Rdng Teacher Cassell & Keller Schls 1965-76; 6th Grade Teacher Crete Elem Sch 1978-80; 5th/6th Grade Teacher Balmoral Elem Sch 1980-; *ai:* Teachers Advisory Bd; Coord Balmorals Young Authors of IL Contest, 5th Grade Sci Inventions; Spon IL 5th & 6th Grade Quiz Bowl Team; NEA, IL Ed Assn, Crete Monee Ed Assn; *office:* Balmoral Elem Sch 701 W Monee Rd Crete IL 60417

CHOATE, CAROLYN HANNAH, English Teacher; *b:* Munday, TX; *c:* Stefani Choate Ernst, Bryan G.; *ed:* (BS) Piano, Hardin-Simmons Univ 1950; (MED) Rdng, Univ of TX El Paso 1985; Counseling, Univ of Houston 1976; *cr:* Teacher Lubbock Ind Sch Dist 1952-58; Cnslr Mental Health Unit 1975-76; Teacher Ysleta Ind Sch Dist 1977-; *ai:* Natl Jr Honor Society Spon; Rdng Dept Chairperson; Liaison Partners in Ed; Youth Oppurtunities Unlimited Comm; NCTE 1985-; Assn Prof Educators 1980-; Intnl Rdng Assn 1985-, Teacher of Yr 1989-; AAUW 1988-; Womens Political Caucus 1978-80; El Paso Historical Society 1988-89; Charter Fellow W TX Writing Project.

CHOPONIS, RICHARD JUSTIN, Jr/Sr HS Mathematics Teacher; *b:* Reed City, MI; *m:* Wendy Lynn Smith; *ed:* (BA) Phys Ed, Olivet Coll 1980; HS Math Cert, IA 1988; *cr:* Instr Seymour Cmmty Schls 1980-; Adult Ed Instr Indian Hill Comm Coll 1986-; *ai:* HS Bsbl, Jr HS Boys Bsktbl Coach 1980-; Phase III Comm 1987-; Sports Ofcl 1982-; Babe Ruth Bsbl Coach 1982-; IA HS Bsbl Coaches Assn 1982-, Nom Dist Coach 1988; Assembly of God Church Sunday Sch Supt 1985-87, 1989-; Gideons Intnl 1986-; *office:* Seymour Cmmty Schls Park & Main St Seymour IA 52590

CHOULETT, HARRY E., Chemistry Teacher; *b:* Downing, MO; *m:* Jane Louise Collins; *c:* Renee, Raymond; *ed:* (BSED) General Sci/Chem, NE MO St Teachers Coll 1956; (MS) Organic Chem, IA St Univ 1960; *cr:* Teacher Queen City HS 1954-57; Sci Dept Chm Berkeley HS 1965-79; Teacher Berkeley HS 1960-, Univ of CA 1985-; *ai:* Berkley HS Senate Mem at Large 1980-; CA Sci Teachers Assn (Treas 1965-70, Mem 1961-); Berkeley Fed of TZeachers 1960-; CA Assn of Chem Teachers 1985-; Coord Chem-Study NSF Inst Univ of CA 1965-72; Scientific Articles Published; Amer Chemical Society Western Regional Awd in Teaching 1981; *office:* Berkeley HS 2246 Milvia St Berkeley CA 94704

CHOW, HOMER QUON, Biological Science Teacher; *b:* San Francisco, CA; *m:* Shirley Lew; *c:* David, Matthew, Kevin; *ed:* (AA) Ornamental Horticulture, City Coll of San Francisco 1962; (BS) Ornamental Horticulture, 1966, (BS) Bio/Chem, 1988 CA St Polytechnic; Stan Teaching Credential; Specialization in Scndry Teaching, St of CA San Francisco Univ 1969; *cr:* Auto Mechanic Union 76 1956-60; Landscape Designer Nisel Gardens 1960-66; US Army Army Medical Corp 1966-68; Pipefitter US Navy 1968-69; Teacher San Francisco Unified Sch Dist 1969-; *ai:* Little League Bsbl; Bio & Math Tutor; Jr & Sr Class, Family Life, Diving, Fishing Adv; AFT 1970-; CA Acad Sci 1980-; Math Teacher Assn 1972-; San Francisco Medical Society 1988-; CA Poly Alumni Assn 1966-; Vietnam Veteran Bronze Air Medal Accommendation & Good Conduct Medal; Outstanding Teacher Woodrow Wilson HS; *office:* Phillip & Sala Burton HS 45 Conkling St San Francisco CA 94124

CHOY, LUCILLE CHING, 2nd Grade Teacher; *b:* Honolulu, HI; *m:* Dexter J. L.; *c:* Christopher, Ryan; *ed:* (BED) Elem, Univ HI 1966; (MED) Elem, Univ HI 1971; *ai:* Teacher of Teachers Awd 1972; *office:* King William Lunallo Elem Sch 810 Pemehana Honolulu HI 96826

CHOY, MARGARITA LOZANO, Second Grade Teacher; *b:* Leon, Mexico; *m:* Jose L.; *ed:* (BA) Elem Ed, Coll of ID 1975; Bi-Ling Ed; *cr:* Kndgtn Teacher 1975-76; Migrant Summer Sch Teacher 1975-83; 1st Grade Teacher 1977-80; 2nd Grade Teacher 1981- Van Buren Sch; *ai:* Caldwell Ed Assn; ID Ed Assn; NEA; Cath Church CCD Teacher 1983-84; *office:* Van Buren Sch 1109 Denver St Caldwell ID 83605

CHOY, PATSY H. Q. YOUNG, Program Resource Teacher; *b:* Honolulu, HI; *m:* Joseph S.; *c:* Leslie Choy Schaefer, Claudia, Justine; *ed:* (BA) Speech/Drama, Univ of HI 1952; Teaching Credential San Francisco St Univ 1971; (MA) Learning Disabilities/Spec Ed, Univ of San Francisco 1980; *cr:* Eng As Second Lang/Prgm Resource Teacher San Francisco Unified Sch Dist 1972-; *ai:* Assembly & Tutoring Prgm Coord; Dist Inservices Participant & Instr; Theatrical Productions Dir; TESOL (Convention Comms Chairperson, Conference Comms Chairperson) 1988-; Sigma Omicron Pi (Pres 1990, VP 1988-); CATESOL (Elem Chairperson 1980, Convention Comms Chairperson, Conference Comms Chairperson, Mem 1972-); Diamond Hts Neighborhood Assn (VP, Comm Chairperson, Secy) 1963-; *office:* A P Giannini Mid Sch 3151 Ortega Street San Francisco CA 94122

CHRIN, TED S., 5th Grade Teacher; *b:* Frackville, PA; *m:* Karen; *c:* Nicole, Tyler; *ed:* (BS) Elem Ed/Soc Stud, Kutztown Univ 1972; Trained to Teach Skills for Adolescence & Growing; Drug & Alcohol Prgms from Lions Guest Intnl; *cr:* 5th/6th Grade Elem Teacher N Schuylkill Sch Dist & Frackville Elem Center 1972-; *ai:* Pres & Coach of Tamaqua Area Jr Bowlers Assn; Sch Newspaper; PSEA, NEA 1972-; *home:* RD 1 Box 1033 Barnesville PA 18214

CHRISMAN, WESLEY STEVEN, Science Teacher/Coach; *b:* Roswell, NM; *m:* Cheryl Ann (Price); *ed:* (BS) Phys Ed, Wayland Baptist Univ 1979; (MS) Scndry Admin, TX A&I Univ 1983; *cr:* Teacher/Coach La Vernia Ind Sch Dist 1980-86; Coach Roswell Ind Sch Dist 1986-89; Teacher/Coach Medina Ind Sch Dist 1989-; *ai:* Coach HS Ftbl/Defensive Coord; Var Girls Track; Nation Strength/Conditioning Coaches Assn 1984-; NM HS Coaches Assn 1986-89; TX HS Coaches Assn 1989-; Article Published in Journal of Natl Strength & Conditioning Coaches Assn 1989; *home:* PO Box 1381 Medina TX 78055

CHRISS, SANDRA WALKER, English Teacher; *b:* Warsaw, VA; *c:* Bryant, Kiana; *ed:* (BA) Eng, VA St Univ 1970; Grad Stud Trinity, Georgetown Univ; *cr:* 9th Grade Eng Teacher Roper Jr HS 1974-75; 10th Grade Eng Teacher H D Woodson Sr HS 1975-76; Eng/Hum Teacher Spingarn Sr HS 1976-; *ai:* Its Academic Coach; Coord Hum Prgm; NCTE, Natl Cncl of Negro Women Inc; DC Public Schls Writing Prgm Consultant; Acad of Hum Curr Planner; Supts Teacher Incentive Awd 1986-87; *office:* Spingarn Sr HS 26th & Bennind Rd NE Washington DC 20002

CHRISTENSEN, CAROLEE CUNNINGHAM, Fifth Grade Teacher; *b:* Pocatello, ID; *m:* Gary T.; *c:* Gary L., Joseph; *ed:* (BA) Elem Ed Boise ST Univ; (MA) Elem Ed, Western MT; *cr:* 2nd Grade Teacher Washington Sch 1962-64, Idaho Falls ID 1964-65; 1st Grade Teacher 1965-77, 4TH Grade Teacher 1977-86; 5th Grade Teacher 1986- West Yellowstone Elem; *ai:* Asst Vlybl Coach; MEA-NEA; West Yellowstone Teachers Assn; Beta Sigma Phi Pres 1986-; *office:* West Yellowstone H S Po Box 460 West Yellowstone MT 59758

CHRISTENSEN, CLAUDIA GLYNN, Head Teacher; *b:* Murray, UT; *m:* Robert D.; *c:* Glynn, Shawnee Anderson, Jason, Monique, Jared, Jordan; *ed:* (BS) Elem Ed, UT St Univ; *cr:* 1st Grade Teacher Westside Dayton Elem 1983-85; Math/Eng/Quest/Drama Teacher Westside Jr HS 1985-; *ai:* Musical & Drama Dir; Yrbk & Newspaper Adv; NCTM, NCTE; Westside Ed Assn (Pres 1986-88, VP 1985-86); Teacher of Yr 1988-89; Published in Whittenbergers Writers.

CHRISTENSEN, GAIL MARIE REISENAUER, Guidance Counselor; *b:* Milwaukee, WI; *m:* David Allen; *ed:* (BS) Ed, Univ of WI Oshkosh; (MS) Guidance/Counseling, Univ of WI Whitewater; *cr:* Eng Teacher Wilmot Union HS 1978-81, West Allis Nathan Hale HS 1981-82; Guidance Cnslr J I Case HS 1984-85, Kettle Moraine HS 1985-86, Central HS 1986-; *ai:* Pom Pons; WI Ed Assn 1978-; Amer Assn Guidance Counseling 1982-87; Amer Sch Cnslr Assn 1982-87; NCTE 1978-81; PTA 1986-; *office:* Cntrl HS 8516 W Lincoln Ave West Allis WI 53227

CHRISTENSEN, JAMES WILLIAM, Science Teacher; *b:* Stromsburg, NE; *m:* Kimberly Lou Waller; *c:* Korey; *ed:* (BA) Soc Sci, Northwestern Coll 1979; (MA) Elem Curr/Instruction, Univ of SD 1988; Instrument Pilot Rating 1989; *cr:* 6th Grade Teacher Wall Lake Cmmty Sch 1979-82; 6th Grade Sci/Lang Teacher 1982-89, 6th-8th Grade Sci Teacher 1989, Galva-Holstein Mid Sch; *ai:* HS Var Girls Vlybl & Head Track Coach; NSTA 1985-86, 1989; Aviations Creative Educators for Sci 1988-; *office:* Galva-Holstein Mid Sch Galva IA 51020

CHRISTENSEN, PERRY OWEN, Elementary School Principal; *b:* Moroni, UT; *m:* Carolyn Menzies; *ed:* (BS) Elem Ed, UT St Univ 1970; (MED) Ed Admin, Brigham Young Univ 1987; Certified Outcome Driven Developmental Model Trainer; Grad Stud Snow Coll; *cr:* Teacher Moroni Elem 1970-73, Mt Pleasant Elem 1973-80; Teaching Prin Fountain Green Elem 1980-87, Moroni Elem 1987-; *ai:* Dist Math Coord, Career Ladder Comm, Trng Comms; NEA 1973-; UT Ed Assn 1970-82; UT Assn Elem Sch Prins 1982-, Nom UT Prin of Yr 1988-89; UT Rural Schls Assn Outstanding Elem Prin 1986-87; Fountain Green Elem Governors Awd 1985; *office:* Moroni Elem Sch 98 N 200 W Moroni UT 84646

CHRISTENSEN, RILEY EUGENE, Jr/Sr HS Science Teacher; *b:* Maywood, NE; *m:* Mary Elaine Watlington; *c:* Mary M. Green, Karen E., Cody H., Rory E., Kameesha M., Rocky P.; *ed:* (BS) Bio, 1965, (MS) Microscopic Anatomy, 1968 CO St Univ; Scndry Counseling, Henderson St Univ; *cr:* Sci Teacher Isaac Newton Jr HS 1967-72; Eng Teacher 1972-73, Sci Teacher 1973- Hatfield Public Sch; Adjunct Faculty Rich Mountain Comm Coll 1985-; *ai:* Faith Chrstn Church Minister; Pioneers for Christ Philippine Mission Chm Bd of Dir.

CHRISTIAN, BILLY JOE, 3rd Grade Teacher/Principal; *b:* Washington, DC; *ed:* (BA) Elem Ed, Marshall Univ 1984; *cr:* 5th Grade Teacher 1984-85, 6th Grade Teacher 1985-88, 1st Grade Teach Er/Prin 1988-89, 3rd Grade/Prin 1989- Fez Elem; *ai:* Patrol Spon; PTO Treas; Lincoln Cty Teacher or Yr 1989-; Master Teacher Awd 1988-89; Lincoln Cty Teacher of Month 1989; *home:* 1145 9th Ave Apt 3 Huntington WV 25701

CHRISTIAN, ELDA RAMOS, Math/Science Teacher; *b:* Roma, TX; *m:* Bruce; *c:* Teresa, Jessica, Elizabeth; *ed:* (BA) Bio, St Marys Univ 1977; *cr:* Teacher St Mary Magdalen 1977-78, Canterbury Sch 1982-83, Edinburg Jr HS 1983-84, St Joseph Sch 1984-; *ai:* Stu Cncl Spon; Religious Act; Beta Sigma Phi Secy 1982-85; *home:* 1817 Wendy Edinburg TX 78539

CHRISTIAN, POLLY GAEBE, Elem Physical Educ Teacher; *b:* Belleville, IL; *m:* Fred D.; *c:* Michael, Laura, Thomas; *ed:* (BS) Phys Ed, 1970, (MS) Elem Admin, Univ of OK 1988; Elem Ed Cert; *cr:* Kndgtn Teacher Nashville Grade Sch 1970-71; 2nd Grade Teacher 1972-81; Phys Ed Teacher 1982- Cleveland Elem; *ai:* Dist Budget/Salary Comm; Mem Election Comm of Pen; Rep Cncl Pen; LEA/NEA 1970-71; Pen Pep Cncl 1972-; OEA/NEA 1972-; Alpha Phi Alumni (Chapter Adv 1971-74) St Outstanding Alumni 1972; Untd Cerebral Palsey Assn (Exec Bd Liason Ofc for Ind Living Prgm 1980-85); Mcfarlin Meth Church Comm; Working Mother of Yr Awd 1988; *home:* 2626 Brentwood Dr Norman OK 73069

CHRISTIANA, JOSEPH JOHN, 8th Grade Amer History Teacher; *b:* East Hartford, CT; *m:* Susan Loftus; *ed:* (BA) His/Ed/Russian Stud, Univ of Cntrl FL 1980; Working Towards Masters Educl Leadership, Nova Univ 1989-; *cr:* Teacher Robinswood Jr HS 1980-81, South Seminole Mid Sch 1981-; *ai:* South Seminole Mid Sch Building Comm; Oviedo HS Jr Var Soccer Coach; Little League Bsbl Coach; Historical Comm & Chess Club Chm; Seminole Ed Assn 1981-; FL Teaching Profession, NEA; Natl Historical Society, Audubon Society 1981-; St Margaret Mary Cath Church 1967-; *office:* South Seminole Mid Sch 451 S Winter Park Dr Casselberry FL 32707

CHRISTIANSEN, DAVID JON, Advanced Placement Bio Teacher; *b:* Providence, RI; *ed:* (BS) Bio, Transylvania Univ 1976; Ed, Univ of KY; *cr:* Advanced Placement Bio Teacher George Rogers Clark HS 1978-; *ai:* Curr Comm; Academic Team Moderator; ASCD; *office:* George Rogers Clark HS 620 Boone Ave Winchester KY 40391

CHRISTIANSEN, EVAN CARL, Aerospace Sci Dept Teacher; *b:* Springfield, MN; *m:* Kaycharlet Waller; *c:* Kevan C., Kit C., Sylvia F.; *ed:* (AA) General Stud, Univ of NY 1974; (BA) General Stud, 1974; (MA) Comm, 1975 Plattsburgh St Univ; Pilot Trng Navigator Trng Squadron Officers Sch; Air Command & Staff Coll; Industrial Coll of Armed Forces; *cr:* Professor/Dept Head Baptist Coll 1977-79; Teacher/Dept Chm Deland HS 1979-; *ai:* Air Force Jr ROTC Spon; Kitty Hawk Air Society Spon; Model Rocket Club Adv; Rotory Club Fund Chm 1977-79; Kiwanis Club Act Dir 1979-; Shriners Club 1980-; *home:* 185 Lone Tree Trl Deland FL 32724

CHRISTIANSEN, JUDY ROBERTSON, 4th Grade Teacher; *b:* Quincy, IL; *m:* Gary H.; *c:* Richard, Dennis, Brent; *ed:* (BA) Elem Ed, Buena Vista Coll 1967; 3-Year Registered Nurse Diploma, Evangelical Sch of Nursing 1962; Addl Studies, Ed; *cr:* 6th Grade Teacher 1967; Kndgtn Teacher 1967-68; 7th Grade Eng 1968-70 West Ridge Sch; 5th Grade 1970-75; 1st Grade 1975-83 New Park Sch; 4th Grade West Ridge Sch 1983; *ai:* Bldg Plan Comm; 4th Grade Rep K-12 Sci Comm; NEA/ISEA/HEA 1967-; ICTM 1989-; IAS 1988-; Lioness Club VP 1978-79; AAUW 1977-79 1989-; Harlan Cmmnty Lib Brd 1979-86 VP and Pres; Harlan Cmmnty Lib Fnd Brd 1982-84; UMYF Adv; Choir Mem; Sunday Sch Teacher; Outstanding Young Woman in America 1975; *office:* West Ridge Sch Harlan Comm 19th and Victoria St Harlan IA 51537

CHRISTIANSON, J. DEAN, Chemistry/Biology Teacher; *b:* Chester, IA; *m:* Diane; *ed:* (BS) Bio/Chem Upper IA Univ 1963; (MS) Bio, Mankato St 1965; (PHD) Bio/Ecology, Rutgers Univ 1969; Summer Study Woods Hole MA; *cr:* Ecology Teacher Wagner Coll 1969-75; Bio Teacher Univ of Bridgeport 1975-81; Sci Teacher Brunford HS 1982-83, Thomaston HS 1983-; *ai:* Lions Club; Wagner Coll Outstanding Teacher of Yr 1974; *office:* Thomaston HS Branch Rd Thomaston CT 06787

CHRISTIANSON, ROBERT PETER, History Teacher/Chair; *b:* Strum, WI; *m:* Ruth A. Michels; *c:* Jill, Peter; *ed:* (BS) His, 1960, (MST) Soc Stud, 1968 Univ of WI Eau Claire; Grad Work in His, Winona St Univ; *cr:* Soc Stud Teacher Siren HS 1960-63; His Teacher Gale-Ettrick-Trempealeau HS 1963-; *ai:* High Quiz Coach 1971-; Class Adv; WI Cncl Soc Stud 1989-; NEA, WEAC, CRUE 1960-; Gale-Ettrick-Trempealeau Ed Assn (Pres 1984) 1963-; Church (Bd of Deacons Chm 1974-76, Bd of Trustees Secy 1977-82); His Book Club 1972-; Letter of Commendation for Coaching High Quiz Team 3 Cty Championships; *home:* 219 S 12th St Galesville WI 54630

CHRISTIE, LOUISE T. BERARD, Fourth Grade Teacher; *b:* Woonsocket, RI; *d:* Hugh R.; *c:* Peter; *ed:* (BA) Elem Ed/Psych, RI Coll 1971; (MA) Rdng, Univ of RI 1987; *cr:* 4th Grade Teacher Our Lady Queen of Martyrs Sch 1971-72, St Joseph Elem Sch 1972-73; K-9th Grade Substitute Teacher Groton CT 1974; 6th Grade Teacher Freeman Hathaway Elem Sch 1974-77; 7th-9th Grade Lang Art Teacher Fitch Jr HS 1978-79; 4th Grade Teacher 1980-83, 6th Grade Teacher 1983-84, 4th Grade Teacher 1984- Claude Chester Sch; *ai:* Groton Schls Report Card Revision & Rdng Dev Comm; Cetaceam Research Fieldwork; CT Ed Assn,

NEA, Groton Ed Assn 1974-; Mystic Shell Club Mem 1985-; Conchologists of America Mem 1989-; N Atlantic Marine Mammal Assn Mem 1988-; SE New England Marine Educators Mem 1989-; CT Cetacean Society Mem 1990; Cousteau Society, Greenpeace Mem 1988-; Center for Coastal Stud Mem 1986-; St Marys Roman Cath Church Mem 1984-; RI HS Forensics League 3rd Place Humorous Interpretation St Competition 1967; *home:* 28 Meadow St Mystic CT 06355

CHRISTIE, MARLA COX, English/Journalism Teacher; *b:* Asheville, NC; *m:* Colin Mc Millan; *ed:* (BA) Eng, Mars Hill Coll 1988; *cr:* Eng Teacher Owen HS 1988; Eng/Journalism Teacher Madison HS 1988-; *ai:* Newspaper & Literary Magazine Adv; NCTE Mem 1988-; NCAE Mem 1988; Articles Published; *office:* Madison HS 102 Marshall By-Pass Marshall NC 28753

CHRISTIE, TINA MARIE, Mathematics Teacher; *b:* Massillon, OH; *ed:* (BA) Math, Akron Univ 1987; *cr:* Teacher Buttons & Bows Day Nursery & Pre-Sch; Substitute Math Teacher Lorin Andrews Jr HS 1987; Math Teacher Glen Oak East & West HS 1987-; *ai:* NEA, OH Educl Assn.

CHRISTMAN, DEBORAH ROBERTSON, Project Asst/Resource Teacher; *b:* Lynwood, CA; *m:* Randy; *c:* Noah, Annaliese, Alexandra; *ed:* (BA) Linguistics 1975, (MA) Linguistics, 1980 CA St Univ Fullerton; Math/Science Ed, Fresno Pacific Coll; AIMS Leadership Trainer; *cr:* 2nd Grade Teacher 1976-78, 1st Grade Teacher 1978-80 Glenn Martin Elem; 3rd Grade Teacher South Elem 1980-89; Proj Asst Villalovoz Elem 1989-; *ai:* Math Adv Comm; Sci Fair Comm; Testing Comm; Family Math Organizer for Sch; NSTA 1987-; AIMS Leadership Group 1988-; Elem New Teacher Yr; Mentor Teacher Sci; Mentor Teacher Math; Presentor NSTA 1987-88; *office:* Villalovoz Sch 1550 Cypress Tracy CA 95376

CHRISTMAN, R. TODD, Business Teacher; *b:* Barnesville, OH; *m:* Robin A. Lucas; *ed:* (AA) Accounting/Data Processing, Belmont Tech Coll 1984; (BA) Accounting, Muskingum Coll 1986; Voc Bus Ed Kent St Univ 1986; *cr:* Accounting Instr, Swiss Hills Voc Sch 1986-; *ai:* Bus Prof America; Accounting II Club Adv; Bus Prof America, Swiss Hills Chapt Adv 1988-89; Swiss Hills Adult Instr; Business Prof America 1988- Super Adv 1989; Switzerland OH Ed Assn 1986-; OH Bus Teachers 1986-; *office:* Swiss Hills Vocational Sch 46601 Sr 78 Woodsfield OH 43793

CHRISTMAS, LORA PINKERTON, English Teacher; *b:* Snyder, TX; *m:* Jerry; *c:* Shelley, Chad; *ed:* (BS) Elem Ed, Howard Payne Univ 1970; (MED) Educl Admin, Tarleton St Univ 1983; *cr:* 8th Grade Eng Teacher Early Mid Sch 1970-; *ai:* 7th/8th Grade UIL Spon for Impromptu & Oral Rdng; Effective Schls Comm Mem; TX Classroom Teachers Assn Mid Sch Coord 1985-; *office:* Early Mid Sch P O Box 3315 Early TX 76801

CHRISTOPHEL, PAUL WILLIAM, Science Teacher; *b:* Greencastle, PA; *m:* Shirley Jean Rockwell; *c:* C F. Buterbauch, Paul N., Kelly Jo Buterbaugh, Lori M., Joel D.; *ed:* (BSED) Chem, Shippensburg Univ 1963; *cr:* Sci Teacher Morrison Cove Jr HS 1963-66, James Buchanan Jr/Sr HS 1966-72, Mc Connellsburg HS 1977-; *ai:* 1994 Class Adv; Advanced Placement Comm; Staff Dev Comm; Prof Dev Comm; Lead Teacher Advisory Cncl; PSEA Life Mem; NEA Life Mem; Cntrl Fulton Ed Assn Treas 1977-; Mercersburg Fire Co Fire Police 1988-; Mercersburg Volunteer Amb Squad (Chief 1983-84, Asst Chief 1989, Deputy Chief 1990); BSA Asst Scoutmaster 1973-; CPR Instr Amer Heart Assn 1985-; *office:* Central Fulton Sch Dist 151 E Cherry St Mc Connellsburg PA 17233

CHRISTOPHER, DONNA A., English Department Chairman; *b:* Cullman, AL; *m:* David L.; *c:* Mary-Beth, Julianna, Amy; *ed:* (BS) Elem Ed, St Bernard Coll 1972; Working toward Masters Scndry Lang Art Univ of AL; Received Trng for Advanced Placement Class Univ of AL; *cr:* 4th Grade Teacher Cold Springs Elem Sch 1973-80; 6th Grade Eng Teacher Good Hope Elem Sch 1980-87; Eng Teacher Good Hope Mid Sch 1987-88; 9th/12th Grade Eng Teacher Good Hope HS 1989-; *ai:* NHS, Sr Class, Chrldr Spon; Graduation Accompanist; AEA, NEA 1973-; NCTE 1989-; Lioness Club; FBC Choir & Bell Choir; Young Musicians Choir Dir 1987-; Cullmans Bus Woman of Yr 1979; Guest Soloist at Various Soc Functions in St; *home:* 711 5th Ave SW Cullman AL 35055

CHRISTOPHER, GEORGE JOSEPH, Fifth Grade Teacher; *b:* Newark, NJ; *m:* Mary Ann Lee; *c:* John, Mary; *ed:* (BA) Clem Ed K-8, St Peters Coll 1978; (MS) Ed, Monmouth Coll 1985; *cr:* Teacher Avon by the Sea 978-79, Wayside Sch 1979-87, Ocean Intermediate Sch 1987-; *ai:* Swim Team Coach Avon 1985-88; Ftbl Coach Ocean Township 1980-; Girls Sftbl Coach Avon 1985-89; Avon Fire Company Mem 1974-; Juvenile Comm Mem 1978-79; Welfare Local Asst Bd Mem 1986-; Mem of Affirmotive Action 1980-89; *office:* Township Of Ocean Intermediate West Park Ave 1200 Ocean NJ 07712

CHRISTOPHER, MARY ANN LACOUR, Mathematics/English Teacher; *b:* Wichita Falls, TX; *m:* Charles Hamilton II; *c:* Charles H. III, Thomas E.; *ed:* (BS) Ed Math/Eng, Univ of SW LA 1972; Various Grad Level Courses; Enrolled in Masters of Educl Media; *cr:* Math/Lang Art Teacher Plantation Elem 1972-74; Math Teacher Mc Clellan HS, Pulaski East Jr HS 1975-76; 5th Grade Teacher Charles Thomas Elem 1985-86; Math/Rdng Teacher Rumble Jr HS 1986-87; Math/Eng Teacher Yellow Springs Jr/Sr HS 1988-; *ai:* Odyssey of Mind Coach St Luke; NEA, OEA, YSEA Building Rep 1988-; PAGE 1986-87; NCTM, OCTM 1989-; Greene Cty Career; Nom Pres Awd Excl in Teaching; Panel CEAO Mem; *office:* Yellow Springs HS 720 E Enon Rd Yellow Springs OH 45387

CHRISTOPHERSON, MARY BETH BARTTER, Second Grade Teacher; *b:* Duluth, MN; *m:* Nels; *c:* Andy, Alison; *ed:* (BA) Philosophy/Religion/Elem Ed, Cornell Coll 1964; N MI Univ; *cr:* 4th Grade Teacher Whitman Sch 1964-66; 3rd Grade Teacher South Range Sch 1966-68, Stewartville Elem Sch 1968-69; 2nd/3rd Grade Teacher Lake Linden Elem 1969-; *ai:* Porf Dev Rep; Gifted & Talented Prgm; Copper Cty Art Cncl; MI Ed Assn; *home:* 1280 Hickory Ln Houghton MI 49931

CHRISTOPHERSON, STEVEN DOUGLAS, Math Teacher; *b:* San Antonio, TX; *m:* Leslie K. Lawhorn; *ed:* (BS) Psych/Math, Univ of Houston 1981; Addl Studies Masters Math Ed; *cr:* Math Teacher Sam Rayburn HS 1981-; *ai:* Spon SADD; Youth for Christ; KYSSED (Voluntary Drug Testing), VIL Number Sense; VIL Calculator Applications; Academic Decathalon Math Coach; Cheerleading Support Crew; Peer Support Coord; Golf Coach; Kung Fu Instr; *office:* Sam Rayburn HS 2121 Cherrybrook Pasadena TX 77502

CHRISTRUP, ERIC LEE, Science Teacher; *b:* Grand Rapids, MI; *m:* Elaine Rae Vredevoogd; *c:* Faith, Seth; *ed:* (BS) Geology/Earth Sci, Grand Valley St Univ 1973; Approved Prgms; *cr:* Sci Teacher Coopersville Area Public Schls 1974-; *ai:* Sci Olympics Coach; Sci Club & Games & Strategy Club Adv; MI Earth Sci Assn, Natl Earth Sci Teachers Assn 1974-; W MI Sci Teachers Coalition 1988-; Church Sch Bd Pres 1980-86; Grand Valley St Univ Geology Dept Honors Recipient; *office:* Coopersville Jr HS 198 East St Coopersville MI 49404

CHRISTY, RACHEL TAYLOR, Fourth Grade Teacher; *b:* Park Hall, MD; *m:* S. Stanley; *c:* Anthony; *ed:* (BS) Elem Ed, Bowie St Teachers Coll 1963; Advanced Prof Certificate; *cr:* 2nd Grade Teacher White Marsh Elem 1963-64; 3rd Grade Teacher Frank Knoxs Elem 1965-66, Pasadena Elem 1966-68; 4th Grade Teacher Cape St Claire Elem 1969-; *ai:* NEA 1963-; MSTA 1963-; TAAC 1966-; Tanager Forest Civic Assn 1974-.

CHRONISTER, KAY LANDIS, 5th Grade Teacher; *b:* York, PA; *c:* Drew; *ed:* (BA) Elem Ed, York Coll of PA 1973; *cr:* 5th Grade Teacher 1973-78; 4th Grade Teacher 1979-81; 6th Grade Teacher 1981-88 Orendor Elem; Mount Wolf Elem 1988-89; 5th Grade Teacher Conewago Elem 1989-; *ai:* Church Bell Choir; Deacon-Comm Work at Church; Instr Water Aerobics Class; Asst Bsktbl Team & Little League Bsbl Team; NEA; PSEA; Northeastern Ed Assn Bldg Rep; *home:* 1642 5th Ave York PA 17403

CHRZANOWSKI, RONALD F., Social Studies Teacher; *b:* Buffalo, NY; *m:* Anne F. Slominski; *c:* Daniel; *ed:* (BA) Philosophy, St Hyacinth Coll 1969; (MRED) Ed, Loyola Univ 1978; *cr:* Teacher Kolbe HS 1969-70, Archbishop Curley HS 1974-77, Bishop Turner HS 1979-81, Byron-Bergen Cntrl 1982-; *ai:* Scholastic Quiz Team; Soc Stud Travel Club; Substance Abuse Advisory Comm; Rochester Cncl Soc Stud, NY St Cncl Soc Stud; Byron-Bergen Faculty Assn VP 1988-; Univ of Rochester Scndry Teaching Excl Awd 1990; *office:* Byron-Bergen Cntrl Sch Townline Rd Bergen NY 14416

CHUBBUCK, JANICE FULCHER, Physical Ed Dept Chairperson; *b:* Augusta, GA; *d:* Larry J.; *c:* Alycia D.; *ed:* (BS) Phys Ed, GA Southview 1969; (MS) Phys Ed, Univ of SC; *cr:* Phys Ed Teacher/Coach Glenn Hills Jr HS 1969-70, Lucy C Laney HS 1970-79, Lexington HS 1979-; *ai:* Girls Bsktbl & Track Coach; NEA, SCEA, Lexington Ed Assn Rep 1989-I SCAHPERD 1979-; Outstanding Young Women of America 1974; *office:* Lexington HS 2463 Augusta Hwy Lexington SC 29072

CHUITES, SHEPHERD JOHNSTON, French Teacher; *b:* Spartanburg, SC; *m:* Michael Douglas; *c:* B. Shepherd, Thomson C., Carson A.; *ed:* (BA) Fr, Mary Baldwin Coll 1972; (MAT) Fr, Univ of GA 1976; *cr:* Eng Teacher Hardaway HS 1972-73; Fr Teacher Kendrick HS 1973-86, Columbus HS 1986-; *ai:* Fr Club Spon; Fr Honor Society; AATF (GA Dir Natl Fr Test 1982-85, Co Dir 1986-); FLAG/PAGE/SCOLT 1975-; Edgewood Presbyn Church Session Mem 1985-88, 1990; *office:* Columbus HS 1700 Cherokee Ave Columbus GA 31906

CHUN, WENDI M. Y., Physics Teacher; *b:* Honolulu, HI; *m:* Darren T.K.; *ed:* (BS) Physics, 1986, (PD) Sci Ed, 1987 Univ of HI Manoa; *cr:* Physics Teacher Roosevelt HS 1987-; *ai:* Roosevelt HS Solar Car Team Adv; *office:* Roosevelt HS 1120 Nehoa St Honolulu HI 96822

CHUNG, NORMAN, Biology Teacher; *b:* Los Angeles, CA; *m:* Paula Weaver; *ed:* (BA) Phys Ed/Bio, CA St Univ Long Beach 1973; (MS) Ed, APU 1989; *cr:* Teacher Poindexter Elem Sch 1973-79, Moorpark HS 1979-; Coach CA Luth Univ 1982-; *ai:* Coaching & Fishing Club; *office:* Moorpark HS 4500 Tierra Rejada Moorpark CA 93021

CHURCH, BETH MOORE, First Grade Teacher; *b:* Dumas, AR; *m:* Paschal C.; *c:* Charles T., Janet A.; *ed:* (BA) Speech/Elem Ed, Ouachita Baptist Univ 1951; Univ of AR Little Rock, Univ of Cntrl AR, Ouachita Baptist Univ; Numerous Inservice Wkshps; *cr:* 1st Grade Teacher Pulaski Cty Spec 1951-52; Teacher Perryville AR 1952-53, Camp Taylor Sch 1953-58, Pulaski Cty Spec 1961-; *ai:* 1st Grade Team Leader; Church Act; AEA, NEA, PACT; North Pulaski Chamber of Commerce Exemplary Service Awd 1987.

CHURCH, CONNIE HOOKER, English Department Chair; *b:* Herrin, IL; *m:* Charlie; *c:* Stephanie, Dennis; *ed:* (BS) Speech/Eng, 1970, (MS) Gifted Ed, 1988 S IL Univ; *cr:* Eng Teacher Wright City HS 1970-71; Speech/Theatre/Advanced Placement Eng Teacher Carterville HS 1973-; *ai:* Theatre Class; Scholar Bowl; Stu Olympiad; JETS; Gifted Coord; NCTE, IL Ed Assn, NEA; Grand Avenue Baptist Church Trustee; Gifted & Talented Fellowship; Direct Showcase for IL HS Theatre Festival; Annual Presenter at Conferences & Wkshps; *office:* Carterville HS 816 S Division Carterville IL 62918

CHURCH, JANET COUCH, 4th Grade Teacher; *b:* Covington, KY; *m:* James E.; *ed:* (BA) Concentration Elem Ed 1968; (MA) Lib Sci 1973 Morehead St Univ; *cr:* 3rd Grade Teacher Covington Ind Schls 1968-74; 5th Grade Teacher 1974-77/1987-88; 6th Grade Teacher 1977-89; 4th Grade Teacher 1989- Owingsville Elem Sch; *ai:* KY Ed Assn; NEA; Bath Cty Educl Assn; *office:* Owingsville Elem Sch Main St Owingsville KY 40360

CHURCH, KELLYE NEEDLES, Spanish Teacher; *b:* Fort Worth, TX; *m:* Donald Roussel Jr.; *c:* Amanda; *ed:* (BGS) Intnl Bus Relations, TX Tech Univ 1983; Teacher Cert, Univ of N TX 1987; *cr:* Span Teacher Liberty Chrstn Sch 1984-85, Gee Jr HS 1985-86, Selz HS 1987-; *ai:* Jr Class Spon; Pilot Point Classroom Teachers Assn Building Rep 1989-; TCTA Mem 1987-; Womens Federated Clubs (Pres 1987-89, Mem).

CHURCH, ROBERT W., Sci Chair/Physiology Teacher; *b:* San Francisco, CA; *m:* Shirley I.; *ed:* (BA) Biological Sci, 1961, (MA) Biological Sci, 1976 Western St Coll; Biotechnology & Recombinant, Univ of CA Santa Cruz 1989; *cr:* Physiology/Advanced Bio Teacher/Drama Instr Pioneer HS 1966-; *ai:* Drama Club Adv; Stu Blood Drive Coord; CA Teachers Assn 1966-; CA Sci Teachers Assn, NSTA; Hewlett Packard Mini Grant Biotechnology 1990.

CHURCH, THALIA CAROLYN, Dean; *b:* Norfolk, VA; *ed:* (BS) Elem Ed, Norfolk St Univ 1966; (MA) Elem Ed, 1974, (CAS) Educl Admin, 1984 Hofstra Univ; CAS Certificate of Advance Study; *cr:* Teacher 1966-89, Supvr 1981-, Dean 1989- Public Sch 176 Queens; *ai:* Supvr After Sch Tutorial Prgm 1981-85, Safe Harbor After Sch Recreation Prgm 1985-; Comms; Church Act; Youth Wkshps; VA St Teachers Assn, United Fed of Teachers, NY St Black Educators 1966-; Justice Unity Generousity Service Sargeant at Arms 1988-; Norfolk Club Pres 1986-87; Norfolk St Alumni 1988-; *home:* 130-65 Francis Lewis Blvd Laurelton NY 11413

CHURCHILL, ANTHONY PETER, Mid Sch Teacher & Coach; *b:* Milwaukee, WI; *m:* Michele D. Samuelson; *c:* Vincent M., Kathryn M., Robert A.; *ed:* (BA) Soc Stud Ed, Oral Roberts Univ 1982; *cr:* Teacher/Coach Booker T Washington HS 1982-83, Morgan Park Acad 1983-87, St Margaret of Scotland 1987-88, Morgan Park Acad 1988-; *ai:* Mid Sch Soccer/Bsktbl Coach; Asst Var Soccer Coach; Head Track Coach; Dir Summer Sports Camp; Spon Classic Cinema Wkshp; Track/Bowling Wkshp; Fellowship of Chrstn Athletes Mem; St Pauls Bible Church Trustee 1984-; *office:* Morgan Park Acad 2153 W 111th St Chicago IL 60643

CHURCHILL, NORMAN CLIFFORD, Social Studies Teacher; *b:* Kittanning, PA; *m:* Margie D. Marsh Churchill; *c:* Norman J., Kevin L.; *ed:* (AA) Psych, Univ of Tampa 1975; (AS) Air Traffic Control, Univ of Albuquerque 1976; (BS) Soc Stud, Univ of Ta Mpa 1977; Air Traffic Control Grad 1956; MBO Mgmt Prgm; TERPS; *cr:* Air Traffic Control/Standardization Trng Spec Mac Dill AFB 1975-78; Teacher Soc Stud Madison Jr HS 1978-; *ai:* Chm Sch Mgmt Team; Rep Dist Coop Learning Prgm; HCCM 1978-87; HCCSS 1987-; FTP/NEA/CTA 1978-; F&AM 1987-; Lakeside Village HOA Pres 1984-88; *office:* James Madison Jr HS 444 Bay Vista Tampa FL 33611

CHURCHWELL, RICHARD BRUCE, Fourth Grade Teacher; *b:* Demorest, GA; *ed:* (BA) Ed, N GA Coll 1975; *cr:* Teacher Baldwin Elem Sch 1977-; *ai:* NEA, GAE, HAE 1977-; Baldwin Sch Teacher of Yr 1985-86.

CHUSTZ, LETA HUNTER, Science Teacher; *b:* Midland, TX; *m:* Harris Josheph Jr.; *c:* Nancy E.; *ed:* (BS) Scndry Sci Ed, LA St Univ 1973; (MS) Scndry Sci Ed, FL Intnl Univ 1985; *cr:* Sci Teacher Plaquemine HS 1973-74, Cooper City HS 1974-76, Coral Shores HS 1976-; *ai:* Curr Review Comm; Sci Resource Person Neighborhood Elem & Mid Sch; ASCD; Teacher of Yr Coral Shores HS 1983-84; *office:* Coral Shores H S 89901 Old Hwy Tavernier FL 33070

CHUSTZ, SUSAN RICE, LD Mathematics Teacher; *b:* Kansas City, MO; *m:* Al; *c:* Christopher, Travis; *ed:* (BS) Math Ed 1974, (MED) Scndry Ed, 1990 Univ of SW LA; Spec Ed; *cr:* Math Teacher Acad of the Sacred Heart 1974-75; Math Teacher 1975-83, LD Math Teacher 1987- Acadiana HS; *ai:* S Assn of Colls & Schls Accreditation; Stu Act & Honors Prgm Comm Chm; Prof Improvement Planning Comm; LA Assn of Prof Educators, NCTM, Cncl for Learning Disabilities; *office:* Acadiana HS 315 Rue du Belier Lafayette LA 70506

CHUTE, ALLEN FRANCIS, English Teacher; *b:* New Britain, CT; *m:* Sandra R. Prus; *c:* Patrick; *ed:* (BS) Eng/His, 1970, (MS) Psych, 1975 Cntrl Ct St Univ; (CAS) Educl Fnds, S Ct St Univ 1985; Ed, St Josephs & Fairfield; Ct St Mentor Prgm; *cr:* Teacher Dodd Jr HS 1971-; *ai:* Cmptr Club; Sftbl Coach; Cmptr, Testing, Rdng Comms; Schedule & Newspaper Adv; Cmptr Educator of Ct Assn; Amer Legion, YMCA Indian Guides, Southington S Little League; Regional Cmptr Conference Presenter; Teacher Cmptr Trng Wkshps Facilitator; Supt Awd Excl Cmptr Ed; *office:* Dodd Jr HS 100 Park Pl Cheshire CT 06410

CHVATAL, MARIAN KOSKUBA, Gifted Coordinator; *b:* Chicago, IL; *m:* Fred; *c:* Debra Klosowski, Cynthia; *ed:* (BA) Speech, Northwestern Univ 1949; (MA) Rdng Ed, Natl Coll of Ed 1976; Teaching the Gifted, St of IL; *cr:* Teacher Fox Lake Grade Sch 1963-86; Part-Time Teacher Coll of Lake Cty 1976-85; Gifted Co-Ord Fox Lake Grade Sch 1976-; *ai:* Intnl Rdng Assn 1976-; NEA 1975-; *home:* 9909 Winn Rd Richmond IL 60071

CHWAZIK, THADDEUS PAUL, Social Studies Teacher; *b:* Utica, NY; *ed:* (BA) His, 1969, (MA) His, 1971, Certificate of Specialization in Soviet and E European Stud, 1971 Niagara Univ; *cr:* Teacher Proctor HS 1974-87, Utica Sr Acad 1987-; *ai:* Var Track, Cross Cntry, Bsbl Coach; Utica Teachers Assn; E Utica Optimist (Pres 1981-82, Bd of Dir 1982-89); *home:* 1216 Capital Ave Utica NY 13502

CIARLO, JO ANNE HUBBARD, Eng/Theology/History Teacher; *b:* Middlesborro, KY; *m:* Louis Angelo; *c:* Louis III, Jimmie J.; *ed:* (BS) Ed, Seton Hall Univ 1970; (MA) Eng, William Paterson; *cr:* Elem Teacher Paterson Newark 1959-69, Teacher of Eng Paterson Catholic Reg 1969-70; Trenton Diocese 1970-83; Eng/Sci/Theology/World His Teacher Mary Help of Chrstns Acad 1983-; *ai:* Frosh Moderator Adv; Literary Club & Sch Newspaper Moderator; Photographer for Sch Yrbk; MENSA Society of Geniuses 1972-; NCEA 1959-; *office:* Mary Help of Chrstns Acad 659 Belmont Ave North Haledon NJ 07508

CIARROCCHI, JULIA GRACE (AGOSTINI), Economics Teacher; *b:* Uniontown, PA; *c:* Emilio L. III; *ed:* (BS) Bus Admin, Waynesburg Coll 1967; (ME) Bus Ed, WV Univ, PA Dept of Ed 1979; Certified to Teach Accounting, Mrktg, Ec, Typing; *cr:* Bus Ed Teacher Laurel Highlands Sch Dist, 9th Grade Teacher Laurel Highlands Jr HS 1968-82; 9th-12th Grade Economics & Typing Teacher Laurel Highlands Sr HS 1982-; *ai:* Ec Club; Laurel Highlands Ed Assn Pres 1975-77; PA Bus Ed Assn 1970-; PA St Ed Assn 1968-; Dept of Public Assistance Fayette Cty Bd Mem 1975-79; LHEA Pres 1972-78.

CICALESE, FRANCES ANN, Mathematics Teacher; *b:* Newark, NJ; *ed:* (BA) General Elem Ed, Kean Coll 1964; (MA) Ed/Admin/Supervision of Schls, Seton Hall Univ 1972; Math, Rutgers Univ, University Coll, Kean Coll; Cmptr, NJ Inst of Technology; *cr:* 5th-8th Grade Self Contained Classes Teacher Ann Street Sch 1964-78; Adult Ed/Eng as 2nd Lang Teacher Ann Street Sch & Our Lady of Mt Carmel Sch 1969, 1972; Basic Skills Sch Coord 1988-89; 7th/8th Grade Gifted & Talented Prgm/Rdng/Math Teacher 1978-, Basic Skills Lang/Math Teacher 1987- Univ HS; *ai:* Graduation & Class Trip Coord; 8th Grade Adv; In Charge Yrbk Grade Section; Newark Assn of Math Educators 1990; Our Lady of Mt Carmel Church (Society 1977-, Lector 1980-, Eucharistic Minister 1982-); Internship Evaluator Future Teachers; PTA Lang Art Curr Grant; Textbook Selection Comm; Dist Teachers Health, Math, Sci Wkshp Presenter; *home:* 128 Pulaski St Newark NJ 07105

CICCONE, JANE ELIZABETH ANN, 8th Grade English/Rdng Teacher; *b:* Paterson, NJ; *ed:* (BA) Bus/Ec, Upsala Coll 1971; (MA) Admin/Supervision, Jersey City St 1989; Post Masters Stud Elem Ed; *cr:* 1st Grade Teacher 1971-72, 2nd Grade Teacher 1972-75, 3rd Grade Teacher 1975-79 Charles Olbon; 5th Grade Teacher 1980-85, 7th Grade Soc Sci Teacher 1986-87, 6th Grade Teacher 1987-88 Memorial Sch; *ai:* Curr Comm; Field Trip Spon; Volunteer Chaporing Concerts; Participate for Volley Game Against Stu Vs Teachers; Service for Field Day; Negotiations Comm for Teachers Contract 1988-; PCEA Cty Rep 1980-89; Merit Teacher Awd 1986-87; Co-Headed Revised Code of Conduct Comm Submitted to Bd of Ed & Implemented 1989-; *office:* W Paterson Memorial Sch Memorial Dr West Paterson NJ 07424

CICERO, DOROTHY WALLACH, Sixth Grade Teacher; *b:* Redwood City, CA; *m:* Donald Joseph; *c:* Lindsay; *ed:* (BA) Psych, Univ CA Santa Cruz 1975; Psych, His; *cr:* Spec Ed Teacher Ralston Mid Sch 1975-77; Title I Teacher Nesbit Elem Sch 1977-78; Lang Art/Soc Stud/Lang Teacher 1978-84, Phys Ed Teacher 1984-87, 6th Grade Teacher 1987- Ralston Mid Sch; *ai:* Stu Body Officer & Adv; Cheerleading Adv; Cross Cty Coach; Belmont Faculty Assn Secy 1989-; March of Dimes Mem 1987-88; General Excl Journalism Awd 1985; *office:* Ralston Mid Sch 2675 Ralston Avenue Belmont CA 94002

CICHA, SHARON LARSON, 2nd & 3rd Grade Teacher; *b:* Medford, WI; *m:* James M.; *c:* Andrew, Julianna, David; *ed:* (BS) Elem Ed, Univ of WI Stevens Point 1973; *cr:* 1st-2nd Grade Teacher Amery Sch Dist 1966-68; 2nd/3rd Grade Teacher Ladysmith-Hawkins Sch Dist 1968-; *ai:* NEA, WEA; *office:* Hawkins Elem Sch Main St Hawkins WI 54530

CICHOCKI, SHARON A., Mathematics Teacher; *b:* Buffalo, NY; *m:* Ronald Richard; *c:* Gregory, Cynthia; *ed:* (BA) Math, 1977, (MA) Math Ed, 1981 St Univ of NY Buffalo; *cr:* Math Teacher Queen of Heaven 1970-71, Herbert Coll 1981-82, Hamburg Sr HS 1979-; *ai:* NHS & Service Club Adv; HTA Rep; Stu Recognition, Building, Strategy #11 & Taps Comms; Wkshps in Courses I-IV,C2PC Prgm; NY St Teachers of Math 1987-; Hamburg Bd of Ed 1990, Commendation for Math Teaching; Edited Course II Math Text for Merrill Publishing Co; *office:* Hamburg Sr HS 4111 Legion Dr Hamburg NY 14075

CICKAVAGE, WILLIAM JOHN, Math/Computer Science Teacher; *b:* Frackville, PA; *m:* Elaine Bevan; *ed:* (BS) Ed, PA St 1971; Grad Stud PA St; *cr:* Math/Cmptr Sci Teacher Williams Valley Jr-Sr HS 1971-; *ai:* NCTM 1971-76; Jaycees 1977-79; Elks 1971-; *office:* Williams Valley Jr-Sr HS Rt 209 Tower City PA 17980

CICKELLI, JAMES A., Social Studies Teacher; *b:* Savannah, IL; *m:* Jane N. Vagas; *c:* Jamie; *ed:* (BS) Ed Soc Stud, 1974, (MA) Sports Admin, 1985 Kent St Univ; *cr:* Teacher Lakeview HS 1976-; *ai:* NEA, OH Ed Assn Lakeview Teacher Assn 1976-; Blessed Sacrament Church Mem; *office:* Lakeview HS 300 Hillman Dr Cortland OH 44410

CIGANEK, PAULETTE JACOB, Mathematics Teacher; *b:* Brooklyn, NY; *c:* Thomas, Todd, Kristine; *ed:* (BA) Math 1963, Phys Sci, 1963 Trenton St Coll; *cr:* Math Teacher Watchung Hills Regional HS 1963-65, Pascack Hills Regional HS 1965-67, Lacey Township HS 1985-; *ai:* Schlsp Comm; AMTNJ 1986-89; NCTM 1990; *home:* 16 New Jersey Ave Lavallette NJ 08735

CIMINELLO, SUSAN MARY, Kindergarten Teacher; *b:* Wilmington, DE; *ed:* (BSED) Primary/Kndgtn Ed, Univ of DE 1977; Numerous Courses, Univ of DE, Dept of Public Instr, DE Teachers Center in Lang Art, Math, Sci, Cmptr Ed; *cr:* 3rd Grade Teacher 1977-89, Kndgtn Teacher 1989 Holy Angels Sch; *ai:* Precision Dance Moderator St Marks HS 1984-; Testing Coord Holy Angels Sch; DCTN, NCEA, Kappa Delta Pi, Phi Kappa Phi; *office:* Holy Angels Sch 82 Possum Park Rd Newark DE 19711

CIMINO, JAMES ALLEN, French/German Teacher; *b:* Fairmont, WV; *ed:* (BM) Music Ed/Fr, 1973, (MM) Music Ed, 1975 WV Univ; *cr:* Fr/German/Music Teacher Fairmont Sr HS 1973-; *ai:* NHS Adv; Fr Honorary; European Travel-Study Dir & Co-Founder; AATF, NEA 1973-; AATG 1985-; Elks 1989-; Fulbright Teacher Exch England 1988; *office:* Fairmont Sr HS Loop Pk Fairmont WV 26554

CIMINO, JEANETTE ROSE, 6th Grade Teacher of Gifted; *b:* Los Angeles, CA; *ed:* (BA) Ed, 1964, (MA) Educl Admin, 1981, Admin Credential 1981 CA St Univ Los Angeles; Librarianship Credential 1976; *cr:* 5th Grade Teacher/Media Specialist Cortez Elem 1970-76; ESL Specialist Menlo Avenue 1976-78; 6th Grade Gifted/Mentor Teacher/Gifted Coord Gates St Elem 1978-; *ai:* Math Field Day Coach; Garden Club Dir; Grade Level Chairperson; Steer Comm Rep; Intnl Rdng Assn, NCTE, CA Teachers Assn; Mentor Teacher.

CINNAMON, JOAN PETERSON, Language Teacher; *b:* Savanna, IL; *m:* Oliver N.; *c:* Eric, Shan, Lisa; *ed:* (BA) Span, Western IL Univ 1962; *cr:* Span Teacher Jack London Jr HS 1962-63; Span/Eng Teacher Oak St Jr HS 1966-65; 6th Grade Teacher 1979-81, Jr HS Lang Teacher 1981- Limestone Grade; *ai:* Newspaper Spon; Dance Spon; Cty Spelling Bee Coach; Memory Book Adv; First Baptist Church; Limestone PTA; *office:* Limestone Grade Sch Rt 4 Box 242 A Kankakee IL 60901

CINOTTI, DANIEL A., Science Chair/Teacher; *b:* Newport, RI; *m:* Jeanne M. Boisclair; *c:* Amintha K. Provost, Jeanne M.; *ed:* (BS) Zoology, 1955, (MS) Ecology, 1957 Univ of RI; (MS) Sci Ed, Univ of CT 1962; Radiation Bio, Adelphi Coll; Drug Intern Prgm Yale Univ; *cr:* Teacher Guilford Jr HS 1957-58, Guilford HS 1958-63; Sci Chm/Teacher Guilford HS 1963-74, Guilford Sch Dist 1974-; *ai:* Guilford HS Audubon Club Adv; GEA, CEA, NEA 1982-; GSTA, NSTA 1970-; Guilford Land Trust Dir 1974-79; Menunkatuck Audubon (Dir 1982-85, Ed Chm 1983-89); Nom Sci Teacher Awd 1983, 1984; Wesleyan Univ CT Jr Sci Symposia Sci Research Work Citation; Westinghouse Sci Talent Search Citation; Guide Published; *office:* Guilford HS New England Rd Guilford CT 06437

CINTO, RON, Teacher/Coach/Math Dept Chm; *b:* Aurora, IL; *m:* Kristine K.; *c:* Victoria, Evan; *ed:* (BA) General Study, Waubonsee Comm Coll 1976; (BS) Elem Ed/Math, Aurora Univ 1978; *cr:* Teacher/Coach Saratoga Elem Sch 1980-; *ai:* Head Coach Bsbl, Bsktbl, Track; Math Team Coach; *office:* Saratoga Elem Sch 4040 N Division St Morris IL 60450

CINTRON, NORMA H., Spanish Teacher; *b:* Juana Diaz, PR; *m:* Juan R. Torres; *c:* Rafael R., Alberto, Arnaldo, Maricelis; *ed:* (BA) Span, Univ of PR 1961; *cr:* Teacher Jose Gautier Benitez 1961; *ai:* Safety Comm, Talented Stu Adv; Graduation Act Coord; Delegate Teacher Close Up Group Washngton DC; Teacher of Yr Gautier Benitez HS 1989; *home:* Dalmacia 3 B-19 Villa del Rey Caguas PR 00625

CIPOLLINI, JOSEPH G., Gifted, Sci, Math Teacher; *b:* New Haven, CT; *m:* Carolyn Terese Massaro; *ed:* (BS) Bio, 1980, (MS) Environmental/Sci Ed, 1983 S CT St Univ; Certificate Gifted Ed, Univ of CT 1989; Hypercard Educl Applications, Southern CT St Univ; Cmptr Sci Trng Apple II & Mac Intosh Systems; Admin Cert; *cr:* Grad Teaching Asst S CT St Univ 1980-82; Physics Teacher Lee HS 1982-83; Teacher of Gifted Southington Public Schls 1983-; Gifted Prgms Coord Wallingford Public Schls 1984-; *ai:* Sci Fair Adv Southington Jr HS; Project Oceanology Coord; Home Newsletter Layout Ed; Sch Newspaper Adv De Paolo Jr HS; Spec Ed Prof Dev Comm; Co-Chm Cmptr Curr Comm; Sch Handbook, Teacher of Yr Selection, Gifted & Talented Curr Comm; Supt Advisory Bd; CT Sci Fair Assn Cmptr Operations Chm 1986-; Natl Assn Gifted Children Cmptrs & Technology Comm 1989-; Mathcounts Coach 1988, 3rd Place Team, 1st Pl Ind 1988; CT Assn Gifted Mem 1984-; Blackstone Village Bd of Dir (Treas 1985-86, VP 1987-); Staff Mem Univ of CT Summer Inst for Teachers of Gifted 1984; Coord Wallingford Gifted Prgm 1984-; Presented Wkshps & Inservice Prgms NSTA, Zuni Public Schls, Natl Assn Gifted Children, Univ of CT Thinking Skills Conference, CT Assn of Gifted; *office:* De Paolo & Kennedy Jr HS 49 Beecher St Southington CT 06489

CIRACI, SANDRA ROBERTO, Kindergarten Teacher; *b:* Canton, OH; *m:* Ciro Joseph; *c:* Ciro J. II, Frank A., Sam Roberto; *ed:* (BA) Elem Ed/Early Chldhd, Walsh Coll 1977; Learning Disabilities-Behavior Disorders; *cr:* 3rd Grade Teacher 1960-63, Kndgtn Teacher 1977-83, 1st Grade Teacher 1983-85, Kndgtn Teacher 1985- St Louis Sch; *ai:* Home & Sch Teacher Rep; Self Study Team; Lay Teacher Salary Comm; NCEA 1977-; *office:* St Louis Sch 214 N Chapel Louisville OH 44641

CISNERO, BETTY TREVINO, English Teacher; *b:* Charlotte, TX; *m:* Louis; *c:* Denise, Louis Jr.; *ed:* (BA) Span/Eng, St Marys Univ 1972; Bi-ling Ed, Counseling; *cr:* Span Teacher Pleasanton HS 1972-85; Eng/Speech Teacher Poteet Jr HS 1985-; *ai:* UIL Dir; UIL Oral Rdng & Spelling, Stu Cncl, Drugbusters Spon; Lang Art Dept Chairperson; Campus Comm Leader; GSA (Leader 1977-84, Neighborhood Chairperson 1982-84); *office:* Poteat Jr HS P O Box 138 Poteet TX 78065

CITTY, GAY SMITH, 5th Grade Teacher; *b:* Greensboro, NC; *m:* R. Bruce Jr.; *c:* Robbie, James, Emily; *ed:* (BS) Intermediate Ed, Univ NC 1980; Project Galileo Univ NC; *cr:* Teacher Moss Street Sch 1980-85/1985-, Lawsonville Avenue Sc 1985-86; Moss St Sch 1968-; *ai:* Sci Comm; Sch Leadership Comm; Teacher Differentiated Pay Comm; NC Assn of Ed Faculty Rep 1980-; NEA 1980-; Baptist Temple Church Sunday Sch Dept Dir 1988-; United Way Pacesetter Chm Moss Street 1989-; Bronze Awd 1989-; Reidsville City Schls Teache R of the Yr 1987-88; Reidsville City Schls/Chamber of Commerce Sci Teacher Yr 1986-87; *office:* Moss Street Elem Sch 419 Moss St Reidsville NC 27320

CLAAR, LORI L., Mathematics Teacher; *b:* Alum Bank, PA; *m:* David; *c:* Matthew D.; *ed:* (BS) Math/Sci, Univ of Pittsburgh Johnstown 1983; Working Towards Masters Ed Equivalency; *cr:* Math Teacher Conemaugh Valley Jr Sr HS 1983-; *ai:* Sr Class Adv; Mathcounts Team Coach; PA St Ed Assn 1983-; *office:* Conemaugh Valley Jr Sr HS RD 1 Box 132 Johnstown PA 15906

CLABORN, JIM W., 8th Grade Soc Stud Teacher; *b:* Caddo, OK; *m:* Robin Elizabeth Davis; *c:* Dana T.; *ed:* (AS) General, Walters St Comm Coll 1973; (BSC) Elem Ed, Univ of TN 1975; Adult Ed, TN Tech Univ; Foxfire, Carson-Newman Coll; *cr:* Adult Ed Teacher Hamblen Cty Schls 1980-89; Soc Stud Teacher Meadowview Mid Sch 1975-; Soldier US Army Natl Guard 1976-; Farmer Talbott TN 1980-; Newspaper Columnist Back when Morristown Citizen-Tribune 1988-; Instr Walters St Comm Coll 1989-; *ai:* Faculty Rep Hamblen Cty Ed Assn; NEA, TN Ed Assn, Hamblen Cty Ed Assn 1975-; Hamblen Cty Historical Society Pres 1976-; Decedants of David Crockett 1988-; Crockett Tavern Museum (Dir, His) 1986-; 63rd Volunteer Confederate Infantry 1989-; Natl Endowment for Hum Rutgers Univ; Natl Endowment for Hum Pepsico Harvard; TN Outstanding Achievement Awd 1983; Honorary TN Colonel 1988; TN Teacher Appreciation Awd 1989; Newspaper Columinist Back When Morristown Citizen-Tribune; *home:* 984 Lakeshore Rd Talbott TN 37877

CLAGETT, MILDRED WINTER, Retired 12th Grade Eng Teacher; *b:* Clinton, KY; *c:* William; *ed:* (BS) Eng, 1942, (MA) Eng, 1960 Memphis St Univ; *cr:* 1st Grade Teacher Lauderdale Sch 1949-51; 1st/2nd Grade Teacher Grahamwood Elem Sch 1951-56; 8th/9th Grade Eng Teacher Snowden Jr HS 1956-60; 10th-12th Grade Teacher Cntrl HS 1960-72; 12th Grade Teacher Hillcrest HS 1972-82; *ai:* Eng Club 1941-42; Lindenwood Chrstn Church Chrstn Womens Fellowship Service Chm 1984-86; *home:* 1642 Linden Ave Memphis TN 38104

CLAIBORNE, CAROLYN PALMER, 6th Grade Soc Stud Teacher; *b:* Neosho, MO; *c:* Kevin, Doug, Janet; *ed:* (AA) Fullerton Jr Coll 1956; (BA) Home Ec/Psych, Whittier Coll 1958; (MS) Early Chldhd, La Verne Coll 1975; *cr:* 3rd/4th Grade Teacher Carpenter Elem 1958-61; 1st Grade Teacher Hooker Elem 1963-64; 3rd Grade Teacher Gallatin Elem 1964-65, Magnolia Elem 1967-68; 2nd Grade Teacher Thornton Elem 1968-69; 1st/2nd Grade Teacher Williams Elem 1969-74; 1st/2nd Combination Grade Teacher Rives Avenue Elem 1974-75; 1st-4th Grade Teacher Gallatin Elem 1975-85; 6th Grade Soc Stud Teacher South Mid Sch 1985-; *ai:* Schlsp Club Spon; Dept Head; DEA, CTA, NEA; 1st Baptist Church; PEO Guard 1989-; Womens Club of Downey Teacher of Yr 1979; *office:* South Mid Sch 12500 Birchdale Ave Downey CA 90242

CLAIR, DARYL RICHARD, Reading/Language Art Teacher; *b:* Greensburg, PA; *m:* Grace Ungerman; *c:* Jerilyn, Daniel; *ed:* (BS) Elem Ed/Spec Ed, Slippery Rock Univ of PA 1977; Working Towards Masters Admin; *cr:* 4th Grade Teacher Sunrise Estates Elem Sch 1977-79; 6th-8th Grade Rdng/Lang Art Teacher Trafford Mid Sch 1979-; *ai:* Head Teacher; Talent Show Coord; NEA, PA St Ed Assn, Penn Trafford Ed Assn 1977-; Chrstn Life Church (Deacon 1984-, Treas 1988-); Penn Trafford PRIDE Awd for Excl in Teaching 1987; *office:* Trafford Mid Sch 100 E Brinton Ave Trafford PA 15085

CLAIRBORNE, PAULETTE SMITH, Fifth Grade Reading Teacher; *b:* Lafayette, TN; *m:* Fountain; *c:* Rebecca; *ed:* (BA) His, W KY 1967; Rdng Specialist; *cr:* His Teacher Allen Cty HS 1967-68, Cntrl Mid Sch 1968-82; Rdng Teacher Cntrl Mid Sch 1982-; *ai:* Cntrl Mid Sch Newspaper & His Club; MCEA, TEA, NEA, Intnl Rdng Assn; Long Creek Baptist Church Sunday Sch Teacher 1988-; Cntrl Mid Sch Teacher of Yr 1988; *office:* Cntrl Mid Sch Sycamore St Lafayette TN 37083

CLANCY, JO ANN CORSO, Fifth Grade Teacher; *b:* Brooklyn, NY; *m:* Jack; *ed:* (BA) Elem Ed, 1968, (MS) Elem Ed, 1971 Queens Coll; *cr:* 5th Grade Teacher Abraham Lincoln Sch 1973-80, John F Kennedy Intermediate Sch 1968-73, 1980-.

CLAPP, KATHLEEN LYONS, Mathematics Teacher; *b:* Little Falls, NY; *m:* John M.; *ed:* (BS) Math, Univ of ME Presque Isle 1979; *cr:* Summer Sch Teacher Limestone Sch Dept 1976-77; Substitute Teacher Caribou Jr HS 1978-79; Teacher Bucksport HS 1979-; *ai:* Stu Cncl Adv; Climate, Aspiration Comm; Math Team Coach; BTA Exec Cncl; Bucksport Teachers Assn Exec Comm 1987-; ME Teachers Assn, NEA 1979-; NCTM 1987-; *office:* Bucksport HS PO Box 400 Broadway Bucksport ME 04416

CLAPPER, KEVIN MATTHEW, Sr HS Mathematics Teacher; *b:* Stamford, NY; *m:* Kathleen Marie Kenney; *c:* Katelynn; *ed:* (BS) Math Ed/Statistics, SUNY Oneonta 1978; (MS) Math Ed, SUNY Binghamton 1982; *cr:* Math Teacher Chenango Valley 1978-; *ai:* Coaching Jr HS Bsktbl & Var Ftbl; *office:* Chenango Valley Schls 768 Chenango St Binghamton NY 13901

CLARA, ERIKA E., Language Arts/English Teacher; *b:* Nurnberg, Germany; *m:* Aldo Jr.; *c:* Daniel, Gretchen; *ed:* (BS) Eng, Univ of California PA; Grad Stud Univ of CA, Penn St Univ; *cr:* Eng Teacher Hershey Jr HS 1970-71, Southmoreland Jr HS 1972-; *ai:* Stu Cncl; Yrbk; Alpha Gifted Prgm; Stu Announcers; Lang Art Curr Leader 1988-; NCTE 1989-; Westmoreland Cty Lib Bd 1979-80; *office:* Southmoreland Jr HS Box B Alverton PA 15612

CLARE, MICHELE DI MANTOVA, Foreign Language Teacher; *b:* Bayside, NY; *m:* Frank Russel; *ed:* (BA) Elem Ed/ Span Endorsement, (MS) Comm/Ed, 1989, W CT St Univ; *cr:* Substitute Eng Teacher Brookfield HS 1984; Span Teacher Henry Wells Mid Sch 1984-; *ai:* Foreign Lang Club Adv; Stu of Month Comm Mem; Grade Comm; Gifted & Talented Comm 1989; Brewster Teacher Rep 1988-; Brewster Ed Fnd Grant 1990; Phi Lambda Theta Secy 1988; Brewster Teacher Assn Comm Chairperson; Delta Gamma Intnl Schlsp 1982; *office:* Henry H Wells Mid Sch Rt 312 Brewster NY 10509

CLARE, NANON BIRD, English IV Teacher; *b:* Sublette, KS; *m:* Dale; *c:* Lisa, Lori, Linda; *ed:* (BA) Eng/Speech/Drama, Southwestern Coll 1955; Advanced Placement Eng Instruction; *cr:* Phys Ed Teacher Morristown NJ 1955-57; Speech/Drama Teacher Minneola KS 1965-75; Speech/Eng Teacher Atwood KS 1975-84; Eng IV/Advanced Placement Teacher Scott City KS 1985-; *ai:* Sr Class & Concessions Spon; KNEA 1965-; NCTE 1975-; United Meth Church 1939-; *office:* Scott Cmmty HS 712 Main Scott City KS 67871

CLARK, ALTON BRUCE, 10th-12th Grade His Teacher; *b:* Burlington, NC; *m:* Sondra Cristine Brenner; *c:* Justin; *ed:* (BA) His/Soc Stud, Wingate Coll 1982; *cr:* Stu Teacher/Coach Forest Hills HS 1982; In-Sch Suspension Coord/Coach 1983-85, His Teacher/Coach 1986- King Mountain Sr HS; *ai:* Head Bsbl & Legion Bsbl Coach; Ftbl Defensive Coord; NC Assn of Educators, NEA 1983-; NC Coaches Assn 1982-; 1st Presbyn Church of King Mountain 1984-; Grover Fire Dept Trng Officer 1985-89; NC St 3A Champions Coach 1989; SW 3A Conference Base Coach of Yr 1989; *home:* 609 Ginger Dr Kings Mountain NC 28086

CLARK, ANNE MARIE, Teacher of Gifted & Talented; *b:* San Antonio, TX; *m:* Jimmie Carlton; *c:* Kristi, Traci; *ed:* (BS) Elem Ed/Eng, (MED) Curr/Instr, Our Lady of the Lake Univ; Math Learning Inst St Marys Univ; *cr:* Classroom Teacher James Bowie Elem; 3rd-6th Grade Teacher San Antonio Ind Sch Dist; 1st Grade Teacher 1979-83, 5th Grade Teacher 1983-89 Castle Hills Elem; Part-Time Instr Univ of TX San Antonio 1989-; Teacher of K-5th Grade Gifted & Talented Castle Hills Elem 1990; *ai:* Math & Cmptr Club Spon; Stu Literary Magazine Coord; Writing Comm & Cmptr Comm Chm; Instructional Focus & Campus Goals Comm; Northeast Teachers Assn Prof Dev Comm, San Antonio Teachers Cncl Secy 1970-72; TX Elem Sci Teachers Assn, NCTE; San Antonio Area Cncl Teacher of Eng Contest Chm; Alamo Writing Project Fellowship Trinity Univ; Northeast Writing Wkshp; Northeast Dist Literary Magazine Ed; Natl Sci Fnd; *office:* Castle Hills Elem Sch 101 Honeysuckle San Antonio TX 78213

CLARK, ANNETTE RENFRO, 2nd Grade Teacher; *b:* Batesville, MS; *m:* John William; *c:* Benita L., Randall E.; *ed:* (BA) Bus Ed, 1962, (BA) Elem Ed, 1964 Memphis St Univ; Working Toward Masters; *cr:* Teacher Memphis City Schls 1965-; *ai:* Prin Adv Comm; Curr Coord; NEA Unified 1970-; Samaritan Center Secy 1989-; Achieved Career Ladder III Status 1986; *office:* Whitehaven Elem Sch 4783 Elvis Presley Memphis TN 38116

CLARK, AVA EAKMAN, Retired Teacher; *b:* Austin, TX; *m:* Larry Loy; *c:* Chad C. Houston, Cullen C. Houston; *ed:* (BME) Music Ed, Baylor Univ 1971; (MME) Music Ed, Angelo St Univ 1988; Freiburg Organ Inst Germany 1968; *cr:* Music Teacher Wall Ind Sch Dist 1971-75; Piano Instr Angelo St Univ 1974-75; Choral Dir Jefferson Jr HS 1975-78; Music Teacher San Angelo Ind Sch Dist 1978-81; Choral Dir Glenn Jr HS 1981-; *ai:* Pipe Organ Recitals 1984, 1986; Weddings, Funerals, Civic Affairs, Church Organist; Angelo St Univ Musicals & Stu Recitals Pianist & Accompanist; TX Choral Dirs Assn, TX Music Educators Assn, Assn of TX Prof Educators; Mu Phi Epsilon, Kappa Kappa Iota; *home:* 2010 Rancy San Angelo TX 76901

CLARK, BARBARA JEAN, English Teacher; *b:* El Paso, TX; *ed:* (BA) Eng, W TX St Univ 1988; *cr:* Fr/Eng Teacher Andrews HS 1988-89; Eng Teacher Tucumcari HS 1989-; *ai:* Jr Var & Var Cheerleading Spon & Coach; Princs Faculty Advisory Comm; Natl Teacher Assn 1989-; TX St Teachers Assn 1988-89; Romance Writers of TX Panhandle Pres 1988-89; *home:* 3645 South 5th Tucumcari NM 88401

CLARK, BARBARA JUNE, Fourth Grade Teacher; *b:* Leoti, KS; *ed:* (BS) Elem Ed, 1958, (MS) Elem Ed, 1967 KS St Univ Ft Hays; USD 480s Prof Dev Plan 1980-; *cr:* 4th Grade Teacher Mc Kinley Elem 1954-56, Lincoln Elem 1958-61; 5th Grade Teacher 1961-62, 4th Grade Teacher 1962- Lincoln Elem; *ai:* Soc Stud Textbook Selection Comm 1990; Grade Level Chm 1989-; Monat Evaluation System Intensive Assistance Team; Lesson Plan Design Comm 1989-; Liberal Ed Assn, KNEA, NEA Prof Negotiations Comm 1986-87, Master Teacher 1988-89; Delta Kappa Gamma Recording Secy 1986-88; PTA (Founders Day, Lincoln His) 1980-81, Life Membership 1962; Bus & Prof Womens Club (Pres 1979-80, Treas 1989-), Woman of Yr 1974; Beta Sigma Phi (Treas, Ways & Means Chm) 1981-, Order of Rose 1979; United Meth Women Circle 9 (Recording Secy 1986-88, Youth Act Chm 1988-); United Meth Church (Chancel Choir, Ed Comm); Jr Chamber of Commerce Young Teacher Rep 1962; USD 480 25 Yr Pin 1981; 25 Yr KNEA Certificate 1985; USD 480 Mathfest Chm 1987-88; Wrote Lincoln Sch His 1978; *office:* Lincoln Elem Sch 11th And Calhoun Liberal KS 67901

CLARK, BETTY DEBERRY, Science Teacher; *b:* Russellville, KY; *m:* Joseph Wood; *c:* Austin, Benjamin; *ed:* (BS) Home Ec, Austin Peay St Univ 1970; (MS) Elem Ed, W KY Univ 1978; *cr:* 1st/2nd Grade Teacher South Korea 1970-72; Home Ec Teacher/ 4-H Leader Univ of KY 1972-74; 6th-8th Grade Teacher Chandlers Elem 1974-; *ai:* Sci Fair & Sci Comms; Logan Cty Educl Assn, KY Educl Assn 1975-; Ky Educl Innovation Incentive Fund Grant for Yr 1987; *office:* Chandlers Mid Sch 7815 Chandlers Rd Auburn KY 42206

CLARK, BEVERLY GOODLOE, Second Grade Teacher; *b:* Washington, DC; *m:* Horace Pettibone Jr.; *c:* Horace III, Michael, Patrick, Patricia Daniels; *ed:* (BS) Math, DC Teachers Coll 1943; Writing for Children Inst of Childrens Lit 1974; Society of Childrens Book Writers 1981, Cmptr Logo I 1984, Logo II 1986, Univ of Ca Los Angles Extension; *cr:* Teacher St Gerard Majella Sch 1964-; *ai:* Archdiocesan Educl Cmptr Consortium; LEGO TC Logo User Group; NCEA 1990; NCTM 1983-; Confraternity of Chrstn Doctrine Teacher 1957-78, Diploma 1959; CA Museum Fnd 1989-; Archdiocese of Los Angeles Teacher Recognition Awd 1990; *office:* St Gerard Majella Sch 4451 Inglewood Blvd Los Angeles CA 90066

CLARK, BRENDA HARRISON, Soc Stud Dept Chairperson; *b:* Berea, KY; *m:* George A.; *ed:* (BA) Art/Hist, 1975; (MA) Art, 1978; Scndry Prin/Supervisor Curr, 1980 Eastern KY Univ; KY Intern Teacher; 3 Mellon Fellowships Berea; TESA Prgm; College Summer Prgm; Commonwealth Inst for Teachers; *cr:* Teacher Mc Kee Elem 1975-76; Chm Soc Stud Jackson Cty HS 1976-; *ai:* Jackson Cty Task Force Ed; Governors Scholar Selection Comm; Delta Kappa Gamma 2nd VP 1988-, KEA/NEA 1975-; Beta Club Teacher of Yr; 5th Dist US His Teacher Awd; Louisville Scottish Rite Commonwealth Inst for Teachers; Former Advisory Bd Berea Coll HS Co-Op Learning Prgm; Forward in Fifth Grant; TESA; *office:* Jackson County HS Mc Kee KY 40447

CLARK, BRENDA M., 11th Grade Guidance Counselor; *b:* Nashville, TN; *c:* Raymond, Beth; *ed:* (BS) His, 1967, (MS) Guidance/Counseling, 1981 TN St Univ; Grad Work TN St Univ; *cr:* Eng Teacher East Side Jr HS 1967-68; Soc Stud Teacher Du Pont Sr HS 1968-85; Guidance Cnslr Glencliff HS 1985-; *ai:* Jr Class Adv; Jr/Sr Prom Coord; Unified Teaching Profession, Mid TN Assn Counseling & Dev, TN Sch Cnslrs Assn, TN Career Assn Glencliff Chapter Adv; Delta Sigma Theta; Achieved Career Ladder III Cert Through Evaluation TN St Bd of Ed; *home:* 3856 Cravath Dr Nashville TN 37207

CLARK, CAROL SUE, Orchestra Director; *b:* Cleveland, OH; *ed:* (BS) Music Ed, OH St 1961; (MA) Conducting, Trenton St 1969; Grad Stud OH St Oberlin; WV Univ Ithica, Capital, Eastmen; *cr:* Instr Columbus OH 1961-63; Music Teacher Franklin Township 1963-72, Boardman HS 1972-; *ai:* NSOA Bd Mem; ASTA, OMEA, NEA; Boardman HS Orch Awds & Medals; *office:* Boardman HS 7777 Glenwood Youngstown OH 44512

CLARK, CAROLYN CRAMER, Third Grade Teacher; *b:* Lexington, NE; *m:* Bertram V.; *c:* Crystal K.; *ed:* (BA) Elem Ed, NE St Teachers Coll 1969; Grad Work, Kearney St Coll; *cr:* 4th-6th Grade Teacher Dawson Cty Dist Sch 1954-59; 4th Grade Teacher Mullen Public Schls 1959-61; 3rd Grade Teacher Sumner Public Schls 1961-; *ai:* 4-H Club Stu Leader; 3rd Grade Class Spon; NEA, NE St Ed Assn 1954-; Sumner Eddyville Miller Ed Assn (Pres 1989-) 1961-; 4-H Club Leader 1965-; Extension Club Pres 1990; Teacher of Yr Awd.

CLARK, CENIA BROWN, Retired Elementary Teacher; *b:* Doerun, GA; *m:* Robert Eli; *c:* Lillian E. Bateman, Robert W., Jancy V. Garcia, Louisa A. Whitworth; *ed:* (BAED) Ed, GA St Coll for Women 1952; Post Grad Stud Appalacian St Teachers Coll; Numerous Field Courses & Wkshps for Pinellas Cty Teachers; *cr:* Elem Teacher Sigsby Sch 1937-39, Abram Consolidated Sch 1937-42, Palm Harbor Jr HS 1955-56, Sunset Hills Elem Sch 1961-82; *ai:* Ec Fair Pinellas Cty 2nd Graders; Bus & Lunch Duty; Amer Chldhd Ed, Intnl Rdng Assn 1961-62; FL Ed Assn, PTA, Pinellas Cty Teachers Assn; Alpha Delta Kappa Pres 1972-74; Retired Ed Assn 1952-; Health Care; Devotion 1982-; Friends of Tarpon Springs (Lib Pres 1982-83, Bd of Dirs); Garden Club 1987; Womans Club 1984; Historical Society; Suncoast Evangelizing Assn; Church Womans Circle Pres 1975-78; Teacher of Yr 1979; Sunset Hills Faculty & Staff Certificate of Appreciation; Juror Federal, Tampa & Pinellas Court; Model Awd; Amer Ed Week Appreciation Awd; *home:* 2875 Keystone Rd Tarpon Springs FL 34689

CLARK, CHENELL MELANIE, Chemistry Teacher; *b:* Wellsboro, PA; *ed:* (BA) Chem, 1982, (MED) Sci Ed/Chem, 1990 Univ of S FL; *cr:* Adult Ed Teacher Big Bend Comm Coll 1984-85, City Coll of Chicago Europe 1983-85; Chem Teacher Pasco Cty Schls & Land O Lakes HS 1985-; *ai:* Managing Productive Schls Prgm; Sch Sci Fair Dir; Regional Sci Fair Comm; FL Assn Sci Teachers; NSTA; *office:* Land O'Lakes HS 20325 Gator Ln Land O'Lakes FL 34639

CLARK, DUANE ROBERT, English Teacher; *b:* Chippewa Falls, WI; *m:* Kimberly Mc Knight; *c:* Rodney, Cole; *ed:* (BS) Eng, 1969, (MS) Eng, 1976 Univ of WI Stevens Point; Creative Writing, Poetry, Commercial Arts at Univ of WI Eau Claire & Ft Lewis Coll; *cr:* Eng Teacher Durango Sr HS 1979-85, Univ of WI Eau Claire 1985-87, Chippewa Falls Sr HS 1987-89, Chippewa Valley Tech Coll 1989-; *ai:* Chippewa Falls Sr HS Asst Ftbl Coach; Chippewa Valley Tech Coll Stu Senate Adv; WI Fellowship of Poets 1986-; Amer Acad of Poets 1980-; WI Cncl Teachers of Eng 1985-; Original Poems Published Various Literary Magazines; Book of Poems Published 1979; *home:* Rt 3 Box 229-A Chippewa Falls WI 54729

CLARK, ELANE JANET, 2nd Grade Teacher; *b:* Cumberland, RI; *m:* Guy Auburn; *ed:* (BA) Elem Ed, Parsons Coll 1967; (MS) Elem/Gifted Ed, Western IL Univ 1987; Supervision, Western IL Univ; Spec Ed, Natl Coll of Ed; *cr:* 2nd Grade Teacher Galesburg Cmmty Unit Schls 1967-; *ai:* Gifted Instr Elem Enrichment Prgm 1974-; Regional Spec Ed Fine Arts Bd of Dir 1977-81; IL Math Assessment Comm 1984-87; Alpha Delta Kappa Pres 1984-86 Altruistic 1988; Phi Delta Kappa 1985- Membership 1990; GEA, IEA, NEA Local Treas 1977-80 Membership 1987; Friends Public Lib 1978-; YMCA Bd Volunteer/Instr 1980-; PEO Treas 1989-Teacher of Yr 1974; IL St Bd of Ed Fellowship Grant for Gifted 1985-87; Western IL Youth Univ Prgm 1989-; Speaker IL St Bd of Better Curr 1988-; *office:* Gale Sch 1131 Dayton Galesburg IL 61401

CLARK, EVELYN LAWRENCE, Mid & Elem Cmptr Teacher; *b:* Mc Rae, GA; *m:* Harrison; *c:* Isaac L. Lawrence; *ed:* (BA) Elem Ed, Ft Valley St Coll 1972; (MA) Early Chldhd Ed, E MI Univ Ypsilanti 1980; Specialist Degree Prgm Educl Admin, E MI Univ Ypsilanti; *cr:* 1st Grade Teacher Crawford Cty Elem 1971-74, Inkster Public Sch 1977-84; 6th-8th Grade Mid Sch Teacher 1986-89, K-5th Grade Elem Teacher 1989- Cmptr Applications; *ai:* Career Day Comm; Cmptr Club; Culture Act Spon; Special Events Coord; Behavior Alert Team & Discipline Prgm Recording Secy; Spec Stu Achievement Awd Prgm Coord; ACT Tutoring; Rdng in Mall Newspaper in Ed Week Sch Act; Sch Improvement Team; Sch Choir; MASSAP 1989-; Prof Book Clubs 1971-; Wayne Cty & MI Rdng Cncl 1977-; Delta Sigma Theta (Various Comm Chairperson, Financial Secy) 1987-89; NAACP Mem 1988-; GSA Leader 1972-74; Wayne Cty Intermediate Schls Golden Apple Awd 1988; Blanchette Mid Sch Teacher of Yr 1987-88; YWCA Y-Teens Public Service Awd 1988; *home:* 23511 Broken Stone Ct Novi MI 48050

CLARK, FREDERICK J., 8th Grade Soc Studies Teacher; *b:* Loogootee, IN; *ed:* (BS) Soc Sci Ed, 1969, (MS) Soc Sci Ed, 1974 IN St Univ; Gifted/Talented Endorsement Purdue Univ 1988; *cr:* Teacher Greater Jasper Consolidated Schls 1969-; *ai:* Gifted/ Talented Pull-Out Prgm 7th & 8th Grades Jasper Mid Sch; IN Cncl for Soc Stud Bd of Dir 1989-; NCSS; Society for Constitution; Natl Trust for Historic Preservation; Sierra Club; Wilderness Society; IN Bicentennial Fellow 1988; IN Hum Cncl IN Univ; *office:* Jasper Mid Sch 340 W 6th St Jasper IN 47546

CLARK, GLENN E., English Teacher; *b:* Corpus Christi, TX; *ed:* (BS) Scndry Ed, Univ of N TX 1984; (MS) Sci Ed, Univ of TX Austin 1989; *cr:* Eng Teacher L B Johnson HS 1988-; *ai:* Jr Var Vlybl Coach; *home:* 7033 Hwy 290E #128 Austin TX 78723

CLARK, JACKIE COPE, English Teacher; *b:* Paris, TX; *m:* Johnny Dale; *c:* John D., Amy S.; *ed:* (BS) Ed/Eng, E TX Baptist Coll 1960; (MSE) Ed/Eng, Henderson St 1966; *cr:* Teacher Redwater HS 1960-; *ai:* Sr Class Spon; Long Range Planning Comm; TX St Teachers Assn, NEA; 1st Baptist Church Treas; Redwater PTA (VP, Life Membership).

CLARK, JACQUIE C., English Teacher; *b:* Tonasket, WA; *m:* Ward M.; *c:* Daniel; *ed:* (BA) Drama/Eng, E WA Univ 1972; *cr:* Eng/Journalism Teacher Holy Names Acad 1972-74; 9th-12th Grade Eng/Drama Teacher Kootenai HS 1974-80; Teacher/ Substitute Teacher Grand Coulee Dam Sch Dist 1980-84; 10th-12th Grade Eng Teacher Okanogan HS 1984-; *ai:* Honor Society Adv; ASB Fund Cncl; Lib Advisory Comm; Kootenai Ed Assn (Pres, Secy) 1974-80; Grand Coulee Dam Ed Assn 1982-84; Okanogan Ed Assn Secy 1984-; Delta Kappa Gamma 1987-.

CLARK, JAMES RUSSELL, Mathematics & Religion Teacher; *b:* Whitesville, KY; *m:* Peggy Marie Brant; *c:* Jennifer, Emily, Natalie, Susan; *ed:* (BA) His, Brescia Coll 1973; (MA) Ed, W KY Univ 1979; Endorsement Prin; *cr:* Teacher St Mary of the Woods 1970-76; Head Teacher St Alphonsas Sch 1977-79; Teacher St Mary of the Woods 1979-; *ai:* Trinity HS Bsbl Coach; Stu Cncl Adv; DOCE VP 1984-86; Commonwealth Inst for Teachers 1987; Governors Symposium on Ed 1988; *office:* St Mary of the Woods 10521 Franklin St Whitesville KY 42378

CLARK, JANET E., Fourth Grade Teacher; *b:* Buffington, PA; *m:* Paul A.; *c:* Brian E., Mary B. Tolson; *ed:* (BS) Elem Ed, 1962; (MED) Elem, 1973 CA St Coll; *cr:* 2nd Grade Teacher Lemont Furnace Sch 1962-63; 1st Grade Teacher Lincoln Sch 1963-65; Kndgtn 6th Grade Teacher Uniontown Area Sch 1971-85; 4th Grade Teacher Lafayette Sch 1985-; *ai:* Lincoln Sch Outstandting

New Teacher 1964; Fayette Cty Favorite Teacher 1985; *office:* Lafayette Sch 303 Connellsville St Uniontown PA 15401

CLARK, JENNIFER WELLS, Science Teacher; *b:* Mc Minnville, TN; *m:* Richie Dale; *c:* Amber, Dustin, Ramsey; *ed:* (BS) Home Ec Ed, TN Technological Univ 1981; (MED) Curr/Instruction, Mid TN Univ 1987; *cr:* Teacher Westwood Jr HS 1983-; *ai:* Beta Club Spon; Stu Cncl Adv; Homecoming Coord; *home:* 1503 Sycamore Cir Manchester TN 37355

CLARK, JOHN D., 6th Grade Math Teacher; *b:* Knoxville, TN; *m:* Annette R.; *c:* John B., David L., Kevin M.; *ed:* (BS) Elem Ed, Cumberland Coll 1969; (MA) Ed, Union Coll 1970; Univ of Tn; *cr:* Teacher Burriville Elem Sch 1969-70, Halls Mid Sch 1970-; *ai:* Developer Sub Division; Builder Homes; Smokey Mountain Math; *office:* Halls Mid Sch 4317 Emory Rd Knoxville TN 37938

CLARK, JOHN DAVID, Industrial Technology Teacher; *b:* Cincinnati, OH; *m:* Carol Ann; *c:* John, Kristin, Matthew; *ed:* Industrial Art, W St Coll of CO 1968; (BS) Industrial Technology, 1972-73 Ball St Univ; *cr:* Teacher Pike HS 1972, Ben Davis HS 1972-; *ai:* Var Sftbl Coach; Intramural Dir; Ben Davis Little League Adv 1980-; Cadet Ftbl Adv 1989-; IN Coaches Girls Sports 1986-, Sftbl Awd 1990; Marion Cty Coaches Girls Sports Pres 1990; IN Industrial Technology Assn 1972-; IN Coaches Assn Pres Sftbl Comm; IN Elem Ftbl Assn 1988-.

CLARK, JOHN FRANKLIN, JR., World Geography Teacher; *b:* Sunbury, PA; *m:* Ruth Ann Cooper; *c:* Kristen I., Karen I.; *ed:* (BS) Soc Stud, Mansfield St Coll 1969; PA St Univ; *cr:* 7th Grade World Geography/8th Grade World Cultures/Environmental Topics Teacher Williamsport Area Sch Dist 1969-; *ai:* Mid Sch Ftbl & Track Coach; *office:* Lycoming Valley Mid Sch 1825 Hays Ln Williamsport PA 17701

CLARK, JOSEPH RICHARD, Latin & Psychology Teacher; *b:* Hazleton, PA; *m:* Julianne De Bias; *c:* Joseph Jr., Janine; *ed:* (BA) His, Kings Coll 1970; (MED) Soc Sci/Ed, Bloomsburg Univ 1976; Psych, Marywood Coll; *cr:* Teacher West Hazleton HS 1970-; Adjunct Instr Luzerne Cty Comm Coll 1980-; *ai:* Var W, Jr Statesman, Stand Tall, NHS Club Adv; Athletic Dir; HAEA, PSEA, NEA 1970-; Amer Classical League 1979-; PA Athletic Dir Assn 1987-; Little League (Pres 1982-88, Asst Dist Admin 1982-); Outstanding Scndry Educator in America 1975; *office:* West Hazleton HS 325 North St West Hazleton PA 18201

CLARK, JUDY BORDEN, Teacher/Soc Stud Dept Chair; *b:* Mountain Grove, MO; *m:* Terry L. Claar; *ed:* (BSED) Comprehensive Soc Stud, 1974, (MS) Geography/Ed, 1978, Specialist Ed/Ed Admin, 1988 S MO St Univ; Univ of MO Columbia, Univ of MO St Louis, Drury Coll; *cr:* Adjunct Faculty SW MO St Univ 1983, Drury Coll 1988-, SW MO St Univ 1989-; Teacher Mountain Grove HS 1974-; *ai:* Sr Class Spon; NHS Adv; Dist Career Ladder & Dist Prof Dev Comm; NCSS (Comm Appointment 1974-, Instructional Media & Technology Comm 1986-); Delta Kappa Gamma Pres 1980-; NEA Local Organization VP 1989-; Lioness Pres 1970-; Order of the Eastern Star Past Matron 1972-; United Meth Church.

CLARK, KATHLEEN STEVENS, 8th Grade English Teacher; *b:* Portsmouth, VA; *m:* Ronald A.; *c:* Jon, Bill, Jennifer; *ed:* (BA) Eng, San Diego St Univ 1962; *cr:* Teacher Coronado HS 1963-64; Coronado Mid Sch 1964-; *ai:* Spon - East Coast Fld Trip; Spon - Creative Wrtg Magzn; 8th Grade Adv; Spon - Ski Trip; Adv - Speech Contest & Spelling Bee; CAGS 1989 Teacher of Yr 1989; Greater San Diego Rdng Assn Awd of Excl 1989; Coronado Rotary Club Cmmty Svc Awd 1988; Christ Episcopal Church Vestry Clerk 1987-; Sch Imprvmnt Comm 1985-; Kappa Alpha Theta Alumni Sec 1987-; *office:* Coronado Mid Sch 911 7th St Coronado CA 92118

CLARK, KATHRYN MURPHEY, Math Dept Chair & Teacher; *b:* Greenwood, MS; *m:* Fred Lee; *c:* Kathryn K.; *ed:* (BSE) Math, 1976, (MED) Scndry Ed/Math, 1979 Delta St Univ; *cr:* Metric Information Center Coord Delta St Univ 1976-77; Teacher Indianola Acad 1977-79, Pillow Acad 1979-; *ai:* Jr Class, Jr/Sr Banquet Spon; Mu Alpha Theta Adv; Annual Staff Financial Mgr; Delta Kappa Gamma 1989-; MS Private Sch Assn Dist Math Chm 1978-79; Itta Bena Jr Womans Club (Mem, VP 1980-82, Ed Chm 1988-) 1978-, Club Woman of Yr 1979; Phi Mu Area Alumni Recommendations Chm 1979-; Daughters of Amer Revolution 1990; STAR Teacher 1983, 1988; *home:* PO Box 115 Itta Bena MS 38941

CLARK, LAURA SPENCER, Spanish Teacher; *b:* Harviell, MO; *m:* Jack Dean; *c:* Dean S.; *ed:* (BS) Span Art, 1961, (MAT) Art, 1973 SE MO St Univ; Instituto De Filo Logia Hispanica Saltillo Mexico; *cr:* Teacher Lilbourn HS 1960-61, Poplar Bluff HS & Jr HS 1963-; *ai:* Span Club Spon; Alpha Delta Kappa Altrustic Chairperson 1988-; MO Natl Ed Assn 1963-; Foreign Lang Teachers of MO 1989-; Semo Cncl for the Arts 1985-; MO Cncl Arts 1985-; PEO M F Chapter Guard Historian; Museum Arts & Advisory Bd (Secy 1987-88, Pres 1988-89), 1987-; Poplar Bluff Artists Guild; Friends Margaret Harwell Art Museum; Butler Cty Historical Society; Dist Curr Comm Mem; Dist Teacher Evaluation Comm Mem 1987-; Teacher of Yr Selection Comm Mem 1989-; *office:* Poplar Bluff Jr HS West Lester St Poplar Bluff MO 63901

CLARK, LESLIE ANN (MYERS), Fourth Grade Teacher; *b:* Frostburg, MD; *m:* Ralph James; *c:* Amie H.; *ed:* (BS) Elem Ed, 1974, (MS) Elem Ed, 1979 Frostburg St Univ; *cr:* 4th Grade Teacher New Creek Elem 1974-75, Ridgeley Primary & Mid Sch 1975-; *ai:* Asst Intramural Coach; Cty Curr Rep; *home:* 8 Oakview Dr Cumberland MD 21502

CLARK, LINDA KAY (RILEY), Fourth Grade Teacher; *b:* Springfield, MO; *m:* Roy S.; *c:* Ryan, Stephanie; *ed:* (BS) Elem Ed, IL St Univ 1970; Grad Stud; *cr:* 4th/5th Grade Teacher Garfield Sch 1970-80; 4th Grade Teacher Jefferson Sch 1980-89, Wilson Sch 1989-; *ai:* 1st-4th Grade Tutor; Alpha Theta; IEA, NEA, EAP Building Rep 1989-; Civic Chorus 1989; PTA Mem; *home:* 314 Linden Pekin IL 61554

CLARK, MARCIA IVORY, Second Grade Teacher; *b:* Manila, Philippine Isl; *m:* James K; *c:* John M., Thomas G.; *ed:* (BA) Elem Ed, Northern AZ Univ 1970; (MA) Elem Ed, Univ of AZ 1977; Post Master Studies Classes in Bi-Lingual Ed & Elem Ed; *cr:* 3rd Grade Teacher Coolidge Sch 1970-72; 2nd Grade Teacher Mary Welty Sch 1972-89; *ai:* NEA; AEA 1970-80; Welty Sch Teacher of the Yr 1986; Bus & Prof Womens Club 1972-; *home:* 233 E. La Castellana Dr. Nogales AZ 85621

CLARK, MARIE ISABEL, 6th/7th Grade Science Teacher; *b:* Saint Louis, MO; *ed:* (BA) Ed/Soc Sci, Fontbonne Coll 1968; Grad Stud Earth Sci St Louis Univ & Bridgewater St Coll, Massachusetts Univ of OK & Univ of WY & W WA St Coll; *cr:* 4th Grade Teacher 1961-71, 6th-8th Grade Sci Teacher 1971-73, 6th/7th Grade Sci Teacher 1973- Acad of the Visistation; *ai:* Bsktbl Team Spiritual Guide; Acad of the Visitation Academic Affairs Comm Mem; NSTA Mem 1981-; Visitation of Holy Mary Mem 1957-; Earth Sci Grants; WI & WY Audubon Schlshps; Lesson Published 1988; *home:* 3020 N Ballas Rd Saint Louis MO 63131

CLARK, MARJORIE TRULAN, Teacher; *b:* Houston, TX; *c:* Carol, Virginia; *ed:* (BA) Ger, Rice Univ 1962; (MA) Amer Stud, Univ of Houston 1986; *cr:* US His/Ger Teacher Highlands HS 1962-65; US His Teacher Dulles HS 1979-; *ai:* Academic Decathlon Coach; TX St Teachers Assn 1962-65, 1979; Bluebonnet Cncl for Soc Stud 1989-; GSA 1949-, Thanks Badge 1982; *office:* Dulles HS PO Box 1004 Sugar Land TX 77487

CLARK, MARTHA E., Anthropology Teacher; *b:* Columbus, OH; *ed:* (BAE) Anthropology/Soc Sci Ed, Univ of FL 1972; (MAE) Gifted Ed, Univ of S FL 1978; Working Toward PhD Applied Anthropology, Univ of S FL; *cr:* Teacher Golf Jr HS 1972-73; Cnslr Bayonet Point Jr HS 1973-77; Teacher Hudson HS 1977-83, Dunedin HS 1983-; Instr St Petersburg Jr Coll 1985-; *ai:* Model United Nations Club; Kappa Delta Pi, FL Gifted Assn 1976-; Pi Gamma Mu 1986-; FL Cncl for Soc Sci 1972-; Richey Suncoast Theatre VP 1978-83; Spec Olympics Volunteer 1972-; Very Spec Arts Festival Volunteer 1983-87; Parent Teacher Stu Assn Excl in Teaching Recognition Dunedin HS 1989; Pinellas Cty Schls Service Awd 1988; African Meth Episcopal Church Outstanding Educator 1987; Dunedin HS Stu Cncl Exceptional Contributions Awd 1986; Congressional Awd of Appreciation 1984; Pinellas Cty Ec Fair Ec Teaching Project 3rd Place Awd 1984; Hudson HS Teacher of Yr 1981; 2nd Place Pasco Cty Teacher of Yr 1981; Outstanding Service 1980; *office:* Dunedin HS 2465 Drew St Clearwater FL 34616

CLARK, MARTHA FRANCES, Latin & Spanish Teacher; *b:* Nashville, TN; *ed:* (BA) Span/Eng/Latin, Belmont Coll 1979; Grad Sch Vanderbilt Univ 1980-81; *cr:* Teacher Beech Sr HS 1981-; *ai:* Foreign Lang Club Spon; Jr Classical League Spon 1981-; TN Foreign Lang Teachers Assn; *office:* Beech Sr HS 2136 Long Hollow Pike Hendersonville TN 37075

CLARK, MARY BETH, English Teacher; *b:* Tuscumbia, MO; *m:* Donald Johnson; *c:* Phillip; *ed:* (BSED) Eng, 1965, (MA) Eng, 1971 Univ of MO Columbia; *cr:* Eng Teacher St Elizabeth HS 1965-67; 6th Grade Teacher 1967-69, Eng/Soc Stud Teacher 1969-71 W Plains HS; Eng Teacher Mountain Grove HS 1973-74, Hallsville Mid Sch 1978-; *ai:* MO Assn Teachers of Eng Mem 1985-; Phi Delta Kappa Mem 1986-; MO Ed Assn Mem 1989-; *office:* Boone Cty R-IV Mid Sch Rt 1 Hallsville MO 65255

CLARK, MARY BETH BRUMFIELD, Marketing Education Teacher; *b:* Jackson, MS; *m:* Percy Norman; *c:* George H., Cynthia Gullett, Paul N.; *ed:* (BS) Bus Ed, Univ of SW LA 1953; (MS) Ed, Ball St Univ 1972; *cr:* Bus Ed Teacher Bolton HS 1958-62, Univ HS 1962-63; Distributive Ed Teacher Garinger HS 1964-66; Bus Ed Teacher Fayetteville HS 1966-69; Bus Ed/Mrktng Ed Teacher Ca rmel HS 1969-; *ai:* DECA Spon; Delta Kappa Gamma Pres 1961-; IN Voc Assn; AVA 1971-; Mrktng Ed Assn, IN Mrktng Ed Assn; Outstanding DECA Adv 1980; IVA Awd of Merit 1985; Published Articles; Dist & St Conference Coord for Competitive Events; Natl Competitive Event Chairperson.

CLARK, MARY PROPER, English/Reading Teacher; *b:* Warrington, England; *m:* Harold D.; *c:* M. K., Susen L.; *ed:* (BS) Eng/Rdng, 1967; (MED) Rdng, Rdng Specialist 1969 Clarion Univ; *cr:* Teacher-Cranberry Jr/Sr HS 1967-; *ai:* Sr Class Adv; Asst Adv Model Un; Head Coach-Track & Field 1978-; Vlybl Coach 1973-78; NCTE; IRA; PCTE; Crawford-Venango Cty Vlybl Officials Assn; Franklin-Oil City ASA Umpires; Cranberry Ed Assn Bldg Rep Editor-Assoc Newspaper; *office:* Cranberry Area Jr Sr HS Main St Seneca PA 16346

CLARK, MELBA DEAN, 7th Grade Soc Stud Teacher; *b:* Mc Minnville, TN; *ed:* (BA) Eng, David Lipscomb Coll 1971; (MA) Rdng, TN Technological Univ 1981; Advanced Work Mid TN St Univ; Mid TN Writing Project; Lions Quest Trng Seminar; *cr:* 6th Grade Eng/Rdng/Spelling Teacher North Elem Sch 1971-85; 7th Grade Soc Stud/Rdng Teacher Warren Cty HS 1985-; Eng Instr Motlow St Cmmty Coll 1984-85, 1989-; *ai:* Instr WCJH Lions Quest Prgm; TN Tech Intnl Rdng Assn Sec, Executive Cncl Mem 1980-; Delta Kappa Gamma 1989-; Alpha Delta Kappa 1990; WCEA Secy 1976, 1978; Warren Cty Jr HS Teacher of Yr 1989; Jaycees Outstanding Young Educator 1978; Phi Delta Kappa Schlsp Awd 1980; *office:* Warren Cty Jr HS 504 N Chancery St Mc Minnville TN 37110

CLARK, NANCY A., Mathematics/Chemistry Teacher; *b:* New Castle, IN; *c:* Timothy C. Baker, Elizabeth A. Walker; *ed:* (BS) Math/Chem, (MAT) Math, 1971 Purdue Univ; Chem, Western Univ; Several Wkshps; *cr:* Math/Chem Teacher in Public HS 1960-81, Limestone Cmmty HS 1984-86, Notre Dame HS 1988-; *ai:* Girls Swim Team Coach; Delta Kappa Gamma Research Chm 1975-; NSTA 1988-; Clinton Cty Assn Retarded People Past Bd Mem 1978-81; Natl Sci Fnd Grant; *home:* 1319 W Daytona Dr Peoria IL 61614

CLARK, NANCY A., Third Grade Teacher; *b:* Frostburg, MD; *ed:* (BA) Ed, MI St Univ 1971; (MA) Ed, E MI Univ; *cr:* Elem Teacher Wyandotte Public Schls 1971-; *ai:* Downriver Consortium Prof Staff Dev Teacher Rep; Wyandotte Ed Assn Secy 1982-87; Alpha Delta Kappa Chapter Pres 1988-; Wayne Cty Intermediate Sch Dist Mainstreaming Grant 1980; *office:* Monroe Sch 1501 Grove Wyandotte MI 48192

CLARK, PATCH LEE, Theatre/English Teacher; *b:* Ithaca, NY; *m:* Ronald L.; *c:* Robert E.; *ed:* (AA) Theatre/Television, Marjorie Webster 1967; (BFA) Theatre Ed, 1974, (MFA) Performance/Theatre, 1978 VA Commonwealth Univ; *cr:* Theatre/Eng Teacher Thomas Dale HS 1974-76; Instr VA Commonwealth Univ 1978-80; Creative Art Specialist Woodview Nursing Home 1982-83; Eng/Theatre Teacher Thomas Dale HS 1986-; *ai:* Drama Club Spon; Dance Team Coach & Dir; Cooperative Learning Rep; VA Assn Teachers of Eng; Teacher Incentive Grant VA Commission for the Arts 1989-; Articles Published 1989; Co-Author Book 1985; *office:* Thomas Dale HS 3626 W Hundred Rd Chester VA 23831

CLARK, PATTYE CHANDLER, Social Studies Teacher; *b:* Pine Bluff, AR; *m:* L. Stanley Jr.; *c:* Stan, David; *ed:* (BS) Eng/Soc Stud, AR St Univ 1969; *cr:* Eng Teacher J E Wallace HS 1969-70, Northeast HS 1970-72; Soc Stud Teacher Southeast Mid Sch 1972-88, Pine Bluff HS 1988-; *ai:* Pine Bluff HS Key Club Faculty Adv; Hinman Fellowship Intnl Paper Company; *office:* Pine Bluff HS 711 W 11th Pine Bluff AR 71601

CLARK, RICHARD GEORGE, Curriculum Specialist; *b:* Bakersfield, CA; *m:* Barbara Ann Franklin; *c:* Karen, David, Amy; *ed:* (BA) His, 1972, (MA) Elem Curr/Instr, 1980 CA St Bakersfield; *cr:* Teacher Lincoln Jr HS 1972-79, Golden St Jr HS 1979-80; Curr Spec Curran Jr HS 1980-85, Sierra Jr HS 1985-; *ai:* Phi Delta Kappa; *home:* 5642 Brooks Ct Bakersfield CA 93308

CLARK, ROBERT DONALD, Biology Teacher; *b:* Erie, PA; *m:* Margaret Timashenko; *c:* Laura Mulholland; *ed:* (BS) Scndry Bio, 1968, (MED) Scndry Bio, 1974 Edinboro St Univ; Edinboro St Univ, Gannon Univ, FL St Univ; *cr:* Bio Teacher Saegertown Sch Dist 1968-72, Penncrest Sch Dist 1972-; *ai:* Amer Society of Ichthyologists & Herpetologists, The Herpetologists League, NEA, Pi Delta Kappa, PA St Ed Assn; Penncrest Area Ed Assn (VP 1984-86, Pres 1986-87); *office:* Saegertown HS RD 1 Mook Rd Saegertown PA 16433

CLARK, RON ALAN, Sixth Grade Teacher; *b:* Waterloo, NY; *m:* Donna Butler; *c:* Kirsten, Kelli; *ed:* (BA) His, 1969, (MAT) Ed, 1971 Univ of Redlands; *cr:* Kndgtn Teacher Grand Terrace Elem 1970-72; 1st-2nd Grade Teacher Amer Sch of London 1972-74; 6th Grade Teacher Wilson Elem 1974-; *ai:* Coach Womens Vlybl, Jr HS Bsktbl, Jr Var Wrestling Amer Sch of London; Womens Vlybl Coach Univ of Redlands; Girls Sftbl Coach Colton City League; Assn of Colton Educators Elem Dir 1977-78; US Prof Tennis Assn P-1 1988-; S CA Tennis Assn Girls Tennis Coach; Redlands Racquet Club Pres 1985; *office:* Woodrow Wilson Elem Sch 750 S 8th St Colton CA 92324

CLARK, RONALD DEAN, Social Studies Teacher; *b:* Austin, MN; *m:* Ann Patricia Coleman; *c:* Andrea, Kate, Daniel; *ed:* (AA) Soc/Antero, Carleton Coll 1975; *cr:* Admin Asst Austin HS 1975-76; Child Care Cnslr MN Sheriffs Boys Ranch 1976-77; Teacher Rocori HS 1978-; *ai:* 9th Grade Ftbl Coach; Meet & Confer Comm; Teacher Rights Chm; Rocori Ed Assn Pres 1983-87; *office:* Rocori HS 534 5th Ave N Cold Spring MN 56320

CLARK, RONALD LEE, Science/Phys Ed Teacher; *b:* Gnadenhutten, OH; *m:* Marcia Martin; *c:* Keri S.; *ed:* (BS) Phys Ed, Wilmington Coll 1965; *cr:* 7th/8th Grade Phys Ed Teacher Toledo City Schls 1965-67; 7th/8th Grade Sci/Phys Ed Teacher C R Coblentz Sch Dist 1967-; *ai:* 7th/8th Grade Girls Bsktbl & Track, 7th/8th Grade Boys Ftbl & Track, 5th/6th Grade Girls Intramurals Coach; Sci Fair Coord; NEA; Preble Cty Bass Club; *home:* 207 Wrenn Ave New Paris OH 45347

CLARK, RONALD RICHARD, 8th Grade History Teacher; *b:* Centerville, IA; *m:* Terri Lynn Harl; *c:* Taylor R.; *ed:* (BS) Phy Ed, 1966, (MS) His Ed, Northeast MO Univ 1979; *cr:* 8th Grade Teacher Howard Jr HS 1966-; 1968-70 U S Army; Athletic Dir Howard Jr HS 1986-; *ai:* 7th Grade Boys Bsktbl Coach; 8th Grade Boys Track Coach; Jr HS Athletic Dir; IA Bsktbl Coaches Assn 1972-; IA Athletic Dir Assn 1986-; Centerville City Park Bd Pres 1974-; Amer Legion 1970-; Amer Vets 1970-; Chief Negotiation Centerville Ed Assn 1989-; Pres Elect Centerville Ed Assn 1990; *home:* 802 Drake Ave Centerville IA 52544

CLARK, ROSE MARY, English Teacher; *b:* Kingston ON, Canada; *m:* Bardine J.; *c:* Colin J.; *ed:* (BA) Sociology/Psych, 1978; (MA) Sociology, 1985 Univ of NM; Teacher Ed, Univ of NM 1981-82; *cr:* Eng/Soc Stud/Psych Instr Calhan HS 1982-; *ai:* Forensics Coach; Staff Adv; Faculty Rep; CO Lang Art Society 1982-; *office:* Calhan Sch 800 Bulldog Dr Calhan CO 80808

CLARK, RUTH WESLEY, Science Teacher; *b:* Atlanta, GA; *m:* Alvin; *c:* Alvin W.; *ed:* (BA) Elem Ed, Clark Coll 1957; (MA) Elem Ed, Atlanta Univ 1970; Further Stud Sci & Math; *cr:* Teacher Rose Garden Hills Elem 1957-61, R L Craddock Elem 1961-70, J F Kennedy Mid Sch 1970-79, W A Sutton Mid Sch 1979-81, Ralph J Bunche Mid Sch 1981-; *ai:* Leadership Cncl; House & Team Leader; Sci Contact Teacher; Chm Computation & Environmental Stud Cluster; Atlanta Assn of Teachers, GA Ed Assn, NEA, GA Sci Teachers Assn; Natl Cncl of Negro Women, Delta Sigma Theta, NAACP; Teacher of Yr Craddock Sch 1969-70, Bunche Mid Sch 1985-86; Area Finalist Area I Academic Achievement Incentive Prgm; *office:* Ralph J Bunche Mid Sch 1925 Niskey Lake Rd SW Atlanta GA 30331

CLARK, SANDY K., English Teacher; *b:* Estherville, IA; *m:* Thomas Howard; *c:* Lisa Clark Bingham, Chad R., Daniel E.C.; *ed:* (BA) Eng, Univ of IA 1965; Working Towards Masters of Art, Univ of IA; Elem Level Coursework, N AZ Univ; *cr:* Eng Teacher Mt Vernon HS 1969-70; Kndgtn Teacher Prescott Chrstn Sch 1978-80; Eng Teacher Mesa Public Schls 1981-82, Prescott Chrstn Acad 1985-86, Orangewood Chrstn Sch 1987-; *ai:* Lib Comm; HEAW Fellowship for MAT; *office:* Orangewood Chrstn Sch 1221 Trinity Woods Ln Maitland FL 32751

CLARK, SARA ELIZABETH YOUNG, 2nd Grade Teacher; *b:* Chattanooga, TN; *m:* Walter G.; *c:* Donna Ortiz, Leah Holloway, AaRon, Rachel; *ed:* (BE) Ed, Chicago St Univ 1959; (MS) Sci Ed, Northwestern Univ 1978; Art Ed, Art Institute of Chicago; Sci Ed, De Paul Univ; Cmptr Ed, North IL Univ; Cmptr Ed/Sci Curr Dev, Natl Coll of Ed; Taft Institute of Government, Loyola Univ; *cr:* 1st/4th/7th Grade Teacher Chicago Public Bd of Ed 1959-70; Educl Specialist 1974-76, Elem Teacher 1971-72/1976- Evanston Public Bd of Ed #65; *ai:* Dist Ed Cncl Minority Rep; Dawes Building Leadership Co-Chm; Soc Stud Rep; Chm Evanston Minority Caucus; Dawes Sch/Evanston Township PTA Mem; NEA, IEA Mem 1971-; Evanston Dist Ed Cncl Minority Rep 1984-; Northwestern Univ Chicago Club Mem 1988-; Jr Great Books Dawes Sch Leader 1984-88; NEA North Region Mem 1984-; Evanston Campfire of America Co-Leader 1980-86; Evanston Stu Teacher Cooperating Teacher 1976-; Chicago Area Assn Black Educators Outstanding Educators Awd 1985; Martin Luther King Celebration Recognition Awd-Evanston F J Center Choice 1988; Co-Author Numerous Books; *home:* 2006 Washington St Evanston IL 60202

CLARK, THELMA OLIFF, 3rd Grade Teacher; *b:* Amercius, GA; *m:* Harvey; *c:* Ronald, Nadine; *ed:* (BS) Elem Ed, FL Memorial Coll 1954; Urban Ed, FIU; Univ of Miami, FL Intnl Univ; *cr:* 1st Grade Teacher 1955-64, 2nd Grade Teacher 1964-73 Floral Heights Elem; Rdng Resource Teacher Area Office Curr 1973-76; 3rd Grade Teacher Allapattah Elem 1976-; *ai:* Mc Knight Achievers Society, Amer Red Cross, GSA Spon; Grade Group & Chapter I Chairperson; United Teachers of Dade 1955-; Mc Knight Achievers Honor Society Bd Mem 1989-; Gamma Phi Delta (Youth Dir, 2nd VP) 1984-88, Outstanding Service; Antioch Baptist Church Young Adult Choir Adv 1985-, Outstanding Service; Mc Knight Achiever VP 1989-; Teacher of Yr 1989; Admin Teacher of Yr 1984; FL Reps Awd Outstanding Service to Cmmty 1984; *home:* 3308 NW 53rd St Miami FL 33142

CLARK, WANDA KAY, Second Grade Teacher; *b:* Sparta, GA; *ed:* (BS) Elem Ed, 1972, (MED) Early Childhd Ed, 1979 GA Coll; *cr:* 3rd Grade Teacher 1972-84, 2ndgrade Teacher 1985-, T J Elder Primary Sch; 3rd Grade Teacher Sandersville Elem Sch 1984-85; *ai:* Project Activities Chm for Sch; Steering Comm for PRIDE Prgm; Sch Teacher of Yr for My Sch 1980.

CLARK, WANDA W., Home Economics Teacher; *b:* Laurel, MS; *ed:* (BS) Home Ec Ed, 1974, (MS) Home Ec Ed, 1978 Univ of S MS; *cr:* Home Ec Teacher Crystal Springs Jr HS 1974-76, Crystal Springs HS 1978-81; Extension Home Economist MS Cooperative Extension Service 1981-86; Rehabilitation Teacher MS Voc Rehabilation for the Blind 1986-87; Home Ec Teacher Wesson Attendance Center 1987-; *ai:* Sr Class Spon; FHA & SADD Adv; *office:* Wesson Attendance Center 532 Grove St Wesson MS 39191

CLARK-TYLER, ANN LORENA, French Teacher; *b:* Los Angeles, CA; *m:* Gary L.; *c:* Chelsea, Luke; *ed:* Fr, Univ de Paris/La Sorbonne 1969; (BA) Fr, Univ of CA Los Angeles 1969; Architecture, Univ of CA Berkeley 1970-71; Tissue Culture Technician, Univ of CA Los Angeles & Univ of OR; *cr:* Sci Teacher St Patricks Grade Sch 1982-83; Math Teacher 1988, Ger/Fr Teacher 1989, Fr Teacher 1989- Roseburg HS; *ai:* Fr Club Adv; 2020 Comm Secy; Adult Chaperone to Stu to Germany; IMPACT Team; AATF, COFLT 1987-; Arts Center (Ways & Means Chairperson 1978-81, Arts Festival 1981); *office:* Roseburg HS 547 W Chapman Roseburg OR 97470

CLARKE, JEFFREY KEITH, Dean of Students & Teacher; *b:* Rutland, VT; *ed:* (BA) His, Middlebury Coll 1982; *cr:* Asst Cross Cntry Ski Coach Middlebury Coll 1983-85; Head Cross Cntry Coach MT St Univ 1985-87; Dean of Stus/Teacher Carrabassett Valley Acad 1987-89; Mgr Fischer of America 1989-; *ai:* US Ski Coaches Assn Bd of Dir 1988-; US Ski Assn New England Comm Chm 1989-; US Ski Team Head Coach, Swiss Week 1988; US Ski Team, Staff, World Univ Games, TCH 1987.

CLARKSON, BETTY WEEMS, Fourth Grade Teacher; *b:* Clifton, MS; *m:* N. E.; *c:* Jean Elizabeth, Nancy Ellen; *ed:* (BA) Sociology, Millsaps Coll 1948; (ME) Elem Ed, ME Coll 1966; *cr:* Teacher Watkins Elem 1948-52; Teacher Jackson Acad; Teacher Casey Elem; *ai:* NEA; Alpha Delta Kappa; Kappa Delta Pi; Jacksonians for Public Ed Cerificate of Excl 1973 & 77; Elem Teacher of Yr; *office:* Casey Elem Sch 2101 Lake Circle Jackson MS 39211

CLARSON-KRUSE, NANCY, Fourth Grade Teacher; *b:* Flushing, NY; *m:* William F.; *ed:* (BS) Elem Ed, 1968, (MA) Elem Ed, 1970 Adelphi Univ; Grad Work National Univ of Ireland & Univ Coll Dublin; *cr:* 4th-6th Grade Teacher S Grove Sch 1968-; Research/Dev of Microcompter in Elem Classroom Syosset Cntrl Sch Dist 1980-81; *ai:* Former Math Olympiads Adv; Goudreau Museum of Math in Art & Sci (Museum Store Buyer, Mgr, Bd of Dir) 1986-; *office:* South Grove Sch Colony Ln Syosset NY 11791

CLARY, MARTHA MAE (MILLER), Gifted/Talented Teacher; *b:* Elwood, IN; *m:* Richard Melvin; *c:* Michael R., Sheryl L. Wright, Deanna R. Hockey; *ed:* (BA) Elem Ed, Univ of N IA 1982; Purdue Univ 1962-63; Drake Univ 1975; Grad Stud Drake Univ, Univ of N IA; *cr:* 3rd/4th Grade Teacher St Edwards Elem Sch 1982; Gifted/Talented Resource Teacher Waterloo Cmmty Sch 1990; *ai:* St Edwards Sci Fair Coord 1988-89; 1st-8th Grade Curr Comm; Leadership Dev Prgm; Kappa Delta Pi, Purple & Gold Univ of N IA Meritorius Schlsp 1982; Published Sci Article 1988.

CLASSE, JEANNE SCHAUB, French Teacher; *b:* Summit, NJ; *m:* John Gaither; *c:* Christopher; *ed:* (BA) Fr, Mary Baldwin Coll 1968; (MA) Fr, Tulane Univ 1971; (JD) Law, Birmingham Sch of Law 1980; Inst of European Stud Honors Prgm Paris France 1966-67; *cr:* Teaching Asst Tulane Univ 1968-69, 1970-71; Fr/Eng Teacher Trexler Jr HS 1971-72; Fr Instr Univ of AL Birmingham 1983-85; Fr Teacher Altamont Sch 1972-; *ai:* Fr Club Spon; Awds Day Prgm; AATF (Pres 1985-88, VP 1983-85, Mem 1972-); AL Assn of Foreign Lang Teachers (Pres 1976-77, VP 1975-76, Mem 1972-); Alliance Francaise (Pres 1976-77, VP 1975-76, Mem 1979-); AL St Bar Mem 1981-; AL Heart Assn Dist Captain for Heart Sunday 1987-; Southern Assn of Colls & Schls Visiting Comm Mem 1982, 1986, 1987; Immersion Inst Fr Teacher Co-Dir 1987; Birmingham Sch of Law Amer Jurisprudence Awd in Conflicts 1979; Honor Stu Awd 1980; Outstanding Young Women of America 1983; Hugh Kaul Endowed Chairperson for Teaching Excl 1987; *home:* 1816 Forest Haven Ln Birmingham AL 35216

CLAUS, PAMELA JEANNE, Elem Principal/Program Coord; *b:* Catskill, NY; *s:* S.; *ed:* (BS) Elem Ed N-6, Plattsburgh St 1976; (MS) Admin, St Lawrence Univ 1989; *cr:* 2nd Grade Teacher Kingsbury PS 1976-78; 6th Grade Teacher 1978-88; Elem Prln/K-12 Prgm Coord 1989- Parishville Hopkinton CS; Elem Cty Wide Sci Mentor Boces 1986-89; *ai:* Comm Sp Ed Chm; Dist Coord for Chapter I; PSEN Prgm; Dist Grant Writer; Optical Society Amer Outstanding Sci Teachers NY 1987; Clarkson Univ Sci Teacher of Yr 1988; St Lawrence Teachers Learning Ctr Bd Mem 1987-; Potsdam Canton Hospital Guild Bd Mem; *home:* 6 Meadow E Apt G Potsdam NY 13676

CLAUSSEN, DONALD GORDON, Sixth Grade Teacher; *b:* Thomas, OK; *m:* Glenda Mae Hamar; *c:* La Donna, Brad, Shaun, Scott; *ed:* (BS) Elem Ed, 1966, (MS) Elem Ed, 1971 Southwestern St; *cr:* 6th Grade Teacher Unified Sch Dist #370 1966-69, Unified Sch Dist #361 1969-70; 5th Grade Teacher Barber Cty N 1970-75; 6th Grade Teacher Thomas Public Sch 1980-; *ai:* KSTA 1966-75; OEA 1980-; NEA 1966-75, 1980-; Bethany Brethern in Christ Church Bd 1982-88; Teacher of Yr 1988-89.

CLAUSSEN, VAN EARLE, Elementary Teacher; *b:* Wilson, KS; *ed:* (BA) Elem Ed, 1968, (MA) Elem Ed, 1974 Fort Hays St; Geo & His Studied in all 50 States, Canada, Cuba, Europe; *cr:* 1st-8th Grade Teacher Country Schls KS 1946-51, Big Delta AK Army 1951-53; 5th-6th Grade Teacher Beverly Grade Sch 1953-61; 6th Grade Teacher Downs Grade Sch 1961-78; 5th Grade Teacher Avon Park Mid Sch 1978-; *ai:* Phi Delta Kappa 1974- Outstanding Teacher 1974; KS Congress Outstanding Teacher 1974; Lions Club 1988-; News Week & New Yorker Ad 1974; KS Spelling Bee Champions 3; Sch Stu Teacher Since 1932; *home:* 414 E Oak Avon Park FL 33825

CLAXON, JACALYN ESHAM, Mathematics Teacher; *b:* Portsmouth, OH; *m:* Kenneth Allen; *c:* Kent; *ed:* (BS) Math, 1976, (AMED) Ed, 1981 Morehead St Univ; Resource Teacher Trng 1987; *cr:* Math Teacher Lewis Cty HS 1976-; *ai:* Beta Club Spon; Chm Budget Finance Comm; Staff Dev Rep; Lewis Cty Teacher Assn Building Rep; NCTM 1978-; Commercial Hotel Corporation Secy 1987-; Teacher of Yr 1986; *office:* Lewis Cty HS PO Box 99 Vanceburg KY 41179

CLAXTON, JOHN R., Physics, Bio, Phys Sci Teacher; *b:* Nashville, TN; *m:* Vickie Pack; *c:* Samuel, Amy, Benjamin; *ed:* (BS) Ed/Bio, Univ of TN 1975; (MA) Ed/Admin, Austin Peay St Univ 1988; Elem Ed, OH St Univ; Physics, TN St Univ; *cr:* 6th Grade Teacher Mansfield Christian Sch 1975-83; Sci/Math Teacher Davidson Acad 1983-; *ai:* 7th-8th Grade Boys Bsktbl Coach; 7th-8th Grade Ftlbl & Var Girls Bsktbl Asst Coach; Natl Fed Interscholastic Coaches Assn 1988-; Hendersonville Chapel 1983-; *office:* Davidson Acad 1414 Old Hickory Blvd Nashville TN 37207

CLAY, CELIA ANNE, Science Teacher; *b:* Houston, TX; *ed:* (BA) Scndry Ed, Univ of St Thomas 1981; Grad Stud Psych, Medical Anthropology, Microbiology; *cr:* Sci Chairperson Our Lady of Guadalupe Sch 1982-84, Marian Chrstn HS 1984-86; Sci Teacher Northside Health Careers HS 1987-; *ai:* Human Anatomy & Physiology Textbook Selection Comm Northside Ind Sch Dist 1990; Organized Earth & Wild Week; Sci Teachers Assn of TX, TX Assn of Bio Teacher Mem 1988-89; NABT Mem 1985-86; Research Awd 1989; Participate Grad Prgm Univ of TX Health Sci Center San Antonio; Microbiology Instruction for Scndry Sci Teachers 1989; Article on Sci Teaching & Ethics Published in Newsletter of the TX Assn of Bio Teachers.

CLAY, DOYLE ELLIS, JR., Physical Education Teacher; *b:* Lodi, OH; *m:* Judith Mae Steyer; *c:* Joel D., John D., James W., Dougals E. Myers, Heather R. Myers; *ed:* (BS) Health/Phys Ed, Olivet Nazarene Univ 1967; (MS) Phys Ed, Bowling Green St Univ 1977; *cr:* Teacher/Coach Vanlue Local Sch 1967-69, Fostoria City Schls 1969-; *ai:* Boys Track Coach & Athletic Dir; Registered Ftbl & Track Ofcl; AAHPERD, OAHPERD, NEA, OEA, FEA 1967-; Fostoria Redmen Club (VP, Secy) 1977-86; Fostoria Boosters Club 1969-; Tri Cty Striders Track Club Pres 1990.

CLAY, PRISCILLA BRADLEY, First Grade Teacher; *b:* Corsicana, TX; *m:* James Randall; *c:* James A., Emily C.; *ed:* (BS) Elem Ed/Kndgtn Endorsement, North TX St Univ 1976; Gesell Inst Sch Readiness/Maturation; *cr:* 6th Grade Math Teacher Ennis Mid Sch 1976-77; Kndgtn Teacher Sam Houston Elem 1977-85; Kndgtn Teacher 1985-89, 1st Grade Teacher 1989-90 Wm B Travis Elem; *ai:* Supt Advisory Comm; Univ InterScholastic League Storytelling; Selected to Teach Super Conducting Super Collider Curr; Assn of TX Prof Educators Mem 1978-; TX St Teachers Assn Faculty Rep 1976-78; Beta Sigma Phi (Treas 1989-, VP 1990), Pledge of Yr 1984-85; *office:* Wm B Travis Elem 200 N Shawnee Ennis TX 75119

CLAY, SAMANTHA WILLIAMS, 12th Grade English Teacher; *b:* Knox City, TX; *m:* William L.; *ed:* (BS) Speech/Drama/Eng, Mc Murry Coll 1965; (MS) Speech/Drama/Eng, E TX St Univ 1969; *cr:* Teacher O Donnel HS 1965-67, Bonham Jr HS 1967-70; Teacher/Dept Head Westwood Jr HS 1972-75, Berkner HS 1975-; *ai:* Future Teachers of America; NCTE, TX Joint Cncl Teachers of Eng, Dallas Cncl Teachers of Eng 1972-; RISE Acad Outstanding Teacher of Yr 1980; Westwood Jr HS PTA Life Membership 1974; Berkner NHS Honorary Membership 1985; *office:* Richardson Berkner HS 1600 E Spring Valley Rd Richardson TX 75081

CLAY, WILLIE MAE THOMAS, Science Teacher; *b:* New Orleans, LA; *c:* Schwann, Joseph D. Jr.; *ed:* (BS) Health/Phys Ed/Recreation, Southern Univ 1973; (MS) Adapted Phys Ed/Spec Ed, Univ of New Orleans 1984; *cr:* Teacher/Coach Grace King HS 1974-76, Bonnabel HS 1976-80; Spec Ed Teacher Hahnville Jr HS 1980-84; Sci Teacher/Coach C E King Jr HS 1984-; *ai:* Jr HS Bsktbl, Track, Vlybl Coach; Black His Prgm Dir; Assn of TX Prof Ed 1984-; Alpha Kappa Alpha.

CLAYBROOKS, BEVERLY CALDWELL, 5th Grade Teacher; *b:* Martin, TN; *m:* Walter William; *c:* Carol, Warren, Christie E., Nicole C.; *ed:* (BS) Elem Ed, TN St Univ 1964; Guidance & Counseling, TN St Univ; Music Ed, Univ of TN Martin; TN Career Ladder Level I; *cr:* Teacher Carter Lawrence Elem 1965-68, Turner Elem Sch 1968-70, Percy Priest Elem Sch 1970-73, Sharon Elem Sch 1973-; *ai:* Just Say No to Drugs Prgm Coord; Drug Free TN Governors Alliance; Sharon Sch Goals & Objectives Comm; ASCD, NEA, TN Ed Assn; Alpha Kappa Alpha; Phi Delta Kappa; Obion River Dist Assn Assy Secy 1987-88, 1988-89; Oak Grove Baptist Church (Minister of Music, Church Clerk); Outstanding Educator; *home:* 337 S McComb St Martin TN 38237

CLAYMORE, MARY KAY HUNT, 6th Grade Math teacher; *b:* Philadelphia, PA; *m:* Michael James; *c:* Kathleen; *ed:* (BS) Elem Ed, Univ of ND 1977; (MED) Counseling & Guidance, Univ of ID 1990; *cr:* Kndgtn Teacher 1977-79, Kndgtn/Pre-Sch Teacher 1979-80 Council Bluffs Cmmty Schls; 5th Grade Teacher 1984-89, 6th Grade Teacher 1989-Kellogg Sch Dist 391; *ai:* Dance Squad Adv; WA St Math Cncl 1986-; NEA 1977-80, 1984-; ID Society for Energy & Environmental Ed 1987-; Beta Sigma Phi Treas 1983-; *office:* Kellogg Sch 800 Bunker Ave Kellogg ID 83837

CLAYTON, BRENDA YOUNG, Kindergarten Teacher; *b:* Philadelphia, MS; *m:* N. T. Jr.; *c:* Jonathan; *ed:* (BAE) Elem Ed 1975, (ME) Elem Ed, 1978 Univ of MS; Working on Ed Specialist Degree; *cr:* 1st Grade Teacher 1976-78, 1st-4th Grade Teacher 1978-86, Kndgtn Teacher 1986- Fairview; *ai:* MAE, NAE 1976-; *office:* Fairview Jr HS Rt 1 Box 268 Golden MS 38847

CLAYTON, CHARLES, 6th/7th Grade Soc Stud Teacher; *b:* New River, TN; *m:* Wilma Mae Sharp; *c:* Melinda K. Chitwood Carson, Charles C. II; *ed:* (BS) His, Cumberland Coll 1970; (MA) Admin, TN Tech Univ 1974; Elem Cert, TN Tech Univ 1974; *cr:* Clerk Martain Air Craft 1954-55; Factory Worker Natl Cash Register Company 1955-67; Teacher Oneida Ind Sch 1970-; *ai:* 6th Grade Spon; Textbook Selection Comm; Oneida Ed Assn (Pres 1970-, Exec Comm); TN Ed Assn, NEA 1970-; *home:* RR 1 Box 161-C Helenwood TN 37755

CLAYTON, CONNIE HALEY, 2nd Grade Teacher; *b:* Covington, KY; *m:* Gary Lynn; *c:* Sarah B., James W.; *ed:* (BA) Elem Ed, N KY Univ 1973; (MA) Elem Ed, 1975, (Rank I) Elem Ed, 1980 Morehead St Univ; *cr:* 3rd Grade Teacher Augusta Ind 1973-75; 1st Grade Teacher Brooksville Elem 1975-76; 4th Grade Teacher 1976-89, 2nd Grade Teacher 1989- Taylor Elem; *ai:* KY Ed Assn; Brooksville Chrstn (Mem, Sunday Sch Teacher); *home:* Rt 3 Box 30 A Brooksville KY 41004

CLAYTON, KAREN DARLENE, Physical Education Teacher; *b:* Cleveland, OH; *ed:* (BS) Phys Ed, Bowling Green St Univ 1979; *cr:* Teacher Whitney Young Jr HS 1979-80, Shaw HS 1980-81, Mayfair Elem 1981-83, Caledonia Elem 1984-85, Shaw HS 1985-; *ai:* Jr Var Girls Bsktbl & Sftbl Coach; NEA, OEA 1979-; Service Awds For Teaching Self-Contained Spec Ed Children; *office:* Shaw HS 15305 Terrace Rd East Cleveland OH 44112

CLAYTON-DAVIS, RUTH, English Teacher; *b:* Grinnell, IA; *m:* Michael L.; *c:* Andrew, Kathryn; *ed:* (AA) Mt St Clare Coll 1969; (BA) Eng, Marycrest Coll 1971; Natl Coll of Ed, WIU, Sangamon St; *cr:* Teacher Rockridge HS 1971-; *ai:* Eng Dept Chairperson; Drama Club & Class Spon; NEA, IEA 1971-; Rockridge Teachers Assn Grievance Chairperson 1985-; NCTE; YWCA-Rock Island Bd Mem 1989-; Mt St Clare Natl Alumni Comm 1990; Amer Legion Auxiliary Girls St Staff 1972-; Whos Who in Amer Ed; Escorted Stus to Europe 1988-89, Australia & London 1990; *office:* Rockridge USCD 300 14110 134th Ave W Taylor Ridge IL 61284

CLAYTOR, ERNEST F., 7th Grade Math Teacher; *b:* Toledo, OH; *m:* Barbara J. Hines; *c:* Thomas, May, Adam; *ed:* (BS) Elem Ed, Rio Grande 1966; (MED) Guid & Counseling, Xavier 1972; *cr:* 6th Grade Teacher Heimandale Elem 1965-69; Title I Math Teacher Columbus Bd of Ed 1969-83; 7th Grade Teacher Southmoor Mid Sch 1983-; *ai:* Columbus Ed Assn 1965-; *office:* Southmoor Mid Sch 1201 Moler Rd Columbus OH 43207

CLEAR, GLORIA LEWIS, Second Grade Teacher; *b:* Fort Edward, NY; *w:* George P. (dec); *c:* Ellen Mc Entee; *ed:* (BE) Ed, Oneonta St Teachers Coll 1948; Grad Hrs; *cr:* Elem Teacher Fort Edward Sch 1948-54; Drama Teacher Fort Edward Sch 1952-53; Elem Teacher Rochester Sch System 1954-55, Hudson Falls Central Sch 1957-; *ai:* Sci Comm; Fort Edward Teachers Assn Treas 1950; NYSTA; Widowed Persons Service (Secy, 1988-, Team Leader 1987-); Public Christmas Prgm Maple St Sch 1960-68; Comm Concerning Drop Outs 1975; *home:* 28 Circle Dr South Glens Falls NY 12803

CLEAR, NANCY REED, Fourth Grade Teacher; *b:* Silver City, NM; *m:* Terrye Ray; *c:* Terra R., Tisha A.; *ed:* (BA) Elem Ed, Univ of S CO 1973; Grad Stud; *cr:* 1st Grade Teacher Penrose Elem 1973-74, 1976-79; 4th Grade Teacher 1979-82, 1st Grade Teacher 1983-84, 2nd Grade Teacher 1984-88 Florence Elem; 4th Grade Teacher Penrose Elem 1989-; *ai:* Natl Spelling Bee Competition Spon; All Sch Talent Show Coord; Rdng Comm; *office:* Penrose Elem Sch 100 Illinois Penrose CO 81240

CLEARY, CATHERINE POWELL, Fifth Grade Teacher; *b:* Providence, RI; *c:* Julie Cleary Howland, Anne, Elizabeth; *ed:* (BS) Elem Ed, Chatham Coll 1958; Rdng/Gifted/Talented Ed; *cr:* 1st Grade Teacher West Irondequoit NY 1958-; 5th Grade Teacher Scio NY 1979-; *ai:* Coord Gifted/Talented Ed 1980-88; Scio Teachers Assn 1980-; Allegany Cty Teachers Assn Treas 1984-87; Kanakadea Rdng Cncl 1979-; Lioness Club 1986-; Co Author Ch II Grant Proposal; Co Author of Entry in Kodak CompetitiOn; Presented 2 Workshops at Conf; Supervised Gifted Talented Stu Cty Wide Video Contest; *home:* 3070 Riverside Dr Wellsville NY 14895

CLEARY, KATHLEEN ELLEN, Teacher; *b:* St Paul, MN; *ed:* (BS) Elem Ed, Univ of MN 1971; Working toward Masters; *cr:* Teacher Emmet D Williams Sch 1971-82, Roseville Area Schls 1982-83, Brimhall Sch 1983-; *ai:* Roseville Math Comm; Roseville Curr Cncl; ADL (Recording Secy, His) 1978-; MEA, REA 1971-; Brimhall PTA Adv 1983-; Roseville Outstanding Contributions Awd 1988, 1990; *office:* Brimhall Sch 1744 W Co Rd B Roseville MN 55113

CLEGHRON, DONNA S., Second Grade Teacher; *b:* Arley, AL; *m:* Charles D.; *c:* Christopher, Craig; *ed:* (BS) Elem Ed, Univ of N AL 1970; (MA) Elem Ed, Univ of AL Tuscaloosa 1974; *cr:* 6th Grade Teacher Good Hope HS 1970-71; 1st Grade Teacher Speake HS 1971-72; 1st Grade Teacher 1972-87, 2nd Grade Teacher 1987- Addison Elem Sch; *ai:* Delta Kappa Gamma; PTO VP 1989-; *home:* PO Box 32 Addison AL 35540

CLEM, ADA BEE (HOLT), First Grade Teacher; *b:* Elkmont, AL; *m:* David Rowe; *c:* Rowena Mc Nutt, Ashley, Travis, Curtis; *ed:* (BS) Elem Ed, Athens Coll 1974; (MA) Elem Ed, Univ of N AL 1977; Learning Disabilities, Music, Art, & Drama; Several Wkshps; *cr:* 5th Grade Teacher 1974-75, 1st Grade Teacher 1975- Johnson Jr HS; *ai:* System Wide Policy For Promotion & Retention Comm; NEA, AL Ed Assn, Limestone Cty Ed Assn, PTO 1974-; Wrote 3 Christmas Plays Kndgtn & 1st Grade Performed for PTO; *office:* Johnson Jr HS Rt 1 Box 123 Athens AL 35611

CLEM, SANDRA SUE (SANDAGE), High School English Teacher; *b:* Mt Ayr, IA; *m:* Steven Wayne; *c:* David W., Tami S.; *ed:* (BSE) Eng, NE MO St 1987; *cr:* Substitute Teacher Rockwood Sch Dist, Fox HS; Eng Dept Head Tower Grove Chrstn Sch; *ai:* Cheerleading Coach; Jr Class Spon; NCTE 1988-; Two Poems Published; Critical Paper Prepared for Publication Consideration; *home:* 1252 Trails Dr Fenton MO 63026

CLEMENT, ELLEN THOREN, HS Choral Director; *b:* Marquette, MI; *m:* Clare Jerome; *c:* Karen, Michael, Stephen, James; *ed:* (BME) Music Ed, N MI Univ 1958; (MA) Music His/Lit, Univ of MI 1969; Grad Stud; *cr:* Vocal Music Teacher Marquette Area Public Schls 1969-; *ai:* Marquette Cty Boy Choir Dir & Founder; Marquette Male Chorus Dir & Founder 1981-; Curr Comm; HS Choral Act & Trips; Amer Choral Dir Assn Cntrl Division Chairperson HS Standards & Reportoire 1986-88; MI Sch Vocal Assn Dist 14 Mgr 1982-86, St Honors Choir Dir TTBB 1983; Marquette Ambassadors Good Will Awd 1981; Marquette Kiwanis Thank You Awd 1987.

CLEMENTS, BARRY WILLIAM, Mathematics Teacher; *b:* Detroit, MI; *m:* Linda Diane Knakal; *c:* Kevin, Kristen, Amy; *ed:* (BS) Math, MI St Univ 1974; (MED) Ed, Wayne St Univ 1977; *cr:* Math/Gifted Prgm Teacher Bemis Jr HS 1974-; *ai:* Ftbl Coach; Cmptrs in the Classroom Comm; *office:* Bemis Jr HS 12500 19 Mile Sterling Heights MI 48078

CLEMENTS, CARRIE ANN, 4th-6th Grade Lang Arts & Math; *b:* Lamar, SC; *ed:* (BS) Elem Ed, Francis Marion Coll 1981; *cr:* 4th-6th Grade Lang Arts & Math Teacher James F Byrnes Acad 1983-; *ai:* Vlybl Coach; JV Girls Coach; Co-Chm-Spring Fling; Adv Byrnes Parent Organ; Winthrop Rep Children at Risk; Darlington Police Aux Treas 1981-85; Mid Sch Teacher of Yr 1988-89; *office:* James F Byrnes Acad Rt 6 Ashby Rd Florence SC 29501

CLEMENTS, KAREN MC DANIEL, Second Grade Teacher; *b:* Malvern, AR; *m:* James Wilburn; *c:* Mack D.; *ed:* (BSE) Early Chldhd Ed - Magna Cum Laude, Ouachita Baptist Univ 1978; *cr:* 3rd Grade Teacher 1978-85, 2nd Grade Teacher Glen Rose Elem Sch 1985-; *ai:* Glen Rose PTA Treas 1984-85; *home:* Rt 1 Box 963 Donaldson AR 71941

CLEMENTS, KELLY REED, Social Studies Teacher/Coach; *b:* Provo, UT; *m:* Jeanie Payne; *c:* Angie, Shay, Rindy, Alec; *ed:* (BA) Soc Stud/Phys Ed, BYU 1975; Several Wkshps; Coaching Classes; Clinics; *cr:* Teacher/Coach Springville Jr HS 1975-77, Springville HS 1977-; *ai:* Stu Cncl Adv; Head Bsbl Coach; LIPC Comm; Driver Ed Instr; UT Ed Assn Negotiation Team 1987-88; Teacher of Month Awd 1989; UT Bsbl Coaches Assn, Coach of Yr 1979, 1982, 1987, 1989; Church Leadership Bishopric 1984-88; UT Bowhunters Assn 1987-; Best Teacher Awd BYU; *home:* 844 S 1000 E Springville UT 84663

CLEMENTS, LOUIS J., Social Studies Dept Chair; *b:* Rigby, ID; *m:* Diane Hegsted; *c:* Brad, Shaun, Kristen Hathaway, Kimberly, Leslie; *cr:* Teacher Madison Jr HS 1964-68; Soc Stud Dept Head 1972-Madison HS; *ai:* Stu Government & Literary Club Adv; Home Study Coord; Kiwanis Club Educator of Yr 1989; Jr Chamber of Commerce Teacher of Yr 1968; Upper Snake River Valley Historical Society (Pres 1977-82, Dir 1982-) Historian of Yr 1990; Chamber of Commerce Bd 1988-; Madison Cty Chm ID Centennial 1989-; Rexburg Centennial Chm 1982-83; Chm ID Intl Folk Dance Festival 1988-; Author 7 Books; *home:* 102 W 2000 N Rexburg ID 83440

CLEMENTS, NELDA R., Second Grade Teacher; *b:* Clay Cty, TN; *m:* Mickey Sr.; *c:* Cherry A. Hanks, Mickey Jr.; *ed:* (BS) Elem Ed, TN Tech Univ 1979; Cert in Spec Ed; *cr:* Teacher Red Boiling Springs Sch 1980-; *office:* Red Boiling Springs Sch Hillcrest Dr Red Boiling Spring TN 37150

CLEMENTS-COBB, CYNTHIA A., Business Teacher/Dept Chair; *b:* Chester, PA; *m:* William R.; *c:* Mychal L., Nicole R.; *ed:* (BS) Bus Ed, DE St Coll 1974; Principalship, Widener Univ; Keystone Bus Sch, Wilmington Coll; *cr:* Teacher Darby Township HS 1974-80, Acad Park HS East 1980-83, Acad Park HS 1983-; *ai:* Cheerleading Spon 1987-; Bus Dept Head 1988-; Jr Var Bsktbl Coach 1986-87; Delta Sigma Theta 1973-; US Army Reserves PFC 1976-80; Spencer Memorial Sunday Sch Teacher 1988-; Chester UAME Church (Hardin Youth Choir Adv 1989-, Anniversary Comm Chairperson 1988-); *office:* Acad Park HS 300 Calcon Hook Rd Sharon Hill PA 19079

CLEMENTZ, BETTY MAY, French Teacher; *b:* Sterling, IL; *m:* Thomas F.; *c:* Kimberly; *ed:* (BSED) Latin/Fr, IL St Univ 1964; W IL Univ, N IL Univ, Calvin Coll, Univ of WI Whitewater; *cr:* Teacher Rock Falls HS 1964-; Teacher of Gifted Sauk Valley Comm Coll 1985-; *ai:* Fr Club, Frosh Class Adv; Whittle Channel I Curr, Discipline Review Comm; NEA, IEA 1964-; Rock Falls HS Ed Assn (Secy, Treas, Building Rep, Pres), Mem of Yr 1968, 1986; IL Foreign Lang Teachers Assn 1985-; *office:* Rock Falls HS 101 12th Ave Rock Falls IL 61071

CLEMENTZ, DIANE ROSE KWIECINSKI, 3rd Grade Teacher; *b:* Madison, WI; *m:* Patrick D.; *c:* Joseph, Michael; *ed:* (BSE) Elem Ed, 1972, (MEPD) Elem Ed, 1978 UW Whitewater; *cr:* 1st-4th Grade Teacher Logan Sch 1972-; *ai:* NEA, IL Ed Assn, Belvidere Ed Assn 1972-; Rockford Cmmty Chorale 1976-; *office:* Logan Sch 620 Logan Ave Belvidere IL 61008

CLEMMONS, DIXIE JANE, 2nd Grade Teacher; *b:* Detroit, MI; *m:* Ronald K.; *c:* Adam; *ed:* (BS) Elem Ed, Austin Peay St Univ 1978; *cr:* 2nd Grade Teacher Tennessee Ridge Elem Sch 1978-; *ai:* Chrldr Spon; Sch Fund Raising Comm Chairperson; PTA Treas; *office:* Tennessee Ridge Elem Sch School St Tennessee Ridge TN 37178

CLEMON, BEATRICE HARGROVE, 2nd Grade Teacher/Chairperson; *b:* Atlanta, GA; *ed:* (BA) Psych, Spelman Coll 1963; (MS) Early Chldhd Ed, GA St Univ 1974; Numerous Courses; *cr:* Teacher Atlanta Bd of Ed 1963-; *ai:* NEA, GA Assn of Educators, Atlanta Assn of Educators; NAACP, BSA; Dean Rusk Elem Sch Teacher of Yr 1988-89; *office:* Dean Rusk Elem Sch 433 Peeples St SW Atlanta GA 30310

CLEMONS, MARY GAY, 7th Grade Language Art Teacher; *b:* Mt Sterling, KY; *c:* Jeanne Faulkner, Laura G. Faulkner; *ed:* (AA) Pre-Liberal Art, VA Intermont 1962; (BA) Scndry Ed, Univ of KY 1964; (MA) Scndry Ed, Morehead St Univ 1978; Writing Process E KY Univ; Shakespeare Inst Univ of KY; *cr:* 8th Grade Eng Teacher Mapleton Elem 1964; Eng Teacher Mt Sterling HS 1972-76; Lang Art/Speech/Drama Teacher Mc Nabb Mid 1976-; *ai:* Speech Team Coach; Drama Instr; Youth in Government Spon; Scorekeeper Youth League Bsbl; MCEA, KEA 1976-; KMSA 1983-; Commonwealth Inst for Teachers Charter Mem; Montgomery Cty Teacher of Yr; St Finalist Teacher of Yr; *home:* 33 Samuels Ave Mount Sterling KY 40353

CLEMONS, OWEN, Mathematics Teacher; *b:* Valdosta, GA; *ed:* (BS) Mid Chldhd Ed, Albany St Coll 1979; (MS) Mid Chldhd Math/Sci, Valdosta St Coll 1982; Stu Teacher Services; Data Collector; *cr:* Sci Teacher Lowndes Jr HS 1979-80; Team Leader/Math Teacher 1980-, Bsktbl Coach 1981-87 Lowndes Mid Sch, Lowndes HS 1988-; *ai:* LAE/GAE/NEA 1979-; Yorkrite Mason Sr Warden 1983- Outstanding Leader 1986; Teacher of Yr 1981; *home:* Rt 3 Box 212 Valdosta GA 31601

CLESTER, ROSEMARY DURHAM, Sixth Grade Teacher; *b:* Cardwell, MO; *m:* Morris Ray; *c:* Destry R., Christie M.; *ed:* (BSE) Elem Ed/Jr HS Soc Stud, AR St Univ 1983; Parents as Teachers Prgm; Kndgtn-6th Sci, Math Trng; *cr:* Machinist Ely & Walker 1973-80; Elem Teacher Southland C-9 Sch 1983-; *ai:* Parents as Teachers Instr; Jr HS Cheerleading Spon; Elem Curr Comm Mem; Girls 8-10 Sftbl Team Coach 1984-85; Southlands 1st Elem Sci Fair Co Chairperson; MSTA Mem 1983-; CTA Secy 1987-88; Lioness Club Mem 1986-87; Cardwell-Southland Alumni Assn (Secy, Treas) 1985-89; *office:* Southland C-9 Sch P O Box 47 Cardwell MO 63829

CLEVELAND, ELINOR A., Director of Bands; *b:* Houston, TX; *ed:* (BMED) Music, Univ of Houston 1969; Univ of Houston; *cr:* Dir of Bands Elkhart HS 1969- 7, North Shore HS 1977-; *ai:* Marching Band; Symphonic Band; Musical Orch; Dept Chairperson for Fine Arts; Spon Music Club; TX Classroom Teachers Assn 1977-87; TX Bandmasters Assn 1969-; TX Music Educators Assn 1969-; Region Secy Band 1987-; North Shore HS Teacher of Yr 1988; Elinor Cleveland Awd Elkhart Public Schls 1975; Pilot Club Teacher of Month 1988; TX PTA Life Mem North Shore HS 1988.

CLEVELAND, LIBBY LEIGH, Teacher/Mathematics Dept Chair; *b:* Coleman, TX; *m:* Kenneth; *c:* Beth Cleveland Buckley, Vicki Cleveland Fretwell, Kevin; *ed:* (BA) Elem Ed, Univ of TX 1958; (MS) Math/Eng, W TX Univ 1965; *cr:* 3rd Grade Teacher Sondra Schls 1959-61; 6th-12th Grade Teacher Dimmitt 1961-; *ai:* Jr Spon; Math UIL; Textbook Selection Comm; NAMT; CTA Pres; Math Essay Published; Math Conferences Presenter; *home:* 715 W Grant Dimmitt TX 79027

CLEVENGER, WENDY WARD, 4th Grade Teacher; *b:* Elmhurst, IL; *m:* Walter S.; *c:* Mark; *ed:* (BA) Ed, N IL Univ 1967; *cr:* Elem Teacher Haish Sch 1967-68, Jefferson Sch 1968-; *ai:* Young Authors; Sci Olympiad; Rndg Cncl, Dixon Teachers; DEA Membership; PEO Secy 1980-85; *office:* Jefferson Sch 800 4th Ave Dixon IL 61021

CLEVENSTINE, RICHARD FRANCIS, Biology Teacher; *b:* Ashland, PA; *m:* Barbara Diane Stewart; *c:* Amy N., Beth C., Laura A.; *ed:* (BS) Bio, Bloomsburg Univ 1972; (MA) Scndry Ed, Villanova Univ 1974; (MA) Bio, Westchester Univ 1977; (EDD) Sci Ed, Temple Univ 1984; *cr:* Adjunct Professor PA St Univ 11984; Bio Teacher Ridley HS 1972-; Adjunct Professor DE Cty Comm Coll 1987-; *ai:* Sci Olympiad Coach; Technology & Prof Dev Comm; NSTA, NEA, NABT; Springfield PTA; Impact Teacher Grant, Awd 1989; Videomicroscopy Grant 1987; Sci Articles Published; *office:* Ridley HS 1001 Morton Ave Folsom PA 19033

CLIFFORD, DOROTHY F., Teacher; *b:* Vanceburg, KY; *c:* Jacque Best; *ed:* (BA) Elem Ed, Morehead Univ 1963; Bus, Schwab Bus; *cr:* Teacher Inverness Primary Sch 1972-89; *ai:* Grade Level Chm; Delta Kappa Gamma (Corresponding Secy 1987-88, Secy 1989-); Inverness Primary Teacher of Yr 1980; FL Soc Stud Teacher of Yr 1983.

CLIFFORD, LAWRENCE PAUL, Mathematics Teacher; *b:* Riverside, CA; *m:* Marsha Wright; *c:* Katherine, Elizabeth; *ed:* (BA) Scndry Ed, Univ of KY 1974; (MED) Admin/Curr/Supervision, Wright St Univ 1976; Bus & Cmptr Programming; *cr:* Math Teacher Stivers HS 1974-83; Math/Cmptrs Teacher E J Brown Intermediate Sch 1983-84; Math Supvr Dayton City Schls 1984-86; Math Teacher Patterson Career Center 1986-; *ai:* NEA, OEA, DEA, NCTM; *office:* Patterson Career Center 118 E 1st St Dayton OH 45402

CLIFFORD, MAUREEN, English Teacher; *b:* Newark, NJ; *ed:* (BA) Eng, Newark St Coll 1971; *cr:* Eng Teacher Brick Township HS 1971-89; *ai:* NEA, NJ Educl Assn; Brick Township Educl Assn Building Rep 1980-81; *office:* Brick Township HS 246 Chambers Bridge Rd Brick NJ 08723

CLIFT, BRENDA CRABTREE, Third Grade Teacher; *b:* Baltimore, MD; *c:* Mary E., Margaret L.; *ed:* (BS) Home Ec, TN Technological Univ 1968; *cr:* Eligibility Worker TN Dept of Human Services 1967-68; 6th Grade Teacher 1966-67, 1st Grade Teacher 1971-72, Kndgtn Teacher 1975-77, 1st Grade Teacher 1977-87, 3rd Grade Teacher 1987- Fifth Consolidated Sch; *ai:* Project WRITE; Extended Contract Teacher; Before & After Sch Day Care Prgm; Parents are Teachers Instr 1989; Career Ladder Teacher; Adopt-A-Sch Comm; Supts Advisory Cncl Sch Rep; Alpha Delta Kappa 1988-; Dyer Cty Ed Assn, NEA 1975-; 1st United Meth Church (Pres Status, Role of Women) 1989-; Dyersburg & Dyer Cty Teacher Center Advisory Bd; Nom

Teacher of Yr; *office:* Fifth Consolidated Sch PO Box 1270 Dyersburg TN 38024

CLIFTON, RICHARD W., Elementary & HS Principal; *b:* Mt Pleasant, IA; *m:* Linda Lou Peasley; *c:* Katyryn, Alicia, Andrea, Anna; *ed:* (BA) Soc Stud/Phys Ed, W IL Univ 1968; (MS) Admin, NW MO Univ 1972; *cr:* Teacher/Coach Gladstone Grade Sch 1963-69, Southern 1970-83; Prin/Coach Southern Elem & HS 1984-; *ai:* Stu Cncl Spon; Bsktbl & Ftbl Coach; *office:* Southern Unit 120 37-39 South St Stronghurst IL 61480

CLINE, ALBINA L., Health Teacher 4-6/Phy Ed 1-6; *b:* Meadville, PA; *m:* Robert Eugene; *c:* Deanna; *ed:* (BS) Health/Phys Ed, Slippery Rock St Coll 1975; (MS) Phys Ed, WV Univ 1980; *cr:* Teacher Mineral Wells Elem Sch 1975-; *ai:* Coaching Vlybl; Track; Jump Rope for Heart; OH & WV Vlybl Ofcl; Health Book Selection Comm; Soc Comm; Metropolitan Life Health Awd.

CLINE, JEFFREY L., English Teacher; *b:* Mt Vernon, OH; *m:* Joanna Virgin; *ed:* (BA) Bible, KY Chrstn Coll 1978; (MA) Eng, 1985, (MAE) Scndry Ed, 1986 Morehead St Univ; *cr:* Teacher Olive Hill Elem 1985-86; Eng Teacher Boyd Cty Sr HS 1986-; *ai:* Boyd Cty Writing Project Dir & Coord; HS Literary Magazine Adv; KCTE, NCTE, KEA 1985-; Oak Grove Church of Christ Evangelism Out Reach Comm 1989-; Farmers Chrstn Church Minister 1979-86; Received Writing Project Grant KY Dept of Ed; Whos Who in Amer Ed 1990; Nom Outstanding Young Men of America 1990; *office:* Boyd Cty Sr HS 12307 Midland Trl Rd Ashland KY 41101

CLINE, ROLAND DOUGLAS, Math Dept Chair/Math Teacher; *b:* Hagerstown, MD; *m:* Rebecca Mc Kee; *c:* Matthew, Bradley; *ed:* (BS) Math, Frostburg Univ 1971; (MED) Math, Shippensburg Univ 1976; *cr:* Math Teacher N Harford Jr/Sr HS 1971-73, E Russell Hicks Mid Sch 1973-80; Instructional TV Teacher Bd of Ed Washington Cty 1980-82; Math/Cmptr Teacher E Russell Hicks Mid Sch 1983-; *ai:* Ed Enrichment Newsletters for Elem & HS; Founder Talented & Gifted Math Class; Math Counts Team Coach; NCTM; Partnership for Academic & Creative Excl VP 1980-82.

CLINE, SALLY MYERS, Home Economics Teacher; *b:* Cleveland, OH; *m:* Robert J.; *c:* Christopher; *ed:* (BA) Home Ec, Ball St Univ 1972; (MS) Ed, IN Univ 1982; Quest Intnl 1986; *cr:* Home Ec Teacher Wakarusa Mid Sch 1973-; *ai:* Vlybl Coach; Stu Cncl Adv; United Meth Church 1955-; Psi Iota Xi 1986-.

CLINE, SALLY WILLIAMS, 6th Grade Teacher; *b:* Taplin, WV; *m:* Billy K.; *c:* Shawn E. Cline Riggins; *ed:* (AB) Eng/Soc Stud, Marshall Univ 1973; Cmptr Technology Trng, Logan Cty Bd of Ed; *cr:* Teacher Mallory Elem 1961-; *ai:* Jr Amer Citizen Spon; WV Spec Olympics Spon; WV Ed Assn 1961-; Delta Kappa Gamma Intnl Comm Chairperson 1986-; United Meth Church-Teacher of Young Adults & Youth Cnslr 1969-; Mother of Yr 1984; Logan Cty Teacher of Yr 1977-78; Supervising Teacher 1984; *home:* Box 356 Davin WV 25617

CLINE, SANDRA PARK, 4th Grade Teacher; *b:* Clarksville, AR; *m:* Jack Jr.; *c:* John, Scott; *ed:* (BA) Elem Ed, Univ of Ozarks 1971; Working Toward Masters Counseling, Univ of Cntrl AR; *cr:* 4th Grade Teacher Clarksville Public Schls 1971-74, 1977-; *ai:* Various Act; Calendar & Personnel Policy Comms; AEA Mem 1985-86; 1st United Meth Church Mem; Spotlight Teacher of Month; *office:* Kraus Elem Sch 1901 Clark Rd Clarksville AR 72830

CLINE, WILLIAM R., English Department Chair; *b:* Binghamton, NY; *m:* Elizabeth Anne Rakestraw; *c:* Tracy, Beth, Nicole, Michelle; *ed:* (BA) Eng, SUNY Cortland 1971; Permanent Cert SUNY Cortland; *cr:* 7th-12th Grade Eng Teacher Greene Cntrl HS 1971-; *ai:* 12th Grade Adv; Jr Var Soccer; Var Bowling; Dist Advisory Comm; Eng Curr Revision Comm Dept Chm; Ftbl, Bsbl, Track & Newspaper Coach; Greene Teachers Assn (VP 1973-86, Grievance Chm 1975-86); Greene C&MA Church (Deacon 1983-, Sunday Sch Supt 1986-); Band Boosters Treas 1988; Natl Coaches Assn Awd for Excl; Outstanding Men of America Designation; Yrbk Dedication 1986; *office:* Greene Cntrl HS S Canal St Greene NY 13778

CLINEBELL, SABRENA GIBBS, Science Teacher; *b:* Dodge City, KS; *c:* Nickolaus J., Hannah J.; *ed:* (BA) Chem, Ft Hays St Univ 1978; Lions Quest Skills Adolescence; Microscale Experiments Chem; Physics Demonstration & Laboratory Inst; *cr:* 7th-9th Grade Sci Teacher Ravenna Public Schls 1978-81; 8th-12th Grade Sci Teacher Tescott Public Schls 1982-83; 7th-12th Grade Sci Teacher Republican City Schls 1983-84, Beaver Valley Public Schls 1984-; *ai:* Academic Bowl Team Coach; Class of 1990 Spon 1986-; Slide Presentation 1986-; Altar Society 1986-; Nom Excl in Sci & Math Teaching Awd; Ft Hay St Univ Memorial Union Act Bd; *home:* 1121 Flannery Ave Cambridge NE 69022

CLINGENSMITH, DONALD, Mathematics Teacher; *b:* Butler, PA; *m:* Patricia Schreecengost; *ed:* (BSED) Math, Slippery Rock Univ 1961; Grad Stud Univ of Pittsburgh, Penn St Univ; *cr:* Math Teacher Beatty Jr HS 1961, Mars Area HS 1961-; *ai:* Bsktbl Coach; Math Chm; Prins Advisory Comm; Math Club & 9th Grade Class Spon; NEA, PA St Ed Assn, Mars Area Ed Assn 1961-; Volunteer Fire Dept Treas 1990; Borough Authority Chm 1979-81; Amer Legion Mem 1985-; Natl Sci Fnd Grant; Natl Sci Fnd Inst in Math Augustana Coll 1968; *home:* Box 142 Harmony St Connoquenessing PA 16027

CLINKSCALE, CHELITA ANN, 5th Grade Teacher; *b:* Chicago, IL; *ed:* (BA) His/Elem Ed, Univ of Detroit 1965; (MA) Guidance/Counseling, Univ of MI 1968; *cr:* Teacher Detroit Public Schls 1965-; *ai:* Curr Comm; Service Squad Spon; Delta Sigma Theta, NAACP, YWCA; *office:* Fitzgerald Elem Sch 8145 Puritan Detroit MI 48238

CLINTON, DEBORAH BERRY, Fourth Grade Teacher; *b:* Lubbock, TX; *m:* Kenney W.; *c:* Berry W.; *ed:* (BS) Elem Ed, West TX St Univ 1974; (MED) Rdng, TX Tech Univ 1988; Herman Method Reducing Rdng Failures; Elem Eng As 2nd Lang Trng; Sci TX Tech Univ; *cr:* Remedial Rdng Teacher Hart Elem Rdng Lab 1975-78; 4th Grade Teacher Hart Elem 1978-; *ai:* Leadership Comm; Xi Mu Iota VP 1989-; *home:* Box 603 Hart TX 79043

CLINTON, DONALD CAREY, History and Computer Teacher; *b:* Los Angeles, CA; *m:* Mymie R. Clinton; *c:* Carey, Amy; *ed:* (BS) Psych, Univ of GA 1974; (BSED) Soc Stud, Univ of GA 1980; (MSED) Soc Stud, GA Southern Coll 1985; Ed 5, GA Southern Coll; *cr:* His Teacher J R Trippe Mid Sch1980-; Cmptr Teacher J R Trippe Mid Sch 1986-; *ai:* Y-Club Adv; Newspaper Pub Adv; Elem Homebound Teacher; Bus Coord; Prof Assn GA Ed 1984-; GA Historical Society 1980-; Intnl Childbirth Assn 1986-; Gifted Teaching Wkshp; *office:* J R Trippe Mid Sch 302 W 2nd Street Vidalia GA 30474

CLINTON, JANE ELIZABETH (SWARTZ), Business Teacher; *b:* Everest, KS; *m:* Robert J.; *c:* Bonnie J., Tracy L., Karla S.; Bus Teacher Eudora HS 1977-; *ed:* (BS) Phys Ed/Bus, Emporia St 1967; *cr:* Bus/Phys Ed Teacher Westphalia HS 1967-69; Phys Ed Teacher Burlington HS 1975-76; Bus/Phys Ed Teacher Summerfield HS 1976-77; *ai:* FBLA; Vlybl; Inservice Comm; Cheerleading; NEA, KNEA 1967-; KBEA 1988-; Delta Zeta 1989; Meth Church (Music Comm 1989-, Usher 1984-); *home:* 2905 Chisholm Dr Lawrence KS 66047

CLINTON, JOE, English Teacher; *b:* Detroit, MI; *m:* Jane A.; *c:* Kelly, Michael, Martha; *ed:* (BA) Speech/Eng, 1971, (MA) Soc Stud, 1973 E MI Univ; *cr:* Teacher Mapey Boys Trng Sch 1970, Detroit Redford HS 1971-74, Troy Athens HS 1974-; *ai:* Var Girls Bsktbl, Jr Var Girls Golf, Frosh Boys Bsktbl Coach; NCTE; *home:* 2874 Quail Run Troy MI 48098

CLINTON, LINDA KAY (MORGAN), 8th English Teacher/Dept Chair; *b:* Ada, OK; *m:* Phillip Lance; *c:* Brian L., Charles A.; *ed:* (BSED) Eng, 1970, (MAED) Ed, 1976 E Cntrl St Univ; Admin Cert 1990; *cr:* HS Eng Teacher Hammon Public Schls 1970-71; Jr HS Eng Teacher Valliant Public Schls 1971-73; Sr Rdng Supvr Guthrie Job Corps 1980-81; Jr HS Eng Teacher Guthrie Public Schls 1980-; *ai:* Eng Dept Chairperson; Chapter IV Indian Tutor; Stu Assistance Prgm; Adjunct Instr Langston Univ; OK Cncl Teachers of Eng 1985-; NCTE, OEA, NEA, ASCD; Guthrie Assn Classroom Teachers Negotiations Team; Presidents Honor Roll Cntrl St Univ; Teacher of Yr Hammon Public Schls 1970 & Guthrie Jr HS 1990; *office:* Guthrie Jr HS 705 E Oklahoma Guthrie OK 73044

CLIPPERT, RICHARD JOHN, 6th Grade Teacher; *b:* Ferndale, MI; *m:* Susan Carol Burns; *c:* Jason, Cara; *ed:* (BS) Elem Ed, 1977, (MA) Elem Ed, 1980 Oakland Univ; *cr:* 6th Grade Teacher Sterling Elem 1977-; *ai:* Safety Patrol Supvr; Camp Prgm Coord; *office:* Sterling Elem Sch 12500 19 Mile Rd Sterling Heights MI 48078

CLODFELTER, ANNE EYLER, English Teacher; *b:* Johnson City, TN; *m:* Donald Glen; *c:* William G., Jon E.; *ed:* (BA) Music/Eng, Agnes Scott Coll 1960; (MM) Music Applied Piano, IN Univ 1963; Grad Level Ed; *cr:* 1st-6th Grade Music/7th-8th Grade Eng Teacher Stinesville IN 1962; 7th/8th Grade Eng Teacher Dist 123 1962-65; 10th/11th Grade Teacher Columbus HS 1965-66; 9th Grade Eng Teacher Seymour HS 1984-; *ai:* NCTE, ICTE; Brownstown Presbyn Church (Choir Master 1975-, Organist 1979-); Tri Kappa VP 1971-87; Tesa Trng 1989; TESA Seminar For Trainers 1989; *home:* RR 1 Brownstown IN 47220

CLODFELTER, MARGARET E., Science Teacher; *b:* Decatur, IL; *m:* Donald Vernon; *c:* Susan, Gregory; *ed:* (BS) Elem Ed, Univ of Indianapolis 1962; (MS) Elem Ed, IN Univ 1965; *cr:* 3rd/4th Grade Teacher Indianapolis Public Sch 1962-65; 3rd Grade Teacher Greenwood Cmmty Sch 1965-68, Vigo Cty Schls 1968-70; 8th Grade Sci Teacher Sullivan Jr HS 1978-; *ai:* Yrbk & 8th Grade Class Spon; SWSTA (Building Rep, Delegate) 1980-82; ISTA 1962-70, 1978-; NEA 1978-; Delta Kappa Gamma 1987-; United Meth Church Music Dir 1968-; *home:* PO Box 501 Farmersburg IN 47850

CLOMAN, RITA NELL (LINCOLN), Algebra Teacher; *b:* Fort Worth, TX; *m:* Douglas Eugene Jr.; *ed:* (MS) Math, East TX St Univ 1979; (BS) Math/Phys Ed, ETSU 1972; Math, ETSU & Richland Comm Coll; *cr:* 6th Grade Math Teacher Ennis Mid Sch 1972-76; Geometry Teacher 1976-80, Geometry/Intro Alg II Teacher 1980-85 Ennis HS; Pre-Alg/Alg I Teacher 1985-89; Alg I Teacher 1989- W H Atwell Fundamental Acad; *ai:* FTA/Jr Class Sponsor; Vlybl Coach Asst; Soc Games Club Sponsor; TX Ed Week Comm; Contest Team Class; Math Club Co-Spon; Southwest Vlybl Ofcls Assn Mem 1983-89; TX Ed Assn/NEA Mem 1972-; Womens Intnl Bowling Congress League Secy 1988-; Alpha Kappa Alpha Mem 1971-; Order of Eastern Star Chapter Secy 1988-; Whos Who Among TX Educators; the Most Prominent Ed of TX 1983; *office:* W H Atwell Acad 1303 Reynoldston Ln Dallas TX 75232

CLOONAN, LISA BREAZEALE, Third Grade Teacher; *b:* Lufkin, TX; *m:* John; *c:* Karena, Jana, Shawn; *ed:* (BS) Elem Ed, Stephen F Austin Univ 1970; *cr:* 2nd Grade Teacher 1971-72, 3rd Grade Teacher 1974-76 Hudson Elem; 4th/5th/6th Grade Math Teacher 1978-83, 3rd Grade Teacher 1985- St Patrick Sch; *ai:* Eucharistic Minister; Taught Religion; GSA Leader; Lib Volunteer; Church Head Religious Ed; *home:* 306 River Oak Lufkin TX 75901

CLOSE, GRACE ANN, English Teacher; *b:* Monmouth, IL; *c:* Suzanne L. Millas, Randall A. Millas; *ed:* (BA) Eng, Monmouth Coll 1963; (MED) Sndry Ed/Rdng, Univ of IL 1976; Cooperative Learning, Thinking Skills, Skills for Living; *cr:* Rdng Instr Parkland Comm Coll 1974-81; Drama/Rdng Teacher Orange Grove Jr HS 1981-83; Rdng Instr Pima Comm Coll 1984; Advanced Eng Teacher Canyon Del Oro HS 1984-; *ai:* Sch Poetry Coord; Sch Improvement Comm; Cooperative Learning Wkshp Presenter; Dist Comm Eligibility Requirements; Curr Revision Advanced Eng Skills for Living; Eng Placement Evaluator; Univ of Chicago Outstanding Teacher Recognition 1989; NCTE Mem 1989-; AEA Building Rep 1988-89; Articles Published in N Cntrl Rdng Assn Yrbk; *office:* Canyon Del Oro HS 25 W Calle Concordia Tucson AZ 85704

CLOSE, SOFIA, English Department Chair; *b:* Oakland, CA; *ed:* (BA) Eng/TOEFL, CSUS Sonoma St 1972; Teaching Cert Eng, CSUH Hayward 1985; Admin Credential, CSUH 1989; *cr:* Bi-ling Tutor Sonoma Cty Schls; Eng AS Second Lang Univ of CA Berkeley/Holy Names 1978-79, Eng Lang Acad Japan/Korea 1980-82; Eng Dept Chairperson De Anza HS 1987-; *ai:* Friday Night Live Adv; Bi-ling Adviory Comm; AFS & Global Friends Spon; Academic Senate Curr Writing Comm; ASCD, CATE, RABE Mem 1990; Portfolio Writing Project; *office:* De Anza HS 5000 Valley View Rd Richmond CA 94803

CLOUD, DONNA LEACH, 5th Grade Teacher; *b:* Houston, TX; *m:* Michael Dennis; *ed:* (BA) Elem Ed, Univ of TX 1976; (MED) Elem Admin, Univ of OK 1980; Adult Ed, Univ of OK; *cr:* 4th Grade Teacher Northwood Elem 1977-78; 6th Grade Teacher 1978-88, 5th Grade Teacher 1988- Epperly Heights Mid Del Schls; *ai:* Media Advisory Bd, Sch Improvement, Cmptr Lab, Textbook Adoption Comm; NEA 1977-; OK Ed Assn, Mid-Del ACT 1978-; Epperly Heights Teacher of Yr 1988-89; Mid-Del Dist Teacher of Yr Finalist; OK Librarians Assn Prgm for Encyclopedia; *office:* Epperly Heights Elem Sch 3805 Del Rd Del City OK 73115

CLOUD, JULIANA COLEMAN, 1st Grade Teacher; *b:* Seattle, WA; *m:* Martin John; *c:* Mariesa L.; *ed:* (BS) Elem Ed, OR St Univ 1986; Emphasis in Math; Working Towards Masters in Rdng; *cr:* 1st Grade Teacher Ocosta Elem 1986-89; *ai:* Girls Var Bsktbl; Phys Ed & Cmptr Comm; Little Dribblers K-6th Grade Bsktbl Prgm; *office:* Ocosta Elem Sch Star Rt Westport WA 98595

CLOUGH, DAVID OTIS, Computer Studies Teacher; *b:* Dodge City, KS; *m:* Carol L. Reynolds; *c:* Christina Leuth, David A.; *ed:* (BS) Bus Ed, St Mary of the Plains 1968; Working Towards Masters & St Cmptr Cert; *cr:* Bus Teacher Odin HS 1968-72; Sci/Cmptr Stud Teacher Kennedy Mid Sch 1972-; *ai:* Photography & Spec Cmptr Classes; NEA 1968-; *office:* Kennedy Mid Sch 1309 Fort St Hays KS 67601

CLOUGH, DIXIE LOUISE, Third Grade Teacher; *b:* Warren, PA; *c:* Joshua T.; *ed:* (BAED) Elem Ed, 1972, (MED) Elem Ed, 1979 Edinboro Univ; *cr:* 1st Grade Teacher Youngsville Elem 1973-76; 4th Grade Teacher Sugar Grove Elem 1977; 3rd Grade Teacher Pleasant Township Elem 1977-; *ai:* Soc Stud & Humane Ed Curr Comms; Warren Cty Ed Assn Union Rep 1986-; PA St Ed Assn, NEA 1973-; *home:* Box 196 Pittsfield PA 16340

CLOUGH, JAMES WILLIAM, 6th Grade Teacher; *b:* Hudson Falls, NY; *m:* Judith Leavitt; *c:* Robert J., Tammy J. Estabrook; *ed:* (BS) Ed, 1960; (MS) Ed, 1964 SUNY Oneonta; *cr:* 5th Grade Teacher 1960-64, 6th Grade Teacher 1964-68, 5th Grade TeacheR 1968-79, 6th Grade Teacher 1979- S Glens Falls Cntrl Sch; *ai:* HS Var Sftbl Coach 1980-85; Bldg-Elem Cmptr Coord 1988-; Outdoor Educl Camping Trip 1973-; Sch Drama Club Adv 1960-80; Faculty Assn Treas 1964-66; BSA 1960- (Silver Beaver Awd 1977, St George Awd 1976); BSA Order of Arrow section Adv 1977-88 Distinguished Service Awd 1981; BSA Area Adv 1988-; *office:* S Glens Falls Cntrl Sch Tanglewood Dr South Glens Falls NY 12803

CLOUGH, JOHN L., Fourth Grade Teacher; *b:* Huntsville, TX; *m:* Lillian Lucille Malard; *ed:* (BA) Elem Ed, TX Southern Univ 1971; Working Towards Masters; *cr:* 6th Grade Teacher Alcott Elem 1970-71; 5th Grade Teacher Briargrove Elem 1971-73; 6th Grade Teacher Southmayo Elem 1973-84; 4th Grade Teacher Sanchez Elem 1984-; *ai:* Safety Patrol Spon; *office:* George I Sanchoz Elem Schl 2700 Berkley Houston TX 77012

CLOUSE, JANE MARIE, Fifth Grade Teacher; *b:* Tiffin, OH; *ed:* (BS) Elem Ed, OH St Univ 1984; *cr:* 5th Grade Teacher Sacred Heart Elem 1985; 7th/8th Grade Teacher 1985-86, 5th Grade Teacher 1986- St Wendelin Elem; *ai:* Outstanding Young Women of Amer 1987; Cath Club Youth Dept Area Coord 1986-89; *office:* St Wendelin Elem Sch 300 N Wood St Fostoria OH 44830

CLOUSE, MARY MAHER, Kindergarten Teacher; *b:* Alton, IL; *c:* Candi, Aaron; *ed:* (BS) Elem Ed, S IL Univ Edwardsville 1969; *cr:* 1st Grade Teacher 1969-73, Kndgtn Teacher 1973-79 Godfrey Elem; Kndgtn Teacher Lewis & Clark & Mark Twain 1979-80, Godfrey Elem 1980-81, Mark Twain 1981-; *ai:* Mark Twain IL Network of Accelerated Schls, St Steering Comm; GSA Troop 142

Leader 1989-; BSA Pack 173 Comm Mem 1990; Alton Area Educl Employees Credit Union Bd of Dirs 1989-; *office:* Mark Twain Sch 907 Milton Rd Alton IL 62002

CLOUSE, TRACIE RENEE, Business Teacher; *b:* Pueblo, CO; *ed:* (AA) Bus, Otero Jr Coll 1984; (BA) Bus Ed, NW OK St Univ 1986; *cr:* Bus Instr Healy HS 1987-; *ai:* Soph Class Spon; HS Girls Bsktbl Coach; Jr HS Girls Vlybl, Bsktbl, Track Coach; KS Coaches Assn 1987-; KS Bus Ed Assn 1987-; *office:* Healy HS 410 Main Healy KS 67850

CLOUSER, RALPH CHARLES, JR., HS Mathematics Teacher; *b:* Middletown, PA; *c:* Mary Ruhl, Ralph III, Scott, Matthew; *ed:* (BS) Math, Elizabethtown Coll 1963; Lehigh Univ, Coll of William & Mary, Millersville Univ; *cr:* Math Teacher Elizabethtown Area HS 1963-; *ai:* Yrbk Adv 1969-80; EAEA Local Assn (Pres, Treas 1967-75, Membership) 1963-; PSEA, NEA 1963-; Pre-Teen Bsbl (Coach, Commissioner) 1978-85; NSF Grants Lehigh Univ & William & Mary Coll; *home:* 420 N Lime St Elizabethtown PA 17022

CLOUTHIER, KATHLEEN JOAN (MC GRATH), Mathematics Teacher; *b:* Kenosha, WI; *m:* Peter R.; *ed:* (BA) Math, Dominican Coll 1971; (MS) Math, Marquette Univ 1973; Miscellaneous Credits for Cmptr & Discipline; *cr:* Math Teacher Gifford Jr HS 1974-81, Case HS 1981-; *ai:* Curr Writing in Math & Cmptr Literacy; N Cntrl Evaluation Comm; NEA, WEA 1982-; REA Building Rep 1982-; Assistantship Marquette Univ 1971-73.

CLOWARD, SUSAN LUNDELL, First Grade Teacher; *b:* Spanish Fork, UT; *m:* David D.; *c:* Thomas; *ed:* (BS) Elem Ed, 1972, (MS) Rdng Specialist, 1982 Brigham Young Univ; Slingerland Rdng Instruction, Essential Elements of Ed Trng; *cr:* Grad Asst Brigham Young Univ 1981-82; Teacher/Leader Nebo Dist 1984-86; 1st Grade Teacher Brockbank Elem 1972-; *ai:* Delta Kappa Gamma 1983-.

CLOWER, CHERYL SMITH, Home Economics Teacher; *b:* Knoxville, TN; *m:* Ronald Alan; *c:* Justin A., Kristen L.; *ed:* (BS) Home Ec Ed, 1977, (MS) Home Ec Ed, 1981 Univ of TN Knoxville; *cr:* Home Ec Teacher Forest Park Jr HS 1981-84; Dietitian Metropolitan Hospital 1984-85, Meth & St Jude Hospital 1985-86; Home Ec Teacher Morrow Jr HS & McIntosh HS 1986-; *ai:* FHA Club Adv; Amer Home Ec Assn 1975-; Amer Dietetics Assn 1981-; Meth Church 1968-; FHA Alumni 1989-; Parenting Grant in Ed 1988-; Top 10 Teacher McIntosh HS 1989; *office:* Mc Intosh HS 201 E Walt Banks Rd Peachtree City GA 30269

CLUGSTEN, MELODY SHIFF, Vocal Music Teacher; *b:* Toledo, OH; *m:* Joseph A.; *ed:* (AA) Music, Monticello Coll 1968; (BMUS) Vocal Music, S IL Univ 1972; *cr:* Jr HS Vocal Music Teacher Bethalto Sch Dist 1972-73, Wood River-Hartford Sch Dist 1973-79, 1981-; *ai:* Chorus & Ensemble; *office:* Wood River-Hartford Sch Dist 501 E Lorena Ave Wood River IL 62095

CLUPPER, JO ANN, 2nd Grade/Elem Supervisor; *b:* Pomona, CA; *ed:* (BA) Elem Ed/Psych, Sch of Ozarks 1976; (MA) Elem Ed, Olivet Nazarene 1988; *cr:* 1st Grade Teacher Pensacola Chrstn Sch 1974-76; 2nd Grade Teacher 1976-, Elem Supvr 1984- Grace Baptist Acad; *ai:* Elem Newspaper Ed 1990; Master Teacher Awd 1987; *office:* Grace Baptist Acad 2499 Waldron Rd Kankakee IL 60901

CLUTE-HILL, PATRICIA DIONE (WADE), Second Grade Teacher; *b:* San Jose, CA; *m:* Michael Gary Hill; *c:* Claudia D. Clute-Schroeder; *ed:* (BA) Ed, San Jose St Univ 1959; Sch of Ministery; Church of Religious Sci 1985; *cr:* Teacher Stanford Univ 1964, Cambrian Sch Dist 1959-63, 1965-; *ai:* Suicide & Dropout Prevention; CA Teachers Assn (Past Pres 1974-75, Trainer High Risk Prgm, Womens Caucus Newsletter Ed 1972-81); Cambrian Dist Teachers Assn; United Church of Religious Sci (Practitioner 1979-, Bd of Dir 1984-86); San Jose 1st Church of Religious Sci; Workbook in Arithmetic for Addison Wesley with Todd Hodgon; *home:* 1945 Janet Ave San Jose CA 95124

CLUTTS, LOIS MARY, Language Arts Teacher; *b:* Chicago, IL; *m:* Raymond Walton; *c:* Kathleen A. Evans, Raymond E.; *ed:* (BA) Eng, IL St 1951; (MS) Ed, Gov St 1971; *cr:* Elem Teacher Farren Sch 1951-53, Dunne Sch 1953-57; Lang Art Teacher Brookwood Jr HS 1957-82; *ai:* NEA; Lionesses Pres 1986; League of Women Voters Pres 1972; Literacy Grant; *home:* 426 Arquilla Glenwood IL 60425

COAKLEY, ELIZABETH SUTHERLIN, Special Education Teacher; *b:* Port Arthur, TX; *m:* Ronald Rex; *c:* Martha L., Erin L.; *ed:* (BS) Scndry Ed, Lamar Univ 1973; (MA) Spec Ed, N TX St 1979; Several Trng Courses; *cr:* Teacher Beaumont Ind Sch Dist 1973-74, Grand Prairie Ind Sch Dist 1974-83, Carroll Ind Sch Dist 1983-86, Keller Ind Sch Dist 1987-; *ai:* Asst Soccer Coach 1988; Soph, Jr, Sr Class Spon; Drug Free Schls Advisory Cncl 1988-; Project Graduation 1988-; TSTA Pres 1982-83; Life Improvement Grant 1990; *office:* Keller HS 101 Indian Trl Keller TX 76248

COASTON, GEORGE ELLIS, Science Teacher; *b:* New Orleans, LA; *m:* Shirley Ann Dumas; *c:* Debra A. Coaston Ford, George E., Angela R.; *ed:* (BA) Bio, Dillard Univ 1959; Numerous Univs; *cr:* Technician Medical Research & Nutrition Lab 1960-62, Medical Labs 1962-65; Research Technician Univ of CA Medical Center 1964-69; Teacher Newark Sch Dist 1969-; *ai:* Black Stu Union Club Adv; NEA, CA Teacher Assn 1969-; Newark Teacher Assn 1969-, WHO 1976; Phi Beta Sigma, Aid Assn for Luths Treas 1987-; Dillard Alumni Treas 1985-; *office:* Newark Jr HS 6201 Lafayette Ave Newark CA 94560

COATES, LUCILLE, Teacher; *b:* Bee Spring, KY; *w:* Eugene (dec); *c:* Spencer, Sur M., David; *ed:* (BS) Elem Ed, 1969, (MA) Elem Ed, 1973, (Rank I) Cnslr, 1979 W KY Univ; US Park Ranger Interpreter Mammoth Cave Natl Park; *cr:* 8th Grade Teacher Sunfish Sch 1968-74; 6th Grade Teacher Kyrock Sch 1975-80, Edmonson Cty Mid Sch 1981-; *ai:* Chrldr Spon 1968-73; KEA Delegate 1983-86; *home:* PO Box 441 Brownsville KY 42210

COATNEY, PATRICIA ADAMS, Fifth Grade Teacher; *b:* Lindsay, OK; *m:* Richard W.; *ed:* (BS) Elem 1971, (ME) Rdng, 1976 East Cntrl Univ; *cr:* Rdng Speclst Connerville Sch 1971-78; 5th Grade Teacher Stratford Sch 1978-; *ai:* Spelling Bee Coord; Peewee Spelling Bee Coord; Chm Lang Art Comm; Gifted/Talented Comm; Stratford Ed Assn Pres 1978-; OCA/NEA 1977-; Delta Kappa Gamma Secy 1985-; Phi Delta Kappa 1980-; Natl Guard Family Support Group Chairperson 1989; Stratford Teacher of Yr 1984; Whos Who Among Young Amer Profs 1988-89; *office:* Stratford Elem Sch P O Box 589 Stratford OK 74872

COATS, BARBARA BLACKBURN, High School Math Teacher; *b:* Tampa, FL; *m:* Christopher Vincent; *c:* Amy, Christopher Jr.; *ed:* (BA) Math, Univ of W FL 1983; *cr:* Alg/Cmptr Teacher Washington HS 1983-84; Drop Out Prevention Washington Lee 1984-87; Math Teacher 1987-, Teacher in the Baccalourate 1988- Pensacola HS; *ai:* Alg II Team Coach; Spon Lions Jr Club Called Leo; FL Cncl Teacher of Math 1987-; Escambia Cty Teacher of Math 1987-; NEA 1983-; Franklin D Roosevelt Wives Club Pres 1976-77; Monsanto Teacher in Residence Prgm 1989; Episcopal Diocese of Cntrl Gulf Coast Commission for Spiritual Growth; *office:* Pensacola HS A & Maxwell St Pensacola FL 32501

COATS, JANELLE LAYNE, Reading Teacher; *b:* Winchester, TN; *m:* Thomas Eugene Jr.; *c:* Mary M.; *ed:* (BS) Soc Sci, 1968, (MED) Curr/Instruction, 1971; (EDS) Admin/Supervision, 1988 Mid TN St Univ; *cr:* Soc Stud Teacher Westwood Jr HS 1969-75; 7th/8th Grade Teacher Pelham Elem 1975-76; Soc Stud Teacher Westwood Jr HS 1976-80; 6th Grade Teacher Pelham Elem 1980-85; Rdng Teacher Westwood Jr HS 1985-; *ai:* Yrbk Adv; Teacher Study & Instructional Cncl; NEA; TN Ed Assn 1969-; Manchester Ed Assn Teacher of Yr 1978; Pelham Volunteer Fire Dept Secy 1988-; Book & Research Paper Written; *office:* Westwood Jr HS 505 Taylor St Manchester TN 37355

COATS, RUSSELL CARL, Business Teacher & Coach; *b:* Clinton, OK; *m:* Shirley Karen Coats Ezzell; *c:* Kurtis R.; *ed:* (BS) Phys Ed/Bus Ed, NW OK St Univ 1986; *cr:* Bus Teacher/Bsktbl Coach Terral HS 1986-87, Prairie Valley HS 1988-; *ai:* HS Boys & Girls Bsktbl & Bsbl Coach 1986-87; Jr/Sr HS Boys & Girls Bsktbl Coach 1988-; HS Golf Coach; TX Ed Assn 1988-; TX Assn of Bsktbl Coaches 1989-; *office:* Prairie Valley HS Rt 3 Box 550 Nocona TX 76255

COBB, ANN WEATHERLY, 5th Grade Teacher; *b:* Atlanta, GA; *m:* William Henry II; *ed:* (BA) Art Ed, Stratford Coll 1974; (MED) Elem Ed, GA St Univ 1977; Continious Staff Development 1975; Childrens Lit I, Art Appreciation 1988; Childrens Lit II, Talents 1989; *cr:* Teacher Norton Park Elem 1975-77, Russell Elem 1978-80, 1982-; *ai:* Russell Rdng Comm Coord; Peachtree Presbyn Church; Russell Elem Teacher of Yr 1989; *office:* Russell Elem Sch 3920 S Hurt Rd Smyrna GA 30080

COBB, DEIDRE THOMPSON, Sixth Grade Teacher; *b:* Birmingham, AL; *m:* Fhone Charles; *ed:* (BS) Elem Ed, 1977, (MA) Elem Ed, 1979 AL St Univ; *cr:* 6th Grade Teacher Woodward Elem 1978-; *ai:* Girls 4-H Club Leader; AL Ed Assn, NEA Mem 1978-; AFT Building Rep 1978-; Alpha Kappa Alpha Mem 1978-; *home:* 401 W Smithfield Dr Dolomite AL 35061

COBB, DOLOREZ, 6th Grade Teacher/Team Leader; *b:* Harrisburg, PA; *ed:* (BA) Elem Ed, Howard Univ 1976; Teacher Expectations for Stu Achievement; Ed Admin, Shippensburg Univ; Instrumental Enrichment Wkshp; *cr:* File Clerk AMP Inc 1976-77; Tutor Local Boys Club 1981-82; Spec Events Supvr City of Harrisburg 1989; Teacher John P Scott Intermediate Sch 1990; *ai:* 6th Grade Team Leader; Stu Cncl Adv; Faculty Choir Mem; Delta Sigma Theta 1990; Black Womens Caucus of Harrisburg Asst Recording Secy 1989-; PA Conference on Black Basic Ed Treas 1988-; PTO Mem; Supt Awd Outstanding Contributions Harrisburg Sch Dist 1986; Nominee for Positive Teaching Awd 1986; *home:* 1192 Bailey St Harrisburg PA 17103

COBB, JAKETTA MANGOLD, Biology Teacher; *b:* Cheyenne, OK; *c:* Tyson; *ed:* (BS) Phys Ed/Bio, Univ of TX Austin 1972; Health, Life Sci, Earth Sci; Advanced Trng Gifted & Talented Curr; *cr:* Bio Teacher Palo Duro HS 1972-75; Life/Earth Sci Teacher Bowie Jr HS 1979-84; Bio Teacher Palo Duro HS 1984-; *ai:* Palo Duro HS Activity Coord Comm; Dist Wide Comm Strategic Planning Sch Improvement Prgm; Amarillo Classroom Teachers Assn, TX St Teachers Assn, NEA Mem 1972-75, 1979-; *office:* Palo Duro HS 1400 N Grant Amarillo TX 79107

COBB, MARY STOUT, Librarian; *b:* Kellogg, ID; *m:* Jerry Lee; *c:* Jacob A., Elizabeth M.; *ed:* (BS) Elem Ed, Univ of ID 1970; Ed Media Generalist, Univ of ID 1987; *cr:* 1st/2nd Grade Teacher Elk Creek Elem 1970-73; 1st-3rd Grade Sunnyside Elem 1973-86; Ed Media Generalist Kellogg Mid Sch 1986-; *ai:* Stu at Risk Comm; Delta Kappa Gamma VP 1975-; *office:* Kellogg Mid Sch 800 Bunker Ave Kellogg ID 83837

COBB, PHILLIP H., Mathematics Department Chair; *b:* Cedartown, GA; *c:* Amy, Jeremy, Kyle; *ed:* (BA) Health/Phys Ed, Evangel Coll 1969; (MA) Health/Phys Ed, E MI Univ 1972; Admin, Jacksonville St Univ; TPAI In-Field Evaluator; *cr:* Teacher Clio Mid Sch 1969-70; Teacher/Coach Bentley Mid Sch 1970-78, Carver Mid Sch 1980-81, Elm Street Mid Sch 1981-; *ai:* Mathcounts Coach; Math Dept Chm; NEA, GAE Building Rep; PAE (Pres, Pres Elect, Treas, Building Rep); *office:* Elm Street Mid Sch PO Box 440 Rockmart GA 30153

COBB, RUBY M., Retired Readng Consultant; *b:* Dermott, AR; *c:* Jacqueline Cobb Lewis, Gwen Cobb Ford, Michele Cobb Boyd, Laquitta; *ed:* (BS) Elem Ed, Kent St Univ 1965; (MA) Sch Admin, Clev St Univ; Grad Work Bowling Green St Univ Extensiion 1973; *cr:* Bible Study Leader; Rdng Consultant Cleveland Bd of Ed; *ai:* Volunteer Cnslr for Alternaterm Pregnancy Crisis Center; Alpha Kappa Alpha; Martha Holden Jenning Fellowship Awd; *home:* 5668 Carlton Dr Bedford OH 44146

COBBS, JO BARSH, Third Grade Teacher; *b:* Pine Bluff, AR; *m:* James; *c:* Amy L.; *ed:* (BS) Elem Ed, Univ of AR Pine Bluff 1965; (MED) Elem Counseling, Univ of AR Fayetteville 1974; Univ of NE Omaha; *cr:* Teacher Pine Bluff Public Schls 1965-72, Omaha Public Schls 1973, USDESEA Amer Schls Germany 1973-81, Omaha Public Schls 1987-; *ai:* Clair Memorial Church Finance Comm; Burger King Adopt-A-Sch Comm; Benson West & Hartman Sch PTA; NEA 1965-; NE St Ed Assn 1978-; Omaha Ed Assn 1978-; Omaha Ed Assn Black Caucus 1987-; Sigma Gamma Rho Inc Pres 1965-; *home:* 6425 N 68th St Omaha NE 68104

COBLE, ERIC CLAYTON, Social Studies Teacher; *b:* Denver, CO; *m:* Carolyn Peterson; *c:* Jonathan; *ed:* (BA) Poly Sci - Magna Cum Laude, Yale Univ 1967; Poly Sci, Stockholm Univ, Lund Univ Sweden; *cr:* His Master Fountain Valley Sch 1974-75; Soc Stud Teacher Smoky Hill HS 1975-80, Overland HS 1980-; *ai:* Phi Beta Kappa 1967-; Yale Alumni Schls Comm 1975-80; CO Governers Awd for Excl in Teaching 1985; CO Fnd Awd for Distinguished Teaching 1990; NHS Excl Teaching Awd 1984, 1987; *office:* Overland HS 12400 E Jewell Ave Aurora CO 80012

COBLENTZ, MICHAEL JAMES, Teacher of History/Government; *b:* Peru, IN; *m:* Arlene Virginia Pedersen; *c:* Kelley N., Troy A., *ed:* (BS) Soc Stud, Manchester Coll 1964; (MA) World His, Ball St Univ 1967; Admin & Supervision in Scndry Schls, Ball St Univ 1988; *cr:* His Teacher Peru HS 1964-; *ai:* Mentor Teacher Comm; IN at Ed Prgm; Educl Adv 1990; Sch Corporation Comm For Gifted & Talented; Performance Based Awd Comm; Natl Historical Assn; NEA LifeMem; IN St Historical Society; IN St Teachers Assn; Miami Cty Historical Society Peru Cmmty Ed Assn; Winchester Old Timers Historical Society Life; Kiwanis Pres 1968-69; NRA Life Fireside Art Club; Local Teacher of Yr 1988-89; Nom for Fullbright Fellowship to China 1985; *office:* Peru HS 401 N Broadway Peru IN 46970

COBURN, BARBARA ANN (MOONEY), Chemistry Teacher; *b:* Welch, WV; *m:* William S. Jr.; *c:* Jonathan, Heather; *ed:* (BS) Chem/Gen Sci Ed, Concord Coll 1971; (MS) Safety Ed, Marshall Univ 1982; *cr:* Teacher Cntrl Jr HS 1972-73, Logan Cntrl Jr HS 1973-78, Peterstown HS 1978-; *ai:* Natl Honor Society Adv; NSTA, Delta Kappa Gamma; Natl Assoc Stu Activity Adv; Parent Adv Cncl; Academic Boosters Club; *office:* Peterstown H S Peterstown WV 24963

COBY, REBA JAN, 5th Grade Reading Teacher; *b:* Morgantown, WV; *ed:* (AB) Elem Ed, GLenville St Coll 1975; (MA) Elem Ed, WV Univ 1984; *cr:* Teacher Union Elem Sch 1976; Pleasants Cty Mid Sch 1976-; *ai:* Pleasants Cty Teachers Acad Advisory Comm Chairperson; Homebase Prgm Coord; 5th Grade Teachers Advisory Comm Rep; WV Textbook Advisory Comm 1980-85; WV Assn of Mid Level Educators 1985-; Intnl Rndg Assn, WVRC 1986-; Pleasants Cty Rdng Cncl (VP 1988-, Pres 1990); Alpha Delta Kappa (Mem, Treas 1986-88) 1985-; Teacher of Yr 1988-89; WV Teachers Acad Grad 1987; *office:* Pleasants Cty Mid Sch Box 469 Belmont WV 26134

COCHENOUR, LINDA FEICK, Sixth Grade Teacher; *b:* Charleroi, PA; *m:* Robert John; *ed:* (BS) Ed, 1969, (ME) 1973 CA Univ of PA; *cr:* 5th Grade Teacher Carroll Elem 1969-80, Ginger Hill Elem 1980-85; 6th Grade Teacher Finley Mid Sch 1985-; *ai:* Co-Spon Finley Mid Sch Stu Cncl, Chrldrs; Ringgold Ed Assn 1969-; PA Ed Assn 1969-; NEA 1969-; Finley PTA 1989-; Nom Finley PTA Phoebe Apperson Hearst Outstanding Educators Awd; *office:* Finley Mid Sch Rt 88 Finleyville PA 15332

COCHENOUR, SHARA LEE, English Teacher; *b:* Columbus, OH; *m:* Michael Wayne; *ed:* (BA) Eng, OH St Univ 1986; *cr:* Eng Teacher Westfall HS 1986-; *ai:* Girls Reserve Bsktbl Coach 1986-88.

COCHRAN, BETTY BATES, 7th/8th Soc Stud/Lit Teacher; *b:* Athens, AL; *m:* William F.; *ed:* (BS) Home Ec Ed, Auburn Univ 1973; (MS) Elem Ed, AL A&M 1981; *cr:* Home Ec Teacher Weogulfka HS; Teacher Harvest Sch 1977-; *ai:* Statistician Bsktbl Teams; Past Chrldr & Beta Club Spon; Math Team Coach; NEA, AEA, MCEA 1977-; Nom Jaycees Outstanding Young Teacher of Yr & Harvest Sch Teacher of Yr; *home:* PO Box 193 Madison AL 35758

COCHRAN, BRENDA QUINN, Home Economics Teacher; *b:* Portland, OR; *m:* John Lucas; *ed:* (BA) Home Ec Ed, 1984, (MS) Health Ed, 1990 OR St Univ; *cr:* Home Ec Teacher Crescent Valley HS 1986-; *ai:* Substance Abuse Cncl Mem; Staff Wellness

Month Co-Coord; Menucha Stu Leadership Retreat Staff Rep; FHA Adv; Amer Home Ec Assn; *home:* 742 NW 12th Corvallis OR 97330

COCHRAN, DOT MARTIN, Marketing Teacher/Coordinator; *b:* Mayfield, KY; *m:* J. Ralph; *c:* Kay C. Cayce, James R. Jr.; *ed:* (BS) Distributive Ed, 1956, (MS) Supvr Ed, 1965 Austin Peay Univ; Ed Bus, Murray Univ 1970; Spec Classroom Techniques Courses, Univ of KY; Spec Mrktg Courses, Western Univ; *cr:* Personnel Interviewer USAF 1955-56; Bus Mgr Bethel Coll 1956-64; Mrktg Teacher/Coord Christian Cty HS 1965-; *ai:* Christian Cty HS Advisory Comm; DECA-Mrktg Club Adv; Delta Kappa Gamma Treas 1960-; Kappa Della Pi Pres; Delta Pi Epsilon; Delta Kappa Gamma (Pres, Treas 1970-87); DECA Club Teacher Coord 1965-89, Outstanding Teacher for Region One; Second Dist KY Voc Assn Secy; Bus & Prof Club Schlsp Comm; USAF Recruiting Force Recognition for Outstanding Service 1980; Article Published; *home:* 318 Hillaire Dr Hopkinsville KY 42240

COCHRAN, JANICE MARIE, First Grade Teacher; *b:* Eufaula, AL; *ed:* (AA) Elem Ed, Hillsborough Comm Coll 1978; (BA) Elem Ed, FL St Univ 1980; *cr:* 3rd Grade Teacher 1981-83, 1st Grade Teacher 1983- Mc Donald Elem Sch; *ai:* CTA Mem 1989-; Big Brothers & Sisters, Peer Tutorial Services Teacher 1989-; Mc Knight Achievers Teacher 1986-87; *home:* 3006 46th St Tampa FL 33605

COCHRAN, JEANNE TAYLOR, Spanish Teacher; *b:* Plymouth, MA; *m:* A. Barry; *c:* Alanna, Ryan; *ed:* (BA) Fr/Span, Westminster Coll 1971; Diplome Trimestriel La Sorbonne, Univ of Paris 1970; *cr:* Fr/Span Teacher Cntrl Dauphin Sch Dist 1971-; *ai:* NACEL Host Family 1989; PA St Modern Lang Assn 1988-; *office:* Cntrl Dauphin E HS 626 Rutherford Rd Harrisburg PA 17109

COCHRAN, JOHN ROBERT, US/World History Teacher; *b:* New Orleans, LA; *c:* Kay, John Jr.; *ed:* (BS) Scndry Ed/Phys Ed/His, Univ N AL 1978; *cr:* His Teacher/Coach Hartselle HS 1978-; *ai:* Girls Bsktbl & Sftbl Coach; Fellowship of Chrstn Athletes & Stu Spon; NEA, AL Ed Assn; Hartselle Jaycee Outstanding Phys Educator Awd 1985; Nom for St Awd; *office:* Hartselle HS 604 S Sparkman St Hartselle AL 35640

COCHRAN, MARILYN LERNER, 7th Grade Life Science Teacher; *b:* Kansas City, MO; *c:* Kelli, Matthew; *ed:* (BS) Elem Ed, Univ of KS 1972; Sci/Geophysics, Univ of MO; Grad Stud Geophysics, Energy, Rdng & Intervention Trng; *cr:* 7th Grade Teacher Lincoln Acad 1980-81; 8th/9th Grade Sci Teacher Northwest Mid Sch 1981-84; 8th Grade Sci Teacher Center Jr HS 1984-85; 7th Grade Life Sci Teacher Hocker Grove Mid Sch 1985-; *ai:* Spon Anti Drug Club Choice is Mine; Excl for Ed Comm; NEA 1973-, Excl in Teaching; Ohev Shalom Synagogue (Youth Dir 1990) 1989-; Kehilith Israel Synagogue Teacher of Holocaust 1985-; Dept of Energy Seminar St of TX 1990; Deans List; Scroptimists Schlsp; *home:* 4921 W 64th St Terr Prairie Village KS 66208

COCHRAN, PATRICIA MANN, Secondary Mathematics Teacher; *b:* Fort Smith, AR; *m:* Jim R.; *c:* Amy, Dean; *ed:* (BS) Math, SW OK St Univ 1968; (MS) Math, Tarleton St Univ 1984; *cr:* Math Teacher R L Turner HS 1969-76, Euless Jr HS 1976-77; Cmptr Teacher Upward Bound 1982-83; Math Teacher Stephenville HS 1983-84; Math/Physics Teacher Clarksville HS 1986-; *ai:* Jr Class Spon; Historical Society Spon; Cmptr Math Coach; UIL Calculator Coach; TX Cmptr Educators 1986-; NCTM; ATPE; *office:* Clarkesville HS S Spruce Clarksville TX 75426

COCHRAN, PATSY BURNS, Sixth Grade Teacher; *b:* York, PA; *m:* Robert O.; *c:* Cindy L., Timothy O.; *ed:* (BS) Eng/Elem Ed, York Coll PA 1972; Inst for Personal Effectiveness Marywood Coll; Continuing Ed, Cntrl York Acad; *cr:* 5th Grade Teacher Stony Brook Elem 1973-82; 6th Grade Teacher Cntrl York Mid Sch 1982-; *ai:* All Sch Musical Dir; 6th Grade Dept Chm; Devers PTA Pres 1967-69; Christ Evangelical Luth Pre-Sch Teacher 1966-69; Cntrl York Sch Dist Chm 1984.

COCHRAN, PHILIP CLARK, 6th Grade Teacher; *b:* Twin Falls, ID; *m:* Betty Marie Moldenhauer; *c:* Kathy Cochran Peacock, Mike, Tim, Tom, Richard; *ed:* (BS) Sci, MT St 1952; Elem Ed Cert ID St Univ 1966; *cr:* Teacher Veterans Voc Ag 1952-54; 6th Grade Soc Stud/Math/Sci Teacher Valley Elem 1966-; *ai:* Jr HS Ftbl & Bsktbl Coach 1970-73; Jr HS Ftbl Coach 1974-89; NEA, IEA 1967-; Hazelton City Cncl Valley Booster Club Water Commissioner 1981-85, Youth Service Awd 1989.

COCHRAN, SHIRLEY DAVIS, Instructional Aide; *b:* Dallas, GA; *m:* Bill W.; *c:* Kendall, Darin; *cr:* Instructional Aide Dallas Elem 1979-; *ai:* Whitworth Memorial Baptist Church 1953-; *home:* 1540 Holder Rd Dallas GA 30132

COCHRANE, JUDITH ANNE EKSTRAND, Teacher/Designated Principal; *b:* Winona, MN; *m:* James William; *c:* Steven, Michael, Gregory, Patrick; *ed:* (BA) Ed, MI St Univ 1958; *cr:* 2nd Grade Teacher Lida M Henry Sch 1958-59; 2nd/3rd Grade Teacher Millville Nibley Sch 1960-61; 5th Grade Teacher Idyllwild Elem 1968-70; 2nd-4th Grade Teacher Macdoel Elem 1970-81; Kndgtn Teacher Dorris Elem 1981-89; Teacher/Admin Macdoel Elem 1989-; *ai:* Delta Kappa Gamma 1983-; Butte Valley CTA, NEA (Pres 1986-88, Negotiating Chm 1988-89); Our Lady of Good Counsel Pres 1985-86; Butte Valley Fed Womens Club 1987-88.

COCK, BONNIE KEARLEY, 4th Grade Teacher; *b:* Pensacola, FL; *m:* Hiram Hohnnson Jr.; *c:* Robin, Ryan; *ed:* (AA) General Ed, Pensacola Jr Coll 1970; (BA) Elem Ed, Univ West FL 1971; (MS) Admin/Supervision/Ed, Troy St Univ 1977; Masters Level Ec/Whole Lang/Discipline, Univ of West FL; *cr:* 1st Grade Teacher Myrtle Grove Elem Sch 1971-72; 3rd Grade Teacher Childersburg Elem 1972-73, Rhodes Elem 1976-80; 4th Grade Teacher Berryhill Elem 1980-; *ai:* NEA; SRPE; *office:* Berryhill Elem Sch PO Box 628 Milton FL 32572

COCKERHAM, JUNE W., English Teacher; *b:* Winston-Salem, NC; *m:* Randy H.; *c:* Jessica D.; *ed:* (BS) Eng, ECU 1971; (AG/AP) Eng, Wake Forest Univ 1988; Advanced Placement Eng, Wake Forest Univ; *cr:* 9th-12th Grade Eng Teacher Western Guilford HS 1971-78; Eng Teacher Forsyth Tech Coll 1977-78; 8th/9th Grade Honors Eng Teacher Northwest Jr HS 1984-86; 10th-12th Grade Eng Teacher South Stokes HS 1986-; *ai:* Spon Debate & Spirit Clubs; Steering Comm Southern Assn of Schls & Colls; NC Assn of Educators Career; Assn of Teachers of Gifted Children Mem 1984-; Bus & Prof Womens Assn 1985-; Mem NC Writing Project; *office:* S Stokes Sr HS R 1 Walnut Cove NC 27052

COCKRELL, LISA BOONE, English/His/Theater Teacher; *b:* Wichita Falls, TX; *c:* Jennifer M.; *ed:* (BS) Ed, Midwestern St Univ 1981; *cr:* Eng Teacher Throckmorton HS 1982-85; Eng/His/Theater Teacher Peaster HS 1985-; *ai:* UIL Literary Coach & One-Act Play Dir; Drama Club Spon; NCTE 1982-85; USITT 1988-89; ATPE 1982-86; *office:* Peaster HS PO Box 129 Hwy 920 Peaster TX 76074

COCKRILL, LEE J., English Dept Chairperson; *ed:* (BA) Eng, Univ of MO 1970; (MA) Eng/Ed, Univ of MO Kansas City 1973-74; *cr:* Teacher Caruthersville Sr HS 1970-73; Teacher/Eng Dept Chairperson Harrisonville Sr HS 1973-; *ai:* Dist Curr Comm Mem; Harrisonville Stu Cncl Spon; St of MO Stu Cncl Bd of Dirs 1989-, Camp & St Cnslr, Government Day & Harrisonville City Comm; NEA; *office:* Harrisonville Sr HS 1504 E Elm St Harrisonville MO 64701

COCKS, MARGARET C., Third Grade Teacher; *b:* Morenci, AZ; *ed:* (BS) Elem Ed, N AZ Univ 1978; Grad Work N AZ Univ, Univ of AZ; *cr:* Kndgtn/3rd Grade Teacher Highland Primary Sch 1979-; *home:* Box 15 Snowflake AZ 85937

CODER, SUSAN BRUBAKER, 3rd Grade Teacher; *b:* Marysville, OH; *m:* Larry E.; *c:* Kimberly Godfrey, Douglas L.; *ed:* (BA) Elem, OH St Univ 1964; Teachers Cert, Ashland Coll; *cr:* 4th Grade Teacher Raymond Sch System 1960-61; 3rd Grade Teacher Maryville Exempted Village Schls 1961-; *ai:* Impact Comm; Intervention Comm; NEA 1960-62/1965-; OH Ed Assn 1960-62/1965-; Marysville Ed Assn 1960-62/1965-; Aletheia Society Pres/Secy/Treas 1976-; *home:* 222 Ash St Marysville OH 43040

CODERE, LOIS BAILEY, Math Teacher; *b:* Flint, MI; *m:* John A.; *ed:* (BA) Math 1966, (MA) Math/Ed 1970 Northern MI Univ; *cr:* Math Teacher Calumet Public Schls 1966-68, Lake Linden-Hubbell Public Schls 1968-; *ai:* Coach Jr Varsity Girls Bsktbl; Sch Improvement Comm; NEA, MI Ed Assn, MI Cncl of Teachers of Math; MI Tech Univ Awd of Academic Excl 1984; Scholastic Coach Magazine Natl HS Coaching Awd 1987; Lake Linden Hubbell Public Schls Employee of Yr 1988-89; *office:* Lake Linden-Hubbell Public Sch 601 Calumet St Lake Linden MI 49945

CODIEUX, THOMAS HENRY, 7th Grade Sci/Math Teacher; *b:* New Bedford, MA; *m:* Marilyn T. Freitas; *c:* Aaron D.; *ed:* (BA) His, SE MA Univ 1977; *cr:* 6th Grade Soc Stud Teacher 1978-79, 7th Grade Sci/Math Teacher 1980, 6th Grade Sci/Math/Rdng Teacher 1981-89, 7th Grade Sci/Math Teacher 1990 Dartmouth Mid Sch; *ai:* Dartmouth HS Asst Frosh, Jr Var, Var Ftbl Coach, Asst Var Track Coach 1980-; NEA, MA Teachers Assn 1977-; MA HS Ftbl Coaches Assn 1974-89; MA HS Track Coaches Assn 1980-89; Dartmouth Recreation Supvr 1974-84; Dartmouth Hall of Fame Comm Vice-Chm 1988-; *office:* Dartmouth Mid Sch 529 Hawthorn St Dartmouth MA 02747

CODY, MICHELE L., Seventh/Eighth Grade Teacher; *b:* Staten Island, NY; *c:* Jennifer; *ed:* (BS) Elem Ed, Seton Hall 1970; *cr:* 5th Grade Teacher St Vincent De Paul 1964-66, Blessed Sacrament 1966-70; 7th/8th Grade Math Teacher St John Villa 1970-73, St Charles 1976-; *ai:* Bowling Moderator; Mini Marathon Coord; Fed of Cath Teachers Delegate 1976-; Drug/Alcohol Rehab Ed Volunteer 1986-, Teacher of Yr 1988; *office:* St Charles 200 Penn Ave Staten Island NY 10306

CODY, THOMAS GERALDINE, CSJ, 3rd Grade Teacher; *b:* St Louis, MO; *ed:* (BA) Elem Ed, Fontbonne Coll 1963; (MS) Ed/Spec Ed, IL St Univ 1976; *cr:* 3rd Grade Teacher St Louis Cathedral 1976-83, Teacher Holy Cross 1983-88; Spec Ed Bishop Healy 1988-89; 1st Grade Teacher St Anne 1989-; *ai:* Fund Raising Act for Sch; ASCD 1988-.

COE, SEXTON EARLIE, 7th/8th Grade Teacher; *b:* Dobson, NC; *m:* Brenda; *c:* Lori A., Shannon R.; *ed:* (BS) His, Appalachian St Univ 1970; *cr:* Teacher Copeland Elem 1970-; *ai:* Math Counts Spon; Coaching; *office:* Copeland Elem Sch Rt 2 Box 439 Dobson NC 27017

COEN, LAWRENCE ARTHUR, English Teacher; *b:* Perth Amboy, NJ; *ed:* (BA) Eng, Point Park Coll 1969; Teaching Credentials Point Park Coll; Grad Work Univ of Pittsburgh & Univ of MD; *cr:* Eng Teacher Interboro Sr HS 1972-75, La Plata HS 1975-; *ai:* Classic Cinema Club Spon; MD St Teachers Assn, Educl Assn of Charles Cty; *office:* La Plata HS Box 790 Radio Station Rd La Plata MD 20646

COENEN, MATTHEW JOHN, 6th-8th Grade Math Teacher; *b:* Harlan, IA; *m:* Kaye Ann Fazio; *c:* Matthew, Ann; *ed:* (MSE) Supervision, Drake Univ 1969; (BA) Philosophy, Conception Seminary 1965; *cr:* Teacher Casady Elem 1967-72, Pleasant Hill Elem 1972-83, Mc Combs Mid Sch 1983-; *ai:* Phase III Comm; TA Coord; B/C Co-Chairperson; Team Leader; NEA, IA St Ed Assn, Des Moines Ed Assn 1967-; Norwalk Sch System Sch Bd 1977-; Norwalk Swimming Pool Comm Treas 1989-; Lakewood Benefited Sanitary Dist Treas 1986-; Des Moines Jaycee Teacher Of Yr 1969; IA Assn of Sch Bd Mem; *home:* 4728 Candlewick Dr Norwalk IA 50211

COFER, CATHY SMILEY, 8th Grade Lang Arts Teacher; *b:* Louisville, KY; *m:* William Harold; *c:* Blair, Brad; *ed:* (BS) Elem Ed/Spec Ed, Western KY Univ 1977; (MED) Learning & Behavior Disorders, Univ of Louisville 1980; Admin, Western KY Univ; *cr:* LD Teacher 1977-84, Lang Arts Teacher 1984- Mount Washington Mid; *ai:* Chrldng Coach; Spelling Bee Coord; *home:* 8816 Wood Valley Ln Louisville KY 40299

COFFEY, DONNA HOSKINS, 7th/8th Grade Lang Art Teacher; *b:* Danville, KY; *m:* Donald Stephen; *c:* James S.; *ed:* (BA) Elem Ed, Univ of KY 1970; (MA) Elem Ed, Eastern KY Univ 1976; *cr:* 6th Grade Teacher Vine Grove Elem 1970-72; 6th-8th Grade Teacher Boyle Cty Elem 1972-79, Hustonville Elem 1979-; *ai:* Guidance Comm; 8th Grade Spon; Jr HS & Spelling Bee Coord for Sch; Beta Club Spon 1983-, Awd 1988; Conservation Dist Distinguished Service 1977, 1981-83 & 1989; Boyle Co Dist Outstanding Teacher 1973; Hustonville Baptist Church Childrens Dir 1978-; Lincoln Cty 4-H Ldr 1979-86; Outstanding Alumnus 1983; Cmmty & Church Choir, Ensemble Mem; Soprano Soloist; *office:* Hustonville Elem Sch College St PO Box 6 Hustonville KY 40437

COFFEY, FRANCIS G., Fifth Grade Teacher; *b:* Milford, MA; *m:* Linda Lavell; *c:* Jennifer, Francis; *ed:* (BA) Liberal Art, Worcester Jr 1970; (BS) Elem Ed, Fitchburg St 1973; (MS) Leadership/Admin, Worcester St 1982; *cr:* 5th Grade Teacher Milford Public Schls 1973-; *ai:* Little League Coach 1988-; *home:* 114 Green St Hopedale MA 01747

COFFIN, ELIZABETH GRING, Principal/Teacher/Dir/Owner; *b:* Cambridge, MA; *m:* David Page; *ed:* (BA) Eng Lit/Ed, Mary WA Coll 1971; (Diploma) Nursery & Primary Montessori, St Nicholas/London 1977; Addl Training Early Childhood Ed Amer Univ 1979; *cr:* K & 6th Grade Rdng Teacher Highland Sch 1971-72; Directress the Boxwood Sch 1972-; *ai:* Natl Ctr for Montessori Ed; Keep Fauquier Clean 1989-; VA Adopt a Highway 1989- (1st Sch in Cty); Recognition By Civic Organ Concerned with Environment; Boxwood Sch Invented Litter Lickers; Rally Parents to Help for Spring Clean-Ups; Celebrate Earth Day; Writer of Letters to the Editor; *office:* The Boxwood Sch 507 Winchester St Warrenton VA 22186

COFFMAN, ANNA MARIE, Music Specialist; *b:* Seoul, S Korea; *c:* Coy D.; *ed:* (BA) Music Ed/Piano Performance, Northeastern St Univ 1978; Grad Stud; *cr:* Music Specialist C E Gray Elem & Bixby Public Sch 1979-; *ai:* C E Gray Fine Arts Play, Swing Choir; NEA (Staff Dev Comm 1987-89) 1979-; OK Ed Assn 1979-; Bixby Ed Assn; OK Music Educators Assn, Amer Choral Dirs Assn 1980-; OK Elem Honor Choir 1982, 1984; Amer Choral Dirs Childrens Honor Choir 1983; SAGTA Clinician 1987-; *office:* C E Gray Elem Sch PO Box 160 Bixby OK 74008

COFFMAN, JANET HOLLAR, History Teacher; *b:* Rockingham Cty, VA; *m:* Glenn C.; *c:* Greg; *ed:* (BS) His, JMU 1969; *cr:* Teacher Dayton HS 1946-47; Substitute Teacher Rockingham Cty & Harrisonburg Public Schls 1955-67; Teacher Harrisonburg HS 1967-; *ai:* Jr Class Spon; Excl Comm; NEA, VEA, HEA 1975-; Hospital Auxiliary 1990; *home:* 211 Maryland Ave Harrisonburg VA 22801

COFFMAN, LOUISE WINWARD, English Teacher; *b:* Preston, ID; *m:* Lance; *c:* Kent W.; *ed:* (BS) Phys Ed, Brigham Young Univ 1966; (MED) Phys Ed, Univ of ID 1969; Eng; *cr:* Teacher Snowflake Union HS 1966-67; Teacher/Coach Walla Walla Comm Coll 1967-69; Teacher Crane Elem Dist 1969-76; Teacher/Coach W WY Comm Coll 1976-78; Teacher Crane Elem Dist 1978-84, Yuma HS 1984-; *ai:* Mat Maids Club Adv; Crane Ed Assn Pres 1974-75; NCTE 1988-; NEA, AZ Ed Assn, CTA 1973-; Alpha Delta Kappa Pres 1990; *office:* Yuma HS 400 S 6th Ave Yuma AZ 85364

COFFMAN, PRISCILLA CHAPMAN, 5th Grade Teacher; *b:* Essex, MD; *m:* Dale Lawrence Jr.; *c:* John T., Maria A.; *ed:* (AA) Liberal Arts, Anne Arundel Comm Coll 1964; (BS) Sociology/Math, Univ of MD 1966; (MED) Early Chldhd Ed, Towson Univ 1974; NE MO St Univ, Univ of N IA, Univ of IA, Marycrest Coll; *cr:* Kndgtn Teacher Pumphrey & Linthicum Schls 1966-74; Substitute Teacher Cardinal Schls 1974-79; 5th Grade Teacher Cardinal Cmmty Schls 1979-; *ai:* Speech Contest Coord; Lang Art Curr Comm; Talented & Gifted Support Team; Sci Outdoor Ed Coord; IA Rdng Assn Research Reporter 1988-; NEA; IA St Ed Assn Local Negotiations Comm 1988-89; Eldon Ec Dev Comm Worker; Wapello Cty Hospice (Bd Mem 1977-80, Volunteer 1978-) Service Awd 1980; St Aloysius Church CCD Coord 1979-84, Service Awd 1984; PEO (Guard, Schlsp Chm) 1990; Published Poems in Magazines; *office:* Cardinal Cmmty Schls RR 1 Box 275 Eldon IA 52554

COFFMAN, RONNA LARGE, English/Journalism Teacher; *b:* San Angelo, TX; *m:* Jimmy D.; *c:* Collin, Kellye, Kyle; *ed:* (BS) Eng, Sul Ross St Univ 19 74; Addl Studies Journalism; Eng; Ed; *cr:* Teacher Monahans HS 1981-; *ai:* UIL Coord for Academics; Jouralism Spon; Annual Spon; Literary Criticism Spon; ATEE; NCTE.

COFFMAN, TERRY RICHARD, Soc Stud Teacher/Ftbl Coach; *b:* Lima, OH; *m:* Sally Ann Ferguson; *c:* Cassandra, Jason, Joshua; *ed:* (BSED) Soc Stud, OH Northern Univ 1966; (MSED) Ed, St Univ of NY Potsdam 1988; *cr:* Spec Ed Teacher Perry HS 1966-69; Soc Stud Teacher Carthage Cntrl HS 1969-; *ai:* Head Ftbl Coach; NY St Cncl Soc Stud; Elks 1970-; *office:* Carthage Cntrl HS Martin Street Rd Carthage NY 13619

COFFMAN, TIM J., Science Instructor; *b:* Richwood, WV; *m:* Judith Lynn Green; *c:* Joshua; *ed:* (BA) Bio/General Sci Comp, Glenville St Coll 1978; WV Coll of Grad Stud; *cr:* Teacher Richwood Jr HS 1979-; Professor Whitewater Guide USA Whitewater 1988-; *ai:* Environmental Awareness Club Adv Richwood Jr HS; Explorer Scouts Post Adv; WV Ed Assn 1981-; Richwood Jaycees Treas 1981-83; Issack Walton League 1979-; Summersville Archery Club 1988-; Richwood Archery Club, Wadcutters Pistol Club 1987-; *office:* Richwood Jr HS Valley Ave Richwood WV 26261

COFIELD, LAURA JEAN, Biology/Chemistry Teacher; *b:* Franklin, GA; *ed:* (BS) Bio Ed, Auburn Univ 1979; (MED) Bio Ed, W GA Coll 1985; *cr:* Bio/Chem Teacher Griffin HS 1979-; *ai:* Jr Class Spon; Jr Steering Comm Adv; Phi Delta Kappa 1987-; GA Ed Assn 1979-; Griffin Spalding Ed Assn Treas 1979-; Bus & Prof Womens Club 1984-86; Griffin HS Teacher of Yr 1987-88; *home:* 913 Morningside Dr Griffin GA 30223

COGGIN, DANNY KEITH, Director of Bands; *b:* Madison, TN; *m:* Patricia Bailey; *c:* Andrew, Katie; *ed:* (BS) Music Ed, TN Tech Univ 1979; *cr:* Assoc Dir 1979-88, Dir of Bands 1988- Bradley Cntrl HS; *ai:* E TN Band Assn (Jazz Chm 1988-89) 1979-; TN Bandmasters 1982-; Phi Beta Mu 1986-; Natl Band Assn 1984-; *office:* Bradley Cntrl HS 1000 S Lee Hwy Cleveland TN 37311

COGHLAN, ROSEMARIE M., English Teacher; *b:* Darby, PA; *m:* Raymond; *c:* Raymond, Brigid A.; *ed:* (BA) Eng, Chestnut Hill Coll 1971; (MA) Eng, Villanova Univ 1977; *cr:* Eng Teacher St Huberts HS 1971-72; Eng Substitute Teacher/Lay Reader W Chester Area Sch Dist 1974-76, 1978-83; Eng Instr DE Cty Comm Coll 1981-83; Eng Teacher/Dean of Stus Villa Maria Acad HS 1983-; *ai:* Service Club Asst Moderator; NCTE, PCTE; BSA Troop #149 Treas 1985-89; Incentive Monies Grant W Chester Area Sch Dist; Mid St Steering & Visiting Comm; Whos Who in Amer Ed 1989-; *office:* Villa Maria Acad Green Tree Malvern PA 19355

COHEN, JANET SAMBUCETTI, Science Teacher; *b:* Woodland, CA; *m:* Michael; *c:* Matthew, Annelisa; *ed:* (BA) Sociology, CA St Univ Sonoma 1974; *cr:* Math Teacher Greenfield Sch 1975-78; 4th Grade Teacher 1978-89, Cmptr Specialist/6th Grade Sci Teacher 1989- Gold Trail Sch; *ai:* Track Coach; SIP Phys Ed Component Chm; AIMS Teacher Cty Office; CUE 1989-; CAPHERD, ASCD 1987-; Womens Soccer 1984-; Sftbl Assn 1979-; St Patricks Church 1980-; Mentor Teacher; *office:* Gold Trail Sch 889 Cold Springs Rd Placerville CA 95667

COHEN, JOAN HALLEEN, Mathematics Teacher; *b:* New York, NY; *ed:* (AB) Math, Herbert Lehman of CUNY 1969; (MAT) Math, GA St Univ 1988; Univ of WI 1970-73; Phillips Exeter Acad Math & Cmptr Conferences, 1988, 1989; Duke Univ Teaching Fellow Summer 1989; Woodrow Wilson Natl Fellowship Fnd Princeton 1990; *cr:* Math Teacher Columbia HS 1974-77; Educl Therapist Peachford Hospital 1977-79; Math Consultant Discovery Learning 1980-81; Math Dept Chm Yeshive HS 1982-84; Math Teacher Sequoyah HS & Cross Keys HS 1984-; *ai:* Mu Alpha Theta & Cross Keys Environmental Club Spon; Teaching Assistantship Univ of WI 1970-73; Teaching Fellow Duke Univ TIP Prgm 1989; STAR Teacher 1988; Woodrow Wilson Fellow Summer 1990; *office:* Cross Keys HS 1626 N Druid Hills Rd Atlanta GA 30319

COHEN, JOAN S., Teacher of Mentally Gifted; *b:* Philadelphia, PA; *m:* Stanley E.; *c:* Lori Mandelzweig, Barbara Weinstein, Marci; *ed:* (BS) Elem Ed, 1956, (MED) Elem Ed, 1971 Temple Univ; Psych, Ed of Gifted Children; *cr:* Elem Teacher 1956-74, Teacher of Mentally Gifted 1974- Philadelphia Sch Dist; *ai:* Coach & Judge Odyssey of Mind Teams; Judge De Valley Sci Fair; Teaching Shakespeare for Children Holy Family Coll; PA Assn Gifted Ed; Bnai Brith Educators Lodge 1986-87; Cited by Philadelphia Sch Dist, City Cncl, PA House of Rep, Senate of PA; *home:* 9724 Chapel Rd Philadelphia PA 19115

COHEN, MERYL, Science/Chemistry Teacher; *b:* New York, NY; *m:* Harmon; *ed:* (BS) Chem, Hunter Coll CUNY 1966; (MS) Sci Ed, Syracuse Univ; Prof Diploma Ed Admin, Long Island Univ; Service Courses Madeline Hunter; *cr:* Lab Teacher New York City Public Schls 1966-67; Sci Teacher Jericho Jr/Sr HS 1967-68, Syracuse Public Schls 1968-70; Chem Teacher Riverhead HS 1970-; *ai:* Steering, RCFA Exec Comm Mem; Mid States Evaluation Building Rep; NYSUT, NSTA, SCSTA Mem; *office:* Riverhead HS 700 Harrison Ave Riverhead NY 11901

COHEN, MORLEY JAY, Science Co-Chair; *b:* Los Angeles, CA; *ed:* (BA) Psych, Sonoma St Univ 1972; (MA) Educl Psych/Counseling/Therapy, CA St Univ Northridge 1984; Scndry Ed Sci; *cr:* Sci Chm Pinecrest Intermediate Sch 1980-87; Sci Co-Chm Chaparral Mid Sch 1988-; *ai:* Chess Club Spon; Stock Market Club; Sci Fair Coord 1981-87; CA Sci Teachers Assn, NSTA, CA Teachers Assn 1988-; CA Energy Ed Forum Excl in Energy Research Awd; Naval Civil Engineering Laboratory Perpetual Trophy Awd; *home:* 1338 Calle Crisantemo Thousand Oaks CA 91360

COHEN, NICKI HOROWITZ, Social Studies Teacher; *b:* Patterson, NJ; *m:* William; *c:* Lisa R. Horowitz, Neil S. Horowitz, Adam R. Horowitz; *ed:* (BED) Elem Ed, Univ of Miami 1965; (MED) Scndry Soc Sci, Winthrop Coll 1988; *cr:* 6th Grade Teacher Plantation Park Elem 1965-66; 5th/6th Grade Teacher Gardner Park Elem 1979-82; 9th Grade Teacher Cramerton Jr HS 1983-85, Belmont Jr HS 1985-; *ai:* Soc Stud Dept Chm; Sch Store & Stock Market Game Spon; Gaston Cty Soc Stud Textbook Selection, Economic Ed Advisory Comm 1978-88; Gaston Cty Cmmty Based Alternatives Task Force Chm 1978-80; NCSS, NC Cncl for Soc Stud 1983-; NC Assn of Educators 1979-88; Jr League Gaston Cty 1975-83; Taft Inst Two Party Government Fellow; Article Published by Center for Research & Dev Law Related Ed 1987; *office:* Belmont Jr HS 110 Central Ave Belmont NC 28012

COHN, HOWARD MARTIN, Social Studies Teacher; *b:* Bronx, NY; *m:* Carol Susan Kaplan; *c:* Stephen M.; *ed:* (AA) Liberal Art, Bronx Comm Coll 1964; (BA) His, City Coll of NY 1966; *cr:* Soc Stud Teacher Jr HS 22X 1966-71, Jr HS 144X 1971-80, Jr HS 142X 1980-; *ai:* Knights of Phythias 1968-; *office:* John Philip Sousa Jr HS 142X 3750 Baychester Ave Bronx NY 10466

COKER, ONITA COBB, 3rd Grade Teacher; *b:* Rogers, TX; *m:* Louis V.; *c:* Connie Higdon, Alan, David; *ed:* (BS) Elem Ed, Univ of North TX 1954; (MED) Rdng Ed, TX Womans Univ 1988; *cr:* 3rd Grade Teacher Fort Worth ISD 1954-59; Kndgtn Teacher Richland Hills Baptist Private Sch 1961-62; 4th Grade Teacher 1971-72; 3rd Grade Teacher 1972- Birdville ISD; *ai:* Grade Level Chairperson; NEA 1954-59/1971-; TX St Teachers Assn 1954-59/1971-; Delta Kappa Gamma 1985-; TX St Rdng Assn 1988-; Richland Hills Public Lib Bd (Mem 1984- VP 88); TX Congress PTO Life Mbrshp Awd 85; *office:* Holiday Heights Elem Sch 5221 Susan Lee Ln N Richland Hills TX 76180

COLANGELO, JANET WSZOLEK, 1st Grade Teacher; *b:* Hammond, IN; *m:* Frank A.; *c:* Denise, Jenna; *ed:* (BSED) Elem Ed, Northern IL Univ 1970; *cr:* 3rd Grade Teacher 1970-71, 2nd Grade Teacher 1971-82, 1st Grade Teacher 1983- Wilson Sch; *ai:* AFT Secy 1977-79.

COLARUSSO, KATHERINE M., Physical Education Teacher; *b:* Northampton, PA; *m:* Angelo; *ed:* (BS) Health/Phys Ed, W Chester St Univ 1972; *cr:* Phys Ed Teacher Franklin-Wolf & Washington Building 1972-87, Lehigh Township Sch 1987-; *ai:* Lehigh Ski Club; Northampton Sch Dist Wellness Comm; Amer Heart Assn Ladies Benefit; Golf Tourney Comm; *home:* 5168 Lincoln Ave Whitehall PA 18052

COLASURDO, ANTHONY P., English Dept Coordinator; *b:* Jersey City, NJ; *m:* Pamela Mc Grath; *c:* Anthony, Nicholas; *ed:* (BA) Eng, St Peters Coll 1972; (MA) Rdng, Jersey City St Coll 1976; Working Toward Supervisory Certificate & Prins License; *cr:* Teacher Weehawken HS 1972-; *ai:* Newspaper & Yrbk Adv; Varsity Bsbl Coach; NCTE, NEA, NJ Ed Assn, Journalism Ed Assn; Columbia Scholastic Press Assn; Governors Teacher Recognition Awd 1990; Subject Area Coord; *office:* Weehawken HS 53 Liberty Pl Weehawken NJ 07087

COLATRUGLIO, KENNETH ANTHONY, English Department Chairman; *b:* Tiffin, OH; *m:* Margaret Kirian; *c:* Robert, William, Mary A. Fricker, David; *ed:* (BS) Eng, Bowling Green St Univ 1968; OH Writing Project; *cr:* Eng Teacher Sandusky Public Schls 1968-; *ai:* Var Wrestling Head Coach; SSWOA 1975-; NEA, OEA, NEOTA, SEA 1978-; Amer Legion 1988-; Italian Amer Bro 1990; OH Writing Project Grant; *office:* Sandusky HS 2130 Hayes Ave Sandusky OH 44870

COLAVITO, BARBARA J., Fifth Grade Teacher; *b:* Glens Falls, NY; *m:* Joseph W.; *c:* Katherine A. Colavito De Ninis, Joseph W. II; *ed:* (BS) Elem Ed, SUCO Oneonta 1960; *cr:* 3rd Grade Teacher Binghamton Sch Dist 1961-64; 2nd Grade Teacher 1968, 5th Grade Teacher 1968- Vestal Cntrl Schls; *ai:* Vestal Teachers Assn, NEA; *office:* Vestal Schls Main St Vestal NY 13850

COLBERT, DAVID CHARLES, Fourth Grade Teacher; *b:* Johnstown, PA; *m:* Carol Flook; *c:* Lindsay, Carrie; *ed:* (BSED) Elem Ed, Indiana Univ of PA 1972; PA Sci Teachers Ed Prgm; Drug Ed Trng Prgm; *cr:* Teacher Conemaugh Valley Elem Sch 1972-; *ai:* Conemaugh Valley Youth League 4th-6th Grade Girls Bsktbl Volunteer Coach; PA St Ed Assn, NEA, Conemaugh Valley Ed Assn 1972-; Conemaugh Valley Volunteer Fire Company, Franklinboro Volunteer Fire Company 1966-; Jackson Township Rod & Gun Club 1985-; Conemaugh Township Cambria Cty Assessor 1990; Conemaugh Valley Sch Bd Commendation 1984; Conemaugh Valley Sch Dist House of Rep Awd 1985; *home:* RD 2 Box 94 Johnstown PA 15904

COLBERT, LARRY D., Music Teacher & Band Director; *b:* Athens, GA; *m:* Glenda Haynes; *c:* Kenya N., Khary N.; *ed:* (BSED) Music Ed, Albany St Coll 1974; (MED) Music Ed, GA St Univ 1978; *cr:* Music Teacher Jackson Bd of Ed 1976-78; Music Teacher/Band Dir Monroe Elem Sch 1978-; *ai:* Creative Visions Fnd Treas; Dir of Monroe Elem Band & Chorus; Adv of Monroe Elem Drama Club; GA Music Educators Assn, Music Educators Natl Conference, Walton Assn of Educators, GA Assn of Educators, NEA; Walton Assn of Educators Humanitarian 1988; Sardis Presbyn Church (Secy 1960, Elder 1986-, Treas 1985-); Monroe Elem Teacher of Yr; Superior Ratings Band Performing Groups 10th Dist Festival; *office:* Monroe Elem Sch Bold Springs Ave Monroe GA 30655

COLBERT, NATALIE FISHER, Orchestra Teacher; *b:* Atlanta, GA; *m:* Reginald Raul; *c:* Alexandra, Jonathan; *ed:* (BM) Music Ed, 1979, (BM) Flute Performance 1979 Univ of GA; Orch Teaching Wkshps 1978; Conducting Wkshp Lawrence Univ; *cr:* Elem/Mid Sch Teacher W T Jackson Elem, Sch Orch Teacher E Rivers Elem, Teacher Sutton Mid Sch 1980-; *ai:* Conductor Atlanta Public Schls Youth Orch; Amer String Teacher Assn St Secy 1987-; Natl Sch Orch Assn; Phi Delta Kappa Outstanding Teacher 1988; Atlanta City Schls Outstanding Music Teacher Academic Achievement Awd; Sutton Mid Sch Teacher of Yr 1989; *office:* Sutton Mid Sch 4360 Powers Ferry Rd Atlanta GA 30327

COLBY, GARY ALLAN, Social Studies Teacher; *b:* Springfield, MA; *m:* Tammy Lynn; *ed:* (BA) His Ed, Notre Dame Coll 1985; *cr:* Soc Stud Teacher Franklin HS 1985-; *ai:* Class Adv 1985-89; Jr Var Bsktbl & Var Sftbl Coach; NHS Faculty Cncl; Co-Founder Rallies R Us Pep Rally Duo; NH Soc Stud Cncl 1985-; Yrbk Dedication 1989; *office:* Franklin HS 115 Central St Franklin NH 03235

COLDREN, DOROTHY ANN, Fourth Grade Math Teacher; *b:* Louisville, MS; *m:* Thomas; *ed:* (BA) Elem Ed, E MS Jr Coll 1955; (BSE) Elem Ed, Delta St Univ 1957; (MA) Elem Ed, George Peabody Coll 1963; Industries in Ed, AR St 1985; *cr:* Teacher Hughes Elem Sch 1957-63, Magruder Elem Sch 1963-65, Del Monte Elem Sch 1965-66, Stilwell Elem Sch 1966-67, Hughes Elem Sch 1967-; *ai:* Departmental Math Chm; Personal Policies Comm; York Cty 4th Grade Teachers Chm 1963-64; Grade Level Chm 1988-89; Assn Chldhd Ed Intnl (VP 1980-81, Secy 1978-79); Pro Publicity Chairperson 1974-75; Parent-Teacher Life Membership 1983-84; Delta Kappa Gamma Schlsp 1963; AR Educl Assn, NEA, VA Educl Assn; Delta Kappa Gamma VP 1980-81; Classroom Teachers Assn Pres 1978-79; York Cty Teachers Assn, PTO; 1st Baptist Church Sunday Sch Teacher 1959-62; Outstanding Elem Teacher of America 1973-74; Most Successful Teacher 1989-; Trng Union Teacher 1957-58; *home:* PO Box 601 Hughes AR 72348

COLDREN, IDA FLO, Teacher; *b:* Silsbee, TX; *m:* Bill Lawrence; *c:* Candyce C. Key, Cade L., Kyle L., Cody; *ed:* (BS) Home Ec, TX Chrstn Univ 1951; Elem Cert & Gifted & Talented Cert Courses; *cr:* Teacher Silsbee Ind Sch Dist 1951, Midwest City Ind Sch Dist 1953-55, Amarillo Ind Sch Dist 1959-60, Silsbee Ind Sch Dist 1960-61, Houston Ind Sch Dist 1967-68,Silsbee Ind Sch Dist 1968-72, Van Vleck Ind Sch Dist 1973-80, Silsbee Ind Sch Dist 1980-; *ai:* Teams Coach, UIL Literary, Spelling, Ready Writing, Prose & Poetry Rdng Spon, Accompanist Jr HS Band, UIL Solo & Ensemble; Alpha Delta Kappa Pres 1986-87; Silsbee Womans Club Chorus Accompanist; *home:* PO Box 1402 Silsbee TX 77656

COLDWELL, LOUISE DENNINGTON, Physical Education Teacher; *b:* Springfield, MO; *m:* Stephen Wayne; *c:* Kevin J.; *ed:* (BSED) Health/Phys Ed, SW MO St Univ 1972; Certified CPR Instr; *cr:* 7th-12th Grade Girls Phys Ed/Health Teacher 1972-89, 9th-12th Grade Var Girls Track Teacher 1972- Liberty HS; *ai:* 9th-12th Grade Girls Var Track; 7th Grade Class Spon; BSA (Public Relations 1988-89, Comm Chm 1989-); Chapel Hill Church (Camp Cnslr 1972-80, Asst Clerk 1987-); Outstanding Scndry Educator of America 1974; Outstanding Young Women of America 1976; MO St HS Act Assn MUOA Ofcl 1977-; Dist Track Champions 1986; *home:* Rt 2 Box 2900 Mountain View MO 65548

COLE, CECILIA SANDERS, 6th Grade Teacher; *b:* Lebanon, KY; *m:* Charles W.; *c:* Jonathan, Stephen; *ed:* (AA) St Catharine Jr Coll 1974; (BA) Elem Ed - Magna Cum Laude, Transylvania Univ 1976; (MS) Rdng Specialist, E KY Univ 1978; Rank I E KY Univ 1980; *cr:* 6th Grade Teacher Mercer Cty Elem 1976-; *ai:* 6th Grade Chorus Asst Dir; Magazine Ed; Mercer Cty PTO (Pres 1978-80, VP 1980-82, Spec Projects Chm); Mercer Cty Ed Assn Secy 1988-; KEA Mem; Pioneer Baptist Church Childrens Choir Asst; KY Bus Woman 1980; Whos Who in HS & Jr Coll & Univs; *office:* Mercer Cty Elem Sch Rt 5 Harrodsburg KY 40330

COLE, CHARLES EVERETT, JR., Jr HS History/English Teacher; *b:* Louisville, KY; *m:* Robin Leigh Watkins; *ed:* (BS) His/Scndry Ed, Asbury Coll 1983; Grad Sch Hood Coll; *cr:* Teacher/Coach Jessamine Cty Public Schls 1983-85, Montgomery Cty Public Schls 1985-86, Liberty Chrstn Acad 1986-; *ai:* Var Boys Bsktbl Coach; Asst Athletic Dir; Teacher of Yr 1988-89; *home:* 6744 Centennial Dr Reynoldsburg OH 43068

COLE, DAVID EUGENE, Fourth Grade Teacher; *b:* Centralia, IL; *m:* Peggy Shahan; *c:* Kevin, Kelly, Tricia, Terry; *ed:* (BS) Soc Stud, S IL Univ Edwardsville 1970; (MSB) Ed Admin, IL St Univ 1974; *cr:* 6th Grade Teacher Wilson Elem 1970-76, Washington Intermediate 1976-77; 4th Grade Teacher Sunset Hills Elem 1977-89, Wilson Intermediate 1989-; *ai:* Taught Gifted Prgm; Math, Soc Stud, Dev Math & Rdng Objectives, Newspaper in Ed Comm; NEA; 1st Presbyn Church; Newspapers in Classroom Wkshp Presenter; *home:* 1513 S 8th Pekin IL 61554

COLE, DON, 6th Grade Teacher; *b:* Redwood Falls, MN; *m:* Sally Anne Madson; *c:* Patrick, Jayson, Charles; *ed:* (BS) Elem Ed, Southwest St Univ 1971; (MED) Elem Ed, Univ of MN 1987; *cr:* 6th Grade Teacher Willmar Sch Dist 1971-; *ai:* Asst Var Hockey, Cross Cntry, Tennis Coach; Willmar Ed Assn Secy 1988-; Willmar Hockey Assn VP 1974-76, Parents of Yr 1978; *home:* 521 SW 10th St Willmar MN 56201

COLE, DONNA COPE, English Teacher; *b:* Borger, TX; *m:* H. Donnell; *c:* D Lana C.; *ed:* (AA) Ed, Victoria Coll 1974; (BS) Elem Ed, TX A&M Univ 1977; (MS) Rdng/Lang Art, Univ of Houston 1982; Trainer NJ Writing Project TX; Danforth Leadership Fellow; Strategic Planning; *cr:* 1st Grade Teacher Presbyn Day Sch 1977-78; K-8th Grade Music Teacher William Offer & Dudley Magnet & Mitchell Elem 1978-82; 1st-3rd Grade Teacher of Gifted Talented Shields Elem 1982-84; 6th-8th Grade Choral Dir/Rdng/Eng Teacher Howell Intermediate 1984-89; 10th Grade Eng Teacher Stroman HS 1989-; *ai:* Stu Cncl, NHS, Annual Spon; Danforth, Strategic Planning, Effective Schls Comms; TX Classroom Teachers (Pres 1989-) 1979-; Alpha Delta Kappa (Pres 1982-85) 1982-; Delta Kappa Gamma, Schlsp 1988-; Crossroads Educl Cncl; Victoria Family Outreach Bd Mem; Jr League Public Relations Dir 1980-; Victoria Symphony Bd Prgm Chm 1979-; Victoria Symphony Guild Ticket Chm 1979-85; Kappa Delta Pi; Chm Bd Dirs KAVU-TV; TX Classroom Teachers Magazine; *home:* 104 Buckingham Victoria TX 77904

COLE, GEORGIA ECHOLS, Third Grade Teacher; *b:* Moulton, AL; *m:* Wilberforce; *c:* Patshenia S., Katernia W.; *ed:* (BS) Elem Ed, AL St Univ 1958; (MS) Elem Ed, Univ ND; *cr:* Teacher Lauderdale Cty HS; West End HS; Lexington HS; *ai:* Textbook Comm; Rdng Tutor for Children with Problems; AEA; NEA; Local NEA; Rdng Prgm; *home:* Rt 3 Box 404 Killen AL 35645

COLE, GRACE NANCE, 7/8th Soc Stud/Science Teacher; *b:* East Chicago, IN; *m:* Charles Donald Jr.; *ed:* (BA) Scndry Soc Stu Teaching, 1983, (MA) His, 1988 Purdue Univ; *cr:* 8th/11th Grade Soc Stud Teacher, Whiting Jr/Sr HS 1985-; 6th-8th Grade Soc Stud/Sci/Health Teacher/Jr HS Div Chairperson Saints Peter & Paul Sch 1985-; *ai:* Spon for Sci Fair/His Day; NCSS 1983-; Saint Mary Church 1985-; Natl Wildlife Fed 1988-; World Wildlife Fund 1986-; Jr HS Div Chairperson 1986-; *home:* 735 N Ernest Ave Griffith IN 46319

COLE, IRENE LANIK, Kindergarten Teacher; *b:* Bentleyville, PA; *m:* Ronald S.; *c:* Virginia Vasko, Joseph; *ed:* (BS) Elem, CA St Teachers Coll 1959; *cr:* 4th Grade Teacher 1959-60, 6th Grade Teacher 1960-68 Bentleyville Elem; Kndgtn Teacher Bentworth Sch Dist 1968-; *ai:* BEA, NEA 1959-; PSEA 1959-, 30 Yr Certificate 1989; 4-H 1968-; PA Farmers 1985; PA Wool & Sheep Assn 1987; *home:* Rd 1 Box 211 Lanik Rd Bentleyville PA 15314

COLE, JAMES RICHARD, Social Studies Dept Chair; *b:* Peoria, IL; *c:* Matthew, Benjamin; *ed:* (BA) His, W IL Univ 1968; (MA) His, Loras Coll 1980; Doctorate Prgm IL St Univ; *cr:* Teacher Central Grade Sch 1968-70 & 1971-; *ai:* NHS Adv; Cedarville Area Historical Society Pres 1988-; IL St Grant for Grad Stud 1985-86; *office:* Freeport Sr HS 701 W Moseley Freeport IL 61032

COLE, JANE ELIZABETH SWITZER, Soc Stud Teacher/Dept Chm; *b:* Kokomo, IN; *m:* Jack R.; *c:* Rachel Elizabeth, Sarah Ewing; *ed:* (BS) Secondary Ed/Soc Stud, Ball St Univ 1970, (MA) Sociology, 1976, (EDS) Sch Superintendency; *cr:* Soc Stud/Eng Teacher Elwood Haynes Mid Sch 1970-71;. Sub Teacher Valparaiso IN; Soc Stud Teacher Redkey HS 1973-75; Soc Stud Teacher/Dept Chm Jay Cty HS 1975-; *ai:* JCHS Stu Cncl Adv; Curr Comm; Co-Spon Sr Class; Chairperson St & Regional; Faculty Mem on Appeals Bd; Accreditation of HS; PBA; NCA; Natl Assn Stu Cncl; NCSS; IN NCSS; Psi Iota Xi Philanthropic Psi Ote of Yr; Altrusa; *office:* Jay County H S RR 2 Hwy 67 Portland IN 47371

COLE, KADY EUNSON, Sixth Grade Teacher; *b:* Schenectady, NY; *m:* Michael David; *c:* Nicholas R., Sarah E.; *ed:* (AS) Ed, Ferrum Jr Coll 1970; (BS) Elem Ed, 1972, (MS) Elem Admin/Elem Supervision, 1979 Radford Univ; *cr:* Teacher Rural Retreat Elem 1972-; *ai:* OM Coach; Cmptr Coord; 6th & 7th Grade Math Chm; *home:* PO Box 33 Sunsetview Rural Retreat VA 24368

COLE, M. MARTHA FURNISH, Jr HS Language Arts Teacher; *b:* Switzerland Cty, IN; *w:* William R. (dec); *c:* Carl W., Clara M. Blanton; *ed:* Teacher Cert Elem Ed, Hanover Coll 1936-38; Cntrl Normal Coll 1939; IN Univ 1954-57, 1960-62; Purdue 1969-70; *cr:* Elem Teacher Rural Schls 1938-44; Soc Stud Teacher/Girls Bsbl Coach Sopchoppy HS 1944-46; Elem Teacher Switzerland Cty-Jefferson Craig 1946-68; Eng Teacher/Dept Head Switzerland Cty Jr HS 1968-; *ai:* Jr HS NHS Spon; Asst Drama Dir; 8th Grade Class Spon; ISTA SE Division Dept Chairperson 1963; Switzerland Cty CTA Pres; IN Cty Teachers of Eng; Order of Eastern Star; Kappa Kappa Kappa (Pres, Corresponding Secy, Recording Secy); Julia L Dumont Club Pres; Switzerland Cty Mental Health Assn Ed Dir; Amer Legion Auxiliary Pres Teacher of Yr 1983; Mt Sterling Baptist Church (Teacher, Youth Dir, Choir Dir); Honorable Mention Pacesetter Awd 1973; Semi Finalist Teacher of Yr 1985-86; Directory of Distinguished America 1981; Poetry Published 1974; Hoosier Teacher of Eng 1981; Switzerland Cty Fnd Vevay Secy 1979; *home:* Rt 2 Box 52 Vevay IN 47043

COLE, NORMAN WILLIAM, 5th Grade Teacher; *b:* Arcata, CA; *m:* Sheila Ann Tucker; *c:* Tulli O., Nora A., Tucker W.; *ed:* (BS) Health/Phys Ed/Elem Ed, TN Wesleyan Coll 1975; *cr:* Teacher Tellico Plains Elem 1976-; *office:* Tellico Plains Elem Sch PO Box 179 School Hill Tellico Plains TN 37385

COLE, PAMELA BURRESS, English Teacher; *b:* Richlands, VA; *m:* Rocky Dean; *c:* Rocky T.; *ed:* (BA) Eng, Emory & Henry Coll 1982; (MS) Eng, Radford Univ 1984; Lib Media Specialist, Clinch Valley Coll 1988; *cr:* Health/Phys Ed Teacher 1981-83, Eng Teacher 1983- Whitewood Elem; *ai:* Oral Comm Seminar Spon; Forensics Coach; Academic Excl Dir; Buchanan Ed Assn, VA Ed Assn 1981-; Buchanan Cty Industrial Planning Comm Mem; *home:* PO Box 115 Whitewood VA 24657

COLE, PATRICIA ANN (ALUISE), Fifth Grade Teacher; *b:* Huntington, WV; *m:* Dennis Franklin; *c:* Dennis F. Jr.; *ed:* (BA) Elem Ed, 1980, (MA) Elem Ed, 1986 Marshall Univ; *cr:* 2nd Grade Teacher 1980-81, 5th-8th Grade Math/5th-6th Grade Sci Teacher 1981-82, 5th Grade Teacher 1982-84, 5th/7th/8th Grade Math/Sci/Soc Stud/5th Grade Eng Teacher 1984-85, 5th Grade Teacher 1985- Our Lady of Fatima Sch; *ai:* Cabell Cty Rdng Cncl Sch Rep; Math Olympiad Coach & Moderator; Assisted Spec Olympics; Kappa Delta Pi, NCEA, PTO; Huntington Womans Club Jr Dept (Chm Art 1983, 1985, Treas 1984, Soc Chm 1986, 3rd Vice Chm 1987, 2nd Vice Chm 1988, 1st Vice Chm 1989, Chm 1990) Bd Mem of Yr 1988, Outstanding Comm Chm 1983, 1985; Saint Stephens Cath Church; Nom Ashland Oil Teacher Achievement Awd; Outstanding Young Woman of America; *home:* 308 W 9th Ave Huntington WV 25701

COLE, RITA R., English Teacher; *b:* Winnfield, LA; *m:* Ronald E.; *c:* Kelly, Lauren; *ed:* (BA) Eng Ed, NE LA Univ 1978; (MA) Eng Ed, LA Tech Univ 1982; *cr:* Teacher Webster Jr HS 1979-82, Zwolle HS 1982-; *ai:* Yrbk & Jr Class Adv; Prom Coord; Teacher Inservice Trainer; Master Teacher 1990; Sabine Parish Teacher of Yr 1988; *office:* Zwolle HS PO Box 188 Zwolle LA 71486

COLE, SAMUEL LANDIS, Technology Teacher; *b:* Mc Caysville, GA; *m:* Pam J.; *c:* Seth A.; *ed:* (BSED) Industrial Arts, Univ of GA 1975; (MA) Technology Ed, WV Univ 1978; Advanced Study in Technology WV Univ 1978-80; *cr:* Teacher Forsyth Cty HS 1975-77; Grad Asst WV Univ 1977-80; Teacher Cheat Lake Mid Sch 1980-81, N Forsyth Mid Sch 1981-; *ai:* Technology Stu Assn Adv; Little League Bsbl Coach; Phi Delta Kappa, Epsilon Pi Tau, AVA, TSA, GVA, PAGE, GITEA; Ducktown Masonic Lodge #572; Explorations in Technology Grant St of GA; *office:* N Forsyth Mid Sch 3645 Coal Mt Dr Cumming GA 30130

COLE, SHARON CARRICKHOFF, 6th Grade Teacher; *b:* Lexington, NC; *m:* Richard M.; *c:* Jonathan, Erin; *ed:* (BS) Elem Ed, Appalachian St Univ 1969; *cr:* 6th Grade Teacher Dunbar Intermediate Sch 1969-70; 5th/6th Grade Teacher Boomer Ferguson Elem 1973-74; 8th Grade Rdng Teacher Lexington Mid Sch 1977-78; 4th/5th/6th Grade Teacher South Gastonia Elem 1979-; *ai:* Lang Arts Steering Comm; MAC Cmptr Mgmt Prog; NEA; NCAE; *office:* South Gastonia Elem Sch 3005 S York Rd Gastonia NC 28052

COLE, SHIRLEY DANIELS, Fourth Grade Teacher; *b:* Roby, MO; *m:* James J.; *c:* Cynthia, Phyllis Cole Fattmann; *ed:* (BA) Elem Ed, Univ of MO Kansas City 1968; Univ of MO Kansas City; IN Univ Ft Wayne; NW MO St Univ Maryville; Pittsburgh St Univ; *cr:* 3rd-5th Grade Teacher Bloodland C-7 Sch Dist 1953-55; 3rd/4th Grade Teacher N Kansas City Sch Dist 1968-72; 4th Grade Teacher St Joseph Sch Dist 1975-79; 3rd/4th Grade Teacher Neosho R-5 Sch Dist 1980-; *ai:* 4th Grade Store Spon; MSTA, IRA; NCTA Building Rep; Northside Baptist Church (Sunday Sch Teacher 1985-, Pianist 1981-); Gideon Auxiliary (Pres 1985-87, VP 1990); *office:* Central Sch W Hickory Neosho MO 64850

COLE, TERRY R., Physical Education Instructor; *b:* Waynesburg, PA; *m:* Jane Sveom; *c:* Shane, Dirk; *ed:* (BA) Geography/Geology/His/Phys Ed, Univ of WI Superior 1965; Univ of MN 1969; *cr:* Wrestling Coach Univ of WI Superior 1964-65; Geography Teacher/Coach Hibbing HS 1965-71; Coach Hibbing Jr Coll1969-71; Phy Ed Teacher/Coach Waynesburg Jr HS 1971-; *ai:* Waynesburg Freestyle Wrestling Club Coach; Mid Sch Intramural Dir; Ph y Ed Dept Chm; AAHPER; Lions Club; Moose Club; Greene Cty Historical Society VP 1985-86; *home:* RD 1 Box 98 Pine Bank PA 15354

COLE, WINELL, Third Grade Teacher; *b:* Addison, AL; *m:* Robert W.; *c:* Karen Cole Cochran, Suzie Cole Clayton; *ed:* (BS) Elem Ed, Samford Univ 1958; *cr:* 5th Grade Teacher Alice Byrne Sch 1958-59; 4th Grade Teacher Valley View Sch 1959-60; 7th-8th Grade Eng Teacher Addison HS 1960-61; 1st Grade Teacher 1963-64, 4th Grade Teacher 1964-66 Addison Elem; 3rd Grade Teacher Hackleburg Elem 1972-; *ai:* AL Ed Assn 1960-; NEA 1958-; PTO 1972-; *home:* PO Box 183 Hackleburg AL 35564

COLE, YVONNE E., Biology Teacher; *b:* St Louis, MO; *m:* Robert Harold Sr.; *c:* Robert II, Ryan P.; *ed:* (BS) Bio, 1968, (MS) Bio, 1978 St Louis Univ; *cr:* Bio Teacher Lindbergh Sr HS 1968-; *ai:* Flyerette Pom Pon Squad Dir; Positive Stu Action Comm Spon; AFT 1975-85, 1989-; NEA 1985-89; MO Area Pom Pon Assn (Co-Founder, Past Co-Pres); MO St HS Acts Assn Advisory Bd; *office:* Lindberg HS 4900 S Lindbergh Saint Louis MO 63126

COLEBANK, HARRIET SCOTT, Mathematics Teacher; *b:* Morgantown, WV; *m:* Phillip W.; *c:* Elizabeth, Craig, Brook, Laura; *ed:* (BS) Math Ed, WV Univ 1969; Post Grad Work at WV Univ; *cr:* Math Teacher Rivesville HS 1967-68, Cass Dist Jr HS 1970-81, Westover Jr HS 1983-84, Morgantown HS 1984-85, University HS 1985-; *ai:* Chrldr & Jets Team Coach; SADD & Class of 1992 Spon; Phi Delta Kappa; WV Ed Assn, NEA, Monongalia Cty Ed Assn 1970-; Cheat Lake Friends of the Lib 1981-; Woodland United Meth Chruch Trustee 1987-; Local Sch Improvement Prgm Recipient; Attended WV Leaders of Learning, Monongalia Cty Teachers Acad; *home:* Rt 4 Box 149 Morgantown WV 26505

COLEBANK, SHARON TUTWILER, First Grade Teacher; *b:* Winchester, VA; *m:* Lyle David; *c:* Joshua; *ed:* (BA) Elem Ed, Shepherd Coll 1972; *cr:* 1st Grade Teacher John J Cornwell Elem 1972-73, Augusta Elem 1973-; *home:* RFD 1 Box 89A Augusta WV 26704

COLELLA, PHILLIP JAMES, Retired; *b:* Rochester, PA; *m:* Ann Lucille Tomei; *c:* Phyllis M. Bates, Christie A. Bates; *ed:* (BA) Eng, St. Bonaventure 1949; (MA) Pittsburgh Univ 1970; *cr:* English Teacher Ambridge Area Schls 1967-69, Moon Area Sch Dist 1969-88; *ai:* Asst Ftbl Coach, Benedictine HS, Ambridge HS, Moon Area Schls, St Bonaventure Univ; NEA 1967-88; PSEA 1967-88; MEA 1969-88; PASR 1969-88; City Recreation Supt 1964-67; Adult Educ Instr 1976-78; *home:* 241 La Rue Dr Coraopolis PA 15108

COLEMAN, ALMA JAMES, English Resource Specialist; *b:* Laurel, MS; *c:* Jamica, Falana, James Jr.; *ed:* (BA) Eng, Alcorn Univ 1973; Early Chldhd & Spec Ed Univ of S MS & MS St Univ; *cr:* Teacher Five Cty Child Dev 1973-78, Laurel Cty Schls 1978-; *ai:* CEC; Delta Sigma Theta; *office:* R H Watkins HS 1100 W 12th St Laurel MS 39440

COLEMAN, ANNA RODICHOK, Biology Teacher; *b:* Harrisburg, PA; *m:* Mark Edwin; *c:* Mark T.; *ed:* (BS) Ed/Bio, Elizabethtown Coll 1967; *cr:* 7th Grade Sci Teacher 1967-70, 10th Grade Bio/Advanced Bio/Botany Teacher 1970- Williams Valley Jr/Sr HS; *office:* Williams Valley Jr/Sr HS Rt 209 Tower City PA 17980

COLEMAN, ANNE JOWERS, English Department Chair; *b:* Atlanta, GA; *m:* Randall; *c:* Christopher; *ed:* (BS) Speech/Drama, Univ of S AL 1970; (MED) Eng, GA St Univ 1983; Data Collector/Peer Teacher; *cr:* Teacher Morrow Sr HS 1980-86, Stockbridge Sr HS 1986-; *ai:* Sr Class Spon; Prins Advisory, Teacher of Yr, Grading Policy Comms; Stockbridge Lang Art Dept Chairperson; Prof Assn GA Educators 1985-; NEA 1980-85; Stockbridge Teacher of Yr 1988-89; Clayton Cty Educator of Week 1986; Southern Assn of Coll & Schls Visitation Comm; Writing Across Curr Speaker; *office:* Stockbridge Sr HS 109 Lee St Stockbridge GA 30281

COLEMAN, BELINDA LA VERNE, Third Grade Teacher; *b:* Winston-Salem, NC; *ed:* (BS) Intermediate Ed, Winston-Salem St Univ 1974; (MA) Early Chldhd Ed, Fayetteville St Univ 1988; *cr:* 2nd-5th Grade Teacher Scurlock Elem Sch 1974-; *ai:* 3rd Grade & Scurlock Sch Hospitality Chairperson; Senate Bill 2; Differentiated Pay & New Sch Specifications Comm; NC Assn of Educators (Sch Rep 1987) 1974-; NEA 1974-; PTA Advisory Bd; Hoke Cty Teacher of Month 1989; Scurlock Sch Teacher of Yr 1978; NC Center for Advancement of Teachers 1988; *office:* Scurlock Elem Sch Rt 2 Box 505 Raeford NC 28376

COLEMAN, CHARMAINE YANEK, Language Arts Teacher/Chairman; *b:* Du Bois, PA; *c:* Shawn J.; *ed:* (BS) Lang Art, PA St Univ 1964; Grad Stud Clarion St Coll, Edinboro St Coll, PA St Univ; *cr:* Eng Teacher Du Bois Area Sr HS 1964-67, St Charles Borromeo Sch 1972-75; Eng Teacher/Dept Chm Our Lady of the Valley Grammar Sch 1978-; *ai:* 8th Grade Yrbk Club Adv; NCEA 1978-; PA St Alumni Assn 1975-; Cub Scouts (Den Mother, Moderator) 1976-80.

COLEMAN, DIANE S., Fifth Grade Teacher; *b:* Paterson, NJ; *m:* Charles Rogers; *c:* Charles R.; *ed:* (BA) Elem, Paterson St Coll 1967; *cr:* Teacher Alps Road Sch 1967-70, Mt View Sch 1970-76, J F Kennedy Sch 1976-; *ai:* Environmental Camping Adv; Earth Day Coord; NJ Ed Assn, Wayne Ed Assn; *office:* John F Kennedy Elem Sch 1310 Ratzer Rd Wayne NJ 07470

COLEMAN, EDREL, Retired Teacher; *b:* Covington Cty, MS; *m:* Victor Sherral; *c:* Janet C. Mitchell; *ed:* (BS) Ed, KS St Univ 1962; Math, Univ of OK; Journalism, Univ of Ak; *cr:* Elem Teacher OK 1962-63, AL 1963-66, AK 1960-70, FL 1972-84; *ai:* Pres of Charlotte Cty Retired Educators Assn; Mgr Volunteer Salvation Army Thrift Shop; Volunteer Worker 1990 Census, Earth Day, Amer Heart Assn, Fund Raising; Charlotte Cty Retired Educators Pres 1988-; Amer Assn Retired Persons Certificate Outstanding Service To CmmtyAwd 1990; Right to Brethe VP 1980-85; Mem FL Retired Educators Cultural Affairs Comm Mem; Teacher of Yr Neil Armstrong Elem Sch 1980; Founder & Grants of Help Educate Little People About Drugs, Alcohol, Nicotine Honored at White House; Toured with Art Linkletter About Drugs; Military Wife of Yr; *home:* 1451 Hayworth Rd Port Charlotte FL 33952

COLEMAN, GARY L., Counselor; *b:* Mc Alester, OK; *m:* Cheryl K. Wendland; *c:* Sarah; *ed:* (BA) Soc Stud, Oral Roberts Univ 1976; (BSED) Elem, 1978, (MED) Guidance/Counseling, 1979 Northeastern Univ; Grad Stud Univ of Tulsa, Northeastern Univ; *cr:* 5th Grade Teacher 1978-82, Cnslr 1982- C E Gray Elem Sch; *ai:* Tutorial Prgm; Sunday Sch Teacher; Prin & Supt Advisory & Curr Dev Comms; N Cntrl Steering Comm Chairperson; OK Ed Assn, NEA, ASCD; Optimist Club Pres 1986-87, Key Man Service Awd 1983-85, 1987-88; *office:* C E Gray Elem Sch P O Box 160 Bixby OK 74008

COLEMAN, GAYLE D., Mathematics Teacher; *b:* Georgetown, SC; *m:* Roosevelt Jr.; *c:* Crystal, Cameron, Clifton; *ed:* (BA) His/Psych, SIU Edwardsville 1975; (MAT) Math/Cmptr Sci, Webster Univ 1986; Cnslr Ed Stud, Dept of Ed, S IL Univ Edwardsville; *cr:* HS Soc Stud Teacher Sch Dist #189 1976-79; HS Math Teacher St Louis Public Schls 1981-; Math Tutor Upward Bound Prgm St Louis Univ 1987-88; Adjunct Instr/Dept Math & Basic Skills Teacher Harris Stowe St Coll 1989-; *ai:* Chairperson Annual

Scndry Math Contest St Louis Public Schls; Southwest HS Math Team Spon; Participant St Louis Public Schls Partnership Prgm; NCTM 1990; MO Cncl of Teachers of Math, IL Cncl of Teachers of Math, Math Educators of Greater St Louis, Urban Math Collaborative of St Louis Exec Cncl Mem 1986-; Benjamin Banneker Assn 1990; 1st Place Teacher Cmptr Learning Month St Louis Public Schls Division of Technology Dev; *office:* Southwest HS 3125 S Kingshighway Saint Louis MO 63139

COLEMAN, JACQUELINE B. WIGGINS, Social Studies Teacher; *b:* Tampa, FL; *m:* Ronald L.; *ed:* (BA) Sociology, Miles Coll 1974; (MED) Admin, Univ of Tampa 1980; Cert/Ed, Univ of S Fl 1975; *cr:* Hillsborough Cty Sch Syst; Soc Stud Teacher W Tampa Mid Sch; Amer Government/Ec Teacher Greco Jr HS; *ai:* Alpha Kappa Alpha, Inc Ivy Leaf Reporter 1984-85; Women in Touch with Society Corr Secy 1981-87; Natl Soc Stud Cncl, Classroom Teachers Assn, PTO, Natl Jr Honor Society Faculty Cncl, Cultural Brain Bowl Spon, Teacher Adv Steering Comm, Mid Sch Task Force, Trinity CME Church, Alpha Kappa Alpha, Women in Touch with Society, Bay Cmmty Players Theatrical Troupe; Outstanding Young Women of America Meritorious Awd, Alpha Kappa Alpha Inc Letter of Appreciation Tampa Parks & Recreation, Jr Achievement Service, Cultural Brain Bowl Service, UNCF Meritorious Awds; Delta Sigma Theta Meritorious Awd & Cert of Appreciation FL Dept of Corrections; *office:* Greco Jr HS 6925 Fowler Ave Tampa FL 33617

COLEMAN, JAMES BERNIS, Assistant Prin of Instruction; *b:* Lumberton, NC; *m:* Linda West; *c:* Kristin M., James H., Tiffany L.; *ed:* (BA) His, 1977, (MA) Ed, 1984 Pembroke St Univ; Numerous Trng Courses; *cr:* Classroom Teacher Spaulding Monroe Mid Sch 1977-87; Part-Time Instr Robeson Comm Coll 1985-; Asst Prin of Instruction Spaulding-Monroe Mid Sch & E Arcadia Sch & Booker T Washington Sch 1987-; *ai:* Young Astronaut Club Spon; Southern Assn of Coll & Schls Steering Comm Chm Spaulding-Monroe Mid Sch; NEA, NC Assn of Educators Mem 1977-; Aerospace Ed Fnd Life Mem 1989-; Robeson Cty Schls Bd Mem 1986-89, Vice Chm 1986; Air Force Assn Life Mem 1974-; USAF 1971-75; NC Sch Bds Assn Achievement Awd 1988-89; Bladen Cty Teacher of Yr 1981; NC Mid Grades Law Project 1988; *home:* Rt 5 Box 569 Lumberton NC 28358

COLEMAN, JAMES JOSEPH, 8th Grade English Teacher; *b:* Buffalo, NY; *m:* Peggy Williams; *c:* Jason, Sara, Ben; *ed:* (BA) Eng, St John Fisher 1969; (MA) Eng, St of IL Univ Carbondale 1971; Human Sexuality, Parent Effectiveness Trng, Teacher Self Assessment, Competency Based Ed, KS St Univ; *cr:* 8th-9th Grade Eng Teacher Vandalia Jr HS 1972-77; Spec Ed Teacher KS St Univ 1988; 8th Grade Eng Teacher Manhattan Mid Sch 1977-; *ai:* Track & Intramural Ftbl Coach; Sch Improvement Plan Comm; Vlybl & Beginning Guitar Club; Teacher & Adv Coord 1980-83; Manhattan Recreation Volunteer Ftbl Coach 1980-87; *office:* Manhattan Mid Sch 901 Poyntz Manhattan KS 66502

COLEMAN, JANINE MARIE, Spanish Teacher; *b:* Appleton, WI; *m:* Jeff; *c:* Thomas; *ed:* (BS) Span/Scndry Ed, Univ of WI Whitewater 1979; *cr:* Span Teacher Parkview Jr HS 1980-82, Portage HS 1983-; *ai:* Portage Ed Assn 1983-; *office:* Portage HS 2505 New Pinery Rd Portage WI 53901

COLEMAN, JEAN CHERRY, Second Grade Teacher; *b:* Mansfield, TX; *m:* Thomas Allen; *c:* John T., Bruce A.; *ed:* (BS) Elem Ed, TX Wesleyan Coll 1951; Grad Stud North TX St Univ & TX Wesleyan Coll; *cr:* 4th Grade Teacher 1951-52, 2nd Grade Teacher 1952-54 R Vickery Elem Sch; 2nd Grade Teacher S S Dillow Elem Sch 1954-55, Ben Milam Elem Sch 1955-56, L A Mills Elem Sch 1965-; *ai:* Univ Interscholastic League Meet Dir 3rd Grade Spelling for UIL Meet in MISD Dist 1980; Curr Comm & Prin Selection Comm; TX St Teachers Assn, NEA (Treas 1969) 1965-89; South Dallas/Ellis Cty Rdng Cncl 1983-87; Assn Childhood Ed (Parliamentarian) 1951-55; Ladies of Leaf Fed Womens Clubs 1976-; PTA 1965-; 4th Generation Teacher; *home:* Box 737 Midlothian TX 76065

COLEMAN, JERRY, 5th Grade Classroom Teacher; *b:* Battle Creek, MI; *m:* Kim Butterfield; *c:* Ann, Laurie; *ed:* (BA) Elem Ed, 1974, (MA) Teaching Mid Sch, 1983 W MI Univ; *cr:* 6th Grade Teacher Lake Center Elem 1975; 7th Grade Teacher 1976-79, 5th Grade Teacher 1979- Marshall Mid Sch; *ai:* 7th-8th Grade Boys & Girls Bsktbl Coach; Christmas Basket Collection Chm; MI Educl Assn Humanitarian Awd 1988; *home:* 280 Borden Dr Battle Creek MI 49017

COLEMAN, JERRY LEE, Physical Education Teacher; *b:* Kansas City, MO; *m:* Beverly Ann Howe; *c:* Jennifer, Cari; *ed:* (BS) Phys Ed, 1975, (MS) Scndry Admin, 1983 Cntrl MO Univ; *cr:* Teacher Ft Osage Sch Dist 1977-; *ai:* IMS Comm; Jr/Sr HS Track & Field Coach; MAPHERD Mem 1987-; CEA, MSTA 1977-; Cntrl Assembly of God Mem 1981-; Ft Osage Mid Sch Educator of Yr 1980-81; *home:* 1311 N Elsea Smith Rd Independence MO 64056

COLEMAN, KAREN HULBURT, English Department Chair; *b:* Youngstown, OH; *m:* Ron J.; *ed:* (BSED) Eng, Youngstown St Univ 1971; (MED) Eng, Westminster Coll 1977; Working Towards HS Prin Certificate Scndry Admin; *cr:* Eng Dept Teacher 1971-, Chm 1982- Cardinal Mooney HS; *ai:* Sr Class & Literary Magazine Adv; Eng Dept Chairperson; Phi Delta Kappa, NCTE; *office:* Cardinal Mooney HS 2545 Erie St Youngstown OH 44507

COLEMAN, LELA DUKES, Social Studies Teacher; *b:* Marianna, AR; *m:* Llewellis E.; *c:* Charmane S., Myreon D.; *ed:* (BS) Comp/Soc Sci, Coll of the Ozarks 1970; (MS) Sociology, AR St Univ 1990; *cr:* Teacher Lee Sr HS 1970-; *ai:* Stu Cncl, Ladies of Tomorrow, Sr Class Spon; Young Men Soc Organization; AR Educl Assn, NEA, Lee Cntry Educl Assn; Delta Sigma Theta; *home:* PO Box 782 Marianna AR 72360

COLEMAN, LINDA KAY, Chorus Teacher; *b:* Kokomo, IN; *ed:* (BS) Music Ed, 1985, (MS) Music Ed, 1988 Univ of IL; *cr:* Choral Teacher Roosevelt Mid Sch 1986, Pontiac Township HS 1985-87; Teaching Asst Univ of IL 1987-88; HS Choral Teacher Plainfield HS 1988-; *ai:* Madrigal Singers & Spring Musical Dir; ACDA, MENC, Phi Delta Kappa; *office:* Plainfield HS 612 Commercial St Plainfield IL 60544

COLEMAN, LINDA MARIE CITIZEN, 1st-4th Grade Phys Ed Teacher; *b:* Kinder, LA; *m:* Eric Mark; *c:* Ginger S.; *ed:* (BS) Health/Phys Ed, Grambling Coll 1973; (MED) Prin/Supervisor of Instr, Mc Neese St Univ 1976; *cr:* Teacher Oakdale Jr HS 1974-88; Teacher Oakdale Elem Sch 1988-; *ai:* Spec Olympics Coach; Sch Float & Assertive Discipline Comm; Allen Parish Assn of Ed (Pres 1987-89) Membership 1988-; LA Alliance Health, Phys Ed, Recreation & Dance Backbone 1988-89; Minority Affairs Comm Chm 1987-89; Delta Sigma Theta; Allen Action Agency Secy 1988-; Allen Cncl on Aging Chm 1989-; *home:* PO Box 322 Oberlin LA 70655

COLEMAN, LYNDA KELSO, English Department Chairperson; *b:* Benton, KY; *m:* William Mac; *c:* Trevor, MacRae, Whitney; *ed:* (BS) Bio/Eng, 1971, (MS) Scndry Ed, 1978 Murray St Univ; Additional Hours on Scndry Ed, Murray St Univ 1979; *cr:* Teacher Calloway Cty HS 1973-; *ai:* Book Ed; Resource Teacher; NCTE 1980-; KY Hum Cncl Grant; Commonwealth Inst of Teachers; *office:* Calloway Cty HS 2108 College Farm Rd Murray KY 42071

COLEMAN, MARGARET MC CONNELL, English Teacher; *b:* Kingsport, TN; *m:* Geoffrey M.; *ed:* (BA) Eng Ed, VA Polytechnic & St Univ 1976; Extensive Trng Gifted Ed; *cr:* Eng Teacher Shoemaker Elem Sch 1976-83; Shoemaker Jr HS 1983-84; Gate City HS 1984-; *ai:* Sr Class Co-Spon; Mem Sch Advisory Comm; Gifted Stu Ace Comm; Cty Gifted Stu ACE Comm; SAT Test Site Proctor; VEA; NEA; SCEA; Gate City HS Teacher of Yr 1986-87; Yrbk Dedication 1988; Gate City HS Teacher Month 1989; *office:* Gate City H S 127 Beech St Gate City VA 24251

COLEMAN, MARGARETTE CANDI, First Grade Teacher; *b:* Elkhorn City, KY; *c:* Gary Jr.; *ed:* (BS) Elem Ed, Pikeville Coll 1968; (MA) Elem Ed, 1975, (Rank I) Elem Ed, 1986 Morehead St Univ; *cr:* Teacher Elkhorn City Schls 1968-74; Homebound Teacher Mullins HS & Feeder Schl 1974-77; Teacher Mullins Sch 1977-89, Pikeville Coll 1985; *ai:* Elkhorn City Little League & Jr HS Cheerleading Spon; Prgm Chairperson Spring Festival 1987; SCH Chairperson Keep Pike Cty Beautiful; PCEA (Sch Chm 1977-87) 1968-89; PTO Pres 1980-81; Jaycees Mem 1980-81, Outstanding Jaycee Wife; KY Colonel Honorary Colonel 1976-89; Pritcher Ed Comm Helped Organize 1st Town Meeting; Tuscon Early Ed Model 3rd Grade 1969-74; Received Grant KY Ed Fnd 1987; Commonwealth Inst Teachers 1987; Pilot Teacher Ec for Elem 1990; *office:* Mullins Sch 1265 N Mayo Trl Pikeville KY 41501

COLEMAN, MARTA JO, English Teacher; *b:* Denver, CO; *w:* Charles S.D. Crawshaw (dec); *ed:* (BA) Eng/Scndry Ed, ID St Univ 1979; (MA) Eng/Comm Arts, Western St Coll of CO 1985; Phd Prgm Memphis St Univ 1988; Emt Intermediate; *cr:* Teacher/Coach Grace HS 1980-81; Teacher Rifle HS 1981-86, Glenwood Springs HS 1986-87, Rifle HS 1987-, CO Mountain Coll 1985-, Leysin Amer Sch Switzerland 1990-; *ai:* Speech/Debate Asst Coach; CO Lang Arts Society 1981-; World Cncl on Gifted & Talented 1984-; NEA; Rifle Volunteer Ambulance Service Emt 1989-; Rifle Cncl for the Arts 1983; Climax Molybdenum Schlsp For MA; RHS Teacher of Yr 1988.

COLEMAN, MARY SUE VAUGHN, 7th Grade Lang Arts Teacher; *b:* Milledgeville, GA; *m:* J. Craig; *c:* Wendy A., Susan V.; *ed:* (BS) Elem, 1971, (MED) Mid Grades, 1976, (EDS) Mid Grades, 1985 GA Coll; *cr:* Teacher Carver Elem Sch 1974-88; Part Time Instr GA Coll 1985-; Team Leader/Teacher Boddie Mid Sch 1988-; *ai:* Team Leader Boddie Mid Sch; Lib Media Comm; Jr Beta Club Spon; Phoenix Literary Magazine Spon; Writing Coord Boddie Mid Sch; Prof Assn of GA Educators 1983-; Ga Cncl of Teachers of Eng 1981- Mid Sch Teacher of Yr 1989; NCTE 1988-; Delta Kappa Gamma Society Intnl-Beta Chapter1989-; GA Colls Ed Cncl Mem; 4-H Volunteer (Pres 1975-) Volunteer of Yr 1977; Hardwick Baptist Church Trustee of Mt Nebo Cemetary 1986-; PTA Baldwin HS 1985-; Carver Elem Teacher of Yr 1987; Baldwin Cty Teacher of Yr 1987; Semifinalist GA Teacher of Yr 1988; Article Published Journal Mid Sch Prin; Article Published in Mid Sch Journal; Boddie Mid Sch Teacher of Yr 1989; *office:* Boddie Mid Sch 1340 Orchard Hill Rd Milledgeville GA 31061

COLEMAN, MICHELLE CLAY, Speech/Theatre Arts Teacher; *b:* Tyler, TX; *m:* Ronald C.; *c:* Sanchelle; *ed:* (BS) Speech/Theatre, E TX St Univ 1976; (MFA) Theatre, Trinity Univ 1979; *cr:* Prof Apprentice/Journeyman/Actress Dallas Theater Center 1976-79; Creative Arts Teacher Alpha Kappa Alpha Day Care Center 1980; Theatre/Speech Teacher Franklin D Roosevelt; *ai:* Roosevelt Homecoming Act, Sr Class, Debate Team, Speech & Theatre Team Spon; Dallas Ind Sch Dist Tribute to Martin L King, Asst of Entertainment, Theater Arts Textbook, TX Speech Textbook Comms; Zakat Temple Masion Talent & Schlsp Pagent Dir; TX Teacher Assn, Natl Thespian Society, Classroom Teachers of Dallas, Bishop Dunne Alumni, Dallas Speech Teacher Assn, TX Forensic Assn, Delta Sigma Theta, Dallas Black Bus & Prof Women; Cedar Crest Chrstn Meth Evangelistic Church (Theatre Arts Guild Dir, Evangelistic Choir Secy, Sunday Sch Teacher, Youth Dir); Nom Jack Lowe Awd & Teacher of Yr; Theater Gold Mask Awd; UIL One Act Play Contest Winners 1986; TX Teaching Certificate; *office:* Franklin D Roosevelt Sch 525 Bonnieview Rd Dallas TX 75203

COLEMAN, OLIVIA PATRICIA JACKSON, Spanish Teacher; *b:* Selma, AL; *m:* Harry T. Jr.; *c:* Brian, Chandra; *ed:* (BA) Modern Foreign Lang, Fisk Univ 1969; (MA) Span/Linguistics, Vanderbilt Univ 1978; MI St Univ Madrid Spain; Memphis St Univ; *cr:* Span Teacher Nashville-Davidson Cty Sch System 1970-71; 6th Grade Teacher Escondido Sch Dist 1971-73; Span Teacher Memphis City Schls 1981-; *ai:* Span Club Spon; Stu Cncl Faculty Co-Spon; Guidance Comm Mem; White Station Educl Fund Bd of Dir-Faculty Rep; NEA, TEA, MEA 1981-; AATSP 1981; TFLTA Wkshp Collaborator 1981-; Memphis-in-May Inc Bd of Dir 1989-; The Links Inc Chapter Treas 1985-, Service Awd 1989; Alpha Kappa Alpha Inc 1966-, Service Awd 1969; Rotary Fnd Teacher Initiative Grant Recipient; Life Blood Certificate of Merit; Foreign Lang In-Service Wkshp Presenter; Foreign Lang Curr Dev Team & Staff Dev Comm; Validation Study Team for NTE; WTEA Foreign Lang Chairperson; *home:* 2221 Thornwood Ln Memphis TN 38119

COLEMAN, PATRICIA ANN, 6th Grade Teacher; *b:* Binger, OK; *m:* Clyde; *c:* Brooke Lipscomb, Shalyn Markle; *ed:* (BA) Elem Ed, Southwestern St 1963; *cr:* 4th Grade Teacher Hereford TX 1964-67; 1st Grade Teacher OK City Sch 1969; 7th/8th Grade Math/Sci Teacher Putnam Schls 1970; 2nd Grade Teacher Stillwater Public Schls 1971; 6th Grade Teacher Duncan Public Schls 1972-; *ai:* Math Team, Jr Police, Newspaper, Just Say No Spon; Sci Fair, Spelling Bee & Artist in Residence Coord; NEA, OK Ed Assn, Duncan Educators Assn; OK Geographic Alliance, Natl Geographic Alliance Mem; Marlow Chamber of Commerce, Emergency Food Bank Mem; Hemophiliac Drive Co-Chm; Red Cross, United Fund Volunteer; Duncan Teacher of Yr 1988; *home:* Rt 4 Box 35 Marlow OK 73055

COLEMAN, PENNY MARTIN, Second Grade Teacher; *b:* Zanesville, OH; *m:* George A.; *c:* Rob, Brooke; *ed:* (BS) Elem Ed, 1976, (MA) Elem Ed, 1982 OH St Univ; *cr:* 2nd Grade Teacher Heath City Schls 1976-; *ai:* Yrbk; Heath Ed Assn; *home:* 987 Terrace Dr Heath OH 43056

COLEMAN, RONALD EARL, Fourth Grade Teacher; *b:* Logan, UT; *m:* Joann Eckersley; *c:* Renalee, Kevin; *ed:* (BS) Elem Ed, Weber St 1966; (MED) Elem Admin, BYU 1973; Wkshps Coll Classes; *cr:* 5th Grade Teacher Edison Elem 1966-67, Lynn Elem 1967-68, Mountain View 1968-70; 4th-6th Grade Teacher Gramercy 1970-; *ai:* Bsktbl & Sftbl Coach; Sci Projects & Rocket Rock Clubs Chm; Dance Club Teacher; OEA Person; Ogden Ed Assn (Rep, Leader); BSA (Asst Leader 1963-64, 1988-89, Leader 1988); Cub Scouts (Comm Chm, Cubmaster 1980-85, Religious Leader 1985); Boys St (Political Office 1956, Leader 1956); Democrats Political Leader 1970-; *office:* Gramercy Elem Sch 1270 Gramercy Ogden UT 84404

COLEMAN, VERNA WHITE, Fifth Grade Teacher; *b:* Evergreen, AL; *c:* Cynthia C. Patterson, Denise L. Patterson, Joseph D., Timothy J., Robert R.; *ed:* (BS) Elem Ed, AL St Coll; Working Towards Masters; *cr:* Teacher Whitley Elem Sch 1958-60, A F Owens Elem Sch 1963-70, Orchard Elem Sch 1973-; *ai:* Grade Level Chairperson; Talent Unlimited; Adopt-A-Sch & Drop-Out Prevention Comm; Me-ology Coord; AFT 1975-; Vigor Band Mother 1988-; Vigor PTA 1976; NAACP; Environmental Club Pres 1988-; Neighborhood Guards Pres 1987-; Usher Club Mem 1988-; The Whitley Club; Cancer Fnd; Safety Patrol, Pleasant Hill Humanitarian Awd; *office:* Orchard Elem Sch Howells Ferry Rd Mobile AL 36618

COLEMAN, VICKY LYNN, Fourth Grade Teacher; *b:* Mesa, AZ; *c:* John S., Bradley A., Mark D.; *ed:* (BA) Elem Ed, AZ St Univ 1965; Grad Stud AZ St Univ 1965-79; *cr:* 3rd Grade Teacher Barcelona Elem 1965-73; Pre-Sch Instr Colemans Ed House 1978-81; Teacher of Gifted & Talented 1981, 2nd Grade Teacher 1982-84, 4th Grade Teacher 1984- Salk Elem; *ai:* Red Mountain HS Booster Club Exec Bd; AZ Jr Golf Assn Volunteer; MEA 1981-; AEA 1981-; LDS Church Instr 1978-; BSA Merit Badge Cncl 1989-; *home:* 2132 N 63rd Pl Mesa AZ 85205

COLEMAN, WANDA JOY, Gifted/Talented/Eng Teacher; *b:* Salem, IL; *m:* Charles G.; *ed:* (AA) Eng, Lindsey Wilson 1964; (BA) Eng, W KY Univ 1967; Grad Stud & AAT Credit; *cr:* Eng Teacher Hiseville HS 1967-69, West Jr HS 1969-70, Carlsbad Jr HS 1971-72, Columbia-Brazoria Ind Sch Dist 1978-; *ai:* Lang Art Comm; Eng Dept Head 1984-86; Alpha Delta Kappa (VP 1990, Sargent At Arms 1988-, Mem, Officer); Life Fellowship Dir; Chrstn Center W Columbia TX Mem; *office:* Columbia-Brazoria Ind Sch Dist Box 154 West Columbia TX 77486

COLES, DEBORAH CALLOWAY, Language Arts Teacher; *b:* Pittsylvania Cty, VA; *m:* Milburn Lester; *c:* Shane L., Alethia M.; *ed:* (BS) Elem Ed, St Pauls Coll 1979; *cr:* Lang Art Teacher Louisa Cty Intermediate Sch 1979-84, Louisa Cty Mid Sch 1984-; *ai:* Girls Bsktbl Coach; SCA Spon; Yrbk Adv; LAMMP Coord & Instr; Summer Sch Instr; NCTE, LCEA 1989-; Rising Sun Baptist Church Youth Leader 1989-; CADRE Bd of Dir 1990; MACAA Teacher of Yr Awd 1989; *office:* Louisa Cty Mid Sch P O Box 448 Mineral VA 23117

COLES, EDWARD L., 6th Grade Teacher; *b:* Tacoma, WA; *m:* Frances Hobbs; *c:* Togo, Stephanie; *ed:* (BA) Elem Ed, Concordia Coll 1974; *cr:* Teacher Christ Memorial Luth 1978; *ai:* Coach Girls Sftbl; Boys Bsktbl; *office:* Christ Memorial Lutheran Sch 5719 N Teutonia Milwaukee WI 53209

COLES, MELLISSA KNEECE, English-History Teacher; *b:* New Orleans, LA; *m:* Rupert D.; *ed:* (BA) His/Eng, Centenary Coll; (MED) Elem Ed, S Meth Univ; Grad Stud Centenary Coll, LSUS, LA Tech, Northeast Univ; *cr:* His/Sci Teacher Thomastown HS 1980-83; Rdng Teacher Lowe Mid Sch 1983-85; Eng Teacher Princeton Jr HS 1985-86; Eng/His Teacher Logansport HS 1986-; *ai:* Yrbk Spon; NEA, LEA, DEA; Comwolei Pres 1987-89; United Meth Women Chm 1987-89; Desoto Parish Jr HS Teacher of Yr 1988-89.

COLEY, GWENDOLYN DARNELL, Chapter I Teacher; *b:* ALexander City, AL; *m:* George F. Sr.; *c:* Undrea, Kimberly, Darnell, George Jr.; *ed:* (BS) Elem Ed, AL A&M 1963; (MA) Elem Ed, AL St Univ 1973; *cr:* 3rd Grade Teacher 1963-66, Music Teacher 1966-70 Edward Bell Sch; Chapter I Teacher Alexander City Sch 1970-76; 1st Grade Teacher Jim Person Sch 1976-; *ai:* NEA, AL Ed Assn; Amer Red Cross Bd; Pensions & Security Bd; Beautification Bd; Whos Who Among Amer Colls & Univs 1963; Spec Service to Cmmty Awd 1989; Chrstn Mother of Yr 1979; *home:* 1405 I Street Alexander City AL 35010

COLGLAZIER, CATHERINE CLARK, English Teacher; *b:* Los Angeles, CA; *m:* E. William Jr.; *c:* J. Geraldine, William C.; *ed:* (BA) Eng, Univ of CA Los Angeles 1967; (MS) Ed, Univ of TN 1986; CA St Los Angeles, Univ of VA, Univ of MT, Harvard Univ; *cr:* Eng/His Teacher Rosemead HS 1968-71, Mt Pleasant HS 1971-73, Lawrence HS 1973-76; Geography Teacher Milham Ford Great Britain 1975; Substitute Teacher Missoula Cty Schls 1977-78; Eng Teacher Brookline HS 1978-83, Webb Sch of Knoxville 1983-84, Oak Ridge HS 1984-; *ai:* Grad Speaker Comm Chairperson; NHS; SACS Ed; NCTE (Presentations 1988) 1970-; Alpha Kappa Gamma 1988-; LWV, Sierra Club; Instr at Gov Acad for Teachers of Writing, Presentations at NCTE 1988; Inst on Moral & Civic Ed Harvard 1983; Knox Cty Inservice 1988-89; Outstanding MA Grad 1986; *office:* Oak Ridge HS Providence Rd Oak Ridge TN 37830

COLIHAN, BARBARA D., Math Dept Chair/Teacher; *b:* Washington, DC; *c:* Michael, Christopher; *ed:* (AA) Ed, Wharton Cty Jr 1983; (BS) Math Ed, Univ of Houston 1984; Grad Stud Univ of Houston; *cr:* Classroom Teacher/Dept Chairperson Lamar Jr HS 1984-; *ai:* Jr NHS Spon; Pass the Torch Mentorship Comm; Lamar Classroom Teachers Assn; Delta Kappa Gamma 1989-; TX Assn for Gifted & Talented 1990.

COLLAZO, JOSE ALFONSO, Bilingual Biology Teacher; *b:* Humacao, PR; *m:* Lizette M. Diaz; *c:* Maraliz, Jose C., Enid I.; *ed:* (BA) Bio, Univ of PR 1977; *cr:* Bi-Ling Bio Teacher 1977-86, Sci Dept Chairperson 1986-87, Dean of Stus 1987-89, Bi-Ling Bio Teacher 1989- Kelvyn Park HS; *office:* Kelvyn Park H S 4343 W Wrightwood Chicago IL 60639

COLLER, GEORGE PATRICK, Science Teacher; *b:* Spokane, WA; *m:* Jane Raugust; *c:* Misty, Eddie; *ed:* (BA) Industrial Technology, E WA St Coll 1970; (MED) Industrial Ed, E WA Univ 1978; *cr:* Teacher Mead Sch Dist 1972-; *ai:* WA Sci Teachers Assn 1980-; WA Grange 1989-; WA Dept of Wildlife Grant 1989; *office:* Northwood Jr HS N 13120 Pittsburg Spokane WA 99208

COLLETT, BETTY (GREEN), Kindergarten Teacher; *b:* Muldrow, OK; *m:* Dean; *c:* Paula Goff, Mary Heard, Elizabeth Frederick; *ed:* (BS) Ed, Univ of AR 1976; *cr:* Teacher Our Redeemer Luth Pre-Schl 1970-75, Beard Elem 1976-; *ai:* Lead Teacher; Curr & Selection Comm; NEA, AR Ed Assn; Fort Smith Classroom Teachers Assn Faculty Rep; ACEI; PTA Pres 1969-70, Lifetime Membership Pin 1984-85; Helped Develop Fort Smith Kndgtn Guide; Pilot Sch for Early Prevention of Sch Failure; *home:* 1821 Vicksburg Fort Smith AR 72901

COLLETT, EUNICE JANE MOSLEY, Business Dept Chairperson; *b:* E Mc Dowell, KY; *m:* Roy; *c:* David R., Eric W.; *ed:* (BS) Bus, 1970, (MS) Bus, 1978 Morehead St Univ; *cr:* Bus Teacher Morgan Cty HS 1975-; *ai:* Established Commercial Bank Within HS With Stus as Bank Personnel; FBLA Adv; 4-H Cncl (VP 1983-85, Secy 1985-87) Leadership 1985, 1987; *home:* Rt 1 Box 82 West Liberty KY 41472

COLLETTI, HELEN PERINO, Second Grade Teacher; *b:* Princeton, IL; *m:* Jerome J.; *c:* James, Jerome, Gina; *ed:* (BA) Eng, St Xavier 1969; *cr:* 1st/2nd Grade Primary Teacher St William 1975-; *ai:* Jr Great Books Prgm Leader; Primary Unit Leader; Extended Day Prgm; NCEA; St Wiliam Literary Team 1980-; *home:* 7131 W Altgeld Chicago IL 60635

COLLEY, KATHLEEN PITTMAN, Fourth Grade Teacher; *b:* Madisonville, TN; *m:* Joseph Sheldon; *c:* Stewart, Joseph; *ed:* (BA) Elem Ed, Clinch Valley Coll & Univ of VA 1970; Rdng, Math, Soc Stud & CPR Undergraduate & Grad Level Taken for Re-Cert Purposes; *cr:* 3rd Grade Teacher Haysi Elem Sch 1968-69; 4th Grade Teacher Sandlick Elem Sch 1970-; *ai:* Spelling Bee, Sci, Sci Fair Comm, 4-H Club Adv; Dickenson Ed Assn, VA Ed Assn, NEA 1968-; *home:* Rt 2 Box 583 Haysi VA 24256

COLLIER, CRYSTEL S., 1st Grade Teacher; *b:* Ft Meyers, FL; *m:* Walter Russell; *c:* Paige Suzanne, Kelly Georgia; *ed:* (BS) Elem Ed, Austin Peay St Univ 1979; *cr:* 2nd Grade Teacher 1979-83; 1st Grade Teacher 1983-87; 2nd Grade Teacher 1987-88; 3rd Grade Teacher 1988-89; 1st Grade Teacher 1989- Waverly Elem; *ai:* NEA/TEA 1979-84; Warrioto Chapter Intnl Rdng Assn 1984-; Home Demonstration Club Sec/VP/Pres 1970-; *office:* Waverly Elem Sch 110 Veterans Pl Waverly TN 37185

COLLIER, JANE WRIGHT, Mathematics Department Head; *b:* Auburn, KY; *m:* Bennie E.; *c:* Martin E.; *ed:* (BA) Math, W KY Univ 1964; *cr:* Teacher Logan Cty Sch System; *ai:* Natl Beta Club Spon; NEA, KY Ed Assn, Logan Cty Ed Assn; Delta Kappa Gamma Society 1982-88; Outstanding Educator Awd by Editorial Bd of W KY Univ Coll of Ed 1976; *home:* 119 Cumberland Cir Russellville KY 42276

COLLIER, JANET OWEN, 7th Grade Language Arts; *b:* Youngstown, OH; *m:* J. B.; *ed:* (BA) Elem Ed, Grove City Coll 1963; (MA) Eng, Westminster Coll 1965; *cr:* Teacher 1963-, Lang Art Coord 1976- Boardman Glenwood Mid Sch; *ai:* Course of Study Revision, Composition, Rdng Competency Comm; Eng Festival; Mentor Prgm for New Teachers; Intnl Rdng Assn Building Rep 1976-; Delta Kappa Gamma Secy 1984-85; Jennings Scholar; Articles Published Monthly in Parent Newsletters; Grant to Develop Glenwood News Bureau; *office:* Boardman Glenwood Mid Sch 7635 Glenwood Ave Youngstown OH 44512

COLLIER, KIM JENNINGS, English Teacher; *b:* Mc Allen, Tx; *m:* Forrest Blair; *ed:* (BBA) Mrktg, 1985, Teaching Cert Eng Composition, 1987 TX A&M; Teaching Asst TX A&M; *cr:* Eng Teacher Snyder HS 1988-; *ai:* Drug Free Organization Spon; NCTE 1985-; *office:* Snyder HS 3801 Austin Snyder TX 79549

COLLIER, LAWRENCE RICHARD, 7th Grade Life Science Teacher; *b:* Barberton, OH; *m:* Rose M.; *c:* Richard, Laura; *ed:* (BS) Earth Sci, 1972, (MS) Phys Ed, 1978 Univ of Akron; *cr:* Sci Teacher Green Mid Sch 1972-; *ai:* Reaching Into Stu Kliques; After Sch Kids; Summer Enrichment Cmptr Wkshp; *office:* Green Mid Sch 1711 Steese Rd Greensburg OH 44232

COLLIER, PATRICIA ANN, Third Grade Teacher; *b:* Windber, PA; *m:* Charles Robert; *c:* Amy M., Scott T.; *ed:* (BS) Elem Ed, Indiana Univ of PA 1971; *cr:* 3rd Grade Teacher New Paris Elem 1971-; *ai:* Lead Teacher Facilitator; Cmptr Coord; PSEA, NEA; Chestnut Ridge Alumni Assn Pres 1983-85, 1987-89; *office:* New Paris Elem RD 2 Box 148 Fishertown PA 15539

COLLIER, SHARON ANITA (RISINGER), Speech Teacher; *b:* San Antonio, TX; *c:* Cindy, Charlie; *ed:* (BS) Scndry Ed/Eng/Speech, TX A&I Univ 1966; Prof Wkshps; Teaching at TX Educl Theatre Conventions; *cr:* Eng Teacher Memorial Jr HS 1966-67, Gregory Portland Jr HS 1967-68; Speech Teacher Arnold Jr HS 1984-; *ai:* Off Broadway Bucs Drama Club, Silent Illusions Mime Troupe Spon; Take Stu to Tournaments; 3 Drama Productions a Yr; TX Educl Theatre Assn 1984-; Huntwick Womens Club Pres 1979-80; Bible Study Fellowship Leader 1978-83; Wrote 3 Plays; *office:* Arnold Jr HS 11111 Telge Rd Houston TX 77040

COLLIER, VICKY G., Chemistry Instructor; *b:* Holden, WV; *c:* Amy E., Brandon J.; *ed:* (AS) Medical Laboratory Technology, S WV Comm 1977; (BA) Chem Ed, Marshall Univ 1979; (MA) Scndry Ed, Morehead St 1983; PRISMS Teachers Physics & Advanced Placement Chem; *cr:* Chem Instr Sheldon Clark HS 1980-; *ai:* Sci Club Spon; Sheldon Clark HS & Martin Cty Sci Fair Coord; Sci Dept Chairperson; KY Ed Assn, NEA, Amer Chemical Society; Mapco Teacher Achievement Awd 1985, 1988; Leadership Wkshp KY Sci & Technology Cncl Participant 1989; *office:* Sheldon Clark HS Rt 40 Inez KY 41224

COLLIER, VIOLA CHRISTINE, Fourth Grade Teacher; *b:* Okmulgee, OK; *m:* Eddie B.; *ed:* (BA) Elem Ed, Tulsa Univ 1968; (MA) Rdng Specialist, Northeastern St Univ 1972; *cr:* 3rd-4th Grade Teacher 1968-69, 6th Grade Teacher 1969-70, 2nd Grade Teacher 1970-71, 4th Grade Teacher 1971- Patrick Henry Elem Sch; *ai:* Pres of Young Adult Missionary Society; St John Baptist Church; Pres of Colliate Dist Young Adults; Tulsa Classroom Teachers Assn 1968-; OK Ed Assn 1968-; NEA 1968-; *home:* 3753 N Lansing Pl Tulsa OK 74106

COLLING, MARK EUGENE, 6th Grade Teacher; *b:* Compton, CA; *m:* Kathleen Margret Shea; *c:* Timothy, Matthew, Mary K.; *ed:* (BA) Elem Ed, Univ of AK 1981; *cr:* 5th/6th Grade Teacher Hunter Elem 1981-; *home:* 4093 Stillwater Ct Fairbanks AK 99709

COLLINGE, PAMELA JEAN, 4th Grade Teacher; *b:* La Junta, CO; *m:* Michael Alan; *c:* Aubrey, Glen, Leslie; *ed:* (BA) Elem Ed, 1979, (MS) Psych, 1982 Emporia St Univ; Early Chldhd Cert 1979; *cr:* 4th Grade Teacher Mulberry Elem Sch 1979-; *ai:* NEA 1987-; KNEA 1979-82, 1987- Teacher of Yr 1982; Delta Kappa Gamma 1988-89; Soil Conservation Service Conservation Teacher of Yr 1988-89; Greenwood Cty Cattlewomens Assn 1979-; Amer Assn of Univ Women Pres 1979-82; Nom Outstanding Young Women in America 1980; *office:* Mulberry Elem Sch 201 N Mulberry Eureka KS 67045

COLLINS, AMY BERNIECE MARCUM, Principal; *b:* Frankfort, IN; *m:* Richard Dale; *c:* Matthew, Allison; *ed:* (BA) Elem Ed, Ball St Univ 1970; (MS) Elem Ed, IN Univ 1972; Spec Ed, IN Univ & Ball St 1972; Real Estate, Purdue 1976; *cr:* EMR-Primary Teacher Kokomo Public 1970-75; 1st-5th Grade Teacher 1981-87, 1st-12th Grade Prin 1988- Heritage Chrstn; *ai:* Detentions, Curr, Graduation Requirements; IN Assn for Ed of Young Children; ASCD 1989-; ASCI 1988-; *office:* Heritage Chrstn Sch 7350 Kennedy Ave Hammond IN 46323

COLLINS, BETTY GOWER, 5th Grade Teacher; *b:* Norman, OK; *m:* John David; *c:* Christopher, Clayton; *ed:* (BS) Elem Ed, OK St Univ 1972; KS Sch Team Trng Prevention of Substance Abuse; *cr:* 6th Grade Teacher 1972-77, 3rd Grade Techer 1978-80, 5th Grade Teacher 1980- Caney Valley Unified Sch Dist; *ai:* Substance Abuse Prevention Sch Team Mem; Just Say No Club Spon; Mem Steering Comm North Centrl Evaluation; Lang Arts Curr Comm Mem; Cmptr Curr Comm Mem; Caney Valley Teachers Assn, NEA; *office:* Lincoln Memorial Grade Sch 1st & High Sts Caney KS 67333

COLLINS, BRUCE DWAIN, Band Director; *b:* Lubbock, TX; *m:* Julie Linn Smith; *ed:* (BMED) Music, 1978, (MA) Music, 1984 W TX St Univ; *cr:* Asst Dir Robert E Lee HS 1978-79, 1984-85; Dir of Bands Alamo Jr HS 1979-84, Gruver Ind Sch Dist 1985-86, Pampa Mid Sch 1986-; *ai:* Band Act Including Marching, Concert Performances, Contests; TX Music Educators Assn 1978-, Honor Band Finalist 1988; TX Band Masters Assn 1978-; *office:* Pampa Mid Sch 2401 Charles Pampa TX 79065

COLLINS, CAROL J., Spanish/French Teacher; *b:* Morristown, NJ; *c:* Jonathan K. Saxe, Holly H. SaxE; *ed:* Sorbonne 1951-52; (BA) Romance Lang-Cum Laude, Harvard/Radcliffe 1953; (MA) Fr Montclair St 1967; Span, NOEA Inst 1963; Fr, Middlebury Coll 1974; *cr:* Fr/Span Teacher Sparta HS 1961-66; Fr Teacher Mountain Lakes HS 1967-80; Span Teacher Marlboro Mid Sch 1983-85; Fr/Span Teacher Lakewood HS 1985-; *ai:* Span Club & Fr Honor Society Adv; Lakewood Ed Assn Faculty Rep; Liaison to Supt; Foreign Lang Educators of NJ 1980-; Amer Assn Teachers of Span & Port 1987-; NY Alliance Francaise 1967-; NJ Harvard Club (Schls Comm 1973- , Exec Bd 1978-80); Rider Coll Grant; Total Immersion Prgm in Span 1989; *office:* Lakewood H S 7th St And Somerset Ave Lakewood NJ 08701

COLLINS, CAROLINE CLEVELAND, Fourth Grade Teacher; *b:* Webster City, IA; *m:* Richard Lee; *c:* Aaron, William; *ed:* (BA) Spec Ed/Elem Ed, 1973, (MA) Elem Ed, Univ of KY; Rank I/ Supervision/Admin, Eastern KY Univ; *cr:* 2nd Grade Teacher Hearn Elem 1973-76; 4th Grade Teacher 1989-Bridgeport Elem; *ai:* Organize Yearly Sci Fair; Franklin Cty Ed Assn Treas 1990-; PTO Teacher Rep; Nom & Received a Teacher of Yr Awd 1975; *office:* Bridgeport Elem Sch Rt 2 Frankfort KY 40601

COLLINS, CHARLES, JR., Piano & Vocal Music Teacher; *b:* Pontiac, MI; *m:* Claraniece Monette Hogan; *c:* Aisha M., Christian K., Christoffer K., Charles III; *ed:* (BS) Music Ed, TN St Univ 1978; *cr:* Fine Art Cnslr Oakland Univ 1976; Teacher Dalewood Jr HS 1978-86, Hixon Jr Hs 1986-87; Fine Art Instr univ of TN 1987, TN St Univ 1977-; Teacher Brainerd Sr HS 1987-; *ai:* Southeast Inst for Music Ed; E TN Vocal Assn, NEA 1978-; Orchard Knob Baptist Church Minister of Music; Coach of Yr 1979, 1981, 1984; Six Flags Choral Competition Best in Class 1986-87, 1990; CLinician for City/Cty Music Teachers Wkshp; Dir of All City Chorus; Composer & Arranger of Choral Music; Minister of Music at Orchard Knob Baptist Church; Music Educators Natl Conference 1976 ; *office:* Brainerd Sr HS 1020 N Moore Rd Chattanooga TN 37411

COLLINS, CHARLES ALLEN, Soc Stud/Cmptr Sci Teacher; *b:* Stuart, VA; *m:* Pamela Ann Wilson; *ed:* (BA) His, Lynchburg Coll 1969; (MS) Educl Supervision/Mid Sch Curr, Averett Coll 1983; Univ of VA; *cr:* 5th/6th Grade Teacher Figsboro Elem Sch 1976-83; 7th Grade Soc Stud Teacher Bassett Mid Sch 1984-85; Soc Stud Teacher Laurel Park HS 1985-87; Soc Stud/Cmptr Sci Teacher G W Carver Mid Sch 1988-; Cmptr Sci/Bus Teacher Natl Bus Coll 1988-; *ai:* Head Ftbl Coach Hardin Reynolds Sch; Jr Var Head Coach Laurel Park HS; Asst Head Track Coach Laurel Park HS; Patrick Cty Ed Assn Treas 1970-71; Henry Cty Bd Assn Ec Benefits Chm 1974-78, 1989-; Patrick Cty Jaycees St Dir 1970-75, Officer of Yr 1973; VA BASS Fed Regional Dir 1984-87; Ed & Publisher 1986-87; *home:* 106 Autumn Dr Collinsville VA 24078

COLLINS, CYNTHIA GUILLORY, English I Teacher; *b:* Alexandria, LA; *m:* Charles A.; *c:* Cyd, Charles, Curtis; *ed:* (BSE) Speech, Delta St Univ 1978; *cr:* Eng I Teacher St Joseph HS 1988-; *ai:* Stu Cncl Adv; *home:* 486 Goldfinch Dr Greenville MS 38701

COLLINS, DEBORAH JUNG, English Department Chair; *b:* Bellevue, IL; *m:* Chip; *c:* Christine, Dale; *ed:* (BA) Speech/Drama/Eng, Marquette Univ 1971; *cr:* Teacher 1974-; Chairperson/Eng Teacher 1982- Holy Spirit HS; *ai:* Dir Sch Musical 1975, Religious Retreat Dramatic Stations; Homecoming Queen Contest Moderator; NCTE; Marquette Univ Coll of Speech & Theatre Outstanding Stu 1971; *office:* Holy Spirit HS Rt 9 & California Absecon NJ 08201

COLLINS, DORIS TALLEY, Math Teacher; *b:* South Boston, VA; *m:* Donald G.; *c:* Shelly; *ed:* (BS) Chem, Math, Betty Coll 1969; (MED) Secondary Math, GA St Univ 1976; *cr:* Teacher East Rome Jr HS 1969-72; Lawranceville Mid Sch 1972-75; Trickum Mid Sch 1975-76; Parkview HS 1976-; *ai:* Math Team Spon; St Math Tournament Co-Chair; Mu Alpha Theta Spon; GA Cncl Teacher Math; NCTM; GAE; NEA; *office:* Parkview HS 998 Cole Dr Lilburn GA 30247

COLLINS, GWEN WILLIAMS, Fourth Grade Teacher; *b:* Texarkana, TX; *m:* Jake C.; *c:* Kirk, Michelle Collins Anderson; *ed:* (BA) Ed/Eng, Hardin-Simmons Univ 1954; Post Grad Work; *cr:* 3rd Grade Teacher Seminole Ind Sch Dist 1955-60, 1970-81; 4th Grade Teacher Ector Cty Ind Sch Dist 1981-84, Reagan Magnet Sch 1984-; *ai:* UIL Spelling Team Coach; Campus Improvement Team; Grade Level Chm; Delta Kappa Gamma Chm of Prof Affairs 1971-; TX St Teachers Assn 1955-81; TX Classroom Teachers Assn 1981-; Hardin Simmons Univ Cowgirls VP 1953-54; Jr Study Club VP 1964-66; Leader of ECIDS Inservice Wkshps; Career Ladder III; *office:* Reagan Magnet Elem Sch PO Box 3912 2321 E 21st Odessa TX 79760

COLLINS, HORTENSE DAVIS, Pre-Kindergarten Teacher; *b:* Nacogdoches, TX; *m:* Charles R.; *c:* Seth; *ed:* (BS) Elem Ed, TX Southern Univ 1972; Bi-Ling Ed Houston Baptist Univ 1974-76; Supervisor Tx Southern Univ; *cr:* Nursery Teacher TX Southern Univ 1971-72; 6th Grade Teacher Our Lady of Guadelupe Sch 1972-73; Kndgtn Teacher Alamo Elem 1973-78; 1st Grade Teacher 1978-85, Pre-K Teacher 1985- Alcott Elem; *ai:* Ridgegate Civic Club Block Leader; NAEYC Bldg Rep 1985-; HFT 1980-; Twice Nom Outstanding Young Educator Alamo Elem 1974/1976; *office:* Alcott Elem Sch 5859 Bellfort Houston TX 77033

COLLINS, IDA LOU BERLY, First Grade Teacher; *b:* Paris, TX; *m:* Donald R.; *c:* Don, David; *ed:* (AA) Music Ed, Paris Jr Coll 1954; (BA) Music Ed, Austin Coll 1956; Elem Ed, TX Womens Univ; *cr:* Elem Music Teacher Sherman Public Schls 1956-58; 4th Grade Teacher 1958-64, 1st Grade Teacher 1976- Grand Prairie Ind Sch Dist; *ai:* Chm of Campus Beautification Textbook Selection Comm; Former Grade Level Chm; Grand Prairie Classroom Teachers Assn, TX Classroom Teachers Assn; PTA (Character & Spiritual Growth 1989-, 1985-87, Parliamentarian 1987-89, 1990, VP 1983-85, Prgm Chm 1983-85), TX Life Membership 1989-, Service Awd 1986-87; Outstanding Teacher 1988-89; *home:* 1513 Danish Dr Grand Prairie TX 75050

COLLINS, JAQUELINE WIGHT, Sr HS Guidance Counselor; *b:* New Rochelle, NY; *m:* Le Roy M.; *c:* Le Roy Wight, Laurie A.; *ed:* (BMED) Music Ed, Syracuse Univ 1952; (MS) Guidance, Hofstra Univ 1971; *cr:* Caseworker Westchester Cty Dept of Child Welfare 1952-54; Teacher Memorial Jr HS 1954-59, 1968-70; Guidance Cnslr Roosevelt Jr/Sr HS 1970-; *ai:* Educl Coord Summer Sch; Coord Sch Dist 15 & EOP; Church Organist; Choir & Musical Dir for Local Theatre Groups; Adult Ed & Piano Teacher; Part Time Employment Volunteer Work; LIPGA, NYSGPA Mem; PTA Past Pres 1967-68; Suburban League (Past Pres, Mem) 1961-; Alpha Kappa Alpha; Amer Field Service Bd of Dir; Five Towns Child CareCenter (Bd Mem, VP) 1987-89; Jenkins Awd; Whos Who Among American Women 1989; *home:* 456 Barnard Ave Cedarhurst NY 11516

COLLINS, JENNIFER, Volleyball Coach; *b:* Chicago, IL; *ed:* (BA) Journalism/Eng, 1986, (MA) Sport Admin, 1989 OH St Univ; *cr:* Asst Coach OH St Univ 1987-89; Vlybl Coach Northwestern Univ 1989-; *ai:* Mens Club Vlybl Team & YMCA-Park Dist Children Coach; Spec Olympic Volunteer; Amer Vlybl Coaches Assn 1989-; US Vlybl Assn 1985-; *office:* Northwestern Univ 1501 Central St Evanston IL 60201

COLLINS, JOYCE KITCHEN, 5th-6th Grade Math Teacher; *b:* Ironton, OH; *m:* Joe Edward; *c:* Jodee, Jan, Joel, Jerel; *ed:* (BA) Elem Ed, Rio Grande Coll 1964; Cmptr; *cr:* Teacher Lawrence Cty OH 1958-66, Gallia Cty Local Sch Dist 1967- /1973-; *ai:* Spelling Bee Adv Grades 5 & 6; Charity Fund-Raiser Chairperson; OEA/NEA 1973-; OCLEA 19730-; Local Newsletters Publications; Selected Poems Under Advisement for Publication; *office:* Hannan Trace Elem Sch Rt 1 Crown City OH 45623

COLLINS, JOYCE MORROW, Business Teacher; *b:* Grenada, MS; *m:* Alan B.; *c:* Linda G., Wesley A.; *ed:* (AA) Bus Ed, Freed-Hardeman Coll 1971; (BS) Bus Ed, 1973, (MED) Bus Ed, 1976 MS St Univ; Cmptr Sci; Grad Stud Holmes Jr Coll 1981-86; *cr:* Bus Teacher Grenada Lake Acad 1974-77; Bus Teacher/Dept Chairperson Kirk Acad 1973-74, 1977-84; Bus Teacher Grenada HS 1984-; *ai:* Bus Club & Co-Ed-Y Spon; Former Paper Staff & Jr Class Spon; NBEA, MBEA 1977-; MPSEA (Mem, Dist Chairperson 1983, VP 1982) 1973-84; MS Ec Cncl Delegate 1983; MEC STAR Teacher 1975, 1977; Curr Folio Reviewer for St Dept of Ed 1990; *office:* Grenada HS Fairground Rd Grenada MS 38901

COLLINS, KAREN KROPINICKI, 5th Grade Teacher; *b:* Bethlehem, PA; *m:* Wallace Craig; *c:* Teresa, Christopher, Matthew; *ed:* (BS) Elem Ed, Bloomsburg St Coll 1973; (MA) Counseling, Univ North FL 1978; *cr:* 6th Grade Math Teacher 1973-78, Gifted/Talented Teacher 1978-80 Lakeside Mid Sch; 5th Grade Teacher Olympia Elem 1980-81; 4th Grade Teacher 1981-, 5th Grade Teacher 1987 Converse Elem ; *ai:* Lord of Life Luth Church Center for Child Dev Bd Chairperson 1990; *office:* Converse Elem Sch 102 School St Converse TX 78109

COLLINS, KATHY L., Elementary Guidance Counselor; *b:* Salem, OH; *c:* Megan E.; *ed:* (BS) Elem Ed, Kent St Univ 1971; (MS) Guidance/Counseling, Youngstown St Univ 1976; Various Courses & Wkshps; *cr:* 3rd Grade Teacher 1971-74, Career Ed Coord 1974-76, Elem Cnslr 1976-79, 6th Grade Teacher 1979-89, Elem Cnslr 1989- Boardman Schls; *ai:* Facilitator Evening Parenting Sessions; Drug/Alcohol & Gifted/Talented Comm Mem; NEA, OH Ed Assn; Boardman Ed Assn (Past VP 1982-84, Uniserv Rep 1987-) 1971-; PTA 1971-; Jennings Scholar 1978-79; *office:* Boardman Schls 5555 Market St Youngstown OH 44512

COLLINS, KATIE NORTON, Seventh Grade Science Teacher; *b:* Laurel, MS; *m:* Dwight Freeman; *c:* Joey S. Matthews, Leigh D.; *ed:* (BS) Elem Ed, 1968, (MA) Elem Ed, 1977 William Carey Coll; *cr:* Teacher Calhoun Elem Sch 1969-; *ai:* MS Assn of Educators (Government Relation 1989-, Chm Jones Cty, Mem 1969-); MS Sci Teachers Assn; *home:* 4404 Forest Dr Laurel MS 39440

COLLINS, LINDA BUTLER, Science Teacher; *b:* Quincy, FL; *m:* J. Milton Jr.; *ed:* (BA) Psych/Sociology, Tift Coll 1971; *cr:* Fairmount Elem 1971-73; Fayette Mid Sch 1984-; *ai:* Sci Club Spon; Sci Olympiad Team Asst Coach; NSTA, GA Sci Teacher Assn 1986-; *office:* Fayette Mid Sch 450 Grady Ave Fayetteville GA 30214

COLLINS, LISA ROYAL, 3rd Grade Teacher; *b:* Jesup, GA; *m:* Norwood A.; *ed:* (BS) Early Chldhd, GA Southern 1980; Teacher Screven Elem Sch 1980 -; *ai:* Sch Planning Comm; PAGE; Screven First Bapt Church Nom Comm Teacher 1989-; *office:* Screven Elem Sch PO Box 159 Screven GA 31560

COLLINS, LORA CHAFFINS, Kindergarten Teacher; *b:* Mousie, KY; *m:* Morrell; *c:* Lutrena Slusser, Amain; *ed:* (BS) Kndgtn, Elem, Univ of Ada 1968; *cr:* Kndgtn Teacher Parkway Bd Ed 1964-; *ai:* NEA 1964-; OH Ed Assn 1964-; Parkway Ed Assn 1964-; Univ Womens Club 1975-; *home:* 1708 Nagel St St Marys OH 45885

COLLINS, MARIA COLASUONNO, Life Science Teacher; *b:* New York, NY; *c:* Kevin, Christy; *ed:* (BS) Bio, Marietta Coll 1963; (MA) Sci Ed, Teachers Coll Columbia Univ 1965; Grad Stud Sci, Math, Ed; *cr:* 7th/8th/10th Grade Sci Teacher Bronxville HS 1963-67; 9th Grade Sci Teacher Clarkstown Sr HS 1967-69; 7th Grade Sci Teacher Felix Festa Jr HS 1974-; *ai:* Rockland Teachers Center Dial-A-Teacher Prgm; NYSUT, Clarkstown Teachers Assn; *office:* Felix V Festa Jr HS South Parrot Rd WEST Nyack NY 10994

COLLINS, MORRIS LYNN, Art Teacher; *b:* Kansas City, KS; *m:* Loretta Mae Derritt; *c:* Christa, Seth, Barbara, Sarah; *ed:* (BS) Art Ed, Cntrl MO St Coll 1969; (MS) Art Ed, Cntrl MO St Univ 1973; Grad Stud; *cr:* Elem Art Teacher Warrensburg Sch Dist R-VI 1969-; *ai:* Dist Performance Based Teacher Evaluation, Stu Advisory, Dist Curr Advisory Comm; Cmmty Leadership for Alcohol & Substance Abuse Prevention Team; MO St Teachers Assn; NAEA; Warrensburg Teachers Assn Pres 1973-74; Johnson Cty Bd of Services Pres 1980-; Industrial Services Contractors Inc VP 1985-86; Mid MO Artist Incorporated Art Achievement Awd; Warrensburg Jaycees Outstanding Educator Awd; Nom Warrensburg Sch Dist Teacher of Yr; *office:* Martin Warren Elem Sch 105 S Maguire Warrensburg MO 64093

COLLINS, NETTIE HOLLOWAY, History Teacher; *b:* Prentiss, MS; *m:* Jessie J.; *c:* James L.; *ed:* (BA) Sociology/Soc Work, Jackson St Univ 1971; Grade Level Ed Courses, Univ of S MS Hattiesburg; *cr:* Soc Worker Amer Red Cross 1971, Jackson Cty Welfare Dept 1973-77; Teacher Moss Point Schls 1977-; *ai:* Youth Legislature Co-Spon; Curr, Rdng, Discipline Comms; NCSS; Alpha Kappa Alpha Basilieus of Theta Zeta Omega 1977; *home:* 5764 Eastwood Dr Moss Point MS 39563

COLLINS, PAMELA WILSON, 6th Grade Math & Sci Teacher; *b:* Martinsville, VA; *m:* Charles A.; *ed:* (AS) Ed, Patrick Henry Comm Coll 1974; (BS) Ed, Averett Coll 1976; Grad Stud Averett Coll; *cr:* Teacher Richard H Clarke Elem 1976-86, John D Bassett Mid Sch 1986-; *ai:* Monitor Math Team; Henry Cty Sci Advisory & Cty Wide Soc Stud Comm; Pen-Pal Club Spon; Henry Cty Ed Assn 1989-; *home:* 106 Autumn Dr Collinsville VA 24078

COLLINS, PHYLLIS VARNEY, 8th Grade Teacher; *b:* Huddy, KY; *m:* Bruce; *c:* Margaret A., Bruce II; *ed:* (BS) Elem Ed, Pikeville Coll 1970; (MS) Elem Ed, Morehead St Univ 1978; KY Cert Math & Sci; *cr:* 1st-8th Grade Teacher Woodman Elem 1963-66; 3rd/4th Grade Teacher Eden Elem 1966-68; 8th Grade Teacher Phelps 1968-69, South Williamson Elem 1969-; *ai:* Var Cheerleading Spon; Var Boys Bsktbl & Minor League Boys Bsbl Coach; NEA, KY Ed Assn, Delta Kappa Gamma; PCEA Building Rep; *home:* PO Box 8 Railroad St Huddy KY 41535

COLLINS, RUBIE M. (BROWN), Science Teacher; *b:* Columbia, LA; *m:* Le Roy; *c:* Cedric, Carol Every, Pamela, Carone, Shonteez; *ed:* (BS) Bio, Grambling St Univ 1964; (MED) Ed/Physics, Sci Ed, 1979 Northeast Univ; Master Teacher Trng for Teacher Evaluation Prgm 1990; *cr:* Teacher Mayfield HS 1964-68, Bastrop Jr HS 1969-81, Lee Jr HS 1981-; *ai:* Church Deacones & Youth Group; Co-Spon Schls Sci Club; Academic Achievement & Natl Jr Honor Society Comm; Master Teacher Evaluation Team; LA Ed Assn, NEA, Monroe City Assn of Educators Mem 1964-; Alpha Kappa Alpha Pres 1990-92; Teacher of Yr; *home:* 202 Keeble Dr Monroe LA 71202

COLLINS, SUSAN E., Language Arts Teacher; *b:* Oneida, TN; *m:* Jimmy A.; *c:* Everett, Melanie; *ed:* (BS) Eng Ed, UTC 1972; (MED) Eng Ed, 1979, (SPED) Eng Ed, 1989 W GA Coll; *cr:* Teacher Whitfield Cty Schls 1972-; *ai:* PAGE, GA Cncl of Eng Teachers; Schlsp W GA; *office:* Northwest Whitfield HS 1651 Tunnel Hill Varnell Rd Tunnel Hill GA 30755

COLLINS, TERESA WOOD, Instrumental Music Teacher; *b:* Russellville, KY; *m:* Murrell Carmen; *c:* Ryan C.; *ed:* (BA) Music Ed, 1982, (MA) Scndry Sch Guidance, 1989 W KY Univ; *cr:* K-6th Grade General Music/6th-12th Grade Instrumental Teacher Gamaliel Sch System 1983-85; K-6th Grade General Music/7th-12th Grade Instrumental Teacher 1985-88, 5th/6th Grade General Music/9th-12th Grade Instrumental Teacher 1988-89, 5th-8th Grade General Music/6th Grade Instrumental Teacher 1989- Monroe Cty Sch System; *ai:* KY Educators Assn, KY Music Educators Assn 1983-; KY Band Masters Assn 1986-87; 3rd Dist Band Dir Assn 1983-; *home:* 534 E Main St Gamaliel KY 42140

COLLINS, WANDA ABBOTT, English Teacher; *b:* Wetumpka, AL; *m:* Michael Edward; *c:* Michael J.; *ed:* (BA) Bio/Microbiology, 1983, (BS) Speech/Theatre, 1983, Ed/Chem/Span, 1983 SD St Univ; *cr:* Span/Eng Teacher Floodwood Public Schls 1985-87; Eng Teacher Silver Lake Public Schls 1987-; *ai:* Fall Play, One-Act Competition, Childrens Play Drama Dir; Drama/Speech Club, 8th Grade Class Adv; Speech & Asst Sftbl Coach; MN Ed Assn (Pres 1989) 1985-; Hutchinson Art Guild 1987-; GSA Brownies Asst 1986-87; Summer Arts Prgm Dir 1985-87; Taught Cmmty Ed Classes GED, Aerobics, Creative Dance for Children; Coached Synchronized Swim Clubs; Outstanding Young Women of America 1982, 1984; Sftbl Coach Summer Prgm; *office:* Silver Lake Public Sch 229 Lake St Silver Lake MN 55381

COLLINS-COLE, VIVIAN JOYCE, Mathematics Teacher; *b:* Brooklyn, NY; *m:* Bernard; *ed:* (BA) Sociology/Math, Herbert H Lehman Coll 1984; (MS) Math Ed, Long Island Univ 1990; *cr:* Teacher A B Davis Mid Sch 1984-86, Mt Vernon HS 1986-; *office:* Mount Vernon HS 100 California Rd Mount Vernon NY 10552

COLLOM, BETTE GIBSON, English Teacher; *b:* Owosso, MI; *c:* Donald, Jeffrey, Samantha; *ed:* (BA) Rhetoric/Public Address, 1964, (MA) Comm, 1968 MI St Univ; PHD Candidate MI St; *cr:* Grad Teaching Asst MI St 1965-69; Eng Teacher Massapequa HS 1970-; *ai:* WMHS Radio Club, Debate Club Adv; Yrbk Co-Adv; Massapequa Teacher Center M-TRACT Bd Mem 1987-; Massapequa Fed of Teachers Ed of Union Paper 1979-, Several Journalism Awds; NCTE 1985-; *office:* Massapequa HS Merrick Rd Massapequa NY 11758

COLLUM, JANET FISHER, Theatre Art & Eng Teacher; *b:* Hot Springs, AR; *m:* Harold Bruce; *c:* Mary, James L., Jesstin K., Jessica L., Justin W. (dec); *ed:* (BSE) Theatre Art/Eng Oral Comm, 1975, (MSE) Theatre Art/Oral Comm, 1976 Henderson St Univ; Cmptr Ed, Desktop Publishing, Photography, Instrumental, Vocal Music, AR Writing Project; *cr:* Speech/Theatre Art Curr Teacher Garland Cty Comm Coll; Eng/Oral Comm/Theatre Art/Journalism Teacher Mountain Pine HS 1975-88; Theatre Art/Journalism Teacher Hot Springs HS 1988-; *ai:* Trojan Speakers Forensics Team Coach; Thespian Troupe 78 & Quill & Scroll Spon; Act & Textbook Comms; Adv Old Gold Book; Red Ribbon Anti Drug Prgm; NEA, AEA, CTA, Amer Scndry Curr Assn, ASCA, Scholastic Press Assn, AR Press Assn, Associated Press Assn, SSCA, Columbia Press Assn; Alpha Delta Kappa, Art Cncl Hot Springs, Spec Olympics; Hot Springs Arrt Center Bd Dirs; Hot Springs Fine Art Center Pres Performing Art Comm 1989-; Theatre Arts Prgms Dir; Fine Arts Summer Enrichment Prgm; Amer Coll Theatre Festival Bd Mem; *office:* Hot Springs HS 701 Emory St Hot Spgs Natl Pk AR 71913

COLLUM, MARY JO RHOADS, Fourth Grade Teacher; *b:* Iowa City, IA; *m:* David E.; *c:* Jared D., Justin P.; *ed:* (BA) Elem Ed, William Penn Coll 1970; Grad Work Univ of IA, Drake Univ; *cr:* 3rd Grade Teacher 1970-86, 4th Grade Teacher 1987- BGM Cmmty Schls; *ai:* Renewed Service Delivery System & Teacher Advisory Comm Mem; Mainstreaming, BGM Writing Project, BGM Rdng Comm; ISEA, NEA, BGMEA 1970-; IRA 1980-; Natl TTT Society Pres 1984-86; BGM Excl Ed Awd; *home:* 610 West St Brooklyn IA 52211

COLMAN, LINDA KUESTER, Chemistry Teacher; *b:* Yoakum, TX; *m:* Gary R.; *c:* Sarah, Elizabeth, Catherine, Christopher; *ed:* (BSED) Math/Chem, 1976, (MS) Chem, 1978 SW TX St Univ; *cr:* Phys Sci Teacher Victoria HS 1978-80; Chem Teacher Cuero HS 1988-; *ai:* UIL Sci Coach; TX Assn Gifted & Talented, TX St Teachers Assn, TX Math & Sci Coaches Assn; Alpha Epsilon Xi (VP 1984-86, Treas 1984-85, Pres 1986-88), Woman of Yr, Sweetheart 1986-87.

COLOMB, IRENE GODZIK, 5th Grade Teacher; *b:* Rutland, VT; *m:* Reggie M.; *c:* Jennifer A., Christopher J.; *ed:* (BA) Elem Ed, Univ of VT 1976; Addl Studies Castleton St Coll; Coll of St Joseph the Provider; *cr:* 3rd Grade Teacher Northwest Elem Sch 1976-77; K Teacher Park Street Sch 1977-78; 1st Grade Teacher Limestone Elem Sch 1978-79; 3rd Grade Teacher Damon Elem Sch 1979-82; 5th Grade Teacher Poultney Elem Sch 1982-; *ai:* NEA 1976-; VEA 1982-; Immaculate Heart of Mary Religious Ed Teacher 1976-78; Teacher of Yr Nom 1981; *office:* Poultney Elem Sch Allen St Poultney VT 05764

COLSON, CHARLA RUTH, 4th Grade Teacher; *b:* Hotchkiss, CO; *c:* Jeffrey D.; *ed:* (BA) Soc Sci, Univ of S CO 1968; Several Elem Ed Courses at Numerous Univs; *cr:* 3rd Grade Teacher Garnet Mesa Elem 1970-79; 4th Grade Teacher Lincoln Elem 1979-89; *ai:* Multiple Sclerosis Read-A-Thon Dir 1978; Awd for Collecting most Money in CO Schls; *home:* 721 Howard St Delta CO 81416

COLTRANE, PATRICIA BRANCH, Science Department Chair; *b:* Providence Forge, VA; *m:* Richard Brooks Jr.; *c:* Cary R. Kimball, Richard B. III, Laura L.; *ed:* (AB) Bio, Randolph-Macon Womans Coll 1961; (MED) Bio, Coll of William & Mary 1977; Advanced Placement Bio; *cr:* Teacher Osbourne HS 1961-62, Denbigh HS 1968-70, Orcutt Baptist Sch 1974-77, Carver Elem 1977-78; Dept Chairperson Warwick HS 1978-; *ai:* Parent Advisory & Sci Self Study Comms; NABT 1988-; VA Jr Acad of Sci, Amer Jr Acad of Sci 1984-; Orcutt Baptist Sch Bd 1980-83; Randolph-Macon Alumnae Assn VP 1965-67; Mellon Grant; Warwick HS Teacher of YR 1989; Newport News Scndry Teacher of Yr 1989; Nom Presidential Awd for Excl in Sci Teaching; *office:* Warwick HS 51 Copeland Ln Newport News VA 23601

COLVARD, MARY PAGE, Science Teacher/Chairperson; *b:* Sidney, NY; *c:* Jeffrey T., Craig S., Matthew D.; *ed:* (BSED) Scndry Bio, St Univ NY Geneseo 1968; (MSED) Scndry Bio, St Univ NY Onenta 1988; *cr:* Sci Teacher Sidney Cntrl Sch 1969-; *ai:* Sci Club Adv 1971-; NY St Electric & Gas Educl Consultant 1981-; Instr Adult Ed The Hospital 1982-; Cmptr Software & Sci Adv 1983-; Sci Dept Chairperson; Sidney Teachers Assn (Secy, Building Rep, Grievance Comm 1983-); NY St Regents Bio Comm 1985-; Sci Teachers Assn of NY St Finance Comm 1986-; Catskill Leatherstocking Section of STANYS Secy 1986; Sidney Cntrl Sch Safety Comm 1987-; Cornell/Howard Hughes Biomedical Grant

Comm 1989-; Sidney HS Faculty Advisory Cncl 1989-; Sci Teachers Assn of NY St; Phi Delta Kappa; Optical Society of America; NABT;l Sigma Xi; Item Writer NY St Regnts Bio Examination 1985-, Schlshp Examination 1988-; St Univ of NY Oneonta Math & Sci Project Consultant & Instr 1986-88; Co-Dir & Instr Sci Ed 494 Energy Concepts Societal & Technological Issues; Author Several Articles 1986-89; Presented Various Study Courses 1977-82; Ostego Sigma Xi OUtstanding Scvi Teacher 1984; *office:* Sidney HS 95 W Main St Sidney NY 13838

COLVIN, CLARENCE LEROY, English Teacher; *b:* Erie, PA; *m:* Susan K. Allen; *c:* Robert, Stephen, Katy, Colleen; *ed:* (BA) Eng, Gannon Univ 1966; (MED) Eng, Edinboro Univ 1970; Grad Stud Sch Admin; *cr:* Eng Teacher Erie Memorial Jr HS 1966-72; Curr Writer Erie Mid Sch Task Force 1972-73; Project Dir Erie Gridley Mid Sch 1973-74; Eng Teacher Erie Tech Memorial HS 1974-82, Roosevelt Mid Sch 1982-; *ai:* Implementation within Erie Sch Dist; AFT Faculty Rep 1966-69; Erie Ed Assn Faculty Rep; PSEA, NEA; St Matthew Church Parish Cncl 1976-80; Summit Township Water & Sewer Authorities 1980-85; Roosevelt Teacher of Yr 1987-88; Cooperating Teacher for Stu Teachers; *office:* Roosevelt Mid Sch 2300 Cranberry St Erie PA 16502

COLVIN, LORRAINE WALTERS, Third Grade Teacher; *b:* Kansas City, MO; *m:* Laurance Dale; *c:* Joshua A., Leah R.; *ed:* (AA) Liberal Art, Chrstn Coll 1971; (BS) Elem Ed, Univ of MO Columbia 1973; *cr:* 2nd Grade Teacher 1974-75, Kndgtn Teacher 1975-86, 3rd Grade Teacher 1986- Lathrop R-II Sch Dist; *ai:* Teacher Assistance Team Co-Chm 1989-; Career Ladder Comm Mem; MO St Teachers Assn 1974-; Lathrop Little League Bd Mem 1987-; Chrstn Church Life Mem; *office:* Lathrop Elem Sch 700 Center St Lathrop MO 64465

COLVIN, ROSEMARY MOOSBURNER, Fifth Grade Teacher; *b:* New York, NY; *m:* Raymond J.; *c:* Rosemary Wynne, Rita Buciovaz, Roberta Giberti, Regina Garceau, Raymond, Ronald; *ed:* (AA) Liberal Arts-Summa Cum Laude Massasoit Comm Coll 1970; (BS) Elem Ed- Summa Cum Laude, Bridgewater St 1972; Ed; *cr:* 6th Grade Elem Teacher St Colman 1972-74; 4th/5th Grade Elem Teacher Perkins Sch 1974-75; 4th-6th Grade Elem Teacher Oscar F Raymond Sch 1975-; *ai:* City Elem Lang Arts Comm Mem; BEA Mem, MTA Mem 1972-; NEA Mem 1974-; Safety Trng Dynamics Pres 1983- *office:* Oscar F.Raymond Sch 125 Oak St Brockton MA 02401

COLVIN, RUTH, Resource Teacher; *b:* Fayetteville, NC; *ed:* (BS) Elem Ed, Fayetteville St Univ 1958; Urban Ed Certificate, Univ of Hartford 1982; Grad Stud Univ of NC Greenville, Cntrl CT St Univ, Univ of Hartford; *cr:* Teacher NC Sch Systems 1958-68; Summer Prgm Project Jog 1975-83; Resource Teacher Hartford Bd of Ed 1968-; Coord Summer Prgm St Monicas Tutorial 1983-; *ai:* Drama, Video, Chrldrs & Sci Club Adv; Adv to Debating Team; Delta Sigma Theta Mem; Circle of Friends Pres 1984-88; Les Ames (Pres 1985-88, Mem); PTA Secy 1988-; Iota Phi Lamdba, Apple for Teacher Plaque 1988; St Monicas Episcopal Church (Vestry, Parish & Stewardship Comms, Pre-Teen Youth Group, Coord, Stewardship, Choir; Democratic Party of Bloomfield 1985-; My Sisters Place Volunteer 1975-87; Mt Siani Hospital Volunteer 1975-88; Outstanding Elem Teacher America 1975; Multi Culture Ethnic Week Plaque 1986-87.

COLWELL, CAROL ANN, Biology Teacher; *b:* Brady, TX; *m:* Brent T.; *ed:* (BS) Bio/Health, TX Tech 1985; Genetics, Univ of St Thomas; Kids in Need of Direction Houston; Cmptr Literacy; *cr:* Bio/Chem/Life Sci/Health Teacher Lefors Ind Sch Dist 1985-86; Bio Teacher Pampa Ind Sch Dist 1986-; Microbiology Clarendon Coll 1988-; *ai:* Band Spon; Kids in Need of Direction Co-Coord; Tutorial Comm; STAT; *office:* Pampa HS 111 E Harvestor Pampa TX 79065

COLWELL, GWENDOLYN D., English Teacher; *b:* Richland, GA; *m:* Jack V.; *c:* Gail Colwell Slater, Clark N., Laura M.; *ed:* (BA) Eng, Shorter Coll 1961; *cr:* Teacher Long Creek Elem Sch 1962-63, Highland Elem Sch 1970-72, Johnston Cty Schls 1972-76, Pennville Elem Sch 1977-86, Chattooga HS 1986-; *ai:* Pennville Elem Chorus & Classroom Music Volunteer Dir 1980-84; Chattooga HS Choral Music Prgm Dir, Organizer, Developer, Musical Plays Dir 1986-; NEA 1972-82; PAGE (Building Rep 1984-86) 1983-; Kappa Kappa Iota 1985-88; Benson Elem Sch Teacher of Yr 1975; Chattooga HS Outstanding Teacher 1987-88; *office:* Chattooga HS Lyerly Hwy Summerville GA 30747

COLWELL, PATRICIA T., Second Grade Teacher; *b:* Atlanta, GA; *w:* George (dec); *ed:* (AB) Eng, GA St Univ 1964; *cr:* Teacher Guice Elem Sch 1964-79, Beaverbrook Elem 1979-; *ai:* Yrbk Adv; Math, Soc Stud Curr, Calendar Comm; Morning Devotion Spon; NEA, GAE 1964-; GSAE 1979-; Stewart Avenue United Meth Church 1942-; PTA Parliamentarian; Atlanta & Griffin Sch Teacher of Yr; Leon Hoover-Fulton HS STAR Teacher 1970; *home:* 1404 Parkway Dr Griffin GA 30223

COMB, DARREL WAYNE, High School Band Director; *b:* Lafayette, LA; *m:* Betty Ann Langlinais; *c:* Rene P., Andre C., Stephan J.; *ed:* (BME) Instrumental Music, 1975, (MME) Instrumental Music, 1978, Admin, 1990 Univ of SW LA; Supervision of Stu Teaching; Admin Cert; *cr:* Band Dir Acadia Parish 1975-79, Lafayette Parish 1979-; *ai:* Fine Arts Dept, Music Act Prgms Chm; Marching, Jazz, Concert, Guard & Percussion Dir; SLBDA (Treas 1981-84, Pres 1984-87); LA Jaycees VP 1980-81; Lions Club; *home:* Rt 1 Box 563 Breaux Bridge LA 70517

COMBEST, BOBBIE REED, English/Reading Teacher; *b:* Tulia, TX; *m:* Wallace Andrew; *c:* Debra L. Murphy, Janna L. Davis, Kevin A.; *ed:* (BS) Ed/Eng, Sul Ross St Univ 1957; Grad Level Eng & Ed; *cr:* 5th Grade Teacher East Elem 1957-59; Eng Teacher Alpine HS 1959-63; 5th Grade Teacher Bluebonnet Elem 1965-66; Eng Teacher Snyder Jr HS 1966-69, 1971-; *ai:* Spelling Bee Coach; NEA; TX St Teachers Assn Life Mem; TX Classroom Teachers Assn Treas 1968-69; NCTE; Eng Dept Head Snyder Jr HS; Educl Excl Awd from Cncl for Educl Excl 1990; *office:* Snyder Jr HS 2901 37th St Snyder TX 79549

COMBS, BETTY JO, Elementary Teacher; *b:* Elizabethton, TN; *m:* Jack; *c:* Lewis; *ed:* (BS) Health/Lang/Elem, 1956, (MA) Elem Ed, 1981, Elem Ed, 1984 E TN Univ; Several Wkshps Elem Ed; *cr:* 1st Grade Teacher Lowndes Cty Elem Sch 1958-60; 6th Grade Teacher Chinquapin Sch 1962-68; 5th Grade Teacher Bluff City Elem Sch 1968-; *ai:* TEA, SCEA, NEA; PTA Lifetime Mem 1975; Eastern Star (Matron 1977, Grand Comm 1982-85); 4-H Club Spon Outstanding Leader Awd 1974; Young Democrats of TN (Pres, Secy); *office:* Bluff City Elem Sch Box 280 Bluff City TN 37618

COMBS, JACK E., Physical Education Teacher; *b:* Boone, NC; *m:* Mary Jo Cudd; *c:* Marc, Jacquelyn, Julie; *ed:* (BS) Phys Ed/ Health, Appalachian St Univ 1960; (MAT) Soc Stud, Converse Coll 1973; (MA) Admin, Appalachian St Univ & Univ of SC 1989; *cr:* Teacher/Coach Caroleen Elem Sch 1960-62, Chase HS 1962-64; Phys Ed Teacher Jesse Boyd Elem Sch 1964-; *ai:* Coaching; Southern Assn & Various Sch Comms; Sch Improvement Cncl; NEA 1960-; NC Ed Assn 1960-64; SC Ed Assn 1964-; SC Assn of Health Phys Ed Recreation 1964-; First Baptist Church of Spartanburg Sunday Sch Teacher 1973-; *office:* Jesse Boyd Elem Sch Fernwood & Glendale Rd Spartanburg SC 29302

COMBS, LANA SUTTON, HS & Mid Sch Choral Director; *b:* Lexington, KY; *m:* Robert; *c:* Matthew B., Jordan G.; *ed:* (BME) Music Ed, Cumberland Coll 1971; (MM) Music/Piano, Morehead St Univ 1973; Rank I & Elem Teaching Certificate Morehead St Univ; *cr:* 1st-5th Grade Music Teacher Henry Cty Schls 1971-72; 1st-8th Grade Music Teacher Flemingsburg 1972-74; 6th Grade General Classroom Teacher 1974-83, Spec Ed/LDH Teacher 1983-86 Ewing; 1st-8th Grade Music Teacher Flemingsburg 1986-88; 7th-12th Grade Music Teacher Fleming HS 1988-; *ai:* Show Choir; Madrigals; Vocal Coach; Morehead Youth Soccer League (Secy, VP) 1985-; *office:* Fleming Cty HS/Simons Mid Sch Elizaville Rd Flemingsburg KY 41041

COMBS, MARY-JO CUDD, Business Education Teacher; *b:* Mayo, SC; *m:* Jack E.; *c:* Marc, Jacqui, Julie; *ed:* (BA) Bus/Ed, Limestone Coll 1959; (MAT) Soc Stud, Converse Coll 1971; (MS) Admin, Appalachian St Univ, Univ of SC, Clemson Univ 1989; Grad Stud; Trng in Real Estate; *cr:* Bus Ed Teacher Boiling Springs HS 1959-; *ai:* Boiling Springs Jr Class & Ring Spon; Natl Voc Honor Society Spon & Chm; Co-Spon of BLT Club; Bus Ed Dept & Prom Chm; St Voc Audit, Southern Dept Assn Comms; Sch Improvement Cncl; NEA, SC Ed Assn, SC Bus Ed Assn 1959-; 1st Baptist Church of Spartanburg Sunday Sch Teacher 1973-; Alpha Delta Kappa 1978-; Teacher of Yr 1989 Boiling Springs HS 1989; *office:* Boiling Springs HS PO Box 16130 Boiling Springs Station Spartanburg SC 29316

COMEAUX, BARBARA W., Biology Teacher; *b:* Columbia, TN; *m:* Jim; *c:* Shelly, Jeff; *ed:* Sci Ed, Univ of TN 1967; *cr:* Teacher Christenberry Jr HS 1968-77, Bearden Jr HS 1977-; *ai:* Stu Government Assn Adopt-A-Sch Comm Spon; Knox Cty Ed Assn, TN Ed Assn 1968-; NEA, Natl Assn of Stu Cncls 1986-; Natl Assn of Wkshp Dirs 1988-89; Amer Diabetes Assn Bd of Dirs 1986-88; *office:* Bearden HS 8352 Kingston Pike Knoxville TN 37919

COMEAUX, LOYCE WILLIAMS, English Department Chair; *b:* Port Arthur, TX; *ed:* (BA) Eng/Fr, Huston-Tilloson Coll 1975; (MED) Sch Admin, Lamar Univ 1985; *cr:* Eng Teacher Thomas Edison Mid Sch 1971-80; Realton Century 21 1979-81; Lab Technician Texaco Research 1980-81; Eng Teacher/Cnslr Port Arthur Adult Sch 1982-88; Eng Teacher/Dept Chairperson Stephen F Austin HS 1981-; *ai:* UIL Spelling, Ready Writing Spon; TX St Teachers Assn, NEA, Port Arthur Classroom Teachers Assn, PTA 1971-; Alpha Kappa Alpha 1970-; Negro Bus & Prof Women 1989-; Citizens Concerned for Promoting Cultural Awareness 1990-; Teacher of Yr Stephen F Austin HS 1987-88; TX Excl Awd for Outstanding HS Teachers from Univ of TX at Austin 1989; Level 3 Career Ladder Teacher; *home:* 3603 75th St #607 Port Arthur TX 77642

COMER, GARY LYNN, Mathematics Department Teacher; *b:* Statesville, NC; *c:* Teresa L., Mindy B.; *ed:* (BA) Health/Phys Ed, Appalachian St 1976; (BA) Math, Lenoir Rhynne 1984; Cmptrs; *cr:* Phys Ed Teacher/Coach Alexander Cntrl HS 1976-77; Phys Ed/Math Teacher/Coach E Alexander Jr HS 1977-83; Math Teacher/Coach Alexander Cntrl HS 1983-; *ai:* Var Ftbl Asst Coach; Local Sports & HS Bsktbl Officiate; Jr Var Bsbl Head Coach; Intramurals Club Spon; Jr Class Prom Comm Head; NEA, NCCA 1976-; NCCOA 1980-; Cty Recreation Ofcl Pres 1975-; Career Level II; Ftbl, Bsbl Conference Championships; *home:* PO Box York Rd Stony Point NC 28678

COMER, LES, 6th Grade Teacher; *b:* Three Forks, MT; *m:* Patricia L.; *c:* Vicki, James; *ed:* (BA) Elem Ed, W MT Coll 1963; Grad Stud; *cr:* 6th Grade Teacher Bozeman Schls 1963-; *ai:* MT Ed Assn, MT Rdng Cncl; MT Cncl Soc Stud Bd of Dir; Masons, Shriners; De Molay Boys (Advisory Bd 1980-, Dad Adv 1988-), Cross of Honor 1989; Rainbow Girls Dad Adv; *home:* 1120 N 9th Bozeman MT 59715

COMER, MAXINE RAY, Choral Director; *b:* Union Church, MS; *m:* Thomas L.; *ed:* (BME) Music Ed, MS St Coll for Women 1965; (MAT) Rollins Coll; *cr:* Elem Music Teacher Eustis Elem 1965-70, Choral Dir Eustis Mid Sch 1970-; *ai:* Eustis Mid Chorus Spon; Lake Cty Ed Assn Sch Rep 1984-89; FL Ed Assn 1969-; MENC 1965-70; *office:* Eustis Mid Sch 1731 E Bates Ave Eustis FL 32726

COMER, ROSALYN SUE, Mathematics Teacher; *b:* Philadelphia, PA; *c:* Rayna, Jeff; *ed:* (BS) Scndry Ed/Math, Temple Univ 1972; (MA) Educl Admin/Supervision, Rider Coll 1979; *cr:* Teacher Cheltenham HS 1972-; *ai:* Track, Sftbl, Gymnastics, Dance Coach; NEA; *office:* Cheltenham HS Rices Mill Rd & Carlton Ave Wyncote PA 19095

COMERFORD, DANIEL J., III, 7th Grade Soc Stud Teacher; *b:* Brooklyn, NY; *m:* Katie Wiener; *ed:* (BA) His/Ed, St Univ of NY New Paltz 1968; (MA) Black Stud/Soc Issues, 1970, (MA) Medieval His/Ed, 1973 St Univ of NY Stony Brook; (DED) Curr/ Instruction/Scndry Ed/Research/Methodology/Instrument Design/Evaluation, NY Univ 1983; *cr:* Soc Stud Teacher/Team Coord 1968-72, Disruptive/Unmotivated Stus Spec Prgm Dir 1974-82, Soc Stud/Honors Prgm/Skills Level Courses Teacher 1982-, Mentor-Intern Prgm Evaluator 1987-, Personnel Assoc 1988- Three Village Cntrl Sch Dist; Adjunct Professor St Univ of NY Stony Brook 1988-; *ai:* Amer Red Cross Cmmty Blood Drive Chm; Three Village Teachers Assn Grievance Chm; Early Amer Industries Assn Pres Patent Research Grant-in-Aid 1987; NERA, ASCD, NCSS; AERA Annual Meeting Presenter 1985, 1987; NEERO Annual Meeting Presenter 1985, 1986, 1988; British-Amer Rhykenological Society; Phi Delta Kappa 1979; NYS Mid Sch Assn Annual Meeting Presenter 1985; Natl Organization of Legal Problems in Ed; NY ST Outstndng Teacher of Amer History By DAR; Whos Whos in Amer Ed 1988, 1989; Three Village CSD Instructional Recogaition Awd 1987 & Teacher of Yr 1979-80, 1972-73; US Dept of Ed Scndry Schls Recognition Prgm Teacher Rep & Co-Editor 1984; Outstanding Scndry Educators of Amer 1973, 1975; Article Published 1989; *office:* R C Murphy Jr HS Nicolls Rd Setauket NY 11733

COMERRO, JOHN BURNS, English Department Chairman; *b:* Paterson, NJ; *m:* Katherine Robin Cleary; *c:* Thomas, Hope; *ed:* (BA) Eng Lit, Rutgers Univ 1971; (MS) Rdng, Russell Sage Coll 1981; *cr:* Eng Teacher 1976-, Eng Dept Chm 1979- Berlin Cntrl Sch; *ai:* NY St Eng Cncl Teacher of Excl Awd 1986; *office:* Berlin Cntrl Sch Rt 22 Cherry Plain NY 12040

COMFORT, ROSANNE ELIZABETH (DORSEY), Retired English Teacher; *b:* Mountain View, CA; *m:* Paul Anthony; *ed:* (BS) Eng/Philosophy, Willamette Univ 1983; (MA) Eng/Modern Fiction, Univ of Exeter England 1990; Curr Dev & Literary Criticism, Auburn Univ; *cr:* Eng Teacher Archbishop Milty HS 1984-85, St Francis HS 1986-89; *ai:* Asst Speech & Debate Team, Inter-Act Club, Campus Ministry Retreats; NCTE, NCEA, CA Assn Teachers of Eng; St Pius X Church Parish; Rotary Fnd Grad Schlshp 1985; Ca Assn of Teachers Conference 1987; Natl Endowment for Hum Grant 1989; Published & Directed Eng Teachers Sourcebook 1988; Literary Criticism Conferences; *home:* 5381 NW Deerfield Way Portland OR 97229

COMO, FLORENCE J., Fifth Grade Teacher; *b:* Fall River, MA; *c:* Jennifer; *ed:* (BS) Ed, 1959, (MS) Ed, 1962 Bridgewater St; (MA) Eng, Univ of RI 1968; Grad Courses Boston Univ & Brown Univ; *cr:* Teacher Fall River Public Schls 1959-66, Lincoln Public Schls 1967-; *ai:* Lang Art Curr Comm; MA Teachers Assn, Natl Teachers Assn; Kappa Delta Pi, Delta Kappa Gamma; *home:* 134 Tower Rd Lincoln MA 01773

COMPTON, CLEO RICHARDSON, Retired Elem Supvr; *b:* Pryor, OK; *m:* Kenneth D.; *c:* Joan Quiring; *ed:* (BS) Elem Ed, Northeastern St Coll 1940; (MS) Elem Ed, Univ of OK Norman 1956; Working on Cert to Teach Educable Mentally Handicapped, Univ of Tulsa & Univ of Denver; Many Wkshps & Seminars; *cr:* Elem Teacher Rural Schls Mayes Cty 1937-40, Papago & Navajo & Choctaw Schls 1950-56; Teacher of Educable Handicapped/ Elem Teacher Tulsa Public Schls 1956-75; Elem Teacher Temple Chrstn Sch 1975-77; Elem Supvr Bible Fellowship Learning Center 1977-85; *ai:* Kappa Delta Pi 1956; NEA, OK Ed Assn, Tulsa Classroom Teachers Assn 1956-75; *home:* 2127 S Delaware Ct Tulsa OK 74114

COMPTON, MARCIA ROBERTSON, Second Grade Teacher; *b:* Saginaw, MI; *m:* Dana B.; *c:* Zachary, Jennifer; *ed:* (AA) Delta Coll 1971; (BS) Ed/Eng/Art, E MI Univ 1973; (MA) Elem Ed, Cntrl MI Univ 1978; *cr:* Art/Elem Ed Teacher 1973-79, Classroom Teacher 1979- Freeland Cmmty Schls; *ai:* Wellness & Lib Comm; NEA, MI Ed Assn; Freeland Ed Secy 1975-76; Kappa Delta Gamma 1988-89; Saginaw Choral Society (Corresponding Secy 1978, Chamber Choir 1989-); Freeland HS Commencement Keynote Speaker 1989; *office:* Freeland Elem Sch 710 Powley Dr Freeland MI 48623

COMPTON, PENNY DORNBUSCH, Instrumental Music Teacher; *b:* New Braunfels, TX; *m:* William Robert; *c:* Courtney E., Christopher R.; *ed:* (BMED) Music Ed, TX Luth Coll 1979; Working Toward Masters in Music Ed; *cr:* Band Dir Krueger Mid Sch 1979-81, Garner Mid Sch 1982-; *ai:* Mid Sch Jazz Band, Orch & Musical Productions; Adult Band; TX Music Educators Assn, TX Bandmasters Assn 1979-; TX St Teachers Assn, NEA; *office:* Garner Mid Sch 4302 Harry Wurzbach San Antonio TX 78209

COMSTOCK, VERLA MAE (SCHROEDER), 3rd/4th Grade Teacher; *b:* Twin Falls, ID; *m:* Ross E.; *c:* Edward, Kevin, Albert; *ed:* (BS) Elem Ed, Concordia Teachers Coll & WI Univs 1970; *cr:* 2nd/3rd Grade Teacher 1953-56, 3rd Grade Teacher 1857-59

Immanuel Luth Parochial Sch; 2nd Grade Teacher St Johns Luth Sch 1960; 3rd-5th Grade Teacher Portage Cmmty Schls 1967-89; *ai:* Winnebago Ridge Runners Snowmobile Club Treas; St Johns Luth Sunday Sch Mailing Secy; *home:* W 8502 Lock Rd Portage WI 53901

CONANT, GRACE ARLENE, 4th Grade Teacher; *b:* Zenith, KS; *m:* Eldon Carroll; *c:* Merrill R., Ferrill R., Tamsel A. Kuhns, Kevin C., Quentin E.; *ed:* (BS) Home Ec, 1956, (BS) Elem Ed, 1966 Ft Hays St Univ; Summer Grant Concordia Teachers Coll 1966; *cr:* Home Ec/Eng Teacher Waldo HS 1956-58; 8th Grade Teacher Ingalls Jr HS 1962-64; 4th Grade Teacher Ingalls Elem Sch 1965-70, Cimarron Elem Sch 1970-; *ai:* Jr Class Spon; Curr Comm; Negotiation Teams; KEA (Pres, Secy, Building Rep, Assn Rep); NEA Life Membership; Natl Rdng Teachers Assn; Delta Kappa Gamma 1978-; Chamber of Commerce 1988-; Soc Stud Youth Teacher & Teen Spon; Jacksonian Newspaper Woman of Month 1980; Arthritis Fnd Chairperson Gray Cty 1972; Natl Rdng Conference 1986.

CONAR, LUCY C., 5th Grade Teacher; *b:* Niota, TN; *m:* Thomas Earl; *c:* Thomas E. Jr., Stephen C., Michael F.; *ed:* (BA) Ed, TN Wesleyan Coll 1969; (MS) Curr/Instruction, Univ of TN Knoxville 1985; *cr:* Teacher Ingleside Elem Sch 1969-; *ai:* Steering Comm Sch of Excl Appliation Chairperson; Mentor Teacher; Athens Ed Assn IPD Comm 1969-; TN Ed Assn, NEA 1969-; Keith Memorial United Meth Church Many Offices 1960-; Career Ladder III; Ingleside Teacher of Yr; Athens City Sch Teacher of Yr; Grant With Co-Teacher; *office:* Ingleside Elem Sch Guille Athens TN 37303

CONARD, BILLIE BOYD, Health/Physical Ed Teacher; *b:* Waynesville, NC; *m:* Jeffrey Lee; *c:* Jarrod Boyd; *ed:* (BS) Phys Ed, Mars Hill Coll 1979; *cr:* Teacher/Coach Tuscola HS 1979-; *ai:* Amer Bus Womens Assn, NC Alliance for Health, Phys Ed, Recreation, Dance; *home:* 266 Pisgah Dr Canton NC 28716

CONATSER, MARGUERITE HOLLAND, 5th Grade Teacher; *b:* Nashville, TN; *m:* Bob; *c:* Joseph Bob, Daniel Glenn, Holly Amanda Conatser Powers; *ed:* (BS) Elem Ed/Phys Ed, Mid TN St Univ 1955; *cr:* K/6th Grade Teacher Phys Ed 1955-56, Phys Ed Teacher Bordeaux 1956-59/1960-65; 3rd/4th Grade Teacher Kings Lane 1959-60; Phys Ed/4th/5th Grade Teacher Ashland City 1976-79; 5th Grade Teacher Harpeth 1979-87; Pegram Elem 1987-; *ai:* Faculty Advisory 1987-88; Teacher of Yr Program Sch 1988-89; Harpeth Yrbk Dedication; Park Ave Baptist Church Mem 1950-; *office:* Pegram Elem Sch Dogwood Ln Pegram TN 37143

CONAWAY, DIANNE E., 4th Grade Teacher/Dept Chm; *b:* Mechanicsburg, PA; *M:* John T.; *ed:* (AA) Elem Ed, Harrisburg Area Comm Coll 1972; (BS) Elem Ed, PA St Univ 1974; Admin, Western MD; Project Weild & Project Learning Tree; Environm Ental Ed Trng; EEI & TESA Trained; *cr:* Teacher 1974-75; Teacher/Dir 1975-79; Carlisle Cmmty Nursery; Teacher Green Park Elem 1980-83; Techer/Dept Chm Blain Elem Sch 1984-; *ai:* Sch Improvement Comm Pres; PTO Teacher Rep, Past Pres (2 Yrs) Treas (3) Girls Sftbl Coach; Mentor; ASCD 1988-; Natl Cncl for The Soc Stud 1988-; PA Cncl for Soc Stud 1988-; 4-H Leader 1884-; 4-H Advisory Cncl 1989-; Dickinson Presbyn Adult Fellowship Pres 1987-; Church Ed Comm; Chm of Dist Environmental Ed Prgm; Chm of Soc Stud Curr Dev; Developed Mentor Prgm; *home:* 1755 Pine Rd Newville PA 17241

CONAWAY, REBECCA GOLT, Third Grade Teacher; *b:* Wilmington, DE; *m:* William Edmond; *c:* Teresa Conaway Mason; *ed:* (BS) Elem Ed/Geography, Salisbury St Univ 1970; Advanced Prof Certificate with Masters Equivalent 1980; *cr:* 3rd Grade Teacher Snow Hill Elem Sch 1970-; *ai:* Film Festival Stu Adv; After Sch Tutor; Cooperating Teacher for Salisbury St Univ, Trng Teachers; Sch Improvement Advisory Comm Mem; NEA, MSTA, WCTA; *office:* Snow Hill Elem Sch 5708 Coulbourne Lane Dr Snow Hill MD 21863

CONAWAY, TRUDI, 7th Grade Basic Ed Teacher; *b:* Los Angeles, CA; *m:* Victor Allen; *ed:* (BA) Soc Sci, San Diego St Univ 1971; (MS) Ed, US Intnl Univ 1979; *cr:* 3rd/4th Grade Teacher Sunset Beach Elem 1971-73; 3rd-5th Grade Teacher Westwood Elem 1973-79; 7th Grade Teacher Meadowbrook Mid Sch 1979-89, Bernardo Heights Mid Sch 1989-; *ai:* Proficiency & Remediation, Stus At-Risk Coord; Associated Stu Body, Newspaper Adv; Rancho Bernardo Girls Sftbl (VP, Mgr) 1976-84; Prgm Improvement Plan Teacher, Grant; *office:* Bernardo Heights Mid Sch 12990 Paseo Lucido San Diego CA 92128

CONDE, A. RICHARD, Spanish Teacher; *b:* Massillon, OH; *m:* Karen S. Cahill; *c:* Adam, Amanda; *ed:* (BA) Span/Eng, Malone Coll 1966; (MA) Span, Univ of AZ 1968; *cr:* Teacher Springboro HS 1968-; *ai:* Peer Counseling; Clearcreek Schls Wellness Comm; OH Ed Assn, NEA, Clearcreek Ed Assn, Modern Lang Assn, Amer Assn Teachers of Span & Portuguese 1968-; Church; BSA; Span Honorary; Educator of Yr 1989; *office:* Springboro HS 1605 S Main St Springboro OH 45066

CONDE, VERONICA (GURAUSKAS), Multi-lingual Cultural Teacher; *b:* Gary, IN; *m:* Francis A.; *ed:* (BA) Eng, Ball St Univ 1962; (MAT) Fr, IN Univ 1969; *cr:* Eng/Fr Teacher Emerson HS 1962-71; ESL Teacher Lew Wallace HS 1971-73; Fr Teacher Brussels Amer HS Belgium 1973-74; Multi-Lingual Cultural Teacher Lew Wallace HS 1974-; *ai:* Delta Kappa Gamma Pres 1984-86; NEA Life Mem; IN St Teachers Assn; *office:* Lew Wallace HS 415 W 45th Ave Gary IN 46408

CONDER, RA NAE NAYLOR, Fifth Grade Teacher; *b:* South Jordan, UT; *m:* Neldon; *c:* Sharlene Conder Barton, Robert N., Carol A. Conder Nuttall, Bradley G.; *ed:* (BS) Elem Ed, Univ of UT 1968; *cr:* 3rd Grade Teacher Midvale Elem 1968-80, Welby Elem 1980-89; 5th Grade Teacher Welby Elem 1989-; *ai:* Alpha Delta Kappa (Secy 1976-78, Pres 1990-, Chaplain 1980-82, Pres Elect 1988-); NEA, UT Ed Assn, Jordan Ed Assn; Outstanding Teachers of America Awd 1974; Teacher Leader 1986-87; *office:* Welby Elem 4130 W 9580 S South Jordan UT 84065

CONDON, LINDA LEE, Reading/French Teacher; *b:* Chicago, IL; *ed:* (BSED) Elem Ed, N IL Univ 1977; (MA) Elem Ed, Governors St Univ 1986; *cr:* Kndgtn Teacher 1977-78, 5th Grade Teacher 1978-84 Fernway Park Elem; Rdng/Fr Teacher Grissom Jr HS 1984-; *ai:* NHS, Fine Arts Club Spon; Outdoor Ed Comm Sch Dist 140 Founding Mem; Alpha Delta Kappa St Recording Secy 1988-; Intnl Rdng Assn, IFT, AFT; Alpha Xi Delta, Phi Kappa Phi, Mortar Bd; Golden Apple Awd, Master Teacher Nominee; *office:* Grissom Jr HS 17000 S 80th Ave Tinley Park IL 60477

CONDON, PATRICIA ELIZABETH HEATON, French Teacher/Dept Chair; *b:* St Paul, MN; *m:* Joseph L.; *c:* Nicholas, Colleen, Timothy; *ed:* (BA) Fr, Univ of MN 1970; Cert Metro St Coll 1984; *cr:* Teacher/Dept Chairperson Arapahoe HS 1984-; *ai:* Fr Club; Soc Comm; Wild Warrior Women; CARE Team Group Facilitator; Kappa Delta Pi 1985-; CCFLT 1984-; *office:* Arapahoe HS 2201 E Dry Creek Rd Littleton CO 80122

CONE, DAWN CLIFTON, Sixth Grade Teacher; *b:* Altoona, AL; *m:* Charlie L.; *c:* Allison, Christopher; *ed:* (BS) Scndry Ed/Math, Jacksonville St Univ 1969; (MA) Elem Ed, Univ of AL 1978; *cr:* Math Aide NASA 1966/1967; Math Teacher Hokes Bluff HS 1969-71; 6th Grade Teacher Cleveland HS 1974-; *ai:* 4-H Club Spon; Just Say No Club Spon; 6th Grade Adv; Altoona 1st United Methodist Church Lay Delegate/Sunday Sch Teacher; Clevland Band Boosters Secy 1986; AL St Soc Stud Fair Judge; Teacher Hall of Fame Nom Blount Cty; *home:* Rt 1 Box 60B Altoona AL 35952

CONEY, ELAINE MARIE, Span, French & Latin Teacher; *b:* Magnolia, MS; *ed:* (BA) Span, Millsaps Coll 1974; (MA) Span, 1975, (PHD) Span, 1977 Universidad Interamericana; (MED) Scndry Ed, Univ of S MS 1979; *cr:* Eng Teacher Liberty Attendance Center 1976-77; Span/Fr Teacher S Pike HS 1977-; *ai:* Foreign Lang Club Spon; MS Assn of Educators, S Pike Assn of Educators, MS Foreign Lang Assn 1977-; MS Assn Women in Ed Leadership VP 1988-; Substance Abuse Policy Cncl Appointed by Governor Mabus 1988; Teacher of Yr 1988; Bd of Examiners Natl Cncl for Accreditation in Teachers Ed; Bd of Examiners Natl Cncl for Accreditation in Teachers Ed; *home:* PO Box 208 Magnolia MS 39652

CONGER, ROBERT BRIAN, Band Director; *b:* Wilkes Barre, PA; *m:* Julie Hewit Delcamp; *ed:* (BM) Music Ed, E Carolina Univ 1975; (MM) Music Composition, Northwestern Univ 1976; (DMA) Trombone Performance, N TX St Univ 1983; *cr:* Band Dir Hartsville Jr HS 1977-80; Trombone Prof Miami Univ 1983-84; Trombonist Glenn Miller Orchestra 1984; Band Dir Meadowbrook Mid Sch 1984-; *ai:* Television, Media Teacher, Chess Club Spon; Golf Coach; Intnl Trombone Assn 1980-; Music Educators Natl Conference 1975-; FL Bandmasters Assn 1984-; *office:* Meadowbrook Mid Sch 6000 North Ln Orlando FL 32808

CONGER, RONALD JESSE, NJROTC Associate Instructor; *b:* Savannah, GA; *m:* Martha Jean May; *c:* Charles E., James A.; *ed:* (AS) General Stud, Mohegan Comm Coll 1984; Occupational Ed, S IL Univ; Curr Dev & Cnslr Trng, US Navy; *cr:* Chief Radioman US Navy 1967-87; Instr Fleet Trng Center 1984-87; NJROTC Assoc Instr Gaithersburg HS 1987-; *ai:* NJROTC Drill Team & Color Guard Coach; Veterans of Foreign Wars Mem 1987-; Distinguished Instr Awd 1985; Course Supvr Designation Teletype Maintenance Course 1985-87; Designated Curr Dev Specialist 1986-87; *office:* Gaithersburg HS 314 S Frederick Rd Gaithersburg MD 20877

CONKLIN, WARREN GEORGE, Econ/Criminal Justice Teacher; *b:* Brooklyn, NY; *ed:* (BA) His, Hobart Coll 1976; (MS) Ed, Elmira Coll 1981; Criminal Justice, Ec Courses, Corning Comm Coll; *cr:* Teacher Horseheads HS 1976-; Adjunct Professor Corning Comm Coll 1988-; *ai:* Var Soccer, Sftbl Coach; Ed Cncl; Teacher/Mentor Comm; Taft Inst; *office:* Horseheads HS Fletcher St Horseheads NY 14845

CONLEY, BETTY NEWLAND, Language Arts Teacher; *b:* Piqua, OH; *m:* Earl; *c:* Christopher A., Patricia A. Spradlin; *ed:* (BS) Ed, OH Univ 1966; *cr:* Teacher Portsmouth City Schls 1968-; *ai:* HS Newspaper Spon 1989-; Schlsp Team Coach 1985-; Portsmouth City Schls Competency Test Comm 1985; Portsmouth City Schls Ed Assn 1968-; OH Ed Assn, NEA; Melton Fnd Awd Berea Coll 1986, 1988, 1989; OH St Schlsp Test Comm 1985; *office:* Portsmouth City Sch Marshall & Farney Ave Portsmouth OH 45662

CONLEY, ELAINE HIGGINS, English Teacher; *b:* Lakeview, IA; *m:* Larry Marvin; *c:* Patrick, Kristin; *ed:* (BA) Eng, Univ of IA 1965; Working Towards Masters Eng, His, Ed; *cr:* Eng Teacher Foothill HS 1965-68; Core Teacher Woodbrook Jr HS 1968-69; Eng Teacher Foothill HS 1969-, Bakersfield Coll 1986-88; *ai:* Wrting Proficiency Comm Mem; CA Schlsp Fed Adv; Mentor Teacher Selection Comm Mem; CA Assn Teachers of Eng 1987-; NEA 1965-; CTA 1969-; Kern HS Dist Mentor Teacher 1988-89; Outstanding Teacher 1978; Teacher of Month 1987; *office:* Foothill HS 501 Park Dr Bakersfield CA 93306

CONLEY, JERRIE CHILDRESS, K-1st Grade Music/Art Teacher; *b:* Memphis, TN; *c:* Robin Conley Baker, Carol Conley Workman, Robert M. Jr.; *ed:* (BS) Elem Ed, 1966, (MA) Curr/Instruction, 1987 Univ of TN Martin; *cr:* 1st/2nd Grade Teacher S Fulton Elem 1966-67; Teacher Martin Elem 1967-79, Martin Primary 1979-; *ai:* Martin Elem After Sch Day Care Dir; WCEA Faculty Rep & Delegate; Intnl Rdng Assn Pres 1990; Alpha Delta Kappa Pres 1986-88; Pilot Club Pres 1980-81, Pilot of Yr 1980; W Weakley Cancer Organization Secy 1988-; Center of Excl for the Enrichment of Sci & Math Ed Awarded PTO Schlsps; *home:* 325 S College Martin TN 38237

CONLEY, MELAINE ANN, Middle School Science Teacher; *b:* Charleston, WV; *m:* Robert B.; *ed:* (BS) Bio, 1982, (MS) Bio, 1986 Morehead St Univ; *cr:* 6th-8th Grade Sci Teacher Ironton Jr HS 1983-; *ai:* Ironton HS Var Chrldr Adv; Math & Sci Ed Advisory Commission OH St Bd of Ed; *home:* 1033 Mc Cown St Russell KY 41169

CONLIN, JAMES DONALD, Business Department Chair; *b:* Pawtucket, RI; *m:* Martha Charlotte Price; *c:* Andrea C. Conlin Martin, Jeffrey P.; *ed:* (BS) Bus Admin/Accountancy/Finance, Bryant Coll 1950; (MED) Bus Ed, Shippensburg Univ 1968; Grad Courses Cmptr Programming & Supervision; *cr:* Systems Salesman Remington Rand Corporation 1950-54; Teacher Mercersburg Acad 1954-70, Mid Township HS 1970-; *ai:* Stu Act Coord; Adv to Club & Class Advs; Conduct Sr Trip, Baccalaureate & Graduation; Mid Township Teachers Assn, Cape May Cty Teachers Assn, NJ Teachers Assn 1970-; NJ Bus Teachers Assn 1986-; Natl Assn Stu Act Advs 1984-; ASCD 1990; Atlantic Comm Coll Advisory Bd-Accounting 1986-; Cape May Cty Voc Tech Sch Advisory Bd 1987-; Stone Harbor Bd of Ed VP 1987-; Participated Teacher in Space Prgm 1985-86; Mid Township HS Teacher of Yr 1986-87; *office:* Middle Township H S 212 Bayberry Dr Cape May Crt Hse NJ 08210

CONNELL, JULIE HOLLAND, Mathematics Teacher; *b:* Mankato, MN; *m:* Thomas Robert; *ed:* (BA) Math, St Olaf Coll 1983; *cr:* Math Teacher Duluth Cathedral Sch 1983-85, Central HS 1985-; *ai:* Prom; Swing Choir Choreographer; CEA, MEA, NEA Mem 1985-; *office:* Central HS 531 Morse St Norwood MN 55368

CONNELL, LAURA BURNS, Social Studies Teacher; *b:* Niagara Falls, NY; *c:* M. Shawn, Maureen Survant; *ed:* (BA) His, Niagara Univ 1950; His, Niagara Univ; Rdng, Syracuse Univ; *cr:* Intel Analyst MIT 1956-58; Substitute Home Instruction Teacher Holy Spirit Sch 1961-68; Soc Stud/Rdng/Ed Consultant NY St 1971-78; Soc Stud/Rdng Teacher Our Lady of Mt Carmel Sch 1979-.

CONNELLY, KEVIN MARK, Computer Science Teacher; *b:* Newark, NJ; *m:* Tacie K.; *c:* Mark, Eric, Andrew; *ed:* (BA) Bio, Univ of DE 1975; (MA) Cmptr Ed, Columbia Univ 1989; Admin & Supervision, Loyola Coll; *cr:* Research Specialist Univ of PA 1975-80; Teacher Rising Sun HS 1981-86, Perryville HS 1986-; *ai:* Instr Appleworks for Educators; Gifted & Talented Seminars; Testing Supvr Univ of DE; Mid Sts Evaluation Team; Chm Perryville Technology Use Support Team; MD Sch Performance Prgm; Olympics of Mind; MSTA, CCCTA Sch Rep 1982-83; NAUG; Glasgow Reformed Presbyn Church; Articles in Immunology of Breast Milk & Secretory Immunity & Infection; *office:* Perryville HS 1696 Perryville Rd Perryville MD 21903

CONNELLY, MARGARET MARGITTNY, 6th Grade Teacher; *b:* New York, NY; *m:* Lawrence A.; *c:* Marcia Connelly Eggleston, Susan Connelly Griffin, Anne, Mary; *ed:* (BS) Home Ec, Plattsburgh St 1957; (BS) Elem Ed, Potsdam St 1965; *cr:* Home Ec Teacher Madrid Waddington Cntrl 1959-62; 6th Grade Teacher Norwood-Norfolk Cntrl 1970-; *ai:* 5th/6th Grade Olympiad Contest Spon; Delta Kappa Gamma 1987-; Church of Visitation Rosary Society (Trustee 1989-, Secy 1965-72); Chosen to Accompany Guidance Cnslr St Wide Wkshps; *home:* 4 Morris St Box 22 Norfolk NY 13667

CONNELLY, PATRICIA SWAIN, English Teacher; *b:* Spartanburg, SC; *m:* Wesley; *c:* Craig, Kevin, Hugh; *ed:* (BA) Eng, Furman Univ 1964; (MAT) Eng, GA St Univ 1989; *cr:* Eng Teacher Pickens HS 1964-66, Fayetteville HS 1967, Walton HS 1986-; *ai:* Sr Class Spon; Walton STAR Teacher; *office:* Walton HS 1590 Bill Murdock Rd Marietta GA 30062

CONNER, ALMA GAYLE, Fourth Grade Teacher; *b:* Vanderbilt, TX; *ed:* (BS) Elem Ed, Sam Houston St Teachers Coll 1964; (MED) Counseling, Prairie View A&M Univ 1979; *cr:* Elem Teacher Blum Ind Sch Dist 1964-67, Coolidge Ind Sch Dist 1967-70; Jr HS Teacher/Coach 1970-74, Elem Teacher 1974-Acad Ind Sch Dist; *ai:* Univ Interscholastic League Coach Picture Memory; Assn of TX Prof Educators; *office:* Academy Elem Sch Rt 2 Temple TX 76502

CONNER, ANNE REMBERT, Kindergarten Teacher; *b:* Myrtlewood, AL; *m:* John Wesley Jr.; *c:* Marcus, Kristi; *ed:* (BS) Early Chldhd Ed, AL St Univ 1975; Grad Stud Livingston Univ, Univ of AL; *cr:* 3rd/4th Grade Teacher 1975-76, Kndgtn Teacher 1976- Sweet Water HS; *ai:* Little League Ball Team Spon; AL Ed Assn, NEA 1975-87; New Hope 1 Baptist Church Choir Dir 1960-; Matrons/Bible Sch (Prgm Chm, Teacher) 1980-; Daughter Elks 1985-86, Sweet Heart 1985; New Hope #1 Nursery Dir 1990; *office:* Sweet Water HS P O Box 127 Sweet Water AL 36782

CONNER, DENNIS W., Sci Teacher/ Sci Dept Chair; *b:* Lafayette, IN; *m:* Carolyn Rose Hasty; *c:* Christine; *ed:* (BS) Chem, 1972, (MS) Ed Admin, 1979 Purdue Univ; Telecommunications On-Line Searching, Project INSITE Grant; Gifted Ed Endorsement, Purdue Univ; *cr:* Chem Teacher Haworth HS 1972-74; Sales Engineer Kunkle Valve Co 1974-75; G Sci Teacher/Coach De Kalb Jr HS 1975-78; Gifted Sci/Gifted Phys Sci Teacher/Coach Sunnyside Mid Sch 1978-; *ai:* 8th Grade Ftbl & 6th-8th Grade Bsktbl Coach; Academic Coord; Fundraising Coord; Hoosier Assn of Sci Teachers 1988-; NEA 1978-; Lafayette Ed Assn Comm Work 1978-; IN HS Athletic Assn Licensed Ofcl; North Cntrl Evaluations 1976, 1987, 1989.

CONNER, JENNY ELAINE (TATE), Health Teacher; *b:* Dahlonega, GA; *m:* Donald R.; *c:* Jarad C.; *ed:* (AS) Secretarial Sci, 1975, (BS) Comprehensive Bus Ed, 1982, (MS) Mid Grades, 1985 N GA Coll; *cr:* Health Teacher Lumpkin Cty Mid Sch 1982-; *ai:* Honor Roll & Beta Club Spon; Prof Assn of GA Educators Building Rep 1983-; *office:* Lumpkin Cty Mid Sch 200 School Dr Dahlonega GA 30533

CONNER, LARRY WALTER, Elementary Media Specialist; *b:* Danville, KY; *ed:* (BS) Elem Ed, Campbellsville Coll 1972; (MS) Media Specialist, E KY Univ 1980; *cr:* Teacher Mc Kinney Elem 1972-77, Hogsett Elem 1977-85; Media Specialist Toliver Elem 1985-; *office:* Toliver Elem Sch Maple Ave Danville KY 40422

CONNER, MARJORIE FLETCHER, Fifth Grade Teacher; *b:* Mobile, AL; *m:* Amos Jr.; *c:* Amos T., Marlon D.; *ed:* (BA) Elem Ed, AL St Univ 1968; (MS) Admin Supervision, Nova Univ 1977; *cr:* 5th Grade Teacher Glendale Elem 1968-69; 4th/5th Grade Teacher Tropical Elem 1969-; *ai:* AL St Alumni; Christ The King Afro-Amer Comm; *office:* Tropical Elem Sch 4545 SW 104th Ave Miami FL 33165

CONNER, PAULETTE A., Principal; *b:* Greenville, PA; *m:* James C.; *c:* Brett M., Christopher A.; *ed:* (BS) Elem Ed, Univ of Pittsburgh 1970; (MS) Educl Psych, 1974; (EDS) Admin, 1989 Butler Univ; *cr:* Elem Teacher St Barnabas Sch 1975-89; Prin St Michael Sch 1989-; *ai:* Soccer Club; Sch Promotional Comm; Bd of Ed; Home Sch Assn; APA; NCEA; Phi Beta Kappa; *home:* 8552 Trails Run Rd Indianapolis IN 46217

CONNERLEY, HAROLD ALLEN, Mathematics Teacher; *b:* Grenada, MS; *m:* Lu; *c:* Robert, Allen; *ed:* (BS) Math Ed, MS St Univ 1965; (MED) Math Ed Auburn Univ 1974; Educl Specialist; *cr:* Teacher/Coach Cross Keys HS 1965-71; Tucker HS 1971-75; Berman HS 1971-75; Asst Prin Trickum Mid Sch 1975-76; Teacher/Coach Norcross HS 1977-87; Peachtree HS 1977-87; *ai:* Ftbl Coach; BSA Troop Comm 1978-; *office:* Columbia H S 2106 Columbia Dr Decatur GA 30032

CONNOLLY, CARMEL, First Grade Teacher; *ed:* (BA) Elem Ed, Incarnate Word Coll 1970; (MS) Ed/Rdng/K-12, Fordham Univ 1982; Scripture/Theology/Liturgy & Catechetics/Certified Catechetical Teacher; *cr:* K-5 Grade Teacher Archdiocese San Antonio TX 1962-75; K-3rd Grade Teacher Archdiocese NY 1975-; *office:* Visitation Sch 171 W 239th St Bronx NY 10463

CONNOLLY, CONNIE ARLEN, Mathematics Teacher; *b:* Dubuque, IA; *m:* Allan P.; *c:* Patrick, Margaret; *ed:* (BA) Math, Edgewood Coll 1972; (MEPD) Math, Univ of WI Platteville 1979; *cr:* Jr HS Math Teacher 1973-78, HS Math Math Teacher 1978- Dubuque Cmmty Sch; Part Time Math Teacher Loras Coll 1986-; *ai:* ICTM, NCTM; DEA Secy 1978-80; ISEA, NEA; Natl Sci Fnd Grants 1988, 1989; *office:* Dubuque Sr HS 1800 Clarke Dr Dubuque IA 52001

CONNOLLY, MICHAEL JAMES, Eighth Grade History Teacher; *b:* Pawtucket, RI; *m:* Susan; *c:* Michael Jr.; *ed:* (BA) Ed/ Soc Stud, Univ of RI 1972; (MED) Cnslr Ed, Providence Coll 1978; Taft Inst RI Coll; *cr:* 8th Grade His/Civics Teacher Slater Jr HS 1972-73; *ai:* Stu Cncl & 9th Grade Class Adv; Project Pass Teacher; Ftbl, Bsbl, Intramural Coach; AHEPA 1975-81; Assumption Church (Pres 1978-80, Bd Mem 1975-80, 1987-); Northeast Soc Stud Conference Speaker 1989; *office:* Slater Jr HS 281 Mineral Spring Ave Pawtucket RI 02861

CONNOLY, ALICE LANGSTON, Retired Teacher/Substitute; *b:* Johnston Cty, NC; *m:* John Leo Jr.; *c:* Maura K., Margaret Connelly Glenn, John M.; *ed:* (BA) Soc Stud, Atlantic Chrstn Coll 1950; Elem Ed, Campbell Univ & East Carolina Univ; *cr:* Teacher Harnett Cty Schls 1950-53, Wake Cty Schls 1953-55, Chowan Cty Schls 1955-57, Onslow Cty Schls 1957-59/1970-71/1962-68/ 1974-84, Colwyn PA 1959-60, Parochial Schls 1972-74; *ai:* 1950-53 Erwin HS Girls Bsktbl Coach/Monogram Club Spon; 1955-57 Pres Chowan Cty Ed Assn; 1966-68 Secy of PTA; 1972-73 Spon Annunciation Sch Newspaper; 1973-74 Annunciation Sch Chairperson of Rdng Prgm; 1975-80 Bell Fork Elem Chairperson of Steering Comm Accrediation; NEA, NCEA, CTA; *home:* 1115 Hendricks Ct Jacksonville NC 28540

CONNOR, JUDY BARTELT, 6th Grade Reading Teacher; *b:* Geneva, IL; *m:* Robert R.; *c:* Sean; *ed:* (BS) Elem Ed, N IL Univ 1972; Mid Sch Trng, National Coll; *cr:* 4th Grade Teacher Dean Street Sch 1972-77; 6th Grade Teacher Clarence Olson Sch 1980-83; 3rd Grade Teacher Dean Street Sch 1983-88; 6th Grade Teacher Clarence Olson Sch 1988-; *ai:* Pep Club Adv; Women of Moose; *office:* Clarence Olson Sch 720 W Judd St Woodstock IL 60098

CONNOR, PAULINE DUMAS, Classroom Teacher; *b:* Woonsocket, RI; *m:* James David; *c:* James R.; *ed:* (BA) Elem Ed, RI 1974; Candidate Rotarian Fellowship Eastern St 1974; Grad Work Cath Univ & MD Univ & RI Coll; *cr:* Teacher 1957-; Cooperating Teacher RI Coll & Univ of RI 1979-; *ai:* Stu Adv; Bernon Heights Sch Primary Grades Curr Coord; Delta Kappa Gamma (Pres 1979) 1977-79; Teachers Guild (Steward 1990) 1988-; Rotary Club 1974-76, Art Grant 1974; Teachers Forum (Pres 1986) 1986-87; Teacher of Yr, Natl Teacher of Yr 1975; *home:* 3690 Mendon Rd Cumberland RI 02864

CONNOR, STEVEN MORLEY, English Teacher; *b:* Columbus, OH; *m:* Nancy Ester Wiggand; *ed:* (BA) Eng Ed, Mt St Marys 1966; (MA) Admin, Xavier Unit 1978; *ai:* Golf Team Coach; Jr Honor Society Adv; Lang Art Dept Chm; OH Ed Assn 1966-; Lakewood Teachers Assn 1968-; Federal Grant.

CONNORS, PATRICK JAMES, 8th Grade Science Teacher; *b:* Waltham, MA; *m:* Jeanne; *c:* Brian, Jill; *ed:* (BS) General Sci/ Scndry Ed, Westfield St 1971; (MS) Sci Teaching, Amer Intnl 1975; Post Grad Course Work in Admin, Westfield St; *cr:* Sci Teacher Powder Mill Mid Sch 1971-; *ai:* Southwick Ed Assn VP 1980-81, MA Teachers Assn, NEA; BSA Cncl Mem; Parish Church Eucharistic Minister; *office:* Powder Mill Mid Sch 94 Powder Mill Rd Southwick MA 01077

CONOVER, MITSUYE HAMADA, Social Studies Teacher; *b:* Manzanar, CA; *m:* Neal G.; *c:* Shawn D.; *ed:* (BA) Soc Stud, Ca St Univ 1965; *cr:* Soc Stud/Eng Teacher Stephens Jr Hs 1965-70; De Mille Jr HS 1970-72; Soc Stud Teacher Madison Jr HS 1973-79; Eng Teacher Bartlesville Mid HS 1983-84; Eng/Soc Stud Teacher Central Mid Sch 1984-; *ai:* Supt Comm Cncl; Bartlesville Sch Fdtn; Dept Chm Soc Stud; Long Beach Ca NEA 1965-72; Bartlesville Ed Assn 1973-; OK Ed Assn 1973-; NEA 1973-; OK Soc Stud Cncl 1988-; NCSS 1985-; *office:* Central Mid Sch 900 Cherokee Bartlesville OK 74003

CONRAD, BRIAN LYNN, Mathematics Teacher; *b:* Hinsdale, IL; *ed:* (BA) Phys Ed, Univ of Pacific 1971; *cr:* Math Teacher John Marshall Mid Sch 1972-; *ai:* Math Team Adv; *office:* John Marshall Mid Sch 1141 Lever Blvd Stockton CA 95206

CONRAD, CAROL RUTH, 1st Grade Teacher; *b:* Akron, CO; *ed:* (AA) Gen, Indian Hills Comm Coll 1972; (BA) Kndgtn/Elem Ed, Northeast MO St Univ 1975; *cr:* Kndgtn Teacher 1975-79, 1st Grade Teacher 1979 Van Buren Cmmty Sch; *ai:* Served on Negotiations 1987-89; Membership Chm IA Rdng Cncl Jefferson; Jefferson/Van Buren Cncl; IA Rdng Assn 1975-; IA Cncl Teacher Math 1988-; *office:* Van Buren Cmmty Sch Mc Kinley & Beswick Stockport IA 52651

CONRAD, DARLENE JOYCE, History Teacher; *b:* Baltimore, MD; *c:* Michelle Kulp; *ed:* (BA) Soc Stud, 1968; (MED) Rdng Remediation, 1976 Salisbury St Univ; *cr:* Teacher Pocomoke HS 1968-69; Pocomoke Mid Sch 1969-71; Snow Hill HS 1972-; *ai:* Legal Intern Adv; Jr Class Prom Adv; Sr Class Act Spon; Cmmty Service Coord; Delta Kappa Gamma 1988-; Worcester Cty Teachers Assn Rep 1972-85; Treas 1986-; MSTA/NEA 1968-; Soroptimists 1987-; Kidney Fnd Trustee 1987-; Nom for Worcester Cty Teacher of the Yr 1989; Contributor to Ctr for Reasearch & Dev in Law-Related Ed; *home:* 107 S. Church St #B Snow Hill MD 21863

CONRAD, JILL KAY, Mathematics Teacher; *b:* Albion, NE; *m:* Chris; *c:* Carrie, Abbie; *ed:* (BS) Math, Univ of NE 1981; Working Towards MAT Math; *cr:* Teaching Asst Univ of NE 1980-82; Teacher Crete Public Schls 1983-; *ai:* Natl Assn Teachers of Math 1983-; NEA; NE Math Scholars Fellowship 1986-89.

CONRAD, JOAN HOLLENBECK, History Government Teacher; *b:* Hallstead, PA; *m:* David Carl; *c:* Michelle, Jeffrey, Jonathan; *ed:* (BS) Elem Ed, Bob Jones Univ 1965; (MA) Spec Ed/Mentally Retarded, W MI Univ 1971; *cr:* 2nd Grade Teacher L'anse Cruese Sch System 1965-66, Greenville Sch System 1966-67, Pennfield Sch System 1968-69; Jr/Sr HS Teacher Ms Valley Chrstn Sch 1978-; *ai:* Tutoring; J A, Teen Group, Bicentennial Contests, DAR Contest, VFW Voice of Democracy Contest Spon; Government Fellowship in Spec Ed to Get Masters; Stu Won N Cntrl Division of Bicentennial Contest 1990; *home:* 3955 Laverne Alton IL 62002

CONRAD, RHONDA MORGAN, Mathematics Teacher; *b:* Panama City, FL; *m:* John Devoe; *c:* Kelly, Johnny, Casey, Chris; *ed:* (AA) Pre-Bus, Gulf Coast Jr Coll 1975; (BS) Elem Ed, Univ of W FL 1977; *cr:* Teacher Everitt Jr HS 1978-86, Mosley HS 1986-; *ai:* Cheerleading Spon for Var Squad; Bay Dist Math Cncl Treas 1989-; *office:* A C Mosley H S 3418 N Palo Alto Ave Lynn Haven FL 32444

CONRAD, RICHARD LEE, Math Teacher/Team Leader; *b:* Anamosa, IA; *m:* Kathleen Susan Gaffney; *c:* Scott, Sara; *ed:* (BA) Ed/Math, Univ of N IA 1972; *cr:* 6th-8th Grade Math Teacher Willow Cmmty Schls 1972-76; Math Teacher Harding Mid Sch 1976-; *ai:* 7th Grade Interdisciplinary Team Facilitator; 7th Grade Girls Track & Bsktbl Coach; IA Cncl Teachers of Math 1980-; IA St Ed Assn, NEA 1972-; Natl Marriage Encounter Area Pres 1988-89; Knights of Columbus Cncl Grand Knight 1985-87; Nom Presidential Awd for Excl in Teaching Math & Sci 1989-; Nom for US West Outstanding Teacher Awd 1989; Article Printed; *office:* Harding Mid Sch 4801 Golf St NE Cedar Rapids IA 52402

CONRAD, TRACEY BRANSON, Science Teacher; *b:* St Louis, MO; *m:* Robert; *c:* Rachel, Kristin; *ed:* (BS) Sci/Ed, Univ of MO Columbia 1985; General Sci Cert; *cr:* Sci Teacher Sturgeon R-V Sch 1985-; *ai:* 8th Grade Class Spon; Faculty Adv Comm; Career Ladder Assessment Comm; MSTA 1985-; CTA VP 1988-89; CTA 1985-; PTSO 1988-89; *office:* Sturgeon R-V Sch PO Box 248 Sturgeon MO 65284

CONREY, PATRICIA ANN, Biology I & II Teacher; *b:* Navasota, TX; *m:* Clifford Martin; *c:* Christopher, Melissa, Meredith; *ed:* (BAT) Bio, 1969, (MED) Bio, 1971 Sam Houston St Univ; *cr:* Bio I & II Teacher Conroe HS 1971-72; Bio/Anatomy/ Physiology Teacher Lumberton HS 1972-74; Bio I & II Teacher Klein HS 1974-77; Bio I & II/Anatomy/Physiology Teacher Cypress Creek HS 1980-; *ai:* Sci Symposium Coord; Sci Fair Spon & Adv; NSTA 1984-; NABT 1987-; CAST 1983-; ATPE 1980-; Teaching Fellowship Sam Houston St Univ; Outstanding Teacher of Yr Lumberton HS; Special Projects in Bio; Publication; *office:* Cypress Creek HS 9815 Grant Rd Houston TX 77070

CONRO, JAMES PHILIP, Mathematics Teacher; *b:* St Charles, IL; *m:* Elizabeth A. Simon; *c:* Laura, Daniel, Kevin; *ed:* (BSED) Math, N IL Univ 1972; *cr:* Math Teacher Burlington Cntrl HS 1973-; *ai:* Stu Cncl Adv; Curr, Sch Improvement, Discipline, Election Comm; Local Ed Assn (Pres 1978-82, 1984, VP 1984-) Outstanding Local Leader 1987; Nom Kane Cty Educator of Yr; *office:* Burlington Cntrl HS P O Box 396 Burlington IL 60109

CONROE, JANE E., Science Teacher; *b:* Cleveland, OH; *m:* Douglas E.; *c:* Deborah, Michael, Patricia; *ed:* (BA) Chem, Kent St Univ 1972; (MSED) Chem, St Univ Coll Fredonia 1989; *cr:* Chem/Physics Teacher Aurora HS 1972-74; Chem/Physics/Earth Sci Teacher Chautauqua HS 1984-89; Sci Teacher Maple Grove HS 1989-; *ai:* 8th Grade Class, Sci Club Adv; IMPACT Team Co-Chm; NSTA, Southern Tier Sci Teachers Assn 1988-; SS Peter & Paul Church (Religious Ed Instr 1989-, Spec Minister 1987-); Empire St Challenger Fellowship 1988-89; *home:* PO Box 137 Maple Springs NY 14756

CONROY, CATHERINE FUNKHOUSER, Teacher of Gifted; *b:* New Kensington, PA; *m:* Richard L.; *c:* Heather J., Matthew R., Nathan M.; *ed:* (BSED) Ed/Math, IN Univ of PA 1970; Educl Support Team Trng Stu Assistance St Vincent Coll; Services for Teens Risk Tier II Trng W Psychiatric Inst; *cr:* Math Teacher Burrell Jr HS 1970-84; Teacher Burrell Sch Dist 1970-; Teacher of Gifted/Remedial Math Burrell HS 1984-; *ai:* Stu Cncl Adv; Math Team Coach & Spon; Burrell Ed Support Team; Burrell Ed Assn Treas; PA St Ed Assn, NEA, PA Assn for Gifted Ed; Burrell Chemical Abuse Reduction Through Ed Teacher Rep 1986-; Strongland Chamber of Commerce Ed Task Force Chairperson 1989-; St Alphonsus Adult Choir (Pres, Librarian) 1966-; Henry C Frick Fnd Grant; *office:* Burrell HS Puckety Church Rd Lower Burrell PA 15068

CONROY, LYNDON R., History Teacher; *b:* Harlowton, MT; *m:* Sandra Baker; *c:* Jennifer; *ed:* (BA) Soc Stud, Concordia Coll 1982; *cr:* Teacher Colstrip HS 1985-; *ai:* Horsepower Club Spon; Asst Ftbl & Track Coach; Mid Sch Bsktbl & Vlybl Coach; MT Coaches Assn 1988-; Moose Club 1990; *office:* Colstrip HS Pine Butte Dr Colstrip MT 59323

CONTI, JACKLYN MARIE, Kindergarten Teacher; *b:* Youngstown, OH; *m:* Joseph R.; *ed:* (BSED) Elem Ed, 1964; (MSED) Elem Ed 1973 Youngstown ST; Post Masters Studies Stu Teaching Evaluation Course; Chem for Chldrn Course; Babes Trng Prgm; Sci is Fun to Teach for Elem Teachers; *cr:* 2nd Grade Teacher, Bd of Ed, 1964-66; Kindergarten Teacher 1966- Market Street Elem Sch; *ai:* Market Street Steering Comm, Right to Read Comm; Phi Delta Kappa; Delta Kappa Gamma; OH Ed Assn; Bdman Ed Assn; NEA; Eastern OH Encl of Teachers of Math; Intnl Rdng Assn; Natl Pan Hellenic Schlsp Chm 1987-89; OH ST Grants for Lang Arts; Nutrition Grants Youngstown Univ 1979-81; Natl Sci Recipient 1985; Martha Holden Jennings Grant for Sci 1989; *office:* Market Street Elem Sch 5555 Market St Youngstown OH 44512

CONTI, JUDTIH HOGAN, 7th Grade Art Teacher; *b:* New Kensington, PA; *m:* Neil A.; *ed:* (BS) Art Ed, 1974, (MA) Fine Arts, 1983 IN Univ PA; *cr:* Jr HS Art Teacher Punxsutawney Area Schls 1974-; *ai:* Art Club; Yrbk Photographs & Layout; NEA 1975-; PSEA 1975-; Natl Organization for Women 1989-; Intnl Society for Animal Rights 1986-; Humane Society 1985-.

CONTRERAS, DAVE, Social Studies Chair; *b:* Los Angeles, CA; *m:* Noralee Goodwin; *ed:* (BA) His, C S Los Angeles 1971; (MA) Multicultural Ed, San Diego St 1979; *cr:* Teacher Cathedral HS 1971-74, Frohne Sch 1974-75, Santa Barbara HS 1976-78, San Diego HS 1978-79, Hoopa HS 1979-; *ai:* Athletic Dir; Bsbl Coach; Anti-Substance Abuse Club Adv; CA Athletic Dir Assn 1988-; Humboldt Historical Soc 1985-; Kide Public Radio Bd Chm 1980-86; Excl in Teaching Humboldt Cty Schls 1987; Outstanding Teacher Awd Hupa Bus Cncl 1988-87; *office:* Hoopa Valley HS PO Box 1308 Hoopa CA 95546

CONWAY, ANN F., Social Studies Teacher; *b:* Schenectady, NY; *ed:* (BA) His/Intnl Stud, Siena Coll 1986; (MS) Rdng, St Univ of NY 1988; *cr:* Soc Stud Teacher Waterford Halfmoon Cntrl Sch 1986-87, Shenendehowa Cntrl Schls 1987-; *ai:* Club Adv Speech & Debate Team;Coaching-Jr Var Field Hockey; NY St Cncl of Soc Stud Teachers 1986-; *office:* Shenendehowa Cntrl Sch 970 Rt 146 Clifton Park NY 12065

CONWAY, BEVERLY FLUTH, 5th Grade Teacher; *b:* Mitchell, SD; *m:* Edward S.; *ed:* (BA) Music Ed, Sioux Falls Coll 1954; (MSED) Ed/End/Counseling, Canisius Coll 1966; Prof Growth, Univ of CA Riverside, CA St Hayward, Univ of SD; *cr:* Scndry Music Ed Teacher SD Schls 1954-60, Dept of Defense Schls 1960-63, Tonawanda NY 1963-64, Fairfax Cty 1966-67, Anne Arundel Cty 1967-68; Elem Teacher St Dept Schl Liberia Africa 1969-70, Dept of Defense Sch 1973-78; Adult Ed Teacher Fitzsimmons Medical Center 1978-80; Elem Teacher Hemet CA 1981-; *ai:* NEA, CA Ed Assn 1983-; HTA (Exec Bd 1984-, Poly Action Chairperson) 1983-; Phi Delta Kappa; Democrat St Cntrl Comm (Delegate 1988-, Vice Chairperson 1989-, Exec Bd 1987-88); Teacher of Yr 1985; *home:* 41641 Fulton Ct Hemet CA 92344

CONWAY, CAROL M., English Teacher; *b:* Evergreen Park, IL; *ed:* (BA) Eng, St Mary of Woods Coll 1971; (MA) Eng, Chicago St Univ 1977; *cr:* Eng Teacher Morgan Park HS 1971-77, Hyde Park Career Acad 1977-88; Eng Dept Chairperson Hyde Park Career Acad 1980-87; Eng Teacher Morgan Park HS 1988-; *ai:* NCTE 1978-; Chicago Teachers Union 1971-; AFT 1971-; St Linus Parish (Liturgy Coord, Lector, Adult Catechist, Eucharistic Minister) 1983-; Work at Homeless Shelter; Mellon Fellowship in Multi-Ethnic Literacy 1990; Fry Fnd Fellowship in Writing 1990; Many Poems Published; *office:* Morgan Park HS 1744 W Pryor Ave Chicago IL 60643

CONWAY, DONALD PURNELL, Elem Phys Ed Teacher/ Coach; *b:* Hyattsville, MD; *m:* Joyce Patricia Turner; *c:* Darryl P.; *ed:* (BS) Health/Phys Ed, DE St Coll 1964; (MA) Phys Ed, George Washington Univ 1969; Grad Stud MD Univ, Bowie St Univ, Azusa Pacific Coll; *cr:* Teacher Glenarden Woods Elem 1964-70, Holly Park Elem 1964-66, Bladensburg Elem 1981-82, Thomas Stone Elem 1982-83, Ridgecrest Elem 1970-; *ai:* Dr Martin Luther King Jr. Black His Prgm, Ben Franklin Stamp Club Teacher Spon; Asst Bsbl Coach; Jr Babe Ruth Head Bsbl Coach; NEA, MD St Teachers Assn; Amer Alliance for Health, Phys Ed, Recreation & Dance; Prince Georges Cty Educators Assn, Natl Fed Interscholastic Coaches Assn, MD Assn for Health, Phys Ed, Recreation & Dance; MD PTA; Metropolitan WA YMCA Aquatics Volunteer Certificate of Appreciation 1984; Calverton Recreation Cncl Coach 1975-81, Hall of Fame 1989; Calverton Citizen Assn (2nd VP 1979-80, Bd of Dir 1976-80, Public Service Chm 1978-80); Silver Spring YMCA (Team Rep, Meet Mgr) 1982-85; Prince Georges Cty Babe Ruth League Inc VP 1990; Certifcates of Recognition for 10, 15, 20, 25 Yrs of Service in Ed Prince Georges Cty MD; Certificate of Appreciation for Addressing Langley Park Kiwanis Club 1981; Appreciation Awd Plaque for Continuous Dedication to Youth of Calverton 1978; Appreciation Awd Plaque for Service to Stus Ridgecrest Elem Sch 1976; *home:* 3411 Dunnington Rd Beltsville MD 20705

CONWAY, LUVERNE BOWEN, Mathematics Dept Teacher; *ed:* (BS) Math, Univ of Montvallo 1966; (MED) Math, Auburn Univ 1981; *cr:* Teacher Lowndes Cty HS 1966-69, Ft Dale Acad 1969-72, 1979-84, 1984-; Instr Wallace Coll 1986-; *ai:* Sr Spon; Math Team; Sci & Beta Club; Alpha Delta Kappa; AL Cty of Teachers of Math.

CONYERS, LYNN HILTON, 3-D Art & Photography Teacher; *b:* St Paul, VA; *m:* T. Scott; *c:* Thomas H.; *ed:* (BFA) Art Ed, VA Commonwealth Univ 1971; (MFA) Ceramics, James Madison Univ 1986; Arrowmont 1971, TX Technological Univ 1975, Univ of VA 1973, 1975; *cr:* Art Teacher Wise Jr HS 1971-72, Ferrum Coll 1976-77, Mary Baldwin Coll 1988-, Waynesboro HS 1973-; *ai:* Craft & Photography Guild & Natl Art Honor Society Spon; VA Art Ed Assn (Membership Chm 1980, Archivest 1988-), Art Teacher of Yr 1984; NAEA 1970-; Amer Craft Cncl 1980-; Shenandoah Valley Art Center (Steering Comm 1985-86, Standards Comm 1988-); VA Museum of Fine Arts; Best in Show Art Work 1970, 1985; Exhibited Art Work Fine Art Galleries, Various Univs.

COOK, ANN SHACKELTON, Gifted Education Specialist; *b:* Joliet, IL; *c:* Kimberly A., Lauren Ordway, Jody Harris; *ed:* (BA) Eng, Northwestern Univ 1965; (MS) Counseling, Shippensburg Univ of PA 1985; Advanced Seminars Drug & Alcohol Counseling & Gifted Ed; Inst on Thinking, Grad Sch of Ed Harvard Univ; *cr:* Gifted Ed Specialist Carlisle Area Schls 1979-; *ai:* Mid Sch Hockey & YMCA Competitive Swim Team Coach; Leader of Mid Sch COA Counseling Group; NEA, PA St Ed Assn 1981-; Natl Assn of Alcohol & Drug Abuse Cnslrs 1990; Carlisle YMCA (Bd of Dir 1982-89, Pres of Bd 1980-83), Service to Youth 1989; Carlisle United Way Bd of Dir 1979-86, Leadership 1985-86; *office:* Carlisle Area Sch Dist 623 W Penn St Carlisle Barracks PA 17013

COOK, BARBARA HELMS, Kindergarten Teacher; *b:* Monroe, NC; *m:* James Bradford; *c:* Steven Bradford, Brian Hartsell; *ed:* (BS) Secretarial Admin, Univ of NC Greensboro 1953; Early Chldhd Ed, Univ of MD; Univ of DE; Salisbury St Univ; *cr:* Kndgtn Teacher Ridgely Elem Sch 1966-67, Greensboro Elem Sch 1967-; *ai:* Kndrgtn Team Leader; Comm Mem Greensboro Sch Lib Media Prgm Comm; Alpha Delta Kappa (Pledge Chm, Treas, Chaplain) 1970-; NEA; MD St Teachers Assn; Caroline Cty Teachers Assn; Caroline Health Services Inc Bd of Dir 1980-88; Town & Cntry Club Greensboro Pres 1965-66; Panelist 28th Annual Convention MD Assn Bd of Ed - Coping with Demands on Teachers; *office:* Greensboro Elem Sch Rt 1 Box 32 Greensboro MD 21639

COOK, BEVERLY ANNE, Government & History Teacher; *b:* Cripple Creek, CO; *ed:* (BA) Poly Sci, CO St Univ 1962; Prof Ed Certificate Univ of Denver; Grad Stud Univ of CA Los Angeles, Loyola Marymont; *cr:* His Teacher R-3J Weld Cty JR/Sr HS 1964-65; Substitute Teacher Denver Public Schls 1965-68; 1th-9th Grade His Teacher Henry Clay Jr HS 1968-80; Government/His Teacher Bell HS 1980-; *ai:* Sch Site Leadership Cncl Co-Chairperson; Bell HS Bd of Dir Union Rep; Yr Round Schls United Teachers LA; UTLA Bd of Dir 1968-; CTA, NEA St Cncl 1986-; CFT, AFT 1986-; Natl Yr Round Ed 1984-; St Democrat Comm of 57 (Secy 1984, Dem Ad 1958), Democrat of Yr 1988; Articles on Yr Round Ed; *office:* Bell HS 4328 Bell Ave Bell CA 90201

COOK, CAROL EILEEN GRILE, 3rd Grade Teacher; *b:* Celina, OH; *m:* Le Roy; *c:* April Coram; *ed:* (BS) Elem Educ, Mid-Amer Nazarene Coll 1972; Ed Courses Northeast MO St Univ; *cr:* 3rd Grade Teacher Northwestern R-1 Schls 1972-; *ai:* Chm Salary Comm Cmmnty Teachers Assn; MO St Teachers Assn 1972-80; Cmmnty Teachers Assn 1972-; MO Assn Rural Ed 1989-; Northeast Sci Co-Op 1985-86; Church of Nazarene Choir Dir 1972-; Church of Nazarene (Youth Pres 1973 Sunday Sch Teacher 1972-75); *home:* R R 3 Box 413 Brookfield MO 64628

COOK, CATHY BROWN, Second Grade/Contact Teacher; *b:* Louisville, KY; *m:* James Gilbert Jr.; *c:* James G., Matthew S.; *ed:* (BS) Elem Ed, 1971, (MA) Elem Ed, 1975 E KY Univ; Rank I Elem Sch Admin, 1979; *cr:* Elem Teacher 1971-, Contact Teacher 1979- Shelby Cty Bd of Ed; *ai:* Stu Cncl Adv; Sch Newspaper Co-Editor; Math Curr, Staff Dev, Calender, Parenting & Family Life, Guildance Comms; Shelby Cty Ed Assn (Secy 1976-77, Mem 1971-); KY Ed Assn, NEA 1971-; KY Assn Sch Admin 1981-84; Henry Clay PTA (Treas 1987-88, Mem 1974-); Eastern Star 1968-; Outstanding Elem Teachers of America 1975; *home:* Rt 3 Box 483A Shelbyville KY 40065

COOK, CHARLES WAYMON, Math/Science Teacher; *b:* Blaisville, GA; *m:* La Verne Young; *c:* Christina R.; *ed:* (BS) Mid Grades Ed, North Ga Coll 1961; (MED) Sci Ed, 1968 Adm/ Supvr, 1972 Univ of GA; *cr:* Math Teacher Woody HS Gap 1961-63; Math/Sci Teacher Willingham Jr HS 1963-68; Audio/ Visual Dir Bibb Cty Schls 1968-72; Math/Sci Teacher Westfield Sch 1972-; *ai:* Elem Prin Westfield Schls; Coaches Elem Sports Bibb Cty Schls; Curr Comm; Phi Delta Kappa 1972-74; Holiday Ramblers St Chaplain 1989-; RV Travel Club GA; Mem of United Meth Mens Organization; Write Poetry; *home:* 3542 Jones Rd Macon GA 31206

COOK, CHELSEA CARROLL, Principal; *b:* Marysville, CA; *m:* Carol Sue Brannon; *c:* Christopher, Cari Cook Smith, Jeremy; *ed:* (BA) Music Ed, 1960, (MT) Music Ed, 1966 Cntrl St Univ; Grad Stud; Teaching Certificates; *cr:* Instrumental/Vocal/General Music Teacher Peru Public Schls 1961-62; Maintainance Supvr Swedlow Plastics 1962-63; Instrumental/Vocal Music Teacher Wetumka Public Schls 1963-65, Cleveland Public Schls 1965-66; Band Teacher Wewoka Public Schls 1966-74; Instrumental/ Vocal/General Music Teacher New South Wales Australia 1975-75; Band Teacher 1975-80, Elem Teacher 1980-83 Wewoka Public Schls; Elem Prin 1983-86, Mid Sch Prin 1986- Henryetta Public Schls; *ai:* OK Ed Assn, NEA 1966-83; Wewoka Ed Assn Pres 1979-80, Teacher of Yr 1980; Lions 1972-74, 1983-85; BSA (Asst Scoutmaster 1974-, Camp Scoutmaster 1983, Cubmaster 1977-78, 1983-84, Troop Comm 1985-) Top Scouter 1981; GSA Advisory Comm 1987-; Articles Printed; *office:* Henryetta Mid Sch 505 N 7th Henryetta OK 74437

COOK, CONNIE MENDENHALL, Fourth Grade Teacher; *b:* Nampa, ID; *m:* Mel M.; *c:* Chad J., Rhett M.; *ed:* (BA) Elem Ed, Boise St Univ 1978; Numerous Univs; *cr:* 1st Grade Teacher Garfield Elem 1978-85; 1st Grade Teacher 1985-87, 2nd Grade Teacher 1987-88, 4th Grade Teacher 1988- Koelsch Elem; *ai:* NCTM, ID Cncl of Rdng, ID Ed Assn, Boise Ed Assn, Snake River Personnel & Guidance Assn, ID Society Individual Psych, NEA; Church (Youth, Relief Society, Act Coord); 1st Grade Materials Author 1985-87; *office:* Koelsch Elem Sch 2015 N Curtis Boise ID 83706

COOK, DENNY GENE, Algebra Teacher; *b:* Belleville, IL; *m:* Connie L Toliver; *c:* Amy B., Jodi K.; *ed:* (BS) Math/Amer His, Murray St Univ 1970; (MS) Educl Admin, S IL Univ Edwardsville 1988; *cr:* Teacher West Mid Sch 1970-85; Instr Lewis & Clark Comm Coll 1985-; *ai:* Stu Pride Spon; Minority Excl Math & Sci; NCTM, ICTM, IL Sci Teachers Assn 1988-; Mid Sch Wkshps; Dist Math Contest Organizer; Trigonometry With Model Rocketry; *office:* Alton HS 2200 College Ave Alton IL 62002

COOK, ELIZABETH ANN (BANDY), English, Govt, Comp Teacher; *b:* Windsor, VT; *m:* Joel Robert; *c:* Erin M., Colin C.; *ed:* (BS) Ed, Univ of VT 1971; Bible Temple Baptist Inst; *cr:* 3rd/4th Grade Teacher Union Dist 37 1971-73, 3rd/4th Grade Teacher 1981-84, 5th/6th Grade Teacher 1984-86, Jr/Sr HS Eng/ Government/Cmptr Teacher 1986- Temple Chrstn Acad; Eng Instr Temple Baptist Inst 1989-; *ai:* Honor Society & Jr/Sr Class Spon; Testing & MS St Honor Coord; Girls Bsktbl Coach; Whos Who in Amer Ed 1989; *office:* Temple Christian Acad 14190 Dedeaux Rd Gulfport MS 39503

COOK, FRANCES LOWERY, Mathematics Department Chair; *b:* El Dorado, AR; *m:* Charles William; *c:* Charles Jr., Robert L.; *ed:* (BS) Eng/Math, S AR Univ 1954; (ME) Scndry Ed, Southern Meth 1957; *cr:* 7th-9th Grade Math Teacher El Dorado Jr HS 1954-55, Gaston Jr HS 1955-63; 7th-8th Grade Math Teacher Cary Mid 1978-79; Tutor Argyle Mid Sch 1979-80; 7th-8th Grade Math Teacher Gaston Mid Sch 1981-84; 9th-12th Grade Math Teacher Lincoln HS 1984-86; 9th Grade Math Teacher Thomas Jefferson 1986-; *ai:* Key Club & Math Contests Spon; Greater Dallas Cncl Math Teachers, Classroom Teachers of Dallas, TX St Teachers Assn; NCTM, NEA; *office:* Thomas Jefferson HS 4001 Walnut Hill Ln Dallas TX 75229

COOK, JANICE J., English Chair/Jr Eng Teacher; *b:* Brady, TX; *m:* Ronnie L.; *c:* Amy, Ryan; *ed:* (BA) Eng, Univ of TX Arlington 1968; (MED) Scndry Ed, N TX St Univ 1981; *cr:* Eng Teacher Ferris HS 1968-70, Grapevine HS 1971-; Dept Chairperson Grapevine HS 1987-; *ai:* NHS Adv; NCTE, TX Joint Cncl Teachers of Eng 1975-; Delta Kappa Gamma 1982-; Phi Delta Kappa 1984-; Amer Cancer Society Secy 1980-; Grapevine Public Lib Bd Secy 1985-; *office:* Grapevine HS 3223 Mustang Dr Grapevine TX 76051

COOK, JOEL EDWIN, Lang Arts/Math Teacher; *b:* Summerville, GA; *ed:* (BS) Bio, 1977, (MED) Mid Grades, 1979 Berry Coll; *cr:* Sci Teacher Pennville Elem Sch 1977-84; Math Teacher Westside Mid Sch 1984-85; 7th Grade Lang Arts & Math Teacher Lyerly Elem 1985-; *office:* Lyerly Elem Sch Church St Lyerly GA 30730

COOK, JOSEPH H., Social Studies Teacher; *b:* Sewickley, PA; *m:* Judy Black; *c:* Gregg, Sue Fox, Charles Fox; *ed:* (AA) His, Trenton Jr Coll 1963; (BA) His/Ec, Waynesburg 1970; Grad Stud CA St Coll; Environmental Seminar, Univ of WI; Calculator & Cmptr Technology, PA Dept of Ed; His Ed, PA St Univ; *cr:* Fitter Helper Ambridge US SteeL 1960; Artillery Fire Direction & Intelligence 25th US Army Vietnam 1966; Teacher Cntrl Greene Sch 1969-; *ai:* Drama Coach; Audio & Video Coord; Curr Coord Mid Sch Soc Stud; W PA His Society; Greene Cty Museum (Building & Grounds Chm, Bd of Dir) 1970-80; Knapps Battery Civil War Re-Enactment Supply Sargent 1970-75; Newspaper Observer & Reporter; *office:* Cntrl Greene Sch Dist 126 E Lincoln St Waynesburg PA 15370

COOK, JUDY HOOD, Sixth Grade Teacher; *b:* Amarillo, TX; *m:* Tony Jay; *c:* Judd, Cody; *ed:* (BS) Elem Ed, W TX St Univ 1964; *cr:* 6th Grade Teacher Houston Ind Sch Dist 1964-65; 2nd Grade Teacher Lubbock Ind Sch Dist 1965-67; 5th/6th Grade Teacher Mansfield Ind Sch Dist 1967; 6th Grade Teacher Eminence R-1 1980-; *home:* PO Box 52 Eminence MO 65466

COOK, KELLY L., English/Spanish Teacher; *b:* Bryan, OH; *ed:* (BA) Scndry Ed, Huntington Coll 1983; (MS) Scndry Ed, IN Univ 1988; *cr:* Eng/Span Teacher Waldron HS 1983-87; Span Teacher 1985-87, Eng/Span Teacher 1987- Camden HS; *ai:* Span Club; Kappa Delta Pi Mem 1987-; *office:* Camden-Frontier HS 4971 Montgomery Rd Camden MI 49232

COOK, KENNETH HERSCHEL, 7th-8th Grad Soc Stud Teacher; *b:* Montgomery, AL; *c:* Amber E. Harris, Lane K.; *ed:* (BS) Phys Ed, CA St Coll 1970; (MA) Safety Ed, Auburn Univ 1976; (MA) His, Univ of Montevallo 1983; Working on Admin Cert Univ of Montevallo; *cr:* 7th/8th Grade Teacher/Ftbl/Bsbl Coach Autaugaville HS 1970-72; 7th-8th Grade Teacher/Ftbl/ Bsbl/Wrestling/Track Coach Lake Placid HS 1972-74; 7th/8th Grade Teacher/Ftbl/Bsbl Coach Autaugaville HS 1974-75, Marbury HS 1975-77, Dallas Cty HS 1981-88; 7th/8th/10th Grade Teacher Keith HS 1988-89; 7th/8th Grade Teacher Brantley Mid Sch 1989-; *ai:* Mid Sch Bsktbl Coach; Soc Stud Club Spon; AL Cncl for Soc Stud 1989-; Ftbl Coach of Yr Awd Advertiser Journal 1974; *office:* Brantley Mid Sch 5585 Water Ave Selma AL 36701

COOK, LA VERNE YOUNG, Fifth Grade Teacher; *b:* Macon, GA; *m:* Charles Waymon; *c:* Christina R.; *ed:* (BS) Elem Ed, N GA Coll 1962; (MED) Elem Ed, Univ of GA 1967; *cr:* 1st Grade Teacher 1962-63, 4th Grade Teacher 1963-68 Dr John H Heard Elem; 5th Grade Teacher Westfield Schls 1972-; *ai:* Sch Coord Outdoor Environmental Classroom.

COOK, LAURA CATHERINE, English Teacher; *b:* Rochester, NY; *ed:* (BA) Eng, Univ of Buffalo 1987; Working Towards MA Lit, Bread Loaf Sch of Eng Middlebury Coll; *cr:* Eng Teacher Midlakes HS 1987-; *ai:* Co-Adv Sch Store; Class Ranking Comm; Appreciation & Recognition Comm Chm; Empowerment Comm; Organized Teachers Writing Group; Phi Beta Kappa 1987; NCTE Mem 1989-; Rural Teacher Schlsp Bread Loaf Sch of Eng 1989; *office:* Midlakes HS Rt 488 Clifton Springs NY 14432

COOK, MARY JANE (GLOVER), English Teacher; *b:* Springfield, MA; *m:* James; *c:* Christopher Dunn, Michael Dunn, Lisa Dunn; *ed:* (BA) Sociology, 1972, (MA) Eng, 1989 Amer Intnl Coll; *cr:* Eng Teacher Chestnut Street Jr HS 1974-85, HS of Commerce 1985-; *ai:* Jr Class Adv; Faculty Advisory Comm; Horace Mann Mentor & Drama Teacher; MA Teachers Assn, Springfield Ed Assn 1974-; Prgms for Gifted & Talented Articles Printed; Natl Endowment of Hum Grant; *home:* 1223 Longmeadow St Longmeadow MA 01106

COOK, NANALEE LARSEN, 4th Grade Teacher; *b:* Spanish Fork, UT; *m:* Mark Evan; *c:* Stephanie C. Stevens, Valerie, Heath, Kevin, Austin, Joseph; *ed:* (BS) Elem Ed, Brigham Young Univ 1965; *cr:* Teacher Lafayette Elem 1965-67; 1968-69, 1981- Moroni Elem; *ai:* Career Ladder Steering Comm Mem; NEA, UEA, North Sanpete Assn; LDS Primary Pres 1986-; PTA VP 1976-77; Stake Relief Society 1974-76; Stake Primary 1972-74; Core Team Dist; ODDM Comm & Trainer; Yr Round Sch Comm; *home:* 12 E Main Moroni UT 84646

COOK, NANCY STEPAN, Spanish Teacher; *b:* Vicksburg, MS; *w:* Randall S. (dec); *ed:* (BA) Span, 1957, (MA) Span, 1963 Univ of N TX Denton; Benedict Sch Lang Las Palmas Canary Islands 1986; *cr:* Span/Eng Teacher Robert Driscoll Jr HS 1957-59; Span/Fr Teacher All Saints Episcopal Jr Coll 1959-61; Span/Eng Teacher Rugby Acad 1961-62; Span/Grad Teaching Asst Univ of N TX 1962-63; Span/Fr/Eng Teacher Lake Highlands Jr HS 1965-74; Span/Fr Teacher Richardson HS 1974-; *ai:* Span Club

Spon; Amer Assn Teachers of Span & Portuguese; *office:* Richardson HS 1250 W Beltline Rd Richardson TX 75080

COOK, SANDY GUY, World Studies Teacher; *b:* Newnan, GA; *m:* Russell H.; *c:* Misty, Mandy, Rusty; *ed:* (BA) His, 1977, (MED) Soc Stud/Ed, 1979 W GA Coll; *cr:* Teacher Madras Elem Sch 1977-78, Troup Jr HS 1979-86, Troup HS 1986-; *ai:* Y-Club & Sr Class Adv; PAGE 1987-; La Grange Crisis Pregnancy Center Bd of Dir Secy 1989-; Rosemont Baptist Church Youth Sunday Sch Worker 1987-; Nom Teacher of Yr Troup Jr HS & Troup HS; *office:* Troup HS 1920 Hamilton Rd La Grange GA 30240

COOK, SARAH, 2nd Grade Teacher; *b:* Deering, MO; *m:* Donald Ray; *c:* Douglas, Randall, Curtis, Christopher; *ed:* (BSED) Elem Ed, Univ of MO 1958; (MAT) Early Chldhd, Webster Univ 1990; *cr:* 1st Grade Teacher Oakville Elem 1958-61; 3rd Grade Teacher 1977-82, 2nd Grade Teacher 1982- Point Elem; *ai:* Mentor Teacher 1988-89; NEA, MNEA 1977-; *home:* 2614 Baltusrol Dr Saint Louis MO 63129

COOK, SARAH ANN, Fifth Grade Teacher; *b:* Waynesboro, TN; *m:* Thomas E.; *c:* Gary; *ed:* (BS) Elem ED, Univ of North AL 1979; *cr:* Teacher Frank Hughes 1979-; *ai:* TN Teacher Assn 79-; Natl Teacher Assn 1979; Democrat Women PTO; Eastern Star; United Meth Women Chm of Comm 1989; Clifton United Meth Choir; *home:* Rt 1 Box 207 Waynesboro TN 38485

COOK, SARAH W., English Teacher; *b:* Carrollton, MS; *m:* Joseph S.; *c:* Melinda, Jeffrey, Jennifer; *ed:* (BA) Eng, Delta St Univ 1966; (MED) Eng Ed, Univ of MS 1976; *cr:* Eng/Speech Teacher Winona HS 1966-67; Eng/Sci Teacher Jones Road Sch 1967-70; Eng/Fr Teacher Lee Acad 1970-72; Eng Teacher W P Daniel HS 1973-77, Washington Sch 1978-; *ai:* Cheerleader, 9th Grade, Literary Magazine, Asst Drama Spon; MS Private Sch Assn Dist Eng Chm 1990; MS Cncl of Teachers of Eng; Pilot Club; Greenfield Baptist Church Pianist 1986-; *home:* 135 Teresa Dr Greenville MS 38701

COOK, WILLIAM LEE, Social Studies Teacher; *b:* Aberdeen, SD; *m:* Julia Marie Wiese; *c:* Heather M., Shalan L., Ashley C.; *ed:* (BA) His, Univ of N IA 1975; *cr:* 7th/8th Grade Soc Stud Teacher Waverly Shell Rock Jr HS 1975-; *ai:* Head Frosh Girls Bsktbl, Asst Var Ftbl, Girls & Boys Track Coach; *office:* Waverly-Shell Rock Jr HS 215 3rd NW Waverly IA 50677

COOK-JOHNSON, JANICE MARIE, College Life Director; *b:* Battle Creek, MI; *ed:* (AGS) General Stud, 1984, (AAS) Electronics Technology, 1984, (AS) Engineering, 1985 Kellogg Comm Coll; (BGS) Poly Sci/Sociology, Univ of MI 1987; Working on Masters in Public Admin, W MI Univ Kalamazoo; *cr:* Upward Bound Prgm Asst 1988-89, Coll Life Facilitator 1990- Kellogg Comm Coll; *ai:* Charon Assoc of Battle Creek Employability Dev Plan Specialist 1985-86; Jr Achievement of S Cntrl MI Center Mgt for Night Prgm 1983-85; Safe Place of Battle Creek (BD Chairperson for Public Relations, Bd Mem) 1989-; Instituted Attendance Policy; Authored Major Proposal for Pres of Coll; Submitted & Helped Implement Changes in Saturday Component of Upward Bound Prgm; Office of Ethics & Religion Univ of MI Ann Arbor 1985-87; *office:* Kellogg Comm Coll 450 North Ave Battle Creek MI 49017

COOKE, EILEEN FRANCIS MARIE, Religion Teacher; *b:* Philadelphia, PA; *ed:* (BA) His, Chestnut Hill 1972; (MA) Scndry Ed/His, Villanova 1980; Nurses Asst; Working towards Masters Theology, La Salle Univ 1991 *cr:* 1st Grade Teacher Nativity BVM 1976-80; 6th Grade Teacher St Helena 1980-84; 5th-8th Grade Teacher Our Lady of The Rosary 1984-88; 9th-12th Grade Teacher W Cath HS 1988-; *ai:* W Cath HS Cmmty Service Corporation Moderator; Chldrs Moderator 1988-89; Archdiocesan Soc Stud Comm; Natl Assn Soc Stud Teachers; Philadelphia Soc Stud Cncl; Articles for Encyclopedic Dictionary of Religion; Book Consultant for Holt; Designer of Soc Stud Curr K-3rd Grades; *office:* West Cath HS 4501 Chestnut Philadelphia PA 19139

COOKE, JENNIFER HAINES, 6th Grade Teacher; *b:* Los Angeles, CA; *ed:* (BA) Ed, Univ of La Verne 1983 *cr:* Teacher Murray Elem 1983-; *ai:* Christmas Prgms; Sci Fairs.

COOKE, JOY DARVEL, Geometry Teacher; *b:* Somerset, KY; *m:* Barry Robin; *ed:* Bus/Offices, Somerset Voc Sch 1977; (AS) Math, Somerset Comm Coll 1987; (BA) Math Ed, E KY Univ 1988; Working Towards Masters Math Ed, E KY Univ; *cr:* CIMM Prgm Math Tutor Somerset Comm Coll 1987; Stu Teacher Somerset HS 1988; Summer Sch Math Teacher Pulaski CtY HS 1988; Math Teacher/Math Dept Chairperson Rockcastle Cty HS 1988-; *ai:* KY Educl Assn, NCTM; Somerset Chrstn Women Club (Project Adv 1980-83, Prayer Adv 1983-85); Woodstock Baptist Church 1969-; Mini Grant for Math Games Forward & 5th; *home:* 4531 Hwy 39 Somerset KY 42501

COOKE, MARY LOIS, Fifth Grade Teacher; *b:* Statesville, NC; *ed:* (BS) Intermediate Ed, Appalachian St Univ 1973; (MS) Ed, Univ of NC Charlotte 1978; Working Towards AG Cert; *cr:* 4th/5th Grade Teacher Mt Mourne 1973-74; 5th/7th/8th Brawley 1974-; *ai:* Supt Advisory Cncl Mem; Sch System Calendar & Textbook Comm Mem; NCAE, NEA; Bethesda Presbyn Church Elder 1990-; Sch Annual Dedication 1981, 1986; Brawley Sch Teacher of Yr 1986; *office:* Iredell Cty Schls/Brawley Rt 7 Box 259 Mooresville NC 28115

COOKE, NADA GARBER, Sixth Grade Teacher; *b:* Waynesboro, VA; *c:* Laura Cooke Rathbone, Matthew A.; *ed:* (BA) Religion/Philosophy, Greensboro Coll 1958; (MAED) Elem Ed, 1982, (EDS) Lang, 1986 W Carolina Univ; *cr:* Kndgtn Teacher Beaverdam Sch 1971-73; Kndgtn Teacher 1973-78, 5th Grade Teacher 1978-88, 6th Grade Teacher 1988- Clyde Elem; *ai:* Olympics of Mind Teams Coach; Teach Lit & Creative Writing Wkshps on St, Regional, Local Levels; Intnl Rdng Assn Pres 1981-83; Phi Delta Kappa, Kappa Delta Pi Mem; Haywood Cty Teacher of Yr 1981-82; Recipient of Reeves Memorial for Drop Out Prevention 1989; *home:* PO Box 244 Lake Junaluska NC 28745

COOKE, NELLIE, English Teacher; *b:* Birmingham, AL; *ed:* (BA) Eng/Speech, D C Teachers Coll 1973; (MS) Vocational Ed/Admin, VA Polytechnic Institute & St Univ; Open Space Ed; Cmptr Literacy Drug Prevention Ed; *cr:* Teacher Shaw Jr HS 1974-; *ai:* Dean of Stu Affairs; Prgm Coord Black His Prgm/Sr Awd Day, Administrative Team; Public Relations/Correspondence Comm; Shiloh Baptist Church Woman of Yr 1989; Potomac Links Torchlighter Awd 1989; WA Post Magazine Outstanding Teacher DC Public Schls 1989; NAACP Mem 1983-; Amer Red Cross Mem 1984-; WTU-WA Teachers Union 1975-; Bd of Advisors-Young Writers Contest Fnd; Daughters of Mary Mc Cloud Bethune; Outstanding Teacher Washington Post 1989; *office:* Robert Gould Shaw Jr HS 10th & Rohde Island Ave Nw Washington DC 20001

COOKE, PATRICIA BRIDWELL, English Teacher; *b:* Greenville County, SC; *m:* Dan G.; *c:* Bucky, Danielle; *ed:* (BA) Eng, 1968, (MA) Eng, 1977 Furman Univ; Converse Coll; Univ of SC Spartanburg, Furman Univ; *cr:* Eng Teacher Travelers Rest HS 1968-72, Eastside HS 1972-73, Blue Ridge HS 1978-; *ai:* Academic Team Co-Spon; Sr Class Adv; SC Teachers of Eng 1985-; Greenville Cty Teachers of Eng 1982-; *office:* Blue Ridge HS 2151 Fews Chapel Rd Greer SC 29651

COOKE, PATRICIA KUCHA, Learning Disabilities Teacher; *b:* Scranton, PA; *m:* Joseph J.; *c:* Shaun, Nicholas; *ed:* (BA) Spec Ed/Elem Ed, Marywood Coll 1977; *cr:* Substitute Teacher 1977-80, Elem Teacher 1980-81, HS Teacher 1981- Scranton Sch Dist; *ai:* Spec Ed Curr Comm 1983, 1986; ARA Food Services Comm 1989-; Tech HS Soc Comm 1987-88; Cntrl City Little League Treas 1986-88; *home:* 416 Marion St Scranton PA 18509

COOKE, ROSEMARY REILLY, Writing Process Teacher; *b:* Morristown, NJ; *c:* Robert; *ed:* (BA) Early Chldhd/Gen Elem, Newark St/Kean Coll 1973; (MA) Letters Drew Univ 1981; Writing Institute, Columbia Univ 1989-; *cr:* Kndgtn Teacher St Bernards 1965-66; 5th Grade Teacher Holy Trinity 1966-69, Our Lady of Peace 1971-74, Our Lady of Lourdes 1974-76; 4th/5th Grade Teacher Southern Blvd Sch 1976-84; 5th Grade Teacher Chatham Mid Sch 1984-; *ai:* House Leader 5th Grade; Curr Planning Comm For L A; Assn of Chatham Teachers, Articles Instr Magazine 1982 & 1987; Sch Advisory Panel; Silver Burdet Co 1985; *office:* Chatham Mid Sch 480 Main St Chatham NJ 07928

COOKMAN, JAY PRESTON, Guidance Counselor; *b:* Mason City, IA; *m:* Annette Maria Fraizer; *c:* Jaynette, Jeffrey; *ed:* (BS) Health/Phys Ed, 1960, (MS) Counseling/Guidance, 1963 Drake Univ; Counseling & Guidance Inst Univ of SD 1965; *cr:* 8th Grade Soc Stud Teacher 1961-63, Ftbl Coach/Girls Bsktbl Coach/7th-12th Grade Guidance Cnslr 1963-69 Johnston HS; *ai:* Valley HS Fellowship of Chrstn Athletes & Ambassador Club Spon; Facilitator Valley HS Support Group; ISEA, NEA 1961-; Drake D Club Pres 1978-80; NDEA Summer Guidance & Counseling Summer Inst Univ of SD Dr E Gordon Pohling 1965; *office:* Valley HS 1140 35th St West Des Moines IA 50265

COOKSEY, ALAN R., Social Studies Teacher & Chair; *b:* Barberton, OH; *m:* Rosemary Ruth Barkhurst; *c:* Joanna, Melinda; *ed:* (BA) His, Coll of Wooster 1962; (MA) His, Kent St Univ 1966; *cr:* Teacher Portage Jr HS 1962-66, Barberton HS 1966-70; Teacher/Chm Medina HS 1970-; *ai:* Project Series Coord; Head Ftbl Coach; Soc Stud Chm; NCSS; Medina City Teachers Assn (VP, SECY); Asian Inst Grant; Firestone Scholar; Dow Chemical Teacher of Yr; Published Clearing House; Jennings Fnd Scholar; *office:* Medina HS 777 E Union St Medina OH 44256

COOLEY, BLANCHE B., Third Grade Teacher; *b:* Sandusky, OH; *ed:* (BS) Elem Ed, Bowling Green St Univ 1961; Grad Work Edinboro St Univ; *cr:* Elem Teacher Furry Elem 1958-59, 1961-63; Jr HS Phys Ed Teacher Perkins Jr HS 1963-67; Elem Teacher St Road Elem 1967-; *ai:* Jr HS Cheerleading Adv 1963-67; Perkins Ed Assn VP 1961-67; OH Ed Assn 1958-; NEA 1967-; Kappa Phi Chaplain 1960-61; *office:* State Road Elem Sch 4200 State Rd Ashtabula OH 44004

COOLEY, LOUISE ARTHUR, Mathematics Teacher; *b:* Birmingham, AL; *m:* Andy; *c:* Christopher, Patrick, Andrea; *ed:* (BS) Elem Ed, Univ of AL Bessemer 1979; *cr:* Teacher Bessemer St Tech Coll 1977-79, Jefferson Cty Bd of Ed 1979-; *ai:* Math Dept Head; Founder & Spon Peer Tutoring Prgm; AEA, NEA, AFT; *office:* Mc Adory HS 4800 Mc Adory School Rd Mc Calla AL 35111

COOLEY, MARGIE ELAINE (BURTON), Second Grade Teacher; *b:* Columbia, KY; *m:* Charles Michael; *ed:* (AA) Ed, Lindsey Wilson Coll 1963; (BS) Elem Ed, Campbellsville Coll 1965; (MED) Mental Retardation/Ed, Univ of Louisville 1970; *cr:* 2nd Grade Teacher 1965-68, Teacher of Educable Mentally Handicapped 1969-83, 4th Grade Teacher 1984-85, Teacher of Educable Mentally Handicapped 1986-87, 2nd Grade Teacher 1988- Sanders Elem Sch; *ai:* Easter Seal Sch Chairperson; PTA Photographer 1983-86; KY Congress Parents & Teachers Life Membership Awd 1984; *office:* L Max Sanders Elem Sch 8408 Terry Ln Louisville KY 40258

COOLEY, MARTHA TEINERT, English Teacher; *b:* Copperas Copve, TX; *m:* Charles O.; *c:* Liesien Bouvette, Terasa Cooley; *ed:* (BA) Eng, Univ of TX Austin 1963; (MA) Eng, Univ of TX San Antonio 1988; Grad Stud Various Univs; *cr:* Primary Teacher Immanuel Luth Sch 1955-57; Eng Teacher Alvin HS 1963-84, St Anthony HS Seminary 1988-; *ai:* TX St Teachers Assn 1963-; Alvin Teachers Assn Pres 1973-74, Teacher of Yr 1979, 1982; NEA 1963-84; Amer Assn of Univ Women Pres 1967-69; Delta Kappa Gamma 1969-86; NCTE 1963-85; *office:* St Anthony HS Seminary 3200 Mc Cullough Ave San Antonio TX 78284

COOLEY, TIMOTHY JACK, English Teacher/Coach; *b:* De Ridder, LA; *m:* Rhonda Kay; *c:* Caleb J.; *ed:* (BS) Health/Phys Ed, 1983, (MS) Health/Phys Ed, 1986, Supervision/Admin, 1990, Mc Neese St Univ; Supervision for Stu Teachers Course; *cr:* Eng Teacher/Coach Leesville Jr HS 1984-85, E Beauregard HS 1985-; *ai:* Class Spon; 5th-8th Grade Girls & Boys Bsktbl Head Coach; HS Boys Asst Bsktbl Coach; LA HS Coaches Assn, Natl HS Coaches Assn 1986-; Assn Prof Educators LA 1987-; Friendship Baptist Church (Sunday Sch Supt 1986-, Deacon 1988-); E Beauregard PTO Parliamentarian 1987-; *home:* Rt 1 Box 290 De Ridder LA 70634

COOLMAN, RAND WILLIAM, Marketing Teacher/Coordinator; *b:* Escanaba, MI; *m:* Joanne Finlan; *c:* Tyler; *ed:* (AB) Hotel/Restuarant Mgt, Lansing Comm Coll 1979; (BAED) Mrktg Ed, CO St Univ 1982; US Air Force Tech Sch Air Transportation Grad Wrk; *cr:* Mrktg/Coord Teacher Northglenn HS 1982-; *ai:* DECA & Ski Club Spon; Intramural Bsktbl Dir; DECA St Advisory Comm; NEA 1985-; CO Ed Assn 1985-; CO Mrktg Ed Assn 1982-; AVA 1982-89; CO Voc Assn 1982-; CO St Ed Grant Dev Hotel/Motel Mgt; Adams Cty Sch Dist #12 Voc Teacher of Yr 1989; Delta Nu Alpha/Denver Transportation Club Teacher of Yr 1990; *office:* Northglenn H S 601 W 100th Pl Northglenn CO 80221

COOMBES, GEORGE WILLIAM, History Department Chairman; *b:* North Hollywood, CA; *m:* Elise Turner; *c:* Will; *ed:* (BA) Eng, S Meth Univ 1969; Lib Art, SMU 1971-72; His, Univ of TX of the Permian Basin 1989-; *cr:* Athletic Dir Cistercian Prep Sch 1969-73; Athletic Dir/Admissions Dir/Dean of Stu/His Dept Chm/Eng Instr Trinity Sch 1973-; *ai:* Coach Ftbl Team & Girls Bsktbl Team; Work with Fine Art Dept in Producing Sch Plays; Asst Stu Cncl; Confederate Air Force Squadron Leader 1987; Hi-Sky R/C Club Pres 1980; *office:* Trinity Sch 3500 W Wadley Midland TX 79707

COOMBS, EARL S., Biology Teacher; *b:* Salt Lake City, UT; *m:* Dianne F.; *c:* Steven, Kierstina, Jennifer, Brienne; *ed:* (BS) Phys Ed, 1972, (MS) Human Physiology, 1979 Univ of UT; (EDS) Educl Leadership, Brigham Young Univ 1987; Various Wkshps & Advanced Placement Bio; Sports Medicine; *cr:* Sales Consultant Commercial Supply Company 1971-74; Bio Teacher East HS 1974-77, Cyprus HS 1977-; *ai:* Track & Field Coach; Morale Comm Chm; Accreditation Comm Mem; Article Published; Writing Work-A-Text Human Physiology; Curr Writer Dist Bio Courses; *office:* Cyprus HS 8623 W 3000 S Magna UT 84044

COOMER, BOBBIE POWELL, First Grade Teacher; *b:* Columbia, KY; *m:* Russell; *c:* Mark; *ed:* (AA) Elem Ed, Lindsey Wilson Coll 1973; (BS) Elem Ed, 1975, (MA) Elem Ed, 1979 W KY Univ; (Rank I) W KY Univ 1981; Admin Endorsement Elem Sch Prin; Endorsement for Supvr of Instruction; *cr:* 1st Grade Teacher Colonel William Casey Elem Sch 1976-; *ai:* Adair Cty Gifted Ed Comm; Teacher Ed Advisory Cncl Lindsey Wilson Coll; Adair Cty Ed Assn Treas 1984, 1985; KY Ed Assn St Delegate 1984, 1989; Mid Ed Assn Regional Delegate 1988, 1989; KY Ed Assn Mem 1976-; NEA; Freedom Church of God Ladies Auxiliary (Pres 1987, 1988, Secy 1989-); KY Teacher Internship Prgm Resource Teacher & Observer; Commonwealth Inst for Teachers 1988-89; KY Arts Cncl Co-Writer Grant; Forward in the 5th Co-Writer Mini Grant; *home:* 9495 Russell Springs Rd Russell Springs KY 42642

COOMER, JOAN CALVERT, Spanish Teacher; *b:* Greenville, SC; *m:* James Claudus; *c:* Sharon C. Mattingly, James C:, Jeffrey C.; *ed:* (BA) Fr/Span, Berea Coll 1963; (MACT) Span, Western KY Univ 1970; Rank I-Scndry Admin Wky 1985; *cr:* Span/Eng Teacher Brodhead HS 1963-64; Span/Fr/Eng Teacher Temple Hill Sch 1965-73; Span/Fr Teacher 1973-84, Span/Chm of Dept 1984- Barren Cty HS; *ai:* Foreign Lang Club; Coord of Exch Stu Prgm; Chairperson of Foreign Lang Dept; Barren Cty Ed Assn; KY Ed Assn; NEA 1964-; KY Cncl on Teaching of Foreign Lang; Amer Cncl on the Teaching of Foreign Lang 1973-; KY Assn of Teachers of Span & Portuguese; Amer Assn of Teachers of Span & Protuguese 1973-; *home:* 8265 Tompkinsville Rd Glasgow KY 42141

COON, MARY LEMME, 2nd Grade Teacher; *b:* Meadville, PA; *m:* Lawrence Henry Jr.; *c:* Allison, Karen, Anne, Samuel; *ed:* (BS) Ed, Indiana Univ of PA 1969; (MS) Ed, Univ of Edinboro 1971; *cr:* 2nd Grade Teacher Conneaut Valley Elem 1969-; *ai:* PSEA, NEA; *home:* RD 4 Box 322 Meadville PA 16335

COONEY, JOAN C. (DALEIDEN), 8th Grade Math/Religion; *b:* Chicago, IL; *m:* John Joseph; *c:* Eileen Brieno, Colleen, Maureen Kopanski, John; *ed:* (PHB) Ed, De Paul Univ 1963; (MA) Rdng Specialist, Cardinal Stritch Coll 1967; Grad Courses Comm/Eng at Numerous Univs; *cr:* 1st/2nd Grade Teacher St Mary 1950-57; 1st/5th Grade Teacher St Theresa 1957-59; 6th Grade Teacher St Mary 1959-60; 5th/6th Grade Teacher St Francis 1960-62; 7th Grade Teacher Holy Trinity 1962-64; 5th-8th Grade Music/Eng Teacher Notre Dame 1964-66; Supervising Rdng Consultant Chicago Archdiocese 1967-69; 10th-12th Grade Psych/Speech/Eng/Band/Chorus Teacher Cathedral HS 1969-71; Coord Deaf &

Hearing Schls/7th-8th Grade Teacher Holy Trinity 1971-73; Remedial Rdng & Psych Teacher/Prin Cook Cty Jail 1971-80; Prin St Benedict Sch 1973-77; 8th Grade Math/Religion Teacher All Saints 1984-; *ai:* Dir Class Plays Cathedral HS 1969-71; ASCD 1989-; Awd of Excl IL Math & Sci Acad 1989; Outstanding Teacher St Ignatius Coll Prep 1989; *office:* Queen Of All Saints 6230 N Lemont Chicago IL 60646

COONFIELD, JAMES DEE, Art Instructor; *b:* Rocky Ford, CO; *m:* Shirley Ann Brown; *c:* Sheryl A. Jack, Debra D. Toller, James G.; *ed:* (AA) Fine Art, Otero Jr Coll 1973; (BA) Art Ed, 1975, (MA) Art Ed, 1977 Adams St Coll; Type D Admin Certificate, Denver Univ 1986; *cr:* Teacher Carson Jr HS 1975-89, Carson Mid Sch 1989-; *ai:* Honor Organization Dir; Soc Acts Spon; Peer Assessment Team Mem; Fellowship Chrstn Athletes Spon; Sch Dist Credit Union Comm Mem 1988-; Denver Art Guild 1961-, CO Stu 1st Place 1961; Southwest Art Guild (VP 1969-70, Pres 1970-71), Leaders Trophy 1971; Church (Sunday Sch Supt 1968-71, Bd Finance Dir 1987-89); Whos Who in Amer Colls & Univs 1975; Magazine Article Published 1978; Newspaper Articles Published; *office:* Carson Mid Sch Bldg 6200 Fort Carson CO 80913

COONROD, LARRY D., Drafting Department Chairman; *b:* Emmett, ID; *m:* Sharon; *ed:* (BA) Ed, 1961, (MA) Voc Ed, 1962 Univ of CA Chico; Univ of CA Berkely, San Francisco, Fresno, Milwaukee Tech Coll; *cr:* Teacher Ukiah HS 1962-67; Drafting Instr Sierra Comm Coll 1979-; Drafting Teacher Rio Americano HS 1967-; *ai:* Key Club Adv 1967-75; Cty Fair Voc Ed Drafting Chm 1975-; Voc Ed St Frameworks Comm 1975-; Epsilon Pi Tau Pres 1982-84, Laureate 1984; CTA, NEA, CIEA 1962-; Elks 1990; Dist Teacher of Yr 1976, 1989-; Teacher Service Awd 1977, 1980-81; Masonic Lodge Teacher Awd of Excl 1980; Favorite Teacher 1972, 1974, 1977, 1980, 1987; *office:* Rio Americano HS 4540 American River Dr Sacramento CA 95864

COOPER, BARBARA MAYO, 5th Grade Teacher; *b:* Delhi, LA; *m:* Richard; *ed:* (BA) Elem Ed/Spec Ed, 1980, (MS) Elem Ed, 1987 NE LA Univ; *cr:* 6th/7th Grade Math Teacher Rayville Jr HS 1980-82; 5th Grade Lang Art/Math Teacher Start Elem Sch 1982-; *ai:* Richland Parish Task Force 1987-; LA Tip & La Tep Staff Dev/Prof Improvement Comm Mem 1989-; Richland Parish Teacher of Yr Evaluation Comm; Kappa Delta Pi 1987-; Alpha Delta Kappa 1987-; Teacher of Yr Start Jr HS & Richland Parish Jr HS 1987, Start Elem 1986; *home:* Rt 7 Box 571 Monroe LA 71203

COOPER, CATHY MARIE, Mid Sch Math Teacher; *b:* Oak Hill, OH; *ed:* (BS) Math-Magna Cum Laude, Rio Grande Coll 1973-; *cr:* Jr HS Math Washington C H; 5th Grade Teacher; HS Math Teacher; 6th Grade Teacher; Mid Sch Math Teacher Jackson City Schls; *ai:* Former Safety Patrol Adv; Former Olympics of the Mind Coach; Curr Comm; Competency Testing Comm; Txtbk Selection Comm; OH Teachers of Math 1986-; OEA/NEA/JCEA 1974-; Chi Beta Phi 1972- Honer Lifetime; Delta Kappa Gamma Sec 1978-81; Nom for Ashland Oil Teacher of Yr 1988; Ranatra Fusca; *home:* 32 Green Meadow Ct Jackson OH 45640

COOPER, DENNIS ALLEN, 7th/8th ESOL/Spanish Teacher; *b:* Melbourne, Australia; *m:* Janet Liao; *c:* Laura Durrenberger, Dennis C., Chrissie, Carla; *ed:* (BA) Span, TX Western 1966; (MED) Admin, N TX St Univ 1982; *cr:* Span Teacher Goliad Ind Sch DiSt 1966-67, Ysleta Ind Sch Dist 1967-76; Coach/Teacher Gary Ind Sch Dist 1977-79; ESOL Teacher Dallas Ind Sch Dist 1979-; *office:* L V Stockard Mid Sch 2300 S Ravinia Dallas TX 75211

COOPER, ELEANOR JACKSON, First Grade Teacher; *b:* Athens, GA; *m:* Johnny Howard; *c:* Lisa A.; *ed:* (BS) Elem Ed, 1958, (MS) Elem Ed, 1977 N GA Coll; *cr:* Teacher Jones Elem 1958-; *ai:* Facilities & Staff Dev Unit Comm; HCEA Building Rep 1970-72, 1989-; NEA, GAE 1958-; Hoschton United Meth Church (Teacher, Choir Dir, Choir Mem) 1961-85; Teacher of Yr Jones Sch 1969, 1981; *office:* Sylvester B Jones Elem Sch 6th St Chicopee Gainesville GA 30505

COOPER, HERMAN WILLIAM, Teacher-Dept Head; *b:* Paterson, NJ; *m:* Barbara Whitaker; *c:* Kevin, Kathleen Clark, Karen, Donna Sarte, Lisa Fusciello, Valerie Lynn, Janine, Deborah; *ed:* (BA) General Arts, Bergen Jr Coll 1953; (BA) Bio, Fairleigh Dickinson Coll 1955; (MS) Bio, Union Coll 1968; NSF Univ of MD & Stockton St Coll; Supervision Cert Monmouth Coll; AEC Electric Power Generation Drexel Univ; Seton Hall Univ; Rutgers Univ; Trenton ST; Glassboro St; Jersey City St; *cr:* 1st Lieutenant U S Marine Corps 1955-57; Sci/Math Teacher Saddle Brook HS 1958-60; Chief Naturalist Island Beach St Park 1970-83; Bio/Marine Sci Dept Head Cntrl Regional HS 1960-; *ai:* Jr Var Bsktbl/Bsbl Coach; NHS Adv; Natl Marine Educators Assn Life Mem; Amer Littoral Society; NJ Sci Supervisors Assn; NJ Sci Teachers Assn; NJ Bio Teachers Assn; NSTA, NABT, NEA, NJ Ed Assn; Ocean Cty Cncl of Ed Assns; People To People, Citizen Ambassador Prgm, Biological Exch to People's Republic of China 1988; Knights of Columbus (Past Grand Knight, 4th Degree Past Faithful Navigator) Family of Monty 1989; Ancient Order of Hibernians; Lacey Detachment Marine Corps League Life Mem; NJ Ed Assn Environmental Ed Comm; Corporate Mem Bermuda Biological Station for Research; Co-Founder & First Pres NJ Marine Ed Assn; Co-Author Decision-Making for Coastal Zones; Author Twenty Common Shells of NJ; Articles in Atlantic Flyway Review; NJ Assn for Environmental Ed Quarterly; Berkeley Township Bd of Ed 1963-64; Ocean Cty GSA Bd of Dir 1970-71; Ocean Cty Dept of Ed Instr-Ocean Bay Beach Project 1969-70; *office:* Central Regional HS Forest Hills Parkway Box C Bayville NJ 08721

COOPER, JACK E., Science Teacher; *b:* Willis, TX; *m:* Margaret Sue Pruitt; *c:* Christy M.; *ed:* (BA) Physics, 1971, (MED) Physics/Math/Ed, 1980 Sam Houston St Univ; Medical Technology; *cr:* Lab Instr Sam Houston St Univ 1969-71; Teacher Ennis HS 1971-; Part Time Instr Navarra Coll 1980-; *ai:* Jr Engineering Tech Society Adv; Univ Interscholastic League Coach; Superconducting Super Collider Curr Comm; TX St Teachers Assn VP 1971-; AAPT 1979-89; Acad of Sci 1988-; Dallas Regional Sci Fair Outstanding Sci Teacher 1986-87; TX Energy Sci Symposium Teacher Spon; *office:* Ennis HS 1405 Lake Bardwell Dr Ennis TX 75119

COOPER, JAN MORRISON, Teacher-Coordinator; *b:* Meridian, MS; *m:* Danny B.; *c:* Clayton S., Clinton L.; *ed:* (MED) Bus Ed, Delta St Univ 1977; (BS) Bus Ed, MS St Univ 1973; Mrktg Ed; Cmptr Courses; *cr:* Teacher Bus & Commerce Center 1973-75, Joe Barnes Voc Complex 1977-84; Teacher/Coord Cleveland Voc Complex 1984-; *ai:* DECA Club Spon; Adopt-A-Sch Rep; Delta Kappa Gamma Publicity Chm 1986-; MS Assn of Mktg Teachers 1973-; *office:* Andrews Mid Sch 405 NW 3rd St Cleveland MS 38732

COOPER, JANE KIZER, Sixth Grade Teacher; *b:* Maryville, TN; *m:* Kenneth W.; *c:* Joel W., Leslie E.; *ed:* (BS) Ed, Univ of TN Knoxville 1966; (MED) Elem Ed, Winthrop Coll 1973; Working Towards Ed Specialists Degree; Prgm for Effective Teaching; Teacher Incentive Prgm; *cr:* 3rd-5th Grade Teacher 1971-73, 5th Grade Teacher 1973-87, 6th Grade Teacher 1987- Lancaster Sch Dist; *ai:* Academic Tutoring Lab-Leader; Parenting Ed Spon; Palmetto St Teachers Assn 1987-, St Service Awd 1989; PSTA Pres 1988-; 1st Pentecostal Holiness Church (Womens Ministry, VP, Childrens Church Dir) 1990; *home:* PO Box 262 Lancaster SC 29721

COOPER, JESSIE BLAKE, Fourth Grade Teacher; *b:* Patterson, GA; *cr:* Teacher Pierce Cty Trng, Patterson Jr HS, Patterson Elem Sch.

COOPER, KENNETH PETER RUSSELL, His/Religion Teacher Chair; *b:* New York, NY; *ed:* (BA) Sociology, Manhattanville Coll 1980; (MA) Spec Ed, Boston Coll 1982; (MRE) Theology, Cath Univ 1989; Iona Coll 1982; *cr:* Teacher St Augustines 1983-84, Cardinal Hayes 1984-86; Teacher/Chm Brother Rice HS 1986-; *ai:* Var Bsbl Coach; Peace & Justice Seminar & Project Supvr; NCEA; Chrstn Brothers 1982-; Natl Recognition of Chrstn Service Peace & Justice Seminar; Kids in Harlem Volunteer; *office:* Brother Rice HS 74 W 124th St New York NY 10027

COOPER, LENORA ANN BONNER, 6th Grade Teacher; *b:* Cleveland, OH; *m:* James; *c:* Leernette; *ed:* (BA) Elem Ed, Lincoln Univ 1970; (MA) Ed, SIU Edwardsville 1979; Pars Cmptr Trng; *cr:* Oral Lang Teacher Project Speak 1970-77; 1st Grade Teacher Hawthorne Elem 1977-78; 6th Grade Teacher Lilly-Freeman Elem 1978-; Reservation Sales TWA; *ai:* Lilly-Freeman Sch Jr Beta Club Spon; Jail & Jill of America, Delta Sigma Theta & Kappa Delta Phi Comms; Delta Sigma Theta 1970-; Kappa Delta Phi 1978-80; St Luke Ame Church; Urban League Guild Membership 1974-78, Service Awd 1974; Outstanding Young Women in America, Kappi Delta Phi Honor Society in Ed 1978.

COOPER, LESLIE ELLEN, English/Spanish Teacher; *b:* Seattle, WA; *ed:* (BA) Eng, 1969, (MA) Eng/Ed, 1970 Univ of OR; Advanced Span Courses, CA St Univ Sacramento; *cr:* Teacher Casa Roble Fundamental HS 1970-; *ai:* AFS Adv; Schlsp Comm; San Juan Teachers Assn, Foreign Lang Assn Greater Sacramento; North Ridge Golf & Cntry Club Team Captain 1989-, Club Champion 1989-; San Juan Unified Sch Dist Mentor Teacher 1986-; *office:* Casa Roble Fundamental HS 9151 Oak Ave Orangevale CA 95662

COOPER, LINDA WITHAM, Third Grade Teacher; *b:* Jamestown, KY; *m:* Roger David; *c:* Jason, Jeremy; *ed:* (AA) Elem Ed, Lindsey Wilson Jr Coll 1967; (BS) Elem Ed, 1969, (MA) Elem Ed, 1970 W KY Univ; (Rank I) Elem Ed, E KY Univ 1980; *cr:* 6th Grade Teacher 1969-70, 3rd Grade Teacher 1970- Union Chapel Elem; *ai:* NEA, KY Ed Assn, Russell Cty Teachers Assn 1969-; Union Chapel PTO 1982-; Campbellsville Coll Excl in Teaching Awd 1989; *home:* Rt 1 Box 239-D Russell Springs KY 42642

COOPER, LOIS MOORE, Fifth Grade Teacher; *b:* Glenville, WV; *m:* James Ernest; *c:* James A., Melinda C. Osborne; *ed:* (BA) Elem Ed, Glenville St Coll 1964; (MS) Speech Comm, WV Univ 1984; WV Teachers Acad Grad 1989-; *cr:* 7th Grade Teacher 1964-66, 3rd Grade Teacher 1966-76, 4th Grade Teacher 1976-77 Mabscott Elem; 5th Grade Teacher Hollywood Elem 1977-; *ai:* Soc Stud Fair Sch, WV Childrens Book Awd Prgm Sch Coord; NEA, WV Ed Assn, Raleigh Cty Ed Assn 1964-; Intnl Rdng Assn 1985-; Alpha Delta Kappa Honorary Teacher 1988-; Teacher of Yr Raleigh Cty 1988-89; WV Teachers Acad Grad 1988-89; WV Ed Fund Inc Mini Grant 1988-89; Raleigh Cty Mini Grant 1988-89, 1989-.

COOPER, MICHAEL HOWARD, Jr HS Principal; *b:* Gatesville, TX; *m:* Cheryl Mae Rusk; *c:* Candice L., Colleen B.; *ed:* (BS) Scndry Ed, Baylor Univ 1980; (MS) Ed, Tarleton Univ 1986; All Level Cert, TX A&M 1981; *cr:* Elem Phys Ed Teacher Midway-Hewitt Elem 1981-82; Jr HS Teacher/Coach 1982-86, Jr HS Asst Prin 1986-89, Jr HS Prin 1989- Midway Jr HS; *ai:* TX Assn of Scndry Sch Prins, NASSP, ASCD, TX Coaches Assn, TX Girls Coaches Assn Mem; *office:* Midway Jr HS 9101 Woodway Dr Waco TX 76710

COOPER, NORMAN L., 6th Grade Teacher; *b:* St John, KS; *ed:* (BS) Elem Ed, 1974, (MS) Elem Ed, 1980 KS St Univ; *cr:* 2nd Grade Teacher 1976-83, 6th Grade Teacher 1983-85, 5th Grade Teacher 1985-86 R V Phinney Elem; 6th Grade Teacher Northside Elem 1986-; *ai:* Sci Club; Ft Larned KNEA (VP 1978-79, Negotiations Chm 1988-89, Rep Assembly Delegate 1983-89); KS Assn Teachers of Sci; Intnl Rdng Assn; Eden Valley Church of the Brethren (Mem 1966-, Mission Commission 1984-87, Usher); Unified Sch Dist 495 Master Teacher 1990; *office:* Northside Sch 16th & State Larned KS 67550

COOPER, PATRICIA SANDERS, Talented/Gifted Teacher; *b:* Fort Benning, GA; *m:* Calvin R.; *c:* R. E.; *ed:* (BS) Elem Ed, SC St Coll 1979; (MS) Elem Sch Admin, the Citadel 1986; Program for Effective Teaching; Great Books; Project Wild; *cr:* 4th Grade Teacher 1979-80; 3rd Grade Teacher 1980-85 Berkeley Elem; Talent/Gifted Teacher Ready/Cross Schls 1985-; *ai:* Honor Society Adv; Health Club Adv; Ace Club Activity Spon; SC Ed Assn Mem; NEA Mem; Daughters of Allen VP 1989-; Womens Club Pres 1989-; *office:* Ready Intermediate/Cross Elem PO Box 608 Moncks Corner SC 29461

COOPER, RAMONA S., Second Grade Teacher; *b:* Sallisaw, OK; *m:* Richard L.; *ed:* (BA) Elem Ed, Panhandle St Univ 1965; Mem of Metropolitan Instructional Leadership Prgm; *cr:* 2nd Grade Teacher Shell Rock IA 1965; 1st Grade Teacher 1966, 3rd Grade Teacher 1968-69, 2nd Grade Teacher Gardner KS 1966- *ai:* Mem of Supt Cabinet; Gardner Edgerton Teachers Assn; KS NEA; Outstanding Elem Teachers of Amer; *home:* Rt 1 Box 95A Edgerton KS 66021

COOPER, RICHARD H., Mathematics Teacher/Dept Chair; *b:* Mt Pleasant, MI; *m:* Cynthia L.; *c:* Rheanna L., Christa S.; *ed:* (BS) Math, Cntrl MI Univ 1978; *cr:* 7th/8th Grade Math Teacher Cass City Intermediate 1978-79; Math Teacher Pewano-Westphalia HS 1979-81, Sacred Heart Acad 1981-, Mid MI Comm Coll 1990-; *ai:* Math Dept Head; Soph Class Adv; Master Schedule for HS; Kappa Mu Epsilon; NCTM; Phi Epsilon Kappa; *office:* Sacred Heart Acad 316 Michigan St Mount Pleasant MI 48858

COOPER, ROBERT LEWIS, Mathematics Teacher; *b:* Pittsfield, MA; *ed:* (BA) Math, N Adams St Coll 1959; (MS) Math, Univ of Buffalo 1976; *cr:* Math Teacher Taconic HS 1969-; *ai:* Radio Station WTBR-FM; Quiz Team; DJ Entertainer; *office:* Taconic HS 96 Valentine Rd Pittsfield MA 01201

COOPER, SHERRY DAHRENS, Jr HS Counselor; *b:* Portland, OR; *m:* Jerome Stephen; *ed:* (BS) Ed, 1966, (MS) Educl Counseling, 1970 OCE; Personnel Certificate Counseling, 1973; *cr:* Sci/Phys Ed/Math Teacher/Cnslr Rowe Jr HS 1966-; *ai:* OEA, NEA; Orton Dyslexia Society; *office:* Rowe Jr HS 3606 SE Lake Rd Milwaukie OR 97222

COOPER, SHIRLEY BROWN, Business Teacher; *b:* Newark, NJ; *m:* James Thomas; *c:* Travis, Traci, Christel; *ed:* (BS) Bus Ed, Fayetteville St Univ 1987; *cr:* Secy Household Finance 1978-80, Fayetteville St Univ 1980-87; Teacher Clinton HS 1987-; *ai:* NC Bus Ed Assn, NC Educators Assn, Pi Omega Pi 1988-; *office:* Clinton HS 1201 W Elizabeth St Clinton NC 28328

COOPER, TOM W., Biology Teacher; *b:* Wetumpka, AL; *m:* Nancy Hurston; *c:* Debbie Jarrett, Susan Stokes, Jill; *ed:* (BS) Bio/His, Auburn Univ 1971; *cr:* Sci Teacher Arab HS 1971-72, Brewton Mid Sch 1972-75; Bio/His Teacher Lineville HS 1976-; *office:* Lineville H S Lineville AL 36266

COOPER, VALERIA FREDERICK, English Department Chairman; *b:* Warsaw, NC; *m:* Larry James; *c:* Tiffany C., Frederick C.; *ed:* (BA) Eng, NC Cntrl Univ 1975; Working Towards Masters Eng; *cr:* Cnslr James Sprunt Comm Coll 1975-82; Cnslr/Admin Extended Day Sch 1982-83; Eng Dept Chairperson Clinton HS 1983-; *ai:* Clinton HS Ebony Club & Ensemble Spon; Steering, Guidance, Editing, Concerned Stu, Eng, Textbook Selection Comm; Soph & Hospitality Club Adv; NCTE 1975-; NC Eng Teachers Assn 1989-; Clinton Area Fnd for Ed 1985-; Delta Sigma Theta Chairperson of Public Relations 1973-75; GSA Troop Leader 1986-; Wednesday Lib Club (Founder, Pres) 1988-; Mt Zion Holy Church Financial Secy 1977-; Prayer of Faith Youth Dir 1984-; Mellon Fellowship Recipient NCCU Lib Sci 1975; Cape Fear Writing Project Fellowship UNC-W for Writing Consultant 1985; Clinton City NCAE Teacher of Month Recognition 1989; Management Certificate from Atlanta Univ 1980; *home:* PO Box 433 610 W Plank Rd Warsaw NC 28398

COOPER, VIRGINIA TURBERVILLE, Retired 3rd Grade Teacher; *b:* Marmaduke, AR; *m:* V. G.; *c:* Bonnie Manning, Phyllis Pankey, Jackie; *ed:* (BA) Elem Ed, 1960, (MS) Elem Ed, 1973 AR St Univ; Cmptr & Typing; Vo Tech Cmptr Literacy; Short Courses Rdng Skills, Classroom Art & News Media; *cr:* 2nd Grade Teacher 1956-70, 3rd Grade Teacher 1970-89 Marmaduke Elem; *ai:* AEA, NEA 1958-83; Alpha Delta Kappa (VP, Chaplain) 1960-85; Classroom Teachers Assn 1985-89; Retired Teachers Assn 1989-; *home:* 501 N 4th Marmaduke AR 72443

COPAS, LINDA BRETTMANN, Fourth Grade Teacher; *b:* Elmhurst, IL; *m:* Michael R.; *c:* Michael, Melissa; *ed:* (BS) Elem Ed, 1973, (MEPD) Gifted & Talented Ed, 1982 Univ of WI Stevens Point; *cr:* K-12 Grade Gifted & Talented Coord 1975-85, Elem Head Teacher 1985-86, Elem Teacher 1973- Tri Cty Area Sch Dist; *ai:* Chapter 2 Coord 1984-; WI Cncl for Gifted & Talented; WI St Rdng Assn; Delta Kappa Gamma Comm Chairperson 1984-; Phi Delta Kappa 1989-; NEA, WEAC,

CWUC Public Relations Comm 1989-, WEAC Outreach 1989; Tri-Cty Ed Assn (Pres, Secy) 1987-; WI Assn of Educators (Past St Secy, Bd of Dir) Plainfield Womens Club GFWC Pres 1982-84; Eastern Star Worthy Matron 1984-86; United Meth Church Secy of Bd of Trustees 1984-86; Listed in Personalities of America 1985-86; Outstanding Practitioner Ed Awd Univ of WI Stevens Point 1983; CESA 7 Rural Ed Gifted/Talented Liaison Rep Awd 1980;CESA 7 Gifted & Talented Teacher of Yr Awd 1979; *office:* Tri-Cty Area Sch Dist PO Box 67 Plainfield WI 54966

COPASS, BARBARA GUMM, 4th & 5th Grade Teacher; *b:* Fountain Run, KY; *m:* Billy; *c:* Bretta, Benjamin; *ed:* (BS) Elem Ed, 1968-71, (MA) Elem Ed, 1971-74 Western KY Univ; *cr:* Elem Teacher Fountain Run Elem 1971-; *ai:* Monroe Cty Teachers Assn; PTO; *home:* 7670 Austin Tracy Rd Fountain Run KY 42133

COPE, LINDA ONKS, 9th Grade English Teacher; *b:* Johnson City, TN; *m:* Ted E.; *c:* Edwin, Aaron; *ed:* (BS) Eng/Speech, 1965, (MA) Rdng, 1976, (MA) Supervision/Admin, 1988 E TN St Univ; *cr:* Eng Teacher Rogersville HS 1969-79; Cherokee Comprehensive HS 1980-; *ai:* Local Newspaper Stu Writers & Sch Newspaper Facuty Spon; Southern Assn Steering Comm Class Spon; Sch Musicals Prompter; Stu Intern from Walters St Comm Coll 1990; Delta Kappa Gamma (Recording Secy 1985-86, Corresponding Secy 1986-87, Election Chairperson 1989-); NCEA (Secy 1987-89, Rep 1985-86); Big Creek Baptist Church Youth Teacher 1987-; *office:* Cherokee Comprehensive HS Rt 7 Rogersville TN 37857

COPE, LOU ANN J., Science/Biology Teacher; *b:* Chadron NB, CANADA; *m:* Wayne P.; *c:* John W., James P.; *ed:* (BS) Bio, 1962, (MS) Bio, 1967 Chadron St Coll; Grad Study Univ of WY, Univ of SD Spearfish, Univ of SD Vermillion; *cr:* Jr-Sr HS Sci/Bio Teacher Todd cty HS 1962-64; Bio Teacher Newell HS 1964-66; Jr/Sr HS Sci/Bio Teacher Lyman HS 1966-67, Oelrichs HS 1968-73, 1975-; *ai:* Soph, Jr, Sr Class Spon; Rodeo Club; Mothers Day Tea; Oelrichs Ed Assn; Order Eastern Star; Chadron St Coll Grad Asst 1967-68; *home:* HC 46 Box 4 Oelrichs SD 57763

COPE, MARY ELIZABETH CASH, First Grade Teacher; *b:* Gainesville, GA; *m:* Stephen Earl; *c:* Jill, Chad; *ed:* (BS) Elem Ed, Brenau Coll 1969; (MED) Early Chldhd Ed, N GA Coll 1976; *ai:* Sci Curr Comm; Phi Delta Kappa, Prof Educators Assn of GA; Whos Who in Amer Colls & Univs 1969; *office:* Enota Primary Sch Enota Dr Gainesville GA 30501

COPE, NANCY R., Social Studies Teacher/Chair; *b:* Newark, NJ; *m:* Samuel E.; *c:* Jeffrey E., Julia A.; *ed:* (BA) Soc Stud, Wake Forest Univ 1964; (MAT) US His, Univ of NC Chapel Hill 1968; Canadian Stud Duke Univ 1978, 1985; Univ of MN; Advanced Trng Mentor Trainer NC St Univ 1985-; *cr:* Teacher Piedmont HS 1964-66, Aycock Jr HS 1966-68, Southwest Jr HS 1969-70, Russell Jr HS 1970-75, Greenwood Sch 1975-76, Broadway HS 1976-77; Teacher/Dept Chm Lee Cty Sr HS 1977-; *ai:* Mock UN; Close Up; Mentor Trainer & Network; Sch Planning Comm; NCSS 1985-88; NCAE (Treas, Pace Comm, Retirement Comm, Newsletter) 1965-, Merit Awd 1988; NEA; NC Cncl Soc Stud Bd of Dir 1986-89, Meritous Services 1989; NC Assn Gifted & Talented 1985-88, Outstanding Ag Teacher 1984; Habitat for Humanity 1989-; BSA Cncl Advisory Bd 1987-; St Lukes United Meth Church 1976-; Appointment St Prof Review Commission 1985-88; Governors Awd Excl 1988; Outstanding Young Educator 1978; Teacher of Yr Lee Cty 1980; Yrbk Dedication 1980; NEH Grant 1987; Kodak Grant 1985; *office:* Lee Cty Sr HS 1708 Nash St Sanford NC 27330

COPELAND, ALFRED LEE, Art & Ceramic Teacher; *b:* Pickens, OK; *m:* Juanita Jean Bedwell; *c:* Amy L. Johnson, Lance E.; *ed:* (BS) Art Ed, 1967, (MS) Art Ed, 1971 Univ of OR 1971; Various Art Classes; *cr:* Art Teacher Joseph Lane Jr HS 1967-88; Art/Ceramics Teacher Roseburg HS 1988-; *ai:* Head Cross Cntry & Asst Track Coach; Roseburg Ed Assn, OR Ed Assn, NEA 1967-; Roseburg Rotary Teacher of Month; *office:* Roseburg HS 547 W Chapman Ave Roseburg OR 97470

COPELAND, BEVERLY JONES, Kindergarten Teacher; *b:* Littlefield, TX; *m:* Joe Dean; *c:* William F, Clayton D., Kay Garvin; *ed:* (BA) Elem Ed, Univ of Guam 1970; (MA) Spec Ed, AZ St Univ 1974; Grad Stud Early Ed, TX Tech Univ 1976; *cr:* Spec Ed Teacher Anderson Elem 1969-72; Emotionally Handicapped Teacher Franklin Elem 1972-73; Kndgtn Teacher Borden County Ind Sch Dist 1973-; *ai:* Kndgtn Teachers of TX 1978-; TX St Teachers Assn 1975-; Whos Who Among Stu in Amer Univ 1969-70; Governors Comm for Spec Ed 1970-72; Spec Olympics Dir 1971; Article Published 1956; *office:* Borden Elem Sch Box 95 Gail TX 79738

COPELAND, HARRIETT MARTIN, Principal; *b:* Martinsville, VA; *m:* Paul Kenneth Sr.; *c:* J. Whitney, P. Kenneth Jr., M. Brooke; *ed:* (BS) Elem Ed, Averett Coll 1975; (MED) Elem Ed, Univ of VA 1977; Rndg Specialist Cert Admin & Supervision; *cr:* Classroom Teacher Collinsville Primary Sch 1975-81; Rdng Curr Specialist Sch Bd Office 1981-82; Asst Prin Mt Olivet Elem Sch 1982-83; Prin Mary Hunter Elem Sch 1983-86; Asst Prin Bassett Mid Sch 1986-87; Prin Ridgeway Elem Sch 1987-89; Dir of Elem Ed Sch Bd Office 1990; *ai:* NEA, VEA 1975-81; NAESP 1986-89; *office:* Ridgeway Elem Sch Church St Ridgeway VA 24148

COPLEY, JAMES WILSON, Language Arts Teacher; *b:* Centerville, TN; *m:* Cathie Diane Chessor; *c:* David, Rebecca; *ed:* (AS) Health/Phys Ed, Columbia St Comm Coll 1968; (BS) Health, 1974, (MA) Health, 1978, Austin Peay St Univ; *cr:* Elem Phys Ed Teacher Centerville Elem Sch 1968; Jr HS Health Teacher 974-76, 7th Grade Sci/Math Teacher 1976-77 Hickman Cty Jr HS; 6th Grade Sci/Health/Math Teacher 1977-88, 7th Grade Math Teacher 1988-89, 6th Grade Lang Arts Teacher 1989- Hickman Cty Mid Sch; *ai:* Admin Peer-tutoring Prgm; Spon & coach Math Team; Sales Comm; Sch Discipline Comm; Hickman Cty Ed Assn VP 1982; Hickman Cty T-Pac Chm 1984-85; Hickman Cty Ed Assn Spec Services Chm 1983-84; Outstanding Young Educator 1975; Most Distinguished Classroom Teacher Hickman Cty Mid Sch 1990; *home:* Rt 2 Box 131 Lyles TN 37098

COPLEY, LAURENS WINDSOR, Science Department Chairman; *b:* Wheatland, WY; *m:* Pamela M.; *c:* Windsor, Erin; *ed:* (BS) Applied Bio, UT St Univ 1978; (MS) Natural Sci, Univ of WY 1988; *cr:* Physics/Earth Sci Lyman HS 1978-79; Summer Instr Univ of WY 1986-87; Sci/Math Teacher Lyman Mid Sch 1979-; *ai:* Head Vlybl & Mathcounts Coach; Sci Fair Spon; NSTA 1980-; WY Sci Teachers Assn (WY St Sci Fair Coord, Bd of Dir Mem) 1980-.

COPLEY, WANDA SUE, Fifth Grade Teacher; *b:* Ashland, KY; *ed:* (AB) Elem Ed, 1976, (MA) Elem Ed, 1978, (Rank I) Elem Ed, 1980 Morehead St Univ; *cr:* 3rd Grade Teacher Louisa Elem Sch 1976; 5th Grade Teacher Louisa Mid Sch 1977-; *ai:* Asst Bstkbl & Academic Team Coach; Stu Cncl Spon; Yrbk & Safety Patrol Adv; Lawrence Cty Teacher Assn, KY Ed Assn 1976-; Lawrence Cty Org Assn 1985-; Order of Eastern Star; *office:* Louisa Mid Sch Box 567 Louisa KY 41230

COPLING, DONALD RALEIGH, Physical Ed Teacher/Coach; *b:* Saint Louis, MO; *m:* Shelly Kay Strick; *c:* Trenton; *ed:* (BS) Phys Ed, Sch of Ozarks 1981; *cr:* Phys Ed Teacher/Health Joel E Barber C-5 1981-; *ai:* Coaching Boys Ftbl 7th & 8th Grade; Girls 7th & 8th Grade Bsktbl; Boys 7th & 8th Grade Bsktbl; 6th Grade Bsktbl Coach; 7th & 8th Grade Boys & Girls Track; Schlsp Comm; MSTA 1982-; *office:* Joel E Barber C5 Rt 2 Box 85 Lebanon MO 65536

COPNEY, BARBARA LOUISE, Elementary Teacher; *b:* Brooklyn, NY; *c:* Dawn M. Robinson; *ed:* (BA) Elem Ed, Brooklyn Coll 1974; (MS) Spec Ed, 1980; Working Towards Specialist Degree Soc Stud, W GA Coll; *cr:* Pre-Sch Teacher Georgia-Livonia Day Care Center 1975-80; Elem Teacher Brooklyn Temple 1980-83; Teacher Montauk Jr HS 1983-86, Ralph Mc Gill Elem Sch 1986-; *ai:* Good Friend Prgm; Teacher of Yr Awd.

COPP, WILLIAM FREDERICK, Fourth Grade Teacher; *b:* New Carlisle, IN; *m:* Margaret Ann; *c:* Bradley, Marcia Stevenson, Rebecca Phillips; *ed:* (BA) Elem Ed, 1973, (MS) Elem Ed, 1977 IN Univ South Bend; *cr:* 4th/5th Grade Teacher Jimtown Elem Sch 1973-; *ai:* Elem Boys Bsktbl & Elem Girls Intramural Vlybl & Bsktbl Coach; *home:* 63171 Cedar Rd Mishawaka IN 46544

COPPEDGE, PENNY S., English/Geography Teacher; *b:* Florence, AL; *c:* James K. Isom, W. B. Isom; *ed:* (BS) Elem Ed, 1972, (MED) Rdng, 1982 Winthrop Coll; Summer Writing Inst 1983, Hum Writing Inst, Winthrop Coll 1984; *cr:* 2nd Grade Teacher Richmond Drive Sch 1972-78; 5th Grade Teacher Sunset Park Sch 1979-81; 6th Grade Teacher Richmond Drive Sch 1981-84; 7th-9th Grade Teacher/Develomental Eng Lab Sullivan Jr HS 1984-; 7th Grade Teacher Sullivan Mid Sch 1990; *ai:* Organized & Sponsored First Young Writers Club, Co-Spon Litwits Society Sullivan Jr HS; SC Intnl Rdng Cncl Co-Chairperson Parents & Rdng Comm 1984-85; Palmetto Rdng Cncl Treas 1983-85; Winthrop Summer Fellows Pres 1985-87; Phi Kappa Phi, Kappa Delta Pi 1972-79; Amer Assn of Univ Women 1990; Winthrop Alumni Schlsp 1976; Ed Improvement Act Teacher Grant 1984; Coord Winthrop/Observer Writers Conference 1985-; *office:* Sullivan Mid Sch 1825 Eden Terr Rock Hill SC 29730

COPPES, JEFFERY WAYNE, Teacher of the Gifted; *b:* Lock Haven, PA; *m:* Joan Lenore De Arment; *c:* Caitlin M.; *ed:* (BS) Elem Ed, Lock Haven Univ 1977; (MED) Educl Admin, 1984, Elem/Scndry Principalship 1989 Penn St Univ; *cr:* 3rd Grade Teacher 1977-80, 1st Grade Teacher 1980-81 Smithfield Elem; 1st-5th Grade Teacher of Gifted Alfarata Elem 1981-; *ai:* Regional Dir, Bd Mem, Coach PA Odyssey of the Mind; Co-Dir New Visions Camp; PA Assn for Gifted Ed 1981-, Teacher Achievement Awd 1988; Volunteer for Huntingdon Cty Easter Seal Society 1980-; *home:* 1531 Oneida St Huntingdon PA 16652

COPPLE, PRISCILLA SUSAN, Phys Ed/Health Teacher; *b:* Idaho Falls, ID; *m:* Brent O.; *c:* Errin, Emily, Naomi, Joshua; *ed:* (BA) Elem Ed/Health Ed, Augustana Coll 1980; Phys Fitness Instr Cert IDEA; First Aid Cert Red Cross; Lifesaving, Water Safety Instr Red Cross; *cr:* 6th-8th Grade Soc Stud Teacher Dirksen Jr HS 1980-81; Soc Worker Will Cty Cmmty Action Agency 1981-83; 5th-12th Grade Phys Ed/Health Teacher 1988-, Cross Cntry Coach 1990 Aurora Chrstn Sch; *ai:* 5th-12th Grade Cross Cntry Coach; 10th Grade Class Spon; Amer Heart Assn Jump for Heart Coord; Maple Lawn Chrstn Church Ladies Friendship Pres 1985; Birthright of Joliet (Volunteer, Cnslr) 1987-; Maple Lawn Chrstn Church Jr HS Sunday Sch Teacher 1987-; Will Cty Running Club Treas 1981-83; *home:* 11235 Arbeiter Rd Minooka IL 60447

CORA, SPIRO PETE, His Teacher/Soc Stud Chair; *b:* Greenville, MS; *m:* Virginia Lee Brothers; *c:* Michael S., Catherine A., Christopher S.; *ed:* (BA) His, 1963, (MA) His, 1970 MS Coll; AAA Teaching Certificate His; *cr:* Soc Stud Teacher Immokalee HS 1963-66, Enochs Jr HS 1966-69, Wingfield HS 1969-; *ai:* Soph Class Spon; Close Up Fnd Spon & Area Admin; Local Shared Governance Comm; Dist Soc Stud Chm Jackson Public Schls; NCSS 1963-; MS Cncl for Soc Stud Bd Mem 1984-88; Greek Orthodox Church Holy Trinity & St John Theologan Treas 1978-80; R J Reynolds Ec Inst Univ of NC Chapel Hill 1979; MS St Soc Stud Textbook Selection Comm 1983; *office:* Wingfield HS 1985 Scanlon Dr Jackson MS 39204

CORAM, MARY A., Second Grade Teacher; *b:* Moline, IL; *ed:* (BS) Elem Ed, W IL Univ 1977; (MA) Elem Ed, NE MO St Univ 1987; *cr:* 3rd Grade Teacher 1977-86, 2nd Grade Teacher 1986- Kendall Sch; *ai:* IA Cncl Teachers of Math 1985-; NEA 1977-; Drake Avenue Chrstn Church (Deaconess, Bd Mem, Sunday Sch Teacher) 1981-; PTO Treas; *office:* Kendall Elem Sch 701 Washington Ave E Albia IA 52531

CORBELL, BERMAN DALTON, Social Studies Teacher; *b:* Snyder, TX; *m:* Dawn Marie English; *c:* Kenyon, Stacy Crawford; *ed:* (BA) Phys Ed, Univ of TX El Paso 1957; *cr:* Head Ftbl Coach Mc Collum HS 1969-73; Sales Rep 1973-85; Teacher Terrell Wells Mid Sch 1985-86, Cole HS 1986-; *ai:* Golf, Ftbl, Bsktbl, Track, Bsbl Coach; TX St Teachers Assn 1957-73, 1986-; TX St Coaches Assn 1957-73; Lions Club 1965-69; Keller HS Yrbk Dedication 1965; Head Ftbl Coaching Record; *home:* 13727 Winding Hill San Antonio TX 78217

CORBETT, COZETTE P., Third Grade Teacher; *b:* Lee City, KY; *m:* Joseph E.; *c:* Timothy, Kevin, Jeffrey; *ed:* (BA) Elem Ed, Morehead St Univ 1953; (MS) Early Chldhd, S CT St Univ 1976; *cr:* Teacher Columbus Public Sch System 1953-56, Wallingford Public Schls 1967-; *home:* 19 Stillwood Rd Wallingford CT 06492

CORBETT, GERRI M., Middle School Math Teacher; *b:* Bessie, OK; *m:* Bill; *c:* Charles Anderson, Cheryl C., Steven Anderson; *ed:* (BA) Math, OK City Univ 1963; (MED) Counseling-Ed, SE OK St Univ 1980; *cr:* Cmptr Programmer Federal Aviation Agency 1965-76; Math Teacher Kingston Mid Sch 1976-; *ai:* 7th/8th Grade Statewide Math Competitions; *office:* Kingston Mid Sch PO Box 370 Kingston OK 73439

CORBETT, JOAN P., Kindergarten Teacher; *b:* Brooklyn, NY; *m:* Edward B.; *c:* Tracey, Christopher; *ed:* (MS) Guidance/Counseling, Bklyn Coll 1989;(BA) Early Chldhd, Bklyn Coll 1962; Adv Cert Ed/Guidance/Counseling; Brooklyn Coll 1990; *cr:* Kndgtn Teacher 1962-84;Peer/Staff Developer 1984-85; Kndgtn Teacher 1985- Weeksville Sch; *ai:* Mem Weeksville Heritage Luncheon Comm; UFT 1962-; AACD 1986-; NAACP 1966-; AKA 1960-; Sandy Ground Historical Society 1980-; *home:* 982 Park Pl Brooklyn NY 11213

CORBETT, JOAN RIDDLE, 3rd Grade Teacher G/T; *b:* Vernon, TX; *m:* Bailey Lee Jr.; *c:* Kay Spark, Kim Martin, Nancy Johnson, Bailey III; *ed:* (BS) Elem Ed/Eng, Midwestern St Univ 1958; (MS) Management, Univ of Houston CLC; Gifted & Talented/NASAS Teachers of Space Tech/Sci Inst; *cr:* 3rd Grade Gifted Teacher Williams Elem 1959-62; 2nd-3rd Grade Teacher Pearl Hall Elem 1979-81, Mae Smythe Elem 1981-; *ai:* Gifted Talented Curr Comm; Strategic Planning Comm; Greater Houston Rdng Cncl; Mu Alpha ESA Pres/All Offices 1963-; Camp Fire Girls Inc Adult Trainer of Yr 1976; Parkview Estates Civic Cncl Bd Mem 1984-; South Main Baptist Church; TX Career Ladder III; Kappa Kelta Pi NHS for Ed; TX Electric Outstanding Ed Stu Awd; Phi Beta Kappa; *office:* Mae Smythe Elem Sch 2202 Pasadena Blvd Pasadena TX 77502

CORBETT, PETER RAMSAY, Drivers Ed & Phys Ed Teacher; *b:* Hyannis, MA; *m:* Kathleen Gardner; *c:* Peter, Kristopher; *ed:* (BA) Health/Phys Ed/Recreation, Kings Coll 1976; (MS) Safety, 1979, (MS) Sports Medicine, 1984 Marshall Univ; Natl Emergency Medical Technitian; CPR Instr; Nationally Registered Notory Public; *cr:* Phys Ed Teacher Bridge Elem & Kenton Elem 1977-79; Ftbl/Bsktbl Coach Stonewall Jackson HS 1977-79; Drivers Ed/Phys Ed Teacher Herbert Hoover HS 1979-89, George Washington HS 1989-; *ai:* Ftbl, Bsktbl, Track Coach; Certified Athletic Trainer 1984; Teacher In Space Candidate; Semi Pro Ftbl Player; Kanawha Cty Coaches Assn Treas 1988-; Kanawha S Bsktbl Ofcls; WV Coaches Assn Mem; Bible Center Church (Soloist, Ensemble Mem) 1976-; WV Textbook Adoption Comm; Guest Speaker St Drivers Ed Conferences; *office:* George Washington HS 1522 Tennis Club Rd Charleston WV 25314

CORBETT, SUE-ANN, Physical Education Teacher; *b:* Rockford, IL; *ed:* (BSE) Phys Ed, N IL Univ 1959; *cr:* Phys Ed Teacher Galena HS 1959-; *ai:* Color Guard, Pirettes, Chrldr Adv; AFT, IL Fed of Teachers, Galena Fed of Teachers; Save Turner Hall Fund Inc, Galena Art Theatre Past Pres.

CORBIN, NEIL W., Biology Teacher; *b:* Brockway, PA; *m:* Susan Ragan; *c:* Christine, Neil, Susan, Robert, Lisa; *ed:* (BS) Bio, CA St Univ 1963; (MNS) Bio, Univ of OK 1969; *cr:* Bio Teacher Charleroi HS 1963-64, Scottsdale HS 1964-83, Brophy Coll Prep 1983-84, Saquaro HS 1984-86, Brophy Coll Prep 1986-; *ai:* Ftbl Coach; Lettermens Club Spon; NBTA 1964-; Amer Legion Post 44 1974-; Natl Sci Fnd Univ of OK Masters Prgm 1967-69; *office:* Brophy Coll Prep 4701 N Central Ave Phoenix AZ 85012

CORBY, TIMOTHY RICHARD, Seventh Grade Soc Stud Teacher; *b:* Evanston, IL; *m:* Regina Rivera; *c:* Kyler R.; *ed:* (BA) His, Univ of CO Boulder 1982; Grad Study Instructional Technology, Univ of CO Denver 1982-87; *cr:* 7th Grade Academics Teacher Aurora Hills Mid 1982-; *ai:* Head Wrestling & Odyssey of the Mind Coach; Membership of Accountability; North Cntrl Visitation; Building Cncl; Soc Discipline; Dist Soc Stud Curr Standing Comm; Aurora Ed Assn 1982-; CO Awds Ed & Civic Achievement Honorable Mention Distinguished Teacher 1989; Aurora Hills PTSA 1982, 1985, 1988, 1989; *office:* Aurora Hills Mid Sch 1009 S Uvalda St Aurora CO 80012

CORCORAN, DEE ANN, Retired Teacher; *b:* Bay City, MI; *m:* Patrick J.; *c:* Megan M. Tourda; *ed:* (AA) Bay City Jr Coll 1957; (BS) Elem Ed, W MI Univ 1959; (MA) Elem Admin, MI St Univ 1972; Curr Study; *cr:* 4th/5th Grade Teacher Wheat Sch 1959-62, Greenwood Sch 1962-66; 4th Grade Teacher Parkview Elem 1962-64; 6th Grade Teacher Washington Intermediate 1967-79; 5th Grade Teacher Mc Alear Saw Den Elem 1979-89; *home:* 4680 Foxcroft Dr Bay City MI 48706

CORDER, BARBARA RIGGLE, Second Grade Teacher; *b:* Pulaski, VA; *m:* Daniel Duane; *c:* Michael S. Price, Christopher R. Price; *ed:* (BS) Early Chldhd Ed, Radford Coll 1974; Grad Stud; *cr:* Elem Teacher Draper Elem 1974-; *ai:* Directing & Managing Extra Act; Admin Asst; Authored Genelogy Book; *office:* Draper Elem Sch Rt 1 Draper VA 24324

CORDER, GAIL SINGLETON, French Teacher; *b:* Orange, TX; *m:* Michael; *c:* Brian, Cassidy; *ed:* (BA) Fr, Univ of TX Arlington 1980; *cr:* Scndry Fr Teacher Trinity Valley Sch 1981-; *ai:* Fr Exch Prgm Coord; SADD Faculty Adv; AATF 1983-; TX St Teachers Assn 1980-83; NHS Alpha Chi 1978-80, Phi Sigma Iota in Foreign Lang Secy 1978-80; Certified Superior Oral Proficiency by Modern Foreign Lang Assn; *office:* Trinity Valley Sch 6101 Mc Cart Ave Fort Worth TX 76133

CORDER, JULIE FLECK, Fourth Grade Teacher; *b:* Elkhart, IN; *m:* Eddie Charles; *ed:* (BA) Early Chldhd Ed, Appalachian St Univ 1973; Radford Coll & Surry Comm Coll; NW NC Regional & Mt Airy Sch System Staff Dev Courses; *cr:* 1st Grade Teacher 1973-81, 1983, Kndgtn Teacher 1982, 4th Grade Teacher 1984- Mt Airy City Schls; *ai:* NCAE Secy 1976; NEA Mem 1974-; NCAE Mem; Teacher of Yr 1974-75, 1987; Primary Rdng Prgm Initial Teacher 1976-82; Primary Rdng Prgm Staff Dev Leader 1978; *office:* Tharrington Elem Sch 315 Culbert St Mount Airy NC 27030

CORDES, JOHN BRUCE, Fifth Grade Teacher/Asst Prin; *b:* Marshall, MO; *m:* Nancy Soldwisch; *c:* Katherine Mick, Paul, Karl; *ed:* (BA) Elem Ed, 1960, (MA) Elem Ed, 1968 Concordia Univ; (MS) Sch Admin, De Paul Univ 1971; Eng/His, Oxford Univ Oxford England 1983; Sci, De Paul Univ; Music, Concordia Univ; *cr:* 3rd/4th Grade Music Teacher St Paul Luth Sch 1960-65; 4th/5th Grade Head Teacher John Laidlaw Sch 1965-72; Title I Dir Western Springs Public Schls 1968-80; 5th Grade Teacher/ Asst Prin Field Park Sch 1972-; Minister of Music Trinity Luth Church 1982-; *ai:* Sci Comm; Sci Coord; Western Springs Ed Assn Pres 1972-74, 1976; IL Ed Assn Treas 1973-74; NEA Delegate to Rep Assembly 1972, 1980, 1990; St Johns Luth Church Chm of Elders 1977-79; St Paul Luth Church (Organist, Choir Dir) 1960-65; Grace Luth Church (Organist, Choir Dir) 1965-75; Hope Luth Church (Organist, Choir Dir) 1976-78; *office:* Field Park Sch 4335 Howard Ave Western Springs IL 60558

CORDREY, LEE O., Science Teacher; *b:* Cincinnati, OH; *m:* Nora A. Knowles; *c:* Alexander, Anne; *ed:* (BS) Scndry Ed, Univ of Cincinnati 1970; Counseling; *cr:* Sci Teacher Mt Healthy City Schls 1971-; *ai:* Stu Cncl; Boomerang & Rocket Club; Newspaper; Athletic Coord; NEA, OH Ed Assn; Mt Healthy Teachers Assn (Pres 1980-81, Treas 1982-88); Cmptr Users Group 1987-; Local News Coverage Boomerang Club Carried by Associated Press; Negotiations Team; Supt Advisory Cncl; Building Advisory Cncl Pres, Secy; *office:* Mount Healthy Schls 1917 Miles Rd Cincinnati OH 45231

CORELLA, CHARLOTTE, Teacher; *b:* Hilo, HI; *c:* Michal J.; *ed:* (BA) His, Pepperdine Univ 1968; (MA) Ed, Univ of HI 1982; *cr:* Teacher Waiakea HS 1988, Pahoa HS 1981-88; *ai:* Follies & Awds Assembly Adv; Citizen Bee Coach; Mock Trial 3rd Pl St Trophy 1986.

COREY, JUDITH ANN SPRINGSTON, Fifth Grade Teacher; *b:* Peoria, IL; *m:* Thomas William; *c:* John W., Jeffrey M., Gregory L., Mark A.; *ed:* (BA) Bus Ed, Marycrest Coll 1960; (BA) Guidance & Counseling, Bradley Univ 1972; Cert Elem Ed 1963; Various Courses, Wkshps & Univs; *cr:* 2nd Grade Teacher Riverview Sch 1960-61; 1st Grade Teacher Lincoln Sch 1963-64; Cnslr Bradley Univ 1972-73; Dean of Stu Morton HS 1974-85; 5th Grade Teacher Lettie Brown Sch 1985-86, Jefferson Sch 1986-; *ai:* Paperwork Reduction Comm Chm; Morton Ed Assn (Secy, Cncl Mem, Building Rep, Newsletter Ed) 1973-; IL Ed Assn, NEA 1973-; IL St Deans Assn (Historian 1982-84, Membership Chm 1984-85) 1974-86; Mental Health Assn of Illinois Valley 1977-; Multi-Cty Juvenille Officers League 1978-85; Amer Personnel & Guidance Assn, Tri-Cty Guidance Assn 1973-80; Amer Mental Health Cnslrs Assn 1978-80; Labor Management Team 709 Mem 1989-; Outstanding Young Women of America 1973; *home:* RR 1 N Tennessee Ave Morton IL 61550

COREY, MICHELE, Spanish Teacher; *b:* New Kensington, PA; *ed:* (BA) Span, Indiana Univ of PA 1968; Grad Stud Univ of Valladolid Spain & Univ of WV; *cr:* Span Teacher Burrell HS 1969-; *ai:* Span Club & Jr Class Adv; St George Church Bible Team Coach 1986-89, 1st Place Awds 1986-89; *office:* Burrell HS Puckety Church Rd Lower Burrell PA 15068

CORKREAN, JOHN PATRICK, 4th Grade Teacher; *b:* Winterset, IA; *ed:* (BA) Elem, Simpson Coll 1976; Grad Studies; *cr:* K-12 Stu Winterset Cmmty Sch 1959-72; Coll Stu Simpson Coll 1972-76; Teacher Winterset Cmmty Sch 1976-; *ai:* Jr HS Boys Bsktbl; Little League Bsbl; WCEA Exec Bd 1984-86; Jaycees Pres 1974-81, Outstanding Jaycee 1980; Optimist Club 1986-; Mens Club Pres 1987-88; *home:* 831 S 6th Ave Winterset IA 50273

CORLEY, BARBARA PURCELL, Speech/Drama Teacher; *b:* Louisville, KY; *m:* William H.; *c:* Elizabeth De Witt, Robert P., William H. Jr., Christy R.; *ed:* (BA) Eng/Speech/Drama, 1957; (MA) Ed, 1959 Univ of KY; Drama/Eng/Spch/ Austin Peay St Univ 1962-64; *cr:* Teacher Bryan Station Jr 1957-60; Midway Jr Coll 1967-69; Sallie P Durrett 1960-63; Clarksville HS 1969-89; *ai:* Drama Club; Thespians; Speech Team; Natl Forensics League; Dance Team; Dir All Plays; Sch Beauty Pagent Dir; Dir Cty Wide Summer Show; NEA; Natl Eng Teachers; Theatre of Amer; Kappa Delta Phi; Yrbk Dedication; Career Level 3; *office:* Clarksville H S Richview Rd Clarksville TN 37043

CORLEY, LARRY DALE, Mathematics Department Chair; *b:* Paris, AR; *m:* Carol Sue Nichols; *c:* Joshua; *ed:* (BS) Math, Northeastern St 1965; (MS) Guidance/Counseling, OK St Univ 1977; OK Provisional Scndry Prin & Supt Certificates; *cr:* Math Teacher Haskell Public Schls 1965-68; Lt US Navy 1969-71: Math Teacher/Admin Coweta Public Schls 1972-81; Math Teacher Ft Gibson Public Schls 1982-; *office:* Ft Gibson HS PO Box 280 Fort Gibson OK 74434

CORMIER, BEAULAH EDWARDS, 7th Grade Eng/Rdng Teacher; *b:* Crowley, LA; *m:* Herbert; *c:* Renwick, Quincy; *ed:* (BS) Eng, Southern Univ 1970; *cr:* Teacher St Theresas 1967-69, Midland HS 1971-72, Lake Arthur HS 1972-73, Carencro Elem 1973-74, Northside HS 1973-74, Comeaux HS 1974-75, Crowley Jr HS 1975-; *ai:* Southern Univ Alumni Secy; LA Ed Assn, NEA; St Theresas Worship Commission Chairperson; St Theresas Parish Cncl Asst Secy.

CORMIER, EDDIE JOSEPH, Mathematics Teacher; *b:* Breaux Bridge, LA; *m:* Giselle A. Naomi; *c:* Tonya, Casey, Jessica; *ed:* (BA) Elem Ed, 1975, (MS) Admin/Supervision, 1981 Univ of SW LA; Spec Educl Services; *cr:* Phys Ed/Lang/Soc Stud Teacher Stephensville Elem 1975; Sci Teacher St Martinville Jr HS 1975-76; Math Teacher Breaux Bridge Jr HS 1976-; *ai:* 4-H Spon; Breaux Bridge Jr HS Tutoring Prgm Chm & Coord; Math Self Study, St Jude Mathathon Chm; Bstkbl Coach; Math Dept Rep; Textbook Adoption & Philosopohies/Objective Comm; Sch Enrichment & Remediation Prgm Coord; St Martin Assn of Educators, LA Assn of Educators, Natl Assn of Educators Mem 1975-; Knights of Columbus Inside Guard 1988-89; Parks Jaycees Past VP 1978-79; St Bernard Home Sch Assn Mem 1979-; Amer Bowling Congress Mem 1980-; Breaux Bridge Jr HS Teacher of Yr 1988-89; St Martin Parish Jr HS Teacher of Yr 1988-89; Co-Author St Martin Parish Math Criterion Test; Co-Author LEAP Remediation Study Guide; *office:* Breaux Bridge Jr HS Main & Martin Sts Breaux Bridge LA 70517

CORMIER, IRENE WATSON, Third Grade Teacher; *b:* Baton Rouge, LA; *m:* Roy Pierre; *c:* Ronald Eisley, Fairlane Eisley, Cherry Harris; *ed:* (BA) Elem Ed, 1964, (ME) Elem Ed, 1971 Southern Univ; Plus 30 Elem Ed, Univ of SW LA 1974; Prof Improvement & Right to Read Prgm; Lang Experience Approach to Rdng; *cr:* Teacher East St Louis 1964-65, St Martinville 1965-81, Westside Elem 1981-; *ai:* Visiting Comm Southern Assn of Colls & Schls Accrediting Public & Private Schls; Natl Assn of Univ Women, Southern Univ Alumni VP 1967-69; Lafayette Parish Assn of Classroom Teachers; Cmmty Action Anti-Poverty Prgm; Church Mission Society; Appointed Comm Chm of St Adopted Textbooks, Math, Rdng, Stu Dictionaries; *home:* 223 Montreal Dr Lafayette LA 70507

CORMIER, MADELEINE TUFTS, Fourth Grade Teacher; *b:* Greenwich, CT; *m:* Gene; *c:* Laura; *ed:* (BA) Early Chldhd Ed, Wheelock Coll 1966; (MED) Cmmty Counseling, Salem St Coll 1984; *cr:* Nursery Sch Teacher German-Amer Presch 1967-69; 5th Grade Teacher Liverpool Elem Sch 1969-70; 9th-13th Grade Teacher Lawn Upton Mid 1985-86; 4th/5th Grade Teacher Bell Sch 1970-; *ai:* Stu Assistance Team; NEA, MA Teachers Assn, Marblehead Ed Assn; Wheelock Coll Alumni Assn Pres 1988-, Centennial Alumni Awd 1989; Horace Mann Grant Teacher 1987-88; Fulbright Exch Oxford England 1985-86; *office:* Bell Sch 40 Baldwin Rd Marblehead MA 01945

CORMIER, STEVEN A., Social Studies Teacher; *b:* Jennings, LA; *m:* Faye Underwood; *c:* Michael; *ed:* (BA) Soc Stud Ed, Mc Neese St Univ 1972; (MA) His, Old Dominion Univ 1982; *cr:* 2nd Lieutenant USAQMC Ft Lee VA 1973, Ft Carson CO 1973-75; Teacher Lloyd C Bird HS 1978-; *ai:* Lloyd C Bird HS Var Debate Team Coach; Chesterfield Ed Assn Faculty Rep 1980-; Richmond Civil War Roundtable 1984-; Author 1989; *home:* 14102 Granite Pointe Ct Chesterfield VA 23832

CORN, DARREL LEE, Social Studies Teacher; *b:* Oakland City, IN; *m:* Rena Mae; *c:* Geoffrey, Darren; *ed:* (BA) Soc Stud, Oakland City Coll 1970; (MS) Soc Stud, IN St Univ 1975; Admin, Evansville Univ; Drivers Ed, Auctioneering, Real Estate, Insurance Courses; *cr:* Teacher SW Dubois HS & Mid Sch 1970-; *ai:* NEA, ISTA; E Gibson Little League 1965-; Princeton Little League Coach 1960-63; Oakland City Judge & Councilman at Large; Outstanding Young Man Awd.

CORN, RANDALL A., English Teacher; *b:* Marion, IN; *m:* Cindie L. Childs; *c:* Benjamin, James; *ed:* (BS) Eng, Ball St Univ 1983; Working Towards Masters IN Univ, Purdue Univ; *cr:* Teacher Brownsburg HS 1984-; *ai:* Acad Competition & Honors Lit Seminar Dir; In-Service Trng Comm; Alternative Ed Comm Chm 1987-88; Project XL Organizational Comm 1988-; *office:* Brownsburg HS 1000 S Odell St Brownsburg IN 46112

CORNALI, ROBERT LOUIS, Social Studies Teacher; *b:* Greensburg, PA; *m:* Pamela Kubjalko; *c:* Brian, Benjamin, David; *ed:* (BS) Comprehensive Soc Stud, Clarion Univ of PA 1965; *cr:* Teacher Norwin Sch Dist 1965-; *ai:* AFS Stu Adv; Stu Asst Prgm; World Affairs of Pittsburgh; Norwin Ed Assn Grievance Chm; Huntingdon Township Planning Commission 1987-; *office:* Norwin Sch Dist 257 Mc Mahon Dr North Huntingdon PA 15642

CORNELIOUS, BONNIE MARTIC, 7th Grade English Teacher; *b:* Findlay, OH; *w:* Warren (dec); *c:* Scott, Philip; *ed:* (BS) Elem Ed, Bowling Green S Univ 1977; (MS) Elem Ed, 1983, (MS) Counseling, 1990 Shippenburg Univ; *cr:* Teacher James Buchanan Mid Sch 1979-; Adjunct Professor Wilkes Coll 1984-; *ai:* Tuscarora Ed Assn Pres 1989-; Franklin Cty Sch Management Assn 1983, Outstanding Educator 1983; *office:* James Buchanan Mid Sch 5191 Fort Louden Rd Mercersburg PA 17236

CORNELIUS, CATHY SUHRHEINRICH, Teacher/ Counselor; *b:* Huntingburg, IN; *m:* Jeff; *ed:* (BS) Sci, IN St Univ Evansville 1980; (MS) Cmmty Cnslng, Univ of Evansville 1981; *cr:* Teacher Mitchell Cmmty Sch 1982-85; Teacher/Cnslr Tecumseh Jr-Sr HS 1986-; *ai:* Spon Stu Chrstn Club; Jr HS Track Coach; Academic Team Coach; IN St Teacher Assn; Huntingburg United Meth Church Mem; Delta Zeta Alumni; *home:* 205 S Washington St Huntingburg IN 47542

CORNELIUS, DONNA NETHERTON, First Grade Teacher; *b:* Cullman, AL; *m:* Jerry D.; *c:* Kari, Matthew; *ed:* (BS) Elem Ed, Athens St Coll 1976; (MS) Early Chldhd Ed, Univ of AL Birmingham 1980; *cr:* 1st Grade Teacher Susan Moore HS 1976-77, Fairview HS 1977-; *ai:* Sch Improvement Comm 1988-; NEA, AEA, CCEA 1977-; Church Sunday Sch Teacher 1989-; Delta Kappa Gamma 1982-85; *home:* Rt 8 Box 1180 Cullman AL 35055

CORNELIUS, ROSE ANGELA, Psychology/Sociology Teacher; *b:* Temple, TX; *m:* William; *c:* Angela, William; *ed:* (BS) Psych/Sociology, Mary Hadin Baylor Univ 1981; *cr:* Teacher Temple HS 1984-; *ai:* Psych Club; TSTA, NEA 1984-; Jr League 1990; *office:* Temple HS 415 N 31st St Temple TX 76504

CORNELL, GENEVE SMITH, 5th Grade Teacher/Director; *b:* Santaquin, UT; *w:* Charles Leroy (dec); *c:* Joan C. Walston, Douglas, Carolyn C. Layton, Louise, Kathryn C. Boone, Lasca C. Rose, Jared, Roger, Ralph, David; *cr:* Asst Dir 1980-83, Teacher 1971-, Bd of Trustees Mem 1975-, Dir 1983- Amer Heritage Sch; *ai:* Graduation Comm; Writer, Dramatic Coach, Costume Mistress Annual Patriotic Prgm; Poly Party (Dist Chm 1960-66, St Delegate 1960-76); St Republican Women (4th VP, Pres) 1966-70; Amer Fork HS PTA (Pres, Cncl Bd Mem); Amer Fork Cultural Club Pres; Amer Fork Lady Lions Club Pres; Pres Cncl of Cultural Clubs Pres; Church of Jesus Christ of Latter Day Saints (Teacher, Leader); Amer Fork Outstanding Young Mother of Yr Nom 1965; Natl His Day Nom Columbus Inst 1990; Daughters of Amer Revolution; Outstanding His Teacher of Yr UT 1988; Honor Certificate for Patriotic Prgm Script & Admin Awd Nom 1990; *office:* Amer Heritage Sch 125 N 100 E Pleasant Grove UT 84602

CORNELL, PAUL ROBERT, Mathematics Dept Chair; *b:* Chicago, IL; *m:* Renee Rodecap; *c:* Ryan, Chad, Kaitlyn; *ed:* (BA) Math/Scndry, 1974, (MA) Scndry/Math Ed, 1978 AZ St Univ; *cr:* Math Teacher 1974-, Math Chm 1975- Paradise Valley HS; *ai:* Math Club Spon; NCTM, AZ Assn of Teachers of Math 1980-; Paradise Valley Sch Dist Learning Leader Awd 1988; *office:* Paradise Valley HS 3950 E Bell Rd Phoenix AZ 85032

CORNFORTH, ULLAH DELLE, Third Grade Teacher; *b:* Lincoln Park, MI; *ed:* (BS) His/Elem Ed, 1949, (MS) Scndry Ed, 1982 Baylor Univ; *cr:* His Teacher Rockport HS 1949-51; 3rd Grade Teacher Moody Elem Sch 1952-; *ai:* PTA (VP 1961-62, Mem 1952-); TSTA Secy 1952-; AAUW Pres 1967-68; Teacher of Yr 1988-89; Career Level Three; *home:* Box 39 Eddy TX 76524

CORNILS, JAY ALBERT, English Teacher; *b:* Aurora, IL; *ed:* (BA) Speech/Drama, Concordia Univ 1972; (MAT) Hum, CO Coll 1981; Admin Cert, Denver Univ; Writin Lit Inst Univ of CO; *cr:* Dir of Drama Concordia Coll 1972-73; Eng Teacher Seroul Jr HS 1973-79, Widefield HS 1979-; *ai:* Advanced Placement Coord; Natl Interscholastic Athletic Admin Assn 1986-; ASCD 1988-; Natl Fed of Interscholastic ofcls Assn St Dir 1984-; Intnl Assn of Approved Bsktbl Ofcls St Pres Elect; Published 3 Times; St of CO Track Rules Interpreter; *office:* Widefield HS 615 Widefield Dr Security CO 80911

CORNISH, CHARLOTTE YOUNG, Teacher of Gifted; *b:* Ackerman, MS; *m:* Carroll Jr.; *c:* Kim, Charlie; *ed:* (BS) Elem Ed, MS St Univ 1970; *cr:* Teacher of Gifted Ackerman Elem 1980-; *ai:* Coach Future Problem Solving Team; Sch Paper Spon; MS Prof Educators, MS Assn for Talented & Gifted; Band Boosters Treas 1988-; Twentieth Century Club; *home:* Box 434 Ackerman MS 39735

CORNWELL, DEBRA HOOVER, First Grade Teacher; *b:* Columbia, SC; *m:* Chris B.; *c:* Kasey N.; *ed:* (BA) Early Chldhd, W Carolina Univ 1974; *cr:* Kndgtn Teacher 1974-76, K-1st Grade Teacher 1976-78, 1st Grade Teacher 1978- Asbury Elem; *ai:* Stu Based Support Team; NCAE Faculty Rep 1988-89; PTA Faculty Rep; Roger City Meth Church Childrens Ministries 1985-; *office:* Asbury Elem Sch 310 Salem Rd Lincolnton NC 28092

CORNWELL, DIANE ANDERSEN, 6th Grade Math/Science Teacher; *b:* Amityville, NY; *m:* Randy L.; *c:* Melissa, Kasey, Kyle; *ed:* (AA) Music Ed, Palm Beach Jr Coll 1971; (BA) Music Ed, 1973, (BA) Elem Ed, 1977 Lenoir-Rhyne Coll 1977; *cr:* 5th Grade Teacher 1974-80, 6TH Grade Teacher 1980-84 Cntrl Elem, G E Massey Elem 1984-88; North Brook Elem 1988-89; 6th Grade Math/Sci Teacher West Lincoln Mid Sch 1989-; *ai:* NCAE

1974-78/1989-; Sci Fair Comm 1987-88; Sci/Math Fair Coord 1988-89; *home:* Rt 1 Box 251-A Lincolnton NC 28092

CORNWELL, JEANNIE DUKE, Humanities Teacher; *b:* Meridian, MS; *m:* Dale B. Sr.; *c:* D. Bruce Jr., D. Brian; *ed:* (BS) Scndry Soc Stud, 1978, (MED) Scndry Ed/Remedial Rdng, 1983, (MA) Poly Sci, 1988 MS St Univ; *cr:* CETA Teacher Newton Cty Schls 1978-80; Remedial Rdng Teacher Pioneer Cntrl Schls 1983; Teacher Lauderdale Cty Schls 1980-82, 1984-; *ai:* Jr HS Chrldrs, Newspaper, Stu Cncl, Citizen Bee, MS Model Security Cncl Delegations, Jr & Sr Prom Spon; Lauderdale Cty Fed of Teachers Pres 1986-, Outstanding Service Awd 1986-88; NCSS Membership Comm 1989-; MS Cncl Soc Stud Exec Comm Dist 3 1988-; Amer Bus Womens Assn Various Comm 1984-; Pi Sigma Alpha 1988-; Governors Speakers Bureau Ed Reform Speaker 1989; 1st Baptist Church of Marion 1985-; Fulbright to Pakistan 1988; NCSS Fellowship to Germany 1990; Korean Stud Cncl Intnl Fellowship to Korea 1990; MS Power Fnd Grant 1989; Yrbk Dedication 1988-89; Fellow Taft Inst Two Party Government 1985; *home:* Rt 5 Box 554 Meridian MS 39307

CORNWELL, MARY HUDDLESTON (TURNER), Fifth Grade Teacher; *b:* Roanoke, VA; *m:* Barkley Alan; *ed:* (BS) Elem Ed, James Madison 1967; (MED) Elem Ed, Univ of VA 1973; *cr:* 4th Grade Teacher Anne E Moncure 1967-68; 3rd/4th Grade Teacher Bel Air Elem 1968-71; 5th Grade Teacher Dale City Elem 1971-74, Kerrydale Elem 1975-83, Lake Ridge Elem 1983-; *ai:* Prince William Ed Assn, VA Ed Assn, NEA 1968-; *office:* Lake Ridge Elem Sch 11970 Hedges Run Rd Woodbridge VA 22192

CORNWELL, NANCY LANDRUM, Guidance Counselor; *b:* Fountain Run, KY; *m:* Clovis Joe; *c:* Nancy J.; *ed:* (BS) Bus Ed, 1962, (MA) Cnslr Ed, 1967 W KY Univ; Rank I Cnslr Ed; *cr:* Jr HS Math Teacher 1962-65, HS Bus Teacher 1966-67 Austin Tracy Sch; HS Cnslr 1967-74; Elem Cnslr Austin Tracy/Park City 1974-; *ai:* South Cntrl Assn Cnslr Dev, KY Personnel & Guildance Assn, KY Ed Assn 1962-; KY Gifted & Talented Assn 1986-; NEA Life Mem 1962-; *home:* 12220 Brownsford Rd Fountain Run KY 42133

CORONADO, JUANITA MARGARITA, Assistant Principal; *b:* Laredo, TX; *ed:* (BS) Ed, 1980, (MS) Ed, 1982 Laredo St Univ; Cert in Mid Management 1984, Supervision 1983, Spec Ed & Bi-ling 1982; *cr:* 5th Grade Teacher 1980-83, Spec Ed Resource Teacher 1983-89 Don Tomas Sanchez Sch; Asst Prin Farias Elem Sch 1989-; *ai:* Paisano Rdng Cncl, TX Elem Prin & Supvrs Assn 1989; TX St Teachers Assn Pres Elect 1989-; Laredo Chamber Meritorious Teacher Awd 1989; *home:* 1111 Clark Laredo TX 78040

CORRALES, MARINA, Social Science/Spanish Teacher; *b:* Tijuana, Mexico; *m:* Enrrique; *c:* Ennrique Jr., Andre D.; *ed:* (BA) Liberal Art/Soc Sci, 1978; (MA) Span 1980, Sch of Ed Soc Sci/ Span, 1981 SD St Univ; *cr:* Teacher SD St Univ 1980-83; Substitute Teacher Montgomery HS 1982-84, Teacher ACCESS 1983-84; Mentor Teacher Sweetwater Union HS Dist 1988-89; Teacher Natl City Jr HS 1984-; *ai:* Span Club Adv; Teachers Treat Co-Spon; Natl City Jr HS Teacher of Yr 1986-87; *office:* National City Jr HS 1701 O Avenue National City CA 92050

CORRELL, KENNETH ROBERT, Sixth & Seventh Grade Teacher; *b:* Erwin, TN; *m:* Gina M. Bennett; *c:* Amy C., Kenneth R. II; *ed:* (BS) Elem Ed, E TN St Univ 1978; Working Towards Masters Bus Admin; *cr:* 6th/7th Grade Teacher Love Chapel Elem 1979-; *ai:* Love Chapel Elem Jr Beta Club Spon; PTA Life Membership 1985; Southern Sensations Magazine 1989; *home:* 302 Mountain View St PO Box 436 Erwin TN 37650

CORRELL, MICHAEL JAMES, 5th Grade Teacher; *b:* Hayward, WI; *M:* Rita Robey; *c:* Jamie, Jonathan; *ed:* (BS) Spec Ed/Elem Ed, Univ of WI Eau Claire 1982; Physiological Trng Specialists, USAF; *cr:* Classroom Teacher Chileda Inst 1983, Cameron Elem Sch 1983-; *ai:* JV Bsktbl Coach 1983-88; Maranatha Evangelical Free Church Chrstn Ed Dir 1986-89; *office:* Cameron Elem Sch 600 Wisconsin Ave Cameron WI 54822

CORRIGAN, WENDY COTTON, HS Mathematics Teacher; *b:* Colon, Panama; *m:* Dennis M.; *c:* Denise, Casey, Sean; *ed:* (MED) Educl Technology, 1989, (BS) Math, 1972 AZ St Univ; *cr:* Math Dept Chairperson/Teacher Dysart HS 1972-83; Cmptr Coord Dysart Unified Sch Dist 89 1983-89; Math Teacher Dysart HS 1989-; *ai:* NHS Spon; Cntrl Assn Steering Comm Chairperson; Principals Teacher Comm Mem; NEA; AZ Assn for Teachers of Math 1972-; AZ Alliance for Sci & Math 1985-; Sun Valley Cmptr Cncl Chairperson 1985-86; BSA Pack 263 Treas 1971-73; *office:* Dysart HS 11405 N Dysart Rd Rt 1 Box 703 Peoria AZ 85345

CORRIHER, CAROLYN TREECE, Honors English Teacher; *b:* Albemarle, NC; *m:* Mark B.; *c:* Brad M.; *ed:* (AB) Eng/Ed, Catawba Coll 1972; Various Curr, In Service Wkshps; *cr:* Eng Teacher Davie HS 1972-; *ai:* NCTE; Selected Young Teacher of Yr; *office:* Davie HS 1200 Salisbury Rd Mocksville NC 27028

CORROA, ANTHONY JOHN, Band Director; *b:* New Orleans, LA; *m:* Jeanine Troxclair; *c:* Kevin M., Elise N., Danielle T.; *ed:* (BM) Music, 1969, (MM) Music, 1971 LA St Univ; *cr:* Band Dir Episcopal HS 1971-72, White Castle HS 1973-78, St Thomas More 1978-86, Parkview Baptist HS 1982-84, Parkview Baptist HS 1985-87, Tara HS 1988-; *ai:* Marching Band; Jazz Ensemble; Concert Band; LA Music Educators Assn, LA Band Masters Assn, Intnl Assn Jazz Educators, Baton Rouge Musicians Union, Music Educators Natl Conference; Buddy-Lee Dance Orchestra 1975-; Baton Rouge Symphony Orchestra 1968-; *home:* 3425 Ridgemont Dr Baton Rouge LA 70814

CORSE, RALPH WILLIAM, K-12th Grade Science Coord; *b:* Cape Girardeau, MO; *m:* Cindy; *c:* Ralph, Iris, Ryan; *ed:* (BED) Bio, SE MO St Univ 1970; (MA) Scndry Admin, Univ of MO Kansas City 1986; *cr:* Sci Teacher Puxico HS 1970-78, Independence Chrstn Sch 1980-84; Sci Resource/Classroom Teacher 1986-89, Sci Coord 1990 Kansas City Sch Dist; *ai:* Dist Sci Coord; NSTA, Natl Sci Supvrs Assn, Sci Teachers of MO; *home:* 113 N Holder Independence MO 64050

CORSON, JANET L. (SMITH), Foreign Lang Dept Chairperson; *b:* Gloversville, NY; *c:* Katherine A., J. Kenneth; *ed:* (BA) Fr, Beaver Coll 1964; (MA) Fr Literature, Univ of MD 1971; Fr Western Reserve Univ; Towson St Univ; Loyola Coll; Johns Hopkins Univ; *cr:* Fr Teacher Cleveland Hts 1964-65, Binghamton Public Schls 1965-66; Fr/Speech Teacher Maryvale Preparatory Sch 1978-79; Fr Teacher Baltimore Cty Public Schls 1980-; *ai:* Spon Foreign Lang Club; Mem Values Comm; Minority Achievement Participation Success Comm; Teachers Assn Baltimore Cty 1980-; AAWw (2nd VP/Mem 1981-); *office:* Holabird Mid Sch 1701 Delvale Ave Baltimore MD 21222

CORTELLESI, DEBRA JEAN, Educational Evaluator; *b:* Charleroi, PA; *m:* Michael; *c:* Erik; *ed:* (BA) Elem Ed, CA St Univ 1979; (MA) Gifted Ed, WV Coll Grad Stud 1990; *cr:* 2nd/3rd Grade Teacher Panther Elem Sch 1979-81; 2nd Grade Teacher Bartley Elem Sch 1981-83; 4th Grade Teacher Gary Elem Sch 1983-84; Gifted Teacher Voc Tech Center 1984-89; *ai:* Womens Club 1980-81; *office:* Welch Elem Sch 30 Central Ave Welch WV 24801

CORTEZ, DAVID, Mathematics Teacher; *b:* Elsa, TX; *m:* Carmen Peralez; *c:* Marco A., Petra P., Mario A., Miguel A.; *ed:* (BA) Government, Pan American Coll 1971; (MSW) Soc Work, W MI Univ 1974; (MED) Counseling, Pan Amer Univ 1985; Mid Management Cert; *cr:* Teacher Edcouch-Elsa Ind Sch Dist 1971-72; Cnclr Fennville Public Schls 1974-75; Teacher/CNslr/ At-Risk Coord/Discipline Mgr/Drug Coord Monte Alto Ind Sch Dist 1975-; *ai:* LPAC, Drug Ed, Discipline Comm, Promotion/ Retention Comm; Lions Club (Secy, Treas 1987-88); MLK Schlrshp W MI Univ; Pan Amer Univ Bi-Ling Grant; *office:* Monte Alto Ind Sch Dist Rt 1 Box 116 Edcouch TX 78538

CORTEZ, ESPERANZA HOPE, Elementary Counselor; *b:* San Antonio, TX; *ed:* (BS) Ed, 1973, (MED) Ed, 1975 Sul Ross St Univ; (MED) Scndry Ed, Stephen F Austin St Univ 1983; Cert Spec Ed Cnslr UTPB 1988; Mid-Management Admin SFASU 1983; Supvr SFASU 1983; Cnslr UTPB 1982; *cr:* Teacher 1973-79; Kndgtn Bi-ling Teacher 1979-83 Zavala Elem; Bi-ling Supvr Summer Prgm 1985-88; Cnslr Ector Cty Ind Sch Dist 1983; *ai:* Campus Action Team for Fannin-Lamar Early Ed Center; Coach After Sch Sftbl & Vlybl; In Schl Services; Head Teacher Adult Ed Prgm Odessa Coll 1975-78; TX St Teachers Assn Faculty Rep 1974-83; Odessa Classroom Teacher Assn Faculty Rep 1976-78; NEA 1978; Phi Delta Kappa 1982; TX Assn of Bi-ling Educators 1975-82; TX Personnel & Guidance Assn 1984-86; Permian Basin Cnslrs Assn 1983-; TX Assn for Counseling & Dev 1983-; Elem Counselors Handbook of Guidance Act Related to TX Essential Elements Co Author; *office:* Fannin/ Lamar Early Ed Center PO Box 3912 Odessa TX 79760

CORTEZ, GERRE L., History Teacher/Coach; *b:* Topeka, KS; *ed:* (BS) Phys Ed/His, Univ of TX Arlington 1983; *cr:* Teacher/ Coach Jackson Mid Sch 1983-88, South Garland HS 1988-; *ai:* Frosh & Jr Var Girls Bsktbl Team Coach; Asst Var Coach; TX HS Girls Coaches Assn, TX St Teachers Assn, Garland Ed Assn 1989-; TX Assn of Bsktbl Coaches 1989-; *office:* South Garland HS 600 Colonel Dr Garland TX 75043

CORTEZ, JAMES A., Science Teacher; *b:* Jacksonville, FL; *m:* Emilie Olsen; *c:* Katherine, David; *ed:* (BS) Chem, Spring Hill Coll 1970; Chem, TX A&M Univ 1972; (MS) Scndry Sci Ed, Univ of N FL 1984; *cr:* Instr The Bolles Sch 1975-; *ai:* Cmptr Acts Comm; Amer Chemical Society Alternate Councilor 1986-, Outstanding Teacher 1988; NE FL Engrs Society 1989, Outstanding Teacher; Cross Cntry AA FL Coach of Yr 1980; Articles Published 1986-88; Roeder Advanced Placement Chem Exam 1989-; *office:* The Bolles Sch 7400 San Jose BLvd Jacksonville FL 32217

CORTEZ, MILDRED S., Fifth Grade Teacher; *b:* Church Point, LA; *m:* Hubert N.; *c:* Claire C. Daly, Kathleen C. Whipp, Carolyn C. Artall; *ed:* (BA) Upper Elem Ed, Univ of SW LA 1955; (MED) Supervision & Admin, LA ST Univ 1961; *cr:* 5th/7th Grade Teacher Eunice Elem Sch 1954-56; 7th Grade Teacher Market Street Elem 1956-63; Supervising Teacher Univ of SW LA 1970-86; 5th/6th Grade Teacher Grolee Elem Sch 1965-; *ai:* NEA; LA Ed Assn; St Landry Assn of Ed Outstanding Elem Teacher; Delta Kappa Gamma; Catholic Daughters of Americas Vice-Regent 1987-; *home:* Rt 2 Box 49-D Opelousas LA 70570

CORVASCE, FRANCES DIANE, English Teacher; *b:* Brooklyn, NY; *ed:* (BA) Eng, Brooklyn Coll 1971; (MA) Eng Lit, 1973, (PHD) 18th Century British Lit 1976 NY Univ; *cr:* Instr Manor Jr Coll 1977-78; Teacher Edward Shallow Jr HS 1978-80, Louis Armstrong Mid Sch 1980-; *ai:* Mainstream Comm Supvr Stu TeacHers; Yrbk, Literary Magazine Adv; Debate Team Coach; Arista-Honor Roll Adv; Eng Dept Chairperson; Graduation Adv; UFT Consultation Comm; Sch Congress Rep; ASCD 1990; NYCTE 1980-; NY Cncl Teachers Eng; Nom NY St Teacher of Yr 1984; Book Satire Trillium Press 1986; Mid Sch Journal Article 1987; *office:* Louis Armstrong Mid Sch 32-02 Junction Blvd East Elmhurst NY 11369

CORWIN, NORMA BAUM, Band Director; *b:* New Castle, PA; *c:* Abbi Rabeneck; *ed:* (BME) Piano/Woodwinds, Westminster 1962; (MS) Bus Ed, Robert Morris 1984; *cr:* HS Band/Elem Music Teacher New Castle Schls 1962-63; Choir/General Music Teacher 1969-85; Instrumental Music/Band Teacher 1985- Montour Schls; *ai:* Jazz Ensemble; Accelerated Fine Arts Enrichment Prgm; MENC, MFT; *home:* 291 Noble Ave Pittsburgh PA 15205

COSAND, SANDRA RAY, 5th Grade Teacher; *b:* Lansing, MI; *m:* Paul N. Jr.; *ed:* (BA) Elem Ed, Univ of AZ 1970; Univ of AZ Grad Sch; *cr:* 5th & 6th Grade Teacher Eloy Intermediate Sch 1970-80; 6th Grade Teacher Ajo Public Sch 1980-81; 5th Grade Teacher Loving Elem Sch 1981-; *ai:* Spon Elem Sch Stud Senate; Stamp Club Adv; Eloy City Council Person 1979-80; Pi Lambda Theta 1973; Alpha Alpha Delta Kappa 1990; Leaders of Amer Elem Ed 1971; Coord Eloy Curr 1979-80; *home:* 1005 Irum Carlsbad NM 88220

COSBY, ANNA MARIE, Mathematics Teacher; *b:* Greenville, KY; *m:* Cletus Jewell; *c:* Stephanie, Sarah; *ed:* (AB) Math, 1972, (MA) Guidance/Counseling, 1974 W KY Univ; (Rank I) Guidance/Counseling, 1977; *cr:* Math Teacher Central City HS 1972-; *ai:* Soph Class Spon; Prins Cncl Cntrl City HS; Math Comm Muhlenberg Cty Schls; Cntrl City Ed Assn Secy 1984-86; Muhlenberg Cty Ed Assn Building Rep 1987-88; KY Ed Assn, NEA, Kenlake Cncl of Math Teachers, NCTM; Greenville Band Boosters Treas 1989-; Cumberland Presbyn Women Pres 1984-; W KY Univ Alumni Assn Schlsp Chm 1977-; Cumberland Presbyn Choir; Greenville Elem PTO.

COSBY, JEAN BURNS, Second Grade Teacher; *b:* Louisville, KY; *m:* James E. Jr.; *c:* Thomas E., Mary J. Nave, James A.; *ed:* (BA) Elem Ed, 1955, (MA) Elem Ed/Lib Sci 1959 Mid TN St Coll; *cr:* 3rd Grade Teacher 1950-60, 2nd Grade Teacher 1968- Pulaski Elem Sch; *ai:* Calendar, TAB, Grade Level Comm Mem; Delta Kappa Gamma 1955-59, 1986-; First Baptist Church 1944-; *office:* Pulaski Elem Sch 606 Cedar Ln Pulaski TN 38478

COSGROVE, DONNA KOLB, Secondary School Counselor; *b:* Aurelia, IA; *c:* Kristin, Will, Wade; *ed:* (BA) Eng, Buena Vista Coll 1973; (MS) Guidance/Counseling/Personal Services, Univ of SD 1985; Grad Stud Substance Abuse Prevention, Eating Disorders, Elem Counseling; *cr:* Eng Teacher Aurelia Cmmty HS 1973-85; Guidance Cnslr Marcus Cmmty Schls 1985-87, Maurice-Orange City HS 1987-; *ai:* Amer Field Service & Jr Class Spon; Faculty Advisory Comm; Area Ed Agency 4 Cnslr Advisory Comm Secy; IA Assn of St Counseling & Dev (Secy, Treas) 1985-; IA Sch Cnslrs Assn (Secy, Pres) 1985-; IA St Ed Assn Pres Elect 1973-83; NEA Pres Elect 1987-; Faith Luth Church (Choir Mem, Bible Sch Chairperson, Teacher) 1987-; *office:* Maurice-Orange City HS 615 8th St Se Orange City IA 51041

COSIANO, GAYTANA IACANO, 3rd Grade Teacher; *b:* Cleveland, OH; *m:* Ralph V.; *c:* Angela, Martha Considine, Patricia, Joanne, Mary Fazekas, Patrick; *ed:* (BS) Elem Ed, OH Univ 1959; Ursuline Coll; *cr:* 1st Grade Teacher Warrensville Heights Sch System 1957-59; 2nd Grade Teacher 1976-89, 3rd Grade Teacher 1989- St Charles Sch Cleveland Cath Diocese; *ai:* Intnl Rdng Assn; *office:* St Charles Sch 7107 Wilber Ave Parma OH 44129

COSNER, MARGARET GARNAS, Third Grade Teacher; *b:* Northwood, IA; *m:* Gordon Lewis; *ed:* (AA) Ed, Waldorf Coll 1945; (BS) Ed, Wartburg Coll 1961; *cr:* 4th Grade Teacher Dumont Sch 1945-47; 3rd Grade Teacher Longfellow Sch 1947-48; 3rd Grade Teacher Aplington Sch 1948-50; 3rd Grade Teacher Parkersburg Sch 1950-; *ai:* ISEA/NEA 1945-; Local PEA Sec/ Treas; Parkersburg Historical House Society 1975-; Mem of Northwood Luth Church; *home:* 401 Bethel Parkersburg IA 50665

COSS, BARBARA JOAN ATWOOD, Kindergarten Teacher; *b:* Waterbury, CT; *m:* William Francis Jr.; *c:* Maryanne Struble, William III, Barbara Lawless, Elizabeth De Santo, Cynthia Roberts; *ed:* Cycle of Dev Gisell Inst; Sci Trng for Early Chldhd, Tucott Mountain; Religious Stud, Math Their Way, St Joseph Coll; *cr:* Rdng Specialist Reading Research Center 1966-75; Kndgtn Teacher St Marys Grammar Sch 1976-; *ai:* Kndgtn Curr Comm Archdiocese of Hartford; Faculty Adv Home & Sch Assn; Kndgtn Teachers Assn of CT, NCEA; Rainbows Society for Soc & Emotional Problem Stu in Cath Schls; Orton-Gillingham Society; *office:* St Marys Grammar Sch 43 Cole St Waterbury CT 06702

COSSEL, DONNA ANN, Fifth Grade Teacher; *b:* Warner Robins, GA; *ed:* (BS) Elem Ed, Northern AZ Univ 1976; (MED) Elem Ed, 1985; (EDS) Educl Admin, Univ of AZ; Cooperatv Learning Trng Johnson & Johnson Prgm 1989; Essential Elements Effective Instrctn Madeline Hunter 1990; *cr:* 5th Grade Teacher Tanque Verde Unified Dist 13 1978-; Mgr/Waitress Gaslight Theatre 1980-; *ai:* HS Chrlr/Songleader Spon; Essential Skills Comm; Curr Dev Comm; Teacher Asst. Trng Team Ldr; Mentor Teacher Prgm (Mentor Teacher); Cum Laude Honors Achvt Excl 1977; NEA/AEA/TVTA Var Comm Rep 1976-; Tanque Verde Home Owners Bd Mem 1983-86; 3rd St Kids Chairperson 1987-88; Big Bro & Sis Vlntr 1987-; *office:* Agua Caliente Elem Schl 11420 E Limberlost Tucson AZ 85749

COSTA, ALICIA CHRISTINA, SSF, Mathematics Dept Chairperson; *b:* New Orleans, LA; *ed:* (BS) Math, Loyola Univ 1978; (MED) Scndry Sch Admin, Univ of New Orleans 1983; *cr:* Office Clerk Regina Caeli HS 1969-70; Teacher All Saints Sch 1973-75, St Francis Xavier 1975-77; Teacher/Dept Head Holy Rosary Inst 1988-89; Teacher/Dept Head St Marys Acad 1978-90; *ai:* Academic Games League; Mu Alpha Theta Club Adv;

Disciplinary Coord; NCTM 1978-89; Greater New Orleans Teachers of Math 1979-; Sisters of Holy Family 1969-.

COSTA, CAROL ANNE, History/Economics Teacher; *b:* Providence, RI; *ed:* Assoc Liberal Arts/Psych, RI Jr Coll 1980; (BA) Liberal Arts/His, RI Coll 1983; Advance First Aid Cert, CPR Instr, Certified Coach; *cr:* Bus Owner Back Court Pub 1984-86; Tournament Staff Intnl Tennis Hall of Fame 1984-; Teacher/Athletic Dir Bishop Keough Regional HS 1987-; *ai:* Yrbk Adv; Tennis, Bsktbl, Sftbl Coach; Athletic Dir; RI Athletic Dirs Assn, RI HS Sftbl Coaches Assn, RI HS Bsktbl Coaches Assn 1986-; RI HS Girls Tennis Coaches Assn Pres 1986-; Glocester Democratic Town Comm (Treas 1985) 1984-; Coach US His Class to St Championship on Constitution & Bill of Rights/Will Represent RI in Natl Finals 1990; *home:* 12 Brook Hill Rd North Scituate RI 02857

COSTA, JOANNE MARIE, Computer Teacher; *b:* Chicago, IL; *m:* Joseph N.; *ed:* (BSED) Mrktg/Bus Ed, Northern IL Univ 1981; Cmptr Programming/Counseling/Ed Admin; *cr:* Mrktg Vocational Coord Teacher Bloomington Area Vocational Center 1981-84; Cmptr/Typing Teacher Lockport East HS 1984-85; Cmptr Teacher Prairie Cntrl HS 1985-; *ai:* Sr Class Spon; Natl Honor Society Selection Comm; Cmptr Curr Comm-Secy; ICVECA 1981-84 Tenacity Rapport Initiative Perseverance Awd 1984; Mrktg Ed Assn Alumni Adv 1982-85; IL Bus Ed Assn 1981-; Onarga Womans Club 1985-88; Developed & Implemented New Course for Cmptr Curr; Presenter for Prgm at IL St Bus Ed Conference; North Cntrl Evaluation Visiting Team Mem; *home:* PO Box 34 Fairbury IL 61739

COSTA, JOHN JOSEPH, Technology Education Teacher; *b:* Meriden, CT; *m:* Judy Ann Downing; *ed:* (BS) Industrial Art, Teachers Coll of CT 1957; (MS) Industrial Art, Cntrl CT St Coll 1962; Guidance & Counseling Univ of CT 1971; Safety Ed Southern CT St Univ 1979; *cr:* Teacher Lyman Hall HS 1957-; *ai:* CT Technology Stu Assn Club Adv; Cmmty Ed Work Cncl Mem; Wallingford Ed Assn CT & Natl Ed Assn; CT Driver & Safety Ed Assn (Treas & Secy); CT Technology Ed Assn Life Mem; CT Technology Ed Leadership Cncl; New England Assn of Technology Teachers Life Mem; Intnl Technology Ed Assn Life Mem; Epsilon Pi Tau; Appreciation for Dedication & Commitment to Driver Ed & CT Driver Safety Ed Assn 1984; Bd of Ed Staff Mem Recognition Awd 1989-; Recognition Awd for 26 Yrs of Service to CT Technology Ed Leadership Cncl 1990; *office:* Lyman Hall HS Pond Hill Rd Wallingford CT 06492

COSTA, MARY-ELLEN, Health Teacher; *b:* New Bedford, MA; *ed:* (BS) Phys Health Ed, Bridgewater St Coll 1985; *cr:* Health Educator New Bedford HS 1985-; MA Migrant Ed Summer Prgm 1987-; *ai:* Varsity Vlybl Coach Bristol-Plymouth Rgnl HS 1987-; Intramural Dir/Coach, Ford Mid Sch 1988-; NEA 1985-; Teachers Assn 1985-; New Bedford Ed Assn 1985-; *office:* New Bedford HS 230 Hathaway Blvd New Bedford MA 02740

COSTA, RENAE MARGARET (EGGE), Chapter One Teacher; *b:* Mayville, ND; *m:* Richard R.; *ed:* (BA) Elem/Spec Ed, Univ of ND 1973; Univ of ID, E WA Univ; *cr:* Spec Ed Teacher Silver King Elem 1973-75; Kndgtn Teacher 1975-84, 2nd Grade Teacher 1984-88 Pinehurst Elem; Chapter I Teacher Kellogg Mid Sch 1988-; *ai:* Phi Delta Kappa Research Rep 1989-; Delta Kappa Gamma Legislative Chairperson 1978-; W Shoshone Ed Assn (Pres, VP, Treas) 1973-; ID Ed Assn Bd of Dirs 1985-89; Kootenai Cty Democrats Precinct Person 1986-; Beta Sigma Phi Pres 1977-82, Sweetheart 1982; Amer Assn of Univ Women 1974-82; Panhandle Rdng Cncl 1986-; NEA Internship for Women & Minorities; PTA Nominee for Natl Teacher of Yr; *home:* 3309 W Pine Hill Dr Coeur D Alene ID 83814

COSTELLO, AQUINAS RICHARD, OP, Religion Department Chair; *b:* Lincoln, NE; *ed:* (BS) Eng, 1955, (MA) Eng, 1961 Univ of NE; (BPh) Philosophy 1965, (STB) Theology, 1968, (MDiv) Theology 1968 St Alberts Coll; Theology St Alberts Coll; *cr:* Eng Dept Chm Marston Jr HS 1957-62; *ai:* Campus Minister; Chrstn Service Organization Moderator; Religion Dept Chm; New Teachers & Classroom Management Supvr; Brother of St Patrick Chaplain; Phi Delta Kappa, NCTE, CA Teachers of Eng 1955-83; Dedication to Eng Discipline Honor Awd 1962; M/Sgt US Army 1950-52 Sgt Major of 108th AAA Brigade; *office:* Pater Noster HS 2911 San Fernando Rd Los Angeles CA 90065

COSTELLO, DANIEL, US History Teacher; *b:* Pittsburgh, PA; *ed:* (BA) Soc Sci, 1962, (BS) Soc Sci, 1963 MT St Univ; Scndry Ed, Grad Sch CA St Univ Fresno; *cr:* Teacher Fowler HS, Bullard HS; Ftbl Asst Coach CA St Univ Fresno; *ai:* Sch Building Comm; Head Ftbl Coach Fowler HS; Asst Ftbl Coach Bullard HS & CA St Univ Fresno; NEA, CTA, Fresno TA; *office:* Bullard HS 5445 N Palm Ave Fresno CA 93704

COSTELLO, FRANK THOMAS, Music Teacher; *b:* Hoboken, NJ; *m:* Claire Wraga; *c:* Lauren; *ed:* (BA) Music Ed, 1971, (MA) Music Ed, 1973 Jersey City St Coll; Cert Admin/Supervision, NJ 1975; *cr:* Music Teacher Secaucus Public Schls 1971-; *ai:* Marching, Concert, Jazz Band Dir; Musical Dir Sch Productions; MENC, NJMEA 1971-; NAJE 1987-; Secaucus Ed Assn VP 1987-; Guest Conductor Jersey City St Coll 1989, Hudson All-Cty Concert Band 1982, N Jersey Band Festival 1981; *office:* Secaucus Mid/Scndry Sch Millridge Rd Secaucus NJ 07094

COSTELLO, GEORGIANA M., Math Specialist; *b:* Mt Vernon, NY; *ed:* (BS) Elem Ed, 1943, (MA) Elem Admin, 1946 Teachers Coll Columbia Univ; Grad Work Columbia Univ & Fordham Univ; *cr:* 1st 2nd Grade Teacher Nathan Hale Elem Sch 1939-57; 3rd Grade Teacher Wm H Holmes Elem Sch 1957-79; 3rd Grade/Hum/2nd 6th Grade Math Specialist Columbus Elem Sch 1980-; *ai:* NY St Teachers Assn Mem 1939-; Mt Vernon Teachers Assn Treas 1946-47; Mt Vernon Fed of Teachers Mem 1970-; Delta Kappa Gamma Mem 1959-85; Alpha Delta Kappa Mem 1988-.

COSTELLO, KATHERINE NAJAIM, Sixth Grade Teacher; *b:* Syracuse, NY; *m:* Andrew J.; *c:* Katherine Costello Franco, Andrew G.; *ed:* (BS) Ed, NY St Univ Oswego 1956; *cr:* 1st Grade Teacher Sch 16 1956-57, Mamoran Act Ave Sch 1957-58; 3rd Grade Teacher St Augustine Cath Sch 1966-67; 6th Grade Teacher Roosevelt Elem Sch 1968-; *ai:* Curr Comm; Sponsorship Class Trips; New Bruns Ed Assn, NBEA; NJ Ed Assn, NEA; Sci Grant St of NJ 1971; Governors Awd Outstanding Teacher Recognition NJ 1989-; Governors Teacher Recognition Awd.

COSTELLO, MICHAEL JOHN, English Teacher/Dept Head; *b:* Philadelphia, PA; *m:* Ellen Mary Hannus; *c:* Clare E. Wojtosik, Christine E. Mc Dermott, Mary M. O Shea, Catherine M. Hoffman, Anna M., Amy B.; *ed:* (BS) Eng, St Josephs Coll 1958; (MED) Classroom Eng Teaching, Temple Univ; *cr:* Spec Ed Teacher Sheridan Elem Sch 1958-61; Eng Teacher Edward Bok AVT Sch 1961-; *ai:* Class of 1991 Spon; Athletic Finance Mgr; Assembly Prgms Chm; NCTE; *office:* Edward Bok AVT Sch 8th & Mifflin Sts Philadelphia PA 19148

COSTELLO, PATRICIA POCKETTE, English Teacher; *b:* Rutland, VT; *m:* Brian P.; *c:* Jacqueline B., Patrick Jr., Cara; *ed:* (BS) Eng, Univ of VT 1969; North Adams St 1971; Castleton St Coll 1974-; Coll of St Joseph 1983-;Southern VT Coll 1985; Lesley Coll 1987--89; *cr:* Sub Teacher Rutland Jr & Sr HS 1971-76; Eng Teacher Rutland JR HS 1976-89; Rutland HS 1989-; *ai:* Mem Project Web; Local Recert Agency-Screening Comm; Rutland Ed Assn; VEA & NEA; NCTE; Phi Beta Kappa-Elected 1969; Kappa Delta Pi-Elected 1968; *office:* Rutland H S Library Ave Rutland VT 05701

COSTEN, JOYELINE STEARNS, 4th Grade Teacher; *b:* Tipton, OK; *m:* Joe K.; *ed:* (BA) His, OK Coll for Women 1947; (MLS) Liberal Stud, Univ of OK 1978; Eastern NM Univ His 1959; Rdng 1981/84/85; TX Tech Univ Cmptr Sci 1984; Johnson St Coll Gifted/Talented Ed 1980; Wayland Bapt Univ Eng 2nd Lang 1988; *cr:* HS His/Eng Teacher Laing Sch 1947-48; 4th Grade Teacher Mountain Park Sch 1948-51; 3rd Grade Teacher Friona Sch 1953-55; 4th Grade Teacher Mary De Shazo Sch 1955-; *ai:* De Shazo Sch Support Teachers Chm; Mary De Shazo Sch Teacher Grants Chm; Muleshoe TX St Teachers Assn VP 1988-; Muleshoe TX Classroom Teacher Assn Pres 1964-65 Schlrsp 1974/76; Amer Assn of Univ Women Pres 1956-61 Outstanding Woman of TX 1981; TX Congress of Parents/Teachers Honorary Life Mem 1978; Teacher Essay Contest Clark Fnd Schlrsp; Delta Kappa Gamma Society Intnl Schlrsps; Nom West TX Univ Awd Women for Distinguished Svc; *home:* P O Box 202 Muleshoe TX 79347

COSTNER, STEPHEN MONROE, Chemistry/Biology Teacher; *b:* Newport, TN; *m:* Beverly Gwen Ramsey; *ed:* (BS) Scndry Sci Ed, TN Tech 1969; (MA) Ed, Union Coll 1978; *cr:* Teacher Northport Elem Sch 1969-71; Chem Teacher Parrottsville HS 1971-72; Chem/Bio Teacher Cocke Cty HS 1972-; *ai:* Cocke Cty HS Golf Coach; Key Club Adv; NSTA, Sci Assn of TN 1978-89; Kiwanis Club Honorary Mem 1981-; Smoky Mountain Cntry Club (Pres 1978-79, Bd of Dir 1990); *home:* 1111 Woodlawn Ave Newport TN 37821

COSTON, GENE ARMSTRONG, 4th Grade Teacher; *b:* Tidioute, PA; *m:* Richard E.; *c:* Renee Patterson, Michele Longabaugh, Matthew; *ed:* (BRE) His/Religious Ed, Baptist Coll of PA 1963; (MSED) Ed, SUNY Cortland 1965; Spec Ed, SUNY; *cr:* 4th Grade Teacher Harry L Johnson Sch 1963-; *ai:* Coached Odyssey of Mind Teams; Supervise 4th Grade Job Squad Groups; Johnson City Teachers Assn Secy 1977-79; NYEA, NEA; Trng Teachers Around Cntry in Outcomes Based Ed Effective Schls Prgms as Rep of Johnson City Sch System; *office:* Harry L Johnson Sch 235 Harry L Drive Johnson City NY 13790

COSTOPOULOS, JOHN THEODORE, Biology Teacher; *b:* Chicago, IL; *ed:* (BS) Bio, Univ of IL Chicago 1985; Grad Work Ed, Univ of IL; *cr:* Substitute Teacher Oak Park Elem 1986; Bio Teacher Steinmetz Academic Centre for Wellness & Sports Sci 1987-; *ai:* Sch Sci Fair Coord; *office:* Steinmetz Academic Centre 3030 N Mobile Chicago IL 60634

COSTOPOULOS, LEONARD, Social Science/English Teacher; *b:* Chicago, IL; *m:* Joanne Tomas; *c:* Stacy, Melissa; *ed:* (BS) Soc Sci, IL St Univ 1964; (MA) Urban Stud, Roosevelt Univ 1975; *cr:* Jr HS Soc Sci Teacher Oak Park Elem Sch Dist 1964-67, 1969-76; Psych Teacher Dist 218 1976-78; Psych/Eng/His Teacher Riverside-Brookfield HS 1978-; *ai:* Various Curr Review Comm; Various Stu Government Spon; NEA, IL Ed Assn, Riverside-Brookfield Ed Assn; *office:* Riverside-Brookfield HS Forest Ave & Golf Rd Riverside IL 60546

COTA, LISA FOLEY, Amer History/Sociology Teacher; *b:* Hartford, CT; *m:* Samuel Flores; *c:* Steven S., Samantha C.; *ed:* (AA) Liberal Arts, Broward Comm Coll 1975; (BAE) Soc Stud Ed, FL Atlantic Univ 1977; (MED) Scndry Rdng Ed, AZ St Univ 1982; Grad Stud Ed, Counseling Classes; *cr:* Rdng Teacher Apollo HS 1978-81; Soc Stud Teacher Deer Valley HS 1981-; *ai:* Class of 1993 Spon; Skyhawk Staff Organization Mem; Assembly Comm Mem; Ethnic/Minority Stud; Natural His 1980-83; Native Amer Heritage Assn 1974-77; NEA St Delegate 1983; Royal Palms Baptist Church 1977-; *office:* Deer Valley HS 18424 N 51 Ave Glendale AZ 85308

COTE, LEO F., Social Studies Teacher; *b:* Glens Falls, NY; *m:* Diana Daggett; *c:* Mary B., David; *ed:* (BA) His, Siena Coll 1966; (MA) Teaching, 1968, (MS) Ed Psych/Statistics, 1970 St Univ NY Albany; Cert Adult Grad Study Ed Admin, Castleton Coll 1982; *cr:* 5th-7th Grade Teacher St Michaels Sch 1968; Teacher Schodack Cntrl 1968-70, Whitehall Jr/Sr HS 1970-; Dean of Discipline Whitehall 1990; Coord of Enrichment Prgms 1990; *ai:* Soc Stud Dept Chairperson; Horizons Enrichment Prgm; NY St Cncl of Soc Stud, NCSS Pres 1970; Adirondack Mountain Club Pres 1985; Adirondack 46er Pres 1989; NY St Grant for Curr Project 1969; Academic Affairs Dir Whitehall 1984-86; Whitehall Teachers Union Pres 1980-82; *office:* Whitehall Jr/Sr HS Buckley Rd Whitehall NY 12887

COTE, LETHA J., Latin Teacher; *b:* Ismay, MT; *ed:* (BE) Latin/Fr/Eng, Univ of WI La Crosse 1937; (MA) Speech, Univ of WI Madison 1942; Grad Stud at Various Univs; *cr:* Latin I-IV/Fr/Eng as 2nd Lang I HS Teacher Gays Mills WI 1937-41, Sparta WI 1941-49, La Crosse WI 1949-50, Palm Springs CA 1950-; *ai:* CA Teachers Assn Delegate 1950-; NEA Mem 1950-; Vergilian Society of America Mem 1955-; Amer Classical Assn; WI Teachers Assn Pres; Fulbright Scholar US Government Amer Acad Rome 1955; 1st Prize Italian Universita Stranieri Perugia; 1st Prize Fr Universite Lausanne Switzerland.

COTE, RICHARD G., Mathematics/Physics Teacher; *b:* Manchester, NH; *m:* Claudette Bergeron; *c:* Tawnia L., Sarah A.; *ed:* (BA) Math, St Anselms Coll 1968; (MBA) Ec/Management, 1981, (PHD) Ed, Univ of S FL; *cr:* Teacher Parkside HS 1969-79, Springstead HS 1979-; *ai:* Ftbl & Golf Coach; Class Adv; NSTA, FL Coaches Assn; Hermando Cty Acad of Teachers; Article Published; Inst for Intnl Research & Practice; *home:* 9338 Elida Rd Spring Hill FL 34608

COTHRAN, RUSSELL RANDLE, 6th Grade Teacher; *b:* West Point, MS; *m:* Glenda Carolyn Reeves; *c:* Angie C. Tunnell; *ed:* (AA) Gen Ed, Itawamba Jr Coll 1969; (BS) Ed Psych, MS St Univ 1971; (MED) Educl Admin, MS Univ 1977; Drug Ed Seminars & Wkshps; *cr:* Jr HS Teacher/Coach Houlka HS 1971-73; Drug Ed Specialist/Asst Bsbl Coach Chickasaw City Schls 1973-77; Elem Prin/Teacher Houlka Attendance Center 1977-84; Classroom Teacher Houlka Mid Sch 1984-; *ai:* Beta Club Chaperone; MS Prof Educators 1983-; Itawamba Comm Coll Alumni Assn Pres 1990; *home:* Rt 2 Box 293 Houston MS 38851

COTHRAN, SUSAN WALKER, Mathematics Teacher; *b:* Durant, OK; *m:* Charles Earl; *c:* Kandie, Kassie; *ed:* (BS) Math/Elem Ed, 1970, (MS) Elem Ed, 1975 S OK St Univ; Cmptrs; *cr:* Math Teacher Coleman 1970-75; Elem Teacher Ravia 1975-76; Math Teacher Caddo 1976-82, Kingston 1982-84, Tishomingo 1984-; *home:* HC 30 Box 218A Durant OK 74701

COTO, RENE ANTHONY, 4th Grade Mathematics Teacher; *b:* Tampa, FL; *m:* Mary Jean Pawelkop; *c:* Jeremy, Sarah; *ed:* (BA) Elem Ed, Univ of S FL 1974; (MED) Mid Grades Ed, GA St Univ 1985; *cr:* Teacher Dunbar 6th Grade Center 1974-75; 5th Grade Teacher Mango Elem 1975-76; Teacher Dunbar 6th Grade Center 1976-79; 4th-6th Grade Math Teacher Woodridge Elem 1979-; *ai:* Sci Textbook Selection Comm 1989; Bd Scholars Chm 1990; Patrol Spon; GA Math League Comm; Martins Crossing Home Owners Assn Swim Team Adv 1987-; Stone Mountain Youth Soccer Assn Coach 1989-; *home:* 808 Greenhedge Way Stone Mountain GA 30088

COTSIS, VIRGINIA MARY, English Department Chair; *b:* Biddeford, ME; *m:* Richard Mohney; *c:* Nicholas R. Mohney; *ed:* (BA) Eng/Fr, San Diego St Univ 1974; (EDM) Prgm Evaluation, Harvard Univ 1982; San Diego Area Writing Project 1979; CA Lit Project 1985; *cr:* Eng/Fr Teacher Jonul Mid Sch 1976-80; Research Asst MA Dept of Ed; Eng/Journalsim Teacher San Marcos HS 1982-84; Eng Teacher/Dept Chairperson/K-12th Grade Lang Art Coord Fillmore Unified Sch Dist 1985-; *ai:* Cty/St Lang Art Conferences & Wkshps Presenter & Speaker; CA Dept of Ed Mentor Teacher 1987-89; NCTE 1985-; Amer Assn of Univ Women Schlsp 1982; Harvard Univ Grant 1982; CA St Schlsp 1974-75; *office:* Fillmore HS 555 Central Ave Fillmore CA 93015

COTTEN, RICHARD L., Mathematics Teacher; *b:* Buffalo, NY; *m:* Carole J. Yusten; *c:* Kristin L., Shannon L.; *ed:* (BA) Elem Ed, St Univ Coll Brockport 1965; Scndry Math, St Univ Coll Fredonia 1972; *cr:* Elem Teacher Frewsburg Cntrl Sch 1965-66, Iroquois Cntrl Sch 1966-67; Math Teacher Ripley Cntrl Sch 1967-68, Westfield Cntrl Sch 1968-79, SW Cntrl Sch 1981-; *ai:* Gymnastics Coach; NY St Mid Sch Assn, NY St Math Teachers Assn; *office:* Southwestern Cntrl Sch 600 Hunt Rd Jamestown NY 14701

COTTEN, SHIRLEY ANN (AYER), Second Grade Teacher; *b:* Crawford, CO; *m:* Orval Lee; *c:* Clinton, Mitchell, Sheldon; *ed:* (AA) Elem Ed, Mesa Jr Coll 1956; (BA) Elem Ed, W St Coll 1963; Kids at Risk, Essential Elements of Instruction, World Conference on Gifted & Talented; *cr:* 3rd Grade Teacher Delta Elem Sch 1956-58; 2nd Grade Teacher Kodiak Elem Sch 1963-67; 1st/2nd Grade Teacher Cedaredge Elem Sch 1967-71; 2nd Grade Teacher Paonia Elem Sch 1971-; *ai:* Outdoor Ed Project Wild, Project Learning Tree Coord; Delta Kappa Gamma Pres 1982-84; Phi Delta Kappa; Delta Cty Ed Assn VP 1989-; Elks Emblem Club Historian 1987; Crawford United Meth Church Trustee 1988-; Cmmty Concert Assn Bd Mem 1986-; *home:* 2295 77 1/2 Rd Crawford CO 81415

COTTER, SUE, Fr Teacher/Foreign Lang Chair; *b:* New York, NY; *m:* John V.; *ed:* (BSED) Scndry, St Univ Coll of NY Buffalo 1974; (MA) Fr Lang/Culture, Univ of CA Santa Barbara 1987; Oral Proficiency Inst SW TX St Univ 1988; Advanced Placement

Regional Wkshp 1986; *cr:* Fr/Span Teacher Buffalo Public Schls 1975-77; Fr Teacher/Dept Chairperson Round Rock HS 1978-; *ai:* Foreign Lang Dept Chairperson; Sr Class, Fr Club, Natl Fr Honor Society Spon; Dist Textbook & Curr Revision Comm; TX Foreign Lang Assn, Amer Cncl on Teaching Foreign Langs, SW Conference Lang Teaching, TX Fr Symposium, AATF; St of Tx Grant 1988; Oral Proficiency Inst 1988; Nom Dist Fr Teacher of Yr 1984; *office:* Round Rock HS 300 Lake Crk Round Rock TX 78681

COTTINGHAM, WALTER LEE, JR., 8th Grade His & Lit Teacher; *b:* Valdosta, GA; *m:* Karen L. Szabla; *c:* Benjamin W.; *ed:* (BA) His, 1974, (MA) Ed Rdng, 1982 Furman Univ; *cr:* Teacher Travelers Rest Correctional Ctr 1975-81, Grad Courses Furman Univ 1984-; 8th Grade Teacher NW Mid Sch 1975-; *ai:* Soc Stud Dept Chm; Magazine Ed; SC Cncl of Soc Stud 1988-; Intnl Rdng Assn; Greenville Cty Historical Society; Upcountry Friends 1989-; Kappa Delta Pi; Northwestern Mid Sch Teacher of Yr 1985-86; DAR Outstanding Teacher of Amer His 1986; *office:* Northwest Mid Sch 1606 Geer Hwy Travelers Rest SC 29690

COTTLE, MICHAEL WADE, Teacher & Principal; *b:* Tuscon, AZ; *m:* Julie Ann Barney; *c:* Seth, Nicolas, Brittany, Jacqlyn; *ed:* (BS) Finance, Brigham Young Univ 1980; *cr:* LDS Seminary Teacher Barlow HS 1984-85; LDS Seminary Teacher/Prin Oregon City HS 1986-; *ai:* Gresha & Oregon Region Quality Circle Chm; BSA Comm Mem 1989-, On My Honor Adult; Little League Commissioner Bd Mem 1988-; *office:* Oregon City HS LDS Seminary 1220 13th St Oregon City OR 97045

COTTON, HELEN MANAGO (STOVALL), Teacher; *b:* Atlanta, GA; *m:* Anderson Clarence; *c:* Sharon Stovall Jackson, Roderick A. Stovall Sr.; *ed:* (BS) Elem Ed, Morris Brown Coll 1961; (MA) Elem Ed, GA St Univ 1972; Reid Bus Coll; Beautmont Sch of Nursing; *cr:* Teacher Thomas H Slater 1961-68, Lester Brewer 1968-83, C M Pitts 1983-; *ai:* Conducted Creative Writing Wkshp; Soc Stud Exhibits & Young Authors Sch Wkshp Chm; Atlanta Assn of Educators, GA Assn of Educators, NEA 1961-; Carroll Height Cmmty Club Secy 1969-79; Toastmistress Club (Pres, Treas) 1980-85; Ministers Wives Financial Secy 1985-; Star Teacher Fulton HS; Recipient of Incentive Proposal Excl in Teaching; Teacher of Yr 1984-85, 1987-88 C M Pitts Elem Sch; Jr League Grant-in Aid For Excl, Creativity in Teaching; Grant-in Aid for Math Project; *home:* 3343 Adkins Rd NW Atlanta GA 30331

COTTRELL, DOUGLAS E., 4th Grade Instructor; *b:* Russellville, AR; *m:* Karen Wyers; *c:* Kathryn, Julia; *ed:* (BS) Elem Ed, 1978, (MED) Elem Ed, 1985 Univ of AR; *cr:* Instr Cedarville Elem 1979-; *ai:* AR Ed Assn Chairperson Human Relations Comm 1983-84; Cedarville Ed Assn Pres 1982-84; NEA 1979-; Article Published AR Soc Stud Teacher; *office:* Cedarville Elem Sch P O Box 97 Cedarville AR 72932

COTTRILL, RUTH HOLT, Mathematics Teacher; *b:* Louisa, KY; *m:* William E.; *ed:* (BS) Math, Univ of KY 1965; Grad Work Univ of KY; *cr:* Math Teacher Fairview HS 1965-66, Paul Blazer HS 1966-68, Chillicothe City Schls 1968-; *ai:* HS Math Curr Comm; Chillicothe Ed Assn 1989-, Treas 1986-87; OH Ed Assn 1989-90; NEA; *home:* 18 Tecumseh Dr Chillicothe OH 45601

COUCH, DEBORAH KAREN, Business & Office Teacher; *b:* Sassafras, KY; *ed:* (BS) Bus Ed, 1971, (MBE) Bus Ed 1975 Morehead St Univ 1975; Bus Ed, Voc Ed Conferences; Competency Based Voc Ed; Several Cmptr Wkshps & Classes; *cr:* Bus Teacher Carl D Perkins Area Voc Ed Center 1971-; *ai:* FBLA Club Adv; KBEA, NBEA 1971-; KEA, NEA 1988-; AVA, KVA, UKRVA (Secy 1984-85) 1971-88; Phi Kappa Phi 1975-; Eastern Star 1989-; Thesis Published; *office:* Carl D Perkins A V E C HCR 60 Box 1100 Hindman KY 41822

COUCH, EYA, Second Grade Teacher; *b:* Greeneville, TN; *ed:* (BS) Elem Ed, E TN St Univ 1971; *cr:* Teacher Mosheim Elem Sch 1969-; *ai:* Delta Kappa Gamma, TN Ed Assn, NEA; Greene Cty Ed Assn VP 1988-89; PTO VP 1984-85; Cty & Dist Teacher of Yr 1987; TN Teachers Study Cncl Pres 1985-87; St Basic Skills Force for Math 1986.

COUCKE, HENRY RADFORD, 6th-8th Grade Teacher; *b:* Detroit, MI; *ed:* (PHB) His, 1958, (MA) His, 1963 Univ of Detroit; Law Sch Univ of Detroit; Sci Courses, MI St Univ; *cr:* 7th/8th Grade Teacher St Michaels 1959-64; Instr Macomb Comm Coll 1964-65; 6th-8th Grade Teacher Holy Name Sch 1965-; *ai:* Brother Rice HS Asst Frosh Ftbl Coach; *office:* Holy Name Sch 680 Harmon Birmingham MI 48009

COUDERT, DONALD JULES, JR., Mathematics Dept Chair; *b:* Pittsfield, MA; *ed:* (BS) Math, Univ of MA Amherst 1970; (MED) Ed/Teacher Cmptr Sci, N Adams St Coll 1987; Additional Credits Univ of MA, Univ of Hartford & N Adams St Coll; *cr:* Math Teacher 1970-, Math Chm 1980- St Joseph Central HS; *ai:* Sci Club, Sch Newspaper, Photo Club & Quiz Team Adv; Advanced Placement Coord; NCTM 1975-; Natl Cncl of Supvr of Math 1989-; Mathwest 1989-; BSA Troop 66 Scoutmaster 1970-Dist Awd of Merit 1973; Pittsfield Cmmty Cable Broadcasting Inc Dir 1990; Amateur Radio Emergency Service 1978-; General Electric STAR Teacher 1986; Phi Kappa Phi Honor Society 1970; Outstanding Young Men of America 1973; G E/PIMMS Fellowship Math 1987-; *office:* St Joseph Central HS 22 Maplewood Ave Pittsfield MA 01201

COUDERT, SHARON, Phys Ed Teacher/Coach; *b:* Port La Vaca, TX; *ed:* (BSED) Phys Ed, SW TX St 1983; *cr:* 1st-12th Grade Phys Ed Teacher San Marcos Treatment Center 1983-86; Jr HS/HS Phys Ed Teacher/Coach Venus HS 1986-; *ai:* Girls Bi-Dist Champion Vlybl 1986-89; Boys Dist Runner-Up Tennis Coach 1990; Johnson Cty Newcomer Coach of Yr 1986; Service Awd Amer Red Cross; Volunteer Exhibit Dallas Museum of Natural His; *office:* Venus HS PO Box 364 Venus TX 76084

COUGHANOUR, SARA ANN HALL, English/Journalism Teacher; *b:* Tucson, AZ; *m:* Arthur Craig; *c:* Kelly, Davis, Aaron; *ed:* (BS) Journalism Ed, 1970, (MA) Teaching of Soc Sci, 1979 N AZ Univ; *cr:* Journalism/Eng/Soc Stud Teacher Kofa HS 1970-75; Public Information Officer N AZ Univ 1975-80; Journalism/Eng/Soc Stud Teacher Flagstaff HS 1980-81; Journalism/Eng Teacher Glendale Union HS Dist 1982-; *ai:* Yrbk Adv; Bsktbl Scorekeeper; Sch Effectiveness Team; Soph Eng Team Leader; NEA, AZ Ed Assn 1970-; Local Sch Ed Assns; Finalist Apollo HS Achievement Above All Teaching Awd 1988-, Nominee 1984-85; Nominee AZ Journalism Teacher of Yr 1984; Apollo HS Co-Favorite Sr Teacher 1988-89; Flagstaff HS Mrs Faculty Homecoming Awd 1981; Flagstaff HS Favorite Sr Teacher 1980-81; AZ Interscholastic Press Assn Stu Newspaper General Excl 2nd Place Awd; *office:* Apollo HS 4625 W Sunnyside Dr Glendale AZ 85304

COUGHENOUR, SALLIE (FOUST), Chemistry/Mathematics Teacher; *b:* Windber, PA; *m:* Thomas Lee; *c:* Benjamin; *ed:* (BS) Chem/Math, Penn St Univ 1970; Grad Stud Univ of Pittsburgh, Penn St Univ, IN Univ of PA, WV Univ; *cr:* Math Teacher Conemaugh Township Area Sch Dist 1970-75, Forrest Hills HS 1980-81; Chem/Math Teacher North Star HS 1981-; *ai:* Chrstn Discussion Club Adv; NEA, PA St Ed Assn, NSTA 1980-; Cub Scouts Asst Leader 1982-85 Natl Sci Fnd Participant 1985; Mellon Fnd Grant 1990; *office:* North Star HS 400 Ohio St Boswell PA 15531

COUGHLIN, MAUREEN ELIZABETH, Theology Teacher; *b:* Cleveland, OH; *ed:* (BA) Comm, John Carroll Univ 1979; Grad Stud, John Carroll Univ; Ursuline Coll; Notre Dame Coll; *cr:* Theology Teacher St Augustine Acad 1980-83, Lumen Cordium HS 1984-85; Dir of Religion/Theology Teacher/Youth Minister Annunciation Cath Church 1985-88; Theology Teacher Padua Fraciscan HS 1988-; *ai:* Womens Tennis Coach; Jr Class Moderator; Diocese of Cleveland Religious Ed Dept 1986; Service Cert Devoted Service in Religious Ed; Cert Lay Pastoral Minister Diocese of Cleveland 1988; *office:* Padua Franciscan HS 6740 State Rd Parma OH 44134

COULSON, BARBARA SALE, Third Grade Teacher; *b:* Sewickley, PA; *m:* David Edwin; *c:* Kelly E.; *ed:* (BS) Elem, Slippery Rock Univ 1974; Working Towards Masters PA St univ; *cr:* 3rd Grade Teacher Richard J Hyde Elem 1974-81, Bon Meade Elem 1981-84; 1st Grade Teacher 1984-86, 3rd Grade Teacher 1986- Richard J Hyde Elem; *ai:* Sftbl Coach; Talent Show Spon; NEA, PA St Assn, Moon Ed Assn; Moon Staff Dev Prgm; *office:* Richard J Hyde Elem Sch 110 Wallridge Dr Coraopolis PA 15108

COULSON, KAREN PETERSON, Third Grade Teacher; *b:* Orleans, MI; *m:* Robert; *c:* Christopher, Craig, Kimberly; *ed:* (BA) Art/Sci/Soc Sci, W MI Univ 1968; (MS) Elem Ed, MI St Univ 1970; *cr:* Substitute Teacher Ionia Cty Cntry Schls 1961-67; Kndgtn Teacher 1967-68, Transition Room 1-A Teacher 1968-75, 3rd Grade Teacher 1975- Saranac Comm Schls; *ai:* Math Comm; *home:* 30 Vosper St Saranac MI 48881

COULSTON, JANE NEEDLER, 3rd Grade Teacher; *b:* Salida, CO; *m:* Robert M.; *c:* Christina S.; *ed:* (BA) Elem Ed, Purdue Univ 1966; (MS) Elem Ed, Butler Univ 1969; *cr:* 4th/5th/6th Grade Teacher Garden City Elem 1966-79; 3rd Grade Teacher Chapel Glen Elem 1979-; *ai:* Wayne Township Aids Adv Cncl; Coop Learning Wkshp Facltr; WTCTA 1966-; Olive Branch Chrstn Church; Chapel Glen PTO Bd Mem 1981-86; Chapel Glen Elem Teacher of Yr 1990; *office:* Chapel Glen Elem Sch 701 Lansdowne Rd Indianapolis IN 46234

COULTER, JAMES DONNIE, 4th Grade Teacher; *b:* Lebanon, KY; *ed:* (AA) His, St Catharine Jr Coll 1972; (BS) Sociology, Campbellsville Coll 1974; (MA) Elem Ed, Eastern Ky Univ 1978; *cr:* 3rd/4th/5th Grade Teacher Mackville Elem Sch 1974-76; 3rd/4th Grades Teacher Willisburg Elem Sch 1976-77; 6th/7th/8th Jr High Teacher 1977-88; 4th Grade Teacher 1988 Mackville Elem Sch; *ai:* Ket Coord Mackville Elem Sch; Chapter Leader Young Astronaut Club Mackville Elem; Mem WA Cty Ed Assn; Textbook Adoption Comm; WA Cty Ed Assn 1974-; KY Ed Assn 1974-; NEA 1974-; Building Rep WA Cty Ed Assn; Treas WA Cty Ed Assn; *home:* Lebanon Rd Po Box 215 Springfield KY 40069

COULTER, MARY RAUH, First Grade Teacher; *b:* Spring Valley, IL; *m:* Michael; *c:* Erinn; *ed:* (AA) Liberal Art, IL Valley Comm Coll 1969; (BA) Elem Ed, IL St Univ 1971; Grad Stud Educl Field; *cr:* 3rd Grade Teacher 1971-84, 1st Grade Teacher 1984- Ladd Cmmty Consolidated Sch; *ai:* Discipline Comm; PTO; *office:* Ladd Cmmty Consolidated Sch 232 E Cleveland St Ladd IL 61329

COUNCIL, JANIE MAE MABRAY, 1st Grade Teacher/Chairperson; *b:* Salters, SC; *m:* James Edward; *c:* Beverly C. Graham, Della Mae C. Hill; *ed:* (BA) Elem Ed, Benedict Coll 1955; Early Chldhd, Univ SC Columbia 1975; Early Chldhd Ed, SC St 1988; Media Ed, Williamsburg Tech; *cr:* Teacher Cades Elem 1967-70, St Mark Elem 1970-; *ai:* Pageant, May Day Chairperson; Sch & Cmmty Beautification; SCEA, NEA, WCEA Mem 1970-; ZOB Holder of Blue Box; OEA (Worthy Matron 1984-, Dist Secy 1981-); St Mark Elem Teacher of Yr 1980-81, 1986-87; Cty Recognition Teacher of Yr 1980, 1987; Service Awd 1982; Dirs Awd of Choirs 1977, 1988; *home:* Rt 2 Box 70 Salters SC 29590

COUNTS, ARTHUR WILLIAM, Art Instructor/Dept Chairman; *b:* Akron, OH; *m:* Jill Block; *c:* Jessica, Daniel; *ed:* (BA) Art Ed, Capital Univ 1978; (MA) Curr/Instruction, 1984, (MA) Scndry Admin 1984 Ashland Coll; *cr:* Art Instr Olentangy HS 1978-, OH Wesleyan Univ 1986-; *ai:* Art & Photography Club; Art Curr Guide K-12; Bexley Area Art Guild Pres 1978-; OH Art Ed Assn 1978-; Columbus Chippers 1988-, AARONS Awd 1988; DE Cultural Art Center Bd Mem 1988-; Natl Wood Carvers Assn 1988-; Cntrl OH Outstanding Art Teacher; *office:* Olentangy HS 814 Shanahan Rd Delaware OH 43015

COUNTS, JEANNINE GRAHAM, Fourth Grade Teacher; *b:* Jacksonville, FL; *m:* William A.; *c:* Hilary; *ed:* (BS) Elem Ed, FL St Univ 1959; (MS) Elem Ed, Nova Univ 1985; *cr:* Teacher Alta Vista Elem Sch 1959-61, 1965-67, Wilkinson Elem Sch 1968-; *ai:* 4th Grade Level Chairperson; Sch Based Management Cncl Communication Comm Mem; Sch Bd of Sarasota Cty Certificate of Recognition; *office:* Wilkinson Elem Sch 3400 Wilkinson Rd Sarasota FL 34231

COURCHESNE, ROBERT EUGENE, Fr Teacher/Foreign Lang Coord; *b:* Worcester, MA; *m:* Sandra Gagnon; *c:* Christophe, Renee; *ed:* (BA) Divisional Fr/Span, St Marys Coll 1968; (MAT) Romance Lang, Clark Univ 1970; Teaching Proficiency, FLES Mid Sch Foreign Lang, Fr Immersions; Scndry Sch Admin, Rdng in Content Area, Meeting Spec Needs Regular Classroom, Theatre & Culture Paris; *cr:* Instr/Asst Fr/Theatre Professor Leicester Jr Coll 1970-75; Fr/Hum Teacher 1975-, Foreign Lang Coord 1986- Martinson Jr HS; *ai:* Sch Wide Interdiscipliary Foreign Lang Week Coord; Martinson Jr HS Art & Hum Comm Mem; Marshfield Teachers Assn Negotiating Team Mem 1986-; South Shore Foreign Lang Assn Pres 1987; Amer Cncl Teaching Foreign Lang Mem 1970-; AAFT Mem 1980-; MA Foreign Lang Assn (Mem, Bd of Dir 1984-88, 2nd VP 1989, 1st VP 1990, Conference Chairperson 1990) 1975-; Marshfield Chamber of Commerce Spec Projects Awd 1987; Horace Mann Grant 1987, 1988; Apple for Teacher Awd 1988; MA Dept of Ed Working Groups on Cert Mentoring;Pre-Conference Wkshp Presenter; Creator St Foreign Lang Poster Contest; *home:* 56 Stagecoach Dr Marshfield MA 02050

COURREGES, JEAN MAY, Fifth Grade Teacher; *b:* New Orleans, LA; *ed:* (BS) Elem Ed, Univ of TN 1959; *cr:* Teacher Duval Cty Sch System; *office:* Southside Estates Elem Sch 9775 Ivey Rd Jacksonville FL 32216

COURSEY, CHARLES CHESNUT, Social Studies Teacher; *b:* Bedford, IN; *m:* Debra Fredenhagen; *c:* Rachel, Chas, Olivia, Fred; *ed:* (AA), St Johns River Jr Coll 1964; (BA) His/Art, Stetson Univ 1967; (MA) Admin/Supervision, Nova Univ 1980; *cr:* Teacher Palatka Jr HS 1967-71, Central Acad 1968-69, Palatka HS 1971-81; Admin Palatka HS 1981-83; Teacher Lake Mary HS 1983-; *ai:* His Club Spon 1967-68; Sr Class Spon 1971-83; Acad Coach Palatica HS 1982-83, Lake Mary HS 1983-; Putnam Fed of Labor (Pres 1972-74, Mem 1974-81; Seminole Ed Assn Mem 1983-; *office:* Lake Mary H S 655 Longwood-Lk Mary Rd Lake Mary FL 32746

COURTER, JAMES ROBERT, 5th Grade Teacher; *b:* Holland, MI; *m:* Christine; *c:* Jason, Jeffrey, Jennifer; *ed:* (BA) Bio, Hope Coll 1974; (MA) Teaching of Sci Western MI 1978; *cr:* Teacher Godfrey-Lee Public Schls 1974-; *ai:* Sci Olympiad Coach; Safety Spon; *office:* Lee Elem Sch 1335 Lee St Wyoming MI 49509

COURTNEY, ALMA L., 7th/8th Grade Teacher; *b:* Colorado Springs, CO; *m:* David John; *ed:* (BA) Math, Ft Lewis Coll 1974; Early Chldhd, CA St Dominques Hills 1977-78; *cr:* 7th-9th Grade Teacher West Jr HS 1974-76; 7th Grade Teacher Edison Jr HS 1976-77; 6th-8th Grade Teacher Hillel Hebrew Acad 1977-78; 7th-8th Grade Teacher Summerville Elem 1978-; *ai:* Girls Vlybl; Math Curr; Math Teams Statistics; Bsbl, Bkstbl Lib Math Related Books, Math Textbook Comm; NCTM; CAPHERD; CTA; NEA; Church Sunday Sch Watch; St Judes Math-A-Thon; Girl & Boy Scouts.

COURY, AUDRAE ROCHELLE, Eng as Second Lang Teacher; *b:* Luverne, MN; *c:* Christopher, Timothy; *ed:* (BS) Elem Ed, 1965, (MED) Spec Ed/Eng as Second Lang, 1985 Univ of MN; TESOL Summer Inst OR St Univ 1984; Eng as Second Lang Trng, Hamline Univ; Ger Stud, Univ of Vienna 1966; *cr:* 3rd Grade Teacher Columbia Heights Public Schls 1965-68; Eng as Second Lang Teacher Minneapolis Public Schls 1969-77; Amer Village USA 1989, 1990; Eng as Second Lang Teacher Roseville Area Schls 1977-; *ai:* Cross Cntry Ski Coach Roseville Area HS 1986-89; Instructional Effectiveness Building Trainer 1983-86; Bicycle Club Adv 1985-89; MN TESOL (Pres 1987-88, VP 1986-87, Bd Mem 1984-86); TESOL (Scndry Ed, Steering Comm) 1988, 1989; Minneapolis Ski Club USSA 1986-, Natl Masters Team 1989; Gopher Wheelman Cycling Club USCF 1984-, Natl Road Race Champion, World Masters Cycling 2nd Place 1988; MN Dept of Ed, China Teacher Exch to Hangzhou Foreign Lang Sch 1989-; MN TESOL Summer Inst Schlsp 1984; *home:* 1736 Pleasant St Saint Paul MN 55113

COUSAR, TARAH FAITH, English Teacher/Dept Chair; *b:* Florence, SC; *ed:* (BA) Eng Ed, Benedict Coll 1986; Rdng Ed, Univ of SC; *cr:* After-Sch Activity Coord Kinder Care Learning Center 621 1985-87; Eng Teacher Mayewood HS 1986-; *ai:* Valhallan Yrbk Staff, Drama Club Adv; SACS Comm Mem; Dept Chairperson Eng/Lang; NEA, SC Ed Assn Mem 1988-; Delta

Sigma Theta (Pres 1984-85) 1983-; SACS Comm Mem 1990; *office:* Mayewood HS Rt 10 Box 310 Sumter SC 29150

COUSER, CARL ANDREW, Sixth Grade Teacher; *b:* Lynwood, CA; *m:* Ann Finne; *c:* Haley, Noah, Lindley; *ed:* (BA) Eng/Ed, Whittier Coll 1974; Post Grad Pepperdine Univ, Univ of ID; Exch Stu Univ of Copenhagen 1974; *cr:* 6th Grade Teacher Washington ELem Sch 1975-80, Sorensen Elem Sch 1980-87, Lakes Mid Sch 1987-; *ai:* 6th Grade Ftbl, Bsktbl, Bsbl, Soccer Coach; *office:* Lakes Mid Sch 15th & Hastings Coeur D'Alene ID 83814

COUSINS, CATHERINE WORTHINGTON, Seventh Grade Math Teacher; *b:* Lenoir Cty, NC; *m:* Bonner Lee; *c:* Connie Cousins Rink, Terri L.; *ed:* (BS) Grammar Ed, E Carolina Univ 1969; *cr:* Math Teacher Kinston City Schls 1969-; *ai:* Rochelle Mid Sch Planning & Kinston City Schls Senate II Bill Comm Mem 1989-; NC Assn of Educators, NEA Mem 1969-; NCTM Mem 1989-; NC Assn Educators Local Treas 1972-73; S Assn Accreditation Kinston Schls Comm Mem 1980-; Wheat Swamp Chrstn Church (Sunday Sch Teacher 1974-77, 1980-83, Chrstn Ed Dept Chairperson 1978-81, Stewardship Dept Chairperson 1981-); Wheat Swamp Chrstn Church (Deaconess 1981-82, 1984-85, 1990, Bd Mem 1978-, Vice Chm of Bd 1990); Chrstn Womens Fellowship Treas 1977-; St Jude Childrens Research Hospital (Math-A-Thon Chairperson 1983, Co-Chairperson 1984); Math Dept Chairperson 1974-86; *home:* 106 Springwood Ln Kinston NC 28501

COUSINS, JACKIE HATCHER, Reading/Language Arts Teacher; *b:* Columbus, OH; *m:* John Bertram; *c:* Melanie A.; *ed:* (BS) Elem Ed, OH St Univ 1983; (MS) Curr Dev, Ashland Univ 1988; *cr:* 7th Grade Eng Teacher 1984-85, 8th Grade Rdng/Eng Teacher 1985-86, 8th Grade Eng/9th Grade Rdng Teacher 1986-88, 8th Grade Rndg/Eng Teacher 1988- Newark City Schls; *ai:* Newark City Schls Chairperson; Lang Art Curr Dev & Competency Based Ed Steering Comm; Curr Coordinating Cncl; OH Cncl Teacher of Eng/Lang Art, NCTE, Newark Organization Teachers of Eng 1986-; Commission of Rdng Sch Study Cncl & OH Eng/Lang Art Teacher Leader Network Appointments; *office:* Newark City Schls 471 E Main St Newark OH 43055

COVINGTON, CAROL CREWS, Mid Sch Admin/English Teacher; *b:* Childress, TX; *m:* Samuel Parks Jr.; *c:* Samuel P. III, James F., Sheri P.; *ed:* (BA) Eng, TX Tech Univ 1959; Alphabetic Phonics Therapist, Basic Principles & Multisensory Techniques for Teaching Rdng; *cr:* 7th Grade Eng/Rdng/TX His Teacher Smylie Wilson Jr HS 1959-63; Pre Sch Teacher St Lukes United Meth 1974-79; 7th-12th Grade His/Government Teacher Western Hills Baptist Acad 1979-80; Eng/Rdng/Lit/His Teacher 1980-, Mid Sch Coord 1987-89, Mid Sch Admin 1990 All Saints Episcopal Sch; *ai:* Stu Handbook; Interdiscipline & Academic Affairs Comm; Stu Records & Progress Reports; Honor Roll; Teens of Month; Academic Lang Therapy Assn 1989-; Mortar BD 1958-; Kappa Kappa Gamma (Pres, Schlsp Chm 1958) 1957-; PEO Sisterhood Pres 1973-75; Phi Theta Kappa; Rdng Therapist; *office:* All Saints Episcopal Sch PO Box 64545 3222 103rd St Lubbock TX 79464

COVINGTON, JUANITA CRAWFORD, Biology Teacher; *b:* Elkton, KY; *m:* William Wayne; *ed:* (BS) Bio, Austin Peay St Univ 1964; *cr:* Teacher Ringgold Jr HS 1963-66, New Providence Jr HS 1966-68, Clarksville HS 1968-70, Northwest HS 1970-; *ai:* Sr Spon; Prins Advisory Comm; Advanced Placement Adv; Beta Beta Beta 1959-64; NEA, TEA 1964-78; Political Action Comm 1976-80; Beta Sigma Phi 1960-65; Clarksville & Montgomery Cty Outstanding Sci Teacher 1984, Teacher of Yr 1983, 1990; St of TN Career Ladder Evaluator 1985; *office:* Northwest HS 800 Lafayette Rd Clarksville TN 37042

COVINGTON, JUDITH LIVINGSTON, Fifth Grade Teacher; *b:* Columbia, SC; *m:* John Dantzler Sr.; *c:* John D. Jr., Wesley A.; *ed:* (BA) Elem Ed, Univ of SC 1972; (MSED) Elem Ed, SC St Coll 1988; *cr:* Teacher Swansea Mid Sch 1972-74, 1975-79, Carver-Edisto Mid Sch 1979-81, 1984-; *ai:* Lib In-Service Comm Mem; Palmetto St Teachers Assn; Norway Matrons Club; Presidential Awds for Excl in Sci & Math Teaching Nom 1990.

COWAN, BRENDA MAYS, Fifth Grade Lang Art Teacher; *b:* Washington, GA; *m:* George A. Jr.; *c:* Ryan A.; *ed:* (BA) Elem Ed, Morris Brown Coll 1974; *cr:* Teacher Washington Wilkes Primary Sch 1974-78; Substitute Teacher Montgomery Sch System 1978-79; Teacher Washington Wilkes Mid Sch 1979-; *ai:* Lead Teacher 5th Grade; GA Assn of Educators, NEA; Order of Eastern Star; *home:* 212 Lexington Ave Washington GA 30673

COWAN, FRANCES (JONES), English Teacher; *b:* Barnsdall, OK; *m:* Donnie Earl; *ed:* (BA) Eng Ed, NSU Tahlequah 1984; *cr:* Eng Instr Locust Grove HS 1985-; *ai:* Jr Class Spon; Comm for Excl in Ed; Asst Play Dir; OK Ed Assn 1988-; Staff Dev 1984-87; NCTE 1985-87; Academic Excl Awd 1984; Dept Arts & Letters NE OK St Univ Tahlequah; *home:* Rt 2 Box 450 Salina OK 74365

COWAN, GARY ALAN, Latin/English Teacher; *b:* New Castle, IN; *ed:* (BA) Eng/Latin/Soc Stud, 1974, (MA) Eng/Latin/Soc Stud, 1977 Ball St; Scndry Sch Guidance; *cr:* Latin/Eng Teacher Bluffton HS 1977-78, Rockville HS; *ai:* Jr HS & Var Boys & Girls Cross Cntry Coach; Jr HS Boys Bsktbl Coach; Jr HS Girls Track; Jr/Sr HS Acad Team Coach; Sch Improvement Team Mem; Prin Advisory Comm Mem; Chosen Mentoring Prgm 1987-88; IN Bsktbl Coaches Assn 1979-; IN Academic Coaches Assn 1987-; Assn for Curr & Dev 1989; IN Classical Conference 1988; N Cntrl Assn Evaluating Teams Mem; Jr Classical League 1975-85; *office:* Rockville Jr/Sr HS 506 N Beadle St Rockville IN 46135

COWAN, LINDA BARNETT, Seventh Grade Teacher; *b:* Henderson Cty, NC; *m:* William J.; *c:* Jill, Janice, James; *ed:* (BS) Elem Ed, 1959, (MA) Elem Ed, 1965 W Carolina Univ; *cr:* 7th Grade Teacher Lexington Jr HS 1959-61; 6th-8th Grade Teacher Etowah 1961-63, Mills River 1963-65; 7th/8th Grade Teacher Jackson Cty Schls 1966-76; 6th-8th Grade Teacher Rugby Jr HS 1976-78; 7th/8th Grade Teacher Fairview Elem Sch 1978-; *ai:* Jackson Cty Senate Bill 2 Steering Comm; NEA 1959-; NC Ed Assn Building Rep 1959-; Alpha Delta Kappa (Past Pres 1986-88) 1965-; *home:* PO Box 207 Webster NC 28788

COWAN, MEL L., Band Director; *b:* Bellville, TX; *m:* Sammy Nickols; *c:* Mel III, Amy; *ed:* (BMUSED) Music Ed, Sam Houston St Univ 1966; (MS) Ed, Tarleton St Univ 1976; Band Instrument Repair Course Red Wing Tech; *cr:* Band Dir Gorman Public Schls 1963, Stephenville Public Schls 1964-66, Clifton Public Schls 1967-73, Mansfield Public Schls 1973-76, Victoria Public Schls 1976-; *ai:* TX Bandmaster Assn, TX Music Ed Assn; Univ Interscholastic League Competition 1st Division Ratings.

COWAN, MOSDAL, Second Grade Teacher; *b:* Rapelje, MT; *m:* A. Gordon; *c:* Marti Cowan De Wolf; *ed:* (BS) Elem Ed, E Mt Coll 1952; Fresno St Univ, Fresno Pacific Coll; *cr:* Teacher Cntry Day Sch 1962-64, Escuela Lincoln 1966-68; Resource Teacher Sun Empire Sch 1968-79; Teacher Cantua Elem Sch 1979-; *ai:* CA Teachers Assn 1980-; *home:* 14120 W Clinton Ave Kerman CA 93630

COWAN, PENNY TAYLOR, Mathematics Department Chair; *b:* Washington, NC; *m:* Richard Danie; *ed:* (BS) Math Ed, NC St Univ 1982; *cr:* Math Teacher D N Hix Sch 1983, S Granville 1983-84, Mattamuskeet HS 1984-86; Math Dept Chairperson Columbia HS 1987-; *ai:* Stu Cncl Co-Spon; Math Club Spon; Teacher of Yr, Teaching Fellowship Comm; NCCTM, NCTM 1984-; Roanoke Island Presbyn Church 1989-; Presidential Awd for Excl in Teaching Math & Sci Nom 1989 & 1990; *home:* Rt 1 Box 1423 Manteo NC 27954

COWAN, RENEAN BALKE, Algebra II Teacher; *b:* Austin, TX; *m:* Jessie Wayne; *c:* Casey W.; *ed:* (BA) Math, Univ of TX Austin 1970; (MS) Mid Management/Sch Admin, TX A&I 1985; Cmptr Literacy; TX Math Staff Dev Module; *cr:* Scndry Math Teacher Natalia Ind Sch Dist 1970-74, Anderson-Shiro CISD 1974-80; Math Dept Head Natalia Ind Sch Dist 1980-89; Algebra II Teacher Hondo Ind Sch Dist 1989-; *ai:* UIL Number Sense & Calculator Applications Coach; TMSCA 1985-; CAMT, TCAMT 1972-; TSTA (VP 1972-73) 1970-75, 1987-88; ATPE 1975-87, 1989-; Order of Eastern Star Worthy Matron 1986-87; TX Career Ladder Level Three; *home:* Rt 1 Box 140 B Devine TX 78016

COWARD, EARLENE WARD, Sci Dept Chm/8th Grade Teacher; *b:* Washington, NC; *m:* William Allen; *c:* Barbara Lucas, Michael; *ed:* (BS) Music/General Sci, NC Cntrl Univ 1957; Sci, NCSU; Mid Sch Cert, Univ of HI; *cr:* Teacher Lenoir Cty 1957-63, Doe of HI 1965-66, Lenoir Cty 1966-; *ai:* Sci Club Spon; Sci Dept Chm; Sci/Math Leadership Mem for Sch & Cty; NC Ed Assn Rep 1977-; NC Sci Teachers 1972-; NSTA 1984-; Alpha Kappa Alpha Hodecus/Parliamentarian 1984-; Alphabettes (Pres 1984-86, Secy 1982-85); Savannah Teacher of Yr 1977 & 1985; Bd of Dir for Green Lamp; *office:* Savannah Mid Schl Rt 2 Box 275 Grifton NC 28530

COWART, CAROL JORDAN, First Grade Teacher; *b:* Jackson, MS; *m:* Carl Milton Jr.; *c:* Catherine E., Carl Milton Trey III, Christina J.; *ed:* (BS) Elem Ed, MS St Coll for Women 1969; Working Towards Masters, MUW 1972, AL A&M Univ 1978-79; *cr:* 1st Grade Teacher 1969-70, 3rd Grade Teacher 1970-72 Decatur City Schls; 3rd Grade Teacher 1973-75, 1st Grade Teacher 1975- Morgan Cty Schls; *ai:* Cub Scout Den Leader St Anns Sch 1990; AEA, NEA, Morgan Cty Teachers 1969-; Pilot Club (VP 1983-84, Mem 1983-, Membership Chm 1984-85, Ed Chm 1985-) Pilot of Yr 1984; *office:* Priceville Sch Rt 4 Box 114 Decatur AL 35603

COWART, DAVID MIKE, Teacher/Sci Dept Chm; *b:* Holdenville, OK; *m:* Judith Ann Johnston; *c:* Sean, Brian; *ed:* (BA) His/Geography 1969, (MAED) Ed 1974, (BS) Bio, 1983-84 East Cntrl St; Post Masters Work OK Univ, OK St Univ, Tulsa Univ; *cr:* Teacher Holdenville Sch System 1969-78; Teacher 1981-, Dept Chm 1982-, Seminole Public Schls; *ai:* Seminole Conservation & Seminole Sci Club; Faculty Advisory Comm; OEA, NEA 1969-; Lions Club 1986-88; Natl Sci Fnd Grants; St of OK Candidate Awd of Excl 1986; Seminole Schls Teacher of Yr 1987; *office:* Seminole HS PO Box 1031 Seminole OK 74868

COWART, MELINDA TRICE, ESOL Teacher/Asst Professor; *b:* Fort Worth, TX; *m:* Ronald E.; *c:* Adam; *ed:* (BS) Elem Ed, Univ TX Austin 1975, (MED) Bi-ling Ed, 1977, (EDD) Supervision/Curr/Instruction, 1982 E TX St Univ; *cr:* Teacher Dallas Ind Sch Dist 1975-79; Instr E TX St Univ 1980-82; Teacher Dallas Ind Sch Dist 1982-; Adjunct Asst Professor TX Womans Univ 1984-; *ai:* Eng as 2nd Lang Consultant; Tennis Club Spon; Explorer Post 111 Cmmty Government Co-Spon; Special Observances Comm Mem; Asian Week Act Coord; Asian Amer Advisory Comm 1982-; Dallas Cty Historical Society SE Asian Exhibit 1989-; Highland Park Baptist Church; Title VII Doctoral Fellow 1979-81; Excl in Teaching Perot Awd 1988; Eng as 2nd Lang Teacher of Yr Finalist 1990; DISD Leadership Dev Acad Mem 1989-; *home:* 4925 Worth Dallas TX 75214

COWART, RHONDA WINDHAM, Fourth Grade Teacher; *b:* Reform, AL; *m:* Bobby William; *c:* Jason R., Kari L.; *ed:* (BS) Elem Ed, 1975, (MA) Elem Ed, 1978 Univ of AL; *cr:* 1st Grade Teacher 1975-82, 3rd Grade Teacher 1982-88, 5th/6th Grade Teacher 1988-89, 4th Grade Teacher 1989 Gordo Elem; *ai:* Pickens Cty Ed Assn, NEA; Mem Gordo United Meth Church; *office:* Gordo Elem Sch P O Drawer J Gordo AL 35466

COWDEN, MARJORIE ROBERTSON, 4th Grade Teacher; *b:* Burgettstown, PA; *m:* William Kline; *c:* Sherry L. Karas, William H., Kevin A. (dec); *ed:* (BS) Elem Ed, CA Univ 1954; *ai:* Eastern Star; Eldersville Meth Church (Organist, Pianist); *home:* RFD 4 Box 35 Burgettstown PA 15021

COWDREY, JOHN LEE, Stu Assistance Cnslr; *b:* Gallup, NM; *m:* Kim Lenae Sumption; *c:* Anthony J., Erin M., David C. Lee, Shealee L.; *ed:* (BS) Elem Ed/Soc Stud, 1969, (MA) Educl Admin, 1975 NM St Univ; Certified Alcoholism Cnslr; Guidance & Counseling Western NM Univ; *cr:* Teacher Bradley Elem 1969-71, White Sands Missile Range Jr HS 1971-79, Gallup Mid Sch 1980-89; Cntrl Office/Stu Assistance Cnslr Gallup/Mc Kinley Cty Public Schls 1989-; *ai:* Substance Abuse Advisory Comm Mem; Alateen, Emotions Anonymous Spon 1989-; Gallup Public Schls Task Force Cntrl Office Rep 1989-; NEA, Las Cruces Ed Assn 1969-75; Alanon 1989-; *office:* Gallup/Mc Kinley Public Schls 700 S Boardman Dr PO Box 1318 Gallup NM 87305

COWELL, SEVERNA (JOHNSON), 5th Grade Teacher; *b:* Mc Gregor, IA; *m:* James Leroy; *c:* Linda L. Miller, Jeffrey J.; *ed:* Stan Elem Ed, IA St Teachers Coll 1953; Univ of MN, Mankato St Teachers Coll, Upper IA Univ, Drake; *cr:* 1st Grade Teacher W Union Public Sch 1953-54; 2nd Grade Teacher Luana Public Sch 1954-56; 1st Grade Teacher Riverside Elem 1956-58; 3rd-5th Grade Teacher Mar Mac Cmmty Sch 1962-; *ai:* NEA, IA St Ed Assn, Mar-Mac Ed Assn; Delta Kappa Gamma Society Intnl 1981-; *home:* 815 Walton Ave Mc Gregor IA 52157

COWEN, JILL DOBIE, Careers/Computers Teacher; *b:* Philadelphia, PA; *m:* Joseph; *c:* Todd Heacock; *ed:* (BA) Elem Ed, 1965, (MA) Elem Ed, 1978 Glassboro; Cmptr-Writing Wkshp; Early Chldhd, Open Ed, Environmental Ed, Leadership & Negotiations; Working Toward PhD; *cr:* 1st-3rd/5th Grade Teacher Riderwood Mid Sch 1965-66, 1970-72, Cape May 1966-68; IV Coord/6th-6th Grade Careers/Cmptrs/Creative Writing Teacher Woodlynne 1972-; *ai:* Sftbl Negotiations; Soccer Coach; Spring Concerts Costume Design & Dance Dir; Lydia, WEA Secy; Wrangle Hill Assn Block Leader; Funding for Vocations; *office:* Woodlynne Public Sch Front & Elm Avenues Woodlynne NJ 08107

COWETT, MARK, Head of Upper School; *b:* Cincinnati, OH; *m:* Joan Yukich; *c:* Mark Jr., Megen; *ed:* (BA) His, Lawrence Univ 1973; (MA) His, Univ of Chicago 1974; (MAT) Univ of Chicago 1976; (PHD) Amer His, Univ of CT 1981; *cr:* Chm His Dept Keith Cntry Day 1982-86, Flintridge Preparatory 1986-88, St Louis Cntry Day 1988-; Head of Upper Sch Harley Sch 1990; *ai:* Responsible for Curr Instruction; Amer Historical Assn, Organization of Amer His 1980-; Univ of AL Press 1986, Rabbi Morris Newfield & AL 1895-1940; *office:* Harley Sch Rochester NY 14604

COWLE, PAUL BERNARD, Physical Education Teacher; *b:* Kansas City, MO; *m:* Mary Louise Black; *c:* Mary A. Paulsell, Paul B. II; *ed:* (BS) Phys Ed, AR Polytech Coll 1965; (MA) Phys Ed, SE MO ST Univ 1971; Certified Hunter Safety Instr MO Dept of Conservation; Certified Casting Instr Amer Casting Assn; *cr:* Phys Ed Teacher Hillsboro Elem Sch 1965-71, Hillsboro Sr HS 1972-; Dept Chairperson/Phys Ed Dept Teacher Hillsboro HS 1978-; *ai:* Womens Track Head Coach; MO Assn Health, Phys Ed, Recreation & Dance 1975-; MO St Teachers Assn 1965-; MO St Dept of Ed (Appointed Mem, Ad Hoc Curr Dev Comm, Phys Ed Curr, Health Curr); Elks 1985-; Head Instr of Casting & Angling Outdoor Ed Wkshps MO St Dept of Ed.

COX, ANNIE MAY, 1st Grade Teacher; *b:* Woodbury, TN; *w:* Sanford H. (dec); *c:* Nancy Hale Young; *ed:* (BS) Elem Ed, A&Y St Coll 1948; George Peabody Coll, Mid TN St Univ; *cr:* Teacher 1948, Prin 1967-75 Woodbury Elem Sch; Teacher/Vice Prin Westside Sch 1975-; *ai:* Bsktbl Coach PJU Cannon Cty Teachers Assn Sftbl Coach; Delta Kappa Gamma Mem 1987-, Key Awd 1988; Univ Woman Mem 1988-; Farm Bureau Bd Mem 1985-; Caney Fork Dev Bd Mem; Woodbrous Housing Bd Mem 1980-; Teacher of Yr 1987-88; Selective Service Bd Presidental Awd 1976; *office:* Westside Sch Murfreesboro Hwy Readyville TN 37190

COX, CAROL W., English Teacher; *b:* Wilson, NC; *m:* Larry V.; *c:* Renee, Stephanie, Larry Jr.; *ed:* (BA) Eng, Bob Jones Univ 1964; Post Grad Courses; *cr:* Eng Teacher Ringgold HS 1964-67, Farmville Cntrl HS 1970-78, Fellowship Chrstn Sch 1979-80, Carrington JR HS 1980, Mountain View Chrstn Sch 1981-83, Emmanuel Baptist Acad 1983-86, Mt Calvary Chrstn Sch 1986-; *ai:* Newspaper Adv; Bsktbl Statistician; Keystone Chrstn Ed Assn 1981-; *office:* Mt Calvary Chrstn Sch Holly St & Hillside Ave Elizabethtown PA 17022

COX, CASEY EDVARD, Agriculture Instructor; *b:* Tacoma, WA; *m:* Melanie L. Parker; *c:* Gunnar L.; *ed:* (AA) Anthropology, Ft Steilacoom Cmmty 1985; (BS) Agriculture Ed, WA St Univ 1987; Beginning ITIP; Effective Classroom Management; Curr Dev For Voc Ed; Research Methods in Continuing & Voc Ed; Cooperative Ed; *cr:* WSU Asst Stu Dir WA St Univ 1986; Supt of Public Instruction Intern WA St FFA Convention 1987; Stu Teacher Yelm HS 1987; Sci/Agriculture Instr Tenino HS 1987-; *ai:* FFA Adv; Sftbl Asst & Jr Var Coach; WVATA Dist 3 Pres 1987-90, Rookie of Yr 1987; WVA, NVATA Mem 1987-; WEA, NEA, TEA Mem 1987-; *office:* Tenino HS PO Box Z Tenino WA 98589

COX, DALE SOREN, History/English Teacher; *b:* Provo, UT; *m:* Rhoda E. Rogers; *c:* Rebecca, Timothy, Heather, Anna; *ed:* (BA) His, Brigham Young Univ 1981; (MED) Ed Admin, AZ St Univ 1987; Chinese Grad Stud; *cr:* Teacher 1981-, Summer Sch Prin 1986- Mesa Unified Schls 1986-; *ai:* Career Ladder Trainer & Liaison; Former Intramural Coach; ASCD Mem 1989-; Phi Kappa Phi Mem 1981-; Church Lifetime Mem; Presenter at Several Regional & St Ed Conferences & Dist In-Service Wkshps; *office:* Poston Jr HS 2433 E Adobe Mesa AZ 85203

COX, DEBRA C., Mathematics Teacher; *b:* Morehead, KY; *ed:* (BA) Scndry Ed/Math, Transylvania Univ 1980; (MA) Scndry Ed/Math, 1983, (Rank I) Scndry Ed, 1987 Morehead St Univ; *cr:* Math Teacher Fleming Cty Mid Sch 1980-85, Fleming Cty HS 1985-; *ai:* Asst Coach Academic Team; Co-Spon Jr Beta Club; KEA, FCEA; *office:* Fleming Cty HS Rt 2 Flemingsburg KY 41041

COX, DEE M., 6th Grade Math Teacher; *b:* Water Valley, MS; *m:* Bobby J.; *c:* Joe, Dee A. Cox Doom, Callie; *ed:* (BS) Bus Ed, 1962, (BA) Elem Ed, 1976 Univ of MS; *cr:* Bus Ed Teacher West Memphis HS 1962-64, Oakland HS 1966-68; 2nd Grade Teacher Sledge Elem Sch 1971-72; 1st Grade Teacher Smithville Elem Sch 1972-73; 6th Grade Math Teacher Water Valley Elem Sch 1976-; *ai:* Water Valley Ed Assn, MAE, NEA; Pilot Club Intnl Secy; Yalobusha Cty Cancer Society Ed Comm; *home:* 309 Panola St Water Valley MS 38965

COX, DORIS ANN PATE, General Music Teacher; *b:* Charleston, SC; *m:* David Wesley Sr.; *c:* David W. Jr., Pate S., Michelle L., Lara K.; *ed:* (BA) Psych/Music, Columbia Coll 1962; (MED) Elem Ed, Univ of SC 1980; *cr:* Psych Teacher A C Flora HS 1962-64; Music Teacher Charleston Cty Schls 1969-71, Oak Grove Elem Sch 1974-; *ai:* SC Ed Assn 1962-64, 1987-; Music Educators Natl Conference 1980-; Main St United Meth Church 1960-; *office:* Oak Grove Elem Sch 479 Oak Dr Lexington SC 29072

COX, ESTELLA MEGGETT, 3rd Grade Teacher; *b:* Idisto Island, SC; *m:* Norman W.; *c:* Norman W., Dawn I.; *ed:* (BA) Elem Ed, Savannah St Coll 1959; (MS) Ed, SC St Coll 1964; Univ of Miami; Barry Univ; *cr:* Teacher Robert Smalls Jr HS 1959-63; Smith-Brown Elem 1963-68; Dorsey Jr HS 1968-70; Seminole Elem 1970-; *ai:* Girl Scout Troop Leader; Youth Group Zeta Phi Beta-Beta Tauzeta Chapter; United Teacher of Dade 1968-; FL Ed Assn 1963-; Zeta Phi Beta Inc (Phylacter 1983-88 Zeta of Yr 1983 Amenities Chm 1983); Meritorious Service 1986; Natl Assn for Advancement of Colored People 1987-; Miami North Western HS PTA; Seminole Teacher of Yr 1984; Outstanding Service & Dedication to Youth of Seminole 1985; Appreciation for Support & Interest in Saturday Classes from Charles R Drew PTA 1987; *home:* 1634 NW 85th St Miami FL 33147

COX, FRANK WILLIAM, Spanish Teacher; *b:* Racine, WI; *c:* Janeen, Lori, Jeff, Doug; *ed:* Peace Corps Trng 1964-66; *cr:* Span Teacher Marquette Univ 1966-67, Marquette HS 1967-79, Brophy Coll Preparatory 1979-; *ai:* Jr Var Bsbl; Intramurals; Hiking Club; Yrbk Moderator; Mexican Trips Leader; AATSP 1970-; AFLA 1982-; *office:* Brophy Coll Preparatory Sch 4701 N Central Ave Phoenix AZ 85012

COX, GARY WAYNE, 4th Grade Teacher; *b:* Carmi, IL; *m:* Judy; *c:* Megan, Emily; *ed:* (BA) Elem Ed, Mc Kendree Coll 1976; *cr:* 3rd Grade Teacher Hickory Bend Sch 1976-78; 4th Grade Teacher Sparta Primary 1978-85, Sparta Lincoln 1985-; *ai:* Sparta Ed Assn, IL Ed Assn, NEA; Sparta Cmmty Chorus Dir 1985-; *office:* Sparta Lincoln Sch 200 N St Louis Sparta IL 62286

COX, HAZEL CROFT, Teacher; *b:* Dade City, FL; *m:* Tillery F.; *ed:* (BS) Primary Ed, Pembroke St Univ 1973; *cr:* Teacher Homosassa Sch 1949-52, Baltimore Cty Schls 1958-63, Citrus Cty Schls 1963-65, Richmond Cty Schls 1965-; *ai:* NCAF Secy 1965-; NEA 1975-; Chapter 65 Order of the Eastern Star Cordova PTO 1944-.

COX, JAMES DALE, Science Department Chairman; *b:* St Charles, IL; *m:* Barbara Coulter; *c:* Andrew, Kevin, Emily, Nathaniel; *ed:* (BA) Bio, Greenville Coll 1972; (MA) Admin, Northern IL Univ 1978; Sci Courses, Teacher Trng, Curr Dev; *cr:* Teacher/Coach/Dept Chm Batavia Jr HS 1972-89; *ai:* 7th/8th Grade Wrestling, Ftbl Coach; Sci, Gifted, Instructional Advisory Cncl, Dept Chm, Comms; Batavia Ed Assn; IL Ed Assn; NEA; IL Sci Teachers Assn; NSTA; Friends of Fermilab-curr Consultant 1984-; Fermi Lab Sci Center Advisory Bd 1988-; Kane Cty Jr HS Teacher of Yr 1978; Recognized Outstanding Sci Teachers 1989-91; Published-Consultant/Author-Friends of Fermilab Ed Prgm; Project Dir Mid Sch Summer Sci Inst; Writer MASER Corp Sci Activity Cards; *office:* Batavia Jr H S 10 S Batavia Ave Batavia IL 60510

COX, JEANA K., Elem Music/Jr HS Math Teacher; *b:* Poplar Bluff, MO; *m:* John Charles; *c:* Mitchell; *ed:* (BME) Music, Cntrl Meth Coll 1975; *cr:* Elem Music Teacher 1975-, Jr HS Math Teacher 1981- Lincoln R II; *ai:* 8th Grade Spon; Accompanist for HS Music Dept; MMEA; Trustee Meth Church; *office:* Benton County R-II Schls Lamine St Lincoln MO 65338

COX, JEANNINE ZURELDA (LEACH), 2nd Grade Teacher; *b:* Lyman, NE; *m:* Arlyn W.; *c:* Arlys, Tonya; *ed:* Elem Ed, McCook Comm Coll 1958; (BA) Elem Ed, Kearney St Coll 1967; *cr:* K-2nd Grade Teacher Wauneta Grade Sch 1958-67; 1st Grade Teacher 1967-68, 2nd Grade Teacher 1968- Imperial Grade Sch; *ai:* Chase Cty Ed Assn 1958-67; Imperial Ed Assn 1967-; NEA 1967-; NSEA 1967-; *home:* RR 1 Box 9 Champion NE 69023

COX, JOHN ROGERS, MS His/Amer His Teacher; *b:* Jackson, TN; *ed:* (AA) Ed, Northwest Jr Coll 1972; (BA) His, Delta St 1974; Certificate Ec Ed & Newspaper in Classroom; Geography Field Wkshp; *cr:* Teacher Carver Mid Sch 1974-78, Oakland Jr HS 1978-80; Interviewer/Cnslr MS Job Service 1980-81; Teacher Grenada Jr HS 1984-; *ai:* Grenada Jr HS Stu Cncl Spon; His Club Spon; His Bowl Team Coach; MS Assn of Educators 1978-80; MS Jr Historical Society Bd Mem 1989-; Impact Awd Winner 1989; *office:* Grenada Jr HS Jones Rd Grenada MS 38901

COX, JON L., US History Teacher; *b:* Marshall, TX; *m:* Donna Kaye Mc Cray; *c:* Felicia, Cedric; *ed:* (BS) Soc Sci, Wiley Coll 1971; (MS) Educl Admin, East TX St Univ 1974; Attended Free Enterprise Institute 1981; *cr:* 5th Grade Teacher Huntington Elem 1971-72; Soc Stud Teacher Marshall HS 1972-; *ai:* Spon Marshall HS Chess Club; Co-Spon Future Teachers of America; Bus Driver Marshall Ind Sch Dist 1973-; TX Classroom Teachers Assn 1976-; Harrison Cty Historical Society 1988-; Marshall-Wiley Alumni Club; H B Pemberton Reunion Assn Co-Chm 1976 & 1981; *home:* 15 Yvonne Marshall TX 75670

COX, JOYCE TUCKER, K-12th Grade Counselor; *b:* Birmingham, AL; *ed:* (BSME) Music Ed Piano, Samford Univ 1970; (MA) Counseling, Univ of AL Birmingham 1978; Psychometrist; Cert in Elem Ed; *cr:* Counselor Jackson Area Career Center 1982-86; Teacher Greenwood Mid Sch 1986-88; Counselor Bullard Havens Voc Tech Sch 1988-89, Isabella Sch 1989-; *ai:* Newspaper, SGA & Beta Club Spon; Amer Guidance Assn 1982-86; Jackson Assn Guidance Public Relations 1984-85; Kappa Delta; Prof Womens Organization 1975-76; *office:* Isabella Sch Rt 2 Box 239 Maplesville AL 36750

COX, KAYE, Mathematics/Computer Teacher; *b:* Oklahoma City, OK; *ed:* (BS) Math, OK St Univ 1971; *cr:* Teacher Douglass HS 1971-; *ai:* Chairperson Awds, Faculty Advisory Comm; Tutoring Coord; Math Team Coach; Soph Class, Math Club Spon; OK Cncl of Teachers Math; AFT; Calculus, Cmptrs, Tutors Grants; *office:* Douglass HS 900 Martin Luther King Ave Oklahoma City OK 73117

COX, LEE RANDOLPH, English Literature Teacher; *b:* Rochester, NY; *m:* Jodi Ann Simpson; *c:* Perrin, Hayley; *ed:* (BA) Eng, Univ of CA Santa Barbara 1969; (MA) Hum/Scndry Ed, S OR St 1978; Univ CA Santa Barbara 1970-71; *cr:* Eng Lit Teacher Rio Mesa HS 1971-; *ai:* Sch Improvement Prgm Mem & Faculty Rep 1987-; AFT 1980-; *office:* Rio Mesa HS 545 Central Ave Oxnard CA 93030

COX, LINDA MARIE, Sixth Grade Teacher; *b:* Bainbridge, GA; *ed:* (BS) Elem Ed, Albany St Coll 1974; (MED) Elem Ed, GA St Univ 1980; Data Collection; Supervision of Stu Teachers; *cr:* Teacher Bainbridge Elem; *ai:* Chrldr Spon; Stu Support Team; NEA, GA Educators Assn 1975-; Decatur Cty Educator Assn 1977-; Albany St Coll Alumni Assn (Pres, Secy) 1977-81, Achievement Plaque 1987; Univ of GA Alumni Assn 1980-; Natl Assn Advancement of Colored People 1985-; Teacher of Yr Bainbridge Elem 1985; *office:* Bainbridge Elem Sch 1417 Dothan Hwy Bainbridge GA 31717

COX, MARCIA SMITH, Elementary Teacher; *b:* Louisville, KY; *m:* Terry Gene; *ed:* (BS) Elem Ed, Belmont Coll 1983; *cr:* 4th-8th Grade Teacher Davidson Acad 1983-88; 4th-5th Grade Teacher Calera Elem 1988-89; *ai:* HS Speech & Drama Dept Forensics Coach; Chorus Dir; *home:* Rt 2 Box 760 Calera AL 35040

COX, MARY LOU, Third Grade Teacher; *b:* Jumping Branch, WV; *ed:* (BS) Elem Ed, Concord Coll 1962; (MA) Elem Ed, Shippensburg Univ 1969; Rdng Ed, WV Coll of Graduate Stud; *cr:* Teacher Harpers Ferry Elem 1962-69; Jumping Branch Elem 1969-; *ai:* WVEA; NEA; SCEA Treas 1970; Alpha Sigma Tau Chaplain 1961; Kappa Delta Pi 1961; Cardinal Key 1961; Alpha Beta Alpha Pres 1959-62 Whos Who Among Students in Amer Coll & Univ Sec/Treas 1962; Schlrshp to Convervation Wkshp; Summers Cty Rep Conservation Wkshp; *home:* 86 St Rt Box 9 Junping Branch WV 25969

COX, MAUDRY JOYNER, Primary Specialist; *b:* Panama City, FL; *m:* James Clifford; *c:* Stephen; *ed:* (BA) Elem Ed, Univ of W FL 1974; (MS) Elem Ed, FL St Univ 1986; Peer Teacher; *cr:* 3rd Grade Teacher 1975-86, Primary Specialist 1987- West Bay Elem; *ai:* Bay Cty Rdng Assn Pres 1989-; FL Rdng Assn Dist Dir 1989-; IRA 1986-; Bch Optimist Club 1989-; West Bay Sch Teacher of Yr 1984; *home:* 8009 Temple Ave Panama City FL 32413

COX, NANCY ORREN, Sixth Grade Teacher; *b:* Elizabethton, TN; *m:* Luther; *c:* Danny, Susan; *ed:* (BS) Elem Ed, E TN St Univ 1981; *cr:* Rdng Teacher 1982, Home Ec Teacher 1983-84, 6th Grade Teacher 1985- Happy Valley Mid Sch; *ai:* Former 4-H Club; Beta Club Spon; *office:* Happy Valley Mid Sch Rt 11 Box 3400 Elizabethton TN 37643

COX, PATRICIA LEE STAVRAKIS, Teacher/Mentor-English; *b:* Steubenville, OH; *m:* Ronald C.; *c:* William R., Stephen J.; *ed:* (BS) Eng/Ed, Youngstown Univ 1961; (MS) Ed, Westminster Coll 1965; Sign Lanaguage for Deaf, Gallaudet Coll; Economics, OH Univ; Composition Through Cmptrs,Kent St Univ; Advanced Amer His Courses, Akron Univ; His Classes, Baldwin-Wallace Coll; Mentorship Teacher Trng, Cleveland St Univ; *cr:* Teacher Youngstown City Schls 1960-63, Liberty Local 1963-64, Austintown-Fitch HS 1964-66; Elem Teacher Towslee Elem 1967-68; Amer His Teacher Willetts 1972-81;Math/Eng Teacher Crestview Elem 1981-83; Amer His Teacher Willetts-Brunswick 1983-85; Eng Teacher Brunswick HS 1985-; *ai:* Eng Dept Curr; Wrote & Helped Administer Amer His Tests of Scholastic Achievement for OH Dept of Ed 1988-; Trained & Helped Implement 1st Mentorship Prgm in Sch System 1989-; Brunswick Ed Assn Trustee of Defense Fund 1985-; Medina Cty Democratic Party Precinct Commiteeperson 1983-86/1990; *office:* Brunswick H S 3581 Center Rd Brunswick OH 44212

COX, PAULYN M., Third Grade Teacher; *b:* Oberlin, OH; *ed:* (AAS) Nursery Ed, St Univ of NY 1953; (BA) Citizenship Ed, Ithaca Coll 1957; Methods Teaching Elem Ed Coll of ST Rose 1969; *cr:* 5th Grade Teacher East Carlisle 1964-65; 8th/9th Grade Teacher Midview Sch 1966-67; 5th Grade Teacher St Columbus 1968; 3rd Grade Teacher Fonda/Fultonville Central Sch 1969-; *ai:* PTA; Teachers Assisting Teachers; NY St United Teachers; Amer Fed of Teachers; Baptist Retirement Ctr Volunteer 1988-; Bed/Bread Club of City Mission 1987-; Amnesty Intl USA 1987-; Deaf Ctr 1970-; Hamilton Hill Arts/Craft Ctr 1970-; Mem Schenectady Young Womens Assn; Lupus Fnd of Amer, Inc 1982-; Literacy Volunteer in "Each One Teach One" Prgm 1975-77; Cancer Fund 1989; Choir Mem & Soloist at Woestina Reformed Church 1958-; Secy of Bd of Dir Carver Commty Ctr 1959-62; Pearl S Buck Fnd Spon; *home:* 1561 Main St Rotterdam Junction NY 12150

COX, SHIRLEY ANN, Fourth Grade Teacher; *m:* Arthur D.; *c:* Paula Hutchcraft, Michael D., Michelle L. Christain; *ed:* (BS) Elem Ed, 1979, (MA) Elem Ed/Rdng, 1984 SE MO St Univ; *cr:* 4th Grade Teacher Dexter Public Schls 1980-; *ai:* MSTA Treas 1983-86; *office:* Cntrl Elem Sch Market & Elm St Dexter MO 63841

COXE, ELOISE AMENTA, Supervisor Enrichment/Gifted; *b:* North East, PA; *ed:* (BS) Ed, Villa Maria Coll 1962; (MS) Ed, Cleveland St Univ 1983; Ed, Cleveland St Univ 1983-86; Ed, Kent St Univ 1985/1987; Ed, FL St Univ 1988; *cr:* Teacher Grades 4th/8th/9th St Gregory Schls 1960-62; Teacher Grade 4 Lindberg Sch 1962-64; Teacher Grade 6 Noble Road Sch 1964-67; Teacher Grade 8 West JR HS 1964-89; Supv Ashtabula Area City Schls 1989-; *ai:* Chairperson, Parent Adv Comm for Gifted Ed; Coord, Dist Young Astronaut Chapters; Coord, Stock Mrkt Game; Dist Mrktg-Our-Schls Comm; NEA; Assn for Supvsn & Curr Dev; OH Assn of Elem Sch Admin; Natl Assn for Gifted Children; OH Assn for Gifted Children; Consortium of OH Coord for The Gifted; Intnl Rdng Assn; Amer Assn of Univ Women Sec/VP/Pres 1967-Membrshp Awd 1974; YMCA-WCA Locl Bd of Dir 1979-81; Martha Holden Jennings Schlr, 1976; St of OH Excl in Ed Grant, 1983-84; *home:* P O Box 2975 Ashtabula OH 44004

COXON, ROBIN C., English Department Chair; *b:* Mesa, AZ; *m:* James F.; *c:* Cortney, Scott; *ed:* (BA) Elem Ed, 1971, (MA) Elem Ed, 1974 Univ of AZ; N Cntrl Accredidation Evaluator; Teacher Residency Prgm Mentor Teacher; Chem Dependency; Red Cross Lifesaving & CPR; *cr:* 4th Grade Teacher 1971-72, 6th Grade Teacher 1973-74 Mammoth Elem; 7th Grade Teacher Gardner Mid Sch 1975-76; 8th Grade Eng/Journalism/Phys Ed Teacher Marana Jr HS 1977-; *ai:* Yrbk, Newspaper, Peer Counseling, Tutoring Adv; Var Club Spon; 8th Grade Girls Vlybl & 7th Grade Boys Bsktbl Coach; Dist Athletic & Extracurricular Comm; Mentor Teacher; NEA; LDS Church Primary Secy 1988-Marana Jr HS Faculty Service Awd 1988; *office:* Marana Jr HS 11279 W Grier Rd Marana AZ 85653

COY, ELSIE MAY COOPER, 4th-8th Grade Head Teacher; *b:* Ewing, NE; *m:* Sylas Eugene; *c:* Marsha Drury; *ed:* (BA) Elem Ed, Wayne St Coll 1975; *cr:* K-8th Grade Teacher Dist #86 1952-54, Dist #88 1954-56, Dist #65 1956-60, DIst #30 1960-64, Dist #42 1964-65; 5th-6th Grade Teacher Ewing Public Schls 1965-66; 4th-8th Grade Teacher Dist #46 1966-; *ai:* Local NE St Ed Assn Treas; Rural Educators of Holty Cty Treas 1989-; *home:* RR 1 Box 32 Ewing NE 68735

COYLE, LINNA ANN, 8th Grade Earth/Space Science; *b:* Winchester, KY; *m:* Gary W.; *ed:* (AB) Psych/Bio, Asbury Coll 1976; (BS) Elem Ed, 1978, (MA) Elem Ed, 1979, (Rank I) Rdng Specialist, 1981 E KY Univ Richmond; Admin Cert Elem Prin, Supvr, E KY Univ Richmond 1985; Trng IBM Cmptr Wkshps; Moonrock Cert & Rocketry, KY Space Ed Prgm Trng; *cr:* 5th/6th Grade Teacher Providence Elem 1978-87; 8th Grade Sci Teacher Belmont Mid Sch 1987-; *ai:* Coach Academic Teams; Clark Cty Evaluation Comm Mem; Chairperson Sci Dept; Trainer Camcorder & Videographer Stus Taping Sch Events; Clark Cty Ed Assn, KY Ed Assn, NEA Building Rep 1978-; Delta Kappa Gamma Secy 1983-; KY Math & Sci Alliance 1987; NSTA, ASCD 1989-; Providence Elem Rep Teacher Awd Recognition Dinner 1985; GTE Sci & Math Grant; KY Math & Sci Alliance Minigrant; Belmont Nom Outstanding Mid Grade Math & Sci Prgm; S Cntrl Bell Adopt a Sch Grant; Nom Ashland Oil Teacher of Yr 1990; *home:* 2105 Mt Sterling Rd Winchester KY 40391

COYLE, NANCY TOMASSO, 7th Grade Teacher; *b:* Elizabeth, NJ; *m:* John; *c:* John, Allyson; *ed:* (BA) Elem Ed, Georgian Court Coll 1984; *cr:* Supplemental Teacher Osborneville Sch 1984-85; 5th Grade Teacher 1985-86, 7th Grade Teacher 1986- Manchester Mid Sch; *ai:* Rdng Evaluation Comm; Intnl Honor Society 1983-84; *office:* Manchester Mid Sch 2759 Ridgeway Rd Lakehurst NJ 08733

COYLE, RITA STEVENS, 4th/5th Grade Teacher; *b:* Grayson, KY; *m:* Bob Wayde; *ed:* (BA) Ed, Morehead St Univ 1974; (MAED) Ed, 1978, (Rank I) Ed, 1984 W KY Univ; *cr:* Teacher Battletown Elem Sch 1974-; *ai:* Ed & Publisher of Local Sch Newspaper Sch Busters; Talent Coord Sch Plays; KY Ed Assn 1975-; Won St Energy Contest Twice; *home:* 165 Wilma Ave Radcliff KY 40160

COYNE, JAMES MICHAEL, Principal; *b:* Roanoke, VA; *m:* Darla Dietz; *c:* Brody A.; *ed:* (BA) Elem Ed, Lynchburg Coll 1974; (MA) Elem Admin, Glassboro St Coll 1986; Grad Work Lynchburg Coll 1974-76, Univ of VA 1976; *cr:* Teacher Rustburg Mid Sch 1974-78; Math Teacher Bridgeton HS 1978-79; 4th Grade Teacher Cherry Street Sch 1979-86; Prin Buckshutem Road Sch 1986-87, Cherry Street Sch 1987-; *ai:* Bridgeton Cooperative Relations Project Mem; Bridgeton Ed Assn 1978-86, Teacher of Yr 1984; Assn of Bridgeton Admin Pres 1986-; Big Brothers 1982-85; Kiwanis Club 2nd VP 1987-89; Governors Teacher Recognition Awd; *office:* Cherry Street Sch Cherry St Bridgeton NJ 08302

COZORT, ELDEN MANN, Mathematics Teacher; *b:* Thermopolis, WY; *ed:* (BS) Math, Grand Canyon Coll 1972; (MA) Math Ed, AZ St Univ 1977; Advance Placement Wkshps in Calculus & Cmptr Sci; Numerous Cmptr Sci Classes; *cr:* Math Teacher Saguaro HS 1972-73, Chaparral HS 1973-76, Saquaro HS 1976-; *ai:* Mem Management Team; Scottsdale Ed Assn Treas 1988-; NCTM Speaker; *office:* Saguaro HS 6250 N 82nd St Scottsdale AZ 85253

COZZENS, REBECCA AUSTIN, Kindergarten Teacher; *b:* Springfield, VT; *m:* David Douglas; *c:* Justin, Joshua; *ed:* (BS) Elem Ed, Castleton St Coll 1971; Grad Stud Ed, Univ of VT; *cr:* 1st Grade Teacher 1971-85, 1st/2nd Grade Teacher 1985-87, Kndgtn Teacher 1987- Brewster Pierce Memorial Sch; *ai:* Baptist Church Deacon 1988-; Cub Scouts Den Leader 1988-; Social Learning 1985 & Kids Kitchen 1989 Incentive Grant; *home:* Box 1258 Huntington VT 05462

CRABB, BETTY CARNES, 6th-8th Grade Math Teacher; *b:* Alex, OK; *m:* Alton Flemon; *c:* Joyce N. Balzhieser, Larry A., Deborah L. Johnson; *ed:* (BS) Elem Ed, OK Coll of Liberal Arts 1970; (MA) Rdng, Univ of CO Colorado Springs 1975; *cr:* K-8th Grade Substitute Teacher Fairbanks AK 1970-71; 3rd Grade Teacher Roosevelt Elem 1971-76, Rush Springs Elem Sch 1976-79; Math Teacher Rush Springs Mid Sch 1979-; *ai:* Stu Cncl Spon; Bookkeeper Jr & Sr Bsktbl Games; Mathcounts Club Coach; OK Ed Assn 1976-; NCTM 1980-; Grady Cty Ed Assn (Secy, Treas) 1990; Rush Springs PTA (Secy 1988-89, Membership Chairperson 1989-); *home:* Rt 2 Box 60 Rush Springs OK 73082

CRABB, VIRGINIA LEE COMSTOCK, Business Ed/Voc Dept Chair; *b:* Muskogee, OK; *m:* William; *ed:* (AS) Bus/Eng, Decatur Jr Coll 1963; (BS) Bus/Eng, Wayland Baptist Coll 1965; Working Towards Masters, Sam Houston St Univ, Univ of Houston; *cr:* Teacher Fredericksburg HS 1965-67; Teacher/FBLA & Stu Cncl Club Spons Furr HS Ind Sch Dist 1967-; *ai:* Voc Dept Chairperson; Prom, Stu Cncl Spon; Faculty Advisory Comm; TBEA 1967-80; HEA 1967-83; Local Teacher Union 1983-89; Houston Square & Round Dance Cncl (Secy 1987-88, Treas 1988-89, Dist Rep 1986-87); Public Service Awd Veterans Hospital, Spec Olympics; *home:* 211 Holyhead Dr Houston TX 77015

CRABBS, CATHERINE LOUISE, 7th Grade Language Art Teacher; *b:* Richmond, IN; *m:* Dean R.; *c:* R. Scott Sivulich, Jamison J. Sivulich; *ed:* (BS) Scndry Ed/Eng, 1970, (MS) Scndry Ed, 1982 IN Univ; Various Courses; *cr:* Eng Teacher Griffith HS 1970-74, 1978-82; 7th Grade Lang Art Teacher Wasilla Jr HS 1983-; *ai:* Cross Cntry Running, Track & Field Coach; Hockey Chrldr Spon; Lang Art Curr Comm; AK Teachers of Eng; NCTE; *office:* Wasilla Jr HS 650 Bogard Rd Wasilla AK 99687

CRABTREE, CAROLYNN KEENY, Lang Art/Computer Sci Teacher; *b:* Chico, CA; *m:* William; *c:* Corinne; *ed:* (BA) Eng, 1970, (MA) Ed/Rdng Specialist, 1976 CSUS; *cr:* Rdng Teacher Rio Linda Jr HS 1970-75; Rdng/Eng Teacher Glen Edwards Intermediate Sch 1975-; *ai:* Rdng Dept, Mentor Teacher Comm, Western Placer Unified Sch Dist Rdng Proficiency Comm Chm; Delta Kappa Gamma; Intnl Rdng Assn; Cmptr Using Educators; Western Placer Teachers Assn (Pres 1984, 1986, Negotiator); CTIIP Grant; Mentor Teacher; *office:* Glen Edwards Intermediate Sch 204 L Street Lincoln CA 95648

CRABTREE, MARGARET ANN, Elementary Teacher; *b:* Bethany, MO; *m:* Edward J.; *c:* Pamela K. Pankau, Teresa A.; *ed:* (BS) Elem Ed, MO Western St Coll 1972; *cr:* 6th Grade Teacher Rushville Elem 1972-76; 5th/6th Grade Teacher 1976-77, 6th Grade Teacher 1980-84, 1st Grade Teacher 1984-89 Winston Elem; *ai:* MO St Teachers Assn; *home:* 216 S Nettleton Cameron MO 64429

CRABTREE, ROBERT ALLEN, Fourth Grade Teacher; *b:* Syracuse, NY; *ed:* (BA) Elem Ed, SUNY Fredonia 1971; (MS) Ed, SUNY Cortland 1975; *cr:* 5th Grade Teacher Pitcher Hill Elem 1971-77; 2nd/5th Grade Teacher Main Street Elem 1977-80; Elem Math Specialist N Syracuse Cntrl Schls 1980-83; 3rd/4th Grade Teacher Bear Road Elem 1983-; *ai:* Adv Bear Road Stu Cncl; Facilitator Roxboro Road Career Day; Coord Bear Road Sci Exhibition; Facilitator N Syracuse Cntrl Sch Dist Elem Sci Comm; NYSUT 1971-; NCTM 1976-; Math Teachers Assn of NY ST; Sci Teachers Assn of NY St Spec Area Rep 1984-; ASCD 1987-; We Care Telephone Suicide Prevention 1989-; PTO, PTA VP 1971-, Honorary Life Mem 1978; Walk to Save the Cty Coord 1981-; Teacher of Yr N Syracuse Cntrl Sch 1987; NY St Assembly Resolution Significant Contribution Cmmty, Schls; CNY Teaching Center Grant 1988; N Syracuse Mini Grants 1987-89; Instr Syracuse Univ; Sci Mentor N Syracuse Cntrl Schls; Elem Sch Recognition Prgm Author 1987; Elem Math Curr Writer; Elem Sci Testing Prgm & Curr Writer 1985-87; Cooperative Learning Instr 1990; Michael Bragman Grant N Syracuse Sch Dist Shared Decision Making; *office:* Bear Road Elem Sch 5590 Bear Rd North Syracuse NY 13212

CRABTREE, ROY H., Life Science Teacher; *b:* Des Moines, IA; *m:* Sandra Parker; *c:* Kristen Jones, Kimberly, Kirk; *ed:* (BS) Bio, 1961, (MA) Bio, 1968, (MSE) Admin, 1986 Drake Univ; *cr:* Sci Teacher Martinsdale Cmmty Sch 1961-62; Instr Des Moines Area Comm Coll 1970; Teacher Ankeny Cmmty Sch 1962-; *ai:* Var Girls Cross Cntry 1979-88, Var Girls Track 1979-; Chm Health Curr Comm 1981-82, 1987-; Vertical Sci Curr Comm 1988-; Sci Dept Chm; NEA, IA St Ed Assn 1961-; Ankeny Ed Assn (Schlsp, Insurance, Building Rep) 1962-73; Polk Suburban Uniserve Unit, St Track Coaches Assn 1976-; Natl Fed Interscholastic Coaches Assn 1985-; United Meth Church 1962-; Masonic Lodge 1965-; Lambda Chi Alpha 1958-; Natl Sci Fnd Grant 1965-68; St Dept of Ed Substance Ed & Life Skills Curr Project 1988; IA St Univ Quality Circle Project Master Teacher 1987-; North Cntrl Steering Comm Track Coach of Yr 1981; Ankeny Schls Task Force; Dist Track Coach of Yr 1981-82; Dist Cross Cntry Coach of Yr 1981; Hawkeye Sci Fair St Judge; *office:* Ankeny Jr HS 105 NW Pleasant St Ankeny IA 50021

CRAFT, LINDA CLARK, Mathematics Teacher; *b:* Green Cty, KY; *m:* Prentiss N.; *c:* (BS) Elem Ed/Math, Campbellsville Coll 1963; (MA) Scndry Ed/Math W KY Univ 1967; *cr:* Math Teacher La Rue Cty HS 1964-77, La Rue Cty Jr HS 1977-; *ai:* Math Dept Chm; Math & Sci Club Spon; NEA, KY Ed Assn 1964-; NCTM 1988-89; United Meth Women VP 1989-; *home:* 795 Greensburg Rd Hodgenville KY 42748

CRAFT, ROSE MARY DAMORE, Science & Physical Ed Instr; *b:* Saginaw, MI; *m:* Daniel E.; *c:* Todd, Tina, Caryn; *ed:* (BS) Phys Ed, Cntrl MI Univ 1972; Post Grad Work Cntrl MI Univ 1976; Continuing Dual Cert Elem Ed, MI St Univ 1977-85; MI Comprehensive Ed Prgm Instr 1989; *cr:* Instr YWCA Aerobic/Fitness 1972, Our Lady of Perpetual Help 1972-73, St Casimir Sch 1973-74, St Paul Sch 1974-; *ai:* Coord Natl Geography Bee Local Level; Young Astronaut Club Adv; 7th-8th Grade Vlybl Coach; First Aid Instr; Beginning First Aid & Human Sexuality Curr Comm; MI Sci Teachers Assn 1989-, Nom Elem Sci Teacher of Yr Awd 1990; MI Health, Phys Ed, Recreation, Dance Assn 1972-; MI Athletic Assn 1980; NCEA, MI Cath Ed Assn 1972-; Amer Red Cross 1986-; Amer Legion Auxiliary 1983-; YMCA, YWCA 1986-; Alpha Gamma Delta House Chm 1970-; Athletic Assn Recognition Awd 1984; Girls Vlybl Coach of Yr Cath Lansing Youth League 1981; *office:* St Paul Sch 718 W Main St Owosso MI 48867

CRAFTON, GARY WAYNE, World History Teacher; *b:* Cape Girardeau, MO; *m:* Claudia Susan Eddington; *c:* William, Laura; *ed:* (BA) His/Soc Stud, Oral Roberts Univ 1973; (MA) His, Univ of Tulsa 1978; Doctoral Work Occupational & Adult Ed, OK St Univ; *cr:* Soc Stud Teacher Tulsa Chrstn Schls 1974-76; His/Hum Instr 1976-82, Coord Dept of Continuing Ed 1982-87 Oral Roberts Univ; Soc Stud Teacher Union HS 1987-; *ai:* Coach Academic Team; Spon NHS; Union Classroom Teachers Assn, OK Ed Assn, NEA 1987-; Civitan Intnl; Lions Intnl; *home:* 10905 S 85 East Ave Tulsa OK 74133

CRAIG, CLIFFORD, Team Leader Phys Ed Dept; *b:* Dayton, TN; *ed:* (BSED) Health, Phys Ed, 1978; (MED) Phys Ed, 1984 Univ of GA; *cr:* Phys Ed Teacher Greene Cty Sch System 1978-79; Phys Ed Teacher/Coach Madison Cty Sch System 1979-; *ai:* Page 1979-; US Navy 1969-73 Sailor Month 1972; Organizer and Coord of Madison Cty Novice Tennis Tournament 1984-1988; Coach of HS and Mid Sch Ftbl Bsktbl Track and Tennis Teams; Head Mid Sch Phys Ed Prgm; Masters Thesis; *office:* Madison County Mid Sch Comer Rd Danielsville GA 30633

CRAIG, DENISE SUZANNE, Teacher; *b:* St Louis, MO; *ed:* (BS) Phys Ed/Health, Cntrl MO St Univ 1982; *cr:* Stu Teacher Janet Marquis 1981-82, Slater Sch Dist 1982-84, Ft Osage Sch Dist 1984-; *ai:* Booster Club; IMS, Public Relations, Salary Comm; IMS & Curr Guide; PEM Club Officer in Coll, NEA, MAHPERD; Booster Club, Public Relations Comm; Adopt-A-Sch Prgm; Coaching Act; Stride-For-Life; Teacher of Yr 1989-; Outstanding Young Women of America 1988-89; Presidential Awd MAHPERD 1989; Dr Elois Pelton; Proclamations; Fall Convention Teacher of Yr; *home:* 1933 C Swope Independence MO 64057

CRAIG, DICIE W., Math Teacher; *b:* Athens, AL; *m:* Harvey J.; *c:* Waiian Q., Rhega V.; *ed:* (BS) Math, 1963; (MS) Math, 1973 AL A&M Univ; Math, Univ of AL; *cr:* Math Teacher New Hope Jr HS 1963-70; Clements HS 1970-; *ai:* Spon Jr Chrldr; NEA 1963-; AL Ed Assn 1963-; Limestone Cty Ed Assn Sec 1963-; AL New South Coalition Secy 1987-; Granted Battelles Summer Associateship HS Math Teachers; *home:* 912 Lucas St Athens AL 35611

CRAIG, EDNA BROWN, Word Processing/Cmptr Teacher; *b:* Eclectic, AL; *m:* Dan J. Jr.; *c:* Dan III, Dawna; *ed:* (BS) Bus Ed, AL A&M Univ 1968; (MS) Bus Ed, Hunter Coll 1977; (MS) Cmptr Ed, C W Post 1988; Theology, Bethel Bible Inst; *cr:* Teacher Mark Hopkins Ind Sch 33 1969-70; Adult Ed Teacher New Frontier Baptist Church 1975-76; Teacher Metropolitan Career Inst 1984; Adult Ed Teacher Uniondale HS 1986-87; Teacher J M Campos Ind Sch 71 1970-; *ai:* Prgms & Seminars Coord; Intnl Cncl for Cmptrs in Ed, Assn of Cmptr Educators Inc, Natl Cncl of Negro Women, Nassau Cty Bd of Elections; New Frontier Baptist Church (Bible Ed Teacher, Choir Mem); Town of Hempstead NY Town Supvr Candidate Election of 1989; *home:* 86 Elmwood Ave Hempstead NY 11550

CRAIG, JEFFERY ALAN, 5th Grade Teacher; *b:* Youngstown, OH; *ed:* (BS) Elem Ed, 1980, (MS) Elem Admin, 1984 Youngstown St Univ; *cr:* 4th-5th Grade Teacher Prospect Elem Sch 1980-; *ai:* HS Ftbl Coach; Jr HS Boys Bsktbl; Jr HS Girls Track; OH Ed Assn 1980-; NEA 1980-; Salem Ed Assn Pres 1988-89; 4-H Adv 1978-; *office:* Prospect Elem Sch 838 Prospect St Salem OH 44460

CRAIG, JENNIFER MANN, 11th Grade English Teacher; *b:* Burlington, VT; *m:* Dane Hamilton; *ed:* (BA) Eng, Univ of TX Arlington 1988; *cr:* Stu Teacher Arlington HS 1988; Eng Teacher Mansfield HS 1988-; *ai:* Key Club; Sr Class Spon; UIL Ready Writing Coach; Jr Class Spon; TSTA 1988-; Teacher of Month Twice; *office:* Mansfield H S 1520 Walnut Creek Dr Mansfield TX 76063

CRAIG, LANA ROBB, Spanish Teacher; *b:* East Liverpool, OH; *m:* Ronald; *ed:* (BA) Span, SUNY Cortland 1970; (MA) Span Lit, CA St Univ Los Angeles 1987; *cr:* Span Teacher Livonia HS 1970-73; Span Teacher/Chairperson Alverno HS 1975-88; Span Teacher Upland HS 1988-; *ai:* Span Club; NHS Faculty Selection Comm; *office:* Upland HS 564 W 11th St Box 1239 Upland CA 91786

CRAIG, MARTHA ELIZABETH, Chemistry Teacher; *b:* Danville, VA; *ed:* (AS) Sci, Danville Comm Coll 1983; (BS) Chem/Bio, Averett Coll 1986; *cr:* Chem/Bio Teacher Gretna HS 1986-; *ai:* Head Coach Gretna Sftbl Team; Stu Act Comm; Jr Class Spon; Sci Comm; NSTA 1985-; VA HS Coaches Assn; Spec Olympics Volunteer; *home:* Rt 2 Box 102-B Chatham VA 24531

CRAIG, PAT M., Reading/English/Speech Teacher; *b:* Akron, OH; *c:* John S.; *ed:* (BA) Elem Ed, Univ of Akron 1965; Upper Division in Lang Art & Mastery Teaching; *cr:* 4th Grade Teacher Hill Top Elem 1971-74; Basic Rdng/Eng Teacher Los Altos Jr HS 1974-76; 6th Grade/St Government Teacher Los Nogales Elem Sch 1976-81; Rdng/Eng/Speech Teacher Las Colinas Mid Sch 1981-; *ai:* Public Speaking Club Adv & Coach; AAUW 1972-; Optomist Club, Cmmty Service 1990; *office:* Las Colinas Mid Sch 5750 Fieldcrest Ave Camarillo CA 93010

CRAIG, VERNA PETRY, Home Economics Teacher; *b:* Houston, TX; *m:* Acie E. Jr.; *ed:* Julie A., Jennie L.; (BAT) Home Ec, Sam Houston St Univ 1971; *cr:* Home Ec Teacher Waller HS 1971-; *ai:* FHA Adv & Alumni/Assocs Adv; Campus Improvement Comm Mem; Voc Home Ec Teachers Assn of TX; St Paul Luth Church Sunday Sch Secy 1986-; Waller Ind Sch Dist & Voc Home Ec Teacher Assn of TX 15 Yr Service Awds; *office:* Waller HS 2402 Waller St Waller TX 77484

CRAIG, WILLIAM GORDON, JR., Jr HS Science Teacher; *b:* Flint, MI; *m:* Marie J. Young; *c:* William G. III, Heather J.; *ed:* (BS) Bio, Spring Arbor Coll 1969; (MA) Admin, Univ of MI 1977; Grad Stud ITIP, Clinical Supervision, Assertive Discipline, TET; *cr:* 9th Grade General Sci/General Math Teacher Mt Morris Consolidated Schls 1969-70; US Army 1971-73; Mid Sch Team Teacher 1974-77, Jr HS Sci Teacher 1978- Mt Morris Consolidated Schls; *ai:* Sch Improvement Comm; Chess Coach; Mt Morris Ed Assn Pres 1985-89; NEA Delegate 1990; MI Beekeepers Assn 1974-; Mt Morris Cntrl Fire Dept Mem 1984-87; Church (Treas, Trustee, Choir Mem); Precinct Delegate 1988; Parent-Teacher League Secy 1990; MI Grant Sch Energy Research; Journal of Bacteriology Article; *office:* Mt Morris Jr HS 12356 Walter St Mount Morris MI 48458

CRAIN, CATHEY MC GUIRE, Second Grade Teacher; *b:* Arcadia, LA; *m:* C. D. Jr.; *c:* Stacey M., Sean N.; *ed:* (BA) Elem Ed, 1979, (MA) Elem Ed, 1986 LA Tech Univ; LA Teacher Evaluation Prgm Assessors Trng; LA Teacher Evaluation Prgm Asst Trainers Prgm; *cr:* Teacher Crawford Elem Sch 1979-; *ai:* Admin Advisory Comm; Bienville Parish Pupil Progression Comm; Multiple Sclerosis Read-A-Thon Chairperson; Master Teacher Evaluation Prgm; 1st Grade Choir Dir 1988-; Child Care Comm Vice Chairperson; NEA, LA Assn of Educators 1979-; Delta Kappa Gamma Corresponding Secy 1985-; Service Club VP 1983-86, Outstanding Young Woman Jaycee Awd 1990; PTO Faculty Rep; Teacher of Yr Crawford Elem Sch 1982-83, 1986-87, 1989-; Teacher of Yr Bienville Parish Elem Division 1989-; *home:* 901 N Myrtle St Arcadia LA 71001

CRAIN, LOUISE KEMP, Second Grade Teacher; *b:* Franklinton, LA; *m:* Sedgie; *c:* James S. Slocum; *ed:* (BA) Elem Ed, Southeastern Univ 1955; Advanced Rdng Courses, Prof Courses; *cr:* 2nd Grade Teacher Delmont Elem 1955-57; 3rd Grade Teacher Almano Elem 1957-58; 2nd Grade Teacher Island Elem 1959-66; 1st Grade Teacher 1966-69, 2nd Grade Teacher 1969- Pine HS; *ai:* LTA Building Rep; Honors Comm & LA Rdng Sch Comm Chm; LA Rdng 1987-89; LA Teacher 1966-; NEA 1956-; PTA Membership Chm; *home:* Rt 8 Box 631 Franklinton LA 70438

CRAIN, PAMELA K., Business Teacher; *b:* Oklahoma City, OK; *m:* Earnest W.; *c:* Misti D., Jami L.; *ed:* (BA) Bus Ed, Cntrl St Univ 1983; Cmptr Applications; *cr:* Teacher Bishop McGuinness HS 1984, Choctaw HS 1984-86, Midwest City HS 1986-; *ai:* Chrldr, Stu Cncl, FCA, Jr Class Spon; OEA 1984-; OEBA 1988-; Teacher of Yr Choctaw HS 1985-86; *office:* Midwest City HS 213 Elm St Midwest City OK 73110

CRAIN, SUSAN KOHUTEK, Counselor & English IV Teacher; *b:* San Angelo, TX; *m:* Kenneth; *c:* Kelli, Kacy; *ed:* (BA) Eng/Poly Sci, 1972, (MA) Eng/Spec Ed, 1977, (MA) Guidance/Counseling, 1987 Angelo St Univ; Cert Lib Sci, TX Womans Univ; Drivers Ed, Hardin-Simmons Univ; *cr:* Eng Teacher Divide Sch 1973-75; Eng/Drivers Ed Teacher Blackwell HS 1975-77; Spec Ed Teacher Edison Jr HS 1977-82; Eng IV Teacher/Cnslr Cntrl HS 1982-; *office:* Cntrl HS 100 Cottonwood San Angelo TX 76901

CRAMBLIT, SHARON PARNELL, 5th Grade Soc Stud Teacher; *b:* Ironton, OH; *w:* Jack L. (dec); *c:* Amy J., Samuel T., Kerri L.; *ed:* (BS) Elem Ed, OH Univ 1973; (MA) Rdng Specialist, Marshall Univ 1977; Impact Trng Drugs & Alcohol; *cr:* Teacher St Lawrence Elem, Ironton City Schls; *ai:* Drug Free Schls Campbell Coord; IEA, NEA, OEA; *home:* 213 Means St Ironton OH 45638

CRAMER, ANN M., Social Studies Teacher; *b:* Findlay, OH; *ed:* (BS) Soc Stud Ed, OH St Univ 1971; (MA) Geography, 1977 Bowling Green Univ; Bus Courses, Bowling Univ; *cr:* Teacher Hopewell Loudon Sch 1971-; *ai:* 7th Grade Class Adv; OEA; *office:* Hopewell Loudon Sch Box 400 Bascom OH 44809

CRAMER, DEBORAH JEAN HENRIS, Primary Spec Ed Teacher; *b:* Morristown, NJ; *m:* William M.; *c:* Gary, Paula, Robert, Brian, Jared; *ed:* (BA) Speech/Lang Pathology, 1978; (MS) Comm Disorders, 1979 William Paterson Coll; Cert Spec Ed Montclair St Coll 1982; Cert Clinical Competence in Speech-Lang Pathology Amer Speech Lang Hearing Assn 1988; *cr:* K-8th Grade Speech Lang Therapist Liberty Twp Ind 1978-84; Allamuchy Sch 1978-84; Primary Spec Ed Allamuchy Twp Elem Sch 1984-; *ai:* Gymnastics Coach & Teacher Allamuchy; Amer Speech Lang/Hearing Assn Mem 1988-; Cncl Exceptional Children Mem 1982-88; Ortonbyslexia Society NJ Mem 1985-; 1986 Warren Cty Teacher of Yr; 1st Runner-Up NJ Teacher of Yr; *office:* Allamuchy Elem Sch P O Box J Allamuchy NJ 07820

CRAMER, LAURA SHELLEY, Principal; *b:* Antioch, CA; *m:* Rockwell C.; *c:* Michael P., Catherine; *ed:* (BA) Eng/His/Anthro, Univ of CA-Berkeley 1958; (MA) Ed, CA St Univ-Sacramento 1968; Ed Admin; *cr:* Teacher DOD Schls 1959-63, OEO Migrant Childrens Schls 1964-66, DOD HS 1973-75, St Louis HS 1976-78, Fairfax Cty Schls 1978-80, Radford Sch 1981-85; Admin Radford Sch 1985-; *ai:* Varsity Chrldr Spon; Assn for Supervision & Curr Dev; NASSP; Bus & Prof Women; *office:* Radford Schl 2001 Radford St El Paso TX 79903

CRAMER, LYNN, Math Teacher, Admin Assistant; *b:* Lamar, CO; *m:* Lillie Marie Jenkins; *c:* Jennifer, Jeffrey, Jeremy, Jeanna; *ed:* (BS) Math, Panhandle St Univ 1974; *cr:* Math Instr Campo Sch Dist RE-6 1974-; *ai:* Athletic Dir; Accountability/Planning Comm; Class Spon; Campo Parks & Recreation Dist Treas 1988-; *office:* Campo Sch Dist RE-6 PO Box 70 Campo CO 81029

CRAMER, VICKI MARIE (LOGAN), Mathematics Department Chair; *b:* Concordia, KS; *m:* Carl R.; *c:* Luke W.; *ed:* (BS) Scndry Ed/Math/Chem/Physics, 1985, (MS) Scndry Ed/Math, 1988 KS St Univ; *cr:* Math/Physics Teacher Blue Valley HS 1985-; *ai:* Chrldr & KS Jr Acad of Sci Spon; NCTM, KS Assn of Teachers of Math; ASCD 1987-89; NEA 1985-89; 7 Dolors Cath Church Mem; Phi Delta Kappa; Phi Kappa Phi; Tandy Cmptr Grant; *home:* 1408 Beechwood Terr Apt 9 Manhattan KS 66502

CRAMPTON, FRANK ROTZ, 5th Grade Teacher; *b:* New Brunswick, NJ; *m:* John E. Sr.; *c:* John E. Jr.; *ed:* (BA) Elem Ed, Glassboro St Coll 1961; (MS) Elem Math, St Francis Coll 1974; *cr:* 2nd Grade Teacher Sunnymead Sch 1961-62; Orland Sch 1962-63; 1st Grade Teacher Sunnymead Sch 1963 & 1964; K/5th Grade Teacher Bourbon Schl 1966 & 1974; 5th Grade Teacher Bethpage Sch 1976-; *ai:* Stu Cncl Rep Spon; Cty Math ReP; SCEA; NEA; TEA; Chaired Cty Math Curr; *office:* Bethpage Elem Sch 420 Old Hwy 31E Bethpage TN 37022

CRANCH, CEDRIC DARYL, Reading/English Teacher; *b:* Abington, PA; *m:* Jeri Jones; *c:* Chesley Brook; *ed:* (BA) Soc of Religion, Amherst Coll 1970; (MA) Elem Ed, 1972, (EDD) Ed Admin, 1990 N AZ Univ; *cr:* Phys Ed Dir Bryn Athyn Church Elem Sch 1970-71; 4th Grade Teacher Catalina Foothills Schls 1973-74; Asst Dean of Stus E AZ Coll 1974-76; Teacher Safford Jr HS 1976-; *ai:* Ftbl Coach; Yrbk, Journalism, Photography Adv; Dist Curr & Mid Sch Transition Comms; Cmptr Instr; Bryn Athyn Fire Dept Lieutenant 1964-72, Outstanding Fireman 1967; Girls ASA Sftbl Coach 1987; *office:* Safford Mid Sch 734 11th St Safford AZ 85546

CRANDALL, ARLENE B., School Psychologist; *b:* Brooklyn, NY; *ed:* (BA) Psych, Marywood Coll 1978; (MS) Sch Psych, St Johns Univ 1983; (PHD) Educl Admin, Long Island Univ 1989; *cr:* Teacher Holy Trinity HS 1978-82; Sch Psychologist The Shield Inst 1983-85, Smithtown HS East 1985-; *ai:* Sr Class Adv; Var Badminton Coach; Crisis Intervention Team Mem; NY Assn of Sch Psychologists (Pres Elect 1987-88, Pres 1988-); NY St Cncl of Pupil Services (Delegate 1988-89, Pres 1989-); Natl Assn of Sch Psychologists Nationally Certified Sch Psychologist, Amer Assn of Suicidology, Assn for Curr & Dev, Amer Assn of Univ Women, Natl Assn of Female Execs, Nassau Cty Psychological Assn; Natl Organization for Women; Article Published in Eric 1987; Phi Delta Kappa, Psi Chi, Kappa Gamma Pi, Alpha Mu Gamma, Delta Epsilon Sigma; *home:* 26 Smith St Glen Cove NY 11542

CRANDALL, CLAUDE, JR., Social Studies Teacher; *b:* Greenville, NC; *m:* Teddie H.; *ed:* (BA) Amer His, 1975, (MA) Amer His, 1977, (TC) Soc Stud, 1978 NC Cntrl Univ; Grad Stud Duke Univ 1981, Appalachian Univ 1983; *cr:* 9th-12th Grade Soc Stud Teacher Hillside HS 1979-; *ai:* Home Sports Ticket Seller; Jr Achievement; Chess Club Adv 1987-89; Asst Coach Sftbl 1984-85, Girls Tennis 1985-86; NEA 1979-; Cubs Scouts Cub Master 1981-88; Tennis Club Secy 1982-89; PTSA Secy 1982-83; *office:* Hillside HS 1900 Concord St Durham NC 27707

CRANDALL, DAVID C., 5th/6th Grade Teacher; *b:* Susanville, CA; *m:* Pamela Lynn Bernal; *c:* Seanna, Daman; *ed:* (BA) Psych, CA St Univ Chico 1966; *cr:* 4th/5th Grade Teacher Parkview Elem 1967-73; 4th/5th/6th Grade Teacher Marigold Elem 1973-80, Neal Dow Elem 1980-; *ai:* Stu Government Adv; Yrbk Adv; Master Teacher in Teacher Trng Prgm; Lead Teacher Neal Dow Sch; NEA 1967-; CA Teachers Assn 1967-; Chico Unified Teachers Assn 1967-; Chico Youth Soccer League Coach 1980-84; Chico Youth Soccer League Bd Secy 1984-86; *home:* 2640 San Jose St Chico CA 95926

CRANDALL, MAURICE EMIL, Secondary English Teacher; *b:* Indianapolis, IN; *m:* Betty L. Schmidt; *c:* Laurice K. Cowan, Melody L., Starla M.; *ed:* (BMUSED) Music Ed, Andrews Univ 1963; Grad Work Eng, Lib; *cr:* 7th-10th Grade Music Teacher Indianapolis Jr Acad 1958-62; Music Teacher/Lib Mt Ellis Acad 1963-68, Milo Acad 1968-73; Eng/Music Teacher Enterprise Acad 1973-80; Eng/Bible Teacher Bass Acad 1980-83; Eng Teacher/Lib Blue Mountain Acad 1983-; *ai:* Band Supvr; Sr Class Spon; Curr Comm; Eng Dept Head; NTE 1989-; ASDA 1985-; Teacher Certificate Awd.

CRANDALL, RONALD W., History Teacher/Dept Head; *b:* Springfield, MO; *m:* Vivien A.; *c:* Elizabeth, Courtney; *ed:* (BSED) His, 1966, (MSED) Scndry Ed/His, 1976 SW MO St; Grad Stud; *cr:* 7th/8th Grade Teacher Sullivan Public Schls 1966-70, Owensville Public Schls 1970-79, Logan Rogersville 1979-; *ai:* MO St Teachers Local Pres 1978-79; Wesley United Meth Church Society Comm; Logan-Rogersville Teacher of Yr 1987-88; *office:* Logan-Rogersville Schls 208-212 Mill St Rogersville MO 65742

CRANDELL, SHARON MARIE, 5th-8th Grade Math/Cmptr Sci; *b:* St Louis, MO; *c:* Brent; *ed:* (BS) Elem Ed, E Cntrl Univ 1982; Cmptr Technology & Child Care; *cr:* 6th Grade Rdng/Sci/7th Grade Math Teacher Purcell Mid Sch 1982-87; K/7th/8th Grade Math Teacher 1987-88, 7th/8th Grade Math Teacher 1988-89, 7th/8th Grade Math/Rdng/Spelling Teacher 1989- Pittsburg Public Sch; *ai:* Gifted & Talented Coord; Frosh Spon; OEA 1982-; *office:* Pittsburg Public Sch PO Box 200 Pittsburg OK 74560

CRANE, BRIAN WILLIAM, Mathematics Dept Chair; *b:* Syracuse, NY; *m:* Victoria Elizabeth Suplee; *c:* Matthew; *ed:* (BS) Math/Scndry Ed, Towson St Univ 1974; Masters Equivalent/Ed 1980; Several Courses, Wkshps; *cr:* Teacher Severn River Jr HS 1974-78; Math Teacher/Dept Chm S River Sr HS 1978-82; Math Resource Mem Anne Arundel Cty Bd of Ed 1982-83; Teacher S River Evening HS 1980-88, S River Summer Sch Center 1980-; Math Teacher/Dept Chm Broadneck Sr HS 1983-; Cmptr/Bus/Math Instr Anne Arundel Comm Coll 1984-; *ai:* Math Club Adv; MD Math League Coord; Church Contemporary Music Singer 1987-; Newmast Honors Teacher NASA Summer 1987; Nominee Presidential Awd for Math Teacher; Geometry/Elem Functions-AB-BC Calculus Curr Comms; *office:* Broadneck Sr HS 1265 Green Holly Dr Annapolis MD 21401

CRANE, ELIZABETH ANN, Third Grade Teacher; *b:* New York, NY; *ed:* (BA) Biological Sci, 1966, (MA) Early Chldhd Ed, 1978 San Jose St Univ; Math, Cmptr, Sci Inst San Jose St Univ 1984; Self-Esteem & Responsibility Seminar Frank Siccone & Jack Canfield 1987; Intnl Congress of Math Educators Brisbane Australia 1984 & Budapest Hungary 1984, 1988; Bill Martin-Literacy for Learning Conference Boston 1989; *cr:* 2nd Grade Teacher 1967-79, 1st-2nd Grade Combination Teacher 1979-80, 2nd-3rd Grade Combination Teacher 1980-81, 3rd Grade Teacher 1981- Baker Sch; *ai:* Written Lang, Mentor Teacher Selection, Spelling, Math, New Teacher Interviewing, Lang Arts, Sch Site Cncl, Discipline Handbook Comms; Santa Clara Valley Math Assn Elem Exec Rep to Bd 1979-83; Local & St Natl Teachers Assn, Math Groups, Intnl Rdng Groups Mem; St Self-Esteem Group, Local Critical Thinking Group Mem; Homeowneres Assn (VP, Pres) 1983-84; *office:* Gussie M Baker Elem Sch 4845 Bucknall Rd San Jose CA 95130

CRANE, MERRELL C., JR., Third Grade Teacher; *b:* Bluefield, WV; *ed:* (BS) Geography, 1974, (BA) Elem Ed, 1976 Brigham Young Univ; (MA) Curr/Instruction, 1983, (CAGS) Admin, 1989 VA Tech; *cr:* 6th Grade Teacher Richlands Mid Sch 1976-78; 2nd Grade Teacher Dudley Primary Sch 1979-80; 4th Grade Teacher 1981-87, 5th Grade Teacher 1988-89, 3rd Grade Teacher 1990- Springville Elem; *ai:* PTA Exec Bd; Part Time Travel Cnslr Bluefield AAA; Mem Springville Boosters Club; Tour Guide for Historic Bramwell Homes Tour; VA Ed Assn 1976-; NEA 1976; Tazewell Ed Assn Exec Bd 1989-; *home:* Rt 4 Box 519a Bluefield WV 24701

CRANE, THOMAS RICHARD, 9th Grade Soc Stud Teacher; *b:* Camden, NJ; *ed:* (BS) Soc Stud, 1963, (MA) General Prof Ed, 1968 Seton Hall Univ; *cr:* His Teacher 1963-67, Asst Prin Mc Clenaghan HS 1967-69; Prin West Florence 1970-72; His Teacher Washington Township HS 1973-; *ai:* Dist Comm of TN; Former Bsktbl & HS Academic Bowl Coach; SC Ed Assn 1963-71; NASSP 1969-72; NEA, NJEA, WTEA 1972-88; SC Bsktbl Coach of Yr 1967; NJ Teacher of Yr 1986-87; *office:* Washington Township HS Hurffville Cross Keys Rd Sewell NJ 08080

CRANE, WILLIAM BRUCE, History Teacher; *b:* Preston, ID; *m:* Shauna Rae Thomas; *c:* Bethany R.; *ed:* (BS) Scndry Ed/His/Span, UT St Univ 1985; *cr:* His Teacher Logan HS 1987-; *ai:* Asst Academic Olympiad & Academic Decathalon Coach; Mission Statement Comm; Logan Ed Assn, UT Ed Assn, NEA 1987-; Study at Natl Hum Center 1989; Rep Dist Conference Coalition for Essential Schls 1988; *office:* Logan HS 1 W 1 S Logan UT 84321

CRANFIELD, SUSAN BATEMAN, English Department Chair; *b:* Montgomery, AL; *m:* Alvin Eugene; *c:* June Lambert, Jim Searcy; *ed:* (BS) Eng/Scndry Ed, Huntington Coll 1966; (MED) Eng/Scndry Ed, Auburn Univ 1972; *cr:* Teacher Baldwin Jr HS 1966-68; Cnslr AL Voc Rehabilitation Service 1968-71; Teacher Prattville HS 1973-; Adjunct Instr Auburn Univ 1980-; *ai:* Chairperson Steering Comm Accreditation Self-Stud; Cty Textbook Comm; Sch Advisory Cncl; Judge Fitzgerald Museum Contest; Autaugo Cty Teachers Assn (Mem 1972-, Editing Constitution 1989); Prattville Service League Sustaining Mem 1972-78; St Marks Church (Altar Guild 1987-) 1971-; *home:* 217 Wetumpka St Prattville AL 36067

CRANFILL, JEFFREY HAMILTON, Director of Bands; *b:* Atlanta, GA; *m:* Saundra Jenyce Brett; *ed:* (BM) Instrumental Music, 1985, Master of Music Instrumental Music, 1990 GA St Univ; *cr:* Orch Asst Dir 1983-87, Brass Instr 1981- 1st Baptist Church; Band Dir Colonial Hills Chrstn Sch 1984-; *ai:* Exec Comm Colonial Hills Chrstn Schls; Phi Beta Mu Outstanding Instrumental Music Ed Awd 1985; Chrstn Instrumental Dir Assn, GA Music Educators Assn, Music Educators Natl Conference 1984-; Omicron Delta Kappa 1985-; 1st Baptist Church (Sanctuary Orch 1979, Pres 1988-89) Tara Winds Cmmty Bands Mem; *office:* Colonial Hills Chrstn Sch 2134 Newman St East Point GA 30344

CRANFORD, AARON REESE, Earth/Life Sci Teacher/Coach; *b:* San Angelo, TX; *m:* Merilyn Loyd; *c:* Bruce, Stacy Cranford Shepherd, Del, Layne, Kelly; *ed:* (BA) Phys Ed, TX Western Coll 1963; *cr:* Sci Teacher Lockhart Jr HS 1986-; *ai:* Ftbl, Bsktbl, Track Coach; TX HS Coaches Assn 1986-; TX Classroom Teachers Assn, Sci Teachers Assn of TX; Lions 1989; *home:* 911-B S Medina Lockhart TX 78644

CRANFORD, RODNEY LYNN, HS Mathematics Teacher; *b:* Gadsden, AL; *m:* Judy Fleming; *c:* Tracy, Brian; *ed:* (BS) Bus Ad, Jacksonville St Univ 1976; Working Towards Masters Sch Admin, Pensacola Chrstn Coll; *cr:* Teacher/Admin Coosa Chrstn Sch 1982-; *ai:* HS Bsktbl & Girls Bsktbl Coach; Beta Club Spon; *office:* Coosa Chrstn Sch Rt 3 Box 140 Gadsden AL 35901

CRANOR, ELS GRIJSEELS, Geography Teacher; *b:* The Haque, Netherlands; *c:* Jim, Bert, Earl; *ed:* (BS) Elem Ed, 1966, (MS) Elem Ed, 1967 St Teachers Coll Haque Netherlands; (BS) Elem Ed, A S Jonesboro AR 1982; *cr:* Teacher Haque Public Schls 1967-71, Forrest City Sch Dist #7 1982-; *ai:* Fr Foreign Lang Teacher; AR Cncl for Soc Stud Mem 1989-; *office:* Forrest City Mid Sch 1133 N Division Forrest City AR 72335

CRAVENS, DORCAS WILLIAMS, English Teacher; *b:* Indianapolis, IN; *m:* Mark A. Jr.; *c:* John E. Johnson Jr., Mark A. V; *ed:* (BA) Eng, IN Cntrl Coll/Univ of Indianapolis 1956; (MS) Ed, IN Univ 1967; *cr:* Eng Teacher Crispus Attucks HS 1959-65, Sch #56 1965-71, Sch #81 1971-73, Shortridge HS 1973-80, George Washington HS 1980-; *ai:* IN Ed Assn, IN Eng Teachers Assn, NCTE; *office:* George Washington HS 2215 W Washington Indianapolis IN 46222

CRAVENS, MICKEY B., Teacher; *b:* May, TX; *m:* H. L. Jr.; *c:* Lamar, Vikki; *ed:* (BS) Elem Ed, 1956, (MED) Scndry Ed, 1957 Howard Payne Univ; Working Towards Doctorate Univ of N CO 1959-; *cr:* Teacher Star Ind Sch Dist 1957-58, May Ind Sch Dist 1959-61, Brownwood Ind Sch Dist 1979-; *ai:* Textbook Selection, Curr, Sch Calendar Comm; TX Classroom Teachers Assn, Amer Assn of Univ Women; *home:* 2108 Southside Dr Brownwood TX 76801

CRAVER, JUDY FOSTER, Mathematics Teacher; *b:* North Wilkesboro, NC; *m:* Herman Glenn; *c:* Nathan Glenn; *ed:* (BS) Math, Appalachian St Univ 1972; *cr:* Teacher Welcome Elem Sch 1972-82, Cntrl Davidson Sr HS 1982-; *ai:* High IQ, Math Team, Quiz Bowl Coach; Prom Spon; SAT Improvement Comm; NC Assn of Gifted Teachers 1989-; NC Cncl Teachers of Math 1972-; NC Creative Writing Summer Inst; Logo Summer Inst; *office:* Cntrl Davidson Sr HS Rt 6 Box 2265 Lexington NC 27292

CRAWFORD, ANN JONES, 7th/8th Grade Teacher; *b:* Rockville Centre, NY; *c:* John, Patrick; *ed:* (BA) His, St Marys Coll 1972; (MS) Ed, Purdue 1980; *cr:* 1st Grade Teacher St Vincents Sch 1972-73; 7th-8th/11th-12th Grade Soc Stud Teacher Bishop Noll Inst 1973-79; 7th-8th Grade Soc Stud/Lang Art Teacher Olph Sch 1985-; *ai:* Jr HS Level Coord 1968-89; Various Fundrasing Act Chm 1986-89; Video News Prgm Spon; NCEA; Woodmar Child Dev Center VP 1982-85; Citizens for Crawford Treas 1975-89; *home:* 9133 Foliage Ln Munster IN 46321

CRAWFORD, ANTHONY D., History Teacher/Athletic Dir; *b:* Lynnwood, CA; *m:* Betty L. Engblom; *c:* Sarah A., Douglas L.; *ed:* (BS) Elem Ed, OR Coll of Ed 1980; Working Towards MS Portland St Univ; *cr:* 6th Grade Teacher Knight Elem Sch 1980-85; Teacher/Athletic Dir Ackerman Jr HS 1985-; *ai:* Supts Advisory & Sch Dist Bi-ling Ed Comm Rep; Drug & Alcohol Crisis Intervention Team Rep; Japanese Exch Stus Host Coord; Canby Ed Assn Rep 1983, 1989; Williamette River League Pres; St Vincent de Paul Society Pres 1988-; St Patricks Ed Dept Teacher-Rep 1982-; Canby Booster Club Mem 1983-; Participant Olympic Torch Relay 1984; Ten Yr Service Pin Canby Elem Sch Dist; - *office:* Ackerman Jr HS 350 SE 13th AVe Canby OR 97013

CRAWFORD, CAROL RUTH (HOLLE), Kindergarten Teacher; *b:* Chicago, IL; *m:* Brian G.; *c:* Chad; *ed:* (BS) Elem Ed, NW MO St Univ 1977; *cr:* 4th-6th Grade Summer Sch Teacher NW MO St Univ Lab Sch 1977; Kndgtn Teacher Pleasant Hill Primary Sch 1977-; *ai:* Pleasant Hill Cmmty Teachers Assn (Secy

1988-89, Mem 1977-); MNEA 1977-; Pleasant Hill PTA Lifetime Membership; *office:* Pleasant Hill Primary Sch Eklund Dr Pleasant Hill MO 64080

CRAWFORD, CAROL VEAZEY, Science Teacher; *b:* San Diego, CA; *m:* Robert Ervin; *c:* Chelsea; *ed:* (BS) Sci/Elem Ed, Univ of TN Knoxville 1978; (MED) Sci Ed, 1980, Sci Ed, 1986 Memphis St Univ; *cr:* Teacher Millington Cntrl Elem 978-; *ai:* Sci Fair; TN/NASA Space Week; NSTA 1988-; 1989-90 TEA/NASA Space Week Winning Sch; Career Level III (Master Teacher) 1986-; *office:* Millington Central Elem Schl 4954 Easley Millington TN 38053

CRAWFORD, CATHY JO, Mathematics Dept Head/Teacher; *b:* Borger, TX; *ed:* (BS) Math, 1980, (MST) Math, 1985 Tarleton St Univ; Grad Stud; *cr:* Teacher Godley HS 1980-83; Teaching Asst Tarleton St Univ 1983-85; Teacher Springtown HS 1985-; *ai:* Spon Jr Engineering Tech Society; UIL Coach/Sci; Textbook Comm; ATPE, STAT, AAPT, NSTA; *office:* Springtown HS 100 Pojo Dr Springtown TX 76082

CRAWFORD, CHARLOTTE AYERS, Sixth Grade Teacher; *b:* Hancock Cty, TN; *ed:* (BA) Elem Ed, 1962, (MA) Elem Ed, 1964 W Carolina Univ; *cr:* Teacher Aycock Elem Sch 1962-66, Vance Elem Sch 1967-71, Tryon Elem Sch 1971-74, Hill Street Mid Sch 1974-; *ai:* Yrbk Staff; Faculty Cncl; NEA, NC Assn of Educators 1962-; *office:* Hill Street Mid Sch 125 Hill St Asheville NC 28801

CRAWFORD, DAVID PAUL, Dept of Eng-Teacher/Counsel; *b:* Mc Keesport, PA; *c:* Dylan, Jessica; *ed:* (BA) Eng/Literature Ed, 1970, (BS) Bus Admin, 1971 Morehead St Univ; (MA) Counseling & Guidance, Xavier Univ 11987; Rdng in Remedial Ed; Rdng Consultant Ed; *cr:* Eng Teacher Piketon HS 1971-74; Rdng Consultant Western Local Schls 1975-76; Eng/Literature/Rdng Teacher 1983-, Cnslr 1987 Piketon HS; *ai:* Class Adv; Future Teachers of Amer Adv; Stars Core Adv; OTEA 1983-; OSCA 1987-; Right to Read (Dir 1984) 1983; Masonic Lodge 1986-; Shrine 1987-; Articles and Poems to Scholastic Publications; *office:* Piketon H S West St Piketon OH 45661

CRAWFORD, DORIS GREER, Teacher of Gifted; *b:* Philadelphia, MS; *m:* Therman C.; *ed:* (BS) Elem Ed, Jackson St Univ 1961; (MS) Elem Ed, Prairie View A&M Univ 1978; Gifted Courses, TX Women Univ & Univ of Tx; Several Wkshps; *cr:* 1st/2nd Grade Teacher Neshoba Cty Schls 1961-67; 5th Grade Teacher 1969-76, Gifted Teacher 1976-89, Gifted Resource/Catalyst Teacher 1989- Dallas Ind Sch Dist; *ai:* Cochran Sch Soc Comm Chairperson; Demonstration Classroom Teacher for New Teachers of Gifted Dallas Ind Sch Dist 1986-89; Classroom Teachers of Dallas 1969-; NEA Life Mem; TX St Teachers Assn; Gifted Children Monthly, Quarterly, Understanding our Gifted; Cedar Crest Evangelistic Church (Circle Leader 1985, Supervisor of Acolytes 1988-); Cochran PTA Prgm Dir; Outstanding Teacher 1980-81; Cochran Sch Teacher of Yr 1981-82; The Bulletin Bd Shop 1989-; *home:* 3424 Kiesthill Dr Dallas TX 75233

CRAWFORD, ELIZABETH WEBB, Eng Teacher/Forensics Coach; *b:* Atlanta, GA; *m:* Brent Overman; *ed:* (BA) Eng/His, Agnes Scott Coll 1986; Teaching Cert W GA Coll 1989; Working Towards MA in Eng, W Ga Coll; Ger Cert Coursework Berry Coll 1990; *cr:* Teacher Coosa HS 1987-; *ai:* Forensics Coach; Jr Class Spon; GA Assn of Educators, NEA 1988-; Floyd Cty Republican Party Vice Chairwoman 1988-; 7th Dist Republican Party Dist Comm Mem 1989-; St Republican Party Comm 1989-; Sara Hightower Regional Lib & Floyd Cty Lib Bd of Dir 1989-; *office:* Coosa HS 4454 Alabama Hwy Rome GA 30161

CRAWFORD, JANE THROWER, Reading Teacher/Dept Chairman; *b:* Wilmington, DE; *m:* Jack Eidson; *c:* Jennifer A., Jacob A., J. Seth; *ed:* (BA) Eng, Winthrop Coll 1974; Working Toward Masters in Educl Admin; *cr:* Remedial Rdng Teacher Gaffney HS 1974-75, Cherokee HS 1978-80; Eng Teacher Boiling Springs HS 1975-78; Rdng Teacher Newberry Jr HS 1980-; *ai:* Rdng Dept Chm; Newberry Jr HS Grant Comm; Newberry Cty Lang Arts Comm; Technology Comm of Newberry Cty; NEA, SC Ed Assn 1986-; SC Rdng Assn 1987-; Mt Hermon Luth Church (WECLA Pres 1983-89, Cncl 1989-); *home:* PO Box 215 Peak SC 29122

CRAWFORD, JANET WILLIAMS, Guidance Counselor; *b:* East Orange, NJ; *c:* Dennis Jr., Robyn, Robina; *ed:* (BA) Psych. Caldwell Coll, Kean Coll 1977; (MED) Counseling/Spec Service Trenton Coll 1980; *cr:* Supv Cnslr New Well Drug & Rc Ab Center 1978-79; Adult HS Cnslr E O Bernie L Edmunson Ct 1979-84; Guidance Cnslr Orange HS 1985-; *ai:* Stu Cncl Adv 1987-89; 12 Together Prgm Facilitate 1988-90; Caldwell Coll EOF Adv Bd 1984-; NJ Guidance Cnslr Assn 1984-; New Urban League Chapter; Who Whos Young Amer 1988.

CRAWFORD, JENNELL M., 5th Grade Teacher; *b:* Lafayette, AL; *m:* George R.; *c:* Kelvin, Kristie; *ed:* (AA) Sci, Gibbs Jr Coll 1965; (BA) Phys Ed & Health, Talladega Coll 1967; (BA) Elem Ed, GA St Univ; Addl Studies GA St Univ; *cr:* 5th Grade Teacher 1967-70; 2nd Grade Teacher 1971-72 Eastisde Elem; Phys Ed Teacher Mount Carmel Elem 1973-76; Phys Ed/5th Grade Teacher L W Burnett Elem 1978-; *ai:* 4-H Club Local Adv; GA Assn of Ed; NEA; Douglas Cty Assn of Ed; NAACP; L W Burnett Teacher of Yr; *office:* L W Burnett Elem Sch 8277 Connally Dr Douglasville GA 30134

CRAWFORD, LIBBY BYARS, 1st Grade Teacher; *b:* Woodruff, SC; *m:* Ted Lee; *c:* Amy, Kim; *ed:* (BA) Elem Ed, N Greenville 1971; (BS) Elem Ed, Lander 1973; (ME) Ed, Converse 1983; *cr:* 3rd Grade Teacher FL St Sch 1973-74; 1st Grade Teacher Ford Sch 1979-; *ai:* Palmetto St; *home:* Rt 1 Box 186 Enoree SC 29335

CRAWFORD, LINDA CARTER, Literature/Reading Teacher; *b:* Marion, SC; *m:* William E.; *c:* Frances, Carroll, Jobey; *ed:* (BS) Elem Ed, Univ of SC 1978; *cr:* Secy Brunson Elem 1968-75; Teacher Hampton Elem 1978-; *ai:* Evergreen Garden Club Pres 1968-78; Brunson Civic Club 1970-71; *home:* 304 Railroad Ave Brunson SC 29911

CRAWFORD, MARILYN LONG, Guidance Counselor; *b:* Sheffield, AL; *m:* Clifford Orr; *c:* Regina C. Golden, Yolanda K.; *ed:* (BS) Bus Ed, TN St Univ 1956; (MED) Office Ed, 1968, Guidance, 1979 Memphis St Univ; *cr:* Bus Ed Teacher Woodstock HS 1956-65; Voc Office Ed Teacher Mitchell HS 1965-71; Cooperative Office Ed Teacher Hillcrest HS 1971-; *ai:* Stu Cncl & Stu Leadership Group Spon; Adopt-A-Sch Coord; Guidance, Prof Leadership, Faculty Advisory Comms; Memphis Ed Assn Teacher Study Cncl Regional Secy 1985-86; Delta Phi Epsilon Secy 1980-81; Memphis Guidance Assn Chm 1986-87; NEA, TN Ed Assn; TN Guidance Assn Dropout Prevention Comm; Memphis Black Bus Assn Bd of Dir; Memphis Mental Health & Drug Abuse Cncl; Delta Sigma Theta Parliamentarian 1985-86, Service Awd; Phi Delta Kappa 1987-89; St Augustine Parish Cncl 1987-88; Book Published; Memphis Rotary Teacher Initiative Grant; *home:* 1880 Fairmeade Ave Memphis TN 38114

CRAWFORD, MARY RANDLEMAN, Fourth Grade Teacher; *b:* Weiser, ID; *m:* Chester P.; *c:* Cheryl A. Tveidt, Mary F. Pederson; *ed:* (BS) Elem Ed, Univ of ID 1969; Grad Stud Boise St Univ, Brigham Young Univ, Univ of ID; *cr:* 3rd/4th Grade Teacher North Elem 1969-70; 1st Grade Teacher New Plymouth Elem 1970-71; 1st/3rd/4th Grade Teacher North Elem 1971-74; 4th Grade Teacher Base Intermediate 1974-75; Kndgtn/4th Grade Teacher West Elem 1976-; *ai:* NEA, ID Ed Assn, Mountain Home Ed Assn 1969-; Mountain Home Hospital Auxiliary 1985-87; *office:* West Elem Sch 415 W 2nd N Mountain Home ID 83647

CRAWFORD, REBECCA ANN, Consumer/Homemaking Dept Chair; *b:* Baton Rouge, LA; *ed:* (BA) Home Ec Ed Teacher, Univ of Houston 1976; (MED) Home Ec Ed, Sam Houston St Univ 1981; Early Chldhd Ed; *cr:* Teacher Sam Rayburn HS 1976-; Part Time Instr San Jacinto Coll 1983-; *ai:* FHA; Sr Class Spon 1981-; Voc Home Ec Teachers Assn of TX 1985-; Delta Kappa Gamma 2nd VP 1990; *office:* Sam Rayburn HS 2121 Cherrybrook Ln Pasadena TX 77502

CRAWFORD, RUBY BARKER, Kindergarten Teacher; *b:* Reed, OK; *ed:* (BS) Home Ec, OK Coll for Women 1963; (MS) Elem Ed, SW OK St Univ Weatherford 1966; Family Finance, OK Univ; Early Chldhd/Elem Ed, OK Univ & Cameron Univ; *cr:* Voc Home Ec Teacher Canute Public Sch 1963-66, Checotah Public Sch 1966-70; Kndgtn Teacher L Mendel Rivers Elem 1970-; *ai:* Child Dev Lab & Health Ed Related Occupations Advisory Bd; In-Service Meetings Departmental Chm; Supvr of Stu Teachers; OK Natl Ed Assn, Jackson Cty Ed Assn (Mem, VP, Secy, Treas, Delegate at Large) 1976-83; USAO Alumni Assn Life Mem; Altus Ed Assn Building Rep; PTA Mem; Amer Bus Womens Assn (VP, Secy, Historian, Bulletin Chm) 1976-85; Jackson Cty Extention Dept Advisory Bd; Kappa Kappa Iota; 4-H Exhibit Judge; Cancer Bazaar, Cystic Fibrosis Fund Drive; Sunday Sch Teacher; Teacher of Yr 1980; Bus & Prof Womens & Metropolitan Life Schlsps; *home:* 2504 Pawnee Altus OK 73521

CRAWFORD, THERESA F., Third Grade Teacher; *b:* Harrison, TX; *m:* Prince L.; *c:* Debra, Terry, Larry, Ricky, Christopher; *ed:* (BA) Eng, Wiley Coll & Pepperdine 1949; *cr:* Substitute Teacher Immaculate Conception 1967-69, Blessed Sacrament 1967-69; Teacher Immaculate Heart of Mary Sch 1969-; *ai:* Soc Stud Sci Coord; Church (Secy 1983-89, Church Bd Treas 1987-); After Sch Girls Bsktbl Awd 1978-82; *office:* Immaculate Heart of Mary Sch 1055 N Alexandria Los Angeles CA 90029

CRAWFORD, TRACEY C., Mathematics Department Chair; *b:* Aberdeen, SD; *ed:* (BA) Psych, Univ of CA San Diego 1982; Math, San Diego St Univ 1984; Grad Courses Math; *cr:* Math Instr San Diego City Schls, Merced Coll; Math Dept Chairperson Le Grand HS; *ai:* NCTM.

CRAWFORD, WALLIE M., Science Teacher; *b:* Houston, TX; *ed:* (BSE) Bio, S AR Univ 1966; (MS) Interdisciplinary Stud, E TX St Univ Texarkana 1984; *cr:* 7th-12th Grade Sci Teacher Harmony Grove HS 1966-67; 7th-8th Grade Sci Teacher Webster Jr HS 1967-75; 7th-9th Grade Sci Teacher Stanton Jr HS 1976-77; 8th Grade Sci Teacher Aransas Pass Jr HS 1979-80; Chem/Physics/Phys Sci Teacher De Kalb HS 1980-; *ai:* Stu Cncl Adv; UIL Sci, Calculator, Number Sense Spon; Dept Head; E TX St Univ Texarkana Stu Teacher Supvr; Assn of TX Prof Educators; Sci Teachers Assn of TX; TX Excl Awd for Outstanding HS Teachers; *office:* De Kalb HS 421 SW Fannin St De Kalb TX 75559

CRAWLEY, OLIVIA PRESTWOOD, Second Grade Teacher; *b:* Roeton, AL; *m:* Larry; *c:* Jaine; *ed:* (BS) Elem Ed, Troy St Univ Troy 1966; (MS) Elem Ed, Troy St Univ Dothan 1989; *cr:* Teacher Mixson Elem 1966-68, Ariton HS 1968-; *ai:* Chrldrs Spon 1986-87; NEA, AL Ed Assn 1966-; *home:* Rt 2 Box 258AA Brundidge AL 36010

CRAYCROFT, PETER RAMBICUR, Journalism Teacher; *b:* Sherman, TX; *m:* Karen Ann Casaday; *c:* Katie L., Greg, Brenna; *ed:* (BJ) Journalism, Univ of TX Austin 1979; *cr:* Journalism Teacher John Marshall HS 1981-84, Sidney Lanier HS 1984-; *ai:* Jr Var Bsbl Coach & Asst Var Bsbl Coach; Young Life Faculty Spon; TX Assn of Journalism Educators St Dir 1982-83; Young Life Austin Comm Mem 1986-; Sunday Murray TX St UIL Champion Headline Writer 1987; Pat Murray ILPC Tops in TX Feature Story 1984; Anne Frahm ILPC Tops in TX Page 1 Design 1985; Michelle Regnier ILPC Tops in TX Editorial 1985; *office:* Lanier HS 1201 Peyton Gin Rd Austin TX 78758

CRAYTON, DARRELL KEITH, Mathematics Teacher; *b:* Austin, TX; *ed:* (BA/AS) Math/Occupation Ed, SW TX St Univ 1985; Grad Stud Scndry Admin Ed TESA; *cr:* Substitute Teacher Austin Ind Sch Dist 1982-85; In Sch Suspension Monitor Anderson HS 1985-86; Scndry Math Teacher Rice Scndry Sch 1986-88, LBJ HS 1988-; *ai:* Teenage Mathematicians Club; Asst Ftbl, Track, Soccer Coach; Head Wrestling Coach; TX St Teachers Assn 1985-; TX HS Coaches Assn 1987-; YOUTH Inc (Founder, Dir) 1986-, Yes-Villager 1988; Travis Cty Pop Warner Ftbl Pres 1989-; NE Austin Capital City Youth Bsktbl Commissioner 1987-; Outstanding Young Men of America 1985; Tracor Incorporated Scholar Awd; Certificate of Citation St of TX House of Rep; AISD Drop Out Prevention Certificate; Good Neighbor of Week Austin Amer Statesmen; *office:* Lyndon Baines Johnson HS 7309 Lazycreek Dr Austin TX 78724

CREECH, DEE MULLINS, 12th Grade English Teacher; *b:* Nixon, TX; *c:* Griffin M., Suzannah K.; *ed:* (BS) Fr/Speech, Univ of TX Austin 1968; (BS) Eng, Univ of TX San Antonio 1982; Foreign Lang Sch Eurocentre, Lausanne, Switzerland 1970-71; Advanced Writers Prgm Writing Project, Writing in Northside Local; *cr:* Fr/Speech Teacher Georgetown HS 1968-69; Eng/Fr Teacher Travis HS 1969-70; Fr Teacher Roosevelt HS 1971-72; Eng/Journalism Teacher Sam Rayburn Mid Sch 1972-73; Fr Teacher John Marshall HS 1973-74; Eng Teacher W H Taft HS 1987-; *ai:* Sr Class Asst Spon; TX St Teachers Assn, NEA 1968-; San Antonio Area Teachers of Eng 1987-; TX St Teachers Assn Austin Chapter Secy 1968-69; Taft HS Sr Class Favorite Teacher 1990; Articles Published; *office:* William Howard Taft HS 11600 FM 471 W San Antonio TX 77825

CREEK, BONDELYN ANN, Fifth Grade Teacher; *b:* Thompson, PA; *m:* Raymond S.; *c:* Leslie, Tobin; *ed:* (BS) Ed, E Stroudsburg St Coll 1961; Russian Stud, Colgate Univ; *cr:* Teacher NY & Germany 1961-68; 2nd-5th Grade Teacher Japan & KY & Okinawa & TX & NC Public Schls 1975-; *ai:* 5th Grade Level & Math Comm for Accreditation Chairperson; Civic Oration Contest Adv; NEA 1981-; NCAE; Officers Wives Club 1967-85; Morganton Road Teacher of Yr 1985; *home:* 3014 Ravenhill Dr Fayetteville NC 28303

CREEKMORE, HENRIETTA HOOD, Math/Sci/Pre-Algebra Teacher; *b:* Johnson Cty, NC; *m:* James Harvey Jr.; *c:* Mitzie, Julietta; *ed:* (BA) Math/Bio, Atlantic Chrstn Coll 1959; *cr:* Teacher Smithfield-Selma Mid Sch; *ai:* Drop Everything & Read Club Adv; NEA, NCEA 1977-; *office:* Smithfield-Selma Mid Sch PO Box 2270 Smithfield NC 27577

CREEL, MARGARETT SANFORD, Third Grade Teacher; *b:* Hattiesburg, MS; *m:* Charlie Thomas Sr.; *c:* Charlie T. Jr., Ike S.; *ed:* (BS) Elem Ed, William Carey Coll 1973; *cr:* Teacher Petal Public Schls 1973-; *ai:* Rdng, Great Books Comm; PMS PTA Officer; Petal AFT, ADK; Carterville Baptist Church; *office:* W L Smith Elem Sch 400 Hillcrest Loop Petal MS 39465

CREESE, JERI LYNNE, 5th Grade Teacher; *b:* Walnut Creek, CA; *m:* Brent; *c:* Jerod; *ed:* (AA) Nursery Sch Asst, Diablo Valley Coll 1977; (BA) Liberal Stud, Chico St 1981; *cr:* 4th Grade Teacher Mission Elem; 5th-6th Grade Teacher Kimball Elem; *ai:* Stu Cncl Adv; Sci & Math Textbook Selection Comm.

CRENETI, FRANK JOSEPH, Assistant Athletic Director; *b:* Philadelphia, PA; *m:* Judith Parkes; *c:* Janice, Tod; *ed:* (BS) His/Poly Sci Ed, Bloomsburg Univ 1962; Grad Sch Temple Univ; *cr:* His Teacher/Coach Woodrow Wilson HS 1962-65, Ben Franklin HS 1965-68, Bristol HS 1968-70; His/Government Teacher/Coach Fort Hunt HS 1970-85; Asst Athletic Dir/Coach W Springfield HS 1985-; *ai:* Head Ftbl Coach; N VA Ftbl Coaches Assn (Secy, Treas) 1975-; VA HS Coaches Assn; 1st United Presbyn Church Elder 1973-80; N Region Coach of Yr Twice; Gunston Dist Coach of Yr 6 Times; VA HS League All Star Coach 1981; *office:* W Springfield HS 6100 Rolling Rd Springfield VA 22152

CRENSHAW, JEANNINE CLAIRE, Math Teacher; *b:* New Orleans, LA; *ed:* (BA) Bus Admin, Furman Univ 1983; Grad Work Ed, Univ of S FL; *cr:* Teacher Charlotte HS 1984-; *ai:* Jr Var Girls Bsktbl & Vlybl Coach; Teacher Adv Prgm Comm Mem; FL Cncl Teachers of Math; *office:* Charlotte HS 1250 Cooper St Punta Gorda FL 33950

CRENSHAW, MARCELLA MATTINGLY, Second Grade Teacher; *b:* Corbin, KY; *m:* Rick; *c:* Brooks, Andrew; *ed:* (BS) Elem Ed, 1972, (MA) Elem Ed, 1978 W KY Univ; *cr:* Elem Teacher Bardstown Elem Sch 1973-75, 1978-; *ai:* Bardstown Ed Assn (Secy 1979-81) 1973-75, 1978-, KY Ed Assn, NEA 1973-75, 1978-; New Salem Baptist Church (Various Teaching Positions, Offices) 1973-86; Bardstown Baptist Church (Various Teaching Positions, Offices) 1986-; Grant Recipient Bardstown Fnd for Excl Public Ed Cook Nook Project; NCTE Center for Children at Risk Candidate 1990; KY Teacher Inst Ed 1990; *office:* Bardstown Elem Sch 420 N 5th St Bardstown KY 40004

CRENSHAW, MARGARET ALICE, Fifth Grade Teacher; *b:* Sedalia, MO; *ed:* (BSED) Elem Sch, Cntrl MO St Coll 1971; (MSED) Elem Sch Admin/Supervision, Cntrl MO St Univ 1975; *cr:* Elem Teacher Benton Cty R-I Sch 1971-; *ai:* Jr & Sr HS

Cheerleading Spon 1973-81; Sr HS Pep Club Spon 1973-75; MO St Teachers Assn 1971-; Cmmty Teachers Assn (VP 1975-76, Treas 1973-75, Grade Sch Rep 1976-77) 1971-; Teachers Admin Sch Bd Mem 1979-81; Parent Teachers Club 1971-; *office:* Benton Cty R-I Sch 500 S Kenney St Cole Camp MO 65325

CRENSHAW, MELVIN ALEXANDER, SR., Guidance Counselor; *b:* Chester, VA; *c:* Melvin A. Jr., Marvin P.; *ed:* (BS) Voc Ed, 1959, (MS) Scndry Guidance, 1974 VA St Univ; Scndry Admin; *cr:* Teacher St Emma Military Acad 1961-69; Guidance Cnslr Richmond Public Schls 1969-; *ai:* Awds Comm Mem; Athletic & Teachers Advisory Prgm Comm; Multicultural Counseling Treas 1985-87; Richmond Personnel Guidance Asst; VA Personnel Guidance Assn (Presentor, Asst); Scndry Prin Assn Presentor; Alpha Phi Alpha (Pres, Secy) 1980-86, Certificate 1986; Prince Hall Mason Worshipful Master 1976-78, Certificate 1978; Sherwood Park Civic Assn; *home:* 1500 Little John Rd Richmond VA 23227

CRENSHAW, MELVIN L., Curriculum Coordinator; *b:* Santa Ana, CA; *m:* Kathy Wiltse; *ed:* (BA) Psych/Educ, Chapman Coll 1972; (MA) Sch Admin/Curr, Univ of La Verne 1985; *cr:* Teacher/Rdng Specialist Salmon Sch Dist 1975-78; Teacher 1978-88; Mentor Teacher 1987-88; Curriculum Coordinator 1988- Victor Elem Sch Dist; *ai:* Stu Act: Jr Olympics; Bsktbl; Soccer; Sci Fairs; Young Author's Conf; Curr Dev Soc Sci & Phys Ed; *office:* Victor Sch Dist 15579 8th Street Victorville CA 92392

CRETTI, BONNIE ELIZABETH BIRMINGHAM, Social Studies Teacher; *b:* New Haven, CT; *m:* Clark; *c:* Elizabeth, Caroline; *ed:* (BA) His, Wellesley Coll 1971; (MA) His/Ed, Univ of WI Madison 1975; Grad Stud Numerous Univs; *cr:* Soc Stud Teacher Malcolm-Shabazz HS 1974-75; Spec Ed Teacher Southern Hills Jr HS 1975-77; Soc Stud Teacher Roaring Fork HS 1977-; Teacher of Gifted/Talented 1988-; *ai:* Stu Cncl Spon; Soc Stud Dept Chairperson; NCSS 1988-; Carbondale Cncl Arts & Hum (Mem 1978-, Bd Mem 1979-81); Roaring Fork HS Teacher of Yr 1982; L S Wood Teacher of Yr 1985; *office:* Roaring Fork HS 180 Snowmass Dr Carbondale CO 81623

CREVIA, DEBRA SONEFELD, Junior High Reading Teacher; *b:* Saginaw, MI; *m:* Kip; *c:* Melissa, Stephanie; *ed:* (BA) Music, 1979, (MAT) Rdng, 1990 Saginaw Valley St Univ; *cr:* Elem Vocal Music Teacher 1979-81, Jr HS Vocal Music Teacher 1981-, Jr HS Rdng Teacher 1988- Saginaw Public Schls; *ai:* Sch Improvement & Lang Art Curr Comm; Spon Rdng Room; Intnl Rdng Assn, MI Rdng Assn, Saginaw Area Rdng Cncl; *office:* South Intermediate Sch 224 N Elm Saginaw MI 48602

CREW, MARY HELEN SIMS, 3rd/4th Grade Teacher; *b:* Chicago, IL; *m:* Ernest Samuel; *c:* Stephanie L., Adrienne M.; *ed:* (BA) His/Ec, Coll of St Francis 1954; (MA) Ed/Art, Azusa Pacific 1972; Grad Stud; *cr:* Teacher Mason Elem 1960-61, John Farren Elem 1961-63, Thomas Jefferson Sch 1963-74, San Rafael Sch 1975-; *ai:* Faculty Rep Sch Improvement Comm; Phi Delta Kappa 1987-; St of CA Mentor Teacher 1985-88; Pasadena-Altadena Links Pres; Nom CA Teacher of Yr Prgm 1984-85; *office:* San Rafael Sch 1090 Nithsdale Rd Pasadena CA 91105

CREWS, JESSE ANDREW, JR., Physical Education Chair; *b:* Folkston, GA; *m:* Joan Canaday; *c:* Ansley, Tye, Hayley, Spencer; *ed:* (AA) Brewton Parker Jr 1973; (BSED) Health/Phys Ed, S GA Coll 1975; (MED) Admin/Supervision, Valdosta St Coll 1982; *cr:* Teacher/Coach St George Sch 1975-81, Charlton Cty HS 1981-; *ai:* Bsktbl Head Coach St George 1976-81, Charlton Cty 1981-; Athletic Dir Charlton Cty 1989-; GA Assn of Educators (Pres 1982-83) 1987-; Charlton Assn of Educators Pres 1989-; Charlton Bd of Commissioners (Chm 1983, Vice-Chm 1984); Elected as Outstanding Young Man of America 1986-; Waycross Journal-Herald Bsktbl Coach of Yr 1988, 1990; Region 2A GA Coach of Yr 1990; Natl HS Coaching Awd 1988; *home:* PO Box 206 Saint George GA 31646

CREWS, TAMMY THOMPSON, American History Teacher; *b:* Century, FL; *m:* William H.; *ed:* (BS) Soc Stud/Amer His, GA Southwestern 1987; *cr:* Amer His Teacher Dougherty HS 1988-; *ai:* Dougherty HS Co-Ed Y-Club Adv; GA Assn of Educators; *office:* Dougherty HS 1800 Pearce Ave Albany GA 31705

CREWS, VICKI JEANES, Third Grade Teacher; *b:* West Palm Beach, FL; *c:* Joanna, Caroline; *ed:* (BSED) Early Elem Ed, GA Southern 1969; (MS) Early Elem Ed, Berry Coll 1979; *cr:* 1st Grade Teacher Broad St Sch 1969-70; 2nd Grade Teacher Sylvania Elem Sch 1970-72; 1st-3rd Grade Teacher Armuchee Valley Elem 1972-85; 3rd Grade Teacher N La Fayette Elem 1985-; *ai:* NEA, GAE; WAE Secy 1977-78; *office:* North La Fayette Elem Sch 610 Duke St La Fayette GA 30728

CRICK, WAYNE DALE, Science Teacher; *b:* Poplar Bluff, MO; *m:* Margaret Hollembeak; *c:* Ryan W., Aaron K., Amanda L.; *ed:* (BA) Phys Ed/Bio, 1973, (MS) Guidance/Counseling, 1987 Western St Coll; *cr:* Sci Teacher Buchanan Jr HS 1973-77, Delta Mid Sch 1977-; *ai:* Mid Sch Ftbl, Boys Bsktbl, Girls Bsktbl & Track Coach; Delta HS Booster Club (VP, Secy) 1988-; *office:* Delta Mid Sch 822 Grand Ave Delta CO 81416

CRIM, JANET FALK, English Department Head; *b:* Hagen-Haspe, Germany; *c:* Samuel, Margaret, Barbara Crim Macomb; *ed:* (AB) Ger, Mercer Univ 1972; *cr:* Eng Teacher Fort Valley Mid Sch 1973-74, Monroe Acad 1974-; *ai:* Sr Beta Club Spon; Macon Civic Chorale Singer 1985-; *office:* Monroe Acad Rt 3 Box 4 Forsyth GA 31029

CRIPLIVER, THOMAS L., English Teacher; *b:* Hammond, IN; *ed:* (BA) Soc Stud/Eng Teaching, Purdue Univ 1984; (MS) Scndry Ed, 1988 Sc Ndry Level Prin License, 1989 (EDS) Specialist Degree IN Univ (Anticipated 1991); Cmptrs for The Classroom Programs; Lions of Amer Organization Spon of the Quest Prgm; Lifeguard/Swimming Instr/Coach; *cr:* Substitute Teacher Hobart Township Cmmty Schls 1979-84, Merrillville Sch Corporation 1979-84; Lifeguard/Swim Instr Lake Station Parks Dept 1979-85; Eng Teacher Lake Station Cmmty Sch Corporation 1984-; *ai:* Stud Cncl Spon; Auditorium Dir; SADD Co-Spon; Asst Ftbl Jr HS Level Coach; Assoc Ftbl Coach Vars Level; Jr HS Head Wrestling Coach; Play/Musical Dir; NASSP Mem 1988; NCTE 1984-; IN Cncl for Teacher of Eng 1985-; M L McClellan Lodge #357 Organist 1983-; Amer Red Cross Chm Water Safety Services 1982-84; Amer Red Cross Volunteer of the Yr 1987-88; *home:* 2480 Union St Lake Station IN 46405

CRIPPEN, DORIS BINDER, Chapter I Reading Teacher; *b:* Hays, KS; *m:* Donald E.; *c:* Galen, Jerry, Jeff; *ed:* (BS) Ed, Fort Hays St Univ 1971; *cr:* 4th Grade Teacher Lenora Grade Sch 1951-52; 1st Grade Teacher 1972-85, Chapter I Rdng Teacher 1985- Hill City Elem Sch; *ai:* KNEA Local Pres 1980-81; NEA; Meth Church; *home:* 611 N 7th Hill City KS 67642

CRISANTI, GARY A., Chemistry/Physics Teacher; *b:* Bridgeport, CT; *m:* Lynne Marie Landry; *ed:* (BS) Chem, 1984, (MS) Chem, 1991 S CT St Univ; *cr:* Sci Teacher Seymour HS 1984, Trumbull HS 1984-; *ai:* Frosh Boys Track Head Coach; *office:* Trumbull HS 72 Strobel Rd Trumbull CT 06611

CRISCOLO, JOHN THOMAS, Regents Biology Teacher; *b:* Bronx, NY; *m:* Peggy Ann Ingino; *c:* John T. III; *ed:* (BS) Biological Sci, C W Post Coll 1963; (MS) Bio/Ecology, Long Island Univ 1966; Admin, Supervision, Educl Law, St Johns Univ; *cr:* Bio Teacher Hicksville Sr HS 1963-; *ai:* Amateur Radio, Aviation, Ecology, Ski Club Adv; Soph & Jr Class Faculty Adv; Ftbl & Bsktbl Events Supervision Admin Adv; NEA Mem 1963-; ASCD Mem 1989-; Aircraft Owners & Pilots Assn Mem 1977-; Fire Island Natl Seashore (Ranger Naturalist, Ecological Adv); Author; *home:* PO Box 283 East Setauket NY 11733

CRISLIP, DIANNA BRICKLE, English Teacher; *b:* Augusta, GA; *m:* Steve; *ed:* (BS) Eng Ed, Univ of GA 1971; Grad Hrs, Augusta Coll; *cr:* Eng Teacher Josey HS 1971-72; Eng/Span Teacher ARC 1972-75; Eng Teacher Butler 1975-77; Eng/Span Teacher Forest Park Sr HS 1977-79; Eng Teacher Thomson HS 1979-88, Lakeside HS 1988-; *ai:* Sr Class Adv; Soph Class Stu Cncl; Tennis Team Coach; Chm SACS Comm; Stu Affairs; NCTE; GA HS Assn Coach Region Tennis Champs 1989; Thomson HS Yrbk Dedication 1988; Lakeside HS Yrbk Most Sch Spirited Teacher 1990; *office:* Lakeside H S 533 Blue Ridge Dr Evans GA 30809

CRISPIN, GEORGE ATWOOD, English Teacher; *b:* Philadelphia, PA; *c:* Deborah Crispin Dominy, Karen D.; *ed:* (BS) His/Phys Ed, Temple Univ 1962; (MA) His, 1976, (MS) Eng, 1981 Glassboro St Coll; (EDD) Ed, Temple Univ 1987; *cr:* His Teacher 1962-82, Eng Teacher 1982 Washington Township HS; Part Time Eng/Comm Teacher Glassboro St Coll 1987-; *ai:* Washington Township HS Class Adv 1962-68; Newspaper Adv 1968; Cross Cntry Coach 1967-74; Chm Eng Evaluation Comm for Mid St Evaluation 1974; NEA, NJ Ed Assn, Gloucester Cty Ed Assn, Washington Township Educl Assn 1962-; Woodbury Friends Meeting Bd of Trustees 1970-; Westtown Friends Sch Bd of Trustees 1983-; Mullica Hill Friends Sch Bd of Trustees 1982-; Woodstown Friends Home for Aged Bd of Trustees 1969-80; *home:* Box 127 Harrisonville NJ 08039

CRISS, SHARON CANDACE (GREENLEAF), 5-6th Grade Eng/Spell Teacher; *b:* Harmony, WV; *m:* Patrick M.; *c:* Stacy L., Anthony; *ed:* (BA) Soc Stud/Elem Ed, Glenville St Coll 1968; (MA) Elem Ed, WV Univ 1975; *cr:* Teacher Mineral Wells Sch 1968-; *ai:* Group Counseling-Grade 6; Lang Art Textbook Adoption Comm; Mem St Francis Xavier Cath Church; *home:* 36 Oakwood Estates Parkersburg WV 26101

CRISTILLO, FRANK D., JR., Computer Programming Instr; *b:* Altoona, PA; *ed:* Voc I Cmptr Programming, PA St 1990; Bus Ed, PA St; *cr:* Post Scndry Instr Johnstown Area Voc Tech 1978-85; Programmer/Analyst Link Cmptr Corporation 1985-87; Instr Altoona Area Voc Tech 1987-; *ai:* Teachers Assn Soc Comm Chm 1989-; Public Relations Comm Mem 1988-; Voc Industrial Clubs of America (Mem 1989-, Club Adv); *office:* Altoona Area Voc-Tech Sch 1500 4th Ave Altoona PA 16603

CRISWELL, MELVIN DANIEL, 6th Grade Math Teacher; *b:* Covington, GA; *m:* Ruth Anglin; *c:* Evans A.; *ed:* (BS) Soc Stud, Univ of GA 1954; (MED) Math, West GA Coll 1975; (EDTS) Math, Jacksonville St Univ 1978; *cr:* Teacher/Coach Newton Cty 1957-68; Teacher/Prin Pickens Cty 1966-69; Teacher Newton Cty 1969-72, Polk Cty 1972-; *ai:* Bsktbl, Ftbl, Bsbl Coach Jr HS; Managed Little League Bsbl Teams; Coached Midget Ftbl; Scout Master; NEA; GAE; Lions Club; DAV; Teacher of Yr Cedar Hill Mid Sch 1987-88; *office:* Cedar Hill Mid Sch E Ellawood Ave Cedartown GA 30125

CRITES, BARBARA GROTHOUSE, Learning Disabilities Teacher; *b:* San Diego, CA; *m:* Larry J.; *c:* Austin J., Zachary A.; *ed:* (BS) Ed, 1980, (MS) Ed, 1984 Butler Univ; Completing Dir of Spec Ed License, Butler Univ; *cr:* Multi-Categorical Spec Ed Teacher Washington Elem 1981; Teacher of Mentally Handicapped Tipton Mid Sch 1981-84; Teacher of Learning Disabilities Northwestern Jr/Sr HS 1984-87, Northwestern Elem 1987-; *ai:* Learning Disabilities Assn; Kokomo Greek Club Secy 1988-; *home:* 1364 N 550 W Kokomo IN 46901

CRITES, CHARLOTTE BARNES, Home Economics/Reading Teacher; *b:* Columbus, OH; *m:* Kelley L.; *c:* Lee A. Carroll, Sue Berry, Gerry, Karen, Kathy; *ed:* (BA) Home Ec, Otterbein Coll 1971; (MA) Ed, Coll of Mt St Joseph 1985; *cr:* Teacher Madison Plains Mid 1971-73, Westfall Mid Sch 1976-; *ai:* Future Problem Solvers Coach; OH Future Problem Solvers Evaluator; Cty Curr, In-Service Comms; *office:* Westfall Mid Sch 19545 Pherson Pike Williamsport OH 43164

CRITTENDEN, GAYBROOKE GARRETT, Reading Resource Teacher; *b:* Middlesex Cty, VA; *m:* Thomas S.; *c:* Debra C. Cantrell, Richard, Robert; *ed:* (BA) Psych, Mary Washington Coll 1952; (MS) Ed, Old Dominion Univ; *cr:* 2nd/3rd Grade Teacher 1966-72, Title I Rdng Teacher 1973-75 Hidenwood Elem; 1st/2nd Grade Teacher Hilton Elem 1972-73, 1976-85; 3rd Grade Teacher Riverside Elem 1975-76; Rdng Resource Teacher Hilton & Saunders & Watkins Elem 1985-; *ai:* Watkins Advisory Comm; Watkins Sch Volunteers Faculty Rep; Newport News Rdng Cncl (Building Rep) 1977-, Teacher of Yr 1981-82; N Riverside Baptist Church Dir Homebound Ministry 1985-; Watkins Elem Sch Teacher of Yr 1989-; *office:* Watkins Elem Sch 21 Burns Dr Newport News VA 23601

CRITTENDEN, TERRIE ANN (WEBB), Teacher/Assistant Principal; *b:* Austin, TX; *m:* Frank Wilson; *ed:* (BA) Elem Ed, Univ of Mary Hardin-Baylor 1978; *cr:* Teacher/Asst Prin Great Hills Chrstn Sch; *ai:* Stu Cncl Elem Spon; *home:* Rt 1 Box 54C-1 Dale TX 78616

CRITTENDON, MARY TOM, Social Studies Teacher; *b:* Elberton, GA; *ed:* (BS) Soc Sci 1966, (MED) Soc Sci 1972 Univ of GA; *cr:* Teacher Blackwell Jr HS 1970-75, Elbert Cty Mid Sch 1975-; *ai:* Soc Stud Departmental Chairperson; Pod Leader; Mem of Building Comm; Prof Assn of GA Educators; Delta Kappa Gamma; Pilot Club Bd of Dir 1987-89; *office:* Elbert Co Mid Sch 45 Forest Ave Elberton GA 30635

CRITZ, JANICE LACKEY, 5th Grade Teacher; *b:* Martinsville, VA; *m:* James Russell; *c:* Jamie; *ed:* (BS) Elem Ed, Averett Coll 1973; *cr:* Teacher Campbell Court 1973-; *ai:* Self Study, Child Study Comms; Family Life Teacher; Delta Kappa Gamma 1984-; *home:* Rt 7 Box 457 Martinsville VA 24112

CRIVELLO, MICHAEL ANTHONY, AP English Teacher; *b:* Milwaukee, WI; *ed:* (BA) Eng, Marquette Univ 1974; (MA) Eng, Univ of N TX 1983; Dallas Inst of Hum & Culture 1985-86; Harvard Univ 1988; Univ of N TX 1989; Hum Ind Study Fellowship 1989; *cr:* Teacher Dominican HS 1974-79, Lewisville HS 1979 ; *ai:* Academic Decathlon Team Spon; TX St Teachers Assn, NEA; Knights of Columbus; Lewisville HS Teacher of Yr 1989; *home:* Flower Mound TX 75028

CRNKOVICH, ROSE A., English Teacher; *b:* Aurora, IL; *ed:* (BA) Scndry Ed Eng, Northeastern IL Univ 1979; (MA) Eng Lang/Lit, Univ of Chicago 1987; *cr:* Eng Teacher Trinity HS 1980-; *ai:* Yrbk Adv; NCTE; ASCD; *office:* Trinity HS 7574 W Division St River Forest IL 60305

CROCHET, SUZANNE THERESE, Fifth Grade Teacher; *b:* Houma, LA; *ed:* (BA) Elem Ed, Northwestern St Univ 1965; (MED) Spec Ed, Southeastern ST Univ 1971; Grad Stud LA St Univ; Nichollas St Univ; Tulane Prof Improvements Prgm, St of LA; *cr:* 3rd/4th/6th Grade Teacher Elysian Fields Elem 1965-82; 5th Grade Teacher Mulberry Elem 1982-; *ai:* Terrebonne Assn of Educators, LA Assn of Educators, NEA Building Rep 1965-; Civitan 1989-; Kappa Kappa Iota Pres 1978-; Ladies Carvinal Club Bd Mem 1970-; Nom Terrebonne Parish Teacher of Yr 1986; *office:* Mulberry Elem Sch 450 Old Bayou Du Large Rd Houma LA 70360

CROCKARELL, MARY TRINKLE, Third Grade Teacher; *b:* Palmyra, TN; *m:* Charles Wesley Sr.; *c:* Charles W. Jr.; *ed:* (BS) Elem Ed, 1974, (MS) Early Chldhd Ed, 1981 Austin Peay St Univ; Admin/Supervision, Austin Peay St Univ 1983; *cr:* 1st-8th Grade Teacher Chestnut Grove Sch 1948-50; 5th Grade Teacher 1970-71, 3rd Grade Teacher 1972- Dover Elem; *ai:* Stewart Cty Teachers Assn, Mid TN Ed Assn, TN Ed Assn, NEA; Stewart Cty Historical Society; Career Ladder I; *home:* PO Box 12 Dover TN 37058

CROCKER, J. W., III, History Teacher; *b:* Altus, OK; *m:* Lona Faye Karnes; *c:* Candy Jordan, Rocky Dub, Dusty Bill; *ed:* (AA) Hill Coll 1969; (BA) Soc Sci, TX Chrstn Univ 1971; (BBA) Gen Bus, TX Wesleyan Univ 1975; (MED) Admin, Tarleton St Univ 1980; Numerous USAF Trng Prgms 1958-61; *cr:* Spec Agent USAF 1945-68; Stu Coll 1968-71; Admin Teacher/Coach Alvarado HS 1971-78; Admin Teacher Joshua Ind Sch Dist 1978-; Part Time Teacher Hill Coll 1978-; *ai:* HS Track, Bsktbl, Ftbl Coach; TX St Teachers Assn 1971-78, 1989; Masonic Lodge Jr Warden 25 Yr Awd; Teacher of Yr 1975-76; Government Teacher of Yr 1973-74; All Air Force Ftbl Team 1955-56; Natl Service Champs; All Navy Ftbl Team 1948; TX Chrstn Univ Lettered 1945; *home:* 104 Hopper St PO Box K Alvarado TX 76009

CROCKER, SHERRY DARLENE, Teacher; *b:* Aberdeen, WA; *m:* Don; *c:* Chad, Matt; *ed:* (AA) Elem Ed/Eng, Gray Harbor Coll 1963; (BA) Elem Ed/Eng, W WA St Coll 1965; *cr:* 3rd Grade Teacher Sedro Wooley Sch Dist 1963-65; 1st-4th Grade Pre Sch Teacher Hoquian Sch Dist 1973-; *ai:* Vlybl Coach; Sch Entertainment Chm; Beta Tau Chapter, Delta Kappa Gamma Cooresponding Secy 1988-; Hoquiam Teachers Assn; Polish Womens Organization.

CROCKETT, ANN GRAHAM, English Teacher; *b:* Kansas City, MO; *m:* James F.; *c:* Louis T. Hurt Jr. Jeffrey S. Hurt; *ed:* (BA) Ed, Univ of CA Santa Barbara 1957; (MS) Rdng, Cntrl MO St Univ 1975; IA St Teachers Coll; *cr:* Nurses Aide Cottage Hospital 1951-57; Teacher Willard Jr HS 1957-59, Sumner HS 1960-62, Paseo HS 1963-; *ai:* Spon Yrbk, Honor Society, Horizon Club, Y-Teens; *office:* Paseo HS 4747 Flora Ave Kansas City MO 64110

CROCKETT, GEORGIA MADELEINE, Librarian; *b:* Williamstown, MO; *w:* Norman L. (dec); *c:* Stephen L.; *ed:* (BSE) Elem Ed, 1963, (MA) Elem Admin, 1966 NE MO St Univ; Various Wkshps & Correspondence; *cr:* 3rd Grade Teacher 1963-66, 4th Grade Teacher 1966-70, Part-Time Elem Prin 1970-82, Librarian 1982- Adair Cty R-II Sch; *ai:* Co-Spon Intramural Academic Bowl; Prof Dev Comm Chm; Career Ladder & Review Comm; Alps Adv Bd; NE Dist Librarians, ADK, Local CTA; Meth Church (Parish Cncl, Ed Comm, Lay Speaker) 1970-; PTA; Grant Geography Inst, Sci Inst, Missourianna Tour Grant; *home:* PO Box 141 Brashear MO 63533

CROMER, FRANCES ALBA, Sixth Grade Teacher; *b:* Bluefield, WV; *m:* Charles B. Jr.; *c:* Suzanne G. (Dec), Michele L.; *ed:* (BS) Ed, Concord Coll 1963; (MS) Ed, WVCOGS 1989; Teacher/Writing Consultant Mercer Cty Schls Summer Inst 1984; RESAI Teacher Acad 1989; *cr:* Substitute Teacher Mercer Cty Schls 1974-75; Adjunct Instr Concord Coll 1989; Teacher Whitethorn Elem 1975-; *ai:* Coach Whitethorn Math Field Day Team; Safety Patrol Adv; Mercer Cty Ed Assn Teacher of Yr 1987; Alpha Delta Kappa Pres 1982-84; Trinity United Meth Church (Admin Bd, Circle Leader) 1990; *home:* 2000 Whitethorn St Bluefield WV 24701

CROMER, FREDA WARTHIN, First Grade Teacher; *b:* Chambersburg, PA; *m:* R. Boyd; *c:* Robert W., Ann C. Gray, Barbara, Timothy B., Ned M.; *ed:* (BS) Elem, 1952, (MS) Elem, 1976 Shippensburg Univ; *cr:* 6th Grade Teacher 1952-55, 2nd Grade Teacher 1955-56 Fort Littleton Elem; 2nd Grade Teacher 1964-65, 1st Grade Teacher 1965-77, 3rd Grade Teacher 1977-86, 1st Grade Teacher 1986- Forbes Road Sch Dist; *ai:* Lead Teacher in Elem Building; Forbes Road Ed Assn Secy 1984-87; PA St Ed Assn; NEA; Fulton Cty Lib Bd 1979-80; Fulton Cty Childrens Services Advisory Bd 1988-; United Presbyn Church (Deacon 1979-85, Elder 1988-).

CROMWELL, RICHARD LEE, Social Studies Teacher; *b:* Ft Worth, TX; *m:* Maureen Gallaher; *c:* Sarah, Jesse; *ed:* (BA) Bible/Religion, WV Wesleyan Coll 1970; (MTH) Theology, Southern Meth Univ 1973; (MAT) His, Boston Coll 1977; Grad Stud Univ of TX; *cr:* Psych/His/Eng Teacher Notre Dame HS 1975-77; Psych/His Teacher Perry Sch 1977-79; Geography Teacher/Coach Reagan HS 1980-84; Psych/Soc Stud/Government/His Round Rock HS 1984-; *ai:* Amnesty Intnl Club Adv; Faculty Rep Supt Cncl; United Meth Church Ordained Minister 1974-; Round Rock HS Teacher of Yr 1988-89; *office:* Round Rock HS 300 Lake Creek Dr Round Rock TX 78681

CRONA, JAMES EDWARD, Sixth Grade Teacher; *b:* Colorado Springs, CO; *m:* Julia Mary Connor; *c:* Daniel, Meghan, Kathleen, Kevin; *ed:* (AS) General Stud, Arapahoe Jr Coll 1968; (BA) Phys Ed/Elem Ed, Univ N CO 1970; (ME) Cmptrs in Ed, Lesley Coll 1983; US Soccer Fed D Coaching License; *cr:* 5th Grade Teacher Sun Valley Elem 1972-79; 5th/6th Grade Teacher John C Shaffer Elem 1979-87; 6th Grade Teacher Coronado Elem 1987-; *ai:* Club Soccer Coach; Building Level Cmptr Coord; Jeff Cty Ed Assn, NEA 1972-; PTSA 1972-; Columbine HS Boosters 1989-; *office:* Coronado Elem Sch 7952 S Carr St Littleton CO 80123

CRONE, KATHY ELIZABETH, Third Grade Teacher; *b:* Frederick, MD; *m:* Dwight Thomas; *c:* Todd A., Emily E.; *ed:* (BS) Early Chldhd Ed, Towson St 1971; (MA) Humane Sci/Math & Sci, Hood Coll 1980; Numerous Educl Wkshps from Frederick Cty; *cr:* Teacher Brunswick Elem Sch 1971-; *ai:* 3rd Grade Team Leader; 2nd Yr Teacher Plus Position; Cooperating Teacher for Stu Teachers; Lang Art Rep; Brunswick HS Parent Advisory Comm 1990; NEA, MD St Teacher Assn, Frederick Cty Teacher Assn 1971-; Delta Kappa Gamma 1975-; GSA 1989-; Bethany Luth Church Choir 1962-; Brunswick Historical Society 1980-; Brunswick Elem PTO (VP 1985-87, Secy 1987-); Teacher Plus Awd 1988-; Writing Comprehension Curr for Brunswick Elem Sch; *home:* 1925-A Point of Rocks Rd Knoxville MD 21758

CRONIN, JAMES THOMAS, English Teacher; *b:* San Diego, CA; *m:* Sonia Ellen; *ed:* (BA) Journalism, CA St Fullerton 1984; Teacher Preparation Prgm/Eng, Univ of La Verne 1985; *cr:* Eng Teacher 1986-, Journalism Adv 1989- Montclair HS; *ai:* Journalism, Environmental Club, Frosh Class Adv; *office:* Montclair HS 4725 Benito St Montclair CA 91763

CRONIN, MARGARET ABAYES, 2nd Grade Teacher; *b:* Aliquippa, PA; *m:* Joseph D.; *ed:* (BS) Elem Ed, Geneva Coll 1961; Chrstn Ed, Nyack Missionary Coll; Post Grad Univ of Pittsburgh; *cr:* 5th Grade Teacher Fair Oaks Elem 1961-64; 5th/6th Grade Combination Teacher Amberg Germany 1964-65; 2nd/4th/5th/6th Grade Teacher Aliquippa Elem 1965-; *ai:* Amer Ed Comm; Aliquippa Ed Assn, PA St Ed Assn, NEA 1961-; AARP, NRTA; US Navy Yeoman 2nd Class 1952-57, Good Conduct Medal, Korean War Medal 1957; Waves (Honor Guard 1954, Drill Team); Mem Planning Comm; Awarded Mini-Grant to Purchase Sch Lib for Class 1990; *office:* Aliquippa Elem Sch 21st St Aliquippa PA 15001

CRONIN, MARY LIPPINCOTT, 5-7th Grade Math Teacher; *b:* Marlton, NJ; *m:* Thomas P.; *c:* Dennis, Kimberly Harty; *ed:* Eng, Univ of MD; (BS) Elem Ed - Summa Cum Laude, West Chester St Coll 1972; (MA) Gen Ed - Summa Cum Laude, Villanova Univ 1977; *cr:* 3rd/4th Grade Teacher 1973-74; 5th/6th Grade Teacher 1974-78 Hillside Elem; Valley Forge Elem 1978-79;2nd/3rd Grade Teacher Hilltop Sch 1979-; 4th-7th Grade Teacher Mountain View Sch 1979-; *ai:* Chief Negotiator Mendham Borough Ed Assn 1989-1991; Mendham Borough Ed Assn Secy; Girl Scout Ldr; Schlot Realtors Referral Assoc; Basking Ridge Presby Chch Mem; Whos Who Among Stu in Amer Univ & Coll 1972-73; NJ Govrnrs Teacher Recog Awd 1988; *office:* Mountain View Mid Sch Dean Rd Mendham NJ 07945

CRONINGER, CATHY LE, Kindergarten Teacher; *b:* Wauseon, OH; *ed:* (BS) Elem Ed, Bowling Green St Univ 1971; (ME) Early Chldhd Ed, Univ of Toledo 1978; Post Grad Courses, Univ of Toledo; Attended Several Classes & Wkshps Early Chldhd Ed; *cr:* Kndgtn Teacher Wauseon Schls 1971-; *ai:* K-2nd Grades Building Resource Person Math; Math Fine Art Curr Comm Mem; Soc Comm Chairperson for Elm Street Sch; Wauseon Ed Assn Pres 1981-82; OH Ed Assn, NEA; Delta Kappa Gamma; Wauseon BPW 2nd VP 1990-; Maumee Valley Civic Theatre; Received OH Teacher & Unit Grant 1979; Invited to Fulton Cty Schls Invitational Acad for Teacher Excellency; *office:* Elm Street Sch 440 E Elm St Wauseon OH 43567

CRONK, KATHLEEN CHERRY, Second & Third Grade Teacher; *b:* Eagle River, WI; *m:* Kleon R.; *c:* Kevon R.; *ed:* (BS) Elem Ed, 1969, (MS) Elem Ed, 1983 Univ of WI Superior; *cr:* 3rd-5th Grade Elem Teacher Richland Sch 1960-62; 1st-2nd Grade Elem Teacher Lake Nebagamon Sch 1963-65; 1st-3rd Grade Elem Teacher Stone Lake Elem Sch 1965-; 1st-3rd Grade Elem Teacher Stone Lake Elem Sch 1965-; *ai:* Sci Comm Secy; *office:* Stone Lake Elem Sch Stone Lake WI 54876

CROOK, JUANITA MARIE YOHO, Teacher; *b:* Akron, OH; *m:* Philip N. Sr.; *c:* Eleanor A. (Dec), Philip N. Jr.; *ed:* (BSED) Elem Ed, Youngstown St Univ 1972; Grad Work; *cr:* Teacher LaBrae Local Bd of Ed 1966-; *ai:* LaBrae Teachers Assn, NE OH Teachers Assn, OH Teachers Assn, Nation Teachers Assn 1966-; BSA (Den Mother & Merit Badge Cnslr 1955-57, Dist Mem at Large 1960-77); Grange 1951-54; Amer Red Cross (First Aid Instr 1967-78, 1990) 1987-; GSA 1960; Church of God (Young Adult Sunday Sch Teacher 1960, Trustee, Choir Mem); Animal Welfare League; YWCA; Block Watch Unit 6-K; Precinct Comm Woman Rep Party.

CROOKS, EVELYN ISENHOUR, Fifth Grade Teacher; *b:* Conover, NC; *m:* James Vaughn; *c:* Jason W., Justin G.; *ed:* (BS) Elem Ed, Appalachian St Univ 1967; *cr:* 6th Grade Teacher Oxford Elem 1967-69; 4th Grade Teacher St Stephens Elem 1970-76; 4th/5th Grade Teacher Webb A Murray Elem Sch 1976-; *home:* Rt 1 Box 684 Claremont NC 28610

CROOM, LORENE PAYNE, Retired Elementary Teacher; *b:* Pikeville, TN; *w:* Fred M. (dec); *c:* Howard L. Martin, Diane Martin Cheves, Alfred T. Martin; *ed:* (BSE) Elem Ed, Univ of AR Fayetteville 1971; Grad Stud Ouachita Baptist Univ, Hampton Inst, Univ of AR Little Rock; *cr:* Primary Teacher Pulaski Cty Spec Sch Dist 1971-84; *ai:* AR Polytechnic Univ Advisory Bd 1975-78, Awd 1978; Blue Cross/Blue Shield Advisory Bd 1978-; Pulaski Cty Spec Sch Dist Awd 1984; Little Rock Retired Teachers Assn; UMW Lakewood United Meth Church VP 1988-; Ivy Book Club Pres 1987-89; N Little Rock Womans Club 1984; *home:* 4606 Crestline North Little Rock AR 72116

CROSBY, ANNE SEWARD, English Teacher; *b:* Quincy, IL; *ed:* (BS) Eng, Univ of NE 1964; (MS) Ed, Wilkes Barre Univ; *cr:* Eng/Soc Stud Teacher Bellevue Jr HS 1964-65; Eng Teacher Memorial Jr HS 1968-70, Medill Bair HS 1971-74, Charles Boehm HS 1974-; *ai:* Gifted Stu Spon Drama Competition; Stu Assist Prgm; PA & Pennsbury Ed Assn, NEA; *office:* Pennsbury Sch Dist Medill Bair HS 608 S Olds Blvd Fairless Hills PA 19030

CROSBY, EMILY JEAN HARRIS, Retired Teacher; *b:* Ellicottville, NY; *c:* Douglas H., J. Bryan; *ed:* (BA) Soc Sci/Ed, Houghton Coll 1948; (MSED) Ed, SUNY Fredonia 1960; Admin/Supervision, St Bonaventure 1968; Counseling, Liberty Univ; *cr:* Teacher/House Parent E TX Acad for Boys 1953; Teacher/Admin Tournavista Sch 1954-55; Elem Teacher Randolph Cntrl Sch 1956-88; *ai:* Soc Stud, Rdng, Math Curr, Dist Wide Eng Curr, Cmptr Ed, Faculty Advisory Comms; After Sch Study Prgm; NY St SW Region 9 Retiree Organizing Comm; ASCD Mem; NY St United Teachers Assn (Pres, Secy, Grievance Chm, Negotiations) 1962-; NY St AFT Comm; United Meth Church (Admin Bd, Jr/Sr Choir, Sunday Sch Teacher) 1960-80; Order of Eastern Star (Matron, Dist Deputy) 1967-87; Baptist Church (Choir, Sunday Sch Teacher, Womens Group Pres) 1986-; *home:* 519 Fair Oaks St Little Valley NY 14755

CROSBY, FRANCES MC CORD, 5th Grade Science Teacher; *b:* Shellknob, MO; *m:* Wilford E.; *c:* Debbie, Connie; *ed:* (MA) Elem, 1980, (BS) Elem, 1970 Cntrl St Univ; Grad Stud; *cr:* 2nd Grade Teacher Wilson Elem 1971-72; 2nd Grade Teacher 1972-80, 5th Grade Teacher 1980- John Glenn Elem; *ai:* Kappa Kappa Iota Treas 1981-82; Western Heights Sch Dist Teacher of Yr 1979; *office:* John Glenn Elem Sch 6500 S Land Oklahoma City OK 73159

CROSBY, JOSEPHINE MECHAM, English Teacher; *b:* Grand Junction, CO; *m:* Rodney Lewis; *c:* Brett, Casey, Chris, Scott; *ed:* (BS) Sociology, Brigham Young Univ 1969; (MA) Sec Ed/Learning Disabilities, Univ of N CO 1974; *cr:* Continuing Ed Teacher Vista HS 1969; Eng Teacher Vernal HS 1969-70; Diagnostician/Spec Ed Teacher Hayden Jr/Sr HS 1970-73; Diagnostician/Spec Ed/Eng Teacher Provo Canyon Bays Sch 1973-74; Spec Ed/Eng Teacher Pleasant Grove Jr HS 1974-77; Eng Teacher Lovell HS 1977-; *ai:* Class Spon; Eng Dept & Lang Art HS Curr Chm; NEA, Lovell Ed Assn, WY Ed Assn; Cowleys Day Comm Book/Cmptr Spec 6; Latter Day Saints Church (Primary Pres, Sunday Sch Teacher, Pianst, Choir, Young Womens Pres, Visiting Teacher); *home:* Box 112 Cowley WY 82420

CROSBY, JUDY GIBBS, Art/Math Teacher/Librarian; *b:* Oak Ridge, TN; *m:* Philip E.; *c:* Casandra A., Philip A., Marianne J.; *ed:* (BS) Art Ed, 1975, (MS) Art Ed, 1987 Univ of TN Knoxville; Working Toward Elem Cert Univ of TN 1990; *cr:* 3rd Grade/HS Teacher Knoxville Baptist Tabernacle 1976-81; K-12th Grade Art Teacher 1986-, HS Art/Math Resource Teacher/Librarian 1990 Temple Baptist Acad; *ai:* Sr Class & Cheerleading Spon; *home:* 5760 Acapulco Ave Knoxville TN 37921

CROSBY, KATHY JEAN, English Department Chairperson; *b:* Gary, IN; *m:* Lawrence Gordon; *ed:* (BA) Eng/Journalism, Valparaiso Univ 1975; (MS) Eng/Journalism, IN Univ 1981; *cr:* Eng Teacher Benton Cntrl HS 1975-80, Hobart HS 1980-81; Eng Professor IN St Univ 1980-81; Eng Teacher/Dept Chairperson Kankakee Valley HS 1981-; *ai:* Quill & Scroll, Yrbk, Newspaper Spon; Dept Chm; Curr & Textbook Adoption Comm; IN Teachers of Writing 1987-; NCTE, NEA, IN Ed Assn, IN HS Press Assn, Columbia Scholastic Press Assn, Natl Scholastic Press Assn; Union Fire Auxiliary 1989-; Vidette Messenger Writer & KV Teacher Recognition Awds; *office:* Kankakee Valley HS Box 182 Rt 3 Wheatfield IN 46392

CROSBY, PEGGY FAYE, 4th Grade Teacher; *b:* Albany, GA; *ed:* (BS) Elem Ed, GA St Coll for Women 1954; (MA) Elem Ed, 1971, (EDS) Elem Ed, 1973 Univ of GA; *cr:* Teacher Thomas Elem 1954-55, Lindsey Elem 1955-64, Parkwood Elem 1964-; *ai:* Houston Cty Assn Ed Secy Thank You 1954-; GA Assn of Ed, NEA 1954-; PTA (Secy, Teacher Rep) Thank You 1954-; Teacher of Yr.

CROSBY, ROSE (RANIERI), Mathematics Teacher; *b:* Brooklyn, NY; *m:* Fred; *ed:* (BS) Math, 1968, (MS) Math, 1972 Brooklyn Coll; *cr:* Teacher F D Roosevelt HS; *ai:* Math Team Coach; Advanced Placement Math Teacher; MAA, Assn of HS Math Teachers, NCTM Mem; *office:* F D Roosevelt HS 5800 20th Ave Brooklyn NY 11204

CROSBY, WILLIAM LARRY, Math Teacher; *b:* Lexington, TN; *m:* Mary L. Blackwood; *c:* Meredith, Leslie, Audra; *ed:* (BS) Ag, 1971; (MS) Curr/Instr 1975 Univ of Tn; *cr:* Math Teacher Riverside HS 1972-; *ai:* Mu Alpha Theta Spon; Math Competition Adv; Decatur Cty Ed Assn (VP) 1988 Outstanding Teacher Awd 1987.

CROSLAND, BARKSDALE JOHNSTON, First Grade Teacher; *b:* Jackson, MS; *w:* Robert M. Jr. (dec); *c:* Robert M. III, Emmet C., Emily Crosland Dixon; *ed:* (BA) Ed, Millsaps Coll 1953; *cr:* 1st Grade Teacher St Andrews Episcopal Day Sch 1953-54, Cleveland Avenue Sch 1954-56; 2nd Grade Teacher Mc Clatchey 1956-57; Kndgtn Teacher 1968-71, 1st Grade Teacher 1972- Jackson Acad; *ai:* MS Private Sch Ed Assn; Jr League of Jackson 1958-70; *office:* Jackson Acad 4908 Ridgewood Rd Jackson MS 39211

CROSLEY, ELOISE WIESE, Second Grade Teacher; *b:* Bloomfield, NE; *m:* Paul N.; *c:* Dawn; *ed:* (BAE) Elem Ed, Wayne St Coll 1966; *cr:* 7th Grade Core Teacher Valley View Jr HS 1966-70; 5th-6th Grade Combination Room Teacher Jefferson Elem 1970-73; 5th-6th Eng Teacher Bloomfield Cmmty Sch 1973-74; 2nd Grade Teacher Creighton Cmmty Sch 1980-90; *ai:* SAT Team; NEA, NSEA, CTA 1980-; Center Lib Bd (Treas 1989-, Mem 1984-); Center Town Bd Mem 1980-83; *office:* Creighton Comm Elem Sch Redick Ave Creighton NE 68729

CROSS, JO ANN MATHEWS, Mathematics Department Chair; *b:* Bonham, TX; *m:* Ben W.; *c:* Carol C. Wise, Cheryl C. Oliver, Jeanne K.; *ed:* (BS) Math, 1959, (MED) Math, 1960 E TX St Univ; Univ of Dallas, Univ of TX Tyler; *cr:* Math Teacher/Dept Head Mesquite HS 1960-; *ai:* Destination Mars Project & Delphi Club Spon; NCTM 1970-; TX Assn of Gifted/Talented 1989-; TX St Teachers Assn 1960-; Mensa 1970-; Intertel 1975-; Tandy Technology Scholar; TX Excl Awd Outstanding HS Teachers Univ of TX Austin; *office:* Mesquite HS 300 E Davis Mesquite TX 75149

CROSS, LINDA GORDON, Second Grade Teacher; *b:* Detroit, MI; *m:* Robert L.; *c:* Jason, Nathan; *ed:* (BS) Elem Ed, Southeast MO 1967; *cr:* 2nd Grade Teacher 1967-69, 4th Grade Teacher 1969-84, 2nd Grade Teacher 1984- Century Elem; *ai:* Jr HS Track Coach 1985-89; Century Ed Assn 1967-89; IL Ed Assn 1967-89; Beta Sigma Phi Pres 1986-87; *home:* Rt 1 Box 43A Ullin IL 62992

CROSS, MARCIA A., Reading Consultant; *b:* Providence, RI; *m:* Steven T.; *c:* Sarah A.; *ed:* (BA) Scndry Ed/Eng, 1974, (MED) Rdng Consultant, 1980 RI Coll; *cr:* Elem Teacher Holy Name Sch 1976-77; Eng Chairperson/Rdng Consultant St Xavier Acad 1978-85; Rdng Consultatn Johnston HS 1985-; *ai:* In-Service Trng Thinking, Writing, Study Skills & Standardized Testing Prgm; NE Scndry Schls Accreditation Steering Comm Mem; *office:* Johnston HS 345 Cherry Hill Rd Johnston RI 02919

CROSS, PHYLLIS ANN (GARVIN), Mathematics Teacher; *b:* Paducah, TX; *m:* Billy Joe; *c:* Ben A., Brad A., Brent A.; *ed:* (BS) Math, Wayland Baptist Univ 1978; (MED) Ed/Scndry W TX St Univ Canyon 1983; Self Study in Cmptr Literacy For Endorsement Testing; Problem Solving Math, Applied Problems & Statistics Math, Wayland Baptist Univ 1987; Advanced Academic Trng Motivating Reluctant Learner 1990; *cr:* Math Teacher Floydada Jr HS 1978-79, Estacado Jr HS 1979-; Part-Time Teacher Adult Learning Center 1983-; *ai:* Organized 1st Math Cmptr Labs Estacado 1980-82; Hospitality Comm Estacado 1988-; UIL Calculator, Number Sense & Math Jr HS Coach 1978-; Comm for Grouping Stu in Plainview Ind Sch Dist 1988-89; Seminar for Drugs & Suicide Among Youth, Teens, Young Adults 1988; Comm Estacado for Locating & Serving Stus with Drugs and/or Suicidal Problems/At-Risk Stus 1988-89; TX St Teachers Assn 1978-83; TX South Plains Cncl Teachers of Math 1989-; Gamma Iota 1986-88; TX Classroom Teachers Assn (Secy, Treas 1979-81) 1978-; Conference for Advancement of Math Teaching; Interview for Wayland Baptist Univ, 1988, Effort to Eliminate Failure Problems; *home:* 1413 W 26th St Plainview TX 79072

CROSS, RONALD GARY, Science/Phys Ed Teacher; *b:* Andrews, NC; *m:* Janet Kammerer; *c:* Maggie, Lindsay; *ed:* (AA) Brevard Coll 1969; (BS) Health/Phys Ed, E Carolina Univ 1971; (MA) Mid Ed/Sci, W Carolina Univ 1979; *cr:* Teacher/Coach Nantahala Sch 1971-; *ai:* Boys Vlybl & Bsktbl Coach; NCAE; Smoky Mountain Conference Coach of Yr; Far West Conference Coach of Yr; Teacher of Yr; *home:* Star Rt Topton NC 28781

CROSS, VERSIA WILLIAMS, Sixth Grade Teacher; *b:* Poplar Bluff, MO; *m:* John Marque; *c:* Marque, Tambra, Tanya, Ki Ara; *ed:* (BA) Ed, Lincoln Univ 1966; (BA) Ed, North East MO St 1977; (MA) Ed, National Coll of Ed; *cr:* Teacher St Louis Bd of Ed 1966-68; EastSt Louis Bd of Ed 1968-71; Normandy Sch Dist 1971-; *ai:* Youth Dir Baptist Church of Holy Communion; Dir Teacher-Child-Parent Organization; Adv Girls Club; Delta Sigma Theta 1966-; PTA President 1977-78; Neighborhood Assn Youth Cnslr 1978-90; Vacation Bible Sch Dir 1977-; Grant (Teacher-Child-Parent Interaction); TESA Awd, ITE Awd Normandy Sch Dist; *home:* 6847 Raymond St Louis MO 63130

CROSSETT, BECKY FORBES, Dept Chair for Gifted Center; *b:* Williamston, NC; *m:* David A.; *c:* Shawn, Kenya, Kevin; *ed:* (BA) Music Ed, E Carolina Univ 1963; (MA) Ed, Coll of William & Mary 1980; *cr:* Choral Dir Churchland Jr HS 1963-65; Teacher Tabb Elem Sch 1980-82; Dept/Chairperson/Teacher Extend Center 1982-; *ai:* HS Extend Prgm Coord; Odyssey of Mind, Future Problem Solving Team Coach; Delta Kappa Gamma 1988-89; Sigma Alpha Iota Choral Dir 1962-63; Seaford Yacht Club 1982-; Article Published in Soc Ed 1981; Teacher of Yr York Cty Public Schls 1987-88; *office:* Extend Center 9300 George Washington Mem Hwy Yorktown VA 23692

CROSSLIN, RICK, 4th Grade Teacher; *b:* Albuquerque, NM; *m:* Brenda Burnette; *c:* Whitney G., William T.; *ed:* (BA) Elem Ed, IN St Univ 1976; (MS) Elem Ed, IN Univ 1981; IN Writing Conference 1986; Hoosier Assn of Sci Teachers St Conferences 1984-; NSTA Regional Conference 1987; MSD Wayne Township Teacher Inservice 1976-; MSD Wayne Township Teacher Evaluation Comm 1984 & Outdoor Ed Comm 1990; ISTA Spring Teacher Trng Inst 1989; IN Elem & Mid Sch St Prin Convention 1989; IN Rdng Conference 1986; Ind Learning Fair 1989; IN Inst for New Bus 1990; NASA Lewis Research Center 1985; *cr:* 4th Grade Sci Exploration Teacher IN St Univ 1975; Teaching Asst IN Boys Sch IN Dept of Corrections 1980; 3rd-6th Grade Teacher Cairo-Amer Coll 1981-83; Instr IUPUI Young Scholars Prgm 1989; 3rd/4th Grade Teacher Chapel Glen Elem 1976-; Resource Instr Indianapolis Childrens Museum Early Chldhd Prgm 1978-; Aerospace Ed Instr IUPUI Grad Course 1986-; Teacher Indianapolis Childrens Museum 1989-; Aerospace Ed Specialist ARAC 1990; *ai:* Suburban West Optimist Soccer Club Founder & Mem 1976-; Adult Soccer Club Mgr, Player, Coach; Girls Summer Sftbl League Coach 1979-80; Cub Scout & 4-H Prgms 1976-; Indianapolis Youth Soccer Peace Games Team 1976-; Pan Amer Games X Soccer Volunteer; Model Teacher 1988; Phi Delta Kappa, Hoosier Assn of Sci Teachers, NSTA, IN St HS Athletic Assn, MSD Wayne Township Classroom Teachers Assn, Natl Friends of Minearolgy, Mid-America & IN Paleontology Society, Indianapolis Aquarium Society, Freflight Fellowship, Natl Audubon Society, IN Aerospace Ed Cncl, Educators Aerospace Ed Assn; Chapel Glen PTO Mem; St Friends of Minearolgy; Deans & Governors List IN St Univ 1975; Distinguished Stu Teaching Awd IN St Univ 1976; Optimist Club & Gleaners Food Band Service Awds 1978; Amer Red Cross Citation 1979; IN Dept of Ed Distinguished Teaching Awd 1985; IN Space Prgm Alternate NASA Teacher 1985; Leonhardt Fellow Earthwatch Expedition 1986; Natl Ed Commission of St Natl Teachers Forum St Rep 1986; MSD Wayne Township Academic Excl Awd 1986-89; *office:* Chapel Glen Elem Sch 701 Lansdown Rd Indianapolis IN 46234

CROSTHWAIT, LINDA (CONNER), 1st/2nd Grade Teacher; *b:* Effingham, IL; *m:* Larry; *c:* Brock, Jennifer; *ed:* (BS) Elem Ed, S OK St Univ 1977; *cr:* Music Teacher Graham HS; 5th/6th Grade Rdng Teacher 1986-88, 1st Grade Teacher 1977-, 2nd Grade Teacher 1980-81, 1988- Graham Elem; *ai:* Staff Dev Comm; Outstanding Young Women of America; *home:* Hoxbar Rt Box 171 Ardmore OK 73401

CROTEAU, GALE HARPER, Secondary Sod Stud Teacher; *b:* Keene, NH; *m:* Brenda Flanders; *c:* Jason A., Sarah Croteau Gallo; *ed:* (BE) Ed/His, Keene St Coll 1964; Working Towards Masters Ed, Keene St Coll 1966; His/Intnl Relations, W CT St Univ; *cr:* Soc Stud Teacher Farmington HS 1964-65, Lebanon Jr HS 1965-66, E Ridge Jr HS 1967-69, John Jay Jr HS 1969-; *ai:* Re-Organization Comm John Jay Jr HS; NEA, Katonah Lewisboro Teachers Assn 1969-; Elks 1989-.

CROTTS, JUDY E., Chapter I Reading Teacher; *b:* Winston-Salem, NC; *m:* Charles M.; *c:* Charles M. Jr., James H. II; *ed:* (AA) Liberal Art, Gardner Webb Coll 1967; (BS) Elem Ed, E Carolina Univ 1969; (MS) Elem Ed/Rdng, NC A&T Univ 1984; *cr:* 6th Grade Teacher Oak Grove Elem Sch 1969-70; 4th Grade Teacher Merrick Moore Elem Sch 1970-72; 7th/8th Grade Teacher Brown Mid 1975-; *ai:* Tutor At Risk Stus; NC Educl Assn 1969-72, 1975-; *office:* E Lawson Brown Mid Sch 1140 Kendall Mill Rd Thomasville NC 27360

CROUCH, CONSTANCE RATLEFF, Language Arts/Soc Sci Teacher; *b:* New Orleans, LA; *c:* Denise Gonzales Bonner, Curtis B. Gonzales Jr., Kyle Crouch Smith; *ed:* (BA) Elem Ed/Eng, Xavier Univ 1953, Grad Stud Admin, Xavier Univ; *cr:* 2nd Grade Teacher New Orleans LA 1953-61, 1st-3rd Grade Teacher Hays Elem Sch 1961-74; 3rd-4th Grade Teacher Hartwell Sch 1974-77; Rdng Resource Teacher George Washington Sch 1977-78; Rdng Resource/Master Teacher A J Bell Mid Sch 1978-80; 6th Grade Teacher Washburn Elem 1980-; *ai:* Discipline Comm; Entry Level Comm Co-Chairperson; Cincinnati Fed of Teachers Area Coord 1985-; Alpha Kappa Alpha Pres 1976-77; *office:* Washburn Elem Sch 1425 Linn St Cincinnati OH 45214

CROUCH, NANCY LEE, 7th Grade TX History Teacher; *b:* Gorman, TX; *c:* Jana L., Julie A.; *ed:* (BS) Bus Ed, TX Chrstn Univ 1958; (MAT) Eng, Tarleton St Univ 1973; His Cert 1977; *cr:* 8th Grade Eng/Lang Art Teacher Ft Worth Ind Sch Dist 1960-62; 7th/8th Grade Amer/TX His Teacher Stephenville Ind Sch Dist 1974-; *ai:* Lakeside Tours Incorporated Dir; Stu Tour Washington DC; Amer Inst of Foreign Study Dir; Adopt-A-Museum Coord; Museum Maintenance Fund Raising Benefit; TX Classroom Teachers Assn 1974-; St Historical Assn 1988-; Stephenville Historical Museum Bd VP 1986-; Cross Timbers Fine Art Cncl 1980-; Kappa Alpha Theta; Panhellenic Cncl Co-Chm 1985-89; Erath Cty Historical Commission CItation for Appreciation; Delta Kappa Gamma Preservation of TX His Awd; St of TX Historical CommissionOutstanding TX His Teacher Awd; Nominee Daughters of Republic of TX Outstanding Teaching of TX His; *office:* Stephenville Ind Sch Dist 1067 W Jones Stephenville TX 76401

CROUCH, PHIL, Mathematics & Computer Teacher; *b:* Glenrock, WY; *m:* Dolores Kowlok; *c:* Carolyn, Robert, Michael; *ed:* (AA) Pre Engineering, Casper Coll 1959-62; (BS) Ed, Black Hills Teachers Coll 1962-64; Univ of UT, Southwestern St of OK, Univ of WY; *cr:* Sci Teacher/Coach Delavan HS 1964-66, Greybull HS 1966-69; Math Teacher/Coach Starrett Jr HS 1969-; *ai:* Mathcounts & Team; Ftbl, Bsktbl, Wrestling, Track; NCTM, WCTM, LEA; Elks; Selection Comm NSF Insts; *office:* Starrett Jr HS 863 Sweetwater St Lander WY 82520

CROUCH, WANDA FAYE, Mathematics Teacher; *b:* Paris, AR; *m:* Ronald Dean; *c:* Rhonda, Ashley; *ed:* (BSE) Math/Bus Ed, 1973, (MED) Voc Bus Ed, 1975 Univ of AR; Grad Study Math/Cmptr Sci; *cr:* Math Teacher Bergman HS 1966-67, 1974-77; Bus/Math/Sci/His Teacher St Joe HS 1967-74; Math Teacher Harrison HS 1977-83; Math/Cmptr Sci Teacher S Garland HS 1983-; *ai:* TEAMS Coach; Bengalette Drill Team; Curr Guide Comm; UIL Calculator Teacher; Phi Beta Lamba Charter Mem; TX Ed Assn, NEA 1983-; AR Ed Assn 1969-83; NCTM 1969-; Heart Assn Subdivision Collector 1979-; March of Dimes Chairperson 1974-77; Eastern Stars (Rebekah, Nobel Grand) 1966-; Hyer Scholastic Schlsp; Food Drive Christmas; Outstanding Young Women of Amer; Commencement Speaker; Guest Presenter AR St Bus Teachers; Article on Articulation Between HS & Coll Accounting; Inservice Presenters; Taught Teachers Use of Cmptr Through E TX Univ; *home:* 1234 Sicily Dr Garland TX 75040

CROUSE, CAMELLIA MILLER, Biology Teacher; *m:* Howard Perry; *c:* Cheyenne C.; *ed:* Grad Stud Sci, Ed; *cr:* Teacher Oceana HS 1975-; *ai:* Jr & Soph Class Adv; Sci Club, Quiz Bowl, Scores Spon; WV Ed Assn 1975-; WV Sci Teachers Assn 1980-; Big Cub Missionary Baptist Church Youth Spon; *office:* Oceana HS P O Box 310 Oceana WV 24870

CROUSE, CATHERINE S., Second Grade Teacher; *b:* Hartford City, IN; *ed:* (MS) Educl Admin, Purdue Univ 1981; Grad Work Educl Admin; IMPACT Trng Drug Free Schls; *cr:* 2nd-4th Grade Teacher Coolspring Sch & MI City Area Schls 1971-; *ai:* Core Team Leader; Just Say No Club Spon & Adv; Co-Spon, Co-Presenter Classroom Self-Esteem Wkshps; Phi Delta Kappa 1975-; Alpha Delta Kappa Corresponding Secy 1986-; IN Prof Educators 1988-; Intnl Rdng Assn 1973-; League of Women Voters 1979-; Volunteer Adult Literacy Prgm; *office:* Coolspring Sch 9121 W 300 N Michigan City IN 46360

CROUSE, CHARLES FRANKLIN, Lead Teacher of Mathematics; *b:* Cainsville, MO; *m:* Wanda Jane Jones; *c:* Kevin F., Todd A., Andrea R., Harry S.; *ed:* (BA) Math/Industrial Art, Univ of MO Maryville 1962; (MS) Guidance/Counseling, IA St 1980; *cr:* Teacher North Cty Cmmty Sch 1962-63; Teacher 1963-70, Teacher/Math Dept Head 1970-83, Lead Teacher of Math 1983- Thomas Jefferson HS; *ai:* Ftbl & Bsktbl Scorer & Time Keeper 1964-; IA Cncl Teachers of Math 1970-; NCTM 1985-; NEA, IA St Ed Assn 1963-; St Math Meetings Presenter; SW IA Math Teacher of Yr; Adult Ed Teacher; *home:* 657 Spencer Ave Council Bluffs IA 51503

CROUSE, DALE, Business Education Teacher; *b:* Gary, IN; *m:* Jeanette Smith; *c:* Andrew, Amy; *ed:* (BS) Bus Ed, E IL Univ 1967; (MS) Bus Ed, S IL Univ 1971; *cr:* Bus Ed Teacher Belleville East HS 1967-; *ai:* AFT Local 434 Treas 1972-74, 1978-; Delta Pi Epsilon; SWABEA; 1st Baptist Church; *office:* Belleville East HS 2555 West Blvd Belleville IL 62221

CROUSE, DEBRA SMITH, Third Grade Teacher; *b:* Zanesville, OH; *m:* Daryl Lawrence; *c:* Erin, Wesley; *ed:* (BA) Early Chldhd Ed, Warren Wilson Coll 1979; *cr:* 3rd Grade Teacher Bethel Elem 1979-; *ai:* Sch Based Comm Chairperson; NEA, Intnl Rdng Assn, NC Assn of Educators 1979-; Snow Hill United Meth (Choir Mem 1980-, Jr Choir Accompanist 1987-); Nom Sch Teacher of Yr 1989; *office:* Bethel Elem Sch Rt 3 Box 256 Waynesville NC 28786

CROVO, NILA J., Fourth Grade Teacher; *b:* Robbins, TN; *m:* Peter M.; *c:* Peter D., Michael; *ed:* (BA) Soc Services, Barrington Coll 1970; Teaching Certificate Glassboro St 1973; *cr:* Teacher Micro Social Learning Center 1971-73; 3rd Grade Teacher Marie Durand Sch 1973-78; 4th Grade Teacher Max Leuchter Sch 1980-; *ai:* The Exchange Club of Vineland Educator of Yr Awd Receipient 1990; *home:* 3323 Swan Dr Vineland NJ 08360

CROW, CHERYL ANNETTE, 8th Grade Math Teacher; *b:* Dallas, TX; *m:* Tony; *c:* Candace, Landon; *ed:* (BS) Math, E TX St 1979; Cmptr Cert; *cr:* 6th Grade Teacher 1979-80; 8th Grade Math Teacher 1980- Winnsboro Ind Sch Dist; *ai:* UIL Number Sense Spon 5th-8th Grades; Budget Comm Math Mid Sch; Chrldr Co-Spon; CTA; *office:* Winnsboro Memorial Mid Sch 505 S Chestnut Winnsboro TX 75494

CROW, CLIFTEEN J., Vocational Business Teacher; *b:* Atoka, OK; *m:* Billy Frank; *c:* Tanya, Lindley, Valerie Rodriguez; *ed:* (BS) Bus Ed, SE OK 1971; (BS) Elem Ed, SE OK St Univ 1971; Voc Bus; *cr:* 1st Grade Teacher Denison Public Schls 1971-80; Voc Bus Teacher Atoka HS 1980-; *ai:* FBLA; Sr Class Spon; AVA, OK Voc Assn, Natl Bus Assn, OK Bus Assn; First Baptist Church; *office:* Atoka HS 800 Greathouse Dr Atoka OK 74525

CROW, V. ESTELL MC LEROY, Remedial Math/Reading Teacher; *b:* Olney, OK; *m:* David Glen; *c:* Terry A. Wyche, Dianna R.; *ed:* (BA) Elem Ed, E Cntrl Univ 1969; *cr:* 6th Grade Teacher 1969-80, 4th Grade Teacher 1980-85, Title V/Tutor 1985-89, Remedial Math/Rdng Teacher/Title V Tutor 1989- Tupelo Elem Sch; *ai:* Coal Cty Teachers Assn, OK Ed Assn, NEA 1969-; Dist Child Abuse Prevention Task Force; *office:* Tupelo Elem Sch P O Box 310 Tupelo OK 74572

CROWDER, JAMES DAVID, Dept Chairman/Ag Sci Teacher; *b:* Sherman, TX; *m:* Peggy Lois; *c:* Kenneth, Kristin, Kurt; *ed:* (BS) Ag Ed, TX A&M 1970; (MED) Ag, Stephen F Austin St Univ 1973; *cr:* Ag Sci Teacher Mc Gregor HS 1970-71, Kilgore HS 1971-77; Dept Head/Ag Sci Teacher Calallen HS 1977-; *ai:* Adv Calallen FFA; Sr Class Party Spon; Natl Voc Ag Teachers Assn, Voc Ag Teacher Assn of TX 1970-; Area Ag Teacher Assn (Honorary St Farmer, Past Pres); Disabled Amer Veterans 1970-; Past Pres Nueces Cty A&M Club; Applicant for Outstanding Voc Ag Teacher of Yr Awd 1989-; *office:* Calallen HS 4001 Wildcat Dr Corpus Christi TX 78410

CROWDER, KENNETH ROBERT, 8th Grade Soc Studies Teacher; *b:* St Louis, MO; *ed:* (BS) Ed, 1971, (MED) Scndry Ed, 1976 Univ MO; *cr:* 8th Grade Teacher Ritenour Mid Sch 1972-; *ai:* Spon Yrly Canned Food Drive for Needy; Active in Teacher Mentor Prgm; NEA Mem 1972-; *office:* Ritenour Mid Sch 8740 Forest Overland MO 63114

CROWDER, PAMELA MC CRORY, Fifth Grade Teacher; *b:* Parris Island, SC; *m:* Joseph Walton; *c:* Heather; *ed:* (BS) Elem Ed, 1970, (MA) Rdng Specialist, 1974 Univ of Tulsa; Admin, Univ of Tulsa 1982; OK St Univ 1989; *cr:* 2nd Grade Teacher Revere Elem 1970-72; 2nd-5th Grade Teacher Cooper Elem 1972-; *ai:* MMICRO Rdng Management Coord; Safety Poster Contest, Safety Patrol Spon; Teacher in Charge; Staff Dev, Building Evaluation, Prins Advisory Comm Chm; Academic Freedom, Sch Improvement Plan, Holt Math Management Prgm, On-Site Budget, Sch Effectiveness, 6 Yr/60000 Mile Warranty Comm; Supervised & Trained Intern Teachers; Grade Level Chm; Creative Writing Cadre; Elem Task Force; Phi Delta Kappa; Tulsa Classroom Teachers Assn, OK Ed Assn, NEA; Delta Kappa Gamma Schlsp 1980; Kappa Kappa Iota Pres; Kappa Delta Pi; Intnl Rdng Assn; Tulsa Cty Rdng Cncl Rep 1989-; OK Rdng Cncl; Ed Admin Alumni Assn Univ of Tulsa; Tulsa Cncl Teachers of Math; ASCD; Evening Pilot Club of Tulsa Pres 1984-85, Pilot of Yr 1987; Broken Arrow United Meth Church; Amer Cancer Society; Amer Arthritis Fnd; PTA; Educator of Week by Facet Enterprises & Radio Magic 99 1989; Featured in Tulsa World for Newspapers in Ed Week 1989; Interviewed on KOTV-TV for Teacher Appreciation Day 1986; 1st Teacher of Week 1989; Provide Entertaining Material Pediatric Ward; *office:* Cooper Elem Sch 1808 S 123 E Ave Tulsa OK 74128

CROWDIS, RHONDA NARAMORE, HS English & French Teacher; *b:* Ft Gaines, GA; *m:* John Arthur; *c:* Levi, Jordana; *ed:* (BA) Eng, 1975, (MA) Ed, 1979 GA SW Coll; *cr:* Teacher Crisp Acad 1973-74, Clay Cty HS 1974-75, Sumter Cty Mid Sch 1975-80, Calhoun Cty HS 1980-87, Early Cty HS 1987-; *ai:* Literary Coach; Oral Interpretation; One Act Play; Sch Newspaper Adv; NCTE 1988-; United Meth Women 1988-; Pi Delta Phi, Order of the Gown; *office:* Early Cty HS 420 Columbia Rd Blakely GA 31723

CROWE, ANNE EVARD, Assistant Principal; *b:* Fort Wayne, IN; *m:* Joseph B.; *c:* Michael, John, Mary A., Elizabeth, David; *ed:* (BA) His, St Mary of the Woods Coll 1959; (MED) Admin, Xavier Univ 1990; *cr:* 7th Grade Teacher Assumption Sch 1959-60; 8th Grade Teacher 1981-87, Asst Prin 1987- St Bartholomew Consolidated Sch; *ai:* Discipline Comm; Rainbows for Gods Children Counseling; NCEA; ASCD; *office:* St Bartholomew Consolidated 9375 Winton Rd Cincinnati OH 45231

CROWE, CLEMENTS, Social Studies Teacher; *b:* Philadelphia, PA; *m:* Mary Dee Humes; *c:* Gregory, Jennifer Trautwein; *ed:* (BA) His, Trinity Coll 1958; (MA) His, Univ of PA 1960; St Univ of NY Albany & Plattsburg; *cr:* Teacher Molly Stark Jr HS 1959-61, Cambridge Cntrl Sch 1961-; *ai:* NY St United Teachers; Cambridge Public Lib Bd (Treas 1961-88, Pres 1988-); Grant to Natl Defense Ed Act Inst in European Cultural His 1968; Fulbright Fellowship to Teach Anglo-Amer Exch Teacher Prgm 1966-67; *office:* Cambridge Cntrl Sch 24 S Park St Cambridge NY 12816

CROWLEY, BETH M., Mathematics Dept Head/Teacher; *b:* New York, NY; *m:* Guy D.; *c:* Samuel D., Lauren E.; *ed:* (BA) Industrial Engineering, Southern Tech Inst 1985; *cr:* Math Teacher Harvester Acad 1985-; *office:* Harvester Acad 4650 Flat Shoals Pkwy Decatur GA 30034

CROWLEY, MARGIE ROSS, 8th Grade Earth Sci Teacher; *b:* Camden, SC; *m:* William Oliver; *c:* Sheila Crowley Moore, Sharon A.; *ed:* (BA) Elem Ed, Furman Univ 1958; Univ of SC, Clemson Univ; Wm Glasser Tecniques, La Verne Coll Center; *cr:* 1st Grade Teacher Pine Tree Hill Elem 1959-60; 7th Grade Teacher Davenport Jr HS 1960-70; 5th Grade Teacher Fairview Elem 1970-84; 8th Grade Teacher Greer Mid Sch 1984-; *ai:* Local & Regional Conservation Energy Coord; Energy Club Adv; PTA, Civic, Garden Club Speaker; Sci Fair Judge; Christmas Parade Entries Organizer; Palmetto St Teachers Assn (Rising Pres 1981-, Pres Elect 1989-); St PTA Honorary Life Mem 1971, Outstanding Teacher of Yr 1988; Delta Kappa Gamma (Mem, Past Pres) 1970-; Furman Univ Panel for Prins Mem 1988; Governor Riley Educl Forum Steering Comm Mem 1988; PET Trng 1987; QUEST Prgm Trng; Supvr Stu Teachers Various Univs; SCETV Participant 1988; Alliance for Quality Ed Grants; EIA Grant; Initiated Transition from Mid Sch to Prgm; Life Underwriters Assn Dist Wide Subsance Abust Awds; Greenville Cty Conservation Teacher of Yr 1986; Greenville Cty Teacher of Yr 1989-; Finalist SC Teacher of Yr 1990; *office:* Greer Mid Sch 301 Chandler Rd Greer SC 29651

CROWLEY, SHERRY, Library Media Specialist; *b:* West Point, MS; *m:* William Paul; *c:* Kimberly, Anna Laura; *ed:* (BA) Lib Sci, Wood Jr Coll 1975; (BS) Lib Sci/Eng, 1977, (MS) Lib Sci 1982 MS St Univ; *cr:* Lib Media/Spec/Eng Teacher East Webster HS 1977-; *ai:* Lib Club Spon; Homecoming Dir; *office:* East Webster H S Rt 2 Box 468 Maben MS 39750

CROY, ANN STRUCHER, Kindergarten Teacher; *b:* Jerome, ID; *m:* John; *c:* Brandon, B Ennett, Kyle; *ed:* (BS) Elem Ed, Univ of ID 1977; Grad Stud; *cr:* 1st Grade Math Teacher Gooding Elem 1977; 2nd Grade Teacher Valley Sch Dist 1977-78; Kndgtn Teacher 1978-79, 2nd Grade Teacher 1981-82, Kngtn Teacher 1983- Kuna Sch Dist; *ai:* Math Curr & Schlsp Comms; Kuna Ed Assn, NEA 1988-; *home:* 10262 Countryman Boise ID 83709

CROZIER, NANCY JOYCE (MILLIKEN), Third Grade Teacher; *b:* Millbury, MA; *m:* George H.; *c:* David, Martha, Peter; *ed:* (BS) Ed, Univ of MO 1979; Lindenwood Coll; Northeast MO St Coll; *cr:* Teacher Lincoln Cty R2 Sch Dist 1980-; *ai:* Cmmty Teachers Assn (Pres 1987-88/VP 1986-88); Univ of MO Alumni Assn; Phi Kappa Phi; Lake St Louis Chamber of Commerce Outstanding Educator 1988; Williams Memorial Meth Church Mission Comm; Named Christa Mc Auliffe Fellow By US Dept of Ed; Received Grant to Implement Cmptr Enhanced Instruction Prgm Grades 2-3-4 in Sch Dist; *office:* Lincoln Cty R2 Sch Dist Sanderson & Welch Elsberry MO 63343

CRUISE, KAREN ASHBY, Fourth Grade Teacher; *b:* Staunton, VA; *m:* Ronald Eldwin; *c:* Justin, Jordan; *ed:* (BS) Elem Ed, VA Polytechnic Inst/St Univ 1975; Developmental Skills Inst Trng; Higher Level Thinking Skills; Curr Dev Math; *cr:* Kndgtn Teacher Boiling Spring Elem 1975-76, Cntrl Elem 1976-80; 4th Grade Teacher Callaghan Elem 1981-; *ai:* PTA; Grant Awarded By Covington/Alleghany Ed Assn 1989; *home:* Rt 2 Box 154A Covington VA 24426

CRUM, AVAFLORENCE POWELL, Mathematics Teacher; *b:* North Fork, WV; *m:* George V.; *c:* Louise C. Goode, Jaye P.; *ed:* (BA) Math, 1956, (MA) Math Ed, 1958 Marshall Univ; Marshall Univ, WV Coll of Grad Stud, WV Univ; *cr:* Teacher Thomas Jefferson Jr HS 1957-62; Teacher/Math Chairperson Stonewall Jackson HS 1962-71, Winfield HS 1971-; Realtor P M Properties 1985-; *ai:* Mu Alpha Theta Spon; Adopt A Cmptr Chairperson; Partnership In Ed Faculty Rep; Math Learning Outcomes Comm; WV Cncl Teacher of Math, 1981-, WV Outstanding Math Teacher 1983; NCTM Referee 1984-; Math Assn of Amer; Putnam Cty Chamber of Commerce Outstanding Educator 1988; NSF Summer Inst 1983; Presidential Awd for Excl in Teaching Math; WV Math Teacher of Yr 1983; WV Ed Fund Merit Awd 1987; Putnam Cty Merit Awd 1988; Putnam Cty Teacher of Yr; *home:* 126 Oakwood Ests Scott Depot WV 25560

CRUM, JO ANN COOK, Sixth Grade Teacher; *b:* Graham, TX; *m:* C. D.; *c:* Carole Roberts, Teresa Odom; *ed:* (BS) Elem Ed, Angelo St Univ 1970; *cr:* 5th Grade Teacher Belaire Elem 1970-73; 6th Grade Teacher Rush Elem 1975-; *ai:* Stu Cncl Spon; City, Regional, St Judge; WRITE Lead, Teacher Trainer; Odyssey of Mind; Future Problem Solving Coach; Textbook Advisory, Curr Writing, Thematic Curr Writing Comm; NEA, TX St Teachers Assn 1970-; Lubbock Educators Assn 1975-; TX Classroom Teachers Assn 1970-; Lubbock Classroom Teachers Assn 1975-; Alpha Delta Kappa (Recording Secy 1986-88, VP 1988-); Caprock Area Writing Project; *office:* Rush Elem Sch 4702 15th St Lubbock TX 79416

CRUM, KATHERINE GONIS, Third Grade Teacher; *b:* San Mateo, CA; *m:* Gordon Wright Sr.; *c:* Scott, Gordon Jr., Stuart, JoeL; *ed:* (BA) Ed, San Francisco St 1955; *cr:* 1st Grade Teacher Martin Sch 1956-57; 4th Grade Teacher Craig Sch 1974-78; Kndgtn Teacher Wimbish/Swift 1981-82; 5th Grade Teacher 1982-88, 3rd Grade Teacher 1988- C B Berry; *ai:* Sunshine Chm C B Berry Sch; TX St Teachers Assn 1981-; Intnl Rdng Assn; C B Berry Teacher of Yr 1988-89; *office:* C B Berry Elem Sch 1800 Joyce St Arlington TX 76010

CRUM, THERESA LEE, Biology Teacher; *b:* Wetumpka, AL; *m:* Bob M. Sr.; *c:* Bob M. Jr.; *ed:* (BS) Bio, Tuskegee Univ 1969; (MED) Bio Ed, Auburn Univ 1977; *cr:* Bio Teacher Wetumpka HS 1969-; *ai:* Spon Sci Club & Stu Cncl; Club Builder Jr Civitan Club; Presenter Effective Sch Inservice Prgm; AL Ed Assn, NEA, Elmore Cty Ed Assn 1969-; Teacher of Month 1989; Wetumpka Civitan Club Secy 1989- Club Builder 1989; Tuskegee Univ Summer Sci Prgm; Coll Bd Advanced Placement Bio Inst Univ of AL; Mellon Grant to Attend A P Ins t; Mem Accreditation Visiting Comm Jeff Davis HS; CMEE Exam Evaluation for Sci; *office:* Wetumpka HS 1251 Coosa River Pkwy Wetumpka AL 36092

CRUMB, CANDACE HERTNEKY, English Teacher; *b:* Goodland, KS; *m:* Dewayne; *c:* Brenda Wolfe, Nancy Pellow; *ed:* (BA) Amer His, CO Coll 1962; *cr:* Eng Teacher Russell Jr HS 1974-86, Palmer HS 1986-; *ai:* Womens Var Bsktbl & Track Head Coach; NEA, CEA, CSEA 1974-; Amer Assn of Univ Women 1962-; *office:* Palmer HS 301 N Nevada Ave Colorado Springs CO 80903

CRUMBLEY, ESTHER (KENDRICK), Mathematics Teacher; *b:* Osceola, FL; *m:* Chandler Jackson; *c:* Pamela Crumbley Conner; Chandler A., William J.; *ed:* (BSE) Math, GA Southern 1966; Licensed Realtor; Grad Work Math Jacksonville Univ; *cr:* Classroom Teacher St Mary Elem 1958-66; GA Licensed Realtor Watson Realty Co 1986-; Math Camden HS 1966-; *ai:* Past Beta Club Adv; Textbook & Lib Comm; Graduation & Prom Comm; GAE (Pres, Sec, Treas) 1966-70; GMA/Camden (Chairperson, Sec, Treas 1979-88) Yrs of Service 1988); PAGE Bldg Rep 1986-; Camden Bd of Realtors (Top Sales listing 1983) 1986; Gual Society Prgm Chm 1984; Camden Cancer Drive Chairperson Fund Drive 1966; Historic Preservation Youth Center Fund Chm 1983-88; St Marys City Cncl Person 1979-88; St Marys City Cncl 1979-88; Post 6 Major Pro Term 1983-88; Chairperson Budget, City Property, Recreation, Charter & Zoning Comms 1979-88; *home:* 211 N Julia St Saint Marys GA 31558

CRUMBLEY, VERA H., English Department Chairman; *b:* Santa Rita, NM; *m:* Bud; *c:* Janean, Jeffrey; *ed:* (BA) Eng/His, 1965; (MA) Eng/Speech, 1967; (MA) Eng/Cmptr Sci, 1989 Western NM Univ; *cr:* Eng/His Teacher C C Snell Mid Sch 1965-; *ai:* Chm Eng Dept; Delta Kappa Gamma; Cobre Ed Assn; NEA; *office:* CC Snell Mid Sch Hwy 180 Bayard NM 88028

CRUMBLY, JOHNETTA WILLIAMS, Business Teacher; *b:* Forrest City, AR; *m:* Jack Bernard Sr.; *c:* Jack B. Jr., Jalandra B., Juanita B.; *ed:* (BS) Bus Ed, Univ of AR Pine Bluff 1970; (MSE) Bus Ed, 1975, Specialist Comm Coll Teaching, 1982 AR St Univ Jonesboro; *cr:* Elem Teacher Stewart Elem Sch 1971-75; Eng Teacher Forrest City Mid Sch 1975-77; Bus Teacher Forrest City HS 1977-; Typing Instr E AR Comm Coll 1989-; *ai:* AR Ed Assn Human Relations Comm Mem; Building Rep for Local Assn; Forrest City Ed Assn Building Rep 1971-; AR Ed Assn Human Relations Comm 1988-; NEA 1971-; Alpha Kappa Alpha Secy 1984-85, Ed 1981; Semper Fidelis Federated Club Reporter 1987-89; Ec Ed-Sears Fellowship 1974-75; Suggested Criteria for Selection of Textbooks Bus Ed Forum 1983; *office:* Forrest City HS 467 Victoria St Forrest City AR 72335

CRUMP, BERNADETTE, CSU, Retired Mathematics Teacher; *b:* South Boston, MA; *ed:* (AB) His, Regis Coll 1954; Grad Stud for Math Cert; *cr:* 3rd Grade Teacher St Matthew 1938-50, St John 1950-55, Immaculate Conception 1955-58; 3rd/6th Grade Teacher St Angela 1958-64; 6th/7th Grade Teacher St Pius V 1964-67; 5th-8th Grade Math Teacher St Paul 1967-73; 7th/8th Grade Math Teacher Sacred Heart 1973-88; *ai:* NCTE, NCMT, New England Cncl of Math Teachers 1988; *home:* 93 Bethany Rd Framingham MA 01701

CRUMP, CHARLES WINSLOW, Retired English Teacher; *b:* Watertown, WI; *m:* Carol Lou Black; *c:* Mike, Bill, Ann, David; *ed:* (BS) His/Eng, Univ WI Madison 1950; (MS) Admin, Univ WI Milwaukee 1972; *cr:* Primary Teacher Savan City Schls 1953-56; Intermediate HS Teacher Williams Bay Schls 1956-64; Teacher Whitnall HS 1964-88, MATC 1976-80; *ai:* Wrestling & Vlybl Coach; Newspaper & Creativie Writing Adv; Rotary Intnl 1987-89; Lions Club 1957-63; Deutschtadt Fnd Secy 1987-; BSA; Founded WI Ed Insurance Trust Secy/Treas; Village of Germantown Pres 1987-; *home:* 178W 9754N Riversbend Cir W Germantown WI 53022

CRUMP, JOANN WHISENANT, First Grade Teacher; *b:* Moulton, Lawrence; *m:* Billy R.; *ed:* (BS) Elem Ed, Athens St 1964-68; *cr:* 1st Grade Teacher W Morgan Sch 1968-; *ai:* Promotion & Retention Policy Comm; AL Ed Assn, NEA 1968-; A-Vote Local Assn 1968-; Nom Outstanding Amer Teacher in America 1983; Nom Outstanding Young Women of America; *office:* W Morgan HS Rt 2 Box 218 Trinity AL 35673

CRUMP, SCOTT, Social Studies Teacher; *b:* Newport, RI; *ed:* (BA) His/Poly Sci, 1976, (MED) Educl Admin, 1980 Brigham Young Univ 1980; Law Grad Trng; Prof Admin Cert, Univ of UT; *cr:* Teacher Bingham HS 1977-; *ai:* Stu Government Adv; Honors His Teacher; Advanced Placement Government & Politics Teacher; Mock Trial Adv; UT Law Related Ed Coord; UT Cncl for Soc Stud Pres 1988-89; UT Ed Assn Faculty Rep 1977-; Riverton City Historical Society Pres 1988-; Author of 2 Local His Books Copperton UT & Lark UT; *office:* Bingham HS 2160 W Miner Mile South Jordan UT 84065

CRUMPTON, REBECCA A., Mathematics Teacher; *b:* Double Springs, AL; *c:* Sarah Crumpton Merritt; *ed:* (BS) Math, Univ of AL 1957; (MA) Math, Univ of N AL 1971; *cr:* Teacher Haleyville HS 1957-61, Winston Cty HS 1961-; *ai:* Beta Club & Soph Class Spon; Cty Sch Calendar Comm; Scholars Bowl Coach; NEA, AEA; WCEA Pres 1970.

CRUSE, EDNA M., Third Grade Teacher; *b:* Magnolia, KY; *w:* Harold T. (dec); *c:* Stephen T.; *ed:* (BS) Elem Ed, W KY St Univ 1963; *cr:* Teacher Upton Elem Sch 1959-; *ai:* Prof Dev Comm Hardin Cty Bd of Ed; Whiz Kids Competition Coach Upton Elem Sch; NEA, KY Ed Assn 1959-; Hardin Cty Ed Assn 1968-; Certificate of Merit Outstanding Teacher KY Congress Parents & Teacher 1989; Outstanding Performance Awd Hardin Cty Bd Ed 1980; *home:* 279 Peachtree St Upton KY 42784

CRUSE, SHARON JONES, Business Teacher; *b:* Louisville, KY; *m:* Gary L.; *c:* Chase M.; *ed:* (BS) Bus Ed, W KY Univ 1974; (MA) Bus Ed, E KY Univ 1977; (Rank I) Guidance Counseling, W KY Univ 1981; *cr:* Teacher Hardin Cty Schls 1974-; *ai:* FBLA Spon; NEA 1974-; PTA VP 1990; *home:* PO Box 93 Upton KY 42784

CRUTCHFIELD, KATHERINE MOORE, Third Grade Teacher; *b:* Tifton, GA; *m:* Wade Vernon; *c:* Luanne, Brian; *ed:* (AA) Liberal Art, VA Intermont 1968; (BS) Elem Ed, Univ of GA 1970; Certificate Renewal Longwood Coll, Univ of VA; *cr:* 5th Grade Teacher 1970-71, 3rd Grade Teacher 1971-74 Hanahan Elem Sch; 4th Grade Teacher 1978-82, 3rd Grade Teacher 1982- La Crosse Elem Sch; *ai:* Sch Young Authors Contest Chairperson; Grade Chm; Lang Art Adoption Comm; Southside Cncl of Rdng Educators Cty Membership Chm 1989-; VA St Rdng Assn; Delta Kappa Gamma 1987-; Jr Womans Club VP 1979-80, Outstanding Young Woman 1980; Outstanding Young Women of America 1979; *home:* 732 Holmes St South Hill VA 23970

CRUZ, DEBRA SMITH, Fifth Grade Teacher; *b:* York, SC; *m:* Hector; *c:* Jonathan Wayne, Tiffany Autumn; *ed:* Religious Ed, Bethany Bible Coll 1989; *cr:* Elem Teacher Blessed Hope Bapt Sch 1977-; *ai:* Scholastic Awd Bethany Bible Coll; *office:* Blessed Hope Baptist Sch 410 Blessed Hope Rd York SC 29745

CRUZ, MARIA REYNOSO, Sixth Grade Mentor Teacher; *b:* Cocotitlan, Mexico; *ed:* (BA) Eng Lit, 1972, Teaching Credential, 1973 San Diego St Univ; Prof Dev Trainer; Fellowship San Diego Area Writing Project UCSD; Bi-ling Cluster Leader, San Diego St Univ; *cr:* Writing/Rdng Teacher/Leader Fine Arts Lincoln Acres 1981-83; Writing/Geography/Mentor Teacher Natl Sch Dist 1984-88; Bi-ling Cluster Leader San Diego St Univ 1988-89; Cluster Leader Natl Sch Dist 1989-; 6th Grade Teacher Lincoln Acres 1990; *ai:* San Diego St Univ & Lincoln Acres Adoption Act Coord; Advisor Supt Comm; GSA; Lang Art Pilot Teacher; Point Loma Coll Ed Dept Mexican Amer Stud Instr; San Diego Sci Educators Assn Mem 1989-; Big Sister Assn; Head Start Volunteer; AIMS Trng in Sci; *office:* Lincoln Acres Elem Sch 2200 Lanoitan Ave National City CA 92050

CRUZEN, RALPH DAVID, Retired Teacher; *b:* Harwood, MO; *ed:* (BA) Elem Ed, Pittsburg St Univ 1959; (MA) Elem Ed/ Admin, MO Univ 1967; Grad Stud Ed, CMSU, UMKC, Mc Pherson Coll; *cr:* 1st-8th Grade Teacher E Washington Sch 1952-53; 6th-8th Grade Teacher Metz Public Sch 1953-57; 7th-8th Grade Teacher Schell City Public Sch 1957-58; 6th Grade Teacher Belton Public Schls #124 1964-88; 5th-7th Grade Teacher Pilot Grove Public Schls 1958-64; *ai:* NEA; MNEA (Treas 1978-81, Building Rep 1974-88); PTA (Safety Leader 1980-88, Life Mem 1976); Belton Meth Church (Devotional Chm, Youth/Adult Coord, Ed Chm); Nom for Natl PTA Phoebe Apperson Hurst Outstanding Educator of Yr; Nom for Excl in Teaching Awd 1987-88; *home:* 805 Stacey Belton MO 64012

CRYDER, CAROL MEERHOFF, Kindergarten Teacher; *b:* Union City, PA; *m:* Robert William; *c:* Brent C., Allyson N.; *ed:* (AS) Medical Secretarial Field, Robert Morris Coll 1969; (BS) Elem Ed, 1974, (MA) Early Chldhd/Elem Ed, 1978 Edinboro Univ; Trng Through Gesell Inst; *cr:* Dental Asst Dr William D Hustead 1969-72; Kndgtn/Remedial Rdng Teacher 1974-75, Kndgtn Teacher 1974- Northwestern Elem Sch; *ai:* Alpha Delta Kappa (VP 1980-82, Historian 1990-); 51 Club Womans Organization 1983-; *office:* Northwestern Elem Sch John Williams Ave Albion PA 16401

CRYTZER, LYNN CAROL (BROZENICK), Choral Director, Music Teacher; *b:* Pittsburgh, PA; *m:* Glenn Paul; *c:* Glenn P. II; *ed:* (BM) Music Ed, Grove City Coll 1974; Univ of Pittsburgh 1975-77, Youngstown St Univ 1989-; *cr:* Music Teacher/Elem Orch Dir Mt Lebanon Sch Dist 1976-78; Choral Dir/Scndry Music Teacher Butler Area Sch Dist 1978-; *ai:* Dist V PMEA Honors Chorus Chm 1989, 1990; HS Musical Vocal Dir 1990; HS Musical Orch Dir 1983, 1984; Private Instruction Piano, Voice, Cello 1975-; Music Educators Natl Conference, PA Music Educators Assn 1975-; NEA, BEA 1977-; Natl Sch Orch Assn 1989-; PA St Ed Assn, Butler Ed Assn; Butler Symphony (Mem, Cellist) 1987-; *office:* Butler Intermediate HS 151 Fairground Hill Rd Butler PA 16001

CUCOLO, NICHOLAS FRED, HS English Teacher; *b:* Glen Ridge, NJ; *m:* Nancy Cox; *c:* David; *ed:* (BA) Eng, Montclair St Rutgers Univ 1974; (MBA) Marketing, Seton Hall Univ 1975; *cr:* Eng Teacher Essex Cty Tech & Voc Schs 1977-, Newark Tech 1977-85, Bloomfield Tech 1985-; *ai:* Sch Newspaper Ed-in-Chief; Grad Assistantship Seton Hall Univ 1974-75, Schlsp & Stipend to Pursue Grad Stud.

CUCOZZELLA, JOSEPHINE MARY, 7th Grade Teacher; *b:* Newark, NJ; *ed:* St Cert, Villa Walsh Normal Sch 1944; (BA) Amer His/Eng, GA Cty Coll 1945; (MA) Soc Stud, Columbia Univ 1949; Numerous Courses & Wkshps in Religious Stud & Soc Stud; *cr:* Elem Soc Stud Teacher Holy Rosary Sch 1937-44, St Marys Sch 1944-49; Soc Stud Teacher Villa Walsh HS 1949-51, Villa Victoria Acad 1951-54; Prin St Anthony Regional HS 1954-56, Holy Spirit Elem 1956-66; 7th-8th Grade Soc Stud Teacher Our Lady of Mercy Sch 1966-77, St Bartholomew Sch 1981-89; 7th Grade Chrstn Doctrine/Soc Stud Teacher, Villa Walsh 1990; *ai:* Religious Group Club Adv; Moderator of Sodality Mems Who Visit Nursing Homes & Orphanages; Forum Club & Forensics Moderator; Tower Hill Remedial Rdng Summer Sch 1966-68; Sunday Sch Teacher 25 Yrs Awd; *office:* Villa Walsh Acad Villa Walsh Western Ave Morristown NJ 07960

CUDDY, MEREDITH FINK, English Teacher; *b:* Parkersburg, WV; *m:* Russell Dale; *c:* Barbara Dale; *ed:* (BS) Eng, California Univ of PA 1957; Univ of Pittsburgh, Univ of VA; *cr:* Teacher Fellowfield Twp 1957-60, La Plata MD HS 1961-62; Teacher 1963-68, 1979- James Monroe HS; *ai:* NHS Adv; NCTE; AAUW 1964-74; *home:* 110 Goodloe Dr Fredericksburg VA 22401

CUFF, ALVIN J., Science Dept Chm/Teacher; *b:* Philadelphia, PA; *m:* Jeanne Mapp; *c:* Maureen, Kimberly, A. Jeffrey, Dwayne; *ed:* (BA) Bio, Lincoln Univ 1953; (OD) Optometry, PA Coll of Optometry 1958; Scndry Cert Ed, Temple Univ 1959-65; Ed, Univ of PA; Sci, Rutgers Univ; Cmptr, Univ of DE, Beaver Coll, Philadelphia Coll of Textile; *cr:* Teacher Stoddart-Fleisher Mid Sch 1959-; *ai:* Sci Dept Chm; Sci Curr Comms; Sch Treas; Cmptr Coord; Intnl Lions Club (Pres, Past Master) Pres Awd 1978-79; Natl Optometric Assn VP, Optometrist of Yr 1977, Founders Awd 1982; Natl Sci Fnd Grants Rutgers, Temple, Univ of DE; Author Articles PA Optometrist; PA Coll of Optometry Recognition Awd 1987.

CULBERTSON, CANDACE K., Math & Computer Sci Teacher; *b:* Wooster, OH; *ed:* (BA) His, 1970, (BS) Cmptr Sci, 1984 Univ of Akron; *cr:* Teacher Waterloo Mid Sch 1972-; *ai:* Mathcounts Coach; Portage Cty Math Curr Comm; OH Cncl Teachers of Math, OH Ed Assn, NEA; *office:* Waterloo Mid Sch 1776 St Rt 44 Randolph OH 44265

CULBERTSON, M. JEAN, Mathematics Teacher/Dept Head; *b:* Maywood, CA; *ed:* (BA) Math, Univ of S CA 1964; Eng & Scndry Cert UT St Univ 1983; *cr:* Math Teacher/Coord of Gifted Begg Sch 1969-72; Math Teacher/Dept Head Center Intermediate Sch 1972-80; Math Instr UT St Univ 1980-83; Math Teacher/ Dept Head S Cache Mid Sch 1983-; *ai:* Supervise Homework Helpers; Volunteer Peer-Tutoring Group; UT Cncl Teachers of Math; 4-H Horse Club Asst Leader 1985-; Center Sch Teacher of Yr 1979; Cache Cty Sch Dist 1988, Teacher of Yr 1989-; *office:* S Cache Mid Sch 29 N 400 W Hyrum UT 84319

CULBRETH, GAIL RITCEY, Mathematics Teacher; *b:* Toccoa, GA; *m:* Harold; *c:* Daniel; *ed:* (BS) Math, Piedmont Coll 1985; Working Towards Masters Math Ed, N GA Coll 1990; *cr:* Math Teacher Charlton Cty Sch System 1985-86, Pickens HS 1986-; *ai:* Fellowship of Chrstn Athletes Co-Spon; PAGE; *office:* Pickens HS 670 W Church St Jasper GA 30143

CULLEN, MARY ANNE, Fifth Grade Teacher; *b:* Providence, RI; *m:* Daniel Patrick; *c:* Andrew B., Aaron B.; *ed:* (BS) Elem Ed 1973, (MED) Elem Ed, 1979 RI Coll; *cr:* 3rd Grade Teacher 1973-81, 5th Grade Teacher 1981- St Bartholomew Sch; *ai:* Home-Sch Assn Mem; Invent America Prgm, Holy Childhood Assn, Book Fairs, St Vincent De Paul Walk for Homeless, Parish, Survival Kits for Homeless Chm; Spelling Bee Chairperson; NCEA Mem 1973; CYO Adv 1977-81; CCD Prgm (Teacher Volunteer 1971-85, Coord Volunteer 1985-86); *office:* St Bartholomew Sch 315 Laurel Hill Ave Providence RI 02909

CULLIGAN, SHARON LEE, Second Grade Teacher; *b:* Spokane, WA; *ed:* (BS) Sociology, Gonzaga Univ 1961; Ed, E WA St Univ; *cr:* 1st/2nd Grade Teacher Lamont Elem Sch 1963-71; 1st-3rd Grade Teacher Sprague Elem Sch 1972-; *ai:* WA Ed Assn 1963-; Sprague Lamont Ed Assn (Secy, Treas 1986-88, Treas 1988-); *office:* Sprague Elem Sch 5th & F Street Sprague WA 99032

CULLMAN, LORETTA L., 8th Grade Language Teacher; *b:* Cleveland, OH; *m:* Alvin O.; *ed:* (BA) Elem Ed, Kent St Univ 1968; (MS) Curr/Instruction, Univ of WI Milwaukee 1976; *cr:* 5th/6th Grade Teacher John Glenn Sch 1968-72; 4th/5th Grade Teacher Thorson Elem Sch 1972-86; 5th-8th Grade Teacher Webster Transitional Sch 1986-; *ai:* Forensics Judge; Drama Club Adv; Rdng & Lang Comms; Delta Kappa Gamma Pres 1986-88; WI St Rdng Assn 1980-; WA Ozaukee Rdng Assn 1980-; Crossroads Presby Church (Elder, Music Comm Chm) 1985-.

CULMER, OLLIE MILLER, Fourth Grade Teacher; *b:* Augusta, GA; *m:* Hubert Miller; *c:* Rene M. Miller; *ed:* (BS) Elem Ed, FL A&M Univ 1954; (MS) Art Ed, FL Intnl Univ 1985; *cr:* Elem Teacher 1955-85, Art Teacher 1986-87, 4th Grade Teacher 1987- Broward Cty Sch System; *ai:* Intermediate Specialist; PTA 1955-; NAEA 1985-89; Women in the Arts Charter Mem 1985; Nom Teacher of Yr; Broward Cty Sci Fair 1st Place Awd 1989-; Certificate of Awd for Dedicated Service 1974, 1976; *home:* 2511 NW 28th Terr Fort Lauderdale FL 33311

CULOTTA, JOSEPH, JR., Chemistry & Physics Teacher; *b:* Grand Rapids, MI; *m:* Miriam Ann Arcoleo; *c:* Kim M. Culotta Sager, Karen A. Culotta Mc Cord, Joseph III; *ed:* (BA) Sci, Tulane Univ 1964; *cr:* Southern Regional Supvr LA Dept of Veterans Affairs 1956-84; Chem/Adult Sci Instr Tulane Univ 1964-82; Talk Show Host WTIX & WNOE Radio 1965-; Chem/ Physics Teacher Pope John Paul II HS 1984-; *ai:* Sci Club Monitor; LA Broadcasters Assn 1971-, Broadcaster of Yr 1972, 1985; Editorials Published 1972, 1981; LA St Univ Medical Schls Deans Comm 1978-85; *office:* Pope John Paul II HS 1901 Jaguar Dr Slidell LA 70461

CULP, BARBARA CLARK, Mathematics Teacher; *b:* Hallettsville, TX; *m:* Charles Linden; *c:* John D., Brian C.; *ed:* (BS) Bio/Math/Psych, 1966, (MS) Bio, 1969 Stephen F Austin St Univ; Univ of Houston Clear Lake, St Thomas Univ, Lamar Univ, Rice Univ; *cr:* Math Chm/Sci/Math Teacher Horace Mann Jr HS 1966-80; Gifted Math Teacher Cedar Bayou Jr HS 1980-82; Teacher/Math Chairperson Gentry Jr HS 1982-85; Math Teacher Ross S Sterling HS 1985-; *ai:* Stu Take Action Not Drugs Spon; Stu Assistance Prgm; Core Team; Univ of Interscholastic League; Number Sense Coach; Baytown Classroom Teachers (Teacher Admin of Yr Comm Chm 1986-87), Teacher of Yr 1985; Baytown Ed Assn Treas 1984-85; TX St Teachers Assn Regional Elections Comm 1984-86; Delta Kappa Gamma (Secy 1984-86, Treas 1986-88, VP 1988-; Pres 1990; Tri-Cities DeMolay Mothers Club Pres 1988; Rice Univ Math Project 1988; Woodrow Wilson Inst Univ Houston 1989; Nom for Presidential Awd for Excl Teaching Math & Sci 1990; *home:* 4905 St Andrews Baytown TX 77521

CULP, CAROLYN M., Spanish Teacher; *b:* Gettysburg, PA; *m:* Wayne L.; *c:* Gregory, Bradley; *ed:* (BA) Span/Fr, Shippensburg Coll 1966; (MA) Urban Ed, Trenton St Coll 1983; *cr:* Span Teacher Cncl Rock HS 1966-; *ai:* Drama & Span Club; Natl Assn of Teachers of Span & Portuguese 1985-; *office:* Council Rock HS Swamp Rd Newtown PA 18940

CULP, DANNY RAY, Fourth Grade Teacher; *b:* Sylacauga, AL; *ed:* (BA) Broadcast/Film Comm, Univ of AL 1977; (MA) Elem Ed, Univ of Montevallo 1983; *cr:* 4th Grade Teacher Pinecrest Elem 1979-; *ai:* Pinecrest Safety Patrol, Bsbl Card Club, Weather Watchers Spon; Local 4-H Club Leader; Pinecrest Young Astronauts Founder & Leader; Pinecrest Intramural Bsktbl Prgm Coach; Southern Assn of Colls & Schls Evaluation Comm; Textbook Adoption Comm; Yrbk Photographer; 1st United Meth Church Admin Bd; St Semi-Finalist Amer Teacher in Space Prgm; 4-H Salute to Excl Natl Rep 1984 & Outstanding St Leader 1983; Nom Outstanding Young Educator of Yr 1985; *office:* Pinecrest Elem Sch Rt 4 Box 300 Sylacauga AL 35150

CULP, EVELYN BENNETT, 5th Grade Teacher; *b:* Richmond, KY; *m:* Ralph Albert Jr.; *c:* Emily R.; *ed:* (BA) Elem Ed, 1971, (MA) Elem Ed, 1977 Univ of KY; *cr:* 4th Grade Teacher Fayette Cty Schls 1971-72; 5th-6th Grade Teacher Mercer Cty Elem 1972-; *ai:* Academic Coach 1986-89; Mercer Cty Ed Assn Secy 1974; KY Ed Assn, NEA; *office:* Mercer Cty Elem Sch Tapp Rd Harrodsburg KY 40330

CULP, MARGARET A. TRAMEL, 6th Grade Teacher; *b:* Richard City, TN; *c:* Robert L., Michael T.; *ed:* (BS) Elem Ed, Mid TN St Univ 1957; Counseling, Univ of MS & Memphis St Univ; *cr:* 5th Grade Teacher Donelson Elem 1957-58; 7th-9th Grade Eng/Soc Stud Teacher Mc Laurin Jr HS 1959-64; 8th-9th Grade Eng Teacher Atlanta GA 1965-67; 6th Grade Teacher Sharp Elem 1968-70; Lead Teacher Sch for Pregnant Girls 1970-77; 6th Grade Teacher Hamilton Elem 1977-; *ai:* Chrldr Spon; Y-Teens; Sch Newspaper; Art & Creative Writing Club; Assertive Discipline Comm Chairperson; Idlewild Presbyn; *home:* 1391 Vinton Ave Memphis TN 38104

CULPEPPER, JACQUELYN MC CLAIN, English/Speech Teacher; *b:* Houston, TX; *m:* R. Alan; *c:* Erin, Rodney; *ed:* (BA) Eng/Speech, Baylor Univ 1967; (MED) Rdng, Univ of Louisville 1986; Rdng Specialist Endorsement; Volunteer Rdng Teacher Mayfield Sch Cambridge England 1979-80; *cr:* Math Teacher Fairdale HS 1967-68; Eng Teacher Western HS 1968-70, Creedmoor Jr HS 1970-74; Writing Teacher Southern Baptist Seminary 1980-85; Eng Teacher Sacred Heart Model Sch 1985-87, Oldham Cty HS 1987-; *ai:* Yrbk Adv; Speech & Debate Coach; Devotional Group Spon; NCTE 1967-74, 1986-; Sigma Tau Delta 1966-; Baptist Seminaries & Baylor Univ Grad Sch of Religion Style & Form Guide Co-Author 1986; *office:* Oldham Cty HS Box 187 Buckner KY 40010

CULPEPPER, JULIA GAYE, Computer Lab Teacher; *b:* Fort Worth, TX; *ed:* (BS) Elem Ed, TX Wesleyan Univ 1972; (ME) Supervision/Elem Ed, TX Womens Univ 1981; *cr:* Early Chldhd Teacher 1972-78, 3rd Grade Teacher 1978-82, 5th Grade Teacher 1982-85 Bess Race Elem; 6th Grade Teacher Sycamore Elem 1985-86; Lab Teacher Meadowcreek Elem 1986-; *ai:* TX St Teacher Assn Building Rep 1974-76; TX Prof Educators Assn 1978-; PTA (2nd VP 1981-82, Publicity Chairperson 1982-83, Hospitality Chairperson 1986-87) Life Membership 1983, Terrific Teacher 1984, Character, Spiritual Life 1982; Outstanding Young Women of America 1973; *office:* Meadowcreek Elem Sch 2801 Country Creek Fort Worth TX 76123

CULVER, BARBARA RHEA BRITTON, 4th Grade Teacher; *b:* Odessa, TX; *m:* James Willie; *c:* Joe T., John G., Jamilyn R.; *ed:* (ABS) Elem Ed, Odessa Jr Coll 1957; (BS) Elem Ed, 1959, (MED) Elem Ed, 1964 TX Technological Univ; Elem Admin, TX Technological Univ 1966; *cr:* 6th Grade Teacher Rankin Public Schls 1959; 1st Grade Teacher Cooper Rural Schls 1960-61, Levelland Ind Sch Dist 1961-67; 5th Grade Teacher 1970-72, 6th Grade Teacher 1972-74 Brownfield Ind Sch Dist; 1st Grade Teacher 1974-78, 4th Grade Teacher 1978- Fredericksburg Ind Sch Dist; *ai:* 3rd-5th Grade Tutor; TX St Teachers Assn, PTA 1959-; Tx Cmptr Assn 1986-; Taught GIs Univ of MD Nuremburg Germany 1959-60; *office:* Fredericksburg Ind Sch Dist 202 W Travis Fredericksburg TX 78624

CULVER, CARLENE SCHROEDER, Third Grade Teacher; *b:* Freedom, OK; *m:* Ronal C.; *c:* Ronda F. Perry, Carri J.; *ed:* (BS) Elem, NWOSU 1964; (MS) Rdng Spec, NWOSU 1972; Pittsburg Univ-Perception; KS St Teachers Coll-Sci; St Marys of PlainsMath; Panhandle St Univ-Sci, Rdng & Math; *cr:* 1st Grade Teacher 1964; 2nd Grade Teacher 1967; 3rd Grade Teacher 1968-Ashland Elem Sch; *ai:* NEA KNEA 1964-; Ashland Educators Assn (Pres 1964-; Treas 1989-); Selected Outstandng Teacher-Ashland HS 1988; *home:* PO Box 667 547 W 7th St Ashland KS 67831

CULVER, MARILYN ANN (BUCK), Chapter I Math Teacher; *b:* Garden City, KS; *m:* James Virgil; *c:* Jamie, Casey; *ed:* (BS) Elem Ed, Bartlesville Wesleyan Coll 1977; *cr:* 3rd Grade Teacher 1977-78, 2nd Grade Teacher 1978-79 Bowline Elem; 4th Grade Teacher Will Rogers 1979-86; 3rd Grade Teacher Wilson 1986-88; Math/Chapter I Teacher Wilson & Jane Phillips 1988-; *ai:* Bartlesville Ed Assn, OK Ed Assn, NEA 1977-; Alpha Delta Kappa 1984-86; 1st Wesleyan Church (Bd Mem, Bible Sch Arts & Crafts Dir); Chrstn Youth Crusaders (Chaplain, Teacher, Summer Camp Cnslr); *home:* 4700 Melody Ln Bartlesville OK 74006

CUMBERFORD, STARLA KENTON, 1st Grade Teacher; *b:* Lexington, MO; *m:* William E. Iii; *c:* Ashley J.; *ed:* (BS) Elem Ed, 1978; (MSE) Learning Disabilities, 1982 Central MO ST Univ; *cr:* 2nd Grade Teacher Leslie Bell Elem 1978-86; 2nd Grade Teacher 1986-87; 1st Grade Teacher 1987-88 James Lewis Elem.

CUMBIE, BOBBY POPE, Fourth Grade Teacher; *b:* Greenville, AL; *w:* James Kenneth (dec); *c:* Susan Barganier, Mollie Gardner, Kenneth P.; *ed:* (BA) Soc Stud/Eng/Piano, Huntingdon Coll 1950; Renewal of Certificate Troy St Univ 1964; Sci, Geography, FL St Univ & IN Univ; *cr:* 3rd/4th Grade Teacher Chapman Elem & Jr HS 1964-67; 6th Grade Teacher Greenville Jr HS 1967-72, Greenville Acad 1972-76; 4th Grade Teacher Ft Dale-South Butler Acad 1976-; *ai:* Elem Spelling Bee Coach; Asst Adult Teacher; AEA Mem 1962-73; NEA Mem 1972-; All Private Sch Assn (Mem 1972-, Seminar Leader 1988, 1990), Nom Teacher of Yr 1989-; AL Teachers of Soc Stud; AL Archive & His Former Mem; AARP; Bolling United Meth Church (Organist, Pastor Relations Comm Chairperson, Secy, Asst Adult Teacher); Ft Dale-South Butler Teacher of Yr 1989-; Open Court Publishing Company Seminar Leader; *office:* Ft Dale-South Butler Acad P O Box 777 Greenville AL 36037

CUMBIE, CAROL GAVIN, English Teacher; *b:* Brooklyn, NY; *m:* James R.; *c:* James Consiglio, Robert Consiglio; *ed:* (AA) Eng, Rockland Cmmty Coll 1967; (BA) Eng, St Thomas Aquinas 1969; (MA) Eng, Wm Paterson Coll 1972; *cr:* Eng Teacher Spring Valley HS 169-82, Cairo HS 1983-86, Fallsburg Cntrl 1986-; *ai:* NCTE 1986-; *office:* Fallsburg Cntrl Sch Brickman Rd Fallsburg NY 12733

CUMMINGS, AUDREY JEANE, English-Social Science Teacher; *b:* Logan, WV; *m:* Forrest Herman; *c:* Alexis E.; *ed:* (BA) Lang Arts/Soc Sci, Morris Harvey Coll 1971; (MA) Admin, WV Univ 1975; WV Coll of Grad Studs, Marshall Univ; *cr:* Teacher Martin Elem 1968-69, Fez Elem 1696-72; Teacher/Prin Martin Elem 1972-75, Fez Elem 1975-77; Prin Ranger Elem 1977-79; Teacher Griffithsville Elem 1979-81; Teacher/Prin Woodville Elem 1981-83; Teacher Hamlin HS 1983-; *ai:* Elem & Jr HS Cheerleading Coach; WV Challenge Coach; Peer Pressure Group Cnslr; WV Ed Assn 1968-71; WV Elem Sch Prin Assn 1971-79; Natl Elem Sch Prin Assn 1975-79; PTA 1988-89; Hamlin Athletic Boosters Club 1989-; 4-H Leader 1969-72; Hamlin HS Faculty Choir 1989-; *office:* Hamlin HS Gen Del Hamlin WV 25523

CUMMINGS, ERNEST L., Elem Phys Ed Teacher; *b:* Upton, WY; *m:* Judy A.; *c:* Scott; *ed:* (BS) Phys Ed, Black Hills St Coll 1970; *cr:* 6th Phys Ed Teacher Jr HS 1970-71; 1st-6th Phys Ed Teacher Eastside Elem Schl 71-79; K-6th Phys Ed Teacher Meadowlark Elem Sch 79-; *ai:* Jr HS Track 1970-73; Elem Intramurals 1971-88; Hlth-Comm 1988-89; Jump Rope for Heart St Adv 1989-90; NEA 1970-85; WY Alliance for Hlth Phys Ed & Dance Rec 1975-90; Jump Rope for Heart Amer Heart Assn Cty St-Coord 1988-89 Outstanding Service 1989; *office:* Meadowlark Elem Sch 816 E 7th Gillette WY 82716

CUMMINGS, IRIS REECE, Mathematics Teacher; *b:* Stanberry, MO; *m:* Walter E. Jr.; *c:* Cynthia Edwards, Thomas, Loretta Dinstel, Sue Williams; *ed:* (BS) Math/Bus, NW MO St 1956; Grad Work Math Ed, KS St Univ Manhattan, CSC Chadron NE; *cr:* Jr HS Math/Sci Teacher Parnell MO 1955-56; Rural Teacher Valley & Howard Cty NE 1963-66; Jr HS Math Teacher Ainsworth NE 1966-69, Mc Cook NE 1969-72, Alliance NE 1976-; *ai:* Mathcounts & Quiz Bowl Coach; NEA, NE St Ed Assn, Alliance Ed Assn, Mc Cook Ed Assn; Alpha Delta Kappa (Pres 1988-, Pres Cncl St Bd Rep 1990); Natl Sci Fnd Grant KS St Univ 1969-72.

CUMMINGS, JO ANN (BELY), Jr HS Math/English/Art Teacher; *b:* Chamberlain, SD; *m:* Edward J.; *c:* Micheal, Cynthia Halderman; *ed:* (BA) Elem Ed, Dakota Wesleyan Univ 1972; SD St Univ Brookings, Univ of SD Vermillion, Black Hills St Coll; *cr:* 8th Contained Classroom Pukwana Public Sch 1957-72; 7th/8th

Grade Eng Teacher Chamberlain Public Sch 1972-76; Eng/Art/Math Teacher Stanley Cty Sch 1976-; *ai:* Jr HS Cheerleading Adv; 8th Grade Class Act Spon; Artists in Schls Coord; Delta Kappa Gamma 1982-; SDEA, NEA, SCEA Mem; Local Teachers Organizations Officers; United Church of Christ Deacon; *home:* 1209 Edgewater Dr Pierre SD 57501

CUMMINGS, JOSEPH MICHAEL, Lang Art/Soc Stud Teacher; *b:* Jersey City, NJ; *m:* Betty Rainey; *c:* Lindsay, Katherine; *ed:* (BS) Scndry Ed, 1971, Elem Ed, 1973 N TX St Univ; *cr:* 6th Grade Teacher Brownsville Ind Sch Dist 1971-72, Edgewood Ind Sch Dist 1972-; *ai:* Level Chairperson; Academic Comm; 6th Grade Soc Stud Club Spon; Sch Public Relations Rep; Edgewood Classroom Teachers Assn 1972-89, Campus Teacher of Yr; TSTA, NEA; PTA Lifetime Membership Awd; US Table Tennis Assn; San Antonio Table Tennis Club Pres 1988-, TX Amateur St Champion 1974; Chosen Represent My Campus With Supt; Wrote Lang Art & Rdng Curr for Grades 4-6 Edgewood Sch Dist; *office:* Stafford Elem Sch 611 SW 36th St San Antonio TX 78237

CUMMINGS, JOSEPHINE SCOTTO, English Teacher; *b:* Brooklyn, NY; *m:* James Joseph; *c:* John, Michele; *ed:* (BA) Eng, St Joseph Coll 1964; *cr:* Teacher St Savior HS 1964-66; Teacher 1966-69, Chairperson 1981-86, Teacher 1987- St Joseph by the Sea; *ai:* Literary Magazine & Open House Comm Moderator; NCTE, Fed of Cath Teachers, NCEA.

CUMMINGS, MARGARET JONES, Department Chair/Teacher; *b:* Scottsburg, IN; *m:* Thomas P.; *c:* Isaac Stearns, Sarah Gorman, Mark, Karen, Benjamin, Daniel; *ed:* (BS) Ed, 1971, (MS) Ed, 1974 IN Univ SE; *cr:* Teacher Parkview Jr HS 1971-79, River Valley Mid Sch 1979-85; Teacher/Dept Chairperson William Chrisman HS 1985-; *ai:* Drill Team Spon; Dist Trainer-Effective Instruction; MO Ed Assn Government Relations Chairperson 1987-89; Phi Delta Kappa 1983-; Metropolitan Effective Instruction Cadre 1987-; ASCD 1990; Suzuki Parents Assn (Pres 1988, Treas 1989-); Fairview Chrstn Church Deacon; *office:* William Chrisman HS 1223 N Noland Rd Independence MO 64050

CUMMINGS, MARY VOIGT, Guidance Coordinator; *b:* Eagle Grove, IA; *m:* William Grosvenor Jr.; *c:* William G. III, Grace A., Mary J., Margaret L., Nancy E.; *ed:* (BS) Ed, Northwestern Univ 1959; (MA) Counseling, Univ of S FL 1977; Seminars; Staff Dev; TET I & II; *cr:* Cnslr Pinellas Park HS 1977-84; Guidance Coord Clearwater HS 1984-; *ai:* Curr Dir & Crisis Intervention Comm; Dept Chm; Phi Delta Kappa, Delta Kappa Gamma, Amer Assn of Counseling & Dev, Phi Kappa Pi; Jr League Pres 1975-; Master Teacher Awd; Non-Educl Clearwaters Outstanding Young Woman 1975.

CUMMINGS, OLIVIA COX, Third Grade Teacher; *b:* Wythe Cty, VA; *m:* Ernest W.; *c:* Robert Dake, Robert, Susan; *ed:* (BS) Elem Ed, TN Wesleyan Coll 1970; MS Curr/Instruction, Univ of TN 1976; *cr:* K-4th/6th Grade Teacher E K Baker Sch 1970-; *ai:* Various Comm for Southern Assn of Schls; Evaluation at Building Level; Mc Minn Cty Ed Assn, E TN Ed Assn, TN Ed Assn, NEA 1970-; TN Assn for Young Child Bd of Dir; Phi Kappa Phi Mem; Listed in Outstanding Leaders in Elem & Scndry Ed; *office:* E K Baker Elem School Rt 3 Box 300 Athens TN 37303

CUMMINGS, SHAREE ANN (CREAGH), Biology Teacher/Coach; *b:* Dublin, TX; *c:* Dustin C. *ed:* (BA) Phys Ed/Health/Recreation/Bio/Earth Sci, Univ of TX Arlington 1976; TX Public Sch Law, Abilene Chrstn Univ; Geology, W TX St Univ; *cr:* Phys Ed/Health Teacher Amarillo Ind Sch Dist 1976-; Bio I/II Teacher Breckenridge Ind Sch Dist 1978-; *ai:* Head Vlybl & Jr HS Track Coach; Stu At Risk, Textbook, Sci Dept Comms; Civic Clubs Speaker; Assn of Prof Teachers & Educators 1980-89; TX Girls Coaching Assn Regional Comm 1976-; First Presbyn Church Breckenridge; Spec Olympics Vlybl, Tennis, Metroplex All Star Vlybl Players Coach Coach of Yr Awd; *home:* 216 W Williams Breckenridge TX 76024

CUMMINGS, SHARYL VIRGINIA, Mathematics Teacher; *b:* Eureka, KS; *m:* Steve Jerome Blomquist; *ed:* (BS) Math/Phys Ed, KS St Teachers Coll 1971; (MS) Ed/Admin, Univ of AZ 1982; Kent St Univ; Several Wkshps, Tucson Unified Sch Dist, Cntrl Bureau of London, Wooster City Sch Dist; *cr:* Health Teacher Wooster HS 1971-72; Math/Phys Ed Teacher Utterback Jr HS 1972-77; Math Teacher Pistor Jr HS 1977-81; Math/Phys Ed Teacher Moseley Park Sch 1987-88; Math Teacher Mansfeld Mid Sch 1982-; *ai:* Mansfeld Advisory Comm & 7th Grade ITO; Tucson Ed Assn Comm Mem 1972-; AZ Ed Assn (Mem, Delegate) 1972-; NEA Mem 1971-; West Ridge HO Assn (Treas 1976, 1980) 1975-; KXCL 1989-; ASBA Golden Bell Awd 1985; 2nd Place Prgm to Reduce Test Anxiety; Math Teacher of Yr 1985; AZ Cncl of Engineering & Scientific Assn; Fulbright Teacher Exch USIA & Cntrl Bureau of UK 1987-88; *office:* Mansfeld Mid Sch 1300 E 6th St Tucson AZ 85719

CUMMINGS, STEVEN WALTER, History/Social Studies Teacher; *b:* Mora, MN; *m:* Jody Ann Isaacson; *c:* Brittany, Derek, Ethan; *ed:* (BAA) His, Univ of MN Duluth 1977; *cr:* Soc Stud Teacher Mc Gregor HS 1977-; *ai:* Defensive Coord Var Ftbl; Asst Var Boys Bsktbl; Learners at Risk Comm Mem 1989-; *office:* Mc Gregor Jr/Sr HS PO Box 160 Mc Gregor MN 55760

CUMMINS, CURTIS LEIGH, JR., Earth Science Teacher; *b:* Richmond, VA; *m:* Gay Duck; *c:* Tripp Bradley, Tiffany Bradley; *ed:* (AS) Sci, Chowan Coll; (BS) Psych, (MS) Educl Psych, Univ of AL; *cr:* Unit Psychologist Partlow St Sch 1973-75; Teacher Westlawn Jr HS 1975-79; Eastwood Mid Sch 1979-; Museum Naturalist AL Museum of Natural His 1980-; *ai:* Sci, Sch Comm, Sci Textbook Selection, Stu Act Prgm Comms; Faculty Self Study Chairperson; NEA, AL Ed Assn, Prof Educators of Tuscaloosa, 1984-; PTA 1986-; *office:* Eastwood M S 2301 14th E Tuscaloosa AL 35404

CUMMINS, DALE LEWIS, Retired Teacher; *b:* Belmore, OH; *m:* Jo Ann; *c:* Mark (dec), Marla F. Fair; *ed:* (BA) Soc Stud/Admin, Univ of Dayton 1949; (MS) 6th Grade Elem Ed, Univ of Wittenburg 1963; Lib Sci, Kent St & Miami Univ; *cr:* Teacher Germantown HS, Bethel HS, W Milton Jr HS, Cookson Elem; *ai:* OH Ed Society, Natl Ed Society 1949-64; Western OH Society 1953-63; BSA Scoutmaster 1945-63, Silver Beaver Awd 1957.

CUMMINS, JANET LEIGH, 8th Grade Lang Art Teacher; *b:* Berea, KY; *ed:* (BA) Eng, Berea Coll 1981; MA Scndry Counseling, E KY Univ 1991; *cr:* Eng Teacher Lee Cty HS 1983-84; Eng/Drama Teacher Clark Moores Mid Sch 1984-; *ai:* Drama Instr; Cheerleading Coach; KY Ed Assn, NEA; *home:* 1658 Foxhaven Box 3 Richmond KY 40475

CUMMINS, NORMA GRIES, 6th Grade Study Skills Teacher; *b:* Corsicana, TX; *ed:* (BS) Scndry Ed/Bus, 1956, (MED) Elem Ed, 1959 N TX St Coll; *cr:* Elem Teacher Lee Elem Sch 1956-65; Bus Teacher Corsicana HS 1965-70; Teacher Hubbard Elem & Hubbard HS 1970-80; 6th Grade Study Skills Teacher Drane Mid Sch 1980-; *ai:* NHS & Faculty Advisory Comm; UIL Coach Listening; NEA, TX St Teachers Assn 1956-; Corsicana Ed Assn 1956-70, 1980-; Alpha Delta Kappa Charter Mem; Cancer Crusade United Fund Fine Art Volunteer; St Lukes United Meth Church (Womens Society of Chrstn Service Life Mem, Founder Frances Burns Circle, Ed Commission Chm); Outstanding Young Women of America 1967; Teacher of Yr Nominee 1963; Outstanding Elem Teachers of America 1973; Teacher Who Contributed Most to Sch Life 1970; *office:* Drane Mid Sch 100 S 18th St Corsicana TX 75110

CUMO, PHILOMENA ANN, French Teacher; *b:* New Castle, PA; *c:* Christopher; *ed:* (BSED) Fr, Indiana Univ of PA 1962; (Ma Equivalent) Teacher Cert Fr, St of PA 1988; Rassias Trng; *cr:* Fr/Span Teacher Dade Cty 1963-65; Fr Teacher Carlynton Sch Dist 1965-; *ai:* Fr Club Spon; Carlynton Long Range Planning Comm; Mid St Evaluating Comm; PA St Modern Lang Assn 1965-, Seminar Presenter 1988; AATF 1965-, Seminar Presenter 1989; Allegheny Foreign Lang Assn 1987-; St Clair Hospital Auxiliary 1988-; Grad Asst Univ of Miami 1962-63; Commonwealth Partnership Fellow 1988; *office:* Carlynton Jr-Sr HS 435 Kings Hwy Carnegie PA 15106

CUNNINGHAM, ALAN LEE, Mathematics Department Head; *b:* Russell, KS; *m:* Kim Joy Lange; *c:* Abigail, Lauren; *ed:* (BS) Math Ed, KS St Univ 1983; *cr:* Math/Bio Teacher Clifton-Clyde HS 1983-84; Math Teacher Silver Lake HS 1984-; *ai:* Boys Head Bsktbl & Bsbl Coach; NEA 1983-; KS Bsktbl Coaches Assn 1984-; KS Assn of Bsbl Coaches 1990; *office:* Silver Lake HS Box 39 Silver Lake KS 66539

CUNNINGHAM, ALSIA SAULSBERRY, Curriculum Coordinator; *b:* Springfield, AR; *m:* Huie D.; *ed:* (BA) Math, Philander Smith 1968; (MA) Scndry Ed, 1975, Scndry Admin 1989 U of MO KC; *cr:* Scndry Math Teacher Southeast Mid 1968-87; Jr HS Math Coord KC MO Sch Dist 1980-81; Resource Teacher 1987-89, Curr Coord 1989- Southeast Mid; *ai:* Spon Jr Honor Society; Spon Local Math Counts; Mem Sch Improvement Plan; Phi Delta Kappa 1988-; NCTM 1987-; ASCD 1989; MO Mid Sch Assn 1989-; *office:* Southeast Mid Sch 6410 Swope Pkwy Kansas City MO 64132

CUNNINGHAM, DAVID EARL, Dean; *b:* Evergreen, AL; *m:* Mollie Ruth Bradley; *c:* Fatima, Anne M., David A.; *ed:* (BS) His/Poly Sci, AL A&M Univ 1980; (MS) Educl/Leadership, Nova Univ 1989; Certified FL Performance Measurement System; *cr:* Soc Stud Teacher Eustis Mid Sch 1983-88; Dean of Stu Leesburg HS 1988-89, Eustis Mid Sch 1989-; *ai:* Discipline Comm Chairperson; Stu Cncl Vlybl Coach Spon; Phi Delta Kappa 1988-; Natl Arbor Day Society; Criterion Service Club Outstanding Educator Awd; *office:* Eustis Mid Sch 1801 E Bates Ave Eustis FL 32726

CUNNINGHAM, DEBORAH WRIGHT, 7th Grade Mathematics Teacher; *b:* St Louis, MO; *m:* Jack; *c:* Melissa, Sarah; *ed:* (BS) Math/Ed, 1973, (MS) Math/Ed, 1987 Univ of TN Martin; *cr:* 8th Grade Math/Algebra I Teacher Bolivar Jr HS 1974-79; 7th Grade Math Teacher Union City Mid Sch 1981-; *ai:* Career Level Tutoring Prgm; S Assn Chairperson for Schls Accreditation; Book Adoption Comm; NCMT, NCTM; TN Valley Authority Prgm for Math & Sci Spon Univ of TN; *office:* Union City Mid Sch 1111 High School Dr Union City TN 38261

CUNNINGHAM, EARL GUY, Bus Law & Marketing Teacher; *b:* La Porte, IN; *m:* Faye Ann Mc Donald; *c:* Dace, Ranell; *ed:* (BS) Bus Ed, Oakland City Coll 1969; (MA) Educl Psych, Valparaiso Univ 1972; Sch Law; *cr:* Teacher Elston HS 1969-71, Rogers HS 1971-; *ai:* Bsktbl, Ftbl, Track, Tennis Coach; Exch Prgm US Information Agency in Africa 1988; Area Coach of Yr Awd 1984, 1986; *office:* Rogers HS 8466 W Pahs Rd Michigan City IN 46360

CUNNINGHAM, EDWARD JOHN, English Teacher; *b:* Philadelphia, PA; *m:* Dolores Melanie Porrmann; *ed:* (BS) Eng/Philosophy Scranton Univ 1961; MALS Prgm, Dartmouth Coll 1974; *cr:* Eng Teacher Carteret Prep 1967-68; Eng/Drama Teacher Dunellen HS 1968-70; Eng Teacher Southside HS 1970-80, Science HS 1980-; *ai:* Drama Dir; NCTE 1988-; Inst for Judeau Chrstn Stud Seton Hall Univ (Past Secy 1980, Bd Trustees 1981-).

CUNNINGHAM, GEORGE S., Physical Education Teacher; *b:* Franklin, NC; *m:* Faye Bonds; *c:* Tera, Stuart, Celeste; *ed:* (BS) Phys Ed/Soc Stud, Piedmont Coll 1959; (MA) Recreation, Univ of GA 1965; *cr:* 5th Grade Teacher Hazel Grove Elem 1959-61; 7th-8th Grade Teacher Baldwin Elem 1961-65; Rdng Teacher S Habersham HS 1965-70; Phys Ed Teacher S Habersham Jr HS 1970-; *ai:* Ftbl & Bsktbl Coach; Letter Club; HEA, GEA, GA HS Assn; Natl Coaches Assn 25 Yr Pin; Teacher of Yr 1986; Natl Sci Grant Univ of GA 1964-65.

CUNNINGHAM, GINA MARLENE STRICKLAND, 7th/8th Grade TAG/Sci Teacher; *b:* Canal Zone, Panama; *m:* Stephen R.; *ed:* (AS) Bio, Cntrl TX Coll 1980; (BS) Bio/His, Univ of Mary Hardin-Baylor 1982; *cr:* 6th Gen His/7th Grade His & Life Sci Teacher 1982-83; 6th Grade Gen His/7th Grade Life Sci/8th Grade Amer His Teacher 1983-84; 6th Grade Gen Sci/7th Grade Life Sci Teacher 1984-85; 6th Grade Gen Sci/8th Grade TAG Earth Sci Teacher 1985-87; 6th Grade Gen Sci/7th Grade TAG Life Sci/8th Grade TAG Earth Sci/8th Grade Earth Sci Teacher 1987-88; 7th Grade TAG Life Sci/8th Grade TAG Earth Sci/8th Grade Earth Sci 1989 Rancier Mid Sch; *ai:* Sci Fair Spon; Phi Delta Kappa; TX Classroom Teachers Assn; TX Assn Gifted & Talented; Sci Teachers Assn of TX; *office:* Rancier Mid Sch 3301 Hilliard Ln Killeen TX 76543

CUNNINGHAM, HUNTER DU BOIS, Jr HS Band Director; *b:* Goliad, TX; *m:* Sara Rucker; *c:* James R., Judith Cunningham Thomas; *ed:* (BM) Music, Stephen F Austin St Univ 1959; Masters Work at Stephen F Austin St Univ, Sam Houston St Univ, Univ of Corpus Christi, E TX St Univ; *cr:* Band Dir Alto HS 1959-62, Kountze HS 1962-65, Goliad HS 1965-72, Taft HS 1972-78, Baytown Jr HS 1978-82, Cedar Bayou Jr HS 1982-; *ai:* Jr Class Spon; Taught Choir & Amer His; TX Bandmasters Assn, TX Music Educators Assn, TX Classroom Teachers Assn; TSTA Cty Pres; *office:* Cedar Bayou Jr HS 2610 Cedar Bayou Rd Baytown TX 77521

CUNNINGHAM, IRA WAYNE, Teacher & Coach; *b:* Cordell, OK; *m:* Nancy Ann Mather; *c:* Christa L., Susan J.; *ed:* (BS) Industrial Art/Phys Ed, 1971, (MS) Educl Admin, SW OK St Univ; *cr:* Elem Phys Ed Teacher Gotebo Sch 1971-76; Teacher/Girls Coach Dill City Sch 1979-82; Teacher/Coach Felt Sch 1985-88; *ai:* Washita Cty Winning Girls Coach 1982; KI-WASH Conference VP 1982; United Meth Youth Dir 1985-87; *home:* Route 1 Box 37A Dill City OK 73641

CUNNINGHAM, JAMES JOSEPH, Geography/History Teacher; *b:* Chicago, IL; *m:* Anne M. Marneris; *ed:* (AA) Liberal Art, Joliet Jr Coll 1973; (BS) His, IL St Univ 1975; Geography, Chicago St Univ; *cr:* Grad Asst Chicago St Univ 1985-86; Substitute Teacher Chicago Public Schls 1985-86; Teacher Amundsen HS 1986-; *ai:* Close Up Prgm for New Amers; Bicycle Club; Prof Personnel Advisory & Extracurricular Athletics Fundraising Comm; Ftbl & Track; Chicago Teachers Union 1987-; Geographic Society of Chicago; Sierra Club Life Mem 1982-; Nature Conservance 1983-; Chicago Area Runners Assn 1988-; Perfect Attendance Awd Amundsen HS 1986-87, 1989-90; *office:* Amundsen HS 5110 N Damen Ave Chicago IL 60625

CUNNINGHAM, JENNIFER BIEL, English Teacher; *b:* Evanston, IL; *m:* Michael Patrick; *ed:* (BS) Eng Ed, IL St Univ 1986; *cr:* Eng Teacher Woodland Jr HS 1986-87, Hephzibah HS 1987-; *ai:* Jr Stu Cncl Co-Spon; Spelling & Oral Interpretation Coach; Faculty Chorus Mem; NCTE Mem 1986-; Augusta Opera Chorus Mem 1990; Augusta Choral Society Mem 1987-; Church of Good Shepherd Mem 1987-; Veterans Admin Hospital Volunteer 1987-; *home:* 4033 Rio Pinar Dr Augusta GA 30906

CUNNINGHAM, LESLEY ELDER, Sixth Grade Teacher; *b:* Lexington, KY; *m:* Bobby R.; *c:* Christopher; *ed:* (BS) Elem Ed, Pikeville Coll 1972; (MA) Ed/Elem, Morehead St Univ 1975; *cr:* 6th Grade Teacher Pikeville Elem Sch 1973-; *ai:* 6th Grade Team Leader; Chm of Retired Teachers Comm; Pikeville Ed Assn (VP, Building Rep) 1980-84, 1990; KY Ed Assn, NEA; *office:* Pikeville Elem Sch 187 Chloe Rd Pikeville KY 41501

CUNNINGHAM, NANCY ANN MATHER, 4th Grade Teacher; *b:* Sergeant Bluff, IA; *m:* Ira Wayne; *c:* Christa L., Susan J.; *ed:* (BS) Soc Stud, 1970, (MS) Elem, 1983 SW OK St Univ; *cr:* Asst Instr OK St Univ Tech 1976-77; 2nd Grade/Chapter I Teacher Dill City Elem 1981-85; 5th/6th Grade/Chapter I Teacher Felt Elem 1985-88; 4th/6th Grade Teacher Dill City Elem 1988-; *ai:* 4-H Leader; United Meth Youth Dir 1985-87; United Meth Church Children Coord 1982-85; *home:* Rt 1 Box 37A Dill City OK 73641

CUNNINGHAM, RHONDA FRYER, Kindergarten Teacher; *b:* Claremore, OK; *m:* Dearl Gene; *c:* Ty, Wade, Clint; *ed:* (BS) Elem Ed, 1977, (MS) Rdng, 1985 Northeastern St Univ; *cr:* 4th Grade Teacher 1978-79, 5th Grade Rdng Teacher 1979-87, 2nd Grade Teacher 1987-89, Kndgtn Teacher 1989- Jay Public Schls; *ai:* 4-H Leader; OK Ed Assn, Jay Prof Assn of Classroom Teachers; Jay Livestock Booster Club.

CUNNINGHAM, RONALD KEITH, US History Teacher; *b:* Lebanon, IN; *m:* Sarah Chavers; *c:* Christopher, Joseph; *ed:* (BA) His, Hanover Coll 1969; (MS) Ed, IN Univ 1972; *cr:* Teacher Indianapolis Public Sch System 1969-72, Southport HS 1972-73, Perry Meridian HS 1973-; *ai:* Foreign Stu Club Spon; Evaluation, Prom, Gifted & Talented Comm; IN Cncl of Soc Stud, NEA, ISTA, PEA; Kiwanis Club Outstanding Teacher 1987-89; *office:*

Perry Meridian HS 501 W Meridian School Rd Indianapolis IN 46217

CUPPY, BARBARA ELLIS, Mathematics Teacher; *b:* Pueblo, CO; *m:* Douglas W.; *c:* Michael, Jennifer; *ed:* (BS) Math, Univ Southern CO 1973; Grad Stud; *cr:* Math Teacher Excelsior Mid Sch 1973-76, Canon City Jr HS 1984-85, Canon City HS 1985-; *ai:* Frosh Class Spon; NCTM 1988-; Canon City Ed Assn, Pikes Peak Ed Assn, CO Ed Assn, NEA 1986-; Co Cncl Teachers of Math 1988-; *office:* Canon City HS 1313 College Ave Canon City CO 81212

CURD, CONNIE SUE, Third Grade Teacher; *b:* Johnson City, TN; *ed:* (BA) Psych, Milligan Coll 1972; (MAT) Elem Ed, E TN St Univ 1974; *cr:* 4th Grade Teacher Stratton Elem 1974-75; 3rd Grade Teacher King Springs Elem 1975-; *ai:* Excell Teacher 1985; *office:* King Springs Elem Sch 1201 King Springs Rd Johnson City TN 37601

CURFMAN, BARBARA THAYER, French/Spanish Teacher; *b:* Atchison, KS; *m:* Bruce Albert; *c:* Anna, Katherine; *ed:* (BS) Span/Eng, 1968, (BA) Ed, 1969 Univ of KS; *cr:* Span/Eng Teacher De Soto Jr HS 1969-71; Eng Teacher Wichita HS 1971-75; Span/Fr/Eng Teacher Coleman Jr HS 1978-88; Span/Fr Teacher Wichita HS 1988-; *ai:* Fr Club Spon; Advisement Bd; CCD Instr; Wichita NEA; Neighborhood Cancer Chm; GSA Daisy & Brownie Leader; PTA (Bd, Elem Foreign Lang Instr); *office:* Wichita Heights HS 5301 N Hillside Wichita KS 67219

CURKENDALL, SUSAN MERRIAM, Mathematics Teacher; *b:* Geneva, OH; *m:* Thomas E.; *c:* Kelly, Brad; *ed:* (BA) Math Ed, Lake Erie Coll 1971; Grad Work; Several Wkshps; *cr:* 7th/8th Grade Math Teacher Riverside HS 1971; 7th Grade Math Teacher Madison Mid Sch 1971-77; Math Teacher Madison HS 1981-; *ai:* MEA, OEA, NEA; United Church Modern Literary Forum 1984-; *office:* Madison HS 3100 Burns Rd Madison OH 44057

CURLEY, JOANNE C., Kindergarten Teacher; *b:* Williams, AZ; *m:* Perry; *c:* Michelle, Regina; *ed:* (BA) Elem Ed, N AZ Univ 1980; *cr:* 5th Grade Teacher 1980-85, Kndgtn Teacher 1985- Seligman Schls; *ai:* HS Girls Bsktbl Coach; Hands Across the Border & Media Coord; *home:* 313 W Chino Seligman AZ 86337

CURLEY, MARY HENDRICKS, Sixth Grade Teacher; *b:* Riceville, IA; *m:* Robert R.; *c:* Michele Larche, Sheryl Grisamore; *ed:* (BA) Ed/Poly Sci/Soc Sci, Upper IA Univ 1957; (MA) Spec Ed, ST Univ of IA 1970; *cr:* 4th Grade Teacher Socorro NM Schls 1957-58; Jr HS Sci/Math Wayland Cons Schls 1959-60; Spec Ed Teacher Joint Cty Schls 1961-69; 6th Grade Teacher Highland Comm 1970-; *ai:* Skills for Adolescent Teacher; NEA/ISEA/HEA VP/Secy/Treas; IRA Secy; Delta Kappa Gamma 1965-; Catholic Daughters of the Americas 1960-; *office:* Highland Comm Sch Ainsworth IA 52201

CURNOW, GARY WILLIAM, Fifth Grade Teacher; *b:* Dover, NJ; *m:* Barbara Schubert; *ed:* (BA) Health/Phys Ed, E Stroudsburg St Coll 1966; (MA) Environmental Stud, Montclair St Coll 1984; Elem Ed Courses; *cr:* Elem Phys Ed Teacher Parsippany Schls 1966-70; 5th Grade Teacher Northvail Sch 1970-; *ai:* Trainer & Facilitator Dist Cooperative Relationships Poject; Parsippany Troy Hills Ed Assn, NJ Ed Assn, NEA 1966-; Phi Kappa Phi 1984-; Lake Musconetong Anglers Club Pres 1968-75; Natl Woodcarvers Assn 1970-; Rotary Club Man of Yr 1987; NJ Governors Recognition Awd 1989; NSTA Convention Rep 1990; *office:* Northvail Sch 10 Eileen Ct Parsippany NJ 07054

CURNUTTE, DELLA MATHER, Health Services Teacher; *b:* Huron, SD; *m:* Ivan M.; *c:* Anthony E., Michael D.; *ed:* (BS) Voc Ed, 1974, (MA) Health Ed, 1985 W KY Univ; Nursing Diploma, St Joseph Hosp Sch of Nursing 1956; Emergency Medical Technician Cert 1987; *cr:* Dir of Nurses Jane Todd Crawford Memorial Hospital 1963-64; Office Nurse KJS De Simone Md, Surgeon 1964-67; Sch Nurse Green Cty Bd of Ed 1967-68; Teacher Green Cty AVEC 1968-; *ai:* HOSA Club Adv; KY Industrial Ed Assn 1985-; Green Cty Cancer Society VP 1986-89; Lifeline Home Health Bd Mem 1986-; Health Careers Task Force Mem 1990; Most Significant Contribution to Health in KY 1969-70; Regional Prgm of Yr in Voc Ed 1986; Nominee Regional Voc Teacher of Yr 1990; *office:* Green Cty AVEC Carlile Ave Box H Greensburg KY 42743

CURRAN, MATTHEW CHARLES, Campus Minister; *b:* New York, NY; *ed:* (BA) Psych/Philosophy, Cathedral Coll of Immaculate Conception 1986; Additional Stud in Counseling, Fordham Univ; *cr:* 7th Grade Teacher Sts Peter & Paul Elem Sch 1986-87; Religion Teacher/Campus Minister St Vincent Ferrer HS 1987-; Group Leader/Head Cnslr Badger Sports Club 1987-; *ai:* Coach Womens Var Bsktbl; Stu Cncl Adv; Dir Religious & Stu Act; NY St Coaches Assn 1990; John J Duffy Awd for Creative Curr Materials 1987; *home:* 60 E 19lth St #4B Bronx NY 10468

CURRI, THETA SWINTON, Retired Teacher; *b:* Ticonderoga, NY; *m:* Thomas E.; *c:* Thomas S., Kristen, Mark, Lonnie, Theta J.; *ed:* (BS) Elem, SUNY Cortland 1954; Teacher In-Service Seminars; *cr:* Elem Teacher Cortland Public Schls 1954-56, 1960-68; 3rd/6th Grade Teacher Syracuse Public Schls 1958-60; 5th Grade Teacher Hague Cntrl Public Schls 1975-79; 3rd/4th Grade Teacher Ticonderoga Public Schls 1980-86; *ai:* AAUW 1968-70; Religious Ed Teacher; Bolton Cancer Drive Co-Chm; NYSTA 1975-86; Cornell Cooperative Ext Warren Cty Bd of Dirs 1983-; Bolton Historical Society Pres 1988-; Bolton Volunteer Firemen Auxiliary 1988-; GSA Leader; *home:* Valley Woods Rd Bolton Landing NY 12814

CURRIE, JOHN N., English Teacher; *b:* Geneva, NY; *m:* Maureen Neff; *c:* Benjamin; *ed:* (BA) Comparative Lit, Hobart Coll 1978; (MFA) Eng, Univ of IA 1981; Admin Certificate SDA; *cr:* Instr Univ of IA 1979-81; Faculty Tutor Empire St Coll 1982; Spec Lecturer St John Fisher Coll 1982-84; Eng Teacher W Irondequoit HS 1984-; *ai:* Acad Decathlon Coach; Mem Ted Sizer Comm; Phi Beta Kappa Mem 1978-; *office:* W Irondequiot HS 260 Cooper Rd Rochester NY 14617

CURRIE, JUANITA, Teacher/Counselor; *b:* Bads Hersfeld, West Germany; *m:* H. L.; *c:* Eric Burdette; *ed:* (BA) Sci/Bio, AM&N Coll 1968; (MED) Ed/Counseling, Univ of AR 1975; Sci & Counseling Wkshps; *cr:* Probation Officer Jefferson Cty Juvenile Court 1973-78; Soc Worker SE AR Mental Health 1978-80; Teacher Southeast Mid Sch 1980-; *ai:* Personnel Policy & Curr Dev Comms; PBEA, NEA; Alpha Kappa Alpha; *office:* Southeast Mid Sch 2001 Ohio St Pine Bluff AR 71603

CURRIE, KATHRYN MARTYN, Science Dept Chair/Teacher; *b:* Los Angeles, CA; *m:* William Charles; *ed:* (BA) Chem, CA St Univ Fullerton 1978; Continuing Ed, CA St Univ Fullerton 1979, CA St Univ Long Beach 1987-89, Univ of San Diego 1988-89; *cr:* Math Teacher Santa Fe HS 1979-80; Chem Teacher Bellflower HS 1980-81; Research Chemist Hills Brothers Chemical Company 1981-86; Chem Teacher Los Alamitos HS 1986-; *ai:* Sch Site Cncl; Attendance Review Comm Dept Chairperson; Academic Cncl; Academic Decathlon & ACS Team Coach; SB1882 Inservice Grant Team Mem; Amer Chemical Society 1988-; NSTA 1989-; NEA 1986-; Nom Presidental Awd of Sci Teaching; Los Alamitos Ed Fund Grant 1989-; *office:* Los Alamitos HS 3591 Cerritos Ave Los Alamitos CA 90720

CURRIE, WILLIAM RONALD, 6th-7th Grade Teacher; *b:* Lumberton, NC; *ed:* (BS) Soc Sci Ed, Campbell Coll 1970; (MED) Counseling, Univ of NC Chapel Hill 1976; *cr:* 4th Grade Teacher S Pines Mid Sch 1970-72; 4th Grade Teacher/Asst Prin S Pines Elem Sch 1973-74; Cnslr 1974-78, Asst Prin 1977-79 Carthage Elem Sch; 6th/8th Grade Sci/Cmptr Laboratory Teacher S Pines Mid Sch 1978-; *ai:* Sch Cmptr Coord; Cty Cmptr Advisory Comm; Supts Summer Enrichment Prgm Teacher; Cmptr Inservice Instr; NC Assn of Educators, NEA 1970-; S Pines Jaycees Outstanding Young Educator 1972; *office:* Southern Pines Mid Sch 255 S May St Southern Pines NC 28387

CURRIER, ARLENE MARIAN, HS His/Government Teacher; *b:* Grand Junction, CO; *ed:* (BA) His, Ottawa Univ 1964; *cr:* Teacher Elk Valley HS 1965-; *ai:* Jr Class Spon.

CURRIER, BARBARA (SHAPPARD), Mathematics Teacher; *b:* Indianapolis, IN; *m:* Robert M.; *c:* Thomas M.; *ed:* (BS) Math, Washburn Univ 1971; (MS) Math, 1973, (PHD) Math, 1976- Univ of MO Kansas City; *cr:* Math Lecturer Washburn Univ 1971-72; Math Grad Teachers Asst Univ of MO Kansas City 1974-75; Asst Math Professor Rockhurst Coll 1975-78; Math Teacher Amer Sch of Paris 1980-84, Greenhill Sch 1984-; *ai:* Math Team Spon; Mathematical Assn of America, NCTM, N TX Area Assn of Advanced Placement Math Teachers, Delta Kappa Gamma; Natl Sci Fnd Fellowship 1972-75; Articles Published; Math & Math Ed Conference Talks; *office:* Greenhill Sch 14255 Midway Rd Dallas TX 75244

CURRIER, NANCEE CLARK, Head of Lower School; *b:* La Crosse, WI; *m:* Richard Denny; *c:* Todd, David, Richard; *ed:* (BS) Ed, Univ of IL 1959; Cmptr Ed; Lower Sch Head-Summer Course; Dir of Admission-Summer Course; *cr:* Kndgtn Teacher Montague Sch 1959-61; Pre-K/Kndgtn Teacher Newburgh Kndgtn 1966-70; 3rd Grade Teacher 1970-86, Lower Sch Head/Dir of Admission 1984- Evansville Day Sch; *ai:* Admissions, Admin, Curr Comm; Cncl for Amer Private Ed 1988-; IN Assn for Ed of Young Children 1990; Delta Kappa Gamma 1978-; Natl Assn of Ind Schls; Ind Schls Assn of Cntrl Sts; Network of Evansville Women 1987-; Evansville Coalition on Adult Literacy Bd Mem 1988-; Evansville Area Rdng Cncl 1980-; *office:* Evansville Day Sch 3400 N Green River Rd Evansville IN 47715

CURRIN, JAMES H., History Teacher; *b:* Harnett Cty, NC; *m:* Elaine H.; *c:* Bethany, Matthew, Rachel; *ed:* (BS) His, 1974, (MED) His, 1989 Campbell Univ; *cr:* Teacher Dunn HS 1974-85, Triton HS 1985-; *ai:* Close Up Club Adv; Voter Registration for Stu; Advanced Placement Courses; NC Assn of Ed 1974-; Harnett Cty Bd of Elections Chm 1990; Iredell Fellowship 1989; *office:* Triton HS R R 1 Box 210 Erwin NC 28339

CURRY, BARBARA C., Business Teacher; *b:* Florence, AL; *m:* Larry J.; *c:* Amy, Joel; *ed:* (BA) Bus Ed, Florence St Univ 1965; Grad Stud AL A&M Univ; *cr:* T M Rogers HS 1965-66; Bus Teacher Buckhorn HS 1966-67; Eng Teacher Wilson HS 1967-68; 5th Grade Teacher New Hope Elem 1968-69; Eng Teacher Davis Hills Mid Sch 1969-72; Bus Teacher Johnson HS 1973-; *ai:* Jr Class Spon; Bus Dept Chairperson; Faculty Advisory & Sch Task Force Comm; Adopt-A-Sch Coord; Accreditation Team; NEA, AL Ed Assn; Huntsville Ed Assn Delegate 1990; Huntsville Bus Ed Assn Pres 1989; Huntsville Historic Fnd; MADD; Interfaith Mission Service; Salvation Army Volunteer; *office:* Jo Johnson HS 6201 Pueblo Dr Huntsville AL 35810

CURRY, ERIC OMAR, Physics Teacher; *b:* Riverton, WY; *ed:* (BS) Bio, 1981, (MS) Physics, 1987 S IL Univ; *cr:* Physics Teacher O Fallon HS 1987-; *ai:* Swim Coach; Jets Team Spon; Amer Inst of Physics Pres 1985-87; Mc Donnell Douglas Awd of Distinction; *office:* O Fallon HS 600 South Smiley O'Fallon IL 62269

CURRY, GARY VERNON, 7th Grade Soc Stud Teacher; *b:* Fort Knox, KY; *m:* Peggy Ann Keltner; *c:* Gary J.; *ed:* (BS) His, Campbellsville Coll 1973; (MAE) Ed, 1978, Admin, 1981 Western KY Univ; *cr:* Teacher Adair Cty Bd of Ed 1973-; *ai:* KEA 1974-; *office:* Adair Cty Bd of Ed Greensburg St Columbia KY 42728

CURRY, JANET, Teacher; *b:* St Louis, MO; *m:* Terrence; *c:* Crystal, Mia, Terri; *ed:* (BA) Elem Ed, 1971, (MS) Cnslr Ed, 1976 S IL Univ Edwardsville; *cr:* Teacher Morrison Sch 1971-; *ai:* Alpha Kappa Alpha; Jack & Jill of America; Prof & Bus Women Assn; *office:* Morrison Elem Sch 630 N 59th St East Saint Louis IL 62203

CURRY, JANET EDWARDS, Correlated Lang Arts Teacher; *b:* Fairmont, WV; *m:* Roger D.; *c:* Timothy; *ed:* (BA) Scndry Ed, Fairmont St Coll 1974; (MA) Rdng WV Univ 1981; Post Masters Studies WVU; *cr:* 7th/8th Grade Eng/Soc Stud Teacher Grafton Mid Sch 1975-; *ai:* Staff Relations Comm; Taylor Cty Ed Assn 1975-; WVEA 1975-; Taylor Cty Outstanding Teacher Awd 1988; *office:* Grafton Mid Sch 225 W Washington St Grafton WV 26354

CURRY, MATTIE ELIZABETH, Remedial Reading Teacher; *b:* Sandersville, GA; *c:* Mykhandria; *ed:* (BA) Eng, Mercer Univ 1987; *cr:* Teacher Central HS-Lanier A 1987-; *ai:* GAE, NEA, BAE 1987-; Outstanding Young Women of America 1986; NAACP Service Awd 1982; *office:* Central HS 751 Hendley St Macon GA 31204

CURRY, ROBERT ALAN, Music Teacher; *b:* La Porte, IN; *m:* Vicki Madaras; *c:* Arica, Christian; *ed:* (BM) Music Ed, Butler Univ 1974; (MA) Music Ed, Brigham Young Univ 1980; Various Music & Ed Classes, Univ of UT; *cr:* Teacher Adams Cty Sch Dist #50 1975-77, Northwest Intermediate Sch 1977-84, Highland HS 1984-; *ai:* Curr Comm 1988-; Music Prgm Study & Teacher Valuing Comms 1989-; UT Music Educators Assn 1976-80; UT Ed Assn 1977-; Received Grant from Highland Assocs & Salt Lake Ed Fnd to Commission Composition for Highland HS Orch 1988; *office:* Highland HS 2166 S 1700 E Salt Lake City UT 84106

CURRY, VIRGINIA HARRINGTON, Sixth Grade Language Teacher; *b:* Bennettsville, SC; *ed:* (BA) Eng, Morris Coll 1972; *cr:* Teacher Pageland Elem Sch 1973-74, Bennettsville Elem Sch 1974-84, Bennettsville Mid Sch 1984-; *ai:* Stu Cncl Adv; Discipline Comm; MCEA, SCEA, NEA; *home:* Rt 4 Box 286 Bennettsville SC 29512

CURRY, WYLENE FENDLEY, Physical Education Chairperson; *b:* Cuthbert, GA; *m:* Chester H.; *c:* Chad H.; *ed:* (BSED) Health/Phys Ed, GA Southern Coll 1961; Grad Stud GA Southwestern 1979-81; Staff Curr Dev 1981-83; *cr:* 8th Grade Sci/Health Teacher Mitchell Cty HS 1962-63; Phys Ed Teacher Albany HS 1963-71; Health/Phys Ed Teacher Randolph Comprehensive HS 1971-80, Randolph-Clay HS 1980-86; Health Issures Randolph-Clay HS 1986-; *ai:* 10th Grade Adv Curr Comm; Dept Chairperson; Graduation Coord; Assist Coordinating Testing & Attendance Records & Report Card Procedures; Alcohol & Drug Awareness Prgm Coord; Full Time Equivalent Comm; Prof Assn GA Educators Building Rep; Camellia Garden Club Pres 1977-81; United Meth Women; GA St Patrol Public Service Awd 1988; Top Teacher 1986; Plaque in Appreciation for Sch Beautification 1985-86; *home:* Rt 1 Box 91 Coleman GA 31736

CURTICE, BRENT ALLAN, Physical Education Dept Chair; *b:* Denver, CO; *m:* Lisa Marie; *ed:* (BA) Phys Ed/Health, Univ of Northern CO 1982; Quest Prgm Teacher Expectation Stu Achievement; Madeline Hunter Teacher Evaluation System; Adolescent Chemical Prgm Johnson Inst; *cr:* Phys Ed/Health Teacher Jackson HS 1982-87, Hotchkiss HS 1987-; *ai:* Head Vlybl, Asst Bsktbl, Head Track Coach; H-Club Class Spon; Dist Health Comm; Drug Free Communities Adv; Nom Teacher of Month 1982 Jackson HS; Nom US West Teacher of Yr 1990; Nom Capher Teacher of Yr 1990; Excl Ed Awd 1987 Jackson HS Staff; Nom 1984-86 3A Vlybl Coach of Yr WY; Nom 1986 3a Vlybl Coach of Yr; Nom ALLSTAR Vlybl Coach WY 1986, Salt Lake City UT 1989; Nom 1989 Gunnison Valley League Vlybl Coach of Yr; Published Articles Fly Fishing, Co-Author Book; *office:* Hotchkiss H S 3535 J60 Rd Hotchkiss CO 81419

CURTIN, BRIAN MICHAEL, High School English Teacher; *b:* Dearborn, MI; *m:* Michelle R.; *ed:* (BA) Eng, Lake Forest Coll 1980; (MS) Ed, Natl Coll of Ed 1987; *cr:* Teacher/Coach Zion Benton Township HS 1980-; *ai:* Var Soccer & Asst Hockey Coach; Athletic Advisory Comm; NCA Athletic Comm Mem & Curr Self Study Comm Chm 1988; IL HS Soccer Coaches Organization Mem; Zion Benton HS Outstanding Teacher of Yr 1985; *office:* Zion Benton Township HS 3901 21st St Zion IL 60099

CURTIN, GLORIA MARIE, Jr HS Social Studies Teacher; *b:* Jackson, MI; *m:* Paul R.; *c:* Mary E. Agnew, Julianne Fowler, Margaret Stitt, Martha J. Andrews; *ed:* (BS) Chem, Marygrove Coll 1947; Ed Courses & Seminars; *cr:* Medical Technician Providence Hospital 1948-49, Mercy Hospital 1949, St Marys Hospital 1949-50, Providence Hospital 1951-55; Jr HS Teacher St Andrew Elem Sch 1971-; *ai:* Stu Cncl Spon; Morning Announcements; NCEA 1988-; DAV Auxiliary 1988-; AARP 1984-; NCCW 1950-; *home:* 1709 Overlake Ave Orlando FL 32806

CURTIS, DEBORAH A., Science Teacher; *b:* Haleyville, AL; *m:* Michael H.; *ed:* (BS) HPER, Univ of N AL 1975; (MA) Bio, Univ of AL Birmingham 1984; *cr:* Teacher Lynn HS 1978, Addison HS 1980-81, Winston Cty HS 1981-; *ai:* Jr/Sr Prom & Jr Class Spon; Teacher Extended Day Prgm; Winston Cty Ed Assn Faculty Rep 1987-88; Phi Kappa Phi, Kappa Delta Pi 1975; AL Ed Assn, NEA

1980-; *office:* Winston Cty HS P O Box 549 Double Springs AL 35553

CURTIS, DEBRA DUNGAN, HS History & English Teacher; *b:* Richmond, TX; *ed:* (BSED) Speech & Hearing Therapy/Eng/His, Stephen F Austin St Univ 1976; Working Towards Masters in Ed, Stephen F Austin St Univ; *cr:* Speech Therapist Mt Pleasant Ind Sch Dist 1976-78; Eng Teacher Beeville Public Schls 1978-80; Eng/His Teacher Woden Ind Sch Dist 1980-; *ai:* Jr Class & Pep Squad Spon, Textbook & Campus Plan Comm; Gifted & Talented Liaison; His Team Coach; UIL Spelling & Ready Writing Coach; Assn of TX Prof Educators Pres 1983-; Nom Outstanding Young Women of America 1985; *office:* Woden HS P O Box 100 Woden TX 75978

CURTIS, DELORES ANDERSON, Science Teacher; *b:* Clarksdale, MS; *m:* David Lee; *c:* David L. Jr., Demetria; *ed:* (AA) Elem Ed, Coahoma Jr Coll 1980; (BS) Elem Ed, MS Valley St Univ 1983; *cr:* Teacher Brooks Elem Sch 1983, Immaculate Conception Sch 1983-84, W Dist Mid Sch 1984-; *ai:* W Tallahatchie Ed Assn; *office:* W Dist Mid Sch P O Box 189 Sumner MS 38957

CURTIS, DOROTHY MARIE, Retired Elem Music Teacher; *b:* Bonne Terre, MO; *c:* Kelly M.; *ed:* (BSE) Music/Ed/Soc Sci, AR St Univ Jonesboro 1960; *cr:* 1st-4th Grade Teacher Rush Tower Sch 1950-51, Telegraph Sch 1951-52; 3rd-4th Grade Music Teacher Jefferson R-7 Sch 1952-53; 1st-8th Grade Music/Band Teacher Windsor C-1 Sch 1953-56; 1st-8th Grade Music Teacher Antonio R-4 Sch 1956-66, Windsor C-1 Sch 1966-86; Part-Time Elem Music Teacher Dunklin R-5 1988-89; *ai:* Private Piano Stu & Entertain Sr Citizens; Jefferson Cty Retired Teachers Assn, MO St Teachers Assn; 1st Baptist Church (Asst Organist, Pianist, Choir); Jefferson Cty Music Club Prgm Dir; *home:* 1009 Taylor Ave Crystal City MO 63019

CURTIS, HILDA VIRGINIA (FINLEY), 6th Grade Teacher; *b:* Rome, GA; *m:* Elihue C.; *c:* Santhia, Byron, Lendl; *ed:* (BS) Poly Sci, TN St Univ 1968; (MED) Elem Ed, W GA Coll 1977; Various Courses; *cr:* Teacher Summerville Elem Sch 1968-70, Rome City Schls 1970-; *ai:* Rome Says No To Drugs Club Adv, 6th Grade Main Elem; RAE Assn Rep 1988-; GAE, NAE 1970-; GAE (Delegate 1988-89, Alternate 1989-); Sch Teacher of Yr Main Elem 1979-80; *home:* 2107 Kingston Hwy NE Rome GA 30161

CURTIS, JAMES WILLIAM, Teacher; *b:* Port Royal, SC; *m:* M. Elizabeth; *ed:* (BA) Soc Sci Ed, Univ Cntrl FL 1985; *cr:* Math/Eng Instr Eustis Mid Sch 1985-86; Eng/Soc Sci Teacher Eustis HS 1986-; *ai:* Bsbl Coach; Sr Class Spon; *office:* Eustis HS 1300 E Washington Ave Eustis FL 32726

CURTIS, JOAN ALLEN, 4th Grade Teacher; *b:* Clarkesville, GA; *m:* Kenneth L.; *ed:* (BA) Elem Ed, Piedmont Coll 1968; (MED) Ed, Univ of GA 1976; *cr:* (1) 4th/5th Grade Teacher White Creek Sch 1968-69; (2) 2nd/3rd Grade Teacher Habersham Cty Sch Sys 1970-95; (3) 4th/8th Grade Teacher White Cty Mid Sch 1975-89;(4) 4th Grade Teacher White Cty Elem Sch 1990; *ai:* GA Assn of Ed; White Cty Assn of Ed; NEA; White Cty PTO; Star Teacher 1985/1988/1989; *office:* White County Elem Sch Rt 5 Box 5041 Cleveland GA 30528

CURTIS, NANCY S., 7th Grade Language Art Teacher; *b:* Lebanon, KY; *m:* Charles; *c:* Tom, Tiffany, Teddy; *ed:* (BS) Elem Ed, Spalding Univ 1972; (MA) Rdng Specialist, Univ of Louisville 1986; Louisville Writing Project; *cr:* 6th/8th Grade Teacher St Bartholomew 1972-78; 7th/8th Grade Teacher Holy Spirit 1978-81, St Athanasius 1981-86; 6th-8th Grade Teacher Mt WashiNgton Mid Sch 1986-; *ai:* Speech Coach; Consultant Bullitt Cty Writing; Stu Cncl Asst; Academic Writing Team Coach; NCTE, KEA; Helped Write Bullitt Cty Teachers Writing Process Grants; Published Article in Courier Journal; *office:* Mt Washington Mid Sch PO Box 99 Water St Mount Washington KY 40047

CURTIS, PETER M., Mathematics Teacher; *b:* Punxsutawney, PA; *c:* Tricia K.; *ed:* (BS) Math, 1976, (MS) Curr/Instruction 1982 MI St Univ; *cr:* Math Teacher Beecher Cmmty Schls 1967-80, Richmond HS 1980-; *ai:* Var Bsktbl & Jr Var B-Ball Coach; Class Spon; Stu Cncl Adv; NCTM, MCTM; Phi Kappa Phi 1982-; *office:* Richmond HS 35320 Division Richmond MI 48062

CURTIS, RAMONA, Assistant Principal; *b:* Seattle, WA; *ed:* (BED) Phys Ed, 1972, (MED) Ed, 1972 W WA Univ; Curr Instr, N IL Univ; *cr:* Asst Prin Hawthorne; Sci/Technology Specialist/Classroom Teacher Seattle WA; Outdoor Teacher Ed N IL Univ; Phys Ed Specialist Seattle WA; *ai:* Citizens Comm for Academic Excl 1982; Excl in Ed Awd 1984; Taft Campus Awd; Leadership in Outdoor Ed 1980; Danforth Fellow in Educl Admin 1989-; *home:* 3031 NE 137th #214 Seattle WA 98125

CURTIS, TIMOTHY J., Physics/Chemistry Instructor; *b:* Chillicothe, OH; *m:* Jan Elise Shanks; *c:* Kerri; *ed:* (BS) Biological Sci, OH Univ 1980; *cr:* Physics/Chem Teacher Sheffield Lake Schls 1980-81; General Sci Teacher 1981-84, Coord of Talented & Gifted 1984-85, Chem/General Sci Teacher 1985-86 Scioto Schls; Physics/Chem Teacher Huntington Jr/Sr HS 1986-; *ai:* Huntington HS Sci Day Co-Coord; Union Scioto Ed Assn Rep 1983-86, Teacher of Yr 1986; Huntington Local Ed Assn Pres 1988-89, Teacher of Yr 1988; NSTA; Natl Aeronautic & Space Admin; Natl Air & Space Museum Stars & Planets Symposium 1983; Industry Teachers Honors Wkshp Miami Univ 1989-; *office:* Huntington HS 188 Huntsman Rd Chillicothe OH 45601

CURVIN, LINDA G., Third Grade Teacher; *b:* Gadsden, AL; *m:* Freddie Ray; *c:* Julie; *ed:* (BS) Ed, Jackson St Univ 1972; Chrstn Ed Seminars; Pensacola Chrstn Coll, Pensacola FL; ACEA Ed Seminars 1975-; *cr:* Teacher Trinity Chrstn Acad 1975-; *ai:* Choir & Solo Duet; Childrens Choir Dir WMU; AL Chrstn Ed Assn 1975-; W Weaver Baptist Church (Mem, Sunday Sch Teacher, Bible Sch Dir, Teacher); AL Chrstn Ed Assn Outstanding Teacher Awd 1980; *office:* Trinity Christian Academy 1500 Airport Rd Oxford AL 36203

CUSHING, GALE KEATING, Assistant Principal; *b:* Bronx, NY; *m:* William P.; *c:* Robbie, Lindsey; *ed:* (BS) Elem Ed, 1974, (MED) Curr, 1977 VA Commonwealth Univ 1977; Public Sch Admin; *cr:* 5th Grade Teacher Franklin Elem 1975; 4th Grade Teacher Enon Elem 1975-80, Chalkley Elem 1980-81; Asst Prin Hopkins Elem 1981-86, Robious Elem 1986-; *ai:* Steering Comm Mem; Delta Kappa Gamma 1st VP 1983-; VA Assn Elem Sch Prin 1981-; Stanhope Jr Womens Club 1983-87; Bon Air Presbyn Church 1984-; VA Commonwealth Univ Adjunct Faculty Mem 1979; *office:* Robious Elem Sch 2801 Robious Crossing Dr Midlothian VA 23113

CUSICK, THOMAS PATRICK, Guidance Counselor; *b:* Red Bank, NJ; *m:* Valerie Miick; *c:* Nicole, Sean; *ed:* (BA) Eng, Montclair St Coll 1972; (MA) Cnslr Ed, Kean Coll 1986; *cr:* Eng Teacher Christian Brothers Acad 1972-76, Thorne Jr HS 1976-79, Middletown HS South 1979-88; Guidance Cnslr Middletown HS North 1988-; *ai:* Little Silver Recreation Bsktbl, Bsbl & Soccer Coach 1987; NJ Profession Cnslr Assn 1986-; Monmouth Cty Guidance Assn 1988-; *office:* Middletown HS North 50 Tindall Rd Middletown NJ 07748

CUSSEN, ANNE, Primary Class Teacher; *b:* Lawrence, MA; *ed:* (BA) His/Ed, Merrimack Coll 1965; (MED) Ed of Deaf, Smith Coll 1966; *cr:* Primary Teacher 1966-70, Mid Sch Teacher 1970-74 Beverly Sch for Deaf; Speech/Hearing/Lang Impaired Teacher Concord Public Schls 1974-78; CASE Collaborative 1978-; *ai:* CASE Prof Assn Pres 1987-; *office:* Case Collaborative-Alcott Sch Laurel St Concord MA 01742

CUSTODERO, THERESA LA FACHE, Fifth Grade Teacher; *b:* Utica, NY; *c:* Kristin M., Kathryn E.; *ed:* (BS) Elem Ed, St Univ of NY Oswego 1965; Grad Stud Syracuse, St Univ of NY Oswego; *cr:* 2nd-5th Grade Teacher Columbus Sch & Hughes Sch & Albany Schls 1965-70; Cnslr Oneida Cty Summer Youth Employment Prgm 1985-86, 1989; Teacher/Instr Mohawk Valley Comm Coll 1971-; *ai:* NY St Teachers Assn, Utica Teachers Assn, AFT 1965-; Clinton Cmmty Choir 1977-78, 1984; Albany Sch PTA Teacher Liason 1985-86; GSA Cookie Chairperson 1986; Soc Stud, Writings, Lang Art, Eng Curr Comm; CIMS Math Rep; *home:* 193 Welsh Bush Rd Frankfort NY 13340

CUTCHALL, CRAIG CLARTON, Fifth & Sixth Grade Teacher; *b:* Mc Connellsburg, PA; *m:* Barbara Black; *c:* Cortney; Corryn; *ed:* (BS) Health/Phys Ed, Slippery Rock 1973; (BS) Elem Ed, Shippensburg 1974; *cr:* Teacher Forbes Road Elem 1974-; *ai:* Girls Varsity Bsktbl Coach; Girls Jr HS Bsktbl Coach; Boys Track Coach; Amer Alliance of Health Phys Ed/Dance; Womens Bsktbl Coaches Assn; Lions Club Pres 1984; Fairview United Meth Church Layleader 1987-; *office:* Forbes Road Elem Sch HCO 1 Box 222 Waterfall PA 16689

CUTFORTH, NANCY BOHNE, Reading Teacher/Gifted Program; *b:* Evergreen Park, IL; *m:* Lorelle V.; *c:* Zachary, Joselyn; *ed:* (BS) Ed, 1970, (MA) Eng Lit, 1972 Chicago St Univ; (EDD) Ed, N IL Univ 1980; Fine Art, La Salle Univ; Gifted Ed, Univ of N CO; *cr:* 2nd/3rd Grade Teacher Sch Dist 135 1970-78; Rdng Instr Trinity Chrstn Coll 1978-80; Composition Instr Chicago St Univ 1981-82; 4th Grade Teacher Sch Dist 135 1981-82; Composition Instr Moraine Valley Comm Coll 1980-; 2nd-6th Grade Teacher of Gifted Sch Dist 135 1982-; *ai:* Intnl Rdng Assn 1987-; Childrens Rdng Round Table (Chm Ways & Means 1977-78, Pres 1976-77); Kappa Delta Pi 1970; Orland Park United Meth Church (Organist 1986-, Trustee 1986-89, Ed Comm Chm 1986, Vacation Bible Sch Dir 1986); St Alexander Church Organist 1963-70; Speaker Intnl Rdng Assn 1986; Article Published 1984; Speaker IL Assn Teachers of Eng 1980; Poetry Published 1969; *home:* 16624 Parker Rd Lockport IL 60441

CUTLER, GAYLE A., English Teacher; *b:* Newark, NJ; *c:* Cindy; *ed:* (BS) Ed, Boston Univ 1959; Grad Stud Eng, Rutgers Univ; *cr:* 4th Grade Teacher Bowen Sch 1959-60; 3rd Grade Teacher Irwin Sch 1960-63; 5th Grade Teacher A R Knight Sch 1971-81; Eng Teacher Carusi Jr HS 1981-; *ai:* Literary Magazine Adv; Cherry Hill Zoning Bd of Adjustment 1978-81; *office:* Carussi Jr HS Roosevelt Dr & Jackson Rd Cherry Hill NJ 08002

CUTLIFF, BARBARA DAVIS, Fifth Grade Teacher; *b:* Cario, IL; *c:* Drew, Todd; *ed:* (BA) Elem Ed, Memphis St Univ 1971; (MA) Admin/Supvr, Trevecca 1989; *cr:* Teacher Hamilton Elem 1971-73, Evans Elem 1973-75, Balmoral Elem 1979-; *ai:* Southern Assn Steering Comm Chm; Memphis Arts Cncl Artist in the Classroom; Public Relations Liasion Sch Cmmty Basic Skills First Lead Teacher; Delta Kappa Gamma Secy 1988; Memphis Ed Assn, TN Ed Assn, NEA 1980-; Rotary Awd for Teacher Excl (Secy 1989-), 1984-; *office:* Balmoral Elem Sch 5905 Grosvenor Ave Memphis TN 38119

CUTRER, KENNETH E., Social Studies Teacher; *b:* Plainfield, NJ; *m:* Gretchen Vaas; *ed:* (BA) Ed/Geography, Univ of KY 1975; (MA) Geography/Ed, E KY Univ 1976; (MA) Religion, Ashland Theological Seminary 1989; *cr:* Teacher/Coach Boyle Cty HS 1976-82; Minister of Ed & Admin Northlake Baptist Church 1982-84; Teacher/Coach Ashland HS 1985-; Youth Minister Trinity Luth ChUrch 1987-; *ai:* Huddle Coach for Fellowship of Chrstn Athletes; Ftbl Team Chaplain; OH Ed Assn 1985-; Ashland City Teachers Assn 1985-; NEA 1985-; World Wildlife Fund & Greenpeace 1989-; *office:* Ashland HS 1440 King Rd Ashland OH 44805

CUTTER, PORTIA L. GREENE, Geometry/Algebra Teacher; *b:* New York, NY; *m:* James Allen Sr.; *c:* James A. Jr., Michelle D.; *ed:* (BA) Math, Hunter Coll 1961; (MST) Math Ed, Memphis St Univ 1972; Post Grad Stud in Math Ed, Memphis St Univ; *cr:* 7th Grade Teacher Del Norte Elem Sch 1961-62; Algebra I Teacher Vanguard Jr HS 1963-64; 7th Grade Math Teacher Klondike Elem Sch 1965; 7th Grade Sci Teacher Humboldt Jr HS 1966-68; 7th/8th Grade Math Teacher Georgian Hills Jr HS 1968-71; Geometry/Algebra I/Pre-Algebra Teacher 1971-, Math Dept Chairperson 1986- Kingsbury Jr HS; *ai:* Cmptr Club & Honor Society Spon; Mathcounts Coach; Natl Jr Honor Society; NCTM, NEA, Memphis Ed Assn 1968-; Memphis Area Teachers of Math VP 1970; Greater Faith Baptist Church (Sunday Sch Teacher, Financial Secy, Choir Treas, Bowling League Secy 1977-80) 1972-, Outstanding Secy 1979; Nom Career Ladder II Partners in Excl Awd 1989; *office:* Kingsbury Jr HS 1276 N Graham Memphis TN 38122

CUTTER, SAULA LESLIE, Sixth Grade Teacher; *b:* Trenton, NJ; *ed:* (BA) Elem Ed, Trenton St Coll 1969; (MA) Curr/Supervision/Admin, Georgian Court Coll 1990; *cr:* 3rd/4th/6th Grade Elem Teacher Mc Galliard Sch 1969-; 6th Grade Teacher Grice Mid Sch 1975-; *ai:* Environmental Ed Dist, After Sch Testing Preparation Prgm Coord; Effective Schls, Amer Ed Week, Dist Screening Comms; NEA (Delegate 1985-) 1969-; NJ Ed Assn (Elections Comm Mem 1989-, Educator 1981-85, PAC Comm Chairperson 1989, Mem 1969-); Hamilton Township Ed Assn (Pres 1988-, VP 1986-88, Rep Cncl 1975-86, Poly Action 1982-, IPD Comm 1986-87, Liaison Comm Chairperson 1987-88, MCEA Rep 1985-88); Hamilton Township Ed Assn (Action Planning Comm Mem 1980-84, Action Planning Comm Chairperson 1985-88) 1969-; NJ Governors Grant 1989-; NJ Governors Teacher Recognition Awd 1985-86; Mercer Cty Soil Conservation Dist Conservation Teacher of Yr 1986; *home:* 11 Bradford Ave Apt 11 Trenton NJ 08610

CUTTS, JESSIE B., Business Teacher; *b:* Vaiden, MS; *M:* De Witt; *c:* La Wanda Sue Tarver, Timothy De Witt; *ed:* (BS) Bus Ed, MS St Univ 1967; Counseling, Bible Ed, Cmptr Cert; *cr:* Bus Teacher Weir Attendance Ctenter 1968-; *ai:* Teach Self Improvement Course Jr HS; Prof Educators Mem 1980-; NBEA 1980-85; MS Bus Ed Assn 1968-89; Bethsaida Bapt Church 1974-; Dow Jones Newspaper Wkshp Grant; *office:* Weir Attendence Center P O Box 98 Weir MS 39772

CUTTS, PEARL, 3rd Grade Teacher; *ed:* (BA) Elem Ed, David Lipscomb 1958; *cr:* 3rd Grade Teacher Mt Laurel Township Schls 1958-; *ai:* NEA, NJ Ed Assn, Burlington Cty Ed Assn, Mt Laurel Ed Assn 1958-; *office:* Fleetwood Sch Fleetwood Ave Mount Laurel NJ 08054

CYR, PAUL TURGEON, Jr/Sr HS Mathematics Teacher; *b:* Crookston, MN; *ed:* (BS) Phys Ed, Univ of MN Morris 1978; (MS) Math Ed, Bemidji St Univ 1989; Theology St, Johns Univ; *cr:* Math Teacher New Richland-Hartland HS 1986-; *ai:* Head Wrestling, Asst Sftbl, Asst Ftbl Coach; *home:* 421 1st St SW Box 212 New Richland MN 56072

CYTERSKI, NORBERT A., 5th-8th Grade Guidance Cnslr; *b:* Erie, PA; *m:* Dorothy Anderson Freeman; *c:* Linda Noble, Jackie Freeman, Beverly Freeman; *ed:* (BA) Soc Stud, Gannon Univ 1953; (MA) Guidance, Allegheny Coll 1960; Edinboro Univ, Behrend Coll Penn St Branch; *cr:* His/Span Teacher Ft Le Boeuf HS 1955-66; Elem Guidance Teacher Ft Le Boeuf Sch System 1966-71; 5th-8th Grade Guidance Cnslr Ft Le Boeuf Mid Sch 1971-; *ai:* Jr HS & Var Bsktbl Coach 1955-57; Jr HS Ftbl Coach 1955-88; PSEA Local Branch VP 1961; *office:* Ft Le Boeuf Mid Sch Cherry St Waterford PA 16441

CZECH, MARYA, Science Teacher/Academic Dean; *b:* Luneburg, Germany; *ed:* (AB) Ed, Mary Manse Coll 1973; (MA) Bio, Ball St Univ 1981; Scndry Teachers Biotechnology Trng, Georgetown Univ 1988; *cr:* Jr HS Teacher Toledo Diocesan Elem Schls 1967-75; Sci/Math Teacher Notre Dame Acad 1975-86; Adjunct Bio Instr Notre Dame Coll Toledo 1982-; Sci/Math Teacher St Joseph Cntrl Cath 1986-; *ai:* Biotechnology Inservice Wkshps for Bio Teachers; NHS Adv; Toledo Diocesan Liturgical Commission Mem; Sisters of Notre Dame Justice & Peace Comm; NABT, Amer Inst of Biological Sci; NABT Conventions Biotechnology Presentations Asst; *office:* St Joseph Cntrl Cath HS 702 Croghan St Fremont OH 43420

CZEMSKI, ANTHONY JOSEPH, Social Studies Teacher; *b:* Chicago, IL; *m:* Margaret Ann Stanley; *c:* Jean; *ed:* (BS) His, N IL Univ 1968; Yearly Wkshp & Conferences; *cr:* Teacher Red Hill Sch 1967-; *ai:* Headscore Keeper; Discipline Comm; IL Ed Assn (Building Rep 1989-, Regional Rep 1974-76); Elks 1974-; *office:* Red Hill Jr HS 110 W Locust Sumner IL 62466

CZEMSKI, MARGARET ANN STANLEY, 6th Grade Teacher; *b:* Olney, IL; *m:* Anthony J.; *c:* Jean; *ed:* (BA) His, N IL Univ 1967; Rdng; *cr:* 6th Grade Teacher Silver Cntrl Grade Sch 1967-76, Calhoun Grade Sch 1976-77; 7th/8th Grade Rdng/Soc Stud Teacher East Richland Mid Sch 1977-81; 6th Grade Teacher Calhoun Claremont Grade Sch 1982-83, E Richland Mid Sch 1983-; *ai:* Cheerleading Spon; Problem Solving, Bsktbl, Track Coach; Phi Delta Kappa Charter Mem 1980; *office:* East Richland Mid Sch 1099 N Van St Olney IL 62450

CZERENDA, JULIE ANN, Art Teacher-Art Chairperson; *b:* Amsterdam, NY; *m:* Michael; *ed:* (BS) Art Ed, Coll of St Rose 1981; (MS) Ed, Elmira Coll 1986; *cr:* 7th-12th Grade Art Teacher 1981-; Dept Chairperson 1981-Candor Central; *ai:* Jr-Sr Play Dir 1989-; Boys Varsity Track 1989; NY St Art Teachers Assn; *office:* Candor Central H S P O Box 145 Candor NY 13743

CZERNIAK, CHARLENE M., Assistant Professor; *b:* Toledo, OH; *m:* David J.; *ed:* (AS) Ed, Monroe Cty Comm Coll 1977; (BA) Ed/Elem Sci, Univ of Toledo 1978; (MED) Ed/Sci, Bowling Green St Univ 1983; (PHD) Ed/Elem Sci, OH St Univ 1989; *cr:* 5th Grade Teacher St Clement Sch 1979; 5th/6th Grade Teacher Bowling Green City Schls 1979-89; Grad Teaching Assoc OH St Univ 1986-87; Asst Professor Univ of Toledo 1989-; *ai:* Provide Sci Ed Wkshps; Sci Ed Consultant; Sci Fairs & Sci Olympiads Asst; Univ Comms; NSTA, Sci Ed Cncl of OH 1984-; Natl Assn Research in Sci Teaching 1986-; Assn for Supervision Curr & Instruction 1989-; Phi Delta Kappa Research Awd; Univ of Toledo Womens Club 1989-; Childrens Sci Book Author & Illustrator; Sci Ed Articles Published; Marine Sci Grant; Dir of Excl in Ed Grants; Dissertation Research Awd; Jenning Scholar; Bowling Green St Univ Annual Research Awd; *office:* Univ of Toledo Coll of Ed 2801 W Bancroft St Toledo OH 43606

CZIRR, MARY STENGLE, Fourth Grade Teacher; *b:* Seneca Falls, NY; : Robert E.; *ed:* (BS) His/Poly Sci, Le Moyne Coll 1961; (MS) Ed, St Univ of NY Geneseo 1967; *cr:* Soc Worker Monroe Cty Dept of Soc Welfare 1961-62; 6th Grade Teacher Romulus Cntrl Sch 1962-65; 4th Grade Teacher Main Street Sch 1965-83, Bear Road Sch 1983-; *ai:* NY St United Teacher 1965-; AFT 1975-; Valley Forge Freedom Fnd; Honorable Mention for Teacher of Yr Awd 1982-83; *office:* Bear Road Sch 5590 Bear Rd North Syracuse NY 13212

D

DABBS, LORETTA YOUNG, Fourth Grade Teacher; *b:* New York, NY; *m:* Henry E.; *c:* Lisa; *ed:* (BFA) Fashion Design, Pratt Inst 1959; (BA) Elem Ed, Jersey City St 1969; (MA) Elem Ed, Trenton St 1989; *cr:* Elem Teacher Public Sch 191 1966-67, Lafayette Mills Sch 1967-; *ai:* Newsletter Ed; Chrldr Coach; Affirmative Action, Lang Art, Report Card, Rdng Comms; Cncl of Negro Women, Natl Assn for Advancement of Colored People 1970-; Natl Alliance of Black Sch Educators 1989-; Governors Teacher Recognition Grant NJ 1987; Author of Booklet 1988; *office:* Lafayette Mills Sch Maxwell Ln Manalapan NJ 07726

D'ABREU-RODDIN, DEBORAH, English Teacher; *b:* Brooklyn, NY; *m:* Gerald; *ed:* (BA) Scndry Eng Ed, SUNY Cortland 1972; (MED) Rdng, Cntrl St Univ 1979; Eng as Second Lang, St Edwards Univ, Univ of TX Austin; *cr:* Eng Teacher Frederick Douglass HS 1976-79; Rdng Teacher St Edwards Univ 1981, Anderson HS 1981-83; Eng/Rdng Teacher Croughton Amer HS 1983-86, W T Sampson HS 1987-; *ai:* Liason Officer; Booster Club; Schoolwide Enrichment Prgm Coord; Forensics Spon; Overseas Educators Assn 1987-; Intnl Rdng Assn 1986-; Officers Club Advisory Bd 1987-; *home:* Box 84 US Naval Base Fleet Br Norfolk VA 23593

DACUS, JEFFREY RAY, 8th Grade Teacher; *b:* Vancouver, WA; *m:* Mary Elizabeth Heurung; *ed:* (BA) Elem Ed, Portland St Univ 1982; (MAT) Soc Stud, Lewis & Clark Coll 1986; *cr:* 8th Grade Teacher Covington Jr HS 1982-83; 7th Grade Teacher Lewis Jr HS 1983-84; 8th Grade Teacher Mc Loughlin Mid Sch 1984-; *ai:* Intramural Spon; 8th Grade Boys Ftbl Coach; 7th Grade Boys & Girls Bsktbl Coach; Marine Corps Historical Fnd 1987-; Naval Inst 1984-; Tailhook Assn 1989-; Museum of Flight Mem 1988-; Friends of The Amer Fighter Aces 1987-; The Air Museum 1984-; *office:* Mc Loughlin Mid Sch 5802 Macarthur Blvd Vancouver WA 98661

DACUS, JULIE, Computer Literacy/Math Teacher; *b:* Fort Worth, TX; *m:* Mike; *c:* Casey, Cori; *ed:* (BS) Math/Poly Sci, TX Wesleyan Coll 1972; Cmptr Literacy Trng-Sam Houston St; Math Sam Houston St; Master Teacher Acad; *cr:* HS Math Teacher Mansfield HS 1972-73; 8th Grade Math Teacher Irving Ind Sch Dist/Travis Jr HS 1973-75; 8th Grade Cmptr Literacy Teacher Navasota Jr HS1978-; *ai:* Number Sense Coach; UIL Dist Literary Meet Coord; Career Leader Comm Rep; TX Cmptr Educators Assn 1984-; Girl Scouts Leader 1986-88; *office:* Navasota Jr H S P O Box 511 Navasota TX 77868

DACUS, MARTHA BARNETTE, English Teacher; *b:* Greer, SC; *m:* Edwin C.; *c:* Michael E., Reba E.; *ed:* (AA) Liberal Art, Mars Hill Coll 1956; (BA) Eng, Furman Univ 1958; (MRE) Youth Ministry, S Baptist Seminary 1962; (MAED) Eng, E Carolina Univ 1982; Various Wkshps; Spec Trng Paideia Prgm UNC Chapel Hill 1989; *cr:* Eng Teacher Blue Ridge HS 1958-60, Smithfield HS 1967; 3rd Grade Teacher S Columbia Elem 1967-68; Eng Teacher ahoskie HS 1970-72, 1985-88; Teacher of Academically Gifted Conway Elem 1978-85; Eng Teacher Hertford Cty HS 1988-; *ai:* Discipline Comm; Literary Club & Magazine Spon; NC Assn of Gifted & Talented Ed 1980-89, Teacher of Yr Region III 1985; NEA, NC Ed Assn, Hertford Cty Ed Assn 1986-; Northampton Hertford Parents for Advancement of Gifted Ed Pres 1983-; 1st Baptist Church Ahoskie (Deacon, Youth Coord, Adult Sunday Sch Teacher) 1980-; Melrose Womens Club Secy 1972; Alliance for Gifted (VP, Bd of Dirs) 1986-87; Teacher of Yr Hertford Cty HS 1988-89, Conway Elem Sch 1982-83; *home:* 919 W Richard St Ahoskie NC 27910

DADE, VICKEY GALE, Third Grade Teacher; *b:* Longview, TX; *ed:* (BS) Elem Ed, TX Womans Univ 1978; *cr:* 3rd Grade Teacher Longview Ind Sch Dist 1978-; *ai:* Soc Stud Curr Guide & Univ Interscholastic League Spelling Comm; TX St Teachers Assn, NEA; Alpha Kappa Alpha, Cmmty Challenge; *home:* 17 Wylie St Longview TX 75602

DAGNE, DONALD RAY, Act Dir/Soc Sci Dept Chm; *b:* Los Angeles, CA; *m:* Pamela Jayne Damico; *c:* Cherish A., Christopher D.; *ed:* (BA) Music, 1971, Credential Standard Elem/Scndry, 1972, Credential Counseling, 1976 CA St Univ Los Angeles; ROP Credential Bus & Retail Sales; *cr:* Tennis Coach/His Teacher 1972-76, Band Dir 1971-77 Monrovia HS; Eng/His/Career Teacher 1977-89, Band Dir/His Teacher 1989- Clifton Mid Sch; *ai:* Leadership & 8th Grade Class Spon; Band, Orch Act Dir Stu Cncl, Drill Team, Banners, Tall Flags & Mascot Dir/Teachers Leadership Rep; Stu Study Team; Electives & His Dept Chm; Music Educators Natl Conference Mem 1972-77; CA St Framework Assn; CA Soc Sci Framework Mem 1983-89; Distrubutive Ed Clubs of America Dir 1981-86; CA Act Dir Assn Mem 1988-; Parents Without Partners Youth Dir 1979-81, Leader of Yr 1980; Church (Youth Dir, Music Dir) 1966-; Amer Stu Travel Tour Guide 1984-, Best Leader 1989; San Gabriel Valley 1979- Teacher of Month & 1980 Teacher of Yr; Golden Apple Awd 1986; Distinguished Service Awd 1990; Annual Yrbk Dedication 1990; *office:* Clifton Mid Sch 226 S Ivy Ave Monrovia CA 91016

DAGRO, CARYL JO, Jrnlsm/English/Reading Teacher; *b:* Chicago, IL; *ed:* (BS) ED, Speech/Journalism/English Eastern IL Univ 1969; (MA) Reading Northeastern IL Univ 1979; Post Masters Studies Northwestern Univ; Northern IL Univ; St Xavier Coll; *cr:* Speech Teacher Proviso West HS 1969-70; 3rd Grade Teacher Nash Elem Sch 1970-77; Reading Specialist Teacher Cooper Jr HS 1977-78; Journalism/English/Reading Teacher Stevenson HS 1978-; *ai:* Newspaper Adv, Yrbk Adv, Quill & Scroll Spon; North Central Evaluation Steering Comm, Ed Assn Executive Bd; Journalism Education Assn; IL Assn of Teachers of Eng; IL Reading Assn; Contributor to Scholastic Journalism Textbook, Co-Author of Study Skills Book, Monthly Study Skills Column in Daily Herald Newspaper, Super Patriot Award; *office:* Stevenson H S 16070 W Hwy 22 Prairie View IL 60069

DAHL, BRENDA SUE, First Grade Teacher; *b:* Guymon, OK; *ed:* (BS) Elem Ed, SW OK St Univ 1981; *cr:* Resource Teacher 1981-82, 5th-8th Grade Math Teacher/7th-8th Grade Girls Coach 1984-88 Skellytown Elem; 1st Grade Teacher Graver Ind Sch Dist 1988-; *ai:* Coached UIL Number Sense, Girls Bsktbl & Track, Calculator , Oral Rdng, Sch Graduations & Musicals; Skellytown Textbook Comm; Gruver United Meth Church 7th-8th Grade Choir Leader 1989-; St Andrews United Meth Church (Childrens Choir, Youth Dir 1987); *office:* Gruver Elem Sch Box 265 Gruver TX 79040

DAHL, ROGER JOHN, World History/Soc Stud Teacher; *b:* Duluth, MN; *m:* Suzanne Marie Fjellman; *c:* Benjamin, Jonathan; *ed:* (BA) His, Bethel Coll 1974; (MA) Ed/Soc Stud, St Thomas 1975; (MA) Mid European His, Univ of MN 1983; *cr:* World His Teacher Blaine Sr HS 1974-79; Soc Stud Teacher Intnl Sch of Disseldorf 1979-81; Advanced Placement/World His Teacher Blaine Sr HS 1981-; *ai:* Elim Baptist Church Several Offices 1984-; Teacher Inventive Grant; Graduating Class Honors Luncheon Speaker; Best Teacher Awds; *office:* Blaine Sr HS 12555 University Ave NE Blaine MN 55434

DAHLBERG, PATRICIA TOCZEK, Jr HS Reading Teacher; *b:* Blue Island, IL; *m:* Robert; *ed:* (BA) Eng, 1972, (MS) Learning Disabilities/Behavior Disorders, 1981 Rosary Coll; *cr:* 7th/8th Grade Lang Arts Teacher St Nicholas & St Louis 1972-73; Substitute Teacher St John, St Charles, St Bernardine 1973; 7th/8th Grade Lang Arts/Rel Teacher St Bernardine 1974-77; 6th-8th Grade Rdng/Eng Teacher 1977-79, 6th-8th Grade Rdng Teacher 1980- Our Lady of the Ridge; *ai:* Sch Newspaper Moderator; Unit Leader; Intnl Rdng Assn 1988-; *office:* Our Lady of the Ridge Sch 10859 S Ridgeland Ave Chicago Ridge IL 60415

DAHLEN, DAVE W., Mathematics Teacher; *b:* Thief River Falls, MN; *m:* Carol Opdahl; *c:* Rachel, Travis; *ed:* (BS) Math, Bemidji St Univ 1974; *cr:* Math Teacher Goodridge HS 1985-; *ai:* Knowlege Bowl Coach; Jr Class Adv; MEA 1985-; Lions Secy 1982-84; Masons Jr Warden 1987-; Northern Navigators (Secy, VP, Pres) 1983-, Leadership Service 1989; *office:* Goodridge HS P O Box 195 Goodridge MN 56701

DAHLEN, JEFFREY JOHN, Sixth Grade Teacher; *b:* Hayfield, MN; *ed:* (BA) Elem Ed, Winona St Univ 1972; (MA) Elem Ed, Univ of MN 1990; *cr:* 6th Grade Teacher Caledonia Public Sch 1974-; *ai:* Sch Patrol Adv; Prin Advisory, Curr, Dist Long Range Planning Comm; River Valley Teachers Pres 1988-; Caledonia Ed Assn Negotiator 1984-; Caledonia Lions VP 1990; Caledonia Charities Bd Mem 1989-; *office:* Caledonia Public Sch W Main St Caledonia MN 55921

DAHLGREN, DENIS ANDREW, 3rd Grade Teacher; *b:* Wellsville, NY; *m:* Colleen R.; *c:* Jonathan, Christopher; *ed:* (BA) Ed, St Univ Coll Geneseo 1976; *cr:* Elem Teacher Wellsville Cntrl Schls 1977-; *ai:* Key Club; Prin Advisory Comm; NY Ed Assn Delegate 1980-; NEA St Delegate 1989-; Kiwanis Club Dir 1985-; PTA Life Mem Teacher of Yr Awd 1985; *office:* Wellsville Central Schls 98 School St Wellsville NY 14895

DAHLKOETTER, DEBRA DYKSTRA, Biology Teacher; *b:* Sioux City, IA; *c:* Cole; *ed:* (BA) Phys Ed, Mt Marty Coll 1973; (MS) Bio/Earth Sci, Univ of SD 1985; Grad Stud Sci & Effective Teaching Classes; *cr:* Sci Teacher West Jr HS 1981-82; Sci/Math Teacher/Coach Emerson-Hubbard HS 1982-84; Sci Teacher/Coach Homer HS 1984-85; Sci Teacher North HS 1985-; *ai:* Effective Schls Cadre Chm; Vlybl Coach; NABT, NSCE; *office:* North HS 4200 Cheyenne Blvd Sioux City IA 51104

DAHLQUIST, DAVID ALLEN, English Department Chair; *b:* Tracy, MN; *ed:* (BA) Eng, Macalester Coll 1964; *cr:* Eng Teacher Lyle HS 1964-; *ai:* Drama Dir; Speech Coach; Yrbk & 8th Grade Class Adv; NEA, MEA 1964-; LEA (Pres, VP, Secy, Negotiating Team) 1964-; Summerset Theatre Bd 1980-; Matchbox Childrens Theatre Bd 1975-; Lions Club 1964-75; *office:* Lyle HS Rt 1 Lyle MN 55953

DAHLQUIST, DAVID C., Choral Director; *b:* Salt Lake, UT; *m:* Maria Elena Mc Curdy; *c:* Kristiana, Rebekah, Jenny, Ryan, Sean; *ed:* (BM) Music Ed/Choral, Univ of UT 1975; *cr:* Choral Dir Payson HS 1975-; *ai:* Chm Fine Art Dept & Grad Comm; Dir Trouveres, Concert Choir, Jr Choir, Soph Choir; Nebo Ed Assn Pres 1985-87; Bonneville Uniserv Pres 1987-88; Payson Civic Chorale (Musical Dir, Conductor) 1981-; Payson Cmmty Theatre Artistic Dir 1989; Payson City Outstanding Citizen of Yr 1985; *office:* Payson HS 1050 S Main Payson UT 84651

DAHMER, CHERYL LYNN, 3rd Grade Teacher; *b:* Petersburg, WV; *ed:* (BA) Elem Ed-Cum Laude, Shepherd Coll 1974; (MA) Elem Ed, WV Univ 1982; *cr:* 3rd Grade Teacher Brandywine Elem 1974-; *ai:* VP of Brandywine Sch Assn; Chairperson Intl Relations Comm of Delta Kappa Gamma Society; Responsible Rdng is Fundamental Prgm; Building Rep Pendleton Cty Ed Assn; Alpha Kappa Chapter Delta KappA Gamma Society Intnl 1984-; Bus & Prof Women VP 1986-88; Mem Phi Alpha Theta 1973; MN Legislative Comm INtnl; *office:* Brandywine Elem Sch Rt 3 Brandywine WV 26802

DAIBERL, RICHARD JOSEPH, Jr HS Social Studies Teacher; *b:* Evanston, IL; *m:* Linda Joyce Cook; *c:* Luke, Shannon, Tessa; *ed:* (BS) Soc Stud, OH St Univ 1968; Grad Stud His; *cr:* 6th Grade Teacher 1968-83, Jr HS Soc Stud/Lang Art Teacher 1984- Park View; *ai:* Evans Scholars Alumni Assn Secy 1974; Nom Kohl Intnl Awd Exemplary Teaching 1989; *office:* Park View Sch 6200 W Lake St Des Plaines IL 60016

DAIL, EDITH JACQUELINE, 7th Grade Teacher; *b:* Cullman, AL; *ed:* (BA) Music Ed, Univ of AL 1964; (MED) Admin, Univ of GA 1972; Rdng Practicum; Working Towards Elem Cert Ed; *cr:* Music Teacher George Fox Jr HS 1964-66; 5th Grade Teacher Whitesburg Elem 1966-67; Music Teacher 1967-72, 7th Grade Teacher 1972- Flat Shoals Elem; *ai:* Grade Chairperson; Choral Dir; Drama Club; Tutorial Prgm; Head of Faculty Discipline Comm; PTA Lifetime Mem; Outstanding Young Women of America; Article Published 1971; *office:* Flat Schoals Sch 3226 Flat Shoals Rd Decatur GA 30034

DAILEANES, KOSTAS, English Teacher; *b:* Lowell, MA; *m:* Elaine Mandragouras; *c:* Steven, Martha; *ed:* (BED) Elem Ed, Univ of NH Plymouth St Coll 1963; (MED) Ed/Counseling, Rivier Coll 1968; Grad Work Eng; *cr:* 5th/6th Grade Teacher Parker Sch 1963-65; Combined Stud Teacher Diamond Jr HS 1965-66; 6th Grade Teacher Maria Hastings Sch 1968-68; 7th/8th Grade Teacher Muzzey Jr HS 1968-80, Clarke Jr HS 1980-86; Eng Teacher Lexington HS 1986-; *ai:* MA Teachers Assn, Lexington Teachers Assn, Natl Teachers Assn 1967-; *office:* Lexington HS 251 Waltham St Lexington MA 02173

DAILER, JAY, Biology Teacher; *b:* Wheeling, WV; *m:* Jill Jordan; *c:* Meg, Besse; *ed:* (BS) Ed, 1973, (MA) Scndry Ed, 1978 WV Univ; *cr:* Sci Teacher Suncrest Jr HS 1973-79; Bio Teacher Elkins HS 1979-; *ai:* Boys & Girls Bsktbl, Boys & Girls Tennis Coach; SADD Spon; Partners in Ed & New Sch Design Lead Teacher; WV Ed Assn, NEA; Conference Coach of Yr; *office:* Elkins HS 1400 S Davis Ave Elkins WV 26241

DAILEY, BARBARA BENTLEY, 2nd/3rd Grade Teacher; *b:* Royal Oak, MI; *m:* Donald L.; *c:* Maureen Dailey Parmann, Lawrence M.; *ed:* (BS) Bio/Speech Drama, Central MI Univ 1969; Postmasters Degree Rdng Instruction, Wayne State Univ; Learning Disability Cert Trng, Wright Univ; *cr:* 4th Grade Teacher Gull Lake Commty Schls 1966-70; Ld Tutor Dayton Pub Schls 1972-74; Rdng Teacher St Clair Cty Interm Sch Dist 1975-77; Rdng Teacher Capac Public Schls 1980; Elem Teacher Yale Public Schls 1981-; *ai:* Gifted & Talented Prgm Teacher; Curr Comm for Soc Stud & Rdng; Prof Dev Comm; Blue Water Rdng/MI Rdng Assn/NRA Correspond Sec 1977-78; Celebrate Literacy Awd 1989; Alpha Psi Omega Sec 1959-61; Signa Kappa Sor 1958-; Youth for Understanding Intl Exch Prgm Field Mgr 1977-; Most Valuable Volunteer 1986; St Clair Cty Rdng Comm for Implimentation (And Trng of Teachers) for MI Model of Rdng 1988-; *office:* Avoca Elem Yale Pub Sch 8751 Willow Avoca MI 48006

DAILEY, JUNE SAUER, Retired Second Grade Teacher; *b:* Fort Lupton, CO; *m:* Richard J. (dec); *c:* Myrna, Prentice, R.R.; *ed:* (BA) Elem Ed, CO St Coll of Ed 1952; Elem Ed; *cr:* 3rd/4th/5th Grade Teacher St Vrain Sch 1940-42; 6th Grade Teacher Fruitdale Elem Sch 1942-43; 3rd/4th Grade Teacher Platteville Elem Sch 1943-46; 2nd Grade Teacher Fort Lupton Public Schls 1950-84; *ai:* NEA Life Mem; CO Ed Assn 1940-84; Fort Lupton

Ed Assn Pres 1961-62; Delta Kappa Gamma Society Intnl; Article in Delta Kappa Gamma Bulletin 1961.

DAILY, SUSIE BARTLEY, Seventh Grade Math Teacher; *b:* Bessemer, AL; *m:* Bill; *ed:* (BS) Elem Ed, Jacksonville St Univ 1972; (MA) Elem Ed, 1984, (EDS) Elem Ed, 1985 UAB; *cr:* Teacher Jackson Elem 1973-85, Arrington Mid Sch 1985-; *ai:* Coach Academic Bowl, Math Team, Forensics Team; Poetry Festival Spon; Beta Club Adv; NEA, AEA, BEA, NEA, Al Ed Assn, Birmingham Ed Assn; Kappa Delta Pi; Instructional Excl Awd 1990; Teacher Recognition Prgm Top 10 Mid Sch Teachers; *home:* 1932 Longview Dr Hueytown AL 35023

DAI ZOVI, LONNIE GAULT, Spanish Teacher; *b:* Clinton, IA; *m:* Robert; *c:* Dino, Michela; *ed:* (BA) Span, Univ of IL 1973; Spec Ed Bilingual Children Xalapa, Mexico; Impact Training for Drug Educators; *cr:* Bi-ling Teacher K-3 Onarga Elem Sch 1973-75; Bi-ling Teacher 4-5 Waukegan Public Schls; Biling Teacher 7-8 West Chicago Jr HS 1976-83; ESC Teacher System Training to Saudi Arabians 1985-86; Span Teacher 9-12 Manzano HS 1986-; *ai:* Span Club Spon; Core Team Mem (Comm of Staff Actively Working Toward Drug-Free Campus); Amer Cncl of Teachers of Foreign Lang 1987-; NM Organ of Lang Educators 1989-; Albuquerque Lang Teacher Organ, Nominated Teacher of Yr 1986-; AFT 1987-; Author "Spanish Alive for Children" Series; Author "Cantos, Ritmas, y Rimas"; *office:* Manzano H S 12200 Lomas NE Albuquerque NM 87123

DAKEWICZ, HELENE POWARZYNSKI, 5-6th Grade Soc Stud Teacher; *b:* Chicago, IL; *m:* Anthony J.; *c:* Kristen, Kevin; *ed:* (BA) Elem Ed, St Xavier Coll 1988-89; Teacher Prof Dev Prgm, St Xavier Coll 1988-89; *cr:* 3rd Grade Elem Teacher Riley Sch 1965-67; 7th Grade Elem Teacher Oliver W Holmes 1967-73; 4th Grade Elem Teacher Jesse Sherwood 1978-80; 6th Grade Elem Teacher Adam Clayton Powell 1980-; *ai:* Intermediate Grade Chm; Pension Rep; Intnl Rdng Assn; *office:* Adam Clayton Powell Jr H S 7530 S South Shore Dr Chicago IL 60649

DAKIS, MIKE NICK, Vice-Principal/P E Instructor; *b:* Hiner, UT; *ed:* (MS) Scndry Ed, Westminster Coll 1958; (MAED) Coll of ID 1962; (PHD) Ed, Brigham Young Univ 1963-; Ed, Humboldt St Coll 1972; Math Specialist, San Jose St Coll 1975; Phys Ed & Mental Health Coll of Redwoods 1985; *cr:* Eng Teacher/Journalism Adv Coach Nampa HS 1959-61; Super & Prin Leadore Sch Dist 1961-65; Supt Hoehne Sch Dist 1965-68; Vice Prin/Phys Ed Instr Mc Kinleyville Jr HS 1968-; *ai:* Mc Kinleyville Sch Attendance Review Bd; Intmural Prgm, Athletics Adv; CO Sch Admin Assn 1965-68; Fisher Peak League Admin Assn Pres 1966-68 Honorary Awd 1968; CA Teachers Assn 1969-; FFA Service Awd 1966; Hoehne Athletic Assn Service Awd 1967; PTA Honorary Awd 1976; Mc Kinleyville Youth Ftbl Coach 1984 Service Awd 1984; Summa Cum Laude 1958; ID Yesterdays Magazine Published Articles 1962-65; Math Teacher Summer Fellowship 1971-74; *office:* Mc Kinleyville Jr H S Central Ave Mc Kinleyville CA 95521

DALE, ALBERTA DIXON, Elem Cnslr & Gifted Ed Teacher; *b:* Quanitco, VA; *m:* Earl R.; *c:* Jack R., David R., Rebekah A.; *ed:* (BA) Elem Ed, 1971, (MS) Elem Psych/Counseling, 1989 TN Tech Univ; *cr:* Kndgtn Teacher Rickman Elem 1971-77; 2nd Grade Teacher Livingston Elem 1977-86, a H Roberts 1986-89; Elem Cnslr/Gifted Ed Overton Cty Sch System 1989-; *ai:* Parental Involvement Prgm; Volunteer Parent Exch Club; Church of Christ Sunday Sch Teacher; Natl Teacher Org TN Assn for Counseling/Dev; TN Ed Assn; Delta Kappa Gamma; *home:* 625 4th St Livingston TN 38570

DALE, ROBERT EUGENE, JR., Sixth Grade Teacher; *b:* Saint Louis, MO; *m:* Alice Lorraine Carlson; *c:* Tammy S., Dale Peterson, Michelle, Scott A.; *ed:* (BA) Liberal Stud/Meteorology, CA St Univ Dominguez Hills 1978; (MA) Admin/Sch, 1984, (MA) Curr, 1984 Univ of La Verne; Prgm Evaluation; US Soccer Fed Trng; Teaching Advanced Math Stu; Commercial Pilot Trng FAA; Sch Admin Trng; *cr:* Prgm Dir Sugar Ray Robinson Youth Fnd 1973-78; Educator Los Angeles Unufied Sch Dist 1978-81, Victor Elem Sch Dist 1981-; *ai:* Stu Cncl Adv; Safety Patrol Adv; Soccer, Bsktbl, & Track Coach; CA Teachers Assn 1978-; NEA 1978-; Adaptive Phys Health & Recreation Assn 1986-87; Victor Elem Teachers Assn 1981-; San Bernardino Cty Sheriffs Aviation Division Reserve Pilot 1986-89; Victor Elem Sports & Academic Service Awd; Coach of Yr Awd 1984/1986; Sugar Ray Robinson Achievement Awd; Book-Manuel Phys Ed for Elem Classroom Co-Author; *office:* Irwin Elem Sch 15907 Mojave Victorville CA 92392

DALESSIO, ELIZABETH A., MPF, 8th Grade Computer Teacher; *b:* Hoboken, NJ; *ed:* (BA) Elem Ed, Coll of St Elizabeth 1973; (MA) Dogma, St Josephs Seminary 1985; Cmptr Literacy Stud & Inservice Wkshps; *cr:* Dir/6th-8th Grade Math Teacher/Coord Head Start Summer Prgm 1971-73; 9th-12th Grade Math/Phys Ed Teacher/10th Grade Sci Teacher/10th Grade Drivers Ed Teacher Villa Walsh Acad 1973-79; 6th-8th Grade Math/Sci Teacher/Coord Our Lady Queen of Peace 1979-80; 9th10th Grade Teacher/Dept Chairperson Villa Walsh Acad 1980-81; Theology Dept Chairperson/Athletic Dir Villa Victoria Acad 1981-84; 6th-8th Grade Math/Sci Teacher/Cmptr Literacy Coord Holy Trinity Parish 1984-; *ai:* Religious Ed, Youth Group, Adult Ed Dir; NCTE Mem 1981-; Beta Beta Beta; Religious Ed Dir; RCIA Prgm Dir; *office:* Holy Trinity Sch 375 Exchange Pl Long Branch NJ 07740

DALEY, ELIZABETH A., Social Ministry Temporary; *b:* Heckscherville, PA; *ed:* (BS) Ed, Chestnut Hill Coll 1972; (MA) Ed, Shippensburg Univ 1978; Basic Cmptr Literacy Course; Cert Gregg Shorthand II; Wkshp & Seminars; *home:* 518 Valley St Orange NJ 07050

DALL, CAMERON MITCHELL, Director of Bands; *b:* Chicago, IL; *ed:* (AA) Liberal Arts, Santa Ana Coll 1983; (BME) Instrumental Music, Butler Univ 1985; IN Univ; Ball St Univ; *cr:* Dir of Bands Wm H Harrison HS 1986-; *ai:* Marching Band, Pep Band, Pit Orch; Natl Band, IN Bandmasters Assn; Detroit Concert Band Society; Arbeitskreis Militarmusik; *office:* Wm H Harrison HS 5700 North Rd 50 W West Lafayette IN 47906

DALLAS, JAMES ROBERT, Counselor/Science Teacher; *b:* Mason City, IA; *m:* Molly; *c:* Erin; *ed:* (BA) Zoology/Chem, 1969, (MAT) Botany/Sci Ed, 1968, (MA) Sch Counseling/Stu Dev 1979 Univ of IA; *cr:* Teacher Oak Park & River Forest HS 1968-70, Malaysia Peace Corps 1970-72; Teacher/Dir Dakota Wesleyan Univ 1980-82; Teacher/Cnslr Alief Ind Sch Dist 1982-; *ai:* Sci Club; Academic Decathlon; TSTA 1982-; NEA 1982; APGA 1980-82; Baylor Coll of Medicine Grant; Outstanding Suburban HS Sci Teacher; *office:* Alief Elsik HS P O Box 68 Alief TX 77411

DALLISON, BELVA ANN, Kindergarten Teacher; *b:* Beaumont, TX; *m:* N. K.; *c:* Tanya, Everett, Gralin, Anthony; *ed:* (BA) Elem Ed, 1976, (MA) Elem Ed, 1988 Lamar; *cr:* 5th Grade/Kndgtn Teacher Fletcher; *ai:* TSTA, BTA; *office:* Fletcher BISD 1050 Ave E Beaumont TX 77701

DALLMANN, CAROL SUNDRY, Kindergarten Teacher; *b:* Wanamingo, MN; *m:* Dwayne D.; *ed:* (BS) Kndgtn-6th Grade, Mankato St Univ 1956; Univ of WY; Mankato St Univ; St Cloud Univ; *cr:* Kndgtn Teacher Willmar Public Schs 1956-58; 1st Grade Teacher Wapato WA 1958-60, Trois Fontain France 1960-61:Kndgtn Teacher Richfield MN 1961-63; Hutchinson MN 1963-64; St Louis Park MN 1964-; *ai:* Staff Dev 3 Years; Class Act Awd SD Innovative Caring Accepting Master Teacher Nov 1988; Certificate Appreciation Recognition Contribution Your Time/Expertise Staff Dev May 1982; *office:* Aquila Primary Sch 8500 W 31st St Saint Louis Park MN 55426

DALMOLIN, JO ANN DELL, Spanish Teacher; *b:* Greensburg, PA; *m:* Horace; *c:* Justin, Kristen, Jonathan; *ed:* (BA) Scndry Ed/Span, 1970, (MAT) Scndry Ed/Span, 1972 Univ of Pittsburgh; Instituto de Cultura Hispanica, Duquesne Univ; *cr:* Span Teacher Comm Coll of Allegheny Cty 1985-86, W Allegheny HS 1970-; *ai:* Span Club Adv; NHS Faculty Advisory Comm; Allegheny Foreign Lang Assn, PA St Ed Assn, NEA, PA St Modern Lang Assn; Gift of Time Honoree Awd 1990; *office:* W Allegheny HS Box 409 W Allegheny Rd Imperial PA 15126

DALMUT, FRANK, JR., Social Studies Teacher; *b:* Fort Smith, AR; *m:* Eleanor Flores; *c:* Dena K., Frank M.; *ed:* (BSE) Phys Ed/Soc Stud, 1972, (MED) Phys Ed, 1975, Admin Certificate HS Admin, 1989 Univ of AR; *cr:* Soc Stud Teacher/Coach Judson HS 1972-74, Greenland HS 1975-76, Lincoln HS 1976-81; Soc Stud Teacher/Asst Prin/Transportation Supvr Prairie Grove HS 1981-; *ai:* Scott Hi-Q Academic Faculty Adv; Knowledge-Master, AR Quiz Bowl, Citizen Bee Spon; Presidential Scholars & Distinguished Teacher, NEA Distinguished Teacher 1988; *home:* Rt 2 Box 282-B Prairie Grove AR 72753

DALPIAZ, NANCY K. (RINEHART), Business Ed Teacher; *b:* La Harpe, IL; *m:* Gary; *c:* Brian, Kevin; *ed:* (BS) Bus Ed, W IL Univ 1965; *cr:* Teacher Beardstown HS 1965-; *ai:* Bus Club & Jr Class Spon; IBEA, NBEA, IVA; Beardstown Ed Assn Secy 1985-87; *office:* Beardstown HS 200 E 15th St Beardstown IL 62618

DAL PORTO, DAVID N., Teacher; *b:* San Francisco, CA; *m:* Sonja; *c:* Steven, Janine, Scott; *ed:* (BA) Soc Sci, San Francisco St Univ 1958; *cr:* Teacher Overfelt HS 1963-65; Dept Head 1970-89, Teacher 1965-, Mentor Teacher 1990 Mt Pleasant HS; *ai:* Mock Trial Team Coach; In Service Comm; CA Teachers Assn 1963-; CA Cncl Soc Stud 1980-; Author Several Historical Simulations; Publisher His Simulations; *office:* Mt Pleasant HS 1750 S White Rd San Jose CA 95127

DALRYMPLE, DOROTHY MORAN, Retired Second Grade Teacher; *b:* Warren, OH; *m:* Carl J.; *ed:* (BS) Ed, Kent St Univ 1953; Grad Classes Rdng, Lang Art, Math, Sci & Audio Visual Aids; *cr:* 2nd Grade Teacher Horace Mann Elem Sch 1953-83; *ai:* NEA, OEA, WEA 1953-83; ORTA, TRTA 1983-; Emblem Club 397 Trustee 1975-; Designed & Organized Phonics Prgm; Supervised Trng of Stu Teachers; *home:* 350 Marwood Dr SE Warren OH 44484

DALTON, CARY J., Director of Bands; *b:* Houston, TX; *ed:* (BS) Music, Lamar Univ 1988; *cr:* Dir of Bands Kountze HS 1986-88, Hull-Daisetta HS 1988-89, Groveton HS 1989-; *ai:* Marching, Concert & Jazz Bands; TX Music Educators Assn St Coll Stu Division Chm; Natl Assn Military Marching Bands; Natl Assn Women Band Dir ; TX Bandmasters Assn; Tau Beta Sigma Delta Omicron Secy 1985 Active of Yr; *office:* Groveton H S Box 728 Hwy 94 Groveton TX 75845

DALTON, LOIS EGGERT, 5th Grade Teacher; *b:* Nebraska City, NE; *m:* Don J.; *c:* James F.; *ed:* (BA) Elem Ed, Wayne St 1979; Grad Stud; *cr:* 5th Grade Teacher Bellevue Public Schls 1979-; *ai:* Leave Policy Comm; Double-Dutch Jumprope for Boys; NEA, NE St Ed Assn, Bellevue Ed Assn 1979-; PTA 1979-; *office:* Ft Crook Elem Sch 12500 S 25th St Omaha NE 68123

DALTON, PATRICIA LYNCH, Jr HS Eng/Amer His Teacher; *b:* Chicago, IL; *m:* Gerald J.; *c:* John G., Kevin M., Cynthia Dalton Young; *ed:* (BAED) Ed, Chicago St Univ 1963; Eng, Governors St Univ; *cr:* 6th Grade Teacher Lathrop Sch 1963-64; 8th Grade Teacher 1970-77, 7th-8th Grade Teacher 1977-80 St Denis Sch; Jr HS Teacher St Michael Sch 1980-; *ai:* Safety Patrol & Newspaper Moderator; 7th Grade Chm; Yrbk Moderator & Co-Moderator; 8th Grade Play Dir; Eng & Soc Stud Comm Chm; NCTE 1980-; NCSS 1978-; NCEA; St Ignatius HS Outstanding Teacher Awd 1984; Sci Fair Judge Certificates 1975-; *office:* St Michael Sch 14355 S Highland Orland Park IL 60462

DALTON, PAULA SCHOONOVER, 8th Grade Science Teacher; *b:* Phoenix, AZ; *m:* Charles; *c:* Brady, Genevieve; *ed:* (BA) Elem Ed, 1973, (MA) Sci Ed, 1986 AZ St Univ; *cr:* 6th Grade Teacher Black Mountain 1980-88; 8th Grade Teacher Desert Arroyo 1988-; *ai:* Ecology Club & Stu Cncl Spon; Prof Growth Comm; AZ Ed Assn 1983-; NSTA 1985-; AZ Assn for Learning About Environment; Mid Sch Teacher of Yr; *office:* Desert Arroyo Mid Sch PO Box 426 Cave Creek AZ 85331

DALTOSO, MICHAEL JOSEPH, Jr HS Teacher; *b:* Walla Walla, WA; *M:* Karen; *c:* Nicole, Nick; *ed:* (BA) Health & Phys Ed, Cntrl WA Univ 1981; *cr:* 6th Grade Teacher Heathwood Elem 1981-82; 9th Grade Health Teacher Covington Jr HS 1982-83; 9th Grade Math Teacher WY East Jr HS 1983-84; 9th Grade Gealth & His Teacher Pacific Jr HS 1984-; *ai:* Girls Bsktbl; Boys Ftbl; Track; Bsktbl; *office:* Pacific Jr H S 2017 Ne 172nd Ave Vancouver WA 98684

DALY, SALLY LOUISE, 7th Grade His/Lit Teacher; *b:* San Diego, CA; *c:* John H. IV, Jennifer L.; *ed:* (BSED) Eng/His, SW TX St Univ 1967; Grad Hrs Rdng & Exceptional Children, Chapman Coll; *cr:* Asst Teacher SW TX St Univ 1967-68; 7th-12th Grade Speech/Kndgtn Teacher Prunedale Chrstn Acad 1979-81; His/Lit Teacher St Anns Acad 1981-; *ai:* Safety Patrol Spon; Tutor; 7th Grade Homeroom; NCEA 1981-; Natl Assn for Female Execs 1989-; Archdiocese of WA 1981-; St James Episcopal Church Chrstn Ed Supt 1980-81; *office:* St Ann's Acad 4404 Wisconsin Ave NW Washington DC 20016

DAMA, JO ANN ADAMS, Second Grade Teacher; *b:* Youngstown, OH; *m:* Donald; *ed:* (BSED) Elem Ed, 1964, (MSED) Curr, 1977 Youngstown St; *cr:* K/1st Grade Teacher Sexton Street Sch 1964-68; 1st Grade Teacher Highland Avenue Sch 1968-71; 2nd/4th Grade Teacher Center Street Sch 1971-78; 2nd/3rd/5th/6th Grade Teacher Lyon Plat Sch 1978-; *ai:* Struthers Ed Assn Building Rep; OH Ed Assn, NEA; Fraternal Order of Eagles Treas 1987-; *office:* Lyon Plat Sch 520 9th St Struthers OH 44471

DAMBOWY, ROSELLA, Third Grade Teacher; *b:* Little Falls, MN; *ed:* (AA) General Ed, Univ of MN 1956; (BS) Elem Ed, 1968, (MS) Elem Ed, 1976 St Cloud St Univ; Working Beyond Master of Sci, Grantley Hall Yorkshire England; Lang & Culture, Jagellonian Univ Krakow Poland; *cr:* 2nd Grade Teacher Dos Caminos 1968-71; Preschool/6th Grade Substitute Teacher San Diego CA 1980-81; Fulbright Exch Teacher Poppleton Road Primary Sch 1984-85; 3rd Grade Teacher Riverside Sch 1971-80, 1981-84, 1985-; *ai:* Started Riverside Review Sch Newspaper & 1st Annual Ethnic Festival; Brainerd Ed Assn, MN Ed Assn, NEA; Intnl Trng Comm Club (Pres 1987-88, Cncl I Secy 1989-); Fulbright Exch Teacher to York England 1984-85; Assn of Overseas Educators; Volunteers in Partnership; Written & Adapted Stores Into Plays PTA Prgms; *office:* Riverside Elem Sch 220 NW 3rd St Brainerd MN 56401

D'AMBRA, JOSEPH SALVATORE, Fifth Grade Teacher; *b:* Worcester, MA; *m:* Deborah Eckland; *c:* Shannon, Kelly; *ed:* (BS) Elem Ed, Worcester St Coll 1980; (MA) Elem Ed, GA St Univ 1986; Certificate Educl Admin & Supervision; *cr:* 4th Grade Teacher 1980-87, 5th Grade Teacher 1987- Snapfinger Elem Sch; *ai:* Discipline Comm Chairperson; Vlybl Team & 8th Grade Bsktbl Coach; GA PTA Lifetime Membership; *office:* Snapfinger Elem Sch Snapfinger Rd Decatur GA 30032

DAMBROSIO, ELLEN CHRISTENSEN, Computer Teacher; *b:* San Francisco, CA; *m:* Michael; *c:* Laura, Kevin; *ed:* (BA) Liberal Stud, San Francisco St Univ 1979; Wkshps & Classes on Effective Teaching Methods & Use of Cmptrs in Ed; *cr:* Cmptr Consultant Stanislaus Cty Dept of Ed 1983-87; Mentor Teacher Empire Unified Sch Dist 1986-88; Teacher Empire Union Sch Dist 1981-; Lecturer 1988-, Cmptr Teacher 1990 CA St Univ Stanislaus; *ai:* Dist Educl Technology Comm; Cmptr Using Educators 1985-; *office:* Teel Mid Sch PO Box U Empire CA 95319

DAME, STEVEN, 6th Grade Teacher; *b:* Spanish Fork, UT; *m:* Sherrie Tucker; *c:* Shannon, Nathan, Tamara; *ed:* (BS) Elem Ed, Univ UT 1978; (AS) Data Processing, 1985, (BS) Cmptr Sci, 1988 Weber St Coll; *cr:* 5th-6th Grade Teacher J A Taylor Elem 1982-; *ai:* Marketing Educl Software; Created Software Cmptrs/Gradebook; Mgr Grading Prgm for Teachers; Paret-teacher Conference Scheduler; Schedule Classes in Scndry Schls; *home:* 1351 27th St Ogden UT 84403

DAMIAN, CAROL G., Physics Teacher; *b:* Salem, OH; *m:* Aurel; *c:* Carol J., Cameron, Cathy Damian Granitto, Vicki Damian Pesa, Steven; *ed:* (BS) Chem/Physics Ed, 1976, (MA) Chem/Physics Ed, 1984 OH St Univ; Grad Stud OH St Univ, Univ of IA, Ashland Univ; *cr:* Physics/Chem/Bio Teacher Licking Heights HS 1976-80; Physics/Chem Teacher Dublin HS 1980-; *ai:* Physics Club Adv; Sci Fair Consultant & Judge; OH Tests of Scholastic Achievement & JETS/TEAMS Tests Academic Coach; Sci Ed Cncl of OH Dist Dir 1988-; Delta Kappa Gamma Secy

1985-88; Amer Assn of Univ Women Dublin Branch VP 1989-; Dublin Plus Parent, Teacher, Stu Organization Mem Bd of Dir 1988-; Jennings Scholar 1985; Dublin HS Annual Hall of Fame Awd 1986; Sherex Chemical Company Teacher/Scholar Awd 1989; *office:* Dublin HS 6780 Coffman Rd Dublin OH 43017

DAMIAN, PATRICIA RE, English Teacher/Eng Dept Chair; *b:* Somerville, MA; *m:* Antonio J.; *c:* Andrea, Mark, Christopher, Robert, Steven, Carla, Luke; *ed:* (BA) Psych, Regis Coll 1962; Master Teachers Prgm, Archdiocese of Boston; *cr:* 3rd Grade Teacher Cummings Sch 1962-64; Substitute Teacher Somerville & Medford Elem Sch 1970-79; Pre Sch Teacher Six Acres Nursery Sch 1979-82; 5th Grade Teacher 1982-84, Eng Teacher 1984- St Clement; *ai:* Lang Art Curr Dev; NCEA 1982-; St Josephs Mothers Club 1982-; *office:* St Clement Sch 589 Boston Ave Somerville MA 02144

DAMICO, ANTHONY PAUL, 8th Grade Language Art Teacher; *b:* Woodbury, NJ; *m:* Margot P. Faith; *c:* Teresa A., Anthony; *ed:* (BA) General Elem, 1969, (MA) Advanced Elem Ed, 1971 Glassboro St Coll; *cr:* 4th Grade Teacher Crescent Park 1969-70; Grad Asst Teacher 1970-71, 4th Grade Teacher 1971-72 Campus Sch; 3rd/5th/Cmptr Ed/8th Grade Teacher Gloucester Township Sch System 1972-; *ai:* Gloucester Township Ed Assn, Camden Cty Ed Assn, NJ Ed Assn, NEA; St Anthony Beneficial Society Secy 1990; *office:* Charles W Lewis Mid Sch Davistown Erial Rds Blackwood NJ 08012

D'AMICO, SANDRA MARIE, Business Education Teacher; *b:* San Diego, CA; *m:* Sam; *c:* Nicole; *ed:* (BA) Bus Ed, CA St Univ Los Angeles 1968; Grad Work, CA St Univ Los Angeles 1968-69; *cr:* Bus Ed Teacher Edison HS 1969-81; Bus Ed Teacher 1981-, Bus Ed Coord/Word Processing Teacher 1982- Huntington Beach HS; *ai:* Bus Ed Dept Coord; DEA, CTA, NEA 1969-; *office:* Huntington Beach HS 1905 Main St Huntington Beach CA 92648

DAMICO, WAYNE GILLESPIE, 8th Grade Science Teacher; *b:* Nashville, TN; *ed:* (AS) Ed, Columbia St Comm Coll 1968; (BS) Scndry/Elem Ed, Univ of TN 1980; Training in Travel Agency Work; *cr:* Teaching East Hickman; Asst to Personnel Dir-Part Time Cain Sloan of Nashville TN; *ai:* Boy Scout Leader 1970-73; Outstanding 4-H Volunteer Leader 1985; Shady Grove Exec 1988-; Comm Center Comm/Treas 1986-88; Shady Grove Church Christ Minster 1985-; *home:* Rt 1 Box 33 Primm Springs TN 38476

DAMOUR, BLITHE REED, English Teacher; *b:* Waverly, NY; *m:* William L.; *ed:* (BA) Eng, New England Coll 1970; Grad Courses Eng, Writing, His; *cr:* English Teacher Hopkinton HS 1970-79, Bishop Brady HS 1979-82, Londonderry HS 1982-84, Bishop Brady 1984-; Writing Instr New England Coll 1985-; *ai:* Folk Group, Curr Comm Brady; New England Coll Alumni Bd; Prom Dance Comm John Stark HS; NCEA 1979-82, 1984-; NEA, NHEA 1970-79, 1982, 1984; Hopkinton Womens Club Antique Show Comm 1990; Henniker Evening Fellowship Pres 1989-; Congregational Church (Choir, Dance Choir) 1970-; Parent & Teachers of Henniker 1988-; Henniker Sch Bd (Chairperson 1981-82) 1979-82; Ed/Writer Manchester Magazine 1986-, NH Times Newspaper 1984-86; Copy Ed/Writer NH Profile 1980-84; *office:* Bishop Brady HS 25 Columbus Ave Concord NH 03301

DAMSCHRODER, LOUIS G., Agriculture Ed Instructor; *b:* Bowling Green, OH; *m:* Valerie Kay Moosmann; *c:* Stephanie K., Kyle A.; *ed:* (BS) Ag Ed, 1976, (MS) Ag Ed, 1978 OH St Univ; Annual Ag Tech Updates, Farm Bus Planning & Analysis Cert Course, OH St Univ 1980; *cr:* Ag Ed Instr Oak Harbor HS 1976-; *ai:* FFA Chapter Adv; OH Voc Assn Mem 1976-, Young Mem 1984; OVATA Dist Chm 1989-, Outstanding Prgm 1987, Young Teacher Awd 1982-83; NVATA; St Peter Luth Church Deacon 1979-; Ottawa Cty Livestock Comm Chm 1989-, Outstanding Prgm 1987; *office:* Oak Harbor HS 11661 W St Rt 163 Oak Harbor OH 43449

DANCE, NOBEL SYLVESTER, Chapter I Math Teacher; *b:* Trenton, TN; *c:* La Shay, Tiffany, Azusa, David, Akilah, Larissa, James; *ed:* (BS) Elem Ed, TN a & I St Univ 1972; Motorcycle Repair, North Amer Sch of Motorcycle Repair 1983; Cert TN Wild Life Resource Agency 1984; Cert TN Instructional Model, TN Public Schls 1985; Addl Studies, Elem Ed, Nazarene Coll; *cr:* Chpt I Math Teacher Chattanooga Public Sch System 1972-; Hunter Safety Instr TN Wildlife Resources Agency 1984-; *ai:* Rep Amer Red Cross 1981-89; Certificate of Appreciation-Chatta Brd of Ed-1989- Bus Basics/Jr Achievement 1989; Safety Awd Exxon Co USA-1987.

DANEKER, MARLENE M., Teacher of Gifted; *b:* Williamsport, PA; *m:* Jack O.; *c:* Deborah Daneker Leyshon, Diane Daneker Stanzione, David, Daniel; *ed:* (BA) Music, 1953, (BS) Eng/His, 1954 Lycoming Coll; (BS) Elem Ed Lock Haven Univ 1979; *cr:* 4th Grade Teacher Becht Sch 1954-55; 1st-6th Grade Music Teacher Jersey Shore Elem 1970-73; 1st-6th Grade Teacher of Gifted Locust St Elem 1980-; *ai:* Odyssey of Mind Coach 1990; Jr Service Group 1957-60; Federated Womens Club (Secy, Pres) 1960-77; Bicentennial Pagent Dir 1976; Dir of Church Choirs 1950-87; *office:* Locust St Elem Sch Locust St Jersey Shore PA 17740

DANFORTH, ROBERT MAX, HS Social Studies Teacher; *b:* East Jordan, MI; *m:* Deanna Derenzy; *c:* Robin, Cayne, Rhona, Palowski; *ed:* (BS) His, 1962, (MA) His, 1965 Cntrl MI Univ; *cr:* HS His Teacher Merritt Consolidated HS 1962-63, Ellsworth HS 1963-65, Vestaburg HS 1965-70, Gladstone Area Schls 1970-; *home:* 1024 Michigan Ave Gladstone MI 49837

DANFORTH, SANDRA DOBBS, English Teacher; *b:* Houston, MS; *m:* Frederic A.; *c:* Robyn Skelton, Jill Skelton; *ed:* (MED) Eng, MS St Univ 1966; Grad Stud Univ of MS; *cr:* Teacher Shannon HS 1966-; *ai:* Annual Adv; MS Prof Educators; *home:* 1200 Jeb Stuart Tupelo MS 38801

D'ANGELO, RICHARD LOUIS, Basic Skills Teacher; *b:* Orange, NJ; *ed:* (BA) Elem Ed, Kean Coll 1973; *cr:* 6th Grade Teacher 1971-80, 8th Grade Teacher 1980-86, Basic Skills Teacher 1986 Mc Kinley Sch; *ai:* Newark Teachers Union Building Rep 1971-; Safaru Club Intnl Tri-St Ed Dir 1988-.

DANHAUER, MARY T., Mathematics/Science Teacher; *b:* Owensboro, KY; *ed:* (BS) Chem, Brescia Coll 1976; (MA) Ag, Murray St Univ 1984; CPR Instr; EMT Certificate; Working on BSN Degree; *cr:* Sci Teacher Mt St Joseph Acad 1976-77, Lourdes Cntrl HS 1977-79, Mt St Joseph Acad 1979-83; Math/Sci Teacher Owensboro Cath HS 1987-; *ai:* Soph Class Spon.

DANIEL, CAROL BARRASS, Math Teacher; *b:* Long Beach, CA; *m:* John Lee; *c:* Sheree D., Marian E. Keown; *ed:* (BA) Elem Ed, KY Wesleyan Coll 1969; (MA) Elem Ed, 1975, Elem Ed, 1980 Western KY Univ; Mid Sch Math Endorsement KWC; *cr:* Teacher Hartford Jr HS 1968-71; OH Co Mid Sch 1971-; *ai:* Math Coach of KY Governors Cup Competition; Academic Sch Coord; Academic Boosters Comm to Honor Stu; OH Cncl Ed Assn Secy/Pres Elec/Pres 1969-70/1971-73; KY Cncl Teachers of Math 1988-, Nom Outstanding Math Teacher Top Ten 1988-89; Alpha Delta Kappa Historian 1987-; The Courthouse Players Co-Chairperson 1982-87; Fort Hartford Womens Club 1987-; Hartford Baptist Church Sunday Sch Teacher; Nom Outstanding Teacher OCEA Spon 1969; Nom Outstanding Teacher OCMS Stud 1973; Dist/St/Natl Rep to Delegate Assemblies; Coord of City/Cty Sponsored Bicentiennial Ball 1988; *home:* Rt 2 Box 297 Hartford KY 42347

DANIEL, CAROLYN MC CLURE, 8th Grade Lang Art Teacher; *b:* Kingston, TN; *m:* Thomas Wayne; *c:* Tracy D. Sloan, Margaret D., Tom; *ed:* (BS) Scndry Ed, TN Tech 1963; (MED) Admin/Supervision, Mid TN St Univ 1981; *cr:* Teacher West Jr HS 1963-65, Coffee Cty Jr HS 1974-; *ai:* Stu Cncl Spon; Power of Positive Stus Comm; TN Ed Assn, NEA 1974-; TN Mid Sch 1989-; 1st Chrstn Church 1964-; *home:* 214 Sharondale Dr Tullahoma TN 37388

DANIEL, DELBERT L., Elementary Principal; *b:* Winfield, KS; *m:* Cecile Fern Wallace; *c:* Ted Keehn, Jay Keehn, Cecile Patton, Mike, Ralph; *ed:* (BA) Elem Ed/Music, Emporia St Univ 1963; (MSED) Elem Ed, NW OK St Univ 1987; *cr:* Dist Dir of Soc Services Cowley Cty 1967-80; Elem Prin/Teacher Marland Public Schls 1981-86; Elem Prin Prue Public Schls 1986-89, Garber Public Schls 1989-; *ai:* Dir Elem Prgms & Field Trips; OEA, NEA; *home:* 2600 N 5th #103 Ponca City OK 74601

DANIEL, JACKIE LOUISE, Third Grade Teacher; *b:* Greenwood, SC; *ed:* (BA) Ed/Religion, Columbia Coll 1963; (MED) Ed, (SPED) Educl Admin 1978 Univ of GA; *cr:* Teacher Goose Creek Elem, Powder Springs Elem; Dean of Women Univ of GA; 2nd/3rd Grade Teacher Pinecrest 1971-; *ai:* Greenwood Ed Assn Pres 1984; NEA Delegate; Phi Beta Kappa Mem; Greenwood Womens Club; GA Teacher of Yr 1966; *home:* 958 Sunset Dr Greenwood SC 29646

DANIEL, KELLY JANE (KUESTER), 4th Grade Teacher; *b:* Rockledge, FL; *m:* John Richard; *ed:* (AA) General Ed, Brevard Comm Coll 1972; (BA) Elem Ed, FL St Univ Tallahassee 1974; (ME) Early Chldhd, GA St Univ Atlanta 1983; *cr:* Teacher Four Oaks Elem 1974-75, Steele Elem 1977-82, Atherton Elem 1982-; *ai:* Grade Level Chairperson; Fernbank Sci Center Rep; PTA; Quail Hollow Homeowners Assn Pres 1988-; *home:* 2851 Herron Cir Snellville GA 30278

DANIEL, LINDA MARTIN, Dean of Stu/Soc Stud Teacher; *b:* Cleveland, OH; *m:* Perry Daniel; *ed:* (BS) Ed/Soc Stud, 1983, (BA) Psych, 1983 Concord Coll; (MA) Counseling, Univ of WV Coll of Grad Stud 1985; *cr:* Adjunct Faculty S WV Comm Coll 1988-89; Soc Stud/Sci Teacher Marsh Fork Mid Sch 1984-; *ai:* Track & Cheerleading Coach; NHS & Stu Cncl Spon; *office:* Marsh Fork Mid Sch Naoma WV 25140

DANIEL, PAT LIFSEY, Spanish Teacher; *b:* Barnesville, GA; *m:* Jay Hugh; *c:* Keith, Matthew, Allison; *ed:* (BA) Span, Guilford Coll 1957; *cr:* Music Dir Shallowford Road Kndgtn 1975-79; Span Teacher Forrest Hills Chrstn Sch 1979-81, Mt Vernon Chrstn Sch 1982-86, Stockbridge Jr HS 1986-; *ai:* Spon for Chrstn Union; Part Time Pianist for Church; *office:* Stockbridge Jr H S Old Conyers Rd Stockbridge GA 30281

DANIEL, PHYLLIS EDWARDS, Asst Principal/English Teacher; *b:* Hollywood, FL; *m:* Edward Lorenzo; *ed:* (BA) Eng Ed, Spelman Coll 1979; (MED) Speech Pathology/Ed, 1985, L-5 Cert Admin, 1989 GA St Univ; *cr:* Eng Teacher Henderson HS 1979-80, Deerfield Beach HS 1980-81, Stone Mountain HS 1981-; Asst Prin Stone Mountain HS 1989-; *ai:* Educl Partnership Coord; Stu Mentor; Homework Helpline Volunteer; Supervise All Stu Act; Chairperson Attendance Comm; Dekalb Schls Curr, Prof Leave & Travel Comm; NEA, NCTE, GA Cncl Teachers Of Eng, NASSP; Alpha Kappa Alpha 1990; Sr Sunday Sch 1985-; Saint Peter & Paul (Bd of Ed 1990, Womens Organizations Mem 1985-); Adv of Yr Jr Civitan Clubs; Rep GSA To Ghana Africa; Teacher of Yr Stone Mountain II Jr HS.

DANIEL, ROBERTA STINSON, Mathematics Lab Teacher; *b:* Gay, GA; *ed:* (BS) Elem Ed, Albany St Coll 1966; (MED) Mentally Retarded Ed, W GA Coll 1973; *cr:* Kndgtn/Pre-Sch/2nd Grade/EMR Meriwether Cty 1966-74; 5th Grade/Math Lab Teacher De Kalb Cty 1974-; *ai:* Chairperson Black His Act; Cmmty Bible Chapel Ed Comm 1983-84; Assoc Professor Berean Bible Coll; Teacher of Yr Gresham Park Elem 1983; *office:* Gresham Park Elem Sch 1848 Vicki Ln Atlanta GA 30316

DANIEL-TYSON, CAMILLE, Soc Stud/Govrnmnt/Econ Teacher; *b:* Sandersville, GA; *m:* Dylan Alan; *ed:* (BS) His, 1987, (MS) Soc Sci, 1970 GA Coll; *cr:* Government/Ec Teacher Washington Cty HS 1987-; *ai:* Mock Trial, Stock Market Game, Free Enterprise Day, Arrive Alive Spon; Soc Stud Project Coord; *home:* Rt 1 Box 550 Harrison GA 31035

DANIELE, NEIL ANTHONY, 5th Grade Teacher; *b:* Long Branch, NJ; *m:* Phyllis M.; *c:* Darrell, Deanna; *ed:* (BA) Eng/ Journalism, San Jose St 1956; (MA) Ed, Univ of San Francisco 1972; Teaching Credential; *cr:* Teacher Soquel Elem Sch Dist 1968-; *home:* 529 Pine St Aptos CA 95003

DANIELLI, LOLA LYNNE, Spanish Teacher; *b:* Santa Rosa, CA; *ed:* (BA) Span, 1960, (MA) Span, 1963 Univ of CA Berkeley; Working toward PHD in Span, Cal Berkeley; *cr:* Span/Latin Teacher Campolindo HS 1963-; *ai:* Span Club Adv; Foreign Lang Dept Chm; Phi Beta Kappa 1960-; Pi Lambda Theta 1961-; Teacher of Yr 1988; *office:* Campolindo HS 300 Moraga Rd Moraga CA 94556

DANIELS, AUBREY LAVON, Assistant Principal; *b:* Jacksonville, FL; *m:* Loraine P.; *c:* Debrina, Taron, Toni, Corey; *cr:* Teacher Ft Myers HS 1974-75, Riverdale HS 1975-79, Dunbar Mid Sch 1979-89; Asst Prin Michigan Elem 1989-; *ai:* Dunbar Mid Intramural Dir; Dunbar Mid Vlybl & Bsktbl Coach; Lee Cty Mentor Prgm Coord 1987-89; Lee Cty Sch Bd 1986-87, Nom Teacher of Yr; Kappa Alpha Psi 1987, Educator of Yr 1987; Omega Psi Phi VP 1989-; Whos Who Among Amer Educators 1990; *office:* Michigan Elem Sch 4812 Michigan Ave Fort Myers FL 33905

DANIELS, BONNIE JEAN, Composition Teacher; *b:* Carleton, MI; *m:* Troy; *c:* Lonnie, Terri, Amy; *ed:* (BS) Soc Stud, E MI Univ 1974; *cr:* Teacher Cadillac Elem Sch 1974-75; Lang Art Teacher Woodhaven Mid Sch 1975-76, Patrick Henry Mid Sch 1976-; *ai:* Natl Jr Honor Society & Newspaper Adv; *office:* Patrick Henry Mid Sch 24825 Hall Rd Woodhaven MI 48183

DANIELS, CATHERINE LOPRETE, Science Teacher; *b:* New York, NY; *m:* John G.; *c:* Cristian G.; *ed:* (BS) Geology, Brooklyn Coll 1960; (MA) Geography, Columbia Univ 1964; Grad Stud; *cr:* Lecturer Brooklyn Coll 1961-64, St Johns Univ & Queens Coll 1964-69; Vol Teacher Environmental Center 1978-81; Teacher Jr HS 1981-; Teacher Trainer New York City Teachers Consortium 1988-; *ai:* Adv Small Animal Care Club; Leader Inventing Prgm; Mid Sch Formation Comm Mem; Mid Sch Curr Comm Secy; Assn Supervision & Curr Dev 1988-; Cath Teachers Assn 1982-; Various Sci Groups; Floral Park Civic Cncl (Secy, Ed Dir) 1976-; Queens Cty Farm Museum 1981-; Society of Women Geographers Fellowship Columbia Univ; *office:* J H S 172 81-14 257th St Floral Park NY 11004

DANIELS, CHARLES WESLEY, Eighth Grade English Teacher; *b:* Longview, TX; *m:* Nancy Sue Morrow; *c:* Dana, Donna Daniels Roberts; *ed:* (BS) Eng/Phys Ed, 1964, (MED) Guidance/ Counseling, Stephen F Austin; Eng, Univ of Houston Clear Lake & Stephen F Austin; *cr:* Coach Danforth 1964-66, Roosevelt Wilson 1966-76; Eng Teacher Blocker Mid Sch 1976-; *ai:* NEA, Alpha Chi, Kappa Delta Pi, Phi Betta Kappa 1964-; First Baptist Church Teacher 1976-80; *office:* Blocker Mid Sch 500 14th Ave N Texas City TX 77590

DANIELS, DEBORAH KEEN, Biology/Physics Teacher; *b:* Wayne Cty, NC; *m:* Linnie Gerald; *c:* Leslie G., Jason B.; *ed:* (BS) Sci/Bio, 1972, (MA) Sci/Bio, 1987 Ec Univ; Physics, Ecology, Organismic Bio, Biochemical Bio; *cr:* Sci Teacher S Wayne Sr HS 1973-; *ai:* Sci Club Adv; Sci Fair Chairperson; Sci Dept Co-Chairperson; Awds & Honors Comm; NEA, NCEA 1976-; Governor & Businessmens Awd 1984; NC Sci Teachers Assn 1973-; NC Model Prgm Awd 1985, 1987; Model Prgm Trifolds for St 1985-86; Math/Physics Activity Book Co-Author 1986; *office:* S Wayne Sr HS Rt 4 Box 55 Dudley NC 28333

DANIELS, EDITH COUNCIL, Kindergarten/1st Grade Teacher; *b:* Oak City, NC; *c:* Ben, Bill; *ed:* (BS) Early Chldhd, 1976, (MAED) Ed, 1987 E Carolina Univ; *cr:* Rdng Lab Teacher W Martin Sch 1976-81; 2nd Grade Teacher 1981-84, 1st Grade Teacher 1984-89, K-1st Grade Combonation Teacher 1989- N Everetts Sch; *ai:* 5 Yr Interim Review; NCAE Mem 1976-; Southern Assn Chm; *office:* N Everetts Sch PO Box 278 Everetts NC 27825

DANIELS, HELEN HICKS, Language Arts Teacher; *b:* Hemphill, TX; *m:* William R.; *ed:* (BS) Elem Ed, Wiley Coll 1977; (MS) Guidance & Counseling, Prarie View; *cr:* Teacher Midway Jr HS 1977-78, Jackson Intermediate Sch 1978-79, Taylor Ray Intermediate Sch 1979-80, George Jr HS 1980-85, Meyer Intermediate Sch 1985-; *ai:* LCTA Teacher of Yr 1989-; Ft Bend Cty Realtor 1989-; Delta Sigma Theta VP 1976-77; *office:* Meyer Intermediate Sch 930 Meyer Rd Richmond TX 77469

DANIELS, JOHN W., Assistant Principal; *b:* Baconton, GA; *m:* Minnie B. Forte; *ed:* (BA) Criminology, St Leo Univ 1981; (BS) Sociology, Univ of MD 1982; (MA) Ed Admin, Fayetteville St Univ 1987; Ed Specialist Campbell Univ; Pursuing Doctoral in Ed Admin, Campbell Univ; *cr:* Teacher DOD Schls 1977-85, E E Smith Sr HS 1986-88; Asst Prin Anne Chestnutt Jr HS 1989-; *ai:* Sr HS ROTC Instr; NCAE 1986-89; NASSP, APAP 1989-; Mason J Warden 1973-; Shriner C Rabban 1973-; *home:* 107 St Marys Pkwy Fayetteville NC 28303

DANIELS, LEE ANN, Biology/Phys Sci Teacher; *b:* Russellville, AR; *ed:* (BS) Phys Ed, 1973, (MS) Phys Ed, 1979 AR Tech Univ; *cr:* Teacher/Coach Fordyce HS 1973-85; Teacher Russellville HS 1985-; *ai:* Sr Class Spon; Building Adv Comm; REA Building Rep; Sch Crisis Team; All Star Spon; Russellville Ed Assn, AR Ed Assn, NEA; *office:* Russellville HS Hwy 7 T Russellville AR 72801

DANIELS, NANCY DIANNE, Spanish Teacher; *b:* Vienna, GA; *ed:* (BS) Scndry Ed/Span, Valdosta St Coll 1984; (MS) Eng 2nd Lang, Nova Univ 1989; Post Grad Stud Colegio Mara Spain; *cr:* Span Teacher Charlton Cty HS 1984-85, Leesburg HS 1985-; *ai:* Span Club Adv; Ecology Fair Comm; FL Foreign Lang Assn, Amer Assn of Teachers in Span & Portuguese 1985-; Natl Wildlife Fed 1986-; Center Marine Conservation 1987-; *home:* 1112 W Main St J-6 Leesburg FL 34748

DANIELS, NORMA JEAN (LISTEN), Third Grade Teacher; *b:* Edmond, OK; *m:* James; *c:* Vernon, Doris Garrido; *ed:* (BS) Elem Ed, Cntrl St Univ 1954; Grad Work; Numerous Wkshps & Inservices; *cr:* 6th Grade Teacher Lone Jack Elem Sch 1967-69; 5th/6th Grade Teacher 1972-89, 3rd Grade Teacher 1989- Mulhall-Orlando Elem Sch; *ai:* Staff Dev Chairperson; NEA, OEA 1972-; Mulhall-Orlando Ed Assn (Secy, Treas); Orlando Chrstn Church 1973-.

DANIELS, SHIRLEY ANDREWS, HS Social Studies Teacher; *b:* Tignall, GA; *m:* Robert C.; *c:* Charlander; *ed:* (BA) US His, Paine Coll 1976; (MA) Soc Sci Ed, Univ of GA 1984; *cr:* Teacher Washington Wilkes Comprehensive HS 1976-78, Oglethorpe Cty Mid Sch 1978-85, Cedar Shoals Comprehensive HS 1985-; *ai:* Lib/Media Advisory Comm 1989-; Natl Assn of Educators 1976-; Teacher of Yr Oglethorpe Cty Sch System 1983; Teacher of Yr Cedar Shoals HS 1987; *office:* Cedar Shoals HS 1300 Cedar Shoals Dr Athens GA 30607

DANIELSON, BARBARA, 9th Grade English Teacher; *b:* Kane, PA; *c:* Terri Dodge, Lori, Debbie Chapman, Daniel; *ed:* (BS) Ed/Eng, Clarion St 1973; (MED) Ed/Rdng, Univ of Pittsburgh 1979; *cr:* Personnel Secy Bovaird & Seyfoung Manufacturing 1968-71; Eng Teacher Bradford Area Schls 1974-; *ai:* Drama Club Adv; Passion Play Chorus Mem; Dir Sch Productions; Dist Mentor Teacher; NCTE; Act 178 Comm Mem; Bradford Area Ed Assn Building Rep; Emanuel Luth Church Dir of Music; Cmmty Chrstn Choir (Organist, Choir Dir, Mem); Keynote Chorus (Mem, Accompanist); *home:* 32 Rosedale Ave Bradford PA 16701

DANNER, ALICE MAE, Attendance Clerk/Secretary; *b:* Sargent, TX; *m:* Thomas Lynn; *c:* Mary A., Timothy L., Lynda; *cr:* Teacher Little Rock Ind Sch Dist 1952-56; Attendance Clerk Mexia Jr HS 1980-; *office:* Mexia Jr HS PO Box 2000 Mexia TX 76667

DANNER, LARRY CLINTON, 8th Grade Instrumental Teacher; *b:* Ducktown, TN; *m:* Terrisa Anne Diggs; *c:* Michael, Christen, Shannon; *ed:* (BS) Music Ed, Univ of TN 1970; Univ of TN; *cr:* Instrumental Teacher Knox Cty Schls 1970-; *ai:* Farragu Mid Fund Raising Coord; Natl Band Assn 1981-; Music Educators Natl Conference 1970-; E TN Band & Orch Assn 1970-; Karns Cmmty Club (VP 1981-82, Pres 1983); Farragut Mid PTA Citizenship Chm 1985-; Concord United Meth Church Brass Choir; TN PTA Life Mem; *office:* Farragut Mid Sch 200 W End Ave Knoxville TN 37922

DANTZLER, SHARON ANN, Fifth Grade Math Teacher; *b:* Leland, MS; *ed:* (BSE) Elem Ed, 1971, (MED) Elem Ed, 1977 Delta St Univ; Cmptr Sci; *cr:* 5th Grade Teacher Leland Consolidated Schls 1971-; *ai:* 5th Grade Math/Soc Stud Chm; Editor Cmptr Generated Sch Newsletter; D esigner/Compiler of Cmptr Generated Awd Day Material; NCTM 1988-; MS Cncl Teachers of Math 1988-; Whos Who Amer Ed 1989-; Michael E Sistrunk Good Apple Awd 1989; *office:* Leland Mid Sch 408 4th St Leland MS 38756

DANZE, NICHOLAS ANTHONY, Theology Teacher; *b:* Gioiosa Marea, Italy; *m:* Nancy M. Forgione; *c:* Nicholas J., Stefanie A.; *ed:* (BS) Poly Sci/His/Scndry Ed, St Josephs Univ 1976; (MS) Religious Stud/Scripture, St Charles Seminary 1990; *cr:* Substitute Teacher Bishop Neuman HS 1976; Teacher Archdiocese of Philadelphia 1977-85, Archdiocese of Camden 1985-; *ai:* Gloucester Cath HS Girls Soccer Head Var Coach; Gateway Regional HS Girls Bsktbl Asst Var Coach; Holy Family Coll Womens Sftbl Head Coach; NCEA; Woodbury Heights Boys Club (Pres, Bd of Dir) 1978-84; Woodbury Heights Borough Councilman 1984-86; *office:* Gloucester Cath HS 333 Ridgeway St Gloucester City NJ 08030

DANZIGER, AILEEN JOAN, English Teacher; *b:* Vineland, NJ; *ed:* (BA) Eng, Long Island Univ 1969; (MA) Sch Public Relations, 1975, Prin/Supervisory Cert, 1977 Glassboro St; *cr:* Teacher Vineland Sch System 1969-72; Dept Head/Personnel Cnslr Oxford Personnel Co 1972-73; Teacher Vineland Sch System 1973-; *ai:* Yrbk Adv; Eng Club Co-Chairperson; Yrbk Dedication 1981; *office:* Vineland HS 3010 E Chestnut Ave Vineland NJ 08360

D'ARCONTE, JEAN ANN, Business Dept Chairperson; *b:* Ringtown, PA; *m:* Gary R.; *c:* Jodi; *ed:* (BS) Bus, Susquehanna Univ 1963; Cmptr Courses; *cr:* Bus Teacher Salisbury HS 1963-; *ai:* FBLA; NEA, PA St Ed Assn, Lehigh Northampton Bus Teachers Assn, PA Bus Ed Assn; *office:* Salisbury HS 500 E Montgomery St Allentown PA 18103

DARDEN, JAMES MELTON, Principal/Math/Sci Teacher; *b:* Los Angeles, CA; *m:* Alice Gail; *c:* Daniel, Andrew; *ed:* (BA) Scndry Ed, Ouachita Baptist Univ 1977; (MED) Bible/Sci, Ezra Bible Inst 1989; Working Towards CAS Chrstn Ed, Calvary Baptist Seminary 1990; ACE Admin; Chrstn Law Assn Natl Legal Seminar; VIP Cmptr Trng; Regional Consultant Prgms; *cr:* Prin/Teacher 1st Church of God Acad 1978-83, Ezra Chrstn Sch 1983-; *ai:* Sr HS Bsktbl & Track Coach; St Convention Head Platform, St Stu Convention, Youth, Music Dir; ACE Consultant 1984-89, Model Status 1980-; Reformers Trophy; Outstanding Coach of Yr 1989; 4 Time St Convention Academic Awd; Model Status Certificate.

DARDEN, JUDY BASS, Teacher; *b:* Hickory, NC; *m:* David H.; *c:* Andrew, Kristen; *ed:* (MED) Elem Ed, Milligan Coll; (BS) Elem Ed, W Carolina Univ; Working Towards Masters; Cmptr Technology; Educl Testing Services 1988; *cr:* 1st Grade Teacher Miller-Perry Elem 1970-72, 1976-80, Rock Springs Elem 1980-84; *ai:* Sullivan Cty Cultural Art Chm 1985-86; Miller-Perry Elem Art Prgm Dir 1984-85; Gamma Delta 1969-71; GSA Day Camp Dir 1982; BSA Day Camp Skills Dir 1981; Tiger Cubs Dir 1982; Colonial Heights Chrstn Church Youth Choir Dir 1979-86; Levittown Chrstn Church 1987-89; *home:* 1024 Rotherwood Dr Kingsport TN 37660

DARDEN, MARTHA BATTS, Mainstream Public Sch Teacher; *b:* Wilson, NC; *m:* Marion Hughes; *c:* Susan Hughes; *ed:* (BA) Elem Ed/Hearing Impaired, Atlantic Chrstn Coll 1960; Grad Work, E Carolina Univ, Univ of NC Greensboro; *cr:* 7th/8th Grade Math Teacher Fremont Graded Sch 1960-62; 4th Grade Teacher Winstead Elem Sch 1962-67; 7th Grade Math Teacher Morningside Sch 1967-70; 1st-8th Grade Teacher E NC Sch for the Deaf 1970-; *ai:* Taught Swimming Classes & Produced Several Television Prgms at E NC Sch Dist; Curr Dev Comm; Alexander G Bell Assn 1960-70; NC St Employees Assn 1978-85; *office:* E NC Sch for the Deaf Hwy 301 N PO Box 2768 Wilson NC 27894

DARDEN, MARY PALMER, 5th Grade English Teacher; *b:* Woodville, MS; *m:* John Paige Sr.; *c:* John Paige Jr., Kent J.; *ed:* (BS) Eng, Alcorn St Univ 1959; (MS) Ed/Hum Stud, Marywood Coll 1979; *cr:* 9th Grade Eng Teacher Sadie V Thompson HS 1959-61, Furness Jr HS 1961-62; 5th/6th Grade Teacher Philadelphia Sch Dist 1962-; *ai:* Prince Hall Sch Writing Team Mem & Leader 1988-89, Rdng Comm Mem; Philadelphia Fed of Teachers 1965-; Urban League of Philadelphia 1989-; *office:* Prince Hall Sch Gratz & Godfrey Ave Philadelphia PA 19141

DARDEN, ROBERT FULTON, JR., Science Teacher; *b:* Beaumont, TX; *m:* Jo Ann Owens; *c:* Robert F. III, Steven L., Danni L. Darden Grayson; *ed:* (AA) His, Lamar Coll 1951; (BSE) His, Univ of Omaha 1962; Military Sci & Tactics, Air Command & Staff Coll 1966; (MED) Ed, American Univ 1974; Sch Law, Baylor Univ Grad Sch; *cr:* Pvt Colonel US Air Force 1951-81; Government/Poly Sci Teacher Wayland Baptist Univ 1975-85; Teacher Metro Learning Center 1981-85; Sci Teacher Carver 6th Grade Sch 1985-; *ai:* Block Leader; Daedalions; Phi Delta Kappa; US Air Force (Legion of Merit 1975, 1981, Bronze Star 1970, Meritorius Service Medal 1969); Soldiers Medal DC 1986; *home:* 4825 Scottwood Dr Waco TX 76708

DARDIN, BASIL MAXWELL, Fourth Grade Teacher; *b:* Elkton, KY; *m:* Larry; *c:* Susan Maxwell; *ed:* (BA) Elem Ed, 1964, (MS) Elem Ed, 1989 W KY Univ; *cr:* 8th Grade Teacher Caneyville KY 1964; 3rd Grade Teacher Kyrock Elem 1964-69; 4th Grade Teacher Brownsville Elem 1969-; *ai:* TESA Coord; Drug Awareness Chm; Career Ed Leader; Writing Project Mem 1989-; NEA, KY Ed Assn, Edmonson Cty Teacher Assn 1964-; Edmonson Cty Womans Club 1980-84; Friends of Lib 1980-85; Teacher of Yr 1984; *home:* 126 Main St Box 281 Brownsville KY 42210

DARDING, ALVERTA LOUISE (EVANS), First Grade Teacher; *b:* Mowrystown, OH; *m:* Roger Lee; *c:* Daniel L., Rebecca L.; *ed:* (BS) Elem Ed, OH St Univ 1965; (MA) Elem Ed, Univ of KY 1967; Rdng Specialist, Univ of IL; Elem Guidance, E IL Univ; *cr:* 1st Grade Teacher Fayette Cty Schls 1965-66; 1st/3rd/5th Grade Teacher Champaign Schls 1968-70; 1st Grade Teacher Carl Sandburg 1970-81; 1st-3rd Grade Teacher Mark Twain 1981-89; 1st Grade Teacher Lincoln Elem 1989-; *ai:* Cmptr Coord Lincoln Sch; Elem Curr Cncl Mem Charleston Unit Schls; Sch Family Liason, Guidance, Counseling for Critically & Terminally Ill Children; Rdng Cncl 1970-; Charleston Ed Assn, NEA, IEA Building Rep 1970-; Phi Delta Kappa 1985-; Sharing our Support Pres 1980-; Hospice Worker Trainer; *office:* Lincoln Sch 4 Madison Charleston IL 61920

DARGAN, MARY KAY MACKEN, Advanced Placement Eng Teacher; *b:* Cleveland, OH; *m:* Charles; *c:* Charley, Chris, Patrick, Daniel; *ed:* (BA) Eng, Notre Dame Coll; (MA) Eng, CA St Univ; Admin Credential Univ of CA Irvine; Theater in England Study of Shakespears Works Cambridge Univ England; Shakespears World Summer Seminar; OR St OR Shakespeanean Festival; *cr:* Teacher Tustin Unified Sch Dist 1968-72, Capistrano Unified Sch Dist 1972-; *ai:* Comm Mem on Capestran Valley Sch Discipline Policy; Comm Mem on Cmmty Relations Sch/Parents; Coaching-Advanced Placement Students Eng; Capistrano Unified Educl Sch Rep 1988-90; CA Teacher Assn; NEA; Teacher of Yr Capistrano Valley HS 1982; Grant Seminar OR St Coll for HS Eng Teachers 1988; *office:* Capistrano Valley H S 26301 Via Escolar Mission Viejo CA 92692

DARIS, PATRICIA JACKSON, English I/Drama Teacher; *b:* Hope Mills, NC; *m:* William Raeford; *c:* Dougetta Corney, Dori Cameron, Frederick Canady, Billy Jr., John-Fairley; *ed:* (BA) Grammar, Fayetteville Meth Coll 1965; (MS) Ed, Pembroke St Univ 1981; Cert Admin, Pembroke St Univ & E Carolina Univ 1983; Educl Specialist, E Carolina Univ; *cr:* 2nd Grade Teacher Montclair Elem 1965-68; 5th/6th Grade Teacher Legion Road Elem 1968-72; 7th Grade Teacher Sherwood Park Elem 1972-75; 7th-9th Grade Teacher South View Jr HS 1975-; *ai:* 7th/8th Grade Lang Art & Eng Departmental Chairperson; Drama Club Spon; Forensics Coach & Judge; Young Philosophers Club Spon; NC Assn of Educators, NC Eng Teachers Assn Mem; United Meth Church Adult Teacher; Democratic Women Mem; Natl Grand Prize Awd; Mem NC Writing Fellows; *office:* South View Jr HS Elk Rd Hope Mills NC 28348

DARLING, MARY JAREMA, 7th Grade Soc Stud Teacher; *b:* Takoma Park, MD; *m:* Paul S.; *c:* Nellie; *ed:* (BA) Psych/Elem Ed, Coll of William & Mary 1978; Instrumental Enrichment Problem Solving, Colby Coll, Univ of S ME; *cr:* 6th Grade Teacher Brentsville Dist Sch 1979-80; 7th Grade Teacher Bonny Eagle Jr HS 1982-; *ai:* Model United Nations, Hiking Club, Debate, Phys Fitness Club, Sci Club, Natl Jr Honor Society Spon; Soccer Coach; Gifted/Talented, Media Comm; Natl His Day; PDK VP 1977-78; ME Audubon Loon Count Area Coord 1982-; TN Toxics Company 1980-82; PDK 1977-79; *office:* Bonny Eagle Jr HS RR 1 Box 430 West Buxton ME 04093

DARMAN, LAURIE THAYER, Sixth Grade Teacher; *b:* Hartford, CT; *m:* Alan Paul; *c:* Shawn P., David T.; *ed:* (BS) Elem Ed, Southern CT Univ 1967; NEH Fellowship Miami Univ OH; *cr:* 6th Grade Teacher Colledge Sch 1967; 4th Grade Teacher La Grange Elem 1968-70; 6th Grade Teacher Boca Raton Acad 1978-; *ai:* Young Astronauts Spon; Elem Teachers of Classics VP 1989-; FL Rdng Assn 1988-; FCIS-Hooker Fnd Fellowship 1989; Founder, Ed Classics Club; Chairperson Natl Mythology Exam; Ed Fnd of Pompano Beach Cty Grants 1984, 1986; *office:* Boca Raton Acad 2700 St Andrews Blvd Boca Raton FL 33434

DARNALL, GLORIA MEYER, 6-12th Vocal Music Teacher; *b:* Reedsburg, WI; *m:* Bruce A.; *c:* Sarah, Mark; *ed:* (BME) K-12 Vocal Music, UW Eau Claire 1973; Addl Studies Music/Drama UW Eau Claire; Vandercook Coll of Music; UW Whitewater; Eastern IL Univ; UW Marinette; *cr:* Church Organist WI Dells/Lake Mills Marinette 1965-; 6th/8th Vocal Music Teacher Marinette Mid Sch 1973-79; 6th-12th Vocal Music Teacher Lake Mills Public Schls 1979-; *ai:* HS Show Choir Dir; Musical Dir; Drama Club Adv; Mid Sch Handbell Choir Dir; WCDA 1974-; ACDA 1974-; Amer Choral Dir Assn; MEA 1973-79; WEA 1973-; NEA 1973-; CPA Bd Dir 1984-86; IMEA 1979-; *office:* Lake Mills Mid Sch 615 Catlin Dr Lake Mills WI 53551

DARNELL, BARBARA KENNEDY, 3rd-12th Grade Reading Teacher; *b:* Denver, CO; *m:* James N. Jr.; *c:* Leanna J., Stacey L., James F.; *ed:* Music Ed, UNC of CO 1962-64; Water Safety Instr UNC of CO 1964-80; *cr:* Water Safety Instr Meeker & Grand Junction Pools 1965-83; Music Dir Monument Chrstn Acad 1980-; Eng/Audit Teacher 1987-, Asst Music Dir 1988- Life Acad; *ai:* Jubilee-Acappelle Singing Group Dir; Youth Who Care Fight Against Drugs Spon; Sr Class Spon 1988-89; Tau Beta Sigma Music Club UNC of CO 1962-64; Sigma Kappa UNC of CO 1962-64; Amer Red Cross (Instr, Life Guard) 1965-80; Youth Who Care Spon Life Act 1989-; Church Youth Group Teacher Cnslr Church of Christ 1969-; *office:* Life Acad 636 29th Rd Grand Junction CO 81504

DARNELL, KAREN FENELON, Speech/Drama Teacher; *b:* Rockford, IL; *m:* Dennis George; *c:* Pete J.; *ed:* (BSED) Speech/Drama, SE MO St Univ 1971; (MSE) Scndry Curr & Instruction Gen, Drake Univ 1979; *cr:* Eng/Speech/Drama Teacher Sullivan HS 1971-73; Eng Teacher Mulvane HS 1973-74; Eng/Speech/Drama Teacher Lafayette HS 1974-75, Valley HS 1975-80; Speech Teacher Kennedy HS 1980-81; Eng Teacher University HS, SE MO Univ 1981-83; Eng/Speech/Drama Teacher Southeast Polk HS 1983-86; Speech/Drama Teacher Lafayette HS 1986-; *ai:* Drama Dir for Extracurricular Productions; Jr Class Spon; Prof Dev Cmmty for Lafayette HS Pres 1988-; MO St Teachers Assn Welfare Rep 1989-; Phi Delta Kappa 1988-; Theatre Ed Assn 1987-; Frederick Boulevard Baptist Church (Mem, Youth Sunday Sch Teacher) 1987-; Fellowship of Chrstn Athletes Co-Leader MO Western St Coll 1988-; Teacher of Yr Sullivan HS 1972; Sch Dist Tinking Skills Trng Team; Staff Person of Month 1989; Teacher of Yr Nominee Top 7 Finalist 1987; Chosen to be Commencement Speaker Lafayette HS 1990; Alumni of Yr SE MO St Univ 1983; *office:* Lafayette HS 412 Highland Saint Joseph MO 64505

DARNELL, ROSALIND MICHELE DOLOVY, Third Grade Teacher; *b:* Youngstown, OH; *ed:* (BSED) Elem Ed, Youngstown St Univ 1972; Kent St Univ, Youngstown St Univ; *cr:* 3rd Grade Teacher Market Street Sch 1972-; *ai:* 3rd Grade Teacher of Gifted & Talented; Steering Comm Grade Rep; Sci Curr Comm; Alcohol & Addiction Basic Ed Stud; Personal Awareness & Living Skills Teacher; Intnl Rdng Assn; Jennings Scholar 1984-85; Martha Holden Jennings Fnd; *office:* Market Street Elem Sch 5555 Market St Boardman OH 44512

DARNELL, VIRGINIA WILLETS, 8th Grade Mathematics Teacher; *b:* Edgecombe Cty, NC; *c:* Liza; *ed:* (BA) Ed, 1968, (MED) Ed Admin, 1981 Duke Univ; *cr:* 5th Grade Teacher Westminster Schls; Mid Sch Chm/5th-7th Grade Teacher River North Acad; 6th Grade Teacher Clisby Sch for Fine Arts; 7th-9th Grade Teacher Githens Mid Sch; *ai:* Advisory Comm Mem; Policy-Making Comm; Durham Cty Schls Teacher Cncl; Durham Symphony (Bd Dir, Chm, Family Concert) 1989-; 1st Presby Church Bd of Deacons 1989-; GSA Regional Co-Chm 1990; NC MSEN Prgm Teacher of Yr 1988; VFW Outstanding Educator in Cmmty Service 1989-; *office:* Githens Mid Sch 6800 Chapel Hill Rd Durham NC 27707

DARNUTZER, DEBRA HEBERT, Second Grade Teacher; *b:* Lake Charles, LA; *m:* Ronald John; *c:* Stephan, Abram; *ed:* (BA) Elem Ed, Univ of Toledo 1977; *cr:* Elem Teacher Grand Lake Sch 1979-; *ai:* Rdng Textbook Adoption Comm; Sch Climate Comm; Graduated Magna Cum Laude Univ of Toledo; *office:* Grand Lake H S Rt 2 Box 360-B Lake Charles LA 70605

DARONATSY, ARAM R., English Teacher; *b:* Gary, IN; *ed:* (BS) Eng/Soc Stud, 1967, (MS) Eng/Soc Stud, 1972 IN Univ; *cr:* Eng Teacher Gavit Jr/Sr HS; *ai:* NCTE; *home:* 1824 N Lincoln Park W Chicago IL 60614

DARPINO, VICTORIA GNOJEK, Elementary Vocal Music Teacher; *b:* Great Falls, MT; *m:* Fred Joseph; *c:* Julian; *ed:* (BA) Music Ed, 1975, (MME) Music Ed, 1979 Univ of N CO 1979; Grad Courses Adams St Coll, Univ of CO, CO Springs, Lesley, CO St Coll; *cr:* Gen Elem Music Teacher Keenesburg & Prospect Valley Elem Schls 1975-78; Asst Teacher Univ of N CO 1978-79; Vocal Music Teacher Horace Mann Jr HS 1978-84, Anna M Rudy Elem Sch 1984-; *ai:* Choir; Renaissance Festival & Social Comm; Performing Arts for Youth Organization Bd of Dirs 1990; CO Springs Ed Assn, CO Educators Assn, NEA, CO Music Educators Assn 1975-; *office:* Anna M Rudy Elem Sch 5370 Cracker Barrel Cir Colorado Springs CO 80918

DARRAGH, MARION WARD, Teacher; *b:* Bellingham, WA; *m:* E. Paige; *ed:* (BA) Elem Ed Math/Sci/Soc/Anthro Art, 1961; (MEd) Mid Sch/Jr HS Math, 1968 Western WA St Univ; Math/Cmptrs/Cooperative Learning/ITIP/Counseling; *cr:* Teacher North Auburn Elem 1961-67, Cascade Jr HS 1967-68, Spiritridge Elem 1969-70; Teacher/Math Dept Head Ringdall Mid Sch 1970-86; Teacher Tyee Mid Sch 1986-; *ai:* St Advisory Comm for Mathcounts; Tyee Spirit Club Adv; Math Club Coach; SLO Comm For Evaluating/Rewriting 6-8 7th Curr; Self-Study Comm for Advisory Prgm; Puget Sound Math Cncl; WA St Math Cncl; NEA/WEA/BEA; Bronze Medallion 1985-89; Natl Awd from The Appaloosa Horse Club for COmpetitive Trail Riding 1985-89; NSF Grant for Statistics Ed Univ of IL 1990; NSF Grant Teaching for Conceptual Understanding in Math Univ of WA 1986; St Coach for Mathcounts Team 1986; *office:* Tyee Mid Sch 13630 SE Allen Rd Bellevue WA 98006

DARRAH, VICKI-ANNE R., First Grade Teacher; *b:* Portland, ME; *m:* Alan; *c:* Lisa, Brian; *ed:* (BS) Elem Ed, Univ of ME Orono 1977; *cr:* Teacher Assoc Hartland Elem 1977-78; 1st Grade Teacher Eastland Elem 1978-; *ai:* ME Teachers Assn, NEA; Beta Sigma Phi (VP, Recording & Corresponding Secy) 1985-; *office:* Eastland Sch Box 411 Corinna ME 04928

DARRENKAMP, MICHELE ANNE, Mathematics Teacher; *b:* Lancaster, PA; *ed:* (BS) Math, Shippensburg Univ 1972; (MED) Math Ed, Millersville Univ 1976; Grad Work Lehigh Univ 1975-76; Grad & Undergrad Work Cmptr Sci, Millersville Univ 1983-86; *cr:* Math/Cmptr Sci Teacher Cedar Crest HS 1972-; *ai:* NHS Adv; Cntrl PA Math Assn, PA Cncl Teachers of Math, NCTM, Lebanon Cty Educl Honor Society; Pilot Club 1988-; Millersville Univ Chms & Dept Honors Lists 1984-85; Ferraniti Educl Systems Video Disc Authoring Team 1987, Math Consultant 1989-; *office:* Cedar Crest HS 115 E Evergreen Rd Lebanon PA 17042

DARSEY, JOSEPH LUTHER, Teachers Aide; *b:* Dublin, GA; *ed:* (BSED) Art, GA Southern Coll 1976; (MED) Mid Grades, GA Coll 1979; *cr:* Teacher Southwest Elem 1977-86, West Laurens Jr HS 1986-; *ai:* Jr HS Wrestling Coach; *office:* West Laurens Jr HS Rt 5 Dublin GA 31021

DARTON, ROBERT JOSEPH, Social Studies Teacher; *b:* Englewood, NJ; *c:* Achilles; *ed:* (BSED) Soc Stud, Defiance Coll 1966; NDEA Inst Chinese Lang, Seton Hall 1967; *cr:* Teacher Bradford HS 1967-70, Jackson Memorial HS 1971-; *ai:* Adv NHS; Asst Field Hockey Coach; Teacher of Yr Jackson HS 1987; Chief Negotiator Jackson Ed Assn 1989-; Jackson Day Comm 1985-; NEA Rep Assembly 1989-; *office:* Jackson Memorial HS Don Connor Blvd Jackson NJ 08527

DA SILVA, GERALDINE MARY, CSFN Religion & Fine Art Teacher; *b:* Victoria, Hong Kong; *ed:* (BA) Elem Ed, Univ of Dallas 1970; (MA) Art Ed/Admin, N TX St Univ 1983; Teachers Certificate, Northcote Trng Coll Hong Kong 1951; TX Teacher Certificate, Dallas 1970; TX Examination of Current Admin & Teachers 1986; *cr:* Elem/Scndry Teacher Maryknoll Convent Sch 1952-59; Elem Teacher St Luke Cath Sch 1959-61; Jr HS Teacher St Thomas Aquinas Sch 1963-65; Jr HS Music/Art Teacher St Luke Cath Sch 1965-69; Jr HS Soc Stud/Art Teacher St Thomas Aquinas Sch 1969-71; Jr HS Math/Religion/Art Teacher St Andrew Sch 1971-73; Jr HS Art/Music/Soc Stud/Girls Choir Teacher 1973-75, Prin 1975-78 St Luke Cath Sch; Jr HS Religion/Art/Sci/Girls Choir Teacher Holy Family of Nazareth Cath Sch 1979-83; Jr HS Religion/Art Teacher 1983-, Asst Prin 1985- St Thomas Aquinas Sch; *ai:* Diocese of Dallas Art Curr Comm; Moderator of Stu Cncl at Holy Family & St Thomas Aquinas; Confraternity of Chrstn Doctrine; Sunday Classes St Thomas Aquinas; Religious Coord, Diocesan Comm Mem; NCEA (Teacher 1959-75, 1979-, Prin 1975-78); Red Cross Church Organizations Hong Kong 1951-59; Wrote an Art Curr for Diocese of Dallas 1983; Received Awds in Hong Kong for Services Rendered Public Services; Awarded Grant for Fine Art Work Done St Thomas Aquinas Sch 1988; *home:* 3717 Abrams Rd Dallas TX 75214

DAUB, LOUISE WENGER, 4th Grade Teacher; *b:* Columbia, PA; *m:* Miles D.; *c:* Rebecca B. Wenger; *ed:* (BS) Elem Ed, Millersville Univ 1960; Post Grad Stud Elizabethtown Coll, Beaver Coll; *cr:* Teacher Manheim Township Sch Dist 1960-68, Elizabethtown Area Sch Dist 1978-; *ai:* PA St Ed Assn, NEA 1960-68, 1978-; Elizabethtown Area Ed Assn 1979-; Antique Automobile Assn of America 1960-; Hershey Region Secy 1975; *office:* Rheems Elem Sch School Ln Rheems PA 17570

DAUGHERITY, WANDA BOLINGER, Language Arts Teacher; *b:* California, MO; *m:* James; *c:* Jennifer, Dan; *ed:* (BSE) Eng, Central MO St Univ 1973; *cr:* Teacher Meadville HS 1973-74, Brookfield Jr HS 1975-77, Northwestern HS 1977-; *ai:* Spon Academic Bowl Teams; Gifted Prgm; Northwestern CTA 1977-; NSTA 1977-; *home:* Rt 1 Sumner MO 64681

DAUGHERTY, EDWIN LEE, Mathematics Teacher; *b:* Gate City, VA; *m:* Betty Cassell; *c:* Anita, Renee; *ed:* (AA) Math, Hiwassee Coll 1956; (BS) Math, 1958, (MA) Ed, 1961 E TN St Univ; Additional Math, ETSU & Univ TN Knoxville 1970; *cr:* Math Teacher Ketrin HS 1958-80, Sullivan North HS 1980-; *ai:* Key Club & Bet Club Spon; Yrbk Adv; NEA, TN Ed Assn 1958-; Sullivan Cty Ed Assn Treas 1975-80; Sullivan Cty Employees Credit (Union Bd of Dir 1988-, Treas 1990); Natl Sci Fnd Univ TN Knoxville 1963-64; Natl Sci Fnd ETSU 1969-70; Teacher of Yr Sullivan Cty 1984; *home:* 1516 Bloomingdale Pike Kingsport TN 37660

DAUGHERTY, MARY E. (HOWE), 6th Grade Teacher; *b:* Galesburg, IL; *c:* Timothy, Colleen Criste, Suzanne; *ed:* (BA) Soc Sci, ASU 1971; *cr:* Pre-Sch Teacher Woodland Chrstn Sch 1974-77; 5th/6th Grade Teacher Plainfield Elem Sch 1977-87; 6th Grade Teacher Rhoda Maxwell Elem Sch 1989-; *ai:* Lang Art; All Dist Comm Asst Prin; Woodland Ed Assn; Bus & Prof Women, PTA; Mentor Educator D/A; Phys Ed, Art, D/A Grants; WSUSD Outstanding Educator; *home:* 1505 Camino Way Woodland CA 95695

DAUGHTERY, JAMES FRANKLIN, Choral Director; *b:* Waynesboro, VA; *m:* Joan Edith Michaels; *c:* Ryan, Eric; *ed:* Cert Music, Staatlische Hochschule Fuer Musik Berlin Germany 1969; (BA) Music, Maryville Coll 1970; (MED) Ed, Univ of VA 1973; (MA) Philosophy, Columbia Univ 1978; MDiv Religion, Union Theological Seminary 1976; *cr:* Teacher Buford Jr HS 1970-73, Powell Valley HS & Powell Mid Schls 1981-; Adjunct Faculty Mt Empire Comm Coll 1989-; *ai:* Big Stone Gap Sch Cmmty Chorale Conductor; VA Choral Dir Assn Dist Chm 1985-87, 1989-; VA Music Educators Assn St Cncl 1985-87, 1989-; Amer Choral Dir Assn; Citizen of Yr Big Stone Gap VA 1987; Excl in Ed Awd VA Tech & St Univ 1989; Articles Published; *office:* Powell Valley HS Rt 1 Big Stone Gap VA 24219

DAUKANTAS, CYNTHIA POCHINI, Assistant Principal; *b:* Fitchburg, MA; *m:* Timothy James; *c:* Cesira J.; *ed:* (BS) Elem Ed, Fitchburg St Coll 1970; Grad Work Educl Leadership, Fitchburg St Coll; *cr:* Kndgtn Teacher 1970-87, Asst Prin 1987- Lunenburg Public Schls; *ai:* Testing, Strategic, Planning Task Force, Horace Mann Selections Comm; Lunenburg Ed Assn Pres 1979-86; ASCD 1987-; MATE 1988-; MA Teachers Assn 1970-; *office:* Thomas C Passios Elem Sch 1025 Massachusetts Ave Lunenburg MA 01462

DAULTON, SHERILL HOBGOOD, Chapter I Reading Teacher; *b:* Henderson, KY; *m:* Gary R.; *c:* Eric, Leslie, Vanessa; *ed:* (BS) Elem Ed, Western KY Univ 1973; (MS) Elem Ed, Eastern KY Univ 1982; *cr:* 4-6 Grade Teacher Burnside Elem Sch 1973-75; 1st & 5th Grades Chapter I Teacher Nancy Elem Sch 1975-; *ai:* Elem Acad Team Coach; Coord of Pops; VP Intnl Rdng Assn; Chapter I Prgm Dev Comm; IRA VP 1989-; NEA 1974-; Nancy Elm PTA Sec 1978-; Pulaski Cty Homemakers Nutrition Chairperson 1975-; Innovation Incentive Grant for Ed; *home:* 2067 Prather Dr Nancy KY 42544

DAVENPORT, ALENA CLARK, Mathematics Teacher; *b:* Globe, AZ; *m:* Richard E.; *c:* Jarrod, Jolene; *ed:* (BA) Phys Sci, N AZ Univ 1972; (MS) Physics, Univ of WY 1974; Post Grad Work in Math; *cr:* Project Engr Sperry Flight Systems 1977-78; Math Teacher Deer Valley HS 1983-86, Goldwater HS 1986-; *ai:* Natl Honor Society Adv; Mu Alpha Theta Co & Jr Class Co Spon; AEA, NEA 1987-; NCTM 1988-; ASCD 1990; PTA 1st VP 1988-; BSA (Cub Pack 722 Treas 1987-89, Scout 365 Comm Mem 1989-); Natl Sci Fnd Fellowship for Math & Sci Univ of WY; Bd of Regents Math Inst Univ of AZ; Natl Sci Fnd Discrete Math Inst N AZ Univ; *office:* Goldwater HS 2820 W Rose Garden Ln Phoenix AZ 85027

DAVENPORT, BILL, History Teacher; *b:* Eureka, KS; *c:* Dwayne, Lisa K.; *ed:* (BA) His, Univ of NM 1962; (MA) Scndry Ed, CA St Univ Northridge 1972; Abilene Chrstn Coll 1962; Pepperdine Univ 1966; *cr:* Teacher Fowler Public Schls 1962-65, Valley View Jr HS 1965-; *ai:* Yrbk & Newspaper Adv; Soc Stud Task Force; Soc Stud Dept Chm; NEA 1962-; CA Teachers Assn; Semi Educators Assn (Bargaining Team Chm 1988-, VP, Bd of Dir, Pres) 1965-; NCSS 1970-; Teacher of Month 1989; We Honor Ours Awd; *office:* Valley View Jr Hs 3347 Tapo St Simi Valley CA 93065

DAVENPORT, CHARLENE FOX, Third Grade Teacher; *b:* Raleigh, NC; *m:* Conley Dean; *c:* Stephen D., Catherine R.; *ed:* (BA) Elem Ed, Meredith Coll 1959; Graduate Ed, Univ NC 1971; Graduate Ed, Univ Central FL 1981; Human Dev Univ VA 1964-65; Rdng in Elem Sch Univ of Greensboro Grad Sch 1971; First Aid, CPR, Creative Writ, Seminole Comm Coll 1979; Sci Teacher Methods; Earth/Phys Sci/Pract Sci, Inst Univ Cen FL 1984; *cr:* 1st-3rd Grade Teacher Public Sch 1954-70; Enlisted Personnel Fort Story 1960; 4th Grade Teacher Seira Elem Sch 1970-74; 8th Grade Teacher Post Grads Oak Ridge Military Acad 1975-76; K & 1st & 4th Grade Teacher Lawton Elem 1980-; *ai:* Co-Chm Lang Arts Comm; TABS; SCLAC Teacher Rep 1989-; Cty Rdng Cncl Secy 1987-89; Teacher of Yr 1986; SSAT FL Writing Team; *home:* 630 E Chapman Rd Oviedo FL 32765

DAVENPORT, CULLEN BRUCE, Social Studies Dept Chairman; *b:* Washington, DC; *c:* Tracy; *ed:* (BA) Sociology, Cntrl St Univ 1968; (MA) Counseling/Psych, Federal City Coll 1975; *cr:* Teacher Evans Jr HS 1968-73, Douglass Jr HS 1973-76, Winston Educl Center 1976-; *ai:* Stu Cncl Spon; Dept Chairperson; Bsktbl Coach; DC Cncl of Soc Stud Teachers 1983-; Alpha Phi Alpha 1966; Helped Write DC His Text; *office:* Winston Educl Center 3100 Erie St SE Washington DC 20020

DAVENPORT, DELRAY S., Spanish/English Teacher; *b:* Idaho Falls, ID; *m:* Tamera Blanchard; *c:* Joshua D., Elizabeth, Rebecca, Amy M.; *ed:* (AA) Eng, Ricks Coll 1984; (BA) Eng, UT St Univ 1987; *cr:* Teacher/Foreign Lang Dept Chm South Fremont HS 1987-; *ai:* Span Club & Jr Class Adv; NCTE 1986-; FEA, NEA Building Rep 1989-; BSA Explorer Adv 1987-; *office:* South Fremont HS 550 N 1st W Saint Anthony ID 83445

DAVENPORT, JUDITH SCOTT, Team Leader-Teacher; *b:* New Haven, CT; *m:* Rodney J.; *c:* Rodney Jr., Scott A.; *ed:* (BS) Elem Ed, Univ North TX 1968; (ME) Elem Ed, 1973; *cr:* Teacher Dallas IND Sch 1968; Dept of Defense Germany 1974-76; Greenville 1977-; *ai:* Dept Head-Soc Stud; Team Leader; TX St Teachers Pres 1984-85; ASCD 1987-; Teacher-Inter 1988-89 Teacher of Yr; Mary C Webb Schlsp NTSU; *home:* 2400 Kent Cir Greenville TX 75401

DAVENPORT, LINDA CARTER, 4th Grade Teacher; *b:* Fort Sam Houston, TX; *m:* Don A.; *c:* Kevin T.; *ed:* (BS) Elem Ed, Southwest TX St Univ 1977; Advanced Academic Trng; *cr:* 4th Grade Teacher Taylor Ray Inter 1979-; *ai:* TX Classroom Teachers Assn 1979-; Level II Career Ladder 1988-; *office:* Taylor Ray Inter 2611 Ave N Rosenberg TX 77471

DAVENPORT, ROBIN DOUGLAS, 4th Grade Teacher; *b:* Virginia Beach, VA; *ed:* (BA) Elem Ed, VA Wesleyan Coll 1974; (MS) Elem Ed, Old Dominion Univ 1978; Post Masters Studies Elem Admin Endorsement ODU 1980; *cr:* 3rd Grade Teacher 1974-79; 4th Grade Teacher 1979- Woodstock Elem; *ai:* SCA Comm Adv; NEA 1979-; VA Ed Assn 1979-; VA Beach Ed Assn 1979-; Phi Delta Kappa 1989-; PTA Treasureer 1979-81, VP 1982-83; Ruritan Natl Creeds Treasurer 1982, Secretary 1983, VP 1984, Pres 1985, Zone Governor 1988; Parents & Teachers Lifetime Mem 1978; Man of the Yr 1986; Outstanding Zone Governor of Holland Dist; The Marquis Who's Who in South & Southwest 1982-83; Woodstock's Teacher of the Yr 1981 & 1984; Ruritan Family of the Yr 1989; *office:* Woodstock Elem Sch 6016 Providence Rd Virginia Beach VA 23464

DAVENPORT, STEPHANNE ALLEN, Spanish Teacher; *b:* Xenia, OH; *c:* Shaun D.; *ed:* (BA) Span, Mt Vernon Nazarene Coll 1979; *cr:* Span Teacher Highland HS 1979-85, Mt Vernon HS 1985-; *home:* 7 Monroe St Mount Vernon OH 43050

DAVID, BETTY ASWELL, First Grade Teacher; *b:* Ruston, LA; *c:* Robert M.; *ed:* (BA) Elem Ed, 1968, (MA) Elem Ed, 1975 LA Tech Univ; Grad Stud Elem Ed, LA Tech Univ 1986; *cr:* Kndgtn Teacher Choudrant Elem 1968-71; 4th Grade Techer Hillcrest Elem 1971-72; 2nd Grade Teacher 1973-76, 1st Grade Teacher 1976- Choudrant Elem; *ai:* Choudrant Elem PTC; LA Ed Assn 1968-85; Assn of Prof Educators Sch Rep 1986-; Delta Kappa Gamma 1988-; Choudrant Elem Sch Teacher of Yr 1987-88; *office:* Choudrant Elem Sch P O Box 360 Choudrant LA 71227

DAVID, CONNIE JENE, Physical Education Teacher; *b:* Tulsa, OK; *ed:* (BS) Phys Ed, TX Tech Univ 1980; (MED) Counseling, N TX St Univ 1988; *cr:* Phys Ed Teacher Carter HS 1981-; *ai:* Head Vlybl Coach; Bsktbl & Track Asst Coach; Assn of TX Prof Educators 1982-; Amer Assn of Counseling & Dev 1987-; Arlington Coaches Assn VP 1987-; *office:* Carter Jr HS 701 Tharp Arlington TX 76010

DAVID, LISA JOHNSON, Physical Education Teacher; *b:* Bakersfield, CA; *m:* Keith Du Wayne; *c:* Travis, Samantha; *ed:* (AA) Phys Ed, Bakersfield Coll 1978; (BS) Phys Ed, CA Poly San Luis Obispo 1980; *cr:* Special Day Palm Avenue 1981-83; Phys Ed Teacher Norris Mid Sch 1983-; *ai:* Girls Vlybl Coach; Athletic & Intramural Dirs; Teacher of Yr 1988; *office:* Norris Mid Sch Rt 11 Box 258 Bakersfield CA 93312

DAVID, PEGGY SPITZIG, 5th Grade Teacher; *b:* Chicago, IL; *m:* Lance J.; *c:* Dawn M., Katie A.; *ed:* (BS) Elem Ed/Spec Ed, Western IL Univ 1978; *cr:* LD Self Contained Classroom Teacher 1978-79, 5th Grade Classroom Teacher 1979- Westfield Sch; *ai:* Winthrop Harbor Lions Club 1989-; Winthrop Harbor Teacher of Yr 1988-89; *office:* Westfield Sch 2309 9th St Winthrop Harbor IL 60096

DAVIDOVICH, ROBERT D., Principal; *b:* Chicago, IL; *m:* Gerda; *c:* Heide Ferranti, Kristin Laas, Susan Koestering, Jon Koestering; *ed:* (BS) Geography, 1973, Teaching Cert Elem Ed, 1975 Carroll Coll; (MS) Educl Admin, Univ of WI Madison 1984; *cr:* 2nd-5th Grade Teacher Meadow View Sch 1976-87; Resource Teacher Park Lawn Elem Sch 1987-89; Prin Ixonia Elem Sch 1989-; Staff Dev Coord Oconomowoc Area Sch Dist 1989-; *ai:* HS Track & Cross Cntry Coach 1987-89; Oconomowoc Ed Assn Pres 1985-86; Phi Delta Kappa, ASCD 1988-; *home:* 7830 Norwegian Rd Oconomowoc WI 53066

DAVIDS, CHERYL EVE, Third Grade Teacher; *b:* Jeffersonville, IN; *m:* Gerald E.;; *ed:* (BA) Elem Ed, 1970, (MS) Elem Ed, 1973 in Univ; *cr:* 3rd Grade Teacher Galena Elem Sch 1970-; *ai:* IN St Teachers Assn 1970-; *office:* Galena Elem Sch 6697 Old Vincennes Rd Floyds Knobs IN 47119

DAVIDSON, ALICE SAARI, Mathematics Department Chair; *b:* Cordova, AK; *m:* Philip C.; *c:* Karen Davidson Esparza, Gretchen A., Philip E.; *cr:* N CA Math Project 1986, Cmptrs in Ed 1982-84 Univ of CA Davis; Supplementary Courses Math Ed 1958-; Teacher Highline Sch Dist 1958-62, Loretto HS 1968-69; Teacher 1969-, Math Dept Chairperson 1976- Mills Jr HS; *ai:* Past Yrbk & 9th Grade Class Adv; NEA 1958-; NCTM; Sacrament Area Math Educators Pres 1989-; Faith Luth Church Alter Guild Secy; Folson-Cordova Sch Dist Mentor Teacher; N CA Math Project Fellow; *office:* Mills Jr HS 10439 Coloma Rd Rancho Cordova CA 95670

DAVIDSON, ANNE R. (FISHER), Spanish Teacher; *b:* Detroit, MI; *c:* Nathan, Micah; *ed:* (BA) Span, 1968, (MS) Span/Bio/Ed Magna Cum Laude, 1986 Butler Univ; *cr:* Span/Eng Teacher St Agnes Acad 1968-69, Lincoln HS 1971-72; Substitute/Tutor 1972-83; Span/Eng Teacher Scecina HS 1983-87; Span Teacher Warren Cntrl HS 1987-; *ai:* Speech, Debate, Natl Forensic League, Spanish Club Coach; Grade Sch Enrichment; Work with Exchange Stu; Coord Cadet Teaching & Strategic Teaching Comm; Phi Delta Kappa 1988-; Amer Assn of Teachers of Span & Portuguese 1989-; NEA, Warren Ed Assn 1988-; Full Schlsp to Butler Univ; *office:* Warren Cntrl HS 9500 E 16th St Indianapolis IN 46229

DAVIDSON, CECELIA ANNE, Principal; *b:* Augusta, GA; *ed:* (BS) Sci Teaching, Clemson Univ 1980; (MED) Educl Admin, Augusta Coll 1984; (EDD) Educl Admin, SC St Coll 1989; *cr:* Sci Teacher Lucy Laney Comprehensive HS 1980-84, N Augusta Mid Sch 1984-87; Asst Prin Hammond Hill Elem 1987-89; Prin N Augusta Elem 1989-; *ai:* Admin Assn 1987-; ASCD 1988-; Whos Who-Amer Educators 1989; Delta Kappa Gamma 1988-; Phi Delta Kappa 1989-; *office:* North Augusta Elem Sch 400 E Spring Grove Ave North Augusta SC 29841

DAVIDSON, CONNIE M., 5th Grade Lang Art Teacher; *b:* Conyers, GA; *m:* Larry Wade; *c:* Keeli L., Ali E.; *ed:* (BS) Elem Ed, 1979, (MS) Elem Ed, 1989 Jacksonville St Univ; *cr:* Chapter I Rdng/Math Teacher 1979-80, 7th Grade Lang Teacher 1980-84, 6th Grade Lang Teacher 1981-84, Chapter I Math Teacher 1984-85, Chapter I Lang Teacher 1985-86, 5th Grade Lang Teacher 1986- Oxford Mid Sch; *ai:* Oxford Ed Assn, NEA 1979-; *office:* Oxford Mid Sch 1401 Caffey Dr Oxford AL 36203

DAVIDSON, JOETTA MAE (GARRETT), Third Grade Teacher; *b:* Anadarko, OK; *:* Harvey L.; *c:* Douglas W., Sharon K. (dec), Karen J. Davidson Winkler; *ed:* (BS) Elem, Chickasha OK 1955; Grad Work on Masters Southwestern OK St Univ; *cr:* 2nd/3rd Grade Teacher 1955-56, 1st/2nd Grade Teacher 1957-58 Amber Sch; Kndgtn Teacher First Baptist Kndgtn 1964-67; 3rd Grade Teacher Amber Pocasset Sch 1967-; *ai:* Spon for Field Trips; Dir for 3rd Graders Christmas Prgm; Sell Tickets for Ball Games; Work in Concessions; OEA, NEA; Rdng Cncl; Mem First Baptist Church Pocasset Sunday Sch Teacher, Certificates of Awd; Poem Published in OK Reader 1979 & 81; Ran for Cty Teacher of Yr 1977 & 82; Writer for Christmas Prgm 1978; *home:* Box 102 Pocasset OK 73079

DAVIDSON, LINDA JOHNSON, Kindergarten Teacher; *b:* Newport, TN; *m:* Steve Alan; *c:* Brad, Brian; *ed:* (BS) Elem Ed, Carson-Newman Coll 1976; Renewing Teaching Certificate Tusculum Coll, TN Tech; *cr:* Kndgtn Teacher Edgemont Sch 1976-; *ai:* Alpha Delta Kappa (Recording Secy 1984-86, Chaplain 1986-88): Cocke Cty Ed Assn, TN Ed Assn, NEA; *home:* Rt 6 Box 497 Newport TN 37821

DAVIDSON, MARK DANIEL, Physics/Science Teacher/Coach; *b:* Bishopville, SC; *ed:* (BS) Bio/Psych, Francis Marion Coll 1985; Working Towards Masters Scndry Ed, Sci; *cr:* Teacher/Coach Bishopville HS 1986-; *ai:* Head Jr Var Ftbl, Asst Var Ftbl, Asst Var Bsbl Coach; Amer Bsbl Coaches Assn 1987-; SC Coaches Assn 1986-; *office:* Bishopville HS 321 Roland St Bishopville SC 29010

DAVIDSON, MIKE R., Mathematics Instructor; *b:* Southgate, CA; *m:* Ellen K; *c:* Sarah, Andrea; *ed:* (BS) Engineering, Univ of Redlands 1969; Cmptr Circuit Design, Network Design & Programming; *cr:* Security Tech US Army 1969-72; Electronics Engr TRW 1973-75; Sci/Math Teacher Mt Whitney HS 1976-78; Math Teacher Golden West HS 1978-80, Green River HS 1983; *ai:* Soph Class & Academic Decathlon Spon; WY Cncl Teachers of Math 1981-; Math Assn of America 1984-89; Natl Sci Fnd Grant 1977; *office:* Green River HS 300 Monroe Ave Green River WY 82935

DAVIDSON, NATHAN ROYAL, General Music/Band Director; *b:* Preston, MN; *m:* Denise R. Abrath; *ed:* Bus/Mrktg, Winona Voc 1970; (AA) Music Ed, Rochester Comm Coll 1973; (BS) Music Ed, Winona St Univ 1975; *cr:* Instrumental Music Teacher Independence HS 1975-77, NW Webster 1977-78, Grand Meadow HS 1978-; *ai:* Class Adv; Pep & Jazz Band; Contest Preparation; Music Contest Judging; Organized Band Parents; Worked Dist Level, Planning, Evaluating & Reporting Comm; NEA 1975-; MN Ed Assn 1978-; WI Sch Music Assn 1975-77; IA Bandmasters Assn, N Cntrl Bandmasters Assn 1977-78; Music Educators Natl Conference 1978-; Intnl Musicians Union 1986-; Assn of Concert Bands Inc 1987-; Intnl Assn of Jazz Educators, Twin Cities Jazz Society 1988-; *home:* Rt 2 Box 151 Grand Meadow MN 55936

DAVIDSON, NELDA M., Fashion Merchandising Teacher; *b:* Meridian, MS; *m:* Woodie; *c:* Tyler; *ed:* (BS) Distributive Ed, 1981, (MA) Voc Ed, 1985 MS St Univ; *cr:* Mrktg/Fashion Merchandising Teacher Ross Collins Voc Center 1981-; *ai:* Meridian HS Fashion Bd Spon 1986-89; MS Assn of Distributive Ed Teachers 1981-; AVA 1981-; 4-H Clothing Advisory Cncl Comm Mem 1985-87; Distributive Ed Clubs of America Club Adv 1981-, Adv of Yr 1988, MS St Univ Schlsp 1979; Nom Young Educator of Yr Meridian MS; *office:* Ross Collins Voc Center 2640 24th Ave Meridian MS 39301

DAVIDSON, ROSEMARY PEARSON, 2nd Grade Teacher; *b:* Atlantic, IA; *m:* A. V.; *c:* Kenneth, Roger; *ed:* (BA) Elem Ed, NWMSU 1975; Addl Studies, NWMSU; Drake Univ; *cr:* 3rd Grade Teacher Jackson Sch 1958-60; 2nd Grade Teacher Cumberland Elem 1964-; *ai:* CMEA Pres/Sec 1964-; ISEA 1964-; NEA 1964-; Delta Kappa Gamma Prof Affairs 1985-; Lib Bd 1964-82; LWML Pres/Sec 1961-; Amer Legion Aux Teacher of Yr 1986; *office:* Cumberland-Massena Schs Cumberland IA 50843

DAVIDSON, STEVE ALAN, Principal; *b:* Charleston, WV; *m:* Linda Sue Johnson; *c:* Bradley, Brian; *ed:* (BS) Music Ed, Carson-Newman Coll 1977; (MED) Admin/Supervision, East TN St Univ 1986; *cr:* General Music Teacher Newport Grammar Sch 1977-78; Elem Teacher Edgemont Sch 1978-85; Prin Bridgeport Sch 1985-; *ai:* Bsktbl Coach; Cocke Cty Elem Schls Athletic Assn Pres; Phi Mu Alpha 1975-; Phi Delta Kappa 1986-; NAESP 1990; Newport Rescue Squad Historian 1978-83; Natl Fed of Interscholastic ofcls Assn 1981-; Amer Radio Relay League 1988-; Published Educl Articles Local Newspaper; *office:* Bridgeport Sch Rt 4 Box 107 Newport TN 37821

DAVIDSON, TOM, 6-8th Grade Teacher of Gifted; *b:* Louisville, KY; *ed:* (BA) Ed, Univ of Louisville 1975; (MA) Ed, 1978, (Rank I) Gifted Ed, 1985 Univ of Western; *cr:* 6th Grade Teacher Maryville Elem 1975-79, Bullitt Lick Mid 1979-87; 8th Grade Teacher Frost Mid Sch 1987-88; 6th-8th Grade Teacher of Gifted & Talented Bullitt Lick Mid 1988-; *ai:* Academic Team; KY Youth Assembly; Drama Coach; Wkshps for Teachers In-Service Rep; Yrbk Spon; Guest Speaker KY Academic Conferences; Yrbk Awd Grants; *office:* Bullitt Lick Mid Sch 1080 W Blue Lick Rd Shepherdsville KY 40165

DAVIDSON, VERVON EUGENE, HS Speech/English Teacher; *b:* Lu Verne, IA; *m:* Gloria; *c:* Cathi, Ralph; *ed:* (BA) Speech Ed, Memphis St Univ 1960; (MA) Tech Theatre, Univ of N IA 1971; Newspaper Fund Fellowship Journalism Univ of IN; *cr:* Teacher Adel HS 1960-68, IA Falls HS 1968-; *ai:* Contest Speech & Drama Act; N Hardin Cty Curr Planning Steering Comm; Local Ed Assn Pres 1971-76; IA Comm Assn Pres 1972-74; US Jaycees (Local Pres 1962-64, St Comm Dev 1965, Natl Dir 1966), Outstanding Young Man of America 1967; Toastmasters Intnl Pres; Local Airport Commission Chm & Licensed Pilot; Outstanding IA Natl Guardsman 1980; *home:* 2412 Linden Iowa Falls IA 50126

DAVIES, BEVERLY JEAN, 2nd & 3rd Grade Teacher; *b:* Sidney, OH; *m:* Daniel M.; *c:* Sarah, Paula, Danika; *ed:* (BS) Elem Ed, Bowling Green St Univ 1973; (MS) Interdisciplinary Stud, Univ of Dayton 1980; Cmptrs Univ of Dayton; Lib Sci Bowling Green St Univ; *cr:* Teacher Anna Local Schls 1973-; *ai:* NEA 1973-; OH Ed Assn 1973-; Anna Local Teachers Assn 1973-; Delta Kappa Gamma 1989-; *office:* Anna Local Schs 1 Mc Rill Way Anna OH 45302

DAVIES, LINDA PETERSEN, Soc Stud Department Teacher; *b:* Denver, CO; *m:* Stephen; *ed:* (BS) His, Univ of Denver 1985; Grad Stud Various Colls & Univs; *cr:* Soc Stud Teacher Sierra HS 1985-; *ai:* Jr Class Spon; NEA; Sierra Pride Awd.

DAVIES, LINDA WILSON, Kindergarten Teacher; *b:* Steubenville, OH; *m:* Richard J.; *c:* Brett, Brian, Brittany; *ed:* (AB) Early Chldhd Ed, Glenville St Coll 1974, (MA) Early Chldhd Ed, WV Univ 1979; *cr:* Kndgtn Teacher Elizabeth Elem 1974-; *ai:* Handwriting Book Selection Comm; In Charge of Arbor Day Celebration; Dir of Christmas Prgm; Hop-A-Thon for Muscular Dystrophy Spon; WV Ed Assn; Order of Eastern Star, Amer Baptist Women; WV Minigrant Kndgtn Learning Lib Project; WV Grant Pre-Sch Orientation Prgm; *office:* Elizabeth Elem P O Box 220 Elizabeth WV 26143

DAVIES, MARILYN, English Teacher; *b:* St Paul, MN; *c:* Laura, Gina, Joseph, Joann; *ed:* (BS) Eng Ed, 1976, (MA) Curr & Instruction, 1987 Univ WI Milwaukee; *cr:* Eng Teacher Mukwonago HS 1976-; *ai:* Yrbk Adv; Sr Banquet Spon; NEA Mem; Kappa Delta Pi (VP 1976-72, Pres 1977-78); Sigma Tau Delta 1976-; NHS Ed; Natl Eng Honor Soc; Mukwonago Lions Club Awd Dedicated Service to Ed 1983; *office:* Mukwonago H S 605 W School Rd Mukwonago WI 53149

DAVILA, YOLANDA C., 8th Grade English Teacher; *b:* Laredo, TX; *ed:* (BA) Eng, Span, TX A&I Univ 1969; (MAIS) Psych, Sociology, Span, Laredo St Univ 1990; Amer Coll of Real Estate - Realtor; *cr:* Teacher Lamar Mid Sch 1969-; *ai:* Sch Spon Webb Cty Spelling Bee; TSTA Life Mem; Laredo Ed Assn 1969-; TX Realtors Assn 1980-87; St Joseph Parish Cncl Pres 1984-86; Religious Ed Coord 1979-; St Joseph Parish Catechist 1969-; Democratic Party Precinct Chairperson; Precinct Election Judge; Teacher of Month/Sch; Webb Cnty Historical Commission Mem; *home:* 1706 Guatemozin Laredo TX 78043

DAVIS, ALICE, 5th Grade Teacher; *b:* Geneva, AL; *ed:* (BS) Eng, AL St Univ 1969; (MS) Elem Ed, Troy St Univ 1976; *cr:* Teacher Mulkey Elem Sch 1969-; *ai:* Church Youth Leader; YAC Club Spon; NEA, AEA, Geneva City Ed Assn; Zeta Phi Beta; 4-H Club Leader Volunteer & Leadership Awds 1982; *office:* J A Mulkey Elem Sch 800 W Meadow Ave Geneva AL 36340

DAVIS, ANNE PARHAM, Sixth Grade Teacher; *b:* Knoxville, AL; *w:* John C. (dec); *c:* Denise Davis Alexander, Deborah Davis Alexander; *ed:* (BA) Elem Ed, IL St Univ 1964; (MA) Counseling, Governors St Univ 1976; Cmptr Literacy Trng; *cr:* Telephone Operator IL Bell 1963-64; Elem Teacher Harvey Sch Dist 152 1964-; *ai:* Honor Stus Annual Recognition Banquet Coord; Safety Patrol Prgm & Stu Cncl Spon; IL Ed Assn Region Chairperson 1985-; IL Teachers Retirement Sys Trustee 1980-; Riley Sch PTA (Teacher Liason, Parliamentarian) 1982-88, Special Teacher Recognition 1984; Parent, Teacher Forum 1985-; Harvey Area Cmmty Organization 1976-81; Curr Mini-Grant in Soc Stud; Congressional Lobbyist for Ed; Participant Educl Testing Service Comm; *home:* 15344 Winchester Harvey IL 60426

DAVIS, ANNETTE CORDER, English Teacher; *b:* Dillon, SC; *m:* James R.; *c:* Daniel, David; *ed:* (BS) Eng/Ed, Univ of North TX 1971; (MA) Eng, S Meth 1977; *cr:* Coll Eng Teacher Cedar Valley Comm Coll 1977-87; 10th Grade Eng Teacher Duncanville HS 1978-; Coll Eng Teacher Mountain View Comm Coll 1987-; *ai:* 10th Grade Level & Spon; NCTE; *office:* Duncanville H S 900 W Camp Wisdom Rd Duncanville TX 75116

DAVIS, ANNIE PAUL, 6th Grade Teacher; *b:* Jonesville, LA; *c:* Tracie Ann Espenan; *ed:* (BA) Elem Ed, Northeast LA Univ 1964; (ME) Elem Ed, Univ of Southern MS 1975; Studies Elem Ed, Univ of Southern MS 1977; *cr:* Secy Dean of Women NLU Natchitoches 1947-50; Steno/Clerk La Dept of Labor 1951-60; Teacher Cathedral Sch 1962-63, Ferriday Elem Sch 1 964-81, Huntington Sch 1981-; *home:* 323 Woodland Ave Ferriday LA 71334

DAVIS, BARBARA CALVERT, Jr HS Lang Arts/Soc Stud Tchr; *b:* Morehead, KY; *m:* James Adair; *c:* Leigh A. Huffman, Christi A.; *ed:* (BA) Elem Ed, Morehead St Univ; *cr:* 1st-12th Grade Fr Teacher Prichard HS 1963-66; Fr/Eng Teacher KY Chrstn Coll 1971-73; 7th-8th Lang Arts/Soc Stud Teacher Star Elem 1975-; *ai:* Academic Team Coach; Outstanding Young Woman 1969; *home:* PO Box 575 24 Sundown Rd Grayson KY 41143

DAVIS, BARBARA COLVARD, Teacher; *b:* Jefferson, GA; *m:* Thomas G.; *c:* Durin, Brian, Russ; *ed:* (BS) Early Chldhd Ed, 1981; (MS) Rdng Ed, 1985, (EDS) Rdng Ed, 1989 Univ of GA; *cr:* Rdng Teacher Madison Cty Schl 1981-; *ai:* Adopt-a-Sch Comm Chairperson; Intnl Rdng Assn, GA Rdng Assn, NE GA Rdng Assn, PAGE 1988-; Phi Kappa Phi, Alpha Upsilon Alpha; *office:* Madison Cty Mid Sch PO Box 690 Danielsville GA 30633

DAVIS, BARBARA LEE, Middle School Teacher; *b:* Florence, SC; *m:* Lawrence E.; *c:* Felicia, Robert; *ed:* (BA) Sociology, Univ of NC-Greensboro 1969; (MED) Ed, East Carolina U 1986; Teachers Coll Columbia Univ; *cr:* Teacher Guilford Cty Sch System 1969-71; Amer Intl Sch of Kabul Afghanistan 1977-79; Carteret Cty Sch System 1979-89; Houston Cty Sch System 1989-; *ai:* NCAE 1983-89; NCCTM 1987-; *office:* Pearl Stephens Alternative Sch Reid St Warner Robins GA 31088

DAVIS, BARBARA SUTTON, Mathematics Teacher/Dept Chair; *b:* Charleston, WV; *m:* Marion H. Jr.; *c:* Susan, Tim, Matt, Stephen; *ed:* (BA) Math, Univ of NC Greensboro 1967; (MAED) Math Ed, E Carolina Univ 1987; Ag Cert; *cr:* Math Teacher Whiteville HS 1967-68; Real Estate Broker Century 21-HomeOwners Realty 1979-82; Math Teacher P S Jones Jr HS 1983-; *ai:* Coach Math Counts 1983-88 & Algebra I & Geometry Teams 1983-; NC Cncl Teachers of Math; WA Bd of Realtors Secy, Treas 1980-81, Realtor of Yr 1981; Math Study Schlsp; Math Study Grant; *office:* P S Jones Jr HS 820 Bridge St Washington NC 27889

DAVIS, BENJAMIN FRANKLYN, JR., Principal; *b:* Atlanta, GA; *ed:* (BA) His, Gettysburg Coll 1967; (MED) Scndry Ed, Temple Univ 1970; Grad Stud Admin; *cr:* Teacher Yeadon Jr/Sr HS 1967-72; Asst Prin Interboro Jr HS 1972-78, Interboro Sr HS 1978-82; Prin Tinicum Sch 1985-; *ai:* DE Cty Prins Assn, PA Assn of Scndry Elem Prins, NASSP, NAESP 1972-; Phi Delta Kappa 1970-; *office:* Tinicum Sch 1st & Seneca Aves Essington PA 19029

DAVIS, BERTHA BRIDGES, 7th Grade Soc Stud Teacher; *b:* Demopolis, AL; *m:* Charles Stanley; *c:* Benjamin C.; *ed:* (AA) Ed, Univ of AL; (BS) His/Phys Ed, Livingston Univ 1969; (MS) His, Jacksonville St Univ 1975; *cr:* Teacher Dar Sch 1969-72; Teacher 1974-82, Asst Prin 1982-83, Teacher 1983- Carlisle Park Mid Sch; *ai:* NEA 1969-; Guntersville Classroom Teachers Pres 1974-75; AL Ed Assn 1969-; Alpha Delta Kappa 1976-80; Pilot Club 1985-88; Jacksonville St Teachers Hall of Fame Nom; AL Teacher of Yr Nom; Americanism Awd; AL His Teacher of Yr; Natl His

Teacher of Yr Nom; *office:* Carlisle Park Mid Sch 801 Sunset Dr Guntersville AL 35976

DAVIS, BILLIE JEAN (PIERCE), 4th Grade Teacher; *b:* Lamar, OK; *m:* Rex; *ed:* (BS) Elem Ed, Grand Canyon Univ 1955; (MS) Elem Ed, W OR St Coll 1962; Seattle Univ, Seattle Pacific Univ, Portland St Univ; Dist Inservice; *cr:* 3rd Grade Teacher Longview Sch Dist 1955-57, Salem Sch Dist 1957-60; Trng for Hearing Impaired OR St Sch for Deaf 1960-61; Pre-Sch/7th Grade Teacher OR St Sch for Deaf 1961-65; Tutor Univ of VA Speech & Hearing Center 1967; Pre-Sch Cnslr for Deaf Portland Public Schls 1969-70; Homemaker 1970-78; 4th/5th Grade Teacher Longview Sch Dist 1978-; 4th Grade Teacher Columbia Valley Gardens Sch 1990; *ai:* WA St Soc Stud Guidelines Writing Team & Reactor Review Panel; Soc Stud Curr, Dist Health Review, Longview Centennial Comm; NEA, WA Ed Assn, Longview Ed Assn, Intnl Rdng Assn, WA Organization for Rdng Dev, Cowlitz Rdng Cncl, WA St Cncl for Soc Stud; Longview Presbyn Church Deacon 1988-; WA St Historical Society; Cowlitz Cty Historical Society; Historic Tour of Longview Leader; Wrote & Designed Various Books.

DAVIS, BOBBIE MORTON, First Grade Teacher; *b:* Vernon, TX; *m:* Bob; *c:* Jennifer, Erin, Matthew; *ed:* (BSED) Elem Ed, SW MO St Univ 1975; Grad Stud Drury Coll, Univ of MO Columbia; *cr:* Teacher of EMH 1975-78, 2nd Grade Teacher 1978-81 Lucy W James Elem; K/Teacher of EMH-Learning Disability Resource Oak Hill R-1 1981-84; Remedial Math Teacher Salem R-80 1984-85; 1st Grade Teacher Lucy W James Elem 1985-; *ai:* Sick Leave Comm Chm; Sci Curr Comm; MO Natl Ed Assn 1985-; St James GFWC Jr Club (Pres 1989-91, VP 1988-89); *office:* Lucy Wortham James Elem Sch 314 S Jefferson Saint James MO 65559

DAVIS, C MICHAEL, Principal/Mathematics Teacher; *b:* Gadsden, AL; *m:* V. V.; *c:* Joel, Hannah; *ed:* (BS) Accounting, Jacksonville St Univ 1979; (MS) Educl Admin, Pensacola Chrstn Coll 1987; Grad Stud His Ed, Univ of AL; *cr:* Teacher 1981-82, Prin/Teacher 1982- Coosa Chrstn Sch; *ai:* Math Club Adv; Sr Class Spon; Assn for Curr Dev 1989-; Whites Chapel Baptist Church (Deacon, Finance Comm) 1980-; *office:* Coosa Chrstn Sch Rt 3 Box 140 Gadsden AL 35901

DAVIS, CAROL SALMONS, English Teacher/Librarian; *b:* Hinton, WV; *m:* Rodney Lee; *c:* Courtney, Ryan; *ed:* (BS) Eng/ Lib Media, Concord Coll 1979; Grad Stud Univ of WV; *cr:* ESEA Title I Rdng Teacher Hinton HS 1980-84; Eng Teacher/Librarian Talcott Schls 1984-; *ai:* Spring Dance Comm Adv & Chaperone; Class Trip Fund Raisers Chm; Eng Dept Chm; NCTE 1983-84; Summers Cty Rdng Cncl Treas 1989-; *home:* 402 Cedar Ave Hinton WV 25951

DAVIS, CELIA MC CLELLAN, 5th/6th Grade Teacher; *b:* Haleyville, AL; *m:* James W.; *c:* Stephanie; *ed:* (AA) Certificate; (BA) His/Poly Sci, 1971, (MA) Elem Ed, 1974 Univ of AL Birmingham; *cr:* 5th Grade Teacher Rutledge Jr HS 1971-76; 4th Grade Teacher Minor Chrstn Sch 1982-83; 4th-6th Grade Teacher Warrior HS 1983-; *ai:* System-Wide Sch Calenden Comm; Plan & Present Honor Roll Pgrm; Help with Honor Club Tapping & Reception; Philosophy & Goals Accrediation Comm; Chldrens Theatre Field Trip Spon; AL Ed Assn; Jefferson Cty Ed Assn; NEA; Warrior PTA; Bragg Jr HS PTA; *home:* 4931 Holly Ln Gardendale AL 35071

DAVIS, CHARLENE PEEBLES, Retired Teacher; *b:* Augusta, AR; *m:* John Edward; *c:* Jim Foster; *ed:* (BSE) Elem Ed, Univ of Cntrl AR 1962; Baylor Univ, Univ of TX; *cr:* 2nd-4th Grade Augusta Schls 1953-58; Teacher Ft Smith 1958-59, Lampasas 1960-61, 1966-72, La Vega 1962-72, Augusta Elem Sch 1973-89; *ai:* Delta Kappa Gamma 1966-; Regional Ed Service Center Shift of Emphasis Project Univ of TX; Tutor Dyslexis Children Scott & White Hospital; Tutor at Risk Stus; *home:* 612 S 3rd Augusta AR 72006

DAVIS, CHARLES HAMILTON, Mathematics Teacher; *b:* Savannah, GA; *m:* Ann Richardson; *c:* Rhett, Christy; *ed:* (BS) Recreation, GA Southern Coll 1969; (MED) Admin, Valdosta St Coll 1977; Guidance & Counseling Cert; *cr:* Soc Worker St of FL 1974-77; Mental Health Cnslr Apalachee Mental Health Services 1977-79; Executive Dir Wayne Cty Skills Inc 1979-86; Teacher Mc Intosh Cty Acad 1986-; *ai:* SAT Study Group; Teacher Recruitment Comm; Homework Assistance Comm; Troubled Children Comm; Stu Support Team; Stu Cncl Adv; Team Leader Mid Sch Math Curr; Prof Assn of GA Educators 1990; Mc Intosh Clean & Beautiful Bd of Dir 1987-89; Mental Health Bd of Dir 1990; TN Valley Assn of Recyclers Pres 1985-86; Mc Intosh Cty Teacher of Yr 1989; *home:* 206 Ft King George Dr Darien GA 31305

DAVIS, CLYDE NEWTON, Earth Sciences Teacher; *b:* Paris, TX; *m:* Anna Sue Hicks; *c:* Russell W.; *ed:* (BS) Soc Sci 1969, (MS) Earth Sci 1986 East TX St Univ; *cr:* Teacher/Coach West Hardin Ind Sch Dist 1971-72, Prairieland 1972-74, Paris 1974-79, Prairieland 1979-80, Paris 1980-; *ai:* Acad, Ftbl, Track & Field Coach; Earth Sci; Univ Interscholastic League Competition; TX Classroom Teachers Assn Treas 1977-78; Assn of TX Prof Educator VP 1988-89; Teacher of Yr Crockett Mid Sch 1989-; Tree Preservation Comm Paris City Cncl 1978-80; *office:* Crockett Mid Sch 655 S Collegiate Dr Paris TX 75460

DAVIS, CYNTHIA ROSE (WESTAFER), English/Spanish Teacher; *b:* Huntington, IN; *m:* Mark Lloyd; *c:* Miriam L., Mark L. II; *ed:* (AB) Eng, IN Wesleyan Univ 1969; Eng, Calvin Coll; *cr:* 2nd Grade Teacher Sts Peter & Paul Elem 1969-70; Eng/Span Teacher Hudsonville HS 1983-; *ai:* Debate & Forensics Coach; Class Spon; *office:* Hudsonville HS 5037 32nd Ave Hudsonville MI 49426

DAVIS, DAISY CAMPBELL, Teacher; *b:* Birmingham, AL; *m:* Howard L.; *c:* Sharon Smith, Rhonda E.; *ed:* (BA) Ed, Tuskegee AL 1946; (MA) Ed/Curr, Southwest TX Univ 1973; Post Grad Ed Supervision, SWTS Univ 1978; Earth/Life Sci, St Marys Univ 1979; Gifted/Talented, Trinity Univ 1981, Career Dev Center 1981; *cr:* Teacher Dept of Defense Overseas Schls, GA, AL 1946-48, 1958; Sci Teacher Neil Armstrong 1968-75/1976-79; Rdng Supvr South San Antonio 1975-76; Teacher San Antonio Ind Sch Dist Hawthorne Elem 1979-; *ai:* Sch Advisory Comm Chapter I Evaluator; Sch Safety Patrol Adv; Gifted/Talented Teacher; Sci Fair Sch Coord; Phi Delta Kappa VP/Treas 1974- Educator of Yr 1976/1982; NEA/TX St Teachers 1974-; Top Ladies of Distinction 1985-; GSA 1958-64 Thanks Badge 1963; Alamo Area Teacher Center Policy Bd; Democratic Women of Bexar Cty Legislative Chair; TX St Teacher Political Action Comm Chair 1981-82; Neil Armstrong PTA VP; Veteran of Foreign Wars Teacher of Yr 1978; Academic Schlsp Tuskegee; Natl Sci Fnd Grant; Outstanding Leaders in Elem/Sec Ed Awd 1976; Listed/ Pictured in TX Politics Today Maxwell/Crain; *home:* 149 Village Green #204 Universal City TX 78148

DAVIS, DANIEL ROBERT, Teacher; *b:* Deerborn, MI; *m:* Mildred Leonhart; *c:* Sherise, Curtis; *ed:* (BS) Chem, E MI Univ 1960; (MA) Sci Teaching, Univ of NM 1965; *cr:* Teacher Seaholm HS 1962-64, Francis Poly Technic HS 1965-; *ai:* UTLA, AFT; NSF Summer Research & Acad Yr Grant; *office:* Francis Poly Technic HS 12431 Roscoe Blvd Sun Valley CA 91352

DAVIS, DARRELL EDWARD, II, Business Education Teacher; *b:* Dover, OH; *m:* Jane A. Doan; *c:* Bryce, Holly, Ammie, Jay; *ed:* (BS) Phys Ed/Bus, Dakota St Coll 1972; *cr:* Mgr Trainee L&K Restaurants 1972-73; Teacher/Coach Barnesville HS 1973-; *ai:* Asst Ftbl Coach; Asst Wrestling Coach; Head Girls Track Coach; Varsity B Adv; Head Chm Class of 1991; BEA/EOEA 1973-; OEA 1973-; NEA 1973-; Head Coach Barnesville HS Wrestling Class AA St Champions 1984; Coach Barnesville Wrestling Team to OVAC Over All Champions 1985; Barnesville Wrestling Team 5th Pl St 1985; *office:* Barnesville H S 910 N Shamrock Dr Barnesville OH 43713

DAVIS, DEANNA H., English Teacher & Dept Chair; *b:* Johnson City, TN; *m:* Robert M.; *c:* Crystal, Laurel; *ed:* (BS) Eng, 1968, (MA) Eng, 1974 E TN St U; *cr:* Substitute Teacher Primasens Amer Schl 1968-69; General Sci Teacher Boones Creek Mid Sch 1969-74; Eng Teacher Daniel Boone HS 1974-; *ai:* Beta Club Spon; Eng Dept Chm; Cty Curr Comm & Instructional Prof Dev comm Mem; TN Ed Assn 1969-74; NCTE 1980-; TN Cncl Teachers of Eng 1986-; Snow Memorial Baptist Church (Youth Teacher, Organist) Task Force for Educl Excl/sch-Coll Collaborative Mem; Articles Published in TN Teachers Magazine & Points of Departure; Building Teacher of Yr 1986; *office:* Daniel Boone HS Rt 16 Box 267 Gray TN 37615

DAVIS, DEBORAH LAYTON, Third Grade Teacher; *b:* Noblesville, IN; *m:* Jack I.; *c:* Amanda, Robert; *ed:* (BA) Elem Ed, Anderson Coll 1972; (MAE) Elem Ed, Ball St Univ 1975; *cr:* 3rd Grade Teacher 1972-73, 4th Grade Teacher 1973-74, 3rd Grade Teacher 1974- Lapel Sch; *ai:* ISTA 1972-; *home:* 15138 E 176th St Noblesville IN 46060

DAVIS, DONNA K., Life Science Instructor; *b:* St Louis, MO; *ed:* (BS) Bio/General Sci, Univ of MO Columbia 1965; (MS) Bio/ Physiology, S IL Univ Edwardsville 1970; *cr:* Sci Teacher Cahokia HS 1966-68; Assoc Scientist Med Research Dept Mead Johnson & Company 1968-69; Bio/Health Instr Belleville Area Coll 1980-82; Sci Teacher Cahokia HS 1970-; *ai:* AFT, NABT, NSTA; Sierra Club Treas 1974-75; Distinguished Teacher Awd W IL Univ 1988; *office:* Cahokia HS 800 Range Ln Cahokia IL 62206

DAVIS, EDNA MC COURT, Retired Elementary Teacher; *b:* Near Cambridge, OH; *m:* Roy Stewart; *c:* Roy M., Stewart L.; *ed:* Ed, Muskingum Coll & Akron Unin; *cr:* Elem Teacher Guernsey Cty 1929-35, Summit Cty 1935-38; Elem/Substitute Teacher 1938-81, Free Volnteer Aide 1981 Muskingum Cty; *ai:* Volunteer Aide Perry Sch; Adv Benjamin Franklin Stamp Club; Asst Vacation Bible Schls; Secy & News Reporter Sonora Sr Cit; Oh Ed Assn; St Teacher Retirement System OH 1981-; Musk Cty Retired Teacher Assn 1981-; AARP of OH 1985-; OH Schls Volunteer 1989-; Public Employees Inc 1981-; Plaque-30 Yrs Service To East Muskingum Local Sch Dist & Recognition & Appreciation 50 Yrs of Dedicated Service to EM Schls 1989; Plaque-OH Schls Volunteer Prgm 1989; Recognition House of Reps 118th General Assembly of OH 1989; *home:* 1015 Arch Hill Rd Zanesville OH 43701

DAVIS, EDNA THOMPSON, English Teacher; *b:* Memphis, TN; *c:* Rhonda Anita Corsey, Frank Terrell; *ed:* (BA) Ed, Le Moyne Owens 1956; (MS) Ed, Memphis St 1971; *cr:* Teacher Memphis Bd of Ed 1956-; *ai:* Majorette Spon 1980-87; Adv Natl Jr Honor Society; Textbook Comm 1988-89; Memphis Ed Assn 1958- Outstanding Woman in Ed 1987; TN Ed Assn 1958-; NCTE 1987-; Alpha Kappa Alpha 1989-; NAACP 1970-; Nom for Memphis Partners Inc Teacher/Cnslr Exemplary Awd 1989.

DAVIS, EDWARD L., Retired Phys Ed Coach; *b:* Biddeford, ME; *w:* Elizabeth N. M. Prentiss; *ed:* (BS) Phys Ed/His/Eng, Univ of ME Orono 1958; (MS) Guidance, St Univ of NY Albany 1963; WSI Red Cross Water Safety Instr; *ai:* Teacher/Coach Patten Acad 1958-59; WSI Eastern Summer Camps 1958-70; Teacher Coach Glenns Falls Mid Sch 1959-86; Glens Falls Public Schls Tackle Ftbl; Instr Eastern Bsktbl & Swimming Clinics; Foothills Cncl Sports Chm 1972-82; Northern Conference Sports Chm 1968-71; BSA Swimming Instr 1959-82; Red Cross WSI 1958-82; Coach Awds & Championships Glens Falls Var Bsktbl Teams 1964-82; *home:* 61 Coolidge Ave Glens Falls NY 12801

DAVIS, EILEEN P. (SCHIPPER), 7th Grade Language Art Teacher; *b:* Enumclaw, WA; *m:* Mitchell Evan; *ed:* (BA) Lang Art/Soc Sci, Pacific Luth Univ 1980; *cr:* Eng Teacher Marysville Jr HS 1983-89; 7th Grade Lang Art/GEO Teacher Valley View Jr HS 1989-; *ai:* Drill Team & ASB Adv; Sftbl Coach; Recognition Assembly Chairperson; Talent Show Comm; Natural Helpers; ADK 1989-; MEA (Secy, State Delegate) 1986-89; NCTE 1990; WEA & NEA 1983-; *home:* 4938 Narbeck Ave Everett WA 98203

DAVIS, FRANCES MC KIBBIN, Retired Elementary Teacher; *b:* Audubon Cty, IA; *m:* Marvin S.; *c:* Jerry A., Rex A.; *ed:* (BS) Eng/Rdng/Soc Sci, Drake Univ 1967; Continuing Ed; *cr:* Elem Teacher Audubon Cty Rural Schls 1945-53; K-2nd Grade Elem Teacher Audubon Cmmty Schls 1953-87; *ai:* Rdng & Curr Guide Comm; NEA, ISEA, AEA 1953-87; 1st Presbyn Church; *home:* Rt 2 Audubon IA 50025

DAVIS, GAIL OSBORNE, Fifth Grade Teacher; *b:* Willow Springs, MO; *m:* John A.; *c:* Kelly, Kyle Davis Van Vliet, John Jr.; *ed:* (BA) Elem Ed, Wichita St Univ 1974; *ai:* Patrol Spon 1988-; Substance Abuse 1989-; Cooperating Teacher WSU 1977-89; WFT; Victorian Society Secy 1988-; *office:* Carter Elem Sch 4640 E 15 Wichita KS 67208

DAVIS, GAIL STEWART, Business Education Teacher; *b:* Atlanta, GA; *m:* Jeffrey Lynn; *c:* Jeffrey Jr., Joshua, Jarrett; *ed:* (BS) Bus Ed, 1975, (MS) Bus Ed, 1980 GA St Univ; EDS in Bus Ed, West GA Coll 1991; *cr:* Bus Ed Teacher Marietta Jr HS 1975-79, South Cobb HS 1980-; *ai:* FBLA Co-Spon; Bus Ed Dept Chm 1982-; *office:* S Cobb Comprehensive HS 1920 Clay Rd Austell GA 30001

DAVIS, GAYE CHRISTIANSON, Home Economics Teacher; *b:* Winona, MN; *m:* Dwayne F.; *c:* Melissa, Courtney; *ed:* (BS) Home Ec Ed, Coll of St Torosa 1968; *cr:* Sr HS Home Ec Teacher/ Head of Dept Mauston Area HS 1968-78; Jr HS Home Ec Teacher Winona Jr HS Dist 861 1985-86, Gale Ettrick Trempealeau Sch Dist 1986-; *ai:* WI Home Ec Assn Mem 1987-; WI Ed Assn, NEA; *office:* GET Jr HS Grove Trempealeau WI 54661

DAVIS, GEORGIA ANN, Second Grade Teacher; *b:* Dover, DE; *m:* John W. Sr.; *c:* John W. Jr., Vincent W.; *ed:* (BS) Elem Ed, DE St Coll 1977; Cert Early Chldhd, 1984; Working on MA in Ed; Taking Courses in Math; *cr:* 2nd Grade Elem Teacher Smyrna Sch Dist 1977-; *ai:* Soc Comm; NAEYC 1989-; Clayton Fire Company Ladies Auxiliary Secy 1981-84; Delta Kappa Gamma Society Intnl 1990; *office:* Smyrna Elem Sch School Ln Smyrna DE 19977

DAVIS, HELEN ANDERSON, Sixth Grade Teacher; *b:* Center, CO; *m:* Marvin L.; *c:* Janet Spruce, Daniel, Cynthia Huffstetler; *ed:* (BA) Elem Ed/Eng 1969, (MA) Elem Ed, Adams St Coll; *cr:* 2nd Grade Teacher 1969-74, 5th Grade Teacher 1974-84, 6th Grade Teacher 1984- Sargent Elem; *ai:* Cardinel Key Club 1966-69; Phi Delta Kappa 1977-; Sargent Ed Assn (Pres 1977-78) 1969-; *office:* Sargent Elem Sch 1967 E Hwy 374 Monte Vista CO 81144

DAVIS, HESTER HAGY, French & Latin Teacher; *b:* Richlands, VA; *m:* Gerald Gordon; *c:* Elizabeth, Ellen; *ed:* (BA) Fr, Radford Univ 1960; Post Grad Work Clinch Valley Coll, Univ of VA, Radford Univ; *cr:* Fr/Eng Teacher Grundy HS 1960-64; Eng/Fr Teacher Grundy Jr HS 1965-77; Latin/Eng/Fr Teacher Grundy Sr HS 1982-85; Latin/Fr Teacher Richlands HS 1985-; *ai:* Spon Fr/Latin Club; Philosophy, Objectives, Governers Sch Candidates Comms; NEA, VEA, TEA Mem; Buchanan Cty Chamber of Commerce Bd of Dir 1977-84; *office:* Richlands HS Rt 460 Richlands VA 24641

DAVIS, INEZ, Mathematics Instructor; *b:* Johnson City, TN; *c:* Carole Thompson; *ed:* (BA) Math, Carson-Newman Coll 1967; (MS) Math, Mid TN St Univ 1981; Ec, Princeton Univ 1974; *cr:* Asst Dir of Alumni Affairs George Peabody Coll for Teacher 1975-76; Math/Lang Art Teacher Apollo Jr HS 1976-81; Math Instr TN St Univ 1981-84, NC Sch of The Arts 1984-; *ai:* Faculty Evaluations & All Sch Benefits Comm; NCCTM, MAA; *office:* NC Sch of The Arts 200 Washington St Winston-Salem NC 27117

DAVIS, ISABEL KINNETT, English Teacher; *b:* Macon, GA; *m:* Malcolm Cole; *c:* M. Cole Jr., W. Ken, Holly Davis Oxford; *ed:* (AB) Eng, 1952, (MED) Eng, 1976 Mercer Univ; *cr:* Eng Teacher Mary Persons HS 1973-76, Bay Springs HS 1976-78, Henry Cty HS 1978-80, Claxton HS 1981-83, Putnam Cty HS 1983-; *ai:* Stu Cncl Spon; Prof Assn of GA Ed, Delta Kappa Gamma; STAR Teacher 1977-78, 1986-87, 1988-89; *office:* Putnam Cty HS 140 Sparta Hwy Eatonton GA 31024

DAVIS, JAMES E., Science Department Chair; *b:* Orange, TX; *m:* Anna K. De Ornellas; *c:* Blake, Kristin, Michael, Paul, Timothy; *ed:* (AA) Health/Phys Ed, Pearl River Coll 1966; (BSE) Health/Phys Ed, Delta St Univ 1969; (MSE) Bio, William Carey Coll; Pre-Doctrate Stud Delta St Univ & Univ of MS; *cr:* Instr Copial Lincoln Comm Coll 1979-86; Teacher/Chm Adams Cty Chrstn Sch 1979-86; Instr Hinds Comm Coll 1986-; Teacher/Chm Hillcrest Chrstn Sch 1986-; *ai:* Ftbl, Bsbl, Bsktbl Coach; Stu Cncl, Beta Club, NHS Adv; Class Spon; MS Private Sch Assn 1979-; NSTA 1973-; Ftbl Schlsp; Deans List Stars Teacher; St Teacher of Yr; Local Teacher of Yr; *office:* Hillcrest Chrstn Sch 4060 S Siwell Rd Jackson MS 39212

DAVIS, JANE SCHNEIDER, 7th Grade Mathematics Teacher; *b:* Winchester, VA; *c:* Lawrence, Anne Nelson, Jeffery, Kim; *ed:* (BS) Chem, Madison Coll 1951; (MAED) Curr/Instruction, VPI & SU 1988; *cr:* 5th Grade Teacher Rappahannock Cty Elem 1964-65; 7th Grade Math Teacher Frederick Cty Mid Sch 1965-; *ai:* Young Historians Club Spon; Frederick Cty Ed Assn 1965-; VA Ed Assn 1970-; NEA 1976-; *office:* Frederick Cty Mid Sch 441 Linden Dr Winchester VA 22601

DAVIS, JANICE KAY, 6th Grade Teacher; *b:* Bentonville, AR; *m:* Robert Wayne; *c:* Tom, Amy; *ed:* (BA) Eng, 1972, Elem Credential, 1973 CA St Chico; Quest Trng Drug Ed; Heres Looking At You 2000 Drug Ed; *cr:* 6th Grade Teacher Rosedale & Parkview Elem 1975-; *ai:* Sunday Sch Teacher; Little League Girls Sftbl Coach; Mem Drug & Alcohol Task Force; *office:* Rosedale Elem Sch 100 Oak Chico CA 95928

DAVIS, JEANNE MARIE (BALL), 8th Grade Social Stud Teacher; *b:* Scranton, PA; *m:* Lester; *c:* Jeffrey, Lester Jr.; *ed:* (BS) Elem Ed, West Chester St Teachers Coll 1959; *cr:* 4th Grade Teacher Lake Consolidated Sch 1959-62; 5th Grade Teacher Ocean Springs Elem Sch 1962-63; Media Center Coord Tinker Elem Sch 1975-77; 7th Grade Teacher Western Wayne Jr HS 1978-82; 8th Grade Teacher Lake Mid Sch 1982-; *ai:* Girls Bsktbl Coach 1959-62; PTA 1959-63, 1969-; NEA, PSEA 1978-; Maplewood United Meth Church (Communion Steward 1978-, Pastor 1978-, Parish Relations Chm 1978-, Secy-Treas 1978-, Trustee 1987-, Admin Bd Secy 1989-); *home:* RD 2 Box 89 Lake Ariel PA 18436

DAVIS, JENNIFER WEBSTER, High School English Teacher; *b:* Knoxville, TN; *ed:* (BS) Eng, Cumberland Coll 1970; *cr:* Eng Teacher Karns HS 1970-77; Boutique Owner Jen Davis Hays 1978-79; Buyer Millers 1980-81; English Teacher Karns HS 1982-; *ai:* Local KCEA; *office:* Karns HS Byington Solway Rd Knoxville TN 37931

DAVIS, JOANNE QUETSCHKE, Kindergarten Teacher; *b:* Toledo, OH; *c:* Sue A.; *ed:* (BED) Ed, 1960, (MED) Early Chldhd, 1973 Univ of Toledo; Career Specialist; *cr:* Kndgtn Teacher Navarre Sch 1960-; *ai:* Navarre Sch Career Specialist; Eng Textbook Study & Kndgtn Rdng Assessment Comm; PTA Treas 1987-88; *office:* Navarre Sch 410 Navarre Ave Toledo OH 43605

DAVIS, JOHN LEO, Sixth Grade Science Teacher; *b:* Binghamton, NY; *m:* Priscilla Ann Watson; *ed:* (AAS) General Bus, Corning Comm Coll 1964; (BS) Bus Ed, Ball St Univ 1968; (MA) General/Experimental Psych/Cmmty Services Counseling, 1970, Elem Conversion, 1974 Ball St Univ; *cr:* Teacher Parker City Elem Sch 1969-83; Instr Ball St Univ 1989; Teacher Monroe Cntrl Elem Sch 1983-; *ai:* All-Sch Sci Fair Coord; NSTA 1980-; Hoosier Assn of Sci Teachers Incorporated Bd of Dir 1980-; Articles Published; *office:* Monroe Cntrl Elem Sch RR 1 Box 17B Parker City IN 47368

DAVIS, JUANITA (RHODES), History Teacher; *b:* Deport, TX; *m:* James A.; *c:* Jay, Dickie; *ed:* (BA) Eng/Hist, Univ of TX at Arlington 1970; *cr:* History Teacher Prairiland CISD 1974-; *ai:* UIL Tutor; ATPE 1976-; Nominee TX Hist Teacher of the Year 1989 George Washington Stell Chpter Daughters of Republic of TX; *office:* Prairiland CISD Box 218 Deport TX 75435

DAVIS, JUANITA BERNARD, Third Grade Teacher; *b:* Bryn Mawr, OH; *m:* Edsel; *c:* Cindy Davis Oleynik, Mark Duane, Diane Davis Haynes, Natasha; *ed:* (BA) Ed, Wilmington Coll 1969; *cr:* 1st Grade Teacher Wilmington City Schls 1954-55; 2nd Grade Teacher 1957-59, 2nd Grade Teacher 1966-67, 3rd G De Teacher 1967-74 & 1975- Sabina Elem; *ai:* Comm for Text Book Selection & Curr Dev; Brownie & Girl Scout Leader 1964-66; PTO Secy 1965; Womens Society of Christian Service (Pres 1962/Mem 1956-); Richland Methodist Church 1945-; *home:* 5084 Peele Rd Sabina OH 45169

DAVIS, JUDY CREWS, Fifth Grade Teacher; *b:* Harmony, NC; *m:* Raymond R.; *c:* Chris, Laura; *ed:* (BA) Elem Ed, Guilford Coll 1972; (MA) Elem Ed/Math Concentration, Appalachian St Univ 1981; *cr:* Teacher Asst South Park Sch 1972-73; 4th/5th Grade Teacher West Yadkin Sch 1973-75, Courtney Sch 1977-78; 5th Grade Teacher West Yadkin Sch 1978-; Effective Teacher Trng Instr Surry Comm Coll 1985-; *ai:* Gamma Nu Schlsp Comm Chm; Drug-Free Week Co-Chairperson; NEA 1977-; NC Assn of Educators (Pres 1983-84) 1977-, Teacher of Yr 1984; Alpha Delta Kappa Historian 1985-; Starmount Band Boosters 1989-; *office:* W Yadkin Sch Rt 3 Box A Hamptonville NC 27020

DAVIS, KATHRYN WALKER, Third Grade Teacher; *b:* Palo Alto, CA; *m:* Joseph C.; *c:* Michael, Elena; *ed:* (BS) Child Dev, CA Poly San Luis Obispo 1975; Teaching Credential CA St Univ Chico 1980; *cr:* 3rd/4th Grade Teacher Pioneer Elem 1980-; *ai:* NSTA, NCTM; Venture Club 1981-85; *office:* Pioneer Elem Sch 175 N Mill Creek Rd Quincy CA 95971

DAVIS, KATHY MC WATERS, Chemistry & Phys Sci Teacher; *b:* New Orleans, LA; *m:* William Louis; *c:* Charles, Jean; *ed:* (BS) Voc Home Ec Ed, 1969, (MS) Voc Home Ec Ed, 1970 LSU; *cr:* Sci Teacher False River Acad 1976-78, Livonia HS 1978-80; Phy Sci/Enviromental Sci Teacher St James HS 1980-82; Earth Sci Teacher St Amant Elem 1982-88; Chem/Phys Sci Teacher St Amant HS 1988-; *ai:* Sci Club Spon; Alpha Delta Kappa Pres 1988-; Delta Kappa Gamma 1986-; NSTA 1977-; LSTA (St Membership Chairperson 1990-, HS Rep 1988-); NEA, LEA, LESTA, NESTA; Academic Booster Club Chem Grant 1990; *office:* St Amant HS 12035 Hwy 431 Saint Amant LA 70774

DAVIS, KEITH, Social Studies Teacher; *b:* Scranton, PA; *m:* Marion Jurnack; *c:* Paul, Gregory; *ed:* (BS) Ed/Soc, Stud Univ of Scranton 1961; Grad Work Cornell Univ, SUNY Oswego; *cr:* Soc Stud Teacher Weedsport Jr/Sr HS 1962-; *ai:* Sr Class Adv; Jr Var & Var Ftbl Coach; Hugh O Brian Leadership Awd Coord; Weedsport Teachers Assn Contract Negotiations Team; Yrbk Dedication; St Nicholas Orthodox Church (VP, Asst Treas) 1965-; *office:* Weedsport Jr/Sr HS E Brutus St Weedsport NY 13166

DAVIS, KEITH JERRY, Sixth Grade Teacher; *b:* Detroit, MI; *m:* Carol Ann Oleksiak; *c:* Jeffrey, Gregory, Kevin, Abigail; *ed:* (BS) Sci, E MI Univ 1968; *cr:* 5th Grade Teacher 1968-74, 6th Grade Teacher 1975- Lowrey Sch; *ai:* Stu Cncl Adv; Safety Patrol Dir; Veterans Day Ceremony Chm; Little League Coach; Trip Coord; MI Fed of Teachers Mem 1968-; Dearborn Fed of Teachers Building Rep 1986-; Museum of Sci & Industry Mem 1984-; Lowrey PTA VP 1982-84; Dearborn PTA Mem 1968-, Distinguished Service Awd 1982; Grant from Saudia Arabia to Promote Trip for 5th & 6th Grade Stus; *office:* Lowrey Sch 6601 Jonathon Dearborn MI 48126

DAVIS, LARRY ANDREW, 7th Grade English/His Teacher; *b:* Lawrenceburg, TN; *m:* Sharon Annette White; *c:* Shannon R., Nicholas T.; *ed:* Assoc Degree His, Columbia St Coll 1972; (BS) His/Phys Ed/Elem Ed, Mid TN St Univ 1975; (MED) Elem Admin/Supervision, Univ of N AL 1980; Trng in Teaching Effectively Using TN Instructional Model; *cr:* Factory Worker Murray OH Manufacturing Co 1972-73; Asst Eng Monsanto Chemical Co 1974; Teacher/Coach Lawrence Cty Bd of Ed 1975-; *ai:* Knowledge Bowl, 7th-8th Grade Girls Bsktbl, Loretto HS Asst Bsbl Coach; Supts Advisory Bd Chairperson Sch Staff & Admin Comm; LCEA, TEA, NEA; *home:* 602 2nd Ave S Loretto TN 38469

DAVIS, LARRY RAY, Aerospace Sci Instr USAF JROTC; *b:* Cardwell, MO; *m:* Beverly Lee Nelson; *c:* Larry S., Nelson R.; *ed:* (BS) Bus Personnel Management, Univ of MO 1965; (MS) Government, 1973, (MA) Poly Sci, 1974 W KY Univ; USAF Command & Staff Coll; Industrial Coll of Armed Forces; *cr:* F-4 Pilot Camranh Bay Vietnam 1969-70; Air Liaison Officer 101st Air Mobile Division 1972-74; F-4 Instr Pilot Cntrl Instr Sch 1977-79; Cntry Mgr Egypt USAF Intnl Prgm Division 1979-83; Cntry Mgr-El Salvador Secy of Defense Security Assistance Agency 1983-86; Aerospace Sci Instr John Foster Dulles HS 1986-; *ai:* NHS Spon; Air Force Assn Bd of Dir 1965-; Rotary Bd of Dir 1987-; VFW Officer 1986-; Civil Air Patrol Operations Officer 1988-; Air Force JROTC Instr of Yr 1987-88; Distinguished Flying Cross; Air Medal with 8 Oak Leaf Clusters; Secy of Defense Superior Service Medal; Combat Readiness Ribbon; Purple Heart; Humanitarian Service Medal; Natl Defense Service Medal; Meritorious Service Medal; Vietnam Service Medal; *home:* 1755 Creekside Dr Sugar Land TX 77478

DAVIS, LAURA WHITE, Music Specialist; *b:* Andrews, SC; *m:* Bennie J.; *c:* Ellen Stalvey, Deborah Healey, James; *ed:* (BAE) Music Ed, Univ of N FL 1978; Orff Cert; *cr:* Dir of Music/ Organist Arlington Presbyn Church 1974-79; Dir of Music Coral Isles Church 1979-89; Music Specialist Key Largo Sch 1979-; *ai:* Key Largo Childrens Chorus; Alpha Delta Kappa 1986-; Amer Guild of Organists 1970-89; FL Elem Music Educators 1979-; FL Vocal Assn 1989-; Whos Who Among Stus 1979; Teacher of Yr Key Largo Sch 1982, 1985; *office:* Key Largo Sch Rt 1 Box 195 Key Largo FL 33037

DAVIS, LEE ALLEN, Math Teacher; *b:* Brentwood, TN; *c:* Ray, Traci; *ed:* (BS) Elem Ed/Eng, Howard Pay Univ 1966; Scndry Ed/Math, 1975, (MED) Ed/Counseling Cert, 1978 Sul Ross; *cr:* Elem Teacher Brownwood ISD 1966-68; Jr HS Math Teacher Balmorhea ISD 1968-74, Pecos ISD 1974-75; Mid Sch Math Teacher Fort Stockton ISD 1975-; *ai:* Univ Intersholastic League Dir; Delta Kappa Gamma Treas 1987-88; West TX Frontier Math Cncl 1987-; TX St Teachers Assn 1966-; *home:* 1501 N Colpitts Fort Stockton TX 79735

DAVIS, LINDA HYAMS, First Grade Teacher; *b:* Hopkinsville, KY; *c:* Benjamin F., Felicia R.; *ed:* (BS) Elem Ed, 1974, (MA) Elem Ed, 1976 Austin Peay St Univ; *cr:* 1st Grade Teacher Elkton Elem 1974-88, North Todd Elem 1988-; *ai:* Todd Cty Ed Assn (Secy 1978-79, 1988-, Treas 1984-85); Delta Kappa Gamma Society Personal Growth Chm 1988-; *office:* North Todd Elem Sch 7300 Greenville Rd Elkton KY 42220

DAVIS, LINDA KAY, Accounting/Eng/Yrbk Teacher; *b:* Saginaw, MI; *m:* Glenn S.; *c:* Meghan L.; *ed:* (AA) Liberal Art, Delta Coll 1974; (BS) Voc Ed/Bus, Univ of MI Flint 1977; (MBA) Bus, Saginaw Valley St Univ 1984; *cr:* Voc Coord Birch Run, Bridgeport, Frankenmuth Schls 1977-79; Classroom Teacher Birch Run HS 1974-; *ai:* Yrbk Adv; NEA, MI Ed Assn 1979; Birch Run Ed Assn (Treas 1980-), 1979; Altrusa Club of Saginaw (Pres 1985-87), Mem 1978-; Dist 5 Altrusa Intnl Prgm Coord 1988-; *office:* Birch Run HS 12450 Church St Birch Run MI 48415

DAVIS, LINDA POWELL, Algebra I Teacher; *b:* Mobile, AL; *m:* James A.; *ed:* (BS) Scndry Math Ed, 1982, (MED) Scndry Math Ed, 1988 Univ of S AL; *cr:* Teacher Mary G Montgomery HS 1983-; *ai:* Algebra I Team Spon; Asst Yrbk Adv; NCTM, Kappa Delta Pi 1983-; Mobile Cty Educators Assn 1988-; *office:* Mary G Montgomery HS 4275 Snow Rd Semmes AL 36575

DAVIS, LOIS ANN BROUSE, 2nd Grade Teacher; *b:* Media, IL; *m:* Frank; *c:* Amy Fairfield, Mary Ann Whiteman; *ed:* (BA) Elem Ed, Western IL Univ 1972; *cr:* 3rd Grade Teacher 1972-76; 2nd Grade Teacher 1976- Southern Unit #120; *home:* Box 779 Media IL 61460

DAVIS, LOWELL DALE, Teacher; *b:* Elkhurst, WV; *m:* Constance Lockhart; *c:* Christopher; *ed:* (BS) Phys Ed, WV Inst of Technology 1962; (MA) Scndry Ed, WV Univ; Grad Stud; *cr:* Teacher 1962-72, Vice Prin 1972-73, Prin 1973-74, Teacher 1974- Clay Cty HS; *ai:* Boys Bsktbl Head Coach; Athletic Dir; Fellowship of Chrstn Athletes Adv; WV Ed Assn, NEA 1962-; Fairview Baptist Temple Deacon 1974-.

DAVIS, LYNN COMSTOCK, French Teacher; *b:* Lakewood, NJ; *m:* William H. Jr.; *c:* William III, Benjamin, Jessica, Jeremy, Andrew, Daniel; *ed:* (BA) Fr, Cntrl Coll 1971; (MS) Foreign Lang/Ed, St Univ of NY Buffalo 1975; Certificate Cours de Civilisation, Francaise Sorbonne Paris *cr:* Fr Teacher Toms River HS 1971-73, S Park Prep 1973-; *ai:* Western NY Foreign Lang Teachers Assn, NY St Foreign Lang Teachers Assn 1975-; AATF 1971-80; *home:* 5335 E River Rd Grand Island NY 14202

DAVIS, MARGARET RIDALL, Teacher of Gifted; *b:* Elmira, NY; *ed:* (BS) Ed, Syracuse Univ 1959; (MS) Ed, Elmira Coll 1968; Insts on Gifted Ed; *cr:* 2nd Grade Teacher 1959-61, 4th Grade Teacher 1961-66 Sch 7; 6th Grade Teacher 1966-, K-6th Grade Teacher of Gifted 1978- Horseheads Cntrl Sch Dist; *ai:* Dist Curr Comm; AGATE-NY St; Delta Kappa Gamma; NSTA; Natl Assn for Gifted Children; SPCA Bd of Dirs 1986-87, Teacher of Yr 1989; Wkshps Conducted & Presentations Given on Gifted Children & Appropriate Programming; Dist In Service Courses; *office:* Horseheads Cntrl Sch Dist Sing Sing Rd Horseheads NY 14845

DAVIS, MARILYN JEAN, Fourth/Fifth Grade Teacher; *b:* Eugene, OR; *c:* Pamela K., Michael S.; *ed:* (BA) Elem Ed, Boise St Univ 1978; *cr:* 4th Grade Teacher 1987-88, 4th/5th Grade Teacher 1988- Joplin Elem; *home:* 3411 Apple Blossom Ln Boise ID 83705

DAVIS, MARTHA DEMETER, Teaching Assistant Principal; *b:* Uniontown, PA; *c:* Gary, Elaine J.; *ed:* (BSED) Elem Ed, CA Univ of PA 1970; (MAED) Rdng Specialist, WV Univ 1975; Grad Stud Loyola Coll; *cr:* Teacher Connellsville Area Sch Dist 1970-74; Teacher 1974-89, Teaching Asst Prin 1989- Harford Cty Bd of Ed; *ai:* MD ASCD, Natl Assn of Elem Sch Prin 1989-; St of MD Intnl Rdng Cncl 1985-; Alpha Delta Kappa 1988-.

DAVIS, MARY LESLIE (SARVER), 3rd Grade Teacher; *b:* Louisville, KY; *m:* Leon; *c:* Margaret L., Clarissa L.; *ed:* (BA) Elem Ed, Campbellsville Coll 1971; (MS) Elem Ed, 1979, (Rank I) Elem Ed, 1985 W KY Univ; Grad Stud; *cr:* 1st Grade Teacher 1971-75, Rdng Teacher 1975-76, 3rd Grade Teacher 1976-89 Clarkson Elem; 3rd Grade Teacher H W Wikey 1989-; *ai:* Cheerleading Spon; Building Comm; Textbook Comm; Participant in Outdoor Theatre Production 1987-89; Article & Pictures Published 1989.

DAVIS, MARY SARTOR, Retired; *b:* Roberts, MS; *w:* Clarence Calhoun (dec); *c:* Gary, Bettie R.; *ed:* (BS) Elem Ed, Univ of Southern MS 1974; *cr:* Clerk/Steno Brookley Field 1944-45; 8th Grade Eng/Amer His/Typing/Bus Teacher Clara HS 1940-42; Salesperson/Bookkeeper Lott Furniture Co 1964-66; Clerk/cashier Rainer Drugs 1966-67; 3rd Grade Teacher Clarke Acad 1970-86; *ai:* Womens Auxiliary Mem 1970-86; Teacher of Week; Pachuta Progressive Womens Club Reporter 1974- Outstanding Dist Report Ribbons; Pachuta Meth Church Pianist & Communion Steward; Pachuta Garden Club Mem 1986-; United Meth Women Mem 1986-; Pachuta Lib Commission Mem; Village Election Commission Mem; Pachuta Bicentennial; Pachuta Meth Church Nominating Comm Mem; *home:* Rt 1 Box 1 Pachuta MS 39347

DAVIS, MELODY TJOSSEM, Second Grade Teacher; *b:* Marshalltown, IA; *m:* Durwood D.; *c:* Leann Kay Smith, Lana Sue; *ed:* (BS) Ed, Drake Univ 1965; 2 Yr Pre-Professional Certificate Simpson Coll; *cr:* Kndgtn Teacher 1957-60/1967-72, 2nd Grade Teacher 1960-66/1984-, Kndgtn Teacher 1967-72, 1st Grade Teacher 1972-84 South Toma Cty Comm; *ai:* Rdng Comm; Critical Skills Curr Comm; Phase III Steering Comm; ISEA Bldg Rep 1957; NEA 1957-; IRA; ICTM 1988; Order of Eastern Star 1959-; PEA Recording Secy 1988-; Church Choir Church Pianist 1978-88; Charter Mem Jaycee Cites 1960-61; *home:* 1203 S Broadway Toledo IA 52342

DAVIS, MONICA DENISE, Phys Ed/Phys Sci Teacher; *b:* Anderson, SC; *ed:* (BS) Phys Ed, Erskine Coll 1988; *cr:* Phys Ed/ Phys Sci Teacher Dixie HS 1988-; *ai:* Var Vlybl & Bsktbl, Jr Var Vlybl & Sci Team Coach; SC CAWS, SCBA 1988-; Region I-A Vlybl Coach of Yr; *office:* Dixie HS PO Box 158 Due West SC 29639

DAVIS, MORRIS ANTHONY, JR., Teacher/Head Coach; *b:* New Orleans, LA; *m:* Charisse Payne; *c:* Marisa A., Lindsey A.; *ed:* (BS) Health/Phys Ed, Xavier Univ 1979; US Army Transportation Sch; Working Towards Masters Scndry Sch Prin, Xavier Univ; *cr:* Sergeant US Army Reserve 1986-; Camp Dir New Orleans Recreation Dept 1987-89; Teacher/Coach Eleanor Mc Main Magnet Sr HS 1987-; *ai:* Head Mens Bsktbl & Track Coach; Jr Class of 1991 Spon; NFICA, LABC; Phi Beta Sigma Financial Secy 1984-89; Prince Hall Mason; City of New Orleans Service Awds 1981; Outstanding Young Men of America; *office:* Mc Main Magnet Sch 5712 S Claiborne Ave New Orleans LA 70125

DAVIS, NANCY HALLBERG, Mathematics Teacher; *b:* Valparaiso, IN; *m:* Bruce; *c:* Bruce, Brian, Dan; *ed:* (BS) Elem Ed, 1961, (MS) Ed, 1979 Valparaiso Univ; *cr:* 2nd Grade Teacher South Sch 1961-62; 1st Grade Teacher Foreman Sch 1962-63; 3rd Grade Teacher Quantico Sch 1963; 2nd Grade Teacher N Terrace

Sch 1963-65; 1st Grade Teacher Kouts Elem 1965-66; 2nd Grade Teacher Tarawa Terrace Sch 1966-67; 6th Grade Math Teacher Portage Schls 1977-; *ai:* 6th Grade Academic Math Team Spon 1980-; *office:* Willowcreek Mid Sch 5962 Central Ave Portage IN 46368

DAVIS, NANCY SURRATT, Mathematics Teacher; *b:* Savannah, GA; *m:* Darrell M.; *ed:* (BS) Math, MS Coll 1973; (MED) Ed/Math, MS St Univ 1980; *cr:* Math Teacher Clinton Jr HS 1973-81, Morton Attendance Center 1981-82, Madison Ridgeland Acad 1982-84, Wingfield HS 1984-; *ai:* Academic Coach; Class Spon; NCTM; *office:* Wingfield HS 1985 Scanlon Dr Jackson MS 39204

DAVIS, NORMAN ALAN, 7th Grade Team Leader; *b:* Birmingham, AL; *m:* Julia Wyatt; *c:* Robert, Steven; *ed:* (BA) Music Ed, 1967, (MS) Admin Higher Ed, 1971 Univ AL; Misc Coursework Univ S MS, Nova Univ; *cr:* Band Dir Demopolis HS 1967-69; Cnslr Dothan AL City Schls 1970-71; Teacher Horace O Bryant Mid Sch 1972-; *ai:* KTV Stu Produced TV Show; Horace O Bryant Mid Sch Teacher of Yr 1987-88; *office:* Horace O Bryant Mid Sch 1105 Leon St Key West FL 33040

DAVIS, PATRICIA ANN, Phys Ed Coach/Health Dept Chm; *b:* San Antonio, TX; *ed:* (BS) Health/Phys Ed/Recreation, TX Womans Univ 1972; EMT Paramedic; *cr:* Ferris HS 1972-75; Teacher/Coach/Dept Chairperson Hutcheson Jr HS 1975-; *ai:* Coached Vlybl, Cross Cntry, Track, Bsktbl; Health Textbook Comm Chm; Health Curr Comm; Sch In-Service Meetings Leader; Lead 1st Aid Sessions for Local & St Health, Phys Ed, Recreation Conventions Univ of TX Arlington; Arlington Coaches Assn 1988-; Amer Red Cross Volunteer Instr 1982-; Teacher of Yr 1988-89; Developed & Wrote New Prgm for Hutchesons Phys Ed Dept; *office:* Hutcheson Jr HS 2101 Browning Dr Arlington TX 76010

DAVIS, PATRICIA BRITTON, Sixth Grade Teacher/Coord; *b:* Chillicothe, OH; *m:* James R.; *c:* Carla J. Ross, Mark R., Myra J. Cryder, Curt P., Beth A. Carter, Jan B.; *ed:* (BS) Elem Ed, OH Univ 1972; (MS) Ed, Mt St Joseph 1985; *cr:* Teacher Union Scioto Schls 1967-; *ai:* 4-H Adv 1973-; *office:* Union Scioto Sch 1432 Egypt Pike Chillicothe OH 45601

DAVIS, PEGGY RUTH, Physical Education Teacher; *b:* Lubbock, TX; *ed:* (BS) Phys Ed, Bio, Hardin-Simmons Univ 1967; Grad Work, Sam Houston St Univ; *cr:* Teacher/Coach Petersburg Ind Sch Dist 1965, Lubbock Ind Sch Dist 1971-81, Hobbs Ind Sch Dist 1981-83, Lubbock Ind Sch Dist 1983-; *ai:* 10th-12th HS Girls Cross Cntry & Track Coach; Lubbock Fed of Teachers; Lubbock Ed Assn Building Rep 1980; TX Assn of Health, Physical Ed, Recreation & Dance Registration Comm: ST Convention 1990; TX HS Girls Coaches Assn Chaperone All Star Track Team 1988; Outstanding Young Women of America 1979; *office:* Lubbock HS 2004 19th St Lubbock TX 79401

DAVIS, PHYLLIS MURDOCK, English Teacher; *b:* Tusculum, TN; *m:* Ronald L.; *ed:* (BS) Eng/His, E TN St Univ 1971; (MAED) Ed, Tusculum Coll 1989; *cr:* Eng Teacher Greeneville Mid Sch 1971-84, Greeneville HS 1984-; *ai:* Sr Class Spon; Dr Hal C Henard Schlsp & Greeneville City Sch System Calendar Comm Mem; Greeneville Ed Assn, TN Ed Assn 1971-; E TN Ed Assn 1971-80, 1985-; NEA 1975-; Delta Kappa Gamma Recording Secy 1989-; *office:* Greeneville HS Tusculum Blvd Greeneville TN 37743

DAVIS, RACHAEL BRANNON, Science Teacher; *b:* Mobile, AL; *m:* Hezekiah Jr.; *c:* Johnny Brannon, Sherrica Denise, Ashley Renee; *ed:* (BS) Bus Admin/Bio, Mobile Coll 1973; Univ of South AL; *cr:* Teacher Mobile Bus Coll, Most Pure Heart of Mary Sch, Mobile Co Sch Bd Semmes Mid Sch; *ai:* Astrobiophysical Sci Club Spon; MCEA; AEA; NEA; *home:* 557 Azalea Rd #117 Mobile AL 36609

DAVIS, RACHEL BROWN, English Department Chair; *b:* Washington, DC; *m:* Phillip James; *c:* Rebecca, Amanda; *ed:* (BA) Eng/Dramatic Arts, Lynchburg Coll 1971; Eng/Ed, Univ of VA & Cath Univ & James Madison Univ & Lynchburg Coll; *cr:* Eng Teacher W T Woodson HS 1971-80; Eng Dept Chairperson Seven Hills Sch 1987-; *ai:* Admissions Comm 1987-; Academic Policies 1988-; Cnslr Bd Adv 1990; 8th Grade Class Spon; NCTE, VAIS 1987-; PEO VP 1971-; Bedford Hills Elem PTA Pres 1990; *office:* Seven Hills Sch 2001 Rivermont Ave Lynchburg VA 24503

DAVIS, ROBERT JOSEPH, Biology Instructor; *b:* North Adams, MA; *m:* Patricia M. Murphy; *c:* Brandon; *ed:* (BA) Bio, N Adams St Coll 1969; (MS) Bio, S CT St Univ 1975; *cr:* Bio Instr Trumbull HS 1969-; *ai:* Adv Trumbull HS Outdoors Club & Environmental Newspaper Magazine; Trumbull Ed Assn 1969-; *office:* Trumbull HS 72 Strobel Rd Trumbull CT 06611

DAVIS, ROBERTA, 7th Grade Science Teacher; *b:* Alliance, OH; *ed:* (BA) Elem Ed, Mt Union Coll 1981; *cr:* Sci Teacher Olentangy Local Schls 1982-85, Worthington City Schls 1985-; *ai:* Vlybl Coach; NSTA; *office:* Mc Cord Mid Sch 1500 Hard Rd Worthington OH 43235

DAVIS, ROBERTA LEE (COWLING), Second Grade Teacher; *b:* Wabash County, IL; *m:* Jimmie Martin; *c:* Ginger R. Links, Martin D., Derry T.; *ed:* (BA) Elem Ed, Eureka Coll 1959; (BA) Elem Ed, Western IL Univ; *cr:* 2nd Grade Teacher Jefferson Park Sch 1957-58; 1st Grade Teacher Streator Sch Dist 45 1961, Abingdon Grade Sch 1962; 2nd Grade Teacher Avon Elem Sch 1964-; *ai:* IL Ed Assn 1967-69; Literacy Volunteers of Amer Inc 1986-; *home:* 500 W Latimer Abingdon IL 61410

DAVIS, RUBY MAE (MOUNT), Fifth Grade Teacher; *b:* Kensett, AR; *m:* John Willie; *c:* Arthur Stearns II; *ed:* (BA) Elem Ed, AR Baptist Coll 1964; (MS) Elem Ed, Harding Univ 1975; Cmptrs in Ed; *cr:* Teacher Castelar, Saratoga, Lothrop & Jefferson Elem Schls 1964-; *office:* Jefferson Elem Sch 4065 Vinton St Omaha NE 68105

DAVIS, SANDRA BELL, Math & Social Studies Teacher; *b:* Martin, TN; *m:* Jerry D.; *c:* Leigh A., John A.; *ed:* (BS) Health/Phys Ed/His, Univ of TN Martin 1963; *cr:* Girls Phys Ed Instr Dyersburg HS 1963-64; Girls Phys Ed/Amer His Teacher Haywood Cty HS 1964-65; Girls Phys Ed/His Teacher Obion Cty Cntrl HS 1965-69; Math/Soc Stud Teacher Union City Mid Sch 1984-; *ai:* Chrldr Spon; *office:* Union City Mid Sch 1111 High School Dr Union City TN 38261

DAVIS, SARA ROGERS, Elementary Music Teacher; *b:* Columbia, SC; *m:* Ricky Kyle; *c:* Benjamin, Patrick; *ed:* (BS) Early Chldhd Ed, W Carolina Univ 1977; Working Towards BS Music Ed; *cr:* 1st Grade Teacher Stecoah Sch 1977-88; Music Teacher Robbinsville Elem & Stecoah Elem 1988-; *ai:* NCAE 1977-; *home:* Rt 2 Box 123-A Robbinsville NC 28771

DAVIS, SHELVA JONES, History Teacher; *b:* Snow Hill, NC; *m:* Melvin; *ed:* (BA) His, 1975, (MA) His, 1981 Kean Coll; *cr:* Soc Stud Teacher Frank H Morrell HS 1976-; *ai:* Adv African-Amer His Club; Comm Mem NHS; Church Lectures & Public Speaking; Historical Society 1975-79; Bd Christian Ed Dir Cultural Affairs 1985-; Irvington Ed Assn Rep 1978-79; *home:* 358 Jackson Ave Scotch Plains NJ 07076

DAVIS, SHERRON PRICE, Second Grade Teacher; *b:* Anniston, AL; *m:* Gregory Alfred; *ed:* (BS) Elem Ed, 1972, (MS) Elem Ed, 1977 Jacksonville St Univ; *cr:* 5th Grade Teacher Fort Mc Clellan Elem Sch 1972-77; 2nd Grade Teacher Centre Elem Sch 1977-; *ai:* Adopt a Sch Comm; AEA Legislative Contact Team; Cherokee Cty Ed Assn (VP, Secy, Treas) 1977-; AL Ed Assn, NEA 1973-; Alpha Delta Kappa (Pres, VP, Secy) 1979-; Beta Sigma Phi (Pres, VP, Secy, Treas) 1973-77, Calhoun Cty Girl of Yr Awd 1977; Centre Elem Sch PTO; Cntrl Presbyn Church Mem; *office:* Centre Elem Sch 725 E Main St Centre AL 35960

DAVIS, SHERRY KIDD, 7th/8th Grade Lang Art Teacher; *b:* Hampton, VA; *m:* Caldwell; *c:* April, Kris; *ed:* (BS) Home Ec Ed, Univ of TN Martin 1974; Endorsement, Lambuth Coll 1983; (MED) Admin & Supervision, Trevecca Nazarene Coll 1989; *cr:* 6th Grade Teacher Trinity Chrstn Sch 1974-75; Nutrition Consultant Head Start 1976-79; 6th Grade Teacher 1981-83, Jr/Sr HS Teacher 1983- Frank Hughes Sch; *ai:* Yrbk Spon 1985-89; TEA, NEA 1987-; *office:* Frank Hughes Sch PO Box A Clifton TN 38425

DAVIS, SPRIGG DIX, Biology Teacher; *b:* Provo, UT; *m:* Mary Lynn Randall; *c:* Mitchell A., Michael L., Lora L., Suzanne E., Kristen L., Randall S., Gregory R.; *ed:* (BS) Ag Ed, Univ of CA Davis 1956; (MA) Bio, CA St Humboldt 1966; *cr:* Ag Teacher Mt Whitney HS 1958-61; Bio Teacher Poway HS 1961-; *ai:* Sci Club Adv; Needy Children Fund Spon; Substance Abuse Comm Mem; PFT Mem; BSA (Scout Master 1971-73, Webelos Leader 1988-); Latter Day Saints Church Bishop 1983-87; Teacher of Yr 1967, 1968; Natl Sci Fnd Grants 1963-66, 1971, 1984; Poway Teachers Assn Pres 1966-67; *home:* 3020 Bernardo Ave Escondido CA 92025

DAVIS, STANLEY JOHN, English Teacher; *b:* Portland, OR; *m:* Theresa Kuvara; *c:* Kassandra, Krishna, Jody, ChriS; *ed:* (BA) Eng, Eastern WA Univ 1965; (Ed Cert) Gonzaga Teachers Prgm, 1966, (MA) Curr & Supervision, 1990 Gonzaga Univ; Neurolinguistic Programming; *cr:* Teacher Spec Ed Otis Orchards Elem 1967-69, East Valley Jr HS 1970-72; Eng/Soc Stud Teacher East Valley Mid Sch 1972-; *ai:* Head Ftbl Coach Mid Sch; Head Girls Bsktbl; Coach Mid Sch; Coord Peer Helpers EUMS; NEA 1967-; NVEA 1974 (Pres 1970, VP 1969, Treas 1968, Negotiater 1969-81); Teacher of Yr 1984; Spokane Foster Parents Assn Pres 1972-73; *office:* East Valley Mid H S N 4920 Progress Spokane WA 99216

DAVIS, STEVE, Fifth Grade Teacher; *b:* Belcourt, ND; *ed:* (BSED) Elem Ed, Univ of ND 1978; *cr:* 4th-6th Grade Teacher Basic Skills 1978-80, 4th-6th Grade Teacher 1980-82, 4th & 5th Grade Teacher 1982-83, 5th Grade Teacher 1983- Turtle Mountain Cmmty Sch; *ai:* Step I Comm Designed to Assist Teacher to Teach Stu Having Academic/Social or Emotional Problems; ND Indian Ed Assn 1977-; Turtle Mountain Pow-Wow Assn (VP 1984/1985-88, Treas 1988); Knights of Columbus 1988-; Turtle Mountain Historical Society 1988-; Turtle Mountain Tribe Public Service Awd 1989; Outstanding Young Men of America 1988; *home:* Box 207 Belcourt ND 58316

DAVIS, SUSAN LYNN, Art Teacher; *b:* Abington, PA; *ed:* (BS) Art Ed, 1972, (MED) Art Ed, 1983 Millersville Univ; *cr:* Art Teacher Garden Spot HS 1972-81; Art Teacher 1981-85, Hum Team Leader/Teacher 1985-88, Art Teacher 1988- Garden Spot Jr HS; *ai:* Var Cheerleading Coach; Jr HS Girls Track Asst Coach; PSEA 1972-; ELCEA Secy 1986-89; Phi Delta Kappa 1983-85; Lancaster Art Assn 1990; Poetry Published; *home:* 1047 Main St Box 219 Blue Ball PA 17506

DAVIS, TERRY ALAN, 7th/8th Social Studies Teacher; *b:* Portsmouth, OH; *ed:* (BS) His/Poly Sci, OH Univ 1974; (MA) Compentency Based Ed, Mount St Joseph Coll 1988; *cr:* Educator Chillicothe City Schls 1974-; *ai:* Title IX Comm; Educator Mentorship Comm; Talent Show Dir; Soc Stud Curr Review Comm; Smith Advisory Cncl; Chillicothe Ed Assn/OH Ed Assn/NEA/Cntrl OH Teachers Assn 1974-; Sisters Cities Bd Mem 1990; Scioto Valley Arts Cncl Bd Mem 1982-88; Ross Cty Black Coalition Chairperson 1986-87; Ross Cty Youth Services Bd; Co Author Outdoor Pageant Bicentennial of Chillcothe; Co Author of Phamplet 1987; Bd of Contributors Chillcothe Gazette; Featured in 2 Articles; *office:* Smith Mid Sch 345 Arch St Chillicothe OH 45601

DAVIS, THADDEUS LEONARD, Sixth Grade Teacher; *b:* Lakeland, FL; *m:* Bessie Bostic; *c:* Courtney L., Jeanese L., Thaddeus L. Jr.; *ed:* (BA) Elem Ed, Univ of S FL 1976; *cr:* 6th Grade Teacher Eagle Lake Elem 1976-; *ai:* Positive Action Coord; Grants Comm Mem; Grade Chm; Youth Pastor; Stu Cncl Adv; Prison Ministry FL St Correctional Inst; Effective Sch Mem; Curr Comm Mem; FL Army Natl Guard 1985-; Teacher of Yr 1988; *home:* 2782 Frazier St Bartow FL 33830

DAVIS, THOMAS JOHN, 5th Grade/Elem Science Coord; *b:* Wilkes Barre, PA; *m:* Mary W.; *c:* Thomas J., Jennifer W.; *ed:* (BS) Elem Ed, Bloomsburg St 1963; Grad Stud Oneonta St, Cortland St, Syracuse Univ; *cr:* Asst Prin 1978-79, Sci Coord 1988-, 5th Grade Teacher 1963- Perry Browne Elem; *ai:* Dist Health/Safety Comm; Norwich St Sci Mentor; NY St Sci Teachers Assn 1980-; NY St Teachers Assn, NEA 1963-; Norwich Elks 1965-75, 1989-; Emergency Operations Center 1980-; NY St PTA Life Mem; *office:* Norwich City Schls Beebe Ave Norwich NY 13815

DAVIS, THOMAS WILLIAM, Latin Teacher; *b:* Indianapolis, IN; *m:* Barbara Beasley; *ed:* (AB) Latin, Wabash Coll 1983; Teacher Cert, Butler Univ 1985; *cr:* Latin Teacher Shelbyville HS 1986-; *ai:* Academic Team Coach; Latin Club Spon; IN Classical Conference VP 1989-; Amer Classical League; Classical Assn of Midwest & South 1986-; Participant NEH Inst; *office:* Shelbyville HS 2003 S Miller St Shelbyville IN 46176

DAVIS, THURMAN BLANTON, Advanced Placement/His Teacher; *b:* Lebanon, KY; *m:* Mary Gayle Pettyjohn; *c:* Elizabeth, Catherine; *ed:* (BA) His, Univ of KY 1965; (MED) Ed, Lynchburg Coll 1969; Grad Stud Univ of VA; *cr:* Historical Interpretation Appomattox Natl Historical Park 1978-79; Teacher Lynchburg Public Schls 1966-; *ai:* His Club; Academic Competition for Excl; Prin Advisory Comm; Jesse Stuart Fnd 1989-; Civil War Roundtable 1978-82; Natl Parks Consesrvation Assn 1990; Governors Sch Outstanding Educator 1989; Lynchburg Public Schls Career Ladder 1989; Heritage HS Brotherhood Awd 1989; *home:* Rt 1 Box 127 Monroe VA 24574

DAVIS, VALENCIA LA SHON, Mathematics Teacher; *b:* Tampa, FL; *ed:* (AA) Liberal Art, Darton Coll 1985; (BA) Math, Albany St Coll 1988; *cr:* Math Tutor Darton Coll 1984-85, Albany St Coll 1985-88; Math Teacher Darsey Private Sch 1988-; Asst Math/Lab Dir Darton Coll 1989-; *home:* 3317 Twin Flower Rd Albany GA 31707

DAVIS, WANDA SUE, Mathematics Dept Chairperson; *ed:* (BA) Math, Shorter Coll 1972, (MED) Math, W GA Coll 1977; Techniques of Teacher Evaluation; Math Curr Revision & Textbook Selection; *cr:* Teacher Calhoun HS 1972-85; Math Dept Chairperson Gordon Cntrl HS 1985-; *ai:* Girls Bsktbl & Sftbl Coach; Trainer for All Sports; Math & Chess Club Spon; Homecoming Chairperson; NHS Advisory Comm; Chrldr Spon; CVAE Team Teacher; GA Assn of Educators Treas 1972-85; Prof Assn of GA Educators, Gordon Cty Credit Union 1985-; Winners Club 1984; Kappa Kappa Iota Tau Conclave Treas 1982-84; Textbook Reviewer for Merrill Publishing Company; Teacher of Yr Nominee; Excl in Teaching Math Nom; *office:* Gordon Cntrl HS 335 Warrior Path Calhoun GA 30701

DAVIS, WILETHA BUSHART, Fifth Grade Teacher; *b:* Sullivan, IL; *m:* Arthur R.; *c:* Arthur; *ed:* (BS) Elem Ed, Eastern IL Univ 1972; *cr:* Elem Teacher West Richland Elem 1972-; *ai:* West Richland Ed Assn (Pres 1975-76; Sec-Treas 1976-77; Pres 1984-85); Sailor Springs Vice Pres 1989-; Amer Legion Aux; *home:* 8 Keiffer Dr Olney IL 62450

DAVIS, ZEHLINE RUSH, 4th Grade Teacher; *b:* Charleston, WV; *m:* Homer R. Sr.; *c:* Karen R., Homer Jr.; *ed:* (BA) Ed-Deans List, Westfield St Coll 1971; Natl Sch of Bus; *cr:* Teacher Tapley Elem 1970-76; Mo Pottenger Elem 1976-; *ai:* Chorus-4th Grade Directress; Curr Comm-Lang Arts Dept of Eng 1973-74; Secretary Faculty Rep Springfield Ed Assn; Mentor Teacher 1973-; NEA Mem 1972-; Springfield Ed Assn Mem/Delegate 1972-; MA Teachers Assn Delegate 1977; Natl Assn Female Executives 1990; NCO Wives Club Itley Pres 1966-67; MA Teachers Assn/NEA/SEA Delg Bd Mem 1976-77; Natl Assn Female Execs 1990; Protestant Women of the Chapel Italian Division Pres; Delegate-Democratic Natl Convention 1976; Black His Postal Stamp Awd Recognition of Teachers February 1988; Team Leader for Career Opportunity Prgm for Aides-Univ of MA; *office:* Mary O Pottenger Sch 1435 Carew St Springfield MA 01104

DAVRAN, ANN, Social Studies Teacher; *b:* Istanbul, Turkey; *ed:* (BA) His, 1983, (MA) Soc Stud, 1985 SUNY Albany; *cr:* Teacher Saratoga Jr HS 1985-86, North Warren Cntrl Sch 1986-; *ai:* Adv Natl Honor Society; Chairperson & Stu of Month Comm; Grant Summer 1990 Endowment For Hum Seminar Columbia Univ; *office:* North Warren HS Main St Chestertown NY 12817

DAWES, EDWARD ALLEN, Auto Mech/Small Engine Teacher; *b:* Hamilton, MT; *m:* Patricia M.; *c:* Raymond, Denise, Christopher; *ed:* (BS) Voc Ed Teaching, N MT Coll 1970; Briggs & Stratton; General Motors EFI & SFI; General Motors Spec Electronics Trng; Ford Electronic Engine Control IV; *cr:* Voc Ed

Teacher Capital HS 1974-; *ai:* VICA Club Adv 1975-77; Plymouth Troubleshooting 1975-77; Voc Ed Curr Dev 1982; MT Ed Assn 1974-; Voc Leadership Conferance Washington DC 1981; *office:* Capital HS 100 Valley Dr Helena MT 59601

DAWKINS, RICK, Assistant Principal; *b:* Shawnee, OK; *m:* Gloria; *c:* Linsey; *ed:* (BS) Elem Ed, 1976, (ME) Admin, 1984 Cntrl OK St Univ; *cr:* Teacher Sooner-Rose Elem 1976-87; Asst Prin Epperly Heights 1987-; *ai:* NAESP, OK Assn of Elem Sch Prin, Mid-Del Assn of Elem Sch Prin 1987-; *office:* Epperly Heights Elem 3805 Del Rd Del City OK 73115

DAWKINS, TERRY ALLEN, Math/Geography Teacher; *b:* El Paso, TX; *ed:* (BSE) Soc Stud/Geography, Univ of Cntrl AR 1985; *cr:* Coach/Math Teacher Griffithville HS 1985-87; Math/Geog Teacher Kensett HS 1987-; *ai:* Beta Club & Sr Class Spon; Personnel Policy Comm Chm; Asst Coach Bsbl; *home:* PO Box 32 Kensett AR 72082

DAWSEY, KIM BARATTINI, Band Director; *b:* New Orleans, LA; *m:* Mark E.; *ed:* (BA) Music Ed, Univ of S MS 1984; *cr:* Band Dir Monticello Jr HS 1984-86, Richton HS 1986-88, Sumrall Attendance Center 1988-; *ai:* Natl Band Dir Assn 1988-; Tau Beta Sigma Pres 1982-84, Outstanding Bandswomen Awd 1983; Delta Kappa Gamma 1990; Hattiesburg Concert Band 1989-.

DAWSON, BETTY GAIL, Second Grade Teacher; *b:* Spencer Cty, KY; *m:* Dennis A.; *c:* Mitchell, Kimberly, Kelli; *ed:* (BS) Elem Ed, Spalding Coll 1968; (MA) Elem Ed, 1978, (Rank I) Elem Ed, 1986 Univ of Louisville; *cr:* 1st-3rd Grade Teacher Bullitt Cty Schls 1969-; *ai:* Grade Level Chairperson; NEA, KY Ed Assn, Bullitt Cty Ed Assn 1969-; Bullitt Cty Teacher of Yr 1978-79; *office:* Mt Washington Elem Sch Old Mill Rd Mount Washington KY 40047

DAWSON, BETTY RUTH WALLACE, Elementary Teacher; *b:* Gary, IN; *m:* R. A.; *ed:* (BS) Elem Ed, St Josephs Coll 1964; (MS) Elem Ed, Univ of Bridgeport 1974; *cr:* Teacher Morningside Elem Sch; *ai:* Adjunct Instr Nova Coll; Coord of Soc Stud; Curr Guide for Soc Stud; Peer & Coord Teacher; FL Rdng Cncl 1987; Phi Delta Kappa 1990; NAACP, Democratic Womens Club 1987; Prof Bus Womens Assn 1989.

DAWSON, BEVERLY JOAN SMITHEY, 4th Grade Teacher; *b:* Birmingham, AL; *m:* Frank J.; *ed:* (BS) Elem Ed, Jacksonville St Univ 1963; (MA) Elem Ed, 1974, (AA) Elem Ed, 1978 Univ of AL Birmingham; 0 *cr:* 7th Grade Teacher Laurel Ridge Elem 1963-64; 6th Grade Teacher Episcopal Day Sch 1964-65; Piano Teacher Cordova AL 1965-67; 4th Grade Teacher Leeds Elem 1967-; *ai:* Young Authors, Sci, Music Comms; In-Service, Empathy Fund Chm; AL Ed Assn 1967-; Natl Assn for Advancement of Humane Ed 1980-; Birmingham Humane Society Humane Ed Teacher of Yr 1980; Humane Society of US Humane Ed Teacher of Yr 1981; Ruffner Mountain Nature Center (CO-Founder, Secy, Mem) 1979-; Wildlife Rescue Service 1980-; Leeds Music Study Club (VP, Mem) 1968-; Jefferson Cty Bd of Ed Curr Writer Exemplary Teacher 1989; *office:* Leeds Elem Sch 201 Ashville Rd Leeds AL 35094

DAWSON, DOROTHY JEAN SMITH, 5th Grade Teacher; *b:* Longview, TX; *m:* James; *c:* Rosalyn P.; *ed:* (BS) Elem Ed, Wiley 1962; (MS) Elem Ed, Prairie View A&M Univ 1978; Eng as Second Lang, Math, Soc Stud; *cr:* Teacher H S Thompson Elem 1962-71, William M Anderson Elem 1972-73, Rufus C Burleson Elem 1973-; *ai:* Gifted Talented, Prin Advisory, TX Public Schls, America Ed Week, Cinco De Mayo, Big Brother & Sister Comm; Classroom Teachers Mem 1962-87; FHA Mem 1960-80; *office:* Rufus C Burleson Elem Sch 6300 Elam Rd Dallas TX 75217

DAWSON, GEORGIA MURPHY, Supervisor; *b:* Memphis, TN; *m:* Robert Shelton; *c:* Rob, David, Hunter; *ed:* (BS) Elem Ed - Cum Laude, 1975, (MED) Educl Admin/Supervision, 1984 Memphis St Univ; *cr:* Teacher Millington Cntrl Elem 1975-85; Supervision Shelby Cty Schls 1985-; *ai:* NEA, TN Ed Assn 1975-; Phi Delta Kappa 1984-; Kappa Delta Pi 1983; Munford Elem PTO (Pres 1990, Secy 1987-88); Munford Meth Church Librarian 1987-; TN Early Chldhd Task Force 1988; *home:* Rt 1 Box 100 Cole Rd Atoka TN 38004

DAWSON, JOHN FRANCIS, Mathematics Department Chair; *b:* Port Henry, NY; *m:* Janice A. Deresky; *c:* John Jr., Jennifer, Jamie; *ed:* (BA) Math, St Michaels Coll 1964; Grad Sch of Math Univ of MA; Grad Sch of Ed St Univ of NY Plattsburgh; *cr:* Teacher Champlain Cntrl Sch 1966-72, Empire St Coll 1989; Math Teacher/Dept Chm Northeastern Clinton HS 1972-; *ai:* Champlain Cntrl Teachers Assn Pres 1967-68; NYS Assn Math Teachers Cty Chm 1987-88; NYTA NE Zone 2nd VP 1968-69; Champlain Village ZBA Chm 1987-; NE Clinton FCU Treas 1972-; *home:* PO Box 271 Champlain NY 12919

DAWSON, JUDY RAIZOR, Classroom Teacher; *b:* Louisville, KY; *c:* Michael, Sara; *ed:* (BS) Elem Ed, 1983-, Elem Ed, 1988 Univ of Louisville; *cr:* Mid Sch Eng & Math Teacher Lynnvale Elem/Mid Sch 1984-; *ai:* Stu Cncl Spon; Acad Coach; East View Baptist Church (Sunday Sch Dir 1988-89 Adult Ss Teacher 1988-Pianist 1989-); *home:* 9526 Leitchfield Rd Cecilia KY 42724

DAWSON, LINDA LEE, 6th Grade Mathematics Teacher; *b:* Saginaw, MI; *m:* Don; *c:* Ryan, Tyler; *ed:* (AS) Math/Sci, Delta Coll 1969; (BS) Math/Sci, 1971, (MA) Rdng/Specialist, 1975 MI St Univ; *cr:* Math/Sci Teacher Carrollton Public Schls 1971-72; Math/Sci/Soc Stud Teacher Charlotte Public Schls 1972-; *ai:* Jr HS Math Dept Head; Math Competition Coord; MI Cncl Teachers of Math 1975-; MI Assn Cmptr Users in Learning 1987-; *office:* Charlotte Jr HS 301 Horatio Charlotte MI 48813

DAWSON, PATRICIA MERCHANT, 6th Grade Elementary Teacher; *b:* Waterloo, IA; *m:* Larry P.; *c:* Jennifer L.; *ed:* (Ba) Elem Ed/Lang Art/Elem Vocal Music, Univ of N IA 1970; Grad Work Drake Univ, NW MO St Univ, NE MO St Univ; *cr:* Lower Elem Teacher Fisher Elem Sch 1970-75; Elem Music Teacher Marshalltown Cath Schls 1975-78; 5th-8th Grade Teacher Lakota Cmmty Schls 1978-80; 4th/5th Grade Teacher N Kossuth Cmmty Sch 1980-81; 6th Grade Teacher Chariton Cmmty Schls 1981-; *ai:* NEA Public Relations Rep 1986-87; Amer Assn of Univ Women Public Relations Rep 1980-; Delta Kappa Gamma Ed Society 1987-; *home:* 326 Elm Milo IA 50166

DAWSON, RICHARD GLEN, Biology/Futuristics Teacher; *b:* Columbia, MO; *m:* Eleanor Louise Webster; *c:* Andrea Dawson Webster, Carolyn Webster; *ed:* (BA) Bio, Carleton Coll 1957; (MS) Bio, Univ of MI 1958; Various Univs; *cr:* Teacher Shawnee Mission North HS 1958-68; Dir Kansas City Environmental Sci Camps 1960-78; Teacher Shawnee Mission South HS 1968-; *ai:* Environmental Action Club Life Spon; NABT Outstanding Bio Teacher Awd 1968; KS Assn Teachers of Sci Editor 1964-69; Greater Kansas City Sci Teachers Assn Secy 1989-; NSTA; MO Prairie Fnd (Secy, Ed) 1965-75, Prairie Conservationist 1980; Burroughs Audubon Society Pres 1964-66, Conservation Educator 1982; All Souls Unitarian Church Bd Secy 1976-82; Lincoln Magnet Sch Advisory Cncl Secy 1978-81; Phi Beta Kappa; Poems Published; Natl Sci Fnd Fellowship; KS Master Teacher; Kansas City Excl in Teaching & Environmental Leadership Awd; Mayors Earth Day Comm Chm; MO Conservation Educator Awd; Governors Task Force on Environmental Impacts; *office:* Shawnee Mission South HS 5800 W 107th St Overland Park KS 66207

DAWSON, SANDRA LOUISE, Vice Principal; *b:* Holyoke, MA; *ed:* (BA) Sociology, Coll of Our Lady of Elms 1967; (MA) Guidance/Psychological Service, Springfield Coll 1978; Amer Intnl Coll Educl Admin Prgm; *cr:* Teacher 1967-88, VP 1988-Selser Sch; *ai:* Chicopee Educl Assn VP 1975-77; MIA, NEA 1967-; City Democratic Comm 1984-; *office:* Selser Memorial Sch WAFB Chicopee MA 01022

DAY, ANN (NAGLE), English Teacher; *b:* Bloomington, IL; *m:* Terance; *c:* Joshua, Joel; *ed:* (BA) Eng, Hanover Coll 1961; (MED) Ed, CO St Univ 1986; *cr:* Eng Teacher Jackson Township 1962-63, Gibson City Schls 1963-64, Littleton HS 1964-68, Park R-3 1975-; *ai:* Class Spon; N Cntrl Steering Comm; NCTE, CO Lang Art Society; CO Lang Art Society Convention Presenter; Park R-3 Dist Teacher of Yr 1980; *office:* Park HS PO Box 1140 Estes Park CO 80517

DAY, BETTY JUNE REED, 6th-8th Grade Art Teacher; *b:* Harrodsburg, KY; *c:* Deidre J., Kimberly D.; *ed:* (BA) Art/Eng, 1958, (MAED) Art, 1980 E KY Univ; Several Painting Classes & Painting Sessions with some KY Foremost Artists; *cr:* Eng Teacher Jefferson HS 1958-59, Jefferson Township HS 1959-64; Eng/Speed Rdng Teacher Franklin HS 1966-68; Eng Teacher Eubank HS 1968-70; Honors Eng Teacher Tates Creek HS 1970; Psych/Sociology/Art Teacher Lebanon HS 1970-71; Head Resident Mens Dormitory/Secy Athletic Dept Cumberland Coll 1970-71;Substitute Teacher Fayette Cty Lexington 1971-72; Art Teacher Bourbon Cty Jr HS 1972-88, Bourbon Cty Mid Sch 1988-; *ai:* Art & Speech Club; Sr Play; Chrldr & Homeroom Spon; Taught Several Teachers Art Wkshps Inservice Cmmty Night Classes for Adults in Art; Art Dept Chm; Cntrl KY Ed Assn, KY Ed Assn 1968-; NEA 1958-; *office:* Bourbon Cty Mid Sch 3343 Lexington Rd Paris KY 40361

DAY, EDWIN LOUIS, Sixth Grade Teacher; *b:* Moline, IL; *m:* Gloria Lea Ewing; *c:* Mark L., Scott M.; *ed:* (BA) Geology, 1959, Elem Ed, 1963 Augustana Coll; Blackhawk Coll; Marycrest Coll; Univ of IL; *cr:* 6th Grade Teacher Rockridge Cmmty Unit Schs 1959-63, Blackhawk 1963-87, Roosevelt 1987-; *ai:* Sports Prgms; Search of New Texbooks Comm; Moline Ed Assn Mem Chm 1967-68; IL Ed Assn; NEA; *home:* 511 25th Ave Moline IL 61265

DAY, GAIL ARMSTRONG, Teacher; *b:* Corinth, MS; *m:* Danny G.; *c:* Adam, Alicia; *ed:* (BA) Eng, Union Univ 1972; *cr:* Teacher Selmer Mid Sch 1972-; *ai:* Chrldr & Newspaper Spon; Lang Art Chairperson; NCTE 1989-; Mc Nairy Cty Ed Assn (Rep 1988-, Pres Elect 1990); Gravel Hill Baptist Church Organist 1970-; Initiated 7th/8th Grade Advanced Lang Art Prgm.

DAY, GLORIA JEANNE, Music Specialist; *b:* Sioux City, IA; *ed:* (BA) Music Ed, Univ of AZ 1979; Addl Studies/Univ of AZ; *cr:* Music Teacher Butterfield Elem 1979-; *ai:* Chorus Grades 4th/5th/6th; Music Ed Natl Conf 1976-; Delta Kappa Gamma 1988-; AZ Ed Assn 1979-; Marana Dist Teacher of Yr Awd 1988-89; Top 10 Ed in AZ 1988-89; *office:* Butterfield Elem Sch 3400 W Massingale Tucson AZ 85741

DAY, JUDITH WEIGAND, 4th Grade Teacher; *b:* Ellsworth, KS; *c:* Andrew, Joel, Kelly Day Stewart; *ed:* (BSED) Elem Ed, KSTC Emporia 1958; (MSED) Elem Ed, Emporia KS St Coll 1976; (EDS) Rdng, Emporia St Univ 1984; *cr:* 4th Grade Teacher 1958, 1st Grade Teacher 1958-60, Washington Sch; Part Time Eng Teacher ACMS & ACHS 1960-67; 3RD/4th Grade Teacher Adams Sch 1967-73; Ch I Rdng Teacher 1974-80, 4th Grade Teacher 1980-84, Washington Sch; 4th Grade Teacher ISL Sch 1984-; *ai:* Lang Art Dept Head USD 470; Facilities Comm; Curr Comm Secy; ACT Assn Pres 1983-84; Outstanding Teacher Affiliate for Work in Amer Ed Week 1983; Walnut Valley Uniserv Secy 1986-; KNEA/NEA 1957-; Cowley Cty IBA Mem 1989-; Outstanding Assn Mem 1988; Delta Kappa Gamma (1st VP 1988-, Pres 1990-); 1st Baptist Church Child Chm Sunday Sch Teacher 1960-; Educl Schlsp Delta Kappa Gamma 1984; Master Teacher Awd from Emporia St Univ 1990; *office:* IXL Elem School Rt 4 Arkansas City KS 67005

DAY, LINDA LORRAINE, English Teacher/Dept Chair; *b:* Luling, TX; *c:* Lauren A.; *ed:* (BA) Eng/His, Univ of TX 1970; Counseling & Guidance; *cr:* Eng Teacher La Marque HS 1971-79; Hartman Mid Sch 1979-82; Jones HS 1982-; *ai:* Prom; Sr Trip; *office:* Jesse H Jones Sr HS 7414 St Lo Houston TX 77033

DAY, M. JO ANN, Fourth Grade Teacher; *b:* Protection, KS; *m:* Bill J.; *c:* Camille, Melissa; *ed:* (BS) Ed, Bethel Coll 1962; *cr:* 2nd Grade Teacher Valley Center Ind Sch Dist 1962-67; 4th Grade Teacher Amarillo Ind Sch Dist 1981-; *ai:* ACTA, TSTA, NEA 1981-89; AFT 1989-; Beta Sigma Phi Treas 1975, Outstanding Girl 1976; Amarillo Symphony Guild, Amarillo Art Alliance; Amarillo Little Theatre Bd Mem; *office:* Windsor Elem Sch 6700 Hyde Parkway Amarillo TX 79109

DAY, NADINE E. (VOPAT), Retired Second Grade Teacher; *b:* Tolstoy, SD; *m:* Orris; *c:* David, Roger; *ed:* Elem Ed, Northern Normal 1941; (BA) Elem Ed, Huron Coll 1973; *cr:* 1st-8th Grade Teacher Franklin Sch 1942-43; Weiss Sch 1946-47; Bramhall Sch 1965-70; 2nd Grade Teacher Highmore Elem 1970-88; *ai:* NEA; HEA Secy; Meth Church Treas; Amer Legion Aux Chaplain Past Pres; Order Eastern Star Sr Center Past Matron; *home:* 515 W 2nd St Highmore SD 57345

DAY, PAMELA JUNE, Drama Teacher; *b:* Baton Rouge, LA; *c:* Sara N. Brown; *ed:* (BS) Elem Ed, N LA Univ Monroe 1977; Ed, Theatre, LA St Univ, N LA Univ; Bob Brooks Sch of Real Estate; *cr:* Teacher Northwestern Mid Sch 1977-80, Teacher Asst NE LA Univ 1982; Teacher Istrouma Mid Magnet 1980-; *ai:* Dir Daytime Players; Homeroom Pres Club, 4-H Club, Jr Beta Club Spon; NEA, LAE, EBRAE 1977-87; Speech Comm Assn 1977-80; Amer Alliance for Theatre & Ed 1990; Baker Little Theatre Bd Mem 1979-85, Best Supporting Actress 1981, Best Character Actress 1982; East Baton Rouge Parish Teacher of Week 1980-81, 1982; Cnslr Summer Youth Employment Prgm 1977-; Outstanding Young Women of America 1985; *home:* 2807-A Garfield St Baker LA 70714

DAY, ROBERT JOHN, Mathematics Dept Chairman; *b:* Fitchburg, MA; *m:* Jane Marie Badagliacca; *c:* Jamison, Colleen; *ed:* (BS) Math, 1968, (MED) Math, 1983 Fitchburg St Coll; *cr:* Teacher 1968-85, Math Dept Chm 1985- N Middlesex Regional HS; *ai:* Head Boys X-Cntry, Indoor Track, Spring Track Coach; Math Team Coach; Local Coord New England Math League Contest; Math Olympiad & Elizabeth Haskins Math Contest; NCTM 1980-; ASCD 1985-; NEA, MA Teachers Assn 1968-; Cntrl MA Track & Field Ofcls Assn 1968-; Guest Speaker MA Scndry Sch Prins Assn Seminar; Prof Dev Grant MA Dept of Ed Project Title Curr Validation; Track Coach of Yr 1979-81; Scholastic Coach Magazine Gold Medal Awd Winner 1988; *office:* N Middlesex Regional HS Main St Townsend MA 01469

DAY, WANDA HUNTER, Teacher of Gifted & Talented; *b:* Metamore, IN; *m:* Ronald L.; *c:* Angela, Ryan; *ed:* (BSE) Elem Ed/Spec Ed, Memphis St Univ 1979; Grad Stud Memphis St Univ; *cr:* Clue Teacher Memphis City Schls 1979-; *ai:* Ridgeway Elem Sci Fair Coord; Inservice Wkshps Presenter; Clue Liaison Memphis Pink Palace Museum; TN Assn for Gifted; W TN Assn for Gifted Publicity Chm 1981-83; Natl Assn for Gifted Children; Career Ladder Teacher.

DAY, WILLIAM DOUGLAS, Social Studies Teacher; *b:* Erwin, TN; *m:* Ethel Marie Williams; *c:* Todd, Matt; *ed:* (BS) Poly Sci, E TN St Univ 1979; *cr:* Teacher Bean Station Schls 1980-; *ai:* Girls Bsktbl Coach; Asst Ftbl & Boys Bsktbl Coach; TEA, NEA 1980-; Ruritan-Bean Station Pres 1987; *office:* Bean Station Elem Sch Rt 1 Hwy 11 W Bean Station TN 37708

DAYAP, JUANITA VALORIA, Fifth Grade Bilingual Teacher; *b:* San Juan, Philippines; *m:* Jose Fabelinia; *c:* Jason V., James P.; *ed:* (BA) Elem Ed, N Luzon Teachers Coll 1968; (MA) Curr & Instruction/Bi-ling Ed, Univ of the Pacific 1984; Bi-ling/Bi-Cultural Teaching Strategies Span Prgm Univ of Pacific 1981-85; High Intensity Lang Trng Span Univ of Pacific 1987; Several Wkshps; *cr:* Pre-Sch Elem Substitute Teacher Stockton Unified Sch Dist 1974-79; Bi-ling Teacher Van Buren Elem Sch 1980-; *ai:* Chm Decorations, Mem Liaison Comm; Classroom Supvr; AFAE Schlsp Spon; Assn of Filipino Amer Educators Secy 1984-86; CA Teachers Assn, NEA, Stockton Teachers Assn Mem 1980-; San Marcelinean USA Mem 1989-; Bi-ling Ed Schlsp 1980-84; Sch Prgm Quality Review Mem 1988; Exemplary Service Team Participation 1983; Exemplary Service Compensatory Ed Project Writing 1984; Excl Educl Awareness Madison Sch 1977; Excl Educl Services Taylor Sch 1978; Spec Ed Awareness 1981; *office:* Martin Van Buren Elem Sch 1628 E 10th St Stockton CA 95206

DAYTON, CONSTANCE E., Language Arts Teacher; *b:* Rockville Centre, NY; *m:* Richard E.; *ed:* (BA) Eng/Elem Ed, Sacred Heart Univ 1971; (MS) Ed, Dowling Coll 1985; *cr:* 1st Grade Teacher St Brigid Sch 1968-69; 1st/3rd/6th Grade Teacher/7th-8th Grade Lang Art Teacher Infant Jesus Sch 1972-; *ai:* Eng, Rdng, Spelling Bee, Sch Newsletter Coord; NCEA, NCET; *office:* Infant Jesus Sch 110 Myrtle Ave Port Jefferson NY 11777

DEADRICK, THOMAS KENT, Sci Teacher/Sci Dept Chm; *b:* Petersburg, WV; *m:* Margaret Jane Osburn; *c:* Douglas K.; *ed:* (AB) Ed/Comprehensive Bio, Fairmont St Coll 1970; (MA) Scndry Sci/Classroom Teacher, WV Univ 1974; Grad Stud Scndry

Admin Cert; *cr:* Teacher E Fairmont HS 1970-; *ai:* Sci Honorary Spon; E Fairmont HS Advisory Cncl Mem, Faculty Staff, Flower Fund Chm, Dress-An-Angel Prgm Chm, Improvement Team Mem; Partners in Ed Comm Mem; Sr Awds Comm Mem; NHS Selection Comm; Cty Ed Assn Comm; Marion Cty Schls Curr, Staff Dev Cncl & Calendar Comm Mem; Marion Cty Ed Assn Past Pres 1970-; WV Ed Assn, NEA 1970-; Phi Delta Kappa 1974-; WV Sci Teachers Assn 1987-; Marion Cty Rdng Cncl 1989-; Marion Cty Sch Employees Federal Credit Union (Loan Comm 1989-, Bd of Dir 1990); Watson Elem Sch Advisory Cncl Short Term Goals Comm Chm 1989-; WV Advisory Cncl on Prof Dev Mem; Presidential Awd Excl Sci & Math Teaching St Awd Winner 1989; Peer Elected Position; WV St Dept On-Site Evaluation Team Mem; E Fairmont HS Positively Bee Awd Winner; WV Univ Benedum Project Prof Dev Schls & Pedagogy Comm; *office:* E Fairmont HS 1 Orion Ln Fairmont WV 26554

DEAL, EDWIN E., English Teacher; *b:* Butler, PA; *m:* Mary Lou Dyke; *c:* Jonathan, David; *ed:* (BA) Eng, Westminster Coll 1962; Grad Stud Westminster Coll & Slippery Rock Univ; *cr:* Instr Shenango HS 1962-; *ai:* NHS Adv; PSEA, NEA 1962-; Shenango Ed Assn (Pres 1967-68, VP 1966-67); 3rd Presbyn Church Deacon 1980-84, 1986-89; Outstanding Scndry Educators of America 1975; Leaders of Amer Scndry Ed 1971.

DEAL, JANET PLYLER, Language Arts/Soc Stud Teacher; *b:* New London, NC; *m:* Charles N.; *c:* George N., Iris Lemmer, Beverly; *ed:* (BS) Elem Ed, 1970, (MS) Elem Ed, IN Univ NW; *cr:* 6th Grade Teacher Foreman Elem Sch 1970-85; Lang Art/Soc Stud Teacher Hobart Mid Sch 1985-; *ai:* Supts Symposium Comm; Hoosier Histrionics Spon; Hobart Teachers Assn Exec Bd Lobbyist 1970-; NEA 1970-; Ogden Dunes Presbyn Church 1970-; Audubon Society; HIEDC; Hobart Gazettes Woman of Yr 1989.

DEAL, PATRICIA JEAN, HS Counselor; *b:* Long Beach, CA; *m:* Richard Stuart; *ed:* (AS) General Ed, Citrus Coll 1978; (BS) Psych, Univ of La Verne 1980; (MS) Counseling, CA St Fullerton 1983; Pupil Personnel Services, CA St Fullerton 1983; Counseling Enrichment Prgm, Azusa Pacific Univ 1989; *cr:* Workmens Compensation Cnslr Occupational Support Services 1984-86; Career Ed Teacher CA St Fullerton 1985; Cnslr Charter Oak HS 1986-; *office:* Charter Oak HS PO Box 9 Covina CA 91723

DEAL, SHIRLEY MAYBERRY, Marketing Ed Teacher; *b:* Statesville, NC; *m:* Blake F. Jr.; *c:* Blake F. III, Darron M., Michael D., Vicky Deal Wilson; *ed:* (AA) Bus, Mars Hill Coll 1955; (BS) Bus, Pfeiffer Coll 1959; (MA) Mrktg Ed, Univ of NC Charlotte 1975; Metrolina Consortium 1981; *cr:* Bus Ed Teacher Hillsborough HS 1959-63; Mrktg Ed Teacher Garinger HS 1963-72, N Mecklenburg HS 1972-; *ai:* DECA Adv; NC Mrktg Educators Outstanding Mem 1986-87; NC Vocational Assn (Pres, Prof Div 1986); Amer Voc Assn St Pres 1987; DECA Adv of Natl Officer 1965; Hillsborough HS Bus Teacher of Yr; N Mecklenburg Teacher of Yr; Charlotte-Mecklenburg 1st Union Outstanding Educator of Yr; Mrktg Resource Center Natl Model Prgm; *office:* N Mecklenburg HS 11201 Old Statesville Rd Huntersville NC 28078

DE AMATO, LORRAINE THERESA, Science Teacher; *b:* Boston, MA; *ed:* (BA) Bio, 1973, (MED) Natural Sci, 1973 Boston St Coll; Patterns in Life, Prgm Simmons Coll 1986-87; Aids Prevention Prgm for Youth; Amer Red Cross Massachusetts Bay 1988; *cr:* Laboratory Technician Boston St Coll 1973-82; Sci Teacher St Mary Jr/Sr Regional HS 1982-; *ai:* NHS & Soph Class Adv; NCEA 1982-; Museum of Sci Boston 1986-; Sweet Adelines Incorporated bd Mem 1987; Natl Sci Fnd Prgm 1986-87; Lynn Bus Ed Fnd Incorporated Grant 1987; *office:* St Mary Jr/Sr Regional HS 35 Tremont St Lynn MA 01902

DEAN, ANNIE BLAKE, 8th Grade Reading Teacher; *b:* Monticello, FL; *c:* Kechia A.; *ed:* (BS) Phys Ed/Health, FL A&M Univ 1973; *cr:* Phys Ed Teacher Greenville HS 1973-75; Rdng Teacher Greenville Mid Sch 1975-; *ai:* Chrldr, Yrbk Staff, Stu Cncl Spon; FL Ed Assn 1973; Greenville Mid Sch Teacher of Yr 1987-88; *office:* Greenville Mid Sch PO Box 428 Greenville FL 32331

DEAN, AUBIE MAE, Retired Teacher; *b:* Henagar, AL; *w:* David Daniel (dec); *c:* Carolyn Chambers, Mary Sayers, Charles, Beverly Corjulo, Rachel Plunkett; *ed:* (BS) Elem Ed, Jacksonville St Coll 1951; Extra Classes Jacksonville Univ; *cr:* Teacher Sylvania HS 1944-50, Ider HS, Williams Avenue Elem Sch, Adamsburg HS 1963-88; *ai:* 4-H Club; Head Start; Lead Teacher; NEA, AL Ed Assn, De Kalb Ed Assn 1944-88; Alpha Delta Kappa (VP, Pres, Chaplain, Treas) 1974-, Perfect Attendance; Gareet Avenue Church Sunday Sch Teacher BYU 1958-: Azalea Garden Club (VP, Pres) 1980-; *home:* 1406 S Grand Ave Fort Payne AL 35967

DEAN, BUENA KAY, Instructional Consultant; *b:* Kermit, TX; *m:* James Ronald; *c:* Deonna K., Bryan H.; *ed:* (BS) Phys Ed/Bio, SW TX St Univ 1967; (MA) Counseling & Guidance, Univof TX Permian Basin 1978; Gifted & Talented Ed; Counseling; *cr:* Teacher San Marcos Ind Sch Dist 1967-, Midland Ind Sch Dist 1977-81; Teacher of Gifted & Talented Greenwood Ind Sch Dist 1981-86; Counselor Ector Cty Ind Sch Dist 1987-88; Instructional Consultant Region 18 Ed Service Center 1988-; *ai:* Delta Kappa Gamma Parliamentarian 1986-; Phi Delta Kappa 1989-; TX Assn for Gifted & Talented (Region Rep 1986-, Prof Staff Dev Comm Chairperson); Beta Sigma Phi (Pres, Secy, Treas) 1985-86, Girl of Yr 1986; PTA Lifetime Membership Awd 1980; *office:* Region 18 Ed Service Center 2811 La Force PO Box 60580 Midland TX 79711

DEAN, DEBORAH NELSON, 7th Grade Teacher/Team Leader; *b:* Atlanta, GA; *m:* Oscar E. Jr.; *c:* Jody, Whitney; *ed:* (BSED) Jr HS Ed, 1972, (MED) Soc Sci, 1976, (BED) Soc Sci 1983 GA Southern Coll; *cr:* Teacher Riverdale Jr HS & Warner Robins Mid Sch 1972-; *ai:* Cheerleading Spon; Mid Sch Comm for Houston Cty; Team Leader; GAE, NEA, PAGE; Church Recording Secy 1989-; *office:* Warner Robins Mid Sch Mary Ln Warner Robins GA 31088

DEAN, GEORGE XAVIER, English/Writing Teacher; *b:* Jersey City, NJ; *m:* Joyce; *c:* David, Cathleen, Karin; *ed:* (BA) Eng, Fordham Univ 1966; (MAT) Eng, Fairleigh Dickinson Univ 1967; Teachers Coll Columbia Univ; *cr:* Teacher Princeton Univ Mid Sch Summer Prgm 1987-88, N Bergen HS 1967-; Lead Teacher Princeton Univ Mid Sch Summer Prgm 1989-; *ai:* Staff Dev Comm Mem; AFT 1970-; Ringwood Bd of Ed (Pres, VP, Mem) 1980-86; Princeton Univ Teacher of Yr Candidate; *home:* 173 Skylands Rd Ringwood NJ 07456

DEAN, HOWARD STOKES, Soc Stud Teacher/Athletic Dir; *b:* Middlesboro, KY; *m:* Patsy G.; *c:* Jeffery, Paul; *ed:* (BS) Phys Ed, Grand Canyon Univ 1958; (MA) Phys Ed, N AZ Univ 1965; *cr:* Teacher/Athletic Dir/Coach Santa Cruz Valley Union HS 1958-; *ai:* Natl Interscholastic Athletic Admin Assn 1985-; *office:* Santa Cruz Valley Union HS 9th & Main St Eloy AZ 85231

DEAN, JULIE ANN, Dir Of Dramatics & Lang Arts; *b:* Benton Harbor, MI; *c:* Erika K., J. Hunter; *ed:* (BA) Scndry Ed/Speech, Univ of AZ 1970; Grad Work Scndry Ed, Univ of S CO, Adams St Coll, Univ of N CO, CO St Univ 1981-; *cr:* Eng Instr US Peace Corps 1971-73; Admin Asst Northwestern Univ 1973-76; Stu Union Mgr Univ of AZ 1976-79; Lang Art/Dir of Dramatics Canon City HS 1983-; *ai:* Dir Tiger Theatre Dramatics Productions; Head Spirit Spon; Pom Pons & Chrldrs; CO Lang Art Society 1985-; Delta Delta Delta 1965-; *office:* Canon City HS 1313 College Ave Canon City CO 81212

DEAN, LARRY CLYDE, 5th Grade Teacher; *b:* Oklahoma City, OK; *m:* De Anna S. Bullock; *c:* Carrie M., Ryan A., Bryan M.; *ed:* (BS) Elem Ed, 1971; (MED) Elem Ed, 1975 Central St Univ; *cr:* Teacher Putnam City Sch/Coronado Elem 1971-; *ai:* Staff Dev Cmptr Instr; Teach Cmptr Skills & Software Packages to Teachers in Dist; Served As Dept Chm; Curr Comm; *office:* Coronado Elem Sch 5911 N Sapalupa Oklahoma City OK 73112

DEAN, MARYELLEN, Third Grade Teacher; *b:* Needham, MA; *ed:* (BS) Elem Ed, Coll of St Teresa 1980; Coaching, Winona St Univ 1980; Master Degree Prgm Basic Sign Lang, Univ of MN; *cr:* Long Term Substitute Teacher Winona Public Schls 1980-81; 4th Grade Teacher 1981-88, 3rd Grade Teacher 1988- Rushford Public Schls; *ai:* MEA, REA Treas 1983; *office:* Rushford Elem Sch 102 N Mill St Rushford MN 55971

DEAN, RHONDA SHELENE, English Teacher; *b:* Fairmont, WV; *m:* Daniel Kevin; *c:* Elijah L.; *ed:* (BA) Eng/Journalism Ed, Fairmont St Coll 1981; *cr:* Journalism Teacher N Marion HS 1981-83; Eng Teacher Ellicott Baptist Sch 1983-84, Calvary Baptist Chrstn Acad 1985-86; Journalism Teacher Grafton HS 1986-88; Eng Teacher N Marion HS 1989-; *ai:* Yrbk & Newspaper Spon; Quill & Scroll Adv; CSPA Gold Crown Yrbk Adv 1983; *office:* North Marion HS Rt 1 Box 100 Farmington WV 26571

DEAN, SANDRA POWERS, English Teacher/Dept Chair; *b:* Cleveland, MS; *m:* Donald E. Jr.; *c:* Michael, Amanda; *ed:* (BA) Eng, Delta St Univ 1970; (MED) General Stud, Houston Baptist Univ 1987; NJ Writing Project in TX; *cr:* Teacher Woodson Jr HS 1970-73, Blair Sr HS 1973-77, Hastings HS 1977-; Dept Chairperson Hasting HS 1985-; *ai:* Dist Eng Curr, Gifted & Talented Scndry Level Comm; Co-Organizer Awds Night; NJ Writing Project in TX Dist Summer Inst Trainer; Alief Ed Assn, TX St Teachers Assn, NEA 1984-; TX Joint Cncl Teachers of Eng, NCTE, Assn for Scndry Curr Dev 1988-; Beta Sigma Phi (Recording Secy, Pres) 1975-81, Outstanding Young Women 1977; Jaycettes 1975-77, Forrest Cty Young Woman of Yr 1978; Hastings HS North Teacher of Yr 1987; Book Review 1989; *office:* Hastings HS 12301 High Star Houston TX 77072

DEAN, WILLIAM ALBERT, English Teacher; *b:* Atlantic City, NJ; *ed:* (BA) Eng Ed, 1971, (MED) Eng Ed, 1975 Rutgers Univ; Temple Univ, San Francisco St Univ; *cr:* Eng Teacher Camden HS 1971-84, Eng Instr Camden Comm Coll 1982-83; Eng Teacher Clark HS 1984-85, Carlmont HS 1985-; *ai:* Carlmont HS Math Engineering Sci Achievement Prgm & Newspaper Adv; NEA, NCTE 1971-; CA Ed Assn 1984-; Natl Assn for Advancement of Colored People 1985-; Magazine Articles Published.

DEANE, MYRA UPCHURCH, Health Occupations Teacher; *b:* Durham, NC; *m:* Charles B. Jr.; *c:* Bennett, Winston, Matthew, Jason; *ed:* Bio/Ed, Wake Forest Univ; (ADN) Nursing, Sandhills Comm Coll 1974; *cr:* Registered Nurse Richmond Memorial Hospital 1974-88; Teacher Richmond Sr HS 1988-; *ai:* Health Occupations Stus of America Adv; NCAE 1989-; NCTUA 1990-; Jr Womans Club Pres 1970-80, Woman of Yr 1974; NC Novice HOSA Adv of Yr 1989; *office:* Richmond Sr HS PO Box 1748 Rockingham NC 28379

DE ANGELUS, GLENDA SIMPSON, Physical Education Dept Chair; *b:* Rome, GA; *m:* Ronald Louis; *c:* Jeffrey, Ginger; *ed:* (BS) Math/Phys Ed, Berry Coll 1974; (MED) Mid Grades W GA Coll 1986; CPR; First Aid; AIDS; *cr:* Math/Phys Ed Teacher E Rome Jr HS 1974-; *ai:* Spon Fellowship of Chrstn Athletes; Ftbl & Bsktbl Chrldrs, Girls Bsktbl & Track Coach; Prof Assn of Educators 1986-; *office:* E Rome Jr HS 415 E 3rd Ave Rome GA 30161

DEANS, BARBARA JAMES, Science Teacher; *b:* New York City, NY; *ed:* (BS) Bio, Bennett Coll 1967; (MA) Human Resources, Pepperdine Univ 1980; Grad Stud SC St Coll; *cr:* Teacher Burke HS 1967-72; Public Affairs US Marine Corps 1972-80; Teacher Ridgeland HS 1981-82, Beaufort Jr HS 1982-84; *ai:* Bio Teachers of America, SC ACAD of Sci, SC 2 1984-; Natl Sci Fnd Grant Clemson Univ 1986; Submitted Article Teacher Magazine 1990; *home:* Rt 4 Box 210 Burton SC 29902

DEAR, LINDA BARLOW, Bsktbl Coach/8th Grade Teacher; *b:* Jackson, MS; *m:* Phil; *c:* Brandi, Travis; *ed:* (BS) Elem Ed, Belhaven Coll 1975; *cr:* Teacher/Coach Rankin Acad 1975-77; Union Acad 1978-86; Simpson Cty Acad 1986-; *ai:* Coaching Pee-Wee Bsktbl; Coaching Jr HS & Varsity Girls Bsktbl & Track; Spon Stud Cncl; Harrisville Youth Assn 1988-; *home:* Rt 2 Box 220-A Florence MS 39073

DEARIN, J. D., French Teacher; *b:* Ames, IA; *m:* Christy Lynn Cox; *ed:* (BA) Fr, 1988, (MED) Ed, 1989 Harding Univ; *cr:* 9th-12th Grade Fr Teacher Mars Hill Bible Sch 1989; *ai:* Yrbk Teacher & Spon; Fr Club Spon; Study Hall Supvr; *office:* Mars Hill Bible Sch Cox Creek Pkwy Florence AL 35630

DE ARMAS-DUCROS, ELIZABETH ROSA, Sixth Grade Teacher; *b:* New Orleans, LA; *ed:* (BA) Ed/Elem, St Marys Dominican Coll 1973; (MED) Educl Admin, Univ of New Orleans 1975; *cr:* 5th Grade Teacher St Matthias Sch 1965-68; 6th Grade Teacher Andrew Jackson Elem 1968-71, 1973; 4th Grade Teacher Bauduit Elem Sch 1974; 5th Grade Teacher John J Audubon Elem Sch 1974; Spec Ed Teacher Mc Donogh #26 Spec Sch; 6th Grade Teacher Terrytown Elem Sch 1978-86, Geraldine Boudreaux Elem Sch 1987-; *ai:* Stu Cncl Spon; Presidential Academic Fitness Prgm Awd; Young Authors of America Prgm Adv; Kappa Delta Pi 1975; Phi Kappa Phi 1976-; Phi Delta Kappa 1975-; ATF 1978-; St Bernard Historical Society of LA 1968-; New Orleans Museum of Art 1990-; Sch Authorship Philosophy; *office:* Geraldine Boudereux Elem Sch 950 Behrman Hwy Gretna LA 70056

DEARRING, GLORIA DELORES, 5th Grade Teacher; *b:* Kingstree, SC; *m:* Charles H.; *c:* Debtonia, Shiellynn, Charles II; *ed:* (AA) Elem Ed/Eng, Kellogg Comm Coll 1964; (BA) Elem Ed/Eng, 1967, (MA) Classroom Ed, 1978 MI St Univ; *cr:* 4th Grade Teacher 1967-71, 3rd/4th Grade Teacher 1971-72, 5th Grade Teacher 1972-85, 6th Grade Teacher 1985-87, 5th Grade Teacher 1987- Dudley Sch, Eng Comm Kellogg Comm Coll 1990; *ai:* Girls After Sch Coach 1971-72; Math Chairperson; Stu Cncl 1984-; 6th Grade Grad Prgm Head; Dir Kellogg Comm Coll Childrens Prgm; Mid Sch Staff, Staff Dev, Dist Effective Sch Comms; Chm Dudley Sch Effective Sch Comm; Coord Sch Store 1984-, Upperlevel Rdng, 6th Grade Girls Health & Beauty Prgm, Style Show; Battle Creek Ed Assn (Rep 196870, Bd Mem 1967-70); MI Ed Assn 1967-; NEA 1967-; Assn of Amer United Women 1972-73; Urban League Guild 1977-78; Urban League 1985-87; Natl Assn for Advancement of Colored People 1986-87; *home:* 145 E Northside Dr Battle Creek MI 49017

DE ARROYO, MERCEDES M., School Director; *b:* Corozal, PR; *m:* Juan Orestes Arroyo; *c:* Grace B., Gloria Platt, Juan O., Maria T., Peter J., Michelle; *ed:* (BA) Ed, 1956/1962, (MA) Educl Admin, 1976, (MS) Spec Ed, 1979 Univ of PR Bridgeport; Working Toward ED in Educl Admin 1983; *cr:* Teacher Academia San Jose-Colegio San Benito 1957-69; Sch Dir Colegio San Benito 1970-84; Founder Colegio Nuestra Senora Del Perpetuo; Dir Socorro 1984-; *ai:* Caguas Cath Schls Cncl of Supervision Mem; Pi Lamda Theta; ASCD, Natl Geographic Society Mem; Altrusas Club Distinguished Citizen Ed 1990; Nom NCEA Distinguished Prin; Recognition as Distinguished Citizen by PR Senate 1990; *office:* Colegio Nuestra Senora Carretera 908 Km 02 Tejas-Humacao Humacao PR 00661

DEARSTONE, JANET HELM, 6th Grade Teacher; *b:* Augusta, GA; *m:* Doug; *c:* Kip Corbin, Dave; *ed:* (BFA) Commercial Art, Univ of GA 1968-69; (MED) Ed, Augusta Coll 1977; *cr:* 5th Grade Teacher Grovetown Elem Sch 1973-77; 5th/6th Grade Teacher Way Chrstn Sch 1977-78; 6th Grade Teacher Norris Mid Sch 1982-; *ai:* Lang Art Dept Chm; Lang Art Textbook Adoption; Curr Dev Comm; PAGE Mem; *office:* Norris Mid Sch 899 Harrison Rd Thomson GA 30824

DEARTH, RUTH ANN, Fifth Grade Teacher; *b:* Logan, OH; *m:* Leslie C.; *c:* Janet Beach, Laura Schoff, Creig H., Kevin, Linda, Kara Thompson; *ed:* (BS) Early & Mid Childhood Ed 1973, (MA 1979 OH St Univ; Cmptr Methods; PASCAL; Fund of Cmptr Applications in Ed & Logo; *cr:* 5th Grade Teacher Fredericktown Schls 1973-; *ai:* Cmptr Club Adv; Jr Great Books; Cmptr Wkshps Graphics Logo; Phi Delta Kappa SecY 1989-; InTNl Rdng Assn 1985-; NCTM 1987-; Bellville Village Cncl 1985-; Recognition Exemplory Service Sch 1988; *home:* 252 Markey St Bellville OH 44813

DEARWESTER, JAMES EDWARD, HS Soc Stud Teacher; *b:* Bellefontaine, OH; *m:* Cynthia Lou Shultz; *c:* Michelle R., Jennifer Jo.; *ed:* (BS) Comprehensive Soc Stud, Urbana Coll 1971; (MS) Sci Teaching, Univ of Dayton 1982; *cr:* Teacher/Coach Triad HS 1971-73, Riverside HS 1973-76, Beavercreek HS 1976-; *ai:* Head Intramural & Patriotism Week Dir; Track Coach; Discipline Comm; OH Cncl Soc Stud, OEA, NEA 1971-; *office:* Beavercreek HS 2940 Dayton-Xenia Rd Beavercreek OH 45385

DEATHERAGE, RONNIE WAYNE, 7th/8th Grade His/math Teacher; *b:* Mt Clemens, MI; *m:* Linda Barnes; *c:* Kevin, Kelly; *ed:* (BS) His/Poly Sci, 1979, (MS) His/Ed, 1988 E KY Univ; *cr:* 7th/8th Grade Teacher Broughtontown Elem 1980-85, Highland Elem 1985-; *ai:* Lincoln Cty Var Ftbl Coach; Lions Club; *home:* 140 Edgewood Dr Stanford KY 40484

DEATON, DAVID F., 5th Grade Teacher; *b:* Scottsburg, IN; *m:* Elizabeth Carol Baker; *c:* Shane, Kristen; *ed:* (BS) Elem Ed, IN St 1973; (MS) Elem Ed, IN Univ 1975; Grad Stud IN Univ; *cr:* 5th Grade Teacher Austin Elem Sch 1973-; *ai:* Little League, Babe Ruth, Jr HS Track, Jr HS Cross Cntry, Elem Bsktbl, 8th/9th Grade Coach; HS Bsktbl & JV Bsbl Asst Coach; Austin Bsbl Assn Pres 1980-; *home:* RR 1 Box 461A Austin IN 47102

DEATON, GARY, Jr HS Language Arts Teacher; *b:* Oneida, KY; *m:* Ruby Stacy; *c:* Gary W.; *ed:* (AA) Ed, Lees Jr Coll 1970; (BA) Elem Ed, 1972, (MA) Ed, 1981 Morehead St Univ; Rank I 6 Yr Prgm Cert Elem & Scndry Principalship; *cr:* 4th/6th Grade Math/Sci/Rdng Teacher Walton-Verona Ind Schls 1972-74; 7Th/8th Grade Rdng/Phys Ed Teacher South Lebanon Elem Sch 1974-75; 7th/8th Grade Lang Arts Teacher Owsley Cty HS 1975-; *ai:* Archery Club Spon; Co-Spon Project Graduation Sr Alcohol/Drug-Free Party; Masonic Lodge; Owsley Cty Saddle Club & Sportsmans Club; *home:* Box 44 Ricetown KY 41364

DEATON, MARSHA GRANT, 2nd Grade Teacher; *b:* Odessa, TX; *m:* Tilmon; *c:* Brad, Jill; *ed:* (BS) Ed, 1971, (MS) Interdisciplinary, 1983 East TX St Univ; *cr:* 1st Grade Teacher Crestview Elem 1971-73; 1st/2nd & 4th Grade Teacher Avery Elem 1973-; *ai:* TSTA 1971-; PTA-PTO 1973-; Avery Garden Club (1st VP) 1985-; *home:* Rt 1 Box 183 Avery TX 75554

DEATON, MARY LOUISE ATTAYEK, Mathematics Teacher/Dept Chair; *b:* Raleigh, NC; *m:* Robert Wayne; *c:* Thomas Attayek, Nicholas E.; *ed:* (BA) Math, Univ of NC Wilmington 1978; (MED) Math, Campbell Univ 1985; *cr:* Teacher W Harnett HS 1978-85; Teacher/Dept Chm Smithfield-Selma HS 1985-; *ai:* Jr Class Spon; Schlsp Comm; Bridge Club; NC Math Teachers Schlsp; *office:* Smithfield-Selma HS Bookerdairy Rd Smithfield NC 27577

DEATON, ROBERT ALLEN, Band Director; *b:* Charlotte, NC; *m:* Debra Mc Neil; *c:* Marta, Tracy; *ed:* (BM) Instrumental Music, Appalachian St Univ 1972; *cr:* Band Dir Howe Hall Mid Sch 1972-73, Middleton HS 1973-76, South Point HS 1979-; *ai:* Marching, Concert, Jazz Bands; Amer Sch Band Dirs Assn 1984-; South Cntrl Band Masters Chm 1986-88; Phi Mu Alpha; Mulberry Baptist Church Deacon; Guest Conductor Charlotte Jr Honor Band; *office:* South Point HS 906 South Point Rd Belmont NC 28012

DEATRY, CRYSTAL LEE CAMPBELL, Art/Mathematics Teacher; *b:* Tremonton, UT; *m:* Jerry Clark; *c:* Heather D., Brandyn, Jeremy; *ed:* (BS) Elem Ed/Early Chldhd Endorsement, 1972, (MED) Art/Creativity/Classroom Management, 1978 UT St Univ; Dist & UT St Univ Wkshps; *cr:* 4th Grade Teacher Mc Kinley Elem 1972-82; 3rd Grade Teacher Honeyville Elem 1982-83; 6th-8th Grade Teacher Bear River Mid Sch 1983-; *ai:* Graphic Art Specialist; Dist Curr Comm Mem; 6th Grade Adv & Math Chm; Delta Kappa Gamma Secy 1973-80; Alpha Delta Kappa Secy 1984-; Tremonton Civic League (Secy, Chm) 1978-; Amer Legion Auxiliary 1989-; Parent Child Tutorial Book.

DEAVERS, BETTY LOU BRISTER, 4th/5th Grade English Teacher; *b:* Lawrence Cty, MS; *m:* Denson Earl; *c:* Cynthia L. Alford, Denson B.; *ed:* (BS) Elem Ed, USM 1970; (MSE) Elem Ed, William Carey 1979; *cr:* 6th Grade Eng/Sci Teacher Sumrall Attendance Center 1970-78; Elem/Jr HS Eng Teacher Topeka-Tilton Sch 1978-; *ai:* MS Assn Educators 1970-84; MS Prof Educators 1984-; Delta Kappa Gamma 1985-; *home:* Rt 2 Box 174 B Jayess MS 39641

DEBERRY, SHARIS KYMBLE, Social Studies Teacher; *b:* Jackson, TN; *ed:* (BS) Poly Sci/Sociology, 1976, (BS) Accounting, 1986 Lambuth Coll; (MED) Counseling/Personnel Services, Memphis St Univ 1977; *cr:* Classroom Teacher Tigrett Jr HS 1977-; *ai:* Mayors Advisory Cncl Faculty Rep; Just Say No Club Coord; Jackson Ed Assn Faculty Rep; Alpha Kappa Alpha; *office:* Tigrett Jr HS 716 Westwood Ave Jackson TN 38301

DEBERTIN, RICHARD HAROLD, Agricultural Education Teacher; *b:* Parshall, ND; *m:* Rosemary; *c:* Tanya, Kyle, Tamara; *ed:* (AS) Sci, NDSF-Bottiuar 1962; (BS) Ag Ed, 1967, (MS) Ag Ed, 1983 NDSU-Fargo; *cr:* Ag Ed Teacher Berthold Public Sch 1967-; *ai:* FFA Adv; Sr Slides Adv; NEA 1967-; NDEA 1967-; NDVATA Pres 1967- Teacher of Yr 1983; NVATA 1967-; NDVA 1967- Teacher of Yr 1985; *office:* Berthold Public Sch Box 185 Berthold ND 58718

DEBEVEC, GARY RAYMOND, Mathematics/Science Teacher; *b:* Big Falls, MN; *m:* Loretta Dion; *c:* Heather, Nicole, Joseph; *ed:* (BS) Elem, Bemidji St 1964; Elem, MI St, E MI; *cr:* Teacher/Gifted Prgm Flint Cmmty Sch 1964-; *ai:* Ligon Environmental Steering Comm; Outdoor Ed Week Camping; MAGTC 1980-; MI Assn of Cmptr Users Learner 1985-; Mini Grant Flint Public Schls; *home:* 417 Carrie Dr Flushing MI 48433

DEBEVEC, MARY SULLIVAN, Soc Stud/Home Ec Teacher; *b:* Virginia, MN; *m:* Raymond A.; *c:* Tony, David; *ed:* (BS) Home Ec, 1964, (BS) Soc Stud, 1985 Univ of MN; *cr:* Home Ec Instr White Bear Lake Jr HS 1964-65; Home Ec/Soc Stud Teacher Chisholm Jr/Sr HS 1965-; *ai:* Sch Dist Staff Dev Comm; Jr Class Adv; Pres of Local Teacher Fed; AFT, MN Fed of Teachers 1964-; Chisholm Fed of Teachers Pres 1990-91; Amer Home Ec Assn, MN Home Ec Assn 1964-; MN Cncl for Soc Stud 1990-91; Amer Cancer Society; St Louis Cty Historical Society; St Planning Comm for Voc Home Ec; Natl Geographic Society Summer Inst 1990; Great Lakes Area Union Leadership Inst; *office:* Chisholm Jr/Sr HS 3rd St & 3rd Ave Chisholm MN 55719

DE BIASE, JEAN M., Mathematics Teacher; *b:* Philadelphia, PA; *m:* Peter P.; *c:* Vincent; *ed:* (BA) Scndry Math Ed, 1979, (MED) Scndry Math Ed, 1983 Temple Univ; *cr:* Math Teacher Stoddart Fleisher Jr HS 1979-83; Math Teacher Alternate for Mid Yrs 1983-; *ai:* Mathletes Spon; Pre-Algebra Club; Sch Enrichment Comm; *office:* AMG II Mid Sch 13th & Susquehanna Ave Philadelphia PA 19122

DE BOER, KAREN L., History Teacher; *b:* Sheffield, AL; *m:* David; *ed:* (BA) His/Geography, Univ of TX Austin 1968; (MLA) Liberal Arts, Southern Meth Univ 1982; TX Alliance Geographic Ed at Univ of TX Arlington 1989; St Bar of TX Law & Hum Inst 1989, Law & Ec 1988; Parent Effectiveness Trng 1974; Dallas Ind Sch Dist US His Wkshp 1986; Grad Stud Univ of TX Arlington 1984, 1986, Univ of Houston Clear Lake 1976, S TX Coll of Law 1970; LTV Making of Defense 1987; NICEL Practical Law Seminar 1986; Friendswood Ind Sch Dist Linguistics Seminar 1969; *cr:* Friendswood Ind Sch Dist 1968-76; Temporary Teacher 1968-81; Substitute Teacher Richardson Ind Sch Dist 1976-77; Dallas Ind Sch Dist 1977-; *ai:* Mock Trial Competition Spon; Southern Assn Evaluation Comm Chairperson; NHS Faculty Cncl 1987-89; Departmental Lead Teacher 1985-87; Whiz Quiz Coord 1982-84; Faculty Advisory Cncl Departmental Rep 1979-84 & Building Rep 1973-76; Bus Magnet Center Close-Up Prgm Spon 1983-84; Newspaper in Ed Participant 1981-87; Magnet Scholastic Competition Spon 1980; Dallas Ind Sch Dist Textbook Comm Chairperson 1984; Friendswood Ind Sch Dist TX His Textbook Comm 1970-71; NCSS, TX Alliance for Geographic Ed; TX St Teachers Assn Life Mem; Natl Cncl for Geographic Ed 1986-88; Classroom Teachers of Dallas Building Rep 1981-82; TX Cncl for Soc Stud (Exec Bd 1987-, St Membership Comm 1987-) 1968-; Richardson Ed Assn 1976-77; Dallas Cncl for Soc Stud (Treas 1985-87, Membership Chairperson 1985-87, St Bd Rep 1987-) 1985-; Gamma Theta Upsilon; SMU Natl Trial Lawyers Assn Mock Trial Judge 1984-86; Bus & Management Center Teacher of Yr 1988-89; Law Focused Ed Leon Jaworski Awd Teaching Excl 1984; Nom Amer Lawyers Auxiliary HS Teacher of Yr 1985; *office:* Bus Magnet Center 2218 Bryan St Dallas TX 75201

DE BOIS, THELMA INGRAM, English Teacher; *b:* Beulah, ND; *m:* Oran P. Jr.; *c:* Lynnette Debois Okola, Drew S.; *ed:* (BA) Home Ec/Eng, CSULB 1973; Post Grad Stud Ed; *cr:* Home Ec Teacher 1974-82, Eng Teacher 1982- Downey HS; *ai:* Omicron Nu, Phi Kappa Phi, Kappa Delta Pi, NEA, CTA, PTA; *office:* Downey HS 11040 Brookshire Avde Downey CA 90241

DE BONIS, MICHAEL JOSEPH, History Teacher; *b:* Troy, NY; *m:* Marilyn M. Zelsnak; *c:* Michael, Theresa, Robert; *ed:* (BA) His, 1959, (MA) His, 1961 Albany St Teachers Coll; *cr:* His Teacher Hudson HS 1959-60, Maine-Endwell HS 1961-; *ai:* NHS Comm; NEA 1961-.

DE BONO, CARL ANTHONY, English Teacher; *b:* Trinidad, CO; *ed:* (AA) Ed, Trinidad St Jr Coll 1964; (BA) Eng Ed, Univ of N CO 1966; (MA) Eng Ed, Adams St Coll 1969; Grad Stud; *cr:* Eng/Drama Teacher Trinidad HS 1966-; Theatre Arts Teacher Trinidad St Jr Coll 1990; *ai:* Eng Dept Chm; Trinidad HS Performing Arts Chm; Honor Society Spon; Written Several Plays & Book; *home:* 722 San Juan Trinidad CO 81082

DE BORD, HAROLD WEBB, 6th Grade Soc Stud/Rdng Teachr; *b:* Johnson City, TN; *ed:* (BS) Elem Ed, 1966, (MA) Elem Ed/Admin, 1973 E TN St Univ; Several Wkshps; *cr:* 5th Grade Teacher Indialantic Elem Sch 1966-67; 5th/6th Grade Teacher Chapel Hill Elem Sch 1967-69; 6th Grade Teacher 1969-73, Prin 1973-81 Henry Johnson Elem Sch; 5th/6th Grade Teacher Cherokee Elem Sch 1981-87; 7th Grade Vice Prin Liberty Bell Jr HS 1987-88; 6th Grade Vice-Prin 1988-89, 6th Grade Teacher 1989- Liberty Bell Mid Sch; *ai:* Soc Stud Re-Evaluation Study Southern Assn Coll & Schls Review; NEA 1966-; TN Ed Assn, Johnson City Ed Assn 1969-; TN Assn of Mid Schls 1989-; TN Elem Assn Southern Assn of Colls & Schls Delegate 1979-82; Kappa Delta Pi, Phi Delta Kappa 1986-; Excel Outstanding Teacher Awd, TN Classroom Teacher of Yr Awd & Liberty Bell Mid Sch Steering Comm Staff Dev 1985-86; TN Congress Parents & Teachers Life Membership Awd 1974; *home:* 404 Oak Ln-Tanglewood Johnson City TN 37604

DE BRABER, LEONARD DAVID, Soc Stud Teacher & Dept Chm; *b:* Grand Rapids, MI; *m:* Dianne Nyhuis; *c:* Andrew, Sandra; *ed:* (BS) Soc Stud, Grand Valley St Univ 1969; (MA) Counseling/Personnel, W MI Univ 1972; Ec, Olivet Coll, Grand Valley St Univ, W MI Univ; Soc Stud, MI St Univ; *cr:* Teacher/Cnslr Sparta Mid Sch 1969-80; Teacher Sparta HS 1980-; *ai:* Soc Stud Dept Chm; Girls Var Bsktbl Coach; NEA, MEA, SEA 1969-; Amer Psych Assn 1984-; MHSAA & BCAM 1980-; Sparta Ed Assn VP; Fairview Ref Church Elder 1975-; Fairview Chrstn Chld Care Center Bd Chm 1989-; Jr Achievement (Teacher, Consultant) 1986-; Jr Achievement Outstanding Ec Educator 1990; *office:* Sparta HS 480 S State St Sparta MI 49345

DE BROUX, RICHARD THEODORE, 8th Grade Science Teacher; *b:* Kaukauna, WI; *m:* Evelyn Marie Berg; *c:* Dean, Scott, Faye, Jeffrey; *ed:* (BA) General Sci, Univ of WI La Crosse 1964; (MS) Sci/Geology, Union Coll 1970; Grad Stud UT St Univ, E NM Univ, Univ of WI Stevens Point, Univ of WI Oshkosh; *cr:* Math/Sci Teacher Lincoln Jr HS 1964-; Sci Teacher Madison Sr HS 1964-; *ai:* Appleton Ed Assn Pres 1975-76, Recognition 1979; WI Ed Assn Cncl Sch Bd of Dir 1979-85; NEA, WI Sci Teachers Assn; Appleton City Cncl (Alderman 1985-, Cncl Pres 1989); Appleton Teachers Credit Union (Bd of Dir, Chm of Bd); Natl Sci Fnd Grant; *office:* Madison Jr HS 2020 S Carpenter Appleton WI 54915

DE BRUCE, MICHAEL LAWRENCE, Special Ed Dept Chair; *b:* Chicago, IL; *c:* Lawrence Young, Tricha A. Randolph; *ed:* (AA) Math, Parkland Coll 1978; (BA) Ed, Lane Coll 1980; Spec Ed, GA Southwestern; Adult Literacy Cert; *cr:* Asst Prin Byromville Elem 1985-87; Dept Chm Dooly Cty HS & Mid Sch 1987-; *ai:* Local Coord Spec Olympics Act; Girls Bsktbl Coach & Asst Coach; NEA, Dooly Cty Educators Assn 1982-88; GA Math Teachers Assn 1981-; Dooling City Cncl Councilman 1989-; *office:* Dooly Cty Mid & HS Hwy 41 N Vienna GA 31092

DE BRUYCKERE, ARLYN MATTHEW, Chemistry/Physics Teacher; *b:* Marshall, MN; *m:* Kimberly D. Hasz; *ed:* (BS) Chem/Phys Sci, Moorhead St Univ 1983; Univ of N IA, Gustavus Adolphus Coll, Moorhead St Univ; *cr:* Chem/Physics/Phys Sci Teacher Shanley HS 1983-87; Guest Instr/Chem Teacher Gustavus Adolphus Coll 1987-88; Chem/Physics Teacher Hutchinson 1988-; *ai:* Jr HS Girls Bsktbl; Drivers Ed; SADD; NHS; Amer Chemical Society, NSTA, AAPT; *office:* Hutchinson HS Roberts Rd Hutchinson MN 55350

DE CAPRIO, JUDITH LA VORGNA, Social Studies Teacher; *b:* New Haven, CT; *m:* John Anthony; *c:* John, Jeffrey, Jenine, Joseph; *ed:* (BA) Ed, 1961, (MS) Spec Ed, 1971 S CT St Univ; *cr:* 4th Grade Teacher Pine Orchard 1961-63; 8th Grade Soc Stud Teacher Branford Intermediate 1978-; *ai:* Prof Dev Comm; Cooperating Teacher Prgm Beginning Educator Support & Trng Prgm; Branford Ed Assn Building Rep; NEA; Faculty Excl Awd 1984; *office:* Branford Intermediate Sch 185 Damascus Rd Branford CT 06405

DECKARD, LINDA M., Kindergarten Teacher; *b:* Princeton, WV; *m:* Timothy J.; *c:* Sherlyn, Amber; *ed:* (BA) Elem Ed, Hobe Sound Bible Acad 1969; Concord Coll, Indian River Cmmty Coll; *cr:* Elem Teacher Hobe Sound Bible Acad 1970-; Coll Instr Hobe Sound Bible Coll 1982-; *ai:* Yrbk Adv; Field Day, Safety Patrol Prgm, Church Vacation Bible Sch Prgm Coord; Hobe Sound Bible Coll/Acad Alumni Assn Treas 1978-89; Sch Paper Contributing Ed; Statewide Educl Wkshps; Childrens Winter Retreat; *home:* 9286 Karin St Hobe Sound FL 33455

DECKER, ARLO A., Sci/Health Teacher/Admin Asst; *b:* Los Angeles, CA; *m:* Marcia Dalley; *c:* Allan, Gillian; *ed:* (BS) Phys Ed, Boise St Univ 1972; (MED) Admin, Univ of ID 1989; *cr:* Teacher New Plymouth Jr-Sr HS 1972-; *ai:* Adv 8th Grade; Jr HS Stu Cncl; Ftbl & Track Coach; Dist Discipline & Evaluation Comm; ID Sci Teachers Assn, IAHPERD, NASSP, Dist III Coaches Assn; *office:* New Plymouth Jr-Sr HS 208 S Plymouth Ave New Plymouth ID 83655

DECKER, DANIEL E., Head Football Coach; *b:* Lock Haven, PA; *m:* M. Elizabeth Pokorney; *ed:* (BA) Scndry Ed, Lock Haven Univ 1975; *cr:* Teacher/Coach Nazareth Area HS 1975-77; Ftbl Coach Lock Haven Univ 1977-82; Landscaper Bus Owner 1977-; Ftbl Coach Bald Eagle Nittany HS 1987-; *ai:* Lock Haven Jaycees (Pres 1980-, Ambassador 1987); Outstanding Young Man of America 1985; *home:* 260 Hogan Blvd Mill Hall PA 17751

DECKER, DREW LEROY, Physical Ed/Math Teacher; *b:* Flint, MI; *m:* Karen Anne Stockwell; *ed:* (BA) Health/Phys Ed/Recreation/Bus Admin, Aquinas Coll 1982; Math, Univ of MI 1985; *cr:* Bus Teacher Marksville IA 1983-84; Math/Phys Ed Teacher Tawas Area 1985-; *ai:* Var Bsktbl Coach; Honors Awd Comm; Bsktbl Coaches Assn of MI 1984-; *office:* Tawas Area Jr HS 255 M-55 Tawas City MI 48763

DECKER, ELIZABETH, Social Studies Teacher; *b:* Hilo, HI; *ed:* (BA) Eng Lit, 1974, (BA) Poly Sci, 1989 Univ of HI; Working Towards Prof Certificate Prgm; Lions Club Drug Ed Prgm; *cr:* Lang Art Teacher St Joseph HS 1975-78, Hilo HS 1979-82, Mt View Elem-Intermediate 1980-81; Lang Art/Soc Stud Teacher Waiakea Intermediate 1982-; *ai:* Soc Stud Dept, WASC Accreditation, WIS Homeroom Prgm Chm; Constitution By-Law Adv; Coordinating Comm Mem; Study Skills Cadre Mem; NCTE 1989-; HSTA, NEA 1979-; Intl Rdng Assn (Pres 1984-85, VP 1983-84); Holy Apostles Church Layreader 1986-; Whos Who Amer Coll Stu 1989; Initiated Project Bus Waiakea Intermediate Sch; Co-Authored Waiakea Intermediate Sch Research & Prgm Book; Whos Who in Amer Coll Stu; *office:* Waiakea Intermediate Sch 200 W Puainako St Hilo HI 96720

DECKER, EVA, Fourth Grade Teacher; *b:* Murphy, NC; *m:* Billy M.; *c:* Davia C. Decker Gordon, Darren B.; *ed:* (BS) Mid Grades Ed, 1980, (MED) Mid Grades Ed, 1985 North GA Coll; *cr:* 4th Grade Teacher Union Cty Elem Sch 1980-; *ai:* Leadership Comm; Chm Tardies & Early Dismissals Comm; Delta Kappa Gamma Mem 1985-; PTA Secy 1987-88; Order of Eastern Star Mem; Butternut Creek Ladies Golf Assn (Mem, Secy); *office:* Union Cty Elem Sch Rt 2 Box 3000 Blairsville GA 30512

DECKER, GEORGE RUSSELL, English Teacher; *b:* Curwensville, PA; *m:* Diane Renee Woodel; *c:* Jennifer, Janessa; *ed:* (BS) Eng/Rdng, Clarion St Coll 1967; *cr:* Eng/Rdng Teacher Upper St Clair Sch Dist 1967-68; HS Eng Teacher Curwensville Area Sch Dist 1968-; *ai:* Stage Crew Adv; Bsktbl Ofcl Scorer; PSEA, NEA; Curwensville Lions Club Secy 1988-; *office:* Curwensville Area HS 650 Beech St Curwensville PA 16833

DECKER, MARILYN LOUISE, Foreign Lang Dept Head-French; *b:* Indianapolis, IN; *m:* David Mark; *c:* Jaime N., James B.; *ed:* (BA) Fr Ed, Bradley Univ 1974; Sorbonne Universite De Paris 1972-73; Graduate Work in Adult Ed/Bi-ling; *cr:* Fr Teacher East Anchorage HS 1977-; *ai:* Spon Spec Classes; Spon Intnl Club 1977-87; NEA 1977-79/1986-; Amer Scandanavian Stu Exch Area Rep 1986-; Amer Field Service & ASSE Liason & Area Rep; *office:* East Anchorage H S 4025 E 24th Anchorage AK 99508

DECKER, WILLIAM L., JR., English Teacher; *b:* Hardinsburg, KY; *ed:* (BS) Ag Ec, Univ of KY 1983; (BS) Elem Ed, W KY Univ 1988; *cr:* Self Employed Family Farm 1978-85; Extension 4-H Agent Univ of KY Extension Service 1985-86; Teacher/coach Irvington Elem 1989-; *ai:* 6th-8th Grade Girls & Boys Bsktbl Coach; Breckinridge Cty HS Girls Sftbl Asst Coach; Breckinridge Cty HS Ftbl Part Time Asst Coach; Goshen Baptist Church Asst Teacher/Life Mem; Breckinridge Baptist Athletic Assn League Dir 1987-; Gideons Mem 1990; *office:* Irvington Elementary Sch Rt 2 Box 90 Irvington KY 40146

DE CONNA, THOMAS, English Teacher; *b:* Plainfield, NJ; *m:* Sheryl; *c:* Christian; *ed:* (BA) Eng, 1975, (MAT) Scndry Ed, 1976 Seton Hall Univ; *cr:* Teacher St Marys Grammar Sch 1976-78, Byram Elem 1978-84, Rangeview HS 1984-; *ai:* Aurora Ed Assn 1990; CO Ed Assn 1984-; *office:* Rangeview HS 17599 E Iliff Ave Aurora CO 80013

DECSI, RITA, Second Grade Teacher; *b:* Buffalo, NY; *m:* Nandor; *ed:* (BA) Ed, D Youville Coll 1970; (MS) Ed, Canisius Coll 1972; Math, Whole Lang, Learning Styles; *cr:* 1st Grade Teacher Parochial Sch 1964-70; 2nd Grade Teacher Hamburg Cntrl Schls 1973-; *ai:* Math, Rdng, Curr Comm; Rdng Act Unit Planning Dir; Hamburg Teachers Assn, NY St United Teachers 1973-; Hamburg Cntrl PTA (Secy 1975-76) 1973-; *home:* 8868 Back Creek Rd Boston NY 14025

DE CURTIS, ANTHONY PHILLIP, English Teacher; *b:* Philadelphia, PA; *m:* Flora Sonia; *c:* Daria, Anthony Jr.; *ed:* (BS) Ed/eng, St Josephs Univ 1970; (MA) Theatre, Villanova Univ 1980; *cr:* Eng/Soc Stud Teacher St Donato Sch 1967-70; Eng Teacher St Thomas More HS 1970-75, Cardinal O'Hara HS 1975-; Eng Professor Widener Univ 1985-; *ai:* NCTE 1981-; Natl Soc His Theatre Pres 1984-86; Alpha Psi Omega 1974-77; Chi-rho Pres 1972-74; Italian Amer of Delaware Cty Pres 1988-, Service Awd 1988; Selected Dept Chm Eng 1974-75; Ed Financial Text Published 1987; *office:* Cardinal O'Hara HS 1701 S Sproul Rd Springfield PA 19064

DEE, RICHARD R., Biology Teacher; *b:* Buffalo, NY; *m:* Wanda L. Steenbergen; *c:* Sandra Bookmiller, Richard R. II, Leslie D.; *ed:* (BS) Bio/Chem, 1963, (MS) Bio, 1963 W KY Univ; Grad Work Canisius Coll, St Univ of NY Buffalo; *cr:* Grad Asst W KY Univ 1962-63; Bio Teacher Maryvale HS 1963-; *ai:* Photography; Building Rep 1986-88; Salary Negotiation Chm 1987; *office:* Maryvale HS 1050 Maryvale Dr Cheektowaga NY 14225

DEEL, CECIL, Seventh Grade Teacher; *b:* Clintwood, VA; *m:* Teresa; *c:* Christina, Philip, Marcus; *ed:* (AA) Ed, Lees Jr Coll 1967; (BS) Soc Sci, Cumberland Coll 1969; (MA) Ed, Morehead St Univ 1973; Grad Stud Univ of VA; US Army Medical Corps; *cr:* Teacher Clinchco Elem 1969-; *ai:* SCA Spon; 4-H Adult Leader; NEA 1973-; SW VA Teachers of Math 1980-; *home:* Rt 1 Box 490 Clintwood VA 24228

DEEMER, A. LISETTE PEREZ, Music Teacher; *b:* Lincoln, NE; *m:* Gary Lynn; *ed:* (BM) Music Ed, Union Coll 1983; (MM) Vocal Performance/Choral Conducting, Univ of NE Lincoln 1986; *cr:* Grad Asst Univ of NE Lincoln 1983-86; Vocal/Instrumental Music Teacher Lincoln 7th Day Adv Schls 1985-; *ai:* Soph Class & Extracurricular Spon; Touring Vocal Groups; NE Adv Schls Music Festival Clinician 1986-88; *office:* Helen Hyatt Elem Sch 5240 Calvert St Lincoln NE 68506

DEEP, ANNORA RODGERS, Fourth Grade Teacher; *b:* Pittsburgh, PA; *m:* Donald; *c:* Colleen, Kelly L., Donny; *ed:* (BS) Elem Ed, Duquesne Univ 1964; Grad work towards MS, Duquesne Univ; *cr:* 6th Grade Teacher North Hills Schls 1964-67; Compensatory Ed Teacher Ridgewood Schls 1976-79; 4th-5th Grade Teacher South Side Schls 1981-; *ai:* SSEA, PSEA, & NEA; *office:* South Side Sch Dist RD 1 Box 410 Hookstown PA 15050

DEERING, GALE POWELL, Sixth Grade Teacher; *b:* Jacksonville, FL; *m:* John Arthur Sr.; *c:* John Jr., Angela; *ed:* (BS) Elem Ed, Jacksonville Univ 1970; *cr:* 6th Grade Teacher Merrill Road Elem 1970, Arlington Annex Elem 1970-72, Susie E Tolbert Elem 1972-73; 5th/6th Grade Teacher Walton Ferry Elem 1973-; *ai:* PTA (Treas 1974-75, 2nd VP 1979-80); PTO Secy 1989-; Teacher of Yr Building Level 1988; *office:* Walton Ferry Elem Sch 732 Walton Ferry Rd Hendersonville TN 37075

DEERING, HILARY J., Science Department Chair; *b:* Carlow, Ireland; *ed:* (BSC) Physics/Chem/Math, Univ Galway Ireland 1942; (MS) Admin, Immaculate Coll Hollywood 1952; *cr:* Instr 1948-53, Prin 1953-60 St Monica HS; Teacher 1960-69, Prin 1969-83, Teacher 1983- Pater Noster HS; *ai:* Bus Mgr; Natl Sci, Natl Math 1950-; CA Interscholastic Assn 1970-80; *office:* Pater Noster HS 2911 San Fernando Rd Los Angeles CA 90065

DEERMAN, VAN MICHAEL, Eng/Physical Education Teacher; *b:* Anniston, AL; *m:* Susan Ann O'Rourke; *c:* David M., Susan M., Matthew S.; *ed:* (BS) Phys Ed, 1970, (MS) Scndry Ed/Phys Ed, 1975 Jacksonville St Univ; *cr:* Eng/Phys Ed Teacher/Coach Weaver HS 1970-; *ai:* W Club; Bsktbl & Asst Ftbl Coach; St Lukes Church Jr Warden 1983-86; Calhoun Cty Coach of Yr 1985-88; *home:* 1898 Hwy 21 N Jacksonville AL 36265

DEES, ROBBIN MARGARETTE, Home Economics Teacher; *b:* Dublin, GA; *m:* James Louie Jr.; *ed:* (AS) Psych, S GA Coll 1983; (BS) Home Ec Ed, GA Southern 1986; *cr:* Home Ec Teacher Lyons Jr HS 1986-; *ai:* FHA Adv; GAWE 1985-89; PAGE 1989-.

DEES, RUTH SAMPLE, Retired Fifth Grade Teacher; *b:* Fredericktown, MO; *m:* Fred; *ed:* (BS) Elem Ed, SE MO St Univ 1958; Correspondence & Extension Classes; *cr:* Teacher Madison Cty Schls 1939-84; *ai:* Classroom Teachers, MO St Teachers Assn; Alpha Delta Kappa (VP 1980-82, Historian 1982-84); NRTA, Meth Church (United Meth Women, Sunday Sch Teacher); *home:* 713 S Maple Fredericktown MO 63645

DE FAZIO, ALICE BARBERIO, Kindergarten Teacher; *b:* Clarksburg, WV; *m:* Mark; *c:* Maria, Anthony; *ed:* (BA) Early Chldhd Ed, 1976, (MA) Early Chldhd Ed, 1980 WV Univ; Grad Work Early Chldhd Ed, WV Univ; *cr:* Kndgtn Teacher West Milford Elem 1976-; *ai:* Bus Partnership Comm; Coord of Ed Fair; NEA, WVEA, HCEA; Alpha Delta Kappa; *home:* 1514 Gould Ave Clarksburg WV 26301

DE FELICE, MICHAEL JOE, Phys Ed Teacher/Dept Chair; *b:* Colorado Springs, CO; *m:* Joyce Dexter; *c:* Laura, James; *ed:* (BS) Phys Ed, E OR St Coll 1977; Advanced Grad Stud Guidance/Counseling, Univ of CO; Univ of N CO; *cr:* Head Bsbl Coach Elgin HS 1977; Phys Ed Teacher Sproul Jr HS 1978-; *ai:* Stu Cncl Spon; Intramural Dir;Coaching Boys Bsktbl, Girls Track; Past Bsbl, Ftbl, Wrestling Coach; Walk for Mankind Faculty Spon; CO Sch Cnslr Assn 1988-89; PTO Pres 1987-89.

DE FEO, BARBARA A., Third Grade Teacher; *b:* Glen Cove, NY; *m:* Richard K.; *c:* Kristen, Ricky; *ed:* (BA) Elem Ed, 1972, (MA) Elem Ed, 1976 St Univ NY Cortland; *cr:* 4th Grade Teacher 1972-74, 6th Grade Teacher 1975-76 Owego North Elem Sch; 4th Grade Teacher Owego North Elem & Apalachin Elem 1976-89; 3rd Grade Teacher Apalachin Elem Sch 1989-; *ai:* Owego-Apalachin Teachers Assn, NY St United Teachers 1972-; *office:* Apalachin Elem Sch Pennsylvania Ave Apalachin NY 13732

DE FILIPPO, CYDNEY ZYLO, Social Studies Teacher; *b:* Washington, PA; *m:* Wallace; *c:* Lauren; *ed:* (BS) Scndry Ed/Soc Stud, Clarion Univ 1971; Insurance License St of NJ; NJ Realtors License; Working on Masters; *cr:* Teacher 1971-88, Career Coord 1978-88 Horace Mann Sch; Teacher Mary Jane Donohoe Sch 1988-; *ai:* Stu Cncl Adv; Peer Teacher; City Schls of Excl CORE Team Sub-Comm Chairperson; NJ Geographical Alliance 1988-; NJ Cncl Soc Stud 1980-89; St Henrys Rosary Society Pres 1989-; St Henrys Parish Spiritual Life Comm 1980-, Veterans Recognition Awds 1988; Bayonne Bd of Ed Designed Dist Awd Winning Display for Convention 1988-89; WOR-TV A Plus for Kids Awd 1989-; Dist Mini-Grant Winner 1988-; Bicentennial of Constitution Dist Elem Rep 1988; NJ Governors Teacher Recognition Awd 1990; *office:* Mary Jane Donohoe Sch E 5th St Bayonne NJ 07002

DEFOE, NANCY L., Second Grade Teacher/Elem Prin; *b:* Hallock, MN; *m:* Joe; *c:* Megan, Matthew, Nicole; *ed:* (BS) Elem Ed, Mayville St Univ 1974; *cr:* Kndgtn Teacher/Basic Skills Aetna Public Sch 1974-75; Supvr University Care Center 1975-76; 3rd/4th Grade Teacher Milton Public Sch 1976-78; 2nd Grade Teacher Pembina Public Sch 1978-; *ai:* ND Cncl of Sch Admin 1988-; Welca Luth Church Secy 1989-.

DE FONDE, AGNES MURPHY, Third Grade Teacher; *b:* Monaca, PA; *m:* Raymond; *ed:* (BS) Elem Ed, Muskingum Coll 1962; (MA) Elem Ed, Univ of Pittsburgh 1967; *cr:* 4th Grade Teacher Beaver Area Sch Dist 1962-66; 3rd Grade Teacher Ellwood City Area Sch Dist 1967-; *home:* RD 2 Box 319 Portersville PA 16051

DEFORD, JO ANN, French/Spanish Teacher; *b:* Saginaw, MI; *ed:* (BSED) Span, Cntrl MI Univ 1970; *cr:* Foreign Lang Teacher Arthur Hill HS 1970-; *ai:* Modern Foreign Lang Club; Pom Pon Coach; Pep Club; Sch Trips; Modern Foreign Lang Assn 1985-; Saginaw Ed Assn, MEA, SEA 1970-; *office:* Arthur Hill HS 3115 Mackinaw Saginaw MI 48602

DE FORD, LINDA EHRIGSON, Social Studies Chairperson; *b:* Houston, TX; *ed:* (BS) US His, Sam Houston St Univ 1971; *cr:* Teacher Splendora HS 1971-89; *ai:* Sr Class Spon; Natl Honor Society Adv.

DE FRANCISCO, MICHAEL ANTHONY, Counselor; *b:* Jamestown, NY; *m:* Darlene Suzanne Hill; *ed:* (AA) Hum, Jamestown Cmmty 1974; (BA) Eng Ed, St Univ of NY Oneonta 1976; (MS) Ed/Counseling, 1981, Advanced Certificate of Specialization Sch Counseling, 1981 St Bonaventure Univ; *cr:* Eng Teacher Panama Cntrl Sch 1978-79; Guidance Cnslr Falconer Cntrl 1982-85; Homelife Cnslr Leelanau Sch 1986-87; Guidance Cnslr Bradford Cntrl 1987-88, Jamestown HS 1988-; *ai:* Schlsp Chairperson; Kappa Delta Pi Mem 1981-; *home:* Rt 2 Box 184 Sinclairville NY 14782

DE GAY, JEANNINE CHIPOULET, French Teacher; *b:* Albi, France; *m:* Windell Wayne; *c:* Jean D., Jean L.; *ed:* (BA) Philosophy, Univ of Toulouse 1958; (BA) Ed, Univ of Paris 1960; (MED) Foreign Lang/Fr, Univ of GA 1985; Kndgtn-12th Grade Inst of Foreign Lang Univ of GA 1989; *cr:* 6th-8th Grade Teacher 1956-58, K-3rd Grade Teacher 1958-59, 6th-8th Grade Teacher 1959-63 Vitry Le Francois Marine France; 9th-12th Grade Teacher Newton Cty HS 1986-; *ai:* Thespian Troop NCHS Ass Dir; Flag Mem 1987-; AATF Mem 1988-; Stu Achievement Awd Article Published.

DEGENHARDT, ELIZABETH ANN (MULLEN), 8th Grade Reading Teacher; *b:* South Amboy, NJ; *m:* Steven; *c:* Matthew; *ed:* (BA) Elem Ed, 1973, Eng, 1973 Coll of St Elizabeth; Numerous Grad Courses in Ed, Trenton St Rutgers Univ; *cr:* 4th Grade Teacher St James Elem Sch 1973-74; 6th Grade Teacher Samuel Shull Sch 1974-75, W C Mc Ginnis Sch 1975-; *ai:* Yrbk & Newspaper Staff Adv; Perth Amboy & Middlesex Cty Teacher of Yr 1984; *office:* William C McGinnis Sch 271 State St Perth Amboy NJ 08861

DE GENNARO, ANTHONY RAY, Chemistry/Physics Teacher; *b:* Oberlin, OH; *m:* Gayle L. Geistweite; *ed:* (BS) Sci Ed, 1980, (MA) Math, 1985 OH St Univ; Working Towards PhD Industrial Engineering, OH St Univ; *cr:* Teacher Reynoldsburg HS 1980-83; Grad Teaching Asst of Math OH St Uni v 1983-87; Teacher Reynoldsburg HS 1987 -; *ai:* Gifted Grant Comm; Math Assn America 1985-; Reynoldsburg Academic Boosters Spec Person 1989; Finalist Outstanding Teacher Asst OH St Univ 1985; *office:* Reynoldsburg HS 6699 E Livingston Ave Reynoldsburg OH 43068

DEGLER, JUDITH HUCKABY, 1st Grade Teacher; *b:* Daytona Beach, FL; *m:* George W.; *c:* Greg; *ed:* (BA) Elem Ed, 1976; (ME) Elem Ed, Rdng Specialist, 1982 Univ of Central Fl; *cr:* 2nd Grade Teacher Port Orange Elem 1976-80; 1st Grade Teacher Spruce Creek Elem 1984-; *ai:* Literary Magazine Comm Mem; Kappa Delta Phi; Cty 1st Grade Task Force Mem; Advisory Bd; Mem St Comm Set Standards for Beginning Teacher Exam; Narrated Video for Volunteers; Practice Ctr Wkshp Leader; *office:* Spruce Creek Elem Sch 642 Taylor Rd Port Orange FL 32127

DE GRAAFF, ERWIN, 1st-8th Grade Head Teacher; *b:* Hollandia, West New Guinea; *ed:* (BA) Elem Ed, Pedagogische Academie Rehoboth 1975; Home Study Intnl/Columbia Union Coll; *cr:* 3rd-6th Grade Teacher Maliebaanschool Utrecht Netherlands 1975-84; 1st-8th Grade Head Teacher Endless Mountains SDA Sch 1984-86, Lancaster SDA Sch 1986-; *ai:* Teaching Photography; Prin Cncl Vice Chm 1989-; *office:* Lancaster Seventh-Day Adventst 1721 Conard Rd Lancaster PA 17602

DE GRAAFF, HELEN GOYDICH, Kindergarten Teacher; *b:* Passaic, NJ; *m:* Robert P. Sr.; *c:* Nicholas, Robert Jr.; *ed:* (BA) Early Chldhd, Wm Paterson Coll 1975; *cr:* Teacher Our Lady of Sorrows Sch 1975-; *ai:* NCEA 1975-; *office:* Our Lady of Sorrows Sch 30 Madonna Pl Garfield NJ 07026

DE GROOT, DONNA VAN ROEKEL, Fifth Grade Teacher; *b:* Oskaloosa, IA; *m:* Howard; *c:* Karen, Lynn; *ed:* (BA) Elem Ed, William Penn Coll 1971; (MSE) Teaching Effectiveness & Elem Curr, Drake Univ 1988; Elem Classroom, Whole Lang, Rdng Comp, Assertive Discipline, Childrens Lit, Aerospace, Study Skills; *cr:* 5th Grade Teacher Whittier Elem 1972-; *ai:* Teach Summer & After Sch Classes in Cmptr Keyboarding; Crisis Team, Wellness Comm, Health Comm, OEA Negotiations Comm, AEA Media Selection Comm Mem; Soc Stud Comm Chairperson; Delta Kappa Gamma (Secy 1988-, 1st VP 1990-92); NEA, ISEA, OEA 1972-; Chrstn Opportunity Center (Vicar 1989-, Bd Mem 1987-); Cntrl Reformed Church (Sr High Youth Leader, Calvinette Leader, Womens Work, Jr HS Sunday Sch Teacher); *office:* Whittier Elem Sch 604 North B Street Oskaloosa IA 52577

DE HART, SCOTT DAVID, Physical Ed Teacher/Coach; *b:* South Bend, IN; *m:* Joan Marie Gregorowicz; *ed:* (BS) Phys Ed, St Josephs Coll 1985; (MS) Scndry Ed, IN Univ 1990; *cr:* Soc Stud Teacher St Jude Sch 1985-87; Ftbl/Wrestling/Bsbl Coach Marian HS 1985-87; Health Teacher/Coach Delta HS 1987-88; His/Phys Ed Teacher/Coach Wawasee HS 1988-; *ai:* Ftbl & Wrestling Coach; NCA/PBA Review; IN St Teachers Assn; IN Ftbl Coaches Assn New Membership Chm 1986; IN Wrestling Coaches Assn; *office:* Wawasee H S 1 Warrior Path Syracuse IN 46567

DE HERNANDEZ, FRANCES NOCHERA, Art/English Teacher; *b:* San Juan, PR; *m:* Jaime Hernandez-Circuns; *ed:* (BA) Fine Arts, 1966, (MA) Translation, 1981 Univ of PR; Ceramics & Calligraphy, Univ of PR; *cr:* Art Teacher Academia Perpetuo Socorro 1966-67, Baldwin Sch 1967-69; Art/Eng Teacher Antilles Mid Sch 1969-; *ai:* Literary Magazine Spon 1986-87, 1987-88; Discipline Comm 1988-89, 1989-; Prof Translators Assn Treas 1982-84; NAEA, NEA; Supts Awd 1987; *home:* 1403 St Moritz Ave San Patricio Caparra PR 00920

DEIBEL, PAULA M., 2nd Grade Teacher; *b:* Effingham, IL; *ed:* (BA) Elem Ed, 1977, (MS) Guidance/Counseling, 1989 E IL Univ; *cr:* 1st Grade Teacher Paxton Elem 1977-80; 2nd Grade Teacher Newton Cntrl 1980-; *office:* Newton Cntrl Sch 100 Maxwell St Newton IL 62448

DEIBLER, R. BLAKE, Middle School Mathematics; *b:* Lancaster, PA; *m:* Lisa Burkhart; *c:* Bree Ann M.; *ed:* (BS) Elem Ed, Millersville Univ 1978; *cr:* 5th Grade Teacher Drumore Elem 1978-82; Block Stud/Math Teacher Swift Mid Sch 1982-; *ai:* Boys & Girls Bsktbl, Bsbl Coach; Yrbk; Memorial United Meth Church (Sunday Sch Supt, Choir Mem, Youth Coord); *office:* Swift Mid Sch 1866 Robert Fulton Hwy Quarryville PA 17566

DEICHLER, JAMES KENNETH, Mathematics Teacher; *b:* Pittsburgh, PA; *m:* Karen Weber; *c:* Kimberly, Jason, Kristin, Kari A.; *ed:* (BS) Scndry Ed/Math, Duquesne Univ 1971; Grad Stud Univ of Pittsburgh, California St Coll of PA; *cr:* Adjunct Professor

Comm Coll of Allegheny Cty 1974-, Univ of Pittsburgh 1983-; Math Teacher S Fayette HS 1971-; *ai:* St Luke Mens Club 1976-; *office:* South Fayette HS R R 2 Box 207a Mc Donald PA 15057

DEINES, DIXIE SNYDER, Eng as Second Lang Teacher; *b:* Hutchinson, KS; *m:* Richard S.; *c:* Kelly, Timothy; *ed:* (BA) Elem Ed, Bethany Coll 1963; (MS) Curr/Instruction/Eng as Second Lang, Univ of WI Milwaukee 1988; Grad Stud Univ of WI Milwaukee; *cr:* Classroom Teacher Kansas City Public Schls 1975-80, Classroom Teacher 1986-88, Eng as Second Lang Teacher 1988- Milwaukee Public Schls; *ai:* Multi-Cultural Comm; Lao Dance & Hmong Dance Club Asst; MTEA 1986-; Habitat for Humanity 1980-; *office:* Story Elem Sch 3815 W Kilbourne Milwaukee WI 53208

DEINES, JUDY SNELL, French Teacher; *b:* Mason City, IA; *m:* Donald; *c:* Benjamin, Joseph, Sarah; *ed:* (BA) Fr, Luther Coll 1967; Grad Stud Winona St Univ; *cr:* Fr Teacher F B Kellogg Sr HS 1967-71, Johns Adams & Kellogg Jr HS 1982-85, John Marshall Sr HS 1985-; *ai:* Fr Club; AATF, MN Cncl Teaching of Foreign Lang, MN Ed Assn; *office:* John Marshall Sr HS 1510 NW 14th St Rochester MN 55901

DEITER, BONITA K., Biology/Chemistry Teacher; *b:* Wamego, KS; *c:* Tarra; *ed:* (BS) Biological Sci, KS St Univ 1971; (MA) Chem Ed, Wichita St Univ 1976; Medical Technology Sch, Providence-St Margaret Health Center; Numerous Wkshps, Act; *cr:* Sci Teacher Hope HS 1972-73, Andale HS 1973-77, Lakewood Jr HS 1977-78, Jefferson W HS 1979-; *ai:* KS Future Educators, FRIENDS, Class, Pep Club Spon; Sch Improvement Team Mem; Frosh, Jr Var & Var Vlybl Teams, Inservice Chairperson; JWEA (Mem, Pres, Secy) 1983-; KATS Newsletter Ed 1987-; Teacher of Month 1989; St Aloysius Cath Church Ed Cncl 1988-; Beta Sigma Phi 1987-; *office:* Jefferson West HS P O Box 268 Meriden KS 66512

DEITZ, MARTHA M., Mathematics Teacher; *b:* Tuscaloosa, AL; *m:* Freeman J. Jr.; *c:* Edward, David; *ed:* (BS) Math, Univ of AL 1963; (MS) Math Ed, LaGrange Coll 1978; *cr:* Teacher Lee HS, Rule HS, Handley HS, Somerset HS; *ai:* Teens Who Care; Delta Kappa Gamma, NCTM; Somerset Womans Club; *office:* Somerset HS 305 College St Somerset KY 42501

DE JESUS, CHRISTOPHER, Mathematics Teacher; *b:* New York, NY; *m:* Wilma Mendoza; *c:* Inez, Evita; *ed:* (BA) Ed/Scndry Math, Rider Coll 1984; Sch Admin, Rider Coll; *cr:* General Math Teacher Trenton Adult Evening HS 1984-88; 9th-11th Grade Remedial Math Teacher Trenton Bd of Ed 1984-88; Frosh Algebra Teacher Trenton St Coll 1989; 8th/9th Grade Pre-Algebra/Algebra I & II/Geometry/General/Math/Remedial Math Teacher Grace A Dunn Jr HS 1983-; Eng as 2nd Lang Teacher Trenton Bd of Ed 1989-; *ai:* Math Clinic; Stock Market Club; Gifted & Talented Prgm Curr, Math Curr, Essay Contest Gifted & Talented Prgm, Stu Admission, Attendance Policy, Grading System Comms; Trenton Dropout Prevention Collaborative; NCTM, NEA, NJ Ed Assn, Mercer Cty Ed Assn, Trenton Ed Assn, ASCD; Puerto Rican Cmmty Day Care Inc (Treas Bd 1983-88, Chm Bd 1989-, Pres 1988-); Winner Stock Market Game; Certificate of Participation Stock Market Game NJCEE 1986, 1988; Stock Market Game Awd 1986; Certificate of Accomplishment HSPT Inst Prgm 1986; Certificate of Merit Outstanding Service Trenton Public Schls 1988; Teacher of Yr 1988-89; NJ Cncl Ec Ed Stock Market Champion 1988; Certificate of Appreciation Faithful Service Trenton Public Schls 1989; *home:* 24 Peartree Ln Levittown PA 19054

DE JONG, C. MARIE NIKKEL, First & Second Grade Teacher; *b:* Sally, IA; *m:* Nicholas Peter; *ed:* Elem Ed, Cntrl Coll 1950-53; *cr:* K-8th Grade Teacher Pleasant View Rural Sch 1953; 1st Grade Teacher Oskaloosa Chrstn Sch 1963-74; 1st/2nd Grade Teacher Peoria Chrstn Sch 1974-; *ai:* HS Sunday Sch Class & Daily Vacation Bible Sch Teacher; *office:* Peoria Chrstn Sch RR 2 Pella IA 50219

DEKKER, GARY, 8th Grade Math/Algebra Teacher; *b:* Sheboygan, WI; *m:* Pamela Joy Eckhardt; *c:* Tracy A.; *ed:* (BS) Math, Univ of WI Oshkosh 1973; Grad Work; *cr:* Teacher St Clements Elem Sch 1974-76, Horace Mann Mid Sch 1978-; *ai:* Sch Effectiveness Team Comm; Math Tutor; NEA, Sheboygan Educl Assn 1978-; *office:* Horace Mann Mid Sch 2820 Union Ave Sheboygan WI 53081

DE KUNDER, ELLA JEAN, Teacher of Gifted/Talented/Eng; *b:* San Antonio, TX; *m:* Alan; *c:* Michael, Mark; *ed:* (BSED) His, SW TX Univ 1966; *cr:* Teacher E Central HS 1984-; *ai:* Spon Frosh Class; Coach Academic Decathlon & Octathlon Teams; Soc & Hospitality Comm; San Antonio Cncl Teachers of Eng; NCTE Publicity Chm 1984-; TX Assn Gifted & Talented 1988-; Autism Society Pres 1978-79, Service Awd 1984; Aggie Moms Club; *office:* E Central HS 1713 FM 1628 San Antonio TX 78263

DE LA CAL, LOURDES, Bilingual 4th Grade Teacher; *b:* Havana, Cuba; *ed:* (BA) Fr, Univ of S C 1978; *cr:* 1st-4th Grade Teacher Wilmington Park Elem Sch 1979-; *ai:* Mem Hispanic Month Comm; Honorary Assn for Women in Ed (Membership 1981) 1981-82; Bi-ling Bicultural Prgm 1980; Recognition of Outstanding Achievement USC Sch of Ed; Mentor Teacher 1987-; *office:* Wilmington Park Elem Sch 1140 Mahar Ave Wilmington CA 90744

DE LA COVA, GLORIA GRANA, Math Department Chairperson; *b:* Bayamo, Cuba; *m:* Nicolas P.; *ed:* Gloria De La Cova Muniz, Nicolas F., Jorge R., Rose M.; (DR) Chem/Physics, Univ Havana 1953; (MS) Math Ed, FL Intnl Univ 1974; *cr:* Chem/Physics/Math Teacher Colegio Del Apostolado 1954-61; Math/Chem/Span Teacher/Math Dept Chairperson Cardinal Gibbons Hs 1964-73; Math/Span Teacher/Math Dept Chairperson Archbishop Curley HS 1973-76; Math Dept Chairperson/Math/Physics Teacher St Brendan HS 1976-; *ai:* Math Club, Mu Alpha Theta Adv; Mem Academic Cncl; NCTM 1971-; NCEA 1987-; Assn Supervision Curr Dev 1990; Chrstn Family Movement Span 1968-; Nom Teacher of Yr, Presidential Excl & Outstanding Teacher Awds; Tandy Technology Scholors; Wkshp Math Teachers Diocese Miami 1989; *office:* St Brendan H S 2950 SW 87th Ave Miami FL 33165

DE LACRETAZ, CHERYL DIANE, English Teacher; *b:* Garden City, KS; *m:* James Larry; *c:* Nathan, Vanessa, Ryan; *ed:* (BA) Eng, NE OK St Univ 1971; Grad Stud Univ of OK, E Cntrl Univ, Univ of TX El Paso; *cr:* Eng/Math/Dance Teacher Seminole HS 1980-85; Eng Teacher Andress HS 1985-; *ai:* Academic Decathlon, High Q, Young Scholars Bowl, Brain Bowl, Citizen Bee Coach; Interscholastic League Teams Ready Writing, Literary Criticism, Spelling; NCTE 1989-; TX Joint Cncl Teachers of Eng, Paso Del Norte Cncl Teachers of Eng 1986-; Grant to Attend W TX Writing Project Univ of TX El Paso 1987; Awarded Stipend from Mellon Fnd to Attend Advanced Placement Summer Teaching Inst 1990; *office:* Andress HS 5400 Sun Valley Dr El Paso TX 79924

DELAHANTY, EILEEN M., Social Sciences Teacher; *b:* Limestone, ME; *ed:* (BS) Scndry Ed, Univ of NE Omaha 1988; *cr:* Soc Sci Teacher Bellevue Chrstn HS 1988-; *ai:* Cheerleading Coach; Homecoming Adv; *office:* Bellevue Chrstn HS 1722 S 16th St Omaha NE 68108

DE LAMAR, MICKEY, Head Coach/Government Teacher; *b:* Camden, AR; *m:* Mary Elizabeth Garner; *c:* Cody, Jaci; *ed:* (BSE) His/Phys Ed 1970, (MSE) Poly Sci, 1976 Ouachita Baptist Univ; *cr:* Teacher/Coach Mesquite HS 19970-75, Richardson HS 1976-86, Mesquite HS 1987-; *ai:* Head Coach & Athletic Dir Mesquite HS; TX HS Coaches Assn 1970-; Richardson Ed Assn 1976-86; Mesquite Ed Assn 1987-; Coach of Yr TX UIL Dist 9-AAAAA 1988-89; TX HS Coaches Assn Bd of Dir Alternate 1989-; *office:* Mesquite H S 300 E Davis St Mesquite TX 75149

DELANDE, DANIEL DALE, Seventh Grade Teacher; *b:* Bridgeport, OH; *m:* Connie Jafrate; *c:* Gina M.; *ed:* (BS) Elem Ed, OH Univ 1972; (MS) Elem Ed, Univ of Dayton 1977; *cr:* Teacher/Prin Blaine Elem 1971-74; Phys Ed Coord Bridgeport Exempt Village Schls 1974-75; Teacher South Jr HS 1975-80; Teacher/Substitute Prin Elm Elem 1980-; *ai:* Newspaper, Yrbk, Stu Cncl Adv; Washington DC, Sch Picnic, Math-A-Thon, Right-to-Read Coord; Math Curr Comm; OH Ed Assn, NEA, Martins Ferry Ed Assn 1975-; Bridgeport HS Band Boosters Pres 1989-; OH Valley Bsktbl Ofcls Bd VP 1989-; OH HS Bsktbl Ofcl, WV HS Coaches Ofcl 1976-; *office:* Elm Elem Sch Euclid Ave Martins Ferry OH 43935

DELANEY, BETTY G., Chapter 1 Resource Teacher; *b:* San Francisco, CA; *ed:* (BA) Psych, Univ of CA Los Angeles 1971; (MA) Ed, San Francisco St Univ 1978; Multicultural Ed, Eng as 2nd Lang Techniques; *cr:* 2nd-6th Grade Classroom Teacher 1973-88, Chapter 1 Resource Teacher 1988- Jefferson Sch Dist; *ai:* Stu & Sch Site Cncl; His, Soc Sci, Lang Art Mentor Teacher for Dist; PDK 1975-; CA Rdng Assn 1988-, Outstanding Rdng Specialist Awd 1989; Amer Bus Womens Assn Pres 1986, Woman of Yr 1987; *office:* George Washington Elem Sch 251 Whittier St Daly City CA 94014

DELANEY, DAVID ALLAN, Choir Director; *b:* Houston, TX; *ed:* (BM) Music Ed/Sacred Music, Houston Baptist Univ 1982; (MM) Choral Conducting, Baylor Univ 1989; *cr:* Music Assn Westbury Baptist Church 1982-84; Choir Dir Pasadena HS 1985-; *ai:* Principals Advisory Comm; TX Music Ed Assn, TX Choral Dirs Assn, Amer Choral Assn 1985-; *office:* Pasadena HS 206 S Shaver Pasadena TX 77506

DELANEY, ELAINE HEILIG, Third Grade Teacher; *b:* Rome, NY; *m:* Edward A.; *c:* Michael, Thomas; *ed:* (BA) Elem Ed, St Univ of NY Oswego 1973; Grad Stud Rdng; *cr:* 3rd Grade Teacher Lura Sharp Elem Sch 1975-; *ai:* Alpha Delta Kappa 1984-; Parent Teacher Group 1987-; *office:* Lura Sharp Elem Sch 7319 Lake St Pulaski NY 13142

DELANEY, JUDITH LYLE, Science Department Chair; *b:* Chattanooga, TN; *m:* Wesley Ray; *c:* Mary Lyle Huff, Susan B. Lyle; *ed:* (BS) Sci Ed, Univ of Chattanooga 1961; (MS) Spec Ed, 1976, (EDS) Educl Admin/Supervision, 1986 Univ of TN Knoxville; Chem, Astromony, Wkshps; Advanced Placement Chem; *cr:* 7th-9th Grade Sci Teacher Tyner Jr HS 1961-63; 8th-12th Grade Sci Teacher Midway HS 1974-80; Bio/Chem/Phys Advanced Placement Chem Teacher Roane Cty HS 1980-; *ai:* Academic Decathlon Team Coach; Sci Olympiad Team; Scholars Bowl Team; Sci Bowl Team; Sci Club Spon; Delta Kappa Gamma; Roane Cty Ed Assn (Pres 1980-, Chief Negotiator 1982-83); TN Ed Assn, NEA, Chem Ed Division; *office:* Roane Cty HS 535 W Cumberland St Kingston TN 37763

DELANEY, KATHRYN GOLDEN, English Teacher; *b:* Everett, MA; *m:* Paul J.; *c:* Katy Even, Sheila, Paul, Christopher; *ed:* (BA) Eng, Coll of New Rochelle 1962; Grad Courses Boston Coll; In-Service Courses; *cr:* Eng Teacher Parlin Jr HS 1962-63; Substitute Teacher Watertown Schls 1973-74; Eng Teacher West Jr HS 1975-81; Real Estate Sales Gallery Realty 1981-82; Eng Teacher Watertown HS 1982-; *ai:* Lecture Series Comm Chairperson; Liaison Teacher Parent Teacher Stu Organization; Eligibility & Schlsp Comm; Watertown Teachers Assn, MA Teachers Assn, NEA 1975-; NCTE 1988-; League Women Voters 1970-; Local PTA 1970-89; Parish Organizations 1970-89; CCD Teacher 1970; Elected Town Meeting Mem; *office:* Watertown HS 51 Columbia St Watertown MA 02172

DELANEY, MAUREEN ANNE, OP, Science Teacher; *b:* Paterson, NJ; *ed:* (BA) Ed/Religion, Villanova Univ 1960; (MAT) Sci, 1972, (MS) Sci, 1972 Oh Wesleyan Univ; Grad Stud for Cert; *cr:* 9th-12th Grade Sci Teacher NY, NJ, Puerto Rico 1960-75; Vice Prin/Academic Dean NJ 1975-78; 9th-12th Grade Sci Teacher Newark NJ 1979-; *ai:* Sci, Newark & Service Club; NJ Sci Teachers Assn, NJ Sci Supvr Assn 1973-; NSTA 1965-; Natl Sci Supvrs Assn, ASCD 1975-; Amer Assn Adv of Sci, Amer Chemical Society, Irish Amer Inst 1980-;NSTA Official Evaluator 1972-, Awd 1968; NJ Sci Teachers Newsletter Ed 1973-78; Natl & St Pux Christi 1978-; Natl & St Network 1980-; Univ of Manchester England Grant 1979; 3rd Intnl Environmental Conference Rep 1989; Natl Sci Fnd Grants 1973, 1966-; NJ Sch Dist Master Teacher 1985-88.

DELANEY, PHYLLIS ELIZABETH, English Teacher; *b:* Quincy, MA; *m:* Timothy J.; *c:* Kevin M., Michael J., Mark P.; *ed:* (BA) Eng, Bridgewater St Coll 1970; Working Towards Masters Rdng Ed, Bridgewater St Coll; *cr:* Rdng Teacher North Jr HS 1970-75; Teacher MS 1981-83, Resource Teacher 1983-86 MA Migrant Ed Prgm; Eng Teacher Brockton HS 1986-; *ai:* NEA, MA Teachers Assn 1986-89; Intnl Rdng Assn 1990; Brockton Youth Soccer Assn Secy 1984-85; Goddard Kndgtn Parent Advisory Cncl Treas 1980-81; 2 Yr Wkshps Participant 1987-88, 1988-89; *office:* Brockton HS 470 Forest Ave Brockton MA 02401

DELANEY, STELLA O'CONNOR, Mathematics Teacher; *b:* Belfast, N Ireland; *m:* Joseph; *c:* Kieran, Conor; *ed:* (BS) Math, 1983, (MS) Math, 1989, Univ of IL Chicago; *cr:* Math Teacher Sacred Heart Acad 1984, Kelly HS 1984-85, Benito Juarez HS 1985-; *ai:* BS With Univ Honors & Distinction in Math; *office:* Benito Juarez HS 2150 S Laflin St Chicago IL 60608

DELANEY, TERRENCE P., Mathematics Teacher; *b:* Chicago, IL; *m:* Shirley L. Stark; *c:* Shane P., Brandon L.; *ed:* (AA) General Ed, Long Beach City Coll 1968; (BA) Health Ed, CA St Univ Long Beach 1973; Bio, Math, General Sci, Public Safety, Driver Ed; *cr:* Teacher Long Beach Poly HS 1973, CA St Long Beach Univ 1975-76, Meridian Jr HS 1984, Kuna Jr HS 1986-; *ai:* Jr HS Ftbl, Bsktbl, Weight Trng, Wrestling, Track Coach; Little League & Babe Ruth Bsbl Coach; NCTM 1989-; NEA, ID Ed Assn, Kuna Ed Assn 1986-; Ducks Unlimited Comm Mem 1983-; Natl Rifle Assn 1968-88; Meridian Amer Legion Bsbl (VP, Bd Mem) 1990; *office:* Kuna Jr HS 441 Porter Rd Kuna ID 83634

DE LA PENA, JULIO, Fifth Grade Teacher; *b:* San Antonio, TX; *m:* Jean M. Nelson; *c:* Joan, Jim; *ed:* (BA) Bus Admin, 1968, (MAT) Teaching, 1970 NM St Univ; Working Towards Educl Specialist Admin; *cr:* Teacher Washington Elem 1970-73, Conlee Elem 1974-; *ai:* Spelling Bee Spon; Assn of Classroom Teachers 1974-; Bontam Weight Sports Assn 1968-88; PTA 1974-, Nom Natl Phoebe Apperson Hearst Outstanding Educator Awd 1986; Semi-Finalist US WEST Outstanding Teacher Prgm 1988; *office:* Conlee Elem Sch 1701 Boston Dr Las Cruces NM 88001

DEL CAMPO, CHRISTOPHER, English Teacher; *b:* Yonkers, NY; *m:* Maria Teresa Biancardi; *c:* Teressa R.; *ed:* (BA) Eng, St Univ of NY New Paltz 1976; Grad Stud Eng, St Univ of NY New Paltz; *cr:* Eng Teacher Roosevelt HS 1978-79, Mahopac HS 1979-; Eng Adjunct Instr Marist Coll 1987-; *ai:* Advanced Placement Planning Comm; Pride Task Force; NCTE 1978-; E Fishkill Recreation 1989-; *home:* 6 Marion Ave Wappingers Flls NY 12590

DELCARPIO, KATHRYNE COOPER, English/Spanish Teacher; *b:* Wichita, KS; *m:* Joseph B.; *c:* Kathryne, Thomas; *ed:* (BA) Speech/Drama/Eng, Southwestern Coll 1974; *cr:* Teacher Joseph S Clark HS 1974, Margaret Haughery Sch for Teen-Aged Expectant Mothers 1974-79, Pearl River HS 1979-; *ai:* ITS Drame Club; Positive Action Spon; SAPE Team Chairperson; NCTE.

DEL CHIARO, DIDI J., Third Grade Teacher; *b:* Berkeley, CA; *m:* Larry; *c:* Brenton, Kristen, Lauren; *ed:* (BS) Phys Ed, Ca Polytechnic 1977; Phys Ed, 1977; Ed, 1979 St Marys Coll; Addl Studies Administrative Ed Credential, Admin Ed Post Masters Studies 1990; *cr:* Phys Ed Instr, Garin Sch; Edna Hill Sch 1978-79; 5th Grade Instr Garin Sch 1979-86;3rd Grade Instr Brentwood Sch 1987-; *ai:* Site Mentor Phys Ed 1988-89; 4th Grade Phys Ed Coord 1989-90; Grade Level Chairperson 1989-90; Dist Salary Comm Chairperson 1989-90; CA Teachers Assn 1989-90; *office:* Brentwood Elem Sch 929 2nd St Brentwood CA 94513

DE LEON, JORGE G., Spanish Teacher; *b:* Havana, Cuba; *m:* Mirta C. Gandon; *c:* Daniel A., Carlos J.; *ed:* (BA) Span, FL Intnl Univ 1981; *cr:* Span Teacher Hialeah-Miami Lakes Sr HS 1985-; *ai:* Span Honor Society Club Spon 1986-; Faculty Cncl 1987-; Foreign Lang Teachers Assn Span SVP 1987-89; Amer Assn of Teachers of Span & Portuguese 1986-; Verbum Incorporated (Literary Adv, VP) 1980-; Radical Hermeneutics Incorporated VP 1988-; *office:* Hialeah-Miami Lakes Sr HS 7977 W 12 Ave Hialeah FL 33014

DE LEON, MARIA ELVA PEREZ, 3rd Grade Teacher; *b:* Mc Allen, TX; *m:* Ramiro; *c:* Marlena, Rogue, Max; *ed:* (BA) Elem Ed, UT-Pan Amer Univ 1973; *cr:* Teacher Westaco ISD 1973-74; Hidalgo ISD 1974-76; Pickering LA Parish 1976-78; Mission ISD 1978-80; Mc Allen ISD 1980-; *ai:* Church Groups & Org; CTA.

DELGADO, HECTOR, Social Studies Teacher; *b:* Juncos, PR; *m:* Gloria M. Vigil; *c:* Cecilia D. Delgado Kahle, Raymundo C.; *ed:* (BA) Span/His, 1970, (MA) Span, 1972, (PHD) Span, 1990 Univ of NM; Bi-ling Ed, Effective Teaching, Cmptr Trng; *cr:* Instr Rutgers Univ 1974-76; Teacher Hoover Mid Sch 1979-89, Wilson Mid Sch 1989-; *ai:* Span Club; AATSP Mem 1970-74; *office:* Wilson Mid Sch 1138 Cardenas Dr SE Albuquerque NM 87108

DELGADO, LORENZO ARAIZA, Spanish Teacher; *b:* Calexico, CA; *m:* Deborah Lynn; *c:* Jacob R., Joshua P.; *ed:* (BA) Span, Univ of CA Riverside 1983; (MS) Sch Counseling, Univ of LA Verne 1988; *cr:* Span Teacher Hemet HS 1984-; *ai:* Sch Schlsp Comm; *office:* Hemet HS 41701 E Stetson Hemet CA 92344

DELINSKY, NANCY DAVIDSON, Spanish Teacher; *b:* Terre Haute, IN; *m:* Joseph L.; *c:* Cindi, Karen, Kathy; *ed:* (BA) Span/Latin/Vocal Music, IN St Univ 1966; (MED) Span, Bloomsburg St Univ 1973; NDEA Inst for Span Teachers, Knox Coll 1966, Wichita St Univ-MX 1967, Univ of Madrid; *cr:* Span Teacher La Porte Cmmty Schls 1966-67, Lebanon Sch Dist 1967-68, Abington Heights Sch Dist 1968-71, Tunkhannock Area HS 1987-; *ai:* Co-Adv Foreign Exch Club; AATSP 1967-74; PTO (Secy, Pres, Publicity) 1978-85; New Cmmty Singers Pres 1978-85; Philharmonic Chorus; Oratorio Society of Wyoming Valley Parish Singers 1985-; *office:* Tunkhannock Area HS 120 W Tioga St Tunkhannock PA 18657

DELK, DARRELL D., 7th Grade Soc Stud Teacher; *b:* West Milton, OH; *m:* Jennie Lee Groff; *c:* Gladden, Velvet Delk Des Jardins; *ed:* (BS) Soc Sci, Manchester Coll 1961; Lake Forest Coll, Miami Univ; *cr:* 7th Grade Teacher Deer Path Mid Sch 1961-62; HS Teacher Trotwood-Madison Public Schls 1962-68; Jr HS Teacher Northmont City Schls 1968-.

DELK, JENNIE LEE GROFF, Fourth Grade Teacher; *b:* Dayton, OH; *m:* Darrell Dean; *c:* Gladden Groff, Velvel L., Delk Desjardins; *ed:* (BS) Ed, Univ of Dayton 1964; Grad Stud Wright St Univ 1984; *cr:* 6th Grade Teacher Trotwood Madison Schls 1964-67; 4th Grade Teacher Arcanum Butler Schls 1969-; *office:* Arcanum Butler Sch N Main St Arcanum OH 45304

DELL, JOHN ROBERT, Fifth Grade Teacher; *b:* Port Huron, MI; *m:* Carole Lynn; *c:* Erin, Jonathan, Breanna, Jeffrey; *ed:* (BA) Elem Ed, 1972, (MA) Classroom Teaching, 1975 MI St Univ; *cr:* 4th/5th Grade Teacher Harrison Elem 1972-; *ai:* Elem Rep Port Huron Area Sch Dist Cmptr Comm; Parent Teacher League Teacher Rep; Port Huron Ed Assn; Clyde Township Planning Commission 1989-; Honorable Mention Wellness Competition Proposal 1989; *office:* Harrison Sch 55 15th St Port Huron MI 48060

DELLEY, VERNELL VIOLETA HENDERSON, 4th Grade Teacher; *b:* Kilgore, TX; *m:* John A.; *c:* John A. Jr., Felisha D., Shelley S.; *ed:* (BA) Elem Ed, TX Coll 1952; (MA) Elem Ed, TX Southern Univ 1966; *cr:* Teacher Crane Ind Sch Dist, Tyler Ind Sch Dist 1961-; *ai:* Youth Promotions of TX Pageants Dir; Top Ladies of Distinction VP 1985-, Cmmty Service Awd 1988-89; Negro Bus & Prof Women 1988-, Cmmty Service Awd 1986-87; Whos Who Among TX Teachers; Nom TX Women Hall of Fame; Nom Women of Yr City of Tyler; *home:* 2719 N Whitten St Tyler TX 75702

DELLIFIELD, DENNIS L., Conductor of Bands; *b:* Oberlin, OH; *m:* Marilee F. Hefner; *c:* David, Jonathan; *ed:* (BA) Music Ed/Speech/Drama, Bluffton Coll 1971; (MSED) Music/Supervision/Curr, Univ of Dayton 1975; Advanced Stud Univ of MI; *cr:* Asst Dir Bluffton HS 1967-68, Elida HS 1968-71; Conductor of Bands Allen East HS 1971-; *ai:* MUSTANG Marching Brass, Concert, Var Pep Band; Jr Class Adv & Play Dir; HS Musical Dir; MENC, OMEA 1967-; NBA 1973-; Lafayette Cmmty Chorus Dir 1975-; Drug Abuse & Awareness Mem 1981-88; Bd of Public Affairs Mem 1980-81; Allen Cty Outstanding Young Educator of Yr Awd; Book Author; Articles Submitted to Music Publication Journals; *office:* Allen East HS 105 N Washington Lafayette OH 45854

DELLINGER, HELEN EDDLEMAN, Retired Teacher; *b:* Mena, AR; *w:* Phil (dec); *c:* D'Ann Dellinger Verkamp; *ed:* (BSE) Elem Ed, Univ of Cntrl AR 1953; (MA) Elem Ed, George Peabody Coll for Teachers Vanderbilt Univ 1958; Grad Stud E NM Univ, NM St Univ; *cr:* 3rd Grade Teacher Cntrl Sch 1947-54; 1st Grade Teacher Broadmoor Sch 1954-61; 6th Grade Teacher Broadmoor & Stone Elem 1963-89; *ai:* Sci Fair Building Rep; Hobbs Ed Assn Treas 1973-74; NM Ed Assn Delegate 1973-76; Delta Kappa Gamma (Treas 1971, Membership Chm 1986-89); Hobbs Democratic Women 2nd VP 1989-; Nom Teacher of Yr Broadmoor Faculty; *home:* 2624 Propps Hobbs NM 88240

DELO, DONALD A., English Teacher; *b:* Jersey City, NJ; *m:* Patricia; *c:* Jason; *ed:* (BA) Eng, Jersey City St Coll 1968; New Sch for Soc Research, Waiters Wkshps; *cr:* Eng Teacher Dwight Morrow HS 1969-75, Waldwick HS 1975-79, Devonshire Prep Sch 1979-83, Snyder HS 1983-88, Academic HS 1988-; *ai:* Literary Magazine Adv; Carnegie, CETA Grant; Governors Teacher Recognition, Princeton Univ Distinguished Teacher Awd; *office:* Academic HS 16 Bentley Ave Jersey City NJ 07304

DE LOACH, LOUISE J., Even Start Director; *b:* Estill, SC; *m:* Otis; *c:* Delcena D., Otis Jr.; *ed:* (BA) Elem Ed, Voorhees Coll 1971; Additional Stud Early Chldhd Ed/Rdng, Univ of SC; *cr:* 1st/2nd Grade Teacher Estill Elem 1971-89; Even Start Dir Hampton Dist 2 1990; *ai:* Even Start Parenting Prgm Dir; NEA, SC Educl Assn, Intnl Rdng Assn; Estill Elem Sch Improvement Cncl & PTA Coord; 1st Grade Chairperson; Kids Connection Sch Newspaper; Puzzle of Parenting Supvr; Governors Hum Project; Supt Comm Chairperson; Sch Improvement Chm; Tutor 1st Grade Stus; *home:* PO Box 812 Estill SC 29918

DE LOACH, MARY ELAINE (ESSNER), Mathematics/Science Teacher; *b:* Cape Girardeau, MO; *m:* Paul Howard; *ed:* (BS) Physics/Math, SE MO St 1976; (BS) Mechanical Engr, Univ of MO Rolla 1981; *cr:* Math Teacher Cntrl HS 1976-77; Sci Teacher North Cty HS 1977-79; Oil Field Engr Schlumberger 1982-84; Math/Sci Teacher Waldo HS 1984-; *ai:* Stu Cncl Adv; 7th Grade Spon; PTO Planning Comm; Personnel Planning Comm; *home:* 407 N Oakland Magnolia AR 71753

DE LOATCH, ELIZABETH ROBINSON, Bio Teacher & Sci Dept Chair; *b:* Littleton, NC; *w:* Herolin S. (dec); *c:* Herolin S., Robert S.; *ed:* (BA) Phys/Health Ed/Recreation/Bio, Hampton Univ 1949; (MA) Phys Admin/Health Ed, NY Univ 1951; (MA) Ed/Bio Concentration, Hampton Univ 1967; Numerous Classes, Univ of VA, Hampton, Old Dominion, Norfolk St Univ, William & Mary; AIMS Wkshp; *cr:* Female Act Dir Police Athletic League 1949-51; Phys Ed/Health Teacher Hampton Univ 1951, Norfolk St Univ 1951-52; Sci Teacher 1963, Teacher/Sci Dept Chairperson 1976- Portsmouth City Schls; *ai:* Tutoring; Sci Club Spon; Parent, Stu, Teacher Assn Mem; Sci Fair Adv; Sch Sci Fair Chairperson; City Sci Fair Comm; Scndry Registration Chairperson; Tidewater Sci Fair; Sch Participation Adv; City Educl Fair; Sci Dept Rep; Sch Testing Comm Co-Chairperson; City Sci Dept Chairpersons Comm Mem; AP Bio Wkshp Old Dominion Univ Sch & System Rep 1988-; VA Assn of Sci Teachers Conference Sch & System Rep 1989; NSTA Conference Sch & System Rep 1990; Portsmouth Ed Assn, VA Ed Assn Mem 1963-; VA Assn of Sci Teachers Mem 1971-; Tidewater Assn of Sci Teachers Mem 1988-; NSTA 1972-88; St James Episcopal Church; Jacks & Jills Inc Co-Founder; YWCA Bd Mem 1955-60; Delta Sigma Theta Inc; Epicureans Inc Charter Mem; Moles Inc Inactive Mem; Woodrow Wilsons HS Teacher of Yr 1989-; Trophy City Parent, Stu, Teachers Assn; Portsmouth City Schls Apple Medal; Governors Sch for Hum Univ of Richmond; Presidental Citation Awd Inspiring Gifted & Talent Stu; Sci Prgm Dedication Leadership Plaque 1988; City Textbook Selection Comm Mem 1976-; City Curr Writing Team; City Bio Competency Test Co-Writer & Evaluator; Supervising Sci Teacher Stu, Teachers, Observers; Natl Sci Teachers Assessment Wkshp; *office:* Woodrow Wilson HS 3701 Willett Dr Portsmouth VA 23707

DE LOGE, ALICE (STRADCZUK), Principal; *b:* Norwich, CT; *c:* Daniel; *ed:* (BS) Ed, E CT St Coll 1972; (MAT) Ed, Sacred Heart Univ 1990; *cr:* 3rd/7th/8th Grade Teacher St Marys Sch 1972-76; CCD Coord St Marys Church 1977-80; 6th/8th Grade Teacher St Joseph Sch 1980-81; 5th/7th/8th Grade Teacher 1981-89, Prin 1989- All Hallows Sch; *ai:* All Hallows Sch Bd & Home-Sch Assn; St Judes Math-A-Thon Sch Coord; *office:* All Hallows Sch 120 Prospect St Moosup CT 06354

DE LONG, DAVID ALDEN, Fourth Grade Teacher; *b:* Weirton, WV; *m:* Susan Lynn Mouser; *c:* Bryan; *ed:* (BA) Elem Ed, Glenville St Coll 1975; (MA) Elem Ed, WV Univ 1980; H & R Block Basic Tax Course 1981; *cr:* Math Teacher Belington Mid Sch 1975-77; Teacher Belington Elem Sch 1977-; *ai:* Barbour Cty Fed of Teachers Treas; Philippi Cub Scout Pack 63 Den Leader 1990; Philippi Baptist Church Financial Secy 1985-87; *home:* Rt 2 Box 125 A Philippi WV 26416

DE LONG, DAVID CLARENCE, Dir of Bands/Music Dept Chair; *b:* Sellersville, PA; *m:* Kathy A. Ciampa; *ed:* (BS) Music Ed, West Chester Univ 1982; Grad Stud West Chester Univ; *cr:* Dir of Music Caesar Rodney Sr HS 1983-; *ai:* Dir of Marching Band, Concert Band, Jazz Ensemble, Brass Quintet; 9th Grad Bsktbl Coach; DSEA, DE Music Ed Assn 1983-; Phi Mu Alpha 1980-; Dover Symphony 1985-; WY Church Choir 1986-; Signa Phi Epsilon Service Chm 1982; Firestone Awd of Excl; *office:* Caesar Rodney Sr HS 239 Old North Rd Camden-Wyoming DE 19934

DE LONG, JAMES WILLIAM, JR., 4th Grade Teacher; *b:* Chicago, IL; *m:* Mary Elizabeth; *c:* Jennifer A., Amy M., Erin N.; *ed:* (AA) Phys Ed/General Ed, Elgin Comm Coll 1973; (BSED) Elem Ed, 1974, (MSED) Admin, 1979 Northern IL Univ; Performance Learning Systems; STET Alden Inst; *cr:* 1st Grade Teacher Parkview 1974-75; 3rd-5th Grade Teacher Fairview Elem 1975-81; 4th Grade Teacher Golfview Elem 1981-; *ai:* Coach Soph Sftbl, Ftbl; Sci Coord; Health & Drug Rep; Ed Assn Dundee Bldg Rep 1985-86; VFW & Amer Legion; PTC Fairview Pres; Viet Nam Army Veteran 1969-71; *office:* Golfview Elem 124 Golfview Ln Carpentersville IL 60110

DELONG, JANICE AYERS, Assistant Professor; *b:* Bedford, VA; *m:* Robert E.; *c:* Beth, Michael, Lynne, Kara; *ed:* (BA) Sociology, 1965, (MED) Guidance Counseling, 1970, (MED) Rdng Specialist, 1987 Lynchburg Coll; Shenandoah Coll & Conservatory; East TN ST Univ; *cr:* Elem Teacher Thaxton Elem 1965-67; Longwood Avenue Chrstn Sch 1975-80; Jr HS Teacher Timberlake Chrstn Sch 1980-85; Instr Liberty Univ 1985-; *ai:* Kappa Delta Pi 1985-; VA St Rdng Assn 1985-; NAPPS 1989; Gideon Auxiliary 1984-; Masterplots Ii; *office:* Liberty University Box 20000 Lynchburg VA 24506

DE LONG, MARJORIE LOUISE, English Teacher; *b:* Hesperia, MI; *ed:* (BA) Bible/Eng, Bob Jones Univ 1956; (MA) Ed, MI St Univ 1971; Linguistics; *cr:* Jr HS Teacher Hesperia Public Schls 1956-58, 1968-69; Elem Teacher/Scndry Intern Missionary Kent Acad & O Kene Sch of Commerce & Kaltungo Teacher Trng Coll 1958-78; Jr/Sr HS Eng Teacher White Lake Chrstn Sch 1979-; *ai:* Drama Dir; Class Spon; *office:* White Lake Chrstn Sch 5280 Dowling Montague MI 49437

DE LONG, SHAYNA J., Business Teacher; *b:* Defiance, OH; *m:* Alan K.; *c:* Chris, Lindsey, Scott; *ed:* (BS) Bus Ed, Defiance Coll 1972; Univ of Toledo/Univ of MO; *cr:* Bus Teacher Hicksville HS; *ai:* OEA/NEA; YMCA; YWCA; United Meth Church; Van Wert Area Swim Team Boosters Secy; Majestic Baton Boosters Secy; Crestview Comm Assn; *home:* Rt 3 Box 83 Van Wert OH 45891

DE LOS SANTOS, RUDY M., 500 W Hobbs; *b:* Roswell, NM; *m:* Nellie Gomez; *c:* Aaron, Andrea, Ryan; *ed:* (BS) Psych, E NM Univ Portales 1978; Working Towards Counseling Degree; *cr:* Cnslr/Athletic Dir Lake Arthur Schls 1978-82; Cnslr/Supvr Roswell Job Corps 1982-85; Cnslr Roswell HS 1985-; *ai:* Natl Guard SFC Sr Instr 1982-; *office:* Roswell HS 500 W Hobbs Roswell NM 88201

DEL TORO, DOLORES TRAVIS, Fifth Grade Teacher; *b:* Honolulu, HI; *m:* David; *c:* Christopher, Matthew; *ed:* (BA) Elem Ed, NMHU Las Vegas 1978; *cr:* 5th Grade Teacher Clardy Elem 1978-; *ai:* Super Scholars, Math Club, Spelling Bee Spon; *office:* Clardy Elem Sch 5508 Delta El Paso TX 79905

DE LUCA, DEBORAH SANTAMONT, Business Teacher; *b:* Massena, NY; *m:* Ronald A.; *c:* Dominic; *ed:* (BS) Bus Ed, 1982, (MS) Voc-Tech Ed, 1984 SUNY Utica-Rome; Interactive Telecomm Network Trng; Cmptr Trng; *cr:* Secy to Dir/Office Mgr Northwest Tech 1971-80; Bus Teacher Gouverneur Cntrl Sch 1980-86, Heuvelton Cntrl Sch 1986-; Adjunct Professor SUNY Oswego 1985-; *ai:* Soph Class Adv; St Raphaels Altar & Rosary Society VP 1989-; Article Published; *office:* Heuvelton Central Sch 100 Washington St Washington St Heuvelton NY 13654

DE LUCA, JOSEPH AUGUST, Spanish Teacher; *b:* St Louis, MO; *ed:* (BA) Latin Amer Stud, 1970, (BS) Ed, 1970 NE MO St Univ; (MA) Span, Univ of MO Columbia 1973; Grad Work Various Univs; *cr:* Span Teacher Univ of MO Columbia 1970-72, Linn HS 1972-73, Hannibal HS 1973-; *ai:* Foreign Lang Club; Youth For Understanding Exch Prgm; MO Ed Assn Congressional Contact Team 1980-; Amer Assn Teachers of Span & Portuguese 1970-; Hannibal Public Lib Trustee 1980-; Hannibal Arts Cncl Secy 1974-; Hannibal Concert Assn 1980-; Fulbright-Hays Schlsps 1981, 1983, 1990; Natl Endowment for Hum 1985, 1988; Title VI Fellowship Univ of Fl to Brazil 1982; Intnl Rotary Club Schlsp Costa Rica 1969; *home:* 510 Central Ave Hannibal MO 63401

DELUCCIA, LYNNE LENCHES, Social Studies Teacher; *b:* Elizabeth, NJ; *m:* William P.; *ed:* (BA) His, Rutgers Coll 1984; Masters Degree Prgm, Seton Hall Univ; *cr:* Soc Stud Teacher Mendham HS 1984-87, Hillsborough HS 1987-; *ai:* Stu Cncl & Band Front Adv; NJ Ed Assn, NEA, NJ Cncl For Soc Stud, Hillsborough Ed Assn; Muscular Dystrophy Special Olympics; Natl Endowment for Hum Grant; Research Role of Constitution in Modern Political Thought; *office:* Hillsborough HS Raider Blvd Belle Mead NJ 08502

DE LUTIS, EVELYN EKBERG, Kindergarten Teacher; *b:* Brockton, MA; *m:* Donald B.; *c:* Stephanie Ryan, Donald Jr., David; *ed:* (BS) Elem Ed, Bridgewater St Coll 1963; *cr:* Kndgtn Teacher Dr A F Hunt Sch 1968-; *ai:* Pre-Cana for Engaged Couples at Church; MA Teachers Assn, NEA 1968-.

DE MARAIS, NORMAN CHARLES, English Department Head; *b:* Cambridge, MA; *ed:* (AB) Hum, Merrimack Coll 1964; (MED) Lang Arts/Rdng, St Coll at Salem 1967; Lang Arts; Gifted/Talented Elem Schls; Cert Leader Great Books Fnd; *cr:* Teacher Tewksbury Jr HS 1964-69; Dept Head Eng Chelmsford Jr HS 1969-78; McCarthy Mid Sch 1978-; *ai:* Dir Stu/Faculty Variety Show for Stu Enrichment Act; Organizing & Chaperoning Ed Field Trips; Coord Lang Arts Related Assemblies; Chelmsford Fed of Teachers Sec 1989-; MA Cncl of Teachers of Eng; NCTE; Teen Theater Wrkshop Fnd/Dir 1970-81; Interfaith Choir Dir 1980-; Confraternity of Chrstn Doctrine (Teacher 1968-78 Pres 1975-76); Notre Dame Acad Musicals Dir 1978-; Organist/Choir Dir St Williams Chrch 1972-; Adv of Lit Magazines Nwspr & Drama Clubs; Sch Eval Teams; Nom Man of Yr By JCs 1973; Commendation from Brd of Selectmen for Work with Teens 1971; Guest Condctr Methuen/MA/Music Dept Town Wide Concert 1990; *office:* C Edith Mc Carthy Mid Sch 250 North Rd Chelmsford MA 01824

DE MARCO, RICHARD JOHN, Social Studies Teacher; *b:* Derby, CT; *m:* Stephanie B. Parniawski; *ed:* (BA) Ed, 1967, (MA) Guidance, 1970 Univ of Bridgeport; *cr:* Salesman/Technician Royal Typewriter Co 1950-67; Teacher Harding HS 1967-68, Hillcrest Mid Sch 1968-; *ai:* Audio-Visual Dept; Coach Tennis, Ftbl, Bsktbl; NCSS 1985-; Smithsonian Mem 1987-; Celebration of Excl Winner 1987, 1989; *office:* Hillcrest Mid Sch 530 Daniels Farm Rd Trumbull CT 06611

DEMAREE-COHEN, COTT, Home Economics Teacher; *b:* Binghamton, NY; *m:* Joel L.; *c:* Matt; *ed:* (AAS) Sullivan Cty Cmmty 1971; (BS) Home Ec, KS St Univ 1974; (MS) Educl Admin, Univ of Scranton 1979; Culinary Coll Sicily; *cr:* Teacher Binghamton HS, North HS, Mac Arthur Jr HS; *ai:* Home Ec Teachers Assn; NY Teachers Assn; Rape & Abuse Crisis Center (VP, Bd) 1985-86; SOS Shelter for Battered Women 1981-83; Hospice; Nom Outstanding Women Broome Cty 1989; *office:* Binghamton HS 31 Main St Binghamton NY 13905

DEMAREO, MARK, Music Director; *b:* Woodbury, NJ; *ed:* (BM) Music, Westminster Choir Coll 1978; (MA) Human Dev/Ed Admin Fairleigh Dickinson Univ 1980; Music Fellowship Northwestern Univ; 1st Recipient NJ 1986; *cr:* Choral Dir Thompson Jr HS 1978-81; Music Dir 1981-; Acting Asst Prin 1988-89; Middletown HS North; *ai:* Music Dir Musical Prod HS

North; Asst Choral Dir St Patricks Cathedral NYC 1986-89; Completed TESA Prgm; 3yr Staff; NJEA 1978-; Phi Delta Kappa 1985- ; Amer Society of Notaries/Notary Public; Music Ed Natl Conf 1978-; NJ All-Shore Chorus Pres 1984; Gov Teacher Recognition Awd 1988; Music Fellowship Awd Northwestern Univ 1986; Guest Conductor NJ All-Shore Chorus 1985; Guest Speaker NJEA Teachers Convention Atlantic City 1983; *office:* Middletown HS North 63 Tindall Rd Middletown NJ 07748

DEMAREST, SONJA ANN, Third Grade Teacher; *b:* Nashville, TN; *m:* Joseph R. Sr.; *c:* Joseph R. Jr., Angela D., Stephanie L.; *ed:* (BA) Ed, Austin Peay St Univ; *cr:* 2nd Grade Teacher 1977-78, 3rd Grade Teacher 1978- Hendersonville Chrstn Acad; *ai:* Chrldr & Pep Club Spon; *office:* Hendersonville Christian Acad 355 Old Shackle Island Rd Hendersonville TN 37075

DEMARKOWSKI, CARL JOHN, English Teacher; *b:* Toledo, OH; *m:* Paulette Palmentera; *c:* Gina, Melissa, Renee, Anne M.; *ed:* (BS) Eng, Xavier Univ 1967; (MA) Eng, 1969, (PHD) Amer Lit, 1980 Univ of Toledo; *cr:* Grad Asst/Part Time Instr Univ of Toledo 1967-69, 1971-75; Teacher/Coach St Johns HS 1974-; *ai:* Sr Moderator, Jr/Sr Prom Moderator; Asst Var Ftbl Coach; St Johns Faculty Rep to Pres for Finances; OH HS Ftbl Coaches Assn 1980-; Cath Ed Assn, Jesuit Scndry Ed Assn; Gesu Grade Sch, Sch Bd Pres 1984-87; NW OH Outstanding HS Eng Teacher 1987; Outstanding Teacher St Johns HS 1979; Articles Published; *office:* St Johns HS 5901 Airport Hwy Toledo OH 43615

DE MARTINO, LINDA DON DIEGO, Mathematics Teacher; *b:* Newark, NJ; *m:* Alfred W.; *ed:* (BA) Math, Newark St Coll 1970; (MA) Math, Kean Coll; Grad Stud; *cr:* Research & Dev Programmer Bell Labs 1970-71; Math Teacher Wayne Township 1971-; *ai:* Class Adv 1992; NEA, NJEA, NCTM, NJ Math Teachers; Delta Kappa Pi Honor Society; *office:* Wayne Valley HS 551 Valley Rd Wayne NJ 07470

DEMCHIK, MICHAEL JOSEPH, Chemistry/Physics Teacher; *b:* Pottsville, PA; *m:* Virginia Carol Felosa; *c:* Michael, Stephanie; *ed:* (BS) Sci Ed, Kutztown St Univ 1959; (MA) Sci Ed, 1963, (EDD) Sci Ed, 1973 WV Univ; Numerous Univ; *cr:* Ed/Sci Specialist Regional Ed Service Agency V 1974-75; Chem Teacher/Admin Boone Cty Schls 1975-84; Asst Professor WV Univ 1984-85; Chem/Physics Teacher Jefferson HS 1985-; *ai:* Sci Fair, Mac Gyver Club, Aquarium Club, JETS Spon; AAPT App Section VP for Schls 1989-; NSTA 1969-, Sheldon Laboratory Awds 1985, Gustav Ottaws Awd 1971, Amer Gas Awd 1989; Phi Delta Kappa 1963-; NEA 1959-; Cncl of Elem Sci Intnl 1984-; WV Sci Teachers Assn 1985-; Authored Papers & Articles; Co-Recipient Sci Ed Search for Excl 1982; *office:* Jefferson HS Rt 1 Box 83 Shenandoah Jct WV 25442

DEMKO, OLIVE SUTTON, Kindergarten Teacher; *b:* La Crosse, WI; *m:* Daniel; *c:* Daniel J., Julie A., Michael P.; *ed:* (BS) Ed, Univ of WI La Crosse 1954; MI St Univ 1971-74; Lake MI Coll 1970; Univ of WI La Crosse 1969; *cr:* 1st Grade Teacher La Crescent MN 1954-55; Pre-Sch Teacher Congregational Nursery Sch 1963-66; Substitute Teacher Niles Cmmty Schls 1970-71; 3rd Grade/Kndgtn Teacher St Marys Sch 1971-; *home:* 309 Shillelagh Niles MI 49120

DEMMEL, SHEILA WRIGHT, 4th Grade Teacher; *b:* Des Moines, IA; *m:* Wayne Ellis; *c:* Jodi L. Demmel Weber, Leanne K.; *ed:* (BS) Elem Ed, Mount Mary Coll 1975; Grad Work, Marycrest Coll, Drake Univ, Univ of IA Iowa City; *cr:* 1st Grade Teacher Danville Schls 1956-59, Mt Pleasant Schls 1959-60; 3rd Grade Teacher Winfield Schls 1960-61; 1st Grade Teacher Wilton Schls 1961-62; Kndgtn Teacher Shellsburg Schls 1971-74; 4th Grade Teacher Cntrl Luth Schls 1976-77, Atkins Elem 1977-; *ai:* Soc Stud Curr Comm; Atkins Elem Building; Campbells Soup Labels Educl Coord; Grant Wood AEA Needs Assessment Comm; IA Rdng Assn; Salem United Meth Church (Sunday Sch Teacher, Bd Mem, Nom Comm, Chm of Bazaar); Van Horne Cmmty, Benton Boosters Club; Fine Art Promotors; Brownie Scout Leader; *home:* 602 3rd Ave Box 24 Van Horne IA 52346

DEMMEL, WAYNE E., US History Teacher; *b:* Mt Auburn, IA; *m:* Sheila Kay Wright; *c:* Jodi L. Weber, Leanne K.; *ed:* (BA) His/Phys Ed, IA Wesleyan 1960; Univ of IA, Univ of N IA, Drake Univ; *cr:* Teacher/Coach Wilton Cmmty Sch Dist 1967-69, Benton Cmmty Sch Dist 1969-; *ai:* Head Girls HS Track & Field; Phase III Payment Comm & Soc Stud Curr Chairperson; IA Assn Track Coaches Regional Coach Awd 1978; Smithsonian Intnl; City of Van Horne (Councilmen 1972-76, Mayor 1984-); United Meth Church (Trustee, Bd Mem); Benton Athletic Boosters; Fine Arts Promoters Mem; Published in Magazines; *office:* Benton Cmmty Sch 400 1st St Van Horne IA 52346

DE MUNDA, RICHARD, Mathematics Teacher; *b:* Philadelphia, PA; *m:* Anita M. Farella; *c:* Christina, Maria; *ed:* (BA) Math, Univ of Buffalo 1962; (EDM) Ed/Math, St Univ of Buffalo 1965; Certificate of Advanced Study Math, Wesleyan Univ 1968; *cr:* Math Teacher Niagara Falls HS 1963-; *ai:* Key Club Adv; Act Coord; Building Plan & Building Comm; NYSUT; AFT 801 Local Scndry Dir 1989-; Natl Sci Fnd Awd 1967-68; *office:* Niagara Falls HS Pine Ave & Portage Rd Niagara Falls NY 14301

DE MUTH, RENO BEN, Speech Teacher; *b:* Evansville, IN; *m:* Florence Ellis; *c:* Sherry, Pamela, Alison; *ed:* (BA) Health/Phys Ed, Univ of Evansville 1961; (MS) Health/Phys Ed, IN St 1971; *cr:* Teacher Fulton Elem Sch 1961-68, Cntrl HS 1968-; *ai:* Ftbl Coach; Fellowship of Chrstn Athletes; Class Spon; Textbook Selection Comm; Curr Writing; Track Clerk; Evansville Teachers Assn Sch Rep 1986-87; IN Teachers Assn, IN Teachers of Eng 1961-; Civitan Chaplin 1980-83; Meth Church Youth Minister 1961-; *home:* 4914 Cynthiana Rd Evansville IN 47712

DEMYANOVICH, KAREN BERLIN, Eng Teacher; *b:* Oil City, PA; *m:* Mark Edward; *c:* John, Mark II; *ed:* (BS) Comprehensive Eng, Indiana Univ of PA 1971-; (MS) Rdng Specialist, Clairon Univ 1975-; Learning Strategy Wkshp; *cr:* Rdng Teacher Keystone HS 1971-73, Cameron Cty HS 1973-80; Eng Teacher Clark HS 1980-81; Instr St Marys Univ 1982-83; Eng Teacher Alvirne HS 1983-; *ai:* Grading Comm; AFT 1984-; Merrimack Cmmty Band 1990; *office:* Alvirne HS Derry Rd Hudson NH 03051

DENARI, ROBERT JOHN, Biology Department Teacher; *b:* New York, NY; *m:* Nancy Anne Porter; *c:* Chris, Thomas, Susan Mc Cullough, John, Steven; *ed:* (BS) Ed, IN Univ 1955; (MED) Ed, Miami Univ of OH 1968; IN Univ, Butler Univ, Wittenberg Univ; *cr:* Teacher/Coach Washington Township Sch 1957-58, Covington Schls 1958-60, Cath HS 1960-65, Tallawanda HS 1965-67, Troy HS 1967-74, Northfield HS 1974-77, Westfield HS 1977-; *ai:* Golf Head Coach; Former Head Bsktbl Coach; OH Bsktbls Coaches Assn 1957-74, Hall of Fame 1967; Natl Assn of Bsktbl Coaches 1960-; IN Bsktbl Coaches Assn 1974-, Century Awd 1977; NEA 1957-; Phi Epsilon Kappa 1953-; Westfield Ed Grant 1989; Nom Westfield HS Teacher of Yr 1989; Nom Westfield HS Natl Sci Teacher of Yr 1990; 4 Coaching Booklets Published; *office:* Westfield Washington HS 326 W Main Westfield IN 46074

DENGES, ETHEL LYNN KRUMME, American History Teacher; *b:* Pittsburgh, PA; *m:* Robert Alan; *c:* Julie L., Mark P.; *ed:* (BA) His/Comprehensive Soc Stud, Muskingum Coll 1970; John Carroll, Kent St, OH Univ; *cr:* Teacher General Sherman Jr HS 1970-71, Warrensville Jr HS 1971-72, Dodge Mid Sch 1983-; *ai:* 8th Grade Team Leader; CARE Comm; United Meth Women Past Pres 1975-77, Pin 1980; Beta Sigma Phi VP 1981-; *office:* Dodge Mid Sch 10225 Ravenna Rd Twinsburg OH 44087

DEN HERDER, BARBARA ANN, First Grade Teacher; *b:* Newark, NJ; *c:* Beth A., Robert A.; *ed:* (BA) Elem Ed, William Paterson Coll 1958; Grad Stud Philosophy for Children; *cr:* 1st Grade Teacher Brookside Sch 1958-64; 1st/2nd Grade Teacher Franklin Sch 1973-74; 1st Grade Teacher Washington Park Sch 1976-; *ai:* Dev Natl Teachers Exam Participant; NEA, NJ Ed Assn, Totowa Ed Assn; Governors Teacher Recognition Prgm 1987.

DENI, ROSEANN PERRELLO, Band Director; *b:* Buffalo, NY; *m:* Lawrence J.; *ed:* (BFA) Music Ed/Music Performance Clarinet, St Univ of NY Buffalo 1980; *cr:* Band Dir Frontier Cntrl HS 1980-81, West Seneca West HS 1981-; *ai:* HS Marching Band Dir West Seneca West; Erie Cty Fair Marching Band Dir; Erie Cty Music Educators Assn 1980-; NY St Band Dir Assn 1987-; NY St Sch Music Assn, MENC 1980-; Principle Clarinet Cheektowaga Symphony & Erie Cty Wind Ensemble; Substitute Clarinet Buffalo Philharmonic Orch; Prof Chamber Group Mem; *home:* 4930 S Freeman Rd Orchard Park NY 14127

DENICE, MARCELA LOUISE, English II Teacher; *b:* Springer, NM; *c:* Lisa M., Edward M.; *ed:* (BA) Eng, OLLU 1971; Working Toward Masters Cnslng; Management Certificate; Licensed Practicing Cnslr; *cr:* Teacher La Coste Mid Sch 1973-74; Teacher/Coach Anson Jones Mid Sch 1974-80, Alamo Hts 1980-82; Teacher Lackland Defense Lang Inst 1982-83; Teacher/Coach Davis Mid Sch 1983-84, Burbank HS 1984-; *ai:* HS Bsktbl, Cross Country & Track Coach; Volunteer Amer Cancer Society; Reach for Recovery; Amer Cancer Society Speakers Bureau Co-Chm & Speaker; AFT VP 1985-; PTA 1973- Schlsp 1979; *office:* Burbank HS 1002 Edwards St San Antonio TX 78204

DENICOLA, MARIAN P., English Teacher; *b:* Bethlehem, PA; *ed:* (BSED) Eng, Univ of California PA 1963; (MA) Eng, John Carroll Univ 1973; Kent St Univ, Ashland Univ, Mount St Joseph Coll, Findlay Coll, Baldwin Wallace Coll; *cr:* Eng Teacher Warren City Schls 1963-69, Lakewood City Schls 1969-; Part Time Eng Teacher Cuyahoga Comm Coll 1976-; *ai:* Lang Art Cncl; advanced Placement Comm; 12th Grade Eng Teachers Group Leader; Lakewood Teachers Assn, Cleveland Teachers of Eng 1969-; OH Ed Assn, NEA 1963-; NCTE (Essay Contest Adv) 1969-; Jennings Scholar Jennings Fnd 1969; Whos Who In Amer Ed 1989; Educl Testing Service Advanced Placement Grader 1989-; *office:* Lakewood HS 14100 Franklin Blvd Lakewood OH 44107

DE NICOLA, RICHARD VINCENT, Chemistry Teacher; *b:* Hamden, CT; *m:* Lorraine Reilly; *c:* Joseph, Anthony, Angela; *ed:* (BA) Zoology, Univ VT 1962; (MA) Cytology, Univ CT 1964; Admin/Supvr, S CT St Univ 1975; *cr:* Teacher/Coach Hopkins Grammar Sch 1965-71; Teacher Ridgefield HS 1971-78; Teacher/Coach Amity HS 1979-; *ai:* Environmental Club & Bermuda Ind Study Spon; Frosh Ftbl; PDK 1975-87; PTA 1972-89; NSF Yale Univ 1967; Hamden Police Citizen Awd 1977; *office:* Amity HS 25 Newton Rd Woodbridge CT 06525

DENISE, ROBERT JOSEPH, Business Education Teacher; *b:* Brockton, MA; *m:* Elizabeth Marie Magaldi; *c:* Michael, Mark; *ed:* (AS) Sales/Mrktg, Burdett Coll 1965; (AB) Bus/Ed, Curry Coll 1967; (MED) Scndry Sch Admin, Bridgewater St 1975; *cr:* Bus Ed Teacher Foxborough HS 1967-68; Substitute Work 1968-69; Bus Ed Teacher Middleborough HS 1969-; *ai:* Supply Coord; Class Adv; Bldg Needs Comm; In-Sch Suspension Comm Chm; Activity Adv; Head Bsbl, JV Bsbl, Frosh Bsbl, Var Ladies Bsktbl, Frosh Girls Bsktbl, Var Golf Coach; Batting Instr Ted Williams Camp; Bridgewater St Asst Sftbl & Vlybl Coach; MA Teacher Assn 1969-; EMAIFO Pres 1967-89; IAABO Exec Bd 1965-89; MA Bsbl Coaches 1967-89; Middleboro Cable Advisory Comm 1985-86; Middleboro Babe Ruth Pres 1977-85; Middleboro Little League Player Agent 1979-82; Referee Shriners Ftbl Classic 1989; Middleboro HS Curr Developer; Sch Evaluation Philosophy & Objectives Comm; Ftbl Superbowl Ofcl 1980; *office:* Middleborough HS 71 E Grove St Middleboro MA 02346

DENIZ, NATALIE CRUZ RODRIGUEZ, Counselor; *b:* Yancey, TX; *m:* Johnny Albert; *c:* Angela; *ed:* (AA) Ed, Fresno City Coll 1964; (BA) Span, Fresno St 1967; Pupil Personnel Services Pupil Counseling; Specialist Teaching Bi-ling/Cross Cultural; Certificado De Filosofia Y Letras Universidad De Valencia Spain; *cr:* Kndgtn Teacher Dixieland Elem Sch 1967-72; K-12th Resource Teacher Migrant Ed Region III 1972-73; K-6th Grade Teacher Washington Elem Sch 1974-75; 7th-8th Grade Cnslr Thomas Jefferson Jr HS 1975-89; 9th-12th Grade Cnslr Madera Adult Ed 1989-; *ai:* Affirmative Action Comm; Madera HS Advisory Comm; Madera Unified Sch Dist Screening Comm; Stu Study Team Facilitator; Madera Unified Teachers Assn Rep 1968-70; Assn of Mexican-Amer Educators Pres 1976; Madera Youth Ftbl Bd VP 1987-89; Young Ladies Inst Pres 1977; Amer Cancer Society Bd 1990; St Joachims Parents Club Pres 1982; Fresno City Coll Bi-ling Bicultural Advisory Comm; Channel 18 Bd of Management; St Joachims Sch Bd; *office:* Madera Adult Ed 130 Santa Cruz Madera CA 93637

DENMAN, DANNETTE DANIEL, Third Grade Teacher; *b:* Hyattsville, MD; *m:* Andrew Jackson Jr.; *c:* Andrew B.; *ed:* (BS) Elem Ed, Univ of GA 1968; Grad Stud Gifted; *cr:* 3rd Grade Teacher W C Britt Elem 1968-71; 2nd Grade Teacher Lake Drive Elem 1971-72; 3rd Grade Teacher Heard-Mixon Elem 1972-74, Livingston Elem 1974-; Teacher of Gifted Newton Cty Schls 1980-89; 3rd Grade Teacher Porterdale Elem Sch 1989-; *ai:* NEA, GA Assn of Educators 1968-; Newton Cty Assn of Educators 1972-, Educator of Yr; Alpha Delta Kappa (Photographer 1988-) 1987-; Newton Cty 4-H Club Adult Leader; Livingston Elem Teacher of Yr 3 Times; Porterdale Elem Teacher of Yr; *office:* Porterdale Elem Sch 45 Ram Dr Covington GA 30209

DENNEHY, CAROLYN ANN, Bio Teacher/Scndry Sci Coord; *b:* Corsicana, TX; *ed:* (BA) Bio, N TX St Univ 1974; (MSSE) Bio/Sci Ed, 1982, (PHD) Kinesiology/Exercise Physiology, 1989 TX Womans Univ; Certified Exercise Test Technologist, Amer Coll of Sports Medicine; *cr:* Phys Sci Teacher Dallas Ind Sch Dist 1975, Arlington TX Ind Sch Dist 1975-83; Phys Ed Teacher TX Womans Univ 1987-88; Biological Sci Teacher Weld Cty Sch Dist 1983-; *ai:* Teacher on Spec Assignment Scndry Sci in Charge of Organizing & Facilitating Sci & Health Restructuring; NSTA, Amer Alliance of Health, Phys Ed, Recreation & Dance; Amer Coll of Sports Medicine; Greeley Teachers Assn; CO Ed Assn; NEA; Mem Book Selection Comm; Excl in Sci Task Force, Alliance for Sci Grant Mem Univ of CO 1985-; Curr Dev Dist 6; Dev & Wrote Anatomy & Physiology Curr Upper Division Bio Stu; Curr Revision Comm, Provided Dist Wide Inservice for using the Revision; Dev Pilot Prgm for Talented & Gifted Stus; Wrote & had Approved a Microbiology Curr for 1 Semester Bio Class 1988; Served on Technology Vision Building Task Force 1989; K-12 Sci/Health Budget, Educl Reform Comm in Biological/Phys Sci Univ N CO 1989; Proposed, Designed, Organized In-Service to Develop Level Outcomes K-12 Sci/Health/Phys Ed Prgm Greeley Sch Dist 1989; *office:* Weld Cty Sch Dist #6 811 15th St Greeley CO 80631

DENNEY, ELISABETH BISHOP, 2nd Grade Teacher; *b:* La Fayette, AL; *m:* Clifford G.; *c:* Christopher; *ed:* (BS) Family/Child Dev, 1976, (MED) Early Chldhd Ed, 1981 Auburn Univ; (EDS) Early Chldhd Ed, W GA Coll 1989; *cr:* Home Ec Teacher Hogansville HS 1977-81; 2nd Grade Teacher Crocker Primary Sch 1981-; *ai:* System Coord Young GA Authors Writing Exposition; Educl Technology Comm; GA Teacher Performance Instrument Peer Data Collector; NEA, GA Assn of Ed 1977-89; Hogansville Assn of Educators Secy 1977-89; Prof Assn of GA Educators 1989-; Hogansville 1st United Meth Church Sunday Sch Teacher 1980-; Pilot Club Secy 1985-88; United Meth Women Circle Leader 1988-; System Teacher of Yr 1984.

DENNEY, SANDRA LEE, 6th Grade Teacher; *b:* Wilmington, DE; *ed:* (BS) Elem Ed, 1967, (MA) Art His, 1969 Univ of DE; Post Grad Stud N Italy/Florence Syracuse Univ 1978 & S Italy/Rome Vergilian Society 1977; *cr:* Part-Time Lecturer Washington Coll 1968-69, Univ of MD Extension Division 1968-71; Part-Time Instr Univ of DE Extension Division 1970-72, 1977-82; Coord Warner Center for Adult Ed 1980-82; Teacher Red Clay Consolidated Sch Dist 1969-; *ai:* Art His Clubs Spon; NY, Philadelphia, Washington DC Museum Trips Lecturer & Guide; Skyline Mid Sch 6th Grade Team Leader; DSEA, NEA; Kappa Delta Pi 1966; Phi Kappa Phi 1967; PA Acad of Fine Art Publication 1973; DE Hum Forum Speakers Bureau Participant 1984-87.

DENNIE, EDNA PINKSTON, Third Grade Teacher; *b:* Montgomery, AL; *c:* Deidre Tatum, Michael, Daryl; *ed:* (BS) Elem Ed, AL St Univ 1962; Teaching the Gifted Natl Coll of Evanston; *cr:* Librarian Lanier HS 1968; 3rd Grade Teacher Irving Elem Sch 1969-73; 4th-6th Grade Teacher Robert E Lucus Intermediate Sch 1973-78; 3rd Grade Teacher Springdale Elem 1979-; *ai:* Rdng Cncl Rep; Eunice Combs Rdng Cncl 1986-; OH Ed Assn, Princeton Assn of Classroom Educators 1973-; Tutorial Ministry Secy 1988-; Springdale PTA Bd Mem; Nom Outstanding Teacher of Yr 1989-; *office:* Springdale Elem Sch 350 W Kemper Rd Cincinnati OH 45246

DENNIE, LEE D., Earth Science/US His Teacher; *b:* Muncie, IN; *m:* Mary Elizabeth O'Donnell; *c:* Jaclyn, Katharine; *ed:* (BS) Poly Sci, Ball St Univ 1979; (MS) Ed/US His/Sci, IN Univ South Bend 1990; *cr:* Jr HS Sci/Soc Stud Teacher Todd Cty HS 1979-82; HS Sci/Soc Stud Teacher Laville Jr/Sr HS 1982-; *ai:* HS Sci Club; HS Asst Coach Ftbl; Head Coach Var Girls Track;

Laville Sch Improvement Comm; NEA, ISTA; Grants in Cmptr Consortium, Weather Station; *office:* Laville Jr/Sr HS 69969 US 31 S Lakeville IN 46536

DENNING, LYNDA WALKER, 3rd Grade Teacher; *b:* Newnan, GA; *m:* William W.; *c:* Christopher W.; *ed:* (BS) Elem Ed, W GA Coll 1968; *cr:* 2nd Grade Teacher 1968-71, 3rd Grade Teacher 1971-74 Hickory Hills Elem; 2nd-5th Grade Remedial Math Teacher Allgood Elem 1974-75; 5th Grade Teacher 1978-86, 3rd Grade Teacher 1986- CLarkdale Elem; *ai:* Teacher Rep Health; Marietta Ed Assn VP 1973-74; GEA; PTA Treas 1984-85; Nom Teacher of Yr 1982; *home:* 4557 Eugenia Pl Austell GA 30001

DENNIS, DONALD A., Science Teacher; *b:* Kingston, PA; *m:* Peggy Price; *c:* Kari, Kyle; *ed:* (BS) Scndry Ed/Earth Sci, Bloomsburg Univ 1971; Rider Coll/Temple Univ/Lamar Univ/Penn St; *cr:* Sci Teacher Upper Moreland Jr HS 1970-71, Newtown Intermediate Sch 1971-75, Holland Jr HS 1975-; *ai:* 9th Grade Bsktbl Coach; Athletic Dir; Buck Cty Jr HS Athletic Dir Pres 1979-; PA St Athletic Dir Assn 1980-; PA Interscholastic Athletic Assn 1971-; Tri-Township Sports Sftbl Dir 1989-; Natl Sci Fnd Grant 1971; Philadelphia Electric Jr HS Energy Proj-Temple Univ 1977-78; *office:* Holland Jr H Sch 400 E Holland Rd Southampton PA 18966

DENNIS, DORRIS STRAUGHAN, Fourth Grade Teacher; *b:* Dallas, TX; *m:* Arvin H.; *c:* Melinda Kooi *ed:* (BS) Elem, TX Wesleyan Coll 1954; *cr:* 2nd Grade Teacher Hawkins Elem 1954-55; 2nd Grade Teacher 1955-56, 3rd Grade Teacher 1956-77 Cntrl Elem; 4th Grade Teacher Shive Elem 1977-; *ai:* ATPE 1987-; TX St Teachers Assn 1954-87; Jaycettes VP 1962-69, Jaycettes of Yr 1964-65; *office:* Shive Elem Sch 3130 Bacon Vernon TX 76384

DENNIS, JAMES L., Social Studies Teacher; *b:* Marietta, OH; *m:* Bonnie Hasley; *ed:* (BA) His, Marietta Coll 1975; (MA) Ed, Salem Coll 1985; *cr:* Soc Stud Teacher Parkersburg South HS 1978-; *ai:* NHS Faculty Cncl; Published Book 1986; Wrote Historical Articles 1990; *office:* Parkersburg South HS 1511 Blizzard Dr Parkersburg WV 26101

DENNIS, KATHLEEN MURPHY, Spanish Teacher; *b:* Robbinsdale, MN; *m:* Nelson Errol; *c:* Lucas, Patrick; *ed:* (BS) Span, Univ of MN 1974; (MS) Scndry Ed, E TX St Univ 1989; Working Towards PhD; *cr:* Substitute Teacher 1978-80; His Teacher Saltillo Ind Sch Dist 1980-84; Span Teacher Sulphur Springs Ind Sch Dist 1984-; *ai:* HS Span Club Spon; Church (Finance Comm Secy 1987-, Sunday Sch Teacher 1985-); BSA Den Mother 1981-.

DENNIS, MARY LOU SPRING, First Grade Teacher; *b:* Dennison, OH; *m:* Robert William; *c:* Craig A., Jeffrey R., Sarah J.; *ed:* (BA) Elem Ed, Kent St Univ 1973; *cr:* 3rd Grade Teacher 1973-75, 1st Grade Teacher 1975- Westgate Elem; *ai:* Harrison Hills Teacher Assn, OEA, NEA 1973-; *office:* Westgate Elem Sch 730 Peppard Ave Cadiz OH 43907

DENNIS, MELINDA MULLIS, Sophomore English Teacher; *b:* Mc Rae, GA; *m:* Ronnie William; *ed:* (AA) Ed, Mid GA Coll 1985; (BS) Eng Ed, 1987, (MED) Eng Ed, 1989 GA Southwestern Coll; Working on Ed Specialist Degree; *cr:* Teacher Dodge Cty HS 1987-; *ai:* Anchor Club Adv; Sch Vitality & Homecoming Comm; Literary Coord; Asst Sftbl Coach; Prof Assn of GA Educators, Dodge Assn of Educators, NCTE 1987-; Eastman Jr Womens Club; Plainfield Baptist Church; *office:* Dodge Cty HS Rt 2 Cochran Rd Eastman GA 31023

DENNIS, SHARON MAE, Math/Physics/Chem Instructor; *b:* Madison, WI; *m:* Patrick William; *c:* Shawn; *ed:* (BA) Math/Physics, Greenville Coll 1964; Numerous Univs; *cr:* Physics/Chem Instr Cascade HS 1964-67; Physics Instr Lower Columbia Coll 1972-74; Jr HS/HS Teacher 1974-, Highly Capable Coord 1984- Wahkiakum Sch Dist; *ai:* NASTA, WSTA; *office:* Wahkiakum HS Box 398 Cathlamet WA 98612

DENNISON, TERRY KING, World Geography Teacher; *b:* Hastings, MI; *ed:* (BS) Soc Stud, 1962, (MA) Geography Ed, 1963 Univ of MI; *cr:* Teacher Niles Cmmty Schls 1963-; *ai:* Ring Lardner Jr HS Stu Cncl; Russian & Scottish Dance Club; Niles Cmmty Schls Teacher of Yr 1982-83; *home:* 622 1/2 N 13th St Niles MI 49120

DENONCOURT, LEO PAUL, Principal/Teacher; *b:* Goffstown, NH; *m:* Monique Frebet; *c:* Myriam, Aline, Daniele, Benedicte; *ed:* (BA) Fine Arts, Bellarmine Coll 1966; (MAT) Elem Ed, Spalding Univ; Elem Trng Montessori Method; *cr:* Prin/Teacher Hayfield Montessori Sch 1967-; *office:* Hayfield Montessori Sch 2000 Tyler Ln Louisville KY 40205

DENSMORE, VIRGINIA NOLTING, Elementary Music Teacher; *b:* Chattanooga, TN; *m:* Gene; *ed:* (BME) Music Ed, 1962, (MME) Music Ed, 1967 FL St Univ; Orff Level Trng I, II, III, IV; *cr:* Elem Music Teacher Sabal Palm Elem Sch 1962-67; Elem Music Professor Developmental Research Sch FL St Univ 1967-; *ai:* Amer Orff Schulwerk Assn (Pres, Founder 1983-85) 1980-; Music Educators Natl Conference; FL Music Educators Assn Music Ed Day Chm 1990; FL Elem Music Ed Assn (Pres 1973-75) 1967-, Outstanding Research 1976; Delta Kappa Gamma Mu St (Pres 1982-84) 1976-; Capital City Cmmty Band 1966-; Developmental Research Sch Teacher of Yr 1988; *home:* 9713 Waters Meet Dr Tallahassee FL 32312

DENSON, JENETTE LEE (MATHIOT), Substitute Teacher; *b:* Billings, MT; *m:* Harry Scott; *c:* Rick F.; *ed:* (BSED) Bio, E MT Coll 1987; Grad Stud Univ of MT; *cr:* Sci Teacher Custer Cty HS 1987-89; Substitute Teacher Malta HS; *ai:* Custer Cty HS Soph Class Spon 1987-89; MT Ed Assn, NSTA 1987-; US Naval Reserves Rank LTJG 1976-; Youth Group Dir 1989-; Univ of MT Sci Inst Schlsp 1988-; *office:* Malta HS Box 1737 Malta MT 59538

DENSON, SHARON KAY, English & Journalism Teacher; *b:* Oxford, MS; *m:* W. Lloyd; *c:* Beth, Christopher; *ed:* (BA) Journalism, Univ of MS 1984; *cr:* Eng Teacher Sylva-Bay Acad 1985-; *ai:* Retrospect Annual Staff Spon; Pageant Dir; Stu Government Spon 1986-1986-88; Silva Bay Speaks Newspaper Spon; *office:* Sylva-Bay Academy Po Drawer J Bay Springs MS 39422

DENSTAEDT, LINDA MITCHELL, English Teacher/Dept Chair; *b:* Minneapolis, MN; *m:* John Michael; *c:* Geoffrey M., Scott J.; *ed:* (BA) Eng, 1968, (MAT) Rdng, 1975 Oakland Univ; Instrumental Enrichment, Gifted, Self Esteem; *cr:* 5th Grade Teacher Pine Knob Elem 1968-69; 9th Grade Teacher Sashabaw Jr HS 1969-71; Teacher Clarkston HS 1971-; Rdng Coord Clarkston Cmmty Schls 1989-; *ai:* Clarkston Writers; Yrbk; Substance Abuse Comm Chairperson; Subject Area Coord & K-12th Grade Comm; Female Faculty Support Group Leader; Level II USVBA Vlybl Coach; MRA 1989-; *office:* Clarkston Cmmty Schls 6595 Middle Lake Rd Clarkston MI 48016

DENT, BERDINE CLOUD, Sixth Grade Teacher; *b:* Columbus, OH; *m:* Carl David; *c:* Carol, Cathleen Beck, Carl D. Jr.; *ed:* (BA) Eng, 1977, (MA) Eng, 1984 CA St Univ Northridge; *cr:* Asst Spec Ed Teacher Burbank Boulevard Elem Sch 1971-79; Teacher Pinecrest Sch 1979-; *ai:* PTA (Historian, Art Dir) 1961-72, Honorary Life Membership 1972; Campfire Girl Leader; Co-Producer Public Service Video for Homeless; *office:* Pinecrest Elem Sch 14111 Sherman Way Van Nuys CA 91405

DENT, EUNICE SIMMONS, Reading Teacher; *b:* Brooklyn, NY; *m:* Frederick W. III; *c:* Cynthia Simmons, Janice Simmons, Tasha Simmons, Nikki Simmons; *ed:* (BS) Elem Ed, Medgar Evers Coll 1975; (MED) Elem Ed, Mc Neese St Univ 1982; *cr:* Educl Assoc PS 83 1964-78; Teacher WEL-MET Summer Camp 1974, PS 262 Summer Sch 1975-78, Adams Children Ctr 1976-78; Teacher Ray D Molo Mid 1978-83, 84-; Teacher Hamilton Elem 1983-84; Teacher Combre Elem 1984; Teacher Adult Ed Ray D Molo Middle 1984-; Teacher St Martin Deporres Residential Ctr Halfway House for Prisoners 1989-; *ai:* Chrldr & Stu Cncl Spon; CAE Building Rep 1982-83; LAE, LAPCAE; League of Women Voters; *office:* Ray D Molo Mid Magnet 2300 Medora St Lake Charles LA 70601

DENT, SHELDON RALPH, Business Education Teacher; *b:* Upland, PA; *m:* Gertrude Helene Hoffman; *c:* Michelle J. Guthrie, Stephen J.; *ed:* (BS) Bus Admin, Elizabethtown Coll 1959; Temple Univ, Univ of DE; *cr:* Soc Stud Teacher Aberdeen HS 1961-63; Bus Ed Teacher Claymont HS 1963-67, Sharon Hill HS 1967-82, Acad Park HS 1982-; *ai:* Bsktbl & Bsbl Head Coach; Head of SE Delco Teachers Assn; SE Bus Ed Assn, PA St Bus Assn; Prof Bsbl Player 1959-62; Longview Farms Civic Assn Treas 1970-76; Brandywine Cncl Civic Assn Highway Planning Commission; *home:* 1115 N Overhill Ct Wilmington DE 19810

DENT, WANDA PRESSLEY, English Teacher; *b:* Greenville, SC; *m:* Glenn M.; *ed:* (BA) Eng, Lee Coll 1975; Grad Stud Ed Prgm Tusculum Coll 1991; *cr:* 5th Grade Teacher Hopewell Elem 1975-79; Eng Teacher Cleveland HS 1979-; *ai:* Academic Contests Drama Coach; Sch Newsletter Ed; Textbook & Sacs Comm; NCTE 1988; Volunteer Tutor 1988-89; *office:* Cleveland HS 850 Raider Dr Cleveland TN 37311

DENTON, CYNTHIA DILLON, Business Education Chair; *b:* Miles City, MT; *m:* Joseph Larry; *ed:* (BS) Bus, 1969, (MS) Bus Ed, 1974, (MS) Phys Ed, 1986 MT St Univ; *cr:* Chm Bud Ed Dept 1969-; *ai:* Yrbk; WBEA, NBEA, MT Ed Assn, Hobson Ed Assn 1969-; Judith Cultural Comm (Founder, Pres) 1985-88; *home:* 201 3rd Ave E Hobson MT 59452

DENTON, ELIZABETH BASS, Home Economics Teacher; *b:* Sayre, OK; *m:* Larry; *c:* Michael, John D.; *ed:* (BS) Home Ec Ed - Cum Laude, Baylor Univ 1973; Grad Stud TX Womens Univ & W TX St Univ; Certified Instr Model Effective Teaching & Supervision; *cr:* Teacher T C Wilemon Jr HS 1974-76, Lancaster HS 1976-79, Humble HS 1979-80, Borger HS 1980-; *ai:* FHA Adv; Teacher Organization Rep to Supts Comm for Positive Results; Inservice Constructor for Effective Schls Trng; Borger Classroom Teachers Assn (Treas 1986-88, Pres 1988-); Delta Kappa Gamma (VP 1990, Comm Chm 1988-); Huthinson Cty Unit of Amer Cancer Society (VP, Mem); Gateway Booster Club (Corresponding Secy 1988-, Pres 1990), Great Amer Smoke-Out 1989; Natl Recognition St Winner 1986, 1989; *home:* 221 Tumbleweed Borger TX 79007

DENTON, ELIZABETH WIMBERLY, Mathematics Teacher; *b:* Rock Hill, SC; *m:* Wayne Woodrow; *ed:* (BS) Scndry Ed/Math, Univ of SC 1972; (MAT) Ed/Math, Winthrop Coll 1975; Mentor Teacher Trng 1986-87; *cr:* Math Teacher Lancaster Hs 1972-78; Math Teacher/Math Dept Chm Barr Street Jr HS 1978-79; Math Teacher E Lee Cty Jr HS 1979-; *ai:* NC Cncl Teachers of Math 1979-, Presidential Awd Excl in Teaching St Nom 1989; NCTM 1981-; E Lee Teacher of Yr 1986-87, 1987-88; *office:* East Lee Cty Jr HS 1337 Broadway Rd Sanford NC 27330

DENTON, J. LARRY, History Teacher; *b:* Billings, MT; *m:* Cynthia F. Dillon; *ed:* (BA) His, 1969, (MS) Scndry Ed, 1975 MT St Univ; *cr:* Soc Stud Teacher Hobson Public Sch 1969-; *ai:* NHS Adv; 8th Grade Class Spon; NEA, MT Ed Assn 1969-; Hobson Ed Assn Pres 1975-83; Judith Basin Cultural Comm 1986-; Served on Hobson City Government Study Commission; *office:* Hobson HS P O Box 410 Hobson MT 59452

DENTON, LINDA ALICE, Fourth Grade Teacher; *b:* Jefferson City, TN; *ed:* (BS) Music Ed, Carson-Newman Coll 1967; (MS) Music, Univ of TN 1982; Post Grad Work Ed, Univ of Cincinnati 1969, Univ of GA 1972, Columbus Coll 1974, 1976; *cr:* Music Ed Teacher Sevier Cty Schls 1967-69; 3rd Grade Teacher Liberty Union Sch Dist 1969-70; 5th/6th Lang Art Teacher Henry Cty Schls 1970-73; Title I Rdng Teacher Muscogee Cty Schls 1976-79; 5th Grade Teacher La Grange City Schls 1979-80; 4th Grade Teacher East Knox Cty Elem 1980-; *ai:* Public Relations Comm; 4th/5th Grade Chorus Asst; Intnl Rdng Assn 1976-; Knoxville Intnl Rdng Assn Treas, ASCD 1988-; TN Rdng Assn, E TN Ed Assn 1980-; Amer Cancer Society Public Ed Comm 1988-; Church of Good Shephard (Altar Guild Chairperson 1982-, Choir 1984-); Nom Teacher of Yr 1987; Knoxville News Sentinel Golden Apple Awd 1986, 1987; Teacher of Month 1989; *office:* East Knox Cty Elem Sch 9315 Rutledge Pike Mascot TN 37806

DENTON, LOUISE WILLIS, 7th-8th Grade Math Teacher; *b:* Grenada, MS; *m:* Charles G.; *c:* Fanesta, Charles; *ed:* (BS) Elem Ed, Jackson St Univ 1961; (MS) Supervision of Instruction, Concordia Coll 1980; Cmptr Sci, Trng Teacher Expectancy Stu Achievement Prgm, Trng Teaching Integrated Math/Sci Prgm Natl Sci Fnd 1985-86; *cr:* Teacher Broad Street HS 1961-62, Mason Primary Sch 1963-68; Adjunct Teacher Triton Coll 1982-84; Teacher Irving Elem Sch 1968-; *ai:* 6th-8th Grade Gifted Math Teacher; Cmptr Comm; Lab Asst Teaching Integrated Math & Sci; Math Comm Dist 89; Cmptr Resource Teacher; Teacher in After-Sch Tutoring Prgm; IL Math Cncl 1985, Nom for Math Teacher of Yr 1986; IL Fed 1968-; Maywood Beautification Secy 1982-88, Appreciation Awd 1988; Maywood United Way Budget Chm 1984-, Appreciation Awd 1986; Maywood Youth Commission Secy 1982, Dedication Awd 1982; Judge for Math & Sci Fair Concordia Coll; *office:* Irving Elem Sch 805 S 17th Ave Maywood IL 60153

DENTON, OLGA GRESH, 2nd/3rd Grade Teacher; *b:* Johnstown, PA; *m:* H. Dean; *ed:* (BA) General Elem, Biola Univ 1962; Grad Stud Pepperdine Univ, Pacific Chrstn Coll, CA St Fullerton; *cr:* 2nd-5th Grade Teacher Commonwealth Elem Sch 1962-; *ai:* Fullerton Elem Teachers Assn Sch Rep 1985-87; CA Teachers Assn, NEA; Cmmty Bible Church Sunday Sch Supt 1974-80; Commonwealth Sch Key Planner for St Review; *office:* Commonwealth Elem Sch 2200 E Commonwealth Fullerton CA 92631

DENTON, SANDRA ELIZABETH, English Teacher; *b:* Kansas City, MO; *ed:* (BA) Eng Lang/Lit, 1969, (MA) Scndry Ed, 1976 Univ of MO; Rdng Cert, OH St Univ 1990; *cr:* Eng Teacher Kansas City MO Sch Dist 1969-84; Editor Lang Art Merrill Publishing Company 1984-86; Eng Teacher Columbus Public Schls 1986-; *ai:* Class & NHS Spon; Comm Dept Chairperson; NCTE; Alpha Kappa Alpha; Jennings Scholar; Advanced Placement Reader Educl Testing Service; Educator of Yr 1988, Nom 1989, 1990; *office:* East HS 1500 E Broad St Columbus OH 43205

DENTON, THOMAS JOHNS, Social Studies Teacher; *b:* Zanesville, OH; *m:* Rebecca S. Milstead; *c:* T. J.; *ed:* (BSED) Soc Stud Comprehensive, OH Univ 1973; Working Towards Masters in Ed & Supervision, Ashland Coll; *cr:* Teacher/Coach Tri-Valley HS 1973-; *ai:* Cross Cntry Coach; Teacher Advisory Cncl; OH Cncl for Soc Stud; Tri-Valley Ed Assn, OH Ed Assn, NEA; ZDGA Secy 1986-; MAGA Secy 1986-89; *office:* Tri-Valley HS 46 E Muskingum Ave Dresden OH 43821

DE PALMA, JOHN, Mathematics Teacher; *b:* Newark, NJ; *m:* Rosemary Vella; *c:* Lisa, John; *ed:* (BA) Elem Ed, 1969, (MA) Early Chldhd Ed, 1972 Kean Coll; *cr:* Rdng Teacher Newark Bd of Ed 1969-77; Math Teacher Randolph Bd of Ed 1977-; *ai:* Stu Government Assn, Yrbk, Intramural Adv; NEA, NJ Ed Assn Mem 1977-; NJ Mid Sch Teachers Assn Charter Mem; Mine Hill Bd of Ed Mem 1981-85; Roxbury Drug Cncl Charter Mem 1988-; *office:* Randolph Intermediate Sch 507 Millbrook Ave Randolph NJ 07869

DE PANTIGA, MARICEL HERNANDEZ, Science Teacher; *b:* Santurce, PR; *m:* Guillermo Pantiga Alonso; *c:* Guillermo R. Pantiga, Maria E. Pantiga; *ed:* (BA) Hum/Ed, Univ of PR 1970; (MA) Ed Admin/Supervision, Inter-Amer Univ of PR 1989; Modern Sci Seminary, Turabo Univ 1985; *cr:* 1st Grade Span/Soc Stud/Math Teacher Rosabel Sch 1974-76; 4th Grade General Sci Teacher 1978-81, 5th Grade General Sci Teacher 1978-85, 9th Grade Phys Sci Teacher 1986-88, 6th Grade General Sci Teacher 1978-, 8th Grade Earth Sci Teacher 1981-, 7th Grade Biological Sci Teacher 1988- Academia del Sagrado Gorazon; *ai:* Elem By-Laws Revision Comm Mem 1989-; Faculty By-Laws Revision Comm Mem 1988-; PTA Secy 1989-.

DE PERROT, LUCY MUSSELMAN, 3rd Grade Teacher; *b:* Vernfield, PA; *m:* John; *c:* Bradley Brubaker, Becky Wagner, Andrew Brubaker; *ed:* (BS) Elem Ed, Elizabethtown Coll 1953; *cr:* Teacher Lower Salford Elem Sch 1953-56; Teacher Lititz Elem 1956-; Teacher Kissel Hill 1968-; *ai:* NEA; PSEA; WEA Building Rep 1988-; Lititz Church of Brethren; Teacher Exch Prgm Japan Summer 1988; *home:* 240 Landis Valley Rd Lititz PA 17543

DE PINA, BARBARA L., Teacher; *b:* New Bedford, MA; *c:* Judy Dufour, Jo A. Roberts, Joyce, Joseph Gomes; *ed:* (AS) Mental Health, BBC Fall River 1972; (BA) Sociology, SMU Dartmouth 1976; Cert Ed, SMU 1977; *cr:* Teacher Aide 1972-75, Teacher 1978- New Bedford Sch Dept; *ai:* RISE Dropout Prevention Prgm 1988-89; Merchant Mariners Soc Club Trustee 1987-; Deans List SMU 1975-77; Hum Awd BBC 1972; *office:* Normandin Jr H S 240 Tarkiln Hill Rd New Bedford MA 02745

DE POLO, CAROL DAVENPORT, First Grade Teacher; *b:* Kingston, PA; *m:* Charles H.; *c:* Christopher, Carlton; *ed:* (BA) Elem Ed, Bloomsburg St Coll 1963; *cr:* Kndgtn Teacher 1963-66, 1st Grade Teacher 1972-77 St Clair Elem Sch; 1st Grade Teacher Dr D Kistler Elem Sch 1977-; *ai:* PA St Ed Assn, NEA; *office:* Dr David Kistler Elem Sch 301 Old River Rd Wilkes-Barre PA 18702

DE POLO, ROBERT JOHN, Chemistry Teacher; *b:* Windber, PA; *m:* Kathleen Pierre; *c:* Kristine, Robert; *ed:* (BSED) Chem/ Phys Sci, 1962, (MED) Chem/Phys Sci, 1969 Indiana Univ of PA; *cr:* Chem Teacher Seneca Valley HS 1962-; *ai:* Sci Dept Chairperson; Seneca Valley Ed Assn Pres 1970-71; PA St Ed Assn, NEA; *office:* Seneca Valley HS 124 Seneca Rd Harmony PA 16037

DEPPEN, DAVID M., 5th Grade Teacher; *b:* Danville, PA; *m:* Debra D. Starr; *c:* Heidi, Tony, Andy; *ed:* (AS) Harrisburg Area Comm Coll 1969; (BA) Elem Ed, 1971, (MA) Elem Ed. PA St Univ 1979; *cr:* 5th Grade Teacher Line Mountain Elem Sch 1972-; *ai:* Yearly Trash-A-Thon; Line Mountain Educl Assn, PSEA & NEA 1972-; Gratz Boro Cncl Pres 1980-; US Army Reserves 1968- Dining Facility Manager; 5th Grade Class Won Outstanding Youth Organization Environmental Awd 1981.

DE PUTRON, DAVID B., 4th Grade Teacher; *b:* Staten Island, NY; *m:* Christine Turbet; *c:* Jenna, Shane, Scott; *ed:* (BA) Ed, St Univ Coll Cortland 1974; Grad Stud ED; CPR Certified; First Aid Cert; *cr:* 5th Grade Teacher 1974-76, 4th Grade Teacher 1976- Seymour Smith Elem Sch; *ai:* Recreation Dir Field Hockey, Ftbl, Soccer, Bsktbl, Summer Sports & Acts; Sports Reporter; Pine Plains Recreation Comm 1976-; NYSUT, Pine Plains Ed Assn, PTA 1974-; Teacher Recognition Awd WCZX Radio Station; *office:* Seymour Smith Sch Academy St Pine Plains NY 12567

DEPUY, CYNTHIA PARKER, 6th Grade English Teacher; *b:* Kingston, PA; *c:* Guy M., Craig S.; *ed:* (BA) Fr, Wilson Coll 1954; Italian, Creative Writing Wkshps; Grad Work Ed, Cornell Univ; Permanent Cert K-6; *cr:* 4th-6th Grade Teacher Poolville Sch & Earlville Cntrl 1954-55; 6th Grade Teacher Hamilton Cntrl Sch 1955-56; 4th-5th Grade Teacher Cayuga Hts & Ithaca Cntrl Sch 1956-58; 2nd Grade Teacher Clinton Cntrl Sch 1966-72; 3rd/5th/ 6th Grade Teacher Fonda-Fultonville Cntrl Sch 1972-; *ai:* Big Brothers/Sisters (Bd Mem, Big Sister) 1983-89; Local, St, NTA, Membership; Colonial Little Theater Stage Work 1977-87; Episcopal Church Altar Guild 1988-; Hospice Fund Raising 1988-89; Coterie Study Club 1978-; Burroughs Nature Study Club (Pres 1975-76) 1974-; Ger Singing Group 1977-87; Presbyn Church Deacon 1972-76; *office:* Fonda-Fultonville Cntrl Sch Cemetary St Fonda NY 12068

DE QUINTERO, MYRIAM, Elementary School Teacher; *b:* Lajas, PR; *m:* Juan G. Quintero Ponce; *c:* Leslie C., Ineabelle, Gilberto, Laura X.; *ed:* (BA) Elem Ed, Cath Univ of PR 1966; *cr:* Teacher Dr Jose C Barbosa Sch; *ai:* Faculty Mem 1985-86; PR Fed of Teachers Mem 1968-; Best Teacher of Yr 1985; *home:* Ave Fagot Esq Obispado M26 Ponce PR 00731

D'ERAMO, MARGARET MARY, Counselor; *b:* Beaver Falls, PA; *c:* Francis, Patrice; *ed:* (BS) Elem Ed, Geneva Coll 1972; (MED) Scndry Cnslng, Westminster Coll 1976; (MED) Elem Cnslng, Duquesne Univ 1986; *cr:* 6th Grade Teacher 1972-86; Elem & Mid Sch Cnslr 1986 Southside Area Sch Dist; *ai:* Spon Stu Cncl; Strategic Planning Comm; PA St Chair-Ethics Comm 1980-85; Ed Assn Bd of Dir 1985-; NEA Bd of Dir 1985-; League of Women Voters; Rep Teachers with Exchange to Omiya Japan 1989; *office:* South Side Mid Sch Rd 1 Box 410 Hookstown PA 15050

DERDERIAN, MICHAEL JAMES, Earth Science Teacher; *b:* Bellville, IL; *m:* Vicki Lynn (Havlen); *c:* John M., Bryanna; *ed:* (BA) Elem Ed, 1970, (BA) Bio, 1972, (MED) Admin 1985 Trinity Univ; Bi-Ling Endorsement to Prof Certificate 1978; *cr:* Teacher Regency Place Elem 1973-79; Teacher/Admin Aide East Terrell Hills Elem 1979-82; Teacher Coker Elem 1982-85, Ed White Mid Sch 1985-; *ai:* Natl Jr Honor Society Spon; Bus Supvr; Campus Team Leader of Writing Skills Across the Curr; Presentor/ Facilitator for Campus/Dist/St; Inservice for Teachng Writing Skills Across the Curr; Assn of TX Prof Educators 1985-; ASCD 1990; Sci Teachers Assn of Tx 1985-; Intnl Plastic Modelers Society 1971-87; Teacher of Month at Ed White Each Yr Since 1985; Faculty Rep North East Teachers Assn 1974-78; Grad Scholars Grant Trinity Univ Full Schlsp 1979-81; Supts Awd North East Ind Sch Dist 1989; *office:* Edward White Mid Schl 7800 Midcrown San Antonio TX 78218

DERDERIAN, VIOLET E., Fifth Grade Teacher; *b:* Lowell, MA; *m:* Mike; *c:* Edward, Mary Peloian, Michael; *ed:* (AA) Elem, Reedley Coll 1969; (BA) Elem, Univ of Fresno 1973; Counseling Young Stu; CPR Trng; *cr:* 6th Grade Teacher 1973-74, 5th Grade Teacher 1974-, 3rd Grade Teacher 1990 Wilson Sch; *ai:* Mr & Mrs Club Yettem Corresponding Secy; Tulare Cty Horseless Carriage CA; Safety Patrol Chm Wilson Sch; Womens Trade Club Tulare Cty; Dinuba Teachers Assn Secy 1973-; Dinuba Negotiation Team 1980-85; Ladies Society Secy 1963-66; Daughters of Vartan (Treas 1985-86, Secy 1986-87); St Mary Armenian Church & Choir; Armenian Olympics San Francisco Awd 1972; Sunday Sch Teacher Yettem 1954-59; *office:* Wilson Elem Sch 305 E Kamm & Greene Dinuba CA 93618

DEREMER, EMILY MOORHEAD, 5th Grade Teacher; *b:* Osterburg, PA; *m:* Clyde; *c:* Glenn, Carol Deremer Horner, Scott; *ed:* (BS) Elem Ed, Lock Haven Univ 1957; (MLS) Lib Sci, Univ of Pittsburgh 1970; PA St Univ, Univ of Pittsburgh, Villanova Univ, Millersville Univ; *cr:* 4th Grade Teacher Bedford Intermediate Sch 1957-59; 5th Grade Teacher Manns Choice Elem Sch 1961-62; 4th Grade Teacher Chestnut Ridge Cntrl Elem 1962-66; Elem Librarian Chestnut Ridge Sch Dist 1967-79; 5th Grade Teacher New Paris Elem Sch 1979-82, Chestnut Ridge Mid Sch 1982-; *ai:* Benjamin Franklin Stamp Club Adv; NEA, PA St Ed Assn 1957-, Life Mem Awd; Chestnut Ridge Ed Assn (Pres 1969-70, VP 1983-85); Gideons Auxiliary VP 1989-; Delta Kappa Gamma (Pres 1980-82, Treas 1970-78) 1967-, Summer Study Schlsp 1970; *home:* RD 2 Box 154 New Paris PA 15554

DERGANTZ, SUSAN KAYE, Language Art Teacher; *b:* Hibbing, MN; *c:* Jennifer J.; *ed:* (BA) Eng/Math, Mankato St Coll 1973; Grad Stud; *cr:* Teacher St Francis Mid Sch 1973-; *ai:* Co-Facilitated a Concerned Persons Group; Nom MEA Teacher of Yr Sch Dist; *office:* Saint Francis Mid Sch 23026 Ambassador Blvd Saint Francis MN 55070

DERIEUX, JUDY KILLIAN, Teacher; *b:* Birmingham, AL; *m:* James Robert III; *c:* James R. IV; *ed:* (BA) Eng, AL Coll 1962; (MA) Spec Ed, Univ of AL 1966; *cr:* Lang/S S Teacher Baker Jr HS 1962-63; Teacher of Gifted & Talented Elyton Elem 1963-73, Robinsin Elem 1974-77,W J Chrstn Sch 1978-; *ai:* Honor Society (Academic & Bowl Coach), Debate Team, Speech & Interpretation, Spelling Bee, Geography Bee, Poetry Festival, 8th Grade Spon; Washington DC & NY Trip Spon; NEA, AEA, BEA, VTP; Birmingham Bd of Ed Teacher of Yr 1990; *home:* 3553 Laurel View Ln Birmingham AL 35216

DE RITA, JANET A., Social Studies Teacher; *b:* Pittsfield, MA; *ed:* (BA) His, C W Post Coll 1964; Working Towards Masters Lesley Coll; *cr:* 7th Grade Soc Stud Teacher Crosby Mid Sch 1964-85; 8th Grade Soc Stud Teacher Herberg Mid Sch 1985-; *ai:* Class & Cheerleading Adv; MA Cncl Soc Stud Mem 1965-; Pittsfield Fed of Teachers Mem 1975-; *office:* Herberg Mid Sch 501 Pomeroy Ave Pittsfield MA 01201

DERITIS, JOYCE MARIE, Head School Nurse/Teacher; *b:* Binghamton, NY; *m:* Armand L. Jr.; *c:* Mark J., Bruce A.; *ed:* Nursing, C S Wilson Mem Sch of Nursing 1952; (BS) Health Ed, SUNY Cortland 1970; *cr:* Staff Nurse C S Wilson Mem Hospital 195-65; Staff SNT Binghamton City Sch Dist 1966-83; Head SNT Binghamton City Sch Dist 1983-; *ai:* Co-Chairperson Comprehensive Health Advisory Comm; Dist Safety, PACT, Adol Com Project Comm; EAP-Wellness Comm Co-Chairperson; HS Boosters Club; NYS Fed of Prof Health Educators (Secy 1984-88, Pres 1988) Distinguished Service 1983; NYS Nurses & NYS Sch Nurses Assn; Dist 5 Nurses; Natl Assn of Sch Nurses; Amer Red Cross Youth Chairperson 1970- National Service Awd 1984; Broome Cty Cncl Alcohol Bd 1984-; Amer Heart Assn Broome Cty 1980-; *office:* Binghamton City Sch Dist 98 Oak St Binghamton NY 13905

DERKS, PAULINE MEYER, Fourth Grade Teacher; *b:* Clyde, MO; *m:* Vincent H.; *c:* Paul, Connie Wilson, Jo Beth Mendoza; *cr:* Rural Teacher Mozingo Valley 1939-45; 3rd Grade Teacher 1961-73, 4th Grade Teacher 1973- St Gregory Barbarigo; *ai:* NCEA; *office:* St Gregory Barbarigo Sch 315 S Davis Maryville MO 64468

DERNAY, DOROTHY J. (FEDOR), Reading Tutor; *b:* Hammond, IN; *m:* William J.; *ed:* (BS) Elem Ed, St Josephs Coll 1972; (MS) Elem Ed, Purdue Univ 1977; Rdng Endorsement K-12; *cr:* 4th Grade Teacher Holy Trinity Elem Sch 1973-74, St Thomas More Elem Sch 1977-79, St John Evangelist Sch 1982-87; Rdng Tutor St John Evangelist Sch 1987-; *office:* St John The Evangelist Sch 9330 Wicker Ave Saint John IN 46373

DERNER, JANET MARY, English Teacher/Dept Head; *b:* Mankato, MN; *ed:* (BA) Eng, Mt Mary Coll 1969; (MA) Eng, Creighton Univ 1974; Additional Courses in Admin; *cr:* Eng Teacher St Marys 1971-76, Loyola HS 1976-78; Prin St Marys 1978-84; Eng Teacher/Dept Head Trinity HS 1984-; *ai:* Speech Contest Dir; NCTE 1987-88; Natl Assn of Pastoral Musicians 1987-; Wrote & Directed Church Centennial Pageant 1985; *office:* Trinity HS Empire Rd & 8th Ave W Dickinson ND 58601

DEROMEDI, EDDI ZACHARIN, Elementary Principal; *b:* Oakland, CA; *m:* Dennis Allen; *c:* Adam, Lia; *ed:* (BA) Child Dev, 1975, (MA) Ed, 1988 CA St Univ Chico; *cr:* 4th/5th Grade Teacher Chico Unified Sch Dist 1977-78; Teacher Lang Handicapped Mt Diablo Unified Sch Dist 1978-79; Eng Teacher Durham Unified Sch Dist 1979-80; 6th Grade Teacher 1981-89, Elem Prin 1989- Corning Union Elem Sch Dist; *ai:* Gifted & Talented Ed Prgm Coord; Phi Delta Kappa, Assn of CA Sch Admin 1989-; *home:* 1660 Bidwell Ave Chico CA 95926

DE ROSA, PATRICIA LEASON, Teacher of Disabilities; *b:* Youngstown, OH; *m:* Joseph; *c:* Joseph M., Robert T.; *ed:* (BA) Elem Ed, Youngstown St 1973; K-12th Grade Rdng, Learning & Behavior Disabilities Cert; *cr:* Teacher Diosese of Youngstown 1974-80, Lowellville Village Schls 1980-; *ai:* Leetonia Ed Assn Curr Comm; Kappa Delta Phi 1973; LEA, OEA, NEA 1980-; Lowellville Athletic Boosters Secy 1970-; Leetonia Bd of Ed Employee of Month 1990; *office:* Orchard Hill Sch 450 Walnut St Leetonia OH 44431

DE ROSE, AGNES JOAN, Second Grade Teacher; *b:* Astoria, NY; *c:* Philip A. Messina; *ed:* (BA) Eng - Cum Laude, Coll of Mount St Vincent 1958; (MS) Elem Ed, Univ of Bridgeport 1969; *cr:* 3rd Grade Teacher PS 110 GreenPoint 1958-59, Kennedy Sch 1959-60; Substitute Teacher Port Chester Public Schls 1961-66; 5th Grade Teacher Kennedy Sch 1966-73; 1st-2nd Grade Teacher Park Avenue Sch 1973-; *ai:* Sunshine Fund Chm Park Avenue Sch; AFT; NYSTA; Port Chester Teachers Assn; Boys Town of Naples Secy 1977-.

DEROUEN, DEBORAH WEBSTER, 2nd Grade Teacher; *b:* Jennings, LA; *m:* John Cordell; *c:* Laurel, Heather, Kelly; *ed:* (BA) Elem Ed, Mc Neese Univ 1972; PIPS; Utilizing Cmptrs in Ed; *cr:* 2nd Grade Teacher Our Lady Immaculate 1972-73; 4th Grade Teacher Kinder Elem 1975; 7th/8th Grade Teacher Welsh Roanoke & Northside Jr HS 1976-77; 2nd Grade Teacher Welsh Elem 1978-; *ai:* Associated Prof Ed of LA; Jeff Davis Assn Teachers of Math; Church Parish Cncl Worship Commission 1988-; Church Choir; *home:* 102 Providence Welsh LA 70591

DERREBERRY, LYNDA ANN, Science Teacher; *b:* Jefferson City, TN; *ed:* (BA) Sociology, Carson Newman Coll 1964; (MED) Ed, TX A&M Univ 1971; Numerous Univs; *cr:* Teacher Columbia HS 1964-67, Lanier Jr HS 1968-70, Ballard Hudson Jr HS 1970; Teacher/Dept Chm Southwest HS 1971-88; Teacher Southeast HS 1988-; *ai:* Stu Assistance Prgm; Ftbl Team Trainer; PAGE, PDK; Red Cross Disaster Team, Pins; Natl Sci Fnd Schlsps; STAR Teacher; Dept of Human Resources Schlsp; McKibbon-Lane Awd Nominee Guest Speaker; Stu Teachers Supvr Writer of Educl Materials; Presenter at ACS Meetings; *home:* 2721 Alta Vista Ave Macon GA 31211

DERRICK, ALICE MEADE, French/Spanish Teacher; *b:* St Paul, VA; *m:* Gary Henderson; *c:* Derek S. Upchurch; *ed:* (BS) Fr, Radford Univ 1966; (MA) Rdng, E TN St Univ 1979; Univ of TN, Towson St Univ; *cr:* Fr/Span Teacher Balto Cty Schls 1966-72; Fr Teacher 1972-73, Rdng/Lang Art Teacher 1973-89, Fr/Span Teacher 1989- Kingsport City Schls; *ai:* Intnl Club Co-Spon; NEA, TEA 1972-; KEA Sr HS Rep; James B Stokely Fellowship; *office:* Dobyns-Bennett HS 1800 Legion Dr Kingsport TN 37664

DERRICK, ANNIE, Biology Teacher; *b:* Sharon, MS; *ed:* (BS) Bio, 1969, (MS) Bio, 1974 Jackson St Univ; Marine Bio, Univ Southern MS 1980; *cr:* Bio Teacher Allen Carver HS 1969-70; Bio & Chem Teacher Durant Attendance Center 1970-73; Bio Teacher Crystal Springs Sr HS 1974-; *ai:* Stu Cncl Adv; Coord of Sci Fair; MS Sci Teacher Assn 1974-; NSTA Review Panel for Scope Mag 1981-83; MS Assn of Ed 1975-; *office:* Crystal Springs H S 211 Newton St Crystal Springs MS 39059

DERRICK, KATHRYN FISK, Media Center Director; *b:* Cincinnati, OH; *m:* J. Andrew; *c:* Ellen, Andrew; *ed:* (BSED) Eng, Univ of Cincinnati 1970; (MED) Educl Media, Xavier Univ 1990; *cr:* Eng Teacher Reading HS 1970-71, Port Hacking HS 1971-73, Reading HS 1973-74; Eng Teacher/Media Specialist Mount Notre Dame HS 1987-; *ai:* Cath Lib Assn; Archdiocese of Cincinnati Ed Commission; *office:* Mount Notre Dame HS 711 E Columbia Ave Cincinnati OH 45215

DERRICK, SANDRA WHALEY, Teacher; *b:* Dalton, GA; *m:* Sid; *c:* Lindsey; *ed:* (AA) Liberal Arts, Dalton Coll 1974; (BSHE) Home Ec/Fashion Merchandising, 1976, (MED) Home Ec Ed, 1980, Univ of GA; *cr:* Home Ec Teacher North Whitfield Mid Sch 1978-; *ai:* FHA Past Adv 1978-86; Phi Upsilon Omicron 1975-; Delta Kappa Gamma (Secy, Historian) 1986-; GAE, NEA, WEA 1978-; GHEA 1981-; Kappa Delta Pi 1980-; PTA (Secy 1979-80, Mem 1978-); United Scleroderma Fnd 1985-; Recipes Published 1987; Articles Published Various Magazines 1984, 1988; *office:* N Whitfield Mid Sch 3264 Cleveland Rd Dalton GA 30720

DERRICKSON, DENISE A., Social Studies Teacher; *b:* Seaford, DE; *ed:* (BS) General Sci/Scndry Ed, James Madison Univ 1978; Working Towards MED Counseling, Human Dev, George Mason Univ 1990; Mediation Coord Trng; *cr:* Teacher Brentsville Dist HS 1978-; *ai:* Model United Nations Club Spon; Sr Class Spon; Love Life Day Chairperson; Drug Free Zone Celebration Consultant; NEA, VEA, PWEA 1978-; AACD, VCA, NVCA, Amer Assn for Curr Dev 1988-; Kappa Delta Phi; Helpline Volunteer 1988-; Childrens Hospital Volunteer 1983-86; Whos Who in Amer Colls 1973; Governors Sch Outstanding Educator 1990; *office:* Brentsville Dist HS Aden Rd Nokesville VA 22123

DERRYBERRY, SYLVIA GAIL, 7th Grade Teacher; *b:* Yazoo City, MS; *m:* James Foreman; *c:* Carrie Lynn Henley; *ed:* (BA) Mid Grades Phys Ed, Univ of Southern MS 1975; (MED) Elem Ed, MS Coll 1989; *cr:* 6th & 7th Grade Phys Ed Teacher Pendorff Elem 1975-77; 7th & 8th Grade Math/Sci/Phys Ed Teacher Crystal Springs Jr HS 1977-78; 4th Grade Math Teacher Crystal Springs Elem 1978-84; 7th & 8th Grade Math Teacher Northeast Jones Jr HS 1984-85; 7th Grade Eng & 8th Grade His Teacher Florence Mid Sch 1985-; *ai:* Coaching-7th & 8th Grade Girls Bsktbl & Track; 7th Grade Chairwoman; Natl Assn of Coaches 1986-.

DE SADIER, DEANAIE TITUS, Health/Social Studies Teacher; *b:* Chicago, IL; *ed:* (BA) Phys Ed/Health, Coll of Mt St Joseph 1979; (MS) Motor Behavior, Univ of IL Chicago; First Aid & CPR Instr; WSI; Certified Aerobic Instr; *cr:* 9th-12th Grade Phys Ed/Health Teacher Percy L Julian HS 1979-80; Grad Teaching Asst Phys Ed Univ of IL Chicago 1980-81; 9th-12th Grade Phys Ed/Health Ed Teacher Percy L Julian HS 1981-84; Phys Ed/Health Teacher St Bartholomew Cath Sch 1985-86; Interim Status/Health Ed Teacher Piper HS 1986; Phys Ed/ Health Ed Teacher Deerfield Beach HS 1986-; *ai:* Deerfield Beach

HS Var Vlybl Coach & Asst Athletic Dir 1988-89, Head Cheerleading Coach & Var Athletic Trainer 1987-88, Girls Jr Var Bsktbl & Cheerleading Coach 1986-87; St Barthelomew Cath Sch Girls Vlybl Coach 1985; Percy L Julian HS Var Vlybl & Girls Track Coach 1982-84, 1st Asst Boys Var Bsktbl 1981-82, Statistician Boys Var Bsktbl & Girls Track Coach 1979-80; Intercollegiate Swim Team 1975-79; USVBA Vlybl 1979-84; AAHPERD 1975-; Natl Assn Sports & Phys Ed, Natl Assn Girls & Womens Sports, Womens Sports Fnd, Amer Vlybl Coaches Assn, Natl Strength & Conditioning Assn, FL Athletic Coaches Assn; Phys Ed Majors Club, Coll Recreation Assn 1975-79; Stu Government Assn, OEA, NEA, Resident Asst 1978-79; Coll Hearing & Appeals Bd 1976-77; Jane Cuni Armstrong Awd Academic Deligence; Zeal, Inspiration, Perserverence Awd; Swim Team Athletic Awds Banquet 1975-79; Most Improved Swimmer 1979; *office:* Dillard HS 2501 NW 11th St Fort Lauderdale FL 33311

DE SALME, JOHN WILLIAM, SR., Music Department Chair; *b:* Corpus Christi, TX; *m:* Margaret B.; *c:* John W. Jr., Robert E., Suzanne E. de Salme-Priester; *ed:* (BM) Music, 1957, (MA) Music, 1960, (MFA) Music Performance, 1967 Univ of IA; *cr:* Band Dir Orange Grove HS 1957-59, IA Valley Cmmty Schls 1960-62, IA City Cmmty Schls & West HS 1962-; *ai:* Jazz, Marching, Pep Band; Music Contest Adjudicator; MENC, NEA, ISEA, ICEA, IBA, NFMA; N Cntrl Assn Evaluation Team Mem; IA Cmmty Band Guest Conductor: Corpus Christi TX Symphony Orch Trombonist; *office:* West HS 2901 Melrose Ave Iowa City IA 52246

DE SANTIS, JAMES LEE, History Teacher; *b:* Pottsville, PA; *m:* Suzette Canese;; *c:* Amy, Joseph, Katie; *ed:* (BS) Geography/ Soc Stud, Lock Haven St Coll 1977; *cr:* Teacher/Coach Socorro Jr HS 1981-83; Teacher Socorro HS 1983-84, Campestre Sch 1984-89, Cooper Sch 1989-; *ai:* Stu Cncl Adv; Campus Comm Cncl; Dist Grading Comm; Horizon City Fire Dept Firefighter 1985-; SW Bsktbl Ofcls Assn Referee 1987-; Socorro Ind Sch Dist Employee of Month 1987; ARCOM 1981; *home:* 16013 Keno El Paso TX 79927

DE SANTIS, MARY WILL HALL, Biology Teacher; *b:* Grayson, KY; *m:* Nicholas T. II; *c:* Mary C., Scott, Nina M., Nicholas T. III; *ed:* (BS) Health/Phys Ed/Bio, E KY Univ 1953; (Rank II) Ed, 1980, (Rank I) Ed, 1985 Morehead KY Univ; *cr:* Health/Phys Ed Teacher Maysville HS 1953-55, Greenup HS 1955-57, Raceland HS 1957-61, Prichard HS 1961-72; Bio Teacher East Carter HS; *ai:* Track, Tennis, Golf, Chrldrs Coach; 4-H Club, Sci Club, Pep Club, Tumbling Teams Spon; Raceland Ed Assn Past Pres; Carter Cty Ed Assn 1987-; NEA, KY Ed Assn Building Rep 1987-; Natl Fed of Women Club 1987-; Garden Club; Beta Sigma Pi; *home:* 595 Sunset Hill Grayson KY 41143

DESCHER, JOHN DANIEL, Mathematics Teacher; *b:* Portland, OR; *m:* Kathy Harden; *c:* Kyle, John; *ed:* (BA) Math Ed, Cntrl WA St Coll 1975; (MA) Math Ed, Cntrl WA Univ 1980; Seattle Pacific Univ, OR St Univ, St Martins Coll; *cr:* Teacher Hoquiam HS 1976-89, Grays Harbor Coll 1989-; *ai:* NCTM, WA Cncl Teachers of Math, WA Math Teachers of Comm Coll; *office:* Grays Harbor Coll Edward P Smith Dr Aberdeen WA 98520

DE SHIELDS, INEZ DENT, Mathematics Teacher/Dept Chair; *b:* Hattiesburg, MS; *m:* Kenneth Simmons; *c:* Kenneth II, Danielle P.; *ed:* (BS) Math, 1974, (MED) Math Ed, 1986 Univ of S MS; *cr:* Teacher Quitman Jr HS 1973-75, Ed Mayo Jr HS 1975-77; Teacher 1977- Dept Chairperson 1984- Moss Point HS; *ai:* Career Beginnings Inc, Modeling Squad & Sr Class Spon; Staff Dev Comm; Moss Point Assn of Educators, MS Assn of Educators 1978-; NEA 1973-; Natl Cncl Teachers of Math 1978-; Alpha Kappa Alpha 1986-; *office:* Moss Point HS 4924 Church St Moss Point MS 39563

DE SIMONE, LOUIS J., Science Teacher; *b:* Long Branch, NJ; *m:* Karen Mason; *c:* Nicole, Brad; *ed:* (BS) Scndry Ed/Sci, Monmouth Coll 1974; *cr:* 7th Grade Sci Teacher Memorial Sch 1974-75; 9th/10th Grade Sci Teacher Red Bank Cath HS 1975-78; 9th Grade Sci Teacher Cntrl Regional HS 1978-79; 8th Grade Sci Teacher Lacey Township Mid Sch 1979-.

DES PAIN, ARVIA SMITH, Fifth Grade Teacher; *b:* Paducah, KY; *m:* Ronald L.; *c:* Teri, Timothy, Todd, Tricia; *ed:* (BA) Elem Ed, Panhandle St 1962; Emporia St Univ; *cr:* 5th Grade Teacher Guymon OK 1962-63; Liberal KS 1963-71; Chptl Rdng Teacher Monte Vista Co 1973-75; 5th Grade Teacher Highland Park ISD 1978-; *ai:* Just Say No Club; Schlsp Comm; Highland Park Eductors Faculty Comm; Highland Park Educators Sec 1979-80; TX St Teachers Assn; NEA; Beta Sigma Phi; Order of Eastern Star; Hi-Plains Promenaders Square Dance Club.

DE STEIGUER, MARY JO JO (DEEM), 8th Grade Lang Arts Teacher; *b:* Tahlequah, OK; *m:* John R.; *c:* John R. Jr., Mary B., Sande; *ed:* (BS) Home Ec, 1956, Masters of Teaching Elem Ed, 1962 Northeastern St Univ; Supervision of Teachers; *cr:* 1st Grade Teacher Celia Clinton Elem 1956-59, Zilker Elem 1963-64; 3rd/ 5th Grade Teacher Neutra Elem 1968-70; 7th Grade Life Sci Teacher 1976-80, 8th Grade Speech Teacher 1985-88, 8th Grade Lang Arts Teacher 1978- Tahlequah Jr HS; *ai:* Spon TJHS Stu Cncl 1978- & HS S Club 1978-86; TJHS Speech Coach 1985-; NJHS Faculty Advisory Cncl; Tahlequah Ed Assn Building Rep 1976-; OK Ed Assn Communications Comm 1976-; NEA 1976-; Phi Delta Kappa Membership Comm 1985-; Tahlequah Church of Christ (Bible Class Teacher 1971-75, 1977-, Dept Coord 1971-75, Seminar Teacher 1985); Amer Legion Auxiliary 1950-; Democrat Party Mem; Soroptimist Club (Past VP, Chm Intnl Affairs Comm, Mem 1977-89); Northeastern St Univ Alumni Assn (Life Mem, Bd of Dirs, Mem 1982-87); Univ of OK Alumni Assn Life Mem; Gladiolus Garden Club Mem 1980-; Cherokee Cty Bd of Health (Mem, Chm) 1978-; Northeastern St Univ Stu Secy Assn Annual Banquet; Teacher of Yr 1989; Amer Legion Natl Ed Prgm Awd 1988; Sertoma Teacher of Month 1986-87; *office:* Tahlequah Jr HS 400 W Morgan Tahlequah OK 74464

DE THOMAS, CAROLYN R., Science Department Chairman; *b:* Springfield, MA; *m:* Anthony V.; *ed:* (BS) Chem, Cntrl CT St Coll 1962; (MA) Chem, St Joseph Coll 1968; *cr:* Chem/Bio Teacher Windsor Locks HS 1962-65; Chem/Bio Teacher 1965-68, Sci Chairperson 1969- Plainville HS; *ai:* Musical Pianist; Ed Assn of Plainville Pres 1968-69; CT Sci Supvrs Assn, CT Sci Teachers Assn; Womens Coll Club of Bristol; Manufacturing Chemists Assn HS Chem Teacher Awd 1970; Sigma Xi Research Society; Univ of CT Teacher Awd 1988; Charles Pfizer Research Grant 1988; Du Pont Mini Grant, Microchemical Journal Publication 1971; *office:* Plainville HS Robert Holcomb Way Plainville CT 06062

DE TIEGE, FRANK J., Sixth Grade Teacher; *b:* Monroe, LA; *m:* Sylvia Spencer; *c:* Frank III, James, Jessica; *ed:* (BS) Elem Ed, Grambling St Univ 1978; Grad Stud Ed; *cr:* Teacher Monroe City Schls 1978-; *ai:* Monroe Fed of Teacher, LA Fed of Teachers 1980-; *office:* Carver Elem Sch 1700 Orange St Monroe LA 71201

DETLEFSEN, WANDA KELLY, Teacher; *b:* Baltimore, MD; *m:* Peter C.; *c:* Christian; *ed:* (BA) Eng/His/Psych, Erskine 1966; Admin/Supervision, Tampa Univ 1975; *cr:* Teacher Calhoan Falls HS; Dean of Stu/Teacher Gulf HS; *ai:* Teachers as Adv; Steering Comm; Delta Gamma Pres 1988-, Teacher of Yr 1984; Past Pres of Teachers Union; *office:* Gulf HS 5355 School Rd New Port Richey FL 34652

DETOFSKY, LOUIS BENNETT, Geology & Biology Teacher; *b:* Philadelphia, PA; *ed:* (BA) Natural Sci/Geology/Bio, Rutgers Univ 1968; (MA) Geology, Glassboro St Coll 1976; Various Colls & Univs; *cr:* Earth Sci/Geology/Bio/Anthropology Instr Washington Township HS 1968-; *ai:* Washington Township HS Geology Club Adv 1968-; NSTA, Amer Assn for Advancement of Sci 1978-; Natl Assn of Geology Teachers 1980-; Geological Assn of NJ, Natl Earth Sci Teachers Assn 1982-; NJ Earth Sci Teachers Assn 1984-; Bnai Brith Corresponding Secy 1987-; Explorer Scouts Adv to Explorer Post 8; Several Published Books Focusing on Geology of Natl Parks & Enviroment 1989; *office:* Washington Township HS Hurfville-Cross Key Rd Sewell NJ 08080

DE TORO, JAMES P., Eighth Grade Math Teacher; *b:* Youngstown, OH; *m:* Susan Blystone; *c:* Michael, Carla, Thomas; *ed:* (BA) Comp Soc Stud, Youngstown St Univ 1977; Scndry Math Cert, Youngstown St Univ 1978; *cr:* Math Teacher Liberty HS 1978-81; 8th Grade Math Teacher 1981-, 7th Grade OH His Teacher 1987- W S Guy Sch; *ai:* Liberty HS Asst Ftbl Coach; Mathcounts Adv, Trumbull Cty Math Course of Study Comm; NE OH Cncl of Teachers of Math 1981-; OH HS Ftbl Coaches Assn, Trumbull Cty Coaches Assn 1978-; PTA 1988-; *home:* 423 Forest Hill Dr Youngstown OH 44515

DETTER, CARLA RENEE, Lang Arts/Soc Stud Teacher; *b:* Lincolnton, NC; *ed:* (BS) Intermediate Ed, Gardner Webb Coll 1982; (MHDI) Intermediate Ed, UNCC 1985; Mentor Trng; Teacher Performance Appraisal Trng; *cr:* 6th Grade Teacher Northbrook Elem 1982-83; 4th Grade Teacher Love Memorial Elem 1983-84; Migrant Recruiter Clerk/Teacher Lincoln Cty Schls 1984; 6th Grade Teacher North Brook Elem 1984-85; 7th-9th Grade Lang Arts Teacher 1985-86; 7th/8th Grade Lang Arts Teacher 1986-87; 7th Grade Lang Arts Teacher 1987-88; 7th/8th Grade Lang Arts Teacher 1988-89 East Lincoln Jr HS; 7th Grade Lang Arts/Soc Stud Teacher East Lincoln Mid 1989-; *ai:* Spelling Bee Coord; NEAE; NEA; Locla UMW Pres 1982-84; Rhyne Heights UM Chruch Lay Leader 1990; Nom for NC Bus Awd; *office:* East Lincoln Mid Sch Rt 1 Box 365 Iron Station NC 28080

DEUEL, NED, Social Studies Teacher; *b:* Gloversville, NY; *m:* Wendy Deuel Thowdis; *c:* Jason, Jeremy, Mollie; *ed:* (BS) Scndry Soc Stud, 1964, (MS) Scndry Soc Stud, 1968 St Univ Coll Cortland; Certificate of Advanced Stud Sch Admin; *cr:* Teacher Westhill Jr/Sr HS 1964-68; Admissions Cnslr St Univ Coll Plattsburgh 1968-69; Teacher Cicero-N Syracuse HS 1969-; *ai:* Developed Curr Challenges of 70s & 80s; Jr Var Bsktbl & Frosh Ftbl Coach; Tutorial Prgm Cicero HS 1973-83; Teacher Evaluation Comm Chm 1973-75; N Syracuse Cntrl Schls Dist Steering Comm 1988-89, Advisory Cncl 1985-88, Inservice Comm Chm 1974-75, Stage & Real Food Coop; Onondaga Cty Teachers Assn Pres 1979-, Spec Service Awd Contribution to Teaching Profession 1990; N Syracuse Ed Assn VP 1973-; US & NY St Handball Assn; NY St United Teachers Ed Confernce Chm 1981; Syracuse YMCA Bd of Mgrs 1979-; Cath Charities Day Care Division Bd of Dir 1973-76; Cntrl NY Volunteer Center Bd of Dir 1978-80; United Way Fund Drive Cntrl NY Ed Campaign Chm 1984; Dev Individualized Instruction Prgm; Teacher-To-Teacher Wkshp Instr; Supervision/Trng Stu Teachers 1972-; *home:* 866 Ackerman Ave Syracuse NY 13210

DEUTCH, JANET LEE, Sixth Grade Teacher; *b:* Chicago, IL; *ed:* (BS) Elem Ed, N IL Univ 1971; (MED) Instruction/Curr, Natl Coll of Ed 1989; *cr:* 3rd-6th Grade Teacher 1974-89, At-Risk Teacher 1990 Mitchell Sch; *ai:* Stu Cncl Teacher Spon; Joyce Fnd Grant; *office:* Ellen Mitchell 2233 W Ohio St Chicago IL 60612

DEUTH, ALLEN, Social Studies Teacher; *b:* Jackson, MS; *ed:* (BS) His, 1971, (MED) Scndry Ed, 1973 Stephen F Austin St Univ; *cr:* Teacher Cherry Creek Schls 1972-74, Jefferson Cty Schls 1974-.

DEUTMEYER, MARY A., Mathematics Teacher/Dept Chair; *b:* Dubuque, IA; *ed:* (BA) Math, Briar Cliff Coll 1971; (MA) Curr/Instruction, Chicago St Univ; Ed Courses, IL Renewal Inst & Chicago St Univ; *cr:* Mercy Mission; St Francis De Sales HS 1976-85; Lourdes HS 1986-87; Math Teacher/Dept Chairperson Seton Acad 1987-; *ai:* Math Club Scheduling, NHS Selection, Curr, Faculty Rep Leadership Comm; NCTM, NCEA; ICTM 1989, Excl Teaching Awd 1989; Dolores Kohl Ed Fnd Awd 1989; Chicago NCA Convention Speaking Conflict Resolution Panel Mem 1990; *office:* Seton Acad 16100 Seton Rd South Holland IL 60473

DEUTSCH, GERALD DAVID, Science Teacher; *b:* New York, NY; *m:* Trudy S. Nagler; *c:* Jonathan, Daniel, David; *ed:* (BA) Earth/Space Sci, 1973; (MA) Liberal Stud, 1976 SUNY; *cr:* Earth Sci Teacher Brentwood Public Schls 1973-75; Hunterdon Cntrl HS 1975-77; Earth/Gen Sci Teacher F H Morrell HS/ Myrtle Ave Mid Sch 1978-; *ai:* Teach After-Sch Astronomy 7th/ 8th Graders; *office:* Myrte Ave Jr HS 255 Myrtle Ave Irvington NJ 07111

DE VAZQUEZ, NANCY ANN LINDERT, Spanish Teacher; *b:* Elgin, IL; *m:* Rafael; *c:* Raquel, Veronica, Andres; *ed:* (BA) Span, Rockford Coll 1971; (MA) Span, UNAM Mexico City 1984; Concordia Coll; *cr:* Bi-ling Ed, Dist 300 1969, 1972, 1973; Dist U-46 1973-74; Span/Eng Teacher St Edward HS 1983-; *ai:* Span Club; Thanksgiving All-Sch Food Drive; Tidal Wave Volunteer; AATSP Mem 1989; Well Child Conference Bd of Dir 1982-83; *office:* St Edward Cath HS 335 Locust St Elgin IL 60123

DEVENA, BARBARA ANN, High School Bus Teacher; *b:* Galesburg, IL; *m:* William; *c:* John, Jeff; *ed:* (BS) Bus Ed, 1970, (MS) Bus Ed, 1982 W IL Univ; Coursework Human Relations, Teaching Stragegies, Cmptrs, Univ of IL & N IL Univ; *cr:* Instr Warren HS 1970-78, Instr Galesburg HS 1978-; Extension Instr N IL Univ 1985-; *ai:* Spon & Trainer Chemical Assistance Reaching Everyone; Personal & Prof Growth Comm; Chrysalis; In-Service Trainer; Stu Mentor Spon; Referendum Steering Comm 1989; Delta Kappa Gamma Treas 1982-; W IL Area Bus Educators 1970-; Knoxville Meth Church HS Sunday Sch Teacher 1990; Phi Delta Kappa Outstanding Educator Awd 1989; Delta Pi Epsilon; *office:* Galesburg Sr H S 1135 W Fremont Galesburg IL 61401

DEVER, ANNIE GRACE, 5th Grade Teacher; *b:* Ocilla, GA; *m:* William L. Sr.; *c:* William Jr., Donald, Keith Womack, Frederick, Karen E. Womack Palori; *ed:* (BA) Elem, Univ S FL 1968; (MED) Admin, Univ of Tampa 1976; Clinical Teaching & Ec Ed, Univ of S FL; Math Summer Prgm Part 1; *cr:* 3rd-6th Grade Teacher Kingswood Elem 1968-; *ai:* Kappa Delta Pi (VP 1984, Cnslr 1986-88, Pres 1985); Alpha Delta Kappa (Chaplain 1986-87, Pres 1988-); Intnl Rdng Cncl; Hillsborough Cncl of Math Teachers; St Andrews United Meth Pre Sch Bd Mem 1980-; FL Cncl Ec Ed Educator of Yr Co Winner 1982-83; Contributing Author of Book; *office:* Kingswood Elem 3102 S Kings Ave Brandon FL 33511

DEVER, PATRICIA SIMMONS BROWN, Assistant Principal; *b:* Pineland, TX; *m:* Wayman T. Sr.; *c:* Lenice Delmarshea Brown, Aliza Y. Brown Burgess; *ed:* (BS) Phys Ed, 1968, (MED) Elem Ed, 1970 Prairie View A&M Univ; Spec Ed Mental Retardation, Bio Health, Mid Management & Rdng Specialist Cert ; *cr:* Teacher Prairie View Laboratory Trng Sch 1968-70, Jasper Ind Sch Dist 1970-74, Holleman Elem Waller Ind Sch Dist 1975-78, Waller Mid Sch 1978-83, Waller Jr HS 1983-85; Asst Prin Waller Jr HS Ind Sch Dist 1985-; *ai:* Drug Awareness Coord; TX St Teachers Assn 1968-; NEA; Waller Cty Teachers Assn Pres 1984-85; Phi Delta Kappa 1976-; Prairie View A&M Univ Natl Alumni & Local Alumni; Tx Assn of Scndry Sch Prin; Tx Executive Women in Ed; Weekly Articles for Local Newspaper Author 1986-88; *home:* 724 Meadow Ln Box 875 Prairie View TX 77446

DEVER-MILES, MARILYN ANN, Eng/Speech/US His Teacher; *b:* Marion, IN; *m:* Bernard L.; *c:* Judith R. Dever; *ed:* (BA) Eng, Marian Coll 1960, (MAT) Eng, IN Univ 1964; Speech; *cr:* Teacher Bennett HS 1960-62, Manual HS 1962-; *ai:* Stu Affairs Bd & Stu Cncl Co-Spon; Sr Banner & Armbands Coord; Sr Spon Mentor Teacher; Supt Advisory Cncl Manuals Rep; Eng Club of Greater Indianapolis, Corresponding Secy 1970; IN Cncl Teachers of Eng; NCTE, Indianapolis Ed Assn IN St Teachers Assn, NEA; Chamber of Commerce Outstanding Volunteer Service with Partner 1983-88; Church Lector; Facilities Task Force Cmmty Meeting Sch Speaker 1981; Project Bus; Nom Teacher of Yr; Hoosier Eng Teacher of Yr 1984; City of Indianapolis Outstanding Excl in Ed Awd for Histlish All Cty Competition 1984; Consultant on Frosh Level MC Dougal Littell Lit Book; Article Published; Marian Coll Outstanding Young Woman of America 1970; *office:* Manual HS 2405 Madison Ave Indianapolis IN 46225

DEVEREAUX, STEWART TRENT, Industrial Art Teacher; *b:* Saginaw, MI; *m:* Christine Ann Maike; *c:* Mark, Miranda; *ed:* (BS) Health/Phys Ed/Recreation, Cntrl MI Univ 1973; Grad Stud Saginaw Valley St Univ; *cr:* Industrial Art Teacher Arenac Eastern HS 1974-; *ai:* Soph Class Adv; Boys Var Bsktbl Coach; Athletic Boosters Pres; *office:* Arenac Eastern HS 200 Smalley St Twining MI 48766

DEVERS, THOMAS OLIVER, 4th Grade Teacher; *b:* Dayton, OH; *m:* Suzanne Barbara West; *c:* Emily; *ed:* (AA) Sinclair Cmmty 1973; (BS) Elem Ed, Univ Dayton 1979; Learning Disability Cert 1980; Cmptr Ed 1986; *cr:* L D Tutor Westbrook Village & T M Jr HS 1979-80; L D Teacher Townview Elem 1980-81; 3rd-4th Grade Teacher Bro Admoor Elem 1981-; *ai:* In Charge of Morning Announcements By Stu Cncl; Dist Cmptr

Comm; Trotwood-Madison Ed Assn 1979-; Trotwood-Madison His Society 1986-; Dayton Buckeye Model a Ford Club 1980-; *office:* Trotwood-Madison City 701 E Main St Trotwood OH 45426

DE VILBISS, BETSY KORB, Mathematics Teacher; *b:* Burlington, IA; *m:* Larry; *c:* Joshua, Samantha; *ed:* (BA) Math, St Ambrose Coll 1975; Grad Work St Ambrose Univ; *cr:* Math Teacher Alleman HS 1975-88, North HS 1988-; *ai:* NHS Selection Comm; RSCMSTA Exec Cncl 1978-80; ICTM 1988-; OLV Ladies Cncl Treas 1987; Alleman HS NHS Katherine Warwick Memorial Awd for Excl Teaching; *office:* North HS 626 W 53rd St Davenport IA 52806

DEVINCENZI, JOHN MICHAEL, Social Science Dept Chair; *b:* San Francisco, CA; *m:* Carol Guisti; *c:* Tina A., Anthony; *ed:* (BA) His, San Francisco St Coll 1965; *cr:* 7th-8th Grade Teacher K R Smith Sch 1967-68; Soc Sci Teacher Crestmoor HS 1968-80; Soc Sci/Stu Government Teacher Capachino HS 1980-83; Soc Sci Dept Head Burlingame HS 1984-; *ai:* Leadership Club & Stu Store Adv; Staff Dev Comm; Soc Sci Curr Cncl; CA Teachers Assn Building Pres 1970-71; CA Assn Dir of Act Stu Government Adv; Teacher of Yr Crestmoor HS 1971, 1974, 1977, 1979-80, Capuchino HS 1981, Burlingame HS 1985, 1987, 1989; Mentor Teacher 1988-; *office:* Burlingame HS Carolyn & Oak Grove Burlingame CA 94010

DEVINE, DENNIS THOMAS, United States History Teacher; *b:* San Mateo, CA; *m:* Marney Moeller; *c:* Jennifer, Christopher; *ed:* (BA) Soc Sci, Univ of AZ 1966; Grad Stud San Jose St Univ; *cr:* Teacher Awalt HS 1967-81, Mountain View HS 1981-; *ai:* Girls & Boys Springboard Diving Coach; Dist Teachers Assn Building Rep 1986-89; Mentor Teacher 1989-; Stanford Univ Study of Scndry Schls 1986; *home:* PO Box 404 Moss Beach CA 94038

DEVINE, GERRY O'HARA, Retired Elementary Teacher; *b:* De Smet, SD; *w:* Phillip Jr (dec); *c:* Kelley, Cathy Ganschow, Kaye KEnnedy, Patricia Lund; *ed:* (BA) Elem Ed, 1965, (MA) Elem Ed, 1975 Univ SD Vermillion; Assoc Degree Elem Ed, N SC Univ Aberdeen 1946; *cr:* Rural Elem Teacher Day Cty Sch Dist 1943-44; 7th Grade Teacher Clear Lake Sch Dist 1945-46; 5th Grade Teacher Benson 1947-50; 5th Grade Teacher/Forensics Teacher Wakonda Sch Dist 1951-89; *ai:* SD Rdng IRA St Coord; SD Ed Assn St VP; SD Rdng Cncl (Coord 1988-), St Literacy 1989; Outstanding Teacher 1973; *home:* 2904 W 33rd Sioux Falls SD 57105

DEVINEY, SUSAN KAY SILCOTT, First Grade Teacher; *b:* Hardtner, KS; *m:* David A.; *c:* David W., Sheila, Jack; *ed:* (BS) Elem Ed, East Cntrl Univ 1982; *cr:* Remedial Lang Arts Teacher Paoli Public Sch 1982; 3rd Grade Teacher 1982-84, 1st Grade Teacher 1984- Maysville Elem Sch; *ai:* Staff Dev Comm; Maysville Assn Classroom Teacher (VP 1983-84, 1989-, Building Rep 1985-86, 1988-89, Negotiations Team 1987, Delegate Assemby 1988-, Secy 1984-85, Pres 1991-93),Rookie Teacher of Yr 1983-84, Teacher of Yr 1989-; Delta Kappa Gamma 1989-; St Catherines Womens Auxiliary 1987-; *office:* Maysville Elem Sch 9 Williams PO Box 780 Maysville OK 73057

DE VITO, MARIE CASCIANO, Third Grade Teacher; *b:* Hillside, NJ; *m:* Carmin John; *c:* Lori, Virginia De Vito Mc Neil, Patricia L.; *ed:* (BS) Elem Ed/Speech Handicapped, Kean Coll 1950; Grad Stud Kean Coll 1987; *cr:* 3rd Grade Teacher A P Morris Elem Sch 1950-53; Speech Therapist North Plainfield Elem Schls 1956-57; 2nd Grade Teacher St Bartholomews Sch 1957-58, Evergreen Sch 1971-78; 3rd Grade Teacher J Ackerman Coles 1978-; *ai:* J A Coles Sch Building Facilitator 1984-86; Scotch Plains-Fanwood Ed Assn Sr Building Rep; Natl Society of Prof Engrs Auxiliary Chm 1978-79; *office:* J Ackerman Coles Sch Kevin Rd Scotch Plains NJ 07076

DE VOE, THOMAS ELLIOTT, History Teacher; *b:* Phillipsburg, NJ; *m:* Linda-Gail Hildebrant; *c:* Mandee M.; *ed:* (BA) Scndry Ed/Soc Stud, IA Wesleyan 1967; (MA) Human Dev, Fairleigh Dickinson 1982; *cr:* His Teacher West Morris Regional HS 1967-68, Mt Olive Upper Elem Sch 1972-; *ai:* Cross Cntry Coach; NEA, NJ Ed Assn, Ed Assn of Mt Olive; Company of Military Historians; Society of the War of 1812; Napoleonic Society of America; Revolutionary, Civil War & Napoleonic Re-Enactment Organization Mem; Brigade of Amer Revolution, Volunteer Living His Morristown Natl Historical Park; Outstanding His Teacher NJ; Sr Ed & Co-Founder Bi-Monthly Napoleonic Journal; 14 Yrs Author over 500 Military & Historical Articles; *home:* 17 Ridge Rd Budd Lake NJ 07828

DEVOR, ROBERT PHILLIP, Science Teacher; *b:* Fayetteville, AR; *m:* Anna Gunn; *c:* Michelle, Christin; *ed:* (BS) Bio, Univ of UT 1973; (MS) Life Sci, LA Tech Univ 1975; Cmptr Wkshp HS Bio Teachers; *cr:* Microbiologist Public & VA Hospital 1975-84; Sci Teacher Houston Ind Sch Dist 1985-87, Humble Ind Sch Dist 1987-; *ai:* Honor Roll & Cmptr Club Spon; Dist & St Textbook Adoption Comm; NSTA 1985-; *office:* Humble HS 1700 Wilson Rd Humble TX 77338

DEVORE, D. HAL, Teacher/Department Chair; *b:* Burlington, IA; *m:* Eunice Maxine Cook; *c:* David, Lori Devore Dryg; *ed:* (BS) Soc Sci, 1959, (MS) Amer His, 1966 W IL Univ; *cr:* Teacher/Librarian Mt Olive HS 1959-62; Teacher Farmington HS 1962-66, Galesburg HS 1966-; Dept Chm Galesburg HS 1971-; *ai:* Ftbl Coach Monmouth Coll; IL Ed Asn, NEA 1959-; NCSS; Cable TV Commission 1980-86; Natl Endowment of Hum Constitution Conference Teaching Consultant; *home:* 1071 Sweetbriar Pl Galesburg IL 61401

DEVORE, JANICE FICHTNER, English Teacher; *b:* Steubenville, OH; *m:* Kenneth E.; *ed:* (BS) Eng/Instructional Media, Kent St Univ 1974; Grad Stud Scndry Ed, Eng, Sports Medicine; *cr:* Eng Teacher Nordonia HS 1974-; *ai:* Girls Track Coach 1976-81; NEA, OH Ed Assn, Nordonia Hills Ed Assn; *office:* Nordonia HS 8006 S Bedford Rd Macedonia OH 44056

DE VORE, LINDA WALTERS, Second Grade Teacher; *b:* Tacoma, WA; *m:* John Daniel; *c:* John M.; *ed:* (BA) Ed, 1968, (MA) Sci Ed, 1975 Univ of Puget Sound; *cr:* Elem Teacher Tacoma Public Sch Dist 10 1968-; *ai:* Lyon Sch Sci Coord; Teaching Team Univ of Puget Sound Natl Sci Fnd; *office:* Mary Lyon Emel Sch 101 E 46th St Tacoma WA 98404

DE VOSS, ANGELA CICANESE, AP Calculus Teacher; *b:* Fremont, OH; *m:* Mark Douglas; *ed:* (BS) Math, FL Southern Coll 1985; *cr:* Teacher Astronaut HS 1985-; *ai:* Asst Track Coach; Brevard Cty Teachers of Math 1989-; Mu Alpha Theta Spon; *office:* Astronaut HS 800 War Eagle Blvd Titusville FL 32796

DEVOTI, JANIS A., Sixth Grade Teacher; *b:* Albuquerque, NM; *ed:* (BS) Elem Ed, 1972, (MA) Ed Admin, 1982 Univ of NM; Grad Stud Curr Instruction Multicultural Teacher Ed; *cr:* 4th/5th/6th Grade Teacher Atalaya Elem 1972-86; Elem Clinical Supvr Univ of NM 1986-88; 6th Grade Bi-ling Teacher Pinon Elem 1988-; *ai:* Sch Improvement Core Team Mem; Mentor Teacher Pinion Sch; Dist Math Curr Comm; Just Say No Club Spon; Phi Delta Kappa Historian 1986-; Assn of Teacher Educators 1986-88; PTO 1972-; Santa Fe Jaycees Educator of Yr 1981; One of 10 Who Made A Difference in Santa Fe 1985; Graduated with Distinction; *office:* Pinon Elem Sch/SFPS 2921 Camino de Los Caballos Santa Fe NM 87505

DE VRIES, JAMES H., English/Social Studies Teacher; *b:* Murdo, SD; *m:* Lynn Ecklund; *c:* Mark, John, Peter, Timothy; *ed:* (BA) Eng, Sterling Coll 1970; Black Hills St Coll; Boise St Univ; *cr:* Teacher Sunshine Bible Acad 1970-75, Cole Chrstn Sch 1978-81, 1983-89, Greenleaf Friends Acad 1989-; *home:* 11004 Powderhorn Boise ID 83704

DEW, IDA LOUISE, Social Studies Teacher; *b:* Rocky Mountain, NC; *ed:* (BA) Ed, Univ of NC Chapel Hill 1974; Advanced Trng in Ec & Counseling; *cr:* 5th Grade Teacher Annie W Holland Sch & Rocky Mountain Schls; 9th Grade Teacher Nash Cntrl Jr HS; *ai:* Chrldr Coach; Future Teachers of America Club Adv; Soc Stud Dept Chairperson; Cty In-Service Planning Comm Mem; NCAE (Dist Pres 1989, Local Pres 1980, Minority Affairs St Chairperson 1990); NEA Delegate to Natl Convention; NCSS; VISIONS Bd of Dir; Teacher of Yr 1989; *office:* Nash Cntrl Jr HS Rt 5 Box 10 Nashville NC 27856

DEWALT, KAREN SUE, Computer Coordinator; *b:* Uniontown, PA; *c:* Kevin M., Craig G.; *ed:* (BA) Lib Sci, Kutztown Univ 1968; (MS) Educl Technology, Lehigh Univ 1987; *cr:* Elem Librarian Reading Sch Dist 1969-70; Mid Sch Librarian Muhlenberg Sch Dist 1974-89; Part Time Instr PA St Univ 1988; Kndgtn-12th Grade Cmptr Coord Twin Valley Sch Dist 1989-; *ai:* Mem Long Range Technology Planning Comm; PAECT 1989-; Cmptr Users of PA 1989-; Bus Women Berks Cty Schlsp; Teachers Advisory Bd Mem; Teaching & Cmptrs Article Published.

DEWBERRY, DOTTIE MAXEY, Jr HS English & Math Teacher; *b:* Holcomb, MS; *c:* Spencer D., Deirdre D.; *ed:* (AA) Ed, Wood Jr Coll 1967; (BS) Elem Ed, 1969, (MED) Elem Ed, 1974 MS St Univ; *cr:* Teacher Oktibbeha Cty Schls 1972-; *ai:* Y-Teen Adv; Functional Literacy Tutor; Jr Class Spon; Homecoming, Jr Prom Chm; Flower, Sch Soc Comms; PTO VP; Maben Garden Club Pres 1972, 1990; Garden Clubs of MS HS Garden Chm; Maben Chamber of Commerce Pres 1979, Outstanding Civil Servant 1981; Oktibbeha Cty Lib Bd 1990; Sturgis Teacher of Yr 1987; *home:* Rt 1 Box 541 Maben MS 39750

DEWEES, ALICE BALDWIN, Social Studies Teacher; *b:* Frankfort, IN; *m:* Carroll N.; *ed:* (BA) Elem, 1970, (MS) Elem, 1975 Ball St Univ; Grad Stud Tulsa Jr Coll & OK St Univ; *cr:* Teacher Twin Lakes Schls 1970-77, Tulsa Public Schls 1977-; *ai:* Red Cross & Yrbk Spon; Foster Mid Sch Advisory Comm; Tulsa Classroom Teacher Assn Delegate 1977-89; Lions Quest Skills for Adolescent Trng; Impact Trng; Curr Writing for Skills Enrichment & Homebase Guidance Prgm; *office:* Foster Mid Sch 12121 E 21st St Tulsa OK 74129

DEWEY, PAULETTE BAKER, English Teacher/Dept Chair; *b:* Evansville, IN; *m:* John Charles; *c:* Joel C., Rachel D., Joshua S., Noel; *ed:* (BA) Eng Lit, Univ of Evansville 1968; (MA) Eng Lit, Univ of Toledo 1975; IDEA Critical Thinking Inst; Great Books Leadership Trng; *cr:* Eng Teacher Washington Cath HS 1968-69, De Villoiss HS 1972-74; Eng Teacher/Dept Chm Rogers HS 1974-; Co-Dir Toledo Area Writing Project 1988-; *ai:* Co-Adv NHS & Future Teachers of America; Rogers HS Public Relations Comm Mem; Academic Banquet Planning Comm Mem; NCTE 1980-; Phi Delta Kappa 1987-; Toledo Area Writing Project Newsletter Ed; NEH Summer Inst Fellow 1985; OH Teacher Leader Network 1988-; Martha Jennings Conference Presenter 1989; Toledo Public Schls Career Ladder Teacher 1989-; *office:* Robert S Rogers HS 5539 Nebraska Ave Toledo OH 43615

DEWITT, HELEN REEVES, Math/Sci/Computer Teacher; *b:* Toronto ON, Canada; *m:* Willard; *c:* Jaymie, Nicole; *ed:* (AB) Bio, 1970, (MA) Sci Ed, 1976 Olivet Nazarene Univ; (MA) Educl Computing, Governors St Univ 1986; *cr:* Teacher Kennedy Upper Grade 1973-; *ai:* System Operator for Dist Telecommunication System; Software Reviewer for NSTA; 2 Articles Pending Publication; NSTA, CESI; ISTA Environmental Ed Assn of IL; TCTM; Delta Kappa Gamma Treas 1980-; Church (Missionary Pres, Church Bd, Childrens Cncl, Guide for Caravans); Governors Master Teacher Awd 1984; Excl in Sci Teaching Awd ISTA 1986; Selected Outstanding Elem Sci Teacher 1989-; *office:* Kennedy Upper Grade Center 1550 Calista Kankakee IL 60901

DE WITT, SUSAN MARIE, Third Grade Teacher; *b:* Rock Springs, WY; *ed:* (AA) General, W WY Coll 1978; (BA) Elem Ed, Univ of WY 1980; *cr:* Kndgtn Teacher Arapaho Sch 1980-81; 3rd Grade Teacher Southside Elem 1981-; *ai:* Lang Art, Staff Dev, Restructuring, Friendship, Sch Awds Comm; Humane Society Mem 1984-; WY Outdoor Cncl Mem 1981-.

DE WOLF, MARGARET JANE EVANS, Mathematics Department Chair; *b:* Coral Gables, FL; *m:* Dennis Keith; *c:* Jennifer, Wendy, Dennis Jr.; *ed:* (BA) Ed, Univ of FL 1966; (MA) Ed, W Carolina Univ 1978; *cr:* Math Teacher Rockway Jr HS 1966-72, Highlands Sch 1977-; *ai:* Jr Class & Chess Club Spon; Swim Team Coach; NC Teachers of Math; *office:* Highlands HS School St Highlands NC 28741

DEXTER, COEN RAYE, Chemistry Teacher; *b:* Amelia, NE; *ed:* (BS) Math/Chem, Kearney St 1967; (MS) Physics, Univ of ID 1976; *cr:* Teacher Burwell HS 1966-67, Hebron HS 1967-72, Julesburg HS 1972-75, Weiser HS 1975-76, Cntrl HS 1976-; *ai:* Track Coach; Jr Class Spon; MVEA, CEA, NEA 1976-; Grandvalley Audubon Society VP 1989-; CO Field Organization Bd of Dirs; CO Breeding Bird Atlas Regional Coord 1987-.

DEXTER, SONDRA DIANE, Science/Health Teacher; *b:* St Louis, MO; *ed:* (BA) Elem Ed, Harris Teachers Coll 1966; (MA) Elem Ed, Univ of AK Anchorage 1976; Significant Trng in Gifted & Talented Ed; *cr:* 2nd/7th/8th Grade Teacher Webster Elem Sch 1966-70; Rdng/Math/Health/Sci Teacher Wendler Jr HS 1970-; *ai:* Scndry Sci Curr Comm; Sci Health Dept Head; AK Sci Teachers Assn (Pres 1976-78, Ed 1978-82); NSTA (Awds Comm 1977-79, Publications Comm 1988-) Sci Teaching Achievement Awd 1981; Natl Sci Supvrs Assn; AK Sci Fair Planning Comm (Engineering Awds 1982-89, Registration 1982-); Nature Conservancy Planetary Society; Anchorage Teacher of Yr 1979; Anchorage Sch Dist Teacher of Month 1981; Presidential Awd Excl Sci Teaching 1983; *office:* Wendler Jr HS 2905 Lake Otis Parkway Anchorage AK 99508

DEY, SHARON L., Math/Computer Teacher; *b:* Sedalia, MO; *ed:* (AB) Poly Sci, Marquette Univ. 1968; Mid Sch Math Cntrl MO St Univ; *cr:* Teacher Milwaukee Public Schls 1968-71; Math Teacher Sedalia Public Schls 1971-76; Math/Cmptr Teacher Sacred Heart Jr & Sr HS 1976-; *ai:* Jr & Sr HS Math Clubs; Cmptr Club; MCTM 1985-; NCTM 1989-; Participant Southwest Baptist Univ Grant Curr Dev & Methodologies Cmptr Sci; *office:* Sacred Heart Sch 416 W 3rd Sedalia MO 65301

DEYO, PAUL ARTHUR, Academic Dean; *b:* Keokuk, IA; *ed:* (BA) Eng, St Ambrose Univ 1971; (STB) Theology, Univ of St Thomas Aquinas 1976; (MA) Ed Admin, NE MO St Univ 1989; *cr:* Teacher/Dean Notre Dame Intnl Sch Rome Italy 1972-76, St Mary HS Clinton IA 1976-78, Notre Dame Intnl Sch Rome Italy 1978-84, Assumption HS Davenport IA 1984-; *ai:* IA HS Athletic Assn/Athletic Dir 1985-88; Diocesan Advisory Comm (Chm, Ed Comm) 1987-; *office:* Assumption HS 1020 W Central Park Ave Davenport IA 52804

DE YULIUS, SALVATORE, 4th Grade Teacher; *b:* Spangler, PA; *m:* Donna Marie George; *c:* Vanessa; *ed:* (BS) Elem Ed, St Francis Coll 1970; (MA) Ed, Penn St 1976; *cr:* 4th-8th Grade Teacher Colver Elem 1970-72; 4th Grade Teacher Cntrl Cambria Elem 1972-; *ai:* Elem Boys Bsktbl Coach; PSEA, NEA; Cntrl Cambria Ed Assn Building Rep 1974-75, 1989-; Cresson Jaycees Dir 1978; Amer Legion Bowling League (Secy, VP) 1985-86; *home:* 11 Fairway Dr Cresson PA 16630

DEZENDORF, JEANNINE GAY, Kindergarten Teacher; *b:* Ruston, LA; *ed:* (BA) Kndgtn/Primary 1973, (MED) Elem Teaching/Early Chldhd, 1975 Northwestern St Univ; Grad Stud Continuing Ed; *cr:* Grad Asst Northwestern St Univ Laboratory Schls 1973-75; Kndgtn Teacher Oak Hill HS 1975-; *ai:* Hospitality Chm; Sch Building Level, Parish Kndgtn Curr, Stu at Risk, Rapides Parish & Textbook Adoption Comms; LTA Sch Rep 1980-85; LEA Sch Rep 1985-88; A&PEL Sch Rep 1990; ADK Historian 1986-88; Alpha Delta Kappa Chaplain 1990; United Meth Women (Circle VP 1980-85, Pres 1985-87), Pin 1985; Comm Wrote Kndgtn Curr Rapides Parish Schls 1981; Whos Who Among Outstanding Women of America; *office:* Oak Hill HS 7364 Hwy 112 Elmer LA 71424

DEZERN, KAY LANGLEY, Teacher; *b:* Portsmouth, VA; *w:* William W. Sr. (dec); *c:* Helen, Bill; *ed:* (BS) Psych, Milligan Coll 1979; (MSED) Counseling, Old Dominion Univ 1983; *cr:* Teacher Crestwood Elem 1979-84, Deep Creek Intermediate 1984-; *ai:* Child Study Team; Stu Assistance Prgm Comm; Phi Delta Kappa 1984-; Chesapeake Ed Assn (Bd of Dir, Poly Action Comm Chairperson, Faculty Rep) 1979-, Distinguished Service Awd 1988; VA Ed Assn (Legislative Contact Team, Candidate to Leadership Acad, Peace & Soc Justice & Collective Bargaining Coalition Steering Comm, Dist S Secy, VA Ed Assn Convention Delegate 1979-; NEA (Natl Convention, Minorities & Womens & Mid Atlantic Conference Delegate, Peace Caucus) 1982-; Chesapeake Cmmty Services Bd Chairperson 1984-89; VA Assn of Cmmty Services Bd Chairperson 1987-88; Pilot Club (Bd, Secy) 1984-86; PTA (Faculty Rep, Bd of Dir); Outstanding Stu Teacher Milligan Coll 1979; Natl Deans List Old Dominion Univ 1983; Chairperson Mayors Task Force on Drugs 1987-89; Article Virginian Pilot Newspaper 1984; Whos Who in Americas Colls &

Univs 1979; Whos Who in the South 1991; *home:* 817 George Washington Hwy N Chesapeake VA 23323

D'HONT, KIM WALLIOR, Spanish/English Teacher; *b:* Aberdeen, SD; *m:* Dennis; *c:* Matthew; *ed:* (BS) Span, Univ of SD 1977; *cr:* Span/Eng Teacher 1977-79; Title I Eng Tutor Wolf Point HS; Span/Eng Teacher Hill City HS 1984-; *ai:* Span Club Adv; Natl Honor Society Adv; Soph Class Adv; SD Foreign Lang Assn 1984-; SD Eng Teacher of Yr Nom 1987-88.

DIAL, CARROL WAYNE, Principal; *b:* Groveton, TX; *c:* David, Denny, Dale; *ed:* (BS) His, Sam Houston St Univ 1963; (MS) Admin, Lamar Univ 1981; *cr:* Teacher/Coach Lovelady Ind Sch Dist 1965-66, Groveton Ind Sch Dist 1966-68; Teacher Central-Nederland Ind Sch Dist 1971-78; Teacher 1979-83, Prin 1983- Helena Park Elem Sch; *ai:* TX Elem Prins Supvrs Assn 1983-; Natl Elem Prins Supvrs Assn 1987-; Teacher of Yr Nederland Ind Sch Dist 1977; Nominee Teacher of Yr Nederland Ind Sch Dist 1983; *home:* 319 35th St Nederland TX 77627

DIALS, RITA THOMPSON, Home Ec Teacher/Dept Head; *b:* Maysville, KY; *m:* Randall; *c:* Ryan Clark, Robbie; *ed:* (BS) Voc Home Ec, 1974, (MS) Voc Ed, 1977, (Rank I) Scndry Ed/Home Ec, 1980 Morehead St Univ; *cr:* Home Ec Teacher Fleming Cty HS 1975-; *ai:* FHA Adv; Sr Class Spon; KY Assn of Home Ec Teachers 1975-; Beta Sigma Phi (Past Pres, Past Treas) 1980-.

DIAMANTOPOULOS, DALE MITCHELL, Phys Ed/Health Teacher; *b:* Winchendon, MA; *m:* Susan Gentile; *c:* Krita, Michael; *ed:* (BS) Health/Phys Ed, Springfield Coll 1979; (MED) Ed/Admin, Fitchburg St Coll 1986; *cr:* Adaptive Phys Ed Teacher Murdock HS 1979-80; Health/Phys Ed Teacher Turkey Hill Mid Sch 1981-; *ai:* Lunenburg HS Head Ftbl Coach 1986-; Lunenburg Teachers Assn 1981-; Mid-Wach Div C League Ftbl Coach of Yr 1989; Boston Univ Shriners All-Star Ftbl Game Coach 1989; *office:* Turkey Hill Mid Sch Northfield Rd Lunenburg MA 01462

DIAMOND, ELAINE DIANE, Social Studies Teacher; *b:* Gary, IN; *ed:* (BS) Ed, 1971, (MS) Ed, 1976, IN Univ; *cr:* Teacher Beckman Mid Sch 1972-; *ai:* NCSS, IN Cncl of Soc Stud, Gary Rdng Cncl, Gary Classroom Teacher AFT #4 1972-; *home:* 954 Pawnee Dr Crown Point IN 46307

DIAZ, GRACE SALAS, Tutoring; *b:* Dumangas, Philippines; *ed:* BSE) Home Ec/Sci, Philippines Union Coll 1941; Law, Philippines Cntrl Univ 1963; (MA) Counseling, Loma Linda Univ 1968; Spaulding Method in Rdng, Spelling, Writing, Riggs Inst 1988; Span Classes, Signing Class for Deaf; *cr:* Teacher Philippines Union Coll 1941-42, Philippines Public Schls 1945-46. 1963,64. W Visayan Acad 1948-51, Upper Columbia Conf of SDA 1968-86; Adult Ed Teacher Oregon Conference of SDA 1987-88; Tutor Clackamas Comm Coll 1987-; Private Tutor 1987-; *ai:* Rivergate SDA Sch Soc, Sch Annual Comm Mem; General Sabbath Sch Secy, Sch Annual Comm Mem. Church Choir Phil Union Coll; Clackamas Cty Soc Service Volunteer 1987-88; Loma Linda Univ Lib 1966-67; 7th Day Adventist (Credential, Missionary Mem) 1968-86.

DIAZ, JOSE M., Spanish Teacher; *b:* Gibara, Cuba; *ed:* (BA) Span Lit, Hunter Coll 1976; (MA) Span, Columbia Univ Teachers Coll 1978; *cr:* Span Teacher Walden Sch 1977-83, Fieldston Sch 1983-84, Hunter Coll HS 1984-; *ai:* 8th Grade Adv; Faculty Cncl Mem; Amer Assn Teachers of Span & Portuguese (Honorarium & Finance Comm Mem, Metropolitan NY Chapter Pres, VP); Amer Cncl Teaching of Foreign Lang NY St Gifted & Talented Comm Co-Chm; Northeast Conference Teaching of Foreign Lang (Dir, New York City Local Comm Mem); Natl Span Examinations Leadership Awd 1984, 1986; Natl Endowment for Hum/Span Lit Performance Univ of VA Charlottesville; Theodore Heubener Awd 1987; *office:* Hunter Coll HS 71 E 94th St New York NY 10128

DIAZ, SUE A., Music Teacher; *b:* Chico, CA; *m:* Rudy A.; *c:* Gregory; *ed:* (BA) Music/Art, CA St Chico 1966; *cr:* Teacher Winship Jr HS 1967-; *ai:* Cheerleading, Spirit Club, Pep Club Sch Spirit Act; Eureka Teachers Assn, CA Teachers Assn, Natl Teachers Assn 1967-.

DI BATTISTA, ANTHONY PAUL, History Teacher; *b:* Newark, NJ; *m:* Rosemary Genova; *c:* Anthony; *ed:* (BA) His, 1977, (MA) Medieval His, 1987 Rutgers Univ; *cr:* Teacher Mendham HS 1979-; *ai:* Stu Cncl & NHS Adv; NJ Cncl Soc Stud 1980-; Fulbright Fellowship, Natl Endowment for Humanities Fellowship; *office:* Mendham HS E Main St Mendham NJ 07945

DIBELLA, MARGARET TOMPKINS, 8th Grade Science Teacher; *b:* Lowell, MA; *m:* Alfred Jr.; *ed:* (BS) Elem Ed/His, Lowell St Coll 1975; (MED) Sch Counseling, Northeastern Univ 1989; *cr:* 2nd-3rd Grade Teacher Pine Glen Elem 1976-81; 7th Grade Math Teacher 1981-82, 8th Grade Sci Teacher 1982-Marshall Simonds Mid Sch; *ai:* Peer Leadership Adv; NEA, MA Teachers Assn 1976-; MA St Cnslrs Assn 1989-; Kappa Delta Pi 1988-; Phi Kappa Phi 1989-; Horace Mann Grants 1986-87; *home:* 77 Patrick Rd Tewksbury MA 01876

DIBERT, ANN ELIZABETH (ROSKO), Business Education Teacher; *b:* Johnstown, PA; *m:* Wayne Edward; *c:* Amy E., Scott E.; *ed:* (BS) Bus Ed, Indiana Univ of PA 1972; *cr:* Bus Ed Teacher Shade HS 1972-83, Johnstown Chrstn Sch 1983-; *ai:* Sr Class & Yrbk Adv; *home:* 1084 Tener St Johnstown PA 15904

DI BIASE, JAN B. DE WAELSCHE, English/Composition Teacher; *b:* Grosse Pointe, MI; *m:* Ronald; *c:* Daniel; *ed:* (BA) Hum, 1971, (MA) Soc Sci, 1976 Univ of Detroit; *cr:* 2nd Grade Teacher 1968-71, 7th Grade Teacher 1971 Divine Child Elem Sch; 8th Grade Teacher Woodhaven Sch Dist 1971-76; 5th Grade Teacher Erving Elem-Woodhaven 1976-78; 8th Grade Teacher Patrick Henry Mid Sch 1978-; *ai:* Yrbk Adv; 8th Grade Essay Contest Coord; *office:* Patrick Henry Mid Sch 24825 Hall Rd Woodhaven MI 48183

DI CAPRIO, ELIZABETH ANNE GARGIULO, 5th Grade Reading Teacher; *b:* Amsterdam, NY; *m:* Robert C. Sr.; *c:* Lisa, Mara Buchanan, Robert Jr., James, David; *ed:* (BS) Music Ed - Magna Cum Laude, 1958, (MS) Elem Ed - Magna Cum Laude, 1976 Coll of St Rose; Childrens Lit, Dept of Rdng Various Coll 1986-; *cr:* Pre K-6th Grade Music Teacher Gloversville Elem Schls 1958-59; Part Time Music Teacher New Hanover Townships Schls 1961-62, Fonda-Fultonville Cntrl Sch 1966-68;6th-8th Grade Music Teacher Estee Mid Sch 1972-74; 4th Grade Teacher 1974-81, 5th Grade Rdng Teacher 1982- Fonda-Fultonville Cntrl Sch; Childrens Lit Adjunct Professor Fulton-Montgomery Comm Coll 1990; *ai:* Sch Improvement & Rdng Comm: Grade Chm; NY St Rdng Assn, Montgomery-Fulton Rdng Cncl 1974-; NY St United Teachers 1972-; Coll of St Rose Alumni Assn 1958-; SOFCO Incorporated Bd of Dir 1983-; Schlsp Fnd (Bd of Dir, VP, Secy) 1987-; Sacred Heart (Organist, Liturgy Dir 1966-, Parish Cncl 1981-) 1966-; PTA Faculty Coord 1974-; Presented Seminars on 5th Grade Whole Lang Rdng Prgm Natl Lit Conference 1990; *office:* Fonda-Fultonville Cntrl Sch Cemetary St Fonda NY 12068

DI CARLO, ROSEMARIE IANNUCCI, Kindergarten Teacher; *b:* New York, NY; *m:* Anthony; *c:* Anthony M., Daniel R.; *ed:* (BA) Speech/Theatre, Iona Coll 1982; Ed, Coll of New Rochelle 1987; *cr:* Asst Teacher White Plains Childrens Center 1982-83; 7th/8th Grade Sci/Math Teacher 1983-86, 2nd Grade Teacher 1985-88, Kndgtn Teacher 1988- St Anns; *home:* 50 N Broadway 5M White Plains NY 10603

DI CARO, DIANNA M., Mathematics Teacher; *b:* New Brunswick, NJ; *ed:* (BA) Math Ed, Rider Coll 1983; (MA) Ed Admin, Kean Coll 1989; *cr:* Math Teacher Manalapan HS 1983-; Adjunct Math Teacher Middlesex Cty Coll 1983-; *ai:* NJEA, NEA Mem 1983-; St Marys Church Parishioner 1961-; *office:* Manalapan HS Church Ln Englishtown NJ 07726

DI CICCO, BARBARA ANNE, Basic Skills Teacher; *b:* Newark, NJ; *ed:* (BA) Elem Ed, Georgian Court Coll 1973; Addl Studies Georgian Court Coll; Rutgers Univ; *cr:* 7th-8th Grade Eng Teacher 1973-87; Basic Skills Teacher Lakehurst Sch 1987-90; *ai:* Safety Patrol Adv; Publicity Chairperson; Yrbk Adv; Asst Intramural Sports Adv; Lakehurst Ed Assn (President Treasurer) 1981; Ocean Cty Ed Assn 1973-; MJ Ed Assn 1973-; NEA/PTA 1973-.

DI CICCO, ROSEMARIE TERESA, 8th Grade English Teacher; *b:* Philadelphia, PA; *m:* Stephen D.; *c:* Anna, Stephen, Nicholas; *ed:* (BA) Eng/Ed, La Salle Coll 1978; (ME) Eng/Ed, Temple Univ 1981; *cr:* Bus Teacher W Philadelphia Cath HS for Girls 1978; 9th Grade Eng Teacher Arch Prendergast HS 1978; Eng Teacher Lower Moreland HS 1978-79; 8th Grade Teacher Holy Cross Sch 1979-85; 8th Grade Eng Teacher Resurrection of Our Lord Sch 1985-; *ai:* Organizer Literary Magazine; *office:* Resurrection of Our Lord Sch 2020 Shelmire Ave Philadelphia PA 19152

DI CIOCCIO, JOSEPH N., Mathematics Teacher; *b:* Ossining, NY; *m:* Eleanore A.; *c:* Katherine L., Jospeh J.; *ed:* (BS) Math, St Bonaventure Univ 1973; (MS) Scndry Math Ed, W CT St Univ 1978; *cr:* Math Teacher Mahopac Cntrl Schls 1973-; *ai:* Jr Var Soccer, Asst Var Bsbl Coach; NY Assn of Math Teachers 1990; NCTM; *office:* Mahopac HS Baldwin Place Rd Mahopac NY 10541

DICK, BARBARA B., Elementary Music Teacher; *b:* Somerset, KY; *m:* Gary; *c:* Keri, Lindsay, Wesley; *ed:* (BME) Music Ed, E KY Univ 1975; (MA) Counseling, W KY Univ 1978; *cr:* Music Teacher Wayne Cty Elem #1 & #3 1975-85, Wayne Cty Mid 1985-87; Teacher of Gifted & Talented Wayne Cty Elem #1 1988-89; Teacher of Music/Gifted & Talented Wayne Cty Elem #1, #3 & Mid 1989-; *ai:* KEA 1975-; *office:* Wayne Cty Mid Sch 314 Albany Rd Monticello KY 42633

DICK, JEAN BERTRAM, Substitute Teacher; *b:* Long Beach, CA; *w:* Ralph L. (dec); *c:* Mary L. Bennett, Lawrence, Susan Kinsey, David, Douglas; *ed:* (BA) Elem Ed Eng, IA St Teachers Coll 1944; *cr:* 4th Grade Teacher Zearing Consolidated Schls 1944-46, Storm Lake Public Schls 1946-47; 5th Grade Teacher Mt Olive Luth Sch 1962-70, First Luth Sch 1970-88; *ai:* IA St Teachers Assn 1944-47; Luth Womens Missionary League Pres 1953-55; First Luth Choir; San Fernando Valley Chorale Costume Chm 1989-; *home:* 14230 Raven St Sylmar CA 91342

DICK, LINDA WRIGHT, Teacher of Gifted & Talented; *b:* Jackson, MS; *m:* R. Dean; *c:* Ryan, Kerri, Jennifer; *ed:* (BA) Eng Ed, 1972, (MS) Spec Ed/Gifted & Talented, 1989 LA Tech; *cr:* Lang Art Teacher Ridgewood Jr HS 1972-73, Walnut Hill Jr HS 1973-76; Soc Stud Teacher Summerfield HS 1984-86; Teacher of Gifted & Talented Ruston Jr HS 1986-; *ai:* Sch Newspaper & Academic Pentathlon Team Spon; Coord Annual G/T Spring Trip; APEL 1986-; Alpha Delta Kappa 1976-; *office:* Ruston Jr HS 1400 Tarbutton Rd Ruston LA 71270

DICKENS, DOLLY CLARK, English/Spanish Teacher; *b:* Wilson, NC; *m:* Charles Douglas; *ed:* (BS) Eng, E Carolina Univ 1979; Foreign Lang Inst, NC Sch of Drugs & Alcohol; *cr:* Lang Art Teacher Jones Jr HS 1979-82; Eng/Span Teacher Jones Sr HS 1982-85, South Lenoir HS 1985-; *ai:* Span Club & Honor Society Adv; Media Advisory & Southern Assn Steering Comm; Word of Day Spon; Amer Assn Teachers of Span & Portuguese; Lenoir Cty Eng Teachers Assn Secy 1989-; Literacy Project; Teacher of Yr 1981-82, 1989-; Published in Literary Magazine; *home:* Rt 3 Box 377A-5 La Grange NC 28551

DICKENSHEETS, PATRICIA LAMBERT, Fourth Grade Teacher; *b:* Longmont, CO; *m:* Frederick E.; *c:* Janice, David; *ed:* (BA) Elem Ed, UNC 1957; *cr:* 4th Grade Teacher Platteville Elem Sch 1957-59; K-12th Grade Music Teacher Gateway CO 1970-76; 2nd/4th/5th Grade Teacher Broadway Elem 1976-; *ai:* Intnl Rdng Assn 1975-; Delta Kappa Gamma Pres 1986-88; First Presbyn Church (Handbell Dir, Youth Choir Dir) 1985-; *home:* 528 Foy Dr Grand Junction CO 81503

DICKENSON, MARY MARGARET P., Junior HS Teacher; *b:* Glendale, CA; *m:* Keith; *c:* John; *ed:* (BA) Poly Sci, 1975, (MA) Near Eastern Lang/Cultures, 1977 Univ of CA Los Angeles; Masters Stud Scndry Ed, CA St Univ; *cr:* Teacher San Gabriel Mission HS 1977-79, St Francis of Assisi Sch 1980-83, Our Lady of Perpetual Help Sch 1983-85, Notre Dame Des Victoires Sch 1985-; *ai:* Stu Cncl Moderator; Talent Show, Sci Fair Coord; CA Math Cncl 1985-; San Mateo Cty Sci Teachers 1988-; NCTM 1985-; Mid East Stud Assn 1976-; Assn of Catholic Stu Cncls 1985-; NDEA Title VI Fellowship Study of Non-Western Lang 1975-77.

DICKERSON, BELINDA GAIL, English/Journalism Teacher; *b:* Cherry Point, NC; *ed:* (BS) Math/Eng, Baptist Coll Charleston 1976; Eng/Ed, Univ of SC; *cr:* 6th-7th Grade Lang Art Teacher Jasper Mid Sch 1978-85; 9th-12th Grade Eng Teacher Jasper Cty HS 1985-; *ai:* Yrbk, Newspaper, Photography, Sr Adv, Steering Comm SACS; Intramural Scorekeeper; NEA, SCEA, JCEA Treas 1983, 1989-; Port Royal Baptist Church (Organist, Sunday Sch Teacher) 1979-86; *home:* PO Box 25 Port Royal SC 29935

DICKERSON, BERNADINE MARIE, 7th Grade English Teacher; *b:* Grand Rapids, MI; *c:* Jack, Jane King, Mary; *ed:* (AS) Sci, Grand Rapids Jr Coll 1947; (BA) Eng, Grand Valley St 1978; Grad Courses Rdng & Ed; *cr:* 5th Grade Teacher Grant Elem 1970-71; 7th Grade Eng Teacher Kent City Schls 1971-; *ai:* Eng Curr & Foreign Lang Curr Comm.

DICKERSON, COTY DARNELL, JR., Health/Physical Ed Teacher; *b:* Christiansburg, VA; *m:* Carolyn Turner; *c:* Chris, Timmy, Joey; *ed:* (BS) Health/Phys Ed, VA Tech Blacksburg 1968; Drug Ed, Media, Ec, Coaching Clinics; *cr:* K-7th Grade Health/Phys Ed Teacher Prices Fork Elem 1968-69; 7th-12th Grade Health/Phys Ed Teacher Shawsville HS 1969-73; 8th/9th Grade Phys Ed Teacher Appomattox Int Sch 1973-74; 9th Grade Phys Ed Teacher Appomattox HS 1974-75; 7th/8th Grade Phys Ed/Health Teacher Appomattox Mid 1975-; *ai:* Var Ftbl & Track Asst Coach; Intramurals Spon Appomattox Mid Sch; VA HS League Ofcl Bsktbl & Bsbl; Natl HS Coaches Assn, VA HS Coaches Assn 1968; NEA, VEA, AEA; Appomattox PTA Mid Sch Teacher of Yr 1987-89; Mountain Empire Bsktbl Coach of Yr 1971-73; Seminole Dist Bsbl Coach of Yr 1977-78; Seminole Dist Bsktbl Coach of Yr 1980-81; *home:* Box 301 Appomattox VA 24522

DICKERSON, ERNEST RICHARD, JR., Health/Phys Ed Teacher; *b:* Bluefield, WV; *ed:* (BS) Health/Phys Ed, Concord Coll 1972; (MS) Phys Ed, VPI & SU 1974; *cr:* Ftbl Grad Asst VPI & SU 1972; Health/Phys Ed Teacher Pulaski Mid Sch 1974-; *ai:* Boys & Girls Bsktbl Coach; Athletic Dir; Intramurals; VA Mid Sch Assn 1989-; VA HS Coaches Assn, Natl HS Athletic Coaches Assn 1974-; *office:* Pulaski Mid Sch 500 Pico Terr Pulaski VA 24301

DICKES, SYLVIA PEARSON, Retired 4th Grade Teacher; *b:* Dixon, NE; *m:* Erwin P.; *c:* Tom, Richard, Dan, David, Jean, Jim; *ed:* (BA) His, Wayne St 1942; Spec Ed, Univ of SD; *cr:* 4th Grade Teacher St Michael 1960-84.

DICKEY, JACK S., Middle School Principal; *b:* Berlin, PA; *m:* Janice F. Walker; *c:* Cathy, Jill, John; *ed:* (BS) Bio, Juniata 1952; (MED) Ed/Supervision, Univ of WV 1965; *cr:* Teacher Forbes HS 1954-73; Prin Forbes HS & N Star 1973-89; Acting Supt N Star 1989-; *ai:* Somerset Cty Prin Pres 1983-84; PA Assn Scndry Sch Prin, NASSP 1974-; Masonic Lodge 1978-; PA Interscholastic Athletic Assn Inc; *office:* N Star Mid Sch Kantner PA 15548

DICKEY, KRISTEN ALESIANI, Kindergarten Teacher; *b:* Monessen, PA; *m:* John Michael; *c:* John; *ed:* (BA) Early Chldhd/Elem Ed, CA Univ 1981; (MS) Curr/Instruction, Univ of S FL 1984; *cr:* 5th Grade Teacher 1981-86, Kndgtn Teacher 1986-Lecanto Primary 1986-; *ai:* Math & Sci Team Leader; Lang Art Media & Soc Stud Comm; Wkshps Presenter for Faculty Gudiance Comm; NEA, CCEA; *office:* Lecanto Primary Sch 3790 W Educational Path Lecanto FL 32661

DICKEY, RONALD NEAL, History Department Chairman; *b:* Selmer, TN; *m:* Judy Lynn Davis; *c:* Ryan, Evan; *ed:* (BS) Scndry Ed, Memphis St Univ 1974; Elem Endorsement; *cr:* Teacher Selmer Mid Sch 1975-; *ai:* Beta Club & Stu Cncl Spon; His Dept Chm; His Competition Comm; TN Ed Assn 1975-; *home:* Rt 2 Box 566 Selmer TN 38375

DICKEY, ROSA LEE, Retired; *b:* Lynchburg, SC; *ed:* (BA) Elem Ed, Soc Stud, Morris Coll 1949; Addl Studies, SC St Coll; *cr:* Teacher St Mark Elem Sch 1949 -84; Asst Prin 1980-84 St John Elem Sch; *ai:* Tutoring Sumter Sch Dist 2; Brownie Girl Scout Leader; Morris Coll Alumni 1985; Natl Cncl Negro Women; OES Skyway Am 1970-.

DICKEY, ROXANN SARLO, Second Grade Teacher; *b:* Ft Myers, FL; *m:* Carl James; *c:* Susan Dickey Stouffer, Ted, John, Dan; *ed:* (BA) Elem Ed - Magna Cum Laude, Univ of S FL 1977; Grad Rdng Certificate 1986; Working Towards Masters; *cr:* 2nd Grade Teacher St Francis Xavier Cath Sch 1977-79; 2nd/3rd Grade Teacher Tropic Isles Elem Sch 1979-85; 2nd/4th Grade Teacher Orangewood Elem 1986-; *ai:* Phi Kappa Phi 1977-; Delta Kappa Gamma; *office:* Orangewood Elem Sch 4001 Deleon St Fort Myers FL 33901

DICKEY, TERESA ALICE, English Teacher; *b:* Los Angeles, CA; *ed:* (BA) Eng, 1982, (MA) Eng, 1984 Loyola Marymount Univ; *cr:* Teaching Asst Loyola Marymount Univ 1982-84; Eng Teacher Saint Francis HS 1984-86, Our Lady of Corvallis 1986-87, Saint Monicas Cath HS 1987-; *ai:* Sr Class Moderator 1988-; CATE 1990; NCTE 1987-; Area 3 Writing Project Fellow 1985; Los Angeles Archdiocesan Teacher Incentive Grant; *office:* Saint Monicas Cath HS 1030 Lincoln Blvd Santa Monica CA 90403

DICKINSON, CATHY JONES, Third Grade Teacher; *b:* Los Angeles, CA; *m:* William C.; *c:* Laurel, Curt, Sarah; *ed:* (BS) Elem Ed, Univ TN Martin 1970; (MS) Spec Ed, Univ of TN 1972; Grad Work Spec Ed & Related Fields; *cr:* Teacher Obion Cty 1970-72; 3rd/4th Grade Spec Ed Teacher Fort Craig 1972-; *ai:* Cncl for Exceptional Children Pres 1980-81; Maryville Ed Assn Treas 1983-85; NEA, TN Ed Assn; Alpha Delta Kappa; Maryville Music Club (Pres 1987-89, Treas 1983-85); TN Governors Writing Acad; Jaycees Teacher of Yr 1974; *office:* Fort Craig Elem Schl 520 Washington Maryville TN 37801

DICKINSON, DONALD C., English Teacher; *b:* Wilkes-Barre, PA; *m:* Linda Naugle; *c:* Matthew, Todd, Beth; *ed:* (BS) Eng/Speech Ed, Shippensburg Univ 1970; Shippensburg Univ; *cr:* Teacher of Eng Chambersburg Area HS 1970-72, Faust Jr HS 1973-83, Chambersburg Area HS 1984-; *ai:* Forensics Dir; PA St Ed Assn, NEA 1987-; Natl Forensic League 1987-, Degree of Excl 1990; *office:* Chambersburg Area HS 511 S Sixth St Chambersburg PA 17201

DICKINSON, GREGORY DENNIS, Mathematics Teacher; *b:* La Puente, CA; *m:* Linda Susan Morgan; *c:* Alyssa; *ed:* (BS) Phys Ed/Math, CA St Polytechnic Univ Pomona 1985; Univ of CA Riverside, Chapman Coll; *cr:* Math/Phys Ed Stu Teacher Lorbeer Jr HS 1986; Math/Phys Ed Teacher Hesperia HS 1986-; *ai:* Var Ftbl & Sftbl Coach; *office:* Hesperia HS 9898 Maple St Hesperia CA 92345

DICKINSON, JANET KEROHER, English Teacher; *b:* San Diego, CA; *m:* Evan Theodore; *ed:* (BS) Eng/Bus Ed, UT St Univ 1967; (MA) Personnel Services/Counseling , Montclair St 1975; *cr:* Eng Teacher Boonton HS 1967-69, Mt Olive Upper Elem 1969-73, Long Valley Mid Sch 1973-; *ai:* Newspaper, Pep Club, Stu Cncl Adv; 8 Yrs Stu Trips Abroad; Geraldine Dodge Fnd Grant; NJ Field Rep Amer Ccsl for Intnl Stud; *office:* Long Valley Mid Sch West Mill Rd Long Valley NJ 07853

DICKINSON, RAE ANN MC LEAN, Fourth Grade Teacher; *b:* Muscatine, IA; *m:* Richard E.; *c:* Katy, Sara; *ed:* (BA) Elem Ed, William Penn Coll 1974; *cr:* 4th Grade Teacher East Cntrl Schls 1975-; *ai:* Religious Ed Teacher; Jackson Cty Conservation Ed Assn; GSA Volunteer; Cystic Fibrosis Bike-A-Thon Chairperson; Jackson Cty Democratic Party; St of IA Fire Dept Fire Safety Awd; *office:* East Cntrl Schls Broad St Sabula IA 52070

DICKSON, JAMES HOWARD, Literature Teacher; *b:* Grants Pass, OR; *m:* Cheryl Lee Jamieson; *c:* Susan M. Clark, Sara A., Shay C.; *ed:* (BSED) Elem Ed, S OR St Coll 1964; (MED) Remedial Ed, Univ of OR 1968-; Continuing Ed, Portland St Coll & Western OR St Coll; *cr:* 4th-6th Grade Teacher Forest Grove Public Sch 1964-77; Supervising Teacher Aloha Chrstn Acad 1978-83; Jr HS Teacher Yamhill Grade Sch 1984-; *ai:* HB 2020 Site Comm Mem; Title 1 ESEA Prin for Educationally Disadvantaged Forest Grove Dist 7; Yamhill Grade Sch Bsbl Coach 1985-86; Drama Teacher; Pilot Teacher Talented & Gifted Prgm Forest Public Schls 1970-71; Rendezvous I & II; Cmmty Sch Partnerships 1988-; NEA Life Mem; Yamhill Ed Assn (Secy, Treas 1986-87); Yamhill Teachers Assn 1984-; Natl Inventive Thinking Assn 1989-; Forest Grove Ed Assn Pres 1965-66; BSA Explorer Leader 1964-67; GSA Leader 1969-70; OR Hunting Safety Instr 1970-; OR Wildlife Fed 1988-; Forest Grove Police Reserves Captain 1968-75; US Dept of Ed Experienced Teacher Fellowship Awd 1967-68; Published Article 1970; *office:* Yamhill Grade Sch 310 E Main Yamhill OR 97148

DICKSON, JOHN R., English Department Chairman; *b:* Fairbury, NE; *ed:* (BS) Lang Art Ed, 1956, (MS) Lang/Art Ed, 1965 Univ of KS; Numerous Grad Courses & Wkshps; *cr:* Eng Teacher Topeka HS 1957-60, W Platte HS 1960-67, Technical HS 1967-68; Eng Teacher/Dept Chm Atchison HS 1968-; *ai:* Dept Chm; Curr Comm; ANEA; KNEA; NEA; Amer Legion; *home:* 1037 Laramie Atchison KS 66002

DICKSON, JOHN ROBERT, III, 4th Grade Teacher; *b:* Nashville, TN; *ed:* (BA) Ec, Rhodes Coll 1968; (MED) Scndry Ed, Memphis St Univ 1977; Ed Prgm, Memphis St Univ 1978; *cr:* Branch Officer 1st Tennessee Bank 1969-74; Teacher Christ Meth Day Sch 1974-78, Shelby Cty Schls 1978-; *ai:* Soccer & Womens Sftbl Coach; Cmptr Club Spon & Adv; Shelby Cty Ed Assn Faculty Rep 1985-87; Curr Writer Shelby Cty Schls Cmptr 1983, 1988-89, Soc Stud 1984-, Eng 1986; Natl Sci Fnd Grant 1981; Chrstn Brothers Univ Sci Grant 1986; *office:* Millington East Elem Sch 6467 Navy Rd Millington TN 38053

DICUS, JULIANNE, Counselor; *b:* Los Angeles, CA; *ed:* (BA) Eng, 1964, (MA) Eng, 1967 Univ of S CA; General Pupil Personnel Credential; Admin Credential; General Scndry Credential; *cr:* Eng Teacher 1965-68, Cnslr/Eng Teacher 1968-72, Work Experience/SCROC Coord/Eng Teacher 1972-73, Eng Teacher 1973-78, Cnslr 1978- Hawthorne HS; *ai:* CA Schlsp Fed Recordkeeper; CA Assn Teachers of Eng 1964-79; CA Assn Counseling & Dev 1970-; Pi Lambda Theta 1964-; Parent Teacher Stu Assn Founders Service Awd 1988; Centinela Valley Scndry Teachers Assn Secy 1966-67; Univ of S CA Pres Circle 1980-; *office:* Hawthorne HS 4859 W El Segundo Blvd Hawthorne CA 90250

DIDAWICK, CYNTHIA FINLEY, Sixth Grade Teacher; *b:* Dalls, TX; *m:* David William; *c:* Dustin W.; *ed:* (BA) Elem Ed, Bridgewater Coll 1977; Minor Gifted Ed, James Madison Univ 1980; *cr:* 1st Grade Teacher A R Ware Elem 1977-78; 5th Grade Teacher Thomas Jefferson Grammar Sch 1978-79, T C Mc Swain 1979-83; Teacher of Gifted Staunton City Schls 1983-88; 6th Grade Teacher T C Mc Swain 1988-; *ai:* Delta Kappa Gamma Comm Chm 1988-; *home:* 205 Oak Ridge Cr Staunton VA 24401

DI DONATO, JEANETTE SERABIAN, Vocal Music Teacher; *b:* Cherry Point, NC; *m:* Daniel A.; *c:* Lauri, Karen, Jennifer; *ed:* (BA) Music Ed, Goucher Coll 1973; Music Ed, Towson St Univ; *cr:* Vocal Music Teacher Sudbrook Jr HS 1973-74, Ridgeway Jr HS 1974-75, Lakewood Jr HS 1975-76, Marlton Mid Sch 1976-; *ai:* MMS Show Biz Kids; Small Ensemble; MMS Show Choir Performance in Disneyworld & Canada; NJEA 1975-; MENC 1990; Fred Waring US Chorus Accompanist Penn St Univ; Show Biz Kids & Show Choir 1st Place Superior Ratings Hershey Music in Parks Festival; Show Choir Outstanding Rating Music Maestro Please Inc 1988; *office:* Marlton Mid Sch Tomlinson Mill Rd Marlton NJ 08053

DIEBALL, JUDITH COLE, 4th Grade Teacher; *b:* Dayton, OH; *m:* Dennis Sr.; *c:* Dennis Jr., Ernest; *ed:* (BA) Ed, Toledo Univ 1976; Grad Stud Univ of Toledo; *cr:* 5th Grade Teacher Clinton Massie Schls 1964-67; 3rd-7th Grade Teacher Sherman Sch 1975-79; 4th Grade Teacher Edgewater 1980-; *ai:* Delta Kappa Gamma (Membership, VP) 1987-; PTA Rep, Teacher of Yr 1984; Young Astronauts (Chapter Leader, NW OH Rep, St Steering Comm); Inservice Teacher in Math & Sci 1990; Fellowship on Writing Project Univ of Toledo; Presenter Educl Symposium; Teacher of Yr 1984-85; 4th Grades Math Teachers Inservice TPS; Whos Who in Amer Ed 1984.

DIEBEL, MURIEL DAVIS, French Teacher; *b:* New Holstein, WI; *c:* Nathan, Mariah, Alicia, John; *ed:* (BA) Fr, Kent St Univ 1970; Grad Level Courses, Univ of Vt, Augusta Coll; *cr:* Teacher Main Street Sch 1971-76, Davidson Sch of Art 1980-83, Topeka KS 1983-84, Thomas Dale HS 1984-; *ai:* Adv Fr Club; Mem Volunteer Comm; Faculty Rep PTSA; Faculty Comm Mem; Crisis Team Faculty Rep; NHS; Teacher Trainer Chesterfield Cty; Spon Societe Honoraire de Francais; AATF 1984-; Parent Teacher Stu Assn Faculty Rep 1988-; *office:* Thomas Dale HS 3626 W Hundred Rd Chester VA 23831

DIEHL, ALTA A., Second Grade Teacher; *b:* Lurgon, PA; *m:* Jack E.; *ed:* (BS) Sci Ed, 1973, (MS) Ed, 1981 Bowling Green St Univ; Grad Stud Elem Ed; *cr:* Kndtn Teacher 1974-75, 2nd Grade Teacher 1975- South Main Elem; *ai:* Career Dev Chairperson; Martha Weber Rdng Cncl, Oh Cncl of Rdng, OH Ed Assn, NEA, Bowling Green Ed Assn Schlsp Comm; Meth Church (Comm Chairperson, Church Sch Dir 1989-, Church Choir Mem); South Main Elem Teacher of Yr 1988; Martha Holden Jennings Fnd Scholar 1988-89; *office:* South Main Elem Sch 437 S Main St Bowling Green OH 43402

DIEHL, CLARENCE HAROLD, Retired Teacher; *b:* Rapid City, SD; *m:* Agnes Marie Westbrook; *c:* Thomas D., Yolanda K. Diehl Obenour; *ed:* (BSE) Elem Ed, 1973, (MED) Elem Ed, 1979 Cntrl St Univ; *cr:* US Military Forces 1944-70; 6th Grade Teacher 1973-74, 5th Grade Teacher 1974-86 Tinker Elem Sch; *ai:* Girls Vlybl, Sftbl, Track Teams Coach; Textbook Review Comm; Kappa Delta Pi 1972-82; Alpha Chi 1973-74; PTA Mem; Disabled Amer Veterans Sr Vice Commander 1988-; Reserve Officers Assn 1979-.

DIEHL, GARY EDWARD, Eng/Creative Writing Teacher; *b:* Marshalltown, IA; *m:* Roberta A. Cross; *c:* Benjamin; *ed:* (BA) Music, 1961, (MA) Music Ed, 1964 UCLA; *cr:* Orchestra/Band Dir Buena HS 1964-70; Soc Stud Teacher De Anza Jr HS 1971-72; Eng Teacher Buena HS 1972-; *ai:* Spon Lit Mag Pawprint; Co-Coach for Knowledge Bowl Team; Chm for Writing Contest; Phi Delta Kappa 1972-; Fellow of South Coast Writing Proj 1980; Fellow in Lit South Coast Writing Proj 1989; Published As Free Lance Writer Natl Newspapers; *office:* Buena H S 5670 Telegraph Rd Ventura CA 93003

DIEHL, JOHN L., Business Education Chair; *b:* Salem, OH; *m:* Sharon L. Gintert; *c:* Chris, Mike; *ed:* (BA) Bus, Mt Union 1978; (BA) Math, Youngstown St 1982; *cr:* Bus Chm Bristol HS 1978-; *ai:* Boys Bsktbl & Girls Sftbl Head Coach; *office:* Bristol HS 1845 Greenville Rd Bristolville OH 44402

DIEHL, MARY JANE, Physical Education Teacher; *b:* Clearfield, PA; *ed:* (BS) Phys Ed, Slippery Rock Univ 1965; (MS) Phys Ed/Athletic Admin, W MD Coll 1988; Coaching/Physiology, Univ of IA 1971; *cr:* Teacher/Coach Curwensville Area Sch Dist 1969-72, Carlisle Area Sch Dist 1972-; *ai:* Bsktbl & Running Club Spon; Intramurals Indoor & Outdoor Track & Field Coach; Carlisle Sch Dist Athletic Cncl; Amer Bus Womens Assn 1989-; S PA Chapter Hall of Fame 1984-, Outstanding Coach 1987; US Field Hockey Assn Mid East Umpiring Chairperson 1980-84; Harrisburg Bd of Ofcls Interpreter 1980-86; Cntrl PA Ofcls Interpreter 1986-; Carlisle Area Ed Assn Building Rep 1978; ITEC Grant; *office:* Carlisle Area Sch Dist 777 S Hanover St Carlisle PA 17013

DIEHL, PENNY SUE (RUCH), Science Teacher; *b:* Sunbury, PA; *m:* Bradley Harold; *c:* Timothy, Johanna; *ed:* (BA) Bio, Shippensburg Univ 1981; Green Cntry Sci Teachers Wkshp 1987-; Continuing Ed, Bartlesville Wesleyan 1986-87, OK Univ 1986, Rodgers St Coll 1988; *cr:* Sci Long Term Substitute Teacher Shippensburg Sch Dist 1982; Dyeing Apprentice Richard Textiles 1982-83; Scndry Sci Teacher Copan Public Sch 1985-; *ai:* Copan Sci Fair Scndry Coord; 8th Grade Class Spon; Dist, St, Intnl Sci/Engineering Fair Teacher Spon; NSTA 1986, 1988-; OK Sci Teachers Assn 1989-; Oak Park United Meth (Church Ed Chairperson 1987-, Treas 1985-87); Scientific Academic Excl Washington-Nowata Cty Medical Society; OK Jr Acad Sci 1989, Intnl Sci & Engineering Fair Teacher Awd 1988; *office:* Copan Public Schls P O Box 429 Copan OK 74022

DIEKROEGER, KIMBERLY ANN, 7th/8th Social Studies Teacher; *b:* Pueblo, CO; *ed:* (BS) His, Eastern IL Univ 1982; *cr:* Soc Stud Teacher Vandalia JR HS 1985-; *ai:* Stu Cncl Spon; Jr HS Girls Track; HS Tennis; *office:* Vandalia Jr H S 1017 W Fletcher Vandalia IL 62471

DIELEMAN, EDWIN DEAN, 8th Grade Mathematics Teacher; *b:* Oskaloosa, IA; *m:* Marcia Ann Whitehead; *c:* Douglas, Deanne, Melanie; *ed:* (BA) Phys Ed, Univ of N IA 1967; Grad Stud Math & Sci; *cr:* Teacher/Coach Alburnett HS 1967-70, Twin Cedars HS 1970-80, Oskaloosa Jr HS 1980-; *ai:* 7th Grade Ftbl, Var Girls Track, 8th Grade Math Quiz Coach; ISEA, NEA 1967-; ICTM 1980-; *home:* 312 North D Street Oskaloosa IA 52577

DIENER, LARRY LINFORD, K-12 Vocal Music Teacher; *b:* Buffalo, NY; *m:* Doris Lucille Steiner; *c:* David, Deborah, Elizabeth; *ed:* (AA) Liberal Art, Hesston Coll 1969; (BA) Music Ed, Goshen Coll 1972; (MM) Music Ed, Cntrl MI Univ 1980; *cr:* K-12th Grade Vocal Music Teacher Choctaw Cntrl Schls 1972-77, Fairview Area Schls 1977-; *ai:* Vocal Soloists & Ensembles Coach; MI Sch Vocal Assn 1980-; Amer Choral Dir Assn 1990; United Meth Church Minister of Music 1976-77; Fairview Mennonite Church Minister of Music 1983-; Nom Outstanding Young Educator Awd Neshoba Cty 1976; Selected as Dir of Dist 9 All-Star Choir 1985, 1987; *home:* 2600 Oaks Rd Fairview MI 48621

DIENGER, JOSEPH EDWARD, Seventh Grade Teacher; *b:* Cincinnati, OH; *m:* Denise Ann Potticary; *c:* Ellen M., Stephen P., Amy E., Shawn J.; *ed:* (BS) Elem Ed, 1977, (MS) Ed, 1984 Xavier Univ; Cmptr Maintenance; *cr:* 6th/7th Grade Teacher All Saints Sch 1977-; *ai:* Sci Fair Coord; Trip Tour Dir; Catholic Youth Organization Referee; Ed Commission Rep; NCEA 1977-; *office:* All Saints Sch 8939 Montgomery Rd Cincinnati OH 45236

DIERCKS, DANIEL PAUL, English/Journalism Teacher; *b:* Greenville, SC; *m:* Rebecca Louies Jones; *c:* Allison C., Christopher K.; *ed:* (MS) Instructional Systems Technology, 1976, (BS) Journalism, 1972 IN Univ Bloomington; Post Grad Work Ball St Univ Munice, IN Univ East Richmond; *cr:* Teacher Hagerstown Jr-Sr HS 1976-; *ai:* Yrbk & Newspaper Adv; IN HS Press Assn VP 1984-85, 1976-, IN Journalism Teacher of Yr 1986; IN Cncl Teacerhs of Eng 1980-; Quill & Scroll Society 1976-; Hagerstown Lib Bd of Trustees 1987-; Hagerstown Bd of Zoning Appeals Pres 1980-; Hagerstown Plan Commission VP 1980-88; IN Dept of Ed Teacher of Yr Finalist 1990; IN HS Press Assn Journalism Teacher of Yr 1986; Articles Published; IN Univ HS Journalism Inst; *office:* Hagerstown HS 701 Baker Rd Hagerstown IN 47346

DIESENHOUSE, ARLENE PASTERNACK, Mathematics Teacher; *b:* New York, NY; *m:* Sheldon I.; *c:* Samantha, David; *ed:* (BA) Math, Coll of City of NY 1968; (MS) Admin/Supervision 1987, (CAS) Sch Bus Admin, 1989 St Univ of NY New Platz; *cr:* 7th-9th Grade Math Teacher South Jr HS 1968-69; 6th-9th Grade Math Teacher IS 320 Brooklyn 1969-73; Math Instr Orange Cty Comm Coll 1985-86; 9th-12th Grade Math Teacher Washington HS 1974-; *ai:* Academic Awds Ceremony; AMTNYS 1980-; Pine Bush Bd of Ed Mem 1985-; *office:* Washingtonville HS 54 W Main St Washingtonville NY 10992

DIETRICH, BETSY B., English as 2nd Lang Teacher; *ed:* (BA) Government/Fr, Smith Coll 160; (MAT) Scndry Ed, NY Univ 1961; Certificate Universite de Paris; Eng as 2nd Lang, Brown Univ; Dartmouth Coll; Universite de Strasbourg; Universite de Fribourg; *cr:* Fr Teacher Lexington Jr HS 1961-64; FR/His Teacher Providence Hebrew Day Sch 1976-84; Eng as 2nd Lang Teacher Providence Public Schls 1984-; *office:* Nathanael Green Mid Sch 721 Chalkstone Ave Providence RI 02908

DIETRICH, DENNIS EDWARD, Social Studies Teacher; *b:* Buffalo, NY; *m:* Linda Ann Helmer; *c:* Timothy M., Leigh A.; *ed:* (BA) Soc Stud/Scndry Ed, NE St Teachers Coll 1968; (MS) Soc Stud Ed, Buffalo St Teachers Coll 1973; Staff Dev Trng; Admin/Supervision Courses; *cr:* Teacher Buffalo City Schls 1968-78, Buffalo Traditional Sch 1978-87, Hutchinson Cntrl Tech HS 1987-; Part Time Staff Developer Buffalo Public Schls 1987-; *ai:* Track & Field Ofcl; Stu Government Adv; Project Bus Jr Achievement; Career Awareness Coord; ASCD Mem 1986-; Natl Cncl Staff Dev Mem 1986-; NEA Mem 1968; Buffalo Teachers Fed Delegate 1968-72; NYS Staff Dev Cncl 1987-; Buffalo Sch Masters Assn 1968-; Parent Teacher Cncls All Schls 1968-; VP Morningside Homeowners Assn 1982; Honorary Mem Kappa Sigma Phi; Hutchinson Cntrl Tech HS Won Natl Schls for Excl Awd 1988-89; Various Curr Comm for Buffalo City Schls;

Presenter at NYS Staff Dev Conference 1990; *office:* Hutchinson Cntrl Tech HS 256 S Elmwood Ave Buffalo NY 14202

DIETRICH, JUDITH MORGENSTERN, Spanish/Comm Skills Teacher; *b:* Cleveland, OH; *m:* John Michael; *c:* Julia A., Dennis M.; *ed:* (BS) Scndry Ed, OH Univ 1970; (MS) Ed, IN Univ 1980; La Universidad Veracruzana Xalapa Mexico 1969; Process Writing Trng, St of IN; Trainer for TESA Prgm; *cr:* Span Teacher Wyoming HS 1971-72; Span/Comm Skills Teacher Meridian Mid 1975-; *ai:* TESA Trainer; Process Writing Prgm Coord; IN Teachers of Writing 1988-; NEA 1985-; Perry Local Educators Pres 1976-80; Crisis Pregnancy Center Cnslr 1988-; Presbyn Church (Sunday Sch Teacher, Youth Camp Cnslr) 1986-89; Eli Lilly Grant 1989-; WRTV Teacher of Week 1990; Author of Process Writing Curr 1991; *office:* Meridian Mid Sch 8040 S Meridian Indianapolis IN 46217

DIETRICH, MICHAEL STEVEN, Mathematics Teacher; *b:* Cumberland, WI; *m:* Debra Renee Johnson; *ed:* (BA) Math Ed, Univ of WI Eau Claire 1987; Transition to Coll Math & Algebra Accents Seminars; *cr:* Math Teacher Berlin HS 1987-; *ai:* Jr Var Bsbl Coach; Frosh Bsktbl Coach; Math Team Adv; AODA Co-Facilitor; Ski Club Adv; Gifted & Talented Comm Mem; Curr Comm; Berlin Little League & Bsktbl Prgm Coach 1989-; *office:* Berlin HS 289 E Huron Berlin WI 54923

DIETZ, ELIZABETH ANN, Junior HS Vocal Music Teacher; *b:* Bethlehem, PA; *ed:* (BS) Music Ed, West Chester St 1968; Teaching Courses; Stu Assistance Prgm Trng; *cr:* Elem Music Teacher 1968-69, Jr HS Vocal Teacher 1969-76, Elem Music Teacher 1976-81, Jr HS Vocal Teacher 1981- Boyertown Sch Dist; *ai:* Girls, Mixed, Male Chorus; Var Singers Show Choir; Musical Dir; Asst Lacrosse Coach; Amer Choral Dirs Assn, Music Educators Natl Conference; Boyertown Ed Assn; Cedarville United Meth Church Choir Dir; Ocean Grove Campmeeting Assn (Youth Dir, Choral Dramatics) 1985-; *office:* Boyertown Area Sch Dist 2020 Big Rd Gilbertsville PA 19525

DIETZ, GEORGE A., Chem Teacher/Asst Prin; *b:* Stuttgart, West Germany; *m:* Diana Bearder; *c:* Christopher; *ed:* (BS) Bio, GA Inst Technology 1976; (MED) Mid Sch Ed, GA St Univ 1978; *cr:* Math/Sci Teacher 1977-80, Sci Teacher/Asst Prin 1980- Woodward Acad; *ai:* Var Girls Soccer Coach; NSTA 1977-; *office:* Woodward Acad 1662 Rugby Ave College Park GA 30337

DIETZE, JUDY HUFFHINES, Third Grade Teacher; *b:* Port Arthur, TX; *m:* Robert Lee; *c:* Cathy, Deborah; *ed:* Elem Ed, TX Womens Univ 1964; *cr:* 3rd Grade Teacher Wallace Elem 1964-69, Brentfield Elem 1979-; *home:* 604 Westwood Richardson TX 75080

DIEZ, MARGO WILSON, Spanish Teacher; *b:* Bluefield, WV; *m:* Pablo; *c:* Beatriz, Emily; *ed:* (BS) Span/Ed/Eng, OH St Univ 1971; Ofcl Sch of Lang 1974-75; TESA 1982; *cr:* Span/Eng Teacher St Francis De Sales HS 1971-74; Eng Teacher Mater Salvatoris 1974-81; Span/Eng Teacher Mifflin Mid Sch 1981-84; Span Teacher St Francis De Sales HS 1984-; *ai:* Span Club; Wrestling Stat Adv; Columbus Diocese Ed Assn 1984-; *office:* St Francis De Sales HS 4212 Karl Rd Columbus OH 43224

DIFFIE, JOHN EDWARD, Physics/Physical Sci Teacher; *b:* Little Rock, AR; *m:* Pret Marie Kays; *c:* Donna, Joseph, Colin; *ed:* (BS) Bio/Chem, Univ of AR Little Rock 1964; (MS) Environmental Sci, Univ of TX Dallas 1978; *cr:* Sci/Math Teacher Booker T Washington HS for Performing & Visual Art 1981-; *office:* Booker T Washington HS 2501 Flora Dallas TX 75201

DIFFINE, SUZANNE MICHELE, Curriculum Resource Specialist; *b:* Tonawanda, NY; *ed:* (BA) Eng, 1970, (MA) Eng, 1977 St Univ of NY Buffalo; NY Univ 1971-72, St Univ of NY Buffalo 1982-84; *cr:* 7th/8th Grade Eng Teacher Buffalo Bd of Ed 1977-78, PS #29 1978-81; 5th-8th Grade Teacher Cause Sch 1981-83; 7th/8th Grade Eng Teacher Frederick Law Olmsted Sch 1983-85, 1986-89; *ai:* Natl Jr Honor Society, N Dist Stu Cncl, Olmsted Stu Cncl & Stus Against Doing Drugs Adv; Home Instruction Tutor; Sat Prep Adv; Advocacy for Gifted & Talented Ed Mem; NY Inst for Arts in Ed Mem Teacher Advisory Comm, Albright Knox Art Gallery Mem, Just Buffalo Literary Guild (Cooperating Teacher, Mem) 1988-; Literature on Overrepresentation of Minorities in Handicapped Conditions & Sch Suspensions; Currently Rewriting Eng Curr for Gifted Children; *home:* 45 Guilford Ln #1 Williamsville NY 14221

DI GIESI, JOHN VINCENT, Eighth Grade Teacher; *b:* Philadelphia, PA; *ed:* (BA) Ed/Eng, La Salle Univ 1982; *cr:* 9th/10th Grade Teacher North Cath HS 1982-83; 9th Grade Teacher Father Judge HS 1983-84; 7th Grade Teacher 1984-86, 8th Grade Teacher 1986- Ascension of Our Lord Sch; *ai:* Sch Yrbk Adv; Stu Cncl & Dance Moderator; Lang Art Coord; Christmas Drive Spirit Comm; Teacher of Yr Ascension Sch 1985; *office:* Ascension of Our Lady Sch 735 E Westmoreland St Philadelphia PA 19134

DI GIOVANNI, MARY LOU A., Second Grade Teacher; *b:* Norristown, PA; *ed:* (BS) Elem Ed - Cum Laude, Gwynedd-Mercy Coll 1973; *cr:* 3rd Grade Teacher Worcester Sch 1973-74; 2nd Grade Teacher Audubon Sch 1974-84, Woodland Sch 1984-; *ai:* Evaluating Writing Samples Comm; Writing Assessor for 2nd Grade Wkshp; PA St Ed Assn, NEA, Methacton Ed Assn; Received Letters of Recognition from Asst Supt; Deans List; Received Prof Recognition & Dept Honors; *office:* Woodland Elem Sch Kriebel Mill Rd Fairview Vlg PA 19403

DI GIROLAMO, ROSINA RENA, English Teacher/Dept Chm; *b:* Monterey, CA; *ed:* (AA) Liberal Arts, Monterey Peninsula Coll 1965; (BA) Sociology, CA St Univ 1967; (MA) Curr Dev, CA Poly St 1975; *cr:* 6th Grade Teacher Ord Terrace Elem 1968-69; 5th/6th Grade Teacher Hayes Elem 1969-71; 6th Grade Teacher Marshall Elem 1971-75; Rdng/Eng Teacher King Jr HS 1975-83; Eng Teacher Walter Colton Mid Sch 1985-; *ai:* Stu Act Dir; Sch Improvement Comm; Human Relations Team Adv; Assn Rep; Dept Chm; Newspaper Adv; Sch Report Card Comm; Monterey Bay Teachers Org; Amer Assn Univ Women Cmmty Liason 1989-; CA Assn of Compensatory Ed Treas 1985-87 & Schlrsp 1987-89; *office:* Walter Colton Mid Sch Colton Dr & Via Gayuba Monterey CA 93940

DI GREGORIO, MARY GERVASI, Third Grade Teacher/Religion; *b:* Boston, MA; *ed:* (BS) Ed, St Josephs Coll 1952; Theology Cert Regis Coll 1968-70; (MED) Religious Ed, Boston Coll 1974; (CPE) Pastoral Care, Santa Maria Hospital 1985; Numerous Wkshps; *cr:* Secy/Bookkeeper Prudence & Carter Clothing 1939-42; 1st-6th Grade Teacher Sisters of St Joseph 1944-74; Religious Ed Coord I C Parish 1974-77; Teacher Sisters of St Joseph 1977-; *ai:* CSJ Liturgical Commission & Choir; Eucharistic & Elderly Minister; Conduct Prayer Groups & Recollection Day; Hospital Volunteer; Teacher Trng; NCEA 1977-; S Shore Coords Chairperson 1975-76; Liturgical Commission 1978-; Intnl Rdng Assn 1980-86; Parish Cncl 1972-77; Stoughton Cncl on Aging 1974-77; Stoughton Interfaith 1974-77; MA Citizens for Life 1978-; Radio Broadcasts; Helped Stus Win Awds; *home:* Maria Convent 106 Waban St Newton MA 02158

DI LELLO, ANNETTE J., Mathematics Teacher; *b:* Albany, NY; *ed:* (BS) Bio/Chem, St Univ of NY Albany 1984; Cert Scndry Sch Sci, Univ of S FL 1989; Working Toward Masters Sci Ed, Univ FL St; *cr:* Sci Teacher 1989-, Math Teacher/Goals 1989- Largo HS; *ai:* Sr Class Spon & Adv; Hospitality Comm; Teacher of Week Largo HS 1989; *office:* Largo HS 410 Missouri Ave Largo FL 34640

DI LELLO, ANTOINETTE MARIE, Vice Prin & 5th Grade Teacher; *b:* Yonkers, NY; *ed:* (BA) Fr/Italian/Religion, 1980, (MA) Rdng, 1983 Manhattan Coll; Catechist Formation Prgm Level I & II; *cr:* 5th Grade Teacher 1981-, Vice Prin 1988- St Paul the Apostle; *ai:* Intnl Rdng Assn, Alpha Upsilon Alpha Mem 1989-; Enrico Fermi Ed Fund (Mem, Advisory Bd) 1976-; Manhattan Coll Rdng Cncl Mem 1989-; Enrico Fermi Schlsp Breakfast (Co Chairperson Arrangements 1987, Schlsp & Breakfast Reception 1976-); *office:* St Paul the Apostle 77 Lee Ave Yonkers NY 10705

DILKS, EDWIN KELVIN, History Teacher/Activity Dir; *b:* Ft Worth, TX; *ed:* (BS) Ed/Drama His, Abilene Chrstn View 1986; *cr:* Teacher 1987, Activity Dir 1989- Haltom HS; *ai:* High on Life & Home Ec Dir; 1 Act Play Asst Dir; Asst Class Spon; ATPE Mem 1987-; Alpha Phi Omega 1985-; Outstanding Young Man of America 1990; *office:* Haltom HS 5501 Haltam Rd Haltom City TX 76137

DILL, RICK, Social Studies Teacher/Coach; *b:* Frederick, OK; *m:* Teresa; *c:* Tina, Gina; *ed:* (BA) Health/Phys Ed Recreation/Soc Stud, SW St Univ Weatherford 1970; *cr:* World His Teacher/Head Ftbl Coach Gallup Mc Kinley Cty 1971-73, Valley HS 1973-77; Civics/His Teacher/Asst Ftbl/head Track Coach Bristow Public Schls 1978-; *ai:* Ftbl/Track Coach; Natl Coaches Assn 1971-; OK Coaches Assn, OK Track Coaches Assn 1978-; Regional Track Coach of Yr 1983-84, 1985-86, 1988-89; All St Ftbl Coach 1990; Bristow Public Schls Class of 40 Teacher of Yr 1988; *office:* Bristow Public Schls 109 W 9th Bristow OK 74010

DILLARD, JACK DAVID, Science Department Chair; *b:* Marble, NC; *m:* Janice Spurrier; *c:* Andrew, Jared; *ed:* (BA) Bio/Chem, Sch of Ozarks 1975; Working Towards Masters Bio; *cr:* Sci Teacher Chadwick HS 1976, Hollister HS 1976-81, Sci Teacher/Dept Chm West Plains R-7 1981-; *ai:* Sci Club, Beta Chi Pi, Hamm Radio Club Spon; Sci Symposium Dir; STOM 1985-90; NSTA 1983-91; MSTA 1981-85; Natl Audubon (VP 1987-89, Pres 1989-); Steering Comm Mem for Interface St Dept of Elem Scndry Ed Math & Sci Prgm; Sci Care Competencies Comm St MMAT Test Dev; *office:* West Plains HS 602 E Olden West Plains MO 65775

DILLARD, KIM ZEBULUN, Tennis Director; *b:* Washington, DC; *m:* Zoe Ann Wages; *c:* Ashley, Faye; *ed:* (BS) Phys Ed & Health, High Point Coll 1976; Tennis Team High Point Coll 1976; *cr:* Tennis Dir & Womens Coach Flagler Coll 1977-78; Head Tennis Prof Cardinal Hill Wwim & Racquet Club 1976-85; Vienna Woods Swim & Tennis Club 1985-89; Phys Ed Inst Wolftrap Elem Sch 1978-89; Dir of Tennis Catawba Cntry Club 1989-; *ai:* US Tennis Assn 1976-; US Prof Tennis Assn 1983-; First Presbyn Church 1989-; 2 Articles Published in Tennis Magazine; Current Top Ranked Player in 35 Age Group Doubles FR NC; *office:* Catawba Country Club PO Box 208 Newton NC 28658

DILLARD, SAMUEL O., Physical Education Teacher; *b:* Shreveport, LA; *ed:* (AA) Ed, Crowder Jr Coll 1974; (BS) Phys Ed, Evangel Coll 1977; Grad Stud in Soc Stud & Health Sci; *cr:* Teacher/Coach Cincinnati Chrstn HS 1977-; *ai:* Var Soccer & Bsktbl Coach; SW OH Soccer Coaches Assn 1986-, Coach of Yr 1987; SW OH Bsktbl Coaches Assn 1987-; Cincinnati Post Coach of Yr 1988; *home:* 70 Fawn Dr Apt 2 Fairfield OH 45014

DILLARD, VICKIE ANN (DANIELS), Third Grade Teacher; *b:* Murphysboro, IL; *m:* Gregory Lane; *ed:* Elem Ed, John A Logan Jr Coll 1972; (BA) S IL Univ 1974; *cr:* 3rd Grade Teacher Carrier Mills-Stonefort Unit 2 1976-; *ai:* Church Primary Teacher 1975-; *home:* Rt 2 Box 407 Harrisburg IL 62946

DILLAVOU, ROBERT L., Social Studies Teacher; *b:* Burlington, IA; *ed:* (BS) Speech/Drama/Soc Sci, IL St Univ 1965; Southern IL Univ/Northern IL Univ/Loyola/Univ of Chicago; *cr:* Teacher Forrestville Valley Unit Dist 221 1965-; *ai:* Jr HS Stu Cncl 1970-; Jr HS Sfety Patrol 1965-; Forrestville Valley Ed Assn (Pres 1970-71; Treas 1975-76/1984-85); Forreston Cmmty Club; Forreston Lib Bd (Pres) 1973-89; Mayor of Forreston IL 1989.

DILLENBURG, MICHAEL DAVID, Phys Ed & Health Dept Chair; *b:* Brementon, WA; *m:* Carla Jene Carroll; *c:* Adam, Matt; *ed:* (AA) General, Yakima Valley Coll 1974; (BA) Ed/Health/Phys Ed, 1977, (MED) Health, 1982 OR St Univ; First Aid Instr Red Cross; *cr:* Phys Ed/Health Teacher Brookings-Harbor HS 1977-; *ai:* Head Wrestling, Asst Ftbl & Track Coach; Weightlifting Room Adv; AAPHER, OR Coach Assn 1980; Brookings Ed Assn VP 1988-89; BSA Adv 1986-; Presbyn Church Mem 1980; Nom Teacher of Yr 1986; Wrestling Head Coach of Culture Exch Team to Korea; *office:* Brookings-Harbor HS 625 Pioneer St Brookings OR 97415

DILLER, MARCELLA M., Teacher of Gifted/Talented/Eng; *b:* Sherman Cty, TX; *ed:* (BA) Eng, Mt St Scholastica 1961; (MA) Eng, Notre Dame Univ 1966; Eng, Univ of CO; Theatre Work, Univ of Denver; *cr:* 5th/8th Grade Elem Teacher Various Cath Schls KS 1951-68; Eng Teacher Mullen HS 1968-76; Teacher of Gifted & Talented Pampa Mid Sch & HS 1983-; Personnel Dir St Catherine Hospital; *ai:* Various Competitions; Mid Sch Newspaper; Kappa Kappa Kappa VP 1984-89; Literacy Prgm 1985-; Probation Cnslr 1969-75, Certificate 1973; Eng Teaching Fellowship Univ of CO Boulder 1977-78; *home:* 1105 Charles St Pampa TX 79065

DILLMAN, DAVID KEVIN, Mathematics/English Teacher; *b:* Chicago, IL; *m:* Judith L.; *c:* Katherine, Jennifer, Joshua, Timothy; *ed:* (BS) Math, St Josephs Coll 1972; (MS) Math, IN St Univ 1973; *cr:* Teacher Horicon Jr HS 1973-77, North Division HS 1986-88, Kewaskum HS 1988-; *ai:* Jr Var Boys Bsktbl & Girls Sftbl Coach; Yrbk Adv; Lomira Fire Dept 1983-; *office:* Kewaskum HS 1510 Bilgo Ln Kewaskum WI 53040

DILLMAN, GLEN DEAN, Social Studies Teacher; *b:* Logansport, IN; *m:* Martha Lou Miller; *c:* Alan, Jennifer; *ed:* (BS) Soc Stud, Manchester Coll 1969; (MS) IN Univ 1973; Grad Stud Purdue Univ, Univ of CA Los Angeles, Univ of VA, Univ of Chicago; *cr:* Teacher Carroll Jr-Sr HS 1969-; *ai:* Sycamore His Club & Carroll Historians Spon; Sch Evaluation Comm; Carroll Ed Assn Pres 1977-78; NEA 1975-; Flora Lions Pres 1978-; Flora Lib Bd Pres 1980-89; Carroll Cty Historical Society; IN Historical Society; IN St Teacher of Yr 1984; IN Daughters of Amer Revolution Teacher of Amer His 1984; Eli Lilly Teacher of Creativity Grant 1987; Stratford Hall Monticello Seminar 1988; Sagamore of Wabash; Manchester Alumni Teacher of Yr 1989.

DILLMAN, PAUL D., Teacher/Ind Tech Chairman; *b:* Nitro, WV; *m:* Linda K. Mathes; *c:* Wendy A., Gerald D.; *ed:* (BS) Ind Technology, WV St Coll 1967; WV Univ; Marshall Univ; *cr:* Teacher St Albans HS 1966-73; Spring Hill Jr HS 1973-79; Mc Kinley Jr HS 1979-; *ai:* Head Coach Girls Track; Coach; Jr HS Girls Bsktbl Boys Track & Boys Tennis; Little League Sftbl Baseball; WV Prof Ed 1989-; Mason 1969-.

DILLON, PATRICK JOSEPH, English Teacher/Eng Dept Chair; *b:* Jackson, MI; *m:* Elizabeth Ann; *c:* Matthew, Erin; *ed:* (MA) Sch Admin, W MI Univ 1989; *cr:* Eng Teacher Reading Cmmty Schls 1983-84; Prin St Anthony Elem Sch 1984-85; Eng Teacher Reading Cmmty Schls 1985-; *ai:* Var Bsbl, Asst Var Ftbl, Jr Var Bsktbl Coach; Quiz Bowl; Curr Comm; NCTE 1984-; MI HS Athletic Assn 1983-; MI HS Bsbl Coaches Assn Dist Rep.

DILLS, LINDA A., High School Business Teacher; *b:* Hobart, OK; *m:* Robert E.; *c:* Brandon, Justin, Monty; *ed:* (BS) Psych/Bus Ed, KS St Univ 1972; Grad Stud; *cr:* Bank Teller 1st Natl Bank Lebanon 1964-69; Bank Bookkeeper 1st Natl Bank Mankato 1973; Career Ed Teacher Chaparral HS 1975; Substitute Teacher United Sch Dist 361 1975-81; Bus Instr Chaparral HS 1981-; *ai:* Jr Class & Prom Spon; KBEA; Harper Cty Ed Assn Secy 1987-88; Zoning Appeals Bd Pres 1981-; PEO; Beta Sigma Phi; *office:* Chaparral HS 124 N Jennings Rt 1 Anthony KS 67003

DIMA-FERGUSON, DEBORAH, Language Arts Teacher; *b:* Evergreen Park, IL; *m:* Robert M. Ferguson; *ed:* (BA) Eng, W IL Univ 1972; (MSED) Counseling, IL St Univ 1980; *cr:* Lang Art Teacher Cntrl Jr HS 1973-; *office:* Central Jr HS 17248 67th Ave Tinley Park IL 60477

DI MARTINO, JULIA, Math Teacher; *b:* Mount Holly, NJ; *ed:* (BA) Math, Glassboro St Coll 1986; Counseling, Personnel Services; *cr:* Math Teacher Florence HS 1986-; *ai:* Class Adv; Adult Sch Teach Algebra; Frosh Field Hockey Coach; Liason Comm; After Sch HSPT Prgm; NJEA, NEA 1986-; Golden Eagle Band Inc VP 1987-88; *office:* Florence Memorial H S Front St Florence NJ 08518

DIMICK, PATRICIA BUERKI, Jr HS Home Economics Teacher; *b:* Wichita, KS; *m:* Ken; *c:* Jonathan; *ed:* (BA) Home Ec Ed, Friends Univ 1984; Working Towards Masters Teaching; *cr:* Home Ec Teacher Goddard Jr HS 1984-; *ai:* 9th Grade Vlybl, HS Asst Girls Bsktbl, Jr HS Track Coach; Sex Ed Curr Comm; Outstanding Young Women of America 1985; *office:* Goddard Jr HS 335 N Walnut Goddard KS 67052

DIMMICH, KATHLEEN BROBST, Librarian-HS/Scndry Lib Coord; *b:* Allentown, PA; *m:* Jeffrey Robert; *ed:* (BS) Lib Ed, Kutztown Univ 1970; (MLS) Reference/Tech Services, Univ of Pittsburgh 1971; (MS) Instructional Technology, Shippensburg Univ 1973; Cmptr Technology, Instructional Methods, Lib Sci; *cr:* Dir Curr Lib Shippensburg Univ 1971-73; Elem Librarian Bethlehem Sch Dist 1973-74; Asst Dir of Learning Resource Center Lehigh Cty Comm Coll 1974-76; Reference/IL Librarian Stroudsburg Univ 1976-78; Elem Librarian Cetronia-Parkland Sch Dist 1978-86; HS Librarian Parkland HS 1986-; *ai:* Scholastic Scrimmage, Knowledge Masters Open Adv; PA Sch Lib Organization Treas 1988-; Lehigh Valley PA Sch Lib Assn Treas; PA Lib Assn (BD Mem, Regional Chairperson) 1976-78; Beacham Press Writing Awd.

DIMMICK, CHRISTINA FISCHER, 8th Grade US History Teacher; *b:* Roslyn, WA; *m:* Richard; *c:* Gregory Bramme, David Pottorff; *ed:* (BA) Ed, Cntrl WA Univ 1963; Purkey Class on Inviting Schls; Ed, WA Cntrl Univ; *cr:* 8th Grade Home Ec Teacher 1963-76, 8th Grade His Teacher 1976- Park Mid Sch; *ai:* Mid Sch, Self Study, AODA Steering, Survey Sub, Drug Awareness, Mid Sch 2000, Soc Stud Comms; Drama & Track Coach; Anchor Teacher; Track Meet Announcer; KEA Pres 1963-; NEA, WEA Rep Assembly Delegate 1963-; Delta Kappa Gamma Pres 1975-78; Lang Art Comm Parks Rep; Southwest Uniserv Pres; WA St Sch Employee Credit Union Advisory Comm Mem; Desert Sun Guild; CCD Religious Class Teacher; Nom Teacher of Yr 1988-89; *office:* Park Mid Sch 1011 W 10th Ave Kennewick WA 99336

DIMOS, SHERI BISHOP, English Department Chair; *b:* Indianapolis, IN; *m:* John G.; *ed:* (BA) Eng, 1986, (BA) Span, 1986 Evangel Coll; *cr:* Eng Dept Chairperson Mansfield HS 1986-; *ai:* Foreign Lang Club, Pep Club, Chrldr Spon; Academic Letter, Weighted-Class, NHS Selection Comm; NCTE 1986-89; *office:* Mansfield HS 300 W Ohio Ave Mansfield MO 65704

DINELLI, DONALD RAY, Social Science Teacher; *b:* La Salle, IL; *ed:* (BS) His, Loyola Univ 1966; (MA) Educl Admin, Univ of San Francisco 1984; *cr:* Lang Art Teacher W Madison Jr HS 1966-67; Soc Sci Teacher Mc Clymonds HS 1968-75; Soc Sci Teacher 1976-78, Dir of Stu Act/Testing 1979-81, Soc Sci Teacher 1981- Fremont HS; *ai:* Chm Alternative Schls & Vice Chm Soc Comm; Bay Area Network of Gay & Lesbian Teachers Area Chm 1985-89; Author; *office:* Fremont HS 4610 Foothill Blvd Oakland CA 94601

DINES, ALAN JOHN, History Teacher; *b:* Pittsburgh, PA; *m:* Ruth H. Sommers; *c:* Terrill, Christian, Samuel; *ed:* (BA) Soc Stud, Westminster Coll 1975; Grad Stud Several Colls; *cr:* 9th/10th Grade His Teacher Montour HS 1979-; *ai:* Montour HS Head Var Track Coach; Montour Scndry His Dept Chairperson; Jr Class, Prom, His Club Spon; Jr Var Track Coach; NEA, PSEA, Montour Ed Assn 1979-; Kenmawr United Presbyn Church (Deacon, Elder, Lifetime Mem); Historical Society of W PA Hands on His Awd; Duquesne His Forum Panel Mem; *office:* Montour HS Clever Rd Mc Kees Rocks PA 15136

DINGLE, BECKY BARBOUR, 8th Grade Soc Studies Teacher; *b:* Fayetteville, NC; *m:* Dickey R. Jr.; *c:* Mandy, Walsh, Tommy; *ed:* (BA) His, Erskine Coll 1971; Citadel; *cr:* 8th Grade Teacher Soc Stud Alston Mid Sch 1971-; *ai:* Natl Jr Beta Club Spon; Sunshine Fund; Sch Imprvmnt Cncl; Quest - Coach Acdmc Comptn; Palmetto Teachers Orgnztn Mem 1981-; Alpha Delta Kappa, Historian 1987; Teacher of Yr 1985-86; *office:* Alston Mid Sch 500 Bryan St Summerville SC 29483

DINGUS, RALPH WALDO, 8th Grade Teacher; *b:* Martin, KY; *ed:* (AB) Art, 1970, (MA) Ed, 1973, (Rank I) Ed, 1978, (Rank I) Admin, 1981 Morehead St Univ; KY Intern Teacher Prgm; *cr:* 8th Grade Teacher Martin Elem 1973-74; Art Teacher 1974-78, 7th/8th Grade Teacher 1978- Prestonsburg Elem; *ai:* KY Youth Assembly & United Nations Assembly Adv 1989-; Decoration Comm Christmas & Spring Dances Spon; Sch Annual Designs & Layouts; Prepare Sch Bus & Hall Duty Schedule for Sch Faculty; *home:* PO Box 201 Martin KY 41649

DINH, VAN PHUC, Teacher; *b:* Ninh Binh, Vietnam; *m:* Chanh T.; *c:* Vu P., Van T., Viet P.; *ed:* (BS) Ed, S IL Univ 1964; Licencie Es Lettres-Linguistics, Dalat Univ 1972; (MA) Ed, S IL Univ 1977; ESOL; Bi-ling, Multicultural Ed; *cr:* Instr Natl Military Acad Dalat 1967-73, Dalat Univ 1973-75; TOSA Office of Bi-ling Multicultural Ed 1978-83; Teacher Cole Mid Sch 1983-; *ai:* Teaching Vietnamese Lang & Culture to Vietnamese Children, Sponsoring & Advising the TET Celebration According to Traditional Customs; Vietnamese Buddhist Assn Bd Mem 1980-; Univ of Denver Ethnic Heritage Prgm Chairperson of Advisory Bd 1979-83; Natl Assn for Vietnamese Amer Ed Mem 1979-85; Teaching Assistantship S IL Univ; Intnl Ed SIU Tuition Awd; Article Published 1976; *home:* 3162 Wheeling St Aurora CO 80011

DININGER, EDWARD LOWELL, Mathematics Department Teacher; *b:* Tiffin, OH; *m:* Janet Sauder; *c:* Edward, Tabetha; *ed:* (BA) Physics, Southern Coll 1973; (MA) Educl Policy/Leadership, OH St Univ 1990; *cr:* St of TN 1972-74; OH Conference of SDA 1974-84; Physics/Math Instr Mt Vernon Acad 1984-; *ai:* Sch Bd Chm; Asst to Prin; Public Relations Officer; Stu Assn Spon; Zapara Teaching Excl Awd; *office:* Mt Vernon Acad 15 Fairgrounds Box 311 Mount Vernon OH 43050

DINKFELD, ROBERT CHRISTOPHER, Elem Phys Ed Teacher; *b:* Glendale, CA; *m:* Marsha Lane Hawkins; *ed:* (BS) Phys Ed, Cntrl MI Univ 1970; *cr:* Phys Ed Teacher Shepherd Public Schls 1973-; *ai:* Girls Cross Cntry Coach; MEA 1973-; SEA Negotiator 1976-; *office:* Shepherd Public Schls 238 S Chippewa St Shepherd MI 48883

DINKINS, GLENDA ALLUMS, Third Grade Teacher; *b:* Minden, LA; *m:* Charlie; *c:* Shumon, Shundra; *ed:* (BS) Elem Ed, Grambling St Univ 1964; (MED) Elem Ed, Prairie View A & M 1968; Grad Work; *cr:* Teacher Webster Parish Sch System, Bossier Parish Sch System, Caddo Parish Sch System; *ai:* PTO, Parents, Teachers & Stus Organization; Yeomans Club; NEA, LA Ed Assn; Caddo Ed Assn Rooky Teacher 1966; *office:* Hillsdale Elem Sch 3860 Hutchinson St Shreveport LA 71109

DINSMORE, BETTY ANN (WILSON), 6th Grade Teacher; *b:* Trenton, MO; *m:* William L.; *c:* Deborah L., Steven L.; *ed:* (BA) Ed, William Jewell Coll 1953; (MA) Ed, Cntrl MO St Univ 1974; *cr:* 2nd Grade Teacher N Kansas City Schls 1953-62; Rdng Specialist 1976-, 6th Grade Teacher 1989- Liberty Public Schls; *ai:* Heartland Nursing Home Volunteer; Liberty Sch Dist Lang & Rdng Comm; Alpha Delta Kappa (Pres, Secy, Treas, Pledge Chm) 1953-; NEA Membership Comm Chm 1989-; Wrote Grants for Liberty Dist.

DINSMORE, JOETTA CAROL, English Department Chair; *b:* San Antonio, TX; *m:* Michael O'Neal; *c:* Mayme, Alice A.; *ed:* (BS) Eng/Health/Phys Ed, 1969, (MA) Eng, 1979 Austin Peay St Univ; *cr:* Phys Ed Teacher Montgomery Cntrl Elem 1969; Eng Teacher Montgomery Cntrl HS 1970-; *ai:* Literary Magazine & Sr Class Spon; Eng Dept Chm 1970-83, 1988-; System Eng Dept Chm 1976-80; Delta Kappa Gamma Mem 1970-80; CMCEA Rep 1970-80, 1983-85; *home:* 2779 Palmyra Rd Palmyra TN 37142

DINSMORE, JUDITH SZALL, 8th Grade Math Teacher; *b:* Union City, PA; *m:* William H. Jr.; *c:* Andrew, Nicholas; *ed:* (BS) Psych, Thiel Coll 1969; (MED) Guidance & Counseling/Scndry, Edinboro Univ 1975; *cr:* Spec Ed Teacher Union City HS 1969-70; Ld Teacher IU 5 Northwest Tri County 1972-74; 8th Grade Math Teacher 1974-; Guidance Cnslr 1985 Fort Leboeuf M Id Sch; *ai:* Impact Core Team; Math Counts Coach; PA Math League Adv; St Teresas Church Choir Dir 1985-; Cursillo Movement; *home:* Box 15 Mill Village PA 16427

DINWIDDIE, SUSAN MC DOWALL, Band Director; *b:* Duluth, GA; *m:* Robert G. Jr.; *c:* Robert Gene III, Rebecca Catherine; *ed:* (BMED) Music Ed, 1974, (MMED) Music Ed, 1979 Univ of GA; *cr:* Band Dir Loganville HS 1974-78, Carver Jr HS 1979-; *ai:* Music Act; GA Music Educators Assn Chm 10th Dist 1988-; Atlanta Journal-Constitution Honor Teacher Awd Finalist Mid Sch Level 1985; *home:* 1012 E Church St Monroe GA 30655

DION, DAVID ARTHUR, Business Teacher; *b:* Keokuk, IA; *m:* Elaine Ann Markovich; *ed:* (BS) Bus Ed, 1971, (MS) Bus Ed, 1986 IL St Univ; *cr:* Bus Teacher Brown Cty HS 1972-75, Hamilton HS 1975-; *ai:* Asst Varsity Ftbl Coach; Spon Class of 1990; Mem Cmptr Curr Comm; IL Bus Ed Assn (Exec Bd 1989-) 1972-; Hamilton Ed Assn 1975-; Delta Pi Epsilon 1984-; W IL Area Bus Ed Assn VP 1990; Hamilton Lions Club Trustee 1989-; St of IL Voc Instructor Practicum, 1987 & 1989; *office:* Hamilton HS 1100 Keokuk St Hamilton IL 62341

DION, RAYMOND L., Health Teacher; *b:* Seattle, WA; *m:* Sandra A. Mac Lean; *c:* Melissa, Holly; *ed:* (BAED) Gen Sci, W WA St Coll 1972; (MAT) Integrated Sci, Lewis & Clark Coll 1977; Trainer of Trainers Drug Curr & Refusal Skills; Impact & Insite Drug Intervention Trng; Slavin Model Cooperative Team Learning; *cr:* Sci Teacher Covington Jr HS 1973-74; Sci/Health Teacher Ringdall Jr HS 1974-87; Health Teacher Tyle Mid Sch 1987-; *ai:* Natural Helpers Trainer; NEA, WA Ed Assn, Bellevue Ed Assn; Amer Sch Health Assn; Sch Health Assn of WA Interim Bd Mem 1989-; Comprehensive Health Ed Fnd Experienced Health Educator Fellowship; *office:* Tyee Mid Sch 13630 S E Allen Rd Bellevue WA 98006

DIORIO, JOHN V., American Government Teacher; *b:* New York, NY; *m:* Theresa Grammauta; *c:* Mary-Jean Roamer, Theresa, Stephanie; *ed:* (BA) Philosophy/Psych, St Johns Univ 1959; (MS) Ed/Government, Fordham Univ 1963; *cr:* Government/His Teacher Archbishop Malloy HS 1959-; *ai:* Bsktbl Coach 1964-66; CYO Bsbl Coach 1960-63; Nassau Cty CYO Bsbl Coach 1969-72; Knights of Columbus Mem 1965-; Sons of Italy Mem 1975-; NYC Cty Comm 1961-64; VP Mutual Tickets Agents Union #23293 1976-80; *office:* Archbishop Molloy HS 83-53 Manton St Briarwood NY 11435

DI PASQUALE, SHERRY FADER, Guidance Counselor; *b:* New York, NY; *m:* Paul; *c:* Erik Josowitz, Michael Josowitz; *ed:* (BA) Psych, Georgian Court Coll 1976; (MS) Health Occupations Ed, FL Intnl Univ 1987; Registered Nurse, Beth Israel Hospital Sch of Nursing 1965; *cr:* Registered Nurse Beth Israel Hospital 1965-66, Paul Kimbal Hospital 1969-76; Teacher Ocean Cty Voc Tech 1976-82, Hollywood Hills HS 1982-89; Cnslr Hollywood Hills HS 1989-; *ai:* Chairperson Underclass Awds; Regional Adv HOSA 1986-87; Broward Cty Cnslrs Assn Mem 1990; HOSA Awds; Outstanding Achievement Health Occupations Ed FIU 1988; *office:* Hollywood Hills HS 5400 Stirling Rd Hollywood FL 33021

DI PILLO, MARYLOU DUTKO, Middle Grade Teacher; *b:* Youngstown, OH; *m:* Gary Jay; *c:* David L., Deanna M.; *ed:* (BA) Elem Ed, Mercyhurst Coll 1971; (MS) Master Teacher Rdng, Youngstown St Univ 1988; Enrolled PhD Prgm Akron Univ; *cr:* Elem Teacher St Christine Sch 1971-; Limited Service Instr Youngstown St Univ 1989-; *ai:* Organist for Parish & Sch Functions; Liturgy Comm; Phi Kappa Phi Honor Society 1989-; Phi Delta Kappa, E OH Cncl Teachers of Math; *home:* 2381 Penny Ln Youngstown OH 44515

DIPPOLITO, APRIL FISH, Second Grade Teacher; *b:* Pampa, TX; *m:* Michael J.; *c:* Nicholas; *ed:* (BA) Kndgtn/Primary, Glassboro St Coll 1965; *cr:* 2nd Grade Teacher Lanning Elem 1965-; *ai:* NEA, NJ Ed Assn 1965-; Norristown Area Aquatic Club 1st VP 1989-; *home:* 1119 Doris Ln Norristown PA 19403

DI PRIMA, FLORENCE MARIE, English Teacher; *b:* Utica, NY; *m:* Samuel J.; *c:* Brianne, Mikel; *ed:* (AA) Liberal Arts, Mohawk Valley Comm Coll 1968; (BA) Eng Lit, Utica Coll of Syracuse Univ 1975; Completed Masters Prgm SUNY Cortland 1978; *cr:* Elem Teacher St Marys Sch 1968-74; Eng Teacher Canastota Jr HS 1975-80, Canastota HS 1980-; *ai:* Self-Esteem for Stu Comm; Yrbk 1987-88, Newspaper 1982-83, Cheerleading 1976 Adv; NYSUT, CTA 1975-; Yrbk Dedication by Sr Class 1985; *office:* Canastota HS Roberts St Canastota NY 13032

DI ROCCO, ANTHONY JOHN, European/AP Amer His Teacher; *b:* Homestead, PA; *m:* Mary Joan Szarnicki; *c:* Dominic, Michael; *ed:* (BS) Ed, Duquesne Univ 1968; PA St Univ; CA St Coll; *cr:* His Teacher Lebanon Jr HS 1968-83, West Mifflin Intermediate 1983-88, West Mifflin Area HS 1988-; *ai:* Continuing Prof Growth Comm; Asst Girls Sftbl Coach; *office:* West Mifflin Area H S 91 Commonwealth Ave West Mifflin PA 15122

DI SANTIS, GERALDINE ANN, Second Grade Teacher; *b:* Philadelphia, PA; *ed:* (BS) Elem Ed/Early Chldhd Ed, Cabrini Coll 1983; *cr:* 2nd-5th Grade Teacher Annunciation BVM Sch 1974-87; 2nd Grade Teacher Penrose Elem Sch 1987-.

DISIPIO, ANTHONY JOSEPH, JR., 8th Grade Science Teacher; *b:* Philadelphia, PA; *ed:* (BS) Earth Sci/Scndry Ed, W Chester St Coll 1975; (MA) Scndry Ed Admin, Villanova Univ 1980; ABD Educl Leadership, Univ of PA; Rosemont Coll Cmptr Inst; *cr:* 8th Grade Sci Teacher Octorana Intermediate 1976-; *ai:* Cmptr Club; Intramural Bsktbl; PA St Intern; St Curr Comm; Mentor Teacher; Sci Curr Coord; PA Sci Teachers Assn, NSTA; *office:* Octorara Intermediate Sch Rd 1 Box 65 Atglen PA 19310

DISMUKES, BETH CANTRELL, Kindergarten Teacher; *b:* Camp Breckenridge, KY; *m:* John Terry III; *c:* Justin, Matthew; *ed:* (BS) Elem Ed, Armstrong St 1979; *cr:* 3rd Grade Teacher 1979-80, Kndgtn Teacher 1980- Richmond Hill Elem; *ai:* GA Assn of Ed; *home:* 482 Ft Mc Allister Rd PO Box 622 Richmond Hill GA 31324

DISORBO, RONALD JACK, 8th Grade Mathematics Teacher; *b:* Olean, NY; *c:* Jeffrey, Derek; *ed:* (BS) Math, 1965, (MS) Math, 1984 St Univ Coll Buffalo; *cr:* Teacher Tonawanda Jr HS 1965-; *ai:* Study Skills Comm; Stu Cncl Adv; Tonawanda Ed Assn (Treas 1981-83, Rep Cncl 1978-81, Exec Bd 1984-83), Distinguished Service Awd 1982; *office:* City of Tonawanda Sr HS Fletcher & Hinds St Tonawanda NY 14150

DITCHKOFSKY, MICHAEL PATRICK, English Department Chair; *b:* Philadelphia, PA; *ed:* (BA) Eng, La Salle Univ 1981; (AM) Eng, Univ of Chicago 1982; *cr:* Academic Consultant/Dean of Stu Univ of Chicago 1982-84; Eng Dept Chm Holy Ghost Prep Sch 1984-; *ai:* Amnesty Intnl Moderator; MLA, NCTE 1984-; Outstanding Teacher of Bucks Cty PA 1988-89.

DITHRICH, MARIE, 4th/5th Grade Math/Cmptr Instr; *b:* Pittsburgh, PA; *ed:* (BS) Elem Ed, 1971, (MED) Ed, 1974 Univ of Pittsburgh; Cmptr Trng & Advanced Math Univ of Pittsburgh; Numerous Math & Cmptr Wkshps; *cr:* 4th Grade Teacher 1971-75, 5th Grade Teacher 1975-76 Nineteenth Ave Elem; 4th/5th Grade Math Teacher 1976-, Cmptr Instr/Coord 1983- Barrett Elem; *ai:* Prof Dev Comm; Career Ed Task Force; NEA Negotiating Team 1975-76; PSEA Negotiating Team 1985-86; Steel Valley Ed Assn Negotiating Team 1990; *office:* Barrett Elem Sch 221 E 12th Ave Homestead PA 15120

DITTA, FRANCES MARY, Government Teacher; *b:* Houston, TX; *ed:* (BAT) SED/His/Poly Sci/Eng, Sam Houston St Univ 1986; *cr:* Eng Teacher 1986-87, Government Teacher 1987- Klein Oak; *ai:* Frosh Chrldrs; Jr Class; Honor Society; *office:* Klein Oak HS 22603 Northcrest Dr Spring TX 77389

DITTMAR, DEBORAH JOHN, Lang Art Teacher/Dept Chair; *b:* Chillicothe, MO; *ed:* (BA) Eng/Theatre Art/Speech, Simpson Coll 1974; (MA) Lit, Univ of N CO 1978; CO St Univ; *cr:* Teacher Woodbine HS 1975-77, Bill Reed Jr HS 1977-78, Walt Clark Jr HS 1978-83, Thompson Valley HS 1983-; *ai:* Prof Growth, Earth Week, Thompson Dist Lang Art Curr Comm; People To People Adult Spon; Friendship Caravan Soviet Union; CO Lang Art Society, Thompson Ed Assn 1977-; Sierra Club, Greenpeace, Unitarian Church; Poetry Published; Walt Clark Jr HS Teacher of Yr; CSU Innovator of Yr; Natl Endowment for Hum Grant; *office:* Thompson Valley HS 1669 Eagle Dr Loveland CO 80537

DITTMER, LINDA DILLARD, 6th Grade Math Teacher; *b:* Des Moines, IA; *m:* Dan; *c:* Chad, Jaren, Kyle; *ed:* (BA) Elem Ed, Simpson Coll 1970; Grad Stud Drake Univ & Univ of N IA; *cr:* 1st Grade Teacher North Elem 1970-71; 5th-6th Grade Sci/Math Teacher East Elem 1975-86; 5th Grade Sci/Math Teacher 1986-89, 6th Grade Math Teacher 1989- Indianola Mid Sch; *ai:* Just Say No Spon; K-6th Grade Math Curr Comm Chairperson; Indianola Ed Assn 1986-; IA St Educl Assn, NEA 1970-71, 1975-; Pleasantville Ed Assn Secy 1970-71, 1975-86; Extension Cncl Secy 1972-76; 4-H (Youth Comm 1983-89, Cty Cncl Spon 1986-89); *office:* Indianola Mid Sch 301 N Buxton Indianola IA 50125

DITTO, FLORENCE JEAN, 6th Grade Teacher/Elem Supvr; *b:* Memphis, TN; *m:* John E.; *c:* Jeanna, Jeanette, Jennifer, JeAnelle; *ed:* (BS) Elem Ed, Memphis St Univ 1969; Ed Admin Memphis St Univ; *cr:* Teacher Memphis City Schls 1969-72; Teacher/Prin Oak Crest Chrstn Acad 1972-75; Teacher/Supvr Thrift Haven Baptist Sch 1975-; *ai:* Sci Fair Coord Mid South Assn of Chrstn Schls; Competition Spon; Mid South Assn Chrstn Schls 1975-; TN Assn Chrstn Sch 1975-; Educator of Yr 1983; *home:* 3556 Kallaher Memphis TN 38122

DITTRICH, JULIE ANN, Biology Teacher; *b:* Pittsburgh, PA; *ed:* (BSED) Bio, Indiana Univ of PA 1988; *cr:* Bio Teacher Richland HS 1989-; *ai:* NABT 1989-; *home:* 809 Pictwood Dr Glenshaw PA 15116

DITZEL, THELMA BRADFORD, Retired/Assistant Principal; *b:* Charleston, ME; *m:* Arthur C.; *c:* Arthur, Mary A, Thelma Palermo, Joseph, John, Jane, Ruth Chang, James; *ed:* (BA) Classics & Fr, Univ of ME 1945; (MA) Classics & Fr, Columbia Univ 1946; Several Wkshps; Cert Religious Ed; *cr:* Fr Teacher John Marshall Coll 1946-47; Fr & Latin Teacher Berkley Inst 1946-47; Lang Arts Teacher 1963-88, Asst Prin 1979-88 Mt Carmel Sch; *ai:* Phi Beta Kappa Honor Society 1945; Phi Kappa Phi Honor Society 1945; Nrta Chaplain 1989; Charleston Lib Librarian 1989-; Comprehensive Plan Comm Secy 1988-; Distinguished Teacher NJ 1989; *office:* Mt Carmel Sch 10 County Road Tenafly NJ 07670

DI VACCARO, MARY DIETRICH, 6th Grade Teacher; *b:* Woodbury, NJ; *c:* Kathleen; *ed:* (BA) Elem Ed, 1968, (MA) Rdng Ed, 1973, Ed Specialist, 1974 Glassboro St Coll; *cr:* 3rd Grade Teacher 1968-73, Rdng Specialist 1974-78, 6th Grade Teacher 1979- Costello Sch; *ai:* NEA, NJ Ed Assn, CCCEA; GCEA Secy 1973-74; NFIE Grant; *office:* Mary Ethel Costello Sch Cumberland St Gloucester City NJ 08030

DIVELBISS, RONALD E., Biology Department Head; *b:* Huntington, IN; *m:* Nancy Stauffer; *c:* Robert E., Katrina L, Kara M.; *ed:* St Francis Coll; *cr:* Bio Teacher Leo Jr/Sr HS 1964-; Marine Bio Teacher E Allen Cty Schls 1987-; *ai:* SADD; Prom Comm; Track & Academic Super Bowl Coach; Work with 4-H Youth & Little League; Chaperone FL Keys Trips; Help Plan Plantings Local Park; Organize Blood Collection Amer Red Cross; 4H Leader & Superintendent 4H Fair; ISTA, NEA, EAEA 1964-; Don Crick Memorial Schlsp Chairperson 1990; Leo United Meth Church (Sunday Sch Supt, Ed Comm, Teach Church Sch); Fort Wayne Zoological Society Mem; Bus Week Ed Grant; *office:* Leo Jr Sr HS 14600 Amstutz Rd Leo IN 46765

DI VIA, RICHARD, English Teacher; *b:* Trenton, NJ; *ed:* (BA) Eng Ed, Trenton St Coll 1983; *cr:* Eng Teacher Mc Corristin HS 1987-; *ai:* Soph Stu Cncl Class Moderator; ASCD 1989-; Golden Poet Awd 1989; Poetry Published 1990; *office:* Mc Corristin HS 175 Leanard Ave Trenton NJ 08610

DIVINIA, ETHEL ANN, Assistant Principal; *b:* Kimberly, ID; *m:* Don D.; *c:* Dustin, Darin; *ed:* (BS) Elem Ed, MT St Univ 1962; (MS) Elem Ed, E TX St Univ 1981; *cr:* 5th Grade Teacher St Joseph MO 1962-63; 6th Grade Teacher N Kansas City 1963-64, Midway Island DOD Sch 1964-65, Tainan Tawain DOD Sch 1965-66; 6th-8th Grade Teacher 1975-89, Asst Prin 1989- Quinlan Mid Sch; *ai:* Gifted/Talented & Odyssey of Mind Dist Coord; Phi Beta Kappa, NASSP 1989-; ASCD 1990; Quinlan Classroom Teachers Assn Pres 1981; Most Prominent Educators of TX 1983; *office:* Quinlan Mid Sch Rt 3 Box 18 Quinlan TX 75474

DIXON, BARBARA NANETTE, History Teacher & Dept Chair; *b:* Birmingham, AL; *ed:* (BS) His, AL Coll 1955; (MA) His, Univ of AL Tuscaloosa 1961; *cr:* Teacher Trussville Elem 1955; Gardendale Jr HS 1956-64; Gardendale HS 1965-; *office:* Gardendale HS 850 Mt Olive Rd Gardendale AL 35071

DIXON, DANETTE V., 6th Grade Teacher; *b:* New Orleans, LA; *c:* Mitchell Mc Murren; *ed:* (BA) Scndry Ed/Hum/Music, Dillard Univ 1954; *cr:* 12th Grade Eng Teacher St Helena HS 1955-60; 6th Grade Teacher 1960-63, Music Supvr 1963-68 Buena Vista Elem Sch; 6th Grade Teacher Salina Elem Sch 1968-; *ai:* Salina Elem Sch Choral Dir; Battle of Books Coach; MI St Univ for Prof Service Teacher Preparation Prgm Spec Awd 1973.

DIXON, JANICE CAROL, Teacher; *b:* Durham, NC; *ed:* (BA) Elem Ed, NC Cntrl Univ 1977; Cmptr Literacy & Basic Programming; Effective Teacher Trng; First Aide & CPR; *cr:* Chrldr Coach 1978-, Teacher 1978- Rogers-Herr Mid Sch; Teacher Advisory Group Univ of NC Chapel Hill 1987-; Consultant Southern Assn Creditation & Neal Mid Sch 1990; *ai:* Black His Bowl Coach; Pep Club Spon; NC His Bowl Coach; Glaxo Partner; Dance Troupe Spon; NC Assn of Educators 1985-; Durham City Educl Assn 1985-; Teachers Educl Forum & Exp Teacher Ed Prgm Univ of NC Chapel Hill Group Mem 1987; St John Baptist Church 1987-89; First Aide Club 1987-89; *office:* Rogers Herr Mid Sch 911 W Cornwallis Rd Durham NC 27707

DIXON, JULINDA LEA, 5th-12th Grade Band Director; *b:* Unionville, MO; *ed:* (BME) Instrumental Music/Music Ed, NE MO St Univ 1985; *cr:* Band Dir Schuyler R-1 Schls 1986-; *ai:* Marching, Jazz, Pep, Concert Band Dir; Sr Class Spon; Winter Flags & Drumline; Summer Camp Instr; Solos & Ensembles; All Conference Band Chorus Coord; MO St Teachers Assn, MO Music Educators Assn 1986-; Sigma Alpha Iota Coll Chaplain 1982-85; Fiesta Bowl Parade 1987; *office:* Schuyler R-1 Schls Box 220 Madison St Lancaster MO 63548

DIXON, LINDA LAY, Retired Teacher; *b:* Houston, TX; *m:* Jerry Bell; *c:* Jerri, Kelly Cooksey, Todd, Pamela Wittenhagen; *ed:* (BS) Elem Ed, Black Hills St Coll 1975; Grad Stud Univ of WY; *cr:* Cmmty Ed Teacher 1975-76, Classroom Teacher Newcastle Sch Dist 1 1976-82; *ai:* Sci Camp Cnslr; Elem Lib Advisory Comm; Delta Kappa Gamma Treas 1980-; PEO All Local 1961-; N WY Mental Health Pres 1988-; Republican Women Pres 1986-; *home:* 31 S Summit Newcastle WY 82701

DIXON, M. TODD, Social Studies Teacher; *b:* Norton, VA; *m:* Mary Elizabeth Clayton; *c:* Melissa, Matthew, Nicholas; *ed:* (BA) Geography, 1987, (MED) Soc Stud Ed, 1988 Univ of FL; *cr:* Soc Stud Teacher Palatka HS 1988-; *ai:* Stu Government Spon; Var & Jr Var Girls Vlybl Coach; Palatka HS Sch Based Management Comm Mem; NCSS 1988-; Palatka HS Teacher of Month 1989; *office:* Palatka HS 302 Mellon Rd Palatka FL 32177

DIXON, PATRICIA FRAME, Sixth Grade Eng/Rdng Teacher; *b:* South Charleston, WV; *m:* Thomas Dupuy; *c:* Thomas W., F. F., Elizabeth A.; *ed:* (BA) Math/Eng, Marshall Univ 1957; (MA) Cmptr Ed, Lesley Coll 1989; Grad Stud Marshall Univ, WV Univ, Univ of CO, Univ of WY, E MT Coll; *cr:* Math Teacher Hurricane HS 1957-63; 6th Grade Teacher Paddock Elem 1963-69, Lovell Mid Sch 1971-; Part-Time Cmptr Teacher Northwest Coll 1988-; *ai:* 6th Grade Adv Chm; Needs Assessment Eng & Rdng 1971-; Co-Chm Rdng & Eng Comms; Delta Kappa Gamma (Pres 1981-83, VP 1979-81, Treas 1986-88); WY Assn Mid Schls 1986; Bus & Prof Women 1972-74; After 5 Club 1982-; Lovell Lib Bd Comm Mem 1970-85; Natl Sci Fnd Grant 1960; WY Assn Mid Schls Wkshp Presenter; *home:* 2198 Hwy 310 Lovell WY 82431

DIXON, PATRICK STEWART, Photography Teacher; *b:* Logansport, IN; *m:* Veronica Kessler; *c:* Kessler S., Dylan J.; *ed:* (BS) Spec Ed/Eng, IN Univ 1973; Various Wkshps; *cr:* Spec Ed Teacher Louisville Public Schls 1973-75, Kenai Jr HS 1975-80; Photography/Eng/Journalism Teacher Kenai Cntrl HS 1980-; *ai:* Building Coord Stu Assistance Prgm; NEA 1978-; Kenai Art Guild 1980-, Several Honors & Art Competition; AK Photographers Guild 1988-; 1 Man Show Photography Kenai Peninsula Coll 1989; 2 Man Show Kenai Art Guild 1989; Published AK Fishermans Journal 1989; *office:* Kenai Cntrl HS 9583 Kenai Spur Hwy Kenai AK 99611

DIXON, RICKEY, Band Director; *b:* Orlando, FL; *m:* Frances; *ed:* (BS) Music Ed, AL St Univ 1975; GA St Univ/Univ of Cntrl FL; *cr:* Band Dir Headland HS 1975-78; Math Remediation West Orange HS 1979-80; Band Dir Fulton HS 1981-; *ai:* Marching Band; Black His Chm; Talent Production Chm; All City Honor Band Chm; Homecoming Comm Chm; Phi Mu Alpha Treas 1974-; PTSA Organizing Comm 1990; Teacher of Yr 1986; Star Teacher 1990; Academic Achievement Incentive Awd 1990; Yrbk Dedication 1985; *office:* Fulton H S 2025 Jonesboro Rd Atlanta GA 30315

DIXON, SHARON LYNNE, Learning Center Coordinator; *b:* Memphis, TN; *ed:* (BA) Elem Ed, Union Univ 1980; (MS) Lib Sci, Univ of Houston Clear Lake 1988; *cr:* 3rd Grade Teacher 1981-82, Librarian 1982- Jacinto City Elem; *ai:* His Fair & Book Fair Coord; Teacher Encouragement Comm; Dev Stu Rdng Circle; After Sch Tutor; Assn of TX Prof Educators 1984-; PTA (Local Pres 1984-86, Galena Park Cncl Pres 1989-); TX PTA Life Membership 1986, Teacher Schlsp 1986; Natl PTA Life Membership 1990; *office:* Jacinto City Elem 10910 Wiggins Houston TX 77029

DIZE, JOAN FOUNTAIN, Third Grade Teacher; *b:* Greensboro, MD; *m:* Elmer Thomas; *ed:* (BS) Elem Ed, 1968, (MED) Elem Ed, 1975 Salisbury St Univ; *cr:* 4th Grade Teacher Denton Sch 1968-76; Chapter I Helping Teacher Greensboro & Ridgely Schls 1976-77; 6th Grade Teacher 1977-88, 3rd Grade Teacher 1988- Denton Sch.

DI ZEREGA, EDWARD D., Choral Music Dept Director; *b:* Wichita, KS; *m:* Susie Speckman; *ed:* (BME) Scndry/Elem Vocal Music Ed, Univ of KS 1978; Univ of KS, Ottawa Univ; *cr:* Substitute Teacher Shawnee Mission Sch Dist 1978-81; Scndry Vocal/Music Ed Teacher Jefferson West HS & Mid Sch 1981-; *ai:* Sch Improvement Team; Sr Class, Stu Cncl, Mid Sch Yrbk Spon; HS Musical Dir; Amer Choral Dir Assn 1982-; Amer Jazz Educators Assn 1983-; KS Music Educators Assn, Music Educators Natl Conference 1980-; *office:* Jefferson West HS & Mid Sch PO Box 268 Meriden KS 66512

DOAN, WINIFRED SNYDER, Fifth Grade Teacher; *b:* Middletown, NY; *m:* Reed W.; *c:* Sherry D. White, Debra D. Davenpor, John L., Marcia D. Jameson; *ed:* (BS) Elem Ed, 1964, (MS) Elem Ed, 1974 Mansfield Univ; *cr:* Teacher Northern Tioga Sch Dist 1964-; *ai:* Advisory Bd of Scholastic Mag; PTO Gertrude Case Sch; Band Parents; Headed Trip to WA; PSEA; TASA Bd of Dir; Grange Valley; Church; Knoxville-Peerfield Fire Co Wives; *office:* Gertrude Case Elem Box 149 Main St Knoxville PA 16928

DOBBINS, JAMES J., JR., Earth Science Teacher; *b:* Winthrop, MA; *m:* Maria A. Cassese; *c:* Maria A.; *ed:* (BA) Sociology and Ed, St Anselm's Coll 1968; (MED) Curr, Antioch Univ 1977; *cr:* Sci/Math Teacher 1968-74; Academically Gifted & Talented Teacher 1974-76; Functional Literacy Teacher 1977-80; Asst Prin 1980-81; 7th Grade Earth Sci Teacher City of Peabody 1981-; *ai:* Sch Store Faculty Adv; Boston Museum of Sci Mid Sch Adv Comm; 2 Time Recipient St of MA Horace Mann Grant for Prgm Dev.

DOBBINS, MARINA, Business Dept Chairperson; *b:* Zurich, Switzerland; *m:* Martin F.; *ed:* (BS/BA) Finance, Suffolk Univ 1985; Working Towards Masters with Cert; *cr:* Bus Teacher 1985-88, Dept Chairperson 1988- Mt St Joseph Acad; *ai:* Natl Bus Honor Society & Jr Prom Moderator; Reaccreditation Team Comm Chairperson; New England Assn Bus Educators, MA Educators Bus Assn 1990; NBEA; *home:* 69 Parker St Westwood MA 02090

DOBBS, DARLENE JOHNSON, Fifth Grade Teacher; *b:* Atlanta, GA; *c:* Ashante; *ed:* (BS) Elem Ed, 1979, (MS) Mid Grades Ed, 1984 GA St Univ; Trained Data Collecter, Supervisor Teacher; *cr:* 4th Grade Teacher St Paul of the Cross Elem Sch 1979-80; 4th/5th Grade Teacher Hutchinson Elem Sch 1980-; *ai:* Mem of Sch Leadership Team; Supervise Stu Patrols; Tutor Stus after Sch Prgm; Atlanta Assn Of Ed; GA Assn of Ed; Ga St Univ Alumni Mem 1979-; NW GA Girl Scouts Brownie Leader 1989-; Work Published In Prof Journal 1987; Teacher Of Yr 1986-87; Incentive Teacher Of Yr 1988-.

DOBBS, KATHERINE PURINTON, 6th Grade Mathematics Teacher; *b:* Cambridge, MA; *m:* David Glenn; *ed:* (BS) Elem Ed, Univ of DE 1978; General Math Endorsement; *cr:* 4th Grade Teacher 1978-80, 4th Grade Gifted Teacher 1980-85 J G Hening Elem; 6th Grade Math Teacher Swift Creek Mid 1985-; *ai:* Grade Level Chm 1980-83, 1985; Helping Understand Gifted Stu Rep 1980-85; VA Mid Sch Assn, Greater Richmond Cncl Teachers of Math 1985-; Kappa Delta Pi; *office:* Swift Creek Mid Sch 3700 Old Hundred Rd Midlothian VA 23112

DOBBS, LINDA CAROL, Mathematics Dept Chairman; *b:* Wheeler, TX; *m:* Larry; *c:* Gregory, Stephanie; *ed:* (BS) Ed, MS St Univ 1969; *cr:* Teacher Starkville HS 1977-78; Teacher 1978-, Chairperson 1985- W Clay HS; *ai:* Soph Spon; St Jude Math-A-thon Chm; Curr Comm; Sch Improvement Planning Comm; NEA, MAE (Local VP 1987-88, Pres 1988-89, Local Secy 1990-91) 1984-; NCTM 1988-; Star Teacher 1986; *home:* 422 Sycamore St Starkville MS 39759

DOBBS, ZELDA PATTERSON, Mathematics Teacher; *b:* Holcomb, MS; *m:* Paul; *c:* Kerry, Tonya, Paul A.; *ed:* (BS) Math, Alcorn A&M Univ 1966; (MS) Math, Jackson St Univ 1976; *cr:* Math Teacher Crystal Springs Jr HS 1966-76, Fifth Street Jr HS 1976-; *ai:* Math Club Spon; Textbook Evaluation Comm; Key Teacher; Academics Awds Banquet Co-Spon; NCTM, NEA, MS Educators Assn; Cub Scouts Den Mother 1987-88; Sunday Sch Teacher 1988-; Missionary Society; Spiritual Choir; STAR Teacher 1987-88; Teacher of Month 1989; *home:* Rt 3 Box 81-B West Point MS 39773

DOBRZENSKI, DARRYL THOMAS, Vocational Auto Teacher; *b:* Crystal Falls, MI; *m:* Mary Jo Johnson; *c:* Kathy Vernitles, Cher Schmitzer, Darryl Jr., Marcia Christhoper; *ed:* (AA) General, La Pieree Coll 1968; (BS) Scndry Ed, 1972, (MS) Scndry Voc Ed, 1983 N MI Univ; Ferris St Coll, Delta Coll; N MI Univ, GM Update Wkshp; *cr:* Mechanic Canoga Park Ford 1962-64, Las Virgeries Unified Sch Dist 1964-69; Voc Auto Teacher N MI Univ 1969-72, Gwinn Cmmty Schls 1972-; *ai:* VICA Adv 1973-; MEA 1969-; MI Winter Fowl Assn 1984-; Ducks Unlimited 1989-; Adv of Yr 1980.

DOBSON, CHARLOTTE MC PHERSON, First Grade Teacher; *b:* Mayfield, KY; *m:* Gail Boyd; *c:* Matthew G., Mark A.; *ed:* (BS) Elem Ed, Murray St Univ 1963; *cr:* 1st Grade Teacher Cuba Elem 1963-; *ai:* Future Planning Comm Graves Cty Schls; Teacher Rep Cuba Elem; KEA, NEA, FDEA, GCEA Mem 1970-; Graves Cty Farm Bureau (Womens Comm Chairwoman 1976-, Womens Chairwoman 1979, 1980), Cert of Recognition Womens Comm 1976-, KY Farm Bureau Womens Prgm 1979, 1980; KY Dept of Ed Certificate of Recognition 1984; *office:* Cuba Elem Sch Rt 3 Mayfield KY 42066

DOBSON, DOROTHY LYNN WATTS, Fifth Grade Teacher; *b:* Santa Monica, CA; *m:* J. Cody; *c:* Brandi, Jeremiah, Hannah; *ed:* (BA) Elem Ed/Spec Ed, UT St Univ 1975; (MED) Spec Ed, Univ of UT 1981; *cr:* Spec Ed Teacher Mexican Hat Elem Sch 1974-76; 3rd Grade Teacher Webster Elem Sch 1977-79; 3rd Grade Teacher 1979-81, 6th Grade Teacher 1981-82 Orchard Elem Sch;3rd-5th Grade Teacher Edith Bowen Laboratory Sch 1982-; Instr Classroom Management Courses UT St Univ 1986-; *ai:* Stu Cncl Adv; UT Cncl Cmptrs in Ed 1983-85; Paradise Volunteer Fire Dept 1982-; Natl Arts Cncl Conference Panel Mem; Wrote Curr Guides Incorporating Newspapers 1983; *office:* Edith Bowen Laboratory Sch UT St Univ Logan UT 84322

DOCHERTY, GARY JAMES, English Teacher; *b:* St Paul, MN; *ed:* (BS) Eng Ed, St Cloud St Univ 1973; *cr:* Eng Teacher St Bernards HS 1973-; *ai:* Eng Dept Chm 1981-86; St Bernards HS Teacher of Yr 1986; *office:* St Bernards HS 170 W Rose Ave Saint Paul MN 55113

DOCKEY, JOAN ELIZABETH, 3rd Grade Teacher; *b:* Shamokin, PA; *ed:* (BS) Elem Ed, Millersville Univ 1961; Addl Studies Penn St Univ; Millersville Univ; *cr:* 2nd/3rd Grade Teacher Conewago Twp 1961-65; 2nd Grade Teacher 1965-66; 1st Grade Teacher 1966-67; 7th/8th Grade Teacher Dev Rdng 1971-72; 2nd Grade Teacher 1972-89; 3rd Grade Teacher 1989- Dover Area Schls; *ai:* Faculty Rep PTA; Coord All-Sch Projects; PSEA; DAEA Sec 1966-67; Delta Kppa Gamma (2nd VP/1st VP/Pres) 1988-; The Lehman Ctr Vol 1988-; Union Luth Sop Soloist 1985-; *home:* 11 Weymouth Ct York PA 17404

DOCTOR, ABBY T., Mathematics Teacher; *b:* Brooklyn, NY; *ed:* (BA) Math, Brooklyn Coll 1966; Grad Work Brooklyn Coll; *cr:* Math Teacher Wm E Grady Voc & Tech HS 1966-67, John Jay HS 1967-; *office:* John Jay HS 237 7th Ave Brooklyn NY 11215

DODD, ESTEL MULLINAX, 2nd/3rd Grade Teacher; *b:* Flintville, TN; *:* Kenneth A.; *ed:* (BA) Eng Music, Birmingham Southern 1955; (MA) Elem Ed/Rdng Specialization, AL A&M Univ 1980; *cr:* 7th Grade Teacher Albertville HS 1955-56; 9th Grade Teacher Athens HS 1958-59; 3rd Grade Teacher Arab Elem Sch 1961-64; 2nd/3rd Grade Teacher Joppa Jr HS & Elem Sch 1973-; *ai:* Taught Private Piano Lessons 1966-84; CCEA 1973-; AEA, NEA 1955-; AL St Poetry Society 1980-; Natl Fed of St Poetry Societies 1980-; 1st Baptist Church Choir Arab Soprano Soloist 1959-; Poetry Published; *home:* 201 Brookwood Cir Arab AL 35016

DODD, KENNETH LE ROY, Middle Grades Teacher; *b:* Atlanta, GA; *m:* Jackie Williams; *c:* Michelle, Serena; *ed:* (BA) His, 1974, (MED) Ed, 1978, (SED) Ed, 1983 W GA Coll; Working towards PHD Curr & Instruction, GA St Univ; *cr:* Lang Lab Dir W GA Coll 1973-79; Eng Teacher Waco Elem Sch 1979-80; Teacher Herschel Jones Mid Sch 1980-; *ai:* Spon Chess & His Club; NCSS, Natl Assn Learning Lab Dirs, GA Historical Society, Atlanta Historical Society; Buchanan Lions Club 1978-; Buchanan Masonic Lodge Past Master 1969-; Buchanan Volunteer Fireman 1978-80; Published Limited Edition; Wrote Significant Prelude Portions in His Haralson Cty; Teacher of Yr 1983; *home:* 196 Willie Head Rd Buchanan GA 30113

DODD, LINDA WEINERT, 8th Grade Math/Algebra Teacher; *b:* Kansas City, KS; *m:* Arthur J.; *c:* James C.; *ed:* (BSE) Elem Ed, 1973, (MSE) Curr/Instruction/Math, 1986 Emporia St Univ; Math & Cmptr Courses at KS St Univ, Univ of KS, Avila Coll; *cr:* Teacher Argentine Mid Sch 1973-; *ai:* Athletic Dir; Stu Cncl Adv; NCTM 1980-84; Nom Learning Exch Excl in Teaching Awd 1987, Classroom & Cmptr Learning Magazine Teacher of Yr Prgm 1989; *home:* 10802 Rowland Ct Kansas City KS 66109

DODD, SANDRA (WHITTEN), English Teacher; *b:* Florence, AL; *c:* Donna, Brad; *ed:* (BA) Eng, 1971, (MED) Eng, 1975 Auburn Univ; Advanced Placement Wkshps; *cr:* Speech Teacher Georgia Washington Jr HS 1975-76; Eng/12th Grade Advanced Placement Eng Teacher Jefferson Davis HS 1976-; *ai:* NHS Adv; Sch Improvement Team; NCTE 1975-; AL Cncl of Teachers of Eng 1988-; NEA, AEA, Montgomery Cty Ed Assn; Georgetown Neighborhood Assn; Frazer Memorial Meth Church; Jeff Davis HS Teacher of Yr 1989, Finalist 1990; *office:* Jefferson Davis HS 3420 Carter Hill Rd Montgomery AL 36111

DODDS, CAROLINE COLEMAN, Media Specialist; *b:* Wheeling, WV; *c:* Heather, David; *ed:* (BA) His, Salem Coll 1968; WV Cert in Soc Stud, Lib Sci; *cr:* Media Specialist Woodsdale Jr HS 1968-71; 6th Grade Self Contained Teaacher Sistersville Jr HS 1971-72; Media Specialist Valley View Elem 1972-77, Belington Mid Sch 1978-; *ai:* Media Aide & Office Workers Spon; PTSA Spring Dance Comm; Belington Mid Sch Band Boosters Treas; WV Ed Assn (Building Rep 1986) 1968-; Jr League of Wheeling 1969-75; Order of Eastern Star 1977-; Cub Scouts of America (Summer Cnslr, Volunteer) 1988-89; Think Coll Grant Recipient 1989; *office:* Belington Mid Sch Box 209 Belington WV 26250

DODDS, STAN W., Athletic Director; *b:* Cheyenne, WY; *m:* Adele M. Meyers; *c:* Stacy, Trent; *ed:* (BA) Math, Univ of WY 1970; (MA) Scndry Ed, Adams St Coll 1989; *cr:* Teacher/Coach Laramie HS 1971-78, Arapahoe HS 1978-85; Athletic Dir/Coach Mullen HS 1985-87, Woodland Park HS 1987-; *ai:* Athletic Dir All Sports & Act; Coach Vlybl, Boys Bsktbl & Track; CO Athletic Dir Assn 1985-; Centennial League Coach of Yr 1982; League Championships & St Runner-Up League 1982, 1986, *office:* Woodland Park HS PO Box 99 Woodland Park CO 80866

DODSON, BRENDA LOU, Second Grade Teacher; *b:* Bristol, VA; *ed:* (BS) Elem Ed, E TN St Univ 1970; Grad Stud; *cr:* 2nd Grade Teacher Fairmount Elem 1970-72, Holston View Elem 1972-73, Cntrl Elem 1973-; *ai:* Cntrl Elem Writer for Magazine; Awds Comm; BTEA, TEA, NEA 1970-; *office:* Cntrl Elem Sch Edgemont Ave Bristol TN 37620

DODSON, DANITA JOAN, English and Spanish Teacher; *b:* Morristown, TN; *ed:* (BA) Eng, Lincoln Memorial Univ 1985; (MA) Eng, E TN St Univ 1986; (EDS) Curr/Instruction, Univ of S MS 1989; Study of Span, Madrid Univ 1987; *cr:* His Teacher 1986-87, Eng/Span Teacher 1987- Hancock Cty HS; *ai:* Stu Cncl & Sr Class Spon; Yrbk Adv; NCTE, NEA 1986-; ACTFL 1988-; ASCD 1989-; GFWC 1986-; Hancock Cty Ed Assn Pres 1989-; Phi Delta Kappa 1989-; Mid South Educl Research Assn Conference Presenter 1989; Governors Acad Teachers of Writing St TN Level 1990; Span Cert Madrid Univ; *home:* Rt 3 Box 416 Sneedville TN 37869

DODSON, DARLEE D., Kindergarten Teacher; *b:* Woodbury, TN; *m:* James F.; *c:* Jonathan B., Lance C., Tyson B.; *ed:* (BS) Early Chldhd Ed, TN Technological Univ 1978; *cr:* Kndgtn Teacher Ashland City Elem Sch 1978-79; 1st Grade Teacher 1979-80, Kndgtn Teacher 1980- E Cheatham Elem Sch; *ai:* Parent Ed Class 1989-; Kappa Delta Pi 1977-86; Cheatham Cty Ed Task Force Co-Chm 1985-86; NEA, TN Ed Assn 1977-; Joelton Church of Christ, Youth Comm 1980-; *office:* E Cheatham Elem Sch Rt 2 Bearwallow Rd Ashland City TN 37015

DODSON, LINDA MAE, Secondary Math Teacher; *b:* Roaring Spring, PA; *m:* Lynn C.; *ed:* (BS) Scndry Ed, Penn St Univ 1983; (MS) Ed, St Francis Univ 1988; *cr:* Math Teacher Frederick HS 1983-84, Everett HS 1984-; *ai:* Sr HS Stu Cncl Co-Adv; PA Ed Assn, Everett Ed Assn 1984; PA Assn Stu Cncl 1988-; Everett HS Yrbk Dedication 1988-89.

DOE, NICHOLAS K., Chemistry Teacher; *b:* Los Angeles, CA; *ed:* (BA) Chem, Univ of CA Santa Cruz 1985; (MAT) Ed, Stanford Univ 1986; *cr:* Chem Teacher Hillsdale HS 1986-87, Aptos HS 1987-; *ai:* Academic Peer Tutoring & Ski Club Adv; CA Assn of Chem Teachers 1986-; *office:* Aptos HS 7301 Freedom Blvd Aptos CA 95003

DOEBERL, GAIL L., Foreign Language Teacher; *b:* Plymouth, MA; *m:* Terrence M.; *c:* Kristin; *ed:* (AB) Fr, Middlebury Coll 1973; (MAT) Fr/Span, Colgate Univ 1974; (MA) Intnl Relations, Johns Hopkins 1978; L Univ D Aix Marscille France; *cr:* Fr Teacher Norwich HS 1973-74; Fr/Span Teacher South Windsor HS 1974-75; Fr Teacher Timothy Edwards Mid Sch 1975-76; Fr/Span Teacher Norwalk HS 1978-; *ai:* AFS & Asian Club Adv; Chaperone Annual Trip to France; Prgm Improvement Team Mem; Fr Achievement SAT Course Provider; CT Assn Teachers of Fr Co-Chairperson Natl Fr Contest Admin 1979-83; CT Organization of Lang Teachers; Congregational Church Mem; Middlebury Alumni Area Interviewer 1988-; Phi Beta Kappa; Coll Scholar; *home:* 111 Simpaug Tpk West Redding CT 06896

DOFFIN, SHERI LYNN (COOK), First Grade Teacher; *b:* Anderson, IN; *m:* Gregory M.; *c:* Rebecca, Angela; *ed:* (BS) Elem Ed, Ball St Univ 1976; (MS) Elem Ed, Purdue Univ 1981; Jr Great Books Leader Trng; *cr:* 1st Grade Teacher Fayette Cty Schls 1976-77, North Newton Sch Corporation 1977-; *ai:* NEA 1976-; ISTA 1990; North Newton Ed Assn 1977-; *office:* Lake Village Elem Sch RR 2 Box 4 Lake Village IN 46349

DOGAN, MARY KADEL, Sci Teacher/Department Chair; *b:* Washington, DC; *m:* Anthony N. Sr.; *c:* Adrianne, Neil, Jason, Lalia, Mary J.; *ed:* (BS) Fr, Radford Univ 1969; (MHDL) Sci Ed, Univ of NC Charlotte 1983; Sci Ed, Univ of NC Charlotte; *cr:* Fr/His Teacher Lord Botetourt HS 1969-71; Sci/His Teacher Grier Jr HS 1974-85; Sci/Fr Teacher Mt Holly Jr HS 1985-87; Sci Teacher York Chester Jr HS 1987-; *ai:* Mentor Teacher; NC Sci Teachers Assn (Dist 2 Dir 1979, Membership 1986); NC Ed Assn, NEA 1974-; NSTA Lifetime; GTE Gift Grant 1988-89; Articles Published; NC Center Advancement of Teaching Teacher Scholar in Residence 1987-88; NC Sci Teachers Assn Outstanding Sci Teacher 1988; Governors Bus Awd Excl in Teaching Sci 1987; Outstanding Sci Teacher Regional Nominee 1987; Gastonia City Medal of Achievement 1989; Schiele Museum of Natural His Sci Teacher of Yr 1988-89; Natl Honor Roll Sci Teachers Assn of Sci Technology 1988-89; *home:* 9000 Centergrove Ln Charlotte NC 28214

DOGARIU, JANICE GIROUX, 6th Grade Teacher; *b:* Detroit, MI; *ed:* (BA) Hum, Univ of Detroit 1972; (MA) Rdng, E MI Univ 1978; *cr:* 2nd Grade Teacher St Gabriel Sch 1972-73; Tutor Madonna Coll Psychoeducational Center 1978-79; 2nd/3rd/5th/6th Grade Teacher St Scholastica Sch 1973-; *ai:* Sch Rdng Coord; Newspaper Editor; Intl Rdng Assn, MI Rdng Assn, Wayne Cty Rdng Cncl Presenter 1989; *home:* 14066 Riga Ave Livonia MI 48154

DOHERTY, BARBARA SYKES, HS English/History Teacher; *b:* Wanfried, West Germany; *m:* Thomas David; *c:* Sean D.; *ed:* (BA) Eng, 1970, (MA) Eng/His, 1972 Univ of OK; Working Towards Doctorate in Eng; *cr:* Instr Univ of OK 1970-72; Croupier/Dealer Harrahs Tahoe Casino 1972-85; Teacher Douglas HS 1985-; *ai:* Jr Class Adv Douglas HS; Soc Stud Task Force; Stu Assistance Prgm Facilitator; NCTE Writing Achievement Awds Judge 1988-; NV St Ed Assn, NEA, Douglas Cty Ed Assn 1987-; Consultant for N NV Writing Project; *office:* Douglas HS Hwy 88 Minden NV 89423

DOHERTY, GARY, Music/Band Director; *b:* Vernon, TX; *m:* Janet Louise Claypoole; *c:* Jason, Micah; *ed:* (BME) Music Ed, W TX St 1979; (MED) Instructional Supvr, Sam Houston St 1990; *cr:* Asst Band Dir Vernon HS 1979-80; Band Dir Bowie Jr HS 1980-85, Wunderlich Intermediate 1985-88; Music Dir Brenham HS 1988-; *ai:* All Levels of Music Instruction; TX Music Educators, TX Bandmasters 1978-; TX Classroom Teachers 1988-; Outstanding Bands/Orchestras Nationally Acclaimed Festivals; Published Poet, Writer; Clinician & Adjudicator; *office:* Brenham HS 1200 Carlee Dr Brenham TX 77833

DOIRON, DORIS J. ROBINSON, Teacher of Fine Arts; *b:* Hemphill, TX; *m:* Everett Nolan; *c:* Robert E., Keith D., Gerald P., John L., Phillip B., Melanie A. Doiron Galvan; *ed:* (BS) Art, Univ of Houston 1971; *cr:* 1st Grade Classroom Teacher Head Start Prgm Odem Elem 1953-54; Classroom Teacher 1972-, Art Dept Chm 1974- S Houston Intermediate; *ai:* Teachers Advisory Comm 1986-; Art Curr Comm; Chairperson Textbook Adoption Comm 1979, 1986, Rewriting 8th Grade Curr 1989-; Church of Living Waters (Mem, Visitation/Prayer Group Leaders, Childrens Church Teacher); Teacher & Practicing Artist Faith Sch of Visual Arts; *office:* S Houston Intermediate Sch 900 College South Houston TX 77502

DOLAN, KRISTY WIIK, 7th-10th Grade Teacher; *b:* Orlando, FL; *m:* Gregory Scott; *c:* Jessica M., Gregory S. II; *ed:* (BA) Art, Souther Coll 1979; Grad Stud; *cr:* Scndry Teacher Greeneville Adv Acad 1979-87; 7th-10th Grade Teacher Ft Myers Jr Acad 1987-; *home:* PO Box 51458 Tice FL 33905

DOLAN, MAUREEN THERESE, Sixth Grade Teacher; *b:* Anamosa, IA; *c:* Matthew, Emily T.; *ed:* (BA) Theatre, Ft Lewis Coll 1974; (MA) Speech/Drama, Univ of IA 1979; Working Towards PhD Theatre, Univ of CO Boulder; *cr:* Research Asst Theatre Dept Univ of IA 1978-79; Grad Teacher Univ of CO Boulder 1987-88; Acting Instr Regis Coll 1989; Teacher Flatirons Elem 1981-; *ai:* Drama Club; Various Building & Dist Comm; Speech Comm Assn; Assn for Theatre in Higher Ed; Dramaturg CO Shakespeare Festival 1987-88; Asst Dir CO Shakespeare Festival 1989; Publications 1988-89; CO Cncl of Higher Ed for Grad Stud 1988; *office:* Flatirons Elem Sch 1150 7th St Boulder CO 80302

DOLAN, PATRICIA ANN, Audio-Visual Coordinator; *b:* Champaign, IL; *ed:* (BA) Eng, Emmanuel Coll 1949; (MED) Elem Ed, Univ of NC Chapel Hill 1970; Courses for Cert of Field & Religious Ed; *cr:* 2nd/4th Grade Teacher St Joan of Arc Sch 1945-47, 1967-69; 1st/2nd/4th Grade Teacher St Genevieve of Pines 1949-52, 1965-67; 2nd/3rd Grade Teacher Immaculata Sch 1952-65; 2nd Grade Teacher St Eugene Sch/Asheville Cath Comm 1970-83; Remedial/Audio Visual Coord Asheville Cath Cmmty Sch 1984-; *ai:* Marian Club & Schl Newspaper Adv 1984-89; NCEA 1985-; Religious of Chrstn Ed 1945-; Veterans of Foreign Wars Auxiliary Mem 1975-; St Eugenes Womens Guild VP 1989-; Published Poetry; *office:* Asheville Cath Cmmty Sch 12 Culvern St Asheville NC 28804

DOLAN, TERESA J., Junior HS Gifted Teacher; *b:* Port Jefferson, NY; *ed:* (BS) His, W CT St Univ 1978; QUEST 1990; COPE 1985; *cr:* 6th-8th Grade Teacher Trumbull Cath Regional 1978-80; His Teacher 1980-82, 7th-8th Grade Spec Ed Teacher 1982-84, 7th-8th Grade Lit/His/Gifted Teacher 1984- Kingman Jr HS; *ai:* Child Study Team Co-Chairperson 1988-; 7th Grade SEARCH Spon; Talented & Gifted Prgm 1984-; Substance Abuse Comm Kingman Elem Dist #4; AFT 1984-; Mohave Cty Art Fair 1987, 2nd Place 1987; Kingman Special Olympics Track Coach 1981-84, Coaching Awd 1984; Dial-A-Teacher Homework Hotline 1989-; Mem Kingman Cares Townhall on Substance Abuse; Honorary Judge Andy Devine Days Bicentennial Parade; *office:* Kingman Jr HS 1969 Detroit Ave Kingman AZ 86401

DOLCE, LINDA V., 4th Grade Humanities Teacher; *b:* New York City, NY; *m:* Anthony; *c:* Christopher, Cara; *ed:* (BS) Elem Ed, Fordham Univ 1960; *cr:* 4th Grade Teacher Hamilton Sch 1960-64; 5th Grade Teacher Pennington Sch 1977-78; Transitional Teacher 1978-79, 4th Grade Teacher 1979-85, 4th Grade Hum Teacher 1985- Longfellow Sch; *ai:* NYSUT; AFT; MVFT Delegate Assembly Building Rep 1982-; *office:* Longfellow Sch 625 S 4th Ave Mount Vernon NY 10550

DOLDER, KAREN JONES, English Teacher; *b:* Berkeley, CA; *m:* David Frederick; *c:* Robert W. Grove, Pamela K. Grove; *ed:* (BA) Latin, Univ CA Berkeley 1964; Standard Scndry Life Credential, Univ CA Berkeley 1965; *cr:* Eng Teacher San Leandro HS 1965-; *ai:* CA Schlsp Fed 1989-; NCTE, CATE, CCCTE 1975-; *office:* San Leandro HS 2200 Bancroft Ave San Leandro CA 94577

DOLEJSI, ROSE A. SOUKUP, Retired; *b:* Wagner, SD; *w:* James (dec); *c:* Richard, Arnold, John; *ed:* Elem Educ Southern St Coll 1929-30; 1967-68; 1970; *cr:* 1st-8th Grade Teacher Rural Schls; 1st Grade Teacher Geddes Cmmnty Sch; *ai:* SDEA Mem; Retired Teachers Organization Mem; Extention Club Mem; Civic Club Mem; Amer Legion Aux Mem; United Meth Church Mem; Pioneer Club Mem; Sr Citizen Mem; *home:* Geddes SD 57342

DOLES, GLENDA COLEMAN, French/English Teacher; *b:* Valetta, Malta; *m:* Jack; *c:* Terry, Todd; *ed:* (BA) Eng/Fr, N LA Univ 1974; Attestation Universide De Poitiers Poitiero France 1974; (MED) Scndry Ed, N LA Univ 1984; Fr, Universite De Poitier France; *cr:* Teacher Delhi HS 1976-; *ai:* Fr Club Spon; Stu Assistance Comm; Homecoming Court Adv; Delta Kappa Gamma 1987-89; NEA 1974-; LA Assn of Educators Building Facilitator 1986-; Richland Parish Teacher of Yr Awd 1986-87; *home:* 200 Dilling Lake Monroe LA 71203

DOLL, BARBARA ROMERO, Junior HS Mathematics Teacher; *b:* Lake Charles, LA; *m:* Walter; *c:* Angela, Paul, Erich, Karl; *ed:* (BS) Math, 1961, (MED) Math, 1963 Mc Neese St Univ; *cr:* Math Teacher Jennings HS 1962-65, Ludwigsburg Amer HS 1965-66; 3rd/4th Grade Teacher St Joseph Elem Sch 1975-78; 7th/8th Grade Math Teacher Bremen Sch 1982-; *ai:* Academic Team & Mathcounts Coach; KEA, NEA; *office:* Bremen Consolidated Sch Hwy 81 Bremen KY 42325

DOLL, RUTH M, Fourth Grade Teacher; *b:* Napoleon, OH; *m:* John W.; *c:* Chad A., Kurt E.; *ed:* (BS) Elem Ed, Univ of Akron 1970; (MS) Teacher Leadership, Wright St Univ 1988; Whole Lang Cmptr Classes; *cr:* 3rd Grade Teacher Norton City Schls 1970-72; 4th Grade Teacher Wapokoneta City Schls 1980-; *ai:* Math & Sci Specialist; Alpha Delta Kappa Project Chm 1983-; Instr for Project Wild; *office:* Cridersville Elem Sch 300 E Main St Cridersville OH 45806

DOLLMANN, MARILYNN ZACCARINE, Business Teacher; *b:* Buffalo, NY; *m:* Ronald K.; *c:* Kristine, Mark; *ed:* (BED) Bus, 1966, (MED) Ed, 1971 St Univ of NY; *cr:* Bus Teacher Frontier Cntrl HS 1966-68, North Charleston HS 1968-69, Frontier Cntrl HS 1970-; *ai:* South Town Teachers Center Rep; Building Advisory Comm; Boston Historical Society Secy 1980-89; *office:* Frontier HS Bay View Rd Hamburg NY 14075

DOLMATZ, STEVEN J., English Teacher; *b:* New York, NY; *ed:* (BA) Ed, 1979, (MA) Eng, 1986 W WA Univ; *cr:* Eng/His Teacher Ferndale HS 1979-80; Eng Teacher Lopez HS 1980-84, Bellingham HS 1984-; *ai:* Advanced Placement Eng Teacher; WA St Poets Assn, Pacific NW Writers; Gifted & Talented Bellingham Sch Dist Task Force Mem; Published Poetry; *office:* Bellingham HS 2020 Cornwall Ave Bellingham WA 98225

DOLSAK, DONNA MILLIK, Algebra/Geometry Teacher; *b:* Warren, OH; *m:* Edward J.; *c:* John, Tom, Mark, Melanie, Amy, Emily; *ed:* Curr/Instruction, Youngstown St Univ; *cr:* Ld Tutor/Algebra Teacher Mc Donald HS 1972-82; Limited Service Faculty-Math Dept Youngstown St Univ 1981-84; Algebra Teacher Youngstown East HS 1982-83; Geometry Teacher Youngstown Wilson HS 1984; Algebra/Geometry Teacher Mc Donald HS 1985-; *ai:* NEA 1972-; OH Ed Assn 1972-; NCTM 1982-; Mc Donald Comm Chest 1985-; Coord/Supervisor Basic Skills Tutoring Prgm/Math Enrichment Prgm/Stu Aide Group; *home:* 511 Iowa Ave Mc Donald OH 44437

DOMBI, KATHLEEN KAY, 3rd-5th Grade Teacher; *b:* Mercedes, TX; *m:* Tibor Prince Sr.; *c:* Tibor II, Elizabeth, Matthew; *ed:* (BA) Elem Ed, Univ of TX Pan Amer 1973; Bi-ling Bicultural Ed Trng; TX Math Teacher Trng Modules TEA; Teaching Computational Skills Teaching Sci; Developing Sci Process Skills; *cr:* Teacher Aide 1966-71, 1st Grade Teacher 1971-78 Progreso Ind Sch Dist; LLD/Itn Teacher Edcouch-Elsa Ind Sch Dist 1978-80; 1st Grade Teacher 1980-87, 3rd-5th Grade Math/Cmptr Teacher 1987- Progreso Ind Sch Dist; *ai:* Dist Math Prgm Implementation; Cmptr Coord; UIL Coaching; Supts Advisory Cncl; Campus Improvement Leadership Chm; ATPE 1980-; PTA Treas 1984-; BSA Treas 1984-; GSA Leader 1988-; Youth Soccer 1983-; Supervision & Curr Dev Bd; Meth Church Ed Bd; *office:* Progreso Ind Sch Dist P O Box 613 Progreso TX 78579

DOMER, JAMES ALLEN, Physical Education Teacher; *b:* St Joseph, MO; *m:* Cynthia Kay Gipson; *c:* Allen M.; *ed:* (BS) Phys Ed, N TX St 1982; *cr:* Teacher/Coach Lewisville Ind Sch Dist 1983-; *ai:* Track, Spec Olympics; TAPHERD; *office:* Lewisville HS 1098 W Main Lewisville TX 75067

DOMIN, PAUL P., 5th Grade Teacher; *b:* Hartford, CT; *c:* Stefanie A., David P.; *ed:* (BS) Elem Ed, Cntrl CT St Coll 1961; (MED) Elem Ed, Univ of Hartford 1971; *cr:* 3rd/4th/6th Grade/K-6th Supportive Teacher Simsouri Public Sch 1961-69; 5th Grade Teacher Squadron Line Sch 1970-; *ai:* Stu Cncl Adv; Numerous Ed Comms; Cooperating Teacher; Mentor Teacher Prgm; Phi Delta Kappa 1963-; Simsbury Ed Assn; Intnl Assn of Turtles Incorporated; *office:* Squadron Line Sch 44 Squadron Line Rd Simsbury CT 06070

DOMINGUEZ, DIANA GONZALEZ, 2nd Grade Head Teacher; *b:* Laredo, TX; *m:* Jesus; *c:* Laurie, Jesus Jr., Marco A.; *ed:* (BS) Elem Ed, Laredo St Univ 1973; Bi-ling Ed Cert; *cr:* Kndgtn Teacher 1973-74, 1st Grade Teacher 1974-78, 2nd Grade Teacher 1978- Alma Pierce Elem Sch; *ai:* Grade Level Head Teacher; Sch Sci Fair Coord; Southern Assn of Accreditation Schls Comm Chairperson; Assn of Teachers & Prof in Ed 1987; Alpha Delta Kappa Mem 1988-; San Martin de Porras Church Catechist 1979-; GSA Leader Paisano Cncl 1980-87; A Pierce Sch PTC Treas 1982-83; Nom Teacher of Yr Golden Apple Awd 1987; *home:* 908 La Plaza Loop Laredo TX 78041

DOMINGUEZ, GLORIA ANN, Spanish/Honors Teacher; *b:* Everett, WA; *m:* Juan N.; *ed:* (BA) Span, Univ of WA 1961; Post Grad Stud Span, Interamerican Univ Saltillo Mexico; *cr:* Span Teacher/Dept Head Sunset Jr HS 1961-74; Span/Fr/Journalism/Honors Teacher/Dept Head Cascade Mid Sch 1974-; *ai:* Span Club; Yrbk; Stu Tours Mexico; Dist Comm Writing Curr Foreign Lang & Gifted; Co-Produced 5 Musical Comedies; PTSA 1965-, Golden Acorn 1968; WAFLT St Bd Mem 1972-74; Chairperson of Sch Cultural Fair; *office:* Cascade Mid Sch 11212 10th Ave SW Seattle WA 98146

DOMINGUEZ, ROSA MARTHA, Second Grade Teacher; *b:* El Paso, TX; *c:* Joseph A., Adrian, Yvette; *ed:* (BS) Elem Ed, TX Western Coll of Univ of TX 1965; Amer Government, Free Enterprise Elem Ed & Marilyn Burns Math Solution, W TX St Univ; *cr:* Teacher El Paso Ind Schls 1966-70, Amarillo Ind Schls 1978-; *ai:* Budget & Salary Comm for AISD; Eastridges Stu Recognition Comm; ACTA 1978-; Grant Coll of Ed at W TX St Univ From TX Bureau of Ec 1986-87; Honored by Peers as Rep of Excl in Ed to AISD PTA; Banquet; *home:* 6014 Jameson Amarillo TX 79106

DOMINICK, ROGER E., 7th Grade Mathematics Teacher; *b:* Niagara Falls, NY; *m:* Renee M. Parker; *c:* Michael, Brian, Christopher, Natalie; *ed:* (AS) Math/Sci, Niagara Comm Coll 1969; (BS) Scndry Ed/Math SUC Geneseo 1971; Permanent Cert Cortland St; *cr:* Teacher Port Byron Mid Sch 1971-; *ai:* Boys Var Track & Intramural Coach; Stock Market Game; *office:* Port Byron Mid Sch Maple Ave Port Byron NY 13140

DOMINY, SANDY TAYLOR, Social Studies Teacher; *b:* Hamilton, Bermuda; *m:* Andy; *ed:* (BS) Ed, 1984, (MED) Ed, 1988 GA Southern Coll 1988; *cr:* Soc Stud Teacher Bryan Cty HS 1984-85, Appling Cty HS 1985-; *ai:* Colorguard Bandfront Instr & Spon; Jr Class Spon; Prof Assn of GA Educators; *office:* Appling Cty HS Rt 7 Box 45 Baxley GA 31513

DOMKOWSKI, ALEXANDER JOSEPH, Physics/Biology Teacher; *b:* Amsterdam, NY; *m:* Mary Elizabeth Wofford; *c:* Eric J.; *ed:* (BS) Physics Ed, SUNY Albany 1970; (MS) Physics, Univ of AR 1973; *cr:* Physics Teacher Gloversville HS 1973-75; Tech Machinist Stephen F Austin St Univ 1975-78; Physics Teacher Webb Sch 1978-89, St Marys Hall 1989-; *ai:* Frosh Class & Rocket Club Spon AAPT 1978-; STRIVE 1988; AAPT, NSTA Test Comm Mem; Articles Written; *office:* St Marys Hall 9401 Starcrest San Antonio TX 78217

DONAHOE, LAUREEN KAY (MC DONALD), First Grade Teacher; *b:* Darlington, WI; *m:* Tom; *c:* Shannon, Colette; *ed:* (BS) Elem Ed, Univ of WI Platteville 1974; *cr:* 1st/3rd Grade Teacher Holy Rosary Sch 1976-79; 1st Grade Teacher S S Andrew-Thomas 1979-; *ai:* Choreographer & Dir of Plays; Kndgtn Stus Recruiter; All Day & Every Day Kndgtn Comm Evaluator; St Augustine Church Religious Ed Teacher 1983-; *office:* S S Andrew-Thomas Sch RR 1 Potosi WI 53820

DONAHUE, MARTHA M., 5th Grade Teacher; *b:* Providene, RI; *ed:* (BA) Eng/Ed, Salve Regina Coll 1963; (MED) Elem Ed, RI Coll 1974; *cr:* 6th Grade Teacher Edgewood Highland Sch 1970-87; 4th Grade Teacher 1987-89, 5th Grade Teacher 1989- Garden City Sch; *ai:* Parish CCD Teacher; Intnl Rdng Assn RI St Cncl; Cranston Teacher of Yr 1984; *office:* Garden City Sch 70 Plantations Dr Cranston RI 02920

DONAHUE, SHEILA EDMONDS, Elementary Music Teacher; *b:* Fairfield, TX; *m:* Michael Neal; *c:* Vandon M.; *ed:* (BFA) Music, Stephen F Austin St Univ 1976; (MA) Music, Sam Houston St Univ 1983; Kodaly Certificate Sam Houston; *cr:* Elem Music Teacher Aldine Ind Sch Dist 1978-79, Belton Ind Sch Dist 1979-82; Mid Sch Music Teacher Temple Ind Sch Dist 1984-86; Elem Music Teacher Killeen Ind Sch Dist 1986-; *ai:* Hay Branch Select Choir Dir; TX Music Educators Assn Region Elem Chm 1980-; Kodaly Educators of TX Mem at Large 1986-; Organization of Amer Kodaly Educators Guest Clinician at Natl Conference 1989; PTA Assn Co-Prgms Dir 1986-, Teacher of Yr 1988; Co-Author of Childrens Song Book; Frequent Dir of Inservice Music Teachers Sessions; *home:* 608 N Penelope Belton TX 76513

DONALD, CATHY M., Science Teacher; *b:* Locke, NY; *ed:* (BS) Phys Ed, 1977, (MSED) Bio, 1988 SUNY Cortland; *cr:* Sci Teacher Marathon Cntrl Sch 1982-; *ai:* Jr HS Bsktbl Coach; Mem Negotiating Comm; NEA, NY St United Teachers; *office:* Marathon Cntrl Sch Box 339 Marathon NY 13803

DONALD, KAREN BUMPERS, Kindergarten Teacher; *b:* Jackson, AL; *ed:* (BS) Early Chldhd Ed, 1975, (MED) Early Chldhd Ed, 1979 AL St Univ; *cr:* Title I Rdng Teacher 1975-76, Kndgtn Teacher 1976- Coffeeville Elem; *ai:* Textbook Comm Mem 1980-84; NEA, AL Ed Assn 1975-; Clarke Cty Educators Assn (Secy, Exec Bd Mem 1975-85) 1975-, Teacher of Yr 1983; Women Progressive Club Incorporated Soc Chairperson 1985-; Berrys Chapel AME Zion Church (Secy, Sunday Sch Teacher, Usher, Choir) 1961-; Order of Eastern Star Prgm Comm 1984-; Southern Accreditation Colls & Schls Comm 1983; *home:* West Point Dr Jackson AL 36545

DONALDSOFN, SUSAN J., Home Economics Teacher; *b:* Chicago, IL; *m:* William D.; *c:* Keri L., Kristopher L.; *ed:* (BS) Home Ec, S IL Univ 1971; Bus Cmptr Classes; Certified Food Service Sanitation Inst; *cr:* Home Ec Teacher Carbondale HS, Vandalis Cmmty HS; *ai:* FHA Club Spon; Amer Home Ec Assn, IL Voc Home Ec Assn, AVA; *office:* Vandalia Cmmty HS 1109 N 8th St Vandalia IL 62471

DONALDSON, ANNELLE R., Choral Director; *b:* Bristol, VA; *c:* Lisa Donaldson Brow, Leslie, Rob; *ed:* (AA) Piano Performance, Sullins Jr Coll 1956; (BA) Piano Performance, Milligan Coll 1980; (MM) Music/Choral Conducting, Bowling Green St Univ 1986; Post Masters Courses Westminster Choir Coll, VanderCook Coll of Music, Univ of Toledo; *cr:* Music Teacher Unicoi Cty HS 1980-83; General Music Teacher Toledo Public Schls 1983-84, Choral Teacher Start HS 1984-; *ai:* HS & Show Choir; Start Barbershoppers; Asst Band Dir; OH Music Ed Assn 1983-; Amer Choral Dirs Assn 1986-; Hymn Society of America 1980-; Toledo Fed of Teachers Music Comm; Erwin Presbyn Church (Pianist, Choir Dir) 1969-83; St Lucas Luth Church Choir Dir 1984-; *office:* Roy C Start HS 2100 Tremainsville Toledo OH 43613

DONALDSON, KATHLEEN LOVETT, Sixth Grade Teacher; *b:* Double Springs, AL; *m:* Ray D.; *c:* Maleesa, Linda Stewart, Tamara Boatfield; *ed:* (BS) Scndry Ed Eng, 1964, (BA) Eng, 1964 Jacksonville St Univ; (MA) Elem Ed, Univ of AL 1978; *cr:* HS Eng Teacher Southside HS 1964-65; HS Eng/Span Teacher Gaston HS 1965-70; 4th-5th Grade Teacher 1970-73, 6th Grade Teacher 1973- Carlisle Elem Sch; *ai:* Drama/Skit Dir; Creative Writing Chm; Ed Profession Rep; Etowah Ed Assn Rep 1964-; AL Ed Assn & NEA 1964-; AL Rdng Assn 1977; Gadsden Lib Bd of Dir 1989-; Jacksonville St Univ Continuing Ed Bd of Governors 1988-; Gadsden Beautification Comm 1989-; Etowah Cty Teacher of Yr 1966; AL Rdng Journal Contributing Author; *home:* 131 Brentwood Dr Gadsden AL 35901

DONATO, LINDA WELLS, Eng as Second Lang Teacher; *b:* Tomball, TX; *m:* Rickey De Paul Sr.; *c:* Rickey Jr., Shameka; *ed:* (BS) Elem Ed, Univ of Houston 1979; *cr:* 4th Grade Teacher Atherton Elem 1979-80; 5th Grade Eng as 2nd Lang Teacher Felix Tijerina 1980-; *ai:* Grade Level Chairperson; Sunrise Missionary Baptist Church Drill Team Matron; Eng as 2nd Lang Teacher of Yr 1989-; Teacher of Month 1988; *home:* 3113 Vintage Houston TX 77026

DONAVAN, DEBORAH, Fourth Grade Teacher; *b:* Elizabeth, NJ; *ed:* (BS) Elem Ed, Monmouth Coll 1972; (MA) Georgian Ed, Georgian Court Coll 1989; *cr:* 5th Grade Teacher 1972-80, 5th/6th Grade Teacher 1981-83, 4th Grade Teacher 1983- Bayview; *ai:* Alpha Delta Kappa Historian 1988-; Ronald Mc Donald House Volunteer 1988-; *office:* Bayview Sch 300 Leonardville Rd Belford NJ 07718

DONAVON, PATRICIA MISAVAGE, Teacher; *b:* Toledo, OH; *m:* Patrick Timothy Sr.; *c:* Patrick Jr., Samuel; *ed:* (BA) Eng, Univ of Toledo 1976; Advanced Trng The Wkshp Way Xavier Univ of LA 1980; *cr:* 2nd Grade Teacher St Agatha Sch 1979-81; *ai:* St Rose Parish Mem; *home:* 26 Grieb Trl Wallingford CT 06492

DON CARLOS, ROSANNA PAYSON, Chemistry Teacher; *b:* Macon, MO; *m:* James Noland; *c:* Maggie R., William H., Katie M.; *ed:* (BSED) Bio, 1962, (MSED) Ed Bio, 1964 Univ of MO Columbia; (MA) Bio, Univ of MO Kansas City 1972; *cr:* General Sci Teacher Mulholland HS 1962-63; Sci Teacher Manual HS 1964-65, Northeast HS 1965-; *ai:* NHS Spon; Sch Advisory Comm; Mentor; Cadre for Rdng Comprenension & Cognitive Dev Mem; Mentor Trng for Trainers & Cadre Trng for Trainers Mem; *office:* Northeast HS 415 S Van Brunt Kansas City MO 64124

DONCHE, LOUIS, JR., 6th/7th Grade Science Teacher; *b:* Brownsville, PA; *ed:* (BS) Zoology, Penn St 1969; Scndry Cert Teaching General Sci/Bio, 1971, (MS) Ecology, 1975 Edinboro St; Natl Sci Fnd Grant Environmental & Cmptr Trng; *cr:* Sci Teacher James Parker Mid Sch 1971-; *ai:* NEA, PSEA, GMEA 1971-; *office:* James Parker Mid Sch 11781 Edinboro Rd Edinboro PA 16412

DONCHEZ, ROBERT J., Social Studies Teacher; *b:* Bethlehem, PA; *m:* Jayne A. Miller; *c:* Robert M., Kristen N.; *ed:* (BS) Scndry Ed/Poly Sci, Kutztown St Univ 1973; Grad Stud Poly Sci/Ed, Kutztown St Coll Grad Sch; *cr:* Teacher William Allen HS 1972-; *ai:* Citizen Bee & Class Adv; Faculty Interest Comm Mem; Allentown Ed Assn 1973-; PA St Ed Assn, NEA; St Annes Roman Cath Church (Mem, Holy Name Society Mem, Lector, Usher, Lector Coord, 60th Jubilee Comm Co-Chm 1989); Bethlehem Housing Authority (Mem 1978-82, Chm 1979, Commissioner 1978-82); Bethlehem Zoning Bd (Commissioner 1983-88, Mem 1983-88); Northampton Cty Election Bd Mem 1983-88; Bethlehem Area Housing Dev Corporation 1982-84; Mayors Southside Cntrl Bus Dist Mem 1975; Outstanding Young Men in America 1977-78; *home:* 377 Devonshire Dr Bethlehem PA 18017

DONCKERS, JUDITH LUOMA, Spanish Teacher; *b:* Negaunee, MI; *c:* Jessica, Cristelle; *ed:* (BA) Span/Fr, 1968, (MA) Scndry Ed, 1969 N MI Univ; Study in Finland & Mexico; *cr:* Conversational Finnish Instr N MI Univ 1977-80; Fr Teacher 1978-85, Span Teacher 1973- Marquette Sr HS; *ai:* SADD, Span Club, N MI Univ Stu Ed Adv; Marquette Ed Assn (Pres Elect 1986-87, Pres 1987-88); Upper Peninsula Ed Assn Exec Bd Mem 1987-; US Coast Guard Auxiliary Flotilla Commander 1983-85; *office:* Marquette Sr HS 1203 W Fair Ave Marquette MI 49855

DONE, CATHY JEAN, Mathematics/Science Supvr; *b:* Gouverneur, NY; *ed:* (BA) Psych, SUNY Potsdam 1975; *cr:* Math/Sci Supvr Richville Chrstn Acad 1985-88; *ai:* Church Youth Leader; Sci Dept & Sci Fair Chairperson; 4-H Club Leader; *home:* Rt 1 Box 132 Gouverneur NY 13642

DONEGAN, DEBORAH MEALER, English Teacher; *b:* Chapel Hill, TN; *m:* Tracy Lee; *c:* Brett, Abby; *ed:* (BS) Elem Ed, 1978, (MED) Admin/Supervision, 1988 Mid TN St Univ; *cr:* 7th/8th Grade Math/Eng Teacher Connelly Mid Sch 1978-85; 8th Grade Eng Teacher Harris Mid Sch 1985-; *ai:* 8th Grade Class Spon; TN Ed Assn, NEA 1978-; Kappa Delta Phi 1988-; Bedford Cty Care Comm 1988; S Assn of Coll & Schls Evaluation Comm Mem; Inservice Trainer for Cmptr Skills & Effective Schls; *home:* 209 Idle Dr Shelbyville TN 37160

DONEGAN, MARY E., English Teacher; *b:* Montclair, NJ; *m:* Bernard L.; *c:* Brendan, James, Meghan; *ed:* (BA) Eng, Caldwell Coll 1966; *cr:* Teacher Middlesex HS 1966-68, West Milford Township Adult Sch 1974-77; Basic Skills Tutor 1980-83, Teacher 1983- West Milford Township; *ai:* Attendance Appeals Comm; Supervisor of Eng Dept Bookroom; Organize Dept Wide Field Trips; NCTE; NJ Track & Field Ofcls Assn 1975-; Irish Amer Assn of NW Jersey (Recording Secy 1989-, Corresponding Secy 1990); *office:* West Milford Township HS 47 Highlander Dr West Milford NJ 07480

DONER, JUDY PARKER, Sixth Grade Teacher; *b:* Chicago, IL; *m:* Thomas B.; *c:* Michael, Karen; *ed:* (AB) Elem Ed, Augustana Coll 1967; (MED) Elem Ed, GA St Univ 1980; *cr:* 5th Grade Teacher Davenport Comm Sch 1967-68; 6th Grade Teacher Clinton Comm Sch 1969-72; 5th/6th Grade Teacher DeKalb Cty Sch 1977-; *ai:* Grade Chairperson; Stu Cncl Spon; Soc Stud Comm Mem; DeKalb Assn of Educators; *office:* Laurel Ridge Elem Sch 1215 Balsam Dr Decatur GA 30033

DONG, JEFF WING, History Teacher; *b:* Seattle, WA; *ed:* (BA) His, Univ of WA 1966; Ed Cert Ed, 1967, (MA) His, 1972 Seattle Univ; *cr:* His Teacher Pasco HS 1967-; *ai:* Key Club & Class Adv; Var Tennis Coach; PAE Pres 1967; WEA, NEA 1967; Kiwanis 1968-, Adv 1978; Pasco Booster Club; *office:* Pasco HS 1108 N 10th St Pasco WA 99301

DONGVILLO, DARLENE C., Elementary Principal; *b:* Benton Harbor, MI; *m:* David; *ed:* (BA) Elem Ed, Western Mi 1975; (MA) Classroom Teaching, MI ST 1978; (MA) Guidance & Personnel, Western MI 1982; *cr:* Elem Teacher 1975-82, Jr HS

Cnslr 1982-86, Elem Prin 1986- Watervliet Public Sch; *ai:* Assn for Supervision & Curr Dev 1988-; NAEYC 1986-; MI Elem & Mid Sch Prin Assn (Secy) 1986-; *office:* Watervliet Public Schls E Red Arrow Hwy Watervliet MI 49098

DONLEY, MARLIN BUCKLEY, History Teacher/Guidance Cnslr; *b:* Oak Hill, OH; *m:* Joyce; *c:* Josh, Erica, Nick; *ed:* (BA) Health/Phys Ed/His, Morehead St Univ 1972; (MS) Guidance, Univ of Dayton 1987; *cr:* Teacher/Coach Ironton HS 1972-73; His Teacher/Coach Oak Hill HS 1973-76; Owner Oak Hill Parts 1976-82; His Teacher Jackson City Schls 1982-; *ai:* OH Ed Assn, Jackson City Ed Assn; United Presbyn Church Trustee 1989-; *home:* 738 Antioch Rd PO Box 254 Oak Hill OH 45656

DONLEY, ROSS WENDELL, Exploratories Teacher; *b:* Detroit, MI; *m:* Kimberley A. Ioset; *c:* Ryan W., Keeley A., Reed W.; *ed:* (BSED) Industrial Ed, Cntrl MI Univ 1971; *cr:* Teacher Pontiac Cntrl HS 1969-70, Pontiac Northern HS 1971; Teacher/Coach Mayville Area Schls 1972-74, Ludington Area Schls 1974-; *ai:* Jr Class Adv; 7th-12th Grade Boys & Girls Cross Cntry & 9th-12th Grade Girls Var Track Coach; Rdng Comm; Sch Coaches Assn; MI Interscholastic Track Coaches Assn 1974-, Coach of Yr 1982; MI Coaches Assn 1982-, Coach of Yr 1982; MI Indsutrial Ed Assn 1989-; BSA Cub Master 1982-84; Lakestride Race Comm Finish Line Dir 1979-82; *home:* 7275 W Juanita Ludington MI 49431

DONLEY, WILL, U S History Teacher/Dept Chair; *b:* Bethesda, MD; *ed:* (BS) Ed, TX A&M 1974; (MA) His, Univ of CA San Bernardino 1986; *cr:* Teacher Chaparral Mid Sch 1976-85, Moorpark HS 1986-; *ai:* Key Club Adv; Moorpark Educators Assn Pres 1981, We Honor Ours Awd 1984; Alliance for Venturas Future 1988-; Fellowship Natl Endowment for Hum Univ of CA Berkeley, Woodrow Wilson Inst Princeton Univ; *office:* Moorpark HS 4500 N Tierra Rejada Moorpark CA 93021

DONNELL, LARK WILLIAMS, Math Teacher/Dept Chair; *b:* Dallas, TX; *m:* Roland Gene; *c:* Deanna L., Leslie A., Nathan L.; *ed:* (BS) Math/Eng, E TX St Univ 1972; (MS) Math Ed, N TX St Univ 1978; Working Toward Mid-Management Certificate, E TX St Univ; *cr:* Math Teacher 1973-, Math Dept Head 1981- N Garland HS; *ai:* Academic Coach; Southern Assn, Master Teacher, Cntrl Textbook Comm; Group Leader; Math Club Spon; Participated Local Evaluation Math Dept; NCTM 1973-; TX Cncl Teachers of Math; Phi Delta Kappa 1989-; ASCD, Assn of TX Prof Educators, Garland Assn TX Prof Educators; First Presbyn Church Elder; Chosen Academic Math Coach 1983-87; *office:* N Garland HS 2109 Buckingham Rd Garland TX 75042

DONNELLY, JAMES DAVID, JR., Dean of Students; *b:* Ft Belvoir, VA; *m:* Joanne Lee Kogut; *ed:* (AB) Intnl Relations/Poly Sci, Colgate Univ 1982; (MS) Instructional Design, Syracuse Univ 1988; Ed Admin, Syracuse Univ 1990; *cr:* Soc Stud Teacher NY Mills Jr/Sr HS 1983-84; Regional Ed Planner Jefferson-Lewis Counties NY 1985-86; Dist Coord for Gifted/Talented Herkimer Cntrl Sch Dist 1986-87; Vice-Prin Mohawk Cntrl Sch Dist 1987-; Dean of Stus New Hartford Cntrl Sch Dist 1990; *ai:* Mt Zion Chrstn Fellowship Deacon 1989-; Clinton Lions Club; Oneida Cty Young Republicans Secy; March of Dimes Group Leader.

DONNELLY, MARK J., Physical Education Teacher; *b:* Plattsburgh, NY; *m:* Joyce M.; *c:* Patrick, Erin; *ed:* (BS) Phys Ed/Health Ed, Univ of VT 1974; W Chester St Coll 1979; St Univ of NY Plattsburgh 1974-83; *cr:* Phys Ed Teacher Beckmantown Cntrl Sch 1974-77; Phys Ed/Health Teacher St Johns Cntrl Sch 1977-81; Phys Ed Teacer Plattsburgh HS 1981-; *ai:* Athletic Trainer for All Sports Boys & Girls; Var Boys Track & Field Coach 1981-89; NY St Safety Comm Rep Section 7 Mem 1982-87; Chm Section 7 Boys Track & Field NYS Track Comm 1983-86; Natl Athletic Trainers Assn 1980-; Adirondak Track & Field Officials Organization Pres 1989-; *office:* Plattsburgh HS Rugar St Plattsburgh NY 12901

DONNELLY, ROBERT LOWELL, Science Teacher; *b:* San Diego, CA; *m:* Debbie Zschech; *c:* Deanne; *ed:* (BSED) Phys Ed/Bio, N AZ Univ 1972; Grad Stud Univ of AZ; *cr:* Sci Teacher Palo Verde HS 1972-; *ai:* Jr Var & Var Bsbl, Ftbl, Var Sftbl, Var Golf Coach; NEA, AZ Ed Assn, Tucson Ed Assn 1972-; *office:* Palo Verde HS 1302 S Avenida Vega Tucson AZ 85710

DONOFRIO, ARCHIE, Mathematics Teacher/Coach; *b:* Willimantic, CT; *m:* Kathy; *c:* Shannon, Andy, T. J.; *ed:* (BA) Math, Thiel Coll 1974; Grad Stud Westminster Coll, Youngstown St Univ; *cr:* Teacher Mohawk Area HS 1974-; *ai:* Head Ftbl & Bsbl, 8th Grade Bsktbl Coach; Summer Bsbl Asst Coach; MEA, NEA, PSEA 1974-; PA Sch Ftbl Coaches Assn 1984-; W PA Coaches Assn 1990; Croation Club 1975-; Article For PA Scholastic Ftbl Coaches Assn Magazine; Motivational Speaker Local Civic Groups & Youth Organizations; *office:* Mohawk Area HS Mowawk School Rd Bessemer PA 16112

DONOFRIO, DANIEL JOSEPH, Science Teacher; *b:* Columbus, OH; *ed:* (BS) Elem Ed, OH St Univ 1973; *cr:* 6th Grade Teacher Hanby Sch 1974-89, Heritage Mid Sch 1989-; *ai:* Sci Fair Adv; Westerville Ed Assn (VP 1979-80, Faculty Rep 1976-79, 1986-88); Westerville Teacher of Yr 1981; OH Governors Awd for Sci Ed 1985, 1990; *office:* Heritage Mid Sch 390 N Spring Rd Westerville OH 43081

DONOHIE, JOHN M., College/Career Counselor; *b:* Philadelphia, PA; *ed:* (BA) Philosophy, St Charles Seminary 1961; (MS) Linguistics, Univ of PA 1976; Temple Univ, Bryn Mawr Coll, Cath Univ of PR Ponce; *cr:* Span Teacher Cardinal Dougherty HS 1967-74; Cnslr to Hispanico Cardinal Dougherty & Little Flower & Hallahan & North Cath & Roman Cath Schls 1974-84; Act 101 Prgm Teacher Chestnut Hill Coll 1972-; Cnslr to Hispanico Cardinal Dougherty & Little Flower & Hallahan Schls 1984-; *ai:* Dir Jornada Prgm for Married Couples; Bd Mem Consumider Hispano; Cncl of Span Speaking Organizations; Teachers of Eng as Second Lang 1976-88; Mayors Commission for Span Speaking (Bd, Commission Mem) 1980-85; *office:* Cardinal Dougherty HS 6301 N 2nd St Philadelphia PA 19120

DONOHOE, FRANCIS X., English Teacher; *b:* Philadelphia, PA; *m:* Mary Lou White; *c:* Katharine, Patrick, Michael, Eileen Hedrick, Theresa Mc Dougall; *ed:* (BA) Eng Ed, La Salle Univ 1955; (MA) Ed, St Josephs Univ 1969; *cr:* Teacher Harding Jr HS 1956-63; Instr La Salle Univ 1960-85; Teacher Frankford HS 1963-88, Mount Saint Joseph Acad 1988-; *ai:* Sch Yrbk Moderator; Sftbl Asst Coach; La Salle Univ Alumni Assn Pres 1966-67; *office:* Mount Saint Joseph Acad Wissahickon And Stenton Ave Flourtown PA 19031

DONOVAN, DONNA LEA, CHM, Biology/Earth Science Teacher; *b:* Clinton, IA; *ed:* (BA) Bio, Marycrest Coll 1964; (MA) Bio/Earth Sci, Ball St Univ 1971; Geology, Univ of Notre Dame; Research Assistantship, IA St Univ; *cr:* Sci Teacher St Joseph Jr HS 1966-76; Stu Ball St Univ 1970-71, IA St Univ 1976-78; Sci Teacher Assumption HS 1978-; *ai:* Stu Blood Drive Faculty Moderator; Human Dev Curr Study Comm Mem; Area Ed Agency Media & NHS Selection Comm; NABT, Quad Cities Sci & Math Teachers Assn; Scott Cty Outstanding Teacher Awd 1988; Natl Sci Fnd Academic Yr & Summer Grants.

DONOVAN, JAMES THOMAS, HS Social Studies Teacher; *b:* Chicago, IL; *m:* Carol L. Stout; *c:* Brad; *ed:* (BS) His/Phys Ed, 1973, (MS) Counseling, 1978 E TX St Commerce; Grad Stud Psych, Classroom Management, Cmptrs; *cr:* Coach/Teacher/Cnslr Canadian TX 1975-81; Cnslr Dalhart Tx 1981-83; Teacher/Cnslr San Miguel Philippines 1983-87; Teacher/Coach/Cnslr Wethersfield England 1987-; *ai:* 9th Grade Class Spon; Bsktbl Coach; Pres Sch Advisory Comm; Youth Act Coord; TSTA VP 1975-83; Lions Intnl Sargeant-At-Arms 1975-83; United Fund Pres 1981; VFW 1970-; Vietnam Vets of America 1979-; *office:* Wethersfield Mid Sch P O Box 499 APO New York NY 09120

DONOVAN, KAREN MANZEL, Business Dept Chairperson; *b:* Ann Arbor, MI; *m:* Michael L.; *ed:* (BA) Bus/Journalism, Cntrl MI Univ 1974; *cr:* Bus Teacher Waldron Area Schls 1975-; *ai:* Yrbk Adv; *office:* Waldron Area Schls 1338 Waldron Rd Waldron MI 49288

DONOVAN, MICHAEL E., Fourth Grade Teacher; *b:* Harrisburg, PA; *ed:* (BS) Elem Ed, 1973, (MS) Instructional Comm, 1978 Shippensburg St Coll; *cr:* Teacher Summit Street Sch 1974, Midway Sch 1975-83, E Pennsboro Elem Sch 1983-; *ai:* Cmmty Relations & Retirement Banquet Comm; PTO Faculty Liason 1986-.

DONOVAN, NOREEN, Special Education Teacher; *b:* Jersey City, NJ; *ed:* (BA) Elem Ed, Georgian Court Coll 1976; (ME) Spec Ed, Trenton St 1983; Cert Supervision & Prin Jersey City St; *cr:* Kndgtn Teacher Whiting Sch 1976-81; Adjunct Professor Brookdale Comm Coll 1987-89; Spec Ed Resource Center Teacher Whiting Sch 1981-; *ai:* Whiting Sch Tournament of Champions Coord; Core Team Mem; Asst Prin; NEA, NJEA, MTEA; *office:* Whiting Sch Manchester Blvd Whiting NJ 08759

DOODY, JANICE MARIE, 8th Grade Mathematics Teacher; *b:* New York, NY; *ed:* (BS) Ed, St Johns Univ 1971; (MA) Ed, Seton Hall Univ 1974; *cr:* 1st Grade Teacher St Pius X Sch 1962-67, St Marys Sch 1967-68; 4th-6th Grade Teacher 1968-71, 7th/8th Grade Teacher 1972- St Patrick Sch; *ai:* NCEA 1985-89; Southside Hospital Chaplaincy Prgm 1981-; Good Samaritans Hospital Chaplaincy Prgm 1986-; Hospice of South Shore Mem 1986-; *office:* St Patrick Sch Montauk Hwy Bay Shore NY 11706

DORAN, ANNE MARIE, Fifth Grade Teacher; *b:* Medford, MA; *ed:* (BA) Ed, 1960, (MS) Ed, 1965 St Coll Boston; *cr:* 3rd Grade Teacher Hugh Roe O Donnell Sch 1960-62, Danversport Sch 1962-63; 3rd Grade Teacher 1964-85, 5th Grade Teacher 1985- Hugh Roe O Donnell Sch; *ai:* Individualized Rdng Prgm Coord; Faculty Senate.

DORATI, HENRY M., Sr HS Math Teacher; *b:* Old Forge, PA; *m:* Janet M. Bocker; *c:* Mark J., Donna L. Mundenar, David C., Suzanne M.; *ed:* (BS) Scndry Ed/Math, Wilkes Coll 1969; (MS) Scndry Ed/Math, Univ of Scranton 1973; Mainstreaming Stus, Bloomsburg Univ; *cr:* Math Teacher Wyoming Area Sch Dist 1969-70, Mid Valley Sch Dist 1970-73, Lacka Cty Area Voc-Tech 1973-85, Pocono Mountain Sch Dist 1985-; *ai:* Stu Assistance Prgm Mem; Mid Valley HS Founder & Adv; NEA, PA St Ed Assn, PA Cncl Teachers of Math; NE PA Cncl Teachers of Math Monroe Cty Rep; Cub Scouts of America Cubmaster 1970-73; NE PA Outstanding Educator 1972; Natl Sci Fnd Grad Stud Awds; *office:* Pocono Mountain Sch Dist PO Box 200 Swiftwater PA 18370

D'ORAZIO, JOSEPH, HS Spanish/Mathematics Teacher; *b:* Longmont, CO; *m:* Lola; *c:* Rhonda Adler, Margot Hoffman, Thuy, Franco, Lisa; *ed:* (BA) Span, Univ of CO 1972; *cr:* Mgr BPOE 1055 1965-85; Teacher Loveland HS 1987-; *office:* Loveland HS 920 W 29th Loveland CO 80538

DORCAS, CAROLYN BROWN, English Teacher; *b:* Johnson City, TN; *c:* Kelley, Todd; *ed:* (BA) Eng, Bennett Coll 1958; (MA) Scndry Curr/Instruction, WV Univ 1981; Rdng Ed, Marygrove Coll 1972; Urban Sociology, Wayne St Univ 1970; Ethics in Media, Marshall Univ 1983; *cr:* Teacher Acad of the Sacred Heart 1970-73; Team Leader WVU/KCS Teacher Corps Project 1979-81; Comm Specialist Kanawha Cty Schls/Cntrl Office 1981-87; Teacher Dunbar HS 1987-; *ai:* Sch Newspaper & Natural Helpers Spon; NCTE; Alpha Kappa Alpha Secy 1989-; Kanawha Cty Sherrifs Task Force on Substance Abuse 1989-; Adjunct Faculty WV St Coll & Univ of Charleston; *office:* Dunbar HS 27th St & Dunbar Ave Dunbar WV 25064

DORGELO, CAROLYN EVANS, 4th-6th Grade Science Teacher; *b:* St Joseph, MI; *c:* Pamela, Jeffery, Diana Dorgelo Zwirn; *ed:* (BS) Ed/Eng, E MI Univ 1955; (MA) Teaching Educationally/Economically Disadvantaged, W MI Univ 1976; Sci, MI St Univ, Univ of MI, Notre Dame Univ; *cr:* Teacher Grand Haven Schls 1955-56, Benton Harbor Area Schls 1956-59, 1972-82, Magnet Sch Creative Art Acad 1982-; *ai:* Prof Dev Benton Harbor Schls; Elem Sci Curr & Young Authors Comm; MI Sci Teachers; Nom for Natl Sci Teacher, Natl Sci Fnd 1990; Teacher of Yr Benton Harbor Area Schls 1989; Lakeland Choral Bd of Dirs 1980-88; Pro Musica; Grand Mere Assn Secy 1975-85; Teachers Guide Activity Idea, MI Dept of Ed Mini Grant; Schlsp Amer Society Environmental Engrs; Natl Sci Fnd Grant Note Dame; Grant Project Learning Tree Amer Forest Inst.

DORHOUT, MARLENE SUE (VAN LEEUWEN), Middle School English Teacher; *b:* Everett, WA; *m:* Marlin John; *c:* Bret; *ed:* (BA) Elem Ed/Eng, Dordt Coll 1965; Grad Work Adolescence, Comm; *cr:* Eng Teacher Lake Worth Chrstn Sch 1965-67, Watson Groen Chrstn 1967-68, Denver Chrstn Sch 1971-89; *ai:* Prof Growth & Fine Arts Comm; Parent Seminars; CLAS; 2nd Chrstn Reformed Church; Published Column; *office:* Denver Chrstn Schls 2135 S Pearl St Denver CO 80210

DORN, ROBERT DAVID, Technology Education Teacher; *b:* Philadelphia, PA; *ed:* (BS) Industrial Ed, 1975; (MS) 1980 Millersville Univ; *cr:* Teacher Highland Regional HS 1975-76, Cntrl Dauphin Sch Dist 1976-; *ai:* Photography Club Adv; Head Boys Girls Track Coach; Stage Crew Adv; Yrbk Adv; Area Coord People to People HS Stt Ambassador; TEAP 1975-; EPT 1974-; Central Dauphin Sch Dist Distinguished Service Awd 1989; *office:* Cntrl Dauphin Sch Dist 1101 Highland Oberlin-Steelton PA 17113

DORNHEGGEN, NANCY ROSENBLOOM, 2nd Grade Teacher; *b:* Tarrytwon, NY; *m:* Donald H.; *c:* Sydney, Donald II, Jared; *ed:* (BS) Elem Ed 1971; (MED) Guidance & Counseling, 1973 Univ of Cincinnati; Admin & Supervision, Xavier Univ 1983; Marketing Economics Bus Law & Mgmt Univ of Cincinnati 1976-77; *cr:* 1st Grade Teacher 4th St Elem 1971-73; 2nd Grade Teacher a D Owens Elem 1973-; *ai:* Mem Guidance Comm; Mem Attendance & Academic Incenvitve Comm; Mem Effective Schls Trng Comm; Vlybl & Bkstbl Coach; Designer Parent Volunteer Prgm; Supervised Stu Teachers & Practicum Stus; Newport Teachers Assn Sec/Sch Rep 1973-; Northern KY Rdng Assn 1987-; a D Owens PTA 1973-; Valley Temple Mem 1987-; Red Cross Servicement & Veterans Volunteer 1971-73; Teachers Rep Effective Schools Improvement Team; *office:* A D Owens Elem Sch 11th & York Sts Newport KY 41071

DORSEY, DOROTHY, Mathematics Teacher; *b:* Hazlehurst, MS; *m:* Henry Jr.; *c:* Madra N., Kauwambee; *ed:* (BS) Math, Alcorn St Univ 1970; Grad Stud Jackson St Unvi; *cr:* Math Teacher Crystal Springs HS 1970-77, Hazlehurst HS 1977-88, Alexander Jr HS 1988-89, Hazlehurst HS 1989-; *ai:* Bible Club Spon Crystal Springs HS 1971-74; Y-Teen Club Spon Crystal HS 1974-77; Math Club Spon Hazlehurst Jr HS 1980, Math Dept Chm 1984-88; MS Prof Educators 1987-88, 1987-89; NCTM 1978-84; True Light Chrstn Club Advisory Cnslr 1988-; *office:* Hazlehurst HS 101 S Haley St Hazlehurst MS 39083

DORSEY, JEFF, Vice Principal; *b:* Deerring, MO; *m:* Margaret Westerling; *c:* Jeffrey C., *ed:* (BA) Eng Lit, Univ of Americas 1971; (MA) Ed, Univ of Pittsburgh 1973; Univ of MA; Assumption Coll; *cr:* Teacher/Team Leader Pittsburgh PA 1971-77; Teacher Fitchburg Public Schls 1977-86; Vice Prin Memorial Mid Sch 1986-; *ai:* Commonwealth Futures Exec Comm; Bd Mem Literacy Volunteers; Legislative Comm MA Teacher Assn; NEA 1971-; Minority Affairs 1986-; Literacy Volunteers Bd Mem 1985-; Commonwealth Futures Exec Bd 1988-; *home:* 496 Bullard St Holden MA 01520

DORSEY, LORAINE, English Teacher; *b:* Navasota, TX; *ed:* (BA) Eng, Prairie View A&M Univ 1964; (MA) Eng, TX A&M Univ 1971; Educl Psych; *cr:* Jr HS Lang Art/Span Teacher George Washington Carver Jr HS 1964-68; HS Eng Teacher/Secy George Washington HS 1964-68; Eng Teacher Navasota HS 1968-; *ai:* Future Teachers of America Navasota HS Adv; Building Leadership & NHS Selection Comm; Class Spon; TX St Teachers Assn Dist 6 Secy 1979-80; NEA; Grimes Cty Ed Assn (Pres, Building Rep); Alpha Delta Kappa Corresponding Secy 1986-88; Delta Kappa Gamma; Order of Eastern Star Point on Star; Navasota HS Teacher of Yr 1988-89.

DORTCH, ELLEN GARNER, 1st Grade Teacher of Gifted; *b:* Wichita Falls, TX; *m:* Edward Burl; *c:* Edwin B., Chelsea L.; *ed:* (BS) Elem Ed, NE St Univ 1974; Working Toward Masters Sch Admin; Certified in Administering Dev Testing, Gessel Inst; *cr:* 1st Grade Teacher 1978-81, 1st Grade Teacher of Gifted 1982- Collinsville Public Schls; *ai:* Sch Prom Spon; Collinsville Ed Assn Negotiator 1982-83; PTO Bd Mem 1984-86; Kappa Kappa Iota Pres 1981-82; NEA, OK Ed Assn; Cmmty Church (Pres Womens GrouP 1986, Bd Mem 1985-88, Sunday Sch Teacher 1988-); Teacher of Yr 1987; *home:* 15600 Winding Creek Dr Collinsville OK 74021

DOSS, BARBARA MULL, Biology Teacher; *b:* Memphis, TN; *c:* Benita J.; *ed:* (BS) Bio, 1964, (MST) Chem, 1970, (MS) Cmmty Health, 1979 Memphis St Univ; Advanced Placement Bio Wkshp, Univ of AL; *cr:* Bio Teacher Hamilton HS 1967-70, Wooddale HS 1970-83, Cntrl HS 1983-; *ai:* NHS, Sci Club, Sci Olympiad Team, Schls Sci Fair Spon; Phi Delta Kappa Prgms VP 1990; Rotary 1988-, Outstanding Teacher 1988; Delta Sigma Theta Parliamentarian 1990-; St Paul Baptist Church Ushers Pres 1988-; NSTA; Howard Hughes Biomedical Research Prgm 1989; Career Ladder Level III 1985; *home:* 1754 Foster Ave Memphis TN 38114

DOSSER, MARCIA EDGEWORTH, 1st Grade Teacher; *b:* Kingsport, TN; *m:* James B.; *ed:* (BS) Elem Ed/Minor Math, 1979, (MS) Ed, 1982 East TN St Univ; Working on PhD; *cr:* 3rd/6th Grade Math Teacher 1979-86, 1st Grade Teacher 1989- North Side Elem; *ai:* Chairperson TN Teacher Study Cncl; Chairperson Primary Grade Comm; Odyssey of Mind Coach; Curr Cncl Mem Supts Study Cncl; Chairperson Northside Pepper Rally; Johnson City Ed Assn 1988-89 (Sch Rep, Chairperson-Instructional & Prof Dev 1986-89, Pres 1989-90); Phi Delta Kappa Honor Society 1982-; Earned Schlp Grant 1984 Attend ETSU Math Courses; Awarded Grant Create Pepper Rally Academic Motivation North Side 1989-; Sch Teacher of Yr 1982, Article Math Prgm Local Paper; *office:* North Side Elem Sch 1000 N Roan St Johnson City TN 37601

DOSSEY, JOYCE WALTERS, Resource Teacher; *b:* Gilmer, TX; *m:* Melton L.; *c:* John L.; *ed:* (BS) Elem Ed, 1967, (MED) Rdng, 1976 Stephen F Austin; Herman Rdng Prgm 1988; ECRI Rdng Prgm 1978; *cr:* MR Teacher Galena Park Ind Sch Dist 1967-69, Henderson Jr HS 1970-71; TMR Teacher Cntrl Elem 1971-76; Early Chldhd Teacher 1977-79, MR Teacher 1979-84 Ore City Elem; Resource Teacher Ore City Jr/Sr HS 1984-; *ai:* Spec Olympics Coach; TSTA, NEA 1967-70; CEC 1989-; TX Assn for Children & Adults with Learning Disabilities 1980-; *office:* Ore City Jr/Sr HS P O Box 100 Ore City TX 75683

DOTSETH, ERVIN RICHARD, Math Dept Chair/Cmptr Coord; *b:* Clarkfield, MN; *m:* Marlys Ristau; *c:* Holly, Travis; *ed:* (BA) Math, Gustavus Adolphus Coll 1964; (MS) Math, Mankato St Univ 1971; *cr:* Math/Sci Teacher Elmore HS 1964-67; Math & Cmptrs Teacher Buffalo Ctr/Rake HS 1968-; Math Teacher Osseo HS 1967-68; *ai:* Lifetime Mem NEA 1970-; Local Pres ISEA 1968-; NCTM/ICTM 1968-; NCA Evaluation Team 1974; MAPCO Teacher Achievement Awd N Central IA May 1989; Mem NSCD; Achieved Perfect 800 on Quant Ability Pt of Gre at MSU; *home:* 106 3rd St NE Buffalo Center IA 50424

DOTSON, HARRIET OLIVER, 6th Grade Teacher; *b:* Savannah, GA; *m:* William Horace; *c:* William Horace II, Alanna Lenzer; *ed:* (BS) Elem Ed, Armstrong St Coll 1968; (MS) Ed, Augusta Coll 1978; *cr:* 5th-8th Grade Math/Rdng Teacher JHC Elem 1968; 4th/5th Grade Self Contained Teacher Anderson St Sch 1969-71; 4th Grade Self Contained Teacher Sandbar Ferry Elem 1972-74; 5th-8th Grade Title I Remedial Math Teacher Johnston Elem 1974-76; 6th Grade Math Teacher W E Parker Elem 1978-79; 7th/8th Lang Art/Math Teacher Fairforest Mid Sch 1977-78; 6th Grade Teacher Oxford Elem 1980-; *ai:* Academic Improvement Comm Chm; Art Sch Bulletin Bd; Terry Stanford Awd of Creativity; TAC Teacher Advisory Cncl Sch Rep; IRA 1980; NCAE (VP 1990) 1980-, Human Relations Awd; NCAGT 1987-; NCTM 1988; Alpha Delta Kappa Gamma (Pres Elect 1988-, Charter Mem 1985-); Gamma Rho Pres 1990; Kiln for Sch Art Grant; Teacher of Yr & Outstanding Educator Oxford Elem; Completed Great Books Trng Course; NC Mentor & Support Team Trng Prgm; Cmmty Sponsored Act Comm for Schls; NC Effective Teaching Trng Prgm; Future Problem Solving Trng; Paideia Trng; *office:* Oxford Elem Sch Rt 1 Box 487 Claremont NC 28610

DOTSON, JUDY L., Fifth Grade Teacher; *b:* Vancouver, WA; *ed:* (BA) Elem Ed, Univ of Puget Sound 1962; Cmptr Specialist; *cr:* 3rd Grade Teacher Narrowsview Elem 1962-64, Harmon AFB Newfoundland 1964-65; 3rd Grade Teacher/Asst Prin Hanau Elem Germany 1965-67; 3rd Grade Teacher Wheelus Libya 1967-68; 3rd-6th Grade Teacher Croughton Elem Sch England 1968-; *ai:* Sch Newspaper Spon; Coaching Vlybl, Bsktbl, HS Level Womens Tennis; Coord Cmptr Stud & Usage; Overseas Ed Assn (Sub-Regional Rep, Schl Level Rep) 1985-; Womens Inst Treas 1978-86; Published in Various Conferences; Exceptional Ratings & Sustained Superior Awds; *office:* Croughton Elem Sch Box 552 APO New York NY 09378

DOTSON, PAMELA TESTER, 7th Grade Math Teacher; *b:* Grundy, VA; *m:* Charles Edward; *ed:* (BA) Poly Sci, Emory & Henry Coll 1983; (MA) Ed, Morehead St Univ 1986; General Math, Clinch Valley Coll 1987; Mid Sch Cert, Clinch Valley Coll; *cr:* Paralegal Internship for Vickers & Via Law Offices 1983; Teacher D A Justus Elem 1983-87, Hurley Mid Sch 1987-; *ai:* St Jude Childrens Research Hospital Math-A-Thon 7th Grade Participant; PTA Treas; *office:* Hurley Mid Sch Rt 1 Box 111 Hurley VA 24620

DOTTERWEICH, PATRICK TIMOTHY, 7th Social Studies Teacher; *b:* Baltimore, MD; *ed:* (BA) US His, Univ MD Baltimore Cty 1983; Loyola Coll; *cr:* Teacher Westminster West Mid Sch 1984-; *ai:* Yrbk Adv; Curr Comm; Ski Club Adv; Teacher Evaluation Comm; Carroll Cty Ed Assn; MD St Teachers Assn; Leader Confirmation Group; Our Lady of Grace Church; *office:* Westminster W Mid Sch 60 Monroe St Westminster MD 21157

DOTY, DEBBIE SARGENT, Mid Sch Mathematics Teacher; *b:* Albuquerque, NM; *m:* Gary Dale; *c:* Justin D., Terence W.; *ed:* (BA) Elem Ed, OK Univ 1985; *cr:* Math Teacher Wayne Mid Sch 1985-; *ai:* Staff Dev, Chapter II & Indian Ed Comms; Negotiating Team; Stus Against Drug Spon; OEA, NEA; WACT Pres; *home:* Rt 1 Box 78A Wayne OK 73095

DOTY, LILLIE CARSON, Chemistry Teacher; *b:* Winona, MS; *m:* John David; *c:* Rachele Doty Whitehead, Jon A.; *ed:* (BS) Chem/Bio, MS St Univ 1960; (MCS) Chem/Bio, MS Coll 1976; (PHD) Chem Ed, Univ of S MS 1985; MS St Univ; *cr:* Advanced Placement Chem/Bio Teacher Brookhaven HS; Chem Teacher Starkville HS 1988-89; Chem Teacher The MS Sch for Math & Sci 1989-; *ai:* Chem Club; Sci Ed Yrbk Supvr; Amer Chemical Society 1976-, Outstanding Chem Teacher of Yr 1987; NSTA 1976-, Presidential Awd for Excl in Math & Sci Teaching 1989; MS Sci Teachers Assn Outstanding Chem Teacher 1987; Phi Delta Kappa; Amer Red Cross Water Safety Instr 1972-; GSA, BSA 1959-85; Amer Assn of Biochemist & Molecular Biologist Grant; *office:* The MS Sch for Math & Sci PO Box W-1627 Columbus MS 39701

DOUD, DAVID M., English Department Chairman; *b:* Carbondale, PA; *m:* Gwendolyn Thomas; *c:* David Jr., Kelly Lynn; *ed:* (BS) Scndry Ed/Eng, Univ of Scranton 1974; Working Towards Masters Univ of Scranton; *cr:* Teacher NEIU 19 1974-75; Teacher/Chm Lakeland Jr/Sr HS 1976-; *ai:* Stu Cncl Faculty & 7th-9th Grade Adv; Head Bsbl Coach; Stu Assistance Prgm Mem; Curr Cncl; Prof Dev Comm; NCTE 1983-; Amer Bsbl Coaches Assn 1983-89; Trout Unlimited 1987-; Lacka River Corridor Assn 1989-; Scranton Times Bsbl Coach of Yr 1988-89; *office:* Lakeland Jr/Sr HS RD 1 Box 247 Jermyn PA 18433

DOUGHERTY, CLARENCE CLARK, Fourth Grade Teacher; *b:* York, PA; *m:* Ruth Anna Wantz; *c:* Lori A., Clark A., Jeffrey L., Linda L.; *ed:* (AS) Ed, York Jr Coll 1966; (BS) Ed, Mansfield St Coll 1969; *cr:* 4th Grade Teacher Northeastern Sch Dist Conewago Elem Sch 1969-; *home:* RD 11 Box 90 York PA 17406

DOUGHERTY, ELAINE, Seventh/Eighth Grade Teacher; *b:* Youngstown, OH; *ed:* (BSED) Elem Ed, 1970, (MSED) Elem Curr, 1990 Youngstown St Univ; Great Books Fnd Trng Seminar Leader; *cr:* 7th-8th Grade Teacher St Christine Sch 1974-; *ai:* WSCS News Team & Video Crew Moderator & Adv; Sch Liturgy & Diocese Competency Testing Comm Mem; NCEA, Intnl Rdng Assn 1974-; ASCD 1990; Cath Collegiate; Mahoning Valley Historical Society; Authored Text Chapter to be Published; *office:* St Christine Sch 3125 S Schenley Ave Youngstown OH 44511

DOUGHERTY, JAN ALBERT, 4th Grade Teacher; *b:* Butler, PA; *m:* Ryan Sr.; *c:* Ryan Jr.; *ed:* (BA) Elem Ed, Indiana Univ of PA 1962; (MA) Elem Ed, Trenton St Coll 1967; Univ of WA/WWU/Seattle Pacific Univ; *cr:* 5th/6th Grade Teacher Pennsbury Sch 1962-67; 4th/5th Grade Teacher Everett Sch Dist 1967-; *ai:* Bldg Steering Comm; PTA Teacher Rep; Everett Ed Assn (Bldg Rep); WA Ed Assn; NEA; *home:* 4806 Seahurst Ave Everett WA 98203

DOUGLAS, ALICE HENRY, Mathematics Teacher; *b:* Joplin, MO; *m:* Mike; *c:* Chris, Eric; *ed:* (BS) Elem Ed, Pittsburg St Univ 1967; (MS) Elem Ed, Emporia St Univ 1973; *cr:* Math Teacher Eldorado Jr HS 1967-70; K-6th Grade Math Teacher Cheteau Elem 1970-71; 6th Grade Teacher Lincoln Elem 1971-81; 4th Grade Teacher Moran Elem 1981-85; 7th Grade Math Teacher Independence Mid Sch 1985-; *ai:* Stu Cncl & Math Club Spon; Team Leader; AAUW Mem 1989-; KS Ed Assn, NEA Mem 1967-74; Independence Ed Assn Pres; Up With Downs Parent Organization Pres 1981-; *office:* Independence Mid Sch 300 W Locust Independence KS 67301

DOUGLAS, BENNYE MC NAIR, Lang Art/Lit Teacher; *b:* Pageland, SC; *m:* Charles E.; *c:* Devonne, Dawn; *ed:* (BA) Eng, Fayetteville St Univ 1965; Univ of NM, Univ of Denver; *cr:* Teacher Shaw HS 1965-66, Pageland Mid Sch 1969-72, Van Buren Mid Sch 1978-81, Polk Mid Sch 1981-; *ai:* Lit & Lang Dept Chairperson; Polks Teacher of Yr 1981; *office:* Polk Mid Sch 2220 Raymac Rd SW Albuquerque NM 87105

DOUGLAS, IMO JANE (RODGERS), Business Education Teacher; *b:* Liberty, KY; *m:* C. Marvin; *c:* Debbie Clements, Maleena Streeval, Deena Randolph, Marvetta Overstreet, Michele, Delinda Johnson; *ed:* (BS) Bus, 1956, Bus Ed, 1989 Eastern KY Univ; *cr:* Bus Teacher Middleburg HS 1957-62, Casey Cty HS 1964-70, Casey Cty AVEC 1970-; *ai:* FBLA Adv; KEA/NEA; KVA/AVA; Womans Missionary Society.

DOUGLAS, JOAN BARLOW, Second Grade Teacher; *b:* Charleston, SC; *m:* John J.; *c:* Cathleen Douglas Hemphill, John H., Karen L., Michelle Douglas Heaphy; *ed:* (BS) Home Ec/Ed, Winthrop Coll 1952; Univ of MD, Univ of NM; *cr:* 2nd/3rd Grade Teacher Apache Elem 1971-; *ai:* Grade Chm Apache Elem; NEA Building Chm 1975-76, 1983-84; NM Assn for Ed Young Children 1983-84; PTA Bd Mem 1987-; Citizens Commission on Human Rights Area Rep 1986-; Say No to Drugs Area Rep of Church 1987-; *office:* Apache Elem Sch 12800 Copper NE Albuquerque NM 87123

DOUGLAS, LEROY, Social Studies Teacher; *b:* New Orleans, LA; *c:* Karen, Vasin, Hadya; *ed:* (BS) Art/Soc Stud Ed, Southern Univ 1964; (MA) His, AL St Univ 1988; *cr:* His Teacher B T Washington Sch 1964-; *ai:* Jr Class Adv; Teacher Research Linkar United Teacher of New Orleans; NCSS; *home:* 3334 N Derbigny New Orleans LA 70117

DOUGLAS, LINDA GALE, Science/Reading Teacher; *b:* Lafollette, TN; *m:* James Leland; *c:* Anthony, Devin; *ed:* (BS) Sci/Phys Ed, Univ of TN 1981; *cr:* Rdng Teacher Pinecrest Elem 1981-84; Sci/Rdng Teacher Jacksboro Mid Sch 1984-; *ai:* Stu Cncl Adv; Drama, Bsktbl, Sci Olympiad Coach; Energy Bowl Winners Coach; TEA Mem 1981-; *office:* Jacksboro Mid Sch PO Box 438 Jacksboro TN 37757

DOUGLAS, LYDIA DAVIS, 9th Grade English Teacher; *b:* Vero Beach, FL; *m:* James Paul; *c:* Jamilyn; *ed:* (BA) Mass Comm/Eng, Western KY Univ 1972; *cr:* Eng Teacher Vero Beach Jr HS 1978-; *ai:* Dist Instructional Cncl; VBJHS Goals/Missions, Discipline Comm; VBJHS Teacher of Month; *office:* Vero Beach Jr H S 1507 19th St Vero Beach FL 32960

DOUGLAS, MARK TODD, Chemistry Teacher; *b:* Mountain View, CA; *ed:* (BA) Animal Sci, Univ of CA Davis 1986; *cr:* Chem Teacher Valley HS 1988-; *ai:* Ftbl & Badminton Coach; Living Spring Chrstn Fellowship Missions Comm 1990; *office:* Valley HS 1801 S Greenville St Santa Ana CA 92704

DOUGLAS, SERENA E. YATES, Librarian; *b:* Newport, RI; *c:* Florette, Ramona; *ed:* (BS) Scndry Bio/Phys Ed, Alderson-Broaddus Coll 1963; (MA) Ed Fdn/Lib Sci, Univ of NM 1990; *cr:* Phys Ed Teacher Rogers HS 1963-64; Admin Line Officer US Navy WAVES 1964-70; Librarian Asst Belen Public Lib 1977-84; Sci Teacher 1984-89, Librarian 1990- Belen Jr HS; *ai:* Belen Jr HS Sci Fair Coord 1985-88; Rural Sci Fair Comm Mem 1989; Sftbl Coach 1985-; Dist Curr Comm Mem 1984, 1988; NM Sci Teachers Assn 1984-; NM Lib Assn 1990; 1st Baptist Church of Belen 1971-; Natl Sci Fnd Grant 1987; *office:* Belen Jr HS 429 S 4th Belen NM 87002

DOUGLAS, SHEILA HOLLAND, Science Teacher; *b:* Monroe, LA; *m:* Samuel H.; *c:* Angela, Erica; *ed:* (BS) Bio, 1971, (MAT) Bio Ed, 1980 Grambling St Univ; Additional Stud, LA Tech Univ; *cr:* General Sci Teacher Caddo Parish Sch Bd 1972-73; Bio Teacher Lincoln Parish Sch Bd 1974-75; Math/Sci Teacher Union Parish Sch Bd 1975-79; Bio/Chem/Environmental Sci/Life Sci Teacher Bienville Parish Sch Bd 1979-; *ai:* Sr Class Spon; Sci Dept & Sci Fair Chairperson; NEA 1972-; Bienville Parish Ed Assn Sci Textbook Adoption Comm Mem 1972-; NSTA 1990; Delta Sigma Theta 1971-; *home:* PO Box 564 Stadium Dr Grambling LA 71245

DOUGLAS, VIOLET AARON, 5th/6th Grade Teacher; *b:* Brooklyn, NY; *m:* Harvey C.; *c:* Patricia Leslie Jones; *ed:* Adult Ed, Brooklyn Coll; *cr:* Telephone Operator NY Telephone Co 1950-55; Telephone Operator Brooklyn St Hosp 1958-61, Attendant 1962-63 Brooklyn St Hosp; Telephone Operator Ft Hamilton Army Post 1963-66; 3rd Grade Asst Teacher Bd of Ed 1968-68; Occupational Therapy/Trainee I Developmental Center 1972-74; Teacher Kings Acad 1981-; *office:* The Kings Acad 2341 Third Ave New York NY 10035

DOUGLASS, JAMES GARY, Social Studies Teacher; *b:* Abilene, TX; *m:* Rebecca Cagle; *c:* Michelle, Paul; *ed:* (BS) Soc Sci/Speech, Abilene Chrstn 1975; Taft Seminar Abilene Chrstn Univ; W TX St Univ; *cr:* Teacher Claude HS 1986-; *ai:* Assn of TX Prof Educators Pres 1987-; *office:* Claude HS P O Box 209 Claude TX 79019

DOUTT, TERRY ANN (TEYNOR), Third Grade/Music Teacher; *b:* Wichita, KS; *m:* Joseph Eugene; *c:* James L. A. Fraser, Christopher K., Rebecca E.; *ed:* (BS) Early Chldhd/Elem Ed, Kent St Univ 1974; *cr:* 5th-8th Grade Lang Art Teacher St Joseph Sch 1967-69; K-8th Grade Substitute Teacher Tusc Cty Public Schls 1969-73; 3rd/5th Grade/General Music Teacher St Joseph Sch 1974-; *ai:* Coaching Girls Bsktbl; Drama Adv; Foster Parent Rep; Cheerleading Adv; Natl Cath Teachers Assn, OH Cath Teachers Assn 1967-; Foster Parents Assn; *office:* St Joseph Sch 600 N Tuscarawas Ave Dover OH 44622

DOVE, MARTHA PELLE, First Grade Teacher; *b:* Albany, GA; *m:* Jackie C.; *c:* Jackson G.; *ed:* (AA) Albany Jr Coll 1970; (BS) Ed, 1972; (MED) Ed, 1974 GA Southwestern; *cr:* Teacher Broad Ave Sch 1972-73; Flintside Elem 1973-74; Nashville Elem 1974-; *ai:* St/Local Teachers Organizations; Nashville Untd Meth Church Mem.

DOVE, MILDRED ALLENE POWERS, Fifth Grade Teacher/Dept Chair; *b:* Lansing, NC; *m:* Wilmer; *c:* Debbie Dove Kidd; *ed:* (AA) Lees Mc Rae 1952; (BA) Bible/Chrstn Ed, Flora Mac Donald Coll 1954; Numerous Colls; *cr:* 4th Grade Teacher Converse Elem 1960-61; 2nd Grade Teacher Douglas Valley Elem 1961-62; Music/6th Grade Teacher Converse Elem 1963-67; Music/6th/7th Grade Teacher Ashe Cty Schls 1967-71; 6th Grade Lang Art Teacher Dillon Cty Sch 1971-78; 5th/6th Grade Lang Art/Soc Stud Teacher Lamar Elem 1978-; *ai:* Ben Franklin Stamp Club Organizer & Spon 1978-; Teachers Choral Club Organizer & Dir 1978-; Emphasis on Academics Comm 1989-; Stu Cncl Organizer & Adv 1978-81; Intnl Rdng Assn 1978-; Judson Ed Assn Secy 1965-66; NEA, SC Ed Assn 1972-78; Hartsville Civic Chorale 1980-; Order of Eastern Star (Assoc Conductress, Organist) 1974-77; St Matthews Epsicopal Church (Soloist, Choir Mem) 1979-; Listed in Amer Biographical Inst; Teacher of Yr Gordon Elem 1978; *home:* 262 W Broad St Darlington SC 29532

DOVE, THOMAS LELAND, Computer Coordinator; *b:* Panama City, FL; *m:* Pamela Clarke; *c:* Jennifer Dove Carrita, Alan W.; *ed:* (BS) Zoology, Univ of MD 1963; (MLA) His of Ideas, Johns Hopkins Univ 1972; *cr:* Sci Teacher Anne Arundel Cty Schls 1963-66; Bio/Photography/Graphics/Cmptr Teacher/Boating/Writer Bowie HS 1967-; *ai:* Amateur Radio Club; Desktop Publishing Newspaper & Yrbk Co-Adv; Sch Instructional

Team Mem; MD Assn of Sci Teachers Treas 1970; NEA, MSTA, Prince Georges Cty Educators Assn 1967-; Queens Landing Assn Various Comm 1985-; Queen Anne Chorale, Annapolis Chorale, Singers Madrigale & Other Vocal Music Organizations 1963-; Published Articles, Boating, Regional Magazines & Syndicated Newspaper; US Coast Guard Licensed Captain, Pilot & Amateur Radio Operator; *office:* Bowie HS 15200 Annapolis Rd Bowie MD 20715

DOVE, TIMOTHY MARK, 7th Grade Soc Stud Teacher; *b:* Cincinnati, OH; *m:* Lisa Mosca; *c:* Kathryn Rochelle; *ed:* (BS) Soc Stud Comprehensive, Miami Univ 1980; (MA) Curr & Instruction/Design, OH St Univ 1988 Cmptr/Drama/Soc Issues/ Drama Interdiscrimary, OH St Univ; *cr:* 7th Grade Soc Stud Teacher Perry Mid Sch 1981-86; Worthingway Mid Sch 1986-88; Mc Cord Mid Sch 1988-; *ai:* Model United Nations Adv; Worthington Strategic Planning Team; Dist Technology Cncl; Dist Software Evaluation Team; Soc Stud Sequence & Scope Grade Course Study Review Cncl; Head Track Coach Boys/Girls Mc Cord; NCSS 1980-; OH Cncl Soc Stud Assn 1980-; Worthington Ed Assn Treas Candidate 1981-; NEA/OEA 1981 ; Perry Mid Sch Staff/RVW Team US Dept Ed Scndrt Recog 1985; Worthingway Mid Sch Staff/RVW Team US Dept Ed Scndry Recog 1987; Co-Author the American People; Co-Author How to Use BSW III; Worthington Outstanding Young Educator; Sohio Excl in Ed Awd Curr Dev; *office:* Mc Cord Mid Sch 1500 Hard Rd Worthington OH 43235

DOVER, BARBARA ELLMS, Teacher of Gifted Students; *b:* Dexter, ME; *s:* J; *c:* Jeanie Mc Clellan; *ed:* Art Ed, Pratt Inst 1944-46; (BA) Art Ed, 1970, (MA) Art Ed, Univ of NM 1973; Lang Art, Training for Teaching Gifted; *cr:* Librarian 1962-76, Kndgtn Dept Head/Teacher 1962-79 Sunset Mesa Schls; Gifted Prgm Teacher Ernie Pyle Mid Sch 1981-86, Mc Collum Elem 1986-87, Hayes Mid Sch 1986-89, Tomasita Elem 1987-89, Bandelier Elem 1989-; *ai:* Sch Support Team Head; Teachers Applying Whole Lang Mem 1986-89; NCTE Mem 1988-89; Created Math Prgm for Sunset Mera Kndgtn; Nom NM Teacher of Yr 1976; *home:* 10017 Blume NE Albuquerque NM 87112

DOW, CLISTA MARY ETTA, 6th Gr Gifted & Talented Tchr; *b:* Purcell, OK; *ed:* (BS) Eng/His, Tufts Univ 1953; (MED) Ed, Boston Univ 1954; Univ of CT Teaching the Talented Prgm 1976-79; Univ of HI Comparative Ed Asia 1976; *cr:* Teacher Sharon Public Schls 1954-; Gifted/Talented Prgm Adjunct Faculty Lesley Coll/Fitchburg St/Bridgewater St 1979-; *ai:* Math Olympiad Coach; Gifted/Talented Comm; Study Skills Curr Comm; Math Curr Comm; MA Assn for Advancement of Individual Potential Pres 1984 & 1987 Leadership 1989; NCTA Pres 1972 Awd of Merit & Educators Awd 1974; Sharon Teachers Assn Pres 1959-, Ed Awd; World Cncl for Gifted/Talented; MA Teachers Assn; Cncl for Exceptional Children; Natl Assn for Gifted Children; NEA Life Mem; Boston Edison Scholar Radcliffe Coll; Leader of Amer Elem Ed; Horace Marin Grants for Curr in Womens His; Power Over Words Spelling for Intermediate Grades; *office:* Sharon Mid Sch 75 Mountain St Sharon MA 02067

DOW, PATRICIA K., English Teacher; *b:* Bristol, CT; *m:* Ronald E.; *c:* Amy E., Jeremy G.; *ed:* (BA) Eng, Coll of St Rose 1965; (MA) Scndry Ed/Eng Concentration, Univ of Hartford 1966; Grad Stud NY Univ 1973-75, SUNY Albany 1985-; *cr:* Eng Teacher Memorial Boulevard 1965-68, Selma HS 1968-69, Troy HS 1978-; *office:* Troy HS 1950 Burdett Ave Troy NY 12180

DOW-WILSON, KATHRYN, Orchestra Director; *b:* Kansas City, MO; *m:* John P.; *ed:* (BMED) Music Ed, Cincinnati Coll Conservatory of Music 1979; *cr:* Orch Dir Groveton HS 1979-82, Robinson Scndry 1983-; *ai:* MENC, NSOA 1979-; Fairfax Cty Orch Dirs Assn Treas 1989-; Prin Bassist-Fairfax Symphony Orch 1988-; *office:* Robinson Scndry Sch 5035 Sideburn Rd Fairfax VA 22032

DOWDY, HAZEL BROWN, Teacher/VOE Coordinator; *b:* Philadelphia, PA; *m:* Warren C.; *c:* Patricia, Margo, Thomas, Eugene; *ed:* (BS) Ed/Scndry Bus/Eng 1971, (MS) Bus Ed, 1973 TX A&I Univ; Various Cmptr Wkshps; Cmnty Ed Cmptr Classes; *cr:* VOE Teacher/Coord Gregory Portland HS 1971-78; Voc Bus Teacher Del Mar Coll 1976-78; Teacher/VOE Coord Canyon HS 1978-85, Smithson Valley HS 1985-; *ai:* Spon Bus Prof of America; Natl Ed Agency, TX St Teachers Assn; Voc Office Ed Teachers Assn of TX , AVA 1971-; *home:* Rt 4 Box 405 Canyon Lake TX 78133

DOWDY, MILTON DAVIS, 7th Grade Lang Art Teacher; *b:* Roanoke, VA; *m:* Bonnie Brown; *c:* Aaron, Christopher; *ed:* (AA) Bluefield Jr Coll 1967; (BA) Eng/Scndry Ed, MS Coll 1969; (MED) Eng, VA Tech 1980; Grad Stud for Recertification; *cr:* 10th/12th Grade Eng Teacher Yazoo City HS 1969-70; 6th-8th Grade Eng/Lang Art Teacher William Byrd Mid Sch 1970-; *ai:* Soccer Act Spon; Soccer Coach; Team Chairperson; Bsktbl Clock Keeper; Ed Week Comm; Dist P Assn Teachers of Eng 1970-; VA Assn Teachers of Eng; Big Brothers 1970-80, 10 Yr Awd 1980; Lynn Haven Baptist Deacon 1981-89; Recreation Booster Coach 1970-; Jaycees Outstanding Young Educator 1974; *office:* William Byrd Mid Sch 2910 Washington Ave Vinton VA 24179

DOWELL, KELLY JOHNSON, Theatre Arts Teacher; *b:* Statesville, NC; *m:* Rodney Kent; *c:* Samuel A.; *ed:* (BA) Theatre Art, Winthrop Coll 1985; *cr:* Theatre Arts Teacher S Iredell HS 1985-; *ai:* Drama Club Adv; NC Theatre Conference 1989-; NEA 1985-; Stagefront Music Theatre; *office:* S Iredell HS Rt 10 Box 90-A Statesville NC 28677

DOWELL, OLIVIA SPRUNT, Director of Admissions; *b:* Memphis, TN; *m:* Jack T.; *c:* Ginny, Charlotte; *ed:* (BS) Elem Ed, Butler Univ 1974; *cr:* 3rd Grade Teacher 1979-88, Dir of Admissions 1988- Hutchison Sch; *ai:* Yrbk Adv; *office:* Hutchison Sch 1740 Ridgeway Rd Memphis TN 38119

DOWELL, STEVEN GAINES, Music/Band Director; *b:* Knoxville, TN; *m:* Cinderella Rose; *c:* Lori R., Stanley G.; *ed:* (BS) Ed/Music, 1976, (MA) Admin/Supervision, 1989 TN Technological Univ; *cr:* Music/Band Dir Anderson Cty Schls 1975-78; Music/Band Dir/Music Supvr Jefferson Cty Sch 1978-81; Agent TN Farmers Mutual Insurance Co 1981-83; Music/Band Dir Smith Cty Schls 1983-; *ai:* Southern Assn of Colleges & Schls Evaluator; Prof Musician; Summer Band Camp Clinician; TN Scndry Schls Band Dir Assn Secy 1979-81; NEA, TN Ed Assn; Smith Cty Ed Assn Pres 1987-88; Warren Cty FFA Alumni Pres 1983, Outstanding Service Awd 1982, Honorary Chapter Farmer 1983; New Market Fire Dept Pres 1979-81; Outstanding Young Men of America 1983; Eagle Scout Order of Arrow 1968; *office:* Smith Cty HS College Ave Carthage TN 37030

DOWELL, SUE YORK, Eng/His/Skills for Adolescence; *b:* Las Cruces, NM; *m:* Dallas; *c:* Tiffany, Denton; *ed:* (BS) Soc Stud, Eastern NM Univ 1971; Ed, ENMU; *cr:* Teacher Artesia HS 1971-72, Tucumcari HS 1972-81, Tucumcari Jr HS 198 1-; *ai:* Skills of Adolescence Prgm Lions Quest; Asst Vlybl/Bsktbl Coach; Head Track Coach; Stu Cncl; Annual & Chrldrs; Tucumcari Ed Assn, NM Ed Assn, NEA 1971-; Tucumcari Families in Action Bd Mem 1988-; Teen Pregenancy Task Force Mem 1986-87; *office:* Tucumcari Jr H S 914 S Fourth Tucumcari NM 88401

DOWLESS, MARY BYRD, 8th Grade History Teacher; *b:* Jacksonville, NC; *m:* Terry Blake; *c:* Cameron; *ed:* (BA) Elem Ed, Univ of NC Wilmington 1977; (MAED) Elem Ed, E Carolina Univ 1983; Grad Certificate 4th-6th Grade & Mid Sch; *cr:* 5th Grade Teacher 1977-85, 8th Grade Teacher 1985- Bladen Elem Sch; *ai:* Spon Bladen Elem Jr Historian Club; NC Center for Advancement of Teaching Participant; Co-Chairperson Southern Assn of Schls & Colls; NC Assn of Educators Mem 1977-; Center Road Baptist Church (Youth Dir 1983-85, Sunday Sch Teacher 1977-, Missions Leader 1973-85); Outstanding Young Educator Jaycee Awd 1983; Bladen Cty Teacher of Yr 1987-88; Nom E Carolina Outstanding Alumni Awd; *office:* Bladen Elem Sch P O Box 638 Elizabethtown NC 28337

DOWN, JOYCE, IHM, Fifth Grade Teacher; *b:* Port Huron, MI; *ed:* (BSED) His, Marygrove Coll 1961; (MED) Elem Ed, Wayne St Univ 1972; Cert Supervision/Admin, Univ of FL; Teacher Effectiveness Trng, Barry Univ; Courses in Elem Ed; *cr:* 1st/2nd Grade Teacher St Joseph Sch 1961-65; 2nd/3rd Grade Teacher St Mary Sch 1965-67; 3rd Grade Teacher St Joseph Sch 1967-71; 2nd/6th Grade Teacher Nativity Sch 1972-79; 5th Grade Teacher/Prin St Lawrence Sch 1979-82; 5th Grade Teacher St Anns Sch 1982-; *ai:* Beginning Teachers Prgm Peer Teacher; Teachers Advisory Cncl 1988-89; NCEA; Pine Jog; *office:* St Anns Elem Sch 324 N Olive Ave West Palm Beach FL 33401

DOWNARD, JAMES ROBERT, 8th Grade English Teacher; *b:* Gallipolis, OH; *m:* Aletta Diane Sprinkles; *ed:* (BA) Eng/His, OH St Univ 1971; *cr:* Enlisted US Air Force 1972-76; Lab Technician Austin Powder Co 1977-82; Instr Wellston City Sch System 1984-; *ai:* Adv Jr HS Creative Writing Magazine Sprocket; Jr HS Stu Newspaper Mimeograph-Bulletin; OH Ed Assn 1984-; Wellston Teachers Assn 1984-; Appointed & Served on St Comm to Draft Statewide Proficiency Test in Composition 1988; *office:* Wellston Jr HS 118 S New York Ave Wellston OH 45692

DOWNER, RITA HEARD, First Grade Teacher; *b:* DeKalb Cty, AL; *m:* Larry D.; *c:* Stephanie, Matt; *ed:* (BS) Early Chldhd Ed/ Elem, Univ of TN Chattanooga 1982; Ed Univ TN Chattanooga; *cr:* Head Start Teacher Cmmty Services 1982-83; Teacher Boyd-Buchanan Elem 1983-; *ai:* Faculty Select Comm BBS 1987-; TN Rdng Assn 1983-; *office:* Boyd-Buchanan Elem 4626 Bonnieway Dr Chattanooga TN 37411

DOWNEY, DOUGLAS FRANKLIN, Instrumental Music Chairman; *b:* Glenwood Springs, CO; *m:* Ann E. Francis; *ed:* (BME) Music Ed, Univ of CO 1970; Courses in Ed, Univ of N CO, CO Coll, Univ of CO, Adams St Coll; *cr:* Band Dir Washington Irving Jr HS 1971-75, General William Mitchell HS 1975-82, Cheyenne Mountain HS & Skyway Elem 1982-; Instrumental Chm Cheyenne Mountain Schls 1988-; *ai:* Dept Chair Cncl; CO Music Educators Dist 5 Rep 1978-84; Amer Sch Band Dirs Assn 1977-86, Stanbury Awd Regional Winner 1977, St Winner 1978; Phi Mu Alpha Pres 1969-70; Omicron Delta Kappa Pres 1970; Local Teachers Union Bd, Cavalcade of Music Bd, Pikes Peak Music Educators; Performed for Pres Regan 1986; Statue of Liberty Celebration; *home:* 4955 Granby Cir Colorado Springs CO 80919

DOWNEY, JOHN FRANCIS, III, Latin Teacher/Coach; *b:* Cambridge, MA; *ed:* (BA) Classical Lang, Denison Univ 1984; Working Toward Masters Classical Lang, Harvard Univ; *cr:* Latin Teacher Belmont Hill Sch 1985-86, Berwick Acad 1986-; *ai:* Academic Adv; Soccer, Hockey, Bsbl Coach; Admissions Comm; Head Summer Sch Prgm, Study Skills; Summer Travel Coord; Berwick Fellowship 1989-; *office:* Berwick Acad Academy St South Berwick ME 03908

DOWNEY, MARYANN GIORDANO, Spanish Teacher; *b:* Buffalo, NY; *c:* Jennifer, Kathryn; *ed:* (BSC) Span/Scndry Ed, St Univ Coll Buffalo 1971; (MA) Foreign Lang Ed, OH St Univ 1976; *cr:* Span Teacher Williamsville Cntrl Schls 1971-72, Rush-Henrietta Cntrl Schls 1982-83, Penfield Cntrl 1983-85, Maryvale Schls 1985-; *ai:* Mid Sch Span Club Adv & NY St Comm Foreign Langs; Foreign Lang Steering Comm; W NY Foreign Lang Educators Cncl VP 1987-88; NY St Assn Foreign Lang Teachers 1982-88, Service Awd 1988; PTO 1989-; NY St Span Foods & Nutrition Teaching Grant 1980.

DOWNEY, MICHAEL JOHN, English Teacher; *b:* Berkeley, CA; *ed:* (BA) Political Sci, CA St Univ Hayward 1968; (MDIV) Theology, Nashotam House 1974; *cr:* Teacher San Lorenzo HS 1969-74; Asst to Dean Cathedral Church of St Paul 1974-78; Sacred Stud/Dept Chm St James Sch 1978-80; Teacher Notre Dame HS 1980-; *ai:* Model United Nations; NCEA 1980-; F D Maurice Society 1973-; Nashotah & Anglican Theological Review; *office:* Notre Dame HS 1540 Ralston Ave Belmont CA 94002

DOWNEY, SANDRA LEE, English Teacher; *b:* Harrodsburg, KY; *ed:* (BA) Comm Arts 1973, (MA) Scndry Ed 1976 Georgetown Coll; Teaching Cert Georgetown Coll 1982; *cr:* Teacher Mercer Cty Sr HS 1973-89; *ai:* Jr Class Spon; Former Adv Co-Ed-4 Club & Youth in Government Prgm; NEA 1973-89; KEA 1973-89; Calvary Baptist Church/Church Clerk 1988-89; Commissioned As KY Colonel for Contribution to KY; Youth Through YMCA Youth in Government Prgm; Writing Grant to Implement Process Writing in Sch; *office:* Mercer County H S 937 Moberly Rd Harrodsburg KY 40330

DOWNEY, TIMOTHY JOSEPH, Mathematics Teacher; *b:* Napoleon, OH; *m:* Pamela Ann; *c:* Michael, Benjamin; *ed:* (BED) Math, Univ of Toledo 1976; *cr:* Teacher Napoleon HS 1976-; *ai:* Var Boys Track & Field, Asst Var Ftbl Coach; Var N-Club Adv; Math Dept Chm ; Curr, Cmptr, North Cntrl Evaluation Comm; Napoleon Faculty Assn Negotiator 1979-81; OEA, NEA; Greater Toledo Math Cncl, Natl Math Cncl 1976-; OH Assn Track & Cross Cntry Coaches 1981-; Jaycees Treas 1985; United Way Silver Awd; Constructed Geometry Test OH Test of Scholastic Achievement 1983; *office:* Napoleon HS 44 Briarheath Dr Napoleon OH 43545

DOWNIE, GORDON L., Bus Education Teacher; *b:* Cleveland, OH; *m:* Bonnie M. Evans; *c:* Mark, Matthew; *ed:* (BS) Bus/Ec/ Phys Ed, Heidelberg Coll 1957; (MA) Health Ed, WV Univ 1975; Dayton Univ, Detroit Univ, IN St Teachers, OH Univ, WV Univ; *cr:* Teacher/Coach Wooster HS 1957-69, Wheeling HS 1969-71, Martins Ferry HS 1971-; Instr Belmont Tech Coll 1984-; *ai:* Head Boys/Girls Track Coach; Head OVAC Cross Cntry Comm; Mem OVAC Track Comm; NEA, OH Educl Assn 1972-; OH Track Coach Assn 1957-, Cross Cntry Coach of Yr 1982; Eastern Dist Track Coaches Assn Secy 1972-, Dist Coach of Yr 1976, 1988-89; Vance Church (Elder 1975-78, Deacon 1972-75); Run for your Church Comm Dir 1985-; OH Track Coaches Track Clinic Speaker 1976, 1986; *office:* Martins Ferry HS 910 Hanover St Martins Ferry OH 43935

DOWNING, GWENDA WHATLEY, 4th Grade Teacher; *b:* Temple, TX; *m:* Dub; *c:* John, Douglas; *ed:* (MS) Elem Ed, UMHB 1960; *cr:* Teacher Temple Ind Sch Dist 1960-; *ai:* TSTA, TCTA; Temple Telegram Golden Apple Awd; Laniers Teacher of Yr; *office:* Lanier/Temple Ind Sch Dist 201 N 8th Temple TX 76501

DOWNING, INA WOMACK, 4th Grade/Piano/Music Teacher; *b:* Utica, MS; *m:* Ernest William Sr.; *ed:* (BM) Piano, MS Southern Univ Hattiesburg 1950; (MAED) Elem Ed, MS Coll Clinton 1975; *cr:* Piano Teacher Pachuta HS 1950-51, Quitman HS 1951-52, Glen Allan HS 1952-55, Silver City Sch 1955, Utica HS 1961-68; Music/4th Grade Teacher Rebul Acad 1968-; *ai:* Piano Accompanist; MS Music Teachers Assn, Natl Guild of Piano Teachers, MTNA, MS Private Sch Ed Assn; MS Ec Cncl & St Chamber of Commerce MS Stu-Teacher Achievement Recognition STAR Awd 1981-82; *home:* 4547 Downing Rd Raymond MS 39154

DOWNING, JACK RUSSELL, Physical Education Instructor; *b:* Portsmouth, VA; *m:* Janice Kay Hales; *c:* Stephen R., Curtis H.; *ed:* (BS) Phys Ed, Univ of WY 1961; SD St Univ, OR St Univ, Western St Coll, Eastern MT Coll, Univ of WY; *cr:* General Sci Teacher Laramie Jr HS 1961-63, Rock Spring HS 1963-65; Health/Phys Ed Teacher Laramie Jr HS 1965-66; Phys Ed Teacher Cody Public Schls 1966-; *ai:* Phys Ed Equipment Mgr; Coach Frosh Girls Vybl 1982-, Jr HS Sftbl 1961-63, Wrestling 1961-63, 1965-66, Track 1961-63, 1965-66, 1978-88, Vlybl 1978-82, Ftbl 1965-66; Head Coach HS Wrestling 1963-65, 1966-76; Asst Coach Track 1965, HS Ftbl 1966, Frosh Ftbl 1969; Cody Ed Assn 1966-; WY Ed Assn & NEA 1961-; WY Coaches Assn (St VP 1974) 1966-; WY Wrestling Coaches Assn Exec Bd 1974-75; WY Assn Health, Phys Ed, Recreation 1982-; BPOE Schlsp Comm 1965-; Cody Lions Chm of Sight Comm 1976-78; Natl Sci Fnd Grant SD St Univ 1963; Alumnus of Yr 1969; Co-Alumus of Yr 1975; *home:* 2020 Shoshone Trl S Cody WY 82414

DOWNING, JOHN MICHAEL, History Teacher; *b:* Sheffield, England; *ed:* (BA) Eng, Oxford Univ 1968; Ed, Leeds Univ 1969; (MA) His, Sheffield 1981; Spec Ed; *cr:* Teacher Pudsey Coll of Further Ed 1969-71, Rother Valley Coll Of Further Ed 1971-82, Butts Cty HS 1982-84, Rockdale Cty HS 1984-; *ai:* Philosophy Club; *office:* Rockdale Cty HS 1174 Bulldog Cir Conyers GA 30208

DOWNING, LINDA A. LE COMPTE, First Grade Teacher; *b:* Neptune, NJ; *m:* John H.; *c:* Kelley A.; *ed:* (BA) Sociology/Elem Ed, Upsala Coll 1972; (MS) Ed, Monmouth Coll 1976; Georgian Court Coll; *cr:* 1st Grade Teacher West Dover Elem (Toms River Schls) 1972-85; Lang Dev/Rdng Teacher Cedar Grove Elem 1985-86; 2nd Grade Teacher West Dover Elem 1986-88; 1st Grade

Teacher Beachwood Elem 1988-; *ai:* Treas Sr Rep; Coached Chrldng Elem; Math Comm; Soc Stud Dist Comm; Governors Teacher Recog Awd 1988; Treas 1972-; NJEA-NEA 1972-; GSA Brownie Leader 1987-; *home:* 614 Elmwood St Forked River NJ 08731

DOWNING, PHYLLIS L., First Grade Teacher; *b:* St Louis, MO; *m:* Lowell S.; *ed:* (BS) Elem Ed, S IL Univ 1969; Effective Classroom & Math Their Way Wkshps; *cr:* Kndgtn Teacher 1969-71, 1st Grade Teacher 1971-73, 2nd/3rd Grade Teacher 1973-74, 1st Grade Teacher 1974- Bethalto Unit 8 Sch; *ai:* Sftbl Coach; New Paper Club Adv; Underachievers Tutor; Bethalto Ed Assn Building Rep 1973-75; IL Rdng Assn 1970-; PTA Soc Chm 1976-77; NEA 1970-; Remove Intoxicated Drivers VP 1980-81; Amer Quarter Horse Assn 1970-; Amer Paint Horse Assn 1980-.

DOWNING, SHARON S., Teacher of Gifted; *b:* Nashville, TN; *c:* Leslie Bierman, Britt, Derek; *ed:* (BSE) Phys Ed, Memphis St Univ 1959; Guidance, Memphis St 1979-80; *cr:* Phys Ed Instr Caruthersville HS 1959-60, Portageville HS 1960-63; Soc Stud Teacher Wayne Cty Schls 1965-77; Teacher of Gifted/Soc Stud Teacher Hernando Mid Sch 1983-; *ai:* Soc Stud Dept & Soc Stud Fair Chm; Stu Asst Prgm Team Mem; Adopt-A-Sch Coord; MS Assn of Talented & Gifted 1988-; Sunrise Home for Girls Bd of Dir 1989-; United Meth Church Admin Bd 1989-; Hernando Mid Sch Teacher of Yr 1986; Impact II St Winner 1986; *home:* 371 W Robinson Hernando MS 38632

DOWNING, WAYNE, History Teacher; *b:* Tulsa, OK; *ed:* (BSED) His, 1973, (MA) His, 1982 Univ of Tulsa; (ABD) His, Univ of ND ; Candidate Government, Harvard Univ 1983; Freedoms Fnd Seminar 1987; *cr:* Teacher/Coach John F Kennedy Jr HS 1973-74; Deputy Sheriff Tulsa Cty Sheriff Dept 1975-80; Instr Tulsa Jr Coll 1981-82; Teacher/Coach Yucca Valley HS 1985-; Adjunct Asst Professor Chapman Coll 1987-; *ai:* Asst Ftbl Coach 1973-74, 1985-, Bsbl 1985; Act Dir 1986-87; Model United Nations 1985-87; Phi Alpha Theta Pres 1981-83; NCSS 1989-; Southern Historical Society 1982-; CA Amer Legion 1987, Schlsp to Freedom Fnd 1987; US Jaycees 1984, Outstanding Young Men of America 1984; Carnegie Doctoral Fellow 1982-83; Settle Awd; Outstanding His Stu Univ of Tulsa 1982; Published Encyclopedia Article 1984; Morongo Unified Sch Dist Soc Stud Mentor Teacher 1988-; *office:* Yucca Valley HS 7600 Sage Ave Yucca Valley CA 92284

DOWNS, MICHAEL WILLIAM, First Grade Teacher; *b:* Mishawaka, IN; *m:* Suzanne Stultz; *c:* Kori; *ed:* (BS) Elem Ed, IN St Univ 1974; (MS) Elem Ed, IN Univ 1979; *cr:* 4th Grade Teacher 1974-77, 3rd Grade Teacher 1977-80 La Paz Elem Sch; 2nd Grade Teacher La Paz & La Ville Elem Sch 1980-87; Kndgtn Teacher 1987-88, 1st Grade Teacher 1988- La VilLe Elem Sch; *ai:* IN St Teachers Assn; Masonic Lodge, Eastern Star; *office:* La Ville Elem Sch 12645 Tyler Rd Lakeville IN 46536

DOWNS, SUZANNE (STULTZ), Kindergarten Teacher; *b:* Mc Kees Rocks, PA; *m:* Michael William; *c:* Kori; *ed:* (BS) Elem Ed, IN St Univ 1974; (MS) Elem Ed, IN Univ 1979; *cr:* 4th Grade Teacher 1975-76, 2nd Grade Teacher 1976-84 Lakeville Elem; 2nd Grade Teacher 1984-87, Kndgtn Teacher 1987- La Ville Elem; *ai:* 1st-3rd Grade Summer Enrichment Teacher; Grade-Level Chm; IN St Teachers Assn; PTO (Exec Bd Mem, Teacher Rep); Eastern Star; Psi Iota Xi; Meth Church Womens Circle Secy; *office:* La Ville Elem Sch 12645 Tyler Rd Lakeville IN 46536

DOXEY, JO ANNE ARRIGONI, Teacher of Gifted & Talented; *b:* Santa Rosa, CA; *m:* Robert Mills; *c:* Koryn L.; *ed:* (AA) Liberal Arts, Santa Rosa Jr Coll 1955; (BA) Anthropology, Univ of CA Berkeley 1958; Grad Stud; *cr:* 2nd-3rd Grade Teacher Brookfield Village 1959-68; 3rd Grade Teacher Baywood Sch 1968-70; 5th Grade Teacher Laurel Sch 1972-73; 3rd-6th Grade Teacher Highland Sch 1973-; *ai:* Docent Oakland Museum Natural Sci & Art; Amer Assn of Univ Women, CA Teachers Assn, NEA; Oakland Museum Assn; *office:* Highland Sch PO Box 5000 Hayward CA 94540

DOYE, JOETTE CHERYL (FAULL), English/French Teacher; *b:* Dodgeville, WI; *m:* Arlyn; *c:* Joelle M.; *ed:* (BA) Eng/Fr, Univ of WI Platteville 1967; *cr:* Eng/Fr Teacher Highland Public Sch 1977; *ai:* Frnsc Coach; VFW Oratorical Adv; HOBY Ldrshp Adv; NEA; WEA; HEA; Linden Legion Aux; Dodgeville Meth Church; *office:* Highland Public Sch 526 Isabell St Highland WI 53543

DOYLE, CHARLES F., Science Teacher; *b:* Neptune, NJ; *ed:* (BS) Bio/Bio Ed, Monmouth Coll 1970; (MA) Environmental Sci/Ed, Glassboro St Coll 1972; *cr:* Sonarman/Oceanographer US Coast Guard 1964-70; Chief Naturalist NJ Division of Parks & Forests 1968-75; Life Sci/Environmental Sci Teacher Wall Intermediate Sch 1970-; *ai:* Unit Chairperson; Audio Visual Aids Coord; Tennis Coach; NJ Ed Assn Environmental Comm 1972-, Golden Apple Awd 1990; NJ Sci Teachers Mem 1970-; NJ Assn for Environmental Ed VP 1970-80; NEA 1982; NABT Outstanding Bio Teacher of Yr 1978; Howell Township (Mayor 1985, Committeeman 1984-85, Environmental Commission Chm 1974-82); Regular Column Author; US Environmental Protection Agency Awd of Merit 1979; *office:* Wall Intermediate Sch Allaire Rd Wall NJ 07719

DOYLE, CONNIE MASON, 3rd Grade Teacher; *b:* Ruston, LA; *m:* Robert Michael (dec); *c:* Michael B., Carey D., Betsy A.; *ed:* (BA) Elem, LA Tech Univ 1973; *cr:* Teacher Newellton HS 1973-; *ai:* Boy Scouts; *office:* Newellton H S P O Box 645 Newellton LA 71357

DOYLE, DIANE LEWALLEN, Junior English Teacher; *b:* San Angelo, TX; *m:* Kenneth Wayne; *c:* Will C., Claire C.; *ed:* (BA) Journalism/Eng, Angelo St Univ 1982; *cr:* Eng Teacher San Angelo Cntrl HS 1989-; *ai:* UIL Spelling Coach; NCTE 1989-; Area Eng Cncl Secy; Fiesta del Concho Publicity Chm 1988-89; Tri Com Organization Schlsp Chm 1987-89; Southland Baptist Church (Sunday Sch Teacher, Bible Sch Teacher) 1985-; *office:* San Angelo Cntrl HS 100 Cottonwood San Angelo TX 76901

DOYLE, KATHLEEN KOZAR, Sixth Grade Teacher; *b:* Youngstown, OH; *m:* Robert C. II.; *c:* Katherine, Robert C. III; *ed:* (BS) Elem Ed, Youngstown St 1979; Guidance/Outdoor Ed, Bus; *cr:* Teacher Huntsburg Elem 1979-; *ai:* Outdoor Camp Instr; Hiram Coll Summer Scholars 1988-89; *home:* 15893 Chardon Windsor Huntsburg OH 44046

DOYLE, MARY ANNE CAMPANELLA, Mathematics Teacher; *b:* Albany, NY; *m:* Brian John; *c:* Sean, Erica; *ed:* (BS) Math, 1972, (MS) Math Ed, SUNY Albany; *cr:* Math Teacher Mohonasen HS 1972-74, Burnt Hills-Ballston Lake 1974-; *ai:* Cheerleading & Class Adv; Treas of Teacher Assn; NCTM; Assn of Math Teachers of NY St; *office:* Burnt Hills-Ballston Lake HS Lake Hill Rd Burnt Hills NY 12027

DOYLE, WENDY WARREN, K-5th Grade Computer Teacher; *b:* Waterloo, NY; *m:* Dennis Curtis; *ed:* (BA) His, SUCNY Geneseo 1975; (MS) Elem Ed, Elmira Coll 1978; Ed Admin, Univ of SC; Certified Instr Ombudsman Prgm; Beyond Awareness in Gifted Ed; *cr:* 3rd-4th Grade Teacher La Fayette Elem 1976-80; 5th Grade Teacher Socastee Elem 1983-87, Gordon Elem 1987-89; K-5th Grade Cmptr Teacher La Fayette Intermediate & Skoi-Yase Primary 1989-; *ai:* Inservice Cmptr Ed Wkshps for Elem Teacher; Cmptr Equipment Drive, 5th Grade Overnight Readathon 1987-88; 5th Grade Jog America Prgm 1987-88; Kndgtn/5th Grade Book Budy Prgm 1987-88; Grade Level Soc Comm Rep 1987-88; Dir Play for Bi-Centennail 1987-88; 4th/5th Grade Aerobics Prgm on Field Day 1987-88;Sch Soc Comm Chm 1988-89; Book Buddy Coord 1988-89; Jog America Prgm 1988-89; 5th Grade Pen Pal Prgm 1988-89; Grade Level Chm 1988-89; NEA 1976-; Alpha Delta Kappa (Pres 1985-87) 1985-; NYS Cmptr & Tech Assn 1989-; Natl His Honor Society 1975-; Parent/Teacher Group 1989-; Socastee Elem Teacher of Yr 1986; Bd of Dir Waterloo Ed Resource Center 1990; *office:* Waterloo Cntrl Sch Dist Lafayette Intermediate Skoi-Yase Primary Waterloo NY 13165

DOZIER, MARTHA HOOVER, Art Dept Chair/English Teacher; *b:* Edison, GA; *c:* Gary, Dave, Diana Dozier Collins, Daryl; *ed:* (BA) Creative Art/Eng, GA Coll 1951; *cr:* Art/Eng/His Teacher Morgan Jr HS 1956-57; Art Teacher Calhoun Cty HS 1968-70; Art/Eng Teacher Southwest GA Acad 1970-; *ai:* Spon Yrbk Staff; Stage Productionist Elem & HS Prgms; Art Ed Trips Spon; 4 Seasons Garden Club Pres 1968-; Calhoun Cty Historical Society Pres 1990; Sunday Sch Teacher; STAR Teacher SGA 1989; Articles Published; *office:* Southwest GA Acad Box 99 Hwy 47 Damascus GA 31741

DOZIER-BRYANT, SHARON DIANE, Home Economics Teacher; *b:* Houston, TX; *c:* Ruby; *ed:* (BS) Home Ec, 1977, (MA) Home Ec, 1989 TX Southern Univ; Spec Ed Cert Univ of SW LA; *cr:* Educator Ross Sterling HS 1976-78, The Learning Tree 1978-79, Franklin Jr HS 1979-84, Thomas Jefferson HS 1984-; *ai:* FHA Adv; Sabine Area Home Economist 1984-; Natl Assn of Univ Women 1980-; Delta Sigma Theta 1988-; *home:* 6216 Willow Ave Port Arthur TX 77640

DRAFAHL, ROBERT L., 5th Grade Teacher; *b:* Council Bluffs, IA; *m:* Sara Grindstaff; *ed:* (BA) Eng Lit, 1958, (EDM) Elem Ed, 1959 Boston Univ; Admin & Supervision; *cr:* 6th Grade Teacher Wellesley MA 1959-66, St Petersburg FL 1966-68, Ft Lauderdale FL 1968-70; Curr Resource Teacher St Petersburg FL 1970-79; 5th Grade Teacher St Petersburg FL 1979-; *ai:* Safety Patrol Spon; Teacher Evaluation Comm; Pinellas Cty Teachers Assn, NEA, FL Teachers Assn; Church (Bd Chm, Sunday Sch Teacher, Supt); *office:* Shore Acres Elem Sch 1800 62nd Ave N Saint Petersburg FL 33702

DRAKE, ALLEN TERRANCE, 5th Grade Teacher; *b:* Watertown, NY; *m:* Terry Petranchok; *c:* Brent, Emily; *ed:* (BA) Psych, 1973, (MS) Elem Ed, 1977 Potsdam Coll; Grad Work, St Lawrence Univ; *cr:* 6th Grade Teacher 1974, 4th Grade Teacher 1975-76 Carthage Elem Sch; 5th Grade Teacher Philadelphia Elem Sch 1976-, Indian River Mid Sch 1990; *ai:* Bsktbl Coach 7th/8th Grade 1977-85, Jr Var 1985-88, 5th/6th Grade 1977-; Rotary Club of Theresa (Pres 1987-88) 1982-; Theresa Recreation Comm (Secy 1989-) 1987-; Theresa Zoning Bd of Appeals (Chm 1989-88) 1986-; *home:* 108 Red Lake Rd Theresa NY 13691

DRAKE, BETH WILLIAMS, Social Science/Spanish Teacher; *b:* Dothan, AL; *m:* James D.; *c:* Stacy, Shana. James Jr.; *ed:* (BA) Ed/His, West George Coll 1971; (MA) Ed/His, Troy St Univ 1990; *cr:* Teacher Hogansville HS 1971-73; Dir Hogansville Day Care Center 1973-76; Quality Control Lab Supvr Uniroyal-Goodrich 1977-84; Teacher Hogansville HS 1985-; *ai:* Jr Class Faculty Adv; Var & Jr Var Chrldr; Span Club; Stu Support Team Chm; PAGE 1987-; Carl Vinson Inst Governmental Research Grant 1989.

DRAKE, DEE E., Science Teacher; *b:* Ann Arbor, MI; *m:* Madeline Huebel; *c:* Katharine; *ed:* (BS) Earth Sci, 1977, (MS) General Sci, 1984 E MI Univ; *cr:* Sci Teacher Huron HS 1979-; *ai:* Ftbl Coach; Ski Club Adv; Clinical Assoc; Natl Earth Sci Teachers Assn Cmptr Coord 1983-; MI Earth Sci Teacher Assn Cmptr Coord 1983-, Teacher of Yr 1987; Natl Assn of Geology Teachers Teacher of Yr 1987; First Baptist Church Bd of Chrstn Ed 1989-; Articles Published.

DRAKE, INA RAE (NEES), 8th Grade Lit/Eng Teacher; *b:* Dixon, IL; *m:* Gerald Wayne; *c:* Michael, Bradley; *ed:* (BS) Elem Ed, E IL Univ 1967; (MS) Elem Ed, S IL Univ; Administrative, Classroom, Personnel Management; *cr:* 6th Grade Teacher Lincoln Sch 1967-68; 3rd Grade Teacher North Side Sch 1968-73, 1974-88; 5th Grade Teacher Cener St Sch 1973-74; Classroom Mangement/Lecturer S IL Univ 1986-87; Lit/Educ Instr Frontier Comm Coll 1979-; 8th Grade Lang Art Teacher Center St Sch 1988-; *ai:* NEA, IL Ed Assn 1967-86; Fairfield Ed Assn (VP, Pres) 1968-84; IL Assn of Classroom Teachers 1968-69; Delta Kappa Gamma Legislative Chm 1978-81; Omicron Pres 1968-73; Governors Master Teacher Awd 1987; *office:* Center Street Sch 200 W Center St Fairfield IL 62837

DRAKE, JOHN RICHARD, Teacher/Coach; *b:* Nashville, TN; *m:* Nilgun Tuzuner; *c:* Deniz, Amber M.; *ed:* (BS) His, Mid TN St Univ 1972; Post Grad Work Elem Ed, Phys Ed & Recreation; *cr:* Teacher/Coach Incirlik Amer HS Turkey 1980-83, Zama HS Japan 1983-85, Incirlik Amer HS Turkey 1985-; *ai:* Athletic Dir Incirlik Amer HS 1987-; Coach Boys, Girls Bsktbl, Track & Field, Tennis, Ftbl 1980-; Pi Gamma Mu 1971-; Dodds-Med Region Sustained Superior Performance Awd 1989; *home:* 2107 Riverside Dr Nashville TN 37216

DRAKE, KATHERINE ANN, 5th Grade Teacher; *b:* Albany, GA; *ed:* (BS) Speech/Speech Therapy, Shorter; (MS) Ed, Troy 1976; Minor in Eng; *cr:* Speech/Eng Teacher Cairo HS; 5th Grade Teacher C B Greer Elem; 5th-6th Grade Teacher W Pensacola 1978-; *ai:* 5th Grade Newspaper, Audubon, Campus Pride Spon; Math, Soc Stud, Lang Art, Sci Comms; Escambia Ed Assn Building Rep, Finance, Membership Rep; FL Ed Assn, NEA; Friends of the Lib Mem.

DRAKE, MARY JAMES, English Teacher; *b:* Greenwood, MS; *m:* Beirns Thomas; *c:* Mary N., James W.; *ed:* (BS) Eng, Bethel Coll 1966; Grad Course Work Murray St; *cr:* 7th/8th Grade Teacher Chapman Mid Sch 1966-69; 10th Grade Teacher Lee HS 1970-73; 10th/12th Grade Teacher Butler HS 1977-80; 7th/8th Grade Teacher Huntsville Mid Sch 1980-; *ai:* Spon Sch Yrbk; NCTE 1987-89; Huntsville Jaycettes Regional Speak Up 1975.

DRAKE, PAULETTE BOUDREAU, Chemistry Teacher; *b:* Baton Rouge, LA; *c:* Paul IV, Amber M., Kerri A.; *ed:* (BS) Chem/Zoology, SE LA Univ 1971; Working Towards Masters in Sci Ed; *cr:* Geometry/Physics/Marine Sci/Bio Teacher 1984-85, Chem/Advanced Bio Teacher 1985-86, Chem Teacher 1986- Gulfport HS; *ai:* Career Beginnings Inc & Jr Class Spon; Stu Asst Team Mem; MS Sci Teachers Assn 1989-; Acs Teachers Local 1989-; *office:* Gulfport HS 100 Perry St Gulfport MS 39507

DRAKE, ROBIN ANNEAR, Eng Teacher; *b:* Coon Rapids, IA; *m:* Terry C.; *c:* Trent, Tara, Trey; *ed:* (BA) Eng, Buena Vista Coll 1973; Grad Work Marycrest Coll, Univ of IA, NW MO St, IA St Univ, Univ of NE Omaha; *cr:* HS Eng Teacher Mt Ayr HS 1973-74; 7th-12th Grade Eng Teacher Exira HS 1974-76; 7th/8th Grade Eng Teacher Atlantic Jr HS 1976-88; Eng Teacher Empire HS 1988-; *ai:* Jr Class Play Spon; Empire Ed Assn, NCTE; Beta Sigma Phi, First Chrstn Church; *office:* Empire HS Rt 1 Box 155 Duncan OK 73533

DRALLE, PEGGY ANN, Mathematics Teacher; *b:* Knoxville, TN; *m:* Keith Roy; *c:* Melanie Mateyka, Barbara Rainey; *ed:* (BA) Bio/Math, Lindenwood Coll 1968; (MA) Admin, NE MO St 1984; Admin; *cr:* Math Teacher Ft Zumwalt HS 1968-; *ai:* Dept Chairperson; Math Curr Coord; Jr/Sr Class, Pep Club Spon; MNEA 1975-; NMTC 1968-; *office:* Fort Zumwalt N HS 1230 Tom Ginnever Dr O'Fallon MO 63366

DRANCE, DANIEL A., Teacher/Math Dept Chair; *b:* Jamaica, NY; *m:* Patricia A. Damiani; *c:* Matthew, Rene; *ed:* (BA) Math, SUNY Geneseo 1974; (MA) Math, SUNY Stony Brook 1975; Natl Sci Fnd Fellow Studying Applications of Microcomputer in Traditional Math Classroom, Hofstra Univ 1986-87; *cr:* Math Teacher Great Neck South Jr HS 1974-75, Babylon Jr/Sr HS 1975-; Adunct Professor Polytech Univ 1981-; Math Dept Chm Babylon Jr/Sr HS 1986-; *ai:* Advanced Placement Calculus Instr; Sr HS Math Team Coach; Prins Cabinet Mem & Adv; NCTM (Convention Speaker 1989) 1980-; Suffolk Cty Math Teachers Assn 1977-, Teacher of Yr 1986; NY St Assn of Math Supvrs 1986-; Natl Sci Fnd Fellowship Exemplary Teachers of Math 1986-87; Regional Industrial Tech Ed Comm Awd Teaching Excl Winner 1990; *office:* Babylon Jr/Sr HS 50 Railroad Ave Babylon NY 11702

DRAPER, CLAIRE PERRY, Health Teacher; *b:* Memphis, TN; *m:* Harold E.; *c:* Sharilyn Shanks, Sandra; *ed:* (BS) Health/Phys Ed, TN St Univ 1955; Memphis St Univ; *ai:* Natl Jr Honor Society; Memphis Ed Assn; TN Ed Assn; NEA; *home:* 1982 Clovia Ln Memphis TN 38114

DRAPER, DORIS KING, 4th Grade Teacher; *b:* New Castle, PA; *m:* Arthur; *c:* Jill Draper Cook, Joseph, Anne Draper Niiro; *ed:* (BS) Elem Ed, Univ of MO Columbia 1978; Confratute Univ of Ct Storrs Ct Gifted Ed; MO Writers Project; *cr:* 2nd Grade Teacher 1978-88, 3rd Grade Teacher 1988-89 Hermann Elem Sch; *ai:* Chair Hermann Elem Sch Enrichment Team; Chair Gasconade R 1 Cmmty Teachers Salary Comm; Mem TAB Comm; Gasconade R 1 Teachers Assn Pres 1987-88; Scenic Regional Lib Bd Treas 1986-89; St Paul U C C Church Various Comm 1984-89; *office:* Hermann Elem Sch 328 W 7th St Hermann MO 65041

DRAPER, YVONNE DUNCAN, Second Grade Teacher; *b:* Henderson, KY; *m:* P. Randall; *c:* Duncan A., William R.; *ed:* (BA) Elem Ed, IN St Univ 1977; Endorsement Early Chldhd, KY Wesleyan 1977; (MA) Elem Ed, W KY Univ 1979; Rank I Murray St Univ 1981; *cr:* Kndgtn Teacher Corydon-Smith Mills Elem 1977-88; 1st/2nd Grade Teacher 1988-89, 2nd Grade Teacher 1989- Corydon Elem; *ai:* Teacher Assistance Team; NEA, KEA, Henderson Cty Ed Assn (Mem 1977-, Rep 1987-88); Human Rights Comm Secy/Treas 1989-; Belleview United Meth Church Ed Coord 1984-89; *office:* Corydon Elem Sch PO Box 349 Corydon KY 42406

DRASCH, CATHERINE M. SCHUELLER, Mathematics Teacher; *b:* Milwaukee, WI; *m:* John III; *c:* Jeffrey, Andrew, David; *ed:* (BS) Math Ed, Mt Mary Coll 1983; *cr:* Math Teacher Pius XI HS 1983-; *ai:* Math Club & Mu Alpha Theta Adv; Pius XI NML Coord; WI Math Cncl 1983-; *office:* Pius XI HS 135 N 76th St Milwaukee WI 53213

DRAWDY, PATRICIA WILSON, English Teacher; *b:* Phoenix City, AL; *m:* Kenneth D.; *ed:* (BA) Eng, GA Southwestern 1969; *cr:* Eng Teacher Early Cty 1969-71, Dougherty Jr HS 1971-83, Radium Mid Sch 1983-86, Albany Mid Sch 1986-; *ai:* Y-Club Adv; PAGE, NCTE; *office:* Albany Mid Sch 1000 N Jefferson St Albany GA 31702

DREDSKE, SHARON ANNETTE, 5th/6th Grade Teacher; *b:* Berlin, WI; *m:* Richard James; *ed:* (BS) Univ of WI Stevens Point 1980; *cr:* 5th-6th Grade Teacher 1980-83, 6th-7th Grade Teacher 1983-87, 5th-6th Grade Teacher 1987- Coloma Grade; *ai:* 5th-8th Grade Girls Sftbl Coach; *office:* Coloma Grade Sch PO Box 9 Coloma WI 54930

DREISS, ELENORE OROCCHI, Second Grade Teacher; *b:* Jersey City, NJ; *w:* Richard J. (dec); *c:* Richard, Teri Dreiss Calnan, Thomas, David, Steven; *ed:* (BS) Ed, Jersey City St Coll 1954; Working Towards Masters Ed; *cr:* 1st Grade Teacher Ridgefield Elem Sch 1954-55, Bergenfield Elem Sch 1956-57; Chapter I Teacher 1972-73, 3rd/2nd Grade Teacher 1973- Clarendon Sch; *ai:* Secaucus Ed Assn, NJ Ed Assn, NEA; Secaucus Babe Ruth League Pres 1985-87; Clarendon PTA Pres 1968-70, Life Membership 1970; VFW Auxiliary; *office:* Clarendon Sch 685 5th St Secaucus NJ 07094

DREMANN, BEVERLY HENWOOD, Kindergarten Teacher; *b:* Mt Vernon, OH; *m:* Arthur K.; *c:* Katherine Dremann Brown, Amy Dremann Crispin; *ed:* (BS) Elem Ed, OH St Univ 1972; OH St Univ, Bowling Green St Univ; *cr:* 1st Grade Teacher 1957-58, 3rd Grade Teacher 1958-60, Kndgtn Teacher 1960- Fredericktown Local Schls; *ai:* Schlsp Comm; Teacher Assistance Team; Team Leader; Delta Kappa Gamma 1983-; OH Ed Assn 1957-; NEA; Fredericktown Presbyn Church Ruling Elder 1986-; Martha Holden Jennings Scholar 1980; Teacher of Yr 1979; *home:* 26 Crestview Dr Fredericktown OH 43019

DRENNAN, MITZI JAN, English Teacher; *b:* San Angelo, TX; *m:* Brent; *c:* Kaylee J., Kristi B.; *ed:* (BS) Phys Ed/Eng, Angelo St Univ 1978; *cr:* Eng Teacher/Coach Monahans Jr HS 1978-84; Eng Teacher Reagan Cty HS 1984-; *ai:* Stu Cncl Spon; UIL Coach; ATPE; TX Joint Cncl of Teachers of Eng; *home:* 1104 Ohio Big Lake TX 76932

DRENNAN, NINETTE BURNS, Second Grade Teacher; *b:* Beebe, AR; *m:* Wendy; *c:* Cheryl, Mark; *ed:* (BSE) Elem Ed, UCA 1976; *cr:* 3rd Grade Teacher Ward Elem 1976-77; Teacher Beebe Primary 1977-; *office:* Beebe Public Sch 1201 W Center St Beebe AR 72012

DRENNAN, PEGGY HOLLIS, Music Teacher; *b:* Duncan, OK; *m:* Jerry Dale; *c:* Cohn R., Hollis D.; *ed:* (BS) Ed/Music, 1959, (MED) Counseling, Abilene Chrstn Univ; *cr:* Music Teacher Taylor Elem; *ai:* Choir; Guitar Groups; TX Music Ed Assn, TX Choral Dir Assn; Delta Kappa Gamma, Phi Delta Kappa; Outstanding Supervising Teacher Abilene Chrstn Univ 1990; *home:* 2414 Rountree Abilene TX 79601

DRESNER, DANIEL AUGUST, Biology Teacher; *b:* Chicago, IL; *ed:* (BS) Bio - Honors, Roosevelt Univ 1969; (MA) Marine Bio, Stanford Univ 1973; Doctoral Candidate in Comparative Marine Biochemistry Immunology, Stanford Univ 1969; *cr:* Sci Dept Chm Palma HS 1974; Chem/Algebra Teacher N Salinas HS 1975; Sci/ Math Teacher 1975-82, Sci Dept Chm 1977-79 El Sausal Jr HS; Instr Chapman Coll 1979, Hartnell Jr Coll 1980-82; Bio Teacher Salinas HS 1982-; *ai:* US Academic Decathlon Coach; Renaissance Club Founder & Spon; Master Teacher; Amer Assn for Advancement of Sci 1972-76; Amer Inst of Biological Scientists; Sigma Xi Life Mem; Camerata Singers Pres 1987-89; I Cantori Singers 1989-; Monterey Peninsula Parole Advisory Comm Bd Mem 1971-72; Shinner Scholar Chicago Museum of Natural His; Franklin Honor Society Life Mem; Natl Sci Fnd Honorable Mention; Dietz Fellow Stanford; NDEA Fellow Stanford; *office:* Salinas HS 726 S Main St Salinas CA 93901

DRESOW, JOAN RITA, Fourth Grade Teacher; *b:* New Prague, MN; *m:* Jeffry Scott; *c:* Jason, Samual, Benjamin; *ed:* (BS) Elem Ed/Rdng, St Cloud St Univ 1981; Grad Courses Hamline Univ, Mankato St Univ; *cr:* 5th Grade Teacher 1982-85, 4th Grade Teacher 1981-82, 1985- Jordan Elem Sch; *ai:* Chm of Rdng Comm; MN Ed Assn 1981-; Teacher of Yr 1987; *office:* Jordan Elem Sch 815 Sunset Dr Jordan MN 55352

DRESSEL, CAROL M., Third Grade Teacher; *b:* Springville, NY; *m:* Jack E.; *c:* Kimberlee, Jason; *ed:* (BA) N-9 Sci Ed, Suny Brockport 1963; Grad Stud Elem Ed; *cr:* 5th Grade Teacher 1967-68, 7th Grade Sci Teacher 1970-71 Attica Cntrl Sch; 2nd/ 3rd Grade Teacher Pembroke Sch Dist 1974-; *ai:* Delta Kappa Gamma 1987-; St Paul Luth Church (Church Bd 1985-89, Chairperson of Worship & Music Comm); *office:* Pembroke Sch Dist Allegheny Rd Corfu NY 14036

DRETCH, MARIE MAE, 6th Grade Teacher; *b:* Perham, MN; *ed:* (BA) Elem Ed, Health, Southwest St Univ 1974; *cr:* K-8 Teacher Hyde Cty Schls 1974-76; Asst Placement Cnslr Goodwill Industries 1976-79; Bldg Prin/Title I Teacher 1979-82; 6th Grade Teacher 1982- Waubeun/Omega/White Earth; *ai:* Jr HS Knowledge Bowl; Elem Knowledge Master Bowl Adv; Pep Club, Bomber Booster Club; MM Ed Assn 1979-; Waubun Ed Assn Pres 1988-; *office:* Waubun Ogema White Earth Cmmty Box 98 Waubun MN 56589

DREW, BONNIE W., Business Dept Chairperson; *b:* Springfield, TN; *m:* Jim; *c:* Christopher, Kelley, Kathryn, Jim; *ed:* (BS) Bus Management, Mid TN St Univ 1973; Univ of AL, Univ of MO, IL St Univ; *cr:* Operations Coord First Amtenn Financial Corp 1974-77; Receptionist S Cntrl Bell 1977-78; Bus Dept Chairperson Calvary Acad 1980-; *ai:* Stu Cncl; Prom Adv.

DREW, CECELIA HALE, Science Teacher; *b:* Blakely, GA; *c:* Bruce S., Sharon M.; *ed:* Assoc in Sci/Chem, 1964, (BS) Chem, 1980 Columbus Coll; Educl Courses Columbus Coll; Grad Courses GA S Coll, Columbus Coll, Troy St Univ; *cr:* Bookkeeper/Secy Empire Gas Company 1970-73; Worker Blakely Regional Youth Dev Center 1976-77; Substitute Teacher Early Cty Bd of Ed 1977-82; Sci Teacher Randolph Clay HS 1982-; *ai:* Sci Competition Team Spon; Media Comm; Supervise Experiments in Green House; Pilot Club of Blakely (Chm Projects Comm 1988-89, Dir Exec Comm 1989-); First Baptist Church Sunday Sch Teacher 1978-88, Perfect Attendance Awd 1980-88; Sci & Technology Awd 1988; Nom Presidental Awd of Excl in Sci 1989; Whos Who Among Chrstn Leaders 1989; *home:* 429 Washington Ave Blakely GA 31723

DREXLER, NORA LEE BJALME, 4th Grade Teacher; *b:* Bellefonte, PA; *m:* Raymond G.; *c:* Michelle; *ed:* (BS) Ed/Sci, Villa Maria Coll 1969; (MA) Ed/Soc Sci, Gannon Univ 1974; *cr:* 4th Grade Teacher Montclair Elem Sch 1969-78, Chestnut Hill Elem Sch 1978; *ai:* Drug & Alcohol Abuse Prgms; NEA 1969-; Millcreek Sch Dist Employee of Month 1976/1989; Governors Lead Teacher Prgm; Writer & Illustrator Childrens Material; Write, Dir, Produce Television Prgms; Teacher Enhancement Prgm; *office:* Chestnut Hill Elem Schl 1001 W 54th St Erie PA 16509

DREXLER, THERESA REMBOLD, Language Art Teacher; *b:* Louisville, KY; *m:* David J.; *c:* Mary T., Michelle M., Angela M., Regina M., Christopher D.; *ed:* (BS) Elem Ed, Spalding Coll 1972; (MA) Ed, Univ of Louisville 1983; *cr:* 3rd Grade Teacher St Agnes Sch 1969-72; 6th/7th Rdng/Lang Art & 5th Grade Teacher Most Blessed Sacrament Sch 1972-75; 2nd Grade Teacher St Ignatius Martyr Sch 1975-76; 2nd/4th/6th Grades Rdng & Lang Art Teacher St Bernard 1978-84; 1st Grade Teacher West Point Ind Sch 1984-85; Chapt 1 & 6th Grade Rdng & Lang Art Teacher Samuel V Noe Mid Sch 1985-; *ai:* NEA; KEA; JCTA; *office:* Samuel V Noe Mid Sch 121 W Lee St Louisville KY 40202

DRIGGS, PEGGY EASTON, First Grade Teacher; *b:* Charlottesville, VA; *m:* David Allen; *c:* Katie *ed:* (BA) Early Childhood Ed, Meredith Coll 1974; *cr:* Title I Rdng Jonesboro Elem/Deep River Elem 1974-76; 2nd Grade Teacher 1976-89; 1st Grade Teacher 1989- Deep River Sch; *office:* Deep River Sch 7908 Deep River Rd Sanford NC 27330

DRILLINGER, DAVID WAYNE, High School Band Director; *b:* Springfield, IL; *m:* Gail Francis Plassman; *c:* Eric T.; *ed:* (BM) Music Ed, 1974, (MA) Music Performance, 1975 E IL Univ; *cr:* Band Dir Centralia HS 1975-86; Jazz Band Dir Kaskaskia Coll 1976-77; Band Dir Alton HS 1986-; *ai:* Music Dept Chm; Marching & Pep Band; Madison Cty Band Dirs Assn Secy 1989-; Natl Band Assn, Music Educators Natl Conference, IL Music Educators Assn, Assn of Concert Bands; Alton Symphony Orch Bd of Dirs; Soloist Alton Symphony Orch 1990; Centralia HS Educator of Yr 1984-85.

DRINNON, BOBBIE (NEATHERLY), Consumer & Homemaking Teacher; *b:* Mountain City, TN; *m:* Jerry Bruce; *c:* Kimberly D.; *ed:* (BA/BS) Voc Home Ec/Sociology, Carson-Newman Coll 1971; Home Ec, Univ of TN; *cr:* Teacher Cocke Cty HS 1971-75, Cosby HS 1973, Walters St Comm Coll 1974, Ben Hooper Voc Sch 1976-; *ai:* FHA Adv; Peer Counseling Group Adv & Founder; Cocke Cty Educl Assn, TN Educl Assn, America Educl Assn 1971-; Networking for Children & Families Preventing Teen Pregnancy Chairperson 1983-; Cocke Cty Cntrl Charities VP 1982-; Cocke Cty Chamber of Commerce Chairperson 1988-; Peer Prgm Chosen TN Model Prgm; Bev Hooper Voc Sch Outstanding Teacher; *office:* Ben W Hooper Voc Sch Hedrick Dr Newport TN 37821

DRISCOLL, ANN HARRINGTON, 4th Grade Teacher; *b:* Rochester, NY; *m:* Patrick; *c:* Amanda, Patrick; *ed:* (BS) Elem Ed, St Univ of NY 1972; Grad Work, SUNY Geneseo & Brockport; *cr:* Substitute Teacher Avon Cntrl Sch 1972-73; 4th-6th Grade Elem Teacher Letchworth Cntrl Sch 1973-; *ai:* Grade Level Rep; Avon Preservation & Historical Society 1985-; Avon Cmmty Theater 1989-; *office:* D F Lockwood Elem Sch Jordan Rd Gainesville NY 14066

DRIVER, BRENDA JOHNS, Business Education Teacher; *b:* Lubbock, TX; *m:* William Michael; *c:* Heath, Blake; *ed:* (BBA) Bus Ed, TX Tech Univ 1973; *cr:* Bus Teacher Benjamin HS 1974-78, Moriarty HS 1984-; Bus Instr NMSU Branch 1979-81; *ai:* FBLA Adv; Mem Pilot Prgm New Bus Mrktg Curr; Mem Textbook Selection Comm Bus/Mrktg Curr; NM Bus Ed Assn 1984-; Mountain-Plains Bus Ed Assn 1973-; NBEA 1973-; AVA 1989-; NM Bus Ed Adv of Yr 1989; Wkshp Co-Leader at NM Vocational Conf Summer 1989; Wkshp Leader at Mountain-Plains Bus Ed Assn; *office:* Moriarty H S Po Drawer 20 Moriarty NM 87035

DROWN, TIMOTHY JOHN, Athletic Trainer/Health Instr; *b:* Biddeford, ME; *ed:* (MS) Phys Ed/Athletic Trng, IN Univ 1986; (BS) Phys Ed/Athletic Trng/Psych, Plymouth St Coll 1985; Certified Athletic Trainer; First Aid CPR; Drug Alcohol Reduction Trng; *cr:* Health/Phys Ed Instr Plymouth Area HS 1986-; Athletic Trainer New Hampton Prep Sch 1986-87; Head Trainer Plymouth Area HS 1987-; *ai:* Head Athletic Trainer All Sports & Stu Trainers; Head Adv Class of 1992; Co Dir Peer Aids Ed Prgm; Coached Girls Bsktbl & Bsbl; AAPHERD 1984-; NATA 1984-, Certified Trainer 1986; Kappa Delta Pi Membership 1985-; Lions Club 1990; *office:* Plymouth Area HS Old Ward Bridge Rd Plymouth NH 03223

DROZD, STANLEY J., JR., Social Studies Teacher; *b:* Staten Island, NY; *ed:* (BA) His, 1972, (MSED) Scndry Ed/Soc Stud, 1974 Wagner Coll; *cr:* Soc Stud Teacher St Francis Sch 1974; Lang Art/Soc Stud Teacher St Roccos Sch 1975-79; Soc Stud Teacher Robert R Lazar Mid Sch 1979-; *ai:* Montville Township Ed Assn Pres 1988-89; St Adalberts Church Cncl (VP 1985- Pres 1990); *office:* Robert R Lazar Mid Sch 123 Change Bridge Rd Montville NJ 07045

DRUFFNER, JEAN MARIE, 5th Grade Teacher; *b:* Avoca, PA; *ed:* (BA) His/Elem Ed, Mt St Vincent Coll 1967; (MSED) Environmental Ed, SUNY Cortland 1971; Grad Stud Sci, Lang, Ed, EMT; *cr:* 5th-8th Grade Teacher St Josephs Sch 1967-68; Outdoor Ed Coord Cortland Madison Cty BOCES 1970-71; Asst Prgm Dir Ashokan Outdoor Ed Center 1972-73; 5th Grade Teacher Phoenicia Elem Sch 1968-70, 1973-; *ai:* Environmental Ed Dir Initiated & Directed Prgm Phoenicia Elem 1970-87; Explorer Scout Post 60 Shandaken NY Adv; Guitar Club; Sci, Gifted, Talented Resource Teacher; NSTA 1986-; PTA 1968-, Jenkins Awd 1985; NYS Conservation Commission Bd Mem 1975-85; St Francis De Sales Childrens Choir Leader 1973-; Frost Valley YMCA Co-Leader Wilderness Trips 1976-82; Stu Conservation Assn Co-Leader Wilderness Project 1983; 3 Articles Published Communicator NY St Outdoor Ed Journal; Organized & Led Explorer Scouts in Tropical Forest & Marine Sci Project to Belize; Taught Guitar; *home:* Box 108 Woodland Valley Rd Phoenicia NY 12464

DRUIETT, NANCY JEAN, Third Grade Teacher; *b:* Enid, OK; *ed:* (BS) Elem Ed, OK St Univ 1981; (MED) Elem Ed, Northwestern OSU 1990; *cr:* 2nd/3rd Grade Teacher Garfield Elem Sch 1981-85; 4th Grade Teacher Harrison Elem Sch 1986; 3rd Grade Teacher Mc Kinley Elem Sch 1987-; *ai:* Stu Cncl Spon; Mem of PTA; Private Tutoring; NEA 1981-; OEA/EEA 1981-; Cherokee Strip Rdng Cncl Membership Chm 1982-; Willow View United; Meth Church Childrens Coord 1982-88; *home:* 4109 S La Mesa Apt C5 Enid OK 73703

DRUM, SUE MARTIN, Fourth Grade Teacher; *b:* Mount Airy, NC; *c:* Steven, Amy; *ed:* (BA) Elem Ed, Appalachian St Univ 1972; *cr:* Teacher Jonesville Elem Sch 1972-; *ai:* NCAE 1972-;NEA 1972-;YCAE:1972-; Teacher of Yr Jonesville Sch; *office:* Jonesville Elem Sch 101 Cedarbrook Rd Jonesville NC 28642

DRUMMOND, JAMES WILLIAM, JR., Fifth Grade Teacher; *b:* Melfa, VA; *m:* Hedy Laverne Jamison; *c:* James III; *ed:* (BA) His, Barber Scotia Coll 1969; (MS) Elem Ed, Morgan St Univ 1975; Loyola Coll; *cr:* Teacher John Ruhrah Elem 1969-; *ai:* Liberty Road Bsbl & Bsktbl; Phi Delta Kappa 1988-; Omega Psi Phi 1968-; PTO John Ruhrah Secy 1975-, 15 Yr Pen; *office:* John Ruhrah Elem Sch 701 S Rappolla Baltimore MD 21224

DRUMMOND, JULIA BUTLER, English & Drama Teacher; *b:* Charleston, SC; *c:* William B, Bradley C.; *ed:* (BA) Eng, Winthrop Coll 1965; (MAT) Eng, Converse Coll; Univ of Paris Through Temple Univ/Furman Univ/Clemson Univ/Coll of Charleston/Univ of SC; *cr:* 8th 9th 10th & 11th Grade Eng Teacher Wren HS 1965-66; 9th Grade Eng/Fr Teacher Sans Souci Jr HS 1966-68; 10th & 11th Grade Eng Teacher J L Mann HS 1970; 7th & 8th Grade Eng Teacher Greenville Mid Sch 1970-80; 7th & 8th GradE Fr/Soc Stud/Typing/Speech Home Ec Teacher; 7th & 8th Grade Eng Teacher 1980-; 7th & 8th Grade Fr/Soc Stud/Drama Teacher 1990-Bryson Mid Sch; Eng 101 & 102 North Greenville Coll 1982-84; Eng 100,101,102,235 Greenville Tech Coll 1986-; *ai:* Drama Act; Local Newspaper Contributor; Civic Oration Contest Coord; Essay Contest Coord; Greenville Cty Ed Assn 1970-; SC Ed Assn 1970-; NEA 1970-; Alpha Delta Kappa Sergeant at Arms 1967-; Honorary Teachers; St Ed Improvement Act Grant; Wkshp in Service Leader; Teacher Incentive Prgm Grant; Published Pamphlets Articles; Speaker for Service Clubs Such As Lions Club/Music Club/Rotary Club; *home:* 6 Oak Hollow Ct Greenville SC 29607

DRUMMOND, MABEL S., Fourth Grade Teacher; *b:* Peebles, OH; *m:* Clarence E.; *c:* Stephen E., D. Anthony; *ed:* (BS) Bus Ed, Wilmington Coll 1949; (MS) Elem Ed, Miami Univ 1984; Grad Stu Miami, Mt Saint Joseph; Bus Coll, Buckeye St, Elem Ed, OH Univ & Univ of Cincinnati; *cr:* Bus Teacher Franklin Rural Sch 1945-47, Mc Clain HS 1950-59; 4th Grade Teacher Greenfield

Exempted Village 1968-; *ai:* Greenfield Teachers Assn Secy 1953; OEA, NEA; Delta Kappa Gamma VP 1990; Presbyn Church Womens Assn Mem; *home:* 589 Turkey Ridge Rd Lyndon OH 45681

DRUMMOND, PATRICIA FERGUSON, English/Speech Teacher; *b:* Buckhannon, WV; *m:* Fred Lane; *ed:* (BA) Eng/Speech, Morris Harrey Coll 1964; (MED) Scndry Ed, Marshall Univ 1971; Grad Stud; *cr:* Eng/Speech Teacher Woodrow Wilson Jr HS 1964-89, South Charleston HS 1989-; *ai:* Jr Class Spon; Girls Track Coach; Play Production Adv & Teacher; *office:* South Charleston HS One Eagle Way South Charleston WV 25309

DRY, MARY JO EILERS, Honors & AP English Teacher; *b:* Hallettsville, TX; *m:* James Randall; *c:* Bobbie Walker, Becky Upchurch, Diane Candler, Carol Summers; *ed:* (BSED) Music Ed/Eng, 1958, (MED) Elem Ed, 1967 SW TX St Univ; Grad Stud Spec Ed, Logic; Variuos Wkshps Through Dist Grants; *cr:* 2nd Grade Teacher Garwood Elem Sch 1966-67; 2nd/3rd Grade Teacher Bloomington Ind Sch Dist 1967-71; Spec Ed/Team Leader/Elem Teacher 1971-75, MS Eng/All Level Rdng Lab Teacher 1975-80, HS Eng/Honors Advanced Placement Teacher 1980- Comal Ind Sch Dist; *ai:* CISD Dist Staff Dev Comm Mem; UIL Literary Criticism & Ready Writing Coach; NCTE, TX Joint Cncl Teachers of Eng 1980-; Sts Peter & Paul Cath Church Mem 1971-; Welder Conservation Grant; *office:* Canyon HS 1510 E IH35 New Braunfels TX 78130

DRYDEN, SUSANNAH RODENBERGER, Director of Orchestras; *b:* Salina, KS; *m:* Phil S.; *c:* Edward, Victor Lafond, Paul, Laura; *ed:* (BMED) Music Ed, Univ of AZ 1966; *cr:* Orch/General Music Teacher Sunnyside Jr HS 1966-69; Orch Teacher Winslow Public Schls 1969-72; Elem Vocal Music Teacher Franklin Sch 1972-74, Garfield Sch 1978-79, Chetopa Schls 1979-82; Asst Orch Dir 1982-87, Orch Dir 1987- Dodge City Public Schls; *ai:* Jr/Sr HS Orch Trips & Act; Music Educators Natl Conference, KS Music Educators Natl Conference, Amer String Teachers Assn, KS String Teachers Assn, NEA, KS Ed Assn; First Southern Baptist Church, Amer Diabetes Assn; *home:* 106 W Mulberry Dodge City KS 67801

DRYE, BONNIE TIDWELL, Sixth Grade Teacher; *b:* Kennett, MO; *m:* Charles O.; *c:* Marc, Marcie; *ed:* (BA) Elem Ed, AR St Univ 1958; Elem Ed, Emporia St 1962; *cr:* Teacher Springfield R-12 1987-; *ai:* Advisory & Textbook Comm; SNEA Building Rep; Womens Federated (Pres 1977, Secy 1976), Outstanding Woman of Yr 1971; *office:* Laura Ingalls Wilder Sch 2526 S Hillsboro Springfield MO 65804

DRYE, YVONNE C., Business Education Teacher; *b:* Albemarle, NC; *m:* Tim E. Sr.; *c:* Eddie, Bonnie, Sherrie; *ed:* (BS) Bus Ed, Pfeiffer Coll 1962; (MS) Bus Ed, Univ of NC 1972; Advanced Cert Courses, UNC-G; EDAF 795; KS St Univ; *cr:* Bus Teacher West Stanly HS 1962-64; 7th/8th Grade Math Teacher Ferndale Jr HS 1967-68; Bus Teacher Thomasville HS 1969-; *ai:* Jr Class Adv; Prom Comm Adv; Developed Bus Mgmt Courses NC Presentation Vocational Ed Conf; NCAE/NEA 1962-64 1967-; ASCD 1989-; Steering Comm Chairperson Southern Assn Accreditation Steering Comm 1985; *office:* Thomasville HS 410 Unity St Thomasville NC 27360

DRZAL, ROBERT, English Teacher; *b:* Manhattan, NY; *m:* Valerie Pamlanye; *c:* Justin; *ed:* (BA) Eng, Dowling 1970; (MS) Ed, Suny Stony Brook 1976; *ai:* Coach Track; Coach Yr at Suny Farmingdale Bsktbl; Long Island 1985-89; Region XV 1986/89; NYS Jr College Coach Yr 1989; *office:* Oakdale-Bohemia Rd Jr H S Oakdale-Bohemia Rd Oakdale NY 11769

D'SOUZA, EDWARD JOHN, Science Department Chairman; *b:* Rangoon, Burma; *ed:* (BA) Physics, Grinnell Coll 1984; (MA) Cmptr Ed, Azusa Pacific 1986; Claremont Graduate Sch; Jr Diploma Fr Lalliance Franchise; *cr:* Sci/Math Teacher Kolb Jr HS 1985-87; Chm Sci Dept-Mentor Teacher/Gifted & Talented Ed Coord/Physics/AP Physics/Math Teacher Eisenhower HS 1987-; *ai:* Academic Decathlon Coach Sci/Math; Coord Dist Sci Fair; Concert Pianist/Organist; NEA 1985-; Kiwanis Intnl Mem 1986-88; Mentor Teacher 1989-; CA Teachers Improvement Prgm Grants; *office:* Eisenhower H S 1321 N Lilac Ave Rialto CA 92376

DUAIME, ROBERT E., Mathematics Teacher; *b:* Philadelphia, PA; *ed:* (BS) Math, Univ of Pittsburgh 1972; (MED) Scndry Math Ed, Temple Univ 1975; PA State Univ British Open Style Learning; Shippensburgh Univ Cmptr Assisted Learning; Philadelphia Coll of Textiles Cmptr Lab; Allentown Coll Cmptrs in Classroom; *cr:* Math Teacher Cncl Rock HS 1972-74, Cncl Rock Intermediate 1974-75; Math Dept Chm Cncl Rock Jr HS 1977-86; Co-Curr Team Leader Cncl Rock Intermediate 1978-85; Math Teacher Cncl Rock Intermediate Jr HS 1975-; *ai:* Bucks Cty Teacher of Math Ed Newsletter 1985-88; PSEA Resolutions (Mideast Region CO-Chm 1984-, Asst Chm 1987-); Our Lady of Grace Church (Head Lector 1984-, Captain Cath Charities Appeal 1989-); *office:* Council Rock Jr HS 400 E Holland Rd Holland PA 18966

DUBBS, SHIRLEY ANN MILLER, Social Studies Teacher; *b:* New Paris, OH; *m:* Philip E.; *c:* Patrick E., Allison A.; *ed:* (BA) Soc Sci Comprehensive, 1967, (MED) Curr Supervision, 1976 Miami Univ Oxford; Trng, Wright St Univ & Miami Univ; *cr:* 6th Grade Lang Art Teacher New Madison Local Sch 1970-72; Soc Stud Teacher Tri Village Local Sch 1972-; *ai:* Publications Yrbk & Newspaper; Links After Sch Counseling Prgm; Academic Advisory Comm; TVEA (Recording Secy, Building Rep); OEA, NEA, OH Soc Stud Cncl; United Meth Church; Teacher of Yr 1988; Natl Issues Forum Fellowship; Write Weekly Column for Cty Daily Newspaper; *office:* Tri Village Local Sch Dist S Main St New Madison OH 45346

DUBE, RONALD NORMAN, Science Teacher; *b:* Nashua, NH; *m:* Roseanna Dougherty; *c:* John, Ben, Luke; *ed:* (BA) Bio, Univ of NH 1964; (MS) Bio, Rivier Coll 1970; Credit Courses Taken at Dartmouth & Suffolk Univ; *cr:* Teacher Milford NH Area Sr HS 1969-70, Nashua Sr HS 1970-79, N Middlesex Regional HS 1979-82, Varnum Brook Mid Sch 1982-; *ai:* Curr Dev in Sci Ed N Middlesex Regional Sch System; NEA, MTA, N Middlesex Sch Assn 1979-; Natl Eagle Scout Assn; Returned Peace Corps Volunteers Mem; Part Time News Reporter & Photographer; Named Citizen of Yr by Nashua NH Chapter DAU 1985; *office:* Varnum Brook Mid Sch Hollis St Pepperell MA 01463

DU BOIS, ANN FORGIE, 5th Grade Teacher/Team Leader; *b:* Somerset, PA; *m:* Maurice R.; *c:* Steven M., Ronald A., Carole A.,; *ed:* (BA) Poly Sci, Gettysburg Coll 1958; (MS) Communicative Disorders, Johns Hopkins Univ 1983; Towson St Univ, Johns Hopkins; *cr:* Elem Classroom Teacher Baltimore City Public Schls 1960-64; 4th/5th Grade Teacher Bushy Park Elem 1979-; *ai:* 5th Grade Team Leader; 5th Grade Act Coord; HCEA, NEA; Howard Cty Chamber of Commerce Outstanding Educator Awd 1986; Lang Art Class Produced Film which Won Various Awds; *office:* Bushy Park Elem Sch 2670 Rt 97 Glenwood MD 21738

DU BOIS, KAREN YORK, Business Education Teacher; *b:* Clayton, GA; *c:* Jim; *ed:* (BS) Assoc Bus, Webber Coll 1967; (BS) Bus Admin, Brenau Coll 1985; Ed Courses & Working on Masters Bus Ed, North GA Coll; *cr:* Exec Secy Bowles & Tillinghast Inc 1969-73; Office Mgr Ratchford & Mc Daniel 1974-75; Real Estate Sales 1979-85; Assoc Broker ERA Linda A Durrence Realty 1985-; Bus Ed Teacher Rabun Cty HS 1985-; *ai:* FBLA Adv; Stu Handbook Comm; GA Bus Ed Assn 1986-; Natl Assn of Realtors 1982-; Rabun Cty Bd of Realtors 1985-; *office:* Rabun Cty HS Rt 1 Box 1339 Tiger GA 30576

DU BOIS, NOLA JANE, First Grade Teacher; *b:* Huron, SD; *ed:* (BS) Elem Ed, Hyles Anderson Coll 1977; *cr:* 1st Grade Teacher Hammond Baptist Grade Sch 1977-; *ai:* Active Mem of Worlds Largest Sunday Sch; *office:* Hammond Baptist Grade School 134 W Joliet St Schererville IN 46375

DU BOISE, ROSETTA JENNINGS, 7th & 8th Grade Teacher; *b:* Chattanooga, TN; *m:* Marion Jr.; *c:* Deena R., Terrence M.; *ed:* (BED) Elem Ed, Chicago Teachers Coll 1962; (MA) Rdng, Roosevelt Univ 1988; Career Awareness/Gifted Ed; *cr:* 3rd Grade Teacher Crown Sch 1962-65; 5th Grade Teacher Melrose Park Sch 1965-66; 6th/7th/8th Grade Teacher Garfield Sch 1966-76, Jane Addams Sch 1977-; *ai:* Chairperson of Teacher Educl Dev Comm; Teacher of Extracurricular Class Creative/Critical Thinking Gifted of 4th & 5th Graders; Spon Jane Addams Sch His Fair; IL His Fair-Advisory Bd Mem 1987- Paticiaption Plaque; Intnl Rdng Assn Mem 1988-89 Honor Chapter 1988; Maywood Cncl 1966-, Local 571 Teachers Union; Maywood United Way Bd & Secy 1987- Commendation 1989; John Vaughans Schlsp Fund Ad-HOC Mem 1985- Commendation 1988; Sigma Gamma Rho Mem 1960; Outstanding Young Women of America 1966; Nom Apple Awd Outstanding Teacher Comm on Teaching Excl; Olive S Foster Awd IL St Historical Society; *office:* Jane Addams Sch 910 Division Melrose Park IL 60160

DU BOSE, DIANE MOORE, Second Grade Teacher; *b:* Wilmington, NC; *m:* Jeff; *c:* Kent, Tamara; *ed:* (BA) Early Chldhd, Univ of NC Wilmington 1966; *cr:* 2nd Grade Teacher William H Blount Elem 1973-76, Pine Valley Elem 1976-; *ai:* Soc Stud Contact Person; Interim Review, Soc Stud, Sch & Cmmty Comm; Cooperating Teacher of Univ of NC Wilmington Stu Teachers; NEA, NC Ed Assn 1973-; Assn of Classroom Teachers, Intnl Rdng Assn 1984-; Alpha Delta Kappa 1989-; NC Jr Sorosis 1978-80; Pine Valley Elem Sch Teacher of Yr 1985-86; *home:* 332 Bristol Rd Wilmington NC 28409

DU BOSE, JANET HAYES, 4th Grade Teacher; *b:* Mc Comb, MS; *c:* Stephen; *ed:* (AA) Basic, Copiah-Lincoln Jr Coll 1971; (BS) Elem Ed, 1973, (MS) Elem Ed, 1986 Univ of S MS; Grad Work at S MS & SE LA Univ; *cr:* 7th/8th Grade Teacher Amite Sch Center 1973-78; 6th Grade Teacher Brookhaven Public Schls 1978-79; 4th Grade Teacher S Pike Public Schls 1979-; *ai:* MTAI Peer Teacher Evaluator S Pike Schls; MSTA 1989-; SPAE, MAE, NEA 1984-; DAR Amite River Chapter 1975-; Pike Cty Citizens for Clean Air 1989-; Natl Sci Fnd Grant 1988-89; Chem for Elem Teachers USM; Teacher of Yr Magnolia Elem 1989; Presenter Sci Wkshps; *office:* Magnolia Elem Sch 275 W Myrtle St Magnolia MS 39652

DUBREUIL, PATRICK ROLAND, French/Spanish Teacher; *b:* Manchester, NH; *m:* Diane Bibeau; *c:* Nicole, Elise, Danielle; *ed:* (BA) Philosophy, Univ of Ottawa Canada 1970; (MA) Theology, Univ of Louvain Belgium 1973; *cr:* Parish Priest R C Diocese of Manchester 1975-80; Span Apostolate-Diocese of Manchester 1980-82; Bi-Ling Ed Teacher Leonard Sch 1982-83; Fr/Span Teacher Amherst Mid Sch 1983-; *ai:* NH Assn of Teachers Foreign Lang; Amherst Ed Assn Personnel Policy Chairperson 1989-; *home:* 11 Mulvanity St Nashua NH 03060

DUBUS, CHARLENE MOUTON, Home Economics Teacher; *b:* Abbeville, LA; *m:* Ardie Dubus; *c:* Julie, Jason, Dennis; *ed:* (BA) Home Ec Ed, 1981, (BA) Dieteties, 1981 Univ of S LA; *cr:* Teacher Indian Bayou HS 1981-; *ai:* FHA Adv; 9th Grade Homeroom Spon; Domestic Homemaker; VAE Active Mem 1982-; *office:* Indian Bayou HS Rt 2 Box 249 Rayne LA 70578

DUCAT, CHRISTINE A. (WEINER), Mathematics Department Teacher; *b:* Milwaukee, WI; *m:* Gary G.; *c:* Jason; *ed:* (BSE) Math, Univ of WI Whitewater 1977; Educl Courses, Univ of WI Madison, Marian Coll, Cardinal STritch, Univ of WI River Falls, Univ of WI La Crosse, Univ of WI Stevens Point; *cr:* Math Teacher Fall River HS 1977-; *ai:* Frosh Class Adv; WI Math Cncl 1977-; Fall River Ed Assn Treas; *office:* Fall River HS 150 Bradley St Fall River WI 53932

DUCHARME, JANICE A., English Teacher; *b:* Webster, MA; *ed:* (BA) Psych, Nichols Coll 1975; *cr:* General Mgr Wollborg-Michelson 1976-81; Eng Teacher Bartlett HS 19 82-; *ai:* Jr Class & Graduation Adv; MA Teachers Assn Mem 1982-; Webster Educators Assn Mem 1982-; Whos Who Among Students Amer Univ & Colls 1974; 1st Female Stu Registered Nichols Coll 1971; 1 of 5 Female Graduates Nichols Coll 1975; Nom Nichols Coll Outstanding Female in Bus 1980; *office:* Bartlett HS Lake Pkwy Webster MA 01570

DUCHEK, MARY K., First Grade Teacher; *b:* Belleville, IL; *m:* Ronald W.; *c:* Joseph, Katharine; *ed:* (BA) Eng/Ed, St Louis Univ 1976; (MED) Rdng, Univ of MO St Louis 1983; *cr:* 2nd Grade Teacher Assumption Sch 1976-78; 1st Grade Teacher Francis Howell Sch Dist 1978-; *ai:* Beginning Teachers Mentor; MO Ed Assn Mem 1978-; BSA Den Leader 1989-; Voted Castlio Sch Teacher of Yr 1987; *office:* Castlio Sch 1020 Dingledine Rd Saint Charles MO 63303

DUCKWORTH, KELLY LEE, 6th Grade Teacher; *b:* Cumberland, MD; *ed:* (BA) Elem Ed, Shepherd Coll 1982; Quest Intnl Trng; Project Charlie Trng; *cr:* 6th Grade Teacher John J Cornwell Elem 1984-86; 2nd Grade Teacher 1987; 6th Grade Teacher Romney Elem 1988-; *ai:* Geography Comm 1989-90; Western MD Rdng Assn Cncl 1989-; Kappa Delta Pi 1981-; Phi Apha Theta 1981-; *office:* Romney Elem Sch Scool St Romney WV 26757

DUDA, MIMA M., 4th Grade Teacher; *b:* Davenport, IA; *ed:* (BS) Elem Ed, Northeast MO St Univ 1971; (MA) Elem Ed, Marycrest 1979; *cr:* 4th Grade Sci/Rdng/Lang Teacher 1971-74; 3rd Grade Teacher 1974-75; 4th Grade Sci/Rdng/Lang Teacher 1975-85; 4th Grade Soc Stud/Lang/Rdng Teacher 1986- Alan Shepard Sch; *ai:* Writing Club Adv; Sci Fair Judge Organizer; Invent IA Elem Coord; Tag Shepard Rep; Phi Lambda Theta 1982-; NSEA 1984-85; IRA 1978-83; NSEA 1976; Church Festival Co Chairperson 1979; Lang Wrkshps; Written Whole Lang Curr for 4th Grade; *home:* 835 Hall St Bettendorf IA 52722

DUDEK, SANDRA LOU, English Teacher; *b:* Wauseon, OH; *m:* Frank L.; *c:* Matthew, Joshua; *ed:* (BS) Eng, Kent St Univ 1974; (MA) Ed, Coll of Mt St Joseph 1986; Cmptr Course, Wright St Univ 1989; *cr:* Eng Teacher Warren City Schls 1974-75; Substitute Teacher SouthWestern City Schls & W Jefferson Schls 1975-77; Eng Teacher Vinton Cty Schls 1977-79, Upper Scioto Valley Schls 1979-; *ai:* 9th Grade Class Adv; Lang Art Comm Mem; OH Ed Assn; Univ Club II Historian 1989-; Wkshp Presenter Writing Conference 1988, Ed Symposium 1989; Dedication of Yrbk Awd 1984; *office:* Upper Scioto Valley HS S Courtright St Mc Guffey OH 45859

DUDLEY, ANGELA MAXINE, Home Arts Teacher; *b:* Sumter, SC; *ed:* (BS) Home Ec Ed, SC St Coll 1977; (MS) Home Ec, E MI Univ 1980; Human Sexuality Grad Course; *cr:* Grad Asst E MI Univ 1978-80; Clothing/Fashion Instr Southern Univ 1980-81, Tuskegee Univ 1981-84; Home Art Teacher Haut Gap Mid Sch 1984-; *ai:* 4-H Club; Collegiality Comm; Charleston Cty Ed Assn (Area Rep 1989-) 1988-; NEA 1988-; SC St Alumni (Secy 1987-89) 1984-.

DUDLEY, ANN AUSTIN, Foreign Language Chairperson; *b:* Ware, MA; *m:* Robert John; *ed:* (BA) Fr, Mt Holyoke Coll 1953; (AMT) Fr, Harvard Univ 1954; Univ CT/Trinity Coll/Springfield Coll; *cr:* Fr/Latin Teacher Palmer HS 1954-55; Fr Teacher Tech HS 1955-56; Latin Teacher Longmeadow HS 1956-61; Latin/Eng Granby HS 1961-64; Latin Chairperson Foreign Lang Teacher Longmeadow HS 1988-; *ai:* Comm for Span Textbook Selection Chairperson; Amer Classical League 1964-; Foreign Lang Assn 1988-; Classical Assn of MA 1988-; MA Fed of Womens Clubs Fellowship 1953; *office:* Longmeadow H S 95 Grassy Gutter Rd Longmeadow MA 01106

DUDLEY, CAROLYNN, Sixth Grade Teacher; *b:* Pocatello, ID; *m:* Craig; *c:* Amy L., Christopher T.; *ed:* (BA) Home Ec, ID St Univ 1971; Grad Stud Elem Ed; *cr:* 6th Grade Teacher Indian Hills Elem 1980-; *ai:* Teaching & Advising Youth Group; PTA Teacher Adv 1989-; SE ID Rdng Cncl Public Relations 1988-89; Parent Advisory Comm Teacher Adv 1987-89; Staff Dev, Staff Welfare & Relations Comms; 4 Mini-Grants for Dev Sci & Rdng Curr; Transition Comm for Elem Stu to Jr HS; Mentor for Prof Action to Retain Teacher Novices in Ed.

DUDLEY, DEBRA BASS, Advance-Placement Biology; *b:* El Paso, TX; *m:* Robert B.; *c:* Dominique; *ed:* Bio, Morgan St Univ 1973; (DDS) Dentistry, Univ of MD Sch of Dentistry 1977; Addl Training Ed Credits in Scndry Sci & Gifted FL Intnl Univ 1989; *cr:* Associateship Practitioner Dr Curtis Adams 1977-79; Cororate Private Practice Owner of General Dental Office 1979-84; Instr Coral Park Sr HS 1984-; Teaching Bio AP & Honors Bio; *ai:* Spon of PEP Club; ADA 1977-; NDA 1977-; Natl Assn Advancement of Colored People 1979-; Northeast Regional Bd; Dental License 1977; St of FL Ed Cert; Cert Bio Sci 9-12; *office:* Miami Coral Park Sr H S 8865 Sw 16th St Miami FL 33165

DUDRA, TED E., Science Teacher/Team Leader; *b:* Akron, OH; *c:* Natalie, Stephanie, Tina; *ed:* (BAED) Comprehensive Sci, 1973, (MAED) Ed, 1977 Akron Univ; Numerous Wkshps; *cr:* 7th-8th Grade Teacher Taft Mid Sch 1973-; *ai:* Sci Olympiad Team & Odyssey of Mind Coach; Sci Dept Team Leader; Plain Local Teacher Assn Rep 1984-88; Portage Lakes Historical Society 1984-; Phi Sigma Kappa VP 1969-; *office:* Taft Mid Sch 3829 Guilford Ave NW Canton OH 44718

DUENAS, CECILIA MARIE, Physics Teacher; *b:* Agana, Guam; *ed:* (BS) Biochemistry, Univ of CA Los Angeles 1985; *cr:* Asst Teacher Neuropsychiatric Hospital UCLA 1984-85; Teacher Washington Prep HS 1985-; *ai:* Stu Act Coord; Leadership & Yrbk Adv; Target Sci Teacher; Volunteers of America Upward Bound Teacher 1987-; Unicamp (Head Cnslr 1981-87); UCLA Spec Olympics (Dir, Coach, Volunteer); Chrstn Childrens Fund 1987-; *office:* Washington Prepatory HS 10860 S Denker Los Angeles CA 90047

DUERBIG, ZINA PATRICIA, Teacher of Eng/Gifted/Talented; *b:* Brooklyn, NY; *m:* James; *c:* Melissa; *ed:* (BA) Eng Ed, Fairleigh Dickinson Univ 1976; (MS) Admin/Supervision/Curr, Georgian Court Coll 1990; *cr:* Teacher of Eng/Gifted & Talented Monmouth Regional HS 1976-; *ai:* BRITE & Future Problem Solving Coach; Gifted & Talented & Grades Comms; Monmouth Scholars Adv; Writer for Sch Newsletter; Gifted Educators of Monmouth Exec Comm 1985-; NCTE Mem 1976-; Monmouth Regional Ed Assn (VP, Secy); Governors Exemplary & Demonstration Prgm Grant; *office:* Monmouth Regional HS 535 Tinton Ave Tinton Falls NJ 07724

DUERSTOCK, SABRA CARMACK, 6th/7th Grade Lang Art Teacher; *b:* New Castle, IN; *m:* Marvin A.; *c:* Scott, Gregory, Bradley; *ed:* (AB) Drama, Butler Univ 1963; (MS) Scndry Ed/Concentration Lang Art, IN Univ; *cr:* Eng Teacher Ben Davis HS 1963; Speech/Eng Teacher Lawrence Cntrl HS 1963-65, Avon HS 1977-78; Lang Art Teacher Aurora; *ai:* Annual All Sch Musical Coach & Direct.

DUET, NORMA FAUCHEUX, 6th Grade Teacher/Admin Asst; *b:* Houma, LA; *m:* Calvin Joseph; *ed:* (BA) Elem Grades, 1973, (MED) Rdng Specialist, 1978, (MED) 1984 Nicholls St Univ; LA Prof Improvement Prgm, LA Teacher Internship Prgm/Teacher Evaluation Prgm Assessor; *cr:* Teacher Cut Off Elem 1973-79, Galliano Jr HS 1979-80, Golden Meadow Upper Elem 1980-85; Teacher/Admin Asst Golden Meadow Mid Sch 1985-; *ai:* 4-H Leader; Microcomputer Coord; Testing & Lafourche Parish Personel Accountability Revisions Comm; Lafourche Teachers Inc, Phi Kappa Phi Inactive, Alpha Delta Kappa Historian 1988-; Natl Deans List Grad Sch; Golden Meadow Mid Sch Outstanding Teacher; *home:* Rt 1 Box 171 Galliano LA 70354

DUFEK, DAN MATTHEW, 5th Grade Teacher; *b:* Sturgeon Bay, WI; *m:* Laurie Schmitz; *c:* Eric, Carrie, Melissa, Katie, Matthew; *ed:* Elem Ed, Door-Kewaunee Teachers Coll 1968; (BS) Elem Ed, UW-Oshkosh 1970; *cr:* 5th Grade Teacher Southern Door Schls 1970-; *ai:* Direct Talent Show; Coordinate Drive Cerebral Palsy; Talent Show; Unit Leader 1973-; Lions Club 1977-; Southern Door Teacher of Yr Awd 1982; *home:* Box 124 R 4 Luxemburg WI 54217

DUFF, LEE BELSHEE, Sixth Grade Teacher; *b:* Staunton, VA; *m:* Eugene Adkerson; *c:* Leigh Duff Leist, Thomas B., William S.; *ed:* (BS) Elem Ed, 1970, (MED) Admin/Supervision, 1974 VA Commonwealth Univ; Working Toward Teacher of Gifted Cert Ed of Gifted Stu; *cr:* Teacher Highland Cty Sch Division 1954-55, Chesterfield Cty Sch Division 1970-76, Pulaski Cty Sch Division 1976-; *ai:* Odyssey of Mind Coach; Team Leader; VA Ed Assn, Pulaski Cty Ed Assn, NEA; Outstanding Elem Teacher of America 1972.

DUFF, VICTORIA BURKHOLDER, Third Grade Teacher; *b:* Cincinnati, OH; *m:* David R.; *c:* Gavin, Amanda; *ed:* (BA) Religious Ed, Muskingum Coll 1970; Ed Cert, Georgian Court Coll 1978; *cr:* 1st Grade Teacher St Josephs Elem Sch 1971-72; East Dover Elem 1979-80; 3rd Grade Teacher East Dover Elem 1980-; *ai:* Report Card Comm; Lang Comm; Sci Comm; Prof Dev Chairperson; Trea Elections Chairperson; Trea Sr Bldg Rep; Evaluations Comm; Duplication Comm; Ocean Cty Rdng Cncl 1984-; White Pine Twig-Hosp (Pres, VP, Treas 1988-); Island Hghts Yacht Club (Soc Chm 1988-89, Jr Sailing Chm 1990); 1989 NJ Govrnrs Teacher Recog Awd; 1989 Revision of Grade 3 Spllg Merill Publ Co; *office:* E Dover Elem Schl 725 Vaughn Ave Toms River NJ 08753

DUFFEE, BEVERLY ANN, English Dept Chair/Instructor; *b:* Sharon, PA; *ed:* (BA) Eng, Roberts Wesleyan Coll 1968; (MA) Eng Lit, CA St Univ Fullerton 1973; *cr:* Eng Dept Chairperson/Instr Leffingwell Chrstn HS 1981-; Eng Instr Biola Univ 1984-85; *ai:* Jr Class Adv; Alpha Kappa Sigma 1968-; Whos Who of Amer Women-Biographee 1983-; *home:* 8811 Park St Sp 98 Bellflower CA 90706

DUFFER, JODEANE PATAKI, Fourth Grade Teacher; *b:* Honolulu, HI; *m:* Leslie Milton; *c:* Scott; *ed:* (BA) Elem Ed, Pepperdine Coll 1965; *cr:* Teacher Denker Ave Elem Sch 1965-; *ai:* United Teachers of Los Angeles Rep; Leadership Cncl For Shared-DecisioN Making Co-Chairperson; Alpha Delta KapPA (Secy 1983-84, Historian 1985-86, Pres 1984-85); BSA Parents Comm 1980-; 1st Luth Church of Torrence (Sunday Sch Teacher 1982-85, Ed Comm Mem 1984-86); *office:* Denker Ave Elem Sch 1620 W 162nd St Gardena CA 90247

DUFFEY, GLENDA DIANNE, Teacher; *b:* Griffin, GA; *ed:* (AB) Psych, 1968, (MED) Ed/Soc Stud, 1972 W GA Coll; Working on EDS W GA Coll; *cr:* Teacher Sand Hill Elem Sch 1969-74, Roopville Elem Sch 1974-, Griffin HS 1990; *ai:* Roopville 8th Grade Class Spon; Graduation Coord; Academic Bowl for GLRS W GA Dist & Roopville Sch, Ga His Bowl Coach; Sch & Carroll Cty Soc Sci Fair Coord; Roopville Sch SACS Steering Comm Chairperson. GA Cncl Ec Ed Stock Market Team Spon; Prof Assn of GA Ed Building Rep 1988-; GA Mid Sch Assn 1989-; NCSS 1987-; Natl Assn for Female Execs 1989-; Alpha Delta Kappa Local Pres 1976-; Phi Delta Kappa 1987-; Carroll Cty Teacher of Yr 1982; Participant in Teacher Space Prgm; Sand Hill Sch Teacher of Yr 1972; *home:* 125 Howell Dr Carrollton GA 30117

DUFFNER, NANCY MARIE, H S English Teacher; *b:* Alexandria, VA; *ed:* (BA) Engl, Speech Comm, 1984; (MAT) Engl, UNC 1987; *cr:* Engl Teacher Northern HS 1987 ; *ai:* Spon Northern Lights, Schl Literary Magazine; Chm Sch Comm Improving Critical Thinking Skills/Sat Scores; Asst Sftbl Coach; Durham Assn Teachers of Eng 1988-; NC Assn Teachers of Eng 1989-; NCTE 1989-; Lyndhurst Fellow UNC 1986-87; *home:* 607 N Greensboro St Carrboro NC 27510

DUFFORD, KELLY JO, English Teacher; *b:* Summerville, SC; *ed:* (BA) Scndry Ed/Eng, Clemson Univ 1985; Prgm for Effective Teaching; *cr:* Stu Teacher Dacusville Sch 1985; Teacher Du Bose Mid Sch 1985-; *ai:* Sch Yrbk Adv; Teacher of Adult Ed; *office:* Du Bose Mid Sch 1000 Du Bose Dr Summerville SC 29483

DUFFY, CRAIG STEPHEN, Social Studies Teacher; *b:* Newton, MA; *m:* Catharine Ann; *c:* Shaila, Colin; *ed:* (BAED) Soc Sci, Pacific Luth Univ 1973; *cr:* Soc Stud Kalles Jr HS 1974-75, Ballou Jr HS 1975-82, Ferrucci Jr HS 1982-; *ai:* Var Girls Bsktbl Coach; Discipline Comm Chm; Puyallup Ed Assn Building Rep 1983-87; Summit Uniserve Rep 1987-89; *office:* Ferrucci Jr H S 3213 Wildwood Park Dr Puyallup WA 98374

DUFFY, DORIS REEVES, Spanish Teacher; *b:* Princeton, IN; *m:* Stanley Joseph; *c:* Heather, Brian; *ed:* (BA) Span, 1977, (MED) Ed, 1981 IN St Univ; *cr:* Span/Eng Teacher 1977-88, Span Teacher 1977- Salem HS; *ai:* Span Club Spon; NEA, Salem Classroom Teachers Assn 1977-; GSA (Leader 1989-, Co-Leader 1980-81, 1988-89); *office:* Salem HS N Harrison St Salem IN 47167

DUFFY, JOAN CLARA, 4th Grade Teacher; *b:* Pittsburgh, PA; *m:* Nicholas J.; *c:* Maureen, Sean; *ed:* (BA) Elem, Mercyhurst 1980; *cr:* Clerk Bell Telephone 1960-62; Insurance Adjustor Northwest 1962-66; Teacher Aide Jamestown Elem 1970-75; 4th Grade Teacher St Michael 1978-; *ai:* PJAS Governors Energy Lector Trng; Natl Fuel Advisory Cncl 1987-; St Michael Liturgy Chm 1979-87, Teacher of Yr 1985; Article on Energy; *office:* St Michael Elem Sch 80 No High St Greenville PA 16125

DUFFY, KATHLEEN MORRIS, First Grade Teacher; *b:* Washington Ch, OH; *m:* Donald E.; *ed:* (BS) Elem Ed, OH Univ 1973; *cr:* 3rd Grade Teacher 1973-80, 2nd Grade Teacher 1980-85, 1st Grade Teacher 1985- Medill Elem Lancaster City Sch System; *ai:* OEA, NEA 1973-; Phi Kappa Phi Honor Society; Martha Holden Jennings Scholar 1980-81; Summa Cum Laude Ashland Oil Teacher of Yr Awd Nom; *home:* 5724 Old Logan Rd SE Lancaster OH 43130

DUFFY, ROSEMARY FRATTAROLI, Teacher; *b:* Philadelphia, PA; *m:* Raymond G.; *c:* Michael, Jennifer; *ed:* (BS) Elem Ed, Univ of PA 1971; Grad Stud Elem Ed, West Chester St Univ; *cr:* 1st Grade Teacher Glenolden Elem Sch 1971-79; *home:* 10 Glenmore Dr Glen Mills PA 19342

DUFOUR, JAY, Social Studies Teacher; *b:* Nashua, NH; *m:* Nancy Mullen; *c:* Martha, Matthew; *ed:* (BED) Soc Stud, Keene St Coll 1970; (MED) Scndry Ed, Suffolk Univ 1974; *cr:* Soc Stud Teacher Hooksett Memorial Sch 1971-78, Manchester HS Cntrl 1978-; *ai:* Cross Cntry & Asst Mens Bsktbl Coach NH Coll; MEA, NEA; *office:* Manchester HS Cntrl 207 Lowell St Manchester NH 03104

DUGAN, ALICE BERNICE (FARRIS), Cmptr Resource/Math Teacher; *b:* Darby, PA; *m:* William T.; *c:* Megan, Sean; *ed:* (BA) Math/Physics, Immaculata Coll 1972; (MA) Educl Admin, Villanova Univ 1980; Math, West Chester Univ; Working Towards Masters Cmptr Ed PA Coll Textile & Sci; *cr:* Math Teacher St Maria Goretti HS 1972-75, Archbishop Carroll HS 1975-77, Cardinal O Hara HS 1978-; *ai:* Scott HS Q Team 1985-; Jr Academic Bowl 1987-; Sch Store Mgr 1988-; NCTM, Assn of Teachers of Math in Philadelphia & Vicinity, PA Cncl Teachers of Math; Diocesan Curr Comm 1986-; O Hara Teacher of Yr 1987-88; White House Distinguished Educator 1989; *office:* Cardinal O Hara HS 1701 S Sproul Rd Springfield PA 19064

DUGAN, BILLYANNA POE, Chapter I Reading; *b:* Linton, IN; *w:* Clifford E. (dec); *c:* Clifford E. II, Constance S. Lawson, Cevin L.; *ed:* (BS) Elem Ed, Greenville Coll 1971; (MS) Elem Ed, SIU Edwardsville 1975; Post Grad Work, SIU Edwardsville; *cr:* 4th Grade Teacher 1971-74, 3rd Grade Teacher 1974-75 Jefferson Vandalia #203; Metric Coord Vandalia #203 1975-78; 2nd Grade Teacher Cntrl Vandalia #203 1978-79;5th Grade Teacher Jefferson Vandalia #203 1979-88; Chapter I Rdng Teacher Jefferson Shobonien #203 1988-; *ai:* Vandalia Sch Faculty Cncl; Kndgtn Screening Team; IL Rdng Assn 1989; IEA/NEA Regional Rep 1980-; Delta Kappa Gamma Comm Chm; Vandalia Teachers Assn Neg Team 1971- Certificate of Merit 1986; IL Eng Teachers Assn 1989; United Meth Church Evangelism Comm 1988-; Serendipity Bible Study Pres 1986-; Friendship Class Revolving Teacher 1985-; Eastern Star; Co-Author Metric Curr Kndgtn Primary Upper Primary & Intermediate-Author of Preface; DAR Teacher of Amer His Awd from Local Chapter; *office:* Jefferson & Shoborier Schls 1500 W Jefferson St Vandalia IL 62471

DUGAN, CAROLYN JANE, English Teacher/I TV Coord; *b:* Springfield, MA; *m:* Robert J. Leonard; *ed:* (BA) Eng, Notre Dame Coll 1975; (MS) Comm/Bus, Univ of NH 1984; *cr:* Eng Teacher Central HS 1977-83; Eng Teacher 1984-; Interactive TV Coord 1989 Memorial HS; *ai:* Phi Delta Kappa Public Relations Dir 1987-88; NCTE Mem 1980-; New England Womens Stud Assn Mem 1989-; Friends of Manchester Lib Fundraiser 1989-; Manchester Jr Womens Club Ticket Chm; Mc Fashion Show Schlrsp 1988-; *office:* Manchester Memorial H S S Porter St Manchester NH 03103

DUGAN, MAUREEN J., Biology Teacher; *b:* Boston, MA; *ed:* (BA) Bio, Framingham St Coll 1971; (MED) Ed, Boston Coll 1982; Harvard Mentor Teacher Prgm; Frontiers in Life Sci; *cr:* Bio Teacher Nashoba Regional HS 1971-; *ai:* Dir of Stu Sci Interns; Mem of Schlsp Comm; NEA, MTA, NTA; Bay St Skills Corporation; Bio Technology Grant; *office:* Nashoba Regional HS 12 Green Rd Bolton MA 01740

DUGGER, MARK RANDAL, Mathematics & Science Teacher; *b:* Enid, OK; *m:* Judy W. Thompson; *c:* Chandra, Melissa, Kristen, Miles, Mason; *ed:* (BS) Chem, Ft Lewis Coll 1973; (BA) Theology, Baptist Bible Coll 1978; *cr:* Math/Sci Teacher Mountain States Baptist Acad 1988-; *office:* Mountain States Baptist Acad 8333 Acoma Way Denver CO 80221

DUGGER, SUSAN E., Business Education Teacher; *b:* Somerset, KY; *m:* Clark Edward; *c:* Brandon C., Staci S.; *ed:* (BA) Bus Ed, E TN St Univ 1974; (MS) Bus Ed, E KY Univ 1981; *cr:* Teacher Pulaski Cty HS 1974-; *ai:* Jr Class Prom Spon; FBLA Adv; KY Bus Ed Assn, Somerset Bus Ed Assn, NBEA; Natl Certificate of Appreciation FBLA; *office:* Pulaski Cty HS 511 E University Dr Somerset KY 42501

DUGGER, THOMAS FREDERICK, English Teacher; *b:* Council Bluffs, IA; *ed:* (BA) Eng/Ed, Spring Hill Coll 1971; (MED) Admin, Tulane Univ 1980; Grad Work Eng, Ed, Spec Ed, Sculpture; *cr:* Teacher/Public Relations Dir Brother Martin HS 1971-76; Teacher/Asst Prin Gables Acad 1976-79; Teacher/Eng Dept Chm PGT Beauregard HS 1979-88; Teacher Chalmette HS 1988-; Part Time Faculty St Bernard Comm Coll 1988-; *ai:* Sr Class Spon; Curr Cncl Chm; *office:* Chalmette HS 1100 Judge Perez Dr Chalmette LA 70043

DUHOSKI, JOHN VINCENT, Religion Teacher; *b:* Gaylord, MI; *m:* Bernadette Kowalski; *c:* Nicole, Nicholas, Nathan; *ed:* (MA) Philosophy, Cath Univ 1977; (STL) Theology, Gregorian Univ 1982; Marquette Univ; *cr:* Clergyman Gaylord Diocese 1982-87; Religion Instr Benedictine HS 1987-; *ai:* Campus Cnslr; Basselin Schlsp 1974; Marquette Fellowship 1986-87; *office:* Benedictine HS 8001 W Outer Dr Detroit MI 48235

DUINK, MARIE JONES, Third Grade Teacher; *b:* Utica, NY; *m:* Jerrold Lynn; *c:* Sean M., Nathan L.; *ed:* (AB) Liberal Art, Mohawk Valley Comm Coll 1967; (BA) Ed, 1969, (MS) Ed, 1970 St Univ Coll Oneonta; Cmptr Technology, St Univ NY; *cr:* 4th Grade Teacher 1970-77, 3rd Grade Teacher 1977- Clinton Elem; *ai:* Clinton Teachers Assn (Secy 1973-75, Building Rep 1976-, Soc Chm); PTA Teacher Rep; BSA Cub Scout Den Leader 1984-86; Oneonta Alumni Assn Pres 1980-82, Mem) 1977-87; Frank Schaffers Sch Days; *office:* Clinton Elem Sch 75 Chenango Ave Clinton NY 13323

DUJANOVICH, DEBORAH ANN, 6th Grade Teacher; *b:* Buffalo, NY; *m:* Michael B.; *c:* Lauren, Caryn; *ed:* (BA) Elem Ed, SUNY Fredonia 1973; (MS) Elem Ed, SUNY Buffalo 1976; *cr:* 5th Grade Teacher 1974-77, 2nd Grade Teacher 1977-78, 4th Grade Teacher 1978-81 Charlotte; 6th Grade Teacher Armor 1983-84, 1986-; K-6th Grade Soc Stud Teacher/Coord Hamburg Cntrl Schls 1989-; *ai:* K-6 Grade Soc Stud Coord; Instructional Management Cncl; Decision Making Comm; Girls Intramural Coach; NY St Cncl of Soc Stud, Niagara Frontier Cncl of Soc Stud 1989-; St Stephens Serbian Orthodox Church Mothers Club Mem 1987-; *office:* Armor Elem Sch 5301 Abbott Rd Hamburg NY 14075

DUKAS, GEORGE JOHN, Chemistry/Physics Teacher; *b:* Parkersburg, WV; *m:* Mary E.; *c:* John, David; *ed:* (BS) Chem, 1960, (MS) Organic Chem, 1962 WV Univ; *cr:* Development Chemist Amer Cyana Mid 1963-64; Sci Teacher Hughes Jr HS 1964-71; Chem/Physics Teacher Parker HS 1971-85, Hillcrest HS 1985-; *ai:* Amer Chemical Society; NEA, SC Ed Assn; Sci Teacher Who Contributed Most to Sci Fair 1971; Greenville Cty Teacher of Yr 1984-85; *home:* 60 Briarrun Pl Greenville SC 29615

DUKE, C. JAMES, 5th Grade Teacher; *b:* Pittsburgh, PA; *m:* Dorothy Belle Irvin; *c:* Erin L., Eric J.; *ed:* (BA) Elem Ed/Sci, West Liberty Coll 1963; (MS) Elem Ed, West VA Univ 1969; *cr:* 5th Grade Teacher South Plainfield Public Schls 1963-64; Head of Sci Dept Garwood Public Sch 1965-66; 5th Grade Teacher Hancock Cty Schls 1967-69; Head /5th Grade Teacher Alverda Public Sch 1970-80; 5th Grade Teacher Penns Manor Elem 1980-; *ai:* Model Rocket Club Adv; Bsktbl, Track Coach; Penns Manor Ed Assn Pres 1976-77; PA St Ed Assn 1970-; PA Assn of Retarded Citizens Spon 1976-77; Purchase Line Church of Brethren Asst Supt of Sunday Sch 1984-86; *home:* RD 1 Box 93 Clymer PA 15728

DUKE, CAROLYN HOLLAND, 4th Grade Mathematics Teacher; *b:* Cathage, TX; *m:* William Robert; *c:* John W., Robert M.; *ed:* (BS) Elem Ed, N TX St Univ 1963, (MA) Elem Ed, Stephen F Austin Univ 1976; *cr:* 4th/5th Grade Teacher Rhome Elem 1962-63; 3rd Grade Teacher Oakhurst Elem 1963-64; 4th Grade Teacher Grapevine Elem 1965-66; 3rd Grade Teacher Johnston Elem 1966-68; 4th Grade Teacher Barton Sch 1970-72; 5th Grade Lang Art Teacher 1972-73, 4th Grade Math Teacher 1973- Baker Koonce Intermediate; *ai:* Delta Kappa Gamma (Secy 1987-88) 1986-87; St Classroom Teacher Assn, Carthage Classroom Teachers Sch Rep; Cntrl Baptist Church; *office:* Carthage Ind Sch Dist Sch 1 Bulldog Dr Carthage TX 75633

DUKE, CONWELL, Principal; *b:* York, NE; *m:* Bobbie Jean Lyon; *c:* Van E., Bryand M.; *ed:* (BS) Voc Ed, MS Valley St Univ 1972; (MS) Elem Ed, Univ of MS 1982; Specialist Prgm MS St Univ; Admin Cert Univ of MS 1983; *cr:* Teacher Clark Street Sch 1975-82; Asst Prin 1982-85, Prin 1985-88 Main Street Elem Sch; Prin Pontotoc Jr HS 1988; *ai:* MS Assn of Sch Admin. ASCD; Mc Donald Church (Choir, Sunday Sch Teacher, Sunday Sch Supt); *office:* Pontotoc Jr HS 132 N Main Pontotoc MS 38863

DUKE, DORIS MARION, Fourth Grade Teacher; *b:* Knox City, TX; *M:* William F.; *c:* Marion R.; *ed:* (BS) Home Ec, Abilene Christian 1967; Elem Ed TX Tech; *cr:* HS Homemaking Instr Sweetwater HS 1971-78; 4th Grade Teacher Whitharral Elem 1978-; *ai:* Coach UIL Number Sense Team; Sch Imprvmt Comm; TACS; *home:* 801 N Denver Levelland TX 79336

DUKE, JIM WAYNE, Chemistry & Physics Teacher; *b:* Madisonville, KY; *m:* Faye Burden; *c:* Jerry W., Pamela D.; *ed:* (BS) Bio/Chem/Physics, 1961, (MA) Chem/Physics, 1963, (Rank I) Chem/Physics, 1970, (EDS) Chem/Physics, 1979 W KY Univ; Duke Univ; Murray St Univ; *cr:* Teacher Nebo HS 1958, Madisonville HS 1961, Chrstn Cty HS 1964, Brescia Coll 1982-, Daviess Cty HS 1990; *ai:* Bsbl & Bsktbl Coach; Boys/Girls Weight & Boxing Coach; Dept Chm; KEA, NEA; Buck Creek Baptist Church Deacon 1973-; BSA Leader; Numerous NSF Grants; Dissertation Effects Upon Achievement of Physics Stu; Teach of Yr Hopkins Cty 1963; Teacher of Yr Daviess Cty 1989; *home:* 12360 S Old Livermore Rd Utica KY 42376

DUKE, JOANN D., Gifted Coordinator; *b:* Grove City, PA; *m:* Louis A. III; *c:* Brian Ashley, Timothy Ashley; *ed:* (BS) Elem Ed/Psych, Slippery Rock Univ 1972; *cr:* Rdng/Title I Teacher 1972, Elem Ed Teacher 1973-88, Law Ed Prgm Dir 1977-84, Gifted Coord 1988- Moniteau Sch Dist; *ai:* Academic Games Spon; PJAS Adv; US Academic Decathlon, HS Bowl, Knowledge Masters Coach; Literary Magazine & Ecology Meet Adv; Republican Party Comm Person 1982, 1989; *office:* Monteau Sch Dist RD 2 Box 2035 West Sunbury PA 16061

DUKE, ROBERT ELLIS, Art Teacher; *b:* Gallatin, TN; *m:* Carolyn Faye; *c:* Richard; *ed:* (BS) Art, 1972, (MAT) Hum, 1976 Mid TN St Univ; *cr:* 7th-12th Grade Art Teacher Joelton Jr/Sr HS 1976-79; 7th-8th Grade Art Teacher John Trotwood Moore Jr HS 1979-80; 9th-12th Grade Photography Teacher Hume-Fogg HS 1980-81; 9th-12th Grade Art Teacher East HS 1981-82; 7th-8th Grade Art Teacher Donelson Mid Sch 1982-85, Dupont Tyler Mid Sch 1985-; *ai:* Girls Soccer Coach; Natl Art Educators Assn 1988-; NEA 1986-; Best of Show Vanderbilt Invitational Art Show 1971; Cheekwood Invitational Art Exhibit 1978; Bicentennial Art Exhibition Purchase Awd Painting 1976; Century III Art Exhibit Purchase Awd Painting 1982; *home:* 700 Ermac Dr Nashville TN 37210

DUKE, TOBI, Music Department Chair; *b:* Los Angeles, CA; *ed:* (BM) Music Ed, Univ of Redlands 1983; *cr:* Elem Music Teacher Viewpoint Sch 1984; Itinerant Instr/Music Teacher Oxnard Elem Dist 1984-85; Music Dir Westlake Luth Church 1984-88; Vocal Music Teacher/Dept Chairperson El Camino Real HS 1986-; Music Dir First Luth Church of Northridge 1989-; *ai:* Show Choir Dir; LA Scndry Music Teachers Assn 1987-; S CA Vocal Assn 1988-; *home:* 19400 Wyandotte St #1 Reseda CA 91335

DUKES, MARION, 5th Grade Teacher; *b:* Cincinnati, OH; *ed:* (BA) Elem Ed, KY St Univ 1973; (MED) Spec Ed, Xavier Univ 1978; Post Masters Studies Ed; *cr:* 3rd Grade Teacher Greenhills Forest Park Sch Dist 1973-81; 5th Grade Teacher Greenhills-Forest Park Sch Dist 1981-; *ai:* Prin Lead Team Rep; OEA 1973-; NEA 1973-; GFPTA 1973-; Alpha Kappa Alpha Sorority 1972-; Christ Emmanuel Christian Fellowship 1987-; Ultimate Christian Womens Fellowship 1987-89; *office:* Kemper Heights Elem Sch 924 Waycross Rd Cincinnati OH 45240

DULIN, JOYCE WOMMACK, 6th Grade Teacher; *b:* Commerce, TX; *m:* Leon; *c:* Leigh, Rebekah, Rachel; *ed:* (BS) Elem Ed, N TX St Univ 1961; Working Towards Masters N TX St Univ; *cr:* 1st Grade Teacher Carrollton Elem 1961-62; 5th Grade Teacher West Riverside Elem 1962-63; 3rd Grade Teacher Wimbish Elem 1964-69; 6th Grade Self Contained Teacher Liberty Acad 1978-81; 6th Grade Math/Sci/Soc Stud/Music/Art Teacher Travis Elem 1981-; *ai:* Delta Kappa Gamma 1966-69; Classroom Teachers Assn 1983-89; TX Sci Educators Assn 1987-88; Problem Pregnancy Center 1985-; Republican Party 1960-; First Baptist Church Jail Ministry 1984-; *home:* 2805 Andover Midland TX 79705

DULL, FREDERICK JOHN, Fifth Grade Teacher; *b:* Dunkirk, NY; *m:* Nancy Bauer; *c:* Tami, Karen, Christopher; *ed:* (BA) Elem Ed, SUNY Fredonia 1965; *cr:* 5th Grade Teacher Frewsburg Cntrl Sch 1965.

DUMAS, ROBERT FRANK, 7th Grade Soc Stud Teacher; *b:* Massena, NY; *m:* Theresa J. Roy; *ed:* (BA) His - Magna Cum Laude, St John Fisher Coll 1974; (MA) Ed, St Univ of NY Brockport 1979; Advanced NIH Ec Seminar; Lang Art Prgm; *cr:* 7th/8th Grade Soc Stud Teacher Albion Mid Sch 1974-81; 8th Grade Soc Stud Teacher Merton Williams Mid Sch 1981-82; 7th Grade Soc Stud Teacher Brockport Mid Sch 1982-; *ai:* Brockport Yorkers Club Adv 1983-88; Stu Cncl Adv 1979-81; Directed Stu Landscaping Project for Albion Mid Sch 1981; Chm Albion Cntrl Schls Soc Stud Monitoring, Recorder/Secy Albion Cntrl Schls Problem Learner Comm; Chm His Fair, Awds Assembly Albion Mid Sch; Adv Albion Mid Sch Future Teachers Club; Merton Williams Mid Sch Cmptr Comm; Adv Brockport Mid Sch Newspaper; Wrote Soc Stud Curr Brockport; Phi Alpha Theta VP 1974-; Rochester Area Cncl for Soc Stud 1974-; NY ST Historical Assn Yorkers Club Adv 1983-88; Teacher of Yr Albion Cntrl Schls 1981; St John Fisher John A Murray Awd; Stu Dedication of Yrbk 1980; Natl Endowment for Hum Seminar; Published Article on Medieval England Sigma XI; *office:* Brockport Mid Sch Allen St Brockport NY 14420

DUMBAULD, JAMES ELDON, Sociology & Psychology Teacher; *b:* Fairmont, MN; *c:* Vivien Basom, Sharon Jones, Karen Mast, James C., Mark, Colleen Breitenbach, Teresa; *ed:* (BA) Sociology/Fine Arts, Western WA Coll 1966; (MA) Sociology/Psych, Univ of British Columbia 1969; Multi-Cultural Teacher & Specialist; Cnslr & Stu Adv; *cr:* Teacher Vancouver Schls 1966-68, John Adams Jr HS 1968-69, John Muir HS 1969-; *ai:* Sr Class Adv John Muir; Courtesy Chm; Big Brother; United Teachers of Pasadena Rep 1969-; NEA 1969-; United Nations Rep to World Conference on Russian Relations; Amer Legion Rep to Valley Forge; Teacher of Yr Awd; *office:* John Muir HS 1905 Lincoln Ave Pasadena CA 91103

DUMIRE, PAULETTA JEAN, H S Social Studies Teacher; *b:* Parsons, WV; *ed:* (BS) Comprehensive Soc Stud/Lib Sci, 1972, (MA) Scndry Schl Curr Emphasis/Amer His, 1983 WV Univ; Grad Stud Honors, Acad Marshall Univ; *cr:* Teacher St Josephs Preparatory Seminary 1973-80; Librarian St Josephs Hospital 1975-77; Teacher Ritchie Cty Sch System 1980-; *ai:* Career Club Adv; Frosh Class Spon; Chapter II, Staff Dev, Stu Recogni tion, Frequent Monitoring Comm; Schlrshp Comm 1988-; Jr Amer Citizenship Club; Cty Soc Stud Fairs; Phi Delta Kappa 1983-; Delta Kappa Gamma 1985-; Daughters of Amer Revolution Chapter Regent 1989 Thatcher Awd 1989; Teachers Forum 1989; Guest Prin Acad 1989; Mellon Grant Advanced Placement Summer Teaching Inst 1990; Ritchie Cty Outstanding Teacher of Amer His 1987; Teachers Forum 1989; *office:* Ritchie County H S 135 S Penn Harrisville WV 26362

DUNAVANT, MARY WALL, 5th Grade Teacher; *b:* O Bion County, TN; *m:* Bedford Forrest III.; *c:* Wm. Henry Riley, Ellen Provience, Wm. Ralph Riley, Maria E. Pollard; *ed:* (BS) Ed, Univ of TN 1967, Univ of TN, *cr:* Jr HS Teacher Obion Elem 1966-68, Title I Sup-Teacher Cntrl Office 1968-75; Migrant Ed Obion Cty & Summer Educ 1968-75; Title I & 5th Grade Teacher South Fulton Elem 1975-; *ai:* PTO-South Fulton Elem; Basic Skills Coord-South Fulton Elem; NEA 1966-; Teacher Ed Assn 1966-; West TN Teacher Assn Rep 1966-; Obion Cty Ed Assn Secy 1966-; Assn of Math 1980-; Girl Scouts of America Leader 1962-75; Booster Club 1975-; *home:* 514 Bishop Union City TN 38261

DUNAWAY, SANDRA HURST, 4th Grade Teacher; *b:* Cuthbert, GA; *m:* David; *c:* Dawn Dunaway Ward; *ed:* (BS) Early Chldhd, Huntingdon Coll 1964; *cr:* 8th Grade Teacher Lauvens Cty HS 1966-67; Teacher/Art Dir Stewart Cty Schls 1967-69; 8th Grade Teacher Stewart Cty Jr HS 1969-71; 3rd/4th Grade Teacher Richland Elem 1971-; *office:* Richland Elem Sch P O Box 135 Phillips St Richland GA 31825

DUNBAR, DEBBIE LYNN, Sixth Grade Teacher; *b:* Mc Alester, OK; *ed:* (BS) Elem Ed, 1981, (MS) Elem Ed, 1985 E Cntrl Univ; *cr:* 6th Grade Teacher Krebs Elem 1981-; *ai:* Diamond Jubilee, Staff Dev, Land Run Day Comms; OK Ed Assn, NEA 1981-88; Krebs Classroom Teachers Assn Pres 1985-88; Epsilon Sigma Alpha (Pres 1985, Secy 1988, Ed Dir 1984); *office:* Krebs Elem Sch PO Box 67 Krebs OK 74554

DUNBAR, NANCY MC KINLEY, 2nd Grade Teacher; *b:* Mt Vernon, OH; *m:* Richard Parker; *c:* Molly, Amy; *ed:* (BS) Elem Ed, Muskingum Coll 1963; Grad Classes OH St Univ, Univ of Va, Old Dominion Univ; *cr:* 2nd Grade Teacher Anne Arundel Cty 1963-64, Robert Louis Stevenson 1964-66, Kingston 1978-; *ai:* VA Rdng Cncl 1978-; VA Beach Cncl, VA Beach Math Cncl; Navy Wives Club Pres 1972; Navy Ombudsman 1974-76, Certificate of Commendation 1978; Tidewater Ballet VP Bd of Dir 1986; Kingston Sch Teacher of Yr; *office:* Kingston Elem Sch 3532 Kings Grant Rd Virginia Beach VA 23452

DUNBEBIN, ANNA MAE (GULINELLO), 1st-3rd Primary Unit Teacher; *b:* Pricetown, PA; *m:* Thomas L.; *c:* Thomas J., Annette A. Dunbebin Melgosa; *ed:* (BS) Elem Ed, Columbia Union Coll 1959; (MA) Supervision & Instruction/Ed Psych, Andrews Univ 1971; Prof Courses in Diagnostic Rdng Disability & Integration of Faith & Learning 1982; *cr:* 2nd Grade Teacher 1963-65, 1st Grade Teacher 1965-83, Primary Unit Teacher 1983- John Nevins Andrews Sch; *ai:* Head Teacher Primary Grades; Various Comm; Mid St Assn (Steering Comm, Chm Action Plan & Interum Reports, Sch Evaluator); Articles Published; Published Kndgtn Course 1983-84; Edited Kndgtn Course for SDA Schls 1983.

DUNCAN, DONELLA COLLET, Reading/Social Studies Teacher; *b:* Cadillac, MI; : Billy Milton; *c:* Byron; *ed:* (BA) Soc Stud, Univ of Southwestern LA 1972; Scdry Teaching; Rdng Specializion; *cr:* Teacher Comcoux HS 1972-77; Techer Elem 1982-83; Cecilia Jr HS 1983-89 Breaux Bridge Jr HS 1989-; *ai:* Coach Quiz Bowl Team; LA St Dept Grants-Enrichment for Low-High Achievers 1987-88; at Risk Sstudents 1988-89.

DUNCAN, EDWARD ALLISON, Band Director; *b:* Little Rock, AR; *m:* Dana Horn; *c:* Tanya Crawford, Kia D., Mineka N.; *ed:* (BS) Music Ed, AR AM&N Coll 1965; Univ of Cntrl AR; *cr:* Band Dir M M Tate HS 1964-65, Booker T Washington HS 1965-66, England HS 1968-77, Pulaski Heights Jr HS 1985-88, Forest Heights Jr HS 1988-; *ai:* Omega Psi Phi Vice Basileus 1987-88; *home:* 6310 Shirley Dr Little Rock AR 72204

DUNCAN, GEORGE ERNEST, 5th Grade Teacher; *b:* Slippery Rock, PA; *m:* Diana Sue Cunningham; *c:* Jody, Jacque; *ed:* (BS) Elem Ed, Slippery Rock Univ 1974; (MS) Elem Admin, Westminster Coll 1977; Writing, Cmptr Trng; *cr:* Elem Teacher Slippery Rock Area Schls 1974-; *ai:* Head Teacher of Building; Borough Councilman (VP, Pres) 1978-; PA Dept Ed Writing Teacher; *office:* Portersville Elem Sch RD 1 Portersville PA 16051

DUNCAN, JAMES HARDING, 8th Grade Lang Arts Teacher; *b:* Fairfax, VA; *m:* Cynthia T.; *ed:* (BS) Eng, 1976, (BS) Elem Ed, 1977- Cumberland Coll; (MA) Elem Ed, EKU 1983; Lab Tech, ORNL 1971-72 & BFG 1976-77; *cr:* 4th Grade Teacher Revelo Elem 1977-78; 8th Grade Practical Arts Teacher 1978-79, 6th Grade Teacher 1979-81, 7th Grade Teacher 1981-83, 8th Grade Art/Lang Arts Teacher 1983- Whitley Mid Sch; *ai:* Rocketman; KEA, NEA 1977-.

DUNCAN, JANICE TAYLOR, 4th Grade Mathematics Teacher; *b:* Richlands, VA; *m:* Douglas Andrew; *c:* Susan E., Matthew D.; *ed:* (BA) Eng/His, Emory & Henry Coll 1966; Univ of VA SW Center; *cr:* 3rd Grade Teacher 1966-86, 1st Grade Teacher 1986-89, 4th Grade Teacher 1989- High Point Elem; *ai:* WCEA, VA Ed Assn, NEA 1966-; *office:* High Point Elem Sch Rt 1 Sinking Creek Rd Bristol VA 24201

DUNCAN, JENNIFER LYNN, 8th Grade English/Lit Teacher; *b:* Tulsa, OK; *m:* Michael Eugene; *ed:* (BA) Eng Ed, Northeastern St Univ 1986; *cr:* 10th Grade Eng Teacher Stigler HS 1986-88; 8th Grade Eng/Lit Teacher Stigler Mid Sch 1988-; *ai:* Cheerleading Coach & Spon; Worked With Gifted & Talented Prgm; Stu Senate Adv; Rdng Comm Mem; Mid Sch Eng Dept Chairperson; *office:* Stigler Mid Sch 302 N W E Stigler OK 74462

DUNCAN, JOANNA MIHOK, 6th Grade Teacher; *b:* Pittsburgh, PA; *m:* Richard; *c:* Julianne, Kerry J.; *ed:* (BA) Elem Ed/Psych, Muskingum Coll 1971; (MA) Early & Mid Chldhd, OH St 1975; Merrill Palmer Inst Detroit, OH Univ, Univ of MD; *cr:* Teacher Wilson Elem 1971-; *ai:* Wilson Sch Outdoor Ed Prgm; Right to Read; European Bound Stu; Delta Kappa Gamma 1978-; NEA, OEA, ZEA 1971-; College Drive Church (Chrstn Ed Secy, Sunday Sch Teacher) 1984-; Youth Club Pianist; Academic Grants 1985, 1986; Intnl Fellowship Exch 1987; *home:* 1165 Friendship Dr New Concord OH 43762

DUNCAN, MARLENE VAUGHN, Univ Supervisor-Stu Teachers; *b:* Bartlesville, OK; *m:* L. Dean; *c:* Jennifer, James; *ed:* (BA) Eng/Philosophy, OK St Univ 1960; (MA) Eng, CO St Univ 1968; Trinity Coll Dublin Ireland 1959; *cr:* Eng Teacher Poudre R-1 Sch Dist 1962-78, Colegio Nueva Granada Bogota Colombia 1978-80, Poudre R-1 Sch Dist 1980-87; Instr CO St Univ 1988-; *ai:* CO Lang Art Assn; *office:* Colorado St Univ Fort Collins CO 80523

DUNCAN, SANDY WESTERMAN, Mathematics Teacher; *b:* Paducah, KY; *m:* Joe Frank; *c:* Angela; *ed:* (BS) Math/Psych, Murray St Univ 1974; (MA) Guidance/Cnslr Ed, W KY Univ 1980; Working Towards Rank I Cnslr Ed, W KY Univ; *cr:* Math Teacher Sikeston Jr HS 1974-75, Elkhorn Jr HS 1975-77, Warren Cntrl HS 1977-; *ai:* NCTM 1977-; NEA, KY Ed Assn, Warren Cty Ed Assn; 3rd Dist Ed Assn Math Contest Monitor; Rockfield Meth Church (Church Pianist, Ed Coord, Bd of Trustees) 1987-; Nom Jaycees Outstanding Young Educator Awd 1984; *office:* Warren Cntrl HS 559 Morgantown Rd Bowling Green KY 42101

DUNCAN, WENDY STANFORD, 1st Grade Teacher; *b:* Atlanta, GA; *m:* Pat; *c:* Charlie, Keri; *ed:* (AA) Fr, Young Harris 1964; (BA) Fr/Ed, 1967, (MED) Elem Ed, 1981 GA ST Univ; *cr:* Dir Cerebral Palsy Center 1967; 2nd/4th Grade Title I Teacher Fairview Elem 1967-70; 1st/2nd Grade Teacher Mt Carmel Chrstn Sch 1973-87; Teacher Rockbridge Elem 1987-; *ai:* Grade Level Media Coord; Budget Rep; Book Fair Comm; Mt Carmel Church (Choir Dir 1974-86, Teacher 1968-); Annual Dedication 1987; *home:* 985 Foxfire Dr Lawrenceville GA 30244

DUNCOVICH, MARK RICHARD, Social Studies Teacher; *b:* Amsterdam, NY; *ed:* (BS) His/Ger, US Naval Acad 1979; Cert Scndry Ed, Towson St Univ; Masters Prgm Ec Ed, Johns Hopkins Univ; *cr:* Soc Stud Teacher Fallstaff Mid Sch 1985-; *office:* Fallstaff Mid Sch 3801 Fallstaff Rd Baltimore MD 21215

DUNDEK, JEFFREY M., Biology Teacher; *b:* Chicago, IL; *ed:* (BS) Bio, Univ of IL Chicago 1983; (MS) Bio, Chicago St Univ 1989; *cr:* Bio Teacher Maria HS 1986-, South Suburban Coll 1990; *ai:* NABT 1986-; Chicago Herpetological Society 1985-; *office:* Maria HS 6727 S California Chicago IL 60629

DUNFORD, INA FARMER, Kindergarten Teacher; *b:* Richmond, VA; *m:* Richard L.; *ed:* (BS) Early Chldhd Ed, 1970, (MS) Rdng, 1976 Radford Univ; VA Commonwealth Univ, Univ of VA, VA Polytechnic Inst & St Univ, Hampton Univ; *cr:* 1st Grade Teacher Elliston Lafayette Elem 1971-73; 1st-2nd Grade Teacher 1973-86, Kndgtn Teacher 1986- Margaret Beeks Elem; *ai:* Montgomery Cty Teacher Evaluation Comm Rep 1989-; NEA, VA Ed Assn, Montgomery Cty Ed Assn 1971; New River Valley Rdng Cncl 1989; New River Valley Assn for Ed of Young Children 1989; Blacksburg Intermediate Womans Club Corresponding Secy 1988-; Alpha Delta Kappa (Pres Elect 1986-88, Pres 1988-): Hampton Univ Natl Sci Fnd Grant for Elem Teachers 1989; *office:* Margaret Beeks Elem Sch 709 Airport Rd Blacksburg VA 24060

DUNHAM, DENNIS JAMES, 6th/8th Grade Health Teacher; *b:* Weisbaden, Germany; *m:* Cris Gwin; *ed:* (BA) Health/Phys Ed, Heidelberg Coll 1981; (MS) Educl Admin, Univ of Dayton 1988; *cr:* Teacher Southern Local 1981-; *ai:* Var Girls Bsktbl Coach; Var Ftbl Asst Coach 1981-86; Var Track Asst Coach 1981-88; NEA, OH Ed Assn; Division III Girls Bsktbl Coach of Yr OH 1990; *office:* Southern Local Mid Sch 54 W Main Salineville OH 43945

DUNHAM, DUANE DONALD, Sixth Grade Teacher; *b:* Ogdensburg, NY; *c:* Robert Burns; *ed:* (BS) Ed, Potsdam Coll 1961; *cr:* 4th Grade Teacher Marion Cntrl 1961-63; 4th/6th Grade Teacher Baldwinsville 1963-.

DUNHAM, JANICE FLYNT, Retired Teacher; *b:* Kingston, OK; *m:* Quinton H.; *c:* Connie Gilchrist, James, Richard; *ed:* (BS) Elem Ed, 1959, (MS) Elem Ed, 1962 SE St Univ; OK St Univ; *cr:* Teacher Aylesworth Public Sch 1942-43, Robert E Lee Elem 1959-60, Durant Jr HS 1960-63, Durant Mid Sch 1963-74, Washington Irving Elem 1974-85, SE St Univ 1986-88; *ai:* Pep Club; Boys & Girls Gymnastics; North-Cntrl Accrediting Comm; Bryan Cty Teachers Assn, Durant Teachers Assn; AAUW Secy; Delta Kappa Gamma Secy; B&PW (Secy, Treas); DAR VP; Medical Mission Chm; *home:* 3810 W Main Durant OK 74701

DUNHAM, SALLY ELIZABETH, 5th/6th Grade Teacher; *b:* Omaha, NE; *ed:* (BA) Elem Ed, Hastings Coll 1965; *cr:* Teacher 1965-, Team Leader 1989- Lincoln Public Schls; *ai:* Phi Delta Kappa 1977-; NEA Life Mem 1965-; LEA, NSEA 1965-; NE PTA Life Mem 1965-; PEO Pres 1964-; Kids on Block Puppeteer 1981-; *office:* Norwood Park Elem Sch 4710 N 72nd Lincoln NE 68507

DUNHAM, VERNA BUNNELL, Second Grade Teacher; *b:* Chicago, IL; *m:* Gary Lee; *c:* Kelle Dunham Kelso; *ed:* (BSED) Elem Ed, W IL Univ 1974; Grad Course Stud W IL Univ & Natl Coll; *cr:* Intermediate Teacher Aide Grant Sch 1974-76; 3rd Grade Teacher 1976-87, 2nd Grade Teacher 1987- Gard Sch; *ai:* Stu of Month Comm; Learner Objectives for St Goals Assessment Tests; NEA, IL Ed Assn, Beardstown Ed Assn; PTO, Bus & Prof Womens Club, United Meth Church; *office:* Gard Elem Sch 400 E 15th St Beardstown IL 62618

DUNKER, LUCY MAC NULTY, 5th/6th Grade Lang Art Teacher; *b:* St Louis, MO; *c:* Frank D. III, Barbara D., Nancy Lockburner; *ed:* (BA) Latin/Eng, Coll of St Elizabeth 1942; Grad Stud William Patterson Coll; *cr:* Eng Teacher St Patricks HS 1942-43; Eng/Latin Teacher Netcong HS 1943-45; 7th/8th Grade Lang Art/Latin Teacher 1960-75, 5th/6th Grade Lang Arts Teacher 1975-89 Fredon Township; *ai:* Fredon Ed Assn, NJ Ed Assn, NEA 1960-89; Sussex Cty Ed Assn 25 Yrs of Service; Comm of Ed St of NJ 30 Yrs of Service; *home:* 56 Fredon Marksboro Rd Newton NJ 07860

DUNKIM, WILLIAM EDWARD, III, Mathematics Teacher; *b:* Berkeley, CA; *ed:* (BA) Math, Univ of CA Berkeley 1980; *cr:* Math Teacher Newark Jr HS 1982-85, Bella Vista HS 1985-; *ai:* Math & Math Academic Decathlon Coach; Math Helpline Co-Host; N Ca Math Project 1985; *office:* Bella Vista HS 8301 Madison Ave Fair Oaks CA 95628

DUNLAP, CRYSTAL BONDS, Biology Teacher; *b:* Clinton, SC; *m:* Steven D.; *c:* Kylie B., B. Drake; *ed:* (BS) Bio, Lander Coll 1979; Grad Stud Sci & Ed; Advanced Placement Biology & ATP Teacher Observations Cert; *cr:* Sci Teacher Carver Mid Sch 1980-83; Bio/Physics Teacher Dixie HS 1983-86; Bio Teacher Abbeville HS 1986-; *ai:* SC Jr Acad of Sci Spon; Acad Team Adv & Coach; Sci Fair Project Coach; NABT, SC Sci Cncl 1988-; Abbeville HS & SC Jr Acad of Sci Teacher of Yr 1988-89; *office:* Abbeville HS PO Box 927 Abbeville SC 29620

DUNLAP, JOHN H., Mathematics Teacher; *b:* Menominee, MI; *m:* Linda A. Baribeau; *c:* Michael, Brad; *ed:* (BS) Math, N MI Univ 1973; Marquette Univ, Carthage Coll; *cr:* Teacher Washington Jr HS 1974-82, Green Bay Lombardi Jr HS 1982-84, Green Bay SW HS 1984-; *ai:* 7th & 8th Grade Boys Bsktbl, 8th & 9th Grade Girls Bsktbl Coach; Faculty Advisory; Jr Class Adv; NEA, WEA, GBEA, GBOA, NFIOA; *office:* Green Bay SW HS 1331 Packerland Dr Green Bay WI 54304

DUNLOP, J. CATHERINE BIGGS, English Teacher; *b:* Benton Harbor, MI; *m:* James E.; *ed:* (BA) Eng, Univ of MI 1956; Univ of CA Los Angeles, W MI Coll; *cr:* 7th Grade Teacher St Josephs Cath Sch 1956-58; Eng Teacher Bridgman HS 1958-59, Birmingham HS 1959-; *ai:* Advanced Placement Club Spon; NEA 1956-; *office:* Birmingham HS 17000 Haynes St Van Nuys CA 91406

DUNN, ANDREA CURTIS, HS Mathematics Teacher; *b:* Greenville, KY; *m:* Clarence Dale; *c:* Elizabeth A.; *ed:* (BS) Math, 1981, (MA) Scndry Ed, Murray St Univ; *cr:* Math Teacher Trigg Cty HS 1981-; *ai:* Beta Club Spon; *home:* 111 Sunset Ct Cadiz KY 42211

DUNN, ANN ROSE, English Teacher; *b:* Benton, KY; *m:* Robert Marvin; *c:* Sandi Webb, John, Dwight, Scott, Keith; *ed:* (BA) Eng/His, Murray St Univ 1964; (MED) Rdng Specialist Xavier Univ 1974; (Rank I) Curr Dev, N KY Univ 1984; Teaching Advanced Placement Eng; *cr:* Eng/His/Fr Lone Oak HS 1965-66; Eng Teacher Boone Cty HS 1974-; *ai:* Women of Boone Club Spon; NKEA, NEA 1974-; NCTE 1989-; *office:* Boone Cty HS 7056 Burlington Pke Florence KY 41042

DUNN, ARTHUR JAMES, Science & Mathematics Teacher; *b:* Queens, NY; *ed:* (BS) Soc Stud/Phys Ed/Sci, St Univ Brockport 1971; (MA) Elem Ed/Health Ed/Sci/Math, St Univ Stony Brook 1976; Cert in 7 Subject Areas; *cr:* Phys Ed/Health Ed/Sci/Math/Rdng/Vocabulary/Religion/Soc Stud Teacher Sts Philip & James Sch 1973-; *ai:* Coached Ftbl, Vlybl, Sftbl & Gymnastics; Sci Coord LI, Chaminade & Kellensburg Sci Fairs; Sci Olympiad Team Regent & St & Math Regents; Suffolk Cty Sci Teachers Assn Mem 1987-; Nom Teacher of Yr 1989-; *office:* Sts Philip & James Sch 359 Clinton Ave Saint James NY 11780

DUNN, BRADLEY P., Mathematics Teacher; *b:* Dallas, TX; *m:* Kim Alexander; *c:* Alexander; *ed:* (BS) Math/Bus Admin, William Jewell Coll 1979; (MBA) Bus/Quantitive Analysis, Univ of MO Kansas City 1985; Working Towards Spec Degree Ed, Cntrl MO St Univ; *cr:* Math Teacher Blue Springs HS 1979-; *ai:* Natl Math Exam Spon; Dist Teachers Salary & Welfare & Prof Responsibility Comms; NEA 1989-; NCTM 1982-; Kansas City Teachers of Math 1980-; Gamma Phi Beta 1985-; Sigma Nu Alumni Assn 1984-88; North Cntrl Evaluation Process Curr Selection Chm 1989-; Blue Springs Sch Dist Salary & Welfare Chm 1987-89; Blue Springs HS Teacher of Yr 1984; *home:* 1718 Drumm Independence MO 64055

DUNN, CAROL M., Language Art Chair; *b:* New York, NY; *m:* James W.; *c:* Alan, Diane; *ed:* (BA) Eng, Wm Smith Coll 1955; (MA) Eng Lit, Syracuse 1962; Admin/Supervision Prgm; Summer Stud Oxford; Advanced Placement Eng Seminar, Stetson Univ; NEH Seminar, Emory; *cr:* Jr HS Eng Teacher Marion Cntrl Sch 1955-57; Eng Teacher Seminole HS 1967-81, Osceola HS 1981-; *ai:* Pinellas Cncl Teachers of Eng (Treas 1986-88, Pres 1988-89); Phi Delta Kappa, FCTE, NCTE; GSA Neighborhood & Cncl Responsibilities 1965-; Red Cross (Instr, Stan First Aid, AIDS Educ, Mem Chapter Health & Safety Comm Mem); Natl Endowment Hum Grant Emory Univ 1989; St Teacher Test in Hum Comm Mem; St Teacher Test in Lang Art Comm Mem; St Frameworks Comm for Lit & the Art Mem; *office:* Osceola HS 9751 98th St N Seminole FL 34647

DUNN, CAROLYN MATTHEWS, 6th Grade Teacher; *b:* Cleveland, TN; *m:* Larry W.; *ed:* (BS) ELem Ed, Univ of TN Chattanooga 1978; *cr:* 6th Grade Teacher Hopewell Elem 1978-; *ai:* Sch Improvement & Planning, Handbook Comms; NEA, TEA, BCEA Faculty Rep 1987-; Hopewell Sch Teacher of Yr 1986; *office:* Hopewell Elem Sch 5350 Freewill Rd Cleveland TN 37311

DUNN, CARWIN VINSON, Elementary Counselor; *b:* Morristown, TN; *m:* Eugene C. Jr.; *ed:* (BS) Elem Ed, Carson-Newman Coll 1969; (MS) Ed/Counseling Psych, Univ of TN 1984; *cr:* Teacher 1969-89, Elem Cnslr 1989- Newport Grammar Sch; *ai:* Delta Kappa Gamma Recording Secy 1990; NEA, TN Ed Assn, E TN Ed Assn; Smokey Mountain TN Assn for Counseling & Dev; Local PTA Pres; Univ of TN Outstanding Achievement in Ed & Counseling Psych 1985 & Women of Achievement Awd 1984; *home:* 303 Sequoyah Dr Newport TN 37821

DUNN, CATHY HOEFER, Jr HS Social Studies Coord; *b:* Columbia, SC; *m:* William Lanier; *c:* Carrington, Brooks; *ed:* (BA) His/Span, Columbia Coll 1978; Grad Hrs in Bus, Lib Sci, His & Ed; *cr:* 4th-6th Grade Soc Stud Teacher 1984-87, Soc Stud Coord 1987- St Paul The Apostle; *ai:* Stu Cncl, 8th & 9th Grade Trips; NCEA 1984-; Parish Cncl 1989-; PTO Nominating Chm; Internship With Congresswoman Liz Patterson; Schlsp to Summer Inst for Teachers Law Course; Published 1989; *office:* St Paul The Apostle Sch 152 Alabama St Spartanburg SC 29302

DUNN, CHARLOTTE LUND, 5th Grade Teacher; *b:* Brady, TX; *m:* Thomas N.; *c:* Lisa Dunn Glenn, Keith W., Wade; *ed:* (BS) Ed, 1956, (MED) Ed Methods/Materials, 1976 SW TX St Univ; (EDD) Curr/Instruction, TX A&M Univ 1988; *cr:* Teacher Goodwin Elem 1956-58; Kndgtn Dir/Teacher First United Meth Church 1963-65; Teacher Frazier Elem 1965-; Instr SW TX St Univ 1986-; *ai:* 5th Grade Team Leader; Comal Ind Sci Dist Cmptr Comm & Curr Dev Team; Alpha Chi Honor Society 1954-55; Teacher of Month 1982-83; *office:* Frazier Elem Sch 1441 Hwy 81 E New Braunfels TX 78130

DUNN, CYNTHIA LYNN, 7th Grade Teacher; *b:* Fort Worth, TX; *m:* Alan R.; *c:* Melinda, Wade; *ed:* (BS) Elem Ed, North Tx St Univ 1976; *cr:* Teacher Browning Hts Elem 1977-83, Mulhall-Orlando Schls 1983-; *ai:* Spon Jr HS Honor Society; Spon HS Chrldr.

DUNN, DAVID MITCHEL, Bible Dept Chair/Teacher; *b:* Woodbury, TN; *m:* Trisha Jenkins; *c:* Jennie L.; *ed:* (BA) Speech/Bible, David Lipscomb Univ 1974; (MA) Religion, Pepperdine Univ 1977; *cr:* 5th-6th Grade Teacher Orange Cty Chrstn Sch 1985-86; Teacher/Dept Chm Mid TN Chrstn Sch 1986-; *ai:* Stu Cncl & Jr Class Spon; Golf Coach; Auburntown Volunteer Fire Dept, Auburntown Lions Club 1986-; Auburntown Historical Society VP 1989-; *office:* Mid TN Chrstn Sch 100 MTCS Rd Murfreesboro TN 37130

DUNN, ELIZABETH JOYCE, Fifth Grade Teacher; *b:* Corinth, MS; *m:* Billy E.; *ed:* (BS) Elem Ed, Univ of MS 1972; (MA) Elem Ed, 1976, Specialist Guidance/Counseling, 1990 MS St Univ; *cr:* 5th Grade Teacher Kossuth Elem 1972-; *ai:* Chrldr Spon; Local Sch Test Coord; MS Assn of Educators Officer 1987-89; Amer Assn of Cnslrs, NEA, Horizon, Natl Teachers Assn.

DUNN, ELLA JEAN (MARTIN), First Grade Teacher; *b:* Rutherford, TN; *m:* Jerry S.; *c:* Michael, Mark; *ed:* (BA) Ed, Univ of TN Martin 1982; *cr:* 6th Grade Teacher 1984-85, 6th/7th Grade Lang Art Teacher 1986, 5th Grade Teacher 1987-88, 1st Grade Teacher 1989 Kenton Elem; *ai:* Phi Kappa Phi; Macedonia Baptist Church; *home:* Rt 1 Box 568 Kenton TN 38233

DUNN, JANICE ELIZABETH, Phys Ed/Health Teacher & Coach; *b:* Milan, TN; *ed:* (BS) Health & Phys Educ, Univ of TN at Martin 1969; (MED) Phys Educ, Memphis St Univ 1970; Post Masters Studies Supervision & Admin; *cr:* Instructor/Coach Memphis St Univ 1970-78; Teacher Fairley Elem Sch 1978-81; Teacher/Coach Treadwell HS 1982-; *ai:* Chrm Health and Phys Educ Dept; Coach Varsity Vlybl and Sftbl; Officiate HS and Collegiate Vlybl; NEA 192-; TEA 1982-; MEA 1982-; Exemplary Teacher/Counselor Awd By Memphis Partners, Inc 1986; *office:* Treadwell H S 920 N Highland Memphis TN 38122

DUNN, JOANNA STARNES, 6th Grade Teacher; *b:* Mineola, TX; *c:* Julie Mc Courry, Laurie; *ed:* (BM) Music, Baylor Univ 1956; Advanced Trng North TX St Univ, Mid TN St Univ, TX Tech Univ; *cr:* Music Teacher Mineola Elem Sch 1956-57; 2nd-3rd/5th-6th Grade Teacher hurst Euless Bedford Ind Stu Dist 1958-61/1965-70; 6th Grade Teacher John B Winn Elem 1970-72; 5th Grade Teacher Borman Elem 1972-73; 4th/6th Grade Teacher Trenors Day Sch 1973-77; 5th Grade Teacher Lafayette Mid Sch 1978-79; 6th Grade Teacher Prairie Creek Elem 1979-83, Honey Elem 1983-; *ai:* Lubbock Classroom Teachers; Outstanding Teacher Awd Ross Perot 1981; *office:* Honey Elem Sch 3615 86th Lubbock TX 79423

DUNN, JOSEPH IRVING, History Department Chair; *b:* Tulsa, OK; *m:* Rhonda Jean; *ed:* (AA) Soc Sci, NE OK A&M 1972; (BA) His/Poly Sci, 1974, (MA) His/Ed, 1976 Northeastern St Univ; *cr:* His Chm Okay HS 1977-; *ai:* Sr Spon & Adv; OK Homecoming 1990; His Ed Coord; OK Ed Assn Delegate 1985-86; OKay Ed Assn VP 1988-; *office:* Okay Public Schls P O Box 188 Okay OK 74446

DUNN, KATHLEEN ROSE, English/Business Teacher; *b:* Coffeyville, KS; *m:* Bob; *c:* Julie, Audrey; *ed:* (BS) Bus/Eng, KS St Univ Pittsburg 1963; (MS) Bus, W IL Univ 1971; John Wood Cmmty Coll, Sangamon St Univ, W IL Univ, Quincy Coll, N IL Univ; *cr:* Teacher Cherokee HS 1959-61, Pittsfield HS 1973-; *ai:* Spon Yrbk; Delta Kappa Gamma Secy 1988-; Delta Phi Epsilon 1971-; Article Published; Scientific Literacy Grant; Enterpreneurship Ed Wkshp Presenter; *office:* Pittsfield HS 201 E Higbee Pittsfield IL 62363

DUNN, MARGARET CARTER, History & Government Teacher; *b:* Hattiesburg, MS; *m:* Warren R.; *c:* Deborah, Kim; *ed:* (BA) His, 1965, (MA) His, 1970 Univ of S MS; Grad Stud; *cr:* Teacher Peeples Jr HS 1967-68, Hattiesburg HS 1968-; *ai:* NHS, Presidential Classroom, Teenage Republican, Veterans of Foreign Wars Spon; AFT 1986-; DAR St Teacher 1975; UDC St Teacher 1980; Republican Womens Club 1980-; MS Historical Assn 1989-; Educl Chm US Constitution Comm; Book on Natchez Trace; Statue of Liberty Restoration Chm 1984-86; *office:* Hattiesburg HS 301 Hutchinson Ave Hattiesburg MS 39401

DUNN, MARK D., Social Studies Chairperson; *b:* Miami, FL; *m:* Claire Bardolf; *c:* Katherine, Elizabeth; *ed:* (BS) Soc Stud Ed, FL St Univ 1974; (MS) Admin/Supervision, 1978, (MS) Soc Stud Ed, 1980 FL Intnl Univ; *cr:* Teacher Miami Springs Jr HS 1974-81, Johnson HS 1981-; *ai:* Var Soccer Coach; Jr Class Spon; Phi Delta Kappa; GA Mountains Soccer Assn Incorporated Exec VP 1984-; Global Awareness Grant Miami Springs Jr HS Through FL Intnl Univ; *office:* Johnson HS 3305 Poplar Springs Rd Gainesville GA 30505

DUNN, RITA E., English Department Chair; *b:* Kalispell, MT; *m:* Roger E.; *ed:* (BA) Eng/Ger, W MI Univ 1965; (MA) Eng, Bradley Univ 1973; Educl Admin, Eng Ed, Bradley Univ, IL St Univ; *cr:* Eng Teacher Lathrop HS 1965-67; Eng/Ger Teacher Cntrl HS 1967-69; Lang Art Teacher St Cecilia Grade Sch 1969-70; Eng/Ger Teacher 1970-80, Eng Teacher/Dept Chairperson 1980- E Peoria HS; *ai:* NHS Spon; Literary Art Magazine Co-Spon; Day of Writing Spon & Organizer; NCTE, NEA 1974-; IL Teachers of Eng Assn Peoria Dist Leader 1985-; Delta Kappa Gamma 1985-; Writing Assessment Teacher Trainer IL St Bd of Ed; IL Writing Project Wkshp Leader; *office:* East Peoria HS 1401 E Washington East Peoria IL 61611

DUNN, THOMAS MICHAEL, Admin Asst/Math Dept Chairman; *b:* Spokane, WA; *m:* Deborah Ann Powell; *c:* James, Ezra; *ed:* (BA) Bio, Cntrl WA Univ 1976; (MRE) Admin, Grand Rapids Baptist Theological Seminary 1987; Creation Sci Seminars 1989; Liebenzell Candiate Trng 1985; *cr:* Math/Sci Teacher Amer Fnd Sch of Monterry Mexico 1976-77; Bible/Math/Sci Teacher Sch Damascus Chrstn Sch 1977-; Admin/Dir Outdoor Ed Assn of Portland Area Chrstn Schls 1981-87; Admin Asst Damascus Chrstn Sch 1988-; *ai:* Stu Cncl Adv; Missions Commission Liaison; Bsktbl Ofcl; Assn of Chrstn Schls Intnl 1977-; Inst for Creation Research 1979-; B ible Sci Assn Coord 1989-; Republican Natl

Comm 1980-; Disabled Amer Veterans 1985-; OR Right to Life 1986-; Precinct Comm Person; Outstanding Young Man of America 1982; *office:* Damascus Chrstn Sch 14251SE Rust Way Boring OR 97009

DUNN, TIMOTHY J., Social Studies Teacher; *b:* Morristown, NJ; *m:* Diane Cuchessi; *c:* Melissa, Kevin; *ed:* (BA) His, Montclair St Coll 1973; *cr:* Soc Stud Teacher Randolph HS 1973-74, Williamstown HS 1974-76, George Washington Jr HS 1976-81, Central Sch 1981-84, Dwight D Eisenhower Sch 1984-; *ai:* Adv Academic Quiz Bowl Team; Adv Stock Market Club; Wyckoff Educl Assn Treas 1987-; Governors Teacher Recognition Awd 1990; *office:* Dwight D. Eisenhower Sch 344 Calvin Ct Wyckoff NJ 07481

DUNNAM, BOBBYE LYNNE, History and French Teacher; *b:* Meridian, MS; *m:* H. C.; *c:* Angela Lynn Carraway, Cynthia Diane Beasley; *ed:* (BA) General Liberal Arts, 1985, (MS) Scndry Ed, MS St Univ 1987; Certified Prof Secy; Staff DevCoord; *cr:* Teacher Enterprise HS 1985-; Sec Southern Pipe & Supply Company Inc 1959-82; *ai:* Frosh Class Spon; French Club Spon; Newspaper Adv; Curriculum Coord; Homecoming Comm; MS Professional Educators 1989; NEA 1985-89: Professional Sec Assn Intl; MS Cattlemens Assn; St Boulevard Baptist Church; Simmons Hunting Club; Star Teacher-1989; Teacher of the Year-1986; Top Hat Awd; Published Articles on Genealogy; Sr Adult Choir Dir; *office:* Enterprise H S PO Drawer A Enterprise MS 39330

DUNNIGAN, DEBRA DENICE, Mathematics Teacher; *b:* Chattanooga, TN; *ed:* (BS) Scndry Math Ed, Univ of TN Chattanooga 1982; (MS) Supervision/Admin, Trevecca Nazarene Coll 1989; *cr:* Math Teacher Howard HS 1982-85, Hixson HS 1985-.

DUNNING, DALE JOHN, Mid Sch Geography Teacher; *b:* Dayton, MN; *c:* Laura Srnsky, Kara Ott, Alice; *ed:* (BS) Bio/Geography/Phys Ed/Soc Stud, St Cloud St Univ 1959; *cr:* 8th Grade Geography Teacher Sch Dist 564 1959-; *ai:* NEA.

DUNNING, KEVIN MICHAEL, 8th Grade Teacher/Principal; *b:* Chicago, IL; *m:* Mary Frances; *c:* Jeremy, Maggie; *ed:* (BA) Elem/Scndry Ed, Concordia Univ 1978; (MA) Government/Politics, St Johns Univ 1985; *cr:* Teacher Trinity Luth Sch 1978-81, Redeemer Luth Sch 1981-84, Luth HS 1984-89; Prin/8th Grade Teacher St John Luth Sch 1989-; *ai:* ASCD 1990; Luth Ed Assn 1978-; OH Cncl for Soc Stud 1989-; Taft Seminar for Teachers 1987; *office:* St John Luth Sch 1027 E 176 St Cleveland OH 44119

DUNNING, SUSAN ARLENE (GIBSON), K-8th Grade Teacher; *b:* Valley City, ND; *m:* Charles; *ed:* (DAS) Office Admin, Wahpeton St Sch of Sci 1969; (GCE) Elem Ed, Freedom Univ 1988; Spec Personalized Alpha Omega Publications; *cr:* Private Secy Farmers Union Grain Terminal Assn 1969-76; Secy 1976-78, Teacher 1979- Christ Center Ministries; *ai:* Sch Plays; Christmas Prgm & Music; Church Ministry & Outreach; Church Organist; Freedom Univ Alumni; Schlsp Freedom Univ; *office:* Christ Center Ministries 3801 42nd Ave S Minneapolis MN 55406

DUNPHY, HELENE ELAINE, 6th Grade Teacher; *b:* St Paul, MN; *c:* William E., Eric P.; *ed:* (MS) Counseling, Univ of WI River Falls 1982; (BAS) Elem Ed, Univ of MN Minneapolis 1960; Life Time Teaching Cert, Certified & Licensed Cnslr St of MN; *cr:* 6th Grade Teacher 1960-64, 3rd Grade Teacher 1964-65, 6th Grade Teacher 1965-74, Adult Basic Ed Night Sch Teacher Minneapolis Schls 1966-76, Lead Rdng Teacher 1974-75, Intermediate Grade Teacher 1975-76, Summer Sch Teacher 1969-74, 1978-79, 1989; 6th Grade Teacher Fundamental Elem Prgm Minneapolis Schls; *ai:* Girls Spec Needs Prgm; Continuous Progress Prgm, Developmental Math & Rdng Tutor; Pre 1-6 Summer Classrooms; MN Fed of Teachers Mem 1960-; Telephone Peer Cnslr 1984-85; Parents Only Teacher Rep 1982-89; *home:* 8019 Xerxes Ave S #201 Bloomington MN 55431

DUNSON, JACKIE LEE (EIBLING), Health/Physical Ed Teacher; *b:* Kenton, OH; *c:* Angela J., Derek D.; *ed:* (BA) Health/Phys Ed, OH Northern Univ 1975; (MA) Ed, Coll of Mt St Joseph 1986; Water Safety & Cardiopulmonary Resuscitation Instr; Drug Abuse Prevention; Sexually Transmitted Diseases; *cr:* Health/Phys Ed/Psych/Sociology Teacher/Vllybl/Track Coach 1978-80, Health/Phys Ed Teacher 1978- Upper Scioto Valley HS; *ai:* Upper Scioto Valley Building Cncl Comm; Hardin Cty Staff Dev & Drug Free Schls Grant Comm; USV Mentor for New Teaching; OH Ed Assn, NEA, Dist Assn 1989-; Univ Club II Active Mem 1989-; Upper Scioto Valley Local Schls 10 Yr Service & Hardin Cty STAR of OH 11 Yrs Service Awd Plaque; *home:* 12483 Township Rd 209 Kenton OH 43326

DUNSWORTH, DEBORAH ELLEN, Geometry/Math Analysis Teacher; *b:* St Joseph, MO; *m:* Hayden M.; *c:* Greg, Jody, Orrin; *ed:* (BS) Math Ed, Univ of OK 1972; *cr:* Math Teacher Blanchard HS 1972-79, Newcastle HS 1979-; *ai:* Staff Dev, Textbook NHS Schlsp Comm; Jr/Sr & Pep Club Spon; NEA, OK Ed Assn 1972-; Blanchard Assn of Teachers 1974-79; Newcastle Assn of Classroom Teachers (Treas 1986-) 1979-; NCTM, OK Cncl Teachers of Math; BSA Comm Mem 1988-; Cub Scouts (Comm Mem 1987-, Asst Den Leader 1988-); *office:* Newcastle HS 101 N Main Newcastle OK 73065

DUNWOODY, SUSAN PENELOPE, English Teacher; *b:* Lafayette, IN; *m:* Harry Alan; *c:* Chad, Todd, Beth A.; *ed:* (BA) Eng Ed, 1969, (MS) Eng Ed, 1977 Purdue Univ; *cr:* Eng Teacher Benton Cntrl Jr/Sr HS 1969-71, E Tipp Jr HS 1973-74, Battle Ground Jr HS 1980-84, Harrison HS 1984-; *ai:* Keyette Spon Outstanding Jr-Sr Girls Philanthropic Organization; Tippecanoe Ed Assn, IN St Teachers Assn, NEA, NCTE; Covenant Presbyn Church; Alpha Phi Alumnae.

DU PERIER, SUSANNA CURRIE, Kindergarten Teacher; *b:* Waco, TX; *c:* Courtney, Jason; *ed:* (BS) Elem Ed, Univ of TX 1966; Grad Classes Univ of HI 1966-67; Center Univ CA; *cr:* 1st Grade Teacher Eastside Elem 1966-69; 1st Grade Teacher 1969-71, Pre-K Teacher 1982-84, Kndgtn Teacher 1984-87 St Louis Sch; Kndgtn Teacher Reilly Elem Austin Ind Sch Dist 1987-; *ai:* Assn of TX Prof Educators 1989-; NEA; TX St Teacher Assn; Austin Assn of Teacher 1987-89; TX Classroom Teachers Assn 1983-87; Kndgtn Teachers of TX 1 983-; NEA of Young Children 1984-; Southern Assn on Children Under Six 1984-; Austin Assn of Ed of Young Children 1984-; Jr League of Austin 1976-; Alpha Delta Kappa Honorary Society for Women Educators 1984-; Delta Delta Delta 1963-; Mem Bd of Trustees St Louis Sch 1987-89.

DUPREE, DOROTHEA LEWIS, 8th Grade English Teacher; *b:* Gadsden, AL; *m:* Earnest Welch; *c:* Antione D.; *ed:* (BS) Eng, 1967, (MA) Eng, 1975, (AA) Sch Admin, 1978 AL A&M Univ; Various Courses & Wkshps Univ of AL; *cr:* 8th Grade Teacher Attalla City Bd of Ed 1967-; *ai:* Quest for Excl Coord; Textbook Comm Mem; Attalla Teachers Assn Secy 1971-72; Attalla Ed Assn, NEA Mem; Zeta Phi Beta Chaplain; Boys Clubs of America Bd Mem 1989-, Service 1990; Southern Chrstn Leadership Conference Spiritual Adv 1988-, Dedication 1989; Westside Cmmty Club (Secy, Prgm Dir) 1980-, Service 1985, 1989; *office:* Etowah Mid Sch 429 S 4th St Attalla AL 35954

DUQUETTE, EDWARD JOHN, Science Department Chair; *b:* Long Beach, CA; *m:* Ann Marie; *c:* Aimee, Amanda, John P.; *ed:* (AA) Philosophy, St Edwards Univ 1962; (BS) Microbiology, 1966, (MS) Microbiology/Biochemistry, 1968 St Univ of CA; Biotech Engr, Bus Mgmt, Cmptr Application Engr; *cr:* Application Microbiologist Purex Corporation 1966-681 Fermentation Engr Nutrilite Products 1968-72; Biotechnical Engr 1972-80, Research Applications Coord 1980-86 Anheuser-Busch Industrial Products; Sci Dept Chm Maricopa HS 1988; *ai:* Class & Sci Club Adv; Pupil Study Team Mem; Grad Requirement Comm Mem; CA Bio Ed Assn, NABT, Kern Sci Educators Assn, Society of Industrial Microbiology; Church Act; Numerous Articles Published; *office:* Maricopa HS 955 Stanislaus Maricopa CA 93252

DURANT, JEFFRY LYNN, Fifth Grade Teacher; *b:* Bellaire, OH; *m:* Rosemary Derry; *c:* Jeffry; *ed:* (BS) Elem Ed, OH Univ 1971; (MS) Ed Admin, WV Univ 1974; Post Grad Ed Courses OH Univ/WVU/Dayton Univ/Detroit Univ; *cr:* 7th Grade Teacher Gravel Hill Elem Sch 1971-72; 5th Grade Teacher JeffErson Elem Sch 1972-; *ai:* Shadyside Ed Assn Pres 1975-76/85-86;OH Ed Assn 1971-; NEA 1971-; BPOE (Elks) (Exalted Ruler 1978-79/Dist Deputy 1983-84/ Elk of Yr 1984); Amer Legion 1967; *home:* 4524 Harrison St Bellaire OH 43906

DURANTE, TOM, Director of Bands; *b:* Brooklyn, NY; *ed:* (BMED) Music Ed, N TX St 1983; (MMED) Music Ed, E TX St 1988; *cr:* Dir of Bands Pilot Point HS 1983-85, Kerens HS 1985-87; Grad Asst E TX St Univ 1987-88; Dir of Bands Pocatello HS 1988-; *ai:* Phi Mu Alpha Sinfonia 1981-; Kappa Kappa Psi 1987-; Intnl Clarinet Society 1981-; ID St Cmmty Jazz Band 1988-; *home:* 621 Harrison #8 Pocatello ID 83204

DURBIN, JEFFREY ALLEN, Biology/Chemistry Teacher; *b:* Wheeling, WV; *m:* Charlene Marie; *ed:* (BS) Bio, Muskingum Coll 1982; *cr:* Sci/Bio/Chem/Physics Teacher Buckeye Local Sch Dist 1982-; *ai:* Asst Boys Var Bsktbl Coach; Sci Club & Soph Class Adv; NSTA 1985-; NEA 1983-; OH HS Bsktbl Coaches Assn; Beta Beta Beta; Audubon Society, Nature Conservancy, Natl Wildlife Fed; *home:* RD 2 Box 78 Upland Heights Rayland OH 43943

DURELLI, MONIQUE JUANA, Spanish Teacher; *b:* Buenos Aires, Argentina; *ed:* (BA) Fr, Amer Univ 1968; (MA) Span Linguistics, Cath Univ 1976; *cr:* Teacher Suitland HS 1969-73, Bowie HS 1973-; *ai:* Chairperson; Key Club Spon; *office:* Bowie HS 15200 Annapolis Rd Bowie MD 20715

DURFEE, SANDRA SUNDQUIST, English Department Chairperson; *b:* Manchester, CT; *m:* David Rising; *c:* Susan Durfee Parr, David R. Jr.; *ed:* (BA) Eng Lit, Brown Univ 1957; (MA) Liberal Studs, Johns Hopkins Univ 1987; NY Writing Project; *cr:* Teacher Hamburg HS 1968-78, Edgewood HS 1978-80, St Pauls Sch for Girls 1980-; *ai:* Adv Lit Magazine; Co-Chm Multi-Cultural Assessment Comm; Chm Co-Curr Comm; NCTE 1968-; MD Cncl Teachers of Eng 1981-; Teachers and Writers Collaberative 1989-; Grant Yeats Summer Inst Shgo Ireland 1990; *office:* St Pauls Sch For Girls Brooklandville MD 21022

DURHAM, ALTA HOERBERT, Science Teacher; *b:* Emden, IL; *m:* Louis; *c:* Jude, Paul, William, Roxanne, Andrew; *ed:* (BS)Zoology, Northern IL Univ 1951; Biological Sci, Ed; *cr:* Sci Teacher Richmond Burton HS 1951-53; Toluca Unit Dist 1953-58; Eisenhower HS 1958-60; Toluca Unit Dist 1971-; *ai:* Jr Class Spon; Scholastic Bowl; IL Sci Teachers Assn; IL Chem Teacher; *office:* Toluca Jr Sr H S 306 N Maple Toluca IL 61369

DURHAM, DAVID CRAIG, English/Speech Teacher; *b:* San Angelo, TX; *m:* Jan Burley; *c:* Bart, Darcy, Kelsey; *ed:* (BA) Eng/Phys Ed, 1967; (MA) Eng, 1969 Sam Houston St Univ; TX Tech Univ; *cr:* Fresh/Soph Eng Instr South Plains Coll 1969-72; Recreation Dir/Coach TX Dept of Corrections 1973-82; Eng Rdng Teacher/Coach Van Vleck ISD 1982-84; Kenedy ISD 1984-87; Eng/Speech Teacher/Coach Van Vleck ISD 1987-; *ai:* Asst Ftbl/Bsktbl Coach; Head Track Coach; Class Spon; TX HS Coaches Assn 1967-; TX Assn Bsktbl Coaches; Chm-Ethics Comm 1986 Mem 1982-; TX Assn for Gifted and Talented 1989-; BSA Bd of Dir 1988; Graduate Fellowship Eng Dept Sam Houston St Univ 1967-69; Career Ladder Teacher Recognition Since Inception 1984; *office:* Val Vleck H S 4th St Van Vleck TX 77482

DURHAM, EDNA BROCK, Fourth Grade Teacher; *b:* Murray Cty, GA; *m:* William Q.; *c:* Randall D., Cynthia Williams; *cr:* Teacher Varnell Elem Sch 1957-; *ai:* Whitfield Ed Assn, GA Ed Assn, NEA; Varnell Parent Teacher Assn, Delta Kappa Gamma 1977-; *home:* 112 Lin-Bar Dr Dalton GA 30721

DURHAM, ELSIE MARIE, Retired; *b:* Covington, KY; *ed:* (BS) Elem, Eastern KY Teacher Coll 1947; Cincinnati Bible Seminary; AZ St; *cr:* 1st-8th Grade Teacher Mountain Mission Sch 1948-58; Chrstn Indian Sch 1958-65; 2nd/5th Grade Teacher Camargo Elem 1966-89; *ai:* 4-H Club 5th Grade 1970-89; MCEA Secy 1977; KEA; NEA; Antioch Chrstn Church Children Church Dir 1973-80; Retired with 43 Yrs Work with Children 1989; *home:* 550 Town Branch Jeffersonville KY 40337

DURHAM, JOYCE GOODIN, Business Ed Dept Chairman; *b:* Columbia, KY; *m:* Hunter; *c:* Stacey Durham Wilson, Robert H.; *ed:* (BA) Bus Ed, 1963, (MA) Bus Ed, Univ of KY 1969; Grad Stud Cmptrs; *cr:* Bus Ed Teacher Woodford Cty HS 1964-71, Adair Cty HS 1971-; *ai:* FBLA Adv; Adair Cty Contact Person; Delta Pi Epsilon 1965-; Delta Kappa Gamma 1975-; KY Ed Assn 1963-; KY Bus Ed Assn 1965-; Selected Outstanding Teacher 5th Dist Campbellsville Coll; Selected Outstanding Prof Leader Chamber of Commerce; *office:* Adair Cty HS Greensburg Road Columbia KY 42728

DURHAM, MARILYN FAIRCHILD, American History Teacher; *b:* Beloit, KS; *m:* William F.; *c:* William F. Jr., Doris Durham Denning; *ed:* (MS) Amer His, Pittsburg St Univ 1970; Post Grad Work Effective Schls Trng; Trainer for Other Teachers in N KS City Sch Dist; *cr:* His/Journalism Teacher N KS City HS 1966-79; His Teacher Antioch Mid Sch 1979-; *ai:* The Hornets Buzz Sch Newspaper Spon 1967-79; Mid Sch Stu Newspaper Spon; MO Press Women Assn 1970-79; Delta Kappa Gamma Pres 1984-86; NEA, NKC; Teacher Trainer for NKC Sch Dist Through Prof Dev Grant; Wrote Curr for Dist; Served on Ec Cncl for Rockhurst Coll; *office:* Antioch Mid Sch 2100 NE 65th St Gladstone MO 64118

DURHEIM, LARRY ROBERT, Computer Science Teacher; *b:* Moscow, ID; *m:* Elaine Lucile Pitman; *c:* Crystal D. Hammon, Christine D. Case; *ed:* (BA) Elem Ed, Northwest Nazarene Coll 1967; Cmptr Sci; *cr:* 4th & 6th Grade Teacher 1967-73, Jr HS Math 1973-74 Nampa ID Sch Dist; 6th Grade Teacher Hines Elem Sch 1974-84; K-6 Cmptr Sci Harney Cty Sch Dist #3-Hines Sch 1984-; *ai:* 6th Grade Boys Bsktbl Coach; 5th & 6th Boys/Girls Vlybl Coach; Hines Sch Site Comm Chairperson; OEA/NEA Negotiator 1967-; Nazarene Church Dist Sunday Sch Supt of Yr 1976-77; Nampa ID Jaycees Outstanding Young Educator 1971-72; *home:* 405 N Saginaw P O Box 543 Hines OR 97738

DURKIN, MIKE, English Dept Chair/Teacher; *b:* South Bend, IN; *m:* Diane K. Sutter; *c:* Deborah, Matthew, Bethany; *ed:* (BA) Eng Ed, 1969, (MA) Eng, 1972 W MI Univ; *cr:* Eng Teacher Pennfield HS 1969-; *ai:* Var Bsktbl; Yrbk, Frosh Class Spon; Distance Learning, John Craig Allen Schlsp Comm; Bsktbl Coach of MI Assn Regional Coach of Yr 1981-82; Commencement Addresses; *office:* Pennfield HS 8587 Q Drive N Battle Creek MI 49017

DURNAN, CHARLES DENNIS, 6th Grade Teacher; *b:* Flint, MI; *m:* Ellen Bruce Cloud; *c:* Kelly, Leslie Caterer, Chad, Melissa Caterer; *ed:* Art Ed, Flint Comm Jr Coll 1970; (BS) Elem Ed, Cntrl MI Univ 1972; (MA) Comm Ed/Leadership, E MI Univ 1977; Guided Imagery; Positive Attitude in Ed; Educl Management; Great Books Leader Trng; Instructional Skills Trng; Energy Specialist; Health & Family Planning Ed; *cr:* Teacher Holly Dist Schls 1972-; *ai:* Chm Sch Discipline & Rdng Improvement Comm; Coord Sch Drug Ed Prgm; Cmmty Ed Instr; Bsbl Coach Summer Prgm Youth & Mens Leagues; Positive Living Fnd 1980-; Born to Win for Educators 1986-; Wizard of Oz Club 1980-; Tiger Stadium Fan Club 1989; Outstanding Young Educator Awd Holly Jaycees; *office:* Davisburg Elem 12003 Davisburg Rd Davisburg MI 48019

DURNELL, CAROL JUSTICE, Math Lab-Chapter I; *b:* Logan, WV; *m:* Richard N.; *c:* Thomas A., James E., Suzanne STeinbeck; *ed:* (BA) Elem Ed, Glenville St 1970; (MA) Early Chldhd, WV Univ 1977; WV Univ 1985; *cr:* Teachers Aide Humphrey Elem 1967; 2nd Grade Teacher North Elem 1968; Stu Teaching Belmont WV 1970; 2nd Grade Teacher Belmont Elem 1970-71; 3rd Grade Teacher 1971-76, 1st Grade Teacher 1976-77, 3rd Grade Teacher 1977-79 Criss Elem; Split 3rd/4th Grade Teacher Leachtown Elem 1979-83; 1st Grade Teacher 1983-84, 4th Grade Teacher 1984-88, Chapter I Math Lab Teacher 1988-89, Gihon Elem 1989-; *ai:* Sch Based Assistance Team; PTA Exec Comm; Served on Sch Improvement Comm; WV Ed Assn Mem 1970-; Wood Cty Ed Assn Mem 1970-; Philanthropic Ed Organization Chapter G Ways & Means Chm 1981-89; *home:* Rt 9 Box 216A Parkersburg WV 26101

DUROCHER, CLYDE FRANCIS, 6th Grade Science Teacher; *b:* Freda, MI; *ed:* (BS) Sci, N MI Univ 1961; *cr:* 4th-6th Grade Teacher Novi Cmmty Schls 1961-64; 6th Grade Teacher Calumet Public Schls 1964-65; 5th Grade Teacher Novi Cmmty Schls 1965-66; 6th Grade Teacher Calumet Public Schls 1966-; *ai:* Sci Curr Objectives; Stanton Township Fire Dept Treas 1980-83; *home:* Box 126 Freda Loe Atlantic Mine MI 49905

DURR, SHEILA ANN AVERY, 6th Grade Soc Stud Teacher; *b:* Guys, TN; *m:* Paul E.; *c:* Nikki N., Paul A.; *ed:* (AS) His, Jackson St Comm Coll 1971; (BS) His, Univ of TN Martin 1974; Elem Cert Lambuth Coll & Memphis St Univ; *cr:* Kndgtn Teacher Bethel Springs Elem 1974-75; 5th Grade Teacher 1975-86, 6th Grade Soc Stud Teacher 1986- Selmer Mid; *ai:* Mc Nairy Cty Ed Assn, TN Ed Assn, NEA; United Negro Coll Fund Cty Comm Rep 1988-; St Rest Church (Choir Pres, Youth Dir, Bible Sch Dir, Sunday Sch Teacher); Love & Unity Club Secy 1987-; Ruritan Club Charter Mem; Selmer Mid Sch Teacher of Yr 1989; *home:* Rt 1 Box 118L Guys TN 38339

DURST, HAZEL WILT, Retired; *b:* Amboy, WV; *m:* Lewis A.; *c:* Bradley, Carla Summers, Lewis C.; *ed:* (BA) Elem Ed, Fairmont St Coll 1972; WV Univ; *cr:* Teacher Jerra Alta Elem 1953-54, Aurora Elem 1966-89; *ai:* Cty Curr Comm; Cty Report Card Comm; Sch Calender Comm; PCEA Secy 1972-88; WVEA Mem 1982-88; NEA Mem 1972-88; Amboy United Meth Church (Ch Trustees Church Ladies Aide VP Church Pianist Organist) 1985-92; Cmmnty Choir Dir; PTO Pres of Aurora Sch; Past Mem of Rebecca Lodge; *home:* Star Route Box 21 Amboy WV 26701

DURST, SUSAN RAE, English Teacher; *b:* Boise, ID; *m:* James W.; *c:* Kathryn, Blake; *ed:* (BA) Eng/Ger, ID St Univ 1973; (MA) Eng/Rdng, Boise St Univ 1979; *cr:* Eng Teacher Mc Clintock HS 1973-74, Lackey HS 1974-75, Meridian Jr HS 1975-80, South Jr HS 1980-88, Borah HS 1988-; *ai:* NCEA 1973-; NCTE 1975-; Articles Published ID Journal of Rdng; Wrote Curr for St Adopted Required Course Dev Rdng; Taught 3 Summers Boise St Univ; *office:* Borah HS 6001 Cassia St Boise ID 83709

DUSBIBER, KATHLEEN SMALL, Physical Education Teacher; *b:* San Diego, CA; *m:* Stanton; *ed:* (BA) Phys Ed, Univ of CA Santa Barbara 1954; Working Towards Masters CA St Univ; *cr:* Teacher La Puente HS 1954-55, Temple City HS 1956, La Puente HS 1957-59, Wheelus Air Base Jr-Sr HS 1960, Glendore HS 1961, La Puente HS 1964-; *ai:* AAHPER; *office:* La Puente HS 15615 E Nelson Ave La Puente CA 91744

DUSEK, THOMAS CLAYTON, History Teacher; *b:* Cameron, TX; *m:* Glenda Sue Bales; *c:* Lansing, Thomas; *ed:* (BS) His/Speech, Howard Payne Univ 1962; (MA) His, Sam Houston St Univ 1974; Post Grad Stud His, TX A&M Univ 1977-78; *cr:* Teacher Cameron Ind Sch Dist 1969-76, New Caney Ind Sch Dist 1978-80; Part-Time Instr Temple Jr Coll 1976-88; Teacher Buckholts Ind Sch Dist 1980-; *ai:* One-Act Play Dir; UIL Coord; Teacher Rep for Grievance Comm; Soph Class Spon; *home:* PO Box 563 Cameron TX 76520

DUSSEAU, BETH LABEAU, Eighth Grade Teacher; *b:* Monroe, MI; *m:* Thomas L.; *c:* Jeffrey, Jennifer; *ed:* (BA) Speech/Drama/Eng, Marygrove Coll 1967; Grad Stud Ed, E MI Univ, Univ of Toledo; *cr:* Eng/Speech Teacher Murray-Wright HS 1967-68; 8th Grade Teacher Custer Jr HS 1968-69; Eng Teacher St Mary Acad 1971-72; 8th Grade Teacher St Michael Sch 1975-; *ai:* 8th Grade, Cheerleading, Sch Newspaper Adv; Vlybl & Sftbl Coach; Detroit Fed of Teachers 1968-70; NEA 1980-; St Mary Church Choir Dir 1970-; Monroe Cmmty Players 1974-; Huron Civic Theatre 1986-; *office:* St Michael Sch 510 W Front St Monroe MI 48161

DUSTERHOFF, MARILANE G., Math Coordinator; *b:* Plaguemine, LA; *m:* Jerry; *c:* Jean, Chris, Kurt; *ed:* (BA) Scndry Ed Math, Univ of Dallas 1967; (MA) Scndry Instr, TX A&I Univ 1987; Corpus Christi St Univ; Southwest TX St Univ; *cr:* Math Teacher Irving HS 1967; Bishop Lynch HS 1967-68; Calallen HS 1979-82; Teacher & Dept Chm Chisholm Trail Mid Sch 1982-88; Math Coord Round Rock Ind Sch Dist 1988-; *ai:* NCTM; TX Math Teachers Assn; Austin Area Cncl of Teachers of Math; TX Assn of Supervisors of Math; ASCD; *office:* Round Rock Ind Sch Dist 1311 Round Rock Ave Round Rock TX 78681

DUSZA, CONSTANCE T., Math Dept Chair/Math Teacher; *b:* Altoona, PA; *m:* Daniel J.; *c:* Alexander; *ed:* (BS) Math Ed, Indiana Univ of PA 1972; Grad Classes Indiana Univ of PA, Univ of Pittsburgh Johnstown, Wilkes Coll; *cr:* Math Teacher Bishop Guilfoyle HS 1981-; *ai:* NCTM Mem 1988-; Mellon Fnd Grant for Advanced Placement Course Summer 1990; *office:* Bishop Guilfoyle H S 2400 Pleasant Valley Blvd Altoona PA 16602

DUTTRY, CYNTHIA YOHE, Second Grade Teacher; *b:* Du Bois, PA; *m:* Scott Fredrick; *c:* Leslie, Jimmy, Michael; *ed:* (BS) Elem Ed, Edinboro Univ 1972; Grad Stud PA St Univ, E Stroudsburg Univ, Gannon Univ; *cr:* 2nd Grade Teacher Fox Township Elem Sch 1972-75; Kngtn Teacher S St Marys Elem Sch & Bennetts Valley Sch 1976-80; 1st/3rd-5th Grade Teacher 1981-85, 2nd Grade Teacher 1986- Bennetts Valley Elem Sch; *ai:* PA St Ed Assn Building Rep 1974; Univ Women 1973-80; Eastern Star Pres 1980-81; Bennetts Valley Womens Club 1987-; Shiloh Presbyn Church Organist 1968-81; *office:* Bennetts Valley Elem Sch Rt 255 Weedville PA 15868

DUTY, LYNN ANN (MILLER), Sixth Grade Teacher; *b:* Toledo, OH; *m:* William H.; *c:* Matthew, Stephenen, Katherine; *ed:* (BED) Eng/Soc Stud, Kent St Univ 1968; (ME) Univ of Toledo 1979; St Anns Coll England 1968; E MI Univ 1985; *cr:* 7th Grade Teacher 1968-69, 6th Grade Teacher 1969- Shoreland Elem; *ai:* Safety Patrol Adv & Act Dir; Pi Lamda Theta (VP 1983, Mem 1980-86); NEA, OH Ed Assn 1968-; NCTE, Intnl Rdng Assn 1985-; OH Cncl Teachers of Eng & Lang Art 1987-; Jennings Scholar 1988-89; Oh Teacher Leader Network Mem 1988-; Whos Who in Amer Ed 1989; *office:* Shoreland Elem Sch Suder at E Harbor Dr Toledo OH 43611

DUVALL, JUDITH M., 1st Grade Teacher; *b:* Vancouver, WA; *ed:* (BA) Elem Ed, WA St Univ 1965; (MA) Elem Ed, Central WA St Univ 1970; *cr:* 1st Grade Teacher Chester Valley Elem Sch 1965-70; 1st Grade Teacher 1970-79; 2nd Grade Teacher 1980-84; 1st Grade Teacher 1985- Coll Gate Elem Sch; *ai:* Teacher in Charge; Rdng Pilot Prgm; NEA 1965-; *office:* College Gate Elem Sch 3101 Sunflower Anchorage AK 99508

DUVALL, MARGARET HARELSON, Chapter I Reading Teacher; *b:* Atkins, AR; *m:* Dain; *c:* Jeffrey, Jason; *ed:* (BSE) Elem Ed 1978, (MSE) Elem Ed, 1982 AR Tech Univ; Rdng Specialist, AR Tech Univ 1984; *cr:* 1st Grade Teacher Dardanelle Public Schls 1978-79; 3rd Grade Teacher Ola Public Schls 1979-80, Pottsville Public Schls 1980-84; Chapter I Rdng Teacher Pottsville Public Schls 1984-; *ai:* AAFC 1988-; PAE 1987-; *office:* Pottsville Elem Sch P O Box 70 Pottsville AR 72858

DUVALL, MARY LOUISE HOOD, Fourth Grade Teacher; *b:* Warner, OK; *m:* Robert Lee; *c:* Gary, Terry; *ed:* (AS) Elem, Connors St Coll 1969; (BS) Elem, 1971, (MS) Elem, 1974 Northeastern St Coll; Admin, Northeastern St Univ 1981; *cr:* 3rd-4th Grade Teacher Midway Elem 1971-77; 5th Grade Teacher Dewar Elem 1977-80; Remedial Math Teacher 1980-83, 4th Grade 1983- Midway Elem; *office:* Midway Elementary Box 97 Hitchita OK 74438

DUWE, CYNTHIA KAY, Spanish Teacher; *b:* Fresno, CA; *c:* John, Justin; *ed:* (AA) Span, Reedley Coll 1966; (BA) Span, 1968, Span/Eng, 1969 Fresno St Coll; Span/Eng, CA St Hayward 1975; (MA) Scndry Admin, CA St Fresno 1989; *cr:* 6th Grade Teacher Auberry Elem 1979-84; Eng/Span Teacher Sierra HS 1984-; *ai:* Soph Class Adv; Mentor Teacher 1988-89; WASC Prgm Chm 1989-; St Quality Review Team 1987-88; *office:* Sierra Joint Union HS 33326 N Lodge Rd Tollhouse CA 93667

DUZAN, SUE HEARN, 2nd Grade Teacher; *b:* Paris, IL; *m:* William Austin; *c:* Daniel A., Tricia N.; *ed:* (BS) Elem Ed, 1973, (MS) Elem Ed, 1988 E IL Univ; *cr:* 2nd Grade Teacher Lake Crest Sch 1973-; *ai:* Oaklands HS Chrldrs Spon; Phi Delta Kappa, Alpha Delta Kappa, EIU Rdng Cncl; Oakland Ed Assn VP; Natl Assn for Eastern Star; *home:* RR 2 Box 229 Oakland IL 61943

DUZEN, SUZANNE, SSCM Principal; *b:* Wilkes Barre, PA; *ed:* (BA) Elem Ed, Alvernia Coll 1971; (MED) Rdng, Bloomsburg Coll 1981; (MS) Educl Admin, Univ of Dayton 1986; Several Wkshps; *cr:* 2nd Grade Teacher Holy Name of Jesus Sch 1970-73; 1st/2nd Grade Teacher St Joseph Sch 1973-79; 2nd Grade Teacher Nativity Sch 1979-84; Prin St Andrew Sch 1984-87, St Catherine Laboure Sch 1987-; *ai:* Organized Puppet Ministry Troupe; Give Storytelling & Puppets Wkshps; Produce Original Puppet Shows; NCEA, Fellowship of Chrstn Puppeteers; Intnl Rdng Assn 1989-; Pax Christi 1989-; *office:* St Catherine Laboure Sch 4020 Derry St Harrisburg PA 17111

DVORAK, JANEEN ANN, Fifth Grade Teacher; *b:* Owosso, MI; *ed:* (BA) Upper Elem Ed, 1973, (MA) Upper Elem Ed, 1976 Cntrl MI Univ; Ed Classes, Cntrl MI Univ, Detroit Sch of Bus, MI St Univ; *cr:* 5th-6th Grade Rdng/Lang Teacher 1973-77, 5th Grade Teacher 1977- New Lothrop; *ai:* Gifted & Talented Ski Club; Shiawassee Rdng Assn (Secy, Treas) 1978-83; MI Ed Assn 1973-; Wildlife Recovery Assn 1985-; Shiawassee Road Runners Treas 1978-, Runner of Yr 1982; Red Cross Swimming 1973-75; CETA Supvr 1979; Grant Conservation Sch Higgins Lake MI, Sci Camp Jacksonhole WY; *office:* New Lothrop Elem Sch 9435 Beech St New Lothrop MI 48460

DVORKIN, ROBERT I., 6th Grade Science Teacher; *b:* Poughkeepsie, NY; *m:* Debra Shore; *c:* Michael, Andrew; *ed:* (BS) Elem Ed, Corpus Christi St Univ 1968; Elem Ed/Eng, SUNY New Paltz 1972; *cr:* 5th Grade Teacher 1968-70, 6th Grade Teacher 1970-87, 6th Grade Sci Teacher 1987- Wappingers Cntrl Schls; *ai:* Cmmty Martial Arts Instr 1975-; Civilian Inst of Defensive Tactics 1988-; Karate & Me Summer Childrens Prgm 1988-; Harding Club 1989-; Eastern Tae Kwon Do Union Chm 1989-; *home:* 22 Miller Rd Poughkeepsie NY 12603

DVORSKY, VICTOR F., Mathematics Teacher/Chair; *b:* Lansford, PA; *m:* Mary Ann Mc Gee; *c:* Karen, Kenneth; *ed:* (BA) Philosophy, Stonehill Coll 1963; (MA) Theology, Holy Cross Coll 1968; (MTS) Math, Cath Univ 1972; *cr:* Math Teacher Notre Dame Boys HS 1968-69, Bishop Mc Namara HS 1969-75, Holy Cross Acad 1975-83; Math Teacher/Chm Bullis Sch 1983-; *ai:* Math Club; MD Conference Math Teachers; NCTM; WA Assn of Ind Schls Math Chm; *office:* Bullis Sch 10601 Falls Rd Potomac MD 20854

DWIGHT, TIMOTHY JOHN, Social Studies Teacher; *b:* Burlington, IA; *m:* Nancy Ann Tiemeier; *c:* Shelly, Christine, Timothy, Jason; *ed:* (BA) His/Poly Sci, 1969, (MAT) Soc Stud Ed, 1971 Univ of IA; Grad Stud Scndry Admin; *cr:* Soc Stud Teacher West HS 1971-72, Northwest Jr HS 1972-83, Iowa City HS 1983-; *ai:* 8th Grade Ftbl Coach; BSA Webelos Leader 1988-; *office:* Iowa City HS 1900 Morningside Dr Iowa City IA 52245

DWYER, BARBARA MITCHELL, English Teacher; *b:* Chicago, IL; *m:* Patrick M.; *c:* Morgan M., Devin E.; *ed:* (BA) Eng, 1973, (MA) Lit, 1974 W IL Univ; Sch Admin, N IL Univ; *cr:* Teacher Proviso West HS 1974-77-, Lake Park HS 1977-; *ai:* NEA, IEA 1985-; NCTE, IATE 1974-; Articles Published.

DWYER, DAVID WILLIAM, Math Teacher/Team Leader; *b:* Parsons, KS; *m:* Janiece Ilene Mc Millan; *c:* Jeremy D., Brian C.; *ed:* (BS) Math, KS St Coll Pittsburg 1969; Working on Masters Bus Admin; *cr:* Math Teacher Sharples Jr HS 1969-81, Mc Clure Mid Sch 1981-; *ai:* Stu Store Adv; Math Team Coach; Team Leader; WA St Math Cncl, NCTM, ASCD, Math Assn of America 1986-88; Kenmore Little League Coach 1981, 1988-; WA St Micro-Cmptrs Grant; Seattle City Excl in Ed Awd; Cmptr Prgm Published; *home:* 6129 NE 204th Seattle WA 98155

DWYER, JAMES PATRICK, Mathematics Teacher; *b:* Providence, RI; *m:* Charlene Maclure; *c:* Brenton, Ryan; *ed:* (BA) Scndry Ed Math, 1976, (MED) Urban Ed, 1979 RI Coll; *cr:* Math Teacher Martin Jr HS 1976-; *ai:* RI Ed Assn, EPEA, NCTM 1976-; Little League Coach; *home:* 113 Mac Arthur Rd Woonsocket RI 02895

DWYER, MARGARET MARY, Third Grade Teacher; *b:* New York, NY; *m:* John; *c:* Margaret Minson; *ed:* (BA) Brooklyn Coll 1977; (MSED) Ed, 1979; *cr:* Rdng Teacher 1956-58; 2nd Grade Teacher 1958-60, 3rd Grade Teacher 1960-63 St Francis de Sales Sch; 2nd/3rd Grade Teacher St Camillus Sch 1963-; *ai:* Bus & Prof Womens Organization VP Peninsula Chapter 1985-; *home:* 254 Beach 133 St Belle Harbor NY 11694

DWYER, RICHARD S., Social Studies Teacher; *b:* Boston, MA; *m:* Mary Jane Levine; *c:* Suzanne, Tracey; *ed:* (BS) Soc Stud/Eng, Boston St Coll 1962; Framingham St Coll, Antioch Coll; *cr:* Teacher Algonquin Regional HS , Hollister HS; *ai:* Cmmty Action Prgm Coord; MTA Pres 1978-83; NEA 1962-; *home:* Box 582 York Beach ME 03910

DWYER, SHIRLEY VINEYARD, 8th Grade Math Teacher; *b:* St Vrain, NM; *m:* Parnell R. Jr.; *c:* Vondell Michaels, Lori Carter Marneta; *ed:* (AA) Bus, (BS) Ed, 1973, (MS) Ed, 1979 ENMU; *cr:* Classroom Teacher Berrendo Mid Sch 1974-; *ai:* Coach Mathcounts Teams; Coach Math/Sci Bowl Teams; NCTM 1989-; NEA REA Treas 1980-; Delta Kappa Gamma 1987-; *office:* Berrendo Mid Sch 800 Marion Richards Rd Roswell NM 88201

DWYER, SUSAN L., High School Guidance Counselor; *b:* E St Louis, IL; *m:* Ken; *c:* Julie; *ed:* (BSED) Elem Ed, IN Univ of PA 1970; (MED) Cnslr Ed, Univ of Pittsburgh 1986; *cr:* Teacher 1970-72, 1975-86, Cnslr 1986- Moon Schls; *ai:* Dept Head; Class Spon; Advanced Placement Coord; MEA, PSEA, NEA, ACCA; *office:* Moon Sr HS 904 Beaver Grade Rd Coraopolis PA 15108

DWYER-KUELLER, MARY THERESE, Theology Teacher/Chairperson; *b:* Cleveland, OH; *m:* Thomas D.; *c:* Sean D.; *ed:* (BA) Religious Stud, OH Dominican Coll 1976; (MA) Pastoral Ministry, Boston Coll 1981; *cr:* Teacher Villa Angela Acad 1976-81; Pastoral Minister St William Church 1981-85; Teacher St Joseph Acad 1985-; *ai:* Stu Cncl Moderator; NCEA; Irish Amer Club; *office:* Saint Joseph Acad 3430 Rocky River Dr Cleveland OH 44111

DYAL, BRENDA FAYE, Math Teacher; *b:* Eastman, GA; *ed:* (BS) Math Ed, GA Coll 1969; (MED) Math, GA Southwestern 1976; *cr:* Math Teacher Dodge Cty HS 1969-71/1981-, Lowndes Jr HS 1971-72, Dodge Elem Sch 1973-81; *ai:* Beta Club Adv; Dodge Prof Educators Chapter Pres 1988-89; Prof Assn of GA Educators; Dodge Cty HS Star Teacher 1988; *office:* Dodge County H S Cochran Rd Eastman GA 31023

DYAR, FONDA WILLIAMS, English Teacher/Dept Head; *b:* Greenville, SC; *m:* Ty D.; *c:* J. P., Hillary; *ed:* (BA) Scndry Ed, Clemson Univ 1977; *cr:* Eng Teacher Pendleton Mid Sch 1977-81, Pendleton Jr HS 1981-; *ai:* Eng Dept Chairperson; Stu Incentive Comm; Literary Pamphlet Adv; NCTE, PSTA 1989-; Pendleton Jr Assembly 1990; Pendleton Jr HS Teacher of Yr 1989-; *home:* 320 Spring Ln Seneca SC 29678

DYBING, MYRON JAY, HS Music/Math Teacher; *b:* Harvey, ND; *m:* Pam Lockhart; *c:* Melanie, Kristin; *ed:* (BS) Music, Minot St Univ 1963; (MA) Music, Univ Northern CO 1967; *cr:* Jr HS/HS Music/Math Upham ND 1963-67; Kindred ND 1967-; *ai:* HS Swing Choir; Sr Class Adv; HS Jazz Band; Pep Band Dir; MENC 1963-; NDMENC 1963-; NDEA 1963-; HS Act Adv Bd 1968-70; Natl Street Rod Assn 1967-; Kustom Kemps Amer St Rep 1983-; MN Street Rod Assn; *office:* Kindred HS Hwy 15 Kindred ND 58051

DYE, CAROL LEE (HORTON), 7th/8th Grade Reading Teacher; *b:* Detroit, MI; *c:* Jason K., Joshua K.; *ed:* (BS) Eng Lit/Lang/Elem Ed, E MI Univ 1972; (MAED) Rdng Diagnosis/Remediation, Baldwin-Wallace Coll 1982; *cr:* K-8th Grade Substitute Teacher Sheffield Lake 1974-78; 2nd/3rd Grade Teacher Spring Branch Elem 1978-80; Basic Skills Teacher Litchfield Elem 1980-82; 7th/8th Grade Teacher Cotton Boll Elem 1982-; *ai:* Stu Cncl Adv; 8th Grade Guidance Specialist; Peoria CTA Pres 1984-85; BSA (Advancement Chm 1988-89, Troop Comm 1989-); Article Published in Eng Journal; *office:* Cotton Boll Elem Sch 8540 W Butler Ave Peoria AZ 85345

DYE, LYNETTE MARIE (HOBELL), Rdng Teacher/Chapter I Tutor; *b:* E St Louis, IL; *m:* Michael Warren; *c:* Lindsay C.; *ed:* (BS) Elem Ed, 1981, (MS) Elem Ed/Rdng, 1989 E IL Univ; *cr:* Substitute Teacher Marion Cty Schls 1981-83; Rdng/His Teacher Kinmundy-Alma Jr HS 1983-89; Rdng Teacher/Chapter I Tutor Franklin Park Sch 1989-; *ai:* Beta Club & Cheerleading Spon; *office:* Franklin Park Sch 1325 N Franklin Salem IL 62881

DYE, MARY JANE TRENUM, 6th Grade Soc Stud Teacher; *b:* Keyser, WV; *m:* Herbert Marshall Jr.; *c:* Derek, Kaitlyn; *ed:* (BS) Elem Ed, 1976; (MED) Curr/Instruction, 1985 Frostburg St Coll; *cr:* Teacher Northern Mid Sch 1978-; *ai:* Yrbk Adv.

DYE, PATRICIA BALSLEY, Junior High Science Teacher; *b:* Louisville, KY; *m:* Michael Craig; *c:* Melissa, Stephanie; *ed:* (BA) Elem, E KY Univ 1975; (MS) Elem, Morehead Univ 1985; Wkshps & Conventions; *cr:* Teacher W R Castle Elem 1976-78, Porter Elem 1978-80, Clark Elem 1980-; *ai:* CESI Mem; NSTA, KY Mid Sci Assn, Natl Mid Sch Assn, KY Sci Teachers Assn Mem; Floyd Cty Ed Assn Sick Leave Bank Comm; Floyd Cty Teachers Assn VP 1986-89; KY Ed Assn (Mem 1975-, Delegate 1980-); Delta Kappa Gamma Mem; KY Sci & Technology Cncl Incorporated Grants 1989-; *office:* Clark Elem Sch 140 Clark Rd Prestonsburg KY 41653

DYE, RICHARD ALAN, Guidance Counselor; *b:* Medina, OH; *m:* Susan Marie Corp; *c:* Jessica, Mary, Kali; *ed:* (BS) Health/Phys Ed, Baldwin-Wallace 1972; (MA) Phys Ed, Univ of Akron; Scndry Guidance Cnslr, Univ of Akron; *cr:* Health/Phys Ed/Psych Teacher Elyria HS 1972-73; Teacher Twinsburg City Schls 1973-84; Cnslr Dodge Mid Sch 1984-85, R B Chamberlin HS 1985-; *ai:* Dist Curr Advisory; CARE; Fellowship of Chrstn Athletes Adv; Ftbl & Bsktbl Coach; Phi Delta Kappa 1987-; OH Sch Cnslrs 1985-; NEA 1973-; Twinsburgh Person of Yr 1978; Chagrin Valley Conference Ftbl Coach of Yr 1978; Twinsburgh Young Man of Yr 1975; *office:* R B Chamberlin HS 10270 Ravenna Rd Twinsburg OH 44087

DYE, ROBERT JOSEPH, Eng Teacher/Rdng Specialist; *b:* Philadelphia, PA; *m:* Mary Jane R.; *c:* Robert Jr., Lisa; *ed:* (BA) Ed/Eng, Easter Coll 1961; (MS) Rdng, Univ of PA 1975; *cr:* Teacher Marple Newton Sch Dist 1961-; *ai:* Dir of Music Various Churches; *home:* 475 Parkway E Broomall PA 19008

DYE, SALLY J., Jr High Teacher; *b:* Mount Vernon, IL; *ed:* (BA) Eng, Eastern IL Univ 1972; *cr:* Jr HS Teacher Geff Grade Sch 1972-; *ai:* Scholastic Bowl Coach; Delta Kapa Gamma 1986-; Teachers of Geff Assn Pres 1984-; Wayne Assn of Teachers Chm 1988-; Geff PTO 1972-; Geff Chrstn Church 1963-; Fairfield Lions Club Star Teacher 1987; *office:* Geff Grade Sch Lafayette St Geff IL 62842

DYER, BARBARA ANITA (O'MARA), High School Science Teacher; *b:* Laconia, NH; *m:* Ronald P.; *c:* Stephen, David; *ed:* (BS) Sci Ed, 1969, (MS) Sci Ed, 1974 Fitchburg St Coll; St Johns Hospital Medical Technician; *cr:* Teacher Reingold Elem 1969; Sci Teacher Memorial Mid Sch, Fitchburg HS; *ai:* Fitchburg Gas & Electric Light Company Teacher Adv Panel; Visiting Comm to Westfield HS Accreditation; Sierra Club; Phi Delta Kappa 1978-79; Westminster Mineral Club 1986-88; NE Marine Environmental Inst; Horace Mann Grant; IPS Sci Grant-Gifted/Talented; *office:* Fitchburg HS 98 Academy St Fitchburg MA 01420

DYER, DANIEL OSBORN, English Teacher; *b:* Enid, OK; *m:* Joyce; *c:* Stephen; *ed:* (AB) Eng, Hiram Coll 1966; (MED) Eng, 1971, (PHD) Curr & Instruction, 1977 Kent St Univ; Summer Seminar Natl Endowment for Hum 1990; *cr:* Eng Teacher Aurora Mid Sch 1966-78; Asst Prof Lake Forest Coll 1978-79; Eng Teacher W Reserve Acad 1979-81; Instr Kent St Univ 1981-82; Eng Teacher Harmon Mid Sch 1982-; *ai:* Drama Dir; NCTE, Phi Delta Kappa, NEA; Prof Best Leadership Awd Learning Magazine 1989; Books Published; *office:* Harmon Mid Sch 130 Aurora Hudson Rd Aurora OH 44202

DYER, ERIC B., 6th-8th Grade Art Teacher; *b:* Ancon Canal Zone, Panama; *c:* Marc, Jennifer; *ed:* (BA) Art/Jewelry/Sculpture, 1971, (BFA) Painting & Printmaking, 1971 CA Coll of Arts & Crafts; *cr:* Art Teacher Granada HS 1972-80, Mendenhall Mid Sch 1980-; *ai:* CA St Visual & Performing Arts Curr Dist Comm; Yrbk Illustrations; *office:* Mendenhall Mid Sch 1701 El Padro Dr Livermore CA 94550

DYER, MARGARET GOFF, 10th & 11th Grade Eng Teacher; *b:* Scotts Hill, TN; *m:* Thomas V. Jr.; *ed:* (BS) Ed/Eng, Bethel Coll 1962; *cr:* Elem Teacher Morris Chapel 1957-62; Eng Teacher Scotts Hill 1962-; *ai:* Sr Class & Beta Club; Delta Kappa Gamma (Treas 1982) 1963-; Outstanding Young Educator Awd Scotts Hill Jaycees 1977; Alderperson on Scotts Hill City Bd 1982-; Vice-Mayor 1984-86, 1988-; *home:* Rt 1 Box 83A Scotts Hill TN 38374

DYER-FORKASDI, ELIZABETH ANN, English Teacher; *b:* Phoenix, AZ; *m:* John Tim; *ed:* (MA) Eng, Chapman Coll 1972; (BA) Eng, AZ St Univ Tempe 1965; Coursework Toward Alcohol Counseling Credential Saddlebag Coll; Working Towards Masters Psych, Pepperdine Univ; Life Time Stan Scndry Teaching, Comm Coll Teaching, Rdng K-14, Pupil Personnel, Admin Credentials; *cr:* Eng/Rdng Teacher Foothill HS 1965-70; Eng Instr Coastline Coll 1981-84; Rdng/Study Skills Teacher Golden West Coll 1989; Eng Lit/Amer Lit/Eng/Rdng Teacher University HS 1970-; *ai:* All Sch Rdng Prgm; University HS Proficiency Prgm; Anti-Alcohol & Anti-Drug Presentations, & Counseling University HS; Core Team University HS; Frosh, Eng 3, Advance Eng Composition Prgm; NCTE, Orange Cty Rdng Assn, Intnl Rdng Assn, Irvine Teachers Assn, ASCD, CA Teachers Assn (Dist Secy 1976, St Rep 1977); Creative Alternatives Bd of Dir 1985-87; Whos Who in Amer Ed 1989; *office:* University HS 4771 Campus Dr Irvine CA 92715

DYESS, JEFFREY KEITH, Geometry/Physics Teacher; *b:* Montgomery, AL; *ed:* (BS) Scndry Ed/Math, Univ of S MS 1986; Scndry Ed, Math, William Carey Coll 1990; MS Institutions of Higher Learning Bd of Trustees Physics Wkshp 1989; *cr:* Math Teacher Philadelphia HS 1986-87; Math/Sci Teacher Wayne Cty HS 1987-; *ai:* Physics Club Spon; MS Cncl Teachers of Math 1987-; MS Assn of Physicists 1989-; MS Prof Educators Building Rep 1988-; *home:* Rt 4 Box 585 Waynesboro MS 39367

DYKES, JIM BYRON, Seventh Grade Science Teacher; *b:* Kingsport, TN; *c:* Bo-Jacob, Ashleah; *ed:* (BS) Bio/Health, 1978, (MA) Supervision/Admin, 1980 E TN St; *cr:* Sci Teacher Church Hill Mid Sch 1981-; *ai:* Photography Club Adv; Mid Sch Coach; *home:* PO Box 1347 Church Hill TN 37642

DYKES, RONALD A., History/Biology II Teacher; *b:* Johnson City, TN; *m:* Peggy Taylor; *c:* Chad *ed:* (BS) His/Bio, 1975, (MA) His, 1982 E TN St Univ; *cr:* His Teacher W View Sch 1978-81; His/Bio Teacher 1981-87, Vice Prin 1986 David Crockett HS; Teacher/Vice Prin Sulphur Springs Sch 1987-88; His/Bio Teacher Daniel Boone HS 1988-; *ai:* Washington Cty Mid Sch Scholars Bowl Prgm Coord; Soc Stud, Sci Text Selection Comm; Head Track & Asst Ftbl Coach 1981-87; Washington Cty Ed Assn, TN Ed Assn, NEA 1977-; Teacher of Yr 1982; Sci Teacher of Yr 1987; Washington Cty Nom St Sci Teacher of Yr; Achieved Career Level III Status TN Dept of Ed.

DYMACEK, MERILEE NEIS, Vocal Elem Music Teacher; *b:* Lawrence, KS; *m:* Bill J.; *c:* Kristen, Wendy; *ed:* (BME) Music Ed, KS Univ 1971; *cr:* Vocal Elem Music Teacher Gardner Elem 1971-73, Nottingham Elem 1973-; *ai:* 5th & 6th Grade Honors Choir; NEA 1971-; *office:* Nottingham Elem Sch 15th & Elm Eudora KS 66025

DYNAN, WILLIAM JOHN, Social Studies Teacher; *b:* Summit, NJ; *m:* Virginia Zimnick; *c:* Alan E., Robert J.; *ed:* (BA) Bus Ed, Montclair St Teachers Coll 1956; (MA) Admin/Supvr, Montclair St Coll 1960; Natl Curr Stud Inst ASCD; *cr:* Teacher Forest Avenue Sch 195668, Deerfield Sch 1968-69, South Orange-Maplewood Bd of Ed 1969; Adjunct Prof Seton Hall Univ 1963-69; *ai:* NJ Ed Assn, NEA 1956-; West Orange Rent Leveling Bd Vice Chm 1969-71; West Orange Citizens Advisory Comm Chm 1987-89; Teacher Trng Prgms Study Commission St of NJ; NJ Scndry Sch Improvement of Math Ford Fnd Advisory Group; *home:* 39 Maple Ave West Orange NJ 07052

DYSERT, L. DARYLENE, 1st Grade Teacher; *b:* Klamath Falls, OR; *c:* Barry; *ed:* (BS) Elem Ed, CA St Poly Tech Univ 1964; Grad Stud; *cr:* 6th Grade Teacher Arroyo Grande Mid Sch 1965-66; K-2nd Grade Teacher Macdoel Elem Sch 1966-70; 1st Grade Teacher Henley Elem Sch 1970-71, Peterson Elem Sch 1971-85; 3rd Grade Teacher 1985-86, 1st Grade Teacher 1986-Bonanza Elem Sch; *ai:* 7th Day Adv Sch Bd Mem 1978-80; Klamath Lake Cty Boys Youth Ranch (Bd Mem, Secy-Treas) 1978-; Mini Lab Prgm I Dev Write Up 1978; Cty Curr Comms; *home:* Rt 2 Box 175 Bonanza OR 97623

DYSICK, DORIS BYRD, Social Studies Chairperson; *b:* Spartanburg, SC; *m:* Willie K.; *c:* Alvin F.; *ed:* (BA) Soc Stud, SC St Coll 1964; (MS) Soc Stud, IN Univ 1969; Stu Teacher Services Admin; *cr:* Teacher Carver Jr HS 1964-68, Jenkins Jr HS 168-71; Soc Stud Teacher/Chairperson Jordan HS 1971-; *ai:* Academic Decathlon Team Spon; March of Dimes Team for Walkathon; GA Assn of Educators, Muscugee Assn of Educators 1971-; NEA 1964-; Phi Delta Kappa 1976-; March of Dimes (Bd Mem 1978-, Chairperson Teenage Bd 1980-88), Service 1980; Columbus-Ft Benning Secy Alumni of SC St Coll 1977-; Mentor Teacher Muscugee Cty Outstanding Teacher Awd; *office:* Jordan HS 3200 Howard Ave Columbus GA 31994

DYSON, SILVONIA ALLEN, Mathematics Teacher; *b:* Perry, GA; *m:* Edward James; *c:* Leslie, Shana, Rebecca, Amber; *ed:* (BS) Math, Ft Valley St 1970; (MED) Math, Univ of GA 1971; *cr:* Teacher Northside Jr HS 1971-; *ai:* Houston Educator Assn, NEA Mem 1971-; *office:* Northside Jr HS 500 Johnson Rd Warner Robins GA 31093

DZUBA, JOHNETTE, Third & Fourth Grade Teacher; *b:* Donora, PA; *ed:* (BA) Sociology, La Roche Coll 1972; (MS) Elem Ed, Duquesne Univ 1976; *cr:* 6th Grade Teacher Con-Area Cath 1977-78; 7th/8th Grade Teacher Visitation 1978-85, St Marys 1985-86; 3rd/4th Grade Teacher St Florian 1986-; *ai:* PA Jr Acad of Sci Judge 1983; Parents for Handicapped Persons Arts & Crafts Instr 1982-85; *office:* St Florian Box 188 United PA 15689

E

EADES, ANN JACOBS, Secondary Teacher/H S Coach; *b:* Jacksonville, NC; *m:* Tommy; *c:* Autumn Michelle; *ed:* (BS) Belmont Coll 1975; TN Tch; *cr:* Teacher/Coach Dibrell Elem 1977-80; Warren Cty Jr HS 1980-81; Warren Cty Sr HS 1981-; *ai:* Head Coach Warren Cty Sr HS; Inducted Belmont Coll Hall of Fame 1989; *home:* Box 133 Morrison TN 37357

EADIE, MARY ELLEN, Communications Teacher; *b:* New Castle, PA; *m:* Mary Ellen Theobald; *c:* Colleen P., Donald F., Rory C.; *ed:* (BS) Fr, 1971, (MED) Rdng, 1978 West Chester Univ; *cr:* Fr/Span Teacher Sleighton Sch 1972-76; Stu Skills Instr West Chester St Coll 1980; Rdng Instr PA St Univ 1988; Rdng/Comm Teacher West Chester Area Sch Dist 1978-; *ai:* 8th Grade Team Leader; Correspondent for Newspapers; *office:* Stetson Mid Sch 1060 Wilmington Pike West Chester PA 19382

EADS, CHARLOTTE ELIZABETH, Orchestra Director; *b:* Port Author, TX; *ed:* (BM) Music/Ed, Southern Meth Univ 1983; *cr:* Orch Dir Spring Branch Ind Sch Dist 1983-85, Pasadena Ind Sch Dist 1985-; *ai:* Stu Cncl Spon; TX Music Educators Assn Region Orch Chm 1987-; Delta Kappa Gamma Society Intnl 1990; Music Educators Natl Confernce 1980-; TX Orch Dir Assn 1983-; Natl Sch Orch Assn 1989-; TX Music Educators Conference (St Stu Pres 1981-83) 1980-; TX Music Educators Assn St Stu Secy 1981-82; Amer String Teachers Assn 1987-; Pasadena Philharmonic Orch 1986-; *office:* S Houston HS 3820 S Shaver South Houston TX 77587

EAGAN, CLAUDIA A., English Teacher; *b:* Cranston, RI; *m:* Kevin A.; *ed:* (BA) Eng/Scndry Ed, Univ of RI 1972; (MAT) Eng, RI Coll 1976; *cr:* Eng Teacher Woonsocket HS 1972-; *ai:* Drama Club Adv; Eng Dept Schlsp Comm; Self Evaluation Team Cmmty Relations Chm; *office:* Woonsocket Sr HS 777 Cass Ave Woonsocket RI 02895

EAGLESTON, KENNETH LEE, Chemistry Department Head; *b:* Kenova, WV; *m:* Sherry Berkeley; *c:* Adam T., Candace A., Justin L.; *ed:* (BA) Chem, Marshall Univ 1971; *cr:* Sci Teacher Cammack Jr HS 1971-77; Chem Teacher Huntington HS 1977-; *ai:* Spon SADD; Mem Sch Improvement Comm; Textbook Adoption Comm; *office:* Huntington HS 900 8th St Huntington WV 25701

EAGLIN, MARIE MELANCON, Kindergarten Teacher; *m:* Joseph Mac Arthur; *c:* Darin, Eugene, Sharlotte, Eric; *cr:* Elem/Special Ed Teacher George Washington Carver HS 1963-69; Kndgtn Teacher Grand Coteau Elem Sch 1969-; *ai:* Grand Coteau Elem Planning Comm 1989-; The Littlest Chrldrs Act 1975; Art Exhibit Spon 1962; NEA, LA Ed Assn; Salutatorian Amer Legion Medal 1959; St Landry Civic Club Outstanding Scholastic Awd 1958; World Week Magazine Essay Contest 1957; Outstanding Elem Teacher of America Awd 1975; Zappa Zeta Honor Society 1962; NEA Article 1988; The Morning Star Article 1981-; *home:* P O Box 11 625 Burleigh Ln Grand Coteau LA 70541

EAKER, SALLY BLAYLOCK, Kindergarten Teacher; *b:* Oak Ridge, MO; *c:* Kimberly A. Eaker Groves, Eric D.; *ed:* (BS) Elem Ed, SE MO St 1967; Parents as First Teachers Cert 1985; *cr:* Kndgtn Teacher Scott City R-1 1967-; *ai:* MO St Teachers Assn; Cmmty Teachers Assn Pres 1972; Alpha Delta Kappa 1985-88; Eastern Star (Worthy Matron 1984-85, Dist Deputy 1988-89); *office:* Scott City R-1 3000 Main St Scott City MO 63780

EANES, A. B. BRADY, Principal; *b:* Welch, WV; *m:* June Ellen England; *c:* Tamberlee J., Erin B; *ed:* (BS) Elem Ed, Bluefield St 1970; (MA) Educl Admin, WV Univ Coll of Grad Stud 1985; Supervision Classes, Marshall Univ; Prins Acad; Mastery Teaching; *cr:* 4th-6th Grade Teacher Welch Elem 1970-76; 5th/6th Grade Teacher Fall River Elem 1976-87; 6th Grade Teacher Switchback Elem 1987-89; Prin Anawalt Sch 1989-; *ai:* Bsktbl, Ftbl Coach; Sch Safety Adv; Stamp Club Spon; Soc Stud Fair Coord; Academic Comm Chm; Mc Dowell Cty Inservice Instr; Sch Newspaper Adv & Spon; Sch Inservice Instr; NEA, WV Ed Assn, Mc Dowell Cty Ed Assn, NAESP, WV Assn of Elem Sch Prins, Mc Dowell Cty Admin Assn, Mc Dowell Cty Elem Admin; Welch Elem Teacher of Yr; Fall River Elem Teacher of Yr; *office:* Anawalt Elem Sch Box 230 Anawalt WV 24808

EANNACE, REBECCA S., Math Teacher/Gifted Coord; *b:* Pittsburgh, PA; *m:* Micael A.; *c:* Leda, Vincent, Patrick, Michelle; *ed:* (BS) Math, St Francis Coll 1965; *cr:* Math Teacher 1965-67; Tells HS Math Teacher 1985-86, Math Teacher 1985-; HS Gifted Coord 1986-; Burgettstown Jr-Sr HS; *ai:* ACT 178 Comm; WA Cty Gifted Consortium; NEA 1985-; PSEA 1985-; BAEA 1985-; *office:* Burgettstown Jr-Sr HS 99 Main St Burgettstown PA 15021

EARHART, BRENDA JEAN, 12th Grade English Teacher; *b:* Dover, NJ; *m:* David Brian; *c:* Matthew D., Brett R. Keener; *ed:* (BS) Bus Admin, Rollins Coll; 1983; (MS) Eng, Nova Univ 1986; *cr:* Eng Teacher De Laura Jr HS 1985-86, Palm Bay HS 1985-86, Eau Gallie HS 1986-, Brevard Comm Coll 1987-89; *ai:* Beta Club Spon; Prom Comm; Brevard Cty Guardian Ad Litem Prgm Guardian 1987-; *office:* Eau Gallie HS 1400 Commodore Blvd Melbourne FL 32935

EARL, PEGGY PEELER, Fourth Grade Teacher; *b:* Toluca, NC; *m:* Gary R.; *c:* Lisa, Rebecca; *ed:* (BA) Early Chldhd Ed, 1970, (MA) Rdng, 1977 ASU; *cr:* Kndgtn Teacher Washington Elem 1971-72; 3rd Grade Teacher 1972-78, 4th Grade Teacher 1978- Casar Elem; *ai:* Spelling Bee Chm; Sci Fair Comm; NCAE 1971-; NCCIRA 1976-; ACEI 1986-; GSA (Leader, Asst Leader) 1985-, 5 Yr Pin Awd 1990; Reeps Grove United Meth Church Various Church Offices 1955-; Volunteer Upper Cleveland Area Needs-Day Camp; *home:* 627 Carpenters Grove Church Rd Lawndale NC 28090

EARL, RICHARD JON, 8th Grade English Teacher; *b:* Fostoria, OH; *m:* Pamela Ann Miller; *c:* Shawn M., Katie E.; *ed:* (BA) Eng, Univ of Findlay 1973; (MED) Admin/Supervision, Univ of Toledo 1989; Masters Work Toward Prin Cert; *cr:* Teacher/Coach Emerson Jr HS 1973-; *ai:* Asst Var Ftbl Coach Fostoria HS; NEA, OEA, FEA 1973-; *office:* Emerson Jr HS 140 W High St Fostoria OH 44830

EARLE, BEVERLY ANN, Kindergarten Teacher; *b:* Hemlock, MI; *ed:* (BA) Eng, Cntrl MI Univ 1958; Grad Work Univ of MI; *cr:* Teacher Midland Cty 1952-53, Hemlock Elem 1953-; *ai:* MI Ed Assn 1952-80; AFT 1980-; Hemlock Ed Assn; Hemlock Lib Bd (Treas, Secy, Trustee) 1960-80; Hemlock Brownie Troop (Organizer, Leader) 1955-65.

EARLL, MIKE DEAN, Agriculture Education Instr; *b:* Hawarden, IA; *m:* Mary Jo Breuker; *c:* David M; *ed:* (AA) Ag Ed, Worthington Comm Coll 1977; (BS) Ag Ed, IA St Univ 1979; *cr:* Ag Ed Instr Round Lake HS 1979-80, Sibley Ocheyedan HS 1980-; *ai:* Spon FFA Chapter; Sibley Ocheyeden Ed Assn Pres 1987-88; IA Voc Ag Teachers Assn (Secy, Treas) 1987-88, Outstanding Young Mem 1982-83; ISEA, NEA 1980-; Indian Lake Baptist Church Chrstn Ed Bd Chm 1987-; Osceola Cty Democratic Party/Chm 1988-; Distinguished Educator Morningside Coll 1989; Outstanding Young Men of America 1988; Natl FFA Alumni Washington DC Intern 1985; Honorary IA FFA Degree 1990; *office:* Sibley-Ocheyeden HS 120 11th Ave NW Sibley IA 51249

EARLS, BETSY BURK, 2nd Grade Teacher; *b:* Springfield, MO; *m:* Douglas Roy; *c:* Anna M.; *ed:* (BS) Elem Ed, 1977, (MS) Elem Ed, 1983 SW MO St Univ; *cr:* Elem Librarian MO Elem Sch 1978-79; Substitute Teacher MO R-12 1979-80; 2nd Grade Teacher Jeffries Elem 1980-; *ai:* Pilot Parents 1990; MO Governors Interagency Coordinating Cncl; *home:* 715 W Cambridge Springfield MO 65807

EARLY, CARLA THOMPSON, Math Teacher; *b:* Waynesville, NC; *m:* Russell Lee; *c:* Meredith; *ed:* (BS) Elem Ed, Appalachian St Univ 1975; *cr:* 4th Grade Teacher Bob Mathis Elem Sch 1975-76; 8th Grade Math Teacher Blackburn Mid Sch 1976-; *ai:* Mathcounts Coach; NC Cncl Teachers of Math; Dwight D Eisenhower Math/Sci Grant; *office:* Blackburn Mid Sch Rt 1 Box 231 Newton NC 28658

EARLY, GILBERT NEAL, Social Studies Teacher; *b:* Raleigh, NC; *m:* Barbara Norris; *c:* Joyce A.; *ed:* (BA) His/Poly Sci, Greenville Coll 1964; (MA) Modern European His, E IL Univ 1969; *cr:* Teacher John F Kennedy HS, Singapore Amer Sch 1975-77, Blair HS 1977-79, Seneca Valley HS 1979-; *ai:* Attendance Monitor; Poly Sci Club Spon; NEA Fellowship Gilgamesh Epic 1986; Phi Alpha Theta E IL Univ; Selectee Yale Outreach Seminar & MI Summer Inst on China 1987; *home:* 116 E Church St Frederick MD 21701

EARNEST, BETTIE OSWALD, 5th Grade Teacher; *b:* Greenville, AL; *m:* Ralph Alvin; *c:* Melodie K., Merrie K.; *ed:* (BMED) Music, William Carey Coll 1967; Elem Ed Certificate 1971; Working Towards BS Cmptr Sci 1988-89; *cr:* Music Teacher Mc Kenzie Elem & Georgiana HS 1969-70; 4th Grade Teacher 1970-88, 5th Grade Teacher 1988- East Three Notch Elem Sch; *ai:* Delta Omicron Intnl 1965-; First Baptist Church Greenville Music Dir 1967-69; First Baptist Church Andalusia Music Dir 1970-71; Southside Baptist Church Anadalusia Music Dir 1975-76, 1989-.

EARNEST, JACQUELYN HODGES, English Teacher; *b:* Andalusia, AL; *m:* William Albert Sr.; *c:* William A. Jr., Laura A.; *ed:* (BA) Eng, Huntingdon Coll 1964; (MS) Supervision/Admin, Troy St Univ 1975; *cr:* Exec Secy AL Farm Bureau Fed 1964-69; Teacher Holtville HS 1969-; *ai:* Jr Class & Scholars Bowl Team Spon; Delta Kappa Gamma Secy 1987-88; Elmore Cty Teachers Assn 1974-75; Cains Chapel United Meth Church (Organist, Choir Dir) 1980-; Mellown Grant AP Wkshp; Teacher of Yr Holtville HS; *office:* Holtville HS Rt 2 Box 52 Deatsville AL 36022

EARNEST, JANE CANAL, 5th Grade Teacher; *b:* Camden, NJ; *m:* Joseph C.; *c:* Paul, Lee A.; *ed:* (BA) Sociology, Georgian Court Coll 1966; Ed Gloucester Cty Coll; Ed Glassboro Coll; *cr:* Soc Worker Cath Soc Svcs 1966-68; Asst Teach Kingsway Learning Ctr 1977-82; 5th Grade Teacher Most Holy Reedemer 1982-; *ai:* Sci Coord; Field Trip Coord; Self Study-Steering Comm; NCEA; *office:* Most Holy Redeemer Sch RR 1 Box 596 Delsea Dr Westville NJ 08093

EARNEST, MARTIN LEON, Chem Teacher/Sci Dept Chair; *b:* Alexandria, IN; *m:* Linda Kay Hart; *ed:* (BS) Chem/Math, Taylor Univ 1965; (MA) Chem/Math, Ball St Univ 1971; Cmptr Trng, Ball St Univ; *cr:* Chem/Math Teacher Eastbrook United Sch Corporation 1965-68, Madison-Grant United Sch Corporation 1968-; *ai:* Sci Dept Chm; Campus Life Youth for Christ Spon; NSTA, Hoosier Assn of Sci Teachers 1977-; IN St Teachers Assn, NEA 1965-; Lakeview Wesleyan Church (Youth Group Spon 1968-83, Sunday Sch Teacher 1967-82), Service Awd 1981; IN Academic All Stars Certificate of Merit 1988; *home:* 567 Circle Dr Fairmount IN 46928

EASLEY, JANET LUE, Second Grade Teacher; *b:* Camp Mc Call, NC; *ed:* (BA) Elem Ed, NW Nazarine 1966; Working on Masters in Remedial Elem Math; *cr:* 2nd Grade Teacher Leavenworth Elem 1966-67, Holmes Elem 1967-; *ai:* Wilder Ed Assn Pres 1969-70; IEA, NEA 1967-; PTA Secy 1970; Pet Haven (Wilder Area Rep, Volunteer) 1983-; Beta Sigma Phi (VP, Pres) 1970-71; Nom ASPCA Teacher of Yr 1988; Co-Recipient KIVI-TV Cmmty Involvement Awd 1988; *office:* Holmes Elem Sch Box 488 Wilder ID 83676

EASLEY, SHARON ANN (WELCH), English Teacher/Dept Chair; *b:* Canton, IL; *m:* Donald Edward; *c:* Matthew, Nicholas; *ed:* (BS) Eng, 1975, (MSE) Ed, 1986 Univ of WI Platteville; *cr:* Eng/Journalism Teacher Galena HS 1975-78; Asst Ed Wm C Brown Company 1978-79; Eng/Lang Art Teacher Cuba City Public Schls 1979-87, Rio Jr-Sr HS 1987-89; *ai:* Drama Coach & Adv; Pupil Services Comm; Rndg Curr & Lang Art Curr Co-Chairperson; Dist Long Range Planning, Lib, NHS Selection, Dist Testing Comm; Cuba City HS NHS Honorary Mem; NCTE 1975-78, 1987-; WREA 1990; NEA, WEA, REA 1975-; ITA 1975-78; Evangelism Comm Church (Admin Cncl Recording Secy 1989-, Nominations Secy 1989-, Sunday Sch Teacher 1987-, 1978-82, Pastor & Staff Relations 1984-87) 1987-; Lodi Lib Comm; *office:* Rio Jr-Sr HS Box 275 Church St Rio WI 53960

EASON, JOHN FRANCIS, JR., Fifth Grade Teacher; *b:* South Mills, NC; *m:* Irish Howard; *c:* John III, Sarah; *ed:* (BA) Soc Stud, NC Wesleyan Coll 1964; Grad Study E Carolina Univ; *cr:* Teacher Plymouth HS 1966-68, Alexander Wilson Sch 1968-71, S Graham Elem Sch 1971-; *ai:* PTA Pres 1981-82.

EASON, ROBIN J., Math Teacher; *b:* Granite City, IL; *ed:* (BA) Math, 1986; (MED) Sec Math Ed, 1989 West GA Coll; *cr:* Math Teacher Cntrl HS 1986-; *ai:* Chrldng Spon Ftbl/Bsktbl; Phi Delta Kappa 1989-; Oneicron Delta Kappa 1986-; Phi Kappa Phi 1987; Kappa Mu Epsilon 1986; *office:* Central H S 113 Central Rd Carrollton GA 30117

EASON, TONIA THOMPSON, English Teacher/Dept Chair; *b:* Columbus, GA; *m:* R. Wayne; *c:* Scarlett L.; *ed:* (BS) Eng, Jacksonville St Univ 1969; *cr:* Eng Teacher Johnston Jr HS 1969-70, Cntrl Mid Sch 1970-71, Toulminville HS 1971-81; Eng Teacher/Dept Chairperson Le Flore HS of Comm & Arts 1981-; *ai:* Le Flore Study Club Adv; Le Flore Management Team Mem; Mobile Cty Ed Assn (Secy 1987-89, VP 1988-89, Pres 1989-); AL Ed Assn (Bd of Dirs, Dist I Dir) 1988-; NEA Delegate 1986-; Southeastern Improvement Laboratory AL St Advisory Bd 1987-; Womens Club of Chickasaw 1985-; Chickasaw Bd of Adjustments 1989-; NEA Opportunity Sch Grant Recipient; Mobile Cty Nominee Jacksonville St Univ Hall of Fame; *office:* John L Le Flore HS 700 Donald St Mobile AL 36617

EAST, PATRICIA RAE GOING, Elementary Classroom Teacher; *b:* Stillwater, OK; *m:* Clifford N.; *c:* Stacey Carter, Larry; *ed:* (BS) Elem Ed, OK St Univ 1960; (MS) Elem Ed, Cntrl St Univ 1967; *cr:* 4th Grade Teacher Western Oaks Elem 1961-70; Upper Elem Teacher Apollo Elem 1970-; *ai:* Apollo Jr Police Spon; Soc Stud Vertical Team & System Curr Planning Comm Head; Kappa Kappa Iota Pres 1967-68; Forest Hill Chrstn Church (Sr HS Youth Leader, Choir Accompanist, Financial Secy, Sunday Sch Secy, Teacher, Youth Traveling Choir Spon & Accompanist, Vacation Bible Sch Dir) 1967-80; Choctaw Nazarene Church (Sr HS Spon, Sunday Sch Teacher, Choir Accompanist) 1982-; Putnam City Schls Excl in Ed Golden Apple Awd 1989; Apollo Elem Teacher of Yr 1974-75.

EAST, ROBBIE EZELL, Fifth Grade Teacher; *b:* Birmingham, AL; *m:* David; *c:* James, Sarah Beachboard, Lex Allen; *ed:* (BA) Eng, David Lipscomb Univ 1949; Austin Peay Univ, Univ of TN Nashville, Belmont Coll, Univ of Chattanooga, Trevecca Nazarene Coll, David Lipscomb Univ; *cr:* 1st/2nd Grade Teacher Hillcrest Sch 1949-50; 5th Grade Teacher Boyd Buchanan Sch 1963-66; 6th Grade Teacher Robertson Cty 1966-69; 5th/6th Grade Teacher Goodpasture Chrstn Sch 1969-; *ai:* Media Comm; Delta Kappa Gamma 1st VP 1982-, 1st VP Awd 1990; Extensive Travel US, Europe, Mid East, Australia, New Zealand, Canada, VI; *home:* 101 Keeneland Hermitage TN 37076

EASTER, JUDITH RAE, 7th Grade Eng/Soc Stud Teacher; *b:* Ironton, OH; *ed:* (BS) Elem Ed, OH Univ 1960; OH Univ/Capital/Oh St; *cr:* Teacher Ironton Jr HS 1964-66; Rosemore Jr HS 1966-; *ai:* Adv to Drug Prevention Group; Spon Washington DC Trip Over Spring Break; Whitehall Ed Assn Treas 1969-71; Whitehall Ed Assn Bldg Rep 1971-76; Whitehall Educator of Yr 1989; *office:* Rosemore Jr HS 4735 Rosemore Whitehall OH 43213

EASTER, ROBERT WESLEY, Spanish Teacher; *b:* San Diego, CA; *m:* Edris Susan Kruger; *c:* Colin, Bryce; *ed:* (BA) Span, 1976, (BS) Cmptr Sci, 1982 San Diego St Univ; Advanced Managers Trng; Electronic Data Systems, Dallas TX; *cr:* Teacher Grossmont Union HS 1976-81; Account Operations Mgr Electronic Data Systems 1982-85; Teacher/Dept Chm/Mentor Teacher Poway Unified Sch Dist 1985-; *ai:* Amer Cncl Teachers of Foreign Lang; Mentor Teacher 1989; *office:* Poway HS 15500 Espola Rd Poway CA 92064

EASTERDAY, DANNIE DEAN, History/Geography Teacher; *b:* Chillicothe, OH; *m:* Lisa Colleen Shoemaker; *c:* Nicholas D.; *ed:* (BS) His, Morehead St Univ 1975; (MA) Admin, Univ of Dayton 1985; *cr:* His/Geography Teacher Scioto Valley Local Schls 1975-; *ai:* Asst Var Bsktbl Coach; Soc Stud Curr Supvr; Natl Geography Olympiad Adv; NCSS 1990; OH Assn of Coaches 1975-; Jr HS Soc Stud Chm; Southeastern Jr/Sr HS Teacher of Yr 1990; *home:* 56 Tanager Ct Chillicothe OH 45601

EASTMAN, MARIE MAXINE, Mathematics Dept Chair; *b:* Salamanca, NY; *m:* Lawrence William; *c:* Janice, Holly, Stephen; *ed:* (BS) Elem Ed, Univ of TN Chattanooga 1982; (MA) Supervision/Admin, TN Tech Univ 1990; *cr:* Math Teacher Rhea Cntrl Elem 1982-; *ai:* 7th Grade Floor & Math Head; *office:* Rhea Central Elem Schl 208 E 4th Ave Dayton TN 37321

EASTMAN, SALLY SCHELL, Second Grade Teacher; *b:* Cleveland, OH; *m:* Brett Keating; *ed:* (BS) Elem Ed, OH Univ 1973; (MA) Early Chldhd Ed, GA St Univ 1977; Grad Stud Admin & Supervision; *cr:* 1st-3rd Grade Combination Teacher Oglethorpe Elem 1974-76; Kndgtn Teacher Kindercare 1979-77, Immaculate Heart of Mary 1977; 2nd-4th Grade Teacher East Side Elem 1977-; *ai:* Chi Omega 1973-73; PTA 1977-; *office:* East Side Elem Sch 3850 Roswell Rd Marietta GA 30068

EASTON, JOAN S., Fifth Grade Teacher; *b:* Bronx, NY; *m:* Peter Lowell; *c:* Robert H.; *ed:* (BS) His/Scndry Ed, NY Univ; (MS) Elem Ed, Southern CT St Coll 1978; *cr:* 7th Grade Soc Stud Teacher Jr HS 82 1966-; 6th Grade Teacher Norcross Sch 1966-67; 5th Grade Teacher Fair Haven Mid Sch 1967-71; 6th Grade Teacher Hamden Hall Cntry Day Sch 1978-79; 3rd/5th-7th Grade His Teacher Buckley Cntry Day Sch 1980-; *ai:* Soc Stud Curr Comm; Former Coord of Academic Scheduling; Sch Rep to Herricks Teacher Center; Adv to Buckley Banter; *office:* Buckley Cntry Day Sch I U Willets Rd Roslyn NY 11576

EASTWOOD, MYRNA LOIS, Science Teacher; *b:* Los Angeles, CA; *m:* Bill M.; *c:* Valorie Stewart, Linda Sheeks; *ed:* (BA) Biological Illustration/Teaching Credential/Scndry, Univ of CA Los Angeles 1968; (MA) Cnslr Ed, San Diego St Univ 1976; Classroom Management Trng Wkshps Madelaine Hunter; *cr:* Sci Teacher Oak Crest Jr HS 1968-69; Art Teacher 1969-85, Sci Teacher 1985- Earl Warren Jr HS 1985-; *ai:* Sch Hispanic Tutorial & Recycling Prgms Co-Founder; CTA, SDFA (Secy 1970-71, Rep 1978-79, Negotiation Team 1986-); San Diegudo Womens Sftbl Co-Founder 1974-76; Bobby Sox Mgr 1970-75; Solana Beach Recycling Prgm Co-Founder 1970-71; Womens Sftbl Co-Pres; Mentor Teacher; Dist Teacher of Yr; Developed Right Brain Drawing; Yrbk Dedication; *office:* Earl Warren Jr HS 155 Stevens Ave Solana Beach CA 92075

EATON, ELIZABETH HOPE, English Teacher; *b:* Roswell, NM; *c:* Albert S., Sarah Park; *ed:* (BA) Eng, Univ of OR 1982; (MA) Eng, W TX St Univ 1987; *cr:* Eng Teacher Robert H Goddard HS 1987-; *ai:* Ski Club Spon; NEA, Roswell Ed Assn 1987-; *office:* Robert H Goddard HS 701 E Country Club Roswell NM 88201

EATON, JAMES D., 5th Grade Teacher; *b:* Normal, IL; *m:* Barbara K. Miller; *c:* Andrea; *ed:* (BA) Elem Ed, IL Wesleyan Univ 1981; (MS) Educl Admin, IL St Univ 1987; *cr:* 4th Grade Teacher Oakdale Elem 1981-88; 5th/6th Grade Teacher Glenn Elem 1988-; *ai:* Var Wrestling Coach Normal Cmmty HS; Glenn Building Leadership Team; K-6th Grade Math Study Comm; 5th/6th Grade Math Teams Spon; St Johns Luth Church Cncl 1990; Peoples Bank Geography Contest Consultant 1989; *office:* Glenn Elem Sch 306 Glenn Ave Normal IL 61761

EATON, JERREN UNRUH, 1st Grade Teacher; *b:* Dover, DE; *c:* Paul, Kevin, Anne; *ed:* (BS) Elem Ed, Univ of DE 1974; Grad, Inservice, Continuing Ed Courses; *cr:* 5th/6th Grade Math Teacher Redding Mid Sch 1974-75; Music Teacher 1984-85, 7th/8th Grade Eng/Rdng Teacher 1985-86, 1st Grade Teacher 1986- Holy Cross Elem; *ai:* Drama Club; Yrbk; Christmas Prgm; Chorus; Creative Magazine; Accompaniment for Sch Mass; Positive Teaching Awd Amer Family Inst; *home:* PO Box 99 Odessa DE 19730

EATON, MARGARET ANN, English/ESL Teacher; *b:* Lynwood, CA; *m:* Jerold B.; *ed:* (BA) Span Lang/Lit, Immaculate Heart Coll 1980; (MA) Teaching Eng to Speakers of Other Langs, Monterey Inst Intnl Stud 1983; Teaching Credential Ed, CA St Univ Stanislaus 1985; *cr:* Eng/ESL Teacher La Loma Jr HS 1983-85, Gonzalez Union HS 1985-86, La Loma Jr HS 1986-; Part Time ESL Teacher Modesto Jr Coll 1989-; *ai:* Developed & Organized Dist ESL Curr; CATESOL Mem 1983-; Stanislaus Wildlife Care Center Volunteer 1987-; Developed Dist ESL Curr New Core Lit Prgm 1989; Corrected Essays CA Assessment Prgm 1987-88; *office:* La Loma Jr HS 1800 Encina Ave Modesto CA 95354

EATON, MELINDA GUTH, High School English Teacher; *b:* Baltimore, MD; *m:* Wayne Lee; *c:* Gaelyn E. L.; *ed:* (BFA) Drama Ed, VA Commonwealth Univ 1972; (MSED) Scndry Ed, Old Dominion Univ 1987; *cr:* Drama/Eng Teacher Bethel HS 1971-85; Eng Teacher York HS 1985-; *ai:* Bethel HS Drama Club 1971-80; York HS Class Spon 1985-; Steering Comm 1988-; York Ed Assn 1985-; VA Ed Assn, NEA 1971-; York Cty Shorinkan Karate Mem 1987- Brown Belt; *office:* York HS 9300 G Washington Memorial Hwy Yorktown VA 23690

EATON, MELINDA RINGER, English Teacher; *b:* Tuscola, IL; *m:* Gregory L.; *c:* Laura, David; *ed:* (BSED) Eng, E IL Univ 1972; *cr:* Eng Teacher Wilmington HS 1972-74; Eng Teacher 1974-75, Part-Time Eng Teacher 1983-85, Eng Teacher 1986- Morris Cmmty Sch; *ai:* Yrbk Staff Faculty Adv; NHS Faculty Bd; Quill & Scroll Adv; Presbyn Church of Morris Deacon 1977-; Presbyn Womens Organization VP 1982-83; Presbyn Circle Leader 1987-88; Delta Kappa Gamma Candidate for Membership 1990; *office:* Morris Cmmty HS 1000 Union St Morris IL 60450

EATON, O. LEE, Jr High Social Studies Teacher; *b:* Jenkins, MO; *m:* Bonnie Lou Ford; *c:* Christopher, Lisa Haley, Larry Newman, Mike Newman, Tommy Newman, Betty Newman; *ed:* (BS) Math/Soc Stud, Drury Coll 1974; Grad Cmptr Classes, Drury; *cr:* 1st-8th Grade Teacher High Point Dist 1964-65; 7th/8th Grade Elem Prin Phillipsburg Elem 1965-67; 7th/8th Grade Teacher Cook Sch 1967-68; 7th/8th Grade Elem Prin Gasconade C-4 1968-69; Jr HS Soc Stud Teacher 1975-78, Jr HS Cmptrs/Soc Stud Teacher 1983- Joel E Barber C-5; *ai:* Stu Cncl Co-Spon; Dist Soc Stud Comm Chm; MO St Teachers Assn 1964-; *home:* Rt 1 Box 2345 Phillipsburg MO 65722

EATON, PEGGY RUDOLPH, Algebra/Computer Teacher; *b:* Parsons, KS; *m:* Ronnie Guy; *c:* Ronnie; *ed:* (MA) Math, Univ of AL 1977; (NS) Math/Phys Ed, Univ of Montevallo 1973; Cmptr Sci; *cr:* Teacher Thompson HS 1973-74; Teacher/Coach Mc Gill-Toolen HS 1974-76; Teacher Carver Jr HS 1977-81; Teacher/Coach Jeff Davis HS 1981-; *ai:* Girls Bsktbl, Girls & Boys Tennis Coach; MCEA, AEA, NEA 1977-; *office:* Jefferson Davis HS 3420 Carter Hill Rd Montgomery AL 36111

EAVENSON, MARCIA WHITTEN, Fourth Grade Teacher; *b:* San Antonio, TX; *m:* Harold Wayne; *c:* Tracy, Troy; *ed:* (BS) Elem Ed, Hardin-Simmons Univ 1967; (MS) Elem Ed, East TX St Univ 1981; Gifted Ed Cert; Rdng Regx Service Center; Writing

Improvement Wkshps at Regx Educl Service Center; Effective Teaching Facilitator Trng; *cr:* 4th Grade Teacher Gene Howe Elem 1967-69; 5th Grade Teacher Housman Elem 1970-71; Jane Long Elem 1972-73, 6th Grade Teacher Alta Vista Elem 1973-74; 3rd Grade Teacher 1974-85, 4th Grade Teacher Hartman Elem 1975-; *ai:* UIL Coord; Ready Writing Coach; Team Leader 4th Grade; Sch Rep Faculty Comm Committee; TX St Teachers Assn 1969-; TX St Teachers Assn Faculty ReP 1985-; Classroom Teachers of Wylie VP 1989-; Wylies Teacher of Yr 1986; TX Teacher of Yr Nom 1987; Teaching PhilosoPhy Published in East TX Sch Study Cncl Newsletter 1987; *home:* 1330 Shores Cr Rockwall TX 75087

EAVES, DEBORAH VINCENT, English Teacher; *b:* Greenville, KY; *m:* Charles Rice; *c:* James T., Stacie M.; *ed:* (BA) Bus Ed/Eng, 1973, (MA) Ed, 1980 W KY Univ; *cr:* Teacher Greenville HS 1976-; *ai:* Sr Beta Spon; Yrbk & Newspaper Adv.

EAVES, EMILY P., Jr HS Math/Eng Teacher; *b:* Louisville, MS; *m:* Kenenth E.; *ed:* (BSE) Elem Ed, Delta St Univ 1971; *cr:* Teacher Deer Creek Acad 1971-73, Parks Elem 1973-75; Teacher 1976-81, 1983- Winston Acad; *ai:* MPSEA 1976-; Louisville Jr Auxiliary Pres 1986; Louisville Garden Club 1988-.

EAVES, VIRGINIA STEWART, Mathematics Department Chair; *b:* Baton Rouge, LA; *c:* Ashley Verzwyvelt, Wesley; *ed:* (BS) Eng/Math Ed, LA St Univ 1972; (MED) Mid-Management, Univ of Houston 1980; Sch Math Project, Rice Univ 1988; Univ of St Thomas; *cr:* Math Teacher Houston Ind Sch Dist 1974-77; GED Teacher Windham Sch Dist 1977-80; Math/Dept Chairperson Lamar Consolidated Ind Sch Dist 1980-; *ai:* TX Classroom Teachers Treas, NCTM; Teacher of Yr George JR HS; Rice Univ Sch Math Project Schlsp; *home:* 2016 Tremont Ct Rosenberg TX 77471

EBADI, DEL M., Mathematics Teacher; *b:* Logar, Afghanistan; *m:* Darween; *c:* Hashmatt, Hameed; *ed:* (BS) Math, Kabul Univ 1976; (MS) CSPA, IN Univ 1979; *cr:* Math Teacher Shelbyville Sch System 1979-83; Calculus Teacher 1986, 1988 Washburn Univ; Math Teacher Topeka West HS 1983-; *ai:* Math Club Spon; NEA Executive Bd Mem 1988-; Shawnee Cty Assn Teachers of Math VP 1986-87; IN Teachers Assn Mem 1979-83; Shawnee Cty Assn Teacher of Math Outstanding Teacher Awd 1989; Univ of KS Outstanding Teacher Awd 1987; Univ of Chicago Outstanding Teacher Awd 1988; *office:* Topeka West HS 2001 Fairlawn Rd Topeka KS 66604

EBBERTS, THEODORE EDWARD, JR., Chem Teacher/Sci Dept Chair; *b:* Ogdensburg, NY; *m:* Mary Louise Townley; *c:* Wende E., Theodore E. III; *ed:* (BA) Chem, Williams Coll 1964; (MA) Sci Ed, SUNY Albany 1969; *cr:* 9th-12th Grade Sci Teacher Johnsburg Cntrl Sch 1965-66; Bio/Chem Teacher 1966-69, Chem Teacher 1969-88, Chem Teacher/Dept Chm 1988- Ogdesnburg Free Acad; *ai:* HS Var Golf Coach; Sch Schlsp Comm; Odyssey of Mind Coach; Teacher Negotiating Team; Ogdensburg Ed Assn Pres; Ogdensburg Lions Club BPOE 772 Pres 1973-74.

EBEL, LINDA HARMS, 8th Grade Teacher; *b:* Sioux City, IA; *m:* Elmer W.; *c:* Joy, Matthew, Adam, Jill, Christopher; *ed:* (BA) Fr/Span, Briar Cliff Coll 1970; (MAT) Elem Ed, Morningside Coll 1972; 1 Year Grad Wrk Fr & Span Lit/Stephen F Austin St Univ; *cr:* 6th Grade Teacher Riverview Schl 1971-72; 8th Grade Teacher St Michaels Schl 1973-; *ai:* Coord Service Projects 8th Grade; Modern Lang Assn 1969-82; NCEA 1973-; Sioux City Cmmnty Theatre (Bd Mem 1985-87/Dir Jr Theatre 1983-87); Celebration Choir Core Mem 1986-; Women Aware Nom Women in Excll 1986; Briar Cliff Alumni Bd 1986-; *home:* 511 29th St Sioux City IA 51104

EBERLE, JACQUELINE LEAH, Mathematics Teacher; *b:* Aurora, IL; *m:* Larry Alan; *c:* Staci L.; *ed:* (BA) Span/Math Ed, Heidelberg Coll 1980; (MS) Span/Math Ed, Purdue Univ 1987; *cr:* Math Teacher Waldo Jr HS 1980-83, Sunnyside Mid Sch 1983-; *ai:* Cheerleading Spon; Talent Show (Star Search) Coord/Master of Ceremonies; NEA 1980-; ISTA 1983-; Beta Sigma Phi (Girl of Yr 1988) 1983-; *office:* Sunnyside Mid Sch 2500 Cason St Lafayette IN 47904

EBERLE, SUSANNE FISHER, Social Studies Chair; *b:* Johnstown, PA; *m:* Norman A.; *c:* Elizabeth A., Jeffrey M.; *ed:* (BA) Scndry Ed/Eng, Penn St Univ; (MA) Eng, Ball St Univ; *cr:* Teacher St Coll Sch Dist 1957-60, Dobbs Ferry Sch Dist 1961-62, Marion Sch Dist 1964-66, Lee Cty Sch Dist 1973-; *ai:* Prin Advisory Comm; Soc Stud Dept Head; Lee Cty Cncl of Soc Stud 1985-; NCSS 1986-87; Delta Kappa Gamma 1988-; NEA 1957-; Amer Bus Womens Assn Treas 1985-; Cypress Lake Athletic Boosters (Secy, Co-Chairperson Concessions) 1983-86; Ft Myers Jr Womens Club 1984-87; Lee Cty Mid Schls FL Stud Booklet; Lee Cty Soc Stud Teacher of Yr 1981-82, 1985-86; Daughters of Amer Revolution Outstanding Teacher 1987; *office:* Cypress Lake Mid Sch 8901 Cypress Lake Dr Fort Myers FL 33907

EBERSOLE, JULIE A., Spanish Teacher; *b:* Portland, OR; *m:* David A.; *c:* Hayley E.; *ed:* (BA) Span, W WA Univ 1985; *cr:* Span Teacher North Thurston HS 1985-; *ai:* WAFLT 1985-; Teacher of Yr 1989; *office:* North Thurston HS 600 NE Sleater-Kinney Rd Lacey WA 98503

EBERSOLE, RUTH LONGENECKER, Sixth Grade Teacher; *b:* Hershey, PA; *m:* Gerald R.; *c:* James, Steven, Michael; *ed:* (BS) Elem Ed - Magna Cum Laude, Elizabethtown Coll 1957; (MSED) Elem Ed, Millersville Univ 1980; Rdng Specialist Cert, Millersville Univ; Cert Staff Dev & Clinical Teaching Minton Prgm; *cr:* 5th Grade Teacher Richmond Cty Sch Dist 1957-59; 6th Grade Teacher 1959-60, Chapter I Rdng Teacher 1972-76 Lebanon City Sch Dist; 6th Grade Teacher 1976-77, Rdng Specialist 1977-78, 6th Grade Teacher 1978- N Lebanon Sch Dist; *ai:* Rdng Curr & Faculty Schlsp Comms; PA St Educl Assn, NEA, Lancaster Lebanon Rdng Assn; Lebanon Cty Educl Honor Society Secy 1987-88; Amer Assn of Univ Women; *office:* Jonestown Elem Sch S Lancaster St Jonestown PA 17038

EBERT, JO ANN SCHMIDT, Language Arts Teacher; *b:* St Louis, MO; *m:* Raymond; *c:* Elizabeth, Matthew; *ed:* (BA) Eng, St Louis Univ 1967; Maryville Coll; *cr:* 5th-8th Grade Lang Arts Teacher Immaculate Conception 1964-69; 6th-8th Grade Lang Arts Teacher Sacred Heart 1979-; *ai:* Coach-Bellarmine Speech Team; NCEA.

EBERT, PATRICIA MARSHALL, Language Arts Teacher; *b:* Latrobe, PA; *m:* Gary V.; *ed:* (BS) Eng, Clarion St Univ 1969; Masters Equivalency Certificate PA Dept of Ed 1987; Cmptr Sci, Penn St 1989; Discipline, Carlow Coll 1990; Cmptrs In-Service Trng 1989; *cr:* Teacher Greater Latrobe Jr HS 1969-; *ai:* Faculty Advisory Comm; NCTE 1980-; PA Cncl Teachers of Eng 1985-; Faculty Recognition Awd 1987-88; *office:* Greater Latrobe Jr HS Country Club Rd Latrobe PA 15601

EBESU, DUSTIN Y., Music Teacher; *b:* Honolulu, HI; *ed:* (BED) Scndry Music, Univ. of HI 1984; *cr:* Summer Band Teacher Washington Intermediate Sch 1984-85; Band Chorus Teacher Radford HS 1985-; *ai:* Marching Band and Flag Corps Chm Central OAHU Dist Band Festival; 50 Mem Chorus; Private Tutor Clarinet and Saxophone; OAHU Band Dir Assn Sec 1988-89; HI Music Educators Assn Mem 1986-; Pleasant Peasant Folk Band Clarinetist 1987; Royal Hawaiian Band Part-Time Clarinetist 1984-; *office:* Radford H S 4361 Salt Lake Blvd Honolulu HI 96818

ECENBARGER, GLORIA JEAN, Home Economics Teacher; *b:* Millersburg, OH; *ed:* (BS) Voc Home Ec Ed, Ashland Coll 1973; (MA) Ed, Coll of Mt St Joseph 1986; Trained Quest & Chem Intervention Facilitation; *cr:* Teacher Lehman HS 1973-76, Lehman Jr HS 1976-86; Teacher/Dept Chairperson Mc Kinley Sr HS 1986-; *ai:* FHA & St Officer Adv; Curr & Course of Study Writing; Dept Chairperson; Home Ec Curr Comm; NEA, OEA, CPEA 1973-, Teacher of Month 1976; AHEA, OHEA, SCHEA Stark Nominations 1973-; Kappa Delta Pi 1973-; Delta Kappa Gamma 1988-; Canton First Friends Chrstn Ed 1976-; Canton Coll Club 1973-, Schlsp 1969; Canton City Schls Teacher Grant 1982; Martha Holden Jennings Scholar 1984; *office:* Mc Kinley Sr HS 2323 17th NW Canton OH 44708

ECHAURI, ANITA THERESE, 6th-8th Grade Science Teacher; *b:* Tunis, North Africa; *ed:* (BA) Soc Sci, St Johns Univ; *cr:* Jr HS Teacher St Brigid 1964-86; Sci Teacher Robert F Kennedy Incentive Prgm 1986-; *ai:* Sci Coord; Mid Sts Accrediation Comm.

ECHOLS, JEANETTA SMITH, Social Studies Teacher; *b:* Chattanooga, TN; *m:* Andrew R.; *c:* Andre R., Valyncia J.; *ed:* (BA) Sociology, Knoxville Coll 1969; (MED) Ed, Mercer Univ 1981; *cr:* Soc Stud Teacher Chattanooga HS 1969-71, NE Comprehensive HS 1972-; *ai:* NHS Academic Bowl Club Adv; Coordinate Sch Close Up Prgm; GA Cncl Soc Stud 1981-; Mid GA Cncl Soc Stud Prgm Chairperson 1988, Certificate of Appreciation 1989; Jack & Jill of America Incorporated Ways & Means Chairperson 1988-; United Negro Coll Fund 1983-89; *office:* Northeast Comprehensive HS 1646 Upper River Rd Macon GA 31211

ECHOLS, KAY MANER, First Grade Teacher; *b:* Littlefield, TX; *m:* Tommy; *c:* Perry, Van, Rhonda; *ed:* (BS) Elem Ed, Hardin-Simmons Univ 1962; *cr:* 2nd Grade Teacher Stanfield Elem 1962; Rdng Teacher Jr HS Copperas Cove Public Schls 1963; Phys Ed Teacher/Coach Snyder HS 1965-68; Phys Ed/Coach Travis Jr HS 1974; 1st Grade Teacher East Elem 1975-; *ai:* TX St Teachers Assn 1962-85; TX Classroom Teachers Assn 1962-; *home:* Rt 2 Box 135 Snyder TX 79549

ECHSNER, MARY, Spanish Teacher; *b:* St Louis, MO; *ed:* (BA) Span, St Mary of The Woods Coll 1973; (MS) Scndry Ed/Span, IN Univ 1975; *cr:* Span Teacher Northside Mid Sch 1974-83, Columbus North HS 1984-; *ai:* TX Aerobics Teacher; ISTA, NEA, CEA; Columbus Clogging Company; *office:* Columbus North HS 1400 25th St Columbus IN 47201

ECHTINAW, JAMES R., Math Dept Chair/Cmptr Teacher; *b:* Grand Rapids, MI; *m:* Wendy Anne Ratz; *c:* Brandon, Bre Anne, Michael; *ed:* (BS) Sci, 1970, (MA) Teaching Gifted, 1983 Grand Valley St Coll; Cmptrs; Math; *cr:* Teacher Skamt Shop Scuba Sch 1971-79, Kenowa Hills Public Schls 1970-, Grand Valley St Coll 1981-; *ai:* Building Gifted & Dist Gifted Comm; Math Dept Chm; Lunch Hour Aide; KHEA, KLEA, MEA, NEA, MACUL (Building Rep, Negotiator, Head Negotiator, VP, Grievance Chm) 1978-; *office:* Kenowa Hills Jr HS 4252 3 Mile Rd Grand Rapids MI 49504

ECK, ALBERT JOHN, Earth Science Teacher/Advisor; *b:* Creglingen, West Germany; *m:* Margaret Ann Gibbons; *c:* Christopher, Alan, Michael; *ed:* (BS) Chem/Math, N IL Univ 1970; Geology, NE IL Univ; Working Towards Masters; *cr:* 8th Grade Sci Teacher Schotler Park 1970-79; Sci/Math Teacher Hampshore HS 1979-81; 8th Grade Sci Teacher Perry Mid Sch 1981-83; Sci Teacher Carpentersville Mid Sch 1983-; *ai:* Varsity Soccer Coach; Merit Schlsp Towards Masters Degree; Math Sci Fnd Wkshp to Photograph Geology Western Parks; Distinguished Educator Awd Kane Cty; *office:* Carpentersville Mid Sch 100 Cleveland Ave Carpentersville IL 60110

ECKARD, M. LANA MC NEAL, Gifted & Talented Facilitator; *b:* Alexandria, LA; *m:* Donald J.; *c:* Brian N., Tracy D.; *ed:* (BA) Elem Ed - Cum Laude, LA Tech Univ 1969; (MA) Spec Ed/Gifted & Talented, Univ of AR 1988; *cr:* 4th Grade Elem Teacher Schaumburg Elem 1968-70; 7th/8th Grade Arts Coord St Louis King of France 1970-72; 5th Grade Lang Arts Teacher Old High Mid Sch 1980-82; 10th-12th Grade Gifted-Talented Facilitator/Teacher/Cnslr Rogers HS 1985-; Educl Counsultant Creative Righting Publishers 1985-; *ai:* Reach Club Spon; Model United Nations Spon; Odessey of Mind Coach/Spon; Natl Assn of Gifted Children Wkshp Presenter 1985-; AR for Gifted & Talented Ed Presenter 1984-; Delta Kappa Gamma 1989-; United Nations Assn of USA (Keynote Speaker 1989) 1988-; ASCD 1989-; Rogers/Lowell United Fund Drive Chm 1987-88; Rogers Chamber of Commerce Nice Person/Good Citizen Awd 1989; Author/Published Textbook; AR St Dept Sch/teacher Recognition Prgm Grant for Innovative Curr; Rogers/Lowell United Fund Grant to Publish Reference Book; *home:* 816 Orleans Dr Rogers AR 72756

ECKDALL-ESTABROOK, KAREN CHRISTINE, 6th Grade Teacher; *b:* Emporia, KS; *m:* Robert D.; *c:* Alexander C.; *ed:* (BSE) Elem, KS Univ 1978; Working Towards Masters Equivalent Univ of NV Reno, Truckee Meadows Comm Coll; *cr:* Teacher Asst 1978-79, 5th/6th Grade Teacher 1979-82 Verdi Elem; K-6th Grade Teacher 1982-83, 5th Grade Teacher 1983-84 Veterans Elem; 5th/6th Grade Teacher Katherine Dunn 1984-; *ai:* Intramurals; I am Lovable & Capable Comm; Renaissance Faire; Annual San Francisco Trip; Washoe Cty Teachers Assn, NSEA 1979-.

ECKEL, ROBERT J., Principal; *b:* Oklahoma City, OK; *m:* Ruthann Carson; *c:* Sarah E., Tyler W.; *ed:* (ME) Elem Admin, 1984, (BS) Elem Ed, 1979 Cntrl St Univ; Grad Stud Math & Admin; *cr:* 6th Grade Teacher 1980-89, Prin 1990- OK Chrstn Schls; *ai:* Dir of Sch Transportation OK Chrstn Schls 1987-; Kappa Delta Pi 1984-; Assn of Chrstn Schls Inc 1980-; Ok Historical Society 1985-; Outstanding Young Men of America 1985; *office:* Oklahoma Chrstn Schls PO Box 509 Edmond OK 73083

ECKERLE, BERYL B., Fourth Grade Teacher; *b:* New Orleans, LA; *m:* Frank A.; *c:* Pamela, Deborah Crovetto, Gwen; *ed:* (BS) Elem Ed, Our Lady of Holy Cross Coll 1973; *cr:* Teacher Borgnemouth Elem; *ai:* 4th Grade Chairperson; Curr Cncl & Lead Cncl Co-Chairperson; Sch Proofreader; Curr Cncl Secy; IRA, PTA; S Cntrl Bell Sci Grant 1989-; Borgnemouth Elem Teacher of Yr 1989-; *office:* Borgnemouth Elem Sch 5920 1st St Violet LA 70092

ECKFELDT, FRED W., Chemistry & Astronomy Teacher; *b:* Ambler, PA; *m:* Sandy; *c:* Lee A.; *ed:* (BS) Chem, Univ of DE 1971; (MA) Earth/Space Sci, West Chester Univ 1980; *cr:* Chem/Astronomy Teacher N Penn HS 1971-; *office:* N Penn HS 1340 Valley Forge Rd Lansdale PA 19446

ECKLEMAN, MICHAEL ARNOLD, 7th/8th Language Art Teacher; *b:* Amsterdam, NY; *c:* Keith, Scott; *ed:* (MA) Ed, Manhattan Coll 1968; Working Towards Masters Herbert Lehman Coll 1975; *cr:* Lang Art Teacher Hastings on Hudson HS 1968-; *ai:* Head Coach Var Girls Bsktbl; Jr Var Girls Soccer Coach; Environmental Trip; Graduation Coord; Mem Long Range Planning, Scheduling Comm; Mahopac Sports Assn Coach 1989; Coach of Yr Bsktbl 1990; *office:* Hastings On Hudson HS Farragut Pkwy Hastings On Hudson NY 10706

ECKLEY, MONA NELSON, Sixth Grade Teacher; *b:* Altoona, PA; *m:* Harold F.; *c:* Rhonda, Linda, Tonya; *ed:* (BS) Elem Ed, 1966, (MED) Child Dev/Family Relations, 1970 Penn St; *cr:* 1st Grade Teacher Hollidaysburg Area Sch Dist 1966-67, Bedford Area Sch Dist 1967-69; 1st Grade Teacher 1969-76, 2nd Grade Teacher 1976-81, 6th Grade Teacher 1981- Claysburg-Kimmel Sch Dist; *ai:* Spon & Adv Claysburg-Kimmel HS Concerned Stus; Lead Teacher Facilitator Claysburg-Kimmel Sch Dist; Cmmty Park Planning Comm Park Authority; PSEA 1966-; Claysburg BPW Charter Mem; Delta Kappa Gamma 1981-; Greenfield Township Recreation Bd Secy; *home:* RD 2 Box 1337 Claysburg PA 16625

ECKOFF, RALPH RICHARD, Theology Teacher; *b:* Milwaukee, WI; *m:* Ruth A. Wiesner; *ed:* (BA) Speech, Marquette Univ 1961; Deacon Ordination, Kino Inst; Grad Stud Theology, Loyola; *cr:* Dir Ed Good Shepherd Sch for Girls 1964-67; Theology Teacher Fr Lopez HS 1980-; *ai:* Jr Class & Chrstn Service Club Spon; Faculty Adv Coord; NCEA 1980-; Knights of Columbus 1965-66; *office:* Father Lopez HS 960 Madison Ave Daytona Beach FL 32014

ECKSTEIN, AMELIA MADISON, Study Skills Teacher; *b:* Columbus, MT; *m:* Louis C.; *c:* Mathew R.; *ed:* (BS) Music/Bus Ed, E MT Coll 1959; Bus Ed; *cr:* Music Teacher Park City HS 1958; Bus Ed Teacher 1959-73, Substitute Teacher 1985-89, Study Skills Teacher 1989- Absarokee HS; *ai:* Jr Class 1959-61, Stu Publication 1959-73, Yrbk Publication 1959-73, Pep Club 1959-73, Chrldr 1959-73, Frosh Class Spon 1973; Yrbk Publication Co-Spon 1964-65; Local MT Ed Assn (Secy 1963-64, Pres 1970); NEA, MT Ed Assn 1959-70; Jr Spurs Adv 1957-58; Stu Ed Assn 1957-59; PTA 1959-63; 4-H Leader 1960-61, 1985-; Order of Eastern Star Various Positions 1960-; Order of Rainbow Advisory Bd 1970; Outstanding Young Women of America 1966; Election Bd 1980-; Night Election Counting Bd Chm 1986-; *home:* RR 1 Box 2610 Absarokee MT 59001

EDDINGER, HAROLD WAYNE, Teacher of the Gifted; *b:* Thomasville, NC; *ed:* (AB) Eng/His, High Point Coll 1969; Grad Stud UNC-G; *cr:* 7th Grade Lang Art Teacher N Davidson Jr HS 1969-75; 6th-8th Grade Lang Art Teacher for Gifted 1975-88, 7th Grade Lang Art Teacher for Gifted 1988- Brown Mid Sch; *ai:* Senate Bill 2 Steering Comm; NCAE, NEA; Heidelberg United Church of Christ (Elder, Mem of Consistory) 1989-; Outstanding Young Educator N Davidson Area 1972, E Davidson Area 1979; *home:* 252 Kenn-Myer Cir Thomasville NC 27360

EDDINS, JUDY LOVELACE, Third Grade Teacher; *b:* Florence, AL; *c:* Andrew; *ed:* (BS) Elem Ed, 1969, (MS) Elem Ed, 1979 Univ of N AL; *cr:* Summer Head Start Teacher Lauderdale Cty 1972-77; 3rd Grade Teacher 1972-75, 1st Grade Teacher 1975-78, 3rd Grade Teacher 1978- Central HS; *ai:* NEA, AL Ed Assn; Lauderdale Cty Ed Assn Faculty Rep 1983-84; Lauderdale Cty Outstanding Educator of Yr 1982.

EDDLETON, SUSAN CLARK, First Grade Teacher; *b:* Richmond, VA; *m:* Alan Wayne; *c:* Sara, Margaret A.; *ed:* (BS) Elem Ed, Longwood Coll 1977; *cr:* 1st Grade Teacher Chamberlayne Elem 1977-86, Dumbarton Elem 1986-; *ai:* Baptist Women 1990; *home:* Rt 2 Box 3000 Montpelier VA 23192

EDDY, KATHLEEN ELLIS, 1st Grade Teacher; *b:* Glen Dale, WV; *M:* Gary A.; *c:* Ryan, Seth; *ed:* (BA) Elem Ed, West Liberty St Coll 1973; Elem Educ, Learning Disabilities, WV Univ; *cr:* 1st Grade Teacher 1st Ward Elem Sch 1973-76; Glen Dale Elem Sch 1976-; *ai:* Marshall Cty Rdng Cncl 1978-; Northern Panhandle Math Cncl 1989-; Glen Dale United Meth Church Cncl on Childrens Ministeries 1986-; *office:* Glendale Elem Sch 407 7th St Glen Dale WV 26038

EDDY, SHIRLEY KATHRYN (IDSO), Literacy Program Director; *b:* Sisseton, SD; *m:* William Francis; *c:* Elaine Eddy O Neill, Wayne J., Janelle K.; *ed:* (BS) Ed, SD St Univ 1960; (MS) Ed, OR St Univ 1972; Admin Ed, Univ of OR 1975-76; *cr:* Rural Schls Teacher Robert Cty 1941-48, 1955-57; Primary Teacher Sweet Home Sch Dist 55 1960-67, 1975-83; Home Ec Teacher Sweet Home Jr HS 1967-75; Rdng Specialist Sweet Home Oak Heights Elem 1983-87; Literacy Prgm Sweet Home Literacy Cncl 1987-; *ai:* Tutor Trainer; Tutor & Stu Coord; Summer Sch Remedial Prgm Dir; Sweet Home Ed Assn Pres 1968-69; Amer Assn of Univ Women Local Pres 1969-71; NEA, Laubach Literacy Intnl 1987-; OR St Bus & Prof Women Pres 1973-74, Golden Torch 1982; Delta Kappa Gamma OR Legislative Chairperson 1983-85; OR Democratic Women Pres 1981-85; Linn Cty Retired Sr Volunteer Prgm Pres 1988-; Bus & Prof Women Natl Fnd Financial Aids Comm 1983-86; Natl Bus & Prof Women Elections Chairperson 1975, 1976-80; Sweet Home Women of Yr 1966; Omicron Nu 1972; OR Democratic Party Myrtle Sykes Awd 1982; OR Teacher of Yr Nom Sweet Home Sch Dist 1987; *home:* 610 5th Ave Sweet Home OR 97386

EDELSTEIN, ELEANOR, English Teacher/Computer Coord; *b:* Bronx, NY; *c:* Emily, Adam; *ed:* (BA) Poly Sci, Hunter Coll 1962; (MA) Ed, Richmon Coll CUNY 1972; (AA) Comm/Media, Brookdale Coll 1980; (MED) Rdng, Rutgers Univ 1982; *cr:* 2nd/4th Grade Teacher Public Sch 92 Bronx 1962-68; Rdng Teacher Rahway Jr HS 1981-83, Bureau Non-Public Sch 1983-86; Eng/Comm Art Teacher Paul Robeson HS 1986-; *ai:* Newspaper Adv; Academic Olympics Coach; Cmptr Squad Coord; IRA 1981-; NCTE 1986-; Womens Am O RT (VP Fundraising 1970-72, Chapter Pres 1972-74, Dist VP 1974-76); PTA Appreciation Awd; NY Alliance Public Schls Commendation for Outstanding Teaching; Brooklyn HS Recognition Day Outstanding Prof Service; Certificate of Appreciation Outstanding Dedicated Service; *office:* Paul Robeson HS 150 Albany Ave Brooklyn NY 11213

EDEN, DEANNA MAE, Phys Ed Instructor/Coach; *b:* Beatrice, NE; *ed:* (BA) Phys Ed, NE Wesleyan Univ 1973; (MA) Phys Ed, Kearney St Coll 1979; Acquired Endorsements in Soc Sci & Mid Sch 1989; *cr:* Elem Phys Ed Instr Broken Bow Public Schls 1973-77; 10th-12th Phys Ed Instr Beatrice HS 1977-78; 8th/9th Phys Ed Instr Norfolk Jr HS 1979-; *ai:* 7th Grade Girls Vlybl & 8th Grade Girls Bsktbl Head Coach; Amer Alliance Health Phys Ed & Dance, NE Alliance Health Phys Ed Dance, NE Coaches Assn 1973-; Norfolk City Ed Assn Building Rep 1979-; Delta Kappa Gamma Corresponding Secy 1986-; Outstanding Young Women in America Awd 1976; Staff Mem of Month Distinguished Service Awd 1986; *office:* Norfolk Jr HS 510 Pasewalk Norfolk NE 68701

EDENS, DEBORAH BROWN, Marketing Education Teacher; *b:* Springfield, TN; *m:* Samuel F.; *c:* Amanda; *ed:* (BS) Mrktg Ed, Mid TN St Univ 1989; *cr:* Supvr Kroger 1983-89; Mrktg Teacher Franklin Cty HS 1989-; *ai:* DECA & Sr Spon; TN Ed Assn, MEA 1989-; Franklin Cty Distinguished 1st Yr Teacher Awd 1990; *home:* Rt 2 Box 752-8 Estill Springs TN 37330

EDER, FRANCES ALINE, First Grade Teacher; *b:* Terre Haute, IN; *m:* Jerry Ronald; *c:* Jeffrey, Jennifer Eder Walker; *ed:* (BS) Elem Ed, 1959, (MS) Elem Supervision, 1967 IN St Univ; *cr:* 2nd/3rd Grade Teacher Sandison Elem 1959-61; 1st Grade Teacher Rankin Elem 1966-72, Rio Grande Elem 1972-; *ai:* Delta Kappa Gamma Treas 1972-; Intnl Rdng Assn 1968-; Wabash Valley Cncl Intnl Rdng Assn (Treas, Comm Chairperson) 1968- Outstanding Service Awd 1985; NEA; ISTA; VCTA; Barbour Avenue United Meth Church; Vigo Cty Sch Corporation Excl in Teaching Awd 1987; *office:* Rio Grande Elem Sch R R 52 Box 301-A Terre Haute IN 47805

EDER, JAMES M., Social Studies Teacher; *b:* New York City, NY; *m:* Adrienne Rene; *c:* James A., Lauren Garvey, Andrew Fisher; *ed:* (BA) His/Philosophy, St Johns Univ 1961; (MA) Philosophy, CCNY 1963; Ed Admin, Psych; *cr:* Teacher Jefferson Park Jr HS 1963-65, Wm Couper Jr HS 1965-67, Northport Sr HS 1967-; *ai:* Judo Coach Holder of Black Belt; Amer Psych Assn, NYSCSS Presenter Various Educl Conferences; Published Text; Author of 12 Unpublished Novels; *office:* Northport HS Laurel Hill Rd Northport NY 11768

EDGAR, JUDITH BENSON, Social Studies Teacher; *b:* Chicago, IL; *m:* Frank T.; *c:* Kristine; *ed:* (BA) His, N IL Univ 1962; (MA) His, Univ of CA Berkeley 1964; *cr:* His Instr Oakland City Coll 1964-65, Utica Coll 1967-69, Culver Stockton Coll 1970; Instr John Wood Comm Coll; *ai:* Amer Assn of Univ Women Prgm Chairperson 1969-; MO St Teachers Assn 1987-; NCSS 1989-; Canton Public Lib Bd 1987-; *office:* Wyaconda C-1 Sch Walnut St Wyaconda MO 63474

EDGE, AMY K., Biology/Chemistry Teacher; *b:* Tuscaloosa, AL; *m:* Ted; *c:* Andy, Stephanie; *ed:* (BA) Bio/Sociology, Univ of AL 1968; (MA) Learning Disabilities, Univ of AL Huntsville 1975; *cr:* Learning Disabilities 1975-88, Bio/Chem Teacher 1989- Ardmore HS; Government/Sociology Teacher Huntsville HS; *ai:* Spon Cmptr Club; Scholars Bowl; AL Educl Assn; *office:* Ardmore HS 4th St Ardmore AL 35739

EDGELL, CAROL ASHCRAFT, Fourth Grade Teacher; *b:* Pittsburgh, PA; *m:* Thomas Ray; *c:* Thomas R. II, Janeen M., Amy J.; *ed:* (AB) Ed, Fairmont St Coll 1967; Grad Classes WV Univ & Univ Detroit; *cr:* 4th Grade Teacher Cntrl Elem 1967-72; Substitute Elem Teacher Brooke Cty Schls 1975-78; 4th Grade Teacher Mannington Elem 1979-; *ai:* Sch Coord Soc Stud Fair; WV Ed Assn, NEA 1967-; Colliers Meth Church Family Coord 1978-79; *home:* Rt 1 Box 118 A Worthington WV 26591

EDGERLY, ART CLINTON, Remediation Coordinator; *b:* Yakima, WA; *m:* Irma R.; *c:* Artie D., Therese M.; *ed:* (BA) Ec/Ed, Univ of WA 1981; (MED) Ed Rdng Emphasis, Univ of Portland 1987; Teacher Expectation Stu Achievement, Models of Teaching Trng; *cr:* Classroom Teacher 1981-, Remediation Coord 1989- Battle Ground Sch Dist; *ai:* Amboy Sch Intramural Coord; Amboy Mid Sch Stu Body Adv; Jr Var Girls Bsktbl Coach; *office:* Battle Ground Sch Dist 204 W Main St Battle Ground WA 98604

EDGERTON, JUDI L., Business Teacher; *b:* Westfield, NY; *ed:* (AOS) Secretarial Sci, Jamestown Bus Coll 1980; (BS) Bus Ed, D Youville Coll 1982; (MBA) Mrktg/Management, St Bonaventure Univ 1987; Income Tax Trng Through Level I; *cr:* Scndry Teacher Grover Cleveland HS 1982; Bus Teacher Grand Island HS 1983, Maple Grove Jr/Sr HS 1983-; *ai:* IMPACT Comm Intervention Team; Yrbk, Jr Class, Bus Club Adv; CCBTA Schlsp Chm 1985-; GSA Leader 1984-88, First Class 1976; BSA Leader 1989-; *office:* Maple Grove Jr/Sr HS Rd 1 Dutch Hollow Rd Bemus Point NY 14712

EDGIN, BEVERLY WINN, Mathematics Department Chair; *b:* Deland, FL; *m:* Edward C.; *c:* Edward C. Jr., Susan, Amy; *ed:* (BA) Math Ed, FL St Univ 1963; Post Grad Stud; *cr:* Teacher Satellite Beach HS 1963-65, Portland Jr HS 1972-73, White House HS 1973-74, Hendersonville HS 1974-; *ai:* Beta Club Spon; Mid TN Math Teacher, TN Math Teachers Assn, NCTM; *office:* Hendersonville HS 201 E Main St Hendersonville TN 37075

EDIE, WANDA BEAL, Mathematics Teacher; *b:* Detroit, MI; *m:* Joel W.; *c:* Frank Cona, Deborah Young; *ed:* (BA) Math/Soc Stud, 1955, (MA) Guidance/Counseling, 1972 E MI Univ; *cr:* Teacher Southfield HS 1955-57, Algonac Cmmty Schls 1958-; *ai:* Sch Dist Curr Cncl; Dist Cmptr Comm; MI Assn of Mid Sch Educators 1972-; MI Cncl Teachers of Math, NCTM 1955-; St Catherines Church 1957-; Algonac Lioness 1970-76; Local Golden Apple Awd; *office:* Algonac Cmmty Schls 1216 St Clair Blvd Algonac MI 48001

EDIN, MARSHA RICK, Librarian; *b:* Bellingham, WA; *m:* Darry R.; *c:* Scott, Tammi Edin Marcos, Ken, Rick Gibson, Toby Gibson (dec); *cr:* Spec Ed Aide 1974-77, Librarian 1977- Irene Reither Primary; *office:* Irene Reither Primary Sch 954 E Hemmi Rd Everson WA 98247

EDINGER, SALLY J., Media Specialist/Teacher; *b:* Portland, OR; *m:* Jerome; *c:* Jody A.; *ed:* (BA) Bus Admin/Ec, Whitman Coll 1956; (MED) Ed, Walla Walla Coll 1973; Spec Endorsement Media Specialist, Walla Walla Coll 1973; *cr:* Phys Ed Teacher 1965-70, Media Specialist 1970-80 Cntrl Elem Sch; Media Specialist Columbia Jr HS 1980-; *ai:* Drug & Alcohol Prevention; Onward to Excl Team; Talented & Gifted, Dist Spelling Coord; Raider Club Adv; Sch Swim Team Founder; Co-Chm Float Comm; Milton-Freewater Swim Team 1962-75; NEA, OEA 1970-; MFEA 1970-80; MCEA, OEMA 1980-; Camp Fire Cncl Pres 1960-68, Wakan 1967; Christ the King Luth Church Youth Dir 1968-75; Milton-Freewater (Lib Bd Secy 1966-80, Recreation Bd 1966-69); Outstanding Young Women of America; Recipient of Mountain Goat Tag & Article in Outdoor Life 1966; *office:* Columbia Jr HS Drawer K Irrigon OR 97844

EDINGTON, DARL E., Jr HS Mathematics Teacher; *b:* Safford, AZ; *ed:* (BA) Elem Ed, 1984, (MA) Elem Ed, 1989 AZ St Univ; *cr:* Math Teacher Gililland Jr HS 1984-; *ai:* Ftbl, Bsktbl, Wrestling, Bsbl Coach; Teacher Coord Say No to Drugs Prgm; NCTM Pres 1985; *office:* Gililland Jr HS 1025 S Beck Ave Tempe AZ 85281

EDIXON, FRANCES AILEEN, English Teacher; *b:* Sault Ste Marie, MI; *m:* Douglas A.; *ed:* (BS) Eng Ed, Bowling Green St Univ 1972; Grad Work Kent St Univ, Ashland Coll; *cr:* Eng Teacher Ashtabula Area City Schls 1972-; *ai:* NHS Adv; Advanced Placement Eng Teacher; Textbook Selection Comm; Curr Revision Comm; Delta Kappa Gamma 1990; Ashtabula Area Teachers Assn 1973-; OH Ed Assn 1973-; NEA 1973-; Cedarwood Beach Club Bd of Dir Secy 1985-87; YMCA Fund Raising Comm 1989; *office:* Harbor H S 221 Lake Ave Ashtabula OH 44004

EDMONDS, BETH SAMUELSON, Sixth Grade Teacher; *b:* Seneca, KS; *m:* Wally; *c:* Brock, Kelsey; *ed:* (BS) Elem Ed, 1980, (MS) Curr Instr, 1983 KS St Univ; *cr:* 2nd Grade Teacher Washington Sch 1980-81; 7th Grade Teacher Eng/Soc Stud Jardine Mid Sch 1981-82; 5th/6th Grade Teacher Potwin Sch 1982-; *ai:* NEA, KS Ed Assn 1980-; Topeka Ed Assn 1981-; *office:* Potwin School 208 Elmwood Topeka KS 66606

EDMONDS, CONNIE CAMPBELL, First Grade Teacher; *b:* Jackson, KY; *m:* Gordon Anthony; *c:* Craig A., Christina G.; *ed:* (AA) Elem Ed, Lees Jr Coll 1971; (BS) Elem Ed, E KY Univ 1973; (MA) Elem Ed, Morehead St Univ 1975; Elem Ed, Morehead St Univ 1977; *cr:* 1st-4th Grade Teacher LBJ Elem Sch 1974-; *ai:* Breathitt Cty Ftbl Boosters Club, Breathitt Cty Academic Boosters Club, Dist Textbook Comm, Guidance Comm Mem; Breathitt Cty Teachers Assn, KY Ed Assn, NEA 1985-; Class Valedictorian Less Jr Coll 1971; Outstanding Teacher of Yr 1982-83; Appointed 1st Grade Team Leader; *home:* 1357 Beattyville Rd Jackson KY 41339

EDMONDS, JOAN MARIE, Phys Ed Teacher/Dept Chair; *b:* Webster, SD; *m:* Steve; *c:* Branden, Brittany; *ed:* (BS) Health/Phys Ed, Northern St Univ 1967; (MA) Ed, 1985, Type D Scndry Ed, 1986 Western St Coll; *cr:* Teacher Orchard Mesa Jr HS & 1967-71, Lavaland Elem 1971-74, Cibola HS 1974-78; Teacher/Act Coord Cntrl 1978-; *ai:* Act Coord, Advisory Team, Stu Senate, Sr Class Spon; Grant & Networking Comm; Phys Ed Curr Co-Chairperson, Dept Chairperson; Phi Delta Kappa 1988-; NEA, CEA, MVEA 1978-; Dist 51 Educl Awd 1982; *home:* 551 Eastbrook Grand Junction CO 81504

EDMONDS, LINDA W., Science Department Chair; *b:* Meridian, MS; *m:* James S.; *c:* David R., Ashley B.; *ed:* (BS) Scndry Sci, Livingston Univ 1970; (MED) Zoology, Auburn Univ 1971; *cr:* Sci Teacher Choctaw Cty HS 1970, Lee Acad 1971-73, Sumter Acad 1973-; *ai:* Scholars Bowl Coach; Delta Kappa Gamma (Pres 1988-, Secy 1986-88); AL Private Sch Assn Teacher of Yr 1988; *home:* Rt 2 Box 2 Coatopa AL 35470

EDMONDSON, ADAM RUSSEL, SR., AP Chemistry Teacher; *b:* Hazleton, PA; *m:* Margaret Delmonico; *c:* Adam; *ed:* (AS) Chem, 1968, (BS) Chem, 1971, (MED) Sci Scndry Ed, 1973 PA St Univ; Nuclear & Electrical Engineering; Cmptr Interfacing Techniciques; *cr:* Chem Teacher Hazleton Sr HS 1971-; *ai:* Jr Acad of Sci Adv; Adult Ed Cmptr Specialist; Amer Chemical Society 1970-, Excl Awd 1989; Phi Delta Kappa 1973-; PSTA Presenter 1987-89; Amer Red Cross 1st Aid Instr 1968-79; Hazleton Art League 1968-85; Woodrow Wilson Natl Fellowship Master Teacher 1989; Amer Chemical Society Examintions Comm Form B 1980 Advanced Placement Exam; ; Cmptr Interface Manuel Apple IIe Cmptr 1986; *office:* Hazleton Sr HS 700 N Wyoming St Hazleton PA 18201

EDMONDSON, JOE-ANN, First Grade Teacher; *b:* Mansfield, OH; *m:* Jeffrey Kent; *c:* William R., Jay Scott; *ed:* (BS) Elem Ed, Kent St Univ 1959; Graduate Sch Ashland Univ 1989; *cr:* 4th Grade Teacher 1959-61; 3rd Grade Teacher 1961-62; 6th Grade Teacher 1962-63 Newman Sch; 4th Grade Teacher 1963-64; 3/4 Grade Teacher 1964-65 Montgomery Sch;1st Grade Teacher Grant St Sch 1977-; *ai:* Curr Comm Elem; Curr Advisory Comm; Co-Author & Mem Chemical Awareness Comm; Mem Centennial Prgm Grant St Schls 100th Birthday; Delta Kappa Gamma; Sunday Sch Ed Commission Sunday Sch Teacher Christ United Meth Church; *home:* 1930 Mifflin Ave Ashland OH 44805

EDSTER, PAULETTE EVONNE, 5th Grade Teacher; *b:* Richmond, IN; *m:* Jerry; *ed:* (BS) Ed, OH St Univ 1966; Grad Stud; *cr:* 1st Grade Teacher Overlook Elem 1966-67; 2nd Grade Teacher Berea City Schls 1968-69; Kndgtn/1st Grade Teacher Mad River Township 1969-79; 5th Grade Teacher Mineral Bluff 1979-; *ai:* Spon Mineral Bluff Talent Show; Page Building Rep; Ranger Homemakers Secy 1985-86, Ranger Homemaker of Yr 1985; Teacher of Yr Awd Mineral Bluff Elem 1988; *office:* Mineral Bluff Elem Sch Box 39 Mineral Bluff GA 30559

EDWARDS, ANN SIMPSON, 5th Grade Teacher; *b:* Springfield, MO; *m:* Jack O.; *c:* Karl D. Stout, Karen Stout, Daniel Stout, Joseph; *ed:* (BS) Elem Ed, 1970, (MED) Remedial Rdng, 1975 Univ of MO; Acad for Teachers of Gifted Stu 1988; Mythology Inst 1989; *cr:* 5th Grade Teacher West Boulevard Sch 1968-72; 6th Grade Teacher Maries R-2 Sch 1980-; *ai:* Asst Stu with Natl & St His Day Entries & Discover Early America Map Entries; Math, Sci & Soc Stud Curr, Principals Advisory Comm; MO St Teachers Assn 1968-; Teacher of Yr; Outstanding Teachers of His Day 1984; NEH Fellow Mythology Inst Miami Univ; St Incentive Goat Recipient 1987-88; *office:* Maries R-2 Sch PO Box AC Belle MO 65013

EDWARDS, ARLENE RUTH, 3rd Grade Teacher; *b:* Troy, NY; *c:* Batry D. Cone, Douglas R. Cone; *ed:* (BA) Soc Sci, San Diego St 1972; Addtl Studies, 30 Units; *cr:* Teacher Sitgreaves Sch 1972-74; Teacher Mesa View Elem 1974; *ai:* Dir Sch Chorus; Dev Music Prgm K-6th Grade; ARC 1988-; NM Registry Interpreters for Deaf 1988-; Benevolent Patriotic Order of Does Musician/St

VP 1984; Nom Teacher of Yr Awd 1989; *office:* Mesa View Elem 400 Washington St Grants NM 87020

EDWARDS, ARNOLD, Retired; *b:* Hannah, KY; *m:* Inus Boggs; *ed:* (BA) Ed, Morehead Univ 1962; *cr:* 1-8 Grade Teacher Hurricane Elem 1952-57, Terryville Elem 1957-68; Teacher Blaine Elem 1968-84; *ai:* VP & Pres of Lawrence Cty Ed Assn.

EDWARDS, BARBARA JEAN, Spanish Teacher; *b:* Chicago, IL; *ed:* (BA) Span/Sociology, 1984, Certificate Ed, 1986 Gettysburg Coll; Grad Stud Span, Middlebury Coll; *cr:* GED Span Instr Center for Human Services 1984-68; Span Teacher Hempfield HS 1986-87; Span/Eng as Second Lang Teacher Gettysburg Area Sch Dist 1987-; *ai:* Fellowship of Chrstn Athletes Adv; Mid Sch Feasibility Comm; Phi Sigma Iota 1984-, Membership Awd 1984; NEA 1987-; Living Hope Presbyn Church (World Missions & Evangelism Comm Chm 1987-, Sunday Sch Teacher 1986-); Quincentennial Prgm Grant 1989; Gettysburg Coll Span Achievement Awd 1984; *office:* Gettysburg Jr HS Lefever St Gettysburg PA 17325

EDWARDS, BEVERLY BLOYD, Mathematics Teacher; *b:* Louisville, KY; *m:* Wayne D.; *c:* Sara E.; *ed:* (BS) Math/Eng, Campbellsville Coll 1971; (MA) Math Ed, 1975, (Rank I) Ed/ Admin, 1988 W KY Univ; *cr:* Math/Eng Teacher Elizabethtown Ind Schls 1971-74; 7th/8th Grade Math Teacher Greensburg Elem 1974-77; Math Teacher Green Cty HS 1977-; *ai:* NCTM 1989-; Green Cty Ed Assn 1974-; KY Ed Assn; NEA; *home:* 118 Avery Dr Greensburg KY 42743

EDWARDS, CATHY REYNOLDS, Second Grade Teacher; *b:* Batesville, AR; *m:* Glenn; *c:* Chad, Brian; *ed:* (BSE) Early Chldhd/Elem Ed, AR St Univ 1974; Grad Stud; *cr:* Kndgtn Teacher 1974-81, 2nd Grade Teacher 1981- West Elem; *ai:* Batesville Ed Assn Bd Mem 1987-89; AR Ed Assn, NEA 1974-; Alpha Gamma Delta 1971-74; Alpha Tau Omega Sweetheart 1972; West Baptist Church Childrens Comm; Natl Ec Ed Winner 1988; *office:* West Elem Sch 850 Hill St Batesville AR 72501

EDWARDS, CHARLES H., Social Studies Dept Chair; *b:* Somerset, KY; *m:* Barbara Skaggs; *c:* Darrin, Casey; *ed:* (BS) Soc Sci Area, Campbellsville Coll 1970; (MA) Ed, W KY Univ 1975; *cr:* Phys Ed Teacher/Bsktbl Coach Roby Elem 1970-71; His Teacher 1971-76, Math/Soc Stud Teacher 1976-88 Russell Elem Springs Elem; His Teacher RusseLL Cty Jr HS 1988-; *ai:* Curr Comm; Soc Stud Dept Chm; *office:* Russell Cty Jr HS R R 7 Box 230 Russell Springs KY 42642

EDWARDS, DAVID, Mathematics Teacher; *b:* Benton, KY; *m:* Debra Lynn Irvan; *c:* Deanna; *ed:* (BS) Math, 1974, (MAED) Ed 1982 Murray St Univ; *cr:* Math Teacher Marshall Cty HS 1975-; *ai:* NEA, KY Ed Assn, Marshall Ed Assn; *office:* Marshall Cty HS Rt 7 Benton KY 42025

EDWARDS, DEBI SUE, 6th Grade Mathematics Teacher; *b:* Ft Worth, TX; *m:* Thomas Phillip; *c:* Christopher, Lindsey; *ed:* (MS) Elem Ed, AL A&M 1989; (BS) Elem Ed, Univ of N AL 1979; *cr:* 1st Grade Teacher 1979-81, 2nd Grade Teacher 1981-82 Monrovia Sch; 2nd Grade Teacher Glenwood Sch 1982-83; Learning Disabilities Teacher 1983-84, 8th Grade Math/Eng/Pre Algebra Teacher Riverton Sch 1984-89; 6th Grade Math Teacher Acad for Sci & Foreign Lang 1989-; *ai:* Stu Government Assn; Stu Store; NCTM 1989-; AL Rdng Cncl 1987-; Alpha Delta Kappa Historian 1988-; Pictures, Views Published; Teacher of Yr 1989; Favorite Teacher Runner Up 1989; *office:* Acad for Sci & Foreign Lang 3221 Mastin Lake Rd Huntsville AL 35810

EDWARDS, DOROTHY F., 1st Grade Teacher; *b:* Raleigh, NC; *c:* Morris, Jennifer; *ed:* (BS) Elem Ed, W GA Coll 1962; Rdng, FL St Univ, Univ of GA; *cr:* 1st Grade Teacher Lowndes Cty Sch System 1962-72; Head Start Teacher 1968-71, Summer Sch Teacher 1972 Valdosta City Sch System; 1st Grade Teacher Bleckley Cty Sch System 1975-; *ai:* Private Rdng & Math Tutor; Prof Assn of GA Educators 1976-; GA Assn of GA Educators, Natl Assn of Educators 1962-72; Heart of GA Rdng Cncl Mem 1985-87; Delta Kappa Gamma Mem 1977-79; Most Outstanding Young Educator Valdosta Jaycees 1972; Bleckley Primary Sch Teacher of Yr 1975-79; Bleckley Cty Elem Sch Teacher of Month 1984, Bleckley Cty Elem Sch Teacher of Yr 1987; *home:* 1304 Berkley Rd Cochran GA 31014

EDWARDS, GARY DALE, Social Studies Teacher; *b:* Jackson, MI; *m:* Pamela Ann Davis; *c:* Shana, Crissa; *ed:* (BS) Geography, 1969, (MA) African Stud, 1984 Cntrl MI Univ; *cr:* Teacher Mt Morris Jr HS 1969-70, Meridian HS 1970-71; Grad Asst Teacher Cntrl MI Univ 1971-72; Teacher Meridian HS 1972-; *ai:* Var Sftbl St Championship & League Championships; Bible Study; Prof Study Comm Mem 1982-83; Curr Comm Mem 1989-; MI HS Sftbl Coaches Assn Mem 1987-; MCTV Channel 5 Cameraman 1985-89; Precint Republican Party Delegate 1986-; Class B Sftbl Coach of YR 1987; *home:* 4740 Anna Ln Sanford MI 48657

EDWARDS, GLENDA VAUGHAN, English Teacher; *b:* Dallas, TX; *m:* Bill; *c:* Misty, Farrah; *ed:* (BA) Eng, Univ of TX Dallas 1985; (MS) Admin/Mid Management, E TX Univ 1990; *cr:* Eng Teacher N Mesquite HS 1985-; *ai:* TX Assn of Future Educators Club Spon; Mesquite Ed Assn Faculty Rep 1988-; *office:* N Mesquite HS 18201 LBJ Frwy Mesquite TX 75150

EDWARDS, JAMES E., Mathematics Department Chair; *b:* El Paso, TX; *c:* Christine, Kelly, James, Cindy; *ed:* (BS) Math, Univ of TX 1966; (MS) Oceanography, US Naval Post Grad Sch 1973; *cr:* Instr Heritage Coll 1983-86; Math Dept Chm San Marcos Baptist Acad 1987-; *ai:* Jr Class Chm; Faculty Rep; AAPT 1990; *office:* San Marcos Baptist Acad 2801 Ranch Rd 12 San Marcos TX 78666

EDWARDS, JAMES RAY, Math Teacher; *b:* Memphis, TN; *ed:* (BS) Scndry Ed, Minneapolis St Univ 1973; *cr:* Math Teacher Southern Baptist Ed Ctr 1973-77, Westside HS 1980-; *ai:* Chm Math Dept; Report Card/Scheduler Coord; Sr Class Spon; *office:* Westside H S 3389 Dawn Dr Memphis TN 38127

EDWARDS, JOHN L., 5th Grade Elementary Teacher; *b:* Buffalo, NY; *m:* Lynn Saslawski; *c:* Christine, Robert, William; *ed:* (BS) Elem Ed, 1971, (MS) Ed, 1985, (CAS) Admin, 1986 SUNY Brockport; Grad Stud Permanent Cert; *cr:* Elem Teacher Batavia City Schls 1969-; *ai:* Intramural Bsktbl Adv; Elem Cmptr Coord; Co-Chm St-Wide Planning Comm; Teacher Resource & Cmptr Trng Centers; NY St Staff Dev Cncl 1988-; Assn Supervision Staff Dev 1985-; NY St Hunter Trng Master Instr 1973-; Genesee Region Teacher Center Policy Bd Chm 1987-89; Dist Supt New York Recertification Team Reporter & Teacher Rep; *office:* Jackson Elem Sch 411 S Jackson St Batavia NY 14020

EDWARDS, JUDITH ROSE SHORT, Gifted-English Teacher; *b:* Benton, KY; *m:* James H.; *c:* Jeanene L., Harold L. *ed:* (BS) Eng & History, Murray St 1976; (MA) Ed/Eng, Murray St 1982; Rank I Ed/Eng, Murray St 1985; Gifted Cert Murray St Univ; *cr:* Teacher Reidland Mid; *ai:* Academic Coach; Mc Cracken Cty Ed Assn; KY Ed Assn; KY Gifted Assn; NEA; Westminster Presbyterian Church; Extra Mile Awd from Paducah Chamber of Commerce 1989; *home:* 252 Drawbridge Trace Paducah KY 42003

EDWARDS, JUNE M., English Teacher; *b:* Glendale, CA; *m:* Morgan J.; *c:* Terrill, Elaine Olson, Leslie Phillips; *ed:* (BA) Eng/ Psych, Pitzer Coll 1978; CA St Univ Fullerton; *cr:* Primary Teacher Cypress Jr Sch 1964-74; 7th Grade Eng Teacher Jerry D Holland Jr HS 1984-; *ai:* Yrbk Co-Adv; Stu Act Comm; NCTE; *office:* Jerry D Holland Jr HS 4733 N Landis Ave Baldwin Park CA 91706

EDWARDS, KATHRYN STONE, History Teacher; *b:* Windsor, MO; *m:* Barry; *c:* Spenser; *ed:* (BS) Soc Sci Ed, SW Baptist Univ 1984; Grad Work Soc Sci Ed; *cr:* His Teacher Montrose R-IV 1984-86, Hickory Cty R-I 1987-; *ai:* Class Spon; Certified Teachers Assn 1987-.

EDWARDS, LINDA LEE BOYLES, Chemistry/Mathematics Teacher; *b:* Pittsburgh, PA; *m:* Corwyn R.; *ed:* (BS) Ed, Baylor Univ 1979; Grad Studs Various Colls; *cr:* Math/Chem Teacher Woodland Hills Sch Dist 1979-84; Math Teacher Fox Chapel Sch Dist 1980-81, Gateway Sch Dist 1982; Math/Chem Teacher Hillcrest HS 1985-; *ai:* Math Team & Equestrian Club; GCCTM; Calvary Baptist Church Sunday Sch Teacher 1987-; *home:* 22 Agewood Ct Simpsonville SC 29681

EDWARDS, LOIS JEAN, Fifth Grade Teacher; *b:* Spencer, IN; *ed:* (BS) Elem Ed, Ball St Teachers Coll 1964; (MS) Elem Ed, Ball St Univ 1968; Rdng, Ball St Univ; *cr:* 2nd Grade/Jr HS Lang Art Teacher Elwood Cmmty Schls 1964-68; 2nd Grade Teacher Tipton Cmmty Schls 1968-69, Madison Grant Sch Corporation 1969-70; 5th Grade/Jr HS Lang Art Teacher Indianapolis Public Sch 89 1970-; *ai:* Native Amer Study Group; United Teaching Profession; NEA Life Mem; IN St Teachers Assn Minorit ty Affairs Comm 1983; Natl Assn Prof Educators, IN Prof Educators; Church of Christ 1955; Midwest Cherokee Alliance (Charter Mem, Publications); Amer Bus Womens Assn Mem; Right To Life Organization; Indianapolis Public Sch 89 20 Yrs Service; *office:* Kenneth Walker Sch #89 5950 E 23rd St Indianapolis IN 46218

EDWARDS, MADELINE MOSIELLO, 8th Grade Teacher/ Asst Prin; *b:* New York, NY; *w:* Richard M. (dec); *c:* Susan Zimmer, Gerald A.; *ed:* (BA) Comm Arts, Marymount Manhattan Coll 1951; (MA) Ed, NY Univ 1980; *cr:* Jr HS Teacher/Asst Prin St Joseph HS 1965-; *ai:* Responsible for Act Relating to Jr HS such as Yrbk, Graduation, Ring Ceremony & Sacramental Preparation; Marymount Manhattan Coll Alum VP 1960; NCEA Mem; St Joseph Church Mem 1970; Parish Cncl Mem 1989-91; St Joseph Ed Comm hairperson 1970.

EDWARDS, MARTHA AMOS, Kindergarten Teacher; *b:* De Queen, AR; *m:* Benson; *c:* Joann Counts, Wayne, Joseph; *ed:* (BSE) Elem, 1970, (MSE) Early Chldhd, 1981 AR St Univ; Grad Stud Univ of AR Little Rock; *cr:* Headstart Teacher 1969, 1st Grade Teacher 1970-73 Tuckerman Elem; Kndgtn Teacher Cave City Elem 1973-74; 1st Grade Teacher Salem Elem 1974-75; Kndgtn Teacher Cave City Elem 1975-; *ai:* NE AR Assn for Children Under Six Pres 1982-83; AR Assn of Children Under Six Dist 1 Past Mem at Large, Schlsp Awd 1982, Outstanding Mem 1989; Southern Assn of Children Under Six; Kappa Delta Pi, Phi Kappa Phi; Outstanding Elem Teacher 1972; *home:* Box 448 Hardy AR 72542

EDWARDS, MARY LOU JIMISON, English Teacher; *b:* South Bend, IL; *m:* Marcus J.; *ed:* (BA) Eng, Kent St Univ 1968; (MA) Eng, SUNY Fredonia 1977; *cr:* Teacher Frewsburg Cntrl 1969-; *ai:* Yrbk Adv; HS Bowl Coach; Delta Kappa Gamma, NCTE; Mt Sinai-Mecca Order of Eastern Star Dist Deputy 1984; Graduation Speaker 1982, 1989; *office:* Frewsburg Cntrl Sch Institute St Frewsburg NY 14738

EDWARDS, MICHAEL PAIN, SR., Spanish Teacher; *b:* Richwood, WV; *m:* Linda Elaine Miller; *c:* Michael, William; *ed:* (BA) Span/Eng, Lee Coll 1974; (MA) Speech Comm, WV Univ 1984; Grad Stud; *cr:* Teacher Minnora Elem Sch 1974-76, Calhoun Cty HS 1976-; *ai:* CEA, WVEA, NEA Comm Chm 1976-88; NCTE 1988-89; Lions Club 1987-; *office:* Calhoun Cty HS PO Box 898 School St Grantsville WV 26147

EDWARDS, PHILLIP WILSON, High School Math Teacher; *b:* Lafayette, IN; *ed:* (BS) Math, Stephen F Austin 1988; Ed Admin; *cr:* Math Teacher Aldine Eisenhower 1989; Math Teacher/Coach Edgewood HS 1989-; *ai:* HS & Mid Sch Ftbl, Bsktbl Coach; Mid Sch Track Coach; HS Tennis Coach; Mid Sch Math UIL Instr; TX HS Coaches Assn 1989-; *office:* Edgewood HS Hwy 80 E Edgewood TX 75117

EDWARDS, RANSFORD GEORGE, Math Teacher; *b:* Hanover, West Indies; *m:* Cynthia Evadne Shaw; *c:* Sean, Jodi; *ed:* (BSC) Math, Univ of West Indies 1970; (MSC) Math, Central CT St Univ 1983; Grad Stud Math Ed, Brooklyn Coll; Teachers Diploma, Mico Teachers Coll; *cr:* Math Teacher Kingsway HS Jamaica 1955-57, Kingston Coll HS Jamaica 1970-77; Math Lecturer Mico Coll Kingston Jamaica 1977-82; Math Processor Coll of New Rochelle 1987-88; Math Teacher Prospect Heights HS NY 1983-; *ai:* 7th Day Adv Schl Bd Mem; Linden 7th Day Adv Ed Comm; West Indies Coll Bd 1970-80; Linden 7th Day Adv Church Elder 1987-; *home:* 133-16-224 Street Laurelton NY 11413

EDWARDS, RICHARD C., JR., English Teacher; *b:* Muncie, IN; *m:* Nancy Sonia Baspinairo; *c:* Carlton; *ed:* (BA) Eng, Olivet Nazarene Univ 1954; (MA) Theatre, Governors St Univ 1973; *cr:* Teacher of Eng as Second Lang Amer Consulate Japan 1956-57; Eng Teacher Thornton Fractional North HS 1957-60; Teacher of Eng as Second Lang Colegio Anglo-Americano Oruro Bolivia 1960-64; Eng Teacher Thornton Fractional North HS 1964-66; Speech/Drama Teacher/Fine Art Chm Kankakee Sr HS 1966-; *ai:* Acad Awds Comm; IL Theatre Assn 1975-80; NCTE 1987-; Cmmty Art Cncl Incorporated (Pres 1987-89, Bd of Dir 1978-80, 1989-, Mem) 1975-; IL Office of Ed Evaluation Team Mem for Speech & Drama; IL St Thespian Dir 1975-77; Outstanding Elem & Scndry Educators 1976; Notable Amer 1976-77; Service Leadership Awd; S Interscholastic Conference Assn 1978-80, 1983-84, 1985-87; Amicitia Linguarum Awd; NE Conference on Teaching Foreign Lang 1986; *office:* Kankakee Sr HS 1200 W Jeffery Kankakee IL 60901

EDWARDS, RONALD EUGENE, Senior English Teacher; *b:* Parker, SD; *m:* Sharon Ann; *c:* Mark, Paul, Daniel; *ed:* (BA) Eng/ His/Soc Stud, SD St 1964; (MS) Educl Admin, Chapman Coll 1971; *cr:* 10th-12th Grade Eng Teacher Rutland Public Schls 1964-66; 7th-9th Grade Eng Teacher Buchanan Public Schls 1966-68; 9th Grade Eng Teacher Apollo Jr HS 1968-79; Eng IV Teacher Loara HS 1979-; *ai:* Ftbl, Bsktbl, Wrestling, Dances Supvr; Eng Dept Chm 1969-79; Loara HS PTA, CA Teachers Assn, NEA; Outstanding Teacher of Yr 1977; Nominee Teacher Hall of Fame 1978; Masonic Outstanding Teacher of Yr Awd 1979; PTA Teacher of Yr 1981; *home:* 5542 Tiffany Garden Grove CA 92645

EDWARDS, RUBY YOUNG, K-6th Grade Substitute Teacher; *b:* Tousey, KY; *m:* Cecil; *c:* Lowery, Raymond; *ed:* (BS) Elem Ed, W KY Univ 1963; *cr:* 1st-8th Grade Teacher Rural Schls 1953-60; 4th-8th Grade Teacher/Head Teacher Yeaman 1960-62; 5th Grade Teacher Fordsville 1962-63; 1st-3rd Grade Teacher Caneyville 1963-85; *ai:* Grayson Cty Ed Assn, KY Ed Assn, NEA; *home:* Rt 1 Box 150 Falls of Rough KY 40119

EDWARDS, SHARON ANN, English Teacher; *b:* Spartanburg, SC; *ed:* (BA) Eng Ed, 1976, (MA) Eng Ed, 1984 Univ of SC Spartanburg; Advanced Placement Courses & Applied Comm; *cr:* Eng Teacher Hillcrest HS 1976-77, Hinesville Mid Sch 1977-78, Abbeville HS 1978-79, Cherokee HS 1979-81, Blackburg HS 1981-; *ai:* Co-Spon Sch Newpaper & Anti Drug Abuse Club; Palmetto St Teachers Assn (VP 1989-, Treas 1988-89, Mem 1986-); Teacher of Yr Blacksburg HS 1989-; Honored Teacher Cherokee Cty Chamber of Commerce; Helped Write Lit Curr 1988; *office:* Blacksburg HS Ramseur St Blacksburg SC 29702

EDWARDS, THERESA TUCKER, Educational Diagnostician; *b:* Marshall, TX; *m:* Roy; *c:* Linda Macon, Sandra Richardson, Glenn Johnson, Lydia; *ed:* (BA) Soc Sci, Bishop Coll 1951; (MS) Ed/Spec Ed/Admin, E TX St Univ 1976; Physocology, Cnslr; *cr:* Teacher 1954-84, Diagnostician 1985- Marshall Ind Sch Dist; *ai:* E TX Diagnostician Assn 1985-; TX St Teachers Assn, NEA 1954-; Natl Cncl for Spec Children 1986-; Alpha Kappa Alpha Epistoles 1980-85; *home:* PO Box 771 Marshall TX 75670

EDWARDS, THOMAS BRODERICK, Computer Tech Chair; *b:* Cohosset, MA; *m:* Lois Marie; *c:* Tom, John, Lori M.; *ed:* (BA) St Michaels Coll 1965; (MS) Ed, St Coll Boston 1968; Admin & Supervision 1968; PhD Prgm Auburn Univ; TV Instruction, Cmptr Sci, Information Sci, Systems Analysis USAF Grad Sch; *cr:* Teacher Educable Retarded Boston Public Schls 1965-66; Math/ Eng Teacher Brighton HS 1966-67; Cmptr Sci Instr Maxwell AFB 1967-71; Eng Teacher Whitman Hanson Regional HS 1971-74; Consultant/Dir St Dept of Ed 1974-76; Dir/Mgr Cmptr Randolph Public Schls 1979-; *ai:* Bsktbl Coach; Newspapers; Journals; Adult Prgm, ESL Summer Prgm; USAF (Captain, Acad Liaison Officer); Whos Who in Amer Coll & Univ; Data Auto Proposal 1969, St Dept of Ed; Educl Resource Information Center System 1971; Data Automation Bridgewater St Coll Project Contemporary Competitiveness 1972; Created Nutrition Game 1980, Cmptr Game 1981.

EDWARDS, VIVIAN SKIPPER, Social Studies/Chair; *b:* Loris, SC; *m:* Johnny Brooks; *c:* Samantha, Cameron; *ed:* (BA) His, Pembroke St Univ 1964; E Carolina Univ, Winthrop Coll, Clemson Univ, Univ of SC; *cr:* Teacher Williams Township HS 1968-70, Tabor City HS 1970-72, Loris HS 1965-67, 1973-; *ai:* Club Adv;

Close-up; Model United Nations; Princeton Model Congress; Bridge Club; Golf Coach; Soc Stud Dept Chairperson; Comm of 2000 1989; Cty US His Curr Comm; Organization of Amer Historians 1986-; SC Soc Stud Cncl; NCSS 1987-; Teacher of Yr; Taft Inst Fellowship; Strom Thurmond Inst Fellowship; *office:* Loris HS Heritage Rd Loris SC 29569

EDWARDS, WELDON LYNN, English Department Chair; *b:* Abilene, TX; *m:* Elaine Barr; *c:* Regan, Ashley; *ed:* (BA) Eng, 1968, (MA) Eng, 1971 TX Tech; *cr:* Teacher Mineral Wells HS 1968-69, Breckenridge HS 1972-; *ai:* Ready Writing Coach; *office:* Breckenridge HS 500 W Lindsey Breckenridge TX 76024

EDWARDS, WILLA L., Elementary Teacher; *b:* Grand Island, NE; *m:* Virg; *c:* Chaucey, Jaime; *ed:* (BA) Elem Ed, Kearney St Coll 1966; Grad Work Rdng; *cr:* Teacher Centura Public Schls 1967-70, Mc Cook Public 1971-72, Fort Collins 1972-73, Friend Public 1973-; *ai:* Soc Stud Sch Curr; N Cntrl Curr Comm; NEA 1966-; NSEA; Friend Ed Assn Ed Comm Pres 1975-76, 1979-80, 1982-83; *office:* Friend Public Schls 501 Main Friend NE 68359

EELLS, GLORIA LOUISE, History/Government Teacher; *b:* Iowa City, IA; *ed:* (BA) His, Simpson Coll 1961; (MA) Scndry Ed, Univ of IA 1982; *cr:* SS Teacher Webster City HS 1961-64; Roosevelt Jr HS 1964-67; Washington HS 1967-72; Mc Kinley Jr HS 1972-82; Washington HS 1982-; *ai:* Jr Class-Soph Class Spon; Adastra Honors Society; Delta Kappa Gamma VP; Phi Delta Kappa; Dan Forth Fellow.

EELLS, MURRAY M., Biology Instructor; *b:* Syracuse, NY; *m:* Amelia M.; *c:* Deborah, Pete, Gregory; *ed:* (BS) Bio, CA St Pomona 1961; Bio, Grad Sch; *cr:* Bio Instr Azusa HS 1962-65, Trinity Union HS 1968-70, St Regis Falls Cntrl Sch 1985-; *ai:* Soph Class Adv; Cty Fish & Game Commission Chm; Various Research Assistantships in Mexico & US; Awarded Grant to Study Tropical Bio in Costa Rica 1967; *office:* Saint Regis Falls Cntrl Sch Main St Saint Regis Falls NY 12980

EFINGER, MARILYN LOUISE (GILBERT), Jr High Science & Dept Head; *b:* Sioux City, IA; *m:* Donald L.; *c:* Jennifer; *ed:* (BS) Elem Ed, Drake Univ 1967; Assertive Discipline; Microbio/Physiology/Nutrition; *cr:* 4th-5th Grade Basic Skills Teacher Rice Sch 1967-68; 5th Grade Basic Skills Teacher Mc Kinley 1969-70; 6th-8th Grade Sci Teacher St Bernard 1985-; *ai:* Sci Fair Coord; All Sch Carnival Chairwomen; Corporate Women Officers Small Bus 1976-83; NCEA 1985-; Cursillo Leader 1983; Teens Encounter Christ Engagement Encounter Leader 1984-; *home:* 4949 Grandview Dr Peoria Heights IL 61614

EFRAIN, AVILES LOPEZ, 6th Grade Mathematics Teacher; *b:* Orocovis, PR; *m:* Martinez Acevedo Maria Elena; *c:* Efrain Aviles Martinez, Rosa D. Aviles Martinez; *ed:* (BA) Inter Amer Univ 1972; *home:* Apartado 721 Morovis PR 00717

EGALNICK, DEBORAH SHAWD, Life Management/Skills Teacher; *b:* Houston, TX; *m:* Kenneth A.; *c:* Kristin, Kenny; *ed:* (BS) Home Ec Ed, Univ of Houston 1974; *cr:* Teacher Sugar Land Mid Sch 1975-77 & 1985-87, Hodges Bend Mid Sch 1987-; *ai:* PTO Volunteer; Little League Volunteer 1987-; *office:* Hodges Bend Mid Sch 16510 Bissonnet Houston TX 77083

EGAN, JULANE BARCZAK, English/Social Studies Teacher; *b:* Milwaukee, WI; *m:* Patrick M.; *c:* Katie, Brian; *ed:* (BA) Soc Stud/Lang Art, Univ of WI Milwaukee 1976; *cr:* 7th Grade Soc Stud Teacher St Roman Sch 1976-78; 7th/8th Grade Soc Stud/Lang Art Teacher Holy Spirit Sch 1978-80; 7th/8th Grade Soc Stud/Eng Teacher St Anthony Sch 1986-; *ai:* Stu Government Adv; GSA Leader 1989-; *office:* St Anthony Sch N74 W 13604 Appleton Ave Menomonee Falls WI 53051

EGBERT, PATRICIA ANN (DONHAM), Math Teacher; *b:* Ronceverte, WV; *m:* Daniel Park; *c:* Gretchen Dawn, Derek Ray, Daniel Park II; *ed:* (BAED) Elem Ed, Fairmont St Coll 1980; (MA) Speech Comm, WV Univ 1984; *cr:* Math Teacher Wirt Cty HS 1980-; *ai:* WV Cncl of Teachers of Math; *home:* Rt 1 Box 3A Palestine WV 26160

EGER, GAIL ESSENLOHR, Second Grade Teacher; *b:* Montclair, NJ; *m:* John Edward; *c:* Stacey J., Michael J., Kelly A., Robert L.; *ed:* (BS) Elem Ed, Lock Haven Univ 1974; (MS) Elem Ed, SUC Potsdam 1979; *cr:* 2nd Grade Teacher 1974-86, 1st Grade Teacher 1986-88, 2nd Grade Teacher 1988- Beaver River Cntrl Sch; *ai:* Volunteer Odyssey of Mind Competition; Delta Kappa Gamma 1st VP 1982-; Hospital Auxiliary Twig Treas 1987-; Black River Rdng Cncl 1975-77; Church (Chrstn Ed Comm Mem, Pre-Sch/1st/2nd Grade Sunday Sch Teacher, Church Nursery Supvr, Vacation Bible Sch Teacher); Mentor for 2nd Grade Teachers; *home:* RD 1 Box 191 Castorland NY 13620

EGGEN, PAULANN K., 5th Grade Teacher; *b:* La Crosse, WI; *ed:* (BS) Child Dev, 1970, (MED) Elem Ed, 1979 Univ of AZ; *cr:* Elem Teacher Donaldson Elem 1974-; *ai:* AEA, NEA; PTO Intermediate Rep; *office:* Donaldson Elem Sch 2040 Omar Dr Tucson AZ 85704

EGGERS, DONNA BACKHAUS, Jr HS English Teacher; *b:* Enid, OK; *m:* Rene; *c:* Mona Hein, Geri Long, Jodi Cline, Dana; *ed:* (BS) Elem Ed, OK St Univ 1978; Psych; Eng; *cr:* Eng Teacher Garber Public Sch 1978-; *ai:* Teach Quest Skills for Adolescence Jr HS; 8th Grade Spon; OK Ed Assn, OK Eng Teachers Assn 1978-; Garber Ed Assn (Pres, VP, Secy, Building Rep); Lions Club Youth Dir 1989-; *office:* Garber Public Sch Garber Rd Garber OK 73738

EGGERT, ELEANOR (MOSKAL), First Grade Teacher; *b:* Clayton, WI; *m:* Harold August; *c:* Hope Dietrich, John, Joe; *ed:* 2 Yr Elem, Polk Cty Coll 1953; (BA) Kndgtn/Elem WI St Univ River Falls 1968; *cr:* Rural 1st-8th Grade Teacher Beaver Brook 1953-55, Diamond Grove 1956-57, Jones Creek 1960-62, Clover Leaf 1962-66; 1st Grade Teacher Clayton Public Sch 1966-; *ai:* Inservice Comm; Chaperone Sch Functions; Calendar Comm; Ticket Seller Sch Functions; Faculty Schlsp Participant; Testing Comm; Clayton Sch Dist Lib Media Long-Range Planning Comm; Northwestern Rdng Assn 1966-76; St Croix Valley Rdng Cncl 1976-; AFT Treas 1978-; WI Fed of Teachers; 4-H Leader 1964-76 10-Yr Leadership Awd 1974; Church Ladies Club 1953-; *home:* Rt 1 Box 204 Clayton WI 54004

EGGLESTON, CINDY L., Science Teacher; *b:* Newport, NH; *ed:* (BE) Elem Ed, Keene St Coll 1971; Ed Through Dramatics, Producing Cmmty Theater; *cr:* Sci Teacher Paul Elem Sch 1974-; *ai:* Yrbk Adv; Drama Coach; Wakefield Congregational Church (Organist, Choir Dir) 1980-; Founded Sch Drama Prgm; Produce Talent Show & Major Broadway Musical per Yr; *office:* Paul Elem Sch RR 2 Box 770 Sanbornville NH 03872

EGGLESTON, MARY ANN, Computer/Math Teacher; *b:* Little Rock, AR; *m:* Jerry Jay; *c:* Jennifer, Jonathan; *ed:* (BSED) Math, Cntrl MO St Univ 1971; (MS) Cmptr, NW MO St Univ 1986; *cr:* Teacher Harrisonville Jr HS 1971-74; Spec Ed Teacher Adrian Elem/Jr HS 1978; Teacher Drexel HS 1979-; Adjunct Instr Cntrl MO St Univ 1989-, Longview Comm Coll 1987-; *ai:* Math Club, Quiz Bowl, Jr Class Spon; Cmmty Teachers Assn Pres 1984-85; *office:* Drexel R IV HS 4th & Main St Drexel MO 64742

EGLESTON, GAIL RUTH, Language Arts Teacher; *b:* St Louis, MO; *ed:* (BA) Speech/Drama, Hardin-Simmons Univ 1959-63; (MA) Theatre, S IL Univ 1963-65; (MED) Scndry Admin, Univ of MO St Louis 1983-85; *cr:* Tech Dir Van Ellis Theatre; Speech/Theatre Instr 1966-70, Tech Dir/Asst Professor 1970-72, Acting Dir/Asst Professor 1972-73 Hardin-Simmons Univ; Lang Art Teacher Mehlville Sr HS 1973-; *ai:* Faculty Spon Sch Literary Magazine; NCTE, NEA, MO NEA; Encore Theatre Productions, St Louis Zoo Friends, Audubon Society; Rock Haven Task Force 1989-; Mehlville Cmmty Teachers Assn Negotiations Team; Various Poems Published; Various Acting, Theatre & Literary Awds; *office:* Mehlville Sr HS 3200 Lemay Ferry Rd Saint Louis MO 63125

EGLOFF, DIANE MARIE, Third Grade Teacher; *b:* Denver, CO; *ed:* (BA) Elem Ed/Art/Sci, Univ of N CO 1973; Grad Stud; *cr:* 3rd Grade Teacher Eaton Elem; *ai:* Right to Read, GESA, Lang Art Curr, Staff Morale, Accountability Comm; EEA, IRA; Alpha Zi Delta Exec Cncl 1971; Chapter I Summer Sch Grant 1975; *home:* 200 N 35th Ave #58 Greeley CO 80631

EGNATUK, MARY ANN, Junior High School Teacher; *b:* Homer, MI; *ed:* (BS) Soc Stud, W MI Univ 1963; (MA) General Elem Ed, MI St Univ 1968; *cr:* Teacher Albion Public Schls 1963-68, Homer Public Schls 1968-83; Prin 1986-87; Teacher 1983- Hilltop Chrstn Sch; *ai:* Mission Station Radio; MI Educators Chrstn Fellowship Secy; Alpha Delta Kappa (Corresponding Secy 1985-, Pres Elect 1990); *office:* Hilltop Chrstn Sch Western Indian Ministries Box F Window Rock AZ 86515

EGSTAD, MICHAEL C., Social Studies Dept Coord; *b:* Rice Lake, WI; *m:* Judy Johnson; *c:* Chad, Nicole, Bryan; *ed:* (BA) His, 1968, (MA) His, 1972 Univ of WI Eau Claire; Curr Instruction, Mankato St Univ; *cr:* Soc Stud Teacher Rosemount HS 1974-76, Apply Valley HS 1976-80; Soc Stud Dept Coord Apple Valley HS 1980-; *ai:* Soc Stud Steering, Scope & Sequence Comm; Apple Valley HS All-Sport Booster Club (Secy 1987, VP 1988); Ashland Oil Individual Teacher Achievement Awd 1990; US W MN Teacher of Yr Finalist 1989; Apple Valley HS Favorite Teacher & Yrbk Awd 1980-82, 1984-85, 1987-89; *office:* Apple Valley HS 144450 Hayes Rd Apple Valley MN 55124

EHERENMAN, CHRISTIE E., English Teacher; *b:* Evanston, IL; *ed:* (BS) Eng/Rdng, 1981, (MS) Eng/Rdng, 1985 Ball St Univ; *cr:* Eng Teacher Homestead HS 1981-84, Pike HS 1984-; *ai:* Frosh Cheerleading Squads Coach; PCTA 1985-; ISTA 1981-; Indy Runners 1986-; Tri-Fed USA 1987-; *office:* Pike HS 6701 Zoinsville Rd Indianapolis IN 46268

EHMEN, HARLAN GEORGE, Science Teacher; *b:* Freeport, IL; *m:* Martha Gwendolyn White; *c:* Jeffrey, Rebecca Hoffman, Scott; *ed:* (BED) Ag Ed, 1956, (MED) Ed, 1962 Univ of IL; Certified Endorsement Counseling & Guidance, IL Dept of Ed; NDEA Grand Creighton Univ; *cr:* Voc Ag Instr 1956-72, Guidance & Counseling Instr 1972-77 La Moille HS; Sci Instr Allen Jr HS 1978-; *ai:* FFA; Class Adv; Ftbl & Bsktbl Asst Coach; Curr Comm; IL Assn Voc Ag Teachers 1956-72; IL Counseling & Guidance 1973-77; Elks 1970-; NDEA Grant Creighton Univ 1966; *home:* RR 1 La Moille IL 61330

EHMEN, M. GWEN, Junior High School Teacher; *b:* Chicago, IL; *m:* Harlan G.; *c:* Jeff, Becky Hoffman, Scott; *ed:* (BS) Elem Ed, N IL Univ 1974; *cr:* 5th Grade Teacher Amboy Grade 1974-75; 4th Grade Teacher 1975-85, Jr HS Teacher 1985- OH Grade; *ai:* 6th Grade Spon; Delta Kappa Gamma Intnl (Gamma Phi (Secy 1985-86, VP 1987-88, Pres 1989-); *home:* R 1 La Moille IL 61330

EHREN, WILLIAM JAMES, III, Cmptr/Chem/Physics Teacher; *b:* Sheboygan Falls, WI; *m:* Jocelyn Cabal; *ed:* (BS) Chem Ed, Univ of WI Madison 1965; (MS) Chem Ed, Coll of William & Mary 1970; *cr:* Chem/Physics/Cmptr Programming Instr Luxemburg-Casco Sr HS 1965-; *ai:* NHS Adv; Girls & Boys Golf Coach; Ducks Unlimited Chapter VP 1982-; *home:* Rt 4 Box 291A Luxemburg WI 54217

EHRHARDT, VIRGINIA MC COWAN, Teacher of Gifted/Talented; *b:* Nevada, MO; *m:* Donal Lee; *c:* Robert B. Clements, Melissa Clements Roberts; *ed:* (BSE) Elem Ed - Cum Laude, 1976; (MA) Elem Ed, 1980, (EDS) Elem Admin, 1987 NE MO St Univ; *cr:* IBM Secretarial Temple Stephens Company 1962-66; 4th Grade Teacher S Park 1976-85; 5th Grade Teacher E Park 1985-86; K-6th Grade Teacher of Gifted Moberly Public Schls 1986-; *ai:* Future Problem Solvers Coach; Prof Dev Comm Chairman; Moberly Cmmty Teachers Assn Salary Chm; Vacation Bible Sch Dir; Gifted Assn of MO 1985-; MCTA Moberly Pres 1987-89; Eagles Booster 1986-; MO St Teachers Assn 1976-; Thesis Developing an Academically Gifted Prgm Moberly Public Schls; *office:* Moberty Public Schls 101 N Johnson Moberty MO 65270

EIBELL, MARILYN, 4th Grade Teacher; *b:* Philadelphia, PA; *ed:* (BS) Ed - Cum Laude, 1973, (MS) Ed/Elem Math Concentration, 1978 Temple Univ; Masters Prgm Univ of Arts; *cr:* Teacher 1973-78, Math Teacher/Enrichment Specialist 1978-79. Teacher 1979- Bregy Elem Sch; *ai:* Columbus Forum 1989-; *office:* F A Bregy Elem Sch 17th & Bigler Sts Philadelphia PA 19145

EIBEN, WARNER G., English Teacher; *b:* Knoxville, TN; *m:* Cindy Sue Wakler; *c:* Sara, Sandy; *ed:* (BS) Eng, IL St Univ 1977; Grad Studs Eng, Ed Admin & Cmptr Sci; - *cr:* Eng Teacher Tuscola HS 1977-; *ai:* Lang Art Curr-Learning Assessment Comm; Tuscola Ed Assn (Pres 1982-83) 1977- Tuscola HS Teacher of Yr 1988-89; Participant NASA Teacher in Space Prgm 1985-86; *office:* Tuscola H S 500 S Prairie Tuscola IL 61953

EICHER, ROMA JEAN (DILLER), Piano/Voice/Choral Teacher; *b:* Harper, KS; *m:* Christian Samuel; *c:* Marisa Eicher Rue, Dani Eicher Lack, Jaqui, Tyson, Travis; *ed:* (AA) Music, Hesston Coll 1963; OR St Univ; *cr:* Sch Accompanist OR St Univ 1963-64; Teacher/Admin Conservatory for Music Ed 1986-; Piano Teacher W Mennonite HS 1989-; *ai:* Local Coord Natl Convention Mennonite General Assembly 1991; OR Music Teachers Assn (Mem 1964-, Pres 1987-89); MTNA (Bus Chairperson 1972, Mem 1964), Schlsp; Hesston Coll Regional Dir 1978-84; W Mennonite HS Band (Secy 1982-84, Vice-Chairperson 1984-86, Pres 1986-88) 1982-88; Greater Albany Sch Dist Budget Comm (Mem, Chairperson, Pres) 1984-87; *office:* Conservatory for Music Ed 35355 Eicher Rd SE Albany OR 97321

EICKELMAN, COLLEEN ERIN, Soc Science/Eng Teacher; *b:* Omaha, NE; *c:* M. Scott, Kelli Eickelman Schleisman, Molly M.; *ed:* (BS) Scndry Ed/Soc Sci/Eng, 1980, (MS) Cmptr Ed/Prof Ed, 1990 NE Omaha 1990; Cooperating Teacher Project Bus; Emerging Technology in Ed Cmptr; *cr:* Teacher Mc Millan Jr HS 1981-; *ai:* Cmptr Software Evaluation; Coll Prep Course Author & Teacher; Natl His Day & Future Probe Coach; Totem LIterary Publication Selection Ed; Textbook Selection; NEA, NE St Ed Assn 1980-; NCSS 1985-; Urban League of Omaha 1988-; Project Bus 1985-; Alice Buffett Outstanding Teacher Awd, NCTE Lang Art Merit 1989; NCSS Cert of Merit, Natl His Day Recognition Awd, PTSA St Life Membership Awd 1987; *office:* Mc Millan Jr HS 3802 Redick Ave Omaha NE 68112

EIDSON, FRANCES POOLE, Mathematics Teacher; *b:* Memphis, TN; *m:* H. Daniel; *c:* Amy, Daniel; *ed:* (BS) Math, Memphis St Univ 1970; (MAT) Math, Jacksonville Univ 1975; *cr:* Teacher Treadwell Jr HS 1970-71, Joseph Stilwell Jr HS 1971-72, Highlands Jr HS 1972-78, Ocmulgee Acad 1978-79, Humes Jr HS 1979-80, Munford-Ellis Jr HS 1980-82, Bacon Cty HS 1982-86; Instr Brewton Parker Coll Evening Division 1984-89; Teacher Toombs Cntrl HS 1986; Instr Pikes Peak Comm Coll 1987; Teacher Vidalia HS 1986-; *ai:* NEA 1970-86; PAGE 1986-; DCCTM, GCTM, NCTM 1970-; Wkshp Leader GCTM Regional Convention 1987; *home:* Rt 1 Box 395 Chula GA 31733

EIGENFELD, PETER BILL, Eighth Grade Teacher; *b:* Rushville, NE; *m:* Janice Ruth Blanchard; *c:* Bethany A.; *ed:* (BA) Elem Ed, 1975, (MA) Educl Admin, 1981 Concordia Coll; *cr:* Internship/5th Grade Teacher Trinity Luth Sch 1973-74; 5th Grade Teacher St Peters Luth Sch 1975; 5th/6th Grade Teacher 1975-81, 8th Grade Teacher/Youth Services Dir 1981-87, 8th Grade Teacher/Youth Services Dir/Asst Prin 1987- Immanuel Luth Sch; *ai:* Sci Dept Head; Sci Fair Coord; Boys Sftbl & Bsktbl Coach; Supervising Teacher; Sch Accreditation, Math, Sci, Art Curr Review Comms; Luth Ed Assn 1975-; NSTA 1980-; N IL Dist Luth Church (Stewardship, Life Bd) 1988-; N IL Teachers Conference Bd Resolutions Comm Chm 1985-87; Seminar Leader 1989-; Research Survey & Analysis Article Published 1989; *office:* Immanuel Luth Sch 832 Lee St Des Plaines IL 60016

EIKENBERG, BABETTE METCALF, Principal; *b:* Brownsville, TX; *m:* Ronnie D.; *c:* Christopher A., Amy K.; *ed:* (BA) Phys Ed - Cum Laude, 1980, (MED) Supervision/Bio, 1989 Sam Houston Univ; Life Sci Fellow, Baylor Coll of Medicine 1987; *cr:* Teacher/Coach Conroe HS 1980-89; Prin Sacred Heart Elem 1989-; *ai:* Oversee All Extracurricular Act; NSTA Awds & Recognition Comm 1987-89; ATPE Building Comm 1984, Certificate 1984; Presenter at NSTA Convention 1988; *home:* 3177 E Shore Dr Willis TX 77378

EIKHOF, KATHLEEN JANE, Sixth Grade Teacher; *b:* Jersey City, NJ; *ed:* (BS) Ed, SUNY Brockport 1974; (MED) Ed, SUNY New Paltz 1977; Admin, CAS; *cr:* Teacher Round Hill Elem 1975-; *ai:* HS Cross Cntry & Vlybl Coach; Currently Teaching HS Equivalency Orange Cty BOCES; Union Building Rep; Washingtonvilles NYSUT Dist Rep; *office:* Round Hill Elem Sch Rt 208 N Washingtonville NY 10992

EIKLEBERRY, JANET KAUSKEY, Third Grade Teacher; *b:* Bellaire, OH; *m:* Roy W.; *c:* H. Greg Porter, Clark D. Porter, Scott L. Porter; *ed:* (MS) Elem Ed, OH Univ 1974; (MS) Elem Admin, Univ of Dayton 1985; *cr:* Teacher Beallsville Elem 1974-; *ai:* Parenting Wkshp 1990; *office:* Beallsville Elem Sch St Rt 145 Beallsville OH 43716

EILERS, BARBARA RUTH, Second Grade Teacher; *b:* Pana, IL; *m:* John; *c:* Dee Ann Carroll, Joni White, Nancy Stupek; *ed:* (BA) Elem Ed, Greenville Coll 1968; (MA) Sociology, Sangamon St Univ 1976; *cr:* Kndgtn Teacher Lincoln Sch 1959-61; 1st Grade Teacher 1963-65, EMH Teacher 1965-66, Kndgtn/Remedial Rdng Teacher 1966-67 Tower Hill Elem Sch; 3rd Grade Teacher Rosamond Elem Sch 1967-76; 2nd Grade Teacher Lincoln & Washington Elem 1976-; *ai:* Curr Chairperson; Head Teacher 1984-; Chrstn Cty Sci Resource Person; Pana Ed Assn (VP 1978-79, Pres 1979-80); IL Ed Assn, NEA 1959-; Pana Against Drug Dependency 1983-; *office:* Washington Elem Sch 200 S Sherman Pana IL 62557

EIMERMANN, FREDERICK O., Math/Computer Teacher; *b:* Milwaukee, WI; *m:* Kathryn A. Holzhauzer; *c:* Brett, Dana; *ed:* (BS) Math, Univ of WI Milwaukee 1979; *cr:* Teacher/Coach Pulaski HS 1979-80, Hamilton HS 1980-; *ai:* Head Bsbl Coach; Ftbl & Girls Bsktbl Asst Coach; *office:* Hamilton HS W220 N6151 Town Line Rd Sussex WI 53089

EINHAUS, SANDRA LYNN (GREEN), Fourth Grade Teacher; *b:* Huntington, IN; *m:* John William; *c:* Tyler, Emily; *ed:* (BS) Elem Ed/Phys Ed, Marion Coll 1982; (MS) Elem Ed, Ball St Univ 1989; *cr:* Teacher Napoleon Elem Sch 1982-; *ai:* Stu Cncl, Math-A-Thon Spon; Buddy System Comm; Elem & Jr HS Bsktbl, Vlybl Coach; United Meth Church Outreach Chairperson 1990; *home:* R 2 Box 422 Osgood IN 47037

EINHORN, KENNETH MARK, Health Teacher; *b:* Brooklyn, NY; *m:* Roni; *c:* Nathan; *ed:* (BA) Health Ed, Brooklyn Coll 1972; (MA) Guidance/Psychological Services, Springfield Coll 1973; *cr:* Health Educator New Rochelle HS 1980-82, Iona Coll, 1988-89, Albert Leonard Mid Sch 1977-; *ai:* Zeta Beta Tau Mem 1967-72; *home:* 37 Brewster Woods Brewster NY 10509

EIPPERLE, RUTH E., 4th Grade Teacher; *b:* Ida, MI; *m:* Lauren W.; *c:* Larry (dec); *ed:* (BS) Eng/Soc Stud/Sci/Art, 1960, (MA) Elem Ed, 1965 E MI Univ; *cr:* 4th Grade Teacher Ida Public Sch 1956-; *ai:* IEA (AR Treas); MEA, NEA.

EIRIKSSON, SANDRA BURNS, Science Teacher; *b:* Dover, DE; *m:* Dale; *c:* Amanda; *ed:* (BS) Bio, SW TX St Univ 1980; (MS) Bio, Univ of W FL 1988; Doctoral Prgm Scndry Sci Ed, FL St Univ; *cr:* Teacher/Dept Chairperson Ruckel Mid Sch 1983-89; Teacher Niceville HS 1989-; Assoc Instr Okaloosa-Walton Comm Coll 1989-; *ai:* SECURE Environmental Awarenessw Club, Amnesty Intnl, FL Jr Sci Engineering & Hum Symposium Spon; SOAR Frosh Academic Adv; NSTA 1989-; FL Assn Sci Teachers 1986-; Phi Delta Kappa 1988-; Playground Area YMCA 1990; Northwest FL Track Club 1984-; Pensacola Runners Assn 1987-; FDOE Model Technology Sch Grant 1988; Teacher of Yr Ruckel Mid Sch 1988; Optical Society of America Educators Day Awd 1989; *home:* 398 Lincoln Ave Valparaiso FL 32580

EIS, TERRY, English/Social Science Teacher; *b:* Tacoma, WA; *m:* John M.; *c:* Ashley, Erin; *ed:* (BA) Soc Sci/Eng, Friends Univ 1977; (MA) Liberal Art, Southwestern Coll 1990; *cr:* Eng Teacher Arkansas City HS 1977-79; Soc Sci/Eng Teacher Winfield HS 1979-; *ai:* NEA 1988-; *office:* Winfield HS 300 Viking Blvd Winfield KS 67156

EISELE, DARRYL J., English Teacher; *b:* Burbank, CA; *m:* Judy Johnson; *c:* Joe, John, Jeff, Julie; *ed:* (BA) Eng, CA St Chico 1984; *cr:* Co-Dir N CA Writing Project 1983-; Teacher Paradise HS 1984-; Dir Paradise Project for At-Risk Youth 1989-; *ai:* Future Teachers Club Spon; NCTE 1983-; CA Assn Teachers of Eng 1984-87; *office:* Paradise HS 5911 Maxwell Paradise CA 95969

EISEMAN, JAMES JOHN, High School Principal; *b:* Bismark, ND; *m:* Sharon Entzi; *c:* Kim, Cherre, Trent; *ed:* (BA) Math, Valley City St 1974; (MA) Scndry Admin, Northern St 1985; *cr:* Math Teacher 1974-80, Prin/Math Teacher 1981- Strasburg Public Sch; *ai:* Stu Cncl Adv; ND Assn Scndry Sch Prin 1981-; NASSP 1988-89; City Cncl 1986-; Ec Dev Corporation VP 1989-; *home:* Box 195 Strasburg ND 58573

EISENBISE, JANET MERCER, 2nd Grade Teacher; *b:* Pendleton, IN; *c:* Ruth, Jennifer Blake, Rachel; *ed:* (BS) Elem Ed, 1973, (MA) Ed, 1977 Ball St Univ; *cr:* 3rd Grade Teacher 1973-75, 1st Grade Teacher, 1975-81 Jackson Elem Sch; 1st Grade Teacher 1981-85, 2nd Grade Teacher, 1985- Lapel Elem Sch; *ai:* NEA 1973-; Amer Assn Univ Women (Historian 1985-87, Treas 1989-91); *home:* 2642 W Mercer Dr Pendleton IN 46064

EISENBRAUN, IVA ALBIN, Elementary Substitute Teacher; *b:* Wall, SD; *m:* Reinhold P.; *c:* Barbara Crawford, David, Norman, Ruth Beckwith; *ed:* (BS) Elem Ed, Black Hills St Coll 1973; Refresher Courses/Certificate Renewal Elem Ed; *cr:* K-8th Grade Teacher Rural Schls in Pennington Cty 1940-69, Rural Schls in Wall Dist 1969-83; Substitute Teaching in Wall Dist 1983-; *ai:* Elem Substitute Teacher Wall Sch Dist; Tau Sigma Phi Mem 1939-40 Achievement Pin 1940; Beta Tau Gamma Mem 1939-40 Achievment Pin 1940; 4-H Club Leader 1948-58, Cloverleaf 10 Yr 1958; Luth Sunday Sch Teacher 1956-68, Public Recognition 1968; Grad Black Hills St Coll Cum Laude Honors in SD 1973; *home:* HCR Box C-6 Creighton SD 57729

EISENHOUR, MICHAEL U., Mathematics Department Chm; *b:* Lebanon, PA; *m:* Martha Pollio; *c:* Lyn, Beth; *ed:* (BS) Math, Juniata Coll 1968; (MED) Scndry Counseling, Shippensburg Univ 1973; Prins Cert, Univ of DE 1986; *cr:* Teacher Cntrl Islip HS 1968-78; Teacher/Chm Cape Henlopen HS 1978-; *ai:* Boys Var Bsktbl Coach; Girls Var Field Hockey Asst Coach; Video Club Adv; Honors Comm & Math Dept Chm; Stu Act Coord; Natl Fed of Interscholastic Coaches Assn, Natl Assn of Bsktbl Coaches, Math Assn of America, Assn for Cmptrs in Ed, NCTM, DE Cncl of Teachers of Math; Rehoboth Beach Lions Club, Prof Picture Framers Assn; Nominee Presidential Awd of Excl in Teaching Math 1980, 1988, 1990; Dist Teacher of Yr 1988-89; DDE Title II Grant; *office:* Cape Henlopen HS Kings Hwy Lewes DE 19958

EISENMAN, JOANN L., Mathematics Teacher; *b:* Peoria, IL; *ed:* (BA) Math, 1971, (MA) Curr/Instruction, 1982 Univ of Northern CO; *cr:* Jr HS Math Teacher Weld Cntrl Jr HS 1971-; *ai:* Chrldr, SADD, Class Spon; Girls Bsktbl Scorekeeper; N Cntrl Evaluation Steering Comm; Dist Math Coord; CEA, NEA, WCTA Treas 1971-; PDK, NCTM Mem 1971-; ASCD Mem 1983-; *office:* Weld Central Jr HS 4977 W C Rd 59 Keenesburg CO 80643

EISNAUGLE, MICHAEL LEE, Science Teacher; *b:* Chillicothe, OH; *m:* Angela Dawn Sexton; *c:* Michael A.; *ed:* (BA) Comm/Sci, Capital Univ 1974; (MA) Sch Counseling, Univ of Dayton 1986; *cr:* Teacher/Coach Vinton Cty HS 1974-76, Jackson HS 1976-87; Teacher Lick Mid Sch 1987-; *ai:* Sci Fair Coord; Hi-Y Club Adv; Lick Sch Advisory Bd; JV Bsbl/Sftbl VarSftbl/Bsktbl Jr HS Ftbl Coach; United Commercial Travelers 1980-; Wesley Church Layspeaker 1979- 1986-; Gideons Intnl 1980-; Open Doors Ministry 1981-; Poet; *home:* 240 W Huron St Jackson OH 45640

EK, KAREN ESTHER, Music Department Chair; *b:* Chippewa Falls, WI; *ed:* (BA) Vocal Music, 1964, (MST) Scndry Ed/Music, 1977 Univ of WI Eau Claire; Grad Stud Univ of MN, Hamline Univ, Vandercook Coll, Indianhead Arts Center; *cr:* Vocal Music/Dept Chairperson Ladysmith HS & Ladysmith-Hawkins Public Schls 1964-; *ai:* Sr Class Adv; Swing Choir; SEC Dept Chairperson; Fogarty Schlsp Comm; LHS Fnd Bd; NW WI Ed Assn Pres 1975; Music Educators Natl Conference & WI MEC; Amer Choral Dir Assn, WI Choral Dir Assn WI Bd of Dirs 1984-88; Univ of WI Eau Claire Alumni Assn Pres 1975-76; Dist Teacher of Yr 1978; Outstanding Educator Ladysmith Jaycees 1988; Outstanding Young Women of America 1970; *office:* Ladysmith HS 1700 Edgewood Ave E Ladysmith WI 54848

EKLEBERRY, LEE EDWARD, Art Teacher; *b:* Tiffin, OH; *m:* Nancy Melvin; *c:* Andrew, Sarah; *ed:* (BS) Art Ed, Bowling Green St Univ 1968; (PHD) Art Ed, OH St Univ 1983; OH Peace Officers Certificate Upper Arlington Police Acad 1982; *cr:* Instr O M Scott & Sons 1970-75; Lecturer OH St Univ 1979-81; Art Teacher Grandview Heights HS 1981-; Hum Instr Columbus St Comm Coll 1990; *ai:* NHS Selection Comm; Drug & Alcohol Intervention & Prevention Team; Asst Wrestling Coach; MAT Statistician, Yrbk, Art Club Adv; SADD Founder & Advised Chapter; Led Several Stu Tours Europe & NY; NAEA 1981-; OH Art Ed Assn Regional VP 1982, VIO Awd 1982; NEA, OEA, GNEA 1981-; Upper Arlington Auxiliary Police Assn Treas 1980-, 1st Pl in Police Acad 1982; Martha Holden Jennings Fnd Scholar; Grandview Heights City Schls Teacher of Yr 1989; Served on 6 N Cntrl Evaluation Visitiation Teams; Numerous 1 Man & Juried Art Shows; Illustrated Appalachian Biography Book 1986; Published Article 1989; *office:* Grandview Heights Hs 1587 W 3rd Ave Columbus OH 43212

EKLUND, JANELLE M., English Teacher; *b:* Waco, TX; *m:* Rolf; *c:* Charles, Katie; *ed:* (BA) Eng, Baylor Univ 1955; (MLA) Liberal Arts, TCU 1985; *cr:* Teacher Luth Parochial 1959-61, Richland HS 1969-; *ai:* Whiz Quiz; Delta Kappa Gamma 1988-; NCTE; *office:* Richland HS 5201 Holiday Ln E Fort Worth TX 76180

EKLUND, NANCY RASO, Elementary Phys Ed Specialist; *b:* Austin, MN; *m:* Byron; *c:* Christopher, Lauren; *ed:* (BS) Phys Ed, 1975, (BS) Spec Ed, 1975 St Cloud St Univ; (MS) Early Chldhd/Spec Ed, Univ of N CO 1989; Qualities of Good Instruction, Gesell Inst of Human Dev; *cr:* Spec Ed Teacher Monroe Jr HS 1975-78; Elem Phys Ed Specialist Washington/Roosevelt Sch 1978-; *ai:* Sch Dist #2 Wellness Comm; WY Alliance for Health, Phys Ed, Recreation, Dance (VP Dance 1985-87, Pres 1988-), Honor Awd 1987, Elem Phys Ed Teacher of Yr 1988; NEA, WEA; Amer Heart Assn 1988-; United Way; Roosevelt Sch Teacher of Yr 1988; St & Regional Conferences Presenter; *office:* Washington Roosevelt Sch 750 W 5 N Green River WY 82935

EL-HOSNI, NINA BOND, Substitute Teacher; *b:* Russellville, AR; *m:* Hazim Abdullah; *c:* Rebecca El-Hosni Messner; *ed:* (BS) Elem Ed, Univ of MO Kansas 1968; *cr:* 2nd Grade Teacher 1968-72, 1st Grade Teacher 1972-87 Spring Branch Elem Sch; Substitute Teacher Chapel Hill Early Chldhd Center 1990; *ai:* Independence Teachers Assn, NEA 1968-87; Presbyn Church Lifetime Mem; Spring Branch PTA (Historian 1983-85) 1968-87; Outstanding Elem Teachers of America Awd 1973; *home:* 9717 Timber Meadows Lees Summit MO 64063

EL-KHOURI, BARBARA ANN, Math Teacher; *b:* Andrews, NC; *ed:* (BS) Ed, Western Carolina 1979; *cr:* 9th/10th Grade Remedial Math & Eng Teacher Andrews HS 1979-80; 6th Grade Self Contained 1980-81, 6th-8th Grade Math Teacher & 6th Grade Lang Arts/Health & Phys Ed Teacher 1982-82, 6th-8th Grade Math & 6th Grade Lang Arts & 7th-8th Grade Girls Health & Phys Ed 1982-83, 6th-8th Grade Lang Arts & 6th Grade Health & Phys Ed 1983-84 Peachtree Elem; 8th Grade Math Teacher 1984-88, 7th Grade Math Teacher 1987- Carrington Jr HS; *ai:* Pep Club Adv; Track Scorekeeper; Team Adv; Catholic Young Adults Leader 1987-88; *office:* Carrington Jr H S 227 Mitton Rd Durham NC 27712

ELAM, PAT WAYNE, 1st Grade Teacher; *b:* Dallas, TX; *m:* Debra M. Vickery Elam; *c:* Matthew R., Mark R.; *ed:* (BA) Music Ed, Dallas Bapt Univ 1974; Univ of Houston Clear Lake; *cr:* 4th Grade Teacher Almeda Baptist Sch 1975-76; 3rd Grade Teacher 1976-86; 1st Grade Teacher 1986- Broadway Baptist; *ai:* Minister of Music Broadway Baptist Church; Deacon Broadway Baptist Church; Secy Deacon Body Broadway Baptist Church.

ELAM, REBA J., English Teacher; *b:* Memphis, TX; *m:* W. N.; *c:* Debbie, Brad; *ed:* (BA) Eng, W TX St Univ 1963; Grad Stud W TX St Univ; *cr:* Eng Teacher Caprock HS 1963-68, Tascosa HS 1979-; *ai:* 9th Grade Chrldr, Youth for Christ, TAFE Spon; CARE Bowling Club Team Leader; Cooperative Learning Team; Hall of Fame Comm; Delta Kappa Gamma 1987-; St Stephen Meth Church (UMW Pres 1978-79, Admin Bd, Ed Commission Chm) 1974-; Outstanding Sch Teachers TX Excl Awd; *office:* Tascosa HS 3921 Westlawn Amarillo TX 79102

ELANDER, RODGER F., JR., Mathematics Teacher; *b:* Pleasantville, NY; *ed:* (BA) Phys Ed, Denison Univ 1985; Grad Courses OH St Univ; *cr:* Math Teacher Brookhaven HS 1985-; *ai:* Jr Var Bsktbl Coach; Asst Coach Var Ftbl, Sftbl; Columbus Ed Assn, OH Ed Assn, NEA; Columbus City League Ftbl Coaches Assn; *office:* Brookhaven HS 4077 Karl Rd Columbus OH 43224

ELARDO, ROBERT ANTHONY, Soc Studies/Eng Teacher; *b:* Buffalo, NY; *m:* Rosalie Germain De Reu; *c:* Jason, Justin; *ed:* (BS) His, Canisius Coll 1967; (MA) Amer His, St Louis Univ 1969; (MS) Scndry Ed, Canisius Coll 1971; *cr:* Scndry Teacher Buffalo Public Schls 1969-; Lecturer NY St Univ Buffalo 1989-; *ai:* Var Soccer Coach; Newspaper & Yrbk Adv; Outdoor Ed; Sch Advisory Comm; Buffalo Teachers Fed; Building Delegate; Dept Chm; Soc Stud; SADD Adv; Phi Alpha Theta 1967-70; NEA 1969-; Lake Shore Little League Dir 1982-85; Young Amer Soccer Treas 1983-85; BRIET SUNY Buffalo Clinical Faculty; NEH Collaborative Hum Prgm SUNY Buffalo; NEH Study of Immigration Wells Coll; Buffalo Teacher Center Grant Outdoor Ed; Mentor Teacher Buffalo Public Schls; *office:* Buffalo Alternative HS 280 Oak St Buffalo NY 14203

ELDER, BARBARA ANN, 5th Grade Math Teacher; *b:* Muscatine, IA; *ed:* (AA) Elem Ed, Muscatine Comm Coll 1971; (BA) Elem Ed, Northeast MO St Univ 1974; *cr:* 6th Grade Teacher 1974-75, 5th Grade Teacher 1975-77 Novinger Sch Dist; 5th Grade Teacher West Liberty Comm Schls 1977-; *home:* RR 1 Box 27-A Nichols IA 52766

ELDER, CARLYN LANG, Social Studies Dept Chair; *b:* Cuero, TX; *m:* John Fletcher III; *c:* John F. IV, Scott C.; *ed:* (BA) Ed/Span, 1957, (MA) Ed/His, 1967 S Meth Univ; (DAED) Curr/Cmptrs, George Mason Univ 1988; Video Disk Interactive; *cr:* Teacher Sierra Vista Jr HS 1968-69, Enterprise HS 1969-70; Asst Professor Troy St Univ 1970-74; Teacher/Dept Chairperson Falls Church HS 1974-; *ai:* Natl His Day Adv; Soc Stud Dept Chairperson; Girls Vlybl Coach; NCSS; Annandale United Meth Church Admin Bd Chairperson 1984-87; Delta Kappa Gamma St Nominations 1989-, Schlsp Awd 1985; Capitol Historical Society Outstanding Teacher/Historian Awd; Database & 10 Units in Project Published; Grants for Developing Local His Curr, Cmptrs & Soc Stud Curr; *home:* 3911 Mill Creek Dr Annandale VA 22003

ELDER, JOSEPH DAVID, World/Amer History Teacher; *b:* Heavener, OK; *c:* Jeffrey, Lesley; *ed:* (BA) His, 1972; (MA) His, 1980 Northeastern St Univ; Law, Tulsa Univ; *cr:* Teacher Wagoner HS 1972-75; Union HS 1975-; Tulsa Jr Coll 1989; *ai:* Union His Club; Coaching SocceR; Prin Slection Comm; OK Historical Society 1990; Phi Alha Theta Pres 1972; Union Classroom Teachers Assn Pres 1977-79; Northeastern OK Adult Soccer Assn VP; *home:* 2711 S 119 E Ave Tulsa OK 74129

ELDER, KAREN IONE (SAGEMAN), Earth Science Teacher; *b:* Pasadena, CA; *c:* Kimberly K., Teresa L.; *ed:* (AA) Geology, Glendale Comm Coll 1977; (BS) Geology, 1980, (BS) Scndry Ed, 1980 Univ of ID; ID St Univ, W WA Univ, E WA Univ, Seattle Pacific Univ; *cr:* Math/Sci Teacher Blackfoot Alternative Sch 1981-82; Math Teacher Pocatello-Highland HS 1982-83; Sci Teacher Marysville Jr HS 1983-; *ai:* Phi Theta Kappa 1977; Marysville Rock & Gem Club Treas 1988-; *office:* Marysville Jr HS 1605 7th St Marysville WA 98270

ELDER, MARGO MITCHELL LAWSON, Seventh Grade Teacher; *b:* Upland Township, PA; *m:* Tony D.; *c:* Tony D. II, Daniel N.; *ed:* (BA) Anthropology/Sociology, Univ of IA 1972; (MED) Rdng/Lang Arts, Univ of NC 1978; Cert as Academically Gifted Teacher at Lenoir-Rhyne Coll; *cr:* Classroom Teacher E Franklin Jr HS 1972, J S Spivey Jr HS 1972-76; Chapter I Rdng Teacher 1978-82, Classroom Teacher 1982 Grandview Mid Sch; *ai:* Vlybl Coach 1978-79; Sch Newspaper Spon 1979-80, 1986-87; 7th Grade Team Leader 1988-89; Soc Stud Dept Head 1989-; NEA 1982-; NC Assn of Educators 1982-; Taylorsville Presbyn Church Deacon 1985-87; Attend NC Center for Advancement of Teaching 1988; *office:* Grandview Mid Sch 737 12th St SW Hickory NC 28602

ELDER, NELL ELIZABETH, Fourth Grade Teacher; *b:* Blue Mountain, MS; *ed:* (BS) Bus Ed, Blue Mountain Coll 1960; (MS) Elem Ed, MS St Univ 1968; *cr:* Teacher Braddagico HS 1960-62; Walnut Elem 1962-67; Ripley Elem 1967-; *ai:* Sch Yrbk; 5 Yr Plan Comm; Instrctnl Mgmt Plan Comm; MS Prof Ed Bldg Rep 1986-88; Chickasaw Nations DAR Regent 1988-; Tippah

Historical/Genealogy (Pres, Sec); Kappa Iota Sec 1986-87; Alpha Deta VP 1987-89; Help Write Instrctnl Mgmt Plan; Evaluatn Comm; Outstndng Teacher of Amer 1973; *home:* Rt 1 Box 179 Blue Mountain MS 38610

ELDER, SHIRLEY BROWN, 8th Grade Eng/Soc Stud Teacher; *b:* Paducah, TX; *m:* Isaac; *c:* Ronita, Isaac C.; *ed:* (BA) Music, Prairie View Univ 1957; (MA) Ed, CA St Los Angeles 1981; *cr:* Teacher Snyder TX 1957-59, Blandford Elem 1963-67, Alvarado Intermediate 1967-68, Rincon Intermediate 1968-; *ai:* Mentor Teacher; Academic-Stan, Guidance, Soc Stud Curr Comm; Journalism; Teacher of Yr 1990; *office:* Rincon Intermediate Sch 2800 E Hollingworth West Covina CA 91792

ELDER, VINCENT K., Mathematics Teacher; *b:* Parkersburg, WV; *m:* Tamy R. Ruble; *c:* Megan, Ross; *ed:* Assoc Electrical Engineering, WA Tech Coll 1982; (BS) Math Ed, OH Univ 1986; *cr:* Math Teacher Frontier HS 1986-; *ai:* Frontier HS Head Ftbl Coach 1989; NHS Comm Mem; Sr Class Adv; Marietta Coll 1985-87 & Marietta HS 1988 Asst Ftbl Coach; OH Cncl Teachers of Math, NEA, Frontier Local Ed Assn Mem 1986-; BSA Asst Scoutmaster 1980, Eagle Scout 1976; Amer Ftbl Coaches Assn Mem 1987; OH HS Coaches Assn Mem 1988-; *home:* Gale Ave Box 622 Newport OH 45768

ELDRICH, MICHAEL K., English Chair; *b:* Helena, MT; *m:* Margaret Lynn; *c:* Elizabeth; *ed:* (BA) Eng, Univ of MT 1981; Fellow Ancient World Inst Univ of ID; Grad Stud Speech, Rdng, Lit, Hum; *cr:* Teacher/Chm Timberline HS 1981-85; Kendrick HS 1985-; *ai:* Annual, Newspaper, Drama Club Adv; Eng Curr Comm; St Dept of Ed (Rater of Writing Proficiency 1985-, Table Leader 1987-89); Grace Nixon Schlsp; Fellow Ancient World Inst; Published Poetry; Grant to Modify Eng Curr; *office:* Kendrick HS Rt 2 Box 6 Kendrick ID 83537

ELDRIDGE, EDNA BOREN, Fifth Grade Teacher; *b:* Porterville, MS; *m:* John Bryan; *c:* Angie, Michele; *ed:* (BS) Elem Ed, MS St Univ 1972; *cr:* 2nd Grade Teacher E Kemper Elem 1972-78; 5th Grade Teacher Kemper Acad 1978-; *ai:* MS Private Sch Assn.

ELDRIDGE, HORTENSE BASS, 5th Grade Lang Art Teacher; *b:* Sampson, NC; *m:* Harvey Allen Jr.; *c:* Harvey A. III, Robert S.; *ed:* (BS) Elem, Campbell Univ 1967; *cr:* 5th Grade Teacher Warrenwood Elem 1967-68, Wayne Avenue 1968-69, Harnett Elem 1969-84, Dunn Mid Sch 1984-; *ai:* Lang Art Lead Teacher; 5th Grade Academically Gifted Teacher; Writing Comm Chm; Rdng Assn 1980-; Tuesday Review Book Club Pres 1978-79; Dunn Mid Sch Teacher of Yr 1988-89; *home:* 1009 Westhaven Dunn NC 28334

ELDRIDGE, PENNY SINGLETON, Teacher of Gifted & Talented; *b:* Berkeley, CA; *m:* Ronald Paul; *c:* Toni, Trina, Tammy; *ed:* (BA) Soc Sci, 1977, (BA) Phys Ed, 1978 CUS Dominguez Hills; Working Towards Masters Admin, CUS Dominguez Hills 1991; Gifted & Talented Instr Trng; *cr:* Teacher Compton & Los Angeles Schls & Lynwood SDA Acad 1977-80; Dept Chairperson 1986-89, Teacher 1980-, Mentor Teacher 1989- Hosler Jr HS; *ai:* Curr, Gifted & Talented, PQR Comm; Chrldr Spon; Girls Sports Facilitator; New Teacher of Yr 1980-81; Gifted & Talented Dist Cmmty Appreciation Awd; *office:* Hosler Jr HS 11300 Spruce St Lynwood CA 90262

ELEAZER, RICHARD ELON, HS Mathematics Teacher; *b:* Corpus Christi, TX; *ed:* (BS) Scndry Ed, 1975, (MS) Educl Admin, 1978 TX A&I; Cmptr Programming, Cmptr Technology; *cr:* Teacher Taft HS 1975-; *ai:* Math Club, UIL Number Sense & Calculator Spon; Building & Leadership Team; Career Ladder Comm; UIL Dist Calculator Applications Dir; TMSCA, NCTM 1985-; MAA 1988-; Taft Ind Sch Dist Teacher of Yr 1990; Nominee Univ TX Ex-Teacher of Yr 1986; *office:* Taft HS 400 College Taft TX 78390

ELEBASH, MARIE BLACKBURN, Gifted Social Studies Teacher; *b:* Birmingham, AL; *m:* Albert Parrish Jr.; *c:* John M. Holloway III, Jeffrey W. Holloway, Joseph P., Daniel H.; *ed:* (BS) Eng, 1962, (MED) Admin/Supervision, 1973 Auburn Univ; Gifted Cert, Univ of Cntrl FL 1985; *cr:* Rdng/Eng Dept Head Goodwyn Jr HS 1963-73; Eng/Journalism Teacher Montgomery Acad 1976-83; Remediation Teacher Edgewood Jr HS & Jefferson HS 1983-84; Gifted Soc Stud Teacher Jefferson Jr HS 1984-; *ai:* Future Problem Solving & Knowledge Master Coach; Project Bus Spon; Alpha Delta Kappa (Publicity Chm 1979, Mem) 1969-; Coached St & Intnl Winning Team Future Problem Solving 1988; 1st Place Future Problem Solving Team for FL Will Compete in Intnl Competition; *home:* 1050 Carrigan Blvd Merritt Island FL 32952

ELI, PAUL STEVE, High School Art Teacher; *b:* Herrin, IL; *m:* Palanita Lazorchak; *c:* Megan L.; *ed:* (AA) Commercial Art, 1968, (BA) Art Ed, 1972 S IL Univ; *cr:* Art Teacher Johnston City HS 1972-; *ai:* Homecoming Act Coord; Sr Class Co-Spon; Musicals Stage Crew Mgr & Scenery Designer; NEA Lifetime Mem; IL Educl Assn, Johnston City Ed Assn 1972-; IL HS Rodeo Assn (Public Relations Dir 1978-81, Pres 1981-84); Downstate Art Educators 1988; Certificate Winner IL Teacher of Yr 1987; Nom for Williamson Cty Sch Bell Awds 1989; IL HS Rodeo Assn & Williamson Cty 4-H Service Recognition 1988; *office:* Johnston City HS 1500 Jefferson St Johnston City IL 62951

ELIAS, WILLIAM EDWARD, Spanish Teacher; *b:* Youngstown, OH; *m:* Janet Kay Terlecki; *c:* Holly A., Christopher J.; *ed:* (AB) Span/Eng, 1964, (MSED) Scndry Principalship, 1971 Youngstown St Univ; *cr:* Lieutenant Military Police US Army 1964-66; Eng Teacher Hillman Jr HS 1966-68; Eng/Span Teacher 1968-, 11th Grade Basics Eng Teacher Woodrow Wilson HS; *ai:* Night/Summer Sch Teacher Youngstown City Schls; Steering & Cntrl Evaluation, NHS Comms Mem; NEOTA, OEA, NEA 1982-; YEA Grievance Rep 1982-; *home:* 4800 Pine Trace Dr Youngstown OH 44515

ELIASON, OSCAR R., Science Teacher; *b:* Duluth, MN; *m:* Carole; *c:* Greg, Paul, Wendy, Scott; *ed:* (BS) Biological Sci, Univ of MN Duluth 1962; Univ of MN 1967-68; Mankato St 1980; Univ of MN Duluth; *cr:* Sci Teacher Cromwell HS 1962-; *ai:* Head Girls Bsktbl Coach; Athletic Dir; MN Girls Bsktbl Coaches Assn, MN Sci Teachers Assn, MN Athletic Dir Assn; Cromwell Volunteer Fire Dept 1966-78; *office:* Cromwell HS Hwy 210 & 73 Cromwell MN 55726

ELIOPULOS, BETTY, Spanish & French Teacher; *b:* Marysville, CA; *ed:* (BA) Span, CA St Univ Sacramento 1971; Grad Stud CA St Univ Sacramento, Univ of CA Berkeley, Universidad De Guadalajara Mexico; *cr:* Span/Fr Teacher Jackson HS 1972-77; Span Teacher Extension Prgm San Joaquin Delta Jr Coll 1974-77; Span/Fr/Span Advanced Placement Teacher Lincoln HS 1977-; *ai:* Foreign Lang Club Adv; Schlsp Comm Mem; Advanced Placement Coord; CTA, Foreign Lang Assn of Greater Sacramento, Delta Kappa Gamma; CA St Railroad Museum, Crocker Art Museum Assn, Sacramento Symphony Assn; *office:* Lincoln HS 1081 7th St Lincoln CA 95648

ELIZEY, GEORGIA ROBINSON, Chemistry Teacher; *b:* Magnolia, MS; *m:* William; *c:* Christopher; *ed:* (BS) Bacteriology/Chem, Southern St Univ 1973; (MS) Curr/Instruction, Cleveland Univ 1982; Hope Coll; *cr:* Chem Teacher Shaw HS 1980-; *ai:* Career Awareness Prgm Sci; Scheduling Comm Mem; Phi Delta Kappa 1986-; NSTA 1981-; Sci Ed Cncl of OH 1984-; Martha Holden Jennings 1988, Master Teacher Awd; Cleveland Regional Sci Teachers 1985-.

ELKINS, HOLLIS L., English Humanities Teacher; *b:* Watertown, SD; *ed:* (BA) Eng, Augustana Coll 1967; (MA) Eng, NM St Univ 1970; (PHD) Amer Stud, Univ of NM 1977; *cr:* Eng Instr Univ of TX El Paso 1970-73; Instr Women Stud Univ of NM 1977-79; Eng/Hum Instr Rio Grande HS 1981-; Eng Instr Coll Division Voc Tech Inst 1988-; *ai:* Academic Decathlon Coach; Research Spon 1985-; NM Cncl of Teachers of Eng (Presenter 1986, Conference Evaluator 1987-88) 1983-; Sporting Women, Albuquerque Roadrunners 1987-; Runners & Walkers Club 1989-; Honors Prgm Instrs Chm 1985-; Grad Fellowships NM St Univ; *office:* Rio Grande HS 2300 Arenal Rd SW Albuquerque NM 87105

ELKINS, PATRICIA ANN LAFERLY, Fourth Grade Teacher; *b:* Garrett, KY; *m:* Melvin Douglas; *ed:* (BS) Elem Ed, Pikeville Coll 1965; Morehead St Univ, W MI; Alice Lloyd Coll; *cr:* 4th Grade Teacher Beaver Creek Elem 1965-69; 3rd/4th Grade Teacher Ryan Elem 1969-; *ai:* Bronson Ed Assn, MI Ed Assn, NEA; Amer Cancer Society Reach to Recovery Volunteer; Nom Outstanding Elem Teachers of Amer 1973; *home:* 755 E Chicago Bronson MI 49028

ELKINS, THELMA LUCILLE, Social Studies Teacher; *b:* Bible Grove, IL; *m:* Kenneth W.; *c:* Randall K.; *ed:* (BS) Soc Sci, IL St Univ 1950; (MED) Guidance/Counseling, Univ of IL 1964; *cr:* Soc Stud Teacher Loda Jr HS 1950-52, J W Eater Jr HS 1953-55; 5th Grade Teacher Myna Thompson Elem Sch 1956-57; Soc Stud Teacher/Guidance Cnslr Fisher Cmmty Unit Dist #1 1957-; *ai:* Frosh Class Spon; Jr HS Gifted Prgm; Fisher Ed Assn Pres; IL Ed Assn 1970-78; NEA; Champaign-Urbana News-Gazette & Regional Office of Ed For Champaign-Ford Counties Educators Awd; IL Ed Assn & NEA for Outstanding Service & Contributions to the United Teaching Profession; *home:* 314 E Division St Fisher IL 61843

ELKOWITZ, ANGELA BRADFORD, Business Teacher; *b:* Newport News, VA; *m:* Robert A.; *ed:* (BA) Bus/Distributive Ed, Northwestern St Univ of LA 1987; *cr:* Bus Teacher/Dept Head Hicks HS 1988-; *ai:* Jr/Sr Class & FBLA Spon; NBEA 1988-; LA Bus Educators Assn 1989-; *office:* Hicks HS Gen Del Hwy 121 E Hicks LA 71437

ELKS, ANN PHARR, Elementary Supervisor; *b:* Tar Heel, NC; *m:* William R.; *c:* Marianne Elks Stoudt; *ed:* (BA) Early Chldhd, 1970, Elem Ed, Pembroke St Univ; (MA) Elem Ed, E Carolina Univ 1976; (EDD) Nova Univ 1988; Supt Certificate E Carolina U niv; *cr:* Teacher Bladen Elem Sch 1970-76, Elizabethtown Primary Sch 1976-85; Supvr/Dir Staff Dev Bladen Cty Schls 1985-; *ai:* Elem Curr Supervision; Coord/Dir System-Wide Staff Dev; NC Assn Sch Admins; Phi Delta Kappa; ASCD; NC Assn Gifted Educators, NC Assn of Educators; Delta Kappa Gamma Intnl; GSA Trng Coord; Local Grad Schlsp Grant; Optomist Outstanding Educator Awd; Teacher of Yr Bladen Elem Sch & Elizabethtown Primary Sch; *office:* Bladen Cty Schls PO Box 37 Elizabethtown NC 28337

ELLARD, SANDRA GANDY, History Teacher; *b:* Shreveport, LA; *m:* Hugh P. Jr.; *c:* Samuel B., Benjamin L.; *ed:* (BA) Eng, Millsaps Coll 1981; *cr:* Eng Teacher Mc Adams HS 1982-88; His Teacher East Holmes Acad 1988-; *ai:* Annual Adv; 9th Grade & Beauty Pageant Spon; NCTE 1986-88; Atlala Right to Life Pres 1989-; MS Right to Life Trustee 1989-; 1st Baptist Church (Sunday Sch Teacher, Various Comms) 1982-; STAR Teacher Mc Adams HS 1987; *office:* East Holmes Acad PO Box 247 West MS 39192

ELLEBRACHT, LINDA G. (WALKER), Fifth Grade Teacher; *b:* Abilene, TX; *m:* Dennis S.; *c:* Emily A., John W.; *ed:* (BS) Elem Ed/Eng, Mc Murry Coll 1972; Course Study Psych Human Dev, St Marys Univ; *cr:* Rdng Teacher E Cntrl HS 1976; 4th/5th Grade Teacher Harmony Elem 1976-78, 5th Grade Teacher 1978-, 2nd Grade Teacher 1990 John Glenn Elem; *ai:* St Hedwig Cath Youth Organization Bsbl Coach 1984-85; St Hedwig Cath Youth Organization Leader 1979-; Lone Oak 4-H Spon 1986-88; E Cntrl 4-H & FFA Clubs Fundraisers Comm 1988-; St Marks Luth Church Calling Comm 1989; Beyar Cty 4-H & FFA Fundraisers Comm 1986-; Lone Oak 4-H Pet Clinic 1987; E Cntrl Ind Sch Dist Rdng & Lang Art Curr 1975-78; Assn of TX Prof Educators 1986-; ECTA, TSTA Mem 1976-86; E Cntrl Spec Educators Friends of Spec Ed 1989-; *office:* John Glenn Elem Sch 7284 FM 1628 San Antonio TX 78263

ELLENBECKER, CATHERINE RIEDL, Art Specialist; *b:* Milwaukee, WI; *m:* Thomas L. Sr.; *c:* Mary, Thomas Jr., Timothy, Margaet, Kathleen, Colleen; *ed:* (BS) Art Ed, Mount Mary Coll 1973; (MS) Art Ed, Univ of WI Milwaukee 1982; Grad Stud Various Univ; *cr:* Art Specialist Mother of Good Cncl Sch 1974-80; Art Specialist/Substitute Teaching Ripon Sch Dist & Green Lake Sch Dist 1982-84, Montello Sch Dist 1984-; *ai:* Discipline Comm; Stu Cncl Adv; Dist Art Exhibit & Art Schlsp Fund Drive; Kappa Gamma Pi 1973-; WI Designer Crafts Cncl 1981-; WI Puppetry Guild 1984-; Our Lady of The Lake Religious Ed (Coord 1988-, Instr 9th-12th Grade 1986-); Teacher Recognition Natl Scholastic Art Awds 1987-, & Regional Scholastic Art Awds 1986-; Milwaukee Journal Stu Calendar Art Competition Teacher Recognition 1989-; Five Ctys Prof Art Exhibit; Kohler Art Center Sheboygan WI Juried Entry 1984; WEA Art Showcase, Juried Entry 1989; *office:* Montello Sch Dist 222 Forest Ln Montello WI 53949

ELLER, BRENDA DUNCAN, Fourth Grade Teacher; *b:* Lebanon, TN; *m:* Stephen Brawner; *c:* Mark S., Timothy J., Amy M.; *ed:* (BS) Elem Ed, TN Tech Univ 1976; *cr:* 5th-6th Grade Teacher Pleasant Shade Elem Sch 1967-68; Title I Teacher 1968-69, 4th Grade Teacher 1969- Fairlane Elem Sch; *ai:* Grade Level Chm; Soc Stud Textbook, Spelling Bee, In-Service Comm; TEA, NEA 1967-; MCEA 1968-; Meadorville Missionary Baptist Church 1967-; Career Level III; *home:* Rt 1 Box 22 Pleasant Shade TN 37145

ELLER, LISA OGLE, Math Teacher; *b:* Erwin, TN; *m:* Kevin; *ed:* (BS) Math, 1984, (MED) Scndry Ed, 1988 E TN St Univ; *cr:* Math Teacher Unicoi Cty HS 1984-; *ai:* Math Club, Scholars Bowl, Campus Prayer Group Spon; Math Contest Supvr; TN Teachers Study Cncl System (Chm 1988-, Regional Secy 1988-); Unicoi Cty Ed Assn Treas 1987-88; TN Ed Assn, NEA, Upper E TN Cncl of Math Teachers; Fishery Church Youth Dir 1989-; Unicoi Cty Teacher of Yr 1990; *home:* Rt 1 Box 9A Unicoi TN 37692

ELLERBROCK, SONDRA MARIE, 5th/6th Grade Teacher; *b:* Toledo, OH; *ed:* (BS) Math/Sci/Bus Admin, Aquinas Coll 1981; (MA) Elem Ed, E MI Univ 1986; Regular Participation Wkshp & Prgms To Continue Prof Dev; *cr:* 2nd Grade Teacher 1981-86, Math Tutor 1981-, 5th/6th Grade Teacher 1986- St Mary Sch; *ai:* Math & Sci Dept Chairperson; Sci Fair, Youth Service Coord 1988-; Monroe Cty Dist Sci Fair Steering Comm; NCTM 1983-; Cath Soc Services of Monroe Cty Bd Mem 1986-89; *office:* St Mary Sch 151 N Monroe St Monroe MI 48161

ELLETT, DONNA GEORGE, Retired Teacher; *b:* Los Banos, CA; *m:* Charles Richard; *c:* Robert, Cindi, Kim Galvan, Kris; *ed:* (BA) General Ed, San Jose St 1955; Grad Stud; *cr:* 4th Grade Teacher Robert Bruce Sch 1955-57, 4th Grade Teacher 1957-59, 6th Grade Teacher 1964-67, 5th Grade Teacher 1968-89 Charles Wright Sch; *ai:* AAUW; *home:* 2848 Tahoe Dr Merced CA 95340

ELLING, ANN MARIE EASTMAN, Fourth Grade Teacher; *b:* Rochester, MN; *m:* Michael Frederick; *c:* Sara J., Jesse A.; *ed:* (BS) Elem Ed/Math, 1977, (MS) Teaching/Math 1979 Univ WI River Falls; *cr:* Primary Math Instr Univ WI River Falls Lab Sch 1977-79; Grad Elem Math Instr Univ of WI River Falls 1986-87; 4th Grade Teacher Westside Elem 1979-; *ai:* Math SEC Comm Elem Chairperson; Positive Discipline Comm; Girls 8th Grade Bsktbl Asst Coach; Homework Comm; 4th Grade Dept Unit Leader; WI Ed Assn 1977-; WI Math Cncl; Ezekiel Luth Church Sunday Sch Supvr; River Falls Racquetball & Health Club 1980- Numerous Tournament Awds; Amer Amateur Racquetball Assn; River Falls Days Pageant Comm; River Falls Hosptial Auxillary; Cray Inst Grant Inservice & Materials Restructure Math Teaching; *office:* Westside Elem Sch 1007 W Pine River Falls WI 54022

ELLINGSON, NANCY MAY, English Teacher; *b:* Greenwood, WI; *m:* Donald; *c:* Mary D. Ellingson Du Bois, Laural K. Schindler. Thomas F.; *ed:* (BS) Art/Eng, UW La Crosse 1971; (MS) Art Ed, Winona St Univ 1977; *cr:* Teacher La Crescent Sch Dist 1971, La Crosse Sch Dist 1972-, Winona St Univ 1976-77; *ai:* Adv for Creative Writing Magazine; NEA; WEA; WCTE; NCTE; Kappa Deta Pi; Taught Eng in Poland with UNESCO 1981; Poetry Published in Various Little Literary Magazines; Public Readings of Poetry; Paintings Exhibited Including Milwaukee Art Museum & Rochester Art Center.

ELLIOT, MARY ELLEN, Kindergarten Teacher; *b:* Wichita Falls, TX; *m:* Paul Y. Jr.; *c:* Eric, Nathan, Aaron, Larkin; *ed:* (BA) Music, Midwestern St Univ 1964; Teacher Cert Kndgtn Endorsement, Univ of TX 1974; Rndg, Midwestern St Univ; *cr:* Kndgtn Aubrey Ind Sch Dist 1974-75; Kndgtn 1976-, 1st Grade Music Teacher 1989- Holliday Ind Sch Dist; *ai:* Uil Band Stu Accompanist; Assn of TX Prof Educators; 1st United Meth

Church Chancel Choir; Composed PTA Prgms Songs; *office:* Holliday Ind Sch Dist 751 College St Holliday TX 76366

ELLIOT, MARY WILLIAMS, 6th-8th Grade Reading Teacher; *b:* Monroe, NC; *m:* James E.; *c:* Mario J.; *ed:* (BA) Eng, Barber Scotia Coll 1965; (MA) Ed, Univ of NC Charlotte 1976; *cr:* HS Teacher 1965-66, 8th Grade Lang Arts/Phys Ed Teacher 1966-67 Winchester Avenue Sch; Teacher Monroe Mid Sch 1968-; *ai:* Monroe Schls Drop Out Prevention Prgm Co-Chairperson; NC Teaching Fellows Steering Comm Mem Monroe Schls; Monroe HS Band Nominating Comm; Monroe City Assn of Classroom Teachers (Secy 1977-78, Pres 1978-79, Treas 1980-81); Union Cty Bd of Elections Precinct Judge 1988-89; Initiative Awd for Mid Sch Parent Involvement 1989; *home:* 304 Turner St Monroe NC 28110

ELLIOT, SHERLENE (JOHNSON), Business Teacher; *b:* Tupelo, OK; *m:* Bill; *c:* Donette Johnston; *ed:* (BS) Bus Ed, 1976, (MS) Ed, 1979 E Cntrl Univ; Lib Sci, Voc Office Courses; *cr:* Bus Teacher Pittsburg HS 1976-82; Bus Teacher/Librarian 1982-86, Voc Office Instr 1986- Allen HS; *ai:* Jr Class Spon; FBLA & Yrbk Adv; OK Ed Assn, NEA, OK Bus Ed Assn, OK Voc Assn, NBEA, AVA, Natl Assn of Classroom Educators in Bus Ed; *home:* Rt 1 Box 227 Stonewall OK 74871

ELLIOTT, BARBARA ANN, Fifth Grade Teacher; *b:* San Diego, CA; *m:* James Francis; *c:* Jennifer Marie Elliott Amthor; *ed:* (BA) Soc Sci, San Diego St 1970; (ME) Ed, Pepperdine 1979; *cr:* 5th Grade Teacher Fuerte Elem 1970-; *ai:* Phys Ed Coord; Math Chm; Glee Club Teacher; Site Planning Comm; Phi Delta Kappa 1989-; *office:* Fuerte Elem Sch 11625 Fuerte Dr El Cajon CA 92020

ELLIOTT, CAROLYN SUE (BENNETT), Science Teacher; *b:* Barbourville, KY; *m:* Leonard Charles; *c:* John, Thomas, Donald; *ed:* (BS) Health/Phys Ed, Cumberland Coll 1973; (MA) Ed Health Emp, Union Coll 1976; Rank I in Ed; *cr:* Teacher Jesse D Lay Elem Sch 1974-; *ai:* Beta Club Spon; NEA; KY Ed Assn Delegate 1976; Mem Cntrl Baptist Church; *home:* PO Box 793 Barbourville KY 40906

ELLIOTT, DEB K., Counselor; *b:* Chelsea, MI; *m:* Craig; *c:* Michelle, Heath; *ed:* (BA) Speech Comm, 1980, (MS) Scndry Ed, 1984 Wichita St Univ; Counseling Cert 1989; *cr:* Asst Forensic Coach Wichita St Univ 1980-81; Teacher Goddard HS 1981-82; Teacher 1982-89, Cnslr 1989- Maize HS; *ai:* NHS; Sr Class Spon; *office:* Maize HS 4600 N Maize Rd Maize KS 67101

ELLIOTT, DONNA FLEMING, Kindergarten Teacher; *b:* Grayson, KY; *m:* Lowell T.; *c:* Brad, Mary J.; *ed:* (AB) Elem Ed, 1980; (MAED) Elem and Early Chldhd Ed, 1981 Morehead St Univ; Rank I, Elem Ed; *cr:* 3rd/4th/5th Grade Teacher Blaine Elem Sch 1981-88; K/Kndgtn Teacher Blaine Elem Sch 1988-; *ai:* NEA 1981; KY Ed Assn 1981-; Lawrence Cty Ed Assn 1981 ; Lawrence Cty Organization of Teachers 1987-; *home:* 2249 Sherwood Dr Grayson KY 41143

ELLIOTT, JANE ANN, First Grade Teacher; *b:* Painesville, OH; *ed:* (BA) Elem Ed, OH Univ 1972; (SS) Elem Ed, WV Univ 1976; *cr:* 1st Grade Teacher Mt Pleasant Elem 1972-88, Adena Elem 1988-; *ai:* OEA, NEA 1972-; Order of Eastern Star 1971-; *home:* Box 55 East St Mount Pleasant OH 43939

ELLIOTT, JANICE HAUGHT, First Grade Teacher; *b:* Mannington, WV; *m:* Daniel Peter; *c:* Mary E. Strickland, Dana M., Amy L.; *ed:* (BA) Elem Ed, Fairmont St 1960; (MS) Rdng, Old Dominion Univ 1972; *cr:* Teacher Portlock Elem 1975-; *ai:* Band Parents; Head Chaperone Band Trips; Rdng Cncl; Church Nursery Dept Leader 1980-; *office:* Portlock Elem Sch 1857 Varsity Dr Chesapeake VA 23324

ELLIOTT, JUDITH CAROL, HS English Teacher; *b:* Long Beach, CA; *m:* Damon D.; *c:* James, Devlin; *ed:* (BA) Eng, Univ of WA 1965; Continuing Ed Natl Writing Projects Open Prgm Univ of CA Davis 1987; *cr:* 6th Grade Teacher Incline Village Elem 1969-70; 7th-12th Grade Eng Teacher Capital Chrstn Sch 1986-; *ai:* Jr & Sr Class, Aeronautics Club Adv; Curr Comm; Early Chld Ed Comm Multi-Cultural Comm Chm 1976-77; PTA VP 1977-78; Under 10 Youth Soccer Coach 1980-81; Cmmty Club Chm 1984-85; Care Home Sunday Ministry 1983-; *home:* 14974 Anillo Way Rancho Murieta CA 95863

ELLIOTT, SHIRLEY NICHOLS, English Teacher; *b:* Quincy, IL; *m:* Charles Keith; *c:* David, Teresa Soard, Sharon Hall, Mary B. Harper; *ed:* (BA) Phys Ed, Eureka Coll 1955; Courses Univ of S FL, Miami-Dade Comm Coll, Valencia Comm Coll, Jacksonville Univ; *cr:* 12th Grade Eng/Speech Teacher South Side HS 1963-64; Phys Ed/12th Grade Eng Teacher North Side HS 1964-66; Phys Ed Teacher Carthage Cmmty HS 1967-70; 8th Grade Eng Teacher South West Jr HS 1973-75; Eng/Speech Teacher Lakeland Highlands 1975-78; 9th Grade Eng Teacher Westminster Chrstn Sch 1978-81; 8th Grade Eng Teacher Meadowbrook Mid Sch 1985-; *ai:* Stu Recognition Comm Chm; NEA, CTA, FTA 1985-; Commission of Ministry Secy 1988-; FL Chrstn Womens Fellowship (Study Chm, Dist Coord); *office:* Meadowbrook Mid Sch 6000 North Ln Orlando FL 32808

ELLIOTT, WILMA COOPER, Sixth Grade Teacher; *b:* Harman, WV; *m:* G. Douglas; *c:* Mathew; *ed:* (BA) Phys Ed/Eng, Shepherd Coll 1971; (MA) Health Ed, WV Univ 1976; Elem Ed; *cr:* Eng/Speech Teacher Charles Town Jr HS 1972-75; Eng/Phys Ed Cass Dist Jr HS 1975-76; 6th Grade Teacher Wadestown Grade Sch 1976-; *ai:* 4th/5th Grade Bsktbl Coach; NEA, WV Ed Assn 1972-; Wadestown PTA Secy Lifetime Mem 1982, Phoebe Hearst Awd; *office:* Wadestown Grade Sch R R 1 Wadestown WV 26589

ELLIOTT-BANKS, JANICE DUNLAP, 8th Grade English Teacher; *b:* Washington, DC; *m:* Calvin; *c:* Michelle Elliott, Kimberly Elliott, Charles, Anthony, Charmaine; *ed:* (BS) Eng, DC Teachers Coll 1972; (MAT) Rdng, Trinity Coll 1981; *cr:* Stu Teacher Exch Coord DC Teachers Coll 1972-73; Eng Teacher J Watson Bailey Jr HS 1973-74; Bladensburg Jr HS 1974-77; Greenbelt Mid Sch 1978-; *ai:* Adv Stu Government Assn; Mem Faculty Advisory Comm-Natl Jr Honor Society; Mem Effective Schls Comm; MSTA; Zeta Phi Beta Inc; Tots & Teens Inc; Certificates & Letters of Commendation for Public Service; *office:* Greenbelt Mid Sch 8950 Edmonston Rd Greenbelt MD 20770

ELLIS, ARTHUR FOBES, English Teacher; *b:* Peru, IN; *m:* Viva M. Burket; *c:* Arthur R., Steven D., Ivan L., Peter D., Sylvia Erdile, Rita Kemple, Carolyn S.; *ed:* (BS) Soc Stud/Scndry Ed, Manchester Coll 1949; (MS) Eng Equivalent, Butler Univ 1953; Manchester Coll, In Univ, De Pauw Univ, Ball St Univ; *cr:* Teacher Liberty Sch 1949-50, Peru Cmmty Schls 1950-89; *ai:* Eng Instr of Gifted & Talented; Finish Line Track Coord Drama Wkshp Wabash valley Arts Consortium; IN St Teachers Assn 1949-; NEA Life Mem; Peru Cmmty Ed Assn 1950-; Foresters Vice Chief Ranger 1956-; IN Sheriffs Assn; Natl Rifle Assn; Natl Sci Fnd Wkshp Summer 1959; Natl Sci In-Service Fellowship 1967-68; Math Intensive Wkshp Ball St 1972; *office:* Peru Jr HS 52 E Daniel St Peru IN 46970

ELLIS, BARBARA HUSEMAN, Language/Reading Teacher; *b:* Edna, TX; *m:* Adrian Cecil; *c:* J. R. Mize, Raeanne Mize, BrenT E.; *ed:* (BS) Elem Ed, TX A&I Univ 1967; Gifted Ed Courses; Prof Growth, Advanced Academic Lang Art Trng; *cr:* 4th Grade Teacher Kingsville Ind Sch Dist 1967-68; 1st Grade Teacher Pearland Ind Sch Dist 1968-69; 6th-8th Grade Lang Art Teacher Friendswood Ind Sch Dist 1970-78; 6th Grade Lang Art Teacher 1979-84, 5th/6th Grade Gifted & Talented Lang/Rdng Teacher 1984- Pearland Ind Sch Dist; *ai:* Bay Area Writing Contest Spon; 5th/6th Grade Academic Enterprises Teams, 6th Grade Knowledge Master Open Team, 5th/6th Grade TX Quiz Bowl Team Coach; Gifted & Talented Curr Dev Comm; TX Assn Gifted & Talented 1984-; Alpha Delta Kappa Ways & Means Chairperson 1987-89; Assn TX Prof Educators 1986-; Bay Area Rdng Cncl 1987-; Tri Cty YMCA 1982-; St Stephen Luth Church 1970-; Pearland Area Dads Club Team Mother 1986-; Nom Thanks to Teachers Awd & Pearland Ind Sch Dist Teacher of Yr; Bay Area Rdng Cncl Prgm Presenter; *office:* Jamison Mid Sch 2516 Woody Rd Box 7 Pearland TX 77581

ELLIS, CYNTHIA JANE, Sixth Grade Teacher; *b:* Athens, TN; *ed:* (BA) Elem Ed, TN Tech Univ 1976; Rdng, UT Chattanooga; *cr:* Classroom Teacher South Polk Elem Sch 1976-; *ai:* Spelling Bee Spon; TIP Building Spon from Duke Univ; Polk Cty Ed Assn (Building Rep 1977-80, Exec Bd 1981-82); Polk Cty Ed Assn in Service Cty Wide on Tabsic 1982; in Service Cleveland Comm Coll Lib Skills 1983; *office:* South Polk Elem Schl Rt 1 Old Federal Rd Oldfort TN 37362

ELLIS, ELIZABETH HENDERSON, Third Grade Teacher; *b:* Fort Payne, AL; *m:* Robert Nelson; *c:* Robert II, Paul; *ed:* (AS) Ed, Northeast St Jr Coll 1970-71; (BS) Elem Ed, 1971-73, (MS) Elem Ed, 1975 ISU; *cr:* Teacher Fyffe Elem 1973-; *ai:* PTO Play; Sch Visiting Comm Teams for Evaluating SOU Assn Accred; NEA, AEA, DEA Mem; Delta Kappa Gamma (Recording Secy 1985-86, Membership Chairperson 1989-); *office:* Fyffe Elem Schl P O Box 7 Church St Fyffe AL 35971

ELLIS, GAYLE MC CLYMONT, 4th Grade Teacher; *b:* Richmond, VA; *ed:* (BA) Ed, VA Commonwealth Univ 1965; Grad Courses, VA Commonwealth Univ, Univ of Richmond; *cr:* 4th Grade Teacher Broad Rock & J B Fisher Schls 1965-70, Gill Cntry Day Sch 1970-78, Pearsons Corner Sch 1978-; *ai:* Teacher Advisory, Lib Selection Comm Grade Level Rep; Delta Kappa Gamma (Pres 1980-82, Ellinor Preston Coordinating Cncl Treas 1982-87, Secy 1983-86); NEA, VEA, HEA; PTA, VA Museum Fine Arts; Article Published; Speaker Soc Stud Instrs Conference; *office:* Pearsons Corner Sch 2456 Ashcake Rd Mechanicsville VA 23111

ELLIS, HATTIE MAE, 6th Grade Reading Teacher; *b:* Durant, MS; *ed:* (BS) Elem Ed, Jackson St Coll 1961; (MED) Elem Ed, MS St Univ Starkville 1972; Educl Management, Sch Admin, Head Start Trng Prgm, Rdng Teacher; *cr:* 1st-3rd Grade Teacher Holmes Cty Sch 1951-58; 7th-8th Grade Sci/Math Teacher Goodman Elem Sch 1958-66; 5th-6th Grade Sci Teacher Goodman-Pickens Elem Sch 1966-68; 6th Grade Math Teacher 1968-70, Remedial Rdng Teacher 1970-73, Rdng Teacher 1973-77 Lexington Attendance Center; Pre-Sch/K-8th Grade Homebound Teacher for Handicapped HolmesCty Schls 1977-82; 5th Grade Sci Teacher 1982-84, 5th-8th Grade Remedial Rdng Teacher 1984- Jacob J Mc Clain Mid Sch; *ai:* Holmes Cty Assn of Educators, NAE, NEA (Rep, Asst Secy 1965-80, Chm Teachers Needs Comm 1984-87); MS Rdng Teachers Assn; Order of Eastern Star Worthy Matron 1978-87, Dist Queen 1983; Belmont Baptist Church Secy 1962-; Freedom Democratic Party 1970-; Parents Teachers Stu Organization 1982-.

ELLIS, JAMES F., Health & Phys Ed Teacher; *b:* San Luis Obispo, CA; *m:* Beverly Siple; *c:* Sarah, Leigh A.; *ed:* (BA) Health/Phys Ed, Bridgewater Coll 1967; Health/Phys Ed, James Madison Univ 1973; *cr:* Health/Phys Ed Teacher N River Jr HS 1967-69; Driver Ed Teacher Wilson Memorial HS 1969-70; Driver Ed Teacher 1970-72, Health/Phys Ed Teacher 1970-78 Stuarts Draft HS; Health/Phys Ed Teacher Stuarts Draft Mid Sch 1978-; *ai:* Intramurals Dir; Gifted & Talented Comm.

ELLIS, JANET DE CORTE, Chapter I Reading Specialist; *b:* E Brady, PA; *m:* David C.; *c:* Brian D., Michael A.; *ed:* (BS) Elem Ed/Fr, 1963, (MED) Rdng Specialist, 1972 Slippery Rock Univ; Doctorate Work, IN Univ of PA; *cr:* Fr/Rdng Teacher Center Township 1963-64; Rdng Teacher Butler Area Jr HS 1975-77; Chapter I Rdng/Math Teacher Slippery Rock Mid Sch 1977-; *ai:* Ski Club Adv; Stu At Risk LRPSI Comm Chairperson; PSEA, NEA, Keystone St Rdng Assn, Phi Delta Kappa; Moraine Conservation; SRU Alumni Assn; Ducks Unlimited; Ward Fnd; *office:* Slippery Rock Mid Sch Keister Rd Slippery Rock PA 16057

ELLIS, KAREN FLOREN, Mathematics Teacher; *b:* Miami, FL; *m:* R. Scott; *c:* Kristina M., Erik A.; *ed:* (BA) Math, 1975, (MS) Math Ed, 1976 Univ FL; *cr:* Instr VA Polytechnic Inst & St Univ 1976-77; Teacher Oak Ridge HS 1977-; *ai:* NHS & Ski Club Spon; Various Schlsp Comms; NCTM; Smokey Mountain Math Educators Assn; Oak Ridge Kennel Club Bd of Dirs 1982; Co-Chairperson NCTM Regional Conference; *office:* Oak Ridge HS Providence Rd Oak Ridge TN 37830

ELLIS, LAWRENCE WILLIAM, Mathematics Teacher; *b:* Jacksonville, IL; *m:* Betty Stafford; *c:* Dale Therrien, Doug Therrien; *ed:* (BSED) Math, IL St Univ 1962; (MAT) Math, Tulane Univ; *cr:* Teacher Plainfield HS 1962-79; Ed/Publisher The Enterprise Newspaper 1979-85; Teacher Lisle Jr HS 1985-86, Plainfield HS 1986-; *ai:* Math Club & Asst Academic Scholastic Bowl Spon; Metropolitan Math Club 1987-; Assn of Plainfield Teachers (Pres 1970) 1962-79, 1986-; Plainfield Rotary Club (Treas 1988-) 1984-; Natl Sci Fnd Grant Summer Stud Tulane Univ 1967-69; *home:* 14 W Maple Ct Plainfield IL 60544

ELLIS, LENARY G., English Teacher; *b:* Noxapater, MS; *m:* Harvey Jr.; *c:* Tanya L., Kristin L.; *ed:* (BS) Elem Ed, 1972, (MS) Elem Ed, 1973, (EDS) Elem Ed, 1976 Jackson St Univ; *cr:* Teacher Brookhaven Public Schls 1973-77, Jefferson Parish Public Schls 1977-; *office:* Roosevelt Mid Sch 3315 Maine Ave Kenner LA 70065

ELLIS, LORETTA LINDSEY, First Grade Teacher; *b:* Lakeland, FL; *c:* Lawrin T., Lori E. Ellis Runner; *ed:* (BS) Elem Ed, Univ of FL 1960; Early Chldhd Ed Wkshps & Seminars; *cr:* Teacher Bartow Jr HS 1960-61; 1st Grade Teacher Avon Elem 1964-76, Hopewell Elem 1976-86, Sun'n Lake Elem 1986-; *ai:* Grade Level Chairperson; Peer Teacher to Beginning Teacher; FL Alpha Delta Kappa (Historian 1984-86, Chaplain 1986-88, Recording Secy 1988-, Pres 1990, St Comm Chairperson); Honor Causa 1990; Highlands Cty Ed Assn, FL Teaching Profession, NEA, PTO; Sweet Adelines (Pres 1987-89, Treas 1984-85), Sweet Adeline of Yr 1986; Band Parents Assn Secy 1978-80; Bible Study Teacher; Math Grant; Teacher of Yr & Soc Stud Teacher of Yr.

ELLIS, MARY FRANCES, French/Spanish Teacher; *b:* Springfield, MA; *ed:* (BA) Fr, Coll of Our Lady of The Elms 1972; *cr:* Teacher M Marcus Kiley Jr HS 1975-; *ai:* Springfield Ed Assn; Mem Election Comm; MA Foreign Lang Assn; Delta Kappa Gamma-Alpha Chapter-Chm World Fellowship 1989; *office:* M Marcus Kiley Jr HS 180 Cooley St Springfield MA 01128

ELLIS, MOZELLE WHITESIDE, Soc Stud/Language Arts Teacher; *m:* Ira E.; *c:* Karen J. Stacey, Marion D., Cary D., Leta L., Grace, Kimberly K. Czupryna; *ed:* (BBA) Teaching Commerical Subjects, Stephen F Austin Univ 1952; (MED) Elem Ed, East TX St Univ 1973; *cr:* Teacher Shepherd ISD HS 1952; Kilgore ISD HS 1952-55; Grand Saline ISD Mid Sch 1969-; *ai:* Spon His Day Act; ATPE; *office:* Grand Saline ISD 300 Stadium Dr Grand Saline TX 75140

ELLIS, PATRICIA ANN, Second Grade Teacher; *b:* Tupelo, MS; *ed:* (BA) Sociology, Lane Coll 1970; (MA) Ed, Natl Coll of Ed 1986; *cr:* Paraprofess Aide Benjamin Franklin Elem 1970-74; Teacher Auer Ave Elem 1974-79; Teacher Oliver Wendell Holmes Elem 1979-; *ai:* Inner City Arts Cncl 1971-74; Adult Literacy 1986-88; *office:* Oliver Wendell Holmes Elem 2463 N Buffum St Milwaukee WI 53212

ELLIS, ROBERT EDWARD, JR., Social Studies Teacher; *b:* Honolulu, HI; *m:* Barbara Jinks; *c:* Janice, Robert, Jeffrey; *ed:* (AS) Scndry Ed, Kennesaw Jr Coll 1977; (BS) Scndry Ed, 1982, (MED) Soc Stud, 1985 GA St Univ; Grad Work Spec Ed; *cr:* Msgt USAF Data Processing 1951-71; Operations Analyst Federal Reserve Bank Atlanta 1971-81; Soc Stud Teacher Sprayberry HS 1982-; *ai:* After Sch Study Prgm; *office:* Sprayberry H S 2525 Sandy Plains Rd Marietta GA 30066

ELLIS, ROBERT H., Choral Director; *b:* High Point, NC; *m:* Alma Traynham; *c:* Anne C., Barbara Harvey, Ellen Burt, Scott; *ed:* (BS) Music Ed, High Point Coll 1951; (MA) Music Ed, Appalachian St Univ 1956; (Rank I) Music Ed, Murray St Univ 1983; Choral Wkshps, Univ of NC; Music Ed Wkshps, Appalachian St Univ; Show Choir Wkshp, Ball St Univ, Univ of NC Greensboro; *cr:* Choral/Band Dir Allen Jay Sch 1953-55, Scotland Neck 1956-57, Claremont Cntrl HS 1957-63, Page HS 1963-70; Choral Dir Briarcliff HS 1970-78, Henderson Cty Sr HS 1978-; *ai:* Henderson Cty HS Chamber Singers; KMEA All St Chorus Cahie 1987-89, 25 Yr Service 1986, Nom Teacher of Yr 1989-; All St Chorus & Clinics; Organized TTBB All St Chorus 1987-89; ACDA Choir Performance 1986-89; *home:* 935 Hometead Trl Henderson KY 42420

ELLIS, RUTH ANNE (OLIVE), Fourth Grade Teacher; *b:* Hopewell, VA; *m:* Bruce D.; *c:* Joni, Cindy; *ed:* (BA) Elem Ed, 1965, (MA) Elem Ed, 1985 Wichita St Univ; *cr:* 3rd Grade Teacher Coll Hill 1965-67; 3rd-5th Grade Teacher Allen 1977-; *ai:*

Parents Assn for Hearing Impaired Children Secy 1978-79; *home:* 122 N Parkwood Wichita KS 67208

ELLIS, THELMA LAMBDIN, Fourth Grade Teacher; *b:* Williamsburg, KY; *ed:* (BS) Ed, 1981, (MA) Ed, 1986 U of LA; *cr:* 3rd Grade Teacher 1981-82, 4th Grade Teacher 1982- Mt Washington Elem; *ai:* 4th Grade Chairperson; Philosophy Comm; Steering Comm; KY Ed Assn 1981-; NEA 1981-; Bullitt Cty Teachers Assn 1981-; Artist in Ed Grant; *home:* 2309 Meadowbrook Dr Shepherdsville KY 40165

ELLIS, THERESA TORREGROSSA, Math Teacher & Computer Coord; *b:* Richmond, VA; *m:* Gary Wayne; *c:* Victoria M., Ryan D.; *ed:* (BS) Math Ed, VA Polytechnic Inst & St Univ 1971; Cmptr Sci & Gifted Ed from Univ of VA, Univ of Richmond, VA Commonwealth Univ; *cr:* Math Teacher/Dept Chm Robious Jr HS 1971-75; Math Teacher/Cmptr Coord Midlothian HS 1976-; *ai:* Cmptr Coord for Sch & Club Adv; UTP, NEA, VEA, CEA 1971-89; VA Cncl Teachers of Math; Greater Richmond Cncl of Teachers of Math (Bd Mem 1972-74) 1972-74, 1976-84, 1986, 1988; Womens Club of Walton Park 1977-84; Walton Park Civic Assn (Bd Mem 1978-82) 1977-; Winfree Memorial Baptist Church 1982-; *office:* Midlothian HS 401 Charter Colony Pkwy Midlothian VA 23113

ELLISON, ANNIE EASTERLING, 7th Grade Teacher; *b:* Laurinburg, NC; *m:* James Milton Sr.; *c:* James Jr., Derrick, Tanesha; *ed:* (BS) Home Ec Ed, NC Cntrl Univ 1971; Cert Math/Soc Stud/Lang Art, Bembroke St Univ 1980; *cr:* Home Ec Teacher Calvert Cty HS 1971-73; Math Teacher 1973-77, Math/Lang Art/Rdng/Soc Stud Teacher 1977-89 Fairmont Mid Sch; *ai:* Robeson Cty Math Curr Dev Comm; PSORC Sch Improvement Team; NEA, NC Assn of Ed Building Rep 1974-; Natl Assn of Math Teachers 1988-; Natl Assn for Advancement of Colored People Membership Chairperson 1990; Pines of NC GSA Leader; *office:* Fairmont Mid Sch 402 Iona St Fairmont NC 28340

ELLISON, BETTY DANIEL, Rdng Specialist/Fr Teacher; *b:* Manchester, GA; *m:* Darthus Jr.; *c:* Darthus III, Keith B.; *ed:* (BA) Fr - Cum Laude, Morris Brown Coll 1972; (MA) Rdng Specialist, Atlanta Univ 1975; *cr:* Rdng/Fr Teacher Greenville HS 1972-84; Rdng Specialist/Fr Teacher Central HS 1986-; *ai:* Spelling Bee Chairperson; NEA, Foreign Lang Assn of GA, GA Assn of Educators, ASCD, Intnl Rdng Assn; Zeta Phi Beta; Pi Delta Phi; GA St Teachers Schlsp; Nom Teacher of Yr; Whos Who in Amer Ed 1990; *home:* 88 Johnson Ave Ext Manchester GA 31816

ELLISON, JESSE FLOYD, Health Teacher; *b:* Corbin, KY; *ed:* (BS) Health/Phys Ed, Cumberland Coll 1983; Rank II W KY Univ; *cr:* Asst Bsktbl Coach Georgetown Coll 1983-84, E KY Univ 1984-85; Health Teacher Bowling Green Jr HS 1985-; Asst Bsktbl Coach Bowling Green HS 1986-; *ai:* Asst Bsktbl Coach Bowling Green HS; NEA, KY Ed Assn 1985-; KY HS Coaches Assn 1980-; *office:* Bowling Green Jr HS 1141 Center St Bowling Green KY 42101

ELLISON, JO ELLA JOHNS, Typing Teacher; *b:* Austin, TX; *m:* Robert Sr.; *c:* Gregory A. Johns, Robin C. Ellison Montgomery, Robert Jr., Lloyd B.; *ed:* (BA) Bus Ed, Huston Tillotson Coll 1980; Certified to Teach Office Ed; *cr:* Lib Clerk/Ed Secy 1968-78, Office Duplication Teacher 1982-87, Austin Ind Sch Dist Jr HS 1982-87; Typing/Eng Bus Ed Teacher Austin Ind Sch Dist Kealing 1982-; *ai:* Fine Arts & Black His Comms; Austin Assn of Teachers, TX St Teachers Assn, NEA; Mt Zion Baptist Church Youth Supvr 1968-; Delta Sigma Theta; Natl Cncl of Negro Women; Natl Deans List 1978-79.

ELLMAN, ELAINE NEWLAND, Teacher of Gifted; *b:* Tucson, AZ; *m:* Ronald N.; *ed:* (BA) Elem Ed, Univ of Cntrl FL 1978; (MA) Admin/Supervision, Univ of S FL 1986; Taught Gifted Cert Courses for Cty Teachers St of FL; *cr:* 4th Grade Teacher Wekiva Elem 1978-80; 5th Grade Teacher 1980-82, Teacher of Gifted 1982-83 Eastbrook Elem, Keeth Elem 1983-; *ai:* Odyssey of Mind & Knowledge Master Academic Cmptr Team Coach; Oratorical Contest Coach; Cty Recognition Awd for Advocacy in Gifted Ed; Recognized for Coaching an Academic Cmptr Competition 1st Place FL & 41st in Nation 1990; *home:* 1707 Demetree Dr Winter Park FL 32789

ELLWEIN, BETTY GOETZ, Fourth Grade Teacher; *b:* Loyalton, SD; *m:* Donald D.; *c:* Bruce D., Karen L.; *ed:* Elem Ed, Presentation Jr Coll 1960; (BA) Elem Ed, Pacific Luth Univ 1972; *cr:* 2nd Grade Teacher Miller Public Schls 1960-61; 2nd Grade Teacher Roscoe Public Schls, 1962-63; 1st/2nd/4th/5th/6th Grade Teacher Sumner Sch Dist 1972-; *ai:* PTO Bd Rep for Intermediate Grades; Dist Rdng Curr Mem; Organizational Comm for Our Staff; SEA Building Rep 1986-88; WEA; *home:* 38310 183rd Ave SE Auburn WA 98002

ELMLEAF, JAMES R., Teacher; *b:* Iron River, MI; *ed:* (BA) His, 1960, (MA) His, 1962, MI St Univ; *cr:* Teacher Royal Oak Public Schls 1960-; *ai:* Royal Oak Adult Ed Prgm Building Supvr; MI Cncl Teachers of Math Distinguished Service 1989; Detroit Area Cncl Teachers of Math Treas 1980; NCTM; Guardian Angels Church St Vincent de Paul Society Clawson VP 1988-; *office:* Churchill JR HS 707 Girard Ave Royal Oak MI 48073

ELMORE, CARA ADRIENNE, English Teacher; *b:* Shelby, NC; *ed:* (BA) Eng, Gardner Webb Coll 1975-80; (MA) Eng, Bread Loaf Sch of Eng 1985-; Lincoln Coll Oxford; *cr:* Eng/Drama Teacher Shelby Sr HS 1981-; Eng Teacher Cleveland Comm Coll 1987-; *ai:* Annual Staff; NCAE Pres Elect 1989-; NC Teachers of Eng 1983-; NCTE 1987-; Abuse Prevention Cncl Bd 1987-; Teacher of Yr 1987, 1989; Regional Teacher of Yr 3rd Runner Up; Governors Awd Excl in Teaching; Outstanding Alumni Gardner-Webb Coll; *office:* Shelby Sr HS E Dixon Blvd Shelby NC 28150

ELMORE, DEBORAH LEATHERS, Fifth Grade Teacher; *b:* Tupelo, MS; *m:* Roger Franklin; *c:* Benjamin, Elizabeth, Bryan; *ed:* (BA) Elem Ed, MS Univ for Women 1977; (MS) Elem Ed, Univ of MS 1980; MS Teacher Assessment Instrument Trained Evaluator; Jane Stallings Trng Cycle for Teacher Improvement; Dr Anne Williams Basic Elements Trng Cycles One & Two; *cr:* Kndgtn Teacher 1977-78, 3rd Grade Teacher 1978-79, 4th Grade Teacher 1979-83, 5th Grade Teacher 1983- Tupelo Public Schls; *ai:* Teachers Dist Excl, Staff Dev, Curr Revision Comm Mem; Delta Kappa Gamma Recording Secy 1984-88; NEA, MS Prof Educators Mem; Assn for Excl in Ed Small Grants for Teachers Prgm Coord; Tupelo Pilot Club; Amer Cancer Society Bd Mem; St Dept of Ed Statewide Task Force Mem; Tupelo City Sch Dist Teacher of Yr 1988; *home:* 1226 N Clayton Ave Tupelo MS 38801

ELMORE, MARIA ELIZABETH, Mathematics Teacher; *b:* Geleen, Netherlands; *m:* Charles Steven; *c:* Bryan C., Kevin; *ed:* (BS) Math/Ed, AZ St Univ 1970; (MA) Math/Ed, Univ of TX Austin 1975; Use of Micro Cmptrs in Classroom, Western St Coll; Educating Exceptional Child, CO St Univ; Certified to Teach Advanced Placement Calculus, Millsaps Coll; *cr:* Jr HS Math/Algebra Teacher Madison Sch 1970-72; Teacher Bethesda Chevy Chase HS 1980-81; Tutoring at Home/Substitute Teacher MS & OR & IL; Teacher Heritage Acad MS Univ for Women 1986-; *ai:* Volunteer Work for MS Swimming; Mem US Swimming; Math Assn of America; Swim Columbus (VP Bd 1988, 1990, Treas 1987); MS Economic Cncl STAR Teacher 1987, 1989; MUW Outstanding Math Teacher Awd 1987, 1989; *office:* Heritage Acad 625 Magnolia Ln Columbus MS 39701

EL MOUSSA, DOMINIQUE ANGELIQUE, French/Spanish Teacher; *b:* Anvers, Belgium; *m:* Nabil Kamel; *c:* Angelique, Tarek; *ed:* (BA) Fr/Span, Institut Superieur De Bruxelles 1974; (MS) Fr, CA St Univ Long Beach 1987; *cr:* Legal Secy Shalant Haddock Mc Donough Law Firm 1977-78; Scndry Sch Teacher Whitney HS 1986-; *ai:* Fr Club Adv; *office:* Gretchen Whitney HS 16800 Shoemaker Ave Cerritos CA 90701

ELMQUIST, GARY RAY, Mathematics Teacher; *b:* Longmont, CO; *ed:* (BA) Math, Univ of CO 1972; (MA) Math Ed, Univ of N CO 1980; *cr:* Teacher Widefield HS 1972-73, Mead Jr HS 1973-; *ai:* Math Dept Chm; Sch Improvement, Dist Mid Sch, Dist Curr Comm; NCTM 1972-; Phi Beta Kappa 1971-; Longmont Cty 1st Luth Church Organist 1978-; *home:* 1315 Grays Peak Dr Longmont CO 80501

ELOE, LAURA JANE (SCHNEIDER), Mathematics Teacher; *b:* Albany, NY; *m:* Paul W.; *c:* Nathan W.; *ed:* (BSED) Math/Theology, Univ of Dayton 1984; Working Towards Masters in Theology, Univ of Dayton; *cr:* Math Instr Univ of Dayton 1985-88; Math Teacher Chaminade-Julienne HS 1984-; *ai:* Pastoral Team Mem; Stu Pastoral Team Faculty Adv; Math Dept Soc Chairperson; Liturgical Choir Dir; Math Assn of America 1985; Immaculate Conception Church Folk Choir Dir 1984-; Marianist Ed Consortium Grant, 1986; *office:* Chaminade-Julienne HS 505 S Ludlow St Dayton OH 45402

ELRICK, DONALD, English Teacher; *b:* Cleveland, OH; *ed:* (BA) Eng, Hiram Coll 1964; Grad Work Eng, Univ of Akron; *cr:* Teacher Medina HS 1964-80, Lake Cath HS 1980-81, Lorain Cty Comm Coll 1982-83, Lakewood HS 1983-; *ai:* Honor Day Comm; NEA, OEA, NEOTA, LTA; Coll Entrance Examination Bd Adv Placement Consultant 1980; Educl Testing Service Adv Placement Reader 1976-81; *home:* 1886 W 47th St Cleveland OH 44102

ELROD, PEGGY MARTIN, Fourth Grade Teacher; *b:* Gladewater, TX; *m:* Donald Ray; *c:* Todd M., Eric T.; *ed:* (BS) Elem Ed, Stephen F. Austin St Univ 1961; (MA) Philosophy Analytical Teaching, TX Wesleyan Univ 1986; *cr:* Teacher Arlington Ind Sch Dist 1961-; *ai:* Little Elem 4th Grade Lead Teacher; Supts & Curr Cncl; Tate Springs Baptist Church Mem; Whos Who in Amer Univs 1960-61; Teacher of Yr; Ideas & Articles Published; Sid Richardson Grant; AISD Pyramid Project Grant; *office:* J B Little Elem Sch 4210 Little Rd Arlington TX 76016

ELSON, DONNA RUTH, Sixth Grade Teacher; *b:* De Kalb, IL; *m:* Walter S.; *c:* Anne Crowe, Jay; *ed:* (BS) Elem Ed, Northern IL Univ 1954; (MS) Elem Ed, IL St Univ 1976; Will Complete MS Educl Admin in 1991; *cr:* 1st Grade Teacher Sycamore Public Schls 1954-61; 2nd-6th Grade Teacher Decatur Public Schls Dist 61 1966-; *ai:* Designee; NEA, IL Ed Assn 1954-; Decatur Ed Assn 1966-; Alpha Delta Kappa (Treas 1980-82/1986-88, Pres 1982-84/1988-, Comm Chm) Selected to Represent Stevenson Sch Those Who Excel Prgm 1985; *office:* Stevenson Elem Schl 3900 N Neely Ave Decatur IL 62526

ELSTON, JO ANN FOSTER, 5th Grade Teacher; *b:* Lincoln, NE; *m:* James Foster; *c:* Mark, Lori; *ed:* (BS) Home Ec, 1956, (BA) Elem Ed, 1960 Univ of NV Reno; *cr:* Home Ec Teacher Humboldt HS 1956-57; Sewing Teacher Cntrl Jr HS 1958-60; 4th/5th Grade Teacher Echo Loder Sch 1962-; *ai:* Entomology Teacher of Gifted; Woodworking, Sewing Teacher; WCTA, NSEA 1960-; 4-H (Leader, St Pres), Natl 4-H Alumnus of Yr 1978; UNR Alumni Assn (Homecoming Chairperson, Pres), Outstanding Alumnus 1975; Univ of NV Reno Pres Medal 1989; Grant Buy Equipment Children Intercity Sch; Young Educator of Yr Washoe Cty 1963; NV Teacher of Yr 1977; Reno Chamber Commerce Teacher of Month 1982; *home:* 2345 Armstrong Reno NV 89509

ELY, DEBRA G., Third Grade Teacher; *b:* Rome, GA; *c:* Matthew; *ed:* (BS) Elem Ed, Shorter Coll 1977; (MS) Early Chldhd Ed, Berry Coll 1984; *cr:* Teacher Kingston Elem Sch 1977-; *ai:* Teacher of Yr 1988; *office:* Kingston Elem Sch 90 Main St Kingston GA 30145

EMANUEL, DAVID, JR., Mathematics Teacher; *b:* Lumberton, NC; *m:* Louise Strickland; *c:* Elgin, Daryle, Arlis, David III; *ed:* (BS) Math, 1979, (BS) Math Ed, 1982, (MS) Math Ed 1990 Pembroke St UniV; *cr:* Math Teacher Pembroke Sr HS 1982-83, W Robeson/Purnell Swett HS 1983-; *ai:* Jr Var Bsbl Coach; NEA; Church Brotherhood Pres 1986-; Babe Ruth Pres 1988-, Coach of Yr 1988; Dixie Youth Pres 1989-; Little League Coach 1981-87, Coach of Yr 1982, 1984; *office:* Purnell Swett Sch P O Box 1210 Pembroke NC 28372

EMANUELE, JOSEPH ROBERT, III, Mid Sch Mathematics Teacher; *b:* Amsterdam, NY; *m:* Tina Marie Ripepi; *ed:* (BA) Liberal Art, SUNY Plattsburg 1974; (BA) Math Ed/Sociology/Criminology/Health/Coaching, SUNY Plattsburg 1978; (MS) Spec Ed, SUNY Albany 1987; *cr:* Math/His Teacher St Anne Inst 1979-81; Math Teacher 1988, Part Time Tutor/Math/General Teacher 1981- Amsterdam HS; Mid Sch Math Teacher Fonda-Fultonville 1982-; *ai:* Fonda-Fultonville Cntrl Sch Cmptr Curr & Assertive Discipline Comm; Fonda-Fultonville Sch Natl Jr Honor Society; NY St Math Teachers Assn, NY St United Teachers Union Mem; Natl Rifle Assn, PTA Natl Congress Mem; *office:* Fonda-Fultonville Cntrl Sch Cemetery St Fonda NY 12068

EMERICK, KAREN CRAWFORD, Teacher of Gifted; *b:* East Liverpool, OH; *m:* Jonathan Scott; *ed:* (BS) Elem Ed, Kent St Univ 1979; Gifted & Cmptr Stud; *cr:* Substitute Teacher 1979-80, 1st Grade Teacher 1980-81, 5th Grade Teacher 1981-86, Teacher of Gifted 1986- Carrollton Southern Local; *ai:* Odyssey of Mind Coach; Future Problem Solving Prgm Dir & Coach; Mid Sch Newspaper Adv & Ed; NEA, OH Ed Assn, Carrollton Ed Assn, 1981-; OH Assn of Gifted Children 1986-; Martha Holden Jennings Scholar Kent St Univ 1984-85; *office:* Carrollton Schls 80 3rd N E Carrollton OH 44615

EMERSON, ELLA K., Health/Phys Ed Teacher; *b:* Ft Bragg, NC; *m:* Ray A.; *c:* Avery, Ashlee; *ed:* (BS) Health/Phys Ed/Driver Ed, Radford Univ 1972; (MA) Supervision/Admin, George Washington Univ 1987; *cr:* Health/Phys Ed Teacher Bayside HS 1972-79, Green Run HS 1979-89, Salem HS 1989-; *ai:* Gymnastic Coach; Adopt-A-Sch Comm; Intramural Activity Coord; Career Teacher 1985-; Dept Chairperson 1986-; US Gymnastic Fed 1974-; VA Beach Coaches Assn 1975-; Salem HS Teacher Assn 1989-; City Wide PTA Citizenship Chairperson 1987-88; Tallwood PTA 1989-; *office:* Salem HS 2300 Lynnhaven Pkwy Virginia Beach VA 23464

EMERSON, KAY LEWIS, Gifted & Talented Teacher; *b:* Chicago, IL; *w:* Philip Edward (dec); *c:* Daniel, Susan, Bradford; *ed:* (BS) Ed, IN Univ 1956; (MS) Eng, Wm Carey Coll 1982; Gifted Ed, Univ of S MS Hattiesburg; Grad Courses, Butler Univ; *cr:* Eng Teacher Zionsville HS 1956-59, Sacred Heart Cath Sch 1959-63, 1973-78; Dir Hattiesburg Civic Arts Cncl 1978-79; Gifted/Talented Teacher Forrest Cty Schls 1979-; *ai:* Yrbk, Newspaper, Drama Club Spon; Forensic & Media Dir; City-Wide Ed Comm on Learning Disabilities; MS Prof Assn, Kappa Delta Rho; Jr Auxiliary Secy; Travelers Aid Bd; YWCA Exec Bd; Appointed to Continual Progress Ed Grant Comm; Elected Chm of Forrest Cty Teachers Advisory Cncl; *home:* 404 Kensington Dr Hattiesburg MS 39402

EMERSON, LARRY DOUGLAS, 8th-9th Grade Soc Stud Teacher; *b:* Russell Springs, KY; *m:* Pamela Flanagan; *c:* Jill S.; *ed:* (BA) His, 1971, (MA) Scndry Ed, 1975 W KY Univ; *cr:* His Teacher Russell Cty HS 1971-73; 8th Grade Soc Stud Russell Springs Elem Sch 1974-87; His/Geography Teacher Russell Cty Jr HS 1988-; *ai:* Chm Grad, Awds, Sch Philosophy Comms; NEA, KEA, Russell Cty Ed Assn 1971-; Russell Cty Air Bd Secy 1986-; Russell Cty Tax Appeals Bd 1983-; *home:* Rt 3 Box 228-R Russell Springs KY 42642

EMERSON, STEVEN JOHN, English Teacher/Coach; *b:* Moorhead, MN; *ed:* (BA) Eng, Concordia Coll 1986; *cr:* Eng Teacher/Wrestling & Ftbl Coach East Grand Forks 1986-87; Eng Teacher/Wrestling & Track Coach Medford HS 1987-; *ai:* Head Wrestling & Head Girls Track Coach; NCTE Mem 1986-; *office:* Medford HD 104 2nd St Ne Medford MN 55049

EMERT, LORNA JONES, 5th & 6th Grade Teacher; *b:* Greensburg, PA; *m:* William K.; *c:* Robert, Cheryl Shaffer, David, Chris, Anna Gula, Scott; *ed:* (BS) Elem, CA St 1972; *cr:* Teacher Westmoreland Cty 1963-65, Ligonier Valley 1965-66, Mt Pleasant Area 1966-; *office:* Donegal Elem Sch School House Ln Jones Mills PA 15646

EMERY, DAVID ROLAND, Mathematics Teacher; *b:* New York, NY; *m:* Margaret-Irene Sensenig; *c:* Robert D, James C; *ed:* (BS) Math, Ursinus Coll 1961; (MA) Math, Univ of PA 1963; Grad Work PA St Univ; NSF Cmptrs, Univ of PA; *cr:* Asst Instr Univ of PA 1961-63; Math Lecturer Ursinus Evening Sch 1962-; Teacher Methacton HS 1963-; *ai:* Adv Natl Honor Society; Coach Math Team/Cmptr Team; Exec Dir PA Academic Decathlon; Cmptr Specialist Methaction HS; Methacton Ed Assn, PSEA, NEA, 1963-; ATMOPAV/PCTM 1970-; Cntrl Schwenkfelder Church Audit Comm Chm 1987-; NSF Grant 1967 Summer Inst; US Academic Decathlon Dev Grant 1990; Article in Two Yr Coll Math Journal; *office:* Methacton HS Kriebel Mill Rd Fairview Village PA 19403

EMFIELD, SCOTT DOUGLAS, Soc Stud Teacher/Dept Head; *b:* Santa Monica, CA; *m:* Donna Marie Gunter; *c:* Jared, Anna, Miriam, Rachel, Adam, Paul; *ed:* (BA) His, ID St Univ 1976; (MA) Ancient Stud, Univ of MN 1978; Archeological, Univ of Tel Aviv Israel; Ed, Coll of St Thomas; *cr:* Teacher/Dept Head Canyon View Jr HS 1979-; Part-Time Instr Coll of E UT 1985-; *ai:* Dist Soc Stud & Teachers Handbook Comm; NEA Building Rep 1980-81; Western Boys Bsbl Assn Coach 1986-88; Emery Cty Girls Sftbl Coach 1989-; *office:* Canyon View Jr HS Canyon View Jr H Canyon Rd Huntington UT 84528

EMICK, KRAIG ROBERT, Dir of Bands; *b:* Marshalltown, IA; *m:* Karen Ann Bonefas; *c:* Kristopher, Kirk; *ed:* (BME) Music Ed, Drake Univ 1973; (MA) Music Ed, Univ of N IA 1985; Instrumental Music Clinics, Wkshps; Grad Stud Sch Admin; *cr:* Dir of Bands Jesup Cmmty Schls 1973-; *ai:* Marching, Symphonic, Pep Band; Registered Ftbl & Bsktbl Ofcl; Jr Class Spon; NEA, IA St Ed Assn; Jesup Ed Assn Past Pres; IA Bandmasters Assn, NE IA Bandmasters Assn, Music Educators Natl Conference, IA Music Educators Assn, Natl Assn of Jazz Educators, Natl Band Assn, Amer Sch Band Dir Assn; US Achievement Acad Natl Comm Mem; Pi Kappa Lambda Chapter Pres; Phi Mu Alpha Sinfonia Chapter Pres; Knights of Columbus Acts Chm 1986-; St Judes Fnd Natl Appreciation Awd; Natl Comm Mem US Achievement Acad; Masters Research Paper used Univ of N IA; *office:* Jesup Cmmty HS 531 Prospect Jesup IA 50648

EMIGH, CHARLINDA WALKER, Third Grade Teacher; *b:* Philippi, WV; *m:* Clyde V.; *ed:* (BA) Elem Ed, Alderson Broaddus Coll 1977; (MS) Elem Ed, WV Univ 1983; WV Univ, Goddard Coll; *cr:* 3rd Grade Teacher Junior Elem Sch 1977-; *ai:* Sci Fair Coord; WVEA Building Rep 1977-; Cross Roads United Meth Church (Charge Rep 1985-86, Finance/Admin Cncl 1989-); PTA Life Membership 1985; *home:* Rt 2 Box 95 Philippi WV 26416

EMISON, JULIA REVES, 7th/8th Lang Arts Teacher; *b:* Jackson, TN; *m:* Michael Andrew; *c:* Michael, Matthew; *ed:* (BA) Eng/Scndry Ed, Union Univ 1973; (MS) Curr & Dev, Memphis St 1984; *cr:* Teacher Cntrl Elem 1973-75; Westover Elem 1975-; Part Time Teacher Jackson St Comm Coll 1988-89; *ai:* Coach for Academic Pentathlon Team; Dir of Sch Play; Banquet Spon; Just Say No Sch Spon; NCTE 1987-; W TN Rdng Assn 1989-; 1st Baptist Church Class Pres 1989-; Outstanding Young Educator of Speech 1976; Pres Watertown Ed Assn 1987-88; *office:* Westover Sch Rt 1 Huron TN 38345

EMMER, AGATHA DE PINTO, Dist Math Coord/Math Teacher; *b:* Hoboken, NJ; *m:* James Henry; *c:* Agatha Emmer-Guthrie, Jennifer, Mary, Anna; *ed:* (BA) Math Ed, Jersey City St Coll 1964; Jersey City St Coll & Seton Hall Univ; *cr:* Math Teacher Brandt Sch 1965-69, Hoboken HS 1971-73, Borough Sch 1974-89; Adjunct Faculty Cty Coll of Morris 1981-84; Dist Math Coord/Math Teacher Morris Plains Dist 1989-; *ai:* Annual Math-A-Thon Coord; NJML Competition, AJHSME Coach; Dist Math Comm; Dist Instructional Cncl; Resource & Dev Cncl Rep; ATMNJ, NCTM 1988-; NJEA, NEA 1965-; MCCEA, MPEA 1974-; *office:* Borough Sch 500 Speedwell Ave Morris Plains NJ 07950

EMMERT, CHARLES LEON, Physics Teacher; *b:* Lebanon, IN; *m:* Darlene Duncan; *c:* Gregg A., Vicki L.; *ed:* (BSED) Physics/Chem, Ball St Teachers Coll 1962; (MA) Sci, Ball St Univ 1965; *cr:* Sci/Math Teacher Thorntown HS 1962-64; Physics Teacher Noblesville Sr HS 1964-; *ai:* Sci Club Spon; Natl Honor Society Faculty Cncl; Sci Projects Spon; Team Spon in Tournament for Academic Competition; IN Section Amer Assn of Physics Teachers (VP, Secy, Pres) 1986-89, Outstanding Teacher of HS Physics 1983; AAPT 1964-; NEA; Hoosier Assn of Sci Teachers Inc 1988-; NSTA 1963-; IN St Teachers Assn Local Treas 1962-; IN Childrens Christian Home (Pres 1973-79) 1981-; Cumberland Pike Church of Christ (Deacon, Treas) 1967-; *office:* Noblesville Sr HS 300 N 17th Noblesville IN 46060

EMMET, AUDREY RIGNEY, Mathematics Dept Chairperson; *b:* El Paso, TX; *ed:* (BA) *cr:* Teacher St Louis Cath Elem 1964-77, Reicher Cath HS 1977-; *ai:* Stu Cncl Spon; NCEA, Natl Math Teachers Assn; Historic Waco Fnd; *office:* Reicher Cath HS 2102 N 23rd Waco TX 76708

EMMETT, PATRICIA DRIEHAUS, Third Grade Teacher; *b:* Cincinnati, OH; *m:* Jerome R.; *c:* Anne C. Linde, Denise, Patrick, Julie, Mary, Colleen; *ed:* (BA) Elem Ed, 1981, Spec Rdng Cert 1981 Mt St Joseph; *cr:* 5th Grade Teacher St William Sch 1956-58; 1st Grade Teacher O L Victory 1958-60; 3rd Grade Teacher Resurrection 1977-; *ai:* Jr HS Sftbl Team Coach; PTO Secy 1965-66; *home:* 536 Morrvue Dr Cincinnati OH 45238

EMMETT, WILLIAM ELTON, Mathematics Department Head; *b:* Chattanooga, TN; *m:* Donna Lynn Beason; *ed:* (BS) Bus Management, Auburn 1976; (BS) Math Ed, Univ of TN Chattanooga 1984; *cr:* Classroom Teacher Northwest Georgia HS 1986-; *ai:* Beta Club Spon; Frosh Ftbl Coach; *office:* Northwest Georgia HS 150 Pace Dr Trenton GA 30752

EMMONS, BARBARA R., Basic Skills Teacher; *b:* Philadelphia, PA; *m:* George H.; *c:* Dawn Robertson, Pat, Heather; *ed:* (BS) Elem Ed, E Stroudsburg Univ 1958; *cr:* 1st Grade Teacher Harker Wylie Sch 1958-60; 2nd Grade Teacher Denbo Sch 1962-63, Emmons Sch 1974-75; Basic Skills Teacher Emmons Sch 1975-81; 6th Grade Teacher Creiton Sch 1982-85; Basic Skills Teacher Little Red Sch 1985-89; *ai:* NEA, NJ Ed Assn, Pemberton Township Ed Assn, W Jersey Rdng Cncl; Eastern Star 1983-89; Winnebago Intnl Travelers Club; *home:* 146 Pole Bridge Rd Browns Mills NJ 08015

EMMONS, JERRY, Mathematics Teacher; *b:* Lorain, OH; *m:* Judy Pool; *c:* Amy, Amanda; *ed:* (BSED) Math Sci, OH St 1966; (MSED) Math Ed, W MI Univ 1973; Grad Stud Beyond Masters; *cr:* Math Teacher Eastwood Schls 1966-68, Norwalk HS 1968-; *ai:* NCTM, OCTM; NSF Grant 1971-73; Teacher of Yr Norwalk City Schls 1975; Teacher of Yr OH Cncl Teachers of Math 1985; *office:* Norwalk HS 80 E Main Norwalk OH 44857

EMMONS, REVA LORETTA, Business Teacher; *b:* Calm, MO; *m:* John Wesley; *c:* Jody Morey, John Jr., Carolyn; *ed:* (BS) Bus, W MI Univ 1981; Grad Stud; *cr:* Bus Teacher Parchment HS 1982-89, First Assembly Chrstn 1983-; *home:* 1103 Nichols Rd Kalamazoo MI 49007

EMSWILLER, MARSHA MC ENTIRE, Kindergarten Teacher; *b:* Kittannig, PA; *m:* Bernard C. III; *c:* Kristen M., Bernard IV; *ed:* (BS) Elem Ed, 1968, (MS) Elem Guidance, 1971 Edinboro; *cr:* 3rd Grade Teacher Transfer Sch 1968-76; 1st Grade Teacher Reynolds Elem 1976-79; 3rd Grade Teacher 1979-82, Kndgtn Teacher 1982- Transfer Primary; *ai:* Early Prevention of Sch Failure Team; PA St Ed Assn, NEA; Reynolds Ed Assn Building Rep 1970-72; Kndgtn Booklet; *home:* RD 2 Box 2214 Mercer PA 16137

ENDEL, ELIZABETH ALLENE (EMERSON), 10th Grade English/Lit Teacher; *b:* El Dorado, AR; *m:* Danny Glenn; *c:* Elise D.; *ed:* (BS) Bus Ed/Eng, LA Tech Univ 1979; *cr:* Eng Teacher Junction City HS 1979-; *ai:* Majorette & Sr Class Spon; Chapter I Comm 1980-82; Gifted & Talented Cncl 1983-86; AR Ed Assn, NEA; REA Intnl, Music Evangelism, Church Youth Dir, S AR Cmmty Band; *home:* PO Box 291 Junction City AR 71749

ENDERS, CHRISTINE KESTER, English Teacher; *b:* Chicago, IL; *m:* William; *c:* Rebecca; *ed:* (BA) Eng, Univ of IL Chicago Circle 1976; Working Toward Masters in Ed; *cr:* 4th Grade Teacher 1977-79, Jr HS Eng Teacher 1976-77, 1980-89 Queen of Martyrs; *ai:* Drama Club Chm; Stu Cncl Co-Chm; NCEA 1976-89; Univ of IL Alumni Assn.

ENDICOTT, JILL MC KINNON, Kindergarten Teacher; *b:* Concord, CA; *m:* Edward L.; *c:* Katie, Emily, Phillip; *ed:* (BS) Speech Pathology/Audiology, CA St Univ Hayward 1974; Working Towards Masters Ed/Childrens Lit, CA St Univ Hayward 1991; *cr:* 5th Grade Teacher 1976-84, Kndgtn Teacher 1984- Green Valley Sch; *ai:* Dramatic Coach; Green Valley Cross-Age Drama Productions; Green Valley Sch Accountability Report Card, Childcare Comms; San Ramon Valley Cmmty Advisory Comm Substance Abuse Ed 1986-87; San Ramon Valley Curr Review Comm 1987-88; San Ramon Valley Advisory Comm Curr 1988-89; Green Valley PTA Honorary Service Awd 1978-79, 1985-86; Work Published in Honorary Focus on Fine Arts 1989; *office:* Green Valley Sch 1001 Diablo Rd Danville CA 94526

ENDSLEY, VICKIE ENLOW, 6th-8th Grade Math Teacher; *b:* Fairfield, IL; *m:* Curtis Glen; *c:* Clinton, Lance; *ed:* (AS) Math Ed, Olney Cntrl Coll 1977; (BA) Math Ed, E IL Univ 1978; (MS) Scndry Ed/Emphasis on Math, Univ of S IN 1990; *cr:* 6th-8th Grade Math Teacher Edwards Cty K-12 1979-; *ai:* NEA, IEA 1979-; Edwards Cty Teachers Assn Treas 1979-; Delta Kappa Gamma Intnl 1988-; NCTM, ICTM 1987-; S Cntrl IL Teachers of Math 1988-; Pork Womens Assn Dir 1980-; *office:* Edwards Cty K-12 Sch 361 W Main St Albion IL 62806

ENGEBRETSON, TIMOTHY WILLIAM, Health/Phys Ed Teacher; *b:* Forreston, IL; *ed:* (BS) Phys Ed, W IL Univ 1985; *cr:* Health/Phys Ed Teacher Alden-Hebron HS 1985-87, Knoxville HS 1987-; *ai:* Soph Ftbl & Frosh Bsktbl Coach; IL Assn of Health, Phys Ed, Recreation, Dance 1983-; *office:* Knoxville HS Main & Ontario Sts Knoxville IL 61448

ENGEL, AL E., Social Studies Teacher/Coach; *b:* Independence, KS; *c:* Linda K. Engel Ward, Mark A., Matthew P., Anne M. Engel Gerry, Patrick H., Margaret C. Engel Paddock, Hope E., Faith E., Paul J., Luke A.; *ed:* (BA) His, 1960, (MS) Soc Stud Ed, 1962 Cntrl St Univ Edmond; Grad Fellowship Univ of MS Oxford 1963; Various Wkshps & Seminars; *cr:* Teacher/Coach Bishop Mc Guinness HS 1960-62; Teacher/Coach Mt St Marys HS 1964; Teacher Capital Hill Jr HS 1966; Teacher/Coach NW Classen HS 1967-76, Douglass HS 1978-; *ai:* Fellow Chrstn Athletes Huddle Spon Coach; AFT Charter Mem 1972-; *office:* Douglass HS 900 N Martin Luther King Oklahoma City OK 73117

ENGEL, FRED H., Social Studies Teacher; *b:* Cincinnati, OH; *ed:* (BA) Poly Sci, Univ of CA Berkeley 1966; (MA) Early Modern/Modern European His, San Francisco St Univ 1972; PhD Candidate His, Univ of CA San Diego 1972; Scndry Ed Credential, Univ of CA Berkeley 1969; *cr:* Soc Stud Teacher Cherry Creek HS 1983-; *ai:* Model United Nations Club Co-Spon; Amer Historical Assn, NCSS; Del Amo Fnd Fellowship for Study in Spain 1972-74; Natl Endowment for Hum Fellowship for Summer Seminar in Florence Italy 1988; *office:* Cherry Creek HS 9300 E Union Ave Englewood CO 80111

ENGEL, JEFFREY L., Chemistry/Physics Teacher; *b:* Americus, NJ; *ed:* (BS) Ag, Rutgers 1969; (MED) Sci Ed, 1982, (EDS) Sci Ed, 1988 Univ of GA; *cr:* Chem/Physics Teacher Madison Cty HS 1983-; *ai:* Chess Team; NSTA, GSTA, FAS; *office:* Madison County HS P O Box 7 Danielsville GA 30633

ENGEL, JUDITH S., Mathematics Teacher; *b:* Bronx, NY; *ed:* (BA) Math, 1952, (MA) Math/Ed, 1956 Hunter Coll; *cr:* Math Teacher Bronx Voc HS 1952-53; Acting Chairperson-Math Jr HS 44 1953-55; Math Teacher Bronx HS of Sci 1955-; *ai:* NY Society for the Experimental Study of Ed Math Section VP 1957-58; NCTM, Intnl Alliance for Invitational Ed, Assn Math Teachers NYS, ASCD; Natl Sci Fnd Inst to Study Math at Syracuse Univ 1966 & Drew Univ 1967; NY Writing Project Fellowship Lehman Coll 1983; Article on Teaching Published in Several Journals; AFT Video Series 1986; Bus Week Grant for Innovative Teaching 1990; *office:* Bronx HS of Sci 75 W 205th St Bronx NY 10468

ENGEL, MARLENE MARIE (CLELAND), First/Second Grade Teacher; *b:* Albany, OR; *c:* Lynn, Mark, Lisa; *ed:* (BS) Ed, Concordia Teachers Coll 1964; (MA) Spec Ed, AZ St Univ 1973; Grad Stud Ed; *cr:* Teacher Bethlehem Luth 1962-64, Christ Luth 1974-; *ai:* Christ Caller 1984-88; Stephen Minister 1988-; Pacific SW Teachers Conference Finalist Teacher of Yr Awd 1989; *office:* Christ Lutheran Sch 3901 E Indian Schl Rd Phoenix AZ 85018

ENGEL, TWYLA JOY, Third Grade Teacher; *b:* Hanford, CA; *ed:* (BA) Fine Arts/Elem Ed, Calvin Coll 1977; (MA) Elem Ed, AZ St Univ 1981; Childrens Lit Certificate, 1991; BASIC & LOGO Cmptr Classes, CA St Univ Hayward; *cr:* 2nd Grade Teacher Phoenix Chrstn Grade Sch 1978-82; 4th Grade Teacher Woodlands Chrstn Sch 1982-88; 4th/5th Grade Teacher Annandale Chrstn Australia 1988-89; 3rd Grade Teacher Woodlands Chrstn Sch 1989-; *ai:* Elem Plays & Musicals Dir; Fine Arts & Prof Growth Comm; Lang Art Comm Chm; Contra Costa Cty Rdng Assn 1985-; Intnl Rdng Assn 1989-; Diablo Valley Philharmonic Orch Prin Flautist 1984-87; Berkeley Presbyn Bell Choir Bell Ringer 1989-; Teaching Position Townsville Queensland Australia 1988; *office:* Woodlands Chrstn Sch 2721 Larkey Ln Walnut Creek CA 94596

ENGELAGE, MELNA JEAN BUENEMAN, Fifth Grade Teacher; *b:* Warrenton, MO; *m:* Norman A.; *c:* Darrell, Randall, Cheryl Cunningham; *ed:* (BS) Elem Ed, Lindenwood Coll 1972; *cr:* 6th Grade Teacher 1972-78, 5th Grade Teacher 1978- Wentzville R-IV Sch Dist; *ai:* Micro Cmptr Instructional Adv Comm Wentzville R-IV Dist; MO St Teachers Assn Mem 1972-; Phi Delta Kappa 1987-; Alpha Delta Kappa 1979-; Whos Who in MO Ed 1975; *home:* 601 Stamer Rd Wright City MO 63390

ENGELBRECHT, LYNN MOSER, 5th Grade Teacher/Team Leader; *b:* Oklahoma City, OK; *m:* Donald; *ed:* (BA) Elem Ed, Univ of WY 1968; (MLS) Lib Sci, TX Womans Univ 1986; *cr:* 3rd Grade Teacher Sam Hughes Elem 1968-69; 5th Grade Teacher a H Meadows Elem 1974-75, Jackson Elem 1975-77, AH Meadows Elem 1979-80 & 1981-; *ai:* Assn of TX Prof Ed 1981-; Dallas Needlework & Textile Guild 1978-89; Team Leader; *home:* 2721 Colonial Cir Mckinney TX 75070

ENGELHARDT, GERALD J., Physical Education Dept Chair; *b:* Joliet, IL; *m:* Anne Marie Heinrich; *c:* Rachel, Laura, Sarah, Matthew, Luke; *ed:* (BA) Phys Ed/His, N Cntrl Coll 1970; (MS) Phys Ed, N IL Univ 1973; *cr:* Teacher/Coach Granger Jr HS 1970-75; Teacher/Coach/Dept Chm Waubonsie Valley HS 1975-; *ai:* Intramurals; Bsbl; Dept Chm; Amer Assn of Health, Phys Ed, Recreation 1970-; IL Assn of Health Phys Ed & Recreation 1973-; IL Bsbl Coaches Assn Conference Rep 1975-83; Phi Delta Kappa 1979-; W Suburban Dept Chm Assn 1985-; Yorkville Congregational Church (Bd of Religious Ed Sunday Sch Teacher, Youth Leader) 1978-; Yorkville Park Dist Coach 1985-; Dist 90 Teacher of Yr 1972; Scholastic Coach Article 1974; Fox Valley Bsbl Camp Dir 1978-81; Outstanding Coach Awd 1985; Influential Teacher Awd 1989, 1990; *office:* Waubonsie Valley HS 2590 Rt 34 Aurora IL 60504

ENGELHARDT, PATRICIA ANN (SISCO), 5th Grade Teacher; *b:* Long Beach, CA; *m:* Thomas E.; *c:* Terrance, Timothy; *ed:* (BS) Chldhd Dev, CA St Univ Fullerton 1983; (MA) Ed, Claremont Grade Sch 1985; *cr:* 5th Grade Teacher Elsinore Elem 1983-; *ai:* Claremont Grad Sch Aubrey Douglass Excl Teaching Awd 1984; High Tech Grant Phys Fitness Prgm Awd 1984; *office:* Elsinore Elem Sch 512 W Sumner Lake Elsinore CA 92330

ENGELSMA, DANIEL LEE, Industrial & Tech Teacher; *b:* Grand Rapids, MI; *m:* Sharon Kay De Ulsser; *c:* Cara L., Marcia K.; *ed:* (AS) Bio, Grand Rapids Jr Coll 1970; (BS) Bio, Grand Valley St 1972; (MA) Elem Ed, MI St 1976; Industrial, Technology Ed, W MI Univ; *cr:* 2nd Grade Teacher 1972-74, 4th Grade Teacher 1974-76 Plymouth Chrstn Elem; 7th-12th Grade Teacher Plymouth Chrstn HS 1976-; *ai:* Mission, Acts Comm Chm; Building, Lib Comm; MI Industrial Educl Society (Regional Admin Officer 1989, Industrial Contact Comm Chm) 1987-89, Regional Service Awd 1989; Rehoboth Sch Teaching Adv 1982-86, Outstanding Service Awd 1986.

ENGERSKI, CHERYL JUSTICE, Elementary Counselor; *b:* Brazil, IN; *ed:* (BA) Elem Ed, IN Univ 1978; (MS) Elem Ed, De Pauw Univ 1981; (MS) Elem Schl Counseling, IN St Univ 1989; *cr:* 3rd-5th Grade Teacher 1978-88, Cnslr 1988- Rockville Elem; *ai:* Case Conference & ISTEP Coord; Screening & Awds Prgm Comm Mem; NEA, IN St Teachers Assn 1978-; Grad Asst IN St Univ; *office:* Rockville Elem Sch 406 Elm St Rockville IN 47872

ENGET, MAUREEN SALO, Home Economics Instructor; *b:* Kenmare, ND; *m:* Allie; *c:* Jared, Aaron, Chris; *ed:* (BS) Home Ec Ed, ND St Univ 1965; Grad Stud; *cr:* Home Ec Instr Crosby HS 1965-66, Powers Lake HS 1966-69, Stanley HS 1969-; *ai:* NDVHET (VP 1989-, Exec Cncl); AVA, NDVA, SEA, NDEA, NEA; Natl FHA Team Adv 1985-; FHA Dist & St Adv Adv of Yr 1988; Resource Person Curricular Planning Coll of Home Ec NDSU; Cooperating Teacher NDSU Stu Teachers 1978-; *office:* Stanley HS Box 10 Stanley ND 58784

ENGILIS, SARAH SHELBURNE, English Teacher; *b:* San Francisco, CA; *m:* Dennis; *ed:* (BA) Eng/Writing Emphasis, Dominican Coll 1984; *cr:* Mrktg Investment Public Storage Inc 1985; Teacher Valley HS 1987-; *ai:* Co-Chairperson WASC Accreditation Process; Honors Comm Mem; Future Teachers of America Mentor Spon; Var Bsktbl Booster; Friends for Survival Mem 1987-; *office:* Valley H S 6300 Ehrhardt Ave Sacramento CA 95823

ENGLAND, CAROLYN MC CRAY, Albebra/Geometry Teacher; *b:* Middlesboro, KY; *m:* George A.; *c:* Holly, Angel; *ed:* (BS) Chem, Lincoln Memorial Univ 1986; Certified to Teach Math, Bio, Physics & Chem; *cr:* Math Teacher Upward Bound Prgm, Lincoln Memorial, Powell Valley HS, Claiborne Cty HS; *ai:* Dance Squad & Math Club Spon; *home:* Rt 3 Box 201 Tazewell TN 37879

ENGLAND, JOHN MARK, Science Teacher; *b:* Eugene, OR; *ed:* (BA) Bio, Univ of OR 1981; Cert Ed, William Paterson Coll 1983; Post Grad Stud Ed & Sci; *cr:* Sci Teacher Butler HS 1983-84, Wallkill Valley Regional HS 1984-; *ai:* Ftbl & Swimming Coach; Earth Day Act Coord; NEA Mem 1983-; Amer Swim Coaches Assn Mem 1989-; Mid States Evaluation Comm; *office:* Wallkill Valley Regional HS Grumm Rd Hamburg NJ 07419

ENGLAND, KATIE IRENE, Second Grade Teacher; *b:* Gainesville, GA; *ed:* (BSE) Elem Ed, North GA Coll 1967; (MED) Elem Ed, Univ of GA 1974; *cr:* 2nd Grade Teacher Chestnut Mountain Elem 1967-; *ai:* Hall Cty Ed Assn Treas 1975-77; GA Assn of Educators 1967-; NEA (Natl Convention Delegate 1970, 1975) 1967-; Gainesville Bus & Prof Womens Club 1970-75; *office:* Chestnut Mountain Elem Sch Box 7249 Winder Hwy Chestnut Mountain GA 30502

ENGLAND, PAMELA ANN, Secondary Mathematics Teacher; *b:* Welch, WV; *m:* James William; *c:* James B.; *ed:* (BS) Ed/phys Ed, Concord Coll; (MS) Math, Radford Univ 1971; Cert AP Calculus, Univ of SC 1989; *cr:* Scndry Math Teacher Welch HS 1967-74; Adjunct Math Instr Bluefield St Coll 1978; Scndry Math Teacher Mount View HS 1979-; *ai:* Prom Dir; Administer Amer HS Math Exam; Steering Comm; Math Field Day; Delta Kappa Gamma Society Intnl (Photographer, Music Chm) 1982-; WV Cncl of Teachers of Math 1989-; Mc Dowell Cty Math Teachers Assn Pres-Elect 1989-; NEA, WV Ed Assn, Mc Dowell Cty Ed Assn 1967-; Welch United Meth Church Youth & Chancel Choirs 1953-; Amer Legion Mt View Teacher of Yr Nom 1988-89; Mt View Key Club Teacher of Yr 1988-89; Tandy Technology Scholars OUtstanding Teacher of Math 1989-; *home:* PO Box 91 Welch WV 24801

ENGLAND, SHERYL KAYE, Science Teacher; *b:* Enid, OK; *m:* Bryan Truman; *c:* Brandyn T.; *ed:* (BSE) General Sci Ed, Southern AR Univ 1975; (MSE) Phys Sci, Henderson St Univ 1981; *cr:* Sci Teacher Bradley HS 1975-80, Spring Hill HS 1980-; *ai:* I Now Spon the Sr Class & Beta Club; I Started the Stu Cncl/Beta Club & SADD at Spring Hill; AR Ed Assn 1987-; NEA 1987-; NSTA 1980-82; Beta Chapter Won Competition at Beta Convention Little Rock 1987; Beta Journal Publication Had Two Articles & Pictures About Us Since Own Inception 1984-; Shaver Springs Baptist Church 1971-; I Have Been the Only Sci Teacher for SHS Until this Yr; I Taught All the Sciences Offered Life, Earth, Phys, Bio, Geology, Chem, Physics, Human Anatomy & Physiology Alternating Years; There is Now a Different Life Sci Teacher this Year; Beta Chapter Won Scrapbook Competition at Beta Conven Tion in Little Rock 1987; *office:* Spring Hill R R 1 Box 834 Hope AR 71801

ENGLAND, TIMOTHY EDWARD, Social Studies Teacher; *b:* Detroit, MI; *m:* Theresa Ann Winland; *ed:* (BS) Soc Stud Ed, 1980, (MS) Ed Admin, 1981 Bob Jones Univ; *cr:* Soc Stud Teacher 1983-85; Asst Prin 1985 Licking Cty Chrstn Acad; *ai:* Yrbk Adv; Var Soccer Coach; Jr HS Bsktbl Coach; Debate Spon; Buckeye Chrstn Sch Assn Athletic Adv.

ENGLAND, ZONA MAE, First Grade Teacher; *b:* Auburn, OK; *m:* Jack J.; *c:* Tammy Haynes, C. L., Mark; *ed:* (AA) Elem Ed, SWBC Bolivar 1955; (BS) Elem Ed, MSSC Joplin 1968; *cr:* 1st/2nd/4th Grade Teacher Wheaton RIII Schls.

ENGLE, AMY L., HS Mathematics Teacher; *b:* Hamilton, OH; *m:* John R.; *c:* Jacob; *ed:* (BS) Math Ed, Ball St Univ 1984; Math Ed, Curr, Instruction, Purdue Univ 1989; *cr:* Math Teacher Western Boone Jr/Sr HS 1984-; *ai:* Teacher Appreciation Comm 1990; Teacher Inservice Comm 1989-; Stu Academic Awd Faculty Mem 1990; NEA, IN St Teachers Assn 1985-; Western Boone Teachers Assn Secy 1985-; Mem Math K-12th Grade Gifted & Talented Curr Writing Conference Team Clinton, Boone, Hendricks Cty; Sunshine Society Ideal Lady 1988-.

ENGLE, KAREN ELAINE, Sixth Grade Teacher; *b:* Lewistown, PA; *ed:* (BS) Elem Ed, 1971, (MS) Elem Ed 1975 Shippensburg Univ; *cr:* Elem Teacher Paxtonia Elem Sch 1971-; *ai:* NEA, PSEA, CDEA 1971-; Capital Area Rdng Cncl VP 1990; *office:* Paxtonia Elem Schl 6135 Jonestown Rd Harrisburg PA 17112

ENGLE, STUART L., English-Journalism Teacher; *b:* Fort Wayne, IN; *m:* Rita E.; *c:* Rachel, Kenneth; *ed:* (BS) Journalism/Eng, Ball St 1979; (MA) Ed, IN St 1985; *cr:* Teacher Lewis Cass HS 1980-; *ai:* Tennis & Track Coach; Newspaper Adv; Lions Intnl 1989-; US Prof Tennis Registry 1989-; *office:* Lewis Cass Jr Sr HS Hwy 218 Walton IN 46994

ENGLER, GAIL P. (WEYEL), Mathematics Teacher; *b:* New Braunfels, TX; *m:* Chuck; *c:* Kevin, Gail; *ed:* (BA) Math, Univ of TX Austin 1969; *cr:* Eng/Math Teacher Comal Ind Sch Dist 1970-71, New Braunfels Ind Sch DIst 1971-73; Math Teacher New Braunfels Ind Sch Dist 1984-; *ai:* Twirlers & Soph Class Spon; ATPE 1984-; St Paul Luth Church Membership Comm 1989-; Chrstn Acad 1983, Life Mem 1983; Math & Sci Eisenhower Grant SW TX; *office:* New Braunfels HS 2551 Loop 337 E New Braunfels TX 78130

ENGLHARD, KATHRYN FULLER, Spanish Teacher; *b:* Los Angeles, CA; *m:* Ronald F.; *c:* Michael, Matthew; *ed:* (BA) Span/Speech, Univ of AZ 1966; (MA) Scndry Ed, CA St Los Angeles 1970; *cr:* Teacher Western HS 1966-68, Corona del Mar HS 1968-71, Laguna Hills HS 1980; *ai:* Key Club Adv; Advanced Placement Intnl Baccalaureate Span Teacher; CA Teachers Assn, NEA; Church Vacation Bible Sch Dir 1985, 1988; Kappa Alpha Theta Alumni Club 1970-; Bible Study Fellowship Childrens Leader 1978-80; Saddleback Valley Chamber of Commerce Teacher of Yr 1986; Teacher of Month; *office:* Laguna Hills HS 25401 Paseo de Valencia Laguna Beach CA 92653

ENGLISH, CHARLOTTE PATRICE (STRONG), Interpretation & Debate Coach; *b:* Carthage, TX; *c:* Alexander C.; *ed:* (BA) Comm, Univ of TX Arlington 1976; Grad Work Speech Comm, Ed, Theatre, Univ N TX; *cr:* Speech/Theatre Teacher S Grand Prairie HS 1976-77; Math/Speech/Theatre Dir Winona HS 1977-79; Comm Dept Chm Mac Arthur HS 1979-82; Debate & Speech Coach/Theatre Dir Plano E Sr HS 1982-86; Interpretation/Debate Coach Plano Sr HS 1986-; *ai:* Natl Forensic League Adv & Spon; Oral Interpretation, Duet Acting, Oratory, LD Debate, Stu Congress Coach; Liason Comm for Mid Sch & HS PISD Speech Prgms; TX Forensic Assn (Treas 1983-85, Emeritus Membership Comm Chm) 1979-; TX Speech Comm Assn (Dist 10 Chm 1989-) 1979-; Amer Forensic Assn Mem 1979-; Natl Forensic League (N TX Chm 1986-87) 1979-; Plano Ind Sch Dist (Textbook Comm 1989, Critical Thinking Action Team Mem 1987-88); Outstanding Coach Awd Irving Invitational 1981, Burleson Invitation 1983, Trinity Invitational 1987, 1989; Outstanding Teacher Awd Mac Arhtur 1982, Plano East 1985; Coached 3 Natl Speech Champions, 3 Natl Speech 2nd Places, 11 St Speech Champions; *office:* Plano Sr HS 2200 Independence Pkwy Plano TX 75075

ENGLISH, ELIZABETH SHELL, Business Education Teacher; *b:* Winston-Salem, NC; *m:* Herbert Allen; *c:* Cheli E.; *ed:* (BS) Bus Ed, NC Cntrl Univ 1953; (MA) Bus Ed, Columbia Univ Teachers Coll 1957; Post Grad Stud Wayne St Univ; *cr:* Teacher Detroit Inst of Commerce 1953-56, Dodge Voc HS 1957-; *ai:* Advisory Cncl Chairperson; FBLA Coord; Bus House; Stu Affairs Asst Coord; Bus Ed of Metropolitan NY 1960-; Delta Pi Epsilon; Jack & Jill of America Incorporated (Financial Secy, Pres 1981, Teen Adv 1979-81); Delta Sigma Theta Soc Action Comm 1988-; Outstanding Educator NY Club of Natl Assn of Negro Bus & Prof Womens Clubs Women of Color Awd 1990; *office:* Dodge Voc HS 2474 Crotona Ave Bronx NY 10458

ENGLISH, JENNIFER SULLIVAN, Math Teacher/Dept Chairperson; *b:* Richmond, VA; *m:* Thomas Richard; *c:* Katie, Richard; *ed:* (BS) Math, Mary Washington Coll 1979; *cr:* Math Teacher Lancaster HS 1979-; *ai:* Dept Chairperson Mem of Faculty Advisory Comm; *office:* Lancaster H S P O Box 123 Lancaster VA 22503

ENGLISH, JUDY BETH, Second Grade Teacher; *b:* Abilene, TX; *m:* Jerry Lynn; *c:* Julie, Jay, Jason; *ed:* (BS) Elem Ed, Hardin Simmons Univ 1965; *cr:* 3rd Grade Teacher Bayless Elem 1965-66, Tye Elem Sch 1966-68; Kndgtn/2nd Grade Teacher Faith Chrstn Sch 1977-79; 1st/2nd Grade Teacher Wylie Elem Sch 1979-; *ai:* Assn of TX Prof Educators 1979-; PTA 1978-; Band Booster Club 1983-; Abilene A&M Mothers Club (Publicity Chm, Historian) 1987-; Outstanding Teacher Awd; *home:* 1854 Jackson Abilene TX 79602

ENGLISH, LENA COKLEY, Science Teacher; *b:* Rhems, SC; *w:* Walter Sr. (dec); *c:* Alexandrea, Walter Jr.; *ed:* (BS) Health/Phys Ed/Bio, SC St Coll 1972; Grad Work Univ of SC, Appalachian St Univ, Francis Marion Coll, Coll of Charleston; *cr:* Phys Ed Teacher Evans Jr HS 1973-78; Sci Teacher 1978-79, Phys Ed/Health Teacher 1979-82 Hand Mid Sch; Bio/Phys Ed Teacher C A Johnson HS 1982-83; Sci/Health Teacher Williams Mid Sch 1983-88; Sci Teacher Southside Mid Sch 1988-; *ai:* Stu Incentive Comm; Black His; Sci; NEA, SC Ed Assn 1973-; SC Sci Cncl, NSTA 1983-; Cancer Society; Hospice; *office:* Southside Mid Sch 200 Howe Springs Rd Florence SC 29501

ENGLISH, MARY ELIZABETH, 11th/12th Grade US His Teacher; *b:* Norwich, CT; *ed:* (AB) Government, CT Coll 1956; (MA) Ed, Univ of CT 1961; Content Rdng Including Study Systems, St of CT; *cr:* Soc Sci Instr Norwich Free Acad 1956-; *ai:* NEA, CEA, EANFA, Delta Kappa Gamma; Volunteer & Gift Shop Wm W Backus Hospital 1956-, Service Awd 1987; Charles F Noyes Awd; NFA Service Awd 25 Yrs.

ENGLISH, MAXIE JUNE FOX, Sci Teacher & Sci Chairperson; *b:* Elizabethton, TN; *m:* Eddie Jr.; *c:* Krista J., Johannah L.; *ed:* (BS) Hlth & Phys Ed, East TN St Univ 1968; (MED) Mid Grades Ed - Sci, 1988; (EDS) Mid Grades Ed - Sci 1989 Western Carolina Univ; Fast 1 1986; Fast 2 1987; Fast 3 1988; Effectv Teacher Trng 1987; Proj Wildlf 1984; Aquatic Wild 1989; *cr:* Elem Phys Ed Teacher Washington Cty Sch Sys 1969-71; Marshall HS 1972-73; Sci Teacher Asheville JR HS 1973-; *ai:* NSTA - Evaluator 1984/1990; Mid Sch Task Force 1990; Faclty Cncl 1990; Dept Hd 1990; Southern Assn Evaluation Team Mem; Sch Trip Coord 1984; Txtbk Selctn Comm 1980/1985/1990; Proj Wildlf St Coord; NSTA 1977-; NCSTA 1975-; NCAE/NEA 1976-; Kappa Delta Pi ASCD 1987-; DAR 1987-; NC Dept of Archives Vlntr 1987-; Washington Cty Geneology Assn 1990; Voted As Acadmc All Star Teacher 1985-86; *home:* 28 Edgemont Rd Grove Park Apt 6 Asheville NC 28801

ENGLUND, LINDA TRUMBULL, English Department Chair; *b:* Chicago, IL; *m:* Carl; *c:* Timothy; *ed:* (BS) Eng Ed, Northwestern Univ 1972; (MS) Psych, US Intnl Univ 1975; *cr:* Eng Teacher Mt Carmel HS 1974-; Eng Dept Chairperson Rancho Bernardo HS 1990-; *ai:* Advanced Placement Eng & Mentor Teacher; Drama Dir 1979-81; Poway CA Fed of Teachers, AFT 1974-; Northwestern Alumni Assn 1975-; San Diego Museum of Art 1979-; Old Globe Theater 1972-; Nominations for Poway Teacher of Yr 1989-; *office:* Rancho Bernardo HS 13010 Paseo Lucido San Diego CA 92128

ENGMAN, GILTA CASANOVA, Spanish Teacher/Chair; *b:* Utuado, PR; *m:* Rodney; *c:* Eda M., Herbert N.; *ed:* (BA) Art, Univ of PR 1968; (MS) Foreign Lang, George Mason Univ 1982; *cr:* Linguist Researcher Mc Graw Hill Book Company 1969-70; Span Teacher Woodbridge Sr HS 1973-74, Godwin Mid Sch 1977-, Woodbridge Mid Sch 1988-; *ai:* Foreign Lang Club Spon 1990; Sponsored Stu to Participate Prince William Contest; Stu Organized Trips; Started Exch Stu Prgm 1983-; Dale Cty Span Club Spon 1980-87; NEA, VA Ed Assn 1977-; Sigma Delta Pi 1981-; Dale City Civic Assn Teacher of Yr 1985; *office:* Woodbridge Mid Sch 2201 York Dr Woodbridge VA 22192

ENGRAM, MARVIN C., English Teacher; *b:* Miami, FL; *ed:* (BA) Eng, 1982, (MED) Personnel Admin, 1983 Tuskegee Univ; *cr:* Summer Youth Cnslr Metro Dade Summer Prgms 1984-87; Eng Instr Miami Northwestern Sr HS 1984-; *ai:* Stu Cncl Adv; Kappa Delta Pi 1983; Omega Psi Phi Editor 1986-87; *home:* 2934 NW 66th St Miami FL 33147

ENGRAV, NANCY GAUSTAD, First Grade Teacher; *b:* Caledonia, MN; *m:* Richard; *ed:* (BS) Elem Ed - Cum Laude, Viterbo Coll 1972; *cr:* 1st Grade Teacher St Marys Sch 1972-; *ai:* Mardi Gras Comm; Grandparents Day Comm Chairperson; Parental Rdng Wkshp Comm; NEA 1972-; Kappa Gamma Pi; Jaycee Women 1982-84; Area Arts Cncl Secy 1985-87; Congregation Cncl (Treas, Secy) 1981-; Outstanding Elem Teachers of America 1974; *home:* RR 2 Box 204 Mabel MN 55954

ENGSTRAND, MARGARET ANN, Phase III Coordinator; *b:* Sioux City, IA; *c:* Becci Christensen, Elizabeth Pavone, Jennifer Bliss, Katherine Christensen, David Christensen, Paul Christensen; *ed:* (BS) Elem Ed, Morningside Coll 1973; Grad Stud Univ of IA, Univ of SD, Univ of N IA, Marycrest, Morningside Coll; *cr:* 1st Grade Teacher Northside Sch 1953-56; 2nd-5th Grade Teacher Emerson Sch 1973-88; Phase III Coord Admin Service Center 1988-; *ai:* Facilitator for in Service Course in Integrated Rdng/Writing Process; Phi Delta Kappa, NEA, ISEA, SCEA, IA Women in Ed Leadership, NCTE, IA Rdng Assn & Cherry Plywood Rdng Assn; Adults Children Learning Disabilities Bd Mem 1983-86; Candidate for Teacher of Yr 1985; Presenter at IA St Phase III Ed Conference 1990; Nominee for PTA Phoebe Apperson Hearst Awd 1988; Sioux Citys Outstanding Teacher for Appreciation Week 1985; *office:* Sioux City Cmmty Schls 1221 Pierce St Sioux City IA 51105

ENGSTROM, SUSAN RIVERS, Language Arts Teacher; *b:* Inglewood, CA; *m:* Gorden Cameron; *ed:* (AA) General Ed, Modesto Jr Coll 1977; (BA) Eng, CA St Univ Stanislaus 1979; *cr:* Lang Arts Teacher Mae Hensley Jr HS 1986-; *office:* Mae Hensley Jr H S 1806 Moffett Ceres CA 95307

ENLOE, JOHN TAYLOR, Principal; *b:* Alexandria, LA; *c:* Jennifer L. *ed:* (BA) Eng, Rhodes Coll 1972; (MS) Supervision/Admin, E TN St Univ 1986; Working Towards PhD E TN St Univ; *cr:* 1st-4th Grade Teacher/Prin Benson Elem 1974-75, 7th/8th Grade Teacher/Prin Whites Elem 1975-77, Jones Cove Elem 1979-81; 7th/8th Grade Eng Teacher/Prin Wearwood Elem 1981-; *ai:* 7th/8th Grade Girls & Boys Bsktbl Coach; 8th Grade Trip Chm; Accreditation Comm Chm; Whole Lang Pilot Sch Chm; Phi Kappa Phi Mem 1987-, Academic Awd 1987; Lions Club 1977-; Poems Published; Governors Acad for Teachers of Writing; *office:* Sevierville Intermediate Sch 226 Cedar St Sevierville TN 37862

ENNIS, JENNIFER EDWARDS, 4th Grade Teacher; *b:* Smithfield, NC; *m:* Winfred Craig; *c:* Natalie; *ed:* (BS) Primary Ed, Campbell Coll 1986; Mentor Teacher Trng 1987-88; *cr:* 1st Grade Teacher Clayton Primary 1977-78; 4th Grade Teacher Clayton Elem 1978-; *ai:* Leader & Mentor Teacher; Teacher Assistance & Improvement Team Mem; NEA Mem 1978-; Mt Zion United Meth Church Mem 1978-; Sunday Sch Teacher for Toddlers 1986-; United Meth Women (Treas, Mem) 1986-88; Teacher of Yr 1987-88; *office:* Clayton Elem Sch 105 2nd St Clayton NC 27520

ENNIS, LINDA LARCHE, Mathematics Teacher; *b:* New Orleans, LA; *m:* Ron L. Sr.; *ed:* (BS) Soc Worker, Southern Univ 1974; Elem Cert Elem Ed, LA St Univ 1976; (MS) Elem Ed, E TX St Univ 1986; *cr:* Teacher Roger Q Mills 1976-; *ai:* Act Chm; Sch Cncl & Math Club Co-Chm; Alpha Kappa Alpha 1976-.

ENNIS, LOTTIE STRUM, 5th Grade Teacher; *b:* Rocky Mount, NC; *m:* William Daniel; *ed:* (BS) Interm Ed, Atlantic Chrstn Coll 1982; (MED) Interm Ed, Campbell Univ 1985; *cr:* 7th/8th Grade Teacher Southern Nash Jr HS 1982-86, Springfield Mid Sch 1986-88; 5th Grade Teacher Red Oak Elem 1988-; *ai:* Church Sunday Sch Youth Teacher; Youth Choir Dir; NCAE 1982-;

Springfield Mid Sch Teacher of Yr Candidate; *office:* Red Oak Elem Sch P O Box 70 Red Oak NC 27868

ENNIS, REBECCA LEE, Teacher-Specialist; *b:* New York City, NY; *ed:* (BA) Poly Sci/His, Stephen F Austin St 1975; (MED) Curr/Instruction Soc Stud, Univ of Houston 1981; Amer Economy Inst TX A&M Univ 1983; The Constitution Cntrl MO St Univ 1989; Natl Endowment Hum-Soc His US Carnegie Mellon Univ 1990; *cr:* World/Amer His/Government/Economics Teacher Jack Yates HS 1976-85; Government/Economics Teacher Sharpstown HS 1985-89; Teacher Specialist Project Access 1989-; *ai:* Sharpstown HS Key Club, Sharpstown HS Delegation Houston Area Model United Nations, Stu Congress Legislative Enterprise Spon; Houston Cncl for Soc Stud Bd Mem 1988-; TX Cncl for Soc Stud; Natl Endowment Hum Grant Awd Carnegie Mellon Univ; *home:* 12211 Fondren 808 Houston TX 77035

ENOS, DEBORAH H., Science Teacher; *b:* Louisville, KY; *m:* John; *c:* Ruth A., April E.; *ed:* (BS) Bio, Morehead St Univ 1980; (MA) Ed, N KY Univ 1984; Chem; *cr:* Sci Teacher Campbell Cty HS 1980-81, Gallatin Cty HS 1981-83, Newport HS 1983-; *ai:* Sr Class Spon; NSTA, Natl Teachers Assn, KY Ed Assn, KY Sci Teachers Assn; KY Ed Fnd Mini-Grant Acid Rain; *office:* Newport HS 900 E 6th St Newport KY 41071

ENOS, JAMES THOMAS, Fifth Grade Teacher; *b:* Tullahoma, TN; *ed:* (BS) Ec, 1959, (MA) Curr of Inst, 1967 Mid TN St Univ; Additional Stud; Career Ladder I; *cr:* 4th Grade Teacher Miami Cntry & Resident Sch for Boys 1959-61; 5th/6th Grade Teacher Hickerson Station 1961-62; 6th/7th EMR Teacher Shelbyville Mills 1962-67; 5th Grade Teacher/Asst Prin Westwood Elem 1967-; *ai:* Vice Prin; Manchester Ed Assn (VP 1968-69, Pres 1969-70); TN Ed Assn, NEA 1967-; *home:* 403 N Washington St Tullahoma TN 37388

ENRICO, GARY, Band Director; *b:* Weehawken, NJ; *m:* Madalene Panoforte; *c:* Michele, Desiree, Christine; *ed:* (BA) Music Ed, Mont Clair St 1975; *cr:* Music Teacher D S Kealey Sch 1976-79, T G Connors Sch 1979-82; Band Dir Hoboken HS 1982-; *ai:* In Charge of HS Band; NEA/NJEA/HCEA 1976; *office:* Hoboken H S 9th & Clinton Sts Hoboken NJ 07030

ENSMINGER, BOBBY, Science Teacher; *b:* Baton Rouge, LA; *m:* Patricia Taylor; *c:* Bobby, Joseph, Elizabeth; *ed:* (BS) Construction, 1973, (MED) Scndry Ed, 1986, Sci Ed, 1988 NE LA Univ; 0d Specialist Prgm Sci Ed; Post Grad Work Toward MBA; *cr:* Sci Teacher Ft Necessity HS 1987-; *ai:* SADD, Wildlife Club, Sci Fair Spon; Substance Abuse Prevention Ed Comm Mem; LA Assn of Prof Educators, Kappa Delta Pi; 32nd Degree Mason 1978-; Shriner 1985-; Carnegie Inst for Advancement of Excl in Teaching Natl Teacher Awd 1988; *home:* PO Box 727 Jigger LA 71249

ENSOR, MARY CATHERINE GRACE, Sixth Grade Teacher; *b:* Bristol, VA; *m:* Richard D.; *c:* Emily J.; *ed:* (BS) Elem Ed, 1973, (MA) Ed, 1982 E TN St Univ; *cr:* 6th Grade Teacher Cntrl Elem Sch 1973-78; 3rd Grade Teacher 1978-79, 6th Grade Teacher 1979-81, 4th/5th Grade Teacher 1981-82, 5th Grade Teacher 1982-89, 6th Grade Teacher 1989- Holston View Elem Sch; *ai:* 4th-6th Grade Remediation Tutor; Instr Parents Accent Learning Prgm; Wrote 5th Grade Curr Guide Black His; Lobbyist Nashville Ed Bills; Safety Patrol Spon; Bristol TN Ed Assn Secy 1980-81; TN Ed Assn Delegate 1975-78; Assn Supervision Curr 1988-; PTA (Secy, Parliamentarian) 1976-78; Bristol Jr League 1982-86; Bristol Chamber of Commerce 1983-85; Sullivan Cty Jaycees 1982-83; Rotary Outstanding Teacher Awd 1989; Career Level III Status; Served Various Southern Assn Schls, Coll Evaluation Comm; Whos Who in Amer Colls & Univs; *office:* Holston View Elem Sch 1840 King College Rd Bristol TN 37620

ENSZER, GARY W., 3rd Grade Teacher; *b:* Saginaw, MI; *ed:* (BA) His Teaching, 1972, (MA) Classroom Teaching, 1975 Saginaw Valley St Univ; Ed; *cr:* Teacher Emerson Elem 1973-74, Herig Elem 1974-79, Jerome Elem 1979-; *ai:* Coaching Grades 4th & 6th Boys & Girls Bsktbl; Chrldng/Floor Hockey/Sftbl; 8 Yrs in Row City Champs Floor Hockey; Saginaw Ed Assn 1973-; MI Ed Assn 1973-; NEA 1973-; Friendship Games Coach.

EOFF, DEBBIE MILBURN, 8th Grade English Teacher; *b:* Nocona, TX; *m:* Garry; *c:* Lacie, Carlie; *ed:* (BS) Scndry Ed, Howard Payne Univ 1978; Gifted Ed; *cr:* Eng/Speech Teacher 1978-, Gifted/Talented Teacher 1985- Brownwood Jr HS; *ai:* 7th & 8th Grade Forensics Coach; TX Classroom Teachers Assn 1979-; Brownwood CTA Pres 1981-82; Teacher of Yr 1989-; *office:* Brownwood Jr HS 1200 Avenue D Brownwood TX 76801

EPHRAIM, NORMA LOUISE, History Teacher; *b:* Uvalde, TX; *m:* Jesse Paul Jr.; *c:* Jesse P. III, Kendrich T., Erich Brown; *ed:* (BA) His - Magda Cum Laude, Univ of N TX 1964; Grad Stud TX Womans Univ Denton, OK Univ Norman; *cr:* Teacher Denton Jr HS 1964-66; Teacher/Academic Coach Denton HS 1977-; *ai:* Academic Coach Denton HS Whiz Quiz Team 1977-; Academic Decathlon Coach 1987-89; NHS & Future Teachers Assn Spon; AASS 1977-79; Delta Kappa Gamma (1st VP 1984-88) 1980-; Citizens Traffic Safety Support Commission 1976-79; Teacher of Month 1990; Co-Authored Religious Ed Books; *office:* Denton HS 1007 Fulton Denton TX 76201

EPP, LAURINE QUIRING, Retired Teacher; *b:* Newton, KS; *m:* G. Kenneth; *c:* Deborah Epp Mc Keever; *ed:* (BA) Bible, Bethel Coll 1944; (MA) Chrstn Ed, Northwestern Univ 1948; Elem Ed, Pittsburg St Univ 1964-74; *cr:* 6th Grade Teacher Valley Sch 1940-41; 3rd-5th Grade Teacher North Reno 1941-42; 3rd Grade Teacher Bluemont Elem 1950-51, Mc Kinley Elem 1969-71, Guthridge Elem 1971-85; *ai:* KNEA 1969-; NEA, Parsons Ed Assn 1969-85; PTA 1956-63, 1969-85; Wesley Meth Cncl of Ministries 1987-; Washington Avenue Meth (Commission on Ed Chm, Adult Dept Supt); Stafford 1st Meth Childrens Coord 1953-54; Sacramento 1st Meth Chrstn Ed Dir 1948-50; Artlices, Poetry, Prayer Published.

EPPERSON, ROCHELLE S., Scndry Science Teacher; *b:* Chicago, IL; *m:* Thomas C.; *c:* Kristin, Megan; *ed:* (BS) Zoology/Ed, E IL Univ 1976; Grad Courses E IL Univ; *cr:* Sci Teacher Tower Hill HS 1978-80; Asst Financial Aide Admin Lake Land Coll 1980-83; Sci Teacher Mattoon Jr & Sr HS 1985-; *ai:* E IL Univ Zoology Club; NABT 1987-; NEA 1986-; Peace Meal Service for Sr Citizens 1987-; NOA Schlsp Marine Bio Wkshp 1989; Accent on Ed Grant 1990; *office:* Mattoon HS 2521 Walnut Mattoon IL 61938

EPPLE, DORTHY M., First Grade Teacher; *b:* Fulton Cty, OH; *m:* Paul E.; *c:* Ricky E., Clifford H.; *ed:* (BA) Elem Ed, Fort Wayne Bible Coll 1960; (MS) Elem Ed, St Francis Coll 1965; *cr:* 1st Grade Teacher EAC Schls 1960-62; Substitute Teacher Fort Wayne Consolidated Sch 1971-77; Kndgtn Teacher Ward 1977-79; Kndgtn/1st Grade Teacher Weisser Park 1979-81; 1st Grade Teacher Fairfield 1981-; *ai:* IN St Teachers Assn, NEA 1977-; BSA South Wayne Sch Troop Treas 1979-83; *office:* Fairfield Elem Sch 2825 Fairfield Ave Fort Wayne IN 46807

EPPS, LEE HAMILTON, Eng Teacher/Asst Dept Chair; *b:* Durham, NC; *c:* Le Tanya; *ed:* (BS) Eng, NC A&T St Univ 1968; (MA) Supervision/Human Relations, George Washinton Univ 1984; Cmptr Literacy, Play Production in Schls & Substance Abuse; *cr:* Teacher Henderson HS 1968-69; Cataloguer/Researcher NBC-TV 1969-70; Teacher Hart Jr HS 1970-; Curr Writer Takoma Cmptr Literacy Center 1986, Langdon Instructional Service Center 1958; Coord DC Summer Enrichment Prgm 1989; Teacher Franklin Adult Center 1990; *ai:* Adv Natl Jr Honor Society; Dept Chairperson Eng Dept 1984-89; Founder & Adv of JETS Journal, Sch Newspaper & Morning Broadcast Team; Building & Writing Coord; Asst Coach for Girls Track; Co-Chm for Gifted & Talented; Cafritz Fellow 1988-89 Awd 1988; Inst of Educl Leadership 1989-; NCTE 1968-; DC Cncl Teachers of Eng 1980-; Prophecy Homeowners Assn Block Capt 1985-; Church Act; Washington Post Mini Grant 1985-86; Supts Incentive Awd 1985; Cafritz Fellowship Visited London Schls 1988-89; Published Booklets 1989; Commercial for Ed 1990; Certificates for Judging Bicentennial Essays & Poetry; *office:* Charles Hart Jr H S 601 Mississippi Ave SE Washington DC 20032

EPTING, TAMMYE NISEWONGER, Language Art/Reading Teacher; *b:* Atlanta, GA; *m:* Al; *c:* Drew, Abbye, Ben; *ed:* (BA) Early Chldhd Ed, 1981, (MS) Rdng Specialist, 1982 Univ of GA; *cr:* 6th Grade Lang Art Teacher Oconee Intermediate; 5th Grade Lang Art Teacher Oconee Elem; 6th-8th Grade Rdng Specialist Oconee Intermediate; *ai:* Honors Day Comm; Curr Guides; *office:* Oconee Cty Intermediate Sch Colham Ferry Rd Watkinsville GA 30677

ERAZMUS, CYNTHIA, Second Grade Teacher; *b:* Meriden, CT; *ed:* (BS) Elem Ed, Cntrl Ct St Univ 1973; (MLS) Lib Sci, S Ct St Univ 1978; *cr:* 1st/2nd Grade Teacher St Stanislaus Sch 1975-; *ai:* St Stanislaus Childrens Choir Dir; *office:* St Stanislaus Sch 81 Akron St Meriden CT 06450

ERAZMUS, JANET, 8th Grade Teacher; *b:* Chicago, IL; *ed:* (BSEE) Elem Ed, De Paul Univ 1968; (MED) Curr/Admin, Loyola Univ 1990; *cr:* Teacher St Turibius; *ai:* Testing Coord Drug & Alcohol Pgrm; Coord Math, Rdng, Soc Stud Chairperson; Luturgy Coord Parish & Sch; Kappan 1968-; IEA, NEA, NCEA 1990; St Vincent De Paul Society Distributing Food to Needy 1989-; Nom for Kohl Intnl Teaching AwD; *home:* 5434 S Komensky Chicago IL 60632

ERBE, LEWIS M., US History Teacher; *b:* Tamaqua, PA; *m:* Tana Lynn Boyer; *c:* Lindsay, Adrienne, Lewis B.; *ed:* (BS) Soc Stud, E Strousburg St Coll 1976; (MED) Scndry Ed, Towson St Univ 1982; *cr:* Teacher Rising Sun HS 1977-; Instr Cecil Comm Coll 1990-; *ai:* Girls Head Track Coach; Stus Helping Other People Service Club Shop Adv; St Bsktbl Comm; Regional Dir; *office:* Rising Sun HS 289 Pearl St Rising Sun MD 21911

ERDMAN, WANETA CALLAHAN, Fifth Grade Teacher; *b:* Milford, IL; *m:* Myron; *c:* Ann Meyer, Linda Langel, Mark; *ed:* (BA) Elem, IL St Univ Normal 1947; *cr:* 6th/7th Grade Teacher Tremont Grade Sch 1947-48; 6th Grade Teacher Cessna Park Grade Sch 1948-49; 5th Grade Teacher Fairbury Cropsey 1967-; *ai:* Schlsp & Negotiating Comm; IL Ed Assn, NEA; St Pauls Luth Church Sunday Sch Teacher/Bible Sch Teacher; *home:* RR 1 Box 85 Chenoa IL 61726

ERDMANN, LA DONNA LYNN (BENGE), Mathematics/Computer Teacher; *b:* Kenmare, ND; *m:* Kim Dale; *c:* Robin, Daniel; *ed:* (BS) Math, Minot St Coll 1980; Cmptr; *cr:* Math/Cmptr Teacher Goodrich Public 1980-; *ai:* Frosh Class Adv; Piano Teacher; Tutor; Church (Cncl Treas 1987-, Organist 1989-); Vlybl Team Mem 1981-; *home:* 101 Mc Kinley Ave Box 133 Goodrich ND 58444

ERICKSON, ELLEN COX, First Grade Teacher; *b:* Dodgeville, WI; *c:* Karyle Johnson, Kim; *ed:* Elem Ed, 1950; (BA) Elem Ed, 1952; (MS) Elem Ed, 1988 UW Platteville; *cr:* 1st/8th Grade Teacher Fort Deifnce Sch 1950-52; 1st Grade Teacher Blanchardville Elm Sch 1952-54; 1st/8th Grade Teacher Moscow Center Sch 1954-56; 1st Grade Teacher Mineral Point Elem Dist 1964-; *ai:* Math Comm; At-Risk Teacher Participant; NEA; PTA Swic Teaching Pin 1984; WEA; MPEA; Hidden Valley Rdng Cncl; IA Cty Republicans 1984; Tregoning for Assembly Comm 1985-Treas; *office:* Mineral Point Elem Sch Cothern St Mineral Point WI 53565

ERICKSON, M. DEANE (GUY), Third Grade Teacher; *b:* Camp Le Juene, NC; *m:* David G.; *c:* Megan, Lucas; *ed:* (BS) Family Services 1974, (BS) Elem Ed, 1975 IA St Univ; *cr:* 2nd-4th Grade Teacher Exira Elem 1975-; *ai:* Exira Chrstn Church (Mem, Sunday Sch Teacher) 1984-; Omicron Nu 1973-; IA Federated Womens Club 1977-81; *office:* Exira Elem Sch Washington St Exira IA 50076

ERICKSON, MERLYN S., Physics Teacher; *b:* Estherville, IA; *m:* Maureen Kaphingst Erickson; *c:* Kevin; Kristin Spangrud; *ed:* (BA) Physics/Math, Augustana Coll 1961; (MA) Sci Ed, Univ of MN 1967; San Diego St; Sch of Mines; Univ of MN; *cr:* Physics/Math Teacher Yankton Jr HS 1961-62; Forest Lake Sr HS 1962-67; Stillwater Sr HS 1967-; *ai:* Astronomy Club; SCEA & MEA Gov Rel Chm 1978-84; NSTA 1965-; *office:* Ind Sch Dist 834 523 W Marsh St Stillwater MN 55082

ERICKSON, RODNEY EUGENE, Social Studies Teacher; *b:* Kulm, ND; *m:* Barbara Lou Carlson; *c:* Tammie Junkans, Todd, Tim; *ed:* (BA) His, Bethel Coll 1953; (MA) Ed, St Thomas Coll 1974; *cr:* Teacher Fridley Jr HS 1959-83, Fridley Mid Sch 1983-; *ai:* Adv Odyssey of Mind & Youth in Government; 8th Grade Team Leader; NEA, MEA 1959-; Outstanding Teacher Performance Awd Medtronic 1989; *home:* 2106 Midlothian Rd Roseville MN 55113

ERICKSON, ROY RICHARD, Social Studies Teacher; *b:* St Paul, MN; *m:* Patricia Ann Mc Guinn; *c:* Kathryn A., Meghan P.; *ed:* (AA) Liberal Arts, Lakewood Comm Coll 1976; (BS) Scndry Ed/Soc Stud, 1978, (MA) Psych Ed Stud, 1984 Univ of MN; Attendee Presenter Logo Cmptr Lang Wkshps; Advanced Trng Techniques of Cooperative Ed; *cr:* Spec Ed Teacher 1979-86, Soc Stud/Logo Cmptr Teacher 1987, Soc Stud Teacher 1988- Highland Park Scndry Complex; *ai:* Dain Bosworth Scholastic Achievement Awd 1989; Ecolab incorporated Quest for Excl Ed Grant 1990; *office:* Highland Park Scndry Complex 1015 S Snelling Ave Saint Paul MN 55116

ERICKSON, SANDRA VALERIE, Gifted English Teacher; *b:* Gadsden, AL; *m:* Richard P.; *c:* Christopher; *ed:* (BA) Eng, Univ AL 1965; (MA) Counseling/Guidance 1973, (MA) Gifted Ed, 1982 Eastern NM Univ; Grad Stud Bus Admin Troy St Univ; Advanced Placement Training for Teaching Eng, Univ Cntrl FL, Univ AL & The Citadel; *cr:* Eng Teacher Marshall Jr HS 1972-74, Dept Of Defense Overseas Schls Upper Heyford England 1974-77; Gifted/Teacher Yucca Sch 1977-81; Eng Teacher Tularosa HS 1982-85; Gifted Eng/AP Eng Teacher Lake Brantley HS 1985-; *ai:* Spon Perspectives Sch Literary Magazine; Brain Bowl; Academic Team; Future Problem Solving; Academic Decathlon & Waves of Excl; Seminole Cncl Teachers of Eng 1985; NCTE 1977; Amer Assn of Univ Women 1981; Alamagerdo Jr Womens Club Pres 1981-85; NM Outstanding Volunteer of Yr 1985; Cub Scouts Volunteer of Yr 1979; Gifted & Talented Parents Organization Pres 1983-85; *office:* Lake Brantley H S 991 Sand Lake Rd Altamonte Springs FL 32714

ERICKSON, SONDRA KOERING, English/Journalism Teacher; *b:* Ada, MN; *c:* Carter; *ed:* (BA) Eng, Concordia Coll 1964; Numerous Seminars in Educl Leadership; Elements of Effective Ed, Classroom Management, Clinical Supervision; Working on Masters in Educl at St Thomas; *cr:* Eng Teacher Princeton HS 1964-68, Cambridge HS 1968-69; City Ed Princeton Union Newspaper 1970-71; News Dir WKPM Radio Station 1975-76; Eng Teacher Princeton HS 1976-; *ai:* Scholastic Publications, Newspaper, Yrbk Adv; PEA Secy 1965-68; PEA Teacher of Yr 1978 & 1980; NEA; NCTE, MCTE, JEA; Jam Secy 1968-69; ASCD; Church Cncl 1984-87, 1990; City Planning Commission 1978-81; Rison River Concert Assn Bd Mem 1983-87; Princeton Drama Wkshp Bd Mem 1974-; United Fund 1988-; Excl in Ed Awd 1986; MN Adv of Yr for Scholastic Journalism 1989; Distinguished Service Awd 1982; *home:* Rt 5 Box 11 Princeton MN 55371

ERICSON, EUGENE, Business Education Teacher; *b:* Kewanee, IL; *m:* Muriel Clucas; *c:* Brent, Crystal Sportsman,Carmel Ackman, Bart, Cadi, Cara; *ed:* (BSED) Bus Ed, 1959; (MSED) Bus Ed, 1963 Western IL Univ; (EDD) Ed Admin, IL St Univ 1977; Post Masters Studies Admin Northern IL Univ 1977; Cmptr Software & Application Courses Elgin Cmmty Coll 1987-; *cr:* Bus Chair Yates City H S 1959-61; Manlius H S 1961-63; Voc Office Coord Larkin H S 1963-78; Intern, Division of Adult Voc Tech Ed 1974; Chairperson Applied Arts Streamwood H S 1978-; *ai:* Chair Dist U-46 Cmmty Bus Adv Comm; Coord Dist U-46 Cosmetology Trng; Chair Stu Academic Honors Recog Prgm; Chair Sr Voc Recog Assembly 1989-; IL Bus Ed Assn 2nd V P 1964-65; Assn of Elgin Sch Adm Sec 1983-84; Nat Ed Assn Life Mem; Elgin Jaycees 1968-72; Jaycee of Month 1969; Outstanding Comm Chair 1969; Elgin Fire & Police Commission Sec 1983-85; Chair 1988-; Article Published IL Career Ed Journal 1977; Consultant Model Compentency Based Prgm Prep of Admin of Occupational Career Ed Prgms 1974; *office:* Streamwood H S 701 W Schaumburg Rd Streamwood IL 60107

ERIKSEN, DONNA L., Jr/Sr HS Soc Stud Teacher; *b:* Boelus, NE; *m:* Riley; *c:* Deb Dabbert, Kath Argent, Tim; *ed:* (BA) Elem/Soc Sci, Kearney St Coll 1968; Grad Stud Soc Sci; *cr:* Upper Elem Teacher Ashton Public Sch 1965-66; Lower Elem Teacher Boelus Public Sch 1966-67; Jr/Sr HS Soc Stud Teacher Centura Public

Sch 1967-; *ai:* 8th Grade Class Spon; Jr HS Stu Cncl & Pep Club Spon; NEA, NSEA 1966-; *home:* Rt 1 Box 20A Boelus NE 68820

ERIKSEN, TED DON, II, English Department Chair; *b:* Detroit, MI; *m:* Kimberlee A.; *c:* Zachary, Katherine; *ed:* (BA) Eng Ed, MI St Univ 1976; (MA) Guidance/Counseling, Edinboro St Univ 1982; *cr:* Eng Teacher Susquehanna Valley HS 1976-77, Maplewood HS 1977-83; Dir of Guidance 1983-84, Eng Teacher 1984- Maplewood HS; *ai:* Penncrest Eng Curr Comm; Advanced Writing & Wildlife Habitat Dev Spon Maplewood HS; Penncrest Ed Assn, PA Ed Assn 1977-; Black Ash Sportsmans Club Bd of Dir 1983-; G W Smith Schlsp Comm Chm 1988-; *office:* Maplewood HS RD 1 Guys Mills PA 16327

ERKER, CARMELA MONTAGNA, Retired; *b:* Bufalo, NY; *m:* John Joseph; *c:* Patricia N. Hoffman; *ed:* Elem Ed, Mount St Joseph Coll; *cr:* Elem Teacher St Francis Xavier Sch; *ai:* St Elizabeth Ann Seton Awd; Appreciation Awd Stu of Friends St Francis Xavier 1973; *home:* 238 Laird Ave Buffalo NY 14207

ERNESTI, DONA J., K-8th Grade Resource Teacher; *b:* Broken Bow, NE; *m:* Alvin; *c:* Douglas, Todd, Andrew, Nicholas; *ed:* (BA) Elem Ed, Kearney St Coll 1967; Spec Ed & Mid Sch Endorsements; *cr:* 5th-8th Grade Teacher Howells Public Sch 1967-69; 7th-8th Grade Teacher St John Neumann 1979-88; K-8th Grade Resource Teacher Platte Center Public Sch 1988-; *ai:* NEA; *home:* Rt 2 Box 582 Dodge NE 68633

ERNST, EVAN G., Mathematics Teacher; *b:* Youngstown, OH; *m:* Bonnie Johnston; *c:* Kristy, Kerri, Darin; *ed:* (BS) Math, Youngstown St 1972; *cr:* Teacher Mohawk Area Schls 1972-; *ai:* YEA Adv 1972-75; Math Club Spon 1973-74; Evaluation Steering Comm; PSEA 1972-; Mohawk Ed Assn (Pres 1984-85) 1972-; Westfield Presbyn Church (Trustee, Elder) 1990; *home:* 115 Col New Castle Rd Bessemer PA 16112

ERNSTER, THOMAS JOSEPH, English Teacher; *b:* Waterloo, IA; *ed:* (BA) Eng, AZ St Univ 1973; (MA) Medieval-Renaissance Lit, AZ St Univ COol of Holy Names 1977; Univ CA Berkeley; San Francisco St Univ; Berlitz Sch Intnl Lang; *cr:* Lang Art Teacher Most Holy Trinity Sch 1977-80; Eng Instr Glendale Comm Coll 1977-80; Eng Teacher Sch of Epiphany 1980-, Mercy HS 1984-; *ai:* Epihany Sch Curr Comm; Lang Art Act Adv Epiphany Sch; Textbook Selection Comm Epiphany Sch; NCEA Mem 1980-; Bay Area Writing Pro Mem 1984-; Phi Alpha Theta Mem 1972-; Natl His Honor Society 1972-; Bd of Ed Chairperson 1983-85; Arch of San Francisco Nominating Comm; Recipient Lewis Schlsp in Eng Holy Names Coll 1975; Travel in Europe/Italy/France/Germany; *office:* Sch of the Epiphany 600 Italy Ave San Francisco CA 94112

ERNY, LORI NEAL, Fourth Grade Teacher; *b:* Crawfordsville, IN; *m:* Ken; *c:* Melinda, Stephen; *ed:* (BA) Elem Ed, Cedarville Coll 1979; *cr:* 4th Grade Teacher Faith Chrstn Sch 1979-86; *home:* 16 Seventh Street Fruitport MI 49415

ERREGER, CHARLES JOHN, Social Studies Teacher; *b:* Queens, NY; *m:* Abby T. Stern; *c:* Kevin, Sean; *ed:* (BA) His, Queens Coll 1968; (MA) His, Adelphi 1973; *cr:* Soc Stud Teacher Valley Stream N HS 1968-; *ai:* Var Ftbl, Girls Var Bsktbl, Girls Badminton Coach; Valley Stream Teachers Assn 1968-; St Davids Church Property Comm 1979-; *office:* Valley Stream North HS 750 Herman Avenue Franklin Square NY 11010

ERRICKSON, ROBIN RAE, 7th Grade Soc Stud Teacher; *b:* Newport, RI; *ed:* (BA) His, Western MD Coll 1983; Curr Dev; *cr:* 7th Grade Soc Stud Teacher North Carroll Mid Sch 1983-; *ai:* Carroll Cty Ed Assn Sch Rep 1988-; MD St Teachers Assn Convention Delegate 1989-; *office:* North Carroll Mid Sch Hanover Pike Hampstead MD 21074

ERTEL, CONSTANCE M. SKAHILL, Jr HS Social Studies Teacher; *b:* Dubuque, IA; *m:* Francis Joseph; *c:* Nathan; *ed:* His/Ed, Clarke Coll 1970-73; (BA) His/Ed, KS Newman Coll 1974; (MS) Ed, W IL Univ 1985; *cr:* Soc Stud Teacher/Head Courtland HS 1974-76; 7th Grade Teacher/Soc Stud Head Holy Ghost Sch 1979-81; 8th Grade Teacher/Soc Stud Head St Anne Sch 1981-; *ai:* Rainbows for All Gods Children Facilitator; Jr HS Musical Play Dir; 8th Grade Spon; Washington DC Trip Coord & Chaperone; Assoc Prin; Soc Stud Chairperson; Jr HS Coord; Coll for Kids Instr; Confirmation Teacher; Project Bus Coord; Mem of Cath Schls Week Comm; NCEA 1981-; KNEA 1974-76; Pi Gamma Mu 1974-; St Anne Parish 1981-; IL Math & Sci Acad Awd of Excl 1988; IL St Senate Certificate of Recognition 1988; Speaker for Achievements Project Bus 1990; *home:* 3404 3rd St C East Moline IL 61244

ERVIN, CYNTHIA FORTENBERRY, 4th-6th Grade English Teacher; *b:* Tylertown, MS; *m:* Rodney; *c:* Scott, Lori; *ed:* (BS) K-8th Grade Elem, Univ of S MS 1977; *cr:* 2nd Grade Teacher 1978-80, 4th Grade Teacher 1980-82, 4th-6th Grade Eng Teacher 1982- Dexter Sch; *office:* Dexter HS Rt 2 Box 234 Tylertown MS 39667

ERVIN, WAYNE D., Social Studies Teacher; *b:* Winston Salem, NC; *m:* Kay Virginia James; *c:* Rebecca; *ed:* (AB) His, High Point Coll 1967; (MED) Soc Sci, Univ of GA 1980; (EDSP) Soc Sci, GA Southern Coll 1987; *cr:* Soc Stud Waynesboro HS 1967-69; Traffic Analyst US Army Security Agency 1969-72; Soc Sci Jane Macon Jr HS 1972-75; Soc Stud Brunswick HS 1975-; *ai:* Model United Nations & Natl Forensic League Spon; Glynn Cty Assn of Ed Pres 1976-77; GA Assn of Ed PACE Comm 1977-80; GA Cncl of Soc Sci 8th Dist Dir 1979-80; Natl Forensic League 1985-, Diamond Key Coach 1990; Glynn Cty Mental Health Assn Pres 1985-86; AL GA Egyptian Seminar United Arab Republic 1979; Liberty Bell Awd Glynn Cty Bar Assn 1988; STAR Teacher Brunswick HS 1981, 1984, 1988-; Amer His Teacher of Yr Daughter of Amer Revolution 1983; *office:* Brunswick HS 3920 Habersham St Brunswick GA 31520

ERWIN, KATHY ANN (CHANDLER), English/Phys Ed Teacher; *b:* Hannibal, MO; *m:* David Owen; *c:* Amanda, Ashlee, Zachary; *ed:* (BSE) Phys Ed, 1971, (MA) Health/Phys Ed/Recreation, 1976 NE MO St Univ; *cr:* Phys Ed Teacher Knox Cty HS 1971-75, Grundy Cty R-IX HS 1976-78; 1st-4th Grade Elem Teacher Bible Grove Elem 1979-82; Lang Art Teacher Adair Cty R-II HS 1984-; *ai:* Drama Coach; Spelling Bee Coord; 5th/6th Grade Bsktbl, Summer Little League Bsbl & Sftbl Scorekeeper; MO St Teachers Assn, Cmmty Teachers Assn Pres 1984-; Parent Teacher Stu Organization 1984-, Friendship 1987; *office:* Adair Cty R-II Sch 205 W Dewey Brashear MO 63533

ERWIN, PAULA W., Elem Phys Ed Teacher; *b:* Jackson, OH; *m:* William E. Jr.; *c:* William E. III, Kevin; *ed:* (BS) Elem Ed, Rio Grande 1967-; *cr:* Elem Teacher Vinton Cty Schls 1962-65; Elem Teacher Jackson Schls 1965-; *ai:* Reserve Vlybl Coach; Head Sftbl Coach; VCEA/EA/NEA 1967-; SEOFPCA Sec/Treas 1989-; Jackson Cty Ag Society Treas 1983-; Clerk Scioto Twp Trustee; *office:* Jackson City Sch 379 E South Jackson OH 45640

ERZAR, JAMES STEPHEN, Mathematics Teacher; *b:* Winton, MN; *m:* Constance Kay Boyom; *c:* Kristen, Matt; *ed:* (BA) Math, St Cloud St Univ 1975; *cr:* Teacher Deer River HS 1975-; *ai:* Bsbl Coach; Dept Chm; Bsktbl Ofcl; NCTM 1974-; MSHSCA 1975-; NASO 1984-; *office:* Deer River HS P O Box 307 Deer River MN 56636

ESCALANTE, JAIME ALFONSO, Mathematics Instructor; *b:* Cochabamba, Bolivia; *m:* Fabiola; *c:* Jaime Jr., Fernando; *ed:* (Ms) Advanced Math, CA St Los Angeles; *cr:* Math Instr Garfield HS 1974-; *ai:* Chm Jaime Escalante Math Prgm E Los Angeles Coll; Pres George Bush Advisory Comm in Ed Mem; Presidential Awd Excl in Ed 1988; *office:* J A Garfield HS 5101 E 6th St Los Angeles CA 90022

ESCANDEL, THOMAS RAYMOND, Fourth Grade Teacher; *b:* Bryn Mawr, PA; *m:* RoseAnn Stengele; *c:* Keith W., Lindsey M.; *ed:* (AA) Keystone Jr Coll 1970; (BA) Elem Ed, Mansfield Univ 1972; Permanent Cert Various Area Insts; *cr:* 5th Grade Teacher 1972-80, Chapter I Math Teacher 1980-81, 4th Grade Teacher 1981-, Chapter I Math Teacher 1988-89 Susquehauna Cmmty Elem Sch; *ai:* 4th Grade Environmental Ed & Camping Trip Co-Coord; PA St Ed Assn, NEA 1972-; Harford Cong Church Sunday Sch Teacher 1985-; BSA Cub Master 1983-87; *home:* PO Box 64 Maple St Brooklyn PA 18813

ESCOBAR, PATRICK FREDRICK, Fine Arts Teacher; *b:* San Bernardino, CA; *ed:* (AA) Commercial Advertising, San Bernardino Valley Coll 1958; (BAED) Art Ed, CA Coll of Arts & Crafts 1961; (BA) Span Lang/Mural Design, Univ of Mexico 1976; (MA) Admin, San Bernardino Univ 1978; *cr:* Cnslr Oakland Naval Supply 1968-70; Teacher/Cnslr San Bernardino HS 1974-76; Bi-ling Resource Teacher 1980-81, Teacher of Gifted & Talented/MGM Math Teacher 1981-86 Arrowview Intermediate; Fine Art Teacher Cajon HS 1986-; Fine Art/Math Teacher Pacific HS 1990; *ai:* Pacific HS Golf Coach; SBTA, CTA, NEA; Jr Chamber of Commerce Outstanding Teacher of Yr 1984, 1988; *office:* Cajon HS Cajon 1200 W Hill Dr San Bernardino CA 92407

ESHBAUGH, PATRICIA BOAM, 4th Grade Teacher; *b:* Cleveland, OH; *m:* John R.; *c:* Elaine, Mark; *ed:* (BS) Elem Ed, 1971, (MS) Curr/Supervision, 1980 Wright St Univ; Trng Cmmty Intervention 1985; Trng TASC Inc 1987; *cr:* 1st Grade Teacher Huber Hts Menlo Park 1967-71; 4th Grade Teacher Huber Hts Lamendola 1971-; *ai:* Trainer on Tasc Inc; Huber Hts Ed Assn (VP 1986-88 Sec 1968-69); *office:* Lamendola Elem Huber Hts City 5363 Tilbury Rd Dayton OH 45424

ESHLEMAN, RONALD EUGENE, Chemistry Teacher; *b:* Waynesboro, PA; *m:* Jo Ann; *c:* Ronald, Sharlene; *ed:* (BS) Phys Sci, Millersville St 1961; (MED) Phys Sci, Penn St Univ 1966; Chem, Trenton St 1965, MT St Univ 1971, Hope Coll 1973, Univ of DE 1971-75; *cr:* Chem Teacher Hightstown HS 1961-70, Claymont HS 1970-89, Brandywine HS 1989-; *ai:* Jr Var & Var Bsbl Coach 1961-69; Sci Club Adv 1961-89; NHS Adv 1975-89; Sci Dept Chm 1970-89; Sci Olympiad Spon 1975-89; NEA 1961-; DSEA, BEA 1970-; Bible Baptist Church Bd Pres 1984-87; Bitner Awd Top Phys Sci Stu Millersville 1961; NSF Grants to Penn St, MT St, Hope Coll, Univ of DE; DE St ACS Chem Teacher of Yr 1986-87; *office:* Brandywine HS 1400 Foulk Rd Wilmington DE 19803

ESKOLA, PATRICIA MEYER, 6th Grade Teacher; *b:* Little Rock, AR; *m:* James Ronald; *c:* James T., Jeffrey G., Chad C.; *ed:* (BSE) Elem Ed, Univ of Cntrl AR 1968; Ouachita Univ, Univ of AZ Little Rock; *cr:* 3rd Grade Teacher Shawnee Elem 1968-69; 4th/5th Grade Teacher Marion Elem 1969-71; 4th-6th Grade Teacher Hazen Elem 1971-77; 4th/5th Grade Teacher Baseline Elem 1977-78; 4th-6th Grade Teacher Robinson Elem 1978-; *ai:* AR Ed Assn, NEA, Pulaski Assn of Classroom Teachers; Amer Red Cross CPR Instr; *home:* 4821 Jerry Dr Little Rock AR 72212

ESKOLA, ROBERT EDWIN, Geography Teacher; *b:* Eveleth, MN; *m:* Virginia Mae; *c:* Mark A., Kathryn L. Skubic, Joseph P.; *ed:* (BS) Soc Stud/Math, St Cloud St Teachers Coll 1951; (ME) Geography Ed, Univ of MN Duluth 1976; *cr:* Teacher Toivola-Meadowlands HS 1951-52, Aurora HS 1955-59, Virginia Scndry Sch 1959-.

ESKRIDGE, BETTYE IRVING, Second Grade Teacher; *b:* Collierville, TN; *m:* George U. Sr.; *c:* George Jr., Tarolyn, Shauna; *ed:* (BA) Elem Ed, Lane Coll 1968; (MA) Elem Counseling, W KY Univ 1982; (Rank I) Elem Ed 1987; *cr:* 5th Grade Teacher Rosa Fort Elem 1968-69; 6th Grade Teacher Washington St 1969-72; 6th Grade Teacher Meadows Elem 1973-76; 2nd Grade Teacher Cntrl Elem 1976-87;2nd Grade Teacher James R Allen Elem 1987-; *ai:* KEA, NEA; Alpha Kappa Alpha, PTO; *home:* 3001 Centennial Ave Radcliff KY 40160

ESPINOSA, PETER DAMIAN, 5th Grade Teacher; *b:* Alamosa, CO; *m:* Kim Caird; *c:* Aaron; *ed:* (BA) Elem Ed, Univ of NM 1979; Grad Stud; *cr:* 4th Grade Teacher 1979, 5th Grade Teacher Albuquerque Public Schls 1980-; *ai:* Cross Cntry Ski Instr; *home:* 3409 Marmac NE Albuquerque NM 87106

ESPINOZA, KATHLEEN FANNIN, Physical Education Teacher; *b:* Los Angeles, CA; *m:* Ozzie; *c:* Thomas, Kristina; *ed:* (BA) Phys Ed, CA St Univ Long Beach 1980; Safety Educl Credential, CA St Long Beach; Prof Rescuer Amer Red Cross; *cr:* Teacher Huntington Beach Union HS 1980-83, Sunnyside Union HS 1984-; *ai:* Stu Cncl Frosh Class, Dance Club Spon; Gymnastics Extra-Curricular Act; CAHPERD, AAHPERD, AZ Safety Ed Assn; Red Cross; BSA; *office:* Sunnyside HS 1725 E Bilby Rd Tucson AZ 85716

ESPOSITO, DENNIS JOSEPH, Elementary Guidance Counselor; *b:* Philadelphia, PA; *m:* Bernadette Castor; *ed:* (BS) Elem Ed, Temple Univ 1975; (MA) Counseling, Glassboro St Coll; *cr:* 4th Grade Teacher 1975-85, K-5th Grade Guidance Cnslr 1985- Gloucester Township Public Schls; *ai:* Gloucester Township Recognition Awd 1985, 1989; *office:* Gloucester Twp Public Schls 17 Erial Rd Blackwood NJ 08012

ESPOSITO, WILLIAM MICHAEL, English Teacher; *b:* New York, NY; *m:* Jean Kiliman; *ed:* (BA) Eng, Mt Union Coll 1969; (MED) Eng, Westminster Coll 1982; Grad Stud in Ed, Madeline Hunter; *cr:* Sci Teacher Delehanty HS 1970; Eng Teacher Salem HS 1970-; *ai:* NEA 1970-; NCTE 1989-; Elks 1985-; Jenning Scholar; *office:* Salem HS 1200 E 6th St Salem OH 44460

ESSARY, MACK RAY, Jr High Science-Dept Chairman; *b:* Stilwell, OK; *m:* Nadine G.; *ed:* (BS) Ed, 1954, (MA) Ed, 1960 Northeastern St Coll; *cr:* 6th Grade Teacher Wilson Elem 1957-58; Sci Teacher Winslow Jr HS 1958-; *ai:* Jr HS Bsktbl Coach; Jr HS Track Coach; Co-Spon Winslow HS Indian Club; Sci Decathalon Chairperson; Winslow Sch Employees Federal Credit Union Pres; *office:* Winslow Jr H S P O Box 580 Winslow AZ 86047

ESSARY, PATRICIA ANN (CONNELL), Head Librarian; *b:* Fulton, KY; *m:* Elvis; *c:* Leigh A.; *ed:* (BS) Scndry Ed/Eng/Soc Stud, 1969, (MS) Scndry Ed/Eng/Soc Stud, 1971 Univ of TN Martin; (MLS) Lib Sci, Peabody Coll 1973; *cr:* K-12th Grade Librarian Gibson Cty Bd of Ed 1974-78; 9th-12th Grade Librarian Obion Cty Bd of Ed 1978-83; Eng/Rdng Teacher 1984-88, 9th-12th Grade Librarian 1988- Rutherford Cty Bd of Ed; *ai:* Frosh Class & Lib Club Spon; Faculty Cncl; Rutherford Ed Assn (Cxec Bd 1989-, Facuty Rep 1987-88), Building Level Teacher of Yr 1989-, Distinguished Classroom Teacher 1987; TN Ed Assn, NEA Mem 1974-; Amer Lib Assn Mem 1988-; Delta Kappa Gamma (Mem 1980-, Chapter Pres 1988-); Leadership Rutherford Class Mem 1988; Leadership Rutherford Alumnus 1989-; Rutherford Chamber of Commerce Mem 1988-; Easter Seals Fnd Block Chairperson 1986-; Whos Who in Amer Ed 1987-; Whos Who of Women Exec 1989-; Stokely Fellow Univ of TN Knoxville 1988; TN Governors Acad 1987; *office:* La Vergne HS 250 Wolverine Trl La Vergne TN 37086

ESSELMAN, BARBARA MUNRO, Fourth Grade Teacher; *b:* Peoria, IL; *m:* James H.; *ed:* (BA) Elem Ed, Beloit Coll 1963; Univ of MN; *cr:* 3rd Grade Teacher Roseville Schls 1963-69; 2nd-4th Grade Teacher St Paul Public Schls 1970-; *office:* North End Sch 27 E Geranium St Saint Paul MN 55117

ESSEX, CAROL ALLTON, Fifth Grade Teacher; *b:* Miami, OK; *m:* Lawson M.; *ed:* (BS) Ed, 1974, (MS) Ed, 1980, (EDS) Higher Ed, 1981 Pittsburgh St Univ; Grad Work in Adult Ed, Career Counseling; *cr:* 4th Grade Teacher Fairland Elem 1974-76; 3rd Grade Teacher 1976-80, 5th Grade Teacher 1980- Wilson Elem; *ai:* Miami Assn of Classroom Teachers, OK Ed Assn, NEA Mem 1974-; OK Rdng Assn, Lakeland Rdng Cncl Mem 1989-; OK Ed Assn Excl in Ed Awd for Innovative Classroom Techniques 1989; *office:* Wilson Elem Sch 308 G Northwest Miami OK 74354

ESTABROOK, KAREN J., English Teacher; *b:* Warsaw, NY; *ed:* (BA) Eng Lit, Houghton Coll 1979; (MS) Eng Ed, Alfred Univ 1984; *cr:* Eng Teacher Scio Cntrl Sch 1979-; *ai:* Adv of Tiger Prints Sch Newspaper; Published Nine Articles & Nine Pieces of Fiction Four Intnl Magazines; *office:* Scio Cntrl Sch Washington St Scio NY 14880

ESTER, BEVERLY JEAN FARROW, Business/Secretarial Teacher; *b:* Lawrenceburg, IN; *m:* Eric P.; *c:* Tyler; *ed:* (BS) Bus Ed, Ball St Univ 1984; Pursuing Masters Degree Sncdry Ed/Bus, Ball St Univ; *cr:* Stu Teacher Lawrenceburg HS 1984; Secretarial Teacher Southeastern Career Center 1984-; *ai:* Bus Profs of America & Stu/Sch Representation Spon; Nom & Semi-Finalist IN Teacher of Yr 1989; *office:* Southeastern Career Center Box 156 US 50 Versailles IN 47042

ESTERBURG, ARLENE CATHERINE, 5th Grade Teacher; *b:* Pittsburgh, PA; *ed:* (BS) El Ed, Duquesne Univ 1973; *cr:* 5th Grade Teacher 1974-75; 4th Grade Teacher 1975-79; 6th Grade Teacher Court Sch 1979-80; 6th Grade Teacher 1980-81; 5th

Grade Teacher 1980-86; 2nd Grade Teacher 1986-87; 5th Grade Teacher Carnegie Elem 1987-; *ai:* Spon Talent Show; AFT 1974-; Carlynton Fed Teachers 1974-; Holy Trinity Choir 1975-; Poltava Ukrainian Dance Co 1980-; Holy Trinity CCD 1974-85; *office:* Carnegie Elem Schl Kings Hwy Carnegie PA 15106

ESTES, BETTY BERRY, 2nd Grade Teacher; *b:* Hazlehurst, MS; *m:* Lester A. Jr.; *c:* Ellen, Trey; *ed:* (BS) Elem Ed, MS Coll 1971; (MS) Elem Ed, MS St Univ 1974; *cr:* Elem Teacher Starkville Public Sch 1971-; *ai:* Staff Dev Comm; Curr & Textbook Comm Chairperson; 5 Yr Planning Comm; MS Prof Ed, Kappa Kappa Iota; First Meth Church (Admin Bd, Finance Comm) *office:* Overstreet Elem Sch S Jackson St Starkville MS 39759

ESTES, BOBBIE N., Fourth Grade Teacher; *b:* Uriah, AL; *m:* Darrell; *c:* Michelle, Jason, Sean; *ed:* (BA) Elem Ed, Auburn Univ 1962; (MS) Elem Ed, Univ of S AL 1990; *cr:* 5th Grade Teacher Frisco City Elem 1962-63; 2nd/3rd Grade Teacher Cntrl Park Elem 1963-68; 3rd/4th Grade Teacher St Pius Cath 1974-77; 2nd-4th Grade Teacher E R Dickson 1977-; *ai:* Delta Zeta Alumni Organization; Auburn Univ Alumni Organization; Master Teacher 1988-; *home:* 605 Burlington Ct Mobile AL 36608

ESTES, CAROLYN HULL, Fifth Grade Teacher; *b:* Memphis, TN; *m:* Robert Marion; *c:* Robert F., David C.; *ed:* (BS) Ed, Memphis St Univ 1955; Univ of TN, Natl Coll of Ed, N TX Univ, TX Chrstn Univ, Univ of TX Arlington; *cr:* 4th Grade Teacher Memphis City Schls 1955-57, 1959-66; 6th Grade Teacher Knoxville City Schls 1957-58; 3rd Grade Teacher Admiral Richard Byrd 1968-69; 5th Grade Sci Teacher Ft Worth Ind Sch Dist 1970-; *ai:* Grade Chairperson; Southwest Creek Bank Prgm; Ft Worth Classroom Teacher Assn Faculty Rep 1983-86, Teacher of Yr 1985; TX Cncl PTA Prgm Chairperson 1970-, Life Mem 1984; NEA, TSTA 1970-; Sigma Kappa Alumna Pres 1982-84, Outstanding Alumnae 1983; Daughters Amer Revolution 1977-, Outstanding Amer His Teacher 1988; Ft Worth Genealogical Society Bd of Dir 1989-; Nom Ft Worth Ind Sch Natl Teacher of Yr 1985-86; Adopt-A-Sch Outstanding Teacher 1987, 1989; Book Author; Creativity Awd 1981, 1982, 1984, 1985, 1989; *office:* Westcreek Elem Sch 3401 Walton Ave Fort Worth TX 76133

ESTES, DAVID WAYNE, Algebra 1/Geometry Teacher; *b:* Arab, AL; *m:* Sandra Lynne Powell; *c:* Jacob, Amie, Benjamin; *ed:* (BS) His Ed, Auburn Univ 1981; (MED) Scndry Ed/Math, AL A&M Univ 1989; *cr:* His Teacher/Bsktbl/Ftbl/Sftbl Coach P T Beauregard HS 1981-82; His Teacher/Ftbl/Track Coach 1982-84, Math Teacher/Head Track Coach 1984- A P Brewer HS; *ai:* Var & Jr Var Girls & Boys Head Track Coach; NEA, AL Ed Assn 1982-; Natl Fed of HS Coaches Assn 1984-; New Salem Baptist Church Deacon 1986-; *office:* A P Brewer HS Rt 2 Box 149 Somerville AL 35670

ESTES, JOHN JOSEPH, Junior High School Teacher; *b:* North Adams, MA; *m:* Donna Jolin; *c:* Deron, Amy; *ed:* (BSE) Elem Ed, N Adams St Coll 1971; *cr:* Teacher Clarksburg Sch 1971-; *ai:* Womens/Girls Var Bsktbl Coach Drury Sr HS; MA Teachers Assn, NEA 1971; North Adams Lodge of Elks 1980; Lucretia Crocker Grant 1986; *home:* 5 Carson Ave Clarksburg MA 01247

ESTES, ROBBIE D., Fourth Grade Teacher; *b:* Grenada, MS; *m:* Jap Wade; *c:* Marshall W., Joan Estes Rodgers; *ed:* (BA) Religious Ed, Millsaps Coll 1952; (MA) Elem Ed, Univ of MS 1976; Working Towards Specialist Degree Elem Ed, Univ of MS; *cr:* 5th Grade Teacher Belden 1950-52; 6th Grade Teacher Duck Hill 1955-57, Williams Sch 1957-61; 4th Grade Teacher Grenada Sch Dist 1961-; *ai:* Grenada Cty Teachers Pres 1976-77; MAE, Classroom Teachers 1956-86; Adult Sunday Sch Teacher 1956-; *home:* Rt 2 Box 180 Holcomb MS 38940

ESTEY, BETHANY J., 1st Grade Teacher; *b:* Dover, NH; *ed:* (BA) Elem Ed, Barrington Coll 1972; (MA) Urban Ed, Jersey City Coll 1983; *cr:* 1st-3rd Grade Teacher Chancellor Ave Sch Annex 1972-; Basic Ed Teacher/Cnslr Irvington Adult Sch 1989-; *ai:* Irvington Adult Sch Advisory Comm; Phi Delta Kappa 1983-85; *office:* Chancellor Avenue Annex 255 Chancellor Ave Newark NJ 07112

ESTIN, JOAN M., Teacher; *b:* Los Angeles, CA; *m:* Danny; *c:* Brooke, Brett; *ed:* (BA) His, 1971, Ed, 1972 Univ CA Los Angeles; Gifted; *cr:* Teacher LA Unified 1972, Wilmington 1972-73, Grass Valley Sch Dist 1975-; *ai:* Various Inservices; World Gifted Conference Speaker 1987; CAG Speaker 1988; Nom CA Gifted Teacher Of Yr 1988; *office:* Lyman Gilmore Hwy 20 Grass Valley CA 95945

ESTRADA, JANE MORRIS, Sixth Grade Science Teacher; *b:* Gulfport, MS; *w:* James P. (dec); *c:* Tenderly Dougherty, Angela Moleski, Alison, Jim; *ed:* (BS) Soc Stud Ed, 1958, (MED) Elem Ed, 1971 Univ of S MS; Grad Stud USM; *cr:* 5th-8th Grade Math Teacher Lyman Elem Sch 1973-80; Prin/Math Teacher Coast Episcopal Elem 1980-86; 8th Grade Rdng Teacher 1987-89, 6th Grade Sci Teacher 1989- Michel Mid Sch; *ai:* Builders Club Spon; 6th Grade Chm; Biloxi Schls Sci Curr Comm; Biloxi Ed Assn VP 1989-; MS Assn of Educators Pres 1979-80, Dist 6; MS Assn of Educators Bd of Dir 1978-80; NEA 1978-80, 1989-; Amer Bus Women Assn VP 1988, Woman of Yr; Gold Star Wives of America Secy 1988-; Harrison Cty Assn Pres 1978-80; MS Private Sch Assn Elem Teacher of Yr 1985-86; *home:* 1711 Wisteria St Gulfport MS 39501

ESTRADA, S. D., History Teacher; *b:* Silver City, NM; *ed:* (BA) His, 1975, (MA) His, 1976, (BS) Scndry Ed, 1981 NM St Univ; Grad Work Interdisciplinary Areas of Educl Admin, Bus Admin, Public Admin; *cr:* His Teacher Las Cruces HS 1983-; *ai:* Model United Nations Simulation & Internation Simulation Spon; Las Cruces HS Improvement Comm; Las Cruces Classroom Teachers Assn 1989-; Sigma Nu Pres 1974, Natl Grad Awd 1975; White House Presidential Scholars Distinguished Teacher 1989; NM St Bd of Ed Certificate of Recognition 1989; Nom Las Cruces HS Teacher of Yr 1989-; *office:* Las Cruces HS 1755 El Paseo Rd Las Cruces NM 88001

ESTRADA, SYLVIE CAPLIER, French Teacher; *b:* Paris, France; *m:* Roberto Estrada Jimenez; *c:* Nicolas, Sophie, Caroline; *ed:* (BA) Foreign Lang, Sorbonne Paris 1970; (MA) Amer Stud, Charles V, Paris VII 1971; Fr, Span Teaching Grad Sch of Ed at Berkeley 1980; *cr:* Fr Teacher Pomona Coll 1971-74; Fr/Span Teacher St Andrews Sch 1974-76; Eng Teacher Liceum Francais Kennedy 1976-77, Liceo Franco Mexicano 1977-78; Fr/Span Teacher San Ramon Valley HS 1980-; Fr Teacher Diablo Valley Coll 1989-; *ai:* San Ramon Valley HS Intnl Club Adv 1985-; Mentor Teacher 1989-; EB Bulletin Co-Ed; ECDE BI-ling Berkeley 1987-88; Univ of CA Berkeley Alumni Assn; Fulbright Scholar 1971; Fulbright Fellowship Awarded for Teacher Exch Prgm 1990; *office:* San Ramon Valley HS 140 Love Ln Danville CA 94526

ESTRADA, VICKIE, 7th Grade Geography Teacher; *b:* Norton, KS; *m:* Arthur A.; *c:* Isidra J.; *ed:* (BA) Ed, Emporia St Teachers Coll 1969; (MA) Curr/Ed, KS St Univ 1976; Grad Hours Ed, Geography, Eng as a Second Lang Instruction; *cr:* Adult Ed Teacher AVTS 1980-82; Eng as 2nd Lang Teacher Pioneer Coll 1982-86; Teacher KCK Public Sch 1969-; *ai:* Extra Duty for Concerts & Sport Events & After Sch Act; Soc Chm for Sch; Project Stu Taught Awareness & Resistance Teacher; NEA 1969-; Mid-Tesal; KS Assn Teachers of Eng; Grace Chrstn Fellowship Church; Elem Sci Curr Guide 1978; KS St Grant for Stud 1987; Eng as 2nd Lang Curr, KS His & Government Guides 1990; PTA Lifetime Membership Awd; *office:* Argentine Mid Sch 22nd & Ruby Kansas City KS 66106

ESTREICHER, ALBERT, Third Grade Teacher; *b:* New York, NY; *m:* Sandra Smoller; *c:* Beth, Carolyn, Donna; *ed:* (BS) Ed, 1963, (MS) Ed, 1967 City Univ of NY; Educl Admin & Supervision Advanced Certificate Prgm, City Univ of NY; *cr:* Vacation Playgrounds Teacher New York Public Schls 1962-69; Remedial Rdng/Math Teacher Public Sch 161 & 20 1970-75; Division Supvr Tyler Hill Sleepaway Camp 1982-89; Teacher Public Sch 161 & 32 1963-; *office:* Public Sch 32 32 Elverton Ave Staten Island NY 10308

ESTRIDGE, VICKIE SPURLOCK, Math Teacher; *b:* London, KY; *m:* Larry Hobert; *c:* Rodney H., Ryan H.; *ed:* (BS) Math, 1986, (MA) 1988 Eastern KY Univ; Rank I Admin; *cr:* Math Teacher Jackson Cty HS 1986-; *ai:* Chrldr Spon; Attendance Waiver Comm; *office:* Jackson County H S Rt 421 Mc Kee KY 40447

ETCHASON, REBECCA ANN (BROCKMANN), Business Education Teacher; *b:* St Louis, MO; *m:* Bobby L.; *c:* Adam, Emily, Mark; *ed:* (AA) Secretarial Trng, Cntrl MO St Univ 1972; (BS) Scndry Ed/Bus, SE MO St Univ 1984; *cr:* Bus Teacher Hillsboro HS 1986-; *ai:* MO Voc Assn, NBEA, MO Bus Ed Assn, Jefferson Cty Bus Ed Assn; Redeemer Luth Church Treas 1986-88; Beta Sigma Phi Pres 1982-83; MO St Incentive Grant; *office:* Hillsboro HS 12 Hawk Dr Hillsboro MO 63050

ETCHBERGER, ROBERT DAVID, Sixth Grade Teacher; *b:* Lebanon, PA; *m:* Suellen Marie Emrich; *ed:* (BS) Elem Ed, Lebanon Valley Coll 1971; (MED) Elem Ed, Millersville Univ 1978; *cr:* Teacher Fredericksburg Elem Sch 1971-; *ai:* Elem Intramural Sports Coach; Elem Soc Stud Curr Comm Chairperson; N Lebanon Ed Assn Building Rep; PA St Ed Assn, NEA; Tabor United Church of Christ (Choir Mem, Sunday Sch Teacher, Pres, Church Cncl Treas); BSA Merit Badge Cnslr; Lebanon Cty Historical Society; Natl Railroad Historical Society, Sierra Club, Greenpeace, Appalachian Trail Conference; *office:* Fredericksburg Elem Sch Box 27 Fredericksburg PA 17026

ETHEREDGE, JANET LYNN PHILLEBAUM, Third Grade Teacher; *b:* Hico, TX; *m:* Sam; *c:* David, Jason, Jennifer; *ed:* (BSED) Elem Ed, Abilene Chrstn Univ 1972; (MED) Elem Ed, Univ of N TX 1983; *cr:* 2nd Grade Teacher 1972-73, 3rd Grade Teacher 1973- Otis Brown Elem; *ai:* Math Rep; TX St Teachers Assn 1972-80; Assn of TX Prof Educators (Zone Leader, Building Rep) 1990; Irving Mothers of Multiples 1985-; *office:* Otis Brown Elem Sch 2501 W 10th Irving TX 75060

ETHEREDGE, VANETTA BING, Fifth Grade Teacher; *b:* Allendale, SC; *m:* James William; *c:* Lorna V., William C.; *ed:* (BS) Elem Ed, Claflin Coll 1964; (MAT) Elem Ed, Winthrop Coll 1974; Univ of SC 1978; *cr:* 3rd Grade Teacher Sunset Park Elem 1964-66; 2nd Grade Teacher West End Elem 1966-68; 3rd Grade Teacher Richmond Drive Elem 1968-74; 4th Grade Teacher Edgewood Elem 1974-79; 5th Grade Teacher St Andrews Elem 1979-; *ai:* Jack & Jills of America Incorporated; Links Incorporated; Amer Assn of Univ Women 1980-; Teacher of Month Edgewood Elem Sch; Outstanding Teacher in America; Certificate of Recognition-Teacher of Yr 1984-85; *home:* 2210 Longview Ct Charleston SC 29414

ETHERTON, DE LAYNE NEWSOME, Sixth Grade Teacher; *b:* Fort Payne, AL; *m:* Rickey Coy; *c:* Kathan, Kiley; *ed:* Elem Ed, NE AL St Jr Coll; (BS) Elem Ed, 1973, (MS) Elem Ed, 1976 Jacksonville St Univ; (EDS) Elem Ed, Univ of AL 1978; Completed Space Camp Prgm for Educators 1988; Became Licensed EmergencY Medical Technician 1987; *cr:* 5th/6th Grade Teacher Ider HS 1973-74; 6th Grade Teacher Plainview HS 1975-; *ai:* Sch Newspaper Spon; Asst Sunday Sch Supt; Dir of Childrens Choir at Church & Pianist; De Kalb Ed Organization, AL Ed Assn, NEA 1973-; Church (Asst Sunday Sch Supt, Dir of Childrens Choir, Pianist); Outstanding Young Women of Amer 1986; *home:* Rt 1 Box 281 Sylvania AL 35988

ETHIER, DIANE M., 6th Grade Teacher; *b:* Worcester, MA; *c:* Wayne; *ed:* (BS) Ed, Worcester St Coll 1973; (MEd) Ed, Bridgewater St Coll 1978; Certificate of Advanced Graduate Study, Bridgewater St Coll; *cr:* 4th Grade Teacher 1973-74; 2nd Grade Teacher 1974-79; 3rd Grade Teacher 1979-83; 5th/6th Grade Teacher Soc Stud 1983- Chatham Elem Sch; *ai:* Testing Coord K-6; Intramural Sftbl Coach; Teacher Assist Boys Choir; Kappa Delta Pi 1973; Harwich Cranberry Harvest Festival Comm 1987-; Cape Cod Conservatory Wind Ensemble 1973-86; Harwich Town Band 1973-; Barnstable Town Band 82-; Horace Mann Grant to Enhance US Soc Stud Curr 1984; Horace Mann Grant to Enhance European SS Curr 1985; *home:* 10 Robins Way Harwich MA 02645

ETHRIDGE, CHERYL (COKER), Mathematics Dept Chair; *b:* Georgetown, SC; *m:* Sheldon Dale; *c:* Robert, Ryan, Amanda; *ed:* (BS) Math, Baptist Coll Charleston 1972; (MAT) Math Ed, Citadel 1976; NSF Summer Wkshp, Citadel 1980; Advanced Placement Calculus Endorsement, Citadel 1985; *cr:* Teacher St Andrews Jr HS 1972-74; Teacher/Dept Chairperson Goose Creek HS 1974-81; Math Coord Berkeley Cty Schls 1981-84; Adjunct Professor Coll of Charleston 1982; Teacher/Dept Chairperson Goose Creek HS 1984-; *ai:* Math Dept Chm; Textbook Adoption Comm; Consensus Based Evaluation Team; Math Team Co-Spon; NCTM 1973-; SC Cncl of Teacher of Math 1976-; SC Cncl of Advanced Placement Math Teachers 1980-; Baptist Coll Alumni 1976-78; Berkeley Cty Credit Union Rep 1987-88; Odyssey of Mind Local & St Judge 1983-87; Ed Improvement Act Implementation Cncl 1987-88; 4Rs Grant Participant 1987-89; Published Article Advanced Placement Publication Clemson Univ 1990; HS Teacher of Yr & Berkeley Cty Finalist 1980-81; *office:* Goose Creek HS 1137 Redbank Rd Goose Creek SC 29445

ETHRIDGE, IRIS GAY, Classroom Teacher; *b:* Phil Campbell, AL; *m:* William David Sr.; *c:* Sandra D. Ethridge Huggins, William D. Jr.; *ed:* (BS) Health/Phys Ed/Recreation, Howard Coll & Samford Univ 1958; (MED) Scndry Ed, Univ of S AL 1980; Taft Seminar Auburn Univ; *cr:* Teacher Robert E Lee Elem 1958-59, Baker HS 1960-62, Theodore HS 1962-68, Pillans Mid 1970-85, Mary G Montgomery HS 1985-; *ai:* Jr Class, Agape Chrstn Fellowship, Tennis Club Spon; Boy & Girls Tennis Teams Coach; Mobile Cty Soc Stud Cncl Pres 1988-89; AAHPERD, NEA, AEA, MCEA, ABWA Memberships; Shrine Bowl Stu Coord 1974-79; Skycrest Babe Ruth (Secy, Coach, Mgr) 1981-84; Cottage Hill Little League Coach 1978-80; Presidents Advisory Cncl Univ of S AL; *home:* 3400 Canacee Dr Mobile AL 36693

ETHRIDGE, LINDA KANAS, 4th Grade Teacher; *b:* Fayetteville, NC; *m:* Mark; *c:* Brad Leatherwood, Brooke Leatherwood, Linc Leatherwood; *ed:* (BA) Elem Ed K-4, Mars Hill Coll 1983; *cr:* Teacher Crabtree Elem 1984-85, Bethel Elem 1985-90; *home:* 679 Hillside Terrace Waynesville NC 28786

ETHRIDGE, MARY JANE, 2nd Grade Teacher; *b:* Goose Creek, TX; *m:* Reginald; *c:* Tracy, Keith, Gwen Sonnier; *ed:* (BA) Ed, Baylor Univ 1964; (ME) Ed, Prairie View A&M 1975; *cr:* 1st Grade Teacher Odessa Ind Sch Dist 1964-67; *ai:* Delta Kappa Gamma Mem 1968-; Memorial Baptist Church Life Mem; Outstanding Young Women of America; *home:* 1409 Sherwood Baytown TX 77520

ETIENNE, YVONNE, Kindergarten Teacher; *b:* Mt Pleasant, IN; *ed:* (BA) Elem, St Bens Coll 1965; (MS) Early Chldhd/Guidance, Spalding Coll 1969; *cr:* 1st Grade Teacher St Clements 1964-65; 5th Grade Teacher 1965-66, 1st/7th/8th Grade Home Ec Teacher 1966-74 St Marys; Spec Ed Teacher Memphis TN 1974-76; K-1st Grade Teacher St Simons 1974-; *ai:* 1st/2nd Grade Sacrament Prgm; Talks on Death, Dying, Caring for Aging; Key Club Cmmty Services Awd 1977; Nom Teacher of Yr 1987-89; *home:* 1412 Memorial Washington IN 47501

ETTENSOHN, DAVID ADRIAN, Art Teacher/Fine Arts Coord; *b:* Tell City, IN; *m:* Billie Jo Kessner; *c:* Craig, Brian; *ed:* (BS) Art Ed, Brescia Coll 1964; (MS) Scndry Ed, 1978, (Rank I) Scndry Ed, 1980 Murray St Univ; *cr:* Art Teacher Owensboro Cath HS 1964-66; Guidance Cnslr/Art Teacher Holy Name HS 1966-71; Art Teacher/Fine Arts Coord Henderson Cty HS 1971-; *ai:* Doubledozen, Rewards, Goals, Schlsp, Faculty Advisory, Prof Leave, Foyer & Gym Remodeling Comms; Sr Class Spon; Evaluation Appeals Panel; NEA, KY Ed Assn 1974-; United Way HS Chm 1986-89; *office:* Henderson Cty HS 2424 Zion Rd Henderson KY 42420

ETTER, DANA VERN, Mathematics Teacher; *b:* St Marys, OH; *m:* Gloria Louise Harris; *c:* Brandon, Amanda, Samantha; *ed:* (BS) Math Ed, Univ of Cincinnati 1981; *cr:* Math Teacher Roger Bacon HS 1983-; *ai:* Frosh Wrestling & Var Track Coach; NCEA 1983-; Natl Sci Fnd Grant; *office:* Roger Bacon HS 4320 Vine St Cincinnati OH 45217

ETTER, JULIE MARLEEN (NEIE), Mathematics Teacher; *b:* San Antonio, TX; *m:* Jeffrey A.; *c:* Shannon, Erin; *ed:* (BS) Educl Curr & Instruction, TX A&M 1980; *cr:* Math Teacher Manor Mid Sch 1985-86, Red Oak HS 1986-; *ai:* Sr Class Spon; *office:* Red Oak HS PO Box 160 Red Oak TX 75154

ETZWILER, LINDA FAIRWEATHER, Third Grade Teacher; *b:* Anaconda, MT; *m:* David J.; *c:* Christopher, Michael; *ed:* (BS) Elem Ed, Soc Sci Western Mt Coll 1969; Curr Endorsement 1988; *cr:* Kndgtn-8th Grade Math Teacher 1983-85; Kndgtn-8th Math/Rdng/Eng 1985-86; 3rd Grade Teacher 1986- West Yellowstone Sch; *ai:* Ski Instr Cross Cntry; Vocational Comm; Teacher Rep Interview Comm; West Yellowstone Teacher Assn 1983-; Mt Ed Assn 1983-; Beta Sigma Phi Pres 1986-87 Women Yr 1986; BSA 1983-; Public Lib Bd Mem 1988-; *office:* W Yellowstone Sch Box 460 West Yellowstone MT 59758

EUBANKS, BETTYE HALL, English/Health/Phys Ed Teacher; *b:* Duncanville, AL; *m:* Willie James; *c:* Anthony D., Latonda M., Mark E.; *ed:* (BA) Phys Ed, Stillman Coll 1964; Various Wkshps, Insts, Classes, Univ of AL; *cr:* Teacher Pickens Cty Bd of Ed 1965; Women/Girls Dir Barnes YMCA 1965-66; Teacher Hale Cty HS & Moundville Public 1967-86, Sunshine HS 1986-; *ai:* Univ of AL Bioprep Eng Teacher; Class Co-Spon; Aide Spelling Bee & Shunshine HS Scholars Bowl Spon; AL Ed Assn 1967-; Hale Cty Teachers Assn 1967; NCTE 1985-87; NEA; NEH Participant 1988; St Lang Arts Wkshp in Eutaw 1977; NEH Participant in Afro-Amer Lit 1990; *home:* 2809 22nd St Tuscaloosa AL 35401

EUBANKS, PATRICIA GALE, 6th Grade Art/Soc Stud Teacher; *m:* Gary L.; *c:* Andrew L.; *ed:* (A) Ed, Walker Coll 1975; (BS)ed, Univ South AL 1979; *cr:* 6th 8th Grade SS Art Religion Teacher St Dominics Sch 1979-80; 5th Grade Teacher St Pius Sch 1980-81; 6th/7th/8th Grade Art Teacher Park View Intermediate 1981-; 7th Grade His Park View Intermediate 1981-; *ai:* Spon-Park View Jr Historians; Dept Chm Soc Stud; PTA; South East Cncl for SS; Park View South Civic Club; Park View South Garden Club.

EUBANKS, SUSAN SADLER, 7th Grade Mathematics Teacher; *b:* Houston, TX; *m:* Lloyd; *ed:* (BAT) Math, 1978, (MA) Math/Cmptr Sci, 1988 Sam Houston St Univ; *cr:* Teacher New Caney Ind Sch Dist 1978-79, Huntsville Ind Sch Dist 1979-; *ai:* Chrldr & Stu Cncl Spon; On-Campus & Dist Wide Comm; NCTM, TX Cncl Teachers of Math 1978-; GTE Grant; *office:* Mance Park Jr HS 828 8th St Huntsville TX 77340

EUDY, RUSSELL D., Athletic Dir/Science Chair; *b:* Hot Springs, AR; *m:* Malisa A. Eudy-Wideman; *c:* Candace; *ed:* (BA) Religion, 1986, (BSE) Scndry Ed, 1987 Ouachita Baptist Univ; *cr:* Jr & Sr Girls Bsktbl Coach/Sci Teacher 1987-, Athletic Dir 1989- Abundant Life Schls; *ai:* Sylvan Hills 1st Baptist Church Mem; *office:* Abundant Life Schls 9200 Sylvan Hills Hwy North Little Rock AR 72120

EUELL, THOMAS EDWIN, III, Fifth Grade Teacher; *b:* New York, NY; *m:* Linda Mc Lane; *c:* Kelly, Megan; *ed:* (BE) Ed, Univ of Miami 1969; (MA) Instructional Systems Technology, IN Univ Bloomington 1974; *cr:* 6th Grade Teacher Riley Ave Sch 1969-73, 6th Grade Teacher 1973-79, 5th Grade 1979- P *ai:* NYSTA 1969-; NYS Marine Sci Assn 1981-; NYS Grant for Prgm Stimulation of Natural Aptitude through Photography; Photography Inservice & Parent Wkshps; Chisanbop Math & Drug Alcohol Abuse Trng; *office:* Pulaski Street Elem Sch Pulaski St Riverhead NY 11901

EUGENE, MARION LEE, 8th Grade English Teacher; *b:* New Orleans, LA; *m:* Paul Joseph Sr.; *c:* Susie Foster Harrison, Herbert L. Foster, Harold V.; *ed:* (BA) Eng, Southern Univ New Orleans 1974; (MED) Scndry Sch Admin, Univ of New Orleans 1980; Grad Stud; *cr:* Eng Teacher Lincoln Mid Sch 1975-77, Allen Ellender Mid Sch 1978-; Eng Dept Head Allen Ellender Mid Sch 1980-; *office:* Allen Ellender Mid Sch 4501 Ames Blvd Marrero LA 70072

EVANISKY, JOAN, Fifth Grade Teacher; *b:* Hartford, CT; *ed:* (BS) Ed, Teachers Coll of CT New Britain 1956; (MED) Ed, Univ of Hartford 1962; *cr:* Teacher Emerson Williams 1956-; *ai:* Ed Assn of Wethersfield (Pres 1981-84, Mem 1956-); *office:* Emerson-Williams Sch 461 Wells Rd Wethersfield CT 06109

EVANOFF, JACQUELINE LEMBREE, 2nd Grade Teacher; *b:* Needham, MA; *m:* John G.; *c:* Michael J. Starace, Michele M. Starace; *ed:* (BS) Elem Ed, Gorham St Teachers Coll 1962; Univ of CT; *cr:* 2nd Grade Teacher 1962-65, 1st Grade Teacher 1966-68 South Windsor CT; 1st Grade Teacher Kennedy Sch 1970-71; 1st Grade Teacher 1971-88, 2nd Grade Teacher 1989- Cousens MSAD 71; *ai:* Participant in Mainstreaming all Children; Teacher Consultant-Handwriting; Tactics of Thinking Course; NEA 1962-; ME Teachers Assn 1970-; Assn for Teacher Educators in ME 1985-; Published Blueprint for Excl in Handwriting Performance Objectives; Published Pre-Sch, Pre-Handwriting Guide; *office:* Cousens Sch Day St Kennebunk ME 04043

EVANS, ANN MARIE, English Teacher; *b:* New Martinsville, WV; *ed:* (AA) Eng, Del Mar Comm Coll 1972; (BS) Scndry Ed, 1974, (MS) Speech Comm, 1978 Univ of N TX; Grad Stud Comm, Univ of KS 1977-80; Eng as 2nd Lang/Writing, Corpus Christi St Univ 1982; Coastal Bend Writing Project Grad 1984; *cr:* Eng Teacher S Oak Cliff HS 1975-76; Eng/Speech Teacher Martin Jr HS 1980-88; Eng Teacher Roy Miller HS 1988-; *ai:* Soph Cncl Spon; Teacher of Month Comm; Instructional Leader TX Assessment of Academic Skills Preparation Group; TX Cncl Teachers of Eng; Natl Womens Poly Caucus; Teacher of Month 1990 Miller HS 1990; Teaching Assistantship Univ of KS 1977-79; Grad Fellowship N TX St Univ 1976-77; Dir/Designer Harbour Playhouse 1989; *office:* Roy Miller HS 1 Battlin Buc Blvd Corpus Christi TX 78408

EVANS, ANNETTE BARNES, Fifth Grade Teacher; *b:* Clayton, NC; *c:* Adrienne, Roderick; *ed:* (BS) Comm Art, Fayetteville St Univ 1973; Elem Ed & Mid Sch Lang Art, Univ of SC; *cr:* 6th Grade Teacher N Myrtle Beach Elem 1974-75; 3rd/5th Grade Teacher Woodland Park Elem 1977-83; 6th Grade Teacher Boeblingen Amer Elem 1983-86; 9th-11th Grade Teacher Clayton HS 1987-89; 5th Grade Teacher Westarea Elem 1989-; *ai:* Math Comm; Sci Club; NASA SEEDS; NCTE Mem 1987-; NEA; Sch Advisory Cncl Stuttgart W Germany; *office:* Westarea Elem Sch 941 Country Club Dr Fayetteville NC 28301

EVANS, CARLTON WEBB, Biology Teacher; *b:* CLarksville, TN; *m:* Debora Ann Wright; *c:* Carleigh R.; *ed:* (BS) Bio, 1975, (MA) Supervision & Admin, 1978 Austin Peay St Univ; *cr:* Life Sci/Bio Teacher Montgomery Cntrl HS 1977-78; Bio I/II Teacher Waverly Cntrl HS 1978-; *ai:* Sci Club Spon; Sci Acts Coord; NEA, TN Ed Assn, NSTA 1978-; Audubon 1971-; Natl Wildlife Fed 1976-; Career Ladder Participant Level III; Vanderbilt Univ Sci Teacher of Yr 1986; TN Collaborative for Educl Excl Sci Task Force; *home:* Rt 6 Clarksville TN 37040

EVANS, DAVID ALONZO, History/Philosophy Teacher; *b:* Pittsburgh, PA; *m:* Rosemary Ann; *c:* Erin; *ed:* (BS) Scndry Ed/Soc Stud, CA Univ of PA 1972; Grad Stud Glassboro St; *cr:* Teacher Arthur Rann 1972-76, Notre Dame of Chicago 1976-80, Arthur Rann 1982-; *ai:* Stu Cncl Adv 1983-; Bsktbl Coach 1974-76; NEA 1972-; Galloway Township Assn Building Rep 1988-, Teacher of Yr 1986; US Navy Petty Officer 1965-69, Sailor of Month 1969, Honorary Discharge.

EVANS, DEBORA KERSHNER, Third Grade Teacher; *b:* Springfield, OH; *m:* Dennis W.; *ed:* (BS) Elem Ed, 1981, (MS) Principalship, 1985 Wright St Univ; Various Wkshps; *cr:* 3rd Grade Teacher Cedar Cliff Elem Sch 1981-; *ai:* Cedar Cliff Ed Assn Secy 1989-; *office:* Cedar Cliff Elem Sch PO Box 45 248 N Main St Cedarville OH 45314

EVANS, DENNIS MICHAEL, Principal; *b:* Huntington Park, CA; *m:* Judith Ball; *c:* Laurie, Spencer, Kirk, Brett, Tyler, Katie; *ed:* (BS) Elem Ed, 1974, (MED) Sch Admin, 1979 Brigham Young Univ; *cr:* Classroom Teacher 1974-81, Prin 1981- Taylor Elem Sch; *ai:* AZ Schls Admin Assn 1981-; Natl Assn Elem Schls Prins 1988-; BSA Dist Chm 1990; *office:* Taylor Elem Sch PO Box 1100 Snowflake AZ 85937

EVANS, DON L., English Teacher; *b:* Milton-Freewater, OR; *m:* Shirley J. Layton; *c:* Theresa A., Anthony J.; *ed:* (BS) Eng/His/Ed, Univ of OR 1959; (MA) Ed/Eng, CA St Univ Sacramento 1963; *cr:* Eng Teacher Campos Verdes Jr HS 1959-80; Civics/Soc Stud Teacher Highlands HS 1963-68, Rio Linda Sr HS 1969-74; Eng Teacher Don Julio Jr HS 1981-; *ai:* Speech & Drama Act; Sch & Dist Spelling Bee; NEA Life Mem 1959-; CTA 1959-; PTA Historian 1959-70, Honorary Life Mem 1962; Grant Dist Teachers Assn 1959-, Distinguished Service, Teacher of Yr 1985; N Highlands Park & Recreation 1963-70, Teenage Canteen; Sacramento Cty Finalist 1985; CA Team Teaching Pioneer 1960-65; Grant Dist Eng Dept Head 1964-74; *office:* Don Julio Jr HS 1333 Grand Ave Sacramento CA 95838

EVANS, DONNA HARTER, 1st Grade Teacher; *b:* Peru, IN; *m:* David A.; *c:* Duane A., Darren S.; *ed:* (BS) Elem Ed, 1959, (MA) Elem , 1962 Ball St Univ; Several Wkshps; *cr:* 4th Grade Teacher Mc Kinley Sch 1959-62; 1st Grade Teacher New Lisbon Sch 1962-63, Shadeland Sch 1966-67, Blue River Elem 1973-; *ai:* Book Adoption Technology & Other Building Comms; Henry Cty Rdng Cncl; *office:* Blue River Valley Elem Sch Box 187 Mount Summit IN 47361

EVANS, ELIZABETH ANN MASON, Mathematics/History Teacher; *b:* Florence, AL; *m:* Dwight Lamar; *c:* Kristopher, Lori; *ed:* (BS) Sociology, Univ of N AL 1971; Math Ed; *cr:* General Math Teacher 1988-89, US His/Math Teacher 1989- Tri Cty Bible Sch; *ai:* Jr Class Spon; Math Club Co-Spon; Chorus Co-Dir; Springfest Musical Variety Show Dir; LACE Treas 1985-86; PTF (Historian 1987-89, Parlimentarian 1989-); DCEA Treas 1984-86; Austinville Church of Christ Youth Leader 1987-; *home:* Rt 1 Box 404 Decatur AL 35603

EVANS, GERTRUDE ALICE, V-Principal/4th Grade Teacher; *b:* Woodbury, NJ; *ed:* (BS) Elem Ed, Villanova Univ 1970; (MA) Elem/Scndry Ed/Admin, Glassboro St Coll 1981; *cr:* LPN Salem Cty Memorial Hospital 1941-54; Teacher 1954-, Vice-Prin 1990 St Mary Regional Sch; *ai:* Testing Coord; Admin Hot Lunch Prgm; Teachers Liaison St Mary Regional Bd of Ed; NCEA 1954-; St Marys Guild Pres 1971-73; Pastoral Cncl of Camden Diocese Charter Mem 1970-, Bishops Medal 1982, Humanitarian Awd 1987; Salem Day Care Center (Charter Bd Mem, Secy, Treas); Alpha Sigma Lambda 1967; *home:* 143 Carpenter St Salem NJ 08079

EVANS, GWENDOLYN SAMS, Kindergarten Teacher; *b:* Cave Spring, GA; *m:* William R. Jr.; *ed:* (BA) Elem Ed, Fort Valley St Coll 1970; (MS) Early Chldhd, GA Coll 1979; *cr:* Teacher Hancock Cntrl Elem, L S Ingrahm Pre-Sch, Sparta Elem, M E Lewis Sr Elem Sch; *ai:* GAE Secretary 1971-72; Fort Valley St Alumni Club Sec1973-74; *office:* M E Lewis Sr Elem Sch Rt 2 Box 456 Sparta GA 31087

EVANS, JENNY (POOT), 10th Grade Eng/Rdng Teacher; *b:* De Lier, The Netherlands; *ed:* (BA) Eng, 1970, (MA) Rdng, 1976 W MI Univ; *cr:* Cmptr Rdng Instr Calhoun Area Voc Center 1984, 1985, 1989; Rdng Instr Kellogg Comm Coll 1988-89; Eng Teacher Battle Creek Cntrl HS 1971-; Eng Consultant Charon Assn 1977-; *ai:* Rdng Study Skills Comm Chairperson; Scndry Rdng Comm; Battle Creek Ed Assn (Assn Rep 1980-, Bd of Dir 1988-, Prof Negotiations Team 1989-, Building Assn Rep), Golden Apple 1989; Master Teacher Awd Battle Creek Kiwanis Club 1989; Kellogg Fnd Grant 1990; *office:* Battle Creek Cntrl HS 100 W Van Buren Battle Creek MI 49017

EVANS, JOANNE VOGELSANG, Mathematics Teacher; *b:* Cincinnati, OH; *m:* Randy C.; *ed:* (BSED) Elem, 1972, (MED) Math, 1978 Miami Univ; Additional Courses Calculus, Sch Law, Techniques Improving Scndry Math Instruction, Classroom Cmptrs; *cr:* 5th Grade Teacher C R Coblentz Mid Sch 1972-81; Math Teacher Natl Trail HS 1981-; *ai:* Stu Cncl Adv; Quiz Bowl Team Co-Adv; Faculty Cncl; NCTM 1977-; OH Cncl Teachers of Math; NEA, OH Ed Assn 1972-; Delta Kappa Gamma Society Intnl (Treas 1984-) 1983-; Kappa Delta 1969-; Coblentz Classroom Teachers Assn (Treas 1976-81, 1988-, VP 1983-86); Math Graded Course of Study Comm 1984, 1989; C R Coblentz Mid Sch Faculty Service Awd 1981; Outstanding Young Women of America 1982; Teacher Inservice Metric System (Developer, Dir, Presenter); Elem Advisory Comm Teacher Ed Redesign, Miami Univ 1979-80; *office:* Natl Trail HS 6940 Oxford-Gettysburg Rd New Paris OH 45347

EVANS, LINDSEY (SHELTON), English Teacher; *b:* Huntingburg, IN; *m:* Bruce C.; *c:* Colin; *ed:* (BS) Eng, Purdue Univ 1971; (MS) Ed, Univ of Evansville 1976; *cr:* Speech & Eng Teacher Thornton HS 1971-73; 8th Grade Eng Teacher Southridge Mid Sch 1973-88; 10th Grade Lit & Comp Teacher Southridge HS 1988-; *ai:* Spon Hoosier Spell Bowl Team; Southwest Dubois Classroom Teachers Assn 1973-; IN St Teachers Assn 1971-; IN Teachers of Writing 1988-; Beta Sigma Phi 1974-;Huntingburg Study Club 1988-; *office:* Southridge HS Hwy 231 South Huntingburg IN 47542

EVANS, MARIE LISTER, Assistant Principal; *b:* Lakeland, GA; *m:* Marvin Velton; *c:* Marvin, Theresa Reynolds, Evan, Bruce; *ed:* (BS) Elem Ed, 1972, (MED) Elem Ed, 1976, (EDS) Mid Grades Ed, 1984 Valdosta St Coll; Early Chldhd Ed, Data Collection, Stu Teacher Supervision, Admin & Supervision Leadership; *cr:* Teacher Clyattville Elem Sch 1972-81; Teacher/Team Leader 1981-89, Asst Prin 1989- Lowndes Mid Sch; *ai:* Sch Level Strategic Planning, Emergency Preparedness Comm; Assisted Writing Grant for At-Risk Stu Ed; Lowndes Assn of Educators (Pres Elect 1987-88, Pres 1988-89); NEA; GA Assn Educators Pres Uniserv Cncl 1988-89; ASCD, CEC, GA Cncl Intnl Rdng Assn; GA Mid Sch Assn, Child Abuse Cncl, PTO; Lowndes Mid Sch Teacher of Yr 1987-88; Lowndes Cty Teacher of Yr 1988; Roundtable of Excel Teaching Math; *office:* Lowndes Mid Sch 506 Copeland Rd Valdosta GA 31601

EVANS, MARLENE CRABTREE, Third Grade Teacher; *b:* Vernon, OH; *m:* Eddie Lee; *c:* Tammy L. Davis, Debra K. Marshall; *ed:* (BS) Elem Ed, Rio Grande Coll 1967; *cr:* 3rd Grade Teacher 1963-64, 5th Grade Teacher 1964-65 Decatur-Washington; 3rd Grade Teacher Kenneth W Lewis Elem 1965-; *ai:* Treas Kenneth W Lewis Mothers Club; Rdng Competency Comm; Delta Kappa Gamma Honorary Mem 1977-78; *home:* 311 W Main St Oak Hill OH 45656

EVANS, MATTIE HARRIS, English I Teacher; *b:* Jackson, MS; *c:* Alonzo T.; *ed:* (BA) Lang Art, Jackson St Univ 1962; (BS) Elem Ed, 1979; (MS) 1980; *cr:* Chm Eng Dept/Teacher Harris Jr Coll 1962-66; Eng I Teacher Amanda Elzy HS 1966-; *ai:* Natl Jr Honor Society Adv; Academic Team Coach; City-Wide Eng Prgm Coord; Sigma Gamma Rho; Strangers Home Baptist Church; Summer Writing Fellow; *home:* 701 Bowie Ln Greenwood MS 38930

EVANS, MELVIN JAMES, Third Grade Teacher; *b:* East Stroudsburg, PA; *ed:* (BS) Elem Ed, 1975, (MED) Elem Ed, 1980 E Stroudsburg Univ; *cr:* 3rd Grade Teacher 1977-80, 2nd Grade Teacher 1980-81 Avona Elem Sch; 3rd Grade Teacher Wilson Elem Sch 1981-; *ai:* PSEA, NEA 1977-; Avona Elem PTA PA Congress of Parents & Teachers Honorary Life Membership 1981; *office:* Wilson Elem Sch 21st St & Washington Blvd Easton PA 18042

EVANS, NANCY KING, Spanish & French Teacher; *b:* New Kensington, PA; *m:* Dennis W.; *c:* Bethany, Jonathan; *ed:* (BS) Ed, Clarion Univ 1972; Univ of Valencia, Kent St Univ, Gannon Univ; *cr:* Substitute Teacher Akron City Schls 1973-76; Eng/Span Teacher Cuyahoga Valley Chrstn Acad 1976-78; 5th-8th Grade Teacher St Boniface Sch 1979-80; Fr/Span/Eng Teacher Elk Cty Chrstn HS 1980-; *ai:* Lang Club; Independent Study Span III, Span IV; NCEA 1979-; *office:* Elk Cty Chrstn HS 600 Maurus St Saint Marys PA 15857

EVANS, NANCY WILLIAMS, 2nd Grade Teacher; *b:* Dell Rapids, SD; *m:* Thomas C.; *c:* Erin, Emily; *ed:* (BS) Elem Ed, MO Western Coll 1974; Literature in Classroom; *cr:* 2nd Grade Teacher Ellis Elem 1974-; *ai:* Prin Adv Comm; Intnl Rdng Assn 1986-; MSTA 1974-; Plattsburg Comm Teachers Assn Past Treas 1974-; Presently Writing a Literature Grant; *office:* Ellie Elem Sch 603 Frost Plattsburg MO 64477

EVANS, NED JOHN, 5th Grade Teacher; *b:* Wilkes-Barre, PA; *m:* Rose Ann Moosic; *c:* John, Kyle; *ed:* (BS) Elem Ed, Wilkes Coll 1977; (MS) Elem Admin 1982, (MS) Scndry Admin 1987 Scranton Univ; *cr:* Jr HS Teacher GAR HS 1978-79; K-6th Grade Teacher Dr David Kistler Elem Sch 1979-; *ai:* Boys & Girls Elem Intramural Coach; 5 Gold Medal & 4 Silver Championships; Coord St Judes Hospital Math-A-Thon; Boys-Girls Soccer Coach 1 Silver-1 Gold Medal; PA St Ed Assn Mem 1977-; Wrote Kndgtn Level Play & Directed Year Santa Forgot Christmas 1978-79; *home:* 143 Laird St Wilkes-Barre PA 18702

EVANS, PATRICIA LEE, English/History Teacher/Supvr; *b:* Hammond, IN; *m:* Marley E.; *c:* Melissa, Melinda, Meggin; *ed:* (BS) Music/Eng, Ball St Univ 1967; Grad Stud, St Francis Coll; Admin Seminars, Pensacola Chrstn Coll; *cr:* Music Teacher Manchester Cmmty Schls 1967-70; Eng/Music Teacher Heritage Hall Chrstn Sch 1973-75, Landmark Chrstn Sch 1976-82, Grace Baptist Acad 1982-87; Eng/His/Music Teacher Cornerstone Chrstn Acad 1987-; *ai:* Honor Society Spon; Sci Fair Coord; Prgm Dir; Ed Supvr; Amer Assn of Chrstn Schls; SAI Music Honorary in Coll; E Cntrl Sci Fair Comm 1988-; Graduated on Honors Prgm; Piano & Organ Teacher; Church Choir Dir; Have Performed & Spoken at Conferences & Meetings; Have had St Winners in Music & Natl Winners in Essay Competition; *office:* Cornerstone Christian Acad Sch 1352 Parkway Dr Saint Clair MO 63077

EVANS, PATRICIA MAHFOUZ, Fourth Grade Teacher; *b:* Burkeville, TX; *c:* Cathy D., Mark J.; *ed:* (BS) Elem Ed, Lamar Univ 1973; Inst of Childrens Lit 1980; Several Grad Courses, Lamar Univ; Numerous Wkshps; *cr:* Stenographer to Employment Interviewer TX Employment Commission 1951-60; Secy Engineering Pure Oil Company 1962-63; Secy 1965-71, Teacher 1973- Hillcrest Elem; *ai:* Planning Comm; Teaching 4th Grade Gifted/Talented Pull-Out Prgm & Regular Classroom; PTA Honorary Life Membership 1970; NEA, TSTA, Nederland Teachers Assn 1973-, Dist Teacher of Yr 1983; Intnl Rdng Assn SE TX Cncl; Pilot Club Corresponding Secy 1966-69; Outstanding Young Women of America 1968; Published Article in Early Yrs Magazine 1982; *office:* Hillcrest Elem Sch 220 17th St Nederland TX 77627

EVANS, PAUL M., Speech/Debate Teacher; *b:* Chillicothe, MO; *m:* Carol R.; *c:* Heather R.; *ed:* (BS) Ed/Speech/Theater, MWSC 1977; Grad Stud in Ed, KY Univ, NWMSU, NEMSU; *cr:* Speech/Drama Teacher Bode Mid Sch 1977-81; Teacher/Coach Benton HS 1981-; *ai:* Speech, Debate & Forensics Dir; Speech Club Spon; Curr Comm; NEA 1978-; Speech Theatre Assn of MO 1977-; Natl Forensic League 1981-; Pi Kappa Delta VP MWSC 1975-77, Outstanding Sr 1977; NW Conference Speech of MO VP 1984-86; *office:* Benton HS 5655 S 4th Saint Joseph MO 64504

EVANS, PETER MICHAEL, Social Studies Teacher; *b:* Akron, OH; *m:* Barbara Trout; *c:* Timothy, Christopher, Brooke; *ed:* (BA) His, VA Military Inst 1965; US Army Officers Basic & Advanced Schls; US Army Adjutant Generals Sch; Command & General Staff Mid-Management Trng, Angelo St Univ; *cr:* Commissioned Officer US Army 1965-77; Soc Stud Teacher Pymatuning Valley HS 1979-81, Petrolia HS 1982-84, Terrell Cty Ind Sch Dist 1984-; *ai:* Jr HS & HS Ftbl, Jr Var Girls Bsktbl, Var & Jr HS Tennis Coach; Jr HS Newspaper Adv & Spon St Awd of Achievement; UIL Impromptu Speaking Adv; NEA, OEA Uniserve Rep 1979-81; NEA, TSTA Mem 1982-; Natl Eagle Scout Assn Mem 1986-; Jaycees Mem 1976-80; US Army Reserves Commissioned Officer 1976-; *office:* Terrell Cty Ind Sch Dist Box 747 Sanderson TX 79848

EVANS, RICHARD A., Mathematics Department Chair; *b:* Farragut, IA; *m:* Margaret L. Trembly; *c:* Kelly J. Evans Murphy, Tracy J. Evans Ford, Teresa J. Evans Nixon; *ed:* (BA) Bus Admin/Soc Stud, CSC Greeley 1955; (MA) Math, CSU Fresno 1970; *cr:* Teacher/Coach Laird HS 1955-58, Seibert HS 1958-60, Idalia HS 1960-67, Wray HS 1967-; *ai:* NHS, Fellowship of Chrstn Athletes, Sr Class Spon; Girls Track Coach; NCTM; IAABO Intnl Assn of Approved Bsktbl Ofcls, CO Ftbl Ofcls Assn; KS St Bsktbl & Ftbl Ofcls Assn, NE St Bsktbl & Ftbl Ofcls Assn; NSF Grant Fresno St Coll 1967-70.

EVANS, RICHARD ALLEN, 8th Grade Teacher; *b:* Gary, IN; *m:* A. Jane Parker; *c:* Cory R., Tanya R.; *ed:* (BA) Geography/Sociology, 1969, (MS) Soc Stud, 1975 IN St Univ; *cr:* Teacher Hanover Cntrl HS 1969-70, Hammond Tech/Voc HS 1970-74, H Morton HS 1974-82, H Scott Mid Sch 1982-; *office:* Scott Mid Sch 3635 173rd Hammond IN 46323

EVANS, RICHARD MARK, English Teacher; *b:* Lawrence, MA; *m:* Carol Hoag; *c:* Justin; *ed:* (BA) Eng, Merrimack Coll 1966; *cr:* Eng Teacher Cardinal Cushing Acad 1966-68, Andover HS 1968-; *office:* Andover H S Shawnsheen Rd Andover MA 01810

EVANS, ROBERT CARL, Exceptional Chldhd Ed Teacher; *b:* Hopkinsville, KY; *c:* David, Sarah, Emily; *ed:* (BS) Mental Retardation, Murray St Univ 1970; (MED) Spec Ed, Univ of Louisville 1980; Cert Supervision Spec Ed; *cr:* Teacher Outwood Sch 1965-68, Jefferson Cty Public Schls 1970-; *ai:* Jefferson Cty Teachers Assn Prof Rep; Corporal Punishment Advisory Comm; CEC, Phi Delta Kappa, NEA; Optomist Club Intnl; NEA Elections, Prof Negotiational, Jefferson Cty Teachers Assn Poly Action Comm; Jefferson Cty Teachers Assn Bd of Dir.

EVANS, RONALD JAMES, Band Director; *b:* Fitzgerald, GA; *m:* Karyl Arn; *c:* Kelli S., Shana L.; *ed:* (BMED) Music Ed, Univ of GA 1963; (MMED) Music Ed, Vander Cook Coll 1970; Spec Ed Music Ed, Troy St Univ 1991; *cr:* Band/Choral Dir South Hall HS 1963-73, Johnson HS 1973-86; Instrumental Coord/Band Dir Gainesville HS 1986-; *ai:* Marching Band; Jazz Ensemble; GA Music Educators Assn 1963-; Phi Beta Mu St Pres 1984-86; Amer Sch Band Dir Assn St Chm 1982-; Kiwanis Youth Service Awd Recognized John Philip Sousa Fnd; Citation of Excl Natl Band Assn; Selected Teach Governors Honors Prgm GA; *office:* Gainesville HS 1120 Rainey St Gainesville GA 30505

EVANS, SHARON C., 4-6th Soc Stud Teacher/Homerm; *b:* Greencastle, IN; *m:* Robert W.; *c:* Robert S., Richard B., Scott G.; *ed:* (BS) Elem Ed, IN Cntrl 1969; (MS) Elem Ed, IN Cntrl 1972; Gifted & Talented Endorsement Purdue Univ; *cr:* Sec Coll Life Insurance Co of Amer 1960-65; Admin Asst Ser Vaas & Co 1965-70; 6th Grade Teacher J K Lilly SCh 42 1970-72; Teacher South Putnam Cntrl Elem Sch 1972-; *ai:* Stud Cncl Adv; Hist Club Spon; G/T Curr Comm; G/T Broad-Based Comm; G/T Selection Comm; Swim Team Booster Club Officer/Spon; Chm Prof Affairs 1982-84; 2nd VP 1984-86; 2nd VP 1988-; 1st VP 1990-92 Delta Kappa Gamma Society; IN Prof Educators Mem 1974-; Delta Theta Tau 1987-; Putnam Cty Fnd Life Mem; Putnam Cty Lib Bd (Sec 1978/Member 1976-82/VP 1989/Mem 1988-92); Fnlst IN St Teacher of Yr 1981-82; Natl Sci Fnd Fellowship 1971; *home:* 600 Bloomington St Greencastle IN 46135

EVANS, SHEILA HULLINGER, Drama/English Teacher; *b:* Chicago, IL; *m:* George E.; *c:* Susan, James; *ed:* (BA) Eng/Drama, Alverno Coll 1963; Eng, Univ of IL & Univ of Toledo; *cr:* Eng Teacher Blue Island Dist 218 1963-67; Eng/Drama Teacher Woodruff HS 1967-69; Eng/Teacher of Gifted Clay HS 1976-80; Eng/Drama Teacher Sprayberry HS 1986-; *ai:* Drama Club; Literary Meet Chm; One Act Spon; ITS 1988-; Lassiter HS/Tritt Elem PTA Pres 1983-84; Lassiter Band Booster Club Pres 1986-87; Pope Booster Club Secy 1990; OH Jenning Scholar; Sprayberry HS Teacher of Yr; *office:* Sprayberry HS 2525 Sandy Plains Rd Marietta GA 30066

EVANS, SHIRLEY GOSSETT, 8th Grade Lang Art Teacher; *b:* Centerville, TN; *m:* Howard William; *c:* Kent Mc Clanahan, Todd Mc Clanahan, Zena Mc Clanahan Horn; *ed:* (BS) Scndry Ed/Home Ec, 1960, (MA) Curr/Instruction, 1975 George Peabody Coll for Teachers; Admin, TN St Univ 1986; *cr:* Chem/Bio Teacher Hickman Cty HS 1968; 8th/9th Eng Grade Teacher Hickman Cty Jr HS 1975-77; 7th-8th Grade Sci Teacher 1978-79, 6th Grade Eng/Soc Stud Teacher 1980-86, 8th Grade Lang Art Teacher 1982- Hickman Cty Mid Sch; *ai:* Dropout Prevention & Textbook Comms; Eng Dept Chairperson; NCTE 1976-; Hickman Cty Ed Assn Pres 1982-86; TN Ed Assn Exec Cncl 1982-88, Plaque 1988; NEA St Delegate 1982-88; Cub Scouts of America Den Mother 1965-70; Outstanding Young Women of America 1973; Mothers March of Dimes Past Chairperson Hickman Cty; Natl Sci Fnd Awd; TN Ed Status of Women in Ed Comm; Mrs TN 1st Runner Up 1970; *home:* Buffalo Springs Lobelville TN 37097

EVANS, SONJA HESTER, English Teacher/Dept Chair; *b:* Macon, GA; *m:* Cliff M. Jr.; *c:* Cliff III, Kyle; *ed:* (BA) Eng, Tift Coll 1978; (MED) Eng, Mercer Univ 1986; *cr:* Teacher Mary Persons HS 1978-; *ai:* Jr Class & Prom Spon; Parents Night & Media Comm; NCTE 1987-; Tucker/Jossey Circle of Meth Women 1988-; Monroe Cty Teacher of Yr 1989-; *office:* Mary Persons HS Montpelier Ave Forsyth GA 31029

EVANS, SUNDIAL (STRICKLAND), Third Grade Teacher; *b:* Waynesboro, MS; *m:* Olen; *c:* Keith; *ed:* Elem Ed, Jr Coll 1959; (BS) Elem Ed, Univ S MS 1962; (MA) Elem Ed, Willliam Carey 1978; *cr:* 3rd Grade Teacher Beat Four Sch 1959-; *home:* PO Box 125 Waynesboro MS 39367

EVANS, TIMOTHY FITZGERALD, Biology Department Chairman; *b:* Jackson, MS; *ed:* (BS) Phys Ed, 1985, (BS) Bio, 1985- SW MO St; *cr:* Teacher/Coach Belle HS 1985-; *ai:* Coaching Cross Cntry, Jr Var Bsktbl, Head Track Coach; Sr Spon; Salary Comm; NHS Induction Comm; Track Coaches of MO; Bsktbl Coaches of MO; Lions Club; *home:* PO Box 425 Vichy MO 65580

EVANS, UNA MERLE, Second Grade Teacher; *b:* Sweetwater, TX; *m:* Samuel; *c:* Jonathan, Isha; *ed:* (BA) Elem Ed, Sul Ross St Univ 1974; (MA) Counseling, Univ of TX Port Bolivar; Cert Bus Field; SW Bus Univ TX; *cr:* Receptionist St Joseph Hospital 1968-70; Teacher-Aide Big Springs Sch Dist 1970-73; Receptionist Denver Childrens Hospital 1974-75; Teacher Anson Jones 1975-; *ai:* TX Teachers Assn, Midland Classroom, Teachers Assn 1975-; Delta Sigma Theta Pres 1985-87, Woman of Yr 1986; Links Inc Pres 1980-88; Orgenas Club Inc Secy 1982; *home:* 412 Stoneybrook Midland TX 79703

EVANS, ZORA A. OUTLAW, Retired 2nd-3rd Grade Teacher; *b:* Ralls, TX; *m:* Joe William; *c:* David N., Judith A. Trainor, Paul B., Mary E.; *ed:* (BA) Eng/Psych, Baylor Univ 1947; (MED) Ed, Stephen F Austin St Univ 1961; Grad Work, TX Tech, Univ of Houston; *cr:* Soc Stud Teacher Post Ind Sch Dist 1947-48; Eng Teacher Brownfield Ind Sch Dist 1948-49, Shallowater Ind Sch Dist 1951-52; 4th Grade Teacher Dickinson Ind Sch Dist 1957-59; 2nd/3rd Grade Teacher La Marque Ind Sch Dist 1959-84; *ai:* TX St Teachers Assn; TX Classroom Teachers Local Unit Secy 1983-84; Alpha Delta Kappa (Pres 1980-82, Dist Chm, St Historian 1982-84), AAK of Yr 1982; Daughters of the Amer Revolution Chapter Regent 1989-91; Daughters of 1812 Registrar 1991-93; *home:* 1408 Houston Dr W La Marque TX 77568

EVANS-LOMBE, JUDITH ERROLL, Counselor; *b:* Fremont, NE; *m:* Charles Spencer; *c:* Marianne, Marcia, Michael, Melinda; *ed:* (BS) Elem Ed, Emporia St Univ; (MS) Counseling, Pittsburg St Univ; Prevention/Intervention Wkshp Trainer; *cr:* Kndgtn Teacher Fitzmorris; 1st Grade Teacher Edgewood; 3rd-5th Grade Teacher Cedar Bluff; 4th Grade Teacher Garfield; 4th-5th Grade Teacher Dearing; *ai:* Long Range Planning & USD 445 Ed Comm; Building Leadership Team USD 445; Peer to Peer Spon; KS Assn for Counseling & Dev, Natl Assn for Counseling & Development, Natl Drop-Out Prevention Network, NEA, KS Natl Ed Assn, ASCD, KS Prevention Prof, Natl Prevention Prof; KS Citizens Advisory Bd (Secy, Vice Chairperson, Chairperson) 1982-; KS SE Secy 1988-89; KS Counseling Assn; Coffeyville Public Lib Bd Chm; Montgomery Cty Correction Advisory Bd (VP, Chm); *office:* Roosevelt Mid Sch 1000 W 8th Coffeyville KS 67337

EVANSON, CLIFFORD GEORGE, Air Force JROTC Teacher; *b:* Cleveland, OH; *m:* Diana Delvaux; *c:* Lia; *ed:* BA Equivalent Jr Reserve Officer Trng Corps Curr, USAF Air Trng Command 1985; Outdoor Ed; Non Commissioned Officer Acad 1975; Sr Non Commissioned Officer Acad 1980; Command Non Commissioned Officer Acad 1982; *cr:* Supvr USAF 1959-85; AFJROTC Teacher Plainfield HS 1985-87, Kaiserslautern HS Germany 1987-; *ai:* AFJROTC Drill Team European Champions; British Gliding Assn 1980-; Overseas Educl Assn 1987-; Amer Legion 1987-; Sergeants Assn 1980-; *office:* Kaiserslautern Amer HS APO New York NY 09094

EVARTS, LYNN, English Teacher; *b:* Madison, WI; *m:* Larry Federer; *ed:* (BS) Eng Ed, Univ WI Oshkosh 1985; Lib Sci Degree, Univ WI Madison; *cr:* Eng Teacher Sauk Prairie HS 1985-; *ai:* AODA Group Facilitator; Forensic Coach; SEC Lang Art Chairperson; NCTE 1985-; *office:* Sauk Prairie HS 105 9th St Prairie Du Sac WI 53578

EVE, THERESA OWLETT, Science Teacher; *b:* Pensacola, FL; *m:* Brian Douglas; *ed:* (BS) Bio/Ed, Univ of Cincinnati 1986; *cr:* Sci Teacher Northwest HS 1987-; *ai:* Stu of Month Selection Comm; Frederick B Krecker Awd 1990; *office:* Northwest HS 10761 Pippin Rd Cincinnati OH 45231

EVELAND, JUNE WOLF, Third Grade Teacher; *b:* Laurelville, OH; *m:* Dwight; *c:* Michel, Martin; *ed:* (BA) Elem Ed, OH Univ 1969; *cr:* 3rd Grade Teacher Logan Elem Sch 1961-90; *ai:* Logan Elem Sch Teacher Recognition Awd 1983; *home:* 16108 Maple St Laurelville OH 43135

EVELEIGH, LORRAYNE, Kindergarten Teacher; *b:* Nekoma, KS; *m:* Bob; *c:* Todd, Michelle; *ed:* (BS) Elem Ed, Ft Hays Univ 1960; Gesell Dev Trng; Cooperative Learning; *cr:* Teacher Rude Sch 1951-52; 3rd-5th Grade Teacher Heizer Elem 1952-54; 1st/2nd Grade Teacher Wheatland Elem 1954-64; Kndgtn Teacher Park Elem 1966-; *ai:* Homework Help Teacher; Delta Kappa Gamma Comm 1985-; Great Bend Ed Assn 1956-, Master Teacher of Yr 1984; KS Ed Assn Delegate 1951-, Teacher 1976; NEA 1951-; Ed Home Unit; 1st United Meth Church Youth Dir Many Comms; Received KS Young Bank Officer Sweepstakes Awd 1984 & Regional Awd 1986; *home:* 2110 San Domingo Great Bend KS 67530

EVEN, SHIRLEY ANN (JOHNSON), Teacher of Gifted/Talented; *b:* Louisville, KY; *m:* John P.; *c:* Juliet, Charles, Thomas; *ed:* (BS) Elem Ed, Catherine Spalding Coll 1966; (MED) Scndry Ed, Univ of Louisville 1968; Mid-Management Certifiicate Univ of TX 1989; Advanced Acad Trng Gifted & Talented, Cmptr Sci, Art Northside Sch Dist; *cr:* Elem Teacher Louisville Parochial Schls 1963-66, Jefferson Cty Public Schls 1966-69, Elem Teacher 1969-84, Teacher of Gifted & Talented 1984- Northside Ind Sch Dist; *ai:* TX Marine Bio Assn 1984-; Assn of TX Prof Educators 1977-; TX Archaeological Assn 1987-; NISD Nom Trinity Awd Excl in Ed; *office:* Colonies North Elem Sch 9915 Northampton San Antonio TX 78230

EVENSEN, ELISABETH HILDEGARD, Kindergarten Teacher; *b:* Saint Paul, MN; *ed:* (BS) Nursery Sch Kndgtn Primary, Univ of MN 1963; Addl Studies Graduate Study in Wkshp Way Xavier Univ; Graduate Study Voice Univ of MN; *cr:* 1st Grade Teacher Franklin Elem Sch 1963-64; Kndgtn Teacher Harrison Elem Sch 1965-76; Dayton's Bluff Elem Sch 1976-77; Hayden Heights Elem 1977-; *ai:* Gifted & Talented Comm; Multi-Culture Comm; Delta Kappa Gamma Pres 1973-; Nom Teacher of Yr 1974; Assn for Chldhd Ed Pres 1961-72; Amer Guild of Organists 1971-; Twin City Choirmaster 1975-; Church Musicians & Choir Dir 1985-; Kndgtn Stu Performed & Sang before Voice Teachers from Around the Nation at Univ of MN Vocal Work Shop 1986; Video Taped for Grad Stud Reference; *office:* Hayden Heights Elem Sch 1863 Clear Ave Saint Paul MN 55119

EVERETT, CONSTANCE POWERS, Mathematics Teacher; *b:* Buckhannon, WV; *m:* Delmar; *c:* Scott, Todd, Chad; *ed:* (BA) Math, Muskingum Coll 1960; Kent St Univ, Bowling Green Univ, Ashland Coll; Martha Holden Jennings Fnd Summer Wkshp; *cr:* Math Teacher Parma City Schls 1960-62, Ravenna Chrstn Acad 1981-85, Colonel Crawford Sch Dist 1985-; *ai:* Math Dept Chairperson Colonel Crawford Sch Dist; 7th Grade & Chess Club Adv; OEA, NEA, OH Cncl Teachers of Math 1985-90; NCTM 1986-; *home:* 3100 Lebanon Rd Lebanon OH 45036

EVERETT, DEBORAH STUART, Dir of Comm Soc Teacher & Adv; *b:* Indianapolis, IN; *m:* Christopher J.; *ed:* (BS) Sociology & Soc Wk, Carroll Coll 1973; (MSW) Soc Wk, IN Univ 1977; *cr:* Admission Cnslr Carroll Coll 1973-75; Coord Vol Homebound Sr 1977-79; Admin & Fac Mem Park Tudor Sch 1979-; *ai:* Fac Adv; Box Office Mgr; Case 1979; Jr Leag Church Vocal & Bell Choir Mem Bd Mem 1980-81/83-84; *office:* Park Tudor Mid Sch 7200 N College Ave Indianapolis IN 46240

EVERETT, ELIZABETH LILLY, Biology Teacher; *b:* Hopkinsville, KY; *m:* D. J. III;; *ed:* (BS) Bio Sci, Univ of KY 1966; (MA) Ed, Murray St Univ 1989; *cr:* Teacher/Dept Chm Bryan Station 1966-74; Teacher Hopkinsville HS 1985- *ai:* Head Spon Class of 1993; NSTA 1985-; KSTA 1985; NABT 1985; Widowed Persons Service Bd 1982-85; Chrstn Cty Lib Bd Vice Chm 1988; *office:* Hopkinsville H S 430 Koffman Dr Hopkinsville KY 42240

EVERETT, EVA SAVAGE, Kindergarten Teacher; *b:* Mc Minnville, TN; *m:* Joe M. Sr.; *ed:* (BA) Early Chldhd, Catawba Coll 1984; *cr:* Teacher Asst 1969-71, 1976-84, Teacher 1984- Mocksville Elem; *ai:* Yrbk Adv; Prof Educators of NC 1984-; Friends of NC Symphony 1978-; *home:* 229 Cherry Mocksville NC 27028

EVERETT, GLENDA MC GEE, 5th Grade Soc Stud Teacher; *b:* Port Arthur, TX; *m:* Terry; *c:* Brandon, Lara; *ed:* (BA) Elem Ed, 1978, (MS) Elem Ed, 1981 Stephen F Austin Univ; *cr:* Phys Ed Teacher 1979-80, Math Teacher 1980-85, Soc Stud Teacher 1985 Baker-Koonce; *ai:* Carthage Classroom Teachers 3rd VP 1983; TX St Teachers Assn Treas 1984; *office:* Baker-Koonce Intermediate Sch 1 Bulldog Dr Carthage TX 75633

EVERETT, SHERRY ALLEN, Teacher; *b:* Fort Worth, TX; *m:* James Carter; *c:* Matthew A.; *ed:* (BA) His/Eng, Univ of TX Arlington 1971; Grad Studies; *cr:* Teacher Young Jr HS 1983-; *ai:* Spon NHS; Chm Liaison Comm; TX St Teachers Assn Building Rep; TCSS, NCSS; Teacher of Yr Nominee 1989, 1990; AWARE Finalist Teacher of Yr 1989-; *office:* Charles W Young Jr HS 3200 Woodside Dr Arlington TX 76016

EVERETTS, DANIEL ERNEST, Mathematics Teacher; *b:* Cleveland, OH; *ed:* (BS) Scndry Math Ed, OH St Univ 1985; *cr:* Math Teacher Hamilton Township HS 1985-; *ai:* Bsbl Coach; NCTM, OH Cncl Teachers of Math 1986-; *office:* Hamilton Township HS 4999 Locbourne Rd Columbus OH 43207

EVERHART, CAROL H., 6th Grade Sci/Health Teacher; *b:* Johnson City, NY; *ed:* (BS) Elem Ed, Bloomsburg St Coll 1974; Masters Equivalency Local Colls & Intermediate Unit 1988; Grad Stud Local Colls & Intermediate Unit; *cr:* Substitute Elem Teacher Wyoming Valley West Sch Dist 1974-76; Kndgtn Teacher Charles Street Elem 1976-80; 2nd Grade Teacher State Street Elem 1980-83; 6th Grade Self-Contained Teacher 1983-84, 6th Grade Sci/Health/Math Teacher 1984-88, 6th Grade Sci/Health Teacher 1988- Wyoming Valley West Mid Sch; *office:* Wyoming Valley West Mid Sch Chester St Kingston PA 18704

EVERHART, MADGE COLE, Fourth Grade Teacher; *b:* Topeka, KS; *m:* James L.; *ed:* (BA) Ed, Washburn Univ 1976; (MS) Rdng Specialist Curr/Instruction, Emporia St Univ 1981; *cr:* Substitute Teacher Topeka Unified Sch Dist #501 1976-77; 4th Grade Teacher 1977-87, 3rd/4th Grade Teacher 1987-88, 4th Grade Teacher 1988- Morris Elem Sch; *ai:* NEA 1977-; Cmmty Unity Church (Bd Mem 1987-, Bd Secy 1989-); *office:* Morris Elem Sch 7120 Gibbs Rd Kansas City KS 66106

EVERHART, STEPHEN DANIEL, Mathematics/Algebra I Teacher; *b:* Thomasville, NC; *m:* Carolyn Leonard; *c:* Anna M., Allyson M., Keri J.; *ed:* Grad Courses NC A&T; *cr:* Teacher/Coach East Davidson HS 1973-74, North Davidson Jr HS 1974-; *ai:* Head Coach 9th Grade Ftbl, 7th/8th Grade Boys Bsktbl; NC Coaches Assn 1973-; *office:* North Davidson Jr HS Rt 10 Box 1660 Lexington NC 27292

EVERITTS, DONNA LEE, High School English Teacher; *b:* Washington, DC; *ed:* (BS) Eng, Miami Univ 1968; (MA) Lit, Univ of Redlands 1972; Various Univs; *cr:* Eng Teacher Riverside Unified Sch Dist 1968-71, Ft Lupton Schls 1972-; *ai:* Denver Art Museum, Denver Natual His Museum, CO His Museum; Natl Endowment for Hum 1987; CO Writers Project Instr 1989-; *office:* Ft Lupton HS 530 Reynolds St Fort Lupton CO 80621

EVERLINE, JERI LOUISE, English Teacher; *b:* Rensselaer, IN; *ed:* (BA) Eng, Ball St Univ 1968; (MA) Eng, Butler Univ 1973; Rdng Endorsement; Working towards Gifted Endorsement; *cr:* 9th Grade Eng Teacher South Newton Jr-Sr HS 1968-71; 8th Grade Eng Teacher Fayette Cty Schls 1977-78; 7th Grade Eng Teacher Eastern Hancock Jr-Sr HS 1978-85; 8th Grade Eng Teacher Westfield-Washington Schls 1985-; *ai:* Mid Sch Academic Coach; IN Academic Coaches Assn.

EVERLY, CALVIN JAMES, Sixth Grade Science Teacher; *b:* Farmington, MI; *m:* Anne Marie Luchowski; *c:* Shawn M., Colleen M. Murry, Monet L.; *ed:* (BA) Comm Art/Sci, W MI Univ 1976; Sci Ed in Mid Sch Funded Grants WMU; Hands on Sci St Level Prgm; *cr:* US Navy USS Bigelow DD 942 1959-61; General Laborer Fabricated Steel Corporation Incorporated 1961-66; Prof Fire Fighter South Bend Fire Dept 1966-72; Teacher Lawton Cmmty Schls 1977-; *ai:* Sci Curr Mid Sch & All Earth Day Act Coord; Organized Laser Fund Raiser; MI Sci Teachers Assn 1983-; *office:* Lawton Cmmty Schls 880 2nd St Lawton MI 49065

EVERMAN, NINA NEAL, LBD Special Ed Teacher; *b:* Winchester, KY; *m:* Douglas Arthur; *c:* Khristie, Nicole; *ed:* (BA) Elem/Spec Ed (EMH), 1976, (Rank II) Spec Ed/LD/BD, 1978, (Rank I) Spec Ed Consultant, 1979 E KY Univ; *cr:* EMH Teacher Powell Cty Mid 1976-77; 1st Grade Teacher 1977-80, LBD Teacher 1980- Clay City Elem; *ai:* Spec Olympics Coach; Cheerleading Spon; Pre-Sch Comm; Band Boosters; Honors Banquet; 4-H Leader; KEA 1976-; OEEC; Homemakers 1975-; 4-H Cncl; Young Republicans VP 1970-; *home:* 200 Woody Ware Rd Clay City KY 40312

EVERSOLE, MARGARET (THOMAS), Librarian/Media Specialist; *b:* Muncie, IN; *m:* Arthur Allen Jr.; *c:* Frances M., Alysia A.; *ed:* (BS) Soc Sci, 1966, (MLS) Lib Sci, 1976 Ball St Univ; Courses in Admin & Supervision; Lions Quest Trng; *cr:* Librarian Crooked Creek Elem 1966-67, Makaha Elem 1967-68, Wapahani HS 1968-69; Librarian/Audio Visual Dir Anderson HS 1969-72; Librarian/Media Specialist Pendleton Heights Mid Sch 1972-; *ai:* Spon Alternatives in Motion; South Madison Classroom Teachers Assn Building Exec; CTA Negotiation Team Mem; Pendleton Heights Mid Sch Building Level Improvement Team Mem; Amer Lib Assn 1989-; Assn of IN Media Educators 1966-; NEA, ISTA, SMCTA (Building Rep, Building Exec Negotiations) 1976-; Alpha Delta Kappa (Chaplain, Treas, Pres, Recording Secy) 1980-; Pendleton First United Meth Church; Article & Prof Tip Published; *office:* Pendleton Heights Mid Sch 301 S East St Pendleton IN 46064

EVERSOLE, MARTHA LEACH, Kindergarten/Chapter 1 Teacher; *b:* Pleasant View, KY; *m:* Boyd Lee; *ed:* (BS) Elem Ed, 1983, (MA) Early Chldhd/Elem Ed, 1984, (Rank I) Elem Ed, 1986 E KY Univ; *cr:* Spec Ed Teacher Brodhead Elem 1984-85; 1st/2nd Grade Teacher 1985-86, Kndgtn Teacher 1986-89, Kndgtn/Chapter 1 Teacher 1989- Livingston Elem; *ai:* Phi Kappa Phi, Kappa Delta Pi 1982-; BACUS, KACUS, SACUS 1983-; KY Ed Assn, NEA 1985-; KY Lib Assn 1989-; Rockcastle Lib Trustee 1988-; Campbellsville COll Excl in Teaching Awd 1989; Commonwealth Inst for Teachers 1990; *office:* Livingston Elem Sch P O Box 190 Main St Livingston KY 40445

EVERSON, BARBARA BENNER, Spanish Teacher; *b:* Clarkston, WA; *m:* Gary Lester; *c:* Joseph, David, Brent; *ed:* (BSED) Eng, Univ of ID 1973; Numerous Grad Studs; Trng in Total Phys Response Methodology; *cr:* Eng/Span Instr Coeur D Alene HS 1973-77; Span Instr Canfield Jr HS 1986-87, Coeur D Alene HS 1987-; *ai:* Dept Chairperson; CEA, IEA, NEA 1973-77, 1987-; Trinity Luth Church (Search Bible Study Coord 1980-83, Bd of Ed 1978-81, Sunday School Teacher 1990-); *office:* Coeur D Alene Sr HS N 5530 4th St Coeur D'Alene ID 83814

EVERSON, DAVID PAUL, Biology Teacher; *b:* Arkon, OH; *m:* Norma Jean Regester; *c:* Brian; *ed:* (BA) Scndry Ed, Shepherd Coll 1975; *cr:* Teacher Philip Barbour HS 1977-; *ai:* Ecology Field Day & Sci Fair Coord; Cmptr Technology Comm; Sci Club Advanced Placement Lab; WVEA 1985-; AFT 1977-84; WV Dept of Ed Grant; Barbour Teacher Center Mini-Grants; *office:* Philip Barbour HS Rt 2 Philippi WV 26416

EVERSON, H. LORRAINE ARMSTRONG, 3rd/4th Grade Teacher; *b:* Sidney, MT; *m:* Donald E.; *c:* Steven R., Brian K.; *ed:* (BS) ED/Soc Sci, Drake Univ 1969; Slingerland Seattle Pacific Univ; *cr:* Eng Teacher Open Bible Coll 1969-70; 4th Grade Teacher Crestview Sch 1970-74; Substitute Teacher 1974-77; Elem Teacher Kingsway Acad 1977-78, Arlington Chrstn Sch 1978-; *home:* 6332 176th Pl NW Stanwood WA 98292

EVERT, COLLEEN FINNERTY, Social Studies Chair; *b:* Grand Rapids, MI; *m:* Edward P.; *c:* Kathleen, Jennifer; *ed:* (BA) His, Mercy Coll of Detroit 1962; (MED) Ed, Natl Coll of Ed 1986; Intnl Summer Sch Certificate, Cambridge Univ; *cr:* Asst Dean of Stu Affairs Mercy Coll of Detroit 1962-63; His Teacher St Patricks Acad 1965-69; Teacher/Soc Stud Chairperson Rosary HS 1969-; *ai:* Admin Bd; NCSS 1969-; IL Cncl of Soc Stud 1985-; Organization of Amer Historians 1990; Geneva Historical Society 1980-; Natl Trust for Historic Preservation 1975-; Amnesty Intnl Moderator; Univ of Chicago Outstanding Area Educator; *office:* Rosary HS 901 N Edgelawn Ave Aurora IL 60506

EVERTS, MICHAEL LEA, Math Dept Chairman; *b:* Monohans, TX; *c:* Angie Gilbert, Amy Martin; *ed:* (BA) Chem/Math, Austin Coll 1969; (MED) Mid Management, TX Tech Univ 1979; Wildlife Conservation; Fish & Wildlife Management: Medical/Lab Specialist, US Army; *cr:* Chem Instr South Plains Coll 1969; Math Teacher Levelland HS 1970-83; Adult Ed Teacher Levelland ISD 1974-82; Math Teacher Whitharral HS 1985-; *ai:* Whitharral Sch/Cmmty Improvemement Comm; UIL Math Dir; TSTA-NEA 1971-83; TASB 1988-; US Army 1966-69; DAV 1987-; *home:* 309 14th St Levelland TX 79336

EVES, ADAIR, Reading Department Chair; *b:* Teheran, Iran; *ed:* (BS) Elem Ed, Shippensburg Univ 1973; (MLA) Liberal Art, W MD Coll 1980; *cr:* 4th/5th Grade Surrey Sch 1974-81; 6th-8th Grade Teacher Boonsboro Mid Sch 1981-; *ai:* Odyssey of Mind Judge; Tennis Intramurals Coach; Lang Art Task Force; Evaluation & Concerns Comm; Sch Improvement Team; Washington Cty Teachers Assn 1974-; MD St Teachers Assn, NEA; Natl Organization for Women Washington Cty Chapter Pres 1982-84; League of Women Voters; Parent, Teacher, Stu Assn; Articles Published; *office:* Boonsboro Mid Sch 1 J H Wade Dr Boonsboro MD 21713

EVES, DONNA RAE DAL PONTE, Science Teacher; *b:* Sterling, CO; *m:* Joseph C.; *c:* Joe, Jason; *ed:* (BS) Bio Sci, CO St Univ 1970; (MA) Curr Instructional, Univ of Northern CO 1980; Staff Dev-Peer Coaching; Refusal Skills; Thim Heath Curr; *cr:* 7th Grade Sci Teacher Jerstad-Agerholm 1970-71; 5th/6th Sci Teacher Milliken Mid Sch 1971-73; 4th/5th/6th Grad Sci/Math/Rdng Teacher Sexson Iliff Elem 1976-78; 7th/8th Grade Eng/Sci/Health Careers/Gifted Talented Teacher Sterling JrHHS 1980-; *ai:* Coached Vlybl-Bsktbl-Track-Gymnastics-Sftbl; Health Insurance Comm; South Platte Ed Assn Pres 1988- Outstanding Leadership Awd 1989; *home:* 731 Columbine Sterling CO 80751

EVICK, JOHN ALLAN, Mathematics Teacher & Coach; *b:* Wheeling, WV; *m:* Kimberly Ann Krock; *c:* Jessica, Zachary; *ed:* (BS) Math Ed, OH St Univ 1982; Working Towards Masters Wheeling Jesuit Coll; *cr:* Substitute Teacher Worthington & Upper Arlington Schls 1982-83; Math Teacher Barnesville HS 1983-86, St Clairsville HS 1986-; *ai:* Tennis Coach; NEA, OH Ed Assn, NCTM; *office:* Saint Clairsville City Schls 108 Woodrow Ave Saint Clairsville OH 43950

EVRIDGE, ROBERT JOSEPH, 8th Grade Soc Stud Teacher; *b:* Chicago, IL; *m:* Jan Elizabeth Williams; *c:* Katherine E.; *ed:* (BA) Elem Ed, 1971, (MAT) Elem Ed, 1972 Harding Coll; Ed Admin/Supervision, Univ of TN 1976-83; Cmptr Service Technician 1985; Cmptrs Skills Next 1984-85; *cr:* 6th Grade Teacher Bonny Kate Elem 1972-73; 5th-7th Grade Stu with Learning Problems Teacher 1973-79, 8th Grade Amer His Teacher 1979-85, 8th Grade Amer His/6th-8th Grade Cmptr Skills Teacher 1985- Cedar Bluff Mid Sch; *ai:* Soc Stud Dept Chm; Girls Bsktbl Coach; Cmptr Service Technician; TN Assn for Children with Learning Disabilities 1973-78, Teacher of Yr 1978; NEA 1972-; TN Ed Assn 1972-, Educator of Yr 1989; TN Assn of Mid Schls 1980-; Career Level III Teacher 1985; Jr League Mini Grant 1989; Knoxville Chamber of Commerce Best Awd 1989; Cedar Bluff Mid Sch Teacher of Yr 1989; OH Valley Coll Medal of Merit in Ed 1990; *office:* Cedar Bluff Mid Sch 707 Cedar Bluff Rd Knoxville TN 37923

EWERS, JAMES LEE, 8th Grade Teacher; *b:* Streator, IL; *m:* Jean D. Nielen; *c:* Byron, Brent; *ed:* (BS) Music Ed, Olivet Nazarene Univ 1961; (MA) Sch Admin, Eastern MI Univ 1969; *cr:* Teacher Momence Public Schls 1961-64; Howell Public Schls 1964-69; Huron Valley Schls 1969-; *ai:* Study Skills Class after Schl; NEA; MI Ed Assn; Huron Valley Ed Assn Treas 1974-78; Mott Fdn of Flint MI Grant to Work on Schl Admn Proj; *home:* PO Box 2052 Howell MI 48844

EWIN, BILL E., Mathematics Department Chair; *b:* Chandler, IN; *m:* Jo Ellyn Brandt; *c:* Keith, Daynette France, Brandi; *ed:* (BS) Math, Oakland City Coll 1962; (MS) Scndry Ed, IN Univ 1967; Cmptr Ed Trng, Univ of Evansville; *cr:* Teacher Boonville HS 1962-, Ivey Tech Coll 1980-; *ai:* NHS Faculty Spon; WCCTA, ISTA, NEA, Natl Assn Teachers of Math 1962-; North-Cntrl Assn of HS & Colls Evalutation Teams; *office:* Boonville HS N 1st St Boonville IN 47601

EWING, BETTY LINTON, 5th Grade Teacher; *b:* Clarksville, TX; *m:* Dickie H.; *c:* Kyle, Amy; *ed:* (BS) Voc Home Ec, 1971, (MS) Elem Ed, 1975 E TX St Univ; *cr:* Home Ec Teacher Carrollton-Farmers Branch Ind Sch Dist 1971-72; Kndgtn Teacher 1972-74, 5th Grade Teacher 1974- Clarksville Ind Sch Dist; *ai:* UIL Number Sense Team; *home:* Rt 6 Box 114A Clarksville TX 75426

EWING, C CRAIG, English Teacher; *b:* Lawrence, KS; *c:* Eric, Ryan; *ed:* (BS) Eng, Univ of MO 1972; (MS) Rdng Specialist, Univ of KS 1976; *cr:* Lang Arts Teacher St Charles 1974-75; Rdng Specialist Jackson MS 1975-76; Eng/Rdng Teacher Bishop Miege 1976-88; Eng Teacher St Thomas Aquinas 1988-; *ai:* Boys & Girls Soccer Coach; Scholars Bowl Coach; Coord Sch Bookstore; Northeast KS Soccer Coaches Assn Pres 1988-; KS Teachers of Eng 1984-88; NCTE 1985-89; KS Coaches Assn 1985-; Young Educator of Yr Awd KS City Jr Chamber of Commerce 1985; Excl of Teaching Awd Nom KS City Star 1987/1990; Teaching Excl Awd KS Univ Honors Prgm 1987; *office:* St Thomas Aquinas H S 11411 Pflumm Rd Overland Park KS 66215

EWING, DICKIE HAROLD, Science Teacher; *b:* Clarksville, TX; *m:* Betty Linton; *c:* Amy, Kyle; *ed:* (BA) Ag Ed, 1970, (MS) Ag Ed, 1971 ETSU; Various Wrkshps; *cr:* Ag Teacher R L Turner 1971-72; 5th Grade Teacher Clarksville Intermediate Sch 1972-77; 7th Grade Teacher Clarksville Jr HS 1977-; *ai:* UIL Sci Team Spon; Boys Summer Bsbl Coach 1972-90; Tiger Booster Club Mem; ATPE Mem 1986; TX Teacher Appraisal System High Acad Recognition; Teacher of Yr Awd; *office:* Clarksville Jr HS P O Box 1016 Clarksville TX 75426

EWING, JAMES G, History/Social Studies Teacher; *b:* Waterbury, CT; *m:* Judith E.; *ed:* (BA) His/Hum, Brown Univ 1956; His, Yale Univ 1956-58; His, Northwestern Univ 163-64; His, Univ of Bridgeport 1966-67; *cr:* Teacher Roger Ludlowe HS 1957-66, Kenmore East HS 1967-68; Lecturer Univ of Bridgeport 1965-85; Teacher Stratford HS 1968-; *ai:* CT Ed Assn, Stratford Ed Assn, NEA 1968-; CT Cncl for Soc Stud, CT Assn for Supervision & Curr Dev 1986-; NCSS 1960-; ASCD 1986-; John Hay Fellow 1963-64; *office:* Stratford HS 45 N Parade Stratford CT 06497

EWING, KAY NOZAKI, Language Art Teacher; *b:* Spokane, WA; *m:* Thomas G. Jr.; *ed:* (BA) Eng Lit, 1965, (BE) Ed, 1965 Gonzaga Univ; (ML) Univ of WA 1975; *cr:* Lang Art Teacher Cascade Jr HS 1965-; Adjunct Professor Seattle Pacific Univ 1987-; *ai:* Natural Helpers Prgm Adv; Auburn Sch Dist Cmptr Comm; Mentor Teacher; Steering Comm for Cascades NW Assn of Accreditation Process; NEA, WA Ed Assn, Auburn Ed Assn; Delta Kappa Gamma Intnl Society (Local Chapter Secy 1986-89, 2nd VP 1990; Beta Phi Mu Intnl Lib Sci Honor Society, Intnl Cncl for Cmptrs in Ed, Intnl Society for Technology in Ed, NW Cncl for Cmptr Ed; *office:* Cascade Jr HS 1015 24th NE Auburn WA 98002

EWING, SHERRY J. (BRYANT), 7th-9th Grade Math Teacher; *b:* Mountain Home, AR; *m:* Danny L.; *c:* Joanna; *ed:* (BA) Math/Bus Ed, Harding Univ 1976; Math, Cmptr Courses; *cr:* 8th-12th Grade Math Teacher Caraway HS 1978-81; 7th-9th Grade Math Teacher Douglas Mac Arthur Jr HS 1981-; *ai:* Mathcounts Team Coach; ACTM, NEA, AEA 1978-; JCTA (Treas 1982-83) 1978-; GSA Co-Leader 1989-; Church Bible Class Teacher; *office:* Douglas Mac Arthur Jr HS 1615 Wilkins Jonesboro AR 72401

EWING, STANLEY E., Mathematics Teacher; *b:* Richland Cty, WI; *m:* Janita W. Peckham; *c:* Daniel, Dean, Suzanne, Sheila, Sheryl; *ed:* (BS) Math, Univ of WI Platteville 1962; (MA) Math, W MI Univ 1969; Grad Stud Math, Univ of WI Madison 1962-64; *cr:* Math Faculty Asst Univ of WI Platteville 1962-63; Math

Teacher Parkview HS 1964-68; 5th Grade Math Teacher Platteville Mid Sch 1976-80; Math Teacher Platteville HS 1969-76, 1980-; *ai:* Coach Boys Cross Cntry, Frosh Boys Bsktbl; Drama Set Construction Asst; Platteville Free Meth Church Youth Dir 1975-; Platteville Area Teacher of Yr; W MI Univ Natl Sci Fnd Academic Yr Inst 1968-69; *home:* 2187 Cty Hwy B Platteville WI 53818

EXTON, WILLIAM THOMAS, Math Department Chairman; *b:* Canandaigua, NY; *m:* Beth Ellen Schoenfeldt; *c:* Heather, Dawn, Amber; *ed:* (BS) Math Ed, Geneseo St Univ 1972; *cr:* Math Teacher 1972-77, Math Dept Chm 1977-, AP Math Teacher 1982- Perry Cntrl Sch; *ai:* Head Ftbl & Bsbl Coach; Natl Honor Society Adv; Steering, Ed-Tech, Effective Schls, Marking & Grading Comm; NYS Assn of Math Teachers; United Meth Church Trustee 1978-87; Recipient Univ of Rochester Awd for Excl Public Sch Teaching 1985; Alumni Assn Teacher of Yr 1989; *home:* 3391 Bacon Rd Perry NY 14530

EYL, DAVID E., Business Teacher; *b:* Hamilton, OH; *m:* Shelley R. Newland; *c:* Michael, Ashton; *ed:* (BS) Bus Management, OH Northern Univ 1983; *cr:* Teacher Allen East HS 1983-; *ai:* Boys Var Bsktbl Coach; OH HS Bsktbl Coaches Assn 1983-; *home:* Box 7024 Lafayette OH 45854

EZELL, DORIS AMURR, 7th Grade Lang Art Teacher; *b:* Mc Connells, SC; *c:* Dartinia A., Denikoa A. L. Meeks; *ed:* (BA) Eng, 1973, (MA) Scndry Ed, 1975 Winthrop Coll; CYLUC-E Writing Inst; *cr:* Teacher Indian Land Sch 1973-77, Lewisville HS 1977-78, Chester Jr HS 1978-; *ai:* Chester Jr HS Literary Club Spon; NCTE Mem 1984-; NEA Mem 1980-; Brattonsville Advisory Bd Appointed Mem 1990; SC Arts Commission Teacher Incentive Grants; Poetry Books Author; Chester Jr HS Teacher of Yr 1988-89; Palmetto Rdng Cncl Distinguished Teacher 1988-89; Awarded Bronco Yrbk Dedication Awd 1988; Chester Cty Teacher Incentive Prgm Bonus Cash Awd; Appointed CLASP Guest Speaker Rock Hill Sch Dist 3; *office:* Chester Jr HS Caldwell St Chester SC 29706

F

FABER, FREDDIE JAMES, JR., 7th/8th Grade Science Teacher; *b:* Moline, IL; *m:* Clare M. Clatts; *c:* Freddie J. III, Tammy L. Chamberlain; *ed:* (BA) Scndry Sci, Glassboro St 1972; Comprehensive, NJ Coll; NJ St Certified Paramedic; Advanced Cardiac Life Support Amer Heart Assn; Missile Launcher Tech & Nuclear Submarine Qualified US Navy; *cr:* Torpedoman/Missile Launch Tech US Navy 1959-68; 7th/8th Grade Sci Teacher Cinnaminson Mid Sch 1972-; *ai:* NJ St Assn Mem; NJ Academic Saftey Consortium Mem 1985-; *office:* Cinnaminson Mid Sch Forklanding Rd Cinnaminson NJ 08060

FABIAN, CAROL FLORY, First Grade Teacher; *b:* Defiance, OH; *m:* Jonathan W.; *c:* Natalie J.; *ed:* (BS) Elem Ed, Manchester Coll 1972; (MS) Ed, St Francis Coll 1986; Defiance Cty Schls Staff Dev Prgms; Arts Unlimited, Bowling Green St Univ; *cr:* 1st Grade Teacher Hicksville Elem 1972-; *ai:* Defiance Cty Course of Study Rdng & Hicksville Elem Gradecard Comm; Four Cty Voc HS Early Chldhd Ed Occupations Prgm; Hicksville Ed Assn, OH Ed Assn 1972-; NEA 1974-; Delta Kapa Gamma Society Intnl 1987-.

FABIAN, DEBORAH ENGLE, First Grade Teacher; *b:* Elmira, NY; *m:* Robert; *c:* Allison, John; *ed:* (BS) Elem Ed, SUNY Geneseo 1973; *cr:* 2nd Grade Teacher 1973-82, Kndgtn Teacher 1983-84, 1st Grade Teacher 1984- North Warren Cntrl Sch; *ai:* North Warren PTSA Schlsp Selection Comm; AIDS Awareness Comm; North Warren Teachers Assn Bldg Rep 1989-; Amer Cancer Society Crusader 1978-; *office:* North Warren Central H S Elem Bldg Brant Lake NY 12815

FABISH, CHARLES EDMOND, Physics Teacher; *b:* Peoria, IL; *m:* Pamela Diane Oliver; *c:* Joe, Kristin, Kelly, Mark; *ed:* (BS) Chem, IL St 1969; (MA) Ed Admin, Bradley Univ 1974; Particle Physics Inst; Fermi Lab; Fusion Wkshp; Argonne Lab; Robotics Class IL Cntrl Coll; *cr:* Physics/Chem Teacher Hopedale HS 1969-70; Math Teacher Woodrow Wilson Sch 1971-75; Prin Blessed Sacrament Sch 1976-82; Physics/Chem Teacher Woodruff HS 1983-; *ai:* Acad Team, Scholastic Bowl, Tennis Coach; Phi Delta Kappa 1987-; AAPT, AFT 1983-; Marriage Encounter Bd 1989-; St Marys Sch Bd Pres 1986-87; GSA Service Awd; Author Sci Literacy Grant; Stu Cmptr News-Editor; *office:* Woodruff HS 1800 Perry Peoria IL 61603

FABRICIUS, TERESA (TESNOHLIDED), English/ Communications Teacher; *b:* Caldwell, ID; *m:* Jon; *c:* Marie, Jake, Zack; *ed:* (MS) Ed/Comm, 1982, (MED) Counseling, 1983 Univ of ID; *cr:* Eng/Journalism/Speech/Comm Teacher Genesee HS 1984-; *ai:* Yrbk Adv; NEA Local Pres 1988-; Teaching Excl Awd Univ of ID; *office:* Genesee HS PO Box 98 Genesee ID 83832

FABRIZIO, PATRICIA, English Teacher; *b:* Glen Cove, NY; *m:* Dominick; *c:* Laura S. Gibbs, Nancy A. Staudt; *ed:* (BA) Eng Ed, Georgian Court Coll 1981; (MED) Ed, St Lawrence Univ 1987; Gifted Ed; Process Writing Great Books Prgm; Trng Seminar Tactics for Thinking; *cr:* Eng Teacher 1981-86, Coord of Gifted Ed 1983-86 St Mary Acad; Eng Teacher Indian River Cntrl Schls 1986-; *ai:* Forensics Team Coach; Textbook Selection Comm Mem; K-8th Grade Lang Art; Standarized Test Advisory Comm Mem; ASCD, NY St Rdng Assn; Coord & Developed Curr for Gifted Ed Prgm St Mary Acad; Wrote Curr HS Course Indian River Cntrl; *home:* 184 Dingman Pt Rd Alexandria Bay NY 13607

FACCHIANO, VINCENT ANTHONY, Fifth Grade Teacher; *b:* Bethlehem, PA; *ed:* (BS) Ed, Kutztown St 1964; (MS) Ed, Lehigh Univ 1967; *cr:* 5th Grade Teacher Muhlenberg Elem 1964-75; 5th/6th Grade Teacher Jefferson Elem 1975-79; 5th Grade Teacher Dodd Elem 1979-; *ai:* Dodd Sch Yrbk Photography & Asst Layout 1986-; Allentown Ed Assn Exec Comm 1972-73; ALSAC Charities Chm 1969-70; MDAA Telethon Chm 1978; Allentown Sch Dist Recognition & Achievement in Teaching Awd 1978; *office:* Hiram Dodd Elem Sch S Church & Mohawk Sts Allentown PA 18103

FADALE, WILLIAM F., Fifth Grade Teacher; *b:* Jamestown, NY; *m:* Diane Herbst; *c:* Edward, Michael, Elizabeth; *ed:* (BA) Elem Ed, Fairmont St Coll 1966; (MA) Elem Ed, Univ of Akron 1974; Kent St Univ; *cr:* 4th Grade Teacher 1966-76, 5th Grade Teacher 1976-89 Homewood Elem; *ai:* Cmptr Club Adv; Lorain Ed Assn Building Rep 1970-71; Northeastern OH Ed Assn, OH Ed Assn; Masonic Lodge #145; Shriner; Martha Holden Jennings Scholar; *office:* Homewood Elem Sch Gobel Dr & Charleston Ave Lorain OH 44055

FADGEN, SHEROLYN GOODRICH, Sixth Grade Teacher; *b:* Cortland, NY; *m:* Phillip; *c:* Pamela Fadgen Donlon, Karen; *ed:* (BFA) Art Illustration, Syracuse Univ 1955; (MSE) Sci Ed, Coll of St Rose 1965; *cr:* 1st Grade Teacher Dixon Sch 1957-58; 3rd-5th Grade Teacher Hebrew Acad 1965-67; 5th/6th Grade Teacher Shenendehowa 1968-; *ai:* Mentor Prgm; Curr Instructional Cncl Rep; Buddy Prgm; Dist Cmptr Comm Mem; Scholars Ed Prgm Spon Golub Corporation & NY St Univ; *office:* Shenendehowa Karigon Elem Sch Rt 146 Clifton Park NY 12065

FADUS, MARIE IADAROLA, High School English Teacher; *b:* New Haven, CT; *m:* Richard Fiske; *c:* Richard, Charles, Michael, Joseph, Amy; *ed:* (BA) Eng, Albertus Magnus Coll 1952; *cr:* Teacher Fair Haven Jr HS 1952-56, Dodd Jr HS 1972-73, Wilbur Cross HS 1976-; *office:* Wilbur Cross HS 181 Wilbur Cross New Haven CT 06511

FAGAN, S. MARGARET, IHM, Eighth Grade Teacher; *b:* Philadelphia, PA; *ed:* (BA) Ed/Soc Sci, Immaculata Coll 1985; *cr:* 7th/8th Grade Teacher Annuciation BVM 1977-81; 7th Grade Teacher St Laurence 1984-87, 8th Grade Teacher Sacred Heart 1987-; *ai:* Stu Cncl & Yrbk Adv; Declamation & Spelling Contest Coach; Lang Art Coord; Mid Sts Assn, NCEA; *office:* Sacred Heart Sch 701 Franklin St West Reading PA 19611

FAGAN, SHARON KAE, Elementary Counselor; *b:* Enid, OK; *m:* Dennis L.; *c:* W. Bryan, Shawn, Rebecca; *ed:* (BS) Elem Ed, KS St Teachers Coll 1969; (MS) Guidance/Counseling, N TX St Univ 1974; Child Abuse Prevention Play Therapy; Emotionally Disturbed Children-Parent Ed; Early Chldhd Ed; Eng 2nd Lang; Attention Deficit & Hyperactivity Disorder; Drug & Alcohol Prevention; Reality Therapy; *cr:* 3rd Grade Teacher Oskaloosa KS 1969; 3rd/4th Grade Teacher Shawnee Mission KS 1969-71; Spec Ed Teacher Lancaster TX 1971-74; Elem Cnslr Irving TX 1974-; *ai:* N Cntrl TX Personnel & Guidance Assn Membership Chm 1978-79; TX Assn Counseling & Dev; BSA, Keller HS & Mid Sch Booster Club, Keller Swim Team Mem; Elem Counseling Prgm Mem Received Natl Recognition as Exemplary Elem Guidance Prgm; Certificate of Appreciation VFW #2494 1982-89; Certificate of Appreciation Meadows Fnd Charitable Awds Prgm 1988; Top Tiger Awd Irving HS Stu Cncl 1985-86; Present Prgms & Natl Conventions Concerning Consultation & Parent Ed; *office:* Paul Keyes Elem Sch 115 W Grauwyler Rd Irving TX 75061

FAGERGREN, PETER JONES, Science Department Chair; *b:* Cedar City, UT; *m:* Sheri Ellen Chamberlain; *c:* David, Daniel, Jennifer, Laurie, Erik, Nell; *ed:* (BA) General Sci, 1969, (MA) Bio, 1973 Univ of NE; Grad Courses Univ of AZ 1973-78; *cr:* Ranger Grant Teton Natl Park Service 1971-73; Chemist Univ of AZ Medical Sch 1973-78; Teacher Patagonia Union HS 1978-; *ai:* Var Bsktbl Coach 1978-88; Sci & Hiking Club 1978-; AZ Ed Assn (Pres 1987-88, Pres Elect 1989); BSA Scoutmaster 1986-; North Cntrl Evaluation Team for Accrediation Steering Comm Chm; *office:* Patagonia Union HS PO Box 254 Patagonia AZ 85624

FAGRELIEUS, ERIC WALTER, Science/Math Teacher; *b:* Helena, MT; *m:* Phylis; *c:* Parker A., Jeremy R.; *ed:* (BA) Geology, 1983, Scndry Sci, 1986 Univ of N Co; *cr:* Earth Sci Teacher Eagle Valley Mid Sch 1988-89; Chem/Physics/Earth Sci/Algebra/ Algebra 2 Teacher Ouray HS 1989-; *ai:* HS Bible Study; Rock Climbing & Chess Club; BSA Scoutmaster 1989-; *office:* Ouray Sch P O Box N Ouray CO 81427

FAHY, LESLIE LEIN, Third Grade Teacher; *b:* Los Angeles, CA; *ed:* (BS) Elem Ed, Grand Canyon Univ 1968; (MA) Elem Ed, N AZ Univ 1972; *cr:* Teacher Salome Elem Sch 1971-72, Dept of Defense Dep Schls Germany 1972-75, S Peru Copper Corporation 1975-77, Quartzsite Sch Dist 4 1977-; *ai:* NEA, AEA; *office:* Ehrenberg Elem Sch Box 130 Ehrenberg AZ 85334

FAILLA, DOROTHY CHARAPATA, 5th Grade Teacher; *b:* Crivitz, WI; *m:* Salvatore; *c:* Stephanie, Geoffrey, Pamela, Michael, Janine; *ed:* Nursing, Alverno Coll; (BS) Elem Ed, 1971, (MS) Continuing Elem Ed, 1973 St Univ of NY Stony Brook; *cr:* Elem Teacher Sachem Sch Dist 1972-; *ai:* Cmptrs Task Force Sachem Sch Dist; Half Hollow Hills Sch Dist Cultural Arts Chm 1960; St James Bridge Club Pres 1980; *home:* 19 Musket Pl Setauket NY 11733

FAIR, LINDA ELOIS, Fourth Grade Teacher; *b:* Tuskegee, AL; *m:* James Edward; *c:* Jameson; *ed:* (BS) Elem Ed, Univ of GA 1974; *cr:* Lib Asst Univ of GA Main Lib 1970-72; Corps Intern Teacher Clarke Cty Bd of Ed 1972-74; Teacher Oconee Cty Elem 1974-; *ai:* GA Assn of Ed (Pres 1983-85, Secy 1980-81); Natl Rdng Teacher Assn 1987-; Assn of Classroom Teachers 9th Dist Dir 1983-84; Ebenezer Baptist Church Vacation Bible Sch Dir; Univ of GA Speaker for Lang Arts Teachers 1974; *office:* Oconee Cty Elem Sch Hog Mountain Rd Watkinsville GA 30677

FAIR, WILLIAM R., Drama Teacher; *b:* Plain Dealing, LA; *m:* Darlene Portier; *ed:* (BA) Fr/Elem Ed, 1968, (MA) Educl Supervision, 1978 LA St Univ Baton Rouge; (MA) Elem Ed, Centenary Coll & LA Tech 1984; Cert Elem Sch Counseling; *cr:* 5th-8th Grade Teacher Terrebonne Parish Schls 1968-75; 8th Grade Teacher Holy Rosary Sch 1975-76; 4th Grade Teacher Ingersoll Elem 1976-81; 5th Grade Teacher 1981-88, Drama Teacher 1988- S Highlands Magnet; *ai:* Co-Founder & Spon S Highlands Players; Drama Coord S Highlands Performing Arts Magnet 1981-; S Highlands 5th Grade Trip Organizer 1981-; CAE, LAE, NAE 1976-; St PTA 1976-, Educator of Distinction 1989; Gas Light Players Pres 1977-79; Theatre Arts Guild Bd of Dirs 1978-80; Shreveport Little Theatre Corps of Volunteers 1985-; *home:* 143 E Wyandotte Shreveport LA 71101

FAIRCHILD, ALICE ZACK, Third Grade Teacher; *b:* Detroit, MI; *m:* Kenneth J.; *c:* Russell, Rosanne, Robert, Rachel; *ed:* (BS) Elem Ed, Univ of S CA 1973; (MS) Educl Counseling, Natl Univ 1990; CA Leadership Math Prgm; Mc Crackin Lang Art & Co-Operative Learning Wkshps; QUEST Skills for Growing; *cr:* Teacher Ocean View Sch Dist 1973-; *ai:* Westmont Yrbk Adv; Gifted & Talented Ed Coord; CA Leadership Math Prgm Liason; Stu Study Team; CA Assn of Gifted, Honorary Assn of Women in Ed USC, NEA 1973-; GSA Troop Leader 1989-; BSA Asst Pack Leader 1988-; Luth Womans Missionary League 1985-; *office:* Westmont Elem Sch 8521 Heil Ave Westminster CA 92683

FAIRCHILD, BRENDA DAVIS, 6th Grade Teacher/Group Leader; *b:* Corpus Christi, TX; *m:* Jeffery Max; *c:* Jeffery D.; *ed:* (BS) Elem Ed, Lamar Univ 1976; Working Towards Masters; *cr:* 1st Grade Teacher Bingman Elem 1977; 4th Grade Teacher Vidor Elem 1977-83; 6th Grade Teacher Vidor Mid Sch 1983-; *ai:* Team Leader Responsible for Group 6th Grade Teachers & Act of Group; *office:* Vidor Mid Sch 2500 Hwy 12 Vidor TX 77662

FAIRCHILD, FRANCINE SMITH, Third Grade Teacher; *b:* Saratoga Springs, NY; *c:* Julia, Elizabeth Fairchild Toro, Susan, George, Samuel, Margaret; *ed:* Eng Lit, Brown Univ 1953-55; (BA) Eng Lit, Univ Miami 1956; (MS) Ed, Russel Sage Coll 1969; *cr:* 6th Grade/Adult ESL Teacher Saratoga Springs; 6th Grade Teacher Shenandoah Cntrl; 3rd-5th Grade Teacher Dorothy Nolan Elem; *ai:* Saratoga Springs Teachers Assn Rep; Saratoga Springs Historical Society; Ladies of Charity Bd of Dir; *office:* Dorothy Nolan Sch RD 2 Jones Rd Saratoga Springs NY 12866

FAIRCHILD, LOWELL THOMAS, Eighth Grade Teacher; *b:* Sneedville, TN; *c:* John; *ed:* (BS) Bus Admin, Lincoln Memorial Univ 1962; (MA) Ed, Union Coll 1974; *cr:* Prin Keplar Elem Sch 1962-69, Rock Hill Elem Sch 1969-73; Teacher Surgoinsville Elem Sch 1973-80, Surgoinsville Mid Sch 1980-; *ai:* Hawkins Cty Ed Assn, TN Ed Assn, NEA 1962-; *home:* PO Box 1572 Mt Carmel TN 37645

FAIRCLOTH, CAROL SUTHERLAND, Special Education Teacher; *b:* Uvalde, TX; *m:* Howard Lee; *c:* Victoria A. Bell Schulz, Robert S. Bell, Rebecca D. Bell Miller; *ed:* (BS) Ed, NM St Univ Las Cruces 1972; (MED) Sul Ross Univ 1976; *cr:* EMR Teacher San Antonio Ind Sch Dist 1972-73; EMR/LD Teacher Uvalde Ind Sch Dist 1973-82; LD/VH Teacher Sonora Ind Sch Dist 1982-85; B-Level Teacher Carlsbad Ind Sch Dist 1985-; *ai:* Jr HS Dept Head; Spec Ed; NEA, Phi Kappa Phi 1972-; Beta Sigma Phi 1983-85; *office:* P R Leyva Jr HS 800 W Church Carlsbad NM 88220

FAIRCLOTH, MARGARET WINGATE, Math Dept Chairperson/Teacher; *b:* Macon, GA; *c:* Tony R., Janet F. Jackson; *ed:* (BS) Math, GA Coll Milledgeville 1963; (MED) Ed, Mercer Univ 1982; *cr:* Teacher Southwest HS 1963-88, Southeast HS 1988-; *ai:* Reduction Paper Work & Bibb Cty Textbook Selection Comm Mem; Var & Jr Var Math Team Coach; Dist 8 Scndry Math Teacher; The Math Assn of America, NCTM; GA Cncl of Teachers of Math Life Mem; NEA, GA Assn of Educators, Bibb Assn of Educators; Phi Delta Kappa Rep 1987-88; Church (Sunday Sch Teacher, Youth Group Spon, Asst Supt Sunday Sch, Deaconess, Governing Bd Mem); Cmmty Upward Bound Fed Prgm; Amer Cancer Society Zone Captain Collector; PTA Life Mem; GA Presidential Awd Excl Math Teaching Natl Winner; Woman of Achievement; Roundtable Honors Seminar 1988, 1989; Presidential Awds Excl Sci & Math Teaching 1987;Stu Teacher Achievement Recognition Southeast HS 1990, Southwest HS 1980, 1982-84, 1987, 1990, Bibb Cty & 8th Dist 1980; Bibb Cty Teacher of Yr 1982; Mc Kibben Lane & Gladys Thompson Awd 1983; Gladys Thompson Math Dist Winner 1988; Wiley Murrell Suttles & Scndry Ed Awd 1988; Outstanding Young Educator 1967; *office:* Southeast HS 1070 Anthony Rd Macon GA 31204

FAIRLEY, ETHEL D., Fifth Grade Teacher; *b:* Sweetwater, AL; *c:* Jacquelyn L. Carothers; *ed:* (BA) Elem Ed, AL St Univ 1960; Working Toward Masters, Univ of S AL; *cr:* Teacher Ella Grant Elem Sch 1960-62, Mary Weeks Burroughs Sch 1962-79, Woodcock Elem Sch 1979-; *ai:* Stu Cncl & Safety Patrol Spon; 5th Grade Music Chorus; Mobile Cty Ed Assn, NEA; Mayme Cunningham Federated Club Financial Secy; St James Baptist Church Minister of Music; Teacher of Yr 1980; *home:* 408 Yerby Dr Mobile AL 36617

FAISON, ETHEL SPEIGHT, Teacher; *b:* Snow Hill, NC; *m:* James L.; *ed:* (BS) Elem Ed, DC Teachers Coll 1969; Grad Stud Trinity Coll Home & Sch Inst; Peer Supvr Trng & Teacher Ed Support Trng Univ of DC; *cr:* Supervising Instr Harriet Tubman Elem Sch 1970-73; Art Teacher Summer Sch Prgms 1970; Rdng/Math Summer Sch Teacher Seaton Elem 1972, Marie Reed Elem 1982, Shaed Elem Sch 1983; 6th Grade Teacher Harriet Tubman Elem Sch 1969-; *ai:* Teacher Leveraged Curr Comm; Safety Patrol & Stu Government Spon; Fundraising, Spelling Bee, Safety, Security, Testing Comm; Peer Supervision Team; Teachers Choral Group; DC Black Sch Educators 1988-; Intnl Rdng Cncl 1988-; Dillard Alumni & Friends 1970-; Home & Sch Inst Mem Bd of Dir 1982-83; Perfect Attendance Awd 1985-86; *office:* Harriet Tubman Elem Sch 13th & Kenyon Sts NW Washington DC 20010

FAISON, PEARLENE MILLER, 4th Grade Teacher; *b:* Kenansville, NC; *c:* Linda, Lenward, Crystal; *ed:* (BS) Elem Ed, Fayetteville St Univ 1970; Numerous Wkshps & Seminars; *cr:* Teacher E E Smith HS 1967-68, Branch Elem Sch 1968-69, B F Grady Elem Sch 1969-; *ai:* Grade Coord; Town Beauification, Attendance, Expectation Comm; Duplin Cty Assn Ed (Treas, Pres) 1979-83; NC Assn of Ed Instructional Prof Dev Chairperson 1987; NEA; Terry Sanford Awd Chairperson 1984-89; Salem Lodge 1975; Sunday Sch Teacher 1980-; Daughters of Zion 1980-; B F Grady Teacher of Yr 1981; Certificate of Merit; Duplin Cty Lang Art Governors Excellent Awd 1990; *home:* PO Box 82 Sycamore St Kenansville NC 28349

FALCIONE, ARNOLD M., History Teacher; *b:* Boston, MA; *ed:* (BA) His, 1967, (MA) His, 1972 Univ of NH; *cr:* His Teacher Dover HS 1967-; *ai:* Key Club Adv; NEA 1967-79, 1988-; Dover ABC Comm 1970-; Bentley Coll Excl in Scndry Teaching Awd 1988; *office:* Dover HS Alumni Dr Dover NH 03820

FALCOCCHIO, MARYANNA, Upper Elem Mathematics Instr; *b:* Wilkinsburg, PA; *ed:* (BS) Bus Admin/Bus Ed, Robert Morris Coll 1977; *cr:* Bus Instr Turtle Creek Area HS 1977-79; Upper Elem Math Instr St Agnes Sch 1981-; *ai:* Upper Elem Coord; PA Math League, Johns Hopkins Univ Math & Verbal Talent Search Adv; Stu Cncl Co-Adv; NCEA 1981-; NBEA Awd of Merit 1976-77; St Agnes Parent Teacher Guild 1981-; Phi Theta Kappa Mem; NBEA Awd of Merit Winner 1976-77; Phi Theta Kappa Natl Honor Robert Morris Coll Alumni Grant 1973; *office:* St Agnes Sch 11400 St Agnes Ln North Huntingdon PA 15642

FALGOUT, MARSHALL, Mathematics Teacher; *b:* Southgate, CA; *m:* Mona Dawn Stafford; *c:* Eric, Mark, Amy, Dan, Mandi; *ed:* (BA) Phys Ed/Math, Humboldt St 1968; (MA) Ed, USF 1984; Teaching Credential, Humboldt St 1974; *cr:* Teacher Deep Valley Chrstn Sch 1974-77; Math Teacher Potter Valley HS 1977-87, Ukiah HS 1987-; *ai:* Soph Class Adv; Faculty Cncl; Distinguished Teacher Awd 1989; *office:* Ukiah HS 1000 Low Gap Rd Ukiah CA 95482

FALICKI, MARY NOEL (ANNA S.), Teachers Aide; *b:* Great Meadows, NJ; *ed:* (BS) Soc Stud, Fordham Univ 1952; *cr:* Teacher St Casimir Sch 1926-27; Holy Cross Sch 1928-29; St Anthony Sch 1929-30; Holy Cross Sch 1930-32; St Stanislaus 1932-35; St Josep Sch 1935-37; St Mary Sch 1938-40; St Hedwig 1943-45; Our Lady of Consolation 1945-46; SS Cyril & Methodius Sch 1946-48; St Joseph Sch 1948-49; St Adalbert Sch 1949-52; SS Cyril & Meyhodius Sch 1949-52; Teaching/Prin Immaculate Conception Sch 1953-56; St Mary Sch 1956-59; Teacher St Stanislaus 1962-63; Coord CCD Prgm/Teacher of CCD Pre Schl/Kndgtn; Parish Organist Sacred Heart 1963-66; Teacher/Organist/Catechist Our Lady of Czestoachowa Sch 1966-68; Teacher/Organist/Cathechist Our Lady of Jasna Gora 1968-76; Prin/Teacher St Bernard Sch 1976-78; Teacher/Organist St Hedwig Sch 1978-80; *office:* Our Lady of Czestochowa Sch 1315 Enfield St Enfield CT 06082

FALIN, CAROLYN MURRAY, Teacher; *b:* Waverly, OH; *m:* Paul; *ed:* (BS) Basic Bus/Soc Stud, Cumberland Coll 1968; (MS) Office Admin/Bus Ed, E KY Univ 1972; Prof Cert; Curr Supvr; Scndry Sch Prin; Sch Bus Admin; *cr:* Teacher Whitley Cty HS 1968-77, Pikeville Coll 1977-78, Whitley Cty HS 1978-; *ai:* KEA, NEA, KBEA, NBEA 1968-; Alpha Lambda, ADK Women Educators Treas 1988-; *home:* PO Box 411 Williamsburg KY 40769

FALK, CANDY L., 3rd Grade Teacher; *b:* La Center, WA; *m:* Murray; *c:* Larry Lawson, David, Saundra Hurst, Karen Erschen; *ed:* (BS) Elem Ed, Portland St Univ 1975; (MED) Early Chldhd Ed, Linfield Coll 1990; *cr:* Teacher Aloha Park 1975-; *ai:* Spelling Bee Coord; Beaverton Ed Assn 1975-; Beta Sigma Phi (Secy, VP) 1969-; *home:* Rt 2 Box 363A La Center WA 98629

FALK, CHARLES WILLIAM, English Teacher; *b:* Gallitzen, PA; *m:* Kathleen Marie Anderson; *c:* Melissa L., Warren, Daniel J., Nathan, Bethany A.; *ed:* (BA) Eng Ed, St Univ of NY Fredonia 1965; *cr:* HS Eng Teacher Mayville Cntrl Sch 1965-66; Eng Teacher Lincoln Sch 1966-; *office:* Lincoln School 301 Front St Jamestown NY 14701

FALKENBURG, LIANE M. R., Third Grade Teacher; *b:* New York City, NY; *m:* Donald R.; *c:* David R., Steven J.; *ed:* (BS) Elem Ed, NY St Univ Coll Oneonta 1962; (MAT) Rdng, Oakland Univ 1982; Instructional Skills Trng & 3rd Grade Growing Healthy Trng Oakland Schls; *cr:* 3rd Grade Teacher Brookside Sch 1962-64; 1st/2nd Grade Teacher Norwood-Norfolk Cntrl Sch 1964-66; 3rd Grade Teacher Lander Elem Sch 1966-67; 3rd/5th Grade Teacher H T Burt Elem Sch 1975-; *ai:* Advisory Cncl; Sch Improvement Team; 3rd Grade Gifted & Talented Cluster Teacher; MI Ed Assn, Brandon Ed Assn, NEA 1975-; *office:* H T Burt Elem Sch 209 Varsity Dr Ortonville MI 48462

FALKNER, JAMES WILLIAM, 7th Grade Geography Teacher; *b:* Sparta, WI; *m:* Marcia Ann Bloom; *c:* Jaron, Jason; *ed:* (BS) Bio, Univ of WI La Crosse 1972; Prof Dev; *cr:* 5th-8th Grade Sci Teacher Winter Public Schls 1972-74; 7th/8th Grade Geography Teacher Tomah Public Schls 1974-; *ai:* Oakdale Fire Dept; *home:* Rt 1 Box 369 Tomah WI 54660

FALKNER, NOREEN MARGARET ROMAN, English Teacher/Dept Chair; *b:* Dunkirk, NY; *m:* William Jackson III; *c:* Jessica Hayes; *ed:* (BS) Eng/Art Ed, Univ of Dayton 1966; (MS) Eng Ed/Drama, SUC Buffalo 1971; Various Courses & Writers Wkshp Canisius Coll; *cr:* 7th-9th Grade Lang Art Teacher Clinton Jr HS 1967; 7th Grade Eng Teacher Amsdell Jr HS 1967-68; 10th-12th Grade Eng Teacher Frontier Cntrl HS 1968-; *ai:* Prom & Chrldr Adv; Play Adv & Dir; Eng Dept Chairperson; Dist Dev Cncl; Data Analysis & Natl Amer Society Selection Comm; NCTE 1980-; Niagara Frontier Rdng Cncl 1988-; Eng Dept Chairperson Erie Cty 1986-; NYSUT 1967-; Jr League of Buffalo Comm Work 1981-; Cntrl Park Homeowners Assn Comm Work 1978-; PTSA Frontier Cntrl HS 1968-; Nardin Parent Cncl 1986-; Curr Comm Dist Chm 1980-82; Comm Skills Curr & In-Service Conference for Dist.

FALKNER, WILLIAM JACKSON, Special Educ Coordinator; *b:* Niagara Falls, NY; *m:* Noreen Margaret Roman; *c:* Jessica; *ed:* (BA) Eng, SUNYAB 1970; (MS) Spec Ed, 1978, (CAS) Admin Supvr, 1987 SUCAB; Elements of Instruction; *cr:* Teacher Buffalo Public Schls 1970-; Coord Mc Kinley HS 1989-; *ai:* Very Spec Arts Comm; Academic Cncl; Phi Delta Kappa 1986-; NEA 1970-; Buffalo Teachers Fed 1970-; Nordin Parent Cncl 1986-; Holy Name Society 1977-; NEA Historian 1970-; Alpha Sigma Phi Alumni Assn 1988-; Cntrl Park Homeowners VP 1987-; Veterans of Foreign Wars 1987-; Leo Knights Chairperson 1980-; Co-Authored Philosophy of Ed for Erie Cty Detention Home 1973; *office:* Mc Kinley H S 1500 Elmwood Ave Buffalo NY 14207

FALL, DIANA LYNNE, Fourth Grade Teacher; *b:* Hays, KS; *ed:* (MS) Educl Admin Elem, Ft Hays St Univ 1988; *cr:* 4th Grade Teacher Eastern Heights Elem 1981-; *ai:* Phi Delta Kappa 1988-; Agra Public Lib Bd (Treas, Sec) 1985-; *office:* Eastern Heights Elem Sch Box 145 Kirwin KS 67644

FALLON, BRENDA JEAN, Teacher; *b:* St Cloud, MN; *ed:* (BS) Phys Ed, SE MO St Univ 1987; CPR, Water Safety Instr; *cr:* 9th-12th Grade Phys Ed/Health Ed Teacher Monroe City R-1 HS 1987-89; *ai:* Head Girls Vlybl, Asst Girls Var Bsktbl, Head Girls Jr Var Bsktbl Coach; Ms Club & Cheerleading Spon; Spec Olympics Adv; Health Curr HS Spon 1987-89; MMAPHERD, AAPHERD Mem 1984-; Spec Olympics Volunteer 1984-; Drug Awareness Volunteer 1987-89; HS Lock-In; *home:* 1218 Quantock #10 Saint Louis MO 63125

FALLON, THOMAS TRACEY, Sixth Grade Teacher; *b:* St Louis, MO; *m:* Kathleen Ward; *c:* Meghan, Jonathan; *ed:* (BA) General Elem Ed, 1968, (MA) Comm Coll Ed, 1976 Glassboro St Coll; *cr:* Teacher Charles W Lewis Sch 1968-71; Teacher/Core Leader Glen Landing Mid Sch 1971-; *ai:* Soc Stud Curr Comm; Core Leader; 2nd PA Regiment, Gloucester Cty Historical Society, Woodbury Old City Restoration Comm; Kodak Young Filmakers Awd; Young Peoples Film Festival NJ PBS; Gloucester Township Bd Ed Recognition Awd; NJ Governors Teacher Recognition Awd; Articles Published; *office:* Glen Landing Mid Sch Little Gloucest Rd Blackwood NJ 08012

FALLS, CHERRY VAREE, 3rd Grade Teacher/Math Coord; *b:* Wynne, AR; *ed:* (BA) His, Rhodes Coll 1973; (MED) Elem Guidance Cnslr, Memphis St Univ 1977; *cr:* His/Phys Ed Teacher St Agnes Acad 1973-74; 4th-6th Grade Math Teacher St Agnes 1974-77; 4th Grade Teacher St Marys Episcopal 1977-80; 5th-6th Grade Math Teacher 1980-81, 3rd Grade Teacher 1981- St Marys Episcopal Sch; *ai:* Math Coord Lower Mid Schls; NCTM 1980-; Idlewild Presbyn Church; Creative & Outstanding Teacher Awds; *office:* St Marys Episcopal Sch 60 Perkins Extended Memphis TN 38117

FALLS, MARIANNE BARNETT, 3rd Grade Teacher; *b:* Clover, SC; *m:* Frank C. Jr.; *c:* Travis G., Jessica L.; *ed:* (BS) Elem Ed 1966; (MAT) Elem Ed, 1973 Winthrop Coll; *cr:* 2nd Grade Teacher Mc Clevey Elem 1967-70; Spec Ed Teacher Episopal Church Home for Children 1970-73; 3rd Grade Teacher Bethel Elem 1974-; *ai:* Apt Evaluator; NEA/SCEA Pres 1982-83; Phi Delta Kappa 1987-; YCEA Pres 1967; *office:* Bethel Elem Sch Hwy 55 East Clover SC 29710

FALLS, PATRICIA FREEMAN, English-Debate Teacher; *b:* Sentinel, OK; *m:* Timmy C.; *c:* Scott C., David W., John S.; *ed:* (BA) Speech/Drama, N TX St Univ 1965; (MA) Eng/Speech/Journalism, Univ of TX Tyler 1987; *cr:* Eng/Speech Teacher Chapel Hill HS 1965-66, Elmore Cty HS 1966-68; Eng Teacher Chapel Hill Mid Sch 1975-80; Eng/Debate Teacher Whitehouse HS 1980-; *ai:* Jr Class Spon; Debate & Ready Writing Coach; Campus Beautification, Campus Goals, HS Management Comm; Classroom Teachers Secy 1990; Assn of TX Prof Educators 1985-87, 1989-; Alpha Delta Kappa (Historian 1984-85, VP 1986-88); *office:* Whitehouse HS PO Box 518 Whitehouse TX 75791

FALLU, LESLEY WELDON, Mathematics Teacher; *b:* Brockton, MA; *m:* Real J.; *c:* Daniel, Andrew; *ed:* (BA) Math, Bates Coll 1977; *cr:* Math Teacher Villa Augustina Acad 1977-79, Cntrl HS 1979-; *office:* Manchester Cntrl HS 207 Lowell St Manchester NH 03104

FALSTICH, WILLIAM B., Administrative Intern; *b:* Bethlehem, PA; *m:* Cindy Ann Yary; *c:* William M., Michael T.; *ed:* (BS) Elem Ed, Kutztown Univ 1973; (MED) Elem Ed, Lehigh Univ 1978; Working Towards Cert Elem Sch Prin; *cr:* Elem Teacher 1973-89, Admin Intern 1989- Northampton Area Sch Dist; *ai:* NEA, PSEA 1973-; Lions Club Past Pres 1983-; *home:* 240 N Chestnut St Bath PA 18014

FALZONE, SHIRLEY REVILL, English Teacher; *b:* Big Sandy, TX; *m:* Vincent J.; *c:* Lisa, Michael; *ed:* (BS) Poly Sci, 1977, (MA) Interdisciplinary Stud, 1984 Univ of TX Tyler; Educl Supervision & Educl Admin; *cr:* Eng/Government Teacher Big Sandy HS 1979-82; Eng Teacher John Tyler HS 1982-; *ai:* TISD Supts Faculty Advisory & Steering Comms; NCTE Mem 1982-; Delta Kappa Gamma Mem 1990; Phi Delta Kappa Local Secy 1989-; Conducted Wkshp Region Seven Educl Center; Reviewed Article From Educl Magazine for Publication; *office:* John Tyler HS 1120 North NW Loop 323 Tyler TX 75702

FANIS, JUDY TRANTHAM, Earth Science Teacher; *b:* Greeneville, TN; *m:* Richard Lynn; *c:* Bryan N., Erin M.; *ed:* (BS) Phys Ed, E TN St Univ 1970; (MED) Ed/Phys Ed, Univ of VA 1972; Cert Earth Sci, Univ of VA; *cr:* Teacher/Coach Orange Cty HS 1970-75, Castlewood HS 1975-76, John S Battle HS 1978-; *ai:* Jr Var Girls Bsktbl Coach; Battle Stu Boosters Club Spon; Vlybl Scorekeeper; Hospitality, Textbook Selection, Family Life Ed Planning Comms; VA Ed Assn, NEA 1970-; VA Assn of Sci Teachers 1986-; SW VA Assn of Sci Teachers (Past Coord Earth Sci Section Fall Conference, Planning Comm, Washington Cty Coord) 1986-; Cub Scouts Den Leader-Cubmaster 1985-88; BSA Scout Coord 1986-; Pleasant View United Meth Church Various Comms 1980-; Presentor at SW-Vast Fall Conference 1988; Teacher of Issue for Sch Newspaper 1990; *office:* John S Battle HS Lee Hwy Bristol VA 24201

FANNING, DORIS GRANT, Asst Prin & 6th Grade Teacher; *b:* Chicago, IL; *w:* William P. (dec); *c:* William, Maureen Fanning Pariso, Nancy Fanning Basso, Laura Fanning Saverino, Thomas, Colleen Fanning Gallant; *ed:* (BA) Liberal Arts/Ed/Eng, Univ of Miami Coral Gables 1950; Working Towards Masters Ed, Cath Univ of America Washington DC 1951; *cr:* 4th Grade Teacher St Ferdinands 1952-55, St Giles 1968-70; 4th Grade Teacher 1970-88, 6th Grade Teacher 1988- St John Bosco; *ai:* Asst Prin; Stu Cncl Fund-Raising; Gottlieb Hospital Volunteer Worker 1980-82, 1990; *office:* St John Bosco Sch 2245 N Mc Vicker Chicago IL 60639

FANNON, ADRIAN, Social Studies Chairman; *b:* Brooklyn, NY; *ed:* (BA) His, St Francis Coll 1967; (MA) Soc Stud Ed, NY Univ 1971; Afro-Amer Inst Columbia Univ 1970; Robert A Taft Inst of Goverment Pace Univ 1972; Inst for Prof Dev Rutgers Univ 1983; *cr:* Math/Soc Stud Teacher St Joseph Sch 1958-60, St Mary Star of the Sea 1960-61, St Anthony of Padva Sch 1961-65, Our Lady of Angels Sch 1965-68; Prin St Brigid Sch 1976-78; Prin/Teacher Robert F Kennedy Incentive Prgm 1968-; *ai:* Moderator Math League, Mathcounts, Yrbk, Alumni Coord; NCEA 1970-; NCSS 1974-; ASCD 1981-; *office:* Robert F Kennedy Incentive Pgm 284 Warwick St Brooklyn NY 11207

FARAR, VICKI BAUSKE, Math/Typing Teacher/Drill Team; *b:* Longview, TX; *m:* James W.; *c:* Jacki; *ed:* (AS) General, Kilgore Jr Coll 1968; (BBA) Bus General, Univ of TX 1970; *cr:* Bus Ed Irving HS 1971-76; Bus Ed/Scndry Math Tatun Mid Sch; Tatun HS 1980-; *ai:* Drill Team Dir Tatum Eaglettes 8 Yrs; Jr Class Spon & Chm Jr Sr Prom 2 Yrs; CTA 1980-89; DTDA 1982-; TSTA Life Mem; Rangettes Forever Life Mem; *home:* 201 E Marshall Longview TX 75601

FARBER, MARIAN CLARK, Business Education Dept Chair; *b:* Decatur, NE; *c:* Stuart L. Jr., Nancy L.; *ed:* (BS) Bus Ed, Univ of NE 1957; (MS) Sch Admin/Curr, Pepperdine Univ 1972; Grad Stud Bus Ed at Univ CA Los Angeles, CA St Univ Los Angeles & Long Beach; *cr:* Bus Ed Teacher Fullerton HS 1957-58, Mayfair HS 1958-60, La Mirada HS 1960-; *ai:* FBLA; CBEA 1960-; CVA 1975-; PEO Treas 1987-89; Model Site Team Mem Bus Ed CA St 1984-88; Dev Curr Cmptr Applications Sch Site 1984-; *office:* La Mirada HS 13520 Adelfa Dr La Mirada CA 90638

FARCAS, CLAUDETTE DUSSEAULT, Spanish Teacher; *b:* Somersworth, NH; *m:* Gordon W.; *ed:* (BA) Span, Univ of NH 1970; (MS) Bi-Ling Ed, S CT St Coll 1975; *cr:* Span/Fr Teacher Exeter HS 1970-72; Span Teacher Brookfield HS 1972-80, Marshall HS 1985-; *ai:* Span Club; TX Classroom Teachers Assn 1985-; Foreign Lang Educators E TX Treas 1989; TX Foreign Lang Assn 1988-; Sigma Delta Pi; *home:* Rt 5 Box 411 F Marshall TX 75670

FARINA, MARITZA, Seventh Grade Bi-ling Teacher; *b:* Guantanamo, Cuba; *ed:* (AA) Liberal Art, Union Coll 1982; (BA) Liberal Art/Ed, Kean Coll 1984; Instrucional Theory in Practice Prgm; *cr:* 6th Grade Teacher 1984-89, 7th Grade Teacher 1989- Dayton Street Sch; *ai:* Participated in Summer Sch & After Sch Tutorial Prgm; NTU 1984-; *office:* Dayton Street Sch 226 Dayton St Newark NJ 07114

FARKAL, GEORGE EDWARD, Fourth Grade Teacher; *b:* Pittsburgh, PA; *m:* Kathy Ann Juba; *c:* Christopher; *ed:* (BS) Elem Ed, CA St 1973; (MS) Elem/Admin, Duquesne Univ 1978; *cr:* Elem Teacher Steel Valley Sch Dist; *office:* Park Elem Sch Main And Cambria St Munhall PA 15120

FARKAS, RICHARD DAVID, 5th Grade Teacher; *b:* Northampton, PA; *m:* Debra J. Remaly; *c:* Eric, Ross; *ed:* (BS) Elem Ed, East Stroudsburg Univ 1972; (MS) Elem Ed, 1989; *cr:* 5th Grade Teacher Hereford Elem Sch 1972-73; 4th Grade Teacher Hereford Elem Sch 1973-82; 5th Grade 1982-; *ai:* Audio-Visual Coord 1982-; Peer Coaching 1989-; Cooperating Teacher Kutztown Univ Students Field Prof Semester Experience 1982-; Bsbl Little League Coach 1985-89; Religious Ed Instr 1986-89; Presention PA Mid Sch Conference Creative Motivation Lang Art 1989; Presentation PA St Conference for Mid Schls Creative Motivation for Lang Art 1990; *office:* Upper Perkiomen Mid Sch 201 w Fifth St East Greenville PA 18041

FARLEY, JOHN GILBERT, JR., Science Teacher; *b:* Latrobe, PA; *m:* Josephine Criscuolo; *c:* Matthew, David, William; *ed:* (BS) Bio, 1975, (MS) Environmental Ed, 1986, Scndry Sci Specialist, 1988 S CT St Univ; BEST Assesor CT St Dept of Ed; *cr:* Sci Teacher St Louis Sch 1975-78; Bio Teacher Brien Mc Mahon HS 1978-79; Sci Teacher Johnson Jr HS 1979-80, Flood Jr HS 1980-83, Sleeping Giant Jr HS 1981-83, Hamden Mid Sch 1983-86; Bio Teacher Hamden HS 1986-; *ai:* Hamden HS Class of 1990 Spon; Hamden HS Fascilities Task Force; BEST Assessor St Dept of Ed; CT Sci Teachers Assn 1978-; BSA Scoutmaster 1969-; Rotary Club Awd Top 10 Stu Motivation 1989; *office:* Hamden HS 2040 Dixwell Ave Hamden CT 06514

FARLEY, THOMAS ROSCOE, World History Teacher; *b:* Portsmouth, VA; *m:* Tania Ihlenburg; *ed:* (BA) Eng/His, VA Polytechnic Inst, St Univ 1973; (MSE) Ed, Old Dominion Univ 1983; Grad Stud Old Dominion Univ; *cr:* Teacher Indian River HS 1973-74, Indian River Jr HS 1975-; Geography Instr VA Wesleyan Coll 1986-; *ai:* Spon Natl Jr Honor Society; Chm Sch Video Comm; Mem Faculty Planning Comm; CEA, VEA, NEA, 1973-; ASCAP 1982-; Teacher of Yr 1988; Published 1st Album Songsmyth 1982; Voted Best Acoustic Musician Hampton Roads 1985; Voted Best Rhythm Guitarist Hampton Roads 1987; Odyssey of Mind-Writer Scndry Classroom Activities 1986-89; Published Street Talk Band Album 1985; *office:* Indian River Jr HS 2300 Old Greenbrier Rd Chesapeake VA 23320

FARMER, DEANNA LOUISE, 3rd & 4th Grade Teacher; *b:* Chickasha, OK; *m:* B. D.; *c:* Glenda Friesen, Leon; *ed:* (BA) Elem Ed, Panhandle St Univ of OK 1980; *cr:* 3rd & 4th Grade Adams Elem 1980-; *ai:* Past Spon of 7th & 8th Grade Class; Chrldr Spon; NEA 1980-; AWANA Cubbie Leader 1982-; Sunday Sch Teacher Adams Menn Brethren Church.

FARMER, GINA KAY, English Teacher; *b:* Merkel, TX; *ed:* (BS) Eng/Phys Ed, Mc Murry Coll 1983; (ME) Ed Admin, Abilene Chrstn 1986; *cr:* Eng Teacher/Coach Coahoma HS 1983-86; Teacher/Coach Munday HS 1986-88, Cedar Hill HS 1988-; *ai:* Cross Cntry, Bsktbl, Track Coach; *home:* 2400 Cypresswood Trl #821 Arlington TX 76014

FARMER, MICHAEL H., Science Department Chairman; *b:* Greer, SC; *m:* Kathyrn Truesdale; *c:* Kenley; *ed:* (AS) Chemical Technology, Greenville Tech Coll 1969-70; (BS) 1971-72, (MED) Sci Ed, 1973-74 Clemson Univ; Infrared Spectroscopy Certificate, Greenville Tech Coll 1971; Electronics Certificate, Natl Radio Inst 1972; Chem Safety Course, SC Dept of Labor 1973; Teaching IPS, Univ of GA 1971; NSF Project Physics Grad Credit, Clemson Univ 1974; Seminar Futuristic Sociology Grad Credit, Furman Univ 1980; Advance Programming Apple Cmptr, Sch Dist Greenville Cty 1981; Bell & Howell Microprocessor Theory Course, Greenville Tech Coll 1981; Cmptr Circuit Design & Boolean Algebra, Clemson Univ 1983-84; Grad Credit Using Apple II as Laboratory Instrument, Xavier Coll 1984-85; Modern Applications of Linear Algebra, 1986; Advanced Placement Physics Inst 1986 Clemson Univ; Grad Credit Advanced Placement Chem Inst, Furman Univ 1987; *cr:* Quality Control Supvr General Battery & Ceramics Corp 1961-64; Field Quality Inspector Plastic Products Incorporated 1964-67; Quality Control Analysis Phillips Fiber Research Center 1967-72; Algebra I/Basic Math Instr Greer HS 1972-73; Sci Dept Chm/Chem/Advanced Chem/Advanced Physics Instr Riverside HS 1973-; *ai:* Greenville Tech Stu Body Pres 1966-67, Clemson 1968-69; Comm to Oppose Teaching Creationism SC Schls 1979-; Comm to Upgrade Sci & Math Ed SC Chm 1978; Riverside Faculty Rep on Citizens Advisory Cncl Comm 1979-83; Greenville Cty Food Drive for Needy Chm 1979-80; Riverside HS Sci Fair Spon 1976-; Riverside HS Academic Bowl Team Coach 1978-80; Riverside HS Academic Awds Prgm Spon 1976-; Riverside HS JETS Spon 1978-80; SC Sci Teachers Assn VP 1974-75; Greenville Cty Sci Teachers Assn Pres 1978-79; Greenville Cty Ed Assn Bd of Dir 1979-80; Chem Tech Society Pres 1967-68; SC Sci Cncl (VP 1980-81, Pres 1982-83); Amer Humanist Assn Chm 1982-83; Amer Chem Society Ad Hoc Comm 1978; Greenville Cty Sch Dist Career Ed Advisory Comm 1984-85; SC Congress of Parents & Teachers Honorary Life Time Mem; Western SC Sci Fair Chm Fund Raising Comm 1978-82; Public Speaker Civic Clubs; Clemson Univ & SC Jr Acad of Sci Mini-Research Grants Adv to Stu 1976-; Riverside HS SC Jr Acad of Sci Chapter Adv 1976-; Riverside HS Teacher of Yr 1972-73; SE Regional James Conant Awds HS Chem Teacher by Amer Chem Society 1978; SC Society of Prof Engnrs Educator of Yr Awd 1979; NSTA STAR Awd 1979; Sigma Xi Clemson Univ Outstanding Sci Teacher Awd 1980-81; *home:* PO Box 193 Tigerville SC 29688

FARMER, SHIRLEY ELLEN, Kindergarten Teacher; *b:* Glouster, OH; *m:* James Thomas Sr.; *c:* James Thomas Jr., Rebecca S. Farmer Stegall; *ed:* (BA) Ed, 1972, (MS) Ed, 1974 Wright St Univ; *cr:* K-5th Grade Teacher Centerville City Schls 1972-.

FARNER, THOMAS PATRICK, US History Teacher; *b:* Mt Holly, NJ; *m:* Carol J. Park; *ed:* (BS) Scndry Ed/US His, Mansfield Univ 1969; *cr:* 7th/8th Grade Eng/Soc Stud Teacher Newcomb Mid Sch 1970-85; 11th/12th Grade US His Teacher Pemberton Township HS 1985-; *ai:* Boys & Girls Intra-Scholastic Tennis Coach; Formulated US His Curr; NEA, NJEA; Stafford Township Historic Preservation Comm Resident Historian; NJ St Speakers Bureau 1987-88; Natl, St & Local Level Articles Published; Constitution Bicentennial Competition Natl Judge; Eagleton Inst Fellowship Study Prgm; *office:* Pemberton Township HS II Arneys Mount Rd Pemberton NJ 08068

FARNSWORTH, CONSTANCE KAY, 5th Grade Teacher; *b:* Muskegon, MI; *ed:* (BS) Elem, Olivet Nazarene Coll 1963; (MA) Elem Ed, MI St Univ 1971; MSU; Lansing Community Coll; Western State Univ; Univ of MI; *cr:* Teacher Upper Arlington Schls 1963-64; Teacher Grand Blanc Schls 1964-66; Teacher Dept of Defense Schls 1966-69; Teacher Waverly Community Schls 1960-90; Professor John Wesley Coll 1971-75; *ai:* 15 Yrs-Stu Cncl Adv; Gifted & Talented Coordinator; Chess Club Sponsor; Creater Annual Patriotic Assem; Curriculum Comm Rdng Metric Sys Chm Math Comm Soc Stud Spelling Etc; NEA/MEA/WEA Bldg Rep 1969-; Bus & Prof Womens Cncl Chm 1977-80; Phi Delta Kappa 1973-90; Chrstn Educators Assn Intl 85-; Moral Majority for Freedom 1979-86; MI Comm for Freedom 1983-; Precinct Deleg-Repub 1986-; County Repub-Exec Comm 1986-; MI St Repub Exec Comm 1986-; Right to Life of Lansing; Metric System Spoke to PTO; *home:* 204 Elmshaven Dr Lansing MI 48917

FARNSWORTH, MARGARET MARIE, Business Teacher/Secondary; *b:* Pocatello, ID; *m:* Rick Dale; *c:* Ronald J., Melissa M.; *ed:* (BS) Bus Ed, Univ of ID 1969; Grad Work Cmptrs, Word Processing, Lotus, Electronic Office, Piano; Various Seminars; *cr:* Computerized Accounting Cardinal Thriftway 1975-80; Bus Teacher Aberdeen HS 1980-; *ai:* Jr Class Adv; Bus WeeK Chm; NEA, IEA 1980-; IBEA 1990; Bus Prof of Amer Adv; Beta Sigma Phi (Pres 1986-87, VP 1973-74); *office:* Aberdeen H S 4th & Fremont St Aberdeen ID 83210

FARNUM, BARBARA L., English Teacher; *b:* Appleton, WI; *m:* Randall; *c:* Lisa, Laura O'Shea, Joseph; *ed:* (BA) Eng, Univ of WI Green Bay 1971; *cr:* Eng Teacher Holy Cross Sch 1974-81, St Marys 1983-; *home:* 408 Wood Appleton WI 54911

FARNUM, GEORGE WILLIAM, Fifth Grade Teacher; *b:* Jamaica, NY; *m:* Diane Urevich; *c:* Jennifer; *ed:* (BA) Hum/Eng, Adelphi-Suffolk 1968; (MS) Elem Ed, Adelphi Univ 1972; *cr:* 5th Grade Teacher Gatelot Ave Sch 1969-70, Merrimac Sch 1970-; *ai:* Organized Fund Raising for Sch Beautification Project; Sachem Teachers Assn Building Rep 1984-89; Novel & Short Stories Used in Curr; Current Material used Dist Soc Stud Curr; Lead Teacher Berkeley Health Prgm; *office:* Merrimac Elem Sch 1090 Broadway Ave Holbrook NY 11741

FARR, DIERDRI, Social Studies Teacher; *b:* Boise, ID; *ed:* (BS) History/Phys Ed, Brigham Young Univ 1978; His, Univ of UT; *cr:* His Teacher Amer Fork HS 1978; *ai:* UEA/NEA Rep; UHSAA St Dir; Drill Team/Pep Club Adv; Drill Team Competition; Tennis Coach; Soph Class Adv; Soccer Coach; Alpine Ed Assn Cluster Rep; Alpine Curr Comm Soc Stud; UT Ed Assn Sch Rep 1989-92 Soc Stud Teacher of Yr 1989; Latter Day Sts Church Sunday Sch Teacher; *office:* American Fork HS 510 N 600 E American Fork UT 84003

FARR, JERRY WILLIAM, Health/Phys Ed Teacher; *b:* Grants Pass, OR; *m:* Pamela Joan Packwood; *c:* Michelle, Andrea; *ed:* (BS) Health/Phys Ed, OR St Univ 1971; Teaching Certificate Health/Phys Ed, Portland St Univ 1980; Health & Counseling Grad Stud; *cr:* 9th Grade Health Teacher 1980-81, 9th Grade Health/Drivers Ed Teacher 1981-83, 9th Grade Health/8th-9th Grade Basic Math Recordkeeping Teacher 1983-84, 9th Grade Health/8th Grade Phys Ed Teacher 1984-85, 9th Grade Health/Phys Sci Teacher 1985-86, 9th Grade Health/7th Grade Phys Ed Teacher 1986- R A Brown Jr HS; *ai:* Head 9th Grade Ftbl, 9th Grade Girls Sftbl Coach; Adolescence Against Abuse; Teen Day Mem; 9th Grade Class Adv; Extra Duty Pay Revision Comm; OR HS Coaches Assn 1980-; OR St Univ Alumni Assn 1971-; OR St Club 1989-; *office:* R A Brown Jr HS 1505 SW 219th Ave Hillsboro OR 97123

FARR, LOIS WHITING, Teacher Lang Arts Vice Prin; *b:* Salmon, ID; *m:* David Brown; *c:* David Whiting, Colleen; *ed:* (BA) Eng Ed, BYU 1957; BYU 1970; NAU 1988-89; *cr:* Teacher Carl Hayden HS 1957-58, Springville Jr HS 1960-61, Holbrook HS 1961-64, Cntrl Jr HS 1966-67; Sub-Teacher Lakeside Sch Dist 1967-69; Teacher St Johns Elem 1969-70; Teacher/Vice-Prin Snowflake Jr HS 1970-; *ai:* Coord Teen of Month with Elks Lodge Faculty Advisory Comm; Church of Jesus Christ Auxilliary Teacher & Pres 1957-; (Meeting House Librarian 1985-; 3 Months Stake Mission 1956); CTA 1970-; Delta Kappa Gamma (Secy 1988-/2nd VP 1990-); BPOE Awd for Continued Support of Youth Act 1986-87; Far-West Laboratory for Educl Research & Dev; Published Article About Childrens Book Proj; *office:* Snowflake Jr HS Box 1100 Snowflake AZ 85937

FARRANDS, DENISE ANN, Science & Religion Teacher; *b:* Middletown, CT; *ed:* (BS) Ed, St Johns Univ 1969; (MA) Ed, Fairfield Univ 1973; *cr:* 5th-6th Grade Teacher Nativity BVM Sch 1965-67; 6th Grade Teacher St Thomas the Apostle Sch 1967-69; 5th/7th-8th Grade Teacher our Lady of Victory Sch 1969-; *ai:* Moderator & Founder Reach Out Prgm; Stu Giving Service to Elderly; NCEA 1989; Miriam Joseph Farrell Awd From Ncea Distinguished Teacher Awd; *home:* 634 Jones Hill Rd West Haven CT 06516

FARRAR, RICHARD B., JR., Biology Teacher; *b:* Penn Yan, NY; *m:* Gayle Green; *c:* Michelle Quinn, Marc; *ed:* (BS) Bio, Hougton Coll 1960; (MED) Frostburg St Univ 1990; PhD Candidate Biopsychology, Univ of Chicago 1965-68; Ecology, Western MI Univ 1964-65; Bus Admin, George Mason Univ 1981-82; *cr:* Sci Teacher Concord HS 1962-64; Instr Univ of IL 1966-68; Dean of Stud Golden Hills Acad 1968-69, Woodstock Country Sch 1969-74; Bio Teacher Northern HS 1987-; *ai:* FFA Adv; Lead Teacher in Sci; Faculty Advisory Comm; Rotary Club Treas 1988-89; Governors Natural Resource Cncl 1977-78; Childrens Sci Book Awd 1974-75; Conservationist of Yr, CT River Watershed Cncl 1972; Outstanding Bio Teacher Awd NABT 1971; *office:* Northern HS R R 2 Box 4 Accident MD 21520

FARRELL, KENNETH M., US History Teacher; *b:* Elizabeth, NJ; *m:* Donna Favoriti; *c:* Kaitlin; *ed:* (BA) Soc Stud, Montclair St Coll 1982; (MA) Educl Admin, Kean Coll 1988; *cr:* Soc Stud Teacher Holmdel HS 1982-83, Rahway HS 1983-; *ai:* Key Club Adv 1984-85; Bsktbl 1982-, Sftbl 1985-, Bsbl Asst Coach 1983; NCSS; *home:* 800 Falesky St Rahway NJ 07065

FARRIS, DONALD HERACH, Resource Teacher; *b:* St Louis, MO; *m:* Margarett D. Klassen; *c:* Wendy R., Kimberly D.; *ed:* (BA) Elem Ed, Phys Ed, Tabor Coll 1974; Emporia St Coll; Fresno St Univ; Stanislaus St; Outowa Univ; Fresno Pacific Coll; *cr:* Phys Ed Teacher K-8 Cncl Grove Elem 1974-76; Phys Ed Teacher 1st-6th Redwood Chrstn Schls 1976-77; Phys Ed Teacher/Vice Prin Nazarene Chrstn Schls 1977-80; 6th Grade/Resource Teacher Clovis Unified Sch Dist 1980-; *ai:* Head Ftbl Coach; Head Boys Bsktbl Coach; Head Girls Sftbl Coach; Head Track Coach; Head Paddle Tennis Coach; 1975-76 Ftbl League Champs; 1974-75 Bskbl Girls League; 1982-83 Boy Bsktbl League Champs; 1987-88-89 Paddle Tennis League Champs; *office:* Dry Creek Elem Sch 8098 N Armstrong Ave Clovis CA 93612

FARRIS, JOHN BEN, Physical Education Teacher; *b:* Summerdale, AL; *m:* Priscilla Shaw; *c:* Verina, Velissa, Jahn; *ed:* (BA) Phys Ed, 1978, Scndry Ed, 1980 Morehead St Univ; Lorain Cty Comm Coll; *cr:* Phys Ed Teacher Port Clinton City Schls 1981-; *ai:* Ftbl, Bsktbl, Track Coach; Youth Prgm Head Start Supvr; Saturday Detention Session; NAACP 1989; *home:* 435 Franlin Sandusky OH 44870

FARRIS, SHARON AKERS, Langauge Art/Spanish Teacher; *b:* Beaver, OK; *m:* Duane S.; *c:* Michael G., Mark D., Marlon D.; *ed:* (BA) Eng/Span, NW OK St Univ 1960; Grad Stud; Career Ladder Step II; *cr:* Eng Teacher Arnett HS 1963-64; 6th Grade Teacher 1964-69, HS Eng/Span Teacher 1969-82, Jr/Sr HS Lang Art/HS Span/3rd Grade Span Teacher 1982- Higgins Ind Sch Dist; *ai:* Class Spon; Faculty Comm Mem; TSTA; Whos Who in Amer Colleges 1960; Lipscomb Cty Teachers Organization Pres; *home:* Box 85 Shattuck OK 73858

FARRY, MELINDA (HEUER), English Teacher; *b:* Zanesville, OH; *m:* Joseph William Jr.; *c:* Joseph, Kathleen; *ed:* (BS) Eng Ed, OH St Univ 1978; Eng Ed, OH St Univ 1990; *cr:* Teacher Whitehall-Yearling HS 1978-; Summer Sch Teacher Eastland Career 1986-; *ai:* Dance & Drill Team Coach; Stu Assistance Team; Lang Art Curr Comm; NEA, OH Ed Assn 1978-; Whitehall Ed Assn (Secy 1989-, Building Rep 1987-88); NCTE 1980-89; Showcase Amer (VP 1987-, Secy 1984-87); Educator of Yr 1988; Faculty Cncl 1985-89; Articles Published; *office:* Whitehall-Yearling HS 675 S Yearling Rd Whitehall OH 43213

FARVER, HELEN SCHENCK, Chapter I Reading Teacher; *b:* Kansas City, MO; *c:* Jane Farver Vogt; Anne Farver Reekie; *ed:* (BME) Music/Ed, 1954, (MS) Ed/Rdng/Eng, 1962 Emporia St Univ; Specialist in Rdng, Elem Cert; *cr:* Eng Teacher Burlingame HS 1954-56; Music Teacher Belvoir Elem 1956-57; Eng Teacher James Bowie Jr HS 1958-59, Liberty Jr HS 1959-60, Highland Park HS 1960-62; Eng/Rdng Teacher Shawnee Heights HS 1962-64, Burlingame Schls 1983-; *ai:* Intnl Rdng Assn 1990; KS Rdng Assn 1989; Delta Kappa Gamma 1988-; PEO Chaplain 1983-; Church Organist.

FASANO, JOSEPH ANTHONY, Career Education Coordinator; *b:* Brooklyn, NY; *m:* Daphne Lopez; *c:* Joseph, Athena M.; *ed:* (BBA) Bus Ad, Dowling Coll 1971; (MALS) Ed/Ph, Stony Brook 1973; *cr:* Data Engr Aerospace Avionics 1970-71; Math Teacher St Hugh of Lincoln 1972-73; Marketing Teacher 1973-88, Career Coord 1988- Brentwood HS; *ai:* DECA Adv 1974-87; Sch Store 1974-87; Jr Var La Crosse 1973; DECNY (Bd of Trustee, Mem) 1987-88; Suffolk Cty Employment Day Comm Bus & Industry Chm 1988-; Suffolk Cty Youth Employment Comm 1988-89; Brentwood HS Entenmanns Partnership Advisory Bd, Cablevision Advisory Bd; *office:* Brentwood HS 1st St & 3rd Ave Brentwood NY 11717

FASCHING, JANE HERRMANN, First Grade Teacher; *b:* Shakopee, MN; *m:* Bill; *c:* Michael, Brian, Cole; *ed:* (BA) Elem Ed, Gustavus Adolphus Coll 1976; (MS) Curr/Instruction, Mankato St Univ 1986; Various Wkshps; *cr:* 5th Grade Teacher 1977-81, 6th Grade Teacher 1981-85, 1st Grade Teacher 1985- Central Elem Sch; *ai:* Art & Academic Awds Comm; Elem Math Dept & Assurance of Master Comm Mastery Comm Mem; NEA, MN Ed Assn 1976-; Cntrl Ed Assn (Secy 1989, 1990) 1976-; Cntrl Negotiations Team 1986, 1989; Metro-League Co-Chair 1985-87; Parents Advisory Comm 1988-; Church of Peace All Saints Luth Church Pianist-Organist 1986-; MN Educators Acad 1989; Nom

Teacher of Yr 1987; Thanks to Teachers Awd Semi-Finalist; *office:* Central Elem Sch 210 W 7th St Norwood MN 55368

FAST, PAMELA G., English/Journalism Teacher; *b:* Eldorado Springs, MO; *ed:* (BS) Eng, Cntrl MO St Univ 1986; *cr:* Eng/Journalism Teacher Eldorado Springs R-II Schls 1987-; *ai:* Head Cheerleading Spon; Jr HS Newspaper & Yrbk Adv; Class Spon; Cmnty Teacher Assn; NEA 1987-; NCTE 1990; *home:* Rt 4 Box 48c El Dorado Spgs MO 64744

FATCHETT, PATRICIA ANGELL THOMAS, Lang Art Teacher/Dept Chair; *b:* Peoria, IL; *c:* Melissa A.; *ed:* (ALA) Eng, 1958, (BA) Eng, 1963, (BS) Eng, 1964 Univ of MN; (MALS) Religion/Sci, Hamline Univ 1983; *cr:* 11th/12th Grade Eng Teacher Kirkwood Sr HS 1964-65; 7th/9th Grade Eng/Soc Stud Teacher Portland Jr HS 1965-76; 10th-12th Grade Eng Teacher John F Kennedy HS 1976-; *ai:* Danceline Adv 1976-80; Cheerleading Adv 1982-88; Track Scorer & Announcer 1976-; NCTE, MEA, NEA Mem 1965-80; MFT, AFT Mem 1980-; Alpha Delta Kappa (Chapter Pres 1974-76, St Comm Chm 1970-, Intnl Comm Chm 1976-88) 1968-; Outstanding Young Woman of Yr Nom 1973; Whos Who in American Ed 1989-; *office:* Bloomington Kennedy HS 9701 Nicollet Ave S Bloomington MN 55420

FAUCETT, SHARON LEE, Orchestra Director; *b:* Conway, SC; *ed:* (BA) Music Performance - Summa Cum Laude, 1982, (BS) Music Ed - Summa Cum Laude, Elon Coll 1982; *cr:* Orchestra Dir Cumberland Cty Schls 1982-; *ai:* Orchestra Coach Cello/Double Bass; Cumberland Cty Youth Orch; Awds Coord Cumberland Cty Orchestras; Banquet/Hospitality Chm Cumberland Cty Orchs; Housing/Audition Chm NC All St Honors Orch; MENC 1977-; NSOA Newsletter Ed1990-91; Fayetteville Symphony Prin Cellist 1988-; Cumberland Quartet Cellist; *office:* Hopemills Jr/Southview Sr HS 220 Cameron Rd Hope Mills NC 28348

FAUCETTE, CAROLYN CHAVIS, English Teacher; *b:* Fuquay-Varina, Wake; *c:* Everett, Nathaniel, Brian, Sean; *ed:* (BA) Eng, St Augustines 1964; Working toward MS in Eng NCCU; *cr:* Eng Teacher Vance Cty Schls 1964-; *ai:* Co-Chairperson of Friendship Club; NCAE; Delta Sigma Theta; *office:* Vance Sr HS Rt 6 Box 285 Henderson NC 27536

FAUL, AUDREY ANN (KERR), Chapter I Teacher/Elem Prin; *b:* Grafton, ND; *m:* Dwight; *c:* Joshua, Jared; *ed:* (BS) Elem Ed, Mayville St Coll 1976; (MA) Sch Admin, Univ of Mary 1989; *cr:* 1st/2nd Grade Teacher 1976-87, Elem Prin 1981-, Basic Skills/Chapter I Teacher 1987- Goodrich Public Sch; *ai:* ND Assn of Sch Admin, ND Assn to Elem Sch Prins 1982-; Amer Legion Auxiliary, New Horizons Homemakers; *home:* Box 364 Goodrich ND 58444

FAULCONS BLOUNT, FREYA FALUCON, Business Teacher; *b:* Ahoskie, NC; *m:* Cleveland Augustus Jr.; *c:* Zebrena, Cindi; *ed:* (BS) Bus Ed, Elizabeth City St Univ 1968; Math, East Carolina Univ 1973; Vocational Cert, Elizabeth City St Univ 1987; *cr:* Teacher Robert L Vann Sch 1969-70, Ahoskie HS 1971-85, Murfreesboro HS 1985-88, Hertford Cty HS 1988-; *ai:* FBLA Adv Asst; NCAE 1969-; PACE 1969-; Bus Ed Assn 1989-; *office:* Hertford County H S PO Box 1326 Ahoskie NC 27910

FAULKENBERRY, KATHY DALLEY, Speech/Debate Teacher; *b:* Ft Smith, AR; *m:* Bill R.; *c:* Billy R., Chris H.; *ed:* (BA) Speech Ed, Northeastern St Univ 1966; Univ of Houston; Emporia St Univ; KS St Univ; Rdng; *cr:* Jr HS Speech Teacher Barrett Elem 1967-68; Eng Teacher Univ of OK Norman 1972-73, Univ of Houston 1973-74, Ball HS 1975-76, Clear Creek HS 1976-77; Eng/Speech Teacher Panama HS 1977-81; Speech/Debate Teacher Caney Valley HS 1981-; *ai:* Natl & Catholic Forensic League, Theatre Club, NHS Spon; KNEA, NEA, KS Theatre Assn, KS Speech Assn, Natl Forensic League; Delta Kappa Gamma Prgm Chairperson 1986; Nom KS Theatre Teacher of Yr 1986; Coached Natl Speech Tournaments-Won Natl Awds 1988 & 89; Debate teams Coach; KS St Championshi Speech Tournament Stus Coach; *office:* Caney Valley HS RR 1 Box 67 A Caney KS 67333

FAULKNER, JOHNITA HENDERSON, 6th Grade Reading Teacher; *b:* Mc Crory, AR; *m:* Donnie R.; *c:* Bart, Dustin; *ed:* (BSE) Elem Ed, AR St Univ 1972; Cert in Classroom Management; PET; Assertive Discipline I & II; Rdng Styles & Techniques; *cr:* Teacher Harrisburg Schls; *ai:* Stu Cncl Adv; NEA; AR Ed Assn; Intnl Rdng Assn; Harrisburg Ed Assn; Progressive Century Club Recording Secy-Reporter 1984-; PTA Recording Secy & Treas; United Meth Church Admin Bd; Executive Bd AR Assn of Stu Cncls; *office:* Harrisburg Mid Sch PO Box 47 Harrisburg AR 72432

FAUNT, SHARYN L., English Teacher; *b:* Sault Ste Marie, MI; *m:* William; *ed:* (BA) Eng Lit/Lang, Lake Superior St Coll 1970; (MA) Scndry Ed, N MI Univ 1981; *cr:* Teacher Aide Rudyard HS 1971-73; Teacher Sault Area HS 1974-78, Sault Alternative HS 1978-80, Sault Area HS 1981-; *ai:* Nursing Home & Church Work; NCTE, Upper Peninsula Rdng Cncl; Teacher of Yr 1989; First Woman to Deliver Commencement Address in Sch System 1986; *home:* 1000 Bingham Ave Sault Sainte Marie MI 49783

FAUSEY, JANIS P., Social Studies/Latin Teacher; *b:* Williamantic, CT; *m:* Cary A.; *c:* Joy, Donald; *ed:* (BA) His, Albertus Magnus Coll 1967; (MS) Ed/Soc Sci, 1978; *cr:* Teacher Windham HS 1978-; *ai:* Latin Club Adv; *office:* Windham HS 355 High St Willimantic CT 06226

FAUSHER, JULIANN MARIE LUNDQUIST, Third Grade Teacher; *b:* Minneapolis, MN; *m:* Jim N.; *c:* Traci-Ann, Brett; *ed:* (AA) Secretarial Sci, 1969, (BS) Elem Ed, 1973, (MS) Elem Ed, 1986 Bemidji St Univ; *cr:* 1st Grade Teacher J W Smith Elem 1974-82; 2nd Grade Teacher 1982-88, 3rd Grade Teacher 1988- Northern Elem; *home:* 9670 Irvine Ave NW Bemidji MN 56601

FAUSSETT, RUSSELL WAYNE, History Teacher; *b:* Willows, CA; *ed:* (BA) His, Coll of Pacific 1962; General Scndry Teaching Credential CA; *cr:* Teacher St Marys HS 1962-69, Linden HS 1969-; *ai:* NEA, CTA; *office:* Linden HS 18527 E Front St Linden CA 95236

FAUST, RICHARD F., Assistant Principal; *b:* Port Huron, MI; *m:* Kay Collins; *c:* Aaron, Sarah; *ed:* (BS) Phys Ed, 1969, (MA) Scndry Sch Admin, 1977 MI St Univ; *cr:* Phys Ed Teacher Gardner Jr HS 1969-70, Garfield Jr HS 1970-75; Phys Ed/Math Teacher 1975-89, Asst Prin 1989- Holland Woods Intermediate; *ai:* Boys Ftbl, Bsktbl, Wrestling, Track; Girls Bsktbl & Track; Natl Jr Honor Society Adv; Intermediate Algebra Study Comm; *office:* Holland Woods Intermediate 1617 Holland Ave Port Huron MI 48060

FAVERO, CAROL EBERT, Language Arts Chairman/English; *b:* Ogden, UT; *m:* Daniel; *c:* Kerry D., Jill A., Brad L., Debra K. Favero Meenderink, Craig L. (dec); *ed:* (BS) Scndry Ed, UT St Univ 1961; Post Grad Stud; *cr:* Eng Teacher Ogden HS 1965-66, Fickett Jr HS 1966-67, Highland Jr HS 1967-69, Ogden HS 1969-70, Highland Mid ScH 1971-; *ai:* Sch Newspaper; UT Writing Project, Ogden City Dist Writing, Peer Teachers Comm Mem; Stu Writing Panel UT Teachers Convention; After Sch Writing Class; Printed Books of Stu Creative Writing in Mid Sch; Amer Assn of Univ Women Mem of Presidency 1972-74; Church Positions; PTA Quality Ed to Stus Awd 1978-79; Stu Body Most Favorite Teacher Awd 1978-79; Stan Examiner Awd 1988-89; Highland Mid Sch Teacher of Quarter 1988-89; *home:* 994 Mountain Rd Ogden UT 84404

FAVREAU, ANNE-MARIE, 1st Grade Teacher; *b:* Berlin, NH; *ed:* (BA) Foreign Lang, Rivier Coll 1974; (MED) Elem Ed, Plymouth St 1982; Jr Yr Abroad at Sorbonne Univ Paris; Summer Stud at McGill Univ-Montreal; Montpellier Univ Montpellier France; Univ of Tours & Univ of Dijon France; *cr:* Teacher 1974-75; Bi-Ling Aide 1975-77; Teacher 1977 Berlin Public Sch; *ai:* Mem of Sch Improvement Prgm Brown Sch; AAUW Pres 1988-; St Kieran Parish Cncl Pres 1984-88; Summer Stud Grants at French Univ.

FAWCETT, VIRGINIA CARROLL, Gifted Teacher; *b:* Talara, Peru; *c:* Robert, Alan; *ed:* (BA) Elem Ed, Rollins Coll 1956; (MS) Elem Ed, Nova Univ 1981; Leadership Trng Seminar Univ of S FL Tampa 1988; Ed Courses, Univ of Cntrl FL; *cr:* Teacher/ESE Gifted Ed Teacher Altamonte Elem Sch 1957-; *ai:* Odyssey of Mind Coach; Stu Cncl Spon; Steering Comm for Gifted; Delta Kappa Gamma 1985-; Seminole Ed Assn; Altamonte Elem Sch Teacher of Yr 1984.

FAZENBAKER, ALLEN R., Science Teacher; *b:* Langley Afb, VA; *m:* Deborah Lynn Staudt; *c:* Paula, Amy, Mary K., Rachael; *ed:* (BS) Agronomy, 1975, (MS) Agronomy, 1977 OH St Univ; Grad Work Terrestrial Ecology, Kent St Univ 1978-80; Grad Work Philosophy, Boromeo Coll of OH 1985-86; *cr:* Production Chemist Isolab Corp 1978-79; Research Biologist Union Carbide 1979-80, Diamond Shamrock Corp 1980-84; Teacher Edgewood Sr HS 1986-; *ai:* Head HS Track, Asst Jr HS Wrestling, Asst Cross Cntry Coach; SADD & Exploring Post Adv; NEA 1986-; Audubon Society; Sierra Club; *office:* Edgewood Sr HS 2428 Blake Rd Ashtabula OH 44004

FEAR, MARY SUE POLLARD, Soph Language Arts Teacher; *b:* Evansville, IN; *m:* Loren Ray Jr.; *c:* David W., Sara M., Laura L., Lisa K.; *ed:* (BS) Ed/Art, Eastern IL Univ 1975; Work on Masters, Eastern IL Univ 1986-87; *cr:* 5th-12th Grade Art Teacher C Y Cty CUD #10 1975-78; 2nd Grade Art Teacher St Thomas Catholic Sch 1983-85; 6th-8th Grade Lang Arts, Art Teacher Edwards Cty CUD #1 1986-88; Soph Lang Arts Teacher USD 457 Garden City HS 1988-; *ai:* Chrldr Spon 1975-78/1986-88; NEA, KNEA 1988-; INEA 1975-78/1986-88; Bible Chrstn Church Sunday Sch Supt 1988-89; Plainfield Chrstn Church 1989-; Lead Team Teacher So Lang Arts; *home:* RR 1 Box 152 Hidalgo IL 62432

FEARON, FREDERICK DAVID, 6th Grade Math/Sci Teacher; *b:* Colorado Springs, CO; *m:* Robbie Lynn; *c:* Kacy S.; *ed:* (BA) Sociology, Univ N CO 1975; Elem Teacher Cert, Univ of N CO 1977; *cr:* 2nd Grade Teacher 1977-83, 4th Grade Teacher 1983-86 Burlington Elem Sch; 6th Grade Math/Sci Teacher Burlington Mid Sch 1986-; *ai:* NEA 1977-; Shinpukai Kempo Karate 4th Degree Black Belt 1987; Outdoor & Wildlife Ed Prgms; Dev Implementation; *office:* Burlington Mid Sch 2600 Rose Ave Burlington CO 80807

FEARRINGTON, PRISCILLA EPPS, Second Grade Teacher; *b:* Bryant, VA; *m:* Robert L.; *c:* Deveron W. Reaves; *ed:* (BS) Elem Ed, Coppin St Coll 1963; (MS) Ed, Johns Hopkins 1972; *cr:* Teacher Samuel Chase Elem 1963-64, Elmer Henderson Elem 1964-68, Phelps Lane Elem 1968-70, Sarah M Roach Elem 1970-; *ai:* Sch Planning Team; Sch Budget Advisory; Grade Chairperson; Hospitality Chairperson; Baltimore Teachers Union; Natl Cncl Negro Women; NAACP; Happy Set Incorporated; Teacher of Month; *home:* 7202 Mandan Rd Greenbelt MD 20770

FEATHERSTONE, LILA NILSON, Chemistry Teacher; *b:* York, NE; *m:* Allen M.; *ed:* (BS) Chem, Le Tourneau Coll 1983; (MS) Math, Kearney St Coll 1986; *cr:* Lab Tech II Roman L Hruska Meat Animal Research Center 1983; Math/Chem Teacher Sidney Public Schls 1985-88; Grad Asst Teacher Kearney St Coll 1984-; Chem Teacher Manhattan Public Schls 1988-; *ai:* Oustanding Teacher of Yr 1988; *office:* Manhattan HS 2100 Poyntz Ave Manhattan KS 66502

FEAZEL, BRENDA KAYE MC CASKY, Chemistry Teacher; *b:* Peoria, IL; *m:* Lester Scott; *ed:* (BA) Chem, 1983, (BA) Ed/Physics, 1985 IL St Univ; Grad Teaching Asst IL St Univ; Track, Field, Vlybl, Dance Trng; *cr:* Research Asst IL St Univ 1983; Analytical Chemist Bloomington Normal Water Reclamation Center 1984-85; Chem/Earth Sci Teacher Oregon HS 1985-; *ai:* Drill Team Adv; Vlybl & Track Coach; NEA 1985-; IL Assn of Chem Teachers 1985, 1989; Research Articles Published; *office:* Oregon HS 210 S 10th St Oregon IL 61061

FEDER, HELEN, Mathematics Specialist; *b:* Wustensachsen, Germany; *m:* Daniel; *c:* Robert, Barbara Feder Murdock; *ed:* (BS) Elem Ed, OH St Univ 1946; OH St, Natl Sci & Math Trng; Hofstra Univ Spec Grant; *cr:* Classroom Teacher Canton Public Schls 1946-48, Agudas Achim Pre-Sch 1948-50; Math Specialist Plainedge Public Schls 1970-; *ai:* After Sch Wkshp; Nassau Cncl Math Teacher Assn Math Teacher of Yr 1977; NCTM NY St Awd; Domino Pizza NY St Awd; PTA Pres Life Membership 1968; Teacher Center Grant; Co-Authored Books NY St Dept of Ed; *home:* 303 N Michigan Ave N Massepequa NY 11758

FEDOR, CELIA MAJKA, 4th Grade Teacher; *b:* Utica, NY; *m:* Frederick; *c:* Faith Fedor Russell, Christiana Fedor Rivet; *ed:* (BS) Elem, SUNY Oswego 1960; Grad Courses SUNY Oneonta, SUNY Oswego, SUNY Cortland, Long Island Univ; *cr:* 4th Grade Teacher Yorkville Elem 1960-62; 3rd Grade Teacher Harts Hill Elem 1962-63; 6th Grade Teacher 1964-84, 3rd Grade Teacher 1984-85, 4th Grade Teacher 1985- De Forest Hill Elem; *ai:* St Marys Sch Bd Mem; Niagara Mohawk Energy Corporation Teachers Advisory Panel; Westmoreland Teachers Assn (Mem, Treas); NYSUT 1960-; *office:* De Forest A Hill Elem Sch Rt 233 Westmoreland NY 13490

FEDORKO, JOHN CHARLES, Math Department Chairman; *b:* Johnsonburg, PA; *ed:* (BSED) Math, Clarion Univ of PA 1964; (MST) Math, Rutgers Univ 1971; Grad Work in Math Penn St Univ, Notre Dame Univ, Allegheny Coll; *cr:* Math Teacher St Marys Area HS 1964-; *ai:* PA Cncl of Teachers of Math, Math Assn of America; Natl Sci Fnd Math Grants Rutgers Univ 1968-71; Notre Dame Univ 1979; Distinguished Teacher Honor Stu Awd Penn St Univ 1987.

FEDORYSZYN, EDWARD ALEXANDER, Sixth Grade Teacher; *b:* Brooklyn, NY; *m:* Donna M.; *c:* Evita M.; *ed:* (AS) Liberal Art, Bliss Coll 1969; (BA) Early Chldhd Ed, Univ of ME Machias 1972; (MA) Elem Ed, Russell Sage Coll 1975; *cr:* 6th Grade Teacher Coxsackie Elem Sch 1972-; *ai:* Freelance Magazine Writer; *office:* Coxsackie Elem Sch Sunset Blvd Coxsackie NY 12051

FEDROW, LINDA L., Gifted Ed/Elementary Teacher; *b:* Monongahela, PA; *m:* Gary; *c:* Alison, Abbey, Roxanne; *ed:* (BS) Elem Ed, CA Univ 1972; Numerous Courses Towards Masters; *cr:* 3rd Grade Teacher 1973-74, Corrective Math Teacher 1974-76 Yough Sch Dist; 4th Grade Teacher Lowber Elem 1976-86; Teacher of Gifted Ed Youth Sch Dist 1986-; *ai:* NEA, PA St Ed Assn.

FEE, THOMAS CHARLES, Social Studies Teacher; *b:* Cincinnati, OH; *m:* Libby Linkenfelter; *c:* Jim; *ed:* (BA) Ed, 1965, (MA) Scndry Ed, 1977 Univ of KY; Admin Cert, E KY Univ 1987; *cr:* Soc Stud Teacher KY Village Detention Facility 1970-71, Bryan Station 1971-; *ai:* Spon of Mock Trial Team; KY Jr Historical Society; Mock Congress; Task Force for Soc Stud; Mid Sch Curr Comm; Fayette Cty Soc Stud Assn; KY Cncl for Soc Stud; KY Assn Teachers His Mid Sch Rep 1983-88; Spon of Yr KY Jr Historical Society 1977; Teacher of Yr Bryan Station 1985; *office:* Bryan Station HS 1865 Wickland Dr Lexington KY 40505

FEENEY, THOMAS R., Ag Science/Biology Teacher; *b:* Muncie, IN; *m:* Kimberly Butler; *c:* Marc, Levi, Nathan, Megan; *ed:* (BS) Bio, Purdue Univ 1974; Grad Stud Bio, Ed, Purdue North Cntrl, IN Univ South Bend; *cr:* Teacher South Cntrl HS 1975-76, Elston Jr HS 1976-78, Rogers HS 1978-83, Grimsley HS 1983-; *ai:* Grimsley Jr Jaycees Service Club Adv; NC Assn of Educators 1983-; New Beginnings Evangelical Presbyn Church; Sci Labs & St Guidelines Written & Correlated for Publication & Distribution to Greensboro Teachers; *office:* Grimsley HS 801 Westover Terr Greensboro NC 27408

FEENSTRA, DAVID WAYNE, High School Science Teacher; *b:* Zeeland, MI; *m:* Dawn Marie Saul; *ed:* (BS) Bio/Phys Sci, MI St Univ 1987; Educl Leadership, W MI Univ; Instructional Theory Into Practice; Freedom Seminar Chemical Dependence & Addictions Prgm; Athletic Coaches Ed; *cr:* Teacher/Youth Cnslr Wedgewood Acres Chrstn Youth Homes 1987-88; Teacher Lakeshore HS 1988-; *ai:* Head Jr Var Ftbl Coach; Asst Var Wrestling Coach; Jr HS Track Coach; Young Life Soph Class Adv; Core Group Counseling Discussion Group; Variety Show; MI Sci Teachers Assn 1987-; MI HS Ftbl Coaches Assn 1987-; Tri-County Unit I Fire Dept Volunteer Fireman 1990; Project VIC Video Discs in Classroom.

FEES, RUTH, English Teacher; *b:* Sidney, NE; *ed:* (AA) Span, Northeastern Jr Coll 1972; (BA) Eng/Ed Media, Univ N CO 1974; (MA) Hum, CO Coll 1980; *cr:* Jr HS Eng Teacher Holyoke Jr HS 1974-75; Jr HS & HS Eng Teacher Plainview Sch 1975-; *ai:* Sr Class, Cheerleading, Pep Club, Knowledge Bowl Spon; CEA, NEA, UNISERV, NCTE 1975-: Natl Poetry Anthology Publications 1978-81; Plainview Teacher of Yr 1980; *office:* Plainview HS School House Rd Sheridan Lake CO 81071

FEICK, RAYMOND R., Biology Teacher; *b:* St Louis, MO; *ed:* (BA) Ed/Bio, Harris Teachers Coll 1969; (MS) Bio, S IL Univ 1976; Bio at St Louis Univ, Univ of MO St Louis, WA Univ; Bio Technology DNA, Cold Springs Harbor Research Center; *cr:* Elem Teacher St Louis Public Schls 1969-70; Teaching/Research Asst S IL Univ 1970-72; Bio Teacher Southwest HS 1972-80; Instructional Coord St Louis Public Schls 1980-82; Bio Teacher Acad of Math & Sci 1982-; *ai:* Spon ECO-ACT Prgm; Amer Assn of Cell Biologists 1971-81; Amer Assn Advancement of Sci 1980-; Wild Canid Survival & Research Center (Bd Mem 1975-, VP 1981-83); In Motion Dance Company VP 1989-; J A Druschel Memorial Schlsp 1969; Natl Sci Fnd Grant Microbiology & Human Genetics 1988 & Natl Sci Fnd DNA Biotechnology 1989; Article, Study Guide, Laboratory Manual Published; *home:* 4502 Tower Grove Pl Saint Louis MO 63110

FEIKES, EDWARD LEE, Social Studies Teacher; *b:* La Porte, IN; *m:* Mary Catherine Calvi; *c:* Stephen, Matthew, Regina Hans; *ed:* (BS) Soc Stud, Ball St Univ 1957; (MA) Soc Stud, IN Univ 1960; *cr:* Soc Stud Teacher La Porte Cmmty Sch 1957-68; Soc Stud Teacher/Dept Head Windsor Schls 1970-71; Teacher La Porte Cmmty Schls 1971-; *ai:* Soc Stud Dept Head 1965-67; La Porte Human Relations Cncl 1971-73; Far East Society Grant 1959; Japan Society Grant 1960; *home:* 5206 N 900 E New Carlisle IN 46552

FEINSTEIN, MICHAEL IRWIN, Economics Teacher; *b:* Chicago, IL; *m:* Loretta; *c:* Marta, Lisabeth; *ed:* (BA) His, Univ of CA Los Angeles 1959; (JD) Law, Loyola Univ Law Sch 1966; *cr:* Attorney Private Practice 1968-76; Teacher Los Angeles HS 1960-, Fairfax Cmmty Adult Sch 1967-; *ai:* Los Angeles HS Budget Comm Mem; Los Angeles HS Alumni Assn Distinguished Teacher Awd 1969; *office:* Los Angeles HS 4650 W Olympic Blvd Los Angeles CA 90019

FEIST, EUGENE P., Mathematics Department Chair; *b:* Velva, ND; *m:* Mary W. Mc Closkey; *c:* Margaret, Paul; *ed:* (BA) Math, Minot St Coll 1960; (MS) Physics, Naval Post Grad Sch 1967; Grad Work TX St A&I 1973-74; *cr:* Electrical Technician Navy 1952-56; Naval Officer/Instr US Naval Acad 1967-69; Pilot US Navy 1960-77; *ai:* St Bernard HS Financial Dev Dir; *office:* St Bernard HS 222 Dollison St Eureka CA 95501

FEIST, KATHY ROSS, Fourth Grade Teacher; *b:* Minot, ND; *m:* Myron; *c:* Stephanie; *ed:* (BS) Elem Ed, Spec Ed, Minot St Univ 1978; *cr:* Primary Mentally Handicapped Teacher 1979-81; 4th Grade Teacher 1982- Minot Public Schls; *ai:* Minot Ed Assn Treas 1985-87; ATE Bd Mem 1986-; Phi Delta Kappa; Delta Kappa Gamma Leadership Chairperson 1986-; Sch Aged Child Care Bdmem 1989-; Gifted/Talented Prgm Advisorycomm Mem 1989-; *office:* North Hill Elem 2215 8th St N W Minot ND 58701

FELD, DAVID ALBERT, Aerospace Science Inst; *b:* Paris, KY; *m:* Sandra Kay Kenney; *c:* Deborah Johnson, Cynthia Vetter, Brian; *ed:* (BS) Anthropology, Univ of KY 1955; (MS) Ed, GA St Univ 1984; *cr:* Navigator USAF 1955-76; Garage Mgr Roadway 1976-79; ROTC Instr Morrow HS 1979-; *ai:* Model Rocket Club; Cmptr & Word Processing Spon & Instr; VFW Mem 1979-; Whos Who in GA Dist Citizen & Educator 1984; *office:* Morrow HS 2299 Old Rex Morrow Rd Morrow GA 30260

FELDER, BETTY G., Earth Science Teacher; *b:* Ridgeville, SC; *m:* Wallace Jr.; *c:* Lita, Christy; *ed:* (BS) General Sci, Claflin Coll 1964; Life & Earth Sci, SC St Coll, Univ of SC, Francis Marion Coll; *cr:* Teacher Wilson HS 1965-66, Carver Elem Sch 1967-70, Green Wood Elem Sch 1970-73, Williams Mid Sch 1973-; *ai:* Amer Ed Week Prgm & 8th Grade Graduation Chairperson; SC Ed Assn 1965-; Mc Leod Volunteer 1982-83; *home:* 141 E Wilson Rd Florence SC 29501

FELDER, ISHMELL, Asst Chair-Soc Stud Teacher; *b:* Macon, GA; *ed:* (BA) His, Morehouse Coll 1972; (MED) Soc Stud Ed, Mercer Univ 1982; *cr:* Core Teacher Westport Jr HS 1972-76; 8th Grade Soc Stud Teacher Ballard B Jr HS 1976-85; 9th-12th Grade Soc Stud Teacher Central HS 1985-; *ai:* Debate Team Coach; Detention Mgr; CARE At-Risk Teacher; Asst Soc Stud Dept Chm; Media Center Comm; Prof Assn of GA Educators 1980-; GA Cncl of Soc Stud 1985-; Phi Delta Kappa 1989-; Morehouse Alumni Assn Macon Chapter Secy 1977-; St Luke Baptist Church 1957-, Honorary Day 1984, 1988; *office:* Central HS 751 Hendley St Macon GA 31204

FELDER, PAULETTE MAURIN, Third Grade Teacher; *b:* New Orleans, LA; *m:* Robert; *c:* Margaret, Rob, Andrew; *ed:* (BA) Elem Ed, 1973, (MED) Elem Ed, 1977, Elem Ed, 1985 SE LA Univ; Master Teacher Trng LA Teaching Internship & LA Teacher Evaluation Prgms; *cr:* Classroom Teacher D C Reeves 1973-; *ai:* Assn of Prof Educators of LA 1987-; Holy Ghost Cath Church Parish Cncl Mem; Hammond Area Cancer Society Chm; *home:* 1420 S Elm St Hammond LA 70403

FELDHAUS, KATHY L., Third Grade Teacher; *b:* Sturgis, MI; *m:* Leon H.; *c:* Christy, Chad; *ed:* (BS) Elem Ed, Sioux Falls Coll 1969; *cr:* Kndgtn Teacher 1969, 3rd Grade Teacher 1969- West Cntrl Sch; *ai:* West Cntrl Ed Assn, SD Ed Assn, NEA 1969-; Intnl Rdng Assn 1984-88; *office:* West Cntrl Sch 605 E 2nd St Hartford SD 57033

FELDKAMP, MARY GOODWIN, Science Department Chair; *b:* Rushville, IL; *m:* Wayne Edwin; *c:* Carl L.; *ed:* (BA) Bio, Culver Stockton Coll 1974; KSAM Instr; *cr:* Sci Teacher Laddonia RV 1974-75, Lewis Cty C-1 1976-80, Canton RIV 1980-84, Wyaconda C-1 1985-; *ai:* Sr Class, Sci Club, NHS Spon; Prof Dev Comm; MSTA, CTA; 4-H Horsemanship Leader 1985-; Showboard 1990-; *home:* RR 1 La Grange MO 63448

FELDMAN, RHONDA ANN, Second Grade Teacher; *b:* Little River, KS; *m:* John; *c:* Sean, Bren; *ed:* (AA) Hutchinson Comm Coll 1974; (BA) Elem Ed, Wichita St Univ 1976; Grad Courses Ed; *cr:* 4th Grade Teacher Buhler Grade Sch 1976-77; 2nd Grade Teacher Park Sch 1977-; *ai:* Prof Dev Cncl Mem; K-NEA 1976-; Lyons Unified Teachers Assn (Pres 1980-81, Co-Pres 1989-); 4-H Club Valley Bluebirds Project Leader 1989-; *office:* Park Grade Sch 121 S Workman Lyons KS 67554

FELDMANN, JANE ROGERS, 7th Grade Science Teacher; *b:* Syracuse, NY; *m:* Richard; *ed:* (MS) Health, Phys Ed, 1978, (BA) Phys Ed, 1973 Syracuse Univ; Ad Cert Sci; *cr:* Phys Ed Hazzard Street Sch 1973-78; Sci Teacher Linton HS 1978-82, Bethlehem Cntrl Schls 1982-; *ai:* Adv Leadership Club; Jr Varity Golf Coach Sch Improvement Team; Future Dir Comm; NEA 1982-; Bethlehem Teachers Assn (Secy 1989 VP 1990); Bethlehem Opportunities Unlimited Pres 1984-1986; Delta Kappa Gamma; *office:* Bethlehem Central Mid Sch Kenwood Ave Delmar NY 12054

FELDMANN, RANDY G., Science Teacher/Coach; *b:* Hobart, OK; *m:* Rhonda J. Biddy; *c:* Miranda R., Randall B.; *ed:* (BS) Phys Ed, SW OK St Univ 1987; *cr:* Sci Teacher/Coach Tyrone Public Schls 1987-89, Healdton Public Schls 1989-; *ai:* Jr HS & HS Ftbl, Girls & Boys HS Track Asst; Jr HS Boys Bsktbl Head; OEA; *office:* Healdton Public Schls 624 Carter Healdton OK 73438

FELICE, JOHN STEVEN, Mill Cabinet Instructor; *b:* Salinas, CA; *m:* Karen A. Silacci; *c:* Shannon M., Holly R.; *ed:* (AA) Industrial Art/General Ed, Hartnell Coll 1981; (BA) Industrial Art, CA St Univ Chico 1984; Credential Prgms, Chapman Coll & UCSC; *cr:* Industrial Art Instr Salinas HS 1984-; Mill Cabinet/Construction Tech Instr Mission Trails ROP & Salinas Union HS Dist 1984-; P/PEPSE Teacher in Charge Salinas HS 1989-; *ai:* Pupil/Parent Educl Prgm for Skills Enrichment; Club Adv Voc Industrial Clubs of America; Head Jr Var Ftbl Coach; Faculty Senate & Core Team; CA Industrial & Technology Ed Assn Mem 1984-; Natl Teachers Assn, CAVA Mem 1984-; Dist Employee & Sch Site Employee of Month 1989; *office:* Salinas HS 726 S Main St Salinas CA 93901

FELICE, LUCY ANN, 11th Grade English Teacher; *b:* Syracuse, NY; *ed:* (BA) Eng/Scndry Ed, FL Atlantic Univ 1971; (MS) Rdng, Univ of LaVerne 1982; *cr:* Teacher Miami Springs Sr HS 1971-74; Dept Head 1978-82, Teacher 1974- Hialeah-Miami Lakes Sr HS; *ai:* Alpha Delta Kappa; *office:* Hialeah-Miami Lakes Sr H S 7977 W 12th Ave Hialeah FL 33014

FELICIANO, BLANCA, Science Teacher; *b:* Aguada, PR; *ed:* (BA) Sci Ed, Newark St Coll 1972; (MA) Educl Admin, Montclair St 1988; *cr:* Sci Teacher E Orange Bd of Ed 1972-73, Kearney Bd of Ed 1973-; *ai:* NJEA, NEA, KEA; *office:* Franklin Sch 100 Davis Ave Kearny NJ 07032

FELLENBERG, JAMES E., Technology Teacher; *b:* Libby, MT; *m:* Cheryl Ramona Engle; *ed:* (BA) Scndry Ed, Univ of MT 1980; *cr:* 7th/8th Grade Teacher Orah D Clark Jr HS 1981-; *ai:* Sch Photography Coord; Voc Ed Dept Chairperson; AK St Task Force to Develop Technology Ed Mem; Comm for St Accreditation Mem; AK Dept of Ed Merits Awd; *office:* Orah D Clark Jr HS 150 S Bragaw Anchorage AK 99508

FELLENCER, MARY LOUISE GEORGE, 5th Grade Homeroom Teacher; *b:* Allentown, PA; *m:* Jerome C.; *c:* Barbara, Jeffrey (dec), Alma M., Sally, Dennis; *ed:* (AA) Art, St Genevieve 1949; (BA) Bus Management, Allentown Coll of St Francid De Sales 1985; Completion Alvernia Coll 1985; Grad Stud Penn St, Lehigh Univ, Wilkes Coll, Katztown Univ; *cr:* 4th Grade Teacher Holy Ghost Elem 1966-68; Spec Ed Teacher Mercy Day Sch 1968-69; 4th-8th Grade Teacher St John the Baptist Sch 1969-75, Holy Spirit Mid Sch 1975-; *ai:* Sch Cmptrs; Sch Talent Show & Sci Curr Coord; E PA Cncl Teachers of Math (Exec Bd 1980-88) 1980-; Keystone Energy Ed Network, NCEA; Access Alumni Allentown Coll Exec Bd 1985-; Grants Amer Chemistry Society Allentown Coll 1985-86, PA Office of Energy & VGI Gas Company Penn St Univ 1988, PA General Assembly Lehigh Univ 1985-86; Participate Drug Prgm for Children 1989; *home:* 428 Haines Mill Rd Allentown PA 18104

FELLENSTEIN, TERRY ALLAN, Teacher; *b:* Bedford, OH; *m:* Mary Tgrese Medhurst; *c:* Jeremy, Becky, Caleb, Seth, Rachel; *ed:* Bible, N Cntrl Bible Coll 1977; (MDIV) Theology, Assemblies of God Theological Seminary 1980; *cr:* Teacher Grace Chrstn Acad 1981-; *ai:* Jr Class Adv; Var Ftbl & Bsbl Coach; Var Girls & Jr HS Girls Bsktbl Coach; OK Chrstn Conference Ftbl Coach of Yr 1988-89, 1989-; *office:* Grace Chrstn Acad 4712 S Santa Fe Oklahoma City OK 73109

FELLER, CAROL SCOTT, Fourth Grade Teacher; *b:* Fayetteville, AR; *m:* Brian F.; *ed:* (BA) Upper Elem Ed, Univ of N IA 1977; Grad Stud St Univ of IA, Clark Coll; *cr:* Teacher Bellevue Area Cath Elem Sch 1977-; *ai:* Cheerleading Moderator; Safety Patrol Coord; Bellevue Comm Players Publicity 1989; *office:* Bellevue Area Cath Elem 403 Park St Bellevue IA 5203

FELLER, EMMA VICTORIA, Fifth Grade Teacher; Bucheburg, Germany; *ed:* (BS) Elem Ed/Ger, S IL Univ 196 (MED) Ed, Univ of IL 1971; Advanced Certificate in Ed & Mat Univ of IL 1976; *cr:* 4th Grade Teacher Washington Sch 1968-6 Mark Twain 1969-70, Abraham Lincoln Sch 1970-81; 5th Grade Academics in Fine Arts Magnet Teacher Millie Proegler 1981-; a Drama, Creative Writing, Teaching Ger to Gifted Stu; I Teachers of Math 1974-85; Two Rivers Rdng Assn 1969-8 Urban-Rural Dev Prgm Secy 1973-77; Sch Rep Intnl Rdng Ass NY City & Natl Conference on Open Classroom Denver CC Present Math Approach N IL Univ 1976; *home:* 629 S Harriso Kankakee IL 60901

FELLER, SUSAN KARLENE, Fifth Grade Teacher; *b:* Dayto OH; *ed:* (BS) Soc Stud Ed, 1962, Conversion to Elem, 196 Manchester Coll; (MS) Ed, Purdue Univ 1970; Grad Stud Ed; *c* Elem Teacher Brownsburg Schls 1963-65, Lebanon Cmmty Sc Corporation 1965-; *ai:* Outdoor Classroom Comm Chm; IN Cn for Soc Stud, Intnl Rdng Assn 1990; Clegg Gardens Bd Trustees, Conner Prairie Pioneer Settlement, Tippecanoe Ct Historical Society 1990; *home:* 650 Romig Lafayette IN 47901

FELLERS, LYNNE HERTHUM, Social Studies Chair Teacher; *b:* Baton Rouge, LA; *m:* Clyde E.; *c:* Laurie, Tim; *ed* (BS) Ed, LA St Univ 1962; *cr:* Teacher North Side HS 1962-64 Polytechnic HS 1964-66, Brewer HS 1979-; *ai:* Peer Assistanc Leadership Class Teacher; Sr Class & NHS Spon; Care Team Gifted & Talented Curr Modificatiion, Prin Advisory, Schls Comm; TSTA, NEA, WSCTA 1979-; *office:* Brewer HS 1000 S Cherry Ln White Settlement TX 76108

FELTNER, HAROLD, English Department Chairman; *b* Hazard, KY; *c:* Greg, Gary, David; *ed:* (BA) Eng, Berea Coll 1961; *cr:* Eng Teacher 1961-, Span Teacher 1965-70 Toledo De Vilbiss HS; Eng/Cmptr Teacher Toledo Univ Comm Coll 1968-71; *ai* Adult Evening Sch Instr; Phi Delta Kappa 1962-; NCTE 1990; AFT 1961-; Unitarian Church 1962-; Berea Coll Stu Exch Cuba 1959; NDEA Schlsp OH St Univ 1968; Outstanding Young Men of America 1971; Outstanding Eng Teacher NW OH 1983; Outstanding Citizenship & Writing Awd Sue Bennett Coll 1958; Florence Writing Awd Berea Coll 1961; *office:* Toledo De Vilbiss HS 3301 Upton Ave Toledo OH 43613

FELTON, LLOYD S., Science Teacher; *b:* Hertford, NC; *ed:* (BS) Bio, Elizabeth City St Coll 1969; *cr:* Sci Teacher Perquimans Cty Union Sch 1969-70, Perquimans Cty HS 1970-; *ai:* HS Sci Fair Co-Adv; After Sch Study; The Future Scientists of America 1973-74; NEA 1989-; NC Alliance of Chemistry Teachers 1990.

FELTS, ADELE GOTTHELF, History Teacher; *b:* Yazoo City, MS; *m:* M. Leon; *ed:* (BAE) Soc Stud, 1972, (MSS) His, 1974 Univ Of MS; (AA) Tcaching, Univ of MS; *cr:* IIis Teacher Decatur HS 1975-; Part-Time His Teacher John C Calhoun Comm Coll 1987-; *ai:* Decatur HS Scholars Bowl Team Spon; Delta Kappa Gamma, Decatur Ed Assn, AL Ed Assn, NEA; *home:* 4566 Arrowhead Dr SE Decatur AL 35603

FELTS, KATHERINE CLINARD, Substitute Teacher; *b:* Springfield, TN; *m:* R. Ralph; *c:* Jerry, Marshall; *ed:* Elem Ed, Mid TN St Univ 1937; Extension Courses Austin Peay St Univ; *cr:* 1st Grade Teacher Robetson Cty Schls; *home:* 4058 Hwy 49 W Springfield TN 37172

FELTS, VANETA LOWERY, Third Grade Teacher; *b:* Weatherford, TX; *m:* Milton Felts; *c:* Glenn, Molly; *ed:* (BS) Elem Ed, 1962, (MA) Counseling, Sul Ross Univ; *cr:* Spec Math Teacher 1976-79, 6th Grade Teacher 1979-87, 3rd Grade Teacher 1987- Sabinal Elem Sch; *office:* Sabinal Elem Sch Cullins Sabinal TX 78881

FENCYK, EDWARD W., JR., 8th Grade Counselor; *b:* Detroit, MI; *m:* Geraldine; *c:* John, Maureen; *ed:* (BA) His, Univ of Detroit 1969; (MED) Guidance & Counseling, 1973, (ESP) Gen Admin, Wayne St Univ; *cr:* Teacher Burroughs Jr HS 1970-74; Teacher/Cnslr Wyandot Mid Sch 1974-79; Cnslr 8th Grade Ctr Sch 1979-81; Teacher/Cnslr Iroquois Mid Sch 1981-; *ai:* Stu Cncl Spon Iroquois Mid Sch; Macomb Cty Personnel & Guidance Assn.

FENELEY, KENNETH HOWARD, Band Director; *b:* Engadine, MI; *m:* Judith; *c:* Margaret Van Hoose, Elizabeth Parrish, Jennifer; *ed:* (BME) Music Ed, 1958, (MA) Music Ed, 1962 Cntrl Mi Univ; *cr:* Band Dir/Teacher Mackinaw City Public Schls 1958-59, Engadine Public Schls 1959-60; Grad Asst Cntrl MI Univ 1960-61; Band Dir Gladwin Public Schls 1961-62, Mt Pleasant Jr HS 1962-67, Clare Public Schls 1967-; *ai:* MEA, NEA Local Pres 1972-76; MI Sch Band Orch Assn (Local Pres, St VP 1972-74, 1985-87); Clare United Meth Church; MI Band Dir of Yr 1974; *office:* Clare Public Schls 201 E State St Clare MI 48617

FENIMORE, PATRICIA FLANNERY, Kindergarten Teacher; *b:* Portsmouth, OH; *m:* Carl David; *c:* Jeffrey S., Jamie L.; *ed:* (BS) Ed, OH Univ Athens 1967; Ed, OH Univ Athens 1968-; Grad Stud Xavier Univ 1968; *cr:* Kndgtn Teacher Valley Elem 1964-70, Wheelersburg Elem 1970-; *ai:* NEA, OH Ed Assn; OH Academic Hall of Fame Sch Awd 1988; *home:* 1114 Norwood Ave Rt 5 Wheelersburg OH 45694

FENN, CHARLES G., Technology Teacher; *b:* Schenectady, NY; *m:* Vickie L. Spearance; *c:* Carolyn, Angela *ed:* (AAS) Electrical Tech, Hudson Valley Comm Coll 1962; (BS) Industrial Art, SUCO 1968; Grad Stud SUCO; *cr:* Instr US Army 1964-66;

Technology Teacher Sandy Creek Cntrl Sch 1968-; *ai:* Sch Newspaper Adv; Sandy Creek Teachers Assn, NY Ed Assn, NEA; *office:* Sandy Creek Cntrl Sch Salisbury St Sandy Creek NY 13145

FENNELLY, ROBERT E., 8th Grade Mathematics Teacher; *b:* West Chester, PA; *m:* Judith Ann John; *c:* Scot, Sean; *ed:* (BS) Math, West Chester Univ 1962; Grad Stud West Chester Univ, Villinova Univ, Layfette Coll; *cr:* Teacher Downingtown Jr HS 1962-69, Lionville Jr HS 1970-; *ai:* Asst Math Chm; NEA, PSEA, DAEA; Downingtown Alumni Assn Pres 1967-70; Lafayette Coll Natl Sci Fnd Grant 1970; *office:* Lionville Jr HS 50 Devon Dr Downingtown PA 19335

FENNESSEY, L. COLLEEN, Kindergarten/Chapter I Teacher; *b:* Ottawa, IL; *ed:* (BSED) Ed, N IL Univ 1969; *cr:* Kndgtn Teacher 1969-70, 1st Grade Teacher 1970-71 Jefferson Sch; Kndgtn/Chapter I Teacher Milton Pope Sch 1971-; *ai:* Starved Rock Rdng Cncl 1980-; *home:* 1207 Germania Dr Ottawa IL 61350

FENNESSY, VIRGINIA EVERETT, Gifted English Teacher; *b:* Suffern, NY; *m:* Mark L.; *ed:* (BA) Theatre, 1979, (BA) Eng, 1980 SUNY Buffalo; (MSE) Scndry Ed, SUNY Coll Oswego 1987; *cr:* Eng/Drama Teacher Millard Hawk Jr HS 1981; Jr HS Eng Teacher Myuderse Acad 1981-83; Eng/Latin Teacher Fowler HS 1984-85; Gifted Eng Teacher Nottingham HS 1985-; *ai:* NHS; Drama Club Technical Dir; AGATE 1985-; TANYS 1986-, Best Technical Ensemble Work 1986; Auburn Players Bd Mem 1982-; Grant Awarded Childrens Theatre Production Cayuga Cty 1990; *office:* Nottingham HS 3100 E Genesee St Syracuse NY 13224

FENNIG, FREDERICK MARK, Science Teacher; *b:* Abilene, KS; *m:* Elizabeth Orsi; *c:* Katherine, Paul; *ed:* (BS) Bio, AR Coll 1969; Ed, Astronomy & Physics; *cr:* Classroom Teacher Des Arc HS 1980-; *ai:* 7th Grade Spon; NEA 1980-; DAEA Pres 1983-84; *office:* Des Arc HS Rt 2 Box A Des Arc AR 72040

FENTON, CHRISTINA M., 6th Grade Teacher; *b:* Syracuse, NY; *m:* Michael J.; *ed:* (BA) Eng, Elem Ed, SUNY Potsdam 1969; (MA) Elem Ed, SUNY Brockport 1973; *cr:* 1st Grade Teacher Tappan Zee Elem Sch 1969-70; 6th Grade Classroom Teacher Gates Chili Cntrl Sch Dist 1970-; *ai:* Several Comm Mbrshps; Coach Club; Blood Drive Red Cross; Teach Start Dev Courses Ed Gifted; Delta Kappa Gamma Mem 1987-; Agate 1989; NYS Teacher Yr 1988; Rochester Area Career Ed Cncl Proj Mgr 1987-; Written Several Curr Guides Ed Gifted; Dir Olympics Mind NYS; *home:* 2192 Ridgeway Ave Rochester NY 14626

FENTON, DANIEL JOSEPH, Science Department Chair; *b:* Inglewood, CA; *ed:* (BA) Biological Sci, 1978, (MS) Environmental Stud, 1983 CA St Univ Fullerton; *cr:* Sci Teacher St Angela Merici Sch 1979-84; Sci/Math Teacher De La Salle HS 1984-85; Sci Dept Chm Cathedral HS 1986-; *ai:* Jr Class Academic Cnslr; Sci Club Moderator; Brothers of Chrstn Schls Religious Congregation 1985-; Diocese of Orange Distinguished Teacher Awd 1983; *office:* Cathedral HS 1253 Bishops Rd Los Angeles CA 90012

FENTON, EVELYN LEE (ZURCHER), Second Grade Teacher; *b:* Enterprise, OR; *m:* Robert D.; *c:* Bradley N., Gregory D., Steven M.; *ed:* (BA) Soc Sci, San Diego St Univ 1974; (MA) Ed, US Intnl Univ 1985; *cr:* 2nd Grade Teacher Lakeside Farms Elem 1986-; *ai:* Home Visits Each Family at Beginning of Yr; Yearly Sessions with Gifted Stu; 2nd Grade Chairperson; Various Sch & Dist Comms; Mem Sch Bd & Cncl; Lakeside Teachers Assn, CA Teachers Assn, NEA, PTA 1986-; Carlton Hills Chrstn Elem Sch (Mem of Sch Bd, Secy) 1987-; Schlsp to Natl Univ 1983; *office:* Lakeside Farms Elem Sch 11915 Lakside Ave Lakeside CA 92040

FENTON, THEODORE J., 8th Grade Amer Studies Teacher; *b:* Mount Pleasant, IA; *m:* Leeanne Lachnitt; *c:* Erik A., Susan M.; *ed:* (BA) Soc Sci, Univ of IA 1972; (MA) His, NE MO St Univ 1975; Grad Stud Drake Univ, W IL Univ; *cr:* Teacher Oak Street Mid Sch 1972-; *ai:* Yrbk Adv; Career Ed Teacher; Mid Sch & HS Levels Ftbl, Wrestling Coach; Phi Delta Kappa 1975; ASCD 1986; *office:* Oak Street Mid Sch 903 Oak St Burlington IA 52601

FENTRESS, RUBY P., Mathematics Teacher/Dept Chair; *b:* Sparta, TN; *m:* Gene Austin; *c:* Lorri J. Fentress Mathis; *ed:* (BS) Math, TN A&I St Univ 1961; Master of Ed Scndry Ed, Memphis St Univ 1971; *cr:* Teacher Bolivar Industrial HS 1961-62; Algebra I/II Teacher Hamilton HS 1962-; Lecturer/Developmental Stud Dept St Tech Inst 1975-; *ai:* Les Jeune Dames Spon; NHS & Sr Class Adv; Mr & Miss Hamilton Comm Mems & Math Chairperson for Dept; NEA, TEA, Math Teachers; YWCA; Delta Sigma Theta; Manna Outreach Prgm; Teacher of Yr Awd 1974; Yrbk Dedication; *home:* 6740 Kirby Oaks Ln Memphis TN 38119

FERGASON, NANCY SNIPES, Teacher of 5th Grade Gifted; *b:* Daingerfield, TX; *m:* Charles W.; *c:* Morriss, Rhonda Nekuza, Marc; *ed:* (BA) Elem, N TX Univ 1959; (MS) Elem, E TX Univ 1973; Cmptrs, Gifted Ed, TX Womens Univ 1978; *cr:* 4th Grade Teacher Tisinger Elem 1960-62; 5th/6th Grade Teacher Shands Elem 1964-78; Teacher of 5th Grade Gifted Rugel Elem 1978-; *ai:* Cmptr Sci; Thinking Skills, Math, Gifted Ed Wkshp Conductor; Alpha Delta Kappa 1974-79; Phi Rho Pi VP 1975-, Outstanding Mem 1975; PTA Life Mem 1977; Outstanding Elem Teacher of Amer Awd 1974; *home:* 4319 Live Oak Mesquite TX 75150

FERGERSON, JAMES FREDRICK, Physics/Physical Sci Teacher; *b:* Karnes City, TX; *m:* Mary Merritt; *c:* TaraLeigh, Emily, Alex; *ed:* (BS) Phys Ed/Bio, 1975, Drivers Ed, 1979, Phys Sci, 1987- SW TX St Univ; *cr:* Teacher/Coach Kenedy HS 1975-77, Woodsboro HS 1977-84, Goliad HS 1984-86, Sinton HS 1986-; *ai:* Drivers Ed; Jr Class; ATPE 1986-.

FERGUSON, BONNIE MEYER, 1st Grade Teacher; *b:* Ribolt, KY; *c:* Roger W.; *ed:* (BA) Elem Ed, Morehead St 1963; *ai:* Tollesboro PTO Publicity Chairperson.

FERGUSON, CAROLYN ODOM, First Grade Teacher; *b:* Elizabethton, TN; *m:* Sam Lee; *c:* Carolee, Phillip; *ed:* (BS) Elem Ed, E TN St Univ 1972; E TN St Univ 1973; Applachian St Univ 1977; Cumberland Univ 1990; *cr:* 1st Grade Teacher Cloudland Elem 1972-73, Valley Forge Elem 1974-; *ai:* Textbook Comm; TN Ed Assn 1988-; Heart Assn 1987-88; Career Ladder; *home:* Rt 8 Box 2900 Elizabethton TN 37643

FERGUSON, CELINDA YUNGER, Mathematics Teacher/Dept Chair; *b:* Oklahoma City, OK; *m:* Jerry D.; *c:* Kimberly D. Ferguson Painter, Leesa L.; *ed:* (BSED) Math, Cntrl St Univ 1963; *cr:* Math Teacher Southeast HS 1963-70, Cntrl Jr HS 1970-76, Cntrl Mid HS 1976-88, Math Dept Chairperson Moore HS 1989-; *ai:* NHS Adv; Scholastic Team Coach; North Cntrl Evaluation Comm; Delta Kappa Gamma (Treas 1974-78, Mem 1974-); OEA, MACT (Mem 1963-, Sch Rep); OK Assn of HS Math Teachers 1986-; 1st Baptist Church of Moore 1976-; Moore HS Alumni 1989-; *office:* Moore HS 300 N Eastern Moore OK 73160

FERGUSON, DEAN THORNBURG, Social Studies Teacher; *b:* Hays, KS; *m:* Joanne Leigh; *c:* Keegan, Kelsey; *ed:* (BA) His, Spring Arbor Coll 1983; Teaching Cert, MI St Univ 1985; Working Towards MA His, Cntrl MI Univ; *cr:* Soc Stud Teacher Mt Pleasant HS 1986-; *ai:* Head Coach Var Soccer; Co-Adv Youth in Government Club; Adv Soc Stud Olympiad; *office:* Mt Pleasant HS 1155 S Elizabeth Mount Pleasant MI 48858

FERGUSON, DIANE, 7th/8th Grade Math Teacher; *b:* Dumas, AR; *ed:* (BSE) Soc Stud, Univ of AR Monticello 1969; Grad Stud Univ of Cntrl AR; Cmptrs, AR St Univ Beebe; *cr:* 7th-12th Grade Math Teacher Cotton Plant HS 1969-71; 7th/8th Grade Math Teacher Mc Crory HS 1971-; *ai:* Jr Honor Society & Jr Class Spon; AR Cncl of Math Teachers 1975-89; Watson Meth Church Mem; *office:* Mc Crory HS P O Box 427 Mc Crory AR 72101

FERGUSON, JUDITH GORDON, Health Occupations Instructor; *b:* Croswell, MI; *m:* Dale E.; *c:* Kelly, Dennis; *ed:* Nursing, Port Huron Jr Coll 1965; (BAS) Nursing-Voc Cert, Siena Heights Coll 1987; (MA) Educl Admin, Cntrl MI Univ 1990; Leadership Dev Prgm, Ferris St Univ 1989; *cr:* Office/Registered Nurse D A Smallwood DO Clinic 1974-84; Placement Coord/Instr Sanilac Career Center 1984-; *ai:* Marketing & Recruitment Comm; HOE, MOEA 1984-; Peck Bd of Ed Secy 1990; Sanilac Cty Assn of Sch Bds Pres; *home:* 5740 Hamilton Rd Peck MI 48466

FERGUSON, MARIAN BROWN, Jr High History Teacher; *b:* Amarillo, TX; *w:* Lionel K. (dec); *c:* Michael, David, Ellen; *ed:* Maryville Coll; (AB) Elem Ed, Washington Univ 1957; *cr:* 5th-6th Grade Teacher Webster Groves Sch Dist 1957-65; Substitute Teacher Cmmty Unit Dist 308 1977-82; Jr HS His/Soc Stud Teacher/Dept Chm Our Lady of Good Counsel Sch 1982-; *ai:* Curr Dev Comm; NCEA 1982-; NEA, MO St Teachers Assn 1957-65; *home:* 28 Aldon Rd Montgomery IL 60538

FERGUSON, MAX EUGENE, 7th/8th Grade Soc Stud Teacher; *b:* Newton, KS; *m:* Gail Huschka; *c:* Danny, Alexandra; *ed:* (BA) Ed, Southwestern 1974; (MS) Mid Sch Ed, Wichita St Univ 1982; Trained to Teach Project STAR 1986; *cr:* Jr HS Teacher Medicine Lodge Intermediate Sch 1975-; *ai:* Ftbl, Bsktbl & Track Coach; Athletic Dir; Project Star Coord; NEA, KS Ed Assn 1975-; GHEA Pres 1984-85; KS Coaches Assn, United Meth Church, Cub Scouts Pack 224; Emporia St Univ KS Master Teacher of Yr 1989; *home:* 211 S Oak Medicine Lodge KS 67104

FERGUSON, PENNY BLACKWOOD, English Department Chair; *b:* Nashville, TN; *m:* Sam L.; *c:* Laurie, Julie; *ed:* (BA) Eng, Maryville Coll 1969; (MA) Eng, 1974, (EDS) Curr/Instruction, 1981, (EDD) Eng Ed, 1988 Univ of TN; Numerous Wkshps & Conferences; Governors Sch for Teachers of Writing 1986; *cr:* 7th Grade Eng Teacher John Sevier Elem 1969-70, 11th Grade Teacher Maryville HS 1970-; *ai:* NHS Faculty Advisory Bd; Beta Epsilon & Jr Class Spon; Maryville Scholars & Maryville HS Curr Comm Mem; Eng Dept Chm; Apple of Gold Ed; NCTE, TN Cncl Teachers of Eng; E TN Assn Teachers of Eng Treas 1987-, Eng Teacher of Yr 1985; Delta Kappa Gamma; Bijou Theatre Teacher Advisory Bd; Xi St Doctoral Stud Schlsp; Jaycees Blount Cty Outstanding Young Educator 1975; TN Hum Cncl Outstanding Teacher of Hum 1986; Univ of TN Outstanding Eng Ed Grad Stu 1988; *office:* Maryville HS 825 Lawrence Ave Maryville TN 37801

FERGUSON, TERRI SMITH, First Grade Teacher; *b:* Syracuse, NY; *m:* Harold E.; *c:* Matthew, Andrew; *ed:* (BS) Elem Ed, 1970, (MS) Ed, 1971 St Univ Coll Cortland; Instructional Theory into Practice; SAGE; *cr:* 6th Grade Teacher Westhill CSD 1971-72; 4th-6th Grade Teacher Homer CSD 1972-75, 1980-82; 1st/2nd/5th Grade Teacher Cincinnatus CSD 1982-; *ai:* Cincinnatus Curr & Stu Self-Esteem & Respect Comm; Developmental Ed Task Force; Seven Valley Rdng Cncl, NY St Rdng Assn; Truxton United Meth Church Admin Bd Chm 1987-.

FERGUSSON, DIANNE SMITH, English Teacher; *b:* Laurinburg, NC; *c:* Molly E.; *ed:* (BS) Eng, W Carolina Univ 1966; (MA) Eng, 1971, (PHD) Eng, 1974 Univ of SC; Post Doctoral Coursework; *cr:* Peace Corps Volunteer Burkina W Africa 1967-69; Research Analyst SC Dept of Youth Services 1974-76; Instr Newberry Coll & Midlands Tech Coll 1977-79; Dept Chairperson Midlands Tech Coll 1979-84; Eng/Advanced Placement/Coll Prep Teacher Irmo HS 1985-; *ai:* Sch Newspaper Publications Bd; Sch Literary Magazine Advisory Bd; Graduation Prgm Comm; In-Service Trng Presentations; Modern Lang Assn, NCTE, Prof Writing Consultants; Bus & Prof Womens Club Capital Club Pres 1985-86, Career Woman of Yr 1985; Amer Assn of Women in Cmmty & Jr Colls (St Coord 1983-84), 1980-84; Leadership Dev Acad 1983; Advanced Placement Reader, Eng Examinaton 1988-; Natl Endowment for Hum Summer Fellowship 1990; Book & Article Written; *office:* Irmo HS 6671 St Andrews Rd Columbia SC 29210

FERMON, BENJAMIN FRANKLIN, US/Arizona History; *b:* East Carson City, UT; *m:* Jeanne Marie Hoskins; *c:* Jeffrey A.; *ed:* (BA) Sociology, 1980, Teacher Cert, 1983 Southern UT St; Grad Stud, UT St Univ; *cr:* Phys Ed/Psych Modoc HS 1983-85; Phys Ed/Grad Asst Southern UT St 1985-86; Soc Stud Mohave HS 1986-; *ai:* Head Ftbl Coach 1987-; Head Wrestling Coach, Wrestling Club Adv; Bleacher Creatures Co-Adv; Pep Club; *home:* 971 Bahama Cove Riviera AZ 86442

FERN, TAMI LYNNE, Teacher of Gifted/Talented; *b:* Brooklyn, NY; *ed:* (BS) Soc Sci/Ed, Russell Sage Coll 1966; (MS) Elem Ed, Queens Coll 1970; (EDD) Spec Ed, Teachers Coll & Columbia Univ 1989; *cr:* Adjunct Professor Teachers Coll & Columbia Univ 1989; Teacher Franklin Square Schls 1966-; Adjunt Professor C W Post Coll 1989-; *ai:* Seagate Mem; NAGC, CEC 1988-; AGATE 1985-; Author Project Funny Bone; PTA Awds for Excl Teaching 1971, 1979, 1989; *office:* Franklin Square Schls Washington St Franklin Square NY 11010

FERNANDER, WILLIAM ROBERT, English Teacher; *b:* Sewanee, TN; *m:* Lynda Jean Kiningham; *ed:* (BA) Eng, Univ of South 1975; Additional Ed Courses, Mid TN St Univ, Trevecca Nazarene Coll, Motlow St Comm Coll; *cr:* Eng/Span Teacher Grundy Cty HS 1975-76; Title I Rdng Teacher South Jr HS/Clark Memorial 1976-77; Sales Rep 1977-81; Eng Teacher Franklin Cty HS 1981-; *ai:* Asst Ftbl, Strength & Conditioning Coach; NEA, TEA 1982-; TN Athletic Assn 1987-; Nom Franklin Cty HS Cty Teacher of Yr 1987; *office:* Franklin Cty HS 801 1st Ave Winchester TN 37398

FERNANDES, TERESA ANN, Mathematics Teacher; *b:* Middleboro, MA; *ed:* (BA) Math/Ed, Brown Univ 1985; *cr:* Teacher Brockton Chrstn Regional HS 1986-89, Carver HS 1989-; *ai:* Established Cmmty Ministry Outreach Prgm Brockton Chrstn HS; *home:* 30 N Main St Carver MA 02330

FERNANDEZ, NICHOLAS JOSEPH, HS Social Studies Teacher; *b:* New York City, NY; *m:* Lynn Frances Christian; *ed:* (BA) Labor Stud, Empire St SUNY 1983; (MA) Curr/Teaching, Columbia Univ 1986; MA Phys Ed/Scndry Ed/Soc Stud, Brooklyn Coll 1991; *cr:* Guidance/Teaching Sch Settlement Assn 1982-83; Phys Ed Teacher Borough Hall Acad 1983-84, Day Sch 1985-86, Allen Stevenson Sch 1984-85; Soc Stud/Phys Ed Teacher E Dist HS 1986-; *ai:* Sports Gym, His through Film Club Eastern Dist HS; PTA Mem 1989-; Minority Schlshp; Sports Articles Published in Newspaper; Help Hotline Sch Settlement Assn; *office:* Eastern Dist HS 850 Grand St Brooklyn NY 11211

FERNANDEZ, OTILIA JANES, Foreign Languages Dept Chair; *b:* Philadelphia, PA; *m:* Emilio; *c:* Otilia, Adelaida, Emilio; *ed:* (BS) Architecture, Univ of Havana Cuba 1959; (MED) Counseling, Univ of Cincinnati 1969; Licensed Optician, St of OH; *cr:* Math/Span Teacher 1964- Foreign Lang Dept Chairperson 1987- Woodward HS; *ai:* Span Club; SW OH Opticians Assn 1984-; Real Estate Investors Assn 1989-; North Cntrl Assn Team Evaluator Univ of Cincinnati Cooperating Teacher; *office:* Woodward HS 7001 Reading Rd Cincinnati OH 45237

FERNANDEZ, PRISCILLA PAIG, Sixth Grade Teacher; *b:* Albuquerque, NM; *m:* Peter; *c:* Michael F., Richard J. F., John F.; *ed:* (BA) Elem Ed, NM Highlands Univ 1975; (MA) Elem Ed, Univ of CO 1980; Ed Spec Educl Admin, Univ NM 1990; Instr for Rocky Mt Natl Cmptr Seminar, Newspapers in Ed Wkshp; Admin Intern Univ of NM; *cr:* Inst of Scientific Research NMHU 1973-75; Teacher Denver Public Schls 1975-83, Los Lunas Public Schls 1983-; *ai:* Soccer Coach; NEA 1983-; Phi Delta Kappa 1989-; Delta Kappa Gamma 1988-; 1st Christa Mc Auliffe Fellowship Awd Winner for NM; 1st Elem Distinguished Teacher of Yr; Sch Distinguished Alumni of NMHU-CONAC; Outstanding Hispanic Family Awd; *office:* Daniel Fernandez Intermediate PO Drawer 1300 Los Lunas NM 87031

FERNANDEZ, REBECCA BOND, Home Economics Teacher; *b:* Abbeville, SC; *m:* Robert Joe; *c:* Robert J. Jr., Jennifer K., Joshua S.; *ed:* (BS) Home Ec, Lander Coll 1976; *cr:* Home Ec Teacher Mc Cormick HS 1977-84, Abbeville HS 1985-; *ai:* FHA Club; Yrbk Adv; Technical Asst to St Dept of Ed Home Ec Division; Upper Savannah Health Dist CncL Pres 1987-88; Received 1st Ciritan Grant Awarded in SC to Fund Teenage Implementing Parenting Skills; SCHEA Bd Mem; *office:* Abbeville HS Old Hodges Rd PO Box 927 Abbeville SC 29620

FERNANDEZ, SHIRLY WAGNER, Sixth Grade PEP Teacher; *b:* Tacoma, WA; *c:* Ryan; *ed:* (AA) Ed, Eastfield Coll 1977; (BS) Elem Ed, 1978, (MED) Elem Ed, 1980 E TX St Univ; Curr/Instruction, Univ of S FL; *cr:* 2nd Grade Bi-ling Teacher James Bonham Elem 1978-81; 6th Grade Teacher Wimauma Sch 1982-;

ai: Teach & Coordinate Adult Basic Ed Prgm Beth-El Presbyn Mission 1989-; Peer Facilitator Wimauma Sch 1986-; AFT 1989-; Wimauma PTA Treas 1986-87; Article & Poetry Published; *office:* Wimauma Sch 5709 Hickman Wimauma FL 33598

FERNANDEZ-DUNN, PAULA KATHRYN, Spanish Teacher; *b:* Washington, DC; *m:* Paul Winston Sr.; *c:* Kristina, Paul Jr.; *ed:* (BA) Span - Cum Laude, Georgetown Coll 1974; Masters Equivalency Ed, Xavier Univ 1980; Univ of Madrid Spain 1972; Foreign Lang & Classroom Teachers Wkshps; *cr:* Span Teacher Beavercreek Local Schls 1974-75, Northwest Local Schls 1975-; *ai:* Span Honorary Society; Span Club; PTA Elem Sch Span for Fun Prgms; Foreign Lang Dept Chm; Textbook Adoption & Curr for Foreign Lang, Schlsp Comms; OH Foreign Lang Assn 1974-; Amer Assn Teachers of Span & Portuguese 1989-; GSA Asst Brownie Leader 1987-89; Southern Baptist Church (Sunday Sch Teacher, Youth Dir) 1974-; Natl Hispanic Honorary Society Sigma Delta Pi; *office:* Colerain Sr HS 8801 Cheviot Rd Cincinnati OH 45251

FEROLITO, JOSEPH ANTHONY, Math Teacher/Advisor/Tutor; *b:* Cambridge, MA; *ed:* (BS) Ed/Math/Soc Sci, Boston Coll 1963; (MSW) Boston Univ/Harvard 1974; Stanley Kaplan Sat Prep Instruction; Several Seminars; Coll Adv; Far Eastern Stud Inst of E Traditional Philosophy; Lang, Harvard Univ; *cr:* Teacher/Cnslr Matignon HS 1963-70; Teacher Somerville HS 1970-74; Cnslr Cambridge Youth Resource Bureau 1974-76; Teacher/Adv Cambridge Rindge & Latin Sch 1976-; *ai:* Chinese Culture Club; Coll Planning Adv; Tutor; Recreation Youth Volunteer; Coord Gropp Cnslr; Self-Esteem & Bible Study Wrksp Leader; Garden Club Leader; Teacher Adv; NEA, MA Teachers Assn, Cambridge Teachers Assn 1963-; Maryknoll Mission 1989-; Poulist Cmmty Center; Fulbright Scholar; *home:* 74 Cushing St Cambridge MA 02138

FERRAGANO, DOLORES M., Principal Intern; *b:* New York City, NY; *ed:* (BSED) Elem Ed, Wagner Coll 1969; (MSED) Elem Ed, Richmond Coll 1971; Masters Candidate Admin & Supervision, Bank Street Coll; Selected to Participate in Prins Inst, Bank Street NYC; *cr:* 5th Grade Teacher Public Sch 55 1969-75; 4th/5th Grade/Comm Arts Teacher Public Sch 36 1975-; Prin Intern Public Sch 38 1990; *ai:* Phi Delta Kappa Mem 1989; Staten Island Rdng Assn Mem 1969-; ASCD, United Fed of Teachers; Metropolitan Museum of Art; Museum of Modern Art; Impact II Developer Grant 1985; Teacher of Yr Phi Delta Kappa 1989.

FERRANDO, ANGELA AMANTEA, Assistant Principal; *b:* New York City, NY; *m:* James T.; *c:* Linda, Thomas; *ed:* (BA) Chem, St Josephs Coll 1960; (MS) Admin/Supervision/Scndry Ed, St Johns Univ 1981; *cr:* Chem Teacher Bay Ridge HS 1960-61; Per-Diem Public Sch 23 1966-67; Per-Diem Markham Jr HS 1967-69; Chem Teacher/Asst Prin/Academic Dean St Joseph by the Sea 1970-; *ai:* Jr Class Moderator; Racquetball Coach & Moderator; Fed of Cath Teachers 1972-; Catholic Teachers Assn, NSTA 1970-; NASSP 1989-; Woodrow Civic Assn 1976-; *office:* St Joseph by the Sea HS 5150 Hylan Blvd Staten Island NY 10312

FERRARI, PATRICIA ANN, Asst Principal/Bus Teacher; *b:* Herrin, IL; *ed:* (BS) Bus Ed, 1968, (MS) Bus Ed, 1971 S IL Univ; Cert Educl Leadership Scndry Sch Prin; S IL Univ Carbondale 1984; *cr:* Bus Teacher 1968-, Asst Prin Duquoin HS 1986-; *ai:* Vlybl, Sftbl, Bsktbl, Track Coach; Stu Cncl, Newspaper, Class Spon 1971-76; North Cntrl Comm & Bus Dept Chairperson; Delta Pi Epsilon 1971-; Southern Bus Ed Assn, IL Bus Ed Assn 1968-; DuQuoin Ed Assn (Past Pres, Regional Chairperson); NEA Mem; IL Ed Assn (St Delegate 1979-85, Exec Comm); Booster Club; Khoury League (Coach, Umpire); Perry Cty Counseling Center; IL Master Teacher 1984; St Bd of Ed Comm Mem Consumer Ed 1985; IEA Wkshp Trainer for Personal Skills 1984-86; *office:* Duquoin HS 500 East South St Du Quoin IL 62832

FERRARO, ANTHONY JOHN, JR., Sixth Grade Teacher; *b:* Sioux City, IA; *ed:* (MS) Admin/Supervision Univ of Dayton 1986; *cr:* Teacher Rushmore 1981-82, Shenandoah 1982-87, Weisenborn 1987-; *ai:* HS Var Bsbl & Bsktbl; Staff Dev Comm; Gifted Coord & SOAR Gifted Adv ; Conditioning Coord; NEA, OH Ed Assn 1981-; Miami Valley Coaches Assn 1989-; *office:* Weisenborn Intermediate Sch 6061 Old Troy Pike Huber Heights OH 45424

FERRARO, JOAN HOARLE, Third Grade Teacher; *b:* Jersey City, NJ; *m:* George; *c:* Georgina Ferraro Roy, Frederick V., Maria Ferraro Medlina, Corinna A.; *ed:* (BA) Ed, Amer Intnl Coll 1975; (MA) Ed/Rdng, Worcester St Coll 1980; (AA) Bay Path Jr Coll; *cr:* Actuarial Asst MA Mutual Insurance Company 1960-63; Chapter I Rdng Teacher Sch Union 61 1975-80; 3rd Grade Teacher Wales Elem 1980-; *ai:* Grantwriter Wales Elem; MA Teachers Assn 1985-; Sch Union 61 Teachers Assn Pres 1985-; Wales Arts Cncl 1989-; Wales Lib Trustee 1971-79; *home:* 126 Union Rd Wales MA 01081

FERRARO, LORRAINE, 6th Grade Teacher; *b:* Brooklyn, NY; *m:* Robert Nathan; *c:* Lauren; *ed:* Assoc Advertising Art/Design, Farmingdale St Coll 1970; (BS) Elem Ed, Oneonta St Coll 1972; (MA) Elem Ed/Art Ed, Adelphi Univ 1976; Advertising Art; *cr:* Artist New York NY 1973-76; Teacher Clara Carlson Sch 1977-81, Gotham Avenue Sch 1981-; *office:* Gotham Avenue Sch Gotham Ave Elmont NY 11003

FERREL, SHERRI BARFIELD, Science Teacher; *b:* Bernice, LA; *m:* Gregory Ray; *c:* Casey L., Olivia M., Ashley B.; *ed:* (BS) Geology, LA Tech Univ 1985; Completed Requirements LA Cert; Will Complete MS Sci Ed, May 1991; *cr:* Sci Teacher Simsboro HS 1986-; *ai:* Sci Club; NHS Selection Comm; APEL 1987-89; *office:* Simsboro HS P O Box 118 Simsboro LA 71275

FERRELL, ALICE LAVON (THOMAS), Teacher; *b:* Pickens, SC; *m:* William Edward; *c:* Tiffany, Kinja, Amber; *ed:* (BA) His, Winthrop Coll 1975; (MA) His, Furman Univ 1984; Pursuing Math Cert, Cmptr Information Systems Degree; *cr:* Teacher Better Skills Incorporated 1975-77, Bryson Mid Sch 1978-89, Woodmont Mid Sch 1989-; *ai:* Cmptr Team Spon & Coach; Cmptr Club Spon; NEA, SCEA, GCEA 1978-; Teen Leadership Connection Advisory Bd 1989-; Winthrop Coll Black Alumni Assn Greenville-Spartanburg Chapter VP 1988-; Bryson Mid Sch Teacher of Yr 1980-81; Outstanding Young Woman of America 1983; *home:* 13 Hull Dr Greenville SC 29605

FERRELL, JANICE RENE, Director of Choral Music; *b:* Fort Worth, TX; *c:* Shannon Michelle; *ed:* (BFA) Music, 1979, (MA) Music 1981 Univ of TX; Silverlake Coll/Memphis St Univ; *cr:* Music Teacher Pete & Bell Elem Sch 1979-81; Choral Dir Jacksonville Mid Sch 1981-87, Athens HS 1987-; New England Music Camp 1989-; *ai:* TX Music Ed Assn; TX Music Adjudicators Assn/Adjudicator; TX Conference Choir Clinic Bd Dir 1987-; Amer Choral Dir Assn TX Choral Dir Assn/Organization of Amer Kodaly Educators; Kodaly Edudcators of TX; Intntl Kodaly Society; East TX Amer Guild of Organists Dean 1981-; Palestine Civic Theatre Bd Adjudicators 1987-89; Six Flags Over TX Invitational Choral Festival; 4 Times Best in Class & Judges Discretionary Awd; Choral Numerous Univ Interscholastic League Sweepstakes & Division 1st; Univ of TX Watson W Wise Awd; James H Stewart Presidential Schlrshp; Alpha Chi Honor Society-Pres; *office:* Athens H S 708 E College Athens TX 75751

FERRELL, JEANNE MARIE ANDRIANO, 7th Grade Reading Teacher; *b:* Steubenville, OH; *m:* Michael L.; *c:* Matthew, Ryan, Johanna; *ed:* (BA) Elem Ed/Lang Arts, West Liberty St Coll 1970; (MA) Elem Ed/Lang Arts, WV Univ 1976; Grad Courses, WV Univ; *cr:* 1st Grade Teacher Edgewood Sch 1970-71, Hooverson Heights Primary 1971-75; 3rd Grade Teacher Franklin Primary 1978-84; 7th Grade Rdng Teacher Wellsburg Mid Sch 1984-; *ai:* Personnel & Wellsburg Mid Rdng Book Adoption Comm; WV Ed Assn; PTA; Brooke Cty Ed Assn; Brooke Cty Teachers Acad 1986; WV Ed Fund Grant; *home:* 495 Lee Rd Follansbee WV 26037

FERRELL, PAMELA, 5th Grade Teacher; *b:* Charleston, MO; *ed:* (BS) Elem Ed, SE MO St Univ 1980; NY Sch of Interior Design 1975; *cr:* Teacher of Gifted & Talented 1986-89, 5th Grade Teacher 1980- Warren E Hearns Elem; *ai:* MO St Teachers Assn Dist Nom Chairperson 1980-; MSTA (Dist Nom Chairperson 1987-, Convention Delegate 1985-88); Gifted Assn of MO; Charleston Cmmty Teachers Assn (Pres 1986, VP 1985, Nom Comm 1985, 1990, Salary Welfare Comm 1990) 1980-, Outstanding Mem 1986; Charleston Parent Teacher Assn; 1st Baptist Church; Jr Study Club (Pres 1985) 1970-; Outstanding Young Women America Awd 1986; Mississippi Cty Heart Assn Co-Chairperson; Cancer Fund Volunteer;Mississippi Cty Historical Society Mem; MO Fed Womens Club; *office:* Warren E Hearnes Elem Sch Plant Rd Charleston MO 63834

FERRIS, JEAN MACE, Kindergarten Teacher; *b:* Savanna, IL; *m:* John W.; *c:* Kathryn Ferris Crawford; *ed:* (BSE) Kndgtn/Primary, W IL Univ Macomb 1955; Grad Work at N IL Univ De Kalb, Natl Coll of Ed Evanston, St Coll of IA Cedar Falls; *cr:* 1st Grade Teacher Bushell-Prairie City Schls 1955-57, St Clair Shores Elem 1957-58, Savanna City Schls #71 1958-59, Thomson Consolidated Grade Sch 1960-67, Kndgtn Teacher Savanna Cmmty Unit Dist 300 1967-; *ai:* Spon 5 Young Astronauts Chapters; NEA; Delta Kappa Gamma Various Comm 1968-; NAEYC 1987-89; PEO Pres 1987-89; Savanna Service Club Pres 1979-80; Savanna Township Lib Trustee 1989-; Savanna Train Project Secy 1987-; Little Red Caboose Day Care Pres 1986; Those Who Excel Honorary Mention Awd IL St Bd of Ed 1983; Savanna Chamber of Commerce Awd for Service to Cmmty 1976; Distinguished Alumni Awd Savanna Cmmty Unit Dist 1989; Master Teacher Awd; Governors Awd 1984; *home:* 1602 E Lawn Dr Savanna IL 61074

FERRIS, LORRAINE CATHERINE, English Teacher; *b:* Queens, NY; *ed:* (BA) His, Ladycliff Coll; (MA) Modern European His, Cath Univ 1970; Several Wkshps in Management, Childcare, Teacher Trng; *cr:* 1st-6th/8th Grade Elem Teacher St James Sch 1957-64; 8th Grade Elem Teacher St Matthews Sch 1964-66; Asst Admin Lt Joseph P Kennedy Jr Home 1967-70; Jr HS Teacher St Anthony Sch 1970-; *ai:* 8th Grade Homeroom Teacher; Unofficial Mentor Jr HS & Alumni; Eng Dept Head; Faculty Retreat Coord; Parish Advisory Sch Bd; Steering Comm Sch Accreditation; Competitive Grant Prgm Adv; St Anthonys Teen Club Adv 1980-84; Yrbk & Play Comm 1981-85; *office:* St Anthony Sch 12th & Lawrence St NE Washington DC 20017

FERRIS, RACHEL DE MARIO, Teacher of English Composition; *b:* Welch, WV; *m:* Sam Bird; *c:* Cathy, Diane De Mario Spresser; *ed:* (BS) Soc Stud/Eng, Concord Coll 1946; Univ of KY; Advanced Placement, Concord Coll; Univ of London/Paris/Rome; *cr:* Soc Stud Teacher Gary HS 1947-49; Eng Teacher Trap Hill HS 1969-72, Liberty HS 1982-; *ai:* 11th Grade Class Spon; Creative Arts Festival Liberty HS; Raleigh Cty Comm Curr Dev; WV Ed Assn Mem 1969-; Assn of Supvrs of Curr Dev Mem 1990; Beckly Womens Club (Co-Chm Ed Dept 1987-89, Co-Chm MS Teen Pageant 1986); Raleigh Cty 20 Yrs Teaching Awd; Spon Foreign Exchange Stu; Organizer /Tour Leader of Stu Groups Abroad; *home:* 115 Pine St Beckley WV 25801

FERRITO, ORESTA MARY, Science Teacher; *b:* Paterson, NJ; *ed:* (BS) Scndry Ed/Sci, Seton Hall Univ 1979; Master of Ed Prgm, Montclair St Coll; *cr:* Sci Dept Head Mary Help of Chrstns Acad 1979-89; Sci Teacher Don Bosco Coll 1983-85, De Paul HS 1989-; *ai:* Public Speaking & Debate Coach; NJ Sci League Scndry Bio Team Adv; NJESTA 1986-; NASSP 1983-89; ASCD 1989-; Paterson Diocese Forensic League Dir.

FERRITTO, DORA TURANO, Second Grade Teacher; *b:* Ashtabula, OH; *m:* Thomas B.; *c:* Sharon, Cynthia Wynn, Doreen; *ed:* (BA) Elem Ed, Lake Erie Coll 1965; (MS) Elem Ed, Youngstown St Univ 1985; Numerous Colleges; *cr:* 1st Grade Teacher Kingsville Sch 1965-70; 2nd Grade Teacher Lincoln Sch 1970-81; 3rd Grade Teacher 1981-84, 2nd Grade Teacher 1984, 1989- Ridgeview Sch; *ai:* Public Relations, Right-To-Read, Curr, Conservation, Sci Comm; Rep to Assertive Discipline Seminar; Volunteer March of Dimes, Cancer, Heart Comm; NEA, OH Ed Assn, Northeastern OH Teachers Assn, Buckeye Ed Assn 1965-;Intnl Rdng Assn 1984-; Happy Hearts Sch Bd, OH Schls Bd Mem 1977-83; GSA Leader Brownie Troop 1960-63; Lincoln Sch PTO Secy 1972-73; Ashtabula Womens Club Secy 1986-88; Elks Ladies Assn; St Josephs Church CCD Teacher 1972-73; *home:* 6105 Phillips Dr Ashtabula OH 44004

FERTIG, RALPH A., III, Fourth Grade Teacher; *b:* Pottsville, PA; *m:* Nancy Mc Millen; *c:* Alan L., Betsy Louise Laury; *ed:* (BS) Health/Phys Ed, E Stroudsburg St Coll 1961; (MED) Ed, Lehigh Univ 1964; PA St Univ; *cr:* 6th Grade Teacher Lehigh Elem Sch 1961-63; Phys Ed Teacher Dist Wide Elem 1963-65; 6th Grade Teacher Washington Elem Sch 1965-77; Elem Prin Northampton Boro Schls 1977-81; 4th Grade Teacher Franklin Elem Sch 1981-; *ai:* Astt Var Track Coach; Wellness Comm; Staff Dev Comm; Act 178 Comm; NEA Life Mem; PA St Ed Assn 1961-; PA Assn Supervision & Curr Dev 1975-82; Northampton Area United Way Bd Dir 1990; Lehigh Valley Pops Singers Founder & Dir 1978-; Lions Club 1964-69; *office:* Northampton Area Sch Dist 1617 Laubach Ave Northampton PA 18067

FERTIG, SYLVIA KORTE, Second Grade Teacher; *b:* Highland, IL; *c:* Brian D., Gary A.; *ed:* (BA) Phys Ed/Eng, 1963, (BA) ELem Ed, 1976 Mc Kendree Coll; *cr:* Eng/Phys Ed Teacher Triad HS 1963-68; Elem Phys Ed/Jr HS Eng/2nd Grade Teacher 1976- Lebanon Grade Sch; *ai:* Delta Kappa Gamma 1988-; Lebanon Womans Club 1974-77; Outstanding Young Women of America Awd 1974; *home:* 421 Clover Dr Lebanon IL 62254

FESMIRE, JOYCE NELL (HAYS), Fourth Grade Teacher; *b:* San Antonio, TX; *m:* William David; *c:* Harlan, Barry; *ed:* (BA) Elem, Lambuth Coll 1975; (MS) Curr/Instruction, Memphis St 1983; *cr:* 4th Grade Teacher Westover Elem 1975-; *ai:* Phi Theta Kappa 1973-74; Omicron Phi Tau 1974-75; Delta Kappa Gamma 1982-.

FESSLER, EDWARD JOHN, Social Studies Teacher; *b:* Cheyenne, WY; *m:* Cathy Warren; *c:* Mary Ann; *ed:* (BA) Amer Problems, Univ of WY 1977; (MA) Ed, Lesley Coll 1990; TESA Qualified Instr; *cr:* Houseparent/Cnslr Cathedral Home for Children 1977-78; Teacher Sheridan HS 1978-; *ai:* Class of 1992 Co-Spon; Sheridan HS Attendance Comm 1989-; *office:* Sheridan HS 1056 Long Dr Sheridan WY 82801

FETCHKO, JOHN D., Physics Teacher; *b:* Windber, PA; *:* Shirley Molnar; *ed:* (BS) Physics, Carnegie Mellon Univ 1970; (MED) Physics, Indiana Univ of PA 1975; *cr:* Physics/Math/Cmptr Literacy Teacher Greater Johnstown Area Voc-Tech Sch 1970-; *ai:* Greater Johnstown Voc-Tech Ed Assn, PA St Teachers Assn, NEA 1971-; St Grant for Establishment of Voc-Tech Sch Cmptr Laboratory; Article Published.

FETNER, SANDRA MERRILL, Sixth Grade Teacher; *b:* Birmingham, AL; *m:* James Emory; *c:* Reagan, Lee; *ed:* (BA) Elem Ed, 1974, (MA) Elem Ed, 1977 Univ of AL Birmingham; *cr:* Teacher Chalkville Elem Sch 1975-; *ai:* Chm Self Study Accreditation & 5 Yr Interim Study Comm; Annual Staff Spon; Sch & Cty Instructional Improvement Comm; AL Ed Assn Faculty Rep 1975-78; Charity League 1989; Republican Party 1970-85; Nom Exemplary Teacher 1987; *home:* 6664 Ransom Rd Birmingham AL 35210

FETTER, SANDRA JUNE (KELBLE), Teacher & Coach; *b:* Bryan, OH; *m:* Michael B.; *c:* Robert, Raymond; *ed:* (BS) Math, Defiance Coll 1968; (MED) Phys Ed/Health, OH Univ 1970; Springfield Coll, Sul Ross St Univ, San Antonio Coll, Kilgore Coll; *cr:* Teacher/Coach Fort Stockton Ind Sch Dist 1969-70, Fort Davis Ind Sch Dist 1970-73; Teacher Schertz-Cibilo-Universal City Ind Sch Dist 1974-77, Fort Stockton Ind Sch Dist 1977-78, Happy Ind Sch Dist 1978-79, Union Grove Ind Sch Dist 1980-81, 1985-86; *ai:* Bsktbl/Vlybl Coach; UIL, Number Sense, Slide Rule; Cmmty Bsbl & Bsktbl Coach; TSTA, NEA (Campus Spokesman 1977-78) 1969-86; OEA 1967-68; Beta Sigma Phi (Secy, Treas, VP), Girl of Yr 1973, Ms Congenialty 1982-83; United Meth Church (Mem, Youth Spon, Vaction Bible Sch Teacher, Choir, Sunday Sch Teacher); Beta Sigma Phi; Jeff Davis Cty (Bd of Dir, Bd Mem); *home:* PO Box 59 White Oak TX 75693

FETTERMAN, JOYCE CARNEY, Sixth Grade Teacher; *b:* Colver, PA; *m:* James; *c:* Heather; *ed:* (BA) Elem Ed, 1979, (MS) Elem Math, 1983 Indiana Univ of PA; *cr:* 2nd Grade Teacher Blacklick Valley Sch Dist 1979-80; Remedial Math/Cmptr Teacher 1980-85, 6th Grade Teacher 1985- Penns Manor Area Sch Dist; *ai:* Phi Delta Kappa; *home:* RD 2 Box 166 Clymer PA 15728

FETTERS, CLAUDIA M., Earth Science Teacher; *b:* York, PA; *ed:* (BS) Scndry Ed, Clarion St Univ 1975; Grad Courses in Bio, Chem, Physics, Geology, Astronomy, Cmptr Sci & Ed; *cr:* Sci Chairperson Immaculate Conception Acad 1980-82; Earth Sci Teacher Hayfield Scndry Sch 1982-; *ai:* Astronomy Club Spon;

NSTA; Natl Earth Sci Teachers Assn; *office:* Hayfield Secondary Sch 7630 Telegraph Rd Alexandria VA 22192

FETTIG, ALFRED, Sixth Grade Teacher; *b:* Orrin, ND; *m:* Margaret B.; *c:* Mike, Kristi; *ed:* (BA) Commerce, Dickinson St Univ 1964; 5th Yr Univ of WA 1970; (MA) Seattle Univ 1973; *cr:* Teacher Goodrich ND 1964-66, Alpac Elem 1967-; *ai:* HS Ftbl & Jr HS Bsktbl Coach; Auburn Ed Assn Poly Action 1975-76; Lions Club 1964-66; Elks 1970-85; Knight of Columbus Grand Knight 1987-88, Family of Yr 1988; *home:* 25705 127th SE Kent WA 98031

FETZER, CATHIE MARIE (ROUSE), 6th Grade Teacher; *b:* Newport, OR; *m:* Jay Dean; *c:* Curtis; *ed:* (BA) Elem Ed, OR Coll of Ed 1980; *cr:* 4th/5th Split/5th Grade Teacher Victor Point Elem; ESD Aide-Primary Learning Center Tillamook Cty ESD; 6th Grade Teacher East Elem; *ai:* Eng Lang Art, Onward to Excl Comms; *home:* 606 Cottonwood Tillamook OR 97141

FETZER, KAREN NELSON, Mathematics Teacher; *b:* Akron, OH; *m:* Peter A.; *ed:* (BS) Math, Kent St Univ 1964; Cmptr Programming Classes & Accounting; *cr:* Teacher Stow City Schls 1964-68, Rootstown Local Schls 1968-; *ai:* Math Team Coach; OSAT; RTA Treas 1986-89; *office:* Rootstown Mid Sch 4140 St Rt 44 Rootstown OH 44272

FEUERBACH, TONA BAILEY, Music Teacher; *b:* Burlington, IA; *m:* Keith; *c:* Nathan Fredricksen, Timothy Fredricksen, Kimbery; *ed:* (BS) Phys Ed, 1970, Elem Ed, 1987 Dana Coll; Grad Stud; *cr:* Kndgtn Teacher 1980-86, Kndgtn/Phys Ed Teacher 1985-89, K/1st/2nd Grade/1st-8th Grade Music/K-3rd/6th-8th Grade Phys Ed Teacher 1986-89, K-8th Grade Music Teacher 1989- Zion Luth Sch; *ai:* Athletic Dir; Girls Vlybl, Co-ed Track, Sftbl Coach; Spring Prgm & Youth Choir Dir; Luth Ed Assn 1985-; Pool Bd (Mem, Secy) 1983-85; Church Choir Mem; Luth Womens Missionary League (Prgm Chm 1985-86) 1980-; *office:* Zion Luth Sch 117 E Prairie Wilton IA 52778

FEUERBACHER, JOHN WILLIAM, Science/Computer Sci Teacher; *b:* New York, NY; *m:* Mary Kyle; *c:* John E., Glen Kyle, Kristen Kyle; *ed:* (AS) Bus/Public Relations, Cleveland St 1976; (BS) Ed, Mid TN St Univ 1981; Casio Cmptr Repair Sch; *cr:* Sci/Cmptr Teacher Waldron Jr HS 1983-; *ai:* 3rd-8th Grade Cmptr Enrichment; Certified Scuba Diver; NEA 1983-; Rutherford Ed Assn Public Relations 1990; Geophysics Grant; Lynhurst Fnd Awd; Published & Copyrighted Cmptr Prgm; Co-Author of Phys Sci Booklet; Governors Awd for Excl in Working with Handicapped; *home:* 3028 Thompson Ln Murfreesboro TN 37129

FEURER, ROBERT E., Science Teacher/Dept Chair; *b:* Humboldt, NE; *m:* Julie Ann Horn; *c:* Erin, Cade; *ed:* (BS) Ed/Bio/Phys Sci, 1978, (MS) Ed/Bio, 1986 Kearney St Coll; *cr:* Sci Teacher North Bend Cntrl Jr/Sr HS 1979-; *ai:* Asst Boys & Girls Track; Sci Club & Future Teachers of America Spon; NEA, NE St Ed Assn, North Bend Cntrl Ed Assn (Local Pres, Treas) 1979-; NSTA; NE Scholastic Wrestling Coaches Assn Pres 1988-89; NE Coaches Assn 1979-; North Bend Optimst (Pres 1984) 1984-; Black Masque Chapter Mortar Bd Univ of NE Lincoln Distinguished Teachers Awd 1990; *office:* North Bend Cntrl Jr/Sr HS 13th & Pine North Bend NE 68649

FEWELL, BECKY J., Mathematics Department Chair; *b:* Pampa, TX; *m:* Randy; *c:* Cassie, Stephen; *ed:* (BS) Math Ed/HPE Ed, 1978 W TX St Univ; Cmptr Sci; *cr:* Math Teacher Dalhart HS 1978-86, Olton HS 1986-; *ai:* UIL Number Sense; Soph Class Spon; Fellowship of Chrstn Athletes Spon 1978-; Presidential Awds Excl in Sci & Math; Whos Who Among Young Women; *office:* Olton HS PO Box 667 Olton TX 79064

FEY, PHYLLIS LAMP, Retired First Grade Teacher; *b:* Clinton, IA; *m:* William H.; *c:* William C.; *ed:* (BA) Elem Ed, Marycrest Coll 1981; *cr:* Rural Teacher Washington Township Schls 1943-48; 1st Grade Teacher Northeast Cmmty Schls 1969-89.

FEY, ROSE M., Art Teacher; *b:* Grand Junction, CO; *ed:* (BA) Art, E KY Univ 1968; (MA) Guidance Counseling, Xavier Univ 1970; CO St Univ, Univ of Cincinnati; *cr:* Art Teacher Goshen Public Schls 1968-70, Norwood City Schls 1970-; *ai:* OEA, OAEA, NEA.

FIALKOVICH, STEPHEN GERARD, Religion Teacher; *b:* Allegheny Cty, PA; *m:* Helen Elizabeth Davis; *c:* Megan C.; *ed:* (BA) Philosophy/Religious Stud/His, La Roche Coll 1976; Diocesan Accreditation; Grad Stud Theology, Duquesne Univ; *cr:* Teacher North Cath HS 1976-; *ai:* North Cath HS Spon; Chrstn Life Cmmty Adv 1976-81; Var Girls Sftbl Head Coach 1977-80, 1989-; Pro Life 1988-; Fed of Pittsburgh Diocesan Teachers 1979-; NCEA 1976-; Amer Red Cross 1978-, Outstanding Sch Awds 1978-82, 1988, Outstanding Spon 1984, 1989; Cntrl Blood Bank 1973-; *home:* 7346 Denniston Ave Pittsburgh PA 15218

FIANDT, JANET LOUISE, 3rd Grade Teacher; *b:* Goshen, IN; *m:* Arick Joel; *c:* Beth A. Bowers; *ed:* (BA) Elem Ed, Goshen Coll 1969; (MS) Elem Ed, IN Univ 1972; *cr:* 1st Grade Teacher Model Elem Sch 1969-79; 1st Grade Teacher 1979-88, 3rd Grade Teacher 1988- Chamberlain Elem Sch; *ai:* Chamberlain Sch 5th Grade Girls Club Co-Spon; Goshen Ed Assn, IN St Teachers Assn, NEA 1969-; Intnl Rdng Assn 1972-; Support Our Kids 1989-.

FIANO, PILAR MARIA, Reading/Lang Arts Teacher; *b:* La Coruna, Spain; *ed:* (BA) Elem Ed, Kean Coll 1972; *cr:* Bi-ling Teacher George Washington Sch 1 1972-78; Rdng/Lang Art Teacher William F Halloran Sch 22 1978-; *ai:* Public Relations, EEA Budget, Inservice Wkshp Comm; Elizabeth Ed Assn Exec Comm 1975-; UCEA, NJEA, NEA; Alpha Delta Kappa 1980-; Recipient Various Yrs Local Dist Project Teach Grants; Recipient Governors Teacher Recognition Awd 1989-; *office:* William F Halloran Sch 22 447 Richmond St Elizabeth NJ 07202

FICEK, ERNEST JOSEPH, Phys Education/Health Teacher; *b:* Dickinson, ND; *m:* Vivian C. Hunke; *c:* Christine, Scott; *ed:* (BS) Phys Ed/Psych/Geography, Dickinson St Univ 1965; *cr:* Bio/Geography/Psych Teacher Belfield HS 1967-68; Psych/Life Sci/GeogrAphy Teacher Stanley HS 1968-76; Phys Ed/Health Teacher Hagen Jr HS 1976-; *ai:* Coached HS Track/Bsktbl/Ftbl Belfield HS; HS Track/Jr HS Bsktbl & HS Cross Cntry Stanley HS; Jr HS/Track and Ftbl Hagen Jr HS; NEA; NDEA; DEA; Elks Club; Team Hall of Fame Coll Track Performance.

FICK, BEVERLY J., Language Arts/Reading Teacher; *b:* Three Rivers, MI; *ed:* (BM) Music, W MI Univ 1964; (MA) Rdng Scndry, Cntrl MI Univ 1985; *cr:* Band Dir Otsego Public Schls 1964-65; Band Dir 1965-76, MS Lang Art/Rdng Teacher 1976- Hesperia Cmmty Schls; *ai:* 7th Grade Class Spon; Cmptr, Profession Dev Comms; MI Rdng Assn, Intnl Rdng Assn; Lakeshore Rdng Cncl Pres 1984-85, Honor Cncl 1985; White River Dog Trng (Secy, Treas) 1989-; Elected Teacher of Yr Local System 1986; 25 Yrs of Service 1990.

FICKAU, BARBARA J., 1st Grade Teacher; *b:* Berlin, WI; *ed:* (BS) Elem Ed, UW Stevens Point 1972; Addl Studies Elem Ed Univ of WI Milw; Cardinal Stritch Coll of Milw; Univ of WI Whitewater; *cr:* 2nd/3rd Grade Teacher Prospect Hill Elem Sch 1972-78; 3rd Grade Teacher New Berlin Ctr Elem Sch 1978-79; Orchard Lane Elem Sch 1979-86; 1st Grade Teacher Glen Park Elem Sch 1986-; *ai:* New Berlin Ed Assn Bldg Rep 1974-; WI Ed Assn 1974-; NEA 1974-; WMVS Auction Art Go-Getter/Info Clerk 1976-; Wandering Foot Quilters VP/Secy 1980-; WI Quilters Inc Corresp Secy 1981-; *office:* New Berlin Public Schls 4333 S Sunny Slope Rd New Berlin WI 53151

FICKEN, CONNIE R., English Teacher; *b:* Evanston, IL; *m:* Mark A.; *c:* Ashley, Troy, Brittany; *ed:* (BSED) Eng, Cntrl MO St Univ 1986; Post-Grad Cert Classes in Speech, Drama & Journalism, NWMSU Maryville; *cr:* Eng Teacher King City HS 1988-; *ai:* Journalism Teacher; Yrbk, Newspaper, Stu Cncl Adv; MSTA, NCTE 1988-; CTA (VP, Pres) 1989-; Beta Sigma Phi (Recorder, Historian) 1989-; GSA Leader 1988-89; Prince of Peach Luth Church; *office:* King City HS 300 Grand St King City MO 64463

FICKEN, THERESA LOUISE, Coord of Gifted & Talented; *b:* Laurens, IA; *m:* Randall Ray; *ed:* (BS) Elem Ed, Mankato St Univ 1974; Hofstra Univ, Drake Univ; *cr:* K-6th Grade Coord of Gifted & Talented Nevada Cmmty Schls 1975-; *ai:* Nevada Cmmty Schls Invent IA Spon; Thinking Skills Network; Mentor Prgm; IA Talented & Gifted Assn 1976-; North Cntrl Region Aerospace Ed Assn 1989-; IA Acad of Sci/IA Sci Teachers Section 1988-90; Beta Tau Delta 1989-; Talented & Gifted Instructional Materials Review 1980; Talented & Gifted Curr Guide for NV Schls; *office:* Nevada Cmmty Schls 9th & I Ave Nevada IA 50201

FICKES, KAY NESS, Second Grade Teacher; *b:* Dallastown, PA; *m:* Ralph S.; *c:* Dane S.; *ed:* (BA) Elem, Millersville St 1954; Numerous Ed Courses; *cr:* 1st Grade Teacher Jacob J Devers 1954-57; 2nd-3rd Grade Teacher Jackson Elem 1958-; *ai:* YCEA, PSEA, NEA; PTA 1954-, Life Mem 1987; *office:* Jackson Elem Sch 177 E Jackson St York PA 17403

FIDLER, DANIEL ROSS, 7th/8th Grade Teacher; *b:* Detroit, MI; *m:* Nidya Norma Flores; *c:* Benjamin, Carey, Charlie; *ed:* (BA) His/Art, CA St Polytechnical Univ 1972; *cr:* Teacher Lathrop Sch 1972-74, French Camp Sch 1974-; *ai:* Dist Math Comm; Academic Team, Vlybl, Math Team Coach; Mentor Teacher; NEA, Mantela Educators Assn, CA Teachers Assn 1972-; CA Teachers Instructional Improvement Prgm, AB 803 Grants; Mantela Unified Teacher of Yr 1987-88; Mantela Coach of Yr 1980; *home:* 1616 Meadow Ave Stockton CA 95207

FIDLER, MARCIA LIGHT, History Teacher; *b:* Indianapolis, IN; *m:* Glenn E.; *c:* Mark; *ed:* (BA) His, De Pauw Univ 1971; *cr:* His Teacher 1971-, 7th/8th Grade Team Leader 1987- Orchard Cntry Day Sch; *ai:* Musical Dir; Accreditaiton Comm Chm; Admissions, Advisory-Guidance, Curr, Evaluation Comm; Jr League; *office:* Orchard Cntry Day Sch 615 W 63rd St Indianapolis IN 46260

FIEBIG, CONNIE SHUMATE, Counselor; *b:* Fairfield, TX; *m:* Danny Wayne; *c:* Michael, Matthew; *ed:* (AA) Temple Jr Coll 1968; (BS) Eng, SW TX St 1969; (MS) Guidance, Prairie View A&M 1980; *cr:* Teacher Rogers Ind Sch Dist 1969-74, Bartlett Ind Sch Dist 1974-80; Teacher 1980-89, Cnslr 1989- Salado Ind Sch Dist; *ai:* At Risk Coord; Drug Contact Person; NEA, TX St Teachers Assn, Bell Cty Educators Assn; 1st Baptist Church (Sunday Sch Teacher, Youth Comm, Childrens Comm); *office:* Salado Ind Sch Dist P O Box 98 Salado TX 76571

FIEGEL, COLLEEN GEORGETTE, Biology Teacher; *b:* New Orleans, LA; *ed:* (BS) Health/Safety/Phys Ed, 1976, (Med) Phys Ed/Sci, 1984 Univ of New Orleans; Grad Stud Univ of New Orleans 1989; *cr:* Teacher St Louise De Marillac Sch 1976-77; Teacher/Coach L W Higgins HS 1977-; *ai:* Sci Club Spon; HS Curr Revision & Discipline Comm; NSTA, NABT, LA Sci Teachers Assn; Jefferson Fed of Teachers Exec Cncl 1988-; Jefferson Ofcls Assn Pres 1986-88; Westbank Bus & Prof Women Young Careerist 1985; LA St Finalist & Region Teacher of Yr 1990; Chapter II Video Microscopy Minigrant; *home:* 725 Jefferson Heights Ave Jefferson LA 70121

FIELD, JOHN SAMUEL, III, 5th Grade Teacher; *b:* Madison, IN; *m:* Marita; *c:* Christopher T., Eric M., Jessica E., Craig N.; *ed:* (BS) Elem Ed, 1975, (MS) Elem Ed, 1979 IN St Univ; *cr:* 5th Grade Teacher Sandusky Elem 1975-78, North Decatur Elem 1978-; *ai:* Asst Var Ftbl Coach; Asst Var Bsbl Coach; 7th Grade Boys Bsktbl; IN St Teachers Assn 1975-89; Decatur Cty Ed Pres/VP/Treas/Bargaining Spokesperson 1988-89; Geography Educators Network of IN 1989; *office:* North Decatur Elem School Rr 1 Box 95-A Greensburg IN 47240

FIELD, KATHERINE MARIE (FUHR), 3rd Grade Teacher; *b:* Shenandoah, IA; *m:* Dan; *c:* Christopher, Kelly M.; *ed:* (BS) Elem Ed, NE Wesleyan 1975; Ed Math Prep, Marycrest Coll 1985; Cmptr as a Teaching Tool, Marycrest 1986; Packaging with Pizzaz 1986; Astronomy, Marycrest Coll 1987; Integrating the Cmptr Math/Sci, Marycrest 1987; Elem Math/Sci, IA St Univ 1989; Elem Ed Aerospace Class, San Jose St Univ 1990; Cosm Atari/Pilot/Lang, MarycreSt 1983; Ed Prins of SLD, Wayne St Coll 1980; Ed Human Relationship, Drake Univ 1979; *cr:* 1st Grade Teacher Open Space Wildewood Elem 1975-76, Bancroftt Sch 1976-80; Learning Disability Teacher for Six County Rural Schls Wakefield AEA; 6th Grade Teacher Red Oak IA 1981-83; 1st Grade Teacher 1983-84, 3rd Grade Teacher 1984- Corning Elem; *ai:* Aerospace Project Leader for 4-H; Aerospace Elem Consultant; Creative Corner Presch Bd of Dirs 1984; Adoption Comm for Corning Elem; Spelling 1989, Eng 1984, Math 1986, Sci 1985; Delta Kappa Gamma (Pres 1990-92, VP 1985-); Adams Cty Child Abuse Prevention Cncl Secy 1988-89; NSTA 1989-; IA Acad of Sci 1990; NSEA, ISEA, & CCEA 1982-; Civil Air Patrol 1987-; Founder of Foster Grandparent Prgm for 3rd Grade 1985; Kidcare Adams Cty Child Abuse Prevention Cncl Secy 1988-89; Delta Kappa Gamma Pi Chapter (First VP 1985- , Pres 1990); Adams Cty 4-H Aerospace Project Leader 1990-; Ben Franklin Stamps Club Leader 1988; GSA Leader-Brownie Troop #210 1987-89; Amer Legion Auxiliary Mem 1990; Nom for Presidential Awd for Excl in Sci 1990; Elected Vice Chm IA AcaD of Sci 1990; Elem Sci Teachers; Founder of 3rd Grade Foster Grandparent Prgm 1985.

FIELDER, LINDA SIMS, Second Grade Teacher; *b:* Rocky Ford, CO; *m:* Bill Gaylon; *c:* Kerry, Debi Bryne, Gerared; *ed:* (BA) Ed, Western St Coll 1964; *cr:* 1st/3rd Grade Teacher Muscoy Sch 1964-67; 3rd Grade Teacher Heritage 1967-68; 2nd-4th Grade Teacher Susan B Anthony Sch 1968-.

FIELDS, CAROLE BETH, 8th Grade English Teacher; *b:* Dallas, TX; *ed:* (BA) Eng, Angelo St Univ 1984; Working Towards Masters Ed, Univ of N TX; *cr:* Eng Teacher Bowie Jr HS 1984-; *ai:* Creative Writers Club Spon; Aerobic Instr; *home:* 2916 Forest Pt #1714 Arlington TX 76006

FIELDS, DIANA MARIA, 3rd Grade Teacher; *b:* Chicago, IL; *m:* Willie S.; *c:* Anthony W.; *ed:* (BS) Psych/Ed, Brockport St Univ 1975; (MS) Ed, National Coll 1980; Ed Admin, Early/Pre-Sch Ed, Seminary Sch; *cr:* 2nd/3rd Grade Teacher Rochester Public Sch 1975-77, 3rd Grade Teacher Hickory Bend Sch 1978-; *ai:* Volunteer Homeless Shelter; GEA, IEA, Union 167; NAACP; New Faith Baptist Church Bd of Deacons; *office:* Hickory Bend Sch 600 191st Pl Glenwood IL 60425

FIELDS, DOROTHY MANN, 5th Grade Teacher; *b:* Peterstown, WV; *m:* Joe V.; *c:* Rebekah A.; *ed:* (BSED) Eng & Soc Stud, Concord Coll 1965; WV Univ & WV Coll Graduate Stud; *cr:* Teacher Nicholas Cty HS 1965-71, Peterstown Elem 1981-; *ai:* Lang Arts Curr Comm; Spelling Bee Coord; Young Writers Coord; NEA/WVEA/MCEA 1981-; Delta Kappa Gamma 1972-; Peterstown Baptist Church Teacher/VBS Dir 1979-; Peterstown Academic Boosters 1988-; Peterstown OES #118 1979-; *home:* Box 548 Peterstown WV 24963

FIELDS, FRED R., Accounting Teacher/Coach; *b:* Muncie, IN; *m:* Zoe C. Hash; *c:* Bart H.; *ed:* (BS) Bus Ed, 1973, (MA) Phys Ed, 1978 Ball St Univ; IN Life Insurance License; *cr:* Teacher/Coach Riverview Jr HS 1973-82, Huntington North HS 1983-; *ai:* Var Girls Bsktbl Coach; IN Coaches of Girls Sports Assn 1987-, Coach of St Champion 1990; In Bsktbl Coaches Assn 1973-, St Championship Coach 1990; Twice Nom Huntington Cty Cmmty Sch Corporation Young Educator of Yr; Coaches Choice Poll Coach of Yr 1989; *home:* 4611 N 615 W Huntington IN 46750

FIELDS, JOHN THOMAS, Math Teacher; *b:* Norwich, CT; *m:* Katherine S.; *c:* John, Erin; *ed:* (BA) Math Ed, Villanova Univ 1970; (MS) Math Ed, Univ of CT 1971; *cr:* Teacher Elizabeth St Sch 1971-73; Kelly Jr HS 1973-75; Teachers Memorial Jr HS 1975-; *ai:* Boys Bsktbl Coach 1980-; Tm Challenge Cup Supv; Chf Exmnr Ged Prgm; YMCA Instr 1976- Volunteer of Yr 1984; Sportsman of Yr 1985; Norwich Teacher of Yr 1987; *home:* 89 School St Taftville CT 06380

FIELDS, NANCY FRENCH, Science Teacher/Dept Chair; *b:* Langdale, AL; *m:* Thomas L.; *c:* Trey F., Caitlyn L.; *ed:* (BS) Bio, 1975; (MED) Scndry Sci, 1977 Auburn Univ; *cr:* Sci Teacher Wacoochee Jr HS 1975-; *ai:* Annual Staff Spon 1975-; Chrldr Co-Spon 1980-; Accreditation Comm; Coord Jr Highlights Beauty Pageant; NEA 1975-; PTA Sec 1979-80/1983-84.

FIELDS, RACHEL OUELLETTE, French Teacher; *b:* Van Buren, ME; *m:* S. Ray; *c:* Timothy; *ed:* (BS) Fr, Univ of ME 1973; *cr:* Fr Teacher Limestone Jr/Sr HS 1974-76; Travel Consultant DE Motor Club 1977-80; Sr Secy DE Dept of Agriculture 1983-86; Fr Teacher Lake Forest HS 1986-; *ai:* Fr Club Adv; Foreign Lang Dept Chairperson; DE St Ed Assn 1986-; AATF (Secy, Treas) 1988-; DE Cncl Teachers of Foreign Lang 1987-; Lake Forest Sch Dist Teacher of Yr 1988-89; *office:* Lake Forest HS Rd 1 Box 847 Felton DE 19943

FIELDS, SUSAN ERCANBRACK, Speech & Drama Coach; *b:* Fort Smith, AR; *ed:* (BS) Lang Art Ed, OK Univ 1981; Grad Stud Cntrl St Univ OK; *cr:* Eng/Gifted/Yrbk/Speech/Drama Teacher Noble Schls 1981-; *ai:* Thespian Club; Natl Forensic League; OK Ed Assn; *office:* Noble HS P O Box 519 Noble OK 73068

FIELDS, SUSAN MICHAEL, Home Economics Teacher; *b:* Goshen, IN; *m:* Paul L.; *c:* Bryan; *ed:* (BS) Home Ec Ed, Goshen Coll 1966; (MS) Home Ec Ed, Purdue Univ 1972; *cr:* Teacher Brookdale Jr HS 1966-84, West Side Mid Sch 1984-; *ai:* Impact Team; Sch Improvement Comm; Amer Home Ec Assn 1966-80; *office:* West Side Mid Sch 101 S Nappanee St Elkhart IN 46514

FIELDS-NEW, SUSAN CRAIGE, English Teacher; *b:* Atlanta, GA; *m:* Randy L.; *ed:* (BA) Eng/Classics, Univ of GA 1973; Working Toward Masters GA St Univ, Oglethorpe Univ; *cr:* Teacher North Springs HS 1973-; *ai:* Local Sch Advisory & Curr Revision Comm; PTSA Bd Mem; *office:* North Springs HS 7447 Roswell Rd Atlanta GA 30328

FIENE, JEANNE RAE, High School Principal; *b:* Aurora, IL; *ed:* (BME) Instrumental Music, 1983, (MM) Music Supervision, 1990 Pittsburg St; Grad Stud Math; Educal Admin EDS Specialist, Pittsburg St, N IL Univ, SW MO St Univ; *cr:* K-12th Grade Music Teacher Unified Sch Dist 285 Cedarville KS 1983-84; 8th-12th Grade Math Teacher 1986-88, 9th-12th Grade Prin 1988- Wheaton R-III; *ai:* Sr Class Spon; Overall Act & Athletics; Phi Delta Kappa 1987-; Womens Network 1988-; Sigma Alpha Iota (Pres, Adv) 1980-86, Sword of Honor 1980; Music Educators Natl Conference 1980-86; SE KS Symphony 1980-86; Pittsburg Cmmty Theatre 1981-86; Cmmty Band 1981-86; Various Church (Choir, Quartet, Secy of Cncl) 1970; *office:* Wheaton R-III Schls 116 Mc Call PO Box 249 Wheaton MO 64874

FIFE, DELL SCOTT, Mathematics Department Chair; *b:* Brigham City, UT; *m:* Ruth Spackman; *c:* Brian S., Cindy R. Fife Mc Dougal, Lance D.; *ed:* (BS) Math/Physics, Weber St Coll 1966; (MA) Math, UT St Univ 1970; Math & Ed, UT St Univ; *cr:* Teacher Ogden HS 1966, Sky View HS 1966-; Adjunct Professor UT St 1976-80; Dept Chm Sky View HS 1980-; *ai:* Graduation & Dept Chm; Tutoring Coord; CEA, UEA, NEA (Building Rep, Negotiating Team); UCTM, NCTM; BSA (Troop & Dist Comm) 1976-85; The Church of Jesus Christ of Latter-Day Saints Bishop 1987-; NSF Grants; *home:* 290 N 100 W Box 64 Hyde Park UT 84318

FIGLAR, RAYMOND GREGORY, Social Studies Teacher; *b:* Bridgeport, CT; *m:* Synthia Higgins; *c:* Heather, Nathan; *ed:* (BA) His, Salem Coll 1965; (MA) His, WV Univ 1970; WV Univ Coll of Grad Stud 1989; *cr:* US His/Eng Teacher Martins Ferry HS 1965-66; World His & US His Teacher Fellowsville HS 1967-70; US His/Problems of Democracy/Eng Teacher Valley HS 1970-77; Eng Teacher Hundred HS 1977-80; Advanced Placement Amer His/Psych/Sociology Teacher Magnolia HS 1980-; *ai:* Sr Class Spon; Coached Wrestling; Umpired Var Bsbl; Directed Dramatics Club Plays; Soc Stud Chairperson Valley HS 1970-76; Wetzel Cty Scndry Soc Stud Coord 1973-74; AFT Mem 1989-; WV Ed Assn (Building Rep 1983-85, Mem 1981-88); NEA Mem 1981-88; Wetzel Cty Democratic Exec Comm Mem 1976-80; *office:* Magnolia HS Maple Ave New Martinsvlle WV 26155

FIGLEY, SANDRA LEA SKABO, Biology Teacher; *b:* St Petersburg, FL; *ed:* (AA) St Petersburg Jr Coll 1976; (BSED) Bio Ed, Asbury Coll 1979; Working Towrd MSED with Emphasis in Bio, Univ of FL 1990; *cr:* Sci Teacher Sixteenth Street Mid Sch 1979-84; Bio Teacher St Petersburg HS 1984-; *ai:* Bowling Team Coach; NHS Adv; 9th Grade Transition Team Comm; Pinellas Cty Sci Teachers Assn Exec Bd Mem 1980; Nom Teacher of Yr 1982, 1989; 1st Recipient of Audubon Pin Pinellas Cty Schls Schlsp Awd 1984; *office:* Saint Petersburg HS 2501 5th Ave N Saint Petersburg FL 33713

FIGUEROA, EDNA, Biology Teacher; *b:* Kingsville, TX; *m:* Ben; *c:* Ted, Teri; *ed:* (BS) Bio/Eng, 1967, (MS) Scndry Ed, 1981 TX A&M Univ; Grad Stud Eng Lit, Process Writing, Sociology; *cr:* Eng Teacher Ben Bolt HS 1967-68; Eng/Bio Teacher Tom Browne Jr HS & Carroll HS 1968-70; Sci Teacher San Jacinto Intermediate 1971-73; Eng Teacher Robstown HS 1977-78; Eng/Bio H M King HS 1978-; *ai:* H M King HS Stu Cncl Spon; Natl Assn of Stu Act Adv Mem 1985-; TX Assn of Stu Cncls (Mem 1985-, Spon, Head Teacher Spon 1987-88), 5-Yr Pin 1990, Plaque 1988; TX Parents & Teachers Assn Mem 1980-, Life Membership Awd 1988; Our Lady of Good Counsel Cath Church Religious Ed Teacher 1987-; Kleberg Cty Commissioners Court Resolution 1985; Kingsville Chamber of Commerce Resolution 1990; Article Published on Environmental Ed 1990; *office:* H M King HS 2210 S Brahma Blvd Kingsville TX 78363

FIGUEROA, MARGARITA P., Physical Education Teacher; *b:* San Elizario, TX; *m:* Robert J.; *c:* Robert Jr., Christina M., Jorge L.; *ed:* (AA) Recreation Leadership, El Paso Comm Coll 1981; *cr:* Recreation Leader III El Paso Parks & Recreation 1972-80; Phys Ed Teacher St Pius X Parochial Sch 1980-; *ai:* Vlybl, Bsktbl, Track Coach; 7tH/8th Grade Health Teacher; Faculty Rep Sch Bd; GSA Leader 1975-76; *home:* 10629 Birthstone El Paso TX 79925

FIGUEROA, ROSEMARIE ARMIJO, Business Teacher; *b:* Tucson, AZ; *m:* Jesus V.; *c:* Gabriel J., Imelda I., Christina M.; *ed:* (BS) Bus Ed, Univ of AZ 1975; Grad Stud Univ of AZ; *cr:* Bus Educator Sunnyside HS 1975-80, Desert View HS 1985-; *ai:* FBLA Spon; Schlsp & Graduation Comm Mem; Career Ladder Level III Teacher; AZ Bus Ed Assn 1985-; Tucson Assn for Bi-ling Ed; Univ Hispanic Alumni Assn 1989-; AFT 1987-; US Secy of Ed Natl Outstanding Bus Voc Ed Dept Prgm Awd 1989; FBLA Spon Recognition Awd; *office:* Desert View HS 4101 E Valencia Rd Tucson AZ 85706

FILEMYR, SARA WALKER, Second Grade Teacher; *b:* Norfolk, VA; *m:* Edward Joseph; *c:* Edward, Richard, Ann, Kathryn Bowland, Janet; *ed:* (BA) Latin, Swarthmore Coll 1955; (MS) Elem Ed, Temple Univ 1969; *cr:* Teacher Richboro Nursery Sch 1967-69; Eng as 2nd Lang/Part Time Teacher Lakeshore Tech Inst 1972-80; Part Time Pre-Sch Teacher Cedar Grove Sch Dist 1976-79; 1st/2nd Grade Teacher Random Lake Sch Dist 1973-; *ai:* Random Lake Ed Assn, WI Ed Assn, NEA 1973-; Random Lake Lib Bd Pres 1984-; Friends of Lib (Secy, Treas) 1988-; St of WI Democratic Party Platform Comm 1986-; Random Lake Interfaith Food Pantry Secy 1988-.

FILENE, MYRON, English Teacher Staff Coord; *b:* Alhambra, CA; *m:* Maya Muir; *c:* Simon G. Muir-Filene; *ed:* (BA) Eng Lit, Stanford Univ 1970; (MAT) Eng Ed, Reed Coll 1975; Cert AP Supervision, Brooklyn Coll 1988; *cr:* Eng Teacher Centennial HS 1975-76, Boys & Girls HS 1983-84; Eng Teacher/Staff Coord Brooklyn Tech HS 1982-; *ai:* Steering & Sch Improvement Comm Mem; Experimental & Innovative Prgm Comm Chm; NCTE, ASCD, UFT, AFT; *office:* Brooklyn Tech HS De Kalb Ave & S Elliott Pl Brooklyn NY 11217

FILI, JOSEPH D., English Teacher; *b:* New York, NY; *m:* Elizabeth Marie Jahn; *ed:* (BA) Eng, Fordham Univ 1970; (MAT) Eng, Monmouth Coll 1974; Project Advance, Syracuse Univ; *cr:* Eng Teacher St Benedicts Sch 1970-71; Eng Dept Chm St John Vianney HS 1971-79, Chrstn Brothers Acad 1979-88; Eng Teacher Chrstn Brothers Acad 1988-; *ai:* SAT Preparation Prgm Instr; Sch Literary Journal Adv; Camping Club Moderator; NCEA 1989-; North Easting Camping Center Dir 1985-87; Articles Published on Amer Folk Music & Folk His; Asst Dir Tour Which Made it Possible for Gary Snyder to Bri ng Poetry to Australia; *office:* Chrstn Brothers Acad 850 Newman Springs Rd Lincroft NJ 07738

FILITOR, VERONICA LAPETINA, 2nd Grade Teacher; *b:* New York, NY; *m:* Frederick A.; *c:* Rita J. Filitor Yackanich, Jane F. Hanley, Magee F. Murray, Mary F. Corby, Joann F. Padgett; *ed:* (BA) Eng, Notre Dame Coll 1969; *cr:* 3rd Grade Teacher Our Lady Help of Chrstns 1966-74; 2nd Grade Teacher Reverend George A Brown Sch 1974-; *ai:* Primary Dept Coord; NW Jersey Rdng Assn 1976-81; *office:* Rev Geo A Brown Memorial Sch 294 Sparta Ave Sparta NJ 07871

FILIZETTI, RICKY M., Industrial Tech Teacher; *b:* Marquette, MI; *m:* Sharleen Stine; *c:* Sarah, Brooke, Ricci; *ed:* (BS) Industrial Ed, N MI Univ 1977; Working Toward Masters in Ed; *cr:* I E Teacher Gwinn Area Cmmty Schls 1979-; *ai:* Girls Jr Var Bsktbl Coach; *office:* Gwinn Mid Sch Granite St Gwinn MI 49841

FILKINS, ALICE JEAN, Retired 7th Grade Math Teacher; *b:* Rochester, NY; *ed:* (BED) Elem Ed, Geneseo St Coll 1944; (MED) Ed, Alfred Univ 1957; Grad Stud Geneseo St Coll, Alfred Univ, Syracuse Univ, NY Univ; *cr:* 7th Grade Math Teacher Wellsville Cntrl Schls 1944-89; *ai:* Natl Jr Honor Society Spon; Delta Kappa Gamma Corresponding Secy 1984-; Wellsville Ed Assn Treas; Red Cross Secy; Bus & Prof Women (Secy 1986-87, Treas).

FILLINGAME, BONNIE TWYCROSS, Retired Teacher; *b:* Whittier, CA; *m:* Ralph Alan; *c:* Kari, Michael, Scott; *ed:* (BA) Child Dev, Univ of CA Davis 1975; Teacher Trng Prgm, Univ of CA Davis 1975-76; CA Teaching Certificate; *cr:* 1st Grade Teacher Rincon Valley Chrstn Sch 1976-77, Covenant Chrstn Sch 1977-79, Elkhart Elem 1979-82; *ai:* Lane Cty Medical Auxiliary (Bd Mem 1987-) 1984-.

FILLMER, LESLIE DONALD, Advanced Placement Music Instr; *b:* Birmingham, AL; *m:* Barbara Jane; *ed:* (BM) Applied Music - Cum Laude Univ of AL 1974; Baldwin-Wallace Coll Conservatory of Music; *cr:* Instrumentalist/Arranger USAF Acad Band 1970-72; Eng Horn Soloist/Personnel Mgr AL Symphony Orch 1974-81; Morning Show Host WBHM-FM 1980-; Advanced Placement Music Theory/Lit Teacher AL Sch of Fine Arts 1981-; *ai:* Music Dir/Conductor AL Youth Symphony & Red Mountain Chamber Orch; Adv Birmingham City Stages Jazz Camp & Classical Oasis; Pi Kappa Lambda Mem 1974-; Birmingham Festival of Arts 1982, Silver Bowl Awd 1982; Amer Fed of Musicians 1972-; Conductors Guild 1988-; Johnson Fnd Grant Orchestral Composition 1975; AL St Cncl on Hum Grant 1989; Ind Presbyn Church Commission for Magnificat & NUNC Dimittis 1989; *office:* AL Sch of Fine Arts 820 N 18th St Birmingham AL 35203

FILLMORE, ALVA RUBERT, Fourth/Fifth Grade Teacher; *b:* Chico, CA; *w:* Roland (dec); *c:* Linda Hicks, Kenneth, Deborah Severy; *ed:* (AA) Soc Sci, Taft Coll 1967; (BA) Soc Sci, Fresno St 1969; Life Teaching Credential 1969; Grad Stud 1969-; *cr:* 4th/5th Grade Combination Teacher Mc Kee Sch 1969-; *ai:* Child Study Team; Site Cncl; *home:* 1040 Stevens St Taft CA 93268

FILLYAW, MARY KATHLEEN FREDRICK, 5th Grade Teacher; *b:* Miami, FL; *m:* Charles E.; *ed:* (BS) Elem Ed, FL St Univ 1972; *cr:* CLassroom Teacher Pinellas Cntrl Elem 1972-; *office:* Pinellas Cntrl Elem Sch 10501 58th St N Pinellas Park FL 34666

FILOSE, ELAINE, Third Grade Teacher; *b:* New York, NY; *m:* Donald Staszyn; *ed:* (BS) Elem Ed, 1969, (MS) Elem Ed, 1974 St Johns Univ; *cr:* 3rd Grade Teacher St Helens Sch 1969-74; 1st-3rd/5th Grade Teacher New Hyde Park Road Sch 1974-; *ai:* Sch Store & Stu Cncl Spon; Teachers Union Exec Bd Mem; PTA Jenkins Memorial Awd Lifetime Membership; *office:* New Hyde Road Sch New Hyde Park Rd New Hyde Park NY 11040

FILSON, JOHANNA VARALLO, 7th/8th Grade Math Teacher; *b:* Camden, NJ; *m:* Douglas Joseph; *c:* Serena, Michael; *ed:* (BA) Elem Ed, Glassboro St Coll 1974; Grad Stud; Glassboro St Coll to Ascertain Baccal; *cr:* 6th Grade Teacher Cramer Elem Sch 1974-78; 6th Grade Teacher 1978-89, 7th/8th Grade Math Teacher 1989- E Camden Mid Sch; *ai:* Acad Prgm Mem; Logo Club; *office:* E Camden Mid Sch 3064 Stevens St Camden NJ 08105

FILZEN, KEVIN JOSEPH, Phys Ed/Sci Teacher; *b:* Minneapolis, MN; *m:* Laurie A. Snider; *c:* Spencer J., Mc Kenna A.; *ed:* (AA) Law Enforcement, Normandale Jr Coll 1975; (BS) Phys Ed/Kinesiology, Pepperdine Univ 1980; Supplementary Credential in Sci & Life; Sci, Phys Ed, Ed Classes Univ CA Irvine, Irvine Valley Coll, CA St Coll Northridge; *cr:* Phys Ed Teacher Mountainview Acad 1980-81, Center for Early Ed 1981-83; Phys Ed Teacher/Sci Dept Chair St Margarets 1983-; Athletic Dir Mid Sch; *ai:* Flag Ftbl & Girls Bsktbl Coach; 6th Grade Adv; Teacher of Yr 1990; *office:* St Margarets Sch 31641 La Novia San Juan Capistrno CA 92675

FINANE, NAIDA KAROLY, English Teacher; *b:* New Florence, PA; *m:* William James Jr.; *c:* Benjamin K.; *ed:* (BA) Eng, Chatham Coll 1970; (MS) Eng Ed, Syracuse Univ 1971; Grad Stud Gifted Ed; *cr:* Eng Teacher Waunakee HS 1970-73, Hayward Unified Sch 1978-81; Gifted Teacher Robertsville Jr HS 1981-83; Eng Teacher Oak Ridge HS 1983-; *ai:* Literary Magazine Adv; NCTE Mem, Outstanding Service 1989; SE Consortium for Minorities in Engineering; Montersori Sch Bd Mem 1981-84; Friends of Lib Bd Mem 1984-86; *office:* Oak Ridge HS 27 Providence Rd Oak Ridge TN 37830

FINCH, JEAN, Teacher of Academically Gifted; *b:* Spring Hope, SC; *ed:* (BS) Ed, Atlantic Chrstn Coll 1962; (MED) Ed, E Carolina Univ 1971; *cr:* 4th Grade Teacher 1962-79, Gifted & Talented Teacher 1979- Bailey Elem Sch; Teacher of Gifted & Talented Middlesex Elem Sch 1979-; *ai:* NC Assn of Educators, NEA 1962-; Kappa Delta Phi 1971-; Samaria Baptist Church Teacher; *home:* Rt 1 Spring Hope NC 27882

FINDEISEN, BEN HENRY, Science Teacher; *b:* Texas City, TX; *m:* Sandra Sue Kilbase; *c:* John A., Kelly M.; *ed:* (BS) Ag Ed/Bio, Sam Houston St 1967-79; Composite Sci Certificate; *cr:* Sci Teacher/Dept Chm Splendora HS 1967-; *ai:* Stu Cncl, Just Say No Club Spon; Faculty Rep for HS; TX St Teachers Assn 1967-; FFA & Cub Scouts of America Awds; *office:* Splendora HS P O Box 168 Splendora TX 77372

FINDLEY, DAVID MARTIN, Guidance Counselor; *b:* Canton, OH; *m:* Katherine Quinn; *c:* Elizabeth, Thomas; *ed:* (BA) Journalism, Kent St Univ 1969; Grad Stud Ed, Ashland Univ; *cr:* Elem Teacher Millersburg Elem 1969-74, Lakeville Elem 1974-81; Soc Stud Teacher 1981-88, Guidance Cnslr 1988- West Holmes Jr HS; *ai:* Track Coach; West Holmes Ed Assn Pres 1983-85; West Holmes Sch Dist Teacher of Yr 1988; Martha Holden Jennings Scholar 1990; *home:* 4853 TR 305 Millersburg OH 44654

FINDLEY, JAMES LEE, Humanities Faculty; *b:* West Palm Beach, FL; *m:* Joy Elizabeth Daniels; *c:* David H., William Mc Lean, Addie J.; *ed:* (BA) His, 1968, (MA) His, 1974 Baylor Univ; (JD) Law, Baylor Sch of Law 1977; *cr:* Law Practice Gainesville FL 1977-83; Hum Faculty LA Sch for Math/Sci/Arts 1983-; *ai:* Pre-Law Club Spon; Young Democrats; Sch Coord Close-Up Fnd; FL Bar 1977-; Phi Alpha Theta 1974-; Cncl for Basic Ed Fellow 1989; *office:* Louisiana Sch for Math/Sci/Art 715 College Ave Natchitoches LA 71457

FINDLEY, KATHRYN MARLAR, Math Teacher; *b:* Hope, AR; *m:* Randy D.; *c:* Jessica, Aubrey; *ed:* (BS) Math, 1971, (MS) Math, 1974 E TX St Univ; Abstract Algebra, Univ of TX Dallas; *cr:* Teacher Mesquite Ind Sch Dist 1972-74, Richardson Ind Sch Dist 1974-; *ai:* GOCTM, ATPE, PTA, REA; Canyon Creek Presbyn Church; *office:* L V Berkner HS 1600 E Spring Valley Richardson TX 75081

FINE, JOE THOMAS, Band Director; *b:* Oklahoma City, OK; *m:* Christine Diane Wallace; *c:* Derek; *ed:* (BME) Instrumental Music, Cntrl St Univ 1983; Working Towards MED in 1990; *cr:* Band Dir Sequoyah Mid Sch 1983-; *ai:* Cntrl OK Dirs Assn Jr HS Chairperson 1989-; OK Music Educators Assn; *office:* Sequoyah Mid Sch 1125 E Danforth Edmond OK 73034

FINE, MARJORIE LOUISE, Chemistry/Phys Science Teacher; *b:* Holiday, TX; *ed:* (BS) Bio/Pre-Med, Midwestern St Univ 1955; (MS) Animal Physiology, OH Univ 1957; Certificate Medical Technology, Las Cruses NM 1967; Teacher Effectiveness Trng 1979; Effective Teaching Practices Conferences 1987; Common Sense Discipline 1988; *cr:* Bio/Chem Teacher Petrolia HS 1966-70; 6th-12th Grade Sci Teacher Adrian HS 1970-77, 1980-81; Chem/Phys Sci Teacher Electra HS 1977-80, Brownwood HS 1982-; *ai:* TX Classroom Teachers 1988-; TSTA Oldham Cty Unit Secy 1974-75; Beta Beta Beta 1952-55; Midwestern Univ Cowgirls 1952-55; Teaching Assistantship OH Univ 1955-57; *office:* Brownwood HS 2100 Slayden Brownwood TX 76801

FINKE, FREDERICK JOHN, Science Teacher; *b:* Manhatten, NY; *m:* Meredith Anne Headquist; *c:* John; *ed:* (BA) Bio, Harding Univ 1974; *cr:* Teacher/Coach White Cty Cncl HS 1975-77; FL Cntrl Acad 1979-81; Mt Dora Bible Sch 1982-84; Mt Dora HS 1984-85; Lyman HS 1985-; *ai:* Mens Track, Men & Women Cross

Cntry Head Coach; NEA 1981-; Seminole Ed Assn 1985-; FL Athletic Coaches Assn Cross Cntry Chm 1989-; Athletics Congress Coaching Ed 1985-, Presidents Awd 1988; FL Track Coach of Yr 1983, 1985; South Team Olympic Sports Festival Distance Coach; Articles Published.

FINKLEA, COLEEN WOODHAM, Principal; *b:* Florence, SC; *m:* Allen; *c:* Casey; *ed:* (BS) Psych, Francis Marion Coll 1974; (MED) Ed Admin, Univ of SC 1986; Doctoral Ed Admin, Univ of SC; *cr:* Public Assistance Technician Florence Cty Dept Soc Services 1975-76; Teacher 1976-87, Asst Prin 1987-89 Florence Cty Sch Dist III; Prin St Anthony Cath Sch 1989-; *ai:* SC Assn of Elem Prins, NAESP, ASCD 1987-; NCEA 1989-; Florence Chamber of Commerce 1989-; GSA Asst Leader.

FINLEY, BERNADETTE DE VOE, 4th Grade Teacher; *b:* Charleston, SC; *m:* Joseph L.; *c:* Chantille, Chadera, Charnee; *ed:* (BS) Pre Sch Ed, Elem Ed, SC St Coll 74; (MS) Elem Guidance Cnslr, TheCitadel 1985; *cr:* 1st/4th Grade Teacher Jane Edwards Elem 1974-76; 6th Grade Teacher R D Schroder Mid Sch 1976-79; 4th Grade Teacher Memminger Elem 1980-; *ai:* Black His Chairperson; Drama Club; Discipline Comm; Health Liason; Intnl Rdng Assn 1989-; Lenevar Civic Club 1987-; *home:* 1327 Kiki Way Charleston SC 29407

FINLEY, CAROLYN B., Language Arts Teacher; *b:* Tamaqua, PA; *m:* Russell J.; *c:* Rebecca, Rachel, Russell Jr.; *ed:* (BS) Eng/Scndry Ed, Kutztown Univ 1963; Skills for Adolescence Trng; *cr:* Teacher Tamaqua Area Sch Dist 1964-66, 1977-; *office:* Tamaqua Area Jr HS High St Box 90 Tamaqua PA 18252

FINLEY, PATRICIA J., 6th Grade Mathematics Teacher; *b:* Escanaba, MI; *ed:* (AA) Ed, Bay De Noc Comm Coll 1966; (BA) Ed, 1968, (ma) Ed, 1970 N Mi Univ; Grad Stud Ed & Cmptrs; *cr:* 6th Grade Self Contained/Math/Typing/Quest/Phys Ed, 7th Grade Math/Eng, 8th Grade Math Teacher Armanda Area Schls 1970-; *ai:* Project Pride Sch Awds; Dist Math Comm; *office:* Armada Mid Sch 23550 Armada Center Rd Armada MI 48005

FINLEY, WILLIAM HENRY, American History Teacher; *b:* San Bernardino, CA; *m:* Judy C. Thornton; *c:* Laura A., Patrick M., Sarah K.; *ed:* (BS) His, 1973; (MS) His, 1975 Univ of Southern MS; Curr Instruction Memphis St Univ; *cr:* HS His Marion Cty HS 1975-76; Guidance East Marion HS 1976-77; 7th Grade Soc Stud Woodstock Elem 1978-82; 8th Grade Amer His Shadowlawn Mid Sch 1982-; *ai:* Spon Annual 8th Grade Trip WA DC; Shelby Cty Ed Assn 1978-; TN Ed Assn 1978-; NEA 1978-; Outstanding Teacher Awd Chrstn Brothers Coll 1985; *home:* 5303 Richwood Cove Memphis TN 38134

FINN, DAVID HAL, Teacher of English; *b:* Cheyenne, WY; *m:* Barbara Ruth Mallin; *c:* Elizabeth R., Daniel J.; *ed:* (BA) Eng Lit, CA St Univ Northridge 1981; (MA) Scndry Ed, Univ MO Kansas City 1983; *cr:* Dir of Jewish Ed Avian Air Base 1974-76; Judail His Stud Teacher Temple Ramat Ziaon 1976-79; Eng/Creative Writing Teacher Meadowbrook Jr HS 1981-84; Eng/Stu Leadership Teacher Olathe South HS 1984-; *ai:* Stu Cncl; NCTE 1981-; Olathe Natl Ed Assn Building Rep 1984-; Masonic Lodge 436 1990; Chapter II Grant for Cmptrs Integrated Into Writing; Mini Grant for Writing Across Grade Levels 1-11; *office:* Olathe South 1640 E 151st St Olathe KS 66062

FINN, ELLEN BRADY, English/Latin/History Teacher; *b:* Washington, DC; *m:* Thomas John; *c:* Anthony T., Louise, Lucy Finn Hully, William, Catherine; *ed:* (BA) Classical Archeology, Wellesley Coll 1956; (MAT) Eng, Oakland Univ 1974; Latin, Wayne St Univ; *cr:* Eng/Latin/His Teacher Acad of the Sacred Heart 1974-; *ai:* Adv; Sch Newspaper; Eng Dept Acting Head; Detroit Classical Assn 1989-; Natl Classical League 1989-; Phi Beta Kappa Membership 1956; Numerous Wkshp Grants; Teaching Advanced Placement Courses in Eng & HiS: Teaching of Asian Stud; Global Ed; Teaching of Eng Composition 1974-; *office:* Acad of the Sacred Heart 1250 Kensington Rd Bloomfield Hills MI 48013

FINN, GORDON STEPHEN, Science/Mathematics Teacher; *b:* Oakland, CA; *m:* Judith Ann Mc Knight; *c:* Lori D. Johnston, Michael; *ed:* (BA) Phys Ed, Univ of CA Berkeley 1961; Teaching the Two-Sided Mind; Trng St Marys Coll 1988; Microcmptr Based Lab Trng, Univ of CA Berkley 1988; Producing Capable Young People, Univ of CA Berkley 1987; *cr:* Teacher/Coach Del Valle HS 1962-79; Teacher/Coach/Athletic Dir Acalanes HS 1979-85; Teacher Acalanes HS 1985-; Coach St Marys Coll 1985-; *ai:* Ftbl Coach St Marys Coll; Sr Class Adv; Graduation Coord; Acalanes Dist Sci Curr Comm; Acalanes Impact Trng Comm; CA Teachers Assn, NEA 1979-; Acalanes Ed Assn Crisis Comm 1989-; *office:* Acalanes HS 1200 Pleasant Hill Rd Lafayette CA 94549

FINN, JANET L. (GUILLETT), Science Teacher; *b:* Bay City, MI; *m:* Theodore G.; *c:* Victoria A., Alice C., Susan L.; *ed:* (BS) Ed, 1981, (MEPD) Ed/Concentration Physics, 1987 Univ of WI Platteville; *cr:* Teacher Wauzeka Public Sch 1981-; *ai:* Jr HS Adv; Post Prom Party Organizer; NSTA, WSST, Phi Kappa Phi Mem; Womens Civic Club Secy.

FINN, WILLIAM F., Elementary Principal; *b:* Little Rock, AR; *c:* William T., Jason D.; *ed:* (BA) Elem Ed, Philander Smith Coll 1968; (MS) Elem Admin, Univ of AR Fayette 1975; Grad Stud; *cr:* Teacher Little Rock Sch Dist 1968-73; Dean of Stu Southwest Mid Sch 1973-78; Vice Prin Southwest Jr HS 1978-82; Prin Booker Arts Magnet Sch 1983-; *ai:* Phi Delta Kappa, ASCD 1982-; Little Rock Prin Roundtable 1973-; Natl Assn for Sickle Cell Disease Bd Mem 1975-; Sickle Cell Fnd of AR (Bd Mem 1970-, Pres 1988-) Service Awd 1978; Alpha Phi Alpha 1967-; *office:* Booker Arts Magnet Sch 2016 Barber St Little Rock AR 72206

FINNEGAN, DAWN TURNEY, Fifth Grade Teacher; *b:* Sewickley, PA; *m:* Daniel; *c:* Daniel Jr.; *ed:* (BS) Elem Ed, PA St Univ 1971; *cr:* 4th Grade Teacher 1971-77, 3rd Grade Teacher 1977-79, 6th Grade Teacher 1979-86, 5th Grade Teacher 1986- Highland Sch; *ai:* Sch Newspaper Spon; Head Teacher; Discipline Comm Chairperson; Helped Develop Decision Making Model Highland; Monthly After-Sch Act & Dances Spon; Schls Talent Show Annual Spon; Ambridge Area Ed Assn, PA St Ed Assn, NEA 1971-; Highland Sch PTO Pres 1971-; Pi Lambda Theta 1970; PA St Alumni Organization 1985-; St Veronicas Womens Guild 1980-; Outstanding Young Educator Awd Ambridge Jaycees; *office:* Highland Elem Sch Highland Ave Ambridge PA 15003

FINNEGAN, JOANN SALVINO, Social Studies Teacher; *b:* Brooklyn, NY; *m:* Ronald; *c:* Broc, Jared; *ed:* (BA) His/Poly Sci, 1972, (MS) Scndry Ed, 1973 City Univ of NY; (MA) Rdng, Kean Coll 1976; World His Summer Inst 1988; Ec Summer Inst 1988, 1989; Intnl Baccalaureate Seminars; *cr:* Teacher St Johns Villa Acad 1974-76, E Orange HS 1976-78, Dillard HS 1978-79, Deerfield Beach HS 1979-, Broward Comm Coll 1988-; *ai:* Intnl Baccalaureate Prgm Stu Academic Coach; Amer Teachers Magazine, NCSS; *home:* 8008 SW 29th St Davie FL 33328

FINNEGAN, KATHLEEN ANNE, Mathematics Teacher; *b:* Orlando, FL; *ed:* (BS) Elem Ed/Math, St Bonaventure Univ 1980; (MS) Cmptr Ed, Nazareth Coll 1988; *cr:* 3rd Grade Teacher St Boniface Sch 1980-83; Jr HS Math Teacher Nathaniel Roch Cmmty Sch 1983-; *ai:* Pom Pom Girl Coach; Fashion & Talent Show Dir; NYSUT 1983; Camp Good Days & Spec Times (Cnslr, Dir) 1985-, Teddi Awd 1988; Luekemia Society Volunteer 1987, Volunteer Awd 1989; *office:* Nathaniel Rochester Cmmty Sch 85 Adam St Rochester NY 14608

FINNEGAN, MICHAEL PHILLIP, Fourth Grade Teacher; *b:* Norfolk, VA; *m:* Lessie Scarborough; *c:* Moira, Kellan; *ed:* (BS) Elem Ed, E Carolina Univ 1971; Amer Inst for Foreign Study; *cr:* Teacher Cape Hatteras Sch 1976-; *ai:* Wrestling Coach; NC Assn of Educators Mem at Large 1980-81; Buxton Meth Church Youth Leader 1985-87; Buxton Meth Men; *home:* Box 8 Buxton NC 27920

FINNELL, RUDOLPH ERIC, Instrumental Music Teacher; *b:* Indianapolis, IN; *m:* Evelyn L. Dickerson; *c:* Rudolph Jr., Eloise; *cr:* Music Teacher Westside HS 1969-75, Manual HS 1977-79, Broad Ripple HS 1979-; *ai:* Amer Fed of Musicians Mem 1967-; Natl Assn of Jazz Educators Mem 1984-; IN Educators Assn Mem 1977-; Black Jazz Caucus of NAJE 1985, Outstanding Service 1985; Indianapolis Public Schls Beyond the Call of Duty Awd 1987, 1988 & Outstanding Teacher Awd 1985; *office:* Broad Ripple HS 1115 E Broad Ripple Ave Indianapolis IN 46220

FINNEY, GENEVA B., French-Spanish Teacher; *b:* Summerton, SC; *m:* Ernest A.; *c:* Yolanda Mays, Ernest Jr., Ronald, Robert; *ed:* (BS) Fr/Eng, Benedict Coll 1949; (MS) Ed, SC St Coll 1968; Foreign Lang Inst VA St Univ; Gerontology Wksp Sch of Soc Work Univ SC; Thinking Skills on a Higher Order, SC St Coll; *cr:* Fr/Eng Teacher Scotts Branch HS 1949-54, Whittemore HS 1955-64, Voorhees HS 1965-66; Fr/Span Teacher Felton Laboratory Sch 1968-; *ai:* Stu Cncl, Modern Lang Club Adv; Soc Welfare Comm, Soc Decorum Coord; NEA, AATF 1969-; SC Ed Assn 1949-; Phi Delta Kappa (Secy 1980, 1983) 1975-, Certificate 1980; Stu Ed Assn Adv; Amer Red Cross, Cmmty Improvement Block Captain; Natl Assn Univ Women Pres 1984-; Grant Geriatics, Modern Foreign Lang, Critical Thinking.

FINNIGAN, PATRICK J., Social Studies Teacher; *b:* Nashua, NH; *m:* Dorothy Snow; *c:* Sheila, P. J., Brenda, Mary; *ed:* (AB) His-Bio, St Anselm Coll 1954; (MA) His, Salem St Coll 1969; *cr:* Teacher Central Sch 1956-63; Asst Prin Woodbury HS 1963; Teacher Andover Jr East Doherty 1963-88; Andover Sr HS 1988-; *ai:* NEA 1956-; MA Teachers Assn 1956-; Andover Ed Assn 1956-; CCD Teacher; VFW; Knights of Columbus; *home:* 17 Henry St Salem NH 03079

FINOS, MARLES ANNE, 3rd Grade Teacher; *b:* Martinez, CA; *m:* Mel; *c:* Michelle Finos Schlader, Marcy; *ed:* (BA) Elem Ed - Magna Cum Laude, Univ of Pacific 1962; Grad Stud; *cr:* 3rd Grade Teacher Mc Kinley/Stockton 1962-63; 3rd/4th Grade Teacher Lodi Public Schls 1965-; *ai:* Serve as Mem Various Sch Site Comms; NEA, CA Teachers Assn, Lodi Ed Assn; Omega Nu (VP, Corresponding Secy, Officer, Comm Chm) 1964-84; *office:* Vinewood Elem Sch 1600 W Tokay Lodi CA 95242

FINOTTI, ROGER C., 5th Grade Teacher; *b:* Indiana, PA; *m:* Charlene K. Harvey; *c:* Michele, Matthew; *ed:* (BSED) Elem, Indiana Univ of PA 1968; (MSED) Elem Math, Univ of Pittsburgh 1975; Amer Red Cross Safety; *cr:* Teacher Homer Center Elem Sch 1968-; *ai:* Homer Center HS Head Track Coach 1968-84, Asst Ftbl 1968-74, 1980-85; Childrens Hospital Fund Drive HCEA Treas 1970-; PSEA, NEA 1970-; Boosters Organization, Red Barn Sportmans; *office:* Homer Center Elem Sch S Main St Homer City PA 15748

FINSETH, CONSTANCE E. (ST JOHN), Math Teacher; *b:* Renton, WA; *c:* Tobe, Sami, Jaimie; *ed:* (BA) Elem Ed, Western WA Univ 1969; (MED) Elem, Univ of Pittsburgh 1978; *cr:* Music Teacher Edgewood MD 1969-71; 2nd/3rd/4th Grade Teacher 1971-81, 7th/8th Grade Math Teacher 1981- Pittsburg Public Schls; Quasar Teacher in Residence LRDC Univ of Pittsburgh 1990; *ai:* NCTM; Math Cncl of Western PA; PA Cncl Teachers of Math; Women & Math Ed; Pittsburgh Fed of Teachers; PA Fed of Teachers; AFT; Highland Park Cmmty Club; Appointment Quasar Teacher in Residence; Creative Teacher of Yr Awd 1989; Outstanding Math Teacher Awd 1990; *office:* Univ of Pittsburgh 712 LRDC 3939 O Hara St Pittsburgh PA 15260

FINTON, ESTHER SCHAFER, Second Grade Teacher; *b:* Warsaw, IL; *m:* Daniel; *c:* Deborah Mc Laughlin, Craig; *ed:* (BA) Elem Ed, Carthage Coll 1966; Elem Ed, Western IL Coll; *cr:* Teacher Warsaw Dist 316 1962-; *ai:* Cty Institute; WTA, IEA, NEA; Intnl Rdng Assn; Meth Church; Authored Books of Teacher Material for Classroom Use; Article Published in Childrens Encyclopedia.

FIORICA, CAROLYN J., Social Studies Teacher; *b:* Quincy, FL; *m:* Anthony Michael; *ed:* (BA) Soc Stud Ed, FL St Univ 1971; (MS) Ed Tech/Org Trng, Univ of Miami 1990; *cr:* Classroom Teacher Teague Mid Sch 1976-78, Shaw HS 1978-79, Milwee Mid Sch 1979-84, Lake Howell HS 1984-; *ai:* Tabs Comm; Seminole Ed Assn (Faculty Rep 1981-82, Leg Comm 1980-82); Cert Area Teacher Test Grant Comm; *office:* Lake Howell HS 4200 Dike Rd Winter Park FL 32792

FIPPS, BRIAN WILLIAMSON, Mathematics/Cmptr Prgm Teacher; *b:* Lumberton, NC; *ed:* (BS) Math, Mars Hill Coll 1976; *cr:* Teacher Pine Forest Sr HS 1976-; *home:* 1048-A Andrews Rd Fayetteville NC 28311

FIRDA, EMMA MINEMIER, Second Grade Teacher; *b:* Nanticoke, PA; *m:* Andrew; *c:* Lauren D.; *ed:* (BS) Elem Ed, Wilkes Univ 1958; Addl Studies Trenton ST Coll, Bloomburg ST Coll; Marywood Coll; *cr:* 1st Grade Teacher Oxford Valley Elem, Fallsington Elem, Manor Elem 1958-65; 3rd Grade Teacher Manor Elem 1965-66; 3rd Grade Teacher Oxford Valley Elem 1966-68; 2nd Grade Teacher PA Valley Elem, Oxford Valley Elem 1969-; *ai:* Church Cncl Mem Concentrating Act with Christian Ed Comm; Sunday Sch Teacher for 15 Yrs & Assoc with Ongoing Ed Progms of Church; Pennsbury Ed Assn 1958-; PA St Assn 1958-; Natl Ed Assn 1958-; *home:* 6 Hedge Road Levittown PA 19056

FIREBAUGH, DOUGLAS B., Chemistry/Astronomy Teacher; *b:* Freeport, IL; *m:* Audrey Bessert; *c:* Michele, Dena; *ed:* (MS) Chemical Ed, Univ of UT 1963; (BS) Chem, Manchester Coll 1962; Dickenson Coll, Bowling Coll, Univ of PA, St Cloud St Univ, Rockford Coll, Highland Coll; *cr:* Chem Teacher 1963-, Sci Dept Head 1985- Freeport HS; *ai:* JETS, NHS, Class Adv; Sci Fair Chm; Freeport Ed Assn, IL Ed Assn, NEA 1963-; Church Camp Bd Chm 1975-81; Manchester Coll (Alumni Chm 1973, 1983-, Bd of Dir 1987-), Merit 1973; Article Published; Jaycee Outstanding Educator; Amer Chem Society Teacher Awd; Presidential Teacher Awd; Top 10 Teachers in IL Awd; *office:* Freeport HS 701 W Moseley Freeport IL 61032

FIRESTONE, BARBARA JANE, Fifth Grade Teacher; *b:* Wichita, KS; *ed:* (BS) Elem Ed, Friends Univ 1968; (MS) Elem Ed, Wichita St Univ 1974; Ed, Wichita St Univ; Special Prgms in Citizen Ed Center for Research & Dev Wake Forest Univ Sch of Law/Law-Related & Stud on Constitution; *cr:* 5th Grade Teacher 1968, 6th Grade Teacher 1985-88 McCollom Elem; Adjunct Professor/(Soc Stud Methods) Wichita St Univ 1986-88; *ai:* Teacher in Charge KS Cncl for The Soc Stud Pres; Center for Research & Dev for Law-Related Ed; Bd of Trustees Lang Arts/Soc Stud Comm; Supts Evaluation CncL Prof Review Bd; KS Cncl Soc Stud Bd of Dir; Women in Leadership Prgm; Soc Stud Curr Guide Comm KS Guide; Inservice Presenter Lang Arts/Rndg/Soc Stud; Co-Chairperson Midregional Intnl Rdng Assn Conference Luncheon; Screening Comm for Soc Stud Coord/Prin; KS Cncl for Soc Stud Pres/Bd 1988-89; NCSS Elem SS Teacher of Yr 1989; NEA Various Comm, NEA Elem Teacher of Yr 1989; Wichita Distinguished Teacher of Yr 1989; 1990 KS Teacher of Yr; Good Apple Awd USD 259 1988; Tribute to Teacher KAKE-TV 1984; KS Educl Slate Natl Bicentennial Celebration 1986; Constitutional Sampler; Amer Bar Assn Ed/Bar Partnership Magazine Elem Schls/Courts 1989; Sun Up KS Soc Stud Journal; 5th Grade Class Presents Hamlet; Public Service Announcements We the People Count a Series of 6 PSA Prepared By 5th Graders Televised Channel 2 Wichita KS 1989; *home:* 1404 N Wood Wichita KS 67212

FIRESTONE, MARVEL A., Third Grade Teacher; *b:* York, PA; *m:* Gary A.; *c:* Kelly, Tanya Smith, Jonathan, Chad; *ed:* (BS) Elem Ed, Millersville Univ 1971; Masters Equivalency; *cr:* Substitute Teacher Dover Sch Dist 1959-78, West York Sch Dist 1968-78; Teacher Dover Sch Dist 1978-; *ai:* Rdng Comm; LIU Comprehensive Sch Evaluation Team; DAEA, PSEA, NEA; *home:* 2730 Conewago Rd Dover PA 17315

FIRESTONE, MARY MATTOX, Math Teacher; *b:* Oxford, NC; *m:* Wayne King; *c:* Mason King, Matthew Hunter; *ed:* (BS) His, Jacksonville St Univ 1982, (MA) Math, Univ of AL 1989; *cr:* Math Teacher Southside HS 1983-, Gadsden St Comm Coll 1989; *ai:* SADD Spon; Alpha Delta Kappa 1986-89.

FIRICH, JEAN, English Teacher; *b:* Ambridge, PA; *ed:* (BS) Ed/Eng/Rdng, Slippery Rock Univ 1969; Grad Level Courses Slippery Rock St Coll, Cleveland St Univ; Cmmty Intervention; Leadership Insts; Project Teach; *cr:* Rdng Teacher Center Township HS 1969-71, Sayre Area HS 1971-73; Rdng Teacher 1973-76, Eng Teacher 1976- Bay HS; *ai:* Facilitate After-Care Support Group; Drug-Free Cmmty Comm; NEA 1969-; PA Ed Assn 1969-73; OH Ed Assn 1973-; Bay Teachers Assn (Secy 1977-78, 1989-) 1973-; *office:* Bay HS 29230 Wolf Rd Bay Village OH 44140

FISCH, THOMAS MICHAEL, 8th Grade Soc Stud Teacher; *b:* Huntington, NY; *m:* Kathleen E. Ryan; *c:* Linda, Lauri, Shane R.; *ed:* (BA) Poly Sci, St Michaels Coll 1968; Grad Stud SUNY Plattsburgh 1971-73; *cr:* Scndry Soc Stud Teacher Pius X Cntrl Sch 1968-71; 7th/8th Grade Soc Stud Teacher Saranac Lake Mid Sch 1971-; *ai:* Stu Adv; Jr Var Bsbl Coach; St Bernards Bd of Ed Chm 1972-74; NY Mid Sch Assn 1988-; Santa Clara Town Bd Town Councilman 1984-87; Pee Wee Hockey Assn Coach 1975-78; *office:* Saranac Lake Mid Sch Petrova Ave Saranac Lake NY 12983

FISCHER, BARBARA BUSHMAN, English Teacher; *b:* Lakeland, FL; *c:* Barbara K., Beverlie K., Philip J. II; *ed:* (BA) Eng/Sociology, Univ of AL 1966; Grad Courses 1982-83; *cr:* Teacher Trinity Presbyn Sch 1975-; *ai:* Sr Spon; Tennis Team Mother; Parent Bd Teacher Advisory & Soc Comm; Jr League Bus Mgr 1970 ; Mental Health Bd 1966 69; *home:* 1818 Ridge Ave Montgomery AL 36106

FISCHER, DEBBIE ROTSTEIN, Bus Cooperative Ed Teacher; *b:* Dubuque, IA; *m:* Matt Joseph; *c:* Nicholas; *ed:* (AA) General Ed, FL Jr Coll 1975; (BA) Ed, Univ of FL 1977; (MS) Admin/ Supervision, Nova Univ 1979; Bus Ed, Admin/Supervision, Univ of S FL; *cr:* Secy Douglas Printing Company 1973-77; Teacher Newberry HS 1977-83, Clearwater HS & Adult Ed 1983-84; Bus Cooperative Ed Coord Northeast HS 1984-; *ai:* Homecoming Comm; FBLA Spon & Dist 12 Adv; Pinellas Bus Ed Assn (VP 1985) 1984-; FL Voc Assn 1977-; America Voc Assn 1978-85; Diversified Cooperative Teachers Assn of FL (Secy 1983) 1977-84; Pinellas Adult & Voc Educators 1984-; Alachua Cty Bus Educators (Secy) 1977-84; Northeast HS Teacher of Month; *office:* Northeast HS 1717 54th Ave N Saint Petersburg FL 33714

FISCHER, DONNA POOL, 4th Grade Teacher; *b:* Strasburg, ND; *m:* Wayne; *c:* Peggy Fischer Hildebrandt, Brent; *ed:* (BA) Elem Ed, Northern St Univ 1973; Rdng Specialist; *cr:* Elem Ed Teacher Emmons Cty Rural Sch 1956-57; 3rd/4th Grade Teacher Hazelton Public Sch 1957-58; 4th Grade Teacher Ashley Public Sch 1958-59, Finley Public Sch 1959-60; 1st-6th Grade Teacher Aberdeen Public Schls 1974-; *ai:* Delta Kappa Gamma 1989-; Kappa Kappa Iota 1987-89; Intnl Rdng Assn 1975-80, 1989-; Northern St Univ VP 1969-70; Faculty Wives Pres 1974-75; PTA VP 1970; Baptist Church (Sunday Sch Teacher, Choir, Womens Work); Teacher of Week Awd 1990; *home:* 1727 S 1st St Aberdeen SD 57401

FISCHER, ELLEN THOMPSON, Sixth Grade Teacher; *b:* Noblesville, IN; *m:* Paul John; *ed:* (BS) Elem Ed, IN Univ 1974; (MAE) Elem Ed, Ball St Univ 1977; Quest Intnl Basic Trng 1986, Advanced Trng 1988; *cr:* 6th Grade Teacher Mount Vernon Mid Sch 1974-; *ai:* Summer Sch Teacher; Mount Vernon Classroom Teachers Assn Treas 1981-83; IN State Teachers Assn; NEA; IN Rdng Assn; Psi Iota Ci, Theta Alpha (Treas, Corres Secy 1989-); Kids & Kettles Home Extension Club, Health & Safety Leader 1986-87; Skills for Adolescence Cmnty Informational Panel 1990; Teaching of Parent Seminars 1986-; *office:* Mt Vernon Mid Sch 1862 W Street Rd 234 Fortville IN 46040

FISCHER, FALTON M., Fifth Grade Teacher; *b:* Oconto Falls, WI; *m:* Donna Schnese; *c:* Richard, Jim, Terry; *ed:* (BS) Upper Elem, Univ of WI-River Falls 1961; (MS) Elem Admin, Univ of Wi-Superior 1967; *cr:* 5th Grade Teacher Franklin Sch 1961-64; 5th & 6th Grade Teacher Riverview Sch 1964-; *ai:* Coach Bsktbl/ Ftbl/Track & Vlybl; Safety Patrol Adv; Math & Geography Bowl Adv; NEA 1961-; WEA 1961-; Wausau Ed Assn Bldg Rep/Chrmn Salary Research 1973-74; Lions Club Pres 1978; Lions Club Zone Chm 1973/Membership Devel Awd 1973; Outstanding Young Educator Presented By Jaycees; Outstanding Teacher Awd Presented By Sch Dist; *home:* 3805 Henry St Wausau WI 54401

FISCHER, JOEL BRUCE, Third Grade Teacher; *b:* St Cloud, MN; *m:* Sharon Adelman; *c:* Aaron J., Tanya L.; *ed:* (BS) Elem Ed, 1965, (MS) Elem Ed, 1975, Ed Admin, 1980 St Cloud St Univ; US Navy Advanced Radiomens Sch; *cr:* 6th Grade Teacher 1968-78, 4th Grade Teacher 1978-82, 3rd Grade Teacher 1982- Isanti Elem Sch; *ai:* Bsbl Card Club; Track & Field; Amer Legion 1968-; MN Historical Society Commendation for Excl in Teaching His; *office:* Isanti Elem Sch County Road 5 Isanti MN 55040

FISCHER, KENNETH J., 5th Grade Teacher; *b:* Philadelphia, PA; *m:* Janet A.; *c:* Jennifer, Christine; *ed:* (BS) Psych, 1974, (BS) Ed, 1976 Marymount Coll; (MS) Admin, KS St Univ 1983; *cr:* 6th Grade Teacher St Johns 1976-79; 5th Grade Teacher Beloit Elem Sch 1979-; *ai:* Curr Comm Math & Soc Sci; Earl Mitchell Cty Teachers Assn Secy 1982-83; Coaching T-Ball 1986-89; Coaching Bsktbl 1989; St Johns Church Ushers 1988; *office:* Beloit Elem Sch W 12th & Bell St Beloit KS 67420

FISCHER, KEVIN E., Computer Teacher; *b:* Green Bay, WI; *m:* Debbie Jo; *ed:* (BA) Bus Ed, NW IA Coll 1985; (MS) Cmptr Ed, Barry Univ 1990; *cr:* Cmptr Teacher Mays Mid Sch 1985-; *ai:* Cmptr Club Adv 1985-; Newspaper Adv 1990; ICPSC Cmptr Competition 1988-; CEAI 1984-; YMCA Adult Prgm Dir 1987-88; Vineyard Chrstn Fellowship (Prgm, Youth Dir) 1987-; Grant Recipient Class Cmptr Literacy & Stu Success; Teacher of Yr Mays Mid Sch 1990; Article Published Dade Cty Cmptr Ed Newsletter; *office:* Mays Mid Sch 11700 SW 216th St Miami FL 33170

FISCHER, LYMAN DIXON, Mathematics Teacher; *b:* Winona, MN; *m:* June Emily Witt; *c:* Keith, Kevin; *ed:* (BA) Math, 1964, (MS) Sci Ed, 1974 Winona St Univ; *cr:* Math Teacher Oshkosh-South Park Jr HS 1964-66, Lombardi Mid Sch 1966-; *ai:* Head Cross Cntry & Girls Track Coach Southwest HS; Running Prgm Lombardi Mid Sch; GBEA, WEA, NEA; Mid Sch Teacher of Yr Awd of Excl 1985; *home:* 3249 W Point Rd Green Bay WI 54313

FISCHER, LYNDA PANDOZZI, English Teacher; *b:* Newark, NJ; *m:* Kenneth J. Jr.; *c:* Steven, Lindsay; *ed:* (BS) Ed, Seton Hall Univ 1978; *cr:* Lang Art Teacher Carl Sandburg Mid Sch 1979-81; Rdng Wkshp Teacher Jonas Salk Mid Sch 1981-83; Basic Skills Teacher Cedar Ridge HS 1983-86; Eng Teacher Madison Cntrl HS 1986-; *ai:* 1991 Class Adv; New Stu Orientation Comm Adv; Alpha Delta Kappa 1990; *office:* Madison Cntrl HS 1 Wisdom Way Old Bridge NJ 08857

FISCHER, MAX W., 6th Grade Teacher; *b:* Akron, OH; *m:* Sharon K. Wrather; *c:* Ashley, Abby; *ed:* (BS) Elem Ed, 1974, (MS) Ed, 1981 Univ of Akron; Supervision, Ashland Univ 1985-86; *cr:* 4th/6th Grade Teacher Mapleton Local Schls 1974-77; 5th Grade Teacher Ashland City Schls 1977-81; 5th/6th Grade Teacher Wooster City Schls 1981-; *ai:* Intramurals Dir Kean Sch; Sci Olympiad Coord Kean Sch; Wooster Ed Assn Building Rep/Neotiation 1981-; OEA/NEA 1977-; ASCD 1987; Big Brothers Ashland 1976-81 Merit Service 1981-; Apple Creek United Meth Church Trustee/Lay Speaker 1987-; *office:* Kean Sch 432 Oldman Rd Wooster OH 44691

FISCHER, TED F., Fifth Grade Teacher; *b:* Baltimore, MD; *m:* Claudia Lages; *c:* Matt, Amanda; *ed:* (BS) Elem Ed, Towson St 1971; (MS) Elem Ed, Loyola 1979; Cooperative Learning & Assertive Discipline; *cr:* 6th Grade Teacher 1971-82, 5th Grade Teacher 1983- Norwood; *ai:* Safety Patrol Adv; TABCO (Rep 1971-80) 1981-; *home:* 16 Hapsburg Ct Perry Hall MD 21234

FISCHER, THEODORE, Guidance Counselor; *b:* Passaic, NJ; *m:* Patricia Marzocca; *c:* Denise, Christopher; *ed:* (BS) Bus Ed/ Eng, 1966, (MA) Ed Admin/Supervision, 1973 Seton Hall Univ; Montclair St Coll; *cr:* Eng Teacher 1966-68, Bus Ed Teacher 1967-68, Cnslr 1968-70, 1979-85, 1988- E Rutherford HS; Cnslr 1970-72, Asst Supt 1972-78, Dir 1985-88 Becton Reg HS; *ai:* Var Sftbl Coach; Bergen Cty Ed Assn, Becton Ed Assn, NJEA, NEA 1966-; Norwood Bd of Ed Pres 1976-82; Norwood Recreation Comm 1973-76; Immacutate Conception K of 1985-; *office:* Henry P Becton Regional HS Paterson Ave & Cornelia St East Rutherford NJ 07073

FISCHER, WAYNE THOMAS, Mathematics Department Chair; *b:* Jersey City, NJ; *m:* Silika; *c:* Nathan; *ed:* (BS) Math, IN Univ of PA 1973; Cmptr Courses; Working on MA Kean Coll; *cr:* Peace Corps Sangam HS 1973-77; St Josephs HS 1977-; *ai:* Bowling Coach; Chess Team & Math League Moderator; Assn of Math Teachers of NJ 1985-; Amer Math Society 1989-; US Chess Fed 1984-; Middlesex Cty Coaches Assn; Coach of Yr 1987; *office:* St Josephs HS 145 Plainfield Ave Metuchen NJ 08840

FISHEL, PAULINE DEAN, Mathematics Teacher; *b:* Hill City, KS; *m:* Duane; *c:* Terri, Darren; *ed:* (BS) Math, Ft Hays St Univ 1958; (MS) Math, Emporia St Univ 1976; *cr:* Math Teacher Natoma HS 1958-59, Lakeview HS 1962-63, Bogue HS 1963-68, Kensington KS 1968-69, Hope HS 1969-78, Ft Riley Adult HS 1978-79, Centre HS 1979-82; Instr Marymount Coll 1982-86; Teacher Sacred Heart HS 1986-; *ai:* Frosh Class; Cath Ed Assn; *office:* Sacred Heart HS 230 E Cloud St Salina KS 67401

FISHER, ARLENE K., Science Teacher; *b:* New Castle, PA; *ed:* (BS) Bio, Earth and Space Sci, Clarion Univ 1966; (MED) Gen Sci, Scndry Guidance Cnslr, Westminster Coll 1970; Comparative Ed, Slippery Rock Univ 1988; *cr:* Sci Teacher Riverside Beaver Cty Sch Dist 1966-; *ai:* PSEA; NEA 1966-; *office:* Riverside Mid Sch Rt #2 Country Club Dr Ellwood City PA 16117

FISHER, BETH SWINT, Kindergarten Teacher; *b:* Douglassville, TX; *m:* Pat Odell; *c:* Cynthia C. Cash Bickerdike, Stephanie L. Cash Hodges, William N. Cash, John T. Truett; *ed:* (BS) Elem Ed/Kndgtn, Baylor Univ 1953-55; (BS) Elem Ed/ Kndgtn, E TX St Univ Commerce 1977; *cr:* Teacher Pearsall Elem, Jefferson Elem 1960-61; Teacher Aide Alba Golden Elem 1973-75; Teacher Grand Saline Elem 1977-; *ai:* Sunday Sch Teacher; Soc Stud Dev Leader; Assn of TX Prof Ed 1989-; Beta Sigma Phi; Grand Saline Study Club Pres 1972; Kings Creek 4-H Club (Organizer, Pres, Leader) 1967, Leadership Awd; Service to Care Home Outstanding Awd 1986; NCNB Nom Outstanding Teacher 1989.

FISHER, COLLETTE CROTTY, Health/Home Economics Teacher; *b:* Spencer, IA; *m:* Mark L.; *c:* Molly, Kate; *ed:* (BS) Home Ec Ed, 1979, (BS) Health Ed, Univ of WI-Stout 1979; Working on Masters in Scndry Ed, Drake Univ; *cr:* 7th-9th Grade Home Ec Teacher Evans Jr HS 1979-82; 10th-12th Grade Home Ec Ed Teacher 1982-89, 9th-12th Grade Health Ed Teacher 1989- Ottumwa HS; *ai:* Health Advisory Comm; Ottumwa Sch Dist Curr Coord; Scndry Health Skills for Life Prgm; NEA 1979-; Ottumwa Ed Assn Rep Mem 1979-; Outstanding Young Women of America Awd 1986; St Marys Church Alter & Rosary Society 1979-; Al-Ateen Charter Mem 1982; Alpha Phi Past Pres/Soc Chm/ Rush Chm/Phi Friend; Natl Panhellenic Alumni Cncl Humanitarian Awd 1979; *office:* Ottumwa H S 501 E 2nd Ottumwa IA 52501

FISHER, ELIZABETH GRANT, French/History Teacher; *b:* Fort Jackson, SC; *m:* Jerry; *c:* Elizabeth, Sara; *ed:* (CECF) Fr Civilization, Sorbonne Univ of Paris 1962; (BA) Fr, Winthrop Coll 1963; (CEP) Poly Sci, Inst d Etudes Politiques Paris 1964; (MED) Guidance/Counseling, Coll of William & Mary 1969; Re-Cert Courses, UNC Chapel Hill; *cr:* Fr Teacher W Memphis Sr HS 1965-67, Rose HS 1967-68; Fr/Government Teacher Kecoughton HS 1968-70; Research Asst Univ of NC Chapel Hill 1970-85; Fr/ His Teacher Cresset Chrstn Acad 1985-; *ai:* Foreign Lang Assn of NC; Durham Herald & Sun Newspapers in Ed Teacher of Yr 1989; Article Published 1982; *office:* Cresset Chrstn Acad 3707 Garrett Rd Durham NC 27707

FISHER, ETHEL PAGE, Third Grade Teacher; *b:* Horse Cave, KY; *m:* Kenneth Dewitt; *c:* Kenneth K., Wynecta M., Kevin K.; *ed:* (BS) Elem Ed - Cum Laude, Cntrl St Univ 1955-57; (MS) Elem Ed, IN UNiv 1967-69; Spec Ed, Purdue Univ & IN Univ 1971-73; *cr:* Elem Teacher Hartigan Sch 1957; Elem Sci Teacher Froebel Sch 1958-60; Elem Teacher Horace Worton Sch 1961-72, John H Vohr 1972-; *ai:* 2nd-6th Grade Great Book Leader; Mentor Teacher; Spelling Bee 3rd-6th Grade Coach & City Wide Spon 1972, 1989; Vohr Sch Peer Coach; Vohr STAY Coord; ERD Teacher; Queen of Hearts Bridge Club; Amer Chldhd Assn, Gary Rdng Assn, Soc Stud Assn, PTA; Alpha Kappa Alpha, NAACP, St Timothy Church, IN Univ Alumni, Gary Teachers Union 4; Cntrl St Alumni Beams Pres; AFT Outstanding ERD Work Citation; Nom Certificate Awd Outstanding Teacher; Nom Outstanding Elem Teacher of America 1975; John Vohr Sch Outstanding Service Certificate; *home:* 1580 Wallace Gary IN 46404

FISHER, GAIL E. (STRINGER), 3rd Grade Teacher; *b:* Lincoln, IL; *m:* John F.; *c:* Kevin, Kamia Fisher Hansen; *ed:* (AA) Liberal Arts, Lincoln Coll 1960; (BA) Elem Ed, Carthage Coll 1972; Natl Coll; Northern Il Univ; Governors St Univ; *cr:* 4th Grade Teacher Wauconda Schls 1961-62; 5th Grade Teacher, 4th & 8th Grade Art Teacher Hawthorn Sch 1964-71; 2nd & 3rd Grade Teacher Zion Public Schls 1972-; *ai:* Stu Cncl Adv 1989-; Gifted Teacher of Gifted Stu 1989-; Teacher-Adv Stu Teachers Zion Schls 1989-; Zion Ed Assn Bldg Rep 1989-; Zion Karate Club-Instr 1980-85; Blackbelt 1985; York House United Meth Church Chairperson 1984-86; Magazine Articles Published 1989-; Name Read Into IL Rec St Senate 1988; Outstanding IL Educator; Luncheon Governors Mansion 1988; *office:* West Elem Sch 2412 Jethro Av Zion IL 60099

FISHER, GLENN LOE, Teacher; *b:* New York, NY; *m:* Jill Wilson; *c:* Kimberly; *ed:* (BA) Geography, Univ of CA Los Angeles 1968; (MS) Sch Bus/Admin, Pepperdine 1976; *cr:* Teacher/Pool Teacher Figueroa Street 1968-69, Fries Avenue 1969-70; SPC 5 US Army 1970-72; Teacher Fifteenth Street Elem 1972-; *ai:* Sch Decision Making Cncl Mem; UTLA (Rep 1988, Chapter Chm 1980-86); NEA; LACTMA Finalist Outstanding Elem Math Teacher Awd; *office:* Fifteenth Street Elem Sch 1527 S Mesa St San Pedro CA 90731

FISHER, GRACE KIMBERLY, 3rd Grade Teacher; *b:* Petersburg, VA; *ed:* (BS) Ed, Longwood Coll 1979; Working Towards Masters Rdng; *cr:* 3rd Grade Teacher South Primary Sch 1979-; *ai:* South Primary Youth Advisory Cncl Spon; Richmond Area Rdng Cncl, VA Area Friends of Gifted; Jr Federated Womans Club of Petersburg (Ways & Means Chm, 1st VP, 2nd VP, Pres, St Jr Arts & Crafts Chm 1988-) 1981-, Outstanding Jr 1984; *office:* South Primary Sch 13400 Prince George Dr Disputanta VA 23842

FISHER, HOWARD B., Biology Teacher; *b:* Oceanside, NY; *m:* Caren Benstock; *c:* Justin, Jessica; *ed:* (BA) Scndry Ed/Bio, 1970, (MS) Scndry Ed/Bio, 1973 Univ of Bridgeport; *cr:* Phys & Life Sci Teacher Woodland Jr HS 1970-73; Regents & General Bio Teacher West Jr HS 1974-78; Phys Sci Teacher/Multi-Age Teaming West Mid Sch 1978-85; Regents Bio/General Bio/Sci Teacher Binghamton HS 1985-; *ai:* Coach Odyssey of Mind 1984-, Knowledge Master Open 1987, NY St Sci Olympiad 1985; Marine Bio Instr 1986-; Vesdal Youth Soccer Asst Coach & Mgr 1983-87; SUNY Interns Cooperating Teacher 1985-; NEA Building Rep 1989-; Binghamton City Sch Dist Congruency Comm Mem 1987-; Binghamton HS Athletic Eligibility Review Comm Mem 1987-; Binghamton Teachers Assn Newsletter Co-Ed 1988-; St Univ of NY Binghamton Institutional Bio Safety Comm Mem 1988-; Binghamton City Sch Dist Teacher of Yr 1987; NSTA/NASA SSIP Natl Winner Teacher-Adv 1982, 1983; Mensa Service Awd 1983; Nom Space Educators Awd 1984, 1985; *office:* Binghamton HS 31 Main St Binghamton NY 13905

FISHER, JOYCE HOCKMAN, Fifth Grade Teacher; *b:* Freeport, IL; *m:* Louis W.; *c:* Wendy Slick Kerin, Anthony Y. Slick; *ed:* (BS) Music, Univ of WI Platteville 1963; (MS) Elem Ed, N IL Univ DeKalb 1989; *cr:* Vocal Music Teacher Forreston Grade & HS 1963-65; 3rd-5th Grade Teacher Rockford Public Schls 1970-; *ai:* IEA, NEA 1970-; Kantorei Boys Choir Accompanist 1978-85; Broadway Covenant Church Organist 1978-81.

FISHER, KAREN STONEROCK, Third Grade Teacher; *b:* New Castle, IN; *c:* Amy, Julie; *ed:* (BS) Elem Ed, 1972, (MS) Elem Ed, 1977 Ball St Univ; *cr:* 4th Grade Teacher 1974-78, 3rd Grade Teacher 1978- Spiceland Elem Sch; *ai:* IN St Teachers Assn, NEA 1974-; Delta Kappa Gamma Corresponding Secy 1981-; IN St Rdng Cncl 1988-; *office:* Spiceland Elem Sch Main St Spiceland IN 47385

FISHER, LA JUAN MARTIN, Mathematics Teacher/Dept Chair; *b:* Jacksonville, TX; *m:* Ronald R.; *c:* Victoria A., Christopher M.; *ed:* (AA) Ed, Lon Morris Jr Coll 1974; (BS) Math/Health Ed, E TX St Univ 1976; Advanced Acad Trng; *cr:* Math Teacher Royse City TX 1976-77, Havelock HS 1977-78, West Carteret HS 1978-81, Nimitz HS 1981-82; Math Teacher/ Dept Chm Sam Houston HS 1982-; *ai:* UIL Number Sense & Calculator Math Coach; Super Spon of Yr 1976-77; Positive Reinforcement Contest 1986; Nom TX Excl Awd for Outstanding HS Teachers 1986; STAR Teacher Awd 1986; Nom Presidential Awd for Excl in Sci & Math Teaching 1988-; Nom Tandy

Technology Scholars 1989; Sam Houston HS Teacher of Yr 1989-; Pamphlet Published; *office:* Sam Houston HS 2000 Sam Houston Dr Arlington TX 76014

FISHER, LEONA KENT, Music/Performing Arts Teacher; *b:* Grenada, MS; *m:* Jonathan; *c:* Kent J., Roger F., Nancy M.; *ed:* (BA) Music, Fisk Univ 1957; Post Grad Stud Ed; Sacred Music Wkshps Mary Grove Coll; *cr:* Teacher Dillard HS 1957-58, George & Chaney Elem Sch 1958-61, Burton Elem Sch 1962-69, Courville Elem Sch 1969-; *ai:* Detroit Public Schls Annual Fine Art Festival Coord 1986-88; St Paul United Meth Church Minister of Music 1984-; Hartford Memorial Baptist Church Childrens Choir Dir 1988-89; Delta Sigma Theta Prgm Chairperson 1956-; *home:* 13342 Vassar Dr Detroit MI 48235

FISHER, MICHAEL, Teacher; *b:* Dayton, OH; *m:* Janet Leslie Miller; *c:* Samantha A.; *ed:* (BA) Math/Comm/Ed, Marietta Coll 1972; Continuing Ed; *cr:* Teacher Parkwood Elem/Beavercreek Local Schls 1972-; *ai:* Musical Dir Technical Drama; Comm for Gifted; Technology Comm Strategic Planning for Beavercreek Schls; Natl NEA Convention; Beavercreek Ed Assn (Pres 1988-, Assn Rep 1982-85); OH Ed Assn St Delegate 1988-; Oh Ed Assn, Western Oh Ed Assn, NEA 1972-; Belmont United Meth Church Facilator for Strategic Planning 1989-; Dayton Dog Trng Club Dir of Trng 1987 Instr of Yr 1986; Hawker United Church of Christ Sftbl Team 1976- Player of Yr 1983/87; Nom Beavercreek Teacher of Yr 5 Times; *office:* Parkwood Elem Schl 2940 Dayton-Xenia Rd Beavercreek OH 45385

FISHER, NANCY ANNE, Third Grade Teacher; *b:* Anchorage, AK; *ed:* (BS) Elem Ed, MT ST Univ 1978; *cr:* 3rd Grade Teacher Stevensville Elem 1978-; *ai:* Sci Textbook Selection Comm Co-Chm; Stevensville Booster Club; 3 Yrs As Secy/Treas of Stevensville Teachers Assn; *office:* Stevensville Elem Sch 300 Park St Stevensville MT 59870

FISHER, PAT TWINER, Chem Teacher/Sci Dept Chair; *b:* Kingsport, TN; *c:* Ashley Fisher Mohler, Louie M.; *ed:* (BA) Bio, 1966, (MAED) Media, 1987 N LA Univ; Sci Courses, N LA Univ 1987; *cr:* Bio Teacher Richwood HS 1969-70, Katy HS 1975-77; Chem Teacher Ouachita HS 1982-; *ai:* SGA & Past Honor Society Spon; Teacher of Yr 1987; LA Tech Natl Sci Fnd Chem Cert; Outstanding Teacher Scholars Banquet; *office:* Ouachita HS 681 Hwy 594 Monroe LA 71203

FISHER, PENNY SUMMERS, Assistant Principal; *b:* South Charleston, WV; *m:* Jonathan S.; *c:* Jonathan S. II; *ed:* (AB) Span/Math, 1977, (MA) Curr Mid Sch, 1981 Marshall Univ; Preparing Prospectus for Doctoral Prgm WV Univ; *cr:* Span/Math Teacher 1977-88, Asst Prin 1988- Hurricane Mid Sch; *ai:* Phi Delta Kappa, NASSP, Natl Mid Sch Assn; *office:* Hurricane Mid Sch 518 Midland Trl Hurricane WV 25526

FISHER, ROBERT DOUGLAS, Sci Teacher/Guidance Cnslr; *b:* Charleroi, PA; *m:* Gail Ellen Mc Guire; *c:* Autumn, Jessica, Braden; *ed:* (BS) Earth/General Sci Ed, California Univ of PA 1973; (MS) Educl Admin, Univ of Dayton; Counseling; *cr:* 7th-9th Grade Sci Teacher 1974-86; 7th/8th Grade Sci/Guidance Teacher Buckeye Cntrl Jr HS 1986-; *ai:* Audio-Visual Club Adv; Sci Fair Coord; *home:* PO Box 293 Mount Pleasant OH 43939

FISHER, ROSALYN WHEELER, Elem/Special Education Teacher; *b:* New Rochelle, NY; *m:* William E.; *ed:* (BA) Elem Ed, Shaw Univ 1974; (MS) Learning Disabilities, Coll of New Rochelle 1980; Lib Sci Courses to Work as Media Specialist; *cr:* K-6th Grade Elem Teacher New Rochelle Schls 1974-77; Special Ed Teacher 1977-80, Media Specialist 1980-87 Greenburgh Graham Sch; Elem/Spec Ed Teacher Windermere Elem Sch 1987-; *ai:* Sound Shore Lioness Club Pres 1985-87, Pres Awd 1987; 10 Yrs Outstanding Services for Spec Ed Greenbaugh Graham USFD 1987; *home:* 3033 Golden Rock Dr Orlando FL 32818

FISHER, SUSAN GRADY, English Teacher; *b:* Charleston, WV; *m:* Neal R.; *c:* Laura, Casey; *ed:* (BS) Ed, WV Univ 1974; *cr:* Teacher Fluvanna Cty HS 1974-78, Appomattox Cty HS 1984-; *ai:* Stu Cncl Assn; *office:* Appomattox Cty HS Rt 5 Box 630 Appomattox VA 24522

FISHER, TERESA HAYWOOD, High School English Teacher; *b:* Laurinburg, NC; *m:* Raymond H.; *c:* Matthew, Katherine; *ed:* (BA) His/Eng, Francis Marion Coll 1978; Additional His/Eng Course Work, Univ of SC; *cr:* HS Eng Teacher Emmanuel Baptist Sch 1978-79, Bates Sch 1979-80; Adult Ed Teacher Lexington Cty Dist #2 1979-81; HS His/Eng Teacher Sloans Sch 1981-83; Eng Teacher Emmanuel Baptist Sch 1986-; *ai:* Jr Class Spon; Fine Arts Dir; Pi Gamma Mu; Cmmty Concert Assn; Whos Who in Amer Ed 1989-; *office:* Emmanuel Baptist Sch Rt 1 Box 82 Hwy 15 N Hartsville SC 29550

FISHER, TIMOTHY HYLAND, 5th/6th Grade Teacher; *b:* Dover, NJ; *m:* Robin Du Bosque; *c:* Jason, Michael; *ed:* (BS) Elem Ed, Columbia Union Coll 1978; His; *cr:* Teacher 1978-, Vice Prin 1984- Tranquility Adv Sch; *ai:* Ski Club, Small Engine Club, Historical NJ Club Adv; NJ Ed Assn; NJ Model A Ford Club (Asst VP 1988-89, VP 1989-90, Pres 1990-91); *home:* 111 Wolf Corner Rd Greendell NJ 07839

FISHER, VIRGINIA STARR, Science Teacher/Dept Chair; *b:* Palestine, TX; *m:* James Everette; *c:* James, Jr.; *ed:* (AA) Henderson Cty Jr Coll 1979; (BS) Bio, 1982, (MED) Scndry Ed, 1984 Stephen F Austin St Univ; I Can Zig Ziglar Corporation Dallas TX 1987; Peer Pressure Reversal Trng 1989; Teacher Expectations Stu Achievement 1989; *cr:* Teacher 1983-, Dept Chairperson 1985- Adams Mid Sch; *ai:* UIL Sci Coach; Math/Sci Club Spon; Washington Dc Tour Spon; Supt Faculty Advisory Comm 1986-88; Supvr of Stu Teachers from Univ of TX Arlington; World Baptist Youth Conference Coach; TX Classroom Teachers Assn 1983-; PTA 1983-; Nom Adams Faculty Educator of Yr 1989; Adams Mid Sch Educator of Week 1988; *office:* Adams Mid Sch 853 W Tarrant Rd Grand Prairie TX 75050

FISHER, WILLIAM F., 8th Grade Math/Science Teacher; *b:* New York City, NY; *m:* Janet Pearce; *c:* Michele, Karen, Stephanie; *ed:* (BS) Ed, Seton Hall Univ 1964; (MA) Rdng, William Paterson Coll 1971; Sci NJ Inst of Technology, Rutgers Univ; *cr:* 8th-11th Grade Teacher Emerson Mid Sch & HS 1964-66; 8th Grade Math/Sci Teacher Paramus Public Sch/W Brook Mid Sch 1967-; *ai:* 8th Grade Boys Bsktbl Coach; Young Astronauts Club Adv; W Milford Bd of Ed Chm; Curr & Instr Comm; NJEA, Ed Assn of Paramus, NEA; Girls Bsktbl Assn Coach; Bd of Ed Chm W Milford NJ; Curr & Instr Comm; *office:* W Brook Mid Sch Roosevelt Blvd Paramus NJ 07652

FISHER, WILLIAM PETER, 5th Grade Teacher; *b:* New Brunswick, NJ; *m:* Sheila F. O'Brien; *ed:* (BS) Ed/Elem/Spec Ed, Slippery Rock St Coll 1974; Cmptr Sci Specialist; *cr:* Teacher J C Parks Elem 1974-89, William B Wade Elem 1989-; *ai:* Rdng Curr & Health Curr Comm; Cmptr Curr Comm & Staff Dev Instr; BEACCON Newsletter for Ed Assn of Charles Cty Staff & Mem of Membership Comm; MD St Teachers Assn Convention Delegate 1986; Charles Cty Ed Assn Mem 1989-; NEA Convention Delegate 1989-; Grade Level Chairperson, Team leader; Retired Teachers Converns Comm Mem St Level 1988-; Charles Cty Outstanding Teacher Awd 1984; *office:* William B Wade Elem Sch 5000 Smallwood Dr Waldorf MD 20603

FISHER-GLATT, JILL MEYERSON, 6th Grade English Teacher; *b:* New York City, NY; *m:* Edward Glatt; *c:* Douglas Fisher, Aaron Fisher; *ed:* (BS) Elem Ed, Boston Univ 1958; (MA) Admin/Supervision, Kean Coll 1975; *cr:* 6th Grade Teacher Jackson Avenue Sch 1958-62; 2nd Grade Teacher Hillel Acad 1967-70; 5th/6th Grade Teacher Woodbrook Sch 1970-84; 6th Grade Eng Teacher Woodrow Wilson 1984-; *ai:* ASCD 1985-; NEA 1958-; NJ Ed Assn 1970-; League of Women Voters Edison (Ed Chm 1973-76) 1966-76; Religious Ed Chm 1972-76 *office:* Woodrow Wilson Mid Sch Woodrow Wilson Dr Edison NJ 08820

FISK, DAVID JAMES, History Teacher; *b:* Utica, NY; *m:* Rosemarie Ampula; *c:* David, Nathan, Amanda; *ed:* (BSE) Amer His, 1964, (MAED) Amer His, 1972 SUNY Cortland; *cr:* Teacher Johnson City HS 1964-; *ai:* Frosh Ftbl, Jr Var Bsbl & Var Soccer Coach; Ski Club & Key Club Adv; Johnson City Teachers Assn (VP 1978-79, Negotiating Team 1977-87); *office:* Johnson City HS 666 Reynolds Rd Johnson City NY 13790

FISK, JUDITH ELIZABETH, Principal; *b:* Hollywood, CA; *m:* Wayne M.; *c:* Karen Murphy, Dianna, Michael, John; *ed:* (BS) Ed, OR St Univ 1977; Educl Policy & Management, Univ of OR; *cr:* Teacher Grand Prairie Sch 1977-78, South Shore Sch 1978-89; Prin St Marys Sch 1989-; *ai:* St Marys Day Care Dir; Delta Kappa Gamma 1982-; Beta Sigma Phi 1986-; ASCD 1989-; Democratic Party Cntrl Comm 1988-; *office:* St Marys Sch 815 SW Broadalbin Albany OR 97321

FISK, NANCY DUPUY, 8th Grade Lang Arts Teacher; *b:* Beckley, WV; *m:* James E.; *c:* Eric, Timothy, Andrea; *ed:* (BA) Scndry Sd, Soc Stud, Univ of NC 1963; (MA) European His, Modern Emory Univ 1973; Recertification Elem Ed Winthrop Coll 1979; *cr:* 7th/8th/9th Soc Stud Howard Bishop Jr HS 1964-66; Lecturer-His Belize Teachers Coll 1966-68; 7th/8th/9th Soc Stud Jr Lee 1971-73; 5th Grade Teacher East Elem 1978-85; 8th Grade Teacher Monroe Mid Sch 1985-; *ai:* Jr Beta Club Spon; Sacs Chairperson/Steering Comm-Southern Assn Accreditation Colleges-Schls; Effective Schls Steering Comm Co-Chm Instructional Focus; NCEA Pod Rep 1980-; NEA Mem 1964-; Teacher of Yr East Elem Monroe City Schls 1984; *office:* Monroe Mid Sch 601 Sunset Dr Monroe NC 28110

FISK, WILLIAM ALAN, Science Teacher; *b:* Canton, OH; *m:* Carol Lynn Simmons; *c:* A. J. Molnar, Arnie J. Molnar; *ed:* (BA) Bio, Hiram Coll 1969; (MA) Ed, Coll of Mt St Joseph 1986; *cr:* Sci Teacher Carrollton Exempted Village Sch 1969-73, Hartford Jr HS 1973-; *ai:* 8th Grade Bsktbl Coach; CPEA 1973-; OH Ed Assn, NEA 1969-; *home:* 486 Steubenville Rd Carrollton OH 44615

FISKE, JOHN F., III, Mathematics Teacher; *b:* Lebanon, NH; *m:* Linda Elwood; *c:* Jessica, Annikah; *ed:* (BS) Math Ed, Plymouth St Coll 1973; *cr:* Teacher Lebanon Jr HS 1973-76, Lebanon HS 1977-; *ai:* Indian River Mid Sch Sftbl Coach; Math Topics Team; Lebanon Teachers Assn, NEA, Assn of Teachers of Math 1973-; Intnl Bd of Bsktbl Ofcls 1973-78; NH Bd of Soccer Ofcls 1970-; NH Interscholastic Sftbl Comm 1981-87; Natl Ski Patrol Candidate Trng Officer 1975-; *office:* Lebanon HS 495 Hanover St Lebanon NH 03746

FISTER, MICHAEL JON, Music Teacher; *b:* Allentown, PA; *m:* Barbara Jean Miller; *c:* Sarah E.; *ed:* (BA) Music Ed, Moravian Coll 1980; (MS) Ed, Temple Univ 1985; *cr:* Music Teacher St Elizabeth Sch 1980-; *ai:* Jr Choir & Handbell Dir; Pastoral Musicians Mem 1985-; Municipal Opera Co Dir 1987-; Bethlehem Bach Choir Mem 1980-84; *office:* St Elizabeth Sch 433 Pershing Blvd Whitehall PA 18052

FITCH, SHIRLEY CLANTON, Fifth Grade Teacher; *b:* Terre Haute, IN; *c:* Mary A. Fitch Clegg; *ed:* (BA) Eng, East Cntrl St Coll 1948; Additional Undergraduate, Grad Courses OH St Univ; *cr:* Teacher Duncan City Schls 1950-51, Marion City Schls 1966-; *ai:* NEA, OH Ed Assn, Marion Ed Assn, Intnl Rdng Assn; Amer Bus Women.

FITE, ROBERT WILLIAM, His/Geography Teacher; *b:* Peoria, IL; *m:* Valerie Jeanne; *c:* Lindsay C., B. J., Bradley C.; *ed:* (BA) Scndry Ed/Bible Ed, Maranatha Baptist Bible Coll 1983; *cr:* Teacher/Coach Calvary Chrstn Sch 1983-; *ai:* Sr Spon; Bible Quiz Team; Soccer & Bsktbl Coach; Bsktbl Camps; Youth League Soccer Coach; Church Youth Work; *office:* Calvary Chrstn Sch 1700 Eastland Roseville MI 48066

FITHEN, DONNA S., Spanish/French Teacher; *b:* Wheeling, WV; *w:* Barry G. (dec); *c:* Tara L. Wise; *ed:* (BA) Eng, W Liberty St Coll 1960; (MA) Eng Ed, WV Univ 1968; Cmptr Trng & Word Processing, OH Univ; *cr:* Eng Teacher Brilliant HS 1961-63, Steubenville HS 1970-73, St Clairsville HS 1974-; *ai:* Y-Teen, Soph Class & Cheering Adv; Debate Team Coach; AAUW, NEA, OEA Mem 1974-75; Wheeling Symphony Auxiliary 1970-81; *home:* 111 Orchard Ln Saint Clairsville OH 43950

FITHEN, PAMELA MEYER, Third Grade Teacher; *b:* Steubenville, OH; *m:* John Ross; *ed:* (BS) Elem Ed, Univ of Steubenville 1973; (MS) Admin/Supervision, Univ of Dayton 1975; *cr:* 2nd Grade Teacher Irondale Elem Sch 1973-76; 1st Grade Teacher Edison Elem Sch 1976-87; 3rd Grade Teacher Knoxville Elem Sch 1987-; *ai:* Alpha Delta Kappa Intnl Historian 1983-; NEA, OH Ed Assn, Edison Local Ed Assn 1973-; *home:* RD 1 Box 31A Irondale OH 43932

FITHIAN, GARY D., 8th Grade Science Teacher; *b:* Audubon, NJ; *ed:* (BA) Jr HS Sci/Math, 1973, (MA) Environmental Sci Ed, 1981 Glassboro St Coll; Supvrs, Prin Cert Glassboro St 1981; Drug Free Yrs Wkshp for Parents Certified Teacher 1989; *cr:* Sci Teacher Penns Grove Mid Sch 1973-; *ai:* Just Say No To Drugs, Alcohol & Tobacco Adv; NSTA, NJ Sci Teachers Assn 1985-; NJ Ed Assn, NEA 1973-; Fulbright Teacher Exch Prgm Banbury England 1990; *office:* Penns Grove Mid Sch Maple Ave Penns Grove NJ 08069

FITTS, DAVID WILLIAM, Director of Instrumental Music; *b:* Detroit, MI; *ed:* (BA) Music Ed, MI St 1981; Presently Enrolled in Masters of Arts at MI St; *cr:* Assoc Dir Hunt Mid Sch 1982; Dir of Music Springport Public Schls 1982-84; Dir of Bands Perry Public Schls 1984-; *ai:* Conduct Pep Band; Mid Sch/HS Jazz Bands; Teach Privately; Support Group Leader; Pip Fest Group Facilitator; Presently An MSBOA Adjudicator.

FITTS, MILTON THOMAS, Teacher Social Studies/Coach; *b:* Peacock, TX; *m:* Linda V.; *c:* Jayson, Holly Fitts Parker, Jody, Jon; *ed:* (BA) Phys Ed, W TX St Univ 1960; *cr:* Teacher/Coach Amarillo Schls 1960-61, Tahoka Schls 1961-64, Seminole Schls 1964-80, Midland Schls 1980-; *ai:* Core Team; Ftbl, Bsktbl, Track Coach; *home:* 4020 Livingston Midland TX 79707

FITZGERALD, ANITA BELL, Fifth Grade Teacher; *b:* Mound Bayou, MS; *m:* Joseph; *c:* Paul, Ladi Crimea, Wendell; *ed:* (BSE) Elem Ed, Delta St Univ 1974-75; *cr:* 2nd Grade Teacher Pearman Elem 1976-79; 5th Grade Teacher Cypress Park Elem 1979-; *ai:* MAE, NEA, CAE 1986; NCNW 1980; *home:* 722 Church St Cleveland MS 38732

FITZGERALD, DAVANEL, Second Grade Teacher; *b:* Trinidad, TX; *ed:* (BS) Elem Ed, N TX St 1960; (MED) Spec Ed, TX Womens Univ 1966; Working Towards Doctorate; *cr:* 1st Grade Teacher Edwin J Kiest Elem 1960-67; Spec Ed Teacher 1967-77, 2nd Grade Teacher 1977- S S Conner; *ai:* S S Conner Spec Ed Safety Patrols 1972-76; CARE 2nd Grade Chairperson 1988- & Demonstration Teacher 1989-; United Teachers of Dallas 1980-; PTA (VP 1969-88, Prgm Chm, Historian, Dept of Health & Welfare 1964-66, Dept of Publicity); TX Congress of Parents & Teachers 1960-, St Life Membership 1967; Natl Congress of Parents & Teachers Natl Life Membership 1984; Baylor Medical Center Volunteer 1980-86, Top 10 Awd 1983; Dallas Natl Teacher of Yr Awd 1973; Ross Perot Teacher Awd for Excl 1974; Article Published 1975; *home:* 6925 Clemson Dallas TX 75214

FITZGERALD, FRANKEY LYNN, Third Grade Teacher; *b:* Center, TX; *ed:* 2 Yr Prgm Basic, Panola Jr Coll 1971-73; (BS) Elem Ed, 1975, (MED) Elem Ed, 1977 Stephen F Austin St Univ; *cr:* 3rd Grade Teacher S W Carter Elem 1975-; *ai:* Goals & Textbook Comm; Elem UIL Sponsorship of Listening, Music Memory Dictionary Skills; Assn of TX Prof Educators; Band Boosters Organization Treas 1975-81; Kappa Delta Pi; Inclusion in Most Prominent Educators of TX 1983; Favorite Teacher of TX; Outstanding Contribution to Music Awd 1980; Outstanding Contribution Rendered; Dragon Ftbl Support 1985; *home:* 106 Wildwood Cir Center TX 75935

FITZGERALD, KATHLEEN, Fourth Grade Teacher; *b:* New York, NY; *ed:* (BS) His/Ed, Mount St Vincent 1965; (MS) Elem Ed/Psych, W CT St 1971; Elem Ed Certificates Catechetics, Manhattan Coll; Rdng, Math, Mt St Vincent; Sci, BOCES; Lang Art, Fordham Univ; *cr:* 3rd Grade Teacher St Anthonys 1958-59; 1st/2nd Grade Teacher St Bernards 1959-64; 1st Grade Teacher 1964-82, 6th-8th Grade Teacher 1982-86, 4th Grade Teacher 1986- St Patricks; *ai:* CCD & St Nutritional Services Coord; Bsktbl & Hockey Coach; Parish Cncl Mem; NCEA; *office:* Saint Patricks Sch State Rd Bedford Village Bedford NY 10506

FITZGERALD, MARGARET LOU, Math/Art Teacher; *b:* Denver, CO; *m:* Alan W.; *c:* Kathleen; *ed:* (BA) Liberal Stud, 1982, (MA) Ed, 1986 CA Poly Tech Inst; *cr:* 3rd Grade Teacher 1971-77, 2nd Grade Teacher 1977-81, Vice Prin 1979-81, 1986-89, Math Specialist/Art Teacher 1982- St Christopher Sch; *ai:* Math

Olympiad Moderator; Stu Cncl Moderator 1986-89; *office:* St Christopher Parish Schl 900 W Christopher St West Covina CA 91790

FITZGERALD, PAMELA JEAN COFFELT, English/Journalism Teacher; *b:* Jackson, MI; *m:* Daniel Robert; *c:* Shaunna S. Huling, Chad D.; *ed:* (BA) Eng/Psych, Spring Arbor Coll 1987; Educl Leadership, E MI Univ; *cr:* Eng/Journalism Teacher Jackson HS 1987-; *ai:* Adv Reflector News; Building Comm; MIPA, Quill & Scroll, Natl Curr Cncl, JEA, OMEA, ONEA, ASCD; Cascades Humane Society (Pres 1983-85, Bd Mem) 1979-; 1st United Meth Church (Teen Adv, Cnslr) 1980-84; Distinguished Employee Awd; Academic All Amer 1987; Outstanding Teacher 1988-; *office:* Jackson HS 544 Wildwood Ave Jackson MI 49201

FITZGERALD, PATRICIA EILEEN, Business/Marketing Chairperson; *b:* Camden, NJ; *ed:* (BA) Bus Ed, 1981, (MA) Bus Ed, 1984 Montclair St Coll; *cr:* Acquisitions Ed/Asst Ed/Bus Ed Asst John Wiley & Sons Incorporated 1982-86; Bus/Mrktg Dept Chairperson/Bus Technology Instr/COE Coord/Adult Div Word Processing Supvr/Adult Div Instr Camden Cty Voc & Tech Sch 1986-; *ai:* Camden Cty Voc & Tech Sch FBLA Adv; Lesson Plan; Job Description & Evaluation & Retention Comm; Equity Awds Comm & Improvement Awds Comm Chairperson; NJ Cooperative Office Ed Coord Assn Southern Region (VP, Rep) 1989-; NBEA 1980-, Outstanding Graduating Sr Awd 1981; Eastern Bus Ed Assn, NJ Bus Ed Assn 1980-; Delta Pi Epsilon 1981-; Camden Cty Voc & Tech Sch Teacher of Yr 1990; Articles Published 1990; Louis C Nanassy Grad Awd 1984; M Herbert Freeman Undergraduate Awd 1981; *office:* Camden Cty Voc & Tech Sch 6008 Browing Rd Pennsauken NJ 08109

FITZGERALD, RODGER PIERPONT, Guidance Counselor 9-12; *b:* Richmond, VA; *m:* Fannie Beatrice Wilkinson; *c:* Benita P. Fitzgerald Brown, KiM L.; *ed:* (BS) Chem, VA Union Univ 1955; (MA) Guidance/Counseling, VA Tech 1973; Grad Studies VA Tech & Univ of VA; *cr:* Math/Sci/Chem Teacher Jennie Dean HS 1957-65; Math Teacher 1965-72, 9th-12th Grade Sch Cnslr 1972-Gar-Field Sr HS; Homebound Cnslr 1989; *ai:* Signet Gifted Prgm Screening Comm; Natl Assn Teacher Math; NEA; Natl Sch Counselers Assn; Dale City Lions Pres 1985-86 Lion of Yr 1985-86; Dale City San Dist Advisory Comm Chm 1986-87; Bd of Dir Northern VA Comm Coll Mem 1985-; General Electric Fellowship RPI 1959; NDEA Fellowship Amer Univ 1960; Sunday Sch Teacher; Southern Baptist Deacon; Chm Bd of Dir Manassas Choral Soc Honor Disch USAF 1950-54; Cub Scout Intl Rep; *home:* 14914 Daytona Ct Dale City VA 22193

FITZGERALD, STEPHEN M., HS Mathematics Teacher; *b:* Bernice, LA; *m:* Ruby Ann Manuel; *c:* Steven, Tracy, Kevin; *ed:* (BS) Math, 1965, (MS) Math, 1969 Lamar Univ; *cr:* Math Teacher/Coach Woodville HS 1965-67; Math Teacher Port Neches HS 1967-; *home:* 936 West Dr Port Neches TX 77651

FITZGERALD, WILLIAM FRANCIS, French Teacher; *b:* Troy, NY; *m:* Marylee Casey; *ed:* (BA) Fr Ed, Siena Coll 1982; *cr:* Fr Teacher Albany HS 1983-; Adjunct Professor SUNY Albany 1987-; *ai:* Tutoring Stus; NY St Assn of Foreign Lang Teachers.

FITZ MORRIS, MARY MALONE, Fifth Grade Teacher; *b:* Brooklyn, NY; *m:* Paul; *c:* Christopher, Douglas, David, Maura; *ed:* (BS) Ed - Summa Cum Laude, Fordham Univ 1953; (MS) Ed, Hofstra Univ 1957; Grad Stud C W Post Coll of Long Island Univ; *cr:* Elem Teacher E Meadow Dist 1953-57, Smithtown Dist 1969-; *ai:* 5th Grade Rep Dist Soc Stud Curr Comm; AFT, NYSUT, Smithtown Teachers Assn 1969-; Local Religious Organizations, Political Organizations; *office:* Accompsett Elem Sch Lincoln St Smithtown NY 11787

FITZPATRICK, AL, Teacher; *b:* Widby Island, WA; *ed:* (BS) Poly Sci, 1974, (MS) Soc Sci, 1975 S OR St Coll; Shakespeare Stud Reading Univ Berkshire England; Govt Stud PA St Univ; *cr:* Teacher Mazama HS 1975-78; Government/Law/Communications Teacher Newport HS 1978-; *ai:* Mock Trial, Swimming Coach; Youth Legislature, Sr Class Adv; NCSS Facilitator 1989-; OR Speech Teachers Assn Wkshp Presenter 1985; OR Theatre Arts Assn Treas (1984-87; Wkshp Presenter Exec Bd); Optimists Club Youth Optimist Adv 1989-; YMCA Youth Legislative Adv 1987-; Law Related Ed Project Mock Trial Team Coach 1989-; Republican Natl Convention OR Delegate 1988, 4th Place OR Championships 1990; Keisai Koho Fellowship; US Constitution Bicentennial Commission; Newport HS Yrbk Favorite Teacher 1990, Most Enthusiastic Teacher 1989; *office:* Newport HS 322 NE Eads St Newport OR 97365

FITZPATRICK, DONA FRAN, Mathematics Teacher; *b:* Glenridge, NJ; *ed:* (BS) Math/His, Lynchburg Coll 1972; Working on Masters Degree Supervision; *cr:* Math/His Teacher Father Judge Mission Seminary 1972-73; Math Teacher Dunbar HS 1973-76, E C Glass HS 1976-; *ai:* Jr Class Spon; Cooperative Learning Resource Teacher; Habitat for Humanity; Help Organize Math Contests; Train Stu Teachers; Blue Ridge Cncl Teacher of Math 196-; NCTM 1990; Delta Kappa Gamma Nominating Comm 1989-; Provided Wkshp on Cooperative Learning VA Cncl Teachers of Math Conference 1990; *office:* E C Glass HS 2111 Memorial Ave Lynchburg VA 24501

FITZPATRICK, JAMES C., 6th Grade Teacher; *b:* New Martinsville, WV; *m:* Lana Coomes; *c:* James D., Michael B., Stephen N.; *ed:* (BA) Philosophy, Atanaeum of OH 1965; (MA) Elem Ed, Marshall Univ 1969; *cr:* Teacher Corps Intern Marshall Univ 1967-69; Teacher Bardstown Elem Sch 1969-74; 6th Grade Teacher Wood Cty 1974-76, Nelson Cty 1976-; *ai:* Bookstore Mgr; NEA, KEA, NCEA Unified Membership; Team Leader 1971-72; Intern Prgm Intern Resource Teacher 1987-88; Stu Teacher Supvr 1988-89; *home:* 1995 Lutheran Church Rd Bardstown KY 40004

FITZPATRICK, KAREN A. BOUDREAU, Kindergarten Teacher; *b:* Fitchburg, MA; *m:* Richard O. Jr.; *c:* Kelly A., Ryan M.; *ed:* (BSED) Early Chldhd Ed, Fitchburg St Coll 1974; Post Grad Stud Developing Learning Centers & Use of Manipulatives; Catechist Certificate Religious Ed; Drug Ed Cert; *cr:* Kndgtn-8th Grade Art/Math/Sci Teacher St Joseph Sch 1974-85; Private Tutoring 1975-78; Kndgtn Teacher St Joseph Sch 1974-; *ai:* Write To Read Prgm Primary Grades Dir; Sch Chldhd Olympics Coach; NCEA Mem 1974-; St Joseph Sch Bd Secy 1977-79; St Joseph PTA Mem 1974-; St Joseph Bazaar Comm Booth Chm 1975-; *office:* St Joseph Sch 35 Columbus St Fitchburg MA 01420

FITZPATRICK, MICHELLE MASSICOTTE, 4th/5th Grade Science Teacher; *b:* Providence, RI; *m:* Francis E.; *ed:* (BS) Elem Ed, Lowell St Coll 1970; (EDM) Counseling, Fitchburg St Coll 1976; Cert Elem Prin Univ of Lowell ; *cr:* 4th/5th Grade Teacher Sci/Rdng 1970-; Asst Prin 1978- Kittredge Sch; *ai:* Stu Cncl 5th Grade PTO Liason; Sch Store Adv; Newsletter Editor; ASCD 1989-; North Andover Teachers Assn 1970-; MA Teachers Assn 1970-; NEA 1970-; North Andoves Democratic Town Comm Mem Delegate St Convntns 1980-; *home:* 31 Royal Crest Dr North Andover MA 01845

FITZPATRICK, ROBERT JOHN, Math Department Teacher; *b:* Philadelphia, PA; *m:* Faye Hunt; *c:* Jamie C.; *ed:* (BS) Health/Phys Ed, TN Tech Univ 1974; *ai:* Ftbl Coach 1976-; Jr Class Sp N; *home:* Rt 5 Box 164 Lafayette TN 37083

FITZPATRICK, ROSEMARY, English Teacher; *b:* Newton, NJ; *ed:* (BS) Lang Art, Univ of Albuquerque 1970; *cr:* 6th-8th Grade Teacher St Cecilia Sch 1970-73; 7th/8th Grade Eng Teacher Holy Family Sch 1975-80; 6th-8th Grade Teacher St Cecilia Sch 1981-.

FITZPATRICK, SUE CAROL JOHNSON, 5th Grade Teacher; *b:* Smiths Grove, KY; *m:* Julian A. II; *ed:* (BS) Elem Ed, 1975; (MA) Elem Ed, 1980 Western KY Univ; Cert Supv Endorsement Rank I Western KY Univ; *cr:* 5th Grade Teacher Kyrock Elem Sch 1977-; *ai:* Asst Den Leader Cub Scouts; Edmonson Cty Ed Assn Pres; KY Ed Assn/NEA Mem 1977-; Outstanding Teacher Kyrock Elem Sch 1983-84; *office:* Kyrock Elem Sch Hwy 259 Sweeden KY 42285

FITZRANDOLPH, ROBERT E., Science Department Chair; *b:* Texarkana, AR; *ed:* (BS) Chem, Southern St Coll 1969; (MSE) Phys Sci, S AR Univ 1977; Prgm for Effective Teaching, Youth Empowering Systems; *cr:* Sci/Math Teacher 1969-70, Sci Teacher 1970-85, Sci Dept Chm 1986- College Hill Jr HS; *ai:* College Hill Jr HS N Cntrl Accreditation Steering Comm, Personnel Policy Comm Mem; Scndry Curr Cncl Mem; ASTA, NSTA 1987-; Teacher of Yr 1986-87; *office:* College Hill Jr HS 1600 Forrest Texarkana AR 75502

FITZSIMMONS, JOHN THOMAS, Social Studies Teacher; *b:* Beloit, WI; *m:* Anna Brossard; *ed:* (BS) His, Univ of WI Parkside 1971; *cr:* Teacher Our Lady of the Assumption 1975-79; Cost Estimator Beloit Corporation 1979-83; Mgr Regal Beloit Corporation 1983-86; Teacher Our Lady of Perpetual Help 1987-; *office:* Our Lady of Perpetual Help Sch 3801 N Miller Rd Scottsdale AZ 85251

FITZSIMMONS, KENNETH R., Elementary Principal; *b:* New Kensington, PA; *m:* Debbie G.; *c:* Lucy J., Crystal, Casey; *ed:* (BA) Elem Ed, Edinboro 1973; (MA) Ed Admin, St Bonaventure Univ 1980; NASSP Prin Assessment & Leader Trng; *cr:* Elem Teacher/Elem Prin Warren Cty Sch Dist; *office:* Warren Cty Sch Dist Sugar Grove Elem Sugargrove PA 16350

FITZSIMONS, PATRICIA K., 5th Grade Teacher; *b:* Chicago, IL; *m:* Thomas; *c:* Thomas; *ed:* (BA) Ed, Chicago St 1958; Grad Stud Sci & Math; *cr:* Teacher Lewis-Champlin Elem 1958-59; 8th Grade Sci Teacher/Coord Luella Elem 1959-68; Departmental Math Teacher 1968-75, 5th/6th Grade Teacher 1975- Jane Addams; *ai:* Book Comm; Audio-Visual Coord; Sci Grant; Natl Contest Winner Environmental Awareness.

FITZWATER, HELEN COTRILL, 3rd Grade Teacher; *b:* Pullman, WV; *w:* John L. Jr. (dec); *c:* John III, Franklin, Jann Swiger; *ed:* (BS) Elem Ed, 1970; (MA) Supervision/Admin Elem Sch, 1974 Frostburg St Coll; *cr:* Teacher Red House Sch 1970-72; Dennett Road Elem 1972-; *ai:* GCTA Secy 1988-; MD St Teacher Assn & NEA Delgate to Convention 1989; Garrett Cty Bd Realtors 1980-;Preston Cty Homemakers Secy 1988-; Pythian Sisters 1962-; Poem Published Treasured Poems of America By Sparrowgrass Poetry Forum Inc 1990; *home:* PO Box 248 308 Oakland Dr Oakland MD 21550

FIVUSH, GEORGETTE CYNTHIA, English Department Chairperson; *b:* New York, NY; *m:* Donald; *c:* Adam; *ed:* (BA) Eng/Lang/Lit, City Coll of NY 1962; Ed, Univ of Cntrl Fl; In-ServiCe Trng Orange Cty; *cr:* Math/Eng Instr Castle Hill Jr HS 1962-63; Eng Instr Cntrl Fl Acad 1982-83; Eng Instr 1983-89, Eng Instr/Dept CHairperson 1989- Jones HS; *ai:* FL Future Educators of America Chapter & Literary Magazine Spon; Writing Contests Coord; Teachers as Adv Steering, Rdng, RIF Comm; JEMS; Orange Cty Teachers of Eng, FL Teachers of Eng Mem 1983-; Orange Cty Rdng Cncl Mem 1986-; Metropolitan Orlando Urban League Services for Crime Prevention Essay 1990; Jones HS PTA Mem 1983-; Highland Park PTA Pres 1980-82; FL Future Educators of America St Advisory Bd 1987-; NCTE Literary Magazine Prgm Judge 1989-; Certificate Orange Cty Sch Bd NCTE Awds 1989; *office:* Jones HS 801 S Rio Grande Orlando FL 32805

FIXMAN, ROBERT CHARLES, Teacher; *b:* St Louis, MO; *m:* Linda Ann Rotskoff; *c:* Lisa, Jennifer; *ed:* (BA) Elem Ed, Harris Teachers Coll 1968; (MS) Elem Sch Admin, Univ of MO St Louis 1970; *cr:* Teacher Ashland Sch 1968-70, Weber Sch 1970-82, Claymont Sch 1982-; *ai:* Sci Fair & Aluminum Recycling Chm; Star Night Spon; NSTA 1979-80, 1985; NEA 1990; Pillar of Parkway 1985; Friends of Gifted Teacher of Yr 1982; *office:* Claymont Elem Sch 405 Country Club Dr Ballwin MO 63011

FLACK, CHRISTINE HALL, 4th Grade Teacher; *b:* Cooperstown, NY; *m:* Vern; *c:* Joel M., Shane L.; *ed:* (BS) Elem Ed 1976, (MS) Elem Ed/Rdng, 1980 SUC Oneonta; Cooperative Teaching; Trng Federal Math/Sci Projects; Energy Concepts, Issues, NYSEG Sponsored; *cr:* Teacher/Owner Jack & Jill Nursery Sch 1974-76; 1st Grade Teacher 1977-87, 4th Grade Teacher 1987- Bainbridge/Guilford Sch; *ai:* Building Leadership Team; Ski Club Adv; Curr Comm; Catskill Rdng Cncl 1980-88; Amer Fed of Teachers Educl Research & Dissemenation Prgm 1989-; Bainbridge Guilford Teachers Assn (Secy 1984, Building Rep 1985); St Matthews Episcopal Church Vestry 1987-89; Educl Research/Dissemination Trainer 1989-; Cowrote Parents as Rdng Partner Grant 1990; Presenter of Whole Lang Concepts at MA Rdng Cncl 1982; Summer Whole Lang Conference 1981-83; *home:* RD 1 Box 62A Unadilla NY 13849

FLAISIG, CAROL POPA, Junior High School Teacher; *b:* Cleveland, OH; *m:* William Paul; *c:* Thomas; *ed:* (BS) Ed, Cleveland St Univ 1972; *cr:* 6th Grade Teacher St Paschal Baylon Sch 1972-77, St Francis Sch 1979-81; 3rd/7th Grade Teacher Blythe Elem Sch 1982-84; Jr HS Teacher St Paschal Baylon Sch 1984-; *ai:* Stu Cncl Moderator & Adv; NCEA; Amer Legion Auxiliary Historian 1989-; Excl in Ed Awd 1989; *office:* St Paschal Baylon Sch 5360 Wilson Mills Rd Highland Heights OH 44143

FLAMER, CELESTE ALTHEA, Fifth Grade Teacher; *b:* Lynn, MA; *ed:* (BS) Ed, Wilberforce Univ 1967; *cr:* 6th Grade Teacher Cubberley Sch 1967-68; 3rd Grade Teacher Perry Sch 1968-70; 3rd/6th/5th Grade Teacher Ingalls Sch 1970-; *ai:* Tutor; Volunteer Lynn Hosp 1976-77; Volunteer Family Childrens Service of Greater Lynn 1983-84; Volunteer Hospice-Lynn Visting Nurses Assn 1987-88; *office:* Ingalls Elem Sch 1 Collins St Terr Lynn MA 01902

FLANAGAN, ROSEMARY DEVANEY, Chemistry Teacher; *b:* Methuen, MA; *m:* Joseph; *c:* James, Macaela, Luke; *ed:* (BA) Chem/Math, Emmanuel Coll 1973; Environmental Stud, Chem, VT Coll of Norwich Univ; *cr:* Math/Sci Teacher Fairfax Cty Public Schls 1973-77; Chem Teacher Medomak Valley HS 1986-; *ai:* NEA, Amer Chemical Society, ME Sci Teachers; *office:* Medomak Valley HS Manktown Rd Waldoboro ME 04572

FLANDERS, DORIS SIMMONS, First Grade Teacher; *b:* Alamo, GA; *m:* James Maxwell; *c:* Ellen Rivenbark, Susan Wiley, Jimmy, Jeanie Fields; *ed:* (BS) Home Ec, Univ of GA 1949; *cr:* Home Ec Teacher Lake Park HS 1949-51, Echols Cty HS 1952-53; 4th/5th Grade Teacher Randolph Cty Elem Sch 1957-59; 2nd Grade Teacher Morton Avenue Elem Sch 1967-80; 3rd Grade Teacher 1980-85, 1st Grade Teacher 1985- Lyons Elem Sch; *ai:* NEA, GEA.

FLANIGAN, JAMES ROBERT, English Teacher; *b:* Charleroi, PA; *m:* Ellen Fonner; *ed:* (BA) Eng, Waynesburg Coll 1964; PA St Univ; CA Univ of PA; *cr:* Teacher Waynesburg Cntrl Sch Dist 1965, Frazier Sch Dist 1967, W Greene Sch Dist 1967-68, Mc Guffey Sch Dist 1968-; *ai:* PRIDE Task Force Mem; Yrbk Adv; Stage Mgr 1970-87; NCTE; Thoreau Society Life Mem; NEA, PSEA, MEA 1968-; Claysville VFD (Secy, Treas) 1988-89; Claysville Lodge 447 F&AM Master 1983, 1990; NEH Concord Authors Seminar 1986; Certificate of Recognition PA Sch Press Assn; Outstanding Scndry Educators of America 1973; *home:* RD 2 Box 12 Claysville PA 15323

FLANNERY, AMANDA TALLEY, Second Grade Teacher; *b:* Nashville, TN; *m:* Roger L.; *c:* Laura Flanner Kendrick, Jack, Beth; *ed:* (BA) Elem Ed, David Lipscomb Univ 1961; (ME) Elem Ed, TN St Univ 1989; *cr:* Teacher Metro Nashville Public Schls 1965-67, Shelby Cty Public Schls 1967-68, David Lipscomb Univ Campus Schls 1974-; *ai:* Faculty Financial Assistance Comm; Grade Level Chm; Intnl Rdng Assn; Natl Trust for Historic Preservation; *office:* David Lipscomb Elem Sch Granny White Pike Nashville TN 37203

FLANNERY, BERNITA LYNN, Music Instructor; *b:* Aberdeen, SD; *m:* James; *c:* Corey, Nathaniel; *ed:* (BS) Music, Northern St Coll 1977; *cr:* K-12th Grade Vocal Music Teacher Tri Cty 1977-79; K-6th Grade Vocal Music Teacher St Marys Cath 1979-80; K-12th Grade Music Teacher Hosmer Sch 1983-89; 12th Grade Music Teacher Roscoe Sch 1989-; *ai:* HS Band & Chorus, Soph Class Adv; SAI 1976-; Phi Beta Mu 1988-; Music Service for Cmmty; *office:* Roscoe Sch Main St Roscoe SD 57471

FLANNERY, CARMEL THOMPSON, Retired Teacher; *b:* Landville, WV; *m:* Wm. F. Jr.; *c:* Wm. F. III, Micheal, Patricia L. May; *ed:* (BA) Eng/Elem Ed, Charleston Univ 1966; Grad Stud WV Univ & Marshal Univ; *cr:* Teacher Chrstn Elem 1945; Substitute Teacher Logan Cty 1960-63; Teacher Mallory Elem 1963-85; *ai:* Sch PTA Mem 1963-85, Teacher of Yr 1980, 1985; Cty PTA Mem 1963-85, Teacher of Yr 1980; *home:* PO Box 177 Mallory WV 25634

FLANNIGAN, PATRICIA RUTH, Third Grade Teacher; *b:* Gadsden, AL; *ed:* (BS) Elem Ed, Auburn Univ 1973; (MA) Elem Ed, Univ of AL 1978; *cr:* 3rd Grade Teacher John S Jones Elem 1973-79; Southside Elem 1979-; *ai:* Etowah Ed Assn Rep for 14 Yrs; Etowah Ed Assn Treas 1975-77; AL Ed Assn Delegate to Assembly 1975-78; NEA; Teacher of Yr Southside Elem 1988-89; *office:* Southside Elem Sch Rt 1 Box 721 Gadsden AL 35901

FLATAU, SUSIE KELLY, English Teacher; *b:* Fort Sill, OK; *m:* Jack Peirce; *c:* Jennifer L.; *ed:* (BA) Eng, Sam Houston St Univ 1973; *cr:* Eng Teacher Conroe HS 1973-84, Westlake HS 1984-; *ai:* Tutorial Facilitator; ATPE Rep; Technology Comm; Stu Asst Model-Teacher Rep; TSTA Membership Chairperson 1987-88; ATPE Building Rep 1989-; EEA 1984-87; Key Club Intnl Salute to Teachers Day 1985; Spirit of Ed Awd 1986-87; St Textbook Comm; Nom for Teacher of Yr 1988-; Golden Apple Awd 1989; Coord of Stu Movie for TV 1985; Keywannette Spon; *office:* Westlake H S 4100 Westbank Dr Austin TX 78746

FLAUM, CAROL J, German Teacher; *b:* Dayton, OH; *m:* Steve M.; *c:* Erin R., Heidi M.; *ed:* (BA) German, Wright St Univ 1975; Ger Teacher, Hithergreen Mid Sch 1975-82; Tower Heights Mid Sch 1982-; *home:* 5604 Gander Rd E Dayton OH 45424

FLAUM, STEVE M., Social Science Teacher; *b:* Dayton, OH; *m:* Carol Jean Whisler; *c:* Shannon, Michelle, Erin, Heidi; *ed:* (BA) Comprehensive Soc Stud, Wright St Univ 1968; *cr:* Teacher Centerville City Schls 1968; *ai:* E F Inst Travel Groups Europe Coord; Lead in Kazoo Group; Centerville-Washington Township Ed Fnd 1989; Excl in Ed Awd 1989.

FLEISCHACKER, DONNA M., Health & Physical Ed Teacher; *b:* Atwood, KS; *ed:* (BA) Phys Ed/Health, KS St Univ 1970; (MA) Phys Ed, Fort Hays St Univ 1978; *cr:* 5th/6th Grade Teacher Edson KS 1970-71; 1st-12th Grade Phys Ed Teacher Victoria KS 1971-72; 6th-8th Grade Phys Ed/Health Teacher Kennedy Mid Sch 1972-; *ai:* Jump Rope for Heart Sch Coord; Vlybl Coach; KS Ed Assn 1973-, Master Teacher 1983; Phi Delta Kappa Pres 1977-; Governors Cncl on Fitness 1989; St Dept of Health Cncl 1989-; Phys Ed Cncl 1982-; Phi Delta Kappa Schlsp; Civil Air Patrol 1987-; Trainer of Trainees for Project STAR; *office:* Kennedy Mid Sch 1309 Fort Hays KS 67601

FLEISCHAUR, MICHAEL J., History Teacher; *b:* New Castle, PA; *m:* Jane; *ed:* (BA) His, Waynesburg Coll 1968; (MED) Slippery Rock St Univ 1971; Fulbright Fellowship to India 1973; Indiana Univ of PA TAFT Fellowship 1975; NEH Russian Stud Fellowship 1984; Yale Russian Stud Fellowship 1985; *cr:* World Cultures Teacher N Allegheny Intermediate 1968-79; Amer/Russian Teacher N Allegheny Sr HS 1979-; *office:* N Allegheny HS 10375 Perry Hwy Wexford PA 15090

FLEISHMAN, ALAN RICHARD, Social Studies Teacher; *b:* Brooklyn, NY; *m:* Patricia Schwab; *c:* Sarah, Elizabeth; *ed:* (BA) His, 1969, (MS) Ed, 1971 Queens Coll CUNY; Continuing Ed, SUNY Stonybrook; *cr:* Soc Stud Teacher J F Kennedy HS 1969-; *ai:* Amnesty Intnl Chapter Spon; Natl His Honor Society 1969-; NEH Summer Seminars 1987, 1990; Fulbright Egypt Schlsp 1988; NEH Grant 1989; *office:* J F Kennedy HS 3000 Bellmore Ave Bellmore NY 11710

FLEITZ, PAMELA JEAN, Choral Director; *b:* Louisville, KY; *ed:* (BMED) Music Ed, Univ of Louisville 1982; (MAE) Cnslr Ed, W KY Univ 1988; *cr:* Percussion Instr Univ of Louisville 1982-; Music Teacher Bullitt Cntrl HS 1982-; *ai:* Bullitt Cntrl Choral Dir; Lyre Club Spon; Discipline Comm & Music Dept Chairperson; KY Music Educators Assn (All-St Chorus SABT Coord 1990) 1982-; Music Educators Natl Conference. KY Ed Assn, NEA 1982-; Musicians Union Local 169 1978-; Teacher of Yr Bullitt Cntrl HS 1988-89; *office:* Bullitt Central HS Hwy 44 Shepherdsville KY 40165

FLEMING, BRADLEY D., Admin/High School Teacher; *b:* Bloomington, IL; *m:* Deobrah Mc Lamb; *c:* Joshua, Carrie; *ed:* (BS) Ed, Bob Jones Univ 1976; *cr:* Eng Teacher Hope Chrstn Sch 1976-78; Admin/Teacher Calvary Baptist Chrstn 1978-, Trinity Baptist Sch 1990; *ai:* Church Music Dir & Soloist; ASCD; IL Advisory Comm Non-Public Schls 1988-; *office:* Calvary Baptist Chrstn Sch PO Box 445 Williston VT 05495

FLEMING, COZETT COWAN, US History Teacher; *b:* Lowell, AR; *m:* James H.; *c:* Sandra, Debra Duckering, James, Eric; *ed:* (BED) General Elem, Fresno St Coll 1966; Extention Class Through Many Colls & Univs; *cr:* Teacher Mc Kinley-Roosevelt Sch Dist 1963-65, Fresno Unified Sch Dist 1966-; *ai:* NEA, CA Teachers Assn, Fresno Teachers Assn 1963-; Amer Historical Society of Germans from Russia Corresponding Secy 1980-81; Fresno Philatilic Club 1980-89; *office:* Fort Miller Mid Sch 1302 Dakota Fresno CA 93704

FLEMING, FRANK JOSEPH, Science Teacher; *b:* Yankton, SD; *m:* Diana Sue Welch; *c:* Angelina, Christina, Kevin, Jason, Jeremy; *ed:* (BS) Botany, MT St Univ 1971; *cr:* Teacher Fairfield Dist 21 1971-; *ai:* MT Sci Teachers Assn Mem; MT Traffic Ed Assn St Pres; Fairfield Teachers Assn Past Pres; Amer Driver & Safety Ed Assn Mem; Better Elem Sci Teacher Mem; *home:* RR 1 Box 39 Fairfield MT 59436

FLEMING, JAMES CHRISTOPHER, 8th Grade Soc Stud Teacher; *b:* Ft Leavenworth, KS; *m:* Jamie Denise Duis; *ed:* (BA) Poly Sci, Univ of FL 1980; Teaching Credential Humboldt St Univ 1983; Grad Stud Amer His, Univ of UT; *cr:* 8th Grade Soc Stud Teacher Treasure Mountain Mid Sch 1984-; *ai:* 7th/8th Grade Stu Cncl Adv & Bstkbl Coach; Yr of Earth, Sch Improvement, Career Ladder Comms; Negotiations Team Mem; Park City Ed Assn (VP 1985-86) 1984-; Greenpeace 1988-; Servas 1987-; *home:* PO Box 1568 Park City UT 84060

FLEMING, JOAN VODOKLYS, Third Grade Teacher; *b:* Concord, MA; *m:* John Maher; *ed:* (BS) Ed, Framingham St Coll 1962; Grad Work Univ VA, George Washington Univ, George Mason Univ; *cr:* 4th Grade Teacher Roosevelt Sch 1962-64; 2nd/3rd Grade Teacher Lyles-Crouch 1964-74, Maury 1974-; *ai:* EAA, VEA, NEA 1964-; *home:* 1109 Allison St Alexandria VA 22302

FLEMING, LINDA TEETS, Chapter 1 Resource Teacher; *b:* Cumberland, MD; *m:* Albert John; *c:* Lucinda Davis, Lawre Virts, Lissa, Albert J. II; *ed:* (AA) Elem Ed, Garrett Comm Coll 1974; (BS) Elem Ed, 1975, (ME) Admin/Supervision, 1979 Frostburg St Univ; *cr:* 6th-8th Grade Teacher Route 40 Elem Sch 1975-77; 5th Grade Teacher 1977-89, Teacher-in-Charge 1983-, Chapter 1 Resource Teacher 1989- Dennett Road Elem Sch; *ai:* Rural Sch Enhancement Team Mem; Dennett Road Sch Parent Volunteer, Peer Tutor Coord; Dennett Road Sch Discipline Comm Mem; NEA, MSTA, Garrett Cty Teachers Assn 1975-; Bus & Prof Women Secy 1988-; Camp Agape Day Camp (Founder, Dir) 1980-; Otterbein United Meth Church (Historian, Family Life Coord, Adult Women Sunday Sch Teacher) 1972-; *office:* Dennett Road Elem Sch 1217 Dennett Rd Oakland MD 21550

FLEMING, NORTON B., 5th Grade Teacher; *b:* Louisville, KY; *m:* Frances A. Edwards; *c:* Ricky, Deanna, Monique, Corey, Norton, Scottie; *ed:* (BA) Elem Ed, Drake Univ 1975; (MS) Elem Ed, Western KY Univ; *cr:* Asst Heywood Environmental Sch 1975-76; Phys Ed Instr Luhr Elem 1976-77; 6th Grade Teacher Shaffner Elem 1977-78; 4th/5th Grade Teacher Wilkerson Elem 1978-; *ai:* Coached JV Bsktbl Shawnee HS and Butler HS; Grade Level Chairperson; Sch Planning Comm; Schls Cmptr Team Leader; Jefferson Cty Teachers Rep; Coached Optomist Bsktbl; *home:* 1618-7 Brashear Dr #20 Louisville KY 42010

FLEMING, PEGGY SUE (FRY), 7th Grade Teacher; *b:* Pittsburg, KS; *m:* Robert; *c:* Kyle, Michael, Margaret, Joseph; *ed:* (BS) Elem, Pittsburg St Univ 1972; Natural Family Planning Master Teacher; *cr:* 1st/2nd Grade Teacher W Mineral Attendance Center 1972-73; Spec Rdng Teacher Eugene Fields Elem Ed 1974-75; Jr HS/7th Grade Teacher St Marys Grade Sch 1986-; *ai:* Natural Family Planning Instr; Geography Bd Dir 1988-; Vision & Value Team Mem; PTA Secy 1984-85; St Mary Sch Evaluation Steering Comm Chairperson; *office:* St Marys Grade Sch 213 E 9th St Pittsburg KS 66762

FLEMING, VICKIE L., Chapter 1 Teacher; *b:* Topeka, KS; *m:* Kenneth J.; *ed:* (BS) Elem Ed, Baker Univ 1978; (MS) Master Teacher, Emporia Univ 1984; Rdng Specialist, Univ of KS 1987; Educl Kinesiology I & Beginning Sign Lang Instruction, Marva Collins Teacher Trng Inst; *cr:* 3rd/4th Grade Teacher Unified Sch Dist 346 1978-79; 6th Grade Teacher Unified Sch Dist 342 1979-86; Chapter I Teacher Unified Sch Dist 341 1987-; *ai:* Dist Curr, Screening, Rdng, Kids Need Emotional & Educl Developmental Support Comms; Intnl Rdng Assn 1988-; Alpha Delta Kappa 1986-; NEA 1979-; Oskaloosa Educl Assn 1987-; Edu-Kinesthetics Network of Midland Empire, ASCD, Mc Louth Ed Assn; Apple Cmptr Users Group, Prgm Evaluation Comm Chm; Cmmty Ed Advisory Cncl, Needs Assessment Survey Chm; Co-Author Known & Narrated Stories & Scenes Volume I & II; Co-Writer/Producer Chapter 1 Video; Margaret Mc Namara Certificate of Merit; Whos Who in Amer Ed.

FLEMING-FOSTER, IMA JEAN, Social Studies Chairman; *b:* Madison, AR; *m:* Thomas Lee; *c:* Justin, Jessica,; *ed:* (BA) Hist, Lane College 1973; *cr:* Teacher School Dist 147 1974-79; Teacher/Coach San Elizario ISD 1981-; *ai:* Class Spon, Dist Teacher Comm; Natl Honor Soc, Curr Comm; Craft Club Spon; Cheerleader Spon; Track & Cross Country Coach; Teacher of the Year San Elizario ISD 1986-87; Career Ladder Level III; *home:* 1521 Opossum Cl El Paso TX 79927

FLEMMONS, MARI ROBERTSON, Journalism/Photography Teacher; *b:* Flint, MI; *m:* Kenn; *ed:* (BS) Journalism, AR St Univ 1981; Cert Awarded Univ of Cntrl AR 1986; *cr:* Reporter Helena World 1981-83; Feature Writer AR Democrat 1983-85; Journalism Teacher Parkview 1986-; *ai:* Sr Spon; Sr Publications; Quill & Scroll; Newspaper; Yrbk; Publicity; Tommy Logue Schlsp Selection Comm; Journalism Ed Assn 1986-; Society Of Prof Journalists 1979-; AR HS Press Assn, NEA, AR Ed Assn 1986-; Chi Omega Alumni Assn; Magazine Writer & Ed; *office:* Parkview Arts/Sci Magnet HS 2501 Barrow Rd Little Rock AR 72204

FLESHMAN, THERESA FAZIO, Third/Fourth Grade Teacher; *b:* Oak Hill, WV; *m:* Michael F.; *ed:* (AA) Elem Ed, Beckley Coll 1974; (BA) Elem Ed/Early Chldhd Ed, Marshall Univ 1976; *cr:* Elem Teacher Bellepoint Elem Sch 1977-; *ai:* Whos Who Among Stus in Amer Jr Colls Beckley Coll 1974-75; *office:* Bellepoint Elem Sch Miller Ave Hinton WV 25951

FLETCHER, BARBARA ANN, 5/6th Grade English Teacher; *b:* Livingston, TN; *ed:* (BS) Home Ec Ed/Elem Ed, TN Technological Univ 1971; *cr:* Receptionist Cookeville General Hospital 1971-72; Soc Worker 1972-73, 2nd/4th-6th Grade Classroom Teacher 1973- Baxter Elem Sch; *ai:* Past Mem Textbook Adoption Comm; NEA, TEA. PEAC Mem; *office:* Baxter Elem Sch Baxter TN 38544

FLETCHER, BETTY RAINS, Fourth Grade Teacher; *b:* Alma, GA; *m:* Jimmie; *c:* Robin Ryan, Kimberly Cronk, Jamie; *ed:* (BS) Elem, Marion Coll 1968; (MS) Elem, Ball St 1971; *cr:* 2nd Grade Teacher Hoarce Mann Elem 1968-71, Martin Boots Elem 1971-83; 4th Grade Teacher Center Elem 1983-; *ai:* Teacher Expectation Stu Achievement; Wkshp Way Various Book Adoption Comm; Rdng Guidebook Comm; NEA, IN St Teacher Assn, Marion Teacher Assn; Meth Women Assn (Sunday Sch Teacher, Youth Group Mission Work); *office:* Center Elem Sch 4415 S Nebraska St Marion IN 46953

FLETCHER, CAROL ANNE, Business Teacher; *b:* Monroe, LA; *m:* Bobby W.; *c:* Casey Booth; *ed:* (BS) Bus Ed/Eng, 1979, (MBA) Bus Management, 1982 NE LA Univ; Cmptr Literacy; *cr:* Bus Teacher LA Bus Coll 1978-79; Eng Teacher Bastrop Jr HS 1980; Marketing Rep Xerox Corporation 1981; Bus Teacher Neville HS 1981-; *ai:* FBLA, Class Spon; *office:* Neville HS 600 Forsythe Ave Monroe LA 71201

FLETCHER, CATHY WILSON, Computer Teacher; *b:* Lubbock, TX; *m:* Danny J.; *c:* Jerry, Jay, Jodie; *ed:* (BS) Elem Ed, TX Tech Univ 1971; (MED) Rdng, Univ of TX El Paso 1977; Supervision/Admin; Teacher Evaluation Appraisal Trng; *cr:* 1st Grade Teacher Reese Elem 1971-74; 8th Grade Teacher Frenship Jr HS 1978-79; 2nd Grade Teacher Casey Elem 1979-86; Elem Appraiser Frenship Ind Sch Dist 1986-87; Remedial Rdng Teacher 1987-89, Cmptr Teacher 1989- Casey Elem; *ai:* Cty Spelling Bee Spon; Little Dribblers; FFA; 4-H; Assn TX Prof Educators (Region Dir 1985-89,. Candidate St Treas 1990); Wolfforth Lib Comm Mem; *office:* Casey Elem Sch Box 100 Wolfforth TX 79382

FLETCHER, DONALD F., Retired; *b:* Williamstown, MA; *m:* Joyce Horn; *c:* James W., Jane M.; *ed:* (BA) Eng/Soc Stud, North Adams-St Coll 1964; *cr:* Teacher Half Hollow Hills 1964-69; Ballston Spa Sch Dist 1970-89; *ai:* NEA Life Mem 1964-89; William Lodge AF & AM 1964-; Amer Legion 1945-.

FLETCHER, ERIN BRIGGS, 7th Grade Soc Stud Teacher; *b:* Miami, FL; *m:* Fred S.; *c:* Lillian, Celeste; *ed:* (BS) Elem Ed, 1962, (MA) Elem Ed, 1976, (AA) Elem Ed, 1985 Univ of AL; Natl Geographic Society Summer Geography Inst 1987; *cr:* 7th-9th Grade Eng/Span Teacher Eastwood Jr HS 1962-64; 9th-11th Grade Eng Teacher St James Sch 1965-73; 6th Grade Teacher Westlawn Mid Sch 1974-82; 7th Grade Soc Stud Teacher Tuscaloosa Mid Sch 1982-; *ai:* Team Leader Tuscaloosa Mid Sch; Tuscaloosa Mid Sch Steering Comm Chm; Tuscaloosa Mid Sch Supts Advisory Comm Rep; Celebration 65 Chm; Natl Cncl Geography Ed Regional Comm 1989-; AL Cncl of Soc Stud 1987-; NCSS 1986; Kappa Delta Pi 1984-85; GSA Cncl Nom Women Committed to Excl 1989; Jacksonville St Univ Nom Teacher Hall of Fame 1989; Tuscaloosa Jr League Sustainer; Fulbright Scholar Awd 1990; Geography Teacher Consultant Natl Geographic Society 1987-; AL Teacher of Yr Finalist; Outstanding Grad Stud Fnd of Ed Univ of AL 1984; *home:* 12 Monnish Dr Tuscaloosa AL 35401

FLETCHER, VIRGINIA GREENE, 7th/8th Grade Lang Art Teacher; *b:* Cowen, WV; *m:* Thomas R.; *c:* Paula M., Jo C.; *ed:* (BS) Bio/His, Fairmont St Coll 1969; (MA) Gifted, WV Coll of Grad Stud 1984; Learning Disabilities Cert; Mid Sch Authorization Trng; Elem Cert Through Comprehensive Test; Developmental Guidance/Counseling from Horizon Center; *cr:* Soc Stud Teacher Ravenswood HS 1969-71; 6th Grade Teacher Glade Elem 1979-82; Cty Diagnostician Webster Cty Bd of Ed 1982-84; 7th-8th Grade Teacher Glade Jr HS 1984-86; Teacher of Gifted & Learning Disabilities Glade Jr HS & Elem 1986-89; 7th/8th Grade Teacher Glade Jr HS 1989-; *ai:* Girls Bsktbl Coach 1981-89; NEA, WV Ed Assn 1978-; WV Assn Gifted & Talented 1986-; NCTE 1989-; Extension Homemakers, Cowen Womans Club 1976-; WV Spec Olympics Cty Chairperson 1979-80; WV Literacy Volunteers; *office:* Glade Elem/Jr HS PO Box 218 Cowen WV 26206

FLETCHER, WANDA SUTHERLAND, Fifth Grade Teacher; *b:* Kingsport, TN; *m:* Randy L.; *c:* Kristie L.; *ed:* (BS) Elem Ed, 1972, (MED) Elem Ed, 1983 E TN St Univ; *cr:* Teacher Lebanon Elem 1971-74, Brookside Elem 1974-; *ai:* Annual Spon; Awd Day Coord; Phi Kappa Phi 1983-85; PTA TN Life Mem 1990; *home:* Rt 2 Box 249 Jonesborough TN 37659

FLEURY, RICK LEE, Art Teacher/Art Dept Chair; *b:* Malone, NY; *m:* Lisa Marie Mc Phee; *c:* Andrew J., Erin E.; *ed:* (AAS) Advertising Design/Production, Mohawk Valley Comm Coll 1976; (BS) Art Ed, St Univ Coll Buffalo 1978; (MA) Art Ed, Ball St Univ 1982; Supervising Art Ed Stu Teachers; Assistanship Awd Muncie IN; *cr:* Art Teacher 1978-81, Art Dept Chm 1982- Argyle Cntrl Sch; *ai:* Art Club, Natl Art Honor Society, Frosh Class, Sch Newspaper, Talent Unlimited-Tri Cty Stu Journal, Miss Teen NY St Adv; Art Chm; Negotiations Mem; Stu of Month Comm Mem; Argyle Cntrl Sch Just Say No to Drugs Fund Raiser; Argyle Teachers Assn Negotiations Comm Mem; NY St Art Teachers Assn Mem Honorable Mention Awd; NAEA Mem; Corporate Business Grant Art Facility Expansion; Hyde Museum 2nd Pl Awd Adirondack Regional Show 1982; Implemented Art Curr, Environments Courses Buffalo St; *office:* Argyle Cntrl Sch Sheridan St Argyle NY 12809

FLICK, MARJORIE EBERLE, Computer Coordinator; *b:* Grove City, PA; *w:* James W. (dec); *ed:* (BS) Scndry Ed, Clarion Univ 1952; (MS) Supervision, Duquesne Univ 1977; Elem Prin Cert Duquesne Univ; *cr:* Teacher 1959-74; Head Teacher 1974-85; Cmptr Coord 1985- Riverside Beaver Cty Sch Dist; *ai:* RBCEA; PSEA; NEA; Camp Run VP Church Trustee 1986-; Friendship Circle Treas 1984-; *office:* Riverside Mid Sch Rd 2 Box 4010 Ellwood City PA 16117

FLICKINGER, JODIE NEPHEW, High School Science Teacher; *b:* Warren, OH; *m:* David B.; *c:* Evin, Katie; *ed:* (BS) Medical Technology, Youngstown Univ 1974; Teaching Cert Comprehensive Sci, Toledo Univ 1987; *cr:* Medical Technologist St Vincents Medical Center 1973-88; Bio/Chem/Physics Teacher Evergreen HS 1988-; *ai:* Odyssey of Mind Teams Coach; Minigrants Hands on Sci Labs Fulton Cty Office of Ed; *office:* Evergreen HS 15455 Co Rd 6 Metamora OH 43537

FLICKINGER, MAY O. HUBER, Third Grade Teachers Aide; *b:* Galesburg, IL; *m:* Charles E.; *c:* Kenneth, Karol Smith; *ed:* (BS) Home Ec/Ed, Univ of IL Urbana Champaign 1943; Grad Work Bradley Univ, W IL Univ, S IL Univ; *cr:* 3rd Grade Teacher 1961-86, 3rd Grade Teachers Aide 1987- Brimfield Elem Sch; *ai:* NEA, IL Ed Assn 1961-86; Brimfield Assn (VP 1968, Treas 1969, 1973); Phi Upsilon Omicron Univ of IL; DAR; Amer Legion Auxiliary; 4-H Girls Club Leader; Knox Cty Home Ec Club; United Meth Church; Outstanding Elem Teacher of America 1973; *home:* Box 342 Williamsfield IL 61489

FLICKINGER, TERRI C., History/Civics Teacher; *b:* El Paso, TX; *m:* John H.; *c:* Matthew, Robert; *ed:* (BA) His, 1978, (MA) His, 1982 NM St; *cr:* Teacher Mesilla Valley Chrstn 1980-; *ai:* Sr Class & Yrbk Adv; ACSI; Presbyn Univ (VP 1982-86, Teacher 1986-); *office:* Mesilla Valley Chrstn Sch 2010 Wisconsin Las Cruces NM 88001

FLINN, REBECCA ANN, Teacher/Program Facilitator; *b:* Upland, CA; *c:* Sean; *ed:* (BS) Lit/Lang, CA St Univ Pomona 1969; (MA) Sch Management, Univ of LaVerne 1988; *cr:* Eng Teacher Chino HS 1970-75; Teacher/Gifted Prgm Facilitator Moreno Valley HS 1978-; *ai:* Sch Newspaper Adv; *office:* Moreno Valley HS 23300 Cottonwood Ave Moreno Valley CA 92388

FLINSPACH, URSULA R., Math Teacher; *b:* Washington, PA; *m:* Donald A. II; *c:* Donald A. III; *ed:* (BA) Math, Southern IL Univ 1975; (AS) Cmptr Sci, John Wood Comm Coll 1984; Grad Stud Math; *cr:* Aviation Electronics Tech US Navy 1969-72; Math/Physics Teacher Highland HS 1976-77; Math/Cmptr Sci Teacher Quincy Notredame HS 1977-85; Math/Physics Teacher Homer HS 1986-88; Mt Zion HS 1988-; *ai:* Chrldr Coach; Math Team-Precalc; Teams-JETS Math/Physics; Calculus-AP; IL Cncl Teachers of Math; NCT ; US Navy Aviation Electronics 1969-72 E5 Awd; Honorable Mention-Hero of Yr Champaign Cty 1989; *office:* Mt Zion H S 305 S Henderson Mount Zion IL 62549

FLINT, DIANE, English/Latin Teacher; *b:* Greencastle, IN; *ed:* (BA) Eng, 1969, (MS) Ed, 1972 IN St Univ; *cr:* Teacher Amer Baptist Assembly 1978, Cascade HS 1969-; *ai:* NHS Cascade Chapter Spon; SAT Class Instr; NCTE 1972-; NEA, IN St Teachers Assn 1972-; Mill Creek Classroom Teachers Assn 1969-; Alpha Delta Kappa 1972-; Greencastle 1st Baptist Church 1964-; IN Academic Competitions for Excl Most Influential Teacher Awd 1987, 1989; Whos Who Among America Educators 1990; *office:* Cascade HS PO Box H Clayton IN 46118

FLINT, GEORGE, JR., 7th/8th Grade Teacher; *b:* Englewood, NJ; *m:* Anidelle Tomlinson; *c:* Robert Hershenow, Nicholas Hershenow, Sally Mc Daniel, Thomas Hershenow, Jennifer, Ruthann Codina; *ed:* (BA) Soc Sci/Ec, Bucknell Univ 1952; Various Courses; *cr:* Account Exec Merrill Lynch Pierce Fenner & Smith 1955-62, Sutro & Company 1962-63; 4th/8th Grade Teacher Fresno Unified Sch Dist 1964-; Photographer 1980-; *ai:* Vlybl Coach; Yrbk Adv; Soc Sci Steering Dist Comm; Fresno Teachers Assn, CA Teachers Assn, NEA; Fresno Cmmty Theater, Fresno Childrens Playhouse (Bd Mem, Actor); Westminster Presbyn Church Bd Mem; GSA Golden Valley Cncl; Cntrl CA Photographers Guild, Jeri Nagle Memorial Schlrshp Fund Charter Mem; Fresno Ski Club Pres; BSA (ASST, Scoutmaster, Troop Comm); Nom Fresno Cty Outstanding Educator 1970-71; Fresno Dist Fair Honorable Mention Photography 1989; *home:* 254 W San Bruno Fresno CA 93704

FLINT, RODNEY LEWIS, 6th Grade Teacher; *b:* Shiloh, MI; *ed:* (BA) Industrial Art, San Diego St Univ 1963; Working Towards Masters Counseling; *cr:* 7th-8th Grade Industrial Art/Sci Teacher Lancaster Elem Sch Dist 1964-68; 9th-12th Grade Industrial Art/Sci Teacher Antelope Valley Union Sch Dist 1968-69; 7th-9th Grade Industrial Art/Sci/Math Teacher Wm S Hart Sch Dist 1969-70; 7th-12th Grade Industrial Art Teacher San Bernardino Unified Sch Dist 1971-73; 7th-9th Grade Industrial Arts/Sci Teacher Ontario-Montclair Unified Sch Dist 1973-75; 4th-6th Grade Self Contained Teacher Soledad Union Sch Dist 1977-; *ai:* CA Teachers Assn 1963-; CA Sci Teachers 1980-81; Industrial Arts Assn 1963-78; Soc Stud Assn 1989-; GSA Scout Leader 1978-80.

FLIS, JULIA CALVO, 7th Grade Life Science Teacher; *b:* Yigo, GU; *m:* Robert Joseph; *c:* Cody, Monica; *ed:* (BA) Bio, Univ of GU 1970; ASCP Trng & Cert/Cytotechnology; Graduate Work Rdng & Bio; *cr:* Lab Asst/Cytotechnologist Guam & US 1970-82; Health/Earth Sci/Life Sci Teacher Dededo Mid Sch 1982-; Spec Project Research Asst Univ of GU/Weri 1984-85; *ai:* DMS Sci Fair, Dept Ed Sci Expo Steering, DMS Sci Club Oraganizing, Chamorro Week Comm; NJHS Adv; NSTA 1989; Intnl Rdng Assn 1988-; Cub Scouts Den Mother 1983-85; IRA Grants-Sci Lottery; Current Events Sci Books for Sci Expo; Sci Ta Ped Repeated Rdngs; *office:* Dededo Mid Sch West Santa Monica Ave Dededo GU 96912

FLOM, LARRY JAMES, Soc Stud Chm/History Teacher; *b:* Faribault, MN; *ed:* (BA) His, St Olaf Coll 1957; Univ SD; Univ Northern IA; *cr:* Teacher Riverside HS 1961-72; West HS 1972-; *ai:* Sioux City Cmmty Sch Dist Soc Stud Curr Comm; Co-Writer Curr Course Guides, Amer His II, World His I/II, Accelerated Amer His II; Founder West HS Hall of Fame; Sioux City Ed Assn 1961-; IA Ed Assn; NEA; NCSS; Sons of Norway; Intl Brotherhood Magicians; Omaha Magical Society; Distinguished Educator Awd Morningside Coll 1989; Nom IA Distinguished Teacher Awd 85; US West Outstanding Teacher Awd 1988; *home:* 4110 Peters Sioux City IA 51106

FLOM, SHERMAN H., 5th Grade Teacher; *b:* Glenwood, MN; *m:* Mary Ann Ocenas; *c:* Erica; *ed:* (AA) Elem Ed, NWCC 1964; (BA) Elem Ed, Univ of WY 1969; Cmptr Sci, Ad Ed, Gifted/Talented; *cr:* 5th Grade Teacher Amer Internation Sch 1971-73, Pioneer Park Elem 1973-82, Wind River Elem 1982-89, Jackson Elem 1989-; *ai:* 10 & Under Soccer Coach; Lander Swim Club Bd of Dir; WY Ed Assn Treas; NEA; Phi Delta Kappa Research Chm 1987-88; Elks, Lander Sportsman Club, Old Time Fiddlers; *office:* Jackson Elem Sch 720 W Jackson Ave Riverton WY 82501

FLOOD, JERRY NEIL, Business Education Teacher; *b:* Gary, IN; *ed:* (BS) Scndry Bus Ed, 1966, (MS) Scndry Ed, 1971 IN Univ Bloomington; *cr:* Bus/Eng Teacher Crown Point HS 1966-71; Bus Teacher Boone Grove HS 1971-; *ai:* Class of 1990 & NHS Spon; Performance Based Accreditation Steering Comm; Porter Township Schls Pride Comm; NEA, IN St Teachers Assn, Porter Township Teachers Assn; Winfield Township Advisory Bd 1979-82; *home:* 10115 Clay Crown Point IN 46307

FLORA, JAMES EDWARD, Social Studies Teacher; *b:* Dodgeville, WI; *m:* Linda L. Griswold; *c:* Lisa M., Geoffrey, Matthew; *ed:* (BA) His, Univ of WI Platteville 1967; W MI Univ, De Pauw Univ, Maclaster Coll, Univ of WI Milwaukee, Marquette Univ; *cr:* Teacher New Holstein HS 1967-; *ai:* Dir Ed for Employment & Staff Dev; Asst Athletic Dir; Adv Stu Cncl; Forensic Coach; Sch Nurse; EMT; WCSS Pres 1982-84; Bus World Dir; Chamber of Commerce Pres 1985-87; Dist Teacher of Yr 1985; St Soc Stud Teacher of Yr 1987; Freedoms Fnd Natl Awd 1989; *office:* New Holstein HS 1715 Plymouth St New Holstein WI 53061

FLORES, EMILY LOVERDE, English Department Chair; *b:* San Antonio, TX; *m:* Edward T.; *c:* Eric, Elissa; *ed:* (BA) Eng, St Marys Univ 1971; Writing Trainer NJ Writing Project TX, Instructional Leadership Trng, Clinical Supervision Trng; *cr:* Eng Teacher John Marshall HS 1971-77, Tom Clark HS 1978-80; Eng Teacher 1980-, Dept Chairperson 1983- Coke Stevenson Mid Sch; *ai:* Dist Instructional Policy Handbook & Textbook Adoption Comm; Dist Curr Writing & Revision Team; Dist Inservice Presentor/Facilitator; NCTE, TCTE 1985-; NJWP Trainers in TX 1988-; SAACTE Prgm Chairperson 1987-88; Trinity Univ Excl In Teaching Awd, Learning Magazine Leadership Excl Awd, NCTE Center of Excl for Teaching Eng Nom; *office:* Coke Stevenson Mid Sch 8403 Tezel Rd San Antonio TX 78250

FLORES, HERMINIA SANTIAGO, Spanish Teacher; *b:* Van Horn, TX; *m:* Reuben Reyes; *c:* Alexandra A.; *ed:* (BA) Span, Sul Ross St Univ 1979; *cr:* Teacher Crockett Jr HS 1980-81, Hood Jr HS 1981-; *ai:* Stu Cncl, Core Team Mem, Stu Aasistance Services Spon; TSTA, NEA, TFLA 1989-; TCTA 1981-89; *office:* Hood Jr HS PO Box 3912 Odessa TX 79760

FLORES, JANA SUE, 6th Grade Teacher; *b:* Orange, CA; *m:* Geno J.; *c:* Allyson, Taylor; *ed:* (BA) Sociology, CA St Univ Hayward 1975; *cr:* Teacher Orcutt Union Sch Dist 1981-; *ai:* Mentor Teacher Lang Art; Cty Soc Stud, St Dept of Ed His-Soc Sci CAP Comm; His Project of CA Mem; CA Cncl for Soc Stud Mem 1989-; *office:* Pine Grove Elem Sch 1050 Rice Ranch Rd Santa Maria CA 93455

FLORES, JEAN AGEE, Sixth Grade Math Teacher; *b:* Shamrock, TX; *c:* Marty; *ed:* (BA) Elem Ed, Friends Univ 1970; *cr:* Jr HS Eng Teacher Sublette Jr HS 1971-73; 5th Grade Teacher Lincoln Elem 1973-89; 6th Grade Math Teacher West Mid Sch 1989-; *ai:* Childrens Bible Drill Team Spon; Math Fest Co-Chairperson 1985-86; *office:* West Mid Sch U Sch Dist #480 401 N Kansas Liberal KS 67901

FLORIAN, ELSIE KEADY, Religion Teacher; *b:* Wilkensburg, PA; *m:* John; *c:* Suzanne Bence, Martin, Deborah Smoody; *ed:* (BS) Elem Ed, Duquesne Univ 1976; Religious Ed Prgm Duquesne Univ; *cr:* 3rd Grade Teacher 1970-89, 4th-7th Grade Relgion Teacher 1989-St Theresa Sch; *ai:* Parish Coord Rainbows for All Gods Children Prgm; Lector for Parish Liturgy; *office:* St Therese's Sch 3 St Thurese Ct Homestead PA 15120

FLORIG, SANDRA MARY (HAUBER), Jr HS Sci & Health Teacher; *b:* St Marys, PA; *m:* Kurt William; *c:* Kevin; *ed:* (BS) Bio/General Sci, Clarion Univ 1973; Introduction Cmptr Programming; *cr:* Bio Teacher De Sales HS 1974-75; Jr HS Sci/Health Teacher Queen of the World Sch 1976-; *ai:* Sci Fair Coord; 7th Grade First Aid Instr; Mid St Steering Comm Co-Chairperson; Drug Free Schls Comm Rep; NCEA 1976-; Amer Red Cross 1980-, 5 Yr Service Awd 1990; *office:* Queen of the World Sch 134 Queens Rd Saint Marys PA 15857

FLORIN, SUZANNE M., Mathematics Teacher/Chair; *b:* Chicago, IL; *m:* David; *c:* Adam, Kathy; *ed:* (BS) Math/Physics, 1972, (MS) Math Ed, 1979 Winona St Univ; Math Ed, Univ of MN Minneapolis 1987; *cr:* Math Teacher/Chairperson Cochrane-Fountain City HS 1972-; *ai:* NEA, NCTM 1972-; Natl Ski Patrol 1986-; *office:* Cochrane-Fountain City Schls Box 219 Fountain City WI 54629

FLORKEVICH, JERRY, 7th/8th Grade English Teacher; *b:* Uniontown, PA; *m:* Linda Lujack; *c:* Bryan; *ed:* (BS) Phys Ed/Health/Eng, Salem Coll 1969; Scndry Admin; *cr:* Teacher/Coach Harrison Cty Schls 1969-75, Uniontown Schls 1975-; *ai:* Coaching 7th & 8th Jr HS Ftbl Prgm; *office:* Uniontown Schls 303 Connellsville St Uniontown PA 15401

FLORO, P. THOMAS, JR., Social Studies Teacher; *b:* Toledo, OH; *m:* Lisa Linke; *c:* Zachary Alan; *ed:* (BA) Intensive Soc Stud, Univ of Toledo 1979; (MS) Admin/Supervision, Univ of Toledo 1985; *cr:* Soc Stud Teacher Oak Harbor HS 1981-; *ai:* Frosh Class Advr; Varsity Bsbl Coach; NEA 1981-; *office:* Oak Harbor HS 11661 W St Rt 163 Oak Harbor OH 43449

FLOUNDERS, MARGARET R. MC FARLAND, 6th Grade English/Rdng Teacher; *b:* Media, PA; *m:* Donald C.; *c:* Thomas C., Courtney M.; *ed:* (BS) Elem Ed/Art, Kutztown St Univ 1971; (MED) Ed, Widener Univ 1985; Learning Inst Writing Experience; Wanda Lincoln Bureau of Educl Research Gifted; Roger Taylor Houghton Mifflins Whole Lang Trng; W Chester Univ Teacher Expectations & Stu Achievement Trng 1989; *cr:* 4th Grade Teacher 1971-78, 6th Grade Teacher 1978-82, 5th Grade Teacher 1982-85 Oakmont Elem; 6th Grade Mid Sch Eng/Rdng Teacher Haverford Mid Sch 1985-; *ai:* Organize Sch Halloween Party; Intramural Girls Bsktbl; Mid Sch Steering Comm, Write Eng & Rdng Curr Guides; In Service Dept with the Writing Process Approach & TESA Trng; NEA, PSEA 1971-; HTEA Salary Comm 1975-76; Upper Providence Twp Republican Party Comm Woman 1979-89, Spec Service 1989; Rose Tree Little Leage Team Mother 1990; Rose Tree Media Alumni Assn Bd of Dir 1981-; *office:* Haverford Mid Sch 1701 Darby Rd Havertown PA 19083

FLOURNOY, JAMES ALAN, Science Teacher; *b:* Kansas City, KS; *m:* Luetta Arlene Burger; *ed:* (BS) Scndry Ed, KS St Univ 1978; (MA) Bio, Univ of MO Kansas City 1988; Sci Resource Coord Prgm, North Kansas City Sch Dist; *cr:* Sci Teacher St Stephens Acad 1978-80, St Patricks Sch 1980-; *ai:* 8th Grade & Stu Cncl Moderator; Sci Fair & Sci Curr Coord; Yrbk Moderator; NSTA 1986-; NCEA 1980-; MO Bio Teachers 1989-90; MO Jr Acad of Sci Teacher of YR 1985; Region 7 Teacher of Yr Awd 86; mid West Research Inst Fellowship; *office:* St Patricks Sch 1400 Ne 42nd Terr Kansas City MO 64116

FLOWERS, KARLA MC CARTER, 4th Grade Teacher; *b:* Wichita Falls, TX; *m:* Gary L.; *c:* Ashlee, Saylee Mc Call; *ed:* (BS) Phys Ed, 1983, Elem/Scndry Eng, 1990 WTSU; *cr:* Coach/Phys Ed Teacher 1983-89, 4th Grade Teacher 1989- Spearman; *ai:* UIL Ready Writing; *home:* 1115 S Townsend Spearman TX 79081

FLOWERS, LINDA DOEZEMA, Eng Dept Chair/A P Coord; *b:* Lancaster, OH; *ed:* (BA) Eng, 1970; (MA) Eng, 1972 OH Univ; Univ of South FL 1987; *cr:* Eng Teacher OH Univ 1970-72; HS Eng Teacher Lancaster HS 1972-79; Tampa Cath HS 1979-; *ai:* Literary Club; Chaperone for Sr Events; Curr Coord Comm; Book Selection Comm for Diocese of St Petersburg; Lancaster Classroom Teachers Assoc Negotiations Chm 1970-79; OEA/NEA 1970-79; NCEA 1979-; Teaching Fellowship to OH Univ 1970-72; Jennings Scholar-Outstndg Teaching in OH 1976; Developmental Lang Prgm at Tampa Cath 1986; *office:* Tampa Catholic HS 4630 N Rome Ave Tampa FL 33603

FLOWERS, LINDA KAY, Jr HS English/History Teacher; *b:* Denver, CO; *ed:* Chrstn Ed, TN Temple 1976; Working Towards BS Liberty Univ; *cr:* Teacher Faith Chrstn Sch 1976-81; Teacher/Jr HS Lead Teacher/Supvr Fayette Chrstn Sch 1982-; *ai:* Soc Sci & Sci Fair Prgms Head; Lib Sch Book Fairs & Book Ordering Organizer; *office:* Fayette Chrstn Sch 152 Longview Rd Fayetteville GA 30214

FLOWERS, ROLAND E., 5th Grade Teacher; *b:* San Antonio, TX; *m:* Beverly Ladson; *c:* Jason, Kristin; *ed:* (BS) His/Government, Univ of TX Austin 1972; (MS) Elem Ed, SW TX St Univ 1982; *cr:* Teacher Adams Hill 1973-; *ai:* Edgewood Lions Club Bd of Dir 1984-86; Jack & Jill of America Incorporated 1987-.

FLOYD, BETTYE BYRD, English Teacher; *b:* Tuscaloosa, AL; *m:* David; *c:* Lateisha, Michael; *ed:* (BA) Eng, Stillman Coll 1972, (MS) Troy St Univ 1977; *cr:* Eng Teacher, West Blocton HS 1972-74, Smiths Station HS 1974-; *ai:* NCTE.

FLOYD, MARILYN LOUISE, Substitute English Teacher; *b:* Lesage, WV; *cr:* Prin/1st-8th Grade Teacher Fairview Sch; Teacher Barker Sch; Teacher Coxs Landing 1958-; *ai:* Camp Fire Leader; Camp Cnslr; 4-H Leader; WV Ed Assn, Cabell Cty Rdng Cncl, Math Teachers Organization; Coxs Landing PTA; Cmmtny Srs; Benjamin Franklins Stamp Club; Womans Club of Coxs Landing (Pres, VP, Parlimentarian, Ways & Means Chairperson); General Fed of Womens Clubs of WV St Chairwoman; WV St Teacher of Yr 1968; Governors Beautification Awd; Conservation Educator of Yr 1971; Cabell Cty Sch System Drug Abuse & Prevention Prgm Author & Organizer; 4-H Alumni St Awds; *home:* 6650 Ohio River Rd Lesage WV 25537

FLOYD, WILLIAM ARTHUR, Assistant Principal; *b:* Laurens, SC; *m:* Gracie Seabrooks; *c:* Gregory W., Kenneth W.; *ed:* (BS) Bio, Allen Univ 1965; (MED) Natural Sci, 1975, Admin, 1987 Clemson Univ; Earth Sci Curr Project, FL St Univ; Bio Inst Wilkes Coll; Grad Prgm Clemson Univ; *cr:* Classroom Teacher Riverview HS 1965-67, Westside HS 1967-70; Classroom Teacher 1970-86, Asst Prin 1986- T L Hanna HS; *ai:* Discipline Grades 9 & 11; Textbook Mgr; Emergency Drills Mgr; Mgr & Chm Special Projects & Fund Raisers; Evaluate Teachers & Substitute

Teachers; SC Scndry Sch Prin Assn, NEA 1986-; Anderson Cty Sch Dist 5 Masters 1986-; Univ of SC Minority Bd 1988-; Anderson City Mayors Comm for Handicapped 1988-; Kiwanis Intnl Youth Spon Clubs 1988-; Anderson Cty Recreation Commission 1980-; 1968 FL St & 1969 Wilkes Coll Natl Sci Fnd Grant; Royal Baptist Church Trustee Bd; Anderson Youth Treatment Bd; Anderson Cty Federal Credit Union Bd of Dirs; *office:* T L Hanna HS 2123 Marchbanks Ave Anderson SC 29621

FLOYDS, CAROLYN WILSON, 6th Grade Teacher; *b:* Ft Wayne, IN; *c:* Chavarro; *cr:* Teacher Suttle Elem 1974-75, Marion Elem 1975-76; Truancy Officer Putnam Cty Schls 1976-77; Cnslr FL Sch for Deaf & Blind 1977-78; Teacher Sunshine HS 1978-; *ai:* Elem Dept Curr Coord; Yrbk & In-Service Comms Chm; Hale Cty Ed Assn, AL Ed Assn, NEA; Order of Eastern Star Assn Matron.

FLUD, SHERRIE NUNN, 5th Grade Teacher; *b:* Henryetta, OK; *m:* Jerry; *c:* Starla, Melissa; *ed:* (AS) Elem Ed, Connors St Coll 1972; (BS) Elem Ed, Cameron Univ 1974; *cr:* 4th & 5th Grade Teacher Hanna Elem Sch 1975-82; 5th & 6th Grade Teacher Cooper-McClain Elem Sch 1982-; *ai:* OEA; NEA; 4-H Club Cty Leader; Stamp Club Local Pres; Chrldng Spon; *office:* Eufaula Public Sch 210 High St Eufaula OK 74432

FLUDD, LEON, JROTC Instructor; *b:* Santee, SC; *m:* Ella A. Schuler Fludd; *c:* Sherrie, Princess, Marlena; *ed:* (AA) Bus Mgmt, Los Angeles Comm Coll 1981; (BA) Soc Sci, Coker Coll 1988; Scndry Counseling; Diesel Mechanic Cert; *cr:* Typewriter Technician Smith Corona Merchant 1964-66; Squad Leader 1966-67; Drill Sergeant 1972-76; Instr Primary & Basic NCO 1976-78; Sr Drill Sergeant 1980-82; 1st Sergeant 1982-87 US Army; JROTC Instr Bowman HS 1987-; *ai:* Drill Team Supv; Supply Serge Ant Bi-Racial & Public Relations; Masonic Mason 1973-; Officers Assn 1982-; VFW 1989-; AME Felderville (Steward Board 1984- Class Leader 1982- Finance Comm Sunday Sch 1987-) Certificate 1989; Volunteer for DSS Soc Worker 1987-87; Letter of Appreciation 1987; Cert of Retire-US Army; Natl Defense Service Medal; Army Commendation Medal; Bronze Star Medal; Vietnam Service Medal; Vietnam Campaign Medal W/DVC 60; Vietnam Cross of Gallantry W/Palm; Meritorious Service Medal; Combat Infantryman Badge; Good Conduct Medal; Army Service Ribbon; Overseas Service Ribbon; NCO Prof Dev Ribbon; Drill Sergeant Identification Badge; Overseas Service Bar; *home:* 2198 Whittaker Dr SE Orangeburg SC 29115

FLUHARTY, BARRY LEE, Testing Coordinator; *b:* Fairmont, WV; *m:* Grade Verrier Duffy; *c:* Michael, Randolf, Abner; *ed:* (ABED) Soc Stud Comprehension, Fairmont St Coll 1967; Ed, Univ of VA, George Washington Univ, Univ of MD; Psych, Bowie St Univ; *cr:* Teacher Pine Grove HS 1968, Indian Head Mid Sch 1969-79; Teacher 1979-89, Testing Coord 1988- Waldorf HS; *ai:* Class & NHS Spon; Sch Newspaper; MSTA 1969-88; EACC; Elks Club; Amer Legion Voice of Democracy Awd 1969; European Travel with Stu.

FLUTE, ELEANOR PARKER, Fifth Grade Teacher; *b:* Talbotton, GA; *m:* Louis Randall; *c:* Juan, Deangelo; *ed:* (BS) Elem Ed, Morris Brown Coll 1971; (MS) Mid Grades, Columbus Coll 1979; *cr:* 5th Grade Teacher Cntrl Elem/Mid Sch 1971-; *ai:* Jr Girl Scout Leader 1972-75; GA Assn of Ed Pres 1980-81; NEA Teacher of Yr 1981; Talbotnites Civic & Soc Club Pres 1982-83; *home:* Rt 2 Box 95-B Talbotton GA 31827

FLYNN, GAYLE GUSSMAN, 7th Grade English Teacher; *b:* Washington, DC; *m:* Jack Bonecutter; *ed:* (BS) Elem Ed, 1972, (MS) Equilvalent Elem Ed, 1979 Univ of MD; *cr:* Teacher Tall Oaks Elem 1972-81, Carole Highland Elem 1981-83, Robert Goddard Mid Sch 1983-; *ai:* Future Teachers of America; Thinking Skill Comm; Prince Georges Cty Assn Rep 1972-; MD Teachers Assn, NEA 1972-; Lake Shore Baptist Church 3rd-4th Grade Girls in Action Spon; Annapolis Detention Center Volunteer; Wrote Curr Concerning Higher Level Thinking Skills for Prince Georges Schls; *home:* 8226 Bodkin Ave Pasadena MD 21122

FLYNN, JAMES BENJAMIN, History Teacher & Coach; *b:* Memphis, TN; *m:* Patricia Barner; *c:* Jodi, Quitman Powell, Cindy Powell; *ed:* (BSE) Phys Ed, Delta St Univ 1970; *cr:* Coach Lambert Jr HS 1970-72; Coach/Soc Stud Teacher Hernando Mid Sch 1972-; *ai:* Girls Bsktbl & Track, Boys Ftbl Coach; Lions Club Pres 1988-; Jaycees Pres 1977-78; *office:* Hernando Mid Sch 893 Oak Grove Rd Hernando MS 38632

FLYNN, JEANNE WEBB, 4th Grade Teacher; *b:* Ewing, IL; *m:* John T.; *ed:* (BS) Home Ec, S IL Univ 1952; (MAT) Lang Art, Webster Univ 1970; *cr:* Home Adv Univ of IL Extension Dept 1952-53; Teacher Affton Sch Dist 1954; *ai:* NCTE 1986-89; NEA Life Mem 1954-; MO NEA 1965-; Affton Ed Assn 1954-; Kappa Kappa Iota Pres 1980-82; *office:* Gotsch Intermediate Sch 8348 S Laclede Station Rd Saint Louis MO 63123

FLYNN, LESLIE M., Third Grade Teacher; *b:* Providence, RI; *ed:* (BA) Elem Ed, Mt St Joseph Coll 1974; *cr:* 5th Grade Teacher 1974-75, 2nd Grade Teacher 1975-76, 3rd Grade Teacher 1976- Narragansett Elem Sch; *ai:* HS Drama Club; Narragansett Teachers Assn Exec Bd 1980-; NEA, RI Ed Assn; Amer Red Cross; Civil Defense; *office:* Narragansett Elem Sch 55 Mumford Rd Narragansett RI 02882

FLYNN, WILLIAM JOSEPH, Reading/Writing Teacher; *b:* Paterson, NJ; *m:* Jennifer L. Jobbins; *ed:* (BA) Eng, Montclair St Coll 1968; Numerous Courses; *cr:* Teacher Cntrl Mid Sch 1968-; *ai:* Cooperative Relationships Project; NEA, NJ Ed Assn, Morris Cty Ed Assn, Parsippany-Troy Hills Ed Assn 1968-; NJ St Dept of Ed; Parsippany Jr Chamber of Commerce Teacher of Yr 1972; *home:* RD 4 Box 126D Boonton Township NJ 07005

FLYNT, JAMES PURKS, Fourth Grade Teacher; *b:* Washington, GA; *m:* Julia Howell; *c:* Eddie; *ed:* (BBA) Retailing, 1985, (MED) Elem Ed, 1974 Univ of GA; *cr:* 6th/7th Grade Teacher Main Street Sch 1965-69; 7th/8th Grade Teacher J P Carr Jr HS 1969-74; 4th Grade Teacher Honey Creek Elem 1974-; *ai:* Prof Assn of Ed 1987-; GA Assn of Educators 1965-86; Rockoak Cty Assn of Educators 1965-86; Conyers First Meth Church Kndgtn Comm 1986-; Chancel Choir 1977-; Teacher of Yr 1984; Southern Assn of Coll & Schls Accreditation Steering Comm Chm; *home:* 1291 Shadowlawn Dr Conyers GA 30207

FOAT, SANDY M., Sixth Grade Teacher; *b:* Tomah, WI; *m:* Grant; *c:* Kyle; *ed:* (BA) Spec Ed, Elem Ed, Univ WI 1979; Rdng License Univ WI 1986; *cr:* EMH Teacher CESA 18 1979-84; 6th Grade Teacher Wheatland Ctr 1984-; *ai:* Rdng Curr; Soc Stud Curr; Public Relations Comm 1985-87; Amer Ed Week Chairperson 1986; Sch Inservice Comm; NEA Sec 1984-; Rainbows Prgm Adult Facilitator 1988-; *office:* Wheatland Ctr Sch 6606 368th Ave Burlington WI 53105

FOCHLER, KATHRYN S., 3rd Grade Teacher; *b:* High Point, NC; *m:* Ronald; *c:* Suzanne, Jonathan; *ed:* (BS) Elem Ed, E Carolina Univ 1965; *cr:* 1st Grade Teacher W Edgecombe Elem 1964-65, Bridgeton Elem 1965-66; 2nd Grade Teacher Oak Grove Elem 1966-69; 3rd Grade Teacher Hillandale Elem 1976-; *ai:* 3rd Grade Team Leader; Durham Cty Assn of Educators Membership Chm 1988-; NC Assn of Educators; Alpha Delta Kappa VP; *office:* Hillandale Elem Sch 2107 Hillandale Rd Durham NC 27705

FODOR, MARIANA DUARTE, Sr Practical Nursing Coord; *b:* New York, NY; *m:* Joseph E.; *ed:* (RN) Nursing, NY Univ Bellevue Sch of Nursing 1958; (BA) Bio/Lang, Hunter Coll 1972; (MA) Scndry Ed of Disadvantaged, NY Univ 1975; Defense Information Sch; US Army ARRTC-BTMS Battalion Trng; Defense Strategy Courses; *cr:* Nurse/Teacher DOD Schls Japan 1969-72, New Rochelle HS 1972-74; H C Coord Park E HS 1974-75; Coord Bio-Medical Inst Lehman HS 1977-80; Asst Chief Nurse US Army Ft Totten 1980-86; Jr Practical Nurse/Core Coord 1986-89, Sr Practical Nurse Coord 1989- Mabel Dean Bacon Voc HS; *ai:* E&AP Comm; Mabel Dean Bacon Building Comm; Sr Practical Nursing Adv & Coord; Equal Opportunity Activist in Archaic Organizations; Active Retired Lieutenant Colonel in Many Act; Outstanding Scndry Teachers of America Teacher of Yr 1975; NY Acad of Sci Life Mem 1987-; Staten Island Hospital 1980, Cmmty Service Awd; Reserve Officers Assn Advisory Cncl 1979-; Congress of Intnl Reserve Officers Natl Delegate 1988; Assn of Military Surgeons of USA Exec Cncl 1985-; Meritorious Service Medal 1983; Expert Field Medical Badge Awd US Army 1977; Published Family Life & Sex Ed Curr; Military Order of World Wars Elected Adjutant 1988-; Whos Who of Amer Women 1984; *office:* Mabel Dean Bacon Voc HS 127 E 22nd St New York NY 10010

FOEHRKOLB, SUE BALKAN, Lang Art/Rdng Dept Chairperson; *b:* Moline, IL; *m:* Lawrence C.; *c:* Jamie, Matthew; *ed:* (BA) Speech/Drama, Clarke Coll 1970; Working Towards Masters Ed, Cmptr Applications; *cr:* Lang Art/Rdng Teacher 1970-, Dept Chairperson/Lang Art Teacher 1985- Glenview Jr HS; *ai:* Chairperson Dist Reassessment Learning Objectives 1989-; Dist Rdng Comm 1988-; Coord, Faculty Rep Glenview Jr HS Academic Achievement; Good Citizenship Selection Comm 1985-, Cmptr Curr Comm 1989-; IL Math & Sci Acad, Awd of Excl 1989; NEA, IL Ed Assn, E Moline Ed Assn 1970-; PTA Mem 1970-; BSA Asst Den Leader 1988-; Bd of Ed Outstanding & Dedicated Service Awd Dist 37 1985, Outstanding Achievement Instruction 1984; *office:* Glenview Jr HS 3210 7th St East Moline IL 61244

FOERSTER, ROBERT STEVEN, Principal; *b:* Evansville, IN; *m:* Lauralee Hamilton; *c:* Lisa M., Lorijane; *ed:* (BA) Ed, 1972, (MS) Sci Ed, 1976 Purdue Univ; (PHD) Ed, Butler Univ 1987; Cmptr Use in Schls, Purdue Univ; *cr:* Teacher West Lafayette Schls 1972-88; Prin Burtsfield Sch 1988-; Consultant NASA-Teacher in Space 1985-; *ai:* NASA Space Ambassador; NAESP Mem 1990; Challenger Center Charter Mem 1987-; Air Force Assn Jimmy Doolittle Fellow 1986; Jaycees Outstanding Young Hoosier 1986; Purdue Sch of Hum Distinguished Alumni 1986; Honorary Doctorate Butler Univ 1987; *office:* Burtsfield Sch 1800 N Salisbury West Lafayette IN 47906

FOGARTY, EMILY ST. CLAIR, Mathematics Teacher; *b:* Saranac Lake, NY; *m:* John J.; *c:* Emily, Terence, John; *ed:* (BA) Math, Coll of New Rochelle 1959; (MS) Admin, Plattsburgh St 1987; *cr:* Elem Teacher St Bernards Sch; Math Teacher Tupper Lake Cntrl Sch, Saranac Lake Cntrl Sch; *ai:* 10th Grade Class Adv; St Bernards Sch Bd Pres 1989-; *home:* 37 Riverside Dr Saranac Lake NY 12983

FOGERTY, CHARLES VINCENT, III, 8th Grade Soc Stud Teacher; *b:* Baltimore, MD; *m:* Michelle Marie Hanson; *c:* James P., Clare M.; *ed:* (BS) Soc Sci, Towson St Univ 1984; *cr:* Security Specialist US Air Force 1977-81; Teacher Westminster E Mid Sch 1984-; *ai:* Stu Act & Cmmty Service Adv; Liberty Church of MD Sunday Sch Teacher 1989-; Cncl on Ec Ed MD Honorable Mention Annual Awds 1989, 1990; *office:* Westminster E Mid Sch Longwell Ave Westminster MD 21157

FOGG, ROSA YELLING, Library-Computer Resource; *b:* Atmore, AL; *c:* Stephanie, Connie Fogg Jenkins; *ed:* (BED) Ed, Chgo Teachers Coll 1957; (MS) Natural Sciences, Chgo ST Univ 1967; Post Masters Studies, Administration and Supervision; *cr:* Research Asst Northwestern Univ 1953-56; Teacher Fiske Elem Sch 1957-74; Night Sch Teacher at City Coll 1974-87; Teacher Wacker Elem Sch 1974-; *ai:* Sci Fair Coord, Dram Coach, Family Life Resource Person, Substance Abuse Resource Person, Curr Comm - LSC Chgo Teachers Union 1957-; Amer Assn for Bio Teachers 1965-76; Amer Assn for Adv of Sci 1968-84; Phi Delta Kappa Pres 1974-; Past Pres 1983; Hon Serv Key 1985; Teacher Salem Lutheran Church 1951-; Dist 18 CPS 30 Yr Serv 1987; Teacher Wacker Sch Appreciation 1988; Rosemoor Comm Voter Registration; Schlsp Undergrad Sch 1950, Research Asst Microbiology Northwestern Univ (1953-55) Publ in Scientific Amer, Listed in : Notable Americans of Bicent. ERA 1976-77, World's Who's Who of Women 1978, Who's Who of Community Leaders 1947, Int Reg of Profiles 1981.

FOGLE, DEBORA HENDRIX, First Grade Teacher; *b:* Orangeburg, SC; *m:* Steve R.; *c:* Drew, Ross; *ed:* (BA) Elem Ed, Univ of SC 1974; *cr:* Kndgtn Teacher St Helena Elem 1975; 3rd Grade Teacher Denmark-Olar Elem 1975-78; 1st Grade Teacher Edisto Primary 1978-; *ai:* Orangeburg Cty Ed Assn, SC Ed Assn, NEA 1985-; NAEYC 1988-89; Calvery Baptist Church Sunday Sch Teacher; *office:* Edisto Primary Sch PO Box 69 Cordova SC 29039

FOGLIA, KIM BIANCA, Science Teacher; *b:* Queens, NY; *ed:* (BS) Environmental Sci, 1980, (MPS) Entomology, 1985 Cornell Univ; Ed, Smith Coll; Environmental Sci, SUNY Binghamton; Cert, Cornell Univ; *cr:* Lecturer Cornell Univ 1985-87; Teacher Caroline Elem 1986-87, Chenango Valley HS 1987-; *ai:* Bd of Dir; 9th Grade & Outdoor Club Adv; Cayuga Mature Center (Bd of Dir, Bd Mem) 1989-; Sci Curr Dev Comm 1990; *office:* Chenango Valley HS 768 Chenango St Binghamton NY 13901

FOLDEN, JOYCE WOODHAM, Second Grade Gifted/Talented; *b:* Corrigan, TX; *m:* E. W.; *c:* Cindy Guinn, Larry L., Mindy K.; *ed:* (BS) Elem Ed/Soc Stud/Eng, Stephen F. Austin Univ 1956; Prof Growth Dev Tactics for Learning; Gifted/Talented Ed; Effective Teaching Practices; Learning Styles; *cr:* Private Tutor/Subsitute Teacher Nacogdoches ISD 1956; Jacksonville ISD 1956-65; 3rd Grade Teacher Kurth Elem 1965-66; 5th & 6th Grade Teacher 1966-76; 2nd Grade Teacher 1976- Joe Wright Elem; *ai:* 2nd Grade Gifted/Talented Prgm Dev; UIL Coord Joe Wright Elem Campus; Stu Performance Comm Jacksonville ISD; Lambda Phi Chapt Pres Awd 1989; Delta Kappa Gamma Intnl/Key Women Teachers (Treas 1976-78 2nd VP 1988- 1st VP 1990-); Central Baptist Church Preschooler Teacher; Crestwood Nieghborhood Club; *home:* 2933 Oak Point Dr Lake Jacksonville TX 75766

FOLEY, JUDITH H., French Teacher; *b:* Bethlehem, PA; *ed:* (BS) Fr, Bloomsburg Univ 1968; *cr:* Fr Teacher Delhaas HS 1968-81, Franklin D Roosevelt Jr HS 1981-87, Neil A Armstrong Jr HS 1981-; *ai:* Writing Across the Curr; Elements of Essential Instruction; Dist Foreign Lang Comm; NEA 1968-; PA St Ed Assn 1968-; Bristol Township Ed Assn 1968-; Bristol Township Ed Assn Building Rep 2 Yrs; *office:* Neil A Armstrong Jr H S 475 Wistar Rd Fairless Hills PA 19030

FOLEY, LINDA JOAN, English Teacher; *b:* Evarts, KY; *m:* James Troy; *c:* Glenn, Greg, Suzy; *ed:* (BA) Eng, E KY Univ 1960; (MA) Ed, 1969, (Rank I) Ed, 1981 Union Coll; *cr:* Teacher Evarts HS 1960-63, Corbin HS 1963-; *ai:* Beta Club Spon; In-Service & Teacher Improvement St Dept Comms; NEA, KEA 1960-; NCTE 1970-; Rotary Club Teacher of Yr 1976.

FOLEY, MARY ELIZABETH, Fourth Grade Teacher; *b:* Chicago, IL; *ed:* (BA) Eng, Mundelein Coll 1962; *cr:* Elem Teacher Ryerson Elem 1962-71, Richard Wright Elem 1971-; *ai:* Chicago Teachers Union Delegate 1974-88; Teacher Action Caucus Secy 1983-88; *office:* Richard Wright Elem Sch 627 N Harding Chicago IL 60624

FOLEY, MICHAEL, Marketing Ed Teacher; *b:* Bethesda, MD; *m:* Marykate Maag; *c:* Josh, Erin, Natalie; *ed:* (BS) Ed, 1975, (MS) Ed, 1979 VA Tech; Post Grad Stud George Mason Univ; *cr:* Mrktng Teacher Fauquier HS 1975-79, Osbourn Park HS 1979-; *ai:* Golf Coach; Head Wrestling Coach; DECA Adv; St Officer Adv; Sch Store Spon; Schlsp Comm; VA Assn of Mrktg Educators 1975-; Mrktg Educators of Amer 1975-; VA Ed Assn 1975-; Prince William Cty Chamber of Commerce 1980-; VA DECA Dist Adv; VA DECA Policy & Planning Comm; Nom for VA Mrktg Ed Teacher of Yr; Wrestling Coach of Yr; *office:* Osbourn Park H S 8909 Euclid Ave Manassas VA 22111

FOLK, JOYCE ANN (LIBB), HS Coordinator/Math Teacher; *b:* Salem, IN; *m:* H. Jack; *c:* Stacy, Alyssa; *ed:* (BA) Home Ec, Bowling Green St Univ 1968; Cmptrs/Math/Nutrition; Underachievers/Discipline; Cmptrs Ed; *cr:* Pre K/Kndgtn Teacher 1st Chrstn Church Pre Primary Sch 1974-86; Substitute Teacher 1986-87; HS Coord/Home Ec/Math/Bible Teacher 1987- South Haven Chrstn Sch; *ai:* Yrbk Adv; Coordinate HS Prgm; HS Counseling & Career Planning; Coll Bd Testing Preparations; NHS; Phi Upsilon Omicron 1968-; *office:* South Haven Christian Sch 780 Juniper Rd Valparaiso IN 46383

FOLKMAN, BARBARA BACHNER, Mathematics Teacher; *b:* New York, NY; *m:* Theodore John; *c:* Margaret, Andrea, Teddy; *ed:* (BA) Math, 1966, (MS) Math Ed, 1967 Hofstra; C W Post Cert Teaching Gifted/Talented; Grad Credits in Accounting; Natl Sci Fnd Grants 1986, 1987, 1988; *cr:* Teacher 1966-82, Coord of the Gifted 1982-83, Teacher 1983-86 Grand Ave Jr HS; Teacher Mepham HS 1986-; *ai:* CO Chm Dist Curr Comm; Mathletes Adv Jr HS 1982-; Frosh Class CO Adv; Mentor Li Math Fair Speaker Ncmta Stu Symposium; Nassau Cty Math Teachers Bd Mem 1970-, Teacher of Yr 1989; Math Assn of NY Mem 1968-; Math Assn Amer Mem 1985 -; NCTM Mem 1966-; Brownie Leader

1979; Grand Ave Outstanding Prof Awd 1985; Life Mem Grand Ave PTSA 1986; Published Curr Guides for Dist; *office:* Wellington C Mepham HS Camp Ave Bellmore NY 11710

FOLLETT, CHARLES MICHAEL, Health & Physical Ed Teacher; *b:* Mansfield, OH; *m:* Nancy Lynn; *c:* Katherine, Jacob; *ed:* (BS) Elem Ed, Ashland Coll 1975; (MA) Elem Admin, Bowling Green St Univ 1981; Post Grad Work Ashland Coll; *cr:* 6th Grade Teacher Shiloh Elem 1975-77; 7th-8th Grade Teacher Shiloh Mid Sch 1977-79; 3rd Grade Teacher Plymouth Elem 1979-88; 6th-8th Grade Teacher Shiloh Mid Sch 1988-; *ai:* Teacher Adv to Natl Geographic Society for Teaching of Geography; Faculty Rep for Dev of AIDS Curr; Mem of Richland Cty Republican Cntrl Comm; Precinct Chm Republican Party; Girls Sftbl Assn Pres; NEA, OEA; Natl Geographic Society Teaching Adv 1977-; Natl Wildlife Society 1988-; Lions Club 1978-81, Jaycees (Treas, Pres) 1983-86, Jaycee of Quarter for Region 1985; Developed & Coordinated Local Outdoor Ed Sch Prgm; *office:* Shiloh Mid Sch 20 Mechanic St Shiloh OH 44878

FOLSE, RAPHAEL JAMES, III, English Department Chairman; *b:* New Orleans, LA; *c:* Olivia L. Wells, Chance W.; *ed:* (BS) Eng/Soc Stud/Speech, 1958, (MS) Ed, 1975 LA St Univ; Grad Work 1977, 1979; Grad Work Towards PhD Soc Stud 1982; *cr:* Teacher Lab Sch LSU 1953-54; Postmaster Social Security Office 1954-65; Teacher Marksville HS 1965-80, Carter C Raymond 1980-82, Hicks HS 1982-; *ai:* Eng, Soc Stud, Speech, Psych Rally Coach; Yrbk Spon; Curr in Psych Sch System; Assn of HS Eng Teachers 1965-75; Jaycees 1965-70; Kiwanis Club 1970-72; Fellowship White Horse Beach Playhouse Awd 1954-55; Fellowship Amer Acad of Dramatic Art Awd 1955-56; Most Outstanding Writer of Eng Themes 1957-58; *home:* PO Box 8012 Alexandria LA 71306

FOLTZ, EMILY J., English Teacher; *b:* Terre Haute, IN; *ed:* (BS) Eng, IN St Univ 1983; *cr:* Eng Teacher Monrovia Jr/Sr HS 1983-84, Gladys Porter HS 1985-; *ai:* Sigma Tau Delta, Kappa Delta Pi 1982; Pfennig Scholar Eng IN St Univ; *office:* Gladys Porter HS 3500 International Blvd Brownsville TX 78521

FOLTZ, MADELINE CAROL, Home Economics Teacher; *b:* Findlay, OH; *m:* Donald K.; *c:* Donald K. II, David E., Bryn J.; *ed:* (BA) Home Ec Ed, Bluffton 1973; (ME) Career/Tech Ed, Bowling Green St Univ 1980; *cr:* Teacher Paulding Exempted Vlg 1973-; *ai:* FHA/Home Ec; Related Occupation Adv; Amer Home Ec Assn 1987-; OH Voc Assn 1973-; NEA 1973-; Paulding Ed Assn Secy 1973-; OH Ed Assn 1973-; AVA 1973-; Amer Heart Assn Dev Chm 1987-; Ind Insurance Agents Paulding Cty Schlsp Comm; Certfd Home Ec 1987-; *office:* Paulding Exempted Village Sch 405 N Water St Paulding OH 45879

FOMOUS, CATHY O'DONNELL, Chemistry Teacher; *b:* Claremont, NH; *m:* John M.; *ed:* (BS) Botany, Univ of NH 1974; (MS) Botany, TX Tech Univ 1981; (PHD) Genetics, Georgetown Univ 1988; Trng in Medical Genetics; Licensed Genetic Cnslr; *cr:* Sci Teacher TX Public Schls 1977-79; Electron Microscope Technician TX Tech Univ 1979-81; Pre Doctoral Stu Georgetown Univ 1981-88; Instr Cath Univ 1983; Cytogenetics Lab Dir Columbia Hospital for Women 1988-89; Chem Teacher Oakton HS 1989-; *ai:* Spon Chem II Club; Amer Society of Human Genetics; Best Presentation Jr Scientist 1987; Pre Doctoral Fellowship Georgetown Univ 1982-87; *office:* Oakton HS 2900 Sutton Rd Vienna VA 22181

FONS, SHIRLEY CRANE, Third Grade Teacher; *b:* Hillsdale, MI; *m:* Kenneth F.; *c:* Ellen Burzynski, Jane, Kenneth A., Jody Braxel, Jill Moore, Jackie Solofra, John D.; *ed:* (BS) Elem Ed, Alverno 1972; Real Estate Brokers License; Supportive Consultant; *cr:* Teacher Holy Apostles Sch 1958-64, St Leonards Sch 1964-67, St Marys Sch 1967-; *ai:* Supervisory Teacher, Mentor for Stu Teachers Alverno Coll; Honored by Home, Sch Milwaukee Arch-Diocese Service to Teaching; *office:* St Marys Sch 9553 W Edgerton Hales Corners WI 53130

FONTANA, JANE SARLAS, Kindergarten Teacher; *b:* Chicago, IL; *m:* Bert; *ed:* (BA) Ed, Chgo Teachers Coll 1956; Early Chldhd Ed; *cr:* Kndgtn Teacher Geo B Mc Clellam 1956; Art Music Teacher Spec Ed Holden 1960; Curr Cons Dist II Chgo 1968-71; Prin/Dir St Nicholas Sunday Church Sch 1978; *ai:* Teacher Trng Brookline Seminary; Consulting Teacher Chgo Bd Ed; Spon FTA; Audio-Visual Coord; Il DPC Sec 1971-74; Animal Rescue 1980; DPCA Sec 1968-72; Assn Chldhd Sec 1953-60; AAUW 1980-; Nom Kate Maremount Awd; Short Childrens Story-Published-Young Life; *office:* George Mc Clellan Sch 3527 S Wallace Chicago IL 60609

FONTANI, CAROL GEFFNER, High School Art Teacher; *b:* New York City, NY; *m:* Vittorio; *c:* Marina, Marco, Dario, Roberto; *ed:* (BA) Art His, Sarah Lawrence Coll 1961; (MA) Fine Art, Columbia Univ 1966; Math, Biscayne Coll; *cr:* Art Teacher Joan of Arc Jr HS 1963-65, Great Neck Jr HS & Mac Arthur Sr HS 1965-67; Math Teacher Northwestern Sr HS 1977-78, Homestead Jr HS 1978-80; Math/Art Teacher Killian Sr HS 1980-; *ai:* Class of 1988 Spon; Weldon Mac Intosh Schlsp Fund Chairwoman; Mural Coord; Exceptional Ed Teacher of Yr 1990; *office:* Killian HS 10655 SW 97th Ave Miami FL 33176

FONTES, PATRICIA SANDERS, 7th Grade Teacher; *b:* Burbank, CA; *m:* Joe P. Jr.; *c:* Michael G., Thomas G., Robert W., Gerard J., William G.; *ed:* (BM) Applied Music, Mt St Marys Coll 1955; (MA) Educl Admin, CA Luth Univ 1985; *cr:* Phys Ed/Music/His Teacher Santa Clara HS 1955-57; Music Specialist Santa Clara Elem Sch 1964-67; 6th-8th Grade Jr HS Teacher Our Lady of Guadalupe 1975-; *ai:* Mesa Union Sch Dist Bd Mem 1978-; Legislative Network of Bd Mems CA; ACSD 1986-; Primary Drugs Prevention Comm Mem 1990; Oxnard Union HS Gang Task Force Mem 1990; 4-H (Leader, Club Spon) 1970-78; CA St Writing Fellowship 1978; Whos Who in Amer Ed 1989-; L A Archdiocesan Classroom Grant in Sci; Vice Prin Our Lady of Guadalupe 1984-; *office:* Our Lady of Guadalupe Sch 530 N Juanita Ave Oxnard CA 93030

FONTIS, MATTHEW CHARLES, Humanities Instructor; *b:* Houston, TX; *m:* Donna Elizabeth Copeland; *ed:* (BS) Ec/His, St Johns Univ 1972; (MA) Hum, St Johns Coll 1982; (MLA) Society/Lit, Harvard Univ 1990; Grad Trng Dept of Philosophy St Univ of NY Stony Brook 1982-83; Prof Chefs Diploma Cambridge Cooking Sch; *cr:* Research Assoc Univ of NH & New England Center for Appropriate Tech 1978-80; Writing Specialist/Adjunct Professor of Philosophy & World Lit Salem St Coll 1984-88; Hum Instr The Waring Sch 1988-; *ai:* Adv Coll Bowl Team, Fencing, Project Adventure Act; Coll Advisory & Hum Coordinating Comm; *office:* The Waring Sch 35 Standley St Beverly MA 01915

FOOR, CORINNE ELAINE, Instrumental Music Instr; *b:* Everett, PA; *ed:* (BS) Music Ed, Elizabethtown Coll 1983; (MS) Ed Dev & Strat, Wilkes Coll 1990; *cr:* 6th-8th Grade General Music Teacher Lampeter Strasburg Sch Dist 1984; Jazz Band Dir Elizabethtown Coll 1987-88; HS Band Dir/Inst Music Teacher Elizabethtown Area Sch Dist 1984-; *ai:* HS Marching Band; HS Concert Band; HS Jazz Band; MS Jazz Band; Elem Band; HS Bsktbl Pep Band; PMEA 1984-; MENC 1984-; NBA 1986-; LLMEA Symphonic Band Guest Conductor 1990; Mem Lancaster Brass Quintet 1986-; *office:* Elizabethtown Area S D 600 E High St Elizabethtown PA 17022

FOOTE, NANCI LEE COOK, 5th Grade Teacher; *b:* Seattle, WA; *m:* Thomas Raymond; *c:* Kristi L. Carick, Karin M. Kramer, Kathlee A. Kramer, Dustin T.; *ed:* (BA) Music Ed, CWU 1973; Geology & Earth Sci Courses; At Risk Kids Trng; *cr:* 5th Grade Teacher Mt Stuart Sch 1974-; *ai:* Soccer Coach; After Sch Sci & Art Club; 5th Grade Environmental Outdoor Camp; WASCD Mem 1989-; WSTA Mem 1980-; WA St Sci Teacher of Yr for Elem 1982; WA St Regional Sci Teacher of Yr 1987; *office:* Mt Stuart Sch 705 W 15th St Ellensburg WA 98926

FORAN, LAWRENCE F., Head Teacher/Soc Stud Teacher; *b:* Hazleton, PA; *m:* Dorothy Ann Gochalla; *ed:* (BS) Scndry Ed/Soc Sci, 1968, (MED) Elem Ed, 1972 Bloomsburg Univ; *cr:* Teacher Hazleton Area Sch Dist 1968-; *ai:* Act Coord & Safety Patrol Adv; Greek Cath Union Lodge 989 Pres 1983-84; Greek Cath Lodge 89 (Pres 1985-, Secy, Treas 1990); PTA Stu Adv Awd 1980-81/1981-82; *office:* Locust St Elem Sch 725 N Locust St Hazleton PA 18201

FORBES, CARLA L., Counselor; *b:* Dixon, IL; *ed:* (BS) Ed/Elem, SW MO St Univ 1981; (MA) Counseling Psych/Counseling Ed, Univ of MO Kansas City 1985; Ed Admin, Univ of MO Kansas City 1991; *cr:* 3rd Grade Teacher 1981-82, 2nd Grade Teacher 1982-88 Winnwood Elem; Cnslr Winnetonka HS 1988-; *ai:* Mem Impact Core Team; Support Group Leader; Teacher Spon Peer Helpers; NEA 1988-.

FORBES, DANA A., Math/Phys Ed Teacher; *b:* Paducah, KY; *m:* Mike; *c:* Scott, Karina; *ed:* (BS) Phys Ed, Murray St Univ 1966; (MA) Chrstn Ed, Scarritt Coll 1969; *cr:* Math Teacher North Marshall HS 1967-68; Homemaker/Real Estate Broker Marion IL 1968-79; Math/Phys Ed Teacher Crab Orchard HS 1979-; *ai:* Yrbk, JETS Team, Olympiad, Sr Class Spon; Academic Bowl & Vlybl Coach; Crab Orchard Ed Assn (Pres 1984-85) 1979-; IL Ed Assn, NEA 1979-.

FORCE, CHARLES E., Mathematics Teacher; *b:* Decatur, IL; *m:* Cathy Eileen Brown; *c:* Andrew, Julie; *ed:* (BA) Math, Millikin Univ 1972; (MS) Pure Math, N IL Univ 1974; Natl Sci Fnd Discrete Math Wkshp IL St Univ 1985; Grad Stud Cmptr Prgm Langs, Various Univs; *cr:* Grad Asst N IL Univ 1972-74; Math Instr Millikin Univ 197-78, 1989; Math Teacher Eisenhower HS 1974-; *ai:* Cmptr Club Adv; Math Task Force Comm Calculus Chairperson; IL Comm Sch Math; NEA, IEA; Math Assn of America 1973-75; Decatur Ed Assn (Finance Dir) 1978-; IL Governor Master Teacher 1984; E IL Univ Great Teacher Awd 1985; Eisenhower HS Teacher of Yr 1978, 1984; *office:* Eisenhower HS 1200 S 16th St Decatur IL 62521

FORCIER, HELENE F., English Teacher; *b:* New York, NY; *c:* Jack, Amy, Jeremy, Jeffery; *ed:* (BA) Eng/Ed, 1969, (MA) Eng, 1973 AZ St Univ; Admin Courses; *cr:* Teacher South Mt HS 1970-73; Dept Chairperson/Teacher Greenway HS 1973-80; Teacher Washington HS 1981-; *ai:* Sr Class Adv; Mastery Learning OBI Frosh Team Leader; NEA, AEA, CTA 1970-; NCTE; Articles Published; *office:* Washington HS 2217 W Glendale Ave Phoenix AZ 85021

FORD, AVEARN, 6th Grade Teacher; *b:* Haddock, GA; *m:* Carol Ann Randleman; *c:* Carolyn, Patrick, Ronald; *ed:* (BED) Comprehensive Soc Sci, 1968, Elem Ed, 1971 Univ of Toledo; Grad Work Bowling Green St Univ & Toledo Univ; *cr:* Teacher Toledo Public Schls 1968-; *ai:* Building Comm Mem; Safety Patrols Supvr; Toledo Fed of Teachers Building Comm Mem 1989-; Shiloh Baptist Church (Assoc Minister 1988-, Adult Sunday Sch Teacher 1987-); NAACP Mem; Military Service-Good Conduct Medal, Letter of Appreciation, Letter of Commendation; *office:* Spring Sch 730 Spring St Toledo OH 43608

FORD, CAROLYN DIGGS, Fifth/Sixth Grade Lang Teacher; *b:* Oneonta, AL; *m:* Autrey J.; *c:* Deborar Ford Jackson; *ed:* (BSED) Elem Ed, Jacksonville St Univ 1975; (MA) Elem Ed, Univ of AL 1978; *cr:* 2nd/3rd Grade Teacher 1975-76, 1976-77, 5th Grade Teacher 1977-78, 1985-86, 5th Grade Teacher 1986-87, 5th/6th Grade Lang Teacher 1987- Appalachian Sch; *ai:* Sch Spelling Bee Spon; Local 4-H Leader.

FORD, CYNTHIA RICHARD, Math Teacher; *b:* Baton Rouge, LA; *m:* Michael G.; *c:* Gerard, Alison; *ed:* (BS) Math Ed, Southern Univ 1974; (MED) Math Ed, Univ of Southwestern LA 1979; Univ of Southwestern LA; *cr:* Teacher Breaux Bridge HS 1975-80; Acadiana HS 1980-; *ai:* Sadie Hawkins Dance Comm; LA Assn of Educators 1974-; Lafayette Parish Assn of Classroom Teachers 1980-; LA Assn of Teachers of Math 1988-; Southern Univ Alumni Assn (Sec 1984-88); *office:* Acadiana H S 315 Rue Dubelier Lafayette LA 70506

FORD, HOPE ANN, Third Grade Teacher; *b:* Duluth, GA; *ed:* (BA) Elem Ed, 1975, (MS) Early Chldhd, 1980 N GA Coll; Several Courses & Seminars; *cr:* 2nd Grade Teacher Cumming Elem 1975-76, Mashburn Elem 1976-77; 3rd/4th Grade Teacher Loganville Primary 1977-; *ai:* NEA, GAE (Secy 1983-84) 1975-; Delta Kappa Gamma 1989-.

FORD, JEFF DALE, 7th Grade Sci/Phys Ed Teacher; *b:* Pikeville, KY; *m:* Pamela R. Forsyth; *ed:* (BS) Phys Ed 1980, (BS) Sociology 1981 Pikeville Coll; (MS) Phys Ed, Morehead St Univ 1990; MS Projected Summer 1990; *cr:* 7th Grade Sci Teacher 1982-83/1989, 8th Grade Sci Teacher 1989-; HS Bsbl 1985-86/1989, Jr HS Phys Ed 1982-83/1989-; Asst HS Bsktbl & Jr HS Coach 1982-85 Millard HS; Jr HS Phys Ed; *ai:* Coach HS Bsbl; Power Lifting & Muscle Building Trainer; Pro-Fitness Power Lifting Team VP 1986-; News Express of Pikeville Spotwriter 1980-; Mill HS Boosters Bd Mem 1988-89; Outstanding Coll Grad of America 1980; Outstanding Young Men of America 1980; *office:* Millard HS Millard Hwy Pikeville KY 41501

FORD, JOYCE EAVES, Honors Eng/Eng II Teacher; *b:* Weatherford, TX; *m:* E. Mark; *c:* Armin P., Leah J. Ford Sessum; *ed:* (BA) Eng, 1977, (MAT) Eng, 1979 Tarleton St Univ; Ed Courses Pedagogy, TX St Univ; *cr:* Teacher Mineral Wells HS 1977-; *ai:* Oral Interpretation Prose, Poetry & Literary Criticism UIL Spon; Mineral Wells Ind Sch Dist Career Ladder & Curr Comm; Alpha Delta Kappa Secy 1984-85; TX St Teachers Assn, NEA; Rotary Club Teacher of Month 1986.

FORD, KELLY CURTIS, English Teacher; *b:* Duncan, OK; *ed:* Eng Ed, Cameron Univ 1971; OK Writing Project 1979-; *cr:* Teacher Walters HS 1971-75, Oologah HS 1975-; *ai:* Academic Team Coach; Jr-Sr Class Spon; Oologah-Talala Classroom Teachers Assn (Local Staff Dev Comm 1987-88, Chm 1988); OK Assn of Academic Coaches (Secy, Treas) 1989-; OK Cncl Teachers of Eng (Bd of Dirs 1971-82, Bd Consultant 1983-, 1st VP, 2nd VP, 3rd VP, Pres 1981); OK Ed Assn, NEA, OK Assn for Gifted-Creative-Talented; NCTE (Excl in Stu Literary Magazines Recognition Prmg Judge 1987-, Writing Achievemetn Awds Judge 1988-); St Dept of Ed Lang Arts PublicAtions & Various Comms; *home:* Rt 5 Box 443 Claremore OK 74017

FORD, LORRAINE M., 2nd Grade Teacher; *b:* Colton, NY; *m:* William H.; *c:* Rebecca Ford Stone, Bonnie Ford Dunleavy, Betsy; *ed:* (BA) Elem Ed, 1976, (MA) Elem Ed, 1981 St Univ Coll Potsdam; *cr:* 3rd Grade Teacher 1977-81, 5th Grade Teacher 1981-85, 2nd Grade Teacher 1985- Lawrence Avenue Elem Sch; *ai:* Ed Lawrence Avenue Sch Newspaper 1987-88; Lawrence Avenue Rdng Comm Mem; 1st Place Womens Team Mem Potsdale Coll Sigma Pi Open; NYSUT Mem 1977-; GSA Jr Troop Leader 1972-75; Sunday Rock Musical Participant 1989-; Potsdam Golf & C C Mem 1985-; *office:* Lawrence Avenue Elem Sch Lawrence Ave Potsdam NY 13676

FORD, MARY LOSEY, English Teacher; *b:* Lansing, MI; *m:* Terry Williams; *c:* Teryn, Terry; *ed:* (BA) Phys Ed, MI St Univ 1970; (MS) Phys Ed, E MI Univ 1974; Grad Stud Cmptrs & Comms; *cr:* Teacher Mt Morris Jr HS 1970-; *ai:* MI Ed Assn, NEA; Foster Parents 1972-79; Red Cross Cardio Pulmonary Resusitation Instr 1970-84; BSA Den Mother 1986-87; *office:* Mt Morris Jr HS 12356 Walter St Mount Morris MI 48458

FORD, MARY OCTAVIA (BROWN), Mathematics & Science Teacher; *b:* Charleston, SC; *c:* Tei D., Guenevere; *ed:* (BS) Sci/Math, Claflin Coll 1968; (MAT) Spec Ed, 1976, (MA) Spec Ed/Rdng, The Citadel; Introductory Phys Sci Chrstn Brothers Coll 1972; Phys Sci II, E Carolina Univ 1973; Math, Geometry, The Citadel 1985; Cmptr Math, The Baptist Coll of Charleston 1986; *cr:* Math Teacher B Wilson HS 1968-70; Math/Sci Teacher Gordon H Garrett HS 1970-; *ai:* Awds Chm; Recognition, Fund Raiser Comm Mem; SCTM, CCTM; Delta Sigma Theta 1965-; Natl Sci Fnd Grant for Introductory Phys Sci, Phys Sci II, Geometry & Algebra, Introduction Cmptrs; *home:* 2121 Royal Castle Ln Charleston SC 29414

FORD, MICHAEL DALE, Geography/English Teacher; *b:* Louisville, KY; *m:* Gina Jo Whitaker; *ed:* (BA) Geography, E KY Univ 1983; (MED) Poly Sci, Univ of Louisville 1989; *cr:* Eng Teacher S Dearborn HS 1983-85; Geography Teacher Valley HS 1985-; *ai:* Jr Var Boys Bsktbl & Bsbl Coach; Asst Athletic Dir; Kenwood United Meth Church; KY Poly Sci Conference Budgeting of Public Schls in KY Prof Paper 1989; *office:* Valley HS 10200 Dixie Hwy Louisville KY 40272

ORD, NANCY MOORE, Mathematics Teacher; *b:* ...cksonville, FL; *m:* Richard C.; *c:* Randy, Paige; *ed:* (BS) Bio, 77, (MS) Math, 1988 Univ of S AL; *cr:* Sci Teacher Arnold Sch 78-79; Math Teacher Alba HS 1979-88, Baldwin Cty HS 1988-; Var Chrldr & NHS Spon; NEA 1980-; AL HS Athletic Assn, CTM 1988-; *home:* 308 Brierwood Ct Bay Minette AL 36507

ORD, PAMELA HUNTER, Language Arts Teacher; *b:* ...etroit, MI; *m:* Harold Steele; *ed:* (BA) Scndry Ed/Spec Ed, MI Univ 1974; (MA) Scndry Rdng, Wayne St Univ 1979; *cr:* POHI ...acher Oakman Orthopedic Sch 1974-79; Lang Art Teacher ...ew Mid Sch 1980-; *ai:* Oakman Sch & Drew Sch Guidance ...dvisory Cncl Mem; Co-Spon Natl Jr Beta Club; ASCD Assoc ...em 1988-; MI Rdng Cncl Assoc Mem 1987-; NAACP Mem ...67-; *office:* Drew Mid Sch 9600 Wyoming Detroit MI 48204

ORD, PAUL ROGER, Jr HS Math/Soc Studies Teacher; *b:* ...keville, KY; *m:* Jonnie Chaffin; *c:* Jonathan W.; *ed:* (BS) His, ...keville Coll 1970; Ed, Morehead St Univ 1980; *cr:* Teacher Pike ...ty Bd of Ed 1970-; *ai:* Asst Bsktbl, Track & Field Coach; 4-H ...eader; KY Ed Assn, NEA; PCEA (Mem, Sch Rep) 1985-; Salem ...nited Meth Church (Sunday Sch Teacher, Supt) 1968; Little ...eague Asst Coach 1985; Teacher of Yr Awd Pike Cty 1989; ...ome: Rt 1 Box 900 Pikeville KY 41501

ORD, PHYLLIS HUGHES, First Grade Teacher; *b:* Piney ...ats, TN; *m:* Jerry R.; *c:* Lisa Ford Barnes, Jeri A., Jonathan H.; ...d: (BS) Elem Ed, E TN St Univ 1961; *cr:* Teacher Church Hill ...lem Sch 1958-60, Lake Shipp Elem 1961-62, Blountville Elem ...962-70, Indian Springs Elem 1973-; *ai:* TN Ed Assn, NEA, ...ullivan Cty Ed Assn; PTA VP Life Time Membership 1989; ...ptimist Club Outstanding Young Educator; *home:* 5116 ...Waterford Dr Kingsport TN 37664

ORD, R. DENISE ROBERTS, Math Teacher; *b:* Burlington, ...C; *m:* Bruce D.; *c:* Ashley; *ed:* (BA) Math Ed, Univ of NC ...hapel Hill 1980; *cr:* Math Teacher Courtland HS 1980-88, ...hancellor HS 1988-; *ai:* Tutorial, Courtesy Comm; R2ATM ...984-; PTA 1988 Finalist Teacher of Yr; Tutor Stus in Their ...omes After Sch; *office:* Chancellor H S 6300 Harrison Rd ...redericksburg VA 22401

ORD, SCOTT CLINTON, English Teacher; *b:* Steubenville, ...H; *ed:* (BS) Comp Soc Sci, Elem Ed, OH St Univ 69; (ME) Elem ...dmin, Ashland Univ 1985; *cr:* HS Eng Teacher Benjamamaharaj ...ch Ubon, Thailand 1970-74; Elem Teacher Bronson Sch 1976-81; ...eters Colony Elem Sch 1981-82; Eng Teacher Norwalk Mid Sch ...982-; *ai:* Academic Challenge Team Adv; Sch Play Production ...ir; Newspaper Adv; Treas 1977-79; VP 1982-86; PreS 1987-88 ...orwalk Teachers Assn; Lefty Grove Bsbl Leag (Secy 1984-87, ...ommissioner 1987-); Teacher of Yr-Norwalk Teachers Assn ...981; Distinguished Citizen of Yr-Norwalk Area Chamber ...ommerce 1986; *home:* 57 Baker St Apt 25 Norwalk OH 44857

ORD, THERESA GILLILAND, Health/General Bus Teacher; ...: Roswell, NM; *m:* Roger Dean; *c:* Patricia D., Laura E.; *ed:* (AA) ...ealth Ed/Phys Ed, S Plains Coll 1978; (BS) Health Ed/Phys Ed, ... TX St Univ 1980; *cr:* Teacher Kennedale Jr HS 1981-; *ai:* Just ...ay No Club Co-Spon; TX St Teachers Assn 1982-; Teacher of Yr ...wd 1988-89; *home:* 3000 Woodlark Dr Fort Worth TX 76123

ORD, THOMAS ALFRED, 6th Grade Teacher; *b:* Watsonville, ...A; *m:* Debbie Kay; *c:* Zachariah T., Elijah C., Jessicah E.; *ed:* ...BA) Liberal Stud, CSU Sacramento 1977; *cr:* Classroom Teacher ...alo Verde Union Sch 1977-86; Del Dayo Elem 1986-87; Coyle ...venue Elem 1987-; *ai:* Stu Body Adv; Stu Study Team; Sch Site ...ncl; Math Rep; CTA/NEA; Cub Scouts Cubmaster 1989; Fair ...ak United Meth Church Mem; Carmichael Chamber of ...ommerce; Teacher of Yr Hnrb Mntn 1989; *office:* Coyle Avenue ...lem Sch 6330 Coyle Ave Carmichael CA 95608

FORD, THOMAS LEE, Mathematics Instructor; *b:* West Chester, PA; *m:* Catharine Z.; *c:* Laura C.; *ed:* (BA) Math, Univ of DE 1971; Grad Stud 1973-; *cr:* Math Instr Salesianum Sch 1973-; Asst Professor Goldey Becom Coll 1983-; Math Inst Univ of DE 1983-; Advanced Placement Consultant 1988-; *ai:* Calculus Instr Univ of DE Forum to Advance Minorities Engineering; DE Cncl Teachers of Math 1974-; Sci Alliance 1989-; Advanced Placement Recognition Awd Coll Bd 1989; Presidential Scholars Prgm Selected One of Best Educators in America 1988; Distinguished Teacher; *home:* 3 Paschall Ct Wilmington DE 19803

FORDE, ROGER DEAN, 6th Grade Teacher; *b:* Fargo, ND; *m:* Judy Ystaas;; *ed:* (BS) Elem Ed, Valley City St Univ 1977; Elem Ed, Univ ND Grand Forks &NDSU Fargo; *cr:* 6th Grade Teacher Tolna Public Sch 1977-; *ai:* Tolna Ed Assn Pres 1979-80; ND Ed Assn; Natl Ed Assn; PTA; Tolna Booster Club; *office:* Tolna Public Sch Tolna P O Box Tolna ND 58380

FORE, DEBORAH SHELTON, Business Education Teacher; *b:* Conway, SC; *ed:* (BS) Bus Ed, 1985, (MED) Adult Ed, 1989 Univ of SC; *cr:* Bus Teacher Finklea Career Center 1985-; *ai:* FBLA Adv; Finklea Career Center Public Relations & Sch Improvement Comm Chairperson; Horry Cty Voc Assn (Secy, Treas) 1988-; SC Bus Ed Assn, NBEA 1985-; *office:* Finklea Career Center Rt 1 Box 236 B Loris SC 29569

FORE, DONALD LEE, Algebra II Teacher; *b:* Cameron, MO; *m:* Martha Joan Whiteaker; *c:* Timothy J., Tonni D.; *ed:* (BSED) Math, NW MO St Univ 1964; (MSED) Math, S IL Univ 1972; St & Local Wkshps, Seminars, Conventions; *cr:* Math/Sci Teacher Wm Chrisman Jr HS 1964; Math Teacher Wm Chrisman Sr HS 1964-; *ai:* Beartown Stu Cncl Spon; North Cntrl Re-Evaluation Steering Comm; NHS Supervisory Comm; NEA, MO Ed Assn, MO Cncl Teachers of Math, Kansas City Area Teachers of Math; Oak Grove United Meth Church Bd of Trustees; Oak Grove Public Schls Sch Bd 1989-; *home:* 38105 E Rnd Prairie Oak Grove MO 64075

FORE, JO ANNE MONSON, Fifth Grade Teacher; *b:* Florence, SC; *c:* Lacy T., Judith A., Robert W., Gladys M.; *ed:* (BS) Elem Ed, 1979, (ME) Elem Ed, 1984 Francis Marion Coll; Working Toward Ed Specialist Degree in Admin; *cr:* Teacher Lester Elem 1980-81, Henry Timrod Elem 1981-89, Wallace Gregg Elem 1989-; *ai:* PSTA; *office:* Wallace Gregg Elem Sch Rt 4 Florence SC 29501

FORE, LINDA COMPTON, United States History Teacher; *b:* Los Angeles, CA; *m:* John Wyatt Jr.; *c:* Whitney, Wyatt, Matthew; *ed:* (BS) His/Soc Sci, Longwood Coll 1970; *cr:* Teacher Nottoway Cty HS 1970-71, Cluster Springs Elem Sch 1971-76, Franklin Cty HS 1976-; *ai:* Sch Self Study Steering Comm Co-Chairperson; VA Ed Assn, NEA 1971-76, 1985-; NCSS 1988-; *office:* Franklin Cty HS 506 Pell Ave Rocky Mount VA 24151

FOREMAN, M. JEANNE, COE Coordinator; *b:* Denver, CO; *c:* Michael, Jill, Scott; *ed:* (BA) Bus Ed, CO St Coll of Ed 1956; (MA) Voc Ed, OH St Univ 1982; *cr:* Bus Teacher East HS 1961-64, Linden Mc Kinley HS 1978-83, Brookhaven HS 1983-89; COE Coord Brookhaven HS 1989-; *ai:* CMAC 1989-; Columbus Symphony Orch Tempo Unit 1970-76; Kinder Key 1965-68; Career Ed Dept Chm 1984-89; *office:* Brookhaven HS 4077 Kayl Rd Columbus OH 43224

FOREMAN, MARGERY DOXTATOR, English Teacher; *b:* Waterloo, NY; *m:* Richard A.; *c:* Richard A. III, Lisa Foreman Earl; *ed:* (BA) Eng, Utica Coll 1971; Ed, Syracuse Univ, SUNY Utica-Rome 1974; Various Wkshps in Whole Lang; Effective Essential Elements of Learning Wkshps; *cr:* 6th/8th Grade Teacher Annunciation Sch 1971-83; Lib Asst Frank J Basloe Lib 1983-84; Part-Time Adjunct Teacher Mohawk Valley Comm Coll 1989; 8th/10th Grade Teacher Dolgeville Cntrl Sch 1984-; *ai:* 7th & 12th Grade Stu Cncl Adv; Stu Leadership Comm; Sch Lib Comm Rep & Chairperson 1990; Delta Kappa Gamma Society Intnl 1st VP 1990; Daughters of Founders & Patriots of America St Pres 1984-87; DAR Past Regent-Local Chapter; Herkimer Garden Club Mem; Herkimer Frank J Basloe Public Lib Bd of Dirs; Remedial Rdng Club-8th Grade Mini Grant; *office:* Dolgeville Cntrl Sch Slawson St Dolgeville NY 13329

FORESO, RONALD F., Social Studies Teacher; *b:* Orange, NJ; *m:* Kathleen Marie Winters; *c:* Kate; *ed:* (BA) Soc Stud, Seton Hall Univ 1974; *cr:* Soc Stud Teacher Parsippany HS 1974-; *ai:* Adv Pep Club, Var Club, Interact Club, His Club, Jr Class, Parsippany HS Publicity Cncl; Ftbl Announcer; Girls & Boys Bsktbl Scorer & Timer; Parsippany-Troy Hills Ed Assn 1974-; Natl Assn of Stu Act Advs, Company of Military Historians 1987-; Assn of US Army 1983-; Natl Rifle Assn 1980-; Amer Society of Military Insignia Collectors, Assn of Amer Military Uniform Collectors, Orders & Medals Society of America, Orders & Medals Research Society of Great Britain 1989-; E Militaria Collectors Assn Sergeant At Arms 1979-; Parsippany Jaycees Outstanding Young Person of Yr Awd 1978; US Army Achievement Medal 1984; Parsippany-Troy Hills Township Outstanding Service Awd 1985; Parsippany-Troy Hills Distinguished Faculty Awd 1985; Geraldine R Dodge Fnd Grant 1987; *office:* Parsippany HS Vail And Baldwin Rds Parsippany NJ 07054

FORET, GLORIA KREAMER, Assistant Principal; *b:* Houma, LA; *m:* Donald P.; *c:* Mason E., Jonathan V.; *ed:* (BA) Elem Ed, 1971, (MED) Guidance/Counseling, 1980 Nicholls St Univ; Prof Improvement Prgm; *cr:* 1st Grade Teacher Lacache Sch 1971; 5th Grade Teacher 1972, 3rd Grade Teacher 1973-89 Upper Little Caillou Sch; Asst Prin Lacache Mid Sch 1989-; *ai:* LA Assn of Prins 1989-; Cath Daughters of Amer 1971-; Amer Legion Auxiliary 1987-; St Joseph Parish Cncl 1983-84; Friends of Terrebonne Parish Lib 1988-89; Chauvin Jaycees Incorporated Outstanding Young Educator 1988; *office:* Lacache Mid Sch Rt 1 Box 331 Chauvin LA 70344

FORGE, KATHY HAYE, Math Teacher; *b:* Bryan, OH; *m:* Steven E.; *c:* Taylor; *ed:* (BS) Bio, Manchester Coll 1976; (MS) Bio Sci, Univ of ID 1982; Cmptr-Bus/Problem Solving Techniques; *cr:* Bio Teacher Sacajawea Jr HS 1977-80; 7th/8th/ Alg Math Teacher Sacajawea Jr HS 1982-; *ai:* LEA/IEA/NEA 1977-80/1982; *office:* Sacajawea Jr HS 3610 12th Lewiston ID 83501

FORKENBROCK, JAMES JOSEPH, English Teacher; *b:* Dyersville, IA; *m:* Carol Kay Mousel; *c:* Michael, Thomas, Sandra Watson; *ed:* (BA) Eng, St Marys Univ 1963; Grad Work Univ of IA, Loras Coll, Drake Univ; Lib Sci/Media Specialist, Univ of N IA; *cr:* Media Dir 1968-82, Eng Teacher 1963- Edgewood-Colesburg; *ai:* NHS Advisory Comm; IA Cncl of Teachers of Eng, NCTM, NEA, IA St Educl Assn 1963-; City of Edgewood Mayor 1990; United Way Bd of Dirs 1989-; Greater DE Cty Fnd Bd of Governors 1989-; Cty Teachers Assn Pres of Ed 1979-85; *home:* 307 S Bell Edgewood IA 52042

FORMAN, MARDELLE HOPKINS, Second Grade Teacher; *b:* Weston, WV; *m:* James M.; *c:* Joyce A. Forman Bernatowicz, William J., Robert R.; *ed:* (BA) Music/Elem Ed, Fairmont St Coll 1952; (MA) Music, WV Univ 1957; *cr:* Teacher Bruceton Elem Sch 1952-; *ai:* Kappa Delta Pi; Delta Kappa Gamma (Secy, Music Chm); United Meth Women; Gideons Intnl Auxilary; *home:* Rt 1 Box 375 Bruceton Mills WV 26525

FORMBY, JANE FORD, Teacher of Hearing Impaired; *b:* Natick, MA; *c:* Shannon E., Melissa; *ed:* (BA) Eng, Univ of MA 1969; (MED) Early Elem Ed, Armstrong St Coll 1980; Deaf Ed, GA St Univ; *cr:* 4th Grade Teacher Gateway Regional Sch System 1969-70; 6th Grade Teacher 1970-71, 4th Grade Teacher 1973-75, 2nd/4th Grade Teacher 1981-84, Teacher of Hearing Impaired 1984- Savannah-Chatham Bd of Ed; *ai:* Savannah-Chatham Bd of Ed Hearing Impaired Comm; Exceptional Child Prgm Instr of Hearing Impaired; Chatham Assn of Educators, GA Assn of Educators 1981-; GA Cncl of Hearing Impaired 1989-; PTA Treas 1986-87; St James (Ed Prgm Instr 1980-88, Coord 1986-88); Ballet South (Supporter, Comm Mem) 1989-; Mental Health Assn, Greenpeace, GA Historical Society; AMBUC Schlsp; Savannah-Chatham Cty Public Schls Spec Ed Certificate Awd 1989, 1990.

FORREST, CHRISTOPHER MORTON, Health/History Teacher/Coach; *b:* Florence, AL; *m:* Barbara Ann Leibecki; *ed:* (BS) HPER/His, Univ of N AL 1978; Grad Stud, Univ of Montevallo; *cr:* Substitute Teacher/Coach Lauderdale HS 1982-85; Coach/Teacher Bibb Cty HS 1985-; *ai:* Asst Var Ftbl & Head Var Girls Bsktbl Coach; NEA, AEA, BCAA 1985-; *office:* Bibb Cty HS 214 Birmingham Rd Centreville AL 35042

FORREST, KATHLEEN POHOLEK, Spanish Teacher; *b:* Attleboro, MA; *m:* Wayne James; *ed:* (BA) Span, Wheaton Coll 1977; (MED) Bi-ling/Bicultural Ed, RI Coll 1978; *cr:* Span Teacher Charles E Shea HS 1977-; *ai:* Shea HS Key Club Co-Adv; *office:* Charles E Shea HS 485 East Ave Pawtucket RI 02860

FORREST, MARTHA L., Jr High School Counselor; *b:* Green Bay, WI; *m:* John A.; *ed:* (BA) Span, 1969, (MS) Counseling/ Guidance, 1977 Univ of WI Madison; *cr:* Span Teacher Winnequah Mid Sch 1970-75; Sch Cnslr Jackson Jr HS 1976-; *ai:* Building Leadership Team; Gifted & Talented Comm; Stu Recognition Coord; Crisis Intervention, Stu Assistance, & Child Study Teams; MN Sch Cnslr Assn, MN Assn of Counseling & Dev, Anoka Hennepin Ed Assn, MN Ed Assn, NEA 1976-; *home:* 677 Lake Pine Dr Shoreview MN 55126

FORREST, R. IMOGENE SMITH, Fourth Grade Teacher; *b:* Carbondale, IL; *m:* William W.; *c:* Lori L., Willaim C.; *ed:* (BS) Elem Ed, Siu Carbondale 1960; (MS) Elem Ed Rdng, Siu Edwardsville 1976; *cr:* Kndgtn Teacher Du Quoin Public Sch 1960-62; Murphysboro Public Sch 1962-63; Anna Public Sch 1963-64; 1st Grade Teacher Lick Creek Public Sch 1965-68; Kndgtn/1st/2nd/4th Grade Teacher Granite City Sch Dist #9 1968-; *ai:* Judge Young Authors Cometition; Soc Stud Textbook Review Comm; Lang Art Curr Comm; Kapa Delta Pi; Siu E Alumni Assn; Beta Sigma Phi; Smithsonian Assoc; Outstanding Young Educator Nom Chamber of Commerce; Outstanding Elem Teachers; Outstanding Young Amer Women; *office:* Prather Elem Schl 2300 W 25th St Granite City IL 62040

FORSBERG, DALE R., 5th Grade Teacher; *b:* Burlington, WI; *m:* Nancy Bacheller; *c:* Todd, Jonathan, Kristen; *ed:* (BSED) Elem Ed, Elizabethtown Coll 1970; Grad Stud; *cr:* 6th Grade Teacher Bardonia Elem 1970-71; 5th/6th Grade Teacher Taft Elem 1971-; *ai:* Ages & Stages Pre-Sch & After Sch Prgms Owner; Yrbk & Stu Cncl Adv; NY St United Teachers 1970-; Alert Hook Ladder & Engine Co #1 (Volunteer Fireman, Fundraising Comm Chm, Video Programing Dir) 1972-; Congers United Meth Church Sunday Sch Teacher; *home:* 68 S Harrison Ave Congers NY 10920

FORSBERG, DANN GLENN, Fifth Grade Teacher; *b:* New Ulm, MN; *m:* Claudia Hope Walters; *c:* Rachel, Jana; *ed:* (BA) Elem Ed, Augsburg Coll 1980; *cr:* Title I Teacher Pinewood E 1980-81; 5th Grade Teacher Pinewood W 1981-; *ai:* Rdng, Continuing Ed, Lit Comm Mem; MEA 1980-; PER 1983-86; *office:* Pinewood Elem Sch Hwy 75 Box 897 Monticello MN 55362

FORSBERG, RENIE PAPPAS, 2nd Grade Teacher; *b:* Charleston, SC; *m:* J. Eric; *c:* Tony, Erin; *ed:* (BS) Elem Ed, 1973, (MED) Elem Ed, 1982 Coll of Charleston; *cr:* 2nd Grade Teacher Baxter-Patrick Elem 1973-77, Stiles Point Elem 1977-; *ai:* NEA 1973-; PTA VP 1973-; Greek Ladies Philoptochos Society VP 1986-87; *office:* Stiles Point Elem 883 Mikell Dr Charleston SC 29412

FORSTER, ARDENA LOUISE, 4th Grade Teacher; *b:* Elizabeth, NJ; *ed:* (BS) Ed/His/Psych, Midland Luth Coll 1971; Toms River Instructional Theory Into Practice; Styles of Learning; Networks-Alcohol Substance Abuse Prgm; Cmptr Literacy; *cr:* 6th Grade Teacher 1971-76; 4th Grade Teacher 1976- Cedar Grove Elem Sch; *ai:* Asst Sci Club; Dir Original Opera; NEA 1971-; Battleground Arts Ctr Childrens Drama Teacher 1980-; BAC Summer Drama Camp Mgr 1978-; Order of Eastern Star 1966-; *office:* Cedar Grove Elem Sch Cedar Grove Rd Toms River NJ 08753

FORSYTH, JOHN P., English Teacher; *b:* Parsons, KS; *m:* Gail Mangham; *c:* Janean, Zach, Sam, John; *ed:* (BA) Poly Sci, Stephen F Austin St Univ 1974; (JD) Law, Univ of Ks 1977; Teacher Cert MT St Univ 1984; *cr:* Eng Teacher Cut Bank HS 1985-87, Wilsall HS 1987-; *ai:* Newspaper & Yrbk Adv; Bsktbl & Track Coach; NCTE, MT Assn of Teachers of Eng & Lang Art; Eng Journal Writing Awd; Bread Loaf in Schls Grant; Dow Jones Newspaper Fund Fellowship; IBM MT Teacher of Yr 1989; Numerous Articles; Mem NCTE Comm for Lang Art Rural Schls; *office:* Wilsall HS Hannaford St Wilsall MT 59086

FORSYTH, JOHN W, Teacher, English Dept Chairman; *b:* Mc Keesport, PA; *ed:* (BA) Eng/Soc Stud, Duquesne Univ 1963; Grad Work, PA St Mc Keesport Duquesne Univ, Gannon Coll; *cr:* Athletic Dir 1969-84, Teacher 1963-, Bsbl Coach 1967-69 & 1988-W Mifflin Area Sch Dist; *ai:* Head Bsbl Coach; Service Awd by Three Rivers Athletics Conference; Federal Grant to Gannon Coll 1969; *office:* W Mifflin Area HS 91 Commonwealth Ave West Mifflin PA 15122

FORSYTHE, CHARLES WAYNE, Administrator; *b:* Lester, AL; *m:* Shirley Lewis; *c:* Gregory W.; *ed:* (AA) Liberal Arts, Calhoun Comm Coll 1971; (BS) Scndry Ed/Government, Athens St Coll 1982; (MS) Sch Admin, Pensacola Chrstn Coll 1990; Certificate Educl Admin Assn of Chrstn Schls Intnl; *cr:* Agent NY Life Insurance Company 1971-75, Lincoln Natl Life Insurance Company 1975-81; Teacher Triana Village Sch 1985-85; Asst Prin Westminster Chrstn Acad 1985-87; Admin Highland Chrstn Acad 1987-89; *ai:* NHS Spon; Bd AL Associated Press Broadcasters Assn Bd of Dir Mem; Published Books & Contributed Non-Fiction News Articles; *office:* Highland Chrstn Acad 1827 Mill St Pulaski TN 38478

FORSYTHE, TERRY A., Counselor; *b:* Joplin, MO; *m:* La Donna S. Coleman; *c:* Christen; *ed:* (BS) Bio in Ed, MO Southern ST 1970; (MS) Scndry Cnslng, Pittsburg ST Univ 1978; *cr:* Sci Teacher North Jr HS 1970-71, Wyandotte HS 1971-72; Walker R-IV 19772-78; Cnslr Walker R-IV 1978; *ai:* Natl Honor Society Spon; CTA Mem; WCTA Schlsp Chm; MSTA Mem 1972-; WCTA Mem 1972-; ASCD Mem 1990; Church of God Sunday Sch Teen Teacher 1983-; Develop Local Career Ed Micro View File; the Society of Distinguished Amer HS Stu Natl Ldrshp Awd; *office:* Walker H S PO Box 1050 Walker MO 64790

FORTE, GERALDINE CYNTHIA, Language Art/Soc Stud Teacher; *b:* Novato, CA; *c:* Jonathon; *ed:* (BA) Behavorial Sci, 1973, (MA) Counseling & Guidance Ed, 1973 San Jose St Univ; Master Teaching, Admin & Supervision; *cr:* Cnslr/Soc Stud Teacher Milpitas Unified Sch Dist 1973-; *ai:* Lang Art & Soc Stud Dept Prgm Chairperson; Mentor Teacher; Sch Improvement Plan Prgm Mgr; Washington DC Club Adv; Assn of CA Sch Admin, CA League of Mid Schls 1988-; CA Teachers Assn 1973-; NAACP 1970-; Alpha Kappa Alpha Pres 1979-, Creative Writing 1989; Natl Cncl of Negro Women 1985-; *home:* 2988 Davidwood Way San Jose CA 95148

FORTENBERRY, BETTY P., Reading Teacher; *b:* Bogalusa, LA; *m:* Brewster E.; *ed:* (BA) Elem Ed, USM 1974; (MS) Elem Ed, William Carey 1978; *cr:* 3rd Grade Teacher 1974-80, 4th-8th Grade Rdng Teacher 1980- Dexter Attendance Center; *ai:* MPE.

FORTENBERRY, IMAGENE (WEST), 3rd Grade Teacher; *b:* Haleyville, AL; *m:* Hewett C.; *c:* Kathy Gamble, Karen Knight, Jeff L.; *ed:* (BS) Elem Ed, Florence St Teachers 1952; (MS) Elem Ed, Univ of N AL 1976; Various Wkshps & Study Courses; *cr:* 3rd/4th Grade Teacher Winston Cty Schls 1952-63; 3rd-5th Grade Teacher Decatur City Schls 1963-70; 3rd/4th Grade Teacher Haleyville City Schls 1970-; *ai:* HEA & DEA 1970-; AEA 1952-; NEA 1952-, Life Mem; Haleyville Study Club 1984-86; Amer Legion Auxiliary (Pres, Secy, Treas) 1980-; 1st United Meth Church 1952-; *home:* 3103 17th Ave Haleyville AL 35565

FORTHUM, SHARON ANN MC MANUS, Second Grade Teacher; *b:* Mitchell, SD; *m:* Larry Dean; *c:* Tammie L.; *ed:* (BA) Elem Ed, Dakota Wesleyan Univ 1967; *cr:* 2nd Grade Teacher Battle Creek Cmmty 1967-; *ai:* 10th Grade Concession Mgr; Western Hills Cooperative Curr Dev Project; Soc Stud Curr Team Adv; NEA, ISEA Membership; Battle Creek City Lib (Pres, VP, Secy); *home:* 301 6th Battle Creek IA 51006

FORTMANN, CANDICE J., English Teacher; *b:* Milwaukee, WI; *m:* James; *c:* Peter, Sean; *ed:* (BS) Scndry Ed/Eng, Univ of WI Oshkosh 1971; (MED) Curr/Instruction Natl Coll of Ed 1989; AODA Care Trng; *cr:* HS Eng Teacher Muskego HS 1971-78/1980-81; Mid Sch Eng Teacher Bay Lane Mid Sch 1982-; *ai:* Strategic Planning Comm; Loan Officer Muskego Norway Credit Union 1984-; WI Ed Assn; NEA; ASCD; *office:* Bay Lane Mid Sch S 75 W 16399 Hilltop Dr Muskego WI 53150

FORTNER, ALICE (STOBAUGH), Second Grade Teacher; *b:* Risco, MO; *m:* Royce Wendell; *c:* Angela, Mark, Betsy; *ed:* (BS) Eng/Home Economics, 1967, (BE) Elem Ed, 1977 Semo St Univ; *cr:* K-1st Grade Teacher St James Elem 1967-69; 2nd Grade Teacher Risco Elem 1975-; *ai:* MO St Teachers Orgaznization 1975-; Classroom Teachers Assn Treas 1980-; PTO 1980-; *office:* Risco Elem Sch Box 17 Risco MO 63874

FORTNER, CHARLES R., Spec Ed Dept Coordinator; *b:* Stollings, WV; *m:* Janet Hall; *c:* Charles, Rebecca; *ed:* (BA) Health/Phys Ed/Bus Admin, Marshall Coll 1959; (MA) Spec Ed, Cntrl St Univ 1971; *cr:* Teacher/Coach Greenon HS 1969-77, Lenore HS 1981-83, Logan Jr HS 1983-87; Coord Logan Cty Bd of Ed 1987-; *ai:* Ftbl; AFT; Amer Legion; *office:* Logan Cty Bd of Ed Box 477 Logan WV 25601

FORTNER, MARY MERRITT, Home Economics Teacher; *b:* Denver, CO; *m:* Brian D.; *c:* Danna, Sandy, Kelly; *ed:* (BS) Voc/General Home Ec, 1978, (MS) Scndry Ed, 1981 E NM Univ; *cr:* Home Ec Teacher C V Koolger Jr HS 1979-82, Logan Municipal HS 1983-; *ai:* FHA & 7th Grade Spon; NEA 1978-; NM Voc Home Ec Teachers Assn 1984-; *office:* Logan Municipal HS PO Box 67 Logan NM 88426

FORTNER, NANCY KAYE, 1st Grade Teacher; *b:* Greensburg, IN; *ed:* (BA) Elem Ed, IN Cntrl 1974; (MS) Elem Ed, IN Univ 1977; *cr:* 1st Grade Teacher Rosenmund Elem 1974-; *home:* 25 Ryle Dr Greensburg IN 47240

FORTSON, BARBARA CRAWFORD, Math Teacher/Dept Chairperson; *b:* Lumpkin, GA; *m:* George Arlington; *c:* Kesal P., Kerwin P.; *ed:* (BS) Elem Ed, Albany St 1962; (MED) Elem Ed, Valdosta St 1973; EDS Mid Grades, GA Southwestern; *cr:* 2nd Grade Teacher Lee Cty Trng Sch 1962-65; 1st Grade Teacher Dent-Reynolds Elem Sch 1965-70, Mitchell Cty Primary Sch 1970-72; 7th Grade Math Teacher Radium Springs Mid Sch 1972-; *ai:* YMCA & Math Club Spon; Girls Sftbl Coach; Stu-At-Risk Chairperson; Dougherty Cty Teachers Assn 1972-; Prof Assn of GA Educators 1980-; GA Assn of Educators (Rdng Teachers 1962-89, Arithmetic Teachers 1972-); Jack & Jill of America (Secy 1981-85, Teen Spon 1979-83); Dougherty Cty Math Teacher of Yr 1989-; Sci & Soc Sci Fair Teacher Recognitions; *office:* Radium Springs Mid Sch 2600 Radium Springs Rd Albany GA 31705

FORTUNE, EDDIE LEE, 7th Grade Mathematics Teacher; *b:* Bishopville, SC; *m:* Bonita Frances; *c:* Pierre, Juliette, Emmanuel; *ed:* (BS) Math, Voorhees Coll 1977; (MED) Scndry Ed/Math, TX Southern Univ 1979; *cr:* Teacher Jack Yates Sr HS 1977-78, Lamar Fleming Mid Sch 1978-; *ai:* Seven Elves Club Chm; Athletics TX Youth Acad Dir; Lamar Fleming Mid Sch Chess Instr; Faculty Advisory Comm (Pres 1988-89, Mem 1989-); Windsor Village UMC Traffic Coord 1987-; US Tennis Assn Mem 1988-, 2nd in St 1989; United Negro Coll Fund Building Rep; Nom Outstanding Young Men in America 1988-89; *office:* Lamar Fleming Mid Sch 4910 Collingsworth Houston TX 77026

FOSCHINI, ROSALIE BRANCATO, Bilingual Education Teacher; *b:* Passaic, NJ; *m:* Robert R.; *c:* Robert W., William R., Mark R., Gregory T., Mary J. S.; *ed:* (BA) Span/Accounting, Montclair St Coll 1955; (MA) Urban Ed, William Paterson Coll 1980; Grad Study Middlebury Coll, Jersey City St Coll, Univ of Madrid Spain; *cr:* FLES Teacher Hackensack Public Schls 1955-60, 1963-64; Span Teacher River Dell Regional Jr/Sr HS 1972-74; Bi-ling Ed/Eng as 2nd Lang Teacher Hackensack Public Schls 1975-; *ai:* TESOL 1990; NEA, NJEA, BCEA, HEA Teacher Rep 1955-; Pi Lambda Theta 1981-; Waldwick PTA 1968-76; *office:* Fanny M Hillers Sch Longview Ave Hackensack NJ 07601

FOSS, MARTHA WAGER, First Grade Teacher; *b:* Chicago, IL; *m:* Curtis Henry; *c:* Pamela, Julie Langmade; *ed:* (BA) Elem Ed, Trinity Coll 1960; Ed, Natl Coll of Ed 1990; *cr:* 1st Grade Teacherd Union Ridge 1960-61; 1st-2nd Grade Teacher Durkee Elem 1961-62; Director of Sch Marts 1967-69; 1st Grade Teacher Gavin South 1969-70; 1st & 2nd Grade Teacher B J Hooper 1970-; *ai:* Outstanding Young Educators Awd Jaycees 1969; Exemplary Prof Performance Awd 1988; *home:* 18620 Millburn Rd Wadsworth IL 60083

FOSSEN, SUSAN FRANCYNE, English Teacher; *b:* Wadena, MN; *m:* John Richard; *c:* Michael, Sara, Eric; *ed:* (BS) Eng/Fr, Moorhead St Univ 1965; Working on Masters Degree Scndry Ed AZ St Univ; *cr:* Fr Teacher W Fargo HS 1966-67, Fargo N HS 1967-68, Detroit Lakes HS 1983-84; Eng Teacher Casa Grande Union HS 1985-; *ai:* Casa Grande Union HS Gifted Ed Coord; Natl Honor Society Local Chapter & Games R Us Club Spon; CGEA, AEA, NEA 1985-; AAGT 1988-; Natl Cncl of Teachers of Eng 1989-; Appointed to St Advisory Bd of Gifted & Talented 1989-; Delta Kappa Gamma 1986-; Awarded Ed in Partners Grant for Gifted & Talented Stu in HS 1988-; *office:* Casa Grande Union HS 420 E Florence Blvd Casa Grande AZ 85222

FOSTER, ANDREW THOMAS, History Teacher; *b:* Tuscaloosa, AL; *m:* Vanesa Thomas; *ed:* (BS) HPER, Livingston Univ 1979; *cr:* Teacher/Coach Thomasville Acad 1979-82; Coach Maxwell Elem 1982-83; Teacher/Coach Brookwood HS 1983-; *ai:* Head Bsktbl & Asst Ftbl Coach; Soc Stud Fair Chm; Tucaloosa Cty Ed Assn Building Rep 1983-; AL Ed Assn 1983-; Brookwood Athletic Boosters, Brookwood PTSA 1983-; Coaling Baptist Church Sunday Sch Teacher 1986-88; Rotary Intnl Group Study Exch Germany Mem 1988; *home:* Rt 5 Box 749 Cottondale AL 35453

FOSTER, BARBARA LOU, English Teacher; *b:* Lubbock, TX; *c:* Piper, William; *ed:* (BA) Eng, 1959, (MA) Scndry Ed, 1976 TX Tech Univ; *cr:* Eng Teacher Gallup Jr HS 1969-70, Peach Cty HS 1975-77, Tahoka HS 1977-; *ai:* Jr/Sr One Act Play; UIL Ready Writing Critical Analysis; Jr Class Spon; TX St Teachers Assn Secy 1987-89; Womens Club Schlsp 1990; *home:* 2029 Avenue R PO Box 1423 Tahoka TX 79373

FOSTER, BETTY V., Sophomore English Teacher; *b:* West Monroe, LA; *ed:* (BS) Eng/Scndry, Grambling St Univ 1957; Linguistic, Chicago Teachers Coll 1965, NE LA Univ 1967-68; Guidance/Admin, NE LA Univ 1971-73; *cr:* Teacher Sharkey Cty Trng Sch 1958-60, Dunbar Jr HS 1961-65, Richardson Jr HS 1965-68, West Monroe HS 1968-; *ai:* Ouachita Educl Assn 1965-; LA Ed Assn, NEA.

FOSTER, CONNIE VAN CAMP, Third Grade Teacher; *b:* Batavia, NY; *m:* Riley Edward Jr.; *c:* Mandy, John; *ed:* (BSE) Elem Ed, Univ of AR 1971; *cr:* 2nd Grade Teacher Gladeview Elem 1972-73; 1st Grade Teacher Belle Galde Elem 1973-76; 3rd Grade Teacher James A Garfield Elem 1978-; *ai:* Sci & Lang Art Comms to Write Course of Study; NEA 1978-; OH Ed Assn 1978-; Garfield Ed Assn 1978-; Beta Sigma Phi Pres 1976; United Meth Church Sunday Sch Teacher 1985-; *home:* 4361 Fairground Rd Atwater OH 44201

FOSTER, ELAINE PETERSON, French Teacher; *b:* Boston MA; *m:* Bradford C.; *c:* Eric, Karen; *ed:* (BA) Fr, Univ of MA Amherst 1970; Alps, Dartmouth Coll; *cr:* Fr Teacher Belmont HS 1970-73, Inter-Lakes Jr Sr HS 1981-; *ai:* Inter-Lakes Ed Assn Exec Bd; Meredith Youth Bsktbl Asst Coach; AATF 1970-; Phi Beta Kappa, Phi Kappa Phi 1970-; *office:* Inter-Lakes Jr/Sr HS Rt 25 RR 3 Box 152 Meredith NH 03253

FOSTER, H. EUGENE, History Department Chair; *b:* Saint Joseph, MO; *ed:* (BSED) His, MO Western St Coll 1971; (MA) His, NW MO St Univ 1974; Post Grad Stud Univ of MO Kansas City; Regional 19 Federal Law Enforcement Acad; *cr:* His Chm Plattsburg HS 1972-; *ai:* Positive Club Comm; Plattsburg Service Club; Amer His Society 1978-; St Historical Society of MO 1976-; Natl Center for His; Federal Career Ed Grant; Nom St His Teacher of Yr; St Teacher of Gifted MO Scholars Acad; Historical Research Methods Class Lesson Plans Published; *office:* Plattsburg HS 800 Frost Plattsburg MO 64477

FOSTER, JANICE H., 11th Grade English Teacher; *b:* Paducah, KY; *m:* R. Lynn; *c:* Alan, Michael; *ed:* (BS) Eng, 1963, (MA) Eng, 1965 Murray St Univ; *cr:* Eng Teacher HS 1963-, Newspaper Adv 1975-78, Yrbk Adv 1975- Lone Oak HS; *ai:* Tri Hi Y & Beta Club Spon; *office:* Lone Oak HS College Ave Paducah KY 42001

FOSTER, JEFFREY THOMAS, Principal; *b:* Houston, TX; *m:* Brenda Rankin; *c:* Jon, Jayne; *ed:* (BA) Sociology, 1972, (MA) Guidance/Counseling, 1976, (Rank I) Sch Admin, 1980 W KY Univ; *cr:* Teacher Barren Cty Schls 1972-; Natl Park Service Dept of Interior Mammoth Cave 1974-; *ai:* KEA; NEA; Masonic Mem; *home:* 124 Trappers Trl Glasgon KY 42141

FOSTER, JUDY WEBER, English Teacher; *b:* Fayette, OH; *m:* Roger; *c:* Tamara; *ed:* (BA) Eng/Home Ec, Adrian Coll 1963; *cr:* HS Teacher 1963-64; Jr HS Teacher Oakley W Best 1964-66; Teacher Grand Ledge Public Schls 1967-; *ai:* Building & Dist Effectiveness Team, Grand Ledge Against Drugs Comm Mem; Mid Sch Gifted & Talented Coord; Grand Ledge Ed Assn Public Relation Chairperson 1980-; MI Assn of Mid Schls 1983-, Regional Teacher of Yr 1985; NEA MI Convention Delegate 1980-89; MI Jr Quarter Horse Assn Adv 1987-89, Mother of Yr 1987; Order of Eastern Star 1963-; 4-H Leader 1978-85, Club Leader of Yr 1981, 1982; St of MI Partnership for Ed Awd 1986 & Mini-Grant 1987; *office:* Hayes Mid Sch 12620 Nixon Rd Grand Ledge MI 48837

FOSTER, KAREN KING, English & Reading Teacher; *b:* Lake Charles, LA; *m:* David Ian; *c:* Heather, Jennifer; *ed:* (BS) Eng Ed, 1970, (MED) Scndry Ed, 1975 LA St Univ; Post Grad Work Amer & Eng Lit; *cr:* Eng Teacher Baker HS 1972-75; Instr Mc Neese St Univ 1983; Eng Teacher La Grange Sr HS 1987, Westlake HS 1987-88; Eng/Rdng Teacher Bishop Noland Episcopal Day Sch 1989-; *ai:* Drama Club Adv; Daughters of Amer Revolution Flag Chm 1983-85; *office:* Bishop Noland Episcopal Day 715 Kirkman St Lake Charles LA 70601

FOSTER, LINDA CAVNER, Second Grade Teacher; *b:* Duncan, OK; *m:* Roger D.; *c:* Jeff, Dena Williams, Tim; *ed:* (BA) Chrstn Ed, Bob Jones Univ 1960; Ed, Mercer Univ; Learning Disabilities, Natl Inst of Learning Disabilities; *cr:* Kndgtn Teacher 1971-72, 1st Grade Teacher 1972-85, 2nd Grade Teacher 1985- Stone Mountain Chrstn Sch; *ai:* Curr Comm; Sch Yrbk Dedication 1988-89; *office:* Stone Mountain Chrstn Sch P O Box 509 Stone Mountain GA 30086

FOSTER, MARY LINDA GRISSOM, Mathematics Department Chair; *b:* Sparta, TN; *m:* Douglas Allen; *c:* Mary E., Mark D.; *ed:* (BA) Math, David Lipscomb Univ 1970; (MA) Ed/Psych, George Peabody Coll of Vanderbilt Univ 1971; *cr:* Math Teacher Bellevue Mid Sch 1971-; *ai:* Math Team Spon; Team Leader; Faculty Advisory Comm; UTP 1982-; NCTM 1984-; *office:* Bellevue Mid Sch 655 Colice Jeanne Rd Nashville TN 37221

FOSTER, NANCY MORRIS, Second Grade Teacher; *b:* Acushnet, MA; *m:* Robert William; *c:* Kelly, Erinn; *ed:* (BA) Elem Ed, Univ of MA Amherst 1971; Credits in Ed, Rdng; *cr:* Title I Rdng/Math Tutor 1973-76, 2nd Grade Teacher 1976- Acushnet Elem Sch; *ai:* Rep Sch Improvement Cncl; Schlsp & Lang Art Study Comm; Delta Kappa Gamma Secy 1990-; Teachers Assn (Treas, Building Rep); Town Meeting Mem 1987-88; Unitarian Memorial Church Bd of Governors Clerk 1990; *home:* 17 Cedar St Fairhaven MA 02719

FOSTER, NANCY P., English Teacher; *b:* Warren, PA; *c:* Dean Curtkeith, Karla Keith Kimmy; *ed:* (BS) Scndry Ed/Eng, Edinboro Coll 1983, (MED) Ed/Psych, Edinboro Univ 1987; *cr:* Eng Teacher Corry Ave HS 1984-; *ai:* PSEA 1984-; NCTE 1987-; Wattsburg Youngsville U M Church Sunday Sch Teacher/Organist/Pianist; Outstanding Graduate Stu Awd May 1988; *home:* Rd 2 10053 Hillwood Dr Wattsburg PA 16442

FOSTER, NANCY PARKER, English Teacher; *b:* Wilmington, NC; *m:* Donald S.; *c:* Alison, Chad; *ed:* (BS) Eng, E Carolina Univ 1970; *cr:* Lang Art Teacher Havelock Jr HS 1971-73; Eng Teacher West Craven HS 1973-75, 1979, 1987-; *ai:* Eng Honor Society Sch Literary Magazine Spon; Quiz Bowl Adv; Comm Drawing Up Absentee Policy Chm; Hospitality Comm; NEA, NC Ed Assn 1973-75, 1979, 1987-89; NCTE 1987-; *home:* 125 Robin Hood Rd Greenville NC 27834

FOSTER, PAULETTE HEBERT, Teacher; *b:* Hammond, LA; *m:* Marlon K.; *c:* Kearney, Annette, Aaron; *ed:* (BA) Phys Ed/Eng, 1969, (MED) Supervision/Admin, 1976, General/Elem Ed, 1989 Southeastern LA Univ 1989; Rdng Insts; In Service Wkshps; PIPS Courses; *cr:* Phys Ed/Eng Teacher Springfield HS 1969-78; Phys Ed Teacher Springfield Elem Sch 1978-85; Asst Prin Albany-Springfield Jr HS 1985-86; - 4th Grade Teacher Springfield Elem Sch 1986-; *ai:* COE Task Force; Designated Prin; Fair Comm; Chm Open House Comm; Field Trip Coord; Beta Club Spon 1985-86; Pres Academic Awd Coord 1985-; Remediation LEAP Teacher 1989-; LA Assn of Educators Rep 1988-, Teacher of Yr 1988-89; LA Pem Secy 1967-68; *home:* PO Box 235 Springfield LA 70462

FOSTER, REBECCA HODGES, English Teacher; *b:* Waurika, OK; *m:* Jim; *c:* Krista M., Lisa R.; *ed:* (BS) Voc Home Ec, Abilene Chrstn Coll 1963; (MED) Lib Sci, Mid TN St Univ 1989; Endorsement Eng, N TX St Univ 1970; *cr:* Home Ec/Eng Teacher Dallas Chrstn HS 1963-69; Voc/Home Ec Teacher Garland HS 1971-73; Eng Teacher Corpus Christi Ind Sch Dist 1974-77, Mid TN Chrstn Sch 1984-; *ai:* Sr Beta Spon; Phi Kappa Phi, ASCD, Amer Lib Assn 1989-; NCTE 1984-; Murfreesboro Area Home Ec Assn Treas 1986-87; Chairperson Steering Comm 1988-89; Self-Study for Southern Assn of Colls & Schls; Teacher of Yr 1985, 1987.

FOSTER, RICHARD WAYNE, History Teacher, Coach; *b:* Milan, TN; *m:* Kaye Carter; *c:* Elizabeth, Ryan; *ed:* (BS) Soc Stud/Health/Phys Ed, Bethel Coll 1968; (MS) Univ of TN Martin 1973; *cr:* Prin 1978-79, His Teacher 1968- Lexington HS; *ai:* Girls Bsktbl & Frosh Ftbl Coach; NEA, TN Ed Assn; TN Athletic Coaches Assn Dist Coach of Yr 1984, 1986, 1988.

FOSTER, ROBERT W., History Teacher; *b:* New Bedford, MA; *m:* Nancy Morris; *c:* Kelly, Erinn; *ed:* (BA) His, Univ of MA 1970; (MA) US His, Bridgewater St Coll 1976; *cr:* Soc Stud Teacher Normandin Jr HS 1970-78, New Bedford HS 1978-; *ai:* Asst Girls Bsktbl Coach; Debate Team Adv; Southeastern Cncl for Soc Stud Pres 1989-; MA Bsktbl Coaches Assn Service Above Self Awd 1988-89; Asst Coach of Yr 1988-89.

FOSTER, SALLY YOUNG, Kindergarten Teacher; *b:* Cincinnati, OH; *m:* Steve P.; *ed:* (BA) Elem Ed, Capital Univ 1975; (MED) Teacher Leadership, Wright St Univ 1983; Early Chldhd Ed; Math Their Way; Ec Ed; *cr:* 1st Grade Teacher 1975, Kndgtn Teacher 1975-77 Chillicothe City Schls; 1st Grade Teacher 1977-81, Kndgtn Teacher 1981- Lebanon City Schls; *ai:* Building, Dist, Steering, Staff Dev, Guidance, Health Curr, Dev Rdng Curr, Dev Kndgtn, N Cntrl Evaluation Steering Comm; Drug Care Team; Lebanon Ed Assn, OH Ed Assn, NEA 1977-; *office:* Francis Dunlavy Elem Sch Water St Lebanon OH 45036

FOSTER, SAYDE P., English Department Chair; *b:* Winter Garden, FL; *ed:* (BA) Eng, 1978, (MA) Hum, 1980, (PHD) Hum, 1983 FL St Univ; *cr:* Teacher Hernando HS 1983-; *ai:* Sch Improvement & Cty Eng Curr Comm; Peer Teacher for Beginning Teacher Prgm; Phi Delta Kappa 1987-; Alpha Delta Kappa 1987-89; Presented Papers at Intnl Conference in Madrid Spain 1986 & Yearly at MIFLC in Tallahassee; *office:* Hernando HS 200 Kelly Ave Brooksville FL 34601

FOSTER, SHARON V., Science Teacher; *b:* Jackson, MI; *ed:* (BA) Bio, Austin Coll 1964; *cr:* Teacher Burleson Jr HS 1964-66, Country Day Sch 1966-, Aldercar Sch England 1984-85; Asst Prin Country Day Mid Sch 1973-; *ai:* Stu Asst Prgm; Fulbright Teaching Fellow England 1984-85; *office:* Country Day Sch 4200 Country Day Ln Fort Worth TX 76109

FOSTER, TERRY, Elementary Principal; *b:* Grove Hill, AL; *m:* Marilyn Diane Anderson; *c:* Landon, Diana; *ed:* (BS) Elem Ed, 1974, (MED) Elem Ed, 1975, (EDS) Elem Ed, 1978 Livingston Univ; Cert Sch Admin 1982; *cr:* 3rd-4th Grade Teacher Grove Hill Elem Sch 1974-82; Prin Fulton Elem Sch 1982-85, Grove Hill Elem Sch 1985-; *ai:* Clarke Cty DHR Multi-Disciplinary Child Protection Team; Phi Delta Kappa 1987-; Clarke Cty Ed Assn, AL Ed Assn, NEA, NAESP; AL Assn of Elem Sch Admin (Dist VIII Pres, Dist Rep 1983-86); AL Assn of Sch Office Personnel 1982-; Patrick Henry Jr Coll Alumnus of Yr 1977.

FOTH, MARY GENGLER, Second Grade Teacher; *b:* Elkton, SD; *m:* David F.; *c:* Kathleen, Sarah, Rachel; *ed:* (BA) Elem Ed, Mt Marty Coll 1973; *cr:* 2nd Grade Teacher St John Sch 1973-; *ai:* Sacramental Prgm Dir; Religious Ed Dept Chairperson; Rdng Comm; NCEA 1973-; Diocesan Teaching Corps 1973-74; Chamber of Commerce; Amer Cancer Society; *home:* 414 S Walnut St Bancroft IA 50517

FOUCHER, JOYCELYN OGLE, Sixth Grade Teacher; *b:* New Orleans, LA; *m:* Marcus R. Sr.; *c:* Marcus Jr., Michael; *ed:* (BA) Eng Ed, Xavier Univ 1980; *cr:* Rdng Teacher Xavier Univ Preparatory 1979-80; Teacher Incarnate Word Sch 1980-85; Eng Teacher Blessed Sacrament Sch 1985-86; 2nd Grade Teacher St Jude Sch 1986-87; 6th Grade Teacher Our Lady Star of Sea Sch 1987-; *ai:* Coaching Chrldr; Moderator of Dance Club; *home:* 6439 Derbyshire Dr New Orleans LA 70126

FOUST, BARBARA EDSON, Second Grade Teacher; *b:* Jamestown, NY; *m:* Kenneth W.; *ed:* (AA) Hum, Jamestown Comm Coll 1974; (BA) Eng, Thiel Coll 1976; (MS) Rdng, St Bonaventure Univ 1980; Elements of Instruction; *cr:* 4th Grade Teacher Portville Cntrl 1976-81; Kndgtn Teacher Falconer Cntrl 1981-82; Remedial Rdng Teacher 1982-85, 2nd Grade Teacher 1985- Portville Cntrl; *ai:* Advisory Cncl; S Tier Rdng Assn; Delta Kappa Gamma; PTA Life Membership; 1st Presbyn Church; *office:* Portville Cntrl Sch Elm St Portville NY 14770

FOUST, CAROL LYNN, Teacher/Coach; *b:* Cincinnati, OH; *ed:* (BA) Comp Soc Stud 1981, (BA) Gen Sci, 1981, (MS) Speech & Comm, 1988 Marshall Univ; *cr:* Teacher 1981-, Vlybl Coach 1981- Shady Spring Jr HS; *ai:* Spon Jr Civilian 1988-; Vlybl Girls Coach 1981-; Track Coach 1981-88; WV Ed Assn 1988-.

FOUST, DANIEL G., Mathematics Department Chair; *b:* Bellefonte, PA; *m:* Linda K. Sharer; *c:* Erica; *ed:* (BS) Scndry Ed, 1972, (MED) Math, 1973 PA St Univ; S Meth Univ; *cr:* Math Dept Chm Bullis Sch 1976-80; Math/Cmptr Teacher 1980-87, Math Dept Chm 1987- Fort Worth Cntry Day Sch; *ai:* Mu Alpha Theta & Cmptr Club Adv; NCTM 1976-; TX Cmptr Ed Assn 1980-; BSA Asst Scoutmaster 1980-; Minimam Square Golden Rectangle Disection; Journal Recreational Math; Intnl Cncl for Cmptrs Ed SIGCS Newsletter; *office:* Fort Worth Cntry Day Sch 4200 Country Day Ln Fort Worth TX 76109

FOUST, FRANCES NAPOLITAN, First Grade Teacher; *b:* Sharon, PA; *m:* David; *c:* Julie; *ed:* (BS) Elem Ed, Edinboro Univ 1971; (MED) Early Chldhd Elem, Slippery Rock Univ 1978; *cr:* 5th-8th Grade Eng Teacher 1971-72, 1st Grade Teacher 1972- Msgr Geno Monti Sch; *ai:* NCEA; *home:* 8255 Lincoln St Masury OH 44438

FOUST, HENRY O., Spanish Teacher; *b:* Burlington, NC; *ed:* (BAED) Span Ed, Univ of NC Chapel Hill 1980; *cr:* Rehab Aide Alamance-Caswell Mental Health 1980-84; Span Teacher Northwood HS 1984-; *ai:* Stu Cncl ADV, FCA, Alpha Beta Phi Adv; FLANC 1984-; Carolina Alliance Foreign Lang Teachers Chatham Cty & Northwood HS Teacher of Yr; *office:* Northwood HS Rt 4 Box 61 Pittsboro NC 27312

FOUST, J'AIME L. (MEYER), Social Studies Teacher; *b:* Hollywood, CA; *m:* James E.; *ed:* (BS) Scndry Ed/Soc Stud, Temple Univ 1985; (MED) Adult Ed, Univ of S MS 1988; Pursuing 2nd Masters Degree in Lib Sci, Sch Media, St Univ of NY Albany; *cr:* Drug/Alcohol Cnslr US Navy 1975-80; Soc Stud Teacher Queensbury HS 1985-; *ai:* Class of 1990 Adv; Spirit Week Coord; NCSS 1988-; Queensbury Faculty Assn (Building Rep, Negotiations, Prin Selection Comm); Natl Organization of Women 1982-85; Regional Scholars Recognition Prgm Teacher; *office:* Queensbury HS 99 Aviation Rd Queensbury NY 12804

FOUST, ROBIN K., Teacher/Area Supervisor; *b:* San Antonio, TX; *m:* Douglas W.; *cr:* Teacher Playhouse Day Care Center 1973-84, Castle Hills 1st Baptist Day Care Center 1984-; *ai:* Summer Schedule Coord; Playground Supvr; Church Acts; *office:* Castle Hills Firs Baptist Sch 2220 NW Military Hwy San Antonio TX 78230

FOUST, RUTH ELLEN (BRUMIT), English Teacher; *b:* Mc Leansboro, IL; *m:* Bill S.; *c:* Brad S., Lisa C.; *ed:* (BS) Elem, Oakland City Coll 1962; (MS) Elem, IN St Univ 1965; Grad Stud Eng; *cr:* 4th Grade Teacher Taft Elem 1962-65; 7th/8th Grade Eng Teacher Doolen Jr HS 1965; 7th/8th Grade Eng/Soc Stud Teacher Townsend Jr HS 1977-78; 7th/8th Grade Eng Teacher Magee Mid Sch 1978-; *ai:* Alpha Delta Kappa (Corresponding Secy 1988-, Pres 1990; *office:* Magee Mid Sch 8300 E Speedway Tucson AZ 85710

FOWLER, BETTY L. (OLNEY), Home Economic Teacher; *b:* Harleton, TX; *w:* Robert W. (dec); *c:* Vickie L. Echols, Robert D., Richard E.; *ed:* (BS) Home Ec, 1952, (MED) Scndry Ed, 1975 Stephen F Austin St Univ; Psych, Univ of MD 1954; Free Enterprise, TX A&M Univ 1985; *cr:* Cty Home Dem Agent Center 1952-55; Home Making Teacher Tenaha HS 1956-57; Kndgtn Teacher Intnl Day Care E Pakistan 1959-61; Home Ec Teacher Kilgore HS 1968-; *ai:* FHA Chapter I 1968-; Voc Home Ec St Dir 1968-; Teacher of TX; TX St Teachers Assn Local Pres 1984-85; NEA (Local Voting Delegate 1985) 1968-; PTA VP 1975-76, Honorary Mem 1990; Alpha Delta Kappa (VP, Pres) 1982-84; Natl Arbor Day Fnd Dir 1990; Keep TX Beautiful; 1st Baptist Church (Church Hostess 1976-81, Remodeling Comm Chairperson); Kilgore Jr Coll Occupational Ed Advisory Comm; TX Congress of Parents & Teacher Honorary Life Membership; TX ASSN FHA Honorary Membership; Mrktg Consultant Family Bus; E TX A&M Mothers Club Schlsp Chairperson; *office:* Kilgore HS 711 N Longview St Kilgore TX 75662

FOWLER, PAMELA GAY SAYRE, Teacher of Elementary Gifted; *b:* Euclid, OH; *m:* Frank Andrew; *ed:* (AA) Ed, Martin Coll 1975; (BS) Elem/Early Chldhd, Athens St Coll 1977; (MA) Gifted Ed, Univ of AL 1979; Addl Stud Space Orientation Prof Educators Level I & II, WA DC; Several Wkshps Comptr & Data Base Word Processing; *cr:* Elem Gifted Teacher Limestone Cty Schls 1977-; *ai:* Earth Shuttle Prgm & Co-Ordinated Field Trips; Create Curr Units for Prgms of Study & Parent Circulars; Young Astronaut Prgm & Model Rocketry; Amer Ed Week Comm; Kappa Delta Pi 1979-; NEA 1977-; AL Ed Assn 1977-; Limestone Cty Ed Assn 1977-; Alatag 1977-; Young Astronaut Prgm Coord 1989-; Natl Space Society Mem 1988-; Space Acad Wings 1989; St of AL Name The Orbiter Contest Winners 1989; Teacher in Space Certificate & Patch 1985; *office:* Limestone County Vocational 505 E Sanderfer Rd Athens AL 35611

FOWLER, PHILLIP HENRY, Advanced Biology Teacher; *b:* Waterbury, CT; *m:* Joan Kukoski; *c:* Jeffrey, Mark, Dennis; *ed:* (BS) Bio, 1969, (MS) Bio, 1971 Cntrl CT St Coll; Drug & Advanced Drug Ed Wheeler Clinic; *cr:* Teacher Litchfield HS 1969-; Instr Mattuck Comm Coll 1981-85; *ai:* SADD, Stu Cncl, Sr Class Adv; Boys Soccer & Girls Bsktbl Coach; Kappa Delta Pi Mem 1968-, Honor Society in Ed 1968; Terryville Lions Club 1985-89; Terryville Republican Town Comm 1990; Celebration of Excl 1988, 1990, Finalist 1988, 1990; Univ of CT Alumus Teacher of Yr Awd 1985; *office:* Litchfield HS West St Litchfield CT 06759

FOWLER, SALLY KEITH, 7th-9th Grade Lit Teacher; *b:* Centerville, TN; *d:* Doug; *c:* Jennifer, Jonathan; *ed:* (AS) Elem Ed, Columbia St 1976; (BS) Elem Ed, Mid TN St Univ 1978; Grad Stud; *cr:* 6th-8th Grade Rdng Teacher 1978-79, 7th-9th Grade Grammar/Lit Teacher 1979- Columbia Acad; *ai:* Jr HS Cheerleading & 9th Grade Spon; PTO (Mem 1988-, Liasion Comm 1988-89); Columbia Acad Assoc, Columbia Acad Boosters Mem 1984-; Winner of Ed Awd 1976; *home:* 103 Hilltop Dr Columbia TN 38401

FOWLER, WILLIAM NEWTON, JR., English Teacher; *b:* Ahoskie, NC; *m:* Rachelle Jean Longnecker; *c:* Emily, Claire; *ed:* (BS) Eng, E Carolina Univ 1977; Grad Stud for Academically Gifted Cert; *cr:* Eng Teacher Chocowinity HS 1977-78, E B Aycock Jr HS 1978-; *ai:* Newspaper Adv; Mentor Teacher; Ag Comm Chm; NEA, NCAE Mem; *office:* E B Aycock Jr HS 1325 Red Banks Rd Greenville NC 27834

FOX, BRENDA DIX, Second Grade Teacher; *b:* Rocky Mount, NC; *m:* Raymond Brian; *c:* Dee Ann, Jeanette; *ed:* (BS) Early Chldhd Ed, James Madison Univ 1969; *cr:* Kndgtn Teacher Lynchburg City Schls 1969-70; Teacher Shenandoah Cty Schls 1977-; *ai:* Soc Comm Chm; BiAnnual Sch Plan Comm; *office:* W W Robinson Elem Sch Susan Ave Woodstock VA 22664

FOX, CHARLES DANIEL, Social Studies Teacher; *b:* Saginaw, MI; *m:* Linda Grinnell; *c:* Shelly; *ed:* (BS) Multidisciplinary Soc Sci, 1975, (MLIR) Labor/Industrial Relations, 1978, (MAT) His, 1982 MI St Univ; *cr:* Teacher Eaton Rapids Mid Sch 1975-84, Eaton Rapids HS 1984-; *ai:* Eaton Rapids HS High Potential Youth Prgm Coord; MI Assn Ed Gifted & Talented Children, MI Cncl Soc Stud 1985-; Cmmty Heritage Fnd Eaton Rapids Trustee 1988-; *office:* Eaton Rapids HS 800 State St Eaton Rapids MI 48827

FOX, DAVID D., English Teacher; *b:* Waterloo, IA; *m:* Cheryl A. Calease; *ed:* (BA) Eng Ed, Wartburg Coll 1985; IA Writers Project; *cr:* Eng Teacher Wellsburg Cmmty Sch 1985-86, Steamboat Rock Cmmty Sch 1986-; *ai:* Head Ftbl & Jr HS Track Coach; *home:* 305 N Monroe Wellsburg IA 50680

FOX, DAVID R., Anatomy/Biology Teacher; *b:* Rangely, CO; *m:* Ellen Gail Hoff; *c:* Andy D., Angela D.; *ed:* (AA) Liberal Art, Rangely Jr Coll 1973; (BS) Phys Ed, CO St Univ 1976; Working Towards Masters Univ of NM, Univ of AZ; *cr:* Sci Teacher Shiprock HS 1976-81; Teacher/Coach Fruita Jr HS 1981-83, Fruita Monument HS 1983-; *ai:* Head Girls Bsktbl & Bsbl Coach; SWL League Pres; Mesa Valley Teachers Union 1981-; Bsktbl Coaches Assn; Coach of Yr SW League 1987-; Rocky Mountain News Denver Post Coach of Yr 1989; *office:* Fruita Monument HS 1815 J Rd Fruita CO 81521

FOX, DONNIE LEE, Sixth Grade Teacher; *b:* Williamsburg, KY; *m:* Pamela Gail Brooks; *c:* Jason, Ryan, Brittany; *ed:* (BA) Phys Ed, 1978, (BA) Elem Ed, 1979 Ed, 1985 Cumberland Coll; *cr:* Janitor Liberty Elem 1977-79; Rdng Specialist Boston Elem 1979-80; 4th-6th Grade Head Teacher Jellico Creek Elem 1980-81; 6th Grade Teacher Pleasant View Elem 1981-; *ai:* Ftbl & Boys Bsktbl Coach; Parenting & Family Life Skills, Attendance, Fall Festival Comm Chm; Minor League Bsbl Coach; KEA, NEA 1979-; WCEA 1981-; *home:* Rt 3 Box 217 A Williamsburg KY 40769

FOX, H. JUNE, FM Broadcasting Teacher; *b:* Chestertown, MD; *m:* John Michael Canning; *ed:* (BA) Radio/TV Comm, Univ of MD 1986; (BS) Broadcast Journalism, Univ of MD 1986; *cr:* Teacher Kent Cty HS 1987-; *ai:* Spon Radio Club; Sch Rep for Cty Cncl of PTA; Spotlight on Ed Comm; MD Public Radio Assn Bd of Dir 1987-; AVA 1987-89; Kent Cty HS Sch PTA/Stu Assn 1987-; Baltimore Gas & Electric; MD Sci Supvrs Assn Energy Mini Grant.

FOX, JANE (BOYER), Business Ed/Department Chair; *b:* York, PA; *m:* Terry G.; *c:* Randall, Ryan; *ed:* (BS) Bus Ed, 1965, (MA) Elem Ed, 1968 Shippensburg Univ; *cr:* Teacher Keefauver Elem Sch 1965-66, Gettysburg Sr HS 1966-70, Biglerville HS 1979-; *ai:* Sch Store Adv; NEA, PA St Ed, Upper Adams Ed Assn, NBEA; *office:* Biglerville HS N Main St Biglerville PA 17307

FOX, JOY BOHLEBER, 1st/2nd Grade Teacher; *b:* Evansville, IN; *m:* Robert Harold; *c:* Brian; *ed:* (BS) Elem Ed, IN St Univ 1972; *cr:* Stu Teaching Sacred Heart Cath Sch 1971; 1st/2nd Grade Teacher Oakdale Public Sch 1972-77, Immanuel Luth 1981-; *ai:* Teach Summer Bible Sch Venedy & Sparta IL; Teach 6th/7th Grade Confirmation Class Sparta IL; Lib Bd Mem 1984-; Nom Teacher of Yr 1987; Nom Natl Finalist Teacher of Yr 1987; *home:* Box 343 Coulterville IL 62237

FOX, JOYCE GRANT, Second Grade Teacher; *b:* Indianapolis, KY; *m:* Philipp Jr.; *c:* Philipp B., Dale G., Marcus A.; *ed:* (BA) Elem Ed, 1962, (Rank II) 1987 Union Coll; *cr:* 4th-5th Grade Teacher Harlan Cty Sch System 1962-63; 1st-4th Grade Teacher Bell Cty Sch 1963-64; 2nd Grade Teacher Bourbon Cty System 1964-65; 1st Grade Teacher Georgetown Ind Systems 1968-75; K-3nd Grade Teacher Jesse D Lay Elem 1977-; *ai:* KY Ed Assn 1962-; Delta Kappa Gamma 1985-; Ossoli Club (1st VP, Pres 1985-); Amer Assn Univ Women 1980-84; *home:* 12 Robin Road Corbin KY 40701

FOX, LINDA LENCALIS, Science Teacher; *b:* Hazleton, PA; *m:* James A.; *c:* Heather; *ed:* (BS) Bio, E Stroudsburg Univ 1969; E Stroudsburg Univ; *cr:* Sci Teacher 1969-82, Dept Chairperson 1976-82 East Hills Jr HS; Sci Teacher Freedom HS 1982-; *ai:* Bethlehem Ed Assn, PA Ed Assn, NEA 1969-; NSTA 1988-; Wrote Curr for Honors-Introduction to Chem & Physics Prgm Bethlehem Area Sch Dist; *office:* Freedom HS 3149 Chester Ave Bethlehem PA 18017

FOX, MARK ALLEN, Life Science Teacher; *b:* Two Harbors, MN; *m:* Christine Marie Luudgren; *c:* Caryn; *ed:* (BS) Life Sci, St Cloud St Univ; *ai:* Ftbl, Bsbl, Photo Club Coach; *office:* St Francis Mid Sch 23026 Ambassador Blvd Saint Francis MN 55070

FOX, MARTHA SUE, Biology/Physiology Teacher; *b:* Lawrenceburg, TN; *m:* Ronnie W.; *c:* Brian C., Lawren T.; *ed:* (BS) Bio, 1972, (MS) Bio, 1974 Mid TN St Univ; *cr:* Bio Teacher/Grad Asst Mid TN St Univ 1972-74; Bio Teacher Franklin HS 1974-82; Night Sch Bio Teacher Columbia St Univ 1980; Bio Teacher Brentwood HS 1982-; *ai:* Faculty Sunshine Comm; Foster Childrens Christmas Party & Prom Spon; Brentwood Chrstn Sch Parents Assn Co-Chairperson 1989-; Lead Teacher Bio Dept BHS 1982-84; Level III of TN Career Ladder; Amer Cancer Society Awd; Outstanding Sci Teacher by Sigma Xi Club 1990; *office:* Brentwood HS 5304 Murray Ln Brentwood TN 37027

FOX, MARY LINN, Second Grade Teacher; *b:* Martinsburg, WV; *ed:* (BA) Elem Ed/Lang Art, Shepherd Coll 1976; Grad Work WV Univ, Salem Coll; *cr:* Teacher Pleasant View Elem 1976-; *ai:* Sch Advisory Cncl; Morgan Cty Ed Assn, WVEA 1976-; PTA (Reporter 1988-89, Treas 1989-) 1976-; GSA 1977-81; *office:* Pleasant View Elem Sch Rt 3 Box 365 Hedgesville WV 25427

FOX, MICHAEL ALAN, Sixth Grade Teacher; *b:* Danville, PA; *m:* Bonnie S. Manley; *ed:* (BS) Elem Ed, Bloomsburg Univ 1969; Numerous Courses; *cr:* 6th Grade Teacher 1969-79, 4th Grade Teacher 1979-89 New Albany Elem; 6th Grade Teacher Wyalusing Elem 1989-; *ai:* NEA, PSEA 1969-; *office:* Wyalusing Elem Sch RD 4 Box 8 Wyalusing PA 18853

FOX, REGINALD ALAN, Choral Dir/Cmptr Sci Teacher; *b:* Newport News, VA; *ed:* (BA) Fine/Performing Art, Christopher Newport Coll 1983; (MS) Scndry Music Ed, Old Dominion Univ 1988; Math/Cmptr Cert, CNC 1988; Math/Cmptr Endorsement, Star Schls Telecommunications Project Administrative Courses; *cr:* Choral Dir 1983-, Cmptr Sci Teacher 1987- Bruton HS; *ai:* Theater Asst; Band Auxiliary Unit & Sight & Sound Spon; Coord of Choral Music Acts York Cty Public Schls; Cmptr Software Selection Comm; Cultural Awareness Coord; NEA, VA Ed Assn, York Ed Assn, Music Educators Natl Conference, VA Music Educators Assn 1983-; VA Choral Dirs Assn 1988-; VA Alliance for Arts Ed 1989-; Exch Club of Williamsburg Music Dir; 1st Baptist Church Morrison Minister of Music 1971-; Exch Club of Williamsburg Book of Golden Deed Awd 1987-88; TERC Star Schls Cmptr Prgm; York Cty Teacher of Yr Finalist 1988; York Cty Teacher of Yr 1990; Teacher Incentive Grant VA Commission for Arts 1989; Perfect Attendance Awd York Cty Schls 1988-; *office:* Bruton HS 185 Rochambeau Dr Williamsburg VA 23185

FOX, RONALD JOHN, Mathematics Department Chair; *b:* Sioux City, IN; *m:* Ann E. Werthmann; *c:* Ronald T., Michael A.; *ed:* (BAE) Math, Wayne St Coll 1968; (MA) Math, Univ of SD 1972; Various Ed Courses & Wkshps, Univ of CT; *cr:* Math Instr Akron Cmmty Schls 1968-72, Lewis Cntrl Cmmty Schls 1972, IA Western Comm Coll 1989-; *ai:* K-12th Grade Math Comm Chairperson; Lewis Cntrl HS NCA Comm Co-Chairperson; Track Teams High Jump Coach; Lewis Cntrl Ed Assn (Pres, Pres Elect) 1983-84, HS Teacher of Yr 1984; IA Cncl Teachers of Math St Convention Presentor Nom Presidential Awd for Teaching Excl 1985, 1988, 1990, Semi-Finalist 1985-88; Area 13 Selection Comm Educator of Month 1989; Utilize Technology in Classroom Spec St Comm; Named Person Who Made Difference by Coll of St Mary; *office:* Lewis Cntrl Cmmty Schls Hwy 275 Council Bluffs IA 51503

FOX, SHIRLEY MYERS, Third Grade Teacher; *b:* Salinesville, OH; *m:* Walter J. Jr.; *c:* Phillip J., Gary J.; *ed:* (BA) Elem Ed, Akron Univ 1973; (MS) Ed, Kent St 1978; Kent St, Youngstown St, Mt Union Coll, Akron Univ, Ashland Univ; *cr:* Kndgtn Teacher 1973-78, 2nd Grade Teacher 1978-85, 3rd Grade Teacher 1985-86, 2nd Grade Teacher 1986-87, Kndgtn Teacher 1987-88, 3rd Grade Teacher 1988- Beloit Elem; *ai:* Staff & Classified Comm Person; Local Union Building Rep; Curr Developer Lang Art; WBEA, OEA, NEOEA Mem 1973-; Intnl Rdng Assn 1985-; Sweet Adelines Bd Mem 1989-; Alliance Cmmty Concert 1987-; PTO VP; Martha Holden Jennings Scholar 1978-79, Grant 1989-; *office:* Beloit Elem Sch 17926 E 5th St Beloit OH 44609

FOX, SUSAN C., 3rd Grade Teacher; *b:* Syracuse, NY; *m:* Morton I.; *c:* Amy Mc Kean, Rochelle; *ed:* (BA) Elem Ed, Syracuse Univ 1961; *cr:* Permanent Substitute Teacher Sumner Sch 1963-64; Elem Teacher Heman Street Sch 1969-78, Kinne Street Sch 1978-; *ai:* Lang Art Leader; Drama Club; Creative Writing Classes; NYSTA; Womens Amer ORT Literacy Volunteer; Hum Conference Speaker, Ran Wkshps Involving Lang Art & Other Subjects, Led Sch Wkshps in Lang Art & Art; Currular Writing for E Syracuse Minoa Sch System; *office:* Kinne Street Sch Kinne St East Syracuse NY 13057

FOX, SUSAN CREA, Speech/English Teacher; *b:* Grangeville, ID; *m:* Jerome W.; *c:* James W., Katy A.; *ed:* (BS) Ed/Phys Ed/Eng, Univ of ID 1973; (MED) Ed/Sport Psych, Univ of NE Lincoln 1980; *cr:* Phys Ed/His Teacher Post Falls Jr HS 1973-75, Lewiston HS 1975-79, 1980-81; Grad Asst Univ of NE Lincoln 1979-80; Asst Dir Intramural & Campus Rec Univ of ID 1981-82; Basic Skills Ed Instr Cntrl TX Coll 1983; Speech/Eng Teacher Grangeville HS 1986-; *ai:* Amer Alliance of Health Phys Ed & Recreation 1973-82; Natl Intramural Recreation Sports Assn 1981-82; NCTE 1986-; Grad Asst Univ of NE Lincoln 1979-80; *office:* Grangeville HS 910 South D Grangeville ID 83530

FOX, WILLIAM RAYMOND, 5th Grade Teacher; *b:* Syracuse, NY; *ed:* (BS) Elem Ed, 1976, Permanent Cert Elem Ed/Soc Stud, 1979 Cortland St; *cr:* Elem Teacher La Fayette Cntrl Sch 1976-; *ai:* Bsktbl Coach 7th/8th Grade Boys Modified 1977-88 & 11th/12th Grade Var Girls 1980.

FOXWELL, BETSY M., 7th/8th Grade Teacher; *b:* Chicago, IL; *m:* Warren Roger; *ed:* (BA) Eng, Univ of WI Madison 1960; *cr:* Teacher CPS 1961-; *ai:* Sch Newspaper Spon; Natl Jr Honor Society; FTA Literary Magazine; Chicago Metro His Fair FPSB Coach; NCTE; IL Teacher of Eng; IL Assn of Outlook; Natl Cncl Teachers of Soc Stud; Park Ridge Youth Campus Bd Mem 1987; Kate Maremont Awd; Chicago Fnd Ed Grants; *office:* De Witt Clinton Sch 6110 N Fairfield Chicago IL 60659

FOXWORTHY, BECKY J., French Teacher; *b:* Indianapolis, IN; *ed:* (BA) Fr, 1981, (MA) Fr/Linguistics, 1984 Ball St Univ; (EDS) Gifted Ed, Nova Univ 1988; *cr:* Substitute Teacher Indianapolis Public Schls 1979-83; Eng/Fr Teacher Imperial Point Preparatory Sch 1984-85, Atlantic Cmmty HS 1985-; *ai:* Sr Class Spon 1989-; Soc Comm; Intnl Baccalaurate; FL Foreign Lang Assn 1985-; FL Assn for Gifted 1986-; Intnl Stu Exch Prgm Stu Universite de Franche Comte, Besancon France 1981-82; Eng Speaking Union Schlsp; Univ of London, Oxford Univ 1988; *office:* Atlantic Cmmty HS 2501 Seacrest Blvd Delray Beach FL 33444

FOXWORTHY, DEANNA BARNABO, Fifth Grade Teacher; *b:* Detroit, MI; *m:* Harley; *c:* Richard Smith, Christopher Smith, Jennifer Smith, Erica Smith; *ed:* (BFA) Art, Wayne St Univ 1961; (MA) Scndry Ed, W WV Univ 1988; Cert Wayne St Univ; Sci Cert Glenville St Coll; *cr:* 7th-12th Grade Art Teacher Howell Public Schls 1968-74; Sci/Soc Stud Teacher 1981-85, 2nd Grade Teacher 1985-88, 5th Grade Teacher 1988- Troy Elem; *ai:* Teach Summer Classes Spec Prgm Glenville St Coll; Childrens Coll Sci Classes; Glenville St Coll EPPAC Comm; Intnl Assn for Solar Energy Ed 1990; Photography Awd Honorable Mention Photographers Forum; *office:* Troy Elem Sch Gen Del Troy WV 26443

FOY, ELEANOR DOLTON, 2nd Grade Teacher; *b:* Trenton, NJ; *m:* Donald J. Jr.; *c:* Donald III, Terry Foy Mc Carthy, Brien D.; *ed:* (BA) Primary/Elem Ed, Trenton St Coll 1944; Painting/Drawing, Columbia Univ 1945-46; Studio Study, Princeton NJ Art Assn 1977-80; Painting, Mercer Cty Comm Coll 1980; *cr:* Teacher Trenton Public Schls 1944-47, Robinson Sch 1963-; *ai:* Sch Helper Gifted & Talented; Robinson Sch Rep Governors Teacher Recognition Prgm 1988; Morrisville Trenton Art Group, Princeton Art Assn (Mem, Exhibitor) 1977-80; NJ Story Tellers League 1989-; Hamilton Township Historic Society (Secy, Mayors Comm Treas 1976-; NJ Cultural Affairs Hamilton Township Advisory Comm 1988-; His Grant 1985-86; Travel Articles Published; His Hamilton Township Article Published; Poem & Short Article Published; 1st, 2nd Prizes Painting Exhibits; *office:* Robinson Elem Sch Gropp Ave Trenton NJ 08610

FOY, JAN MILLER, Fourth Grade Teacher; *b:* Tiffin, OH; *m:* Kenneth B.; *c:* Katherine L.; *ed:* (BA) Elem Ed, OH Wesleyan Univ 1977; (MA) Ed/Rdng, Heidelberg Coll 1989; *cr:* Teacher Tiffin City Schls 1977-; *ai:* Various Textbook Selection Comm; Accompanist for Sch Choir; Humane Society Bd Mem 1982-; Eastern Star Officer; Panhellenic Society (Pres) 1977-; Church Organist 1977-; Geneology Society Mem 1983-; YMCA Mem 1983-; *office:* C A Krout Sch Glenn St Tiffin OH 44883

FRADY, TONDA MURR, 8th Grade US History Teacher; *b:* Fredericksburg, TX; *m:* Bobby T.; *ed:* (BS) Elem Ed/His, Sul Ross St Univ 1973; Cooperative Learning Trng, US Constitution & Law, Ysleta Sch Dist Sponsored Wkshps; *cr:* 6th Grade Teacher 1973-77, 4th Grade Teacher 1977-81, 6th Grade Teacher 1981-85 Sageland Elem; 8th Grade Teacher Eastwood Mid Sch 1985-; *ai:* His Club Spon; His Dept Chairperson; Advisory Comm His Tutor; Steering Comm YISD Bicentennial & Sesquicentennial; Assn of TX Prof Educators (Pres, VP, Treas, St Resolutions Comm 1989-) 1980-; El Paso Cncl for Soc Stud (Secy, VP) 1989-; Valley Forge Freedom Fnd Ed Liasion 1990; Kappa Kappa Iota (Pres, VP) 1983, 1985; PTA Secy 1986, 1987; Red Cross Volunteer 1989-; Grace Meth Church Admin Bd 1988-; Teacher of Yr 1976, 1984, 1989; Finalist in Top Ten 1984; George Washington Medal of Honor Valley Forge Freedom Fnd 1989; Summerlee Commission TX His; Nom TX Hum Awd & Scndry Soc Stud Teacher of Yr; Whos Who in TX Ed 1975; *home:* 1913 Anise El Paso TX 79935

FRAELICH, DONNA PHYLLIPS, 5th Grade/8th Grade Reading; *b:* Willard, OH; *c:* Karin, Michael, Michelle, Kenneth; *ed:* (BA) Elem Ed, Bowling Green St Univ 1976; *cr:* 1st Grade Teacher; Substitute Teacher, 5th Grade Teacher Western Reserve Schls; *ai:* 7th/8th Grade Girls Bsktbl & HS Track Coach; Chrldng Adv; OEA, NEA, WRTA Building Rep 1976-; Beta Sigma Phi 1966-86; 4-H Adv; Summer Track & Sftbl Coach; Friends of Library Treas; *office:* Western Reserve Mid Sch 3841 State Rt 20 Collins OH 44826

FRAGETTA, FRANK ANTHONY, III, Fifth Grade Teacher; *b:* Utica, NY; *m:* Laura Rachel Desidero; *c:* Sundy, Adam, Corby; *ed:* (BS) Elem Ed, SUC Geneseo 1970; (MS) Elem Ed, SUC Cortland 1975; *cr:* 5th Grade Teacher New York Mills 1971-; *ai:* Teacher Fellowship PTA NY St 1973; *home:* Box 69 Middle Rd Remsen NY 13438

FRAGOLA, ANTHONY DONALD, Biology-Chemistry Teacher; *b:* Hamden, CT; *m:* Carol Ann Rostkowski; *c:* Mark V., Lisa G. Waterbury, Karen; *ed:* (AA) Sci, Mt San Antonio Coll 1955; (BS) Pharmacy, Univ of CT 1959; (MS) Sci, S CT St Univ 1968; NSF Grants Yale Univ, Fairfield Univ, Cntrl CT St Coll, Bowdoin Coll, S CT St Univ; *cr:* Pharmacist Ligget Drug Chain 1960, Yale New Haven Hospital 1961; Bio/Chem Teacher The Morgan Sch 1962-; *ai:* Ftbl Coach The Morgan Sch 1974-87; Offensive Coord 1987; St Championship Team; CT Pharmaceutical Assn, CT Ed Assn, NEA, Clinton Ed Assn 1990; Pharmacy Lectures Civic Groups; NABT an Outstanding Bio Teacher CT 1971; Ed Assn of Clinton (Pres, VP); *office:* The Morgan Sch Rt 81 Clinton CT 06413

FRAHM, KRISTI, English Teacher; *b:* Harvey, ND; *m:* Donn E.; *c:* Whitney; *ed:* (BS) Eng, Valley City St Univ 1980; *cr:* Eng Teacher/Librarian Regent Public Sch 1980-82; Substitute Teacher Carrington & New Rockford & Sheyenne Public Schls 1982-84; Eng Teacher Carrington HS 1984-; *ai:* Resource Team & Sch Improvement Comm; Dir One-Act Play for Competition; ND Ed Assn 1980-; ND Teachers of Eng 1988-; Church Circle (Secy, Treas) 1987-89; Ladies Golf Club Treas 1988-89; Region 5 Play Dir of Yr 1989; *office:* Carrington HS 100 3rd Ave S Carrington ND 58421

FRAHM, LESLIE EDWARD, 7th Grade Math Teacher; *b:* Manning, IA; *m:* Libby Blackley; *c:* Lindsay D., Leslie A.; *ed:* (BA) Bus/Ec, Belmont Abbey Coll 1970; Certificate Ed, Pembroke St Univ 1975; (MA) Math Ed, NC St Univ 1986; Cmptr Sch, US Army Ft Benjamin Harrison 1971-74; *cr:* US Army Data Analyst MOS 74C40 1971-74; Purchasing Agent Raeford Turkey Farms 1974-75; Dir of Extended Day 1975-, Math Teacher 1975-76 Hoke Cty Schls; Math Teacher/Coach Wake Cty Schls 1976-; *ai:* Girls Bkstbl Coach; *home:* 5932 Crepe Myrtle Ct Raleigh NC 27609

FRAID, COLETTE NELSON, 7th Grade English Teacher; *b:* Denver, CO; *m:* Rod; *ed:* (BA) Eng, Carroll Coll 1982; MS Cmmty Counseling, Univ Of WI Whitewater 1992; AODA Trng; *cr:* Eng Teacher Central Mid Sch 1982-; *ai:* Sch Newspaper Adv; Delta Kappa Gamma 1986-; *office:* Central Mid Sch 400 N Grand Ave Waukesha WI 53186

FRALEY, BETTY NEWMAN, Business Education Chairperson; *b:* Hillsboro, TN; *m:* George W.; *c:* Beri, Beth; *ed:* (BS) Bus Ed, Mid TN St Univ 1955; (MED) Admin/Supervision, TN St Univ 1982; *cr:* Bus Ed Teacher Whitwell HS 1955-57; 7th-8th Grade Teacher East Jr HS 1957-60; Bus Ed Teacher Franklin Cty HS 1969-; *ai:* Franklin Cty Drug Prgm Coord; Peer Counseling Group for Drugfree Youth Stu Volunteers Spon; NEA; Franklin Cty Ed Assn Treas 1980-82; TN Bus Ed Assn, NBEA, TN Ed Assn; Franklin Cty Democratic Exec Comm Secy 1980-89; Level III Career Ladder Educator; *home:* Rt 2 Box 2726 Winchester TN 37398

FRALEY, CHARLES LEE, Psych Teacher/Athletic Dir; *b:* Richmond, VA; *m:* Peggy Ferrell; *c:* Angela; *ed:* (BA) Psych, Randolph-Macon Coll 1979; Working Towards Masters Guidance & Counseling, Radford Univ; *cr:* Psych Teacher/Athletic Dir Narrows HS 1979-; *ai:* Head Var Ftbl & Jr Var Bsktbl Coach; Boys Monogram Spon; VA HS Coaches Assn 1979-, Mountain Empire Dist Coach of Yr 1988, 1989; Weightroom Workers (Secy, Treas) 1989; Narrows HS Teacher of Yr 1981, 1983.

FRALEY, JUDY ROBERSON, Grammar Rules Teacher; *b:* Tiptonville, TN; *m:* Mike; *c:* Shane; *ed:* (BS) Soc Stud/Scndry Ed, 1969, (BS) Eng/Sncdry Ed, 1983 Univ of TN Martin; *cr:* 7th/8th Grade Grammar Rules Teacher Lake Cty Jr HS 1970-; *ai:* Teachers Study Cncl St Level Research Comm; Lake Cty Jr HS Stu & Adventure Class Spon; Delta Kappa Gamma 1988; TEA, Lake Cty Ed Assn; Creative Teaching Mini-Grant; TN St Dept of Ed Self-Esteem Acts Presenter 1989; *office:* Lake Cty Jr HS 200 College St Ridgely TN 38080

FRALICK, MARK D., 8th Grade History Teacher; *ed:* (BS) His, N MI Univ 1974; (MS) Admin, Cntrl MI Univ 1980; *cr:* Teacher Lewis Cass Intermediate Sch Dist 1975, Petoskey Public Schls 1975-; *ai:* 9th Grade Ftbl & 7th-8th Grade Track Coach; Little League (Coach, Officer) 1987-; *office:* Petoskey Mid Sch 601 Howard Petoskey MI 49770

FRAME, JANE THUMA, Third Grade Teacher; *b:* Jamestown, OH; *m:* Arthur Edwin; *c:* Arthur Jr., Catherine Hauser, Peter; *ed:* (BS) Bio, Denison Univ 1954; Ed Courses, Wright St Univ & OH Northern Univ; Working Towards Masters Univ of Dayton; *cr:* 3rd Grade Teacher Wapakoneta City Schls 1969-; *home:* Rt 2 Box 7 Wapakoneta OH 45895

FRANCE, NATALIE O. S., 8th Grade Soc Stud Teacher; *b:* Cheraw, SC; *m:* Aaron Mc Kenneth; *ed:* (BA) Intermediate Ed, Livingstone Coll 1978; Ed Admin, Univ of S MS, Hattiesburg & Univ of NC Greensboro; Guidance Counseling, Akron Univ; *cr:* 1st/2nd Grade Teacher Southfork Elem 1978-79; 5th/6th Grade Teacher Lowrance Intermediate 1979-84; 8th Grade Teacher Kirk Mid Sch 1984-; *ai:* Travel Club Co-Spon; Sch Coord Project Bus Jr Achievement; OH Mid Sch Assn 1987-; Alpha Kappa Alpha (Asst Chairperson, Heritage Comm) 1988-; Bronze Leadership Awd Jr Achievment Incorporated 1989; Teacher of Yr Lowrance Intermediate Sch 1983-84; *office:* Kirk Mid Sch 15305 Terr Rd East Cleveland OH 44112

FRANCE, ROBERT CHARLES, World History/Sports Medicine; *b:* Vancouver, WA; *m:* Sharon K. Wallinder;; *c:* Brian, Allison; *ed:* (BA) Phys Ed/Health, Pacific Lutheran Univ 1976; Emergency Med Tech 1984; Cert Athletic Trainer 1989; Spec Ed & Sci-Med; *cr:* Teacher/Coach Coupeville HS 1976-84; Teacher/Athletic Trainer/Coach Federal Way HS 1984-; *ai:* Athletic Trainer; Head Boys Track Coach; Stu Trainer Adv; WA Coaches Assn 1976-; Natl Coaches Assn 1976-; Amer Ath Trainers Assn 1989-; *office:* Federal Way H S 39611 16th Ave S Federal WA 98003

FRANCE, ROBERTA PAYNE, 4th Grade Teacher; *b:* Canonsburg, PA; *m:* Osborne Davis; *c:* Daniel, Candace Raskin, Linda S. Carter; *ed:* (BS) Elem Ed, OH Univ 1968; (MA) Curr/Supvr, WV Univ 1975; Elem Classroom Teacher Indian Creek & Wintersville Elem 1976-; *ai:* NEA, OEA, ICEA; Beta Sigma Phi Pres 1952-62, Girl of Yr 1960; Steub Womans Club 1988-; Natl Sci Fnd; Author of Gifted Materials; Indian Creek Teacher of Yr 1987.

FRANCIS, JAMES MICHAEL, History Teacher; *b:* Cincinnati, OH; *m:* Karen Leibert; *c:* Kathleen; *ed:* (BA) His, AZ St Univ 1970; (MA) His, Univ of BC 1978; *cr:* His Teacher Shaw HS 1972-75; Jr HS His Teacher 1977-88, Sr HS His Teacher 1988-Idaho Falls Sch Dist 91; *ai:* Idaho Falls HS Outdoor Club Adv & Dir; Shaw HS Honors His Teacher 1972-75; NEA 1979-; Idaho Falls Rotary Club Honary Membership 1988-: Article Published 1981; Idaho Falls Sch Dist 91 Teacher of Yr 1985; Amer Bar Assn Liberty Bell Awd 1988; ID Natl Endowment for Hum Teacher-Scholar 1989-; *home:* 2810 Westmoreland Dr Idaho Falls ID 83402

FRANCIS, JANET KAY RINO, Home Economics Teacher; *b:* Dallas, TX; *m:* Donald Keith; *c:* Jeff, Donna, Scott; *ed:* (BS) Home Ec Ed, N TX St Univ 1967; (MS) Home Ec Ed, E TX St Univ 1985; *cr:* Cons Home Ec Teacher Sam Rayburn Ind Sch Dist 1979, Savoy Ind Sch Dist 1979-; *ai:* 8th Grade Class Spon; FHA Adv; Prgm Coord Gifted & Talented; At-Risk Stu; UIL Academic Competition; Savoy Classroom Teachers Assn (Secy 1988-, Schlsp Comm); TCTA 1988-; VHETAT 1983-; Delta Kappa Gamma, Grayson Cty Home Ec 1985-89.

FRANCIS, MARGARET ALEXANDER, Fifth Grade Teacher; *b:* Bristol, VA; *w:* Edward V. (dec); *c:* Judith F. Parsons; *ed:* (A) Math, VA Intermont 1956; (BS) His, East TN St Univ 1968; (MA) Ed, Union Coll 1979; *cr:* Teacher Anderson Elem 1968-; *ai:* Comm-Prin Adv/Vision/Policy/Stu at Risk/Soc Stud Txtbk; NEA; TEA; Briston TN Ed Assn Treas 1983-84; Pilot Club of Bristol (Pres 1975-77/1988-89 & Treas, 1983-84); United TN Career Ladder Level I; *office:* Anderson Elem Sch 901 9th St Bristol TN 37620

FRANCIS, MARGARET THORNTON, First Grade Teacher; *b:* Killarney, WV; *m:* Harry Mc Donald;; *c:* Margaret E., Rebecca J.; *ed:* Grad Work Univ of VA; *cr:* 2nd Grade Teacher Stoco Elem 1951-55; 1st/2nd Grade Combination Teacher Glen Lyn Elem 1955-59; 2nd Grade Teacher Margaret Beeks Elem 1963-65, Enderly Heights Elem 1967-69; Kndgtn Ed Teacher S Seminary Coll 1969-70; 1st Grade Teacher Marion Primary 1977-; *ai:* NEA 1951-; VA Ed Assn 1955-; Smyth Cty Ed Assn 1977-, 25 Yr Pin 1989, Service Awd 1989; PTO (Treas 1977-79) 1977-; Amer Cancer Society Bd Mem 1985-; Smyth Cty Chamber of Commerce 1970-; Sherwood Anderson Assn 1976-; Holston Hills Cntry Club Ladies Golf Silver Bowl Handicap Champion 1987; Article Published; Supervising Teacher Radford Univ, Emory & Henry Coll; *home:* 1281 Prater Ln Marion VA 24354

FRANCIS, MARIE TERRY, Retired-Third Grade Teacher; *b:* Hopkinsville, KY; *w:* George Jr. (dec); *c:* Delma J., George T.; *ed:* (BA) Eng/Elem Ed KY St Univ 1940; Soc Work, Atlanta Univ; *cr:* Teacher Waynesboro HS, Davistown Elem, Mason Sch, Paint Lick Elem, Lancaster Elem; *ai:* Lancaster PTA Secy; KY Ed Assn, Cntrl KY Ed Assn 151-82; Retired Teachers Assn 1982-; Garrard Cty Ed Assn 1951-82; Elected City Cncl 1983; Ex Mem Lancaster Womans Club, Lancaster Lib Bd.

FRANCIS, REBECCA JANE, Art Department Chair; *b:* Alexandria, VA; *ed:* (BS) Art Ed, James Madison Univ 1984; Recert Classes; *cr:* Art Teacher Plaza Jr HS 1984-; *ai:* Cty Wide Youth Art Month Co-Chairperson 1989; Art Club Spon; Chrldr C oach Awd Best Jr HS Squad NCA Camp 1987; Yrbk Spon 1987-88; Spirit Club Spon; Art Dept Chairperson; PTSA 1984-; NAEA 1983-85, 1989-; Norfolk Jaycees 1989-; Virginia Beach United Meth Church 1985-; Plaza Jr HS Teacher of Yr 1991; VA Commission for Art Grant Awd 1989; St Art Ed Conference Presenter 1988; *office:* Plaza Jr HS 3080 S Lynnhaven Rd Virginia Beach VA 23452

FRANCIS, RICHARD T., Specialist of Gifted Education; *b:* Roxbury, MA; *m:* Agnes Foster; *c:* Richard, Gina; *ed:* (BA) Suffolk Univ 1958; Springfield Coll; Westfield St Coll; Harvard Univ; *cr:* Day Sch Dir Cooper Cmmty Center 1955; 6th Grade Teacher 1958-87; Prin East Longmeadow Public Schls 1964-66; Specialist of Gifted Students 1987-.

FRANCISCO, LESLIE STUART, Earth Science Teacher; *b:* St Clair, MI; *m:* Deborah G. Kauhola; *c:* Jamie; *ed:* (BS) Bio, Cntrl MI Univ 1970; (MAED) Counseling, N MI Univ 1980; *cr:* Chem Teacher Rapid River HS 1970-71; 71P20 US Army RVN 1971-72; Cnslr/Teacher Richmond Cmmty Schls 1974-; *ai:* Sci Olympiad & Vlybl Coach; *home:* 5709 Pt Tremble Algonac MI 48001

FRANCKE, DOROTHY J. DINKELMEYER, Substitute Teacher; *b:* Mineola, NY; *m:* Clayton S.; *c:* Jeryl A. Cosgrove, Mark, Joyce Gabrus, Karen Woska, Gary; *ed:* (BS) Bus Admin, Hofstra Univ 1948; (MS) Elem Ed/Rdng NY New Paltz 1951; Individualized Prgms in Kndgtn, Helping the Slow Learner, Individualized Rdng, Diagnosis, Evaluation & Testing of Rdng Prgms, Soc Stud in Primary Grades; *cr:* 2nd/4th Grade Teacher N Bellmore Public Schls 1948-50; K-4th Grade Substitute Teacher 1954-66, Title 1 Rdng Teacher 1961-68, K-2nd Grade Teacher 1968-82 Wantagh Elem Sch; K-4th Grade Substitute Teacher Woodlawn Elem Schls 1985-; *ai:* PTA (Exec Bd, Teacher Rep) 1970-82, Life Mem 1982; Wantagh United Teachers Exec Bd 1977-82; Bd of Ed Budget Advisory Comm 1982; Whos Who in Amer Univ & Coll; *home:* 315 Lark Ave Sebring FL 33872

FRANCO, AIDA CORIANO, Fourth Grade Teacher; *b:* E Chicago, IN; *m:* Hector L.; *c:* Reinaldo, Hector L., Araceli; *ed:* (BA) Elem Ed, Inter Amer Univ 1976; (MS) Guidance/Counseling, Univ of Bridgeport 1980; *cr:* 1st Grade Teacher 1976-80, 2nd Grade Teacher 1980-84, 3rd Grade Teacher 1984-88, 4th Grade Teacher 1988- Antilles Elem Sch; *ai:* Grade Level Chairperson; Support Team Mem; Staff Dev Comm Mem; Antilles Consolidated Ed Assn, NEA, Overseas Ed Assn 1976-; Sustained Superior Performance Awd; Career Commitment Awd; *home:* Calle Punta Salinas MA-13 Marina Bahia Catano PR 00632

FRANCO, NANCYE (HODGES), Sixth Grade Teacher; *b:* Alexandria, VA; *m:* Robert Peter; *c:* Shawn, Krista, Kara, Seth, Robbie; *ed:* (BS) Elem Ed, Medaille Coll 1972; Post Grad Stud Suny; Group Process in Classroom; Wkshp Teaching Rdng Elem Sch; *cr:* 1st Grade Teacher St John the Baptist Sch 1968-71; 2nd Grade Teacher River Avenue Elem 1974-77; 6th Grade Teacher Smithtown Chrstn Sch 1985-; *office:* Smithtown Chrstn Sch Higbie Dr Smithtown NY 11787

FRANCZAK, WILLIAM J., English Department Chairman; *b:* Buffalo, NY; *m:* Sandra A.; *c:* Dennis W., Andrew J., Eileen K., Jennifer A., Rebecca A.; *ed:* (BA) Eng, St Bonaventure Univ 1962; (MS) Ed, Buffalo St Coll 1968; *cr:* HS Eng Teacher Holland Cntrl Sch 1962-; *ai:* Girls Jr Var & Boys Modified Soccer Coach; Eng Dept Chm; Holland Teachers Assn VP 1972; Town of Holland (Assessor 1969-74, Justice 1975-78, Supvr 1978-89); *home:* 9391 Savage Rd Holland NY 14080

FRANK, CATHERINE DURFEE, Teacher of Gifted; *b:* Salamanca, NY; *m:* Norton M.; *c:* Norton Jr., Martin, Mary B. Palm; *ed:* (BS) Elem Ed, 1968, (MED) Ed/Gifted, 1981 Wright St Univ; *cr:* 2nd/4th/5th Grade Classroom Teacher 1968-84, Teacher of Gifted 1984- Fairborn City Schls; *ai:* Young Authors Comm; Fairborn Ed Assn (Treas 1975) 1968-; OH Ed Assn, NEA 1968-; OH Assn of Gifted Children 1981-85; Friend of the Fairborn Lib (Pres, Secy) 1975-; Phi Delta Kappa 1981-; Smocking Arts Guild of America 1985-; Martha Holdings Jennings Fnd Teachers Grant Fairborn City Schls; Teacher of Yr 1988; *office:* Fairborn City Schls 306 E Whittier Dr Fairborn OH 45324

FRANK, CORTEZ B., Math Dept Co-Chair/Asst Prof; *b:* Lafayette, LA; *ed:* (BS) Math, 1976, (MED) Admin, 1981 Southern Univ; Post Grad Math, LSU & Southern Univ; Doctoral Studs, LSU; *cr:* Teacher E B R Parish Sch SysteM 1976-80; Instr Southeastern LA Univ 1980-84; Asst Prof Southern Univ Laboratory 1985-; *ai:* Yrbk Adv; Drama Club/Beta Club Spon; Discipline Comm Chm; Task Force Chm; Honors Prgm Comm; Stu Act Comm; Handbook Comm Chm; Mu Alpha Theta Co Spon; Phi Delta Kappa Mem 1987-; Kappa Phi Kappa; Save A Youth Cmnty Organization Founder/Pres 1985- Leadership 1986-86; Deltonian Service Club Founder/Pres 1974-75 Leadership 1975 & 1985; Publications 1981; Article in NASSP 1989; PEERS, PULSE & HESTS; Papers Presentations Topics in Math, Time Management, Making Transitions, Deseq In Ed, The Plight of Black Educators; *home:* 6622 Oak Glen Dr Baton Rouge LA 70812

FRANK, DIANE BURKE, Teacher; *b:* Maquoketa, IA; *m:* Steven R.; *c:* Annette, Timothy; *ed:* (BA) Math, Coll of St Teresa Winona 1975; *cr:* Jr HS Math Teacher St James Sch 1975-76; HS Math Teacher Marquette Sch Inc 1976-79; Jr HS Math Teacher Mt Pleasant Cmmty Sch 1979-80; HS Math Teacher Glidden-Ralston Cmmty Sch 1980-81, St Marys HS 1981-89; *ai:* IA Cncl of Teachers of Math; *home:* 1212 N Oneida Storm Lake IA 50588

FRANK, DONALD E., Guidance Counselor; *b:* Johnsonburg, PA; *c:* Kimberly, Donald J., Kerry, Kathy, Krista; *ed:* (BS) Eng/Soc Stud, Clarion Univ 1962; Working Towards Masters St Bonaventure; *cr:* Eng Teacher 1962-89, Guidance Cnslr 1989- Johnsonburg Area HS; *ai:* Ftbl & Wrestling Coach; PSEA, NEA; JEA Pres 1967-68; *office:* Johnsonburg Area HS Elk Ave Johnsonburg PA 15845

FRANK, HELEN C., Mathematics Teacher; *b:* Bronx, NY; *m:* Gary E.; *c:* Ronni, Robert; *ed:* (BA) Math, Queens Coll 1966; Grad Stud; *cr:* Teacher Lake Lehman Jr HS 1980-; *ai:* Jr HS Math Dept Co-Chm; *office:* Lake Lehman Jr HS Lehman PA 18627

FRANK, JULIA DIANE, Health/Physical Ed Teacher; *b:* Indianapolis, IN; *ed:* (BS) Phys Ed, Skidmore Coll 1975; (MS) Scndry Ed, Univ of MO 1981; *cr:* Phys Ed Teacher Southwest HS 1975-80; Phys Ed Teacher Mary Inst 1980-84; Health/Phys Ed Teacher Kirkwood HS 1984-; *ai:* Var Field Hockey; Frosh Class Spon; 9th Grade Class Adv; MO Assn of Health, Phys Ed, Recreation & Dance Mem; Girls Field Hockey Coach of Yr 1979, 1980; *office:* Kirkwood HS 801 W Essex Kirkwood MO 63122

FRANK, NANCY TAYLOR, Social Studies Teacher; *b:* Springfield, OH; *c:* Jessica, Alison; *ed:* (BA) His/Poly Sci, Bellarmine Coll 1978; Univ Louisville Sch of Law & Univ of S FL Grad Sch; *cr:* Adjunct Professor Manatee Comm Coll 1983-84; Dean of Admissions/Prin/Teacher Prew Preparatory Sch 1984-86; Teacher Pine View Sch for Gifted 1986-; *ai:* Class, Key Club, Young Republicans Club Spon; Faculty Liaison to Parent-Teacher Bd; Jr League 1976-; Amer Civil Liberties Union Bd of Dir 1987-88; Brownie Scout Leader Troop #299 1982-84; Venice PTA Pres 1982-84; United Way Private Sch Division Chm 1985; David Anchin Sch Improvement Awd Sarasota Cty Sch System 1st Place 1984; Eng Speaking Unions Competition 1st Place for Summer Enrichment Prgm About Australia; *office:* Pine View Sch For Gifted 2525 Tami Sola St Sarasota FL 34237

FRANK, NEIL HOWARD, Spanish Teacher/Dept Chair; *b:* Cincinnati, OH; *m:* Marlene Schmidt; *ed:* (BA) Span/His, Capital Univ 1979; (MA) Bi-ling Ed, OH St Univ 1982; *cr:* Span Teacher Franklin HS 1979-81, Reynoldsburg HS 1982-83, Turpin HS 1983-; *ai:* Intnl Club Adv; OH Foreign Lang Assn, NEA 1979-; Published Classroom Game Ideas in OH Foreign Lang Assn Journal 1989; OFLA Conference Session on Ideas 1988; Local Inservice on Ideas 1990; *office:* Turpin HS 2650 Bartels Rd Cincinnati OH 45244

FRANK, ROSEMARIE ELIZABETH, Kindergarten Teacher; *b:* Jersey City, NJ; *m:* Steven; *c:* Brandon, Kelly, Kristen; *ed:* (BA) Elem Ed, Trenton St Coll 1970; *cr:* 1st/2nd/4th Grade Teacher 1970-, Kndgtn Teacher 1987- Ella G Clarke Sch; *ai:* Lakewood Ed Assn (Jr Rep 1988-) 1970-; NJ Ed Assn 1970-; Cmmty Relations Comm 1990; *office:* Ella G Clarke Sch Marietta Ave Lakewood NJ 08701

FRANK, STEPHEN EUGENE, 9th Grade Math Teacher; *b:* Altoona, PA; *m:* Janice Stofka; *c:* Kristin, Scott; *ed:* (BS) Math/Ed, IN Univ of PA 1970; Working Towards Masters & Prin Cert in Ed Admin, Penn St; *cr:* Math Teacher T Roosevelt Jr HS 1970-83; Officer US Army 1983-86; Math Teacher T Roosevelt Jr HS 1986-; *ai:* HS Chess Club Co-Adv; Mem Dist Comm of Altoona Profs; NEA, PSEA, AAEA Chm of Spec Services 1987-; Reserve Officers Assn 1970-; Active US Army Reserve Officer-Major TNG Officer 1971-, Many Decorations; *office:* Theodore Roosevelt Jr HS 6th Ave & 15th St Altoona PA 16602

FRANK, VIRGINIA BERKEY, Third Grade Teacher; *b:* Sterling, CO; *m:* Robert L.; *c:* Kristin J., David R.; *ed:* (BS) Elem Ed, Univ of CO 1971; Elements of Instruction, Gifted & Talented, Cmptrs; *cr:* Kndgtn Teacher Wheatridge Pre-Sch & Kndgtn 1972-74; 4th-6th Grade Sci/Eng Teacher Iliff/Caliche Elem 1981-83; 5th Grade Teacher 1983-86, 3rd Grade Teacher 1986-Franklin Elem; *ai:* Franklin Elem Dir of Gifted & Talented Ed; Textbook Selection Curr & Class Size Comm; NEA, CEA, SPEA 1981-; RE-1 Valley Cert of Appreciation Gifted & Talented Commitment 1988-; Excl in Schlsp Citation Univ of CO.

FRANKEL, CAROLE, Mathematics Teacher; *b:* Chicago, IL; *m:* Barry; *c:* Scott, Steve; *ed:* (BSPE) Phys Ed/Math, De Paul Univ 1969; (MED) Math, Northeastern Univ 1971; AZ St Univ; Cmptr Programming & Lang, Univ Ottawa; *cr:* Math/Phys Ed Teacher St Pats HS 1968-69; Phys Ed Teacher Hatch & Mann Elem 1969-71; Phys Ed/Math Teacher Rhodes Jr HS, Powell Jr HS 1976-81; Public Relations Dir Valley Big Brothers/Big Sisters 1982-86; Math Teacher Mesa HS 1986-; *ai:* Optimalearning Core Team Mem; NCTM 1989-; NEA, AZ Ed Assn 1986-; AZ Assn Teachers of Math 1989-; Valley Big Brothers/Big Sisters Bd Mem 1986-87; *office:* Mesa HS 1630 Southern Ave Mesa AZ 85204

FRANKEL, YITZCHOK DAVID, Jewish Studies Teacher; *b:* New York, NY; *m:* Renee Bomstein; *c:* Batya, Moshe, Esther, Shoshana, Avi, Shimon, Elisheva, Mordechai, Shmuel, Ashira; *ed:* (BA) Ec/Math, Brooklyn Coll & Queens Coll 1969; Grad Stud Mesivtha Tifereth Jerusalem Rabbinical Seminary 1970, 1974, Brith Mohel Sch Mt Sinai Hospital 1973; *cr:* Hebrew Stud Instr Torah Acad Greater Philadelphia 1974-77, Yeshiva Univ HS 1977-78,. Torah Acad for Girls 1978-79, Yeshiva Dvar Yerushalayim 1979-80, Hebrew Acad of Five Towns & Rockaway 1980-85, Hebrew Acad Nassau Cty 1985-; *ai:* S Shore Vaad Hakasruth Founding Mem 1989-; Halachic & Non-Halachic Articles Published 1972-75, 1989; *home:* 256 E Walnut St Long Beach NY 11561

FRANKEN, JOLEEN SCHNEIDER, First Grade Teacher; *b:* Keokuk, IA; *m:* Joel D.; *ed:* (BS) Elem Ed, Greenville Coll 1968; (MS) Elem Teaching, NW MO Univ 1986; Sci Ed; *cr:* 1st Grade Teacher Sutherland Comm Schls 1968-70, Spencer Comm Schls 1970-75; 3rd/4th Grade Teacher 1975-77, 1st Grade Teacher 1977 Denison Comm Schls; *ai:* Thinking Skills Comm; Phase III Supplemental Pay Comm; Tabs Comm; Dev Activities Proj Team Leader; AAUW Mem 1970-75 & 1989-; Whos Who of Young Women 1975; Denison Ed Assn 1975-; Service Awd 1984; NEA 1968-; IA St Ed Assn Executive Bd 1987-; Connie Belin Fellowship on Talented & Gifted-Summer 1990; IA Democratic Party-Cty Chairperson; *home:* 608 N Main St Denison IA 51442

FRANKENFIELD, ROBERT BARRY, 4th Grade/Head Teacher; *b:* Easton, PA; *m:* Judy Lee Basta; *c:* Andrea, Jennifer, Amanda; *ed:* (BA) Elem Ed, Morehead St Univ 1974; *cr:* 4th Grade Teacher Williams Township Elem Sch 1974-80; 5th-7th Grade Rdng/Sci Teacher Philip Lauer Mid Sch 1980-83; 4th Grade Teacher 1983-87, 4th Grade/Head Teacher 1987- Wilson Boro Elem Sch; *ai:* Boys Head Bsktbl Coach; Asst Athletic Dir; Summer Playground Dir; PTA (2nd VP 1987-) Life Membership 1985; *office:* Wilson Boro Elem Sch 21st & Washington Blvd Easton PA 18042

FRANKINBURGER, PATRICIA JEAN, English Teacher; *b:* Michigan City, IN; *m:* Bruce; *c:* Christine, Adam; *ed:* (BA) Eng, Ball St Univ 1974; Working Towards Masters at IN Univ; Grad Work Numerous Univs; *cr:* Eng/Spec Ed Teacher Fort Wayne Cmmty Schls 1974-77, Wind River Schls 1977-80; Spec Ed/resource Person Lander Valley HS 1980-86; Eng Teacher La Porte HS 1986-; *ai:* IN St Teachers of Eng 1986-; AFT; Natl Cncl Exceptional Children Convention Presenter 1985; *office:* La Porte HS 602 F Street La Porte IN 46350

FRANKLIN, ALFRED BRIAN, Science Teacher; *b:* West Palm Beach, FL; *m:* Sandra M. Roberts; *c:* Lisa, Bryan; *ed:* (AA) General Ed/Phys Ed, Palm Beach Jr Coll 1964; (BS) Phys Ed/General Sci FL St Univ 1967; (ME) Curr & Instr/Phys Ed, FL Atlantic Univ 1969; *cr:* Phys Ed Supervisor Graham EckeS Private HS 1967-68; Sci Teacher/Coach Howell Watkins Jr HS 1969-; *ai:* Spon-Fellowship Christian Athletes; Coach-Jr HS Swim & Dive Teams; Coach-Jr HS Surf Intramurals; Spon-FL Jr Acad Sci Club; Phi Epsilon Kappa Mem 1967-68; Whos Who in Palm Beach Cty 1981; Palm Beach Cty Amer Red Cross Chm Water Safety Comm 1974-86; Distinguished Svc 1986; Finalist Dwyer Awd Competition; Excl Ed Teacher of Yr Palm Beach Cty; *office:* Howell L Watkins Jr H S 9480 Mac Arthur Blvd Palm Beach Gardens FL 33410

FRANKLIN, CAROLYN LOUISE, English/Theatre Arts Teacher; *b:* Kaufman, TX; *m:* Gene; *c:* Jennifer, Stacy, Carrie; *ed:* (BS) Eng/Speech, E TX St Univ 1975; Gifted & Talented, TX Theatre, At Risk Conference; Several Wkshps; *cr:* Teacher Malakoff Jr HS 1975-76, Kemp HS 1976-78, Walden Oak Private Sch 1978-80, Ross Sterling HS 1980-82; *ai:* UIL Coord & Regional Adv; Chrldr Spon; Gifted & Talented Coord; One Act Play Dir; At Risk Cnslr; Frosh Class Spon; NCTE, TX Ed Theatre Assn 1985-; *office:* Slidell HS P O Box 69 Slidell TX 76267

FRANKLIN, ILENE GREENBERG, Science Teacher; *b:* Brooklyn, NY; *m:* William H.; *c:* Cobi A, Elana L.; *ed:* (BA) Bio/Scndry Ed, Fairleigh Dickinson Univ 1970; Working Towards Masters Bio/Nematology, William Paterson Coll 1970-71; *cr:* Sci Teacher Morrison Jr HS 1972-74, Newman Cntrl Cath HS & St Mary Mid Sch 1974-76; Medical Technologist Wallkill Valley General Hospital 1979-81; Sci Teacher Vernon Township HS 1981-; *ai:* Bus Publicity Mgr for Theatre Arts Dept; NJBTA, NJSTA; Beta Sigma Phi Pres 1988-89; Morrison Music Theatre Assn VP 1978-79; AT&T/NJ Bus Industry Sci Ed Consortium Hnrs Research Grant 1988; Leadership Inst for Teachers Modern Bio Rutgers Univ 1988; Nom Presidential Awd Excl Teaching Sci; Nom Catalyst Awd Excl Teaching Chem; Instr Douglass Sci Inst HS Women Sci 1989-; *office:* Vernon Township HS PO Box 800 Vernon NJ 07462

FRANKLIN, JANET M. WAITKUS, Jr HS Science Teacher; *b:* Springfield, IL; *m:* Larry; *c:* Charles; *ed:* (BSED) Zoology, E IL Univ 1969; W IL Univ, Univ of WI, N MI Univ, Univ of HI; *cr:* Sci Teacher Meredosia-Chambersburg Jr/Sr HS 1969-; *ai:* Soc Class Spon; NHS; Peer-Mentor Teacher; NSTA; IL Sci Teachers Assn 1989-; IL Ed Assn, NEA 1969-; Natl Sci Fnd Grants; *office:* Meredosia-Chambersburg HS Rt 104 Meredosia IL 62665

FRANKLIN, JIM WILLIAM, Social Science Teacher; *b:* Dearing, KS; *m:* Carole O.; *ed:* (BS) Soc Sci/Psych, Univ of WY 1959; Univ of Portland/Portland St Univ & Centrl WA Univ; *cr:* Soc Sci/Eng Teacher Rawlins HS 1961-64; Natrona Cty HS 1964-69; Columbia River 1969-; *ai:* Coached HS Ftbl; Spon Key Club; Natl/St/Local Teacher Organizations; ELKS 1961-; Coach of Yr; *office:* Columbia River HS 800 Nw 99th St Vancouver WA 98665

FRANKLIN, JOAN JACOBSON, Kindergarten Teacher; *b:* Herkimer, NY; *m:* Carlton O.; *c:* Jami B., Robert; *ed:* (AAS) Nursery Ed, SUNY Cobleskill 1962; (BA) Early Chldhd, SUNY Brockport 1964; Inservice Trng; *cr:* 2nd Grade Teacher Clinton Elem 1964-65; 1st Grade Teacher 1965-71, Kndgtn Teacher 1971-Westmoreland Cntrl; *ai:* Oneida Cty Kndgtn Teachers; Alumni Asst; PTO; Band Boosters Secy 1988-89; *office:* De Forest Hill Elem Sch Rt 233 Westmoreland NY 13490

FRANKLIN, LINDA EARLY, 6th Grade Science Teacher; *b:* Bridgeport, TX; *m:* Benjamin G.; *c:* Misty C.; *ed:* (BS) His/Bio/Phys Ed, Mary-Hardin Baylor 1969; (MS) Bio, East TN St Univ 1972; Working Towards Elem Sch Cert; *cr:* HS Sci/Phys Ed Teacher Temple HS 1969-70; Grad Asst East TN St Univ 1970-72; 2nd Grade Teacher Happy Valley Elem 1972-75; 6th Grade Sci Teacher DeKalb Mid Sch 1975-; *ai:* Taught Mini-Courses in Boating Safety, Gymnastics & Cmptrs; Just Say No Club, Quiz Bowl Spon; TN Ed Assn, NEA 1975-; NSTA 1982-; Teacher of Yr 1978-88; Hunters Safety TN Wildlife Resources Agency 1988; My Favorite Teacher Channel 5 1989; *home:* PO Box 482 Smithville TN 37166

FRANKLIN, MELONEE SEAL, English Teacher; *b:* Hattiesburg, MS; *m:* Craig; *c:* Alee B., Alexandra N.; *ed:* (BS) Eng, 1984, (MS) Eng Ed, 1989 Univ of S MS; *cr:* 8th Grade Eng/9th Grade Speech Teacher Picayune Jr HS 1984-86; 12th Grade Eng Teacher 1986-87, 9th Grade Eng Teacher 1987-88, 10th Grade Eng Teacher 1989 Picayune Memorial HS; *ai:* NHS Spon; MS Prof Educators 1988-; NCTE; Teacher of Month; *office:* Picayune Memorial HS 800 5th Ave Picayune MS 39466

FRANKLIN, THOMAS LEE, Language Art Teacher; *b:* Louisville, KY; *ed:* (BS) Elem Ed, 1971, (MA) Elem Ed, 1974 W KY Univ; Gifted Ed; *cr:* 1st/2nd Grade Teacher G C Burkhead Elem Sch 1971-76; 7th-9th Grade Teacher Hardin Cntrl Jr HS 1976-83, Radcliff Mid Sch 1983-86; 6th-8th Grade Teacher Hardin Cntrl Mid Sch 1986-; *ai:* Coach News Quiz Team; Spon Beta Club; Stu Cncl Adv; Intnl Rdng Assn, KY Ed Assn, NEA; Glendale Merchants Assns VP; Former Teachers of Radcliff Prgm Chm; *office:* Hardin Central Mid Sch 3040 Leitchfield Rd Cecilia KY 42724

FRANKO, SUSAN MARIE, 7th/8th Grade English Teacher; *b:* Youngstown, OH; *ed:* (BS) Elem Ed, 1972, (MS) Curr, 1977 Youngstown St Univ; *cr:* 5th-8th Grade Teacher St Brendan 1972-76; 6th Grade Teacher Roosevelt 1976-89; 7th-8th Grade Teacher Mc Donald HS 1989-; *office:* Mc Donald HS 600 Iowa Ave Mc Donald OH 44437

FRANKS, CAROLYN DICUS, 4th/5th/6th Grade Teacher; *b:* Hohenwald, TN; *m:* Grayford Lynn; *ed:* (AS) Bus, Columbia St Comm Coll 1974; (BS) Bus Ed, Univ of North AL 1976; (MED) Elem Counseling, Memphis St Univ 1987; Elem Ed Endorsement; *cr:* 4th-8th Grade Rdng Teacher Pinhook Sch 1976-77; 5th Grade Teacher 1978-80, 4th Grade Teacher 1980-88, 4th/5th/6th Grade Teacher 1988- Frank Hughes; *ai:* Soc Stud Textbook, Career Ladder Planning Comm; Wayne Cty Ed Assn, NEA, TN Ed Assn 1976-90; Order of Eastern Star Ruth 1978-79; 1st Baptist Church 1967-; *home:* RR 2 Box 237 Clifton TN 38425

FRANS, CHARLOTTE COX, Lang Art/Soc Stud Teacher; *b:* Mt Airy, NC; *m:* Robert Mitchell; *c:* Kelly A., Robert S.; *ed:* (BS) Elem Ed, Appalachian St Univ 1973; *cr:* 4th-6th Grade Teacher Westfield Elem Sch 1973-87; 8th Grade Teacher Pilot Mountain Elem Sch 1987-; *ai:* Stu Cncl & Journalism Class Spon; NCAE; PTA; *office:* Pilot Mountain Elem Sch 115 W School St Pilot Mountain NC 27041

FRANSEN, CHRISTINE IRENE, HS Mathematics Teacher; *b:* Chicago, IL; *ed:* (BS) Math Ed, Univ of IL Chicago 1969; (MS) Math, NE IL Univ 1971; NASA Educators Wkshps Newmast 1985; Fermilab Summer Inst 1989; Numerous Advanced Placement Calculus Conferences; *cr:* Math Teacher Senn Metropolitan Acad 1969-; *ai:* Spon of Orchesis Modern Dance Club; Coach of Acad Olympics Dance Team; Asst to Math Contest Club Spon; Comm to Develop a Coll Curr Prgm; IL Cncl of Teachers of Math 1969-; Natl Cncl of Teachers of Math, Metropolitan Math Club of Chicago 1990; Chicago Teachers Union 1969-; Friends of Fermilab 1989-; NASA Educators 1985-NASA Educators Awd 1985; Kate Maremont Awd 1982; Univ of Chicago Dedicated Teacher Awd 1979, 1982, 1983; Blum-Korler Awd 1989; TeachersManual Teaching Algbra I to Limited Eng Stu; Coll Prep Algebra I Course Univ of IL Chicago; *office:* Senn Metropolitan Acad 5900 N Glenwood Chicago IL 60660

FRANZ, DONALD L., Science Teacher; *b:* Liberal, KS; *m:* Joyce M.; *c:* Kathy, Sharon, Alan; *ed:* (BS) Sci, Bethel Coll 1954; (MED) Sci, Wichita St Univ 1962; *cr:* Teacher Pleasant Valley Schls 1954-64, Wichita Public Schls 1964-; *ai:* NEA 1954-; *office:* Wichita Public Sch 2220 W 29th N Wichita KS 67204

FRANZ, GENEVIEVE MAE VANDER TUIN, 4th Grade Teacher; *b:* Grand Rapids, MI; *m:* Henry Braun; *c:* John Paul; *ed:* (BA) Minors, Calvin Coll 1957; Grad Stud Various Courses Natl Coll; *cr:* Kndgtn/3rd Grade Teacher Highland Chrstn Sch 1957-60; 5th Grade Teacher Clearwater Public Sch 1961-62; 3rd/4th Grade Teacher Timothy Chrstn Sch 1965-; *ai:* Voice Solo Work; Choir Dir; Sci & Bible Comms; Choir Dir; Chrstn Ed Assn; *office:* Timothy Chrstn Grade Sch 188 W Butterfield Rd Elmhurst IL 60126

FRANZ, SUSAN TOLSON, Third Grade Teacher; *b:* Salem, OH; *m:* John A.; *c:* Nathan, Whitney; *ed:* (BA) Spec Ed/Elem Ed, Kent St 1976; Grad Stud Rdng; *cr:* 2nd Grade Teacher Lisbon Exempted Schls 1976-78; 3rd Grade Teacher 1978-81, Spec Ed 1981-88, 3rd Grade Teacher 1988 Wadworth City Schls; *ai:* Lib Comm Chairperson; Handicapped Awareness Week Committeeman; *home:* 9260 Deerfield Dr PO Box 306 Westfield Ctr OH 44251

FRANZER, PATRICIA SEVERT, Math/Computer Teacher; *b:* Coldwater, OH; *m:* Michael; *c:* Neal, Greg, Mark; *ed:* (BS) Scndry Math Ed, 1974, (MS) Curr/Supervision, 1986 Wright St Univ; *cr:* 7th/8th Grade Math/Cmptr Teacher Celina City Schls 1974-; *ai:* Scholastic Team Coach; NCTM, OH Ed Assn, OH Cncl Teachers of Math, NEA, Celina Ed Assn VP 1982-84; Coldwater Academic Promoters Secy 1987-; Alpha Delta Kappa (VP 1987- Pres 1990-92); Martha Holden Jennings Scholar 1989-; *home:* 811 S Parkview Dr Coldwater OH 45828

FRANZETTI, ROBERT JOSEPH, Government Teacher; *b:* Austin, TX; *m:* Maureen Walsh; *c:* Julie M., Michelle J.; *ed:* (BA) His/Government, Univ of TX Austin 1963; (MA) His/Government, SW TX St Univ 1970; *cr:* Teacher Harlendale Jr HS 1965, Travys HS 1965-68, Crockett HS 1968-; *ai:* NHS, Close-UP, Stu Cncl Spon; Aviation Club; Austin Assn of Teachers Pres Outstanding Mem 1979; TX St Teachers Assn, NEA; Austin Cncl of Soc Stud Secy 1988-89; Cty of Austin Historic Landmark Commission 1978-79; Textbook Consultant; Test Writer; Written Numerous Lesson Modules; Austin Teacher of Yr 1983-84; Tracor Teaching Excl Awd 1987; *office:* David Crockett HS 5601 Manchaca Rd Austin TX 78745

FRASER, BRIAN STEPHEN, Eighth Grade Teacher; *b:* Waterbury, CT; *m:* Barbara Ann Place; *c:* Rebecca, Heidi, Heather, Jennifer, Jessica; *ed:* (BA) Ec, Univ of CT 1968; Intensive Prgm Coll Grad Elem Ed; Elem Ed, Cntrl CT St Coll; *cr:* 5th Grade Teacher 1968-71, 7th Grade Teacher 1971-78 Sprague Sch; 8th Grade Teacher North End Mid Sch 1978-; *ai:* Waterbury Curr Advisory Comm; Soc Stud Mid Sch Level Rep; Prin Advisory Cncl; Waterbury Teachers Assn Rep; CT Ed Assn, NEA 1968-; Waterville Cncl Pres 1983-85; *office:* North End Mid Sch 534 Bucks Hill Rd Waterbury CT 06704

FRASER, ELSIE WILLIAMSON, 8th Grade English Teacher; *b:* Junior, WV; *m:* Tom; *c:* Sam, Kenneth, Tom, David, Cathy Faron; *ed:* (BA) Ed, Marshall St Univ 1947; (MA) Ed/Psych, OR St Univ 1964; Post Grad Counseling, Univ of CA Los Angeles 1968; CA Realtor License; Soc Case Worker Almatilla Cty; *cr:* Model Sch Teacher Barbour Cty WV 1939-41; Demonstration Teacher Portland OR 1947-48; Trng Teacher OR Coll of Ed 1948-49; Teacher Pendleton Public Schls 1959-66; Mid Sch Teacher Pasadena CA 1966-; *ai:* Yrbk & Sch Paper Adv; United Teachers of Pasadena Rep 1988-; Pasadena Partners Ed Bd Mem 1985-; CATE Past Mem; NEA; AAUW Mem 1975-; S CA Teachers Eng Wkshp & Seminar Conducter; *office:* Washington Mid Sch 1505 N Marengo St Pasadena CA 91103

FRASER, MADELYN C., Third Grade Teacher; *b:* Burwell, NE; *m:* W. Harvey; *c:* Kristine R. Schuetz, Michael W., Kendra K.; *ed:* (BS) Ed, Peru St Coll 1965; Grad Stud Peru St Coll, Kearney St Coll; *cr:* Kndgtn/Pre-Sch Teacher Norris Public Sch 1968-70; 2nd Grade Teacher Odessa Public Sch 1970-71; 6th Grade Teacher 1984-88, 3rd Grade Teacher 1988- Humboldt Public Sch; *ai:* Humboldt Ed Assn Secy 1989-; NSEA, NEA 1984-; Chamber of Commerce 1971-; Hospital Auxiliary 1980-; Amer Legion Auxiliary 1975-.

FRASER, CYNTHIA ANN (SMITH), Third Grade Teacher; *b:* Gloversville, NY; *m:* Scott A.; *c:* Chad, Kerri; *ed:* (BS) Ed/Sci, NY St Univ Oneonta 1970; *cr:* Kndgtn Teacher Park Terrace Sch 1970-72; Kndgtn Teacher 1972-84, 3rd Grade Teacher 1984-88, 6th Grade Teacher 1988-89, 3rd Grade Teacher 1989- Edinburg Common Sch; *ai:* GSA 1985-87; Cub Scout Den Mother 1982-85; *home:* 7 E Sinclair Rd Northville NY 12134

FRASIER, LINDA MARIE, English/French Teacher; *b:* Medina, NY; *m:* David; *ed:* (BA) La Sorbonne Paris France 1971; (BA) Fr, Houghton Coll 1972; (MS) Teaching Rdng, Univ of Geneseo 1983; *cr:* Fr Teacher Plymouth Intermediate Sch 1973-74; Eng Teacher Letchworth Cntrl Sch 1980, Wellsville Cntrl Sch 1981; 7th-12th Grade Eng/Fr Teacher Fillmore Cntrl Sch 1981-; *ai:* Teachers Assn Treas 1985-86; Baptist Church Sunday Sch Teacher; *home:* 11854 Wiscoy Rd Portageville NY 14536

FRASIER, MARTHA M., Fourth Grade Teacher; *b:* Donalds, SC; *m:* Thomas Leroy; *c:* Beverly S. Green, Kerwin T. Smith; *ed:* (BS) Elem Ed, Allen Univ 1952-56; (MED) Ed, Clemson Univ 1975-76; Elem Music; Recertification A&T Univ, Lander Coll, Univ of SC Columbia; *cr:* 5th/6th Grade Teacher Carver Elem 1956-70; 4th Grade/3rd Grade Sci Teacher 1970-74, 5th-7th Grade Lang Art Teacher 1974-78, 4th Grade Teacher 1978-Donalds Elem; *ai:* Supervising Teacher Erskine Stu Teachers; NEA, SC Ed Assn; Abbeville Ed Assn Mem; Zeta Phi Beta Mem 1960-80; Women Involved in Rural Electricity 1984-; African Meth Church (Mem, Organist, Sunday Sch Teacher, Steward) 1956-; Missionary Society; Abbeville Cty Sch Dist Campus Teacher Incentive Awd 1988; Abbeville Cty Teacher of Yr Finalist 1986; Donalds Elem Appreciation Awd Outstanding Dedication 1987; Erskine Stus Teacher Service Awd 1980-; *home:* Rt 2 Box 455 Donalds SC 29638

FRAZER, ANDREA WOOD, Science Teacher; *b:* Otis AFB, MA; *m:* Kenneth H.; *ed:* (BS) Psych, 1982, (BBA) General Bus/Mangement Systems, 1982 S Meth Univ; Grad Stud Astronomy, Univ of TX Austin; Masters Prgm Astronomy, Univ of AZ 1990-93; *cr:* Earth Sci Teacher Longfellow Mid Sch 1985-86; Astronomy/Sci Teacher Theodore Roosevelt HS 1986-; *ai:* Sr Class Spon; Alamo Regional Acad of Sci & Speech Tournament Judge; Wkshp Presenter Conference for Advancement of Sci Teaching 1989-; Project 2061; Roosevelt HS Stu Motivation Comm Chm 1989; Sci Teachers Assn of TX 1985-; Planetary Society 1987-; Assn of TX Prof Educators 1988-; Zeta Tau Alpha 1979-; Greenpeace 1983-; NSF Grant Univ of AZ Prgm Assist to Lead to Masters Degree in Astronomy; *office:* Roosevelt HS 5110 Walzem Rd San Antonio TX 78218

FRAZER, JEFF CLARK, Government/US History Teacher; *b:* Amarillo, TX; *ed:* Soc Stud, Amarillo Coll 1980-82; (BA) Poly Sci, 1984, (MA) Poly Sci, 1985 Baylor Univ; *cr:* Poly Sci Instr Wayland Baptist Univ 1985-86; Government/His Teacher Caprock HS 1986-; *ai:* Soccer Coach; Gifted & Talented Curr Writing Comm; Faculty Advisory Comm Mem; Use of Space Ed in Classroom Space Camp Awd Winner 1990; *office:* Caprock HS 3001 E 34th Amarillo TX 79103

FRAZIER, ANNA MARIE WELLS, Fifth Grade Teacher; *b:* Louisa, KY; *m:* Donald Richard; *ed:* (BA) Elem Ed, 1970, (MA) Elem Ed, 1977 Morehead St Univ; *cr:* 5th Grade Teacher Louisa Mid Sch 1980-; 6th Grade Teacher Louisa Mid Sch & Louisa Elem 1970-80; *ai:* Safety Patrols; Lawrence Cty Teacher Assn 1970-; Lawrence Cty Organization of Teachers 1985-; KY Ed Assn 1970-; Soil Conservation 1980-, Plaque Outstanding Work 1990; *office:* Louisa Mid Sch Box 567 Louisa KY 41230

FRAZIER, BARBARA LANE (PARKER), Journalism Teacher; *b:* Austin, TX; *m:* Ronald D.; *c:* Scott A. Cooper, Annmari L. Bacon; *ed:* (BA) Journalism, Sam Houston St Univ 1974; *cr:* Legal Asst/Law Office Mgr/Legal Secy 1958-; Journalism Teacher Killeen HS 1976-79; Copy Writer/Acting Copy Chief Unicover Incorporated 1979-81; Advertising Production Dir Stewart & Stevenson Intnl 1982-85; Journalism Teacher Mc Cullough HS 1988-; *ai:* HS Newspaper, Yrbk, Photography Adv; Pour le Merite for Excl Awd 1980; Articles Published; *office:* Mc Cullough HS 3800 S Panther Creek Dr The Woodlands TX 77380

FRAZIER, ETTA BROWN, Science Teacher; *b:* Beaumont, TX; *m:* Jeff; *c:* Jalaine R., Jermaine R.; *ed:* (BS) Home Ec, Prairie View A&M Univ 1977; (MS) Prof Services Home Ec, Cntrl St Univ 1982; Cert Skills for Adolescence; Say No To Drugs & Yes To Life; *cr:* Home Ec Teacher Moore Schls 1980-83, Grant HS 1984-85; Sci Teacher Webster Mid 1985-; *ai:* Sci Fair Curr Chairperson; AFT Building Rep 1986-; OK Sci Teachers Assn; *office:* Webster Mid Sch 6708 S Santa Fe Oklahoma City OK 73179

FRAZIER, GERRY LEWIS, Physical Education Teacher; *b:* Trenton, NJ; *m:* Pamela Joanne Panizzi; *c:* Wesley, Shawn, Tricia; *ed:* (BA) Health/Phys Ed, Hope Coll 1976; (MED) Health Ed, Trenton St Coll 1980; PA St & Bloomsburg St Univ; *cr:* Phys Ed Teacher Belmont Hills Elem Sch 1976-; *ai:* Safety Coord; Recreation Supvr; NEA, PA St Ed Assn 1976-; Bensalem Township Ed Assn Rep at Large 1976-; *office:* Belmont Hills Elem Sch 5000 Neshaminy Blvd Bensalem PA 19020

FRAZIER, JANET FRANCES LYNCH, Retired Kindergarten Teacher; *b:* Memphis, TN; *m:* Samuel Jefferson Jr.; *c:* Samuel J. III, Janet Frazier Payne, Judy Frazier Brown; *ed:* (BA) Eng/Soc Stud Ed, Chrstn Brothers Coll 1942; Grad Work KS St Univ, Columbia Univ, AZ St Univ, Univ of AZ, Grand Canyon Univ; *cr:* 2nd Grade Teacher Peabody Sch 1942-45; Pre-Sch Teacher Springfield MO 1945-47; Kndgtn Teacher Church 1959-60; 4th/5th Grade Teacher Alcott 1960-63; 4th Grade Teacher 1963-66, Kndgtn Teacher 1966-82 Encanto; *ai:* Private Piano Teacher 1982-; NEA 1944-82; AEA 1963-82; PTA, Teacher of Yr; Bus & Prof Women VP 1975-82; DAR; N Baptist Church Nutrition Class Teacher 1981-82; Cub Scout Leader; Master Teacher Stu Teacher Trng AZ St Univ 1972-82; Co-Author Kndgtn Manual; Organized First Public Kndgtn in Osborn Sch Dist; *home:* 14625 N 55th Ave Glendale AZ 85306

FRAZIER, JANET LEE, Kindergarten Teacher; *b:* Oneida, TN; *m:* Bill Sebastian; *c:* Kevin, Jonathan Soldner, Daniel Soldner; *ed:* (BS) Elem Ed, E TN St Univ 19776; Kndgtn Endorsement; Various Courses Towards Masters; *cr:* Dir Oak Ridge Church Day Care 1972-74; Kndgtn Teacher Central Elem 1976-; *ai:* Inservice Comm Rep; Lead Teacher Advisory Comm; NEA, TEA Mem; Central Elem Teacher of Yr 1988-89; Morgan Cty Teacher of Yr 1989; Excl in Teaching Awd 1976-86; *office:* Central Elem Sch Hwy 62 Wartburg TN 37887

FRAZIER, LINDA RENEE, 1st Grade Teacher; *b:* Waco, TX; *M:* David P.; *c:* Patrick, Crystal; *ed:* (BS) Elem Ed, Baylor Univ 1976; *cr:* Kndgtn Teacher 1976-84; 1st Grade Teacher 1984- Wortham Elem; *ai:* Spon Little Dribblers; *home:* 5th & Askew St Coolidge TX 76635

FRAZIER, STEVEN LEE, Sixth Grade Teacher; *b:* Mansfield, OH; *m:* Teresa Kasler; *ed:* (BA) Spec Ed/EMR, OH Dominican Coll 1976; (BA) Elem Ed, OH St Univ 1981; Advanced Trng His/Soc Sci, Old Sturbridge Village Teacher Inst; *cr:* EMR Teacher 1976-81, 6th Grade Teacher 1981- Kae Avenue Elem; *ai:* WKAE-TV Channel 3 Producer & Dir; Outdoor Ed Coord; Whitehall Ed Assn Building Rep 1977-80; OH Ed Assn, NEA; Worthington Historical Society Properties Mgr 1978-81; OH Historical Society, Natl Trust for Historic Preservation; Whitehall City Schls Teacher of Yr 1980; *office:* Kae Ave Elem Sch 4738 Kae Ave Whitehall OH 43213

FRAZIER, SUSAN GRUNN, English Teacher; *b:* Strongsville, OH; *m:* John Richard; *c:* Sarah, Jonathan; *ed:* (AA) Liberal Art, Schoolcraft Comm Coll 1969; (BA) Eng Lit/Lang, 1971, (MA) Rdng, 1977 E MI Univ; *cr:* Teacher Fowlerville HS 1973-, Lansing Comm Coll 1985-; *ai:* Eng Dept Chairperson; Dist Eng Curr Cncl Educl Dev & Planning & Dist Planning Comms; Support Group Facilitator; Union Rep; Livingston Cty Rdng Cncl 1975-80; *home:* 535 W Coon Lake Rd Howell MI 48843

FRAZIER, THOMAS GILBERT, Sixth Grade Teacher; *b:* Cleveland, TN; *c:* Jason, Kenny, Amy; *ed:* (AS) Scndry Ed, Cleveland St; (BS) Scndry Phys Ed, (MS) Elem Ed, Univ of TN Knoxville; *cr:* 6th Grade Teacher South Polk Elem 1976-; *ai:* Boys Bsktbl Coach; NEA, TN Ed Assn 1976-; Beech Spring Baptist Church Deacon 1983-88; Polk Cty HS Bsktbl Team Captain 1969-72, Best Defensive Player 1972; Outstanding Young Men of America 1983; *home:* Rt 1 Box 624 Oldfort TN 37362

FRAZIER, VERA STEVENS, Fourth Grade Teacher; *b:* Mayetta, KS; *m:* Roy Everett; *c:* Brenda Eagle, Bruce, Marcia, Rex; *cr:* 1st-8th Grade Pleasant Grove Sch 1945-48, South Cedar Sch 1948-49; 1st/2nd Grade Teacher Denison Elem Sch 1945-55; 4th Grade Teacher Mayetta Elem Sch 1960-; *ai:* NEA 1945-53/1960-; K-NEA 1945-55/1960-; Mayetta OES Worthy Matron 1945-87; Gr Chapter of KS OES Gr Rep of OH/KS 1956-58; Teacher of Yr of USD 337; *home:* PO Box 73 Denison KS 66419

FRECHMAN, ALAN D., Mathematics Teacher; *b:* New York, NY; *m:* Lynn Adams; *c:* Brian, Erica; *ed:* (BS) Math/Physics, 1970, (MS) Math, 1972 Univ of S CA; Grad Stud Univ S CA & CSUN; *cr:* Math Teacher Pacoima Jr HS 1970-72, Audubon Jr HS 1972-, Math Teacher Los Angeles HS 1986-; *ai:* Excl in Math Prgm; *office:* Audubon Jr HS 4120 11th Ave Los Angeles CA 90008

FRECKLETON, JANET ELLEN, Sixth Grade Teacher; *b:* Patterson, NJ; *m:* James Bell; *c:* Iain; *ed:* (BS) Soc Sci, CA Polytechic St Univ 1968; Study Span Lang/Culture/His Abroad; *cr:* 5th Grade Teacher Patterson Road Sch 1969-71; 3rd/5th/6th Grade Teacher Joe Nightingale Sch 1972-85; 5th/6th Grade Teacher Ralph Dunlap Sch 1986-; *ai:* Sch Improvement Plan; Phys Ed Comm; After Sch Enrichment; Gifted & Talented Teacher 1971; Orcott Educators Assn (Rep 1969-, Negotiations 1976); Published Simulation; *office:* Ralph Dunlap Sch 1220 Oak Knoll Santa Maria CA 93455

FRED, CHARLES PATRICK, 6th Grade Mathematics Teacher; *b:* Mineola, NY; *m:* Alison Smith; *c:* Shawn B.; *ed:* (BA) Elem Ed, St Univ of NY Stoneybrook 1975; *cr:* 5th Grade Classroom Teacher St Mary Magdelen 1976-77; 6th-8th Grade Math Teacher St Margaret Mary 1977-79; 6th/7th Grade Math Teacher Jackson Heights Mid Sch 1979-; *ai:* Jackson Heights Sftbl Team Soc Dir; After Sch Tutoring Prgm Supvr; Affective Learning Steering Comm; Fnd for the Advancement of our Cmmty Through Schls, for Outstanding Achievement Through Stu Involvement; Quest Intnl for Affective Learning; Grants for Extra Stu Tutorial Prgm; *office:* Jackson Heights Mid Sch Academy Dr Oviedo FL 32765

FREDE, RONALD L., Music Dept Chair/Band Dir; *b:* St Louis, MO; *m:* Virginia L. Mc Coy; *c:* Holly M. Frede Smardo, Lee G.; *ed:* (BME) Music Ed, Cntrl Meth Coll 1961; (MA) Music Ed, WA Univ 1966; Post Grad Studs, Webster Univ & Univ MO St Louis; *cr:* 5th-12th Grade Music Teacher Pacific MO 1961-65; Dir of Bands Mc Cluer HS 1965-; *ai:* Marching & Pep Band; Jazz Ensemble & Pit Orchestra; Music Educators Natl Conf; Natl Band Assn; MO Music Educators Assn Exec Bd 1985-87; St Louis Suburban Music Educators Assn (Band VP, Festival Chm 1983-85, Pres 1985-87, Outstanding Music Educator 1987); Outstanding Young Men in Amer 1971; Most Outstanding Concert Band in Intnl Band Festival 1973; Ferguson-Florissant Bd of Ed Special Commendation 1983; *home:* 1705 Deborah Dr Florissant MO 63031

FREDELL, CONRADT H., Biology Teacher; *b:* Alamogordo, NM; *m:* Jeri Lyn; *c:* Heidi, Karl; *ed:* (BS) Bio Ed, 1973, (MAT) Bio Ed, 1976 N AZ Univ; Grad Stud Sci; *cr:* Sci Teacher Kingman Jr HS 1973-81; Bio Instr Mohave Comm Coll 1980; Bio/Earth Sci Teacher Clear Creek HS 1981-; *ai:* Ftbl & Ski Team Coach; NEA 1973-; NATB 1981-; Whos Who in the West; Candidate Teacher in Space; *office:* Clear Creek HS 161 Chicago Creek Idaho Springs CO 80452

FREDERICH, THOMAS JOE, Fourth Grade Teacher; *b:* Warsaw, IN; *m:* Lisabeth Ann Perry; *c:* Michael, Jonathan, Mary K.; *ed:* (BA) Elem Ed, Indianapolis Univ 1973; (MA) Elem Ed, Purdue Univ 1978; *cr:* 5th Grade Teacher 1974-76, 4th Grade Teacher 1976- De Motte Elem; *ai:* IN St Teachers Assn 1974-; Kankakee Valley Teachers Assn (Pres, Building Rep, Head Negotiator, VP, Negotiate Team Mem) 1974-86; *office:* Kankakee Valley Sch 1000 S Halleck Demotte IN 46310

FREDERICK, ELEASE, Sixth Grade Teacher; *b:* Enfield, NC; *ed:* (BS) Elem Ed, Winston-Salem St Univ 1971; (MED) Intermediate Ed, NC Cntrl Univ 1977; *cr:* Teacher Halifax Cty Schls 1971-; *ai:* Photography Club Adv; PTA Exec Comm; NC Assn of Educators Faculty Rep 1688-; HC Assn of Educators Treas 1977-78; Natl Assn of Univ Women Treas 1986-; Alpha Kappa Alpha Treas 1988-; Teacher of Yr Nominee 1981; Outstanding Leaders Elem, Scndry Ed 1976; NC Awds Prgms Outstanding Math Teachers 1987, Lang Art Teachers 1988; *home:* Rt 1 Box 225 Enfield NC 27823

FREDERICK, JANE (FINK), 6th Grade Teacher; *b:* Allentown, PA; *m:* Donald P.; *c:* Stephen, Ryan; *ed:* (BS) Elem Ed, E Stroudsburg Univ 1970; (MED) Elem Ed, Lehigh Univ 1974; Peels Prgm Clarion Univ; *cr:* 6th Grade Teacher Cetronia Elem Sch 1970-74; 6th Grade Teacher 1974-83, 5th Grade Teacher 1983-86, 6th Grade Teacher 1986- Ironton Elem Sch; *ai:* Parkland Ed Assn (VP 1986-88) 1970-; PA St Ed Assn, NEA 1970-; St Pauls Luth Church Chairperson Chrstn Ed 1976-82, 1986-; *office:* Ironton Elem Sch 2207 Main St Coplay PA 18037

FREDERICK, KAREN SUSAN (ADIUTORI), Director of Choirs; *b:* Erie, PA; *m:* Ronald A.; *ed:* (BS) Music Ed, Indiana Univ of PA 1979; Grad Stud Ed, Univ of Pittsburgh & Allegheny Intermediate Unit; *cr:* 7th/8th Grade Chorus Teacher MT Royal Jr HS 1980-86; 8th/9th Grade/HS Chorus Teacher Shaler Sch Dist 1986-; *ai:* HS Concert, HS Jazz, 8th & 9th Grade Mixed, Girls & Boys Choirs; HS Womens & Mens Chorus; PA Music Educators Assn, Music Educators Natl Conference; *office:* Scott Ave Jr HS/Shaler Area HS 381 Wible Run Rd Pittsburgh PA 15209

FREDERICK, L. SCOTT, Amer & World Cultures Teacher; *b:* Pittsburgh, PA; *m:* Virginia Ann Ferguson; *c:* Aimee, Kerri, Erin; *ed:* (BS) Ed/Soc Sci, 1976, (ME) Soc Sci, 1983 CAlifornia Univ of PA; *cr:* Instr Soc Stud Ringgold Sr HS 1976-; Instr Geography Washington & Jefferson Coll 1989-; *ai:* Head Boys Track Coach, Boys & Girls Cross Cntry Coach; Soph Class & Cultural Act Club Spon; Mem Cmmty Service Comm; Monongahela Area Lib Bd of Dir Co-Chm Building Comm 1984-89; Mid Mon Valley Transit Authority Bd of Dir Chm Personnel Comm 1986-88; Monongahela City Councilman Dir of Parks & Property Dept 1984-88; Presidential Scholar CA St Coll 1983; *home:* RD 2 105 Sequoyah Ln Monongahela PA 15063

FREDERICK, SUE HAZLETT, 5th Grade Teacher; *b:* Clinton, IN; *m:* Ronald B.; *c:* Carrie R.; *ed:* (BS) Elem Ed, IN St Univ 1972; (MS) Psych, Butler Univ 1975; *cr:* 6th Grade Teacher Acton Elem 1972-76, Franklin Township Mid Sch 1976-77; 5th Grade Teacher Rockville Elem Sch 1977-; *ai:* Textbook Adoption & Awds Comm; Hoosier Girls St Comm Chairperson; Jump Rope for Heart; Chrldr Spon; ISTA 1972-; RTA Secy 1973-74; Amer Legion Auxiliary Ed Chm 1981-; Eastern Star 1968-; Gamma Phi Beta Alumnae 1972-; Rockville PTO; *office:* Rockville Elem Sch 406 Elm Rockville IN 47872

FREDIN, JOHN, Literature/Composition Teacher; *b:* Kansas City, MO; *m:* Sharon Kittelson; *c:* John III, Diana; *ed:* (BA) Eng/Drama, 1958, (MA) Eng, 1965 Wichita St Univ; Numerous Additional Hrs; *cr:* Eng Teacher Wichita HS West 1958-59, Wichita HS South 1959-63, Wichita HS North 1963-; *ai:* Schlsp, Commencement Speakers, NHS Comm; AFT; Wichita Cncl Teachers of Eng Pres 1973-75; Ed Wichita Public Schls City Wide Litrary Magazine 1975-76; Photographer, Poetry, Prose Contributor Wichita Public Schls Literary Anthology 1985; 2 Teacher Recognition Awds Univ of KS 1989-.

FREDRICK, PATRICK J., Art Teacher; *b:* Decatur, AL; *m:* Cheryl Anne Gabrielson; *ed:* (BFA) Art, Abilene Chrstn Univ 1986; Graphics Specialization, Bessemel St Tech Coll; *cr:* Art Teacher Fryeburg Acad 1988-; *ai:* Frosh Class & Art Club Adv; ME Art Ed Assn 1989-; ME Teachers Assn, NEA 1990-; Church of Christ; Independently Commissioned Works of Art Murals or Graphic Design Projects; *office:* Fryeburg Acad 152 Maine St Fryeburg ME 04037

FREDRIKSEN, BETH A. (MC KEOWN), K-7 Grade Chap I Rdng Teacher; *b:* Brookings, SD; *m:* Richard; *c:* Michael, Matthew, Joseph, Mari, Laura; *ed:* (BA) Elem Ed, Mt Marty Coll 1970; Elem Ed Area Curr; *cr:* 3rd Grade Teacher Fort Dodge 1970-71; Kndgtn Teacher Elkton Public Sch 1971-79; Elem K-8th Grade Teacher Brookdale Hutterite Colony Sch 1980-83; Chapter Math Teacher Elkton Public Sch 1983-87; Tutor 1987-88; Chapter Rdng Teacher 1988-; *ai:* SD Rdng Cncl 1989-; SD Ed Assn (Local Pres) 1973-; NEA; Jaycettes (Local/State Ofcs) 1974-84 Key Woman 1983; Cub Scouts (Cub Master/Asst Cub Master 1988-, Den Leader 1984-86).

FREEBERN, JANET FLYNN, Third Grade Teacher; *b:* Glens Falls, NY; *m:* Timothy H.; *c:* Erika, Meredith; *ed:* (BS) Elem Ed St Univ of NY Plattsburgh 1975; *cr:* 3rd Grade Teacher 1976-81, 2nd Grade Teacher 1981-82, 3rd Grade Teacher 1984-86, 3rd Grade Teacher 1988- Wingdale Elem Sch; *ai:* Mid-Hudson Rdng Cncl Mem; *office:* Wingdale Elem Sch Rt 55 Wingdale NY 12594

FREED, KAREN ANN, Second Grade Teacher; *b:* Greensburg, PA; *m:* Wayne H.; *ed:* (BS) Ed, Slippery Rock Univ 1976; (MED) Ed, Indiana Univ of PA 1982; *cr:* 1st-3rd Grade Teacher Jeannette Sch Dist 1977-; *ai:* NEA, PA St Ed Assn, Jeannette Teachers Assn 1977-; Manordale Farms Civic Assn 1988-; Jeannette PTO Guest Speaker; Guest Speaker Rotary Intnl Conference Dist 733; *home:* 2404 Willow Dr Export PA 15632

FREED, SHARON LYNN, First Grade Teacher; *b:* Pittsburg, PA; *ed:* (BS) Elem Ed/Lib Sci, Clarion Univ 1968; (MED) Elem Ed, Univ of Pittsburgh 1971; *cr:* 1st Grade Teacher Carnegie Elem Sch 1968-; *ai:* Carlynton Fed of Teachers; *office:* Carnegie Elem Sch Franklin Ave Carnegie PA 15106

FREEDMAN, ANDREA SUE, Third Grade Teacher; *b:* Buffalo, NY; *ed:* (MS) Ed, US Intnl Univ 1990; (Ba) Soc Sci, San Diego St Univ 1972; *cr:* Teacher Carlton Oaks Elem Sch 1973-; *ai:* Master Teacher; Lang Arts-Rdng Implementation Comm; Sch Improvement Prgm Comm; Curr Adv Cncl; Intnl Rdng Assn 1986-; Greater San Diego Math Assn; PTA 1973-; Sierra Club 1989-; *office:* Carlton Oaks Elem Sch 9353 Wethersfield Rd Santee CA 92071

FREEHAUF, DEANNA SPLITT, Fourth Grade Teacher; *b:* Joliet, IL; *m:* Edward; *c:* Trisha, Scott; *ed:* (BA) Elem Ed, Edgewood Coll 1966; *cr:* 4th Grade Teacher St Patricks Sch 1966-67; 4th Grade Teacher 1967-72, Kndgtn Teacher 1978-82 Lemont Cmmty Consolidated Dist #113; 4th Grade Teacher Lemont-Bromberek Combined Sch Dist #113 1982-; *ai:* Discipline Comm; Lemont Elem Cncl (Pres 1968-69, VP 1979-80); Lemont Snowmobile Club (Treas 1972-73, Pres 1975-76, Co-Pres 1977-78); *office:* Lemont-Bromberek Sch Dist 1130 Kim Pl Lemont IL 60439

FREELAND, JUDITH M., 5th & 6th Grade Dept Teacher; *b:* Hillsboro, ND; *m:* Mervin J.; *c:* Leetha R. Gooding; *ed:* (BS) Elem Ed, Mayville St Coll 1966; Numerous Colls; *cr:* Teacher Bloomfield 3 1951-53, Ervin 3 1955-57, Bloomfield 3 1957-58, Hillsboro Spec Sch Dist 1958-; *ai:* TAT & STEP Facilitator; NEA, ND Educators Assn 1958-; Hillsboro Ed Assn (Pres, Delegate Rep, Secy) 1958-; Writing Fellowship Concordia Coll; Historical Fiction Article Published; *home:* 621 2nd Ave NE Hillsboro ND 58045

FREELAND, PHYLLIS LETBETTER, Computer Teacher; *b:* San Saba, TX; *m:* Billy Bob; *c:* Corey, Paige; *ed:* (BBA) Bus Ed, TX Tech Univ 1970; Math; *cr:* Bus Teacher Crosbyton HS 1970-71, Durham Bus Coll 1971-72; VOE Coord Kaufman HS 1972-75; Bus Teacher East Chambers CISD 1976-77, Anahuac HS 1977-79; Math/Bus Teacher Pasadena Ind Sch Dist 1985-; *ai:* Cmptr Club; Stu & Teacher Awd Comm Mem; Pasadena Ed Assn (Comm Mem 1985-88, Exec Bd 1987); TSTA, NEA 1970-79, AEA Pres Elect 1979; FHA Honorary Life Mem; Anahuac Ed Assn Public Relations Chm; TX St Teacher Assn; Nom Teacher of Yr 1979; Southern Assn for Accrediatation Kaufman HS Chm; Waxahachie HS Bus Dept Southern Accreditation Comm Mem; *office:* Sam Rayburn HS 2121 Cherrybrook Pasadena TX 77502

FREELON, GLADYS WARD, Fourth Grade Teacher; *b:* Salem, AL; *m:* Joe W.; *c:* Joe W. Jr., Gawana; *ed:* (BA) Mental Retardation/Elem Ed, Chicago St Univ 1971; (MS) Urban Teachers Ed/Spec Ed, Governors St Univ 1974; Gifted, Natl Coll of Ed; *cr:* Postal Clerk US Post Office 1959-69; Teacher Dist 89 Maywood IL 1972-; *ai:* 4th-6th Grade Rdng Asst; Gifted Pullout Prgm; Rdng is Fundamental, Curr Improvement, Soc Stud, Black His Chairperson; Alpha Kappa Alpha Black Coll Chairperson

1983, Cmmty Action Awd 1983; Lambda Alpha Omega RIF Chairperson 1989-; IL Rdng Cncl Mem 1984-; Maywood Beautification Comm Pres 1980-88, Maywood Cmmty Service Awd 1989; Maywood Schlsp & Outreach Prgm Pres 1989-; Maywood Against Drugs Corres Secy 1990; Cmmty Action & Service Awd; Accomodations Supt of Dist & Prin of Irving; *home:* 801 S 8th Ave Maywood IL 60153

FREEMAN, DANIEL LEE, Gifted Math Program Teacher; *b:* Detroit, MI; *m:* Terry Jolene Bennett; *c:* Todd, Karen; *ed:* (BA) Math, Spring Arbor Coll 1969; (MS) Math/Ed, E MI Univ 1972; *cr:* Math Teacher Dickinson Jr HS 1969-80, Churchill HS 1980-82, Frost Mid Sch 1982-; *ai:* Livonia Franklin HS Girls Var Bsktbl Coach; Wayne Cty Spec Olympics Coord 1986-, Pentathlon; Livonia Mid Sch Teacher of Yr 1987-88; *home:* 30830 Stephen Ct Westland MI 48185

FREEMAN, DOROTHY LEE, Principal; *b:* Baltimore, MD; *ed:* (BA) Eng, Newman Coll 1971; (MA) Eng, Towson St Coll 1976; (MED) Scndry Ed, Towson St Univ 1979; Advanced Prof Ed in Theology; *cr:* Teacher Sisters of St Francis 1956-71, Archdiocese of Baltimore 1956-, Coll of Notre Dame 1986-89; Prin Archdiocese of Baltimore 1980-84, 1989-; *ai:* Carmelite Yrbk Adv; Natl Cath Teachers Assn 1980-; MD Teachers Assn for Continuing Ed 1988-; Archdiocesan Scndry Sch Prin 1989-; *office:* Our Lady of Mt Carmel HS 1706 Eastern Ave Baltimore MD 21221

FREEMAN, ELLEN REEDER, Second Grade Teacher; *b:* Brigham City, UT; *m:* Alan B.; *c:* Amber; *ed:* (BA) Phys Ed, Ut St Univ 1965; Dual-Certificate Elem Ed, Weber St Univ 1978; (MS) Phys Ed, Ut St Univ 1989; *cr:* Phys Ed Teacher Gerlach HS 1965-67; Bus Teacher Elko HS 1967-70; Phys Ed Teacher Wells HS 1970-77; 2nd Grade Teacher Hervin Bunderson Elem 1978-; *ai:* Leopardettes Drill Team 1970-77; Vlybl, Bsktbl, Track Coach; Chrldrs; Sch Paper 1965-67; Delta Kappa Gamma (VP 1982-84, Pres 1986-88); Ladies Improvement Outstanding Mem 1970; Civic Club; Symphonic Choir; *office:* Hervin Bunderson Sch 641 E 200 N Brigham City UT 84302

FREEMAN, GEORGIA ANN, 6th Grade Teacher; *b:* Charlotte, NC; *ed:* (BS) Elem Ed, 1969, (MS) Media, 1971 Appalachian St Univ; *cr:* 5th Grade Teacher Marie G Davis Elem 1970; 4th Grade Teacher Oak Hill Elem 1972; 5th/6th Grade Teacher Mt View Elem 1973-; *ai:* NC Ed Assn Building Rep 1972-, Nominee Teacher of Yr 1980; NC Cncl Teachers of Math 1987-, Outstanding Elem Math Teacher 1987; NEA; Jaycees Outstanding Young Educator 1979; Outstanding Elem Math Teacher NC Cncl of Teachers of Math 1987; NC Center For Advancement of Teaching Participant; *home:* 236 W Park Dr Morganton NC 28655

FREEMAN, HARRY E., Social Studies Teacher; *b:* Logan, WV; *m:* Ilene L. Lambert; *c:* H. Morgan, Kolena, Jason, Sean; *ed:* (BA) Soc Stud, Marshall Univ 1970; (THG) Theology Degree, Tabernacle Baptist Bible Inst 1979; (MA) Scndry Admin, Marshall Univ 1983; *cr:* Teacher Loredo Lane & Chapmanvllle Grade 1971-74; Teacher/Prin Madison Chrstn Sch 1976-77; Teacher Windsor HS 1978-, Chapmanville Jr HS & Chapmanville HS 1980-; *ai:* Close Up Spon; 1st Baptist Church (Deacon, Trustee) 1976-77.

FREEMAN, JEANETTE LYNN, Third Grade Teacher; *b:* Brewton, AL; *m:* James T.; *c:* Elizabeth; *ed:* (BS) Elem Ed, Univ of TN Chattanooga 1980; Curr & Instruction, Elem Ed; *cr:* 4th-6th Grade Sci Teacher 1980-81, 5th Grade Teacher 1981-84, 6th Grade Teacher 1984-87, 3rd Grade Teacher 1987- Bridgeport Elem Sch; *ai:* Jackson Cty Ed Assn (Faculty Rep 1983-84) 1980-; AL Ed Assn, NEA 1980-; Bridgeport Literary Club Pres 1978-80; Bridgeport Manufacturing Company Inc VP 1968-; Signal Mountain Cmmty Guild 1984-; *office:* Bridgeport Elem Sch Jacobs Ave Bridgeport AL 35740

FREEMAN, JULIANA LASHLEY, Business Education Teacher; *b:* Garysburg, NC; *m:* Waldo; *ed:* (BS) Bus Admin, St Pauls Coll 1981; Provisional Certificate; *cr:* Teacher Brunswick Sr HS 1985-, James Solomon Russell Jr HS 1989-; *ai:* FBLA Sponsorship; Tag Screening Comm; VA Ed Assn, Bus Ed Assn, NEA 1985-; Optimist Club 1989-; *home:* Hwy 46 N Cochran Rd Lawrenceville VA 23868

FREEMAN, K. HELEN, 9th Grade English Teacher; *b:* Wiesbaden AFB, West Germany; *ed:* (BA) Eng, 1975; (MED) Eng Ed, 1978 Valdosta St Coll; (MED) Cmmnty/Sch Cnslng, GA St Univ 1984; *cr:* Eng Teacher, Cook Cty Jr HS 1976-78; Hahira Mid Sch 1978-79; Redan HS 1979-86; Miller Grove Jr HS 1986-; *ai:* Writing Consultant Miller Grove Jr HS; Tutor for Homework Helpline Prgm; NEA/GTE 1981-82; Kappa Delta Pi 1984-; Jr Leag of Atlanta 1986-; Scottish Rite Hosp Aux 1988-; Valdosta St Coll Alumni Assn 1978-; Excl in Eng Awd 1984; Articles and Poem Published 1986 Colleaque; Supervised Stu Teachers Winter Qtr 1980, Winter Qtr 1982; Achieved 4 0 Gpa for Second Masters Degree Awarded Membership Into Kappa-Delta Pi Honor Society; *office:* Miller Grove Jr HS 2215 Miller Rd Decatur GA 30035

FREEMAN, LEZLIE ELAND, Pre-1st Grade Teacher; *b:* Minneapolis, MN; *m:* Joe; *c:* Carisa, Sara, Cody; *ed:* (BSE) Elem Ed, NE MO St Univ 1976; *cr:* Kndgtn Teacher Lockridge Elem 1976-86; 3rd Grade Teacher 1980-81, Pre-1st Grade Teacher 1986- Pence Elem; *ai:* Stu Cncl Spon; Early Chldhd Comm Mem; Intnl Rdng Assn, Delta Kappa Gamma, Fairfield Cmmty Ed Assn; 4-H Leader; *office:* Pence Elem Sch 1000 S 6th Fairfield IA 52556

FREEMAN, LINA LEWIS, Special Ed Dept Chair/Teacher; *b:* Greenville, MS; *m:* Keith E.; *c:* Jalil K., Joshua L.; *ed:* (BS) Ed - Cum Laude, 1979, (MS) Ed - Magna Cum Laude, 1981 Jackson St Univ; ECRI; Diagnostician Trng; *cr:* Behavior Disordered Childrens Teacher Stern Elem 1981-83; Learning Disabled Childrens Teacher Samuell HS 1983-; *ai:* Jr Var Chrldrs; Faculty Advisory Comm Secy; Multicultural Comm Chairperson; Phi Delta Kappa, Phi Kappa Phi, Delta Sigma Theta; CEC Pres 1980-81; PTA, Spec Ed PTA Mem; *office:* Samuell HS 8928 Palisade Dr Dallas TX 75217

FREEMAN, MARCIA DALE, Teacher; *b:* Longview, TX; *m:* Johnny W.; *c:* Richard, Robert; *ed:* (BA) Elem Ed, TCU 1963; *cr:* 3rd Grade Teacher Birdville Ind Sch Dist 1963-; *ai:* PTA Life Membership Service Pin 1987; Assn of TX Prof Educators Building Rep.

FREEMAN, PHYLLIS ANNE, Third Grade Teacher; *b:* Enid, OK; *m:* Paul D; *c:* Justin A., Christopher M.; *ed:* (BSED) Elem Ed, Southwest TX ST 1978; Addl Studies Pursuing Master's Degree in Ed at Southwest TX ST Univ; *cr:* 1st Grade Teacher 1978-83; 2nd Grade Teacher 1983-87; 3rd Grade Teacher Montgomery Elem Sch 1987-; *ai:* Rdng Coord for Montgomery Elem Sch, Chairperson for Parent Ed; Montgomery Elem PTA; World Book Rdng Prgm Spon; Delta Kappa Gamma 1989-; Montgomery PTA Chairperson Parent Ed 1978-; Life Mem 1985; Intnl Rdng Assn 1988-; Kirby Baptist Church Teacher 1974-; Montgomery Elem Teacher of the Yr 1984, 1986; TX PTA Life Mem 1985; Nominee Trinity Prize-Excellence in Teaching 1986; *home:* 7917 Leafy Hollow San Antonio TX 78233

FREEMAN, RACHEL MOODY, Resource Teacher; *b:* Louisville, KY; *m:* Edwin B.; *c:* Ba Shaun, Nikki; *ed:* (BA) Elem, KY St Univ 1974; (MS) Ed, Univ of Louisville 1984; *cr:* Teacher 1974-89, Resource Teacher 1989- Portland Elem; *ai:* Portland Elem Academic Team, Curators Spon; Curr Writing Comm for Jeff Cty Public Sch; Learning Choice Bd Mem for Magnet Sch; Amer Red Cross Rep; Jefferson Cty Teacher Assn 1974-; Hermosuras Club.

FREEMAN, SUSAN MAXWELL, 2nd Grade Teacher; *b:* Lafayette, IN; *m:* Thomas B.; *c:* Anne, Ryan; *ed:* (BS) Elem Ed, IN Univ 1970; (MS) Elem Ed, Purdue Univ 1973; *cr:* 2nd Grade Teacher South Montgomery Sch Corp 1970; Delphi Cmmty Sch 1970-; *ai:* Recording Sec Kappa Kappa Kappa 1974; Investment Club 1988; *office:* Hillcrest Elem Sch Wabash & Vine St Delphi IN 46923

FREEMAN, WOODY RUMPH, 6th Grade Mathematics Teacher; *b:* Fort Valley, GA; *m:* Wayne Oliver; *c:* Wayne II, Christopher; *ed:* (BA) Elem Ed, Talledega Coll 1972; (MA) Mid Grades, Fort Valley St Coll 1975; *cr:* Teacher Fort Valley Mid Sch; *ai:* Fort Valley Mid Sch Drama Dept Dir & Mathemagic Club Founder Adv; GA Assn of Educators; Alpha Kappa Alpha; *home:* 308 Delores Dr Fort Valley GA 31030

FREEMYER, PATSY BENNETT, 9th/10th Grade English Teacher; *b:* N Little Rock, AR; *m:* Wesley Neal; *c:* Norma Edmonds Ortiz, Patti Freemyer Martin, Kenneth W., Emily Freemyer Maggio; *ed:* (BA) Eng/Drama, Hendrix Coll 1953; Gifted & Talented Cert, Univ of AR; AR Writers Project Cert, Henderson Univ; Age of Shakespeare, Univ of Oxford England; *cr:* Teacher Pine Bluff Jr HS 1953-54, Sanford Sr HS 1954-56, N Little Rock Jr HS 1956-58, Cntrl HS 1978-; *ai:* Natl Jr Honor Society & Dionysians Drama & Staff Dev Comm Spon; Discipline Comm; Delta Kappa Gamma VP 1989-; Natl Assn Eng Teachers; United Meth Women Conference Pres 1982-86; Natl Assn Jr Auxiliary Past Pres 1976-77; PEO Sisterhood Educl Chairperson; Teacher of Yr; *home:* 106 Rose Cir Helena AR 72342

FREERS, GARY W., English Teacher; *b:* Muscatine, IA; *ed:* (BA) Eng, Univ of N IA Cedar Falls 1963; (MA) Guidance & Counseling, NE MO St Univ Kirksville 1970; Licensed Funeral Dir in IA & IL; Grad Stud Quad City Grad Center; *cr:* Eng Teacher Rock Island HS 1963-65, 1967-70; Eng Teacher/Cnslr Edison Jr HS 1970-; *ai:* Phi Delta Kappa; *office:* Edison Jr HS 9th St & 42nd Ave Rock Island IL 61201

FREGOSO, MANUEL JESUS, Soc Stud/Bi-ling Teacher; *b:* Tucson, AZ; *m:* Barbara Aguiar; *c:* Monica J., Marie J., Manuel J. Jr., Michael J.; *ed:* (BA) Scndry Ed/Span, 1976, (MED) Bi-ling Ed, 1984 Univ of AZ; *cr:* Migrant Teacher Santa Cruz Valley Union HS 1976-80; Span Teacher Townsend Mid Sch 1980-81; Soc Stud Teacher Safford Magnet Mid Sch 1981-; *ai:* Nom St Bi-ling Teacher of Yr 1989; *office:* Safford Magnet Mid Sch 300 S 5th Ave Tucson AZ 85701

FREIMAN, LELA LINCH, Drama Teacher; *b:* Canton, MS; *c:* Jennifer; *ed:* (BA) Speech/Drama Ed, St Univ of IA 1962; (MEd) Spec Ed, Univ of AZ 1977; Attends Wkshps, Seminars & Conferences; *cr:* Speech/Eng Teacher Sturgeon Bay HS 1962-65; 1st Aid Instr Pima Comm Coll 1974-79; LD/Resource Teacher Naylor Jr HS 1975-83; Drama Teacher Sahuaro HS 1983-; *ai:* Thespian & Travel Troupe Spon; N Cntrl Evaluation Facilities Comm Chairperson; AZ Theatre Educators Assn St Secy 1985-; Natl Theatre Ed Assn 1987-; GSA Trainer 1961-, Thanks Badge I 1976, Thanks Badge II 1988; Luth Scouters Assn Cross & Crown 1983; Univ of AZ Theatre Arts Advisory Cncl 1988-; SW Actors Studio Bd VP 1987-; Assn for Retarded Citizens Mainstream Teacher of Yr 1989-; *office:* Sahuaro HS 545 N Camino Seco Tucson AZ 85710

FREISEN, EDWARD MICHAEL, Ohio History Teacher; *b:* Youngstown, OH; *m:* Sherry Ballas; *c:* Kalin; *ed:* (BS) Health/Phys Ed/His, Youngstown St Univ 1981; Health Ed, Youngstown St Univ; *cr:* Driver Ed Teacher Youngstown East HS 1976-77, South Range HS 1979-81; His Teacher East Palestine HS 1981-82; Health/His Teacher Newton Falls 1983-; *ai:* Frosh Boys Bsktbl Coach; OH HS Athletic Assn Mem; Mahoning & Trumbull Cty Coaches Assn; Mahoning Valley Constitution 1970- 15 Yr Awd 1986; Bsktbl Ofcl Comm Assn Chm 1990 OH HS Athletic Assn; *home:* 2730 W River Rd Newton Falls OH 44444

FREITAG, WALTER FRED, 4th Grade Teacher; *b:* Bristol, CT; *ed:* (BA) Elem Ed, Concordia Coll 1978; (MS) Elem Ed, Cntrl CT St Univ 1983; *cr:* 6th Grade Teacher 1980-81, 4th Grade Teacher 1981-82 Thalberg Sch, 4th Grade Teacher Strong Sch 1982-; *home:* 384 Matthews St Bristol CT 06010

FREITAS, MARIA, Fourth Grade Teacher; *b:* Newark, NJ; *c:* Kim, Dana; *ed:* (BA) Elem Ed, 1977, (MA) Elem Ed, 1981 Georgian Court Coll; *cr:* 3rd Grade Teacher 5 Yrs, 4th Grade Teacher 8 Yrs Southard Sch; *office:* Southward Sch Kent Rd Howell NJ 07731

FREITAS, MARY CUMBEE, Social Studies Teacher; *b:* Whiteville, NC; *c:* Ronald Wayne, Eric Devon, Manuel Glenn; *ed:* (BA) His, Pembroke St Univ 1970; (MAS) Soc Stud, Univ of SC 1975; Ed Specialization Home Economics, Univ of SC 1979; Black Amer Stud; PET; *cr:* US His Teacher 1970-74, Bible Teacher 1971-74 Dillon HS; Soc Stud Teacher Maple Jr HS 1974-; *ai:* Chrldr Spon; Pep Club; HS Stu Cncl; Yrbk Dedication; Jr Amer Citizens Spon; Production Manager Sch Talent Show; NTA 1970-; SCEA SC Ed Assn 1970-; Daughters of American Revolution Regent 1978-; United Daughters Confederacy Pres 1978- Natl Delegate 1984; Black Stud Inst USC 1989; Sch Parent-Teacher Adv; Supt Teachers Comm; *home:* 103 Kay Dillon SC 29536

FREIZE, ARBRA CELESTE, Kindergarten Teacher; *b:* Gainesville, GA; *m:* Clarence T.; *c:* Trampus; *ed:* (BS) Elem Ed, Albany St Coll 1971; (MA) Early Chldhd Ed, Univ of GA 1975; *cr:* 1st Grade Teacher 1971-72, 2nd Grade Teacher 1972-75 Mock Rd Elem; Kndgtn Teacher Morningside 6th Grade Center 1975-82; 5th Grade Teacher 1982-83, 4th Grade Teacher 1983-86, Kndgtn Teacher 1986- New Hope Elem; *ai:* Partners in Progress, Teacher in Workplace Comm; NEA, LCAE, MACUS; Delta Sigma Theta.

FRENCH, ELIZABETH JANE (MOSLEY), 7th Grade Mathematics Teacher; *b:* Bruce, MS; *m:* Robert Clayton; *c:* Martin B., Mary E.; *ed:* (BS) Bio, 1971, (MS) Elem Ed, 1976 Univ of TN Knoxville; Cmptr Sci, Spec Ed, Coll Algebra, Univ of TN Chattanooga; *cr:* 4th/5th Grade Teacher Bradley Cty TN 1971-73; 6th/7th Grade Math Teacher 1977-83, 6th-8th Grade Cmptr Teacher 1984-85, 7th Grade Math Teacher 1985- Farragut Mid; *ai:* United Way Coord for Sch; Invent America Club Spon; Sch Newspaper & Yrbk Staff; CORE Team; Team Leader; Prof Advisory Cncl; Mathcounts, Math Competition Teams, Future Problem Solving Coach; Inservice Needs, Sch Soc, Textbook Selection Comm; Math Curr Revision Chairperson; Knox Cty Ed Assn, TN Ed Assn, NEA, PTA, TN Assn of Mid Schls 1977-; Smoky Mountain Math Educators Assn 1982-; Phi Delta Kappa 1984-; Alpha Chi Omega 1972-; Robert Unger Moms & Pops Ice Skating Fundraising Organization; Invent America Grant; Classroom Management, 7th Grade Math Implementation Inservice Presenter; TAMS Presenter on Cmptr LOGO Lang; Farragut Mid Sch Teacher of Yr; *office:* Farragut Mid Sch 200 W End Ave Knoxville TN 37922

FRENCH, KRISTIN JENNIFER, Mathematics Teacher; *b:* Salem, OH; *ed:* (BS) Math, Ashland Univ 1987; *cr:* Math Teacher Fort Myers Mid Sch 1987-; *ai:* Natl Jr Honor Society Adv; Intramural Vlybl, Bsktbl, Track Coach; Lee Cty Math Cncl 1987-88; *office:* Fort Myers Mid Sch 3015 Central Avenue Fort Myers FL 33901

FRENCH, MARY, English Department Chair; *b:* Chicago, IL; *c:* Ross, Claudia, John, David, Andrew; *ed:* (BA) Eng, Jacksonville Univ 1961; (MA) Eng - Cum Laude, Villanova Univ 1967; Gifted Ed, Curr & Supervision; *cr:* Eng Teacher Inglewood HS 1959-62, Eng Teacher 1963-, Dept Chairperson/Eng Teacher 1982- Downington HS; *ai:* Artists in Residence, Project Discovery, Theme Reader Prgm Coord; Theatre Chair, Visual & Performing Art Curr Advisory Comm; Dist In-Service Comm Mem; NCTE, ASCD; Univ of Chicago Outstanding Teacher Awd 1983; Mid States Self Study Evaluation Chairperson 1988; *office:* Downingtown Sch Dist 445 Manor Ave Downingtown PA 19335

FRENZEL, VICTORIA EBERLE, Mathematics/Soc Stud Teacher; *b:* San Marcos, TX; *m:* Paul Borden; *c:* Christopher, Kimberly; *ed:* (BS) Ed, TX A&I 1962; Univ of Sci & Arts of OK, OK City Comm Coll, OK St Univ; *cr:* Elem Teacher Carrizo Springs TX Schls & Riviera TX Schls 1965-67, Oklahoma City Schls 1965-67, Tuttle Schls 1976-; *ai:* Stu Cncl Spon; Scholastic Meet Math Coach; Tuttle Ed Assn (Secy, Treas) 1980-85; Delta Kappa Gamma VP 1989-; Kappa Kappa Iota VP 1988-; Girls Sftbl Coach 1977-80; Sunday Sch Teacher 1976-85; Tuttle Teacher of Yr 1988; Nom for Presidential Awd of Excl Sci & Math Teachers; *office:* Tuttle Mid Sch Box 780 Tuttle OK 73089

FRERE, KATHY J., English & Physical Ed Teacher; *b:* Charleston, WV; *m:* Raymond; *c:* Corby, Lance, Cindy; *ed:* (BA) Phys Ed/Eng, Univ of Charleston 1962; Working Toward Masters; *cr:* Eng/Phys Ed Teacher Washington Jr HS; Phys Ed Teacher Dover HS; Eng Teacher St Albans HS; Eng/Phys Ed Teacher Danville HS; Teacher St Vincent De Paul Sch; Eng/Phys Ed Teacher East Knox HS; *ai:* BB & Vlybl Coach; OH Ed Assn; East

Knox Ed Assn Pres; NEA; Red Cross Instr; St Vincent Parish Cncl; Bowling League Pres; Martha Holden Jennings Scholar.

FREUND, PEGGY G., 3rd Grade Teacher; *b:* Barkers Creek, NC; *m:* Richard M.; *c:* Joy F. Poppe, Jeffrey I.; *ed:* (BS) Elem Ed, W Carolina Univ 1955; Post Grad Courses; *cr:* 1st Grade Teacher Hamlet Elem Sch 1955; Capt John Smith 1968-71; 2nd Grade Teacher Woodley Hills Elem 1974-78; 2nd-3rd Grade Teacher Markham Elem 1978-; *ai:* Sci Lead Teacher; Annual Operating Plan for Sch; Sch Based Management, Prgm of Stud Implementation, Soc Comm; NEA 1968-; PTA Bd Teacher Rep; Smithsonian Inst Sponsored by Natl Sci Resources Center to Develop Hands-On Elem Sci Projects; *home:* 3406 Wessynton Way Alexandria VA 22309

FREY, MELODY BASCOM, Third Grade Teacher; *b:* Columbus, OH; *m:* Dennis J.; *ed:* (BS) Elem Ed, 1975, (MA) Elem Ed, 1979 OH St Univ; *cr:* Kndgtn Teacher Kirkersville & Etna Elem 1975-76; 2nd Grade Teacher 1976-84 & 1986-88, Gifted Resource Teacher 1984-86, 3rd Grade Teacher 1988- Kirkersville Elem; *ai:* Advisory Comm for Early & Mid Childhood Ed OH St Univ Newark Campus; SW Licking Ed Assn 1975-; OH Ed Assn 1975-; Newark Organization Teachers of Eng 1984-; Martha Holden Jennings Scholar 1980-81; Martha Holden Jennings Grant 1983-84; Delta Kappa Gamma; Phi Kappa Phi 1984; Honored for Teaching Excl & Prof Leadership OSU Fall Convocation 1984; *office:* Kirkersville Elem Sch 215 N 5th St Kirkersville OH 43033

FREY, NANCY BRUBAKER, First Grade Teacher; *b:* Lancaster, PA; *m:* Frederick Moyer; *c:* Carmen F. Rayne, Frederick D.; *ed:* (BS) Elem Ed, Elizabethtown Coll 1956; Millersville St Teachers Coll 1956; Working Towards Advanced Prof Salisbury St Coll 1963-73; *cr:* 1st Grade Teacher Lititz Elem Sch 1956-58; 2nd/3rd Grade Teacher 1959-63, 1st Grade Teacher 1964- Wicomico Bd of Ed; *ai:* NEA, MSTA; *home:* 602 S Kaywood Dr Salisbury MD 21801

FREY-MASON, PATRICIA, Mathematics Dept Chairperson; *b:* New York City, NY; *m:* Hale V.; *ed:* (BA) Math, D Youville Coll 1970; (MED) Math Ed, St Univ of NY Buffalo 1970; Math Ed, Cmptr Ed, Admin; *cr:* 7th Grade Math Teacher Public Sch 43 1970-77; Math/Cmptr Teacher/Dept Chairperson Buffalo Acad for Visual & Performing Arts 1977-; *ai:* Cmptr Club Adv; Sch Advisory Cncl Pres; Comprehensive Sch Improvement Prgm Comm Mem; NY St Assn Math Teachers (Dist Rep 1990) 1987-; NCTM (Manuscript Reviewer 1985-) 1982-; ASCD 1987-; Math Teacher Article 1985; Natl Cncl Excl in Ed Summer Inst 1988; Woodrow Wilson Geometry Inst 1989; *office:* Buffalo Acad for Visual & Perf 333 Clinton St Buffalo NY 14204

FREYMAN, MARY THERESE, BVM, Eighth Grade Teacher; *b:* Dubuque, IA; *ed:* (BA) Sociology/His, Clarke Coll 1966; (MA) Sociology Ed/Religion, N IL Univ 1977; Afro-Amer Stud, Univ of Chicago; Cmptr Programming, Archdiocese of Chicago; Grad Stud Ed, Mundelein, Triton, Univ of Chicago, Loyola Univ; *cr:* 1st-4th Grade Teacher St Gilbert 1955-59; 3rd/4th Grade Teacher St Ellen 1959-64; 7th/8th Grade Teacher St Eulalia 1964-; *ai:* Patrol Supvr; Mission Moderator, Testing Coord; Archdiocesan Teachers Assn, NEA 1964-; PTO 1970-; Maywood Human Relations Cncl Secy 1966-72; Nexus Coffeehouse Ecumenical Congregation Chairperson 1965-70; Proviso Township Mental Health Referendum Dir 1968; St Eulalia Pastoral Cncl Chm 1966-; Archdiocesan Office for Laity 1970-82; Adult Ed Afro-Amer Stud Chicago, Oak Park & Marywood IL; Triton Coll Grant for Teaching Sci Gifted; Spiritual Dir; Christ Renews His Parish; *office:* St Eulalia Sch 815 W Lexington St Maywood IL 60153

FREYMAN, WILLIAM DAVID, Vocational Drafting Teacher; *b:* Baltimore, MD; *m:* Linda Kay Oursler; *c:* Michael D., Kara L.; *ed:* (BS) Ed/Ind Arts, 1969, (MED) Ed/Ind Arts, 1973 Univ of MD; *cr:* Ind Arts Teacher Belt Jr HS 1969-73; Voc Draft Teacher S Garrett HS 1973-; *ai:* Race Team Coach & Spon; Asst Boys & Girls Track Coach; White Water Rafting Club & Ski Club Spon; Garrett Cty Fed of Teachers 1986-; Natl Ski Patrol (Patrol Leader 1979-88, E Division Staff 1984-), Natl 6237 1983, Certified 210 1985, Yellow Merit Star 1985; BSA (Asst Scout Master, Waterfront Dir, Order of Arrow Mem); Coach of US Ski Assn; *office:* Southern Garrett HS 1100 E Oak St Oakland MD 21550

FRIBLEY, DAVID K., US History Teacher; *b:* Ashland, OH; *m:* Sally E. Klein; *c:* Cory B., Laua A., Karla M.; *ed:* (AB) His, Baldwin Wallace Coll 1964; (MAT) His Ed, Miami Univ 1966; *cr:* Soc Stud Teacher Trenton Jr HS 1966-67; US His Teacher/Swim Coach Port Clinton HS 1976-72; Teacher/Coach East HS 1972-; *ai:* Var Head Coach Mens Swimming Team; *office:* East HS 230 S Marr Rd Columbus IN 47201

FRICK, ELIZABETH STECHSCHULTE, Fourth Grade Teacher; *b:* Lima, OH; *m:* R. Stephen C.; *c:* Marna E., Allyson E.; *ed:* (BS) Elem Ed, Bowling Green St Univ 1970; Lib Media Specialist Bowling Green St Univ 1984-86; *cr:* 3rd Grade Teacher 1970-84, Elem Lib Specialist 1984-86, 4th Grade Teacher 1986- Leipsic Local Sch; *ai:* Leipsic Ed Assn, NEA 1970-; OH Ed Assn Treas 1970-; OH Child Conservation League (Secy 1978-79, VP 1981-82, Pres 1982-83, Treas 1989-); Putnam Count Tennis League Secy 1988-89; *home:* 108 Spring St Ottawa OH 45875

FRICKE, DONNA NADEANE SILBERNAGEL, Marketing Teacher; *b:* Bismarck, ND; *m:* Joel; *c:* Jacob D., Adam J.; *ed:* (AA) Management, Bismarck Jr Coll 1982; (BS) Mrktg Ed, Univ of ND 1984; Grad Stud Univ of ND, Minot St, ND St Univ; *cr:* Teachers Aide Wilton HS 1984; Mrktg Teacher Century HS 1984-; *ai:* DECA & Jr Class Adv; ND Voc Assn 1989-, Young Educator Awd 1988; Natl Mrktg Ed Assn 1989-; O M Mager Leadership Awd 1983; Bismarck Jr Coll DECA Pres 1981-82; Bismarck St Coll Alumni Assn Pres Elect 1989-; *office:* Century HS 1000 Century Ave Bismarck ND 58501

FRICKE, GERALDINE SPENCER, Kindergarten Teacher; *b:* Milwaukee, WI; *c:* Kristin Cardwell, Robert J., Derek S.; *ed:* (BA) Elem Ed, Univ of WI 1958; *cr:* 1st Grade Teacher Milwaukee Cty Schls 1958-62, Fairfax Cty Schls 1964-65, 1972-74; Kndgtn Teacher Keswick Chrstn 1977-; *office:* Keswick Chrstn Sch 10101 54th Ave N Saint Petersburg FL 33708

FRICKENSTEIN, CARMEN THOMPSON, Retired; *b:* Brunswick, NE; *m:* Joe; *c:* JoAnn Bergh; *ed:* (BS) Eng/Elem Ed - Cum Laude, Midland Coll 1968; Univ of NE Lincoln, Loyola Univ, Concordia Teachers Coll, Wayne St; *cr:* Teacher Rural Sch 1937-41; Elem Teacher Creighton Cmmty Schls 1957-84; *ai:* Creighton Teachers Organization Past Pres; NE St Teachers Assn, NEA, Intnl Rdng Assn; Ladies Auxiliary VFW #1151 Treas; Creighton Womans Club Treas; Amer Legion Auxilliary Historian; Creighton Tree Bd; Creighton Clean Cmmty Commission Pres; *home:* 1102 Clark Ave Creighton NE 68729

FRIDAY, SUSAN FRESH, 1st Grade Teacher; *b:* Altoona, PA; *m:* W. Kent; *c:* Alan, Laura; *ed:* (BS) Elem Ed, Lock Haven St Coll 1971; Masters Equivalent; *cr:* 4th Grade Teacher Oak Ridge Elem Sch 1971-76; 2nd Grade Techer 1976-79, 1st Grade Teacher 1979- Lincoln Sch; *ai:* 1st Grade Dept Chairperson; Elem & Dist Curr Cncl; PA St Ed Assn, NEA, Tyrone Area Ed Assn 1971-; Cath Daughters of America, Santas Elves of Tyrone, Tyrone Regional Art & Act Cncl Creative Young Actors & Artists Summer Act Dir, Tyrone Cmmty Players Childrens Theatre Exec Comm 1988-; Bicentennial Grant 1976.

FRIDAY, SUSAN GRAVES, English Teacher; *b:* Cleveland, OH; *m:* Beranrd J.; *c:* Keith; *ed:* (BA) Eng, SUNY Albany 1968; Ed, SUNYA; Eng, Russell Sage; *cr:* Eng Teacher Sescutoga Springs Publis Schls 1968-71, Schuylerville Cntrl Sch 1980-81; Greenwich Cntrl Sch 1981-83, Hartford Cntrl Sch 1983-; *ai:* Chaverone Sr Class Trip; NHS Selection Comm; NY St Teachers Assn 1968-; NY St Saddleforge Assn 1960- Service 1986; Amer Morgan Horse Assn Youth Leader 1975-; Ny St Morgan Horse Society Youth Leader 1968-; Natl Leader Morgan Youth Group; 4-H Leader; Instricted Natl Winner 4-H Horse Judging Contestant; *home:* 22 Scout Rd Gansevoort NY 12831

FRIEDERICH, GAIL MILLER, Curriculum Resource Teacher; *b:* Birmingham, AL; *m:* Sheldon K.; *ed:* (BS) Elem Ed, Univ of S MS 1975; (MED) Educl Leadership, Univ of Cntrl FL 1988; *cr:* Classroom Teacher Suwannee Mid Sch 1975-76, Suwannee Elem Sch 1976-78; Classroom Teacher 1978-88, Curr Resource Teacher 1989- Lake Silver Elem; *ai:* Sch Oration Contest; Sch Newspaper; News Liaison; Sch Staff Dev & Additions Coord; Textbook & Partners in Ed Rep; FL Assn of Sci Teachers 1985-88; Kappa Delta Pi 1987-89; PTA Bd Faculty Rep; Environmental Grant Writing Team; St Certified FL Master Teacher; Lake Silver Teacher of Yr 1986; Beginning Teacher Adv 1985-89; Lake Silver Sci Grant Writing Team; Summer Enrichment Sci Prgm Teacher; *office:* Lake Silver Elem Sch 2401 N Rio Grande Ave Orlando FL 32804

FRIEDERS, CAROL MOENNING, 4th Grade Teacher; *b:* Quincy, IL; *m:* Robert; *c:* Michael, Paul, Mary; *ed:* (BSED) Eng/ Elem Ed, Quincy Coll 1954; *cr:* Kndgtn Teacher Oak Park Sch 1954-59; 4th Grade Teacher Holy Angels Sch 1969-; *ai:* NCEA 1969-; *office:* Holy Angels Sch 720 Kengington Pl Aurora IL 60506

FRIEDMAN, HYMAN ALEXANDER, Art Teacher; *b:* Newark, NJ; *m:* Amy Morrel; *c:* Penni D., Sharon Friedman Sweet; *ed:* (BA) Elem Ed, Seton Hall Univ 1957; (MA) Art Ed, NY Univ 1962; *cr:* Teacher Lincoln Sch 1957-60; Art Teacher Lincoln Sch, Locust St Sch, Harrison St Sch, Grace Wildby Sch 1960-75, Abraham Clark HS 1975-; *ai:* Art Club Adv; Hall Duty Monitor; Union Cty Teachers Credit Union Bd of Dirs 1966-; Linden Cmmty Recreation Commission Art Instr 1963-83, Plaque; *office:* Abraham Clark HS 122 W 6th St Roselle NJ 07203

FRIEDMAN, KATHLEEN MAHER, Earth Science Teacher; *b:* Kingston, NY; *ed:* (BA) Sci/Ed, St Univ of NY 1971; (MLS) Medical Librarian, Univ of AZ 1980; Grad Work Geosciences; Working Towards Masters Astronomy, Univ of AZ; *cr:* Phys Sci Teacher Kingston City Schls Consolidated 1972-76, San Manuel Sch Dist 1977-79; Earth Sci Teacher Tucson Unified Sch Dist 1980-81, Tanque Verde Sch Dist 1981-; *ai:* Sci & Engineering Fair Spon; Natl Assn of Geology Teachers, NSTA, AZ Sci Teachers Assn 1989-; Natl Sci Fnd Grant; *office:* Emily Gray Jr HS 4201 N Mel Pomene Way Tucson AZ 85749

FRIEDMAN, LAURA LOUISE, English Teacher; *b:* Dubuque, IA; *ed:* (BA) Eng, IA St Univ 1985; Elements of Effective Instruction Training-Levels I & II; Cooper L Earning Training-Levels I & II; Sch Team Training-Level I; *cr:* 8th Grade Teacher Indian Woods Mid Sch 1985; 9th-12th Grade Teacher Shawnee Prgm Night Sch 1988-, Shawnee Mission Summer Sch 87-89; *ai:* Shawnee Mission Effective Instruction Cadre 1986-; *office:* Shawnee Mission Sch Dist 9700 Woodson Shawnee Mission KS 66207

FRIEDMAN, MADONNA, Third Grade Teacher; *b:* Manchester, IA; *ed:* (BA) Elem Ed, Briar Cliff Coll 1966; Trng for Working with Gifted & Talented; Teaching to Every Learner; Teacher as Leader; *cr:* 1st/2nd Grade Teacher Immaculate Conception Sch 1958-61; 2nd Grade Teacher Sacred Heart Sch 1961-66; 1st-3rd Grade Teacher Immaculate Conception Sch 1966-68; 3rd Grade Teacher St Thomas Aquinas Sch 1968-70, Holy Ghost Sch 1970-79, Sacred Heart Sch 1979-; *ai:* Soc Comm; Parish Cncl Soc Action Comm; Teacher as Leader Prgm; NCEA; Parish Cncl (Chairperson, Liturgy & Spiritual Growth Comm) 1982-86; Common Venture 1969-71; Parish Census Dir 1986; Recognition by Scott Foresman for Tutorial Prgm; *office:* Sacred Heart Sch 234 N Sycamore Monticello IA 52310

FRIEDMAN, SANDRA GOLDMAN, Resource Room Teacher; *b:* New York City, NY; *m:* Robert B.; *c:* Jane; *ed:* (BS) Ed, Univ of PA 1962; (MS) Spec Ed, C W Post Coll 1979; *cr:* 5th Grade Teacher PS 39 1962-64; 4th Grade Teacher PS 2 1964-66; Resource Room Teacher Huntington HS 1978-; *ai:* Orton Society 1982-; Univ of PA Alumni Interviewer 1984-; *office:* Huntington HS Oakwood & Mc Ray Rds Huntington NY 11743

FRIELING, ESTHER BODLING, Retired Teacher; *b:* Vernon, TX; *w:* Oscar H. (dec); *c:* Wanda Frantz, Kenneth; *ed:* (AA) Elem Ed/Parish Worker, St Johns-Winfield 1941; Geography, Concordia Teachers Coll; *cr:* 1st/2nd Grade Teacher Immanuel Luth Sch 1941-46, St Matthews Luth Sch 1946-51; 3rd/4th Grade Teacher 1955-61, 2nd Grade Teacher 1965-86 St Paul Luth Sch; *ai:* Outstanding Luth Educator TX Dist 1982.

FRIEND, CRAIG THOMPSON, 9th Grade Soc Stud Teacher; *b:* Glens Falls, NY; *ed:* (BA) His, Wake Forest Univ 1983; (MA) His, Clemson Univ 1990; *cr:* Soc Stud Teacher Southwest Jr HS 1983-87; Teaching Asst Clemson Univ 1987-89; Soc Stud Teacher Southwest Jr HS 1989-; *ai:* Beta Club Spon; Jr Var Bsktbl Coach; Lander Awd Excl in Study of His Clemson Univ; *office:* Southwest Jr HS 1 Roadrunner Ave Gastonia NC 28052

FRIERSON, CASSANDRA W., Human Resources Director; *b:* Andrews, SC; *m:* James L.; *c:* Angela, Brian; *ed:* (BS) Bio, SC St Coll 1963; (EDM) Educl Admin, Univ of Rochester 1976; Certificate of Advanced Stud Univ of Rochester 1986; *cr:* Sci Teacher 1966-85, Sci Dept Head 1986-88, Human Resources Dir 1988- Rochester City Sch Dist; *ai:* Prism Prgm Bd of Dir; Amer Assn of Sch Personnel Admin; Sch Admin Assn of NY St; Sci Teachers Assn of NY St; Urban League of Rochester; Natl Assn for the Advancement of Colored People.

FRIERSON, DELANEY WALKER, Business Education Teacher; *b:* Houston, TX; *m:* William James Sr.; *c:* Ingra, Taningra, Lula J., William Jr., Kelvin; *ed:* (BA) Poly Sci/Scndry Sci, Prairie View A&M Univ 1975; Working Toward MED, Ed Admin, Univ of SC; *cr:* Teacher Hillcrest HS 1978-; *ai:* Miss Wildcat Pageant Coord 1979-83; Cheerleading Adv 1979-80; FBLA Adv 1984-; Steering Comm for Southern Accreditation Coll & Schls 1989-; Coord Sumter Ctys Star Search 1990; Sing Out Winner 1988-89; SC Ed Assn 1985-; FBLA Alumni 1983-; SC Bus Ed Assn 1988-; SC Cncl for Cmptrs in Ed 1989-; Green Hill Baptist Young Adult Choir Adv 1982-86; Clarendon Cty Beauty Pageant Consultant 1983; *home:* P O Box 615 Manning SC 29102

FRIESEN, MARLENE MAUDE, Music/English/Drama Teacher; *b:* Rosteern SK, Canada; *ed:* (BA) Music Ed, NW Nazarene Coll 1980; *cr:* Teacher Nampa Chrstn Sch 1980-; *ai:* Sch Play Dir, Band Adv 1990; Phi Delta Lambda (Secy, Treas) 1986-88; Amer Choral Dir Assn; Natl Music Educators; Chamber of Commerce Teacher of Month 1989.

FRIGO, ANTHONY T., Band Director; *b:* St Louis, MO; *ed:* (BME) Music Ed, Loyola Univ 1981; Marching Band Drill Design, Instruction, Woodwind Methodology; *cr:* Band Dir River Oaks Acad 1981-82; Woodwind Instr Loyola Univ 1987-88; Head Band Dir Rummel HS 1982-; *ai:* Marching, Symphonic, Jazz Bands; Music Dept Head; LA Music Educators Assn 1979-, Sr High Honor Band Chm Dist VI; LA Band Masters Assn 1981-87; Intnl Assn of Jazz Educators 1981-; Guest Clinician Jr HS Honor Jazz Band 1990; Adjudicator LA Dist Level Lg Ensemble Festivals; Prof Appearances with Bob Hope, Rich Little, Ella Fitzgerald, Temptations; *office:* Archbishop Rummel HS 1901 Severn Ave Metairie LA 70001

FRIMML, MARLYS WERNING, Kindergarten Teacher; *b:* Newhall, IA; *m:* Robert J.; *c:* Linda M. Timm, Jennifer L., Christopher R., Matthew D.; *ed:* (BA) Music/Elem Ed, Wartburg Coll 1962; Univ of IA; *cr:* K-12th Grade Music Teacher Garrison Consolidated Sch 1962-63, Garwin Cmnty Sch 1963-65; K-6th Grade Music Teacher Marion Ind Schls 1965-70; 2nd Grade Teacher 1972-88, Kndgtn Teacher 1988- Benton Cmnty Sch 1988-; *ai:* ISEA, NEA 1962-; Music Ed Assn 1962-70; IA Rdng Assn 1987-; St Bd for Hearing Impaired Secy 1984-88; Conference for Hearing Impaired 1980-; IA Parents of Deaf 1980-; Church Choir Dir; *home:* RR 1 Box 34 Newhall IA 52315

FRISBIE, ANN HERN, Vocational Home Ec Teacher; *b:* Enid, OK; *m:* George R.; *c:* Megan, Eric; *ed:* (BS) Home Ec Ed, OK St Univ 1983; *cr:* Voc Home Ec Teacher Minco Public Schls 1983-; *ai:* FHA Adv; 7th Grade Class Spon; MEA Schlsp Comm; NEA, OK Ed Assn; Minco Ed Assn (Pres 1989, Secy 1988); Amer OK Voc Assn, Amer Home Ec Assn 1983-; Thaita Chi Omega 1989-; Young Homemaker of OK Adv 1983-87; Outstanding Young Women of America; *home:* Rt 2 CW 217 Tuttle OK 73089

FRISBY, DONNA STEVENS, Fourth Grade Teacher; *b:* Vinita, OK; *m:* Joe Wayne; *c:* Sami Jo,; *ed:* (AA) Home Ec Ed, Northeastern Ok A&M 1975; (BS) Family Relations & Child Dev, OK St Univ 1978; (ME) Rdng Northeastern St Univ 1982; *cr:* 2nd Grade Teacher 1978-85, 4th Grade Teacher 1985-1986 Hall Halsell Sch; 4th Grade 1986-87,1988-, 5th Grade 1987-88 Will Rogers School; *ai:* OEA; NEA; Vinita Classroom Teachers Assn; *home:* Rt 1, Box 392 Vinita OK 74301

FRISCH, DENNIS D., 7th/8th Grade Science Teacher; *b:* Davenport, IA; *m:* Judith M. Walker; *c:* Mark S., Todd J., Jill K.; *ed:* (BA) Sci, 1966, (MA) Bio, 1970 Univ of N IA; Grad Courses Univ of IA; *cr:* 9th Grade Sci Teacher Nell-Mc Gowen Jr HS 1966-69; 7th-8th Grade Sci Teacher Wilton Elem 1970-; *ai:* NABT, NEA, IA St Ed Assn 1970-; Durant Volunteer Ambulance Service (Mem, VP 1976, Pres 1977-78, 1989-), 1975-, Advanced Emergency Medical Technicial I-0 1980; Jr HS Sci Teacher of Yr 1978; Natl Sci Fnd Academic Yr Inst Awd 1969-70; IA Teacher Incentive Awd 1976; Article Published 1989; Recipient of Jaycees Cmmy Service Awd 1981-82; IA Governors Volunteer Awd Recipient 1986; *office:* Wilton Elem Sch 201 E 6th Wilton IA 52778

FRIST, BONNIE MAE, 4th Grade Teacher; *b:* Anderson, IN; *c:* Kimberly R. Frist Alexander, Robert D.; *ed:* (BS) Elem Ed, 1971, (MA) Elem Ed, 1975 Ball St Univ; Gifted/Talented Lang Art, Math Classes & Trng; *cr:* 4th Grade Teacher 1971-, Lang Art Gifted/Talented Teacher 1988- Greenfield Cntrl Cmmty Schls; *ai:* ISTA, NEA 1989-; IN Prof Educators; IN Assn for Gifted 1989-; *office:* Eden Elem Schl 8185 N St Rd 9 Greenfield IN 46140

FRITCHEY, JUDD E., Band Director; *ed:* (BS) Music Ed, Clarion Univ 1979; (MS) Sch/Cmmty Counseling, Youngstown St Univ 1989; Higher Ed Counseling, Data Processing; *cr:* Band Dir Rayen HS 1979-80, Hayes Jr HS 1980-; *ai:* All Instrumental Ensembles; Kappa Delta Pi 1978-87; Chi Sigma Sota, Phi Kappa Phi 1989-; Academic Schlsp for Masters Degree; *office:* Hayes Jr HS 1616 Ford Ave Youngstown OH 44504

FRITTS, JANET HICKS, English Teacher; *b:* Corning, AR; *m:* Dwight; *c:* Melissa, Julie; *ed:* (BSE) Eng, AR St Univ 1983; *cr:* Eng Teacher Clarkton Jr/Sr HS 1983-87, Portageville Mid Sch 1987-; *ai:* Spon Natl Jr Honor Society; Spelling Bee, Writing Achievement Contest Coord SE MO Univ; Prof Dev Comm 1987-; MSTA 1983-87; *home:* 209 W 4th Portageville MO 63873

FRITZ, LEAH WERTMAN, First Grade Teacher; *b:* Palmerton, PA; *m:* Robert F.; *c:* Robert C., Brent D.; *ed:* (BS) Elem Ed, Bloomsburg Univ 1951; *cr:* 1st-8th Grade Teacher 1951-55, 1st/2nd Grade Teacher 1955-59 W Penn Township; 1st Grade Teacher Tamaqua Area Sch Dist 1960-; *ai:* Delta Kappa Gamma Chairperson Various Comms; NEA, PA St Ed Assn, Tamaqua Ed Assn; Lioness; Pocahontas Cncl Cnslr 1985, 1990; Luth Church Women Treas 1960-86; *office:* W Penn Elem Sch RD 2 New Ringgold PA 17960

FRITZ, TOMMY G., Mathematics Department Chair; *b:* Fresno, CA; *m:* Ruth L. Mc Nary; *c:* Kerr, Erica; *ed:* (BA) Phys Sci, Fresno St Univ 1958; (MALS) Math, Wesleyan Univ 1971; *cr:* Curr/Project Dir 1986-88, Teacher 1961- Riverdale HS; *ai:* CTA, NEA 1970-; Natl Sci Fnd Grant 1970-71; *office:* Riverdale HS 3086 W Mt Whitney Ave Riverdale CA 93656

FRIZELL, DANIEL, High School English Teacher; *b:* Orrville, OH; *ed:* (BA) Eng Ed, Heidelberg Coll 1981; *cr:* Eng Teacher Smithville HS 1982-; *ai:* Fellowship of Chrstn Athletes & Yrbk Adv; Faculty Cncl Mem; Church of Christ Choir Dir; *office:* Smithville HS 484 E Main St Smithville OH 44677

FRIZZELL, EVERETT RAY, HS Chemistry/Physics Teacher; *b:* Lancaster, NH; *m:* Margaret F.; *c:* Lyle, Lara; *ed:* (BS) Sci/Ag, Univ of NH 1968; (MED) Sci, Univ of VT 1977; Chem, Univ CA Berkely; *cr:* Sci Teacher Colebrook Acad 1968-72, Essex Jr HS 1972-77, Berlin HS 1977-85, Profile HS 1985-; *ai:* Gifted/Talented Comm Mem; NH Sci Teachers Assn 1972-; NSTA 1985-; Town of Stark Sch Bd Chm; Coos Cty Planning Bd Mem; *home:* RFD Box 469 Emerson Rd Stark NH 03582

FRNECH, JACQUELINE MARIE, Elementary Teacher; *b:* Hartford, CT; *ed:* (BS) Phys Ed, Towson St Univ 1979; (MA) Exercise Physiology, Univ of MD 1989; US Field Hockey Olympic Dev Coach; Olympic Trng Center 1980; Level I Certified Coach; *cr:* Phys Ed Specialist Charlotte Latin Sch 1980-83; Asst Field Hockey/Lacrosse Coach/Grad Asst Univ of MD 1983-85; Exercise Physiologist N Arundle Carolina Rehab & Fitness Center 1985-86; Phys Ed Specialist Baltimore Cty Public Schls 1986-88, Howard Cty Public Schls 1988-; *ai:* Before Sch Club Dir; HS Lacrosse Field Hockey Coach; Baltimore Indoor & Baltimore Se I Hockey Player 1980-; Olympic Dev Field Hockey Coach; Jr Hockey & Media Comm; MAHPERD 1977-79, 1988-; USFHA VP Jr Hockey 1989; VP Jr Hockey USFHA 1989; Received Grad Assistantship Univ of MD 1983-85; *office:* Bollman Bridge Elem Sch 9623 Lambeth Ct Columbia MD 21046

FRODEL, EDWARD C., History Department Chair; *b:* Aberdeen, WA; *m:* Ann Marie Sommerseth; *c:* Margaret M., Kara A.; *ed:* (BA) Poly Sci, Univ WA 1958; (MA) His, 1969, (PHD) His, 1974 Univ CO; Ger, Univ of Innsbruck Austria; *cr:* Jr/Sr HS Soc Stud Teacher Tumon HS 1958-60; Jr HS Teacher Army Dept Sch 1960-61; Jr HS Lang Art/Soc Stud Teacher Mc Knight Jr HS 1964-65; His Dept Chm Amer Intnl Sch 1965-68; Western Civics/Russian His Teacher Univ CO Denver 1969-73; World Civics/Russian His Teacher Pacific Luth Univ 1973-74; His Dept Chm/Advanced Placement His Teacher N Kitsap HS 1974-; *ai:* Jr St & Stu Government/Elections Adv; Advanced Placement; Dist Curr Comm; HS Leadership Team; WA St Cncl for Hum, NCSS, WA Ed Assn; Intnl His Honorary; NDEA Honorarium Research Grant for SE Europe; Teaching Associateship Univ CO Denver; NEH Fellowship; Ind Study in Hum; *home:* PO Box 342 Poulsbo WA 98370

FRODGE, PAULETTA SMITH, 4th Grade Teacher; *b:* Burkesville, KY; *c:* Ashley P.; *ed:* (BS) Elem Ed, 1982; (MS) Elem Ed/Rdng Specialist 1984; Elem Ed, 1986 Western KY Univ; *cr:* 4th-6th Grade Teacher Cumberland Cty Elem 1982-; *ai:* Republican Womens Club; Sunday Sch Teacher at Burkesville Church of Christ; Homemakers Club of Burkesville; Burkesville Womens Club; Burkesville Womens Club; Hospital & Nursing Home Volunteer; KY Ed Assn 1982-; NEA 1982-; Alpha Kappa Chapter 1989-; PTA & PTO Cumberland Cty Mem 1981-; Outstanding Service Awd 1983-85; Past VP & Treas of Burkesville PTA; *office:* Cumberland Cty Elem 150 Glasgow Rd Burkesville KY 42717

FROEHLINGSDORF, JOSEPH C., HS Teacher; *b:* Virginia, MN; *m:* Susan Mordini; *c:* Hanns, Peter, Joe Jr., Tommy; *ed:* (AA) Ind Arts, Virginia Jr Coll 1959; (BS) Univ MN 1963; (MA) Ind, Arts Photo, Univ MN 1982; *cr:* Teacher Virginia HS 1963-; *ai:* Mens Swim Coach; Adv Lettermans Club; Amer Red Cross Inst Trainer Natl Coaches Assn; MN Coaches Assn; *home:* 7132 Hwy 53 Britt MN 55710

FROGGE, JAMES LEWIS, Science Department Chairman; *b:* Kankakee, IL; *m:* Margaret Hansen; *c:* Jessica, Sarah, Nathan; *ed:* (BS) Engineering, Yale Univ 1972; (MA) Sci Teaching, Governors St Univ 1982; Chem, Princeton 1982; Math, Univ of IL 1986-88; *cr:* Sci Teacher Bishop Mc Namara 1972-; *ai:* Asst Var Ftbl Coach; Faculty Advisory Bd; NSTA, ACS, AAPT, AAAS; Dreyfus Master Teacher 1982; Governors Teaching Awd 1983; Reviewer J Chem Ed 1980-; *office:* Bishop Mc Namara HS Brookmont at Entrance Kankakee IL 60901

FROLA, CYNTHIA CIPOLLONI, English Teacher; *b:* Masontown, WV; *m:* John L.; *c:* John Jr., Joseph P.; *ed:* (BS) Elem Ed, 1963, (MA) Rdng, 1965 WV Univ; Rdng, Child Dev, Psych, Ed Admin; *cr:* Instr WV Univ 1964-69; Teacher Springfield Local Schls 1980-; *ai:* Rdng, Lang Art Graded Course of Study Comms; Stu Government Adv; Kappa Delta Pi 1963-; Intnl Rdng Assn 1963-87; OH Eng Teachers Cncl; Nativity Church Ed Comm Chm 1984-86; Space Sci Stu Involvement Prgm Dist Winner; *office:* Schrop Mid Sch 2215 Pickle Rd Akron OH 44312

FROM, LORNA SUE, First Grade Teacher; *b:* Maryville, MO; *m:* Ronald Ray; *c:* Lori A., Jeffrey D., Thomas R.; *ed:* (BS) Elem Ed, 1973, (MS) Rdng, 1982 NW MO St Univ; Several Wkshps & Courses in Elem Ed; *cr:* Chapter I Rdng/Math Teacher 1974-76, 1st Grade Teacher 1976- Eugene Field Elem; *ai:* Prof Dev Comm 1988-; Instructional Improvement Cncl; Assn for Child Ed (Pres, VP, Secy) 1980-86; CTA, MO St Teachers Assn (Pres, VP) 1985-87; *office:* Eugene Field Elem Sch 418 E 2nd Maryville MO 64468

FROMAN, MITCHELL LEE, Jr High School History Teacher; *b:* St Louis, MO; *m:* Sandra Shirley Musgrave; *c:* April, Mitchell Jr, Matthew; *ed:* (BS) Soc Stud/Earth Sci, 1974, (MAT) His Scndry Admin, 1980 SE MA St Univ; *cr:* Jr HS Sci Teacher/Coach N Jefferson Mid Sch 1974-76; Sci Teacher/Coach Scott City HS 1976-77; Jr HS His Teacher Greenville HS 1978-; *ai:* His Day Dir; Scholars Bowl Coord , Jr Beta Club Adv; 7th Grade Class Spon; Dist Discipline Code Comm; Dept Curr Comm; Career Ladder Rerite Comm; Asst Elem Bsktbl Coach; Greenville Fed Teachers Salary Comm; Greenville Fed of Teachers Pres 1989-; Amer Historical Assn 1982-84, Certificate of Recognition 1984; MO Historical Society 1981-84; Wayne Cty Historical Society 1988-; Phi Alph Theta 1970-74; Nom Outstanding Teacher MO 1989; Nom E A Richter Awd Excl Citizenship Ed 1989; Greenville Fed Teachers VP 1986-89; Stu Won Dist, St, Natl His Competition Awds & Schlsp; *office:* Greenville HS P O Box 277 Greenville MO 63944

FRONTINO, DOLLY, Elementary & Head Teacher; *b:* Hastings, PA; *ed:* (BS) Elem Ed, St Francis Coll 1967; Masters Equivalent Penn St 1969; *cr:* Elem Teacher 1967-, Head Teacher 1983- Cambria Heights-Bakerton Elem; *ai:* ACT 178 Prof Dev & Cambria Heights Citizens Advisory Comm; PSEA, NEA 1967-; Cambria Heights Ed Assn (Pres Elect 1989-, Pres 1990, Building Rep 1978-); *home:* PO Box 394 Spangler St Hastings PA 16646

FROSCH, CAROL SNOW, Soc Stud Department Chair; *b:* Ponca City, OK; *ed:* Assoc Bus, N OK Coll 1967; (BS) Bus, OK St Univ Stillwater 1969; (ME) Scndry Ed/Soc Stud, Cntrl St Univ Edmomd 1974; (EDD) Scndry Ed, Univ of OK Norman 1980; *cr:* Substitute Teacher Mid-Del Schls 1979-82; Asst Professor/Dept Chairperson OK Baptist Univ 1982-84; Ed Specialist Univ of OK 1984-85; Substitute Teacher Mid-Del Schls 1985-86; Classroom Teacher/Dept Chairperson Choctaw-Nicoma Park Schls 1986-; *ai:* Sch Soc Stud Dept Chairperson; Dist Scndry Soc Stud Chairperson; Dist Textbook Selection Comm; Sch Entry Yr Assistance Prgm Chairperson; NEA, OK Ed Assn, Choctaw-Nicoma Park Assn Classroom Teachers 1986-; OK Historical Society 1989-; Articles Published 1980-84; OK Trivia Contest Consultant 1988; *office:* Nicoma Park Jr HS 1321 N Hickman Nicoma Park OK 73066

FROST, FRANCES MILES, Chemistry Teacher & Dept Chm; *b:* Lake Charles, LA; *m:* Lawrence N. Jr.; *c:* Lawrence III, Christopher, Laura; *ed:* (BS) Bio Ed, Mc Neese St Univ 1970; Grad Work Mc Neese St Univ & LA St Univ; Chem, LSU; *cr:* Teacher Washington HS 1970-76, St Theresa of Avica 1976-77; Teacher/Sci Dept Chm Redemptorist HS 1977-; *ai:* Jr Moderator & Prom Spon; Yrbk Photographer & Asst Moderator; *office:* Redemptorist HS 4000 St Gerard Baton Rouge LA 70805

FROST, FRANK STEVEN, Mathematics/Science Teacher; *b:* Kalispell, MT; *m:* Rayleen J.; *c:* S. Paul, Sara E.; *ed:* (BS) Math/Phys Sci, W MT Coll 1976; *cr:* 5th-8th Grade Math/Sci Teacher Vaughn Sch 1976-; *ai:* Boys Bsktbl, Boys & Girls Track & Field Coach; MSTA; *office:* Vaughn Sch PO Box Vaughn MT 59487

FROST, SHARON ANNE (DAWALD), First Grade Teacher; *b:* Carthage, MO; *m:* Randy D.; *ed:* (BS) Ed, MO S St Coll 1978; *cr:* 3rd Grade Teacher 1978-81, 1st Grade Teacher 1981- Wildwood Elem Sch; *ai:* MO St Teachers Assn (Mem 1978-, VP 1989-); Sarcoxie Cmmty Teachers Assn 1978-; Intnl Rdng Assn Jasper Cty 1986-; Mt Moriah United Meth Church Youth Leader 1985-; Wildwood Elem Teacher of Yr 1982; *home:* Rt 2 Box 123AAA Carthage MO 64836

FROST, SUE LONDON, Art Teacher; *b:* Portsmouth, VA; *m:* John W.; *c:* Megan S.; *ed:* (BFA) Art Ed, Univ of NC 1971; (MS) Counseling, Old Dominion Univ 1976; Art Ed Grad Stud, VCU; *cr:* Art Teacher VA Beach City Public Schls 1981-; Staff Artist Frames Etc Gallery 1985-; *ai:* Adopt-A-Sch Comm; Curr for Art; City Wide Art Show; Zoo Mem 1986-; Civic Club 1976-; Art Center 1971-; VA Museum Fellowship; *home:* 1788 Upper Chelsea Reach Virginia Beach VA 23454

FROSTMAN, SHIRLEY G., 7th Grade Science Teacher; *b:* Washburn, WI; *ed:* (BS) Natural Sci, Univ of WI Madison 1958; (MS) Prof Dev/Natural Sci, Univ of WI Whitewater 1978; Grad Stud Cmptr Sci; *cr:* Sci Teacher Waukesha Public Schls 1958-; *ai:* Sci Tutor; Sci, Chess, Cmptr Club Adv; NASA Orbiter Naming Contest Adv; NEA, WEAC, EAW, Milwaukee Educators Cmptr Assn; *office:* Butler Mid Sch 310 N Hine Ave Waukesha WI 53188

FRUIT, GRACE TUCKER, Art Teacher; *b:* Louisburg, NC; *m:* William Shepherd; *c:* Jean Fruit Smith, Betsy, Bill Jr.; *ed:* (BA) Art/His, Mary Washington 1963; (MA) Hum/Art His, Old Dominion 1983; *cr:* Art Teacher Princess Anne HS 1963-66; 5th Grade Teacher Kempsville Meadows Elem 1967-68, Point-of-View Elem 1968-69; Art Teacher Kempsville Jr HS; *ai:* Stu Cncl & Art Club Adv; Stu Awds Comm Prgm Chairperson; Wellness Comm; Natl Art Ed Assn, VA Art Ed Assn 1984-; VA Beach SPCA (Treas 1982-84) 1974-85; Kempsville Jr HS Teacher of Yr 1989; VA Art Ed Conference Wkshp Leader; Article Published; *office:* Kempsville Jr HS 860 Church Dr Virginia Beach VA 23464

FRUM, ROBERT HAROLD, 6th Grade Teacher; *b:* Athens, OH; *m:* Mary Frances; *c:* Brett M., Cynthia D. Hoke; *ed:* (THB) Theology/Philosophy, Olivet Nazarene Univ 1958; (MS) Elem Admin, Univ of Dayton 1968; *cr:* 6th Grade Teacher Kitty Hawk Elem 1962-65, Monticello Elem 1965-87; Title I Dir/Elem Summer Sch Prin/6th Grade Math/Eng Teacher Weisenborn Intermediate 1987-; *ai:* Huber Heights Ed Assn Pres; Montgomery Cty Ed Assn Pres Elect; Martha Holden Jennings Schlsp Awd; *home:* 575 Pine St Tipp City OH 45371

FRUTCHEY, JAMES ARTHUR, Social Studies Coordinator; *b:* Scranton, PA; *m:* Barbara Melliand; *c:* James J.; *ed:* (BS) His, Union Coll 1964; (MA) His, PA St 1968; Newark St Coll, Seton Hall Univ, E Stroudsburg Univ, Indiana PA Univ, Millersville Univ; *cr:* Sr HS Teacher Fanwood HS Scotch Plains 1965-70, Abington Heights HS 1970-; Soc Stud Coord Abington Heights Sch Dist 1970-; *ai:* Var Sftbl Coach; Tour Cnslr, Stu Groups to Soviet Union or Europe; NCSS, Soc Stud Supvrs Assn; Frank T Dolbear Awd Funds for Travel to Soviet Union 1979; *office:* Abington Heights Sch Dist Abington Heights HS N Campus Noble Rd Clarks Summit PA 18411

FRUTH, KIRK ALLEN, 5th Grade Teacher/Elem Cnslr; *b:* Defiance, OH; *m:* Lynette Ann Moneghan; *c:* Abbey, Jennifer, Ryan; *ed:* (BS) Elem Ed, 1976, (MS) Guidance/Counseling, 1980 Bowling Green St Univ; *cr:* 5th Grade Teacher 1976-, Elem Cnslr 1984- N Richland Adams Sch; *ai:* Intramural Recess Bsktbl & Cty Drug Abuse Prgm; Building Intervention Team Mem & Secy; NEA, Mem 1976-; St Johns United Church of Christ (Chrstn Ed Bd Pres 1982-85, Sunday Sch Supt 1987-89); Martha Holden Jennings Lecture Series Bowling Green St Univ 1979-80; Drug Ed Grant; *office:* N Richland Adams Elem Sch RR 4 Defiance OH 43512

FRY, MARILYN VAN CISE, Biology/Physiology Teacher; *b:* Sharon, PA; *m:* Thomas; *c:* Brett; *ed:* (BA) Bio, OH Northern Univ 1960; (MA) Bio, Univ of Toledo 1967; Univ of Pittsburg, Bowling Green, Dayton Univ, St Francis; *cr:* Sci Teacher Brookfield HS 1960-61, Mc Guffey HS 1962-63, Paulding HS 1963-64, Riverdale HS 1964-69, Paulding HS 1969-; *ai:* Paulding Ed Assn (Pres, Other Office Comms) 1969-; NW OH Ed Assn, NEA ; NSTA; Assistantship to Univ of Pittsburg 1961-62; Univ of Toledo Grants 1969; Outstanding Teacher Awd OH Acad of Sci 1972; Outstanding Educator of America 1973; Teacher Delegate for Youth Sci Exchange to Soviet Union 1989; *home:* 901 Kay Nora Ave Paulding OH 45879

FRY, WALLACE SAMUEL, Science Teacher; *b:* Grand Rapids, MI; *m:* Rosanne Grace Parks; *c:* Christopher, Matthew, Kathleen; *ed:* (BA) Bio Sci, 1964, (MS) Resource Dev, 1979 MI St Univ; Teacher Expectation of Stu Achievement; Effective Teacher Trng; *cr:* Sci Teacher Mason Public Schls 1964-; Adjunct Faculty Mem for Academic Learning Prgm MSU 1984-; *ai:* Staff Dev Comm; Sch Environmental Learning Center Coord; Mentor Teacher for MSU Academic Learning Prgm; MDMEA (Pres 1971-74, Negotiator 1969-74); MEA Rep 1971-72 & 1974; NEA Rep 1972; Central Meth Church Admin Bd 1989-; BSA Sci Cnslr 1984-; Pherisis Donor for Red Cross 1986-; Past Stu Cncl Adv; Past Audio-Visual Dir; Participant in Research for Preconceived Misconceptions MSU Coll of Ed; *home:* 2350 Rolfe Rd Mason MI 48854

FRYE, RUTH CHILTON, Fourth Grade Teacher; *b:* Reidsville, NC; *m:* Joseph F.; *c:* Susan A.; *ed:* (BA) Elem Ed, Elon Coll 1965; (MA) Elem Ed, Fayetteville St Univ; Effective Teacher & Mentor Trng; Cmptrs Level II; *cr:* Teacher Vass-Lakeview Elem Sch 1965-; *ai:* Sch Beautification & Soc Sch Comm; NCAE, NEA Local Rep 1985-87; Intnl Rdng Assn 1988-; Southern Assn Various Comm Chairs 1970-86; PTA Membership Chm Ways-Means; Vass Womans Club (Pres, Secy, VP); Vass Fire Dept Auxiliary Pres; Young Educator of Yr 1970; Best all Around Teacher 1980; *home:* PO Box 336 Vass NC 28394

FRYE, TOM R., Theatre Instructor; *b:* Wichita, KS; *c:* Jeffery, Amy; *ed:* (BA) Theatre, 1971, (MA) Theatre, 1984 Wichita St Univ; *cr:* Sp Ed Teacher Starkey Developmental Ctr 1971-74, Levy Sch 1975-76, Fabrique Sch 1976-78; Theatre Instr Southeast Sch 1979-; *ai:* Thespians; Wichita Music Theatre; Wichita Cmmty Theatre; Crown-Uptown Dinner Theatre; Iron Springs Chateau Dinner Theatre Ex Dir 1976-77; Wichita Childrens Theatre Marple Theatre; Crown Players Pres 1971-72 Best Actor 1976; Crown Players VP 1973-74 Best Supporting Actor 1973; Wichita Cmmty Theatre Bst Supporting Actor 1981; Newton Cmmty Theatre Dir 1981/1983/1984; Camp Wonderful Bd Pres 1978; Camp Wonderful Camp Dir 1973-1977; Assn for Retarded Citzens Volunteer 1970; 1989/1988 Gridiron Dir Prof Journalists Assn Variety Schlrshp Show; Dir Wichita Cmmty Theatre Summer Production Commedia 89; *office:* Southeast H S 903 S Edgemoor Wichita KS 67218

FRYE, WYNONIA TASSELL, Retired Elem & Scndry Teacher; *b:* Atmore, AL; *w:* Sullivan (dec); *c:* Richard A. Freeman, Beverly A. Holman; *ed:* (BS) Home Ec, AL A&M Univ 1958; (MS) Elem Ed, Park Forest Univ 1975; *cr:* Teacher Public Sch 1959, 1986-; *ai:* New Homemakers of America Club Adv; Dancing & Majorettes Instr; Outstanding Teacher Awd 1985; AL A&M Univ Schlsp Awd.

FRYER, JEAN MURDOCH, Fifth Grade Teacher; *b:* Morrilton, AR; *m:* Jefferson R.; *c:* Joe L. Du Vall; Tami Du Vall Mc Farland; *ed:* (BS) Elem Ed, 1977, (MED) Elem Ed, 1985 AR Tech Univ Russellville; *cr:* 5th Grade Teacher Pottsville Elem Sch 1978-; *ai:* Pottsville Salary Comm; AR Ed Assn, NEA 1978-; Pope Cty Marine Rescue Auxiliary (Reporter 1988) 1987-; AR Natl Guard NCO Auxiliary 1982-; Pottsville PTO; Pottsville Elem Assn of Classroom Educators (5th Grade Level Comm Officer, Fund Raising Comm); *home:* 804 NW 2nd St Atkins AR 72823

FRYMOYER, DENNIS CLAYTON, English Teacher; *b:* Reading, PA; *m:* Lora J. Eppihimer; *c:* Scott, Mark; *ed:* (BS) Eng, Bloomsburg Univ 1970; (MED) Rdng Specialist, Kutztown Univ 1974; *cr:* Eng/Rdng Teacher Northeast Jr HS 1970-84; Eng Teacher Southern Jr HS 1984-87, Reading Sr HS 1987-; *ai:* Wrestling Coach; Asst Rdng Sr HS; *office:* Reading Sr HS 13th & Douglas Sts Reading PA 19604

FUCETOLA, MARIE GRACE, Mathematics Teacher; *b:* Hammonton, NJ; *ed:* (BA) Jr HS Ed, Glassboro St Coll 1968; *cr:* Math Teacher Dr J P Cleary Jr HS 1968-71, Hammonton Mid Sch 1971-; *ai:* Asst Yrbk Adv; Vlybl Intramural Coach; Alpha Delta Kappa (Pres, Treas) 1976-; NJ Math Teachers Assn 1985-; NEA, NJEA, ACCEA, HEA 1968-; Hammonton Hawks Assn Mem 1989-; St Martin Rosary Society; St of NJ Governors Teacher Recognition Prgm 1987; *office:* Hammonton Mid Sch Central Ave Hammonton NJ 08037

FUCHS, ENID J., First Grade Teacher; *b:* Marshfield, WI; *m:* Don; *ed:* (BS) Elem Ed, Univ of WI Stevens Point 1975; Grad Stud Univ of WI Eau Claire; *cr:* 1st Grade Teacher Medford Public Schls 1970-; *ai:* NEA, WI Ed Assn; Medford Ed Assn; Medford Ambulance Service Emergency Medical Technican 1977-88; *office:* Medford Elem Sch 1065 W Broadway Medford WI 54451

FUCHS, GERALD R., Science/Social Studies Teacher; *b:* Brenham, TX; *ed:* (BAT) Bio, Sam Houston St 1975; (MED) Soc Stud/His, 1987, Supervision Certificate 1990 Univ Houston/Univ Park ; Mid Management 1991; Grad Stud Univ TX/Austin & TX A&M; TTAS Appraisal Cert; *cr:* Teacher Deer Park Ind Sch Dist 1978-; *ai:* DPEA Treas; Campus Planning Comm; TSTA 1978-; *office:* Deer Park Jr HS 410 E 9th St Deer Park TX 77536

FUCHS, SUSAN MAY, Third Grade Teacher; *b:* New York, NY; *ed:* (BA) Elem Ed, 1971, (MS) Ed, 1974 Herbert H Lehman Coll; Post Masters Stud; *cr:* 5th Grade His/Culture Cluster Teacher Public Sch 154 1971-75; In Excess/Regular Substitute Teacher New York Public Sch System 1975-76; 3rd Grade Teacher Public Sch 159 1977, Public Sch 149 1977-78, Public Sch 159 1978-.

FUCHSGRUBER, BERNICE DAHL, Retired 2nd Grade Teacher; *b:* Osnabrock, ND; *m:* John; *c:* Roger; *ed:* Elem Ed, Minot St 1957; (BA) Elem Ed, Mayville St 1975; *cr:* All Grades Teacher Bethel Sch 1944-46, 7th Grade Teacher Mill City Sch1946-47, All Grades Teacher Metcalf Sch 1947-48, 2nd Grade Teacher Southern Sch Dist 1957-84; *ai:* Substitute Teacher in Cando, Egeland, Rock Lake & Bisbee Schls; NEA 1944-46, NDEA 1957-; Altar Society (Secy, VP); Chrstn Mothers (Pres, Secy); *home:* RR 2 Box 104 Cando ND 58324

FUESHKO, STEPHEN, Fourth Grade Teacher; *b:* Scranton, PA; *m:* Sonja Basalyga; *c:* Susan, Sharon; *ed:* (BS) Elem Ed, 1961, (MS) Elem Admin, 1973 Univ of Scranton; *cr:* 5th Grade Teacher Franklin Twp Sch 1961-64, S Abington Sch 1964-67; 5th Grade Teacher/Prin Newton Ransom Sch 1967-84; 4th Grade Teacher Abington Heights Mid Sch 1984-; *ai:* Elem Sports Prgm; Educl Comm; Little League, Teen-age League Coach 1964-75; PSEA, NEA 1964-; Phi Delta Kappa 1975-; PIAA Ofcl 1964-75; Church Officer Treas 1970-82; *home:* 631 Venard Rd Clarks Summit PA 18411

FUGATE, PEGGY CHENAULT, Second Grade Teacher; *b:* Hazel Green, KY; *m:* Paul; *ed:* (BS) Elem Ed, E KY Univ 1969; *cr:* 2nd/3rd Grade Teacher Campton Elem 1969-; *ai:* Just Say No Club Spon.

FUGATE, ROBERT, JR., Science Teacher; *b:* Jackson, KY; *m:* Eliza Combs; *ed:* (BS) Elem Ed, Eastern Ky Uni V 1969; Ashland Univ; Coll of Mount St Joseph; Kent St Univ; *cr:* Elem Teacher Breathitt Cty Schls 1969-71; Sci Teacher Shelby JR HS 1971-90; *ai:* OEA 1971-90; NEA 1969-90; NSTA 1971-90; NRA 1969-90; *home:* Rd 3 7001 St Rt 61 Shelby OH 44875

FUGITT, DONNA RILEY, Science Teacher; *b:* Delight, AR; *m:* Bobby D.; *c:* David T., Kelly S.; *ed:* (BS) Ed, Univ of AR Little Rock 1974; *cr:* 3rd Grade Teacher 1975-78, 2nd Grade Teacher 1979-84, Sci Teacher 1985- Bryant Sch; *ai:* Nom Presidential Awd Excl in Sci 1990; *office:* Bryant Public Sch 200 NW 4th St Bryant AR 72022

FUHRMAN, ERVIN LESTER, 4th Grade Teacher; *b:* Huntington, IN; *m:* Shirley L. Wygant; *c:* Robin, Nondus Christman, Natilee Kechel; *ed:* (BS) Elem Ed, Huntington Coll 1957; (MS) Elem Ed, St Francis Coll 1968; *cr:* Teacher Washington Center 1957-69, Cntrl Elem/Huntington Cty Cmmty Sch Corp 1969-; *ai:* Whitley Cty Classroom Teachers Pres 1966-67; Huntington Classroom Teachers; *office:* Central Elem Sch 601 N Jefferson St Huntington IN 46750

FUKUMOTO, KEITH MAKOTO, Music Department Chairman; *b:* Honolulu, HI; *ed:* (AA) Liberal Arts, Leeward Comm Coll 1977; (BM) Music, Western WA Univ 1979; (MED) Scndry Ed, Univ of HI Manoa 1988; *cr:* Band Instr Leilehua HS 1980-; *ai:* Gifted & Talented Selection, Onward to Excl, Cntrl Dist Band Festival, 2.0 Comm; Sr Class Adv & Audio Coord; Music Educators Natl Conference 1978-; HI St Teachers Assn, Oahu Band Dirs Assn 1980-; Leeward Symphonic Wind Ensemble Pres 1975-88; Leeward Comm Coll Distinguished Alumni Awd; *office:* Leilehua HS 1515 California Ave Wahiawa HI 96786

FULCHER, MARGARET KLEIN, First Grade Teacher; *b:* North Tonawanda, NY; *m:* William Lewis; *c:* William L. III, Cheryl Cleaver, Mark, Brian; *ed:* (BS) Ed, Univ of NY Brockport NY 1954; Certified Mentor Teacher in NC; *cr:* Teacher Lincoln Sch 1954-55, Clayton Elem 1955-56, JY Joyner 1956-57; Camp Glenn Sch 1957-58, Starpoint Cntrl Sch 1958-64, Ross Corners Ch 1964-68, Swift Creek Elem 1968-; *ai:* Coord of Swift Creek Elem Schls Rdng is Fundamental Prgm; Supervising Teacher of Stu Teachers; Mentor Teacher of Initially Certified Teachers; NY St Teachers Assn 1954-68; NEA 1954-; NC Assn of Educators 1968-; Wake County Assn of Classroom Teacher Sch Rep 1968-; BSA Occoneechee Cncl Den Mother 1968-73, Den Mother of Yr 1972; Ross Corners PTA Co-Pres With Husband 1966-68; Wake Cty Teacher of Yr 1980-81; *office:* Swift Creek Elem Sch 5601 Holly Springs Rd Raleigh NC 27606

FULKERSIN, LORRAINE FERN (ALFORD), ESL Teacher & GT Span Teacher; *b:* Amarillo, TX; *m:* James Wray; *c:* Shane W., Bobby L., Monte J.; *ed:* (BA) Elem Ed/Span, Wayland Baptist Univ 1975; (BA) Elem Span, 1975, Bi-ling, 1978 Plainview; Grad Stud Eng as a 2nd Lang & Linguistics, Tarleton Univ; *cr:* 4th Grade Bi-ling Ed Teacher 1975-76, 3rd Grade Bi-ling Ed Teacher 1976-77 Ft Concho Elem; 3rd Grade Bi-Ling Ed Techer H V Helbing Elem 1977-79; Pre K-5th Grade ESL Teacher 1979-, Gifted & Talented Span Class Teacher 1988- Mineral Wells Ind Sch Dist; *ai:* Childrens Church Coord & 2nd Grade Sunday Sch Teacher Immanuel Baptist Church-Mineral Wells; Delta Kappa Gamma Mem; TX Classroom Teachers Assn Mem 1979-80; TSTA Mem 1975-79; Stu Teacher Awd from Wayland Baptist Coll 1976; Nom for Tarleton St Univ Instructional Awd 1990; Nom for Woman of Year Zonat Club 1990; Highest Class Achievement at H V Helbing Elem Sch 1978-79; *home:* 605 SE 25th Ave Mineral Wells TX 76067

FULKERSON, BARBARA ANN, 11th-12th Grade His Teacher; *b:* Paterson, NJ; *m:* Donald Evan; *c:* Darlene; *ed:* (BA) Soc Sci, Paterson St Coll 1967; Masters Urban Ed, Jersey City St Coll 1981; *cr:* His Teacher West Milford HS 1967-71, Southern Regional HS 1971-; *ai:* Leader of Stu Tours to Europe; Adv Model United Nations, Princeton Model Congress, Jr States Organization; Memof Sch Instructional Cncl; NHS Advisory Comm; Mid States Comm His Chairperson; Teacher of Night Sch Adult Ed; NJ Ed Assn, NEA, NCSS, Southern Regional Ed Assn; Governors Outstanding Teacher 1987-88; NJ St Governors Sch Teacher Scholar Prgm Public Issues 1990; *office:* Southern Regional HS 600 N Main St Manahawkin NJ 08050

FULLEN, BRENDA (SMITH), Business Teacher; *b:* Walnut Ridge, AR; *m:* Charles E.; *ed:* (BSE) Bus Ed, 1977, (MSE) Bus Ed, 1981 AR St Univ; Specialist Degree Bus Ed, AR St Univ; *cr:* Bus Teacher Clover Bend HS 1977-81, Oak Ridge Cntrl HS 1981-83, Ridgecrest HS 1983-; *ai:* Soph Class Spon; *office:* Ridgecrest HS 1701 W Court St Paragould AR 72450

FULLEN, MARY MC CLUNG, 6th Grade Teacher; *b:* Fort Spring, WV; *m:* Floyd D.; *c:* John, Elizabeth; *ed:* Liberal Arts, Greenbrier Coll 1958; (BS) Elem Ed, Concord Coll 1961; *cr:* Eng/Spelling Teacher Greenbrier HS 1961-67; 6th Grade Teacher Lewisburg Intermediate Sch 1978-; *ai:* Partners in Ed Comm; Greenbrier Cty Ed Assn 1978-; WV Ed Assn 1978-; NEA 1978-; Greenbrier Rdng Cncl 1987-90; Greenbrier Cty Youth Camp Trustee 1970-; Asst 4-H Leader 1980-; Greenbrier Cty Choral Society 1971-; United Meth Women 1980-; *home:* Rt 1 Box 312 Fort Spring WV 24936

FULLER, ANGIE PRINCE, Health & PE Teacher; *b:* Tullahoma, TN; *m:* Roy F.; *c:* Monica D., Stephen B.; *ed:* (BS) Health/Phy Ed, 1964; (MA) Health/Phys Ed/Elem Ed, 1965 Mid TN St Univ; Admin/Supervision, TN St Univ 1982; *cr:* Girls Bsktbl Coach MTSU Campus Sch 1963-65; Grad Asst MTSU 1964-65; 8th Grade Teacher/Coach Estill Springs Elem Sch 1965-67; Health/Phys Ed Teacher North Jr HS 1967-; *ai:* Hunter Safety Teacher; Spon 7tt/8th/9th Grade Just Say No Club; Sch Policy and Rules Comm; Parent Teacher Conf Comm; Franklin Cty Ed Assn Sch Rep/Treas; TN Ed Assn Franklin Cty Rep; NEA; Order of Eastern Star (Worthy Matron/Treas 1989-); Lions Club Awd 1987 Dedicated & Outstanding Cmmnty Service; *office:* North Jr H S Hwy 41-A Rt 2 Winchester TN 37398

FULLER, CHARLES HENRY, 4th Grade Teacher; *b:* Coffeen, IL; *m:* Carolyn Lee Hensch; *c:* Serena, Charles II, Rebekah; *ed:* (AB) Modern Lang/Phys Ed, Greenville Coll 1961; (MS) Elem Ed/Admin, S IL Univ 1968; Elem Ed, NE MO St 1986; *cr:* Coach/Lang Art Teacher Miltonvale Wesleyan Coll 1961-62; *ai:* Olympic Spelling Coach; Deer Hill Church Elder 1980-; *office:* Mehlville R-9 Sch Dist 3120 Lemay Rd Saint Louis MO 63125

FULLER, HENRIETTA CHEEK, Fifth Grade Teacher; *b:* Jefferson, NC; *m:* Robert Welton; *c:* Catherine F. Hope, Stephanie Hopkins, Robert W. Jr., Jonathan; *ed:* (BS) Elem Ed, Appalachian St Univ 1969; *cr:* Teacher Dabney Elem Sch 1969-; *ai:* Sch Sci Fair Coord; Sch Phys Ed Contact Person; NEA, NC Assn of Educators 1969-; NC Cncl of Teachers of Math 1985-; Outstanding Elem Math Teacher 1989; *home:* Rt 1 Box 90A Henderson NC 27536

FULLER, JACKIE BALTHROP, Social Studies Teacher; *b:* Slidell, TX; *m:* Radford Aaron; *c:* Ju Lee Fuller Moore, Joel B., Jennifer Fuller Friday, Justin A.; *ed:* (BS) Home Ec Ed, TX Womans Univ 1953; Grad Stud Elem Sci, Scndry Sci, Government, Ed; *cr:* 5th-8th Grade Teacher Keller Ind Sch Dist 1959-68; Teacher of Government/US His/Economics/Gifted & Talented Aubrey Ind Sch Dist 1973-; *ai:* Spon Jr Class; Jr/Sr Prom Adv; Aubrey Ed Assn Pres 1987-88; TX St Teachers Assn 1973-78, 1981-; NEA 1981-; Delta Kappa Gamma 1989-; *home:* Rt 2 Box 243 A D Aubrey TX 76227

FULLER, JIMMY DARYL, 6th-7th Grade History Teacher; *b:* Fedscreek, KY; *m:* Judith Elizabeth Jones; *c:* Claire E., Daryl, Alicia; *ed:* (BA) Elem Ed, 1969, (MS) Elem Ed, 1973, Elem Principalship, 1980 Morehead St Univ; *cr:* 4th Grade Teacher 1969-77, Asst Prin 1977-, 6th/7th Grade His Teacher 1987- Big Rock Elem; *ai:* Little League Bsktbl Coach; NEA, BEA, VA Ed Assn; First Church of God (Bd Mem, Chm, Song Dir) 1980-; BSA Scoutmaster 739; *home:* 676 Fedscreek Rd Steele KY 41566

FULLER, JIMMY LEE, Fifth Grade Teacher; *b:* Cynthiana, KY; *m:* Janet Dennis; *c:* Jan Leigh; *ed:* (BA) Elem Ed, Morehead St Univ 1970, (MS) Elem Ed, 1978; Rank I Elem Ed, 1987 Georgetown Coll; *cr:* 5th Grade Teacher Westside Elem Sch 1971-; *ai:* Gifted Talented Comm; Law Related Ed Comm; Sci Curr Comm; Harrison Co Ed Assn (SEC 1987-88; Pres 1988-89); Cynthiana Elks #438 Exalted Ruler 1989- Elk of Yr 1977-78/1979-80; KY Dir Elks Natl Free Throw Contest 1980-; Cynthiana-Harrison Cty Jaycees Educator of Yr; Nom Ashland Valvoline Teacher Awds; *home:* 122 Battle Grove Ave Cynthiana KY 41031

FULLER, LIZZIE LORAINE, Fifth Grade Teacher; *b:* Mercer, TN; *ed:* (BA) Elem Ed, Lane Coll 1959; (MS) Ed, Univ of TN 1971; *cr:* 2nd Grade Teacher Rosenwald Elem 1959-69; Chapter I Teacher 1969-70, 5th Grade Teacher 1970- Pinson; *ai:* Madison Cty Teachers Assn, TN Teachers Assn, Natl Teachers Assn; *home:* Rt 1 Box 203 Mercer TN 38392

FULLER, MARY E., Principal; *b:* Washington, DC; *m:* Charles H.; *c:* Jeanne Spellman, John, Patricia; *ed:* (BSEd) Fordham Univ 1953; (MSED) 1963, (CAGS) 1989, Bridgewater St Coll; *cr:* Bus Office Supvr NY Telephone Company 1948-53; Teacher 1963-88, Prin 1988- Bourne Sch System; *ai:* Teenage Retreat Prgm ECHO Dir; Cmptr & Inservice Comm; NEA, MA Teachers Assn, MA Rdng Assn, ASCD, Barnstable Cty Ed Assn, Bourne Ed Assn Schlsp Comm; Barnstable Cty Ed Assn; Bourne Cablevision Comm Secy 1987-; Fall River Diocese Youth Ministry 1970-, Bishops Awd; Outstanding Teacher of Yr 1975; Horace Mann Grant 1987-89; Diagnostic Prescriptive Math Horace Mann Grant 1988-89; Articles Published; *office:* Edward C Stone Mid Sch 5400 Lindberg Ave Otis AFB MA 02542

FULLER, OLA PATTERSON, Fourth Grade Teacher; *b:* Shreveport, LA; *m:* Clarence Burney; *c:* Eumeko K.; *ed:* (BS) Ed, Grambling St 1962; (MA) Ed, Southern Univ, Univ of CA, Univ of S IL 1972; Completed LTIP & LTEP Prof Dev Prgm; *cr:* 4th Grade Teacher Greenmore 1962-67, N Highland 1968-72, Summer Grove 1973-77, Claiborne Magnet 1978-; *ai:* GSA Leader Claiborne; Zion Baptist Youth Supvr; Shreveport MetropolitaN Ballet Inc Advisory Bd; Caddo Magnet HS PTSA Corresponding Secy; LAE; CAE Rep 1979-; NEA 1962-; Top Ladies of Distinction Incorporated; Circle 7 Missionary Society; Rdng Grant Univ of IL; Speech Grant Univ of CA Fullerton; Sci Grant Univ of MI.

FULLER, PATRICIA LUCILE DAVENPORT, 7th/8th Grade Teacher; *b:* Dallas, TX; *m:* Charles Neal; *c:* Holly L., Crystal N.; *ed:* (BS) Elem Ed, Univ of TN 1985; (MS) Supervision/Admin, Lincoln Memorial Univ 1990; Cmptr Skills Next; Calculators in Classroom; Whole Lang; *cr:* Sch Secy 1978-85, Chapter I Aide 1979-80 Wearwood Elem; Itinerate Teacher Catons Chapel Elem & Wearwood Elem 1985-86; 7th/8th Grade Teacher 1986-, Asst Prin 1989- Wearwood Elem; *ai:* NEA, TN Educators Assn 1985-; Sevier Cty Teachers Assn 1985-; NCTM 1984-; Wearwood Sch Support Group (Secy, Treas) 1981-; Title IV Grant; *office:* Wearwood Elem Sch Rt 7 Box 181 Sevierville TN 37862

FULLER, WILLIAM HORACE, Retired Teacher; *b:* Hondo, TX; *m:* Elizabeth Johnson; *c:* Eric, Marie; *ed:* (BA) Elem Ed, Denver CA 1958; CO Univ, UNC, Metro St; *cr:* Teacher Kemp Elem 1966-72; Prin Dupont Elem 1972-74; Teacher Kemp Elem 1974-87; *ai:* Coached After Sch Act; Many Comms; CEA Treas 1970; *home:* 2855 Hudson Denver CO 80207

FULLERTON, GEORGINE BONACCI, Second Grade Teacher; *b:* New Rochelle, NY; *m:* John Phillips; *ed:* (BA) Eng, Coll of New Rochelle 1973; (MS) Elem Ed, Fairfield Univ 1980; *cr:* 1st-4th Grade Teacher Columbus Elem Sch 1973-; *ai:* Teacher Act Coord & Fundraiser; Family Math Coord; NYSUT, UFT; NY PTA (Teacher 1989-, Rep 1987-88); *office:* Columbus Elem Sch 275 Washington Ave New Rochelle NY 10801

FULLMER, RICHARD LEE, Math Teacher/Track Coach; *b:* Torrington, WY; *m:* Patricia Kathleen Cook; *c:* Steven R., Michael T., Douglas E.; *ed:* (BA) Math Ed, Univ of WY 1964; Grad Stud Univ of WY; *cr:* Math Teacher Sundance Jr HS 1964-65; Sci Teacher Torrington Jr HS 1965-69; Math Teacher Lingle-Ft Laramie HS 1969-; *ai:* HS Boys Track Coach; Jr HS & HS Athletic Dir; Goshen Cty Ed Assn Pres 1973-74, Teacher of Yr Nom 1971-72; WY Coaches Assn Coach of Yr 1982; Lingle Presbyn Church Elder 1977-87; Track Article Published in Coaching Clinic 1974; *home:* Star Rt Lingle WY 82223

FULMER, BARBARA DELL, Third Grade Teacher; *b:* Santa Rosa, NM; *m:* Richard K.; *c:* Larry, Tracy Fulmer Heller; *ed:* (BS) Elem Ed - Magna Cum Laude, Baylor Univ 1977; *cr:* 2nd Grade Teacher La Vega Ind Sch Dist 1977-78; 2nd Grade Teacher 1978-84, 3rd Grade Teacher 1984- Midway Ind Sch Dist; *ai:* Midway Ind Sch Dist Technology Comm; Assn of TX Prof Educators 1978-; PTA Mini-Grants; *office:* Woodway Elem Sch 9101 Woodway Dr Waco TX 76712

FULMER, KATHLEEN A. (GALLAGHER), Mathematics Teacher; *b:* Bethlehem, PA; *m:* Barry P.; *ed:* (BA) Poly Sci, PA St Univ 1969; (MED) Ed, Lehigh Univ 1974; *cr:* Kndgtn Teacher Joshua Barney Sch 1971-73; Supportive Math Teacher Bethlehem Area Voc Tech Sch 1973-76; Math Teacher E Hills Jr HS & Mid Sch 1981-; *office:* East Hills Mid Sch 2005 Chester Ave Bethlehem PA 18017

FULTON, KAREN E., 4th Grade Teacher; *b:* Monette, AR; *m:* Edward A.; *c:* Melissa, Amy; *ed:* (BS) Elem Ed, S IL Univ Edwardsville 1981; Working Towards Masters Degree; *cr:* Instr Aide Hinchcliffe Sch 1972-74, 1977-80; 5th Grade Teacher 1981-82, 3rd Grade Teacher 1982-87, 4th Grade Teacher 1987- LaVerna Evans Sch; *ai:* PTO VP 1981-82; Teacher Union Building Rep 1984-85; O Fallon United Church of Christ Chrstn Ed Bd Secy; *office:* Estelle Kampmeyer Elem Sch 707 N Smiley St O'Fallon IL 62269

FULTON, KRISTA JAN (TRIMBLE), Third Grade Teacher; *b:* Tipton, IN; *m:* Dwight David; *c:* Amie J., Lee A., Katherine M., Teresa J.; *ed:* (BA) Elem Ed, IN Univ Purdue 1981; (MS) Elem Ed, Ball St 1986; *cr:* 6th Grade Teacher White River Elem Sch 1982-83; 6th Grade Teacher 1983-84, 2nd Grade Teacher 1984-89, 3rd Grade Teacher 1989- Willard Elem Sch; *ai:* 4th-5th Grade Boys & Girls Bsktbl Coach; Co-Chairperson Randolph Cntrl Classroom Teachers Assn; Chairperson Natl Teacher Week Comm; Faith-Trinity United Meth Church 1988-; *office:* Willard Elem Schl 615 W South St Winchester IN 47394

FULTON, LINDA DOWDY, Guidance Counselor; *b:* Jacksonville, FL; *m:* Randy William; *c:* Joshua W., Heath F.; *ed:* (BS) Elem Ed, 1980, (MA) Guidance/Counseling, 1988 SE MO St; *cr:* 4th Grade Teacher Marquand Elem 1981-82; 6th/3rd Grade Teacher Meadow Heights Elem 1982-88; Cnslr Perryville Jr HS 1988-; *ai:* Stu Cncl Dances & Act Chaperone; SE MO Univ Soph Block Prgm Cooperating Teacher 1986-88; MO Sch Cnslr Assn, SE MO Sch Cnslr Assn 1988-; Meadow Heights CTA Secy 1986-88; Patton Meth Church Bible Sch Teacher 1989-; *office:* Perryville Jr HS College at Edwards Perryville MO 63775

FULTON, NADINE HALL, Fourth Grade Teacher; *b:* Cincinnati, OH; *m:* Alvin E.; *c:* Sterling M., Larry, Stacey; *ed:* (BS) Elem Ed, Knoxville Coll 1965; (MS) Spec Ed/LD, SC St Coll 1982; *cr:* 1st Grade Teacher Miles Standish 1965-66; 7th/8th Grade Lang Art Teacher Camilla Consolidated Sch 1966-69; 4thGrade Teacher Chambers Elem Sch 1969-78, Felton Laboratory Sch 1978-79, Whittaker 1979-; *ai:* 4th Grade Level Chairperson 1981-; NEA 1965-; SC Educl Assn 1978-; SC Cncl of Teachers of Math 1988-89; Trinity United Meth Church Sch Teacher 1987-; Alpha Kappa Alpha 1963-; Teacher Incentive Prgm 1987-88; Whittakers Teacher of Yr 1989-; *home:* 473 Meadowlark NE Orangeburg SC 29115

FULTON, PATRICIA ANNE, Biology Teacher; *b:* Wheeling, WV; *m:* Albert Parker II; *ed:* (BS) Comprehensive Bio, Wheeling Coll 1977; (MA) Comm, WV Univ 1984; *cr:* Bio Teacher Mt de Chantal Acad 1978-79, John Marshall HS 1979-.

FULTON, REBECCA JAMES, Dean of Students; *b:* Kingstree, SC; *m:* Joseph Sr.; *c:* Janice F. Redding, Pamela F. Thomas, Joseph Jr., Marlon; *ed:* (BA) Eng, Johnson C Smith Univ 1965; (MA) Urban Ed, Brooklyn Coll 1972; *cr:* Classroom Teacher Public Sch 144 1968-69; Classroom Teacher 1969-85, Dean of Stus 1986- Intermediate Sch 271; *ai:* Arista Honor Society, Future Teachers Club, Sunshine Comm, Remedial & Tutorial Lunch Time Classes Adv; Schls Chief Fundraiser, Disciplinarian, Mediator; Alpha Kappa Alpha Variegated Comm 1985-; Les Congenials Secy 1984-; Church (Secy, Teacher) 1975-, Dedication Awd 1988; Martin L King Center Teacher 1984-85; Long Beach Parents Bd 1974-85; NY Alliance of Teachers Awd 1987; Alpha Phi Alpha Service Awd 1988; Teacher of Yr Awd 1970, 1971, 1974, 1975, 1978, 1980, 1985; Teacher of Dist 1988; *home:* 232 W Hudson St Long Beach NY 11561

FULTS, NANETTA, Curriculum Director; *b:* Ashland, KY; *ed:* (BS) Elem Ed, Rio Grande Coll 1972; (MA) Elem Ed, OH Univ 1975; (EDD) Ed Admin, WV Univ 1989; *cr:* 2nd Grade Teacher 1971-86, Elem Supvr 1986-89, Curr Dir 1989- Jackson City Schls; *ai:* ASCD; Delta Kappa Gamma VP 1988-, Annie Webb Blanton Schlsp 1983; Phi Delta Kappa Historian 1988-; Bus Prof Women, Amer Assn of Univ Women; *office:* Jackson City Schls 379 E South St Jackson OH 45640

FULTZ, BARBARA (RICHARDSON), Sixth Grade Teacher; *b:* Cincinnati, OH; *m:* David; *c:* Lisa Fultz Smith, Jennifer Fultz Mc David; *ed:* (BA) Eng, Morehead St Univ 1966; Elem Endorsement 1976; *cr:* Soc Worker Public Assistance Office 1966-70; Teacher Pathways 1975-77, Carter Cty Bd of Ed 1977-; *ai:* NEA; *office:* Carter Elem Sch General Delivery Carter KY 41128

FULWIDER, CINDY WALKER, Physical Ed/Health Teacher; *b:* Knoxville, TN; *m:* George; *c:* Chad, Derrick, Jace; *ed:* (BS) Health/Phys Ed, Milligan Coll 1972; (MA) Scndry Ed, E TN St Univ 1975; Phys Ed, E TN St Univ 1984; *cr:* Secy Milligan Coll 1970-72; Lifeguard/Swim Instr Elizabethton City Pool 1974-75; Teacher/Coach Happy Valley Mid Sch 1972-; Adult Ed Prgm Instr Elizabethton HS 1982-; *ai:* Aerobic Fitness Instr HS Athletes; Dir Phys Ed Enrichment Act; Jump Rope for Heart Coord; Water Aerobics, Swim, CPR, First Aid Instr; Happy Valley Mid Sch Curr & Disciplinary, Chairperson Handbook Comm; Fitness-Gram Dist Coord; TN Assn of Health, Phys Ed, Recreation & Dance (Chm Scndry Section 1987-88, VP Phys Ed & Dance 1988-89) Nom Scndry Phys Ed Teacher 1989; Amer Alliance of Health, Phys Ed, Recreation, Dance Mem 1972-; Jump Rope for Heart (St Task Force 1984-, Natl Rep 1988); TN Ed Assn, NEA, Natl Assn Sports & Phys Ed; Amer Heart Assn Pres Carter Cty 1987-89; Red Cross 1973-; BSA Water Safety, Swim & Fitness Consultant 1986-; Carter Cty Ed Assn, Womens Sports Fnd; Career Level III Teacher; Coord Top Sch TN Jump Rope for Heart 1986; TN Rep S Dist of Amer Alliance of Health, Phys Ed, Recreation & Dance; Conducts Inservices St & Local Levels; Interviewed for Womens Day Magazine & Womens Weekly Magazine; *office:* Happy Valley Mid Sch Rt 11 Box 3400 Powder Branch Rd Elizabethton TN 37643

FULWOOD, BETTY CROSS, First Grade Teacher; *b:* Braden, TN; *m:* William P.; *c:* William M., Malcolm K., Sandra C. Topping, Mark A.; *ed:* (BS) Curr/Instruction/Elem Ed, 1961, (MS) Curr/Instruction/Elem Ed, 1988 Memphis St Univ; Elem Ed, Memphis St Univ 1990; Gifted Ed/Spec Ed; Taught Apex Grades; *cr:* 4th Grade Teacher 1956-59, 1st Grade Teacher 1959-60 Millington Cntrl; 2nd Grade Teacher 1960-61, 3rd Grade Teacher 1961-62 Millington E; 1st Grade Teacher Scenic Hills 1962-63; 2nd Grade Teacher Bartlett Elem 1963-64; 1st Grade Teacher Millington E 1964-; *ai:* Math Tournament Spon; Stu in Rdng Tutor; Grade Level Chm 1962-; NEA, Shelby Cty Ed Assn 1956-, 25 Yr Pin 1981; TN Ed Assn 1956-, 25 Yr Plaque 1981; Shelby Cty Teacher Study Cncl Secy 1988-; Teacher Study Cncl SW Dist III Chairperson 1989-; Shelby Cty Ed Assn Benefits Educator; PTA Officers Election Chairperson 1988-, Teacher of Yr 1988; Moose Club 1981-; Career Ladder III; Faculty Teacher of Yr 1989; Heart Person 1987; ASAP After Sch Prgm Chairperson 1989-; Probitionary Teachers Mentor 1984-; *office:* Millington E Sch 6467 Navy Rd Millington TN 38053

FUNDAUN, KIM, 8th Grade Science Teacher; *b:* Sioux Falls, SD; *m:* Michele; *c:* Mikaela; *ed:* (BS) Outdoor Ed, Black Hills St Coll 1979; Bio, Insects, Psych of Exceptional Children, Black Hills St Coll; Cmptrs, Seattle Pacific Univ; Sports Medicine, Developing Discipline, Earth Sci, Univ of SD; *cr:* Ftbl Coach 1980-83, Track Coach 1980-86, 7th/8th Grade Teacher 1980-87 Deadwood Jr HS; Track Coach Lead HS 1987-89; 8th Grade Sci Teacher Deadwood Mid Sch 1987-; *ai:* 8th Grade Team Leader; Deadwood Volunteer Fire Dept 1984-; St Patricks Cath Church Finance Officer 1985-; CASA 1988-; Ducks Unlimited, Natl Rifle Assn, Black Hills Fly Fishers, Roubaix Sporting Club Past Pres; *office:* Deadwood Mid Sch 716 Main Deadwood SD 57732

FUNDINGSLAND, MARSHA GAYLE, Fourth Grade Teacher; *b:* Longview, WA; *ed:* (BA) Ed, E WA Univ 1969; (MA) Ed/Rdng, Cntrl WA Univ 1981; Admin Credentials, Prin Pre-Sch-12th Grade; *cr:* 5th Grade Teacher 1969-70, 4th Grade Teacher 1970-80, 3rd Grade Teacher 1980-82, 4th Grade Teacher 1982- Auburn Sch Dist; *ai:* Seattle Pacific Univ Adjunct Faculty Mem; Coordinated Building Young Authors Conference & Speech Contest; Math Olympiad Adv; Dist Inservice Advisory Comm Mem; Sch Accreditation Steering Comm Chairperson; Intnl Rdng Assn; WA Ed Assn, NEA 1969-; United Way Coord Building Campaign 1989-, Crystal 1989-; Seattle Pacific Trainer Teachers Prgm 1988-.

FUNK, FREDERICK JAMES, 8th Grade Teacher; *b:* Plumsteadville, PA; *m:* Carolyn Buck; *c:* Frederick, Stephen; *ed:* (BS) Chem, Gen Sci Phys Ed, West Chester St PA Coll 1955; (MS) Admin, Univ of PA 1960; Univ of PA; West Chester St Coll; *cr:* Teacher Haverford Township Sch Dist 55; Teacher Penn Delco Sch Dist 1955-58; Teacher Upper Darby Sch Dist 1958-; *ai:* Soccer Coach Mid Sch 32 Years; Bsbl Coach Mid Sch 32 Years; Team Leader; PSEA; NEA Lifemem; NSTA; Radnor Township Republican Party Comm 1970-72; Leisure Services Commission Vce Chm 1974- of Marple-Newtown; *home:* 2 Plymouth Rd Newtown Square PA 19073

FUNK, KAREN CORNELL, Physical Education Teacher; *b:* Cortland, NY; *m:* Richard; *c:* Cari; *ed:* (BS) Phys Ed, 1972, (MS) Phys Ed, 1976, (CAS) Admin, 1990 SUC At Cortland; Adolescence Pregnancy Wkshps, AIDS Trng for Curr Dev, Athletic Trng; *cr:* Substitute Teacher 1972-82, Coach 1973- Phys Ed Teacher 1982- Family Life Ed Curr Coord 1985-, Admin Intern 1989- Marathon; *ai:* Jr Var/Var Field Hockey & Modified Sftbl Coach; Class & Youth Speakout Group Adv; Drug Free & Effective Schls Comms; Interscholastic Athletic Conference Field Hockey Chairperson 1983-; ASCD 1989-; Amer Legion Aux Ed Chairperson 1982-; Cortland Bowling Assn, 600 Club 1990; Lions Club Presentation on Drug Free Schls; *home:* RD 2 Box 287A Phillips Rd Marathon NY 13803

FUNK, MICHAEL LEE, US History Instructor; *b:* Watertown, WI; *m:* Jeanne L.; *c:* Robert, Steven; *ed:* (BA) His, 1960, (MST) His, 1971 Univ WI Oshkosh; *cr:* Soc Stud Teacher WI Heights HS 1963-64, Appleton HS West 1965-66, Appleton HS East 1967-; *ai:* Adv Stu Congress-Appleton East; Jobs Daughters Teacher of Yr 1982; *office:* Appleton High School East 2121 Emmers Dr Appleton WI 54915

FUNK, SUSAN SCHUPPEL, Middle School Teacher; *b:* Lansing, MI; *m:* Curt M.; *ed:* (BS) Ed, OR St Univ 1966; (MA) Ed, Lewis & Clark Coll 1981; Numerous Grad Hrs/Various Institutions; *cr:* 4th Grade Teacher West Linn 1966-69, 6th-8th Grade Mid Sch Teacher 1969; *ai:* NEA/OEA/WLEA Secy 1987-89, Aw d; N Cncl Teachers Rdng/Eng; OEA Poly Action Rep 1981-86; *home:* 2680 Gloria Dr West Linn OR 97068

FUNKE, LUANNE RHEINBERGER, Retired/Volunteer Teacher; *b:* Tulsa, OK; *m:* Robert H.; *ed:* (BA) Ed/Eng, Benedictine Heights 1953; (MA) Ed/Psych, Cath Univ 1962; (MA) Theology/Counseling, St John Univ 1968; Sci, Foreign Lang; Drug Ed. WA Univ 1972; Art Museum Wkshp 1973; *cr:* K-8th Grade Teacher St Catherines Sch & Sacred Heart Sch 1948-60; Prin Monte Cassino Sch 1960-70; 4th-6th Grade Teacher Maryland Sch 1970-88; Volunteer Teacher Rockwood Dist 1990; *ai:* MO Ed Assn 1970-88; Tulsa Sch Bd Delegate 1968-70; Little Council OK Ed Commission 1968-70; Teacher Benedictine Heights Coll 1958-59; Cultural Enrichment Summer Field Trips 1984-88; *home:* 2035 Sundowner Ridge Dr Saint Louis MO 63101

FUNKHOUSER, BETTY DRIVER, 10th/12th Grade Eng Teacher; *b:* Rockingham Cty, VA; *m:* Johnny L.; *ed:* (BA) Eng, James Madison Univ 1961; (MED) Eng, Univ of VA 1971; *cr:* 9th Grade Eng Teacher Fairfax HS 1961-62; 9th-12th Grade Teacher Broadway HS 1962-; *ai:* Forensics Coach; Sr Class Spon; Awds Comm; VATE; BPW Secy 1963-70; NDEA Grant Univ of VA 1969; Seminar Appointee James Madison Univ 1989; *office:* Broadway HS P O Box 367 Broadway VA 22815

FUNKHOUSER, LINDA JAHNS, English Teacher; *b:* Queens Long Island, NY; *m:* Jerry; *c:* Nola D. Loup, Audra L.; *ed:* (BS) Elem 8 Ed 1976; (BA) HS Eng, 1987 UT Pan American; *cr:* 5th Grade Teacher El Jardin 1976-79; 6th Grade Sci Teacher Los Fresnos Jr HS 1979; 5th/6th Grade Teacher Perez Elem 1983-86; 9th/10th/11th Grade Eng Teacher Pace HS 1986-; *ai:* Kappa Delta Pi Life Mem 1976-; BISD Teaching Profession 1976- 10 Yr Pin 1990; Cum Laude 1976; *home:* 637 N Indiana Brownsville TX 78521

FUNSTON, BONNIE SUE (HALE), Music Teacher; *b:* Poplar Bluff, MO; *m:* Marck F.; *c:* Jeffrey, Kevin; *ed:* (BME) Music Ed, SE MO St Univ 1971; (MM) Music Ed, S IL St Univ Edwardsville 1988; *cr:* Elem Music Teacher Meramec Valley R-3 1971-74, Dunklin R-5 1974-; *ai:* MO St Teachers Assn Dist 2nd VP 1982-83; Dunklin Cmmty Teachers Assn Pres 1981-82; Music Ed Natl Conf; Grace Church Choir Dir 1980-; S IL St Univ Edwardsville Grad Awd in Music Ed 1988; Scholastic All Amer Collegiate 1988; *office:* Dunklin R-5 Elem Sch 440 Joachim Ave Herculaneum MO 63048

FUQUA, DAVID BERKLEY, Accounting Teacher/Vice Prin; *b:* Caswell Cty, NC; *m:* Sharon Truax; *c:* Susanne, Daniel, Stephanie, David III; *ed:* (BA) Bible, Bob Jones Univ 1974; Bus Courses, Alamance Comm Coll; *cr:* Bible/His Teacher 1978-79, Jr Class Adv/Teacher 1979-82, Sr Class Adv/Teacher 1982-85, Accounting Teacher/Vice Prin 1985- Alamance Chrstn Sch; *ai:* Bible Quiz Team, Sch Testing, Bsktbl Concession Stand, Shar-a-thon, Summer Sch, Hs Chapel Prgms, Hs Awds Day, Guidance Counseling Coord; Florence Baptist Church (Sunday Sch Supt, Asst Pastor); Bus Owner & Operator.

FURBY, CHERYL BELINDA, Biology Teacher/Science Chair; *b:* Baltimore, MD; *ed:* (BS) Bio, Morehead St Univ 1986; Guidance & Counseling, Morehead St Univ; *cr:* Bio Teacher Fleming-Neon HS 1987-; *ai:* Beta Club Adv; Bsktbl Statistician; Academic Team Coach Asst; Cheerleading Coach; NEA, KEA 1989-; *office:* Fleming-Neion HS PO Box 367 Neon KY 41840

FURDA, ALICE, English Teacher; *b:* Johnstown, PA; *m:* Andrew J.; *c:* Emily A.; *ed:* (BA) Eng, Univ of Pittsburgh 1974; *cr:* Eng Teacher Shade Sch Dist 1975-76; Speech/Drama Teacher Johnstown Voc Tech 1978-79; Eng Teacher Johnstown Chrstn Sch 1986-; *ai:* Drama Club & Graduating Class Adv 1991; *office:* Johnstown Chrstn Sch RD Box 166 Hollsopple PA 15935

FURIOLI, HELEN VIRGINIA (WISEMAN), Fifth Grade Teacher; *b:* Wheeling, WV; *m:* William David; *c:* Catherene, Sara, Jenna; *ed:* (BA) Elem, W Liberty St Coll 1971; (MA) Elem Classroom Teaching, WV Univ 1979; Grad Stud; *cr:* 5th Grade Teacher Wellsburg Mid Sch 1971-; *ai:* WVEA, BCEA, NEA 1971-; *office:* Wellsburg Mid Sch 1447 Main St Wellsburg WV 26070

FURLONG, RICHARD ANDREW, Guidance Counselor; *b:* Paterson, NJ; *ed:* (BA) Jr Ed, 1969, (MA) Soc Sci, 1972 William Paterson Coll; (MA) Stu Personnel Services, Montclair St Coll 1974; *cr:* Teacher Ringwood Mid Sch 1969-70, Brooklawn Mid Sch 1970-84; Cnslr Parsippany HS 1985-89, Brooklawn Mid Sch 1984-85, 1989-; *ai:* Soccer Coach; NJ Ed Assn 1969-; NJ Prof Cnslrs Assn 1985-86; ASCA 1987-; Natl Assn of Coll Admissions; *office:* Brooklawn Mid Sch 250 Beachwood Rd Parsippany NJ 07054

FURLOUGH, VICKIE BOWMAN, 7th-9th Grade Science Teacher; *b:* Shelby, NC; *m:* James Edward; *c:* Kristen Greene, Ryan, Taylor, Ariel; *ed:* (BS) Health/Phys Ed, Gardner Webb Coll 1977; Working Towards Masters Mid Grades E Carolina Univ; *cr:* Teacher D F Walker 1978-80, Creswell Sch 1980-; *ai:* Creswell Elem Sch Teacher of Yr 1983; NC Fellowship Math & Sci Teachers; *office:* Creswell HS PO Box 188 Creswell NC 27928

FURMAN, CHERYL BRIDGES, Fifth Grade Teacher; *b:* Orlando, FL; *m:* Richard; *c:* Rick, Charlie; *ed:* (BA) Ed, Univ of FL 1968; (AA) Ed, Orlando Jr Coll 1966; *cr:* 1st Grade Teacher Lanett Jr HS 1968; 3rd Grade Teacher Dover Shores Elem 1969; 1st Grade Teacher Delaney Elem 1969-73; 1st Grade Teacher Windermere Elem Sch 1979; 5th Grade Teacher Lake Highland Prep Sch 1982-; *ai:* Curr & Sch Plant Comm; Cheerleading & Outdoor Games Spon; Natl Assn Storytelling 1989-; Classroom Teachers Assn, NEA 1969-; BSA (Comm, Chm) 1984-; Rotary Spon for Exch Stus 1989; BSA Explorer Post Adv 1988-; Century Club of the Univ of FL 1969-; *office:* Lake Highland Prep Sch 901 N Lake Highland Ave Orlando FL 32803

FURMAN, GEORGE A., Teacher; *b:* Tampa, FL; *m:* Judith A. Weaver; *c:* Kathleen M. Furman Pulido, Cheryl A., Georgina A.; *ed:* (BS) Soc Sci, Univ of Tampa 1984; *cr:* Teacher Van Buren Jr HS 1984-; *ai:* Academic Bowl Coach; Steering Comm Teachers as Advisors Prgm; Coached Ships Bsbl Teams (USS Monticello), Little League Ftbl (YMCA Alachua FL), Little League Bsbl (N Seminole Park Tampa FL); Scouts Troop Ten Tampa FL; Disabled Amer Veterans; Mary Help of Chrstn Church; PTA Van Buren Jr HS; 2 Bronze Stars with Combat V, Navy & Marine Corp Commendation Medal, 3 Purple Hearts, Medal of Honor 2nd Class (Republic of Vietnam), 4 Good Conduct, Presidential Unit Citation, Natl Defense, Vietnam Service, Vietnam Champaign, Expert (Pistol & Rifle) USN; Best Jr HS Teacher (Tampa Bay Magazine); Most Popular Teacher Van Burem 1988; *office:* Van Buren Jr HS 8715 22nd St N Tampa FL 33604

FURNARI, ELAINE DODGE, 8th Grade Mathematics Teacher; *b:* Buffalo, NY; *m:* John J.; *c:* Lia Locklair, Adina S., Elena; *ed:* (BS) Elem Ed, Coll of Charleston 1978; (MAS) Pre-Adolescent Ed/Math, Baptist Coll Charleston 1985; *cr:* 8th Grade Math Teacher Sedgefield Mid 1978-81; 8th Grade Math Teacher/Dept Head 1986-87 Alston Mid; 8th Grade Math Teacher 1978-, Dept Head 1987- Oakbrook Mid; *ai:* Quest & Mathcounts Coach/Spon; Sick Leave Bank; Teacher Incentive Prgm; Mid Sch Organization Comm; NEA, Alpha Delta Kappa; Teacher of Yr Sedgefield Mid 1980, Alston Mid 1984, Oakbrook Mid 1987; *office:* Oakbrook Mid Sch 4704 Old Fort Rd Ladson SC 29456

FURNESS, DORIS TROTH, Retired; *b:* Allen, NE; *M:* Dale F.; *c:* James L.; *ed:* (BA) Elem Ed, Wayne St 1962; Spec Ed, Wayne St 1973; TX His, WTSU 1986; *cr:* Teacher Dist 68 Rural 1938-40; 5th/6th Grade Teacher/Prin Jackson NE 1960-72; 6th Grade Teacher Mid Sch South 1973-75; 2nd Grade Teacher Pampa TX 1976-77; 3rd/6th Grade Teacher 1978-88; *ai:* Currently Sub Teacher Allen NE; NSEA 1963-84; NEA 1963-84; TX S.T.A. 1976-77; Chm Cmmty Outreach Services; Drive Sunday Sch Supt 12 Yr Luth Church; *home:* 120 W 5th Allen NE 68710

FURPLESS, CATHY SEGRAVES, Academically Gifted Teacher; *b:* Southport, NC; *m:* William Price; *c:* Laura E., Catherine A.; *ed:* (BA) Scndry Eng Ed, Univ of NC Chapel Hill 1975; (MED) Scndry Eng Ed, Univ of SC Columbia 1983; Grad Cert Trng Gifted Ed/Admin/Supervision; Advanced Placement Eng; Great Books Fnd; *cr:* Academically Gifted Resouce/Eng Teacher Chowan HS 1977; Academic Gifted Resource Teacher Perquimans Cty Mid Sch 1978; Academically Gifted Lang/ Resouce Teacher Leland Mid Sch 1979-81; Academically Gifted Lang Arts Teacher S Brunswick Mid Sch 1982-85; Academically Gifted/Spec Needs Coord Brunswick Cty Schls 1986-; *ai:* Cheerleading; Drama; NHS; Chorus, Piano; NC Assn for Gifted Ed 1977-, Task Force 1986; Carolina Future Problem Solving Prgm Advisory Cncl 1988-; NC Assn of Educators 1977-85; Trinity United Meth Church (Asst Organist/Pianist, Youth Choir Dir/Pianist) 1981-; Presenter NC Cncl Exceptional Children Conference; Kids Kits Grant Natl Diffusion Network; Adv Local Parents for Advancement of Gifted Ed; Co-Ed Exceptional Children Newsletter; *office:* Brunswick Cty Schls Star Rt Hwy 133 Southport NC 28461

FURROW, MARY CATHERINE, Fifth Grade Teacher; *b:* Rocky Mount, VA; *ed:* (AS) Ed, Ferrum Jr Coll 1974; (BS) Elem Ed, Radford Coll 1976; (MS) Elem Ed, Radford Univ 1982; *cr:* 5th Grade Teacher Rocky Mount Elem 1976-; *ai:* Sch Improvement Comm; Supts Advisory Cncl; NEA.

FURSMAN, JACQUELINE HIBBS, Kindergarten Teacher; *b:* Boston, MA; *m:* John A. III.; *c:* Erika L., Jill A., John A. IV.; *ed:* (BS) Elem Ed, 1976; (MS) Elem Ed, 1982 Emporia ST Univ; *cr:* 6th Grade Teacher 1976-77, 1st Grade Teacher 1977-81 Longfellow Elem; Kindergarten Greeley Grade/Longfellow Elem 1988-; *ai:* Beta Sigma Phi Pres 1980-81, Woman of the Yr 1981; Bus & Prof Women's Young Careerist 1980; *office:* Greeley Grade/ Longfellow Elem W 6th Garnett KS 66032

FURTADO, MAUREEN FAHEY, Third Grade Teacher; *b:* Taunton, MA; *c:* Sarah; *ed:* (BS) Ed, 1970, (MED) Spec Needs, 1978 Bridgewater St; (MED) Educl Technology, Fitchburg 1990; *cr:* 4th Grade Teacher Leonard Sch 1970-72, 4th Grade Teacher 1972-84, 3rd Grade Teacher 1984- Galligan Sch; *ai:* Taunton Girls Club (Bd of Dir, Pres 1978-87), Distinguished Service 1987.

FURTADO, ROBERT A., Biology Teacher; *b:* Somerville, MA; *m:* Sharon Bowness; *c:* Amanda E.; *ed:* (BS) Bio, Boston St Coll 1970; Environmental Sci & ISCS Curr, E Nazarene Coll; Environmental Sci, Boston Univ; Human Genetics & Bioethics, Ball St Univ; Cell Bio, Univ of TX; *cr:* Sci Teacher Quincy Point Jr HS 1970-81; Bio Teacher Pope John Paul II HS 1981-84, Sidney H Lanier HS 1984-; *ai:* Sci Club, Clean Clear CO Sch, Recycle Moderator; Discipline & Teacher of Yr Comm Mem; NSTA 1979-, Cert 1988; NEA, TSTA, AAT 1984-; Amer Diabetes Assn 1989-; Natl Geographic Society 1972-; Natl Wildlife Assn 1976-; PTA Comm Mem Employee of Yr 1989; Tracor Scholar Teacher 1989; TX Med Assn Teacher of Yr Nominee 1990; PTA Employee of Yr 1989; *office:* Sidney H Lanier HS 1201 Peyton Gin Rd Austin TX 78758

FURZE, CHERYL CLARKE, 2nd Grade Teacher; *b:* Fall River, MA; *c:* P. Colin; *ed:* (BFA) Art Ed, SE MA Univ 1972; Psych & Multicultural Awareness; *cr:* 2nd Grade Teacher Davol Sch 1972-; *ai:* Sch Drama Club Co-Dir; Liaison to Calendar Project Adopt A Sch; Sch Improvement Cncl Mem; Fall River Educators Assn Exec Bd 1973-76; Public Relations Comm Mem 1986-87; Art Festival Childrens Chairperson; Art Unlimited (Bd of Dir 1985-, VP 1986, 1990); Art Assn (Bd of Dir 1986-88, Teacher 1986-88); Fall River Public Schls Recognition Awd 1986; Spon B Aetna for Excl in Ed; *office:* Davol Sch 112 Flint St Fall River MA 02723

FUSCO, ANDREW A., Mathematics Dept Teacher; *b:* Amsterdam, NY; *m:* Ellen Newcomb; *c:* Lynette, Adam; *ed:* (BA) Math, SUNY Potsdam 1972; *cr:* 7th Grade Math Teacher/CS I II York Cntrl HS; *ai:* Mod Ftbl Coach; RIT Teacher of Yr Awd 1987; AMTNYS Mem 1986-.

FUSHIMI, CINDY, Biology Teacher; *b:* Salt Lake City, UT; *ed:* (BA) Environmental Ed, 1982, (MA) Sci Ed, 1987 OH St Univ; *cr:* Bio Teacher Troy HS 1983-; *ai:* Gymnastics Coach; Chrldng Adv; OH Ed Assn, Troy City Ed Assn 1983-; Natl Sci Fnd Grant for Courses in Bio & Geology; *office:* Troy HS 151 W Staunton Rd Troy OH 45373

FUSIEK, BONITA PAYNE, Writing Center Dir/Eng Teacher; *b:* Hamilton, OH; *m:* William John; *c:* Agnes; *ed:* (BS) Eng, St Josephs Coll 1976; (MS) Eng, Purdue Univ 1981; Several Wkshps; *cr:* Eng Teacher N White HS 1976, Tippecanoe Jr HS 1976-81, Sunnyside Jr HS 1981-87; Writing Center Dir Jefferson HS 1987-; *ai:* Spon Literary Magazine; Ed Corporation Newsletter; Curr Coord Composition Prgm; Chm Textbook Adoption Comm; Lafayette Ed Assn, IN St Teachers Assn, NEA, IN Teachers of Writing, Phi Delta Kappa, NCTE, ASCD; Grant Tippecanoe Cty Public Schls Fnd 1987; Gem Awd Lafayette Sch Corporation 1984; Golden Apple Nom 1988, Semifinalist 1990; *office:* Jefferson HS 1801 S 18th St Lafayette IN 47905

FUSSELL, FREDDIE M., Kindergarten Teacher; *b:* Patterson, GA; *m:* Charles W.; *c:* Avis, Allen, Charles, Michele; *ed:* (BA) Elem Ed, TX Southern Univ 1973; (MA) Elem Ed/Rdng, Prairie View A&M Univ 1981; Eng as Second Lang; *cr:* Kndgtn Teacher Osbourne Elem 1973-74, Northline Elem 1973-75; Kndgtn/1st Grade Teacher Janowski Elem 1974-; *ai:* Janowski Elem Grade Level Chairwoman; Congress of Houston Teachers 1977-; NEA 1973-77; Houston Sch After Sch Rdng & Spelling Tutorial Services.

FUTRELL, GLENDA J., 1st Grade Teacher; *b:* High Point, NC; *m:* J. Dale; *c:* Tanya; *ed:* (BS) Primary Ed ASU 1967; *cr:* 2nd Grade Teacher Thomasville City 1967-72; 1st Grade Teacher Davidson Cty 1972-; *ai:* Cntrl United Meth Church (United Meth Women Pres 1979-80, Missions Chairperson, Mary Frances Stubbs Circle Pres), Special Missions Pin 1980; Thomasville Mini Grant; Math Article Published in Instr Magazine; *home:* PO Box 715 Denton NC 27239

FUTRELL, TERRIE BRANTHAM, English Teacher; *b:* Goldsboro, NC; *m:* Stephen Jesse; *c:* Ryan L., Katie L.; *ed:* (BA) Eng, 1971, (BS) Scndry, 1971 TN Temple Univ; *cr:* 5th Grade Teacher Bethany Chrstn Schls 1971-73; 5th/6th Grade Teacher Roanoke Valley Chrstn Schls 1973-75; 8th/12th Grade Eng Teacher Cross Lanes Chrstn Schls 1984; 7th/9th Grade Eng Teacher Roanoke Valley Chrstn Schls 1985-89; *ai:* Yrbk Adv 1985-86; *home:* 6419 N Barrens Rd Roanoke VA 24019

FUTYMA, KATHLEEN WALTERS, Spanish Teacher/Dept Chairman; *b:* Arlington, VA; *m:* Anthony J.; *ed:* (BA) Span, Mary Washington Coll 1983; Teaching of Eng As Second Lang, George Mason Univ; Enhancing Stu Motivation, Photography, Teaching Rdng to Second Lang Stu, Enhanced Instructional Process; Curr for The Gifted, Microcmptrs; *cr:* Span Teacher/Dept Chairperson Saunders Mid Sch 1983-86; Itinerant Saunders Mid/Woodbridge Mid 1986-89, Saunders Mid/Lake Ridge Mid 1989-; *ai:* Dept Chairpersons Rep to Cty for Lang Dept; Mid Sch Lang Curr Comm; Team Coord Cncl; Foreign Lang Club Spon; Yrbk Photographer; Cty Foreign Lang Rep to Center for Applied Research & Dev in Ed; Prince William Fed of Teachers AFL-CIO (Admin VP 1986-88, Treas 1984-86/1988-); Greater Washington Area Teachers of Foreign Lang 1986-; Foreign Lang Assn of VA 1988-; Phi Sigma Iota 1980-; Presenter VA St Foreign Lang Conference; Presenter Prince William Co Division-Wide Inservice Fall 1989; Nom GWATFL & FLAVA Outstanding Foreign Lang Educator Awds 1990; *office:* Saunders Mid Schl 13557 Spriggs Rd Manassas VA 22111

G

GAAL, ZOLTAN, JR., 7th/8th Grade Science Teacher; *b:* Komarom, Hungary; *m:* Cathy R.; *c:* Heather Hansen, Ingrid Hansen; *ed:* (BS) Bio, SUNY Coll of Forestry & Environmental Sci Syracuse 1966; (MS) Ed, SUNY Albany 1968; Grad Stud; *cr:* Bio Teacher Gales-Chili HS 1968-70, Service HS 1970-74; Self Employed Forester 1974-82; Bio/Algebra Teacher Service HS 1982-83; Sci/Health Teacher US Hanshew Mid Sch 1984-; *ai:* Boys Soccer Asst Coach; Chess & Juggling Coach; Chess Tournament Dir; Mayfair Comm; AK Ed Assn 1982-89; AK Fed Teachers 1989-; AK Sci Teachers Assn 1985-; Numerous Photos Published in Books, Magazines, Newspapers Photo Researchers Inc; *office:* US Hanshew Mid Sch 10121 Lake Otis Pkwy Anchorage AK 99507

GABBERT, KAY DILL, 2nd Grade Teacher; *b:* Cumberland, MD; *cr:* Teacher Randolph Cty Bd of Ed 1968-69, St Marys Cty Bd of Ed 1969-; *ai:* Primary Level Dept Chm; Sch Improvement Team Mem; Kappa Delta Pi 1967-69; NEA, MSTA 1969-; *home:* 428B Military Ln Great Mills MD 20634

GABERT, JUDY K., English Teacher; *b:* Salmon, ID; *m:* Ron Rush; *c:* Cameron Rush, Adam Rush, Jordan Rush; *ed:* (BA) Eng/ Ed, 1973, (MA) Ed, 1990 Boise St Univ; *cr:* Teacher North Jr HS 1973-77, South Jr HS 1977-84, Boise HS 1984-; *ai:* Stu Assistance Team; Stu At-Risk Comm; Class Adv; Payada Youth-To-Youth; IEA, NEA, BEA Rep 1973-; ICTE Secy 1983-87; At-Risk Stus Grants; *office:* Boise HS 1010 Washington Boise ID 83702

GABLE, FRANCES B., Eng/Spelling/Soc Stud Teacher; *b:* Laurel, MS; *c:* John G., Kay G. Elmore, Ramona G., Jeffrey M.; *ed:* (AA) His, Jones Cty Jr Coll 1960; (BS) His, Univ of S MS 1962; (MA) Elem Ed, William Carey Coll 1979; *cr:* Classroom Teacher Myrick Elem 1962-63, Pleasant Ridge Elem 1963-65, Pascagula Jr HS 1968-70, Myrick Elem 1976-; *ai:* MS Assn of Educators, NEA 1976-; Eastern Star; *home:* Rt 3 Box 255 Ellisville MS 39437

GADD, ROSELYN SIMINI, Fourth Grade Teacher; *b:* Niles, OH; *m:* Alan L.; *ed:* (BS) Elem Ed, 1969, (MS) Teacher/Rdng Specialist, 1970 Youngstown St Univ; Cmptr, NASA Wkshps; *cr:* 6th Grade Teacher 1969-72, 4th Grade Teacher 1972-76, Rdng Specialist 1976-79, 4th Grade Teacher 1979- Mc Donald Local Elem; *ai:* Girls Track Coach St Competition; Mc Donald Ed Assn Secy 1982-; YMCA (Local Bd of Dirs 1977-79, Cty Bd of Dir 1978-79), Mem of Yr 1979; *home:* 619 E Liberty Girard OH 44420

GADDIE, WILMA LESTER, Third Grade Teacher; *b:* Harrodsburg, KY; *m:* George R.; *c:* David, Ray, Janie Dickens, Rebecca Ford; *ed:* (BA) Elem Ed, Campbellsville Coll; Ed, Bowling Green Univ; *cr:* 1st Grade Teacher Mercer Cty 1951; Substitute Teacher Toledo Public Schls 1968-70; EMH 1974-75, 5th Grade Teacher 1975-76, 3rd Grade Teacher 1976- Taylor Cty Elem; *ai:* Active in Church, Sunday Sch, Womans Missionary Society; Bus Prof Women 2nd VP 1974-; Taylor Cty Ed Assn Building Rep 1974-; *office:* Taylor Cty Elem Sch 1100 Lebanon Ave Campbellsville KY 42718

GADDY, CONNIE S., 2nd Grade Teacher; *b:* Brooklyn, NY; *m:* David; *c:* Sean M., Necole; *ed:* (BA) Elem Ed, W NM Univ 1981; Spec Ed, Sci; *cr:* 1st/2nd/5th/6th Grade Teacher Duncan Elem Schls; *ai:* After Sch Gifted Prgm; Liaison Comm; *office:* Duncan Elem Schls Mc Grah Ave Duncan AZ 85534

GADIENT, ELIZABETH L., 7th & 8th English Teacher; *b:* Davenport, IA; *ed:* (BA) Engl, Marycrest Coll 1964; (MS) Counseling Ed, Western IL Univ 1982; *cr:* Eng Teacher John Greer Jr HS 1965-69, Montmorency Cmmty Sch 1969-; *ai:* NCTE; IL Ed Assn; NEA; Montmorency Ed Assn VP/Pres; Fish; *office:* Montmorency Comm Sch 9415 Hoover Rd Rock Falls IL 61071

GADSDEN, BENJAMIN DAN, Band & Choral Director; *b:* Charleston, SC; *m:* Ijuana M.; *ed:* (BS) Music Ed, Grambling St Univ 1984; Numerous Courses & Schls; *cr:* General Music Teacher St James-Santee Elem Sch 1986-88; Band Dir Lincoln HS 1988-; *ai:* Lincoln HS Marching, Concert, Wind Ensembles, Choir; Sr Class Adv; Charleston Cty Band Dir Assn Treas 1990; Percussive Arts Society, SCMEA 1989-; Music Ed Natl Center 1989-; Order of Brotherhood Soc Service Incorporated Regional Public Relations 1984-; Outstanding Young Men of America Awd 1989; *home:* 1735 Ashley Hall Rd #278 Charleston SC 29407

GADSDEN, MARGARET, Fifth Grade Teacher; *b:* Charleston, SC; *ed:* (BS) Elem Ed, 1976, (MED) Early Chldhd Ed, 1990 The Coll of Charleston; *cr:* 1st-5th Grade Teacher W J Fraser Elem Sch 1976-; *ai:* RMUE Church Choir; NEA 1983-; Nominee for Teacher of Yr 1987-88; *office:* W J Fraser Elem Sch 63 Columbus St Charleston SC 29403

GAEDE, JEAN MARALDO, Chair-Liberal Arts Division; *b:* Detroit, MI; *m:* Keith A.; *c:* Elizabeth, Brian; *ed:* (BA) Eng, Saint Xavier Coll 1971; (MA) Educl Admin, Cntrl MI Univ 1982; Additional Stud Univ of MI, MI St Univ; *cr:* Eng Instr Beaverton HS 1975-76, Beaverton Jr HS 1976-86; Eng Instr 1986-88, Chair/ Liberal Arts Division/Instr 1988- Interlochen Arts Acad; *ai:* Stu Life & Master Schedule ComM; Admin Cncl; Coord Teaching Interns inSt of Intnl Ed & Amity Inst; *office:* Interlochen Arts Acad PO Box 199 Interlochen MI 49643

GAFFORD, LYNN (ROBERTS), English Teacher; *b:* Omaha, NE; *c:* Harrison R.; *ed:* (BA) Fr, N TX St Univ 1973; Counseling Services; Cmptr Assisted Instruction; *cr:* 7th-9th Grade Eng Teacher Bowman Jr HS 1973-75; 9th-10th Grade Eng Teacher Williams HS 1975-78; 11th-12th Grade Eng Teacher Plano Sr HS 1979-; *ai:* SAT Prep Course; Teams Tutorial Course; Eng Dept Treas; Delta Kappa Gamma 1990; TX Joint Cncl Teachers of Eng 1975-; Plano Soccer Parents 1984-; Grant TX Writing Project 1983; Teacher of Yr Finalist 1984; Speaker at Writing Wkshps/ Conventions 1975, 1983-84, 1989; *office:* Plano Sr HS 2200 Independence Pkwy Plano TX 75075

GAFFORD, YOULANDA K., Physical Education Teacher; *b:* Clarksville, TN; *ed:* (BS) Health/Phys Ed, Austin Peay St Univ 1970; (MA) Health/Phys Ed/Recreation, TN St Univ 1975; *cr:* Health Teacher Hopkinsville HS 1970-72; Elem Phys Ed Teacher Wade Elem & Jordonia Elem 1972-76; Phys Ed Teacher Mc Gavock HS 1976-82; Elem Phys Ed Teacher Ross Elem 1982-86; Phys Ed Teacher Mc Gavock HS 1986-; *ai:* Girls Var Track Coach; Fellowship of Chrstn Athletes Spon; TN Assn for Health, Phys Ed, Recreation & Dance (Chairperson Dance Section 1989-, Chairperson Sports Section 1987-88); *home:* 420 Walton Ln E23 Madison TN 37115

GAGE, MARYNA MORRIS, 6th Grade Teacher; *b:* Cut Bank, MT, *m:* James Olen; *c:* Raymond E, Robert Hill, Rayfard Hill, Jamie Hill; *ed:* (BA) Elem Ed, Univ of AZ 1963; (MA) Elem Ed, NM St Univ 1975; Numerous Wkshps, Mini Courses; *cr:* 4th Grade Teacher Meadow Elem 1961-62; 6th Grade Teacher Travis Elem 1963-68; 2nd Grade Teacher Van Horn Elem 1968-69; 6th Grade Teacher Bitterroot Elem 1969-70; 3rd/5th/6th Grade Teacher Southern Heights Elem 1970-83; 6th Grade Teacher Coll Lane Elem 1983-90; *ai:* Presentor; Hobbs Dist Sci Fair; Ch Judging Comm Building Chairperson Coll Lane Sch; Ch Coll Lane Girls Tea, Boys Kite Fest 1983-; Ch 6th Grade Tasting Party 1983-; NEA 1963-; Hobbs Teachers Assn Building Rep 1977-80 & 1983-85; Classroom Teachers Assn 1970-89; Delta Kappa Gamma Corresponding Secy 1986-88; Natl Fed Grandmothers of Amer 1st Pl Scrapbooks 1978-83; Intnl Rdng Assn 1982-; Hobbs Dist Teacher of Yr 1986; Coll Lane Elem Master Teacher 1989; Nom Presidential Awds Excl 1990, Fine Arts Awd 1988; Escort Honor Stu Grad 1990; *home:* 4105 N Dal Paso Hobbs NM 88240

GAGE, SANDRA LYNN (TAYLOR), Third Grade Teacher; *b:* Pigeon, MI; *m:* Samuel Mathew; *ed:* (BSED) Elem Ed, Cntrl MI Univ 1974; *cr:* Substitute Teacher Various MI Elem Schls 1974-75; 6th Grade Teacher Ubly Cmmty Schls 1975; 6th Grade Teacher 1976-78, 3rd Grade Teacher 1978- Elkton-Pigeon-Bay Port Schls; *ai:* Adult Church Choir; *office:* Elkton Elem Sch 176 N Main St Elkton MI 48731

GAGNON, DENISE LACROIX, French Teacher; *b:* St Pamphile, PQ Canada; *m:* Roger L.; *c:* Roger D.; *ed:* Math Ed, Laval Univ PQ 1960; (BA) Math Ed, Providence Coll 1972; (MA) Fr, RI Coll 1980; *cr:* Math Teacher St Pamphile 1960-66; Fr Teacher Holy Family 1966-72; Math/Fr Teacher Woonsocket Jr HS 1975-; *ai:* Dauphine Chorale Dir; RI Heritage Commission Mem 1983-; RI Foreign Lang Assn Mem 1989-; Fellowship to Study Fr Dijon France 1979; *home:* 350 New River Road Manville RI 02838

GAGNON, RAY, English Teacher; *b:* Plattsburgh, NY; *c:* Erik; *ed:* (BA) Scndry Ed/Eng, SUNY Plattsburgh 1970; Grad Stud SUNY Plattsburgh; *cr:* 8th Grade Eng Teacher Plattsburgh Mid Sch 1970-; *ai:* Photo Club, Yrbk Staff, Mid Sch Bsbl Card Club Adv; Bsktbl Coach; Sch Spirit & Climate Comms; Plattsburgh Little League Bd of Dirs; Plattsburgh Pioneers; Quebec Major Jr Hockey League Dir of Press 1984; N Cntry Sports Collectors Club Co-Founder 1980; Sports Columnist Plattsburgh Press Republican 1984-; *office:* Ronald B Stafford Mid Sch 17 Broad St Plattsburgh NY 12901

GAGNON, SUSAN MILLER, Teacher; *b:* Brockton, MA; *m:* Carroll P.; *c:* Jane S. Kent, John C.; *ed:* (BS) Ec/Bus, Simmons Coll 1961; (MED) Rdng, Bridgewater St 1981; Grad Work in Cmptrs, Math, Soc Sci; Certified Teacher Quests Skills for Adolescence Prgm; *cr:* Comptrollers Staff NEGEA Service Corp 1961-63; 3rd Grade Teacher Indian Head Sch 1963-64; Parttime Rdng Teacher Maquan Sch 1974-79; Chapter I Teacher South Sch 1979-80; 5th Grade Teacher Intermediate Sch 1980-81; 5th-7th Grade Teacher Mid Sch 1981-; *ai:* East Bridgewater Mid Sch Cmptr Club Adv; East Bridgewater Ed Assn MTA Rep 1987-;MA Teachers Assn, NEA; Rosies Place Volunteer; *office:* East Bridgewater Mid Sch Central St East Bridgewater MA 02333

GAIDOS, WILLIAM MICHAEL, Business Teacher; *b:* Orange, NJ; *m:* Jane Belton Rea; *c:* Selise Gaidos Mc Neill, Michelle Lefong; *ed:* (BS) Bus Accounting, San Jose St Univ 1969; (MS) Bus Ed, James Madison Univ 1977; *cr:* Teacher Rockingham Cty Public Schls 1975-81, Shenandoah Cty Public Sch 1981-; *ai:* FBLA & Photography Club Spon; Jr Class Adv; Prof Comm Chm; *home:* PO Box 327 Edinburg VA 22824

GAIKOWSKI, PATRICIA OSTROWSKI, Science Teacher; *b:* Detroit, MI; *w:* Robert (dec); *ed:* (BS) Bio, Wayne St Univ 1973; Grad Work; Rainforest Research Stud Queensland Australia; Biological Stud Galapagos Islands Ecuador; *cr:* Teacher Sacred Heart Elem 1965-70; Sci Teacher Divine Child Elem 1970-; *ai:* Sci Olympiad Team Coach; Regional & St Sci Olympiad Events Captain; Metro Detroit Sci Fairs Stu Spon; Metropolitan Detroit Sci Teachers Assn; Detroit Archdiocese Sci Curr Comm; *office:* Divine Child Elem Sch 2501 H Weier Dr Dearborn MI 48128

GAIN, BETTY HAMM, Third Grade Teacher; *b:* St Louis, MO; *m:* William Randall; *c:* William R. II, Leonard J., Grace M. Gain Masters; *ed:* (BA) Phys Ed, Culver Stockton 1950; *cr:* Elem Phys Teacher Washington & Lincoln & Harrison 1950-54; 1st Grade Teacher 1969-78, 3rd Grade Teacher 1971- Brown Sch.

GAINES, FRANKIE M., Vocal Music Teacher; *b:* Rochelle, LA; *c:* Zina D. Curlee Paige, Vicki M. Curlee Simmons; *ed:* (BS) Vocal Music/Piano, Grambling St Univ 1961; (MM) Choral Music, Northwestern St Univ 1973; Organ Wkshp, LA Coll; Cmptr, Data Processing, Programming Wkshp, Northwestern St Univ; Real Estate, Market Wkshp, LA Coll; *cr:* Vocal Music Teacher Wright Elem 1961-63, Jones Street Jr HS 1964-69; Vocal Music/Rdng Teacher Brame Jr HS 1969-; Minister of Music Mt Triumph Baptist Church 1987-; *ai:* Gatorettes Show Choir Dir; Flags Corp Marching Unit Spon Brame Jr HS; Music Educators NE 1968-, Choral Superiors 1969-; Amer Choral Dirs 1972-; LA Music Educators Public Relation 1988-, Dist II Superiors 1969-; Alpha Kappa Alpha Corresponding Secy 1988-, Service Awd 1989; Natl Assn of Univ Women VP 1984-86, Woman of Yr 1983; Mt Triumph Baptist Church Minister of Music;Statue of Liberty Ellis Island Centennial Commission 1984, Charter 1984; Links Inc 1990; LA Worlds Fair Gatorettes Perform 1984; Top Ladies of Distinction Inc (Schlsp Chm 1990, De Bose Natl Piano Area Dir 1982-85, Dir Awd 1984; Natl Sandy Lake Show Choir 1987-, Overall Winner 1987-; *office:* Brame Jr HS 4800 Dawn St Alexandria LA 71301

GAINES, JUDY DAVIDSON, Language Arts Teacher; *b:* Fulton, KY; *m:* James Thomas; *c:* Ashley; *ed:* (BS) Elem Ed, 1970, (MS) Remedial Rdng, 1971 Murray St Univ; Post Masters Stud in Gifted Ed; *cr:* Remedial Rdng Teacher Norria City-Omaha-Enfield Sch System 1971-77; Lang Art Teacher Carmi Mid Sch 1979-80, 1981-; *ai:* Gifted Coord; Wabash Valley Rdng Cncl Pres 1974-75; *office:* Carmi Mid Sch 201 W Main St Carmi IL 62821

GAINES, RUTH ANN, Drama Teacher; *b:* Des Moines, IA; *c:* Brandon M.; *ed:* (BA) Drama/Speech Clarke Coll 1969; (MA) Dramatic Art, Univ of CA 1970; Ed, Human Dev & Fine Arts Courses; *cr:* Radio/Tv Announcer WHO TV 1979-86; Drama/ Speech Instr Des Moines Area Comm Coll 1971-; Human Relations Facilitator Heartlund AEA 1979-; Drama Instr East HS 1971-; *ai:* Dir Sch Plays, Mime Group; Spon Thespian Troupe & Drama Club; Phi Delta Kappa 1987-; Delta Kappa Gamma Secy 1986-; Delta Sigma Theta 1988-; NAACP 1982-; Des Moines Tutoring Bd Secy 1987-; Drama Wkshp Bd 1989-; George Washington Carver Awd 1979; Outstanding Young Women of Amer 1977; YWCA Women of Achievement Awd 1987; *office:* East H S 815 E 13th St Des Moines IA 50316

GAINES, WENDY WITTIG, Second Grade Teacher; *b:* Manistee, MI; *m:* Andrew R.; *c:* Caroline; *ed:* (BA) Early Chldhd Ed, Hillsdale Coll 1972; (MA) Elem Ed, MI St Univ 1976; *cr:* 1st Grade Teacher 1972-87, 2nd Grade Teacher 1987- E Bay Elem Sch; *ai:* 2nd Grade Curr Comm; Pi Beta Phi Alumnae Club Secy 1980-83; Cntrl Day Care Center Bd Mem 1985-87; *home:* 277 Knollwood Dr Traverse City MI 49684

GAINES, WILLIAM HENRY, Social Studies Teacher/Chair; *b:* Greenville, SC; *m:* Susan Iler; *c:* William H. Jr.; *ed:* (BA) Scndry Ed/His, 1970, (MED) Scndry Ed/His, 1975 Clemson; Advanced Placement Cert European His; Prgm for Effective Teaching; *cr:* Teacher Southside HS 1971-84, Travelers Rest HS 1984-; *ai:* NHS Spon; Natural Helpers; Soc Stud Dept Chm; Interim Evaluation Comm Chm; City of Travelers Rest Councilman 1979-; Teacher of Yr 1990; *home:* 29 Springdale Dr Travelers Rest SC 29690

GAIPL, LINDA L., 6th Grade Mathematics Teacher; *b:* Pensacola, FL; *ed:* (BS) Elem Ed, 1971, (MS) Elem Ed, 1981 Chadron St Coll; Numerous Courses; *cr:* Teacher Hyannis Elem Sch 1972-77; 6th Grade Teacher N Platte Public Schls 1977-; *ai:* Odyssey of Mind Teams & Math Olympiad Team Coach; N Platte Ed Assn 1977-; Alpha Delta Cappa Pres 1990; Cooper Fnd Grant 1990; *office:* Adams Mid Sch 1200 Mc Donald Rd North Platte NE 69101

GAISER, JANICE WALKER, Second Grade Teacher; *b:* Maysville, MO; *m:* Roger E.; *c:* Vallri A., Vanessa L.; *ed:* (BS) Elem Ed, MWSC 1976; (MS) Elem Ed, NWMSU 1981; Parents at Teacher Educl Conference Trng; Additional Classes; *cr:* 2nd Grade Teacher Maysville R-I Sch Dist 1976-; Parents as Teachers Ed Maysville R-I 1989-; *ai:* Parents as Teacher Educator; Comm Chm for Curr Dev; Served on Several Comms for Elem Curr Dev; MO St Teachers Assn Pres 1985-86; Psi Epsilon VP 1990; PEO Secy 1988-; Church Comm Comm Person 1989-; Teacher of Month 1988; *home:* Rr 1 Osborn MO 64474

GAITAN, EDWARD W., 7th Grade Teacher; *b:* Albuquerque, NM; *m:* La Donna M. Hyder; *c:* Xondria, Brett, Ty; *ed:* (BA) Soc Sci/Phys Sci/Phys Ed/Geography, CA St Univ Fresno 1974; Military; *cr:* K-12th Grade Substitute Teacher 1974-76; 4th-7th Grade Combined Teacher Lakeside Elem Sch 1976-78; 5th Grade Teacher Armona Elem Sch 1978-79; 7th Grade Teacher John C Martinez Jr HS 1979-89; *ai:* 7th/8th Grade Boys & Girls Cross Cntry, Soccer, Track Coach; CA Teachers Assn, Parlier Faculty Assn 1979-89; *office:* John C Martinez Jr HS 13174 E Parlier Ave Parlier CA 93648

GAITHER, GAYLE CALDWELL, English Department Chairperson; *b:* Poteau, OK; *m:* Billy Donald; *c:* Dawn Little, Christopher David, Mary Gaye; *ed:* (BA) Eng Ed, 1968; (MED) Eng Ed, 1973 Southeastern OK St Univ; *cr:* Eng Teacher Durant HS 1968-; *ai:* Coach; Academic Bowl Team; Staff Dev Comm; Chm Eng Dept; NEA 1968-; OEA 1968-; Duvant Ed Assn 1968-; Nom for Teacher Yr Awd ; Ex-Pres Duvant Ed Assn; Ex-Chair Staff Dev Comm; Spon Chldrs; Spon Jr Prom Comm; *office:* Durant HS 8th & Walnut Durant OK 74701

GAJAFSKY, GLORIA JOHNSON, Science/Biology Teacher; *b:* Wausau, WI; *m:* David Lee; *c:* Carrie Jo, Brian Craig; *ed:* (BS) Natural Sci, UW-Madison 1966; (MEPD) Ed Sci, UW-Whitewater 1987; *cr:* Teacher Highland in 1966-67, Louisville KY 1968-70, Gahanna OH 1970-72, Waukesha Schls 1980-; *ai:* Honors Recognition; St Scope & Sequence; Sch Climate; WEA; NEA; Church Choir; Ftbl Booster Treas 1989-; Band Boosters; Honors Grad; *office:* Butler Mid Sch 310 N Hin Waukesha WI 53188

GALANTE, PAOLINA, Spanish Teacher; *b:* Buffalo, NY; *ed:* (BA) Span/Poly Sci, St Univ of NY Fredonia 1983; (MA) Span/ Italian, St Univ of NY Buffalo 1990; Middlebury Intensive Lang Stud, Travel; *cr:* Span Teacher Lakeshore Cntrl Schls 1984-85, Lackawanna HS 1985-; Free Lance Translator 1985-; Travel Consultant Scandia Tours & Travels 1988-; *ai:* Sr Class Adv; Graduation Night Coord; Stu Cncl Co-Adv; Sch Planning Team; NY St Foreign Lang Teacher Assn; Amer Translators Assn; Evans Township Committeeman; BOCES Summer Grant; Outstanding Young Women Awd 1987, 1989; Translator in Europe 1985, 1988; *office:* Lackawanna HS 560 Martin Rd Lackawanna NY 14218

GALARNEAULT, THOMAS RICHARD, World/American History Teacher; *b:* Aitkin, MN; *m:* Carol Ann Leland; *c:* Julie, John; *ed:* (BS) World His/Amer His/Math, Univ of MN Duluth 1965; (MS) World His, Bemidji St Univ 1977; *cr:* Amer His/ World His Teacher Bemidji HS 1967-; *ai:* Northern Town Bd Chm 1980-; *office:* Bemidji HS 201 15th St NW Bemidji MN 56601

GALBRAITH, FRANK P., III, 7th Grade Soc Stud Teacher; *b:* Knoxville, TN; *m:* Cheryl Howard; *c:* Mark, Dayna, Cody, Casey; *ed:* (BA) Geography, E TN St Univ 1965; *cr:* Visitor Relations Rep TN Valley Authority 1965-66; Teacher Halls Mid Sch 1967-70, Farragut Mid Sch 1970-; *ai:* Chess Club, Past Stu Cncl, Pep Club Spon; Admirals Day & Spec Prgms & Assemblies, Heritage Day Comm; Track Coavch; Audio-Visual Club; KCEA, TEA 1967-; Union Cmmty Presbyn Church Dir of Music 1978-; BSA Scout Master Troop 18 1965-74; Halls Mid Sch Teacher of Yr; Farragut Jaycees Outstanding Young Educator Awd; *office:* Farragut Mid Sch 200 W End Ave Knoxville TN 37922

GALBRAITH, NANCY E., Mathematics & Chem Teacher; *b:* Bay City, MI; *ed:* (BS) Math, 1970, (MA) Scndry Ed/Math, 1976 Cntrl MI Univ; *cr:* Teacher Merrill HS; *ai:* Coord Merrill Cmmty Schls Tutoring Prgm; NHS Adv; Bd Dir Midland Camera Club; Merrill Ed Assn (Pres 1974-75, Treas 1985-88); NHS Recognition & Life-Time Membership 1990; *office:* Merrill HS 555 Alice Merrill MI 48637

GALL, JANET KAREN, 3rd Grade Teacher; *b:* Kimball, NE; *m:* Steve K.; *c:* Kenneth, John; *ed:* (BA) Elem Ed, W WA St Univ 1965; (MS) Early & Mid Ed, OH St 1985; *cr:* Speech/Hearing Therapist Heath Public Schls 1965-68; 3rd Grade Teacher N Fork Public Schls 1970-; *office:* Newton Sch 6645 Mt Vernon Rd Newark OH 43055

GALL, STEVE R., Geography Teacher/Dept Chair; *b:* St Paul, MN; *m:* Mary Jane; *ed:* (BA) Soc Stud/Poly Sci, Hamline Univ 1970; (MAED) Soc Stud Ed, Univ of MN 1974; Japanese Culture & Ed; Local Urban Geography; Bus Economics for Jr & Sr HS Stu; *cr:* Geography Teacher Oak-Land Jr HS 1970-; *ai:* Var Bsbl Coach Stillwater HS 1974-80; Cross Cntry Coach Oak-Land J r HS 1978-81; Golf Club; St Croix Valley Ed Assn Building Rep 1986-89; MN Cncl for Soc Stud 1970-; Project Bus of MN 1985-88; Valley Athletic Assn 1970-79; Amer Assn for Individual Investors; Hamline Univ Piper Athletic Assn; Oak-Land Jr HS Natl Sch of Excl Educator Awd; *office:* Oak-Land Jr HS 820 Manning Ave N Lake Elmo MN 55042

GALLAGHER, ANN RAWLINS, Mathematics/Science Teacher; *b:* Los Angeles, CA; *m:* Henry F. Jr.; *c:* Nancy, Thomas, Constance; *ed:* (BA) Zoology/Chem, Pomona Coll 1957; Grad Stud at Various Insts; *cr:* Sci Teacher Shipley Sch 1958-61; Math/Sci Teacher Foothill Cntry Day 1966-; *ai:* In Charge Charitable Outreach for Foothill; Phi Beta Kappa; PEO Pres 1970-72; Claremont Meth Church; Mortar Bd; Written Sci Workbooks; *office:* Foothill Cntry Day Sch 1035 W Harrison Claremont CA 91711

GALLAGHER, PENNY COX, Physical Ed Teacher/Coach; *b:* Philadelphia, PA; *c:* Julie A.; *ed:* (MS) Phys Ed, 1973, (MED) Phys Ed, 1978 Univ of Pittsburgh; *cr:* Teacher/Coach Washington HS 1973-; *ai:* Started Var Prgms Track, Vlybl, Bsktbl Prgms 1974; Track & Vlybl Coach; NEA, PSEA; Washington YMCA Bd of Dirs 1986-; *office:* Washington HS Allison & Hallam Ave Washington PA 15301

GALLAGHER, SHEILA ANN, Fifth Grade Teacher; *b:* Chicago, IL; *ed:* (BS) Elem Ed, KS Univ 1980; Teacher Effectiveness Trng; Teaching Both Sides of Brain; Problem Solving & Math Solution; Cmptrs In Ed; Elem Sci Solutions I & II; Demonstrating Techniques of Sci Ed; AIMS; *cr:* 5th Grade Teacher Our Lady of Unity 1980-82; 5th Grade Teacher 1982-84, 4th-6th Grade/Jr HS Teacher 1984-88 Blessed Sacrament; 5th Grade Teacher William Allen White 1988-; *ai:* Math & Sci Club, Safety Patrol Co-spon; Sci Coord; Regional Sci Convention Hostess 1990; KS Rdng Assn, KS Assn of Teachers of Sci 1988-; Cath Youth Organization Vlybl Coach 1980-88; Big Brothers & Sisters of Kansas City Big Sister 1988-; Southwestern Bell Grant Applicant; *office:* William Allen White Elem Sch 2600 N 43rd Terr Kansas City KS 66104

GALLAGHER, THOMAS A., Mathematics & Physics Teacher; *b:* Washington, IN; *m:* Carolyn S. Riester; *c:* John T., Richard E., Diane E., Karen A., Randy A.; *ed:* (MS) Math, IN St Univ 1960; Grad Stud IN Univ; *cr:* Math/Physics Teacher 1957-, Dir/Summer Driver Ed Teacher 1962- Barr Reeve Cmmty Schls; *ai:* Math Assn of America Mem; Exec Comm of Southern IN Sch Trust; *home:* RR 2 Box 635 Montgomery IN 47558

GALLE, ADELE CUTLER, English Teacher; *b:* Paterson, NJ; *m:* Richard Charles; *c:* Anne F. Galle Kotasak, Bradley Cutler; *ed:* (BA) Eng, Montclair Coll 1957; Grad Stud; *cr:* 8th Grade Eng Teacher Ramsey Jr HS 1957-62; 6th/7th Grade Eng Teacher Anthony Wayne Jr HS 1974-80; 9th/10th Grade Eng Teacher Wayne Valley HS 1980-; *ai:* Newspaper Adv; 1990 Sr Class Adv; Rotating Class Adv 1982-; Wayne Ed Assn Building Rep 1981-; *home:* 80 Fieldstone Pl Wayne NJ 07470

GALLEGOS, JOSE E., Elementary School Teacher; *b:* Palma, NM; *m:* Rosemary Ann Head; *c:* Alicia, Christopher, Lucia G. Benoit, Monica, David; *ed:* (BA) Elem Ed/World His, E NM Univ 1962; Priesthood Stud, Franciscan Order; Adult Basic Ed, Numerous Wkshps & Insts; *cr:* Classroom Teacher 1962-, Adult Ed Instr 1965- Artesia Public Schls; *ai:* NEA 1986-; NM Adult & Continuing Ed Assn (Bd of Dir, Mem) 1965-, Outstanding Teacher Awd 1974; Amer G I Forum Local Pres; Riverside Water Coop (Charter Mem & Pres); BSA Leader 1963-68; 4-H Leader 1968-80; Our Lady of Grace Cath Church (Eucharistic Minister, Mem San Jose Comm, Mem Annual Fiesta Comm, Pres/Mem Pastoral Cncl); Rdng Inst TX Western 1965; Summer Inst Ec Univ NM Albuquerque; *home:* 8 Chalk Bluff Rd Artesia NM 88210

GALLEGOS, TONY ALEX, Teacher; *b:* Nara Visa, NM; *m:* Cheryl Ann Mc Call; *c:* Tamera R., Robbie L.; *ed:* (BA) Math/Sci/Phys Ed, 1960, Sci Ed, 1961-63 CO St Coll; *cr:* Teacher Pierce Consolidated Sch 1960-62, Moffat Cty HS 1963-65; Math Dept Chairperson 1978-86; Teacher Taft Mid Sch 1965-; *ai:* Albuquerque Teachers Fed; GSA Co-Leader 1966-70, Outstanding Leaders Southwest Cncl 1973; New Life of America Youth Group (Dir, Leader) 1971-; Nom for Consideration Presidential Awds for Excl in Sci & Math Teaching Prgm; Semi-Finalist Albuquerque Jaycees Outstanding Young Educator Prgm.

GALLEGOS, VIRGINIA WARZECHA, English IV/IVAPH Teacher; *b:* San Antonio, TX; *m:* Rudy Martinez; *c:* Shayne T., Therese C.; *ed:* (BA) Eng/His, Our Lady of the Lake Coll 1973; (MA) Eng, Univ of TX San Antonio 1979; Advanced Placement Trng Trinity Univ 1983; NJ Writing Project of TX 1985; *cr:* Eng Teacher/Dept Coord Medina Valley Ind Sch Dist 1973-79; Eng Teacher John Jay HS 1980-86; Eng Academic Teacher Wm H Taft HS 1986-; *ai:* UIL Spelling Coach; Literary Magazine Co Spon; NCTE, TX Joint Cncl of Teachers of Eng 1980-88; San Antonio Cncl Teacher of Eng 1980-89; Trinity Univ Advanced Placement Trng Grant; Book Adoption Comm Awd; Providence HS Recertification Panel 1988, Curr Writer for Eng II, II Honors & IV; Curr Writer for Eng II, II Honors & IV; *office:* William Howard Taft HS 11600 Fm 471 W San Antonio TX 78253

GALLERANI, PAUL PETER, American History Teacher; *b:* Newton, MA; *m:* Patricia Grady; *c:* Scott, Brian; *ed:* (BA) Ed His, Norwich Univ 1967; (MAT) Amer His, Bridgewater St Coll 1980; *cr:* Teacher/Coach Weare Jr-Sr HS 1967-69, King Philip North 1969-; *ai:* Coaching; Negotiating Team; Annual Field Trip Washington DC 1977-; MA Teachers Assn, Natl Teachers Assn, Norfolk Cty Teachers Assn; Little League; Horace Mann Grant 1987; *office:* King Philip North Jr HS 18 King St Norfolk MA 02056

GALLICCHIO, BERTILLE COLE, HS English Teacher; *b:* New Haven, CT; *m:* Vincent S.; *c:* Vincent Jr., Lauren; *ed:* (BS) Scndry Ed/Eng/British Lit, 1971, (MS) Scndry Ed/Eng/Amer Lit, 1976 Southern CT St Coll; (Rank I) Admin/Supervision, Eastern KY Univ 1990; Cmptrs in Ed 1984-85; CT Cooperating Teacher Prgm 1986-87; Working on EDD, Curr & Instruction, Univ of KY; *cr:* Eng/Rdng Teacher May V Carrigan Mid 1971-81; Eng Teacher West Haven HS 1981-87, Model Laboratory Sch 1987-; *ai:* HS Drama Coach; Gifted & Talented, Curr Steering, Teacher Ed Admissions Comm; NCTE 1971-; KCTE 1987-; Phi Delta Kappa 1990; Hartland Homeowners, Tates Creek PTA 1987-; Model Parents for Excl 1989-; Citation Commitment to Excl in Ed 1987; Outstanding HS Teacher 1989; Nom for Ashland Oil Teacher Achievement Awd 1989, 1990; Grant KY Arts Cncl Artist in Residence Prgm 1990; *office:* Model Laboratory Sch Donovan Annex Lancaster Ave Richmond KY 40475

GALLIFORD, GEORGE WILLIAM, 4th/5th Grade Teacher; *b:* Batavia, NY; *m:* Vivian Paul; *c:* Gregory, Gretchen, Grant; *ed:* (BS) Elem Ed, 1965, (MS) Elem Admin, 1969 St Univ of NY Genesco; Teaching of Writing Process Approach, St Univ of NY Brockport; *cr:* 5th-6th Grade Teacher Pavilion Cntrl Sch 1965-67; Summer Sch Teacher Jackson Sch 1969-80; 4th-6th Grade Teacher Batavia City Sch Dist 1967-; *ai:* Mid Sch Ski Club Adv; Girls Cross Cntry Coach; Track Ofcls Group Pres; 4-H Sch Dev Comm Building Rep; Unit Leader of Other Teachers; Prin Designee at RM; NYSUT Building Rep 1988-; Kappa Delta Pi Ed Honor SocietY 1964-65; Presenter NY St Eng Teachers Convention, NYSUT at Brockport & Genesee Cty Teachers Conference Day 1982-84; *home:* 2 Narramore Ave Batavia NY 14020

GALLION, LINDA S., Teacher; *b:* Charleston, WV; *m:* James A.; *c:* Andy, Kristi; *ed:* (BA) Soc Stud/Phys Ed, Marshall Univ 1962; Grad Stud Teaching Gifted, Identification, Curr Dev; *cr:* Teacher Northside HS 1962-65, Northside Jr HS 1974-; *ai:* Red Cross Club, GAA, Class Spon; Girls Bsktbl City League Coach; Inservice Comm; NEA, VEA, RCEA, NCSS, VA Cncl Soc Stud; Sunday Sch Teacher 1966-; Church Choir Pres 1978-; Constitution Comm Chm 1988-; Trip to Soviet Union Partial Grant; Conducted Inservices Trip & Presentation at SE Regional Soc Stud Conference; *office:* Northside Jr HS 6810 Northside High School Rd Roanoke VA 24019

GALLIVAN, THERESE THOMSON, 8th Grade Teacher; *b:* Washington, DC; *m:* Gene Mills; *c:* Archie, Mary Kathryn; *ed:* (BA) His/Ed, Longwood Coll 1977; *cr:* 7th Grade Soc Stud Teacher Falling Creek Mid Sch 1977-79; 8th Grade Teacher Our Lady of the Rosary Sch 1986-; *ai:* Cheerleading Adv; Safety Patrol Sponsor; Sch Bd Rep; Field Trip Coord; NCEA 1986; Jr League 1988-; *office:* Our Lady Of The Rosary Sch 2 James Dr Greenville SC 29605

GALLO, CHRISTINE JOHNSON, Educational Coordinator; *b:* Fargo, ND; *m:* Joseph F. Jr.; *ed:* (BS) Eng/Ed, Saint Cloud St Univ 1984; Working Toward Masters Human Dev/Psych, Univ of TX Dallas; *cr:* Lang Art/Rdng Teacher Milaca Mid Sch 1984-85: Lang Art Teacher T J Rusk Mid Sch 1985-89; Ed Coord Brainworks 1989-; *ai:* Pupil Asst Support System Coord 1987-89, Outstanding Pass Team Leader 1988; *home:* 6402 Melody Ln #2122 Dallas TX 75231

GALLO, JOHN CHRISTOPHER, Social Studies Teacher; *b:* New York, NY; *m:* Linda Cullinan; *c:* Christopher, Andrew, Jennie L., Michael; *ed:* (BA) His, 1974, (MA) His, 1975 St Univ of NY Stony Brook; (EDD) Educl Admin/Supervision, St Johns Univ 1986; Prof Diploma Educl Admin/Supervision, St Johns Univ 1979; *cr:* Teacher Nesaquake Intermediate Sch 1975-; *ai:* Yrbk Adv; Bsbl Coach; Evaluation of Prof Staff Dist Comm; NCSS; St Josephs Church (Bd of Dir 1989-, CYO); Western Suffolk Teachers Center Grant Ec Ed 1988; NY St Cncl of Ec Awd Stock Market Activity 1989; Doctoral Thesis St Johns Univ 1986; *office:* Nesaquake Intermediate Sch Edgewood Ave Saint James NY 11780

GALLOWAY, JOAN K., Biology/Chemistry Teacher; *b:* New York, NY; *c:* Robert; *ed:* (BS) Bio, West Chester Univ 1966; (MS) Ed, Villanova Univ 1968; (MS) Phys Sci, 1972 West Chester Univ; *cr:* Phys Sci Teacher/Bio Dept Chm North Jr HS 1966-74; Dept Chairperson/Bio Teacher East Jr HS 1974-76; Bio/CHem Teacher Henderson HS 1976-; Teacher West Chester Univ 1972-74; Bio/Chem Teacher Philadelphia Coll Textiles & Sci 1976-89; *ai:* Ski Club; Riding Teacher; NABT 1975-; PSEA 1965-; NSTA 1968-; NSF Grant Geology ISCS; Schlsp Cath Univ Tissue Culture Course; Nom Outstanding Bio Teacher 1989-; *office:* Henderson HS Lincoln & Montgomery Aves West Chester PA 19380

GALLOWAY, MARIA COX, English IV & Spanish I Teacher; *b:* Tupelo, MS; *m:* William K.; *c:* Daniel; *ed:* (BA) Span/His, Delta St Coll 1973; Eng/Gifted & Talented Courses; *cr:* Eng IV/Span I Teacher S Pontotoc 1974-; *ai:* Beta Club & Sr Class Spon; HS Girls Sftbl Team Coach; Delta Kappa Gamma; MS Prof Educators Pres 1983-84; Star Teacher 1979; *office:* S Pontotoc Attendance Center Rt 5 Box 36 Pontotoc MS 38863

GALLOWAY, MARY, Kindergarten Teacher; *b:* Washington, MO; *m:* Donald Keith; *c:* Suzanne, Don; *ed:* (BA) Elem Ed, William Woods Coll 1966; *cr:* Kndgtn Teacher R #1 N Callaway Dist 1966-68, 1973-; *ai:* Text Books, Christmas, Friends of Ed Comms; MSTA 1966-; CTA (Treas, Building Ref) 1987-88; William Woods (Treas, Pres) 1977-79, Green Owl 1975; Natl Alumna Bd 1978-80; Peo Sisterhood (VP, Guard, Corresponding Secy) 1988-92; Outstanding Young Women of America 1977; *office:* Auxusse Elem Sch Box 8 Auxvasse MO 65231

GALLOWAY, NORMA S., Business & Health Teacher; *b:* Hartford, AL; *m:* Leslie E.; *c:* Colby, Caleb; *ed:* (AS) General, Enterprise St Jr Coll 1967; (BS) Health/Phys Ed, Auburn Univ 1970; (MS) Scndry Ed, Troy St Univ 1976; Certified Amer Heart Assn CPR Instr; *cr:* Phys Ed Teacher Dadeville Elem; Phys Ed/Bus Teacher Misses Howards Sch for Girls; Phys Ed/Health/Bus Teacher Geneva Cty HS; *office:* Geneva Cty H S 201 Lily St Hartford AL 36344

GALLUP, CYNTHIA E., Biology/Phys Sci Teacher; *b:* Miami, FL; *ed:* (BSE) Bio/Earth Sci/Geography, Wayne St Coll 1984; Bio/Earth Sci, Univ of SD; *cr:* Teacher Sioux City Cmmty Schls 1985-; *ai:* NEA, IA St Ed Assn 1985-; *office:* West Mid Sch 1211 W 5th St Sioux City IA 51103

GALLUP, JANICE ELLEN, Physical Education Teacher; *b:* Sleepy Eye, MN; *m:* Lyn Marshall; *c:* Jeff, Jack, James; *ed:* (BS) Phys Ed, 1961, (MA) Phys Ed, 1977 Mankato St Univ; Coaching Certificate; CPR Instr; Curr Dir for Phys Ed & Specialist Dist #77 Schls 1968-; *cr:* 7th-10th Grade Phys Ed Teacher Nicollet HS 1961-66; Elem Phys Ed Teacher Mankato Schls Dist #77 1966-82; 7th-11th Grade Phys Ed Teacher East Jr/Sr HS 1982-; *ai:* K-12th Grade Phys Ed Dept Chairperson & Coord; 7th-8th Grade Intramural Prgm Co-Supvr; Amer Alliance for Health, Phys Ed, Recreation & Dance 1970-, St Winner 1989-; MN Assn for Health, Phys Ed, Recreation & Dance Secy 1961-, Teacher of Yr 1989-; Intnl Assn for Phys Ed & Sports for Girls & Women 1989-; Amer Heart Assn Basic Life Support Instr 1982-; Amer Red Cross Blood Donor; NEA Life Mem; MN Ed Assn Mem 1961-; Mankato Teachers Assn Treas 1980-85; Mankato Teacher of Yr Awd 1981; Co-Writer for PEPI Film; 1976 Bell Awd; Co-Author City Wide Jog N Log Prgm; MN Scndry Phys Ed Teacher of Yr 1989-; Supvr Stu Teachers; *office:* Mankato E Jr/Sr HS 2600 Hoffmann Rd Mankato MN 56001

GALOUGH, JAMIE PEREAU, Human Resource Teacher; *b:* Schenectady, NY; *m:* Mark B.; *c:* Jacob, Kathryn; *ed:* (BS) Home Ec Ed, 1979, (MS) Home Ec Ed, 1983 SUNY Plattsburgh; *cr:* Consultant NY St Ed Dept 1979-; Human Resource Teacher Argyle Cntrl Sch 1979-; *ai:* FHA/HERO, CLass & Yrbk Adv; Family Life Ed Comm Chairperson; Dist Planning Comm; Cheerleading Coach; NY St Home Ec Teachers Assn, Argyle Teachers Assn 1979-; Maple Street PTSO 1989-; Article Published; Wrote Curr NY St Ed Dept; *office:* Argyle Central Sch Sheridan St Argyle NY 12809

GALUSHA, WESLEY JAY, Art Teacher/Project Coord; *b:* Le Mars, IA; *m:* Maybell Marie Christensen; *c:* Sean P., Dail; *ed:* BFA Endorsement Ed/Art, Univ of NE Omaha 1983; Working Towards Masters Degree in Educl Admin/Scndry Ed, Univ of NE; *cr:* Visiting Artist/Ceramics Dept Univ of NE 1984; Art Teacher 1984-, Project Coord 1989- Bryan Jr HS; *ai:* Art Club Adv; Coord Positive Peer Culture; Adopt-A-Sch Partnership Drug Intervention, Stu-At-Risk Prgm, Newsletter, Sch Improvement; Analysis & Evaluation Comm Chm Art Prgm & Phys Ed Prgm; Analysis & Evaluation Comm Mem Art Prgm; Assignment Book Comm Mem; NEA, Omaha Educl Assn, NE Educl Assn 1983-; Certificate Excl Exemplary Achievement in Classroom 1990; Numerous Pottery Shows; Recognition of Merit Awd NW Rotary Club; Foster Parent; Public Service Chicano Awareness Center Mothers South-Cntrl Group; *home:* 8129 Read St Omaha NE 68122

GALVIN, GERALDINE D., Third Grade Teacher; *b:* Buffalo, NY; *m:* James; *c:* Colleen Gyr, Karen Groot, Dean, Patrick, Diane; *ed:* (BS) Phys Ed, Cortland St 1958; Grad Stud Elem Ed 1968; *cr:* Phys Ed Teacher Haverling Cntrl HS 1958-59, Haverling Cntrl Elem Sch 1968-69; 3rd Grade Teacher Vernon Wightman Primary Sch 1972-; *ai:* Rdng Comm; Sci Comm; Mid States Philosophy Comm-Chm; Haverling Teachers Assn; NY St Teachers Assn; St Marys Church; Elks Auxilliary; *office:* Vernon E Wightman Sch Maple Hgts Bath NY 14810

GALVIN, JENE MAURICE, Dean; *b:* Cinti, OH; *m:* Bonita Jean Williams; *c:* Mitch, Lindsey; *ed:* (BS) Eng, 1967, (MED) Guidance/Counseling, 1970 Xavier Univ; *cr:* Teacher W Clermont Schls 1968-69; Teacher/Cnslr Cincinnati Public; Schls 1969-72; Coord New Morning Sch 1972-74; Coordinating Teacher Cincinnati Public Schls 1974-; *ai:* Assemblies & Recruitment Comm Chm; AFT, OH Fed of Teachers, Cincinnati Fed of Teachers 1972-; Clermont Cty Bd of Elections Mem 1988-; Clermont Cty Dem Party Exec Comm 1986, Outstanding Democrat of Cermont Cty; Articles Published; Write Bi-Weekly Column; Clermont Cty Bd of Elections Mem; *office:* HS for the Comm Professions C/O Hughes Center 2515 Clifton Cincinnati OH 45219

GAMACHE, DALE N., Spanish Teacher; *b:* Utica, NY; *m:* Robin Holmes; *c:* Erin D.; *ed:* (BA) Foreign Lang Ed, Univ of Cntrl FL 1980; *cr:* Span Teacher Port Orange Elem 1983-84, Ormond Beach Jr HS 1985-87, Seabreeze Sr HS 1988-; *ai:* Civitan Club; Girls/Boys Diving & Girls Golf Team; Volusia Cty Foreign Lang Teachers Pres 1987-88; FAATSP, AATSP, FFLA; *office:* Seabreeze Sr HS 2700 N Oleander Daytona Beach FL 32118

GAMAGE, JANE ELLEN, English Teacher; *b:* Lebanon, PA; *ed:* (BA) Eng, Univ of ME Orono 1982; *cr:* Substitute Teacher Yarmouth & Cumberland Sch Systems 1982-83; Teachers Aide Westbrook Coll Day Care Center 1983; Teachers Aide/Literacy Volunteer ME Youth Center 1984; Eng Teacher Massabesic HS 1984-; *ai:* NHS, Class, Literary Group Adv; ME Cncl of Lang Art 1988-; ME Literacy Volunteer Tutor 1982-84; *office:* Massabesic HS West Rd Waterboro ME 04087

GAMBATESE, LILLIAN PIAZZA, 4th Grade Teacher; *b:* Jersey City, NJ; *m:* Henry; *ed:* (BA) Elem Ed, Jersey Cty St Coll 1964; Elem Ed, JCSC 1964-69; Princeton; Fairleigh Dickson Univ; Kean Coll; Seton Hall; *cr:* 5th Grade Teacher PS 23 1964-65; 2nd Grade Teacher Millington Sch 1965-70; 1st Grade Teacher Hohenfels Germany DODS 1970-72; 2nd/4th Grade Teacher Millington Sch 1972-; *ai:* Passaic Twp Ed Assn Pres 1979-85; Passic Twp PTO VP 1988-; Mini-Grant Tele Conference Authors Childrens Books; *home:* 449 Mountain Ave Berkeley Heights NJ 07922

GAMBILL, VERNE W., 7th Grade Science Teacher; *b:* Cincinnati, OH; *:* Anita R.; *ed:* (BA) Bio, Olivet Nazarene Univ 1964; (MA) Scndry Ed, MI St Univ 1976; *cr:* HS Bio Teacher Prairie Heights Cmmty Schls 1964-67; Jr HS Sci Teacher Lakewood Schls 1968-69; 7th Grade Life Sci Teacher Lansing Public Schls 1969-; *ai:* Teach Hunter Safety Class; Pattengill Mid Sch Sci Dept Chm 1982-88; NEA 1964-; MI Ed Assn, LSEA 1969-; Lansing Schls Environmental Club 1969-84; MI St Univ Stu Teacher Ed Prgm Recognition; *office:* Pattengill Mid Sch 1017 Jerome St Lansing MI 48912

GAMBLE, LAURA CHRISTINE, Music Teacher; *b:* Easley, SC; *ed:* (BS) Music, SC St 1962; (MED) Music, Wayne St Univ Detroit 1969; Peabody Conservatory; Furman Univ; *cr:* Teacher Bryson HS 1962-69; Bryson 9th Grade Center 1969-71; Hillcrest HS 1971-72; Bryson Mid 1972-; *ai:* Annual Spring Sing Choral Clinic; Sch Musicals; NEA/SCEA 1971-; MENC 1971-; Greenville Chorale (Pres 1981-82/Section Leader 1988-89/Soloist 1987); Teacher of Yr Bryson Mid Sch 1988-89; H & R Block Tax Preparer 1989; *home:* 124 Jackson St Easley SC 29640

GAMBLE, SALLY MILLER, 4th & 5th Grade Teacher; *b:* Louisville, KY; *m:* Llester; *ed:* (BS) Phys Ed 1975, (MED) Coll Stu Personnel 1981 Univ of Louisville; Montessori, Xavier Univ; *cr:* 6th Grade Teacher Dann C Byck Elem 1975-76; 5th Grade Teacher Kerrick Elem 1976-77; 2nd/5th Grade Teacher ColeRidge-Taylor Elem 1978-; *ai:* Spon of after Sch Prgm; JCTA Rep; Southern Assn Comm; Safety Patrol Spon; Field Day Coord; Chicago Schlsp Project; Multicultural Ed Comm; Montessori Ed Comm; JCTA Bd of Dir 1988-; KEA 1975-; NEA 1975-; Outstanding Citizen of Louisville 1976; Awd for Promoting Peaceful Desegregation 1976; Whos Who Among Americas Women 1983/1984; *office:* Coleridge-Taylor Elem Sch 1115 W Chestnut St Louisville KY 40203

GAMBLES, CAMILLE DE ST. JEOR, Sixth Grade Teacher; *b:* Salt Lake City, UT; *m:* Paul Dean; *c:* Robert, Thomas, Jill, Sarah; *ed:* (BS) Elem Ed, 1959, (MS) Lang Art, 1979 Univ of UT; Gifted Endorsement; UT Writers Project; *cr:* Teacher Granite Sch Dist 1959-64; Teaching Fellow Univ of UT 1972-74, 1978; Teacher Granite Sch Dist 1982-; *ai:* Gifted Talented Teachers Upland Terrace Dir; Curr Writer Granite Dist; Fellowship Univ of UT; Nom Teacher of Yr Granite Dist 1988-89; *home:* 3550 Oakview Dr Salt Lake City UT 84124

GAMBLIN, BRENDA FORK, Mathematics Teacher; *b:* Madisonville, KY; *m:* Joseph R.; *c:* Joey, Christa; *ed:* (BS) Math/Accounting, 1972, (MAED) Guidance/Counseling, 1978, Guidance/Counseling, 1980 Murray St Univ; *cr:* Math Teacher Ferndale Baptist Sch, Calloway Cty HS, Providence HS, S Hopkins HS; *ai:* Beta Club Adv; Homecoming Parade Chm; KY Cncl Teachers of Math, NCTM 1986-; KY Ed Assn 1976-; First Baptist Church Sunday Sch Teacher 1977-; Dawson Springs Band Boosters VP 1988-89, G T Wallace Service Awd 1989; GSA Leader 1986-88; BSA Leader 1983-85; *office:* S Hopkins HS PO Box 1611 Nortonville KY 42442

GAMM, ESTHER, 4th Grade Teacher; *b:* Chicago, IL; *m:* Bernard; *c:* Sue, Ira; *ed:* (BA) Ed, 1960, (MS) Ed, 1965 Roosevelt Univ; Advanced Teacher Trng Prgm Inst for Psychoanalysis; *cr:* Kndgtn/1st Grade Teacher Evanston Dist 65 1960-67; Temple Judea 1961-76; Rndg/Writing Teacher Temple Sholun 1965-75; Evening Courses Teacher Northeastern Coll 1970-73; 4th Grade Teacher Skokie Dist 68 1967-; *ai:* Teacher of Great Books at Highland; Master Teacher for Stu Teachers; Worked with HS Stus in Child Dev Prgm; Teacher Rep Prof Action Comm; NEA Mem 1960-; Skokie Ed Assn Pres 1970-74; Phi Delta Kappa 1970-; Lincolnwood Bd of Ed Candidate 1970; Woman of Month Lerner Paper 1970; *home:* 4843 W Lunt Lincolnwood IL 60646

GAMMAGE, SUSAN CAROL, Science Teacher; *b:* Columbus, GA; *ed:* (BS) Biological Scis, Auburn Univ 1972; Post Grad Stud Genetic Engineering, Talented & Gifted; *cr:* Life Sci Teacher Daniel Jr HS 1973-79; Life Sci/Honors Bio Teacher Forest Meadow Jr HS 1979-; *ai:* Girls Tennis Team Coach; Chm Morale Comm; Coord Dist Sci Fair Comm; Mem Faculty Advisory, At Risk, Site Based Management Comm; Delta Kappa Gamma, Assn TX Prof Educators 1985-; NSTA 1972-; PTA, Richardson Ed Assn 1979-; Outstanding Teacher Muscogee Cty Sch Dist; Outstanding Educator of Yr, Phoebe Apperson Hurst Awd Nom, Most Influential Teacher Richardson Ind Sch Dist 1988; *office:* Forest Meadow Jr HS 9373 Whitehurst Dallas TX 75243

GAMMON, GERALDINE CRIDER, Fourth Grade Teacher; *b:* Cullman, AL; *c:* Gene C. Sharpton Jr., John W. Sharpton, Charles W. Sharpton; *ed:* (BS) Elem Ed, St Bernard-Cullman 1973; (MA) Elem Ed, Univ of AL 1979; *cr:* Lib Aide 1966-67; Head Start Teacher 1967-68; 3rd/4th Grade Teacher 1969-71 Dowling Sch; 4th Grade Teacher Addison Sch 1973-; *ai:* Faculty Rep; Rep NEA Rep Assembly; Local Textbook Comm; County Rep Southern Assn of Sch and Colleges; Accreditation Comm; NEA; AEA; WCEA; Treas; VP 1986-88; Pres 1988- Alpha Delta Kappa Sorority for Women Educators; Civitan Intl 2nd VP 1988-; *home:* 1412 Cottonwood Ln Cullman AL 35055

GAMPP, PAMELA SUE, Social Studies Teacher; *b:* Portsmouth, OH; *ed:* (BS) Soc Stud, OH Univ 1972; *cr:* Soc Stud Teacher Bloom Local Sch 1972-73, Minford Local Sch 1974-; *ai:* Jr Class Adv; *office:* Minford HS P.O. Box 204 Minford OH 45653

GANCE, GERALD A., Chemistry Teacher; *b:* Endicott, NY; *m:* Rosemary Cox; *c:* Christopher, Shannon; *ed:* (BS) Chem/Bio, Gannon Univ 1969; Sci Ed, Monmouth Coll; Chem, Rutgers Univ; Cmptr Sci, Kean Coll; *cr:* Chem Teacher Red Bank Regional HS 1969-; *ai:* Coach Head Cross Cntry 1969-73, Bsbl 1972-75, Bsktbl 1974-78, Ftbl 1974-77; Adv Key Club 1970-77, Class 1976, 1983-85; Ski Club 1976-; Amer Chem Society 1985-; Sci Teacher Assn 1987-; Sci Curr & Testing Assn 1987-; Teacher of Yr 1986; Governors Excl Awd 1986; *office:* Red Bank Regional HS 101 Ridge Rd Little Silver NJ 07739

GANDIAGA, BEVERLY REEVES, English/Reading/Art Teacher; *b:* Mackay, ID; *m:* Henry J.; *c:* Gregory, Philip, Laurie; *ed:* (BA) Art, Univ of ID 1953; Teaching Endorsement, ID St Univ 1970; Grad Stud; *cr:* Art Instr Buhl HS 1970-73; 8th Grade/HS Instr Castleford HS 1973-; *ai:* NHS Annual, Soph Class Adv; Negotiations Comm for Teachers Organization 1990; Reader for 11th Grade Writing Proficiency Test St of ID 1988-89, 1989-90; *office:* Castleford HS 500 Main Castleford ID 83321

GANDOLFO, JOSEPH E., English Teacher; *b:* Rome, Italy; *ed:* (BA) Eng, 1971, (MA) Eng/Ed, 1974 CCNY; *cr:* Teacher Jr HS 143 Manhattan 1971-; *ai:* Sr Adv; Yrbk Ed; Curr Writer Acad of Travel & Tourism; Teacher of Non Eng Speaking Adults; *office:* Jr HS 143 515 W 182nd St New York NY 10033

GANDY, CONNIE K., Phys Ed/Head Basketball Coach; *b:* Kansas City, KS; *m:* Ken; *ed:* (BS) Phys Ed, Fort Hays St Univ 1982; *cr:* Sci/Phys Ed Teacher Russell Mid Sch 1983-84; K-6th Grade Phys Ed Teacher Oatville Elem 1984-85, Rex Elem 1985-87; 9th-12th Grade Phys Ed Teacher Campus HS 1987-; *ai:* Head Girls Bsktbl; Weight Room Supvr; Target KS Rep; KS Bsktbl Coaches Assn Coach oF Yr 1989; Natl Fed Coaches; PTA Teacher of Yr Lifetime Mem; *office:* Campus H S 2100 W 55th South Wichita KS 67217

GANDY, MARY ANN SMITH, 4th Grade & Homeroom Teacher; *b:* Albany, GA; *c:* Kevin, Kaira Saran; *ed:* (BA) Fr/Liberal Arts, 1973, Elem Ed, 1975, (MAT) 1982 Wayne St Univ; Licensed Real Estate/Social Worker/Registered Rep; Licensed By SEC; *cr:* Owner Rainbow Childrens Ctr Nursery Sch 1975-80; 1st/6th Grade Teacher Detroit Public Schs 1975-; Founder/Dir Childrens Diognostic Inst of Amer 1979-81; Registered Rep Consolidated Financial Corp 1985-; *ai:* Fr Club; Stu MTH; Super Nice Lunchtime Contest; Local Sch Cmmty Organization; Teacher Rep; Assn of Mental Health Admin; Delta Sigma Theta; *home:* 19964 Spencer Detroit MI 48234

GANDY, MARY DREW, History Teacher; *b:* East Chicago, IN; *m:* Michael E.; *c:* Michael W., Michelle N.; *cr:* His/Eng Teacher Lockney HS 1972-73; His Teacher Pampa Mid Sch 1979-; *ai:* Honors Assembly Comm Chm 1989; NEA, TX St Teahcers Assn 1972-73; Pampa Classroom Teacher Assn 1987-88; Mid Sch Rep Dist Communication Comm 1987-89, Dist Discipline Management Comm 1986-87; *office:* Pampa Mid Sch 2401 Charles Pampa TX 79065

GANDY, SHARRON GRIFFIN, French Teacher; *b:* Quitman, GA; *m:* Bill; *c:* Ryan, Alden; *ed:* (BA) Fr/Span, Valdosta St Coll 1971; Grad Work Univ of GA; *cr:* Teacher Valdosta HS 1976-; *ai:* Spon Fr Honor Society; Foreign Lang Dept Head; AATF 1976-; Foreign Lang Assn of GA 1980-; Academic Alliance of Foreign Lang 1986-; Valdosta Jr Womans Club VP 1976-84; Baptist Young Women Pres 1988-; *office:* Valdosta HS 3101 N Forrest St Valdosta GA 31602

GANGLE, GARY J., Business Teacher; *b:* Veblen, SD; *m:* Karen Weverstad; *c:* Scott, Kiel; *ed:* (MS) Ed, 1973; (BS) Bus Ed, 1969 Northern St Univ; *cr:* Teacher Howard HS 1969-70; Stenographer US Army 1970-72; Teacher Howard HS 1972-73; Mrktg/Admissions Dir Barnes Bus Coll 1973-82; Teacher Sisseton HS 1982-; *ai:* FBLA of Amer, Jr Class Adv; FBLA 1982-; FBLA (Natl Officer Adv 1984-85); St Natl Ed Assn 1982-88; Optimist Intnl 1973-78; Current Adv 3 Time St Champion FBLA 1986-89; *office:* Sisseton HS 16 Walnut St Sisseton SD 57262

GANN, ANDREA FOLSOM, 7th Grade Block Teacher; *b:* Honolulu, HI; *m:* Ronald Wayne; *c:* Joseph F. Woodward; *ed:* (BA) Eng, Univ of WA 1975; (MA) Cmptrs in Ed, Lesley Coll 1990; *cr:* Rdng/Math Teacher Secret Harbor Farms 1976-78; 7th/8th Grade Teacher Lakewood Jr/Sr HS 1979-; *ai:* Jr HS ASB & Leadership Adv; Jr HS Act Coord; Natl Mid Sch Assn, WA St Assn for Mid Level Ed; *office:* Lakewood Jr/Sr HS P O Box 10 Lakewood WA 98259

GANN, RONALD WAYNE, Mathematics Department Chair; *b:* Bryan, TX; *m:* Andrea F.; *ed:* (BA) Math, Univ of WA 1970; (MA) Cmptrs in Ed, Lesley Coll 1990; *cr:* Math Teacher Lakewood Jr/Sr HS 1974-; *ai:* Sci Olympiad Coach; Math Chm; WA St Math Cncl 1982-; Lakewood Ed Assn Pres 1988-; *office:* Lakewood Jr/Sr HS Po Box 10 Lakewood WA 98259

GANNON, JOHN JOSEPH, Social Studies Teacher; *b:* Philadelphia, PA; *ed:* (BA) Poly Sci, Penn St 1972; (MED) Ed, Temple 1976; Curr Supervision, Soc Stud, Penn St; *cr:* Soc Stud Teacher Cooke Jr HS 1975-79, Vaux Jr HS 1979-81, J R Masterman 1981-89; *ai:* Girls Cross Cntry, Boys Var Bsktbl, Girls Var Track & Field Coach; Soph Class Adv & Activity Spon; PA Cncl for Soc Stud 1988-; *office:* Masterman Laboratory Sch 17th & Spring Garden St Philadelphia PA 19130

GANO, JANET ANNE, English Teacher; *b:* Honolulu, HI; *m:* James H.; *c:* Gregory S., Jeffery M.; *ed:* (BA) Eng, Univ of Cntrl FL 1970; *cr:* Eng Teacher Leesburg Mid Sch 1971-72, Auburndale HS 1972-74, Auburndale Jr HS 1975-85, Auburndale HS 1985-; *ai:* BARC Co-Chairperson; Academic Team; Polk Cty Cncl of Eng Teachers VP; Mellon Sch & Auburndale Jr HS Teacher of Yr; Auburndale HS Teacher of Yr; Excl in Ed Awd; *office:* Auburndale HS 125 Prado Ave Auburndale FL 33823

GANS, JOHN THOMAS, Teacher; *b:* Little Rock, AR; *ed:* (BS) Music Ed, Univ of AR 1963; (MS) Master of Arts, Governors St Univ 1976, Roosevelt Univ; Voice Music Ed, Chicago St Univ; *cr:* Teacher Farragut HS 1963-81; South Shore HS 1981-87; Lindblom Tech HS 1987-; *ai:* Concert Choir; Solo Wkshop; Madrigal Singers; Chamber Choir; Music Educators 1964-; Amer Choral Dir 1972-; IL Choral Dir Assn 1972-; *office:* Lindblom Tech H S 6130 S Wolcott Ave Chicago IL 60636

GANT, MORRIS CLYDE, Fourth Grade Teacher; *b:* Seattle, WA; *ed:* (BA) His, Univ of OR 1969; (MA) His, WA St 1972; Curr/Instr, Univ of OR 1973, 1980; Teacher Intern Prgm 1973-74; *cr:* 6th Grade Teacher S Umpqua Schls 1973-76; 4th Grade Teacher Eugene Public Schls 1978-79, Creswell Public Schls 1980-; *ai:* Math & Lane ESD Film Review Comm; OR Ed Assn St Task Force Goal 2 1985; Lane Cty Uniserv (Secy, Treas) 1984-85; Creswell Ed Assn (Co-Pres, VP) 1985, 1988; OR Ed Assn (Local Rep, Officer); Joseph Kinsman Starr Schlsp 1965-69; Fulbright Exch Teacher 1986-87; Oea Bicentennial Task Force 1976; St, Local Rep, Officer or Ed Assn; *office:* Creswell Public Schls 996 West A Street Creswell OR 97426

GANTLEY, JUDY ECKERT, Music/English Teacher; *b:* Belleville, IL; *ed:* (BM) Music, Stetson Univ 1962; (MM) Music, Univ of S CA 1964; Writing Project Univ S CA; Keyboard Prgm, Dick Grove Sch of Music; Lang Art, Pasadena City Coll; *cr:* Teacher Belvedere Jr HS 1966-82; Stu/Substitute Teacher 1983-84; Teacher Walter Reed Jr HS 1985-; *ai:* Impact; Mid Sch Cncl Coord; United Teacher of Los Angeles, NEA, NCTE; Los Angeles Master Chorale; *office:* Walter Reed Jr HS 4525 Irvine Ave North Hollywood CA 91602

GANTT, LLOYD JAMES, JR., Social Studies/Math Teacher; *b:* Quincy, IL; *ed:* (BA/BSE) His, NE MO St Univ 1972; (MA) His/Ed, 1974, (PHD) Ed, 1990 Stanford Univ; Apple Consortium Trng, Cmptr, Infused Classrooms; *cr:* Teacher/Mentor Boys Town 1975-79; Dept Chm/His Teacher Oakwood Sch 1979-80; His Teacher/Dept Chm Menlo Sch 1980-82; Teacher/Mentor Shoreham Wading River Mid Sch 1982-; Professor Adjunct Dowling Coll 1989-; *ai:* Cross Cntry, Cmptr Infused Classrooms Steering, Title IX Dist Comm; Fr Exch; NCSS; Phi Delta Kappa VP 1980-82; NAACP, ACLU; Pres Schlsp; Ford Fnd Grad Fellowship; Guest Ed Soc Stud Review; *home:* 3 Tower Hill Rd Box 824 Shoreham NY 11786

GANTT, RANDI TOLMAIRE, 8th Grade Lang Arts Teacher; *b:* Chicago, IL; *m:* J. Russell; *c:* Jamal Barnes, Mia Barnes, Marci Barnes; *ed:* (BA) Ed, Univ of IL Chicago 1971; *cr:* 3rd Grade Teacher Duffy Sch 1971-72; All-Purpose Teacher W Pullman Sch 1972; Upper Grade Lang Art Teacher Henry R Clissold Sch 1972-; *ai:* Writing Club; Great Books; Delta Sigma Theta Mem 1967-; *office:* Henry R Clissold 2350 W 110th Pl Chicago IL 60643

GANTT, ROSEMARY FAULKNER, First Grade Teacher; *b:* Commerce, GA; *m:* Herbert Carl Sr.; *c:* Carl, Jamila, Akilah; *ed:* (BS) Elem Ed, 1969, (MA) Elem Ed, 1972 Ft Valley St; *cr:* Teacher Hubbard Elem 1969-; *ai:* Natl Teachers Assn; *office:* Hubbard Elem Sch Culloden Rd Forsyth GA 31029

GANTZ, MARILYN KAY, English Teacher; *b:* Walla Walla, WA; *m:* Garey; *c:* Jennifer, Jonathan; *ed:* (BA) Speech, 1969, (BS) Elem Ed, 1969 Walla Walla Coll; (MA) Speech, Univ of WA 1971; *cr:* Eng/Phys Ed Teacher Hoodview Jr Acad 1970-71; 7th Grade Teacher Milton-Stateline Sch 1971-74; Jr HS Eng Teacher Livingstone Jr Acad 1984-85; Eng/Phys Ed/Bible Teacher Emerald Jr Acad 1985-89; Eng/Home Ec/Bible Teacher Livingstone Jr Acad 1989-; *ai:* Drama Club Coach; Newspaper & Annual Adv; Spiritual Act Spon; NCTE, OR Cncl Teachers of Eng, N Pacific Union Conf Teachers.

GANUS, NELDA JEANETTE, Sixth Grade Math Teacher; *b:* Waynesboro, MS; *m:* Harold Jackson; *c:* Daniel J.; *ed:* (BS) Elem Ed, Univ of Southern MS 1973; (MED) Elem Ed, William Carey Coll 1976; *cr:* 4th Grade Teacher Beat Four Elem Sch 1973-80; 6th Grade Teacher Chatom Mid Sch 1980-; *ai:* Faculty Soc Chairperson; Woodworking Class Teacher; Comm Mem Sch Improvement; AEA, WA Cty Teachers Assn 1980-; *home:* Rt 1 Box 229 Millry AL 36558

GAPCZYNSKI, JAMES JOSEPH, Sixth Grade Teacher; *b:* Schenectady, NY; *m:* Regina Mc Manus; *ed:* (BS) Ed, SUNY Buffalo 1970; (MS) Curr Dev, SUNY Albany 1974; *cr:* 5th Grade Teacher Division St Sch 1970-72, Caroline St Sch 1972-74; Asst Prin Caroline St Sch/Sch #4 1974-75; 6th Grade Teacher Caroline St Sch 1975-; *ai:* Chess Club, Kickball Club Adv; Building Rep; Teachers Assn Comm Worker; Saratoga Springs Teachers Assn 1970-; NY St United Teachers 1970-; AFT 1970-; PTA 1970-; Saratoga Springs Summer Beautification Dir Project Dir 1980-89; Honorary Life Membership in Natl PTSA 1977; Saratoga Springs City Cncl Resolution for Outstanding Service Cmnty as Dir Summer Beautification Project 1989; Historic Perservation Fnd

Awd 1988; *office:* Caroline St Sch 310 Caroline St Saratoga Springs NY 12866

GARBAR, JOAN HAYES, English Teacher; *b:* Boston, MA; *m:* Henry J.; *ed:* (BS) Eng Ed, Seton Hall Univ 1962; (MA) Eng, Bucknell Univ 1976; Grad Stud Latin, Immaculate Heart Coll 1961-64; *cr:* Eng Teacher St Luke HS 1956-57, St Anne Sch 1957-61, St Genevieve HS 1961-65; Eng Teacher/Asst Prin/Prin Madonna HS 1965-68; Eng Teacher Clear Lake Jr HS 1968-69, Guilford HS 1969-; *ai:* Curr Revision Comm; Moderator Coll Seminar; NEA, CT Ed Assn, Guilford Ed Assn; NDEA Inst Grant Boston Univ 1965, Bucknell Univ 1967; Bucknell Univ Fellowship 1969; Guilford HS Teacher of Yr 1988; *office:* Guilford HS New England Rd Guilford CT 06437

GARBOWSKI, SABINA PRUSZYNSKI, Algebra I & II Teacher; *b:* Jersey City, NJ; *m:* Stanley A.; *c:* Stanley J., Sabina M.; *ed:* (BA) Math, Jersey City St Coll 1970; Algebra Curr Project Rutgers Coll; *cr:* Math Teacher N Arlington HS 1970-72, St Michaels Sch 1973-76, Linden HS 1980-; Prof of Math Adjunct Union Cty Coll 1989-; *ai:* Math Adv for Minorities in Engineering; Cranford Jr GSA Leader 1987; *office:* Linden HS 121 W St Georges Ave Linden NJ 07036

GARBRICK, GEORGE RICHARD, Language Arts Teacher; *b:* Lancaster, PA; *ed:* (BA) Philosophy, St Francis Coll 1964; Theology, St Francis Seminary; Ed Courses, Millersville Univ; IU-13 Wkshps; *cr:* Eng Teacher St Anne Sch 1966-; *ai:* Sch Literary Magazine Ed; Spelling Bee & Lang Art Coord; NCTE, NCEA 1989-; YMCA 1987-; Lang Art Curr Diocese of Harrisburg 1989-; E F Educl Fnd Foreign Exch Sch; Philadelphia Museum of Art Summer Wkshp Grant; Whos Who in Amer Ed 1990; *office:* St Anne Sch Liberty And Cherry Lancaster PA 17602

GARBUTT, PATRICIA LEAPHART, Physical Education Teacher; *b:* Jesup, GA; *m:* Frank Randall Jr.; *ed:* Advanced Trng Spec Ed, Phys Ed; *cr:* 1st Grade Teacher Walton Cty 1967-68; 1st Grade Teacher 1969-70, 3rd Grade Teahcer 1971-72 Orange Street; 4th Grade Teacher 1974-75, 2nd Grade Teacher 1975-89, Phys Ed Teacher 1989- T G Ritch; *ai:* Own Riding Stable & Teach Riding; NEA, GAE 1985-; SE Saddle Seat Assn VP 1985-; 4-H (Volunteer Leader, Horse Club & Judging Spon); Episcopal Young Churchman Spon; *office:* T G Ritch Elem Sch 420 Cedar St Jesup GA 31545

GARCIA, ANA M. (MEZA), 7th Grade Math Teacher; *b:* El Paso, TX; *m:* Alfredo E.; *ed:* (BS) Ed, Univ of TX El Paso 1986; *cr:* 6th-7th Grade Math Teacher Surratt Elem Sch 1986-87; 7th-8th Grade Math Teacher Clint Jr HS 1987-89; 7th Grade Math Teacher Mountain View Jr/Sr HS 1989-; *ai:* UIL Coach Number Sense & Calculator Appl; Chrldr Spon; Natl Jr Honor Society Cncl Mem; Kappa Delta Phi Mem 1986-87; *office:* Mountain View Jr/Sr HS 14964 Greg Dr El Paso TX 79936

GARCIA, ARMANDO, History Teacher; *b:* San Benito, TX; *ed:* (BA) His, Pan Amer Coll 1968; (MA) Span, TX A&I Univ 1974; *cr:* Span Teacher Mercedes Ind Sch Dist 1968-75; His Teacher Weslaco Ind Sch Dist 1975-78; Span Teacher Progreso Ind Sch Dist 1978-80; His Teacher Santa Maria Ind Sch Dist 1981-; *ai:* Textbook Selection Comm 1984-88; TX Cncl for Soc Stud 1987-89; Mercedes Jaycees Treas 1970-73; Mercedes Ind Sch Dist Bd Mem 1975-78; *home:* 708 S Missouri Mercedes TX 78570

GARCIA, ARTURO, Mathematics Department Chair; *b:* Benavides, TX; *c:* Angela; *ed:* (MS) Mid Management Ed, 1978, (BS) Scndry Ed/Math/His, 1972 TX A&I Univ; Effective Sch Course; *cr:* Math Teacher Brownsville Ind Sch Dist 1972-73, Brooks Cty Ind Sch Dist 1973-78; Math Dept Head Freer Ind Sch Dist 1978-; *ai:* 7th Grade, HS, Number Sense UIL, Calculator UIL Coach; TSTA Pres 1980-81; Lions Club 1978-80; Outstanding Teacher at Freer 1988-89; *office:* Freer HS P O Box 240 Freer TX 78357

GARCIA, AZALIA OLIVEIRA, Social Studies/Science Teacher; *b:* Corpus Christi, TX; *m:* Jesus Omar; *c:* Michelle; *ed:* (BA) Scndry Ed/His/Fine Arts, 1983, (MS) Elem Ed, 1987 TX A&I Univ; *cr:* Elem/Scndry Ed Teacher St Joseph Sch 1983-85; Scndry Ed Teacher Benavides Ind Sch Dist 1985-; *ai:* 8th Grade Sponsorship; Jr HS Stu Cncl, 7th Grade Class, Art Club, Sci Club, HS Chrldr Spon; Deans List Awds A&I Univ; *home:* PO Box 512 Benavides TX 78341

GARCIA, CELINA HINOJOSA, Business Teacher; *b:* Alice, TX; *m:* Jose Amador Jr.; *c:* Joey, Louie, Jacqueline; *ed:* (BBA) Accounting, TX A&I Univ 1984; *cr:* 7th Grade Teacher St Joseph Cath Sch 1985; Bus Teacher Alice HS 1985-; *ai:* Operation Graduation Chairperson; Jr Class & Jr/Sr Prom Spon; ATPE 1989-; Alice HS PTA Mem 1985-; St Joseph Sch PTO (Treas 1987-89) 1983-; Alice Ind Sch Dist Teacher of Month 1990; *office:* Alice HS 1 Coyote Trl Alice TX 78332

GARCIA, EVELYN BELL, 5th Grade Teacher; *b:* Billings, MT; *m:* Arthur B.; *c:* Benjamin, Jake; *ed:* (BA) Elem Ed, Univ of MT 1971.

GARCIA, GLORIA B., Teacher Primary Unit; *b:* Spring Grove, MN; *m:* Frank E.; *c:* Frank Jr., Gloria Servais, Anthony; *ed:* (BS) Elem Educ, Univ of WI 1970; *cr:* 3rd Grade Teacher 1970-83; 1st-3rd Grade 1983 St James Cath Sch; *ai:* Midwest WI Rdng Cncl 1980-; Alpha Delta Kappa 1975-; 20th Century Club 1965-; *home:* 716 Hillview Ave La Crosse WI 54601

GARCIA, JANIE, Counselor; *b:* Laredo, TX; *ed:* (BA) Psych/Eng, 1979, (MS) Guidance/Counseling, 1980 TX A&I Univ; *cr:* Eng Teacher Robstown Ind Sch Dist 1980-84; Eng Teacher/Cnslr Ben Bolt-Palito Blanco CISD 1984-; YOU Prgm Cnslr 1988, JTPA Prgm Cnslr 1989 TX A&I Univ; *ai:* Chrldrs; Pep Squad Drill Team; One-Act Play Dir; Sr Club Spon; Foreign Lang Club; TSTA 1980-83; ATPE 1983-84; Parent Teacher Stu Assn 1987-; *office:* Ben Bolt-Palito Blanco CISD P O Box 547 S Hwy 281 Ben Bolt TX 78342

GARCIA, JOSE AURELIO, Spanish Teacher; *b:* Havana, Cuba; *ed:* (AA) Ed, Miami Dade Jr Coll 1966; Fr, Univ of ME 1968; (BS) Span/Fr, Appalachian St 1968; *cr:* Fr/Span Teacher John Mc Knitt Alexander Jr HS 1968-85; Elem Foreign Lang Lead Teacher Charlotte-Mecklenburg Sch System 1985-87; 10th-12th Grade Span Teacher Garinger Sr HS 1987-88; 7th-9th Grade Span Teacher Randolph Jr HS 1988-; *ai:* Foreign Lang Dept Chairperson; Foreign Lang Comm for Southern Assn Evaluations Chairperson; Foreign Lang Camps Charlotte-Mecklenburg Schls Co-Dir 1979, 1981; Stu Cncl Adv; Stu Publications Annual Sch Newspaper, Foreign Lang Club & Stu Act Spon; Asst Track Coach; AATF, AATSP, CTA, ACTFL; Leadership Wkshps & Seminars; CMSS Oral Proficiency Wkshp Staff Mem; *home:* 2420 Kingsbury Dr Charlotte NC 28205

GARCIA, JUAN DIEGO, Sixth Grade Teacher; *b:* Brownsville, TX; *m:* Rebecca Hinojosa; *c:* Sandra, Erica, Vanessa; *ed:* (BS) Elem Ed, Pan Amer Coll 1970; (MED) Counseling/Guidance, Pan Amer Univ 1977; Metric System Trng; *cr:* Elem Teacher Del Castillo Elem Sch 1987-; *ai:* Mem Campus Plan Comm; *home:* 1837 Wilson St Brownsville TX 78521

GARCIA, KATHRINE LAZARINE, Counselor; *b:* Beville, TX; *m:* Hector Jr.; *c:* Klaire Kathryn, Kamryn Alyse; *ed:* (BS) Elem Ed, 1980, (MS) Guidance/Counseling, 1983 TX A&I Univ; *cr:* Teacher 1980-85, Cnslr 1985- R a Hall Elem Sch; *ai:* Assn TX Prof Educators 1980-; *office:* R A Hall Elem Sch 1100 W Huntington Beeville TX 78102

GARCIA, L. DIANNE NORWOOD, Social Studies Chair; *b:* Jefferson City, MO; *m:* Amancio Jose; *c:* Maria del Mar, John; *ed:* (AB) Span, St Louis Univ 1966; Grad Stud St Louis Univ; *cr:* Span Teacher Parkway Cntrl HS 1966-67, Bowie HS 1967-69; Soc Stud Teacher Holy Infant Sch 1972-; *ai:* Debate Team; NCEA; *office:* Holy Infant Sch 248 New Ballwin Rd Ballwin MO 63021

GARCIA, LUCIA SERNA, 3rd Grade Teacher/Dept Chair; *b:* Seguin, TX; *m:* Simon Guss; *ed:* (BA) Span, 1975, (MA) Elem Ed W/ Bi-Ling Endorse, 1978 Our Lady of the Lake Univ; Educl Research, AM Fed Teacher Ladder Leader Prgm; Gifted & Talented Stu Trng; Eng As Second Lang; Whole Lang; Cooperative Groups; Drug Awareness Laison-SAISD; *cr:* Teachers Aide Wichita Falls Ind Sch Dist 1972-73; Substitute Teacher Edgewood ISD 1973-74; Teacher K-5 San Antonio ISD 1976-; *ai:* Master Teacher Appraisal Adv Comm TX Ed Agency; 3rd Grade Dept Chairperson; Faculty Adv Comm Rep 3rd Grade; AFT 1976-; TX Fed of Teachers 1976-; Bexar Cty Fed of Teachers 1976-; Guadalupe Cultural Arts Center1987-; Bexar CTY Audobon Society 1985-; Smithsonian Institute 1985-; Spon-Gift/Talented Prgm 1983-86; Career Ladder Selection Comm-SAISD; Career Ladder Level III Teacher; Academic Coord/Dept Chairperson; SAISD Textbook Advisory Comm; Sch Patrol Spon; Faculty Advisory Chairperson; Ed Consultant HBJ Pub Co; *office:* Sarah S King Elem Sch 1001 Ceralvo San Antonio TX 78207

GARCIA, MARIA ESTHER, Fourth Grade Teacher; *b:* Ranchos De Taos, NM; *ed:* (BA) Span, Aquinas Coll 1968; (MA) Elem Sch Admin, Cntrl MI Univ 1977; Bi-ling Ed, Saginaw Valley St Univ; *cr:* 1st-5th Grade Teacher St Josaphats, Holy Trinity, Our Lady of Grace, Our Lady of Perpetual Help; Dir of Migrant Ed Prgm Saginaw Public Schls 1972-77; 1st-4th Grade Teacher Fuerbringer Sch 1977-; *ai:* NEA, MT Assn; Saginaw Ed Assn Building Rep 1986-87.

GARCIA, MARY LOU, Social Studies Teacher; *b:* Harlingen, TX; *ed:* (BS) His/Phys Ed, Pan Amer Univ 1980; Edinburg CISD & Assn of Valley Educators TX Ed Agency Effective Teaching Practices 1989; Gifted & Talented Seminar 1987; Center of Free Enterprise TX A&M Summer Session 1984; *cr:* Teacher/Tennis Coach San Benito Consolidated Ind Sch Dist 1980-87; Teacher/Health Coord/Phys Ed Teacher Villa Maria HS 1987-; *ai:* Cheerleading Spon 1981-83, 1985-87, 1988-89; 7th Grade Soc Stud Dept Chairperson; Stu Cncl Co-Spon 1980-82; TX His Textbook Comm 1986-87; Jr Class Spon; San Benito Cmmty Dev Bd 1982-85, Exec Bd 1984; TCTA Mem 1980-87; Boys Club 1983-84; Natl Trust for Historic Prevention 1986-89; *office:* Villa Maria HS 244 Resaca Blvd Brownsville TX 78520

GARCIA, NORMA LUCIA (DE LOS COBOS), Sixth Grade GATE Teacher; *b:* Los Angeles, CA; *m:* Louis Alfonso; *c:* Anna M. Linder, Sylvia Mc Nally, Michael; *ed:* (BA) General Elem, 1964, (MA) Adv Curr, 1976 San Diego St Univ; Admin Work; Cmptr Classes; Completed Competencies Gifted & Talented Ed; *cr:* 5th Grade Teacher Paradise Hills Elem 1966-72; Teacher/Corps Team Leader San Diego St Univ 1972-73; 5th/6th Grade Gifted/Talented Ed Teacher 1973-, Mentor Teacher 1988-89 Gage Elem; *ai:* Gifted & Talented Ed Prgm Team Leader; Cmptr Club Coach; Lang Arts Comm; AFT (Rep 1972) 1972-; San Diego Teachers Assn (Rep 1972) 1966-; PTA 1966-, Life Awd 1988; Certificate of Appreciation Contribution to Racial Integration & Monitoring Effort; *office:* Gage Elem Sch 6911 Bisby Lake Dr San Diego CA 92119

GARCIA, PATRICIA ANNE, Math/Science Teacher; *b:* San Antonio, TX; *ed:* (BS) Math/Sci, UTSA 1987; Cmptr Sci Southwest TX St Univ; *cr:* Stu Teacher Health Careers HS; Teacher Sam Houston HS 1987-; Fox Tech Night Sch 1989-; *ai:* Spon Peers Leadership; Co Spon Engineering Club; after School Tutoring; Ticket Taker Home Sport Events; Special Olympics Vol 1987-; UTSA Alumni Assn 1987-; BATS Vol 1987; Muscular Dystrophy Summer Camp Vol 1987-88; *home:* 11610 Vance Jackson 855 San Antonio TX 78230

GARCIA, RICHARD ORLANDO, Bands Director; *b:* Denver, CO; *m:* Angela; *c:* Luis O.; *ed:* (AA) Music Performance, W WY Coll 1982; (BA) Music Ed, Univ of WY 1983; *cr:* Bands Dir Rawlins Mid Sch 1984-86, Fergus HS 1986-; *ai:* All Music Act; MT Band Masters, MT Ed Assn 1986-; Music Educators Natl Conference (Pres, VP) 1983-84; *office:* Fergus HS 201 Casino Creek Lewistown MT 59457

GARCIA, ROBOT CHARLES, Earth Science Teacher; *b:* San Antonio, TX; *m:* Donna Maxwell; *c:* Katy, Kasey; *ed:* (BA) Elem Ed/Life Earth Sci, Univ of TX Tyler 1981; *cr:* 8th Grade Earth Sci Teacher Marshall Jr HS 1984-; *ai:* Faculty Affairs Comm; Text Book Comm; TCTA Mem 1984-; *home:* 123 Fariview Marshall TX 75670

GARCIA, RONALD JAMES, Industrial Arts Chairman; *b:* Oakland, CA; *m:* Michele Dian Ruth; *c:* Amy, Emily, Bethany, Cody; *ed:* (AA) Drafting Technology, Chabot Coll 1968; (BA) Industrial Arts, San Jose St Univ 1970; *cr:* Teacher Prospect HS 1971-; *ai:* Electronics Commission Adv; Mentor Teacher; Prof Photographers of Santa Clara Valley, Prof Photographers of CA; Campbell Union HS Dist I A Teacher of Yr 1986; Teacher of Yr Prospect HS 1989; *office:* Prospect HS 18900 Prospect Rd Saratoga CA 95070

GARCIA, TIMOTEA PRUNEDA, 1st-5th Grade Phys Ed Teacher; *b:* Bishop, TX; *c:* Pauline P., Luis P.; *ed:* (BA) Elem, 1979, (MA) Bi-ling, 1984 TX A&I; ESL Certificate TX A&I 1985; *cr:* Phys Ed Teacher Robstown Ind Sch Dist 1979-80, Phys Ed/Migrant Teacher 1980-, ESL Teacher 1985- Driscoll Ind Sch Dist; Adult Learning Teacher Driscoll-Bishop 1981-; *ai:* TACAE Mem; *home:* PO Box 385 Driscoll TX 78351

GARD, JEFF RICHARD, Second Grade Teacher; *b:* Cedar Rapids, IA; *ed:* (BS) Elem Ed, 1974, (MS) Educl Admin, 1978 IA St; *cr:* 2nd Grade Teacher Lowell Elem Sch 1974-; *ai:* 2nd Grade Horizontal Comm Recorder; Rdng Vertical & Phase III Steering Comm Mem; Phi Delta Kappa Mem 1978-; Boone Ed Assn (Negotiations Comm 1989-, Mem 1974-); IA St Ed Assn, NEA Mem 1974-; Awana Youth Assn Pal Dir 1980-; Berean Baptist Church Sunday Sch Teacher 1975-; Lowell PTA Mem 1974-; *office:* Lowell Elem Sch 1420 Benton St Boone IA 50036

GARDELLA, PAUL ROBERT, Mathematics Teacher; *b:* Worcester, MA; *m:* Carole Pietrzak; *c:* Dan, Cindy, Amy, Sara; *ed:* (BS) Ed/Math, Worcester St Coll 1967; *cr:* Math Teacher Oxford Mid Sch 1967-; *ai:* Oxford Ed Assn, NEA, MTA 1967-; *office:* Oxford Mid Sch Main St Oxford MA 01540

GARDENER, BERNETTA HARRIS, English Teacher; *b:* Tatum, TX; *m:* Charles James; *c:* Brieonna E. J.; *ed:* (BA) Psych/Sociology, 1972, (MA) Guidance/Counseling, 1974 TX Southern Univ; Grad Stud Eng; Wkshps Eng, Cmptrs; Toured Italy; *cr:* Cnslr Meadowbriar Home for Girls 1974-75; Teacher Shepherd Mid Sch 1982-83, Humble HS 1983-; *ai:* Previously Spon Frosh, Soph, Jr Classes; Chaperon Project Grad; Mem Church Choir; Assn of Tx Prof Educators 1989-; *office:* Humble HS 3701 Wilson Rd Humble TX 77338

GARDENER, KATHLEEN CAROL, 2nd & 3rd Grade Teacher; *b:* Chicago, IL; *m:* Terry; *ed:* (BA) Elem Ed, Cntrl Coll 1971; (MA) Elem Ed/Supervisor, Univ of IA 1 980; Cmptr Ed, Rdng Cert; *cr:* 3rd/5th/6th Grade Teacher Jefferson Elem 197--74; 2nd Grade Teacher Douma Elem 1974 1976; 1st Grade Teacher Wildwood Elem 1987-; *ai:* Peer Observation Prgm Chairperson; Phase III Steering Comm; US West Teacher of Yr Selection Comm; Drama Act Coord of Invent Ottumwa; IA St Ed Assn Executive Bd Mem 1986-92; Ottumwa Ed Assn Hazel Thompson Awd 1979; IA Rdng Assn; ASCD; Alpha Delta Kappa 1980-; Past Pres of Ottumwa Ed Assn; *office:* Pickwick Elem Sch 1306 W Williams Ottumwa IA 52501

GARDINER, ELSADIA DELORES, First Grade Teacher; *b:* Miami Beach, FL; *ed:* (BA) Eng, St Thomas Univ 1978; Working Towards Masters Dev Counseling, St Thomas Univ; *cr:* Teacher St Monica Sch 1979-; *office:* St Monica Sch 3490 NW 191 St Miami FL 33055

GARDNER, ALAN WILLIAM, 6th Grade Teacher; *b:* Baltimore, MD; *m:* Elaine; *c:* Paul Cantezlu, Caryn Cantezlu, James; *ed:* (BS) Ed, Fairleigh Dickenson Univ 1969; IBM Office Products; *cr:* Dept Head IBM 1969-74; 6th Grade Teacher 1974-79, 8th Grade Sci Teacher 1979-85, 8th Grade Sci/Eng Teacher 1984-89, 6th Grade Teacher 1989- Upper Saddle River; *ai:* Band Officer; Super Drug Study Group; *office:* Cavallini Mid Sch 392 W Saddle River Rd Upper Saddle River NJ 07458

GARDNER, BETH EMERSON, Computer Coordinator; *b:* Steuben County, IN; *m:* Larry K.; *c:* Eric, Michael; *ed:* (BS) Bus Ed, 1961; (MA) Guidance/Counseling, 1964 Ball St Univ; Certificate in Cmptr Ed Governors St Univ; Elem Cert N IL Univ, Univ of IL, Joliet Jr Coll, Natl Coll of Ed; *cr:* Cnslr Bremen HS; Classroom Teacher; Elem Teacher/Asst Prin, Cmptr Coord Peotone Dist 207-U; *ai:* Dist Cmptr Comm; Assist with Supervision of Elem Sporting Events; Teach Adult Classes; United Meth Church Bell Choir; Teaching Assoc Univ of IL; *office:* District 207-U Conrad & Mill Peotone IL 60468

GARDNER, DANIEL B., Mathematics Teacher; *b:* Keyser, WV; *m:* Charlotte R. Foster; *c:* Jeremy S., Brian M.; *ed:* (AA) Scndry Ed, Potomac St Coll 1975; (BA) Scndry Ed/Math, WV Univ 1977; *cr:* Math Teacher Wirt Cty HS 1977-79, Union HS 1979-; *ai:* 8th Grade Class Spon; Sch Advisory Comm; NEA, WVEA GCEA 1979-; Keyser Rescue Squad (Pres 1987) 1986-; *office:* Union HS Rt 50 Box 750 Mount Storm WV 26739

GARDNER, DANIEL WAYNE, Mathematics & Science Teacher; *b:* Bend, OR; *m:* Vonna Jean Stewart; *c:* Catherine M., Kenneth D.; *ed:* (BS) Math, Portland St Univ 1962; (MS) Math, Univ of OR 1971; *cr:* Math/Sci Teacher Vale Union HS 1962-; *ai:* Head Coach Boys & Girls Cross Cntry, Wrestling; Adv Sci Club; Vale Ed Assn Pres 1987-; Vale Fire & Ambulance Dept Asst Chief 1988-; City of Vale Mayor 1981-87; *office:* Vale Union HS 505 Nachez St S Vale OR 97918

GARDNER, DIANN STRAUSER, Language Art Teacher; *b:* Pottstown, PA; *m:* Robert Walter Jr.; *c:* Alyson L., Richard M.; *ed:* (BA) Soc Sci, James Madison Univ 1967; Post Grad Courses Radford Univ; *cr:* 7th Grade VA His Teacher Galax City Schls 1967-68; 10th Grade Eng Teacher Carroll Cty Schls 1968-71; 8th Grade Lang Art Teacher Pulaski Cty Schls 1973-; *ai:* Team Leader; Chess Spon; Pulaski Cty Ed Assn 1973-; VA Ed Assn, NEA 1967-; Pulaski Jr Womans Club (Pres 1981) 1973-86, Jr of Yr Awd 1981; 1st United Meth Church (Youth Coord 1973-86, Bd Cncl of Ministeries, Comm on Missions, Substitute Sunday Sch Teacher); *office:* Pulaski Mid Sch 500 Pico Terr Pulaski VA 24301

GARDNER, GINGER, Third Grade Teacher; *b:* Centerville, IA; *ed:* (BS) Elem Ed, Cntrl MO St Univ 1971; (MS) Elem Guidance/Counseling, NW MO St Univ 1976; Psych & Ed; *cr:* Teacher Bessie Ellison Elem Ed 1971-; *ai:* Phi Delta Kappa; CTA Welfare Rep; MO St Teachers Assn St Delegate 1981-; St Joe Cmmty Teachers Assn (Secy, Elem Rep) 1981-83; Allied Arts; PEO Sisterhood; Nom St Joseph Teacher of Yr; *office:* Bessie Ellison Elem Sch RR 1 Saint Joseph MO 64507

GARDNER, JAMES CLARK, Social Studies Chairman; *b:* Stillwater, OK; *m:* Judith Elaine Shaber; *c:* Clark J., Garett J.; *ed:* (BS) Scndry Ed, OK St Univ 1967; (ME) Ed, Wichita St Univ 1975; Grad Work Wichita St, Emporia St, KS St; *cr:* Teacher El Dorado HS 1969-; *ai:* Sr Class Head Spon; Dir of Concessions; Chm Soc Stud; KS Cncl for Soc Stud St Pres 1980; NCSS Delegate 1980; NEA Delegate 1972, 1990; KS Ed Assn St Bd of Dir 1979-82; El Dorado Ed Assn Pres 1973-74, 1990-; KS St Master Teacher 1990; Finalist KS Teacher of Yr 1982; Unified Sch Dist 490 Teacher of Yr 1982, 1990; Outstanding Young Man of America 1973; United Way Ed Division Chm; *office:* El Dorado HS 401 Mc Collum Rd Eldorado KS 67042

GARDNER, JOHN GOODENOUGH, Fifth Grade Teacher; *b:* Manchester, NH; *m:* Jean Lydia Kaufman; *c:* Bill, Karin; *ed:* (BA) CA St Los Angeles 1969; Grad Stud; *cr:* Soldier US Army 1956-59; Checker/Dispatcher May Company 1959-66; Teacher Post Elem Sch 1970-; *ai:* Sch Site Cncl; Prin Designee; World Champion Lapsitter 1975-; City of Garden Grove Certificate of Recognition 1976; Published 1982; *home:* 7559 Paseo Laredo Anaheim Hills CA 92808

GARDNER, MIKE DON, Mathematics Department Chair; *b:* Weiser, ID; *m:* Sheri Linda Lester; *c:* Scott, Mark; *ed:* (BS) Scndry Ed Math, 1974, (MS) Scndry Ed Math, 1977 E OR St Coll; *cr:* Math Teacher Culver HS 1974-84; Math Teacher/Dept Chm Redmond HS 1984-; *ai:* OR Ed Assn; NCTM; OR Cncl Teachers of Math; City of Culver City Cncl 1979-80; Culver Sch Dist Bd Mem 1990-; *office:* Redmond HS 675 SW Rimrock Redmond OR 97756

GARDNER, PAULA LYNN, Seventh Grade Lang Art Teacher; *b:* St Francis, ME; *m:* Gary; *c:* David; *ed:* (BS) Eng, Univ of ME Ft Kent 1974; *cr:* Spec Ed Teacher Cmmty HS 1974-76; K-12th Grade Substitute Teacher SAD 27 1978-81; 6th-8th Grade Tutor 1981-82, 7th Grade Lang Art Teacher 1982- Ft Kent Elem; *ai:* Re-Cert Comm Mem; Speech Coach; *home:* PO Box 381 Lower Main Eagle Lake ME 04739

GARDNER, RUTH ANN MARSHALL, Assistant to Band Director; *b:* Falmouth, MA; *ed:* Dance & Baton Trng; *cr:* Majorette/Color Guard Instr Sandwich HS 1980-83; Color Guard Instr Cape Cod Express Drum & Bugle Corp 1982-83; Color Guard Instr Bourne HS 1986-87; Color Guard Instr Barnstable HS 1979-; Majorette/Color Guard Adv Cmmty of Jesus-Spirit of America Band 1986-; Majorette Adv Falmouth HS 1989-; *ai:* Dir of Cape Cod Classics Color Guard 1985-; Choreographer Jr Miss Pageant Barnstable HS 1989; RI Matadors Drum & Bugle Corp Marching Mem 1987-89, Natl Drum Corp Assn Color Guard Champions 1987, Drum Corp Assn Summer Indoor Color Guard Champions 1989; Time Receipient Hats off Awd Barnstable Public Sch System; *office:* Barnstable HS 744 W Main St Hyannis MA 02601

GARDNER, SANDRA JONES, Primary Specialist; *b:* Stanford, KY; *m:* Edward C.; *c:* Sheri, Kevin; *ed:* (BS) Elem Ed, E KY Univ 1970; Working Towards Admin & Supervision; *cr:* Teacher Tropical Elem 1971-75; Teacher 1976-85, Primary Specialist 1986- Bennett Elem; *ai:* Delta Kappa Gamma, Broward Teachers Union; Mt Olive Baptist Church Elem Stu Volunteer Tutor; Broward Cty Rdng Cadre Mem; Bennett Elem Teacher of Yr 1985; Nom Broward Ctys FL Teacher of Yr; *office:* Bennett Elem Sch 1755 NE 14th St Fort Lauderdale FL 33304

GARDNER, SHARON MARIE, Vocational Home Ec Teacher; *b:* Tulsa, OK; *m:* Randy Gene; *c:* Cassie, Zachary; *ed:* (BS) Home Ec Ed, OK St Univ 1975; Working Toward Masters in Ed Admin; *cr:* Teacher Fairland Public Schls 1975-; *ai:* FHA Adv; Sr Class Spon; OK Ed Assn, OK Voc Assn 1975-; Beta Sigma Phi 1985-.

GARDUNO, YOLANDA RITA GONZALES, Music Teacher; *b:* Las Vegas, NM; *m:* Gerald; *c:* Cruz, Antonio; *ed:* (BA) Combined Foreign Langs, 1974, (MA) Bi-ling Ed, 1979 NM Highlands Univ; *cr:* Elem Classroom Teacher 1976-80, Music Teacher 1980- W Las Vegas Schls; *ai:* Las Vegas Little League Bd of Dir Treas; BSA Troop 102 Comm Mem; N Cntrl NM Music Educators Secy 1983-84; Cub Scout Pack 620 Cubmaster 1984-89; Our Lady of Sorrows Childrens Choir Dir 1985-86; First Lady of Yr; Las Vegas NM Beta Sigma Phi 1989; *home:* 11 Grand Ave Las Vegas NM 87701

GAREY, DIANA JENNINGS, First Grade Teacher; *b:* Wills Point, TX; *m:* Matthew E.; *c:* Alison, Kyle; *ed:* (BS) Elem Ed, SW TX St Univ 1973; Working Towards Masters Univ of Houston, University Park; *cr:* 3rd Grade Teacher Inwood Elem 1973-76, Ermel Elem 1976-77; 1st Grade Teacher Highlands Elem 1977-80, B P Hopper Primary 1980-; *ai:* 1st Grade Team Leader; TCTA, BCTA, Delta Kappa Gamma; *office:* Bonnie P Hopper Primary Sch 405 E Houston Highlands TX 77562

GARGIUL, BELLA DELUCA, Fourth Grade Teacher; *b:* Auburn, NY; *m:* Joseph; *c:* Joseph Jr., Marie Clark, Patrick; *ed:* (BS) Elem Ed, SUNY Buffalo 1954; Grad Stud SUNY Oswego & SUNY Cortland; *cr:* 4th Grade Teacher Auburn Enlarged City Sch Dist 1954-; *ai:* Stamp Club Adv; Auburn Teachers Assn 1954-; AFT, NEA 1974-; NY St United Teachers 1954-; Antique Auto Club of Amer 1988-; Finger Lakes Region Antique Auto Club 1977-; Italian Heritage Society of Auburn 1984-; Casey Park Educl Assn 1954-; *office:* Casey Park Elem Sch Pulaski St Auburn NY 13021

GARGUIL, JOSEPH A., JR., Social Studies Teacher; *b:* Auburn, NY; *m:* Donna M.; *ed:* (MS) Soc Stud Ed, Syracuse Univ 1988; (BS) Comprehensive Soc Stud, Ashland Univ 1981; *cr:* Amer His Teacher Lowville Acad & Cntrl Schls 1985-86; Global Stud I & II Teacher Moravia Jr/Sr HS 1986-; *ai:* Boys Bsktbl & Girls Soccer Jr Var Coach; Var Boys Lacrosse, Var Girls Sftbl; NHS & Soph Class Adv; US Cncl for Soc Stud 1986-; Elks Club 1986-; Teacher of Yr 1988-89; *office:* Moravia Jr/Sr HS 50 S Main St Moravia NY 13118

GARGUILO, MARIA THERESA, Social Studies Teacher; *b:* Bronx, NY; *ed:* (BS) Ed/Soc Sci, St Thomas Aquinas Coll 1971; (MS) Ed, Plattsburgh St Univ 1976; *cr:* 2nd Grade Teacher 1967-68, 3rd Grade Teacher 1968-71, 5th/6th Grade Soc Stud Teacher 1971-73, 7th/8th Grade Soc Stud Teacher 1973-85 Sacred Heart Sch; 11th/12th Grade Soc Stud Teacher Monsignor Scanlon HS 1985-; *ai:* NCEA Mem 1970-; Plattsburgh St Schlsp Study Early His of Champlain Valley; Field Work & Research Fort Ticonderoga; *office:* Monsignor Scanlan H S 915 Hutchinson River Pkwy Bronx NY 10465

GARION, GAIL BEATTY, Second Grade Teacher; *b:* Jamaica, NY; *m:* Terrance; *ed:* (BSED) Elem Ed, SUNY Oswego 1963; *cr:* 2nd Grade Teacher Secatogue Sch 1963-64; 1st Grade Teacher 1964-67, Non-Graded Primary Teacher 1967-71 Longfellow Sch; 1st-2nd Grade Teacher Intervale 1971-76, 1985-86; Kndgtn Teacher 1976-77, 2nd Grade Teacher 1978-84, 1986- Northvail; *ai:* MCEA, NEA, NJEA, PTHEA; NJ Alpha Delta Kappa (Corresponding Secy 1978-80, Pres 1980-82, St Corresponding Secy 1982-84); NJ Schoolwomens Club Trustee 1984-86; Teaneck Teachers Assn (Teacher Admin Conference Team 1969, Co-Chairperson to Prepare Math Kits 1972); PTA; NJ Alpha Delta Kappa (St Pres of Pres Cncl 1980-87, St Parliamentarian 1984-86; Nom Outstanding Elem Teachers of America 1974; *office:* Northvail Elem Sch 10 Eileen Ct Parsippany NJ 07054

GARLAND, ELIZABETH ADAMS, Fourth Grade Teacher; *b:* Mountain City, TN; *m:* Raymond B.; *ed:* (BA) Ed, 1965, (MS) Ed/Supervision/Rdng Specialist 1967-72 Miami Univ; Rdng Specialist K-12th, Miami Univ 1972; *cr:* Kndgtn Teacher Miami Univ 1967-69; 2nd-4th Grade Teacher Preble Shawnee Sch 1969-; *ai:* PSLEA Pres Building Rep; Phi Delta Kappa, Delta Kappa Gamma, OEA, NEA, PSLEA 1969; *home:* 3841 Oxford Millville Oxford OH 45056

GARLICH, MARY MARTHA, CDP, Typing Teacher; *b:* Melbourne, KY; *cr:* Typing Teacher St Camillus Acad 1979-; *ai:* Dir of Boarders; Work With Needy; *office:* St Camillus Acad E Center St Corbin KY 40701

GARMAN, HOWARD D., Jr High Teacher/Admin Asst; *b:* Gravette, AR; *m:* Anita; *c:* Sherry Miller, Randy; *ed:* (BA) Bible AZ Bible Coll 1965; Addl Studies Sch Admin Grace Coll 1978; Computer Trng 1981, Electronics 1982 Glendale Comm Coll; *cr:* Substitute Bible Chapel Chrstn Sch 1964; Teacher Bible Chapel Chrstn Sch 1966-72; Admin/Teacher Western Chrstn Sch 1972-80; Admin Asst Grace Chrstn Sch 1980-86; Teacher/Admin Asst Western Chrstn Sch 1986-; *ai:* Coach Jr Boys Soccer, Sftbl, Yrbk, Stu Cncl Adv; Capt Chrstn Serv Brigade 1963-71; 2nd Grade Boys Sunday Sch Teacher 1960-66; HS & Coll Spon 1966-71; 1975 Teacher of the Yr for Western Assn of Chrstn Sch; VP of AZ Assn of Chrstn Sch.

GARMEN, GREGGORY DAVID, Science Teacher Coach; *b:* St Paul, MN; *ed:* (BS) Phys Sci/Chem/Physics, Mankato St Univ 1986; Grad Work Chem, Physics; *cr:* Sci Teacher Waubun HS 1987-; *ai:* Asst Boys Bsktbl Coach; Girls Tennis Coach; MN St HS Coaches Assn 1990; *home:* Rt 1 Box 169 Waubun MN 56589

GARNEAU, JOHN MICHAEL, 7th Grade History Teacher; *b:* Laconia, NH; *m:* Ellen Flagg; *c:* Derek Welch, Craig Welch, Trent Welch; *ed:* (BA) Phys Ed, 1964, (MS) Sch Admin, 1972 Plymouth St Coll; *cr:* His Teacher Corcoran HS 1964-67; Phys Ed Teacher Burr & Burton Acad 1967-68; Sci/Math Teacher Memorial Mid Sch 1968-69; His Teacher Belmont Jr HS 1969-; *ai:* Var Girls Vlybl Coach; 7th Grade Adv; Winter Carnival Chm; Faculty Advisory Mem; NEA 1976-89; Amer Vlybl Coaches Assn 1980-89, Reg 1 Coach of Yr 1989; NH Coaches Assn (Pres 1987-) 1977-, Coach of Yr 1978, 1980, 1988, 1990; *office:* Belmont Jr HS School St Belmont NH 03220

GARNER, ANNA P., Counselor/Assistant Principal; *b:* Homer, LA; *m:* Henry P.; *c:* Paul; *ed:* (BA) Elem Ed, Northwestern St Univ 1950; (MED) Guidance/Counseling, Nicholls St Univ 1967; Admin, LA Tech 1972; *cr:* 4th Grade Teacher De Quincy Elem 1950-53; 6th Grade Teacher 1967-70; Scndry Teacher 1970-76; Scndry Cnslr 1976-81; Cnslr/Prin 1981- Haynesville HS; *ai:* Sape Dir Grad; NASSP 1985-; Amer Assn Counceling/Dev; LA Assn Counseling & Dev; LA Assn of Ed; NEA; Claiborne Parish Drug Free Sch & Comm Adv Cncl; Delta Kappa Gamma Society Intl; *office:* Haynesville H S 406 1st East St Haynesville LA 71038

GARNER, CAROLYN LARKINS, 5th Grade Teacher of Gifted; *b:* Hoboken, GA; *m:* Jim L.; *c:* Greg, Renee; *ed:* (BA) Elem Ed, GA Coll Milledgeville 1967; Gifted & Talented, FL St Univ; *cr:* Librarian Memorial Drive Elem 1967-68; 6th Grade Teacher 1968-71, 3rd Grade Teacher 1972-89, 5th Grade Teacher of Gifted 1989- Hiland Park Elem; *ai:* Bay Cty Rdng Assn; Bay Dist Sci Cncl (Elem Rep 1988-89, Pres 1989-); FL Assn of Sci Teachers, NSTA; Hiland Park Teacher of Yr 1983 & Sci Teacher of Yr 1988; Bay Cty Math & Sci Presidential Awd 1990; Teacher Enhancement for Math & Sci Grant 1990; *office:* Hiland Park Elem Sch 2507 Baldwin Rd Panama City FL 32405

GARNER, H. WAYNE, Social Studies Teacher; *b:* Rockhill, SC; *m:* Carol Robertson; *c:* Lauren, Mark; *ed:* (BS) Scndry Ed, 1977, (MED) Soc Stud Ed, 1985 Univ of SC; *cr:* Teacher Pine Ridge Mid Sch 1978-; *ai:* SC Ed Assn 1983-; Pine Ridge Ruritan Bd Mem 1989-; Outstanding Young Men of America 1984; *home:* 152 Kings Way Lexington SC 29072

GARNER, KAREN SNELSON, English/Drama/Art His Teacher; *b:* Sewanee, TN; *m:* D. Carter; *c:* Elizabeth L.; *ed:* (BS) Eng, Mid TN St Univ 1977; (MEd) Educl Admin, TN St Univ 1982; Educl Leadership, Peabody Coll Vanderbilt Univ 1983-84; *cr:* Eng Teacher South Jr HS 1978-85; Eng/Drama/Art His Teacher Cmmty HS 1985-; *ai:* Drama Club Spon; Southern Assn Steering Comm; Chairperson Eng Dept; Franklin Cty Ed Assn (VP, Pres) 1980-82; Bedford Cty Ed Assn 1985-; TEA, NEA Mem 1978-; ASCD 1989-; NCTE 1980-; Shriners South Jr HS Teacher Liason 1983, Teachers Appreciation Awd 1984; Peabody Schlsp 1983; Teach Adjunct Mid TN St Univ; *home:* 2210 Oakhaven Dr Murfreesboro TN 37129

GARNER, NANCY CAMPBELL, Mathematics Teacher; *b:* Rockingham, NC; *m:* Ralph Foster; *c:* Stephanie J., George M. (dec); *ed:* (BS) Math, 1976, (MA) Math/Ed, 1990 Pembroke St Univ; *cr:* Math Teacher E Montgomery HS 1976-81; Cmptr Instr Pembroke St Univ 1985, 1986, 1987; Math Teacher Richmond Sr HS 1981-; *ai:* Math Competition Coach & Contest/Exam Mgr; SAT Admin; Sch Improvement Plan Comm Mem; NC Cncl Teachers of Math, NEA, NC Assn of Educators Mem 1976-; The Compassionate Friends Mem 1989-; Schlsp from St of NC 1985; *office:* Richmond Sr HS PO Box 1748 Hwy 1 N Rockingham NC 28379

GARNER, PATRICIA ANN, Life Science Teacher; *b:* Nashville, TN; *m:* Larry Leon; *c:* Larry C., Melynda K. Cundieff, Melyssa G. Crews; *ed:* (AA) Lon Morris Coll 1976; (BSED) Bio/Eng, 1977, (MED) Scndry Ed, 1982 Stephen F Austin St Univ; Post Grad Bio, Stephen F Austin St Univ 1985; Microprocessors, Univ of TX Tyler 1989; *cr:* Medical Technologist Nan Travis Memorial Hospital 1967-73, Childrens Clinic 1973-77; 1st Grade Teacher Jacksonville Elem Sch 1978-79; Sci Teacher Jacksonville Mid Sch 1979-; *ai:* Sci UIL Coach; Spon a Stu to Veterinarian Camp TX A&M Galveston; Spon 16 Stus to Epcot; TX Math & Sci Coaches Assn 1988-; TX Assn For Gifted & Talented 1990; Sci Teachers Assn of TX 1986-; Delta Kappa Gamma 1984-; Alpha Chi 1978; Personality Feature Jacksonville Daily Progress 1990; Employee of Month Jacksonville Ind Sch Dist Sch Bd 1990; *home:* Rt 8 Box 292 Jacksonville TX 75766

GARNETT, CYNTHIA S., Fifth Grade Teacher; *b:* Wisconsin Rapids, WI; *ed:* (BS) Elem Ed, Univ of WI Stevens Point 1976; Grad Courses Mental Health, Writing Process, Teaching Various Learning Styles, Elem Math, Curr Dev, Cmptrs in Ed; *cr:* 4th Grade Teacher Randolph Sch Dist 1976-78; 4th/5th Grade Teacher 1983-85, 5th Grade Teacher 1978- Weyauwega Elem Sch; *ai:* Intnl Rdng Assn, WI Math Cncl, NCTM; Cntrl WI Rdng Cncl (VP 1988-, Pres 1990), Celebrate Literacy Awd 1989; WI St Rdng Assn; Univ of WI Stevens Point Fellowship 1985; Sch Dist Teacher of Yr 1986-87; *office:* Weyauwega Elem Sch PO Box 580 400 Ann St Weyauwega WI 54983

GARNIER, VALERIE BARNES, English/Honors English Teacher; *b:* Dallas, TX; *m:* Tom; *c:* Meredith; *ed:* (BS) His, Baylor Univ 1980; (MS) Ed, N TX St Univ 1984; *cr:* 6th-8th Grade Eng/Publications Teacher Lamar Jr HS 1980-; *ai:* Natl Jr Honor

Society; Textbook Selection Comm; Assn of TX Prof Educators 1981-; TX St Teachers Assn 1980-81; TX Joint Cncl Teachers of Eng 1989-; PTA 1980-; Amer Assn of Univ Women 1982-83; Named Outstanding Young Women of America 1985; *home:* 2822 Lawrence Irving TX 75061

GARNSEY, JANET JO, Third Grade Teacher; *b:* Clio, MI; *ed:* (BA) Ed/Eng/Sci, Univ of MI Flint 1961; (MA) Ed, Eastern Univ 1967; *cr:* 2nd Grade Teacher Clio Area Schls 1961-65; 3rd Grade Teacher Kearsley Cmmty Schls 1965-; *office:* Fiedler Elem Sch 6317 Nigtingale Ln Flint MI 48506

GARNTO, ANGELA B., Kindergarten Teacher; *b:* Dublin, GA; *c:* Joshua; *ed:* (BS) Early Childhood 1976, (MED) Early Childhood 1984 GA Coll; *cr:* Kndgtn T J Elder Primary 1976-; *ai:* Boy Scout Den Mother Pack 74; PTA Secy; *office:* T J Elder Prim Sch 316 Hall St Sandersville GA 31082

GAROFOLO, RONALD JOSEPH, Architectural Drafting Teacher; *b:* Omaha, NE; *m:* Pamela Davis; *c:* Amy, Timothy; *ed:* (BS) Industrial Ed, 1971, (MS) Vocational Ed, 1975 Univ of NE Omaha; Cmptr Aided Drafting & Design; *cr:* Industrial Art Teacher Bryan Jr HS 1971-78; Architectural Drafting Teacher Tech HS 1978-84, Bryan Sr HS 1984-; *ai:* Co-Chm Faculty Courtesy Comm; Tournament Dir Boys & Girls St Tennis; Boys Tennis Coach; Jr Class Spon; Prom Comm Master of Ceremonies; Faculty Auction Coord; Adopt-A-Sch Comm; Letter Winners Club Schlsp Comm; Omaha Ed Assn (Sr HS Rep, Bd of Dir, Building Rep, Captain) 1990; NE St Ed Assn, NEA 1986-; NE Industrial Technology Ed Assn Metro Dist Teacher of Yr 1989; Metropolitan Tennis Coach Assn Pres 1988-; Alice Buffett Outstanding Teacher Awd 1988; *office:* Wm Jennings Bryan Sr HS 4700 Giles Rd Omaha NE 68157

GARONE, FRANK, English Teacher; *b:* Brooklyn, NY; *c:* Elizabeth, Christopher; *ed:* (BA) Philosophy, St Francis Coll 1966; (MA) Philosophy, Duquesne Univ 1968; Eng Grad Courses; *cr:* 7th Grade St Brigids Sch 1965-66; Philosophy Teacher Duquesne Univ 1967-69, Point Park Coll 1968-70; Eng Teacher Long Island Luth HS 1970-74, Oyster Bay HS 1974-88, Vernon Mid Sch 1988-; *ai:* Natl Jr Honor Society Adv; Oyster Bay Rotary Club NHS Honery Membership; *home:* 10 6th St Bayville NY 11709

GARREN, SHEILA JOHNSTON, 4th Grade Teacher; *b:* Roanoke, VA; *m:* Kenneth R.; *c:* David, Steven, Kristine; *ed:* (BA) Ed, Radford Univ 1961; Grad Stud Radford Univ & Univ of VA; *cr:* Teacher Roanoke City Schls 1961-62, Hampton City Schls 1962-65, Roanoke Cty Schls 1980-81, City of Salem 1981-; *ai:* Steering, Textbook Adoption, Gifted Advisory Comms; Pi Gamma Mu; Chi Beta Phi; Kappa Delta Pi; Fortnightly Club; Stonegate Swim Club Bd of Governors; *office:* East Salem Elem Sch 1765 Boulevard Salem VA 24153

GARRET, JENNIFER STOLL, 7th & 8th Grade Math Teacher; *b:* Kansas City, MO; *m:* Edgar Julian Jr.; *c:* Justin, Jordan; *ed:* (AA) Columbia Coll 1973; (BA) Lib Sci, Univ of MO 1975; (MED) Ed, East TX St Univ 1977; Math Cert, Scndry & Elem 1983; *cr:* 4th/5th Grade Teacher Miller Grove Ind Sch Dist 1978-80; Grad Asst Math Dept East TX St Univ 1981-82; Teacher Mid Sch Commerce Ind Sch Dist 1983-; *ai:* NJ HS Adv 1984-; Math Club Spon for UIL Number Sense Contest 1983-; Mathcounts Coach 1989-; Phi Delta Kappa Local Research Rep 1989-; NCTM Classroom Teachers Assn 1985-; PEO Pres 1989-; Thalian Culture Club (VP 1986-87, Pres 1987-88); Resource Speaker at ETSU Spring Seminar for Supervising Teachers 1988-90; Presenter at Conference for Advancement of Math Teachers 1989; Selected to Teach Model Lesson Using Methods of Effective Teaching & Supervision that was Video-Taped & Used Statewide; *office:* Commerce I.S.D.Mid Sch Sycamore Commerce TX 75428

GARRETT, BECKIE COLE, English Teacher; *b:* Hemet, CA; *m:* James; *c:* Joseph T., Brady J.; *ed:* (BS) Eng, San Diego St Univ 1974; Eng/Comparative Lit, Univ of CA Irvine; *cr:* Co-ASB Adv 1985-86, Decision Making Teacher 1988-89, Eng Teacher 1975-San Marcos HS; *ai:* Mid Sch, Curr Dev, Gifted & Talented Ed, Effective Schls Planning, San Marcos HS Schlsp Selection Comms; Disaster Preparedness Team; CA Teachers Assn 1975-; CA Schlsp Fed Teacher of Yr Awd 1986, 1988; Co-Author Nationally Recognized Lang Art Curr; *office:* San Marcos HS 1615 San Marcos Blvd San Marcos CA 92069

GARRETT, ELISA DANIEL, United States History Teacher; *b:* El Paso, TX; *m:* Dennis; *ed:* (BS) Soc Stud, Univ of TX 1979; *cr:* Spec Ed Aid LBJ HS 1979-81; Spec Ed/Math Teacher Manor Jr HS 1981-82; Eng as Second Lang/GED Instr Austin Cmmty Schls 1980-82; Asst Instr Austin Comm Coll 1982-83; Eng/Rdng/Eng as Second Lang/US His Instr Lake Travis Mid Sch 1983-; *ai:* SADD Spon; 8th Grade Academic Adv; Textbook Selection, Former Prin & Supt Advisory, Salary Study Comm; *office:* Lake Travis Mid Sch 3322 RR 620 S Austin TX 78734

GARRETT, GLORIA G., Fourth Grade Teacher; *b:* Olympia, WA; *ed:* (AA) Elem Ed, Centralia Comm Coll 1975; (BA) Lit, Whitworth Coll 1977; Grad Stud St Martins Coll; *cr:* 4th Grade Teacher 1979-86, 5th Grade Teacher 1986-89, 4th Grade Teacher 1989- Elma Elem; *ai:* Supvr of Gifted Hum; Fine Arts Comm; Teacher Assistance Team; Westminster Presbyn Church Elder; Olympia Chorale & Light Opera Bd Mem 1980-; *office:* Elma Elem Sch 30 Elma Monie Rd Elma WA 98541

GARRETT, JAMES MICHAEL, Social Science Depart Teacher; *b:* Santa Rosa, CA; *m:* Roberta Marchioni; *c:* James M. Jr.; *ed:* (BA) Phys Ed, San Francisco St Univ 1971; *cr:* Soc Sci Dept Teacher Benicia HS 1973-; *ai:* Club Adv Block B Lettermans Society; Girls Var Bsktbl Coach; NEA, Benicia Teachers Assn 1973-; Amer Legion; *office:* Benicia HS 1101 Military W Benicia CA 94510

GARRETT, JEWELL JOHNSON, American Government Teacher; *b:* Johnson City, TN; *m:* Marshall E.; *c:* Eddie Jr.; *ed:* (BS) His/Poly Sci/Sociology, E TN St Univ 1968; Aerospace & Rdng Wkshps; *cr:* 7th/8th Grade His Teacher Sulphur Springs Sch 1968-69; 7th/8th Grade His/Geo Teacher Jonesborough Mid Sch 1974-87; 12th Grade Amer Government Teacher Daniel Boone HS 1987-; *ai:* Stu Cncl, Sch Sign, United Nations Security Cncl Model Spon; Academic Scholar Bowl Team Co-Spon; Washington Cty Ed Assn Pres Elect 1989-; TN Ed Assn, NEA 1968-; Civil Air Patrol, Republican Women Organization, VFW Auxiliary; Pi Gamma Mu 1968-; Excell Teacher of Yr 1987-88; Washington Cty Teacher of Yr 1988, 1989; TN Poly Sci Government Certification Test Panel; Southern Assn of Colls & Schls Evaluation His Chm; *home:* 2016 Northwood Dr Johnson City TN 37601

GARRETT, LARRY EUGENE, Band/Orchestra Director; *b:* Deming, NM; *m:* Jennifer Lynne Campbell; *c:* Benjamin, Barry; *ed:* (BMUSED) Music Ed, NM St Univ 1979; (MS) Applied Music, TX Tech Univ; *cr:* Asst Band Dir Estacado HS 1980-81; Band/Orch Dir J T Hutchinson Jr HS 1981-; *ai:* Jr HS Chm All Region Orch; TX Music Ed Assn 1979-, Jr HS Honor Orch 1984, 1986, 1988; *office:* J T Hutchinson Jr HS 3102 Canton Ave Lubbock TX 79410

GARRETT, NANCY FROMME, Second Grade Teacher; *b:* Terre Haute, IN; *m:* William M.; *c:* Bradford, Lu Anne Franklin, Sue Barbarich; *ed:* (BS) Elem Ed, 1951, (MS) Elem Ed, 1967 IN St Univ; Cmptr Trng Purdue; *cr:* 2nd Grade Teacher 1951-53, Kndgtn Teacher 1959-66, 2nd Grade Teacher 1967-88, Primary Substitute Teacher 1988- Otterbein Elem; *ai:* ISTA, NEA, BEA (Life Mem, Secy 1968), Edgar P Williams Outstanding Educator Awd 1986; Dollars for Scholars; BSA Cncl, GSA Cncl; Ventura Club (Pres, Secy) 1951-; United Meth Women; *home:* PO Box 173 Otterbein IN 47970

GARRETT, PATRICIA ANN (VAN WINKLE), Counselor/Secondary School; *b:* Nebraska City, NE; *c:* Richelle Squires, Rachelle; *ed:* (BSE) Spec Ed, 1970; (MSE) Spec Ed, 1979; Sch Guidance/Cnslng, 1985 Univ of Cntrl AR; Cnslng Ecs; Gifted/Talented Areas; Math; Poly Sci; Sci; Ecs; Cmptr Prgmg; *cr:* Spec Ed Elem/Mid Sch Teacher Bryant Public Sch 1970-74; Elem/Scndry Teacher 1974-86; Spec Ed Teacher 1974-86; Scndry Cnslr 1986-90 Harmony Grove Sch; *ai:* Sch Drug Facilitator;past Test Coord; Acad Quiz Bowl Coord/Supv; Citizen Bee Close-Up Fdtn Spon/Coord; Knowledge Master Open Spon/Coord; Past Jr Class Adv/Spon;Past Chrldr Spon; AEA-Harmony Grove Ed Assn Pres 1976-; AEA-Local Assn Comm Mem 1975; AR Learning Disabilities Assn Mem/Presenter 1975-78; CEC Mem 1971; Saline Democratic Womens Comm Mem 1988-; Little Rock Rescue Mission Volunteer 1989; Mid-South Entergy Corp Ldrshp Inst 1989; Purdue Univ Gifted Inst; PCCP-NOVA Prgm 1988; Pulsar-Pals Prgm 1989; Star I & II 1990; *home:* 211 Bass Ln Benton AR 72015

GARRETT, WILLIE F. BIGGERS, Third Grade Teacher; *b:* Center, TX; *m:* Bemon Osby; *ed:* (AA) Elem Ed, Butler Coll 1962; (BS) Elem Ed, TX Coll 1964; Master Teacher Cert Stud; MMSEC Summer Trainers Inst 1989; TAIR Rdng Conference; Sci Teachers Conference 1990; *cr:* 3rd/4th Grade Teacher Red Oak Elem Sch 1964-66; Chapter Read/2nd Grade Teacher Scott Elem Sch 1966-68; 2nd Grade Teacher Woodville Elem 1968-76; 3rd Grade Teacher San Augustine Elem 1976-; *ai:* Mt Horeb Baptist Church; VP Missionary Society; Choir Soloist for ChurCh & Sabine Valley Dist Choir; Johnny Wade Schlsp Comm; Youth Encampment Prgm Adv; Soloist Veterans & Chamber of Commerce Functions; SAE Assn Membership Rep; TSTA, NEA Membership Rep; PTA Mem; Teacher of Month 1989; *home:* Rt 1 Box 446 San Augustine TX 75972

GARRIS, CATHERINE TYNER, Kindergarten Teacher/Dept Chai; *b:* Murfreesboro, NC; *m:* Willie Eugene; *c:* Anita L. Garris Vega; *ed:* (BA) Early Chldhd Ed, Elizabeth City St Univ 1973; *cr:* Teacher Lakeview Elem Sch 1973-; *ai:* Grade Level Chairperson & Statewide Kndgtn Convention Rep; Teacher Advisory Comm Rep; Chairperson Courtesy Comm 1976-77, Prgm Comm 1986-88; Portsmouth Ed Assn, VA Ed Assn, NEA 1973-; Teacher of Month Awd 1990; *office:* Lakeview Elem Sch 1300 Horne Ave Portsmouth VA 23701

GARRIS, KARL JEROME, US History Teacher; *b:* Lynch, KY; *m:* Tara Lynn Edwards; *c:* Chelsey M.; *ed:* (AB) Phys Ed, 1980, (MA) Phys Ed, 1981 Morehead St Univ; *cr:* Health/Phys Ed Teacher Univ Breckinridge Trng 1981-82; Health/Phys Ed/Math Teacher Owen Cty HS 1982-85; US His Teacher Meade Cty HS 1985-; *ai:* Var Bsktbl Asst Coach; Natl Assn of Bsktbl Coaches 1984-; *office:* Meade Cty HS Old State Rd Brandenburg KY 40108

GARRISON, LARRY GAINES, Rdng/Creative Writing Teacher; *b:* Forks, WA; *m:* Sarah L. Clyburn; *c:* Lynsea L.; *ed:* (AA) Gen Ed, Peninsula Cmmty Coll 1966; (BA) Soc Stud, Western WA St Coll 1969; (MED) Rdng, Univ of GA Athens 1978; Eng Lit Western WA St Coll; *cr:* 6th Grade Teacher Blaine Elem Sch 1969-74; Eng Teacher Blaine HS 1975; Rdng Teacher Blaine Mid Sch 1975-80; Rdng/Math Teacher Hydaburg City Schls 1980-81; Rdng/Writing Teacher Valdez City Schls 1981-; *ai:* Downhill Ski Chaperone; Blaine Sch Dist Cross Cntry Running Coach; Hydaburg City Schls; Valdez Rdng Assn Pres 1985-87; AK & IRA 1985-; Elsie Ware Mayer Schlshp Peninsula Jr Coll; Dev Wrap Valdez City Schls;Articles Published in Boating & Sailing Magazines; *home:* PO Box 1691 Valdez AK 99686

GARRISON, LONA M., 8th Grade Lang Arts Teacher; *b:* Sewickley, PA; *m:* Steven D.; *c:* Matthew, Gregory; *ed:* (BFA) Theatre, WV Univ 1977; Teachers Cert, Geneva Coll 1978; GA Southern Coll; *cr:* Teacher 1978-, Lang Arts Dept Chairperson 1987-, Public Relations Coord 1989- Hinesville Mid Sch; *ai:* Comm Club; Alpha Delta Kappa Pledge Trainer 1986-; Coordinate & Write Articles Teaching & About Teachers for Local Paper; *office:* Hinesville Mid Sch 307 E Washington Ave Hinesville GA 31313

GARRISON, MARY SUE FISCHESSER, Assistant Principal; *b:* Rockwood, TX; *m:* James M.; *c:* Jim Ewing, Amy; *ed:* (BS) Scndry Ed/Soc Stud, TN Technological Univ 1967; (MED) Elem Ed, W Ga Coll 1979; (EDS) Admin/Supervision, TN Technological Univ 1984; TN Acad for Sch Leaders; TN Instructional Model; Skills Enhancement Trng; *cr:* 9th-12th Grade Teacher Spring City HS 1967-73; 2nd/7th/8th Grade Teacher Cloverleaf Elem Sch 1974-79; 2nd/4th/7th/8th Grade Teacher Spring City Elem Sch 1979-87; Curr/Instruction Coord Rhea Cty Dept of Ed 1987-89; Asst Prin Rhea Cty HS 1989-; *ai:* TN Cncl for Soc Stud 1984-, Soc Stud Teacher of Yr 1986; NCSS 1984-; ASCD 1984-; TN ASCD 1983-; Rhea-Dayton Ed Assn, TN Ed Assn 1967-73, 1979-; NEA 1967-; Spring City Homecoming Coord 1985-86; Career Ladder III; Outstanding Young Women of America; Bartow Cty Teacher of Yr 1977; Rhea Cty Teacher of Yr 1986; TN Soc Stud Teacher of Yr 1986; *home:* PO Box 25 Laurel Dr Spring City TN 37381

GARRISON, PHILLIP E., Computer Science Teacher; *b:* Jackson, MI; *m:* Julie May Wheeler; *c:* Jon, Ryan, Patrick; *ed:* (AS) Jackson Comm Coll 1964; (BS) Sci Ed, 1966, (MS) Sci Curr, 1971 MI St Univ; *cr:* Teacher Vandercook HS 1966-; *ai:* MACUL; NEA; *office:* Vandercook HS 1000 Golf Ave Jackson MI 49203

GARRISON, PHYLLIS PALOMBI, Social Studies Teacher; *b:* Trenton, NJ; *m:* Joseph Anthony; *c:* Maria; *ed:* (BA) Soc Stud, Montclair St Coll 1971; *cr:* Teacher St Anthony HS 1971-74, Notre Dame HS 1974-88, Hightstown HS 1988-; *ai:* Delta Kappa Gamma 1990; *office:* Hightstown HS Leshin Ln Hightstown NJ 08520

GARRISON, ROBERT JAMES, Science Department Chair; *b:* Omak, WA; *m:* Penny Anderson; *c:* James; *ed:* (ba) Ed, 1969, (BA) Bio, 1972 Cntrl WA Univ; *cr:* Bio Teacher Okanogan HS 1969-; *ai:* Sci Club Adv; WA St Sci Teachers Assn 1987-; City of Okanogan Councilman 1976-82; Okanogan Fire Dept Asst Chief 1982-, Fireman of Yr 1986; Okanogan Ambulance Assn Service EMT 1982-89; *office:* Okanogan HS 411 S 5th Okanogan WA 98840

GARRISSON, F. TERRY, Social Studies Teacher; *b:* Denver, CO; *m:* Venetia; *c:* Terri L. Manson, Valerie Owens, Pamela, Kevin; *ed:* (BA) His, 1962, (MAT) His, 1968 CO St Univ; *cr:* Teacher Denver Public Schls 1962-; *ai:* Boys & Girls Soccer Head Coach; Class Spon 1990; NCSS 1980-; AFT 1962-; CO Cncl Soc Stud 1980-; Coach of Yr Denver Public Schls Soccer 1986; *office:* Manual HS 1700 E 28th Denver CO 80205

GARRITY, DEBBE ANNE, Jr HS Math/Eng Teacher; *b:* Akron, OH; *ed:* (BS) Elem/Music, Malone Coll 1973; (MS) Math Clinician, Kent St Coll 1983; *cr:* 6th Grade Teacher 1974-78, 3rd Grade Teacher 1978-86 B L Miller Sch; Jr HS Eng/Math Teacher Sebring Mc Kinley HS 1986-; *ai:* Jr HS Uniqueness; Sch Wide Grading; NEA, OH Ed Assn 1974-; Sebring Local Ed Assn Pres; NCTE 1990; OH Cncl Teachers of Math 1981-; Greater Canton Teachers of Math 1985-; E OH Cncl Teachers of Math 1984-; NE OH Ed Assn (Exec Comm 1990) 1981-; Jaycees 1984-88; Math Scholar 1990; Outstanding Young Women in America 1985; *home:* 246 Bachtel SW North Canton OH 44720

GARROU, JAN UNDERWOOD, 5th Grade Teacher; *b:* Charlotte, NC; *m:* Arthur Thomas; *c:* Charles M.; *ed:* (BS) Elem Ed, Appalachian St 1971; *cr:* 6th Grade Teacher 1971-88, 5th Grade Teacher 1988- Valdese Elem; *ai:* Stu Cncl Adv; Grade Chairperson; Sch Store Adv; NCAE 1971-87, Burke Cty Human Relations Awd 1985; NCCTM 1988-; PTO Exec Bd & Treas; *office:* Valdese Elem 298 Praley St Valdese NC 28690

GARROW, SHEILA MAY (KANDT), 3rd/4th Grade Teacher; *b:* Calgary AB, Canada; *m:* David Ronald; *c:* Jill, Mark; *ed:* (BSC) Elem Ed, La Sierra Coll 1965; *cr:* 3rd/4th Grade Teacher Santa Monica Jr Acad 1965-67; 6th-8th Grade Teacher Bellflower Adv 1967-68; Librarian Lynwood Acad 1968-69; 2nd/3rd Grade Teacher Conejo Adv 1967-79; 3rd-6th Grade Teacher Roseburg Jr Acad 1979-; *ai:* North Pacific Union of SDA; Curr Honors 1967; Teacher of Yr North Amer Div of 7th Day Adv 1988; *office:* Roseburg Jr Acad 1653 NW Troost Roseburg OR 97470

GARTZ, SUZANNE M., Mathematics Teacher; *b:* Toledo, OH; *ed:* (BA) Math Ed, Univ of Toledo 1964, (MA) Math Ed, E MI Univ 1972; *cr:* Teacher Custer Jr HS 1962-69, Monroe Jr HS 1970-; *ai:* Sch Store Spon; Graduation Requirements & Scndry Math Curr Comms; MI Cncl Teachers of Math 1978-; NEA 1962-; Monroe Citizens Planning Commission 1982-; St Pauls United Meth Church 1970-; Sci Fnd Grant Scndry Math; Monroe Sch Bell Awd 1986; *office:* Monroe Jr HS 503 Washington Monroe MI 48161

GARVEY, ANN, 1st Grade Teacher; *b:* Brooklyn, NY; *m:* James C.; *c:* Michael, Pamela; *ed:* (BS Ed, St Johns Univ 1958; (MS) Ed, Hofstra Univ 1962; *cr:* Teacher Albany Avenue Sch 1958-; *ai:* PTA Major Offices Pres 1958- Life Membership 1965; BSA Mem Merit Badge Comm 1975- *office:* Albany Avenue Elem Sch N Albany Ave Massapequa NY 11758

GARVEY, POLLY FOSTER, 10th Grade English Teacher; *b:* Jacksonville, NC; *m:* Elbert L. Jr.; *ed:* (BA) Journalism, Univ of NC Chapel Hill 1985; *cr:* Teacher Dixon HS 1985-; *ai:* Newspaper & Prom Adv; NCTE 1988-; *office:* Dixon HS Rt 2 Box 322a Holly Ridge NC 28445

GARVEY, SHARON WALTZ, Mathematics Teacher; *b:* Scranton, PA; *m:* David D. Sr.; *c:* David D. Jr.; *ed:* (AB) Math, Marywood Coll 1965; (MS) Math, OH Univ 1971; Cmptr Programming, Marywood Coll 1967; Theology, Boston Univ Sch of Theology 1965-66; *cr:* Math Teacher S Jefferson NJ Schs 1966, Scranton Cntrl HS 1966-68, WY Seminary 1968-70, Onondaga Cntrl Schs 1970-; *ai:* NHS Selection Comm; NYSUT-Onondaga Faculty Assn VP 1987-; St Johns Episcopal Church (Vestry 1988-, Pres Altar Guild 1980-); NSF Grant OH Univ 1968-71; *home:* 101 Barnstable Ct Camillus NY 13031

GARVIN, LINDA D., Spanish Teacher; *b:* Wilmington, DE; *m:* Ricahrd C.; *c:* Jenny, Ricky; *ed:* (BA) Span, Newberry Coll 1967; (MED) Scndry Guidance, Clemson Univ 1973; *cr:* Teacher Seneca HS 1968-73; Cnslr Tri-Cty Tech Coll 1973-84; Teacher West-Oak HS 1984-; *ai:* Foreign Act Club; SC Organization of Lang Teachers; Beta Sigma Phi; Comm Colls & Jr Colls Outstanding Women; *office:* West-Oak HS Rt 5 Box 206 Westminster SC 29693

GARVIN, MADELINE MARCELIA, English Teacher; *b:* Fort Wayne, IN; *ed:* (BS) Fr/Eng, IN Univ Bloomington 1973; (MAE) Guidance/Counseling/Eng, Ball St Univ 1978; Gifted & Talented Endorsement; *cr:* Fr/Eng Teacher 1973-81; Assoc Instr IN Univ 1981-82; Fr/Eng Teacher 1982-85; Assoc Instr African-Amer Stud IN Univ 1986-87; Eng Teacher/Gifted & Talented Coord Wayne HS 1987-; *ai:* Faculty Key Club & Wayne HS Key Club Charter Adv; Creative Writing Competition, Spell Bowl Coach 1989; Gifted & Talented, Lang Art Curr Writing Comm; Eng Textbook Adoption Comm; Organized Remedial Rdng Prgm, Rdng Comm 1976-78; Title IV-C Lang Prgm Comm 1981; Natl Alliance Black Sch Educators, Mary McCleod Bethune Outstanding Teacher Awds 1989; Pi Lambda Theta, Delta Kappa Gamma Membership Chairperson 1988-; NCTE; IN Cncl Teacher of Eng Contact Person; IN Teachers of Writing Assn; FWCS Composition Adoption Comm Secy 1984; Ft Wayne Ed Assn, IN St Teachers Assn, NEA; IU External Affairs, Part-Time Employees Grievance Comm Rep 1986-87; Phi Delta Kappa; Supervision, Curr Dev Assn; Ft Wayne Alliance Black Sch Educators Secy 1984; Natl Alliance Black Sch Educators Life Mem; PTA; 1st Wayne Street United Meth Church Mem; Martin Luther King Montessori Sch Past Mem Exec Bd; Waynedale Kiwanis Club Mem; Kiwanis Youth Services (Coord, Schlsp Comm Mem); Delta Sigma Theta Mem; YWCA Mem; IN Univ Alumnae Assn Life Mem; NAACP Life Mem; Ft Wayne NAACP Ladies Auxiliary Past Pres; IN Dist Key Club Intnl Numerous Certificates, Awds & Recognitions; Outstanding Ed Alumnus Awd IN Univ 1990; Academic Decathalon St Essay Contest Judge 1990; Recognition Certificate Supt Ft Wayne Cmmty Schls, Governor Bayh, St Supt H Dean Evans; IN Univ, Mc Nutt Outstanding-Favorite Instr 1987; Eurilla Wills NAACP Ladies Auxiliary Recognition For Service 1984; Leadership-Membership Team Intake Adv Awd 1983; IN Univ Conference 1982; Ebony Magazine Awd; *home:* 1005 E Hawthorne St Fort Wayne IN 46806

GARVIN, MARSHA JEAN, First Grade Teacher; *b:* Louisville, MS; *ed:* (BS) Elem Ed, MS St Univ 1974; *cr:* 1st Grade Teacher Scott Cntrl Elem 1976-; *ai:* Instruction Management Chairperson Scott Cty 1st Grade Teachers; MS Prof Educators Building Rep 1986-; Scott Cntrl PTO Fund Raising Comm Co-Chairperson 1976-; *home:* Rt 1 Box 96-035 Forest MS 39074

GARVIN, MAVA SHELTON, Librarian/Teacher; *b:* Manchester, TN; *m:* David; *c:* Dwight, Jennifer; *ed:* (BS) Elem Ed, MTSU 1969; (MLS) Lib Sci, Peabody 1970; MTSU 1988; *cr:* Librarian Coffee Cty 1970-71; Librarian/Teacher Lascassas Elem 1972-; *ai:* REA; TEA; NEA; *home:* 7389 Halls Hill Pk Milton TN 37118

GARWOOD, DIANNE THORNTON, Business Education Teacher; *b:* Lafayette, GA; *m:* Glen David; *ed:* (BS) Bus Ed, Western MI Univ 1965; (MS) General Ed, Saginaw St 1979; Word Processing Macomb Comm Coll; Speedwriting Oakland Intermediate Center; *cr:* Bus Educator Teacher Lincoln Sr HS 1966-; *ai:* Class Spon 1990; Steering Comm for North Cntrl Evaluation; Class Spon 1969 & 1979; Stu Cncl & Natl Honor Society; MI Bus Ed Assn; Lincoln HS Teacher of Yr 1990 *office:* Lincoln Sr H S 22900 Federal Warren MI 48089

GARZA, ALBERTO, JR., Theatre Arts Instructor; *b:* Brownsville, TX; *ed:* (BA) Theatre Arts, Univ of TX Pan Am 1979; Grad Stud Costume Design, Tech Design, Directing, TX Chrstn Univ; *cr:* Teaching Asst TX Chrstn Univ 1980-82; Costume Asst Old Globe Theatre 1982-84; Asst Designer South Coast Reperatory Company 1984; Drama Teacher South Jr HS 1985-; *ai:* UIL One Act Play Contest; Drama Club; Solo, Duet & Group Acting Contest; TX Classroom Teachers Assn 1985-; TX Educl Theatre Assn 1987-; Theatre Mc Allen Resident Dir, 1988-; St Troopers Assn 1988-; Teaching Asst TX Chrstn Univ; *office:* South Jr HS 601 W Freddy Gonzalez Dr Edinburg TX 78539

GARZA, DELIA ALCALA, 8th Grade English Teacher; *b:* Brownsville, TX; *m:* Lionel; *c:* Mariana; *ed:* (BS) Eng/Span, TX A&I Univ 1967; Writing Inst 1985; *cr:* Teacher Brownsville Ind Sch Dist 1967-68, Gulfport Ind Sch Dist 1969, Austin Ind Sch Dist 1970-73, San Antonio-Northside Ind Sch Dist 1978-; Dept Chairperson Lang Art 1985-; *ai:* UIL Ready Writing Spon; NEA, TSTA Mem 1970-85; ATPE, NCTE Mem 1985-90 *office:* Sul Ross Mid Sch 3630 Callaghan Rd San Antonio TX 78228

GARZA, ROBERT, Mathematics Teacher; *b:* Baytown, TX; *m:* Minnie Perez; *c:* Robert E., Jessica M.; *ed:* (BA) Math/Span, Univ of Houston 1975; (MA) Math Ed, Univ of Houston Clear Lake 1979; Deaconate Prgm; *cr:* Math Teacher North Shore HS 1975-76, Alvin HS 1976-80, Clear Creek HS 1980-; *ai:* Chess Club Adv; TSTA; St Mary Church Deacon 1984-.

GARZA, SEVERO, Asst High School Band Director; *b:* Brownsville, TX; *ed:* (BA) Music Ed, Corpus Christi St 1985; *cr:* Asst Band Dir Flour Bluff Jr HS 1985-89, Flour Bluff HS 1989-; *ai:* HS Jazz Band Dir; TX Music Educators Assn 1985-; *office:* Flour Bluff HS 2505 Waldron Rd Corpus Christi TX 78418

GARZA, VICTOR ISLAS, Computer Literacy Teacher; *b:* Port Isabel, TX; *m:* Maria del Rosario Ochoa; *c:* Elma T., Carlo J.; *ed:* (BA) Poly Sci, Pan Amer Univ 1978; Working Towards Educl Admin, Univ of TX Pan Amer Brownsville, Mid-Management Certificate; *cr:* Oral Eng/Lang Dev Teacher Cummings Intermediate 1978-79; LD/Spec Ed Teacher Villa Nueva Elem 1979-81; His Teacher 1982-85, Cmptr Literacy Teacher 1985-Faulk Intermediate; *ai:* Golf Coach; Campus Improvement Team; Prin Advisory Comm; *home:* 4823 Paseo del Rey Brownsville TX 78521

GARZAREK, FRANK R., JR., Mathematics Specialist; *b:* Birmingham, AL; *m:* Mary Elizabeth Mackinaw; *c:* Tripp, Todd; *ed:* (BS) Math/Eng, Univ of AL 1966; (MS) Math, Nova Univ 1972; Admin Cert Admin, Univ of AL Birmingham 1980; *cr:* Eng/Math Instr Fairfield Jr & Sr HS 1966-69; Math Instr Apollo Mid Sch 1969-74; Math Specialist Jess Lanier HS 1974-; *ai:* Homecoming Spon; Academic Coach; Sports Artist; Schlsp Cnslr; Beauty Pagaent Master Ceremony; B-Team Ftbl Announcer; St Aloysius Sch Bsktbl Coach 1982-; *office:* Jess Lanier HS 100 High School Dr Bessemer AL 35020

GASAWAY, ZENOVA SCOTT, Second Grade Teacher; *b:* Diboll, TX; *m:* Harold E.; *c:* Byron, Brandon; *ed:* (BS) Elem Ed, Prairie View A&M Univ 1973; Grad Stud Rdng Prairie View A&M, Univ of MO Kansas City; *cr:* 2nd Grade Teacher Diboll Elem Sch 1973-76, Dobbs Elem Sch 1976-; *ai:* Peer Coaching; Grade Level Chm; Instruction Focus Team; Confidential Consultant for My Building; NEA, Intnl Rdng Assn 1976-; PTA Life Time Membership Awd 1979; Second Missionary Baptist Church Sunday Sch Teacher 1990; Tiger Cub (Coord 1988-, Den Mother 1987-); Harmony in Grandview 1990; Nom for Excl in Teaching 1984 & 1990; Nom Dist Teacher of Yr 1989, 1990; *office:* Dobbs Elem CSD #1 9400 Eastern Ave Kansas City MO 64138

GASDICK, MARY ELIZABETH SHEPPARD, Fourth Grade Teacher; *b:* Mc Keesport, PA; *m:* Charles T.; *c:* Holly C., Charles C.; *ed:* (BA) Elem Ed, Mt Union Coll 1973; Masters Equivalency Rdng Specialist , CA Univ of PA 1980; DASH Elem Sci, Univ of HI 1989; *cr:* Title I Rdng Teacher 1974, 3rd Grade Teacher 1975-78, 4th Grade Teacher 1979- Elizabeth-Forward Sch Dist; *ai:* PA St Ed Assn, Elizabeth-Forward Ed Assn; Natl & Cntrl PTA Assn 1981-; Mon Valley Educl Consortium Great Ideas Grants 1988-; *office:* Central Elem Sch 401 Rock Run Rd Elizabeth PA 15037

GASE, MARY ELLEN, Music Teacher; *b:* Saginaw, MI; *ed:* (BMUSED) Theory/Composition, St Mary-of-the-Woods Coll 1959; (MA) Music His, 1978, (MA) Art His, 1981 CA St Univ; Music Ed, Univ of MI, Alma Coll, Calvin Coll, MI St Univ, Delta Coll, Northwestern Univ & Cntrl MI Univ; *cr:* 7th-9th Grade Vocal Music Teacher South Intermediate Sch 1959-81; 3rd-12th Grade Music Teacher Saginaw Sch Dist 1966-80, 1987-; 7th-12th Grade Music Teacher Center for the Arts & Sciences 1981-; *ai:* Choir Performances; Amer Choral Dir Assn, Music Educators Natl Conference, MI Music Educators Assn 1990; Jr League 1962-; St Stephens Church 1959-; Northwestern Univ Fellowship 1984; Music Sch; Articles Published; Guitar Curr Awds; *office:* Center for Arts & Sciences 115 W Genesee Saginaw MI 48602

GASKILL, JEANNE DIPPOLD, Sixth Grade Teacher; *b:* St Marys, PA; *m:* John W.; *c:* Melissa; *ed:* (BS) Elem Ed, Villa Maria Coll 1966; (MS) Ed, Elmira Coll 1973; *cr:* 6th Grade Teacher Harford Cty Schls 1966-70; 5th/6th Grade Teacher Elmira City Schls 1970-73; 4th Grade Teacher Fox Township Elem Sch 1977-81; 6th Grade Teacher St Marys Mid Sch 1981-; *ai:* St Marys Ed Assn, PA St Ed Assn, NEA; St Marys Band Parents Chaperone Chm 1988-; *office:* St Marys Mid Sch 977 S St Marys Rd Saint Marys PA 15857

GASKILL, JULIA REGAN, 6th/7th/8th Grade ESOL Teacher; *b:* Evanston, IL; *m:* Andrew; *c:* Alan, Lauren; *ed:* (BA) Psych/Music, Univ of the Pacific 1972; (MA) Multicultural Ed, Univ of San Francisco 1978; Univ of CA Los Angeles Writing Project 1989; Monterey Inst of Foreign, Asian Stud 1974-75; *cr:* Japanese Bi-ling Teacher San Francisco Unified Sch Dist 1977-78, Alhambra Unified Sch Dist 1978-82; GATE Teacher 1982-83, ESOL Teacher 1987- Alhambra Unified Sch Dist; *ai:* Delta Phi Upsilon 1983-; La Canada Educl Fnd Public Relations 1989-; Chinese Japanese Bi-ling Ed Inst, Seton Hall Univ Schlsps 1976; *office:* Alhambra Unified Sch Dist 409 S Atlantic Blvd Alhambra CA 91803

GASKINS, JOHN DAVID, Biology/Chemistry Teacher; *b:* Harrisburg, PA; *m:* Kathleen Reiff; *c:* Andrew, John, Kristy, Lynn; *ed:* (BS) Bio, Elizabethtown Coll 1967; (MA) Bio, 1976, (MA) Chem, 1989 West Chester Univ; Sci Supervisory Cert; *cr:* Bio Teacher Valley Forge Military Acad 1967-70; Bio/Chem Teacher Downingtown Sr HS 1970-; *ai:* Ecology Club; ACS; *office:* Downingtown Sr HS Manor Ave Downingtown PA 19335

GASKINS, THERESA MAE, 1st Grade Teacher; *b:* Delaplane, VA; *ed:* (BS) Elem Ed, VA Seminary & Coll 1964; (BS) Elem Ed, Coppin St Coll 1979; Univ of VA; James Madison Univ; *cr:* 1st Grade Teacher Northwestern Elem Sch 1964-; *ai:* Soc Stud Rep; Grade Level Chairperson; Leadership Team Chairperson; NEA 1964-; VA Ed Assn 1964-; Fauquier Ed Assn 1964-; *home:* Box 475 Delaplane VA 22025

GASPARD, REGINA BRUNO, Math/Computer Literacy Teacher; *b:* Port Arthur, TX; *m:* Norman James; *ed:* (BA) Scndry Ed Math/Sci/Comp Lit, Lamar Univ 1975; *cr:* Teacher Woodrow Wilson Ind Sch Dist 1979-82, Stephen F Austin Ind Sch Dist 1982-; *ai:* UIL Calculator Spon; TSTA 1979-; Teacher of Yr Stephen F Austin 1989-.

GASPER, WILLIAM JOSEPH, Math & Science Teacher; *b:* Dunmore, PA; *m:* Jeanette Nowak; *c:* Jason; *ed:* (AA) Sci, Keystone Jr Coll 1966; (BS) Sci, Mansfield St Univ 1968; (MED) Sci, PA St Univ 1970; *cr:* Teacher/Coach Chopticon HS 1969-73, Clearwater Cntrl Cath 1974-; *ai:* Coach Bsbl, Ftbl, Bsktbl & Wrestling; Clearwater Times Sportsman of Yr 1979; FL HS Athletic Assn Bsbl Coach of Yr 1979; Pinellas Suncoast Chamber of Commerce Outstanding Educator Pinellas Cty 1976; *office:* Clearwater Cntrl Cath 2750 Haines Bayshore Rd Clearwater FL 34620

GASPERSICH, MARY CECILE, English/Speech/Drama Teacher; *b:* Pittsburgh, PA; *ed:* (BS) Ed/Eng/Lib Sci, Concord Coll 1977; (MS) Eng, Radford Univ 1983; Advanced Placement Trng; *cr:* Eng/Speech Teacher Matoaka HS 1977-89; Eng/Speech/Drama Teacher Princeton HS 1989-; *ai:* Soph Class & Thespian Spon; Delta Kappa Gamma 2nd VP 1988-; WV Ed Assn, WV Lang Art Cncl; Mercer Cty Ed Assn Scndry Teacher of Yr 1984; Princeton Jaycees Outstanding Young Educators Awd 1986; *home:* 1700 Honaker Ave Princeton WV 24740

GASS, CAROL DAVIS, Kindergarten Teacher; *b:* Ft Wayne, IN; *m:* Charles A.; *ed:* (BS) Elem Ed, Univ of TN 1969; (MA) Elem Ed, E TN St Univ 1978; *cr:* Kndgtn Teacher Highland Sch 1969-72, Crescent Sch 1972-78, Alpha Primary 1978-; *ai:* Hamblen Cty Schls Drug Ed Comm; Hamblin Cty Ed Assn Co-VP 1983-84; TN Ed ASsn, NEA; Lakeway Rdng Assn Secy 1988-89; Intnl Rdng Assn; Phi Delta Kappa 1978; Greeneville City Schls Outstanding Teacher of Yr 1976; TN Career Ladder III Teacher; *home:* 2725 Lowe Dr Talbott TN 37877

GASTON, ARDELLA D., Biology/Chemistry Teacher; *b:* Hazelhurst, MS; *m:* Eugene M.; *ed:* (BS) Bio/Chem, Alcorn St Univ 1967-71; (MS) Bio/Chem/General Sci 1981-82, Specialist Bio/Chem/General Sci, 1982-83 Jackson St Univ; Bio/Chem/Human Physiology Murrah HS 1983-; *cr:* Bio/General Sci Instr Canton Public HS 1971-72; Bio/Chem/Physics/Life Sci/General Sci Instr Simmons HS 1972-79; Cnslr/Advanced Stud GED Instr MS Job Corps Center 1980-81, Asst General Sci Instr 1982-83, Environmental Sci Instr 1985 Jackson St Univ; *ai:* Sci Club & Soph Class Spon; Sci Dept Chairperson; Co-Chairperson Math Dept; Star Teacher of Math; Jackson Fed of Teachers Building Rep 1987-; MS Assn of Educators 1983-; MSTA, NSTA Societies Mem; Church Secy 1988-89, Plaque for Dedication & Service 1988; Elite Social & Civic Club Secy 1988-, Certificate for Outstanding Service 1988; Eastern Star Lucy C Holliday Chapter 508; MS STAR Teacher Achievement Awd 1978-79; Greenville Public Sch Dist Outstanding Service Certificate 1978; Natl Registar Outstanding Coll Grad Awd 1982-83; Alcorn St Univ Academic Schlsp 1967; KS St Univ Bio Fellowship 1990; Fellowship to Jackson St Univ 1980-83; *home:* 4746 Old Poplar Rd Jackson MS 39212

GASTON, CAROLYN DUPREE, Spanish/French Teacher; *b:* Beaumont, TX; *m:* Robert; *c:* Elisa, Stacy, Kara; *ed:* (BA) Fr Ed, Mc Neese St Univ 1972; (MED) Eng Ed, Lamar Univ; *cr:* Span/Eng Teacher Barbe HS 1973-74; Span/Fr/Eng Teacher Lumberton HS 1975-78, Beaumont Chrstn HS 1987-; *ai:* Chapel Coord NHS, Fr & Span Club, Sr Class Spon; *office:* Beaumont Chrstn HS 8001 Old Voth Rd Beaumont TX 77708

GATCHELL, SUSAN JEAN, Business Teacher; *b:* Philadelphia, PA; *m:* Richard David; *ed:* (BS) Bus Ed, Bloomsburg St Coll 1971; Masters Equivalent Bus Ed, West Chester St Coll, Temple & Penn St Univs, Widener Univ 1988; *cr:* Bus Teacher Morrisville HS 1971-72, Ridley HS 1972-83, Garnet Valley HS 1983-; *ai:* FBLA Adv; Delaware Cty Bus Ed Curr Comm Mem; SPBEA; NEA, PSEA 1971-; Garnet Valley Sch Dist PA Teacher of Yr Nom 1989; Mid Sts Evaluation Steering Comm Mem 1988-89; *office:* Garnet Valley HS Smithbridge Rd Box 233 Concordville PA 19331

GATELY, JAMES MATHEW, Social Studies Teacher; *b:* Lockport, NY; *m:* Diane R.; *c:* Tammi, Kevin; *ed:* (BA) His, 1967, (EDM) Teaching Soc Stud, 1968 St Univ of NY Buffalo; *cr:* Soc Stud Teacher Starpoint Cntrl Sch 1968-; *ai:* Jr Class & Close-Up Adv; Effective Schls & Foreign Exch Comm; Var Wrestling Coach; Clarkson Leadership; Citizen Bee & Challenge Adv; NY St United Teachers Negotiator 1968-, Leadership Awd 1988; Pendleton Youth Wrestling Coach 1975-85; Cambria Pack 8 Cub Master 1979-83; Starpoint PTA Life Time Mem; USA Wrestling Coach 1970-, Silver Cert 1988; Natl Sci Fnd Inst Univ of MI; Natl

Endowment for Hum Inst Univ of CO; *office:* Starpoint Cntrl Sch 4363 Mapleton Rd Lockport NY 14094

GATES, DEBBIA JENKINS, 5th Grade Teacher; *b:* Crossett, AR; *m:* J. Randy; *c:* Joshua Brandon, Justin Garett; *ed:* (BA) Elem Ed, Univ of AR 1982 Elem Lib Media Specialist 1990; *cr:* 6th Grade Teacher Southside Elem 1982-84; 5th Grade Teacher Westside Elem 1984-; *ai:* NEA; AEA; Landmark Missionary Youth Dir 1988-; Baptist Church; *office:* Hermitage Westside Elem Sch P O Box 38 Hermitage AR 71647

GATES, JAMES EDWARD, Computer Training Specialist; *b:* Indiana, PA; *m:* Ivy Lee Mac Knight; *ed:* (BM) Vocal Music, Grove City Coll 1971; Ed, Music, Indiana Univ of PA & Duquesne Univ; Math, Cmptr Sci, Harrisburg Area Comm Coll & Penn St Univ; *cr:* Vocal Music Teacher West Branch Area Sch Dist 1971-73, Blairsville-Saltsburg Schl Dist 1973-79; Cmptr Sci Teacher West Shore Sch Dist 1984-; *ai:* Cmptr Curr Comm Mem; Cmptr Hardware & Software Trng Specialist; *office:* West Shore Sch Dist 1000 Hummel Ave Lemoyne PA 17043

GATES, MARY SCOTT, Organist/Choir Accompanist; *b:* Warsaw, IL; *m:* Paul L.; *c:* Stephen, Elizabeth Mothersead, Philip, Christopher; *ed:* (BA) Music, Carthage Coll 1952; (MA) Eng, NW MO St Univ 1970; Grad Stud Music, Univ of IA; *cr:* Music/Eng Teach IA & MO Public Schls; Private Piano/Organ Teacher 1953-; Organist/Choir Accompanist Christ Episcopal Church 1988-; *ai:* Amer Guild of Organists, SW MO Museum Assn Keyboard Club; PEO; Staff Organist at Auditorium Independence MO.

GATES, PAUL E., Spanish Teacher; *b:* Middletown, OH; *ed:* (AB) Span, OH Univ 1960; (MA) Span, Miami Univ 1973; *cr:* Teacher Mc Kinley Jr HS & Middletown Sr HS 1960-66, Meadowdale HS 1966-71; Area Coord Miami Univ 1973-74; Teacher Meadowdale HS 1974-77, Adult Basic Ed 1977-82, Meadowdale HS 1982-; *ai:* Boys Tennis Coach; Frosh Class Co-Adv; Chairperson of Faculty & Supt Teachers Cncl; TESA Facilitator; NEA, OH Modern Lang Assn 1960-; Dayton Ed Assn 1966-; Dayton Tennis Commission Past VP; Dayton Amateur Tennis Hall of Fame 1985; Amer Tennis Assn; NDEA Grants 1962-63.

GATEWOOD, PATRICIA A., Social Studies Teacher; *b:* Pueblo, CO; *m:* Donald; *c:* Donald Jr., Jankeith, Kathy, ERic; *ed:* (ME) Ed, CO St Univ 1981; *cr:* Teacher 1971-, Stu Adv 1981- East HS; *ai:* Pep Club Chrldr & Class Spon; CO Ed Assn, NEA; Delta Sigma Theta; PTSA Teacher of Yr Awd 1989-; *office:* East HS 1545 Detroit St Denver CO 80206

GATHEN, BARBARA ANN, 9th Grade English Teacher; *b:* Fountain Hill, AR; *m:* Thomas Louis; *c:* Kristi, Tiffany; *ed:* (BSE) Eng, Univ of AR Monticello 1967; *cr:* Teacher Dermott Public Schls 1967-69, Warren Public Schls 1969-; *ai:* AR Ed Assn 1967-; Warren Certified Teachers Assn 1969-; AR Cncl of Teachers of Eng 1987-; Young Women Civic Club Monticeclo 1972-; Pilgrim Rest Meth Church; *office:* Warren Jr HS 308 W Pine Warren AR 71671

GATHEN, EMMA YORK, English Teacher; *b:* Osceola, AR; *m:* Letroy; *ed:* (BA) Eng, Rust Coll 1972; (MSE) Curr/Instruction, AR St Univ 1989; Grad Work Rdng & Counseling, AR St Univ; *cr:* Teacher Osceola Mid Sch 1972-85, Osceola Jr HS 1985-; Mississippi Cty Comm Coll 1990; *ai:* Teachers Assisting Teachers Team Mem; Comprehensive Outcomes Evaluation Steering Comm Chm & Dist Comm Mem; Osceola Ed Assn Building Rep 1979-83; AR Ed Assn, NEA, ASCD; Iota Beta Zeta (Secy/Treas) 1985-, Mem of Yr 1982; Versatile 25 Club, Natl Cncl of Negro Women; Odyssey of Mind Regional Judge; St Comm for Adoption of St Mandated Achievement Test; Volunteer Tutor Rosenwald Center; *home:* 320 S Broadway Osceola AR 72370

GATTI, CHERYL G., Mathematics Teacher; *b:* Raton, NM; *c:* Laresa Beck, Ginger Beck; *ed:* (BA) Math, Univ of N CO 1967; Grad Stud; *cr:* Teacher Helen Mc Cune Jr HS 1967-69, Heath Jr HS 1969-74, Aims Comm Coll 1973-74; Instr CO St Univ 1988-89; Consultant NE MN Ed Unit 1988-; Teacher Loveland HS 1983-; *ai:* Knowledgebowl Coach; Math, Engineering Sci Achievement Adv; NCTM, CO Cncl Teachers of Math, NEA, CEA 1982-; Phe Delta Kappa 1985-; Presbyn Church Ruling Elder 1983-86; In House Schlsps Loveland HS; Nom Loveland HS Teacher of Yr; Convention Speech Presenter; *office:* Loveland HS 920 W 29th Loveland CO 80538

GATZA, JULIE, SC, 1st Grade Teacher; *b:* Bay City, MI; *ed:* (BS) Elem Ed, Mount St Joseph 1964; (MS) Early Chldhd Ed, Hunter Coll 1972; *cr:* 1st/2nd Grade Teacher St Anthony Sch 1961-65; 1st-3rd Grade Teacher St James Sch 1966-; *ai:* Spring Musical Dir; Primary Dept Coord; Area Faculty Cncl 1987-; Parish Liturgy Commission Chairwoman 1984-; 25 Yrs of Service to Cath Schls Diocese Awd; *office:* St James Elem Schl 715 14th St Bay City MI 48708

GATZKE, CAROL ANN (MORGAN), 7th/8th Grade Science Teacher; *b:* Cleveland, OH; *m:* Ned S.; *c:* Erin M., Gretchen A.; *ed:* (BSED) Soc Stud, Bowling Green St Univ 1967; (MSED) Environmental/Outdoor Ed, N IL Univ 1974; Course Work Kent St Univ, OH Univ, Univ of WI; *cr:* 7th/8th Grade Soc Stud/Sci Teacher W Geauga Jr HS 1967-75; 7th/8th Grade Life & Earth Sci Teacher Sparta Mid Sch 1975-; *ai:* Sci Olympiad Coach; Inter Comm, Mid Sch Transition Comm; Dist Environmental Ed Comm Chairperson; WI Assn of Evironmental Ed 1975-; WI Society of Sci Teachers 1984-; NEA 1967-; WEA 1975-; Selected Sci World Instr 1984, 1987, 1989; NSF Grant Univ of OK 1971, Univ of WI La Crosse 1990; *home:* Rt 5 Box 420 Sparta WI 54656

GATZLAFF, CARYL STEPHENSON, English Teacher; *b:* Sioux Falls, SD; *m:* Gary R.; *c:* John; *ed:* (BA) Eng, Augustana Coll 1967; (MS) Scndry Ed, Univ of N TX 1983; *cr:* Eng Teacher West HS 1967-68, Oscar F Smith HS 1970-74, Armstrong HS 1975-77, Plano Sr HS 1979-; *ai:* NCTE, TX Joint Cncl of Teachers of Eng, Greater Dallas Cncl of Teachers of Eng; *office:* Plano Sr HS 2200 Independence Pkwy Plano TX 75075

GAUGER, IRENE VAUGHN, First & Second Grade Teacher; *b:* Hominy, OK; *m:* Charles Richard; *c:* Christin R.; *ed:* (BS) Elem Ed, NE OK St Univ 1971; *cr:* 1st/2nd Grade Teacher Burbank Elem 1971-; *home:* Rt 3 Box 465 Ponca City OK 74601

GAUGHENBAUGH, KATHLEEN WILLIAMS, Fifth Grade Teacher; *b:* Lancaster, PA; *m:* Donald; *ed:* (BS) Elem Ed, Bloomsburg St Coll 1979; Grad Work Toward Permanent Cert Bloomsburg Univ, Clarion Univ, Millersville Univ, Cntrl Susquehanna Intermediae Unit #16; *cr:* 2nd-8th Grade Teacher St Marys 1979-80; 7th Grade Teacher St Michaels 1980-81; 6th Grade Teacher 1981-89, 5th Grade Teacher St Columba 1989-; *home:* 36 Nicholas Ave Danville PA 17821

GAUGLER, PENNY MOYER, Reading Teacher; *b:* Sunbury, PA; *m:* Marvin; *c:* Kathryn, Kyle; *ed:* (BS) Span Ed, 1979, Rdng Specialist Certificate, 1980 Bloomsburg Univ; *cr:* Rdng Teacher Fred W Diehl Elem 1980-82, Danville Jr HS 1982-88, Danville Mid Sch 1988-; *ai:* Mid Sch Spelling Bee Coord; Prof Dev Comm Chairperson 1989-; Transition Task Force 1987-88; PA Staff Dev Cncl, PA St Ed Assn; Pi Kappa Delta 1977-; *office:* Danville Mid Sch Rte 11 Danville PA 17821

GAUL, MARION MALLEY, 4th Grade Teacher; *b:* Newton, MA; *m:* William H.; *c:* Elizabeth L., Peter M., Robin R., J. Elise; *ed:* (AB) Eng, Manhattanville Coll 1946; Grad Stud in Drama & Readers Theatre; *cr:* Teacher Agnes Irwin Sch 1971-; *ai:* Faculty Rep to Bd of Trustees 1986-89; Cmmty Service Coord; Academic Policy & Ed Comm Mem; *office:* The Agnes Irwin Sch Box 407 Rosemont PA 19010

GAUL, RITA, Sixth Grade Teacher; *b:* Earling, IA; *ed:* (BA) Soc Sci, Alverno Coll 1942; (MED) Ed/Chem, Creighton Univ 1966; HS Chem & Physics; *cr:* Elem Teacher IL & MN & WI 1942-48, Scndry Teacher MN & NE 1948-83; Elem Teacher NE 1983-89; *ai:* Physics & Chem Grants; *office:* Our Lady of Lourdes Sch 2124 S 32nd Ave Omaha NE 68105

GAUL, YVONNE MARIE, Kindergarten Teacher; *b:* Denison, IA; *m:* Larry I.; *c:* Christopher, Douglas; *ed:* (BA) Spec Ed/Elem Ed, Dana Coll 1979; *cr:* Jr HS Teacher 1981-87, Kndgtn Teacher 1987- St Joseph Sch; *ai:* Cath Youth Organization Teacher 1987-; 4-H Asst Leader 1986-; *home:* RR 1 Box 77 Earling IA 51530

GAULDEN, BEATRICE GILLIAM, Elementary Teacher; *b:* Shreveport, LA; *m:* Reuben L.; *ed:* (BS) Elem Ed, 1968, (MS) Guidance, 1979 Grambling St Univ; *cr:* Teacher Kiroli Elem 1968-79, Glenview Jr HS 1979-82, Ruston Elem 1982-; *ai:* LA Ed Assn, Lincoln Parish Teachers Assn, LA Assn of Educators; Alpha Kappa Alpha; *home:* PO Box 453 Grambling LA 71245

GAULDIN, ALICE GALLAWAY, English 10 Honors Teacher; *b:* Beckley, WV; *m:* Luther L.; *c:* Matthew, Jaimee; *ed:* (AB) Ed, Beckley Coll 1968; (BA) Lang Art Comp, WV Institute Tech 197 ; (BA) Writing/Lib Sci, Marshall Univ 1979; Lang Composition Literature; *cr:* Feature Writer Beckley Newspapers 1974-; Book Mobile Librarian Raleigh Cty Public Lib 1975-79; Lang Arts Teacher Clear Fork HS 1979-81; Woodrow Wilson HS 1981-; *ai:* WWHS Cmptr Club Spon 1988-; Honors Banquet Comm Co-Spon; WV Eng Lang Arts Cncl Mem 1980-; NCTE Mem 1979-; Delta Kappa Gamma Chm Personal Growth & Services 1987-; Woodrow Wilson HS Nom Teacher Yr 1986; Published AP Seminar Manual Article on Figuratine Lang/Poetry/Analytical Writing; *office:* Woodrow Wilson H S 410 Stanaford Rd Beckley WV 25801

GAULKE, GLENN W., Phys Ed/Health Teacher; *b:* Marshfield, WI; *m:* Jane L. Kremsreiter; *c:* Erin, Elliott, Eden; *ed:* (BS) Phys Ed/Health, Univ of WI La Crosse 1983; Working Towards Masters Health Ed, Univ of WI La Crosse; *cr:* Teacher Belmont Sch Dist & Darlington Sch Dist; *ai:* Var Boys Bsktbl, Girls & Guys Track Head Coach; Letterwinners & Weight Club Head; Class Adv; *home:* 235 N Penn Belmont WI 53510

GAULT, REBECCA PEARSON, English Teacher; *b:* Woodruff, SC; *m:* Samuel L. Jr.; *c:* S. C., Kimberly L.; *ed:* (BA) Secondary Ed, 1974, (MA) Elem Ed, 1979 Clemson Univ; *cr:* Eng Teacher Mauldin HS 1974-; *ai:* Sr Class Adv; GCTE; *office:* Mauldin H S 701 E Butler Rd Mauldin SC 29662

GAUMER, BETTY JEAN, Chef Instructor; *b:* Portales, NM; *m:* Charles E.; *c:* Jason, Lyle; *ed:* (MA) Voc Ed/Home Ec, CO St Univ 1989; (BS) Home Ec/Sci, E NM Univ 1964; Chef Educator Courses; Johnson & Wales 1989; Amer Chefing Fed; CO Chef de Cuisine; *cr:* Scndry Teacher 1964-87; Chef Twin Brooks Dude Ranch 1969; Catering Chef Luncheon Is Served 1980-84; Food Service Teacher Excelsior HS 1984-85; Chef Instr T H Pickens Tech Center 1985-; *ai:* Home Ec Related Occupations, FHA Adv; Coached Gold Medal Natl Winner; Chrldr Spon; Food Service Instr of CO Gourmet Dinner Chairpersons 1985-; NEA, CO Educl Assn, Aurora Educl Assn Mem; Amer Chefing Assn; Assn of CO Home Ec (Educl Comm, Apprenticeship Comm) 1985-, Certificate of Appreciation 1990; BSA Summer Camp (Asst Dir 1982-, Comm Chm, Scouting Coord), Scouter Awd 1985; Crisco Awd Outstanding Home Ec Stu; Supt Distinguished Service Awd 1964; Educl Fnd NRA Natl Grant Recipient 1987; Articles Published 1986; *office:* T H Pickens Tech Center 500 Buckley Rd Aurora CO 80011

GAUMER, JEAN ERICKSON, English Teacher; *b:* Minneapolis, MN; *m:* Brian; *c:* Lloyd, Laurie, Elizabeth; *ed:* (BS) Ed, LA St Univ 1961; Comm Stud, Univ of MA; *cr:* Eng Teacher Chalmette Jr HS 1961-65, Ridgefield HS 1967-; Adjunct Grad Sch Ed Fairfield Univ 1990; *ai:* Debate & Mock Trial Coach; Greenpeace; Amnesty Intnl; Celebration of Excl Awd 1987; Published Ed Articles; Developed & Wrote Rhetoric & Lit Curr; *office:* Ridgefield HS 700 N Salem Rd Ridgefield CT 06877

GAUNCE, DRONDA WHITE, 8th Grade English Teacher; *b:* Mobile, AL; *m:* Dave; *c:* Denae, Keli; *ed:* (BS) Elem Ed, William Carey Coll 1981; *cr:* 8th Grade Eng Teacher Gautier Jr HS 1984-; *ai:* 8th Grade Citizenship & Teacher of Month Comm.

GAUSTAD, RICHARD HARLEY, Psych Teacher/Soc Stud Chm; *b:* Cokato, MN; *m:* Susan Faye Heinrich; *c:* Elisabeth Ann, Kirsten Ann; *ed:* (BA) Bus Admin/Economics 1972, (BA) Soc Stud, 1973 Concordia Coll; Grad Work Mankato St Univ, Univ of MN & Winona St Univ; *cr:* Teaching Asst Concordia Coll 1972; Soc Stud Teacher 1974-, Soc Stud Dept Chm 1985- Red Wing Cntrl HS; *ai:* Red Wing Sch & Cmnty Long Range Planning Comm Mem; Continuing Ed Comm Mem; Amnesty Intnl HS Adv; Asst Track Coach Boys; Kiwanis Key Club Adv 1984-86; NCSS; United Way Volunteer 1986-; Asst Scoutmaster 1973-74; YMCA Mem; Awd for Chartering HS Kiwanis Educates Youth Club; Achievement Awd for Working With Learning Disabled Stus In Mainstream Classes; Graduation Honor Teacher 1988; *office:* Red Wing Central H S 525 East Ave Red Wing MN 55066

GAUTHIER, RHONDA J., 7th Grade Math Teacher; *b:* Beverly, MA; *m:* Richard A.; *c:* Adrienne, Andrea; *ed:* (BS) Elem Ed, 1973, (MED) Elem Admin, 1979 Salem St Coll; *cr:* 1st Grade Teacher Edwards Sch 1973-74; 4th-5th Grade Teacher Brown Sch 1974-78; 6th Grade Teacher Cove Sch 1978-81; 6th Grade Sci/7th Grade Math Teacher/Gifted & Talented Coord Briscoe Mid Sch 1981-; *ai:* Math Team Adv; Honors Assembly Organizer; Beverly Teachers Assn, MA Teachers Assn 1973-; ASCD 1987-; St Marys Parish Religion Teacher 1989-.

GAUTREAUX, CAMILE A., Math/Cmptr Literacy Teacher; *b:* New Orleans, LA; *m:* Stella Nicholas; *c:* Corey, Robbie, Trevor, Evan; *ed:* (BA) Elem Ed, Nicholls St Univ 1972; Religious Ed, Loyola Univ 1992; Master Cathechist, Diocese of Houma Thibodaux; *cr:* Teacher Larose Elem 1970-71, Larose-Cut Off Jr HS 1972, Larose Elem 1972-81; Teacher/Cmptr Coord Larose Mid Sch 1981-; *ai:* 4-H Club Leader; Parent Teacher Club Rep; LA Rdng Assn 1975-; Nicholls Rdng Cncl (Treas 1984-850 1975-; LA Assn Teachers of Math 1989-; S Cntrl Swim Assn (Secy 4983-88) 1981-89; Our Lady of the Rosary Parish Cncl (VP 1982-86) 1982-; Bayou Civic Club (Parliamentarian 1984-85) 1982-85; Our Lady of the Rosary Cath Church Religious Ed Dir 1985-; Larose Mid Sch Teacher of Yr 1988-89; *home:* 206 W 13th St PO Box 298 Larose LA 70373

GAVAZZI, MARY MARGARET, Seventh Grade Teacher; *b:* Pittsburgh, PA; *m:* Gerald C.; *ed:* (BSED) Scndry Ed, California Coll of PA 1970; PA St Univ; *cr:* Substitute Teacher Burlettstown Area HS 1970-72, 7th Grade Teacher Our Lady of Lourdes Sch 1972-; *ai:* 7th/8th Grade Field Trip Spon; Sch Fund Raiser Coord; NCEA; Washington-Green Drug Prevention Organization; Our Lady of Lourdes Church Eucharistic Minister; *home:* RD 2 Box 16M Burgettstown PA 15021

GAVIN, ALLENE S., 8th Grade Teacher; *b:* Towanda, PA; *m:* T. Edward; *ed:* (RN) Jersey City Medical Center 1945; (BS) Health Ed Sci, 1945, (MA) Rdng, 1966 Jersey City St Coll; (MA) Ed, NY Univ 1968; *cr:* Instr Jersey City Medical Center 1946-49; Health Ed Dir Hudson Cty TB & Health League 1950-60; Teacher Jersey City Public Schls 1960-; *ai:* Snow Geese Dunes Inc & AL-ED Corporation Pres; Jersey City Ed Assn, NJ Ed Assn, NEA, Intnl Rdng Assn; Jersey City Jr Service League Pres 1964-66; Amer Residential Dev Assn; Towanda Gun Club; World Trade Distributors Incorporated (Mem, Bd of Dir); *office:* Public Sch 11 Bergen Ave Jersey City NJ 07306

GAVIN, SUZANNE, Fine, Perform Arts Chairperson; *b:* Brighton, MA; *ed:* (BA) Scndry Ed/Math, Newark St Coll 1971; (MA) Theatre Arts, Montclair St Coll 1975; *cr:* Teacher St Vincent Acad 1971-74; Chairperson De Paul HS 1976-; *ai:* De Paul Theatre Prgm Tech Dir; Drama Coach; De Paul Mock Trial Team; NCEA 1976-; Operation Rescue Mem 1989-; Servants of the Holy Cross Mem 1986-

GAVIN, TWILA EMGE, Mathematics Teacher; *b:* Sioux City, IA; *m:* John E.; *ed:* (BS) Math, Creighton Univ 1980; Grad Patricia Stevens Modeling Sch 1982, Dale Carnegie 1977; Grad Asst Dale Carnegie Courses 1983; *cr:* Math Teacher Mercy HS 1980-82; Actuarial Technician Capitol Life Insurance Co 1982-86; Math Teacher Cherry Creek HS 1986-; *ai:* Jr Class Adv 1986-89; Teens Organized Against Drugs Spon 1988-89; CO Cncl of Teachers of Math 1988-; NCTM 1989-; Church (Lector 1987-89, Music Minister 1987-); Channel 4 Teacher Who Makes A Difference News Awd; Master Teacher Yrbk Awd 1989; *office:* Cherry Creek HS 9300 E Union Ave Englewood CO 80111

GAWRUSIK, PAMELA J., 6th Grade Teacher; *b:* Chicago, IL; *ed:* (BA) Psych, Natl Coll of Ed 1982; *cr:* 7th Grade Rdng/Lang Art/Soc Stud Teacher Chute Mid Sch 1982-89; 6th Grade Rdng/Lang Art/Soc Stud Teacher Nichols Mid Sch 1989-; *ai:* Speech Club; Stu Cncl Adv; Dist 65 Educators Cncl, IL Ed Assn, NEA 1982-; *home:* 8520 Niles Center Rd Skokie IL 60077

GAY, BOBBIE JEAN MOORE, Kindergarten Teacher; *b:* Fort Worth, TX; *m:* Robert M. Sr.; *c:* Melva C. Mc Gowan, Sharon R. Morris, Cheryl R., Robert M. Jr.; *ed:* (BS) Elem Ed, Houston-Tillotson 1953; TX Woman; *cr:* Teacher Ft Worth Ind Sch Dist 1956-; *ai:* TSTA, NEA 1956-; ACE 1956-87; Delta Sigma Theta 1952-; Natha Howell PTA 1981-; Early Chldhd Grant.

GAY, CATHERINE ELIZABETH, Home Economics/English Teacher; *b:* New Orleans, LA; *ed:* (BA) Eng, 1984, (BS) Voc Home Ec, 1984 TX Chrstn Univ; Quest Trng, Sex Respect Trng; *cr:* Lang Art Teacher Tyrone Mid Sch 1985-87; Home Ec/Eng Teacher Seminole HS 1987-; *ai:* Safety Comm; Pinellas Cty Teachers of Eng 1985-; Arts Center 1987-; *office:* Seminole HS 8401 131 St N Seminole FL 34646

GAY, GARY L., 7-8th Language Arts Teacher; *b:* Berea, KY; *m:* Pauline Nantz; *c:* Gena, Selena; *ed:* (BA) Health Ed, Cumberland Coll 1973; Health Ed, Eastern Ky Univ 1983; Elem Ed Union Coll 1990; Psych; *cr:* 7/8th Grade Teacher Sand Gap Elem Sch 1974-76, Mckee Elem Sch 1976-; *ai:* 7-8th Girls Coach; Girls Coach Jackson Cty HS; KEA/NEA 1986-89; Lions Club VP *office:* Mc Kee Elem Sch PO Box 429 Mc Kee KY 40447

GAY, MARJORIE ROSE, Reading Specialist; *b:* Lake City, MN; *c:* Casey; *ed:* Learning Disabilities, Central St 1987; (BS) Elem Ed, Southern Nazarene 1971; (MA) Rdng Specialist, Central St 1984; Deaf Sign Lang; Bi-Ling Ed Trng; Pharmacy Tech; *cr:* Classroom Teacher Red Rock Public Schls 1971-73; Classroom Teacher 1974-89, Rdng Specialist 1990- Enid Public Schls; *ai:* Organized & Taught Deaf Sign Lang; OEA 1971-81; NEA 1971-81; EEA 1971-81; Church of Christ Teacher/Retreat Chm 1978; Taught Deaf Sign Lang to Sch Children; *office:* Enid Public Schls 1500 E Chestnut Enid OK 73701

GAY, MARTHA NEWPORT, Mathematics Dept Chairman; *b:* Jackson, MS; *c:* Nicholas Bailey; *ed:* (BA) Eng/Elem Ed, Baylor Univ 1967; (MA) Diagnostic Remedial Rdng, Univ of TX 1970; Math, Univ of Houston & Rice Unif; *cr:* 4th Grade Teacher Lucy Read Elem 1967-68; Rdng Teacher 1969-70, 4th Grade Teacher 1970-71 Ortega Elem; Rdng Teacher CY-Fair HS 1971-72; His Teacher Duchesne Acad 1973; Math Teacher River Oaks Baptist Sch 1977-80, St Johns Sch 1980-84; Math Teacher/Math Dept Chm Episcopal HS 1984-; *ai:* Master Teacher; Math Tournament Team & Academic Tournaments Spon; ISAS Evaluation Comm Chm; NCTM Mem 1987-; Peabody Coll VAnderbilt Univ Outstanding Teacher 1986; Episcopal HS Master Teacher Awd 1989; *home:* 2307 North Blvd Houston TX 77098

GAYDOSH, GERI, Instructor/Gifted & Talented; *b:* Indiana, PA; *c:* Nicholas B. Mihalko; *ed:* Elem Ed, IN Univ; (BS) Elem Ed/Spec Ed, Univ of NV Las Vegas 1972; (MS) Cmptr Ed, Nova 1986; Grad Stud 1987; *cr:* Substitute in Spec Ed Several Schls 1965-67; Spec Ed Teacher Vegas Verdes 1967-72; 4th Grade Teacher Gene Ward & Lincoln Elem Sch 1972-80; Teacher of Gifted/Talented Oran Gragson & Halle Hewetson & Mount View 1980-; *ai:* NSEA, CCCTA, NEA; Outstanding Teacher in America 1972; *home:* 5122 Tennis Ct Las Vegas NV 89120

GAYNOR, JANICE MARSH, Teacher of Gifted & Talented; *b:* Newton, NJ; *w:* Richard Thomas (dec); *c:* Richard B., Kevin T.; *ed:* (BS) Music, West Chester Univ 1951; (MED) Soc Fnds, Univ of VA 1981; Elem Admin 1982; Gifted & Talented; Grad Stud; *cr:* 1st-8th Grade Music Teacher Dover Public Schls 1951-54; 1st Grade Teacher Lunenburg Schls 1955; Music Teacher Bisbee Warren Lowell Sch System 1955-56; 6th Grade Teacher Arlington Cty Schls 1956-59; 3rd Grade Teacher Westminster Sch 1968-70; 4th-6th Grade Teacher Arlington Cty Schls 1970-; *ai:* Head Teacher Oakridge 1980-88; Safety Patrol Spon; Stu Government; Math Cty Rep; Natl Zoo Prgm Participant; Lawyers of Arlington Court Tour Prgm for 6th Graders; Sci & Lang Art Cty Rep; Arlington Ed Assn, VA Ed Assn, NEA; Sleepy Hollow Civic Assn (Pres, VP) 1980-89; Alpha Delta Kappa (Treas, Secy); 3 Grants From Arlington Dev of Lang Art; Teacher of Yr Arlington Cty 1981; Channel 7 Demonstration Writing Lessons; Math Enrichment Prgm; Ethnic Heritage Grant; *office:* Oakridge Elem Sch 1414 S 24th St Arlington VA 22202

GAYNOR, JOSEPH PATRICK, Science Teacher; *b:* Far Rockaway, NY; *m:* Francine Villano; *ed:* (BA) Politics, St Johns Univ 1983; *cr:* Sci Teacher St Catherine 1985-; *ai:* Stu Cncl Moderator; *office:* St Catherine Of Sienna School 118-34 Riverton St Saint Albans NY 11412

GAYNOR, SHARON ELIZABETH, 2nd Grade Teacher; *b:* Newark, NJ; *m:* Wesley T.; *c:* Wesley Jr., Tia; *ed:* (BA) Elem Ed, Kean Coll 1972; (MA) Teaching, Montclair St Coll 1983; *cr:* Teacher Newark Bd of Ed 1972-; *ai:* NJ Ed Assn, Newark Teachers Assn, Natl Assn of Teachers.

GAZELLA, JOHN MICHAEL, English Teacher; *b:* Owosso, MI; *m:* Christine K. Coller; *c:* Lisa, Katie; *ed:* (BA) Eng, W MI Univ 1968; (MA) Eng/Scndry Ed, MI St Univ 1972; *cr:* Eng Teacher 1968-83, Asst Prin 1983-85, Eng Teacher 1985- Corunna Mid Sch; *ai:* Track & Ftbl Coach; Corunna Ed Assn, MEA, NEA 1968-; *office:* Corunna Mid Sch 300 Comstock St Corunna MI 48817

GEAGAN, SANDRA D'ARIENZO, Teacher of Gifted Children; *b:* Massena, NY; *m:* Thomas F.; *c:* Thomas M., Peter C.; *ed:* (BS) Ed, 1964, (MS) Ed, 1989 Potsdam Coll; Attendance at Confrature Univ of CT; Trng Work with Gifted Children; *cr:* 3rd Grade Teacher Terryville 1964-68; 2nd/4th/5th/6th Grade Teacher 1970-83, 3rd-6th Grade Teacher of Gifted 1983- Massena Cntrl; *ai:* Odyssey of Mind Cty Comm; St Law Valley Teachers Center Vice Chairperson 1988-; Adjunct Professor Potsdam Coll; Teach Grad Level Course on Gifted Children; Several Wkshps & Speeches on Creativity & Giftedness; *office:* Massena Cntrl Sch Dist 290 Main St Massena NY 13662

GEARHART, REBECCA RHUDY, Third Grade Teacher; *b:* Burkes Garden, VA; *m:* George A.; *c:* Keith, Paige; *ed:* (BS) His/Soc Stud, Madison Coll 1959; *cr:* Soc Stud/His Teacher Andrew Lewis HS 1959-60; 3rd Grade Teacher Cave Spring Elem Sch 1961-65, W Salem Elem Sch 1973-83, Fort Lewis Elem Sch 1983-; *ai:* Math Sci Sch Rep; Credit Union Rep; NEA, VA Ed Assn, Roanoke Cty Ed Assn; Blue Ridge Cncl of Math; *office:* Fort Lewis Elem Sch 3115 W Main St Salem VA 24153

GEARIN, DAWN DAVIDSON, English Teacher; *b:* Greenfield, TN; *m:* Ricky Thomas; *c:* Matthew, Whitney; *cr:* Teacher Dresden HS 1977-; *ai:* Beta Club Co-Spon; Class Spon; NEA, TEA, TAACE; WCEA Treas 1981-82; *home:* Rt 2 Box 217 Greenfield TN 38230

GEARY, DOROTHY ANN (GLYNN), Fourth Grade Teacher; *b:* Fullerton, ND; *m:* Christopher Roy; *c:* Sharon Waterson; *ed:* (BS) Soc Sci/Elem Ed, Univ of ND 1961; (MS) Elem Ed, Azuza Pacific Univ 1987; *cr:* 3rd-5th Grade Teacher Forman Elem Sch 1955-57; 4th Grade Teacher Hickcock Elem Sch 1959-60; 6th Grade Teacher Washington Elem 1961-63; 6th Grade Elem Teacher Darmstadt W Germany 1976-77; 4th-6th Grade Teacher Colton Joint Unified 1963-76; *ai:* Church Act; GATE & MGM Adv 1963-89; Mentor Teacher 1985-; Stu Teacher Master Teacher 1972, 1982, 1987-88; Epsilon Sigma Alpha Secy 1961-63, Service Pin 1961-63; Teacher of Yr Nom 1988; Inland Area Writing Project 1980; Math/Sci/Rdng Teacher Project 1986; Sci Companion 1984; East End Sci Consortium 1985; DOD Superior Performance Awd 1976; Photography Magazine 1966; *office:* Abraham Lincoln Elem Sch 444 E Olive St Colton CA 92324

GEBBEN, CHRISTOPHER JAMES, 4th Grade Teacher; *b:* Effingham, IL; *m:* Diane E. Wente; *c:* Eric, Greg; *ed:* (BS) Elem Ed, 1978, (MS) Elem Ed, 1983 E IL Univ; *cr:* 4th Grade Teacher Washington Sch 1978-79; 3rd Grade Teacher 1979-83, 5th Grade Teacher 1983-89, 4th Grade Teacher 1989- Humboldt Sch; *ai:* Mattoon Ed Assn 1983-; Knights of Columbus 1985-; Parish Sch of Religion Dir 1986-89; *home:* 3120 Oak Ave Mattoon IL 61938

GEDDIE, JUDY WALLACE, Fourth Grade Teacher; *b:* Dallas, TX; *m:* James Michael; *c:* Christopher, Patrick, Clay; *ed:* (BS) Elem Ed, 1965, (MED) Supervision, 1968 Stephen F Austin Univ; Advanced Academic Trng; *cr:* 1st Grade Teacher Karnack Ind Sch Dist 1965-66; 5th/6th Grade Teacher W Rusk Ind Sch Dist 1966-68; 5th Grade Teacher Atlanta Ind Sch Dist 1968-70; 2nd Grade Teacher Sabine Ind Sch Dist 1976-78; 5th/6th Grade Teacher Kilgore Ind Sch Dist 1982-89; 4th Grade Teacher Mabank Ind Sch Dist 1989-; *ai:* UIL Oral Rdng Coach & Judge; Dist Dress Code Comm Mem; Campus Prof Academic Comm; CTA, Delta Kappa Gamma; PTA; *office:* Mabank Ind Sch Dist Box C Mabank TX 75147

GEE, CHERYL MAC DONALD, 2nd Grade Teacher; *b:* San Francisco, CA; *m:* Richard W.; *c:* Carla, Pam, Steven, Katie; *ed:* (BS) Bio Sci, CA Poly 1966; Stan Scndry Teaching Credential CA St 1967; Stan Elem Credential Polytechnic Coll 1968; Rdng Specialist Credential San Luis Obispo 1969; *cr:* Rdng Specialist Santa Margarita 1968-70; Teacher Creston 1970-72; 2nd Grade Teacher Santa Margarita 1972-; *ai:* AETA Building Rep; SRT Co-Chairperson; Placment Testing 3rd-6th Grade rdng Groups; CTA, NEA 1968-91; Atascadero Dist Teachers Assn (Secy 1971-72) 1968-; Los Robles De Oro Arabian Horse Assn (VP 1989-) 1980-; Los Robles De Oro Jr Arabian Horse Assn Adult Leader 1988-; Summer Lit Conference; Summer St Rdng Schlsp; Key Planners Wkshps; *home:* 6200 Monterey Ct Atascadero CA 93422

GEE, GLENDA MILLER, Mathematics Teacher; *b:* Nocona, TX; *m:* David; *c:* Stacey, Dava, Stephenie; *ed:* (BSED) Math/Ed, Midwestern St Univ 1966; Grad Stud Ed & Math; *cr:* Math Teacher Henrietta HS 1967-69, Bowie HS 1976-78, Prairie Valley Ind Sch Dist 1978-80, Nocona HS 1985-; *ai:* Mu Alpha Theta Adv; Math Team Coach; Jr Class Spon; NCTM, TSTA Local Pres 1985-; *home:* 604 Montague Nocona TX 76255

GEERS, DIANE, 6th Grade Teacher/Asst Prin; *b:* Chicago, IL; *ed:* (BA) Scndry Ed, Eureka Coll 1978; *cr:* 6th Grade Teacher St David 1978-85, Bridgeport Cath Acad 1985-; *ai:* Vlybl Coach; Sports Comm Mem; Patrol Moderator; Choir Mem; Asst Prin; Teacher of Yr 5th Congressional Dist 1985; Nom Apple Awd 1987; Heart of Sch Awd Archdiocese of Chicago 1989; *home:* 2920 S Emerald Chicago IL 60616

GEHMAN, JUDY KAY, 9th-12th Grade English Teacher; *b:* Kansas City, MO; *ed:* (BA) Eng, Univ of MT 1988; *cr:* Eng/Speech/Drama Teacher First Baptist Chrstn Sch 1988-; *ai:* Coaching; Soph Class Adv; Drama Dir; NCTE 1989-; *office:* First Baptist Chrstn Sch 11400 La Grange Rd Elyria OH 44035

GEIER, MARGARET EVELYN, Fifth Grade Teacher; *b:* Tulsa, OK; *ed:* (BS) Elem Ed, 1975, (MED) Elem Ed, 1980 NE OK St Univ; *cr:* 4th-6th Grade Teacher Garfield Elem 1975-; *office:* Garfield Elem Sch 701 N Roosevelt PO Box 970 Sand Springs OK 74063

GEIER, RUSSELL LEE, Soc Stud/Govrnmnt/Econ Teacher; *b:* Olney, IL; *m:* Iris Dunn; *c:* Dustin, Michael; *ed:* (BS) Soc Sci, 1970, (MS) Ed Admin, 1990 E IL Univ; *cr:* 3rd-5th Grade Teacher West Liberty Sch 1970-73; 6th Grade Teacher Muddy Grade Sch 1973-74; Jr HS Teacher Newton Central 1974-89; Soc Stud/US Government/Ec Teacher Newton Cntrl Jr HS & Newton Cmmty HS 1989-; *ai:* Jasper Cty Ed Assn Past Pres; *home:* Rt 1 Box 110B Hidalgo IL 62432

GEIMEIER, THOMAS EDWIN, Social Studies Teacher/Chair; *b:* Covington, KY; *m:* Mary F. Conway; *c:* Adam, Alexandra, Anna; *ed:* (BA) His/Bio Ed, N KY Univ 19774; (MED) Admin Ed, 1980, (Rank I) Admin Ed 1982 Xavier Univ; *cr:* Sci Teacher 1976-80, Soc Stud Teacher 1981- Ludlow HS; *ai:* Track & Weight Lifting Coach; Class, Play & Sch Newspaper Spon; Curr Cncl Supvr Teacher Internship Prgm; Bone Co Historic Mem 1988-; Preservation Bd; Amateur Athletic Union Co-Chm KY Physique; Outstanding Teacher Golden Apple Awd 1988; *office:* Ludlow HS 524 Oak St Ludlow KY 41016

GEIS, CAROL ANN (FRANCISCOTTI), Teacher/Lang Art Facilitator; *b:* Dodge City, KS; *m:* Gerald W.; *c:* Michelle A. Franciscotti Wallace, Jennifer L. Franiscotti Mobley; *ed:* (BA) Elem Ed, Univ N CO 1964; WY Writing Project; *cr:* 5th Grade Teacher Pleasant View Elem Sch 1964-65; Sci Teacher 1967-68, 3rd Grade Teacher 1968-69 Cooper Elem Sch; Spec Ed Teacher Newcastle Sch 1975-76; 5th Grade Teacher 1977-79, 6th Grade Teacher 1979- Wagonwheel Sch; Lang Art Facilitator Campbell Cty Sch Dist 1986-; Creative Writing Teacher Northeastern Comm Coll 1986-; *ai:* Team Chm; Lang Art Comm; Effective Sch Team; Sch Chm WY Centennial; Curr Cncl; Young Authors Comm; Tulsa Assn of Teachers, OK Ed Assn 1968-70; Campbell Cty Ed, WY Ed Assn, NEA 1977-89; NCTE 1986-; ASCD 1989-; 4-H Leader 1976-82; GSA Leader 1972-82; Camp Fire Girls Leader 1972-76; *home:* PO Box 995 Gillette WY 82717

GEISE, DONNA MASHBURN, English/Art Teacher; *b:* Loretto, TN; *m:* James A. Jr.; *c:* Tyler, Jessi; *ed:* (BS) Eng/Art Ed, 1981, (MA) Eng Ed, 1986 Univ of N AL; *cr:* Eng Teacher Douglas Cty HS 1981-83, Lawrence Cty HS 1985-86; Eng/Art Teacher Loretto HS 1987-; *ai:* Newspaper Spon; NEA, Lawrence Cty Ed Assn, TN Ed Assn 1987-; *office:* Loretto HS 525 2nd Ave Loretto TN 38469

GEISLER, HARRY S., English Teacher; *b:* Pittsburgh, PA; *m:* Diana Avis; *c:* Kim L., Kerry L.; *ed:* (BS) Ed/His/Eng, Kent St Univ 1958; (MA) Gen Prof Ed, Seton Hall Univ 1972; Montclair St Coll, Wm C Paterson Coll, Kent St Univ; *cr:* Teacher Shaw HS 1958-61, Orange HS 1961-64, Chapel Hill Sch 1965-67; Teacher/A-V Specialist/Media Specialist Paramus Public Schls 1967-; *ai:* Drama Group & Spotlighters Adv; NJEA, NEA 1961-; NCTE 1986-; Friend of NJ Literary Hall of Fame 1989-; Educl Film Lib Assn Bd of Trustees 1969-75; Amer Film Festival Juror 1969-75; *office:* Paramus HS E 99 Century Rd Paramus NJ 07652

GEISLINGER, ROBERT ALFRED, Social Studies Teacher; *b:* Watkins, MN; *m:* Diane; *c:* Todd, Chuck, Tom, Kim; *ed:* (BS) Soc Sci, St Cloud St Univ 1971; Post Coll Classes; *cr:* Teacher St Anthony Sch 1971-; *ai:* Jr HS SADD, Sch Patrol, Cmptr Class Adv; Athletic Dir; HS Bsbl Coach; Township Clerk 1977-; Amateur Bsbl Pres 1988-.

GELLERT, THOMAS NEIL, Director of Bands; *b:* Chicago, IL; *m:* Karen Jaye Hansen; *c:* Elyse H.; *ed:* (BM) Music Performance, 1980/1983, (MM) Music Ed, 1984 Manhattan Sch of Music; (CAS) Educl Admin, NY Univ 1990; Wkshp Cmptr Enhanced Music, Assertive Discipline, Prof Inst in Educl Admin, Long Island Univ, NY Univ; *cr:* Exec Dir Music o the Move Inc 1981-83; Master Practicum Half Hollow Hills HS West 1983-84; Admin Intern Babylon Public Schls 1988-89; Dir of Bands Babylon Jr-Sr HS 1984-; *ai:* Dir Marching Band, Jazz Ensemble; Adv Tri-M, All Sch Musical Stage; Music Dir 1985-; Suffolk Cty Music Educators Assn Exec Bd Chairperson, Chorus Band 1986-88; NY St Sch Music Assn Mem; NY St Band Dir Assn Mem; Music Educators Natl Conf Mem; Mid States Assn Colls & Scndry Schls Evaluation Team Mem 1989-; Concert Tour Montreal CN BHS Wind Ensemble 1989; Outstanding Rating BHS Symphonic Band Liberty Bell Festival 1986; *office:* Babylon H S 50 Railroad Ave Babylon NY 11702

GEMAR, MARIE ELAIN, Biology Teacher; *b:* Seattle, WA; *ed:* (BS) Bio, Briar Cliff 1968; (MA) Physiology, St Marys 1975; Sports Injuries Coach; *cr:* Bio/Chem Teacher Aquin HS 1968-72; Bio Teacher Columbus HS 1972-; *ai:* Var Girls Vlybl & Golf Coach; UVBA 1987-; IA Coaches Assn 1989-; *office:* Columbus HS 3231 W 9th St Waterloo IA 50702

GEMMELL, EMMA ALICE AVERA, Kindergarten Teacher; *b:* Smithfield, NC; *m:* Andrew Hamilton; *ed:* (AA) Peace Jr Coll 1966; (BS) Elem Ed, Atlantic Chrstn Coll 1969; *cr:* 3rd Grade Teacher Private Sch 1969-70; Kndgtn Teacher Oaks Elem Sch 1970-72, Wilsons Mills Elem 1972-; *ai:* NC Senate Bill 2 Sch Comm 1989-; NC Assn of Educators 1970-; Down to Earth Garden Club (Mem 1979-80, VP 1980-81, Pres 1981-82); Kndgtn Health Assessment Comm 1989; *office:* Wilson Mills Elem Sch PO Box 176 Wilsons Mills NC 27593

GENCO, STEPHEN H., Science Teacher; *b:* Red Bank, NJ; *ed:* (BS) Comprehensive Sci, WV Univ 1987; Grad Stud Apache Indian Reservation 1987; Working Towards Masters Georgian Court Coll; *cr:* Chem Teacher Alceshay HS 1987; Sci Teacher

Brick HS 1988-; *ai:* Wrestling & Girls Sftbl Coach; Summer Lifeguard; NJEA, BTEA Mem 1988-; Brick Beach Captain 1982-89; *home:* 620 N Lakeshore Dr Brick NJ 08723

GENGE, JEAN ANN (EIDSON), Business Teacher; *b:* Camdenton, MO; *m:* Milton H. Jr.; *c:* Michael, Beth, Robert; *ed:* (BSED) Bus Ed, 1971, (MSED) Office Ed, 1979 Cntrl MO St Univ; Voc Classes Cntrl MO St Univ; Cmptr Classes Univ of MO Kansas City; *cr:* Bus Teacher Lone Jack HS 1971-89, Raymore-Peculiar HS 1989-; *ai:* Sr Class & NHS Spon; Prof Dev Comm; MO St Teachers Assn 1971-; MO Bus Ed Assn 1985-; Lone Jack CTA (VP 1988-89) 1971-89, Teacher of Yr 1988-89; CTA VP; PTA VP, Lifetime Mem Awd 1987; Bsbl Assn of Lone Jack Secy 1990; Nom Kansas City Star Excl in Ed Awd 1987; *home:* 101 W Seigfreid Rd Lone Jack MO 64070

GENGELBACH, FRANCES HARDING, Science Teacher; *b:* Sibley, IA; *w:* Edward R. (dec); *c:* KURT H.; *ed:* (BS) General Sci, IA St Univ 1954; (MA) Ed, Univ of MO-KS City 1969: Ed Cntrl MO Univ 1971-72; Cert Bible Criswell Coll 1975; Phys Sci North TX Univ 1983; Advanced Bio TX Womans Univ 1984; *cr:* Math/Sci Teacher Plattsburg HS 1964-65; Math/Phys Sci Teacher Lees Summit Jr HS 1969-72; Life/Earth/Phys Sci Teacher Dallas ISD 1982-; *ai:* Morale Comm; Finance Comm; Amer Personnel & Guidance Assn 1969-74; NSTA Life Mem 1969-; Youth for Christ Inc 1970-72; United Teachers of Dallas; *office:* Oliver Wendell Holmes Acad 2001 E Kiest Blvd Dallas TX 75216

GENKINGER, A. BRUCE, 4th Grade Teacher; *b:* New Castle, PA; *m:* Sandra Rowland; *c:* Darryl, Dennis, Donald, Sally; *ed:* (BA) Elem Ed, 1972, (MA) Counseling Ed, 1976 Westminster Coll; *cr:* 4th Grade Teacher Shenango Area Sch Dist 1972-; *ai:* Maint Worker Country Club Golf Course in New Castle; NEA; PSEA; SAEA; *home:* 25 Orchard Way New Castle PA 16105

GENNINGS, BARBARA JEAN (O'KELLEY), Fifth Grade Teacher; *b:* Texarkana, TX; *m:* James F.; *c:* Jason; *ed:* (BS) Elem Ed, East TX St Univ 1979; *cr:* 2nd Grade Teacher Vivian Elem Sch 1980-84; 5th Grade Teacher Bloomburg ISD 1984-; *ai:* TX Classroom Teachers Assn; *office:* Bloomburg Sch P O Box 156 Bloomburg TX 75556

GENO, DORTHY DARMER, Mathematics Teacher/Tutor; *b:* Arab, AL; *m:* Rodney Alex; *c:* Christopher, Paul, Aimee; *ed:* (BS) Scndry Math Ed, Auburn Univ 1972; Course Work Columbus Coll, Tarrant Cty Jr Coll; *cr:* Algebra I/Math II/Math III Teacher Kendrick HS 1972-78; Algebra I/Algebra II/Algebra Honors Teacher Everman HS 1978-83, Fort Worth TX 1983-; *ai:* Tutoring Algebra I & II, Geometry, Trigonometry, Elem Analysis, Coll Algebra, 7th/8th Grade Math; Math Club, Future Teachers of America, Fellowship of Chrstn Athletes, UIL Math Contest, Jr & Frosh Class Spon; Math Contest Coord; Prom Comm; TX St Teachers Assn 1978-83; Parent Teacher Stu Assn 1978-83; Seminary Womans Club 1985-; *home:* 5471 Lubbock Ave Fort Worth TX 76133

GENOVA, EUGENE G., Science Dept Chairman; *b:* Brooklyn, NY; *m:* Barbara J.; *c:* Garrett, Glenn; *ed:* (BS) Earth/Space Sci, Waynesburg Coll 1971; (MA) Liberal Stud, Stonybrook Univ; Post Grad Stud; *cr:* Earth Sci Teacher 1972-, Teacher/Sci Dept Chm 1987- Sachem HS; *ai:* Earth Sci Club Adv; NY St Sci Teachers Assn, Suffolk Cty Sci Teachers Assn 1972-; Century Farms Civic Assn Pres 1987-89; Mestrack Mini Grant Awardee 1988-89; *office:* Sachem HS 51 School St Lake Ronkonkoma NY 11779

GENRTY, RITA B., Social Studies Dept Chairman; *b:* Terre Haute, IN; *m:* Terry M.; *c:* Rebecca; *ed:* (BA) His, 1975, (MA) His, 1976, (EDS) Soc Stud, 1981 W GA Coll; Advamced PLACEMENT SEMINAR; *cr:* Soc Stud Dept Chairperson Carrollton Jr HS 1976-88, Carrollton HS 1988-; *ai:* NHS, Prom Adv; Soc Stud Curr Comm; Phi Delta Kappa; NCSS; GA Cncl for Soc Stud; Carrollton City Teacher of Yr 1987; *office:* Carrollton HS 202 Trojan Dr Carrollton GA 30117

GENSOR, LYNNE MARY (WINK), Language & Reading Teacher; *b:* Denver, CO; *m:* Joseph R. Sr.; *c:* Joseph R. II, Keith W., Kara L.; *ed:* (BA) Scndry Ed, Soc Stud Univ of MD Coll Park 1972; Adv Prof Cert; George Washington Univ WA DC; Loyola; Johns Hopkins Univ Balto MD; Univ of MD Coll Park & Balto; *cr:* Lang Art/Soc Stud/Rdng Teacher Southern Mid Sch 1983-; *ai:* Eagles Quill; Calvert Educl Assn (Sch Rep) 1984-; MD Cncl of Teachers of Eng Cty Rep 1988-; Dunkirk Area Concerned Citizens Assn 1985-; Published Articles & Stories Wa Post; Growing Child Humpty Dumpty; *office:* Southern Mid Sch 9615 H G Trueman Rd Lusby MD 20657

GENTILI, DENNIS RICHARD, Principal; *b:* Woonsocket, RI; *m:* Rita Klimasewski; *c:* Jill, Jodi; *ed:* (BA) Ed, Cntrl CT Univ 1971; (MS) Admin, Providence Coll 1977; *cr:* 6th Grade Elem Teacher 1971-85, Prin 1985- Bernon Heights 1985-; *ai:* Former Woonsocket HS Asst Coach Ftbl 1976-85; Woon Admin Pres 1986-; Labor Cncl Sarg at Arms 1988-; RI Admin; *office:* Bernon Heights Elem Schl 657 Logee St Woonsocket RI 02895

GENTRY, BESSIE FRAZIER, 6th Grade Teacher; *b:* Holly Bluff, MS; *m:* Dr. Ruben; *c:* Regina, Reginald, Ressia; *ed:* (AA) Elem Ed, Coahoma Jr Coll 1964; (BS) Elem Ed, Jackson Coll 1966; (MS) Elem Ed, Jackson Coll 1972; (Ed Spec) Elem Ed, Jackson St Univ 1978; *cr:* 3rd/4th Grade Teacher Darkview Elem Sch 1966-70; Math/Rdng Teacher Boyd Elem Sch 1971-73; 6th Grade Teacher Power Elem Sch 1973-81; Barr Elem Sch 1981-; *ai:* Annual 6th Grade Prgm Spon; Chapter 1 Inservice Teacher; PTA Nom Comm; NEA 1966-; Jackson Ed Assn 1971-; PTA Pres 1980-81; Teacher of the Yr 1985-86; Deborah Circle 1988-; *office:* Barr Elem Sch 1593 W Capitol Jackson MS 39203

GENTRY, CARSEY EDWARD, Spanish Teacher; *b:* Springfield, TN; *ed:* (BA) Span/Fr/Eng, Univ of Indianapolis 1961; (MS) Ed, IN Univ 1966; *cr:* Span/Fr/Eng Teacher Plainfield Jr & Sr HS 1961-64; Span/Eng Teacher Northwest HS 1964-66; Span/Dept Chm Emmerich Manual HS 1966-80; Span Teacher Merle Sidner Jr HS 1980-86, IPS #107 & #90 1987, Arlington HS 1988; *ai:* Span & Intnl Club; IPS All-City Curr; Awds & Honors; Gifted Stu; Span Curr; Span City-Wide Testing; IPS Mentor Prgm; Subject Facilitator Leader; IPS Fnd Grant; Teach IPS Prgm; IFLTA St Poster Contest Judge; Sr Schlshp; Partners in Ed; Span Textbook; NEA, IN St Teachers Assn, IN Foreign Lang Teachers Assn, Indianapolis Ed Assn, Society for Intensified Ed; Amer Assn of Teachers of Span & Portuguese (VP & Pres) 1968-71; Pi Lambda Theta; Indianapolis Public Schls Teacher of Yr 1989-; Finalist IN Teacher of Yr; IPS Above and Beyond the Call of Duty Awd; Society for Intensified Ed Outstanding Teacher Awd; *office:* Arlington HS 4825 N Arlington Ave Indianapolis IN 46226

GENTRY, MARY SUTTON, Second Grade Teacher; *b:* Griffithville, AR; *m:* Paul Wesley; *c:* Anita C., Julie A.; *ed:* (BSE) Elem Ed, Univ of Cntrl AR 1959; Early Chldhd Ed, IA St Univ Ames 1961; Biological Sci, Harding Univ 1973, 1980, 1988; Continuing Ed in PET & Classroom Management 1989-; *cr:* 1st Grade Teacher Bauxite Elem 1959-61; 3rd Grade Teacher Vilonia Elem 1962; 2nd Grade Teacher Gideon MO 1962-63; 6th Grade Teacher Georgetown TX 1963-64; Nursery Laboratory Sch Teacher IA St Univ Ames 1961-; 1st/2nd Grade Teacher Searcy AR 1971-; *ai:* Curr, Sci, Discipline Comms; Book Adoptions for Math, Sci, Rdng, Eng; Stu Teachers in Classroom Supvr; Searcy Ed Assn Teacher of Yr 1989; AR Ed Assn, Natl Rdng Teachers; NEA Observance of Amer Ed; 1st Baptist Church Youth & Adult Teacher 1981-; Chrstn Ed Assn 1979-; Amer Bible Society 1964-; Laubach Literacy Tutor 1971-; Stipends for Sci Courses Harding Univ; Teacher Rep for Mc Graw Hill Book Company Comm Developing New Rdng Series Teacher Rep 1988; *office:* Mc Rae Elem Sch 609 Mc Rae St Searcy AR 72143

GENTRY, WILLIAM PARK, Social Studies Teacher; *b:* Louisville, KY; *m:* Linda Reynolds; *c:* Eric, Lauren, Megan; *ed:* (BS) His/Ed/Poly Sci, Murray St Univ 1972; (MA) Ed, 1976, (Rank I) Sch Admin, 1988 W KY Univ; *cr:* Teacher/Coach Owensboro HS 1972-76; Private Bus 1976-83; Teacher/Coach Grayson Cty HS 1986-; *ai:* HS Bsbl Coach; KEA, NEA 1972-76/ 1983-; Rotary Club 1976-82; *office:* Grayson Cty HS 240 High School Rd Leitchfield KY 42754

GENTRY, WILMA LECHLITER, Business Education Teacher; *b:* Chanute, KS; *m:* John Wallace; *c:* Sherry, Jay; *ed:* (BA) Bus Ed, Ouachita Baptist Univ 1969; Bus & Cmptr Courses; *cr:* Bus Teacher Malvern HS 1969-72, Ashdown HS 1975-; *ai:* Sr Class & FBLA Adv; NEA, AR Ed Assn, Classroom Teachers Assn 1969-; AR Voc Ed Assn 1988-; Ashdown Schls Teacher of Yr 1988; *office:* Ashdown HS 751 Rankin St Ashdown AR 71822

GENZANO, KATHLEEN SHELDON, Mathematics Department Chair; *b:* Camden, NJ; *m:* Ernest J.; *c:* Michael, Denyse, Gary; *ed:* (BA) Math, Glassboro St Coll 1964; Math & Supervisory Grad Classes; *cr:* Math Teacher Collingswood Jr HS 1964-66; K-8th Grade Remedial Math Teacher Brooklawn NJ 1975-81; Math Teacher 1982-87, Math Dept Chairperson 1987- Gloucester Cath HS; *ai:* SAT Classes Teacher; Rainbow for Gods Children; NCTM 1985-; AMTNJ 1986-; Delta Kappa Gamma Soc Chairperson 1986-; S Jersey Cath Sch Teachers Organization N Dist Rep 1986-; *office:* Gloucester Cath HS 333 Ridgeway St Gloucester City NJ 08030

GEORGE, ANNE S., Science Teacher; *b:* Baltimore, MD; *c:* Christopher; *ed:* (BA) Bio, Mt St Agnes Coll 1968; (MED) Human Dev, Univ of MD College Park 1975; *cr:* Bio Teacher Western HS 1968-85; Sci Dept Chairperson Baltimore Polytechnic Inst 1985-87; Sci/Math/Cmptr Sci Teacher Montgomery Blair HS 1987-; *ai:* Marine Bio Club Adv; Blair Magnet Prgm; NSTA Dist Dir 1981-83; NABT Convention Field Trip Coord 1985; MD Assn of Sci Teachers Bd of Dir 1975-81; MD Assn of Bio Teachers Bd of Dir 1980-81; Natl Sci Fnd Pres 1985, Presidential Awd for Excl Sci Teaching; NABT 1980, Outstanding Bio Teachers Awd; Loyola Coll Doctor of Humane Letters 1986; Natl Sci Fnd Presidential Awd Grant 1985; Teacher & Leader 1st HS Stu Marine Bio Delgation to USSR 1989; *office:* Montgomery Blair HS 313 Wayne Ave Silver Spring MD 21209

GEORGE, JANICE DREYER, Lang Art/Phys Ed Teacher; *b:* New Lyme, OH; *m:* Malvin L.; *c:* Susan Leeds, Mark, Paul, Timothy, David, Janet Thompson, Melissa; *ed:* (BSED) Elem Ed, OH Northern Univ 1969; (MED) Elem Phys Ed, Bowling Green St Univ 1979; *cr:* 1st Grade Teacher 1962-70, Jr HS Lang Art Teacher 1970-, Elem Phys Ed Teacher 1972- New Knoxville Local; *ai:* Faculty Cncl Mem New Knoxville Local; New Knoxville Ed Assn Pres 1973-74; OH Ed Assn, NEA, Delta Kappa Gamma, OH Cncl Teachers of Eng Lang Art; Jennings Scholar Martha Holden Jennings Fnd 1982-83; *office:* New Knoxville Local Sch 345 S Main St New Knoxville OH 45871

GEORGE, JENNIFER GERMANY, 6th-8th Grade Math/His Teacher; *b:* Columbia, MS; *m:* Gary Dewain; *c:* Devin D., Megan L.; *ed:* (BS) Home Ec Ed, Univ of S MS 1974; *cr:* Teacher North Forrest HS 1974; Secy Parish Natl Bank 1974-77, Magee Finance Service 1977-81; Teacher Annunciation Cath Sch 1981-; *ai:* APTA Teacher Rep; BSA Cub Den Leader; *home:* 204 Cedar Rd Bogalusa LA 70427

GEORGE, JOYCE W., Science Teacher; *b:* Hawesville, KY; *m:* William H.; *c:* Deborah Hill, Dick G., Kenya Thomas; *ed:* (BS) Health/Phys Ed/Sci, E KY Univ 1953; *cr:* Teacher Madisonville HS 1960-70; Owner/Bus 1970-77; Teacher Browning Springs Mid Sch 1977-; *ai:* SDEA; KEA; NEA; *home:* 780 Homewood Dr Madisonville KY 42431

GEORGE, KAREN RENA, English Teacher; *b:* Kennett, MO; *ed:* (AA) Basic Courses, Three Rivers Comm Coll 1982; (BSE) Eng, AR St Univ 1984; Working on Masters Degree in Eng; *cr:* Eng Teacher Pocahontas Mid Sch 1984-85, Southland HS 1986-; *ai:* Cheerleading & Pep Club Spons; Excl in Ed Comm Pres; HS Curr Comm Mem; CTA, MSTA 1986-; Lions Club 1989-; *office:* Southland HS PO Box 47 Main St Cardwell MO 63829

GEORGE, KAY A., Jr HS Teacher; *b:* Dayton, OH; *ed:* (BS) Elem Ed, Univ of Dayton 1955; *cr:* Teacher Our Lady of Mercy Sch 1952-64, Corpus Christi Sch 1964-; *ai:* Stu Cncl Moderator; Sch Safety Patrol Adv; Designated Person in Charge in Absence of Prin; NCEA.

GEORGE, LEANNE TATE, Teacher of Gifted & Talented; *b:* Hamilton, AL; *c:* Andrew; *ed:* (AA) Scndry Ed/Eng, NE MS Jr Coll 1973; (BAE) Scndry Ed/Eng, 1975, (MED) Scndry Ed/Eng, 1978 Univ of MS; Univ of MS, Blue Mountain Coll; *cr:* Eng Teacher Natchez Public Schls 1975; Eng Teacher/Speech Coach Ft Knox HS 1976-78; Teacher Big Bend Comm Coll West Germany 1979; Eng/Speech/Drama Teacher W P Daniel HS 1980-82; Teacher of Gifted & Talented/Eng/Soc Stud New Albany Mid Sch 1982-; *ai:* Stu Cncl Spon; Sch New Reporter; Geography Bee Coord; Homemakers Cncl Art Contest Coord; ASCD 1990; NEA 1980-; MS Assn of Educators 1980-; New Albany Assn of Educators (VP, Pres, Bldg Rep) 1984, 1985, 1988-; MS Assn of Talented & Gifted 1985-; Daughters of Amer Revolution 1981-; Pilot Club 1989-; Amer Assn of Univ Women 1980-83; Mid Sch Teacher of Yr 1990; Union Cty Educator of Yr 1990;Phi Delta Kappa Educator of Yr 1990; Nom MS Teacher of Yr 1990; *home:* Rt 2 Box 126 Myrtle MS 38650

GEORGE, LINDA BURKE, Math Department Chairperson; *b:* Waco, TX; *m:* Robert Alexander; *c:* Cathryn, Michael; *ed:* (BA) Math/Eng, Univ of TX Austin 1963; (MS) Scndry Psych, Univ of TX Dallas 1978; Several Wkshps; *cr:* Teacher Sarah Zumwalt Jr HS 1963-65, Bryan Adams HS 1965-66, J J Pearce HS 1979-; *ai:* Mu Alpha Theta Spon; Currently Helping to Write St Curr Guide Alg I-II; Academic Coaching; Site-Based Management Comm; Dist Curr Dev; Greater Dallas Cncl Teachers of Math, NCTM 1979-; TX Cncl Teachers of Math 1986-; ASCD 1989-; 1st United Meth Church; Voted Most Influential by Graduating Top 10 Srs 1988; Gifted & Talented Ed Gift Fellow 1989-; *office:* J J Pearce HS 1600 N Coit Rd Richardson TX 75080

GEORGE, MARCUS ALLEN, Counselor; *b:* Hogansville, GA; *ed:* (MED) Cnslr Ed, Auburn Univ 1982; Class A Certificate Scndry Sch Admin 1983; *cr:* Teacher Coosa Cty HS 1975-78, Woodland HS 1978-80; Cnslr/Teacher Lee-Scott Acad 1983-85; Cnslr Fulda Amer HS 1985-; *ai:* Head Ftbl, Wrestling Coach; Child Case Study Comm; PTO VP 1986-87; Sch Advisory Comm Mem 1986-87; *office:* Fulda Amer HS USMCA-Fulda Box 345 APO New York NY 09146

GEORGE, MARIE ANN (GENERAL), Jr/Sr High Art Teacher; *b:* Brooklyn, NY; *m:* Bobby Dean; *c:* Wanda J., Michael D.; *ed:* (BSE) Art Ed, 1975, (MSE) Scndry Admin/Curr/ Instruction, 1982 AR St Univ; Cert in Ger; Scndry Guidance/ Counseling; Working Towards Scndry Prin Certificate; *cr:* Elem Art Teacher Gosnell Public Schls 1975-77; K-12th Grade Art Teacher Monette Public Schls 1977-81, Bay Public Schls 1981-84; 7th-12th Grade Teacher Brookland Public Schls 1984-; *ai:* Art Club, Yrbk, SADD Adv; 10th Grade Spon; NAEA 1989-; AR Art Educators (Reorganization Comm 1982) 1989-; NEA, AEA 1984-; Fraternal Order of Police Lodge 8 Supporter 1988-; 4-H, GSA; Teach in Service Wkshps Elem & Scndry Teachers; *office:* Brookland Public Schls School St Brookland AR 72417

GEORGE, MARY BETH BENHAM, First Grade Teacher; *b:* Troy, OH; *m:* Tyler N.; *c:* Adam; *ed:* (BS) Ed, Wright St Univ 1980; *cr:* 1st Grade Teacher Newton Local Schls 1980-; *ai:* OH Ed Assn; Troy 1st Church Nazarene Sunday Sch Bd 1990-; Stu Fund Drive N CA Earthquake Victims Received Red Cross Recognition; NASA Seeds Project; *office:* Newton Local Schls Long St PO Box 68 Pleasant Hill OH 45359

GEORGE, SALLIE J., Business Education Teacher; *b:* Mendenhall, MS; *m:* Aristides; *c:* Idamaria Liddell, Angela Phillips, Aristides Jr.; *ed:* (BS) Bus, Elizabethtowl Coll 1954; (MBA) Bus Admin, Bradley Univ 1955; *cr:* Instr S IL Univ 1956, Piney Woods Jr Coll 1957-74, Hingham HS 1979-81, Colstrip HS 1981-; *ai:* Cooperative Coord; Inservice Comm; Delta Kappa Gamma 1983-; Order of Eastern Star 1984-; *office:* Colstrip HS 5000 Pine Butte Dr Colstrip MT 50323

GEORGIANA, SAMUEL THOMAS, Chemistry/Science Teacher; *b:* Pittsburgh, PA; *ed:* (BS) Ed/Chem, 1973, (MED) Ed/ Chem 1982 California Univ of PA; *cr:* Chem/Bio/Earth Sci Teacher Kent Cty HS 1973-74; Chem Technician US Steel 1976; Mgr Red & White 1976-78; Chem/General Sci Teacher Bethel Park HS 1978-; *ai:* PA Sci Teachers, NSTA; Muscular Dystrophy Assn 1978-88; Prof Enrichment Prgm 1985-86; Summer Inst Teaching Mid Sch Sci 1989; *office:* Bethel Park HS 309 Church Rd Bethel Park PA 15102

GERARD, REBECCA HUDAK, First Grade Teacher; *b:* Akron, OH; *m:* James K.; *c:* Bradley, Erin; *ed:* (BA) Psych/Elem Ed, Coll of Wooster 1977; Cleveland St Univ, Coll of Mt St Joseph, Akron Univ; *cr:* 2nd Grade Teacher Mc Kinley Elem Sch 1978; Insurance Supvr Progressive Casualty Insurance Company 1979; 1st-3rd Grade Teacher Bellflower Elem Sch 1979-83; 2nd Grade Teacher Garfield Sch 1984-86, Orchard Hollow Elem Sch 1988-89; 1st Grade Teacher Hopkins Elem Sch 1989-; *ai:* Soc & Spirit Comms; Stu of Month Chairperson; Phi Beta Kappa 1976-, Key Awd 1976; Martha Holden Jennings Ec Conference Grant 1982-83; Whitney Stoneburner Prize in Ed 1977; *office:* Hopkins Elem Sch 7565 Hopkins Rd Mentor OH 44060

GERARDI, DUCHERE KING, French/English/Lit Teacher; *b:* Pittsburg, PA; *m:* Herbert T.; *c:* Jennifer Roberts, Heidi, Peter G.; *ed:* Grad Stud Cath Univ, Univ of VA, N VA Comm Coll, George Mason Univ, Univ of Lille Boulogne France; *cr:* 7th/8th Grade Teacher Greentree Sch 1957-61; 10th/11th Grade Teacher Robert E Peary HS 1961-63; 7th-9th Grade Teacher Randolph Jr HS 1963-65; 7th/8th Grade Eng/Lit/Fr Teacher St Anthony Sch 1982-; *ai:* Yrbk Spon; Marketing Comm; New Sch Corpus Christi Secy; Natl Assn Teachers of Fr 1985-; Old Town Civic Assn; *home:* 211 Wolfe St Alexandria VA 22314

GERASCH, INEZ JUST, Retired Substitute Teacher; *b:* New Ulm, MN; *m:* Ralph E.; *c:* Paul, Lucinda Cipani, Mari Weidler; 1st-8th Grade Teacher Rural Brown Cty Schls 1946-49; Teacher Rural Schls 1963-65; 1st Grade Teacher St Marys & St Johns 1965-89; *ed:* (BS) Elem Ed, Mankato St Univ 1971; Grad Work Mankato Univ; *ai:* Brown Cty Historical Society; Wanda Gag House Assn; Teacher of Yr 1989; Distinguished Service Awd in Ed 1989; *home:* 904 S Franklin New Ulm MN 56073

GERBER, ELENA HARDEN, Third Grade Teacher; *b:* Terre Haute, IN; *m:* Jeff; *c:* Alex, Ashlee; *ed:* (BS) Elem Ed, 1977, (MS) Elem Ed, IN St Univ; *cr:* 3rd Grade Teacher MSD of Shakamak 1977-; *office:* MSD Of Shakamak R 2 Box 42 Jasonville IN 47438

GERCHMAN, LEROY FREDRICK, Elementary Science Teacher; *b:* Eveleth, MN; *m:* Margaret Strah; *c:* Lori, Heidi, Beth; *ed:* (BS) Elem, 1963, (MA) Curr/Instruction, 1968 Univ of MN Duluth; *cr:* Elem Sci Teacher Virginia Sch System 1963-; *ai:* MN Sci Teachers Assn; Lions Pres 1971-72; Duluth Sci Fellowship 1966-67; Jaycees Young Educator Awd 1970; *home:* 719 S 10th St Virginia MN 55792

GEREN, WANDA HOPE, Fourth Grade Teacher; *b:* Sweetwater, TN; *ed:* (BS) Bio Sci, Univ of TN 1971; Curr/Instr Ed; *cr:* Teacher Daisy Elem 1971-73, Valley View Elem 1973-78, Clinton Jr HS 1979-80, Willowbrook Elem 1980-84, Woodland Elem 1984-; *ai:* Elem Sci Curr & Textbook Comm; Oak Ridge Ed Assn Constitution & Bylaws Comm; Oak Ridge Natl Lab & Natl Sci Fnd Teacher Trng Prgm; NEA 1971-; TN Ed Assn 1971-; Oak Ridge Ed Assn 1980-, Intnl Rdng Assn; Beta Sigma Phi 1981-85; *office:* Woodland Elem Sch 168 Manhattan Ave Oak Ridge TN 37830

GERETY, SHAWN FRANCIS, English Teacher; *b:* Tacoma, WA; *ed:* (BA) Eng, St Michaels Coll 1978; (MAT) Eng Ed, Univ of Chicago 1980; PhD Prgm Eng, City Univ of NY Univ/Grad Center; *cr:* Eng Teacher Berlin Sr HS 1980-81, Winnisquam Regional HS 1981-82, Riverdale Jr HS 1983-85, Seward Park HS 1985-; *ai:* Literary Magazine Adv; NY City Writing Project 1984-86; NEH Comparative Lit Study Grant 1988; *office:* Seward Park HS 350 Grand St New York NY 10002

GERGEN, ROBERT DUMONT, Social Studies Dept Chair; *b:* E St Louis, IL; *m:* Linda Kay Herman; *c:* Janice, Susan Holman; *ed:* (BS) Geography, S IL Univ 1964; (MED) Ed, Univ of IL Champaign 1971; Thesis Submitted for MA Anthropology, Univ of IL Champaign; *cr:* 7th Grade Geography Teacher Kennedy Upper Grade Center 1964-; Instr Kankakee Comm Coll 1989-; *ai:* Geography Club Spon; Frosh-Soph Golf Coach Kankakee Sch Dist; Curr Cncl; Kappa Delta Pi; IL Cncl for Soc Stud; Kankakee Fed of Teachers Pres 1970-72; Kankakee Eve Lions Pres 1978-80, Service 1984, 1987; IL Assn for Advancement of Archaeology Dir 1986-; General Foods Schlsp; DAR His Teacher of Yr; Curator Historical Society of Greater Peotone; Publications; *home:* 362 S Main Ave Kankakee IL 60901

GERHARDT, GUS WILLIAM, Social Studies Teacher; *b:* Billings, MT; *m:* Sharon Dorene Fisher; *c:* Sara, Christopher; *ed:* (BA) His/Poly Sci, Univ of MT 1968; Working Towards Masters Educl Admin; *cr:* Soc Stud Teacher Lovell Mid Sch 1968-; *ai:* Ftbl Coach; Bis Horn Sch Dist Outstanding Young Educator 1974-75; *home:* 86 Wyoming St Lovell WY 82431

GERHART, MARY E., Science Teacher; *b:* Bloomington, IL; *m:* Paul J.; *c:* Joan, John, Julie, Karen; *ed:* (BA) Liberal Art Ed, Marycrest Coll 1960; Grad Work Univ of NE, George Mason Univ, Univ of VA, Univ of NM; *cr:* 3rd Grade Teacher Ridge Public Schls 1960-61; 2nd Grade Teacher Bessemer Public Sch 1961-62; Kndgtn Teacher Agadas Achim Sch 1965-66; Teacher St Leo 1978-80; Sci Teacher Our Lady Fatima 1983-86; Sci/Lang Art Teacher Hayes Mid Sch 1986-; *ai:* Sci Fair Coord; Sch Improvement & 7th-8th Grade Teams; Prof Controversy; Prgm Planning Comm; Albuquerque Sci Teachers Assn 1983-; ASCD 1983-86; NM Assn Mid Schls 1987-; NM Museum Natural His Docent 1985-; NM Kidney Fnd Bd Mem 1989-.

GERKEN, JOAN NICELY, 3rd Grade Teacher; *b:* Defiance, OH; *m:* Henry D.; *ed:* (BS) Ed, St Francis Coll 1963; *cr:* Elem Teacher Wauseon Exempted Village Schs 1958-61; East Allen Cty Schs 1963-68; Continental Local Schs 1968-69; Northeastern Local Schs 1969-; *ai:* Alpha Delta Kappa Courtesy & Telephone Comm Chm; Young Peoples Theater Guild Membership Chm; Local Teachers Assn Prof Rights & Responsibilities Comm; NEA 1957-; OH Assn 1957-; Northeastern Local Teachers Assn 1969-; Young Peoples Theatre Guild Pres 1988-89; VP 1987-88; PTO-Past Treas; *home:* 21319 Whisler Rd Rt 2 Defiance OH 43512

GERLACH, ROB K., Mathematics/Music Teacher; *b:* Cape Girardeau, MO; *m:* Joan Jensema; *c:* Daniel, Brian, Lori; *ed:* (BS) Elem Ed/Music, Concordia 1978; Kodaly Cert Sam Houston St Univ 1986; *cr:* Teacher/Minister of Music Redeemer Luth Church & Sch 1978-; *ai:* Jr Choir Dir; TX Choral Dirs Assn 1983-; Amer Guild of Organists 1980-; N Austin Optomist; Little League Asst Coach 1986-; *office:* Redeemer Luth Sch 1500 W Anderson Ln Austin TX 78757

GERMAK, GEORGE A., English/Latin Teacher; *b:* Edwardsville, PA; *ed:* (BA) Philosphy, Kings Coll 1958; (MA) Eng/Ed, Scranton Univ 1962; St Bonaventure Univ; Penn St Univ; Oxford Univ; *cr:* Teacher Pemberton Boro HS 1958-59; Woodbridge Sch Dist 1960-63; Kingston HS 1963-66; Wyoming Valley West Sch Dist 1966-; *ai:* 1985 Orgnzd the 1st Mid Sch Chapter of Natl JR Honor Socty in Dist/Adv for this Socty; 1st Mid Sch Yrbk Dist & Adv; Dist Curr Comm 5 Yrs. NEA 1958-; PA St Ed Assoc 1963-; NCTE 1958-; Natl Assoc of Stu Act Adv; Slovak Cath Sokol Treas 1970-; Rcvd An NDEA Grant to Study Eng at PA St Univ 1968; 1 of 20 Teachers Stdyg Comparative Ed Oxford Univ England; *home:* 86 Plymouth Ave Edwardsville PA 18704

GERMAN, JAMES DAVID, Mathematics Teacher; *b:* Amarillo, TX; *m:* Debra A.; *c:* Sydni; *ed:* (BS) Scndry Ed, Lubbock Chrstn Univ 1985; *cr:* Math Teacher/Coach Estacado HS 1985-; *ai:* 9th Grade Ftbl & Jr Var Boys Bsktbl Coach; LCTA 1985-; *office:* Estacado HS 1507 E Itasca Lubbock TX 79403

GERMAN, NANCY CHEATHAM, Kindergarten Teacher; *b:* Ducktown, TN; *m:* James William; *c:* James R., Pamela German Hindman, William B.; *ed:* Early Chldhd Dev Courses 1967-; *cr:* Kndgtn Teacher Humpty-Dumpty Kndgtn 1967-; *ai:* MCYCA 1989-; Nom St of TN Young Childrens Awd 1986; Smyrna Baptist Sunday Sch Teacher 1973-; Elected No 1 1983, No 2 1982, No 3 1981 St of TN Kdngtns; *office:* Humpty-Dumpty Kndgtn Rt 1 Box 227 Charleston TN 37310

GERMANN, KENNETH RALPH, Learning Disabled Resource; *b:* Van Wert, OH; *m:* Helen Christine Selberg; *c:* Christina, Kent; *ed:* (BS) Elem Ed, Concordia Teachers Coll 1965; (MS) Elem Ed, IN Univ 1976; (EDS) Learning Disabilities, Ball St Univ 1987; Severely Emotionally Handicapped, Ball St Univ; *cr:* 4th Grade Teacher Redeemer Luth Sch 1965-72; 5th Grade Teacher 1972-80, 4th Grade Teacher 1980-89, Wyneken Memorial Luth; Educl Therapist Charter Beacon Psychiatric Hospital 1987-; Learning Disabilities Resource Teacher Wyneken Memorial Hospital 1989-; *ai:* Talented & Gifted Coord; Christmas & Spring Prgm & Lang Arts Adoption Comms; Choir Dir; Organist; Luth Ed Assn 1965-89; Assn for Children with Learning Diabilities (Pres 1983-85) 1982-; Decatur Luth Chorale Dir 1986-; Preble Cmmty Choir Dir 1984-86; Preble Centennial Comm 1984; 4-H Club Leader 1982-; Sunday Sch Teacher; Ball St Research Writing Style/Form Manual 1985; *office:* Wyneken Memorial Lutheran Sch Rt 1 Decatur IN 46733

GERMANN, MICHAEL, Mathematics Teacher; *b:* Passaic, NJ; *m:* Karen De Simone; *c:* Matthew; *ed:* (BA) Math, William Paterson Coll 1979; (MA) Supervision/Admin, Jersey City St Coll 1990; *cr:* Math Teacher Westwood HS 1979-85, Secaucus HS 1985-; *ai:* Class Adv, Safe Energy Club Adv; Carlstadt Bd of Ed Mem 1988-; *home:* 545 Union St Carlstadt NJ 07072

GERMANY, JAMES L., Teacher; *b:* DeKalb, TX; *m:* Jimmie Ruth Gray; *c:* Anita C. Hicks, Karla S., James C., Jerome L.; *ed:* (BS) Phys Ed, 1970, (MS) Phys Ed, 1973 TX Southern Univ; Cert Ed, East TX St Univ 1980; Corrective Therapy Cert, Tuskegee AL 1970; Cert, Univ of Houston 1980-; *cr:* Research Specialist TX Southern Univ 1970; Supply Clerk Red River Army Depot 1971; Teacher DeKalb Jr HS 1970-; *ai:* TSTA Contact Person Jr HS Campus; Tour Dir Washington DC Tours; NEA 1970-; TSTA Campus Rep 1970-; East TX Legal Svc Bd Mem 1987- Appreciation 1988; Cmnty Cncl Bd Mem 1988-; Soc Service Target Person for Poor 1988-; People Helping People Bd Mem; Fellowship Soc Stud Wkshp at Univ of Houston; Cmnty Services Awds; *office:* De Kalb Jr H S 845 S W South Front St De Kalb TX 75559

GEROLD, DONNA JEAN (JOHNSTON), Elem Teacher/ Computer Coord; *b:* Sandusky, OH; *m:* James P.; *c:* Scott, Craig; *ed:* (BS) Elem Ed, Bowling Green St Univ 1976; Data Processing, Cmptr Sci, Ashland Univ; Gifted Ed, Toledo Univ, Ashland Univ; *cr:* Teacher Aide 1970-75, 5th Grade Teacher 1976-, Cmptr Coord 1985- Margaretta Local Schls; *ai:* Elem Cmptr Coord; Math Curr, Dist, Law in Ed Comm; Delta Kappa Gamma, OH Cncl of Math 1986-; PTO Exec Bd 1988-; Assn of Supvrs & Curr Dirs Natl Meeting, NW ECHO Conference of OH, Cty Cmptr Seminars Speaker; *home:* 5614 Debra Dr Castalia OH 44824

GERON, SYLVIA F., 8th Grade Soc Stud Teacher; *b:* Waco, TX; *m:* Jesse L. Jr.; *ed:* Assoc His, Tarleton St Univ 1956; (BA) His, 1958, (MA) His, 1962 Sul Ross St Univ; Univ of VA; Presidential Classroom; *cr:* 5th Grade Teacher Marfa Elem Sch 1959-61; 4th/ 5th Grade Teacher Buena Vista Elem Sch 1961-62; 5th Grade Teacher Hereford Ind Sch Dist 1962-68; 8th Grade Soc Stud Teacher Brownfield Mid Sch 1968-; *ai:* Tour Dir & Spon Washington DC; TSTA, NEA 1958-; *office:* Brownfield Mid Sch 601 Tahoka Rd Brownfield TX 79316

GERRALD, GWEN WEBB, 11th Grade US History Teacher; *b:* Statesboro, GA; *m:* Terry L.; *ed:* (BSED) Ed, GA Southern Univ 1974; *cr:* Teacher Statesboro HS 1974-; *ai:* Y Club & Stu Assn of GA Educators Adv; Honors Night Spon; Alpha Delta Kappa Pres 1982-84; Prof Assn of GA Educators 1982-; GA Assn of Educators 1974-82; Stu Teacher Achievement Recognition 1989; *office:* Statesboro HS 10 Lester Rd Statesboro GA 30458

GERRITS, MARIANNE C., Sci/Cmptr Sci Teacher; *b:* Green Bay, WI; *ed:* (BA) Math/Elem Ed, St Norbert Coll 1976; Grad Stud Univ of WI Madison, Univ of WI Green Bay, Univ of WI Oshkosh, Univ of WI River Falls; Mendez Drug Ed Trng; *cr:* Math/Sci Teacher Holy Cross Sch 1976-80; Sci/Cmptr Teacher Notre Dame Mid Sch 1980-; *ai:* Vlybl Coach & League Commissioner; Drama Coach; Swing Choir Choreographer; 8th Grade Class Fund Raising & Booster Bingo Coord; NCEA; League Bsktbl Coach of Yr 1980; *home:* 1019 Robin St De Pere WI 54115

GERROND, M. CAROL MILLER, Business Education Teacher; *b:* Kewanee, IL; *m:* John L.; *c:* Jennifer, Jessica; *ed:* (BS) Bus Ed, IL St 1969; Cmptr Applications, Rock Valley Coll; *cr:* Teacher Yorkville HS 1969-70, Rockford Luth HS 1990; *ai:* Class Adv; Pom Pon Coach; PTA (VP, Secy, Treas) 1980-86, Life Membership 1985; Parent Action Network 1987-; *office:* Rockford Luth HS 3411 N Alpine Rd Rockford IL 61111

GERSCH, DIANN, Teacher; *b:* Kingston, NY; *c:* Will, Carl; *ed:* (BS) Recreation Resources Admin, NC St Univ 1970; (MS) Health/Phys Ed, Univ of NC 1971; *cr:* Health/Phys Ed Teacher Raleigh City Schs 1971-73; Sci Teacher Gold Sand HS 1973-77; Health/Phys Ed Teacher Granite Falls Mid Sch 1981-; *ai:* Girls Bsktbl Coach; NEA, NCAE, AAHPERD, NCAAHPERD; Amer Red Cross 1970-.

GERSPACHER, DENISE EILEEN (PERZY), Early Chldhd Ed Instr/Coord; *b:* Cleveland, OH; *m:* Larry A.; *c:* Jessica A., Jonathon A.; *ed:* (BA) Home Ec, Bowling Green St Univ 1973; (MS) Tech Ed, Univ of Akron 1985; Grad Stud Univ of Akron, Ashland Univ, Kent St Univ; *cr:* Asst Buyer Higbee Cty OH 1973-74; Child Care Centers Supvr USAF Wiesbaden Germany 1974-75; Buyer Higbee Cty OH 1975-80; Substitute Teacher 1980-81; Instr/Coord Chldhd Ed Medina Cty Career Center 1981-; *ai:* FHA, HERO Club Adv; OH Ed Assn, NEA, OH Assn Chldhd Ed, NAEYC, OH Assn for Ed of Young Children, Akron Assn for Ed of Young Children; Medina Cty Home Economists; Amer Red Cross (Volunteer, Instr 1982-); Bus & Prof Women Assn 1980-81, Women of Yr 1980; Certified Home Economist Amer Home Ec Assn 1987-; *office:* Medina Cty Career Center 1101 W Liberty St Medina OH 44256

GERTLER, EVELYN FINEBERG, Sixth Grade Teacher; *b:* Chicago, IL; *m:* Alfred Louis; *c:* Fred I., Janet B. Tulk; *ed:* (BMus) Violin, 1946, (BMusED) Elem/Scndry, 1947 Northwestern Univ; Northwestern Univ, Tulane Univ, Loyola Univ, CA St Univ Hayward; *cr:* 1st-3rd Grade Teacher Daniel Boone Chicago 1960-62, Monroe Elem 1962-66; 1st Grade Teacher Rosenwald New Orleans 1966-70; 3rd-5th Grade Teacher Golden Gate Oakland 1970-74; 1st-6th Grade Teacher Sequoia Sch 1974-; *ai:* Chairperson Mentor Teacher Selection Comm; Choir Conductor; Sci, Stu Study Team, Visual/Performing Arts Comm; Stu Cncl Adv; Rdng Assn Mem 1986-; Oakland Youth Orch Bd Mem 1988-.

GERVASI, GINA ANTONIA, Mathematics Teacher; *b:* Detroit, MI; *ed:* (BS) Math, Cntrl MI Univ 1979; (MA) Math, E Mi Univ 1985; *cr:* 7th/8th Grade Teacher Cntrl Intermediate 1980; Math Teacher Sheperd HS 1980-82, Novi HS 1982-; *ai:* Vlybl Coach, Bsktbl Scorekeeper; NCTM, MCTM 1985-; *office:* Novi HS 24062 Taft Rd Novi MI 48050

GERVASINI, MARIE CONSTANCE, Fourth Grade Teacher; *b:* Torrington, CT; *ed:* (BS) Ed, W CT Univ 1957; (MS) Ed, Univ of Hartford 1961; Courses at Univ of RI, Univ of CT, S CT St Univ, Cntrl CT St Univ; *cr:* 2nd Grade Teacher 1957-62, 3rd Grade Teacher 1962-77, 4th Grade Teacher 1977- Riverside Sch; 4th Grade Teacher Forbes Sch 1985-; *ai:* Forbes Sch Leadership, Soc, Sci & Health Comms; Alpha Delta Kappa (Pres 1984-86, VP & Prgm Chm 1982-84); CT Ed Assn; Torrington Ed Assn Corresponding Secy 1960-61; Torrington Teachers Fed Credit Union (Pres 1979-84, Recording Secy 1989-); Beta Sigma Phi Pres 1965-67; St Peters Sch Bd 1989-; Literacy Volunteers; GSA Leader 1963-65.

GERVING, HERMAN JEROME, Mathematics Teacher & Chairman; *b:* Bismarck, ND; *m:* Kathy Hartinger; *c:* William, Corey, Todd, Melissia, Jennifer, Joshua; *ed:* (BS) Math/Bus, Dickinson St 1970; (MS) Math, MT St 1990; *cr:* Math Teacher Streeter Public Sch 1970-71, Braddock Public Sch 1971-74, Trinity Jr HS 1974-79, Wibaux Cty HS 1986-; *ai:* Jr HS & HS Boys & Girls Bsktbl Coach; MT Ed Assn 1986-; Instruct Adult Ed; *office:* Wibaux Cty HS 105 North F Street Wibaux MT 59353

GESALMAN, JACK W., Mathematics Teacher; *b:* Greensburg, PA; *m:* Dorothy Naomi Clouse; *c:* Karen E., Sheri D., Adam S., Brian S.; *ed:* (BS) Scndry Ed/Math, Shippensburg St 1970; Grad Stud PA St Univ; *cr:* Substitute Teacher 1970-72, Math Teacher 1972- Immaculate Conception Sch 1972-; *ai:* Math Coord; Self Study Pgrm Coord Comm: PA Jr Acad of Sci Spon & Judge; NCEA 1972-; BSA (Scoutmaster 1978-, Chm 1974-87), Service to Boyhood 1988, Awd of Merit 1976; Order of Arrow Vigil Mem

1964-, Vigil Mem Awd 1970; Diocese of Greensburg Contributing Author; *office:* Immaculate Conception Sch 302 2nd St Irwin PA 15642

GESEK, LINDA TRIOLA, Social Studies Teacher; *b:* Elizabeth, NJ; *m:* Henry J.; *c:* Andrew, Glenn; *ed:* (BA) Poly Sci, Marymount Coll 1967; *cr:* Teacher Mother Seton Regional HS 1967-70, Union Cath Regional HS 1979-80, Herbert Hoover Jr HS 1982-83; Teacher/Cluster Leader Linwood Mid Sch 1983-88; Teacher Somerville HS 1988-; *ai:* Soc Service Comm Moderator; Spec Olympics Building Coord; NJEA, NEA 1983-; Natl Geographic Society 1980-; Teacher Assn Eagleton Inst 1990; Church Craft Comm Coord 1976-80; Church Sunday Sch Teacher 1976-80; Parktown Outing Coord 1985, Cncl Cert 1985; Church Choir Mem 1976-83; VFW Certificate Oratorical Contest Moderator; Certificate of Commendation Sen Bradley Geography Awarenes Recognition Prgm; *office:* Somerville HS 222 Davenport St Somerville NJ 08876

GETCHY, ELEANORE FLOWERS, Biology Teacher; *b:* Mercer Cty, PA; *m:* William John; *ed:* (BS) Ed/Bio, Thiel Coll 1957; (MS) Ed, Youngstown St Univ 1976; Working Towards Doctrate Akron Univ; *cr:* Bio Teacher Wilmington Area HS 1957-64; 8th Grade Life Sci/Bio Teacher Neshannock Jr/Sr HS 1966-; *ai:* PA Jr Acad of Sci, Environmental Competitions, Bio Olympics Spon; Delta Kappa Gamma Pres 1978-79; Phi Delta Kappa; PSEA, NEA, Neshannock Teachers Organization; Northminster Presbyn Church (Church Sch Teacher, Womens Assn Leader, Synod Leader in Ed); YWCA; Neshannock HS Teacher of Yr.

GETER, NETTIE A., Mathematics Teacher/Dept Chair; *b:* Manchester, GA; *m:* Emanuel; *c:* Dexter; *ed:* (BS) Math, Fort Valley St 1965; (MA) Math, Morgan St Univ 1971; Math, Univ of Cincinnati, Kent St Univ; *cr:* Math Teacher R L Mc Dougald HS 1965-70; Math Teacher/Dept Chairperson Cntrl HS 1971-; Part-Time Math Teacher W Ga Coll 1984-; *ai:* Math Team Spon; NCTM, NEA, GA Assn of Educators, Carroll Cty Assn of Educators, GA Cncl of Math; ASCD 1989; Alpha Pi Chi Corresponding Secy 1989-; Natl Sci Fnd Grant; Teacher of Yr Nom; STAR Teacher Awd 1982; Carroll Cty Most Outstanding Math Teacher 1989; Nom Presidential Awds for Excl Sci & Math Teaching 1990.

GETTLE, DIANE BRUENS, Mathematics Teacher; *b:* Sycamore, IL; *m:* Charles Edward; *c:* Brandon; *ed:* (BS) Ed/Math, SW MO St Univ 1985; Grad Stud; *cr:* Math Teacher Hillcrest HS 1985-; *ai:* NEA 1987-; Phi Delta Kappa 1989-; *office:* Hillcrest HS 3319 N Grant Springfield MO 65803

GETTY, ELLA NABEREZNY, Home Ec Department Team Leader; *b:* Lowell, MA; *m:* Raynard Anthony; *ed:* (AHE) Home Ec/Retailing, 1948, (BS) Home Ec/Ed, 1951 Boston Univ; (MS) Home Ec/Ed, Simmons Coll 1958; Fitchburg St Coll, Bridgewater St Coll, N Adams St Coll, Univ of MA; *cr:* Teacher Adams HS 1951-54; Home Ec Chm Adams Memorial HS 1954-81; Home Ec Team Leader Hoosac Valley HS 1987-; *ai:* Schlsp Comm; Social Act Adv; Graduation Rehearsals Coach; Amer Home Ec Assn Pres Western MA 1970-72; MA Teachers Assn, NEA; Adams Teachers Assn Building Rep 1956-80; Cath Daughters of Americas; Ladies Ste Anne; Notre Dame Church Parish Cncl 1982-; Volunteerism Awd; Chm Crafts & Sewing Church Bazaar 1978-; MA Teacher Ed Comm; *office:* Hoosac Valley HS Rt 116 Adams MA 01220

GETTY, JOSEPH CHARLES, 7th/8th Grade English Teacher; *b:* Glencoe, MN; *m:* Anne Lorey; *c:* Molly, Emily, Joseph; *ed:* (BA) Eng, 1972, (MA) Ed, 1976 Coll of St Thomas; *cr:* Eng Teacher Blaine HS 1975-84, St Louis Park 1985-; *office:* Saint Louis Park Jr HS 2025 Texas Ave S Saint Louis Park MN 55426

GEURIN, RONALD E., Mathematics Dept Chair; *b:* Peoria, IL; *m:* Diane Kathleen Kisling; *c:* Michelle, Brian; *ed:* (BS) Ed/Math/Chem, Bradley Univ 1962; (MA) Ed, Murray St Univ 1966; Grad Work Univ of IL, IL St Univ, La Verne Coll, IL Cntrl Coll; *cr:* Teacher Roosevelt Jr HS 1962-63, Manual HS 1964-; *ai:* Math Dept Chm & N Cntrl Evaluation Team; Spon & Coach Annual HS Math Examination; IL Cncl Teachers of Math Regional Math Contest; Programming Contests; NCTM; ICTM Certificate 1989; NEA/IEA/PEA; Honors Pgm for Minority Stu in Adv HS Math Courses; *home:* RR 5 Metamora IL 61548

GEVING, BERNIS FLATJORD, Sixth Grade Teacher; *b:* Lawler, IA; *m:* Kenneth L.; *c:* Greta Kulju, Ronda, Rana F.; *ed:* (BS) Elem Ed, Univ of MN Duluth 1971; Grad Stud; *cr:* Teacher Grand Meadow Elem 1955-57, Owatonna Elem 1957-58, Rochester Elem 1958-59, Mc Gregor Elem 1967-; *ai:* Tobacco Prevention Prgm; Learners at Risk Team; Long Lake Conservation Center Class Trip Adv; AFT 1967-; MN Fed of Teachers Treas 1967-; Alpha Delta Kappa (Pres, VP, Secy) 1971-; Grace Luth Church; *home:* Box 219 Mc Gregor MN 55760

GEYSEN, THOMAS FRANCIS, English Teacher; *b:* Boston, MA; *m:* Margaret Anna Leonard; *c:* Marybeth, Laurie, Thomas J.; *ed:* (BA) Eng, Boston St 1967; Eng, Rndg, Spec Ed, Admin Courses, Framingham, Boston, Bridgewater St Colls; *cr:* Asst Prin Franklin HS 1987-88; Eng Teacher Horace Mann Mid Sch 1968-; *ai:* Franklin HS Soccer, Bsktbl, Track, Sftbl, Ftbl Coach; Horace Mann Sch Yrbk & Intramural Adv; Sftbl Coach Dean Jr Coll 1990; Franklin Ed Assn (Pres, VP, Building Rep) 1972-74; MTA, NEA; *office:* Horace Mann Mid Sch Oak St Franklin MA 02038

GHEE, MYRTA RAMIREZ, 5-8th Grade Bilingual Teacher; *b:* Caguas, PR; *m:* Brendan; *ed:* (AA) Liberal Arts, Staten Island Coll 1976; (BA) Eng, Richmond Coll 1978; Scndry Ed/Eng, Rivier Coll; Mid Sch, Scndry Ed, Bi-Ling, Salem St & Merrimack Coll; *cr:* 7th/8th Grade Eng Teacher Dr Mercy Soto Private Sch 1979-82; 5th-8th Grade Bi-Ling Teacher Dr A B Consentino Sch 1984-; *ai:* Liason Between Hispanic Parents & Sch Admin; Informal Counseling for Hispanic Stu; Faculty Pres 1981-82; *office:* Albert B Consentino Sch 685 Washington St Haverhill MA 01830

GHENT, ROBERT MITCHELL, Physical Education Chair; *b:* Middlesboro, KY; *m:* Scottye Ann; *ed:* (BA) His, Morehead St Univ 1966; Grad Stud Univ of KY, Morehead St Univ, Univ of Louisville; *cr:* His Teacher/Head Ftbl/Track Coach Millersburg Military Inst 1966-69; His Teacher/Head Ftbl Coach Fleming Cty HS 1967-68; Phys Ed/Bsktbl Coach Carrithers Mid Sch 1973-77, Jefferson Cty Traditional Mid Sch 1977-; *ai:* Filson Club Historical Society 1989-; Jefferson Cty Ed Assn, KY Ed Assn 1970-; St Marks Episcopal Church Vestry 1990; KY Thoroughbred Owners Dir 1988-; *home:* 516 Morningside Dr Louisville KY 40206

GHILARDUCCI, BETH CONROY, Math Teacher; *b:* Evergreen Park, IL; *m:* August C.; *ed:* (BS) Math, St Josephs Coll 1982; *cr:* Summer Sch Math Teacher Lake Forest HS 1983-84; Math Dept Chm 1988; Math Teacher 1984-87 Carmel HS for Girls; *office:* Carmel HS 1 Carmel Pkwy Mundelein IL 60060

GHIRARDINI, CAROL H., Mathematics Teacher; *b:* Plymouth, NH; *m:* John R. Jr.; *c:* John R. III, David P.; *ed:* (BA) Ed, Univ of MA 1962; *cr:* Elem Teacher UT Street Sch Los Angeles 1962-63; 5th Grade Teacher Arlington MA 1964-68; Math Teacher Golfview Jr HS 1980-89; Bear Lakes Mid Sch 1989-; *ai:* Discipline & Internal Mrktg Comms; Classroom Teachers Assn, Palm Beach Cty Teachers of Math, NEA 1980-; *office:* Bear Lakes Mid Sch 3505 Shenandoah Blvd West Palm Beach FL 33409

GHOLSON, JOHN SAMUEL, Curriculum Coordinator Teacher; *b:* Vivian, LA; *ed:* (BA) Soc Sci/Lang Art, Northwestern St Univ 1964; (MA) Supervision/Admin/Soc Stud, LSU 1973; Mid Sch Curr Stud Univ of FL; Mid Sch Cur Stud Univ of Houston; DEH, Univ of Puget Sound; *cr:* Teacher/Lang Coord Broadmoor Jr HS 1964-70; Lang Coord J S Clark Jr HS 1970; Teacher/Asst Head Master/Curr Coord/Geog Instr First Baptist Church Sch 1970-; *ai:* Spon Natl Jr Honor Society; Spon Heart Fund Drive; Literary Cncl of Teachers; Creative Writing Club; Book Club; Stu Cncl; Yrbk Staff 1968-70; Soc Stud Teacher of Yr 1968-69 Plaque; Natl Geog Soc Mem Lifetime; St Spelling Bees Cncl 1970-; Literary Guild Awd 1971-72 Trophy Grant 1971-72; NISA Mem 1973-80; LISA/ACSI Ind Sch 1970-; NAASP Mem; Heart Fund Spon 1978-; DEH Grant for Medieval Arthurian Lit; Outstanding St Soc Stud Teacher 1977; NIC Newspaper Winner Univ of GA 1972-73; *office:* First Baptist Church Schl 533 Ockley Shreveport LA 71106

GHOLSTON, NANETTE NASIF, Teacher; *b:* Vicksburg, MS; *m:* Robert Edwone; *c:* Robert M., John N.; *ed:* (BS) Elem Ed, Univ S MS 1970; (MED) Elem Ed, MS St Univ 1973; *cr:* Teacher Overstreet Elem Sch; Teacher/Consultant MS Writing/Thinking Inst & MS St Univ; *ai:* Delta Kappa Gamma Corresponding Secy 1988-; Phi Delta Kappa; Phi Kappa Phi; Starkville Prof Ed Assn (Pres, VP) 1985-86 Educator of Yr 1987; Kappa Delta Pi 1970; MS Prof Ed Assn 1983-; MS St Univ Writing/Thinking Summer Invitational Inst Fellowship 1989; Starkville Breakfast Exch Club Teacher of Yr & Teacher of Month Awds 1989; *home:* Rt 2 30 Lake Valley Dr Starkville MS 39759

GIAMETTE, NANCY J., English Teacher; *b:* New Haven, CT; *ed:* (BA) Eng Ed, IL St Univ 1984; Gifted Ed; *cr:* 8th/9th Grade Eng Teacher Chiddix Jr HS 1984-; *ai:* Developed 7th/8th Grade Spelling Prgm 1987, Wrote Gifted Act Book 1984-86, Updated 9th Grade Eng Curr for Unit 5 Sch Dist 1990; *office:* Chiddix Jr HS 300 S Walnut St Normal IL 61761

GIANCRISTIANO, THOMAS F., Social Studies Teacher; *b:* Boston, MA; *ed:* (BA) Ed, Boston Coll 1970; (MED) Media, Boston St Coll 1974; *cr:* Soc Stud Teacher East Boston HS 1971-72, J H Barnes Mid Sch 1972-81; Bus Owner Chicago Franks 1981-; Soc Stud Teacher J H Barnes Mid Sch 1984-; *ai:* Stu Cncl; Faculty Senate; Project Bus Coord.

GIANNETTE, HELEN, 1st Grade Teacher; *b:* Conway, PA; *w:* William (dec); *c:* Patricia; *ed:* (BS) Elem Ed, Geneva Coll 1965; (MA) Elem Ed, Slippery Rock 1969; Elem Ed; *cr:* 1st/2nd/3rd Grade Teacher Vanport Elem 1965-76; 1st Grade Teacher Fort Mc Intosh Elem 1976-81; Coll Sq Elem 1981-; *ai:* NEA; PSEA; BAEA Bldg Rep 1988-; Century Club of Beaver Treas 1979/1990; Crimson Line Aux of Beaver Cty Geriatric Ctr 1965-; *home:* 1309 2nd Ave Conway PA 15027

GIANNONE, CAROLYN WESELCOUCH, Second Grade Teacher; *b:* Derby, CT; *m:* Salvatore; *c:* Sara, Garry, Dana Casey, Lee Angeloszek; *cr:* 3rd Grade Teacher 1965-67, 4th Grade Teacher 1967-69, K-6th Grade Remedial Rdng Teacher 1969-71 Center-Annex Sch; 2nd Grade Teacher Maple Street Sch 1971-76, Center-Annex Sch 1976-77, Bungay Sch 1977-; *ai:* Evaluation Comm; SEA (Secy 1965-67, Pres 1975-77); CEA, NEA 1965-; Delta Kappa Gamma 1971-; *office:* Bungay Elem Sch 35 Bungay Rd Seymour CT 06483

GIARRUSSO, JEAN A., Mathematics Teacher; *b:* Providence, RI; *m:* Alexander; *c:* Annette, Peter, Anthony; *ed:* (BA) Math, RI Coll 1968; Currently Enrolled Univ of NH; Natl Sci Fnd Master of Sci in Teaching Math; Polytechnic Inst 1985-86, RI Coll; *cr:* Math Teacher Johnston HS 1968-71, Cumberland HS 1980-81, N Attleboro HS 1981-86, Span River HS 1986-; *ai:* Math Academic Games Spon; NCTM, Palm Beach Cty Teachers of Math 1986-; Mu Alpha Theta Spon; *office:* Spanish River Cmmty HS 5100 Jog Rd Boca Raton FL 33496

GIBBONS, D. MARK, Business/Music Teacher; *b:* Provo, UT; *m:* Julie Weight; *c:* Aubrey, David A., Melodie, Candice, John E.; *ed:* (BS) Music Ed, Brigham Young Univ 1980; Emergency Medical Technician; *cr:* Music Teacher 1980-88, Teacher/Leader 1984-86 Dixon Mid Sch; Curr Leader Provo Sch Dist 1986-88; Bus/Music Teacher Ramah HS 1988-; *ai:* Asst Vlybl Coach; Class Spon; Pep Band Dir; Sch Cooperative Comm; Provo Ed Assn (Secy 1983-85, Pres 1986-87); Phi Delta Kappa Mem 1985-; UT Ed Assn (VP, Local Pres) 1987-88; ASCD Mem 1986-88; Pleasant Grove Ambulance Assn (Pres 1986-87, Mem 1985-88); Ramah Volunteer Fire Dept Emergency Medical Services Dir 1988-; *office:* Ramah HS PO Box 849 Ramah NM 87321

GIBBONS, ELIZABETH WEBER, Substitute Teacher All Grades; *b:* Elsmere, NE; *m:* Harold D.; *c:* Jerry, Wayne, Kristi; *ed:* Ed, 1958, (BA) Ed/Art/Psych, 1988 Chadron St Coll; *cr:* Rural Sch Teacher Cherry Cty Schls 1955-56, 1958-59; Kndgtn Teacher Crawford City Schls 1959-60; Substitute Teacher Dawes & Sioux Cty 1960-; GED/St Patrol Tester Chadron St Coll 1989-; *ai:* Cultural Center 1968-72, Writing 1969, 1971; United Meth Women Extension (Pres, Secy, Bd Mem 1989-91), Spec Membership Pin 1974; 4-H Organizational & Project Leader 1968-, Alumni Dist Winner 1989-; NE Writing Project Chadron St Coll; Published Articles; *home:* HC 76 Box 4 Crawford NE 69339

GIBBONS, JOANNE D., English Teacher; *b:* Key West, FL; *m:* Edmond A. Jr.; *c:* Eddie, Andrew, Matthew; *ed:* (BAAS) Scndry Ed Eng, Univ of DE 1975; Advanced Level 1 Theology, Diocese of Wilmington; *cr:* Substitute Teacher William Penn HS 1975-76; Lang Art Teacher Christ Our King Elem 1976-78, Corpus Christi Jr HS 1978-; *ai:* Fire Prevention Essays; Spelling Contest; Declamation; NCEA 1976-; *office:* Corpus Christi Sch 901 New Rd Elsmere DE 19805

GIBBONS, VICENTA CALZADILLA, Spanish Teacher; *b:* Banes Oriente, Cuba; *m:* John A.; *c:* Elena C., John G.; *ed:* (BS) Span/Ed, Albertus Magnus Coll 1976; (MS) Span, S CT St Univ 1983; Admin, Supervision, S CT St Univ; *cr:* Eng Teacher Adult Basic Ed 1973-76; Span Teacher Coleytown Jr HS 1976-78, Amity Regional Sr HS 1978-; *ai:* HS Staff Dev, Cooperating Mentor Teacher Prgm, Crisis Resource Team, Self-Esteem Chapter Sub-Comm Mem; Staff Dev Hum Coord; Amer Assn Teachers of Span & Portuguese; New England Chapter Latin Amer Stud; Finalist for Rockefeller Fnd Fellowship for Foreign Lang Teachers 1989; 2nd Annual Intnl Study Seminar Mem; Published Article; *office:* Amity Regional Sr HS 25 Newton Rd Woodbridge CT 06525

GIBBS, CAROL GAYLOR, Fourth Grade Teacher; *b:* Trion, GA; *m:* David Timothy; *ed:* (BS) Scndry Ed, 1971, (MS) Curr/Instruction, 1980 UTC; *cr:* 5th Grade Teacher 1971-72, 6th Grade Teacher 1972-89, 4th Grade Teacher 1989- Happy Valley; *ai:* Spelling Bee Spon; Kappa Delta Pi; Delta Kappa Gamma Schlsp 1988-; Articles Published; *office:* Happy Valley Elem Sch 1600 Happy Valley Rd Rossville GA 30741

GIBBS, DOROTHY BURBACH, Language Arts Teacher; *b:* Cuba City, WI; *m:* Tom; *c:* Jennifer; *ed:* (BA) Speech/Drama, Clarke Coll 1959; (MA) Theatre Arts, Univ of KS Lawrence 1967; Ger, AZ St Univ; Gifted Ed, Univ of N IA; *cr:* Eng Teacher Wahlert HS 1959-60; Speech/Drama/Theology Teacher/Drama Chairperson Mt Carmel Acad 1960-62; 8th Grade Teacher/Asst Prin Mt Carmel Elem Sch 1965; Grad Teaching Asst Univ of KS 1965; Theatre Instr Clarke Coll 1966-69; Grad Asst Univ of IA 1969-70; Lang Art Teacher Washington Jr HS 1973-; *ai:* Sch Newspaper Adv; Washington Writers Project & Literary Magazine, Theatre Arts Prgm, Visual & Performing Arts Opportunities Prgm Dir; Speaking & Listening Study, Mid Sch Study, Mid Sch Implementation Study Comms; Teacher Incentive Awd 1974; PTA Lifetime Membership 1974; Sustained Superior Performance Army Commendation 1964; *office:* Washington Jr HS 51 N Grandview Ave Dubuque IA 25001

GIBBS, DOROTHY SCOTT, Latin Teacher; *b:* Chicago, IL; *m:* George Minnis; *c:* Peter; *ed:* (BA) Ger - Cum Laude, Syracuse Univ 1948; (MAT) Fr, Univ of VA 1964; Grad Stud Univ of Dayton, Miami Univ, Wright St Univ; *cr:* Eng Teacher Aoyama Gakuin Univ 1950-51; Eng/Public Relations Teacher Intnl Chrstn Univ 1957-59; Fr Teacher Brookville HS 1960-61; Latin/Fr/Ger Teacher Kettering Fairmont HS 1968-; *ai:* Jr, OH Sr, Natl Jr Classical League Officer Spons; OH Classical Conference Cncl Mem 1980-83, 1986-89, Hildesheim Vase 1975, 1982; OH Foreign Lang Assn 1968-, Leon Glenn Awd for Outstanding HS Teacher 1984; Amer Classical League 1968-, Mc Kinley Schlsp 1985; Kettering Classroom Teachers Assn, OH Ed Assn, NEA 1968-; Delta Kappa Gamma (Membership Chm 1974-76, 1989-) 1972-, Ruth Grimes Schlsp 1985; Alliance Francaise (Treas 1970-72) 1967-78; Tokyo Chrstn Womens Assn Pres 1950-51; Jennings Fnd Scholar 1986-87; Ashland Oil Teacher Excl Awd 1988; Whos Who in the Midwest 1990; Intnl Whos Who of Bus & Prof Women 1990; *home:* 1417 Constance Ave Kettering OH 45409

GIBBS, RONALD KENNETH, Government/History Teacher; *b:* Schenectady, NY; *c:* Melissa Ford, Jeffrey, Daniel; *ed:* (BA) Soc Sci, 1964, (MA) Instructional Media, 1967, (PHD) Curr/Admin, 1972 MI St Univ; *cr:* Teacher Walter French Jr HS 1965-73; Dir Tri-Dist Summer Sch 1970; Coord Career Ed & Cable TV 1973-82; Teacher Everett HS 1982-; *ai:* Effective Schs Comm; Staff Dev Policy Bd; Co-Chairperson Dist Instructional Cncl; N Cntrl Evaluation Team; ASCD; Phi Delta Kappa VP; Phi Mu Alpha; Lansing Concert Band Pres 1987-89; Sons of Amer Revolution; MI St Univ Alumni Band; Speaker & Wkshp Leader; Statewide Consultant; Taught Media Wkshps on Cable-TV in Schs; *home:* 219 S East St Eaton Rapids MI 48827

GIBBS, SHERRY HAMLIN, 7th-8th Grade Teacher; *b:* Mayfield, KY; *m:* Dwain; *c:* Joanna; *ed:* (BA) Elem Ed/Eng 1969, (MS) Ed, Murray St Univ; *cr:* 6th Grade Teacher Lowes Elem 1969-71; 6th-8th Grade Teacher Farmington Elem 1971-; *ai:* Acad Team Spon; Jr Beta Club; Gifted Ed Comm; KY Ed Assn; *home:* Rt 2 Box 192-B Murray KY 42071

GIBBS, TIMOTHY ROBERT, Mathematics Department Chair; *b:* Buffalo, NY; *m:* Beverly Kiksits; *c:* Jonathan; *ed:* (BSED) Math Ed, 1971, (MSED) Math Ed, 1976 Alfred Univ; *cr:* Math Teacher Whitesville Cntrl Sch 1971-80, Scio Cntrl Sch 1980-; Adjunct Asst Math Prof Alfred Univ 1986-; *ai:* Var Bsbl Coach; Jr & Sr Class Adv; AMTNYS 1988-; Yrbk Recognition 1989; *office:* Scio Cntrl Sch Washington St Scio NY 14880

GIBBS, TRINA CRAMER, 8th Grade Amer His Teacher; *b:* Ardmore, OK; *m:* David Arthur; *c:* Kendall A., Claire E.; *ed:* (BA) Phys Ed/His, Univ of TX Arlington 1976; Counseling Theory/ Practice, Group Counseling, Principles/Philosophy of Guidance, Classroom Management, TX Womens Univ; *cr:* Phys Ed/Rdng Teacher Holy Family Cath Sch 1977-79; 8th Grade Girls Vlybl/ Bsktbl/Track Coach/Amer His Teacher 1979-84, 8th Grade Amer His Teacher 1984- Worley Mid Sch; *ai:* Core Team Comm Mem; Assn of TX Prof Educators; Campus Teacher of Yr 1984; Annual Dedication 1985; Amer His Curr Writer for Dist; Co-Writer TX Statewide Curr; *office:* Worley Mid Sch 500 Pleasant Ridge Rd Mansfield TX 76063

GIBNEY, ELLEN, English Department Chair; *b:* Hoboken, NJ; *ed:* (BA) Eng, Cabrini Coll 1966; (MA) Teaching Eng, Columbia Univ Teachers Coll 1972; Kean Coll & Rutgers Univ; *cr:* Eng Teacher Snyder HS 1966-76; Eng Teacher 1976-78, Eng Coord 1978-85, Eng Dept Chairperson 1985- Academic HS; *ai:* Shakespeare Festival; Theatre Club; NY Times Rep; Theatre Festival; NCTE, NJ Cncl Teachers of Eng, NEA, NJ Ed Assn 1976-; Senator Bradleys Young Citizens Awd Comm 1988-; Rutgers Univ Summer Grant 1969; Jersey City Teacher of Yr 1987; Governor Keans Outstanding Teacher Recognition Awd 1986; Teacher Acad Orientation Article; Contributor to Trng Manual; *home:* 675 Summit Ave Westfield NJ 07090

GIBSON, DONNA JEAN STICE, Third Grade Teacher; *b:* La Belle, MO; *m:* Robert Lee; *ed:* (BSED) Elem Ed, 1970, (MSED) Elem Ed, 1988 NW MO St Univ; *cr:* 1st-3rd Grade Teacher Ravanna R-IV 1966-73; 1st/2nd Grade Teacher Wyaconda 1973-74; 4th Grade Teacher 1974-86, 3rd/4th Grade Teacher 1986-87 W Putnam; 3rd Grade Teacher Putnam Cty R-I 1987-; *ai:* Cmmty Teachers Assn (VP 1988-89, Pres 1989-); Supts Advisory Comm Mem 1989-; Ravanna Township Bd Clerk 1987-; Republican Committee Comm Woman 1989-; Mercer Cty Historical 1987-; *home:* R 3 Box 111 Princeton MO 64673

GIBSON, JANICE MC CLAIN, Business Ed/Computer Instr; *b:* Chicago, IL; *m:* Phil; *c:* Brent, Russ; *ed:* (AA) General Ed, N FL Jr Coll 1974; (BS) Area Bus, Oakland City Coll 1976; (MA) Scndry Ed, Murray St Univ 1979; Cashem/Keys Cmptr Inst, Brooks Word Processing Inst, Memphis St Univ 1983; IBM Novell Network Installation Educl Trng, Atlanta 1989; *cr:* Bus Ed Instr Webster Cty HS 1976-; Cmptr Instr Univ of KY & Henderson Coll 1988-; *ai:* FBLA Adv; Trojan Trivia Entrepreneurship Ed Project Founder & Dir; Sr Class Coord; Cheerleading Spon; Teacher In-Service Cmptr Trainer; NEA, KY Ed Assn 1976-; Webster Cty Teachers Assn (Pres Elect 1988-89, Pres 1989-) 1976-; Commonwealth Inst for Teachers, NBEA, KY Bus Ed Assn 1989-; KY Voc Ed Research Grant Entrepreneurship Project; Presentor Numerous Seminars & Conferences; Testimony before Small Bus Task Force for Legislative Sub Comm 1989; Webster Cty Teacher of Yr 1978, 1989; *office:* Webster Cty HS PO Box 267 Dixon KY 42409

GIBSON, JERRY EDSON, Vocal Music Teacher; *b:* Zanesville, OH; *ed:* (BS) Ed, Muskingum Coll 1966; Music Lit for Mid Sch, OH St Univ; Rio Grande Coll; Childrens Theater; Chrstn Ed, George Williams Coll; *cr:* Music Teacher Adamsville Sch Dist 1960-62, Chandlersville Sch Dist 1960-62, W Muskingum Sch Dist 1960-; *ai:* Dir HS Mens Quartet St & Natl Recognition; Mem Cty Curr Comm; Music Educators Natl Conference 1960-; OH Music Ed 1960, 25 Yr Awd 1989; Dist TX Music Ed (Pres, Treas); Muskingum Cty Music Teachers (Pres, VP, Secy, Treas); Thursday Music Club 1987-; New Concord United Meth Church; Leaders of Amer Ed 1971; Jennings Schlsp 1988-89; *office:* W Muskingum Mid Sch & HS 200 Kimes Rd Zanesville OH 43701

GIBSON, JUDY B., Mathematics Teacher; *b:* Denton, NC; *m:* Stephen G.; *c:* Jason, Ryan; *ed:* (BS) Math, East Carolina Univ 1971; *cr:* Math Teacher Anne Chesnutt Jr HS 1971-75, Kings Mountain Jr HS 1979-; *ai:* Math Team Coach; Jr Beta Club Spon; Math, Sci Fair, Core Comm; Mentor Teacher; Young Baptist Women (Pres 1986-88, Mission Action Chairperson 1988-); Dover Sch PTO 1986-88; *home:* 1243 Boyd Ct Shelby NC 28150

GIBSON, KATHLEEN HAMMOND, 5th Grade Teacher; *b:* Lawrence, MA; *c:* David; *ed:* (BS) Ed, Lowell St 1969; (MED)Guidance Cnslng, Salem St 1980; *cr:* 5th Grade Teacher Marsh-Cntrl Elem 1969-85; Gifted & Talented Teache R Tenney Mid Sch 1985-.

GIBSON, MARION SPENCER, Fifth Grade Teacher; *b:* Elizabeth City, NC; *d:* Lee Otis; *c:* Jacqueline G. Gregory, Sharon A., Levora G. Todd; *ed:* (BS) Elem Ed, Elizabeth City St Univ 1962; Math, Norfolk St Univ; *cr:* Teacher Portsmouth City Schls 1962-64, Chapel Hill City Schls 1964-66, Elizabeth City-Pasquotank Schls 1966-; *ai:* United Fund Drive Spon; Conducted Flutophone Band Chapel Hill; NC Assn of Educators, NEA, NC Ed Assn 1964-; Schlsp Received Frosh Yr; *home:* 1201 Mitchell Dr Elizabeth City NC 27909

GIBSON, PREMUEL LOUISE (CROSBY), Physical Education Instructor; *b:* Lexington, SC; *m:* Willie Jerome; *c:* Orentha, Jerome; *ed:* (BS) Phys Ed, Allen Univ 1967; *cr:* Phys Ed Instr Manning Trng & Manning Mid Sch 1967-; *ai:* Mid Sch Bsktbl Coach; Gymnastic Club Adv; SC Ed Assn, NEA 1967-; SC HS League Coaches 1980-; SC Phys Ed, Health, Recreation & Dance Assn 1987-; Ebenezer Baptist Church Mem 1969-; Usher Bd VP; T-Ball & Minor League Bsbl Coach 1988-; Black River Trustee Wives Alliance Treas 1989-; *office:* Manning Mid Sch 311 W Boyce St Manning SC 29102

GIBSON, RAY C., 7th Grade Lit/Eng Teacher; *b:* New Iberia, LA; *m:* Jacqueline M. Lee; *c:* Brady J., Wynton T.; *ed:* (BS) Instrumental Music, Grambling St Univ 1979; (BA) Elem Ed, Univ of Southwestern AL 1989; Ed Admin/Supervision, Southern Univ Baton Rouge; Scndry Teach, USL Lafayette; *cr:* Teacher Jeanerette Mid Sch 1982-; *ai:* Co-Spon Jr Beta Club; Chm Parental Involvement Comm Model Schls Prgm & Open House Comm 1989-; NEA, LA Assn Educators, Iberia Assn Educators 1982-; City of Jeanerette Civil Service Bd 1988-; Iberia General Hospital Cmmty Adv Bd 1990; Free/Accepted Masons Worshipful Master 1986-88; Jeanerette Mid Sch Teacher of Yr 1984 & 1986-88; *home:* 2105 Time St Jeanerette LA 70544

GIDDINGS, ROGER DEAN, Mathematics Teacher; *b:* Oshkosh, WI; *m:* Debra Val Knackstedt; *c:* James D., John A., Paul T.; *ed:* (BS) Math, Univ of WI Oshkosh 1977; Alcohol & Other Drug Abuse Trng; *cr:* Math Teacher Mayville HS 1977-81, Horace Mann HS 1981-84, Winneconne HS 1984-; *ai:* Pep Club & Jr Class Adv; Environmental Ed Comm; Wrestling Coaches Assn, NCTM 1977-87; Kiwanis Club 1984.

GIDEON, FLORENE A., Retired Teacher; *b:* Stella, MO; *m:* Clyde; *c:* Jamie C.; *ed:* (BA) Ed, Tahlequah 1962; *cr:* 1st-8th Grade Teacher Mc Donald Cty 1946-54; Kndgtn Teacher Rio Dell CA 1954-56; 1st Grade Teacher Porterville CA 1956-61; 2nd Grade Teacher Anderson MO 1962-68; 3rd Grade Teacher Neosho MO 1968-87; *ai:* Delta Kappa Gamma 1980; CTA 1954-88; MSTA 1962-; *home:* RR 2 Box 62 Goodman MO 64843

GIDEON, MARK ALLEN, Director of Theatre; *b:* Springfield, MO; *ed:* (BA) Speech/Theatre, Evangel Coll 1978; (MA) Speech/ Theatre, Pittsburg St Univ 1982; *cr:* Teacher Excelsior Springs HS 1979-82, Aurora Gardens Acad 1984-85, Nixa HS 1985-86, Kickapoo HS 1986-; *ai:* Drama Club & Thespians Spon; Direct Fall Musical, Winter 1-Acts, Spring Comedy; STAM 1985-; SMSA VP 1989-; *home:* 516 E Lindberg Pl Springfield MO 65807

GIEBAS, J. MICHAEL, English/Latin Instructor; *b:* Newark, NJ; *m:* Diane Perrine; *c:* Aimee, Amanda; *ed:* (BA) Classical Lang, St Peters Coll 1967; (MA) Ed, Kean Coll 1969; *cr:* Instr St Josephs HS 1968-69, Red Bank Regional HS 1971-73, Marlboro HS 1973-; *ai:* Marlboro HS Honor Society Adv; Natl Assn of Stu Activity Advs 1983-; NCTE, NJ Cncl Teachers of Eng 1973-; *office:* Marlboro HS St Hwy 79 Marlboro NJ 07746

GIEBEL, CATHERINE MC GIL, Language Art Teacher; *b:* Minneapolis, MN; *m:* Arlyn; *c:* Ann M., Kevin E., Mary E., Mary C.; *ed:* (BA) Eng, Coll of St Catherine 1953; Grad Work Gifted & Talented; Great Books Leadership; *cr:* Lang Art Teacher Jordan Sr HS 1953-56, Montgomery HS 1956-57, Northfield Jr HS 1979-82, Northfield Sr HS 1982-; *ai:* Northfield Ed Assn 1979-; St Dominics Church Parish Cncl 1986-89; *office:* Northfield Sr HS 1400 S Division St Northfield MN 55057

GIEGENGACK, EDWARD THOMAS, Mathematics Teacher; *b:* Iowa City, IA; *m:* Teresa Flynn; *c:* Philip, Paul, Daniel; *ed:* (BS) Math Ed, Villanova Univ 1966; (MA) Math Ed, Fairfield Univ 1967; *cr:* Math/Statistics Teacher AL Hikma Univ Baghdad Iraq 1967-69; Calculus/Geometry Instr Deerfield Acad 1969; 5th-9th Grade Math/Sci Instr Staten Island Acad & Greenwich Cntry Day Sch 1970-75; A P Calculus/Geometry/Algebra II Teacher Fairfield Coll Preparatory Sch 1976;Adjunct Professor Calculus/ Finite Math Fairfield Univ 1985-; Teacher of Algebra/Calculus/ Math Anxiety Fairfield Univ Sch of Continuing Ed 1982-; *ai:* Head Coach Fairfield Univ Mens & Womens Cross Cntry Team; Moderator Math Team; Fairfield Prep Rifle Team Adv; *office:* Fairfield Coll Preparatory Sch N Benson Rd Fairfield CT 06430

GIEGERICH, ELISABETH, Vocal Music Teacher; *b:* Chicago, IL; *ed:* (BA) Instrumental Music, Olivet Coll 1978; *cr:* Vocal Music Instr Bessemer Township 1978-79; Vocal/General Music Teacher Benton Harbor Jr HS 1980-82; Vocal Music Teacher Benton Harbor HS 1982-; *ai:* All 9th-12th Grade Choral Music Act; Jr HS Select Ensemble; MI Sch Vocal Assn (Dist Mgr 1982-88, Honors Choir Supvr 1987-89); Amer Choral Dirs Assn (Womens Choir 1989) 1988-; SW MI Womens Poly Coalition, NAACP 1987-; Monday Music Club 1986-; Conducted MI Regional & St Honors Choir 1989-; Select Ensembles Best 12 Choirs in St 1986, 1987; *office:* Benton Harbor HS 870 Colfax Benton Harbor MI 49022

GIESEKE, SHARON JEAN (GUGGISBERG), Math Dept Chm/Physics Teacher; *b:* Redwood Falls, MN; *m:* Sam E.; *c:* Eric, Paul; *ed:* (BA) Math/Physics, Concordia Coll 1972; Graduate Courses for Gifted Students/Mainstreamed Students/Cmptr; *cr:* Math/Physics Teacher Pine City HS 1972-77; Math Teacher Montgomery HS 1977-79, West Luth HS 1979-; *ai:* Stu Cncl Adv Jr Class Adv; Pine City Ed Assn Treas 1976-77; Montgomery Ed Assn Coord 1978-79; *home:* 14706 91st Pl Maple Grove MN 55369

GIESINGER, IMOGENE MOCK, Consultant; *b:* Houston, TX; *m:* Edgar R.; *c:* Gayle Heintz, Judy Farrar, Edgar; *ed:* (BS) Elem Ed, 1960, (MED) Elem Ed, 1965 Sam Houston St Univ; Post Grad Work Sam Houston Univ 1970-77; *cr:* 1st-4th Grade Teacher Klein Common Sch Dist 1958-59; 1st/2nd/8th Grade Teacher Montgomery Elem Sch 1959-69; 5th/7th Grade Teacher Washington Jr HS 1969-74; 5th/6th Grade Supervisor Reaves Intermediate Sch 1974-76; Prin Anderson Elem 1976-78, Rice Elem 1978-87, Reaves Intermediate 1987-88; *ai:* Coord Parents as Teachers Prgm Conroe Ind Sch Dist; TX St Teachers Assn Secy 1962-63; Delta Kappa Gamma 1st VP 1980-82 Achievement 1984; Phi Delta Kappa; Cath Daughters Secy Charter Mem 1954-58; Conroe Assn Prof Secys Boss of Yr Awd 1986-87; Hunanitarian Awd 1975, 1976; Conroe Ind Sch Dist Named New Elem Sch Imogene M Giesinger ELem; *office:* Conroe Ind Sch Dist 702 N Thompson St Conroe TX 77301

GIESMAN, BETH A., Fourth Grade Teacher; *b:* Pittsburgh, PA; *ed:* (BS) Elem Ed, Liberty Univ 1980; Ed, Fitchburg St Coll & Pensacola Chrstn Coll; *cr:* 2nd/3rd Grade Teacher 1980-83, 5th Grade Teacher 1985-87, Elem Supvr 1985-89, Cheerleading Coach 1986-88, Asst Sftbl Coach 1987-88, 4th Grade Teacher 1983-85, 1987- Twin City Chrstn Sch; *office:* Twin City Chrstn Sch 194 Electric Ave Lunenburg MA 01462

GIESSELMANN, DUANE LYLE, 7th & 8th Grade Teacher; *b:* Omaha, NE; *m:* Connie Jo Dyer; *c:* Mark, Gretchen; *ed:* (BS) Ed/ Soc Sci, 1969, (MED) Elem Ed, 1976 Concordia Teachers Coll; *cr:* 3rd-5th Grade Teacher 1969-72, 6th-8th Grade Teacher 1972-77 Our Redeemer Luth Sch; 7th/8th Grade Teacher/Prin 1977-84, 7th-8th Grade Teacher 1984- St PauL Luth Sch; *ai:* Coaching; Cmptr Coord; Seward Cty Teachers Assn Chm 1969-72; MO Luth Prin Conference Treas 1977-84; *office:* St Paul Luth Sch Columbia & Carleton Farmington MO 63640

GIFFIN, PHILIP COOKE, Ohio History/Geography Teacher; *b:* Boston, MA; *m:* Elmeda Schubert; *c:* Timothy, Catherine Cook; *ed:* Educl Trng Kent St Univ; *cr:* 6th/7th Grade Teacher Madison Local Schls 1956-61; 7th/8th Grade Teacher Ontario Local Schls 1961-; *ai:* Ftbl Coach 1961-89; Bsktbl Coach 1968-79, 1983-86; Track Coach 1961-; Cross Cntry 1961-63; OEA Madison Ed Assn (Treas, Pres) 1957-61; OEA Ontario Teachers Assn Treas 1965-70; AFT, Ontario Fed of Teachers Treas 1975-88; *home:* 3612 Milligan Rd Mansfield OH 44906

GIFFORD, PATRICIA MARIE, English Teacher; *b:* Massillon, OH; *m:* Charles J.; *c:* Brian, Scott; *ed:* (BS) Eng, Kent St Univ 1969; Additional Cert Learning Disabilities & Behavior Disorders; *cr:* Eng Teacher Jackson Local Schls 1971-77; LD Tutor 1982-84, Eng Teacher 1984- Massillon City Schls; *ai:* Spelling Bee Chm; Chemical Awareness Prgm Facilitator; Massillon Ed Assn, NEA, OH Cncl of Eng Teachers; *home:* 6307 Harbor Dr NW Canton OH 44718

GIGANTE, DOMENICO ANTONIO, Italian/French Teacher; *b:* Bari, Italy; *m:* Denise Marie Palomeque; *c:* Maria, Eduardo, Elsa; *ed:* (BA) Fr, Le Moyne 1977; (MA) Fr Lit, Syracuse Univ 1981; Italian Stud, St Univ of NY 1984; *cr:* Fr Teacher Jamesville-De Witt Mid Sch 1978-79; Fr/Italian Teacher Henninger HS 1979-; *ai:* Fr & Italian Clubs; Soccer Coach 1982-83; CNY Italian Teachers Assn 1985-; Alliance Francaise Mem 1988-89; Italian Cultural Society Founding Mem 1983-84; Fr Foreign Lang Immersion Prgm 1989; Nom Best Teachers Excl in Teaching 1989-; *office:* Henninger HS 600 Robinson St Syracuse NY 13206

GIGLIO, MARSHA ZAMOSKY, Upper Elementary Teacher; *b:* Pittsburgh, PA; *m:* Michael Guy; *c:* Michael J.; *ed:* (BA) La Roche Coll 1971; (MS) Ed, Duquesne Univ 1977; Personal Advancement Cmptr Course; Continuing Religion Update Courses; *cr:* Elem Sch Teacher Diocese of Pittsburgh 1966-; *ai:* Art & Speech Upper Elem Moderator Clubs; Stu Cncl Newspaper Co-Moderator; NCEA.

GIGLIOTTI, LISA ANN, Science Chair & Teacher; *b:* Philadelphia, PA; *ed:* (BS) Bio, Neumann Coll 1982; Sci Ed, Temple Univ; IPS Course Boston Univ 1985; Cmptrs Scndry Ed, PhiLadelphia Coll of Textiles & Sci 1988-; *cr:* Phys Sci Teacher Cardinal O Hara HS 1983-84; Math Teacher Dickinson Bus Sch 1988; Phys Sci/Bio Teacher 1984-, Sci Chairperson 1988- St Maria Goretti HS; *ai:* Yrbk Moderator; Faculty Coordinating Comm; NCEA, NACST, Assn of Cath Teachers, NABT; Nom Tandy Technology Outstanding Teacher 1990; *office:* St Maria Goretti HS 10th& Moore St Philadelphia PA 19148

GILBEAU, JEANETTE BARNES, Retired Teacher; *b:* Vernon, TX; *m:* Kenneth W.; *c:* Janis A. Lassner; *ed:* (BA) Ed, San Jose St 1964; Grad Stud; *cr:* Teacher Union Sch Dist 1964-81; *ai:* San Jose Museum of Art Lets Look at Art Prgm Docent; Visit Classrooms Teaching Art Appreciation; Amer Assn of Univ Women.

GILBERT, AMELIA RAMBO, Fifth Grade Teacher; *b:* Martin, TN; *m:* Ronald J.; *c:* Jim, Brian; *ed:* (BS) Elem Ed, 1967, (MS) Curr/Instruction, 1980 Univ of TN Martin; Grad Stud; *cr:* Spec Ed Teacher Memphis City Schls 1967-68; 3rd Grade Teacher Hopkinsville City Schls 1970-71; 5th Grade Teacher Weakley Cty Schls-Dresdem Elem 1971-: *ai:* United Teaching Profession; NEA, TN Ed Assn, Weakley Cty Ed Assn 1971-, Lifetime Membership; VP Dresden Elem; TN Career Ladder Level II; *home:* Rt 2 Box 72 Sharon TN 38255

GILBERT, DEAN CRAIG, Biology Teacher/Sci Dept Chair; *b:* Long Beach, CA; *ed:* (BS) Biological Sci, Univ of CA Irvine 1974; (MAT) Biological Sci, CA St Univ Fullerton 1982; Grad Work Univ of CA Irvine, Pepperdine Univ; *cr:* 8th/9th Grade Sci Teacher/Stu Cncl Stephens Jr HS 1975-79; 7th/8th Grade Health/Sci Teacher Washington Jr HS 1975-76; Bio/Marine Bio/ Anatomy & Physiology Teacher Polytechnic HS 1978-86; Bio/ Marine Bio Teacher/Dept Chm Millikan HS 1986-; Health/Bio Instr Long Beach City Coll 1982-; *ai:* Spon Marine Bio Club; Dir Scope Sequence Coordination Sci Project; NSTA 1988-; NEA, CA Teachers Assn 1974-; LA Harbor Lodge Masons 1978-; Grant for Millikan HS Scope Sequence & Coordination Project; Honorable Mention for Role in Sci Dept Self Study/WASC-SDE Accrediation Report 1988-; *office:* R A Millikan HS 2800 Snowden Ave Long Beach CA 90815

GILBERT, JEAN H., Fourth Grade Teacher; *b:* Covington, KY; *m:* Douglas C.; *c:* Jeffrey, Jayne Chamberlin, Jennifer Hopkins, Janine; *ed:* (BS) Ed, Wright St Univ 1969; Guidance & Counseling Univ of Dayton; *cr:* 3rd Grade Teacher 1969-76, 4th Grade Teacher 1977-82, 6th Grade Teacher 1982-86, 4th Grade Teacher 1986- C F Holliday Elem; *ai:* West Carrollton Ed Assn Building Rep 1972-76, 1985-87; OH ed Assn, NEA; Nom Ashland Oil Teacher Achievement Awd 1988-89; Univ of Dayton W OH Ed Assn Teacher of Yr 1989; Dayton Daily News Teacher in Excl 1988; Significant Teacher Awd West Carrollton 1986-89; *office:* C F Holliday Sch 4100 South Dixie Dayton OH 45439

GILBERT, MARGARET MEAD, Teacher of Gifted Education; *b:* Vienna, Austria; *c:* Megan Meyercord; *ed:* (BBA) Advertising 1948, (MED) Elem Ed 1952 Southern Meth Univ; Endorsement in Gifted Ed TX Womans Univ/Univ of TX Austin; *cr:* 5th Grade Teacher 1967-78, Gifted Ed Teacher 1978- Dallas ISD; *ai:* Laureate Screening Chairperson-Julius Dorsey Elem Sch; Gifted Cadre I -DISD; Lambda Delta Pi; Phi Chi Theta Alumnae Pres 1950-; Delta Kappa Gamma 1975-; Natl Assn for Gifted Children 1988-; Phi Sigma Alpha Pres 1985-87 Woman of Yr 1986; Alpha Phi; DISD Teaching Excl Awd 1975; Teacher of Yr Julius Dorsey Elem Sch 1989-; *office:* Julius Dorsey Elem Sch 133 N St Augustine Dr Dallas TX 75217

GILBERT, MARIE BRADY, Transitional Teacher; *b:* New Haven, CT; *w:* Harold Joseph (dec); *c:* Robin Gilbert O Rourke; *ed:* (BS) Elem Ed, S CT St 1967; Rdng, S CT St; *cr:* 3rd-5th Grade Teacher Ferrara Sch; Trasitional Teacher R Vernon Hays Deer Run Sch; *ai:* NEA, CEA, EHEA; CT St Rdng Grant 1976; *home:* 300 Stepstone Hill Rd Guilford CT 06437

GILBERT, MARY JANE, English Teacher; *b:* Jacksonville, FL; *m:* Scott Jon; *c:* Robby, Chris; *ed:* (BA) Eng, Jacksonville Univ 1974; *cr:* 8th Grade Eng Teacher San Jose Cath Grade Sch 1974-77; Eng Teacher Orange Park HS 1977-81, Middleburg HS 1981-; *ai:* Teaching Eng Honors III & II; Wrestling Team Aerobics Coach; Cheerleading, Newpaper, Literary Magazine, NHS Spon; *office:* Middleburg HS 3750 C R 220 Middleburg FL 32068

GILBERT, PATRICIA PRESTON, Principal; *b:* Paris, TX; *m:* Thomas L.; *c:* Norman, Juliet Egler, Lori; *ed:* (BA) Eng/His, 1971, (MED) Elem Ed, 1974 E TX St Univ; Counseling & Mid-Management Cert E TX St Univ; *cr:* Eng Teacher Delmar Ind Sch Dist 1969-72; Elem Ed Teacher De Soto Ind Sch Dist 1972-77; Cnslr Midlothian Ind Sch Dist 1977-88; Prin Greenville Ind Sch Dist 1988-; *ai:* Richardson Region X Educl Consultant; Phi Delta Kappa 1989-; ASCD 1980-; PTA Lifetime Membership; *office:* Bowie Sch 6000 Stonewall Greenville TX 75401

GILBERT, ROXANE, English Teacher; *b:* Chicago, IL; *ed:* (BA) Journalism Ed, N IL Univ 1979; (MA) Rdng, N IL Univ 1989; Laubach Literacy Trng; *cr:* Eng Teacher 1979-, Chapter I Rdng Teacher 1988-89 Zion-Benton Township HS; *ai:* Scndry Rdng League 1987-; IL Assn of Teachers of Eng; Intnl Rdng League; Kenosha Literacy Assn 1989-; Writing Across Curr Co-Coord; *office:* Zion-Benton Township HS 3901 W 21st St Zion IL 60099

GILBERT, SHARON BRUNT, Fourth Grade Teacher; *b:* Bay City, TX; *m:* Bevil Eugene; *c:* Brent, Corey; *ed:* (BS) Elem Ed, Sam Houston St Coll 1964; *cr:* 2nd Grade Teacher 1964-67, 4th Grade Teacher 1968- Angleton Ind Sch Dist; *ai:* 4th Grade Northside Head Teacher; Compensatory Rdng Teacher; Inservice Dev Comm; Project Graduation Entertainment Co-Chairperson; TSTA (Faculty Rep, Life Mem); TCTA; Delta Kappa Gamma 1st VP; Angleton Child Study Club Pres; Wildcat Booster Club; Second Baptist Church (Sunday Sch Teacher, Nominating Comm Dir, Sunday Sch Cncl); *home:* 602 Pecan Estates Angleton TX 77515

GILBERTSEN, KAYRENE MARIE, Correspondence Ed Director; *b:* Portland, OR; *m:* Gary Lee; *c:* Karlin, Gabrielle; *ed:* (BA) Elem Ed, Wellington Teachers Coll 1966; *cr:* 1st Grade Teacher Bluff Elem 1967-70; Kndgtn Teacher Shold Sch 1977-84; Cty Commissioner Wahkiakum Cty 1985-88; Correspondence Ed Dir Calvert Sch Prgm; *ai:* Ombudsman Coord; *home:* 206 E Sunny Sands Rd Cathlamet WA 98612

GILBERTSON, DONNA (SCHMIDT), Sixth Grade Teacher; *b:* Riceville, IA; *m:* Chester J.; *c:* Daniel, Theodore; *ed:* (BAED) Elem Ed, Seattle Pacific Univ 1958; Upper IA Univ, Drake Univ, Bemidji St Univ, Univ of N IA; *cr:* Rural Sch Teacher Howard & Mitchell Counties 1951-56; Elem Teacher Riceville Ind Sch 1959-61; 3rd Grade Teacher Lakewood Elem 1958-59, Mason City Ind Sch 1961-62; 6th Grade Teacher Riceville Cmmty Sch 1962-67; 3rd Grade Teacher Allamakee Cmmty Sch 1967-69; 3rd/ 6th Grade Teacher Riceville Cmmty Sch 1969-; *ai:* Talented & Gifted Selection Comm; NEA Life Mem; Riceville Ed Assn Pres 1970-71; Howard Cty Ed Assn Pres 1963; Riceville Lib Bd Secy 1974-78; Riceville Wa-Tan-Ye 1977-79; Alpha Delta Kappa 1974-79; *home:* 1904 5th Ave SE Austin MN 55912

GILBREATH, BARBARA FASELER, Middle School Counselor; *b:* Hondo, TX; *m:* Tommy Dee; *c:* Dee A. Gilbreath Haffner, Karen F.; *ed:* (BA) Eng/Lib Sci, Sul Ross St Univ 1965; (MA) Prof Counseling, Univ of TX Tyler 1987; *cr:* Eng Teacher Andress HS 1965-67; Librarian Kemp HS 1969-70; Eng Teacher Lamar Jr HS & Snyder HS 1971-73; Coll Bookstore Mgr Lubbock Chrstn Coll 1973-76; Librarian 1978-89, Cnslr 1989- Stewart Mid Sch; *ai:* TX Prof Educators Assn 1984-; Phi Delta Kappa, TX Assn for Counseling & Dev 1989-; Sch Cnslrs Awareness Network Chairperson 1989-; *office:* Stewart Mid Sch 2800 W Shaw St Tyler TX 75701

GILBREATH, JACKIE BEAIRD, Speech-Drama Teacher; *b:* Moline, IL; *ed:* (BS) Speech/Drama, North TX St Univ 1961; (MA) Speech/Drama, Stephen F Austin St Univ 1968; *cr:* Speech-Drama Teacher Wheeler Jr HS 1962-63, Floydada HS 1963-66, Edna HS 1966-67; Speech Teacher AK St Univ 1968-69; Speech-Drama Teacher North Shore HS 1969-74, North Shore Mid Sch 1974-87, Galena Park HS 1987-90; *ai:* Spon Intnl Thespian Society/Drama Club; Coach Univ Interscholastic League Events; Educl Drama Assn Events; Direct 3 Act Play/One Act Play/Talent Show; Intnl Thespian Society 1988-; TX Forensic Assn 1988-; *office:* Galena Park H S 1000 Keene Galena Park TX 77547

GILBREATH, LYNN ANN, Biology Teacher/Coach; *b:* Slaton, TX; *ed:* (BS) Bio, W TX St Univ 1985; *cr:* Life Sci Teacher/Coach Stanton Jr HS 1986-88; Bio Teacher/Coach Hereford HS 1988-; *ai:* Asst Vlybl, 9th Grade Girls Bsktbl, Track Coach; TX Classroom Teacher Assn 1986-88; Eastern Stars; Vlybl Tm Dist Runner-Up 1988; Dist Co-Champion & Area Runner-Up 1989; *home:* 620 Avenue J Hereford TX 79045

GILCHRIST, MICHAEL REED, Science Supervisor; *b:* Montgomery, AL; *m:* Mary John Amason; *c:* Sarah M., Jennifer L., Thomas R.; *ed:* (BS) Bio, TX Chrstn Univ 1974; (BS) General Sci, Auburn Univ 1977; (MED) Bio, AUM 1980; (MED) General Sci, Auburn Univ 1984; Working on Doctorate & Toxicology Specialist, Auburn Univ; *cr:* Toxicologist Smith Kline & French Labs 1975-76; Sci Teacher Jefferson Davis HS 1977-89; Sci Supvr/Teacher in Residence Auburn Univ 1989-; *ai:* Jeff Davis HS Key Club Adv 1981-89; Phi Delta Kappa Treas 1986-; AETS; Amer Chemical Society; NEA Faculty Rep 1981-83; Montgomery Cty Sci Teacher of Yr 1985; Teacher-in-Residence Montgomery Sch System 1989-; *office:* Auburn Univ Montgomery 7300 University Dr Montgomery AL 36117

GILDAY, FREDERICK JOHN, Mathematics Teacher; *b:* Cherry Valley, NY; *ed:* (BA) Math, Hartwick Coll 1962; Math, Oneonta St Univ 1963-67; Inservice Micro-Cmptrs 1981; TESA Inservice 1989-; *cr:* Math Teacher Cherry Valley Cntrl 1962-63, Ft Plain Cntrl 1963-; *ai:* Staff Dev Changing to Heterogeneous Grouping Comm; *home:* 44 Reid St Fort Plain NY 13339

GILDEN, PATRICIA GAGNE, Advanced Placement Teacher; *b:* Franklin, NH; *c:* Michael, Christine; *ed:* (BA) Ed/Fr, Oglethorpe Univ 1968; (MAT) Fr/Poly Sci, GA St Univ 1973; *cr:* Fr Teacher Sandy Springs HS 1968-74; Prgm Dir of Gifted & Talented Riverwood Hs 1974-77; Dept Chairperson/Foreign Lang Teacher Crestwood HS 1977-82; Advanced Placement His & Government Teacher Milton HS 1982-; *ai:* NOW Chapter, Young Democrats, Amnesty Intnl Spon; S Center for Intnl Stud 1990; STAR Teacher 1972-73; Foreign Lang Teacher of Yr 1976; Teacher Honors Prgm 1988, 1990; *office:* Milton HS 86 School Ave Alpharetta GA 30201

GILDEN, ROBIN ELISSA, Fourth Grade Teacher; *b:* Albany, NY; *ed:* (BS) Elem Ed, Penn St Univ 1972; *cr:* 1st Grade Teacher 1972-76, 2nd/3rd Grade Teacher 1976-81, 4th Grade Teacher 1981 Mc Kee Elem; *ai:* Stu Cncl & Yrbk Adv; Childrens Hospital Annual Fund Drive Adv; Building Goals, Act 78, Testing, Grading, Drug & Alcohol Abuse Prevention, Math Curr, Stu Assistance Prgm Comm; NEA; PA St Ed Assn Building Rep 1984-86; PTA 1972-; PA St Alumni Assn 1972-; Speakers Bureau 1987-; Certificate of Particaption in NASAs Teacher in Space Prgm; Nom for Thanks to Teachers Excl Recognition; Mastery Teaching Certificate; *office:* Mckee Elem Sch Rt 978 Oakdale PA 15071

GILES, ANN STIVERS, Fifth Grade Teacher; *b:* Owensboro, KY; *m:* George Hulon III; *c:* Thomas S., Franklin T.; *ed:* (BS) Elem Ed, 1972, (MA) Elem Ed, Murray St Univ; Admin, Murray St Univ; *cr:* Teacher Cntrl Elem 1972-73, Sinking Fork Elem 1973-74, Southern Chrstn Elem 1974-; *ai:* Sch Chm Kroger Food for Thought; Cty In Service & Promotion Remediation Comm; Chrstn Cty Ed Assn 1973-; KY Ed Assn, NEA 1972-; *home:* 1573 Darnell Rd Herndon KY 42236

GILES, GEORGE HULON, Mathematics Teacher; *b:* Hopkinsville, KY; *m:* Ann Stivers; *c:* Scott, Frank; *ed:* (BS) Math, 1972, (MS) Math Teaching, 1978, (MS) Admin/Supervision, 1980 Murray St Univ; *cr:* Math Teacher Hopkinsville HS 1973, Greenwood Jr HS 1973-80, Richview Mid Sch 1980-; *ai:* Math Team Coach; NEA, TEA 1973-; Mathcounts St Coach 1987; Clarksville Montgomery Cty Teacher of Yr 1987-; *office:* Richview Mid Sch 2350 Memorial Dr Clarksville TN 37043

GILFILLEN, RITA (ENDERS), Science, Math Teacher; *b:* Oak Park, IL; *m:* Vernon; *c:* Rex, Ginger Davidson, Mindy, Molly; *ed:* (BS) Ed - Magna Cum Laude, 1971, (MS) Ed, 1978 Wright St Univ; *cr:* 1st Grade Teacher Miami East 1971; 6th-8th Grade Teacher Fairlawn Local 1971-; *ai:* Jr HS Chrldr Adv; OH Acad of Sci Dist 10 Cty Rep 1983-89; Kappa Delta Pi Honor Society. Phi Eta Tau Honor Society 1969-; Governors Awd for Excl in Sci 1987; Jennings Scholar 1986-87.

GILHOOLEY, JAMES W., Vice Principal; *b:* Scranton, PA; *m:* Mary Higgins; *c:* Jamie, Chris, Matthew; *ed:* (BS) Elem Ed, Bloomsburg Univ 1971; (MS) Mid Sch Ed, Marywood Coll 1978; (EDD) Ed Admin, Univ of PA Philadelphia 1985; *cr:* 8th Grade Sci Teacher St Paul Sch 1972-73; 6th-8th Grade Teacher Scranton Sch Dist 1973-89; Vice Prin W Scranton Intermediate Sch 1989-; *ai:* PA Cncl of Math Teachers 1986-; Phi Delta Kappa 1978-; *office:* W Scranton Intermediate Sch Fellows St & Parrott Ave Scranton PA 18504

GILL, CAROLINE RUTH (DAWSEY), 4th Grade Teacher; *b:* Mansfield, OH; *c:* Stephen M.; *ed:* (BA) His, Coll of Wooster 1976; Univ of Akron Ashland Univ; *cr:* 5th Grade Teacher 1976-84; 4th Grade Teacher 1985 Maple Street Elem Sch; *ai:* Coach 4th Grade Sci Olympiad Team; Outdoor Ed; NEA/OEA Bldg Rep 1987-89; Mothers Study Club I Treas 1988-89; Amer Assn of Univ Women Corresponding Secy 1986-87; Martha Holden Jennings Writing Seminar; East OH Gas Co Sunshine Energy Contest; 1989 Teacher of Yr; *office:* Maple Street Elem Sch 215 Maple St Orrville OH 44667

GILL, DANIEL PATRICK, Fifth Grade Teacher; *b:* Oswego, NY; *m:* Darlene R. Withers; *c:* Daniel, Andrew, Erin; *ed:* (AS) Sci, Auburn Comm Coll 1968; (BS) Elem Ed, St Univ NY Oswego 1971; Grad Work St Univ NY Oswego; *cr:* 5th Grade Teacher Cuyler Elem Sch 1971-; *ai:* AV & Sci Coord.

GILL, DAVID P., Mathematics Teacher; *b:* Johnson City, NY; *m:* Christine A. Edson; *c:* Chelsey; *ed:* (BS) Scndry Ed/Math, Univ of Scranton 1985; (MSED) Scndry Ed/Math, SUNY Binghamton 1989; *cr:* Math Teacher Binghamton City Sch Dist 1985-86; Chenango Valley Cntrl Schls 1986-; Binghamton City Sch Dist 1986-89; *ai:* Boys Varsity Swim Team Coach 1986-; NYSUT AFL-CIO Delegate 1989-; Empire St Challenger Schlsp for Teachers; *office:* Chenango Valley Jr/Sr HS 768 Chenango St Binghamton NY 13901

GILL, DEE GIFFORD, High School Science Teacher; *b:* Amarillo, TX; *m:* Susan Creathbaum; *c:* Patrick, Shawn, Heidi; *ed:* (BS) Bio/Chem, W TX St Univ 1974; HS Sci Teacher Carver Learning Center 1974-79; Sci Dept Chm Palo Duro HS 1979-85; Sci Teacher Highland Park HS 1985-; *ai:* Math & Sci Club; Academic Team Competition; Univ Interscholastic League; *home:* 1601 Hillcrest Amarillo TX 79106

GILL, GARY, Soc Sci Dept Chair/Teacher; *b:* Thomaston, GA; *m:* Lori Warren; *c:* Abbey, Briton; *ed:* Working Towards Specialist Ed, GA Coll; *cr:* Teacher 1980-, Soc Stud Dept Chm 1987- Upson Cty HS; *ai:* Key Club Spon; Jr HS Ftbl Coach; Faculty Grievance, Attendance Hearing, Media Center Comm; Upson Historical Society, Sons of Confederate Veterans; Natl Bicentennial Competition System Contact; *office:* Upson Cty HS 101 Holstun Dr Thomaston GA 30286

GILL, GRETCHEN MOORE, 8th Grade Science Teacher; *b:* Rochester, NY; *c:* Charles J., Jonathan W.; *ed:* (AA) Phys Therapy, Endicott Jr Coll 1971; (BS) Health/Phys Ed/General Sci, VA Commonwealth Univ 1973; Grad Courses in Learning Disabilities, Ed; *cr:* 8th Grade Sci Teacher Huguenot Acad 1973-77; 5th-7th Grade Sci Teacher S Hill Acad 1977-78, 1980-81, 1984-85; 8th/11th/12th Grade Eng Teacher 1985-88, K-10th Grade Phys Ed Instr 1988-89, 8th-10th Grade Phys Ed Instr/8th Grade Sci Teacher 1989- Brunswick Acad; *ai:* 10th Grade Class Spon; SADD & Prom Comm; Asst T-Ball Coach; Assn of VA Academies 1973-78, 1980-81, 1984-; S Hill Jr Womens Club (Treas 1979-81) 1977-82, Outstanding Young Woman of Yr 1982; S Hill United Meth Church (Chancel Choir 1982-, Handbell Choir 1986-); *home:* 907 Plank Rd South Hill VA 23970

GILL, J. SCOTT, Science Department Chair; *b:* Dubuque, IA; *m:* Nora M Schumacker; *c:* Elizabeth, Adam; *ed:* (BA) Sociology, 1973, (BA) Sci Ed, 1976 Univ of Dubuque; Psych, Math; *cr:* Sci Teacher Jefferson Jr HS 1978-; *ai:* Camping & Backpacking Club Spon; IA Hunter Safety Course Spon; 7th Grade Girls Vlybl & Bsktbl Coach; IA Acad of Sci 1988-; BSA (Advancement Comm 1987- Scoutmaster 1973-84); Red Cross First Aid Instr 1978-; Sch Effectiveness Team Mem 1989-; *office:* Jefferson Jr HS 1105 Althauser Dubuque IA 52001

GILL, JEFF W., Mathematics Teacher; *b:* East Liverpool, OH; *m:* Kathy R. Lindner; *ed:* (BA) His, 1983, (MS) Math, 1990 Youngstown St Univ; *cr:* Math Teacher Lisbon Exempted Village HS 1983-87, Southern Local HS 1987-; *ai:* Asst Bsktbl Coach; Stu Cncl Adv; Supts Advisory Comm; Amer Mathematical Society, Pi Mu Epsilon 1989-; *office:* Southern Local Sch Dist 38095 State Rt 39 Salineville OH 43945

GILL, JO (MC DOUGALL), Science Teacher; *b:* Sheldon, IA; *m:* Bruce; *ed:* (BS) Ed, Chadron St Coll 1984; Quest Trng Seminar 1987; Post Grad Courses; *cr:* Teacher West Jr HS 1984-; *ai:* Track; Cheerleading; Pep Club; Talent Show; Sci Fair; Chemical Action Team; Building Improvement Comm; Sigma Delta Nu.

GILL, JOYCE ANN, 6th Grade Teacher; *b:* Akron, OH; *m:* Charles Robert; *c:* Dianne, Steven, Erica, Shannon; *ed:* (BA) Elem Ed, Univ of FL Gainesville 1967; Kent St Univ, Univ of Akron; *cr:* 4th Grade Teacher Northfield Schls 1967-68; Substitute/4th-6th Grade Teacher 1968-77, Rdng/LD Tutor 1978-80 Cuyahoga Falls Schls; 6th Grade Teacher Bolich Mid Sch 1983-; *ai:* 6th Grade Math Team Coach; Kappa Kappa Iota (VP 1976-77, Pres 1977-78); Cuyahoga Falls Ed Assn Bldg Rep; ETC All Amer Youth Show Choir Gala Chm 1988-.

GILL, MARIA MARLA, Biology Teacher; *b:* Newnan, GA; *m:* Tim; *c:* John; *ed:* (BS) Bio, Shorter Coll 1980; (MED) Phys Ed, W GA Coll 1984; *cr:* Bio Teacher Trion HS 1981-82, Douglas Cty Comprehensive HS 1985-; *ai:* Douglas Cty HS Renovation Comm; Futurescape Co-Spon; Prof Assn of GA Educators, Douglas Cty Sci Teachers Assn; Amer Red Cross Volunteer; *office:* Douglas Cty Comprehensive HS 8705 Campbellton St Douglasville GA 30134

GILL, MARTIN KENT, Junior HS English Teacher; *b:* Montrose, CO; *m:* Lois Haverland; *c:* Laurie, Kathleen, Charles; *ed:* (BA) Distributed Eng/His/Ed, Univ of CO 1950; (MED) Ed, Univ of OR 1954; (CAS) Eng Ed, Harvard Univ 1969; NDEA Summer Inst, Univ of CA Berkeley 1964; Bay Area Writing Project, Univ of CA Berkeley 1976; *cr:* Jr HS Teacher Del Norte Scndry Sch 1950-51; 7th Grade Teacher Goshen Elem Sch 1951-53; Soc Living Teacher Cal Young Jr HS 1953-58; Eng/His Teacher Davis Jr HS 1958-88; Lecturer/Supvr Stu Teachers Univ of CA Davis 1965-66; *ai:* Local Teachers Assn, NEA Affiliate, NCTE; City of Davis City Cncl Mayor 1964-68; Sierra Club (Dir 1972-78, Pres 1974-76), Colby Awd 1972; Experienced Teacher Fellow Harvard 1968-69; Co-Author Article NCTE 1986; CA St Dept of Ed Writing Dev Team Mem; Area III Eng Project Fellow 1963-69; *home:* PO Box 115 Camp Sherman OR 97730

GILL, PAMELA SIEGER, Chapter I Dir/Elem Rdng Coord; *b:* Rochester, PA; *m:* Robert John; *ed:* (BS) Ed, PA St Univ 1981; (MS) Ed, Westminster Coll 1985; *cr:* 1st Grade Teacher 1982, 3rd Grade Teacher 1983-85, Rdng Coord 1985- Rochester Area Sch Dist; Summer Instr Westminster Coll Grad Prgm 1987-; *ai:* Writing to Read Prgm & Summer Rdng Prgm Coord; Parent Volunteer Prgm Dir; Instructional Steering Service Comm; Beaver Cty Rdng Cncl Exec Bd, Delta Kappa Gamma Social Chm, Kappa Delta Pi; Intnl Rdng Assn, PA Assn Fed Prgm Coord; Rochester United Meth Church Admin Bd; PA Dept of Ed Chapter I Monitor; Have Monitored Sch Dist Across St; *office:* Rochester Area Sch Dist 540 Reno St Rochester PA 15074

GILL, ROBERT J., Learning Disability Teacher; *b:* Wilkes-Barre, PA; *m:* Maribel Rosales; *ed:* (BA) Philosophy, Passionist Monastic Seminary Coll 1969; (MA) Elem Ed, Seton Hall Univ 1971; (EDD) Elem Ed, Rutgers Univ 1982; Learning Disability Teacher Consultant, Kean Coll of NJ 1976; *cr:* Lang Art Teacher Jonas Salk Mid Sch 1970-72, 1982-89; Resourse Teacher Old Bridge Township Public Schls 1973-76; Part-Time Lecturer Rutgers Univ 1986-; Learning Disability Teacher/Consultant Old Bridge Township Public Schls 1976-82, 1989-; *ai:* Girls Mid Sch Bsktbl Coach; Newspaper Adv; Lang Art & Eng Curr Comm; NCTE, Assn of Learning Consultants; Spotswood Township Recreation Comm; *office:* John Glenn Sch Cindy St Old Bridge NJ 08857

GILL, TERESA WHEELER, 7th Grade Mathematics Teacher; *b:* Mayfield, KY; *m:* James Alan; *c:* J. Alan, Tyler; *ed:* (BS) Elem Ed, Mid Tn St Univ 1975; Intermediate Cmptr Sci 1982; *cr:* 7th/8th Grade Math/Sci Teacher Southside Sch 1976-77; 8th Grade Math Teacher 1978-79, 1980-81, 6th Grade Math/Lang/Soc Stud Teacher 1979-80, 7th Grade Math Teacher 1981- Harris Mid Sch; *ai:* 7th Grade Teachers Chm; Math Dept Comm Mem; Mid Tn St Univ Math Contest Coach; Tn Ed Assn, Bedford Cty Ed Assn, NEA 1978; Daughters of Amer Revolution Conservation Comm Chm 1987-; 1st Baptist Church Kitchen Comm Chairperson; Baptist Young Women (Treas, Mission Coord) 1988-; *office:* Sidney W Harris Mid Sch 400 Elm St Shelbyville TN 37160

GILLAM, GREGORY ALAN, Science Teacher; *b:* Bay City, MI; *m:* Linda Mahin; *c:* Mike, Hilary, Kristy A., Justin; *ed:* Assoc Lang, Delta Coll 1967; (BS) Bio, 1971, (MA) Recreation/Outdoor Ed, 1974 Cntrl MI Univ; Human Genetics, Limnology, Outdoor Ed; *cr:* Bio Instr Flushing HS 1971-; *ai:* NABT 1990; MI Sci Teacher Assn 1986; NSF Grant 1989; MI St Bd of Ed Grant; *office:* Flushing HS 5039 Deland Rd Flushing MI 48433

GILLAM, KENNETH, Math/Physics Teacher; *b:* East Chicago, IN; *m:* Jane Leonard; *c:* Kenneth M., Shannon Perry, Scott D.; *ed:* (BS) Physics, Purdue Univ 1968; IL Institute of Technology; Toledo Univ; Southwest MO St Univ; *cr:* Research Engr Universal Atlas Cement 1968-71, Research Mgr Medusa Cement 1972-80; Consultant 1980-87; Math/Physics Teacher Dora RIII 1987-; *ai:* Jr Class Spon; Coach-Boys & Girls Bsktbl Grades 5th-8th; Sci Fair Judge; Dist Church Conference Pres 1988-; Research Paper for Masonry Society 1978; *home:* HC 61 Box 712 Caulfield MO 65626

GILLAND, ANGELA POINDEXTER, English Teacher; *b:* Memphis, TN; *m:* Wayne O.; *c:* Angela C.; *ed:* (BS) Ed, Memphis St Univ 1980; Math & Span Endorsements; *cr:* Eng Teacher Collierville HS 1980-81, Dogwood Elem 1981-87, Germantown HS 1987-; *ai:* Cheerleading Spon; NCTE, NEA, TEA, SCEA, Kappa Delta Pi 1980-; Germantown Baptist Church 1985-; Foreign Lang Inst Grant Memphis St Univ 1988; *office:* Germantown HS 7653 Poplar Pike Germantown TN 38138

GILLASPIE, JANICE BRYANT, Mathematics Teacher/Dept Chair; *b:* Madisonville, KY; *m:* Robert Meredith; *c:* Janna B., Carrie; *ed:* (BS) Math, Union Coll 1968; (MA) Scndry Ed, Murray St Univ 1976; (Rank I) Scndry Ed, 1982; *cr:* Math Teacher Middlesboro HS 1968-70; *ai:* Kenlake Cncl of Teachers of Math 1974-; KY Assn of Gifted Ed 1990; MAPCO Teacher of Yr; Webster Cty HS Teacher of Yr.

GILLERN, BURDELLA BITTERMAN, Third Grade Teacher; *b:* Jamestown, ND; *w:* Eugene Wm. (dec); *c:* Belinda M.; *ed:* (BS) Elem Ed, Valley City St 1966; Grad Stud Geneseo St, St Univ NY Geneseo; *cr:* 3rd Grade Teacher Mc Kinley Sch 1966-68, Nellie Muir Sch 1968-69; 4th Grade Teacher Red Jacket Sch 1969-; *ai:* Red Jacket Faculty Assn (VP 1975-76, Building Rep, Negotiating Team) 1988; Luth Church Educl Ministry (Mem, Chairperson) 1980-; *office:* Red Jacket Cntrl Elem Sch Lehigh Ave Shortsville NY 14548

GILLESPIE, EMILY H., Biology Teacher; *b:* Commerce, GA; *m:* Gary H.; *c:* Shane; *ed:* (BS) Sci Ed, Brenau Coll 1969; (MED) Bio, N GA Coll; *cr:* Teacher McEver Elem Sch 1969-70, South Hall HS 1970-73, Johnson HS 1973-80, E Hall HS 1980-; *ai:* Sr Class Adv; PAGE; STAR Teacher 1985; *office:* E Hall HS 3534 E Hall Rd Gainesville GA 30505

GILLESPIE, KATHRYN LEE, Chemistry Teacher; *b:* Beckley, WV; *ed:* (BS) Ed, Bob Jones Univ 1977; *cr:* Dean/Teacher Dade Chrstn Schls 1977-80, Calvary Chrstn Schls 1980-; *ai:* Beta Club & Stu Cncl Spon; Girls Var Soccer Coach; NSTA 1985-; FL Assn of Chrstn Schls & Colls 1977-; *office:* Calvary Baptist Chrstn Sch 631 S Dillard St Winter Garden FL 34787

GILLESPIE, LINDA, English Teacher; *b:* Brooklyn, NY; *m:* Edward; *ed:* (BA) Eng, St Johns Univ 1968; (MS) Eng, Long Island Univ C W Post 1975; *cr:* Eng Teacher Sheepshead Bay HS 1968-73; 7th/8th Grade Eng Teacher St Martin of Tours 1977-79; Eng Teacher Maria Regina Dist HS 1979-84; Eng Dept Adjunct Teacher C W Post 1984-85; Eng Teacher St Anthonys 1985-; *ai:* Asst Coach Molloy Coll Equestrian Team; *office:* St Anthonyis HS 275 Wolf Hill Rd South Huntington NY 11746

GILLESPIE, NORMA R., First Grade Teacher; *b:* Leckie, WV; *m:* Frank R.; *c:* Charles; *ed:* (BS) Scndry Ed/Speech/Lib Sci, Concord Coll 1971; WV Coll of Grad Stud; Mc Dowell Cty Teachers Acad 1989; Elem Ed Certificate NTE Score; *cr:* Math Teacher Anawalt Elem 1970-71; 4th Grade Teacher Superior Elem 1971-72; 1st Grade Teacher Anawalt Elem 1972-; *ai:* WV Ed Assn, NEA 1970-; Mercer Cty Soccer League (Chm Bluefield Comm 1987-, Cty Secy 1986-88); *office:* Anawalt Elem Sch Box 230 Anawalt WV 24808

GILLESPIE, ROBERT NICHOLAS, Social Studies/English Teacher; *b:* Houston, TX; *m:* Tracy L. Schleper; *c:* Padraic, Timothy; *ed:* (BA) His, Coll of St Thomas 1969; Grad Prgm Ed, Coll of St Thomas; Grad Stud Poly Sci, Univ of Houston; *cr:* Teacher/Coach Marian HS 1974-78, Mt Carmel HS 1978-84, Westbury HS 1985-86, Florence HS 1986-; *ai:* UIL Spon; Lincoln-Douglas Debate Coach; Head Coach Boys Track Team, Cross Cntry Team; FISD Career Ladder Comm Mem; Florence HS Faculty Schlsp & Academic Advisory Comm; THSCA Mem 1974-; TCIL Girls Track Coach of Yr 1978; Mt Carmel NHS Teacher of Yr 1983; Univ of Houston Teaching Assistantship in Poly Sci 1984; Univ Schlsp for Grad Stud Marquette Univ 1969; *office:* Florence HS PO Box 488 Florence TX 76527

GILLETTE, GRACE SCHNIRRING, 2nd Grade Teacher; *b:* Waltham, MN; *m:* Robert Lowell; *c:* Keith Lowell; *ed:* (BS) Elem Ed, Winona St Univ 1960; *cr:* Elem Teacher Hayfield Cmmty Schls; *ai:* Hayfield Ed Assn Treas 1978-82; St MN Sch Bd Assn Dodge Cty Teacher of Yr 1980; Brownsdale Public Lib Bd Pres 1989-; *home:* RR 1 Box 151 Brownsdale MN 55918

GILLHAM, HARRIETT MC DANIEL, English Teacher; *b:* Jacksonville, FL; *m:* David G.; *ed:* (BA) Eng, La Grange Coll 1976; (MED) Eng/Ed, W GA Coll 1983; *cr:* Eng Teacher Douglas Cty HS 1976-85, South Cobb HS 1985-; *office:* South Cobb HS 1920 Clay Rd Austell GA 30001

GILLIAM, FLORENCE COLLINS, 5th Grade Teacher; *b:* Memphis, TN; *m:* Cleophls A.; *c:* Courtney A.; *ed:* (BS) Elem Ed, TN St Univ 1972; *cr:* Reservationist Amer Express 1972-74; Teacher Huges Elem 1974-80, Memphis Bd of Ed 1981-; *ai:* Soc Stud Textbook Comm; Newspaper in the Classroom Wkshp; Huntsville Space Center Field Trips; MEA, TEA, NEA 1973; 1st Baptist Church; GSA Troop Leader 1979-81; *home:* 770 Hale Rd Memphis TN 38116

GILLIAM, KERNIE, Social Studies Chair/Teacher; *m:* Jackie Lynn Welt; *ed:* (BS) Poly Sci, E MI Univ 1977; Counseling, Cntrl MI Univ; *cr:* Teacher Deerfield Public Schls 1977-79, Gladwin Public Schls 1979-; *ai:* Track & Cross Cntry Girls Coach; Track & Cross Cntry Team St Meet Winners; *office:* Gladwin HS 1400 N Spring Gladwin MI 48624

GILLIKIN, CAROL JONES, 5th Grade Teacher; *b:* Beaufort, NC; *m:* Frank S. Sr.; *c:* Frank S. Jr., Benjamin L.; *ed:* (BA) His/Phys Ed/Elem Ed, Atlantic Chrstn Coll 1959; *cr:* Teacher Windsor Woods Elem 20 yrs; Active Teacher 33 yrs; *ai:* Coord Spelling Bee Windsor Woods Sch; PTA; VBEA; VEA; NEA; Tidewater Cncl of Teachers of Math; Rdng Cncl of VA; Career Teacher 1980-83; Honorary Life Mem VA Congress of Parents & Teachers 1988; Mem Sch Self-Study Steering Comm 1976-77; *office:* Windsor Woods Elem Sch 233 Presidential Blvd Virginia Beach VA 23452

GILLILAN, JERRY WAYNE, Science Teacher; *b:* Boaz, AL; *ed:* (BS) Natural Sci, Lee Coll 1969; (MED) Biological Sci, UTC 1981; Doctor of Ed Admin Supervision, Univ of TN; *cr:* Sci Teacher/Dept Head Charleston HS 1970-85; Sci Teacher Bradley Jr HS 1985-87, Sardis HS 1988-; *ai:* ASCD, NSTA, NEA, AL Ed Assn; Ruritans 1979-85; Admin & Spec Ed Inservice Prgms on Cmptr Use; Presentation on Individualized Methods of Study for NSTA & NDN.

GILLINGHAM, DENNIS RAY, Attendance/Science Specialist; *b:* Vancouver, WA; *m:* Janet Ann Morrison; *c:* Matthew, Philip; *ed:* (BS) General Sci, WA St Univ 1969; (MED) Sci Ed, Univ of Portland 1974; Admin; *cr:* Teacher Tahoma Jr HS 1969-73, St Josephs Sch 1973-74, Shumway Jr HS 1974-76, Columbia River HS 1976-88; Vice Prin Fort Vancouver HS 1988-89; Sci Specialist Vancouver Sch Dist 1989-; *ai:* Ftbl & Bsktbl Coach; WA St Sci Teachers Assn 1988-; *office:* Vancouver Sch Dist #37 605 N Devine Rd Vancouver WA 98661

GILLINGS, GARY LEE, Social Studies Teacher; *b:* Prescott, MI; *m:* Barbara Jean O'Farrell; *c:* Cary, Keith, Kris; *ed:* (AA) Flint Comm Jr Coll 1966; (BA) His, Univ of MI 1968; Post Grad Work, Cntrl MI Univ; *cr:* Teacher Whittemore Prescott HS 1968-; *ai:* NHS & Sr Class Adv; NEA, MI Ed Assn 1968-; Whittemore-Prescott Ed Assn (VP, Pres 1989-) 1968-; MI Ed Assn Rep Assembly Delegate 1988-, Gold Apple Awd; *office:* Whittemore Prescott HS 6001 Mills Rd Whittemore MI 48770

GILLIS, CAROL ANN, Math Teacher/Dept Chairperson; *b:* Dover, OH; *m:* James R.; *c:* Brian J., Carrie A.; *ed:* (BA) Math/Scndry Ed, Walsh Coll 1974; (MS) Math/Scndry Ed, St Univ of NY Geneseo 1983; *cr:* Math Teacher Tuscarawas Cntrl Cath HS 1974-76; Math Teacher 1976-, Dept Head 1987- Nazareth Acad HS; *ai:* Yrbk Adv; NHS Faculty Cncl; Assn of Math Teachers of NY St 1986-; Awd for Excl in Teaching 1986; *office:* Nazareth Acad 1001 Lake Ave Rochester NY 14613

GILLIS, VERA ETLING, Kindergarten Teacher; *b:* Ravenna, OH; *m:* Carl; *ed:* (BS) Early Chldhd, Kent St Univ 1966; *cr:* Kndgtn/Head Start Teacher Streetboro-Wise Elem 1966-67; Southeast Primary 1967-89; *ai:* Pre-Sch Parents; Southeast Local Teachers Assn, Northeast OH Educators Assn, OH Ed Ass N, NEA; Various Church Groups.

GILLUM, FRANCES SANDERS, Social Studies Dept Chair; *b:* Ashland, KY; *m:* Robert Edward; *c:* Melinda E., John S., Catherine A.; *ed:* (BA) Elem Ed, Univ of KY 1968; Elem Ed, 1978, (Rank I) Elem Ed, E KY Univ 1988; *cr:* 1st Grade Teacher Crabb Sch 1968-69; Kndgtn Teacher Noche Buena Sch 1969-70; 3rd Grade Teacher Ferguson Elem 1976-78, Hopkins Elem 1978-84; 7th/8th Grade Math & Soc Stud Teacher Meece Mid Sch 1986-; *ai:* Jr BETA Spon; Washington DC Trip Coord; Delta Kappa Gamma, Kappa Delta Pi; *office:* Meece Mid Sch 210 Barnett St Somerset KY 42501

GILLUND, DENNIS LEE, English Teacher; *b:* Torrance, CA; *m:* Barbara Rome; *c:* Thomas, Jon; *ed:* (BS) Eng/Phys Ed, Valley City St Coll 1965; (MED) Eng/Phys Ed, Univ of NE Lincoln 1971; *cr:* Teacher/Coach Cokato Public Schls 1965-68, Wahpeton Sch of Sci 1969-70, Richfield Public Schls 1971-78, Rosemount Public Schls 1978-; *ai:* Girls Soccer, Boys Bsktbl, Track; Human Resources Comm; AFT, MFT 1978-; NEA, MEA 1971-78; MN Coaches Assn 1971-; *office:* Rosemount Sr HS 1445 Diamond Path Rosemount MN 55068

GILMAN, GREGORY JAY, Math/Computer Sci Teacher; *b:* Owatonna, MN; *ed:* (AA) Electronics Engineering Technology, Rochester Comm Coll 1982; (BA) Math Teaching 1986, (BS) Cmptr Sci 1986 Winona St Univ; Specialized Trng with Cmptr Networks; *cr:* Cmptr Operator Winona Natl Bank 1984-86; Houston Cty Group Home 1986; Cmptr Operator Dodge Cty ASCS 1986-87; Math/Cmptr Sci Instr/Cmptr Coord Lake City HS 1986-; *ai:* Lake City Math League Team 1987-, Track 1986-, Bsktbl 1986-87 Coach; Cmptr Coord 1986-; Jr Class Adv 1986-89; NCTM 1988-; Natl Inst of Certified Engineering Technicians 1982-86; Dist Coord for Hiawatha Valley Math League Dist 1988-; Natl Deans List Rochester Comm Coll 1980-81; *office:* Lake City Jr/Sr HS 300 S Garden St Lake City MN 55041

GILMAN, WALLACE LEROY, 7th & 8th Grade Math Teacher; *b:* St Maries, ID; *m:* Hazel Faye Leighty; *c:* Kristine, Jeffery, Scott; *ed:* (BA) Phys Ed, ID St Univ 1960; Post Grad Work Math; *cr:* Phys Ed/Math Teacher Pinehurst Jr HS 1960-69; Math Teacher Wapato Jr HS & Mid Sch 1969-; *ai:* Math Olympic Team Coach; Natl Sci Fnd Grant San Jose St Univ 1968; *office:* Wapato Mid Sch Dove Ln Wapato WA 98951

GILMORE, MARTHA MOORE, 6th Grade Teacher; *b:* Shelby, NC; *c:* Susan E., Richard R. Jr.; *ed:* (BS) Elem Ed, ASU 1964; (MA) Rdng, Univ of NC Charlotte 1984; *cr:* Teacher Valdese Elem 1964-65, Derita Elem 1965-67, Hidden Valley Elem 1967-70, Bain Elem 1979-; *ai:* NCCIRA Presenter 1985; Rdng Conference UNCC Presenter 1984; Teacher of Yr Bain Elem 1989-; *office:* Bain Elem Sch 11524 Bain Schl Rd Charlotte NC 28227

GILMORE-SMITH, EVELYN ELIZABETH GILMORE, English Teacher; *b:* Crockett, TX; *m:* Arthur D.; *c:* Adrian D.; *ed:* (BA) Eng/Speech, 1975, (MED) Curr/Instruction/Rdng, 1978 Univ of Houston; *cr:* Substitute Teacher Houston Ind Sch Dist 1975-76; Eng Teacher M B Smiley HS 1976-79, H Grady Spruce

HS 1979-; *ai:* NHS Adv Comm; Awds Comm Chairperson; Outstanding Apache Chairperson; African Amer His Comm; Alpha Kappa Alpha 1973-; Natl Cncl of Negro Women 1985-; Short Story Article Published in Black Experience Magazine 1975.

GILREATH, DRUE WILLIAMS, Third Grade Teacher; *b:* Atlanta, GA; *m:* Charles Wayne; *c:* Bradley W.; *ed:* Bus Admin, Mid GA Jr Coll 1966-68; (BS) Early Chldhd Ed, West GA Coll 1971; *cr:* Kndgtn Teacher Buckaroo Ranch 1971-72; Paraprofessional M P Word Elem 1972-75; 3rd Grade Teacher Lake Harbin Elem 1973-; *ai:* Clayton Cty Ed Assn 1973-85; NEA 1973-85; Prof Assn of GA Educators 1985-; Fayette Cty Fair 3rd Place Photo Contest 1984; Southern Living Magazine Photo Contest Consolation Prize 1985; Ken-L-Ration Calendar Photo Contest 1988; *home:* 235 Brookshire Dr Fayetteville GA 30214

GILROY, GARY PATRICK, Dir of Bands/Music Dept Chair; *b:* Lancaster, PA; *m:* Dena A.; *c:* Alexandra; *ed:* (BA) Music Ed, San Jose St Univ 1981; (MA) Music Ed, Univ of IL 1989; *cr:* Band Dir Moreau HS 1980-83, Fred C Beyer HS 1983-; Percussion/Music Teacher CA St Univ & Stanislaus 1984-; *ai:* A & B Jazz, Symphonic, Pep, Marching Bands, Wind Ensemble, A & B Winterguard Dir Beyer HS; Dir Percussion Ensemble CSU Stanislaus; W Scholastic Marching Band VP 1981-85; Percussive Art Society 1985-; SCME 1983-; MENC 1980-; CA Music Educators Assn 1980-; Natl Band Assn 1985-; Stanislaus Cty Music Educators Assn 1983-; IAJE 1986-; NBA 1985-; Intl Assn of Jazz Educators 1986-; Citation Natl Band Assn; Beyer HS Teacher Recognition Awd; CMEA Command Performance 1987-; MBA Natl Champion Band 1987; *office:* Fred C Beyer HS 1717 Sylvan Ave Modesto CA 95355

GILSTRAP, ILA M., 4th Grade Teacher; *b:* Tennessee Colony, TX; *m:* Melvin G.; *c:* Melvin Jr., Stacy B., Shelbye D.; *ed:* (BS) Elem Ed, TX Coll 1955; (MA) Early Chldhd Ed, NY Univ 1958; Summer Wkshps; *cr:* Teacher Greenville Ind Sch Dist 1960-; *ai:* Follies, Cotton Jubilee, Democratic Club, Hunt Cty Museum, Greenville Symphony, Drug Free Greenville Mem; TX St Teachers Assn Bd of Dir 1961-; Delta Kappa Gamma 1985-; NEA (Resolution Comm Precinct Chm, Election Judge); Greenville Intnl Series Bd of Dirs 1975-; Chamber of Commerce 1988-; Boys & Girls Club Bd of Dirs 1988-; Greenville Key Communicator Awd.

GILSTRAP, REBECCA ANN, Second Grade Teacher; *b:* Greenville, SC; *m:* Thomas Benjamin; *c:* Lindsey, Katie; *ed:* (BS) Elem Ed, Winthrop Coll 1980; (MS) Elem Ed, Clemson Univ 1984; *cr:* 2nd Grade Teacher Hagood Elem 1980-; *ai:* Church Act; Math Their Way Grant 1989; *office:* Hagood Elem Sch Sparks Lane Pickens SC 29671

GIMLIM, WANDA LOU FLOYD, 11th/12th Grade Teacher; *b:* Bartlesville, OK; *m:* Joe David; *c:* Gwenna L., Deann Gimlin Merciez, Karen D. Gimlin Williams; *ed:* (BS) Ed, 1978, (MED) Ed, 1983 Cntrl St Univ; Nursing Sch St John Sch of Nursing 1950-53; *cr:* Dir of Nursing Oral Roberts Univ 1970-72; Coord Health Occupations Tulsa Skills Center of Voc Ed 1972-73; Instr Allied Health Careers Tulsa Cty Area Voc Tech Schls 1973-; *ai:* Health Occupations Stus of America Adv; Tulsa Assn Voc Tech Classroom Teachers Exec Cncl; Parliamentary Procedures Teams Coach; OK St Voc Tech Allied Health Careers & Respite Care Curr Comm; ; OK Voc Assn 1973-; OK Health Occupation Ed Teachers Assn 1973-, Teacher of Yr 1989; OK Ed Assn (Parliamentarian 1989-, Mem 1973-); Health Occupation Stu America Mem 1985-; AVA 1973-, Health Occupations Teacher of Yr; Skelly Drive Baptist Church 1965-; Amer Red Cross (Volunteer Disaster Nurse, CPR First Aid Instr) 1979-; Natl Assn of Parliamentarians (Pres 1988-) 1979-; OK Voc Assn Health Occupations Teacher of Yr 1989; US Dept of Ed Secy Awd 1988; Outstanding Voc Prgms Awd Developed; *home:* 8219 E 34th St Tulsa OK 74145

GINDLER, PAULETTE S., German Teacher; *b:* Storm Lake, IA; *ed:* Span, Univ of Madrid 1979; (BA) Span/Ger/Eng, Buena Vista Coll 1981; *cr:* Span/Eng Teacher Guthrie Center HS 1981-82; Ger Teacher Mc Allen HS 1982-; *ai:* Eng & Foreign Lang Tutor; Homework Helpline; Sch Plays; ATPE 1982-84; TX Classroom Teachers Assn 1984-; *office:* Mc Allen HS 2000 N 23rd Mc Allen TX 78501

GINGERICH, WILLIAM JOHN, Social Studies Teacher; *b:* Hot Springs, AR; *m:* Kathryn J.; *c:* Joy; *ed:* (BS) Soc Stud, York Coll of PA 1973; *cr:* Teacher Northeastern HS 1974-; *ai:* Golf Coach; Asst Athletic Dir; Equipment Mgr; Hunting Club; PSADA 1987-; PIAA (Registered Ofcl, Pres) 1986-; *home:* 95 Wedgewood Cir Etters PA 17319

GINNANE, LYNNE BEARDSLEY, Business Teacher; *b:* Rochester, NY; *m:* Edwin J. Richter Jr.; *ed:* (AA) Liberal Arts, Monroe Comm Coll 1972; (BS) Bus Ed, 1975, (MED) Ed, 1978 Nazareth Coll of Rochester; *cr:* Bus Teacher Sodus Cntrl Sch 1975-76, Wayne Cntrl Sch 1976-79, Gananda Cntrl & Lyons Cntrl Schls 1979-80, Gananda Cntrl Sch 1980-; *ai:* Yrbk Adv Gananda Cntrl Sch; Scndry Sch Improvement Team & Graduation Awds Comm; *office:* Gananda Cntrl Sch 1500 Dayspring Ridge Walworth NY 14568

GINNETTI, ANTHONY JOSEPH, Fifth Grade Teacher; *b:* New Haven, CT; *m:* Joan Hobson; *c:* Gregory, Carolyn, Kevin, Wendy, Graham, Daniela; *ed:* (BS) Jr HS Ed/Soc Stud, 1967, (MS) Geography, 1977 S CT St Univ; Photo & Map Interpretation, S CT St Univ; CT St Dept of Ed Cooperating Teacher Prgm; *cr:* 5th Grade Teacher Beecher Road Sch 1967-; *ai:* Soc Stud Curr & Supts Problem Solving Comm; Woodbridge Ed Assn Pres 1976-84; Amer Geographical Society 1989-; NCSS 1983-; Woodbridge Recreation Dept Dir Adult Bsktbl League 1976-78; Natl Fed of Interscholastic Ofcls 1982-; Article Published; CT Sci Educators Assn & CT Cncl Soc Stud Incorporated Wkshp Presenter; *office:* Beecher Road Sch 40 Beecher Rd Woodbridge CT 06525

GIOLIGHTLY, PEGGY SUE RIGGS, 9 & 11th Grade English Teacher; *b:* Harriman, TN; *w:* Clarence A. Jr.; *c:* Randolph, Phillip, Carolyn; *ed:* (BS) Scndry Ed, TN Temple Univ 1973; *cr:* Eng/His Teacher Marietta Chrstn Sch 1975-77, Victory Chrstn Sch 1977-78; Eng Teacher North FL Chrstn Sch 1985; *ai:* Jr Class Spon; *office:* North Florida Chrstn Sch 3000 N Merdian Rd Tallahassee FL 32312

GIORGI, JACQUELINE ANN, English Teacher/Eng Dept Chair; *b:* Vineland, NJ; *ed:* (BA) Eng, 1979, (MA) Eng Ed, 1984 Coll of William & Mary; Advanced Courses in Eng Working Towards PhD; *cr:* Eng Teacher Bayside HS 1979-82/1983-; *ai:* Schlsp Comm; Its Academic Eng Dept Chm; Yrbk Spon; Sch Improvement Comm; Forensics Judge; VBEA 1979-; VBATE 1979-; Grad Assistantship-Dr Gulesian Coll of William & Mary; Outstanding Teacher 1989; Governors Sch for The Gifted; *office:* Bayside H S 4960 Haygood Rd Virginia Beach VA 23455

GIOVANNAZZO, DANIEL ELLIS, 7th Grade English Teacher; *b:* Elyria, OH; *m:* Roberta Ralich; *c:* Brian, Elliot; *ed:* (BA) Eng, 1975, (MED) Admin, 1984 Cleveland St Univ; *cr:* 8th Grade Teacher North Ridgeville Mid Sch 1975-83; 7th Grade Eng Teacher North Ridgeville Jr HS 1984-.

GIPSON, PATRICIA MOORE, 6th Grade Science Teacher; *b:* Kingston, TN; *m:* Richard Douglas; *c:* Megan, Callie; *ed:* (BS) Home Ec, David Lipscomb Coll 1967; Elem Ed Cert, Univ of TN Nashville; *cr:* Teacher Fairview Elem 1967-80, Fairview Mid 1981-; *ai:* Cross Cntry Coach; Sci Curr Comm; Stu Cncl Adv; 6th Grade Team Leader; Williamson Cty Ed Assn Grievance Rep; Williamson Cty Ed Assn (Pres 1978-79, Pres-Elect 1977-78, Secy 1976-77); TEA, NEA 1967-; PTA (VP, Faculty Rep); Booster Club VP 1984-85; Project Reach Grant Participant & Comm Mem; Career Level III Teacher; *office:* Fairview Mid Sch 200 Crow Cut Rd SW Fairview TN 37062

GIPSON, VERNON, US History AP Teacher; *b:* Madisonville, KY; *m:* Delorus Ann Cothran; *c:* Watonya B., Kimberly S.; *ed:* (BA) His, 1970, (MA) His, 1978 Western KY Univ; Rank I Scndry Principalship; *cr:* Part Time His Teacher Madisonville Comm Coll Univ of KY 1982-88; His Teacher Madisonville North Hopkins HS 1970-; *ai:* Partisan Rangers Spon; Historical Society of Hopkins Cty VP 1974-76; KY Historical Society Life Mem; Filson Club 1970-; KY Cncl of Soc Stud 1971-; Hopkins Cty Planning Commission Vice-Chm; Hopkins Cty Geneological Society Pres; Pact Dir 1978-86; Earlington General Baptist Church (Choir Dir, Deacon, Sunday Sch Teacher) 1983-; Geography Inst & W MI Univ Grant 1972; Book Published 1978; *office:* Madisonville North Hopkins HS 4515 Hanson Rd Madisonville KY 42431

GIRARD, CHAR, Reading/Language Arts Teacher; *b:* Santa Monica, CA; *ed:* (BA) His, Immaculate Heart Coll 1971; Elem Teaching Creditial; Working toward Masters Self Esteem Person Centered 1990; *cr:* Teacher St Monicas Elem 1964-65, Blessed Sacrament 1966-70, All Souls 1970-71, Emma W Shuey 1971-; *ai:* Drug Ed for Rosemead Sch Dist Coord; Rdng Lang Art & Phys Ed Comms; PTA (Auditor 1980-82, 1986-88), Honorary Service 1984; Article Published; Los Angeles Cty Office Teacher of Yr Rosemead; Citip Awd; Allstate Grant for Film Editing; *office:* Emma W Shuey Elem Sch 8472 Wells St Rosemead CA 91770

GIRARD, LINDA ANN, Transitional 1st Grade Teacher; *b:* New Haven, CT; *c:* Edward, Nicholas, Margaret; *ed:* (BS) Elem/Spec Ed, 1971, (MS) Spec Ed Multi-Discipline, 1976 S CT St Univ; Systematic Trng for Effective Teaching; Heres Looking at You 2000; Developmentally Appropriate Practices K-2; Process Writing; Teaching Self Esteem; Math Problem Solving K-2, Math Manipulatives; Whole Lang, Appleworks for Teachers; *cr:* 3rd Grade Teacher 1971-82, Transitional 1st Grade Teacher 1982-Stanley T Williams Sch; *ai:* Coord 1st Grade Sci Museum; North Branford Ed Assn, NEA, North Branford Fed of Teachers, CT Fed of Teachers, AFT; CT Cncl on Adoption 1988-; CT Parents of Indian Children (Co Founder 1982, Mem) 1982-; Co Author Transitional 1st Grade Prgm 1982; *office:* Stanley T Williams Sch Middletown Ave Northford CT 06472

GIRLUS, KATHLEEN SHUMAN, 1st Grade Teacher; *b:* Corvallis, OR; *c:* Tanya, Sean; *ed:* (BA) Elem Ed, Marycrest 1968; Grad Stud Univ of IA, Marycrest Coll, W IL, Ottawa Univ; *cr:* 2nd Grade Teacher Wilson Elem 1968-71; Substitute Teacher Radcliff Elem Schls 1971, Davenport Schls 1980-81; 1st/4th Grade Teacher St Alphonsus Sch 1981-; *ai:* Rainbow Group Facilitator; St Paul the Apostle Church (CCD Prgm Asst Supvr 1976-81, Bd Mem 1975-78); Nom for Outstanding Teacher of Scott Cty 1989; *home:* 2414 E Garfield Davenport IA 52803

GIROUARD, YOLANDA DOROTHY, 5th Grade Teacher; *b:* Boston, MA; *ed:* (BS) Ed, Lowell St 1967; *cr:* 5th Grade Teacher Town of Wilmington 1967-; *ai:* MA Teachers Assn, NEA.

GIRTON, BARBARA CAROLYN (MAHAN), Fourth Grade Teacher; *b:* Portales, NM; *m:* Myron Robert; *c:* Myra L. Diaz, Steven M., Anthony B., Traci G. Rhoads; *ed:* (BS) Ed, Coll of Southwest 1967; (ME) Ed, Eastern NM Univ 1976; *cr:* 1st Grade Teacher 1968-70, 3rd Grade Teacher 1970-74 Broadmoor Elem; Learning Disabilities Teacher Taylor Elem1974-80; 4th Grade Teacher Broadmoor & Mills Elem 1980-; *ai:* NM Ed Assn, Hobbs Assn of Classroom Teachers; *home:* 1329 Paige Dr Hobbs NM 88240

GISH, DAVID M., Assistant Athletic Trainer; *b:* Dallas, TX; *m:* Karen Padgett; *ed:* (BS) Phys Ed/Health Ed, Univ of N TX 1984; (MED) Health Ed, SW TX St Univ 1990; *cr:* Asst Trainer Univ of SW LA 1984-86; Head Trainer San Marcos HS 1986-; Asst Trainer SW TX St Univ 1990; *ai:* Alamo Area Athletic Trainers Assn 1986-; SW Athletic Trainers Assn 1984-; Natl Athletic Trainers Assn 1980-; Sigma Tau Gamma Alumni Adv; AAU Jr Olympics Athletic Trainer 1989; TX Spec Olympics Athletic Trainer 1989-; Article Published 1989; *office:* SW TX St Univ Dept of Athletics SW TX St Univ San Marcos TX 78666

GISH, PHYLLIS N., First Grade Teacher; *b:* Beardstown, IL; *m:* Duane M.; *c:* Randy, Deborah Kratzer, Jeffrey, Tracy; *ed:* (AA) Ed, Hutchinson Jr Coll 1969; (BS) Elem Ed, Sterling Coll 1972; (MS) Elem Ed, Wichita Univ 1978; *cr:* 4th Grade Teacher 1972-74, 1st/2nd Grade Teacher 1974-76 Bushton Grade Sch; 1st Grade Teacher Quivira Heights Grade Sch 1976-; *ai:* Sch Improvement & Prof Dev Team Mem; NEA; Delta Kappa Gamma; *office:* Quivira Heights Grade Sch Box 248 Holyrood KS 67450

GISSELBECK, EULA GIBBS, Fourth Grade Teacher; *b:* Kansas, OK; *m:* La Vern Peter; *c:* Steven R., Carl P.; *ed:* (BA) Biblical Lit/Theology, Azusa Pacific 1958; (BA) Ed, Sacramento St Univ 1963; (MS) Ed, SW MO St Univ Springfield 1980; *cr:* 5th Grade Teacher N Sacramento Sch Dist 1936-65; 2nd Grade Teacher Castlewood Elem 1965-66; 1st-4th Grade Teacher Indian Diggings Elem 1971-73; 1st-3rd Grades Teacher Swedeborg Elem 1973-75; 2nd/3rd Grade Teacher Joel E Barber 1975-81; 4th Grade Teacher Waynesville R-6 1981-; *ai:* Helped Organize CTA Joel E Barber Sch; Waynesville R-6 CTA Welfare Comm Mem; Joel E Barber Sch 7th/8th Grade Girls Bsktbl Coach; KSAM Lead Teacher; MO St Teachers Union 1975-; Intnl Rdng Assn 1989-; Kappa Kappa Iota 1986-; *office:* Pick Elem Sch Waynesville Schl Dist Waynesville MO 65583

GIST, JUANITA SHEARER, 4th & 5th Grade Math Teacher; *b:* Wilburn, AR; *m:* Grady Lynn Sr.; *c:* Grady Lynn Jr., Grant; *ed:* (BS) Elem Ed, NM St Univ 1969; (MA) Elem Ed, Western NM Univ 1974; Cmptr Trng, Intermediate Math, Intermediate Phys Ed; *cr:* Kndgtn Teacher Loving 1970-71; 5th-6th Grade Teacher Edison Elem 1971-72; 5th/6th Grade Rdng Teacher 1972-73, 4th/5th Grade Math Teacher 1973- Monterrey Elem; *ai:* New Teacher Orientation Comms; Dev of Dist Math; Curr Comm 5th Grade; Security Guard Var Soccer; NEA, NEA of NM 1972; Amer Assn of Univ Women 1973; Cub Scouts Asst Leader 1963; Beta Sigma Phi, Alpha Mu Chapter 1956; Grant Philanthropic Ed Organization; Chapter A Carlsbad NM; Academic Schlsp NM St Univ Carlsbad; *home:* 405 W Riverside Dr Carlsbad NM 88220

GIUS, JO ANNE LYNSKEY, Business Education Teacher; *b:* Camden, NJ; *m:* Gerald M.; *c:* Jennifer; *ed:* (BA) Bus Ed, 1969, (MED) Bus Ed, 1976 Trenton St Coll; Bus Ed; *cr:* Bus Teacher Pemberton HS 1969-77, Audubon HS 1977-78, Millville HS 1978-; *ai:* NJEA, NBEA 1969-; NJBEA Cty Rep 1987-88; Delta Pi Epsilon 1969-; *office:* Millville HS 200 Wade Blvd Millville NJ 08332

GIUSTI, VINCENZA BANDUCCI, Biology Teacher; *b:* Tassignano, Italy; *m:* Joseph; *c:* Elisa, Stefania; *ed:* (BS) Bio, NE IL Univ 1976; Instructional Practices, Behavior Modification; *cr:* Bio Teacher Trinity HS 1979-80, Mother T Guerin HS 1980-82, Resurrection HS 1986; *ai:* Sci Club Moderator 1986-; Sci Fair Spon & Moderator 1986-; Peer Cnslr Critical Thinking Skills 1988-; Facilitator Toward More Positive Behavior 1986-; NSTA, ISTA, NCEA 1979-; Brannigar Estate Cmmty Assn 1988-; Resurrection HS Newcomer Awd 1986-87; Resurrection HS Educator 1987-8 8; *home:* 330 Crest Ave Elk Grove Village IL 60007

GIVENS, GARY FRANKLIN, Principal; *b:* Bloomington, IL; *m:* Carol Ann Burke; *c:* Micah A., Christine D.; *ed:* (BS) Phys Ed, Cntrl MO St Univ 1970; *cr:* 7th-8th Grade Crafts Teacher Maplewood Richmond Hts 1971-74; 7th-8th Grade Home Room Teacher Hillcrest 7th Day Adv Sch 1974-77; 1st-8th Grade Teacher Crestview 7th Day Adv Sch 1977-84, Hamlet 7th Day Adv Sch 1985-87, Grove 7th Day Adv Sch 1987-89; 9th-12th Grade Prin Oklahoma Acad 1989-; *ai:* Elder in Church; Annual Ed & Spon; Exec, Admin, Discipline, Acceptance Comms; *home:* 6011 Academy Ln Harrah OK 73045

GIVENS, RONALD LEE, Assistant Principal; *b:* Kenosha, WI; *m:* Brenda Edmonds; *c:* Brandon, Leigha, Stuart; *ed:* (BS) Bio, Jacksonville St Univ 1968-; (MS) Sch Admin, A&M Univ 1990; *cr:* Classroom Teacher Pisgah HS 1968-83; Classroom Teacher 1983-89, Asst Prin 1989- Woodville HS; *ai:* Sr Spon; AEA, NEA, JCEA 1968-; Woodville HS Jackson Cty Americanism Awd 1986; Pisgah HS Teacher of Yr 1976; *home:* PO Box 96 Grant AL 35747

GIVHAN, REBECCA JOYCE (CURNUTT), Office Ed Teacher; *b:* Canadian, TX; *m:* Claude H.; *c:* Claude D., Rebecca L., Orla B.; *ed:* (BBA) Bus Admin, West TX ST Univ 1969; (MED) Ed/Cnslr, Univ of North TX 1988; Vocational Office Ed Cert; Vocational Cnslr/Prof Cnslr Cert; *cr:* Bus Ed/Office Ed Teacher Pampa Ind Sch Dist 1969-72; Asst Volunteer Coord Mexia St Sch 1972-74; Office Ed Teacher Mexia Ind Sch Dist 1974-81; Executive Secy Soutland Royalty Company 1981-82; Office Ed Teacher Midland Independent Sch Dist 1982-; *ai:* Office Ed Assn Spon; Bus Prof of America Spon; TX Bus Ed Assn 1969-; TX Voc Teachers Assn 1969-; TX Classroom Teachers Assn 1982-; Bus/Prof Womans Assn 1985-87.

GLADD, GLORIA BELSTRA, English Teacher; *b:* Newton, NJ; *m:* Russell W. Jr.; *c:* Dianne, Russell III, Amy Gladd-Herdman; *ed:* (BS) Eng/Scndry Ed, E Stroudsburg Univ 1980; *cr:* Eng Teacher N Warren Regional HS 1982-; *ai:* NCTE, 1989-; NEA 1982-; *office:* N Warren Regional HS Box 410 Lambert Rd Blairstown NJ 07825

GLADDEN, HOPE WELLS, Third Grade Teacher; *b:* Forest City, NC; *m:* Dwight D.; *c:* Jeffery, Jonathan, David, Suzanne; *ed:* (BS) Primary Ed, ASU 1960; *cr:* 6th Grade Teacher 1960-61, 4th/5th Grade Teacher 1961-64, 3rd/4th Grade Teacher 1965-69 Banoak Elem; CETA Rdng Teacher Mountain View Elem 1976-77; 3rd Grade Teacher Banoak Elem 1977-; *ai:* Staff Dev; Contact Teacher; TAC Rep; NCAE, NEA, CCAE; Sardis Women of Luth Church in America Pres 1988-, Woman of Yr 1989; *home:* Rt 3 Box 376 Vale NC 28168

GLADDEN, LUCY EMMALENE, 1st Grade Teacher; *b:* Centre, AL; *m:* Jerry W.; *c:* Jeffrey W., Brandon C.; *ed:* (BS) Elem Ed, Jacksonville St Univ 1975; (MA) Elem Ed, Univ of AL 1978; Various Wkshps; Educl Rdngs; *cr:* Teacher Centre Elem 1975-; *ai:* St Textbook Comm 1987; Personnel Evaluation of Prof Employers Comm 1989-; Faculty Reporter, Treas, Secy, VP, Pres; Various Comm; NEA, AEA 1975-; Cherokee Cty Ed Assn (Reporter, Secy, VP 1989-, Pres Elect 1989-) 1975-; *office:* Centre Elem Sch 725 E Main St Centre AL 35960

GLADDEN, LYNDON K., Math Department Chairman; *b:* Manchester, GA; *m:* Helen Carol; *c:* Samuel; *ed:* (BA) Math, LA Coll 1954; Teaching Sul Ross Univ 1987; Plastics & Electrical Engr, ICS; *cr:* Math Teacher Runnels Jr HS 1985-; *ai:* ATPE; *home:* 600 Highland Big Spring TX 79720

GLADDING, KARIN MORGHEN, Special Education Teacher; *b:* Breitenwang, Austria; *m:* Fred; *c:* Kiersten, Matthew; *ed:* (BS) Ed, Univ of NV Reno 1974; Grad Stud Ed, Counseling; *cr:* Spec Ed Teacher Stead Elem 1974-75, Incline elem 1975-78, Storey Cty Schls 1978-80; 6th Grade Teacher 1980-87, 3rd Grade Teacher 1987-89, Spec Ed/Teacher of Gifted 1989- Gallagher Elem; *ai:* NSEA, PTA; SCEA (Secy, Treas) 1988-; *office:* Gallagher Elem Sch P O Box C Virginia City NV 89440

GLADE, KAREN TRUNICK, Senior English Teacher; *b:* Warren, OH; *m:* Stephen R.; *c:* Rebecca, Logan, Aaron; *ed:* (BS) Eng, Youngstown St 1976; Writing Process, Assertive Discipline Wkshps; *cr:* Eng Teacher Warren City 1976-77; *ai:* Quiz Team Dir; Delta Kappa Gamma 1988-; Tri-Cty Career Ed Mini-Grant 1988-89; *home:* PO Box 313 5738 St Rt 668 Somerset OH 43783

GLADKOSKY, DEBORAH NAGY, Latin & English Teacher; *b:* Logan, WV; *ed:* (BA) Scndry Ed/Latin/Eng, Marshall Univ 1985; NEH Insts Marshall Univ 1989 & E TN St Univ 1990; *cr:* Teacher Chapmanville Jr HS 1986-89, Chapmanville Jr/Sr HS 1989-; *ai:* Natl Jr Beta Club & Jr/Sr HS Level Latin Club Spon; Voting Teacher Parent Advisory Cncl Comm; Natl Competitions in Latin & Fundraising; WV Jr Classical League (Co-St Chm 1989-, St Chm 1990); Amer Classical League Mem; GSA (Mem 1970-, Leader 1985-), 5 Yr Service, 20 Yr Pin 1990; Natl Lation Competition Winners; *home:* Box 1237 Chapmanville WV 25508

GLADWELL, GILBERT WESLEY, Biology Teacher; *b:* Webster Springs, WV; *m:* Mary Ellen Woods; *c:* Gilbert II, Jason, Kerri-Jo; *ed:* (BS) Bio/Phys Ed, Cumberland Coll 1969; (MS) Ed, WV Weselyan 1987; *cr:* General Sci Teacher Cowen HS 1966-69; Sci Lab Teacher Webster Cty Bd of Ed 1969-70; Bio Teacher Cowen HS 1970-74, Webster Cty HS 1975-; *ai:* Asst Ftbl Coach; Jr Class Spon; WV Ed Assn, NEA; Tau Kappa Epsilon; Masons; Educl Grant 1985; *office:* Webster Cty HS Upperglade WV 26266

GLANZMANN, DUANE ALLAN, Mathematics Teacher; *b:* Oakland, CA; *m:* Kay Louise Kirn; *c:* Brett, Todd, Janee; *ed:* (BS) Math, 1956, (MED) Sch Admin, 1965 Univ of NV; *cr:* Math Teacher Carson Jr HS 1960-62; Vice Prin 1970, Guidance Dir 1971-79, Math Teacher 1962- Carson City HS; *ai:* NCTM, NEA, NV St Ed Assn, Ormsky Cty Ed Assn; NV St Teacher of Yr 1976; Carson City Sch Dist Teacher of Yr 1976; Outstanding Teacher Awd Univ of Chicago 1985; Rotary Club Teacher of Month 1989; Presidential Scholar Distinguished Teacher 1988; Independent Insurance Agents Teacher of Month 1976; *office:* Carson City HS 1111 Saliman Rd Carson City NV 89702

GLASCOM, PATRICIA HERTZ, Fifth Grade Teacher; *b:* Allentown, PA; *m:* Gary Mark; *c:* Sarah M., Elizabeth M.; *ed:* (BS) Elem Ed, Univ of Pittsburgh 1970; Master Stud Temple Univ, Penn St Univ, Wilkes Coll, Cedar Crest Coll, Womens Center, Kutztown Univ, Carbon Lehigh Intermediate Unit 21; *cr:* Tutor-Hearing Impaired Allentown Sch Dist 1970; 6th Grade Teacher Springfield Township 1971-73; Remedial Rdng Teacher Stevens & Cntrl 1975-78; 3rd/6th Grade Teacher Cntrl, UT, Mosser Schls 1970-71, 1973-74, 1980; 5th Grade Teacher Jefferson Elem 1980-; *ai:* Eisenhower Sci-Math Grant Comm Representing Jefferson & Allentown Sch Dist; K-5th Grade Lang Art Planned Course Outline Comm Allentown Sch Dist; Nutrition Grant Comm Jefferson; Delta Kappa Gamma, Womens Teachers Club; Congregation Keneseth Israel (Prgm Chairperson 1979-82, Religious Sch Chairperson 1987-); Wkshp Co-Presenter Peer Coaching Jefferson, Make & Take Sci Materials Jefferson 1990; *office:* Jefferson Elem 750 S St John St Allentown PA 18103

GLASER, KAREN WOLF, Coordinator of Gifted/Talented; *b:* Kokomo, IN; *m:* Gerald Frank; *c:* Patricia, Kyle; *ed:* (BS) Ed, W MI 1976; Grad Stud E MI; *cr:* Teacher 1976-87, Coord of Gifted & Talented 1987- Vandercook Lake Schls; *ai:* Natl Academic All Star Team Coach; First Meth Church VP 1988-; *office:* Vandercook Lake Schls 800 E Mc Devitt Jackson MI 49203

GLASER, LOUISE WAGNER, First Grade Teacher; *b:* Abita Springs, LA; *m:* Elton A.; *c:* Elton, Daniel, Cyndie, Karen; *ed:* (BA) Elem Ed, S LA Univ 1972; Spec Ed & L D Cert, UNO; *cr:* Asst Vice Prin St Margaret Mary 1980-; *ai:* SBLC; Rdng Comm; Skating Night Coord; Girl Scout Leader; Stu Cncl Adv; Primary Coord; NCEA, ACLD; SMM Guild; *home:* 990 Audubon St Slidell LA 70460

GLASS, LINDA L., First Grade Teacher; *b:* Ogdensburg, NY; *ed:* (BS) Elem Ed/Psych, Houghton Coll 1979; (MS) Elem Ed, Nova Univ 1983; *cr:* 1st Grade Teacher St Petersburg Chrstn Sch 1979-; *office:* Saint Petersburg Chrstn Sch 2021 62nd Ave No Saint Petersburg FL 33702

GLASS, MARGARET R., English Teacher; *b:* Pittston, PA; *m:* Warren H.; *ed:* (BA) Eng, Wilkes Coll 1969; (MA) Eng, St Univ of NY Stony Brook 1974; Working on 2nd MA in Arts, Hum, St Univ of NY Stony Brook; *cr:* 9th-12th Grade Eng Teacher Newfield HS 1969-; *ai:* Drama Dir Asst Spring Musicals; NY St Eng Cncl 1990-; Natl Organization of Women 1990-; Sigma Tau Delta; *office:* Newfield HS Marshall Dr Selden NY 11784

GLASS, NANCY CAPLINGER, 5/6 Grade Math Teacher; *b:* Columbus, GA; *m:* James Brooks; *c:* Brantley H.; *ed:* (BS) Phys Ed/Math, 1981, (MAT) Phys Ed/Math, 1982 Livingston Univ; *cr:* Teacher Sweet Water HS 1981-; Part-Time Instr Patrick Henry St Jr Coll 1982-84; *ai:* Elem Honor Society Spon; Budjet Comm; Delta Kappa Gamma 1989-; *home:* PO Box 200 Nanafalia AL 36764

GLASS, STEVEN MICHAEL, Business Teacher; *b:* Des Moines, IA; *m:* Sara Silva; *c:* Amy L., Emily N.; *ed:* (BA) Ed, AZ St Univ 1974; *cr:* Asst Mgr Mc Donalds 1977-78; Insurance Agent 1976-77; Accountant Life Care Services 1977; *ai:* FBLA Adv; HS/Jr Coll; PAC-10 Womens Bsktbl Ofcl; NFL Chain Crew Mem for Phoenix Cardinals; NEA 1978-; AZ Ed Assn 1978-; Temple Schls Ed Assn 1978-; Dads Club 1988-; Tempe Diable Teacher of Yr Awd 1988; Consultant for Co-Author Intro Bus Text Southwestern Publishing Company; *office:* Mc Clintock HS 1830 E Del Rio Tempe AZ 85282

GLASSCOCK, PARKER ELLWOOD, Retired; *b:* Troy, TX; *m:* Bettie Jean Drake; *c:* Lanie, Todd; *ed:* (BS) Phys Ed/Health/Recreation, North TX ST Coll 1956; (MED) Adm/Supervision/Ed, North TX Univ 1962; Bio/Elem Sci/Elem Phys Ed/Coaching; *cr:* Phys Ed & Sci Teacher 1978-88, 4th-5th Grade Jr HS Teacher 1988 Acad ISD; *ai:* Active Substitute Teaching K-12; Coaching Little Dribblers Bsktbl; Coaching Little League Bsbl; Temple-Bell Retired Teachers Assn 1988-; Phi Delta Kappa 1990; Amer Legion Post 526 Holland TX 1985-; USAF 1952-56; Korean War or Conflict; *home:* Box 700 Little River TX 76554

GLASSCOCK, SELMA NELLE, Sci Dept Chairperson/Teacher; *b:* Sonora, TX; *m:* Billy Curtis; *c:* Audrey, Jessica; *ed:* (BS) Math, Sul Ross St Univ 1975; (MS) Bio, Angelo St Univ 1989; *cr:* Math Teacher Pecos-Barstow-Toyah Ind Sch Dist 1976-77, Lohn Ind Sch Dist 1977-79; Sci/Math Teacher Paint Rock Ind Sch Dist 1979-80, 1983-; *ai:* UIL Sci Coach & Spon; TX Assn of Cmmty Schls 1983-; *home:* PO Box 272 Paint Rock TX 76866

GLASSER, JANE ELLEN, English Teacher; *b:* New York, NY; *d:* Jessica, Hara;; *ed:* (BA) Philosophy, Sweet Briar Coll 1967; (MA) Hum, 1980, (BS) Scndry Ed, 1984 Old Dominion Univ; Breadloaf Writers Conference 1975; *cr:* Poet-in-the-Schls Virginia Beach Public Sch System 1976-82; Creative Writing Teacher 1981, Visiting Poet 1982 Norfolk Acad; Eng Teacher Norview HS 1983-; *ai:* Norview Lit & Art Magazine Spon; Norview Forensics Team Adv & Spon; VA Assn Teachers of Eng 1983-; NCTE 1990; VA Poetry Society; New VA Review Incorporated (Co-Founder, VP, Bd Mem) 1979-89; Poems Published; Irene Leache Lit Contest Winner; *office:* Norview HS 1 Middleton Pl Norfolk VA 23513

GLAUS, PERRY L., English Teacher; *b:* Durand, WI; *m:* Lola M. Bauer; *c:* Tina, Lori, Travis; *ed:* (BS) Eng, Univ of WI River Falls 1968; *cr:* Eng Teacher Lake Holcombe Public Sch 1968-; *ai:* Lang Art Chairperson Lake Holcombe; Schlsp Comm Mem; *office:* Lake Holcombe Public Sch Box 40 Holcombe WI 54745

GLAZE, ARTHUR IRVIN, JR., Spanish Teacher/Dept Chair; *b:* San Antonio, TX; *m:* Mary Ellen Rogers; *ed:* (BBA) Bus Admin, 1960, (BS) Span, 1964, (MED) Sch Admin/Span, 1967 SW TX St Univ; Univ of Guadalajara; NDEA Lang Inst San Jose St Univ; Grad Stud Gifted Stu Discipline Management; *cr:* Span Teacher Rogers Mid Sch 1962-67; Span Teacher/Dept Chm Highlands HS 1967-70; Span Teacher Robert E Lee HS 1970-77; Span Teacher/Dept Chm Winston Churchill HS 1977-; *ai:* Natl Span Honor Society Spon; Schlsp, Challenge, Climate Comm; Amer Assn Teachers of Span & Portuguese, TX St Teachers Assn, TX Foreign Lang Assn 1962-; Assn of TX Prof Educators 1989-; Alamo Lang Assn; Optimist Club Stu Recognition Comm Chm 1988-; Scholastic Magazine Natl Ed Advisory Staff; Churchill Teacher of Yr 1982, 1983; Univ of TX Outstanding HS Teachers Awd of Excl; Memorable Influence Supt Certificate of Appreciation Awds 1989; *office:* Winston Churchill HS 12049 Blanco Rd San Antonio TX 78216

GLAZE, BOBBY GLENN, Mathematics Teacher; *b:* Newton, MS; *m:* Linda Jean Blackwell; *c:* Christopher; *ed:* (AA) Liberal Art, Clarke Coll 1973; (BS) Phys Ed, MS Coll 1975; (MA) Educl Admin, William Carey 1989; *cr:* Teacher/Bsbl Coach Newton HS 197-80, R H Watkins HS 1980-; *ai:* Head Bsbl Coach; Co-Spon Fellowship of Chrstn Athletes; MS Assn of Coaches 1976-; Amer Bsbl Coaches Assn 1980-; Coached MS HS All Star Game 1989; Team Won St Championship 1989; *office:* R H Watkins HS 1100 W 12th St Laurel MS 39440

GLEASON, DORIS MATSUO, 1st Grade Teacher; *b:* Captain Cook, HI; *m:* David L.; *c:* Mark L., Shari L.; *ed:* (BS) Elem Ed, St Cloud St Univ 1961; *cr:* 2nd Grade Teacher Elizabeth Gardner Sch 1962-64, Hilltop Elem Sch 1964-65, Maple Lake Elem 1969-86; 1st Grade Teacher Maple Lake Elem 1986-; *ai:* Prin Advisory Cncl; Crisis Comm; MN Ed Assn Pres 1980-; NEA 1980-; *home:* Box 4 Howard Lake MN 55349

GLEASON, ELAINE CHAMPLIN, Third Grade Teacher; *b:* Penn Yan, NY; *m:* P. Earle; *c:* Aaron; *ed:* (AS) Liberal Arts, Corning Comm Coll 1969; (BS) Elem Ed, St Univ Coll Brockport 1971; (MS) Elem Ed, Nazareth Coll 1975; Elements of Instruction 1986-87; *cr:* 2nd Grade Teacher Frank Knight Elem 1971-73; 2nd Grade Teacher 1973-76, 3rd Grade Teacher 1976-81, 1st Grade Teacher 1982-85, 3rd Grade Teacher 1985- Penn Yan Elem; *ai:* Inter-Sch Intermediate Cncl 3rd Grade Rep; Keuka Coll Stu Teachers Spon; Penn Yan Teachers Assn Secy 1983-88; St Pauls Luth Church Deacon 1987-; Amer Legion Auxiliary Americanism Chm 1986-88, Mary Smack Awd 1987, Americanism Citation 1986, Chms Awd 1988; Piloted a Unit on US Constitution 200th Anniversary; NY St Soc Stud Convention Speaker 1987; *home:* 1383 Milo Center Rd Penn Yan NY 14527

GLEASON, PAULETTE L. FINN, First Grade Teacher; *b:* Milwaukee, WI; *m:* John S.; *c:* Stephanie, Sarah; *ed:* (BS) Early Childhood Ed, Viterb Coll 1976; *cr:* 1st Grade Teacher St Patricks Sch 1977-; *ai:* NCEA 1977-; Viterbo Coll Alumni Assn 1977-; *home:* Rt 1 Box 157 La Crosse WI 54601

GLEIM, CAROL JANE (HILL), English Teacher; *b:* Ironton, OH; *m:* Galen H.; *c:* Julie A.; *ed:* (BS) Elem Ed, OH Univ 1966; (MA) Elem Ed, Marshall Univ 1976; Grad Stud, OH Univ; *cr:* Eng Teacher Wheelersburg Elem Sch 1966-72, 1975-; *ai:* Writing Consultant Scioto Cty Schls; NEA 1975-; OH Ed Assn, Wheelersburg Ed Assn 1966-72, 1975-; Delta Kappa Gamma (Mem, VP); Alpha Delta St; Coal Grove Memorial Meth Church 1957-; Chm Various Comms; St Research Comm Mem; *home:* 8652 Green St Wheelersburg OH 45694

GLEMMING, PATRICIA REYNOLDS, English Teacher; *b:* Montclair, NJ; *m:* James H. Jr.; *ed:* (BA) Elem Ed, Fairleigh Dickinson Univ 1974; *cr:* 6th - 8th Grade Teacher St Catherine 1974-76; 6th Grade Teacher 1976-79; 6th - 8th Grade Teacher 1980- Cedar Drive Sch; 5th Grade Teacher Atlantic Elem Sch 1976-80; *ai:* Mid Sch Task Force Comm; Lang Arts Curr Comm; Composition & Literature Curr Comm; Instructional Cncl; Colts Neck Teachers Ed Assn Secy 1980-85; NJEA 1976-; PETA Mem; HSUS Mem; *office:* Cedar Drive Sch 73 Cedar Drive Colts Neck NJ 07722

GLENN, ANN (ETSLER), Dir of Childrens Ministries; *b:* Alexandria, IN; *m:* Don A.; *c:* Pamela A., Scott A.; *ed:* (BSED) Music, IN Wesleyan Univ 1957; (MA) Ed, Natl Coll of Ed 1984; Remedial Rdng, Univ of N IA 1972-76; Great Books Cert 1985; *cr:* 7th-9th Grade Lang Art Teacher Lindmoor Jr HS 1963-65; Remedial Rdng Teacher Jack M Logan Jr HS 1970-76; 7th-8th Lang Art Teacher E F Lindop Sch 1980-87; Dir of Childrens Ministries The Wesleyan Church 1987-; *ai:* Lindop Teachers Assn Secy 1985-87; Rdng Teachers Assn; Amer Cancer Society 1985-87; Wesleyan Women Intnl (Local Pres, Asst General Dir, N Cntrl Area Chm) 1959-89; Faithful Service Awd 1989; Book Mother T Biography; Articles for Various Magazines; *office:* The Wesleyan Church 6060 Castleway Dr Indianapolis IN 46250

GLENN, DEBORAH LYNN, Social Studies Teacher; *b:* Memphis, TN; *ed:* (BS) Soc Sci, Bethel Coll 1975; *cr:* Teacher Barrets Chapel Sch 1979-; *ai:* Yrbk Spon; Stu Assistance Prgm; Core Team Mem; Recognition Comm Chm; Pep Club Spon; TEA, Shelby Cty Ed Assn, NEA 1979-; Richland Church Christian Ed Comm Chm 1985-86; Barrets Teacher of Yr 1987; TN Teacher of Yr Candidate 1986, 1990; *office:* Barrets Chapel Sch 10280 Godwin Rd Arlington TN 38002

GLENN, DOROTHY THARP, Office Ed Coordinator; *b:* Green City, MO; *m:* Terry E.; *c:* Stephanie, Brian; *ed:* (BS) Bus Ed 1962; (MA) Bus Ed; 1963 Northeast MO St Univ; Bus & Ed; Vocational Cert; *cr:* Bus Teacher Belton Sr HS 1962-69; Eudora HS 1969-70; Asst/Auditor 1970-71; Accountant 1978-79; Admin/Asst 1979-82 Univ of KS; Teacher/Coord Lawrence Public Sch 1982-; *ai:* Adv Bus Prof of Amer; HS Rep Lawrence Ed Assn; Mem Various Comm Lawrence HS; NEA/KNEA/LEA 1982-; Phi Delta Kappa Treas 1987-89; AVA/KVA 1986-; United Meth Church; *office:* Lawrence HS 1901 Louisiana Lawrence KS 66046

GLENN, GEORGIA STARNES, Biology Teacher; *b:* York, SC; *m:* Simmaul; *c:* Eric, Corey; *ed:* (BA) Bio, Claflin Coll 1963; (MS) Bio, Cntrl MI Univ 1970; Geology, IN Univ 1965; Working Towards Masters Cntrl MI Beaver Island; *cr:* Teacher Choppee HS 1963-64, Wilson Jr HS 1964-65, Emerson HS 1965-70, Lindblom HS 1972-83, Bogan HS 1983-; *ai:* Bio Club Spon; Nat Sci Fnd IN Univ Geology Grant 1965 & Cntrl MI Univ Masters Degree Bio Grant.

GLENN, HELEN J., 4th Grade Teacher; *b:* Vincennes, IN; *m:* Robert A.; *c:* Kris, David, Jennifer; *ed:* (BS) Elem Ed, 1970, (MED) Counseling Psych, 1989 Univ of IL; *cr:* Kndgtn Teacher Round Lake Elem 1970-71; Elem Teacher Decatur IL Dist 61 1971-; *ai:* Decatur Fed of Teachers 1990; Kappa Delta Pi 1988-;

Macon Sch Bd (Pres 1987-91) 1983-; Jr Welfare Assn 1983-; *office:* Johns Hill/Decatur Dist 61 1025 E Johns Decatur IL 62521

GLENN, JUNE BETTON, Choral Director; *b:* Pine Bluff, AR; *c:* Wilford E. Jr., Stephen A., Stephanie R. Glen Tate, Letitia A.; *ed:* (BS) Music Ed, Univ of AR 1961; (MS) Admin/Supervision Trevecca Nazarene Coll 1989; Music Ed Univ of TN; *cr:* Music Teacher Douglass HS 1962-74, Overton HS 1974-75, Northside HS 1975-86, Carver HS 1986-89, Northside HS 1989-; *ai:* Spon All Choral Act; Concert Choir, Chamber Choir, Male Chorus, Female Chorus & Show Choir; W TN Vocal Assn Sr HS Chm 1983-87, Leadership Excl 1985-87; TN Music Educators Assn Bd Mem 1983-87; Music Educators Natl Conference 1968-; Amer Choral Dirs Assn 1980-; Memphis Ed Assn, TN Ed Assn, NEA; Delta Sigma Theta Secy 1964-66, Service 1966; *office:* Northside HS 1212 Vollintine St Memphis TN 38107

GLENN, KATHERINE, Membership Representative; *b:* Harrisburg, PA; *c:* Cynthia L. Bates, Lawrence Landauer, Joy; *ed:* (BS) Home Ed/Art, Drexel Univ 1957; Religious Philosophy, 1965; (MA) Ed/Counseling, UCSD 1976; Montessori Dir 1976; Theology 1965; Steiner 1975; Health, Phys Therapy, Nutrition; *cr:* Teacher Brookhaven Jr HS; Home Ec Teacher Anaheim Sch Dist 1968-69; 7th-12th Grade Home Ec/Adult Ed Teacher San Diego Sch Dist 1969-72; Pre-Sch/Adult Ed Teacher Escondido HS 1975-78; Substitute Teacher/Adult Ed Puyallup HS 1978-81; Instr/Adv Home Sch 1983-86; *ai:* Home Sch Assn Kalispell MT Founder; Amer Home Ec Assn 1966-72; Amer Assn Univ Women 1983-85; NRTA, AARP 1968-; DAR (Indian Affairs Conservation 1990, Public Relations 1960-62); AAA Top Sales Rep Awd; *home:* 38 5th Ave E Kalispell MT 59901

GLENN, SANDRA KAY, English Teacher; *b:* Sulphur Springs, TX; *ed:* (BS) Bus Ed, 1964, (MED) Elem Ed/Eng, 1967 E TX St Univ; Cert Librarian & EMR Spec Ed; *cr:* Teacher Miller Grove Rural HS 1967-72, Sulphur Springs Ind Sch Dist 1972-; *ai:* Jr Class Spon; Mem Attendance Update, Southern Assn Evaluation Comm Chm; Cmmty Ed Prgm; TX St Teachers Assn; *home:* Rt 2 Box 322 Sulphur Springs TX 75482

GLENNON, OWEN G., Math Teacher; *b:* Chicago, IL; *m:* Carlin Marie Schmid; *c:* Carlin M., Owen J.; *ed:* (BS) Math 1975; Juris Doctor Law 1983 Loyola Univ; *cr:* Math Teacher Marist HS 1976-; *ai:* Moderator of Marist HS Math Team; Math Teachers Assn 1976-; IL St Bar Assn 1983-; the Kohl Ed Fnd 1985-; Marist Lay Teachers Assn Pres 1984-; Univ of Chicago Outstanding Teacher Awd 1983-84; Kohl Fnd Awd for Exemplary Teaching 1985; *office:* Marist H S 4200 W 115th St Chicago IL 60655

GLESSNER, THERESA ANN, English/Journalism Teacher; *b:* Chester, PA; *ed:* (BA) Eng/Comm, Lycoming Coll 1982; (MA) Eng, Kutztown Univ 1989; *cr:* Eng/Journalism Teacher Northampton HS 1982-; Adjunct Eng Professor Lehigh Cty Comm Coll 1989-; *ai:* Yrbk, Newspaper Adv; PA Sch Scholastic Press Assn Bd of Judges 1989, All-St Awd 1989; Columbia Scholastic Press Assn Medalist Awd 1988; *home:* 711 10th Ave Bethlehem PA 18018

GLICKMAN, MARSHA, 2nd Grade Teacher; *b:* Philadelphia, PA; *ed:* (BS) Elem Ed, Temple Univ 1964; Grad Stud; *cr:* 3rd/4th Grade Teacher Rowland Elem Sch 1964-77; 2nd Grade Teacher Cheltenham Elem Sch 1977-; *ai:* PSEA, NEA, CEA; *office:* Cheltenham Elem Sch Ashbourne Rd & Front St Cheltenham PA 19012

GLICKSTEIN-SANDY, BARBRA, 6th Grade Teacher; *b:* Buffalo, NY; *m:* David; *c:* Jeff, Kelly, Kevin; *ed:* (BA) Elem Ed, OH Northern Univ 1972; (MS) Admin/Supervision, Univ of Dayton 1976; Discipline Gifted Ed Classes; *cr:* 5th Grade Teacher Elida Elem 1972-81; 6th Grade Teacher Elida Mid Sch 1981-; *ai:* Quiz Bowl Adv; Sch Newspaper Past Adv; Mid Sch Accelerated Prgm; Good Apple Bulletin Bd Book Writer; Books Co-Author; *office:* Elida Local Schls 4500 Sunnydale Elida OH 45807

GLIDDEN, BETTY TIBBETTS, Language Art/Soc Stud Teacher; *b:* Palermo, ME; *m:* Howard E.; *c:* Rodny, Rebeccado, Patricia J., Susan Glidden Leary; *ed:* (BS) Elem Ed, Univ of ME Farmington 1957; Early Chldhd, Mid Sch Concept, Exceptional Stu; Admin, Prin Acad; *cr:* 5th Grade Teacher Huston Sch 1957-58; 6th Grade Teacher Farrington Sch 1958-59; 3rd-5th Grade Teacher 1959-61, Jr Primary Teacher 1962-64 Palermo Consolidated Sch; Jr Primary Teacher China Elem Sch 1964-65, Palermo Consolidated Sch 1965-66; 5th/6th Grade Teacher 1966-67,Elem Teacher 1970-76, 1st/2nd Grade Teacher 1976-79, 1st/2nd Grade Teacher/Prin 1979-82, 1st/2nd Grade Regular Classroom/Lang Art/6th-8th Grade Soc Stud Teacher 1982-88, 7th/8th Grade Lang Art/Soc Stud Teacher 1988-89, 6th-8th Grade Lang Art/Soc Stud Teacher 1989- Palermo Consolidated Sch; *ai:* Spelling Bee, Civic Oration, Educl Fair Coord; Beginning Teachers Support Team; Asst Prin; ME Teachers Assn, NEA 1957-; ME Assn Mid Sch 1986-; Palermo Teachers Assn 1960-; ME Teachers Support Team 1988-; Sheepscot Lake Fish & Game Assn Secy 1965-88; Branch Mills Grange Local St Natl Levels; Palermo Sch Club 1960-; Volumteer Abenaki Cncl GSA 1986-89; Ad Hoc Planning Comm St Dept Soc Stud Publication; Prin Acad; Erskine Acad Advisory Bd & Curr Sub-Comm; Palermo Stu Service Awd; *office:* Palermo Consolidated Sch Rt 3 Palermo ME 04354

GLIDEWELL, JOSEPH WILLIAM, History Teacher; *b:* Elberton, GA; *m:* Jane Balchin; *c:* Joseph, Clarke; *ed:* (BS) Ed/Soc Sci, GA Southern 1972; (MED) Ed/Soc Sci, GA Coll 1979; His, Clemson Univ; *cr:* Teacher Samuel Elbert Acad 1972-75, Boddie Jr HS 1977-79, Elbert Cty Mid Sch 1979-89, Elbert Cty Comprehensive HS 1989-; *ai:* Jr Var & Frosh Bsbl Coach; His Club Spon; GA Assn Educators (Treas 1990) 1989-; Meth Mens Club (VP 1987-88, Pres 1988-89); Pod Leader at Elbert Cty Mid Sch; Nom for Ernest Lander Awd Best His Paper 1987; Articles Published; *office:* Elbert Cty Comp HS 600 Jones St Elberton GA 30635

GLIDWELL, DELRAE BACKUS, Vocal Music Instructor; *b:* Mountain Grove, MO; *m:* Robert D.; *c:* Ryan C., Bock C; *ed:* (BS) Music, Southwest Baptist Univ 1971; *cr:* Music Teacher 1971-1976; Music Teacher 1976-; *ai:* Show Choir; MO St Teachers Assn 1971-; MO Music Educators Assn 1971-; Music Educators Natl Convention 1971-; Kappa Kappa Iota 1984-; Community Concert Assn 1971-; Federated Music Club 1972-89; Chamber Commerce Spec Recog Awd-1982; Music Festival Vienna Austria-1982; *home:* 1110 S Carl Bolivar MO 65613

GLOCK, CAROL THOMAS, French Teacher; *b:* Pittsburgh, PA; *m:* Carl C. III; *c:* Taylor K.; *ed:* (BS) Fr/Eng, Clarion St Coll 1965; (MED) Univ of Pittsburgh 1972; Working Toward Masters Scndry Counseling; Learning Japanese; *cr:* Instr Millvale HS 1965-66, East Deer HS 1966-67, Valley HS 1967-; *ai:* Fr Club Spon; PSEA, NEA, PSMLA; Jr Womens Club; *office:* Valley Sr HS Stevenson Blvd New Kensington PA 15068

GLOCK, DORIS P. HAND, English Teacher; *b:* Liverpool, England; *m:* George N.; *c:* Paul J.; *ed:* (BS) Eng/His, Kent St Univ 1968; Working on PhD; *cr:* Doctoral Candidate Instr 1968-72, Temporary Instr 1975-76 Kent St Univ; Eng Teacher Avondale HS 1976-78, Hoover HS 1978-; *ai:* Kappa Delta Pi Secy 1990; Chrstn Writers Guild 1987-; Phi Alpha Theta 1972-; NCTE 1978-; Published Articles & Poetry; Ashland Oil Company Golden Apple Awd 1988; Copy Ed Acts 29 1983-84; Taught Creative Writing Adult Classes; *office:* Hoover HS Fair Oaks Dr North Canton OH 44720

GLODICH, JAMES THOMAS, Phys Ed Teacher/Coach; *b:* Detroit, MI; *m:* Kimberly Louise Kyner; *c:* James T., John A.; *ed:* (AA) Lib Arts, Macomb Comm Coll 1977; (BA) Ed, Western MI Univ 1980; (MS) Sch Admin, TX A&I Univ 1989; Athletic Trng, Western MI; Cmptr Literacy, Northside Ind Sch Dist; *cr:* Teacher/Coach Warren Fitzgerald HS 1980-82, Anson Jones Mid Sch 1982-85, Hobby Mid Sch 1985-; *ai:* 7th Grade Ftbl, 8th Grade Bsktbl, Track Coach; At-Risk Stu Comm; Coord Mentor Prgm; Assn TX Prof Educators 1985-; *home:* 9142 Autumn Storm San Antonio TX 78250

GLOGOWSKI, DAVID GERARD, English Teacher; *b:* Omaha, NE; *c:* Elizabeth; *ed:* Scndry Ed, 1980, Teacher Ed, 1989 Univ of NE Omaha; *cr:* Eng Teacher Millard Cntrl Mid Sch 1980-; *ai:* Spon for Cntrl Mid Sch Crective Writers Club; Mem of K-12th Composition Comm; *office:* Millard Cntrl Mid Sch 12801 L Street Omaha NE 68137

GLOGOWSKI, MARILYN CIGARSKI, 5th Grade Teacher; *b:* Kingston, PA; *m:* Walter; *ed:* (BS) Elem, Misericordia 1973; (MS) Wilkes; *cr:* Remedial Rdng Teacher 1975-76, 6th Grade Teacher 1976-78, 4th-6th Grade Teacher 1978-82, 5th Grade Teacher 1982- Lake Lehman; *ai:* Harveys Lake Womens Club 1988-; PTA; Teachers Union Pres; *office:* Lehman Jackson Elem Sch Market St Lehman PA 18627

GLORE, MARILYN HILL, Guidance Counselor; *b:* Poplar Bluff, MO; *m:* Daniel C.; *c:* Jamie L., Tara N.; *ed:* (BSED) Math/Eng, 1968; (MAED) Cnslng, 1972 SE MO St Univ; Mathematics T,Jackson HS 1968-71, Guidance Counselor,Fox HS 1971-; *cr:* Math Teacher Jackson HS 1968-71; Guidance Cnslr Fox HS 1971-; *ai:* Advanced Placement Coord Fox HS; Phi Delta Kappa 1986-; Delta Kappa Gamma 1987-; MO Schl Cnslrs Assn 1972-; Jefferson Cty Sch Cnslrs Assn 1971, Secy 1981-81; C-6 Ed Assn, MO Ed Assn, NEA; Ladies Aid Pres 1988-; Sunday Sch Teacher 1987-; *office:* Fox HS 745 Jeffco Blvd Arnold MO 63010

GLOSSENGER, CAROLYN SUE (WEBB), Business Computer Ed Teacher; *b:* Fort Wayne, IN; *c:* Teressa L. Wolf, Debra L.; *ed:* (BS) Bus Ed, 1959, (MS) Bus Ed, 1962, (MS) Guidance/Counseling, 1964 Ball St Univ; Certificate in Bus & Voc Prgms 1971; *cr:* Bus Teacher Niles Sr HS 1959-61, New Castle HS 1961-62; Bus Teacher/Guidance Huntington Township HS 1963-64; Guidance Cnslr Mingo Junction 1967-68, Woodlan Jr HS 1968-69; Bus Teacher Kialua HS 1970-71; Guidance Cnslr New Haven Jr HS 1971-73; Bus Teacher New Haven HS 1973-; *ai:* Building Cmptr Coord; Teacher for Teachers Teaching Teachers; NEA & IN St Teachers Assn 1971-; IN Cmptr Educators 1989-; E Allen Educators Assn 1971-, Golden Apple Awd 1972; Fort Wayne Apple Users Group Pres 1989-; Published Articles; *office:* New Haven HS 1300 Green Rd New Haven IN 46774

GLOWA, DODIE SCHERF, Social Studies Teacher; *b:* Washington, DC; *m:* Daniel S.; *c:* Ben Bradley, Amy L. Bradley; *ed:* (BA) His/Sociology, Columbus Coll 1970; (MS) Guidance/Human Dev, Troy St Univ 1978; TAFT Inst of Government; FL Soc Stud Teachers Wkshp; Gifted Courses for Cert; *cr:* Soc Stud Teacher Pryor Jr HS 1970-72, Niceville HS 1972-73; Soc Stud Dept Chairperson 1981-86, Soc Stud Teacher 1973- Choctawhatchee HS; *ai:* Girls Golf Team Coach; Southern Assn Guidance Evaluation Comm Chairperson; Natl Soc Stud Assn 1988; Phi Delta Kappa Prgm Comm Co-Chairperson 1987; Amer Assn Univ Women Comm Chairperson 1985-87; Okaloosa Cty Mental Health Assn; Work with Gifted Stu Citation; FL Youth in Government Prgm Plaque; Taft Inst Grant; *office:* Choctawhatchee HS 110 Racetrack Rd Fort Walton Beach FL 32548

GLOWACKI, WALTER M., Geography Teacher; *b:* Easthampton, MA; *m:* Jean M. Enko; *ed:* (BS) Ed/Geography, Westfield St Coll 1959; (MS) Ed/Geography, S IL Univ 1962; (MA) Geography, Univ of KY 1971; Grad Stud Univ KY 1969-70; *cr:* Grad Asst S IL Univ 1959-60; Teacher Granby Jr/Sr HS & Granby Mid Sch 1960-; *ai:* Stu Cncl Adv; Personnel Policies Curr, Various Other Comm; NEA, CEA, GEA; Grant Teaching Assistantship S IL Univ 1959-60; Several Articles Published Natl Ed Journals; Best Geography Article Awd 1972; Natl Cncl Geographic Ed Awd 1971, 1974; *home:* 114 Feeding Hills Rd Southwick MA 01077

GLOWSKI, NORMA KAY (BRININGER), American History Teacher; *b:* Fremont, OH; *ed:* (BA) His/Poly Sci, Hiram Coll 1964; (MA) Ed/His, Kent St 1976; *cr:* Teacher James A Garfield HS 1964-66, Cuyahoga Falls HS 1966-; *ai:* Close-Up Club Adv; Soc Stud Dept Chairperson; Staff Sunshine Fund, Staff Morale & Soc Comm Chm; CFEA, OEA, NEOTA, NEA 1964-; Cuyahoga Falls Schls Teacher of Yr 1987; Summit Cty Close-Up Chairperson 1988-; Residents Against Garbage Environments Secy 1988-89; Congressman Sawyers Military Acad Review Bd 1987-; Hiram Coll Alumni Comm Mem 1984-; *office:* Cuyahoga Falls HS 2300 4th St Cuyahoga Falls OH 44221

GLUSS, JACQUELYN S., 4th Grade Teacher; *b:* Mt Vernon, IL; *m:* Raymond; *c:* Tarra; *ed:* (BS) Elem Ed, S IL Univ 1971; Several Wkshps S IL Univ; *cr:* 4th/5th Grade Teacher Scott Sch; *ai:* Chorus Adv Choreographer; *office:* Scott Sch Mannheim Dist 83 2250 Scott St Melrose Park IL 60164

GLYNN, VIOLET MARTINO, Third Grade Teacher; *b:* Chicago, IL; *m:* Donald M.; *ed:* (BA) Psych, Mundelein Coll 1957; (MED) Admin/Supervision, Loyola Univ 1963; *cr:* 1st Grade Teacher Beidler Public Sch 1957-60; 3rd Grade Teacher John Hay Public Sch 1961-68; 2nd Grade Teacher Mc Kinley Public Sch 1969-73; 3rd Grade Teacher Kellar Public Sch 1974-87, Hines Public Sch 1988-; *ai:* Stamp Club; Peoria & IL Fed of Teachers; Peoria Symphony Guild; *office:* Hines Primary Sch 4603 N Knoxville Peoria IL 61614

GNAD, LEROY P., Mathematics Teacher; *b:* Ellis, KS; *m:* Mary A.; *c:* Troy, Dionne; *ed:* (BS) Math/Physics, 1963, (MS) Math, 1969 Ft Hays St Univ; *cr:* Math Teacher Thomas More Preparatory 1964-; *ai:* Asst Ftbl Coach; NCTM 1964-; Knights of Columbus 1960-; Natl Sci Fnd Summer Inst; *home:* 307 E 24th St Hays KS 67601

GNAGEY, PATRICIA ANN (ZAMER), Business Teacher; *b:* Washington, DC; *m:* Keith; *c:* Christopher, Eric; *ed:* (BS) Bus Ed/Secretarial/Typewriting, Indiana Univ of PA 1983; Grad Stud Univ of Pittsburgh, Indiana Univ of PA, Duquesne Univ, CA Univ, Wilkes Coll; *cr:* Substitute Teacher Turkeyfoot Valley Area HS 1980-83; Bus Teacher Meyersdale Area HS 1983-; *ai:* FBLA Adv Meyersdale Area HS; Homecoming Queen Assembly, Contest Act Coord; PSEA, NEA 1983-; United Meth Church Trustee 1984-89; Meyersdale Area Ed Assn Secy; Office of Secy Local Band Boosters Organization; 6-Yr Term of Office Local Township Auditor; *home:* RD 1 Box 195 Garrett PA 15542

GNEITING, BARBARA GOULD, Kindergarten-4th Grade Teacher; *b:* Everett, WA; *m:* Robert Lee; *c:* Heather, Jeremy; *ed:* (BS) Elem Ed, W MT Coll 1978; *cr:* Teacher Rigby Elem 1978-80, Wise River Sch 1980-; *ai:* Track & Swimming Coach; Supervising Teacher; MT Sci Teachers Assn 1986-; MT Grange Exec 1988-; 4-H Cooking Leader 1986-; Crazy Coyote Players Actress 1985-; Selected to Participate in Better Elem Sci Teachers 1989; *home:* Box 7 Melrose MT 59743

GNODTKE, SANDRA KAY (DAHLEN), Kindergarten/Preschool Teacher; *b:* Iola, WI; *m:* Armand E.; *c:* Allan, Jeffrey, Brian, Erin; *ed:* (BS) Elem Ed, Valparaiso Univ 1964; Grad Work Early Chldhd, Andrews Univ; *cr:* 2nd Grade Teacher Galien Township Schls 1964-67; Kndgtn/Pre-Sch Teacher Trinity Luth Sch 1976-; *ai:* Church Organist; *office:* Trinity Luth Sch PO Box 23 Sawyer MI 49125

GOAD, JAMES NELSON, 8th/9th Grade Ag Teacher; *b:* Carroll Cty, VA; *ed:* (AAS) Ag Bus, 1972, (AS) Sci, 1973 Wytheville Comm Coll; (BS) Ag Ed, VPI & SU 1975; *cr:* Ag Teacher Carroll Cty Sch Bd Woodlawn Intermediate Sch 1975-; *ai:* FFA, Young Farmers, SCA; Carroll Ed Assn, NEA, VA Ed Assn 1975-; Southern Sts Cooperative Chm 1988-; *office:* Woodlawn Intermediate Sch Rt 1 Box 6-B Woodlawn VA 24381

GOADE, CHARLES EDWARD, Social Studies Teacher; *b:* Granby, MO; *m:* Barbara Joan Ball; *c:* Lisa A.; *ed:* (AA) Phys Ed, Southwest Baptist Coll 1957; (BS) Phys Ed, SW MO St 1959; (ME) Soc Stud, Drury 1976; Grad Stud; *cr:* Teacher/Coach Goodman HS 1959-66, E Newton HS 1966-73, Highland HS 1973-74, Neosho HS 1974-; *ai:* NHS Adv; *office:* Neosho R-5 Sch 511 Neosho Blvd Neosho MO 64850

GOATES, WAYNE, Science/Communications Teacher; *b:* Wichita, KS; *m:* Janell Ann Mc Dermed; *c:* Angela A., Brian W.; *ed:* (BS) Eng/Chem, 1969, (MA) Counseling/Sch Psych, 1990 Wichita St Univ; *cr:* 7th/9th Grade Sci Teacher Augusta Jr HS 1969-74; 9th Grade Eng/Comm Teacher Goddard Jr HS 1985-88; 7th Grade Sci/9th Grade Comm Teacher Goddard Jr HS 1988-; *ai:* Asst 8th Grade Ftbl Coach; Head 7th Grade Track Coach; Optimist Intnl Oratorical Contest Spon; NEA; KS Natl Ed Assn 1985-; Goddard Ed Assn 1969-74; KS Assn Teachers of Sci 1988-; NSF Grants Univ of KS 1973-74; Track Coach of Yr 1973-74; *office:* Goddard Jr H S 335 N Walnut Goddard KS 67052

GOATLEY, BRENDA PENN, 8th Grade Reading Teacher; *b:* Lynn, AR; *ed:* (BS) Voc Home Ec, Harding Coll 1965; (MA) Comm Art, Webster Univ 1977; Cert Elem Ed; *cr:* Teacher Rietnour Elem 1965-81, Ritenour Mid Sch 1981-82, Ritenour HS 1982-83, Ritenour Mid Sch 1984-; *ai:* 8th Grade Adv; MO St Teachers Assn 1976-; Rush Creek Homeowners Assn (Secy, Treas) 1985-; *office:* Ritenour Mid Sch 8470 Forest Ave Overland MO 63114

GOBBLE, JEFFREY S., 8th Grade Soc Stud Teacher; *b:* Lexington, NC; *m:* Tina Morgenson; *ed:* (BA) His, Univ NC Charlotte 1979; (MS) Intermediate Ed, NC A&T St 1984; Exceptional Children Trng; *cr:* Remedial Aide 1979-80, Soc Stud Teacher 1980-81, Rmedial Aide 1981-84, Exeptional Children & Soc Stud Teacher 1984- N Davidson Jr HS; *ai:* Sch Newspaper Adv; Ebenezer United Meth Church Cncl Ministeries Chairperson 1985-89; *office:* North Davidson Jr HS Rt 10 Lexington NC 27292

GOBEL, CYNTHIA, 4th Grade Teacher; *b:* Colusa, CA; *ed:* (BA) Phys Ed, 1976, (BA) Liberal Stud, 1981 CA St Univ Chico; Driver Trng, CA St Univ Chico 1981; Coaching: *cr:* 8th Grade Teacher Williams Mid Sch; 3rd Grade Teacher Williams Elem Sch 1983-86; 6th Grade Teacher 1986-89, 4th Grade Teacher 1989- Williams Mid Sch; *ai:* Mentor Teacher Selection & Inservice Comm; Driver Trng Prgm Coord; CA Teachers Assn 1981-; *office:* Williams Mid Sch P O Box 7 11th & C Streets Williams CA 95987

GOBEL, DEBRA WRIGHT, 4th Grade Teacher; *b:* Oneonta, AL; *m:* Danny; *c:* Nathan, Nicholas; *ed:* (BA) Elem Ed, 1980, (MS) Elem Ed, 1984 Univ of AL Birmingham; N AL Teacher Exchange Consultant; *cr:* 5th Grade Teacher Southeastern Elem 1980-89; 4th Grade Teacher Blountsville Elem 1989-; *office:* Blountsville Elem Sch PO Box 160 Blountsville AL 35031

GOBER, DEBORAH ANN, Mathematics Teacher; *b:* Chestertown, MD; *ed:* (BA) Math/Scndry Ed, Asbury Coll 1982; *cr:* Math Teacher Freedom HS 1982-; *ai:* Asst Bsktbl & Sftbl Coach; Jr/Sr Prom Coord; NEA; *home:* PO Box 846 Rutherford Clge NC 28671

GOBLE, BETTY MORIN, 6th Grade Teacher; *b:* Waynesboro, VA; *m:* James Thomas; *c:* Kelly, Kimberly A.; *ed:* (BA) Psych/Ed, Mary Washington Coll 1958; *cr:* 6th Grade Teacher Cora Kelly Elem 1958-62, Columbia Elem 1968-69, Hancock Elem 1970-72, Somerset Elem 1972-73, Monroe Elem 1973-74, Loganville Mid Sch 1974-; *ai:* 6th Grade Chm; Walton Assn of Educators, GA Assn of Educators, NEA; Nob Hill Cntry Club Pres 1974; STAR Teacher; Loganville Mid Teacher of Yr; Outstanding Elem Teachers of Amer; Instructional Fair Winner; *home:* 2148 New London Pl Snellville GA 30278

GOBLE, LYLE, English Dept Chair/Teacher; *b:* Colusa, CA; *ed:* (AS) Pre-Engineering, Bid Bend Comm Coll 1965; (BAED) His, Cntrl WA Univ 1967; (MAED) Curr/Instruction, EasterN WA Univ 1991; Univ Innsbruck Austria 1977; Portland St Univ Morocco 1979; *cr:* Hist/Geog Teacher Madras Sr HS 1967-68; His/Eng Teacher Quincy Sr HS 1968-; *ai:* Lib Supvr; Weight Trng Supvr; Class Adv; World Game Team Adv; Phi Delta Kappa; NCTE; Assn for Curr Dev; Mem Faculty Senate; Mem Steering Comm; Sch Self-Study Evaluation for Accrediation; Mem Selection Team for Teacher of Yr; Comm Mem for Writing Curr Guide Eng K-12th; Chm Eng Comm for Curr Self-Study; *office:* Quincy H S 16 6th Ave SE Quincy WA 98848

GODBY, GIOVANNA BURKS, English Teacher; *b:* Glasgow, KY; *m:* Jeffrey L.; *ed:* (BA) Eng 1978; (MED) Eng Ed 1985 Univ of Louisville; *cr:* Eng Teacher Our Lady of Providence HS 1978-81; Asst Dir Cystic Fibrosis Fnd 1981-84; Grad Asst Univ of Louisville 1984-85; Assoc Editor Mountain Spirit Magazine1985-88; Eng Teacher Boyle Cty HS 1988-; *ai:* Advisor SADD; JR Class Spon; NCTE; Phi Delta Kappa; ALAN: KCTE; Kappa Delta Sorority; Article Published in ALAN Review 1989; Nominee Ashland Oil Teacher of Year 1990; Wrote Nomination Pkg Elem Sch 1989-90; Elem Sch Recognition Prgm.

GODDARD, F. HOWARD, Retired Teacher; *b:* San Francisco, CA; *m:* Carol G.; *c:* Glen, Mark, Kirk, Susan, Karen; *ed:* (BA) Eng, St Marys Coll 1950; *cr:* Teacher Merced Union HS 1956-58, Lakeport HS 1958-59, Merced Union HS 1959-89; *ai:* Swim & Jr Var Ftbl Coach 1959-77; Class of 1963 & 1983 Adv; CA Teachers Assn 1956-89; Natl Rifle Assn, Veterans of Foreign Wars 1983-; Amer Legion 1987-; *home:* 2625 E Dunn Rd Merced CA 95340

GODDIN, DEBORAH ELLIS, English Teacher; *b:* Newport News, VA; *m:* Gustavus A. III; *c:* Chris, Paul, Gus, Bob; *ed:* (BA) Eng, Christopher Newport Coll 1973; (MS) Ed/Eng, Old Dominion Univ 1981; *cr:* Eng Teacher Poquoson HS 1973-; Adjunct Eng Teacher Thomas Nelson Comm Coll 1981-; *ai:* Soph Class & Academic Team Co-Spon; Poquoson HS Prof Cncl Secy; Natl Assn of Teachers of Eng 1987-; VA Assn of Teachers of Eng 1987-; Poquoson HS PTO Treas 1983-84; Poquoson Ed Assn Treas 1974-75; Poquoson HS Order of Bullpen 1988; *office:* Poquoson HS 51 Odd Rd Poquoson VA 23662

GODE, ELIZABETH FAYE, Soc Stud Dept Chair; *b:* Blanco, TX; *m:* Robert David; *c:* Shannon, Jackie, Amanda, Abby; *ed:* (BA) His, N TX Univ 1976; Teaching Cert His/Eng, E TX St Univ 1986; *cr:* Scndry Teacher 1986-89, Dept Chairperson 1989- Winnsboro HS; *ai:* Drama Ovation; Literary Criticism Coach; UIL Coord; Faculty Advisory Comm; Phi Alpha Theta 1976-; Kappa Delta Pi 1986-; 4-H Leader 1985-; *home:* Rt 1 Box 79C Como TX 75431

GODFREY, CAROL A., 2nd Grade Teacher; *b:* Saint Johns, MI; *m:* Ronald Leroy; *c:* Amanda, David; *ed:* (BA) Elem Ed/Soc Stud, Cntrl MI Univ 1967; *cr:* 3rd Grade Teacher Greenville Public Schls 1968-69; 2nd/3rd Grade Teacher Belding Public Schls 1969-71; 3rd Grade Teacher 1971-73, 6th Grade Teacher Rdng Prgm 1973-78, 2nd Grade Teacher 1978- Hesperia Cmmty Sch; *office:* Patricia St Clair Elem Sch 96 S Division Hesperia MI 49421

GODFREY, EDWARD J., Mathematics/German Teacher; *b:* Philadelphia, PA; *ed:* (BA) Ger, St Josephs Coll 1974; *cr:* 5th-8th Grade Teacher Our Lady of Good Counsel Sch 1974-84; Teacher Holy Cross HS 1984-; *ai:* Bowling Coach; Ger Club Moderator; AATG Mem 1989-; AMTNJ Mem 1984-; *home:* 227 Rockland Ave Maple Shade NJ 08052

GODFREY, ERNEST E., Biology Instructor; *b:* Cowley, WY; *m:* Marlene; *c:* Kelly Chimienti, David, Teresa Moffat, Lisa Zurcher, Jennifer Schad; *ed:* (BS) Bio Sci/Phys Ed, E MT Coll 1958; (MS) Sci, Syracuse Univ 1965; Grad Work at Several Insts; *cr:* Sci Instr Redway Jr HS 1958-59, Willits HS 1959-65; Bio Instr Cascade HS 1966-; *ai:* Asst Ftbl Coach 1977; Soph Class & Sci Club Adv; NEA 1958-; CA Ed Assn Local Pres 1958-65; OR Ed Assn Local Pres 1966-; Aumsville Fire Dist Bd of Dir 1984-; OR Simmental Assn Bd of Dir 1989-; Nation Sci Academic Yr Grant 1965-66; *office:* Cascade HS 10226 Marion Rd SE Turner OR 97392

GODFREY, SUSAN GAYLE, History Teacher; *b:* Memphis, TX; *ed:* (BS) Ed, W TX St Univ 1978; *cr:* 5th Grade Teacher Oscar Hinger Intermediate 1979-84; His Teacher Valleyview Jr HS 1984-; *ai:* PTA 1984-; NCSS 1990; *office:* Valleyview Jr HS 9000 Valleyview Dr Amarillo TX 79110

GODSEY, LINDA EARNEST, Fourth Grade Teacher; *b:* Winfield, AL; *m:* James R.; *c:* Jeffrey, Robin Shelton, Christopher, Alycia Eady; *ed:* (BS) Elem Ed, 1976, (MA) Elem Ed, 1979 Univ of N AL; *cr:* 4th Grade Teacher Lauderdale Cty HS 1977-; *ai:* 4th Grade Leader for Cty Inservice 1989-; NEA, AL Ed Assn, Lauderdale Cty Ed Assn 1977-; PTA (Secy 1979-80, VP 1984-85); S Cntrl Bell Mini-Grant 1989-; *office:* Lauderdale County HS P O Drawer 220 Rogersville AL 35652

GODSO, CAROL BROWN, Mathematics Teacher; *b:* New York, NY; *m:* Alan Kurt; *ed:* (BA) Scndry Ed, TX A&M Univ 1985; *cr:* Math Teacher Cy-Fair HS 1985-; *ai:* Assn of TX Prof Educators 1986-; *home:* 13007 Lemur Ln Cypress TX 77429

GODT, FRANCES WILSON, Science/Reading Grades Teacher; *b:* Wilmington, DE; *m:* Harry Eugene; *c:* Harry E. Jr., Susan E.; *ed:* (BS) Elem Ed, DE St Coll 1974; Comm, Norfolk St Coll 1976-77; Rdng, Univ DE; Norfolk St Coll; Systematic Trng Effective Teaching; Environmental Conservation Ed Prgms; *cr:* 6th Grade Teacher/Asst Prin Bayard Mid Sch 1971-76; 7th-9th Grade Remedial Math Teacher P S du Pont Mid Sch 1976-81; 1st Grade Teacher Wilmington Manor Elem 1982-83; 5th Grade Sci Teacher Marbrook Elem Sch 1983-; *ai:* Title VII Multi Cultural Summer Sch 1976, Outstanding Teacher 1976; Kappa Delta Pi Charter Mem 1978-; Honor Society of Ed; DE Nature Ed Society Outstanding Environmental Educator Awd 1986; Awarded Grant Red Clay Consolidated Sch Dist Promote Stu Act; Environmental Ed.

GODWIN, GREGORY SHELDON, Science Department Chairman; *b:* High Point, NC; *m:* Darlene Early; *c:* Andrew; *ed:* (BS) Bio, Appalachian St Univ 1984; *cr:* Sci Dept Chm Princeton HS 1984-; *ai:* SADD Adv; Soph Class Lead Teacher & Chm; Schlrsp Comm Mem; NC Wildlife Assn Mem 1985-; Triangle Land Conservancy Mem 1988-; Natl Wildlife Assn Mem 1985-; Nom Teacher of Yr Princeton HS 1987, 1988; Outstanding Teacher Attitude Awd 1986; *office:* Princeton HS Box 38 Old Hwy 70 Princeton NC 27569

GODWIN, JAMIE KEY, Fifth Grade Teacher; *b:* De Queen, AR; *m:* G. Gailon; *c:* Kory; *ed:* (BSE) Elem Ed, Henderson St Univ 1971; Effective Teaching Prgm 1987; Several Wkshps; *cr:* Eng Teacher De Queen Jr HS 1971-72; 5th Grade Teacher De Queen Elem 1972-; *ai:* Cooperative Teacher S AR Univ Practice Teacher Prgm; Sch Policy Comm 1980-81, 1987-88; Southern Baptist (Sunday Sch & Vacation Bible Sch Teacher) 1960-; *home:* Rt 2 Box 623C De Queen AR 71832

GODWIN, KENNETH O., JR., Director of Choral Music; *b:* Grafton, WV; *ed:* (MM) Music Ed, 1968, (BM) Music Ed, 1966 WV Univ; Grad Work WV Univ; Study Overseas; *cr:* Asst Band Dir WV Univ 1966-68; Dir of Choral Music Grafton HS 1968-; *ai:* WV Dept of Ed Music Curr Writing Comm; WV Teachers Forum Planning Comm; WV on Site Review Team; WV Univ Creative Art Center Bd of Advs; Phi Mu Alpha Pres 1966-68; MENC All-St Chorus Chm 1972-74; Kappa Kappa Psi VP 1966-68; US Dept HEW Fellowship; WV Teacher of Yr 1982; ESEA Title C Grant; Jaycees Distinguished Service Awd; *office:* Grafton HS Riverside Dr Grafton WV 26354

GODWIN, VALORIE DAWN, English/Speech Teacher; *b:* Coeur D Alene, ID; *m:* Greg B.; *c:* Seth, John, Amy; *ed:* (BA) Eng, Univ of ID 1970; Grad Stud Ed, Eng, Speech, Comm; *cr:* Eng Teacher Lakeland HS 1970-78; Eng/Speech Teacher Kellogg HS 1987-; *ai:* Cats Who Care, Spec Writing Project, Jr Class Adv; Coach; Speech Arts Act; IEA, NEA 1970-78, 1987-; Phi Kappa Phi 1970-; Sweet Adelines 1986-88; Cath Daughters of America 1986-; *office:* Kellogg HS Jacobs Gulch Kellogg ID 83837

GODWIN, WILLIAM JOSEPH, JR., Advanced History Teacher; *b:* Milford, DE; *m:* Nancy Carter; *c:* Leanne, David, Marc; *ed:* (BA) Ed, Univ of MD 1967; Advanced His Seminars Univ of MD; Required Rdng, Spec Ed Cert Courses; *cr:* His Teacher Glenelg HS 1967-; *ai:* Track Coach; Howard Cty Ed Assn, MD St Teachers Assn, NEA; Distinguished Teacher Awd Western MD Coll; First Intnl Baccalaureate European His Teacher St of MD; *home:* 1925 Bethel Rd Finksburg MD 21048

GOEBEL, NANCY LOU, Third Grade Teacher; *b:* East Tawas, MI; *m:* Brad T.; *c:* Joshua, Brandon; *ed:* (BS) Sci/Math, Cntrl MI Univ 1970; *cr:* 3rd Grade Teacher Birch Run Public Schls 1970-73; 3rd/5th Grade Teacher Delton Kellogg Schls 1974-; *ai:* Building Comm to Build New Library in Delton; *office:* Delton Kellogg Elem Sch 327 N Grove St Delton MI 49046

GOEDKEN, KEITH A., Language Arts Dept Chairman; *b:* Sibley, IA; *ed:* (BA) Eng, Briar Cliff Coll 1973; Grad Stud Univ of N IA; *cr:* Lang Art Dept Chm 1973-, Curr Coord 1989- St Edmond HS; *ai:* Var Girls Track & Bsktbl Coach; Var Ftbl Asst Coach; Frosh Girls Bsktbl Coach; NCTE, IA Cncl of Teachers of Eng 1973-; ASCD 1989-; Knights of Columbus 1973-; N Cntrl Accrediting Assn Evaluation Teams Chm; Dept of Ed Comm to Write St Lang Art Curr; Governors Task Force to Study HS & Coll Articulation Issues; Spec Ed Advisory Bd; Area Ed Agency Bd for Continuing Ed; *office:* St Edmond HS 501 N 22nd St Fort Dodge IA 50501

GOEHRING, REBECCA SUSAN, Elementary Principal; *b:* Chicago, IL; *m:* Allan Frank; *c:* Molly J., Katharine A.; *ed:* (BA) Elem Ed/Phys Ed, Univ of ND 1973; Grad Stud Educl Admin, Univ of ND; *cr:* 5th/6th Grade Instr Lewis & Clark Elem 1973-75; Basic Skills Instr Montpelier Public Sch 1978-80; 5th/6th Grade Instr Nortonville Public Sch 1980-81; 5th/6th Grade Classroom/7th/8th Grade Lang Art Teacher/Elem Prin Wimbledon-Courtenay Public Sch 1983-; *ai:* Girls Bsktbl & Track Coach 1983-86; ND Assn of Elem Prin, NAESP, ASCD 1987-; NEA 1973-89; United Meth Women 1983-; Friendly Femmes Homemakers 1986-; *office:* Wimbledon-Courtenay Public Sch Box 255 Wimbledon ND 58492

GOEMBEL, BETTY LOUISE, Fifth Grade Teacher; *b:* Gibson City, IL; *m:* Philip D.; *c:* Courtney, Natalie; *ed:* (BS) Elem Ed, IL St Univ 1976; Leader Trng & Math Course; *cr:* 6th Grade Teacher Mid Cty Cmmty Sch Dist 1977-78; Co-Teacher Head Start 1978-79; 5th Grade Teacher Melvin-Sibly Cmmty Sch Dist 1980-; *ai:* Sci Consultant for Ford Cty Sci Grant; Ford Cty Gifted Grant; Jr Great Books Wrote & Received Grant *office:* Melvin-Sibley Grade Sch 100 N Franklin St Sibley IL 61773

GOERS, SANDRA LOU, Eng, Span & Reading Teacher; *b:* Chicago, IL; *m:* Jerry Richard Olson; *c:* Jason R. Goers Olson, Jessica R. Goers Olson; *ed:* (BS) Eng/Soc Sci, Winona St Univ 1972; Grad Stud at Various Univs; *cr:* Eng/Soc Stud Teacher St Cloud Mid Sch 1973-74; Remedial/Rdng Teacher Coppinville Jr HS 1974-75; Eng/Speech Teacher Bosworth R-V HS 1976-77; Eng Teacher Bogard R-IV HS 1977-80; Eng/Span/Rdng/Soc Stud Teacher Braymer C-4 HS 1980-; *ai:* Braymer C-4 Curr Comm Mem; Sr Class Spon; Amer Assn of Univ Women Legal Chairperson Chillicothe MO Branch 1983-84; Plymouth Cmmty Center Mem 1985-; Rural Water for WA Township Mem 1989-; *office:* Braymer C-4 HS 1 Bobcat Ave Box 427 Braymer MO 64624

GOES, JOHN ROBERT, 7th Grade Science Teacher; *b:* Chicago, IL; *m:* Judy Prosser; *c:* Steve, Andy; *ed:* (BA) Philosophy, Univ of Notre Dame 1966; (MA) Ed, U WI Milwaukee 1984; *cr:* 5th/7th Grade Teacher St Agnes Sch 1969-75; 7th/8th Grade Math Teacher IJP Sch 1975-77; 7th Grade Sci Teacher Northview Sch 1977-; *office:* Northview Elem Sch 902 Tyler Rd Howards Grove WI 53083

GOETJEN, LINDA JEANNE, Mathematics Dept Chairperson; *b:* Santa Monica, CA; *c:* Sheri Kabonic, John V. W. II; *ed:* (MS) Ed, La Verne 1990; *cr:* Teacher Rosedale 1969-; *ai:* Sch Site Cncl; Drama Coach; Dev of Sch Discipline; ASCD Mem 1989-; Amer Youth Soccer Organization Registrar 1982-; *office:* Rosedale Mid Sch 12463 Rosedale Hwy Bakersfield CA 93312

GOETZINGER, CAROLYN MC KINNEY, Mathematics Teacher; *b:* Okmulgee, OK; *m:* John W.; *c:* Douglas W., Karen J.; *ed:* (BSED) Elem Ed, 1958, (MT) Teaching, 1968 Northeastern St Univ; Various Courses OK Univ, OK St Univ, Langston Univ; *cr:* Phys Ed Teacher 1958-67, 6th Grade Teacher 1967-68 Mc Clure Elem; 6th Grade Teacher Washington Elem 1968-69; 5th/6th Grade Math Teacher Mc Kinley Elem 1981-85; 6th Grade Math/Soc Stud Teacher Richard Kane Elem 1985-86; 6th Grade Math Teacher Cntrl Mid Sch 1986-; *ai:* 6th Grade Team Leader 1986-88; Homework Policy Comm 1989; At Risk Comm 1989-; Various Textbook Comm; Bartlesville Ed Assn 1981-87; OK Ed Assn, NEA, NCTM 1989-; *office:* Cntrl Mid Sch 8th & Cherokee Bartlesville OK 74003

GOFF, GERALDINE GIBBS, 3rd Grade Teacher; *b:* Tifton, GA; *m:* Steve A.; *c:* Steve A. Jr., Benjamin E.; *ed:* (BS) Elem Ed, Valdosta St Coll 1971; *cr:* 3rd Grade Teacher Lake Park Elem 1972-74, Okapilco Elem 1974-75, Wacona Elem 1975-81; 6th Grade Teacher Worth Acad 1981-82; 4th Grade Teacher Sylvester Elem 1982-87; 3rd Grade Teacher Deariso Primary 1987-; *ai:* Many Comms for Bd of Ed; Prof Assn of GA Educators 1987-; GA Assn of Educators, NEA Mem 1972-87; *home:* 105 Pine Point Cr Sylvester GA 31791

GOFF, ROBERTA DIANE, Language Arts Teacher; *b:* Gassaway, WV; *m:* Roger Doy; *c:* Robyn K. M., Rustyn L. D.; *ed:* (AB) Eng/Speech, Glenville St Coll 1975; (MA) Comm Stud, WV Univ 1987; Mid Chldhd Ed Certificate, Rdng Endorsement; *cr:* Eng Teacher Ellsworth Mid Sch 1975-76; Ec Services WV Dept of Human Services 1977-86; Lang Art Teacher Pennsboro Mid Sch 1986-; *ai:* Honor Society, 8th Grade Class, WV Challenge, Yrbk Spon; WV Young Writers Cty Coord; Academic Cncl; Bus Partner Liason with Simonton Building Products; NEA, WVEA, RCEA 1986-; Pennsboro Womens Club Teacher of Yr; *home:* Rt 1 Box 11A Pullman WV 26421

GOFFEE, KIMBERLY DAWN (THORNTON), Mathematics Teacher; *b:* Akron, OH; *m:* Kenneth Jon; *ed:* (BS) Ed/Fr/Math, Univ of Akron 1987; Starting Master Degree 1990; *cr:* Math Teacher Akron E HS 1987-; *ai:* Jr Var Vlybl Coach; *office:* Akron E HS 80 Brittain Rd Akron OH 44305

GOFORTH, D. WAYNE, Guidance Counselor; *b:* Corryton, TN; *m:* Wrena S.; *c:* Anthony, Katie, David; *ed:* (BS) Music Ed, Univ of TN 1970; (MA) Elem Ed, Union Coll 1984; *cr:* 6th Grade Teacher Maynardville Elem Sch 1980-82; Prin Big Ridge Elem Sch 1982-87; Guidance Cnslr Horace Maynard HS 1988-; *ai:* Jr Class Spon; Channel One Review & Human Services Review Comms; Union Cty Ed Assn Pres 1989-; TEA, NEA Mem; Published Music Instruction Books; *office:* Horace Maynard HS PO Box 249 Maynardville TN 37807

GOFORTH, MARY DAVEY, English Teacher; *b:* Barnesville, OH; *m:* Richard Eugene; *c:* Diane L. Goforth Ohning; *ed:* (BMED) Music Ed, Oberlin Coll 1944; (MA) Ed, Coll of Mt St Joseph 1987; *cr:* Music Teacher Leipsic 1944-46; Eng Teacher Stone Creek/Tusacarawas 1946-68, Indian Valley HS 1972-; *ai:* Lang Arts Graded Course of Study Comm; Indian Valley Teachers Assn 1972-; NCTE 1985-87; New Philadelphia Ed Assn Pres 1986-87; OH Ed Assn 1944-; NEA 1944-; Nomination for OH Teacher of Yr 1985; Selected Indian Valley Teacher of Yr 1985; Martha Holden Jenning Schlsp Awd 1985-86; *home:* 2123 E High Ave New Philadlphia OH 44663

GOHLKE, BARB CALHOUN, 7th-8th Grade Teacher; *b:* Freeport, IL; *m:* Richard; *c:* Christina, Brin, Angela; *ed:* (BA) Eng, Wartburg Coll 1966; *cr:* 7th & 9th Grade Eng Teacher Waver Shell Rock Jr HS 1966-69; Newspaper Coorespondent Waterloo Courier 1974-84; 8th & 9th Grade Eng Teacher Waverly Shell Rock Jr HS 1984-; *ai:* Chm K-12th Grade Lang Arts Coord Comm; Head of Jr HS Eng Dept; *home:* 2713 12th St NW Waverly IA 50677

GOHRING, PATRICIA M., Social Studies Teacher; *b:* Michigan City, IN; *m:* William J.; *c:* Jennifer, Sydney, Michael; *ed:* (BED) Soc Stud, Univ of AK; (MA) Amer His, Ball St Univ; *cr:* Teacher Elston Jr HS 1973-75, Shenandoah HS 1978-79, Costa Cath Sch 1984-; *ai:* 8th Grade Homeroom Class Spon; Self Evaluation Comm; Stu Cncl Adv; Soc Stud Dept Head; NCEA 1984-; Beta Sigma Phi Pres 1983-84, Girl of Yr 1984; Ladies Auxiliary Knights of Columbus VP 1986; *home:* 846 N Cherry St Galesburg IL 61401

GOITIA, DANIEL, Admin Asst & Math Teacher; *b:* Brooklyn, NY; *m:* Jane Schurman; *c:* Laura T., Stephen J.; *ed:* (BA) Math, 1974, (MS) Scndry Ed, 1977 St Johns Univ; Prof Diploma Sch Admin, Long Island Univ 1986; *cr:* Math Teacher Islip Jr HS 1974-80, Babylon Jr-Sr HS 1980-; Asst Dir Captree Cntry Day Camp 1981-85; Admin Asst Babylon Jr-Sr HS 1987-; *ai:* Sr Class & Math Team Adv; Admin Asst; Scholastic Awds Comm; Adult Ed Instr; Pi Mu Epsilon, Kappa Delta Pi, NCTM; Knights of Columbus; 3 Village Soccer; *office:* Babylon Jr Sr H S 50 Railroad Ave Babylon NY 11702

GOLD, IRIS, Special Education Teacher; *b:* Bronx, NY; *c:* Paul, Steven; *ed:* (BA) Sociology, 1968, (MA) Ed, 1973 Hunter Coll; Cert in Spec Ed; *cr:* 1st Grade Teacher Public Sch 25 1968-69; 2nd Grade Teacher 1975-81, Spec Ed Teacher 1981- Boyle Road Elem Sch; *office:* Boyle Road Elem Sch 424 Boyle Rd Port Jefferson Stn NY 11776

GOLD, MITCHELL L., Social Studies Teacher; *b:* Monticello, NY; *m:* Rita Iacono; *ed:* (AA) Liberal Arts, Broward Comm Coll 1979; (BA) His/Poly Sci, CA St Univ Dominguez Hills 1987; Working Towards Masters Degree Admin Ed, CA St Univ San Bernadino; *cr:* Teacher Frisbie Jr HS 1988-; *ai:* Asst Coach Boys Bsktbl, Girls Sftbl; GATE Prgm Organizer; Intramural Sports Coord; NEA, CA Teachers Assn Mem 1987-; Rialto Ed Assn Mem 1988-; *office:* Frisbie Jr HS 1442 N Eucalyptus Ave Rialto CA 92376

GOLD, ROSEMARIE, Teacher of Gifted; *b:* Findlay, OH; *m:* Joe Dan; *c:* John D., Jo Marie; *ed:* (BA) Elem Ed, 1983, (MA) Ed, 1989 Morehead St Univ; *cr:* Teacher Fleming Cty Bd of Ed 1983-; *ai:* Governors Cup Academic Coach; Gifted Comm; Pilot Writing Grant Coord; Morehead St Univ Cooperative Learning Labs Consultant; KY Writing Project; KY St Dept of Ed Hosted Write Ideas Star Satellite Channel; One Week Writing Grant Wkshps Consultant Many Ctys; In-Service Comm & Presenter; Guest Lecturer Morehead St Univ Sch of Ed; Delta Kappa Gamma Intnl, NCTE 1989-; NEA, KY Ed Assn 1981-; Phi Kappa Phi Intnl, Fleming Cty Ed Assn, PTA Flemingsburg Elem Sch 1983-; KY Assn Gifted Ed 1983-; ASCD 1990; Flemingsburg 1st Baptist Church, Champions Against Drugs, Inquirers Club, Project Prom Volunteer, Talking with Your Stu About Drugs & Alcohol, Fleming Cty Golf Assn; Phi Delta Kappa Morehead St Univ Teacher of Yr 1990; KY St Dept of Ed Pilot Writing Grant; *home:* 210 Elizaville Ave Flemingsburg KY 41041

GOLDBERG, FRED HOWARD, Fifth Grade Teacher; *b:* Everett, MA; *m:* Roberta Jaffe; *c:* Rachel, Sam Goldberg-Jaffe; *ed:* (BS) Personnel Management, Amer Intnl Coll 1968; Teacher Cert SE MA Univ 1977; *cr:* 5th Grade Classroom Teacher Hawthorne Brook Mid Sch 1979-; *ai:* Juggling Club; Stu Cncl Adv; *home:* 216 Whipple Hill Rd Richmond NH 03470

GOLDBERG, JONATHAN B., Social Studies Teacher; *b:* Boston, MA; *m:* Ursula; *c:* Alexandra, Jamison; *ed:* (AB) His, Vassar Coll 1977; (MA) Philosophy, Teachers Coll Columbia Univ 1982; Admin & Supervision Course Work, Fordham Univ; *cr:* 7th Grade Teacher Carmel Cntrl Sch Dist Mid Sch 1977-88; 9th/12th Grade Techer Carmel Cntrl Sch Dist HS 1988-; Prof Growth Coord Carmel Cntrl Sch Dist 1987-; *ai:* Prof Growth Coord Develops & Administrates; Variety of Staff Dev Options for the Faculty of the Sch Dist; Assn Supervision & Curr Dev, NCSS, Westchester Cncl for Soc Stud, Natl Staff Dev Cncl, NY St Staff Dev Cncl; Kappa Delta Pi, Phi Delta Kappa Ed Honorary; Consultant Thinking In & Writing Across the Curr; *office:* Carmel HS 30 Fair St Carmel NY 10512

GOLDEN, JENNIE DILLY, Business Education Teacher; *b:* Parsons, WV; *m:* Robert W.; *ed:* (BS) Bus Ed, 1972, (MS) Bus Ed, 1974 Youngstown St Univ; Secretarial, WV Bus Coll 1959; *cr:* Secy US Dept of Agriculture 1959-63, G F Bus Equipment 1963-69, Youngstown Univ 1969-71; Teacher Boardman HS 1972-78, Philip Barbour HS 1980-; *ai:* FBLA Club Spon; Barbour Cty Ed Assn, WV Ed Assn, NEA 1981-; Tucker Cty Historical Society 1978-; Amer Revolution Bicentennial Awd 1976; *office:* Philip Barbour HS Rt 2 Philippi WV 26416

GOLDEN, LYNN MC INTOSH, Second Grade Teacher; *b:* Le Mars, IA; *m:* Monte; *c:* Cari; *ed:* (BA) Elem Ed/Psych, Westmar Coll 1975; (MA) Rdng, Sioux Falls Coll 1987; *cr:* Elem Teacher Paullina/Primghar Sch 1975-; *ai:* Delta Kappa Gamma Membership 1985-; Paullina Ed Assn (VP, Membership) 1975-; Beta Sigma Phi (VP, Membership) 1987-; Mariners (Pres, Membership) 1987-; *office:* Paullina/Primghar Sch Box 638 Paullina IA 51046

GOLDEN, MELINDA BARNHART, Chemistry/Science Teacher; *b:* Hagerstown, MD; *m:* Sylvester S.; *c:* Bernie, Sara; *ed:* (BA) Chem/Ed, Mt St Ayers Coll 1969; (MED) Chem/Ed, Shippensburg St Univ 1972; W MD Coll, Cath Univ, WV Univ; *cr:* Teacher North Hagerstown HS 1969-71, Hancock Mid Sr HS 1971-; *ai:* Class Spon; Yrbk, Prom, Stu Cncl Spon; WCTA, MSTA, NEA 1969-; PTSA; St Thomas Episcopal Church; *home:* 6626 Grasan Ln Hancock MD 21750

GOLDEN, ROGER JOEL, Middle School Counselor; *b:* Brooklyn, NY; *m:* Elayne Seiden; *c:* Scott, Brian, Amy; *ed:* (BS) Ed, New Paltz 1961; (MA) Guidance, Albany St 1976; *cr:* 5th Grade Teacher, 1961-62, 6th Grade Teacher 1963-67, 7th/8th Grade Eng Teacher 1968-71, Mid Sch Cnslr 1972- Pine Bush; *ai:* Dir Stu Talent Shows 1970-85; Yrbk Adv 1978-80; Co-Coach Odyssey of Mind 2nd Place Region 1987; Quest Intnl Parents Evening Sessions 1987-; NYSUT 1961-; Orange Cty Guid Assn 1972-; Pine Bush Little League 1963-78; Pine Bush Arts Cncl 1982-87; Pine Bush Kiwanis 1980-; Stu Dir Film Regional Honors 1970; Teacher of Yr Plaque Stu Cncl 1979; *home:* RD 2 Box 306 Pine Bush NY 12566

GOLDING, M. CORRINE, Jr High/HS Teacher; *b:* ColoradO Springs, CO; *m:* David E.; *c:* John, Jason, Justin; *ed:* (BA) Scndry Ed - Eng, Univ Northern CO 1970; *cr:* Teacher Ellicott HS 1972-; *ai:* Coach Forensics Team; Jr HS Cheerleading Spon; Sch Newspaper Supervisor; Sr Class Spon; EEA/CEA/NEA 1985-; CO Lang Arts Society 1987-; *home:* Rt 2 Box 45 Rush CO 80833

GOLDING, PEARL ANN, Second Grade Teacher; *b:* Jerome, ID; *m:* Richard; *c:* Tom; *ed:* (BA) Elem Ed, Boise St Univ 1974; Grad Stud; *cr:* 3rd Grade Teacher 1975-88, 2nd Grade Teacher 1988- Jefferson Sch; *office:* Jefferson Elem Sch 600 N Fillmore Jerome ID 83338

GOLDMAN, JULES A., Marketing Education Coord; *b:* Detroit, MI; *m:* Lauren Jill Golding; *c:* David, Jennifer; *ed:* (BS) Bus/Mrktg, Ferris St 1967; (MS) Mrktg Ed, Wayne St 1969; *cr:* Pres Goldman Advertising 1969-; Novelty Dir Olympia Arenas Incorporated 1978-; *ai:* Distributive Ed Adv; Martin Luther King HS Sr Class Spon; MI DECA Advisory Comm; Distributive Ed 1969, Mrktg Educator of Yr 1983; Detroit Bd of Ed Certificate 1988-89; *office:* Martin Luther King HS 3200 E Lafayette Detroit MI 48207

GOLDMAN, ROBERT CRAIG, Social Studies Teacher; *b:* Chicago, IL; *ed:* (BA) His, Roosevelt Univ 1965; (MA) Amer His, NE IL Univ 1972; Numerous Courses; *cr:* Substitute Teacher Chicago 1965; Teacher Wendell Phillips HS 1965-75, Numerous Summer Schls 1965-, Senn Metro Acad 1975-; *ai:* Advanced Placement Amer His Teacher & Coord; Chicago Teachers Union 1965-; Amer Historical Assn 1971-75; Uptown Chamber of Commerce 1986; Certificate of Appreciation Service & Work; Article Published 1981; *office:* Senn Metro Acad 5900 N Glenwood Chicago IL 60660

GOLDSBERRY, REID, English Department Chairperson; *b:* Tremonton, UT; *m:* Sheryl Anne Watkins; *c:* Brett, Bart, Darin, Brandon, Tai A.; *ed:* (BS) Eng, 1964, (MED) Phys Ed, 1984 UT St Univ; Advanced Placement Eng Wkshps; *cr:* Teacher/Coach Box Elder HS 1963-65, Las Vegas HS 1965-66; Teacher/Coach 1966-, Dept Chm 1985- Box Elder HS; *ai:* Lang Art Textbook Adoption Comm; HS Welfate Comm Chm; Asst Ftbl & Head Boys Tennis Coach; Engl Dept Chm; NEA Life Mem; UT Ed Assn 1963-; NCTE 1985-; *office:* Box Elder HS 380 S 600 W Brigham UT 84302

GOLDSBY, DIANNE SIMPSON, Math Coordinator; *b:* Minden, LA; *m:* John W.; *c:* John K.; *ed:* (MED) Secondary Ed, LA St Univ 1974; *cr:* Math Teacher Del Rio HS 1969-71; Test Admin LA St Univ 1973-74; Pre-Sch Teacher Memorial Baptist Chrstn Sch 1975-80; Math Teacher/Coord Ridgewood Preparatory Sch 1980-; *ai:* Mu Alpha Theta Spon; Math Contest Supv; Dress Code Comm; NCTM; Greater New Orleans Math Teachers; Nom Presidential Awd Excl Sci & Math Teaching; *office:* Ridgewood Prep Sch 201 Pasadena Ave Metairie LA 70001

GOLDSMITH, BILL W., Fourth Grade Teacher; *b:* Burneyville, OK; *m:* Mary Janette Staton; *c:* Darin, Hope, Kieley; *ed:* (BSED) Bus Ed, 1962, (MA) Elem Ed, 1965 SE OK St Univ; *cr:* 6th Grade Teacher Houston Ind Sch Dist 1962-63; 5th/6th Grade Teacher Stony Point Elem 1963-68; 6th Grade Teacher Irving Ind Sch Dist 1968-70; 4th Grade Teacher Devonian Elem 1970-73; 5th Grade Teacher Irving Ind Sch Dist 1973-79; 4th Grade Teacher Kingston Public Sch 1980-; *ai:* Staff Dev Comm; 5 Yr Improvement Plan Mem; NEA 1968-; OK Ed Assn 1980-; Kingston Ed Assn 1980-, Kingston Teacher of Yr 1982-83; *home:* PO Box 713 Kingston OK 73439

GOLDSMITH, MARVIN RAY, Science Teacher; *b:* West, TX; *m:* Naida Russell; *c:* Ron, Lee; *ed:* (BS) Phys Ed, Baylor 1957; (ME) Ed, Sam Houston 1965; Master Work Geology, KS St 1969; Master Work Sci, Univ of Houston 1985; *cr:* Teacher/Coach Marlin Jr HS 1957-58, Penelope 1959-60; US Marines Reserves 1958-64; Teacher/Prin Cranfills Gap 1960-63; Coach Abbott 1963-67; Sci Teacher La Vega 1981-; *ai:* Sr, Fellowship of Chrstn Stu Spon; TX Coaches Assn Mem 1957-83, 25 Yr 1984; TX St Teacher Assn (Local Pres 1988-89, Pres Elect 1987-88); La Vega Classroom Teachers Mem 1981-, Educl Excl 1989; US Marines E5 Forward Observer 1958; Sci Fellowships KS St & Univ of Houston; Track Article Published; *office:* La Vega HS 555 N Loop 340 Waco TX 76705

GOLDSMITH, MARY GILLESPIE, Second Grade Teacher; *b:* Harmony, NC; *c:* Tonya, Delaine Goldsmith Rucker; *ed:* (BS) Educ, Winston-Salem ST 1962; 21 hrs Psych, Wake Forest Univ; *cr:* 1st Grade Teacher Happy Plains Sch 1963-64; 2nd Grade Teacher Unity High Sch 1965-69; Pine Hall Elem 1970-71; King Primary Sch 1971-; *ai:* Stokes Cty Summer Sch Teacher; Tutor Under Achievers; NC Assn of Educators Pres Dist IV 1980; Stokes Cty Assn Educators Pres; Sch Base Comm; Intnl Rdng Assb 1990; NC Cncl Teachers of Math 1988-90; Galilee Bapt Church Public Relations Comm 1979-; Stokes Arts Cncl 1979-90; Tiny Vikings Majorettes Asst Coach 1978-80; Stokes Cty Teacher of Yr 1979-80; *home:* 3101 Airport Rd. N.E. Winston-Salem NC 27105

GOLDSMITH, RICHARD ILES, History Teacher; *b:* New York, NY; *m:* Jane Cave; *c:* Derek, Andrew; *ed:* (BA) Sociology/Anthropology, Long Island Univ 1968; (MS) Educl Leadership, Nova Univ 1990; Mastery Teaching, New York Bd of Ed 1982; *cr:* Teacher Intermediate Sch 33 1969-75, Satellite W Jr Hs 1979-88, Loggers Run Cmmty Mid Sch 1988-; *ai:* Boys Swim Coach; Mrktg, Adv/Advisee, Merit Sch Finance, Sch Spirit Comms; Soc Stud Acad Games Coach; Peer Teacher; FL Cncl for Soc Stud 1989-; Palm Beach Cncl for Soc Stud 1988-; Amer His Teacher of Yr St of FL 1990; Daughters of Amer Revolution 1989, 1990; *office:* Loggers Run Cmmty Mid Sch 11584 W Palmetto Park Rd Boca Raton FL 33428

GOLDSTEIN, AUDREY R. (GORDON), English Teacher; *b:* Boston, MA; *m:* Saul; *c:* Eric R., Sabra B. Sherry; *ed:* (BS) Eng Ed, 1971, (MA) Non Western His, 1972 Salem St Coll; *cr:* Admin Asst USAF 1954-62; Eng/Soc Stud Teacher Marblehead Jr HS 1974-80; Eng Teacher Marblehead HS 1980-; *ai:* Faculty Forum Chairperson; Prin Advisory Comm Mem; ESL Comm; Alan Cashman Schlrshp Fund Chairperson; NCTE, MA Cncl Teachers Eng, NEA, MA Ed Assn; Career Womens Network Bd Mem 1988-; Jewish Fed; *office:* Marblehead HS Lt Duncan Sleigh Sq Marblehead MA 01945

GOLDSTEIN, BARBARA MAE FIGLER, Third Grade Teacher; *b:* St Louis, MO; *c:* Stacy F., Brian; *ed:* (BS) Elem Ed, 1969, (MS) Guidance & Counseling 1971 Univ of MO Columbia; (MS) Remedial Rdng, Univ of MO St Louis 1972; Advanced Psych; *cr:* 3rd Grade Teacher Pattonville Elem 1969-72; Elem Teacher Lakeside Farms 1972-89; Coll Instr San Diego City Coll 1972-89; Elem Teacher Riverview Elem Sch 1989-; *ai:* Lit & Fine Arts Comm; CA Teachers Assn 1972-; San Diego Rdng Assn 1972-; Tri-Penta Honorary Society; *home:* 13933 Carriage Rd Poway CA 92064

GOLDSTEIN, IRVIN L., Intermediate Levels Teacher; *b:* Louisville, KY; *m:* Daisy Baker; *c:* Steven, M. Alan, Lynne Yudewitz, Sara Weinstein; *ed:* (BA) Elem Ed, Univ of KY 1951; (MED) Supervision/Curr, Univ of Louisville 1961; Grad Stud; *cr:* 6th Grade Teacher Longfellow & Hazelwood Schls 1951-55; 4th-7th Grade Teacher Laurier Sch 1955-56; 4th-6th Grade Teacher Hazelwood & Semple Schls 1956-61, Mt Tabor & Slate Run Schls 1961-; *ai:* Book Store, Snack Company, Credit Unions Spon; Floyd Cty Elem Camping Prgm Coord; Sch Sci Fair & Soc Stud Comm; Sch Credit Union Vice Chm; Led Wkshps Ec Ed & Environmental Ed; NEA, ISTA Local Pres 1951-; NATE 1980-, Reform Jewish Educator 1988; Phi Delta Kappa 1970-80; Bureau of Jewish Ed; IN Enviromental Ed Assn 1970-; Bellarmine Coll Leadership Ed 1987-; Exch Teacher to Vancouver 1955-56; Floyd Cty Teacher of Yr 1990; IN Finalist 1990; Series of Articles Published in Magazines; IN Cncl on Ec Ed Grants 1988, 1989; Conservation Teacher 1975, 1987; Valley Forge Freedom Fnd

Classroom Teacher 1963; *office:* Slate Run Sch 1452 Slate Run Rd New Albany IN 47150

GOLDSTEIN, JACK LEON, Art Teacher; *b:* Brooklyn, NY; *m:* Phoebe Magid; *c:* Richard, Bonnie; *ed:* (BA) Art Ed, 1965, (MA) Art Ed, 1969 Adelphi Univ; Grad Stud Art Ed; *cr:* Art Teacher Elmont Memorial HS 1965-; *ai:* Art, Booster Club; Red Cross Drive Drive; Sewanhaka Fed of Teachers Building Rep 1958-60; *office:* Elmont Memorial HS 555 Ridge Rd Elmont NY 11003

GOLDSTEIN, JUDY LYNNE (MONCRIEF), Health/ Physical Ed Teacher; *b:* Toms River, NJ; *m:* Paul Thomas; *c:* Lisa Monath, Stephen Mc Kenzie; *ed:* (AS) Ed, Ocean Cty Coll 1978; (BS) Health/Phys Ed, Trenton St Coll 1980; Drivers Ed Cert 1981; Skills For Adolescence Trng Cert 1986; *cr:* Teacher/Coach Point Pleasant Boro HS 1983-85, Point Pleasant Boro Memorial Sch 1985-; *ai:* Var Field Hockey Coach Point Pleasant HS; Volunteer Phys Ed Instr St Johns Meth Church Prgm; Coach of Yr Ocean Cty 1988, 1989; *office:* Point Pleasant Mid Sch Laural Herbert Dr Point Pleasant NJ 08742

GOLDWASSER, JANET SCHNEYER, Judaic Studies Teacher; *b:* Lutsk, Russia; *m:* Norman; *ed:* (BS) Bio, Towson St Univ 1978; Beth Jacob Teacher Seminary Jerusalem Israel; *cr:* Teacher Seattle Helman Acad 1978-81, Rudlin Torah Acad 1981-88, Beth-El Religious Sch 1983-; Judaic Consultant Hamerkaz Teachers Resource Center 1988-; *ai:* Coalition for Advancement of Jewish Ed; Beth Israel Sisterhood Chaplain 1988-; *home:* 914 Bevridge Rd Richmond VA 23226

GOLEMON, CATHERINE HALL BLAKE, Retired Grade School Teacher; *b:* Nacogdoches, TX; *w:* Robert Bruce (dec); *c:* Patricia, Bobbie Lawless, Tom; *ed:* (BS) His, Stephen F Austin St Univ 1962; *cr:* 1st-4th Grade Teacher Pine Hill Ind Sch Dist 1941-42; Cisco Elem Sch 1961-66; Kndgtn Teacher Ranger Elem Sch 1968-82; *ai:* Delta Kappa Gamma Pres 1974-, Rose Awd; TSTA; 1st Meth Church (Ranger, Cisco Ranger 1942-); Eastern Star 1942-50; United Meth Women (Pres, Mem) 1945-; Woman of Yr Ranger Chamber of Commerce 1982; Mother of Yr Ranger 1968; Rose Awd Delta Kappa Gamma; *home:* 512 Pine St Ranger TX 76470

GOLOMBISKY, LINDA CAROL MINCHEY, Reading Teacher; *b:* Detroit, MI; *m:* Lee Robert; *c:* Leanna M.; *ed:* (BA) Eng, Oakland Univ; Rdng, Learning Disabilities & Several Wkshps; *cr:* Rdng/Sci Teacher St Casmir, St Bartholomew; Rdng/ Religion Teacher/Chairperson of Gifted Shrine Grade Sch; *ai:* Future Problem Solving & Forensics Coach; Stu Cncl; Acad of Gifted; *office:* Shrine Grade Sch Shrine of Little Flower Woodward at 12 Mile Royal Oak MI 48067

GOLYER, LARRY WES, 5th Grade Teacher; *b:* St Helena, CA; *m:* Sandra Kay Rorvick; *c:* Weston, Barrett, Desiree, Shain; *ed:* (BS) Elem Ed, Saint Cloud St Coll 1972-; (MED) Elem Ed, Univ of MN 1981; *cr:* 5th Grade Teacher Ramsey Elem Sch 1975-76; 6th Grade Teacher 1977-79, 5th Grade Teacher 1979- Sandburg Mid Sch; *ai:* Lions; *office:* Sandburg Mid Sch 1902 2nd Ave Anoka MN 55303

GOMBOS, ANGELA KARADY, Social Science/Scndry Teacher; *b:* Budapest, Hungary; *m:* Geza; *c:* Geza M., Emilia, Victor; *ed:* (AA) Liberal Arts, Mount San Antonio Coll 1964; (BS) Soc Sci-His, CA St Polytechnic Univ 1967, (MA) La Verne Univ 1974; (PhD) Curr/Instruction Educl Psych, Univ of S CA 1985; Teachers Scndry Psych, Stanford Univ; *cr:* Engineering Aide Pacific Telephone & Telegraph Company 1960-63; HS Teacher Hacienda-La Puenta Unified Sch Dist 1967-; *ai:* Parent-Teacher Conference Coord; Medical Club Adv; Amer Psychological Assn; NCSS; International Organization Stress & Anxiety; Am Assn Univ Women; Dissertation Presented at APA Convention 1985; Publication-Co Author Intnl Conference Stress & Emotion; Teaching Summer Taiwan 1990; Adult Sch Amnesty Prgm Teacher; *office:* G A Wilson HS 16455 Wedgeworth Dr Hacienda Heights CA 91790

GOMEZ, BLANCA LYDIA, Elementary School Counselor; *b:* Del Rio, TX; *ed:* (BS) Art Ed, 1975, (MS) Elem Ed, 1977, (MS) Guidance & Counseling, 1986 TX A&I Univ; *cr:* 4th Grade Teacher 1975-76, 1st-6th Grade Art Teacher 1976-81, 4th Grade Teacher 1981-82, 6th Grade Eng Teacher 1982-85, 6th Grade Art Teacher 1985-88, 6th Grade Eng Teacher 1988-89, Elem Cnslr 1989- San Felipe Del Rio C Ind Sch Dist; *ai:* Stu Cncl Adv; Advisory Cncl for At-Risk Stu; Assn of TX Prof Educators VP 1982-84; PTA Life Membership 1985.

GOMEZ, SANDRA CORKILL, Reading Teacher; *b:* San Benito, TX; *m:* Antonio; *c:* Cassandra; *ed:* (BA) Span/Eng 1974, (BS) Phys Ed, 1975 Pan Amer Univ; *cr:* Teachers Aide TX Southmost Coll 1970-71; Lib Aide Rangerville Elem 1972-74; Teacher Faulk Intermediate 1974-; *ai:* Pan Amer Stu Forum Spon 1976-87; UIL Spon 1986-; Coached Vlybl, Bsktbl, Track 1976-78; Rdng Comm; Goals-Objections Comm; Curr Comm; Act Comm; Grading Policy Comm; Campus Improvement Team; Bi-Dist Champs 1978; Consolation Trophy 1977; UIL Spelling Coach 1986-; Dept Chairperson Rdng Dept 1987-; *home:* Rt 4 Box 187 San Benito TX 78586

GONCHER, THOMAS JAMES, Fifth Grade Teacher; *b:* Johnstown, PA; *m:* Mary Jane Medvesky; *c:* Andrea, Lynanne; *ed:* (BA) His/Scndry Ed, St Francis Coll 1968; (MED) Elem Ed, Univ of Pittsburgh 1979; *cr:* Teacher Forest Hills Sch Dist 1968-; *ai:* NEA, PA St Ed Assn; Forest Hills Ed Assn Pres 1971-72; PA Jaycees; Johnstown Tribune Democrat Teacher of Yr; Outstanding Young Men of America; *office:* Forest Hills Elem Sch Box 158 Sidman PA 15955

GONDA, MARY GARCAR, Third Grade Teacher; *b:* Youngstown, OH; *m:* William Sr.; *c:* William Jr., Scott; *ed:* (BSED) Elem, Youngstown St 1970; *cr:* 3rd Grade Teacher St Matthias Sch 1979-; *ai:* NCEA, IRA 1979-; *office:* St Matthias Sch 2800 Shady Run Rd Youngstown OH 44502

GONION, LEO BURL, 7th Grade Mathematics Teacher; *b:* Cody, WY; *m:* Sally Marie Haberthier; *c:* Hap, Gay, Cariveux, Chip, Joy; *ed:* (AA) Ag Engr, NWC 1983; (BA) Elem Ed, Jeff Univ of WY 1955; Sci, Math, Eng, Cmptrs, Athletics; *cr:* 6th Grade Math/Eng/His Teacher Big Piney HS 1953-55; 6th Grade Teacher Powell Elem Sch 1955-65; Mid Sch Coach/Sci Teacher Powell Jr HS 1965-70; Mid Sch Coach/Math Teacher Powell Mid Sch 1970-; *ai:* Mid Sch Wrestling Coach; Powell Ed Assn (Pres, Pres Elect) 1955-, Teacher of Yr 1970; Powell Classroom Teachers, (Pres, Pres Elect 1955-65); WY Ed Assn (Pres, Pres Elect 1955-); NEA Life Mem; Powell Chamber of Commerce Teacher of Yr 1982; Army Natl Guard Colonel 1947-88, Legion of Merit 1988; *home:* 1115 Lane 5 Powell WY 82435

GONZALES, DAVID FIDEL, 8th Grade Reading Teacher; *b:* Santa Fe, NM; *m:* Diana Consuelo Charez; *c:* Michael J., David R.; *ed:* (BA) Elem Ed, Coll of Santa Fe 1966; (MA) Liberal Arts, St Johns Coll 1973; *cr:* 5th Grade Teacher Alvord Elem Sch 1966-67; 7th/8th Grade Lang Art Teacher 1967-72, 8th Grade Rdng Teacher Young Jr HS 1972-80; 8th Grade Rdng/Creative Writing Teacher Alameda Jr HS 1980-; *ai:* Stu Cncl Spon 1967-76; AFT Pres 1970-75; *office:* Alameda Jr HS 1300 La Madera Santa Fe NM 87501

GONZALES, JUAN JOSE, Computer Department Head; *b:* San Antonio, TX; *ed:* (BA) Theology/Span, Univ of St Thomas 1976; (MDiv) Theology, Oblate Sch of Theology 1980; Admin Prgm Archdio of San Antonio 1987-89; *cr:* Teacher St James The Apostle 1981-; *ai:* Graduating Class Spon; Stu Cncl Spon/Adv; Standardized Testing Coord; St James Church Religious Ed Teacher 1988-; *office:* St James The Apostle 907 W Theo San Antonio TX 78225

GONZALES, MARIO RICHARD, 7th-8th Grade Teacher; *b:* Los Angeles, CA; *m:* Aida G.; *c:* Mireya, Raquel; *ed:* (BA) Soc Stud/Ed, Whittier Coll 1978; *cr:* Teacher Mulhall 1979-82, Durfee 1982-85, Columbia 1985-; *ai:* Core Teacher; Builders Club Spon; Yrbk; CA Assn for Bi-Ling Ed VP 1987-89; EMETA; CTA.

GONZALES, MARY LINDA, 6th Grade Teacher; *b:* Holton, KS; *m:* Kenneth L.; *c:* David, Nathan, Colin; *ed:* (BA) Elem Ed, Univ of Montevallo 1976; (MS) Curr & Instr, Emporia St Univ 1985; *cr:* 4th Grade Teacher Sacred Heart 1976-78; 2nd Grade Teacher Assumption Sch 1979; 4th/5th & 6th Grade Teacher Piper Elem 1980-; *ai:* ASCD; *office:* Piper Elem Sch 12200 Leavenworth Rd Kansas City KS 66109

GONZALEZ, RICHARD DAVID, Mathematics Teacher; *b:* Albuquerque, NM; *ed:* (BS) Math, NM Tech 1972; *cr:* Math Teacher Lincoln Jr HS 1973-74, Highland HS 1974-; *office:* Highland HS 4700 Coal Ave SE Albuquerque NM 87108

GONZALEZ-HOGAN, GWENDOLYN, Spanish Teacher; *b:* New York, NY; *m:* Richard; *c:* Amanda, Jessica; *ed:* (BA) Span, SUNY Fredonia 1970; (MS) Ed, Niagara Univ 1976; Italian, Cmptr Programing, Word Processing; *cr:* Adjunct Professor Niagara Univ 1988-89; Teacher Lewiston-Porter Mid Sch 1971-; *ai:* Exch Prgm Experiment in Intnl Living Coord; NY St Assn of Foreign Lang Teachers, W NY Foreign Lang Educators Cncl; Lewiston Porter United Teachers Union Rep Cmmty Ambassador Prgm; St Bonaventure Univ Spec Citation Lang Dept Span Clubs; Span Immersion Week; Bd Commendations for Coordinating Children Exch Prgm; *office:* Lewiston Porter Cntrl Sch 4061 Creek Rd Youngstown NY 14174

GOOCH, JOYCE SMITH, Third Grade Teacher; *b:* Bradford, TN; *m:* Clinton Davis; *c:* Sherri Gooch Dodd, Brett D.; *ed:* (BSE) Ed, Memphis St Univ 1970; *cr:* Kndgtn Teacher E A Harrold Elem 1970-72; K-3rd Grade Teacher Millington Cntrl Elem 1972-87; 3rd Grade Teacher Oak Elem 1987-; *ai:* Chairperson Sch Contests; Shelby Cty Ed Assn, TN Ed Assn, NEA 1970-; W TN Rdng Assn 1980-; Raleigh Church of Christ Supvr of Primary Ed 1977-, Ed Supvr of Yr 1978, 1989; *home:* 5300 Virgil Memphis TN 38134

GOOD, KARLEEN WAGNER, 8th Grade Teacher; *b:* Enid, OK; *m:* William Richard; *ed:* (BA) Eng Lit, Fresno St Univ 1969; Family, Child, Marriage Counseling & Writing Wkshps; *cr:* 6th-8th Grade Teacher Stratford Elem 1969; 8th Grade Teacher Akers Elem 1969; 6th-8th Grade Teacher Stratford Elem 1970-71; 6th Grade Teacher 1971-74, 8th Grade Teacher 1974- Akers Elem; *ai:* HS Dist Rep for Articulation; 8th Grade Grad Speech Adv; Stu Study Team & Dist Writing Project Mem; NCTE Mem; CTA Building Rep 1989-; Eng 300 Society Mem; San Joaquin Valley Writers Project Mem.

GOOD, LINDA MOORE, 2nd Grade Head Teacher; *b:* Zanesville, OH; *m:* Larry A.; *c:* Alicia J., Tricia L., Amy J.; *ed:* (BS) Elem Ed, OH Univ Athens 1964; Various Wkshps; *cr:* 1st/ 2nd Grade Teacher Hopewell Sch 1962-64; 1st Grade Teacher Ellis Sch 1964-68; 2nd Grade Teacher Zanesville City Schls 1970-; *ai:* NEA, OEA, 1962-; ZEA (Building Rep 1988-89) 1962-; Trinity Presbyn Church Mem; Whos Who Amer Women; Whos Who in Midwest; *office:* Munson Elem Sch 109 Brighton Blvd Zanesville OH 43701

GOOD, MICHAEL SCOTT, 6th Grade Social Stud Teacher; *b:* Middletown, PA; *m:* Cherryl L.; *c:* Cathleen; *ed:* (BSED) Elem Ed, Millersville Univ 1972; Grad Work Millersville Univ; *cr:* Classroom Teacher Steelton-Highspire Sch Dist 1972-; *ai:* Adv Sch Safety Patrol; Girls Jr HS Bsktbl Coach; Soc Stud Curr Comm; NEA, PSEA, SHEA; Hummelstown Bsbl Assn VP 1974-75; Capital Bsbl Umpires Assn Chief Umpire 1986-; FFO; Church Cncl; *home:* 610 W 2nd St Hummelstown PA 17036

GOOD, RANDAL DEAN, Social Science Teacher/Chair; *b:* Rugby, ND; *m:* Carole Juntunen; *c:* Julian, Paul, Faith; *ed:* (BA) Soc Sci, Mayville St Univ 1980; *cr:* Soc Sci Teacher Dunseith HS 1981-89; *ai:* Soc Sci Chm; Close-Up Adv; Head Wrestling Coach; ND HS Coaches Assn 1984-; Amer Legion Commander 1988-89; *office:* Dunseith HS P O Box 789 Dunseith ND 58329

GOOD, SANDRA MARIE, Science Dept Chair; *b:* Detroit, MI; *m:* William H.; *c:* John, Heather; *ed:* (BS) Bio, Heidelberg Coll 1969; Gifted Cert; Working towards Masters Sci Ed; *cr:* Sci/ Substitute Teacher Berlin-Amer HS 1969-70; Bio/Sci Teacher Gibsonburg HS 1970-72; Earth/Space/Bio Teacher Stranahan HS 1972-74; Life Sci Teacher Leesburg Jr HS 1974-75; Bio/Hum Bio/Anatomy Teacher/Dept Chair 1975- Leesburg HS; *ai:* NHS Spon; Sci Cty Curr Writing Team; Steering Comm Jr Sci & Engineering Symposium Univ of FL; FAST 1984-; Jayceettes VP 1974-76; Honors Bio NSF Grant Univ of FL; *office:* Leesburg HS 1401 W Meadows Leesburg FL 34748

GOOD, VIVIAN D. (DYE), Eng/Theatre/Comm Teacher; *b:* Johnstown, PA; *m:* Charles W.; *c:* Mark C., V. Elizabeth; *ed:* (BS) Eng, Indiana Univ of PA 1960; (MA) Theatre, Villanova Univ 1983; Grad Stud Gifted Children, Syracuse Univ 1961; Eng, West Chester Univ 1969-72; *cr:* 9th-11th Grade Eng Teacher Phoenixville Sr HS 1960-63; 7th Grade Eng/Rdng Teacher North Brandywine Mid Sch 1971; 10th-12th Grade Eng/Theatre Teacher Phoenixville Sr HS 1971-; Amer Lit Instr Delaware Cty Comm Coll 1990; *ai:* Phoenixville HS Musicals & Plays Dir; Paoli Presbyn Church Plays Asst Dir 1987-88; Magnet Sch Visual & Performing Art Planning Consultant; Phi Kappa Phi 1983-; Alpha Psi Omega 1960-; NCTE; Master Singers 1990; Paoli Presbyn Church 1988-; Phoenixville Day Care Bd of Dir 1968-71; Phoenixville Hospital Auxiliary 1968-70; *home:* 301 Albans Ct Malvern PA 19355

GOODALL, SUZANNE HARDY, 9th/10th Grade English Teacher; *b:* Petersburg, WV; *m:* John Mark; *c:* Bryce F. Ritter; *ed:* (BA) Eng, 1981, (MA) Scndry Ed, 1985 WV Univ; Grad Stud Teaching Strategies & Ed Admin; Masters Degree in Ed Admin; *cr:* Teacher of Gifted Jefferson HS 1985-86; Eng Teacher Loundoun Cty HS 1986-87, Petersburg HS 1987-; *ai:* 9th Grade Spon; WVEA 1985-86, 1987-; NEA 1985-; *office:* Petersburg HS Jefferson Ave Petersburg WV 26847

GOODELL, VICTORIA BERNICE, Math/Science Teacher; *b:* Bay City, MI; *m:* James J.; *c:* Nora, Sara; *ed:* (BS) His, 1969; (MA) Elem Teaching, 1974 Cntrl MI Univ; Post Masters Studies Sci Gifted Ed; Natural Sci Cert; *cr:* 2nd Grade Teacher Lincoln Elem 1967-71; 2nd-6th Grade Teacher Coulter Elem, 1971-81; Math/Science Teacher Handley Pcat 1981-; Graduate Instr Cntrl MI Univ 1988-; *ai:* MI Future Problem Solving Prgm; Saginaw Cty Sci & Engng Fair; Math Olympics Coach; Girls Sftbl Coach; NSTA 1982-; Mi Sci Teachers Assn 1982- Elem Sci Teacher of Yr 1983; Saginaw Cty Geog Society 1982- Sci Teacher of Yr 1983; MI Assn Ed of Gifted/Talented/Creative 1980-; 1st Presbyn Church Elder 1988-; Nat Sci Fndtn Awd 1986; NSTA Exemplary Elem Sci Prgm Awd 1983; Published in MI Sci Teachers Assn Journal 1987; *home:* 4825 Century Dr Saginaw MI 48603

GOODEMOTE, BARBARA HOLMBERG, 6th Grade Teacher/Dept Head; *b:* Orange, NJ; *m:* Richard Arthur; *c:* David, Terry, Kevin; *ed:* (BA) Math, St Teachers Coll Brockport & Oneonta; Drug Awareness Prgm ASAPP 1978, 6th Grade Sci Fair 1976, 6th Grade Grade Graduation 1976; *cr:* 3rd-4th Grade Teacher Rock City Falls 1960-62; 2nd Grade Teacher Broadelbin Cntrl Sch 1963-67; 6th Grade Teacher Joseph Henry Elem Sch 1971-; *ai:* Negotiations Team 3rd Contract; Bd of Dir GTA; Women of Moose 1977-; *office:* Joseph Henry Elem Sch Rt 147 Galway NY 12074

GOODES, JANICE WILD, Business Teacher; *b:* Berwyn, IL; *m:* John Michael; *c:* Darcy, Janine; *ed:* (BA) Bus Ed, CA St Univ Northridge 1973; Grad Stud Bus/Ed; *cr:* Bus Teacher Chatsworth HS; Bus Teacher/Dept Chairperson Agoura HS; Bus Teacher Oroville HS; Rop Instr Butte Cty Regional Occupational Prgm; *ai:* Class of 1992 Adv; Discipline, Retirement, Staff Advisory Comm Mem; Oroville Scndry Teachers Assn Building Site Rep, Teacher of Month 1989; *office:* Oroville HS 1535 Bridge St Oroville CA 95966

GOODFELLOW, GEORGE EDWIN, Chemistry Teacher; *b:* Acushnet, MA; *m:* Carolyn Ann Chase; *c:* Heidi, John, Christopher; *ed:* (BS) Chem, Univ of MA Amherst 1968; (MA) Organic Chem, Bridgewater St Coll 1977; Ed, Bridgewater Coll; Cmptr Sci, Fitchburg Coll; Instrumentation Update, Univ of AZ Tucson; *cr:* Chem Instr Bistol Comm Coll 1979-86; Chem/Physics Teacher New Bedford HS 1968-; *ai:* Asst Ftbl & Track Coach; Commonwealth & Byrd Schlsp Comm Mem; New Bedford Educators Assn 1968-; MA Teachers Assn, NEA 1970-; Horace Mann Grant Educl Research 1986; HS Organic Chem Textbook Written & Used; Sigma Psi Awd Outstanding Teacher 1989; New Bedford HS Outstanding Achievement Awd 1990; *office:* New Bedford HS 230 Hathaway Blvd New Bedford MA 02740

GOODIN, JUDITH ANN, 6th Grade Teacher; *b:* Adair County, KY; *m:* Lowell W.; *c:* Shannon Wolfe, Stacey L.; *ed:* (BS) Elem Ed, Campbellsville Coll 1978; (MA) Elem Ed, Western KY Univ 1981; Elem Ed Rank I Prgm Western KY Univ; *cr:* 3rd Grade Teacher 1978-80; 6th Grade Teacher 1980 Shepherd Elem; *ai:* Acadmc Team; Philosophy Comm; Yrbk Spon; Evaluation Comm; Parenting & Family Life Comm; Adair Cty Ed Assn Secy 1979-80; Homemakers Pres 1988-; *home:* 9845 Liberty Rd Columbia KY 42728

GOODING, JOY TACKETT, Language Art Teacher; *b:* Olive Hill, KY; *m:* Larry W.; *c:* Stephanie, Samuel, David, Sarah; *ed:* (BA) Eng/His, 1969, (MA) Eng, 1972 Morehead St Univ; Post Grad Stud in Admin & Eng Rhetoric; *cr:* Lang Art Teacher Clermont NE HS 1970-71, Fleming Cty HS 1972-75, Maysville Comm Coll 1982-85, Fleming Cty HS 1985-; *ai:* Academic Team Coach; Literary Club Spon; Writing Project Coord; Morehead Writing Project Co-Dir; KY Cncl of Teachers of Eng, NCTE (Judge Writing Contest 1988-89) 1985-; Natl Writing Project 1988-; Jesse Stuart Fnd 1989-; HS Teacher 1990; NEA 1985-; KY Pilot Writing Project Grant Recipient 1989; Ashland Oil Teacher Achievement Awd 1989; *office:* Fleming Cty HS Rt 2 Elizaville Ave Flemingsburg KY 41041

GOODING, LINDA CHABERS, 6th Grade Soc Stud Teacher; *b:* Charleston, SC; *m:* Miles Alton Jr.; *c:* Barbara G. Puleo, Teresa G. Varella; *ed:* (AA) General Ed, Anderson Jr Coll 1969; (BS) Elem, GA S Coll 1971; Mid Sch Trng; *cr:* 6th Grade Teacher Dorchester Terrace Elem 1971-73; 4th-7th Grade Teacher Park Circle Elem 1973-84; 5th/6th Grade Teacher Hanahan Mid Sch 1984-; *ai:* Coach Quest Academic Competition Public Speaking Level I; Co-Teacher Lions Quest; Consensus Based Evaluator Berkeley Cty Teacher Incentive Prgm; Phi Beta Kappa Honor Society, Denmark Society, BERD for Eng & Rdng Teachers; Dorchester Road Nazarene Church; PTA Life Membership 1989; Teacher of Yr Park Circle Elem 1975, 1980.

GOODLING, JOHN MELVIN, Science Teacher; *b:* York, PA; *m:* Charlotte Mae Baker; *c:* Amy L. Schriver, Alice A., Andrea J.; *ed:* (BS) Sci Millersville Univ 1960; (MS) Ed, Temple Univ 1967; (MED) Earth Sci, PA St Univ 1971; Natl Sci Fnd Grant Carleton Coll; Planetarium Operation West Chester Coll & Spitz Space Systems 1974-75; *cr:* Teacher Cntrl York Sch Dist 1960-; *ai:* Head Boys, Girls Track Coach; Cntrl York Ed Assn Pres, PA St Ed Assn, NEA 1960-; Hawks Gunning Club 1986-; Sons of Veterans (Soc Mem Commander) 1988; West York VFW 1987-; Natl Sci Fnd Grant Carleton Coll 1965, PA St Univ 1970-71; Several Wkshps Earth Sci; *office:* Cntrl York Sch Dist 300 E 7th Ave York PA 17404

GOODMAN, CHARLES CHRISTOPHER, Principal; *b:* Muncie, IN; *m:* Hazel A. Longshore Goodman; *ed:* (BS) Elem Ed, 1972; (MS) Elem Ed, 1979 Ball St Univ; *cr:* Teacher Albany Mid Sch 1972-73; Albany Elem Sch 1973-82; Prin Andrews Elem Sch 1982-86; Georgetown Central Sch 1986-; *ai:* Sci Fair Spon; Talent Show Dir; 6th Grade Sci Camp Dir; Union 47 Sci Curr Comm; Union 47 Cmptr Comm; NAESP Mem 1981-; ME Assn Elem Sch Prin 1986-; YMCA Bd of Dir 1982-86; *home:* RR 3 Box 436B Wiscasset ME 04578

GOODMAN, DANA RICHARD, English Faculty Teacher; *b:* Eldred, PA; *m:* Laura Catherine Lee; *c:* Andrew L.; *ed:* (BA) Eng/Philosophy, Roberts Wesleyan Coll 1968; (MA) Eng/19th Century British, Purdue Univ 1970; (PHD) Amer Lit, Ball St Univ 1976; *cr:* Asst Professor of Eng Roberts Wesleyan Coll 1970-72; Division Chm/Assoc Professor of Eng/Hum Eureka Coll 1977-86; Eng Faculty IL Math & Sci Acad 1986-; *ai:* NEH Summer Seminar; Case Western Reserve; TX Arts Cncl Poetry Grant; Intro to Sociology & Literary Stud; *office:* IL Math & Sci Acad 1500 W Sullivan Rd Aurora IL 60506

GOODMAN, DEBORAH KAY (CHAPMAN), Honors Government & Economics; *b:* Vernon, TX; *m:* Robert L.; *c:* Nicole A.; *ed:* (BSE) Speech, 1975, (MA) Pol Govt Sci, 1975 Midwestern St Univ; Soc Stud Composite, Midwestern St Univ; *cr:* Pol Sci Teaching Asst, Midwestern St Univ 1975-77; Product Research/Buyer, Office Environment Co-Op 1977-79; His Teacher/Girls Coach, Zundy Jr HS 1979-85; Govt/Economics Teacher Hirschi HS 1985-; *ai:* Supervising Teacher for Stu Teacher; Textbook Comm Economics; Vertical Team for Hirschi HS-Sch Adv; Sponsored Honors Economics Bus HHS Inc Local; Supervised Honors Govt Tours for Elem Tour About Amer Flag; Assn TX Prof Educators 1979; 1st Baptist Church (Singles Assoc Dir 1983-85) 1979-; NALC Womens Auxilary 1986-; Career Ladder II Level Since 1987; Obtained Historical St Recognition for Wichita Falls HS 1986 Paper Submitted to TX St Historical Comm; *office:* John Hirschi H S 3106 Borton Ln Wichita Falls TX 76305

GOODMAN, JAMES D., 7th/8th Grade Math Teacher; *b:* Sheridan, WY; *m:* Adrienne; *ed:* (BS) Math Ed, E MT Coll 1983; (MA) Cmptr Ed, Lesley Coll 1990; *cr:* 7th/8th Grade Math Teacher Clear Creek Mid Sch 1984-; *ai:* Girls Intramural Bsktbl, Asst Track, Mathcounts Coach; NCTM; *office:* Clear Creek Mid Sch 58 N Adams Ave Buffalo WY 82834

GOODMAN, MARY KAY, High School Teacher; *b:* Portales, NM; *m:* James Thomas; *c:* Bertram P., Barton P.; *ed:* (MA) Eng, Eastern NM Univ 1982; *cr:* Teacher Moriarty Mid Sch 1974-77, Moriarty HS 1979-83, Moriarty Mid Sch 1985-88, Moriarty HS 1988-; *ai:* Soph Class & Drama-Theater Club Spon; Speech Coach; NCTE 1985-.

GOODMAN, NANCY FISHER, Chemistry/Physics Teacher; *b:* Chilhowie, VA; *m:* Charles F. Jr.; *c:* J. Christian, A. Baker; *ed:* (BA) Chem, Radford Coll 1964; (MS) Curr/Instruction, VA Tech 1988; *cr:* Teacher Lynchburg City Schls 1964-69, Marion Sr HS 1977-; *ai:* Sci Academic Team Coach; Math Club Spon; NSTA 1986-87; SW VA Dist Sci Teachers 1984-89; Chilhowie United Meth Church 1969-; Chilhowie Garden Club Flower Show Awds; VA Tech Summer Inst for Physics Teachers Participant; *office:* Marion Sr HS 848 Stage St Marion VA 24354

GOODMAN, SHARON LEACH, Second Grade Teacher; *b:* Terre Haute, IN; *m:* Joseph H.; *c:* Parker G.; *ed:* (BS) Elem Ed, IN St Univ 1966; (MS) Elem Ed, IN Univ 1976; *cr:* 1st Grade Teacher 1966-67, 6th Grade Teacher 1967-74 Maconaquah Sch Corporation; Kndgtn Teacher 1981-84, 2nd Grade Teacher 1984- Seymour Jackson Elem Sch; *ai:* Delta Kappa Gamma 1974-; IN St Teachers Assn, NEA 1966-; *home:* 1411 Stadium Dr Seymour IN 47274

GOODMAN, WALLACE ANDREW, Retired Mathematics Teacher; *b:* Amarillo, TX; *m:* Mildred Britton; *c:* Wesley, Jim, Mary K. Bundick; *ed:* (BA) Bus, W TX St Canyon 1949; (MED) Elem Ed, W TX St Univ 1954; *cr:* 5th Grade Elem Teacher Eunice NM 1949-61; 6th-8th Grade Teacher Caton Jr HS 1961-89; *ai:* Coach Ftbl, Bsktbl, Track 1954-70; Insurance Comm Local Ed Assn; NEA; Eunice Ed System Treas 1974-77; Meth Church (Sunday Sch Teacher, Church Choir) 1962-; *home:* 602 Avenue L Eunice NM 88231

GOODMAN, WILLIAM BENNETT, Social Studies Teacher; *b:* Buffalo, NY; *m:* Margaret Mc Namara; *c:* Bill, Thomas, James, Marianne Buttenschon, Kevin; *ed:* (BS) Bus/Economics, Utica Coll 1957; Scndry Ed, Syracuse Univ; *cr:* Soc Stud Teacher Whitesboro Cntrl Sch 1964-; *ai:* Chairperson Soc Stud Dept; . Whitestown Post Amer Legion Vice Commander 1956- Citizen of Yr Awd 1976; Malson Jones Post VFW 1962-; Whitestown Jaycees Distinguished Service Awd; Councilman Town of Whitestown 1968-77; Supervisor Town of Whitestown 1978-; Teachers Medal Valley Forge Freedoms Fnd His Awd; Oneida Cty DAR Oustanding Amer; *home:* 5113 Wilcox Rd Whitesboro NY 13492

GOODNIGHT, JUDY DAVIS, Sixth Grade Teacher; *b:* Concord, NC; *m:* John Steven; *c:* Landra A., Shannon L.; *ed:* (BA) Ed/Early Chldhd Ed, Univ of NC Charlotte 1982; Intermediate with Concentration in Soc Stud, UNC Charlotte 1983; *cr:* 6th Grade Teacher Shady Brook Elem 1982-89, Woodrow Wilson Elem 1989-; *ai:* Mem Task Force for Kannapolis City Schls; Coord Initially Certified Person/Mentor Support Group; Southern Assn Accreditation Comm Mem; Delta Kappa Gamma Society Intnl 1987-; NC Assn for Educators 1983-; Intnl Rdng Assn 1982-; Kannapolis Civics Club 1989-; Shady Brook Sch PTO Teacher ofYr 1987-88; Mentor Teacher; *office:* Woodrow Wilson Sch 800 N Walnut St Kannapolis NC 28081

GOODNO, DEBRA (HUDSON), 7th/8th Grade English Teacher; *b:* Siloam Springs, AR; *m:* Fred M.; *ed:* (AA) Eng, NEO A&M 1977; (BSED) Eng, 1980, (MS) Spec Ed, 1987 Pittsburg St Univ 1987; *cr:* Eng Teacher Uniontown Schls 1980-; *ai:* Yrbk Adv; Local & Cty Spelling Bee Spon; NEA Local Teachers Assn (Building Rep, Public Relations Comm) 1988-89; Sigma Tau Delta 1980-; Poem Published; Anthology Regents Schlsp; *office:* West Bourbon Elem Sch Old Hwy 54 Uniontown KS 66779

GOODREMOTE, CECIL J., JR., Jr HS Science Teacher; *b:* Buffalo, NY; *ed:* (AAS) Ed, Trocaire Coll 1973; Sci Wkshps 1980, 1981, 1985-Canisius Coll; Natl Fnd Sci Wkshp Grant Canisius Coll 1979; *cr:* 5th Grade Teacher 1960-61, 6th Grade Teacher 1961-62, 5th Grade Teacher 1962-66, 7th/8th Sci Teacher 1966-83, 6th-8th Sci Teacher 1983- S S Peter & Paul Sch; *ai:* Quiz Bowl Moderator; Sci Book Selection Comm; Sci Mentor Region 7 1987; Elem Sch Teacher Developer Grant Herbarium 1978; 50 Articles Published; St Elizabeth Ann Seton Awd 1987; *office:* S S Peter & Paul Sch 68 E Main St Hamburg NY 14075

GOODRICH, LINDA A., Third Grade Teacher; *b:* Joplin, MO; *m:* M. C.; *c:* Kendra, Jeffrey; *ed:* (BS) Elem Ed, 1963, (MS) Elem Ed, 1981 Pittsburg St Univ; Rdng Specialist; *cr:* 3rd Grade Teacher Franklin Elem 1963-65; Spec Ed Teacher Baxter Springs Jr HS 1966-67; 3rd Grade Teacher Rockdale Elem 1976-; *ai:* PEO 1973-; *office:* Rockdale Sch 2116 Rockdale Blvd Miami OK 74354

GOODRICH, LOUISE LYONS, Teacher of Phys Handicapped; *b:* Chicago, IL; *w:* Juarez Lamarr (dec); *c:* Richard, Wanda Peete, Cheryl, Rhonda Walker, Michael, Anthony, Juarez III; *ed:* (AA) Child Dev, Loop Coll; (BS) Spec Ed, NE IL Univ; (MS) Learning Disabilities, Chicago St Univ; Spec Ed, Univ of IL Chicago Circle Campus; Bureau of Staff Dev, Chicago Bd of Ed; *cr:* Postal Clerk US Post Office Chicago IL 1959-70; Teacher Aide Wendell Phillips HS 1969-82; Spec Ed Teacher Cather Elem Sch 1982, Spalding HS & Elem Sch 1982-; *ai:* Cooperating Teacher Roosevelt Univ; Stu Teaching & Observation Prgm; Brother Rice HS Mothers Club; CEC 1982-; AFT: Macedonia Baptist Church (Choir Mem 1977-, Young Adult Club Spon 1990); *office:* Primary PH/TMA Teacher 1628 W Washington Chicago IL 60612

GOODRICH, SARA JANE JOHNSON, English Department Chair; *b:* De Queen, AR; *m:* Thomas K.; *c:* Tina, Michael, Lisa; *ed:* (BA) Ed/Speech/Drama, LA Tech Univ 1951; Advanced Wkshps in Theatre; *cr:* Teacher Delhi HS 1951-53; Hostess Jane Goodrich Show KLAR Radio 1953-54; Teacher Chaparral Jr HS 1967-70, Alamogordo Mid HS 1973-; *ai:* Speech Team Coach; Natl Forensic League 1974-90 Diamond Key Coach; NM Speech Assn Dist Chairperson 1979-80, Coach of Yr 1985; SW Theater Assn Mem 1979-; Alpha Chi Omega; St of NM Legislative Commendation 1986; VFW/Voice of Democracy Service Awd 1975-; Optimist Intnl Oratorical Contest Service Awd; Delegate Natl Sch Bd Conference on Merit Pay; NM Governors Comm for K-12th Grade Drama Competencies.

GOODRICH, TIMOTHY WARD, His/Drafting/Chem Teacher; *b:* Norfolk, VA; *m:* Dianne Wise Nicholas; *c:* Stephen, Mary B.; *ed:* (BS) Health/Phys Ed/Driver Ed, VA Polytechnic Inst & St Univ 1972; (MA) Scndry Phys Ed, Hampton Univ 1979; Amer His/Chem; *cr:* Teacher/Coach Thomas Eaton Jr HS 1973-75; Adv/Coach/Teacher Suffolk Chrstn Schls 1975-83; Teacher/Guidance Sheets Memorial Chrstn Sch 1984-; *ai:* Sr Class Homeroom Co-Spon; NHS Spon; Asst Var Bsbl Coach; Awana Youth Club (Commander, Game Dir) 1987-89; Couples for Christ Sunday Sch Class Teacher 1988-; Whos Who in Amer Ed 1988; Natl HS Coachs Awd Bronze Medal Ftbl 1988; *office:* Sheets Memorial Chrstn Sch 307 Holt St Lexington NC 27292

GOODSON, HAROLD GLENN, Electronics Instr; *b:* Griffin, GA; *d:* Theresa May Head; *c:* Mary J.Presley, Elizabeth D. Sampson, Julie A. Greer; *ed:* (AA) Ed, Clayton St 1972; Electronics, Southern Bus Univ 1963-64; Ed, Univ of GA 1968-70 & 1973-75; GA St Univ 1972-73 & 1988-; Electronic & PT Wkshps; *cr:* Instr USAF 1957-61; Avionics Tech Southern Airways Co 1964-73; Instr Macon Area Vo-Tech Sch 1973-85; Griffin HS 1985-; *ai:* NEA 1985-; GA Assn of Educators 1985-; Griffin-Spalding Assn of Educators 1985-; Trade Industrial Educators of GA 1989-; GA Prin of Technology Assn 1987-; Chm Electronics Dept Macon Tech 1975-85; Sch Evaluation Teams; *office:* Griffin H S 1617 W Poplar St Griffin GA 30223

GOODSON, JO BROWN, English Teacher; *b:* Commerce, TX; *m:* W. M. Sr.; *c:* W. M. Jr., Stacie Luke; *ed:* (BS) Eng/Bus, ETSU 1974; ETSU & UT Tyler; *cr:* Eng Teacher Texarkana HS 1974-80, Economics Teacher Robert E Lee HS 1980-85; Eng Teacher Greenville HS 1985-; *ai:* Spon Stu Cncl; Dir Univ Interschlstc Leag Acad Act; Spon UIL Lit Criticism Category; Prin Adv Comm; Pres Assn TX Prof Educators; ATPE Pres 1983-85/1989- Outstanding Leader 1984-85; First Baptist Church; Outstanding Bus Teacher 1984; TX Excl in Teaching of Private Enterprise-1984; Teacher of Yr-Greenville HS-1989; Pub 1988 TX Study of Ed-Research Journal; *office:* Greenville H S 3515 Lions Lair Greenville TX 75401

GOODWIN, GARY LYNN, Fifth Grade Teacher; *b:* Pocahontas, AR; *c:* Brittney, Joey; *ed:* (AA) Ed, Crowleys Ridge JR Coll 1972; (BSE) Phys Ed, OK Chrstn Coll 1974; (MS) Elem Admin, Cntrl St Univ 1981; Effective Schls Research; Skills for Adolescence; *cr:* Phys Ed Teacher 1974-83, 6th Grade Teacher 1983-89, 5th Grade Teacher 1989- Epperly Heights; *ai:* Dist Textbook Selection Comm; Coaching Duties Asst Ftbll/Head Bsktbll/Asst Wrestling/Head Gymnastics; TeachersAdvisory to Supt Comm; Media Advisory Bd; Schl Improvement Comm; *home:* 3704 Mt Pleasant Midwest City OK 73110

GOODWIN, JAMIE LYNNE, Third Grade Teacher; *b:* Oklahoma City, OK; *m:* Tom W. Jr.; *c:* Thomas W. III, Colin J.; *ed:* (BA) Art Ed, 1977, (MED) Elem Ed, 1982 Central ST Univ; Kelwyn Teacher Effectiveness Trng; Whole Lang Inst; Cooperative Learning Groups; Project Wild Environmental Ed; *cr:* 3rd Grade Teacher 1978-79, K-4th Grade Phys Ed Teacher 1979-82, 4th Grade Teacher 1982-87 Bodine Elem Sch; 1st/2nd Grade Teacher Arcadia Elem Sch 1987-89; 3rd Grade Teacher James Monroe Elem Sch 1989-; *ai:* Staff Dev, Stu Recognition, Arts in Ed Comm; OK Ed Assn (Sch Rep 1987-89, Mem 1978-); Received Grants for Grow Lab; Teach Scientific Processes & Novels; Teach Rdng Through Lit; Building Level Trainer for Kelwyn Teacher Effectiveness Trng; Steering Comm Chm for Arcadias N Cntrl Evaluation; Participated in IDEA; Monroe Artist in Residence Writing Grants; *office:* James Monroe Elem Sch 4810 N Linn Oklahoma City OK 73112

GOODWIN, KIT D., Mathematics Teacher; *b:* Gordon, NE; *ed:* (BS) Math, Chadron St Coll 1985; *cr:* Math Teacher Powder River Cty HS 1985; *ai:* Academic Olympics Chairperson.

GOODWIN, SHARON FRINKS, Teacher; *b:* Orangeburg, SC; *c:* Terence Andrew Frinks; *ed:* (BA) Soc Sci, Claflin Coll 1969; (MED) Scndry Ed, Univ of SC 1977; *cr:* Teacher North HS 1969-81, Orangeburg-Wilkinson HS 1981-; *ai:* Sr Class Spon, Chairperson Honors & Awds Prgm; At Risk Coord; Joint Cncl of Soc Stud 1980-; Amer Cancer Society Bd Mem 1980-82, Volunteer 1982; Drop-Out Prevention Grant for At Risk Stus; Teacher Incentive Campus Awd; SC EIA Comm for Teaching of Black His Mem; *home:* 271 Shadow Lawn Dr Orangeburg SC 29115

GOOLSBEY, MARY ANN, Sixth Grade Teacher; *b:* Breckenridge, MN; *ed:* (BA) Ed, Univ of ND 1968; (MA) Curricular/Instructional Systems, Univ of MN 1981; MECC, TIES Technology Trng; *cr:* 6th Grade Teacher Bloomington Public Schls 1968-; *ai:* MN St Dept of Ed Health Conference Planning, St Model Learner Outcomes Test Comm, St Conference Leader & Curr Developer; AFT; Natl Sch of Excl Staff Mem 1986-87; Research & Dev Grant 1990; *office:* Oak Grove Intermediate Sch 1300 W 106th St Bloomington MN 55431

GOOLSBY, MARILU DOSTER, Teacher of Gifted/Food Coord; *b:* Rebecca, GA; *m:* Brooks Nelson; *c:* Charles L., William N., Elizabeth; *ed:* (BS) Elem Ed, Tift Coll 1965; (MED) Elem Ed, 1976, Ed Specialist Mid Grades 1989 Columbus Coll; *cr:* Elem Teacher 1961-78, Teacher of Gifted 1978-, Nutrition Dir 1986- Talbot Cty Sch System; *ai:* Acad Team Spon; Spelling Coach; GA Ed Assn 1961-80; GA Assn of Educators 1980-84; Prof Assn GA Educators 1986-; Pilot Club of Manchester Warm Springs Pres

1989-; Delta Kappa Gamma Outstanding Educator 1990; *office:* Talbot Cty Sch System PO Box 515 Talbotton GA 31827

GOOZEN, BARBARA, German/Mathematics Teacher; *b:* Grand Rapids, MI; *m:* Eric P.; *c:* Paul, Melissa; *ed:* (BA) Ger/ Scndry Ed, W MI Univ 1966; *cr:* Math Teacher Cntrl Jr HS 1966-67, South Lyon Jr HS 1967-71; Math/Ger Teacher Glennallen HS 1975-; Ger Teacher Prince William Sound Comm Coll 1988-; *ai:* Copper Valley Teachers Assn Pres 1985-87; AK Foreign Lang Assn, AATG, AK Ed Assn, NEA; AK Dept of Ed Merit Awd 1986; Goethe Inst Schlsp 1987; Glennallen Teacher of Yr 1980-82; *office:* Glennallen Sch P O Box 66 Glennallen AK 99588

GORA, PATRICK JOHN, SR., English Teacher; *b:* Chicago, IL; *c:* Patrick Jr, Katherine; *ed:* (BA) Eng, St Josephs Coll 1968; (MSED) Ed/Guidance Counseling, Northern IL Univ 1972; *cr:* Eng Teacher Marmion Military Acad 1968-71; Cnslr Fenwick HS 1971-72; Ftbl/Track Coach North Cntrl Coll 1972-; Eng Teacher Wheaton Cntrl HS 1972-; *ai:* Asst Ftbl, Track Coach North Cntrl Coll; Amer Ftbl Coaches Assn 1976-; *office:* Wheaton Cntrl HS 603 S Main St Wheaton IL 60187

GORDON, ANN SUDDUTH, English Teacher; *b:* Jackson, MS; *m:* Luther E.; *c:* Richard L., Kathy L.; *ed:* (AA) Liberal Art, E Cntrl Jr Coll 1960; (BA) Eng, MS Coll 1962; (MA) Eng, MS St Univ 1968; *cr:* Eng Teacher Picayune Memorial HS 1962-67, Provine HS 1968-70, Mc Cluer Acad 1970-85, Cntrl Hinds Acad 1986-; *ai:* Frosh Class Spon; Speech Elem Art; Long Range Planning Comm; MS Private Sch Assn 1970-; STAR Teacher 1989; *office:* Cntrl Hinds Acad Rt 2 Box 211 C Raymond MS 39154

GORDON, LOYD HUSTON, Mathematics Teacher; *b:* Williamsburg, KY; *m:* Vera Schock; *c:* Bradley; *ed:* (BS) Elem Ed, Cumberland Coll 1967; (MA) Admin, Xavier Univ 1977; *cr:* 6th Grade Teacher Wayne Local Sch Dist 1963-65; Math Teacher Valley View Mid Sch 1965-; *office:* Valley View Local Schls 64 Comstock St Germantown OH 45327

GORDON, MICHELE ANN (DE REMER), Elementary Teacher; *b:* Olean, NY; *m:* Glenn Andrew; *c:* Lindsay, Colin; *ed:* (BS) Educ, SUC 1973; (MS) Educ/Rdng Spec, Elmira Coll 1977; *cr:* Elem Classroom Teacher Addison Central Sch Dist 1973-; *ai:* Mem Orchestra for Area Musicals; Addison Teachers Assn (VP 1977, Pres 1978-); Natl Assn Young Children 1987-; *office:* Addison Central Sch Cowell St Addison NY 14801

GORDON, PATRICIA ANN, Second Grade Teacher; *b:* Pittsburgh, KS; *m:* Gary; *c:* Scott; *ed:* (BA) Home Ec, 1970, (MS) Elem Ed, 1980 Pittsburg St Univ; *cr:* Home Ec Teacher Richland MO 1970-71; 1st/2nd/5th/6th Grade Teacher Lamar Elem 1974-; *ai:* MSTA; Jasper Baptist Church (Mem, Pianist, Youth Sundy Sch Teacher); Wrote & Received Math Grant; Math Manipulative Wkshps Presenter; *office:* Lamar Elem Sch 6th & Walnut Lamar MO 64759

GORDON, SHARON YOUNG, English Department Chairperson; *b:* San Antonio, TX; *m:* M. Dale; *ed:* (BA) Eng, Baptist Coll 1973; (MAT) Eng, Citadel 1976; *cr:* Teacher Bonds Wilson HS 1973-77, Winyah HS 1977-84; Adjunct Prof Coastal Carolina 1982-84; Teacher Georgetown HS 1985-; *ai:* Eng Dept Chm; Curr & Schlshp Comm; Delta Kappa Gamma Finance Chm 1987-; NTE, NEA; *office:* Georgetown HS 2500 North St Georgetown SC 29440

GORE, MARGUERITE FLORENCE BARDY, Social Stud Dept Chairperson; *b:* Detroit, MI; *c:* David T. Elias, Julie E. Carion, Kathryn M. Martin; *ed:* (AA) His, Macomb Comm Coll 1968; (BS) His/Soc Stud, 1972, (MA) Guidance/Counseling, 1977 Wayne St Univ; *cr:* Soc Stud/Eng Teacher Warren Woods Schls 1972-82; Soc Stud Teacher 1982-83, Soc Stud Teacher/Dept Chairperson 1983-84, 10th Grade Soc Stud Dept Chairperson/ Cnslr 1984- Regina HS; *ai:* Stu Cncl Adv; NHS Bd; Prins Advisory Bd; Soc Stud Dept Chairperson; Alpha Delta Kappa; Women of Wayne; MI Cath Guidance Assn; Archdiocesan Curr Cncl; Regina HS Steering Comm N Cntrl; N Cntrl Evaluator of Guidance, Soc Stud at Luth HS Westland.

GORE, SHARON LANIER, Sixth Grade Teacher; *b:* Nashville, TN; *m:* Charles Earl Sr.; *c:* Charles E. Jr., Christopher T.; *ed:* (BS) Elem Ed, Mid TN St Univ 1973; Mid Sch Curr & Principles; Philosophy of Ed; Grad Stud in Ed & Curr; *cr:* 5th Grade Teacher 1973-77, 6th Grade Teacher 1978-82, 6th Grade Teacher/Admin Asst 1982-86 Grassland Elem; 6th Grade Teacher Grassland Mid 1986-; *ai:* Stu Newspaper Spon; Girls Bsktbl Asst Coach; Southern Assn Accreditation Comm, Grade Level Chairperson; Natl Jr Honor Society Selection Comm Mem; Williamson Cty Ed Assn (Sch Rep 1974-77) 1973-; Tn Ed Assn, NEA Mem 1977-; Church Choir 1977-; Carnton Cty Cntry Club (Bd of Dir, Secy) 1981-83; *office:* Grassland Mid Sch Hillsboro Rd & Manley Ln Franklin TN 37064

GORENA, ANIBAL, Physical Science CP Teacher; *b:* Edinburg, TX; *m:* Elma Gonzalez; *ed:* (BS) Bio, Pan Amer Univ 1982; *cr:* Phys Sci Teacher 1982-83, 8th Grade Advanced Sci 1983-84 Edinburg Jr HS; Phys Sci CP Teacher Edinburg Frosh HS 1984-89; *ai:* Girls Frosh Vlybl & Boys Bsktbl Coach; TX Classroom Teacher Assn, TX Assn Bsktbl Coaches; *office:* Edinburg Freshman HS 1100 E Ebony Ln Edinburg TX 78539

GORENA, JAIME, Earth Science Teacher; *b:* Mercedes, TX; *m:* Mary L.; *c:* Dede, Carla, Jaime, Mariana, John; *ed:* (BA) Phys Ed, Pan Amer Coll 1957; Bi-Ling Ed Stud, Univ of AZ, Guadalajara Mexico; *cr:* Elem/Scndry Teacher Lyford Consolidated Ind Sch Dist 1959-; *ai:* UIL Sci Team Spon; Assn of TX Prof Educators; Jr Chamber of Commerce Mem; Sch Bd Trustee; Poems Published; *office:* Lyford Consolidated Ind Sch P O Drawer 220 Lyford TX 78569

GORGONZOLA, GALE TERESA, Mathematics Teacher/Dept Chair; *ed:* (BA) Math, NY St Univ Coll Potsdam 1973; (MA) Math Ed, Univ of MN Minneapolis 1980; *cr:* Elem Math/Rdng Teacher 1973-80, Sr HS Math Teacher 1980- Geneva City Schls; *ai:* Girls Var Soccer Coach; AMTNYS, NCTM.

GORIN, BETTY MITCHELL, US/World History Teacher; *b:* Campbellsville, KY; *c:* Mark A., Beth M.; *ed:* (BA) His, 1963, (MA) His - Magna Cum Laude, 1967 Univ of KY; (Rank I) His/ Sch Admin, W KY Univ 1980; Various Seminars & Schls; *cr:* US His/Soc Teacher Lafayette HS 1963-65; US/European His Teacher Lindsey Wilson Coll 1966-69; Eng/World Civilization Teacher Campbellsville Dist 1975-77; US/World Civilization Teacher Taylor Cty HS 1977-; *ai:* Jr-Sr HS KY His Quiz Bowl Team Coach, St Champions; Newsletter Comm; Soc Stud Dept Merit Rating Team; Evaluation Team Campbellsville HS; Commonealth Preservation Cncl; KY Jr Historical Society Taylor HS Spon 1980, Spon of Yr Awd 1984; Green & Nelson Ctys Historical Society; Taylor Cty Historical Society (Pres, Dir); KY Historical Society Exec Comm, Distinguished Service Awd 1982; KY Assn for Teachers of His, KY Cncl for Soc Stud, Certificate of Excl Teaching 1981, 1982; Natl Trust for Historical Preservation, Taylor Cty Ed Assn, KY Ed Assn, NEA; KY Bicentennial Commission 1986-; 125th Anniversary Memorial Celebration for Battle of Tebbs Bend (Dir 1988, Re-Enactment Coord); Friends of the Jacob Hiestand Stone House Visitors Information Center Project Chm 1988; Taylor Cty St Cemetery Project Co-Chm; Friends of the Log House Co-Chm; KY Historical Highway Markers St Advisory Comm; Taylor Cty League of Women Voters (Pres, Voters Service Chm); Campellsville Jr Womens Club; Woman of Achievement Awd Taylor Cty B&PW 1979; Amer Heritage Cup Excl in Teaching Awd 1985; Certificate Appreciation US Postal Service 1985; Ida Lee Willis Memorial Fnd Preservation Awd 1985; Cmmty Service Awd Campbellsville City Cncl 1986; *home:* 112 Kensington Way Campbellsville KY 42718

GORIN, ROBERT MURRAY, JR., Social Studies Teacher; *b:* Mineola, NY; *ed:* (AB/MA) His, Xavier Univ 1970; (MSED) Ed, Hofstra Univ 1974; (MA) Philosophy, Fordham Univ 1978; (PHD) His, St Louis Univ 1980; Grad Studies Gettysburg Coll, St Joseph Univ, Harvard Univ, Yale Univ, Plimoth Plantation Inst, Adelphi Univ, Baruch Coll, Cuny; *cr:* Soc Stud Teacher Bellmore-Merrick Cntrl HS Dist 1974-77, 1978-83, South Side HS 1977-78, Manhasset HS 1983-; Adjunct Asst His Professor Hofstra Univ 1986-; *ai:* Moral Ed, Prof Growth, Faculty Advisory Comms; Manhasset HS NHS; NCSS (Prof Ethics Comm, Acting Chm 1986) 1974-; Long Island Cncl for Soc Stud; NY St Cncl for Soc Stud; Amer Historical Assn; Organizations of Amer Historians & His Teachers Society; ACSD; Phi Alpha Theta; Assn for Preservation of Civil War Sites; Civil War & NY Historical Society; South Street Seaport Museum; Natl Trust for Historic Preservation; Civil War Round Table Assocs; Friends for Long Islands Heritage; Prof Growth Grants 1987, 1988; St Louis Univ Partial Schlsp; Tatf Scholar 1976; Freedoms Fnd Schlsps 1985, 1987; Society Values in Higher Ed Fellow; Yrbk Dedication 1988; Manhasset HS Teacher of Yr 1988; Presented Paper; Whos Who in East; *office:* Manhasset HS Memorial Pl Manhasset NY 11030

GORMAN, ADRIENNE TOPPILA, Fifth Grade Teacher; *b:* Brocket, ND; *m:* James B.; *c:* Kimberley A. Cole, Stephanie M. Provolt, James S.; *ed:* (BA) Ed, Cntrl WA Univ 1954; (MS) Ed, VA St Univ 1973; *cr:* 1st Grade Teacher Harney Sch 1954-56, Kessler Elem Sch 1956-57, Amer Sch 1957-58, Shoreline Elem Sch 1958-59, Amer Sch 1959-60, Du Pont Sch 1960-62, Olympic Elem Sch 1963-64; 4th Grade Teacher Murfreesboro TN Elem Sch 1966-69; 1st Grade Teacher Mint Valley Elem Sch 1969-70, Chesterfield Cty Schls 1970-72; GED Instr US Army Ed Center 1973-76; 4th Grade Teacher Amer Elem Sch 1976-77; 5th Grade Teacher Robert Gray Elem Sch 1977-86; 4th/5th Grade Teacher Olympic Elem Sch 1986-; *ai:* At Risk & Self-Study Comm; Longview Ed Assn Sch Rep 1982-89; WA Ed Assn 1982-89; Toastmistress Intnl; Defense General Supply Center Club Pres 1971-72.

GORMAN, ANGELA CLARE, SP, English Teacher; *b:* Framingham, MA; *ed:* (BS) Ed, Immaculate Heart Coll 1940; (BA) Eng, St Mary of the Woods Coll 1946; (MA) Scndry Admin, Univ of Notre Dame 1965; Numerous Courses; *cr:* 8th Grade Teacher St Mel Grade Sch 1936-40; 8th Grade Teacher/Prin St Anthony Grade Sch 1940-46, 1953-60; Eng/His Teacher St John HS 1960-64; Eng Teacher Bellarmine-Jefferson HS 1967-71, Marywood HS 1971-74, St Genevieve HS 1975-; *ai:* Curr Comm; Booster Club; In Charge Graduation Ceremonies; Personal Counseling; Published Poems & Articles; *office:* St Genevieve HS 13967 Roscoe Blvd Panorama City CA 91402

GORMAN, GENE FRANCIS, Science Teacher; *b:* Pittsburgh, PA; *m:* Mary Catherine O'Toole; *c:* Mary J. Gorman Anderson, Timothy J., Sally A. Gorman Leonatti; *ed:* (BS) Ed, Univ of Pittsburgh 1960; (MS) Scndry Ed, Duquesne Univ 1972; *cr:* Sci Teacher Cntrl Cath 1960-63, Serra Cath 1963-69, S Allegheny Jr/ Sr HS 1969-; *ai:* Asst Coach HS Ftbl, Bsktbl, Bsbl; Head Coach Ftbl & Bsbl; Stu Cncl Spon; PA St Ed Assn 1969-; S Allegheny Ed Assn, NEA; St Joseph Cath Church Confraternity of Chrstn Doctrine Religion Teacher 1975-; *office:* S Allegheny Jr/Sr HS 2743 Washington Blvd Liberty Borough Mc Keesport PA 15133

GORMAN, MARJORIE MARY, Second Grade Teacher; *b:* Cambridge, MA; *ed:* (BS) Elem Ed, 1969, (MED) Early Chldhd, 1975 Boston St Coll; *cr:* 2nd Grade Teacher Hodgekins Elem Sch 1969-71, Powder House Cmmty Sch 1972-; *ai:* Soc Stud Curr Comm; Cmptr Educl Advisory Comm; Boston Univ Educl Consortium; Somerville Teachers Assn, MA Teachers Assn, NEA 1969-; Somerville PTA, MA PTA 1969-; MA Chapter 188 Grant 1989; *office:* Powder House Cmmty Sch 1060 Broadway Somerville MA 02144

GORMAN, PATRICIA ANN (STARR), Third & Fourth Grade Teacher; *b:* Clinton, MA; *m:* Robert D.; *c:* Michael, David; *ed:* (BS) Elem Ed, Worcester St Coll 1969; *cr:* 5th Grade Teacher Florence G Houghton Sch 1969-78; 3rd/4th Grade Teacher St Mary Elem 1983-; *ai:* NCEA.

GORMLEY, JOHN DENIS, Algebra/Physics Teacher; *b:* New York, NY; *m:* Jo Ann Susan Tripken; *c:* Emily J.; *ed:* (BA) Sci, NY Inst of Technology 1986; (MA) Ed, E Stroudsburg Univ 1991; Certificate Organized Crime Control Bureau NYCPD; Letter of Commendation of Academic Achievement John Jay Coll; *cr:* Police Officer NY City Police Dept 1973-83; Teacher Notre Dame HS 1986-; *ai:* Athletic Dir Notre Dame HS; Coach Jr HS Girls Bsktbl & Sftbl Team; PIAA, NAC Exec Comm 1989-; Honor Society NY City Police Dept; NY St Senate Advisory Comm for Ed; Awarded 13 Citations for Excl Police Duty NYCPD; Awarded 2 Citations for Meritorious Actions NYCPD; *office:* Notre Dame HS 60 Spangenburg Ave East Stroudsburg PA 18301

GORNICKI, HENRY A., History/Law Teacher; *b:* Fargniers, France; *m:* Lucyna A. Galarda; *c:* Lisa M. Bolender; *ed:* (AA) Liberal Art, Niagara Cty Comm Coll 1966; (BS) Scndry Ed/Soc Stud, 1968, (MS) His, 1971 St Univ Coll Buffalo; (AAS) Criminal Justice, Niagara Cty Comm Coll 1983; (MS) Criminal Justice, St Univ Coll Buffalo 1986; Law, Univ of Richmond; His, St Univ Buffalo; *cr:* Military US Marine Corps 1960-64; Criminal Justice Teacher Niagara Cty Comm Coll 1986-87; HS Teacher Niagara Wheatfield Cntrl Sch 1969-; *ai:* Stu Cncl Adv; NY St Teachers Assn 1969-; Lions Club 1984-; Amer Legion 1985-; Elks 1988-; *office:* Niagara Wheatfield Cntrl Sch 2292 Saunders Settlement Rd Sanborn NY 14305

GORSKI, LINDA URBALONIS, Kindergarten Teacher; *b:* Haverhill, MA; *m:* Stephen A.; *c:* Alexander, Zachary; *ed:* (BA) Elem Ed, Univ of MA 1971; (MED) Rdng, Salem St Univ 1976; Grad Stud; *cr:* 3rd/4th Grade Teacher 1971-73, 4th Grade Teacher 1973-76 Walnut Square Sch; 5th-8th Grade Rdng Teacher St James Sch 1976-77; 4th Grade Teacher Walnut Square Sch 1977-83; Part Time Public Kndgtn Teacher Early Chldhd Center 1987-.

GORSKI, ROBERT FRANK, JR., History Teacher; *b:* Camden, NJ; *m:* Kellie Ann Peak; *c:* Kristin, Robert; *ed:* (BS) Ed/US His, West Chester Univ 1980; *cr:* His Teacher Washington Township HS 1980-; *ai:* Jr Var Bsbl Coach; Drill Instr Minutemen Marching Band; Course of Stud His Revision Comm; Sch Coord Gloucester Cty Voter Registration; NEA, NJEA, WTEA 1980-; Phi Alpha Theta 1978; Pi Gama Mu, Kappa Delta Pi 1979; *office:* Washington Township HS RD 3 Box 286 Sewell NJ 08080

GORSUCH, BELLVIA L., English Teacher; *b:* Paris, AR; *m:* Steven E.; *c:* Chad, Allyson; *ed:* (BS) Eng, Univ of MO Columbia 1970; *cr:* Eng Teacher Mehlville Sch Dist 1970-77, Mehlville Sch Dist 1987-; *ai:* Girls Cross Cntry Coach; NEA, Mehlville Cmmty Teacher Assn; *office:* Mehlville Sr HS 3200 Lemay Ferry Rd Saint Louis MO 63125

GORTER, GLORIA CALIMPONG, Language Arts Teacher; *b:* Lahaina, HI; *m:* Bram W.; *ed:* (BED) Scndry Eng, Univ of HI Manoa 1971; Working Towards Masters in Ed; *cr:* Teacher Aiea HS 1985-86, Wahiawa Intermediate 1986-87, Mililani HS 1987-88, Waialua HS & Intermediate 1988-; *ai:* Speech Team Coach; Literary Magazine Co-Adv; Spelling Bee Coord; HI St Teachers APC Comm 1989-; *office:* Waialua HS & Intermediate Sch 67-160 Farrington Hwy Waialua HI 96791

GORTON-HORAN, ANN HILBERT, English/Reading Teacher; *b:* New York City, NY; *c:* Gwynne Zisko, Melissa Webb, Lara L.; *ed:* (BSEd) Elem Ed, SUNY 1959; (MSEd) Dev Rdng, Trenton St Coll 1986; Teaching the Gifted; *cr:* 2nd Grade Teacher Mamaroneck Sch Dist/Murray Ave Sch 1959-61; 1st Grade Teacher Raritan Primary Bridgewater Sch Dist 1961-62; Mother/ Tutoring at Home 19 Magda Ln 1962-77; Eng/Rdng Teacher/ Gifted & Talented Branchburg Cntrl Sch/Branchburg Township Sch Dist 1978-; *ai:* Coach for Odyssey of Mind Teams 1980-; Newspaper Adv 1987-89; Consultant/Teacher Project Write Teacher In-services 1985-; Delta Kappa Gamma Publicity Chm 1987-; NCTE Publication Idea Factory Ed Staff 1987, Published 1988; IRA Rdng Assn; NJ Educators for Gifted; ASCD; Cntrl Rdng Cncl Pres Honor Cncl 1987-89; NJ Rdng Assn Elected Bd of Dir 1988-; Hillsborough Township Bd of Ed Mem/VP 1972-89; Dedication of Media Center in my Name 1989; Mem Delta Kappa Gamma Lambda 1987; Teacher of Yr 1985; Citizen of Yr 1972; Trenton St Coll Rdng Advisory Comm as Sch Bd Mem 1988; Ann H Gorton Media Center; *home:* 19 Madga Ln Somerville NJ 08876

GOSENHEIMER, JUDI THOMAS, English Teacher; *b:* Berlin, WI; *m:* Al; *c:* Marie Gosenheimer Lenling, Patricia, Heidi, James, Daniel, David; *ed:* (BA) Eng, Mt Mary Coll 1967; *cr:* Teacher Longfellow Jr HS 1966-67; Substitute Teacher Sussex Hamilton HS 1970-72; Teacher Friess Lake/St Augustine Schls 1973-77, Germantown 1979-; *ai:* Big Band Vocalist for Jazz Ensemble of Stu; Literary Magazine & Yrbk Adv; Forensics; Earth Week Comm; Talent Show; Writing Festival; Write Now;

Public Relations Comm; Earth Week Comm; Talent Show; Writing Festival; Write Now; PTA VP 1972-74; GEA Rep; Church Cncl Ed Comm Chairperson 1976-78; Stu Assistance Prgm Trng Grant to Assist in Drug/Alcohol Prevention Prgms; Articles Published; Teacher Inservice Presenter; Writer Sch News Reporter; Whos Who Amoung Amer Women 1976; Sch Dist Nom Distinguished Service 1986-87; *office:* Washington HS W180 N11501 River Ln Germantown WI 53022

GOSHEN, KATHRYN F., Government Teacher; *b:* Stuart, FL; *m:* Richard T.; *c:* Mark; *ed:* (AA) Liberal Art/His, Sullins Coll 1960; (BA) Poly Sci/His, Stetson Univ 1962; Grad Stud Rollins Coll; *cr:* Teacher Bishop Moore HS 1962-68; Office Mgr CPA Office 1977-79; Teacher Bishop Moore HS 1979-; *ai:* Academic Cncl; Teenage Republican Club, Sr Class, Sr Retreat Spon; NCEA, Natl Soc Stud Assn 1979-; Alpha Xi Delta; *office:* Bishop Moore HS 3901 Edgewater Dr Orlando FL 32804

GOSNELL, KAREN FORD, Social Studies Dept Head; *b:* Pittsburgh, PA; *m:* Wyatt W.; *c:* Douglas, Gregory, Sharon E. G. Green; *ed:* (BA) Soc Stud/Math, PA St Univ 1963; (MA) His, Indiana Univ of PA 1973; Teacher Effectiveness Trng; Assertive Discipline; WWII; Sch Law; Writing Across Curr; Writing for Learning; *cr:* Teacher T Benton Gayle Mid Sch 1974-; *ai:* His Club Spon; Sunshine Comm; NEA, VEA, SEA 1985-; *office:* T Benton Gayle Mid Sch 610 Gayle St Falmouth VA 22405

GOSSETT, LOIS SCOATES, Fifth Grade Teacher; *b:* Jacksonville, FL; *m:* Earl Fowler; *c:* Amelia; *ed:* (AB) Religious Ed, FL Southern 1955; (MA) Chrstn Ed, Scarritt 1957; Ed Courses Univ of AL Birmingham, Birmingham-Southern Coll; *cr:* 6th Grade Teacher Alex Green Sch 1959-60; 5th Grade Teacher Adamsville Elem Sch 1978-; *ai:* Drama Sch Rep; Kappa Delta Pi, Cap & Gown 1954; Sigma Rho Epsilon Pres 1954-55; United Meth Church Admin Bd Mem 1985; *office:* Adamsville Elem Sch Drawer K Adamsville AL 35005

GOSSETT, ROBERT BREEN, English Teacher; *b:* Memphis, TN; *m:* Rita Beaudrot; *c:* Rogers B.; *ed:* (BS) Ger, 1965, (MA) Ger, 1968 Memphis St Univ; (PHD) Ger, Univ of TN 1977; *cr:* Ger Instr W Carolina Univ 1967-70, Univ of Evansville 1970-73; Teaching Asst Univ of TN 1973-77; Eng Teacher Chrstn Brothers HS 1979-; *ai:* Var Golf Coach; Frosh & Jr Var Bsbl Head Coach; Frosh Class Moderator; Spec Consultant Gemart Incorporated; Delta Phi Alpha 1965; Knoxville Ger-Amer Club Awd for Outstanding Contributions to Ger-Amer Cultural Life 1977; *office:* Chrstn Brothers HS 5900 Walnut Grove Rd Memphis TN 38119

GOSSVENER, PENNY STURGEON, Second Grade Teacher; *b:* Oakland, CA; *m:* John Dana Jr.; *c:* Brandon, Heather; *ed:* (BS) Elem Ed, Cntrl St Univ 1970; *cr:* Kndgtn Teacher Jones Public Schls 1970-71; 5th/6th Grade Teacher Lone Grove Public Schls 1971-72; Kndgtn/2nd Grade Teacher Graham Public Schls 1972-76; 2nd Grade Teacher Fox Public Schls 1980-; *ai:* Fox Staff Dev Comm 1984-89; Fox Staff Dev Building Rep 1988-89; Fox Negotiating Team 1989-; OK Ed Assn 1980-; Fox Assn of Classroom Teachers (Treas 1989-) 1980-; Healdton Facility Planning Comm Secy 1989; Healdton Cmmty Ed Advisory Cncl 1987-; *home:* HC 63 Box 9950 Healdton OK 73438

GOTSILL, THOMAS WILLIAM, English Teacher; *b:* Newark, NJ; *m:* Mary Elizabeth Bayer; *c:* Amy E., Carrie A.; *ed:* (BA) Eng, Saint Anselm Coll 1966; (MA) Eng, Seton Hall Univ 1970; *cr:* Eng Teacher/Bsktbl Coach Ridgefield Park HS 1973-77, Summit HS 1977-81; Head Bsktbl Coach Saint Anselm Coll 1981-83; Dept Chm/Head Bsktbl Coach 1983-85, Eng Teacher 1983- Merrimack HS; *ai:* Steering Comm Accreditation by New England Assn of Schls & Colls; Natl Assn Bsktbl Coaches HS Comm 1973-; Natl Assn Teachers of Eng; NH Assn Teachers of Eng; Three Articles Published in Nation Wide Coaching Magazines; Coach of The Yr Awd NJ 1977; Cornaug Awd Summit HS 1981; *office:* Merrimack HS Mc Elwain St Merrimack NH 03054

GOTT, TIM, Mathematics Teacher; *b:* Dayton, OH; *m:* Ellen Clements; *c:* Andrew; *ed:* (BA) Math, 1985, (MA) Guidance Counseling, 1989 W KY Univ; *cr:* Teacher Paducah Tilghman HS 1985-86, W Hardin HS 1986-; *ai:* Fellowship of Chrstn Athletes Spon; Var Girls Track, Frosh Girls Bsktbl Coach; Project Graduation Coord; Cecila Baptist Church Adult Sunday Sch Teacher 1989-; *office:* West Hardin HS 10471 Leitchfield Rd Stephensburg KY 42781

GOTTLIEB, CAROLEE MC NEILL, English Teacher; *b:* Kearny, NJ; *m:* Stephen; *c:* Jennifer, Becki; *ed:* (BA) Eng/Elem Ed, Glassboro St Coll 1963; (BA) Guidance, Montclair St Coll 1967; Grad Stud Monmouth Coll, Montclair St Coll; *cr:* 1st Grade Teacher Washington Sch 1963-65; 7th-9th Grade Teacher W Kinney Jr HS 1965-70; 10th/11th Grade Teacher Jonathan Dayton Regional HS 1970-73; 9th/11th Grade Teacher Immaculata HS 1985-; *ai:* Sch Literary Magazine & Sr Class Adv; 4-H Adv 1979-81; Cath Teachers of Eng 1985-89; Glassboro Alumni Assn 1963-; Hillsboro Dukes Cheerleading Coach 1984; Woodfern Home & Sch (Chairperson, Class Mothers) 1979-84; 4-H Adv 1979-81; Participant Various Eng Wkshps; *office:* Immaculata HS 240 Mountain Ave Somerville NJ 08876

GOTTLOCK, WESLEY GEORGE, 6th Grade Teacher; *b:* Brooklyn, NY; *m:* Barbara Heath; *c:* Allison, Brian; *ed:* (BBA) Bus, 1967, (MS) Ed, 1972 Hofstra Univ; Grad Stud Queens Coll, Bernard Baruch Coll; *cr:* Teacher Manhattan Public Sch 63 1971-; *ai:* Boys Swimming Coach; Lenox Hill Environmental Camp & Sci Fair Coord; Sch Environmental Comm; United Fed of Teachers Chapter Chm 1981-84; PTA Outstanding Achievement Awd 1988; Poet in Schls Grant 1989; *home:* 25 Oakland Pl Nanuet NY 10954

GOTTSCHE, MYRA M., AP & Excel US History Teacher; *b:* Kingsport, TN; *c:* Angela M., Scott M.; *ed:* (BA) Sociology, Agnes Scott Coll 1964; (MA) Admin/Ed, Univ of Southern MS 1989; *cr:* US His Teacher Nichols Mid Sch 1984-87, Biloxi HS 1987-; *ai:* Citizen Bee Dist Coord; Dist Staff Dev, HS Grade Weights Comm; St Bd Mem Soc Stud Input Comm; Star Teacher 1989-; *office:* Biloxi HS 1424 Father Ryan Ave Biloxi MS 39531

GOUCHER, JUDITH A., US History Teacher; *b:* Waterbury, CT; *m:* Randall; *c:* Cynthia, David; *ed:* (BA) His, Assumption Coll 1973; Ed, Univ of NM; Cmptr, W NM Univ; *cr:* Soc Stud/Sci Teacher St Marys Sch 1979-81; Teacher Belen Jr HS 1985-; *ai:* Educl Competency Comm; *office:* Belen Jr HS 400 S 4th St Belen NM 87002

GOUCHER, NORMA LOU (REESE), Third Grade Teacher; *b:* Novinger, MO; *m:* Bobby L.; *ed:* (BS) Elem Ed, NE MO St Univ 1955; *cr:* Teacher Trinity Rural Sch 1945-46, Mc Kim Rural Sch 1946-48, Stahl Rural Sch 1948-50, Green Grove Rural Sch 1950-52; 3rd Grade Teacher Adair Cty Elem Sch 1952-; *ai:* Career Ladder Comm Teacher; MO St Teachers Assn 1945-; PTA Lifetime Mem Teacher of Month; Adair Cty R-1 Sch PTO; Adair Cty R-1 Teachers Assn; Novinger Planned Progress Service Club 1970-; *home:* RR 3 Novinger MO 63559

GOUDSCHAAL, ROGER DEAN, Business Teacher/Coach; *b:* Quincy, IL; *m:* Elizabeth Mary Tollefson; *c:* Sara J., Grant R.; *ed:* (BS) Bus Ed, Western IL Univ 1971; Grad Work at Univ of N IA Drake; *cr:* HS Teacher/Coach Tripoli Cmmty Sch 1972-; *ai:* Asst Bsktbl & Ftbl Coach; Yrbk Spon; Mock Trial Coach; Tripoli Ed Assn Pres 1978-79, 1989-; ISEA, NEIEU, NEA, IBEA 1972-; Maple Hills Cntry Club VP 1988-; Church Cncl VP 1987-; Faith Church Search Comm Chm 1989; *home:* 207 1st St NW Tripoli IA 50676

GOUGEON, RAYMOND JOSEPH, Social Studies Instructor; *b:* Trimountain, MI; *m:* Jo Ann Marie Opatik; *c:* Nicole L., Kimberly A.; *ed:* Suomi Jr Coll 1960-62; (BS) His/Poly Sci Northland Coll 1962-64; (MST) Univ of WI Superior 1969; Grad Stud Viterbo & Univ of WI La Crosse; *cr:* Teacher/Coach Ashland Public Schls 1965-69, Mauston Public Schls 1969-; *ai:* Head Track, Asst Bsktbl, Cross Cntry, Golf Coach; Stu Cncl Adv; Stu Support System; MEA, WEA, NEA Negotiating Team; WI Edonomic Ed Cncl, WI Soc Stud Teachers; Jaycees, Lions Club Former Mem; *office:* Mauston HS Grayside Ave Mauston WI 53948

GOUGH, TERRY JO, Spanish Teacher; *b:* Orange, TX; *ed:* (BA) Elem Ed, TX Tech Univ 1975; Scndry Cert, SW TX St Univ 1985; *cr:* Remedial Rdng Teacher J Frank Dobie Mid Sch 1976-79; Remedial Math Teacher Rosegarden Elem 1980-81; 1st-12th Grade Migrant Ed Teacher Marion Elem Jr HS 1981-83; Span Teacher Kitty Hawk Jr HS 1983-85; Span/Drill Team Teacher Judson HS 1986-; *ai:* Starlite Drill Team Dir; Spon Stu Trips Mexico; *office:* Judson HS 9695 Schaefer Rd Converse TX 78109

GOULARD, MARILYNN HEIDENREICH, Second Grade Teacher; *b:* Walla Walla, WA; *w:* Irving H. Jr. (dec); *c:* William H., Helen Goulard Hagen, Arthur B., Marilyn Goulard Heyde, Terri Goulard Henningson; *ed:* (BA) Home Ec, Walla Walla Coll 1944; Grad Stud Elem Ed, CA St Univ Los Angeles 1970-72; *cr:* Scndry Music/Home Ec Teacher Loma Linda Acad 1944-45; 2nd Grade Teacher San Gabriel Acad Elem 1977-; *ai:* Kappa Delta Pi 1972-; Amer Guild of Organists 1950-75; Violet & Thomas Zapara Teacher of Yr Awd; *home:* 401 W Duarte Rd #2 Arcadia CA 91007

GOULART, EDMOND, JR., Economics Teacher; *b:* New Bedford, MA; *m:* Amy Elizabeth Davis; *ed:* (BS) Marketing, SW MA Univ 1970; (MBA) Suffolk Univ 1977; Advanced Cmptr Stud; *cr:* Econmics Teacher Somerset HS 1970-; *ai:* MA Teachers Assn, NEA 1970-; Dartmouth Agricultural Comm Mem 1989; Horace Mann Teacher 1987-88; Somerset HS Man of Yr 1978; Dartmouth Planning Commission 1980-87; *home:* 64 Tucker Ln North Dartmouth MA 02747

GOULD, JAMES DOUGLAS, Science Teacher/Dept Co-Chair; *b:* Oakland, CA; *m:* Lindsay Allynne Murch; *c:* Tyler, Jonathan, Jason; *ed:* (BS) Bio/Chem, 1977, (MS) Integrated Sci, 1981 OR St Univ; Leadership Skills, W OR St Coll; Modern Methods, Lewis & Clark Coll; *cr:* Sci Teacher Calapooya Jr HS 1977-82, S Albany HS 1982-; *ai:* Dist Sci, Talented & Gifted Steering Comm; Leadership Cadre Linn & Benton Ctys; Improvements Elem Sci Ed Eisenhower Grant; Staff Presenter Elem Teacher Sci Wkshps; OR Sci Teachers Assn (Regional Dir 1989-) 1977-; WA Sci Teachers Assn 1989-; NSTA 1990; Sigma XI 1987, Sci Teacher of Yr; Tektronix/OR Museum of Sci & Industry; Awd for Excl Sci Teaching OR & WA 1990; Action Alliance Excl Ed Linn & Benton Ctys; S Albany HS Distinguished Teacher of Yr 1987; *office:* S Albany HS 3705 S Columbus St Albany OR 97321

GOULD, VIRGINIA CAROL, Third Grade Teacher/Substitute; *b:* Moses Lake, WA; *ed:* (BA) Art, Gonzaga Univ 1980; Post Grad Stud Gifted Ed, Gonzaga Univ, WA Univ, Whitworth Coll; *cr:* 3rd Grade Teacher St John Vianney Sch 1980-88; Art Instr Spokane Art Sch 1988-; 3rd Grade Long Term Substitute Teacher Bemiss Sch 1989-; *ai:* Whitworth Coll Writing Rally Presenter 1988-; Spokane Art Sch Art Reach Prgm 1988-; *home:* E 11516 Fairview Spokane WA 99206

GOULEY, JANICE WADLEY, First Grade Teacher; *b:* Alhambra, CA; *m:* Robert A.; *c:* Andrea R. Hayes, Shawn K., Pierre J.; *ed:* (BS) Elem Ed, S OR St 1955; Kndgtn Certificate, OR Coll of Ed 1955; Attended Seminars & Wkshps in Early Chldhd Music, Math, Writing, Farm Ag; *cr:* Kndgtn Teacher Longview 1955-56, S OR St Coll 1958; 1st Grade Teacher Walker Sch 1959-61, Horace Mann Sch 1961-62, Walker Sch 1962; Kndgtn Teacher Dingle Sch 1970; K-8th Grade Substitute Teacher Davis, Dixon, Winters, Woodland 1973-77; Kndgtn Summer Sch Teacher/Dir 1978-85, 4th Grade Teacher 1980-81, Vice Prin 1980-81, 1988-89, 1st Grade Teacher 1977- Holy Rosary Sch; *ai:* Church Choir; S OR St Coll Robes Womens Honorary Society & Associated Women Stus VP 1954-55; OR Teachers Assn, AAUW, NEA, Childrens Home Society, Cath Ed Assn; OR Shakesperean Tudor Guild 1962-66; *office:* Holy Rosary Sch 505 California St Woodland CA 95695

GOURLAY, LINDA MARIE STROBEL, Level Four Teacher; *b:* Buffalo, NY; *m:* John Porter; *c:* Shannon, Megan; *ed:* (BA) Elem Ed, 1970, (MS) Elem Ed, 1972 Buffalo St Coll; *cr:* Level 5 Teacher Charlotte Ave Sch 1970-75; Level 5 Teacher 1976-81, Level 4 1981- Armor Sch; *ai:* Annual Reviewer; Hamburg-Fredonia Intern Prgm; Phi Delta Kappa Mem 1985-; Variety Club of Buffalo Mem 1974-; Volunteer Work for Childrens Hospital & Other Charities Camp Good Days; *office:* Hamburg Cntrl Sch 5301 Abbott Rd Hamburg NY 14075

GOURLEY, MARY MEINEKE, English Teacher/Dept Chairman; *b:* Hampton, IA; *m:* Dennis; *c:* John, Matthew; *ed:* (BA) Eng/Speech, IA St Univ 1977; Eng/Ed; *cr:* HS Eng Teacher Stratford Cmmty Sch Dist 1977-79; Eng Teacher Allamakee Cmmty Sch Dist 1980-; *ai:* Chrldng Coach; NCTE; NEA; IA St Ed Assn; *office:* Waukon Jr H S 107 5th St NW Waukon IA 52172

GOVER, MARIA RAMOS, English Teacher; *b:* Los Angeles, CA; *m:* Charles Andrew; *c:* Alicia, Hugh, Margaret; *ed:* (BA) Eng, CA St Univ Los Angeles 1974; (MS) Ed, Mt St Marys Coll 1989; Admin Credential; *cr:* Teacher 1975-78, Dept Chm 1977-78, 1983-89, Teacher 1982-, Faculty Dev Dir 1988- Bishop Amat HS; *ai:* Friday Night Live Moderator; Evaluation, Advisory, Curr, Archdiocesan Personnel Practices Comms; NCTE 1985-; ASCD 1988-; Natl Center for Hum Summer Seminar, Milken Fnd Teacher Incentive, Mellon Fnd/Arco AP Teacher Grants; *office:* Bishop Amat HS 14301 Fairgrove Ave La Puente CA 91746

GOVERNALE, JOSEPH ANTHONY, English Teacher; *b:* Brooklyn, NY; *m:* Ann-Marie; *c:* Stacey, Timothy; *ed:* (BA) Eng, 1970, (MS) Ed/Eng, 1974 St Johns Univ; *cr:* Eng Teacher Bishop Loughlin HS 1970-73, Brentwood HS 1973-; Adjunct Instr Suffolk Cty Comm Coll 1989-; *ai:* Teacher of Yr NHS 1986-87; Published Essay 1978; Writing Novel; *office:* Brentwood HS 5th Avenue Brentwood NY 11717

GOWDY, CHARLEY J., Constitution Teacher; *b:* Bristow, OK; *m:* Diane Dietrich; *c:* Kurt, Lynn, Marla Poston, Sherri Poston, Kevin; *ed:* (BS) Soc Sci/Phys Ed, 1959, (MSED) Soc Sci, 1968 Emporia St Univ; *cr:* Teacher/Coach Emporia Sr HS 1959-69; Great Bend Sr HS 1969-; *ai:* Citizen Bee Regional Coord; Close Up KS Coord; Regional Planning & Zoning Commission Chm 1979-; Barton Industrial Comm Economics Partnerships 1989-; KS Tennis Coaches Assn Chm 1967-68; KS St HS Coaches Convention Guest Speaker 1978; KS Wrestling Coaches Hall of Fame; Citizen Bee Natl Steering Comm-Trip to Washington DC Finals 1989; Emporia Gazette Man of Week 1967; *home:* 2508 Pasco Great Bend KS 67530

GOWDY, VALERIE BOLLENSEN, Teacher of Gifted & Talented; *b:* Elgin, IL; *m:* David P.; *c:* Bryan, Jonathan, Jennifer; *ed:* (BS) Elem Ed, Univ of GA 1967; Gifted Ed, Early Chldhd Ed, Univ of S FL; *cr:* Teacher Doraville Elem 1967-69, Morgan Woods Elem 1981-82, E E Just Elem 1982-; *ai:* Red Cross & Safety Patrol Spon; Gifted Team Leader; NCTM, Hills Cty Math Teachers 1986-; Red Cross 1982-; Cancer Society, Heart Assn 1960-; *home:* 6104 Dory Way Tampa FL 33615

GOWELL, CYNTHIA ANN, 5th Grade Teacher; *b:* Scranton, PA; *ed:* (BA) Elem Ed, 1970, (MS) Elem Ed, 1974 Marywood Coll; Real Estate Trng & St Licensed; Educl Research & Dissemination Scranton Fed of Teachers; Foreign Lang Trng Personal Satisfaction & Dev; Course Work Univ of Scranton; *cr:* 5th Grade Teacher Wm Prescott Elem 1970-; *ai:* Schls & Scouts Prgm; Scranton Sch Dist Eng & Sci Textbook Comm; 5th Grade Trip Harrisburg & Washington DC; 5th Grade Graduation Dinner; Phi Delta Kappa Mem; Scranton Fed of Teachers Building Rep 1978-; BSA Asst Den Leader 1989-; Marywood Coll Alumni Assn (Scranton Pres 1977-79, Natl Exec Bd 1985-87, Giving Fund Drive General Co-Chm 1988); Jr League of Scranton (Chm, Membership Dev Comm, Asst Chm Bd) 1974-; Marywood Coll Alumnae Assn Chairperson of Homecoming 1976, 1990; Sr Alumni Dinner 1986, Family Festival Day 1987; NE PA Philharmonic Chorus Singer 1980-; Marywood Coll Singers 1984-87; Standing Room Only (Mem, Actress, Singer, Dancer) 1974-; Marywood Coll Ed Classes Guest Lecturer 1980-; Presentation of Stu Sci Projects to Sci Ed Class; *office:* Wm Prescott Sch 38 Prescott & Myrtle Sts Scranton PA 18510

GOWER, DORTHA SUE, Fourth Grade Teacher; *b:* Rosie, AR; *ed:* (BS) Elem Ed, Grace Coll 1969; (MS) Elem Ed, Purdue Univ 1972; *cr:* Teacher Park Elem 1969-84; Teacher Handley Elem 1984-; *ai:* Statement of Direction for Lang Arts Comm Mem; AFT; PTA Life Mem 1984; Who's Who in American Education 1989-90; *home:* 206 Ohio Street La Porte IN 46350

GRABER, ANN MARKEE, English/Journalism Teacher; *b:* Maryville, MO; *ed:* (BSED) Eng/Journalism, NW MO St 1979; Grad Courses Univ of IA; *cr:* Eng/Journalism Teacher Gallatin HS 1979-81, Pella Cmmty HS 1983-; Yrbk Coord Univ of IA 1986-; *ai:* Yrbk & Newspaper Adv; ISEA, NEA; IA HS Press Assn 1987-89, Kenneth Stratton Awd 1988; League of Women Voters Newsletter Ed 1990; *office:* Pella Cmmty HS E 212 University Pella IA 50219

GRABER, HOWARD S., Mathematics Teacher; *b:* Barrington, IL; *m:* Neva J. Wipf; *ed:* (BA) Math/Sci, Univ of WY 1966; (MS) Math, Univ of NE Omaha 1970; *cr:* Math Teacher Cncl Bluffs Cmmty Schls 1966-; *ai:* Phi Delta Kappa 1973-; Amer Legion; *office:* Abraham Lincoln HS 1205 Bohnam Council Bluffs IA 51503

GRABER, ROBERT CHARLES, Teacher/Bsktbl Coach; *b:* Newton, KS; *m:* Glenna Sue Umholtz; *c:* Kimberly, Christopher; *ed:* (BS) Ind Ed, Bethel Coll 1973; 40 Hrs Toward Grad Degree *cr:* Teacher/Coach Geneseo HS 1973-74, Newton HS/Santa Fe Middle 1974-; *ai:* Coaching Girls Bsktbl; KS Bsktbl Coaches Assn, 5-A Rep 1987-, Coach of Yr 1987-88; NEA 1973-; Church of Christ Deacon 1987-89; Youth Coach-Recreation Commission 1984-; AR Valley League Coach of Yr 1985-88; *home:* 1120 W 9th Newton KS 67114

GRABOWSKI, KATHY LUNDAHL, Fifth Grade Teacher; *b:* Tacoma, WA; *m:* Michael M.; *c:* Kari, Aron; *ed:* (BA) Bio, Fort Wright Coll 1965; (ASCP) Med Tech, Swedish Hospital 1966; (BAED) WA St Teaching Cert, Univ of WA 1973; *cr:* 2nd-6th Grade Teacher Anchorage Sch Dist 1976-; *ai:* NEA Sch Rep 1981-87; PTA; *home:* 12141 Jerome Rd Anchorage AK 99516

GRACE, ALICE CAROL, Home Economics Teacher; *b:* Anderson, IN; *m:* George E.; *c:* Shelley A., Perry L., Eric R. James, Erin R. James, Misty J., Amanda M.; *ed:* (BS) Home Ec, 1969; (MA) Home Ec, 1974 Ball St Univ; Career Equity Trng; *cr:* HS Home Ec Teacher Shenandoah HS 1969-75; Middle Sch Home Ec Teacher Shenandoah Mid Sch 1975-; *ai:* Jr Honor Society Adv Comm; Gifted/Talented Cncl East Central IN; East Side Church of God Music Ministry; St Staff IN DECA Leadership Conf; *home:* 2641 E 450 N Anderson IN 46012

GRACE, ELIZABETH MILLS, ESL Teacher/Department Chair; *b:* Lakewood, CA; *m:* Robert V.; *ed:* (BA) Eng Lit, Univ of CA Santa Barbara 1983; *cr:* Teacher Marshall Mid Sch 1984-; *ai:* Eng 2nd Lang Dept Chairperson; Long Beach Unified Sch Dist LEP Master Plan & Bi-ling Advisory Comms; NCTE 1983-; CA Assn Teachers of Eng to Speakers of Other Lang 1986-; Teachers Assn of Long Beach 1985-; Presbyn Church Deacon 1988-; *office:* Marshall Mid Sch 5870 E Wardlow Rd Long Beach CA 90808

GRACEY, JOHN J., 5th Grade Teacher; *b:* Sheridan, WY; *m:* Mary Jane Mc Hugh; *c:* John W., Jean M.; *ed:* (AA) Ed, Sheridan Jr Coll 1968; (BA) Elem Ed, 1970, (MED) Curr/Instruction 1978, Univ of WY; *cr:* 4th Grade Teacher Eastside Elem 1970-71; 4th-6th Grade Teacher Parkside & Eastside Mid Sch & Southside Elem 1971-; *ai:* Drug & Alcohol Abuse Support Group Asst; Curr Dev Comm; Powell Ed Assn, WY Ed Assn 1971-; NEA 1970-; Powell Elks #2303 (Exalted Ruler 1980-81, Youth Act Chm 1981-88); Union Presbyn Church (Session Mem 1990, Chrstn Ed Co-Chm); Nom Teacher of Yr; *home:* 723 E Madison Powell WY 82435

GRADILLAS, GILBERT F., 6th Grade Teacher; *b:* Phoenix, AZ; *ed:* (BA) Elem Ed, AZ Univ 1968; *cr:* 5th Grade Teacher Dysart Sch 1968-83; 6th Grade Teacher Surprise Elem Sch 1983-; *ai:* Coach Intramurals; Spon Yrbk; Spon Stu Cncl; NEA 1968-; AZ Ed Assn 1968-; Dysart Ed Assn Treas 1968-; *home:* 12545 W Desert Cove Peoria AZ 85345

GRADISHAR, SUSAN CLOR, 9th-12th Grade Math Teacher; *b:* Harbor Beach, MI; *m:* Frederick John; *c:* Daniel, Matthew, Michael; *ed:* (BS) Elem Ed, 1970, (MED) Math Ed, 1982 Univ of DE; *cr:* 4th-6th Grade Math Teacher Dowell Elem 1971-72; 6th-8th Resource Teacher Shue Mid Sch 1972-73; 5th Grade Teacher Medill Elem Sch 1973-76; 7th/8th Grade Math Teacher Magnolia Mid Sch 1979-81; 9th-12th Grade Math Teacher John Carroll Sch 1981-; *ai:* Frosh Class Adv; Faculty Exec Cncl Mem; Discipline Review Bd; Forest Hill Recreation Cncl Tennis Chm 1989-; Southampton Mid Sch PTO Bd of Dirs 1988-; *office:* John Carroll Sch 703 Churchville Rd Bel Air MD 21014

GRADY, ELIZABETHANN ERBIN, World Geography Teacher; *b:* Pittsfield, MA; *m:* Edwin R. III; *c:* Sarah, Andrew; *ed:* (BA) His/Soc Stud, Trinity Coll 1966; George Mason Univ, Univ of VA; *cr:* Soc Stud Teacher Crosby Jr HS 1966-69, Stratford Jr HS 1970-74, Swanson Jr HS 1974-77, Thoreau Intermediate 1986-87; World Geography Teacher Hayfield Scndry 1987-; *ai:* Key Club, Sr Class Spon; Fairfax Ed Assn, VA Ed Assn, NEA, Geography Alliance; Grant to Study in Korea, Korean Stud Cncl Intnl; *office:* Hayfield Scndry Sch 7630 Telegraph Rd Alexandria VA 22310

GRADY, JIM, JR., Government Teacher; *b:* Pensacola, FL; *m:* Deena Walker; *c:* Lisa; *ed:* (BA) Poly Sci, TN St Univ 1965; (MED) Soc Sci, Wayne St Univ 1971; Univ of MI; MI St Univ; *cr:* 7th Grade Geography Teacher Lincoln Jr HS 1967-77; 8th Grade His Teacher Best Jr HS 1978-87; Government Teacher Ferndale HS 1987-; *ai:* Media Center Planning Comm; MI Assn HS Soc Sci Teachers; Auburn Hills Lib Bd 1986.

GRADY, MARY ANNA, Science Teacher & Dept Chair; *b:* Albertson, NC; *ed:* (AA) General Coll, Montreat 1945; (BS) Sci/Health/Phys Ed, 1948, (MA) Scndry Ed, 1953 E Carolina Univ; Grad Work at Numerous Univs; *cr:* Part Time Est Camp Dir GSA; Part Time Adult Ed Teacher James Sprunt Comm Coll; Sci Teacher B F Grady HS 1948-86, E Duplin HS 1962-; *ai:* Adv Future Teachers of America, Sr Class; Duplin Cty Calender Comm; Teacher Recruiter; NEA, NSTA; NC Assn Of Educators Division Pres 1972, Distinguished Service Awd 1971; NC Sci Teachers Assn Dist Dir 1985-86, Outstanding Sci Teacher 1985-86; Delta Kappa Gamma Society Pres 1980, Outstanding Local Mem 1990; Amer Legion Auxiliary; Nature Conservancy; Sierra Club; Grady Otlaw Literary & Historical Assn Pres; Duplin Cty Teacher of Yr 1971, 1986; Outstanding Bio Teacher St Finalist 1969; St Nominee Presidential Awds Excl in Sci Teaching 1986; NC Bus Awds Excl in Sci Teaching 1987; Whos Who in Amer Ed 1988-89; *home:* Box 9 John David Grady Rd Albertson NC 28508

GRADY, MICHAEL JOHN, Superintendent/Principal; *b:* Bend, OR; *m:* Marylin E.; *c:* David, Phillip; *ed:* (BA) Liberal Stud, CSU Hayward 1977; (MA) Admin, St Marys Coll 1987; *cr:* Teacher 1977-89, Prin 1989- Bridgeville Sch; *ai:* ACSA Mem 1989-; *office:* Bridgeville Sch P O Box 98 Bridgeville CA 95526

GRAETTINGER, JANET KAY (THURBER), Vocal Music Director; *b:* Duluth, MN; *m:* Keith Norris (dec); *c:* Karyn Norris, Kimberly Norris, Kyle Norris, Kirt Norris; *ed:* (BME) Music Ed, Drake Univ 1968; Grad Stud Music & Substance Abuse Prevention; Talking with Kids About Alcohol Prgm Certified Trainer; *cr:* K-12th Grade Vocal Music Teacher Graettinger Cmmty Sch 1968-71; Vocal Music Dir Ruthven Ayrshire Cmmty Sch 1979-; *ai:* Staff Dev, Substance Abuse Programming Coord; Mem Lakeland AEA III Drug-Free Schls Consortium, Goals Objectives Comm Chairperson 1984-89; Sr Class Spon; Salary Comm; MENC, Amer Assn of Univ Women 1989-; Drug Free Schls Cmmty Comm (Chairperson 1988, Secy 1989), Volunteer Service to Comm Awd 1989; *office:* Ruthven Ayrshire Cmmty Sch 1505 Washington Ruthven IA 51358

GRAF, EILEEN M., Junior HS Science Teacher; *b:* Burlington, WI; *m:* Thomas A.; *c:* Jarrett, Ryan; *ed:* Certificate Elem Ed, Racine-Kenosha Teachers Coll 1967; (BA) Elem Ed, Corthage Coll 1971; Working Toward Masters Admin Leadership, Univ of WI Milwaukee; *cr:* Teacher Salem Grade Sch 1967-72, Union Grove Mid Sch 1973-75, Yorkville Elem Sch 1975-; *ai:* Alcohol & Drug Prgm Comm Mem; Jr HS Sci Coord; AFT (Treas 1983, Mem 1975-); NEA; Union Grove Biathlon Coordination Comm 1988; Union Grove Town & Cntry Days Run Coordination Comm 1987; Assisted in Developing Outdoor Ed Prgm Yorkville Jr HS; Sci Fellowship 1987-88; *home:* 1404 10th Ave Union Grove WI 53182

GRAFF, DAN L., Coach/Math Teacher; *b:* Larned, KS; *m:* Linda Kay Webb; *c:* Rebecca E. Taylor, Stacy D.; *ed:* (BA) Ed, KS St Teachers Emporia 1967; *cr:* Phys Ed Teacher 1968-75, Elem Teacher 1975-82 Alta Brown Elem USD 457; Math Teacher Kenneth Henderson Mid Sch 1982 ; *ai:* Frosh Vlybl Coach; Head Coach Boys & Girls Track; NEA 1967; KNEA; GCEA 1990; *home:* 1503 Rowland Rd Garden City KS 67846

GRAFF, MAXINE RAE GREER, Retired Teacher; *b:* Nash, OK; *m:* George Jr.; *c:* George R. III, Patricia J. Graff Dollarhide; *ed:* (BS) Bus Ed/Eng/Geography, OK St Univ 1942; (MA) Teaching, Tulsa Univ 1958; Arts/Elem Cert; *cr:* Bus Ed Teacher Crescent HS 1941-42, Nash HS 1944-46; 1st Grade Teacher Riley Elem Sch 1958-63, Carnegie Elem Sch 1963-84; *ai:* Kappa Delta Pi 1952-61; Delta Kappa Gamma Sevy 1962-; Comm Write Non-Graded Curr Tulsa Public Schs; Elem Sch Math Resource Handbook for Teachers; Handbook Ideas for Self-Contained Primary; *home:* 4107 S. New Haven Pl Tulsa OK 74135

GRAFF-RAMIREZ, ROSANN, Honors World His/Psych Teacher; *b:* Los Angeles, CA; *m:* Ricardo; *ed:* (BA) His, Loyola Marymount Univ 1978; (MA) His, Univ of S CA 1980; Seminars Univ of CA Los Angeles, LMU; *cr:* His Teacher Louisville HS 1980; His/Psych Teacher Bishop Amat HS 1980-; *ai:* Advanced Placement European His Tutor; Chrstn Service Project Adopt-A-Grandparent Asst; Personel Practices & Advisory Comm; Pacific British Historical Society, British Historical Society Mem, 1989-; Huntington Lib Reader Researcher 1989-; Natl Endowment for Hum Summer Inst 1990.

GRAGG, DIANE GARMAN, 5th Grade G T Teacher; *b:* Galesburg, IL; *m:* Phillip J.; *c:* Sherry L. Pruitt, Robert R. Pruitt, David S. Pruitt; *ed:* (BS) Elem Ed, Univ of TX El Paso 1969; Graduate Hours Math & Admin; *cr:* Health/Phys Ed Teacher Del Norte Elem 1969-70; Phys Ed Teacher 1977-78; 4th Grade Teacher 1978-82, 3rd Grade Teacher 1982-86, 5th Grade Teacher 1986- Vista Hills Elem Sch; *ai:* Stu Cncl Spon; Spelling Bee Coord-UIL; Gifted & Talented Summer Sch Prgm-Etymology; Grade Level Chm; NEA, YTA, TSTA 1977-; Kappa Kappa Iota Pres 1988-; PTA (VP, Secy 1977-80) TX Terrific Teacher of Yr 1984; Natl Sci Fnd Math Grant; *home:* 3217 Vogue Dr El Paso TX 79935

GRAGG, LYNDA D., 7th/8th Grade Teacher; *b:* Brooklyn, NY; *ed:* (BS) Elem Ed, IN St Univ 1980; Ed, IN St Univ; *cr:* 2nd Grade Teacher 1985, 7th-8th Grade Teacher 1986- Cntrl Sch; *ai:* 7th Grade Spon; NEA 1985-; *office:* Central Sch St Rd S 4 E Switz City IN 47465

GRAHAM, BETTY BLUE, Science/Health Teacher/Coord; *b:* Globe, AZ; *m:* Beverly K.; *c:* Mary, David, Tim, Elizabeth, Martha, Paul, Peter, James; *ed:* (BA) Arts/Crafts/His, NM Highlands Univ 1950; Experimental Sci; *cr:* 3rd Grade Teacher Mountainair Elem Sch 1950-51; 4th Grade Teacher 1966-67, 5th/6th Grade Sci/Health/Art Teacher 1967- E J Martinez Elem; *ai:* Spon Sci & Environmental Sci Clubs 1989-, Recyclers 1988-89; Health Ed Comm Mem; Elem Sci Curr Comm Coord; Sci/Math Learning Center Originator & Coord; NEA Building Rep; NSTA; Cncl of Elem Sci Intnl Bd of Dirs 1986-89; Santa Fe Childrens Museum Volunteer; 1st Prebyn Church Liturgical Arts Chairperson; NM Conservation Service Teacher of Yr; Natl Audubon Society Schlsp Ed Ecology Summer Camp 1986; *office:* E J Martinez Sch San Mateo & Galisteo Santa Fe NM 87501

GRAHAM, CELESTINE MOORE, Third Grade Teacher; *b:* Clinton, NC; *m:* Charles Maynard; *ed:* (BA) Ed, Livingstone Coll 1966; Univ of NC Wilmington; *cr:* 4th/6th/7th Grade Teacher West Pender Elem 1966-68; 2nd-7th Grade Rdng Teacher Rappahannock VA 1968-69; 3rd-5th Grade Teacher Burgaw Elem 1969-; *ai:* Senate Bill Two Comm; Grade Chairperson; NC Ed Assn, NEA 1989-; Math Assn 1988-89; Pender Cty Math Teacher of Yr 1986; Burgaw Elem Sch Teacher of Yr 1985; Math Teaching with Energy Participant 1984; Selected NC Advancement Teacher Center 1988; *home:* 2229 Shirley Rd Wilmington NC 28406

GRAHAM, CURTIS R., English Department Chair; *b:* St Paul, MN; *m:* Esther Tenenholtz; *c:* Susan, Andrew; *ed:* (BS) Eng, Univ of MN 1962; Grad Stud in Amer Stud, Univ of MN; *cr:* Eng Teacher Harding HS 1962-; *ai:* Harding HS Chapter of Amnesty Intnl Adv; St Paul Fed of Teachers, MN Fed of Teachers 1962-; Phi Beta Kappa 1962-; Natl Geographic Society, Smithsonian 1989-; Univ of MN Alumni Assn 1987-; MN Bus Fnd Excl in Ed Awd Nominee; *home:* 633 W Belmont Ln Roseville MN 55113

GRAHAM, IVAN WILLIAM, Wood Processing Teacher; *b:* Midland Cty, MI; *m:* Joy Dorreen Mc Gahan; *c:* Keith, Calvin; *cr:* Maintenance Teacher Shenandoah Valley Acad 1954-57, San Pasqual Acad 1957-62, Platte Valley Acad 1964-66, La Sierra Coll 1966-69, San Pasqual Acad 1969-70; Ranger Pine Springs Ranch 1970-80; Maintenance Teacher Milo Acad 1980-; *ai:* Milo Fire Dept Bd of Dir Mem 1987-; Commissioned Build Camp Haue Ark of Covenant 1985; *office:* Milo Adv Acad P O Box 278 Days Creek OR 97429

GRAHAM, JAMES FRANKLIN, Science Teacher; *b:* Columbia, MO; *m:* P. Christy Groves; *c:* Jess T., Haley-Jane E.; *ed:* (BS) General Stud, 1979, (BSED) Chem/Bio, 1980 MO S St Coll; *cr:* 7th-12th Grade Sci Teacher Summersville R-II 1980; 5th-8th Grade Sci Teacher Goodman Elem 1980-86; 6th Grade Sci Teacher Intermediate Sch 1986-; *ai:* Boys Var Tennis Coach; Math/Sci Club Spon; NEA, MO Ed Assn; Neosho Ed Assn Pres 1985-87; NSTA 1985-; BSA Merit Badge Cnslr; *office:* Intermediate Sch N Wood St Neosho MO 64850

GRAHAM, LAURA WILLIAMS, Teacher; *b:* Tuskegee, AL; *c:* Martez A.; *ed:* (BS) Eng, 1968, (MA) Sch Counseling, 1990 AL St Univ; Grad Stud Sch Counseling 1990; *cr:* Teacher Evergreen HS 1968, Warren City Schls 1970-76, Atlanta Public Sch 1978-84, Macon Cty Bd of Ed 1984-; *ai:* Jr & Yrbk Adv; Courtesy Mem; Stu Handbook Comm Mem; Book Adoption Comm Recorder; AEA, NEA Mem 1978-; Multicultural Counseling Mem 1989; NAACP Mem 1968; Democratic Club Mem 1987; Zeta Phi Beta (Mem, Public Relation) 1988; Band Service Awd; Governor Wallace Meritorious Service Citation; *home:* Rt 3 Box 574 Tuskegee AL 36083

GRAHAM, LELA MC KINNEY, Business Teacher; *b:* Basin, WV; *m:* Danny W.; *c:* Bryan W.; *ed:* (BS) Bus Ed, Concord Coll 1967; (MA) Speech Comm, WVU 1985; *cr:* Bus Teacher Big Creek HS 1967-70, Welch HS 1970-73, Herndon HS 1970-; *ai:* Co-Spon Herndon HS FBLA; WVEA/CEA 1967-; NEA 1967-; *home:* Box 777 Pineville WV 24874

GRAHAM, MARTHA KING, Fourth Grade Teacher; *b:* Milton, FL; *m:* John Herbert; *c:* John H. III, Staci M.; *ed:* (BS) Ed, FL St Univ 1956; Numerous Courses; *cr:* 2nd Grade Teacher Berryhill Elem 1956-59; 3rd Grade Teacher Sidney Lanier Elem 1959-60, Metcalfe Elem 1960-62; 4th Grade Teacher Dunedin Elem 1962-; *ai:* Law Advisory Cncl; Numerous Sch Related Comms; PCTA, FTP, NEA, Delta Kappa Gamma Recording Secy; *home:* 1336 Highfield Dr Clearwater FL 34624

GRAHAM, MICHEAL MC COMB, Vocational Agriculture Teacher; *b:* Converse, LA; *m:* Amy Hodges; *c:* Ashley N., Christopher M.; *ed:* (BS) Agronomy, 1977, (MS) Life Sci, 1988 LA Tech Univ; *cr:* Research Assoc LA St Univ Research Stations 1978-80; Farm Mgr Huber Farm Service Incorporated 1980-82; Regional Agronomist Na-Churs Plant Food Company 1982-84; Sales Consultant Amerisources Bus Systems 1985-87; Voc Ag Teacher Chatham HS 1987-; *ai:* FFA, Literary Rally, 11th Grade Spon; Bsbl Coach; LVATA 1987-; *office:* Chatham HS P O Box 37 Pine St Chatham LA 71226

GRAHAM, PATTI MUSSILL, Spanish Teacher/Counselor; *b:* Grosse Pointe Farm, MI; *m:* Joseph M. Jr.; *c:* Jennifer; *ed:* (BA) Span, Wayne St Univ 1969; Guidance & Counseling Cert 1988; *cr:* Fr/Span Teacher Lakeview HS 1969-83; Span Teacher 1983-, Cnslr 1988- Lutheran HS East; *ai:* Chrldrs; Stu Cncl & Span Club Adv; Sr Class Spon; MI Foreign Lang Assn 1969-; *office:* Lutheran HS East 20100 Kelly Rd Harper Woods MI 48225

GRAHAM, ROBERT TAYLOR, JR., Agriculture Science Teacher; *b:* Zwolle, LA; *m:* Sharon Rockett; *c:* Laura, Rebecca; *ed:* (BS) Voc Ag Ed, 1974, (MS) Botany/Applied, 1978 LA Tech Univ; Working Towards Ed Specialist Admin & Bus Admin Accounting; *cr:* Voc Ag Teacher Mansfield HS 1978-79; Spec Rep Bus Mens Assurance Company 1981-83; Cooperative Extension Agent Caddo Parish 1979-80; Voc Ag Teacher North De Soto HS 1983-; *ai:* FFA Adv; LA Voc Assn (St Officer, Parliamentarian 1989-, Secy 1988-89, Reporter 1987-88, Constitution Chm 1989-, Resolutions Chm 1988-89, Public Relations Chm 1987-88, Membership Dev 1986-89) 1986-; AVA 1986-; Natl Voc Ag Teacher Assn; LA FFA Alumni Assn (Mem 1988-, St Rep Natl Alumi Leadership Conf 1988); LA Voc Ag Teacher Assn (Membership Chm 1986-89, Secy 1989-, Area II VP 1985-89, Legislative Lobby Comm, Mem 1986-89); De Soto Parish (Supt Employee Benefits Comm of Teachers, Mem 1986-); Broadmoor Baptist Church (Mem, Teacher 1979-89); Ted Roberts Senate Campaign Chm 1987-89; Stan Tiner Congress Campaign Staff Mem 1988; Jim Mc Crery Congress Campaign Volunteer 1988-; Dorothy Smith Bd of Elem & Scndry Ed Rep; Mrs Smiths Readers Panel Rep 1988-89, 1989-; Natl Public Affair Intern 1989; *home:* 109 Lucia Ln Shreveport LA 71106

GRAHAM, RUBY, Social Studies Dept Chair; *b:* Trenton, NJ; *ed:* (BA) Sociology, 1947, (MA) Ed, 1957 Howard Univ; (MA) Ed Admin, San Francisco St Univ 1974; NY Sch of Soc Work, Columbia Univ, Trenton St Coll, Rider Coll; *cr:* Soc Worker NJ Neuro Psychiatric Inst 1949-57; Dir Guidance Unit NJ St Home for Girls 1957; Teacher Johnstone Trng & Research Center 1958-60, Hamilton Township Bd of Ed 1960-63, Lompoc Unified Sch Dist 1963-67; Instr Univ of CA Extension Santa Barbara 1966; Teacher San Francisco Unified Sch Dist 1967-; *ai:* Faculty Cncl Mem; AFT, CA Cncl for Soc Stud, ASCD; Amer Civil Liberties Union; Natl Assn for Advancement of Colored People; Valley Forge Teachers Medal 1974; *office:* Luther Burbank Mid Sch 325 La Grande Ave San Francisco CA 94112

GRAHAM, SHIRLEY CYPERT, Business Teacher; *b:* Sheffield, AL; *m:* Harold; *c:* Suzanne Graham Byrom; *ed:* (BS) Bus Ed, Univ of N AL 1957; Ed Courses, Montevallo Univ & Auburn Univ; *cr:* Bus Ed Teacher Lauderdale Cty 1961-; *ai:* Yrbk Adv; Beauty Pageant Dir; AL Ed Assn, NEA, Lauderdale Ed Assn 1961-; AL Press Assn 1975-; *home:* 338 Robinhood Dr Florence AL 35630

GRAHAM, SHIRLEY DE PUE, Junior High Guidance Counselor; *b:* Hamden, OH; *m:* David E.; *c:* Todd, Andy; *ed:* (BA) Elem Ed, 1973, (MSED) Elem Principalship, 1981 OH Univ Athens; (MSED) Guidance/Counseling, Univ of Dayton 1988; *cr:* K/1st/3rd/6th-8th Grade Teacher Vinton Cty Elem Schls 1969-88; Jr HS Teacher/Guidance Cnslr Vinton Cty Jr HS 1988-; *ai:* OSCA, NEA, OEA; Phi Delta Kappa.

GRAHAM, VICKIE LYN (REGISTER), Mathematics Dept Chair/Teacher; *b:* Douglas, GA; *ed:* (BS) Math Ed, Valdosta St Coll 1969; (MA) Math, GA St Univ 1978; *cr:* Teacher/Math Dept Chm Brooks Cty HS 1969-71; Teacher Cartersville Jr HS 1971-72; Tift Cty HS 1972-74; Pebblebrook HS 1975-78; Teacher/Math Dept Chm Colquitt Cty HS 1978-; *ai:* TPAI Evaluator; Staff Dev & Schlsp Comm; Teacher Effective Schls Wkshp for Teachers; PAGE 1980-; GCTM 1978-; *office:* Colquitt Cty HS 1800 Park Ave Moultrie GA 31768

GRAINGER, WILLIAM, Earth Science Teacher; *b:* Mullins, SC; *m:* Marcia Watts; *c:* Moni A., Jodi D.; *ed:* (BS) Elem Ed, Francis Marion 1974; (MED) Scndry Soc Stud, Univ of SC 1984; *cr:* General Sci Teacher Loris Mid Sch 1975; Sci Teacher Dept of Soc Services 1975-76; Earth Sci Teacher Palmetto Jr HS 1977-; *ai:* Gun Safety Club Instr; Future Teachers of America Club & Wildlife Conservation Club Spon; Pee Dee Regional Rdng Assn Mem 1989-; Masonic Lodge 183 Mem 1982-; Completion of Prgm for Effective Teaching & QUEST; *office:* Palmetto Jr HS 305 O Neal St Mullins SC 29574

GRAMBLIN, ELIZABETH ANN, 6th Grade Lang Arts Teacher; *b:* Easley, SC; *w:* George W. III (dec); *c:* George W. IV, Patrick M.; *ed:* (BA) Music, Claflin Coll 1957; (MED) Elem Ed, Clemson Univ 1978; Music Ed Eng SC St Coll; *cr:* Priv Music Teacher 1957-85; Cnslr Share/JTPA 1972-87; Consumer Teacher Appalachian Hlth Cncl 1975-85; *ai:* Chairperson Music Dir Worship-Easley Chapel United Meth Church; Chairperson Young Adult Ministries-Easley Chapel Church Pianist/Organist; NEA/SCEA/PCEA 1960-; Natl Cncl of Negro Women Pres 1984-89; Alpha Kappa 1955-; Teacher of Yr-Pickens Elem 1985; *home:* 202 Jordan Dr Easley SC 29640

GRAMBLING, FLORA G., First Grade Teacher; *b:* Orangeburg, SC; *ed:* (BS) Elem Ed, 1976, (MED) Elem Ed, 1977 Winthrop Coll; Grad Stud Univ of SC; *cr:* 4th Grade Teacher 1977-89, 1st Grade Teacher 1989- Bamberg Elem; *ai:* Rivelon Ladies Sftbl Team; Orangeburg Part Time Players Costume Person 1987-; Cmptr Coord Bamberg Elem; Grants Comm; *office:* Bamberg Elem Sch PO Box 546 Bamberg SC 29003

GRAMLICH, PENNY LEIGH, Assistant Principal; *b:* Norfolk, VA; *ed:* (BS) Elem Ed, 1977, (MS) Educl Admin, 1982 Old Dominion Univ; EdS Prgm, Coll of William & Mary; *cr:* 4th Grade Teacher Hickory Elem Sch 1977-84; Asst Prin Great Bridge Intermediate Sch 1984-; *office:* Great Bridge Intermediate Sch 369 Battlefield Blvd Chesapeake VA 23320

GRAMS, JOAN LEHNUS, Fifth Grade Teacher; *b:* Kankakee, IL; *m:* Robert; *c:* Jason, Amanda; *ed:* (BS) Elem Ed, IL St Univ 1975; (MS) Ed, Natl Coll of Ed 1984; *cr:* Teacher Limestone Sch 1976-; *ai:* Soc Stud & Math Curr Comm; Math Olympiads Spon; Teacher Evaluation Comm; IL Fed of Teachers, AFT Rep 1985-88; St Mark United Meth Church (Chairperson Ed Dept 1986-89, Secy of Staff, Pastor, Parish Comm 1990); Taft PTO Secy 1986-89; Limestone PTA; *office:* Limestone Grade Sch R R 4 Box 242a Kankakee IL 60901

GRANATO, CONNIE, Science Teacher; *b:* San Antonio, TX; *ed:* (BS) Home Ec, Incarnate Word 1964; (MED) Ed, Trinity Univ 1978; *cr:* Home Ec Teacher 1964-82, Life Sci Teacher 1982-87 Escobar Jr HS; Life Sci Teacher E T Wrenn Jr HS 1987-; *ai:* Sci Club & Fair Spon; UIL Sci Coaching; Sch Climate Comm; NEA, TX St Teacher Assn, Edgewood Classroom Teacher Assn; Sci Teachers Assn of TX; *office:* E T Wrenn Jr HS 627 S Acme San Antonio TX 78237

GRANDELL, SARA MC LAUGHLIN, 8th Grade Teacher; *b:* Wilmington, DE; *ed:* (BA) Latin/Classics-Cum Laude, Univ of DE 1976; *cr:* 7th Grade Teacher St Catherine of Siena Sch 1976-84; 8th Grade Teacher St Peter Cathedral Sch 1984-; *ai:* Newsletter Ed; Lang Art Coord; Schls Long Range Planning Comm Mem; Self Study Process for Mid States Evaluation of St Peters Cathedral Sch Chairperson 1986-88; NCEA; *office:* St Peter Cathedral Sch 6th And Tatnall Sts Wilmington DE 19801

GRANDERSON, MARY F., Fifth Grade Teacher; *b:* San Francisco, CA; *m:* Robert C.; *ed:* (BA) His, Dominican Coll 1957; Numerous Classes Above Credential; *cr:* 5th Grade Teacher Lomita Park Sch; 4th-6th Grade Teacher Green Hills Sch; 4th Grade Teacher Bad Nauheim; 4th-5th Grade Teacher Rose Avenue Sch, Sonoma Sch; *ai:* Sonoma Sch Traffic Patrol Head; Served on Several Dist Comms; Modesto Teachers Assn 1968-; NEA, CA Teachers Assn 1958-; St Josephs Church Parish Cncl Secy 1985; *office:* Sonoma Elem Sch 1325 Sonoma Ave Modesto CA 95355

GRANDINETTI, BARBARA ANN, Teacher of Gifted Lang Art; *b:* Binghamton, NY; *m:* Edward Jr.; *c:* Edward III, Michael; *ed:* (BA) Elem Ed, AZ St Univ 1961; Gifted Endorsement; *cr:* Teacher of Gifted in Lang Art Holiday Park Elem; 2nd/4th-6th Grade Teacher Starlight Park Elem; *ai:* Future Problem Solving Prgm Spon; Tutorting Teacher; Supts Cabinet Sch Rep; Co-Dir & Dir Musical Plays; Dist In-Service Presenter; Odyssey of the Mind St Competition Drama Adjunctor; AZ Rdng Cncl, AZ Asson for Gifted & Talented, Delta Kappa Gamma, Phoenix West Rdng Cncl; PTA Secy 1983-; AZ PTA Educator of Yr 1987; Phoenix Arts Commission Grant 1988-89; Whos Who in Amer Coll Women; Theatre Works Bd Mem; AZ St Univ Jr medallion of Merit Awd Presentor; *office:* Holiday Park Elem Sch 4417 N 66th Ave Phoenix AZ 85033

GRANDONE, ROBERTA MAKI, Foreign Lang Dept Chairperson; *b:* Worcester, MA; *m:* Roy F.; *c:* Joseph O.; *ed:* (BA) Latin/Fr, 1958, (MAED) Eng/Ed, 1962 Clark Univ; Advanced Courses Tufts Univ, Worcester St Coll, Simmons Coll; NDEA Inst; *cr:* Latin Teacher Barre HS 1958-60, Wauchusett Regional HS 1960-62; Substitute Teacher 1962-67; Latin Teacher Quabbin Regional Jr/Sr HS 1967-; Foreign Lang Dept Head Quabbin Regional 1973-; *ai:* Latin Club Adv; Chairperson Self Evaluation NEASC Lib Services; Quabbin Regional Teachers Assn; MA Teachers Assn; NEA 1967-; MA Foreign Lang Assn 1979-; Classical Assn of New England 1967-; Pompeianna 1980-; Amer Classical League 1967-; Delta Kappa Gamma (Recording Secy 1988, Mem 1979-); Barrre Womans Club 1967-; Quabbin Cmmty Band Auxiliary 1980-; Grad With Honors in Classics & Cum Laude Clark Univ; NEASC Evaluation Teams; *office:* Quabbin Regional Jr/Sr HS South St Barre MA 01005

GRANDY, BARBARA CURTIS, Retired; *b:* Payson, UT; *m:* Grant P.; *c:* Curtis, Paul, David, Sheila Sharpe, Sherman, Norell; *cr:* 1st Grade Teacher Los Angeles Sch Dist 1945-46; 5th & 6th Grade Teacher Bear Lake 33 1961-88; *ai:* Pocatello Lit Tutors 1989-; Laubach Way to Read; *home:* 442 N 5th St Montpelier ID 83254

GRANER, ANNE HOPEWELL, Teacher; *b:* New York City, NY; *m:* Richard Louis; *c:* Jessica; *ed:* (AA) Oxford Coll of Emory Univ 1977; (BA) Elem Ed, 1979, (MAT) Elem Ed/Supervision, 1982 Emory Univ; *cr:* 6th Grade Rdng Teacher Redan Elem 1979-80; 6th Grade Soc Stud Teacher Mainstreet Elem 1980-86; *home:* 854 Artwood Rd NE Atlanta GA 30307

GRANESE, JUDITH ANN, English Teacher; *b:* Corona, NY; *ed:* (BA) Eng, 1969, (MA) Eng Lit, 1973 St Johns Univ; Primarily Ed Work 1990; *cr:* Eng Instr Sewanhaka Evening HS 1969-77; Substitute Instr Sewanhaka HS Dist #2 1969-77; Eng Instr Valley HS 1977-; *ai:* Key Club Adv; Helping you Helping me Coord; Intnl Baccalaureate Teacher Coord; Curr Commission, Minority Affairs Comm; NV St Cncl of Teachers of Eng Treas 1986-; South NV Teachers of Eng Pres 1987, Outstanding Teacher 1988; NCTE Comparative Lit Comm 1990; Kiwanis 1987-; Key Club Adv Hall of Fame 1987, NV Teacher Yr Nominee 1986-87; LeadersHip Magazine Adv Spotlight 1989; LeadersHip Magazine Article 1989; Amer Poetry Anthology 1987-88; *home:* 3642 Boulder Hwy #312 Las Vegas NV 89121

GRANGER, DEBORAH ANN (WILE), Fifth Grade Teacher; *b:* Lebanon, PA; *m:* Dale; *ed:* (BS) Elem Ed/Spec Ed, 1977, (MED) Elem Ed/Rdng, 1980 Millersville St Coll; Various Wkshps; *cr:* 4th Grade Teacher Southeast Elem 1977-81; 3rd Grade Teacher Southwest Elem 1981-86; 5th Grade Teacher Harding Elem 1986-; *ai:* Mentor & Coach for New Teachers; Teacher Asst Team Mem; Curr Dev Rdng Dist Comm; NEA, PA St Ed Assn, Lebanon Ed Assn 1977; Intnl Rdng Assn 1989-; PTO 1988-; Voted into Lebanon Cty Educl Honor Society for Teachers; *office:* Harding Elem Sch 1000 S 8th St Lebanon PA 17042

GRANGER, JOANNE G., Biology/Chemistry Teacher; *b:* Jersey City, NJ; *m:* Carl V.; *c:* Oliver Champion, Susan Champion, Janis Champion-Weymouth; *ed:* (BA) Zoology, Wellesley Coll 1952; (MS) Bio, Univ of MI 1953; Canisius Coll Buffalo NY 1967-69; St Univ of NY Buffalo 1970; Canisuis Coll Big PIF 1985; *cr:* Research Technician Carnegie Inst Genetics 1953-54; Histology Technician Armed Forces Inst Pathology 1954-55; Bio Instr D Youville Coll 1962-63; Bio/Chem Teacher St Marys Seminary 1963-69, Mt St Mary Acad 1969-; *ai:* Jr Class Adv; NHS Moderator; Ski Club & Sci Fair Co-Moderator; Sci Dept Chairperson; Natl Sci Assn; Buffalo Chapter Links Past Pres; Buffalo Wellesley Club Past Pres; *office:* Mount Saint Mary Acad 3756 Delaware Ave Kenmore NY 14217

GRANIERI, LILIANA L., Spanish Teacher; *b:* Buenos Aires, Argentina; *m:* Hugo J.; *c:* Patricia Mc Latcher; *ed:* (BA) Span/Fr/Latin, Univ of Buenos Aires 1958; (MS) Span/Linguistics, Georgetown Univ 1976; Cntrl St Univ; Curr Dev in Audio-Visual Lang Teaching 1970; Lang/Linguistic Congress, Georgetown Univ 1975; *cr:* Span/Fr Instr Berlitz Sch of Lang 1963-65; Span Lang/Civil Fr Teacher Intnl Sch 1963-76; Span Instr Georgetown Univ 1975-77; Fr/Span Teacher Bishop Mc Guinness HS 1977-79; Latin/Lang Art Teacher John Marshall HS 1979-81; Span Teacher Langham Creek HS 1981-; *ai:* Span Honor Society, Sending Stu to Academic Prgms at Univ of Madrid & Mexico Spon; HS Rep; Personnel Service Comm; AATSP, TFLA, Inst of Hispanic Culture; Sigma Delta Pi Mem 1975; *office:* Langham Creek HS 17610 F M 529 Houston TX 77095

GRANT, DIANE C., Basic Skills Teacher; *b:* Philadelphia, PA; *m:* Robert N.; *c:* Kelli, Zachary; *ed:* (BA) Elem Ed, Georgian Court 1977; Rdng Specialist Cert; *cr:* 1st Grade Teacher 1977-89, Basic Skills Teacher 1989- Lanoka Harbor; *ai:* Schlsp Comm; Rdng Cncl; PTA; *office:* Lanoka Harbor Elem Sch Manchester Ave Box 186 Lanoka Harbor NJ 08734

GRANT, DOROTHY ELCAN, Social Studies Dept Chair; *b:* Covington, TN; *m:* James Oliver; *c:* Ricardo, Tara; *ed:* (BA) Sociology, TN St Univ 1967; (MA) Classroom Teaching, MI St Univ 1982; *cr:* Soc Stud Teacher Washington Jr HS 1968-71, Lincoln Jr HS 1971-72; Federal Project Writer 1972-74, Soc Stud Teacher 1974- Pontiac Cntrl HS; *ai:* Dist Wide Soc Stud Comm; Trinity Baptist Church, Alpha Kappa Alpha 1970-; *office:* Pontiac Cntrl HS 300 W Huron St Pontiac MI 48053

GRANT, KEVIN, Computer Coord/Math Teacher; *b:* Battle Creek, MI; *ed:* (BS) Astrophysics, MI St Univ 1977; (MA) Math, Ball St Univ 1984; *cr:* Math/Physics Teacher Rensselaer Cntrl HS 1977-79; Cmptr Coord/Math Teacher Whitko HS 1979-; *ai:* Academic Team Head Coach; Phi Delta Kappa, NCTM, Intnl Cncl Cmptr Educators; Libertarian Party of IN Chm 1980-82; Most Influential Teacher In Academic All-Stars 1989; *office:* Whitko HS 1 Big Blue Ave South Whitley IN 46787

GRANT, LINDA WEIN, Eng/Psych/Sociology Teacher; *b:* Monahans, TX; *m:* George William; *ed:* (BS) Scndry Ed, TX Tech Univ 1981; Post Grad Work TX Tech Univ, Univ of TX Permian Basin; *cr:* 8th Grade Eng Teacher Perryton Jr HS 1981-82; 11th Grade Eng/Journalism Teacher Perryton HS 1981-84; 10th Grade Eng/Psych/Sociology Teacher 1984-, 9th Grade Honors Eng Teacher 1989- Monahans HS; *ai:* Future Teachers of America, Frosh Class Spon; Univ Interscholastic League Ready Writing Coach; NHS Selection, Gifted & Talented Dist Comms; TX St Teachers Assn (Pres 1987-88, VP 1989-); NEA, NCTE 1981-; TX Joint Cncl for Teachers of Eng 1984-; Delta Kappa Gamma 1988-; Sandhills Archery Club Reporter 1988-89; This West TX Cntry Company Local Theater 1986; First Baptist Church Choir Alto Soloist 1984-; Elected HS Faculty Spokesperson for Sch Bd Meeting; Fellowship Grant to Inst of Gifted TX Tech Univ Cnslr 1989; Outstanding Young Women of America 1987, 1989; *home:* 905 S Gary Monahans TX 79756

GRANT, MARSHA W., Computer Programming Teacher; *b:* New York, NY; *ed:* (BS) Chem ACS, Univ of SC 1961; (MST) Chem/Ed, Memphis St Univ 1965; (AS) Data Processing, St Tech Inst Memphis 1983; *cr:* Chem/Physics/Cmptr Programming Teacher Frayser HS, Humes Jr HS, S Side HS, Northside HS 1964-; *ai:* Cmptr Club; After Sch Homework Center; Math Dept Comm; Cmptr Teachers of Memphis City Sch Past Pres; Memphis Ed Assn, TN Ed Assn, NEA, Memphis Urban Math Collaberitive; Poetry Society of TN 1988 1st Place Poems Published in TN Voices; Mothers March Volunteer; Phi Theta Kappa Project Achieve Mini Grant Recipient.

GRANT, REBECCA FRANKUM, 2nd Grade Teacher; *b:* Hodgenville, KY; *m:* Donald Ruell; *c:* Matthew A., Andrew R.; *ed:* (BS) Elem Ed, Campbellsville Coll 1976; (MA) Elem Ed, W KY Univ 1986; Distar, Forward in the Fifth, KY Teacher Internship Prgm; *cr:* 1st Grade Teacher 1978-80, 3rd Grade Teacher 1980-81, 5th Grade Teacher 1981-82 Taylor Cty Elem; 1st Grade Teacher 1982-89, 2nd Grade 1989- Mannsville Elem; *ai:* Mentor Teacher 1989-; Prof Dev Comm 1982-; Taylor Cty Ed Assn (Secy 1986-87, Mem) 1978-; KY Ed Assn, NEA 1978-; KY Math Teachers 1988-; Sunday Sch Teacher; Mothers March of Dimes; Educl Innovation Incentive Fund; PTSO Teacher of Month 1989; Outstanding KY Teacher Awd 1984.

GRANT, ROBERT S., 5th Grade Teacher; *b:* Winnebago, MN; *m:* Denise Christine Cornish; *c:* Travis, Anthony, Robert, Adam; *ed:* (BA) Elem Ed, Mankato St Univ 1975; Working Towards Masters Elem Admin, Mankato St Univ; *cr:* Title I Teacher Delavan Elem Sch 1975-76, 1977-78; 5th Grade Teacher Granada-Huntley East Chaina 1978-; *ai:* St Marys Church Parish Cncl VP 1987-89; CYO Leader 1982-86; *home:* 338 E Cleveland Ave Winnebago MN 56098

GRANTHAM, REBECCA SHUMAKER, Mathematics Instructor; *b:* Kosciusko, MS; *m:* William Allen; *c:* William B.; *ed:* (BS) Math, 1967, (MED) Guidance, 1970 MS St Univ; Advanced Stud Admin, Math, Voc Guidance, Cmptr Trng; *ai:* Financial Adv; MS Cncl Teachers of Math, NCTM, MS Prof Educators; Delta Kappa Gamma 1986-; Bus & Prof Womens Club (Pres, Treas) 1971-85, Young Career Woman 1971; Daughters of Amer Revolution, Order of Eastern Star, Zeta Tau Alpha Alumnae Adv Univ of MS; Participant MS St Dept of Ed Exec Management Inst; Head Math Dept Batesville Jr HS; Developer Grant; MS Writing & Thinking Wkshp Grant; NCTM & MAA Wkshp Presentor; *office:* S Panola Hs Po Box 600 Batesville MS 38606

GRANTHAM, SHARON, Language Arts Dept Chair; *b:* Little Rock, AR; *m:* Roger; *c:* Brandi George *ed:* (BA) Eng, Tarleton St Univ 1970; TWU, TWC; *cr:* Eng/Span Teacher Seymour HS 1970-71; 8th Grade Lang Art Teacher Granbury Mid Sch 1975-; *ai:* Natl Jr Honor Society Spon; UIL Modern Oratory & Spelling Coach; TSTA Pres Elect 1989-; Delta Kappa Gamma VP 1985-; Gifted & Talented of TX 1986-; *home:* 415 Mountain View Granbury TX 76048

GRAPETHIN, JENNIFER ANNE, Spanish Teacher; *b:* Evergreen Park, IL; *m:* Kurt Dennis; *ed:* (BA) Span Lang/Lit/ Eng, N IL Univ 1984; (MED) Educl Stud, Univ of IL 1987; Working Towards Second Masters Sch Counseling, Roosevelt Univ; *cr:* Span Teacher Schaumburg HS 1984-; *ai:* Schaumburg HS Stu Cncl Head Spon, Ski Club Spon, HS Prins Advisory Bd Mem; *office:* Schaumburg HS 1100 W Schaumburg Rd Schaumburg IL 60194

GRASLEY, KEVIN LOGAN, English Teacher; *b:* Adrian, MI; *m:* Diane M. Holubik; *c:* Corrie, Erick, Jacob, Andrew; *ed:* (BA) Eng/Soc Stud, Adrian Coll 1977; Elem Industrial Arts, Eastern MI 1982; MI Assn of Mid Sch Educators Conferences; Southeast MI Writing Project Inservices; Ropes Trng; Prof Dev Wkshps; Project Wild Trng; MI Outdoor Ed Assn Confrnes; *cr:* Teacher Blissfield Cmmty Schls 1977-; Blissfield Summer Migrant Prgm 1985-86; *ai:* Blissfield Mid Sch Yrbk Adv; North Central Steering Comm Coord Spelling and Geography Bee; 8th Grade Camping Comm; MI Educ Assn 1977-; NEA 1977-; Natl Eagle Scout Assn 1986-; Boy Scouts of America Cubmaster 1986-89 Cubmaster Awd 1989; Girl Scout Cadette Ldr 1988-89; Summer Bsbl Coach 1987-; Fr Canadian Heritage Society Journal Contributor; MI Assn of Mid Sch Educators Conference Presenter & Cert; Lenawee Cty Prof Dev Presenter; Living His Presenter; *office:* Blissfield Mid Sch 1305 Beamer Rd Blissfield MI 49228

GRASLIE, PETER JAMES, English/Social Studies Teacher; *b:* La Crosse, WI; *ed:* (BS) Eng/Scndry Ed, Univ of WI La Crosse 1976; Wartburg Theological Seminary, LA St Univ Alexandria; *cr:* Eng Teacher CEB HS 1980-82; Jr/Sr HS Eng/Rdng Teacher Forest Hill Acad 1982-83; Eng Teacher Oak Hill HS 1983-86; Eng/Soc Stud Teacher Plainview HS 1986-; *ai:* Annual Staff Adv; Eng Dept Chm; Faculty Study Steering Comm; Rapids Fed of Teachers Building Rep 1988-; NCTE 1989-; Gideons Intnl Memorial Bible Chm 1989-; Seibert Fnd Grant to Study Pastoral Ministery Dubuque 1978-79; *office:* Plainview HS PO Box 1057 Glenmora LA 71433

GRASMICK, PATTY A., 9th&12th Eng/Spanish I Teacher; *b:* Greeley, CO; *m:* Ronald S.; *c:* Steven, Stephanie Buck, Melonie Self, Melissa, Todd Barber; *ed:* (BA LA) Eng & Geography, Univ of Northern CO 1971; (MA) Scndry Ed, Adams St Coll 1982; Writing About Literature; *cr:* 7-9 & 12 Grades Eng/Geography Teacher 1972-73, 7-12 Grades Eng Teacher 1973-85 Granada HS; 8-12 Grades Eng Teacher 1985-89, 9-12 Grades Eng/Span Teacher 1989- Mc Clave HS; *ai:* Sr Class Quarterly Newspaper Adv; Jr Class Spon; Sr/Jr Class Play Dir; Phi Delta Kappa 1987-; CO Ed Assn 1979- CEA Robert H John Jr Mem Schlsp 1982; UNC Eleanor S and Alma J Dickerson Schlsp 1970-71; *home:* 110 E Amache Rd Granada CO 81041

GRASSANO, CHARLES A., Language Arts Teacher; *b:* Chester, PA; *m:* Mary Ann Kryka; *c:* Kendra, Jesse; *ed:* (BA) Eng, Widener Univ 1968; (MED) Eng/Ed, Westchester Univ 1978; First Aid; Coaching; Psych; *cr:* Eng Teacher Northley Jr HS 1968-72; Lang Art Teacher Sun Valley HS 1972-; *ai:* Coach Wrestling 1969-, Asst Ftbl 1968-72, Asst Soccer 1978-, Asst Bsbl 1968-69; Stu Senate Adv 1983-; Crisis Intervention Team 1988-; NCTE 1985-, Nom Teacher of Yr 1986; PCTE 1982-, Nom Thanks to Teacher 1990; Various Coaches Organization (Pres, Secy) 1972-, Penn-Delio PD Coach of Yr 1988; Widener Univ (Fraternity Bd, Pres, Secy) 1973-; *office:* Sun Valley HS Pancoast Ave Aston PA 19014

GRASSI, GLORIA G., 4th&5th Gr Math/Soc St Teacher; *b:* New York City, NY; *ed:* (BA) Fr/Ed, Marymount 1957; Addl Studies Inservice Wkshps Brooklyn Diocese; *cr:* 4th/5th Grade Teacher, St Vincent Ferrer 1957-67; St Catherine of Genoa 1967-; *ai:* Chairperson Intermediate Dept; Math Coord; Soc Stud Coord; NCEA 1975-; Young Republicans (Bd of Governors 1958-70 Co-Gov of NY 1966-68/1956-1970).

GRASSIA, ANTHONY JOSEPH, Mathematics Teacher; *b:* New York, NY; *m:* Kathleen Navas; *c:* Craig, Cara; *ed:* (BS) Math/Ed, 1976, (BA) Math, 1973 Lehman Coll; *cr:* Math Teacher Lehman HS 1973-78, O A Todd Jr HS 1978-; *ai:* Math League Adv; Dist Math Comm; Dutchers Cty Math Teachers Assn 1989-; BSA Den Leader 1984-87; Curr Writing Dist Grant Awds; *home:* 13 Queen Anne Ln Wappingers Flls NY 12590

GRASSMANN, DONALD ROGER, Fifth/Sixth Grade Teacher; *b:* Napa, CA; *m:* Carolyn Ann Thibault; *c:* Preston, Kari; *ed:* (AA) Soc Sci, Napa Valley Coll 1967; (BA) Poly Sci/His/ Hum, 1970, (MA) Ed Rdng Specialization, 1976 Sonoma St Univ; *cr:* Elem Teacher Cotati Schls 1970-71, John L Shearer Sch 1971-; *ai:* Sci Coord; Bsbl Coach & Player; Shearer Sch Womens His Chm; Track & Field Sports Coord; Ben Franklin Stamp Cl ub Adv; Racquetball & Weight Trng; CA Teachers Assn Rep 1973, 1986; Napa Valley Rdng Assn, CA Rdng Assn, CA Teachers of Sci; CA Free & Accepted Masons 1976-; CA PTA 1985-; Napa Educl Fnd Grant Sci; SEEDS Project NASA 1990; *office:* John L Shearer Sch 1590 Elm St Napa CA 94558

GRASSO, JEAN GROCHOWSKI, Second Grade Teacher; *b:* Franklinville, NJ; *m:* Vito A.; *c:* Jeanne M.; *ed:* (BA) Elem Ed, Glassboro St Coll 1975; *cr:* Office Mgr Cmmty Oil and Appliances 1951-62; *ai:* Prepare Children for Sacraments of First Communion & Penance; *home:* Judy Ave Franklinville NJ 08322

GRATO, MARIA, Mathematics Teacher; *b:* Jersey City, NJ; *c:* Joseph; *ed:* (BA) Elem Ed, 1983, (MA) Ed, St Peters Coll 1987; Certificate Elem Ed, Math, Data Processing, Supvr & Admin NJ St; *cr:* Self-Contained 2nd Grade Teacher St Ann Sch 1978-81; Substitute Teacher Hoboken Public Schls 1981-82; Self-Contained 3rd Grade Teacher St Ann Sch 1982-83; Substitute Teacher Hoboken Public Schls 1983-84; 3rd-8th Grade Cmptr Teacher St Ann Sch & St Francis Sch & St Joseph Sch & Our Lady of Grace Sch 1984; 7th/8th Grade Pre-Algebra/Lang Art Teacher High Mountain Sch 1984-85; 8th Grade Level Algebra Teacher 1985-88, 8th Grade Level Math Teacher 1988- Memorial Sch; *ai:* NJEA, NEA 1984-; NCTM 1990; *office:* Memorial Sch 294 Totowa Rd Totowa NJ 07512

GRATZICK, GAIL LENTZ, Mathematics Department Chair; *b:* Baltimore, MD; *m:* Edward W.; *c:* Evan B., Ryan K.; *ed:* (BA) Math, W MD Coll 1968; Course Work Cleveland St Univ & Mary Washington Coll; *cr:* Math Teacher John Hay HS 1968-71, 1973-75, Spotsylvania Jr & Sr HS 1977-88; Dept Chm Spotsylvania HS 1988-; *ai:* Faculty Advisory Comm; Math League Adv; Rappahannock Region Assn Math Teachers (Pres, VP, Secy) 1980-; VA Cncl Teacher of Math, NCTM, NEA 1977-; Delta Kappa Gamma 1985-; Rappahannock Swim League Incorporated (Pres, Treas) 1985-88; VA Leadership Conference; Math Colloquium VA Commonwealth Univ; *office:* Spotsylvania HS 8801 Courthouse Rd Spotsylvania VA 22553

GRAUPE, MARK D., Physical Ed/Math Teacher; *b:* Minot, ND; *ed:* (BS) Phys Ed, Univ of ND 1987; Math & Athletic Coaching; *cr:* Phys Ed/Math Teacher Unity HS 1987-; *ai:* Head Var Boys & Girls Bsktbl Coach; Athletic Dir; ND Ed Assn 1987-; ND HS Coaches Assn 1988, Girls Dist Bsktbl Coach of Yr 1989; *office:* Unity Public Sch Box 37 Petersburg ND 58272

GRAUPMANN, KENNETH H., 6th-8th Grade Teacher; *b:* Glencoe, MN; *m:* Mary Kayser; *c:* Andrew, Jessica; *ed:* (BS) Elem Ed, Concordia 1964; (MS) Elem Ed, Bemidji St Univ 1976; Numerous Univs; *cr:* Teacher First Immanuel Luth Sch 1964-79, Longvalley Elem 1982-; *ai:* Ftbl Coach; Outdoor Ed Coord; Math Counts Coach; NCTE 1968-74; Milwaukee Ofcl Assn Pres 1965-82; SD Orinthologist Union Pres 1982-; Inland Bird Banding Assn 1980-; Church (Treas, Elder, VP); Supvr Jackson Cty Soil Conservation Dist; Articles Published; *home:* Box 111 Kadoka SD 57543

GRAUPNER, SHERYLL ANN, Fifth Grade Teacher; *b:* Independence, MO; *ed:* (BS) Ed, Cntrl MO St Univ 1969; (MA) Ed, Univ of MO Kansas City 1972; *cr:* 5th Grade Teacher Blackburn 1969, Proctor 1969-; *ai:* Proctor N Cntrl Chairperson 1982, Co-Chairperson 1989; NEA, Intnl Rdng Assn; Natl Congress Parents & Teachers; MO St Educl Incentive Grant Math Connection 1987.

GRAUTSKI, RONALD PAUL, Anatomy/Physiology Teacher; *b:* Leominster, MA; *m:* Veronica A. Camy; *c:* Christopher, Caitlin; *ed:* (BS) Ed/Bio, 1966, (MS) Bio, 1969 Fitchburg St Coll; Holy Cross, Williams Coll, Lesley Coll; *cr:* Sci Teacher Fitchburg HS 1966-; *ai:* MA Assn Sci Supvrs, NABT; *office:* Fitchburg HS 98 Academy St Fitchburg MA 01420

GRAVES, BELINDA JORDAN, High School/Jr High Librarian; *b:* Corpus Christi, TX; *m:* Wayne Charles Jr.; *c:* Kelly C.; *ed:* (BA) Government/Poly Sci, Lamar Univ 1973; *cr:* Librarian/Yrbk Journalism Teacher Beaumont Chrstn Jr HS & HS; *ai:* Jr Class Spon; Yrbk Adv; TX HS Press Assn 1990; Beaumont Jr Forum 1990; *office:* Beaumont Chrstn HS 8001 Old Voth Rd Beaumont TX 77708

GRAVES, GLENDA COLE, Fourth Grade Teacher; *b:* Milan, TN; *m:* James W.; *c:* Pamela Graves Daniel; *ed:* (BS) Elem Ed, 1963, (MS) Curr/Instruction, 1984 Univ of TN Martin; *cr:* 3rd Grade Teacher Park Avenue Sch 1958-62; 3rd Grade Teacher 1963-66, 5th Grade Teacher 1967-86, 4th Grade Teacher 1987-89 Martin Elem Sch; *ai:* Homeroom Spon; Just Say No Club; Faculty Rep; Alpha Delta Kappa Historian 1987-89; TN Ed Assn, NEA; Weakley Cty Ed Assn T-PACE Pres; Intnl Rdng Assn Univ of TN Martin Area Cncl Pres; *home:* 68 Bradford Hwy Trenton TN 38382

GRAVES, JOHN CYRUS, Social Studies Teacher; *b:* Ukiah, CA; *m:* Christena E. Keszler; *c:* Scott C., Brett M.; *ed:* (BA) Soc Stud, Pacific Union Coll 1967; Grad Stud; *cr:* Teacher Ukiah Jr Acad 1968-71, W Valley Sch 1971-72, Redwood Valley Sch 1972-79, Pomolita Jr HS 1979-; *ai:* 8th Grade Soc Stud Honors Prgm; CA Teachers Assn, Ukiah Teachers Assn, NEA; Ukiah Jr Acad (Sch Bd Mem 1976-79) 1983-86.

GRAVES, LA JOY LYNN (PARRETT), 6th Grade Teacher; *b:* Danville, KY; *m:* Nelson Dean; *c:* Devin, De Jon; *ed:* (BS) Elem Ed, 1978, (Rank II) Elem Ed, 1988 E KY Univ; *cr:* City Clerk Brodhead KY 1978-89; 2nd Grade Teacher 1978-80, 6th Grade Teacher 1980- Livingston Elem Sch; *ai:* 4-H Leader, Various Sch Comm; KY Ed Assn, NEA 1978-; Brodhead Fire Dept Ladies Auxiliary VP 1988-89; PTA 1986-; KY Assn For Gifted Ed, Rockcastle Cty Assn For Gifted Ed 1985-; *home:* RR 1 Box 98 West St Brodhead KY 40409

GRAVES, MARY ANN, 8th Grade English Teacher; *b:* Memphis, TN; *m:* John C.; *c:* Andy, Randy, John P.; *ed:* (BA) Eng, MS Coll 1972; *cr:* Eng/Span Teacher Franklin Chrstn Acad; HS Eng Teacher S Natchez Adams; 8th Grade Eng Teacher Franklin Jr HS; *ai:* Star Teacher; *home:* Rt 1 Box 162-A Roxie MS 39661

GRAVES, NELDA, 3rd Grade G/T Teacher; *b:* Silsbee, TX; *m:* George E.; *c:* Julie Worsham, Scot Graves; *ed:* (BS) Elem Ed, 1975, (MED) Elem Ed/Rdng, 1986 Lamar Univ; Gifted Talented Courses Univ of Houston, Lamar Univ; Supervision Lamar Univ; TX Teacher Apprasial System Lamar Univ; *cr:* Kndgtn Teacher 1975-76, 3rd Grade Teacher 196-88, 3rd Grade Gifted & Talented 1988 Silsbee Ind Sch Dist; *ai:* UIL Storytelling Coach; Gifted & Talented Campus Comm; Teacher Appraiser; TX Classroom Teachers Assn (VP 1986-87, Pres 1987-88); TCTA Reg V VP 1989; Literary Club (VP 1986 Pres 1987); Performing & Visual Arts Cncl Nominations Comm 1987; Bd of Dir Teachers Center-Lamar Univ; *office:* Read-Turrentine Sch 730 S 7th St Silsbee TX 77656

GRAVES, RITA MANZO, 8th Grade Teacher; *b:* Phila, PA; *m:* Roland B.; *c:* Christe, Jaime, Katie, Michael; *ed:* (BA) Sociology, St Marys Univ 1981; Advanced Trng in Religion, Working Towards Masters Pastorial Ministry, Incarnate Word Coll; *cr:* Teacher Our Lady of Calvary 1964-74, St Peters Sch 1981-82, St Lukes Cath Sch 1982-; *ai:* Sch Religion Coord; Alamo Area Eng Teacher 1987-; NCEA 1982-; Schlsp for 2 Yrs St Lukes to Pursue Masters; *office:* St Lukes Cath Sch 4601 Manitou San Antonio TX 78228

GRAVES, SYLVIA MILLS, Music Teacher; *b:* Indianapolis, IN; *m:* Dale Garten; *c:* Maria, Eric; *ed:* (BA) Elem Ed, William Penn Coll 1971; (MS) Elem Ed, Butler Univ 1977; Gifted & Talented Endorsement in Ed; *cr:* 2nd Grade Teacher 1971-73, 3rd Grade Teacher 1973-76, Music Teacher 1976- Neil A Armstrong Elem; *ai:* Local Sch Steering Comm, Gifted & Talented Identification Comm Chm; 5th & 6th Grade Choir Spon; Classroom Teachers (Pres 1981-82, Secy, Building Rep, Negotiations Team); IN Elem Music Educators Assn; Society of Friends Church Conference Exec Comm Chm 1986; PTO (Prgm Chm, Teacher Rep); *home:* 1260 Joppa Rd Mooresville IN 46158

GRAVES, TINA NICHOLS, Mathematics & Health Teacher; *b:* Portales, NM; *m:* Robert G.; *c:* Joe Nichols; *ed:* Assoc Sci, South Plains Coll 1982; (BA) Sci Ed, Lubbock Chrstn Coll 1984; *cr:* Math Teacher Smyer HS 1984-; *ai:* Stu Cncl; Jr/Sr Class Spon; Jr HS Chrldrs; UIL Calculator; TX St Teacher Assn 1988-89; NASSP 1988-; Drug Free Schls Coord 1987-; Teacher of Yr Smyer HS 1984-85; *office:* Smyer HS Box 206 Smyer TX 79367

GRAVES, VIOLA MARIE, English Teacher; *b:* Alexandria, VA; *ed:* (BA) Eng, Mary Washington Coll 1969; (MA) Hum, Univ of Richmond 1974; Cmptr Sci; *cr:* Eng Teacher King George HS 1969-; Cmptr Sci Teacher Germanna Comm Coll 1981-83; Eng Dept Chairperson King George HS 1983-; *ai:* NCTE 1983-; King George Ed Assn (Pres 1987-88, VP 1985-87); *office:* King George HS 9 W Dahlgren Rd King George VA 22485

GRAVES, WILLIAM LAMAR, Social Studies Dept Chair; *b:* Bogalusa, LA; *m:* Slana Mc Murry; *c:* Rachel, Seth; *ed:* (BS) European His, Livingston Univ 1975; (MA) Contemporary US His, AR St Univ 1976; (PHD) Early Modern European His, TX Chrstn Univ 1979; Post Grad Work Ed, Howard Payne Univ 1981; *cr:* Teacher Rochelle Ind Sch Dist 1979-81; US His Teacher Brady Jr HS 1981-85; His/Govt Instr Cntrl TX Coll 1983-; Soc Stud Teacher Brady HS 1985-; *ai:* Stu Cncl & UIL Ready Writing Spon; Amer Legion Oratory Judge; Phi Alpha Theta Pres 1975-79; Phi Kappa Phi 1976-; Kiwanis (Treas, Secy, Pres) 1982-88; Mc Colluch Cty Youth Soccer Coach 1984-88; Daughters of Amer Revolution Ephram Andrews Chapter His Teacher 1985, 1987; *office:* Brady HS 1000 Wall St Brady TX 76825

GRAVITT, DOROTHY BOYD, Retired Second Grade Teacher; *b:* Whitwell, TN; *m:* Herbert L.; *c:* William E., Nancy G. Tankersley, Herbert L. Jr.; *ed:* (BS) Elem Ed, Mid TN St Univ 1973; *cr:* Teacher Hicks Chapel Elem Sch 1946-53; Prin Stanley Elem Sch 1957-59; Teacher Sulphur Springs Elem Sch 1959-60, Whitwell Elem Sch 1960-87; *ai:* Marion Cty Ed Assn, TN Ed Assn, NEA; Capitol Club TN Republican Party; Marion Cty Republicans Womens Club; Amer Assn of Retired Persons; *home:* S Walnut St Whitwell TN 37397

GRAY, ANN BYLER, Third Grade Teacher; *b:* Lake Arthur, LA; *m:* Donald Joseph; *c:* Joey, Jacky; *cr:* 2nd Grade Teacher Cameron Elem 1960-64; 1st Grade Teacher 1965-80, 3rd Grade Teacher 1981- Hackberry HS; *ai:* NEA, LEA 1960-; Nominee for Natl Teacher of Yr; *home:* 570 Everett Vincent Dr Hackberry LA 70645

GRAY, ANNETTE, 7th Grade English Teacher; *b:* Dermott, AR; *m:* Troy; *c:* Angie; *ed:* (BSE) Bus/Eng, AR A&M 1969; *cr:* Teacher Barton HS 1969-70, Dermott Adult Ed 1970-72, Dermott Jr HS 1972-; *ai:* Dermott Jr Beta Club Spon; *office:* Dermott Jr HS Hwy 35 E Dermott AR 71638

GRAY, BECKY AARVIG, HS Mathematics Teacher; *b:* Bismarck, ND; *m:* Terry Lee; *ed:* (BA) Math, Univ of KY 1970; (MED) Math/Ed, Univ of Louisville 1978; *cr:* Teacher Thomas Jefferson HS 1971-82, Teen-Age Parent Prgm 1982-83, Male Traditional HS 1983-; *ai:* Beta Club spon; KEA, NEA 1971-; *office:* Male Traditional HS 911 S Brook St Louisville KY 40202

GRAY, BONITA LYNNE, Fifth Grade Teacher; *b:* Missoula, MT; *ed:* (BA) Elem Ed, 1972, (MS) Elem Ed, Univ of KY; *cr:* 4th Grade Teacher Taylor Mill Elem 1972, 1976-82; Ec Consultant KY Cncl on Ec Ed 1986-88; 5th Grade Teacher T aylor Mill Elem 1973-1975, 1983-; *ai:* Sunday Sch Teacher; Church Pianist; Phi Delta Kappa (Secy/Mem 1979); KY Ed Assn 1972-; KY Ec Educators (Secy 1986-87, Mem 1986-); RJR Nabisco Fellow for Joint Cncl on Ec Ed 1988; St Ec Awd Prgm; *office:* Taylor Mill Elem Sch 5907 Taylor Mill Rd Covington KY 41015

GRAY, CHARLES JOSEPH, Director of Bands; *b:* Heidleberg, West Germany; *ed:* (BA) Music Ed, CA St Univ Fullerton 1984; *cr:* Dir of Bands Rubidoux HS 1985-; *ai:* Jurupa Unified Sch Dist 1989, Teacher of Yr; Jurupa PTA 1989, Teacher of Yr; *office:* Rubidoux HS 4250 Opal St Riverside CA 92509

GRAY, CHRISTOPHER A., Activities Director/Adm Asst; *b:* Albuquerque, NM; *m:* Diane Conilogue; *c:* William, Roxanne, Wendy; *ed:* (BA) General Soc Stud/Scndry Ed, Univ of WY 1981; *cr:* Soc Stud Teacher Glenrock Mid Sch 1981-86; Soc Stud Teacher 1986-89, Act Dir/Admin Asst 1989- Glenrock HS; *ai:* WY Coaches Assn 1983-; WY Ad Assn 1989-; *office:* Glenrock HS Box 1300 Glenrock WY 82637

GRAY, CLAUDETTE GANN, Kindergarten Teacher; *b:* Waco, TX; *m:* Gilbert Lynn; *c:* Jerry, Thomas, Penny, Patricia; *ed:* (BS) Elem Ed, E TX St Univ 1971; Grad Courses, E TX St Univ & TX Womans Univ; *cr:* 1st-2nd Grade Teacher Montague Sch 1971-86; Kndgtn Teacher Bowie Primary Sch 1986-; *ai:* Goals Setting, Gifted & Talented Selection Comm; TX St Teachers Assn Treas 1971-; TX Classroom Teachers Assn 1986-; Order Eastern Star 1981-.

GRAY, FLORA E. PHILLIPS, Retired Teacher; *b:* Summerville, SC; *m:* Robert F.; *c:* Robert F. II, Catherine Marie Fosaaen; *ed:* (BM) Music Ed, Converse Coll 1940; USC; *cr:* HS Choral Teacher Irwin HS/Murphy HS/Travelers Rest HS 1940-45, Fayetteville HS 1948-50, Rosewood Elem 1952-58, Crayton Jr HS 1958-61, Lower Richland HS 1962-72, W a Perry Mid Sch 1973-76, Colonial Chrstn Acad 1978-84; *ai:* CMTA 1989-; *home:* 3405 Mineral Springs Rd Lexington SC 29072

GRAY, GWENDOLYN JILL, Sixth Grade Teacher; *b:* Pine Bluff, AR; *m:* Stephen Roger; *c:* Stephen A., Katie J.; *ed:* (BS) Ed, Univ of AR Fayetteville 1982; *cr:* Elem Teacher Greenville Elem 1983-87, Sam Taylor Elem 1987-; *ai:* 1st Baptist Church Sunday Sch Teacher; Vacation Bible Sch Teacher; Jr League of Pine Bluff 1987-; Hospice Advisory Bd JRMC 1989-; Neighbor to Neighbor; Jr League Hospice Advisory Bd 1987-; Laubach Trng; Prgm for Effective Teaching; Prgm for Assertive Discipline; *home:* 2835 W 40th Pine Bluff AR 71603

GRAY, HOMER RUSSELL, JR., Teacher/Coach; *b:* Harned, KY; *c:* Russell, Jennifer; *ed:* (BS) Health/Phys Ed, Campbellsville Coll 1970; (MA) Ed, (Rank I) Sch Admin, 1980 W KY Union Bowling Green; *cr:* E-5 US Army 1970-72; Teacher/Coach Hardinsburg Elem Sch 1970-; *ai:* Ftbl & Bsktbl Coach Supervise Intramural Track & Sftbl; Coordinate A Saturday Bsktbl League for Boys & Girls 4th-6th Grade; KEA, NEA, KAHPER, KHSAA; Athletic Booster Club (Adv, Treas); Vietnam Veteran Bronze Star; Nom for KY Phys Ed of Yr; Beack Cty Hall of Fame; Honor Gray Day Hardinsburg Baptist Church; *office:* Hardinsburg Elem Sch Box 19-A Ole Hwy 60 Hardinsburg KY 40143

GRAY, IRA JEAN WAFER, 8th Grade English Teacher; *b:* Jacksonville, TX; *m:* James Marvin; *c:* Mitch, Gaby; *ed:* (BA) Eng, Sam Houston Univ 1952; *cr:* 8th Grade Eng Teacher Jackson Mid 1952-53; 3rd Grade Teacher El Paso TX 1957-58, De Zavala Elem 1952-60; 8th Grade Eng Teacher North Shore Mid 1960-66 & 1972-; *home:* 14022 Roundstone Houston TX 77015

GRAY, KAREN RHEA, Third Grade Teacher; *b:* Greenville, TN; *ed:* (AA) Hiwassee Jr Coll 1973; (BS) Elem Ed, 1975, (MA) Rdng, 1981 E TN St Univ; *cr:* 3rd-6th Grade Teacher Baileyton Elem 1975-80; 3rd Grade Teacher Chuckey Elem 1980-; *ai:* Greene Cty Ed Assn, TN Ed Assn, NEA; Delta Kappa Gamma; *office:* Chuckey Elem Sch Rt 1 Box 445 Chuckey TN 37641

GRAY, KEVIN LAWRENCE, Publications Advisor; *b:* Oneonta, NY; *m:* Diane Elizabeth; *c:* Erika, Kyle; *ed:* (BS) Eng, Pittsburgh St Univ, 1976; *cr:* Eng/Journalism Teacher Paola HS 1977-; *ai:* Newspaper Yrbk Spon; KSPA 1977-; JEA 1989-; KNEA 1990-; Cub Scouts (Den Leader 1988-, Cubmaster 1990-), Den Leader Training 1990; First United Presbyn Church 1988-; *office:* Paola HS 405 N Hospital Dr Paola KS 66071

GRAY, MICHAEL BERNARD, Mathematics Teacher; *b:* Mc Allen, TX; *m:* Diana Nordhausen; *c:* Christopher, David; *ed:* (BS) Eng, SW TX St Univ 1968; (MED) Math, Univ of TX 1975; *cr:* Math Teacher/Dept Head W B Ray HS 1968-78; Math Teacher Victoria HS 1978-; *ai:* Math Club; Number Sense UIL; Mu Alpha Theta; *office:* Victoria HS 1110 Sam Houston Victoria TX 77901

GRAY, OLGA R., Retired Third Grade Teacher; *b:* Johnstown, PA; *ed:* (BS) Ed, Univ of GA 1954; (MA) Ed, Univ of TX 1957; *cr:* 1st Grade Teacher Sherman 1955-59; 2nd/3rd Grade Teacher Phillips 1961-65; 3rd Third Grade Fallis 1965-68, Park Hill Elem 1969-; *ai:* DCTA, CEA, NEA; *home:* 6960 E Girard Denver CO 80224

GRAY, PATRICIA ANN DAMPIER, Mathematics Teacher; *b:* Jackson, MS; *m:* Alvin Eugene; *c:* Patrelle, Alvin II; *ed:* (BS) Sociology/Math, Univ of S MS 1971; (MED) Math, William Carey Coll 1980; *cr:* Math Teacher Prentiss Jr HS 1971-89, Prentiss HS 1989-; *ai:* Math-A-Thon Each Yr & Tutoring Service Spon; Coach Mathcounts Competitors; MAE 1987-; Outstanding Young Woman of America; Prentiss Inst Teacher of Yr; In Upward Bound Prgm 1981; *home:* PO Box 685 Prentiss MS 39474

GRAY, RICHARD ALLEN, K-12th Grade Choral Director; *b:* Shelbyville, IN; *ed:* (BS) Music/Piano/Choral, 1972, (MA) Music/Piano/Choral, 1975 Ball St Univ; Additional Piano Trng, Butler Univ; *cr:* Organist/Choir Dir St Lukes Episcopal Church 1972-; Choral Dir SW Consolidated Sch Corp 1973-; Organist 1st United Meth Church 1987-; *ai:* Sr Class & Show Group Spon; Phi Mu Alpha Pres 1970-71, Outstanding Mem 1970-71; Shelly Cty Choral Dir Assn Pres 1980-; Outstanding Music Stu Ball St Univ 1970-71; *home:* 429 W South St Shelbyville IN 46176

GRAY, SUSAN ELIZABETH, 6th/7th Grade Science Teacher; *b:* Indian Head, NY; *m:* James V.; *c:* Kristin E., Mary E.; *ed:* (BA) Bio, Hartwick Coll 1973; (MA) Scndry Sch Ed, George Washington Univ 1978; Working on Phd in Curr/Sci Ed, Univ of MD; Earth Sci, Loyola Univ; *cr:* Sci Teacher Milton M Somers Mid Sch 1973-; *ai:* Natl Jr Honor Society Spon; OM Team Coach; Staff Dev Steering Comm Charles Cty Mem; NSTA 1975-; Assn of Curr Dev 1989-; Sci Fair Assn 1976-; Assn of Engineers & Sci Supvrs 1979, Outstanding Teacher Awd; Personality of South Awd 1976-77; Outstanding Scndry Teacher 1974; Jaycees Outstanding Teacher Awd 1985; New Mast Mem 1989; Various Curr Dev Comm Mem 1975-; Steering Comm for Cty Staff Dev 1985-; Multicultural Ed Grant 1980, 1981; *office:* Milton M Somers Mid Sch Box A La Plata MD 20646

GRAY, WANDA LOWERY, Teacher of Gifted; *b:* Aberdeen, MS; *m:* S. K.; *ed:* (BA) Soc Stud Ed, 1972, (MPP) Poly Sci, 1977 Univ Cntrl FL; *cr:* Teacher Edgewood Jr HS 1973-; *ai:* Stu Cncl Spon; Track Coach; Soc Stud Dept Chm; Future Problem Solving Coach; Odyssey of the Mind Coach; Knowledge Master Open Spon; Edgewood Jr HS Teacher of Yr 1989-; *office:* Edgewood Jr HS 180 E Merritt Ave Merritt Island FL 32953

GRAYSON, CAROLE HAMMER, Mathematics Teacher; *b:* Jersey City, NJ; *m:* Mark; *c:* Jeremy, Rebecca, Ariel; *ed:* (BA) Math, 1965, (MA) Math, 1968 Jersey City St Coll; (MBA) Accounting, Rutgers Univ 1980; Admin Courses Rider Coll; *cr:* Math Teacher Rahway HS 1966-69, Wayne Valley HS 1969-72; Accountant RCA Corp 1980-83; Math Teacher Ewing HS 1983-84; Liquidation Asst FDIC 1985-86; Math Teacher Roselle 1986-; *ai:* Sch Treas; SAT Prep Course; Jr Boosters; Roselle Ed Assn, NJEA, NEA; Congregation Beth Chaim (Treas 1983-85, VP 1985-87); Undergraduate St Schlsp; MBA Prgm Grant; *home:* 9 Candlewood Dr Princeton Jct NJ 08550

GRAYSON, LAURA VELA, World History Honors Teacher; *b:* Nuevo Laredo, Mexico; *c:* Ian; *ed:* (BA) Drama/His, TX A&I 1972; *cr:* Teacher Fort Worth Ind Sch Dist 1972-75, Austin Ind Sch Dist 1975-; *ai:* St of TX Stu Cncl Spon; Textbook Adoption Comm Faculty Rep; Austin Assn of Teachers Faculty Soc Chairperson; Austin Assn of Teachers Rep 1985-89; TSTA, NEA 1980-; Austin & TX Cncl of Soc Stud 1980-; TX A&I Alumni 1985-; Natl Endowment for Hum Grant 1987-88; L B J Teacher of Yr 1988-89; Teaching Excl Awd 1988-89; AISD Creative Teaching Awd 1980.

GRAYSON, MARGARET MAC QUEEN, Latin Teacher; *b:* Sylacauga, AL; *m:* Richard Joseph II; *c:* Margaret, Isabel, Richard III; *ed:* (BA) Latin/Fr, Salem Coll 1959; Working Toward PhD Univ of NC; *cr:* Latin Teacher Hollins Coll 1985-86, North Cross 1972-; *ai:* St Johns Episcopal Church (Layreader, Chalicist); Habitat for Humanity Bd Mem; Shakespeare Club Mem; Natl Endowment of Hum Summer Seminar Schlsp Univ of VA 1989; Italy Summer Fulbright Schlsp 1990.

GRAZIADEI, RAPHAELLE A., Religion Dept Coordinator; *b:* Port Huron, MI; *ed:* (BA) Latin, Nazareth Coll 1970; Grad Work Theology & Religious Stud; *cr:* Teacher 1970-, Dept Coord 1984- Lumen Chrstn HS; *ai:* Religion Dept Coord; Latin Club Moderator; Sch Sacristan; NCEA 1970-; Amer Classical League 1975-; Freedoms Fnd Valley Forge Study Grant 1979; Inst for Study Comparative Politics & Ideologies Univ of CO Boulder 1979; *office:* Lumen Christi HS 3483 Spring Arbor Rd Jackson MI 49203

GRAZIANO, ANTHONY VINCENT, 7th Grade Science Teacher; *b:* Garfield, NJ; *m:* Angela; *c:* Toni A.; *ed:* (BS) Elem Ed, Seton Hall Univ 1969; (MA) Admin, Rutgers Univ; *cr:* Teacher Wanaque Sch 1969-71, Lacey Mid Sch 1971-; *ai:* 7th/8th Grade Girls Bsktbl, 6th-8th Grade Cross Cntry, 9th-12th Grade Girls Var Track Coach; *office:* Lacey Mid Sch Western Blvd Lanoka Harbor NJ 08734

GRAZIANO, JOHN M., Teacher; *b:* Chicago, IL; *m:* Mary K.; *c:* Jill, Joseph; *ed:* (BSE) Eng/Journalism, NE MO St Univ 1975; Journalism, Univ of IA; General Ed, Mary Crest Coll, Drake Univ; *cr:* Eng/Journalism Teacher Ottumwa HS 1975-; *ai:* Yrbk Adv; Lang Art Articulation Comm K-12; AFT, NCTE; Natl Wildlife Fed; *office:* Ottumwa HS 501 E 2nd Ottumwa IA 52501

GRAZNAK, STEPHANIE ANN, Theatre Teacher; *b:* Kansas City, MO; *ed:* (AA) Theatre 1969, (BA) Theatre, Stephens Coll 1971; Gifted Ed, AR St Univ; *cr:* Drama Teacher Spring Garden Mid Sch 1973-76; Dir Funshop 1977-78; Theatre/Speech Teacher Central HS 1978; Drama Teacher AR Governors Sch 1981-85; *ai:* All Plays/Thespians/Speaking Choir/Mock Trial Team/Public Speaking Engagements; AR Ed Assn 1978-; NEA 1978-; Classroom Teachers Assn 1978-; AR Speech/Comm Assn 1978-; *office:* Central H S Caney Park Rd West Helena AR 72390

GREANEY, DONALD ELIAS, Social Studies Dept Chair; *b:* Chicago, IL; *m:* Anne Margaret Collins; *c:* Teresa A.; *ed:* (BSED) Poly Sci, N IL 1965; (MA) Poly Sci, NE IL 1984; Inst Constitutional Rights Fnd 1989; Univ of Chicago Mellon Fellow 1989-; Univ of Chicago His Fellow 1987; Amer Enterprise Fnd De Paul 1984; Robert Taft Inst Loyola 1985; *cr:* Teacher Yale UGC Parker HS 1965-71; Dept Chairperson Soc Stud Gage Park HS 1971-; Mellon Fellow Univ of Chicago 1989-; *ai:* Chm Union Profession Problems Comm; Chicago Teachers Union Delegate 1978-; ASC Dev 1985-; NCSS; Chicago PTA VP 1987, Outstanding Teacher 1986; Local Sch Cncl Bd Mem 1989-; Dedicated Teacher Awd Chicago Public Schls 1990; Dartmouth Coll Cmptr Literacy Inst 1985; Concordia Coll Multi-Cultural Inst; *office:* Gage Park HS 5630 S Rockwell Chicago IL 60629

GREAR, CARL C., JR., Soc Stud/His/Science Teacher; *b:* San Francisco, CA; *m:* Shirley A. Kimbrough; *c:* C. J., Michelle; *ed:* (BA) Theology, Pacific Union Coll 1983; *cr:* 9th-12th Grade Bible Teacher Redwood Jr Acad 1983-85; 7th-10th Grade Bible/His/Rdng/Phys Ed/Sci/Career Ed Teacher San Francisco Jr Acad 1987-; *ai:* Yrbk Adv; Athletic Coach; Cnslr.

GREATHOUSE, BETTY TOLIVER, Fifth Grade Teacher; *b:* Floyd, NM; *m:* Jack A.; *c:* Dan L., Ross C.; *ed:* (BS) Ed, 1973, (MS) Ed, 1986 E NM Univ; *cr:* 5th Grade Teacher R M James Elem Sch 1976-; *ai:* SEEDS Project NASA; 5th Grade Stu Tutor; NEA 1976-; Portales Ed Assn (Pres 1984-85) 1975-; NSTA 1982-; Phi Delta Kappa 1984-; Delta Kappa Gamma 1981-; Chairperson & Co-Chairperson Sch Sci Fairs; Colonel Aide De Camp Awd; Project Up-Lift Spon; Math Team Competition Continental Math League Spon; *home:* 1300 S Globe St Portales NM 88130

GREATHOUSE, CLAUDE DANIEL, Asst Aerospace Sci Instructor; *b:* Eastland, TX; *m:* Marianne; *c:* Lauran Strait, Elaine Weber, John; *ed:* (BS) Petroleum Engineering, Univ of SW LA 1957; (MS) Operations Research, George Washington Univ 1977; (MA) Management, Cntrl MI Univ 1977; Squadron Officers Sch, Industrial Coll of the Armed Forces, Primary/Basic Navigation Sch; *cr:* Flight Crew Mem 1958-64, Engr/Scientist 1964-69, Combat Air Crew 1969-70, Scientist 1971-78 USAF; Instr USAF JROTC 1982-; *ai:* Spon Model Rocket Club & ROTC Color Guards; 4th/6th Grade After-Sch Enrichment Instr; Amer Assn of Math Teachers Mem 1980-; Outstanding Teacher Awd; Adjunct Faculty of Prince George Comm Coll & Emery Riddle Aeronautical Inst; Freedom Fnd Awds; News Release Writer; Article Published.

GRECO, LINDA WINN, Second Grade Teacher; *b:* Fayetteville, AR; *m:* George R. II;; *c:* Danen Jobe, Lori Jobe, Ashley; *ed:* (BA) Elem Ed, Pittsburg St Univ 1967; (MS) Elem Ed, SW MO St Univ 1980; *cr:* 4th Grade Teacher Council Bluffs IA 1967-70; Kndgtn Teacher Raggedy Ann Learning Land 1976-79; 1st/2nd/5th Grade Teacher Duenweg Sch 1980-; *ai:* Primary Grades Sci & Math Books Selection Comm & 2nd Grade Core Competency Comm; NEA, MNEA, JEA 1980-; Chamber of Commerce Golden Apple Awd Nom 1986-87; *office:* Joplin RV III Duenweg Sch 802 Irwin Duenweg MO 64841

GRECO, RAYMOND LOUIS, Science Teacher; *b:* New Kensington, PA; *m:* Catherine M. Bowden; *c:* Katrina, Louis; *ed:* (BS) Bio, St Vincent Coll 1976; *cr:* Research Technician St Vincent Coll 1976-77; Metalurgical Observer 1977-78, Pollution Control Tech 1978-80 US Steel Homestead; Sci Teacher Knoch Jr/Sr HS 1982-; *ai:* Knoch Sci Club Adv; PA Jr Acad of Sci Comm-Man; Knoch Conservation Club Co-Adv; Knights of Columbus; *office:* Knoch Jr/Sr HS Dinnerbell Rd Saxonburg PA 16056

GREDLER, PETER SHEPARD, Social Studies Dept Chairman; *b:* Lexington, MA; *m:* Susan Dale Mc Featers; *c:* Sara K.; *ed:* (BA) Poly Sci, Gordon Coll 1973; *cr:* Teacher New Preparatory Sch 1974-81; Teacher/Soc Stud Dept Chm Cedar Lee Jr HS 1981-; *ai:* Fauquier Cty Soc Stud Curr Comm; Fauquier Ed Assn Pres 1988-; NCSS 1981-; *home:* 1511 Queen Ct Culpeper VA 22701

GREEMON, JOYCE BENFIELD, Business Teacher; *b:* Gastonia, NC; *c:* Greg, Mark; *ed:* (BS) Bus Ed, Appalachian St Univ 1969; *cr:* Sales Secy Akers Motor Lines Inc 1969-71; Typing/Careers Teacher W P Grier Jr HS 1971-85; Waitress Hereford Barn Steak House 1980-; Typing/Accounting Teacher S Point HS 1985-; *ai:* FBLA & Jr Civitan Club Adv; Sr Spon; S Point HS Differentiated Pay & Senate Bill #2 Differentiated Pay Cty Comm; Voc Showcase Cty Chm; NCAE 1971-; Gaston Shaggers Incorporated 1988-; *home:* 2409 Montrose Dr Gastonia NC 28054

GREEN, ALICE, Social Sci Dept Chairperson; *b:* Americus, GA; *m:* David Jr.; *c:* Tawnya, Alicia; *ed:* (BS) Soc Sci, Teacher Lib Svc, Fort Valley St 1967; GA Southwestern Coll; *cr:* Teacher Macon Cty Elem Sch 1967-73; Media Spec Sumter Cty Central Jr HS 1973-80; Teacher North East Elem 1979-81; Soc Sci Teacher/Dept Chm Sumter Cty Comp HS 1982-; *ai:* Sr Class Adv; Acad Bowl; Soc Sci Club; Guidance Support Team; Media Comm; Staff Dev Adv Comm; NEA; GAE; Silver Circle Soc Club Pres 1976-85; Amer Legion Aux; FOG Pres 1990; Order of Eastern Star Asst Secy; GSA Leader; GSA Leader; *office:* Sumter Co Comp HS 101 Industrial Blvd Americus GA 31709

GREEN, ANN SPENCE, 7th Grade Reading Teacher; *b:* Friendship, TN; *m:* Max Holder; *ed:* (AS) Dyersburg St Comm Coll 1978; (BS) Early Chldhd/Elem Ed, 1980, (MS) Curr & Instruction/Rdng, 1986 Univ of TN Martin; Grad Stud; *cr:* 7th Grade Rdng Teacher Dyersburg Mid Sch 1980-; *ai:* Team Leader; Power of Positive Stus Comm; NEA, TN Ed Assn, Dyersburg Ed Assn 1980-; Delta Kappa Gamma 1988-; Farm Bureau Women Pres 1982-89; Teacher of Yr; *home:* RR 2 Friendship TN 38034

GREEN, CATHERINE WALKER, Reading Teacher; *b:* Beaumont, TX; *c:* Tiffani, Austin III; *ed:* (BS) Elem Ed, Bishop Coll 1971; *cr:* Headstart Teacher Kountze Elem 1971-72; 4th Grade Teacher Travis Elem 1974-76; 5th Grade Teacher Lucas Elem 1976-80; 7th/8th Grade Rdng Teacher Henderson Jr HS 1980-; *ai:* Spon UIL Ready Writing 8th Grade; 7th-8th Grade Eng Tutor; NEA; TSTSA; NAACP; *office:* Henderson Jr H S 605 Avenue B China TX 77613

GREEN, CHERLY MASON, Fourth Grade Teacher; *b:* Bluefield, WV; *c:* James Clinton Jr., Samuel Justin; *ed:* (BS) Elem Ed, Bluefield ST Coll 1975; Gifted Ed, Univ of VA; *cr:* 1st Grade Teacher New Hall Elem; 5th Grade Teacher, 2nd Grade Teacher Tazewell Elem; 3rd Grade Teacher Dudley Elem; 3rd Grade Teacher, 4th Grade Teacher Graham Intermediate; *ai:* Comm to Rewrite Standards of Learning for 2nd Grade Teachers; Gifted Adv Comm; Teacher for 3rd Grade; Dean Mother for Cub Scouts; Intern; Taught at CCA for The Gifted/Talented; AAA Poster Contest Cert 1989; Boy Scouts Dedicate Service Pin 1984; *home:* PO Box 462 Rodman St Bluefield VA 24605

GREEN, CHERYL GREEN, Secondary Choral Director; *b:* Beeville, TX; *m:* Cecil; *c:* Lori Green; *ed:* (BME) Music Ed, Sam Houston St Univ 1973; *cr:* Music Teacher Victoria Ind Sch Dist 1973-78, Calhoun Cty Ind Sch Dist 1984-85, Palacios Ind Sch Dist 1985-; *ai:* TX Music Educators Assn, TX Choral Dirs Assn, Sigma Alpha Iota; UIL Region XIII Choir Accompanist 1989-; *office:* Palacios Jr/Sr HS 100 Shark Dr Palacios TX 77465

GREEN, CHRIS EHRECKE, Sixth Grade Teacher; *b:* Davenport, IA; *m:* James E.; *c:* Christopher, Emily, Gabriella; *ed:* (BA) Elem Ed, St Ambrose Coll 1977; Post Grad Stud Rdng, Lang, Math; *cr:* 3rd Grade Teacher John Glenn Elem 1977-78; 6th Grade Teacher Neil Armstrong Elem 1978-; *ai:* Quest Teacher; Math Bee Team Supvr; Coll for Kids Teacher; ISEA, NEA Soc Chairperson 1978-81; Kappa Delta Pi, Alpha Chi; IC2 Convention Presentor; *office:* Neil Armstrong Elem Sch 212 S Park View Dr Eldridge IA 52748

GREEN, DAN G., AP Calculus/Physics Teacher; *b:* Pocatello, ID; *m:* Melissa; *c:* Nicholas, Marcus; *ed:* (BS) Math, ID St Univ 1971; *cr:* Math Teacher/Coach Hawthorne Jr HS 1971-79; Math/Physics Teacher Pocatello HS 1979-; *ai:* Jr Class Adv; Wilderness Club; Faculty Senate; NCTM, NCTP, NEA, Pocatello Ed Assn; ID St Univ Bengal Fnd; Univ of ID Alumni Excl Awd; *office:* Pocatello HS 325 N Arthur Pocatello ID 83204

GREEN, ERNEST A., Mathematics Teacher; *b:* Boston, MA; *m:* Ann Carney; *c:* Colleen, Kathleen, Maureen; *ed:* (BS) Math, Boston Coll 1966; (MED) Ed, Univ of MA 1981; *cr:* Math Teacher English HS 1966-; *ai:* Var Girls Bsktbl Coach 1979-; MA Bsktbl Coaches Assn 2nd VP 1985-, Girls Coach of Yr 1984, 1988; Boston Globe Girls Bsktbl Coach of Yr 1986; *office:* The English HS 144 Mc Bride St Jamaica Plain MA 02130

GREEN, FREDERICK T., Mathematics Teacher; *b:* Thomasboro, IL; *m:* Lona L. Frisbie; *c:* Jody, Jody, Scott; *ed:* (BA) Math, 1961, (MS) Math, 1969 IL St Univ; Univ of IL, IL St Univ, Natl Coll of Ed; Natl Sci Fnd Grant for Summer Sch Carleton Coll; *cr:* Math Teacher Fenton HS 1961-; *ai:* Girls Bowling Coach; Soph Class Spon; NCTM, ICTM, NEA, IEA, FEA 1961-; *office:* Fenton HS 1000 W Green St Bensenville IL 60106

GREEN, JANET CAVETT, Math Teacher; *b:* Cleveland, TN; *m:* Jeffrey L.; *ed:* (AA) Glendale Comm Coll 1972; (BA) Math 1974; (MA) Scndry Ed, 1976 AZ ST Univ 1976; Post Masters Studies, Scndry Ed; *cr:* Math Teacher Marcos De Niza HS 1974-; *ai:* Attendance Comm; Dance Chaperone; Tempe Scndry Ed Assn; AZ Ed Assn; NEA; *office:* Marcos De Niza H S 6000 S Lakeshore Dr Tempe AZ 85283

GREEN, JAYNE DENTON, Spanish/English Teacher; *b:* Detroit, MI; *c:* Colleen Button, Kerry G.; *ed:* (BA) Scndry Ed/Eng, E MI Univ 1954; Grad Stud Wayne St Univ, Univ of Detroit, Oakland Univ, IUPUI; *cr:* 7th Grade Eng Teacher Grant Jr HS 1956-61, Avondale Jr HS 1967-71; 10th-12th Grade Span/Eng Teacher E Detroit HS 1985-86; 7th-9th Grade Span/Eng Teacher Kelly Jr HS 1986-; *ai:* Sch Improvement Comm; Stu Trips to Mexico Spon; Restructuring Comm Team Teaching; MI Rdng Assn, MI Foreign Lang Assn; Public Service Television Volunteer 1980; BSA Den Mother 1970; *office:* Kelly Jr HS 24701 Kelly East Detroit MI 48021

GREEN, JON J., Mathematics Dept Chm/Teacher; *b:* Perryton, TX; *m:* Melanie Davison; *c:* Benjamin R., Gary N., Mary A.; *ed:* (BS) Bio, W TX St Univ 1976; (MED) Bio/Ed, Wayland Baptist Univ 1985; *cr:* Lab Instr W Tx St Univ 1975-77; Sci Teacher Claude Ind Sch Dist 1978-81; Reearch Technician TX A&M 1981-83; Math/Sci Teacher Dalhart Ind Sch Dist 1983-; *ai:* Fellowship of Chrstn Athletes; Beta Beta Beta; Alpha Chi; Local Church (Servant, Teacher) 1983-; Outstanding Young Men of America 1986; Teaching of Bio Classes Local Jr Coll; *office:* Dalhart HS 1801 E 16th Dalhart TX 79022

GREEN, JULIA A. (O'CONNELL), Retired Second Grade Teacher; *b:* Alton, IL; *m:* Warren; *c:* Sylvia Peters, Cheryl Nash, Adrienne Saxen, Laurence; *cr:* 2nd Grade Teacher Little Flower Sch 1959-73, 1977-85; *ai:* Tutor Laurence Adult Center; Public Sch of Religion Teacher; Latchkey Alternative Prgm; Little Flower Church Cath Charities; *home:* 3330 Sheridan Springfield IL 62703

GREEN, KATHLEEN LOUISE (ELY), Computer Sci Teacher/Leader; *b:* Arcata, CA; *m:* Russell L.; *c:* Christina, Angela; *ed:* (BA) Ger/Math/Music, Humboldt St Univ 1968; (MA) Counseling, Ball St Univ 1975; Grad Stud Cmptr Sci, Math, Counseling; *cr:* Math/Music Teacher Watson Jr HS 1969-73, Pirmasens Jr HS Germany 1973-74; Teacher in Charge Army Predischarge Ed Prgm Pirmasens Germany 1974-75; Math/Counseling Teacher West HS 1976-80; Leader/Cmptr Sci Teacher East 1980-; *ai:* Cmptr Club Spon; Amer Cmptr Sci League All-star Team; Super Quest & Teams Coach; Salt Lake Sch Dist Technology Comm; UT Cncl Cmptrs in Ed Scndry Ed Rep 1988-; NCTM 1969-; NEA 1976-; Delta Kappa Gamma Treas 1984-; Kiwanis Teacher of Yr 1979; Nom Teaching Math Presidential Awd 1986; *office:* East HS 840 S 1300 E Salt Lake City UT 84102

GREEN, KATHRYN PARROTT, Biology Teacher; *b:* Portland, OR; *ed:* (BS) Child Dev, 1964, (BS) Bio, 1965, (MS) Zoology, 1967 CO St Univ; Grad Level Wkshps & Courses Numerous Univs; *cr:* Spec Ed Teacher North Albany Jr HS 1967-68; Sci Teacher Tasis Amer Sch of Cyprus 1984-85, Hillsboro HS 1968-84, 1985-; *ai:* Hillsboro HS Parent Newsletter Layout Ed; OR Sci Teachers Assn (Treas 1973-78, Editor 1986-), D Marshall Service Awd 1989; NABT OR Bio Teacher of Yr 1982; NSTA; Amer Rhododendron Society, Audubon Society; Natl Sci Fnd Grant U-REP Prgm Univ of Berkeley; Washington Cty Compact Curr Specialist Washington Park Zoo; Project Ocean Search Cousteu Society; Lab Exercises Published; *office:* Hillsboro HS 3285 SE Rood Bridge Rd Hillsboro OR 97123

GREEN, LEOLA, Elementary Teacher; *b:* Bruce, MS; *w:* Leemon Scott (dec); *c:* Sharon D. Gaines, Pamela L. Jones, Paula S. Green-Smith; *ed:* (BSE) Ed/Elem Ed, 1975, (MSE) Ed/Elem Ed, 1980 Univ of Toledo; Licensed Practical Nurse Macomber-Whitney HS 1968; *cr:* Licensed Practical Nurse St Vincents Hospital & Medical Center 1961-76; Kindergarten Teacher Stickney Sch 1976-80; 6th Grade Teacher Riverside Sch 1980-; *ai:* Toledo Fed of Teachers (Building Comm 1980-, Building Rep 1989-, Riverside Staff Dev Rep 1980-85); Alpha Kappa Alpha Parliamentarian 1984-; Kappa Delta Phi; Natl Assn of Negro Bus & Prof Women (Dir of Ed, 3rd VP) 1978-; Phi Delta Kappa (Regional Conference Chairperson 1985, Chapter Pres 1986-) 1979-; Indiana Baptist Church (Jr Church Dir 1980-, Chrstn Ed Bd Secy 1980-, Nurses Guild Pres 1970-82); Delta Sigma Theta Mother of Yr 1986; *office:* Riverside Sch 500 Chicago St Toledo OH 43611

GREEN, LINDA ROWLAND, 4th Grade Elementary Teacher; *b:* Kingsport, TN; *m:* Jerry G.; *c:* Bryan G.; *ed:* (BS) Elem Ed, 1968; (MA) Elem Ed, 1978 W KY Univ; Advanced Trng Wkshps, Family Life Skills, Drug & Alchohol Abuse, Process Writing; *cr:* 3rd Grade Teacher South Heights Elem 1968-71; 4th/5th Grade Teacher Audubon Elem 1971-73; 5th/6th Grade Teacher South Heights Elem 1975-78; 6th Grade Elem Teacher 1978-89, 4th Grade Elem Teacher 1989- Cntrl EleM; *ai:* Cntrl Sch Comm Prgm Dev-Building Stu Self-Esteem, Stu Recognition Prgms; Cntrl Elem Sch Coord; Calendar Organization Comm Henderson Cty Sch System; KEA, NEA; KY Ed Grant-Study Prgm-Process Writing; KY Grant Schlsp Study Elem Ec wkshp; *office:* Central Elementary Sch 851 Center St Henderson KY 42420

GREEN, LOREN R., Sixth Grade Teacher; *b:* Akron, OH; *m:* Kay; *c:* Todd, Scott, Tyler; *ed:* (BA) Elem Ed, Salem Coll 1964; (MA) Elem Admin, Xavier Univ 1975; *cr:* 6th Grade Teacher Green Local 1965-66, Ashland City Schls 1968-; *ai:* Girls Jr Var Sftbl & Boys Jr Var Golf Coach; *home:* 223 Samaritan Ave Ashland OH 44805

GREEN, PATRICIA HUFF, Seventh Grade Teacher; *b:* Athens, GA; *m:* Terry; *ed:* (BSE) Elem Ed, Albany St Coll 1971; (MED) Elem Ed, Univ of GA 1976; Working Toward EDS Degree Couseling, Univ of GA; *cr:* 2nd Grade Teacher Clarke Cty Bd of Ed 1971-72; 8th-12th Grade Teacher Greene Cty Bd of Ed 1972-79; 7th Grade Teacher Oconee Cty Bd of Ed 1979-; Rdng Instr Univ of GA 1984-89; *ai:* Media & SACS Interim Review Comm; Greene Cty Assn Educators Secy 1973-75; Oconee Cty Assn Educators Pres 1983-84; GA Assn of Ecucators, Natl Assn of Educators; Delta Sigma Theta 2nd VP 1982-84; Athens Neighborhood Health Ctr Secy 1983-85; Cmmty Housing Resource Bd Treasd 1986-88; Outstanding Young Women of Amer 1979; *office:* Oconee Cty Mid Sch PO Box 186 Colham Ferry Rd Watkinsville GA 30677

GREEN, PEARLETTE KINNARD, 6th Grade Teacher; *b:* Franklin, TN; *m:* James J.; *c:* Thomas, Faith, Joy; *ed:* (BS) Bio, TN St Univ 1968; (MED) Guidance & Personnel Svcs, Memphis St Univ 1979; Cert Elem Ed Lane Coll; Post Masters Studies/Univ of TN; *cr:* 3rd/4th/5th Grade Teacher Trinity Elem Sch 1969-70; 6th Grade Teacher Lipscomb Elem Sch 1970-72; 3rd Grade Teacher Bradford Elem Sch 1972-73; East End Elem Sch 1973-81; 6th Grade Teacher Franklin Mid Sch 1981-; *ai:* Girl Scout Adv; Tutoring; 4-H Volunteer Ldr; Dramatics Adv; Franklin Spec Sch Comm Chm; Dist Teachers Assn Minority Comm 1983-85; Natl Teachers Assn 1969-; TN Teachers Assn 1969-; Natl Sorority Phi Delta Kappa 1989-; Delta Sigma Theta Sorority; NAACP.

GREEN, RITA R., English Chairman; *b:* Greensburg, PA; *m:* George O.; *c:* Natalie; *ed:* Grad Stud Miami Univ; Eng Group Dynamics; *cr:* Eng Teacher Ross HS 1967-69, Aberdeen HS 1969-71, St Joseph HS 1976-; *ai:* Lit Magazine, Academic Bowl, Eng Club Adv; NCTE, CCTE; GSA Leader 1982-84; Bd of Lib Dir Oxford; *office:* St Joseph HS 2320 Huntington Turnpike Trumbull CT 06611

GREEN, RUTH RLEE BLYTHE-MC KINZIE, Retired Fifth Grade Teacher; *b:* Wellington, TX; *m:* Wendell A.; *c:* Gerry D. Mc Kinzie, Judy Mc Kinzie Hunt, Syndie Mc Kinzie Bayley, Melanie Mc Kinzie, George W. (dec); *ed:* (BS) Elem Ed, W TX Univ 1967; Abilene Chrstn Univ; Wayland Baptist Univ; TX Tech Univ; NW TX Univ; Natl Coll of Ed; *cr:* 5th Grade Teacher Lockney Ind Sch Dist 1967-69; 6th Grade Teacher Plainview Ind Sch Dist 1969-87; *ai:* Lakeside Jr Historian Spon; TX St Teachers Assn 1966-89; Plainview Classroom Teachers; Supt Advisory Bds 1975-77, 1987-; Delta Kappa Gamma (VP 1986-87) 1975-; Hale Cty Historical Society Bd 1979, Distinguished Service 1981; TX Historical Society Bd 1984, Distinguished Service 1984; Plainview Civic Theater Bd 1984-; Plainview Chamber of Commerce Red Coats 1978-87; Plainview Commty Concert Bd 1989-; TX Congress of Parents & Teachers Honorary Life Membership 1972; TX Jr Historians Advisory Bd 1982; Advisory Bd BSA Service Awd 1970-78; Teacher of Month Plainview Lions Club 1972; Plains Amer Heritage Awd 1972; YMCA Awd 1974; Terrific Teacher Awd Plainview Cncl of PTA 1983; Articles Published; *home:* 901 Itasca Rd Plainview TX 79072

GREEN, SABRINA SERCOMBE, Music Department Chair; *b:* Arcadia, CA; *m:* Garrett; *ed:* (BA) Music, CA St Univ Los Angeles 1978; (MA) Music Ed, CA St Univ Fullerton 1986; *cr:* Inst Music 1979-83, Inst Music/Dept Chairperson 1983- Lathrop Intermediate Sch; *ai:* Spartan Jazz Band; Dist Honor Orch Mgr 1985-; Pi Kappa Lamda Mem; Orange Cty Model T Ford Club Secy 1988-; *office:* Lathrop Intermediate Sch 1111 S Broadway Santa Ana CA 92707

GREEN, SANDRA ACKERMAN, English Department Chairman; *b:* Chico, CA; *m:* Randy C.; *c:* Jennifer, Sean; *ed:* (BA) Eng, CA St Univ Chico 1971; Bay Area Writing Project 1982; *cr:* Eng Teacher Credence HS 1973-83, Golden St Jr HS 1983-86, River City HS 1986-; *ai:* Lang Art Curr Revision Comm, Sch Site Cncl; Eng Dept Chm; CTA, NEA 1973-; Teacher of Yr Masonic Lodge 1982; Poetry Published; *office:* River City HS 1100 Clearendon West Sacramento CA 95691

GREEN, TERRI RAINS, Band Director; *b:* Greenville, MS; *m:* James David; *c:* David I.; Phi Beta Mu Outstanding Young Band Dir in KY 1990; *ed:* (BME) Music Ed, 1983, (MME) Music Ed, 1984 Delta St Univ; *cr:* Band Dir E Hardin HS 1985-86, J T Alton Mid Sch & N Hardin HS 1986-; *ai:* Marching & Concert Bands; Solo & Ensemble Festival Coord; KY Music Educators Assn Dist Rep 1985-; KY Bandmasters Assn Dist Rep 1986-; Natl Bandmasters Assn; Outstanding Young Women of America Awd 1984; Mid Sch Band Invited to Perform St Music Conference 1989; *office:* James T Alton Mid Sch 400 Brown St Vine Grove KY 40160

GREEN, TRUDY COFFEY, Business Teacher; *b:* Ada, OK; *m:* Tim G.; *c:* Joshua, Jaylie; *ed:* (BSED) Bus Ed, 1980, (MED) Scndry Ed, 1982 E Cntrl Univ; *cr:* Bus Teacher Byng HS 1980-; *ai:* Fellowship of Chrstn Athletes & Sr Class Spon; FBLA (Prof Mem, Spon) 1980-; OBEA, OEA, NEA 1980-88; Phi Beta Lambda OK Ms Future Bus Teacher 1980; *office:* Byng HS Rt 3 Ada OK 74820

GREEN, VERA (BROWER), Kindergarten Teacher; *b:* Deedsville, IN; *m:* Marvin E.; *c:* Lana Hudson, Diane Cogdell, Gary; *ed:* (BA) Elem Ed, Manchester Coll 1953; (MS) Elem Ed, Ball St Univ 1967; *cr:* 1st Grade Teacher Waldron Elem 1953-54; 2nd Grade Teacher Liberty Elem 1954-56; 3rd Grade Teacher Converse Sch 1956-57; Kndgtn Teacher Swayzee Elem 1966-; *ai:* Staff Dev Comm for Corporation; Health Comm; Building Rep for Local Building in Corporation; Oak Hill Classroom Teacher Assn 1966-; IN St Teachers Assn, NEA 1966-; Converse Church of Christ (Womens Council Pres 1983-84, Pre-Sch Advisory Bd 1983-, Pierian Study Club Pres 1982-83); Vacation Bible Sch Teacher 1966-; *home:* 8364 W Delphi Pike Converse IN 46919

GREEN, WALTER, 7th Grade English Teacher; *b:* Rensselaer, IN; *m:* Judith Ann Montgomery; *c:* Erin J., Miranda M.; *ed:* (BS) Phys Ed/Health, 1974, (MS) Ed, 1981 IN St Univ; *cr:* Eng Teacher South Newton Sch Corporation 1975-77, Kankakee Valley Sch Corporation 1977-; *ai:* HS Girls Golf Coach; Mid Sch Ftbl, Track, Bsktbl Coach; Book Adoption Comm; IN St Teachers Assn, NEA 1975-; Kankakee Valley Teachers Assn, IN Bsktbl Coaches Assn; *office:* Kankakee Valley Mid Sch R R 3 Box 182 Wheatfield IN 46392

GREEN, WAYNE GORDON, 5th Grade Teacher; *b:* Puyallup, WA; *m:* Layne Harding; *c:* Kristina, Hollie; *ed:* (BA) Phys Ed/Psych Ed, 1969, 5th Yr Ed, 1973 Cntrl WA Univ; Classes for Maintenance of Educl Knowledge; *cr:* Elem Phys Ed Teacher Lister & Bryant & Willard & Boze & Sacred Heart 1969-78; 4th-6th Grade Teacher 1979-83, 6th Grade Teacher 1983-87, 5th Grade Teacher 1987- Lister Elem; *ai:* Discipline & Sci Comm

Lister Elem; DARE Prgm; NEA, WA Ed Assn, Tacoma Ed Assn 1969-; Vashon Educators Club Pres 1986-; Cedar Heights Assn of Music Promoters 1989-; Soviet-Amer Cultural Exch; *home:* 11490 Abbey Ln SW Port Orchard WA 98366

GREEN, WILLIAM HARRY, History Teacher; *b:* Halls, TN; *m:* Lynn M. Egan; *c:* Brendan; *ed:* (BA) His, Northeastern IL Univ 1981; *cr:* Substitute Teacher 1988, CADRE/His Teacher 1988-89, His Teacher 1989- Lane Tech HS; *ai:* Boys Bsktbl League Open Gym Dir; Boys Frosh & Soph Bsbl Coach; Parent Teacher Stu Assn Mem 1990; *office:* Lane Tech HS 2501 W Addison Chicago IL 60618

GREEN, YVONNE DANIEL, Rdng/Math/Soc Stud Teacher; *b:* San Antonio, TX; *m:* Larry; *c:* Joseph, Justin, Andrea; *ed:* (BS) Elem Ed, MS Univ for Women 1977; Grad Stud USM; Several Wkshps & Mini Courses on Teaching Elem Math Classes; *cr:* 1st Grade Chapter I Math Teacher S Forrest Attendance Center 1977-89; Kndgtn Teacher Small World 1983; 5th Grade Teacher S Forrest Attendance Center 1985-; *ai:* MS Cncl Teachers of Math 1987-; Kappa Delta Epsilon 1977-; *home:* 44 Green Rd Hattiesburg MS 39401

GREENAWALT, ETHEL M., Second Grade Teacher; *b:* Abington, PA; *ed:* (BS) Elem Ed, Beaver Coll 1963; (MA) Chrstn Ed, Wheaton Coll 1968; Grad Courses Penn St Univ & Fairfield Univ; Writing Courses Chrstn Writers Inst & Inst of Childres Lit; *cr:* 2nd-3rd Grade Teacher Pine Road Elem Sch 1963-69; Elem Ed Professor Southeastern Bible Coll 1969-73; Nursery Sch Teacher Chelten Nursery Sch 1973-74; 1st Grade Teacher Delaware Cty Chrstn Sch 1974-75; 2nd Grade Teacher Faith Chrstn Sch 1975-; *ai:* ACSI 1982-; NEA 1963-69; Rydal Park Medical Center Volunteer 1988-; Primary Sunday Sch Materials; Books & Articles Published; *home:* 3963 Buck Rd Huntingdon Vlly PA 19006

GREENAWAY, MILLICENT DICKENSON, Principal And Founder; *b:* Antigua, British W Indie; *m:* Simon Peter; *c:* George A. Thomas, Aubrey J. Thomas, Myona Greenaway Innocent; *ed:* (BA) Elem Ed, Spring Gardens Coll 1947; (BA) Early Chldhd, Shaw Univ 1974; (MA) Elem, Clayton Univ 1978; *cr:* Elem/Handicraft Ed Dept Teacher Leeward Islands Antigua 1947-57; Supvr Newark Pre-Sch Headstart Center 1965-68; Head Teacher/Dir Newark Day Care Center 1968-70,New Hope Dev Day Care Center 1970-78; Prin/Founder Aunt Millies Childrens Learning Center Inc 1978-; *ai:* Pres Village Cncl Jennings & Ebenezer Antigua West Indies, Drama Club; Antigua Jennings Peace Unit (Pres, Founder) 1951-57, Certificate 1955; Commission to Save Child Care (Secy, Treas) 1974-78, Emeritus 1977; Mt Carmel Guild Supvr Youths in Career Trng 1973-78, Plaque 1977; Franklin-St Johns Church Pres United Meth Women 1983-84, Certificate Pin 1984; Young Ambassadors of Bank Street NY Exch Stu Leader of Newarks Group of Travelers 1982-86, Honorary Citizen New Orleans 1983; Endorsement Newark Ex-Mayor Gibson 1981, Mayor Sharpe James 1988; Outstanding Cmmty Leader Awd Eastward Councilman Henry Martinez 1979; Book Published; *office:* Aunt Millies Learning Center 15 E Kinney St Newark NJ 07102

GREENBERG, C. SUE (BOCK), 3rd & 4th Grade Teacher; *b:* Des Moines, IA; *m:* Richard Greenberg; *ed:* (BS) Elem Ed, St Cloud St Univ 1969; (AA) Pre-Ed, Rochester Comm Coll 1971; (MS) Elem Ed, Winona St Univ 1975; Grad Studs, Univ of MN; *cr:* 3rd Grade Teacher Bamber Valley Elem Sch 1969-75; Multi-Age Classroom Teacher 1975-86, Thematic Coord 1986-88, Classroom Teacher 1988- Lincoln Mann Elem Sch; *ai:* Lincoln Mann Elem Sch Schlsp Comm; Meet & Confer Cncl Rochester Public Schls; MN Ed Assn Mem 1969-; NEA 1969-; Rochester Ed Assn Secy 1978-80; Rochester Ed Assn VP 1988-90; Rochester Ed Assn Pres 1990; United Way Bd of Dirs 1980-86; NASA Teacher in Space Prgm; Received Presidential Citations Rochester Ed Assn 1978/1988-89; Chaired Ind Sch Dist #535 Comm Curr & Admin Reorganization1989-; *home:* 748 Northern Hills Dr NE Rochester MN 55904

GREENBERG, LEWIS ANTHONY, Art Department Chair; *b:* St Louis, MO; *m:* Judy Golubock; *c:* Clayton; *ed:* (BS) Art Ed, 1965, (MS) Admin, 1971 Univ of MO; *cr:* Art Instr Riverview Gardens Sch Dist 1965-70, Ladue Sch Dist 1970-80, Francis Howell Sch Dist 1980-; *ai:* Dept Chairperson; *home:* 977 Morena Ct Saint Louis MO 63011

GREENBERG, ROBERTA L. (WOLF), English Department Chair; *b:* New York, NY; *m:* Harold Martin; *c:* Wendy, Franci; *ed:* (BA) Eng Lit/Comparative Lit, Univ Of Denver 1965; Grad Stud Comparative Lit, Univ of Denver; *cr:* Instr Univ of Denver 1966-67; Teacher John F Kennedy 1971-72; Teacher/Dept Chairperson/Advanced Placement Coord Machebeuf HS 1985-; *ai:* Advanced Placement Coord; Moderator/Writers Network; Dept Chairperson; Curr Comm; NCTE 1985-; Phi Beta Kappa 1964-; Ford Fellowship/Centennial Scholar Univ of Denver; *office:* Machebeuf Cath HS 1958 Elm St Denver CO 80220

GREENBERRY, TANYA THORNTON, English Teacher; *b:* Magnolia, AR; *m:* Walter; *ed:* (BA) Eng, Univ of AR Pine Bluff 1964; Delta St Univ Cleveland, Univ of AR Fayetteville; *cr:* 8th Grade/Eng Teacher Eliza Miller Jr HS 1964-; *ai:* NEA, AR Ed Assn; Helena-W Helena Classroom Teachers Assn (Recording Secy 1985-, Treas 1990); NCTE; Delta Sigma Theta (Treas 1970-80, Financial Secy 1980-86, Reporter 1986-, Recording Secy 1990), Certificate of Appreciation 1980, 1982, 1987; E S Jennings Lang Art Lab Teacher of Yr 1988-89.

GREENE, ANNA HOLMES, Mathematics Teacher; *b:* Montgomery, AL; *m:* John T.; *c:* Whitney Smith, Karlynn Dolby, Kenneth, Michael, Christopher; *ed:* (BS) Math, Auburn Univ 1963; Grad Stud Univ of TX San Antonio; Math/Marine Bio, TX A&M; Terramar Marine Bio Prgms; *cr:* Math Teacher Columbus HS 1964-65, Pleasanton HS 1969-; *ai:* Head of Soph Class Spon; UIL Calculator Coach; Effective Sch Cadre; Textbook Selection Comm; Adult Tutor; GTE Grant; *home:* 52 Dugosh Pleasanton TX 78064

GREENE, BRENDA CHESTANG, Fifth Grade Teacher; *b:* Mobile, AL; *m:* James Walton; *c:* Quentin, Darius; *ed:* (AA) Elem Ed, Bishop St Jr Coll 1970; (MS) Elem Ed, 1972, (MED) Elem Ed, 1977 AL St Univ; *cr:* Teacher 6th Avenue Elem 1972-73, Gilmore Elem 1973-75, Thomas Elem 1975-; *ai:* Cub Scouts of America Pack 204 Adv; Phi Delta Kappa Inc 1990; Emeralds Inc (Pres, Treas, Bus Mgr) 1975-; Teacher of Yr Mobile Cty Public Schls 1983; *office:* Martha Thomas Elem Sch 743 Alvarez Ave Whistler AL 36612

GREENE, DENISE M. (PATRYK), Fifth Grade Teacher; *b:* Schenectady, NY; *m:* Michael B.; *c:* Zachary; *ed:* (AAS) Nursery Ed, SUNY Cobleskill 1972; (BS) Elem Ed, SUNY Oneonta 1974; (MS) Rdng, Russell Sage Coll 1979; Counseling & Guidance; *cr:* 4th-6th Grade Teacher Duanesburg Elem 1975-; *ai:* Greater Capital Dist Teacher Center Site Facilitator & Building Ambassador; EMT Trainer; Staff Dev Comm; Sch Improvement Team; ASCD 1988-; *office:* Duanesburg Cntrl Sch School Dr Delanson NY 12053

GREENE, ERIE L., Job Placement Teacher/Cnslr; *b:* Troy, NC; *m:* Genevieve; *c:* Erica L.; *ed:* (BA) Sociology, Fayetteville St Univ 1984; Effective Teacher Trng; Alcohol & Drug Defense Prgm; Intervention Trng; *cr:* In-Sch Suspension Teacher Troy Mid Sch 1984-85; Voc Cnslr Job Placement Teacher West Montgomery HS 1985-; *ai:* Troy Mid Sch Asst Ftbl, Track, Jr Var Bsktbl Coach; West Montgomery HS Jr Var Bsktbl, Vlybl, Asst Var Bsktbl Coach; NC Coaches Assn; NC Dropout Prevention Assn Faculty Chm Adv 1988-; Cntrl Tarheel Conference Vlybl Coach of Yr 1989-; *office:* West Montgomery HS Rt 3 Mount Gilead NC 27306

GREENE, GINA MINTON, Foreign Language Chair; *b:* Marietta, GA; *m:* Michael Sherll; *c:* Nicole R.; *ed:* (BS) Eng/Latin Ed, Univ of TN Knoxville 1978; (MED) Foreign Lang Ed, Univ of GA Athens 1987; Captain USAR Transportation Officer; OBC-OAC Quarter Master & Transportation; *cr:* Teacher Sumter Acad 1978-80, Cross Keys 1980-81; Teaching Asst Univ of GA 1981-82; Teacher/Dept Head Loganville HS 1982-; *ai:* Foreign Lang Club; 9th Grade Spon; Var Cheerleading 1978-86; Amer Classical League, GA Classical League 1980-; Loganville HS & Walton Cty Teacher of Yr 1985; *office:* Loganville HS 150 Clark Mc Cullers Dr Loganville GA 30249

GREENE, JOE, English Teacher; *b:* Ruthersford, NJ; *m:* Maryann Rossi; *c:* Dennis, Alison; *ed:* (BA) Eng, Coll of Emporia 1965; (MA) Admin/Supvr, Seton Hall Univ 1971; Grad Stud Rutgers Univ, William Paterson Coll, Jersey City St Coll; *cr:* Teacher S Hunterdon Regional HS 1965-67, Memorial Jr HS 1967-; Adjunct Instr Sussex Cty Coll 1989-; *ai:* NEA, NJEA 1965-; NCTE 1971-; NJ Teacher of Yr; Distinguished Educator Awd; Whos Who in Amer Ed; Young Authors Conference; Meet the Authors; Menlyns Pen; NJEA Review; *office:* Memorial Jr HS Highland Ave Whippany NJ 07981

GREENE, JUDY, English Teacher; *b:* Coal Run, KY; *m:* David Keith; *c:* Keith; *ed:* (BS) Ed/Eng/Poly Sci, Pikeville Coll 1968; (MA) Ed, Morehead St Univ 1978; Grad Stud Writing, Democratic Ed, OH Univ; *cr:* Elem Teacher Pike Cty Schls 1966-67; Eng Teacher Zane Trace Schls 1968-69, Huntington Schls 1969-; *ai:* Huntington Local Ed Assn Building Rep 1980-; Cntrl OH Teachers Assn Exec Comm 1978-, Accolade Awd 1988; OH Ed Assn Exec Comm 1988-; Hazen Fellowship Grant; *home:* 1256 Mingo Rd Chillicothe OH 45601

GREENE, KEVIN ROBERT, English Teacher; *b:* Poughkeepsie, NY; *m:* Anita B. Reina; *ed:* (BA) Eng/Ed, AZ St Univ 1978; (ME) Ed, CO St Univ 1988; *cr:* HS Eng Teacher Deer Valley HS 1982-84, Fredrick HS 1984-86, Highland HS 1986-88, Mohave HS 1988-; *ai:* Bsktbl, Vlybl, Track Asst Coach; CO Ed Assn Mem 1984-88; AZ Ed Assn Mem 1978-82, 1988-; NEA Mem 1978-; Regents Schlsp, Presidential Schlsp; Whos Who in Amer Univ & Coll Deans List 1974-78; *office:* Mohave HS & Mohave Comm Coll 1414 Hancock Rd Bullhead City AZ 86442

GREENE, LEVESTER, Mathematics Teacher; *b:* St Stephen, SC; *m:* Catheia Eaddy; *c:* Sonya L., Cedric L.; *ed:* (BS) Math/Chem, Allen Univ 1967; (MED) Math Ed, Univ of SC 1977; Math, Sci Hampton Inst 1969, 1971; Math, Francis Marion Coll 1985; Ed, Furman Univ 1988; *cr:* Teacher Wilson Jr HS 1967-69, Florence Dist 1 Adult Ed; Teacher/Bus Supvr 1974-87, Teacher 1969- Wilson HS; *ai:* Jr Class Adv; Faculty & Prin Advisory Cncl; After Sch Math Tutor; Florence Dist I Ed Assn, SC Ed Assn, NEA, SC Cncl Teachers of Math 1967-; Sch Improvement Cncl 1987-89; NAACP; Florence Dist I Human Relations Comm 1988-89; SC Assn for Pupil Transportation 1st Runner Up Supvr of Yr 1981-82, 1984-85, 1985-86, Supvr of Yr 1986-87; Florence Dist I Supvr of Yr 1984-85, 1986-87; Wilson HS Teacher of Yr 1988-89; *office:* Wilson HS 1411 Old Marion Hwy Florence SC 29501

GREENE, LOVELACE JOHN, JR., Vocational Agriculture Teacher; *b:* Abbeville, LA; *m:* Gwen Mouton; *ed:* (BS) Vocational Agriculture Ed, SW LA 1980; (MED) Admin/Supervision, Mc Neese St 1988; Ag & Cmptr Ed, SW LA, Mc Neese St, LA St; *cr:* Teacher Jennings HS 1980-82, Pecan Island HS 1982-; *ai:* FFA Adv; 4-H Club Cmmty Leader; Asst Boys Track Coach; Jr Class Spon; Pecan Island HS Master Teacher; Natl Ag Teachers Assn 1982-; LA Ag Teachers Assn 1982-; NEA, Vermilion Assn of America 1988-; LA Assn of Educations; Vermilion Fair & Festival Incorporated VP 1976-86; Vermilion 4-H (Exec Comm, Mem) 1989-; *office:* Pecan Island HS Pecan Island Rt Box 92 Kaplan LA 70548

GREENE, RICHARD LEE, Assistant Principal; *b:* Havre Da Grace, MD; *m:* Shari Elizabeth Johnson; *c:* Shaylah; *ed:* (BS) Phys Ed, Towson St Univ 1980; (MED) Exercise Psych, Temple Univ 1982; Admin, Loyola Coll; *cr:* Phys Ed Teacher Bel Air Mid Sch 1982-88; Health Teacher/Admin Intern 1988-89, Asst Prin 1989- C Milton Wright HS; *ai:* Curr, Reports, Harford Cty Teacher Proficiency Awd, Eligibility Comms; NAASP 1989-; Grad Assistantship, Undergrad Adv Temple Univ 1981-82; *office:* C Milton Wright HS 1301 N Fountain Green Rd Bel Air MD 21014

GREENE, RITA J., Social Studies Teacher; *b:* Terre Haute, IN; *m:* Jerald D.; *c:* Stephen; *ed:* (BS) Elem Ed, 1965, (MS) Ed, 1968 IN St Univ; IN Univ 1982; Jr HS Endorsement Sci & Soc Stud; *cr:* Elem Teacher 1969-81, Northside Mid Sch 1981; *ai:* Columbus Educators Assn, IN St Teachers Assn, NEA, 1965-; Alph Delta Kappa 1982-.

GREENE, SADIE, Fourth/Fifth Grade Teacher; *b:* Georgetown, SC; *ed:* (BS) Elem Ed, SC St 1979; (MED) Elem Ed, Univ of SC 1988; Effective Teaching Prgm; *cr:* Teacher Greenboro Elem 1979-80, Plantersville Elem 1980-; *ai:* Steering Comm; Newsletter; 4th-6th Grade Dept Chairperson; SCEA/GEA/NAACP 1981-; Delta Sigma Theta 1988-; Teacher of Yr Plantersville Elem 1984-85; *home:* Star Rt 1 Box 167 Georgetown SC 29440

GREENE, SUSAN, 8th Grade Mathematics Teacher; *b:* San Diego, CA; *ed:* (BS) Scndry Math Ed, Appalachian St Univ 1974; (MA) Mid Grade Ed, W Carolina Univ 1979; *cr:* 8th Grade Math Teacher Oakley Elem Sch 1974-75; 7th/8th Grade Math Teacher A C Reynold Mid Sch 1975-84, Black Mountain Mid Sch 1984-; *ai:* Beta Club, Yrbk, Schl Improvement Team Chm; Teach Cmptr Competencies to Cty Teachers; Comm for Reviewing Bd Policy; NCAE, NEA 1974-; NCTM, NCCTM 1988-; United Meth Church; Black Mountain Mid Teacher of Yr 1988-89; *office:* Black Mountain Mid Sch 100 Flat Creek Rd Black Mountain NC 28711

GREENE, SYLVIA WOODS, English Teacher; *b:* Peabody, KY; *c:* Sean, Sarah; *ed:* (BA) Eng, Cumberland Coll 1971; (MS) Eng Ed, Univ of TN 1977; *cr:* Eng Teacher Jacksboro HS 1971-73; Rdng Teacher E La Follette ELem 1973-74; Eng Teacher La Follette HS 1974-75, Eng Teacher Campbell Cty HS 1975-87; Eng/Soc Stud Oak Ridge HS 1987-; *ai:* Organize & Teach Young Authors Camp; Delta Kappa Gamma; TN Cncl Teachers of Eng; *office:* Oak Ridge HS 127 Providence Rd Oak Ridge TN 37830

GREENE, TERESA DONNELLY, 3rd Grade Teacher; *b:* St Louis, MO; *m:* Robert; *c:* Melinda, Melissa; *ed:* (BA) Ed, Mid America Nazarene Coll 1977; (MA) Ed Admin, Univ of MO Kansas City 1985; *cr:* 3rd Grade Teacher Bluejacket Elem 1978-83, Flint Elem 1985-; *ai:* Cntry Hill Homes Assn VP; Kansas City Mother of Twins Pres 1985; PTA Citizenship Chairperson; Rising Star PTA Charter Mem; KS Dairy Cncl & PTA Grants; *office:* Flint Elem Sch 5705 Flint Shawnee Mission KS 66203

GREENE, WANDA ROSS, Math Teacher; *b:* Miami, FL; *m:* Gary Boyd; *c:* Andrew, Jessica; *ed:* (AS) Math, Wingate Coll 1976; (BA) Ed, Univ of NC Charlotte 1978; (MA) Ed/Mid Sch Math, Wingate Coll 1988; *cr:* 6th/7th Grade Teacher Smyran Elem Sch 1978-79; Math Teacher Carmel Jr HS 1979-84, Sun Valley Mid Sch 1984-; *ai:* Mathcounts Coach; Math Dept & Grade Level Chairperson; Family Math Night Comm; NC Cncl Teachers of Math 1979-; *office:* Sun Valley Mid Sch 1409 Wesley Chapel Rd Matthews NC 28105

GREENEWALD, BETTY LEE WHITACRE, Life Science/Teacher of Gifted; *b:* Roscoe, PA; *m:* Edward; *c:* Cindy L. G. Bertschinger; Robert E.; *ed:* (BS) Bio, Grove City Coll 1948; Grad Courses Pitt Univ, IN Univ, CA Univ, Shippensburg Univ; *cr:* Teacher Mc Keesport HS 1948-55, Elizabeth-Forward Jr HS 1970-; *ai:* Elizabeth Forward HS Sci, Health, Geography Fairs; Rdng Prgm; Sch Geographic Grant Comm; Coll Club Bd of Dirs; YWCA (Pres Bd of Dirs 1965-67, All Offices 1955-70); Westinghouse Awd Sci Achievements; *office:* Elizabeth Forward Jr HS 401 Rock Run Rd Elizabeth PA 15037

GREENFEATHER, LAURA FAYE, 4th Grade Teacher; *b:* Claremore, OK; *c:* Taylor; *ed:* (BS) Elem Ed, 1974, (MS) Counseling, 1975 Northeastern St Univ; Doctoral Candidate Stu Personnel, OK St Univ; *cr:* Elem Cnslr Sapulpa Elem Schls 1975-76; HS Cnslr Sapulpa HS 1976-78; Spec Ed Cnslr Tri Quad Spec Services 1979-80; 4th Grade Teacher Keystone 1980-; *ai:* OK Personnel & Guidance Assn 1974-; Natl Indian Youth Cncl 1975-78; *office:* Keystone Sch Rt 3 Box 900 Sand Springs OK 74063

GREENFIELD, DEBORAH HALL, 6th-8th Grade Teacher; *b:* Princeton, WV; *m:* John E.; *ed:* (BA) Hum, IN Univ Southeast 1975; Ed, in Univ Southeast, TESA Coord Trng, Las Vegas 1989; *cr:* 7th-9th Grade Gen Sci Teacher/Eng Teacher Orleans Cmmty Schls 1975-77; 9th & 10th Grade Eng Teacher South Harrison Cmmty Schls 1977-79; 9th-12th Grade Eng Teacher Staunton HS 1981-83; 7th & 8th Grade Eng/Gen Sci Teacher 1985-88; 6th-8th Grade Eng Teacher 1988- South Harrison Cmmty Schls; *ai:* Co-Spon New Middletown Outdoor Lab; Lib Comm; Admin Adv Comm; Book Adoption Comm; Spring Act Comm; Coord Career

Week; Winner Harrison Cty Outdoor Lab 1988; Harrison Cty Soil & Water Conservation Teacher of Yr 1989; *office:* New Middletown Grade Sch Gen Del New Middletwn IN 47160

GREENFIELD, VICKI RICHMOND, Fourth Grade Teacher; *b:* Odessa, TX; *m:* Charles Allen; *c:* Chad A., Kayli L.; *ed:* (BS) Elem Ed, TX Tech Univ 1980; Educl Wkshps; *cr:* 4th Grade Teacher 1980-81, 3rd Grade Teacher 1981-82, 4th Grade Teacher 1982- Tatom Elem MWP ISD; *ai:* First Baptist Church Choir; Handbell Choir; Group Ensemble; Dir Mission Friends; Assn TX Prof Educators (Pres 1981-83 Building Rep 1987-88); *office:* Monahans Wickett-Pyote ISD 1600 S Calvin Monahans TX 79756

GREENHALGH, JUDITH BYRNES, German Teacher; *b:* Easton, PA; *m:* George R.; *ed:* (BA) Ger/Ed, Ursinus Coll 1962; (MA) His, Lehigh Univ 1966; Ger, St Josephs Univ; *cr:* Ger Teacher Schwenksville HS 1963-68, Pen Argyl HS 1968-71, Various Adult Sch Prgms 1973-89, Palisades HS 1981-; *ai:* Ger Club; Exch Prgm Krefeld West Germany; Foreign Lang Forensics Tournament Coach; AATG (Treas 1989, Mem 1962-); Modern Lang Assn Philadelphia Vicinity, PA Modern Lang 1989; *office:* Palisades HS Rd 2 Box 1 Kintnersville PA 18930

GREENICH, KARL EDWARD, JR., Sixth Grade Teacher; *b:* Reading, PA; *m:* Mary Ellen; *c:* Susan P., Jonathan R.; *ed:* (BS) Ec, Albright Coll 1964; Ed Cert, Kutztown Univ 1970; (MS) Ed, Temple Univ 1978; PA St Univ, Carlow Coll, Millersville Univ, Wilkes Coll; *cr:* 4th Grade Teacher Conrad Weiser East Elem 1966-71; 6th Grade Teacher Conrad Weiser West Elem 1971-; *home:* 2020 Cypress Ln Wyomissing PA 19610

GREENLAND, GAYNOR DRAPER, Math/Science Teacher; *b:* Birmingham, England; *m:* Roger Alfred; *c:* Amanda, Anthony; *ed:* (BS) Theoretical Mechanics, 1971, (PACE) Ed, 1972 Univ of Nottingham; *cr:* Math Teacher South Wolds Comprehensive Sch 1972-73; Math/Sci Teacher St Joan of Arc Sch 1980-81, Riverside Acad HS 1983-; *ai:* Beta Club Spon; Quiz Bowl Coach; La Beta Club Planning Comm; Beta Sigma Phi Pres 1982-, Pledge of Yr 1982, Woman of Yr 1983, 1989, Sweatheart 1990; *office:* Riverside Acad Rt 2 Box 1070 J Reserve LA 70084

GREENWALT, JOY BOUNDS, 7th Grade Language Art Teacher; *b:* Terrell, TX; *m:* James Leonard Jr.; *c:* Julia Bliss; *ed:* (BFA) Fine Art/Eng Ed, Univ Tx Austin 1976; (MS) Ed/Gifted Child Ed, E TX Univ; Grad Stud Shakespeare & Evaluation Trng Teacher; *cr:* 7th/8th Grade Lang Art Teacher Rockwall Mid 1976-84; 3rd Grade Teacher Royse City Elem 1989; 7th Grade Lang Art Rockwall Mid Sch 1990; *ai:* UIL Literary Events; TSTA, NCTE, Kappa Delta Pi; TX Assn of Gifted & Talented; 1st Chrstn Church (Youth Dir, Pulpit Comm); Gifted & Talented Appointment; *office:* J W Williams Mid Sch Hwy 66 E Rockwall TX 75087

GREENWALT, SUSAN GESS, Fifth Grade Teacher; *b:* Martinsburg, WV; *m:* Robert H.; *c:* Lisa S. Perez; *ed:* (BA) Elem Ed, Shepherd Coll 1969; Grad Stud WV Univ; *cr:* 6th Grade Teacher High Street Elem & Winchester Avenue Elem 1962-63; 2nd/6th Grade Teacher Bunker Hill Elem 1963-66; 6th Grade Teacher Indwood Elem 1969-70; 4th/5th Grade Teacher Valley View Elem 1970-78, Bunker Hill Elem 1978-; *ai:* Pupil Services Comm; Delta Kappa Gamma Schlsp Chairperson 1987-89; Bunker Hill United Meth Church (Lay Leader 1981-83, Admin Bd Chairperson 1984-86, Coord Family to Family Caring/Sharing Prgm 1987-); Caring Educator Awd 1985-86; Elem Lang Art Teacher of Yr 1986-87; Teacher of Yr Finalist 1987-88; Historical Account Published 1982; *home:* PO Box 483 Bunker Hill WV 25413

GREENWAY, ROY WAYNE, Science Teacher; *b:* Metter, GA; *m:* Dowanna Wimberly; *c:* Jessica, Bryson; *ed:* (BSED) Health/Phys Ed Recreation, GA Southern Coll 1984; Sci, GA Southern Coll; *cr:* Sci Teacher Emanuel Cty Inst 1984-; *ai:* Boys Bsktbl Head Coach; Ftbl & Bsbl Asst Coach; Sci Club Adv; GA Assn of Educators, NEA, Emanuel Assn of Educators; Jaycees; *home:* PO Box 243 Carl Durden St Twin City GA 30471

GREENWAY, RUTH ANN STURGELL, 1st Grade Teacher; *b:* Evansville, IN; *m:* Fred K.; *c:* David, Dena; *ed:* (BS) Elem Ed, Alma & Eastern MI Univ 1963; (MA) Elem Ed, Eastern MI Univ 1970; Elem Ed; *cr:* Kndgtn Teacher Selfridge AFB Sch 1963-67; Sub Teacher Elem Schls Utica MI 1967-70; Kndgtn Teacher 1970-78; 1st Grade Teacher 1979- Utica Cmmty Sch; *ai:* Soc Comm Chm Dresden Elem; MI Ed Assn 1963-; NEA 1963-; Utica Ed Assn 1970-; Romeo Art Guild 1974-76; *office:* Dresden Elem Sch 11400 Delvin Sterling Heights MI 48078

GREENWELL, DIANA GARTIN, First Grade Teacher; *b:* Dayton, OH; *m:* Michael; *c:* Aaron, Zachary; *ed:* (BS) Elem Ed, E KY Univ 1975; (MA) Elem Ed, Univ of Louisville 1979; Teacher Meade Cty Schls 1975-86, Jefferson Cty Schls 1986-87, Meade Cty Schls 1987-; *ai:* Delta Kappa Gamma 1989-; *home:* Rt 1 Box 57 A Ekron KY 40117

GREENWELL, ROBIN QUINN, Mathematics Teacher; *b:* Evansville, IN; *m:* John D.; *c:* Loren Q., Whitney L.; *ed:* (BS) Math, 1977, (MS) Scndry Ed, 1979 W KY Univ; (Rank I) Scndry Ed, Murray St Univ 1981; *cr:* Math Teacher Union Cty HS 1977-; *ai:* Math Club Spon; Sturgis Elem Fall Festival Comm; Union Cty Ed Assn, KY Ed Assn, NEA; Cumberland Presbyn Church Elder 1988-; Union Cty Hospice, Sturgis Elem PTO; Union Cty HS Teacher of Month Awd 1990; Sturgis Chamber of Commerce Yard of Month Awd 1990; *home:* Rt 1 Box 300 Sturgis KY 42459

GREENWOOD, BETTY MC CLURE, Second Grade Teacher; *b:* San Antonio, TX; *m:* Ernest Samuel Sr.; *c:* Ernest Jr., Harold, Sylvia Hildebrand; *ed:* (AA) Elem Ed, St Philips Jr Coll 1955; (BS) Elem Ed, Huston-Tillotson Coll 1958; Univ of AK Rdng/Math; AK Meth Univ Rdng/Math; St Philips Jr Coll Tailoring Prgm Completed; *cr:* Sub/1st Grade Teacher Bitburg AFB Germany Dependents Sch 1961-63; Pre-Sch Teacher Crockett Elem 1965-69; 2nd Grade Teacher Mountain View Elem 1969-72; Spec Ed/1st-2nd Grade Teacher Steele Elem 1972-; *ai:* Tutor Remedial Rdng/Math-Carver Lib; Tutor-Maranatha Baptist Church; NEA 1965-; TX St Teachers Assn 1972-; San Antonio Teachers Assn 1972-; Phi Delta Kappa Inc (1st Anti-Basileus 1981-85, Rdng Power Chairperson 1989-) Soror of Yr 1981; Steele Elem PTA (Treas 1983-85) St PTA Life Membership 1985; *home:* 718 Dunwoodie Dr San Antonio TX 78219

GREENWOOD, CLAUDINE JOHNSON, 8th Grade Math Teacher; *b:* West Point, GA; *m:* John W. III; *c:* Arthur; *ed:* (BS) Math, TX Coll Tyler TX 1970; Columbus Coll Columbus GA 1982-84; *cr:* 9th/12th Math Teacher West Point HS 1980-82; 7th Grade Teacher West Point Elem Sch 1984-86; 8th Grade Teacher Whitesville Rd Mid Sch 1986-; *ai:* Media Comm Mem; GA ATE 1980-; Ebonette Civic Club Pres 1985-87; *office:* Whitesville Mid Sch 1700 Whitesville Rd La Grange GA 30240

GREENWOOD, GEANINE KAY, First Grade Teacher; *b:* Lebanon, MO; *m:* James; *c:* Seth, Cassie, David; *ed:* (BS) Child Dev, Southwest MO St Univ 1978; Cert Elem Ed, SMSU 1983; *cr:* Dir As a Child Grows Day Care 1978-83; 5th Grade Teacher 1983, 3rd Grade Teacher 1984-87, 1st Grade Teacher 1987 Joe E Barber C-5; *ai:* Discipline Comm; PR&R Comm; Head Teacher 1988; MSTA 1983-; CTA (Pres 1988 VP 1990); WMUS Soc Comm 1989-; The Early Learning Friends Grant 1988-89; Coach Boys Soccer Team 1990; *office:* Joel E Barber C-5 Rt 2 Box 85 Lebanon MO 65536

GREENWOOD, THERESA WINFREY, Asst Professor Elem Ed; *b:* Cairo, IL; *m:* Charles H.; *c:* Lisa R., Marc C.; *ed:* (BME) Music, Millikin Univ 1959; (MA) Elem Ed, 1963, (EDD) Elem Ed, 1976 Ball St Univ; Soc Psych, Early Chldhd Ed, Gifted Ed; *cr:* Music Teacher E Chicago Public Schls 1959-61; 3rd/4th Grade Teacher Muncie Public Schls 1962-68; Primary Grade Teacher 1979-85, Resource/Gifted & Talented Prgm Teacher 1986- Burris Laboratory Sch; *ai:* Elem Schls Speaker; HS Stus Gifted/Talented Prgm Co-Dir; Assoc Provosts Ad Hoc Comm for Black Faculty Mem; Sigma Alpha Iota Pres 1970-74; League of Amer Pen Women Mem 1974; Amer Red Cross, WIPB TV Bd Mem; NAACP Achievement Awd 1980; Poetry Published Warner Press 1970, 1980, New York 1977, Saturday Evening Post 1975-76; Christa Auliffe Finalist/Alternate 1990; Eli Lilly Creative Teaching Fellowship 1989; Teacher of Yr Runner Up 1982; Ford Fellowship for Doctorate 1975 & 1976; Accomondation Awd Former IN Governor 1982; *office:* Burris Laboratory Sch Ball St Univ 2000 University Ave Muncie IN 47306

GREENWOOD, TINKA KATHLEEN ANN, Sixth Grade Teacher; *b:* Denver, CO; *m:* Clyde R.; *c:* Christine, William; *ed:* (BA) Elem Ed, Univ N CO 1972; Working Toward Masters CO St Univ, Univ of CO; *cr:* Substitute Teacher Poudre R-1 Sch Dist 1980-81; 1st Grade Teacher 1981-82, 6th Grade Teacher 1982-89 Cache La Poudre Elem; 6th Grade Teacher Laurel Elem 1989-; *ai:* Soc Stud Rep; NEA, CO Ed Assn, Poudre Ed Assn; Poudre R-1 Distinguished Teacher Awd 1988; MESA Outstanding Teacher Awd 1990; *office:* Laurel Elem Sch 1000 E Locust Fort Collins CO 80521

GREENWOOD, YVONNE EARL BOONE, Business Dept Chairperson; *b:* Amarillo, TX; *m:* James L. Sr.; *c:* James L. Jr., Brenda Stephenson; *ed:* (BS) Scndry Ed, Univ of N TX 1973; (MBA) Bus Ed, E TX St Univ 1982; *cr:* Teacher/Dept Chairperson Richardson HS 1976-; *ai:* Mock Trial Team; Pre-Law Club; ATPE, PTA 1976-; Delta Kappa Gamma 1980-; Beta Gamma Sigma 1983-; Leon Jaworski Outstanding Soc Stud Teacher Awd 1989; Semi-Finalist Richardsson Ind Sch Dist 1985, 1990; *office:* Richardson HS 1250 Belt Line Rd Richardson TX 75080

GREER, BETTY H., 5th-8th Grades Eng Teacher; *b:* Aberdeen, MS; *m:* David D. Sr.; *c:* Leisa G. Ward, David D. Jr.; *ed:* (BA) Elem Ed, 1968, (MS) Elem Ed, 1976 Univ of MS; *cr:* Elem/Eng Teacher West Union Sch 1968-; *ai:* Jr Beta Club Spon; NCTE 1989-, Kappa Delta Pi Mem 1965-68; Outstanding Elem Teacher 1973-74; *home:* Rt 2 Box 57A Hickory Flat MS 38633

GREER, BETTY VANNATTA, 4th Grade Teacher; *b:* Windsor, MO; *m:* Harold D.; *c:* Leta M., Liska M., Tommy D., Van Nessa K.; *ed:* (AA) Educ, Harris Teachers Coll 1953; (BS) Elem Educ, Central MO Univ 1955; Webster Univ; MO Univ; *cr:* 2nd Grade Teacher Bayless Elem 1955-57; Sub Teacher Germany 1957-59; Kndgtn Teacher Froebel 1959-64; 1st Thru 4th Grade Teacher Mehlville 1964-; *ai:* Mehlville Cmmnty Teachers Assn Bd Dir; Just Say No Club Spon; Parent Advisory Comm Rep Voluntary Interdistrict Coordinating Cncl; Sports Banquet Chm Metro HS; Natl Rdng Assn; NEA; MO Ed Assn; Mehlville Teachers Assn (Secy 1988-, Membership Chm); Mehlville Cmmnty Swim Team USS Registrar 1972-; Compton Hts Bapt Church; WA PTO; Trautwein PTO Mothers Club; Nom Teacher Yr 1980; 20 Yr Awd Mehlville Sch Dist 1987; *home:* 5230 Butler Hill Est Dr St Louis MO 63128

GREER, CONNIE BATTAGLER, Third Grade Teacher; *b:* Orrick, MO; *m:* William Garry; *c:* Michele M., Erin L.; *ed:* (BS) Elem Ed, Cntrl MO St Coll 1962; (MS) Elem Admin, Cntrl MO St Univ 1972; *cr:* Kndgtn Teacher Excelsior Spring MO Sch Dist 1962-77; Kndgtn-3rd Grade Teacher Orrick MO Sch Dist 1977-; *ai:* Orrick Teachers Assn Salary Comm; Techer Mentor; Orrick Elem Newspaper Comm; Delta Kappa Gamma Communication Chm 1987-89; Orrick Teachers Assn Building Rep 1988-89; Orrick Baptist Church Dept Dir 1987-89; *home:* 413 W Elm Orrick MO 64077

GREER, HASKELL HARRISON, US History Teacher; *b:* Nashville, TN; *m:* Mary Beasley; *c:* Sara A.; *ed:* (BS) His, 1967, (MAT) His, 1970, (PHD Arts) His, 1977 Mid TN St Univ; Poly Sci & Admin of Public Ed, Mid TN St Univ, TN Technological Univ, TN St Univ; *cr:* Teacher Irving Coll HS 1967-69, Warren Cty Sr HS 1969-; Adjunct Faculty TN Technological Univ 1973-, Motlow St Comm Coll 1984-; *ai:* Warren Cty Sr HS US His Team Academic Coach & Mock Trial Team Teacher/Adv; TN Ed Assn, NEA 1967-; TN Congress of Amer His Teachers Pres 1984-86; Phi Delta Kappa; NCSS; TN Cncl for Soc Stud, TN Poly Sci Assn; 2 Fellowships to Participate Robert A Taft Inst of Government 1984, 1986; Fellowship to TN Collaborative Acad Univ of TN Knoxville 1988; Outstanding Scndry Soc Stud Teacher in TN Cncl for Soc Stud 1987; Fellow to Jefferson Meeting on US Constitution Nashville TN 1986; *office:* Warren Cty SR HS 200 Caldwell St Mc Minnville TN 37110

GREER, NANCEY NEWLIN, English Teacher; *b:* Cushing, OK; *m:* Robert J.; *c:* Jennifer, Jason; *ed:* (BA) Bus Ed, 1967, (MS) Ed, 1968 W KY Univ; Grad Stud Eng 1982; *cr:* Teacher Butler Cty 1968-69, Red Boiling Springs HS 1982-; *ai:* Chrldr & Jr Beta Spon; Gamaliel Homemakers; *office:* Red Boiling Springs HS Hillcrest Dr Red Boiling Spring TN 37150

GREER, PAMELA PEPPERS, English Teacher; *b:* Covington, GA; *m:* Clark; *c:* Christopher; *ed:* (BSE) Eng, GA Southern Univ 1983; (MED) Eng, Univ of GA 1989; *cr:* Eng Teacher Newton Cty HS 1983-; *ai:* Var & Jr Var Cheerleading Coach; NEA 1983-; Yrbk Dedication & Top Ten Teacher 1985; *office:* Newton Cty HS 140 Ram Dr Covington GA 30209

GREER, PEGGY GARNER, Fourth Grade Teacher; *b:* Old Hickory, TN; *m:* Edward N.; *c:* Laurie Greer Clark, Lisa Greer Walker; *ed:* (BS) Elem Ed, Belmont Coll 1960; Post Grad Stud TN St Univ; *cr:* 3rd Grade Teacher Glengarry Elem 1962-63; 4th-5th Grade Teacher Woodbine Elem 1966-67; 4th Grade Teacher Nannie Berry Elem 1967-74, Wessington Place Elem 1974-; *ai:* Textbook & Curr Dev Comms; Delta Kappa Gamma Membership Chm 1968-75; *home:* 121 Choctaw Dr Hendersonville TN 37075

GREER, PHILIP EDWIN, 5th Grade Teacher; *b:* Mt Vernon, IL; *m:* Eileen Olivia Karcher; *c:* Amy, Emily, Molly; *ed:* (BS) Ed, SW Baptist Univ 1975; (MS) Ed, SW MO St Univ 1985; *cr:* 6th Grade Teacher Sch of Osage1975-78; 5th Grade Teacher Sedalia Public Schls 1978-79; 5th/6th Grade Teacher Aurora Public Schls 1979-; *ai:* 6th Grade Girls Bsktbl Coach 1978; Jr HS Girls Bsktbl Coach 1979-88; CTA (VP 1977, Treas 1985, Secy 1987); Chm of Prof Dev Comm 1989-; MO St Teachers Assn 1975-; Church Choir 1975-; Sunday Sch Teacher 1973-74, 1977, 1988-89; *home:* Rt 1 Box 104 Verona MO 65769

GREER, VICTORIA LEE (BURR), Life Science Teacher; *b:* Port Clinton, OH; *m:* James P.; *c:* Ryan, Tiffany; *ed:* (BS) Bio, Bowling Green St Univ 1974; Grad Work, Univ of Toledo, Bowling Green St Univ; *cr:* Sci Teacher Port Clinton Jr HS 1974-; *ai:* Port Clinton Jr HS Creative Teacher Grant & Eisenhower Grant 1989; *office:* Port Clinton Jr HS E 4th St Port Clinton OH 43452

GREGG, NETTIE W., Retired Teacher; *b:* Randolph Cty, AL; *m:* Emery; *c:* Dale, Gary; *ed:* (BS) Elem Ed, Jacksonville St 1946; *cr:* Teacher Randolph & Clay Ctys 1942-82.

GREGOIRE, BARBARA MANNING, First Grade Teacher; *b:* Nashua, NH; *m:* C. Norman; *c:* Pamela Woodward, Martha Lamothe, Christoper; *ed:* (BED) Elem Ed, Keene St Coll 1945; *cr:* 6th Grade Teacher Enfield Elem Sch 1944-46; 4th Grade Teacher Wilton Elem Sch 1946-48; Kndgtn Teacher Private 1958-60; 1st/2nd Grade Teacher 1966-86, 1st Grade Teacher 1986- Temple Elem Sch; *ai:* NEA, NH Ed Assn, Con-Val Teachers Assn 1972-; *home:* Highland Ave Wilton NH 03086

GREGORIN, THOMAS S., Scndry Mathematics Teacher; *b:* Waukegan, IL; *m:* Marilyn E. Weakley; *c:* Eric T., Aimee L.; *ed:* (BA) His/Math, IA Wesleyan Coll 1971; (MA) Admin/Supervision, Roosevelt Univ 1986; Grad Stud N IL Univ & St Xavier Univ; *cr:* Classroom Teacher/Coach Novak King Elem Jr HS 1971-72; Math Instr/Coach North Chicago HS 1972-82, Adlai E Stevenson HS 1982-; *ai:* Frosh Bsbl Coach; NCTM 1986-; *office:* Adlai E Stevenson HS 16070 W Hwy 22 Prairie View IL 60069

GREGORY, ANN H., 5th Grade Teacher; *b:* Darlington, MD; *m:* George G.; *c:* Pamela G. Cohen, George G. Jr.; *ed:* (BS) Elem Ed, Univ of DE 1960; *cr:* 2nd Grade Teacher Havre de Grace Elem 1960-62; 5th Grade Teacher Meadowvale Elem 1976-; *home:* 4125 Rock Run Rd Havre De Grace MD 21078

GREGORY, ANNETTE, Music/Phys Ed/Health Teacher; *b:* Princeton, IN; *ed:* (BA) Phys Ed/Music, 1972, (MA) Scndry Ed/Phys Ed/Music, 1977 Univ of Evansville; Drug Prevention & Intervention Stu Assistance Prgms Seminar Trng; *cr:* Music/Phys Ed/ Health Teacher Milltown IN 1972-75; Band/Choral Dir/Music/Phys Ed/Health Teacher Lynnville Grade Sch & Tecumseh Jr-Sr HS 1975-; *ai:* Spon SADD, Just Say No, Stu Assistance Prgm; Girls Jr Var & Var Tennis Coach; Alpha Delta Kappa (Recording Secy, VP 1988-89); Daughters of Amer Revolution 1975-; Order of Eastern Star 1972-; Easter Seals & Heart Assn Volunteer; *office:* Lynnville Grade Sch Hwy 68 Lynnville IN 47619

GREGORY, BARBARA BRUNCKHORST, English Teacher; *b:* Cambridge, MA; *w:* Kevin S.; *ed:* (BA) Eng Cum Laude, Boston Univ 1971; (MED) Curr & Instruction/Rdng, Northeastern Univ 1980; Apple Works; Chapter 1 Cmptr Courses; *cr:* Stu Teacher Winchester HS 1971; 7th-8th Grade Soc Stud/Eng Teacher 1971-72, 7th-9th Grade Eng Teacher 1971- Joyce Mid Sch; *ai:* Sch Newspaper Adv; NEA 1971-; MA Teachers Assn 1971-; Woburn Teachers Assn 1971-; Laubach Literacy Tutor; *office:* Joyce Mid Sch Locust St Woburn MA 01801

GREGORY, CAROLYN RUTH (WELLS), English Dept Head; *b:* London, KY; *m:* Ronnie; *c:* Jackie Gwen; Kerry Le Wyn; *ed:* (BA) Eng, Cumberland Coll 1968; Rank II Eng, Eastern KY Univ 1978; *cr:* Eng Teacher Lily HS 1968-70, Bush Jr HS 1977, South Laurel Jr HS 1978-88, North Laurel Jr HS 1988-; *ai:* Spon Drama Club; KY Educl Assn 1968-; Flatwoods Church of Christ.

GREGORY, JANET FAYE (DAUBS), 3-4th Grade Classroom Teacher; *b:* Olney, IL; *m:* Dennis K.; *c:* Heidi, Darren, Justin; *ed:* (BS) Music Ed, Southern IL Univ Carbondale 1971; *cr:* K-8th Grade Music Teacher Meredosia-Chambersburg Sch 1971-74; 6th-8th Grade Lang Arts Teacher Rockford Chrstn Elem Sch 1981-86; 1st/2nd Grade Teacher 1986-87, 3rd/4th Grade Teacher 1987- West Cty Chrstn Sch; *ai:* Coord Music Prgms & Graduation Exercises; NEA/IEA 1971-74; Assn of Chrstn Schls Intnl Mem 1986-; Southside Assembly of God Church 1987-; 1st Assembly of God Church Choir Mem 1984-86; *office:* West Cnty Chrstn Sch 1951 Des Peres Rd Saint Louis MO 63131

GREGORY, KATHY L., 6th Grade Teacher; *b:* Hanford, CA; *m:* Robert A.; *c:* Marcus, Allison, Kendra; *ed:* (BA) Eng, CA St Univ 1971; *cr:* 4th-6th Grade Teacher Laton Elem Sch 1971-; *ai:* Vlybl Coach; Stu Cncl; Area Curr Cncl Rep; Canton Unified Teachers Assn Pres 1971-; *office:* Laton Elem Sch P O Box 7 Laton CA 93242

GREGORY, KATHY RAINS, Sixth Grade Teacher; *b:* Gadsden, AL; *m:* Gerald Jackson; *ed:* (BS) Music Ed, Jacksonville St Univ 1973; (MA) Admin/Supervision, Univ of AL; Elem Ed, Jacksonville St Univ; Sci, Sea Lab Daphne Island Univ of AL; Space Camp for Teachers I & II; *cr:* Teacher John S Jones Elem 1975-79, Southside Elem 1979-; *ai:* Young Astronauts Club Spon; EEA, AEA, NEA 1975-; Lions Club 1988; Theatre of Gadsden Musical Dir 1985-87; *office:* Southside Elem Sch Rt 1 Box 721 Gadsden AL 35901

GREGORY, MARY JANE, Soc Stud Teacher/Dept Chair; *b:* St Joseph, MO; *ed:* (BA) Psych/Ed, Mt St Scholastica Coll 1966; (MED) Sch Admin, Washburn Univ 1971; Numerous Univs; Menning Fnd Excel Incorporated; *cr:* Teacher Christ The King 1955-57, 1965-66, St Josephs 1957-64, Topeka Public Schls 1966-; *ai:* Debate, Forensics & Stress Prevention Team Spon; Soc Stud Dists Evening Prgm Tutor; Sch Curr Monitoring Chm; Sch of Excl Comm; Soc Stud Dept Coord; Textbook Selection Comm; Phi Delta Kappa Historian 1985-88, Outstanding Educator Awd 1985-86; Delta Kappa Gamma 1979-; Amer Psychological Assn HS Affiliate 1980-; Topeka Ed Assn Negotiating Team 1980-82; KS Ed Assn, NEA; KS-Paraguay Partnership 1969-; KS & Topeka Mental Health Assn 1972-; Survivors of Suicide (Co-Founder, Bd Mem) 1982-; Shawnee Cty Mental Health Assn Volunteer of Yr; Topeka Public Schls Cnslrs Outstanding Educator Awd; KS Bar Assns Liberty Bell Awd; Phi Delta Kappa Educator of Yr Awd; *office:* Highland Park HS 2424 California Topeka KS 66605

GREGORY, MELISSA PHILLIPS, Eighth Grade Science Teacher; *b:* Union, SC; *m:* David Joel; *c:* Kevin, Kyle, Kacie; *ed:* (BS) Elem Ed, 1977, (MED) Elem Ed, 1982 Winthrop Coll; Specialist Math St Dept; *cr:* 7th-8th Grade Math Teacher 1978-79, 8th Grade Sci Teacher 1979-80, 7th Grade Sci Teacher 1980-87, 8th Grade Sci Teacher 1987- Sims Jr HS; *ai:* Stu Government Assn Adv; Miss Sims & Talent Show Spon; UCEA, SCEA, NEA, IRA 1988-; Sims Jr HS PTA (VP 1988-89, Pres 1989-); March of Dimes Walk Sch Comm Chm 1989-; Union Dixie Youth Treas 1988-; Jr Charity League 1989-; Excelsior Elem Sch Improvement Cncl 1987-; Sims Jr HS Teacher of Yr 1988-89; *office:* Sims Jr HS Sims Dr Union SC 29379

GREGORY, RUBIE JOHNSON, Elem Basic Skills Teacher; *b:* Grayridge, MO; *m:* James Edward; *c:* Glenn, Curtis, Stan R., James Jr.; *ed:* (BS) Elem Ed, S IL Iniv 1953; Methods Courses, Lincoln Univ 1958; Sci Methods Course, Trenton St Coll 1978; Camping-Environment, Montclair St Coll 1978; Algebra Method Courses, Burlington Cty Coll; *cr:* Teacher Pinhook Elem Sch 1956-58, Hahn AFB Elem 1966-67, N Hanover Township 1967-; *ai:* Sunday Sch Teacher; Travel Consultant; NCTM 1985-; AMTNJ Bd 1987-; NEA, NJEA, BCEA 1970-; Lake Valley Civic Assn VP 1969-71; Lighthouse Church Teacher 1975-, Teacher of Yr 1986; Presidential Awd for Excl Teaching Math 1987; Mt Holyoke Coll Schlsp Summermath for Teachers 1990; *home:* 236 Villanova Ave Pemberton NJ 08068

GREGORY, SARAH LODESTRO, Fourth Grade Teacher; *b:* Jamestown, NY; *m:* Michael William; *c:* Michael Jr., Katherine, Kristine; *ed:* (BS) Elem Ed, St Univ Coll of NY Fredonia 1959; Grad Stud St Univ Coll NY Fredonia; *cr:* 1st Grade Teacher Jamestown Public Sch 1959-61, Ossining Public Sch 1961-63; 3rd Grade Teacher Vestal Public Sch 1964; Kndgtn-6th Grade Substitute Teacher Binghamton & Bemus Point NY 1965-80; 4th Grade Teacher Bemus Point Sch 1980-; *ai:* Gifted & Talented, Textbook Selection Comm; NEA 1980-; Chautauqua Cty Rdng Assn Sch Rep 1980-; NY Ed Assn (Delegate 1988-89) 1980-; Bemus Point Faculty Assn (VP 1986-87, Pres 1987-88) 1980-; Bemus Point Study Club 1975-; Bemus Point PTA 1972-; Our Lady of Lourdes Church 1971-; *office:* Bemus Point Elem Sch Liberty St Bemus Point NY 14712

GREGORY, SHARON MC WHIRTER, Teacher/Counselor; *b:* Birmingham, AL; *m:* Allen Granville Jr.; *c:* Craig B. Adams; *ed:* (BS) Eng, Univ of AL 1970; (MED) Eng Ed, Mercer Univ 1973; Sch Cnslr, GA Southern 1988; *cr:* Eng Teacher Bibb Cty Public Schls 1971-73, 1st Presbyn Day Sch 1977-85; Teacher of Gifted Prgm Monroe Cty Schls 1985-86; Eng Teacher/Jr HS Cnslr 1st Presbyn Day Sch 1986-; *ai:* Literary Team Coord; Edda Adv; GSCA 1989-; STAR Teacher; *office:* First Presbyterian Day Sch 5671 Calvin Dr Macon GA 31210

GREGORY, WINNIE STEWART, Fourth Grade Teacher; *b:* Scottsburg, IN; *c:* Ashley, Bethany; *ed:* (BS) Elem Ed, Ball St Univ 1971; Working on Masters Degree; *cr:* 1st Grade Teacher 1971-73, Kndgtn Teacher 1973 Robertson Cty Schls; 4th Grade Teacher Houston Cty Schls 1974-; *ai:* Sci Adoption Comm 1988; 4th Grade Chairperson 1983, 1986; Stu Support Team Chairperson 1986; Prof Assn of GA Educators 1980-; Oakland Baptist Church Childrens Church Dir 1988-89; Russell Elem Teacher of Yr Awd 1976; *home:* 2630 Elberta Rd Centerville GA 31028

GREGORY, WORSIE TAYLOR, 4th And 5th Grade Teacher; *b:* Dothan, AL; *m:* James M. II; *ed:* (BA) Elem Ed, 1978, (MA) Elem Ed, 1980 MI St Univ; Lansing Sch Dist Leadership Acad; *cr:* Secy Head Start Prgms 1972-73; Accounting Clerk Oldsmobile GMC 1973-80; Inspector Fisher Body GMC 1981-83; Teacher Lansing Sch Dist 1978-; *ai:* Church Youth Group Leader; Tutoring Prgm; Dir Lansing Schls Third World Affairs; Lansing Sch Ed Assn (Dir of Dept 1987-, Sch Rep 1985-87); MI Ed Assn Mem, NEA Mem 1978-; Delta Sigma Theta Mem 1980-; GSA (Co-Leader, Leader) 1980-, Leader of Yr 1987; Gregory Girls Spon 1989-; Teacher Corp Internship 1977-79; *office:* Wainwright Elem Sch 4200 Wainwright Ave Lansing MI 48911

GREIG, CATHERINE BERG, English Teacher; *b:* Elmhurst, IL; *m:* Gary Stanley; *c:* Jonathan; *ed:* (BA) Span/Ed, Eastern Coll 1977; (MA) Eng Lang/Literature, Univ of Chicago 1985; (MA) Theology, Fuller Theological Seminary 1986; *cr:* 5th/6th Grade Teacher Costa Rican Acad 1977-78; Eng Teacher Colegio Metodista 1978-81, Lourdes HS 1985-; *ai:* Comm Mem for Natl Honor Society; *office:* Lourdes H S 4034 W 56th Chicago IL 60629

GREIG, REBECCA LYNNE, Mathematics Department Chair; *b:* Lafayette, LA; *c:* Ross, Ben, Luke; *ed:* (BS) Math Ed, Univ of SW LA 1972; (MA) Ed/Math, N MI Univ 1975; Post Grad Stud; *cr:* Math Teacher Caledonia Jr HS 1972-73, Acadiana HS 1977-78, Longview Prep Inst 1978-80; Math Teacher/Dept Head Our Lady of Fatima HS 1980-82, St Thomas More HS 1982-87; Math Teacher Lafayette HS 1987-88; Math Teacher/Dept Head St Thomas More HS 1988-; *ai:* Mu Alpha Theta Spon; LA Teachers of Math 1989-, Outstanding Math Teacher 1989; NCEA 1980-; *office:* St Thomas More HS 450 E Farrel Rd Lafayette LA 70508

GREIMANN, STEVEN PAUL, Math/Religion Teacher; *b:* Sheffield, IA; *m:* Eaine Carol Waiser; *c:* Rachel A.; *ed:* (BS) Math, Concordia Coll 1979; Skills for Adolescence for Quest Intnl East TX St Univ; *cr:* Prin/Teacher St Paul Luth Sch 1979-83; Teacher KS City Luth HS 1983-84; Athletic Dir/Teacher Luth HS 1944-; *ai:* Athletic Dir Luth HS; Head Soccer, Bsbl Coach; (Dist III AA 1985-89, Pres. VP 1989-) Coach of Yr 1986-88; TX Assn of Private & Parochial Schls Dist II AA (VP 1985-89, Pres 1989) Coach of Yr Bsbl 1986-88; *office:* Lutheran HS 8494 Stults Rd Dallas TX 75243

GRENCHIK, GEORGE J., Junior High School Teacher; *b:* East Chicago, IN; *m:* Marie J. Suguitan; *c:* George G., Daniel Z.; *ed:* (BA) His, St Josephs Coll Calumet 1968; Various Whole Lang Wkshps, Soc Stud Seminars, Religious Ed Trng, Archdiocese of Chicago; *cr:* Permanent Substitute Teacher St Hedwig Sch 1969; Jr HS Teacher St Victor Sch 1969-; *ai:* Vlybl Coach; Faculty Rep Sch Bd; Soc Stud Chm; 8th Grade Play Asst Dir; NCEA Mem 1970-79; St Victor Athletic Assn (Faculty Rep, Pres) 1972-88; St Victor Peace & Justice Comm Mem 1981-87; St Victor Youth Prgm (Co-Dir, Volunteer) 1976-89; *office:* St Victor Sch 548 Price St Calumet City IL 60409

GRENERT, BEVERLY DIANE, Curriculum Supervisor; *b:* Springfield, MA; *m:* William H.; *c:* Laura L.; *ed:* (BA) Bio, Amer Intnl Coll 1960; (MED) Elem Ed, Antioch/NC Grad Sch 1985; Grad Work Sci Ed; *cr:* 10th/11th Grade Bio/Chem Teacher Arlington Sch 1964-66; 7th-9th Grade Math/Sci Teacher Hopkinton HS 1966-71; Self Employed Browsery Gift Shop 1971-82; 7th/8th Grade Math/Sci Teacher Weare Mid Sch 1982-89; Curr Supvr/Health Ed Teacher NH St Dept of Ed 1989-; *ai:* NH Youth Kids At Risk Sub Comm; NH Sch Bd Assn Risk Comm; Durham Public Health Sci & Math Task Force; Pediatric AIDS Task Force; NH ASCD (Secy 1989-, Bd of Dir 1988-89); NEA 1983-; Natl ASCD 1986-; Commissioners Task Force AIDS 1990; NH Sci Teachers Assn Bd Dirs 1986-89; Natl Sci Fnd Grant 1961-62, 1984; Natl Sci Fnd Publiciation 1985; *office:* NH St Dept of Ed 101 Pleasant St Concord NH 03301

GRENFELL, MARY ROBERTA JARBOE, Debate Coach; *b:* Dallas, TX; *m:* Richard W.; *c:* Charles W., Lee R. Graves; *ed:* (BA) Speech/Soc Stud, Univ of Houston 1972; Speech Courses, Univ of Houston; *cr:* Jr HS Teacher Aldine Ind Sch Dist 1972-77; Debate Coach Klein HS 1979-; *ai:* Speech Club Spon; TX Speech Comm Assn; TX Forensic Assn Archivist 1988-; Natl Forensic League Dist Comm Mem 1987-; Delta Kappa Gamma 1990; Diamond Key Coach; *office:* Klein HS 16715 Stuebner Airline Klein TX 77379

GRENGS, BARBARA KRAUSE, 8th/9th Grade English Teacher; *b:* St Cloud, MN; *m:* John G.; *c:* Carrie E.; *ed:* (BS) Eng, WI St Univ River FalLs 1966; (MA) Eng/Amer Lit, St Cloud St Univ 1969; Post Grad Psych & Lit, Univ of MN; *cr:* 11th/12th Grade Eng Teacher Hastings HS 1967; Teaching Asst St Cloud St Univ 1967-68; Resource Center Librarian North Jr HS 1968-69; Lang Art Teacher Roseville Area Schls 1969-; *ai:* Childrens Theatre Asst Stage Mgr Grant; Co-Authored Career Ed Book; *office:* Roseville Area Mid Sch 15 E Cty Rd B-2 Little Canada MN 55117

GRENIER, KENNETH L., 7th/8th Grade Math Teacher; *b:* Worcester, MA; *m:* Cheryl Cobb; *c:* Jacqueline, Kimberley; *ed:* (BS) Ed, Univ of Bridgeport 1966; (MS) Math Ed, W CT Univ 1972; *cr:* 6th-8th Grade Math Teacher Roosevelt Sch 1966-69; 6th Grade Self Contained Teacher Whisconier Sch 1968-72; 8th Grade Math Teacher Brookfield Jr HS 1972-86; 7th/8th Grade Math Teacher Whisconier Mid Sch 1986-; *ai:* Tennis & Bsktbl Coach HS & Mid Sch; Phi Delta Kappa 1987-; Brookfield Ed Assn (Pres, Treas, VP); *office:* Whisconier Mid Sch W Whisconier Rd Brookfield CT 06804

GRENINGER, RICHARD DELANO, 7th & 8th Grade Math Teacher; *b:* Tylersville, PA; *m:* Cynthia Jane Leiby; *c:* Wade D.; *ed:* (BA) Chem/Physics/Math, Lock Haven Univ 1962; *cr:* Math Teacher Lock Haven HS 1962-; *ai:* Clock Operator Jr/Sr HS Boys & Girls Bsktbl, Ftbl, Wrestling, Tra ck 1962-; Sch Photographer; PSEA 1962-; NEA 1968-; Service Awd Lock Haven Booster Club; *office:* Lock Haven HS W Church St Lock Haven PA 17745

GRESH, CAROL STEPHENIE (LONG), Second Grade Teacher; *b:* Johnstown, PA; *m:* John; *c:* Stephen; *ed:* (BA) Elem Ed, Univ of Pittsburgh 1970; (MED) Elem Ed, Indiana Univ of PA 1972; *cr:* Teacher Greater Johnstown Sch Dist 1970-; *ai:* Summit Chapel Choir Pianist; NEA, PSEA, GJEA.

GRESHAM, LYNN E., 1st Grade Teacher; *b:* Chicago, IL; *m:* Harold; *c:* Christopher, Phillip; *ed:* (BS) Elem Ed, Ball St Univ 1970; (MS) Ed, Purdue Univ 1973; *cr:* 1st Grade Teacher Edgewood Sch 1970-77, Knapp Sch 1977-79; 4th Grade Teacher Jefferson Sch 1983; 5th Grade Teacher Eastport Sch 1984; 1st Grade Teacher Knapp Sch 1985-; *ai:* Care; NEA, IN St Teachers Assn 1970-; Intnl Rdng Assn 1985-; Exchangette Club Bd Mem 1987-; *office:* Knapp Sch 321 Bolka Ave Michigan City IN 46360

GRESHAM, MARGARET PATTERSON, Soc Stud/Psych Teacher; *b:* Medford, OR; *m:* James E.; *c:* Thomas R.; *ed:* (AA) Liberal Art, Texarkana Jr Coll 1964; (BS) Scndry Ed, TX Tech 1967; (MS) Scndry Guidance, Memphis St Univ 1974; (PHD) Adult Ed, Univ of S MS 1985; Soc Stud Composite Sul Ross Univ; *cr:* Teacher Bowie Cty Schls 1967-69; Teacher/Cnslr/Admin Memphis City Schls 1969-86; Teacher Socorro Ind Schls 1986-; *ai:* Var Chrldrs; PSI Club; Peer Asst Leadership of Socorro; At-Risk Montwood HS Steering Comm; Stu Act Dir Montwood HS; Phi Delta Kappa (Pres, VP, Secy) 1974-; Kappa Delta Pi 1984-; ASCD 1980-; Bus/Prof Women 1988-; Whos Who in Amer Educators; Teacher of Month Socorro HS; Selected for Competition Christine Mc Caulley Grant & TX Humanities Teacher; *office:* Socorro HS 10150 Alameda Ave El Paso TX 79927

GRESSETT, SUE COOK, 4th Grade Teacher; *b:* Colorado City, TX; *m:* Leroy Donald; *c:* Randy, Tommy; *ed:* (BS) Elem Ed, Hardin-Simmons Univ 1972; Post Grad Stud HSU, ACU; *cr:* 3rd Grade Teacher Northeast Elem 1972-88; 4th Grade Teacher Stanfield Elem 1988-; *ai:* Spelling Bee Spon; TSTA, NEA, CTA 1972-; 1st Baptist Church Youth Leader 1966-80; Upper CO SWCD Outstanding Conservation Teacher 1985; *home:* 3210 42nd St Snyder TX 79549

GRETLER, MARY-ELLEN NICHOLS, Fourth Grade Teacher; *b:* Derby, CT; *m:* Bill; *ed:* (BA) Sociology/Ed, Coll of Our Lady of the Elms 1965; (MS) Ed, S CT 1971; *cr:* 5th Grade Teacher 1965-66, 4th Grade Teacher 1966-67, 5th Grade Teacher 1967-68 Mary Abbott Sch; 2nd-4th Grade Teacher El Toyon Sch 1968-; *ai:* Natl City Elem Teacher Assn (2nd VP, 1st VP, Membership Chairperson); CA Teachers Assn WHO Awd 1983; *office:* El Toyon-Natl Sch Dist 2000 Division St National City CA 92050

GREUTMAN, RICHARD PAUL, Social Studies Teacher; *b:* Williston, ND; *m:* Diane Nordloef; *c:* Chelsea; *ed:* (AA) His, Univ of ND Williston 1973; (BA) His, Univ of ND Grand Forks 1975; *cr:* Teacher Williston Jr HS 1975-; *ai:* 8th Grade Ftbl & 7th-8th Grade Wrestling Coach; Williston Ed Assn Pres 1984-85; ND Cncl for Soc Stud 1984-; Williston Jaycees Pres 1979-80, Keyman Awd 1978; ND Jaycees Dist Dir 1980-81; *office:* Williston Jr HS 612 1st Ave W Williston ND 58801

GREVE, KATHY TEGELER, Music Teacher; *b:* Manchester, IA; *m:* Michael R.; *c:* Hannah, Mason; *ed:* (BA) Music Ed, St Ambrose Univ 1979; *cr:* Music Teacher St Marys Sch 1980-; *ai:* Choir Dir 7th/8th/9th Grade Choir; Music Coord St Marys Parish; *office:* St Mary'S Elem Sch 132 W Butler Manchester IA 52057

GREWE, CONNIE JEAN (KEMNITZ), Ninth Grade English Teacher; *b:* Granite Falls, MN; *m:* Charles N.; *c:* Susan, Kathy; *ed:* (BS) Eng/Lang Art, St Cloud St Univ 1968; *cr:* Eng/Lang Art Teacher White Bear Lake Public Sch 1968-69, Willmar Public Schls 1969-; *ai:* Censorship Comm; MN Cncl Teachers of Eng,

NCTE 1984-; Willmar Ed Assn, MN Ed Assn, NEA; The Barn Cmmty Theatre Pres 1982-85; Calvary Luth Church 1981-; Chairperson of Writing Comm That Developed Dist Writing Pgrm K-12th; Presented Prgm at St Conference; *office:* Willmar Jr HS 201 SE Willmar Ave Willmar MN 56201

GREY, LINDA JOY, Sixth Grade Teacher; *b:* Denver, CO; *ed:* (BA) Bio, Univ of CO 1974; (MAT) Bio/Ed, Duke Univ 1975; Grad Stud; *cr:* Sci Teacher Brewster Jr HS 1974-75; Sci Teacher 1976-83, Gifted & Talented Resource Teacher 1983-87, Lang Art Teacher 1987- East Mid Sch; *ai:* Lang Art Curr Comm; Sign Lang & Homework Clubs; Phi Beta Kappa 1974; Aurora Ed Assn 1976-; PTSA 1976-; Aurora Public Schls Distinguished Teacher Awd 1987; CO St Teacher of Yr Honorable Mention 1987; Aurora Public Schls Apple Awd 1986; Golden Key NHS 1986; Dean List 1974, 1984, 1985; Aurora Ed Fnd Mini Grant 1989-.

GREY, MARIAN PERKINS, 5th Grade Teacher; *b:* New Haven, CT; *m:* Ross M.; *c:* Jennifer, Michael R., Elizabeth Grey Crane, Julie Grey Mac Kay; *ed:* (BA) Elem Ed, 1951, (MS) 1954 S CT St Coll; *cr:* 4th-6th Grade Teacher Center Sch 1951-55; 3rd-5th Grade Teacher Mary Tracy Sch 1960-62; Substitute Teacher Woodbridge Sch System 1960-62; 5th-8th Grade Part Time Rdng Tutor Ansonia Rdng Tutorial Title I Prgm 1968-76; 5th Grade Teacher St Louis Sch 1976-; *ai:* 8th Grade Graduation Prgm Coord; Sch Prgms & Plays Dir; Grandparents Day & Fundraiser Initiator; NCEA, St Louis Sch Bd Teacher Rep; PTA Secy; WFA Pres 1953-55; GSA; St Louis Sch Evaluation & Accreditation Steering Comm Chairperson; *home:* 31 Seymour Rd Woodbridge CT 06525

GREY, MARILYN CRON, Retired Elementary Teacher; *b:* Detroit, MI; *m:* Lawrence Orin; *c:* Michael, Mark, Matthew, Mitchell Cron; *ed:* (BS) Elem Ed, E MI 1950; *cr:* 1st Grade Teacher Jefferson Schls 1950-58, Ramona Elem; Teacher of Spec Ed Walnut Elem; Teacher Midland; *ai:* MI Ed Assn, CO Ed Assn, NEA; Keep CO Beautiful 1980.

GRICE, SUSAN BROOME, 5th/6th Grade Teacher; *b:* Charlotte, NC; *m:* Mc Heron; *c:* Kristen, Karyn; *ed:* (BS) Elem Ed, Appalachian St Univ 1974; *cr:* Classroom Teacher Lingerfeldt Elem Sch 1974-; *ai:* Sch Steering Comm; Spelling Bee Coord; Sch Assistance Team; Media Materials Comm; NC Assn of Ed; NEA; Maylo United Meth Church; United Meth Women 1976- Lifetime Mem Awd 1987; Lingerfeldt Teacher of Yr 1989; Lingerfeldt Human Relations Awd 1979; *home:* 2442 Pebblestone Ct Gastonia NC 28054

GRIDER, CARRIE DE YAMPERT, Home Economics Teacher; *b:* Selma, AL; *c:* Ronald L. II; *ed:* (BS) Home Ec Ed, 1971, (MED) Home Ec Ed, 1975 Tuskegee Univ; (MA) Speech Comm, Univ of Montevallo 1986; *cr:* St Specialist/Instr KY St Univ 1975-77; Teacher Crawford Jr HS 1977-79; Registrar/Admin Cnslr/Instr Concordia Coll 1981-85; Teacher Southside HS 1985-; *ai:* FHA Adv; Voc Dept Chairperson; Courtesy Comm Mem; AVA 1985-; Amer Home Ec Assn 1989-; AL Ed Assn, FHA 1985-; Reformed Presbyn Church Deacon 1985-; Encore Theater Bd Mem 1980-88; Teen Coalition 1987-88; Public Speaking; Low Rdng Level Publications; Article Published; *home:* PO Box 706 Selma AL 36702

GRIDLEY, GAYLE M., English Teacher; *b:* Bayshore, NY; *m:* Richard Courtland; *c:* Barbara, Richard; *ed:* (BA) Eng, 1982, (MS) Eng/Ed, 1987 St Univ of NY New Paltz; Bus Admin, Rider Coll; *cr:* Secy C W Hill Inc 1970-72; Artist 1972-75; Staff Accountant Nelco Inc 1975-80; Eng Teacher Valley Cntrl Mid Sch 1982-85, Valley Cntrl HS 1985-; *ai:* NY St United Teachers; NCTE 1982-; Amer Cncl for Intnl Study Cnslr 1989-; *office:* Valley Cntrl HS 63-75 Rt 17k Montgomery NY 12549

GRIEBENOW, KEITH C., 5th Grade Teacher; *b:* Rochester, MN; *m:* Dawn Lehse; *c:* Grant; *ed:* (BS) Elem Ed, Bemidji St Univ 1977; (MS) Elem Ed/Gifted Ed, Mankato St Univ 1983; Univ of MN, Coll of St Thomas; *cr:* 5th Grade Teacher Mahtomedi Public Schls 1977-78; 4th Grade Teacher Winnebago Public Schls 1978-79; 5th Grade Teacher Lakeville Public Schls 1979-; *ai:* Lakeville Fed of Teachers 1980-; *office:* Orchard Lake ELem Sch 16531 Klamath Trl Lakeville MN 55044

GRIER, JACQUELINE ANN, English/Journalism Teacher; *b:* Grinnell, IA; *m:* Joel Mark; *c:* Bradley, Bret; *ed:* (BS) Eng, Mankato St Univ 1972; *cr:* Eng/Journalism Teacher Monroe Cmmty Sch 1973-87, Prairie City-Monroe Cmmty Sch 1988-; *ai:* Sch Newspaper Adv; NCTE; IA HS Press Assn St Conference Speaker; *office:* Prairie City-Monroe Cmmty Sch Hwy 163 Monroe IA 50170

GRIER, OLIVIA BANKS, Teacher/GED Dir/Data Collector; *b:* Social Circle, GA; *m:* Walter Lewis; *c:* Tonya R., Cheveda D., Dominque M.; *ed:* (BS) Elem Ed, Savannah St 1973; Working Towards Masters Elem Sch Counseling; *cr:* Teacher 1973-, Data Collector 1975-, GED Dir 1988- Social Circle City Schls; *ai:* Curr, Comptr, Textbook Comm; GA Assn of Educators Membership 1973-; Natl Assn of Educators (VP 1975-76, Pres 1976-77, Secy 1977-78, Treas 1978-87) 1973-; PTO Co-Pres Outstanding Work 1983-84; Bus Ladies of Today Mem Outstanding Work Cmmty 1986-87; Soc Circle Elem Sch Teacher of Yr 1983-84; *home:* 60 Otelia Ln Covington GA 30209

GRIES, LARRY FRANCIS, Teacher; *b:* Evansville, IN; *ed:* (BA) Eng, St Edwards Univ 1966; (MA) Art, Schiller Coll 1972; (MA) Amer Stud/Comm Art, Notre Dame Univ 1974; Teacher Certificate S IN Univ 1984; NJ Writing Project; *cr:* Part-Time Teacher Bishop Hendrickson HS 1966-73; Lecturer Johnson & Wales Coll & RI Comm Coll & S IN Univ & Univ of TX San Antonio & Palo Alto Comm Coll 1970-; Teacher John Marshall HS 1990; *ai:* NCTE, TX Joint Cncl Teachers of Eng; San Antonio Cncl of Teachers Eng 1984-; Columbia Univ Press Assn 1st Place Awd 1989; *office:* John Marshall HS 8000 Lobo Ln San Antonio TX 78240

GRIESER, WENDY SUE, Second Grade Teacher; *b:* Buffalo, NY; *ed:* (BS) Elem Ed, SUC Geneseo 1973; (MS) Ed, SUC Buffalo 1978; *cr:* 1st Grade Teacher 1973-78, 2nd Grade Teacher 1978- Maple Street Elem Sch 1978-; *ai:* Satellite Coord for Greater Capital Region Teacher Center; Hudson Falls Teachers Assn Maple Street Sch Building Rep 1989-.

GRIFFEN, CAROL M., Math-Algebra/Cluster Leader; *b:* Hoboken, NJ; *m:* John W.; *c:* Michelle L., Sean W., Casey P.; *ed:* (BA) Math, St Joseph Coll 1968; Math Ed, Salem St Coll; *cr:* Math Teacher Pickering Jr HS 1968-70; Math/Algebra/ Geometry/Algebra II Teacher Eastern Jr HS/Breed Jr HS/Lynn Vocational Tech Jr HS 1970-; *ai:* Cluster Leader; Yrbk Advisor; NTCM 1967/1983; Comm Dev Citizens Adv Bd 1981-88; Fire Relief Fund Chairperson 1983-88; Hidden Valley Assoc Bd of Dir/ Recreation Chairperson 1985-88; Democratic City Comm-Ward V-Chair.

GRIFFIN, CATHERINE ELIZABETH, Mathematics Teacher; *b:* Edgewood, MD; *ed:* (BA) Math/Fr, Calvin Coll 1987; *cr:* Camp Cnslr/Swimming Instr Fair Winds GSA Cncl 1984-86; Mgr of Kick Pool City of Kalamazoo 1987-88; Math Teacher Bronson Jr/ Sr HS 1987-; *ai:* Jr Class Adv; *office:* Bronson Jr/Sr HS E Grant St Bronson MI 49028

GRIFFIN, DONALD LEWIS, Agribusiness Teacher; *b:* Ashland, AL; *m:* Sheila Freeman; *c:* Christopher; *ed:* (BS) Agribusiness Ed, Auburn Univ 1982; *cr:* Teacher Goodwater HS 1982-88, Cntrl HS 1988-; *ai:* FFA Adv 1982-; Coaching 1983-85; AEA, NEA, AVA 1982-; Athletic Booster 1983-85; Abel Baptist Church Teacher 1988-; Coosa Cty Cattlemans Assn 1982-; Honorary St Farmer Degree 1988; Outstanding Young Men of America 1988; Teacher of Yr Goodwater HS; *office:* Central HS Rt 2 Box 62 Rockford AL 35136

GRIFFIN, EDNA KOONCE, Health/Physical Ed Teacher; *b:* Kinston, NC; *m:* Warner S.; *ed:* (BS) Heatlh/Phys Ed, NC Cntrl Univ 1965; *cr:* Teacher Central Acad 1965-66, Campostella Jr HS 1966-70, Rosemont Mid Sch 1970-; *office:* Rosemont Mid Sch 1401 Auburn Ave Norfolk VA 23513

GRIFFIN, JANET KRAMER, Fourth Grade Teacher; *b:* Cleveland, OH; *m:* James B. Jr.; *c:* James III, Genevieve, Rebecca, Charles; *ed:* (BA) Elem Ed, Univ of Edinboro 1954; *cr:* 4th Grade Teacher Tracy Elem Sch 1965-; *ai:* NEA, PA St Ed Assn, Millcreek Ed Assn, Intnl Rdng Assn.

GRIFFIN, JERI LYNN, Teacher/Acting Asst Principal; *b:* Charlottesville, VA; *ed:* (AA) Child Care, Piedmont VA Comm Coll 1976; (BS) Mid Sch, Longwood Coll 1980; (MS) Admin/ Supervision, Univ of VA 1990; *cr:* Teacher 1980-, Acting Asst Prin 1987- Fluvanna Cty Mid Sch; *ai:* At-Risk Coord Fluvanna Cty Mid Sch; Leadership, Faculty Advisory, Task Force Comm; NEA, VEA, FEA 1980-; ASCD 1989-; VMSA 1987-; Teacher of Yr Awd MACCA 1988; *home:* PO Box 432 Fork Union VA 23055

GRIFFIN, JO BETH RITCHIE, Gifted-Teacher; *b:* Griffin, GA; *c:* Beth Story; *ed:* (AB) Psych, Emory Univ 1956; (MED) Elem Ed, Univ of GA 1973; Archaeology, Univ of VA; *cr:* Teacher Putnam Bd of Ed; *ai:* Quiz Bowl; Natl GA Beef Staff Dev; Delta Kappa Gamma Secy; Grant Univ of VA; Archaeology Star Teacher; *home:* 924 Monticello Rd Eatonton GA 31024

GRIFFIN, LINDA B., 1st Grade Teacher; *b:* Pontotoc, MS; *m:* Alvin L.; *c:* Amy, J. D.; *ed:* (BED) Elem Ed, 1975, (MED) Elem Ed, 1976 Delta St Univ; *cr:* 1st-3rd Grade Teacher Oakland Elem Sch 1976-78; 1st Grade Teacher South Pontotoc Sch 1978-; *office:* South Pontotoc Sch Rt 5 Pontotoc MS 38863

GRIFFIN, MARGARET M., Spanish Teacher; *b:* Waterbury, CT; *m:* Barry J.; *c:* Neil L.; *ed:* (BA) Fr/Span, St Joseph Coll 1980; Working Toward Masters Degree in Career Counseling, Cntrl Ct St Univ; *cr:* Teacher Memorial Mid Sch 1981-87, Rochambeau Mid Sch 1989-; *ai:* Cncl of Lang Teachers 1985-87, 1989-; Carter Heights Condominium Assn (Pres 1987, Secy 1989-); *office:* Rochambeau Mid Sch 100 Peter Rd Southbury CT 06488

GRIFFIN, ROBERT JIM, PECE Coordinator; *b:* Columbus, GA; *c:* Robert J. II; *ed:* (BS) Sci Ed, Albany St Coll 1970; Guidance & Cnslng, Univ of GA; *cr:* Child Care Worker Albany Youth Dev Ctr 1965-70; Sci Instructor Columbus Jr HS 1970-72; PECE Coord T H Fort Jr HS 1972-; *ai:* Adv Stud Cncl; Fort Against Drugs; Girls Bsktbl Coach; Mgr Eastern Little League; Muscogee Cty Assn of Educators 1970-; AVA 1972-; GA Assn Educators 1970-; YMCA Mem 1980-85; Kappa Alpha Psi Mem 1963-; NAACP Mem 1983-; Nom Teacher of Yr 1981; Former Chairperson Vocational Dept; Soc Civic 25 Club-Cert of Recognition; *home:* 3561 Hilton Ave C-10 Columbus GA 31904

GRIFFIN, RODERIC B., JR., Spanish Teacher; *b:* Roxboro, NC; *ed:* (BA) Span, Univ of NC Chapel Hill 1963; (MA) Span, Middlebury Coll 1964; (PHD) Span, IN Univ Bloomington 1972; (MA) Fr, Middlebury Coll 1985; Music Theory & Organ, Mc Gill Univ 1979; Art His, Columbia Univ 1977; *cr:* Span Teacher Taft Sch 1964-66; Teaching Assoc IN Univ 1966-68; Span Teacher/ Foreign Lang Chm Person Sr HS 1971-74; Teacher/Foreign Lang Chm/Dir of Stud Verde Valley Sch 1974-85; Teacher/Foreign Lang Chm Canterbury Sch 1985-; *ai:* Mem & Recorder for Faculty Curr Review Comm; Span Club Faculty Spon; Coord for Foreign Lang Festival; Organist; Modern Lang Assn 1969-74; NEA 1970-74; Phi Eta Sigma; Phi Beta Kappa; 1st Presbyn Church Choir 1985-; NDFL Title IV Fellowships 1968-70; Grants to Study Art His, Music Theory, Travel at Verde Valley Sch; *office:* The Canterbury Sch 3210 Smith Rd Fort Wayne IN 46804

GRIFFIN, SUSAN, Health & Phys Ed Dept Teacher; *b:* Rocky Mount, NC; *ed:* (BS) Health/Phys Ed, 1966, (MAED) Phys Ed, 1973 E Carolina Univ; *cr:* Teacher/Coach Charles B Aycock HS 1966-68; Teacher/Coach/Dept Head Greenwood Jr HS 1968-; *ai:* Phys Fitness Club; Concession Stand at Ball Games; Core Chairperson; NCAE, NCAHPERD; *office:* Greenwood Jr HS 3209 E Ash St Goldsboro NC 27530

GRIFFIN, VALERIE ODESSA, Resource Teacher; *b:* Fredricksburg, VA; *ed:* (BA) Elem Ed-Cum Laude, VA Union Univ 1962; (MED) Rdng; Univ of VA 198; *cr:* 3rd-4th Grades Teacher Cavalier Manor Elem 1962-66; 4th Grade Teacher, Union Elem 1966-69; Bowling Green Elem 1969-88; Rdng Specialist Bowling Green Elem 1988-; *ai:* Stu Cncl Prgm Comm Adv; Rdng Comm; Young Authors Comm; Gifted Ed Comm; Writing Comm; Rappalhannock Area Reading Cncl 1987- Caroline Ed Assn 1963-; VA Ed Assn 1963-; NEA 1963-; Bapt Church Chancel Choir Pres 1976-79; Caroline Cty Chamber of Commerce 1984; Distinguished Teacher Awd; *home:* 211 Harris St Fredericksburg VA 22401

GRIFFIN, VIVIAN ANN, Geography Teacher; *b:* Sebring, FL; *ed:* (BS) Soc Stud, FL A&M Univ 1978; *cr:* Teacher Madison HS 1978-80, Lake Placid Mid Sch 1981-; *ai:* Cheerleading Spon; Soc Stud Chairperson Dept Head; Outstanding Soc Stud Teacher Lake Placid Mid Sch 1989-.

GRIFFING, BETTY V., Communications Dept Chair; *b:* Lawn, TX; *ed:* (BS) His, Howard Payne Coll 1961; Speech & Drama, W TX St Univ; Musical Drama TX Advertising; *cr:* 9th-12th Grade Eng Teacher Clint HS 1961-64; Eng/Drama/Speech Teacher Dimmitt HS 1964-67; Speech/Drama/Eng Teacher Socorro HS 1967-69; Speech/Drama/His Teacher Riverside HS 1969-; *ai:* Comm Dept Chm; Youth for Christ Intnl Spon; Speech & Drama Team, Mock Trial, Academic Decathlon Coach; TX Classroom Teacher Mem 1980-; TX Speech Assn 1988-; N Loop Baptist Chm Budget & Finances Comm 1988-; Teacher of Yr 1987; Dist & St Contests in Speech/Drama & Mock Trial Winner; *home:* 8461 Castner #47 El Paso TX 79907

GRIFFITH, HELENE, Counselor; *b:* Birmingham, AL; *ed:* (BA) Bio/Psych, Rhodes 1962; (MA) Counseling, 1965, (MA) Stu Personnel, 1970 Memphis St Univ; Cmptr Trng, St Tech 1985-; Ed/Sociology, Memphis St Univ 1980-81; *cr:* Teacher Humes HS 1962-65; Teacher/Cnslr White Station HS 1965-; *ai:* Beta Club Spon; Memphis Ed Assn, TN Ed Assn, W TN Assn for Counseling & Dev, NEA; *office:* White Station HS 514 S Perkins Memphis TN 38117

GRIFFITH, JAN PRINTUP, Elementary Teacher; *b:* Albany, GA; *c:* Rebecca, Jeremy H.; *ed:* (BSED) Elem Ed, 1968, (MSED) Elem Ed, 1969 GA Southern Coll; *cr:* Phys Ed Teacher GA Southern Coll 1968-69; Teacher Isabella Elem 1969-70, Combs New Heights Elem 1970-85, Wright Elem 1985-86, Combs New Heights Elem 1986-; *ai:* FTP, NEA, OCEA; Jr League Sustaining Mem; Okaloosa Cty Assn for Retarded Citizens; Teacher of Yr Twice; FL Master Teacher 1985-87; *home:* 727 W Sunset Blvd Fort Walton Beach FL 32548

GRIFFITH, JULIA K., Second Grade Teacher; *b:* Hillsboro, OH; *m:* John P. Hiestand; *ed:* (AA) Ed, 1970, (BS) Ed, 1972, (MA) Curr/Instruction, 1976 Univ of Cincinnati; Inservice Trng; *cr:* 1st Grade Teacher Fairfield Schls 1972-73; 2nd Grade Teacher Hillsboro City Schls 1973-; *office:* Webster Elem Sch 265 W Walnut Hillsboro OH 45133

GRIFFITH, MARY CARANO, Third Grade Teacher; *b:* Mc Alester, OK; *m:* Richard H.; *c:* Gina; *ed:* (BA) Foreign Lang, 1973, (MS) Elem Ed, 1980 SE St Univ; *cr:* 7th Grade Teacher 1974-75, 3rd Grade Teacher 1975- Krebs Sch; *ai:* OK Ed Assn, NEA 1974-; *office:* Krebs Sch P O Box 67 Krebs OK 74554

GRIFFITH, MINERVA JO, Mathematics Teacher; *b:* Clay City, KY; *m:* Virgil; *c:* Debra L. Fenwick; *ed:* (BS) Math, Univ of KY 1953; (MTM) Math, Purdue Univ 1961; Grad Stud Purdue Univ 1965; *cr:* Math Teacher Henderson Cty HS 1953-57, Mt Vernon HS 1957-65, Noblesville HS 1968, IN St Univ 1968-70, Mississinewa HS 1976-; *ai:* NEA 1953-; ISTA 1957-; MTA 1976-; Purdue Univ Fellowship 1959-61; *office:* Mississinewa HS 205 E North H Street Gas City IN 46933

GRIFFITH, SHIRLEY MILLER, Second Grade Teacher; *b:* Chillicothe, MO; *M:* Stephen J.; *c:* Jeff, Amy; *ed:* (BS) Elem Ed, 1974; (MA) Counseling, 1979 Univ of MO; Cmptr Coursework-Economics-Writing Instutitute; Effective Schls Madeline Hunter; Staff Dev/Peer Coaching; Assertive Discipline; *cr:* 1st-3rd Grade Teacher Mill Creek Elem 1974-; *ai:* Steering Comm North Central Accreditation; ITV Building Chm; Intnl Rdng Assn; Jaycees Outstanding Young Educator 1st Runner Up 1985; PTA; Chamber of Commerce KC Star Excl Teaching Nom; *office:* Mill Creek Elem Sch 2601 N Liberty Independence MO 64050

GRIFFITHS, DARLENE MULLEK, Fourth-Fifth Grade Teacher; *b:* Royal Oaks, MI; *w:* John (dec); *c:* Fred, Tim, Chris; *ed:* (BS) Ed/Soc Stud, NM St Univ 1979; *cr:* 2nd Grade Teacher 1979-80, 4th-5th Grade Teacher 1980- Roosevelt Elem; *ai:* OM Dir; Talented & Gifted Roosevelt Sch Coord; *home:* 647 Pacific Terr Klamath Falls OR 97601

GRIFFITHS, LINDA LIEDKE, Sixth Grade Teacher; *b:* Pittsburgh, PA; *m:* Stephen R.; *ed:* (BA) Psych/Ed, Seton Hill Coll 1974; (MA) Ed, Temple Univ 1981; Cert Counseling K-12th, Trenton St Coll 1990; Trng in Gifted Ed, Positive Discipline, Outdoor Ed; *cr:* 3rd Grade Teacher 1974-77, 5th Grade Teacher 1977-80, 6th Grade Teacher 1980- Pennsbury Sch Dist; *ai:* Asst Coach Var Girls Track; Coord Wm Penn Yrbk; Chairperson Disaffected Stu Comm; FAD Comm Spon; PEA, PSEA 1974-; AACD 1990; Lake Underwood Club 1982-; Team Leader 1981-; Stu Affairs Comm; *office:* William Penn Mid Sch 600 South Olds Blvd Fairless Hills PA 19030

GRIFKA, DALE JOSEPH, Mathematics Department Chair; *b:* Bad Axe, MI; *ed:* (BA) Math, MI St Univ 1987; Working Toward Masters Admin; *cr:* Math Dept Chm Peck Jr/Sr HS 1987-; *ai:* Asst Athletic Dir, Var Vlybl, Boys/Girls Track Coach; Jr Class, Stu Leadership Adv; Peck Ed Assn Secy; Bad Axe Jaycees Mem 1982-88; Peck Boosters Club Secy; *home:* 385 W Peck Rd Peck MI 48466

GRIGAS, DEBORAH DURAN, 6th Grade Science Teacher; *b:* Boston, MA; *m:* Paul F.; *c:* Dacia L., Dane E.; *ed:* (AA) Liberal Art, Massasoit Comm Coll 1968; (BS) Elem Ed, Bridgewater St Coll 1971; Addl Stud Inst & Organization in Elem Ed, Sci, Related Fields; *cr:* 6th Grade Teacher Highlands Elem Sch 1971-72; 6th Grade Sci Teacher South Mid Sch 1972-79; 5th-6th Grade Sci Teacher Morrison Elem Sch 1979-81; 6th Grade Sci Teacher South Mid Sch 1981-; *ai:* South Mid Sch Stu Cncl Adv; Sch Space Needs & Faculty Advisory Comms; Sch Improvement Cncl; Mem Philosophy Comm for Sch Evaluation; Horace Mann Grant Self Esteem for Mid Sch; *office:* South Mid Sch 232 Peach St Braintree MA 02184

GRIGBSY, JULIE (BUIST), Head Math Dept/Math Teacher; *b:* Columbus, OH; *m:* Michael Jerry; *c:* Casey L.; *ed:* (BS) Scndry Ed Bus/Math, Baylor Univ 1985; (MS) Math, Univ of North TX 1989; *cr:* Teacher Agnew Mid Sch 1986-87; Teacher/Math Dept Head a C New Mid Sch 1987-; *ai:* Stu Cncl, Math Club Spon; PTA Health/Welfare Chm; PTA Welfare Health & Welfare 1986-; Assoc of TX Prof Educators 1986-; Mesquite Ed Assn 1986-; TX Assn Gifted/Talented 1987; NCTM 1985-; *home:* 1402 Bradford Pl Mesquite TX 75149

GRIGGS, DURWOOD WINSTON, JR., Mathematics Department Chair; *b:* Dothan, AL; *c:* Ashley J.; *ed:* (BS) Math, 1967, (MS) Admin/Supervision, 1973 Troy St Univ; Various Wkshps & Conferences; *cr:* Math Teacher Ashford HS 1967-68, Goshen HS 1968-70; Math Teacher/Chm Headland HS 1970-; *ai:* Key Club & Sr Spon & Adv; Henry Cty Ed Assn Treas 1989-; AL Ed Assn Voting Delegate 1987-; NEA, PDK; Masons (Secy, Sr Warden) 1985-; Jaycees (Treas, VP, Pres) 1970-80; Headland City Cncl 1971-80, Mayor 1980-84, Man of Yr 1979; *home:* 504 Peachtree St Headland AL 36345

GRIGGS, GLORIADINE D., Kindergarten Teacher; *b:* La Grange, GA; *c:* Shawn; *ed:* (BS) Ed, Morris Brown Coll 1965; Early Chldhd Ed 1967; Worked Towards Masters Early Chldhd Ed; *cr:* Kdngtn Teacher La Grande Bd ofEd 1965-71, Adamsville Elem Sch 1973; *ai:* Leadership Team; Grade Level Chairperson; Lib Comm; AAE, NEA; Atlanta Assn of Insurance Women Awd 1980-81; Atlanta Bureau of Fire Services Awd 1981-82; *home:* 1981 Woodberry Ave #F3 East Point GA 30344

GRIGGS, HOWARD G., JR., Business Education Chairperson; *b:* Scranton, PA; *m:* Judith Ann Kalinowski; *c:* Jeffrey, Janice; *ed:* (BSED) Bus Ed, 1964, (MED) Bus Ed, 1969 Bloomsburg St Coll; Grad Work beyond Masters; Natl Radio Insts Advanced Radio/Color Television Servicing Course Grad; *cr:* Teacher/Dept Chm Tunkhannock HS 1964-; *ai:* WY Cty Sch Employees Federal Credit Union Treas; Tunkhannock Area Ed Assn, PSEA, NEA, PBEA 1964-; Delta Pi Epsilon 1984-; Glenburn Township Supvr 1985-; *office:* Tunkhannock HS 120 W Tioga St Tunkhannock PA 18657

GRIGGS, JOHN RICHARD, Mathematics Teacher; *b:* Indianapolis, IN; *m:* Traci Devette; *c:* Kelli, Randy; *ed:* (BA) Math, IN St Univ 1975; (MED) Math Ed, NC St Univ 1990; *cr:* Teacher/Coach Speedway HS 1975-77, Apex HS 1977-; *ai:* Fellowship of Chrstn Athletes; Boys Var Bsktbl; NC Cncl Teachers of Math, NCTM 1985-; Phi Kappa Phi 1990; NC Coaches Assn 1977; Apex Jaycees Outstanding Young Educator 1983; Apex HS Outstanding Teacher 1985; Triangle Conference Coach of Yr 1979-88; *office:* Apex HS 1501 Laura Duncan Rd Apex NC 27502

GRIGGS, NANCY ANN WALKER, First Grade Teacher; *b:* Hancock Cty, IN; *m:* Richard D.; *c:* Timothy B. Thomas, Steven R. Thomas, Deborah Dellinger; *ed:* (BS) Elem Ed, 1974, (MS) Elem Ed/Rdng, 1977 IN Univ; Porter Bus Coll 1960-61; *cr:* Kndgtn Teacher Play N Learn Sch 1970-73; 2nd Grade Teacher 1974-75, 1st Grade Teacher 1975- Weston Elem; *ai:* Rdng Fundamental Coord; Ch II, Curr Comm; Alpha Delta Kappa 1990; ISTA, NEA, GCTA 1974-; Jaycees 1962-67; Cub Scouts Den Mother 1969-70; PTA 1967-; Mothers Club/Boys Club 1968-78; *office:* Weston Elem Sch 140 Polk St Greenfield IN 46140

GRIGSBY, LESLIE BUCHANAN, Fifth Grade Teacher; *b:* Morristown, TN; *m:* Samuel Franklin Jr.; *ed:* (AS) Health/Recreation/Phys Ed, Walters St Comm Coll 1976; (BS) Elem Ed, Carson-Newman Coll 1978; Grad Work Carson-Newman Coll; *cr:* Teacher Union Heights Elem Sch 1978-; *ai:* Girls Bsktbl & Scholastic Bowl Coach; HIV-AIDS Curr & Soc Stud Textbook Comm; 4-H Club Spon; Hamblen Cty Ed Assn, TEA, NEA 1978-; Lakeway Rdng Cncl 1988-; Ladies Jr Rdng Circle Grant; *office:* Union Heights Elem Sch 3366 Enka Highway Morristown TN 37813

GRILL, RICHARD WAYNE, Agricultural Science Teacher; *b:* San Antonio, TX; *m:* Latisha L.; *c:* John, Tracy; *ed:* (BS) Agriculature, SW TX St Univ 1983; Agriculature Mechancis, Farm Machinery & Power, SW TX St Univ; Home Horticulature TX A&M Univ; Voc Supervision Tarleton St Univ; *cr:* Agriscience Teacher Burnet C Ind Sch Dist 1983-; *ai:* FFA Adv; Rodeo Club, Sr Class Spon; Voc Ag Teacher Assn of TX (Dist Secy 1983-86, Dist Pres 1986-); Honorary St Farmer Degree; *home:* 109 E Kerr Burnet TX 78611

GRILL, ROBERT GEORGE, Mathematics Teacher; *b:* Clifton, NJ; *m:* Patricia Ann; *c:* Kim Parrish, Mike Parrish, Timothy; *ed:* (BA) K-12th Grade Math Ed, Trenton St Coll 1978; Admin, Georgian Court Coll; *cr:* Teacher Southern Regional HS 1978-79, Toms River HS North 1979-; *ai:* Var Boys & Girls Tennis Coach; Sch Play Dir; *home:* 1284 Deleware Ave Toms River NJ 08753

GRIM, HERSCHEL A., Content Specialist; *b:* Fountail Hills, PA; *m:* Carol Ann Bricker; *c:* D. Scott, M. Todd, Tamara J.; *ed:* (BS) Psych, Ashland Coll 1965; (MED) Math/Ed - Summa Cum Laude, Kent St Univ 1973; (AAS) Mortuary Sci - Summa Cum Laude, Cincinnati Coll of Mortuary Sci 1980; Ec, Cooperative Learning, Cmpt Programming/Comm, Ashland Univ; Comm & Management/Mrktg, FL St Univ; *cr:* Classroom Teacher Oberlin HS 1965-68, Midpark HS 1968-73; Teacher of Math Content Spec Mapleton HS 1973-75; Math Dept Chm/Teacher Math Content Spec Ashland HS 1975-80; Teacher of Math Content Spec Ontario HS 1986-; *ai:* Stu Cncl & Key Club Adv; Ontario Fed of Teachers (VP 1987) 1986-; OH Fed of Teachers 1986-; OH Ed Assn Life Mem; Homer D Leffler Awd Cincinnati Coll 1981; Outstanding Scndry Educator of America 1974; *office:* Ontario HS 467 Shelby-Ontario Rd Mansfield OH 44906

GRIM, RICHARD DAVID, Science & Biology Teacher; *b:* Flushing, NY; *m:* Joan Croce; *ed:* (BS) Ed, Univ of TN Knoxville 1974; Grad Work Univ of TN Knoxville; Many Educl Wkshps, Seminars, Inservices; *cr:* Teacher/Coach Park Jr HS 1979-80, Horace Maynard HS 1980-83; Teacher Maynardville Elem Sch 1983-85; Teacher/Coach Horace Maynard HS 1985-; *ai:* Asst Ftbl Coach; Knoxville Track Club 1970-89; Sierra Club 1980-84; Greenpeace 1989-; *home:* 1716 Woodrow Dr Knoxville TN 37918

GRIMES, CAROL JEAN, Fifth Grade Teacher; *b:* Minneapolis, MN; *m:* Nestle E. Jr.; *c:* Kathryn J.; *ed:* (BS) Elem Ed, 1972, (MS) Elem Ed, 1983 Bemidji St Univ; Elem Ed, Bemidji St Univ; *cr:* 5th Grade Teacher Northern Sch 1972-; *ai:* Delta Kappa Gamma Mem 1985-; Teacher of Month Bemidji Public Schls 1987; *office:* Northern Sch 201 15th St NW Bemidji MN 56601

GRIMES, CHARLOTTE SUSAN, 7th Grade English Teacher; *b:* Pampa, TX; *m:* Mike; *ed:* (BA) Eng, OK Panhandle St Univ 1967; *cr:* 7th/8th/9th Eng Teacher Yukon Jr HS 1967-76; 7th Grade Eng Teacher Independenc Mid Sch 1976-; *ai:* Bldg Coord IMS Sch Spelling Bee; Reg Coord Region 17 Spelling Bee; Test Monitor Scholastic Meet IMS; VP 1974-76; Pres 1979-81 Yukon Prof Educators Assn; Beta Beta Chapter DElta Kappa Gamma Secy 1981-82/1982-86/1987-88; Zeta Rho Chapter of ESA (Sec 1978-79; Pres 1979-80); Cap Clerk 1976-77; Judge for St Spelling Bee; Judge for Pee Wee Spelling Bee.

GRIMES, DAVID LEE, Elementary Principal; *b:* Childress, TX; *m:* Susan Elaine Sims; *c:* Cathy; *ed:* (BA) Eng, W TX St Univ 1972; (MS) Sch Admin, SW OK St 1975; Elem Prin Admin, SW OK St Univ 1990; *cr:* Eng Teacher Southeast Jr HS 1972-88; Prin Will Rogers Elem 1988-; *ai:* ASCD Mem 1988-; PTA Ex-Officio Officer; *office:* Will Rogers Elem Sch 1100 N Forrest Altus OK 73521

GRIMES, ELAINE EVANS, Gifted Teacher; *b:* Sheboygan, WI; *m:* Bobby Lawrence; *c:* Gary, Keith, Cheryl Wood, Mona Burtz, Curtis Holzschuh, Alisa De Monte; *ed:* (BS) Elem Ed, FL Southern Coll 1969-; (MS) Elem Ed, Univ Of South FL 1891; Specialist Level Classes In Cmptr Sci; *cr:* 6th Grade Teacher Crystal Lake Elem 1969-72; Teacher Of Gifted Polk Cty 1972-74; Prin Beacon Hill Elem 1974-78; 5th Grade Teacher Kathleen Elem 1978-79; 6th Grade Teacher 1975-85, Cmptr Teacher 1985-89 Carlton Palmore Elem; *ai:* Effective Sch Comm; Teacher Ed Cncl; Gifted Curr Comm; Scheduling Comm; Inservice Comm; Teaching Night Courses at FL Southern Coll; Part-times Instr For Cmptr Wkshps; Phi Delta Kappa Historian Grants 1987-; Interface Pres/VP 1986- Outstanding Mem 1989; Delta Kappa Gamma Prgm 1989-; Polk Ed Assn Building Rep 1987-89, Achievement 1989; Beta Sigma Phi (Pres, VP, Secy, Treas 1965-85) Woman of Yr 1978; Meth Church Bd of Ed 1960-86; United Way Bd Mem 1974-81; Teacher of Yr Polk Cty Cmptr Teacher of Yr; Excl Grant-Polk Comm Coll; Writing Team Cty Cmptr Curr; Chm of 1st Cty-Wide Cmptr Fair; Mini-Grant on Telecommunications; Technology Task Force; Judge for Natl Cmptr Competition; *office:* Carlton Palmore Elem Sch 3725 Cleveland Hts Blvd Lakeland FL 33813

GRIMES, HOWARD LEE, JR., Band Director; *b:* Louisville, KY; *ed:* (BS) Music Ed - Summa Cum Laude, Troy St Univ 1977; Various Clinics & Seminars; *cr:* Band Dir Telfair Cty HS 1977-81, Glennville HS 1981-83; Asst Band Dir Coffee HS 1984-87; Band Dir Jefferson Davis HS 1987-; *ai:* Band Concerts, Marching Festivals, Jazz Ensemble Act; GA Music Educators Assn Instrumental Solo & Ensemble Chm 1986-; Music Educators Natl Conference 1977-; Phi Eta Sigma 1974; Gamma Beta Phi 1975; Kappa Delta Pi 1976; Stu Music Educators Natl Conference Pres 1976-77; STAR Teacher Telfair Cty HS 1981; Numerous Band Arrangements Performed; *office:* Jefferson Davis HS Broxten Rd Hazlehurst GA 31539

GRIMES, JEAN JONES, Librarian; *b:* Alton, IL; *m:* David P.; *c:* Jacqueline Jean, David A.; *ed:* (BS) Elem Ed, Eastern IL Univ 1970; (MS) Instructional Technology, Southern IL Univ 1985; *cr:* 1st Grade Teacher Grafton Elem Sch 1971-87; Librarian Grafton, East Dow Schls 1987-; *ai:* Cheerleading Spon; Society Sch Librarians; *office:* Grafton Elem Sch Box 205 Main St Grafton IL 62037

GRIMES, JOHNNIE KENNIE, Learning Disabilities Teacher; *b:* Fort Wayne, IN; *m:* Claude; *c:* Tiffini N. S.; *ed:* (BA) Elem Ed, IN St Univ 1976; (MS) Ed/Learning Disabilities, St Francis Coll 1982; *cr:* Elem Teacher 1976-86, Learning Disabilities Teacher 1986- Ft Wayne Cmmty Schls; *ai:* Zeta Phi Beta; Youth Adv; Scouting; Brownies; Lambda Psi Sigma; Zeta Phi Beta (Secy, Publicity) 1982-83, Zeta of Yr 1986; *home:* 5227 Cloverbrook Dr Fort Wayne IN 46806

GRIMES, MABEL P., Retired 2nd Grade Teacher; *b:* Enterprise, AL; *m:* Roy E.; *c:* Felix W., Purvis; *ed:* (BS) Ed, Troy St Teachers Coll 1951; (ME) Ed, Auburn Univ 1962; *cr:* 6th Grade Teacher 1942-43, 2nd Grade Teacher 1943-49, 6th Grade Teacher 1950-53, 7th-9th Grade Eng Teacher 1953-76, 2nd Grade Teacher 1976-83 Goodman Jr HS; *ai:* Coffee Cty Teachers Assn (Secy 1960-61, Mem); AL Ed Assn, NEA 1942-; *home:* Rt 1 Box 439 Enterprise AL 36330

GRIMLEY, CHARLES MICHAEL, English, Speech Teacher; *b:* Boston, MA; *ed:* (BS) Ed/Eng, Boston St Coll 1961; Ed Admin/Supervision, Boston Univ 1961-64; Ed Admin/Supervision, Harvard Univ 1965; Writing, Univ of MO 1983; *cr:* Teacher John Greenleaf Whittier Sch 1961-62, David A Ellis Annex 1963-75; Instr Boston St Coll 1974-78; Teacher David A Ellis Sch 1975-78, St Louis Cntry Day Sch 1979-; *ai:* Speech & Debate Coach; Ftbl & Track Officiating; Judge Interscholastic Debate; 7th & 9th Grade Sponsorship; AFT 1962-79; NCTE 1980-; Amer Society for Curr Dev 1988-; Boston PTA Pres 1977-78; Boston Faculty Senate Pres 1977-79; Outstanding Elem Teacher of Boston 1974; Nom US Teacher of Yr 1976; Walter J Mc Creery Chair of Distinguished Teaching 1985-; *office:* St Louis Cntry Day Sch 425 N Warson Rd Saint Louis MO 63124

GRIMLEY, MARK JAMES, 7th-8th Grade Soc Stud Teacher; *b:* Austin, MN; *m:* Edie; *c:* Bryan, Matthew; *ed:* (BS) Soc Stud, 1979, Phys Ed, 1979 Winona St Univ; Grad Classes Macalester Coll, Univ of MN & Winona St Univ; *cr:* Teacher Pine Island HS 1979-82, Wabasha-Kellogg 1983-; *ai:* Asst Girls Bsktbl; Asst Boys Bsbl; Lake City Cntry Club VP 1990; *office:* Wabash-Kellogg 611 Broadway Ave Wabasha MN 55981

GRIMM, ANGELA IRENE, Social Studies Teacher; *b:* Frostburg, MD; *ed:* (BS) Soc Sci, Frostburg St Univ 1974; *cr:* Soc Stud Teacher St Peter & St Paul Sch 1977-81, St John Neumann Sch 1981-85, Bishop Walsh Mid Sch & HS 1985-; *ai:* Mid Sch Oratorical Contest; Mid Sch Intramurals; *office:* Bishop Walsh Mid/HS 700 Bishop Walsh Rd Cumberland MD 21502

GRIMM, PATRICIA, Sixth Grade Teacher; *b:* Peoria, IL; *ed:* (BS) Elem/Eng, E IL Univ 1973; Grad Stud Elem Ed; *cr:* 4th Grade Teacher Central Sch 1973-76, Eastview Sch 1976-89; 6th Grade Teacher Ingersoll Sch 1989-; *ai:* Canton Ed Assn (VP 1979-80, Pres 1980-81); PEO (Treas, Recording Secy) 1981-; United Way 1981-83; AAUW; *office:* Ingersoll Sch 1605 E Ash Canton IL 61520

GRIMMETT, MICKIE DIANE, 6th Grade Teacher; *b:* Pauls Valley, OK; *m:* Brent; *c:* Angie, Beth, Tyler; *ed:* (BA) Elem 1981, (BS) Home Ec Ed, 1981 E Cntrl Univ; Ed Wkshps & Seminars; *cr:* 6th Grade Teacher Whitebead 1981-; *ai:* Beta Club Spon; Textbook Comm Chm; OK 4 Yr Plan Local Comm Mem; 5th & 6th Grade Cheerleading Co-Spon; Zoney Teachers Meeting Comm Mem 1985-86; NEA, OK Ed Assn; Whitebead Ed Assn (Pres 1986-87, Secy-Treas 1987-89, VP 1989-), Teacher of Yr 1988-89; Beta Sigma Phi (Pres, Secy) 1986-89; *home:* PO Box 420 Pauls Valley OK 73075

GRIMSLEY, NANCY TYSON, First Grade Teacher; *b:* Bainbridge, GA; *m:* John U. III; *c:* John, Sloan; *ed:* (BA) Early Chldhd, Valdosta St 1967; *cr:* 1st Grade Teacher Jefferson Elem 1967-70, Elcan King Elem 1976-; *ai:* PAGE 1988-; Teacher of Yr 1989; *office:* Elcan King Elem Sch 735 Louise St Bainbridge GA 31717

GRINDLE, DEBORAH WHITE, Counselor; *b:* Houston, TX; *m:* Fred; *c:* Jeffrey; *ed:* (BA) Span, 1977, (MED) Counseling, 1983 Univ of N TX; Univ of Salamanca Spain Cursos del Verano; *cr:* Fr/Span Teacher 1978-84, Fr/Span Teacher/Team Leader 1980-84 Wilson Mid Sch; Fr/Span Teacher/Dept Chairperson Shepton HS 1984-85; Cnslr Calhoun Jr HS 1985-; *ai:* Natl Jr Honor Society & Calhoun Hispanic Pride Co-Spon; Assn of TX Prof Educators 1982-; TX Sch Cnslrs Assn 1985-; TX Assn of Counseling & Dev 1985-; Plano Ind Sch Dist Outstanding

Achievement in Mid Sch Teaching 1983; *office:* Calhoun Jr HS 709 Congress St Denton TX 76201

GRINDROD, JOHN JAMES, English Department Chair; *b:* Chicago, IL; *m:* Phyllis Jean; *c:* Shannon L., Kathleen C.; *ed:* (BS) Eng Ed, Miami Univ 1975; (MA) Admin/Supervision, Univ of Dayton 1978; *cr:* Eng/Journalism/Speech Teacher Perry HS 1973-76; Eng Teacher Allen East HS 1977-78, Memorial HS 1979-; *ai:* Perry HS Frosh Bsktbl & Var Ftbl 1973-76; Allen East Frosh Bsktbl & Jr HS Ftbl 1977-78; Memorial Jr HS Bsktbl 1979-80; Martha Holden Jennings Fnd Scholar 1989; *office:* Memorial HS W South St Saint Marys OH 45885

GRINER, LYNN ANN, 6th Grade Teacher; *b:* Vicksburg, MI; *ed:* (BA) Eng Literature, Olivet Coll 1970; *cr:* 4th Grade Teacher 1970-74; 6th Grade Teacher 1974 Mendon Elem; *ai:* Lead Gifted and Talented Math Group; Math Lead Jr Great Books Group; Mendon Ed Assn Secy 1984-87; *home:* 7532 East W Ave Vicksburg MI 49097

GRIPPA, ARDITH CRESPI, Science Teacher; *b:* Carbondale, IL; *m:* Tony R.; *c:* Amilcare; *ed:* (BMUS) Ed, S IL Univ 1972; Inst II Cert, Slippery Rock Univ; *cr:* Instr Math & Sci Inst 1989; Sci Teacher St Titus Sch 1974-; *ai:* Fed of Pittsburgh Diocesan Teachers Schls Outside Allegheny Cty VP 1987-; NCEA; *office:* St Totis Cath Sch 107 Sycamore St Aliquippa PA 15001

GRISCHOW, A. LYNNE STEFFEN, Sociology Teacher; *b:* Rochester, NY; *m:* Andrew Thomas; *c:* Bryan T., Andrew G.; *ed:* (BA) Sociology/Ed/Soc Stud, Mt Union Coll 1970; (MEA) Admin, Kent St 1980; Dale Carneigie Course, Drug & Alcohol Counseling Wkshp; *cr:* Soc Stud/Sociology Teacher Warren Western Reserve HS 1973-; *ai:* SADD. Safe Rides, PANDA, Just Say No Club Spon; Volunteer Prgm & Consolidation Comm for Warren City Schls; WEA 1973-; Delta Kappa Gamma Society Intnl 1989-; Amer Red Cross Youth Chm 1988-, Volunteer of Month of October 1989; *office:* Warren City Schls Monroe St Warren OH 44485

GRISHAM, NANCY BODEN, Chapter I/Math/Rdng Teacher; *b:* Okmulgee, OK; *m:* James Harold; *c:* Melissa Grisham Lish, Mark, Michael; *ed:* (BS) Elem Ed/Speech, Univ of Houston 1977; Grad Courses, Univ of Houston; TESA Trng, TX Technological Univ; *cr:* 5th Grade Teacher Tenic Holmes Elem 1977-78; 6th Grade Teacher 1978-79, 3rd-5th Grade Chapter I Rdng Teacher 1979-80, 5th Grade Rdng Teacher 1980-88, 4th-5th Grade Chapter I Math/Rdng Teacher 1988- Van Vleck Elem; *ai:* A&M Mothers Club Pres 1986-88; Cedar Lane Baptist Church.

GRISHAM, TRUDY CHRISTAKIS, 6th Grade Gifted Teacher; *b:* Waukegan, IL; *m:* John Grisham; *ed:* (BED) Elem Ed, Univ of Miami 1973; (MED) Instructional Strategies For Gifted Stus, Natl Coll of Ed 1983; *cr:* 3rd-5th Grade Teacher Glen Flora Sch 1973-78; 4th Grade Teacher Nurnberg Elem Sch 1978-80; Resource Teacher for Potential Achievers Waukegan Public Schls 1980-81; Project Discovery Teacher West Elem 1981-; *ai:* Writing a Differentiated Curr for Gifted Stus at Intermediate Level; Natl Assn for Gifted Children 1983-; Waukegan Lib Bd 1977-78; Cmptr Programming Fellowship Univ of IL 1985, 1990; *home:* 2405 Dunlay Ct Waukegan IL 60085

GRISIN, SUZETTE ALINE, Jr/Sr HS Band Director; *b:* Johnstown, PA; *ed:* (BS) Music Ed, Indiana Univ of PA 1985; *cr:* HS Music Teacher Greater Johnstown Area Voc Tech Sch 1987-88; Jr/Sr HS Band Dir Conemaugh Township Area HS 1988-; *ai:* Jr/Sr Class Play Asst Dir; Instrumental & Choral Musical Dir; PA St Educators Assn, Music Educators Natl Conference, PA Music Educators Assn 1987-; Delta Omicron 1982-; Church (Choir Dir 1986-, VP 1988-); *office:* Conemaugh Township HS West Campus Ave Davidsville PA 15928

GRISIUS, SHARON TEAHAN, Third Grade Teacher; *b:* Detroit, MI; *m:* Jerold R.; *c:* Robbie, Kelly; *ed:* (BA) Spec Ed, W MI 1971; (MA) Elem Ed, Oakland Univ 1977; *cr:* 3rd Grade Teacher Fiegel Elem 1972-89; 2nd-3rd Grade Teacher Isgister Elem 1989-; *ai:* Girls Swimming Coach; Dist Laurette Comm; Amer Red Cross Instr 1965-, 20 Yr Service Awd 1985.

GRISSETT, GAIL HAMBY, 6th-8th Grade Lit/Rdng Teacher; *b:* Birmingham, AL; *c:* Noel, Albrielle Williams; *ed:* (BS) Elem Ed, 1970; (MED) Lang Arts/Rdng, 1974 Tuskegee Univ; *cr:* Teacher Birmingham City Schls 1976-; *ai:* NEA; AL Ed Assn; *office:* William J Chrstn Sch 725 Mountain Dr Birmingham AL 35206

GRISSO, MIRIAM LOUISE, Band Director; *b:* Delano, CA; *ed:* (BM) Music/Flute Performance, 1974, (MM) Music/Flute Performance, 1976 Univ of S CA; *cr:* Band Dir Bishop Montgomery HS 1983-84; 4th-8th Grade Instrumental Music Instr Wasco Union Elem Sch Dist 1984-; *ai:* 6th-8th Grade Kern Cty Elem Honor Band Chairperson 1987; Childrens Orch 1983, St Peters-by-the-Sea Presbyn Church HS Musical Dir; Volunteer Substitute S Pasedena HS Marching Band 1980; Private Flute Instruction 1976-81; Secy to Dir Univ of S CA Trojan Marching Band 1972-75; S CA Schls Band & Orch Assn, CA Music Educators Assn, Kern Cty Music Educators Assn, Delta Kappa Gamma, Musicians Union Local #47; Winner of Numerous Music Competitions including: Fresno Philharmonic Young Artist Competition Winner 1973, 1976, Orange Cty Young Artist Competition 1975, Royal Arch Masons Young Artist Competition 1971, Kern Cty Philharmonic Sr Young Artist Competition, Musicians Union Schlsp 1970, Philharmonic Jr Young Artist Competition 1966; USC Sch of Music Ensemble Awd Woodwind Chamber Music 1974, TBS Outstanding Marching Band Staff Awd 1972; Bakersfield Civic Light Opera Awd 1973; *office:* Wasco Union Elem Sch Dist 639 Broadway Wasco CA 93280

GRISWELL, ELAINE MOSES, English Teacher; *b:* Utica, NY; *m:* James Edwin; *c:* Jacob E.; *ed:* (BA) Eng, 1974, (MAT) Eng, 1976 GA St Univ; Charleston Area Writing Project Citadel 1987; Seminar Teaching Honors Eng III Carnegie-Mellon Univ 1988; *cr:* Eng Teacher North Clayton Sr HS 1974-78, Thomson HS 1978-80, Putnam Cty HS 1980-81; Eng Teacher/Dept Head GA Military Coll Prep Sch 1981-84; Eng Teacher Stratford HS 1985-; *ai:* NHS Adv; Quest Coach for Composition; Voice of Democracy Contest Coord; NCTE 1988-89; SCCTF 1989-; St James UMC (Youth Coord 1986-87, Comm Chairperson 1987-88); Hunters Woods Civic Assn Treas 1986-88; Hunters Woods Pool Bookkeeper 1986-88; Teacher of Month Thomson HS 1978, Stratford HS 1988; Whos Who in Amer Ed 1989-; *office:* Stratford HS Crowfield Blvd Goose Creek SC 29445

GRIT, RACHEL SMITH, Home Economics Teacher; *b:* N Wilkesboro, NC; *m:* Jeffrey Scott; *c:* Heather L.; *ed:* (BS) Home Ec Ed, Campbell Univ 1983; *cr:* Home Ec Teacher Forbush HS 1983-; *ai:* FHA Co-Adv; Hospitality Comm; NEA, NCAE 1984-; *office:* Forbush HS Rt 2 Box 944 East Bend NC 27018

GRITZMAKER, CRAIG CALVIN, 6th Grade Teacher; *b:* Tecumseh, MI; *c:* Todd; *ed:* (BS) Elem Ed, Cntrl MI Univ 1973; Post Graduate Work CMU; *cr:* 6th Grade Teacher Ithaca Public Schls 1974-; *ai:* Vlybl Coach-Varsity Team Girls; Ofcl Dir-Vlybl Offcl; Heart of MI Assn; Safety Patrol Adv; NEA-MEA 1974-; *office:* South Elem Sch 400 Webster St Ithaca MI 48847

GRIZZARD, BARBARA SOLOMON, Science/Health Teacher; *b:* Paducah, KY; *c:* Teresa Fite, Cliff; *ed:* (BA) Health, Phys Ed & Recreation, Univ of KY 1962; (MA) Scndry Ed, Murray St Univ 1978; *cr:* Phys Ed Teacher Miami Norland Sr HS 1962-63; Elem Phys Ed Teacher, Marshall Cty Elem Schls 1965-72; Sci/Health/Phys Ed Teacher North Marshall Mid Sch 1973-; *ai:* KY Ed Assn Legislative Comm, NEA, Marshall Cty Ed Assn Treas 1985-; *home:* 619 Elder St Calvert City KY 42029

GROANING, JOSEPH GLENN, Chemistry Teacher; *b:* St Louis, MO; *ed:* (BA) Chem, Univ MO St Louis 1987; Grad Ed Maryville Coll; *cr:* Chem Teacher St Thomas Aquinas Mercy 1987-; *ai:* Girls Jr Var Bsktbl & Boys Var Bsbl Coach; Amer Chemical Society 1989-; MO St Bsbl Coaches Assn, Amer Bsbl Coaches Assn 1988-; *office:* St Thomas Aquinas Mercy HS 845 Dunn Rd Florissant MO 63031

GROB, RICHARD JOSEPH, Science Department Chairman; *b:* Wheeling, WV; *ed:* (BA) Eng/Theology, Wheeling Coll 1965; Grad Credits Univ of Detroit; *cr:* 8th Grade Homeroom/Sci Dept Chm St Vincent De Paul Sch 1965-; *ai:* Sch Safety Patrol, Stu Cncl Moderator; Sci Fair Coord; NCEA 1965-; Grant from Diocese of Wheeling-Charleston; Sci Curr Chm-Diocese of Wheeling Charleston; Sci Textbook Evaluation Comm Chm-Diocese of Wheeling-Charleston; *office:* St Vincent De Paul 127 Key Ave Wheeling WV 26003

GROCE, BECKY GILBERT, Mathematics Teacher; *b:* Lewiston, PA; *m:* Wilfred K. Jr.; *c:* Michael, Andrew; *ed:* (BS) Scndry Ed/Math, Lock Haven Univ 1976; Grad Courses Bloomsburg Univ; *cr:* Teacher Lewiston 1977, Shikellany 1978-; *ai:* NEA, PSEA, SEA Faculty Rep; *office:* Sunbury Mid Sch 115 Fairmont Ave Sunbury PA 17801

GROCHOLSKI, LEO N., Business Teacher; *b:* Bay City, MI; *m:* Shirley B.; *c:* Michael, Mary Grappin, Jan, Jason; *ed:* (BS) Bus, 1960, (MA) Sch Admin, 1965 Cntrl MI Univ; Grad Work in Driver Ed, Additional Bus Courses; *cr:* Teacher Chesaning Union Schls 1960-62, Bay City St James Parochial Sch 1962-63, Bay City Public Schls 1963-; *ai:* St George Society; Elected Dept Chm of Bus Dept; *office:* Bay City W HS 500 W Midland Rd Auburn MI 48611

GROCOTT, DOREEN, Departmental English Soc Stud; *b:* Stoke-on-Trent, England; *m:* Francis John; *c:* Steven J., Mark J.; *ed:* Teaching Dip Phys Ed, Stoke-on-Trent & NS Tech 1952; AENU/AENC Athletics, Leshall-Shropshire 1954; AIWAAA/GB Sr WAAA, Natl-Intnl NS Tech Univ/Caulden Coll 1966;Teaching Cert & Olympic Coach Stafforshire; Advanced Stud in Phys Ed All Areas; Coach Natl/Intnl Olympics 1960; Sr WAAA Coach; *cr:* Phys Ed Teacher Queensberry Girls Sch 1952-62, Longton HS 1963-64, Thistley Hough Sch for Girls 1964-65; Athletics Dir Caulden Coll 1965-66, Univ of North Staffordshire 1966-67; Health/Phys Ed Teacher Bensalem HS 1968-69; 5th & 6th Grade Teacher Pen Ryn Private Sch 1969; Substitute Teacher Pen Ryn St Road; 8th Grade Teacher Departmental Soc Stud, Lit/Phys Ed St Pauls 1969-70; 8th Grade Departmental Teacher St Josephs 1970-74; 8th Grade Departmental Teacher Sacred Heart 1975-; 8th Grade Extra Curr Act Supvr, Sports Dir Willingboro Recreation Dept Salem Road-1990; *ai:* Willingboro Recreation Dept Supvr of Gymnastics Girls Sports Dir; VP MCWAAA & Great Britain Plus Commonwealth; Adv to Duke of Edingburgh Awd Scheme for Girls; Womens Amateur Athletic Assn Asst Coaching Organizer 1956 WAAA 1966; British AA Bd UK Coaching Assn BAAB Coach 1952-66 Sr AAAA1 1966; Assessor to His Royal Highness The Duke of Edinburgh for His Doe Awd for Girls 1960-66 D of E Awd 1960; Duke of Edinburgh Scheme for Girls Coach & Dir 1960-66 D of E Awd 1960; WAAA of G Band Common Wed/Th Sr Coach 1960-66 Sr WAAA 1960; AENU England Netball Coach & Refree 1956-66 AENC 1960; Track & Field Trails for Olympics not selected 1948; Cty Netball Player selected For England Trial 1959; Stansmore Middlesex GB Midland WAAA Secy Olympics 1960; Guest of BAAB; DOFE Awd; PE Organizer for Summer Prgrm in Willingboro Sports Dir; *office:* Sacred Heart 250 High St Mount Holly NJ 08060

GRODE, LINDA DOWNING, 5-8th Grade Math Teacher; *b:* Pittsburgh, PA; *ed:* (BA) Elem Ed, Mercyhurst Coll 1973; (ME) Sch Admin, Edinboro St Univ 1978; Elem Prin Cert; *cr:* 3rd Grade Teacher Union City Elem Sch 1973-78; 4th Grade Teacher 1980-86, 5th-8th Grade Math Teacher 1986- St Leo Sch; *ai:* Spon Mathcounts Team; Amer Jr HS Examinations; Math League Contests; Mem Diocese of Pittsburgh Report Card Revision Comm; ASCD; Fullbright Fellowship Newcastle-Upon-Tyne England 1978-79; *home:* 310 Bayne-Wexford Rd Wexford PA 15090

GRODIS, DONALD ANTHONY, Teacher; *b:* W Pittston, PA; *m:* Sondra L. Ludden; *c:* Donna A., Anthony, Andrew; *ed:* (BA) Soc Stud, Mansfield St Coll 1960; Working Towards Masters Ec/Law Stud; *cr:* Teacher/Vice Prin/Interim Supt Bradford Cntrl Sch 1960-; *ai:* Bsktbl Summer Camp; NEA; BTA (Pres 1974-78) 1986-87; *office:* Bradford Cntrl Sch Rt 226 Bradford NY 14815

GRODJESK, KENNETH B., Science Teacher; *b:* Jersey City, NJ; *m:* Carol J.; *c:* Benjamin, Joseph; *ed:* (BS) Phys Ed/Sci, Bradley Univ 1972; (MS) Sci Ed, IL St Univ 1978; Grad Stud Univ of Rochester; Bio-Technology Trng 1986; Bradley Univ Sci Concepts Inst 1983; Bradley Univ Energy Inst 1982; Doctorate Course Work Completed 1989; *cr:* Sci Teacher Broadmoor Jr HS 1973-; Part Time Life Sci Instr IL Cntrl Coll 1978-82; Coord of Physics/Chem Teacher Bradley Inst for Gifted 1984; Consulting Teacher St of IL 1988-89; Instr Northern IL Univ 1984-; *ai:* IL Jr Acad of Sci; Sci Fair Created & Maintain Nature Trail; NEA, NSTA, IL Sci Techers, Sigma Xi Scientific Research Society; ASCD, IL Assn Supervision & Curr Dev; Sci Teacher of Yr Sigma Xi Phi Delta Kappa 1985; *office:* Broadmoor Jr HS 501 Maywood Pekin IL 61554

GRODT, MARGARET KILPATRICK, Third Grade Teacher; *b:* Colfax, WA; *c:* Jo Ann; *ed:* (BA) Elem Ed/Fine Art, WA St Univ 1969; 5th Yr Univ of WA; Classes E WA Univ, Whitworth, Gonzaga, SPU, CWA; *cr:* 3rd Grade Teacher Edmonds Sch Dist 1969-75, Oakesdale Sch Dist 1976-; *ai:* HS Drama Coach 1980-; Chrldr Adv 1981-88; Intnl Order of Rainbow for Girls Mother Adv 1986-, St Officer 1966; Eastern Star Past Matron 1981-82, 1986-87, St Deputy Inst 1987; *office:* Oakesdale Sch Dist 324 PO Box 228 Oakesdale WA 99158

GROETKEN, ALAN LEO, Jr HS Instructor; *b:* Lemars, IA; *m:* Sondra C. Moldenhauer; *c:* Troy, Trent, Lacee; *ed:* (BS) His/Eng, Westmar Coll 1969; (MA) Ed Admin, Univ of SD 1978; Grad Work, Morningside Coll; Area Ed Agency; *cr:* HS Eng Teacher 1969-79; JR HS Instr 1979- Remsen Union; *ai:* Talented & Gifted Comm; Local Ed Assn Pres; NCTE; Masonic Lodge Service Offices; Shrine Temple Wrecking Crew; *office:* Remsen Union Sch 511 Roosevelt St Remsen IA 51050

GROFF, GUY ROBERT, 6th Grade Teacher; *b:* Camden, NJ; *m:* Mary Ann; *c:* Lori, Allison; *ed:* (BA) Elem Ed, Glassboro St Coll 1973; Elem Ed, Glassboro St Coll; *cr:* Spec Services Rdng Teacher Pyne Poynt Mid Sch 1974-76; 6th Grade Teac Her Costello Sch 1976-; *ai:* Geography Club Spon; Environmental Trip Chaperone/Teacher; Gloucester City Ed Assn Treas 1987-; ASCD 1989-; Explorer Post 404 BSA Asst Leader 1973-80; NJ Governors Teacher Recognition Awd 1986; NJ St Ed Dept Grant 1978; NFIE Math Incentive Grant Comm Mem 1989; PSE&G Energy Ed Grant Indiv 1990; *home:* 168 West Ave Pitman NJ 08071

GROFF, SHIRLEY HAND, Fifth Grade Teacher; *b:* Dillon, MT; *m:* Sidney L.; *c:* Delbert Hunt, Marvin Hunt, Michelle Hunt Olsen; *ed:* (BS) Elem Ed, 1968, (MS) Elem Ed, 1975 Western MT Coll; Various Courses; *cr:* 5th Grade Teacher Clancy Sch Dist No 1 1968-71; GED Prgm Teacher Butte Vo Tech 1971-76; 5th Grade Teacher Butte Sch Dist No 1 1971-; *ai:* Delta Kappa Gamma; MT Society DAR St Regent 1988-; Nominee Golden Apple Awd 1990; Article Published 1987; *home:* 3106 Floral Blvd Butte MT 59701

GROGAN, NILA, Spanish Teacher; *b:* St Louis, MO; *m:* C. William; *ed:* (BS) Span Ed, 1971, (MSED) Span, 1977 S IL Univ Edwardsville; *cr:* Span Teacher O Fallon Township HS 1972-; *ai:* Class Spon 1974-77; Stu Cncl Spon 1977-; Discipline Comm; IL Foreign Lang Teachers Assn (Advisory Bd 1979-84, Secy 1985-88, Bd of Dirs 1989-), Foreign Lang Teacher of Yr 1988; Amer Assn of Teachers of Span & Portuguese; Cntrl Sts Conference on Teaching; IL St Bd of Ed Those Who Excl 1980; O Fallon HS Teacher of Yr 1980; Natl Textbook Company IL Foreign Lang Teacher of Yr 1988; S IL Univ Excl in Ed Awd for Foreign Lang 1990; *office:* O Fallon Township HS 600 S Smiley St O'Fallon IL 62269

GROH, PATRICIA ANN, English/German Teacher; *b:* Chicago, IL; *ed:* (BA) Ger, 1972, (MS) Rdng, 1984 N IL Univ; *cr:* HS Eng/Ger Teacher Huntley Sch Dist #158 1974-76, Belvidere Sch Dist #100 1977-; *ai:* Ger Club; *office:* Belvidere HS 1500 East Ave Belvidere IL 61008

GROMAN, JEAN BAUGH, Advisor; *b:* Covina, AZ; *ed:* (BS) Home Ec/Bus, N AZ Univ 1973; (MS) Scndry Ed, Univ of AZ 1984; Working Towards Masters Admin Cert; *cr:* Teacher Flowing Wells Jr HS & Apollo Jr HS 1973-85; Adv Sierra Mid Sch 1985-; *ai:* Peer Mediators Adv & Coord; Pi Lambda Theta, ASCD, AZ Sch Cnslrs Assn Mem; Tucson Neighborhood Watch Leader 1986-; *home:* 3363 N Christmas Ave Tucson AZ 85716

GRONEMEYER, MARJORY BELT, Retired Teacher; *b:* Lake View, IA; *m:* Dale; *c:* Steven, Todd, Sue Beers; *ed:* (BA) Elem Ed, Univ N IA 1947; *cr:* Elem Teacher Whittier Elem 1947-48, Westlake Sch for Girls 1948-49, Lake View IA 1949-53, Odebolt IA 1953-54, Lake View IA 1958-59, Schaller IA 1961-63, Lake View IA 1965-82; *ai:* Amer Legion Auxiliary Pres 1956-58; Delta Kappa Gamma Chapter Pres 1984-88.

GROOM, CARLA ANN (RASTELLO), Fifth Grade Teacher; *b:* Long Beach, CA; *m:* Anthony Joseph; *c:* Christopher, Michael; *ed:* (BA) Spec Ed/Elem, 1980, (MS) Elem Ed, 1984 N AZ Univ; Trng in Health Act Portal Prgm AZ St Univ; *cr:* 4th/5th Grade Teacher Prescott Unified Sch Dist #1 1980-; *ai:* Young Astronauts Co-Leader; Track Coach; Child Study Team Mem; Phi Delta Kappa Treas 1987-; Yavapai Rdng Cncl Building Rep 1984-; Prescott Ed Assn Building Rep 1980-; *office:* Abia Judd Elem Sch 1749 Williamson Valley Rd Prescott AZ 86301

GROOM, DOROTHY JANE (FRAZIER), Third Grade Teacher; *b:* Smithville, TN; *m:* Thomas Preston; *c:* Amanda J., Emily R.; *ed:* (BA) Elem Ed, TN Technological Univ 1974; Head Start Developmental Trng Univ TN Knoxville; Carreer Opportunities Prgm Certificate of Achievement Tn Technological Univ; Advanced Trng Portland St Coll; *cr:* Head Start Aide 1967, Follow Through Aide 1970-74, Elem Teacher 1974- Smithville Elem; *ai:* Faculty Rep; Co-Chm Retirement Comm; Young Womens Club Secy 1987-88; First Baptist Church 3rd/4th Grade Sunday Sch Teacher 1985-; *office:* Smithville Elem Sch 321 E Bryant St Smithville TN 37166

GROOMS, ED RAY, Gifted/Drama Teacher; *b:* Charleston, MO; *m:* Susan; *c:* Katie; *ed:* (BA) Speech/Drama, SE MO St Univ 1970; (MA) Drama, Univ of MO Columbia 1971; *cr:* Drama/Eng Teacher Monroe City HS 1971-75; Drama/Speech Teacher 1975-79, Drama/Gifted Teacher 1979- Nevada HS; *ai:* Drama Productions; Forensic Competitions; Odyssey of Mind; Speech & Theatre Assn of MO Bd of Governors 1990; Intnl Thespian Society MO St Dir 1978-80; Speech & Theatre Assn of MO Outstanding Teacher 1985; MO Scholars Acad Staff 1986-.

GROOS, PATRICIA SMITH, Gifted Teacher; *b:* Riverside, CA; *m:* David Michael; *c:* Wendy L., David M. Jr.; *ed:* (BS) Elem Ed, Univ of TX Austin 1969; Working Towards Masters Nova Univ; *cr:* Math/Cmptrs Teacher Appalachicola HS 1979-83; 8th Grade His/Cmptrs Teacher Port St Joseph HS 1984-85; Teacher Jefferson Davis Jr HS 1985-; *ai:* Spec Ed Dept Chm; Newspaper Spon; Cmptr Ed Stans FL Comm; United Meth Jr Sunday Sch Teacher; Mandarin United Meth Bell Choir; FL-England Connection Modeming Between FL & Eng Schls; *office:* Jefferson Davis Jr HS 7050 Melvin Rd Jacksonville FL 32210

GROOTERS, KATHY RHOTEN, Second Grade Teacher; *b:* Des Moines, IA; *c:* Megan, Lindsey; *ed:* (BA) Elem Ed, Univ of N CO 1973; (MSE) Effective Teaching, Drake Univ 1988; *cr:* 1st Grade Teacher 1975-78, 2nd Grade Teacher 1979- Carlisle Cmmty Sch; *ai:* Health & Soc Stud Curr; Elem Sch Prgm on Drug Abuse; Carlisle Cmmty Ed Assn (Treas 1983-84) 1975-; IA Conservation Ed Cncl 1988-; PTA Treas; IA Runaway Service Volunteer Recognition.

GROSHART, LOUISE JEAN, 3rd Grade Teacher; *b:* Cass Lake, MN; *m:* Warren; *c:* Jerry, Duane, Lindsey; *ed:* (BS) Elem Ed, Eastern MT 1961; Univ of WY; Univ of Northern CO; *cr:* 2nd/3rd Grade Teacher Washakie Cty Sch Dist 1952-; *ai:* NEA; WEA; Intnl Rdng Assn Pres 1988-; Amer Legion Aux Dir of Girls St 1966-79; Bus & Prof Women 1989; *home:* Box 26 Tensleep WY 82442

GROSS, DIANE, Mathematics Teacher; *b:* Berwyn, IL; *ed:* (BS) Math Ed, NE OK St Univ 1983; Working Towards Masters Educl Admin, Wichita St Univ; *cr:* Math Teacher Manhattan Mid Sch 1983-87, Wichita North HS 1987-; *ai:* Jr Var Vlybl, Bsktbl, Sftbl Coach; Fellowship of Chrstn Athletes Spon; NHS & Stu Act Comm; Wichita Coaches Assn Treas 1989-; KS Assn for Math Teachers 1984-; Big Brothers Big Sisters 1989-; *office:* Wichita North HS 1437 Rochester Wichita KS 67203

GROSS, JAMES R., Science Teacher; *b:* Pottsville, PA; *m:* Nora Bauer; *ed:* (AAS) Child Dev, Rdng Area Comm Coll 1978; (BS) Elem/Early Chldhd, 1979, (MED) Elem Supervision, 1983 Bloomsburg Univ; Admin & Personnel Management Certificate; Cmptr Literacy; Advanced Lifesaving & Water Safety Instr; Adult Basic Ed Instruction; *cr:* Soc Worker Supvr Schuylkill Cty Child Dev Prgm 1972-79; Math Teacher Minersville Area Sch Dist 1979-80; Math/Sci Teacher St Francis Sch 1980-84; Sci Teacher Blue Mountain Sch Dist 1984-; *ai:* Blue Mountain Mid Sch Sci Fair Chm; Pottsville City Democratic Comm Secy; PA Sci Teachers Assn 1990; PA St Ed Assn, NEA 1984-; Bloomsburg Univ Alumni Assn 1979-; Pottsville City Democratic Comm Secy; PA City Controllers Assn 1988-; Knights of Columbus 1974-; Blue Mountain Boys Bsktbl League Pres 1989-; City Controller Pottsville PA; Teacher of Yr Awd 1986; PA St System Higher Ed Alumni Appropriation Network; *home:* 215 Timber Rd Pottsville PA 17901

GROSS, LINDA BELL, Fifth Grade Teacher; *b:* Midland, TX; *m:* Jimmy; *ed:* (BS) Elem Ed, Prairie View A&M Univ 1979; *cr:* Teacher Mountainview Elem 1980-; *ai:* Coach Youth Bsktbl Team; Outstanding Teacher Awd Waco Ind Sch Dist 1990; Mountainview Against Drugs Prgm Organizer; Civic Achievement Awd Prgm Instr; *office:* Mountainview Elem Sch 5901 Bishop Waco TX 76710

GROSS, RICHARD ALLEN, Science/Health Dept Chair; *b:* Lima, OH; *m:* Elizabeth Blake Ditto; *ed:* (BA) Sci/Health Ed, Univ of Findlay 1983; Admin, Bowling Green St Univ; *cr:* Sci Teacher Colonel Crawford Schls 1983-84; Dept Chm/Teacher Elmwood HS 1984-; *ai:* Cross Cntry, Wrestling, Track Coach; FCA, Bloodmobile, Sci Fair Adv; Comm Dept Chm; Supt Advisory Comm; NSTA Speaker 1986-89; OH Acad Sci 1986-; OH Energy Cncl 1987-; Norcrest Church Mem 1988-; Governors Awd Excl in Sci Teaching 1985-86, 1987-88; Elmwood Teacher of Yr 1989-; Northwestern OH Teacher of Yr 1987-88; *office:* Elmwood HS 7650 Jerry City Rd Bloomdale OH 44817

GROSS, ROXIE MARCUM, Third Grade Teacher; *b:* Pitts, KY; *m:* John E.; *c:* Emma Gross Ross, Thomas C.; *ed:* (BS) Sci/Elem Ed, Cntrl St Univ 1969; (MS) Curr/Supervision, Wright St Univ 1987; Post Grad Stud Berea Coll; TESA Trng, Assertive Discipline; Young Authors Conference; Critical Thinking Skills; Law & the Classroom; Dr Henry Wong & Dr Purkey Seminars; Art & Sci Conference; GESA Trng & Instruction; Mentor Trng; Wkshp Way; Math Pentathlon Trng; *cr:* Teacher Estill Cty Schls 1954-55; Stu Teacher Fairbrook Elem Sch 1969; Teacher Temple Chrstn Sch 1969-70, Greeneview S Elem Sch 1970-; *ai:* Project Wild Instr; Amer Bus Women Assn; Beta Sigma Phi; TWIGS; NEA, OEA, GEA Past Pres; White Shrine; Eastern Star *home:* 1034 E Richard Dr Xenia OH 45385

GROSS, ROXIE MARCUM, Third Grade Teacher; *b:* Pitts, KY; *m:* John E.; *c:* Emma Gross Ross, Thomas C.; *ed:* (BS) Elem Ed, Cntrl St Univ 1969; (MS) Curr/Supervision, Wright St Univ 1987; Addl Stud Several Wkshps & Seminars; *cr:* Teacher Estill Cty Schls 1954-55, Temple Chrstn Sch 1969-70, Greenview South Elem Sch 1970-; *ai:* Amer Bus Women Assn; Beta Sigma Phi; Phi Beta Kappa; TWIGS; NEA, OEA, GEA Pres; White Shrine; Eastern Star; *home:* 1034 E Richard Dr Xenia OH 45385

GROSS, WILLIAM FREDRIC, English Teacher; *b:* New York, NY; *c:* Michal, Oliver; *ed:* (BA) Eng, St Univ of NY Albany 1967; Certificate Scndry Ed, Univ of London 1977; (MA) Educl Psych, St Univ of NY Buffalo 1983; *cr:* Teacher Gillingham Sch for Girls 1969-74, Sir William Collins Sch 1977-78, Alleghany Cty HS 1978-79, Hamburg HS 1979-; *ai:* Literary Magazine, Amnesty Intnl Sch Chapter Adv; NCTE, W NY Writing Project, Hamburg Teachers Assn; Cmmty Intervention Core Team Mem 1989-; Natl Endowment for Hum Fellowship 1988; Published Articles in W NY Writing Project; *office:* Hamburg HS Legion Dr Hamburg NY 14075

GROSSENBACH, RICHARD TAGGART, Social Studies Teacher; *b:* Ogden, UT; *m:* Cherlyn Van Luyk; *c:* Cindy Nielsen, Andriana, Will, Jill; *ed:* (BS) Psych, Weber St Univ 1966; Constitutional Democracy Political Conflict & Law Wkshp, UCLA 1970; Grad Courses Spec Ed Cert, UT St Univ 1980-83; Geography of UT Wkshp, Univ of UT 1984; *cr:* Soc Stud Teacher/Sch Dir S Ogden Jr HS 1969-74; Spec Ed Teacher/Dept Head 1981-83, Soc Stud Teacher 1984- Sand Ridge Jr HS; *ai:* Weber Ed Assn Bd of Dir 1987-; UT Ed Assn, NEA Mem 1969-74, 1981-; Greater Ogden Chamber of Commerce Mem 1966-69; Homeowners Assn Pres 1990; Clinton Dist #6 Dist Party Chm 1986-; *office:* Sand Ridge Jr HS 2075 W 4600 S Roy UT 84067

GROSSHEIDER, DONNA GLUECK, Resource Teacher of Gifted; *b:* Cape Girardeau, MO; *m:* Don R.; *c:* Abby G., Neal D.; *ed:* (BS) Voc Home Ec, 1979, (MAED) Early Chldhd Ed, 1984 SE MO St Univ; *cr:* Elem Teacher St Augustine Parish Sch 1979-81; Grad Asst SE MO St Univ 1981-82; Sales Casual Corner 1981-83; Resource Teacher for Gifted Scott Cty R-4 Sch 1983-; *ai:* Adv Parent Group of Gifted Children Scott Cty R-4; Cmmty Teachers Assn 1983-; MO St Teachers Assn 1984-88; Kappa Omicron Phi 1979-82; PTO Secy 1979-82; GSA Leader 1989-; Vacation Bible Sch Teacher 1985-; SE MO St Univ Deans List 1983; Researched & Organized Gifted & Talented Prgm Scott Cty R-4 Elem Sch; *home:* RR 2 Box 406 Cape Girardeau MO 63701

GROSSHEIDER, KOENNING, 1st Grade Teacher; *b:* Fargo, ND; *m:* Robert C.; *c:* Gail, Julie; *ed:* (BS) Elem Ed, Moorhead St Univ 1968; *cr:* 2nd Grade Teacher Jackson Elem 1968-69; 1st Grade Teacher Peebles Elem 1969-71; Kndgtn Teacher 1974-83, 1st Grade Teacher 1983- Columbus Elem; *ai:* NEA, MEA; CEA (Pres 1979-80, Treas 1988-); *home:* Rt 1 Box 83 Columbus MT 59019

GROSSHUESCH, CLAYT EMERSON, Guidance Counselor; *b:* Waukon, IA; *m:* Mindy; *c:* Kydie, Kelley; *ed:* (BA) Math, Southern Meth Univ 1976; (MA) Cnslr Ed, N IL Univ 1983; *cr:* Math Teacher 1976-83, Guidance Cnslr 1983- Waubonsie Valley HS; *ai:* Head Golf & Var Bsktbl Coach; Naperville Operation Snowball Dir; Star Raiders Co-Dir; *office:* Waubonsie Valley HS 2590 Rt 34 Aurora IL 60504

GROSVENOR, M. ILDEAN, Fifth Grade Teacher; *b:* Rural Meta, MO; *m:* Harold; *c:* Douglas, Donald, Terry, Susan; *ed:* (BS) Ed, Lincoln Univ 1963; Working Towards Masters Ed; *cr:* 1st-8th Grade Teacher Rural Maries Cty 1944-46; 4th-8th Grade Teacher Rural Miller Cty 1955-60; 5th Grade Teacher Laquey R-5 1960-; *ai:* 5th Grade Money Making Projects Educl Trip & Ben Franklin Stamp Club Spon; Prof Dev Plan Mem; Delta Kappa Gamma Nominating Comm 1988-; Kappa Kappa Iota Secy 1986-88; *home:* Rt 6 Box 127 Waynesville MO 65583

GROTEFEND, TELETE RICHARDS, First Grade Teacher; *b:* Canton, GA; *m:* Richard Frank; *c:* Christell Smith, Richard S.; *ed:* (BA) Elem Ed, Davis & Elkins Coll 1951; Grad Courses PA St Univ, Temple Univ, North GA Coll; *cr:* Kndgtn Teacher Landisville Elem 1961-69; 2nd Grade Teacher 1971-74, Pre-1st Grade Teacher 1974-78, 1st Grade Teacher 1978- Jasper Elem; *ai:* NEA 1961-69/1971-; *home:* Rt 3 Box 116 Jasper GA 30143

GROVE, DOUGLAS EDWARD, Math Teacher; *b:* Hagerstown, MD; *m:* Mary Ellen Lushbaugh; *c:* Douglas, Alex; *ed:* (BS) Psych, Towson St Univ 1974; Advanced Stud Towson St Univ & Hood Coll; *cr:* Math Teacher Peace Corps Liberia 1976-77, North Hagerstown HS 1978-; *ai:* Math Club Adv; NCTM, NEA, WA Cty Teachers Assn; Williamsport Lions Club; *office:* North Hagerstown HS 1200 Pennsylvania Ave Hagerstown MD 21740

GROVE, NILA F., Reading Teacher; *b:* Shippensburg, PA; *ed:* (BSED) Elem, 1967, (MED) Elem, 1969 Shippensburg St Coll; Rdng Cert, Shippensburg Univ 1986; Jr Great Books Leadership Trng Course 1989; *cr:* 5th-6th Grade Lang Arts Teacher W G Rice Elem 1967-75; 6th-8th Grade Rdng Teacher S Middleton Mid Sch 1976-82; 7th/8th Grade Rdng Teacher, TELLS Rdng Teacher, Dist HS Remedial Rdng Teacher 1983- Boiling Springs Jr/Sr HS; *ai:* Curr Comm for Mid Sts Assn Evaluation Chm; Jr HS Literary Journal Adv; Keystone St Rdng Assn, Cumberland Valley Rdng Assn 1988-; S Middleton Ed Assn Dir 1967-; PA St Ed Assn, NEA 1967-; Shippensburg Univ Alumni Assn Phonathon Captain 1985-; Prince Street United Brethren in Christ Church 1955-; *office:* Boiling Springs Jr/Sr HS 4 Forge Rd Boiling Springs PA 17007

GROVER, ARDITH GAYLORD, 8th Grade English/Rdng Teacher; *b:* Denver, CO; *m:* James R.; *c:* Ian, Tristan, Tyson; *ed:* (BA) Ed/Eng/Rdng/Soc Stud, Hamline Univ 1961; (MS) Curr, Natl Louis Univ 1990; *cr:* 1st Grade Teacher Clear Springs Elem Sch 1961-65; 4th Grade Teacher Lincoln Elem Sch 1967-68; Teacher Placencia Belize Peace Corps 1665-67; 8th Grade Teacher Hill Mid Sch 1980-; *ai:* Ski Club; Spelling Bee; Team Leader; Outdoor Ed, TAP Steering, Lang Art Assessment, Interdisciplinary Unit Writing, Assignment Notebook Comm; Indian Prairie Dist 204 Assn, IL Ed Assn, Nea; 1st Chrstn Church of Downers Grove Deaconess 1980-82; Indian Prairie Dist 204 Infulential Teacher Awd; *office:* Hill Mid Sch 1836 Brookdale Rd Naperville IL 60536

GROVER, DAVID ALLEN, Music Department Chair; *b:* Anchorage, AK; *m:* Loraine Kay Hoffman; *c:* Kim, Brandon Jackson, Elise; *ed:* (BA) Music, W Baptist Coll 1972; (MA) Music Ed, San Jose St Univ 1977; *cr:* Dir Music & Youth 1st Baptist Church 1972-74; Music Dept Chm Kings HS 1977-; *ai:* Dir Touring Group Living Faith; Home Church Minister of Music; MENC 1977-; Teacher of Yr 1982, 1988; *office:* Kings HS 19303 Fremont Ave N Seattle WA 98133

GROVES, DIANA COLLINS, Social Studies Teacher; *b:* Winchester, TN; *m:* Gordon Anderson; *c:* Tara E.; *ed:* (BA) Eng/Geography, 1969, (MA) Soc Stud, 1970 George Peabody Coll; TX His, Trinity Univ; Spec Ed, TN His, Government, Mid TN St Univ; Admin & Supervision, TN St Univ; *cr:* His/Government Teacher Robert E Lee HS 1970-71; His Teacher Eisenhower Mid Sch 1971-76; Geography/His Teacher North Jr HS 1979-; *ai:* His Club Spon; After Sch Group Teacher; Write & Publish Sch Newsletter to Parents; Delta Kappa Gamma, TN Ed Assn, NEA; Franklin Ed Assn (Faculty Rep 1983-84, 1986-, TN Ed Rep Assembly Delegate 1983-84, 1986-89, Newsletter Ed 1983-85, Pres 1985-86, VP 1983-84, Negotiator 1987, Chief Negotiator 1987), Best Faculty Rep Awd 1983; Franklin Cty Historical Society (Dir 1982-86, Prgm Chm 1980-86); Governors Acad Teachers of Writing 1986, 1987; Kenneth Cooper Soc Sci Awd Schlsp 1969; Written Articles; Organized Cty Scndry Sch Stu Competition; Presented Inservice Session Teaching Children with Lang Dysfunctions; *home:* 107 Lakeview Dr Rt 1 Decherd TN 37324

GROVES, JOAN BRADLEY, 8th Grade Science Teacher; *b:* Covington, VA; *c:* John F., Julia A., Jaclyn A.; *ed:* (BS) Bio, Emory & Henry Coll 1968; Grad Stud Hollins Coll, Univ of VA, VA Commonwealth Univ, VA St Univ; *cr:* 4th Grade Teacher Green Valley Elem 1968-69; Bio Teacher Glenvar HS 1969-71; 7th-8th Grade Sci Teacher Hidden Valley Jr HS 1972-76; 8th Grade Sci Teacher Northside Jr HS 1977-78, Swift Creek Mid Sch 1983-86, Midlothian Mid Sch 1986-; *ai:* Pep Club Spon; Discipline Comm; Hazard Comm Liaison; NEA, VA Ed Assn 1968-; VAST; VA Acad of Sci Secy 1971; *office:* Midlothian Mid Sch 13501 Midlothian Trpk Midlothian VA 23113

GROZALIS, MARY CAROLAN, Latin & English Teacher; *b:* Englewood, NJ; *m:* Robert H.; *c:* Tara, Robert Jr.; *ed:* (BA) Latin/Eng, Montclair St Coll 1967; Grad Stud in Ed; *cr:* Teacher Wayne Valley HS 1967-68, Ramsey HS 1968-70; Teacher/Dir Ponds Valley Sch 1974-79; Teacher Eisenhower Sch 1979-86, Valley Sch 1979-86, Kinnelon HS 1986-; *ai:* Latin Club & Natl Latin Honor Society Adv; Foreign Lang Educators of NJ, NJ Classical League, Kinnelon Ed Assn, NEA, NJ Ed Assn; Flood Control Comm; Oakland Tennis Club; *office:* Kinnelon HS Kinnelon Rd Kinnelon NJ 07405

GRUB, JOHN GEORGE, Social Studies Teacher; *b:* Haure De Grace, MD; *m:* Deanna Joan Peak; *c:* Todd M., Ariane A.; *ed:* (BS) Elem Ed, Towson St Univ 1970; (MS) Elem Ed, Morgan St Univ 1977; (CASE) Classroom Management Loyola Coll 1981; *cr:* Teacher Havre De Grace Elem 1970-72, Slate Ridge Elem 1972-75, North Harford Mid Sch 1975-; *ai:* Head Varsity Lacrosse Coach North Harford Sr HS; Co-Dir Harford Lacrosse Camp; MD St Teachers Assn 1971-; Towson St Univ Mem Athletic Hall of Fame 1989-; Trustee-Highland Presbyn Church 1986-88; *office:* North Hartford Mid Sch Box 112 Old Pylesville Rd Pylesville MD 21132

GRUBB, A. JILL, 8th Grade Science Teacher; *b:* Zanesville, OH; *m:* William M.; *c:* Andrea, Kyle, Zachary, Sean; *ed:* (BS) Ed, 1978; (MS) Spec Ed, OH Univ; *cr:* Teacher East Muskingum Sch 1978-; *ai:* Dist Cmptr Comm; NSTA 1985-; Sci Educators Cncl of OH 1984-; Natl Energy Ed Dev Prgm 1983 State Winner 1985-89; Gideon Auxiliary Pres 89-; Sunday Sch Suptv 1985-; Battelle/Ackert Outstanding Teacher Awd 1986; Martha Holden Jennings Grant; *office:* East Muskingum Mid Sch 13125 John Glenn School Rd New Concord OH 43762

GRUBB, DAVID G., Chemistry Teacher; *b:* Philadelphia, PA; *m:* Marti Blumenthal; *c:* Denise, Heather, Andy; *ed:* (BA) Ed/Phys Sci, 1971, (MA) Stu Personnel Services, 1977, Prin/Supvr Certificate, 1980- Glassboro St Coll; *cr:* Earth Sci Teacher 1971-73; Chem Teacher 1973- Cherry Hill HS East; *ai:* Ftbl & Track Coach; Dist Sci Curr Comm; Amer Chemical Society 1987-; Medallion Awd Glassboro St Coll; *office:* Cherry Hill HS East Kresson Rd Cherry Hill NJ 08003

GRUBE, DAVID QUINN, Social Studies Instructor; *b:* Ashton, ID; *ed:* (BA) His, ID St Univ 1981; Taft Seminar, Hinckley Inst of Poly Sci; Univ of UT Salt Lake City; *cr:* Soc Stud Teacher Carlin Combined Schls 1984-; *ai:* Drama & Class Adv; Quiz Bowl Coach; Annual Cty Spelling Bee Chm 1986-; Dist Prof Assn Cty Bd of Dirs; Episcopal Church (Lay Reader, Eucharistic Minister); Cmmty Christmas Play 1988; *home:* 336 Oak St Elko NV 89801

GRUBER, BARBARA ROWLANDS, Mathematics Dept Chairman; *b:* Piqua, OH; *m:* Fred J.; *ed:* (BA) Ed, Univ of FL 1970; *cr:* 2nd/5th Grade Teacher Hillsborough Cty Elem Sch 1970-73; 2nd/4th/5th Grade Teacher Seminole Cty Elem Sch 1973-85; 6th-7th Grade Teacher Seminole Cty Mid Sch 1985-; *ai:* Stu Cncl & Safety Patrol Spon; Chm Creative Writing Comm; Dist Comm Mem Cmptr Curr; Team Leader all Grades; Comm Mem Honors Class Curr; Sch Advisory Comm; SCCTM NCTM Rep 1988-89; PTA Bd Mem 1975-78; Rock Lake Mid Sch Math Dept Chm 1988; Teacher of Yr 1989-; FL St Bd of Ed Master Teacher 1985-88; Spring Lake Elem Teacher of Honors Class 1982-84; *office:* Rock Lake Mid Sch 250 Slade Dr Longwood FL 32750

GRUBER, FRED, 5th Grade Teacher; *b:* Jersey City, NJ; *m:* Ellen Jaylow; *c:* Jennifer, Marcie; *ed:* (BS) Elem Ed, Monmouth Coll 1970; Elem Ed, Kean Coll; *cr:* 6th Grade Teacher Long Branch Elem 1970, Navesink Sch 1970-81; 6th Grade Teacher 1981-87, 5th Grade Teacher 1987- Fairview Sch; *ai:* Yrbk Adv; Assn Faculty Rep; Sch Store Adv; Audio Visual Comm; Chm PTO Rules Comm; NEA 1970-; Monmouth Cty Ed Assn 1970-; Middletown Twshp Ed Assn 1970-; NJ Ed Assn 1970-; Wanamassa First Aid Squad Captain 1980 & 1989; Wanamassa Fire Co Secy 1980-89; Jewish War Veterans 1970-; Local Grants for Movie Making;Grow Lab Greenhouse; Middletown Chamber of Commerce Teacher of Yr; Bd of Ed Grant/First Aid Course; *office:* Fairview Sch 60 Cooper Rd Red Bank NJ 07701

GRUBER, JAMES F., Program Coordinator; *b:* Buffalo, NY; *m:* Ann F. Casullo; *c:* Francis X.; *ed:* (BS) Elem Ed, 1962, (MS) Elem Supervision, 1971 St Univ of NY Buffalo; Grad Studl; *cr:* 5th Grade Teacher Buffalo Sch 37 1962-76; 3rd Grade Follow Through Prgm Buffalo Sch 37 1976-79, Buffalo Sch 53 1979-82; Prgm Coord Buffalo Sch 53 1982-88, Buffalo Sch 80 1988-; *ai:* Intramural Bsktbl Coach; 7th & 8th Grade Yoga Club Instr; Buffalo Teachers Fed 1962-; Fredonia Natl Honor Society; Kappa Delta Pi 1961; Natl Sci Fnd Grants St Univ of NY Buffalo; Nom Teacher of Yr Buffalo 1987; *home:* 393 Porter Ave Buffalo NY 14201

GRUBER, JANETTE ASHMORE, Spanish Teacher; *b:* Sioux City, IA; *m:* Richard; *c:* Stacie, Marcie, Jennifer, Amy, Nicole; *ed:* (BA) Span/Bus, Westmar Coll 1969; Elem Foreign Lang & Cmptr; *cr:* West Bend Cmmty Schls 1969-77; Pocahontas Cmmty Schls 1978-80; Gilmore City Bradgate Cmmty Schls 1979-80; Haveloch-Plover Cmmty Schls 1983-86; Twin Rivers Cmmty Schls 1987-; *ai:* Drill Team Dir; Class & Span Club Spon; IA St Drill Team Assn (Bd Mem, 1987-, Treas 1989-), Lifetime Mem Awd 1988; Phi Beta Lambda 1969-73, Shorthand Awd 1988; Alpha Mau Gamma 1970-73; IA Bowling Assn Pres 1986-87; Pocahontas Branch 1989-; IA Lottery Grant Drake Univ 1988; Twin Rivers Cmmty Schls Outstanding Teacher Awd 1987-88.

GRUBER, LARRY LEE, Science Teacher; *b:* Findlay, OH; *m:* Jocele Ann Bargdill; *c:* Tia M., Dax M.; *ed:* (BS) Bio, Bowling Green Univ 1969; (MST) Earth Sci, Wright St Univ 1978; *cr:* Teacher Perrysburg HS 1970-71, Memorial HS 1971-; *ai:* Wrestling Coach; *home:* 111 Nagel St Saint Marys OH 45885

GRUBER, MARY GETTINGS, Fifth Grade Teacher; *b:* Hillsdale, MI; *c:* Shane, Scott, Steve; *ed:* (BA) Elem Ed/Speech/Eng, 1963, (MA) Elem Ed/Rdng, 1970 MI St Univ; *cr:* 5th Grade Teacher Bath Cmmty Sch 1963-65; Elem Teacher Webberville Cmmty Sch 1967-; *ai:* Crop Walk Co-Spon; Intercurricular Prof Comm; MI Rdng Assn, NEA, MEA, WEA 1963-; 4-H Knitting & Crochet Instr 1987-; Meth Church Choir Mem; *office:* Webberville Cmmty Sch 313 E Grand River Webberville MI 48892

GRUBLER, JANET M. (CIRIPOMPA), Spanish/English Teacher; *b:* Wheeling, WV; *m:* William R. Jr.; *c:* Kirk, Corey; *ed:* (BA) Span/Eng - Magna Cum Laude, Bethany Coll 1972; Grad Work Eng, WV Univ; *cr:* Eng/Span Teacher/Foreign Lang Dept Chm Mt de Chantal Acad 1974-83; Eng/Span Teacher Wheeling Cntrl Cath HS 1985-; *ai:* NHS Advisory Comm; Sociedad Honoraria Hispanica Adv; Amer Assn Teachers of Span & Portuguese, WV Foreign Lang Teachers Assn; Church Choir Librarian; Wheeling Symphony Annual Viennese Ball Volunteer; Victorian Wheeling Society Charter Mem; Pi Beta Phi Alumnae Club Secy; Waltz Night Dance Comm; Cmmty Theater Productions; Adult Tap Dancing Classes Instr; Oglebay Inst; Oglebay Inst Intnl Folk Dancers; Annual Stu Winners Bethany Coll Foreign Lang Day; St Winners Natl Span Examination 1982, 1983; Natl Winner AATSP Stu Schlsp 1983; Travel with Stus Mexico 1978, 1980 & Spain 1990; *office:* Wheeling Central Cath HS 14th & Eoff Sts Wheeling WV 26003

GRUCA, DEBORAH HATFIELD, Mathematics/Soc Stud Teacher; *b:* Decatur, IL; *m:* Michael J.; *c:* Christine, Elizabeth; *ed:* (BA) His, W IL Univ 1971; Grad Stud His, W IL Univ; Teaching Methods, S IL Univ; Cmptr, Wabash Valley Coll; *cr:* 6th-8th Grade Soc Stud/Rdng Teacher Holy Family 1971-72; 6th-8th Grade Rdng/Math Teacher Thomas Jefferson Mid Sch 1972-74; Homebound Teacher Dist 348 1974-82; 6th-8th Grade Math/Soc Stud Teacher St Marys Sch 1982-; *ai:* 8th Grade Spon; GSA Service Unit Dir 1982-85; Walsingham Estates Secy 1982-; *office:* St Marys Sch 419 Chestnut St Mount Carmel IL 62863

GRUDIS, CAROL ANN FOGLIANI, Third Grade Teacher; *b:* Scranton, PA; *m:* Thomas Xavier; *c:* Michaelene Rudis Gall, Stephanie; *ed:* (BS) Early Chldhd/Elem Ed, Marywood 1977; Masters Equivalency from Marywood Univ, Wilkes Coll; *cr:* Kndgtn Teacher 1977-78, 2nd Grade Teacher 1978-79 Moscow Elem; 3rd Grade Teacher Elmhurst Elem 1979-87, Moscow Elem 1987-; *ai:* PA St Ed Assn, NEA; PTA VP 1973-75; North Pocono Womens Club VP 1988-; St Marys Villa Auxiliary 1980-; *home:* 11 Beechwood Dr Moscow PA 18444

GRUEBELE, SHIRLEY ANN (HEIM), 3rd/4th Grade Teacher; *b:* New Leipzig, ND; *m:* Edmund J.; *ed:* (BS) Elem Ed, Dickinson St Univ 1971; Geography; Grad Stud Mary Coll Bismarck, Univ of ND Grand Forks, ND St Univ Fargo; *cr:* 8th Grade Elem Teacher Leipzig Sch Dist 14 1954-60; 3rd-6th Grade Elem Teacher New Leipzig Public Sch Dist 15 1960-; *ai:* Team Mem North Cntrl Assn of Colls & Schls Team Mem; NEA, NDEA Mem; Germans from Russia Historical Society Pres 1983-85; Nom US West Outstanding Local Sch Teacher 1987; New Leipzig Local NDEA ND Teacher of Yr 1989; New Leipzig Schls 25 Yrs of Teaching Service Plaque 1979; *office:* New Leipzig Public Sch 21 Tiger Trail Ave Box 50 New Leipzig ND 58562

GRUELL, TODD, US History Teacher; *b:* Connersville, IN; *m:* Kimberly Wagner; *c:* Patrick; *ed:* (BS) US His/Ed, Ball St Univ 1984; *cr:* US/world His Teacher Okeechobee HS 1984-86; US His Teacher Arcanum-butler Sch Dist 1986-; *ai:* Frosh Bsktbl, Mid Sch Track Coach; IN Cncl for Soc Stud 1986-; *office:* Arcanum-Butler Sch Dist U S Rt 127 Arcanum OH 45304

GRUENEICH, MARK ELLIOT, Principal/Teacher/Coach; *b:* Bismarck, ND; *c:* Shane A.; *ed:* (BS) Sci, Minot St Coll 1975; Educl Admin, Univ of ND; *cr:* Teacher Drayton HS 1975-77, Towner HS 1977-86; Prin/Teacher Parshall HS 1986-; *ai:* Stu Cncl, Sr Class, Honor Society Adv; Var Ftbl Coach; NDEA, NEA, NDHSAA 1975-; NDASSP, NASSP 1986-; Quarterback Club, PTA 1986-; *home:* RR 1 Box 68 Parshall ND 58770

GRUENWALD, DEBORAH ANNE, Third Grade Teacher; *b:* Port Washington, WI; *m:* Jon;; *ed:* (BA) Elem Ed, Univ of WI Eau Claire 1979; *cr:* Long Term Substitute Media Specialist Thorson Elem Sch 1980; 5th Grade Teacher 1980-82, Part-Time 2nd/4th/5th Grade Teacher 1982-83 Kennedy Elem Sch; Half-Time Kndgtn Teacher Grafton Elem Sch 1984; 3rd Grade Teacher Kennedy Elem Sch 1984-; *office:* Kennedy Elem Sch 1629 11th Ave Grafton WI 53024

GRUMBLES, CARL E., 6th Grade Teacher; *b:* Hammond, IN; *m:* Donna Jean; *c:* Scot, Chris, Amanda; *ed:* (BA) Ed, Purdue Univ 1965; (MA) Cnslr Elem, NE IL Univ 1976; Grad Stud N IL Univ; *cr:* Elem Teacher Sch Dist 44 1969-; *ai:* Excl Comm; NEA, IL Ed Assn 1969-; Lisle Heritage Society Treas 184-87; Elected to Sch Bd; *office:* Sch Dist #44 Parkview 341 N Elizabeth Lombard IL 60148

GRUNKE, JOHN HERBERT, Mathematics Teacher; *b:* St Paul, MN; *m:* Jennifer K. Junkman; *c:* Lisa, Sara; *ed:* (BA) Math, 1967, (MA) Math, 1974 Univ of WI River Falls; Grad Stud; *cr:* Teacher Johanna Jr HS 1967-68, Highview Jr HS 1968-82, Irondale Sr HS 1982-; *ai:* Sr HS Math Team Coach; Church Cncl Mem 1987-89; *office:* Irondale Sr HS 2425 Long Lake Rd New Brighton MN 55112

GRUSCHOW, MARGARET, Bio/Chem/Physics Teacher; *b:* Lake City, FL; *ed:* (BS) Wildlife Sci, 1975, (BS) Scndry Ed, 1986 UT St Univ; *cr:* Wildlife Biologist US Forest Service 1976-80; Naturalist US Natl Park Service 1980-84; Sci Teacher Many Farms HS 1987-; *ai:* Stu Government Assn & NHS Spon; Vlybl Coach; Wildlife Society 1972-80, Certified Assoc Wildlife Biologist 1978; NSTA 1986-; *office:* Many Farms HS PO Box 307 Many Farms AZ 86538

GRUSY, ELIZABETH BOND, Fifth Grade Teacher; *b:* Galesburg, IL; *m:* Rodney D.; *c:* Brad Welch, Kristin Welch; *ed:* (BS) Elem Ed, IL St Univ 1971; Math Resource; *cr:* 5th Grade Teacher Loucks Elem Sch 1971, Grundy Elem Sch 1971-81, Lincoln Elem Sch 1981-; *ai:* Model Rocket Shoot; Egg Drop Contest; Soc & Study Skills Comm; Gifted Comm & Curr Advisory Cncl Mem; Wrote Criterion Reference Tests Dist; Delta Kappa Gamma (Newsletter Ed 1983-, Chm Intnl Projects 1980-); Morton Ed Assn Cncl Mem 1983-87; PEO 1983-; Morton United Meth Church Bell Choir 1984-88; *office:* Lincoln Elem Sch 100 S Nebraska Ave Morton IL 61550

GUAJARDO, CHARLES, Fine Arts Chairman; *b:* Doucette, TX; *m:* Anne Marie Kaveski; *c:* Rachel, Jessica; *ed:* (BS) Eng/Speech, Lamar St Univ 1960; (MA) Theatre Arts, LA St Univ 1962; *cr:* Instr Starks HS 1959-61, St Marys Dominican Coll 1963-65, Loyola Univ 1985-87, Archbishop Rummel HS 1962-; *ai:* NHS; Genesian Players; NCTE, Speech Assn of America, Southern Speech Assn, Thespians Society, Cath Forensic League, Natl Cath Theatre Conference, NCEA, NEA; *office:* Archbishop Rummel HS 1901 Severn Ave Metairie LA 70001

GUARD, MARSHA R., Mathematics Teacher; *b:* Tullahoma, TN; *c:* Jason; *ed:* (AS) Math, Motlow St Comm Coll 1981; (BS) 7th-12th Ed, Concord Coll 1986; *cr:* Teacher Fulton HS 1986-87, Bearden Mid Sch 1987-; *ai:* Mathcounts 1989-; TN Assn of Mid Schls, Smokey Mountain Math Ed Assn 1987-; NCTE 1985-; Kappa Delta Phi 1986-; PTA 1988-; TN Career Ladder Level 1.

GUARINO, SUSAN SANTORO, 5th-8th Grade Math Teacher; *b:* Waterbury, CT; *m:* Joseph; *c:* Adam; *ed:* (BS) Elem Ed, 1973, (MS) Remedial Rdng, 1980 Cntrl CT St Univ; Grad Stud; *cr:* 4th Grade Teacher St Francis Xavier 1976-81; 5th-7th Grade Math/Rdng Teacher St Josephs 1981-84; 5th-8th Grade Math/6th Grade Homeroom Teacher St Francis of Assissi 1984-; *ai:* Math Comm Mem Archdiocese of Hartford; *office:* St Francis of Assissi 294 Church St Naugatuck CT 06770

GUBERNATH, KATHLEEN GAIL, Fifth Grade Teacher; *b:* Grayling, MI; *m:* George Adam; *c:* Adam, Jason; *ed:* (BS) Elem Ed, 1967, (MED) Elem Ed, 1988 Bowling Green St Univ; *cr:* 4th Grade Teacher Maumee City Schls 1967-70; 5th Grade Teacher Napoleon City Schls 1978-; *ai:* NEA, OH Ed Assn 1967-70, 1978-; Napoleon Faculty Assn 1978-; Child Guidance League 1986-89; Jennings Scholar 1988-89; *office:* Napoleon City Schls Briarheath Dr Napoleon OH 43545

GUCCIARDO, PERMILLA COVINGTON, Retired Eng Teacher; *b:* Kingman, AZ; *m:* John V.; *c:* Mark, Lisa; *ed:* (BA) Elem Ed, Univ of AZ 1960; Grad Stud; *cr:* 3rd Grade Teacher Carmichael Elem 1960-67; 3rd-5th Grade Teacher Village Meadows Elem 1968-85; 7th/8th Grade Eng Teacher Sierra Vista Mid Sch 1985-; *ai:* AZ Ed Assn, NEA 1960-; Kappa Delta Phi 1975-; Beta Sigma Phi 1964-80; Fullbright Fellowship Exch Teacher, England 1979-80; *home:* 3664 E Foothills Dr Sierra Vista AZ 85635

GUDENIUS, BARBARA HAMAKER, English Department Head; *b:* Baltimore, MD; *m:* D. Martin; *ed:* (BS) Eng/Scndry Ed, 1968; (MED) Eng, 1972 Towson St Univ Johns Hopkins Univ; Loyola Coll; Univ of MD Coll Park; Coppin St Coll; Univ of Baltimore; *cr:* Teacher Willows HS 1969-73, Walbrook HS 1974-79; Eng Dept Head Southwestern HS 1979-88, Western HS 1988-; *ai:* Literary Magazine Spon; NCTA, MD Cncl Teachers of Eng Lang Art 1978-; Amer Wine Society 1985-; Dow Newspaper Fund Schlsp 1986; Coppin-Hopkins Hum Project 1988; Fund for Educl Excl Grant 1989; *office:* Western HS 4600 Falls Rd Baltimore MD 21209

GUDZ, BRIGITTE WORDEN, Mathematics Teacher; *b:* Tallahassee, FL; *m:* Martin John; *c:* Adam T.; *ed:* (AA), N FL Jr Coll 1981; (BSED) Math, W Carolina Univ 1983; *cr:* Math Teacher Asheville HS 1983-; *ai:* Tennis Coach; Comm to Score Proofs for St Geometry Exam; Grace United Meth Church Mem 1988-; Received Schlsp for Math Teachers; *office:* Asheville HS 419 Mc Dowell St Asheville NC 28803

GUENTERT, MARYLOU HARRIS, 9th Grade English Teacher; *b:* Yokosuka, Japan; *m:* Elgin Stephen; *c:* Jake, Marsha; *ed:* (BA) Eng, Sam Houston St Univ 1973; *cr:* 9th Grade Eng Teacher Brenham HS 1987-; *ai:* TX Joint Cncl Teachers of Eng 1989-; Article Published 1990; *office:* Brenham HS 1200 Carlee Dr Brenham TX 77833

GUENTHER, PATRICIA J. MAESTAS, 9th-12th Grade English Teacher; *b:* Las Vegas, NM; *m:* Clint W.; *c:* Jordan; *ed:* (BA) Elem Ed/Eng, 1979, (MA) Rdng/Ed, 1984 NM Highlands Univ; Peer Mentoring, Whole Learning Theory; *cr:* Teacher Pecos Ind Sch Dist 1980; Instr NM Highland Univ 1980-81, Springer Municipal Schls 1981-82, Las Vegas Cmmty Schls 1982-; *ai:* Pep Club, Stu Cncl, Yrbk Spon; Budget & Personnel Hiring Comm; NM Cncl Rdng Teachers 1981-; NM Cncl of Eng Teachers 1982-.

GUERRERO, CARLOS ESTEBAN, Math/Cmptr Math Teacher; *b:* Mc Allen, TX; *m:* Elda E. Sanchez; *ed:* (BA) Math/Bus Admin, TX A&I Univ 1979-80; Certified in Cmptr Sci; *ai:* Cmptr Math Team Coach; TEAMS & Cmptr Coord; *home:* 212 1/2 W Bennett Falfurrias TX 78355

GUERRERO, GLORIA TERESA, Science Teacher/Dept Chair; *b:* Pueblo, CO; *m:* Samuel Alfonso Jr.; *ed:* (BS) Bio, Univ of Southern CO 1976; Teaching Health; Cooperative Learning; *cr:* Stu Govt/Algebra I Teacher 1979-85, 6th-8th Grade Sci Teacher 1978- Risley Mid Sch; *ai:* Chairperson Accountability Comm; Sci Dept Chairperson; Spon Risley Mid Sch Academic Letter; Pueblo Ed Assn CO Sci Teacher of Yr Nom 1990; CO Ed Assn Presidential Awd Excl Nom 1990; NEA; NSTA; CO Public Interest Research Group; Holy Rosary Cath Membership; Todays Ed Feature 1984; Article Published in PACE 1984; *office:* Risley Mid Sch E 7th & La Crosse Pueblo CO 81001

GUERRERO, MARIA P., 3rd Grade Teacher; *b:* Miami Beach, FL; *m:* Pedro E. Jr.; *ed:* (BS) Elem Ed/Early Chldhd, Nova Univ 1984; Nova Univ; *cr:* Sub Teacher 1985; 7th Grade Teacher 1985; 3rd Grade Teacher 1985 Our Lady Queen of Martyrs Cath Sch; *ai:* Coord Span Religious Ed Prgm at Our Lady Queen of Martyrs

Church 1982-; *office:* Our Lady Queen of Martyrs Sch 2785 SW 11th Ct Fort Lauderdale FL 33312

GUERRERO, NANCY GILBREATH, Fifth Grade Teacher; *b:* Trion, GA; *c:* Carlos, Nathan; *ed:* (BS) Elem Ed, Jacksonville St Univ 1968; *cr:* 6th Grade Teacher South Rossville Elem 1968-72, Pond Springs Elem 1972-76; 5th Grade Teacher Chattanooga Valley Elem 1980-; *office:* Chattanooga Valley Elem Sch Rt 1 Chattanooga Valley Rd Flintstone GA 30725

GUERRY, PATRICIA MOSS, 5th Grade Teacher; *b:* Rock Hill, SC; *m:* LeGrand III; *c:* Chip, Tish; *ed:* (BS) Elem Ed, 1969, (MED) Elem Ed, 1980 Winthrop Coll; Admin Cert Prin, Supvr; *cr:* 3rd Grade Teacher Mc Celvey Elem 1969-87; 5th Grade Teacher Harold C Johnson Elem 1987-; *ai:* Bus Ed Partnerships Repl Supt Improvement Cncl; Elem Sch Building Comm; Compensatory Comm; TACTICS Trng; Staff Dev Comm; In-Service Comm; Young Authors Dist Coord; Dist Discipline Comm Primary Teacher Rep; Grade Card Evaluation Comm Grade Level; Fine Arts Grant Prgm; Contract Negotiatons Team Rep 1985-89: Title IX Evaluation Dist Coord; Palmetto Rdng Cncl 1988-; Hamilton Cty Teachers Fed (Building Rep, 2nd VP); *office:* Harold C Johnson Elem Sch 400 E Jefferson St York SC 29745

GUESS, GLENDA ALEXANDER, Math Dept Coord/Math Teacher; *b:* Henderson, KY; *m:* James E.; *c:* Dana Guess Whitson, James Bennett; *ed:* (BA) Elem Ed, KY Wesleyan Coll 1960; (MA) Elem Ed, Murray St Univ 1980; *cr:* Jr HS Soc Stud Teacher 1960-62, 4th-8th Grade Elem Fr Teacher 1963-65 Beaver Dam Elem; Jr HS Teacher Weaverton Elem 1965-66; Jr HS Fr Teacher Henderson Cty Mid Sch 1968-76; 4th Grade Teacher E Heights Elem 1976-79; 8th Grade Math Teacher North Jr HS 1979-; *ai:* Cheerleading & Stu Cncl Spon; NCTM, Henderson Cty Ed Assn, KY Ed Assn, NEA; 1st United Meth Church Various Offices; West Home for Girls (Corresponding Secy, Recording Secy); Served Teacher Evaluation, Local Math Textbook, Cmptr & Gifted Ed Comm; Nom Presidential Awd Outstanding Math Teacher; *home:* 227 Kerry Ln Henderson KY 42420

GUESS, VIRGINIA TOWNSEND, Language Arts Teacher; *b:* Salado, TX; *m:* James L.; *c:* Cynthia Guess Felts, David; *ed:* (BA) Eng, Univ of Mary Hardin Baylor 1964; (MED) Ed, Sam Houston St Univ 1972; *cr:* Eng Teacher San Perlita Ind Sch Dist 1961-64, Edcouch Elsa Ind Sch Dist 1964-68, Madisonville Ind Sch Dist 1969-72; Eng/Rdng Teacher Pettus Ind Sch Dist 1972-86; Eng/Rdng/Speech Teacher Salado Ind Sch Dist 1986-; *ai:* UIL Coord; Speech & Drama Club Spon; One Act Play Dir; UIL Speech Coach; ATPE 1975-; TETA 1987-; Baptist Church Pianist; *office:* Salado Ind Sch Dist P O Box 98 Salado TX 76571

GUGALA, KAY IRENE, Spanish Teacher; *b:* Alma, MI; *m:* David A.; *c:* Justin, Lauren; *ed:* (BA) Span, Mercy Coll of Detroit 1970; Grad Work Span, Univ of MI, Scndry Ed, E MI Univ; *cr:* Span Teacher St Alphonsus HS 1970-74; Span/Religion Teacher Divine Child HS 1975-79; Span Teacher/Foreign Lang Dept Head Bishop Borgess HS 1982-; *ai:* Span Club Adv; Amer Assn Teachers of Span & Portuguese; Alpha Delta Kappa; Panel of Amer Women Pres 1987-; Natl Panel of Amer Women Natl Advisory Bd 1989-; *office:* Bishop Borgess HS 11685 Appleton Redford MI 48239

GUGALA, LOTTIE WINIARSKI, Vocal Music Teacher; *b:* Latrobe, PA; *m:* Emil Julian; *c:* Anita M.; *ed:* (BMED) Music Ed, Univ of Detroit 1958; (MMED) Music Ed, Wayne St Univ 1961; Grad Stud Univ of MI & Horache H Rackham Sch 1961-63; *cr:* Teacher Detroit Public Schls 1958-; *ai:* Clark Sch Choral Dir; Music Educators Natl Conference, AFT; Friends of Polish Art; Amer Cncl for Polish Culture; *office:* Clark Sch 15755 Bremen Detroit MI 48224

GUGAT, TERRY MICHAEL, Social Studies Dept Chairman; *b:* San Jose, CA; *m:* Sharmin Ann Mc Dowell; *c:* Scott M., Todd A.; *ed:* (BA) Soc Sci, Mesa Coll 1978; Teaching Certificate Scndry, Univ of N CO 1980; *cr:* Teacher West Jr HS 1981-85, West Mid Sch 1985-; *ai:* 8th Grade Bsktbl Coach; Teach Soc Stud Methods Class; Sch Dist 51 Teacher Excl Awd.

GUGLIELMINO, PATRICIA COULTER, First Grade Teacher; *b:* Longview, WA; *m:* Peter J.; *c:* Tucker J.; *ed:* (BA) Rdng, 1982, (MA) Rdng, 1988 E WA Univ; 5th Yr E WA Univ; *cr:* Chapter I Teacher 1983, 4th Grade Teacher 1983-84, 1st Grade Teacher 1984- Northport Elem Sch; *ai:* Northport Ed Assn Pres; Rdng Resource Specialist; Intnl Rdng Assn, Assn of Rdng Resource Specialists, WA Organization for Rdng Dev; Natl Wildlife Assn; *office:* Northport Elem Sch Box 180 Northport WA 99157

GUICE, MICHAEL DAVID, 8th Grade Soc Stud Teacher; *b:* Oldenburg, MS; *m:* Eva Ann Langford; *c:* Michelle D., Kristi D.; *ed:* (BS) Ed, MS St Univ 1969; (MED) Ed/Admin, Univ of S MS 1972; Sch Admin Univ of S MS; *cr:* Teacher Lillie Mae Bryant HS 1969-70, Franklin HS 1970-82; Supt of Curr Franklin Cty Schls 1982-84; Teacher Franklin Jr HS 1984-89; *ai:* Phi Delta Kappa (Pres, Treas) 1976-89, Certificate of Recognition 1988; MS Prof Ed Assn 1985-89; Gideons Secy 1988-; Amer Achievement Awd Soc Stud 1972; Taft Inst Seminar Awd 1976; *office:* Franklin Jr HS PO Box 643 Meadville MS 39653

GUIDO, LISA MARIA, French/Italian Teacher; *b:* Detroit, MI; *m:* William John Cibulka; *ed:* (BS) Fr, 1983, (BA) Ed, 1983, (MED) Childrens Lit, 1985 Wayne St Univ; Certificate of Studies Fr, Italian: Italian Studs Univ of Rochester; *cr:* Preschool Fr Teacher Mt Clements Montessori 1982-84; Fr Teacher Washington Elem Sch 1984-87, Fernale HS 1986-87; Fr/Italian Teacher Irondequoit HS 1987-; *ai:* WA Safety Patrol Leader; Frosh/Soph Class Adv; Track Coach; Pre-Season Trainor; Coord Sr Citizens Visitation; Awds Comm; AATF 1983-; Italian Teachers Assn 1987-, NY St Assn Foreign Lang Teachers 1987-; Intnl Dance & Exercise Assn; Amer Red Cross 1980- 5 Yrs Service Awd 1985; Develop FLES Prgm Ferndale Mi; Book to Aid Lang Teaching Elem Sch Level; *office:* Irondequoit H S 260 Cooper Rd Rochester NY 14617

GUIDRY, KAY MOREAU, Second Grade Teacher; *b:* Port Arthur, TX; *m:* Michael C.; *c:* Greg, Laura; *ed:* (BS) Elem Ed, Lamar Univ 1969; Grad Stud Univ of St Thomas; *cr:* 5th Grade Teacher Stephen F Austin Elem 1969-70; 1st Grade Teacher Sims Elem 1970-71, Highlands Elem 1977-80; 1st/2nd Grade Teacher B P Hopper Primary 1980-; *ai:* 1st Grade Team Leader 1980-82; Lang Art Team Leader 1986-; TX St Teachers Assn, Baytown Classroom Teachers Assn; *home:* 3724 Autumn Ln Baytown TX 77521

GUILFOYLE, MARGE MARY, English Teacher; *b:* Hammond, IN; *m:* Thomas F.; *c:* David K.; *ed:* (BSED) Speech/Drama, IN St Univ 1970; (MA) Eng, CA Poly Pomona 1981; Rdng, Gifted/Talented Ed; Stracture of Intellect; *cr:* Drama/Speech/Eng Teacher West Chicago Cmmty HS 1970-75, Gavit Jr/Sr HS 1975-76, Damien HS 1977, Barstow Jr HS 1977-78; Eng Teacher Ontario HS 1978-80; Coord of Gifted & Talented Ed/Teacher Chaffey HS 1980-; *ai:* Mentor Teacher; Instr Staff Dev; NEA 1970-; CA Teachers Assn 1980-; NCTE 1984-; Amer Bus Womens Assn VP 1981-87; Amer Assn of Univ Women 1983-84; Oak Tree Parent Support Group (Pres 1989-, VP 1988-89); Keywanettes Outstanding Educator Awd; Mentor Teacher; Teacher in Space Lecturer; *office:* Chaffey HS PO Box 1429 Upland CA 91785

GUILIANO, VIRGINIA A., 4th Grade Teacher; *b:* New Rochelle, NY; *ed:* (BA) Art His, Coll of Mt St Vincent 1948; Fordham Univ Ed Sch; Columbia Univ Sch of Ed; Toured England & Scandinavia Wright Univ Literary Tour; *cr:* Teacher Cntrl Elem 1959-72; 4th-6th Grade Teacher 1972-75, Teacher of Gifted 1975-88, 4th Grade Teacher 1988- N Palm Beach; *ai:* Excl & Math Comm Mem; CTA, NEA 1980-.

GUILLORY, TED DWAINE, 8th Grade Science Teacher; *b:* Mamou, LA; *m:* Gwendolyn E.; *c:* Rebecca; *ed:* (BA) Elem Ed, NE LA Univ 1979; Astronomy, Scuba, Electronics, Small Engines & Motorcycles AMI Daytona Beach; *cr:* 2nd Grade Teacher Jack Hayes Elem 1979-80; 7th-8th Grade Teacher Truman Elem 1980-81; 6th/8th Grade Teacher Armstrong Mid Sch 1981-; *ai:* Astronomy & Scuba Club Spon; LEA Mem 1986-; PADI Open H2O 1985; NASE Instr 1988; *office:* Armstrong Mid Sch 700 West E Rayne LA 70578

GUILTNER, BONNIE IVALENE JOHNSON, Retired 3rd Grade Teacher; *b:* Zion, AR; *m:* Troy B.; *c:* Gregory J., Linda C. Kuehn; *ed:* (BSE) Sci/Soc Stud/Elem, AR St Teachers 1953; (MS) Elem Ed, St Univ of Wichita 1970; Grad Stud Univ of Wichita; *cr:* Teacher Public Sch 1947-55, Plainview HS 1955-57, Elem Sch Wichita KS 1960-85; *ai:* Building Rep; Class Spon.

GUINEE, PATRICIA ANN, French/English Teacher; *b:* Niles, IL; *ed:* (BA) Commerce/Modern Lang 1986, (MA) Ed, 1990 St Francis Coll; *cr:* Fr/Eng Teacher Bishop Carroll HS 1986-87, N Cambria HS 1987-88, Cntrl Cambria HS 1988-; *ai:* Newspaper Adv; Class Spon; Phi Sigma Iota 1986-88; NCTE 1989-; *office:* Central Cambria HS PO Box 800 Rt 422 W Ebensburg PA 15931

GUINN, LISA GARLAND, Chemistry/English Teacher; *b:* Johnson City, TN; *m:* Bobby Joe; *c:* Daniel; *ed:* (BS) Psych, Milligan Coll 1986; *cr:* Eng/Ec Teacher Hampton HS 1986-88; Eng/Chem Teacher Happy Valley HS 1988-; *ai:* NHS Spon; *office:* Happy Valley HS Rt 11 Box 3500 Elizabethton TN 37643

GUINN, RUTH ANN ANN MARION, Substance Abuse Counselor; *b:* Winfield, KS; *m:* Terry S.; *ed:* (BSE) Ed, Emporia St Univ 1980; (MS) Marriage/Family/Child Counseling, CA St Univ Northridge 1990; *cr:* Bus Teacher Unified Sch Dist #368 1981-84; Cnslr West Valley Chrstn Schls 1984-89; Substance Abuse Cnslr Burrell Center 1990; *ai:* Yrbk & Chrldr Adv; CA Scholastic Fed & Class Spon; Western Assn of Coll Admissions Cnslrs 1987-; CA Sch Cnslrs Assn 1987-; Alpha Sigma Alpha Chaplain 1977-; *home:* 2139 N Rogers Springfield MO 65803

GUINTU, RAMONA DABU, Fifth Grade Teacher; *b:* Lubao Pampanga, Philippines; *m:* Lolito R.; *c:* Leslie, Ron Quillo; *ed:* (BSEE) Elem Ed, Guagua Natl Colls 1952; (MA) Guidance & Counseling, Philippine Womens Univ; Elem Math Amer Institution; Span Food & Nutrition, Religion, Soc Stud, Sci & Lang Art; *cr:* 1st Grade Teacher San Pablo Elem Sch 1950-54; 5th Grade Teacher Santa Cruz Elem Sch 1955-70; 5th/6th Grade Teacher All Saints Sch 1972-80; 5th Grade Teacher St Elzabeth Sch 1980-; *ai:* Stanford Achievement Test Coord; NCEA 1972-; *office:* St Elizabeth Elem Sch 1840 N Lake Ave Altadena CA 91001

GUIST, MAYNARD L., Reading/Computer Teacher; *b:* Viroqua, WI; *m:* Cindy; *c:* Chrissy, Nicky, Angie; *ed:* (BA) Sociology, 1974, (BS) Ed, 1975 N IL Univ; (MEPD) Ed, Univ of WI La Crosse 1983; *cr:* Soc Stud/Rdng/Cmptr Teacher Viroqua Mid Schls 1977-; *ai:* Mid Sch Bsktbl & Tennis; HS Golf Coach; Model Rocketry & Radio Controlled Modeling Adv; Team Leader; Rdng Chairperson; Mid Sch Cmptr Coord; Viroqua Ed Assn Officer 1980-; WI Rdng Assn Mem 1983-; Natl Sch Bd Assn Awd 1987; *office:* Viroqua Area Schls Blackhawk Dr Viroqua WI 54665

GULAS, MARLENE SUE (ADRICK), Reading Teacher; *b:* Covington, KY; *m:* Ronald J.; *c:* Steve, Linda; *ed:* (BS) Eng Ed, Bowling Green St *cr:* Rdng & Lang Arts Teacher Bataan Sch 1961-63, Pt Clinton Jr HS 1963-65; Substitute Teacher Pt Clinton City Schs 1975-76; Rdng & Lang Arts Teacher Pt Clinton Jr HS 1976-; *ai:* Consulting Teacher to Intern Teacher; NCTE; Citizens Awareness of Substance Abuse Secy 1985-87; Amer Assn of Univ Women 1977-83; Pt Clinton Jr Womens (Secy 1967-68/His 1968-69); PEO Treas 1973-74; Martha Holden Jennings Scholar 1989-; *home:* 4652 E Terrace Cir Port Clinton OH 43452

GULBERG, E. LAWRENCE, Athletic Dir/Chem Teacher; *b:* Bremerton, WA; *m:* Deborah L. Fine; *c:* Edward R., Sunny D.; *ed:* (BS) Chem, Stanford 1971; (MED) Sci Ed, 1977, (PHD) Analytical Chem, 1980 Univ of WA; *cr:* Chem Teacher Inglemoor HS 1972-83; Chem Instr Shoreline Jr Coll 1980; Instrument Specialist Fisher Scientific Company 1986-87; Athletic Dir Woodinville HS 1983-; *ai:* Golf Coach; Service Club Adv; Dance Supvr; WA Scndry Sch Athletic Admins Assn Mem 1989-; Young Life Volunteer Leader 1968-73, 1989-; Chem Doctoral Research Publications; *office:* Woodinville HS 19819 136th Ave NE Woodinville WA 98072

GULDHAUG, VIOLET M. (HENDRICKSON), Retired Supervisor & Teacher; *b:* Argyle, WI; *w:* Harold (dec); *ed:* (BS) Elem Ed, Univ of WI Platteville 1969; Moody Bible Inst 1942-46; Grad from Missions Course 1946; *cr:* 1st-8th Grade Teacher Grove Rural Sch 1937-42; Missionary Girls Orphanage Killegal S India 1948-51; Jr HS Teacher New Glarus Public Schls 1965-73; Teacher/Supvr New Glarus Chrstn Nursery Sch 1973-76; 3rd-12th Grade Eng/Soc Stud/Lang Art Teacher New Glarus Chrstn Sch 1976-89; *ai:* Postville Bible Church Youth Worker 1954-62; New Glarus Baptist Bible Church Sunday Sch Teacher 1954-80.

GULICK, WILLIAM D., SR., Science Teacher; *b:* Jackson Heights, NY; *m:* Carol Montroy; *c:* Robert, Christine, Wm. Jr., Timothy; *ed:* (BS) Bio, Fairfield Univ 1969; (MA) Liberal Stud, SUNY 1971; *cr:* Sci Teacher Green Meadows Jr HS 1969-79; Sawmill Jr HS 1979-88; Commack Mid Sch 1988-; *ai:* Stu Cncl Adv; Dist Task Force Mid Ed; Dist Historical Comm; Long Island Kickline Assn Dir 1975-; Honorary Life Mem NYS PTA 1979-88; *office:* Commack Mid Sch Vanderbilt Pkwy Commack NY 11725

GULLEDGE, EMILY COGGIN, Second Grade Teacher; *b:* Fayetteville, NC; *m:* Earl Graham; *c:* Elizabeth; *ed:* (BA) Elem Ed, Campbell Univ 1968; *cr:* 2nd Grade Teacher Indian Trail 1968-69, Oaklawn 1969-71; 1st Grade Teacher 1971-76; 2nd Grade Teacher Cotswold 1976-; *ai:* Cotswold Sch Newspaper Comm; Southern Assn Fine Arts Comm Chairperson; Classroom Teachers Assn 1983-; *office:* Cotswold Elem Sch 300 Greenwich Rd Charlotte NC 28211

GULLET, SHARON ODELLA, American History Teacher; *b:* New Albany, IN; *ed:* (BS) Scndry Ed/Soc Sci, 1964, (MS) Scndry Ed/Soc Sci, 1967 IN Univ; Cert in Ed Gifted/Talented; *cr:* Teacher Scribner Jr HS 1961-78, Floyd Cntrl Jr HS 1978-; *ai:* NEA, IN St Teachers Assn, Floyd Cty Ed 1964-; Kappa Delta Pi 1989-; Floyd Cty Theatre Bd 1988-; Floyd Cty Cncl for Arts 1989-, Medici 1989; *home:* 4025 Grant Line Rd New Albany IN 47150

GULLICKS, KRISTINE RONNING, First Grade Teacher; *b:* Powers Lake, ND; *m:* Gary Wayne; *c:* Jacqueline, Kimberly, Jason; *ed:* (BS) Elem Ed, Minot St Univ 1969; *cr:* 2nd Grade Teacher Williston Public Sch 1969-71; 1st Grade Teacher Grand Forks Public Sch 1971-73; Secy Hartl & Orvik Law Office 1973-76; Kndgtn Teacher 1976-81, 1st Grade Teacher 1981- Westhope Public Sch; *ai:* Sunday Sch Teacher; ND Ed Assn; NEA Life Mem; Westhope Ed Assn; Westhope Womens Club Pres 1986-87; Women of Evangelical Luth Church of America; *home:* Box 198 Westhope ND 58793

GULLION, JAMES MADISON, II, History Department Chair; *b:* Wichita, KS; *m:* Letha Cellars; *c:* Kimberly J.; *ed:* (BSE) Phys Ed, E TX Baptist Univ 1982; Grad Stud Phys Ed; *cr:* Educator/Coach Tennyson Jr HS 1982-85; Athletic Dir/Educator Sam Houston Mid Sch 1985-86; Educator/Coach Poteet HS 1986-87, A C New Mid Sch 1987-; *ai:* Coach 8th Grade Ftbl, Head Bsktbl; Sch & Cmmty Involvement Chm; Cluster Comm Mem; THSCA 1983-; ATPE 1985-; TSTA 1982-85; Public Service Awd; *home:* 2129 Smokey Mountain Trl Mesquite TX 75149

GULLO, ANNETTE NORENE, Third Grade Teacher; *b:* Batavia, NY; *m:* Vincent J. Jr.; *c:* Gregory V., Elizabeth A.; *ed:* (BS) Elem Ed, D Youville Coll Buffalo 1962; Advanced Wkshp & Classes Academic Curr Stud & Religious Ed; *cr:* 1st/2nd Grade Teacher St Josephs Sch 1960-61; 4th Grade Teacher Hanahan Elem Sch 1962-64; 1st Grade Teacher Dover AFB Elem 1970-75; 3rd Grade Teacher Sacred Heart Sch 1980-; *ai:* NCEA Teacher Assoc 1980-; *office:* Sacred Heart Sch 250 High St Mount Holly NJ 08060

GULZOW, STEVE KENNETH, Amer His Teacher/Soc Stud Chm; *b:* Grand Island, NE; *ed:* (BA) His, Hastings Coll 1972; (MSE) Amer His, Kearney St Coll 1977; Univ of NE; Concordia Teachers Coll; *cr:* 7th Grade Soc Stud Teacher, 8th Grade Amer His Teacher, 9th Grade World Geography Teacher 1972-75 Chadron Mid Sch; 7th Grade Soc Stud Teacher, 8th Grade Amer His Teacher 1975- Adams Mid Sch; *ai:* 7th Grade Ftbl Coach; 7th-8th Boys-Girls Track; Interdisciplinary Team Leader; North Platte Public Schls Strategic Planning Team; Chm Soc Stud Dept; North Platte Ed Assn 1975-; NE St Ed Assn 1972-; NEA 1972-; NCSS 1980-; NE St Historical Society 1980-; Benovolent-Protective Order of Elks Schlsp Comm 1975; Sons of Amer Legion 1985; Toastmasters Intnl 1988; Teacher of Month

North Platte Public Schls 1984; Outstanding Teacher of Amer His; NE Chapter Daughters of Amer Revolution 1985; 20th Annual Dakota His Conference Awd Winner 1989; Christa Mcauliffe Awd Nom 1988; *office:* Adams Middle School 1200 Mc Donald Rd North Platte NE 69101

GUMBS, MARION LOUISE, Sixth Grade Teacher; *b:* New London, CT; *ed:* (BA) Ed, Kirkland/Hamilton Coll 1978; (MS) Rdng Teacher, Russell Sage Coll 1983; *cr:* 6th Grade Teacher Rensselaer City Sch Dist 1978-; *office:* Rensselaer Jr/Sr HS 555 Broadway Rensselaer NY 12144

GUMM, MICHAEL LYNN, 8th Grade Sci/Math Teacher; *b:* Campbellsville, KY; *m:* Sandra Rafferty; *c:* Steven, Allen; *ed:* (BS) Math/Chem, Campbellsville Coll 1974; (Rank II) W KY Univ 1984; *cr:* Math/Chem Teacher Monticello HS 1974-84; 8th Grade Sci/Math Teacher Campbellsville Mid Sch 1984-; *ai:* Campbellsville Mid Sch Ftbl & Bsktbl Coach 1985-; KY Ed Assn, NEA, Campbellsville Ed Assn; *office:* Campbellsville Mid Sch RR 1 Campbellsville KY 42718

GUMP, LINDA ANN, Spanish Teacher Foreign Lang; *b:* Dallas, TX; *ed:* (BA) Span, North TX St Univ 1969; (MLA) Liberal Arts, Southern Meth Univ 1973; *cr:* Span Teacher Hillcrest HS 1969-86; Foreign Lang Dept Chairperson/Span Teacher Trinity Chrstn Acad 1986-; *ai:* Foreign Lang Dept Chairperson; Honor Cncl Adv; Span NHS Spon; Amer Assn of Teachers of Span/Portuguese; TX for Lang Assn; Ross Perot Awd for Teaching Excl 1976; *home:* 5881 Prestonview #105 Dallas TX 75240

GUNCHUCK, ROBERTA SUE, Behavior Disorder Teacher; *b:* Mount Pleasant, PA; *ed:* (BS) Elem Ed, 1977, (BS/Sp) Spec Ed, 1977 Slippery Rock Univ; (MA) Speech Comm, WV Univ 1983; Journalism, Univ of CT 1979; Chemical Dependency, Charleston Area Medical Center 1988; Creative Writing, Inst of Childrens Lit CT 1979; *cr:* Behavior Disorder Teacher Wood Cty Public Schls 1977-; Donor Recruiter1986-88, Disaster Service 1987-89 Amer Red Cross; Tutor 1980-; Military Service Asst Amer Red Cross 1986-88; *ai:* Spec Ed Advisory Bd; Wood Cty Accreditation Team; WV St Educl Accreditation Team; Natl Writers Assn 1986-; Amer Fed of Teachers Building Rep 1986-; Rdng Cncl 1980-; Natl Advisory Bd Vantage Press 1988-, Creative Writer 1989; Mu Kappa Gamma Music Honorary 1974-; Application Missions 1977-; Democratic Women Inc 1989-; Amer Red Cross 1987-89; Natl Humane Society 1989-; Green Peace 1989-; Amer Campers Assn 1980-; Lector For Educl Wkshp Groups/Univ & Organizations; An Educators Cry Roberta Sue Gunchuck; Golden Poet/Silver Poet Awd; Creative Writer Awd; Tree Shadows published in Amer Best Loved Poems by Roberta Gunchuck; *home:* 4 Wildwood Estates Apt A Parkersburg WV 26101

GUNDACKER, ROSEMARY NIGON, Mathematics Teacher/ Dept Chair; *b:* Rochester, MN; *m:* Erik; *c:* Sara, Craig, Nicole, Kristi; *ed:* (BA) Math, Coll of St Teresa 1968; (MA) Math, AZ St Univ 1971; Univ of N IA, Makato St, Univ of MN; *cr:* Grad Asst AZ St Univ 1969-71; Teacher Ellsworth Comm Coll 1971-72, Waterloo Schls 1973-74, Rosemount Schls 1974-; *ai:* Math Dept Coord; Math Team Coach; NCTM, MCTM; *office:* Rosemount HS 3335 142nd St W Rosemount MN 55068

GUNDERSON, JIM ALLEN, Science/Mathematics Teacher; *b:* Sidney, NE; *m:* Keffenie Kay Wolfe; *c:* Lance, Brandon; *ed:* (BS) Phys Sci/Chem, Kearney St Coll 1978; *cr:* Sci Teacher Wilsonville Public Schls 1978-80; Sci/Math Teacher Elm Creek Public Schls 1980-; *ai:* All Sch Play Dir; Sr Class Spon; Natl Assn of Sci Teachers 1988-; *home:* 4211 Bel Air Dr Kearney NE 68847

GUNDERSON, JOHN ALBERT, 5th Grade Teacher; *b:* La Crosse, WI; *m:* Lynn Gehrmann; *c:* Ryan, Tricia, Timothy; *ed:* (BS) Psych, 1971, Cert Elem Ed, 1976 Univ of WI Eau Claire; Guidance & Counseling, Univ of WI Stout 1972; *cr:* Guidance Cnclr Osseo Elem Sch 1972-74; 4th Grade Teacher Arcadia Schls 1976-77; 5th Grade Teacher Whitehall Schls 1977-79, Altoona Schls 1979-; *home:* 412 W Washington Ave Fall Creek WI 54742

GUNDERSON, MARGARET HAAS, Business Education Teacher; *b:* Baltimore, MD; *m:* John; *c:* Kristen, Jennifer, Mary E.; *ed:* (AA) Exec Secretarial, Bucks Cty Comm Coll 1975; (BS) Bus Ed, 1977, (MED) Bus Ed, 1980 Trenton St Coll; *cr:* Teacher Delhaas HS 1977, Pennsbury HS 1977-84, Lyman HS 1985-; *ai:* FBLA Spon; SEA, NEA, PEA; *office:* Lyman HS 1141 SE Lake Ave Longwood FL 32750

GUNDRUM, ELSA MAY, Business Teacher; *b:* Reading, PA; *ed:* (BS) Bus Ed/Comprehensive Stud, Bloomsburg Univ 1987; IBM & Apple Cmptr Applications, Telecommunications; *cr:* Long Term Sub Bus Teacher Governor Mifflin Sr HS 1987-88; Bus Teacher Oley Valley HS 1988-; *ai:* NHS & FBLA Adv; In Charge of HS Tutoring Prgm; NEA 1988-; Phi Beta Lambda Alumnus 1986-; *office:* Oley Valley HS Jefferson St Oley PA 19547

GUNKLEMAN, BARBARA ANN, Teacher of Gifted Grades 3-6; *b:* Bay Village, OH; *m:* Gary Ray; *c:* Brian, Steven; *ed:* (BS) Elem Ed, 1972, (MED) Spec Ed Gifted, 1989 Kent St; *cr:* 3rd-4th Grade Teacher Liverpool Elem 1971-80; 2nd Grade Teacher Litchfield Elem 1981-82;3rd-6th Grade Gifted Teacher York Elem 1987-; *ai:* Student Cncl Adv 1989-; CEC; NCCG; AFT; Zion Luth Church Sunday Sch Supt 1986-87 & 1990; Valley City Youth Leag Coach 1982; Presenter CEC Natl Convention San Francisco 1989; Jennings Grant for Comm Resource Guide 1988; Teacher of Excl Medina Cty 1984-85; Presenter Martha Holden Jennings Conf 1987 & 1989; *office:* York Elem Sch 6695 Norwalk Rd Medina OH 44256

GUNN, EDNA JEAN, Counselor; *b:* Starkville, MS; *m:* Robert W.; *c:* Rhonda Sharpe, Debbie Sinko, Bill Teague, Margaret; *ed:* (BS) Bus Secretarial Sci, MS St Univ 1952; (MED) Guidance Ed, MS St Univ 1969; *cr:* Exec Secy Deposit Guaranty Natl Bank 1961-68; Remedial Rdng Teacher Newark AR Sch 1969-71; Cnslr Tyronza AR Sch 1971-73; 5th Grade Teacher Lee Acad 1973-74; Cnslr Delta Sch 1975-; *ai:* 10th Grade Spon; Staff Dev Comm; Southeast AR Cnslr Assn; AR Sch Cnslr Assn; ASCD; *office:* Delta Sch P O Box 41 Rohwer AR 71666

GUNN, FRANCENE AMBROSE, English Teacher; *b:* Detroit, MI; *m:* Gerry Arnaz; *c:* Franscile; *ed:* (BA) Eng, Marygrove Coll 1981; Natl Writing Project Fellow 1986; *cr:* Eng Teacher St Marys of Redford HS 1981-83; Substitute Teacher Burroughs Mid Sch 1984-85; Eng Teacher Martin Luther King HS 1985-; *ai:* Jr Class Adv 1989-; Yrbk Adv 1987-; Pep Club Spon 1988-; NCTE, MI Cncl Teachers of Eng 1988-; *office:* Martin Luther King HS 3200 E Lafayette Detroit MI 48207

GUNN, JOE E., Director of Bands; *b:* El Drado, AR; *m:* Sue Norton; *c:* Nikki, Julie; *ed:* (BME) Instrumental Music Ed, Henderson St Univ 1967; (MM) Music Ed, East TX St Univ 1989; *cr:* Jr HS Band Conway Public Schls 1967-69; Assoc Dir of Bands L D Bell HS 1970-72; Dir of Bands Harwood Jr HS 1972-78/ 1981; *ai:* Ftbl Pep Band; Jazz Ensemble; TX Music Ed Assn; TX Bandmasters Assn; Phi Beta Mu; Honorary Life Membeship TX PTA 1987; *home:* 2517 Sunshine Ct Bedford TX 76021

GUNN, KARLENE EDMONDS, First Grade Teacher; *b:* Gladewater, TX; *m:* James H. Jr.; *c:* Gary S., Karla D., Gregory B.; *ed:* (BA) Elem Ed/Eng, TX Chrstn Univ 1959; Grad Stud & Educl Wkshps *cr:* 1st Grade Teacher B H Carroll Sch 1959-62, Kilgore Heights 1972-87, Chandler Elem 1987-; *ai:* 1st Grade Chm 1984-87; Gifted & Talented Rep 1980-83; Classroom Teachers Assn 1980-, TX St Teachers Assn (Soc Comm Chm, Sch Rep) 1972-82; PTA 1968-, Life Membership Awd 1968; Alpha Delta Kappa (Secy 1987-88) 1982-; *office:* Chandler Elem Sch 711 N Longview Kilgore TX 75662

GUNN, LINDA CHILDS, Fourth Grade Teacher; *b:* Ripley, MS; *m:* James Wallace Jr.; *c:* Trey, Kayla; *ed:* (BS) Elem Ed, Blue Mountain Coll 1977; (MS) Elem Ed, 1979, Specialist Elem Ed, 1982 Univ of MS; *cr:* 4th Grade Teacher Falkner Elem Sch 1977-; *ai:* K-5th Grade Sci Fair Coord 1990; Certified MS Teacher Assessment Instrument Supervise Stu Teachers; MS Prof Educators 1988-; Kappa Kappa Iota Teachers 1985-; *home:* Rt 1 Box 344 Walnut MS 38683

GUNN, MELODY ANN, English Department Chair; *b:* Elgin, IL; *m:* James A.; *c:* Joshua, Adrienne; *ed:* (BSED) Eng, IL St Univ 1971; (MAT) Eng, Rockford Coll 1981; Eng Supervisory Certificate; *cr:* Eng Teacher Harlem HS 1971-72, Marshall Mid Sch 1972-75, Harlem HS 1977-; *office:* Harlem HS 9229 N Alpine Rockford IL 61103

GUNN, PAULINE LEVON, English Department Chair; *b:* Greensboro, FL; *ed:* (BA) Eng, Stillman Coll 1973; (MED) Eng, 1976; (MS) Educl Leadership 1989 FL A&M Univ; *cr:* Eng Teacher Carter-Parramore Mid Sch 1973-; *ai:* Brain Brawl Team, Spelling Bee, Declamation Contest, Walt Disney Dreamers & Doers Awd, Philadelphia-NY City Tour, Fashion & Modeling Club Spon; FTP, NEA, GCCTA 1973-; Gasden Mid Sch Cncl (Asst Secy 1988-89, Chairperson 1990); Union Baptist Assn Congress Secy 1976-; Gadsden Rdng Cncl 1987-; *home:* PO Box 411 Greensboro FL 32330

GUNNELS, JANET C., French/English Teacher; *b:* Ord, NE; *m:* David P.; *c:* Melissa, Michael; *ed:* (BA) Eng/Fr Ed, Kearney St Coll 1961; Grad Stud KS St Univ, VA St Univ, VA Commonwealth Univ, Chapman Coll; *cr:* 2nd-8th Grade Eng Teacher Cozad City Schls 1959-60; 1st Grade Teacher Laupahoehoe Elem Sch 1962; Eng Teacher Laupahoehoe HS 1962-63; 3rd Grade Teacher Baumholder Amer Elem Sch Baumholder Germany 1963-64; Eng/Fr Teacher Baumholder Amer HS Baumholder Germany 1964-65; 8th Grade Eng Teacher Faith Sch 1966 & 1968-69; 1st Grade Teacher St Josephs Elem 1973-74; K-3rd Grade Teacher Aschaffenburg Amer Elem Aschaffenburg Germany 1976-78; 7th Grade Eng/Fr Teacher Lakeside Mid Sch 1979-80; 8th Grade Eng Teacher Dinwiddie Jr HS 1980-84; Fr/Eng Teacher Dinwiddie Sr HS 1984-; *ai:* NHS Adv; Odyssey of Mind Judge; FLAVA; Southside VA Writing Project Assoc 1988-; NEH Grant Tufts Univ Amer Civilization 1984; *office:* Dinwiddie Cty HS PO Box 299 Dinwiddie VA 23841

GUNTER, BRENDA KAY, English Teacher; *b:* Paris, TX; *ed:* (BA) Eng/His, 1979, (MED) Elem Ed, 1982 E TX St Univ; Scndry, Higher Ed E TX St Univ; *cr:* Teacher Rivercrest HS 1979-; *ai:* Jr Class & UIL Spelling Spon; Chm Inservice Planning Comm; Assn of TX Prof Educators (Bd of Dirs 1986-, Region Officer 1984-); Delta Kappa Gamma; Kappa Delta Pi, NCTE, TX Assn for Gifted & Talented; Most Prominent TX Educator 1983; *office:* Rivercrest HS P O Box 130 Bogata TX 75417

GUNTER, DIANE M., 3rd Grade Teacher; *b:* Lima, OH; *ed:* (BA) Elem Ed, Findlay Coll 1967; (MED) Diagnostic Ed Rndgs, Miami Univ 1975; Post Masters Studies Wright St Univ; Bowling Green St Univ; Mount St Josephs; OH St Univ; *cr:* 2nd Grade Teacher 1967-72; 1st Grade Teacher 1972-82; 6th Grade Teacher 1982-88; 3rd Grade Teacher 1988- Celina City Schls; *ai:* Past Pres-Celina Ed Assn; Western OH Ed Assn-Instrnl & Prof Dev Comm; Delta Kappa Gamma Society Intl Pres 1976-78; NEA; OH Ed Assn; Celina Ed Assn; Schlr-William Holden Jennings Fnd; OH Ed Assn-Exec Comm 1983-86; Western OH Ed Assn-Exec Comm 1980-86; Celina Ed Assn-Pres 1972/1982-84/1986-87; BEA Rep 1982-86/1988; *office:* West Elem Sch 1225 W Logan St Celina OH 45822

GUNTER, HORACE EDWARD, World History Teacher; *b:* Kansas City, MO; *m:* Virginia Marie Wisby; *c:* Michael Shanks, Jamie Payne, Michelle Blakley, Kellie, Jeff Shanks; *ed:* (AA) His, Longview Comm Coll 1970; (BSE) Soc Sci Ed/His, NM St Univ Kirksville 1972; MA Early European His, Univ of MO Kansas City 1991; *cr:* Teacher/Adult Ed Instr Kirksville Jr HS 1972-78; Cmptr Prgm Writer Kansas City MO Public Schls 1979-82; Teacher Raymore-Peculiar HS 1982-; *ai:* Impact Coord; Chess Club & Model United Nations Spon; Phi Alpha Theta, NEA 1971-; PTO Special Olympics Pres 1979-82; AF&AM Adair 362 1976-; NEH Grant, Cntrl MO St Univ 1988; Various Newspaper Articles Published; *office:* Raymore-Peculiar HS 211 School Rd Peculiar MO 64078

GUNTER, MARGARET BEELER, English Department Chairperson; *b:* Roanoke, VA; *m:* Robert Leon; *c:* Elizabeth; *ed:* (BA) Eng/Ed, Stratford Coll 1972; (MED) Elem Ed, Univ of VA 1982; *cr:* 6th-7th Grade Teacher Samuel H Hairston Elem 1973-78; 6th-8th Grade Eng Teacher J D Bassett Mid Sch 1978-85; 9th-12th Grade Eng Teacher Fieldale Collinsville HS 1985-; *ai:* Soph Class Spon; Newspaper Spon; Delta Kappa Gamma; *office:* Fieldale-Collinsville H S 415 Miles Rd Collinsville VA 24078

GUNTHER, JANICE MORRISSEY, Third Grade Teacher; *b:* Poughkeepsie, NY; *c:* Christine Nelson, Kathy Dassinger, Robert, Lisa Martin, Virginia, Kenneth, Thomas, John, Geraldine; *ed:* (BA) His/Poly Sci, St Joseph Coll 1948; *cr:* Teacher Allenwood Elem Sch 1974-; *ai:* Monmouth Cty Ed Assn, NJ Ed Assn, NEA, Wall Township Ed Assn; PTA; Rosary; *office:* Allenwood Elem Sch Allenwood & Lakewood Rd Allenwood NJ 08720

GUNVILLE, LAWRENCE JOHN, 5th Grade Teacher; *b:* Hibbing, MN; *ed:* (BA) Elem Ed, Bemidji ST Univ 1969; *cr:* 5th Grade Teacher Westview Elem 1969-70; Northview Elem 1970-; *ai:* Sch Patrol Adv; Yrbk Adv; Northview Site Cncl; PTA Bd Teacher Rep; Summer Sch Lead Teacher; Bicycle Safety Coord; Rosemount Fed of Teachers Membership Chairperson 1989-; MN River Valley Kennel Club Secy 1989-; Honeywell Mini-Grant 1987-88; *home:* 13981 Holyoke Path Apple Valley MN 55124

GURGANUS, MARTY CROSSWELL, Jr HS Physical Ed Teacher; *b:* Goldsboro, NC; *m:* Connie Nichols; *c:* Michael B.; *ed:* (BS) Phys Ed, NC Wesleyan 1984; *cr:* Phys Ed Teacher Grantham Sch 1984-; *ai:* Girls & Boys Bsktbl, Girls Sftbl, Asst Ftbl Coach; Adv for Phys Ed Majors & Monogram Club; Mem of Media Comm; K-9th Grade Field Day Spon; Teacher of Yr Grantham Sch.

GURLEY, CHARLOTTE DIANE MC GINNIS, 5th Grade Teacher; *b:* Gadsden, AL; *m:* Don Alan; *c:* Jason A., Jamie E.; *ed:* (BS) Elem Ed, Jacksonville St 1975; Working Toward Masters; *cr:* 5th Grade Teacher Coosa Chrstn 1975-76; 2nd Grade Teacher Striplin Elem 1977-79; 5th Grade Teacher Floyd Elem 1979-84; 2nd Grade Teacher 1984-89, 5th Grade Teacher 1989- Walnut Park; *ai:* Stash & Cultural Arts Chm; Standing Textbook, Clean & Beautiful, Centennial Comms; Writes & Directs Plays; Talent Show Coord; PAGE, NEA, AEA; Coosa Valley Rdng Assn Pres 1983-84; PTA (Pres, 1st VP, 2nd VP); Teacher of Yr; Articles Published; Sing with Steadfast Gospel Trio; *home:* 141 River Oak Dr Gadsden AL 35903

GURULE, JOE, JR., Phys Ed Teacher/Principal; *b:* Santa Fe, NM; *m:* Sylvia; *c:* Joe III, Krista; *ed:* (BA) Elem/Scndry Ed, SW Union Univ 1976; (MA) Ed Admin, Highlands Univ 1988; Grad Stud Highlands Univ; *cr:* 8th Grade Teacher El Rito Elem 1976-78; HS Teacher MESA Vista HS 1978-80; 8th Grade Teacher 1980-81, Teacher/Prin 1981- Ojo-Caliente Elem; *ai:* Athletic Coord Dist Wide Coach; Dist Chm A D 1989-; Church 1st Elder 1976-, Elders Assn 1980; Texico Conference Electing Comm Mem 1989-; Coach Awd 1976-78; *office:* Ojo-Caliente Elem Sch PO Box 50 Ojo Caliente NM 87549

GURULE, MAXIMO, Mathematics Teacher/Dept Chm; *b:* Rio Lucio, NM; *m:* Anita Rodarte; *c:* Annette Sanchez, Michelle Esquibel, Jeffrey, John; *ed:* (BS) Math/Accounting, Univ of Albuquerque 1965; Energy Ed 1975; Ind Stud Math 1980-82, Diagnostic & Prescriptive Rdng 1978; Curr Dev 1982; Summer Inst for Math Teachers 1983; Individual Study & Use of Cmptrs in Teaching Math 1983; Intro to Microcmptrs 1987; Applications of Holomorphic Functions 1984; *cr:* Math Teacher Penasco Jr-Sr HS 1965-; *ai:* Math Olympics Spon; Math Tutor at Picuris Pueblo; Timekeeper & Scorekeeper at Bsktbl Games; Mathcounts Coach; Math Curr Comm Jr-Sr HS; St Math Competencies Dev Comm Mem 1984; St Evaluation Advisory Comm Mem for Adopted Math Textbook Materials 1981; NASA Project to Name the Orbitor Evaluation Mem 1989; Former Instr Hunter Safety Course for Young Sportsmen; St Anthonys Elem Sch Bsktbl Team Coach; AFT Mem; Penasco Fed of Teachers Mem; Standards Comm; *office:* Penasco Jr HS & Sr HS P O Box 520 Penasco NM 87553

GUSICK, BARBARA VELIN, Mid Sch/HS Reading Teacher; *b:* Ironwood, MI; *m:* George A.; *c:* Jay, Julie; *ed:* (BS) Elem Ed, 1960, (MA) Elem Ed, 1966 N MI Univ; Post Grad Stud Univ of WI Oshkosh; *cr:* 6th Grade Teacher Iron Mountain Mid Schls 1960-74; Elem Rdng Specialist Hilbert Joint Sch Dist 1974-77; Mid Sch Rdng Specialist Omro Public Schls 1977-; *ai:* Omro Mid Sch Forensics Head Coach; Mid Sch Builders Club Adv; NEA, WEA, Delta Kappa Gamma; Omro Ed Assn (Pres 1987-88, Treas 1982-83); PEO Sisterhood Pres 1974-75; N MI Univ Alumni Bd of Dir 1961-87, Outstanding Alumni Awd 1985; Presbyn Church

Elder 1976-79; Univ of WI Oshkosh Ed Dept Ad-Hoc Professor; *home:* 1010 Canterbury Dr Oshkosh WI 54901

GUSTAFSON, BETTY JEANE (RYDER), Retired Teacher; *b:* Derby, IA; *w:* Emory R. (dec); *c:* Marvin A.; *ed:* (BA) Elem Ed/Eng/Soc Sci/Sci, Buena Vista Coll 1962; Univ of CO Boulder 1966; Univ of N IA Cedar Falls 1967, 1968, 1971; Open Court Related Lang, Univ of La Verne; *cr:* 7th/8th Grade Teacher Thayer Consolidated 1942-43, Harcourt Consolidated 1944-47; 6th Grade Teacher Prairie Cmmty Schls 1962-70; 5th/6th Grade Soc Stud/6th Grade Home Room Teacher Paton-Churdan Consolidated Sch 1970-73; 6th-8th Grade Teacher Boone Biblical Ministries 1973-74, 1976-78; 5th/6th Grade Teacher Cmmty Chrstn Sch 1978-85; *ai:* Coord Between Sch & Church; Church Secy; Chrstn Educators Fellowship Pres 1965-67; NEA, ISEA 1940-47, 1958-70; Harcourt Covenant Church (Organist 1958-75, Sunday Sch Teacher 1947-62, Womens Pres 1950-57) 1947-75; Covenant Womens St Bd 1954-57; *home:* 1485 21st Ave N Apt C6 Fort Dodge IA 50501

GUSTAFSON, DENNIS KEITH, Biology Teacher; *b:* Detroit, MI; *m:* Margot M. Kerper; *c:* David, Mark, Timothy; *ed:* (BA) Bio, Bethel Coll 1966; (MS) Zoology, 1975, (PHD) Bio, 1985 Univ of WI Milwaukee; *cr:* Bio/Sci Teacher Rufus King HS 1966-76; Teaching & Research Asst Univ of WI Milwaukee 1976-77; Bio Teacher John Marshall & Rufus King HS 1977-; Asst Bio Examiner Intnl Baccalaureate 1988-; *ai:* Yrbk Bus Mgr; NHS Comm; WI Society for Ornithology (Spring Field Notes Ed 1972) 1965-; AWANA Youth Organization Dir 1987-; Published in Univ of WI Milwaukee Field Station Bulletin 1976; Abstract in Bulletin of Ecological Society of America 1977; Co-Author of Bio Lab Manual Milwaukee Public Schls; *office:* Rufus King Sch for Coll Bound 1801 W Olive St Milwaukee WI 53209

GUSTAFSON, DOUG ALLAN, 6th Grade Teacher; *b:* Prosser, WA; *m:* Kathy Yahn; *ed:* (BA) Earth Sci, Eastern WA Univ 1983; *cr:* 8th-12th Grade Math Teacher 1985-86; 7th Grad Phys Ed/Math Teacher 1986-87; 6th Grade Math & Sci Teacher 1987-Kiona-Brenton City Mid Sch; *ai:* Jr Varsity Boys Bsktbl Coach; Jr Varsity Boys Bsbl Coach; *home:* 931 Market St Prosser WA 99350

GUSTAFSON, MARY ANN CRUTCHFIELD, Language Arts Teacher; *b:* Waco, TX; *m:* Bill Lee; *c:* Len, Brent; *ed:* (BS) Elem Ed/Eng, N TX St Univ 1968; Working Toward Counseling Certificate; *cr:* 6th Grade Lang Art Teacher Dallas Ind Sch Dist 1968-69; 2nd Grade Teacher St Elizabeths Cath Sch 1970-71; 7th Grade Lang Art Teacher Dallas Ind Sch Dist 1971-72; 3rd Grade Teacher S Park Ind Sch Dist 1972-73; 6th Grade Math Teacher 1978-82, 7th Grade Lang Art Teacher 1982- Humble Ind Sch Dist; *ai:* Stu Cncl Spon; Humble Ind Sch Dist Technology Comm; ATPE; Humble HS Bsbl Booster Club Bd Mem 1990; Humble Panhellenic VP 1989-; TX Mid Sch Conference Presenter 1988, 1989; *office:* Atascocita Mid Sch 18810 W Lake Houston Pkwy Humble TX 77346

GUSTAFSON, MARY BAILEY, Second Grade Teacher; *b:* Red Wing, MN; *m:* Wayne Carl; *c:* Indeah L.; *ed:* (BS) Elem Ed, Winona St Univ 1969; Masters Equivalency; *cr:* Elem Teacher Red Wing Sch Dist 256 1969-; *ai:* Curr & Activity Comm; Red Wing Ed Assn Cncl Mem 1979-81; Nn Ed Assn 1969-; Chrldr Coach 1970-71/1975-77; Red Wing Ed Assn 1969-; MS Links Golf Club 1990; Sons of Norway 1990; 1st Luth Church; *home:* 118 Roving Hills Dr Red Wing MN 55066

GUTEREZ, CAROLE LYNN BAUSANO, Fourth Grade Teacher; *b:* San Bernardino, CA; *c:* Kristen; *ed:* (AA) Child Dev, Bakersfield Coll 1975; (BA) Liberal Stud, 1977; (MA) Elem Ed, 1982 CSU Bakersfield; Lib/Media Svcs CA St; *cr:* Teacher Kern HS Dist 1976-77; 4th Grade Teacher Richland Sch Dist 1977-; *ai:* Richland Teacher Assn (Mem 1977- & Treasurer 1983-85); Alpha Delta Kappa (Mem 1985- Recrdg Secy 1986-88); Cooperating Teacher with CA St Univ Bakersfield; *office:* Richland Intermediate Sch 331 N Shafter Ave Shafter CA 93263

GUTERMAN, KAYE CANINGTON, Media Specialist; *b:* Donalsonville, GA; *m:* E. M.; *c:* Brett, Cliff; *ed:* (BS) Elem Ed, 1971, (MED) Rdng Specialist, 1974 Valdosta St Coll; (EDS) Media Lib Sci, Univ of GA 1987; *cr:* Classroom Teacher 1971-78, Teacher of the Gifted 1978-85, Media Specialist Lib 1985-Seminole Elem Sch; *ai:* Jr Beta Club Adv; PTA; Sch & Cty Media Comm; Prof Assn of GA Educators Building Rep 1985-; Delta Kappa Gamma Membership Comm 1987-; United Meth Women (Publicity Chairperson 1989-, Librarian 1990); Outstanding Young Women of America; Teacher of Yr; *office:* Seminole Co Elem Sch 800 Spring St Donalsonville GA 31745

GUTH, NANCY ENGLISH, 6th Grade Teacher; *b:* Oil City, PA; *m:* Dwight Harold; *c:* Todd A., Stefanie A.; *ed:* (BS) Elem Ed, Villa Maria Coll 1968; (MS) Elem Sci, Clarion St Coll 1970; Elem Ed, Cmptrs, Sci; *cr:* 5th Grade Teacher Seventh Street Elem 1968-80; 6th Grade Teacher Riverview Elem 1980-89, Oil City Mid Sch 1989-; *ai:* Home Ec, Service, Stamp Club, Chorus, Drama Moderator; Educl Advisory Comm; Stu Asst Prgm Team Mem; GSA Cadet Girls Leader 1968-70; *home:* 107 Hollmarc Blvd Franklin PA 16323

GUTHRIE, DONNA MORTER, English/Journalism Teacher; *b:* Buena Vista, VA; *c:* Benjamin Cook, David Cook, DanNy Cook, Elizabeth Cook, Grant; *ed:* (BA) Philosophy/Religion/Eng, Greensboro Coll 1962; Supervision & Evaluation/Journalism/Eng/Curr; *cr:* Dir of Chrstn Ed South Roanoke Meth Church 1962-65; Eng Teacher RoanokE Public Schls 1968-69; Elem Teacher 1969-72; Mid Sch Teacher 1982-84; HS Eng/Journalism Teacher 1984- Franklin Cty Public Schls; *ai:* Yrbk Adv; Newspaper Adv; Teacher Trainer Cty Supervision & Evaluation Model; Alpha Delta Kappa Recording Secy 1987-; NCTE/VATE/PATE 1986-; Boones Mill United Meth Church (Lay Leader/Chm Pastor/Parish Relations, Adult S S Teacher 1965-; 1st Place Publications-VHSL; *office:* Franklin Cty H S 506 Pell Ave Rocky Mount VA 24151

GUTHRIE, FRANKIE, Math Teacher; *b:* Atlantic, NC; *c:* Cynthia, Leroy, Michael; *cr:* Bus Driver & Lunch Room 1957-70; General Aide 1970-74; Rdng Aide 1974-79; Math Tutorial Aide 1979- Harkers Island Elem Sch; *ai:* Harkers Island Rescue EMT 1977-85; Sunday Sch Teacher 1965-; *home:* Star Rt Box 512 Harkers Island NC 28531

GUTHRIE, SHEILA BAYSDEN, Teacher/Math Dept Chairperson; *b:* Kinston, NC; *m:* Dennis C.; *c:* Jason L.; *ed:* (BSP) Industrial Technology, East Carolina Univ 1975; *cr:* Careers Teacher 1978-85; Cmptrs Teacher 1983-89; Math Teacher 1985-Jacksonville Mid Sch; *ai:* Math Dept Chairperson; Math Counts Coach; Amer Vocation Assn Treas 1979-85; NEA 1988-89; BSA Comm Chm 1988-89; *office:* Jacksonville Mid Sch 401 New Bridge St Jacksonville NC 28540

GUTIERREZ, ANGEL JULIANA, Business Education Teacher; *b:* Santa Fe, NM; *ed:* (BA) Bus Ed/Spec Ed, New Mexico Highland Univ 1986; Grad Stud; *cr:* Spec Ed Teacher Armijo Elem W Las Vegas Schls 1986-87; Resource Room Teacher W Las Vegas Mid Sch 1987-88; Journalism/Newspaper/Cmptr/Ed Teacher 1988, Bus Ed Teacher 1988- Valley Jr HS; *ai:* Valley Jr HS Newspaper Club Spon 1988-; NEA Mem 1988-; AFT Mem 1986-88; 4-H Project Leader 1985-86; *office:* West Las Vegas Sch Dist PO Box Drawer J Las Vegas NM 87701

GUTIERREZ, GEORGE ALBERT, Spanish Teacher; *b:* Los Angeles, CA; *m:* Juana Maria; *c:* Raymond A., Laura E.; *ed:* (BA) Span, 1967, (MA) Ed, 1976 CA St Univ Los Angeles; Guadalajara Mexico Span Linguistics, Univ of San Francisco; Span Rdng, Methology & Culture, Instituto De Huastepec Mexico; *cr:* Teacher CA St Univ 1966-67, Belvidere Jr HS 1970-75; Adviser Los Angeles Unified Sch Dist 1975-80; Teacher El Sereno Jr HS 1980-; *ai:* ESL Foreign Lang Dept Chm; United Teachers of Los Angeles 1970-; NEA 1970-; El Sereno Chamber of Commerce (Pres 1980-84) Outstanding Service 1984; Public Service Awds City Councilman, St Senator; Outstanding Teacher Awd Eng; *office:* El Sereno Jr H S 2839 N Eastern Ave Los Angeles CA 90032

GUTIERREZ, KATHLEEN GALLAGHER, 5th Grade Teacher; *b:* Allentown, PA; *m:* Michael; *ed:* (BS) Math, Muhlenberg Coll 1966; (MS) Ed, Temple Univ 1970; *cr:* Teacher Salisbury Township Sch Dist 1966-; *ai:* St Thomas More Sch Bd Mem; NEA, PSEA, SEA 1966-; Air Products, Rider-Pool Fnd Excl in Classroom Grants 1988, 1989; *office:* Western Salisbury Elem Sch 3201 Devonshire Rd Allentown PA 18103

GUTOSKI, GERALD ROBERT, Geology/Earth Sci Instructor; *b:* Oshkosh, WI; *m:* Mary D. Koelbl; *c:* James R., Jean R., Joseph R. *ed:* (BS) Geology/Bio/Scndry Ed/Earth Sci/ Natural Sci, 1978 Univ of WI Oshkosh; (MS) Prof Dev/Earth Sci, 1988 Univ of WI La Crosse; *cr:* Earth Sci/Geology/Astronomy/Physics Instr New Berlin West HS 1978-; *ai:* Sci Club Adv; Natl Assn of Geology Teachers 1984-, Cntrl Dist Outstanding Earth Sci Teacher of Yr 1983; Sigma Xi Outstanding HS Sci & Math Teacher Awd St of WI 1987; *office:* New Berlin West HS 18695 W Cleveland Ave New Berlin WI 53146

GUY, ELAINE KELLY, English Teacher; *b:* Beech Mountain, NC; *ed:* (BA) Eng Ed, Pembroke St Univ 1987; *cr:* Eng Teacher Seventy First Sr HS 1987-88, Douglas Byrd Sr HS 1988-; *ai:* Forensics, Speech, Debate Coach; *office:* Douglas Byrd Sr HS 1624 Ireland Dr Fayetteville NC 28304

GUYER, ANITA MASSEY, Kindergarten Teacher; *b:* Marks, MS; *m:* David Lewis; *c:* Mark; *ed:* (BA) Elem Ed, Univ of MS 1977; *cr:* 2nd Grade Teacher St Marys Sch 1977-78; 5th Grade Teacher 1979-87, Kndgtn Teacher 1987- Horn Lake Elem; *ai:* MACUS 1990; PTA 1979-; *office:* Horn Lake Elem Sch 6341 Ridgewood Rd Horn Lake MS 38637

GUYER, JANIS MAYRE (JOHNSON), Second Grade Teacher; *b:* Columbia, MO; *m:* Gerald Neil; *c:* Nathan, Jessica; *ed:* (BA) Elem Ed, NE MO St Univ 1976; Whole Lang Method Trng Teaching in Classroom; *cr:* 2nd Grade Teacher Bucklin Sch 1976-78; 1st-3rd Grade Elem Teacher Linn Cty R-I Sch 1978-; *ai:* Teacher Planning & Welfare Comm; MO St Teachers Assn Mem 1976-; Cmmty Teachers Assn (Secy 1978-79, VP 1981-82, Pres 1982-83); 4-H Project Leader 1989-; Linneus Summer Prgm Coach 1988-89; Participant Lit Study Grant 1988-; Geography Grant Comm Mem 1990; *home:* Rt 3 Box 146 Purdin MO 64674

GUYNN, ROD K., Assistant Principal; *b:* Mc Intosh, FL; *m:* Mary; *c:* Sarah, Naomi, Nathan; *ed:* (AA) General Ed, Cntrl FL Jr Coll 1969; (BA) Scndry Ed, 1978, (MED) Scndry Ed, 1979 Univ of FL; *cr:* Supvr/Teacher Westwood Hills Chrstn Acad 1978-79, Fellowship Chrstn Sch 1979-81; Rdng/Bible Teacher Monte Vista Mid Sch 1981-86; Asst Prin Monte Vista Chrstn HS 1987-; *ai:* Boys Var Bsktbl Coach; Boarding Prgm Dir; Santa Cruz Coach of Yr 1989-; *office:* Monte Vista Chrstn HS 2 School Way Watsonville CA 95076

GUYON, NANCY LENT, Social Studies Teacher; *b:* Peekskill, NY; *m:* Robert A. Sr.; *c:* Robert A. Jr., Christine E.; *ed:* Writing Wkshp West Hartford Sch System; Global Geography Wkshp Inst for Learning CT; *cr:* 9th Grade Teacher Copper Beech Mid Sch 1967-70; 8th Grade Teacher 1970-74, 9th Grade Teacher 1976-78 Sedgwick Jr HS; 7th/8th Grade Teacher King Philip Mid Sch 1980-87; 10th Grade Teacher William Hall HS 1987-; World Geography/Afro Asian His Teacher 1990; *ai:* World Affairs Club Adv; NCSS, CT Cncl for Soc Stud 1980-; Natl Cncl for Geographic Ed 1985-, Distinguished Teacher of Yr 1985; Phi Delta Kappa 1985-; SNET Celebration of Excl Current Events Teaching Unit Honorable Mention Awd 1990; Finalist West Hartfords Teacher of Yr 1986; *office:* William H Hall HS 975 N Main T West Hartford CT 06117

GUZMAN, ARTURO DAVID, Theology/Science Teacher; *b:* Bronx, NY; *m:* Jacqueline Sancho; *c:* Phillip A.; *ed:* (BA) Child Dev, CT Coll 1973; (MS) Admin Rec, George Williams Coll 1974; Drug & Alcohol Abuse Trng; Red Cross Emergency Medical Tech; *cr:* Math/Sci Teacher St Pancras Sch 1980-81; Teacher Dickinson Alternative Sch 1981-82; 8th Grade Teacher/HS Guidance Sacred Heart Mid Sch 1982-88; Theology/Sci Teacher St Nicholas of Tolentine HS 1988-; *ai:* Girls Vlybl, Bsktbl, & Sftbl Coach; NCEA 1976-; Organized Cmmty Food Bank for the Elderly & Highbridge Mens Homeless Shelter; Part Time ESL & GED Teacher for Adults; *home:* 3470 Cannon Pl #J42 Bronx NY 10463

GUZMAN, JOSE R., Business Teacher/Bsktbl Coach; *b:* San Benito, TX; *m:* Viola; *c:* Josejulian; *ed:* (BA) Bus Ed/Phys Ed/Health Ed, UTPA 1978; *cr:* Teacher/Coach Donna HS 1979-81; Bus Teacher/Bsktbl Coach Pace HS 1981-; *ai:* Boys Head Bsktbl Coach; *office:* Pace HS 314 W Los Ebanos Brownsville TX 78520

GUZMAN, SHIRLEY PATRICIA (DUKE), English Teacher; *b:* Tamuning, GU; *m:* Robert John; *c:* Christopher, Taryn; *ed:* (AA) Liberal Arts, Long Beach City Coll 1971; (BAED) Scndry Lit, Univ of Guam 1977; Inservice Trng & Wkshps; *cr:* Eng Teacher George Washington HS 1977-; *ai:* Literary Festival Coord; Mem Onward Toward Excl, Co-Chairperson Career Day Exec Planning, Mem 1990 Graduation Comm; Eng Dept Chairperson 1985-87; NCTE, Guam Fed of Teachers; Guam Cncl Teachers of Eng VP 1987-88; *office:* George Washington HS P O Box 24147 Guam Main Facility GU 96921

GUZO, DOREEN KUZMINSKI, Language Art Teacher; *b:* Jersey City, NJ; *m:* Andrew J.; *ed:* (BS) Sociology, St Peters Coll 1969; (MA) Rdng, Montclair St Coll 1979; Neuro-Linguistic Programming; Writing Courses Columbia Univ, Inst of Childrens Lit; *cr:* 6th-8th Grade Lang Art Teacher All Saints Sch & St Patrick Sch 1967-69; Lang Art/Sociology Teacher/Lang Art Chairperson St Joseph HS 1969-73; Lang Art Teacher/Coord St Vincent Acad 1974-78; Lang Art/Rdng Specialist Hanover Park 1978-81, Whippany Park HS 1982-; *ai:* Chm Mid Atlantic Sts Assn; NCTE; NJ Governors Recognition Awd, Teacher of Yr 1989; NEH Grant Study Shakespeare & Milton at Univ of AZ 1989; NEH Grant Study Orpheus Myth in Opera at Univ of AK Fairbanks 1990; Published a Few Minor Pieces; *office:* Whippany Park HS 165 Whippang Rd Whippany NJ 07981

GUZZONE, LUCILLE PAULINE, English Teacher; *b:* Lawrence, MA; *m:* Benjamin Joseph; *c:* Kim Collier, Ben Jr., Kerri; *ed:* (BA) Eng, Merrimack Coll 1963; Span Cert Univ of N FL 1983; *cr:* Eng Teacher Woodbury HS 1963-64, Sandalwood HS 1970-80; Span/Eng Teacher Southside Jr HS 1980-84, Sandalwood HS 1984-; *ai:* Dir & Coord Faculty Follies; Duval Cty Cncl Teachers of Eng 1989-; Christ The King Church Ladies Guild 1980-; Nom Teacher of Yr Southside Jr HS 1983; *office:* Sandalwood HS 2750 John Prom Blvd Jacksonville FL 32216

GWALTHNEY, HELEN (MAC KAY), Latin/English Teacher; *b:* Vineland, NJ; *m:* Frank; *c:* Jonathan, Amy; *ed:* (BA) Latin, Montclair St Coll 1969; *cr:* Teacher Overbrook Regional Sr HS 1969-; *ai:* NCTE, NJ Cncl of Eng Teachers; Judge at ME Writers Conference; *home:* 436 W Centre St Woodbury NJ 08096

GWALTNEY, DELOISE G., 7th Grade Teacher; *b:* Smithfield, VA; *m:* Kennith A.; *c:* Brian, Melynda; *ed:* (BS) Elem Ed, Norfolk St Univ 1978; Grad Stud Old Dominion Univ & Norfolk St Univ; *cr:* Teacher Isle of Wright Schls; *ai:* Sch Newspaper Co-Spon; NEA, VEA; IWEA Secy; GSA Leader; *home:* Rt 2 Box 76 Ivor VA 23866

GWIN, MARY JANE BARNES, 6th-8th Grade Eng Teacher; *b:* Houston, TX; *ed:* (BS) Elem Ed/Eng, Univ of Houston 1970; TX Career Ladder Level II 1984-87, Level III 1987-; *cr:* 6th Grade Eng/Rdng Teacher/Lang Arts Dept Chair S Houston Interm Sch 1970-82; 8th Grade Eng/Eng Dept Chair 1982-, 6th/8th Grade Gifted/Talented Teacher 1983- Queens Interm Sch; Eng Dept Chairperson Pasadena 1973-; *ai:* Textbook Comm; Lang Arts 1971-72, 1985-88; Rdng/Eng Curr 1979, 1982, 1985, 1990, Effective Sch Comm 1990-; Literary Magazine 1988-, Natl Lang Arts Olympiad Spon 1990; Pentathlon Essay Grader 1986; NCTE 1985-; TX Joint Cncl Teachers of Eng 1980-; TX St Teachers Assn 1972-; NEA 1977-; Alpha Phi 1953-; Walnut Hill Civic Club 1985-; Tau Sigma (Secy 1952), 1951-52; Rdng Pilot Prgm; Harper Row 1st Place Winner Rotary Essay Contest 1990; Contribute Monthly Articles & Update Newsletter to Parents of Stu in Sch; Lang Arts Dept Chairperson 1973-; *office:* Queens Intermediate Sch 1112 Queens Rd Pasadena TX 77502

H

HAACKE, VON K., Fifth Grade Teacher; *b:* Idaho Falls, ID; *m:* Sheree L Blackley; *c:* Joshua, Jed; *ed:* (BA) Botany/Zoology, 1975, (BA) Elem Ed, 1978 Weber St Coll; *cr:* 5th Grade Teacher 1978-79, 3rd Grade Teacher 1979-80, 5th Grade Teacher 1980-81 Hooper Elem Sch; 5th Grade Teacher North Ogden Elem 1981-; *ai:* Phys Ed & Technology Coord & Facilitator North Ogden Elem; Cmmty Sch Dir North Ogden Elem; Weber Ed Assn, UT Ed Assn, NEA Mem 1984-; BSA (Scout Master 1976-79, Troop Chm 1979-88, Troop Comm 1988-); *home:* 2549 N 2125 W Farr West UT 84404

HAAG, ALANA Z., French Teacher; *b:* York, PA; *m:* Robert E.; *c:* Mariana, Michael; *ed:* (BS) Fr, 1970, (MA) Fr, 1975 Millersville Univ; *cr:* Fr Teacher Northeastern HS 1970-; *ai:* Foreign Lang Club; Stu Tours of France; PA St Ed Assn, NEA 1970-; *office:* Northeastern HS 300 High St Manchester PA 17345

HAAG, DOROTHY M. (BARBOUR), Retired Elementary Teacher; *b:* Denver, CO; *w:* Edward Wm. Jr.; *c:* Roger B., Valoree R. Sprentall, Regina V. Hoffman; *ed:* (BA) Eng Lit, Univ of CO 1945; (MA) Curr/Instruction, Univ of MI 1969; Many Prof Dev Wkshps; *cr:* Draftsman Babcock & Wilcox Co 1945-47; Substitute Teacher Ann Arbor Public Schls 1962-70; Elem Teacher S Lyon Cmmty Schls 1970-89; *ai:* Prof Staff Dev Policyt & K-12th Grade Lang Art Comm 1981-82; Chm Sci Comm 1970-73; Rep Curr Cncl 1988; Coord Campbells Labels for Ed 1973-89; Kappa Delta Pi 1942 Schlsp Ed; Phi Kappa Phi 1970 Upper Grade Schlsp; Pi Lambda Theta (VP 1972) 1970-73; Eastside Garden Club (VP 1959-60, Pres 1960-61); Newcomers Club Pres 1949-50; Coterie Club Secy; Barberton Womens Club (Finance Secy 1957-58, Chm Parl Law Dept 1960-61); Philosophy for Children Oakland Schls 1988; Beyond Assertive Discipline 1989; Admin Conference Elem Sch Sci Univ of MI Natl Sci Fnd 1973; *home:* 3071 Miller Rd Ann Arbor MI 48103

HAAK, KENNETH J., Social Studies Teacher; *b:* Lockport, NY; *m:* Patricia J. Jordan; *c:* Kenneth Jr., Stephen W.; *ed:* (AA) Liberal Art/Soc Sci, Niagara Cty Comm Coll 1973; (BA) His/Lib Sci, W KY Univ 1975; (MSED) Scndry Ed, Niagara Univ 1980; Additional Grad Credits Scndry Ed Niagara Univ; *cr:* Instr Millersburg Military Inst 1975-76; Teacher Barker Cntrl Sch 1976-; *ai:* Var Bstkbl, Track, Tennis; Yorker Club & Var Club Adv; NY St Cncl of Soc Stud 1979-; Village of Barker Trustee 1988-; PTO Pres 1989-; *home:* 8708 High St Barker NY 14012

HAAN, CANDACE ANN, Fifth Grade Teacher; *b:* Kansas City, MO; *ed:* (BS) Elem Ed, Valparaiso Univ 1981; Luth Teachers Cert Colloquy Prgm, River Forest Concordia Coll 1985; *cr:* 5th Grade Teacher Immanuel Luth Sch 1981-82; 5th/6th Grade Teacher Martin Luther Sch 1982-85; 5th Grade Teacher Christ Luth Sch 1986-; *ai:* Girls Vlybl, Bsktbl, Track, Sftbl Coach; Yrbk Ed; Childrens Choir Dir; Christ Luth Church Handbell Choir (Mem, Part-Time Dir) 1986-; Christ Luth Church Adult Choir (Mem, Part-Time Dir) 1986-.

HAAS, CONSTANCE MORRISSEY, English Teacher; *b:* Chicago, IL; *m:* L. Richard III; *c:* Corinne, Ryan; *ed:* (BA) Eng, IL Coll 1968; Gifted Ed/Educl Psych; *cr:* HS Eng Teacher Lake Park HS 1968-70; 8th Grade Eng Teacher Keller Jr HS 1970-80; 8th Grade Eng Teacher Mead Jr HS 1981-; *ai:* USS Ofcl for Barrington Swim Club; Volunteer-Lutheran Youth/Soccer/Cub Scouts; *office:* Margaret Mead Jr HS 1165 Biesterfield Dr Elk Grove Village IL 60007

HAAS, PAUL THOMAS, Social Studies Teacher; *b:* Akron, OH; *m:* Ann Foster; *ed:* (BSED) His/Eng, Kent St 1967; *cr:* Soc Stud Teacher Stow HS 1967-69, Cuyahoga Falls City Schls 1972-; *ai:* NEA, OH Ed Assn; Cuyahoga Falls Ed Assn VP 1974-75; *office:* Cuyahoga Falls HS 2300 4th St Cuyahoga Falls OH 44221

HAAS, SALLY MARIE, HS Mathematics Teacher; *b:* Lufkin, TX; *ed:* (BS) Applied Mathematical Sci, TX A&M Univ 1985; (MS) Math Teaching, Stephen F Austin St Univ 1990; Teaching Cert, Stephen F Austin St Univ 1987; *cr:* Math Teacher Lufkin HS 1987-; *ai:* Math Club Spon; MAA 1988-; NCTM, TCTA 1987-; Nacogdoches Tennis Assn Publicity Chairperson 1990; *office:* Lufkin HS 900 E Denman Lufkin TX 75901

HAAS, TERRY MICHAEL, Science Teacher; *b:* Kalamazoo, MI; *ed:* (BA) Bio, Phys Ed, W MI Univ 1981; (MS) Phys Ed, OH St Univ 1987; *cr:* Sci Teacher Schoolcraft Schls 1982-86; Grad Asst OH St Univ 1986-87; Sci Teacher Schoolcraft 1987-; *ai:* Ftbl & Weight Trng Coach; Sci Fair Coord; NSTA, MI HS Ftbl Coaches Assn; MI Groundwater Ed; Kalamazoo Cty Grant; *home:* 7860 WX Avenue Schoolcraft MI 49087

HAAS, TRACEY BRISTOW, History Teacher; *b:* Austin, TX; *m:* Gary R.; *ed:* (BA) His, Univ of TX Arlington 1983; *cr:* Teacher Workman Jr HS 1983-; *ai:* Workman Jr NHS Spon; TX Sesquicentennial Time Capsule Comm; TSTA 1988-; *office:* Workman Jr HS 701 E Arbrook Blvd Arlington TX 76018

HAASER, ROBERT JOSEPH, Social Studies Dept Chair; *b:* Little Rock, AR; *m:* Catherine Marie Wangler; *c:* Bobby, Christie, Elizabeth; *ed:* (BA) His, Univ of Dallas 1971; (MA) Amer His, N TX St Univ 1986; *cr:* Coach/Teacher 1971-77, AthletiC Dir/ Teacher 1977-84, Form Master/Teacher 1984-, Soc Stud Teacher/Dept Chm/Form Master 1986- Cistercian Preparatory Sch; *ai:* Soc Stud Club; Citizen Bee Activity Spon; Natl Geography Bee Coord; Phi Alpha Theta, Organization of Amer Historians 1986-; Written 5 Selections Multi-Volume Handbooks of TX 1990; Coach of Yr Irving Ftbl 1980; *office:* Cistercian Preparatory Sch P O Box 160699 Irving TX 75016

HAATVEDT, LESLIE BLAIR, Dir of Guidance & Counseling; *b:* Atlanta, GA; *m:* Loren A.; *c:* Erik, Andrew; *ed:* (BS) Eng/Soc Stud, Butler Univ 1966; (MS) Mental Health Counseling/ Guidance Counseling, Barry Univ 1988; Several Wkshps; Clinical Supervision; *cr:* Eng Teacher Stranahan HS 1966-68; Eng/Soc Stud Teacher Kinloch Jr HS 1968-69; Interior Designer Cameron Interiors Inc 1976-84; Life Skills Teacher Miami Cty Day Sch 1984-87; Dir of Guidance/Counseling/Teacher Life Skills/Psych Cnslr Individual/Group 1987-; *ai:* Creator, Spon, & Dir Miami Days Peer Cnslr Prgm; Wkshp Facilitator Parenting the Adolescent, Developing Childs Self Esteem & Teaching Human Sexuality Values; Amer Assn Counseling & Development; ASGW; ASCD; ASCA; Health Crisis Network; Journal Article Seminar Learning Skills for Life Mid Sch Journal; *office:* Miami Country Day Schl 601 NE 107th St Miami FL 33161

HABER, CATHERINE, First Grade Teacher; *b:* Kingston, NY; *ed:* (BS) Ed, St Univ of NY New Paltz 1964; Home Sch Cmmty Relationship, Principles of Research, St Univ of NY New Paltz; *cr:* 1st Grade Teacher Red Hook Cntrl Sch Dist 1964-65, Marbletown Elem Sch 1965-; *ai:* Rondout Valley Teachers Assn 1965-89; Rondout Valley Fed 1989-; Altar Rosary Society Secy; *office:* Marbletown Elem Sch PO Box 9 Accord NY 12404

HABER, SCOTT A., Soc Stud Teacher/Dept Chair; *b:* Sandusky, OH; *ed:* (BS) Soc Stud, 1985, (MED) Scndry Ed, 1987 Bowling Green St Univ; *cr:* US His Instr J A Smith Mid Sch 1985-86; Grad Teaching Asst Bowling Green St Univ 1986-87; Substitute Teacher Bowling Green City Schls 1987; Soc Stud Teacher/Dept Chm Cabrini HS 1987-; *ai:* Curr Cncl Mem; Spring Soc Stud Tour of Europe Dir; Class Moderator 1988-; Asst Bsktbl Coach; Drama Productions Asst; NCSS, ASCD 1988-; CHA Cnslr 1988-; NCEA 1987-; Grad Teaching Assistantship Awd BGSU 1986-87.

HABERKORN, JEANETTE INNTOA, Eng-Drama Forensics Teacher; *b:* Honolulu, HI; *m:* Ronald R.; *c:* Tiffany, Peter; *ed:* (BA) Speech/Theatre Art, CO St Univ 1973; (MA) Gifted/ Talented, Univ of CO 1987; *cr:* Pera Prof Doherty HS; Teacher Sabin Jr HS 1990; *ai:* Forensics Tournament Coach; Action Comm; Alpha Psi Omega Pres 1973.

HABIBULLAH, GEMMA W., Mathematics Dept Chair; *b:* Mahayag, Philippines; *m:* Rosli; *c:* Monah, Merced; *ed:* (BSE) Math/Physics, Immaculate Conception Coll 1972 Philippines; (BS) Chem, Univ of San Carlos 1978; (MAT) Math, SE MO St Univ 1986; *cr:* Math Teacher Immaculate Conception Coll 1973-75, Sacred Heart Sch For Girls 1975-77, San Jose Recoletos 1977-78, Cebu Intnl Sch 1978-81; Grad Asst SE MO St Univ 1984-86; Math Dept Chairperson St Pius X HS 1986-; *ai:* Math Club, Gifted Math & 1-8-1-8 Prgms St Louis Univ; NCTM; *home:* 207 N West End Blvd Cape Girardeau MO 63701

HACKBARTH, DAVID G., Biology Teacher; *b:* St Joseph, MI; *m:* Nancy Weiner; *c:* Aaron; *ed:* (BA) Bio, Carthage Coll 1971; *cr:* Bio Teacher New Holstein Sr HS 1971-72, Oshkosh North HS 1972-73, L P Goodrich HS 1973-; *ai:* Pep Team Adv; Stu Assistance Prgm Facilitator; NSTA 1985-; WSST 1986-; Challenger Center 1988-; Fond du Lac Scndry Teacher of Yr 1989; Newmast 1989; Sci World 1989; *office:* L P Goodrich HS 382 Linden St Fond Du Lac WI 54935

HACKBARTH, GERALD HENRY, Mathematics & Science Teacher; *b:* Green Bay, WI; *m:* Geraldine Marie Pierce; *c:* Ross, Kim; *ed:* (BS) Math, Univ of WI Oshkosh 1968; (MS) Math, Seattle Univ 1973; *cr:* Teacher Little Wolf HS 1968-; *ai:* Asst Ftbl Coach; Math League Adv; WI Math Cncl 1980-; WI Ed Assn 1968-; Manawa Ed Assn Pres; Manawa Jaycees (Pres, Dir) 1969-81; Natl Sci Fnd Grant; *home:* Rt 1 Box 121 Manawa WI 54949

HACKBRUSH, JERRILYN KUNZE, Science Department Coordinator; *b:* Harvey, IL; *m:* Charles F.; *ed:* (BA) Bio, Monmouth Coll 1966; (MS) Curr/Supervision, IL St Univ 1978; (MA) Admin, Roosevelt Univ 1983; *cr:* Sci Dept Coord/Bio Teacher Westmont HS 1974-; *ai:* NHS Adv; Sch Improvement & Curr Advisory Cncl; Intouch; Stu Intervention Team; Westmont Teachers Assn Pres 1983-85; IL Sci Teachers Assn 1989-; NSTA 1974-; IL Bio Teachers Assn, NABT 1976-; Delta Kappa Gamma Society Intnl 1987-; Awd of Excl IL Math & Sci Acad 1988; *office:* Westmont HS 909 Oakwood Dr Westmont IL 60559

HACKENBERG, ELIZABETH MAE, Foreign Language Dept Chair; *b:* Cleveland, OH; *m:* Jean-Claude Sutra; *ed:* (BA) Latin/ Soc Stud, Miami Univ 1966; (MS) Ed, Cleveland St Univ 1977; Fr Lit/Culture, Sorbonnie Univ of Paris 1983-84; *cr:* TEFL Teacher C C de Keve Togo 1966-68; Teacher Glenville HS 1969-; *ai:* Head Glenville 9th Grade House; Les Amis 1985-; Cleveland Partnership Grant 1989; *home:* 1843 Hampton Rd Rocky River OH 44116

HACKENBRACHT, JOSEPHINE, Fourth Grade Teacher; *b:* Columbus, OH; *ed:* (BS) Elem Ed, OH St Univ 1968; (MED) Classroom Teaching, Wright St Univ 1974; *cr:* Kndgtn Teacher 1961-62, 1st-2nd Grade Teacher 1962-72, 4th Grade Teacher 1972- Urbana City Schls; *ai:* Urbana Assn of Classroom Teachers Secy 1971-73; 4-H (Pocket Animals Adv 1975-77, Sign Lang Adv 1981-82, 1982-83); *home:* 205 Scioto St Apt 4 Urbana OH 43078

HACKETT, CAROLYN EBHARDT, Language Arts Teacher; *b:* Boston, MA; *m:* James Michael; *c:* Brant, Kevin; *ed:* (BA) Eng, St Andrews Presbyn Coll 1967; A/G & Ger Cert; *cr:* 8th/9th Grade Eng Teacher Kiser Jr HS 1967-72; 7th/8th Grade Lang Art Teacher Guilford Mid Sch 1985-; *ai:* At Risk Prgm Tutor; Spelling Bee & Soc Comm Chm; NEA 1985-; PTA Bd Mem 1985-88, Evon Dean Awd 1988; O Henry Teaching Awd 1985; *office:* Guilford Mid Sch 401 College Rd Greensboro NC 27410

HACKETT, CYNTHIA LEE, Chemistry Teacher; *b:* Youngstown, OH; *m:* Patrick; *c:* Colleen, Meghan, Caitlin; *ed:* (BS) Comprehensive Sci, Youngstown St Univ 1981; *cr:* 7th/8th Grade Teacher Beachwood Local Schls 1981-82; 7th-12th Grade Teacher Mc Donald HS 1984-88; 11th-12th Grade Teacher Niles Mc Kinley HS 1988-; *ai:* Amer Chemical Society 1989-; Nom Excl in HS Chem Teaching Catalyst Awd 1990.

HACKETT, JOSEPH LE ROY, JR., World His Teacher/Band Dir; *b:* Millville, NJ; *m:* Jeanne Laws; *c:* Joe III, Jeannette Torres, Judith Whelan, Joanna, Jonathan; *ed:* Bible, Bob Jones Univ 1965; (BS) Chrstn Ed Hyles-Anderson Coll 1989; *cr:* Teacher Hammond Baptist Jr HS 1978-; *office:* Hammond Baptist Jr H S 134 W Joliet Schererville IN 46375

HACKETT, ROIANNE MILLER, Elementary Teacher of Gifted; *b:* Fairfield, IA; *m:* Thomas Bonwill; *c:* Elizabeth Talbott, Katherine, Daniel; *ed:* (BS) Pre-Med, Parsons Coll 1965; (MA) Gifted Ed, WV Univ 1987; Specific Teaching Trng; Jr Great Books Facilitator; Project WILD; *cr:* Elem Teacher of Gifted Upshur Cty Schls 1976-; *ai:* Elem Conservation Clubs Leader & Spon; Cty Gifted Curr Advisory Cncl Mem; Sch Based Assistance Teams Mem; WV Challenge Elem Team Coach; Sci/Soc Stud Fairs Comm; WV Prof Educators Treas 1986-; Amer Assn of Univ Women 1st VP 1989-; WV Gifted Ed Assn 1980-; WV Assn of Sci Teachers 1982-; Upshur Cty Arts Alliance Art Auction Chm 1985-; Episcopal Church Organist 1982-; WV Ed Fnd Mini-Grants for Classrooms Winner 1984, 1989; Soil Conservation Service Conservation Educator of Yr 1979; *home:* 3 Scott St Buckhannon WV 26201

HACKETT-SMITH, JANEIE DALE, 5th Grade Teacher; *b:* Shelbyville, KY; *m:* Larry Gayle; *ed:* (BA) Elem Ed, KY St Univ; (MS) Elem Ed, (Rank I) Elem Ed, Georgetown Coll; *cr:* 5th Grade Teacher Eastern Elem 1982-; *ai:* Gifted Child, Teachers Advisory, Schl Based Planning Achievement Comm; *home:* Hwy 355 Gratz KY 40327

HACKNEY, CALLEEN J., Physical Ed Dept Chairperson; *b:* Salt Lake City, UT; *m:* Gary D.; *c:* Shannon H. Fouratt, Shane T.; *ed:* (BS) Phys Ed, NM St Univ 1977; Aerobics Classes-Certified Aerobics Instr; Jazz Dance; *cr:* Teacher/Coach Alameda Jr HS 1979-85, Sierra Jr HS 1985-88, Onate HS 1988-; *ai:* Head Coach Vlybl; Dept Chairperson Phys Ed; Onate HS & Dance Club Spon; Honors Phys Ed Class; NM Assn of Health, Phys Ed, Recreation, & Dance 1980-, Nom Phys Ed Teacher of Yr 1990; Las Cruces Classroom Teachers Assn 1985-; NM HS Coaches Assn 1987-; Natl Fed Interscholastics Coaches Assn 1987-; Phi Kappa Phi Mem; NM St Univ Honor Grad; Whos Who Among Stus in Americas Jr Colls; Started NM 1st Honors Phys Ed Class Sierra Jr HS; Perform Annual Sports Acrobatics Show; *office:* Onate HS 1700 E Spruce Las Cruces NM 88001

HACKNEY, EVELYN DOLORES, Retired Teacher; *b:* Philadelphia, PA; *ed:* (BS) Elem Ed, Cheyney 1953; (MS) Ed, Coll of New Rochelle 1973; *cr:* Teacher H J Widener Elem Sch 1953-61, Wm Mc Kinley Elem Sch 1961-69, Seely Place Elem Sch 1969-89; *ai:* Volunteer at Riverside Church Food Pantry; Spon Bizarre Bazaar Seely Place Sch; Delta Sigma Theta 1951-; *home:* 119 De Haven Dr Apt 141 Yonkers NY 10703

HACKNEY, GARY D., High School English Teacher; *b:* Enid, OK; *m:* Caleen J.; *c:* Shannon H. Fouratt, Shane T.; *ed:* (BS) Phys Ed, E NM Univ 1970; (MAT) Eng, NM St Univ 1976; *cr:* Teacher/Coach Alamogordo Mid HS 1970-82; Teacher/Coach 1975-82, Teacher 1975- Mayfield HS; *ai:* Mayfield HS Asst Golf Coach; Las Cruces Classroom Teachers Assn 1980-; NM HS Coaches Assn 1970-85; Volunteer Golf Lessons for Sr Citizens; Shakespeare Specialization Awd; NM St Univ Honor Grad; NHS Honorary Mem; *office:* Mayfield HS 1955 N Valley Dr Las Cruces NM 88005

HADFIELD, CORNELIA ANN (CZAJKOWSKI), 7th-12th Grade Math Consultant; *b:* Moosup, CT; *m:* Myron Deane; *c:* Andrew, Jessica; *ed:* (BA) Math, Annhurst Coll 1959; (MA) Univ of CT 1964; 92 Certificate Admin, Sacred Heart Univ 1990; *cr:* Math Teacher Plainfield HS 1959-69, Annhurst Coll 1971-72, Plainfield HS 1976-88; Math Dept Head 1982-89, 7th-12th Grade Math Consultant 1988- Plainfield HS; *ai:* Prof Dev, Evaluation, Career Incentive, Charter Revision Comm; Sr Class Adv 1981-89; Dist Math Curr Coord 1982-83; NCTM, Assn of Teacher Math in CT, Assn of Supvrs in CT; Rotary Pageant Dir 1978-89; Teacher of Yr Nom 1985; Wkshp Presenter 1989-.

HADGIS, THOMAS, Science Teacher; *b:* Cleveland, OH; *m:* Paula Jean Hrusovsky; *c:* Matthew, Elizabeth; *ed:* (BS) Phys Ed/ General Sci, Cleveland St Univ 1978; *cr:* Sci Teacher Brunswick City Schls 1979-82; Phys Ed Teacher Our Lady of Good Cncl 1982-83; Sci Teacher Medina City Schls 1983-; *ai:* Medina Jr HS Sci Olympiad & Wrestling Coach, Sci Fair Dir; NSTA 1983-; Dow Chemical Excl in Teaching Awd; *office:* Medina Jr HS 420 E Union Medina OH 44256

HADINGER, DONNA RUTH, Fourth Grade Teacher; *b:* Alliance, OH; *m:* Larry W.; *c:* Todd, Beth; *ed:* (BS) Ed, Kent St Univ 1965; Grad Credit in Rdng, Childrens Lit, Sci, Nutrition, Gifted & Talented Stus; *cr:* 3rd Grade Teacher 1965-66, 4th Grade Teacher 1975- Waterloo Local Sch; *ai:* Chairperson Critical Thinking Skills Comm; Intnl Rdng Assn 1989-; United Meth Church Organist 1970-85; *office:* Waterloo Local Schls 6660 Waterloo Rd Atwater OH 44201

HADLER, SALLY LORRAINE, Kindergarten-4th Grade Teacher; *b:* Oconto, WI; *M:* James; *ed:* (BS) Ed, Dr Martin Luther Coll 1978; *cr:* 3rd/4th Grade Teacher Reformation Luth Sch CA 1977-78; 1st-8th Grade Teacher 1978-80, 1st-4th Grade Teacher 1980- St Pauls Luth Sch; *ai:* Presentation of Primary Bible His Act.

HADLEY, DAN EDWARD, Industrial Art Teacher; *b:* Bartlesville, OK; *m:* Vicky Lynn Richardson; *c:* Bobbie L., Joni D.; *ed:* (AA) C J C Claremore 1977; (BS) Industrial Art Ed, SW OK St Univ Weatherford 1980; *cr:* Industrial Art Teacher Unified Sch Dist 286 1980-; *ai:* Fr Class Spon; Carl Perkins Grant; *office:* Unified Sch Dist 286 416 E Elm St Sedan KS 67361

HADLEY, DEBRA LYNN, Jr High Language Arts Teacher; *b:* Fairfield, IA; *ed:* (BS) Bible/Elem Ed, Friends Bible Coll 1981; *cr:* Jr HS Lang Arts Dighton Grade Sch 1981-; *ai:* 7th/8th Grade Act Sponsorship Project Success Comm; Mem Lane Cty Spelling Bee Coord; North Cntrl Evaluation Mem 1987; *office:* Dighton Grade Schl 320 E James Dighton KS 67839

HADLEY, DENNIS B., Spanish/English Teacher; *b:* Ogden, UT; *m:* Lana Blanch; *c:* Stephanie, Marnae, Trent, Celeste, Shannon, Landon, Jared; *ed:* (BA) Eng, 1968, (MED) Ed, 1980 Weber St Coll; *cr:* Eng/Debate Teacher Weber HS 1968-70; Eng Teacher Church Coll of New Zealand 1970-74; Eng/Debate/Span Teacher Weber HS 1974-; *ai:* Span Club Adv; Weber HS Debate Coach 1968-70, 1974-88; UT Speech Arts Assn 1968-70, 1974-88; Natl Forensic League Dist Chm 1988-89, 2 Diamonds Awd; Natl Sci Fnd Grant; Eng Dept Head Weber HS 1985-88; Eng Dept Head Church Coll of New Zealand 1973-74; *office:* Weber HS 430 W Weber High Dr Ogden UT 84414

HADLEY, DOROTHY EVANS, 4th Grade Teacher; *b:* Scottsboro, AL; *c:* Felicia; *ed:* (BS) Elem Ed, Morris Brown Coll 1971; (MED) Elem Ed/Rdng, AL A&M Univ 1979; Voice & Theory of Music, Snead St Jr Coll 1989; *cr:* Classroom Teacher Bridgeport Elem; *office:* Bridgeport Elem Sch 704 Jacobs Ave Bridgeport AL 35740

HADSALL, MARTHA KRUS, Third Grade Teacher; *b:* Anthony, KS; *m:* Kenneth L.; *c:* Craig; *ed:* (BS) Elem Ed, OK St Univ 1974; (ME) Elem Ed, NW OK St Univ 1979; Rdng Specialist, Wichita St Univ; *cr:* 6th Grade Music Teacher Blackwell Public Schls 1974-75; 3rd/4th Grade Music Teacher Harper Grade Sch 1975-; *ai:* HCNEA Building Rep; OK St Univ Ed Stu Cncl 1973-74, Top Ten 1974; Kappa Delta Pi 1972-74; Delta Kappa Gamma 1986-; Harper Cty NEA Treas 1975-; Bus Prof Women (Pres, VP) 1981-, Young Careerist 1979; Beta Sigma Phi (Pres, Secy, Treas) 1977-; United Meth Ed Chm 1975-; *office:* Harper Grade Sch 1317 Walnut Harper KS 67058

HAFT, CAROLYN JEAN (CALL), Fourth Grade Teacher; *b:* Everett, WA; *m:* R. Hap; *ed:* (BA) Ed, Humboldt St Univ; Ed, Univ of OR Eugene; Biological Sci, Univ of CA Davis, Ed, Chico St Univ; *cr:* 4th Grade Teacher Lincoln Elem Sch, Marine View Terrace Elem; 5th Grade Teacher, 3rd-4th Grade Teacher Grant Elem Sch; 4th Grade Teacher Woodrow Wilson Sch; *ai:* Master Teacher; Coord, Rep of Gifted Prgm for Dist; Curr Chm; Dist Supts Advisory Bd; Textbook Evaluation & Adoption Comm; Leadership Team; Dist Curr for Math, Prins Advisory, Report Card, Dist Textbook Adoption Comm; Wilson Sch Site Cncl; NEA, CA Teachers Assn; Eureka Teachers Assn Secy; Gridley Teachers Assn, Kappa Kappa Gamma, Beta Sigma Phi; Butte Creek Cntry Club, PTA.

HAFTEL, SANDRA, 7th/8th Grade Soc Stud Teacher; *b:* New York, NY; *m:* Robert; *c:* Hilary, Benjamin, Rachel; *ed:* (BA) Ec, Hunter Coll 1956; (MA) Soc Stud, Teachers Coll Columbia Univ 1958; Elem Ed & Supervisory Cert William Patterson Coll; Holocaust & Genocide, Kean Coll; Taft Inst; *cr:* Soc Stud Teacher Ardsley Jr-Sr HS 1958-59, Isaac E Young Jr HS 1959-62; Instr Valley Forge Military Acad 1973-75; 7th/8th Grade Soc Stud Teacher Brookside Sch 1978-; *ai:* Mock Constitutional Convention; Natl Geography Awareness Week; Bill of Rights Bicentennial Celebration NJ; Civics Club; Earthwatch NJ/Natl His Day; Greater Bergen Cncl for Soc Stud (Pres 1988-89, Ed 1989-); NJ Cncl for Soc Stud VP 1989-; Culture Ramapa Japanese Society Charter Mem 1989-; Temple Beth Or Pres 1985-86; St of NJ Grant; Taft Fnd Fellowship; Fnd for Free Enterprise Israel Freedom Awd 1986; *office:* Brookside Sch Broodside Ave Allendale NJ 07401

HAGADORN, THOMAS W, Mathematics Teacher; *b:* Hornell, NY; *m:* Deborah Fierle; *c:* Kyle, Lindsay; *ed:* (BS) Scndry Ed-Math, SUC Geneseo 1970; *cr:* Math Teacher Haverling Cntrl Sch 1970-; *ai:* Stu Cncl Adv; Boys Var Soccer Coach; Steuben Cty Boys Soccer Chm; Steuben Cty Exceptional Sr Game Coord-Bsktbl, Soccer; Natl Honor Soc Selection Comm; NSCAA 1987-; Bath Hope for Youth Co-Founder/Pres 1975-77; Bath Kiwanis Youth Soccer League Founder/Coord 1983-; IAABO 156 VP 1981-; Village Youth Commission 1975-78; 1989 Nominee-Presidential Awds for Excl; NYS Section V Coach of Yr 1984-89; *home:* 15 Locust St Bath NY 14810

HAGAN, FRANCES THERESA, Religion Teacher; *b:* Brooklyn, NY; *ed:* (BA) His, St Francis Coll 1960; (MA) Sacred Sci, St Bonaventure 1970; St Johns Univ; Fordham Univ; *cr:* 7th Grade Teacher Immaculate Conception 1950-58; 8th Grade Teacher Holy Cross 1958-63, St Marys Nativity 1963-67; Religion Teacher Acad of St Joseph 1967-; *ai:* Adv; Grant-In-Aid Prgm; Conducted Bible Sch 1978; NCEA 1970-; Northport Hotline 1976; Superior of Nurses Maria Regina Home 1968-71; Spiritual Counseling 1970-; Wkshp Morality 1975; Delegate to General Chapter of Congregation 1967-68; *office:* Acad of St Joseph Brentwood Rd Brentwood NY 11717

HAGAN, TIMOTHY CHARLES, Band Director/Department Chair; *b:* Louisville, KY; *m:* Catherine Wentworth De Witt; *c:* Laura M., Rachel L.; *ed:* (BME) Music Ed, E KY Univ 1981; (MME) Music Ed, Murray St Univ 1982; *cr:* Grad Asst Murray St Univ 1981-82; Band Dir Hart Cty HS 1982-85, Eastern HS 1985-; *ai:* Dept Head; Sch Arts Cncl; KY Music Educators Assn 1982-; Phi Beta Mu Bandmasters 1988-; KY Bandmasters Assn Dist Rep 1987-; Middletown Optimist Club Oratorical Competition Chm 1990; Ashland Oil Teachers Recognition Prgm Golden Apple Awd; *office:* Eastern HS 12400 Old Shelbyville Rd Middletown KY 40243

HAGANY, JUDITH MARIE, 7th/8th Grade Math Teacher; *b:* New Brunswick, NJ; *m:* Lawrence Gerard; *ed:* (BA) Ed/Math, 1974, (MA) Ed/Math 1982 Trenton St Coll; NJ Prin & Supvr Certificate 1987; Jersey City St Coll, Kean Coll, Trenton St Coll, St Peters Coll 1990; *cr:* Math Teacher Pine Brook Sch 1974-; *ai:* Coach & Coord Math Challenges Prgm; Coach Math Team, Continental Math League, Mathcounts; Study Skills Curr, Pine Brook Self-Assessment Comm; MEEA, NJEA, NEA 1974-; NCTM, AMTNJ 1976-; MAA, ASCD 1980-; Pine Brook Sch Governors Outstanding Teacher Awd 1987-88; *office:* Pine Brook Sch Pease Rd Manalapan NJ 07726

HAGAR, LYNNE MARIE, English/History Teacher; *b:* Austin, TX; *m:* Vernon M. III; *c:* Michael, Hope; *ed:* (BA) His/Eng, Univ of CA Los Angeles 1976; Grad Stud Hum, Univ of Dallas, Dallas Inst for Hum; *cr:* Teacher West Mesquite HS 1986-; *ai:* Citizen Bee Coach; Gifted & Talented Steering & Curr Comm Mem; Greater Dallas Cncl Teachers of Eng Parliamentarian 1989-; Mesquite Ed Assn 1986-; TX Assn Gifted & Talented 1988-; TX Assn of Prof Educators 1987-; PTA (Exec Comm, Cultural Art Chairperson); Nom Outstanding HS Teacher; TX Excl Awd; *office:* West Mesquite HS 2500 Memorial Pkwy Mesquite TX 75149

HAGEDORN, JULIE ANN, 5th Grade Teacher; *b:* Gothenburg, NE; *m:* Charles M.; *ed:* (BA) Elem Ed, Sioux Falls Coll 1982; (MS) Curr Instr, SD St Univ 1990; *cr:* 5th Grade Teacher Oscar Howe Elem 1982-; *ai:* Mem Sioux Falls Rdng Comm; Teacher Managing Elem Classroom Wkshp; Co-Taught Integrating Lang Arts Wkshp; Intnl Rdng Mem 1988-; NEA Mem 1989-; SDEA Mem 1989-; Nom Sioux Falls Teacher Yr 1990; *office:* Sioux Falls Public Schls 2801 Valley View Rd 57106 Sioux Falls SD 57106

HAGEL, LEONA P., French Teacher; *b:* St Basile, Canada; *m:* Gary J.; *c:* Shawn, Stephanie Hagel Montez; *ed:* (BA) Fr, SW TX Univ 1971; (MA) Elem Ed, TX A&I Univ 1980; Rdng Specialist Degree 1984; *cr:* 3rd-6th Grade Teacher Edmundston & St Leonard 1961-66; 2nd Grade Teacher George West 1971-73; 3rd-8th Grade Teacher Freer 1973-85; Fr Teacher Victoria Stroman HS 1985-; *ai:* Cmmty Prgm Night Adults Continuing Ed Teacher; FTA Spon; Delta Kappa Gamma Finance Chairperson 1982-84; TSTA (Treas, Secy) 1976-78; *office:* Stroman HS 3002 North St Victoria TX 77901

HAGELE, ELAINE (STICKLE), Accounting Teacher; *b:* Lacombe AB, Canada; *m:* Lowell C.; *c:* David L., Gregory M., Charles A.; *ed:* (BS) Homemaking Ed, Pacific Union Coll 1965; *cr:* Home Ec/Bus Ed Teacher Newbury Park Acad 1965-66, Guam Adv Acad 1966-70; Bus Educator Japan Adv Coll 1975-83; Treas/Bus Ed Teacher Coll View Acad 1985-; *ai:* Class Spon; NE Society of Certified Public Accountants 1988-; Lincoln SDA Credit Union Bd of Dir; *office:* College View Acad Sch 5240 Calvert St Lincoln NE 68506

HAGEMAN, COLETTE VAN WAGENEN, Sixth Grade Teacher; *b:* Salt Lake City, UT; *m:* Donald James; *c:* Lissa, Michelle; *ed:* (BS) Elem Ed, Univ of UT 1980; General Ed, Univ of UT, Jordan Sch Dist; *cr:* 4th Grade Teacher 1980-87, 6th Grade Teacher 1988- Welby Elem; *ai:* Spon Sch Natl Geographic Geography Bee & NASA Seeds Project; Sch Advisory Cncl; Mentor for New Teachers; Team Leader; UT Ed Assn 1980-; Salt Lake Jr Acad Home & Sch Bd Mem 1982-83; Nom Jordan Sch Dist Teacher of Yr 1989-; *office:* Welby Elem Sch 4130 W 9580 S South Jordan UT 84065

HAGEMAN, DONALD E., Social Science Chairman; *b:* Iola, KS; *m:* Janice L. Green; *c:* Bryan D., David R.; *ed:* (AA) Allen Cty Cmmty Jr Coll 1967; (BS) Soc Sci, Emporia St Univ 1969; Law in Ed, Career Ed, Several Ec Seminars; Government & Constitution Seminars, Taft Inst; *cr:* Salesman/Stock Clerk J C Penney Company 1967-69; Soc Sci Teacher/Chm/Coach Norcatur HS 1969-70, Hoxie Jr HS 1970-; *ai:* Jr HS Boys Ftbl & Bsktbl Asst Coach; Boys Track Head Coach; Natl Historical Society Founding Mem 1970-; Local Lions Club (Pres 1980-81, Secy 1981-, Dist Drug Awareness Chm 1985-88, Dist Zone Chm 1988-89, Regional Chm 1989-), Certificate of Merit 1985-88; Young Bank Officers KS Ec Excl Awd Playing Stock Market Game 1985; *office:* Hoxie Jr HS Box 969 Hoxie KS 67740

HAGEMANN, NANCY JEAN RICKEL, Kindergarten Teacher; *b:* Detroit, MI; *m:* Herman; *c:* Nancy, Patrick; *ed:* (BA) Elem Ed/Soc Sci, Mercy Coll 1958; Grad Stud; *cr:* 2nd Grade Teacher 1958-59, 2nd/3rd Grade Teacher 1959-60 Selfridge Sch; 3rd/4th Grade Teacher St Marys Sch 1962; 1st Grade Teacher Selfridge Sch 1962-63; 7th/8th Grade Teacher Anchor Bay Cath 1966-68; 3rd Grade Teacher Anchor Bay Elem 1970-74; Kndgtn Teacher Lottie M Schmidt 1974-; *ai:* Alpha Delta Kappa, Early Chldhd Ed Assn; *office:* Lottie M Schmidt Elem Sch 33700 Hooker Rd New Baltimore MI 48047

HAGEN, KIM A., Elementary Principal; *b:* Eau Claire, WI; *m:* Gail Gerdes; *c:* Scott, Trever; *ed:* (BA) Elem/Spec Ed, Univ Of WI Eau Claire 1974; (MS) Ed Admin, Winona St Univ 1980; Specialist Degree Educl Admin, Univ of MN; *cr:* HS Spec Ed Teacher Mc Henry Cmmty HS 1975; 4th Grade Elem Teacher Cleghorn Elem Sch 1975-80; 6th Grade Elem Teacher Lincoln Elem Sch 1980-86; Elem Prin Little Red/Mt Washington Elem 1986-, Manz Elem Sch 1990; *ai:* Eau Claire Dist Math Adoption, Environmental Ed, Dist Wellness Comm; Phi Delta Kappa (Prgm Co-VP 1985-), Membership Awd 1990; NAESP 1986-; Assn of WI Sch Admin 1986-; Peace Luth Church Bd of Elders 1989-; WI Ed Assn Cncl 1982-86; Eau Claire Assn of Ed 1981-84; Excl in Ed Teacher 1985; *home:* 3418 Gerrard Ave Eau Claire WI 54701

HAGEN, NANETTE CHESTNUT, 2nd Grade Teacher; *b:* Wilmington, DE; *m:* Tony; *c:* Tony Jr., Jennifer, Brent; *ed:* (BS) Elem Ed, Cameron Univ 1976; (MED) Guidance/Counseling, SW OK St Univ 1980; *cr:* Teacher Howell Elem 1977-; *ai:* US Senate Flag Day Celebration; Prof Rights & Responbsibilities, Teacher Evaluation Comm; Prof Management Planning Cncl; Aluminum Can Drive for Ronald Mc Donald House; Natl Ed Week Parade Co-Spon; NEA, OEA, PEAL 1977-; St Bible Drill Competition 1989-; B Kids Leader 1989-; Sunday Sch Teacher 1985-89; Bible Sch Teacher 1989.

HAGEN, PATRICIA LANGSDORF, Third Grade Teacher; *b:* Southampton, NY; *w:* James (dec); *c:* Pamela Lysohir, Beth Anderson, James, Paul; *ed:* (BS) Elem Ed, NY St Univ BrockPort 1950; (MS) Ed, Long Island Univ; Grad Stud Long Island Univ, Hostra; *cr:* 2nd Grade Teacher Southold Elem Sch 1950-53, K-3rd Grade/Rdng/Head Start/Follow Through Teacher Riverhead Cntrl Schls 1955-; *ai:* Prin Advisory, Cmmty Relations, Cty Fair, EIC, Curr Dev, Cntry Fair Tercentenery, Math Objectives, Writing Comms; Negotiating Team Secy; Mem 2nd DSAS Team; Exec Bd of Suffolk Rdng Cncl (Past Recording Secy, Past Pres, Past Bd Mem Read-A-Thon; Advisory Cncl for Suffolk; Delta Kappa Gamma (Past Recording Secy, Past VP, Pres); Amer Assn of Univ Women; Multiple Sclerosis Society; St Johns Parish Cncl (Past Pres, Sch Bd Mem, Chm Mem Comm, CCD Teacher); Cntrl Suffolk Hospital Drives Chairperson & Co-Chairperson;GSA; Friends of Lib; East End Art; Led Various Wkshps; Wheels of Mind Grant Proposal Dist Comm; Riverhead Teacher of Yr 1986-87; *office:* Riley Ave Sch Osborne Ave Riverhead NY 11901

HAGENBAUGH, FRANK VAL, World History Teacher; *b:* Wilkes-barre, PA; *c:* Ron, Jodi, Staci; *ed:* (BS) His/Government, Bloomsburg St Pa 1968, (MED) His/Government, Trenton St NJ 1972; (MA) Admin & Supervision Rider Coll NJ 1974; *cr:* Teacher 1968-1979; Supervisor 1979-84 Willing Gro Memorial Jr HS; Teacher John F Kennedy Sr-Jr HS 1984-; *ai:* Public Address Announcers Club; Coord Sch Wide Tutoring Prgm; Spon Number One Club; Coach Soccer/Bsktbl/Sftbl; Dist Curr Comm; WEA 1968-; BCEA 1968-; NJEA 1968-; NEA 1968-; Mount Laurel Planning Bd Chm; Mount Laurel PTO 1979-; Willingboro (NJ) PTA 1968-; Taft Institute of Amer Government; *office:* John F Kennedy Jr H S J F K Way & Levitt Pkwy Willingboro NJ 08046

HAGENBUCH, BETTY JOHNSON, Teacher; *b:* Colfax, WA; *m:* Ralph D.; *c:* David, Aaron, Brian; *ed:* (BAED) Ed/Bio, WA St Univ 1962; (MA) Ed Curr/Admin, Gonzaga Univ 1990; *cr:* HS Sci Teacher Shadle Park HS 1962-64, Evergreen HS 1964-69; 1st/2nd/4th Grade Teacher Pateros Elem 1969-75, 1979-84; Jr HS Math/Sci/Rdng Teacher Pateros 1984-; *ai:* Knowledge Bowl Coach; 8th Grade Adv; Instructional Materials Comm; WA St Teachers of Math; WA Ed Assn 1962-; NSTA; Heart Assn Grant 1969; Pateros Outstanding Teacher 1988; *office:* Pateros Jr HS Box 98 Pateros WA 98846

HAGENBUCH, MARK ODIS, Elementary Principal; *b:* Danville, PA; *m:* Linda Faye Gutshall; *c:* Andrew, Katie, Julie; *ed:* (BS) Elem Ed, Lock Haven Univ 1974; (MSED) Educl Admin, Bucknell Univ 1979; *cr:* 1st Grade Teacher 1975-79, 5th Grade Teacher 1979-87 Dalmatia Elem Sch; K-2nd Grade Elem Prin Northern Elem 1987-; *ai:* Dist Newsletter & Rdng Comm; Dist Heritage Days; NAESP 1987-; Thompson Battalion Memorial Project (Bd of Dir, PHMC Marker Election Treas, PHMC Marker Election Coord); Lions Club Intnl Mem; Trindle Spring Luth Church Mem; Natl Flag Fnd (Flag Research Consultant, Vexillologist Mem, Patriot Articulator, NFF Author), New Constellation Awd 1990; Sigma Pi (Mem, Secy, IFC Rep); Hagenbuch Family Organization (Family Historian, Newsletter Ed, Newsletter Developer); Natl Muzzle Loading Rifle Assn Mem; *office:* N York Cty Sch Dist 657 S Baltimore St Dillsburg PA 17019

HAGENZIEKER, WILLEM PETER, Academic Block Teacher; *b:* Oosterbeek, The Netherlands; *m:* Rachel Ann Karraker; *ed:* (BA) Eng, Fresno St 1976; *cr:* 7th Grade Academic Block Teacher Clark Intermediate Sch 1979-81; 8th Grade Academic Block Teacher Kastner Intermediate Sch 1981-83; Eng Teacher Clovis West HS 1983-84; 7th Grade Academic Block Teacher Kastner Intermediate Sch 1984-; *ai:* Dist Test Comm; Kastner Sch Writing Comm Rep; Cluster Teacher of Yr 1987-88; *office:* Kastner Intermediate Sch 7676 N 1st Fresno CA 93710

HAGER, ARTHUR F., Social Studies Teacher; *b:* Queens, NY; *ed:* (BA) Ec, Queens Coll 1955; (MS) Ed, St Johns Univ 1961; *cr:* Teacher Springfield Gardens Jr HS 1959-62, Bethpage HS 1962-; *ai:* Poly Act Club Adv; Sch Supreme Court Faculty Mem; NCSS.

HAGER, WILLIAM ALAN, Head Teacher; *b:* Oregon City, OR; *m:* Trudy Louise Tucker; *c:* Sarah, Alex, Sydney, Annie; *ed:* (BS) Elem Ed, Walla Walla Coll 1974; Air Traffic Control/Radar, ATC Instr & Controller; *cr:* ATC Controller US Army 1971-73; 5th/6th Grade Teacher Redding Jr Acad 1974-78; 1st-8th Grade Teacher Enterprise SDA Sch 1978-; *ai:* NPUG of Educators Mem 1978-, Teacher of Yr 1988; *office:* Enterprise SDA Sch P O Box N Enterprise OR 97828

HAGERSTRAND, ALLEN FRANK, Physical Education Teacher; *b:* Waukesha, WI; *m:* Diana L. Endicott-Hagerstrand; *c:* Melissa; *ed:* (BA) Phys Ed, 1965, (MA) Phys Ed, 1967 Humboldt St Univ; (MA) Educl Leadership, St Marys Coll 1990; Conflict Resolution, Peer Counseling, Comm Skills; *cr:* Phys Ed Teacher 1965- , Wrestling/Ftbl/Gymnastics/Swim Coach 1965-78, Coord/Supvr 1984- Mount Diablo HS; Teacher Diablo Valley Coll 1987-; *ai:* Coord/Supvr Peer Counseling Prgm; WASC Self Study Coord; Sch Dist Trainer & Coord/Supvr Conflict Management; Sch Dist Phys Ed Curr Comm; NEA, CA Teachers Assn, Mount Diablo Educators Assn; CA Assn Health, Phys Ed, Recreation Assn 1965-; CA Peer Counseling Assn 1988-; Friends of Greeks in Urban Settings Treas 1985-; Conflict Resolution Panels of Contra Costa Cty VP 1984-; Wrestling Coach of Yr San Francisco Bay Area 1971-72, N CA 1972; Conflict Resolution Contra Costa Cty Outstanding Youth Prgm 1988 & Mentor Teacher 1987-89; Articles Published; *home:* 17 Bonnie Pl Pleasant Hill CA 94523

HAGEWOOD, WILLIAM LOWELL, Social Studies Dept Chair; *b:* Nashville, TN; *m:* Amy Boyd; *c:* James Campbell; *ed:* (BA) His, David Lipscomb Coll 1976; (MED) Soc Stud Ed, Vanderbilt Univ 1985; His, Mid TN St Univ; Working on Doctor of Arts Degree His; *cr:* His/Govt Teacher David Lipscomb HS 1976-; *ai:* Weekend Enrichment Prgm Lipscomb-Coord; NCSS 1976-77; DA Summer Fellowship Through Mid TN St Univ 1988-; Colonial Dames of Amer Outstanding Teacher Awd 1988; David Lipscomb HS Teacher Awd 1985; Nashville Chapter Daughters of Amer Revolution; Outstanding Teacher Nominee 1985; *office:* David Lipscomb HS Granny White Pk Nashville TN 37204

HAGGARD, GAIL WELCH, Kindergarten Teacher; *b:* Florence, AL; *m:* Tommy James; *c:* Paula D.; *ed:* (AA) Ed, Hiwassee Coll 1968; (BS) Ed, Univ of TN 1970; (MA) Ed, Union Coll 1975; *cr:* 5th/6th Grade Teacher Wearwood Elem 1971; Rdng Teacher Sevierville Elem 1971-74; Kndgtn Teacher Sevierville Primary 1974-; *ai:* Countywide Kndgtn Curr Comm; Sevier Cty Ed Assn, TN Ed Assn, NEA 1970-; Nom Sevier Cty Teacher of Yr 1987; *home:* 914 Murphy Rd Sevierville TN 37862

HAGGARD, SYLVIA LEE (BOHALL), Sixth Grade Teacher; *b:* Columbus, IN; *ed:* (BA) Bio/Scndry Ed, Franklin Coll 1966; (MS) Elem Ed, IN Univ 1974; Cmptr, Gifted & Talented Adv Course; *cr:* 5th Grade Teacher St Paul Elem 1966-67; 4th Grade Teacher Burney Elem 1967-79; 4th Grade Teacher 1979-82, 6th Grade Teacher 1982- South Decatur Elem; *ai:* Cluster Teacher-Gifted & Talented; Stu Assistance Team; Mem Performanced Based Accreditation Team; Cmptr Helper; *office:* South Decatur Elem Sch RR 5 Box 246 Greensburg IN 47240

HAGGERTY, CHRISTINE LOUISE, Physical Education Teacher; *b:* Montebello, CA; *ed:* (AA) Gen Ed, Rio Hondo Coll 1979; (BA) Phys Ed, CA St Univ 1981; *cr:* Phys Ed Teacher & Coach Schurr HS 1982-; *ai:* Head Varsity Sftbl Coach; Frosh/Soph Vlybl Coach; First Aid Disaster Preparation Team; Montebello Teachers Assn 82-; Nea 82-; Dept Head Girls Phys Ed; Master Teacher; *office:* Schurr HS 820 Wilcox Ave Montebello CA 90640

HAGLUND, ROGER E., Mathematics Teacher; *b:* Fergus Falls, MN; *m:* Margaret Mills; *c:* David; *ed:* (BA) Math/Physics, Concordia Coll 1964; (MSE) Math, Moorhead St Univ 1975; Cmptr Sci, Moorhead St Univ 1985; *cr:* Math/Physics Teacher North Cntrl HS 1964-65; Math Teacher Talented Youth Math Project Univ of MN 1985-86; Math/Physics/Cmptr Teacher Borup HS 1965-; *ai:* Educl Computing Services Coord; Sci Fair & Jr Class Adv; Borup Ed Assn (Pres, VP, Secy, Treas), Teacher of Yr 1979; NCTM, MN Sci Teachers Assn; Natl Audubon Society; Fargo-Moorhead Kennel Club Treas; Siberian Huskey Club of America; MN St Sci Fair Judge 1987; Intnl Sci & Eng Fair Finalists Coach 1986, 1987; *home:* 6304 NW 4th St Moorhead MN 56560

HAGUE, ELSIE ANN CORDES, Third Grade Teacher; *b:* Seymour, IN; *m:* Bill Max; *c:* John, Kristin; *ed:* (BS) Elem Ed, FL Southern 1957; (MS) Elem Ed, IN Univ 1967; *cr:* 3rd Grade Teacher W Palm Beach 1958-59; 4th Grade Teacher Oaklandon 1959-63; 2nd Grade Teacher Columbus 1963-65; 3rd Grade Teacher Seymour 1965-66, 1973-; *ai:* Asst Supt Sunday Sch; SEA Building Rep 1982-84, 1988-; Supt Sunday Sch 1972-73; Psi Iota Zi Treas 1974-76; Girls Club Bd 1965-75; Humane Society (Life Mem, Bd Mem) 1978-79.

HAGUE, MICHALENE E. PATTI, English Teacher; *b:* Beverly, MA; *m:* Robert C.; *c:* Stacy M.; *ed:* (BA) Eng, 1968, (MAT) Eng/British Lit, 1972 Salem St Coll; Various Courses; *cr:* Eng Teacher Veterans Memorial HS 1968-; *ai:* Past Adv Sch Newspaper, Chess Team; Founder Interscholastic Chess League; Various Sch Graduation Requirement Comms; Chm Sch Drama & Communications Dept Re-Evaluation Comm 1987-89; MA Cncl Teachers of Eng Mem 1987-; Peabody Fed Teachers (Dir Public Relations, Newsletter Ed) 1976-80; N Shore Civic Ballet Co Bd of Assoc 1984-; Best Bet, Horace Mann Grants; *office:* Veterans Memorial HS 485 Lowell St Peabody MA 01960

HAGY, WINI OLSON, Third Grade Teacher; *b:* Chippewa Falls, WI; *m:* Franklin R.; *c:* Christopher L., Todd N.; *ed:* (BA) Elem Ed, Univ of S FL 1970; Math Specialist, Certified for Mid Sch; *cr:* 4th Grade Teacher V M Ybor Elem Sch 1970-71; 3rd Grade Teacher Riverview Elem Sch 1971-72; 6th Grade Teacher S Frederick Elem Sch 1977-78; 6th Grade Teacher 1981-87, 3rd Grade Teacher 1987- Pershing Elem Sch.

HAHN, JANIS STEPHENS, World History Teacher; *b:* Decatur, TX; *ed:* (BS) Ed, TX Tech Univ 1965; (MLA) Liberal Arts, SMU 1976; Region X Leadership Trng; *cr:* Teacher Robert E Lee Jr HS 1966-67, Laurel Jr HS 1967-70, O L Slaton JR HS 1970-72; Teacher 1972-85, Facilitator 1985-86, Teacher 1986- Mac Arthur HS; *ai:* NHS; Instructional Productivity Cncl; Sr Class Spon; Faculty Planning Comm; Booster Club; Phi Delta Kappa; Alpha Delta Kappa Pres 1983; TX Prof Educators Assn Pres 1986-87, Scndry Teacher of Yr 1984; TX Cncl of Soc Stud; Plymouth Park Youth Cnslr 1983-; United Meth Park Sunday Sch Teacher; SMU Outstanding Teacher; Jim Collins Educl Excl Awd; Irving Ind Sch Dist Teacher of Yr, Employee of Month; *office:* Mac Arthur HS 3700 N Mac Arthur Blvd Irving TX 75062

HAHN, LYNN D., Mathematics Teacher; *b:* Chillicothe, MO; *c:* Betsy, Shane; *ed:* (BA) Math/Fr, William Jewell 1975; Grad Stud; *cr:* Math Teacher Linn Cty R-1 1975-76, Brookfield R-3 1976-; *ai:* CTA Planning Comm Mem; MSTA 1975-; MO Mid Sch Assn 1989-; Laclede Recreation Assn (Secy, Treas) 1987-.

HAHN, W. TODD, 4th Grade Teacher; *b:* Rochester, NY; *m:* Andrea Reid; *c:* Chad; *ed:* (BS) Ed, St Univ Coll Geneseo 1967; Grad Work, St Univ Coll Geneseo; *cr:* 5th Grade Teacher Barker Road Elem 1967-84; 4th Grade Teacher Thornell Road Elem 1984-; *ai:* Asst Var Bsktbl & Jr Var Tennis Coach; NY St United Teachers, Pittsford Dist Teachers Assn 1967-; East Rochester & Pittsford PTSA; East Rochester Recreation Commission Vice Chm 1983-; East Rochester Youth Bsbl Bd of Dir 1985-; WHEC-TV Heroes in our Schls; *home:* 914 Main St East Rochester NY 14445

HAHN, WILLIE MC CRAY, History Teacher; *b:* Bellville, TX; *m:* Roy B. Sr.; *c:* Nicole, Sonya K., Roy Jr.; *ed:* (BS) Phys Ed/His, 1969, (MS) His, 1974 TX Southern Univ; Various Seminars & Wkshps; *cr:* Teacher Charles Milby 1970-; *ai:* Archonette Spon & Schlsp Comm Zeta Phi Beta; Schlsp Comm St Agnes Baptist Church; Houston Fed of Teachers; Houston Cncl of Soc Stud Teachers; Zeta Phi Beta; *office:* Charles H Milby 1601 Broadway Houston TX 77012

HAIGH, NANCY CLARK, 8th Grade Teacher; *b:* Washington, NC; *m:* P. Edward; *c:* Tiffany L.; *ed:* (BS) Ed, Appalachian St Univ 1970; *cr:* Teacher Collettsville Sch 1970-; *ai:* Annual Spon; NC Senate Bill 2 Comm; Teen Scene Adv; NCAE, NEA; Southern Assn Comm Chm; Teacher of Yr Collettsville Sch 1978, 1984, 1983; Educator of Yr Ruritan Club 1985; *home:* 203 Old Well Rd Hudson NC 28638

HAIGH, SHIRLEY BALL, Third Grade Teacher; *b:* Portageville, MO; *m:* Howard L.; *c:* Reid, Tom, Terry, Sandra; *ed:* (BA) Elem Ed, SE MO St 1973; *cr:* 3rd Grade Teacher Hayward Elem 1954-60; 6th Grade Teacher St Theresas 1966-67; 5th Grade Teacher Peach Orchard MO 1967-68; 6th Grade Teacher Martelle IA 1968-70; 3rd/5th/6th Grade Teacher Central City IA 1970-; *ai:* CCEA (VP 1971-77, Pres 1972-73); ISEA, NEA; *office:* Cntrl City Cmmty Sch Barber St Central City IA 52214

HAIGHT, THOMAS C., Bus Ed Instructor/Swim Coach; *b:* Cedar Rapids, IA; *m:* Susan Derby; *ed:* (BBA) Bus Ed, Univ of IA 1971; (MA) Bus Ed, Univ of N IA 1976; *cr:* Bus Ed Teacher/Swim Coach East Leyden HS 1971-74; Dist Ed Teacher/Swim Coach Marshalltown HS 1974-85; Swim Coach/Mktg Dir St Peter Aquatics 1982-85; Bus Ed/Swim Coach Seminole HS 1983-; *ai:* Head Coach Boys & Girls Swim Teams; NEA, FL Bus Ed Assn; Pinellas Assn Voc Ed; Pinellas Bus Ed Assn; Amer Swim Coaches Assn; Natl Inter Swim Coaches Assn; FL Swim Coaches Assn; US Swimming; Pinellas Cty Swim Coach of Yr 1983-85, 1989-90; FL Swimming All Star Team Head Coach 1983-85; FL Swimming Age Group Chm 1983-85; Teacher of Yr Nominee 1986; *office:* Seminole HS 8401 131st St N Seminole FL 34646

HAIGLER, RHONDA SUE, Computer Teacher; *b:* Odessa, TX; *ed:* (BS) Math, Southwestern OK ST Univ 1986; (MS) Curr & Instruction Emphasis in Math OK ST Univ 1988; *cr:* Computer Teacher Killeen Ind Sch Dist 1988-; *ai:* Sr Spon, Co-Spon Key Club; NCTM 1987-88; Circle K Charter Mem 1986; Summer Mission Dir, Dir of Puppet Team Baptist Stu Union 1987-88; One of 100 to Win Sallye Mae 1st Yr; Teacher Awd in the Nation; Outstanding Young Woman of Amer 1987; *office:* Killeen Ind Sch Dist 909 Elms Killeen TX 76542

HAIL, J. SHARON, Psychology Teacher; *b:* Somerset, KY; *ed:* (BS) Sociology/Psych, Campbellsville Coll 1971; (MA) Ed, Union Coll 1978; *cr:* Sch Soc Worker 1971-78; Headstart Teacher Summer 1973 & 1974 Pulaski Cty Bd Ed; Math/Soc Stud/Psych Teacher Eubank HS 1978-81; Psych/Sociology/Citizenship Teacher Pulaski Cty HS 1981-; *ai:* Girls Assn Bsktbl Coach 1979; Appsals Comm 1987-89; KY NEA Mem 1978-; NEA Mem 1978-; Pulaski Cty Ed Assn Mem 1978-; Pulaski City Historical Society; Easter Seal Society 1971-78; Lake Cumberland Writers League; *home:* Rt 7 Box 149 A Somerset KY 42501

HAILES, KAY S., Reading/Language Arts Teacher; *b:* Meridian, MS; *m:* James D.; *c:* Shelley, Andrew; *ed:* (BS) Elem Ed, Univ of S MS 1976; *cr:* 3rd Grade Teacher Quitman Elem 1976-77; 7th-8th Grade Teacher Quitman Jr HS 1978-79; 4th Grade Teacher Quitman Elem 1980-; *ai:* MS Jayceets 1976-80; Clarke Cty Rdng Cncl Mem; *home:* 417 Church St Quitman MS 39355

HAINER, CAROLYN CORNELIUS, Sixth Grade Teacher; *b:* Ravenna, OH; *m:* James; *c:* Cara; *ed:* (BA) Elem Ed, OH St Univ 1969; Nova Univ, OH St Univ Columbus, Otterbein Coll; *cr:* 5th/6th Grade Teacher W Broad Elem 1969-77; 5th Grade Teacher Chicago Elem 1978-79; Tutor Amer Heritage Sch 1980-81; 6th/7th Grade Teacher Hilltonia Alternative Mid Sch 1983-; *ai:* Amer Intnl Youth Stu Exch Cnslr; NEA, OEA; CEA Alternate Governor 1975-76; Lincoln Chrstn Ed Assn Secy 1976-77; Lincoln Baptist Church Chrstn Ed Bd 1989-; Aided in Founding a Respected Childcare Center; *office:* Hilltonia Alternative Mid Sch 2345 W Mound St Columbus OH 43204

HAINES, CATHY MOORE, Orchestra Director; *b:* Philipsburg, PA; *m:* Don R.; *c:* Cole; *ed:* (BA) Music Ed, Univ Mary Hardin Baylor 1973; (MA) Music Theory, 1982, (MA) Ed Admin, 1990 Univ of LA; Admin Endorsement; Madeline Hunter Levels I/II Presenters Trng; *cr:* Teaching Asst Univ of LA 1971-72; Orchestra Dir Pulaski Cty Cmmty Sch 1978-81, Cedar Rapids Cmmty Sch Dist 1981-; *ai:* Phase III Steering Comm; Building Extended Learning Prgm; Rep Cncl Buiilding Rep; Past Mem Dist Fine Arts Curr Comm; Natl Sch Orch Assn Exec Sec/Mem 1989-; Menc; Ascd; IA City Comm String Orch Treas 1986-88; Civitan Mem; Natl Cncl for The Arts Midwest Issues Forum; Article LA Menc Journal; Article OH Menc Journal; Article IA Dept of Ed Position Paper; Prof Violinist; Played Joffrey Nutcracker; *office:* Harding Mid Sch 4801 Golf St Ne Cedar Rapids IA 52402

HAINES, DONNA BELLE WILSON, Substitute Teacher; *b:* Benkelman, NE; *m:* Marvin Ellis; *ed:* (BSED) Elem Ed, Chadron St Coll 1970; Grad Stud Chadron St Coll, Kearney St Coll, Hastings Coll; *cr:* K-8th Grade Teacher Dundy Cty 1944-48; 3rd-8th Grade Teacher Max Public Schls 1948-53, 1958-69; 2nd-4th Grade Teacher Benkelman Elem Sch 1955-58, 1970-85; *ai:* Max HS Pep Club Spon; NE Ed Dept Mem; Cambridge Public Schls Evaluation Comm; Benkelman Schls Evaluation of Curr Steering & Soc Stud Curr Writing Comms; 4th Grade Head Team Teaching Mem 1972; NEA Life Mem 1944-; NSEA 1944-85; Benkelman Ed Assn Treas; Delta Kappa Gamma Finance Chairperson; Eastern Star Worthy Matron 1964; Presby Church; Alpha Phi Sigma 1970; Chadron St Coll Deans List 1970; NE ETV Network Educator of Month 1972; Valley Forge Classroom Teachers Medal Awd 1963-64; Outstanding Elem Teachers of Amer Nom 1973; *home:* 1213 B St Benkelman NE 69021

HAINES, GAYLORD W., JR., Social Studies Teacher; *b:* Washington, PA; *m:* Helen; *c:* Shannon M., William A.; *ed:* (BA) Comprehensive Soc Stud, Pitt 1974; *cr:* Teacher Trinity Mid Sch 1975-84; Trinity HS 1984-; *ai:* Trinity HS Girls Soccer Coach & Soccer Coord; SADD Adv; PA St Soccer Coaches Assn; Natl Soccer Coaches Assn; *office:* Trinity HS Park Ave Washington PA 15301

HAINLIN, NANCY EVANS, 4th Grade Teacher/Sci Chair; *b:* Raleigh, NC; *c:* David E., Ella K. Bardugon; *ed:* (BA) K-8 Art Ed, 1952, (MS) K-8 Art/Eng, 1956 Auburn Univ; Adult Ed Cert; Master Teacher Cert; Teacher Cert Prgm; *cr:* Jr HS Eng/Art Teacher Salt Lake City Schls 1957-60; HS Art Teacher Delta Sch Dist 1955-56; 4th Grade Teacher Henry Cty Schls 1961-; *ai:* Chm Sci Dept; Smith-Barnes Elem Sch Master Teacher; Regional Assessment for Beginning Teachers; Kappa Kappa Iota Pres 1980-; NS DAR 1980-; Magna Carter Legatee; the Mayflower Society Legatee; Stockbridge Elem Sch Teacher of Yr 1982-83; Smith-Barnes Elem Sch Teacher of Yr 1986-87; *office:* Smith Barnes Elem Sch 147 Tye St Stockbridge GA 30281

HAIR, KITTIE ELLEN, World History Teacher; *b:* Denver, CO; *ed:* (BA) Poly Sci, Brigham Young Univ 1971; (MA) US Soc His, Univ of NV Las Vegas 1988; *cr:* Teacher Hyde Park Jr HS 1972-77, Eldorado HS 1979-; *ai:* Helping You Helping Me Adv; HS Stu Tutoring Grade Sch Stu; Teacher Advisory Comm; NEA 1979-; NCSS 1985-88; Clark Cty Classroom Teachers Assn 1979-; Peace Corps Health Educator 1971-72; Phi Kappa Phi, Phi Alpha Theta Honor Societies; Nom for NV Soc Stud Teacher of Yr 1988-; Outstanding Faculty Awd 1990; *office:* Eldorado HS 1139 N Linn Ln Las Vegas NV 89103

HAIRSTON, ELEANOR SWOOPE, Jr High English Teacher; *b:* Columbus, MS; *m:* Nicholas Edward Jr.; *c:* Virginia C., Nicholas E. III; *ed:* (BS) Eng, MS Univ for Women 1964; *cr:* Teacher Joe Cook Jr HS 1964-67, Heritage Acad 1968-83, Oak Hill Acad 1985-; *ai:* Oak Hill Anchor Club Spon; *home:* 270 Swoope Rd N Columbus MS 39701

HAIRSTON, KATHEY NEELY, 5th Grade Teacher; *b:* Milan, TN; *m:* David Lee; *c:* Andrew, Emory; *ed:* (BS) Elem Ed, 1974, (MED) Elem Ed, 1975, (EDS/AA) Elem Ed, 1981, 1984 Univ of Montevallo; *cr:* 4th-8th Grade Teacher Center Street 1975-89, Glen Iris 1989-; *ai:* Delta Kappa Gamma Mem 1986-; *office:* Glen Iris Elem Sch 1115 11th St S Birmingham AL 35205

HAJEK, MARGARET ASHCRAFT, Fourth Grade Teacher; *b:* Hays, KS; *m:* Robert Frank; *ed:* (BA) Elem Ed, 1970, (MS) Elem Ed, 1974 Purdue Univ; *cr:* 3rd-5th Grade Elem Teacher Knox Cmmty Sch Corporation 1971-; *ai:* Cty Spelling Bee 5th Grade Judge; Historic Fort Wayne Field Trip & Spring Book Fair Comm; Delta Kappa Gamma 1977-; NEA, ISTA; Knox Classroom Teachers Assn (Membership Chm 1977-78, Building Rep 1972-74, Treas 1976-77); Tri-Kappa 1976-81; PEO Chaplain 1976-77;

Merry Moderns Home Ec Club 1977-82; *home:* Box 222 North Judson IN 46366

HAJEK, WILLIAM ANTON, Science/Computer Teacher; *b:* Moulton, TX; *m:* Magdalan A. Novak; *c:* Kevin S.; *ed:* (BS) Ag Ed, TX A&M Univ 1971; Natl Sci Fnd Earth Sci Teacher Trng TX A&M Univ; *cr:* Voc Ag Teacher Columbia-Brazor Ind Sch 1971-73; Farmer 1974-76; Voc Ag Teacher Industrial Ind Sch Dist 1977-79; Farmer 1980-87; Sci Teacher Industrial Ind Sch Dist 1987-; *ai:* Model Rocket Club; 4-H Leader; Ag Teachers Assn Mem 1971-73, 1977-79; *home:* PO Box 4 Lolita TX 77971

HALBERT, BILLIE MACKEY, Honors World His Teacher; *b:* Dallas, TX; *m:* Robert Allen; *c:* Jarrod, Tuesdee, Kauli; *ed:* (BA) His/Span, 1968, (MED) Supervision, 1982 San Angelo St Univ; Leadership Trng for TX Appraisal System; *cr:* 7th-9th Grade Soc Stud Teacher Glenn Jr HS 1968-70; 10th/11th Grade Soc Stud Teacher Cntrl HS 1970-72; 7th-9th Grade Substitute Teacher Edison Jr HS 1972-74; 6th-8th Grade Soc Stud Teacher Lincoln Jr HS 1974-76; 7th-9th Grade Soc Stud Teacher Lee Jr HS 1976-79; Soc Stud Teacher Cntrl HS 1979-; Soc Stud Supvr/World His Teacher San Angelo Ind Sch Dist 1986-; *ai:* Lincoln & Lee Jr HS Chrldr Spon; Cntrl HS Jr Prom Spon 1980-82 & Pre-Classroom Prgm 1986-; San Antonio Cncl for Soc Stud Secy 1976-78; TX Cncl for Soc Stud 1968-; ASCD 1986-; Phi Delta Kappa 1983-; Amer Assn of Univ Women 1979; Delta Kappa Gamma 1980-82; Kappa Kappa Iota 1978-80; Developmental Ec Ed Prgm Dist Coord; Region XV Service Center Media Advisory Comm; Nom Admin of Yr Awd 1990; *office:* Cntrl HS 1621 University San Angelo TX 76904

HALBGEWACHS, CYNTHIA H. TAYLOR, 8th Grade Teacher; *b:* Macon, GA; *m:* Howard L.; *c:* Ellen, Chris Taylor, Joanne, Lara Taylor, David Taylor; *ed:* (BA) Eng, Valdosta St Coll 1970; *cr:* 12th Grade Teacher Valdosta HS 1969-70; 8th Grade Lang Arts/Soc Stud Teacher Whigton Public Sch 1980-89; *ai:* Beta Club Adv; PTO Pres GAE/NEA 1980-89 Whigham Sch Teacher of Yr 1983-84; Whigham Cmmty Dev Cncl 1988-89; 4-H Volunteer Leader 1986-89 Volunter Leader of Yr 1986; 2nd Place St GA His Lesson Plan Contest 1983.

HALBMAN, ROBERT ALAN, Chair Military Science; *b:* St Louis, MO; *m:* Diane L. Wyrick; *c:* Robert A. Jr., Tayve L. Gifford; *ed:* (BS) Industrial Technology, SW MO St 1960; (MS) Ed, NE LA Univ 1971; US Army Command & Staff Coll, Flight Sch; *cr:* Military Sci Asst Professor NE LA Univ 1970-73; Military Sci Dept Chm W KY Univ 1977-80; Military Sci Chm Bowling Green HS 1980-; *ai:* Coach & Spon Drill Team, Color Guard, Honor Guard; Academic Cncl Mem; *home:* 1603 Campbell Ln Bowling Green KY 42104

HALCOMB, BOBBIE S., 6th-8th Grade Reading Teacher; *b:* Cody, KY; *m:* Truman; *c:* Patricia K., Melissa J.; *ed:* (BS) Elem Ed, Eastern KY Univ 1962; (MA) Elem Ed, Morehead St Univ 1979, 1981; Resource Teacher for KY Teacher Internship Prgm; Teacher Expectation for Stu Achievement Trng; *cr:* 4th/5th Grade Teacher Altro Sch 1961-62; 5th Grade Teacher Carr Creek Elem 1962-64; 6th-8th Grade Remedial Rdng/Creative Writing Gifted Teacher Whitesburg Mid Sch 1964-; *ai:* Yrbk Spon; Chairperson Graduation Comm; Comm Mem Chapter I Parental Involvement, In-Service; Supvr Letcher Cty Teachers Credit Union; KY Ed Assn, NEA 1961-; Letcher Cty Teachers Organization 1964-; *office:* Whitesburg Mid Sch Park St Whitesburg KY 41858

HALE, BOBBY JEAN, 3rd Grade Teacher; *b:* Pyramid, KY; *m:* Edgar; *c:* Gwendolyn Harmon, Anita, Edwynna; *ed:* (BA) Elem Ed, Pikeville Coll 1970; (MA) Ed, Morehead St Univ 1975; Art; *cr:* 1st/8th Grade Teacher Flyd Cty Rural Sch 1949-56; Art Teacher Clark Elem Sch 1971-74; 7th Grade Teacher 1974-75; 3rd Grade Teacher 1975- Prestonsburg Elem; *ai:* Comm Acad Improvement; FCEA; KEA; NEA; Fitzpatrick 1st Baptist Church Sunday Sch Supt 1973-74; Girl Scouts Leader 1967-68; *home:* PO Box 1208 Prestonsburg KY 41653

HALE, CHARLENE AARON, Second Grade Teacher; *b:* Jamestown, KY; *m:* Don; *c:* Charles, Anthony, Michael; *ed:* (BA) Elem Ed, Campbellsville Coll 1963; (MA) Elem Ed, 1979, (Rank I) Elem Counseling, 1981 W KY Univ; *cr:* Eng Teacher Russell Cty HS 1963-66; 2nd Grade Teacher Russell Springs Elem Sch 1977-; *ai:* NEA, KEA; Russell Cty Ed Assn Bd Mem 1983-86; 1st Baptist Church Mem.

HALE, DOROTHY L., Third Grade Teacher; *b:* Montezuma, TN; *m:* Alfred; *c:* Debra L., Terri S. Swan; *ed:* (BSE) Elem Ed, AR St Univ 1964; *cr:* Teacher Marked Tree Elem 1961-.

HALE, EILEEN V., 4th Grade Teacher; *b:* Youngstown, OH; *m:* Larry; *c:* Joelle, Alison; *ed:* (BA) Ed, Sonoma St Univ 1969; *cr:* 2nd-6th Grade Teacher 1969-83, GATE Teacher 1983-85, 4th Grade Teacher 1985- Prestwood Sch; *ai:* Prins Advisory, Environmental, Outdoor Ed Comm; Intergenerational Project; Site Cncl; CA Assn of Gifted 1982-; VMTA 1969-; *office:* Prestwood Elem Sch 343 E Mac Arthur Ave Sonoma CA 95476

HALE, JACK E., 4th Grade Teacher; *b:* Beacon, NY; *m:* Jody Winter; *c:* Jack R.; *ed:* (BS) Elem Ed, 1967, (MS) Elem Ed, 1973 St Univ New Paltz; *cr:* 5th Grade Teacher Rombout Mid Sch 1967-70, Myers Corners Elem 1971-76; 4th Grade Teacher Fishkill Elem 1976-; *ai:* Intramural Dir Soccer, Bsktbl, Sftbl; Soccer & Bsbl Cmmty Teams Coach; *office:* Fishkill Elem Sch Church St Fishkill NY 12524

HALE, JANET BENNETT, Reading Recovery Teacher; *b:* Ironton, OH; *m:* Jerry E.; *c:* Ellisha S.; *ed:* (BA) Elem, OH Univ 1975; Rdng Recovery, OH St; *cr:* Chapter I Rdng Teacher 1975-77, 1st Grade Teacher 1978-89, Rdng Recovery Teacher 1989- Symmes Valley #2; *ai:* Highway Baptist Chapel Church Sunday Sch Teacher of Teens 1975-; Jennings Scholar 1988-89; *home:* Rt 2 Box 202 Kitts Hill OH 45696

HALE, JANICE J. (ADAMS), Third Grade Teacher; *b:* Hartsville, SC; *m:* Donald E.; *c:* Anthony; *ed:* (BA) Ed, Trevecca Coll 1963; WV Univ; *cr:* 6th Grade Teacher Williams Sch 1963-65; 4th Grade Teacher Stanford Sch 1966-67; 3rd Grade Teacher Mineral Wells Sch 1967-; *ai:* WV Assn, NEA, Rdng Cncl; Church of the Nazarene Bd of Dirs; *home:* PO Box 61 Mineralwells WV 26150

HALE, MARY AUXIER, English Teacher; *b:* Paintsville, KY; *c:* Mary-Anne Hale Morgan, Cynthia E.; *ed:* (BS) Eng, Pikeville Coll 1961; E KY Univ, Morehead Univ, Univ of KY; *cr:* 1st-8th Grade Teacher Corn Fork 1955-56; Art Teacher Johns Creek Elem 1958-59, Prestonsburg Elem Sch 1959-62; 9th/10th Grade Eng Teacher Prestonsburgh HS 1962-63; 12th Grade Eng/Appalachian Stud Teacher Burnside HS 1963-81; 7th-9th Grade Teacher Burnside Jr HS 1987-; 9th Grade Eng Teacher Southern Jr HS; *ai:* Southern Jr HS Debate Club; NEA Life Mem; E KY Teachers Network 1986-; KY Ed Assn; Pulaski Cty Ed Assn 1963; *office:* Southern Jr HS 4050 Enterprise Dr Somerset KY 42501

HALE, PATRICIA BOWLING, Fifth Grade Teacher; *b:* Radford, VA; *m:* Stephen Donald; *c:* Emily E., Brady B.; *ed:* (BS) Elem Ed, Radford Univ 1973; MS Upper Elem Ed, Radford Univ; *cr:* 5th Grade Teacher Snowville Elem Sch 1973-; *ai:* Sci Coord; 4-H Club Leader; PCEA 1973-; Phi Delta Kappa; Snowville PTA 1973-; Newbern PTA 1986-; Mt View Meth Church; *office:* Snowville Elem Sch Rt 1 Box 186 Hiwassee VA 24347

HALE, PATRICIA JEAN, Fourth Grade Teacher; *b:* Chicago, IL; *c:* Juanita, Jatasha, Lori Booker; *ed:* (BS) Elem Ed, S IL Univ 1968; (MS) Human Learn/Dev, Governors St 1976; Grad Stud Elem Ed Sci, IIT, Univ of Chicago; *cr:* 4th Grade Teacher Nansen; 4th/5th Grade Teacher Hopkins Elem; 3rd Grade Teacher Betsy Ross; *ai:* After Sch Rdng Tutoring; Soc Center Teacher Act in Drama; Spelling Bee Spon; Assembly Performances Chairperson; *home:* 1009 W 129th Pl Chicago IL 60643

HALE, RITA LOIS, Second Grade Teacher; *b:* Richlands, VA; *ed:* (AS) Ed/General Stud - Summa Cum Laude, SW VA Comm Coll 1977; (BS) Ed - Magna Cum Laude, Clinch Valley Coll 1979; (MA) Ed, VA Polytech Inst & St Univ 1986; *cr:* 3rd Grade Teacher 1979-84, 2nd Grade Teacher 1984-88, 1st Grade Teacher 1988-89, 2nd Grade Teacher 1989- Honaker Elem Sch; *ai:* Phi Kappa Phi 1987-; Intnl Rdng Assn, VA St Rdng Assn 1989-; Honaker Elem PTA Secy 1980-81; *home:* Rt 2 Box 495 Honaker VA 24260

HALE, SAMUEL STEPHEN, Sci/Social Studies Teacher; *b:* Pontiac, MI; *m:* Marilyn Rose Paulson; *c:* Ralph S., Lisbeth L. Hale Gagner; *ed:* (BS) General Bus, W MI Univ 1950; (MAT) His, Univ of WI Superior 1971; *cr:* Sales Standard Oil 1950-55; Pharmaceutical Sales Mead-Johnson & Company 1955-60; Warner Chilcott Lab 1960-66; Teacher Winter Schls 1967-74, 1976-; *ai:* NHS & Jr Natl Honor Society; Environmental Facilitator; Projects Wild Aquatic Facilitator; WI Society of Sci Teacher Mem 1985-; BSA Asst Scout Master 1967-76, Eagle Scout 1944; Free Accepted Masons Master of Lodge 1956; *home:* Rt 1 Box 67 Couderay WI 54828

HALE, SHARON FREEMAN, First Grade Teacher; *b:* Memphis, TN; *m:* Joseph David Sr.; *c:* Joseph D., Emily A.; *ed:* (BA) Early Chldhd, Univ of MS 1980; *cr:* 1st Grade Teacher 1980-82, 3rd Grade Teacher 1982-84 Bovina Elem; 1st Grade Teacher Greenville Chrstn 1984-85, Bovina Elem 1985-; *ai:* PTO Treas; MEA, NEA 1985-88; Red Carpet Rdng Club; GSA Leader 1989-; *office:* Bovina Elem Sch Box 100 Bovina School Rd Vicksburg MS 39180

HALE, SHERRY HOFFER, Third Grade Teacher; *b:* Hallettsville, TX; *m:* William Michael; *c:* Heath; *ed:* (BS) Elem Ed, Univ of Houston Victoria 1976; *cr:* 3rd Grade Teacher Sacred Heart Sch 1977-.

HALEY, JUDY ANN (PATTERSON), Kindergarten Teacher; *b:* St Louis, MI; *m:* Leo M.; *c:* Bryan M., Shawn P.; *ed:* (BA) Ed/Soc Sci/Eng, Alma Coll 1970; (MS) Early Chldhd, Cntrl MI Univ; Gosell Pre-Sch Trng; *cr:* 2nd Grade Teacher South Bendle Elem Sch 1956; Kndgtn Teacher 1967-68, 1st Grade Teacher 1968-69, Kndgtn Teacher 1969- Merrill Elem Sch; *ai:* Math, Sci & Rdng Comm; Effective Schls Comm; NAEYC 1987-; MI Ed Assn (Secy, Treas, VP, Building AR) 1967-; NEA 1967; Headstart Comm 1987-88; Co-Author Elem Handbook Comm 1989; *office:* Merrill Cmmty Schls 345 W Alice Merrill MI 48637

HALEY, MARILYN WAGONER, 7th Grade Science Teacher; *b:* Clovis, CA; *m:* Royce W. Jr.; *c:* Alicia, Jeanette; *ed:* (BA) Elem Ed, Fresno St Coll 1954; Numerous Univs; *cr:* Teacher San Leandro Sch Sch Dist 1954-56, AFB 1956-57, Army Base 1957-58; Substitute Teacher Chicago Sch Dist 1959; Teacher Lncolnwood Sch 1959-61, AFB 1961-65,Richmond Sch Dist 1971-; *ai:* Elem & Jr HS Sci Olympiad Coach 1987-89; Organized & Advised Stu Patrol Lakenheath Sch England 1963; MEA; NEA; REA 1975-; Nom Overseas Teacher of Yr 1964; *home:* 9750 Puttygut Richmond MI 48062

HALEY, PRISCILLA LEMNERTZ, Language Arts & Speech Teacher; *b:* Clearwater, FL; *c:* Tamara L.Hall; *ed:* (AA) St Petersburg Jr. College 1964; (BA) Speech/Eng Ed., Univ of South Fl 1967; Works in Cty for Dropout Prevention; *cr:* Speech/LA Teacher King HS 1968-69; 6th Grade Teacher Okaloosa Elem 1969-70; Speech/LA Teacher Kennedy Mid Sch 1975-76; Speech/LA Teacher Tarpon Springs Mid Sch 1976-; *ai:* Advisor for 8th Grade Field Trip, 8th Grade Dance, Spelling Bee for 10 yrs, Talent Show for 5 yrs, 7th Grade Trip for 3 yrs; Pinellas Cncl Teachers of Eng; Pinellas Classroom Teachers Assn Faculty Rep 1988-; *office:* Tarpon Springs Middle School 501 N. Florida Ave Tarpon Springs FL 34689

HALEY, RICHARD JOHN, Director of Instrumental Music; *b:* Buffalo, NY; *m:* Andrea R. Levitt; *ed:* (BM) Music Ed, St Univ Coll Fredonia 1982; (MS) Ed, Coll of Saint Rose 1989; *cr:* Band Dir Liberty Cntrl Schls 1983-84: Inst Music Dir New Berlin Cntrl Schls 1985-; *ai:* Dir 7-12 Concert Band, 5-6 Elem Band, 7-12 Jazz Ensemble, 6-12 Marching Band; MENC; NYSSMA; ACAMT Treas 1987-89; NYSSMA Certified Adjudicator; Chenango All Cty Jazz Dir; Outstanding Band Mohawk Pageant of Bands 1986 & 1988; *office:* New Berlin Central 1 School St New Berlin NY 13411

HALFWASSEN, BILL, Band Instructor; *b:* Omaha, NE; *m:* Caroline Boening; *c:* Scott, Gretchen Paddock, Brian, Sara; *ed:* (BA) Liberal Arts/Music, Univ IA 1962; Grad Stud at San Jose St, Univ of CA Santa Cruz, Santa Clara Univ, Chapman Coll; *cr:* Band Instr Miles Cmmty Schls 1962-67, Newman HS 1967-68, Vinton Cmmty Sch 1968-70, Moss Landing Mid Sch 1970-; *home:* 43 O Connor Cir Salinas CA 93906

HALL, AGATHA MORTON, 7th Grade English Teacher; *b:* Boaz, AL; *m:* Billy Franklin; *c:* Susan, Shannon; *ed:* (BS) Eng/Phys Ed, 1967, (MS) Phys Ed, 1974 Jacksonville St; *cr:* Eng Teacher 1967-71, Phys Ed Teacher 1967-72 Albertville HS; Eng Teacher Alabama Avenue Sch 1977-; *ai:* GAMA BELLS & Cmmty Ed Rep; Curr Comm; AL Ed Assn, NEA 1977-; Albertville City Ed Assn 1985-; Vacation Bible Sch Prin 1980-89; Church Choir Dir 1981-; Outstanding Teacher of Yr 1984-85; Teacher of Yr Awd 1987-88; *home:* Rt 6 Boaz AL 35957

HALL, BETTY JANE WALTZ, Mathematics Teacher; *b:* Troy, PA; *m:* James Scott; *c:* Christopher, Dennis; *ed:* (BA) Math Ed, Mansfield Univ 1970; Elem Ed, Marywood Coll 1973; Working Toward Masters Math Ed; *cr:* Elem Teacher 1970-1985, Scndry Math Teacher 1985- Elk Lake Sch Dist; *ai:* NE PA Cncl Teacher of Math 1989-; *home:* RD 1 Box 212 Springville PA 18844

HALL, BRAXTON B., History & Government Teacher; *b:* Morehead City, NC; *ed:* (BS) His, E Carolina Univ 1973; E Carolina Univ 1973-74; Mentor Cert 1987; *cr:* Teacher Cape Hatteras Sch 1974-; *ai:* Spon Stu Government, Drama Club, NHS, Quiz Bowl Team; Team Approach for Better Schls, Fine Arts Curr Comm; Cty Leadership Team; NC Assn of Educators (Dare Cty Pres 1986-88, Dist Pres 1987, St Communications Chairperson Commission for Instruction & Prof Dev 1989-); NEA 1974-: Dare Cty Teacher of Yr 1986; Dare Cty Terry Sanford Awd for Creativity 1984; Teacher Recruiter NC Dept of Public Instruction; *office:* Cape Hatteras Sch P O Box 948 Buxton NC 27920

HALL, BRENDA DICKERSON, Fourth Grade Teacher; *b:* Dothan, GA; *m:* William; *c:* Salaam; *ed:* (BS) Eng Ed, Tuskegee Univ 1971; (ME) Elem Ed, 1980, (EDS) Mid Chldhd Ed, 1986 Valdosta St Coll; *cr:* Eng Teacher Appling Cty HS 1971-72; Teacher Morton Avenue Elem 1973-; *ai:* Certified Cadre Leader for Effective Schls Prgm; Systemwide Book Adoption Comm Mem; Waycross Assn of Ed, GA Assn of Ed, NEA 1973-; Waycross City Schls Teacher of Yr 1979-80; Phi Delta Kappa Outstanding Teacher Awd 1983; Magazine Articles Published 1981-83; Articles Reprinted 1988; Diploma Inst of Childrens Lit 1982; *office:* Morton Avenue Sch 701 Morton Ave Waycross GA 31501

HALL, CAROLYN RUTH, Sixth Grade Teacher; *b:* Baltimore, MD; *m:* Victor W.; *c:* Jason, Jenna; *ed:* (BS) Elem Ed, Towson St Univ 1980; (MS) Comm Disorders, Johns Hopkins Univ 1985; *cr:* 3rd Grade Teacher Van Bokkelen Elem Sch 1980-81; 6th Grade Teacher Pershing Hill Elem Sch 1981-; *ai:* Pershing Hill Human Relations Comm Mem; Stu Cncl & Drama Club Spon; Prof Tutoring; Anne Arundel Comm Coll Cont Ed Gifted & Talented Prgm Teacher; Delta Kappa Gamma Mem 1988-; Wesley Chapel United Meth Church (Co-Choir Dir, Co-Organist) 1982-; Curr Writing Math Dept 1987; 1st Place St Film Festival 6th Grade Video 1984; *office:* Pershing Hill Elem Sch 29th Division Rd Fort George Meade MD 20755

HALL, CAROLYN SUE, Fourth Grade Teacher; *b:* Martin, KY; *ed:* (BA) Elem Ed, 1977; (MA) Guidance/Counseling, 1981-83 Morehead St Univ; *cr:* Teacher Oil Srpings Sch 1978-; *ai:* Guidance Comm; KEA 1978-82/1985-; *office:* Oil Springs Sch Rt 40 Oil Springs KY 41238

HALL, CLARICE, First Grade Teacher; *b:* St Louis, MO; *ed:* (BA) Ed, Harris/Stowe St Coll 1957; *cr:* 1st Grade Teacher Waring Elem Sch 1957-60, Banneker Elem Sch 1960-; *ai:* Teacher in Charge Acting Prin 1975-; Supervisory Teacher, Apprentice Teacher Trng; Dir & Spon Banneker Symphonettes Rhythm Band; Individual & Group Cnslr; Coord Bus & Lunchroom Management & Supervision; Career Opportunities Prgm Supervisory Teacher; Effective & Efficient Schls Admin Leadership Prgm Chm; Lower Primary After Sch Prgms Spon & Adv; NEA 1960-; Intnl Rdng Assn 1979-; MO St Teachers Assn 1960-; St Louis Teachers Assn 1980-; Harris/Stowe Allumni Assn Mem 1985-; St James AME Church Mem 1961-; NAACP Mem; Master Teacher Awd 1974, 1975; Lifetime Teacher Appreciation Awd 1976-77; Dir Presenter of Inservice Wkshps Prin & Classroom Teachers; *office:* Banneker Sch 2840 Sam Shepard Dr Saint Louis MO 63103

HALL, CYNTHIA JEAN, Music Teacher Chairperson; *b:* Toledo, OH; *ed:* (BM) Music, OH Wesleyan Univ 1972; (MM/MED) Music Theory Comp/Music Ed, TX Tech Univ 1979; Eastman Sch of Music; UCLA; *cr:* Teacher Isbell Mid Sch 1979-; Organist/Childrens Choirs Dir Camarillo United Meth Church 1980-; *ai:* Chorus; Drama Club; Recorder Club; Mu Phi Epsilon 1968-; AGO 1965-; AAUW 1973-; CCG 1985-; Guest Lecturer-Presenter for Music Ed Wkshps Throughout Southern CA 1983-; Sip Grant 1985; Composer-Arranger-Guest Artist; *office:* Isbell Mid Sch 221 S 4th St Santa Paula CA 93060

HALL, DAISY RUTH, Mathematics/Science Teacher; *b:* Waco, TX; *ed:* (BS) Elem Ed, 1971, (MS) Elem Ed, 1977 TX Southern Univ; *cr:* 2nd Grade Teacher 1971, 3rd Grade Teacher 1971 72 J H Hampton Elem Sch; 5th Grade Teacher E Houston Elem Sch 1973-; *ai:* Sigma Gamma Rho (Adv, VP 1986-, SW Region Membership Chairperson 1988-), Regional Soror 1988, Soror of Yr 1988; TX Assn of Adult Ed 1980-; Natl Women of Achievement VP 1988-; AFT N Forest Treas 1987-, Achievement 1988; GSA Co-Leader; E Houston Elem Sch Teacher of Yr 1989-; *office:* E Houston Elem Sch 8115 E Houston Rd Houston TX 77028

HALL, DANITA TUBBS, Third Grade Teacher; *b:* Sergent, KY; *m:* Freddie Wayne; *c:* Sonja Grimm, Gregory; *ed:* (BA) Elem Ed, 1970, (Rank II) Elem Ed, 1975 Morehead St Univ; Presently Working on Rank I Morehead St Univ; *cr:* Phys Ed Teacher Fleming-Neon Elem 1971-72; 1st Grade Teacher Kingdom Come Settlement Elem 1975; 3rd Grade Teacher Martha Jane Potter Elem 1975-; *ai:* Pom-Pon Girls Adv; KEA, NEA, LCTO, PTO; Order of Eastern Star; Fleming-Neon HS Bsktbl Boosters Secy 1989-; Meth Church Treas 1988-; *home:* Rt 1 Box 35-C Jenkins KY 41537

HALL, DEBBIE MORGAN, Media Specialist; *b:* Welch, WV; *m:* Van C.; *c:* Levi C., Logan H.; *ed:* (BA) Phys Ed/Lib Sci, Concord Coll 1980; Scndry Ed, Coll of Grad Study 1988; Athletic Training Classes, Red Cross Water Safety Instr; *cr:* Phys Ed Teacher 1980-89, Media Specialist 1989- Baileyville HS; *ai:* Baileysville HS Var Girls Bsktbl & Sftbl Coach 1981-84; Pep Club Spon 1984-; WVEA; *office:* Baileysville HS Rt 97 Brenton WV 24818

HALL, DEBORAH A., Social Studies Teacher; *b:* Louisville, KY; *ed:* (BA) His, Eastern KY Univ 1974; (MA) His, Western IL Univ 1975; Ed, Univ of KY 1980; Univ of KY; *cr:* Instr Shelby Cty HS 1975-; *ai:* Spon Co-Ed Y Service Club; Girls Sftbl Coach; Delta Kappa Gamma 1st VP 1985-87; KY Cncl for Soc Stud; Commonwealth Inst for Teachers 1984; Visiting Teachers Inst of KY 1989; HS Teacher of Yr 1982; Eastern KY Univ Autobiography Inst 1986; *office:* Shelby County HS Box 69 Shelbyville KY 40065

HALL, DEBORAH JEAN, Mathematics/Chemistry Teacher; *b:* Niceville, FL; *ed:* (BS) Math, David Lipscomb Univ 1986; Math, MTSU; *cr:* Teacher Glencliff Comprehensive HS 1986-; *ai:* Chrldr Spon; Math Club; Mid TN Math Teachers Assn 1988-.

HALL, DENISE DOVE, Media Coordinator; *b:* Fayetteville, NC; *m:* James E. III; *c:* Elizabeth; *ed:* (BA) Ed, Univ of NC Chapel Hil; 1981; (MLS) Lib/Information Sci, NC Cntrl Durham Univ 1989; *cr:* 4th/5th Grade Teacher 1981-82; 6th Grade Teacher 1982-85; Media Coord 1985- Rockfish Elem; *ai:* Media Club Adv; *office:* Rockfish Elem 5736 Rockfish Rd Hope Mills NC 28348

HALL, DERYL ANN (DUNAGAN), Third Grade Teacher; *b:* Big Spring, TX; *m:* Marvin Eugene; *c:* Allison, Ashley; *ed:* (BS) Elem Ed, Angelo St Univ 1972; *cr:* 1st Grade Teacher 1972-73, 3rd Grade Teacher 1973- Fannin Elem; *ai:* Assn of TX Prof Educators Mem; *home:* 2501 Oxford San Angelo TX 76904

HALL, ETHEL STEVENS, 8th Grade Teacher; *b:* Newnan, GA; *m:* Kurt I.; *c:* Douglas, Beth; *ed:* (BS) Soc Stud, GA Coll 1972; (MED) Elem Ed, W GA Coll 1976; *cr:* Teacher Coweta Cty Bd of Ed 1972-82, All Hallows Sch 1985-; *ai:* 8th Grade Class Spon; Yrbk & Newspaper Adv; Natl Cath Educl Assn 1985-; VFW Auxiliary Secy 1986-87; E Killingly Fire Dept Auxiliary Treas 1986-87; Pres of Coweta Assn of Educators 1981-82; *home:* 779 Bailey Hill Rd Dayville CT 06241

HALL, FRANCES JACKSON, Third Grade Teacher; *b:* Greenwood, MS; *m:* Buddie L.; *c:* Joseph, Cedric; *ed:* (BS) Elem Ed, 1971, (MS) Elem Ed, 1982 MS Valley St Univ; *cr:* Teacher Humphreys Cty Elem Sch; *ai:* Caterer; MS Assn of Educators Building Rep Certificate 1985; NEA; Parthers for Improved Nutrition & Health Adv; MS St Assn of Elk Act of Kindness Asst Directress; Brownie Troop Leader; MS Valley St Univ Alumni Assn Secy; Church (Clerk, Choir Mem, Sunday Sch Teacher); *home:* 209 Roosevelt St Belzoni MS 39038

HALL, GAIL WEST, 6th-12th Grade Music Teacher; *b:* Kershaw, SC; *m:* Benny W.; *c:* Deborah G. Davis, Kevin F. Horton, Julie D. Horton, Ben W. Jr.; *ed:* (AB) Music Pedagogy/Music Ed Coker Coll 1969; Grad Stud; *cr:* Music Teacher Bethune Elem, Mid, HS 1962-76, Robert E Lee Acad 1977-80, Bethune Mid & HS 1980-; *ai:* Sch Annual, Beta Club, Glee Club Spon; Sr Class Adv; Kershaw Cty Music & Arts Grant Writing Comm; Sch Arts In-Sch Coord; Music Educators Natl Assn, SC Music Educators Assn 1969-; Piano Teachers Intnl Lib of Music 1967-; Kershaw Cty Teachers Cncl 1987-; Delta Kappa Gamma 1986-; Bethune HS Booster Club 1980-; Kershaw Cty Teacher of Yr 1988; SC Outstanding Teacher 1986; *home:* 104 Mary Dell Dr Bethune SC 29009

HALL, GARY O., Business Department Chairman; *b:* Los Angeles, CA; *c:* Christopher W.; *ed:* (BA) Bus, 1962, (MBA) Bus, 1966, (EDD) Bus/Ed, 1972 AZ St Univ; *cr:* Teacher Los Angeles City Schls 1962-63; Professor Maricopa Jr Coll Evening Division 1965-75, AZ St Univ 1979-78; Teacher/Dept Chm Tempe HS 1963-; *ai:* Curr Comm & Advisory Cncl Mem; NBEA, WBEA, ABEA 1963-; NEA, AEA, TSEA Pres 1968; Delta Pi Epsilon Pres 1966, Phi Kappa Sigma; Jr Chamber VP Internal Out Speak Up; Fed Fly Fishers Cncl Mem; Published Ed & Fly Fishing Articles; *office:* Tempe HS 1730 S Mill Ave Tempe AZ 85281

HALL, GENIE CALLAHAN, Second Grade Teacher; *b:* Laurel, MS; *m:* Joe F.; *c:* Robin R., Rana J.; *ed:* (BS) Elem Ed, 1974, (MS) Elem Ed, 1976 MSU; *cr:* Teacher Neshoba Cntrl Elem 1974-; *ai:* Kappa Kappa Iota 1984-; *home:* Rt 6 Box 311 Philadelphia MS 39350

HALL, GLADYS MARIE, Business Education Teacher; *b:* Painesville, OH; *ed:* (BS) Comprehensive Bus Ed, Ft Valley St Coll 1974; Add on Certificate Adult Basic Ed; Grad Stud GA Southwestern Coll, GA Southern Univ; *cr:* Bus Ed Teacher Dodge Cty HS 1974-80, Telfair Cty HS 1980-; Adult Ed Teacher Telfair Cty Adult Ed Center 1985-89; Part Time Night Bus Ed Teacher Ben Hill-Irwin Tech 1982-; *ai:* NEA, GA Assn of Educators 1974-; Telfair Assn of Ed Secy 1986-87; Ladies of Profession Club 1974-; Regenerating Academics thru Scholastics Secy 1988-; Telfair Area Ft Valley St Coll Alumni Chapter Secy 1974-; Ft Valley St Coll Natl Alumni 1974-; *office:* Telfair Cty HS 1900 S 3rd Ave Mc Rae GA 31055

HALL, HAROLD DAVID, Biology/Chemistry Teacher; *b:* Welch, WV; *m:* Ginger Lane Durham; *c:* Amanda; *ed:* (AB) Bio, Berea Coll 1967; (MSST) Bio, Amer Univ 1971; Grad Work Beyond Masters Howard Univ, Univ of VA; *cr:* Phys Sci Teacher Osbourn Sr HS 1967-68; Bio/Chem Teacher Stonewall Jackson Sr HS 1968-; *ai:* Sci Fair Adv; Tennis Coach 1968-76; PWEA, NEA, VEA 1967-; NSF Grant for Grad Work at Amer Univ & Howard Univ; VA Dept of Ed Self Study Evaluation Comm Mem 1989; *office:* Stonewall Jackson Sr HS 8820 Rixlew Ln Manassas VA 22110

HALL, JAMIE L., English Teacher; *b:* Dover, OH; *c:* Matt, Jennifer, Mike; *ed:* (BS) Eng/Theatre, Bowling Green St Univ 1968; Eng, OH St Univ; *cr:* Eng Teacher Maumee HS 1968-71, Cardington HS 1979-; *ai:* Drama Coach; Sr Class Adv; OEA, NEA, Local Assn; *office:* Cardington Lincoln HS 349 Chesterville Ave Cardington OH 43315

HALL, JAN STANDLEY, Physical Education Dept Chair; *b:* Twin Falls, ID; *ed:* (AA) Phys Ed, Cottey Coll 1974; (BS) Phys Ed, Boise St Univ 1975; Grad Stud Coll of ID; *cr:* Teacher 1976-79, Athletic Dir Bonners Ferry 1981-85; Teacher Buhl 1985-86, Kimberly 1986-; *ai:* Vlybl & Bsktbl Coach; Chrldr Adv; Class Spon; Natl HS Athletic Dir 1981-85; Natl Coaches Assn 1976-; Womens Golf Assn Pres 1983-84; Whos Who in Amer Women Recognition for Cmmty Service; *office:* Kimberly Sch Dist PO Box O Kimberly ID 83341

HALL, JENNIE ANDERSON, Teacher; *b:* Nacogdoches, TX; *c:* Zenna M.; *ed:* (AA) S TX Jr Coll 1972; (BA) Elem Ed, 1974, (MS) Admin, 1976 TX Southern Univ; Rdng; *cr:* Bookkeeper Houston Federal Credit Union 1968-70; Substitute Teacher North Forest Ind Sch Dist 1970-74; Secy New Macedonia Baptist Church 1959-89; Teacher North Forest Ind Sch Dist 1974-; *ai:* Matron for Singing Group; Tidwells Cheer Fund Pres; TX St Teachers Assn, Sigma Gamma Rho; Greater Houston Rdng Cncl; Adopt Black Children Comm Incorporated; Tidwell Elem Teacher of Yr 1989-.

HALL, JERRE JACKSON, 7th/8th Grade Eng/Rdng Teacher; *b:* Plainview, TX; *c:* Vicky K. Longcrier, B. Howard; *ed:* (BS) Elem Ed, W TX St Univ 1970; Geography & Scndry Cert; Ed & Eng; *cr:* 5th Grade Lang Art/Soc Stud Teacher Rockwall Elem 1970-71; 6th Grade Lang Art/Soc Stud Teacher Highland Park Elem 1971-80; 7th/8th Grade Soc Stud/Eng/Rdng Teacher Highland Park Jr HS 1980-; *ai:* Natl Jr Honor Society Adv; NHS Co Adv; 8th Grade Class Spon; UIL Spelling/Ready Writing/Dictionary Skills; Spec Ed Advisory Bd Comm; TX Assn for Gifted & Talented 1990; TX St Teachers Assn 1970-; Highland Park Educators Treas 1988-; TX Alliance for Geographic Ed 1990; NEA; Lake Tanglewood Cmmty Church Bd Chairperson 1987-89; Highland Park Schls Employee of Yr 1985; Participate in Geographic Inst SW TX St Univ 1990; *home:* Box 50534 Amarillo TX 79159

HALL, JOHNNIE MELVIN, Fourth Grade Teacher; *b:* Myra, KY; *m:* Joyce Robinson; *c:* Rhoda L., John L.; *ed:* (AB) Ed, 1961, (MA) Ed, 1969 Morehead St Univ; *cr:* Teacher Jenkins Ind Schls 1960-66, Hazel Park Sch Dist 1966-; *ai:* MI Ed Assn 1966-; NEA 1960-; Hazel Park Ed Assn (Building Rep 1977-) 1966-; *office:* Roosevelt Elem Sch 24131 Chrysler Dr Hazel Park MI 48030

HALL, JULIE TRAPNELL, First Grade SIA Teacher; *b:* Metter, GA; *m:* Robert Clark; *c:* Travis; *ed:* (AA) Ed, Stephens Coll 1966; (BS) Early Chldhd Ed, Univ of GA 1968; (MS) Early Chldhd Ed, Armstrong St Coll 1980; *cr:* 1st Grade Teacher Watkinsville Elem 1968-69, Gould Elem 1969-70, 5th-8th Title I Rdng Teacher Collins Elem 1977; 1st Grade Teacher David Emanuel Acad 1978-88; 1st Grade/SIA Teacher Metter Primary Sch 1988-; *ai:* David Emanuel Acad Jr Y Club Adv; Sr Y Club Co-Adv; PAGE; *home:* 443 Preston St Metter GA 30439

HALL, KEVIN BARRY, Social Science Dept Chair; *b:* New York, NY; *m:* Ellen Marie Tirone; *c:* Kelsey A.; *ed:* (BA) Sociology/Anthropology, Occidental Coll 1981; Grad Sch of Ed Occidental Coll; *cr:* Teacher/Coach Damien HS 1981-85, San Marino HS 1985-; *ai:* Var Head Coach Boys Bsktbl, Boys & Girls Track & Field; Moderator Model United Nations; Honors, AP His Teacher, Dept Chm; SCIBA 1989-; *office:* San Marino HS 2701 Huntington Dr San Marino CA 91108

HALL, LANNA PENDLETON, Art Teacher; *b:* Bryan, OH; *m:* Clarence J.; *ed:* (BSED) Art Ed, Univ of Toledo 1972; (MA) Art/Painting, 1982, (MFA) Art/Painting, 1984 Bowling Green St Univ; *cr:* Art Instr Edon Northwest Local Schls 1972-80; Grad Teaching Asst Bowling Green St Univ 1980-81; Art Instr Edon Northwest Local Schls 1981-; *ai:* Art Classes for Sr Citizens; Honor Roll Stus & NHS Selection Comm; OH Art Ed Assn, NAEA 1983-; OH Ed Assn, NEA 1972-; Toledo Museum of Art 1972-; Exhibitor Toledo Area Artists Exhibition Toledo Museum of Art 1989; Honorable Mention Painting & Prints Ft Wayne Artists Guild 1989; Best of Show Tri-St Artists Incorporated Annual Show & Sale 1989; *office:* Edon Northwest Local Schls Box 188 W Indiana St Edon OH 43518

HALL, LINDA LIPPS, 2nd Grade Teacher; *b:* Ashtabula, OH; *m:* Jim; *c:* Kristi, Joshua; *ed:* (BA) Early Chldhd, Kent St Univ 1970; Grad Work; Several Wkshps; *cr:* 4th Grade Teacher 1969-70, 3rd Grade Teacher 1970-72, L D Tutor 1978-79, 3rd Grade Teacher 1979-80, 2nd Grade Teacher 1980-81, 1st Grade Teacher 1981-82, Kndgtn Teacher 1982-83 Jefferson Elem; 6th Grade Teacher Rock Creek Elem 1984-86; 2nd Grade Teacher Jefferson Elem 1986-; *ai:* PTO Secy; Safety Patrol & Stu Cncl Adv; Negotiations, Academic Awds, Levy Comm; 4-H Adv 1980-82; Church of Christ (Sunday Sch Teacher, Youth Choir Dir, Many Comms, Youth Adv); *home:* 963 R 307 E Jefferson OH 44047

HALL, LLOYD KENNETH, Social Studies Teacher; *b:* Greer, MO; *m:* Nan Lou Wynn; *c:* Wynn M., Ayra L., Tray G.; *ed:* (AA) Sci, Sch of the Ozarks 1964; (BSE) Soc Stud, Ouachita Baptist Univ 1968; (MSE) Counseling, AR St Univ 19 4; *cr:* Soc Stud Teacher Winona MO HS 1968-69; Served in Vietnam 1969-71; Sci Teacher Winona HS 1971; Soc Stud Teacher Alton HS 1971-; *ai:* Mgr of Concession Stands; MO St Teachers Assn Pres 1988-; First Baptist Church (Deacon, Sunday Sch Teacher) 1973-; Veterans of Foreign Wars 1974-; Alton City Alderman 1977-79; Worked Toward Federal Grant for Elem Building; *home:* Rt 2 Box 2133 Alton MO 65606

HALL, MARY ANITA TIBBITS, Spanish-English Teacher; *b:* Crawford Cty, AR; *c:* Glenda; *ed:* (AA) Span, Westark Comm Coll 1968; (BA) Span, 1970, (MA) Span, 1972 Univ of AR; Summer Inst, Univ of Madrid 1970; *cr:* Grad Teacher Asst Univ of AR 1970-72; Teacher Roland HS 1972-; Instr Westark Comm Coll; *ai:* Span Club Spon; Adult Ed Night Sch Teacher; Homebound Stu Teacher; Class Spon; NEA, OEA, RCTA 1972-; NFLTA; *home:* Rt 2 Box 695-1 Muldrow OK 74948

HALL, MILDRED JOHNSON, Health Occupations Teacher; *b:* Kingsport, TN; *w:* Virgil C. (dec); *c:* Ricky Alan, Rebecca Lynne; *ed:* Nursing, Johnston Mem Hosp Sch of Nursing 1953; Ed Univ of TN 1976-82: Ed East TN St Univ 1964-68; Nursing & Health Classes Local Hospital/East TN St Univ; *cr:* RN Holston Valley Cmmty Hospital 1954-61; Indusustrial Nurses Holston Defense Corporation 1961-69; North Electric Company 1972-75; Teacher Daniel Boone HS 1976-; *ai:* Spon HOSA; Red Cross Bloodmobile Volunteer; WA Cty Ed Assoc 1976-; TN Ed Assoc 1976-; NEA 1976-; Teacher of Yr Awd 1984; Gray Ruritan Club; TN Health Occupations Teacher of Yr 1983; *office:* Daniel Boone H S Rt 16 Box 267 Johnson City TN 37615

HALL, NANCY ELIZABETH SKINNER, First Grade Teacher; *b:* Anderson, IN; *m:* Bobbie Jack; *c:* Eric, Brian; *ed:* (BS) Elem Ed, Ball St Teachers Coll 1963; (MA) Elem Ed, Ball St Univ 1966; *cr:* Art Teacher Anderson Township Schls 1963-64; 2nd Grade Teacher Anderson Cmmty Schls 1964-67; 1st Grade Teacher South Madison Cmmty Schls 1974-; *ai:* 1st Grade Coord 1974-83; Outdoor Lab Comm Mem; IN St Teachers Assn, NEA 1964-67/1974-; South Madison Classroom Teachers Assn Building Rep 1974-; South Madison Area Rdng Cncl; Prof Dev Grant Featherboys Fables Sci 1987 & Sci Adventurers 1990; *office:* East Elem Sch 893 E US 36th Pendleton IN 46064

HALL, PEGGY TINSLEY, Mathematics Teacher; *b:* Newnan, GA; *m:* Gary Michael; *c:* Brittainy J., Christopher M.; *ed:* (AA) Math, Mid GA Coll 1976; (BS) Ed, 1979, (MA) Ed 1982 W GA Coll; Grad Stud Math; *cr:* Jr HS Math Teacher O P Evans 1979-87; Math Teacher Newman HS 1987-; *ai:* Sunshine Comm; MAO Adv; GAE 1989-; *home:* 5 Oak Hill Dr Newnan GA 30263

HALL, REITA JANE, English Department Chairperson; *b:* Mannington, WV; *ed:* (BA) Eng, Bryan Coll 1954; Grad Stud Fairmont St Coll, TN Wesleyan Coll, Univ of KY, Univ of TN Chattanooga; *cr:* Asst to Dean of Women Bryan Coll 1954-56; 11th/12th Grade Eng Teacher Ben Lippen Sch 1956-67; 12th Grade Eng Teacher 1967-, Dept Chm 1972- Mc Minn Cty HS; *ai:* Honor Society Asst Adv; Academic Competition Team Coach; Eng Dept Chairperson; NEA, TEA 1967-; MCEA Many Comm 1967-; ETATE 1975-; 1st Baptist Church; Outstanding Scndry Teacher & Teacher of Yr Awd; *office:* Mc Minn Cty HS 2215 Congress Pkwy Athens TN 37303

HALL, RICHARD D., Mathematics Teacher/Coach; *b:* Monticello, IL; *m:* Dolores A Beedy; *c:* Bryan, Elisabeth, Shelley; *ed:* (BA) Phys Ed, Millikin Univ 1966; Grad Stud Coaching, Math, Cmptr, Driver Ed; *cr:* Math/Coaching Teacher Harvey

Public Schls 1966-72; Math/Coaching/Drivers Ed Teacher Stoughton Public Schls 1972-; *ai:* Girls Head Var Bsktbl Coach; Drivers Ed Behind the Wheel; WI Bsktbl Coaches Assn 1972-; Stoughton Ed Assn 1972-, Teacher of Yr 1982-83; NEA 1966-; WI Educl Assn 1972-; Rainy Day Food Coop 1980-; Downtown Rivatalazations 1989-; Friends of the Lib 1988-; *office:* Stoughton HS 1600 Lincoln Ave Stoughton WI 53589

HALL, RITA FIRESTONE, 7th Grade Mathematics Teacher; *b:* Roanoke, VA; *m:* Thomas E.; *ed:* (BA) Sociology, 1971, (MED) Early Chldhd Ed, 1979 Lynchburg Coll; Math Cert, Roanoke Coll 1986; *cr:* K/1st/3rd-5th Grade Teacher Buchanan Elem 1974-86; Math Teacher Botetourt Intermediate Sch 1986-; *ai:* Botetourt Intermediate SCA Spon; Botetourt PTA 2nd VP.

HALL, ROBERT GERARD, Spec Ed/Math/English Teacher; *b:* Dorchester, MA; *m:* Joan Iafolla; *c:* Sondria; *ed:* (BA) Spec Ed/ Elem Ed, Boston Coll 1973; Berklee Coll of Music 1974-75; *cr:* Resource Room Aide Norwood Public Schls 1976-79; Jr HS Sp Ed Instr Boston Sch Randolph 1979-87; North River Collabortive Alternative HS Prgm 1987-89; Sp Ed Instr/Coord Norfolk Cty Agricultural HS 1989-; *ai:* Mem of Top 40 Band Drummer; Pitcher for Amer Lunch Team Under Control of Norwood Sftbl League; Proficiency Awd Berklee Coll of Music; Percussion Instr Awd 1976; *home:* 33 Green St P O Box 188 Sheldonville MA 02070

HALL, SALLY GALE, 6th Grade English Teacher; *b:* Houston, TX; *c:* Lance Franklin, Elaine Franklin Davis; *ed:* (BS) Elem Ed, Lamar Univ 1961; (MED) Ed, Stephen F Austin Univ 1976; *cr:* 4th/5th Grade Teacher Neches Ind Sch Dist 1962-63; 4th Grade Teacher 1963-65, 5th/6th Grade Music Teacher 1973-80, 6th Grade Eng Teacher 1980- Henderson Ind Sch Dist; *ai:* TX Prof Educators Assn Treas 1981-82; NCTE; 1st Presbyn Church Elder; Henderson Civic Theater Bd of Dirs 1989-; *home:* 1411 Briarwood Trl Henderson TX 75652

HALL, SARA B., Science Teacher; *b:* Dekalb Cty, GA; *m:* James J. Jr.; *c:* Jackie, Jeff, John, Jay; *ed:* (BA) Bio, Emory Univ 1959; (MED) Scndry Sci, GA St Univ 1980; *cr:* Research Technician Center For Disease Control 1959-64; Sci Teacher J P Carr Jr HS 1977-78, Heritage HS 1978-; *ai:* Spon Sci Club; Coach & Spon Sci Bowl, Sci Olympiad, Academic, High Q Teams; NSTA 1979-; GA Sci Teachers Assn 1981-; Sci Teachers of Rockdale & Dekalb 1983-; GA Acad of Sci 1988-; GA Ornothological Society 1980-; Heritage HS, Rockdale Cty Star Teacher 1985; *office:* Heritage HS 2400 Granade Rd Conyers GA 30207

HALL, SHERMAN E., Science Teacher; *b:* Ocilla, GA; *ed:* (BA) Elem Ed, Fort Valley St Coll 1976; Valdosta St Coll; *cr:* Sci Teacher Bacon Cty Mid Sch 1976-; *ai:* 7th Grade Chairperson; Honor Club Adv; GAE/NEA 1976-; Bacon Cty Assn of Ed 1976-; Teacher of Yr 1983-84; Bacon Cty Mid Sch Teacher of Yr 1988; Bacon Cty Assn of Ed Secy 1981-82; NAACP 1986-; Progressive Mens Club 1978-; Amer Heart Assn Cert of Appreciation Volunteer Svc 1988; Amer Cancer-Cert of Appreciation Volunteer Svc 1980; *home:* PO Box 242 Alma GA 31510

HALL, SHERRY DAVENPORT, Science Teacher; *b:* Uvalde, TX; *m:* Alvin Jr.; *c:* Brandy, Trey, Samantha; *ed:* (BS) Bio, Sal Ross St Univ 1971; Alternative Cert Prgm, San Antonio TX Region XX; *cr:* Billing Clerk Rio Grande Electric Cooperative 1973-74; Office Clerk Ag Sterlization & Conservation Service 1982-85; Sch Teacher Pryor Sch Dist 1985-; *ai:* Jr HS Sci UIL & Stu Cncl Spon; Jr/Sr HS Sci Fair Coord; *office:* La Pryor HS P O Box 519 La Pryor TX 78872

HALL, SHIRLEY DANTZLER, Second Grade Teacher; *b:* Orangeburg, SC; *m:* James S. Jr.; *c:* Sheryl D., Karen J.; *ed:* (BS) Elem Ed/Early Chldhd, Claflin Univ 1973; (MS) Elem Ed, SC St Coll 1976; Prgm for Effective Teaching, Assessment of Performance in Teaching; *cr:* 4th/5th Grade/Lang Art Teacher Edisto Mid Sch 1974-75; 4th Grade Teacher St George Elem Sch 1976-78, Bowman Elem Sch 1978-86; 2nd Grade Teacher St Paul Primary Sch 1986-; *ai:* Sch Improvement, Dist Math Curr, St Textbook Adoption Comms; Clarendon Cty Ed Assn 1986-; SC Ed Assn, NEA 1974-; Zeta Phi Beta 1973-; Book Published 1988; *home:* 484 Flamingo Dr NE Orangeburg SC 29115

HALL, STEVEN RICHARD, Eighth Grade Teacher; *b:* Seattle, WA; *m:* Linda Joy; *c:* Sybil, Jared; *ed:* (BA) Psych, 1971, (MS) Ed, 1978 Cntrl WA Univ; Environmental Ed; Cmptr Ed; *cr:* 6th Grade Teacher Morgan Mid Sch 1971-78; 5th Grade Teacher Mt Stuart Elem 1978-82; 8th Grade Teacher Morgan Mid Sch 1982-; *ai:* Honors Stu Camp Dir; HS Head Golf Coach; Sch Newspaper Adv; WA Ed Assn, Ellenburg Ed Assn 1971-; Kittitas Audubon Society Pres 1989-; Initiative 89 St Comm, Cty Chm 1978; Book Illustrator; *office:* Morgan Mid Sch 400 E 1st St Ellensburg WA 98926

HALL, SUSAN JANE, Fifth Grade Teacher; *b:* Macomb, IL; *ed:* (BA) Elem Ed, Parsons Coll 1965; Math, Sci, Soc Stud, Hum, Whole Lang; *cr:* 2nd Grade Teacher Stratmoor Hills Elem; 3rd Grade Teacher Bricker Elem; 6th Grade Teacher Pikes Peak Elem; 5th Grade Teacher Bricker Elem; *ai:* Sci, Rdng, Lang Comm; Dist Chm; Curr Cncl; Harrison Ed Assn Bd; Regional PACE Bd; *office:* Bricker Elem Sch 4880 Dover Dr Colorado Springs CO 80916

HALL, THOMAS J., English Teacher; *b:* Elmira, NY; *m:* Geraldine C.; *c:* John M., Alexandra M.; *ed:* (AB) Eng Lit, Union Coll 1963; (MA) Amer Lit, Purdue Univ 1969; *cr:* Eng Teacher Ernie Davis Jr HS 1963-66, Portsmouth HS 1967-68; Eng Teacher/Dept Chm Southside HS 1969-; *ai:* Oratorical Competition Adv; Liasion Comm Teacher & Admin; NCTE; Mark Twain Society VP 1983-86; Natl Endowment for Hum Inst Mentor Teacher 1988; NEH Huck Finn Summer Seminar 1989; *office:* Southside HS 777 S Main St Elmira NY 14904

HALL, TOMMY A., English Teacher; *b:* Joplin, MO; *m:* Ann Estes; *c:* Debbie Pender, Tommie Baker; *ed:* (BA) Phys Ed/Eng, Hendrix Coll 1955; (MED) Phys Ed/Admin, Univ of AR 1956; Prin Certificate; *cr:* Teacher/Coach St Elizabeth Public Schls 1956-59, Richland Public Schls 1959-68; Classroom Teacher Springfield R-12 1968-; *ai:* MATE, LAD, MSTA, SEA, NEA, MNEA, SNEA; Springfield Public Schls Teacher of Yr Candidate; *home:* 3840 Queens Ct Springfield MO 65807

HALL, VA DONNA C., High School Counselor; *b:* Savannah, GA; *ed:* (BA) Phys Ed, Southwest St Univ 1973; (MS) Phys Ed, KS St Univ 1979; (MS) Cnslr Ed, IA St Univ 1986; *cr:* Coach/ Phys Ed Teacher Bradley HS 1973-74; Teacher/Coach Colfax Cmmty Sch 1975-78; Teacher/Wm Athletic Dir/Coach Upper IA Univ 1980-82; Cnslr/Coach Chariton Cmmty Sch 1986-; *ai:* NHS; Asst Girls Bsktbl; Head Boys Golf; Stu Assistance Prgm; Prin Advisory Comm; Chariton Cmmty Ed Assn, NEA 1986-; Kiwanis 1988-; Order of Eastern Star 1973-; Outstanding Young Women of America 1987.

HALL-LOCKE, TEDDIE, Media Specialist; *b:* Barstow, CA; *m:* Norman; *ed:* (AA) E Cntrl Jr Coll 1973; (BS) Lib Sci, MS St Univ 1975; (MA) Educl Media & Technology, Univ of S MS 1986; *cr:* Media Specialist Mc Laurin Jr HS 1976-81, Burnsville Sch 1981-; *ai:* Beta Spon; Sr Class Spon; Jr Beta Spon; MS Lib Assn 1874-83; Pilot Club of Iuka 1983-861 Attorney Generals SWEEP Comm 1990; Friends of Lib 1988-; STAR Teacher 1988; *office:* Burnsville Sch Drawer A Burnsville MS 38833

HALLER, ANN CORDWELL, Science Teacher; *b:* Denver, CO; *m:* Frederick Ray; *c:* Michael, Lori; *ed:* (BA) Pre-Med, Univ of MT 1966; (MA) Anatomy, Univ of ND Med Sch 1969; (PHD) Anatomy, LA St Univ Med Sch 1975; Nationally Certified By ASPO to Teach Lamaze Childbirth Classes; *cr:* Instr Univ of ND 1968, LA St Univ New Orleans 1973-74; Teacher Kellogg HS 1980; *ai:* Soph, Jr, Sr Class Adv; NHS Co-Adv; PEO Guard 1990; Sigma Xi 1970-; Delta Kappa Gamma 1990; Amer Society Psychoprophylaxis in Obstetrics 1976-; Natl Inst of Health Centennial Teacher ID; Dist I Teacher Achievement Awd 1988, 1989; *office:* Kellogg HS Jacobs Gulch Kellogg ID 83837

HALLER, NORMA RAE, Third Grade Teacher; *b:* Frederick, MD; *ed:* (BA) Elem Ed, 1974, (MA) Elem Ed, 1976 Frostburg St Coll; Advanced Prof Certificate; *cr:* 3rd Grade Teacher Waverley Elem 1974-; *ai:* Cooperative Learning Cadre; Gifted & Talented Rep; Cmptr Grant; *home:* 2153 Wainwright Ct #1-B Frederick MD 21701

HALLICK, MARY PALOUMPIS, Eighth Grade Teacher; *b:* Minonk, IL; *m:* Constantine (dec); *c:* Constance Ramskugler, Athanasia; *ed:* (BS) Elem Ed, IL St Univ 1946; (MA) Curr/ Supervision, Univ SD 1966; (EDD) Curr/Instr, Marquette Univ 1974; *cr:* Teacher/Prin Benson Elem Sch 1944-48; 6th Grade Teacher Sioux City Public Schls 1963-68; 8th Grade Teacher Hamilton Sch Dist 1968-; *ai:* Dist Teacher Evaluation & Supervision Comm; Phi Delta Kappa; Zoning Appeals Bd Chm 1982-; BSA 1970-; Author: Book of Saints, Sowing Seeds, Teachers Guides; Mem of Natl Curr Comm Creek Orthodox Church; *home:* N76 W14720 North Point Dr Menomonee Falls WI 53051

HALLING, STANLEY D., Life Science Teacher; *b:* Cando, ND; *m:* G. Alice Keller; *c:* Amy J., Melissa J.; *ed:* (BS) Ed Sci, Valley City St 1959; Grad Stud Sci; *cr:* 7th Grade Teacher New Salem Public Schls 1959-63; 7th Grade Life Sci Teacher Hughes Jr HS 1963-; *ai:* Hughes Sci Dept Chairperson; Sci Olympiad Co-Adv; Sci Standing & Sci Curr Writing Comm; Bismarck Ed Assn Building Rep 1980; ND Ed Assn Part-Time Field Rep 1975-81; Elks 1960-; Presbyn Church Session Mem 1965-; Steering Comm ND Sci Curr; Schlsp Comm Public & Private; Hughes Teacher of Yr 1986; Represented Hughes Teachers At Rose Garden Washington DC for Exemplary Awd; *home:* RR 2 Box 315 Bismarck ND 58504

HALLMAN, NANCEY FORD, Rdng/Lang Art/Math Teacher; *b:* Louisville, KY; *m:* Douglas; *c:* Ross, Clay; *ed:* (BS) Elem Ed, W KY Univ 1964; (MS) Elem Ed, IN Univ 1971; *cr:* 5th Grade Teacher Portland Elem 1964-70; 4th-6th Grade Lang Art Teacher Mc Cullough Elem 1970-71; 5th Grade Teacher Eastlawn Elem 1972-75; Rdng Teacher Chapter I 1976-83, Lang Art/Math Teacher 1984- St Leonard Sch; *ai:* Math Bowl & Mathcounts Teams 1985-87, 1990; NCTM; *office:* St Leonard Sch 440 Zorn Ave Louisville KY 40206

HALLMAN, NORMA TROXEL, Remedial Rdng/Lang Art Teacher; *b:* Quay, OK; *m:* D. Daryl; *c:* Norman D.; *ed:* (BS) Elem Ed, Cntrl St Univ 1954; (MS) Elem Ed/Rdng Specialist, OK St Univ 1970; Grad Stud; *cr:* 3rd Grade Teacher Blackwell Public Schls 1952-53, Bartlesville Public Schls 1954-57, Arkansas City Public Schls 1957-59; 2nd/5th Grade Teacher 1966-, 5th-8th Grade/Remedial Rdng/Lang Art Teacher 1989- Perkins-Tryon Public Schls; *ai:* Perkins-Tryon Ed Assn (Mem 1966-, Secy, VP 1975-80, Pres); First Baptist Church (Deacons Wife, Vacation Bible Sch Teacher); Kappa Pi Honorary Art.

HALLMAN, ROBERT RICHARD, Eng/Creative Writing Teacher; *b:* Allentown, PA; *m:* Sally Gray; *c:* Gregg, Todd; *ed:* (BA) Eng, Le High Univ 1970; (MA) Eng, Kutztown Univ 1976; *cr:* Eng Teacher 1974-, Creative Writing Teacher 1986-, Literature of the Amer Wilderness Teacher 1989- Nazareth JrHS; *ai:* Sierra Club 1989-; Lehigh Valley Faculty Partnership Local HS & Coll Educators Develop Innovative Curr Models; *home:* RD 6 Box 6042 Stroudsburg PA 18360

HALLMARK, LAWANTA M., Fifth Grade Teacher; *b:* Caddo, OK; *m:* Alton B.; *c:* Bob H., Ken, Jo Lynn Butler; *ed:* (BS) Elem Ed/Eng, 1972, (MED) Elem Ed, 1983 E TX St; Doctorial Prgm, E TX St Univ; *cr:* 4th/5th Grade Teacher Garland Ind Sch Dist 1972-; *ai:* PTA 1968-, Honorary Life Membership 1983; *home:* 3901 Castle Dr Rowlett TX 75088

HALLOCK, DONALD JAMES, Mathematics Teacher; *b:* Pittsburgh, PA; *m:* Deborah Jean; *c:* Jessica R.; *ed:* (BS) Ed/Math, Penn St 1973; Grad Courses Child Dev, Child & Adolescent Psych, Math; *cr:* Math Teacher J Frank Faust Jr HS 1973-; *ai:* Develop Mentor Teacher Prgm Comm; Chess Club Adv; Phi Kappa Phi 1972-; Road Runners of America Mem 1985-; Staff Derv Comm Outstanding Teacher; *office:* J Frank Faust Jr HS 1957 Scotland Ave Chambersburg PA 17201

HALPERN, JEAN KAMMEN, English Teacher; *b:* Indianapolis, IN; *m:* Stephen J.; *ed:* (BS) Geography, Columbia Univ 1964; (MA) Eng Ed, City Univ of NY 1970; Inst for Moral Dev, Moral Ed Harvard Grad Sch of Ed 1983; NY Shakespeare Inst 1988; *cr:* Eng Teacher Jr HS 22 1967-69, Jr HS 117 1970-71, Gorton HS 1971-; *ai:* Var Academic Bowl Team Coach; Mid St Steering Comm; *office:* Charles E Gorton HS Park Ave & Shonnard Pl Yonkers NY 10703

HALPERN, LINDA ANN, Mathematics Teacher; *b:* New York, NY; *m:* Martin S.; *c:* Robert, Ellen; *ed:* (BA) Chem, Hunter Coll 1958; (MA) Chem, Columbia Univ 1959; *cr:* Sci Teacher Walt Whitman Jr HS 1974-75, Commerce Jr HS 1975-76; Math Teacher Emerson Jr HS 1977-86, Hawthorne Jr HS 1986-; *ai:* Sch Bulletin Contributor; Peer Tutoring Prgm; PTA; Phi Beta Kappa; Finalist Yonkers Teacher of Yr; *office:* Hawthorne Jr HS 350 Hawthorne Ave Yonkers NY 10705

HALPIN, DEE, 5th Grade Teacher; *b:* Newark, NJ; *ed:* (BA) Sociology/Ed, NE IL Univ 1975; *cr:* Teacher Christa Mc Auliffe & St Damian & St Agnes & St Joseph & St Raymonds; *ai:* Discipline & Stu of Month Comm; Sch-Cmmty Athletic Spon; AFT; Rainbows Peer Group Support Coord & Facilitator 1985-; *office:* Christa Mc Auliffe Sch 8944 W 174th Tinley Park IL 60477

HALQUIST, SHAWN ALLEN, Director of Instrumental Music; *b:* Kane, PA; *m:* Deanna Neubauer; *ed:* (BA) Trumpet Performance, Edinboro Univ 1982; (MM) Trumpet Performance, SUNY Binghamton 1984; Teaching Cert Music, Edinboro Univ 1984; *cr:* Instrumental Music Teacher Millcreek Township Sch Dist 1985-; *ai:* Marching & Jazz Band; Phi Mu Alpha Sinfonia, Natl String Orch Assn, Intnl Trumpet Guild, Music Educators Natl Conference; Outstanding Young Men of America 1988; *office:* Mc Dowell HS 3320 Caughey Rd Erie PA 16506

HALSAC, CYNTHIA K., Teacher; *b:* Wrightsville, PA; *m:* Ronald W.; *c:* Ashley E., Hillary K.; *ed:* (BA) Elem Ed, Geneva Coll 1971; (MS) Guidance/Counseling, Youngstown St Univ 1974; Advanced Trng in Processed Approach to Writing; *cr:* Teacher Todd Lane Elem 1971-; *ai:* Phi Kappa Phi Membership 1974-; *home:* 355 E 2nd St Beaver PA 15009

HALSEY, BETTY RITCHIE, Spanish/French Teacher; *b:* Beckley, WV; *m:* Fred C.; *c:* Andrea; *ed:* (AB) Eng/Span/Scndry Ed, 1971, (MA) Span Ed, 1974 Marshall Univ; *cr:* Classroom Teacher Oceana HS 1971-; *ai:* Span & Fr Clubs; Span & Fr Honor Society; NHS; Scrapbook Adv; Sr Class Spon; WV Foreign Lang Teachers Assn 1971-; Natl Assn Teachers of Span & Portugese 1971-; Delta Kappa Gamma (Recording Secy 1978-80, Pres 1980-82); Oceana HS Teacher of Yr 1986; *office:* Oceana HS Box 310 Oceana WV 24870

HALSEY, JULIE MICHELLE, French Teacher; *b:* Chateauroux, France; *c:* Christopher; *ed:* (BSED) Scndry Ed/Fr, Univ of MO Columbia 1983; (MA) Fr, Middlebury Coll 1985; *cr:* Fr Teacher Oak Park HS 1985-; *ai:* Fr Club Spon; Leader of Stus Traveling to France; NEA 1986-; Kappa Delta Pi, Pi Lambda Theta 1982-; Group Teacher Grant; Satellite Dish Usage Foreign Lang Ed; Certificate of Proficiency Fr Pronunciation Middleburg Coll; *office:* Oak Park HS 825 NE 79th Terr Kansas City MO 64118

HALSTEAD, BETTYE VINES, Counselor/French Teacher; *b:* Birmingham, AL; *m:* Caleb B.; *c:* C. Brandon, Catherine E.; *ed:* (BS) Eng/Fr, Univ of AL 1965; (MED) Guidance/Counseling, Univ of GA 1971; CEEB & ACT Wkshps; *cr:* Cnslr Robert Toombs Chrstn Acad 1975; Eng Teacher Vestavia Hills HS 1978; Cnslr/Fr Teacher Briarwood Chrstn HS 1978-; *ai:* Amer Assn for Counseling & Dev, AL HS Cnslrs Assn 1980-; Southern Assn of Coll Admin Cnslr 1985-; Univ of AL Birmingham Cnslrs Advisory Bd 1986; Samford Univ Cnslrs Advisory Bd 1988; Phi Mu (Alumnae Club, Advisory Bd); Green Valley Baptist Church; Whos Who in the South & Southwest; Whos Who Amoung Human Service Profs; *office:* Briarwood Chrstn HS 6255 Cahaba Valley Rd Birmingham AL 35242

HALSTEAD, JUDY C., Business Teacher; *b:* Berea, KY; *m:* Gary E.; *c:* Paula Johnson, Robyn Johnson; *ed:* (BS) Bus Ed, 1974, (MA) Bus Ed, 1978, (Rank I) Bus Ed, 1984 E KY Univ; *cr:* Bus Teacher Rockcastle Cty Voc Sch 1975; Part-Time Bus Teacher E KY Univ 1978; Bus Teacher Madison Cntrl HS 1979-88, Madison Southern HS 1988-; *ai:* Chrldr, Drill Team, Sr Class Spon; NEA, KY Ed Assn, MCEA; Berea Younger Womens Club (Mem, Pres

Elect 1990); *office:* Madison Southern HS 213 Glades Rd Berea KY 40403

HALSTED, NATALIE KOWALSKI, Social Studies Teacher; *b:* Chicago, IL; *m:* Donald L.; *c:* Benjamin, Alicea; *ed:* (BA) His/Ed, Douglass Coll 1968; (MA) Soc Sci, Montclair St 1971; (MA) Admin/Supervision, Kean Coll 1978; Natl Inst for Drug Abuse, Trng as Peer Pressure Cnslr; *cr:* 7th Grade Soc Stud Teacher Conackamack Jr HS 1968-71; 7th/8th Grade Soc Stud Teacher T Schor Mid Sch 1971-; *ai:* Stu Cncl Adv; Prin Prgm Improvement Comm Mem; NEA, NJEA, PTEA, MTEA 1968-; PTA 1975-; Grade Level Adv 1974-75; Curr Dev Comm 1969-; *office:* Theodore Schor Mid Sch No Randolphville Rd Piscataway NJ 08854

HALVERSON, JACK E., Science Teacher; *b:* Kansas City, MO; *c:* Lea, Ray; *ed:* (BA) Elem Ed, Univ of AZ 1979; ESL Endorsement; *cr:* 6th Grade Teacher 1979-80, Head Teacher 1980-81 Pearce Elem Sch; Head Teacher Cochise Elem Sch 1981-84; Sci Teacher Paul H Huber Jr HS 1984-; *ai:* Kiwanis Builders Club; Sch Liaison/Adv; DEA, AEA, NEA 1987-; Amer Legion 1984-; BPOE Elks 1988-; Fleet Reserve Assn 1980-; USN 20 Yrs before Teaching; *office:* Paul H Huber Jr H S 15 & Washington Ave Douglas AZ 85607

HAM, BERTIE MATEER, Substitute Teacher; *b:* Wayne County, IL; *m:* Curt D. (dec); *c:* John, Judy Andrews, Janice Aycock; *ed:* Elem Ed, Eastern IL 1936; Grad Stud Rend Lake Coll, Southern Univ Carbondale; *cr:* 4th Grade Teacher Mt Vernon City Schls 1936-40; Kndgtn Remedial Rdng Teacher Summersville Sch 1970-80; *ai:* Jr Womens Club Pres 1939; NRTA; Home Extension 1st Baptist Church; Published Cookbook 1989; Sunday Sch Teacher; Tutor Young & Elderly; *office:* 1812 Isabella Mount Vernon IL 62864

HAM, THOMAS E., French Teacher; *b:* Kingston, NY; *ed:* (BA) Fr, St Lawrence Univ 1965; (MS) Fr Ed, SUNY Potsdam 1970; NDEA Inst St Lawrence Univ 1966 & Univ of OR 1967; Fr Canadian Inst for Lang & Culture SUNY Plattsburgh 1984; *cr:* Adjunct Professor SUNY Potsdam 1987-89; Fr Teacher Potsdam Cntrl Sch 1965-; Asst Fr Canadian Inst for Lang & Culture SUNY Plattsburgh 1985-; *ai:* Whiz Quiz & Fr Club Adv; NY St Assn of Foreign Lang Teachers, AATF, NY St United Teachers; Music Theatre North Bd of Dir 1979-89; Fruma Awd 1979, 1980; Trinity Episcopal Church Vestry 1980-83, 1984-87; Foreign Lang Dept Recipient of NYSAFLT James E Allen Awd 1990; *home:* 29 Pleasant St Potsdam NY 13676

HAMANN, EMIL ELMER, Science Instructor; *b:* Albany, MN; *m:* Mary Lou Jane Lund; *c:* Catherine, Michele, Daniel, Andrea; *ed:* NSF Institutes at Southwest St Univ; Winona St Univ; Coll of St Teresa; MN Sci & Math; *cr:* Instr Clarissa HS 1960-61, Zeeland HS 1961-63, Benson HS 1965-; *ai:* MN Ed Assn/Benson Ed Assn/NEA Negotiator 1978-84; MSTA St Comm Mem 1982-84; St Marks Lutheran Church Chm 1987-; Benson Police Auxiliary Officer 1971-80; NSF Grant for Academic Yr Inst; Univ of ND; *office:* Benson HS 1400 Montana Ave Benson MN 56215

HAMBERGER, NAN MARIE, 11th Grade English Teacher; *b:* York, PA; *ed:* (BA) Eng Ed, Western MD Coll 1975; (MA) Rdng Specialist, Hood Coll 1980; (ED) Ed Policy/Planning & Admin, Univ of MD-College Park 1990; Doctoral Dissertation, Univ of MD 1990; Dissertatation Topic Values in Lit Textbooks; *cr:* 7th Grade Teacher 1975-79, 5th & 6th Grade Teacher 1979-84 Western Heights Mid Sch; 9th & 11th Grade Eng Teacher South Hagerstown HS 1984-; *ai:* Seniors Club Adv Literary Magazine; Cmptr Comm; NEA 1975-; NCTE 1975-; MD St Teachers Assn Chm Task Force on Stu Evaluation 1986-89; *home:* 408 Pangborn Blvd Hagerstown MD 21740

HAMBLIN, EDNA HENDRICKS, Retired-Vice Principal; *b:* Diboll, TX; *m:* Melvin M.; *c:* Don, Ron, Ron Laxson, Don Laxson, Janet Hart-Laxson; *ed:* (BS) General Sci, TX Womans Univ 1947; (MED) Ed, Univ of Houston 1958; Univ of TX; Southwest TX St Univ; St Marys Univ; Our Lady of Lake; *cr:* Teacher 1949-50; 1952-53 Kileen ISD; Houston ISD 1955-59; North East ISD 1960-72; Teacher/Vice Prin Corbett Jr HS 1972-89; *ai:* TX St Teachers Assn; NEA; Killeen Teachers Assn; Houston Teachers Assn; North East Teachers Assn; Cibolo Valley Ed Assn; TX Assn of Scndry Sch Prin; VP PTA Mac Gregor Elem Sch 1957-58; Teacher Adv PTA Mac Gregor Elem Sch 1958-59; Secy Stillwell Elem Sch 1959-60; Secy Northview Elem Sch 1973-74; VP PTA Northview Elem Sch 1974-75; Chm Nom Comm CVEA 1974-75; Mem Consultation Study Comm CVEA 1974; Chm Teacher Personnel Svcs CVEA 1975-76; Faculty Rep CVEA O Henry Sch 1977-78; Delg to TSTA St Convention Houston 1978-79; Mem St Math Convention 1983; *home:* Rt 3 Box 179AB Cibolo TX 78108

HAMBRICK, PENNY SHARP, Senior English Teacher; *b:* Baytown, TX; *ed:* (BA) Scndry Ed/Eng, Sam Houston St Univ 1973; (MS) Supervision, Univ of Houston Clear Lake 1979; Advanced Placement; Instructional Leadership; Dyslexia; TX Teacher Appraisal System; Gifted & Talented; *cr:* Eng/Rdng/Speech Teacher Goose Creek Consolidated Ind Sch Dist 1973-74; Eng Teacher Port Arthur Ind Sch Dist 1974-76; Eng I & II Teacher Devine Ind Sch Dist 1976-77; Rdng Teacher Pasadena Ind Sch Dist 1977-78; Eng I/II/IV Teacher Deer Park Ind Sch Dist 1978-; *ai:* Drug Free Club Spon; Deer Park Ind Sch Dist Discipline & Dress Code Comm; TSTA, NEA 1973-; Deer Park Ed Assn 1978-; Alpha Delta Kappa Historian 1987-; *office:* Deer Park HS South 201 Ivy Deer Park TX 77536

HAMBY, DALE D., Teacher; *b:* San Marcos, TX; *m:* Carolyn Stuckey; *c:* Laura A.; *ed:* (BS) Ed, Tarleton St 1958; (BS) Ed, Univ of N TX 1960; (MED) Ed, Hardin-Simmons Univ 1971; *cr:* Teacher Robert Lee Ind Sch Dist 1960-71, Canyon Ind Sch Dist 1971-77, Roby Ind Sch Dist 1977-78, Snyder Ind Sch Dist 1978-; *ai:* CTA 1989-; Eastern Star Masons Worthy Patron 1967-; Snyder Century II Leadership; *home:* 4108 Jacksboro Snyder TX 79549

HAMBY, JOANN RICH, Social Studies Teacher; *b:* Blairsville, GA; *m:* Glenn Leon; *c:* Royce G., Teresa A. Hamby Shook; *ed:* (BS) Scndry/Soc Stud, Brenau 1986; (MED) Scndry/Soc Stud, N GA Coll 1989; Cmptrs in the Classroom; Data Collection; *cr:* Para-Prof Migrant Ed Union Cty Sch System 1979-85; 8th-12th Grade Soc Stud Teacher Woody Gap Sch 1986-; *ai:* Jr-Sr Prom Spon 1989; Sr Spon 1989-; Media Center Comm 1987-; Philosophy & Objectives Comm 1987-88; Soc Stud Curr Comm 1987-88; GA Assn of Ed, NEA 1980-; GA Cncl of Soc Stud, NCSS 1987-; Phi Alpha Theta His Cncl 1986-; *home:* PO Box 687 Blairsville GA 30512

HAMELMANN, NORMA RUTH, Math Teacher; *b:* Alton, IL; *ed:* (BS) Math Ed, 1967, (MS) Math Ed, 1974 SIL Univ-E; *cr:* Math Teacher Roxana Jr HS 1967-78, Roxana Jr-Sr HS 1978-85, 1985- Roxana Sr HS; *ai:* Jr Class Spon; NEA; IEA; ICTM; NCTM; REA 2nd VP 1972-73; Alton-Wood River Zonta Club Treas 1987-89; *office:* Roxana Sr H S 401 N Chaffer Ave Roxana IL 62084

HAMES, KAREN LUDDEKE, English Dept Chair; *b:* Sedalia, MO; *m:* A. Franklin; *c:* Kasey, John; *ed:* (BS) Speech, SW TX St Univ 1976; *cr:* Teacher E Cntrl HS, Highland Park HS 1981-84, Griffin Mid Sch 1984-; *ai:* Natl Jr Honor Society Spon; TX Spelling Bee Preparatory Coach; TX Joint Cncl of Teachers of Eng 1988-; NCTE 1988-; Assn of TX Prof Educators 1984-; Cncl on Ministries Family Life Chairperson 1985-; *office:* Griffin Mid Sch 5105 N Colony Blvd The Colony TX 75056

HAMES, LYNN VIEL, Fifth/Sixth Grade Teacher; *b:* Fresno, CA; *m:* Steve; *c:* Matthew, Curtis, Kyle, Kevin; *ed:* (AA) Ed, Citrus Jr Coll 1974; (BA) Liberal Stud, Cal Poly San Luis Obispo 1976; *cr:* 6th Grade Teacher Rio Vista Sch 1976-78; 5th Grade Teacher Monterey Road Sch 1978-86; 5th/6th Grade Teacher Lewis Avenue Sch 1986-; *ai:* Gifted & Talented Class Facilitator; Stu Cncl Adv; *office:* Lewis Ave Elem Sch 6495 Lewis Ave Atascadero CA 93422

HAMIL, LYNN RAY, Science Department Chairman; *b:* Kingsley, IA; *m:* Lori; *c:* James, Steven; *ed:* (BS) Bio/Chem/Psych, Morningside Coll 1974; Teacher Cert Courses 1984; Physics, Morningside Coll & Univ of N IA 1987, 1988; Cmptrs, Sioux Falls Coll 1988; *cr:* Sci Instr Spalding HS 1986-; *ai:* Jr Class, Prom Decorations, Stu Cncl Moderator; NHS Comm; Salary Negotiator; Nom Presidential Awd Excl in Sci Teaching 1990.

HAMILTON, BARBARA ANN (VARGO), Religion/History/Lit Teacher; *b:* South Bend, IN; *m:* Thomas E.; *c:* Christopher, Michael, Mary; *ed:* (BA) His/Eng, CA St Fullerton 1975; Credential CA 1976; Admin CA St Fullerton; Theology Univ of Notre Dame; Working Towards Masters Theology Mt St Marys; *cr:* 5th Grade Teacher Holy Cross 1957-58; 4th Grade Teacher Holy Family 1958-59; 1st-8th Grade Teacher/Sch Religion Coord St Pius V 1960-; *ai:* Yrbk, Liturgical Dancer, Choir; NCEA; Father Grimes Awd Outstanding Teacher Orange Diocese 1989; *office:* St Pius V Sch 7681 Orangethorpe Ave Buena Park CA 90621

HAMILTON, BARBARA JO RALEY, 5th/6th Grade Teacher; *b:* Lebanon, KY; *c:* Alana J.; *ed:* (BS) Elem Ed, 1979; (MAED) Elem Ed, 1982 Eastern KY Univ; Rank I, Elem Ed, Eastern KY Univ 1983; *cr:* 5th Grade Teacher Phillips Elem 1979-; *office:* Phillips Elem Sch Hwy 70 Liberty KY 42539

HAMILTON, DEBORAH ANN JENNINGS, Chemistry Teacher; *b:* Brooklyn, NY; *m:* Wirt Henry III; *c:* Mercedes, Wirt Henry IV, Amanda; *ed:* (BS) General Sci, VA Polytechnic Inst & St Univ 1972; (MS) Ed/Scr Curr Specialist, Longwood Coll 1988; *cr:* Teacher US Virgin Islands 1972-73; Lab Technician UPI & SU 1973-75; Teacher Mecklenburg Cty Public Schls 1982-; *ai:* Stu Cncl Assn Co-Spon; Session Leader 10th Annual N VA Cncl Gifted & Talented; Sci Fair Judge; Mecklenburg Ed Assn (Pres 1984-85, Treas 1988-); Lioness Club 2nd VP 1990; St Dept of Educ Task Force on Exceptional Children Mem 1984-85; Teacher of Yr Bluestone Sr 1990; Article Published 1984; *office:* Bluestone Sr HS Rt 1 Box 96-C Skipwith VA 23968

HAMILTON, DEIDRE LENZINI, Language Arts Chair; *b:* Walsenburg, CO; *m:* Duane K.; *c:* Taryn, Rory; *ed:* (BA) Eng, Univ of N CO 1971; (MS) Gifted & Talented, Western St 1988; *cr:* Eng Teacher Walsenburg HS 1972-74; Eng/Soc Stud Teacher John Mall HS 1979-83; Lang Art/Yrbk Teacher Walsenburg Mid & John Mall HS 1984-; *ai:* Walsenburg Mid Sch Newspaper & Spelling Bee; Lang Arts Curr, Discipline & Climate, Hiring New Teachers, Soc Comms; Yrbk Walsenburg Mid Sch & John Mall HS; CEA, NEA, CO Assn Mid Level Schls, NCTE, CO Lang Art Society, Walsenburg Classroom Teachers Assn; Alpha Delta Kappa Secy 1982-, SW Regional Schlsp 1988; CO HS Publications Assn 1972-74, 1989-; SW Regional Schlsp ADK; Deans Honor Roll; *office:* Walsenburg Mid Sch 415 Walsen Walsenburg CO 81089

HAMILTON, ELEANOR AYDELOTT, English/Accounting Teacher; *b:* Hickman Cty, TN; *c:* Shirley Hamilton Butler, Glenda K.; *ed:* (BS) Bus Ed, 1962, (MA) Ed, 1973 Austin Peay St Univ; Cmptr & Income Tax Wkshps; *cr:* Eng Teacher Hickman Cty Jr HS 1962-67; Accounting/Eng Teacher Hickman Cty HS 1968-; Off-Campus Instr/Classes Columbia St Comm Coll 1982-; *ai:* Soph Class Spon; Governors Study Partner Prgm; S Regional Ed Bd; Cmptr Comm; Hickman Cty Ed Assn (Exec Comm 1983-84, Public Relations Comm 1983-88) 1962-; TN Ed Assn (Advisory Comm 1983-84) 1962-; NEA 1962-; Columbia St Cmmty Coll Advisory Comm Office Admin 1988-; Volunteer Income Tax Assistance Prgm 1983-; Integrative Technology Advisory Comm Hickman Cty 1990; Hickman Cty Teacher of Yr 1988-89; TN Most Distinguished Classroom Teacher Hickman Cty Rep 1988-89; Outstanding Teacher Awd Univ of TN Martin 1990; *office:* Hickman Cty HS 1645 High School Rd Centerville TN 37033

HAMILTON, JAMES CLAIR, 6th Grade Teacher; *b.* Cannonsburg, PA; *m:* Betty L. Hammack; *c:* Beth, Chris; *ed:* (BS) Elem Ed/His/Eng, WV St Coll 1970; (MA) Elem Ed Admin, WV Coll Grad St 1978; Dr William Glassers Behaviorl Prgm; Youth Empowering System; NTA Assoc Substance Abuse Prgm; *cr:* Classroom Teacher Belle Elem 1970-74, Richmond Elem 1974-; *ai:* Safety Patrol Organizer; Just Say No Club Spon; Math Field Day Rep & Organizer; Sch Spelling Bee Coord; Sch Based Assistance Team & Core Team Mem; Annual 6th Level Trip Spon & Organizer; Safety Team Mem; Budget Helper; WVEA 1970-75, 1989-; 4-H Active Spon; *office:* Richmond Elem Sch 4620 Springhill Ave South Charleston WV 25309

HAMILTON, JAMES EUGENE, Science Teacher; *b:* Inglewood, CA; *m:* Gayle Cruse; *c:* Cardiff; *ed:* (MS) Ed, Ca St Fullerton 1984; CA Sch Leadership Acad 1990; *cr:* Teacher Alta Loma HS 1980-83, San Marcos Jr HS 1983-; *office:* San Marcos Jr HS 650 W Mission Rd San Marcos CA 92069

HAMILTON, JOSEPH ELROY, Jr/Sr HS Bible Teacher; *b:* Asheboro, NC; *m:* Tina Lackey; *c:* Jonathan K., Heather J.; *ed:* (THB) Bible, Piedmont Bible Coll 1973; *cr:* Pastor Valley View Baptist Church 1974-77; Pastor Calvary Baptist Church 1978-; Teacher Southview Chrstn Sch 1980-; *office:* Southview Christian Sch R R 16 Box 57 Statesville NC 28677

HAMILTON, KENNETH LEE, Science Teacher; *b:* Quakertown, PA; *ed:* (BS) Scndry Ed/Earth & Space Sci, Penn St Univ 1984; Working Toward MA Environmental Ed; *cr:* Sci Teacher Cntrl Bucks Sch Dist 1985-86, Souderton Area Sch Dist 1986-; *ai:* Ftbl, Bsktbl, Bsbl Coach; Youth to Youth Drug & Alcohol Group, Young Astronauts Group, Oceanography Organization Adv; Run Summer Environmental Camp; NSTA, NEA Mem; Drug & Alcohol Resistance Team Mem; *office:* Souderton Area HS 41 W School Ln Souderton PA 18964

HAMILTON, LORRAINE MYERS, English Teacher; *b:* Sumter, SC; *m:* Danny R. Jr.; *c:* Lynn H. Hughes, Danny III, Jenny; *ed:* (BA) Eng/His, Francis Marion Coll 1981; *cr:* Teacher Dillon HS 1981-; *ai:* Sch Adv Comm; Prom Comm; NEA; SCEA; DCEA; Mc Arthur Ave Players 1989-; Dillons Jr Miss Young Woman of Yr Schlsp Prgm 1990; Phi Kappa Phi Honor Society; Pi Gamma Mu Honor Society; Grad Magna Cum Laude-1981; Received Eng Awd FMC 1981; *home:* 103 S Carolina Ave Dillon SC 29536

HAMILTON, MARGARET NEWCOMER, Advanced Placement Teacher; *b:* Xenia, OH; *m:* Kenneth N.; *c:* Laura; *ed:* (BA) His, 1966, (MA) His, 1967 OH Univ; Teacher Ed, West Liberty St Coll; Guidance, WV Univ; *cr:* Instr Old Dominion Univ 1968-69; Teacher/Dept Chairperson Union Local HS 1973-84, UMS-Wright Preparatory 1985-; *ai:* Chess Team Coach; Alpha Xi Delta Natl VP 1978-80; Alpha Xi Delta Fnd Trustee 1976-78; Outstanding Young Woman of Amer 1979; Distinguished Teacher Presidential Scholar 1989; Freedoms Fnd Schlsp Summer Seminar 1990; *office:* UMS-Wright Preparatory Sch 65 N Mobile St Mobile AL 36607

HAMILTON, MARY ELIZABETH (CAIN), Kindergarten Teacher; *b:* Longview, TX; *m:* Gary Dennis; *c:* Lauren E.; *ed:* (BS) Elem Ed/Elem Phys Ed, E TX St Univ 1974; IBM-Write to Read Dist Coord Class 1987; *cr:* Kndgtn Teacher Springlake-Earth Ind Sch Dist 1974-77; 1st/2nd Grade Teacher 1977-83, Kndgtn Teacher 1983- Crane Ind Sch Dist; *ai:* TX St Teachers Assn, TX Classroom Teachers Assn; *office:* Crane Ind Sch Dist 300 W 7th Crane TX 79731

HAMILTON, RICHARD CURTIS, Mathematics Teacher/Dept Chair; *b:* Warren, PA; *m:* Nancy C. Kahl; *c:* James, David; *ed:* (BS) Scndry Ed, Penn St Univ 1953; (MED) Teaching of Math, Temple Univ 1959; NSF Inservice Math Inst, Albright Coll 1959-60, 1962-63; NSF Summer Math Inst, Hunter Coll 1960; *cr:* Math Teacher Perkiomen Sch 1953-54; Electronics Maint Officer USAF 1954-57; Math Teacher Antietam Jr/Sr HS 1957-; *ai:* Math Dept Chairperson; NCTM 1957-; PA Cncl of Teachers of Math 1985-; PA St Educl Assn, NEA 1957-; *office:* Antietam Jr/Sr HS 100 Antietam Rd Reading PA 19606

HAMILTON, ROSA LEE, Second Grade Teacher; *b:* Mc Dowell, KY; *m:* John Edward; *c:* Jodi, Bobbi, Jonda; *ed:* (BSED) Elem Ed, OH Univ 1972 ; Grad & Undergrad Courses; *cr:* 1st Grade Teacher 1968-69, 3rd Grade Teacher 1969-70, 2nd/3rd Grade Teacher 1970-73, 2nd Grade Teacher 1973- Huntington Elem; *ai:* Tutoring Prgm; Pride Comm Home Ec; NEA, OH Ed Assn, Ross Cty Ed Assn 1968-; MADD 1990; *office:* Huntington Elem Sch 188 Huntsman Rd Chillicothe OH 45601

HAMILTON, SUZANNE D., English Teacher/Dept Chair; *b:* Schenectady, NY; *m:* Alan G.; *c:* Meredith, Emily; *ed:* (BA) Eng, Emory & Henry Coll 1974; *cr:* Eng Teacher Culpeper Cty HS 1974-76, Louisa Cty HS 1976-; Clinical Instr Univ of VA 1985-; *ai:* Paw Prints Sch Newspaper Spon; Academic Achievement Comm; Governors Sch for Gifted Selection Comm 1989, 1990; Eng Teacher Kigoma Tanzania E Africa Spec Assignment Missionary 1988; *office:* Louisa Cty HS P O Box 328 Mineral VA 23117

HAMLIN, ELIZABETH FORREST, Fr Teacher/Foreign Lang Chair; *b:* Hillsborough, NC; *m:* Thomas Montague; *c:* Jeffrey Forrest, Stephen Flint; *ed:* (BS) Fr, W Carolina Univ 1971; Effective, Mentor, Supervising Teacher Trng; *cr:* Fr Teacher Stanford Jr HS 1972-83, Orange HS 1983-; *ai:* Inst for Foreign & Amer Cncl for Intnl Stud Cnslr; Fr Club Adv; Foreign Lang Inter-Club Cncl Spon & Week Coord; Mentor & Supervising Teacher; Senate II Bill & Schlsp Comm; Comm Task Force; NC Teaching Fellows; Southern Assn Reaccrediation Steering Comm; FLANC 1973-; Carolina Alliance of Foreign Lang Teachers 1984-; Alpha Kappa Delta 1990; Orange Athletic Boosters 1988-; Caldwell Cty Club Treas 1976; Orange Ed Fnd 1987-; Orange HS & Cty Teacher of Yr 1989-; *home:* 5801 Sneed Rd Rougemont NC 27572

HAMLIN, MICHELLE SPARRE, Mathematics Teacher; *b:* Los Angeles, CA; *m:* Edmund G.; *c:* Jayme A., Jennifer L., James E.; *ed:* (BA) Math/Ger, St Josephs Coll 1969; Graduate Work Math/Cmptr Sci Univ of Me; *cr:* Math Teacher Brunswick Hs 1970-72; Math Teacher Fryeburg Acad 1973; Audio/Visual Dir/ Librn ME Sch Admin Dist 72 1974-75; Math Teacher Westbrook HS 1975-76; Math Teacher Kennett HS 1976-; Math Instr Sch for Lifelong Learning/UNH 1983-; *ai:* Adv-Math Team; Chm Steering Comm; Advisor-Sr Class; Child Study Team; Natl Honor Society 1st Faculty Mem Inducted at KITS; NCTM 1985-; ME Sch Bd Assn 1975-; Bd of Dir/MSAD 72 Chm 1975-; Brownfield Public Lib Vp/Lib 1979-; North Cumberland Mem Hosp Incorporator 1982-; Newmast 1989; *office:* A Crosby Kennett H S Main St Conway NH 03818

HAMM, BILLY M., JR., 8th Grade Soc Stud Teacher; *b:* Snow Hill, NC; *m:* Denise Bowen; *ed:* (BA) Eng, Atlantic Chrstn Coll 1983; Working Towards MA E Carolina Univ; *cr:* Teacher Woodington Mid Sch; *ai:* SCA Spon; His Bowl Spon & Coach; NC Cncl Teaching Soc Stud 1986-; Atlantic Chrstn Coll Full Schlsp; *office:* Woodington Mid Sch Rt 5 Box 274 Kinston NC 28501

HAMM, DEBORAH JOY REYHER, Math Teacher; *b:* Goshen, NY; *m:* Dawson G.; *c:* Kyle D.L.; *ed:* (BS) Scndry Ed Math, Kutztown ST Coll 1972; (MED) Ed, Lehigh Univ 1978; Post Masters Studies Stu Asst Prgm Trng ST of PA Trng; *cr:* Math Teacher Emmaus HS 1972-74; Howard A. Eyer Jr HS 1974-85; Emmaus HS 1985-; *ai:* Kid to Kid Adv (Drug & Alcohol); SAP CORE Mem; Natl Cncl of Teachers of Math 1987-; PA Cncl of Teachers 1987-; Eastern PA Cncl of Teachers of Math 1987-; Outstanding Teacher of Yr Awd from East PA Sch Dist in 1984-85; *office:* Emmaus H S 851 North St Emmaus PA 18049

HAMM, DOUGLAS WAYNE, SR., Computer Instructor; *b:* Coeburn, VA; *m:* Patricia Sue Nickels; *c:* Douglas W. Jr., Carol L.; *ed:* (BS) Elem Ed, 1975, (MA) Elem Ed, 1977 E TN St Univ; Data Processing Tri St Voc Tech Sch; *cr:* Teacher Kingsley Elem Sch 1975-80, Ketron Mid Sch 1980-; *ai:* Sullivan Cty Ed Assn Faculty Rep; Odyssey of the Mind Group Coach; PTSA 1st VP; Ftbl Asst Coach; NEA 1975-; TN Ed Assn, Sullivan Cty Ed Assn Rep 1986-; Parent Teacher Stu Assn 1975-;, Life Mem 1986-87; Ketron Mid Sch Teacher of Yr 1987-88; *office:* Ketron Mid Sch 3301 Bloomingdale Pike Kingsport TN 37660

HAMM, FRANCES JAYNE (MOTE), English/Art Teacher; *b:* Vernon, TX; *m:* Ronald E.; *c:* Mitchell K., Amy K.; *ed:* (BS) Ed, Univ of N TX 1957; Brevard Comm Coll, Univ of Cntrl FL; *cr:* Art/Lang Art Teacher Forest Oak Jr HS 1957-60; Rdng/Eng Teacher Harrington Jr HS 1960-63; Eng/Art Teacher De Laura Jr HS 1972-83; 6th Grade/Music/Art Teacher Northside Sch 1983-84; Adjunct Eng Teacher Vernon Regional Jr Coll; Eng/Art Teacher Vernon HS 1984-; *ai:* Natl Art Honor Society Co-Spon 1984-; Jr Class Spon 1991; 9th-12th Grade Eng Tutor; Summer Sch Eng Teacher; Assn of TX Prof Educators (Mem, Secy 1985-86) 1983-; Delta Kappa Gamma Society Intnl (Mem, Secy 1990, Membership Chm 1988-) 1985-; Delta Gamma Alumna; Amer Assn of Univ Women 1988-; Wilbarger Cty Historical Commission 1989-; 1st Baptist Church Womens Missionary Union (Personnel Comm Secy 1987-89, Adult Choir Treas 1990, Sunday Sch Teacher 1985-); Wilbarger Cty Family His Book Comm Chm & Proofreader 1986; *office:* Vernon HS 2102 Yucca Ln Vernon TX 76384

HAMM, JOANN ELLIS, Eng & Public Speaking Teacher; *b:* Rochester, NY; *c:* Tobin, Scott; *ed:* (BS) Eng/Elem Ed, SUNY Geneseo 1962; (MA) Eng, SUNY Brockport 1986; *cr:* 6th Grade/ Eng/Public Speaking Teacher Pittsford Cntrl Schls 1962-69; Eng Teacher John C Fremont HS 1969-70; Eng/Public Speaking Teacher Westmont HS 1970-81; Eng/Soc Stud Teacher John Marshall HS 1981; Eng/Public Speaking Teacher Webster HS 1981-; Eng Asst/Adjunct Professor Monroe Comm Coll 1987-; *ai:* Speech Team, Brainstormers, Morning TV Show News Anchors, Forensics, Commencement Speakers Coach; Genesee Valley Forensic League Pres 1989-; Natl Forensic League 1970-; NY St United Teachers 1981-; NEA Fellowship 1981-; Personalities of West & Midwest; Yrbk Dedication Pittsford Cntrl Sch 1968 & Westmont HS 1978; PTSA Westmont HS 1977; NY St Eng & Drama Cncl Teacher of Excl 1983; The World Whos Who of Women; *home:* 300 Rock Beach Rd Rochester NY 14617

HAMM, TERESA TERRELL, 8th Grade English Teacher; *b:* Quanah, TX; *m:* James O.; *c:* Blake, Erin; *ed:* (BS) Scndry Ed, TX Tech Univ 1967; (MSED) Counseling, Baylor Univ 1972; *cr:* Teacher Univ Jr HS 1975-76, Parkhill Jr HS 1983-85, A Maceo Smith HS 1984-85, Lake Highlands Jr HS 1985-; *ai:* Stu Cncl Spon; All Stars Wkshp Consultant; NCTE 1984-; Natl Assn of Wkshp Dir 1986-; TX Assn of Stu Cncls 1983-; TX Society of Prof Educators 1986-; Jr League of Dallas 1984-86; Young Life Ed Bd 1987-89; Leadership Consultant TASC; LHSH & PTA Life Memberships; Articles Published; RISD Teacher Cadre; *office:* Lake Highlands Jr HS 10301 Kingsley Rd Dallas TX 75238

HAMMACK, JUDY V., English Department Chair; *b:* Woodville, MS; *ed:* (BA) Eng, 1974, (MA) Eng, 1978 MS Univ for Women; Bay Area Writing Project; Foxfire Trng; *cr:* Eng Teacher Montebello Jr HS 1975-78; Rdng/Eng Teacher/Lab Dir Hapeville HS 1978-83; Eng Teacher/Dept Chairperson Palmetto HS 1983-; *ai:* Jr Class Spon; Teacher Cncl; Amer Lit Curr & Curr Steering Comm Chairperson; Transition Team; NCTE 1975-; Natl Endowment for Hum Fellowship; Teacher of Yr; STAR Teacher; Numerous Presentations Natl, St & Local Levels; *home:* 757 Grant St SE Atlanta GA 30315

HAMMACK, WILLIAM STEVEN, Physics/AP Biology Teacher; *b:* Little Rock, AR; *ed:* (BS) Zoology, 1979, Teaching Credential Scndry Sci, 1980 Univ CA Davis; *cr:* Sci Teacher Countryside Preparatory Sch 1980-82; Chem/Physics/Advanced Placement Bio Teacher Los Gatos HS 1984-; *ai:* Key Club & SAVE Adv; Schlsp Comm; AAPT 1985-; Yrbk Dedication 1988; *office:* Los Gatos HS 20 High School Ct Los Gatos CA 95032

HAMMAN, JOHN B., 6th Grade Teacher; *b:* Shelby, OH; *m:* Barbara Stanford Shelton; *c:* Stephen Shelton, Brian Shelton; *ed:* (BA) Behavioral Sci, CA Poly Pomona 1981; CA Teaching Credential Multiple Subjects 1982; *cr:* Teacher Ontario-Montclair Sch Dist 1983-; *ai:* Chm Sch Site Cncl, Key Planning Comm; Sci Facilitator; Ontario-Montclair Teachers Assn; Greenpeace, Earthwatch; *office:* Corona Elem Sch 1140 N Corona Ave Ontario CA 91764

HAMME, RONALD EDWARD, Fine Arts/Humanities Teacher; *b:* Carlisle, PA; *m:* Virginia Langenhop; *c:* Christopher Friedrich; *ed:* (BA) Art Ed, Penn St 1970; Working Towards Masters in Hum, Penn St; *cr:* Art Teacher Upper Dauphin Area 1970-; *ai:* UDA Prof Dev Comm Co-Chm; Art Club, Advance Placement Studio Art, Art His Adv; UDA Ed Assn Pres 1985-87; PA Art Ed Assn; Millersburg Art Assn 1984-; Local Teachers Assn Pres; Juried Art Shows 1st Place; Writing Hum Textm Text; *home:* Mayfield St Elizabethville PA 17023

HAMMELRATH, CATHERINE BLACKMAN, Spanish Teacher; *b:* Las Vegas, NV; *m:* William S. Jefferson; *c:* Damon, Leah, Erin W., Rachel EManuel; *ed:* (BA) Scndry Ed/Span, Univ of NV Las Vegas 1970; (MA) Span/Scndry Ed, N AZ Univ 1976; Lit in Spain with Univ of N IA; *cr:* 6th-8th Grade Eng/Span Teacher Burkholder Jr HS 1971-82; US Hist/Span Teacher Adult Evening HS 1978-82; Span Teacher Las Vegas HS 1982-; *ai:* SW Conf Lang Teachers/Advisory Cncl 1989-; Clark Cty Lang Teachers, CCCTA, NEA 1972-; Excl in Ed Awd Clark Cty Sch Dist 1987; Attend Univ of VA 1989; Natl Endowment for Hum; *office:* Las Vegas HS 315 S 17th St Las Vegas NV 89101

HAMMER, CHRISTINE ANN, English Teacher; *b:* Toledo, OH; *m:* Peter T.; *c:* Peter M., Craig L.; *ed:* (BA) Eng, Adrian Coll 1967; Advanced Placement Eng Lang/Lit Semnr, Albion Coll 1987; Univ of Mi/Eastern Mi Univ/Cntrl Mi Univ Rdng/ Writing/Lit Grad Courses; *cr:* HS Eng Teacher Clio HS 1967-; *office:* Clio H S 1 Mustang Dr Clio MI 48420

HAMMER, SHARON CICCOLELLA, Speech/Language Pathologist; *b:* Steubenville, OH; *m:* Gene Scott Jr.; *c:* Toni M., G. Scott III; *ed:* (BS) Speech Pathology/Audiology, 1976, (MS) Speech Pathology, 1977 WV Univ; Pre-Sch Handicapped & Learning Disabilities; *ai:* WV Speech, Lang, Hearing Assn; Amer Speech, Lang, Hearing Assn 1977-; AFT 1990; GSA (Service Unit Dir 1988-, Troop Leader 1986-); Natl Reference Inst 1986, Whos Who in Human Services Profs 1986; Co-Authored WVSEERS Grant Hardy Cty Schls 1988; Directed Hardy Cty Pre-Sch Screening Clinics 1979-85; *office:* Hardy Cty Schls 400 N Main St Moorefield WV 26836

HAMMER, SUZANNE CHAMBERLIN, Fifth Grade Teacher; *b:* Lansing, MI; *m:* Thomas Edward; *c:* Jeffrey, Christopher; *ed:* (BA) Elem Ed, Univ of IA 1970; Working Towards Masters, Univ of IA; *cr:* 4th Grade Teacher 1970-82, 5th Grade Teacher 1982-Louisa-Muscatine Cmmty Schls; *ai:* Phase III Curr Dev Comm; NCTM, NEA, ISEA, Pi Lambda Theta; *office:* Louisa-Muscatine Cmmty Sch Grandview IA 52752

HAMMERLE, STEPHEN HELMS, Govt Teacher/Activity Director; *b:* Dallas, TX; *ed:* (Ba) Poly Sci, TX A&M 1977; (MED) Counseling, Univ of N TX 1989; *cr:* Soc Stud Teacher Garland HS 1978-80, Webb Mid Sch 1980-81, Garland HS 1981-; *ai:* Bell Guard, Jr Class, Sr Class Head Spon; Youth & Government, Key Club; Dist Textbook Comm; Act Dir; Garland Soc Stud 1985-; TX Soc Stud, NCSS 1978-; Garland Ind Sch Dist HS Teacher of Yr 1986-87; *home:* 1218 Clinton St Garland TX 75040

HAMMERSLA, JEFFREY WARD, 2nd Grade Teacher; *b:* Cumberland, MD; *m:* Frances Margaret; *ed:* (BA) Eng Western MD Coll 1975; *cr:* 1st Grade Teacher Mt Harmony Elem Sch 1976-85; 2nd-3rd Grade Teacher 1986-87; 2nd Grade Teacher Mutual Elem Sch 1987-; *home:* PO Box 181 St Leonard MD 20685

HAMMERSMITH, DOROTHY C., Sixth Grade Teacher; *b:* Albany, NY; *ed:* (BA) Elem Ed, SUNY Geneseo 1965; *cr:* 6th Grade Teacher Canajoharie Cntrl 1965-; *ai:* Elem Math & Math Contest Adv; *office:* Canajoharie Cntrl Sch Burch St Canajoharie NY 13317

HAMMERT, MARIAN DIECKMAN, Kindergarten Classroom Teacher; *b:* Independence, MO; *m:* Fredrick B.; *c:* Lisa; *ed:* (BS) Elem Ed, Cntrl MO St Univ 1961; (MLA) Ed, SMU 1971; Early Chldhd Cert; *cr:* 2nd Grade Teacher Luff Elem 1961-64, Ludwigsburg & Karlsruhe Germany & Seoul Elem Korea 1964-68; 1st Grade Teacher Seagoville Elem & Darrell Center 1968-72; 2nd Grade Teacher Allgood Elem 1972-76; Kndgtn Teacher Lakewood Elem 1978-; *ai:* PTA (Pres 1989-, Bd Mem 1980-89), Natl Honorary Life Membership 1990, TX Honorary Life Membership 1985; Assn TX Prof Educators Building Rep 1985-; ACEI VP 1977; Alumni Assn of Cntrl MO St Univ (VP, Pres-Elect) 1988-; Dixon Branch Homeowners Assn; Church Cncl Bd of Ed; Teacher of Yr 1983; Outstanding Stu Teacher 1961.

HAMMETT, MARY WEIN, First Grade Teacher; *b:* Anniston, AL; *w:* Charles T. (dec); *c:* Charles T. Jr., Terri H. Thomas; *ed:* (BS) Elem Ed, Jacksonville St Univ 1954; (MA) Ed, Univ of AL Birmingham 1978; *cr:* 5th Grade Teacher Woodstock Elem 1954-56; 1st Grade Teacher Cedar Springs 1958-61, Center Point 1963-; *ai:* Teachers Helping Teachers Task Force Mem; Project LIFE; United Way Rep; AL Ed Assn, NEA 1954-; Jefferson Cty Ed Assn Rep 1963-; Alpha Delta Kappa (Corresponding Secy, VP, Pres Elect) 1977-; *office:* Center Point Sch 2209 Center Point Rd Birmingham AL 35215

HAMMETT, VICKIE STAMPS, 6th Grade Teacher; *b:* Parsons, KS; *c:* Jason, Reece; *ed:* (BSED) Elem Ed, 1977, (MA) Elem Ed, 1989 Pittsburg St Univ; *cr:* 6th-8th Grade Teacher Mc Cune Elem Sch 1978-80; 6th Grade Teacher Edna KS 1982-; *ai:* NEA 1978-80, 1983-84; St Johns Episcopal Church 1977-; Parsons Humane Society Bd of Dirs 1984-86; Iron Horse Historical Society 1989-; Teacher of Yr 1988-89; *home:* Rt 2 Box 258A Parsons KS 67357

HAMMILL, CLEO M. BLACK, Second Grade Teacher; *b:* Clinton, MO; *m:* Charles R.; *ed:* (BA) Ed, Cntrl WA Coll 1958; Grad Stud Univ of WA 1959-61; Cntrl WA Coll; *cr:* 1st Grade Teacher Whitman Elem Sch 1958-60, Woodridge Elem Sch 1960-61; Kndgtn/1st Grade Teacher Munich Elem Sch 1961-68; 2nd/3rd Grade Teacher Bad Toelz Elem Sch 1968-; *ai:* WA St Ed Assn 1958-61; NEA 1958-; Overseas Ed Assn 1961-; ASCD 1986-88; Sch Advisory Comm Mem 1985-86; *home:* Box 632 New York NY 09050

HAMMOCK, MAMIE BROWN, Physical Education/Coach; *b:* Shreveport, LA; *m:* Carl Stewart; *c:* Carl S. Jr., Kristen B.; *ed:* (BS) Health/Phys Ed, LA Tech Univ 1976; (MS) Sports Admin, Grambling St Univ 1980; *cr:* Phys Ed Teacher/Coach Simsboro Sch 1978-86, Ruston Jr HS 1986-; *ai:* Girls Bsktbl Coach; AFT 1987-; Sigma Gamma Rho; *office:* Ruston Jr HS 1400 Tarbutton Rd Ruston LA 71270

HAMMOCK, MAUREEN BURKE, English Teacher; *b:* San Diego, CA; *m:* Steven Michael; *ed:* (BA) Eng, Univ of San Diego 1984; Eng, Univ of San Diego 1990; *cr:* Eng Teacher Mira Mesa HS 1984-; *ai:* Class of 1989 Adv; *office:* Mira Mesa HS 10510 Reagan Rd San Diego CA 92126

HAMMOND, CONSTANCE CARPENTER, Retired Teacher; *b:* Cooperstown, NY; *m:* Dale Arthur; *c:* Frieda Hammond Matties, Jonathan F. C.; *ed:* (AAS) Nursery Ed, NY St Univ Cobleskill 1954; (BA) Elem Ed, NY St Univ Plattsburgh; Grad Work Open Ed, London England; *cr:* K-7th Grade Teacher Kingstation Sch 1954-56; Kndgtn Teacher Schuylerville Cntrl 1957-88; *ai:* NY St United Teachers (Secy 1975-76) 1957-88; Assn of Amer Univ Women 1975-82; Schuylerville Cmmty Theatre Bd of Dir 1988-; Salvation Army Chm 1975-; Battenkill Cntry Club Mem 1985-; *home:* 151 Beaver St Schuylerville NY 12871

HAMMOND, DALE HARLEY, Science Teacher; *b:* Alamosa, CO; *m:* Pamela Tjarks; *c:* David B., Christine M.; *ed:* (BS) Veterinary Sci, 1976, (BS) Bio, 1977, (BS) Bacteriology, 1977 Univ of ID; Various Courses Phys Geology, Cmptr Sci & Teacher Ed; *cr:* Sci Teacher Valley HS 1977-; *ai:* Newspaper Adv; Academic Decathlon Coach; Dist Cmptr Coord; NSTA, Intnl Cmptr Educators; Univ of ID Teaching Excl Awd 1989; *office:* Valley Jr/Sr HS 882 Valley Rd S Hazelton ID 83335

HAMMOND, FAITH LOUISE, English Teacher; *b:* Wilkes-Barre, PA; *m:* Michael William; *c:* David, Joy; *ed:* (BA) Elem Ed, Cedarville Coll 1970; *cr:* Eng/Math Teacher Stateline Chrstn Sch 1976-79, Fulkerson Park Baptist Schls 1979-83; Eng Teacher Grace Chrstn Sch 1983-; *ai:* Cheerleading Spon; Short-Term Missions Trip Spon & Coord; Chosen to Teach 2 Summers in Dominican Republic Seminar Teaching Natl Teachers; *home:* 2006 Ontario Rd Lot 75 Niles MI 49120

HAMMOND, JAMES MICHAEL, Mathematics/French Teacher; *b:* El Paso, TX; *ed:* (BA) Elem Ed/Fr, Univ of TX Arlington 1979; Grad Stud Ed, Univ of N TX 1985; Ed/Rdng, TX Wesleyan Univ 1985, 1988; Fr, Univ of AR Fayetteville 1989; *cr:* 4th Grade Teacher South Birdville Elem 1979-82; 5th Grade Teacher 1982-83, 6th Grade Teacher 1983-89 Smithfield Elem; Math/Lang Art/Fr Teacher Smithfield Mid Sch 1989-; *ai:* Stu Cncl Spon; Kappa Delta Pi Pres ELect 1978-79; Outstanding Young Men of America 1988; General Ed Diploma Teacher Ft Worth Ind Sch Dist 1987-; Fr Teachers Summer Inst Univ of AR

1989; *office:* Smithfield Mid Sch 8400 Main St Smithfield TX 76180

HAMMOND, JOANNE KELLIHAN, Biology Teacher; *b:* Cerro Gordo, NC; *m:* Troy M Jr.; *c:* Dale McDuffie; Summer Inst Univ of NC, Appalachian St Univ, Natl Sci Fellowship Grad Stud; *ed:* (BS) Sci, Pembroke St Univ 1961; (MA) Bio, Appalachian St Univ 1967; *cr:* Teacher Chadbourn Sch 1961-65, W Columbus HS 1965-; *ai:* Class, Club, Act, Dept Head Spon; NEA, NCAE 1961-; NCST; *office:* W Columbus HS P O Box 130 Cerro Gordo NC 28430

HAMMOND, NELLIE VIERA, ESOL Tutor/Clerk I; *b:* Havana, Cuba; *m:* Guy William Jr.; *c:* Guy W. III, Catheryn Carnesella, Jane Henhoeffer, Scott; *ed:* (AA) Ed, S FL Comm Coll 1986; *cr:* Tutor/Aide/ESOL/Bi-ling Teacher Lake Placid Elem Sch 1978-88; Office Clerk I Lake Cntry Elem Sch 1988-; *ai:* Lake Placid Garden Club (Publicity Chm, Corresponding Secy, 1st VP, 2nd VP) 1973-; Lake Placid Womans Club (Recording Secy, Parlimentarian, 2nd-3rd VP) 1982-; Greater Lake Placid Historical Society Charter Mem 1982-; GSA (Dist Chm 1958, Troop Leader 1956-62); Expect Best Awd Supt of Highlands Cty Schls 1986-87; Dir Latch Key Soroptomist After Sch Prgm Lake Placid 1985-86; *office:* Lake Cntry Elem Sch 516 Cty Rd 29 Lake Placid FL 33852

HAMMOND, PATRICIA JEAN, Elementary Librarian; *b:* Trenton, NJ; *ed:* (BS) Lib Sci, Millersville St Coll 1970; (MS) Lib Sci, Drexel Univ 1974; Bucks Cty Comm Coll, Trenton St Coll, Marywood Coll; *cr:* Part-Time Instr Holy Family Coll 1989; Librarian Pennsbury Sch Dist 1970-; *ai:* Pennsbury Rdng Comm; NEA, PA Ed Assn, Pennsbury Ed Assn; Guardian Circle of World Wildlife Fnd; Bucks Cty Free Lib Volunteer; *home:* 19 Misty Pine Rd Levittown PA 19056

HAMMOND, RALPH JEFFREY, Science Teacher; *b:* Louisville, KY; *cr:* Sci Teacher Silver Creek Jr/Sr HS 1982-89; *ai:* Cross Country & O M Coach; NSF Microbiology Inst St of IN Univ; *office:* Silver Creek Jr HS 495 N Indiana Ave Sellersburg IN 47172

HAMMOND, STEPHEN E., Jr HS Science Teacher; *b:* Louisville, KY; *ed:* (BA) Elem Ed, N KY St Univ 1974; (MA) Spec Ed, NE IL Univ 1985; *cr:* 7th/8th Grade Teacher St Johns Sch 1974-77; 7th/8th Grade Sci Teacher St Andrew Sch 1977-78; Enrichment Teacher Koscinsko Elem 1978-79; 7th/8th Grade Sci Teacher St Viator Sch 1979-; *office:* St Viator Sch 4140 W Addison St Chicago IL 60641

HAMMONDS, JAY A., Department Chair, Teacher; *b:* Conshohocken, PA; *m:* Susan Ann Earl; *c:* Elizabeth; *ed:* (BSED) Scndry Ed/Soc Sci, 1965, (MED) Soc Sci, 1971 West Chester St Coll; Grad Courses Univ DE; *cr:* Teacher Felton Public Schls 1965-67, P S Dupont HS 1967-78; Teacher/Dept Chm Glasgow HS 1978-; *ai:* Co-Chm Mid St Accreditation Steering Comm; Cooperative Teacher Univ of DE Clinical Studs Prgm; Felton Ed Assn Pres 1966-67; NEA, DSEA, Christina Ed Assn; DE Cncl Soc Stud; NCSS; Amateur Radio Asst Emergency 1985-87; Emergency Service Coord; BSA Merit Badge Cncl 1963-70; Eastern Coll Amer Stud Fellow 1987; Robert A Taft Government Stud Fellow 1989; Teacher of Yr 1987; Christina Sch Dist HS Teacher of Yr 1987; *home:* 1314 Sherwood Dr West Chester PA 19380

HAMMONDS, MARY ELLEN, 4th Grade Teacher; *b:* Elizabeth, NJ; *m:* William; *c:* Kimberlee, Rebecca; *ed:* (BA) Elem Ed, Lynchburg Coll 1970; (MED) Elem Ed, Georgian Court Coll 1979; *cr:* 4th Grade Teacher E Dover Elem 1970-83; 6th Grade Teacher 1983-89, 4th Grade Teacher 1989- Cedar Grove Elem; *ai:* NEA, Toms River Ed Assn 1970-; GSA Co-Leader 1989-; *office:* Cedar Grove Elem Schl Cedar Grove Rd Toms River NJ 08753

HAMMONDS, MARYLYN R., Third Grade Teacher; *b:* Evansville, IN; *m:* Robert F.; *c:* Nicole; *ed:* (BS) Elem Ed, Oakland City Coll; (MS) Elem Ed, Univ of Evansville; Guidance, Comptr Courses; *cr:* 5th Grade Teacher Francisco Elem Sch; 3rd Grade Teacher Northside Elem Sch & N Madison Elem Sch; *ai:* NEA, ISTA, MCTA; *office:* Mooresville-N Madison Elem Sch 2732 Hadley Rd Camby IN 46113

HAMMONS, BURNETTA HUBBARD, 5th Grade Teacher; *b:* Walker, KY; *m:* George F.; *c:* Frankie Jozell, Caleb Burnell; *ed:* (BS) Elem Ed, 1973, (MS) Elem Ed, 1976 Union Coll; Grad Stud; *cr:* Remedial Math Teacher 1975-82, 5th Grade Teacher 1982- Boone Elem; *ai:* KY Ed Assn 1975-; Forward Fifth Mini Grant 1989; Boone Elem Teacher of Yr Awd 1989; *home:* Box 283 Barbourville KY 40906

HAMMONS, GAYLE L., English Teacher; *b:* Pasadena, CA; *m:* Kenneth J.; *c:* Shanna J.; *ed:* (BA) Eng, Humboldt St Univ 1973; (MAT) Teaching Eng, Univ of AK Juneau 1977; Clinical Teaching; Project TEACH Performance Learning Systems Instr; Teaching Through Learning Channels; Trng in Peer Coaching; Test Dev; Analytical Writing Assesment; *cr:* Teacher Sitka HS; *ai:* Yrbl Adv 1976-80; Mathcounts Adv 1980-; NHS Adv 1988-89; Natl Maids Adv; Sch Service, Improvement, Prof Leave In-Service Comm; Dist-Wide Assessment Team 1983-; Peer Coaching; NCTE 1987-; JEA 1990; NEA; Sitka Ed Assn (Delegate, Pres, Secy, Building, Negotiations Team); Initiated Christmas Card Prgm Sitka HS; Teaching Teachers Classes in Analytical Assessment & Verbal Skills; *office:* Sitka HS 1000 Lake St Extension Sitka AK 99835

HAMMONS, JANET TRUDEAU, First Grade Teacher; *b:* Jeffersonville, IN; *m:* Sharold David; *c:* Sharra C., Matt; *ed:* (BS) Elem Ed, 1969, (MA) Elem Ed, 1973, Rdng Specialist, 1973 Union Coll; *cr:* 1st Grade Teacher 1969-70, Teacher of Perceptually Handicapped 1970-72 Eisenhower Elem; 1st Grade Teacher Gridler Elem 1972-; *ai:* Outstanding Young Women of America 1982; *home:* HC 83 Box 176 Cannon KY 40923

HAMMONS, MERRILL R., English Teacher; *b:* Bowling Green, KY; *ed:* (BA) Eng, Univ of KY 1979; (MA) Ed/Eng, W KY Univ 1982; *cr:* Teacher Cntrl Intermediate 1981-86; Part Time Teacher TX Southmost Coll 1983-84; Teacher Pace HS 1986-; *ai:* NHS Club Adv; Var One-Act Play, Ready Writing, Academic Decathlon Team Coach; Phi Delta Kappa 1980-; Assn of Brownsville Educators, TX St Teachers Assn, NEA 1983-; Camille Lightner Playhouse Actor 1986-; San Benito Cmmty Theater (Actor, Play Selection Comm) 1987; *office:* Pace HS 314 W Los Ebanos Brownsville TX 78520

HAMMONTRE, SIDNEY JEAN, Science/Latin Teacher; *b:* Monahans, TX; *m:* Thomas M.; *ed:* (BA) Anthropology, Univ of TX 1969; Sci Composite, TX Tech; *cr:* Teacher Different Schls San Antonio TX 1976-80, Permian HS 1980-84, Capitan HS 1988-; *ai:* Capitan Assn of Classroom Teachers.

HAMNER, STEVE CARL, 5th Grade Teacher; *b:* Marshall, MN; *m:* Janet C.; *ed:* (BS) Elem Ed, Southwest St Univ 1979; Mankato St Univ; *cr:* 5th Grade Teacher Medford Public Sch 1979-; *ai:* Asst Head Wrestling Coach; Elem Newsletter Adv; Fine Arts Curr Comm; NEA 1979-; Medford Boosters Club Dir Youth Act 1984-89; *office:* Medford Public Sch Box 38 Medford MN 55049

HAMPP, MICHAEL ALLAN, Band Director; *b:* Zanesville, OH; *m:* Shelley Ann Pritchard; *c:* Andrew, Emily; *ed:* (BM) Music Ed, Kent St Univ 1974; Bowling Green St Univ; *cr:* Band Dir Tiffin Columbian HS 1974; Low Brass Instr Heidelburg Coll 1981-; *ai:* Marching & Pep Band; Girls Bsktbl 1974-76; Natl Band Assn 1980-; OH Music Ed Assn 1974-; Dist II Music Festival Chm 1989-; Tiffin Exchange Club Stu of Month Chm 1984-88 Service Awd 1988; *office:* Tiffin Columbian H S 300 S Monroe St Tiffin OH 44883

HAMPSON, SHARON K. GIBSON, Counselor; *b:* Waterloo, IA; *m:* Fernie; *c:* John, Christopher; *ed:* (BA) Elem Ed, Univ of N IA 1974; (MA) Counseling/Sch Psych, Mac Quarie Univ 1981; *cr:* Spec Ed Teacher 1974-78, Cnslr/Psychologist 1978-81 New S Wales Dept of Ed; Cnslr S Tama Mid Sch 1981-; Cnslr/Teacher of Gifted & Talented Stu Wilton Elem Sch 1985-; *ai:* Drug Free Schls, At-Risk, Early Chldhd, Sch Climate, Phase III Sch Reform, Wellness Comm; Amer Assn for Counseling & Dev 1989-; IA Assn for Counseling & Dev 1981-; IA Talented & Gifted 1985-; Wilton Ed Assn (Pres 1989-, VP 1988-89, Teachers Rights 1987-88); NEA, ISEA; IA Democratic Party 1981-; St Conference for IA Assn for Counseling & Dev Presenter 1988; *office:* Wilton Elem Sch 201 E 6th St Wilton IA 52778

HAMPTOM, MARGARET MOSES, 7th/8th Grade Teacher; *b:* Sumter, SC; *m:* Harold; *c:* Darrell; *ed:* (BS) Elem Ed, Barber-Scotia Coll 1965; (ME) Ed, SC St 1976; Univ SC, Sumter Area Tech Coll; *cr:* 3rd Grade Teacher Taliaferro Cty Sch 1965-67; 5th Grade Teacher Alcolu Elem Sch 1967-76; 7th/8th Grade Teacher R E Davis Elem 1976-89; *ai:* Lead Math Teacher; SC Ed Assn; NEA; *home:* Rt 1 Box 50 Mayesville SC 29104

HAMPTON, CAROLYN CARR, First Grade Teacher; *b:* Anadarko, OK; *m:* Hardy Blair; *c:* Kathryn F., Penny K.; *ed:* (BS) Elem Ed, (MS) Guidance/Counseling, Tarleton St Univ; *cr:* 3rd/4th Grade Teacher Tolar Elem 1967-68; 1st Grade Teacher Stephenville Ind Sch Dist 1968-; *ai:* Assn of Prof Educators (Building Rep 1980-, Local Officer); PTA (VP 1968-78, Local Officer); Classroom Teachers Assn Local Officer; Delta Kappa Gamma 1987-; PTO Parliamentarian 1979-; First Baptist Church Various Offices 1952-; Elected & Appointed Offices Through Sch Various Comms; *home:* 1410 Kaylock Stephenville TX 76401

HAMPTON, JOAN MARKES, HS Mathematics Teacher; *b:* Enid, OK; *m:* Joe Neal; *c:* Jason N., Jennifer D.; *ed:* (BA) Math, OK St Univ 1972; Post Grad Work OK St Univ & Phillips Univ; *cr:* HS Math Teacher Pawnee OK 1972-73; 8th Grade Math Teacher 1974-76, Remedial Math Teacher 1979-80 Emerson Jr HS; HS/Mid Sch Math Teacher Waukomis 1983-; *ai:* Academic Coach; Jr Class Spon; OEA, NEA, NCTM, OCTM; Sunday Sch Teacher St Josephs Cath Church Bison; Local Teachers Assn, (Pres, Treas) Twice Local Teacher of Yr; *home:* RR 2 Box 34 Waukomis OK 73773

HAMPTON, MINA MAYTON, Retired; *b:* Durham, NC; *m:* Thomas H.; *c:* Charlotte A., Thomas Jr.; *ed:* (BA) Primary Ed, Meredith Coll 1951; Early Chldhd Ed Univ NC; *cr:* 1st/3rd Grade Teacher Creswell HS 1951-57; 3rd/4th Combination Teacher Columbia Elem 1958; 2nd/4th Grade Teacher Creswell HS 1958-64; 6th Grade Teacher Holt Elem Sch 1964-74; Kndgtn Teacher Lakeview Sch 1974-82; Hillandale Sch 1982-85; *ai:* NC Assn Educators (Resolution Chm) 1975-76; Durham Cnty Unit NCEA (Pres) 1979-80; Durham Cty/Cty Retired Sch Personnel (Pres) 1987-89; Delta Kappa Gamma (Pres) 1970-72/1984-86; Friends of West Point Eno 1987-; St Philips Episcopal Church Chrstn Ed Dir 1983-; Kiwanis Club Citizen-Teacher Awd 1970; Durham Cty Teacher Yr 1978; *home:* 147 Argonne Dr Durham NC 27704

HAMPTON, PAULA SCHIMMELS, English Teacher; *b:* Shawnee, OK; *m:* Tony; *c:* Alyssa; *ed:* (BA) Speech Comm, Wheaton Coll 1982; *cr:* Speech Coach Wheaton Cntrl HS 1981-82; Jr HS Teacher Tidewater Chrstn Acad 1983-84; Eng/Speech Teacher Alliance Chrstn HS 1984-87, 1989-; *ai:* Jr Class Spon; Yrbk Adv; Speech Team Coach; NCTE 1984-87; Co-Dir IL St Championship Readers Theater 1982; *office:* Alliance Chrstn Sch 5809 Portsmouth Blvd Portsmouth VA 23701

HAMRICK, CHRISTINA ANN, Sophomore English Teacher; *b:* Monroe, MI; *c:* Jarrett, Lindsay; *ed:* (BA) Eng, Cntrl MI Univ 1968; (MA) Eng, St Univ of NY Potsdam 1990; *cr:* Eng Teacher Midland Public Schls 1968-69, Crestwood Sch Dist 1969-75, Colon Cmmty Schls 1984-87, Norwood-Norfolk Cntrl Schls 1987-; *ai:* Soph Class Adv; Sr Play Adv & Dir; NCTE; *office:* Norwood-Norfolk Cntrl HS R R 56 Norwood NY 13668

HAMRICK, VIRGIE LOUISE WATSON, Behavioral Intervention Coord; *b:* Ironton, OH; *c:* Bradley A., Kesha L.; *ed:* (BS) Elem, Rio Grande Univ 1966; (MS) Spec Ed, 1969, Specialist Early Chldhd, 1975 Univ of Toledo; Working Toward Doctorate; *cr:* 4th-8th Grade Teacher of Gifted 1981-83, 7th/8th Grade Developmental Rdng Teacher 1983-89, Substance Abuse Coord 1986-, Behavioral Intervention Coord 1989- Washington Local Schls; *home:* 811 Gribbin Ln Toledo OH 43612

HAMROCK, ANGELA SALRENO, Fourth Grade Teacher; *b:* Youngstown, OH; *m:* Aloysius Thomas; *c:* Marilyn Hamrock Pagliara, Margaret Hamrock Gram; *ed:* (BA) Elem Ed, Kent St Univ 1943; (MS) Elem/Exceptional Children, Westminster Coll 1964; *cr:* Sch Secy 1938-40, Elem Teacher 1940-43 Youngstown Public Sch System; Admin Asst Civilian Personnel Branch War Dept Ft Bragg NC 1943-46; Substitute Teacher Youngstown Public Sch System 1948-57; 4th Grade Teacher Boardman Sch Dist 1957-; *ai:* Robinwood Lane Sch Head Teacher; Composition Competency & Amer Heart Assn Collection Comm; Soc Stud & Individualized Rdng Wkshp Presenter; Boardman Ed Assn, OH Ed Assn, NE OH Ed Assn 1957-; OH PTA Life Membership 1985; Nom OH Teacher of Yr; Martha Holden Jennings Awd; Freedom Fnd Teacher Awd; Intnl Yr of Child Grant; 1st Prize 4th Grade Commercial Awd; *home:* 538 6th St Campbell OH 44405

HAMS, BETTY ROSSER, Teacher of Gifted & Talented; *b:* Hannibal, MO; *m:* Jack L.; *c:* William, Robert; *ed:* (BS) Elem Ed, Culver-Stockton 1965; (MA) Elem Curr, NE MO Univ 1980; Gifted Ed, Univ of MO; *cr:* 5th Grade Teacher Mark Twain Elem 1965-68; Vocal Music Teacher Hannibal Elem Schls 1968-69; 6th Grade Teacher Mark Twain Elem 1969-85; Gifted Resource Teacher Hannibal Mid Sch 1985-; *ai:* Odyssey of Mind Team & Future Problem Solving Team Coach; Gifted Assn of MO Bd Mem 1986-87; Hannibal Ed Assn Pres 1970-71; Gifted Ed Seminar Grant; *office:* Hannibal Mid Sch 4700 Mc Masters Hannibal MO 63401

HANBY, DONNA (WEISS), Teacher of Talented & Gifted; *b:* Hamilton, OH; *c:* Christopher; *ed:* (BS) Elem Ed, OH St Univ 1973; Grad Stud Wright St Univ, Univ of Cincinnati, Miami Univ; *cr:* 6th Graded Teacher 1973-79, Teacher of Gifted & Talented 1978- Fairfield City Schls; *ai:* Odyssey of Mind Region 5 Dir, Fairfields Coord, Regional Dir 1988-; Advanced Curr, Primary Gifted, Talented & Gifted Curr Comm; CEC 1988-89; OAGC Regional Rep 1979-81, TAG 1988-89; NEA, OEA, FCTA 1973-; NAGC 1989-; OH Assn for Gifted Children Presenter; OH Teacher Grant 1978; Article Published; Created Nationwide Magazine for Gifted & Talented Stus; Began Saturday Prgm for Gifted Stus Miami Univ Hamilton; Participated in Ohio St Bd of Ed "Classrooms of the Future".

HANCOCK, CONNIE STAUDE, 1st Grade Teacher; *b:* Ft Atkinson, WI; *m:* Billy H.; *c:* Darryl Lacy, Kathy, Chad, Tammy; *ed:* (BS) Elem Ed, Austin Peay 1974; (MED) Elem Ed, 1978, (Rank I) Elem Ed, 1980 Murray St; *cr:* 5th/6th Grade Teacher 1974-75, 1st Grade Teacher 1975- Lacy Elem.

HANCOCK, FINETTA GRAVES, Social Studies Teacher; *b:* Smithfield, KY; *m:* Donald C.; *c:* Kim, Dean; *ed:* (BA) Elem Ed, Georgetown Coll 1952; Working Towards MED Univ of Louisville; Hours Earned as Teacher Trainee at Child Guidance Clinic; *cr:* 3rd Grade Teacher Bethlehem Sch 1949-51, Cane Run Elem, Kennedy Elem 1952-61; 5th Grade Teacher Glenn Hills Baptist 1973-79, Curtis Baptist 1979-82; 6th Grade Teacher Hillcrest Baptist 1982-; *ai:* Data Collector, Assessing Teachers for Cert; Asst Prin; Kappa Delta Pi 1955-61; Delta Kappa Gamma (Corresponding Secy 1986-88,VP 1988-); Fellowship to Child Guidance Clinic as Teacher Trainee 1956.

HANCOCK, KENNETH LEE, Computer Education Teacher; *b:* Keota, OK; *m:* Leigh Ann Shaddox; *c:* Kenneth J. D.; *ed:* (BS) Elem Ed, 1972, (MA) Educl Leadership, 1977 Univ of Tulsa; Working Towards PhD Educl Admin, Univ of Tulsa; *cr:* Teacher/Coach Owasso Public Schls 1972-75; Teacher/Coach/AD Acad Cntrl 1975-79; Prin Keystone Public Sch 1979-81; Dir of Purchasing/Cmpt Ed Teacher Union Public Schls 1981-; *ai:* Kappa Delta Pi, Cooperative Cncl of OK Sch Admin, AASA, OK Assn of Sch Bus Ofcls, ASCD; Union Optimist Club (Selection Comm, 1st Mid Amer Bowl) 1985; New Home Free Will Baptist Church (Sunday Sch Supt 1982-88, Minister of Music 1984-89); Freewill Baptist Masters Men Organization; Write Competency Test for OK Cmptr Cert Comm Mem; *home:* 1721 S Olympia Tulsa OK 74107

HANCOCK, LOUIS JOSEPH, Dir of Bands/Music Dept Chair; *b:* Pitcairn, PA; *ed:* (BS) Music Ed, Gettysburg Coll 1974; Penn St, Univ of WI, Duquesne Univ; *cr:* Band Dir Norwin Jr HS West 1974-76; Dir of Bands Norwin Sr HS 1976-; Adjunct Prof

Duquesne Univ 1983-87; *ai:* Dir of Bands, Music Dept Chm; Mentor Teacher Prgm; Asst Wrestling Coach; PMEA, Music Educators Natl Conference; NEA, PSEA, NEA; Guest Conductor Various Cty & Honor Bands; Exec Secy 1984-89; Bands of America Contest Commission Clinician, Consultant PA Fed of Contest Judges; Bands of America; *office:* Norwin Sch Dist 251 Mc Mahon Rd North Huntingdon PA 15642

HANCOCK, MARIE A., Kindergarten Teacher; *b:* Brooklyn, NY; *m:* Philip H.; *c:* Philip D., Steven M.; *ed:* (BS) Ed, St Univ of NY Cortland 1962; Gifted Ed, Univ of CT Storrs 1981, 1982; *cr:* 6th Grade Teacher Shenendehowa Cntrl Schls 1962-64; 6th Grade Teacher 1964-65; 5th Grade Teacher Ballston Spa Cntrl Schls 1966-70; Kndgtn Teacher 1971-75, 1st Grade Teacher 1975-80, Gifted/Talented Dist Prgm Teacher 1980-85, Kndgtn Teacher 1985- Burnt Hills-Ballston Lake Cntrl Schls; *ai:* PTA Rep; Taught After-Sch Enrichment Class; Chairperson Mentor/Intern Prgm Dist Comm; Building Advisory Cncl; Welcoming & K-1st Dist Comm; Delta Kappa Gamma Society Intnl Mem 1985-; Dist Mini Grant Sci Project; *office:* Francis Lewis Stevens Elem Sch Lakehill Rd Ballston Lake NY 12019

HANCOCK, STEPHEN PAUL, History Department Chair; *b:* Warsaw, IN; *m:* Suetta Kay Board; *c:* Thomas, Charity; *ed:* (BA) His, Cedarville Coll 1980; Working Toward Masters of Religious Ed Degree; *cr:* Teacher Seaford Sr HS 1980-83; Teacher/Dept Chm 1983-, Asst Admin/Teacher 1990 Seaford Chrstn Acad; *ai:* Asst Soccer, Strength & Conditioning Coach; Amer Security Cncl 1980-83, 1989-; First Baptist Church (Trustee 1980-86, 1988-, Sch Bd 1980-83, Deacon 1986-); Supts Prof Staff Advisory Cncl; *office:* Seaford Chrstn Acad 110 Holly St Seaford DE 19973

HANCOX, GREGORY LEE, Mathematics Department Chair; *b:* Knoxville, TN; *m:* Elizabeth Charae Whitehead; *c:* Zachary C.; *ed:* (BS) Ed, Univ of TN Knoxville 1980; *cr:* Math Teacher Thomson HS 1983-86, Harlem HS 1986-87, Harrison-Chilhowee Baptist Acad 1987-; *ai:* Tennis Team; Music Club; Math Assn of America 1989; NCTM 1987-; Everett Hills Baptist Church (Discipleship, Trng Dir) 1989-; *office:* Harrison Chilhowee Baptist Sch 202 Smothers Rd Seymour TN 37865

HAND, BOB FREDERICK, English Teacher; *b:* Washington, DC; *ed:* (BS) Phys Ed, Pfeiffer Coll 1965; (MA) Ed, Univ of VA 1972; *cr:* Teacher Hammond HS 1969-71, Howard Mid Sch 1971-72, Madison HS 1972-77, Lake Braddock Scndry Sch 1977-78, Herndon HS 1978-; *ai:* Head Var Wrestling Coach; VA HS Coaches Assn 1969-89; *office:* Herndon HS 700 Bennett St Herndon VA 22070

HANDEL, ANNE KENYON, 6th Grade Teacher; *b:* Oakland, CA; *m:* Raymond D.; *c:* Rae A. Federas, Mitchell; *ed:* (BS) Elem Ed, CA St Univ Hayward 1963; Certified Travel Cnslr 1987; *cr:* 6th Grade Teacher Anderson Elem 1963-68; 1st Grade Teacher 1968-69, 5th Grade Teacher 1969-85 Verde Vale; 6th Grade Teacher Anderson Elem 1985-; *ai:* Exploratory World Travel Enrichment; Anderson Cascade Teachers Assn Pres 1963-; CA Teachers Assn (Statewide Task Force Chairperson 1973-75) 1963-, We Honor Ours 1981; NEA (Congressional Contact 1977-80) 1963-; Amer Assn Univ Women 1966-; St Cncl of Ed 1971-80, 1982; *home:* 7101 River Crest Dr Anderson CA 96007

HANDLER, LORI ALLEN, Curriculum/Staff Dev Coord; *b:* Mason City, IA; *m:* Timothy; *c:* Graham; *ed:* (BSED) Elem Ed, Bowling Green St Univ 1977; (MED) Curr/Instruction, Miami Univ 1989; Gifted Ed; *cr:* Kndgtn Teacher 1977-78, 3rd/4th/6th Grade Teacher 1978-88, 2nd/3rd Grade Teacher of Gifted 1988-89, Curr/Staff Dev Coord 1989- Mt Healthy City Schls; *ai:* Curr Revision & Grading Comm; Writing to Read Supvr; Dist Technology; TESA Coord; OEA, MHTA Rep 1980-81; *office:* Mt Healthy City Schls 7615 Harrison Ave Cincinnati OH 45231

HANDLEY, RICHARD DALE, Social Studies Teacher; *b:* Portland, OR; *m:* Louise Johnson; *c:* Beth Handley-Merk, Richard Jr., Jennifer, Michael; *ed:* (BA) His, 1962, (MAT) Soc Stud, 1972 Lewis & Clark Coll; *cr:* Soc Stud Teacher Grant HS 1962-63, Ukiah HS 1963-64, Bandon HS 1964-68, Rockwood Jr HS 1968-72, North Bend Jr HS 1972-74, Bandon HS 1974-; *ai:* Track Coach; NHS Adv; Coll Coord; Dist Accountability Prgm Comm HS Rep; NEA, OEA; Julian Virne Inst for Ec Ed Fellowship 1984; Taft Inst for 2 Party System Fellowship 1985; *office:* Bandon HS 550 9th St SW Bandon OR 97411

HANDLEY, ROBERT W., Eng Dept Chair/Mentor Teacher; *b:* Detroit, MI; *m:* Pam Shirakawa; *c:* Kyle, Scott; *ed:* (BS) Speech Comm/Eng E MI Univ 1972; (MA) Ed Admin, CA St Univ Fresno 1980; Grad Stud Eng Lit, CA St Univ Fresno 1987-88; *cr:* Eng Teacher Fresno Unified Schls 1976-80; 11th/12th Grade Eng Teacher Firebaugh HS 1980-83; 8th Grade Eng/9th-11th Grade Teacher/Eng Dept Chm 1983, Mentor Teacher 1989- Edison-Computech HS; *ai:* Teachers of Tomorrow Club Adv; Ftbl, Bsktbl, Miscellaneous Act Announcer Edison HS; Fresno Area Cncl Eng Teachers Mem 1985-; CA Assn Teachers of Eng Chm Presentor 1987-; Fresno Little League System Head 1988-; Short Story Publications; Mentor Teacher; *office:* Edison HS 540 E California Ave Fresno CA 93706

HANDLY, LINDA PHILLIPS, Guidance Counselor; *b:* Knoxville, TN; *m:* Gustave Miller Jr.; *c:* Christopher; *ed:* (BS) Home Ec Ed, 1969, (MS) Spec Ed, 1973 Univ of TN; Cert in Educl & Counseling Psych 1989; *cr:* Teacher South Jr/Sr HS 1970-76, South-Young HS 1976-89; Cnslr South-Young HS 1989-; *ai:* Co-Coord Jr Class; Core Team Mem; Group Leader Tuesday Club; NEA, TEA, KCEA; KEA Bd Dir 1983-84; *office:* South-Young HS 3900 Decatur Rd Knoxville TN 37920

HANDSBOROUGH, DORIS JEAN, Teacher; *ed:* (BA) Elem Ed, Prairie View A&M Univ 1981; *cr:* Scndry Ed/Rdng Teacher Univ of TX Tyler 1987-88; *ai:* Beta Club Co-Spon; Stu Advisory Comm & 8th Grade Spon; Dir 8th Grade Graduation; TX Ed Teachers Assn 1986-; *home:* Rt 1 Box 1488 Centerville TX 75833

HANDSHOE, GARRY, Teacher; *b:* Hueysville, KY; *m:* Barbara Ann Hall; *c:* Leslie, Tiffany; *ed:* (BA) Art, Morehead St Univ 1969; *cr:* Teacher Boyd Cty HS 1969-70, Arcanum HS 1970-; *ai:* Sch Yrbk Adv; Local Teachers Assn (Pres 1981-83, Head Negotiator 1981-82); Dist Teacher of Yr 1990; *office:* Arcanum HS 310 N Main St Arcanum OH 45304

HANDY, BARBARA BUCCIFERRO, Business Teacher; *b:* Amsterdam, NY; *m:* Douglas J.; *ed:* (BS) Bus, Alfred Univ 1982; (MS) Bus Ed, St Univ of NY Albany 1985; *cr:* Bus Teacher Sharon Springs Cntrl Schl 1982-; *ai:* FBLA, Class, Book Store Adv; Delta Phi Epsilon, NYS Bus Teachers Assn 1985-; *office:* Sharon Springs Central Schl Rt 20 Sharon Springs NY 13459

HANDY, RAEANN ASHLEY, Kindergarten Teacher; *b:* Temple, TX; *m:* Charles Edward; *c:* Jennifer, Jeffrey; *ed:* (BAT) Elem Ed, Sam Houston St Univ 1975; Elem Music Ed, Gifted & Talented; *cr:* 1st Grade Teacher 1975-80, Kndgtn Teacher 1983- Ore City Ind Sch Dist; *ai:* Sch Bd Advisory Comm; Kndgtn Lead Teacher; TSTA Secy 1989-; Kndgtn Teachers of TX; PTA; Teacher of Yr 1975-76; *office:* Ore City Ind Sch Dist P O Box 100 Ore City TX 75683

HANDY, RUBY HUDSON, 7th-8th Grade Reading Teacher; *b:* Alto, LA; *m:* Edward Mc Kinley; *c:* Carolyn, Lucille Robinson; *ed:* (BA) Elem Ed, Southern Univ 1959; (MED) Rdng Specialist, Northeast LA Univ 1973; Advanced Trng Elem Ed; *cr:* Teacher Alto HS 1960-70, Mangham Elem Sch 1971-82, Mangham HS 1982-86; Rdng Sp Mangham Jr HS 1986-; *ai:* Chm Sch Building Level Comm; Dir Basic Skills & Tutoring Prgm; LEA/NEA Rep 1986-; Richland Parish Jr HS 1987-88 Teacher of Yr 1987-88; RPEA Assn 1959-; St Matthew BC Asst Clerk 1985-; Richland Parish Democratic Asst Secy 1988-89; LA Fed of Teachers Mem 1989-; Grant for Writing Proposal for Drop Out Prevention Prgm; *office:* Mangham Jr H S PO Box 428 Mangham LA 71259

HANES, LARRY F., Mathematics Teacher; *b:* Hughes Springs, TX; *ed:* (BBA) General Bus, Sam Houston St Univ 1972; (MED) Scndry Ed, Stephen F Austin St Univ 1979; (BS) Cmptr Sci, LSU Shreveport 1985; (MS) Cmptr Sci, Univ TX Tyler 1988; *cr:* Math Teacher Weskom HS 1979-82, Marshall HS 1983-; *ai:* Math Team & Cmptr Programming Team Spon; Marshal HS Math Dept Chm; *office:* Marshall HS 1900 Maverick Dr Marshall TX 75670

HANESS, ROSEMARY, Art Teacher; *b:* Union City, NJ; *m:* Salvatore Guadagnino Jr.; *ed:* (BA) Art Ed, 1964, (MS) Art Ed, 1971 Montclair St Coll; Eng Cert Drew Univ; Jewelry Design/Fabrication, Parsons Sch of Design; Grad Stud Art Ed, NY Univ; *cr:* 1st-6th Grade Art Teacher Linden Public Sch 3 & 5 1963-64; 1st-8th Grade Art Teacher Hillview Sch 1964-68; 9th-12th Grade Art Teacher New Providence HS 1968-; *ai:* Yrbk Adv 1983-; Natl Art Honor Society Adv 1988-; Stage Mgr 1988-; Set Design Coord for HS Musicals 1988-; New Providence Ed Assn, NJ Ed Assn, NEA, NAEA 1964-; Historical Society of Plainfield Publicity 1986-88; Plainfield Cultural/Heritage Preservation Comm Yrbk Ed 1985-87, City Commendation 1987; Plainfield Historic Comm Chairperson 1981-88, Cty Commendation 1987; Hillside Avenue Historic Dist Chairperson 1980-88; Joys of Yesteryear Chairperson 1984-88; New Providence Sch Dist Teacher of Yr 1989-; Union Cty Teacher of Yr 1989-; City of Plainfield 300 Yr His Ed in Chief, Photographer, Layout Designer; *office:* New Providence HS 35 Pioneer Dr New Providence NJ 07974

HANEY, BONNIE BASTIN, 5th/6th Grade Teacher; *b:* Hopkinsville, KY; *m:* Michael; *c:* Elizabeth Hancock, Philip Tillman; *ed:* (BS) Elem Ed, Austin Peay St Univ 1972; (MA) Elem Ed, Murray St Univ 1977; *cr:* 5th Grade Teacher Booker T Washington Mid Sch 1972-74; Kndgtn Teacher Holiday Elem Sch 1977-78; Kndgtn Teacher 1978-86, 5th/6th Grade Teacher 1986- S Chrstn Elem Sch; *ai:* Family Life Ed Comm Mem; Teaching your Stu about Alcohol Participant; KY Educl Assn Mem, Chrstn Cty Educl Assn, NEA 1978-; Hopkinsville HS (Choral Booster 1989-, Ftbl Booster 1990); BSA Supporter 1985-; *office:* South Christian Elem Sch Hwy 117 Rt 1 Herndon KY 42236

HANEY, CHARLES, 7th Grade Science Teacher; *b:* Ironton, OH; *m:* Debra Lynn Birkel; *c:* Heather R.; *ed:* (AB) Geography, Morehead St Univ 1972; (MA) Sch Admin, Marshal Univ 1980-; *cr:* Teacher Dawson-Bryant Intermediate 1972-; *ai:* Head Ftbl, Weight Trng, Asst Track Coach; *office:* Dawson Bryant Intermediate Sch 222 Lane St Coal Grove OH 45638

HANEY, DAVID ALLAN, Science Teacher; *b:* Waynesville, NC; *m:* Janie Carpenter; *c:* Wren, Weston; *ed:* (BSED) Health/Phys Ed/Sci, W Carolina Univ 1978; *cr:* Teacher/Coach Robbinsville HS 1978-84, Owen HS 1984-86, Murphy HS 1986-87, Robbinsville HS 1987-; *ai:* Jr Var Head Ftbl Coach; Var Ftbl Asst Line Coach; Head Wrestling & Bsbl Coach; Fellowship of Chrstn Athletes & Stu Cncl Spon; Natl Coaches Assn 1986-87; Gideons 1988-; Smoky Mountain Conference Wrestling Coach of Yr 1988-; *office:* Robbinsville HS P O Box 625 Robbinsville NC 28771

HANEY, ELIZABETH HIFNER, 5th Grade Teacher; *b:* Independence, MO; *m:* Carl Ray; *c:* James, Jerry, Terry; *ed:* (BS) Elem Ed, 1970; (MS) Elem Super & Admin, 1977 Cntrl MO St Univ; *cr:* 1st-8th Grade Teacher Buckner R-1 1949-52; 3rd Grade Elem Teacher Oak Grove MO 1967-68; 5th-8th Grade Elem Teacher/Prin Strasburg 1968-75; 5th Grade Elem Teacher Odessa R-7 1975-; *ai:* Mentor Teacher; Textbook Comm; Delta Kappa Gamma 2nd VP 1988-; MO St Teachers Assn 1968-; Caring Chrstn Clowns 1985-; Whos Who in MO Ed 1975; *home:* RR 2 Box 123B Odessa MO 64076

HANEY, LEONARD FRANCIS, Mathematics Teacher/Chairman; *b:* Huntington, WV; *m:* Donna Marie; *ed:* (BS) Mining Engineering, WV Inst of Technology 1982; (BS) Math Ed, Marshal Univ 1988; *cr:* Math Teacher Burch Jr/Sr HS 1983-; *ai:* Chm Math Dept; Head Ftbl & Asst Bsktbl Coach; Var Bsbl Umpire; Phi Beta Kappa, Amer Inst of Mine Engrs 1979-82; Math Teachers of Amer 1985-; Ragland Little League Coach 1987-88; WVEA 1984-; Nom Ashland Teacher of Yr Awd; *office:* Burch Jr HS General Delivery Delbarton WV 25670

HANF, RICHARD W., English Teacher; *b:* Elmhurst, IL; *m:* Nancy Demsyn; *c:* Michael, Daniel; *ed:* (BS) Teacher of Hearing Impaired, Trenton St Coll 1980; Scndry Cert; *cr:* Teacher of Hearing Impaired Bayonne Sch System 1980-81; Eng Teacher Kearny Chrstn Cmmty Ed Center 1981-; *ai:* Yrbk Adv; Curr Planning; NCTE Mem 1990; *office:* Kearny Chrstn Cmmty Educl Ctr 151 Midland Ave Kearny NJ 07032

HANIFAN, MARJORIE J. JOHNSON, Retired; *b:* Fenton, IA; *w:* Forrest (dec); *c:* Barbara Zander; *ed:* (AA) Elem Primary, 1941, (BA) Elem Primary, 1963 Univ of Northern IA; Grad Work Univ of IA; *cr:* 1st Grade Teacher Fenton IA 1943-49, Dunkerton IA 1949-51, Dysart IA 1951-57; 2nd Grade Teacher Toledo IA 1957-65; 1st Grade Teacher Knoxville IA 1965-83; *ai:* Bus & Prof Women Pres 1960-62 & 1978-80; Amer Assn of Univ Women; Delta Kappa Gamma Pres 1970-72; Mentor Study Club Pres 1988-89; PEO Pres 1976-78; Bus & Prof Woman of Achievement 1981; *home:* 702 E Cronkhite Knoxville IA 50138

HANING, JANET MC DONALD, 5th Grade Teacher/Head; *b:* Herrin, IL; *m:* Joe Edmund; *ed:* (BS) Elem Ed/Phys Ed, Murray St Univ 1969; *cr:* 6th Grade Teacher Edwardsville Sch Dist 7 1969-70; Lincoln Elem Dist 27 1970-87, 5th Grade Teacher 1987; *ai:* Young Author Spon; Head Teacher of Northwest Sch; Building Rep; Cntrl IL Rdng Cncl 1987-89; Lincoln Elem Ed Assn 1970-; IL Ed Assn 1970-; NEA 1970-; Lintiquers Antique Organization 1989-; Alpha Delta Pi 1st VP 1967-; Article Published in Mailbox Magazine; Dir of Stu Opportunity for Active Reinforcement; Presenter at Quincy Statewide Conference 1974; Rdng Evaluator for Office of Supt of Public Instruction; Adult Ed Phys Fitness Instr 1970-72; *office:* Northwest Elem Sch 506 11th St Lincoln IL 62656

HANIS, KEVIN CHARLES, Mathematics/Phys Ed Teacher; *b:* Seattle, WA; *ed:* Masters Prgm Ed Admin, Univ of WA; *cr:* Math/Eng/Soc Stud Teacher Kentridge HS 1984-88; Math/Phys Ed Teacher Stadium HS 1989-; *ai:* Head Ftbl & Asst Track Coach; Ftbl Club Adv; *office:* Stadium HS 111 North E Street Tacoma WA 98403

HANKA, DEBORAH RAE (HEIRONIMUS), 8th Grade US History Teacher; *b:* Washington, DC; *m:* Edward Alan; *ed:* (BA) Soc Sci, Towson St Coll 1972; Grad Stud; *cr:* 7th Grade Core Teacher Kent Jr HS 1972-73, Martin Luther King Jr HS 1973-74; 9th Grade Civics/Contemporary Issues Teacher 1974-82 Martin Luther King JR HS; 8th Grade US His Teacher Martin Luther King Jr HS 1974-; *ai:* Team Leader; Sch Improvement, Sch Based Management Comm; Chairperson of Effective Schls Subcommittee Stu Staff Advisory Comm; Human Relations Contact Person; Odyssey of Mind & Academic Coach; Prince Georges Cty Educators Assn (Faculty Rep 1981-83, Mem 1972-); MSTA, NEA 1972-; Natl Organization of Women 1975-; Outstanding Teacher Historian for Prince Georges Cty 1988; NCSS Notable Childrens Trade Book; St ITV Comm on Environmental Ed 1980; *office:* M L King Jr Academic Center 4545 Ammendale Rd Beltsville MD 20705

HANKIN, ANNETTE E., English-Drama Teacher; *b:* Chicago, IL; *ed:* (BA) Eng, Univ of IL 1956; Adv Theater Trng; *cr:* Teacher Farragut HS 1964-67, Roosevelt HS 1967-; *ai:* Photography Adv; Drama Dir; Project Eng Northwestern Univ; Scholastic Publications; *office:* Roosevelt HS 3436 W Wilson Chicago IL 60657

HANKINS, A. C., Mathematics Teacher; *b:* Dawson Springs, KY; *m:* Joyce Lane Sirls; *c:* Jennifer, Allen; *ed:* (BS) Math, 1970, (MA) Math, 1972 Murray St Univ; Working on PHD Math, Univ of MO Rolla; *cr:* Grad Asst Murray St Univ 1970-72, Univ of MO Rolla 1972-73; Math Teacher Calloway Cty HS 1974-75, Caldwell Cty HS 1976-; *home:* 1485 Logan Rd Dawson Springs KY 42408

HANKINS, BARBARA SMALL, Dept Chair/Business Teacher; *b:* Philadelphia, PA; *m:* Richard; *c:* Matthew; *ed:* (BS) Bus Ed, Madion Coll 1969; (MAD) Voc Ed, VPD-SU 1975; Grad Stud Cmptr Related Courses; *cr:* Bus Teacher Hayfield Scndry 1970-74, Lake Braddock Scndry 1974-75; Stu Act Asst Dir Hayfield Scndry Sch 1975-78; Dept Chairperson/Cooperative Office Ed Coord Fairfax HS 1978-84; Dept Chairperson/Teacher Chantilly HS 1984-; *ai:* FBLA Local Adv & VA Regional Dir; Bus Ed Teachers of America (Pres 1985-86, Secy 1984-85); VA Bus Ed Assn Mem-at-Large 1978-79, Nom Bus Ed Teacher of Yr 1990; Nom Fairfax Cty Outstanding Teacher 1988-89; Career Level II Fairfax Cty; Peer Observer Fairfax Cty; *office:* Chantilly HS 4201 Stringfellow Rd Chantilly VA 22021

HANKINS, ELIZABETH PORTER, AP English/Spanish Teacher; *b:* Oxford, MS; *ed:* (BS) Eng/Span, 1966, (MED) Span, 1974, (MA) Eng/Creative Writing, 1986 Memphis St Univ; *cr:* Span Teacher Whitehaven HS 1966-69; Lang Methods Teacher

Memphis St Univ 1988; Eng/Span Teacher Germantown HS 1971-; *ai:* Writers Guild & Span Club Spon; Coach Wordsmith Team; Shelby Cty Ed Assn 1971, Schlsp Awd 1973; TN Ed Assn, Shelby Memphis Teachers of Eng 1980-; Natl Assessment of Educl Progress Team Master Teacher Awd 1985; Published Poetry/Scholarly Articles; Bread Loaf Writers Conference 1988; *office:* Germantown HS 7653 Old Poplar Pike Germantown TN 38138

HANKINS, HILDA MOORE, Tenth Grade Biology Teacher; *b:* Altavista, VA; *m:* James Poindexter Jr.; *c:* Laura L. Chandler, Anne Hankins Moore, J. P. III; *ed:* (BA) Bio, Westhampton Coll & Univ of Richmond 1950; Longwood Coll & Univ of VA; *cr:* Bio Teacher Savannah HS 1960-61, Halifax Cty HS 1962-70; 4th-9th Grade Teacher Halifax Acad 1970-72; Bio Teacher Culpeper HS 1972-74; 5th-7th Grade Teacher St Andrews Episcopal Day Sch 1974-78; 4th-9th Grade Teacher Halifax Acad 1978-79; Bio Teacher Halifax Cty HS 1987-; *ai:* Halifax Ed Assn, VA Ed Assn, NEA 1987-; *home:* 325 Mountain Rd Halifax VA 24558

HANKINS, ROBERT M., Science Teacher; *b:* Hays, KS; *m:* Margaret Ann Martin; *c:* Andrea Marxen, Mike, Max, Mark; *ed:* (BS) Sci, 1967, (MS) Curr & Instruction, 1984 KS St Univ; Energy Ed; Aerospace Prgm; Summer Sci Acad; *cr:* Teacher/Coach Saints Peter & Paul 1967-69; Teacher/Athletic Dir Robinson Mid Sch 1969-; *ai:* Stu Cncl Adv; KS Assn Teachers of Sci 1970-; Curr Dev Small & Rural Schls 1985-; Teacher of Yr 1987; Curr Stud 1984-; Summer Sci Acad Grant; *office:* Robinson Mid Sch Box 68 Robinson KS 66532

HANKINS, SUSAN SATTERFIELD, English Teacher; *b:* Columbia, SC; *m:* Richard B.; *ed:* (BS) Eng, Univ of S MS 1983; (MA) Eng, Univ of MS 1986; *cr:* Instr Univ of MS 1984-85, Dekalb Coll 1985-86; Teacher N Clayton HS 1986-; Clayton St Coll 1987-; *ai:* NHS & Newspaper Spon; Public Relations Contact Person; Clayton Cty Ed Assn PAC Chm 1990; MS Philological Assn Presentation 1985; GA St Writing Conference Presentation 1990; *office:* N Clayton HS 1525 Norman Dr College Park GA 30349

HANLON, DANIEL P., Physics Teacher; *b:* Philadelphia, PA; *m:* Lacey L. Croco; *c:* Marc, Eric, Suzanne, Mathew, Julie; *ed:* (BS) Math/Physics, 1961, (MS) Physics, 1966 Temple Univ; Physics, Trenton St; Sci, Penn St Univ; *cr:* Teacher/Math Dept Chm Riverside HS 1961-71; Teacher Neshaminy HS 1971-; *ai:* Sch Newspaper Photography Adv; Natl Fnd Summer Schlsps; *home:* 234 Alden Ave Morrisville PA 19067

HANLON, ROBERT JOHN, English/Latin Teacher; *b:* New York, NY; *m:* Denise Kristman; *ed:* (BA) Philsolphy, Cathedral Coll 1960; (STB) Theology, Cath Univ of America 1964; (MA) Interdisciplinary Hum, San Francisco St Univ 1970; *cr:* Parish Priest R C Diocese of Brooklyn 1964-67; Part-Time Hum Instr San Francisco St Univ 1969-70; Part-Time Comm Coll Instr San Joaquin Delta Coll 1975-76; Teacher Lincoln HS 1970-; *ai:* Mentor Teacher; Amer Classical League 1981-; NCTE 1974-; CA Assn Teachers of Eng 1980-; NEH Fellowship Skidmore Coll 1987; *office:* Lincoln HS 6844 Alexandria Pl Stockton CA 95207

HANN, EDWIN CRAIG, 5th Grade Teacher; *b:* Columbus, OH; *ed:* (BS) Elem Ed, Oh St Univ 1974; Early Chldhd Ed; *cr:* Elem Teacher Hamilton Local Schls 1974-; *ai:* Cmptr Comm; Bsktbl Coach; *office:* Hamilton Local Schls 1105 Rathmeu Dr Columbus OH 43207

HANNA, ENOCH HAMILTON, 6th Grade Math/Science Teacher; *b:* Jackson County, FL; *ed:* (BS) Elem Ed, FL St Univ 1956; *cr:* Teacher Blountstown Elem Sch 1956-; *ai:* Math Olympics; Asst Sch Admin; Peer Teacher Beginning Teacher Prgm; Teacher Ed Ctr Bd Mem, Panhandle Area Educl Cooperative; Phi Delta Kappa 84-; Calhoun Cty Sch Bd Teacher of Yr 1972/1973/1974; Calhoun/Liberty Employees Credit Union Bd Dir Sec 1974-89; Altha 1st Bapt Church Deacon 1968-; *home:* Rt 2 Box 331 Altha FL 32421

HANNA, LARRY JOE, Biology Teacher; *b:* Amherst, TX; *m:* Judy Ann Williams; *c:* Larry S., Tommy K., Timothy R.; *ed:* (BS) Phys Ed, Univ of NM 1974; (MED) Admin, SW Ross St Univ 1988; *cr:* Life Sci Teacher/Coach PetersbUrg Jr HS 1975-77; Phys Sci Teacher/Coach Denver City HS 1978-79; Health Teacher/Athletic Dir Petersburg HS 1980-82; Bio Teacher/Coach Monahans HS 1983-; *ai:* Var Ftbl & Track Coach; Assn of Prof Ed 1978-; TX HS Coaches Assn 1975-; *office:* Monahans HS 809 S Betty Monahans TX 79756

HANNA, MARLYCE ELAM, Kindergarten Teacher; *b:* Vandalia, IL; *ed:* (AB) Art, Lincoln Chrstn Coll 1960; (BS) Elem Ed, Greenville Coll 1963; (MS) Elem Ed, 1967, (PHD) Early Chldhd Ed, 1980 IN St Univ; Doctoral Teaching, IN St Univ 1967-70; *cr:* Kndgtn Teacher Westside Chrstn 1960-61, Highland Cmmty Schls 1961-65, MSD Washington Township 1965-67, MSD Pike Township 1970-; *ai:* NEA Delegate 1983, 1985, 1986; IN St Teachers Assn Dist Cncl 1965; Pike Classroom Teachers Assn (Pres, VP, Negotiations Comm) 1970-; NAEYC Natl Conferce 1976-1979; Alpha Delta Kappa Secy 1980; *office:* Cntrl Elem Sch 6801 Zionsville Rd Indianapolis IN 46268

HANNA, ROBERT CONRAD, English Dept Chairman; *b:* Evanston, IL; *m:* Lesley Hart Barnett; *c:* Charlotte, Emily; *ed:* (BA) Eng, Lake Forest Coll 1974; (MM) Organization Behavior, Northwestern Univ 1976; (EDS) Educl Admin, Coll of William & Mary 1990; *cr:* Eng Teacher Lake Forest Acad 1984, St Margarets Sch 1984-; Eng Dept Chairman Gaston Day Sch 1990-; *ai:* Drama; Sch Newspaper & NHS Spon; Drama Dir, Sr Class Spon; VA Assn of Teachers of Eng (Publications 1986, Annual Conference 1986) 1985-; NCTE 1986-; Natl Cncl Accreditation of Teacher Ed 1983-85; NC Eng Teachers Assn; Kappa Phi Kappa Chapter Pres 1983-84; Kappa Delta Pi 1987-; Various Papers Published; Resources In Education; *office:* Gaston Day School 2001 Gaston Day School Rd Gastonianock NC 28054

HANNAFORD, BUDDY, Director of Instrumental Music; *b:* Marshall, MO; *m:* Karla Allison; *ed:* (BM) Music Ed, Missouri Valley Coll 1967; (MSE) Music Ed, Cntrl MO St Univ 1977; Univ of WI Whitewater, Univ of MO St Louis, NE MO St Univ Kirksville, NW MO St Univ Maryville, Univ MO Kansas City; *cr:* Vocal/Instrumental Music Teacher Adrian R-III Sch Dist 1967-69; Dir of Instrumental Music Trenton R-IX Sch Dist 1969-; *ai:* Instrumental Music Considered Extra Duty in Sch Dist; MO St Teachers Assn, Music Educators Natl Conference, Natl Bandmasters Assn, MO Music Educators Assn, MO Bandmasters Assn, Natl Fed of Interscholastic Act Assn,Phi Beta Mu; Outstanding Young Men of America 1974; Key to City of Trenton 1986; MO House of Rep Resolution Recognition of Outstanding Participation in Bluebonnet Bowl & Cotton Bowl 1987; Outstanding Alumnus Awd MO Valley Coll 1987; Recipient of Incentive Grant for Use in Instrumental Music Dept; *office:* Trenton HS 1415 Oklahoma Ave Trenton MO 64683

HANNAH, CHARLES AUSTIN, Tenth Grade English Teacher; *b:* Louisville, KY; *m:* Barbara Beckmann; *c:* Allison; *ed:* (BS) Eng Ed, 1975, (MS) Eng Ed, 1978 Auburn Univ; Specialist Cert Eng Ed, Auburn Univ 1984; *cr:* 7th-8th Grade Eng Teacher Opelika Jr HS 1975-84; Grad Teaching Asst Auburn Univ 1984-85; 10th Grade Eng Teacher Opelika HS 1985-; *ai:* Literary Magazine Perspectives Spon; NHS Adv; Writing Cncl; Phi Delta Kappa, NCTE; Phi Gamma Delta (Purple Legionnaire Adv 1978-84, Secy House Corporation 1984-), Outstanding Grad Brother 1982; Sun Belt Writing Conference 1981; Natl Endowment for Hum Inst in Literary Criticism 1987; *office:* Opelika HS 1700 Lafayette Pkwy Opelika AL 36801

HANNEMANN, JANALEE ANN (SMITH), 1st Grade Develpmnt Teacher; *b:* San Antonio, TX; *M:* Paul F.; *c:* Don, Jill; *ed:* (BS) Elem Ed, TX A&m Univ 1975; (MED) Elem Ed, Southwest TX St Univ 1979; *cr:* Kndgtn Teacher Fredericksburg ISD 1975-79; Lib Aide South Knoll Elem 1979-80; Kndgtn Teacher 1980-85, Dev 1st Grade Teacher 1985 Fredericksburg ISD; *ai:* TX St Teachers Assn; Kndgtn Teachers of TX; Supt; *office:* Fredericksburg Primary Sch 202 W Travis Fredericksburg TX 78624

HANNON, ELIZABETH JANE, Anatomy & Physiology Teacher; *b:* Evanston, IL; *ed:* (AA) Lib Art, Richland Coll 1981; (BA) Phys Ed, UTA 1983; Grad Stud U of Houston, TX Petroleum Institute, UTD; *cr:* Bio Teacher David W Carter 1983-85; Anatomy/Physiology Teacher W T White HS 1986-; *ai:* Var Boys & Girls Tennis Coach; Drill Team Spon; Dallas Tennis Assn Area Coord 1988-, USTA Schls Contribution 1990; Dallas Coaches Assn 1988-, TX Coaches Assn 1990, US Tennis Assn Dallas Area Schls Coord 1988-, Public Service Awd 1990; Dallas Jr League Sectional Umpire 1989; TX Petroleum Institute Sun Oil Grant; *office:* Warren Travis White HS 4505 Ridgeside Dr Dallas TX 75244

HANSBURRY, KATHLEEN HAAS, Assistant Principal; *b:* Philadelphia, PA; *ed:* (AA) Elem Ed, Bucks Cty Comm Coll 1974; (BS) Elem Ed, Jacksonville Univ 1976; (MED) Admin/Supervision, Univ of N FL 1986; Prin Intern Prgm, St Johns Cty; *cr:* Classroom Teacher Arlington Elem Sch 1977-78, Julington Creek Elem Sch 1978-87; Prin Intern Crookshank Elem Sch 1987-88; Asst Prin Evelyn Hamblen Elem Sch 1988-, Ponte Vedra-Palm Valley Elem 1990; *ai:* Delta Kappa Gamma Recording Secy 1990; Phi Delta Dappa Mem 1988-; AWARE Mem 1989-; M S Society Mem 1988-; *home:* 1169 Wards Pl Jacksonville FL 32259

HANSELL, BONNIE UMBERGER, Middle School Teacher; *b:* Port Arthur, TX; *m:* Warwick Craig; *c:* Connor, Frazier; *ed:* (BS) Ed, Brigham Young Univ 1973; (MA) Spec Ed/Gifted, Univ of UT 1989; *cr:* 5th-6th Grade Teacher Duchesne UT 1973-74, Oakdale Elem 1974-79; Eng/Rdng/Soc Stud/Phys Ed/Health Teacher Eastmont Mid Sch 1979-; *ai:* Stu Body Officer & Natl Jr Honor Society Adv; UT Mid Sch Assn; United Cncl Teachers of Eng; UT Assn of Gifted Ed; Parent Teacher Stu Assn Teacher of Yr 1989-; *office:* Eastmont Mid Sch 10100 S 13th Sandy UT 84070

HANSEN, ANDREA SUSAN, Religion Department Chair; *b:* Cleveland, OH; *m:* William A.; *ed:* (BA) Elem/Spec Ed, Fairmont St Coll 1979; (MA) Religious Ed, Wheeling Jesuit 1988; *cr:* Religion Dept Chairperson/K-12th Grade Teacher 1987-, Religion Teacher 1986- Harrison Cty Cath Schls; *ai:* Key Club Adv; Bishops Evaluation of Catechism for Universal Church Comm; Global Horizons; Hermits Hollow Land Trust Acting Pres 1987-; Teacher of Yr 1989.

HANSEN, BARRY BRACKEN, Sixth Grade Teacher; *b:* Salt Lake City, UT; *m:* Barbara Conrad; *c:* Matthew, Nicole, Natalie; *ed:* (BA) Elem Ed, S UT St 1976; (MS) Curr Dev, Univ of UT 1984; *cr:* Teacher Terra Linda Elem 1976-84, Columbia Elem 1984-; *ai:* Head of Stu Cncl & Intramural Prgm; Choir Dir; Extended Contract Teacher; Part-Time Cntry Music Entertainer & Songwriter; *home:* 2350 Providence Cir South Jordan UT 84065

HANSEN, CAROL ANN, Art Supervisor/Art Teacher; *b:* Sioux Falls, SD; *ed:* Cottey Jr Coll 1953; (BA) Ed/Nursery Sch/Kndgtn/Primary 1955, (BA) Art Ed, 1962 Univ of MN; (MA) Teaching, Augustana Coll 1974; Univ of SD & SD St Univ 1980; *cr:* Kndgtn Teacher Mound MN 1955-62; Art Teacher 1962-77, Art Teacher/Supvr 1977- Sioux Falls SD; *ai:* Delta Kappa Gamma 1969-; Phi Delta Kappa 1979-; ASCD 1982-; SD Art Assn (Pres, VP) 1963-; SD Ed ASSN 1962-; NEA 1955-; Sioux Falls Ed Assn 1962-; NAEA; ASCD; Sioux Falls Civic Art Center; SD Arts Cncl; PEO Sisterhood; St Art Ed Assn Pres 1964-68; Conduct Big Apple Wkshp for Public Sch Staff Dev Office; Adult Ed Drawing & Painting Instr; Initiated Teaching Art Classes at Primary Level by Art Specialists 1979; Started Kndgtn Art Classes 1981; Participant in Conference Curr Instruction Dev in Art Ed 1966-67; SD Art Ed of Yr 1989; Annie D Talent Club 1980; George Washington Medal Valley Forge Fnd for Teaching Patriotism 1970; *home:* 2913 E 12th St Sioux Falls SD 57103

HANSEN, CAROLYN PARKERSON, Gifted Social Studies Teacher; *b:* Eastman, GA; *m:* James M.; *c:* Paul, Jon; *ed:* (BS) Elem Ed, Tift Coll 1961; (MED) Mid Sch, Univ of GA 1980; *cr:* 5th Grade Teacher Schaffner Elem 1961-62; 6th Grade Teacher Somerville Rd Elem 1962-65; Lang Art Teacher 1974-84, Gifted Teacher 1984- Oconee Intermediate; *ai:* Prof Assn GA Educators; OUS PTO VP 1987-88; NCSS; Holy Cross Luth Church; Teacher of Yr Oconee Intermediate, Cty 1989; *office:* Oconee Intermediate Sch Colham Ferry Rd Watkinsville GA 30677

HANSEN, DARREL CHANCY, Earth Sci/Geography Teacher; *b:* Lewisville, ID; *m:* Lisa Young Mc Carrey; *c:* Julie Hansen Taylor, Steven R., Eric D., Wayne K.; *ed:* (MS) Geography, Brigham Young Univ 1971; Geography, CO Univ 1971-72; Teaching Cert, Brigham Young Univ 1972-73; USAF Pilot Trng 1955-56, Aircraft Maintenance Officer Course; Grad Stud Brigham Young Univ, CO Univ 1971-73; *cr:* Pilot/Aircraft Maintenance Officer 1955-66, Civil Service 1966-70 USAF; Teacher Shelley Jr HS 1973-; *ai:* Re-Cert Classes; NEA, IEA, SEA Pres 1975-76; Sigma Gamma Upsilon Mem 1954; Gamma Theta Upsilon Mem 1971; Reserve Officers Assn Pres ID Dept 1980; USAF Acad LO SE ID Region 1980-86, Meritorius SM 1983; USAFR Mobilization Designee 1978-83, Region X Outstanding Mobilization Designee; BSA (Scoutmaster, Comm Chm); Teaching Associateships BYU & CO; Whos Who in West Editions 15-22; *office:* Donald J Hobbs Jr HS 350 E Pine Shelley ID 83274

HANSEN, DOROTHY ELIZABETH, English Teacher; *b:* Silt, CO; *ed:* (AA) Speech/Drama, Mesa Jr Coll 1954; (BA) Speech/Drama, 1957, (MA) Speech/Drama, 1960 Univ of N CO; Post Grad Stud Univ of N CO, Univ of WY, Western St Coll; *cr:* Teacher Padroni Public Sch 1957-78, Telluride Public Sch 1958-60, Newcastle 1961-62, Hayden Public Schls 1962-65, Battle Mtn HS 1962-65; Teacher/Dept Chairperson Treasure Valley Comm Coll 1968-75; Teacher Delta Mid Sch 1975-; *ai:* Delta Cty Schls Policy Comm; Delta Psi Omega 1969-; CO Speech Assn 1960-; CO Eng Assn 1976-89; Drug Free CO, Drug Free Delta 1988-; Delta Mid Sch Yrbk Dedication Supporting Actress Treas Valley Comm Coll 1970; *home:* 620 Sloan Delta CO 81416

HANSEN, EDWARD WILLIAM, 7th-8th Grade Science Teacher; *b:* Deer Lodge, MT; *m:* Ruth M. Kunda Hansen; *ed:* (BA) Ed, Pacific Luth Univ 1973; Ed Curr, Eastern MT Coll; Ed Sci, MT St Univ; *cr:* K-8th Grade Teacher Yaak Elem 1973-74; 4th-6th Grade Teacher Sumner WA 1974-79; Jr HS Sub-Teacher Libby MT 1981-82; Elem/Jr HS Teacher Wibaux MT 1982-; *ai:* Sci Comm; Soc Stud Comm; Sci Fair Coord; Coach Jr HS Ftbl-Bsktbl & Track; Wibaux Ed Negotiator 1989-; MT Ed Assn 1982-; NEA 1982-; 1985 Env Ed Awd; US Dept of Ag Assn Supv & Curr Dev 1989; *home:* PO Box 112 Wibaux MT 59353

HANSEN, HELEN STEFURA, 7th Grade Dev Lang/Reading; *b:* Elizabeth, NJ; *m:* Robert V.; *c:* Nadine Clanirocca, Cynthia Peed; *ed:* (BA) Elem Ed, Newark St Coll 972; (MA) Rdng Specialist Kean Coll 1978; Supervisory Cert 1980; *cr:* 2nd/4th Grade Teacher St Cecelia S Parochial 1969-72; Title I Teacher 1972-76; 6th Grade Teacher 1976-81; 7th Grade Rdng 1981-Woodbride Twp Sch Dist; *ai:* Site Base Mgmt Comm Iselin Mid Sch; Woodbridge Twp Teachers Assn Corresp Sec 1984-87; NJ Governors Teacher Recognition 1989-; *office:* Iselin Mid Sch Woodruff St Iselin NJ 08830

HANSEN, JUDITH C., Sixth Grade Teacher; *b:* Mount Vernon, NY; *m:* Richard E.; *ed:* (BS) Elem Ed, St Univ Oneonta 1969; (MS) Ed, Western CT 1973; *cr:* 6th Grade Teacher Mahopac Cntrl Sch Dist 1969-; *ai:* Jr Var Field Hockey Coach; Jr HS Field Hockey Intramurals; *office:* Mahopac Jr H S Baldwin Pl Rd Mahopac NY 10541

HANSEN, JUNE BLANK, First Grade Teacher; *b:* Rosalia, WA; *m:* Don; *c:* Gary, Wendy Hansen Nist, Sheri Hansen Schell; *ed:* (BA) Elem Ed, E WA Coll 1943; Elem Ed; *cr:* Teacher Oakesdale Sch 1943, 1972-; *ai:* Delta Kappa Gamma; Eastern Star; *home:* Box 215 Oakesdale WA 99158

HANSEN, KATHLEEN BLACK, Mathematics Teacher; *b:* Utica, NY; *w:* Stephen D. (dec); *ed:* (BS) Math/Ed, Oswego St 1983; *cr:* 7th/8th Grade Math Teacher St John Villa Acad 1983-84; 9th-12th Grade Math Teacher Wayne Hills HS 1984-; *ai:* Asst Track Coach; Cheerleading Adv; *office:* Wayne Hills HS 272 Crest Lake Dr Wayne NJ 07470

HANSEN, SANDRA LOUISE, Sixth Grade Teacher; *b:* Hoquiam, WA; *ed:* (BS) Soc Stud, Grays Harbor Jr Coll 1970; (BS) Elem Ed, Cntrl WA St Coll 1970; Rdng/Lang/Soc Stud; 5th Yr Cntrl WA St Coll; Further Stud E WA St Coll; *cr:* 6th/7th Grade Teacher Park Mid Sch 1970-; *ai:* Academic Coach; Anchor Teacher; Mid Sch, Rdng, Park Mid Sch Self-Study Comm; Young Authors Coord; Drama Dir; Annual Adv; Kennewick Ed Assn Secy 1973-76; SISU Secy 1984-86; Delta Kappa Gamma 1978-81;

Veterans of Foreign Wars Teacher of Yr 1988; SEEK Awd 1982; *office:* Park Mid Sch 1011 W 10th Ave Kennewick WA 99336

HANSEN, STEVE GORDON, Third Grade Teacher; *b:* Fallon, NV; *c:* Dale T., Trisha D.; *ed:* (BA) Phys Ed, 1968, Elem Ed, 1978 Univ of NV Reno; *cr:* 7th-12th Grade Phys Ed/Soc Stud Teacher Amer Sch of Aberdeen Scotland 1976-77; 3rd Grade Teacher West End Sch 1978-; *office:* West End Sch 280 S Russell St Fallon NV 89406

HANSEN, THORVAL A., 4th Grade Teacher; *b:* Grand Rapids, MI; *m:* Jacqueline A. De Graaf; *c:* Peggi De Graff, Kerri Pattison, Kristi; *ed:* (BA) Eng, Hope Coll 1960; (MA) Elem Admin, W MI Univ 1970; Educl Courses; *cr:* Teacher Rockford Public Schls 1960-61, Godfrey-Lee Public Schls 1961-65; Prin Jenison Public Schls 1967-70; Teacher Jenison Public Schls 1965-; *ai:* Jenison Public Schls Outdoor Ed Prgm; NEA 1970-; MEA 1960-; MI Assn Environment Outdoor Ed 1980-; Project Lakewell Bd of Dirs 1988-; *office:* Bauerwood Elem Sch 1443 Bauer Rd Jenison MI 49428

HANSFORD, JEANNIE MARIE (DILLINGHAM), Substitute Teacher; *b:* Nashville, TN; *m:* Fred Leonard; *ed:* (BS) Elem, Mid TN St Univ 1980; (MS) Elem Curr/Instruction, Univ of TN Martin 1987; *cr:* 6th Grade Teacher Fort Campbell Mid Sch 1982-85; Teaching Asst Univ of TN Martin 1985-87; Substitute Teacher/Home Instr E Clinton Schls 1989-; Substitute Teacher Hickman Cty Mid Sch 1990; *ai:* Kappa Delta Phi 1987; Gamma Beta Phi 1978-80; Articles Published; *home:* Rt 1 Box 122 Duck River TN 38454

HANSKE, ROBERT WILLIAM, JR., Eng Teacher/Coord Gifted Prgms; *b:* Chicago, IL; *m:* Peggy Charlene Mc Intire; *ed:* (BA) Eng, 1972-73, (MS) Ed, 1981 W IL Univ; *cr:* Eng Teacher 1973-, Gifted & Talented Coord United Township HS 1987-; *ai:* Spring Play, Fall Play, Musical Dir; Poetry Club Spon; Home Ftbl & Bsktbl Games Field & Floor Announcer; Church World Services Crop Walk Organizer 1987-; Educl Service Center 8 IL; Rdng & Lang Art Task Force Chm 1987, 1988; Educl Consultant; *office:* United Township HS 1275 42nd Ave East Moline IL 61244

HANSMANN, PATRICIA J., Vocal Music Instructor; *b:* Belleville, KS; *c:* Tony, Tonya; *ed:* (BMED) Music Ed, Marymount of Salina 1970; (MS) Ed, KS Univ 1983; Grad Stud WSU, Emporia St Univ, Ft Hays Univ; *cr:* Vocal Music Instr Solomon Unified Sch Dist #393 1970-; *ai:* Extra Curricular Music Act; KMEA, MENC 1970-; KNEA 1970-86; Ec Ed Awd; 20 Yr Service Awd.

HANSON, DONALD CHRISTIAN, Mathematics Teacher; *b:* Sherwood, ND; *m:* Joan Ann Beckedahl; *c:* Kerry Grochow, Perry, Sherry, Merry; *ed:* (BS) Phys Ed/Math, Minot St 1964; Masters Work at ND St & Univ of ND; *cr:* Teacher New Salem HS 1964-67, Mandan HS 1967-; *ai:* Head Boys Bsktbl Coach at New Salem & Mandan; ND Ed Assn 1964-; NEA, ND Math Teachers 1967-; ND Coaches Assn 1964-, Coach of Yr 1981; 1st Luth Church Cncl 1988-; Elks 1967-; Eagles 1989-; ND Officials Assn 1962-88; Natl Sci Fnd Grant; Write ND Boys Bsktbl Preview; Jaycees Phys Ed Awd; *office:* Mandan Sr HS 905 8 Ave NW Mandan ND 58554

HANSON, EDWARD ALLAN, Aerospace Science Instructor; *b:* Coulee Dam, WA; *m:* Ellen Jeannette Owings; *c:* Lisa E. Hanson Lee; *ed:* (BS) Phys Sci, WA St Coll 1958; (MS) Poly Sci, Auburn Univ 1970; Squadron Officers Sch, Air Command & Staff Coll, Industrial Coll of Arm Forces; *cr:* Flight Trng Instr/Pilot/TACRECON Pilot/Fighter Interceptor/Air Operations Officer USAF; *ai:* Hunter Ed Instr St of TX; Daedalians Provost Marshall 1971-; Air Force Assn 1960-; Amer Rifle Assn 1959-; TX St Rifle Assn 1980-; TX Assn of Aerospace Teachers 1983-; Assn of TX Prof Educators 1983-; Rotary (Secy, Treas) 1978-88; VFW 1983-; Silver Star, Distinguished Flying Cross, Meritious Service & Air Medal, Pres Unit Citation, Air Force Commendation & Outstanding Unit Awd with Large V Device; Natl Defense Service & Vietnam Service Medal; Air Force Overseas Short & Long Tour, Longevity Service Awd, Small Arms Expert Marksmanship, Air Force Trng Ribbons; The RVN Gallantry with Palm Republic Vietnam Campaigne Medal; *home:* 408 Enchanted Way Del Rio TX 78840

HANSON, HERBERT HAROLD, Social Studies Chair; *b:* Minneapolis, MN; *m:* Ivanette M. Callies; *c:* Darrick, Calisa; *ed:* (BS) Soc Stud, Bemidji St Univ 1963; Grad Stud Bemidji St Univ & Univ MN Duluth; *cr:* Soc Stud Teacher Mass HS 1963-66, Lincoln Jr HS 1966-; *ai:* Boys B Squad Bsktbl Coach; 10th-12th Grade Class Adv; NEA Life Mem; Elks, Hibbing Curling Club; Natl Rifle Assn Life Mem.

HANSON, JERROLD S., History Teacher; *b:* Eau Claire, WI; *m:* Mary S.; *c:* Jaime, Laura, Justin; *ed:* (BA) His/Poly Sci, Univ of WI 1968; (MA) Curr/Instruction, Univ of WI Madison 1969; Grad Stud Univ of WI Whitewater, Univ of WI Milwaukee, FL St Univ; *cr:* Intern Teacher Kaukauna HS 1968; Teacher Kosciuszko Mid Sch 1969-82; Resource Teacher Cntrl Office MPS 1983-84; Teacher Bell Mid Sch 1984-; *ai:* Debate & Forensics Coach; Williamsburg/Washington DC Sch Trips Group Leader; Milwaukee Teachers Ed Assn Building Rep 1985-; WI Debate & Forensics Coaches Assn 1985-; WI Cncl for Soc Stud 1980-; WI Cncl for Gifted & Talented 1989-; Hosted Japanese Educator in Sch & Family Setting; Host Sch for St Level Forensics Tournament; Chairperson US His Text Selection Comm; *office:* Bell Mid Sch 6506 W Warnimont Ave Milwaukee WI 53220

HANSON, KATHLEEN ANN, Mathematics Teacher; *b:* Berkeley, CA; *ed:* (BA) Math, Univ of CA Santa Barbara 1974; (MA) Scndry Sch Admin, Univ of N CO Greeley 1989; *cr:* Math Teacher John Evans Jr HS 1978-87, Greeley Cntrl HS 1987-; *ai:* Stu Referral Team; Bsktbl & Swimming Scorekeeper; Schlsp & Revision of Math Objectives Comm; Kappa Delta Pi 1976-; CCTM, NCTM 1989-; GEA, CEA, NEA 1978-; Star Venture Grant; *office:* Greeley Cntrl HS 1515 14th Ave Greeley CO 80631

HANSON, LINDA HOPPE, First Grade Teacher; *b:* Riverdale, ND; *m:* Kenneth J.; *c:* Teio, Tomi L.; *ed:* (BS) Ed, Minot St Univ 1973; *cr:* Kndgtn Teacher S Prairie Elem 1973; 1st Grade Teacher Dakota Elem 1973-75, Bel Air Elem 1975-; *ai:* ND Ed Assn, ND Rdng Assn, Delta Kappa Gamma.

HANSON, MARY LOU CALDWELL, Second Grade Teacher; *b:* Chandler, OK; *m:* Robert H.; *c:* Jim L.; *cr:* 1st Grade Teacher Kingfisher Public Schls 1951-52; 1st Grade Teacher 1952-85, 3rd Grade Teacher 1959-61, 2nd Grade Teacher 1961- Guthrie Public Schls; *ai:* OEA, NEA 1951-; GACT 1990; *home:* Rt 4 Box 394 A Guthrie OK 73044

HANSON, PEG VANGSNES, Choral Director; *b:* Rugby, ND; *m:* Tom; *ed:* (BS) Vocal Music, Univ of ND 1972; Grad Stud Music Ed, Choral Conducting, Various Colls & Univs; *cr:* Vocal Music Teacher Crosby-Ironton Schls 1972-74; Choral Dir Sage Valley Jr HS 1974-; *ai:* Musical & Show Choirs Dir; WY Music Educators Scndry VP 1987-; Amer Choral Dirs Assn; WY Music Educators Scndry VP 1987-; *office:* Sage Valley Jr HS 1000 Lakeway Rd Gillette WY 82716

HANSON, POLLY SUE, Physical Science Dept Chair; *b:* Merrill, WI; *ed:* (BA) Natural Sci, Coll of St Scholastica 1987; Environmental Research, WI Valley Improvement Company; *cr:* Scndry Ed/Physical Sci Teacher Green Lake HS & Jr HS 1987-; *ai:* Cheerleading, Asst Sftbl, Soph Class, Prom, Ski Club Adv; Sci Olympiad Co-Coach; WEAC, GLEA, NEA; GSA Leader 1989-; Aoda Jr HS Coord 1988-; *home:* 716 Central St Oshkosh WI 54901

HANSON, RANDALL JON, Coord of Gifted & Talented; *b:* Appleton, WI; *m:* Charlotte Ann Arseneau; *c:* Jason J.; *ed:* (BS) Ed/Eng, Univ of WI Madison 1971; Gifted & Talented Ed; Great Books Discussion Leader; Teacher Effectiveness Trng; *cr:* Teacher St Johns Elem Sch 1971-75; Teacher/Coord Menasha Public Schls 1975-; *ai:* Employee Asst Prgm; Rdng Assessment, Effective Schls Advisory, Environmental Ed, High Risk Stu, Wellness, Gifted & Talented Advisory, Natl Jr Honor Society Faculty, Battle of Books Comm; Odyssey of the Mind Coach; Paper Arts Festival & Fox Valley Writing Project Advisory Comm; Academic Orientation Comm; NCTE, WI Cncl Teachers of Eng, WI Assn of Ed for Gifted & Talented; Mid Sch Teacher of Yr 1985; Traveled to Washington DC to Accept US Dept of Ed Scndry Sch Awd 1986-87; Published Author & Co-Author; Articles Published; *office:* Butte Des Morts Jr HS 501 Tayco St Menasha WI 54952

HANSON, SHIRLEY JEAN, Music Teacher; *b:* Hibbing, MN; *m:* Tyrone; *c:* Michael, Kara, Taryn; *ed:* (BS) Music, Bemidji St Univ 1972; Post Graduate Work Music Performance & Music Ed; *cr:* Vocal Music Teacher Greenbush Public Schls 1972-77, Barrett Public Schls 1979-83, Starbuck Public Schls 1984-; *ai:* All Vocal Music Act; Swing Choir; MN Music Educators Assn 1972-; MN Educators Assn 1972-; MN Elem Music Educators Dist Rep 1987-89; MN 4-H Leader 1989-; Church Organist 1972-; *office:* Starbuck Public Schls 500 John St Starbuck MN 56381

HANSON, TONI DRACOS, English Teacher; *b:* Ft Walton Beach, FL; *m:* Doug; *ed:* (BA) Eng/Poly Sci - Summa Cum Laude, FL St Univ 1985; *cr:* Eng Teacher Clay HS 1985-; *ai:* Yrbk Adv; Photography Club Spon; Southern Assn of Colls & Schls Chm; Clay HS Self Study 10 Yr Accreditation Review; NCTE, Clay Cty Rdng Cncl; Clay HS Teacher of Yr 1990; Chamber of Commerce Spotlight Teacher of Month 1989; Supts Excl Awd 1988; *office:* Clay HS 2025 Hwy 16 W Green Cove Springs FL 32043

HANSSEN, RUTH M., Retired Teacher; *b:* Bridgewater, SD; *m:* Harry; *c:* Brenda Gulbranson, Darwin, Cindy Speck; *ed:* (BSED) Elem Ed, Dakota Wesleyan 1971; Refresher Courses 1976, 1981; *cr:* Teacher Mc Cook & Hanson Cty Rural Schls 1943-67, Emery Elem Sch 1967-86; Substitute Teacher/Aide Emery Public Sch 1986-; *ai:* PTO Pres 1975-76; *home:* Box 262 Emery SD 57332

HANZELON, LEE RUTH PETERSON, 5th Grade Teacher; *b:* Chicago, IL; *m:* Robert J.; *ed:* (BS) Elem Educ, Northern IL Univ 1963; (MS) Elem Counseling, IA St Univ; *cr:* 4th Grade Teacher Eisenhower 1963-64; Kndgtn Teacher Army Base Hochst Germany 1964-65; 7th/8th Grade Teacher Mc Kinley 1965-66; 6th Grade Teacher South 1966-68;Hillside 1968-71; Stilwell 1971-73; 5th Grade Teacher Fairmeadows 1973-; *ai:* Sci Chairperson Elem Bldg; Staff Dev Instr; St Comm Elem/Scndry Cert Advisory Comm; Delta Kappa Gamma Recording Secy 1984-; NEA 1963-; IA West Des Moines Ed Assn 1973-; IA Acad Sci 1988-; Hospice Vol 1980-; West Des Moines Jaycees Outstanding Young Educator 1973; IA Teacher Yr 2nd Runner Up 1984-85; *home:* 210 E Ridge Dr West Des Moines IA 50265

HAPER, KATHRYN ANN, First Grade Teacher; *b:* Seymour, IN; *m:* Jerry; *c:* Timothy; *ed:* (BS) Ed, Ball St 1968; (MS) Ed, IN Univ 1972; *ai:* Psi Iota Xi Pres 1980; *office:* Margaret R Brown Sch 550 Miller Ln Seymour IN 47274

HARA, MONITA G., Teacher of Hearing Impaired; *b:* Memphis, TN; *m:* Raymond L.; *c:* Emily J.; *ed:* (BS) Elem Ed, Univ of AL Birmingham 1978; (MA) Deaf Ed, Univ of AL Tuscaloosa 1979; (MS) Educl Admin, CA St Univ Northridge 1988; Amer Sign Lang, Signing Exact Eng; *cr:* Outreach Teacher for Deaf/Blind Children Univ of AL Tuscaloosa 1978-79; Parent Cnslr Chauncey Sparks Dev Center 1979; Tutor CA St Univ Northridge 1988; Hearing Impaired Stus Teacher Hewitt-Trussville HS 1980-; *ai:* Spon Stu Organization for Deaf Awareness; AL A G Bell Assn Membership Chairperson 1987-89; Greater Birmingham RID Pres 1985-87; Cncl of Organizations Serving Deaf Alabamians, Convention of Amer Instr of Deaf, Natl A G Bell Assn; CA St Univ Northridge Fellowship Educl Admin; *home:* 43 Moonglow Dr Birmingham AL 35215

HARALSON, LAURA JORDAN, Science Dept Chair/Teacher; *b:* Johnson AFB, Japan; *m:* Kevin J.; *ed:* (BS) Ed/Bio, TX Tech Univ 1982; *cr:* Honors Life Sci Teacher J T Hutchinson Jr HS 1982-83; Sci Dept Chairperson/Teacher Nocona HS 1984-; *ai:* NHS, UIL Sci Team, Soph Class Spon; ATPE 1984-; *office:* Nocona HS P O Box 210 Nocona TX 76255

HARASIKA, ELENA LOPATKA, 6th Grade Gifted Teacher; *b:* Wilmington, DE; *m:* Michael Jr.; *c:* Michael III, Teresa L., Kimberly A. Gentry; *ed:* (BSED) Math, Univ of DE 1965; Grad Courses Gifted Ed, Cmptrs; *cr:* 6th Grade Teacher Darley Rd Sch 1965-68; Gifted Resource Teacher Claymont Sch Dist 1976-78; 4th-6th Grade Gifted Teacher New Castle Cty Dist 1978-79; 1st-3rd Grade Gifted Teacher 1979-80, 6th Grade Self Contained Gifted Teacher 1980- Brandywine Sch Dist; *ai:* St Wide Math & Dist Soc Stud Comm; NEA, DSEA; Statewide Advisory Cncl for Gifted 1989-; Taught Consulting Bus; DE Cncl Ec Ed Awds; Wrote Article Univ of DE Newspaper; *office:* Harlan Elem Sch 36th & Jefferson Sts Wilmington DE 19802

HARAUGHTY, CANDY GONZALEZ, Sixth Grade Lang Art Teacher; *b:* Mayaguez, PR; *m:* Roger Wayne; *c:* Christian, Heather; *ed:* (BSED) Span, OK Univ 1971; (MSED) Rdng, Cntrl St Univ 1976; *cr:* Teacher Webster Mid Sch 1971-; *ai:* Team Leader; Faculty Advisory Comm Chairperson; NEA, OK Ed Assn; St James Cath Church Woman of Yr 1989; St James Bd of Chrstn Ed Secy 1988-; *office:* Webster Mid Sch 6708 S Santa Fe Oklahoma City OK 73119

HARBAUGH, LOIS JENSEN, Science Department Chair; *b:* Elmhurst, IL; *m:* L. W. Jr.; *c:* Michelle, Bill; *ed:* (BA) Psych, Wheaton Coll 1964; (MAT) Sci Ed, Univ of TX Dallas 1978; *cr:* Teacher Troy Mills Cons Sch 1965-66, Richardson Jr HS 1969-71; Sci Chairperson/Teacher First Baptist Acad 1975-81, Lake Highlands Jr HS 1981-; *ai:* Sci Fair Hall Duty; Natl Sci Supvrs Assn Secy 1987-; NSTA 1978-; Assn of TX Prof Educators 1979-; Sci Teachers Assn of TX; TX Earth Sci Teachers Assn; Crisis Pregnancy Center Bd Mem 1982-88; Christa Mc Auliffe Fellowship Dept of Ed 1988; NSF Inst NRAO Greenbank 1988; NEWMAST Kennedy Space Center 1989; TX St Textbook Comm Scndry Sci 1990; RISE Fnd Grant 1988; *office:* Lake Highlands Jr HS 10301 Kingsley Rd Dallas TX 75238

HARBERTS, WILLIAM, Science Dept/Biology Teacher; *b:* Oakland, CA; *ed:* (BS) Entomology, Univ of CA Davis 1968; (MS) Genetics, 1974, (PHD) Entomology, 1983 WA St Univ; *cr:* Teacher Crenshaw HS 1985-; *ai:* Calendar Comm; Curr Cncl; *office:* Crenshaw HS 5010 11th Ave Los Angeles CA 90043

HARCAR, RAYMOND ANDREW, Instrumental Music Teacher; *b:* Cleveland, OH; *m:* Janis Lee Blinkie; *c:* Kristen, Joel; *ed:* (BS) Music Ed, 1968, (MMED) Music Ed, 1971 Kent St; *cr:* Band Dir Perry Local 1969-71, Field Local 1971-72, Waterloo Local 1972-; *ai:* Stage Band; Majorettes; Flag Corps; Concert & Marching Band; Privatge Instr Kent City Schls; Waterloo Ed Assn (Treas 1981-86, 1988-); Music Educators Natl Conference, OH Music Educators Assn; Consistent I Ratings District Band Contest; *office:* Waterloo Local Schls 1464 Industry Rd Atwater OH 44201

HARCROW, DORTHA (STONE), Jr HS Science Teacher; *b:* Buffalo, TX; *m:* C. O.; *c:* Tanya Wright, Justin Roach; *ed:* (BS) Phys Ed/Health/Sci, 1956, Elem Ed, 1966 Sam Houston Univ; Advanced Academic Trng Sci 1988-; *cr:* Jr HS Teacher Wichita Falls Ind Sch Dist 1956-57, Schulenburg Ind Sch Dist 1957-58, Oakwood Ind Sch Dist 1962-63, Buffalo Ind Sch Dist 1964-; *ai:* UIL Sci & Sci Fair Coach; TSTA, NEA 1965-; Career Ladder; Leon Cty Retired Teachers Spec Recognition Sci Teacher Awd; *home:* Rt 2 Box 5 Buffalo TX 75831

HARD, JODY PLOTNER, 4th-5th Grade Teacher; *b:* Indianapolis, IN; *m:* Loren M.; *c:* Kelly Jo; *ed:* (BA) Elem Ed, 1971, (MED) Elem Ed, 1973 Ball St Univ; Butler Univ; *cr:* 3rd Grade Teacher 1971-73, 1st Grade Teacher 1973-74, 4th Grade Teacher 1974-82 Delaware Trail Elem; 4th-5th Grade Teacher Greenbriar Elem Sch 1982-; *ai:* Unit Leader; Soc Comm Chm 14 Yrs 1989; Historian 2 Yrs; Prgm Improvement Comm Rep 1989-; Largest Grant Washington Township Thematically Integrated Play 1989; Thank A Teacher Awards 1988-; *office:* Greenbriar Elem Sch 8201 Ditch Rd Indianapolis IN 46260

HARD, SUSAN SCHOTT, Math & Computer Sci Teacher; *b:* Chicago, IL; *m:* Peter Jason; *c:* Janine, Kathleen, Colleen; *ed:* (BA) Math, William Paterson Coll 1972; Basic, Pascal, Advanced Data Structures; *cr:* Math Teacher Westwood Regional HS 1972-74, 1977-78, 1979-80; Math & Cmptr Sci Teacher Pascack Valley HS 1981-; *ai:* Cmptr Articulation Comm; Prof Dev Fund Sorting Procedures in Cmptr Sci; *office:* Pascack Valley HS Piermont Ave Hillsdale NJ 07642

HARDEN, BETTIE M., Counselor; *b:* Atlanta, GA; *m:* Julius; *c:* Bertran, Jumill; *ed:* (BS) Morris Brown Coll 1960; (MA) Ed/ Psych, NY Univ 1963; Certificate Counseling, Atlanta Univ 1968; GA St Univ, Univ of GA, W GA Coll; *cr:* Spec Ed Teacher Lena Campell 1960-66; Teacher Coan Mid Sch 1968-71; Elem Cnslr Ed S Cook 1971-74; Cnslr Fulton HS 1974-78; Mid Sch Cnslr C W Long 1978-; *ai:* Natl Jr Beta Club, Wellness Club March of Dimes Spon; Tennis Club; Youth NAACP Adv; AFT GA Sch Cnslrs Soc 1988-89; Natl Cncl of Negro Women; AKA Chairperson, Plaque 1987-; Amer Bridge Assn Scholarship Fund; United Presbyn Women Mem; Alliance Theatre Volunteer; GSA; YWCA Adv; *office:* Crawford W Long Mid Sch 3200 Latona Dr SW Atlanta GA 30354

HARDEN, KAREN ENTSMINGER, English Dept Chair/ Teacher; *b:* Covington, VA; *m:* Franklin D.; *c:* John, Steven, Jami, Amity; *ed:* (BA) Eng, NC St Univ 1974; (AA) Journalism, Jefferson St 1981; *cr:* Teacher S Chrstn Acad 1975-77, E Cary Jr HS 1977, Luray HS 1982-, Jostens Publishers Summer Wkshps 1989-; Scholastic Yrbk Judge Columbia Scholastic Press Assn 1989-; Ged Instr Page Cty Schls Associated Services 1989-; *ai:* MORP; VFW Speech Contest; Creative Writing Spon; Yrbk; Literary Magazine; Folklore Booklet; Page Cty Ed Assn 1982-, Distinguished Educator in Scndry Hum 1989; VA HS League 1986-; Scholastic Publications Advisory Comm; Luray HS Stu Cncl Best All Around Teacher 1989; Shenandoah Valley Folklore Society Teacher of Yr 1985; *office:* Luray HS 14 Luray Ave Luray VA 22835

HARDEN, M. JEAN, 6th Grade Teacher; *b:* Almeria, NE; *m:* Lyle Charles; *c:* Cindee Glidden, Jennifer, Randy; *ed:* (BA) Elem Ed, 1972, Elem Ed, 1979 Kearney St Coll; *cr:* Kndgtn Teacher Liberty Dist #7 1950-52; K-8th Grade Teacher West End #12 1953-54, Liberty Dist #7 1969-72; 4th-6th Grade Teacher Loup Cty Public Sch 1972-; *ai:* NSEA (Comm Chm 1985-, Sandhills Dist Pres Elect 1990); Loup Cty Promotion Assn, Historical Society, Clever Clique Ladies Club, NE Quilters Guild Mem; Taylor United Meth (Organist, Treas) 1970-; Alpha Delta Kappa (St Chaplain 1984-86, Pres 1985-86, St Pres Elect 1990, St Recording Secy 1986-88); Mid NE Literacy & St Arboretum Awds; *home:* HCR 66 Box 27 Taylor NE 68879

HARDEN, MARTHA ROSS, History Teacher/Senior Sponsor; *b:* Troy, AL; *m:* Glenn P.; *c:* Jabe, Jennifer; *ed:* (BS) His, 1979, (MS) His, 1989 Troy St Univ; *cr:* Sci Teacher 1979-87, His Teacher 1987- Pike Cty HS; *ai:* Sr Class & Citizen Bee Spon; Mount Zion Baptist Church; *office:* Pike Cty HS S Main St Brundidge AL 36010

HARDER, KENNETH J., Math Department Chairperson; *b:* Jackson, MS; *m:* Patricia C.; *c:* Page; *ed:* (BS) Math/Sci, MS St Univ 1961; Natl Sci Fnd Math Courses 1963 & 1965; *cr:* Math Teacher Pascagoula Jr HS 1962-65; Math Teacher 1965-88, Math Dept Chair 1988- Bay HS; *ai:* Cmptr Wrkshp for Teachers Instr; NCTM; Knights of Columbus; MS STAR Teacher 1969/1979 & 1983; Teacher of Yr 1985; US Patent for Algebra Bd Game 1982; Article in Math Teacher & IA Math Journal; *office:* Bay Sr H S 105 Blue Meadow Rd Bay Saint Louis MS 39520

HARDER, ROMY DEITCH, English Teacher; *b:* New York, NY; *m:* Patrick; *c:* Lee Felling, Kris Felling; *ed:* (BA) Elem Ed, Univ of AZ 1973; Eng 1987, Working on MA Eng Lit, N AZ Univ; *cr:* 2nd/5th Grade Teacher Holy Angels 1973-75; 5th Grade Teacher E Globe 1975-77; 7th/8th Grade Eng/Hum Teacher Globe Jr HS 1977-87; Eng Teacher Globe HS 1987-; *ai:* Class Spon; Globe Teachers Assn Secy 1990; USA Wrestling St Secy 1989-; Teacher of Yr 1986-87 Globe Sch Dist; *home:* 1011 E Skyline Globe AZ 85501

HARDERT, LINDA BLALOCK, Extended Learning Prgm Teacher; *b:* Quincy, IL; *m:* Ronald A.; *ed:* (BA) Elem Ed, AZ St Univ 1966; Grad Stud AZ St Univ 1966-75; Gifted Ed Seminars, Classes, Inservices, St & Natl Conferences; *cr:* 5th Grade Teacher Saguaro Sch 1966; 4th/5th Grade Teacher Edison Sch 1966-73; 5th Grade Teacher 1975-77, 3rd-6th Grade Extend Learning Prgm Teacher 1977- Booker T Washington Elem Sch; *ai:* NEA, AZ Ed Assn, Mesa Ed Assn 1966-; AZ Assn for Gifted & Talented, Natl Assn for Gifted Children 1975-; Math Prgm & Grad Study Sabbatical Leave Grants; St Gifted Conferences, AZ St Univ, Churches, Peace Organizations Presentations; Co-Edited Book; *office:* Booker T Washington Elem Sch 2260 W Isabella Mesa AZ 85202

HARDIMAN, MICHAEL KIRBY, 7th/8th Grade English Teacher; *b:* Birmingham, AL; *m:* Rhonda Gayle Dickey; *c:* Kevin, Brandi; *ed:* (BS) Ed/Phys Ed, St Bernard Coll 1972; (MS) Ed/ Phys Ed, Univ of AL Birmingham 1976; *cr:* Phys Ed Coach/ Teacher Spalding Sch 1972-73; Eng Teacher Warrior Mid Sch 1973-; *ai:* 4-H Spon; AFT, AL HS Athletic Assn 1973-; Summer League Bsbl Coach 1977-89; *home:* 932 Valley Ridge Rd Warrior AL 35180

HARDIN, BARBARA ANNE, Latin Teacher; *b:* Great Bend, KS; *m:* Charles T.; *ed:* (MED) Ed Admin/Supervision, Memphis St Univ 1985; *cr:* Fr/Span Teacher Park Hill Jr HS 1975-78; Fr/ Span Teacher/Foreign Lang Coord The Auburndale Sch 1980-85; Latin Teacher/Foreign Lang Dept Chairperson Germantown HS 1985-; *ai:* Germantown HS Jr Classical League, W TN Area Jr Classical League, Latin Honor Society Spon; Foreign Lang Dept Chm; Amer Classical League 1985-; TN Foreign Lang Teachers Assn 1979-; TN Classical Assn 1985-; Vergilian Society 1989-; Mc Kinlay Schlsp 1990; Nom Germantown HS Outstanding Teacher 1987-88; Presidential Scholars Prgm Outstanding Teacher 1988, 1990; Governors Acad 1989; *office:* Germantown HS 7653 Old Poplar Pike Germantown TN 38138

HARDIN, KATIE (FRAZER), Third Grade Teacher; *b:* Tioga, WV; *m:* Gary L.; *c:* Christy S.; *ed:* (BA) Elem Ed, Glenville St Coll 1965; (MA) Elem Ed, WV Univ 1972; *cr:* 5th/6th Grade Teacher Murphytown Elem 1965; 1st Grade Teacher Roosevelt Sch 1965-67; Kndgtn Teacher Pirmasens Amer Sch 1967-68; 4th Grade Teacher Roosevelt Elem 1968-70; 1st-3rd Grade Teacher Greenmont Elem 1970-; *ai:* Amer Assn of Univ Women (Pres 1989-91, 1st VP 1972-74, 1986-88, Chairperson 1986-88, St Wkshps, Natl Convention) 1972-89; Delta Kappa Gamma 1987-89. Sunshine Awd; Alpha Delta Kappa (Pres, VP, Historian, Chaplain) 1972-; NEA, WV Ed Assn 1965-89; Wood Cty Ed Assn (VP 1978-88, Chairperson, Faculty Rep) 1965-89; *home:* Valley Manor Dr Williamstown WV 26187

HARDIN, MARY LUE, Counselor; *b:* Limestone, AL; *ed:* (BA) Elem Ed/Bio, Morehead St Univ 1973; (MS) Ed, Univ of Louisville 1984; *cr:* Teacher Hazelwood Elem Sch 1973-75, Middletown Elem Sch 1975-81; Sci Teacher 1981-89, Counselor 1989- Thomas Jefferson Mid Sch; *ai:* Natl Mid Sch Assn Steering Comm; KY Mid Sch Assn 1986-; Highview Optimist Club Outstanding Teacher 1987; *office:* Thomas Jefferson Mid Sch 4401 Rangeland Rd Louisville KY 40219

HARDIN, SUSAN ROYCE, English Teacher; *b:* Ripon, WI; *m:* Elbert A.; *c:* Nathan, Kyle; *ed:* (BA) Eng, CO Coll 1979; Grad Stud Various Univs; *cr:* 7th-8th Grade Rdng/Eng Teacher Plains Mid Sch 1983-86; 9th-10th Grade Eng Teacher Caron City HS 1986-; *ai:* Speech & Debate Asst Coach; NCTE, CLAS, NEA; *office:* Canon City HS 1313 College Ave Canon City CO 81212

HARDING, DOROTHY HOLLELY, 4th-6th Grade Science Teacher; *b:* Brooklyn, NY; *m:* Donald F.; *c:* Barbara Andersen, Alyson Wallace; *ed:* (BA) Bio, Hofstra Univ 1959; Grad Stud Hofstra Univ, St Univ of NY Oneonta; *cr:* Bio/General Sci Teacher Union Free Sch 1959-64; Elem Teacher Sharon Springs Cntrl Sch 1975-; *ai:* Sharon Springs PTO Treas 1982-; CIMS Sci Project Dev & Revision Team 1982-89; *office:* Sharon Springs Cntrl Sch Rt 20 Box 218 Sharon Springs NY 13459

HARDING, EDWARD WAYNE, Mathematics Instructor; *b:* Clinton, IA; *m:* Nancy K. Phillip; *c:* Sara, Adam, Aaron; *ed:* Scndry Admin, Supervision, NW MO St Univ 1990; *cr:* Math Instr Glenwood Cmmty HS 1973-; *ai:* Past HS Golf Coach; NEA, Glenwood Ed Assn; *home:* 117 Hillcrest Glenwood IA 51534

HARDING, LLOYD EMERY, Chemistry, Physics Teacher; *b:* Chariton, IA; *m:* Constance; *c:* Martin L., Tori J.; *ed:* (BS) Physics, OK Univ 1964; (MS) Sci Ed, Emporia St Univ 1968; Numerous Seminars & Wrkshps; *cr:* Math/Sci Teacher 1964-69, Asst Prin 1967-68 Moscow KS; Math/Sci Dept Chm 1970-79; Dist Curr Cncl Chm 1973-74, Chem/Physics/PreCalc Teacher 1969-Independence KS; *ai:* Sci & Chess Club Spon; Organized Field Trips; NSTA 1975-; NEA Local Rep Natl Convention 1961-; Independence NEA (Pres 1976, Salary Chm 1974, Insurance Chm 1987, 1988, Building Rep 1988, 1989); Masonic Lodge (Master 1984, 1987, 1989, Ed Chm 1980-); Univ of KS HS Teacher Recognition Awd 1984.

HARDING, MARITA MOSEMAN, Fourth Grade Teacher; *b:* Springfield, OH; *m:* Charles E.; *c:* Jeffrey, Christopher; *ed:* (BS) Liberal Art, 1965, (MS) Zoology, 1967 Univ of TN; *cr:* Research Asst Oak Ridge Natl Lab 1968-70; Instr Bio Univ of TN Martin 1972-74; 4th Grade Teacher Kenton Sch 1974-; *ai:* Sci Textbook Adoption Comm 1986; Rdng Textbook Adoption Comm Chm 1989; Phi Kappa Phi 1974-; 1st Meth Church Admin Bd 1987-; TN Ed Assn Rep 1987-89; TEA Rep Assembly Delegate 1988; Career Ladder III Cert 1986-; *office:* Kenton Elem Sch College St Kenton TN 38233

HARDING, RICHARD G., JR., Sixth Grade Teacher; *b:* Greensboro, NC; *m:* Diane Ruth Maynard; *c:* Summer, Kristin, Haley; *ed:* (BS) Elem Ed, Auburn Univ 1974; (MS) Admin, Troy St Univ 1983; Master Cert Elem Ed, Troy St Univ; *cr:* 5th Grade Teacher 1974-75, Phys Ed Teacher 1975-80 Pine Street Elem; 5th Grade Teacher 1980-88, 6th Grade Teacher 1988- Pinedale Elem; *ai:* Schls & Cmptrs Articles Published; *office:* Pinedale Elem Sch Dothan Hwy Enterprise AL 36330

HARDISON, GRAY MAYNARD, 1st Grade Teacher; *b:* Raleigh, NC; *c:* Seth, Alison; *ed:* (BA) Early Chldhd Ed, Univ of NC Chapel Hill 1974; *cr:* Classroom Teacher Wake Cty Schls; *ai:* Grade Chairperson; Rdng Recovery Tutor; PALS Prgm Volunteer; NEA, Intnl Rdng Assn 1974-; Church (Adult Choir Mem 1975-89, Childrens Bible Drill Leader 1986-, Childrens Choir Dir 1985-); Outstanding Young Educator 1975; Nom Teacher of Yr 1989; Wake Cty Ed Fnd Creative Grants 1987-.

HARDMAN, LULA MAE, Social Studies Instructor; *b:* Big Fork, AR; *m:* Paul X.; *c:* Ann, Troy; *ed:* (BSE) Soc Stud, Henderson St Univ 1971; (MSE) Adult Ed, CMSU 1984; *cr:* Teacher Wood Jr HS 1971-84, Waynesville HS 1984-; *ai:* Phi Delta Kappa (Secy, Pres) 1977-; MCSS Awds Comm 1980-; NCSS 1984-; CTA, MSTA; Waynes Park Bd Secy, Planning & Zoning Comm Chm; Most Caring Teacher 1989; Nom MCSS Teacher of Yr 1990; *office:* Waynesville HS 1001 Bus 66 Waynesville MO 65583

HARDT, SANDRA KAY (RUDIE), Kindergarten Teacher; *b:* Madison, WI; *m:* Richard S.; *c:* Ryan, Karissa K.; *ed:* (BS) Elem Ed/Spec Ed, UW Oshkosh 1971; Addl Studies Early Chldhd Exceptional Ed Needs Univ WI; *cr:* Kndgtn Teacher Tullar Elem Sch 1971-; *ai:* Human Growth & Dev Adv Comm; Hlth Curr Comm; NEA 1971-; WI Ed Assn 1971-; Appleton Alliance Church Childrens Church Ldr 1988-89; American Red Cross Vlntr 1982-; Teacher of Yr Nom By Prin 1988; Kohl Teacher Fellowship Nom 1990; *home:* 1610 E Robin Way Appleton WI 54915

HARDWAY, ALAN WAYNE, Social Studies Teacher; *b:* Richwood, WV; *m:* Sharon Kay Watson; *ed:* (AB) Elem Ed, Fairmont St Coll 1976; (MA) Curr/Instruction, WV Univ 1983; *cr:* Teacher Terra Alta Elem, Ritchie Cty Schls; *ai:* Ritchie Cty Soc Stud Coord; Asst Ftbl Coach Pennsboro Mid Sch; Asst Bsktbl Coach Ritchie Cty HS; WV Comm St Soc Stud Learning Outcomes; WV Ed Assn, WV Cncl for Soc Stud; WV 4-H All-Stars; Phil M Conley Awd Outstanding Service to Golden Horseshoe Prgm 1987; *office:* Pennsboro Mid Sch 104 School Dr Pennsboro WV 26415

HARDWICK, DOROTHY CHANDLER, Third Grade Teacher; *b:* Pollock, LA; *c:* Keith, Lise, Gregg; *ed:* (BA) Elem Ed, Northwestern St Univ 1958; (MED) Counseling, LA Tech Univ 1980; Admin, Supervision LA Tech Univ 1986; *cr:* 4th Grade Teacher Calcasieu Parish Schls 1958-61; 1st-3rd Grade Teacher Bossier Parish Schls 1976-; *ai:* Grade Level Sr Teacher; Parish Research & Staff Dev Comm Sch Rep; Sch Building Level Comm; Project STAR Coord; Assn of Platt Teachers Pres 1985-86, Teacher of Yr 1985; Bossier Assn of Teachers, LA Assn of Teachers, Natl Assn of Teachers, NW LA Rdng Cncl 1984-; Natl Assn of Curr Admin 1989-; Alpha Delta Kappa 1982-; Gamma Beta Phi 1984-; Natl Mental Health Assn, NW LA Mental Health Assn 1986-; Whos Who in Amer Ed 1987-89; LA Project STAR Grant 1987-; *office:* Platt Elem Sch 4680 Hwy 80 E Haughton LA 71037

HARDWICK, MARIETTA CARTER, Fifth Grade Teacher; *b:* Valdosta, GA; *m:* Eugene; *ed:* (BS) Elem Ed, Savannah St Coll 1971; (MA) Ed, Armstrong Savannah St Joint Grad Prgm 1975; *cr:* 5th Grade Teacher Hahira Elem Sch 1971-72; 6th Grade Teacher Hinesville Elem Sch 1972-74; 5th Grade Teacher Carrie E Gould Elem Sch 1977-; *ai:* Asst Chairperson Steering Comm For S Assn of Colleges; Chatham Assn of Educators, GA Assn Of Educators, NEA 1977-; PTA 1971-, Life Certificate 1985; Lowndes Assn of Educators Delegate; Gould Staff Dev Rep; *office:* Carrie E Gould Elem Sch 4910 Pineland Dr Savannah GA 31405

HARDY, ADA HARRELL, 2nd Grade Teacher/Elem Prin; *b:* Jackson, MS; *m:* Henry Wilson Sr.; *c:* Mary Hardy Kelly, Henry W. Jr.; *ed:* (BA) Elem Ed, Belhaven Coll 1952; Rdng Methods, Theories & Methods, Assertive Discipline, Univ of MS; *cr:* 4th Grade Teacher Canton Public Schls 1952-58; Store Owner & Mgr Variety Shop 1963-64; 2nd Grade Teacher Mc Cluer Acad 1968-70, Tri Cty Acad 1975-; *ai:* Art Contest MPSEA; Christmas Project; Elem Spon for Child Abuse Posters; Duty Schedules for Elem Teachers; MS Private Sch Ed Assn 1975-; First Presbyn Church (Elem Teacher 1953, Sunday Sch Teacher 1955); Edgewood Presbyn Church (VP, Teacher of Womens Group 1970-71), Cntrl Presbyn Church (Women ofChurch, Sunday Sch Teacher) 1960-65; Heart Fund Dist Chm 1962-64; Service Awd for Betterment of TCA 1988; Teacher of Month Tri-Cty Acad 1986-87; *office:* Tri Cty Acad Box K Flora MS 39071

HARDY, BROOKE D., Fifth Grade Teacher; *b:* Brooklyn, NY; *m:* Alice Lorraine Lasewicz; *c:* Derek, Heather; *ed:* (BS) Elem Ed, in St Univ 1967; *cr:* Rdng Specialist 1967-69, 4th Grade Teacher 1969-76, 5th Grade Teacher 1976- Cozy Lake Sch; *ai:* Sch Safety Patrol Adv; Rocket Prgm Coord; Jeff Twsp Sci Comm Rep; Tech Adv Sch Prgm; Jefferson Township Ed Assn (VP 1980-84, Ed Assn Pres 194-86); Jefferson Arts Comm Mem 1987-; Jeff Highlights Tv Production Host 1984-; Annual Jeff Twsp Day Emcee 1986-; White Rock Lake Assn Pres 1989-; NJ Governors Teachers Recognition Awd 1987; Mayors Civic Awd 1987-88; *office:* Cozy Lake School Cozy Lake Rd Oak Ridge NJ 07438

HARDY, DEBRA ROSS, Science Department Chairperson; *b:* Roswell, NM; *c:* Lyndsey Lane, Lauren Marie; *ed:* (BM) Music Ed, Mars Hill Coll 1978; (MA) Ed, Western Carolina Univ 1987; Math & Sci; *cr:* Piano Teacher Home 1977-; Organist Various Denominations 1977-; Elem Music Teacher Mc Dowell Cty 1978; Chorus and Handbell Choir East Rutherford HS 1982; Math & Sci Teacher East Mc Dowell Jr HS 1985-; *ai:* Music Club Spon; Leadership Team Mem for Sch; Sci Dept Chairperson; Chrldng Coach for Jr Pro Bsktbl; Chrstn Womens Club 1987-88; Outstanding Sci Teacher 1988-89; Appointed Dept Chm 1988-; *home:* 908 Oak St Marion NC 28752

HARDY, JENA D., Reading Teacher; *b:* Bloomington, IL; *ed:* (BA) Elem Ed, Lamar Univ 1983; *cr:* Rdng Teacher Woodrow Wilson Mid Sch 1984-; *ai:* TX St Teachers Assn, NEA 1984-; Rdng Curr Guide, Daily Rdng Drills Port Arthur Ind Sch Dist; *office:* Woodrow Wilson Mid Sch 1500 Lakeshore Dr Port Acres TX 77640

HARDY, MARY CIVILS, 1st Grade Teacher; *b:* Kinston, NC; *m:* Kirby J. III; *c:* Kirby J. IV, Mary Kathryn; *ed:* (BS) Elem Ed, Atlantic Chrstn Coll 1972; *cr:* 1st Grade/3rd Grade Teacher Southeast Elem 1972-76; 1st Grade Teacher Teachers Mem Sch 1976-; *ai:* Mentor Teacher; Grade Chm; NCAE; Delta Kappa Gamma; *home:* Rt 10 Box 260 Kinston NC 28501

HARDY, NELWYN A., Home Economics Teacher; *b:* Houston, TX; *ed:* (BS) Home Ec, Sam Houston St Coll 1967; (MED) Home Ec, Sam Houston St Univ 1971; Enhancing Nutrition Ed, Impact Adolescent Chemical Dependency; *cr:* Home Ec Teacher Aldine Ind Sch Dist 1967-71, Lumberton Ind Sch Dist 1971-74; Adj Instr Lamar Univ 1976-79; Home Ec Teacher/Dept Chairperson Lumberton Ind Sch Dist 1980-88; Home Ec Teacher Cypress-Fairbanks Ind Sch Dist 1988-; *ai:* FHA & Hero Adv; Safe Ride Advisory Bd Mem; Sr Class Spon; Amer Home Ec Assn, TX Home Ec Assn 1986-; Voc Home Ec Teachers Assn of TX 1989-;

TX St Teachers Assn 1967-; AVA 1989-; Sabine Area Home Economists Pres 1978-79; Immanuel United Church Board (VP 1989, Financial Secy 1990); Most Prominent Educators of TX 1983; Tri Club Schlsp 1967; TX Assn of Young Homemakers Honorary Membership; Outstanding Scndry Educators of America 1974; *office:* Cypress Creek HS 9815 Grant Rd Houston TX 77070

HARDY, SAM R., Fourth Grade Teacher; *b:* Compton, CA; *c:* Jennifer; *ed:* (BS) Elem Ed/His, 1965, (MA) Ed, 1968 Murray St Univ; (Rank I) Sch Leadership, W KY Univ; *cr:* Teacher Owensboro Public Schls 1965-; *ai:* Sci Textbook, Curr, Report Card Study & Design Comm; Green River Therapeutic Riding Prgm Bd Mem 1986-; Theater Wkshp of Owensboro Tech Assist 1987-; Honor Grad Murray St Univ; Whos Who Among Stud of Amer Colls & Univs; *office:* Sutton Elem Sch 2060 Lewis Ln Owensboro KY 42301

HARDY, VALERIE WALTERS, Social Studies Teacher; *b:* Philadelphia, MS; *m:* Tony; *c:* Jess, Tyler; *ed:* (BS) Scndry Ed/Soc Stud, MS St 1981; *cr:* Tutor/Cnslr Bureau of Indian Affairs 1984-85; Upward Bound Instr MS Band of Choctaw Indians 1984-86; Teacher Neshobo Cntrl HS 1982-; *ai:* Neshobo Cntrl Sch Insurance Comm; Natl Mid Sch Assn 1988-; NCSS 1985; AFT 1988; MS Prof Educators 1985; Futura Club GFWC 1989-.

HARE, ROBERT S., JR., 7th-8th Grade Math/Sci/Cmptr; *b:* Canton, OH; *m:* Paula J. Frank; *c:* Patrick; *ed:* (BA) Accounting/ Elem Ed, Walsh Coll 1969, (MED) Admin, Xavier Univ 1973; Cmptr Sci, Ashland Univ; *cr:* 7th-8th Grade Math/Sci/Health/ Cmptr Sci Teacher St Joseph Sch 1969-; *ai:* Sch Math-Sci Dept Head; Asst Prin; Math Counts Coach; Math-A-Thon Adv; Sci Ed Cncl OH 1981-; Our Lady of Peace Sch Advisory Bd 1988-; Distinguished Teaching Awd Diocese of Columbus 1986; *office:* St Josephs Elem Sch 600 N Tuscarawas Ave Dover OH 44622

HAREMSKI, MARCIA J., English Teacher; *b:* Henry Cty, KY; *m:* Michael; *ed:* (BA) Eng, E KY Univ 1972; (MED) Eng Ed, GA St Univ 1984; AP Eng, Oglethorpe Univ; Natl Gallery of Art; *cr:* Teacher Madison Cty KY 1972-74, Henry Cty GA 1978-81, Gwinnett Cty 1982-; *ai:* Gwinnett Assn of Educators Exec Comm 1989-; GA Assn of Educators; NEA; *office:* Brookwood HS 1255 Dogwood Rd Snellville GA 30088

HARGEST, CHRISTINE ACKELSON, Fourth Grade Teacher; *b:* Pittsburgh, PA; *c:* Patrick, Joshua, Sarah; *ed:* (BSED) Elem Ed, Edinboro Univ of PA 1973; *cr:* 3rd Grade Teacher Klein Sch 1975-76; 4th Grade Teacher 1976-85, 1st Grade Teacher 1985-86, 4th Grade Teacher 1986- Clark Sch; *ai:* Booster Club; Harbor Creek Educl Grant 1989; *office:* Clark Elem Sch 6375 Buffalo Rd Harborcreek PA 16421

HARGETT, LINDA LARKAN, English Teacher; *b:* Galveston, TX; *c:* Leslie L.; *ed:* (BA) Eng/Journalism/Ed, Baylor Univ 1964; *cr:* Eng Teacher Stovall Jr HS 1970-71, Papillion Mid Sch 1971-74, Stovall Jr HS 1975-76, Westbriar 1982-83, Dean Intermediate 1983-; *ai:* Advisement Comm; Eng Tutor; Assn of TX Prof Educators Building Rep 1989-; *office:* Dean Intermediate Sch 14104 Reo Houston TX 77040

HARGIS, DEBBIE PRICE, U S History Teacher; *b:* Pampa, TX; *c:* Amy, Courtney, Emily, Brian; *ed:* (BS) Acad of Freedom, Speech/Drama, Ed, Howard Payne 1974; *cr:* Teacher Permian HS 1987-; *ai:* Pepette Spon; H G Mac Donald Schlsp Comm Mem; TX Cncl Soc Stud, Kappa Kappa Iota 1987-; *office:* Permian HS 42nd & Dawn Odessa TX 79762

HARGRAVE, VIRGINIA ENGLISH, 8th Grade Teacher; *b:* Oneida, NY; *m:* Victor; *c:* James, Charles; *ed:* (BA) Music, Wilmington Coll 1956; Addl Studies, Reg Classroom, OH Univ; Eastern KY; *cr:* Vocal Music Teacher London Public Schls 1956-57; Vocal/Instrumental Music/Band Dir, Reesville Elem 1957-65; Sabinia HS 1957-65; Mid Sch Teacher Sabina Mid Sch 1969-; *ai:* Stu Cncl Adv; Served on Cty Comm; Helped Write Curri Guides; Wilmington Coll Chamber Orchestra 1975-; Fayette Cty Cmmty Band 1988-; Outstanding Alumni Educator Awd Ed Dept Wilmington Coll 1989; *home:* 277 W Washington St Sabina OH 45169

HARGRAVES, LUCY A., English Teacher; *b:* South Kingstown, RI; *ed:* (BA) Eng, RI Coll 1968; (MA) Counseling, Univ of RI 1972; *cr:* Eng/Rdng Teacher Chariho HS 1968-69; Eng Teacher Coventry Jr HS West 1969-79, Coventry HS 1979-; *ai:* 9th/10th Grade Eng Curr Dev; Cheerleading Tryouts Asst Judge; RICTE 1988-; Charlestown Ordinance Comm Secy 1980-; *office:* Coventry HS Club House Rd Coventry RI 02816

HARGRO, ORETHA WILSON, Mathematics Mentor Teacher; *b:* Portsmouth, VA; *m:* Wendell Lorenzo; *c:* Trecia La Vene; *ed:* (BA) Math, Hampton Univ 1971; (MS) Ed, Univ of Guam 1973; (MS) Bus Management, Troy St Univ 1979; Ed, Univ of Guam; Equals, Univ of CA Berkeley; Bus, Troy St Univ, AA Eng, ERAU; Scndry Ed, Univ CA Sacrmento; *cr:* Math Teacher Dededo Jr HS 1970-73, Prep Sch 1973-74, ERAU/Univ of MD/CC Chicago 1977-84; 2nd Grade Teacher Zaragoza Spain/Lakenheath England 1979-84; *ai:* Sftbl Coach; Mentor Teacher; Math Curr Comm; Equals Assoc Staff Mem; Access & Equity; Math Society Mem 1987-; NCTM Reader 1979-; CA Math Cncl Prgm Chairperson 1989-; Natl Cncl Negro Women 1988-, Effort Outstanding 1990; ASCD 1988-, Outstanding Service 1989-; IBM Sales Awd Systems Analyst; *office:* Armijo HS 824 Washington St Fairfield CA 94533

HARGROVE, BARBARA ANN, Mathematics Teacher; *b:* Cameron, TX; *m:* Kenneth Wayne; *c:* Holly, Heather, Hope, Hailey; *ed:* (MS) Ed, Baylor 1975; (AA) Temple Jr Coll 1980; (BS) Math/Chem, Mary Hardin Baylor 1981; *cr:* Math Teacher Lamar Jr Hs Temple 1972-74; Math Teacher 1975-85, Asst Prin 1985-88, Math Teacher 1988- Rockdale HS; *ai:* NHS & Frosh Class Head Spon: Effective Sch Comm Person; Math Help Prgm Tutor; TCTA, NCTM, Delta Kappa Gamma; Honorary Chapter Farmer Rockdale HS FFA; *office:* Rockdale HS 1205 Murray Rockdale TX 76567

HARGROVE, DORIS ELAINE HUTCHINGS, Guidance Counselor; *b:* Brooklyn, NY; *m:* Charles D.; *c:* Lisa Tolliver, Robert Tolliver; *ed:* (BA) Eng, Hunter Coll 1963; (MS) Rdng, 1973, (CAS) Sch Counseling, 1983 Hofstra Univ; (PD) Sch Admin/Supervision, C W Post & Long Island Univ 1985; *cr:* Teacher PS 145 & Jr HS 142 1963-67; Eng Teacher Roosevelt Jr-Sr HS 1967-70; Eng/Rdng/Span Teacher 1970-85, Admin Intern 1984-85 Turtle Hook Jr HS; Guidance Cnslr Uniondale HS 1985-; *ai:* Future Teachers of America Club Adv; Big Brothers/Big Sisters Spon; Cnslr for Minority Prgms; Inroads Coord; Cnslrs Alumni Assn of Hofstra Univ 1983-; ASCD 1985-; Coalition of Uniondale Black Profs 1980-; *office:* Uniondale HS Goodrich St Uniondale NY 11553

HARGROVE, GLENDORA SMALL, Team Leader/Math Teacher; *b:* Henderson, NC; *m:* Harold E.; *c:* Harold Jr., Michelle, Steven, Michael; *ed:* (BA) Ed, NC Cntrl Univ 1985; *cr:* Teacher Eaton-Johnson Mid Sch 1985-; *ai:* Stu Cncl Spon & Adv; NC Cncl Teachers of Math, NC Assn of Educators; *office:* Eaton-Johnson Mid Sch 500 W Rockspring St Henderson NC 27536

HARGROVE, JOE C., English/Reading Teacher; *b:* Miami, OK; *m:* Elaine Mc Ilroy; *ed:* (BA) Sociology, 1976, (MAT) Elem Ed, 1978 OK City Univ; *cr:* Rdng Teacher 1979-80, Soc Stud Teacher 1980-83, Lang Art/Soc Stud Teacher 1983-86, Lang Art/Sci Teacher 1986- Rogers Mid Sch; *ai:* Girls Bsktbl Coach; Metro Church of Spencer Humanitarian Awd 1990.

HARGROVE, THOMASINA GRAHAM, 6th Grade Teacher & Chair; *b:* Bonifay, FL; *c:* Cynita Hargrove Mathews, Carlton, Cedric, Colynda Hargrove Medlock; *ed:* (BS) Elem Ed, FL A&M Univ 1965; (MS) Elem Ed, Nova Univ 1989; Numerous Wkshps; *cr:* 2nd Grade Teacher Braithwaithe Elem 1965-66; 5th Grade Teacher Dunbar Elem 1966-67; 4th Grade Teacher Buena Vista Elem 1967-71; 4th-6th Grade Teacher Floral Heights Elem 1971-; *ai:* 6th Grade Group Chairperson; 6th Grade Promotional Act Chairperson; Leadership Cncl Mem; Partners in Ed Mem; United Teachers of Dade 1965; FL Teachers Assn 1985; Iota Phi Lambda Treas 1969-72; Newway Missionary Baptist Church 1966-; FL A&M Alumni; Teacher of Yr 1976-77; Various Service Certificates & Trophies; *office:* Floral Heights Elem 5120 NW 24th Ave Miami FL 33142

HARGROVE, WILLIE CHARLES, Language Arts Teacher; *b:* Gary, IN; *ed:* (BS) Eng, 1971, (MS) Eng, 1974 IN Univ; *cr:* Eng Teacher Gary Cmmty Sch Corporation 1971-; *ai:* Building Comm; *office:* Dunbar-Pulaski Mid Sch 1867 Georgia St Gary IN 46407

HARKE, BONITA, 5th Grade Teacher; *b:* Enid, OK; *m:* Eugene; *c:* Diana Edwards, Kelby; *ed:* (BS) Home Ec, Panhandle St Univ 1961; (MS) Elem Ed, Adams St Coll 1964; Advanced Ed, KS Univ, OK St Univ, Panhandle St Univ; *cr:* Home Ec/Phys Ed Teacher Pritchett Elem 1961-63; Home Ec/Elem Teacher Elkart Elem 1963-72; Elem Teacher Tyrone Elem 1974-; *ai:* Spon 4-H Club; NEA, OK Ed Assn; TX Cty Teachers Assn VP 1975-76, 1989-; Delta Kappa Gamma 1988-; *home:* Rt 1 Box 21 A Tyrone OK 73951

HARKENRIDER, CARLA PACKER, Sr HS English Teacher; *b:* Wellsville, NY; *m:* David; *c:* Mark; *ed:* (BA) Eng, Potsdam St Coll 1973; (MS) Scndry Eng Ed, St Univ Coll of Arts & Sci Genesso 1976; (MS) Cnslr Ed, Alfred Univ 1989; *cr:* Scndry Eng Teacher Richburg Cntrl Sch 1973-; *ai:* Sr Class & Food Booth Adv Cty Fair; NHS, Cultural Awareness Club Comm Mem; Chairperson Selection Comm Anthony Toporas Memorial Schlsp; First Teacher to Direct Musicals & Start Schls Newspaper; Wellsville HS Alumni Assn Incorporated (Corresponding Secy, Recording Secy) 1984-; *office:* Richburg Cntrl Sch Main St Richburg NY 14774

HARKER, JAY L., Industrial Arts Teacher; *b:* Jasper, IN; *m:* Debra Ann Scott; *c:* Kyle; *ed:* (BS) IED, 1979, (MS) EDAD, 1989 Ball St Univ; *cr:* Teacher Hammond City Sch 1979-; *ai:* Gladiator Press Club 1979-; Class Spon 1986; Jr NHS 1981-84; Yell Men 1983-87; Phi Delta Kappa 1989-; Munster Kiwanis (Secy 1985-87, Pres 1987-88); *office:* Donald E Gavit Jr/Sr HS 1670 175th St Hammond IN 46324

HARKINS, MARJORIE DAVIS, Fifth Level Teacher; *b:* Weston, WV; *m:* Samuel G.; *c:* Charles G. Petty; *ed:* (BA) Elem Ed, Marshall Univ 1968; Mastery Learning & Cooperative Learning; Cooperative Integrated Rdng & Composition; Experienced in Congruency & Soc Comm; Sch Improvement Team; *cr:* Elem Teacher Davis Creek Elem 1966-72, Pratt Elem 1974-; *ai:* Curr Leader for Sch; Congruency Comm; Sch Improvement Team; Soc Comm; Cabell Teachers Assn, Kanawha Teachers Assn, WV Ed Assn, NEA 1966-; *office:* Pratt Elem Sch P O Box 278 Pratt WV 25162

HARKLEROAD, CHARLOTTE DALTON, Business Teacher; *b:* Piney Flats, TN; *m:* Herman Earl; *c:* Christa; *ed:* (BS) Bus Ed, E TN St Univ 1959; Grad Classes E TN St Univ, Milligan Coll & Univ of TN; *cr:* Teacher Bluff City HS 1959-68, Sullivan East HS 1968-; *ai:* NBEA 1980-; NEA, TN Ed Assn, Sullivan Cty Ed Assn 1959-; Piney Flats United Meth Women (Pres, VP, Secy) 1975-; Piney Flats United Meth Choir (Pianist, Asst Organist) 1975-; *office:* Sullivan E HS 4180 Weaver Pike Bluff City TN 37618

HARKLESS, JUDITH ANN DIETRICH, Third Grade Teacher; *b:* Van Wert, OH; *m:* David A.; *c:* Lisa A. Mitchell, Lane A., Lori E.; *ed:* (BS) Elem Ed, 1980, (MS) Elem Ed, 1984 IN Univ; Growing Healthy Trng Ball St UNiv; TESA; Critical Elements of Instruction; Project Learning Tree; *cr:* 1st/2nd Grade Teacher Bethlehem Luth Sch 1965-66, 1968-70; Kndgtn Teacher Imanuel Luth 1967; 3rd Grade Teacher Ossian Elem Sch 1980-; *ai:* Staff Dev, Extracurricular, Gifted & Talented Comm; Young Author Coord; IN Rdng Assn, ASCD, Phi Delta Kappa, IN Univ Alumni Assn, IN St Teachers Assn, Norwell Teachers Assn; LWML (Pres, Secy) 1970-; PTO (Secy, Rep) 1976-88; Bethlehem Ladies Aid, Bethlehem Choral Society 1970-; IN Dept of Ed Prime Time Grant; IN Consortium for Cmptr & HS Technology Ed Grant; Whos Who Among Students in Amer Univ & Coll 1979-80; Natl Deans List 1978-79; *office:* Ossian Sch 213 S Jefferson Ossian IN 46777

HARLAMERT, MARY JO WALLACE, English Teacher; *b:* Urbana, OH; *m:* Dean Lee; *c:* Lesley, Ryan; *ed:* (BS) Interpersonal Comm, OH Univ 1970; *cr:* Eng Teacher New Bremen HS 1970-73; Phys Ed Teacher St Mary Sch 1983-85; Eng Teacher Urbana HS 1985-89; *ai:* Speech Comm Assn of OH; OH Cncl Teachers of Eng, Lang Art; *home:* 120 Stone Ridge Rd Eufaula AL 36027

HARLAN, DALE JAY, Assistant Principal; *b:* Marion, IN; *m:* Gina Marie Gibson; *ed:* (BA) Pastoral Stud, 1983, (MA) Bible, 1985 Bob Jones Univ; Grad Work Algebra, Pre-Calculus, Clayton St Coll 1989; *cr:* Bible/Math Teacher 1987-89, Asst Prin/Teacher 1989- Fayette Chrstn Sch; *ai:* Fayette Chrstn Sch Girls Sftbl Coach; Fayette Baptist Tabernacle Youth Pastor; *office:* Fayette Chrstn Sch 152 Longview Rd Fayetteville GA 30214

HARLAN, JOHN S., Chairman Science Department; *b:* Compton, CA; *m:* Sarah Combs; *ed:* (BS) Phys Sci, CA Polytechnic St Univ 1961; Grad Ed Courses CA & OR; *cr:* Research Test Engr Rocketdyne Canoga Park CA 1961-68; Sci Teacher Newbury Park HS 1973-, Chm Sci Dept 1986- Benson Polytechnic HS; *ai:* NW Sci Olympiad & Physics, Olympics of Mind-Physics Coach; Dist Sci Course Curr Comm; PAVTECT Mem; OSTA Mem 1986-; Author Rocket Theory Handbook; *office:* Benson Polytechnic HS 546 NE 12th Ave Portland OR 97232

HARLAN, TANYA PRICE, 3rd Grade Teacher; *b:* Dallas, TX; *m:* Lendal Lon; *c:* Tiffany, Chelsea; *ed:* (BS) Elem Ed/Rdng, TX Womens Univ 1975; Brokers & Real Estate License; *cr:* Teacher Brownfield Consolidated Ind Sch Dist 1975-; *ai:* ATPE Pres 1977-78, Finalist Teacher of Yr 1988; Chamber of Commerce (Red Skirt 1984-, Chamber Queen Mother 1984); 1st Meth Church (Youth Chm, Choir, Advisory Cncl, Nominations) 1977-; Outstanding Young Woman of America 1984; Nom Readers Digest Hero in Ed 1989; Author & Publisher of Childrens Games 1986-; *office:* Oak Grove Sch PO Box 145 Brownfield TX 79316

HARLESS, SUSAN LOUISE, Seventh Grade Teacher; *b:* San Francisco, CA; *ed:* (BA) Psych, Univ of San Francisco 1969; *cr:* 8th Grade Teacher St Paul Intermediate Sch 1971-83; 7th Grade Teacher St Brigid Sch 1983-; *ai:* Religion Coord; Teachers Enrichment Assn, NCEA 1983-; *office:* St Bridig Sch 2250 Franklin St San Francisco CA 94109

HARLEY, JOYCE LEE, Language Art Teacher; *b:* Norfolk, VA; *m:* Gerald L.; *c:* Gregory, Benjamin; *ed:* (BS) Elem Ed, James Madison Univ 1958; Classes Univ of Toledo; *cr:* 4th Grade Teacher Little Creek Elem 1958-59; 5th Grade Teacher Cherry Sch 1959-64; Adult Ed Hoag Center 1973-76; 7th/8th Grade Lang Art Teacher Jones Jr HS 1976-; *ai:* Sch Newspaper Adv; Asst Dir Sch Musical; Dir Sch Play; Toledo Fed of Teachers, OH Fed of Teachers; Ladies Oriental Shrine (Directress Egats 1977-78, Secy, Treas Egats 1985-, Asst to Recorder 1988-); Martha Holden Jennings Scholar 1985-86; Bowling Green St Univ; Outstanding GED Teacher Awd Adult Ed 1976; *home:* 3231 Astor Toledo OH 43614

HARLEY, NADI WILLIAMS, Mathematics Teacher; *b:* Paragould, AR; *c:* Amber M., Kaytie J.; *ed:* (BSE) Math, Arkansas St Univ 1969; CMSU Warrensburg, MO; Univ of MO; Lincoln Univ; *cr:* 6th Grade Math Teacher Dupo-Hough Elem; Math Teacher Columbia HS, Lake Ozark HS, Twin Rivers HS, Corning HS, Corning, AR; *ai:* NHS Adv 6 Yr Sch/Cmmty Evaluation Comm; Drug/Alcohol Advisory Comm; Schl Evaluation Peer; Gifted/Talented Adv Isory Comm; Class Adv; NEA 1970-; NEACTM 1982-; CEA 1982-; AEA 1982-; ACE 1987-; AGATE 1986-; NCTM 1982-; ACTM 1982-; Beta Sigma Phi 1979-; North Central Evaluation Team; *home:* PO Box 7 Corning AR 72422

HARLIN, BOB F., Principal; *b:* Billings, MT; *m:* Sharon Jean Cook; *c:* Robert P., Michael J.; *cr:* Teacher 1962-70, Cnslr 1971-72, Vice Prin 1973-75 Hardin HS; Teacher/Cnslr 1976-87, Prin 1988- Harding Mid Sch; *ai:* Stu Cncl; NASSP 1987-; Elks Club Schlsp Chm 1985-; Big Horn Cty Parks Commission Secy 1980-; *office:* Hardin Mid Sch 611 W 5th St Hardin MT 59034

HARLOW, JUNE BAILEY, English & Journalism Teacher; *b:* Oolitic, IN; *m:* John B.; *c:* Jennifer Hartman, Julie Springer; *ed:* (BA) Eng, IN Univ 1951; (MA) Eng, Univ of AZ 1959; Numerous Univs; *cr:* Eng/Journalism/Newspaper Teacher Rocky Ford HS 1951-53; Eng/Newspaper Teacher Monroe City HS 1953-54;

Eng/Remedial Rdng Teacher Tucson Sr HS 1954-61; Eng/Soc Stud/Yrbk Teacher Escuela Campo Alegre 1962-63; Eng/Soc Stud/Literary Magazine Teacher Oak Grove Intermediate 1968-77; Eng/Journalism/Newspaper Teacher Connersville HS 1977-79; Eng/Yrbk/Newspaper Teacher W Washington HS 1979-82, Melbourne HS 1984-; *ai:* Yrbk & Newspaper Adv; Brevard Cncl Teachers of Eng, Brevard Fed of Teachers, AFT, 1984-; NEA Past Mem; Pi Lambda Theta 1959; Columbia Scholastic Press Assn 1977-78, 1985-86, 1988-, 1st Place 1978, 1988; FL Scholastic Press Assn 1989-; AAUW Mem; Various Church Organizations; Runner-Up Teacher of Yr Rocky Ford HS; *office:* Melbourne HS 74 Bulldog Blvd Melbourne FL 32901

HARMAN, BETH, 5th Grade Teacher; *b:* Bellefontaine, OH; *m:* Steve; *c:* Jason, Wesley, Erin, Joe; *ed:* (BS) Elem Ed, Bowling Green 1978; (MA) Elem Ed, Wright St 1989; *cr:* 3rd Grade Elem Teacher 1978-80, 2nd/3rd Grade Teacher 1980-84, 3rd/4th Grade Teacher 1984-89, 5th Grade Teacher 1989- Southeastern Elem; *ai:* Chrldg Adv Bellet HS 1980-81; Southeastern Stu Cncl Adv 1984-; Math Wizards Coord 1987-89; *office:* Southeastern Elem Bellefontain Colton & Hamilton Sts Bellefontaine OH 43311

HARMAN, SCOTT JAMES, 5th Grade Teacher; *b:* Lykens, PA; *ed:* (AS) Elem Ed, Harrisburg Area Comm Coll 1968-70; (BS) Elem Ed, Penn St Univ & Harrisburg Coll 1970-72; Teacher Expectation & Stu Achievement, Essential Elements of Instruction, Cooperative Learning; *cr:* Elem Teacher Halifax Area Sch Dist 1973-; *ai:* Asst HS Bsbl Coach 1976-83; Head HS Bsbl Coach 1985-86; Elem Advisory Comm Chm 1989-; Peer Coaching Exec Cncl Pace Chm; Math Curr Comm; Soc Stud Teachers 1987-; Tri-Cty Teener Bsbl League Pres 1972-78; Gift of Time Awds 1988, 1989, 1990; *office:* Halifax Area Sch Dist 3940 Peters Mtn Rd Halifax PA 17032

HARMANOS, STEPHEN ANDREW, Social Studies/AP Instructor; *b:* Exeter, PA; *m:* Kathleen Novak; *c:* Michael, Kyra; *ed:* (BS) Ed/His, 1971, (MED) Ed/His, 1976 Bloomsburg Univ; La Salle Univ, Univ of Scranton, Wilkes Univ; *cr:* Scndry Teacher Wyoming Area HS 1971-; *ai:* Key Club Adv 1980-; NCSS 1986-89; PA St Ed Assn 1971-; Pittston Kiwanis Club Pres 1990; PA Kiwanis Key Club Comm Mem 1984-; PA Key Club, Key of Honor 1987-88; Mellon Fnd Awd AP Study in US Govt 1988 & US His 1990; *office:* Wyoming Area HS Memorial Ave Exeter PA 18643

HARMER, RICHARD M., 5th/6th Grade Math Teacher; *b:* Gouverneur, NY; *m:* Karen Ann Hurley; *c:* Scott, Todd, Bryan; *ed:* (AAS) Bus Admin, Canton Coll 1961; (BS) Elem Ed, SUNY Brockport 1964; (MS) Elem Ed, Potsdam Coll 1972; *cr:* 5th/6th Grade Elem Teacher 1964-86, 5th/6th Grade Elem/Head Teacher 1982-84 Knox Memorial Cntrl Sch; 5th/6th Grade Elem Teacher Edwards Knox Cntrl Sch 1986-; *ai:* 5th/6th Grade Boys Bsktbl & Knox Memorial Sch Var Boys Bsktbl Coach; NEA; Russell Volunteer Fire Dept; Edwards Telephone Company Dir; Hermon Cemetery Assn Pres; *home:* Rt 1 Box 5 Russell NY 13684

HARMON, GERALD EDWARD, Math & Computer Teacher; *b:* Detroit, MI; *m:* Diane M.; *c:* Heather M., Bryan S.; *ed:* (AA) General, Schoolcraft Comm Coll 1971; (BA) Soc Sci/Math, W MI Univ 1973; (MA) Educl Admin, E MI Univ 1977; Cmptr Analyst Trng, MI Bell; *cr:* Math Teacher Wayne-Westland Schls 1973-83; Cmptr Teacher Oakland Comm Coll 1983; Cmptr Analyst MI Bell Telephone 1984; Math/Cmptr Teacher Wayne-Westland Schls 1984-; *ai:* Admin Sch Cmptr Network; Dist Cmptr Comm; Wrestling, Bsbl, Track Coach; Stu Cncl & NHS Adv; MEA 1973-; MACUL 1985-; BSA 1961-73, Eagle Boy Scout 1969; Presbyn Church Deacon 1983-; Project Metric Wrote Metric Act Book; *home:* 46890 Cidermill Novi MI 48050

HARMON, JANE E. SHORES, Third Grade Teacher; *b:* Florence, AZ; *m:* Rodney D.; *c:* Lindsey A., Trenton H.; *ed:* (BA) Elem, Univ of AR 1980; Principles of Effective Teaching; *cr:* 3rd Grade Teacher R E Baker Elem 1980-; *ai:* N Cntrl Accreditation Report Lang Art Self-Evaluation 1981-82, Learning Media Services Self-Evaluation Comm 1987-88; Sci Comm 1983-84; Presented Inservice Sci Act 1989,Handwriting Lesson 1989; Handwriting Comm 1988-89; Develop Dist Rdng Curr Guide Comm 1987-88; Dist Comm for Updating Report Cards 1985-86, 1989-; GSA Co-Leader 1988-; Church Sunday Sch Teacher 1986-; *office:* R E Baker Elem Sch 301 NW 3rd Bentonville AR 72712

HARMON, JANE SCHMITT, Second Grade Teacher; *m:* Tom; *c:* Mark; *ed:* (BS) Elem Ed, S IL Univ 1973; *cr:* 2nd Grade Teacher 1973-79, 3rd Grade Teacher 1980-84, 2nd Grade Teacher 1985- Shawneetown Grade Sch; *ai:* Shawneetown Lib Bd Trustee 1987-; St Marys Church (Music Dept, Parish Cncl); Showtime & Story Hour Cmmty Act; *office:* Shawneetown Grade Sch 120 E Logan Shawneetown IL 62984

HARMON, KEVIN WEBSTER, Social Studies Teacher; *b:* Topeka, KS; *m:* Jeannine A. Hinther; *c:* Ryan W., Jennifer C., Daniel L.; *ed:* (BSE) Soc Stud/Eng, Emporia St Univ 1977; Washburn Univ, KS St Univ, Ft Hays Univ, Emporia St Univ; *cr:* 7th/8th Grade Teacher Unified Sch Dist #449 1978-; *ai:* 7th/8th Grade Class Spon; 7th/8th Grade Ftbl, Boys, Girls Bsktbl, Track Coach; 7th/8th Grade Soc Stud Curr & Textbook Selection; NEA (Local Pres 1986-87, 1989- Mem) 1978-; Optimists Intnl (Mem 1987-88, Girls Bsktbl Clinic 1990, Bsbl Coach 1987-); Pi Gamma Mu Stu Senator for Emporia St Univ; *office:* Easton-Salt Creek Mid Sch Easton KS 66020

HARMON, SHIRLEY TURNER, Third Grade Teacher; *b:* Belington, WV; *m:* William Wilson; *c:* J. P. Hymes, Melissa Hymes; *ed:* (BA) Elem Ed/Eng, Alderson-Broaddus 1972; (MA) Curr/Instruction, WV Univ 1979; Course Work for Masters in Speech Comm; *cr:* Teacher Beards Fork Elem 1976-77, East End Oak Hill Elem 1977-78, Mt Hope Elem 1978-; *ai:* Delta Kappa Gamma Secy 1987-; Fayette Cty Rdng Cncl 1985-; Amer Assn Univ Women VP 1976-78; NEA, WVEA 1976-; PTO; Mt Hope Federated League (Pres, Secy) 1980-, Club Women of Month 1989; Parent Advisory Cncl 1988-; Band Boosters Publicity Chm 1983-87; Appointed to Leaders of Learning Conference; *home:* 211 Bluestone Rd Mount Hope WV 25880

HARMON, VICKI DAROUGH, Fifth Grade Teacher; *b:* Pell City, AL; *m:* Eldred Randall; *c:* Randall L., Christian H., Dorian N.; *ed:* (BS) Elem Ed, Univ of AL Birmingham 1980; *cr:* 5th Grade Teacher Walter M Kennedy Sch; *ai:* Delta Kappa Gamma Society; AL Ed Assn; *home:* 114 West St Pell City AL 35125

HARMS, M. SUSAN ARNOLD, First Grade Teacher; *b:* Savannah, GA; *ed:* (BA) Elem Ed, Mt St Agnes 1965; (MED) Rdng Specialist GA St Univ 1974; Ed Admin, GA Southern Univ & Univ of Dayton; *cr:* 2nd Grade Teacher St Josephs 1965-66; 1st Grade Teacher St Ignatius 1966-68; Our Lady of Assumption 1968-73; Nativity of Our Lord Sch 1973-; *ai:* Deanery Lang Arts Curr Comm 1985; Self-Study Religion Comm 1985-87; Self-Study Lang Arts Comm 1985-87; Chairperson Rdng Guide Comm 1988; Coord Parish 1st Holy Communion Prgm; NCEA; Mercy El Ed Network; Savannah Chapter of DAR; Sisters of Mercy of Amer; St Vincents Alumnae Chorus; *office:* Nativity Of Our Lord Sch 7020 Concord Rd Savannah GA 31410

HARMS, MEG STEINKAMP, Kindergarten Teacher; *b:* Loup City, NE; *m:* Gar; *c:* Seth, Abby; *ed:* (BA) Early Chldhd, Univ of Northern IA 1971; *cr:* Kndgtn Teacher Wellsburg Comm Sch 1971-; *ai:* Speech Coach 1982-86; Pine Lake Archers Secy 1976-; DAP Leadership Conference; Published Early Yrs 1979; *office:* Wellsburg Comm Sch 609 S Monroe Box 188 Wellsburg IA 50680

HARMS, NANCY ELLEN (GUNN), Second Grade Teacher; *b:* Cape Girardeau, MO; *m:* Frederick J.; *ed:* (BS) Elem Ed, Western IL Univ 1967; *cr:* 2nd Grade Teacher Ingersoll Elem Sch 1967-77, Eastview Elem Sch 1978-; *ai:* Young Authors Comm; PTA 1967-; Canton Ed Assn 1967-; IL Ed Assn 1967-; Amer Assn Univ Women Secy 1968-69; *home:* Rt 5 Oak Park Rd Canton IL 61520

HARMSTON, TERRY MICHAEL, Teacher/Coach; *b:* Chicago, IL; *m:* Anne Schlueter; *c:* Greg, Matt; *ed:* (BS) Eng/Phys Ed, 1965; (MS) Phys Ed, 1970 Northern IL Univ; Cert to Teach Gifted; *cr:* Teacher/Coach Stillman Valley HS 1965-70; Grad Asst Northern IL Univ 1970-71; Asst Ftbl Head Wr/Asst Athl Dir Univ WI 1971-74; Teacher/Coach/Athl Dir Leaf River HS 1974-80; Teacher/Coach Stockton HS 1980-; *ai:* Asst Varsity Ftbl Line Coach Stu Cncl Spon; IEA/NEA (VP/Pres 1982-86 Regional Rep Exec Bd 1985-); IFCA 1974-; Lions 1976-80; Christ Luth Church Deacon 1984-88; Stockton Little Leag Coach 1981-84; IEA St Teachers Schlsp Comm 1988-; Chm IEA St Teachers Schlsp Comm 1989-; Elected Rep IEA/NEA St Assembly 1983-; *office:* Stockton H S 500 Rush St Stockton IL 61085

HARNED, MELISSA FARMER, Science Teacher; *b:* Nashville, TN; *m:* Kelly; *ed:* (BS) Elem Ed, 1980, (MED) Admin/Supervision, 1981 Mid TN St Univ; (EDD) Admin/Supervision, TN St Univ 1990; Recycling Wkshp Instr; Completing CPR Instr Trng; *cr:* Sci Teacher Page Mid Sch 1981-; *ai:* Mid TN Electric Membership Corporation Evaluate & Improve 6th Grade Curr & Cty Electric Projects; *office:* Page Mid Sch 6262 Arno Rd Franklin TN 37064

HARNER, LOUELLA SAUBLE, Third Grade Teacher; *b:* Taneytown, MD; *w:* Elwood James (dec); *c:* Linda Harner Frankhouser, Dennis J.; *ed:* (BA) Ec, Hood Coll 1949; Masters Equivalency Stud in Elem Ed, W MD Coll Westminster, Towson St Univ; *cr:* 3rd Grade Teacher Westminster Elem Sch 1963-65, Robert Moton Elem 1965-75, William Winchester Elem 1975-; *ai:* Delta Kappa Gamma (Corresponding Secy 1982-84), 1980-; MD St Teachers Assn Life Mem; NEA, Carroll Cty Ed Assn Mem; Trinity Luth Church (Church Cncl, Sunday Sch Teacher); *office:* William Winchester Elem Sch Carroll St Ext Westminster MD 21157

HARNESS, TIM D., Fourth Grade Teacher; *b:* Elkhart, IN; *m:* Cindy L. Kessler; *c:* Laura, Nathan, Julie; *ed:* (BA) Psych, Univ of MI 1977; (MS) Elem Ed, IN Univ 1987; *cr:* Elem Teacher Elkhart Cmmty Schls 1978-; *ai:* Elem Ftbl & Bsktbl Coach; Cmptr Coord; Outdoor Sci Lab Adv; Instructional Technology Advisory Cncl; Budget Comm; Amer Red Cross Instr 1978-85; Article Published; *office:* Mary L Daly Elem Sch 1735 Strong Ave Elkhart IN 46514

HARNESS, WILLIAM WYATT, 10th/12th Grade Eng Teacher; *b:* Harrison, AR; *c:* Tiffany; *ed:* (BA) Eng, Sch of the Ozarks 1982; *cr:* Eng/Speech Teacher Valley Springs HS 1981-; *ai:* Sr Spon; Valley Springs Baptist Church Youth Instr; *office:* Valley Springs HS PO Box 86 Valley Springs AR 72682

HARNETIAUX, D. MIKE, 6th Grade Teacher; *b:* Highland, IL; *ed:* (BSE) His/Ed, Greenville Coll 1970; Elem Ed; *cr:* 5th Grade Teacher 1970-73, 6th Grade 1973- Greenville Elem; Tree Nursery Mgr Harnetiaux Evergreen Nursery 1977-; *ai:* Greenville Ed Assn Building Rep 1970-; IL Ed Assn 1970-; NEA 1970-; Amer Assn of Nurserymen 1981-88; IL Assn of Nurserymen 1981-88; 1 of 30 to Receive Grant to Participate in Sic Process Wkshp Eastern IL Univ Summer 1989; *office:* Greenville Elem Sch RR 2 Box 190 Greenville IL 62246

HARNETT, JOAN M., OP, Director of Programming; *b:* Bronx, NY; *ed:* (BA) Math, Le Moyne Coll 1975; (MS) Cmptr Sci, NY Inst of Technology 1985; Applied Math/Operations Research, SUNY Stony Brook; *cr:* Teacher St Jude Sch 1975-76; Math Teacher 1977-83, Cmptr Dept Chairperson 1983-88, Dir of Programming 1988- Dominican Comm HS; *ai:* NCEA 1977-; Designed & Established Cmptr Dept 1982-83; *office:* Dominican Commercial HS 161-06 89th Ave Jamaica NY 11432

HARNISCH, ROBERT W., English Teacher; *b:* Chicago, IL; *c:* Scott; *ed:* (BA) Eng, Univ of WI Superior 1968; (MA) Eng, Univ of WY 1971; Univ of WI Stout 1974; Univ of WI Madison 1977; Univ of AZ 1979-80; *cr:* Eng Teacher Antigo HS 1968-70; Graduate Teaching Asst Univ of WY 1970-71; Eng Teacher Roseau HS 1971-72, D C Everest HS 1972-73; Scndry Eng Teacher WI St Pris N Waupun 1973-79; Eng Teacher Birchwood HS 1982-; *ai:* Bsktbl & Forensic Coach; Freedom Jaycees Outstanding Young Educator Awd 1978; Graduate Teaching Assistantship Awd Univ of WY.

HARO, ROSEMARY MEIER, Spanish Teacher; *b:* Greensburg, IN; *m:* James L.; *c:* Angelia, Andrew, Arica; *ed:* (BA) Span, IN Univ 1971; (MA) Ed/Span, NY Univ 1974; *cr:* Span Teacher Bartholomew Consolidated Sch Corporation 1971-; *ai:* Span Club; Columbus 1989-; *home:* 2321 Pearl St Columbus IN 47201

HAROLD, JOSEPH E., Geography Teacher; *b:* Canton, OH; *m:* Cinda Gonser; *c:* Lindsy, Cortney, Jacob; *ed:* (BS) Elem Ed, Malone Coll 1977; Additional Studs Univ of Akron, OH Univ Belmont, Kent St Univ, Malone Coll; *cr:* 6th Grade Soc Stud Teacher Pfeiffer Mid Sch 1977-82; 8th Grade Amer His Teacher Edison Jr HS 1982-83; 5th Grade Teacher Northwood Elem Sch 1983-85; 7th/8th Grade Sci Teacher Conotton Valley HS 1985-88; 6th Grade Teacher Bell-Herron Mid Sch 1988-89; 7th Grade Geography Teacher Louisville Jr HS 1989-; *ai:* Head Coach Boys Bsktbl; *office:* Louisville Jr HS 1201 S Nickelplate St Louisville OH 44641

HARP, ROSE MARIE, Lead Government Teacher; *b:* Austin, TX; *m:* James Franklin; *c:* Wylie B.; *ed:* (BS) Bus Ed, Northern MI 1961; (MAIS) Interdisciplinary, Univ of TX 1980; *cr:* Admin Dept of Defense 1957-59; Teacher St Xaviers Sch 1962-63, Sumter Ind Sch Dist 1963-66, Dept of Defense 1966-68, Richardson Ind Sch Dist 1976-; *ai:* Mock Trial Team; Pre Law & Young Politicians Club; NCSS, TCSS 1980; NEA, TSTA 1976; Sogetsu Intnl 1980-; Law Related Ed Seminar; *office:* J J Pearce HS 1600 N Coit Rd Richardson TX 75080

HARPE, BETTY VANCE, Fifth Grade Teacher; *b:* Meridian, MS; *m:* Ellis C.; *c:* Spencer, Tracy; *ed:* (BA) Elem Ed, Belhaven Coll 1969; (MED) Elem Ed MS Coll 1974; *cr:* 3rd Grade Teacher Stne Mountain Elem Sch 1969-70; 4th Grade Teacher Florence Elem Sch 1970-77, Richland Elem 1980-84; 5th Grade Teacher Richland Mid 1985-; *ai:* Jump Rope for Heart Coord ; Drug Rep Just Say No; MS Prof Ed 1987; Kappa Delta Epsilon 1967-69; Alpha Delta Kappa 1970-77; 1st Presbyn Church; Teacher Yr 1987 Richland Atten Ctr; Teacher Yr Runner-Up 1987 Rankin Cty; MTAI Evaluator; *office:* Richland Mid Sch 175 Wilson Dr Richland MS 39218

HARPER, ALMETA POWELL, First Grade Teacher; *b:* Grand Rapids, MI; *m:* E. Harold; *c:* Julie Harper Dean, David E.; *ed:* (BA) Elem Ed, W MI Univ 1954; (MA) Curr/Instruction, Concordia Coll 1989; *cr:* 1st Grade Teacher Hazlett Public Schls 1956-58; 3rd Grade Teacher 1976-89, 1st Grade Teacher 1989- Washington Sch; *ai:* Dist Rep NWACC Math Comm; Itasca Ed Assn, IL Ed Assn, NEA; *office:* Washington Sch 301 E Washington Itasca IL 60143

HARPER, ANTONY J. D., Science Teacher; *b:* Belfast, N Ireland; *m:* Joan Doris; *c:* Colin A.; *ed:* (BS) Bio/Chem, IN St Univ 1966; (MS) Zoology, Univ of IA 1968; Vertebrate Paleontology & Functional Morphology, Univ of IL Chicago; *cr:* Sci Teacher Glenbrook North HS 1969-71, St Benedicts HS 1978-79, New Trier HS 1979-; *ai:* Head Girls Swim, Boys Swim Coach 1988-; Asst Girls Swim Coach 198-87; Asst Boys Swim Coach 1984-87; New Trier Critical Thinking Comm Mem; NEA, IEA, Local Assn 1980-; NABT 1980-; Natl Assn of Geology Teachers 1989; Amer Natl Assn for the Advancement of Sci 1980-; *office:* New Trier HS 385 Winnetka Rd Winnetka IL 60093

HARPER, ARLISTER WASHINGTON, Mathematics Teacher; *b:* Tyler, TX; *c:* Johnny Paul Jr., Arlistel De Schaunn; *ed:* (BS) Math, TX Coll 1960; TX Southern Univ Houston; *cr:* Teacher Booker T Washington HS 1960-70, Atlanta HS 1970-74, Atlanta Jr HS 1974-; *ai:* Atlanta Ed Assn 1970-; TX St Teachers Assn 1960-; *home:* 2114 N Bois D Arc Ave Tyler TX 75702

HARPER, BARBARA JEAN, Second Grade Teacher; *b:* Port Chester, NY; *ed:* (BA) Psych, Hunter Coll 1953; (MA) Early Chldhd, Columbia Teachers Coll 1959; Various Inst 1987; *cr:* 1st/2nd Grade Teacher King Street Sch; *ai:* NY St United Teachers; Delta Kappa Gamma (Secy, Membership Chm); Port Chester Teachers Assn 1953-, Teacher of Yr 1987; NSDAR (Membership Chm, Historian); Mayfair Volunteer 1978-; Cmmty Chest Volunteer 1958-60; PTA Life Membership 1959, 1988; *home:* 65 Wesley Ave Portchester NY 10573

HARPER, DONALD DEAN, Seventh Grade English Teacher; *b:* Zanesville, OH; *m:* Patricia Jean Abele; *c:* Doug W., Jill C.; *ed:* (BS) Eng, OH St Univ 1972; (MED) Guidance, Xavier Univ 1976; *cr:* 9th Grade Eng Teacher Milford Jr HS 1972-75; 7th Grade Eng Teacher Duncan Falls Jr HS 1975-; *ai:* Journalism Adv; NCTE

Natl Convention Speaker 1972-; Optimist Club 1987-; PTO 1972-; *office:* Duncan Falls Jr HS PO Box 368 Duncan Falls OH 43734

HARPER, KARIN WILLIAMS, Science Dept Chairperson; *b:* Baton Rouge, LA; *m:* Reginald Robert; *ed:* (BS) Microbiology, SE LA Univ 1980; (MS) Sci Ed, Univ of S MS 1990; *cr:* Chem/Physics Instr Natalbany Chrstn Sch 1980-81; HS Sci Instr Southwood Acad 1981-86; Sci Dept Head/Instr Ponchatoula HS 1986-; *ai:* Parish Sci Textbook Adoption Comm; Parish Sex Ed Curr Steering Comm; Sigma Society Adv; Sci Dept Head; Ponchatoula HS Sci Club; Selected as Outstanding Teacher by HS Key Club; *office:* Ponchatoula HS PO Box 454 Hwy 22 E Ponchatoula LA 70454

HARPER, MARY RECKTENWALD, Spanish Teacher; *b:* Iowa City, IA; *c:* Mary J.; *ed:* (BSE) Span, 1974, (MSE) Comparative Lit Span/Eng, 1979 NE MO St Univ; *cr:* Span/Eng Teacher Camanche Cmmty Schls 1975-80; 7th-12th Grade Span Teacher Eddyville HS 1983-; *ai:* Span Club; Phase III Comm; Spaea Foreign Lang Advisory Comm; NEA, ISEA; EEA Pres 1985; OES, Amer Legion Auxiliary, IFLA; Stipend to Univ of N IA 1987 Through Dept of Foreign Lang of IA; *office:* Eddyville HS R R 1 Eddyville IA 52553

HARPER, PATRICIA SMITH, 5th Grade Teacher; *b:* Quitman, MS; *m:* James B.; *c:* Sha, Jim; *ed:* (BS) Elem Ed, MS Univ for Women 1970; *cr:* 5th Grade Teacher Poplar Springs Elem 1970-; *ai:* Delta Kappa Gamma Recording Secy 1977-79; Teacher of Yr 1988; *office:* Poplar Springs Elem Sch 4101 27th Ave Meridian MS 39305

HARPER, PEGGY MARY, 10th Grade Honors Eng Teacher; *b:* Dubuque, IA; *m:* Sidney Calvin; *c:* Matthew T., Megan M.; *ed:* (AA) Liberal Art, Valley Coll 1976; (BA) Communication Art, Univ of W FL 1980; Certificate in Bus & Eng; *cr:* Teacher Rutherford HS 1983-84, Hook Jr HS 1984-85, Hesperia HS 1985-; *ai:* Writing Celebration Coord Grades 9-12; Hesperia Unified HS Union Rep at HS Site; Academic Decathlon Tutor for Entrants; CA Teachers Assn, NCTE, Hesperia Educators Assn Union Rep 1984-89; Teacher of Yr 1988-89; Whos Who in Amer Ed 1989; *office:* Hesperia HS 9898 Maple St Hesperia CA 92345

HARPER, SHARON MURPHY, Teacher of the Gifted; *b:* Wheeling, WV; *c:* Andrew; *ed:* (BA) Speech/Drama, W Liberty St Coll 1969; (MA) Classroom Teaching, WV Univ 1980; Grad Work WV Univ; *cr:* Teacher Newport HS 1970-72; Substitute Teacher Centerburg HS 1972-73; Teacher Follansbee Mid Sch 1973-81, Brooke HS 1981-; *ai:* SADD Spon; Academic Team & Quiz Bowl Team Coach; Mime Troupe, Medieval Feast, Club Review & Fall Play Dir; NEA 1974; Brooke Cty Ed Assn Pres 1974-; WV Gifted Ed Assn 1981-; Brooke Hills Playhouse (Founder, Managing Dir) 1972-; Wellsburg Shakespeare Club Pres 1975-; Brooke Cty Museum Commission Pres 1981-; Brooke Cty Teacher of Yr 1987-88; WV Ed Fund Grants 1987, 1989; WV Arts & Hum Grants 1986-89; WV Teachers Acad 1988; Articles Published; *office:* Brooke HS RD 3 Box 610 Wellsburg WV 26070

HARPER, SHERRY EDWARDS, Language Arts Dept Chair; *b:* Anniston, AL; *m:* Truman E. Jr.; *c:* Andrew, Laurel; *ed:* (BA) Eng, Birmingham S Coll 1974; (MLA) Lib Art, S Meth Univ 1989; *cr:* Eng Teacher Homewood HS 1975-79; Eng Teacher/Lang Art Dept Chairperson N Garland HS 1984-; *ai:* Eng Adv Serendipity Fine Arts Publication; Faculty Spon Literary Club; Phi Delta Kappa 1989-; *office:* N Garland HS 2109 W Buckingham Garland TX 75042

HARPER, SHIRLEY LOUISE, Social Science Teacher; *b:* Los Angeles, CA; *ed:* (BA) Foreign Lang, 1954, (MA) Foreign Lang, 1956 Univ CA Los Angeles; (MA) His/Poly Sci, CSUN 1970; Grad Stud European His, Asian Intellectual His, US His & Poly Sci Stanford, Berkeley Univ CA Los Angeles; *cr:* Asst Teacher Univ CA Los Angeles Italian Dept 1954-56; Teacher Reseda HS 1957-60, Taft HS 1960-; *ai:* Adv Placement Class Preparation; Acad Decathlon Teams Asst Coach; Poly Sci & His 1957-; Alpha Mu Gamma 1952- Top Linguist 1952; *office:* WM H Taft Sr.H S 5461 Winnetka Ave Woodland Hills CA 91364

HARPER, WILMA FAYE CRAIG, 4th Grade Teacher; *b:* Lovington, NM; *m:* James Wilbur; *c:* Cheri D. Hukins, Shara D. Hukins, Craig J.; *ed:* (BA) Ed, 1961, (MS) Ed, 1982, (MS) Ed, 1989 Eastern NM Univ; Rdng, Gifted, Cmptr, Spec Ed, Cultural Awareness, Counseling, Sch Finance; *cr:* 4th Grade Teacher Eunice Public Schls 1961-62, Hobbs Public Schls 1963-; *ai:* Church of Christ; Girl Scout Leader 1971-73; Bobby Sox Sftbl Mgr 1973-75; Hobbs Ed Assn; NM Assn; Taylor PTA VP; United Fund 1975-; 4-H Club Leader 1971-77; Free Enterprise Educator of Yr 1987; *office:* Taylor Elem Sch 1520 N Breckon Dr Hobbs NM 88240

HARPER-GIARDINA, JANET CARLSON, Psychology Teacher; *b:* Hartford, CT; *m:* Vincent J. Jr.; *c:* Christopher, Jennifer; *ed:* (AA) Eng, Hartford Coll for Women 1967; (BA) Eng, Univ of Hartford 1970; (MA) Cnslr Ed, Kean Coll of NJ 1989; Here Looking at You 2000 Drug/Alcohol Ed; *cr:* Eng Teacher St Marys HS 1979-85; Eng/Adjunct Professor Kean Coll 1989; Psych/Eng Teacher/Guidance Cnslr Roselle Cath HS 1985-; *ai:* Peer Group Counseling & Trng; Coll Fair Co-Chairperson; NJCTE, NJPCA 1988-; NJCAC 1987-; Internship with Steps Recovery Centers Drug & Alcohol Rehabilitation 1990; Speaker Self Esteem Youthfest 1990.

HARR, RAMONA GAMINDE, Mathematics Teacher; *b:* Iaeger, WV; *m:* Jon Paul; *ed:* (BA) Math/Ed, Emory & Henry Coll 1986; *cr:* Teacher Sullivan East HS 1986-; *ai:* Girls Bsktbl Team Asst Coach; NHS Spon; *office:* Sullivan East HS 4180 Weaver Pike Bluff City TN 37618

HARRE, JAMES H., Tech Physics Teacher; *b:* Camden, NJ; *m:* Jane G.; *c:* Dawn, James III, Wendy; *ed:* (BA) Hum, Rutgers 1961; Post Grad Glassboro St Coll; Monmoth Coll; Marywood Coll; *cr:* Teacher Swedesboro HS 1961-63, Delhaas HS 1963-80, Harry S Truman HS 1980-; *home:* 516 Democrat Rd Gibbstown NJ 08027

HARRELL, BARBARA L., Business Department Chair; *b:* Brownsville, TX; *m:* David W.; *c:* Amy L.; *ed:* (BS) Bus Ed, SW TX St Univ 1968; Scripsit Word Processing Operating Theory Course; Supervision of Teacher Effectiveness Practices Trng; Free Enterprise Seminars on Teaching Methods & Materials; *cr:* Teacher Brownsville HS 1969-71, Round Rock HS 1980-81, Westwood HS 1981-; *ai:* UIL Accounting Coach; FBLA Adv; TX Bus Educators Assn 1981-; NBEA 1985-89; TX St Teachers Assn 1987-; FBLA Prof Mem; Univ of TX Austin Free Enterprise Internship Chairperson 1990; *office:* Westwood HS 12400 Mellow Meadow Austin TX 78750

HARRELL, FRANK BARNES, Assistant Principal; *b:* Baton Rouge, LA; *m:* Mary Eileen Cheadle; *c:* John, Brian, Kristen; *ed:* (BMED) Instrumental Music, LA St Univ 1971; (MED) Supervision/Admin, 1979, Ed Specialist Supervision/Admin, 1984 Mc Neese St Univ; *cr:* Band Dir Redemptorist Jr/Sr HS 1970-73, Westlake HS 1973-; Asst Prin Sam Houston HS 1990-; *ai:* Sam Houston HS Lit Rally Team spon; Southern Assn Steering Comm Chm; Dist V Band Dirs (Pres, VP, Secy, Treas) 1973-89, Outstanding Mem Awds 1975, 1980, 1985; Apel 1990; NASSP 1989-; Kiwanis Club 1989-; BSA Den Leader 1987-89; Church Choir Dir 1976-; Articles Published; Citizen of Week Westlake 4 Times; Band Dir of Yr 3 Times; *home:* Rt 7 Box 920 Lake Charles LA 70611

HARRELL, GLORIA SEALE, 8th Grade Reading Teacher; *b:* Ravenna, KY; *c:* Peggy L.; *ed:* (BA) His, KY Wesleyan Coll 1951; (MA) Ed, Morehead St Univ 1972; Grad Stud E KY Univ; *cr:* Secy/Pres KY Wesleyvan Coll 1951; 2nd Grade Teacher Daviess Cty Public Schls 1951-52; Typing/Office Practice Teacher Pike Cty Schls 1952-54; 1st/2nd Grade Teacher Shelby Cty Schls 1960-67; Head Start Teacher Morehead St Univ 1967-72; 8th Grade Rdng Teacher Clark Cty Schls 1972-; *ai:* NEA, KEA; *home:* 26 Holiday Rd Winchester KY 40391

HARRELL, MARTHA ANN, 12th Grade Lang Art Teacher; *b:* Blackston, VA; *ed:* (BAE) Eng Ed, Univ of N FL 1976; Spec Courses Learning Disabilities, Speech; *cr:* 7th-9th Grade Eng Teacher Callahan Intermediate 1976-79; 7th-9th Grade Eng Teacher Callahan Jr HS 1980-81; 10th-12th Grade Eng Teacher Andrew Jackson Sr HS 1981-; *ai:* Newspaper Ed; Tapp Comm Drug Substance Abuse Prevention; Advanced Placement Eng Instr; PTSA 1981-85; Sierra Club Newsletter Ed 1988, Sierra Honor Awd 1989; *office:* Andrews Jackson Sr HS 3816 Main St Jacksonville FL 32208

HARRELL, VIRGINIA PERSINGER, Mathematics Teacher/Dept Chair; *b:* Ashtabula, OH; *c:* Sara E., Jeffrey R.; *ed:* (BSED) Math, Kent St Univ 1973; Cmptr Wkshps, Kent St Univ, Akron Univ; *cr:* Math Teacher Brown Jr HS 1973-81; Math Teacher 1981-, Math Dept Chairperson 1987- R B Chamberlin HS; *ai:* Sr Class Adv; Prom Chairperson; OH Ed Assn 1973-; Twinsburg Ed Assn 1981-; OH Cncl of Teachers of Math 1982-; Chagin Valley Math Teachers 1989-; Kent Jr Mothers Club (Pres 1983-84, Treas 1982-83) 1979-; Kent Safety Sch Chairperson 1983-85; Cmptr Mini Grants; *office:* R B Chamberlin HS 10270 Ravenna Rd Twinsburg OH 44087

HARRELSON, ANN, English Teacher; *b:* Haralson, GA; *ed:* (BA) Speech & Eng, Mercer Univ 1962; (MRE) Youth Work, Southern Baptist Theo Sem 1966; (MS) Eng, Troy St Univ 1977; Summer 1968 OH Univ; 1975-76 Evenings Columbus Coll; *cr:* Eng Teacher Hawkinsville HS 1962-64, Fort Valley/Peach Cty HS 1966-76; Eng or Speech Instr Enterprise St Jr Coll/Wallace Coll/Troy St Univ 1977-84; Eng Teacher Early Co Mid Sch 1978-; *ai:* GA Speech Assn VP 1967-68; GA Speech Assn 3rd Dist Dir 1966-67; GA Speech Teacher of Yr 1968; NEA/GEA/ECEA 1978-; Early Cty Assn of Educators Pres 1984-85; Cardinal Key Honorary Society 1960-62; Phi Kappa Delta 1977-79; Analysis of Non-Comm Stu in HS Speech Class 1968; *office:* Early County Middle Schl 413 Columbia Rd. Blakely GA 31723

HARRIGAN, ANN FRANCES, Secondary Science Teacher; *b:* Fort Smith, AR; *m:* Brian Francis; *c:* Cody L., Casey F.; *ed:* (BS) Bio, 1980, (MA) Ed, 1990 Boise St Univ; *cr:* Bio Teacher Borah HS 1981; Earth Sci Teacher Hillside Jr HS 1981-82; Dir of Ed ID Botanical Garden 1988-89; Life Sci/General Sci Teacher North Jr HS 1982-; *ai:* Earth Week Comm Adv 1990; Landscape Project Adv; ID Sci Teachers Assn 1982-; ID Earth Sci Assn 1988-89; Amer Assn of Botanical Gardens & Arboreta 1989-; ID Botanical Garden 1988-, Volunteer Service Awd 1989; ID Christa Mc Auliffe Fellowship 1988-89; *office:* North Jr HS 1105 N 13th St Boise ID 83702

HARRILL, PETER JOHN, K-6th Grade Phys Ed Teacher; *b:* Cairo, Egypt; *ed:* (BA) Health/Phys Ed, TN Wesleyan Coll 1972; (MS) Admin, Union Coll 1973; (EDS) Admin, TN Tech Univ 1979; *cr:* Phys Ed Teacher Ingleside Elem Sch 1972-; *ai:* Intramural, Vlybl, Track Coach; 5th & 6th Grade Sch Camp; *office:* Ingleside Elem Schl 600 Guille St Athens TN 37303

HARRINGTON, CATHERINE ROUSE, Third Grade Teacher; *b:* Eastman, GA; *m:* W. D.; *c:* Wil, Ellen; *ed:* (BA) Early Chldhd Ed, Univ of GA 1979; (MS) Early Chldhd Ed 1982; *cr:* 3rd Grade Teacher Eastman Elem Sch 1979-; *ai:* 3rd Grade Teachers Chairperson Eastman Elem; Media Comm; Certified Data Collector; Instr for Stu Teachers; PAGE 1980-; Dodge Pro of Educators (Secy/Pres) 1986-, Distinguished Service Awd 1990; Jr Womens Club Pres 1985; Ft Meth Church (Childrens Coord, Admin Bd); Dodge Cty Runner Up Teacher of Yr 1986; *home:* Rt 6 Box 375-C Eastman GA 31023

HARRINGTON, CHARLES EDWARD, 7th Grade Biology Teacher; *b:* Brooklyn, NY; *m:* Bloneva; *c:* Brandon; *ed:* (BS) Health Sci, 1969, (MS) Emotionally Handicapped Ed, 1984 Brooklyn Coll; Supervision Prgm, Brooklyn Coll; *cr:* Paraprofessional Teacher Public Sch 45K 1977-78; Paraprofessional of Deaf Children Public Sch 286K Center for Multiple Handicapped 1978-80; Teacher/General Sci Hyde Jr HS 240K 1980-; *ai:* St Philips Church & Big Apple Games Bsktbl Coach; BSA Asst Scoutmaster & Eagle Scout; HANAEC Evening Center Teacher in Charge 1984; After Sch Recreational Prgm Gym Teacher & Recreational Therapist 1981-84; Bushwick Youth Support Prgm Gym Teacher 1982, Summer Prgms 1981-82; Maxwell Voc HS Math & Sci Tutor 1980-81; Bushwick Neighborhood Youth Corps Sr Cnslr 1977-78; Camp DeWolfe Sr Cnslr & Cnslr Trainer 1973-74; BSA Life Mem; St Philips Vestry Mem; St Philips Church Alcolyte 1972-80; *office:* Hudde Jr HS 240 2500 Nostrand Ave Brooklyn NY 11210

HARRINGTON, KATHLEEN M., Spanish Teacher/Foreign Lang; *b:* Cleveland, OH; *ed:* (BA) Eng, Ursuline Coll 1966; (MA) Prof Ed, John Carroll Univ 1973; Admin & Supervision, John Carroll Univ; *cr:* Span Teacher/Foreign Lang Dept Chairperson St Augustine Acad 1966-; *ai:* Chalta (Pres 1974-76, VP 1972-73, Secy 1971-72); Diocesan Foreign Lang Assn, NCEA; Ursuline Coll Alumni Assn, St Joseph Acad Alumni Assn; *office:* St Augustine Acad 14808 Lake Ave Lakewood OH 44107

HARRINGTON, MARY GRACE (JOHNSON), Second Grade Teacher; *b:* Yakima, WA; *m:* Timothy P.;; *ed:* (BA) Elem Ed/Speech Therapy, WA St Univ 1974; (MA) Elem Ed/Curr/Instruction, Univ of WA 1987; Coord & Instr Trng Teacher Expectations & Stu Achievement; Staff Dev Trng & Ed; *cr:* Speech Therapist Richland Sch Dist 1974-77; 1st Grade Teacher Lewis & Clark Elem 1977-78; Jefferson Elem 1978-86; 2nd Grade Teacher Redmond Elem 1987-; *ai:* Master Teacher & Supvr for Stu Teacher; Intnl Rdng Assn (VP 1983-84, Pres 1984-85), Certificate 1985; ASCD Past Mem; WA Ed Assn, Lake Washington Ed Assn; Kndgtn Early Entrance Screening Team; Offered Sch Readiness Wkshps; *office:* Redmond Elem Sch 16600 NE 80th Redmond WA 98052

HARRINGTON, PHIL J., Physics Teacher; *b:* Britt, IA; *ed:* (BS) Physics, IA St 1987; *cr:* Physics Teacher Harlan Cmmty 1987-; *ai:* Sr Class Spon; Frosh Class Adv; Negotiation & Sci Curr Comms; Cadre Mem Stu Assistance Team; Optimist Club 1988-89; Toastmasters 1990; *office:* Harlan Cmmty HS 2102 Durant Harlan IA 51537

HARRINGTON, ROBERT PAUL, Sixth Grade Teacher; *b:* Wilkes Barre, PA; *ed:* (BA) His/Russian Stud, Muhlenberg Coll 1971; (MED) Elem Ed, Lehigh Univ 1972; Advanced Trng Cmptr Basic, Cmptr Literacy Instruction; *cr:* Career Dev Specialist Hazleton Area Voc-Tech Sch 1972-74; 5th/6th Grade Teacher Drums Elem Sch; *ai:* Co-Chm Awds/Achievement Advisory, Teachers Improvement Comm; Lang Art Curr Comm; HAEA, PSEA, NEA 1972-; Hazleton Jaycees Legislative Laison Comm Co-Chm 1981, Nom Outstanding Young Teacher 1979; Author ESEA Title IV-B Grant 1980-83; Developed Elem Comm Arts Multi-Media Lib Learning Center; Helped Initiate Dist Elem Cmptr Prgm; Instructional Packet Author; *office:* Drums Elem Sch RR 3 Box 750 Drums PA 18222

HARRIS, ALCESTER BRYANT, Fifth Grade Teacher; *b:* Cove City, NC; *m:* Jesse Ray Sr.; *c:* Jesse Jr., David B.; *ed:* (BA) Elem Ed, St Augustines Coll 1967; (MS) Ed, E Carolina Univ 1981; *cr:* 4th Grade Teacher Mineola Elem 1967-69; Resource Teacher Pamlico Mid Sch 1969-70; 5th Grade Teacher Duffy Field, F R Danyus 1970-85, Benvenue Elem 1986-; *ai:* Sch Base Comm; Accreditation Steering Comm; Assistance Team; PTO Exec Bd; NEA, NC Assn of Educators Asst Secy 1968-69; F R Danyus Sch 1983-84, Educator of the Month; *office:* Benvenue Elem Sch 2700 Nicodemus Rocky Mount NC 27804

HARRIS, ANN NYQUIST, English, Math Teacher; *b:* Duluth, MN; *m:* Wallace Bailey; *c:* Brandon, Brett, Jaclyn; *ed:* (BA) Eng, Univ of MN Duluth 1969; Math, Marshall Univ 1989; *cr:* Teacher Hibbing MN 1969-70, Ceredo-Kenova WV 1971-72, Milton WV 1987-; *ai:* Mu Alpha Theta Chapter Milton HS Spon; Math Field Day Team Coach.

HARRIS, ANNE MARIE EGGER, Physical Ed & Health Teacher; *b:* Marshfield, WI; *m:* Terry Joseph; *c:* Tricia M., Michael J.; *ed:* (BS) Phys Ed/Health, 1976, (MS) Elem Phys Ed, 1983 Univ of WI La Crosse; *cr:* K-8th Grade Phys Ed Teacher 1976-88, K-5th Grade Phys Ed/7th-8th Grade Health Teacher 1976- Cuba City Elem/Jr HS; *ai:* Coach Jr HS Bsktbl 1988, Jr HS Vlybl, Bsktbl, Track, Cheerleading 1976-84, 5th/6th Grade Girls Bsktbl 1977-81; WAPHER Mem 1985-; GSA Asst Leader 1989-; Emergency Medical Technician 1977-82; Jaycees Activity Dir 1986-88; Nom WI Teacher of Yr 1978-79, 1980-81; 3rd Place Dubuque Marathon 1978; 1st Place Platteville Art Fest 5 Mile Run 1979; *office:* Cuba City Elem Sch 518 W Roosevelt St Cuba City WI 53807

HARRIS, ANTOINETTE MACEO, English Teacher; *b:* Dayton, OH; *m:* James William; *c:* Aaron; *ed:* (BS) Eng Ed, Wright St Univ 1981; *cr:* Eng Teacher Trotwood-Madison HS 1981-; *ai:* Yrbk & Newspaper Adv; NEA, OH Ed Assn 1981-; Trotwood-Madison Ed Assn (Building Rep 1982-84, VP 1985-86); Delta Sigma Theta (Corresponding Secy 1989-, Projects Chairperson 1988-); Dow Jones Newspaper Fund Fellowship 1985; *office:* Trotwood-Madison HS 221 E Trotwood Blvd Trotwood OH 45426

HARRIS, AUBREY EUGENE, Assistant Principal; *b:* Mobile, AL; *M:* Betty Shoots Harris; *ed:* (BA) Elem Ed, 1963; (MA) Ed, 1975 AL St Univ; *cr:* Teacher Ella Grant 1964-71, Nan Gray Davis 1971-79, Council Elem Sch 1979-86; Asst Prin Semmes Mid Sch 1986-; *ai:* Mobile Cty Ed Assn Bldg Rep 1980-86 Cmmty Chm Comm 1985-86; AEA/NEA; Neighborhood Block Club VP 1985-; Teacher of Yr Awd 1978-79.

HARRIS, BETTYE HANNAH, Business Department Chair; *b:* Altheimer, AR; *m:* Eugene L. Sr.; *c:* Doina; *ed:* (BS) Bus Ed, Univ of AR Pine Bluff 1969; (MBEA) Bus Ed, E MI Univ 1975; Effective Instruction Trng Cmptr Seminars Radio Shack; *cr:* Bookkeeper/Payroll Clerk Legal Aid Society 1969-70; Bus Teacher Flint Cntrl HS 1971-; *ai:* Bus Prof of America Youth Club Cntrl HS Spon; Faculty Advisory Comm; MI Bus Ed Assn Mem 1971-; Bus Prof of America Adv 1980-; Instructional Strategies for Bus Curr Planning Project Mem 1986-; 1st Union Baptist Church Mem 1975-; Bus & Office Ed Clubs Adv 1980-, 5 Yr Service Awd 1984; Recognition For Help In Textbook Revision; *office:* Flint Cntrl HS 601 Crapo St Flint MI 48503

HARRIS, BEVERLY MC GLASSION, 5th/6th Grade Math Teacher; *b:* Neosho, MO; *m:* John W.; *c:* Timothy J.; *ed:* (BS) Elem Ed, SW MO St Univ 1963; (MA) Elem Ed, Drury Coll 1975; *cr:* Teacher Springfield Public Schls 1963-65, 1968-; *ai:* Springfield Ed Assn, MO Cncl of Math Teachers, Intnl Rdng Assn, Kappa Delta Pi, Delta Kappa Gamma; *home:* 2506 S Catalina Springfield MO 65804

HARRIS, BRIAN LLOYD, Social Studies Chair; *b:* Decatur, IL; *m:* Carol; *ed:* (BS) Ed, Univ of IL 1987; (MS) Ed Admin, N IL Univ; *cr:* Soc Stud Teacher Waterman HS 1987-; *ai:* F-S Bsktbl; Jr HS Track; Jr Stu Cncl; Waterman Ed Assn Chief Negoiator 1989; *office:* Waterman Jr Sr HS 425 S Elm Waterman IL 60556

HARRIS, CAROL L., Middle School Teacher; *b:* Prairie Grove, AR; *ed:* (BA) Eng/Lang, Northeastern St Coll 1968; (BS) Elem Ed, 1976, (MS) Lib Sci, 1976 NE St Univ Tahlequah; Rdng Diagnostics, Harding Univ; Soc Stud, Univ of AR; Kndgtn Screening, Gesell Inst of Human Dev; *cr:* Mid Sch/HS Teacher Talihina Public Schls 1968, Stilwell Public Schls 1968-69; 1st/2nd Grade Teacher Green Cntry Chrstn Acad 1977-89; Mid Sch Teacher Wright Chrstn Acad 1989-; *ai:* Academic Advisory Comm; Green Valley Bible Camp Cnslr & Cook; Class Spon; NEA, OK Ed Assn Mem 1966-69; NCTE Mem 1966-68; SW Chrstn Schls Mem 1979-89; Green Cntry Chrstn Acad (Teacher 1977-89, Admin 1979-80), Teacher of Yr 1984, Outstanding Service Awd 1979-80; Dir Wkshps Primary Teachers SW Chrstn Schls Conferences; *home:* 7618 S 234 E Ave Broken Arrow OK 74014

HARRIS, CAROLE BRISCOE, 5th Grade Teacher; *b:* Hannibal, MO; *m:* Lars L.; *c:* Brian, Mindy; *ed:* (BS) Elem Ed, NE MO St Univ 1963; (MA) Elem Guidance, NE MO St Univ 1967; *cr:* 1st-8th Grade Teacher Millard Sch 1963-64; 4th Grade Teacher Pettibone Elem 1964-68; 5th Grade Teacher Starkey Elem 1968-70, Bauden Elem 1977-78, Haber Hunt 1978-80; Horace Mann 1980-; *ai:* SCEA Building Rep; Secalia Cmmty Ed Assn 1980-; MO Natl Ed Assn 1988-; Amer Cancer Society 1988-.

HARRIS, CHARLES BENSON, JR., Mathematics/Science Teacher; *b:* Louisburg, NC; *m:* Beverly Anne Wimberly; *c:* Jodi A., Sandy W.; *ed:* (BS) Bus Admin, Campbell Univ 1968; *cr:* Teacher Edward Best HS 1968-73, Spaulding Sch 1975-80, Southern Nash Jr HS 1980-; *home:* Rt 2 Box 334 Spring Hope NC 27882

HARRIS, DANIEL JOSEPH, Mathematics Teacher; *b:* Bakersfield, CA; *m:* Lynn Teresa Henry; *c:* Malia, Kelliann; *ed:* (BS) Nautical Industrial Technology, CA Maritime Acad 1981; *cr:* Chief Mate Digicon Geophysical Corporation 1981-83; Intern Cntrl Cath HS 1984-85; Instr Thomas Downey HS 1985-; *ai:* Frosh/Soph Boys Water Polo & Var Womens Soccer Coach; Cntrl CA Math Project 1990; *office:* Thomas Downey HS 1000 Coffee Rd Modesto CA 95355

HARRIS, DIANNE B., English III Teacher; *b:* Clarksville, TN; *ed:* (BS) Art, Austin Peay St Univ 1966; (MA) Ed, Trevecca Nazarene Coll 1989; Eng, Austin Peavy St Univ 1969-70; *cr:* 7th Grade Art Teacher Howell Sch 1966-68; 7th-9th Grade Art Teacher New Providence Jr HS 1968-69; 11th Grade Eng Teacher Northwest HS 1970-; *ai:* Jr Class Spon 1970-; Steering Comm Southern Assn Evaluations 1981-82, 1987-88; NCTE 1988-; WA Youth Tour Cnslr 1979-; Honorable Mention Cntrl South Exhibition; Awarded Plaque for Exemplary Teaching 1983; *office:* Northwest HS 800 Lafayette Clarksville TN 37040

HARRIS, DON F., 7th-8th Grade Teacher Gifted; *b:* Phoenix, AZ; *ed:* (BA) Elem Ed, AZ St Univ 1959; Endorsement-Gifted 1987; *cr:* 6th Grade Teacher 1959-63, 8th Grade Teacher 1963, 7th Grade Teacher 1964, 8th Grade Teacher 1965-75, Teacher of Gifted 1975- Grandview Osborn Dist; *ai:* St Exec Secy Stu Cncl; 1st Commissioner Youth Soccer; AZ Assn for Gifted & Talented 1976-; *office:* Osborn Sch Dist #8 1226 W Osborn Phoenix AZ 85013

HARRIS, DORIS ANN, Business Dept Chairman; *b:* Sand Gap, KY; *c:* Katie M.; *ed:* (BS) Bus Ed, 1972, (MS) Bus Ed, 1978, (Rank I) Bus Ed, 1985 E KY Univ; *cr:* Soc Worker Dept for Human Resources 1972-73; Bus Teacher Jackson Cty HS 1973-; *ai:* FBLA Spon; *office:* Jackson Cty HS Hwy 421 Mc Kee KY 40447

HARRIS, EMILY C., Third Grade Teacher; *b:* Mound Bayou, MS; *m:* Jesse L. Harris; *c:* Jesse V., Kwame S., Nia M.; *ed:* (BA) Ec/Bus Admin, Tougaloo Coll 1966; Elem Ed, Chicago St 1972; (MS) Elem Ed, Delta St Univ 1979; Spec Ed, Delta St; *cr:* Teacher John F Kennedy HS 1966-70; Elem Teacher Bryn Mawr Elem 1970-72; Secy/Bookkeeper North Bolivar Dev Corporation 1972-76; Teacher I T Montgomery Elem 1977-; *ai:* I T Montgomery Lang Comm; MAE Secy 1985-87; NAE Mem 1977-; *home:* PO Box 31 Mound Bayou MS 38762

HARRIS, EMMA WILLIAMS, Fifth/Sixth Grade Teacher; *b:* New Orleans, LA; *m:* Aaron Sherman; *c:* Errin, Eron; *ed:* (BA) Elem Ed, 1968, (MED) Spec Ed, 1970 Univ of New Orleans; Dr Spencer Kagans Cooperative Learning & Advanced Cooperative Wrkshp; *cr:* 3rd-6th Grade Classroom Teacher 1968-70, Spec Ed Teacher 1970-71 Orleans Parish Public Schls; Spec Ed Teacher 1971-77, 4th-6th Grade Classroom Teacher 1979- Prince Georges Cty Public Schs; *ai:* Stephen Decatur Mid Schl PTA Public Relations, James Ryder Randall Crisis Intervention Team, Lang Art, Sch Spirit Chairperson; NEA, Prince Georges Cty Educators Assn, MD St Teachers Assn 1971-; Chrstn Cmmty Church Mem 1983-; James Ryder Randall PTA Mem 1989-; *office:* James Ryder Randall Sch 5410 Kirby Rd Clinton MD 20735

HARRIS, ERNEST C., Social Studies Teacher; *b:* New Haven, CT; *m:* Shirley Ranney; *c:* Christopher, Jonathan; *ed:* (BA) His, Syracuse Univ 1967; (MS) Scndry Soc Stud Ed, SUNY Cortland 1987; Grad Stud SUNY Oswego; *cr:* Soc Stud Teacher Cntrl HS 1967-70, Auburn HS 1970-74, East Mid Sch 1984-; *ai:* Stu Government Organization Adv; Dist Effective Schls & Mainstreaming the Handicapped Comm; Auburn Teachers Assn, NY St United Teachers, AFT 1967-; Knights of Columbus 1986-; NY Cncl for Hum His Teacher Inst Grant; *office:* East Mid Sch 159 Franklin St Auburn NY 13021

HARRIS, ETHEL SWITZER, Retired; *b:* Bucklin, MO; *m:* Darrel M.; *c:* Karen, Bruce E. H., Pamela K. Resnick; *ed:* (MA) Lang Arts, Webster Coll 1965-71; Lang Arts Webster Coll 1979-80; *cr:* 4th Grade Teacher 1964-65; 2nd Grade Teacher 1965-75 Keysor Sch; 2nd Grade Teacher 1975-79; 3rd Grade Teacher Westchester Sch; *ai:* Kirkwood Teachers Organization Salary Comm 1980-83; Worked on Comm of Teachers Organization & Grade Level Meetings & Courses Involved Implementing New Way; *office:* Westchester Elem Sch 1416 Woodgate Kirkwood MO 63122

HARRIS, GEORGIA JEAN (HOFF), Mathematics Teacher; *b:* Gary, IN; *m:* David Eugene; *c:* Rick, Shelly Baldwin, Mike, Tavis; *ed:* (BSED) Math, SW MO St Univ 1969; *cr:* Teacher Wright City MO 1969-72, Walnut Grove R-V 1972-76, 1982-; *ai:* Math Club & 8th Grade Spon; Career Ladder Revision & CTA Soc Comm; MCTM, NCTM, SWDAMT 1987-; VFW Ladies Auxiliary 1983-; *home:* RR 2 Box 76 Walnut Grove MO 65770

HARRIS, GWENDOLYN TIPP, First Grade Teacher; *b:* Sharon, PA; *w:* Arthaniel E. (dec); *c:* Arthaniel E. Jr., Adalynn E.; *ed:* (AB) Music/Eng, Livingstone Coll 1953; (MED) Elem Ed, Duquesne Univ 1965; Tuskegee Inst, Murray Univ, Western Univ; Summer Sch Tuskegee Univ 1968-69; *cr:* Teacher Pittsburgh City 1961-66, Macon Cty 1966-70, Hopkins Cty 1970-74, Teachers Memorial Sch 1974-84, Murph Sch 1984-85, Clara J Peck Schls 1985-; Summer Sch Teacher Guiford Cty Detention Center 1986-; *ai:* NEA & NCSTA Local Comm; GSA Tutor; PACE Organist St August Amez Church, Butler Chapel AME Zion, St Phillips AME Zion Church; Pearson Memorial; NCAE, NSTA, NCSTA Mem 1966-; NEA (Mem, Building Rep, Delegate 1989); Delta Sigma Theta Mem, Trinity AME Zion Church Political Mem; Presider NCSTA Conference 1989; GSA Leader; GSA Triad Cncl; Natl Sci Conference Delegate 1990; St Augustus AME Zion Church Outstanding Woman 1989; Chrstn Service Awd 1983; *office:* Clara J Peck Elem Sch 1601 W Florida St Greensboro NC 27403

HARRIS, H. DAVID, Social Studies Teacher; *b:* Evansville, IN; *m:* Madeline Thrall; *c:* David, Amanda; *ed:* (BS) Sociology, St Benedict Coll 1970; (BA) Scndry Ed, Univ of Evansville 1973; (ME) Scndry Ed, IN St Univ 1980; *cr:* Teacher/Cnslr St John The Baptist; *ai:* Vlybl Coach; Amer Red Cross (WSIT, LGIT); BSA Natl Aquatic Sch Staff; *office:* St John The Baptist Cath Sch 725 Frame Rd Newburgh IN 47630

HARRIS, JAMES D., Physical/Life Science Teacher; *b:* Panama City, FL; *m:* Kathy S. Sanders; *c:* Shenna K., Elizabeth L.; *ed:* (BA) Sci, Northeastern OK A&M;(BA) Phys Ed, Central St Univ 1981; Psychiatric Aid Eastern St Hosp; Addl Studies Ed Community Jr Coll; *cr:* Educator/Athletic Trnr; Bishop Mc Guiness HS 1981-83; Educator/Coach Del Crest Jr HS 1983-; *ai:* Coach 8th Grade Ftbl; Head Jr HS Wrestling Coach; Jr Varsity Bsbl Coach Del City HS; Pep Club Spon; Scholastic Tournament Spon; Fellowship of Chrstn Athlete Spon; Bldrs Club Spon; Youth Advisement Cncl; Spencer Church Leag, Leag Pres 1981-83; FCA/Hd Athletic Trnr 1982; Kiwanis Club Mem 1988- Service Awd 89; Del Crest Jr HS Stu Cncl Teach Er 1983- Favorite Teacher 1986-89; Red Cross-Public Svc Awd Envolvement; Sunday Sch Teacher for Handicapped; *office:* Del Crest Jr H S 431 Judy Drive Del City OK 73115

HARRIS, JAMES LOUIS, Fifth Grade Teacher; *b:* Livingston, TN; *m:* Leretha Huddleston; *c:* David, Bruce; *ed:* (BS) Elem Ed, TN Tech Univ 1958; (MA) Admin/Supervision, W MI Univ 1965; *cr:* Teacher Lakeview Schls 1958-69; Prin Wilson Elem 1969-70; Teacher Rickman Elem 1970-; *ai:* Overton Cty Ed Assn Pres 1978-79; Mid TN Ed Assn, TN Ed Assn, NEA; 4-H Club Adv Teacher of Yr 1988; *home:* R 3 Box 254 Livingston TN 38570

HARRIS, JERILYN ROLINSON, Biology Teacher; *b:* Cleveland, OH; *m:* Michael Ford; *c:* Kelli, Ryan; *ed:* (BS) Biological Sci, 1964, (MS) Biological Sci, 1966 Univ of CA Los Angeles; Grad Work; *cr:* Sci Teacher Beverly Vista Sch 1965-70, Pomolita Mid Sch 1978-83; Bio Teacher Ukiah HS 1983-; *ai:* SADD Adv; Lawrence Holly Sci Grand Prize Winning Team Coach; NSTA 1978-; CA Sci Teachers Assn 1980-; Women Appointees Cncl 1984-; Mendocino Cmmty Hosp Chm of Bd 1983-86; Sun House Guild Founder 1985-; Amer Assn of Univ Women 1976-; CA Commission on Teacher Credentialing Commissioner; CA Teachers at Presidential Inauguration Rep 1989; Sunset Review Comm St of CA Chm; Stu Choice Awd; Distinguished Adv.

HARRIS, JOSIE EVANS, English Teacher; *b:* Randolph, AL; *m:* Jack A.; *c:* Lisa J. Mask, John M.; *ed:* (MED) Eng Ed, 1983; (BS) Eng Ed, 1989 Auburn Univ; *cr:* 10th-12th Eng Teacher Bibb Graves HS 1983-85;7th-12th Eng Teacher Mellow Valley HS 1985-; *ai:* Spon Pine Yrbk & Sr Girls 4-H Club; Sigma Tau Delta; Kappa Delta Pi; Phi Theta Kappa; Bibb Graves HS Teacher of Yr 1985; Mellow Valley HS Faculty Favorite 1988; *home:* Rt 2 Box 86 Wadley AL 36276

HARRIS, JUANITA KING, Fourth Grade Teacher; *b:* Winter Garden, FL; *m:* Leroy; *c:* Bernard, Roy, Ron, Juandolyn; *ed:* (BS) Phys Ed, FL Memorial; (BS) Elem Ed, FL A&M Univ; Faculty Study 1987; Elem Curr 1987-88; *cr:* 6th Grade Teacher 1987-88, 4th Grade Teacher 1988- Maxey Elem Sch; *ai:* Big Sisters Club Adv 1987-88; NEA 1987-88; TTA, FTA 1988-89; CTA 1989-; Most Positive Teacher Awd & Teacher of Yr Maxey Elem Sch 1987; *home:* 1030 Maxey Dr Winter Garden FL 34787

HARRIS, LINDA GILMORE, 5th Grade Teacher; *b:* Newport, AR; *m:* Alvis Jr.; *c:* Robert L., Holly A., Brett A.; *ed:* (BSE) Elem Ed, AR St Univ 1964; *cr:* 3rd Grade Teacher Gosnell Elem 1965-68; 2nd/4th Grade Teacher Luxora Elem 1968-70; 3rd Grade Teacher Franklin Elem 1970-71; 5th Grade Teacher Cntrl Elem 1971-; *ai:* 5th grade Chairperspn; Personnel Policy Comm; Teacher Assistance Team; Partners in Ed Aerospace Class Teacher of 6th Grade Gifted & Talented Stu 1990; *office:* Cntrl Elem Sch Division at Moultrie Sts Blytheville AR 72315

HARRIS, LINDA RICHARDSON, 7th Grade Math/Science Teacher; *b:* Hopkinsville, KY; *m:* Wm. E. Jr.; *c:* Laurel, Jill, Adam; *ed:* (BS) His, 1967, Elem Ed, 1985- Austin Peay Univ; *cr:* 6th Grade Teacher 1967-72, 7th Grade Teacher 1972-78, 5th Grade Teacher 1978-84 Ashland City Elem; 7th Grade Math/Sci Teacher Sycamore Mid Sch 1986-; *ai:* Stu Cncl Spon; Coach & Spon Math Team; 7th Grade Level Math Teacher for Adult Ed Prgm; Faculty Adv Comm; Sch Annual, Chrldr, Stamp Club Spon; Cheatham Cty Curr Cncl 1971-75; Delta Kappa Gamma Treas 1972-75; Mid TN Math Teachers 1988-; TN Assn for Sch Curr Dev 1989 ; NSTA 1987-; Cheatam Cty Ed Assn (Treas 1968, Pres 1976-77); Bus & Prof Womens Club 1972-74; Natl Assn of Wkshp Dir 1989-; Teacher of Yr 1989; *home:* 1070 Floyd Hudgens Rd Ashland City TN 37015

HARRIS, LOUISE TAYLOR, Kindergarten Teacher; *b:* Waverly Hall, GA; *m:* James Jr.; *ed:* (BA) Elem, Clark Coll 1963; (MA) Early Elem, Atlanta Univ 1972; Inservice Courses; *cr:* 1st Grade Teacher 1964-66, Kndgtn Teacher 1966-72 James L Mayson Elem; Kndgtn Teacher R N Fickett Elem Sch 1972-; *ai:* Consultant Kosmeo Lady Love Cosmetics; Atlanta Fed of Teachers Local 1565 1968-; Matron Circle VP 1963-65; Les Fleurs Soc/Civic Club (Pres, VP) 1982-84, Plaque 1984; Class of 1958 Financial Treas 1988-; Family Circle Travel Club (Pres, VP) 1987-89; 1st Corinth Missionary Baptist Church Active Mem; Teacher of Yr 1979-80; Achievement of Perfect Attendance 1986-87; *home:* 625 Church St NW Atlanta GA 30318

HARRIS, MARTHA JANE (BURKE), 7th-8th Grade Rdng/Sci Teacher; *b:* Okmulgee, OK; *c:* Burke L., Dustin L.; *cr:* 6th Grade Teacher Collinsville OK 1965; 3rd Grade Teacher Chetopa KS 1965-66; 6th Grade Teacher Lamar MO 1966-67; 5th Grade Teacher 1967-68, 7th-8th Grade Teacher 1968- Morris OK; *ai:* MACT Schlsp Comm; OEA; *office:* Morris Mid Sch 6th & Ozark Morris OK 74445

HARRIS, MARY ROUSH, Teacher of Gifted Education; *b:* Miami, FL; *m:* Jim R.; *c:* Hunter H.; *ed:* (BA) Elem Ed, SE LA Univ 1971; Grad Stud; *cr:* Classroom Teacher Kemp Elem 1971-74, Southern Heights Elem 1974-83, Coll Lane Elem 1983-89; Teacher of Gifted Ed Will Rogers Elem 1990; *ai:* Hobbs Ed Assn Treas 1980; Intnl Rdng Assn (VP 1987, Pres 1988); NEA; Cub Scout Leader 1984-87; PTA Mem 1974-; TX Folklore Society (Mem, Cnslr 1989-91) 1973-; Delta Kappa Gamma Secy 1987-.

HARRIS, MICHAEL ALONZO, HS Mathematics Teacher; *b:* Morganton, NC; *m:* Janette; *c:* Andrew, Faith; *ed:* (BS) Bible, 1981, (BSED) Math Sci, 1981 Pillsbury Baptist Bible Coll; Cmptr & Fire Fighter I Course, W Piedmont Comm Coll; *cr:* Teacher/Coach Tabernacle Chrstn Sch 1981-; *ai:* Asst Soccer Coach; Oak Hill Volunteer Fire Dept 1988-; Tabernacle Baptist Church Sunday Sch Dir 1986-; *home:* Rt 7 Box 367 Morganton NC 28655

HARRIS, MICHELLE GEOFFROY, French Teacher; *b:* Herington, KS; *m:* Gregory A.; *c:* Adrienne, Aaron, Zachary; *ed:* (BA) Fr, MI St Univ 1975; Scndry Ed, IN Univ; Summer Inst for Teachers of Fr, Angers France; *cr:* Fr Teacher Edison Mid Sch 1982-, Adams HS 1988-; *ai:* Foreign Lang Textbook Adoption Comm; Elem Foreign Lang Task Force; Foreign Lang Dept Head 1985-87; MI Alliance of Foreign Lang Profs 1988-; *office:* Edison Mid Sch 2701 Eisenhower Rd South Bend IN 46615

HARRIS, PAMELA BURNETTE, 5th-6th Grade Teacher; *b:* Rocky Mount, NC; *m:* Vincent; *c:* Tommy, Amy; *ed:* (BS) Intermediate Eng/Scndry, Atlantic Chrstn Coll 1975; *cr:* 4th-5th Grade Teacher Gold Sand Elem; *ai:* Adv for Alpha Club; Math Chm; Life Lab Teacher; Cmptr Coord; NC Math Assn; Won Teacher of Yr 1987-89, Math Teacher of Yr GSE 1988-89; *home:* Rt 2 Box 767 Louisburg NC 27549

HARRIS, PATRICIA PONDANT, English/Speech/Lang Teacher; *b:* Youngstown, OH; *m:* Carlton J.; *c:* Robert A., Violanda M., Carlton II, Patti M.; *ed:* (BS) Speech/Drama, TX Womans Univ 1961; NY Dramatic Wkshp; Grad Work Stephen F Austin St Univ; *cr:* Eng/Speech/Drill Team Teacher Mt Pleasant HS 1968-69; Summer Repretory Drama Appreciation Teacher Stephen F Austin St Univ 1983-84; Eng/Speech/Drama/Cmptr Literacy Teacher Wells HS 1986-89; Eng as 2nd Lang Lufkin Ind Sch Dist 1989-; *ai:* Stu Cncl, UIL Competitions, Sr Class Spon Wells HS 1986-89; Phi Delta Kappa 1989-; TX Assn of Bi-ling Educators Secy 1989-; TX Classroom Teachers Assn 1989-; *home:* PO Box 362 Nacogdoches TX 75963

HARRIS, PAULETTE ABBOTT, Second Grade Teacher; *b:* Humboldt, TN; *m:* Chester T. Jr.; *c:* Chandra C., Chester T. III; *ed:* (BS) Elem Ed, Univ of TN Martin 1974; *cr:* 2nd/6th Grade Teacher Dyer Elem 1974-; *ai:* Advertising Section Yrbk Adv 1980-81; Basic Skills Dev, Standardized Test Scores Assessment Comm Mem; Gibson Cty Ed Assn, TN Ed Assn, NEA, PTO 1974-; Dyer CME Church (Secy of Rossie T Hollis, Stewardship) 1975-; St Jude Bike-a-Thon (Aide, Volunteer) 1988-89; Dyer Station Celebration Cats from Many Lands Display Dyer Elem 1989; World Day of Prayer Ecumenical 1986; Decorative Art Awd 1987; Lang Art Teacher of Poetry Winner 20th Century Club Contest; *office:* Dyer Elem Sch 322 E College St Dyer TN 38330

HARRIS, RETTA IRENE (BRYANT), First Grade Teacher; *b:* Booneville, MS; *m:* Gregory; *c:* Tyler; *ed:* (BA) Elem Ed, Mac Murray Coll 1975; *cr:* 1st Grade Teacher Woodland Sch 1975-79, Le Vasseur Sch 1979-; *ai:* Memory Book, Village of Reade s & Writers Comm; Two Rivers Rdng Cncl 1979-; Bourbonnais Ed Assn Secy 1981-82; Church Organist.

HARRIS, RHONETTE LYLES, Second Grade Teacher; *b:* Birmingham, AL; *m:* Robert; *c:* Cathy Harris Armstrong; *ed:* (BA) Elem Ed, St Bernard 1976; (MA) Elem Ed, Univ of AL 1979; *cr:* Teacher Cleveland Sch 1976-; *ai:* AL Ed Assn, NEA 1976-; *office:* Cleveland Sch PO Box 127 Cleveland AL 35049

HARRIS, RITA DELL PETTY, Science Teacher; *b:* Dallas, TX; *ed:* (BS) Phys Ed, TX Wesleyan Coll 1966; *cr:* Phys Ed/ Geography/Amer His Teacher/Bsktbl Coach Meridian Elem 1966-67; Elem/Scndry Phys Ed/Remedial Rdng Teacher/Vlybl Coach Reagan Cty Elem Mid & HS 1967-71; Gross Motor Skills Dev Haggerman Elem 1971-72; Geography/Health/Phys Sci/ K-8th Grade Phys Ed/6th Grade Sci & Earth Sci Teacher/Bsktbl Coach Reagan Cty Elem Mid & HS 1972-; *ai:* Jr HS & HS Vlybl, Jr HS Bsktbl; Jr HS & HS Boys & Girls Tennis Coach; Chrldrs & Pep Club Spon; Univ Interscholastic Leag Sci Advisory Comm; Assn of TX Prof Educators, TX Math Sci Coaches Assn, NSTA; Bethel Baptist Church; *office:* Reagan Cty Mid Sch 500 Pennsylvania Big Lake TX 76932

HARRIS, ROBERT D., Computer Instructor; *b:* Houston, TX; *ed:* (BS) Office Management, Univ of Houston 1987; Masters Prgm Adult Trng & Ed, Univ of Houston; *cr:* Admin Asst A-Rocket Moving Company 1981-84; Houston Ind Sch Dist 1985-88; Cmptr Instr Furr St HS 1988-; *ai:* Cmptr Club Spon; Attendance Comm Mem; *office:* Furr Sr HS 520 Mercury Dr Houston TX 77013

HARRIS, ROGER ALAN, First Grade Teacher; *b:* Harrah, OK; *m:* Jimmie Kay Flournoy; *c:* Joshua C. A.; *ed:* (BS) Elem Ed, 1978, (MED) Early Chldhd Ed, 1985 Cntrl St Univ; Positive Reinforcement Teaching Strategies for Educators, Skills for Growing Teacher Trng; *cr:* 5th Grade Rdng Teacher 1978-79, 5th Grade Sci Teacher 1979-80, 5th Grade Self Contained Teacher 1980-81, 3rd Grade Self Contained Teacher 1981-87 Russell Babb Elem; 1st Grade Self Contained Teacher Clara Reynolds Elem 1987-; *ai:* Local Staff Dev Planning; Chairperson Sch Soc Comm; Contract Negotiator & Pres Local Teachers Union; ACT Pres 1990; Harrah Dept of Parks & Recreation Vice-Chairperson; Local Dist Teacher of Yr 1985; *office:* Clara Reynolds Elem Sch 701 S Harrison Harrah OK 73045

HARRIS, ROSEMARY SILVESTRI, Kindergarten Teacher; *b:* Albany, CA; *m:* James Edward; *c:* Thomas, Audrey; *ed:* (BA) Elem Ed, Dominican Coll of San Rafael 1961; Grad Units Ed, Various Insts; *cr:* 1st-3rd Grade Teacher Falls Sch 1961-63; 1st/ 2nd Grade Teacher Mare Island Sch 1964-65; Kndgtn Teacher Napa Junction Sch 1965-73, St Basils Sch 1975-; *ai:* Stu Cncl Secy & Moderator; Summer Sch Teacher; Cath Ed Assn of America; Intnl Arabian Horse Assn; Arabian Horse Registry; Vintage Arabian Horse Assn (Secy 1987-89, VP 1990); *office:* St Basils Sch 1230 Nebraska St Vallejo CA 94590

HARRIS, RUBY NELL THRASH, Third Grade Teacher; *b:* Red Oak, MS; *m:* Mike; *c:* Marie Whitfield, Irwin, Michael; *ed:* (BS) Ed, MS Coll 1964; *cr:* Elem Teacher Pearl River Cntrl Sch; *ai:* Adopt A Sch & Playground Improvement Comm; Sunshine Sch Comm & 3rd Grade Chairperson; *home:* PO Box 206 Mc Neill MS 39457

HARRIS, SANDRA KAUFMAN, Elementary Classroom Teacher; *b:* Virginia, MN; *m:* Allen J.; *ed:* (AA) Math & Pre Ed, Mesabi St Jr Coll 1961; (BS) Elem Ed, Univ of Mn 1963; (MS) Curr & Instruction, Univ of Mn 1973; Educl & Research Dissemination; Human Relations & Comm Skills; Coaching Teacher Higher Levels of Effectiveness; Skills for Adolescence; Peer Coaching & Teacher Mentoring; *cr:* 5th Grade Teacher Brem Elem Sch 1963-67, Pratt Elem Sch 1967-70; Demonstration Teachers/Stu Teaching Supervisor 1970-71, Teaching Asst 1970-71 Univ of MN Minneapolis; Intermediate 4th-6th Grade Teacher Motley Elem Sch 1971-74; 5th/6th Grade Teacher 1971-75, 5th/6th Grade Prgm Coord 1975-77 Anwater Mid Sch; 5th Grade Teacher Barton Fundamentals Sch 1977-82, Burroughs Fundamental Sch 1982-87; Mentor Teacher Minneapolis Public Sch 1987-89; 4th-5th Grade Teacher Burroughs Fundamentals Sch 1989-; *ai:* Sci Curr Liaison; World Lang Comm; MN Teachers Fed; Bnai Emet Synagogue (Bd of Trustees, Ed Couples Club Newsletter); Hadassah (Governing Bd of Dir, Publicity Chairperson; Chevra Bikkur Holim Affiliate Bnai Emet Synagogue Society Visiting III; Commendation Excl Fire Prevention Ed Minneapolis Fire Dept 1987; Nom Woman of Achievement Twin West Chamber Commerce 1985; Selected Outstanding Young Women of Amer 1971; Authored a Publication on Creative Dramatics for The Elem Classroom Teacher Published MN Public Schls 1966; *home:* 11315 46th Ave N Minneapolis MN 55442

HARRIS, SANDRA TRAVER (AEBERLI), 6th Grade Teacher/Team Leader; *b:* Middletown, NY; *m:* Barron M. Jr.; *c:* Gregory, Stephen; *ed:* (AA) Lang Arts/Soc Sci, Delta Coll 1974; (BA) Lang Arts, MI St Univ 1976; (MA) Counseling, Western St Coll 1984; Prof Writer Institute of Childrens Literature 1987; *cr:* 6th Grade Teacher Bullock Creek Mid Sch 1975-76; 3rd Grade Teacher Kings Highway Elem 1976-77; 5th Grade Teacher Morgan Elem 1979-80; 6th Grade Teacher Reij Sch Dist 1980-; *ai:* Spec Grants Comm; Team Leader; Comm Cncl Rep; UVEA Assn Rep 1986-88 Outstanding Assn Rep 1987; CEA; NEA; Phi Kappa Phi 1976; Article Purchased for Publication By the Friend 1987; *office:* Columbine Mid Sch PO Box 1329 Montrose CO 81401

HARRIS, SHARON A., Mathematics Dept Chairperson; *b:* Enid, OK; *m:* Jerry J.; *c:* Tracy Harris Peters; *ed:* (BS) Natural Sci, Cntrl St Univ 1961; (MA) Math, N AZ Univ 1966; Cmptr Sci, Univ of OK; *cr:* Teacher Grandfield HS 1961-63; Math Dept Chairperson Tuba City HS 1963-68, Midwest City HS 1968-82; Teacher 1984-, Math Dept Chairperson 1988- Choctaw HS; *ai:* Gifted & Talented Math Prgm Midwest City HS; Advanced Placement Calculus Choctaw HS; NCTM; 1st Baptist Church Choctaw Organist 1979-; Various Math, Sci, Cmptr Sci Insts; *home:* 19100 SE 29th St Harrah OK 73045

HARRIS, THERESA SMITH, 4th Grade Teacher; *b:* Hazlehurst, MS; *m:* John Allen Jr.; *c:* Jessica, Jennifer; *ed:* (AA) Elem Ed, Copiah Lincoln Jr 1978; (BA) Elem Ed, Univ of Southern MS 1980; *cr:* Teacher Crystal Springs Elem 1980-; *ai:* Co-Chm of Courtesy Comm; AFT 1987-; PTA 1980-; Crystal Springs Jr Auxilary 1987; Selected Teacher of Month 1989; *home:* PO Box 85 Crystal Springs MS 39059

HARRIS, VICKI HENRY, Business Education Teacher; *b:* Bernice, LA; *m:* William Ronnie; *c:* Robert B., Monica; *ed:* (BSE) Bus Ed, 1977, (MS) Bus Ed, 1981 S AR Univ; *cr:* Keyboarding Instr S AR Univ 1988; Bus Ed El Dorado HS 1978-; *ai:* El Dorado HS FBLA Adv; El Dorado HS AR Bus Exec Game Team Spon; Delta Kappa Gamma Alpha Chapter Recording Secy 1988-; NEA, AR Ed Assn, Classroom Teachers Assn, AVA, AR Voc Assn, AR Bus Ed Assn; Bernice HS Band Parents Club 1987-; Bernice HS Athletic Assn Recording Secy 1986-88; Livestock Club Recording Secy 1987-; El Dorado HS Parent Teachers Assn Secy 1981; Whos Who in Stu Amer Colls & Univs 1977; *home:* Rt 2 Box 149 Bernice LA 71222

HARRIS, VIRGINIA ROBINSON, 8th Grade English Teacher; *b:* Monongahela, PA; *m:* Calvin Jerry; *c:* Whitney Bolt, Carter Bolt; *ed:* Amer Stud, Sweet Briar 1959; Brenau Coll; Oglethorpe Coll; GA St Univ; *cr:* Lang Art Teacher Forsyth Cty Ed System 1971-77, Griffin Mid Sch 1977-; *ai:* Oratorical Contest Optimist Club Spon & Adv; *home:* 4510 River Rill Ct Atlanta GA 30327

HARRIS, WILLIAM H., Math Teacher/Math Dept Chm; *b:* Bedford, IN; *M:* Gail D.; *c:* Kyle N., Kari L.; *ed:* (BS) General Sci/Math 1970, (MS) Scndry Ed, 1974 IN Univ; *cr:* Math Teacher/Ftbl Coach Springs Valley HS 1970-; *ai:* Head Ftbl Coach; Jr Class Spon; Math Dept Chm; ISTA VP 1988-; IN Ftbl Coaches Assn 1984; Dist IX Coach of Yr 1989; 1st Baptist Church Trustee 1979; Article Published Grid Magazine 1988.

HARRISON, ADOLPH CHARLES, JR., American Government Teacher; *b:* San Francisco, CA; *m:* Dolores Marie; *c:* Adolph III, Mary D., Terrence M., Cheri L.; *ed:* (BS) Poly Sci, 1956, Gen Scndry Teaching Credential Ed, 1957, (MA) Ed/Poly Sci, 1968 Univ of San Francisco; *cr:* Amer Government Teacher/ Dir of Act Capuchino HS 1957-66, Burlingame HS 1966-; *ai:* Dir of Act; Stu Government Adv; CTA, NEA 1957-; SM UHSD Teacher Assn 1957-, Teacher of Yr 1978; Burligame Lions Club Bd of Dirs 1966-69; San Mateo Cty Supvr 1966; Burlingame City Councilman 1974-78, 1989-, Mayor 1977-78; City of Burlingame Planning Commissioner 1986-89, Lib Bd Trustee 1984-86, Civil Service Commissioner 1981-83; *home:* 376 Lexington Way Burlingame CA 94010

HARRISON, DEBRA ANN (YOUNG), Secondary English Teacher; *b:* Biloxi, MS; *m:* Walter R. Jr.; *c:* Tasha D.; *ed:* (BS) Eng Ed, Jackson St Univ 1974; (MA) Eng Ed, Southern Univ 1983; *cr:* Eng/Rdng Teacher St Martin Jr HS 1974-79, Bitburg HS 1979-81; Eng as Second Lang Teacher/Adult Ed ND 1981-83; Eng Teacher St Martin HS 1984-; *ai:* Jr Class Spon; Youth Drama Group Dir; Church Choir; *office:* St Martin HS 10800 Yellow Jacket Ocean Springs MS 39564

HARRISON, ESTHER COX, Fifth Grade Teacher; *b:* Gladewater, TX; *m:* Guy T. Jr.; *c:* Misty M.; *ed:* (BS) Elem Ed, Univ of TX 1969; Cncl for Advancement of Math Teaching Summer Trng Wkshp; Region VII Educl Service Center Summer Wkshps; *cr:* 7th-8th Grade Math Teacher Irving Ind Sch Dist 1969-71; 5th Grade Teacher Shelbyville Ind Sch Dist 1972-; *ai:* Jr HS Chrldrs; 2nd-12th Grade Academic UIL Coord; Academic UIL Coach Number Sense; Various Comms; TX St Teachers Assn 1969-; Meth Church (Sunday Sch Supt 1978-84, Advisory Bd 1978-); Shelbyville PTO; Shelbyville Athletic Booster Club; Coach Region III AA First Number Sense Academic Team; Dragon Athletic Supporter Awd; Building & Dist Planning Comms S W Carter Elem Sch; *home:* PO Box 408 Shelbyville TX 75973

HARRISON, GWENDOLYN GREER, Social Studies Teacher; *b:* Richland Parish, LA; *m:* James L.; *c:* Jason L., Jesse N.; *ed:* (BA) Soc Stud, 1970, (MED) Soc Stud Ed, 1978 NE LA Univ; *cr:* Teacher Logtown Sch 1970, Calhoun HS 1970-72, 1973-88, Ouachita HS 1988-; *ai:* Soc Stud Fair Co-Dir 1988-; Kappa Kappa Iota (Secy 1987-88, VP 1988-89, Pres 1990); Calhoun HS Teacher of Yr 1987-88; *office:* Ouachita Parish HS 525 N Millhaven Rd Monroe LA 71203

HARRISON, JAMES LOUIS, III, Biology Teacher; *b:* Sheboygan, WI; *m:* Barbara C. Krings; *c:* William J., Stephan J.; *ed:* (BS) Bio, 1968, (MS) Curr/Supervision 1981 Univ of WI Oshkosh; Several Wkshps Univ of Wi Green Bay, Univ of WI Madison; *cr:* Bio Teacher Winneconne HS 1968-; *ai:* HS Track Coach; Academic Bowl Adv; AODA Facilitator; WI Ed Assn, NEA, WI Society of Sci Teachers 1968-; Univ of WI Oshkosh Alumni Assn Bd of Dir 1970-; AFS Club Adv 1975-; NE WI Sci Forum 1985-; Article Published; Wrote Curr Human Growth & Dev; WI St Sci Teachers Convention Presenter; *home:* 229 N 7th Ave Winneconne WI 54986

HARRISON, JESSE WILLIAM, Fourth Grade Teacher; *b:* San Isidro, NM; *m:* La Homa Cravatt; *c:* Cynthia Ann; *ed:* (BS) Phys Ed, NM St Univ 1960; Grad Stud Ed & Phys Ed, Univ of NM Albuquerque, NM St Univ University Park; *cr:* Cnslr/Recreation Leader Childrens Asthma & Research Inst 1960-63; Teacher BIA Civil Service 1963-65, Albuquerque Public Schls 1965-; *ai:* Support Team Sch Level Comm Teacher; Safety Comm; NEA 1965-80, 1984-; Albuquerque Public Schls 20 Yrs Service Certificate of Appreciation 1985.

HARRISON, LINDA GUIDRY, Language Arts Teacher; *b:* Houston, TX; *m:* David H.; *c:* Troy, Tray; *ed:* (BS) Ed, Univ of Houston 1972; (MS) Ed, Univ of Houston Clear Lake 1978; *cr:* 2nd Grade Teacher Carpenter Elem 1972-74; 7th Grade Teacher Deepwater Jr HS 1975-77; 6th-8th Grade Teacher Bonnette Jr HS 1978-; *ai:* Chrldr Coach; Pep Squad Spon; Intnl Rdng Assn 1976-; TX Joint Cncl of Teachers of Eng 1989-; TSTA, NEA 1972-; Natl Assn of Stu Activity Advs; Freeway Amer Little League (Secy 1986-87, Pres Ladies Auxiliary 1988); *office:* J P Bonnette Jr HS 5010 Pasadena Blvd Deer Park TX 77536

HARRISON, MARION L., Psychology/Biology Teacher; *b:* Beckley, WV; *ed:* (BS) Biological Sci/General Sci Comp, Marshall Univ 1972; Vertebrate Natural His, Entomology, Marshall Univ; Several Speech Comm Classes, WV Univ; Seminar Environmental Ed; Seminar Teaching Psych; *cr:* Bio Teacher Sherman HS 1972-79; Psych Teacher Woodrow Wilson HS 1979-; *ai:* Homebound Teacher; Dept Chairperson 1974-79; Boone Cty Ed Assn, WV Ed Assn, NEA 1972-77; Amer Psychological Assn 1979-; NSTA 1974-78; Raleigh Cty Jaycees 1981-83; Delta Kappa Gamma Personal Growth Chairperson 1988-; Nom Teacher of Yr Twice; *office:* Woodrow Wilson HS 410 Stanaford Rd Beckley WV 25801

HARRISON, MILDRED GARNER, First Grade Teacher; *b:* Traverse Cty, MN; *w:* Earl Lawrence (dec); *c:* Linda F. Myers, Leslie A.; *ed:* (BS) Elem Ed, Moorhead 1974; Coll Courses, Wkshps, Inservice; *cr:* Teacher Dist 11 1940-42, Dist 10 1942-45, 5th-8th Grade Teacher Dist 56 1959-66; Teacher Browns Valley Elem 1966-; *ai:* BVEA Secy; GFWC Progress Study Club (Secy, Treas); Luth Church Women Mem 1959-; Teacher of Yr 1980; *home:* PO Box 354 Browns Valley MN 56219

HARRISON, NADINE GILLISPIE, Math Dept Chairperson-Teacher; *b:* Arbovale, WV; *m:* James C.; *c:* Jennifer, Jan; *ed:* (BA) Math/Phys Sci, Glenville St 1966; (MED) Public Sch Admin, NTSU 1987; Grad Stud Numerous Colls 1970-84; *cr:* 8th-9th Grade Math Teacher Clarksburg Mid Sch 1966-67; 9th-12th Grade Math Teacher Huntington HS 1967-70; 8th-9th Grade Math Teacher Trewyn Mid Sch 1971-72; 9th-12th Grade Math Teacher Anderson HS 1972-74; 9th-12th Grade Sci/Math Teacher Western HS 1974-75; 9th-12th Grade Math Teacher Lake Highlands HS 1975-76; 9th-10th Grade Math Teacher 1976-, Dept Chairperson 1979- Vines HS; *ai:* Curr Advisory Comm; Insurance Benefits, Discipline Management, Failure Comm; *office:* Vines HS 1401 Highedge Plano TX 75075

HARRISON, NANCY THOMPSON, Health/Phys Ed Teacher; *b:* Indianapolis, IN; *m:* Daryl E.; *c:* Molly A.; *ed:* (BS) HPER Normal Coll AGU of IN Univ 1968; (MS) Health/Safety, IN Univ; Elem Phys Ed, Scndry Health, Swim; *cr:* WLE/Phys Ed/ Scndry Health/Swim Teacher Speedway Schls 1968-; *ai:* HS Swim Teach Coach; Jr HS Pool Dir; Cmmty Swim Prgm; NEA, SCTA, SPT; Amer Red Cross Volunteer; Speedway Hall of Fame Swim Team St Championship; *office:* Speedway Sch 5357 W 25th St Speedway IN 46224

HARRISON, PATRICIA, Science Teacher; *b:* Ft Knox, KY; *ed:* (BS) Bio, Univ of KY 1977; (MED) Scndry Ed, Univ of Louisville 1989; *cr:* Sci Teacher St Romuald Interparochial Sch 1981-; *ai:* NHS Adv; *office:* St Romuald Interparochial Sch N Main St Hardinsburg KY 40143

HARRISON, PHILIP MICHAEL, Health Department Chairman; *b:* Houston, TX; *m:* Jennifer Jordan; *ed:* (MA) Health/ Phys Ed, Lamar Univ 1983; Working Towards MS in Scndry Ed, TX A&I Univ; *cr:* Teacher/Athletic Trainer Fox Tech HS 1983-; *ai:* Fellowship of Chrstn Athletes Spon; Peer Assistance, Leadership Teacher & Spon; Insurance & Health Dept Coord; Textbook Comm; Dist CPR Instr; Crockett Elem Slow Rdng Prgm Asst; Natl Athletic Trainers Assn 1983-; Alamo Area Athletic Trainers Assn Hospitality Chm 1985-; PTA Mem 1983-; Area Sports Clinic 1987-; *office:* Fox Tech HS 637 N Main Ave San Antonio TX 78205

HARRISON, RANDELL EDWARD, US History Teacher; *b:* Maysville, KY; *m:* Jacqueline Sue Applegate; *c:* Joy N., Natalie S.; *ed:* (BA) His/Scndry Ed, 1975, (MA) His/Scndry Ed, 1976 Univ of KY; Rank I His/Scndry Ed, Morehead St Univ; *cr:* US His Teacher Tollesboro HS 1977-; *ai:* Boys Bsktbl Head Coach 1984-; Athletic Dir; Spirit Club & His Club Spon; KY Ed Assn 1980-; Lions Club (Pres 1989-, Secy 1988-89) 1978-; De Kalb IOOF 1978-; *home:* PO Box 95 Tollesboro KY 41189

HARRISON, ROSETTA, Fourth Grade Math Teacher; *b:* Parkins, AR; *ed:* (BS) Bus Ed, Rust Coll 1962; (MBE) Bus Ed, Jackson St Univ 1974; (ME) Elem Ed, MS St Univ; *cr:* Bus Teacher/Secy West Dist HS 1962-67; Prgm Developer/Asst Dir Mid St Opportunity 1965-73; Prin/Clerk MS Employment Security Service 1974-75, 1977-78; Bus Teacher MS Industrial Coll 1975-77; 4th Grade Math Teacher Tie Plant Elem Sch 1978-; *ai:* Grenada Assn of Ed, MS Assn of Ed 1978-; NEA 1962-; Natl Assn Advancement of Colored People 1970-; First New Hope M B Church Youth Dir 1986-; MS Industrial Coll Teacher of Yr 1977; Tie Plant Elem Teacher of Month 1990; *home:* 1054 Fox St Grenada MS 38901

HARRISON, SANDRA JUNE, Fifth Grade Teacher; *b:* Bastrop, LA; *ed:* (BA) Elem Ed, Northeast LA Univ 1978; Ed-Lang Arts; *cr:* Instructional Aide 1971-75, Spec Ed Resource Teacher 1978-79 Lincoln Elem; 3rd Grade Teacher Jackson Elem 1979-80; 5th Grade Teacher Port Hudson Elem 1980-81, Beechwood Elem 1981-; *ai:* Sch Comm Stu Cncl Spon; CRT Coord; Textbook Comm; Sci Fair Comm; Soc Stud Comm; Newspaper in Ed Person; Honor Roll/Birthday Comm; S S R Comm; Capitol Area Rdng Cncl 1980-; LA Rdng Assn 1980-; Intnl Rdng Assn 1980-92; Teacher Applying Whole Language 1989-; PTA 1978-; *home:* 6112 Bentley Dr Baker LA 70714

HARRISON, SHEILA BRITT, Spanish & English Teacher; *b:* Newton, NC; *m:* Michael; *ed:* (BS) Eng, 1981, (MA) Rdng Ed, 1983 Appalachian St Univ; Span, Appalachian Univ; *cr:* Grad Teaching Asst Appalachian St Univ 1982-83; Span/Eng Teacher Bunker Hill HS 1983-; *ai:* Adv Sch Newspaper & Jr/Sr Prom; Co-Adv Span Club; Chairperson Staff Dev; Mem Media Advisory & Soc Comm; Sigma Delta Pi 1989-; Gamma Beta Phi 1979-81; Alpha Chi 1980-82; *office:* Bunker Hill HS Rt 1 Box 130 Claremont NC 28610

HARRISON, ZITA ELLEN, Third Grade Teacher; *b:* Rice Lake, WI; *m:* Jack E.; *ed:* (BS) Elem Ed, Univ of WI Madison 1970; (MSE) Elem Ed, Univ of WI Platteville 1984; Univ WI Platteville/Univ WI Stevens Point; *cr:* 3rd Grade Teacher Everest Elem Sch 1970-72, 4th Grade Teacher 1972-78, 3rd/4th Grade Teacher 1978-85, 3rd Grade Teacher 1985 Belmont Grade Sch; *ai:* Phi Lambda Theta; WI Assn for Environmental Ed.

HARROLD, MARGARET SPELLMAN, Math Teacher/ Spanish Teacher; *b:* Stamford, NE; *m:* Allen K.; *c:* Allen J., William J.; *ed:* (BA) Math/Span, NE St Coll 1947; (MAT) Math, Univ of NE Lincoln 1974; Lib Sci, Univ of WY Laramie 1963; Univ of NE 1964; *cr:* 8th Grade Teacher Remmers Rural Sch 1942-43; Math Teacher Newman Grove Public Sch 1947-50; Math/Span Teacher Adams Public Sch 1960-; *ai:* NCTM & NEA LIFE MEM; Assn of Teachers of Span & Portuguese 1970-; All St Groups Math/Span Ed; Adams Presbyn Church SS Teacher Purdue Natl Womens Meeting 1976; BSA (Den Mother, Merit Cnslr 1964-); Nom Teacher of Yr 1978-79; Honor & Leters from Former Stu; Wrote His OF Adams Sch Gage Cty His Book; *home:* 848 Cherry St Adams NE 68301

HARRYMAN, F. ALLEN, Mathematics Department Chair; *b:* Holtville, CA; *m:* Janice Catherine Imwalle; *c:* Catherine A., Erica C., Margaret A.; *ed:* (BA) Phys Sci, Chico St Univ 1967; Working Towards Masters in Educl Admin & Preliminary Admin Services Credential Prgm US Intnl Univ; *cr:* Phys Sci Teacher 1968-78, Sci/Math Teacher 1979-80, Math Teacher 1981- Washington Jr HS; *ai:* Salinas Union HS Dist Teachers Assn Pres 1990.

HARRYMAN, MARILYN BURNS, Home Economics/Health Teacher; *b:* Ottumwa, IA; *m:* Merlin Dean; *ed:* (BS) Home Ec Ed, IA St Univ 1965; IA St Univ; *cr:* Home Ec & Sci Teacher Fox Valley Cmmty Schls 1965-72; Home Ec & Health Teacher Van Buren Cmmty Schls 1972-; *ai:* FHA Adv; NEA/ISEA & Local 1965-; Delta Kappa Gamma Treas-Secy 1973-; Amer Home Ec Assn 1976-86; PEO Chaplain 1989-; Christ United Meth Church Mem Chm 1955-; *office:* Van Buren H S 4th & Chestnut Keosauqua IA 52565

HARSHBARGER, ARLENE RECORD, Guidance Counselor; *b:* Forest, IN; *m:* George E.; *c:* Tim, Cindy; *ed:* (BS) Home Ec, 1957, (MS) Guidance, 1960 Purdue Univ; *cr:* Home Ec Teacher Frankfort HS 1957-67; Home Ec Teacher 1967-77, Guidance Cnslr 1977- Northwestern HS; *ai:* Stu Cncl & Design Success Spon; At Risk Comm; NEA, ISTA, NCEA 1957-75; Delta Kappa Gamma (Schlsp Comm 1960-70, Secy 1970-78); Crippled Childrens Assn Pres 1960-63; Howard Cmmty Womens Center Volunteer 1988-; Kokomo Chamber of Commerce 1989-; *home:* 6305 Windwood Dr Kokomo IN 46901

HARSHMAN, STEPHEN DOUGLAS, Scndry Social Studies Teacher; *b:* Tacoma, WA; *m:* Suzanne Parker Raines; *ed:* (BAED) Soc Sci/Phys Ed, 1971, (MA) Soc Sci, 1975 Pacific Luth Univ; Certified CPR Instr; *cr:* Soc Stud Teacher Issaquah HS 1974-76; Soc Stud/Phys Ed Teacher/Dept Chm Liberty HS 1977-87; Soc Stud Teacher Bennington HS 1987-; *ai:* Soph Class Adv; Asst Ftbl & Head Track Coach; NEA 1974-; *office:* Bennington HS 156th & Bennington Rd Bennington NE 68007

HARSTAD, LOIS ANDERSON, Fourth Grade Teacher; *b:* Rail Prairie, MN Morrison; *m:* Arlen B.; *c:* Steven, Cindy St Claire, Kim, David, Daniel, Gail Wiebolt; *ed:* Rural Sch Ed 1952, Stand, 1963 Valley City St Univ; (BA) Elem Ed, Moorhead St Univ 1973; *cr:* Rural Sch Teacher Laketown 1952-53; Spec Ed/4th/5th Grade Teacher Waubun Public Sch 1963-; *ai:* Rep MN at Statue of Liberty Centennial Celebration NY Christa Mc Auliffe Awd 1986; *office:* Waubun H S P O Box 98 Waubun MN 56589

HART, BRENDA LEE, Mathematics/Science Teacher; *b:* Valparaiso, IN; *ed:* (BS) Physics, 1980, (MA) Physics, 1982 Ball St Univ; (BS) Music Ed, Bob Jones Univ 1985; *cr:* Music Teacher Temple Chrstn Sch 1985-87; Math/Sci Teacher Faith Chrstn Sch 1987-; *ai:* Math Olympics & Sci Fair Coord; Elem Prgm Dir; *office:* Faith Chrstn Sch Russ Rd Greenville OH 45331

HART, BRUCE W., Seventh/Eighth Grade Teacher; *b:* Hot Springs, NM; *c:* (AA) Bus, Sacramento City Coll 1970; (BS) Biological Sci/Natural Resources Humboldt St Univ 1972; *cr:* Teacher Fieldbrook Sch 1974-; *ai:* Girls Boys Bsktbl Coach; Athletic Dir; Stu Cncl Adv; Ballroom Dance Instr; CA Math Cncl Far North Treas 1986-89; Fieldbrook Volunteer Fire Dept Firefighter 1976-; Humboldt Cty Teacher of Yr 1987; Finalist CA Teacher of Yr 1987; *office:* Fieldbrook Sch 4070 Fieldbrook Rd Arcata CA 95521

HART, CLARE, Fourth Grade Teacher; *b:* Detroit, MI; *ed:* (BS) Ed/Music, Mt St Joseph Coll 1952; (MS) Ed/Music Xavier Univ & Univ of Cincinnati 1960; *cr:* Music Teacher Shrine of Little Flower 1970-77; 4th/5th Grade Teacher St Mary 1977-; *ai:* Choir; Band; Organist; Intermediate Chm; *home:* 7279 Wildcat Rd Jeddo MI 48032

HART, INEZ ASKEW, Math Teacher; *b:* Gold Hill, AL; *m:* Franklin; *c:* Fritz; *ed:* (BS) Math/Sociology, AL A&M Univ 1965; (MED) Math/Ed, Univ of Montevallo 1975; Auburn Univ; AL St Univ; *cr:* Teacher Pike Cty HS 1965-73; B B Comer Mem HS 1973-; *ai:* Beta Club Spon; Math-A-Thon Coord; Schlrshp Comm Mem; Grade Chm; Mem Prin Adv Comm; NASSP; AL Ed Assn; NEA; Talladega Cty Ed Assn Exec Bd 1989-; NAACP; St John Bapt Church (VP Choir 1989- Chm Pastors Aid 1990 Deaconess 1989- & Teacher 1984-); Auburn Univ Adult Ed Grant; AL St Natl Sci Fnd Grant; Religious Public Speaker; *home:* Rt 3 Box 4007 Sylacauga AL 35150

HART, JACQUELINE EILEEN (NORRIS), School Counselor; *b:* Connellsville, PA; *m:* Charles Douglas; *c:* Crystal, Charla, Chad; *ed:* (BA) Elem Ed, Fairmont St 1972; (MS) Counseling/Guidance, WV Univ 1978; *cr:* Sch Librarian 1972-73, 4th Grade Teacher 1974-78 Anna Jarvis Elem; Teacher of Gifted Taylor Cty Elem Schls 1978-79; Teacher of Gifted 1979-80, Sch Cnslr 1980- Grafton Mid Sch; *ai:* WV Sch Cnslrs Assn; Licensed Prof Cnslr; *home:* Rt 1 Box 327 Independence WV 26374

HART, JOYCE ELAINE, Fifth Grade Teacher; *b:* Kane, IL; *c:* Tad, Jason; *ed:* (BS) Elem Ed, S IL Univ Carbondale 1962; *cr:* 2nd Grade Teacher Emerson Sch 1962-69; Remedial Rdng Teacher East Alton Schls 1972-78; 5th Grade Teacher Eastwood Sch 1978-; *ai:* Gifted Comm; E Alton Ed Assn Pres Elect 1988-; Delta Kappa Gamma; Amer Assn Univ Women Pres 1988- Schlsp Name Grant 1983.

HART, JOYCE ELCHERT, Second Grade Teacher; *b:* Fostoria, OH; *m:* Michael J.; *c:* Dennis M., Gary C.; *ed:* (BA) Elem Ed, Mary Manse Coll 1962; *cr:* 2nd/3rd Grade Teacher Fostoria City Schls 1962-64; 2nd Grade Teacher St Marys 1966-67, 1969-; *ai:* Heidelberg Coll Teachers Advisory Comm; *office:* St Marys Elem Sch 75 S Sandusky Tiffin OH 44883

HART, JUDITH ANN, Second Grade Teacher; *b:* Troy, NY; *ed:* (BS) Elem Ed, the Coll of St Rose 1971; (MS) Elem Ed, 1972, (MS) Remedial Rdng, 1979, Russell Sage Coll; Bachelor of Smiles Clownology, Hudson Valley Comm Coll 1985; Ceramics, Iannone Studio 1978-; Grad Stud Elem Ed, Russell Sage Coll; *cr:* 2nd Grade Teacher St Josephs 1965-66; 5th Grade Teacher 1967-68, 6th Grade Teacher 1968-69, 4th Grade Teacher 1969-70 Sch 3; 2nd Grade Teacher Sch 3 & Watervliet City Sch Dist 1970-; *ai:* Home Tutoring; Comm to Select Asst VP; Stu Teacher Cooperating Teacher; Sch Cabinet; Mission Statement, Report Card, Sch Improvement Comm; PTA (Pres, VP, Treas, Publicity) 1967-, Life Membership; AARC, NYSUT, AFT; St Josephs Eucharistic (Minister, Reader, Lector, Sch Bd); St Rose Alumni Assn, Russell Sage Alumni Assn; Columbiettes Rosary Society; Russell Sage Alumni Assn; Columbiettes Rosary Society; PTA Fellowship; *office:* Watervliet City Sch Dist 10th Ave & 25th St Watervliet NY 12189

HART, LACIE ANN LESTER, Seventh Grade Teacher; *b:* Chilhowie, VA; *m:* Ray; *c:* Alan R., Betty Hart Bays; *ed:* (BA) His/Fr/Span, Emory & Henry Coll 1951; Grad Studs; *cr:* 7th Grade Teacher Wallace Elem 1951-52; Eng/His/Span Teacher Hamilton HS 1954-57; 4th Grade Teacher 1964-68, 7th Grade Teacher 1968- High Point Elem; *ai:* Yrbk Staff; Grade Group Chm; Teach Gifted Lang Arts; *home:* 118 Mc Cray Dr Abingdon VA 24210

HART, LINDA J., 4th Grade Teacher; *b:* Cleveland, OH; *m:* Steven M.; *c:* Christopher; *cr:* Remedial Rdng Mayfield Hts Sch System 1974-75; 4th Grade Teacher St Gregory the Great Schl 1975-; *ai:* Testing Coord for Sch; Adv to Stu Cncl.

HART, MARILYN LANDRY, Jr HS Language Arts Teacher; *b:* Kentwood, LA; *m:* Herbert M. Jr.; *c:* Benjamin H.; *ed:* (BA) Soc Stud, USL 1963; (MED) Guidance & Counseling, SIU 1971; *cr:* Teacher Spring Creek HS 1963-81, Sumner HS 1981-84; Teacher/Cnslr Kentwood Learning Center 1984-88; Teacher Oak Forest Acad 1988-; *ai:* Jr Class Spon; MPSEA 1988-; Co-Authored Book 1975; *home:* 610 Avenue G Kentwood LA 70444

HART, ORRIN MICHAEL, Student at Risk/Dept Chm; *b:* Billings, MT; *m:* Kathleen A. Mc Guire; *c:* Mitchell, Helen; *ed:* (AA) General Stud, SUNY Albany 1974; (BS) Ed, E MT Coll 1984; *cr:* Teacher Lame Deer Jr HS 1985-87, Monument Valley HS 1988-; *ai:* Governing Bd Awd for Excl Kayenta Unified Sch Dist 1990; *office:* Monument Valley HS P O Box 337 Kayenta AZ 86033

HART, PENNY WARREN, Mathematics Teacher; *b:* Newellton, LA; *m:* Robert Dennis; *ed:* (AS) Aviation, 1979, (BA) Liberal Arts/Aviation, 1981 NE LA Univ; *cr:* Math Teacher Bastrop HS 1984-87, Athens HS 1987-; *ai:* TX Assn Future Educators Spon; TX Classroom Teachers Assn 1987-; *office:* Athens HS 708 E College Athens TX 75751

HART, ROSE (COLETTA), First Grade Teacher; *b:* Rochester, NY; *m:* Joseph Patrick; *c:* Nicholas, Patrick, Charles; *ed:* (BA) Elem Ed/Span, St Univ of NY Brockport 1979; *cr:* 2nd Grade Teacher 1979-, 1st Grade Teacher 1989- Mother of Sorrows Sch; *ai:* Primary Grade Testing & Dept Coord; *office:* Mother of Sorrows Sch 1777 Latta Rd Rochester NY 14612

HART, SUZANNE CASGRAIN, Retired French Teacher; *b:* Quebec City PQ, Canada; *m:* Douglas Gordon; *c:* Christine, Joy, Suzy Fels; *ed:* (BA) Cum Laude, Laval Univ 1942; (BA) Foreign Lang, Furman Univ 1969; Grad Stud; *cr:* HS Eng Teacher Couvent De Longueuil 1963-65; Fr/Eng Teacher Bryson & Hillcrest HS 1969-70; Fr/Latin Teacher Southside HS 1970-77; Fr Teacher Travelers Rest HS 1985-89; *ai:* Taught Rdng to Adults & in Public Schls; Modern Lang Assn 1969-; NEA, Palmetto Translators & Interpreters Assn 1989-; Greenville Unitarian Universalist Fellowship Secy 1979-80; Active Mem Youth Organization Charge Summer Camp Disadvantaged Children 1946-49; St Lambert Town Planning Comm Pres; *home:* 117 Knollwood Ln Greenville SC 29607

HARTEL, GREGORY JOHN, Biology/Ecology Teacher; *b:* Milwaukee, WI; *m:* Rita D. Hahn; *c:* Tara M., Kristina L.; *ed:* (BA) Wildlife Management, Univ of WI Stevens Point 1971; (MS) Sci Teaching, Univ of NE 1977; Grad Stud Univ of NE Omaha & Lincoln; *cr:* 7th/8th Grade Sci Teacher St John Vianney 1972-73; Bio/Ecology Teacher Bellevue East HS 1974-; Teacher NE Scholars Inst Univ of NE 1986-; *ai:* Set Design & Construction for Schls Musical & Plays; Bellevue Ed Assn, NE Ed Assn 1974-; Murray Volunteer Fire Dept, Ducks Unlimited 1988-; Natl Wildlife Ed 1975-; *office:* Bellevue East HS 1401 High School Dr Bellevue NE 68005

HARTENSTEIN, PATRICIA ANN, First Grade Teacher; *b:* Wheeling, OH; *ed:* (BA) Elem Ed, OH Univ 1969; (MS) Elem Ed, WV Univ 1976; *cr:* 3rd Grade Teacher South Elem 1969-72, Mackey Elem 1972-75; 1st Grade Teacher North Elem 1975-; *ai:* PSI Chapter Delta Kappa Gamma; 1st Presbyn Church Deacon/ Elder 1980-; *home:* 911 Monroe St Martins Ferry OH 43935

HARTER, CHARLOTTE ANN KASSABAUM, Fifth Grade Teacher; *b:* Bonne Terre, MO; *m:* Orvall D.; *c:* Chad C., Marc B.; *ed:* (BS) Elem Ed, Flat River Jr Coll/MAC 1961; (BS) Elem Ed, Southeast MO St Univ 1963; Post Masters Studies Cntrl MO St Univ; MO Univ Columbia; *cr:* 5th Grade Teacher Mehlville; 5th Grade Teacher; 6th/8th Grade Rdng Teacher Cntrl R 3; Remedial Lang Arts; 5th Grade Teacher Sedalia 200; *ai:* Career Ladder Comm; Exec Bd Mem; SCEA; Lang Arts Comm; Bldg Rep Young Authors Conf; SCEA TEPS Chairperson 1987-; MSTA 1977-; PTA 1978-; Alpha Delta Kapp Membership Chairperson 88-; BPW 10 Yrs; 1st Bapt Church 3rd Grade Dir 11 Yrs; Listed Whos Who in Amer Ed; Teacher of Week; Presented Writing Across Curr St/Local Meetings; *office:* Whittier Sch 907 E 16th St Sedalia MO 65301

HARTER, DONALD L., Principal; *b:* Troy, KS; *ed:* (AA) Elem Ed, Highland Jr Coll 1957; (BS) Elem Ed, Mount St Scholastica Coll 1966; (MS) Elem Ed/admin, Northwest MO St Univ 1973; Working on Specialist Degree in Ed, NW MO St Univ; *cr:* Cordonier Sch 1957-59; Fanning Sch 1959-60; Troy Schls 1960-; *ai:* Ftbl, Boys & Girls Bsktbl, Track Coach; United Sch Admin of KS, KS Assn of Elem Sch Prins, KS Assn of Mid Level Ed, ASCD, Intnl Rdng Assn 1989-; Reorganized Church of Jesus Christ of Latter Day Saints Elder; Highland Comm Coll Bd of Trustees Secy.

HARTER, MOLLIE HAAS, English Teacher; *b:* Bloomsburg, PA; *m:* Richard S.; *c:* Rod A., Jeff R., Louise M.; *ed:* (BS) Bus/Eng, Bloomsburg Univ 1955; PA Soc Stud Cert 1961; Arts in Ed; *cr:* Bus Teacher Bloomsburg HS 1955-56; Eng/Teacher of Gifted Danville Jr HS 1958-82; Eng Teacher Danville Sr HS 1983-; *ai:* Danville Youth Ed Assn Adv; Wellness Comm; Ad Hoc Prof Dev Comm Mem; Meet & Discuss Chairperson; Danville Ed Assn Pres 1978-; PA St Ed Assn Leadership Dev Comm 1980-, Innovative Teaching Awd 1973; NEA St Contact Person for PA 1979-89; NCTE 1975-; Beta Sigma Phi (Pres, Mem) 1952-; Code Appeals Bd for Town of Bloomsburg Chairperson 1982-; Bloomsburgs 3rd Ward Democratic Comm Person 1984-; BSA Merit Badge Certifier 1980-; Alpha Psi Omega; Columbia City Historical Society Mem; Presenter at PA NE Region Key Local Leadership Conference; Bd of Contributors for Danville News; *home:* 319 East St Bloomsburg PA 17815

HARTFIELD, CHARLES VERNON, Mathematics Department Chair; *b:* Miami, FL; *m:* Sadie Bertha Bush; *c:* Charles, Darrell, Patrick, Brian, Gary, C. D., Christopher; *ed:* (BS) Math, Southern Univ 1962; (MA) Curr/Instruction, Northern CO Univ 1975; (EDS) Voc/Tech Ed, Nova Univ 1979; *cr:* Math Chairperson Brownsville Jr HS 1965-67, Allapattah Jr HS 1968-71; TSA Allapattah Jr HS 1972-85; Math Chairperson Northwestern Sr HS 1986-; *ai:* Math Club Spon; Curr Cncl; SAT Tutorial Club; Stu Advisory Comm; DCTM, NCTM 1965-; Miami Chamber of Commerce 1985-; YMCA, Big Brothers of Greater Miami Mem 1970-; Kappa Alpha Psi, Masonic Order Brother 1970-; Ger Lang & Math Exch Stu Awd 1959-60; Natl Sci Fnd Grant to Study Advanced Courses & Methods for Teaching Math; Allapattah Jr HS & Miami NW Sr HS Teacher of Yr;TEC Grant to Study Methods of Improving Math Instructions; Univ of Miami Outstanding HS Teacher Awd; *office:* Miami Northwestern Sr HS 7007 NW 12th Ave Miami FL 33150

HARTIN, HALJEAN WARD, English Teacher; *b:* Durant, OK; *m:* Ronald P.; *c:* Gary Spoon, Brent, Ashleigh, Kara; *ed:* (BA) Eng, 1980, (MS) Eng, 1985 SE OK St Univ; *ai:* OK Ed Assn, NEA; *office:* Durant HS 8th & Walnut Durant OK 74701

HARTL, ROSEMARY SCHINDERLE, Fifth Grade Teacher; *b:* Fond Du Lac, WI; *m:* Michael Anthony; *c:* Marie Hartl Johnson, Patricia Hartl Chamberland, Kathleen; *ed:* (BS) Elem Ed/Bio, Univ of WI Milwaukee 1955; Grad Stud Religion Teacher; *cr:* 5th/6th Grade Teacher Tippecanoe Sch 1955-60; 5th Grade Teacher St Peters Cath 1973-80, Unified Cath Parish Sch 1980-; *ai:* Curr Writing Comm Mem; Math Curr Comm Chairperson; WI Ed Assn 1955-60; NCEA 1980-85; WI Math Cncl 1987-; St Peters Parish Cncl (Vice Chairperson 1982-84, Chairperson 1984-86); St Peters Spiritual Life Comm Chairperson 1982-84, 1986-88; Milwaukee Archdiocesan League of Cath Home & Sch Assn Outstanding Educator Awd 1989-; *home:* 405 Walnut St Beaver Dam WI 53916

HARTLE, SALLIE NOLF, English Teacher; *b:* New Kensington, PA; *m:* William A.; *c:* Megan L., Robin C.; *ed:* (BS) Comprehensive Eng/Rdng, Clarion Univ 1967; (MS) Comm/Rdng, Penn St Univ 1970; *cr:* Eng/Journalism Teacher Kiski Area HS 1967-69, Eng/Journalism/Teacher of Gifted Ed Elizabeth Forward HS 1969-; *ai:* Natl Academic Games Project Coach; Journalism Ed Assn St Dir 1969-78; PA Assn Gifted Ed 1979-; Natl Academic Games Project Dir PA St Lang Art 1979-, Jim Davis Outstanding Coord 1983; *office:* Elizabeth Forward HS 1000 Wiegles Hill Rd Elizabeth PA 15037

HARTLEY, CHRISTINE V., Mathematics Teacher of Gifted; *b:* Elmhurst, IL; *ed:* (BS) Ed, 1974, (MED) Ed, 1978 Miami Univ; *cr:* 7th Grade Math Teacher Fairfield Jr HS 1974-77; Grad Asst Miami Univ 1977-78; 7th/8th Grade Math Teacher 1978-81, 6th-8th Grade Math Teacher of Gifted 1981- Fairfield Mid Sch; Teacher Miami Univ 1986-; *ai:* Odyssey of Mind Coach; NCTM; Greater Hamilton Civic Theatre Bd Mem 1985-; Fairfield City Schls Math Teacher of Yr 1986; Work for Miami Univ Teacher Ed Grant; *office:* Fairfield Mid Sch 255 Donald Dr Fairfield OH 45014

HARTLEY, JEANNE SHULL, Science Teacher Dept Chair; *b:* Columbia, SC; *m:* Douglas Charles; *c:* Brad, Trevor, Peyton; *ed:* (BS) Bio, 1974, (MAT) Bio, 1976 Univ of SC; SC Electric & Gas Energy Ed Wkshp 1982; Univ of SC Environmental Ed Wkshp 1984; Univ of SC Prof Dev Prgm Earth Sci 1986; *cr:* Sci Teacher Hanberry Jr HS 1976-78, Lexington Mid Sch 1978-; *ai:* Sci Dept Chairperson; Coord of Sch Sci Fair; Sch Improvement Cncl; Dev & Maintenance of Outdoor Center; Spon Sch Sci Club & Young Astronaut Club; Lexington Cty Beautification Comm; SC Sci Cncl, SC Earth Sci Teachers Assn; Lexington Soil & Water Conservation Dist Teacher of Yr 1986, 1990; Dev of Outdoor Ed Center Lexingtons Lion Club Awd; SC Telephone Pioneers Awd; SC Ed Grant to Develop Learning Centers 1987; *office:* Lexington Mid Sch 702 N Lake Dr Lexington SC 29072

HARTLEY, JOHN F., JR., 7th Grade Reading Teacher; *b:* La Porte, IN; *m:* Rebecca A. Pollitt; *c:* Bryce L.; *ed:* (BA) His, Cntrl MI Univ 1977; (MS) General Ed/Rdng Concentration, Grand Valley St Coll 1985; *cr:* Teacher New Buffalo Area Schls 1978-; *ai:* 7th Grade Girls Vlybl Coach; Natl Rdng Assn, MI Ed Assn, NEA; New Buffalo Ed Assn Treas 1985-86; *office:* New Buffalo Area Schls 222 S Whittaker St New Buffalo MI 49117

HARTLEY, MARGARET D., Math Teacher; *b:* Sunbury, PA; *m:* William M.; *c:* Diane, Rae Jean; *ed:* (BS) Sci/Math, Bloomsburg Univ 1956; Bucknell Univ/Miami Univ of OH; *cr:* Teacher Selinsgrove PA 1956-57, Los Nietos CA 1957-58, Englewood OH 1958-59, W Milton OH 1960-66, Milton PA 1966-; *ai:* Drama Club; Math Counts; NEA; PSEA Comm Mem; Local MAEA Sec/VP/Pres; Natl Sci Fnd Grant 1963; *home:* 114 Armory Blvd Lewisburg PA 17837

HARTLINE, BETTY MAGILL, First Grade Teacher; *b:* Denton, TX; *m:* James Hilman; *c:* Karen R. Hartline Thomason, Sandra K.; *ed:* (BS) Elem Ed, 1953, (MED) Elem Ed, 1968 Univ of N TX; *cr:* 4th Grade Teacher Argyle Elem 1953-54; 3rd Grade Teacher Sam Houston Elem 1954-58; 3rd-5th Grade Teacher Woodrow Wilson Elem 1961-64; 3rd/6th Grade Teacher Sam Houston Elem 1967-70; 3rd Grade Teacher 1976-82, 1st Grade Teacher 1982- Newton Rayzor Elem; *ai:* TX St Teachers Assn, NEA 1954-89.

HARTMAN, ANITA MAE, English Department Chair; *b:* Shawano, WI; *ed:* (BS) Eng, Univ of WI Oshkosh 1953; *cr:* Eng Dept Chairperson Bonduel HS 1953-; *ai:* Newspaper Adv; Amer Assn of Univ Women 1985-; NCTE, WI Cncl Teachers of Eng 1953-; Delta Kappa Gamma 1962-; Bonduel Ed Assn 1964-66; VFW Voice of Democracy Coach; Amer Legion Oratory Coach Outstanding Friend; Dept of Public Instruction Colonial Games Essay Contest Letter of Commendation; *office:* Bonduel HS 400 W Green Bay Bonduel WI 54107

HARTMAN, ARNOLD RICHARD, Chemistry Teacher; *b:* Brazil, IN; *ed:* (BS) Chem, 1983, (MS) Math, 1985 IN St Univ; *cr:* Chem/Math Teacher Lafayette Jefferson HS 1983; Chem Teacher Owen Valley HS 1983-; *ai:* Boys HS Track Coach; Sci & Chess Club Adv; *office:* Owen Valley HS RR 4 Box 13 Spencer IN 47460

HARTMAN, BRENDA W., Social Studies Teacher; *b:* Frankfort, KY; *m:* Barry; *c:* Robbie, Leslie; *ed:* (BA) Area Soc Stud, 1971, (MA) Ed/His, 1974 E KY Univ; *cr:* 5th Grade Teacher Silver Creek Elem 1971-72; 7th-9th Grade Teacher Conner Jr HS 1973-; *ai:* Stu Cncl Co-Spon; Cty Evaluation, Sch Discipline, Cty Mid Sch Comm; NEA, KEA; Boone Cty Ed Assn Secy 1979-80; KCSS Steering Comm 1987-, Outstanding Soc Stud Teacher 1987; KATH; NCSS 1987-; Boone Cty Historical Preservation Bd Bd Mem 1988-; *office:* Conner Jr HS 3300 Cougar Path Hebron KY 41048

HARTMAN, JULIE L., Physical Education Teacher; *b:* Douglas, NE; *ed:* (BS) Ed, Peru St Coll 1980; Grad Work, Univ of NE Omaha & Lincoln, Wayne St Coll; *cr:* Teacher/Coach Creighton Cmmty Sch 1981-88, Elkhorn Mid Sch & HS 1988-; *ai:* Head Vlybl Coach; Health Curr Comm Mem; Drug Ed Comm; NEA, NSEA 1981-; AAHPEDRD, AVCA 1987-; Fellowship of Chrstn Athletes Co-Spon 1988-89.

HARTMANN, DOLORES O'CONNOR, Teacher of Gifted & Talented; *b:* New York, NY; *m:* William Edward; *c:* Christopher, Anthony, Gregory; *ed:* (BS) Mrktg, Fordham Univ 1949; (MS) Ed, St Univ of NY New Paltz 1963; (MS) Spec Ed, C W Post Univ 1978; Hofstra Univ; Joseph Renzulli Confratute for Gifted Ed, Univ of CT; *cr:* Office Mgr Richard Bandler Co 1949-57; 3rd Grade Teacher Uniondale Sch Dist 1964-66; 6th Grade Teacher 1969-79, Teacher of Gifted & Talented 1979- Bethpage Sch Dist; *ai:* Society for Gifted & Talented Children Secy 1978-83; *home:* 60 Cedar Ave Bethpage NY 11714

HARTMANN, MARA ZARINS, Mathematics Teacher; *b:* Latvia, Europe; *ed:* (BS) Elem Ed, Univ of Rochester 1967; Math, S OK Coll 1981; *cr:* 6th Grade Teacher Pittsford Sch System 1967-69; 2nd/3rd Grade Teacher Antilles Consolidated Schls 1970-74; Title I Math Teacher Marietta Sch System 1974-81; 7th-9th Grade Teacher Ector Cty Ind Sch Dist 1982-; *ai:* Math Coach Academic Decathlon; *office:* Ector Jr HS Crane-Clements Odessa TX 79763

HARTMANN, SANDRA HORNBY, Social Studies Teacher; *b:* Passaic, NJ; *m:* William A.; *c:* Jennifer; *ed:* (BS) Soc Sci, Fairleigh Dickinson Univ 1969; (MA) Anthropology, Montclair St Coll 1978; Cmptr In-Service; *cr:* Teacher Christopher Columbus Mid Sch 1969-84, Clifton HS 1984-; *ai:* Sr Class Adv; Curr Revision; Advanced Placement Curr; Gifted & Talented Honors Classes; Clifton Jr Womens Club (VP, Pres, Mem) 1977-84; West Paterson Lib Bd Secy 1986-; *office:* Clifton H S 333 Colfax Ave Clifton NJ 07013

HARTNESS, ROBERT ARNOLD, JR., Science Teacher; *b:* Woodville, MS; *m:* Linda Adele Ellerbe; *c:* Robert III, Jason B.; *ed:* (BS) Ag Eng Tech, MS St 1968; General Ed, Southern MS; *cr:* Jr HS Math/Sci Teacher Woodville Attendance Center 1968-70; Voc Math Teacher Wilkinson Cty Voc Center 1972-76; Voc Ag Teacher 1981-84, Jr HS Math/Sci/Phys Sci Teacher 1985- W Feliciana HS; *ai:* Jr/Sr HS Boys & Girls Bsktbl, HS Bsbl Coach; LA Fed Teachers; Woodville Jaycees VP 1970; *office:* West Feliciana HS P O Drawer 580 Saint Francisville CA 70775

HARTNETT, ELIZABETH ANNE HUTCHISON, English/History Teacher; *b:* Wilmington, DE; *m:* Maurice A. III; *c:* Anne Hartnett Grego; *ed:* (BA) Scndry Ed/Eng, Cabrini Coll 1961; *cr:* Teacher Claymon HS 1961-64, St Josephs on the Brandywine 1964-65; Vice Prin 1984-86, Teacher 1965- Holy Cross; *ai:* Eng Dept Chairperson; *home:* 144 Cooper Rd Dover DE 19901

HARTSOE, SHERRIE DIANNE, English Teacher; *b:* Lenoir, NC; *ed:* (AA) Pre-Teaching, Caldwell Cmmty Coll 1978; (BA) Eng, Univ NC Charlotte 1980; Cert for Academically Gifted 989; *cr:* Eng Instr Caldwell Cmmty Coll 1980-; Eng Teacher West Iredell HS 1987-; *ai:* Spon of Future Teachers of Amer; Teacher Recruiter for The St of NC; Homecoming Dir; NCAE/NEA 1981-; NCTE 1988-; NCGT 1989-; BPW 1989- Young Careerist 1989; Southern Highlands Institute for Educators 1987 & 1988; Writing Project 1989; Articles in Family-Cmmnty-Work & AWP; *office:* West Iredell H S Rt 6 Box 13 Statesville NC 28677

HARTT, JO HERRINGTON, Language Arts Teacher; *b:* Garrison, TX; *m:* Steve Edward; *c:* Steven, Kip; *ed:* (BS) Elem Ed, Stephen F Austin Univ 1963; Lamar Univ, Univ of Houston, W MI Univ; *cr:* Teacher Kurth Elem 1963-65, Lumberton Mid Sch 1965-; *ai:* Lions-Quest Prgm; Positive Youth Dev; Skills for Adolescence; Lumberton Classroom Teachers Pres 1972-73; Lumberton Ed Assn Pres 1977-78, 1979-80; TX St Teachers Assn Life Mem; *home:* 1330 Keith Lumberton TX 77656

HARTWELL, EILEEN ATKINSON, Teacher of Academically Gifted; *b:* Asheville, NC; *m:* Warren David; *c:* Kathryn E., Zachariah S.; *ed:* (BS) Mid Grade Ed, 1971, (MAED) Ed, 1974 W Carolina Univ; *cr:* 5th Grade Teacher Laurel Creek Elem 1971-72; 3rd-5th Grade Teacher Rankin Elem 1972-75, Newton Open Concept Sch 1975-78; Teacher of Academically Gifted Eno Valley Elem 1978-; *ai:* Eno Valley Swim Club Bd of Dirs; Teacher Cncl; NEA, NCEA Mem 1971-; NCAGT Mem 1984-; ADK Mem 1990; PDK Mem 1985-; *home:* 1836 Forest Rd Durham NC 27705

HARVARD, WILLIAM K., Mathematics Teacher; *b:* Newark, NJ; *m:* Claudia J. Lloyd; *c:* Richard, John, Tim; *ed:* (BA) Sociology, Univ of Redlands 1972; *cr:* Math Teacher Clement Jr HS 1973-78, Redlands HS 1978-; *ai:* Ftbl Coach; Mentor Teacher; Bsbl Coach City of Redlands Youth; *office:* Redlands HS 840 E Citrus Ave Redlands CA 92373

HARVEY, ANITA BENNETT, English Teacher; *b:* Gastonia, NC; *m:* Edward Hardin; *c:* Brad, Cameron; *ed:* (BA) Eng, 1965, (MAT) Ed, 1974 Winthrop Coll; *cr:* Teacher Clover HS 1965-; *ai:* Sr Class Spon; Chosen Outstanding Young Educator 1976; *office:* Clover HS 1625 Hwy 55 Clover SC 29710

HARVEY, DONALD LEROY, Science Department Chairperson; *b:* Ashland, KY; *m:* Shirley Dawn Habada; *c:* Tammra M., Kevin M.; *ed:* (BA) Bio, Walla Walla Coll 1973; (MS) Bio, Andrews Univ 1982; *cr:* Sci/Math Teacher Reading Jr Acad 1973-77, Greater Baltimore Jr Acad 1977-83; Sci Chm Bass Memorial Acad 1983-; *ai:* Acad Standards Comm; Curr Comm & Lib Comm; Jr Class Spon; Sr Class Spon; Jets Teams Coach; NSTA 1983-; Amer Assn for Advancement of Sci 1988-; Teacher of Yr Awd 1984; Thomas & Violet Zapara Awd of Recognition for Excl in Teaching 1989; *office:* Bass Memorial Acad Rt 2 Lumberton MS 39455

HARVEY, KEITH R., 6th Grade Teacher; *b:* Scranton, PA; *ed:* (BA) Elem Ed, 1964, (MS) Elem Ed, 1976 Univ of Scranton; Grad Work SUNY at Stony Brook, Adelphi, NY Univ & Queens Coll; *cr:* 6th Grade Teacher Mid Cntry Cntrl Sch Dist #11 1964-75, N Pocono Sch Dist 1975-; *ai:* Sch Newspaper Adv; Gifted Prgm Teacher - Russian; Phi Delta Kappa, NCSS, NYSTA, PSEA, NEA; Laurel Garden Club Pres; *office:* North Pocono Mid Sch Church St Moscow PA 18444

HARVEY, LINDA COOK, Kindergarten Teacher; *b:* San Antonio, TX; *m:* Bobby; *c:* Rob, Jeff, Lynsey; *ed:* (BA) Curr/Instruction, TX a & M Univ 1973; *cr:* Spec Ed Teacher Gonzales Spec Ed Co-Op 1974-75; 1st Grade Teacher Smiley Elem 1975-78, Nixon Elem 1978-81; Kndgtn Teacher Nixon Elem 1981-; *ai:* Kndgtn Teachers of TX; TX Classroom Teachers Assn; Nixon-Smiley Mustang Booster Club-Pres 1986-; *home:* HCR 40 Box 148 Nixon TX 78140

HARVEY, NANCY CASH, 3rd Grade Teacher; *b:* Tuscaloosa, AL; *m:* James T.; *c:* Bryan T., Brandon A.; *ed:* (BSE) Elem Ed, Delta St Univ 1980; *cr:* 4th Grade Teacher 1980-83, 3rd Grade Teacher 1983-88 Hope Sullivan Elem; *ai:* Kappa Delta Pi Honorary Treas 1979-80; NEA 1981-82; MS Prof Educators 1985-86.

HARVEY, PEGGY S. HERBERT, Third Grade Teacher; *b:* Enid, OK; *m:* Don Kent; *c:* Tiffany, Tonya; *ed:* (BA) Elem Ed, OK St Univ 1980; *cr:* 1st Grade Teacher Garber Elem Sch 1980-81; 3rd Grade Teacher Chisholm Elem 1981-; *ai:* OK Ed Assn, Kappa Kappa Iota, Cherokee Strip Rdng Cncl; OK Best Dedicated to Ed Excl Awd Nom 1989; *office:* Chisholm Elem Sch 300 Colorado North Enid OK 73701

HARVEY, SHERRIE FRANKLIN, Earth Science Teacher; *b:* Buffalo, NY; *m:* Patrick Lee; *c:* Patrick, Ryan; *ed:* (BS) Earth Sci, St Univ of NY Brockport 1978; *cr:* Earth Sci Teacher Floydada Jr HS 1978-81, Somerset HS 1981-84, Jefferson Davis Mid Sch 1984-; *ai:* Newspaper Editor; Chrldr Spon; Talent Show Organizer; UIL Coach; NSTA 1986-; Sigma Xi Outstanding Teacher Nominee; *office:* Jefferson Davis Mid Sch 4702 E Houston St San Antonio TX 78220

HARVEY, VICKI BACHMAN, 2nd Grade Teacher; *b:* Columbus, OH; *m:* Allan H.; *ed:* (BA) Elem Ed, W KY Univ 1968; (MED) Elem Ed, Univ of Louisville; *cr:* Teacher Zachary Taylor Elem 1968-83, Dunn Elem 1983-; *ai:* Participatory Management Comm; Jefferson Cty Teachers Assn Dir; KEA, NEA, KY Assn for Gifted Ed; Louisville Jaycees Dir 1980; Louisville Jaycettes Pres 1979; *office:* Ruth Dunn Elem Sch 2010 Rudy Ln Louisville KY 40207

HARVIE, WILLIAM STUART, Physics Teacher; *b:* Alhambra, CA; *ed:* (BA) Physics, Univ of CA Irvine 1976; (MS) Earth Sci, Univ of CA San Diego 1980; (MAT) Physics, Univ of CA Los Angeles 1982; *cr:* Teaching Assoc Univ of CA Los Angeles 1980-82; Physics Teacher Torrey Pines HS 1983-; *ai:* AAPT 1984-; Phi Beta Kappa 1974-; Articles Published; *office:* Torrey Pines HS 710 Encinitas Blvd Encinitas CA 92024

HARVIEL, JOLETE FUQUAY, Language Arts Teacher; *b:* Burlington, NC; *m:* Ernest J.; *c:* Jennifer, Carrie; *ed:* (BS) Elem Ed, 1971, (MA) Intermediate Ed, 1972 Appalachian St Univ; Certified Academically Gifted 1988; *cr:* 4th Grade Teacher 1972-77, 3rd Grade Aide 1982-83 Grove Park Elem; 6th Grade Teacher 1983-86, 6th Grade Teacher of Academically Gifted 1986- Turrentine Mid; *ai:* Yrbk Comm; Burlington City Assn of Educators 1973-77, 1983-; NC Assn of Educators 1973-77, 1983-; NC Assn for Gifted & Talented 1986-; Democratic Women of Alamance Cty 1st VP 1983-84; *office:* Turrentine Mid Sch 1710 Edgewood Ave Burlington NC 27215

HARWELL, LOUISE DRUMMOND, 8th Grade Earth Sci Teacher; *b:* Atlanta, GA; *m:* Nat; *c:* Francie, Christie, Davis; *ed:* (BS) Therapeutic Recreation, 1974, (BS) Ed, 1977 GA S Coll; St of GA Mid Grades Teacher Cert; NASA Educl Wkshp for Math & Sci Teachers; *cr:* 8th Grade Earth Sci Teacher 1977-82, 1984-, 6th-8th Grade Gifted Sci Teacher 1990- Sharp Mid Sch; *ai:* GA Teacher Practices Assessment Instrument; Mentor Teacher & Data Collector; Prof Assn of GA Educators 1984-; NEA 1977-82; United Meth Women 1977-; Sharp Mid Sch Teacher of Yr Awd 1988-89; Natl Sci Teachers Assn Convention Presenter 1989; Atlanta NSTA Convention Presenter 1990; NASA Natl Resource Person 1986-; *office:* Sharp Mid Sch 3135 Newton Dr NE Covington GA 30209

HARWELL, REBECCA DUNCAN, 7-8th Grade/Lang Arts Teacher; *b:* Savannah, TN; *c:* Christopher Duncan; *ed:* (BS) Mrktng & Retailing, Florence St Univ 1970; (MS) Ed, Tusculumn Coll 1989; *cr:* Classroom Teacher Walnut Grove Elem 1967-72; Librarian Maryville HS 1973-74; 1st/3rd Grade Dir Media Center Sevier Co 1974-75; Prin Whites Elem Sch 1975-76; Classroom Teacher Northview Elem 1976-; *ai:* Drama Club Adv; Ski Club Adv; Dir 8th Grade Prom & Graduation Banquets; Textbook Comm; Dev of Cty Wide Grade Card; NEA 1970-; TEA 1970-; SCEA 1974-; Finalist Teaching Exch Prgm with Australia; *office:* Northview Elem Sch Rt 1 Kodak TN 37764

HARWICK, LARRY K., 6th Grade Teacher; *b:* Cheyenne, WY; *m:* Judith K.; *c:* Viki Winfield, Laura Roth, Jeanni Stewart, Craig, Kristen; *ed:* (AA) Elem Ed, Mc Cook Jr Coll 1959; (BS) Elem Ed, 1964, (MS) Elem Ed, 1966 Kearney St Coll; Grad Stud Adams St Coll, Univ of N CO, CO St Univ; Partners Prgm Chico St; *cr:* 7th Grade Teacher Grant Elem 1959-63; 6th Grade Teacher Arriba-Flagler Consolidated Sch Dist 20 1965-; *ai:* Asst Ftbl Coach 1959-63, 1968-70; Asst Bsktbl Coach 1959-63, 1965-66; NEA 1965-; CO Ed Assn (Pres, Secy) 1965-; Flagler Ed Assn 1989-; Lions Club; Volunteer Fireman Secy 1970-80; Volunteer Ambulance 1970-80; Flagler Teacher of Yr 1973; *home:* 326 Ouray Flagler CO 80815

HARWOOD, CAROLYN FITE, Fifth Grade Teacher; *b:* Shelby, NC; *m:* Johnny F.; *c:* Tracey, Mark; *ed:* (BS) Elem Ed, Appalachian St Univ 1971; *cr:* Teacher Jackson Park Elem 1971-; *ai:* NCAE 1971-89; Delta Kappa Gamma Secy 1986-89.

HARWOOD, JEAN DE VOTIE, Guidance Counselor; *b:* Banner Elk, NC; *m:* Thomas E.; *ed:* (BS) Gen Sci/Psych/Bio, 1974; (MA) Scndry Guidance Cnslr 1984 East TN St Univ; Quest Drug Resistence Ed; Suicide Wrkshp; *cr:* Jr HS Sci Teacher Fall Branch 1975-85; Sr HS Guidance Cnslr Daniel Boone HS 1985-; *ai:* Chrldr Spon; Natl Jr Honor Socty Spon; 7th Grade Sci Curr Chm; WA Cty Ed Assn 1975-;TEA 1975-;NEA 1975-; Poem Publ in Amer Anthology Poetic Voices of Amer June 1990; Teacher of Yr at Sch 1978; *office:* Daniel Boone H S Rt 16 Box 267 Gray TN 37615

HARWOOD, PEGGY MOHR, First Grade Teacher; *b:* Maquoketa, IA; *m:* Paul Duane; *c:* Arla R.; *ed:* (BSED) Elem Ed, NW MO St Univ 1978; *cr:* 2nd Grade Teacher John Glenn 1978-79; 5th/6th Grade Teacher Osborn R-0 1979-81; Jr HS Math Teacher 1981-84, 1st Grade Teacher 1984- Maysville R-1; *ai:* Teacher Support Team Alternative Intervention Strategies; Drug Ed, Rdng Textbook Selection, Teacher/Welfare/Salary Comm; MO St Teachers Assn 1978-; Maysville Educators Cmmty Teacher Assn Pres 1987-88; *office:* Maysville R-1 Sch 601 W Main Maysville MO 64469

HARWOOD, SHERRY JOHNSON, 1st Grade Teacher; *b:* Granite, OK; *m:* William H.; *c:* Jackie, Christa, Peggy; *ed:* (BS) Elem Ed, 1968; (MS) Rdng Spec, 1973 OK St Univ; *cr:* 1st/2nd Grade Teacher Happy Valley Sch 1968-84; 1st Grade Teacher Stroud Elem Sch 1984-; *ai:* 4-H Leader; Staff Dev Comm; Sci & Rdng Curr Comm; NEA; OK Ed Assn 1968-; Stroud Ed Assn VP 1986 Outstanding Svc 1989; Immanuel Luth Church Sunday Sch Supv 1986-87; *office:* Stroud Elem Sch 501 N 1st Ave Stroud OK 74079

HARWOOD, WILLIAM HENRY, Science Teacher; *b:* San Antonio, TX; *m:* Sherry Johnson; *c:* Jackie, Christa, Peggy; *ed:* (BS) Sci Ed, OK St Univ 1970; *cr:* Math/Sci Teacher Glenco OK 1970-72; 7th/8th Grade Teacher Happy Valley 1972-84; Sci Teacher Stroud Public Schls 1984-; *ai:* Sr Class Spon; Academic Club; Coach; Staff Dev Comm; Sci Dept Head; NSTA; OK Sci Teachers Assn Dist Rep 1990 Outstanding Svc 1990; NEA; OK Ed Assn; Immanuel Luth Ch Elder 1988-; Gideons Intl; Fnd Scholar OK Medical Research Fnd; Comm Evaluate Teacher Testing Prgm; Sigma XI Outstanding Sci Teacher 1989; *office:* Stroud Public Schls 212 W 7th St Stroud OK 74079

HASE, JAMES ROBERT, United States History Teacher; *b:* Cleveland, OH; *m:* Gail Ellen Pannent; *c:* Lauren, James Jr.; *ed:* (BS) Comprehensive Soc Sci/His, Findlay Univ 1975; (MS) Rdng Specialist Cleveland St Univ 1981; Grad Classes Kent St, Bowling Green, Ashland, Mt St Joseph, Baldwin Wallace, OH Univ; *cr:* 7th/8th Grade Soc Stud Teacher W Muskingum Schls 1975-77; 8th Grade Summer US His Teacher N Olmsted Schls 1976; 7th/9th Grade Soc Stud/Rdng Teacher N Ridgeville Schls 1977-; Coll Inst Coll of Mt St Joseph 1986; *ai:* Head 8th Grade Ftbl & Head 7th & 8th Grade Girls Track Coach; Soc Stud Dept Spokesman; Building Scheduling Comm; Building Involvement Team Mem; NEA, OH Ed Assn 1975-; North Ridgeville Ed Assn Ex Building Rep 1977-, 2 Mini Grants 1988-89; Kiwanis Intnl 1977-79; OH Athletic Assn 1975-; OH Hot Stove Bsbl Former Local Head Umpire 1971-; North Ridgeville Teacher of Yr 1978-79; OH Jaycees Teacher of Yr 1979, Nom 1977-; North Ridgeville UNICEF Dir; Joint OH Teacher Grants; Individual OH Teacher Grant; *office:* North Ridgeville City Sch 35895 Center Ridge Rd North Ridgeville OH 44039

HASELSCHWERDT, ROSANNE GUTTRICH, English/Speech Teacher; *b:* Gladwin, MI; *m:* Richard; *c:* Jay, Lee; *ed:* (BA) Eng, MI St Univ 1966; *cr:* Teacher/Adv Lakeview HS 1966-67; Teacher Hillsdale Mid Sch 1968; Teacher/Adv Osborne Jr HS 1968-72; Teacher Hazelwood Jr HS 1972-75, Nimitz HS 1982-83, Countryside HS 1983-; *ai:* Bsktbl Team Academic Adv; Youth Bsktbl Class Instr; Teacher Evaluation Comm; Peer Teacher/Beginning Teacher Prgm; GA PTA Honorary Life 1972; NEA, PCTA, PCTE, PTA 1983-; Northwood Presbyn Church 1978-; Countryside HS Teacher of Yr 1985; Optimist Club Outstanding Teacher 1972; *office:* Countryside HS 3000 State Rd 580 Clearwater FL 34621

HASKIN, SUSAN ALICE, Sixth Grade Teacher; *b:* Seattle, WA; *m:* Errol V. Dye; *ed:* (BA) Elem Ed, WA St Univ 1974; (MA) Educl Admin/Ed Psych, Pacific Luth Univ 1985; Working Towards Doctorate Educl Leadership, Seattle Univ; *cr:* Interim Prin Pioneer Sch Dist 1987-88; Eng/His/Geography/Drama/Rdng/Career Planning Teacher Tumwater Mid Sch 1974-87, 1988-; *ai:* Stu Government, Chrldrs, Drama Adv; ASB Act Coord; EPAW 1986-; Phi Delta Kappa 1984-; Alpha Chi Omega Alumni; WSU Alumni; Olympia Yacht Club; Power Squadron; Kiwanis; Tumwater Ed Assn Pres 2 Yrs; *home:* 3414 Mud Bay Rd NW Olympia WA 98502

HASKINS, ELIZABETH PARKER, History Teacher; *b:* Ahoskie, NC; *m:* John Joseph; *ed:* (AB) His, Guilford Coll 1976; (MAT) Ed, Duke Univ 1978; *cr:* 8th Grade US His Teacher N Davidson Jr HS 1977-78; His Teacher Northampton Cty HS East 1978-85, Queen of Peace HS 1986-; *ai:* Human Rights Week Moderator; *office:* Queen of Peace HS 7659 S Linder Ave Burbank IL 60459

HASSACK, JUDY CAROL (STEVENSON), Office Education Teacher/Coord; *b:* Amarillo, TX; *m:* Klaus M.; *c:* Steven B., Kimberly R.; *ed:* (BBA) Bus Ed, W TX St Univ 1968; (MED) Scndry Ed, Univ of N TX 1985; TX Ed Agency Prof Improvement Conference,1984-; St & Natl Leadership Conferences for Office Ed 1984-; Various Prof Seminars & Conferences Bus Field 1984-; *cr:* Bus Teacher Plano Sr HS 1981-83; Office Ed Teacher Plano Sr HS 1984-; *ai:* Bus Prof of America Spon; Campus Whos Who Selection Comm Mem; Plano Ed Assn, TX Ed Assn, NEA, VOE, TAT 1984-; Natl Charity League 1989-; Zeta Tau Alpha Soroity 1965-; Jr League of Richardson 1975-83; Beginning Teacher of Yr Plano Sr HS 1981-82; *office:* Plano Sr HS 2200 Independence Pkwy Plano TX 75075

HASSEL, HELEN FEULNER, Third Grade Teacher; *b:* Evansville, IN; *c:* Kimberly, Holly, John; *ed:* (BA) Elem Ed, Univ of Evansville 1973; (MS) Elem Ed, IN St Univ 1976; *cr:* Teacher Holy Spirit Sch & Corpus Chrstn Sch & St Benedicts Sch 1965-67, 1971-75, Chandler Elem Sch 1975-; *ai:* Kndgtn-3rd Grade Curr Coord; IN St Teachers Assn Building Rep 1985-87; Holy Redeemer Cath Church Volunteer Religious Ed Teacher 1982-84; IN Gov Orrs Talks with Teachers Task Force 1987; Outstanding Young Educator Awd Chandler Jaycees 1979; *home:* 1270 Cross Gate Dr Evansville IN 47710

HASSELMAN, SHARON MINNICK, 6-8th Grade Soc Stud Teacher; *b:* Saint Marys, PA; *m:* Randall J.; *ed:* (BS) Scndry Soc Stud, Clarion Univ 1977; Cert Credits Clarion Univ, Gannon Univ, PA St Univ; *cr:* 6th/8th Grade Soc Stud Teacher Queen of the World Sch 1977-; *ai:* Stu Cncl, Safety Patrol Adv; *home:* 213 Martin Rd Saint Marys PA 15857

HASSELSCHWERT, MARY, 1st Grade Teacher; *b:* Defiance, OH; *ed:* (BS) Elem Ed, 1974; (MS) Elem Ed, 1975 St Francis Coll; *cr:* 1st Grade Teacher St John Grade Sch 1974-; *ai:* NCEA 1974-; Weight Watchers Lecturer 1985-87; RCIA (Spon Adv 87-89 Coord 1989-); *office:* St John Grade Sch 110 N Pierce St Delphos OH 45833

HASSIG, ROBERT M., Social Studies Teacher; *b:* Kansas City KS; *m:* Ronda E. Richardson; *ed:* (BS) Soc Stud, Univ of KS 1975 Univ of KS, KS St Univ, St Josephs Univ, NM Highlands Univ Univ of MO Kansas City, Santa Clara Univ; *cr:* Teacher Lawrence HS 1975-81, Baldwin HS 1981-82, Sumner Acad of Arts & Sc 1982-; *ai:* Track & Ftbl Coach; Soph Class Spon; Natl Geographic Society; Phi Delta Theta; Teacher of Yr; Young Bankers of KS E Ed Awd; *office:* Sumner Acad of Arts & Sci 8th & Oakland Kansas City KS 66101

HASSLER, ARLENE IZZI, Fourth Grade Teacher of Gifted; *b* Newark, NJ; *m:* George S.; *c:* Brian; *ed:* (BA) Elem Ed, Cath Univ of America 1964; Grad Stud; *cr:* Classroom Teacher Greenville Elem Sch 1964-67, Spruce Street Sch 1967-68, 1970-; *ai:* NEA NJEA; OCCEA Cncl Rep 1983-; Lakewood Ed Assn Secy 1983- Alpha Delta Kappa (VP 1980-84, Historian 1984-); Teacher of Yr 1983; *home:* 454 Bennetts Mills-Hyson Rd PO Box 909 Jackson NJ 08527

HASSO, SUSAN MARIE, English Teacher; *b:* Oskaloosa, IA *ed:* (BA) Eng, Marycrest Coll 1971; (MA) Eng, Drake Univ 1981 *cr:* Eng Teacher Holy Family Sch 1971-; *ai:* 8th Grade & Sch Newspaper Adv; Bd of Discipline Mem; Diocen Sch Comm 1987- NCEA 1985-; Kappa Gamma Pi 1988-; Church Choir 1985- *home:* 1533 1/2 W Lombard Davenport IA 52804

HASTINGS, PAMELA BARRON, English Teacher; *b* Huntsville, AL; *m:* Bob L.; *c:* David, John; *ed:* (BA) Soc Stud 1968, (MA) Eng, 1970 Athens St Coll; *cr:* Eng Teacher Prospect HS 1967-69, Whittle Springs Jr HS 1969-70, Ardmore HS 1971- *ai:* Jr Class Spon; Prom Adv; Lang Dept Textbook & Lang Art Curr Dev Comm; NEA 1968-; AEA, LCEA 1971-; PTA Secy 1978-79; Ardmore City Recorder 1980-81; Alpha Delta Kappa 1972-73; *office:* Ardmore HS PO Box 609 Ardmore AL 35739

HASTINGS, ROBERT OLIN, Principal; *b:* Jacksonville, FL; *m* Gloria O.; *c:* James, Rod, Angel; *ed:* (BS) Animal Sci, Mid TN St Univ 1971; (MS) Admin, Nova Univ 1987; *cr:* Sci Teacher 1981-89, Admin Asst 1987-89, Prin 1989- Bronson Mid Sch; *ai* Varsity Bsbl & Head Jr Vars Ftbl Coach; Pres of FFA Alumni Staffing Coord for ESE Prgms; Gulf Marine Educl Fnd (Dir Treas) 1987-; Implemented & Established Ag Prgm at Bronson & Helped Write Curr GuideLines for Course; *office:* Bronson Mid Sch 350 School St Bronson FL 32621

HASTINGS, RONNIE JACK, Physics & Adv Math Teacher; *b* Ranger, TX; *m:* Sylvia L. Hart; *c:* Daniel, Chad; *ed:* (BS) Physics 1968;(PHD) Physics, 1972 TX A&M Univ; *cr:* Regnl Sci Adv Univ of TX 1972-73; Physics Instr 1973-; Advd Math Instr 1973- Sci Dept Chr 1978-85 Waxahachie HS; *ai:* Sci & Math Club Phlsphy Club; Sci Fic & Fantasy Club; Amer Assn of Physics Teachers Outsndng Physics Teacher Awd 1988; Natl Assn of Geology Teachers Pres TX Section 1988-89; Natl Ctr for Sci Ed Bd Mem 1990; North TX Skeptics Pres 1984-88; Sigma Xi Sc Resrch Socty Awd - 1986; Senate Proclmtn, St of TX Recog - 1988; Publ in Journal of Geological Ed; Creation/Evolution Journal, Perspectives in Sci & Chrstn Faith; *office:* Waxahachie HS 1000 Dallas Hwy N Waxahachie TX 75165

HATCH, DONALD J., Computer Science Teacher; *b:* East Orange, NJ; *m:* Janice Nee Gaffga; *c:* Susan O Dowell, Steven; *ed* (BS) Bus Admin, Bloomfield Coll 1961; (MA) Ed, Seton Hall Univ 1967; *cr:* Teacher Madison Avenue Sch; Cmptr Sci Teacher Grove Street Sch; *ai:* Affirmative Action & Job Bank Officer Cmptr Curr Guide Comm; NEA, NJ Ed Assn 1962-; Irvington Ed Assn (Building Rep 1970-75) 1962-; Union Cty Cmptr Users Club Pres 1984-85; 2nd Place Natl Cmptr Learning Month 1988; *office* Grove Street Sch 610 Grove St Irvington NJ 07111

HATCH, HAZEL RATCLIFF, First Grade Teacher; *b:* Houston TX; *m:* Ollie Sr.; *c:* Ollie Jr., Huey T.; *ed:* (BA) Elem Ed, Prairie View A&M Univ 1955; (MS) Elem Ed, TX Southern Univ 1961 SW TX St Univ San Marcos, Univ of TX Austin; *cr:* 2nd Grade Teacher Randolph Elem Sch; 1st-3rd Grade Teacher Austin Ind Schls; *ai:* Assn of Improvement for Rdng, NEA, NAACP NAGAT, TX Classroom Teacher Assn; AAT Sch Rep; GSA Leader; Teaching Disadvantaged Pupils SW TX St San Marcos Grant; Winn Elem Teacher of Yr; *home:* 4507 Kitty Ave Austin TX 78721

HATCH, IVALVE NIELSEN, English Teacher; *b:* Malad, ID *m:* Dale S.; *c:* Chris, Heidi; *ed:* (BA) Home Ec, ID St Univ 1971 Numerous Lit Classes, ID St Univ 1988-89; *cr:* 7th/8th Grade Teacher Mc Cammon Elem 1971; Eng/Home Ec Teacher North Gem HS 1972; 7th Grade Eng Marsh Valley Mid Sch 1981; *ai* NCTE Mem; Latter Day Saints Church; *home:* 45 High St PO Box 132 Arimo ID 83214

HATCH, SAMUEL MARK, English Teacher; *b:* Lodi, CA; *m* Elizabeth Carey; *ed:* (AA) Eng, San Joaquin Delta Coll 1970 (BA) Eng, Univ of CA Davis 1972; (MA) Eng, Univ of CA Los Angeles 1975; 3 Writing Project Summer Inst 1986; Scndry Teaching Credential, CA St Univ Sacramento 1978; *cr:* Eng Teacher Galt Joint Union HS 1979-81, Tokay HS 1981-; *ai* NCTE 1981-; CATE; Area 3 Writing Project (Consultant Presenter) 1986; CA Assessment Prgm Writing Dev Team 1987-88; Lodi Unified Sch Dist Curr Cncl; Alternative Assessment Strategies for New Teachers of Eng; Phi Beta Kappa; AFT 1989- Tokay HS Teacher of Yr 1987; Supts Awd for Contributions Lang Art 1988; Honor Grad Univ CA Davis 1972; St Grad Fellowship Univ UCLA 1972-74; Univ of CA Davis Schlsp 1970-72; Frontier Awd S J Delta Coll 1972; Honor Grad San Joaquin Delta Col 1970; *office:* Tokay HS 1111 Century Ave Lodi CA 95240

HATCH, STEPHEN DANIEL, 5th Grade Teacher; *b:* Lewiston, ME; *m:* Barbara Hinckley; *c:* Abigale, Jennifer, Joselyn; *ed:* (BS) Elem Ed, Univ of ME Farmington 1976; *cr:* 6th Grade Princeton Elem 1976-77; 7th Grade Teacher 1977-79, 5th Grade Teacher 1979- Clinton Elem; *ai:* Math Curr Comm; Girls Coach Elem Bsktbl & Jr Hs Sftbl; NEA, ME Teachers Assn 1976-; Veterans Foreign Wars, Amer Legion 1972; *office:* Clinton Elem Sch Morrison Ave Clinton ME 04927

HATCHER, BARBARA K., Sixth Grade Teacher; *b:* Sevierville, TN; *m:* Joe; *c:* Greg; *ed:* (BS) Elem Ed, Univ of TN 1983; *cr:* 6th Grade Teacher Doyle Mid Sch 1983-; *ai:* Adopt-A-Sch Liaison; KCEA, TEA, NEA 1983-; Smoky Mountain Educl Assn, NCTM 1987-; *office:* Doyle Mid Sch 2021 Tipton Station Rd Knoxville TN 37920

HATCHER, BETTY JOE, Science Teacher; *b:* Cleveland Township, NC; *ed:* (BA) Bible/Bio, Flora Mac Donald Coll 1956; (BS) Sci, Appalachanian Coll 1957; (MS) Sci, Univ of NC Chapel Hill 1961; *cr:* Teacher Red Springs HS 1957-60, 71st HS 1961-62, Millbrook HS 1962-64, Cleveland HS 1964-69, Clayton HS 1969-; *ai:* Magazine Sales; Beautification Club; Jr-Sr Prom; NCEA St Ethics Comm 1962-63; Local NCEA, NCSTA; Eastern Star; Cleveland Fire Dept Bd of Dirs 1982-; NSF Academic Year Schlsp to Attain Masters Degree 1960-61; *home:* 2115 Allen Rd Clayton NC 27520

HATCHER, LINDA DEAN, Science Dept/Science Teacher; *b:* Atlanta, GA; *ed:* (BA) Natural Sci, Shorter Coll 1978; (MED) Mid Grades, Berry Coll 1987; Admin, Jacksonville St Univ; *cr:* 8th Grade Science Teacher Elm Street Mid Sch 1978-80, 1982-; *ai:* Referee HS Bsktbl, Sftbl, Soccer, Vlybl; Polk Assn of Ed, GA Assn of Ed, NEA 1984-; *home:* PO Box 5721 Rome GA 30161

HATCHETT, LOUISE GLASBY, First Grade Teacher; *b:* Yale, OK; *m:* Jay Lynn; *c:* Jason, Janette; *ed:* (BS) Elem Ed, OK St Univ 1968; (MA) Elem Ed, N AZ Univ 1987; Eng as 2nd Lang Endorsement; *cr:* 1st Grade Classroom Teacher Mannford Elem 1968-74, Tuba City Primary 1974-; *ai:* Phi Kappa Phi, Delta Kappa Gamma; *office:* Tuba City Primary Sch Box 67 Tuba City AZ 86045

HATFIELD, BONITA MATTINGLEY, Science Teacher; *b:* Evansville, IN; *m:* James T.; *c:* Carl, Jason; *ed:* (BS) Home Economics, Univ of KY 1965; (MS) Ed, 1980, Ed, 1987 Murray St Univ; *cr:* Nutritionist Eastern St Hosp 1965-67; Chldrns Hosp 1967-69; Sci Teacher Marion Jr HS 1971-72; Home Economics Teacher Crittenden Cty HS 1972-73; Sci Teacher Crittenden Cty Mid 1973-; *ai:* Speech Coach; Bldg Coord; KEA 1971-; NEA 1971-; Marion Womans Club 1972-80; *office:* Crittendon County Mid Sch Salem Rd Marion KY 42064

HATFIELD, SANDRA BALLARD, Music Teacher; *b:* Biloxi, MS; *m:* Donald R.; *c:* Catriona, Emery, Daniel; *ed:* (BS) Music Ed, SW MO St Univ 1969; Working Towards Masters in Ed; *cr:* Elem Music Teacher Mountain Grove Elem 1969-73; Pre-Sch Teacher Dunoon Scotland 1974-75; HS Vocal Teacher Mountain Grove HS 1976-85; HS Instrumental/Vocal Teacher Skyline HS 1985-88; Private Teacher 1988-; *ai:* Band Boosters; 9th & 10th Grade Spon; CTA (Secy, Insurance Comm) 1977-78; Kappa Kappa Iota 1971-78; KKI, MSTA 1969-85; *home:* PO Box 87 Buffalo MO 65622

HATHAWAY, LANA KRAUSE, Seventh Grade Reading Teacher; *b:* Brenham, TX; *m:* Earl T.; *c:* Kate, Kari; *ed:* (BS) Ed/Curr/Instruction, TX A&M 1977; (MS) Ed/Rdng Specialization, 1984; Writing Process Inst; *cr:* 7th Grade Rdng Teacher Brenham Mid Sch 1977-; *ai:* Rdng Dept Chm; Past Chrldr Spon; Discipline Management & Curr Dev Comm; TX Classroom Teachers; *office:* Brenham Mid Sch 1600 S Horton Brenham TX 77833

HATHEWAY, MARGARET COFFEY, Third Grade Teacher; *b:* Springfield, MA; *m:* Robert J.; *c:* David, Kate; *ed:* (BSE) Elem Ed/Spec Ed, 1969, (MSED) Spec Ed, 1975 Westfield St Coll; *cr:* 1st Grade Teacher 1969-76, Resource Room Teacher 1977-79, 1st Grade Teacher 1979-88, 3rd Grade Teacher 1988- C M Granger Sch; *ai:* Curr Steering Comm Town of West Springfield; Granger Sch Improvement Cncl; *home:* 50 Bretton Rd West Springfield MA 01089

HATHORN, CAROLYN WATTS, English Teacher; *b:* Prentiss, MS; *m:* C. Allen; *c:* Sylvia R. Terreo L.; *ed:* (BA) Eng, MS Industrial 1969; MS St Univ; Univ Southern MS; *cr:* Eng Teacher Alexander HS 1969-79; Bassfield HS 1980-; *ai:* Gulf Pines Girl Scouts Leader Cncl Service Team 1988; Jeff Davis Cty Neighborhood Cookie Chm; MS Assn of Educators Building Rep 1985-; Gulf Pines Girls Scout Cncl (Service Team 1988, Dir) Magnolia Awd 1988; *home:* Rt 1 Box 228A Prentiss MS 39474

HATHORN, E. JOAN INGERHAM, Third Grade Teacher; *b:* Pawnee, OK; *m:* Fields; *c:* Mary B. Hathorn Costello; *ed:* (BS) Elem Ed, OK St Univ 1955; (MA) Elem Ed, George Peabody 1957; OK St, NM St; *cr:* 3rd Grade Teacher Guymon OK 1955-56, Hooker OK 1956-57; 3rd-6th Grade Teacher Nashville TN 1957-59; 5th Grade Teacher Hominy OK 1959-65; 3rd/5th/6th Grade Teacher Alamogordo NM 1965-; *ai:* Delta Kappa Gamma 1965-; Hominy Ed Assn Pres 1962-64; Alamogordo Ed Assn 1980-81; Kappa Kappa Iota; *home:* 1004 Juniper Dr Alamogordo NM 88310

HATHORN, GEORGE GUNTER, Science Department Chairman; *b:* Alexandria, LA; *ed:* (BS) Math Ed, 1974; (MS) Math Ed, 1980 Northwestern LA; Post Maters Studies Natl Sci Fnd Physics Class 1975 LSU & Northwestern St in LA; *cr:* Teacher Buckeye HS 1974-89; Adjacent Instructor Northwestern St 1981-88; *ai:* Spon Sci Club; Coach of Golf Team; Amer Math Assn 1987-88; Amer Physics Teachers Assn 1978-81; Amer Chemical Society 1988-89; Asstship 1979-80 Northwestern St Univ; *office:* Buckeye H S General Delivery Buckeye LA 71321

HATLEY, GINGER KAY, Mathematics Teacher/Dept Chair; *b:* Indianapolis, IN; *c:* Jack, Bill, Brian, Lisa; *ed:* (BS) Math/Psych, 1974, (MA) Adult Ed/Math, 1977, (MS) Accounting, 1983 Ball St; *cr:* Teacher W Cntrl Cmmty Schls 1974-79, New Castle Schls 1979-80; Teacher/Coach Anderson Cmmty Schls 1980-; *ai:* Dept Chairperson; NCTM, AFT, IN Fed of Teachers 1974-; IN Cncl of Math 1978-; Anderson Fed of Teachers Treas 1980-; Beta Gamma Sigma, Daughters of Amer Revolution 1984-; Outstanding Young Women of America IN St Schlsp.

HATLEY, MELANIE RENEE, First Grade Teacher; *b:* Piggott, AR; *m:* John Fesmire; *c:* John M., Andrew H.; *ed:* (BS) Home Ec/Early Chldhd Ed, Univ of TN Martin 1976; Several Trng Prgms; *cr:* Pre-Sch Teacher Univ of TN Martin Lab Sch 1976-77; 1st Grade Teacher South Haven Elem 1977-83, Westover Elem 1983-; *ai:* Penthalon Speech Judge; High Five Club Spon & Adv; Phi Kappa Phi 1975-; Phi Upsilon Omicron 1973-; TN Ed Assn 1977-; Henderson Cty Ed Assn Secy 1982; Woodland Baptist Church 1977-; Birth Choice 1989-; *home:* 5 Wild Valley Dr Jackson TN 38305

HATTAWAY, ANNE DRAKE, Learning Disabilities Teacher; *b:* Donalsonville, GA; *ed:* (BSED) Spec Ed, Univ of Ga 1978; (MED) Learning Disabilities, Valdosta St Coll 1984; *ai:* Kndgtn-5th Grade Learning Disabilities & Behavior Disorders Teacher 1978-87, Teacher of Learning Disabilities 1989- Early Cty HS; Prof Assn of GA Educators.

HATTON, CHERYL DENISE, Spec Ed Resource Rm Teacher; *b:* Detroit, MI; *m:* Winfred Burns III; *c:* Charisse, Whitney; *ed:* (BS) Special Ed, 1975, (MA) Special Ed, 1978 Univ of Mi; *cr:* Teacher Acad for Gifted 1975; Sub Teacher Detroit Public Schls 1975; Spec Ed Teacher Northville Public Schls 1975-84, Detroit Public Schls 1984-; *ai:* Jr Class Spon; Social Comm Chairperson; Assn for Severely Handicapped 1976-84; Cncl for Exceptional Children 1976-; Alpha Kappa Alpha 1972- Outstanding Service 1975; Jack & Jill of America Inc 1987-; NAACP; Advisory Bd Mem Schoolcraft Coll; *office:* Osborn H S 11600 E Seven Mile Detroit MI 48205

HAUBERT, MICHELLE RE, Mathematics Teacher; *b:* Kingston, NY; *m:* Tyrus S.; *ed:* (BS) Math, St Univ of NY Cortland 1969; Grad Courses St Univ of NY Brockport, Elmira Coll, Mansfield St Univ, FL Atlantic Univ; *cr:* Teacher R L Thomas HS 1969-73, Mansfield Jr Sr HS 1974-80, Ft Pierce Cntrl 1980-85; Part Time Teacher Indian River Comm Coll; Teacher Martin Cty HS 1985-; *ai:* Math Club Calculus Coach; SAT & PSAT Coord; SAC Math & Ed Prgms Chm; Peer Teacher FL Beginning Teacher Prgm; Mansfields Teachers Union HS Assn Pres 1980; *office:* Martin Cty HS 2801 S Kanner Hwy Stuart FL 34994

HAUG, MARY ANN SCHOETTLY, Sci Dept Chair/Biology Teacher; *b:* Elizabeth, NJ; *m:* Andre C.; *c:* Mary L., Patricia, Daniel; *ed:* (BA) Bio, Coll of St Elizabeth 1964; (MA) Sci, Montclair St Coll 1971; (MA) Admin/Supervision, Jersey City St Coll 1983; *cr:* Bio/General Sci Teacher Edison Jr HS 1965-66; Bio/Drivers Ed Teacher Marylawn HS 1966-70; Anatomy/Psych Teacher Coll of St Elizabeth 1977-78; Bio Teacher 1979-,Bio Teacher/Dept Chairperson 1983- Newton HS; *ai:* Stu Against Violating the Environment Adv; NJ St Sci League Team Coach; K-12th Grade Sci Coord; Natl Bio Teachers Assn, NSTA, NJ Sci Teachers Assn 1979-; Freedom Twsp Bd of Ed Pres 1984-; Newton Memorial Hospital Victim Advocate 1987-; St Joseph Church Confirmation Teacher 1987-; NASA Contest Adv NJ Winning Team 1988-89; *office:* Newton HS 44 Ryerson Ave Newton NJ 07860

HAUGER, JAMES R., Math Dept Chair & Teacher; *b:* Freeport, IL; *m:* Shirley Ann Norvell; *c:* Sandy Laney, Andrew, Jerry Laney, Randy Laney, Michael, Christopher; *ed:* (BS) General Sci/Math, Manchester Coll 1965; (MS) Sch Counseling, Univ of La Verne 1983; Grad Work Univ of CA Davis, Sacramento St Univ, Mc Pherson Coll, Univ of CA Santa Clara; *cr:* Math/Sci Teacher Rio Tierra Jr HS 1965-69; Math Teacher Foothill Farms Jr HS 1969-; *ai:* Math Mentor; Set Comm; N CA Math Project; NEA, GTA, GDEA 1965-; NCTM; Gideons 1988-; Liberty Towers Sch Bd 1981-; N CA Math & CA Academic Partnership Project; Grant Dist Area Chm Jr HS Math; CA Math Initiative Leader; *home:* 4122 Gothberg Ave North Highlands CA 95660

HAUGHEY, CYNTHIA DAWN (HOLMES), Fifth Grade Teacher; *b:* Hammond, IN; *c:* Evan M., Matthew I.; *ed:* (BS) Eng/Sci/Elem Ed, W MI Univ 1978; (MA) Elem Classroom Teaching, MI St Univ 1981; *cr:* Kndgtn Stu Teacher Munich Intnl Sch 1977-78; Kndgtn Teacher New Troy Elem Sch 1978-79; 4th Grade Teacher 1979-80, 5th Grade Teacher 1980- Chikaming Elem; *ai:* 5th-6th Grade Spelling Team; Trinity Luth Church (Sunday Sch Teacher 1978-, Youth Group Leader 1989-); *office:* Chikaming Elem Sch Rt 1 Box 526 Sawyer MI 49125

HAUGLIE, JOSEPH W., ESOL/Foreign Lang Dept Chm; *b:* Flint, MI; *m:* Angela Rose Nottozi; *ed:* (BA) Eng Ed, MI St Univ 1986; Dallas Theological Seminary 1989-; *cr:* ESOL Instr 1989-89, ESOL/Foreign Chm 1989 Sunset HS; *ai:* NCTE 1986-88, 1990; St & Local Wkshps Presenter; ESOL Stu Needs; Response Based Instruction; *office:* Sunset HS 2120 W Jefferson Blvd Dallas TX 75208

HAUKE, WILLIAM A., 6th Grade Mathematics Teacher; *b:* Maysville, KY; *m:* Barbara A. Perry; *c:* Carrie, Christopher; *ed:* (BA) Elem Ed, Moorehead St Univ 1971; (MS) Elem Ed, Univ of Cincinnati 1976; Ec, Univ of Cincinnati; *cr:* 5th/6th Grade Teacher Fincastle Elem 1968-69; 7th/8th Grade Teacher Maysville Jr HS 1970-71; 2nd/3rd Grade Teacher Ebon C Hill East Elem 1971-74; 6th Grade Math Teacher Bethel tate Mid Sch 1974-; *ai:* Georgetown Ex Village Sch Bd Mem 1982-; S OH Teacher of Yr 1984-85; *office:* Bethel Tate Mid Sch Fossyl Dr Bethel OH 45106

HAULER, LAWRENCE ALBERT, 3rd Grade Teacher; *b:* Newtown, PA; *M:* Ruth M.; *c:* Jack L. O. D., Jeff E., Glenn E., Valerie J.; *ed:* (BS) Elem Ed, Lock Haven Univ 1957; PA Law, Marywood Coll; Sexual Abuse, PA St Univ; Natural His of Piedmont, PA St Univ; Using the Outdoors As a Classroom PA St Univ; *cr:* Phys Ed/Rdng Teacher 1958-59, 5th Grade Teacher 1959-63 Woodward Twp Elem Sch; 3rd-5th Grade Teacher Cncl Rock Sch Dist 1963-; *ai:* Elem Ftbl & Bsbl Coach; Bowling Coach; Sfty Cnslr; Grade Level Chm; Chess Club; CREA Rep; NEA 1957-; PSEA 1957-; PACE 1957-; CREA 1957-; Netown Performing Arts VP 1987-; Bux/Mont Bowling League Pres 1970-; Newtown Masonic Lodge 427 1963-; WA Crossing United Meth Church 1983-; VOSH Intnl 1990; *home:* 51 Cloverly Dr Richboro PA 18954

HAUN, RITA NAVE, English/Speech Teacher; *b:* Norfolk, VA; *c:* James C. Jr, Elizabeth H. Neely, Carl A., Teresa H. Battestin; *ed:* (BA) Lang Arts, Concord Coll 1968; Addl Studies Univ of VA; West VA Univ; *cr:* Eng Teacher Montcalm H S 1968-69; Eng/Drama/Speech Teacher Pacahontas H S 1969-; *ai:* Sr Class Spon; Drama Club Spon; Forensics Spon; Asst Coach Girls Varsity Bsktbl Team; Girls Jr Varsity Bsktbl Team NEA/VEA/TEA 1968-; Delta Kappa Gamma 1972-; West VA Easter Seal Society Mem 1974-; Easter Seal Camp for Adults Dir 1980-86; Mercer Cty Easter Seal Society Pres 1984-; Beta Sigma Phi Treasurer 1985-.

HAUPT, BRENDA PRITCHETT, Kindergarten Teacher; *b:* Hawkinsville, GA; *m:* Samuel L.; *c:* Sam; *ed:* (BS) Elem Ed, Univ of GA 1967; *cr:* Rdng Teacher 1967; 4th Grade Teacher 1968-70; Kndgtn Teacher 1976- Bleckley Elem; *ai:* Delta Kappa Gamma Chm of Music 1981-; Gideons Auxillary Chaplain Mem 1987-; Tabernacle Baptist Church Organist & Sunday Sch Teacher 1975-; Bleckley Cty Sch System Teacher of Yr 1981; *home:* 1005 Crest Drive Cochran GA 31014

HAUPT, PEGGY ANN (EIDEMILLER), Art Teacher; *b:* Dayton, OH; *m:* John Daniel; *ed:* (BS) Art Ed/Media Specialist, 1975, (MS) Ed/Curr Supervision, 1986 Wright St Univ; Springfield Museum of Art, IN Univ, Univ of Dayton; *cr:* 7th-12th Grade Art Teacher Miami East Jr/Sr HS 1975-87; 9th-12th Grade Art Teacher Miami East HS 1987-; *ai:* Art Club Adv; W OH Watercolor Society Membership Comm Mem 1990; *office:* Miami East HS 3825 N St Rt 589 Casstown OH 45312

HAUSAUER, DENISE FLYNN, Business/Mathematics Teacher; *b:* Reno, NV; *m:* Mark Ellis; *ed:* (BS) Bus, Univ of NV Reno 1983; *cr:* Teacher Sparks HS 1985-; *ai:* Natural Helpers; Participate in Drama; Score Keeper Bsktbl, Ftbl, Track; Jr Class Adv; Washoe Cty Teachers Assn, NEA, NV St Ed Assn; Nom Outstanding Stu Teacher of Yr, Outstanding Teacher of Yr; *office:* Sparks HS 820 15th St Sparks NV 89431

HAUSER, LINDA SUTTON, 6th Grade Sci/Reading Teacher; *b:* Amarillo, TX; *m:* Ray; *c:* Neal, Dean; *ed:* (BS) Elem Ed, West TX Univ 1971; Advanced Grammar, WTSU; Sci Curr Guide Trng; Region XVI Service Ctr; *cr:* 2nd Grade Teacher 1971-72; Chapter I Aide 1983-84 Stratford Elem; 6th Grade Teacher Stratford Mid Sch 1985-; *ai:* UIL Coach 1985-; Band Booster Mem 1989-; TSTA 1971-72; 1st Chrstn Church (Worship Chm 1985-86, S S Supt 1988-89); the Pantry Bd Bd Mem 1988-; 5-Year Service Awd - Stratford Sch; *office:* Stratford Mid Sch 503 N 8th Stratford TX 79084

HAUSMAN, MICHAEL L., Biology Teacher; *b:* Cincinnati, OH; *ed:* (BSED) Bio Ed, Miami Univ 1984; Working Towards Masters Bio 1990; *cr:* Bio Teacher Mt Healthy HS 1985-; *ai:* Sci Club; High Adventure Explorer Post; NABT; BSA 1968-, Eagle 1979; Sierra Club; *office:* Mt Healthy HS 2046 Adams Rd Cincinnati OH 45231

HAUSMANN, JOHN W., Social Studies Dept Chairman; *b:* Goliad, TX; *m:* Jean E.; *c:* Jason, Jered; *ed:* (BS) His, 1963, (MS) His, 1969 SW TX St Univ; Post Grad Work; *cr:* Teacher Ingleside Ind Sch Dist 1963-64, Anstwell-Tivoli Ind Sch Dist 1964-67; Dept Chm/Teacher Goliad Ind Sch Dist 1967-; *ai:* Natl Soc Sci Honor Society, TX St Teachers Assn; William R Coe Fellowship Awd 1990; *home:* Rt 3 Box 302-A Goliad TX 77963

HAVASY, JUDITH ESTHER, Head Librarian; *b:* Washington, PA; *m:* Richard Alexandria Sr.; *c:* Richard A. Jr.; *ed:* (BS) Lib Sci, 1964, (BA) Eng, 1964 Clarion Univ; PA St Univ, Drexel Inst of Technology, Univ of VA, Brigham Young Univ; *cr:* Librarian Abington Sch Dist 1964-66, Beaver Sr HS 1966-68; Prin Abundant Life Acad 1979-84; Eng Teacher 1987-88, Librarian 1988- Louisa Cty HS; *ai:* Academic & Achievement Comm; HS Lib Club Spon; HS Literary Magazine Co-Spon; N Hundington Sch Dist Self Study Evaluating Comm; Amer Lib Assn 1964-; VA Ed Media Assn 1987-; ACSI 1980-84; ASCD 1988-; Chrstn Ed Assn 1989-; NCTE 1988-; Citizenship Awd.

HAVEL, EDDY, History Teacher; *b:* Refugio, TX; *m:* Patricia Ann Pepper; *c:* Kimberly, Katherine; *ed:* (BS) Scndry Ed, TX A&I Univ 1971; *cr:* Teacher/Coach Somerset Jr-Sr HS 1971-75; Teacher E M Pease Mid Sch 1975-; *ai:* Northside Soc Stud Organization, Natl Assn of Soc Stud, Assn of TX Prof Educators; *home:* Rt 2 Box 144 BC Hondo TX 78861

HAVEL, PATRICIA PEPPER, Mathematics Teacher; *b:* San Antonio, TX; *m:* James E.; *c:* Kimberly A., Katherine L.; *ed:* (BS) Scndry Ed, TX A&I Univ 1970; (MA) Ed Admin, Univ of TX 1976; Cmptr Literacy Univ of Northern CO 1984; *cr:* Teacher Alice ISD 1970-71; Northside ISD 1971-78; Sabinal ISD 1979-81; Lackland ISD 1981-; *ai:* Spon UIL Number Sense/Calculattor; Spon Math/Sci Club; Tech Plan Dist Comm; Calendar-Dist Comm; Lackland Teachers Assn Pres 1986-87; NEA/TX St Teachers Assn; Alamo Dist Cncl Teachers of Math; TX CTM/Natl CTM; GTE Growth Initiatives Teachers Grant; Conf Advancement of Math Teaching Spkr.

HAVELKA, DIANE MARIE, Mathematics Teacher/Coach; *b:* Georgetown, TX; *ed:* (BS) Phys Ed, Southwestern Univ 1980; *cr:* Math Teacher/Coach St Paul 1981-82, St Rose 1982-87, Brazos Jr HS 1987-89, St Rose 1990; *ai:* Bsktbl, Track, Sftbl Coach.

HAVEN-O'DONNELL, RANDEE P., Sixth Grade Teacher; *b:* New York, NY; *m:* Gerard O'Donnell; *c:* Aran; *ed:* (BA) Elem Ed, St Univ of NY Stonybrook 1973; Working Towards Mastes Teacher Research, Mid Sch Math, Teaching of Writing, Univ of NC Chapel Hill; *cr:* 4th/5th Grade Teacher Brooklyn Friends Sch 1976-77; 5th/6th Grade Teacher Frank Porter Graham Elem Sch 1978-89; 6th Grade Teacher Culbreth Sch 1989-; *ai:* Center for Peace Ed & Child Advocacy Rep; Rainbow Soccer & Math Bowl Coach; Culbreth Sch Garbology Recycling Activity Group; NC Assn Ed Pres 1985-86; Phi Delta Kappa Mem 1989-; NC Assn of Educators; NC Recycling Assn Bd Mem 1989-; Explore Grant Impact II 1989; Travel Grant; Orange Cty Soil & Water Conservation Teacher of Yr 1989; Various Articles Written; *office:* Culbreth Sch 225 Culbreth Rd Chapel Hill NC 27516

HAVENS, BONNIE WORLEY, Second Grade Teacher; *b:* York, PA; *m:* Dan E.; *c:* Sean R.; *ed:* (BS) Elem Ed, James Madison Univ 1972; Univ of VA; *cr:* 1st/2nd Grade Teacher Ashlawn Elem Sch 1972-89; *ai:* Gifted & Talented Contact Teacher; Childrens Choice Spon; Volunteer Coord; Hospitality Comm; Delta Kappa Gamma 1984-; Innovative Awds; Washington Post Grants; Human Relation Grants; Book Reviews in Arithmetic Teacher; Gifted & Talented Outstanding Achievement by Arlington Co; Gifted & Talented Outstandng Teacher of Gifted by Northern VA Cncl; *office:* Ashlawn Elem Sch 5950 8th Rd N Arlington VA 22305

HAVENS, RICHARD HARLEY, Mathematics Department Chm; *b:* Ashtabula, OH; *m:* Kay Brenneman; *c:* Greg, Bradley, Kara; *ed:* (BS) Math, Wheaton Coll 1969; (MAT) Math, Bowling Green St Univ 1974; Cmptr Sci, Youngstown St Univ; *cr:* Math Teacher Lake Park HS 1969-72, Ivory Coast Acad 1972-73, Painesville Riverside 1974-75, Jefferson Area HS 1975-; *ai:* Var Head Bsbl Coach; 8th Grade Bsktbl Coach; NCTM 1979-; Dorset First Baptist Church Pastor 1987-; Jefferson Memorial Field Bd 1987-; Amer Family Assn Pres 1989-; Nom for Presidential Awd Excl 1990; Commodore Cmptrs Grant Curr Dev; *office:* Jefferson Area HS 125 S Poplar St Jefferson OH 44047

HAVENS, SHERRILL JANE (LYNCH), Third Grade Teacher; *b:* Canton, IL; *m:* Larry J.; *c:* Jeff, Brad; *ed:* (BS) Elem Ed, IL St Univ 1963; *cr:* Kndgtn Teacher Loucks Grade Sch 1963-65; 3rd Grade Teacher Anderson Grade Sch 1965-66, Mc Call Grade Sch 1967-77, Lincoln Elem Sch 1977-; *ai:* Supts Cabinet; Various Soc Comms; IL Ed Assn, NEA, Canton Ed Assn 1963-65, 1968-; Canton Ed Assn Building Rep; *office:* Lincoln Elem Sch 20 Lincoln Rd Canton IL 61520

HAVER, DEBORAH TODD, Mathematics Teacher; *b:* Patuxent River, MD; *m:* Willard Anthony; *c:* Patricia K., Christina A., Kathleen E.; *ed:* (BA) Math Ed, 1975, (MS) Ed, 1983 Old Dominion Univ; Educl Specialist Prgm, George Washington Univ; *cr:* Teacher Great Bridge Jr HS 1975-87; K-12th Grade Instructional Specialist Math/Sci Sch Admin 1987-88; Instr Tidewater Comm Coll 1985-; Teacher Great Bridge HS 1988-; *ai:* Chm Study Skills Prgm, Math Month; Effective Schls Comm & Jr Class Team Mem; Great Bridge Jr HS Math Dept Head; Tidewater Cncl of Teachers of Math (Treas 1988-, VP 1990); March of Dimes Luekemia Society, Heart Fund; Drillers First Base Co-Ed Sftbl; Great Bridge Jr HS Teacher of Yr 1986; Outstanding Young Women of America 1985; *office:* Great Bridge HS 301 Hanbury Rd Chesapeake VA 23320

HAVERLAH, DOUGLAS GERALD, 5th Grade English Teacher; *b:* Dallas, TX; *m:* Heidi Kubala; *c:* Katie, Kevin; *ed:* (BA) His, TX Luth Coll 1977; Teacher Cert, SW TX St Univ 1980; *cr:* 5th Grade Teacher Floresville Intermediate Sch 1980-; *ai:* Univ Interscholastic League Coach Spelling & Ready Writing; Grade Level Rep To Supt; ATPE Campus Rep 1980-; Wilson Cty Sheriffs Reserve Pres 1981-; *office:* Floresville Intermediate Sch 1200 5th St Floresville TX 78114

HAWK, JOYCE L., Chapter 1 Teacher; *b:* Woodville, GA; *m:* Robert P. Jr.; *c:* Paul, Hollie; *ed:* (BS) Elem Ed, GA Coll 1971; (MED) Early Chldhd Ed, Univ of GA 1979; Microcomputers in Ed; *cr:* 1st-3rd Grade/Chapter 1 Rdng & Math Teacher/Testing Coord Union Point Elem 1971-; *ai:* Stu Support Team Comm; Support Teacher Evaluator; GA Assn of Educators 1971-78; Prof Organization of GA Educators 1986-; *office:* Union Point Elem Sch Witcher St Union Point GA 30669

HAWKINS, ALAN RAY, Texas History Teacher; *b:* Plainview, TX; *m:* Trudy Renee Brazell; *c:* Kyle, Alex, Jennifer Mulanax, Dustin Mulanax; *ed:* (BS) Ed/U S His, West TX St Univ 1966; (MA) Scndry Ed/His, Univ of CO 1977; Youth & the Law; Teacher At-Risk Stus; TX Southwest & Co His; Writing Improvement to Jr HS Stus; Sch Improvement & Effectiveness; *cr:* Teacher Crowell HS 1966-67, Gorman Jr HS 1967-72, Air Acad Jr HS 1972-84, Dumas Jr HS 1984-; *ai:* Time & Score Keeper Vlybl & Bsktbl Games; Tutorials TX & U S His; Stu Cncl Spon 1984-85; Assn of TX Prof Ed 1984-; *home:* 110 Chelsea Dumas TX 79029

HAWKINS, ANN JONES, Home Economics Dept Teacher; *b:* Danville, KY; *m:* Ronald Wayne; *c:* Ronald W. II, Hollan P.; *ed:* (BS) Home Ec Ed, KY St Univ 1977; (MA) Home Ec Ed, E KY Univ 1983; *cr:* Home Ec Teacher Bardstown Bd of Ed 1977-; *ai:* FHA Adv; Bardstown Ed Assn, KY Ed Assn, NEA 1977-; KY St Univ Alumni 1985-; Alpha Kappa Alpha; *office:* Bardstown HS 400 N 5th St Bardstown KY 40004

HAWKINS, CHARLES H., History Teacher; *b:* Tiffin, OH; *m:* Sharon; *c:* Jennifer, Jason; *ed:* (BS) His, OH ST Univ 1966; Bowling Green ST Univ/Dayton Univ; *cr:* His Teacher North Union HS 1970-77, Ada HS 1978-; *ai:* Sr Class Adv; Jr HS Bsktbl Coach; Ada Ed Assn Pres 1978-; Ada Lions Club Pres 1978-; *home:* 0097 State Rt 309 Alger OH 45812

HAWKINS, CYRIL A., JR., Assistant Principal; *b:* Petersburg, VA; *m:* Audrey T.; *c:* Michael, Gregory; *ed:* (BS) Soc Stud, WV St Coll 1959; (MED) Admin/Supv VA St Univ 1973; (EDS) Admin/Supv 1983, (EDD) Ed Admin 1988 Univ of VA; Cpr Trng; *cr:* Deputy Dir United States Army 1977-80; Sr Army Instr Franklin Military Sch 1980-83; Petersburg HS 1983-89; Asst Prin Petersburg HS 1989-; *ai:* Participated Five Self-Study Comm; Serve Dropout Prevention Comm; Serve Drug Abuse Comm; Phi Delta Kappa Mem 1985-; Ascd Mem 1990; Masonic Lodge 43 Mem 1989-; Omega Psi Phi Mem 1957-; Distinguished Instr Awd U S Army; Quartermaster Sch 1973; Doctoral Dissertation Analyzing JROTC Cadets & Studs; Whos Who Among Studs Amer Universities & Colleges 1958-59; *office:* Petersburg High Schl 3101 Johnson Rd Petersburg VA 23805

HAWKINS, DELORES MERRITT, Kindergarten Teacher; *b:* Memphis, TN; *m:* Emmett Louis Jr.; *c:* Dietra Diane, Emmett Louis III, Robin Michelle; *ed:* (BS) Elem Ed, 1970, (MA) Early Chlhd, 1974 Memphis St Univ; Career Ladder I 1985; Career Ladder II 1989; *cr:* Kndgtn Teacher 1975-, 2nd Grade Teacher 1971-75, 5th Grade Teacher 1973-74, 7th/8th Grade Teacher 1970-71, 5th Grade Teacher 1969-70 Riverside Elem; *ai:* Annual Staff Spon; TN Ed Assn 1989-; Shelby Cty Ed Assn 1989-; Natl Ed Assn 1989-; Delta Sigma Theta Memphis St Univ Secy 1968-69; *office:* Riverdle Elem School 7391 Neshoba Rd Germantown TN 38138

HAWKINS, DONNA-MARIE NELSONEA, Sixth Grade Teacher; *b:* Washington, DC; *m:* Bennie Thompson; *c:* Desiree M., Christian P., Gayla M.; *ed:* (BA) Elem Ed, 1969, (MED) Educl Technology, 1977 Howard Univ; *cr:* 2nd/6th Grade Teacher Bustleton Elem 1969-72; 3rd Grade Teacher Sembach Elem 1972-76; 5th/6th Grade Teacher Ramstein Elem 1977-; *ai:* Music Comm; Assn for Educl Comm & Technology 1977-80; Kappa Delta Pi 1977; Sembach Cmmty Childrens Choir (Founder, Dir) 1974-76; Multi Ethnic Stud Coord 1974-76, 1990; *home:* Ramstein Box 7071 APO New York NY 09012

HAWKINS, JOY LEANNE, 7th-8th Lang Arts/Lit Teacher; *b:* Albany, OR; *ed:* (BS) Soc Sci/Corrections/Psych, 1974, (BS) Scndry Ed/Soc Sci, 1975 OR Coll of Ed; (MAT) Lang Arts, Lewis & Clark Coll 1980; *cr:* 7th-12th Eng Grade Teacher Dayton Jr/Sr HS 1975-84; 9th-12th Eng Grade Teacher Cntrl HS 1984-85; Lang Arts/Lit Teacher Cntrl Linn Mid Sch 1985-; *ai:* Dist Lang Arts Comm; Wellness Team 1990; NEA, OEA, DEA, CEA, CLEA 1975-; 4-H (Judge, Educator); Jr OR Suffolk Breeders Assn (Leader, Organizer) 1985-88; OR Purebred Sheep Breeders Assn (VP 1990, Pres 1991-92); *office:* Cntrl Linn Mid Sch 239 W 2nd St Halsey OR 97348

HAWKINS, MARY JANE SHIRLEY, Fourth Grade Teacher; *b:* Anderson, SC; *m:* George A.; *c:* Amy, Anna, Allen M., Adrienne; *ed:* (AA) Bio, Anderson Coll 1967; (BS) Ed, Lander Coll 1969; (MED) Ed, Clemson Univ 1972; Grad Stud Sci Leadership Educl Prgm Specialist Degree 1989-; *cr:* 5th Grade Teacher Homeland Park Elem 1969-70; 6th Grade Teacher Six Mile Elem 1970-72; 5th/6th Grade Teacher Cleo Bailey Elem 1973-75; 3rd/4th Grade Teacher Homeland Park Elem 1979-; *ai:* Assessments of Performance in Teaching to Assess Stu Teachers & 1st Yr Teachers Observer; NEA, SCEA 1989-; SC Sci Cncl 1988-; Sci Steering Comm Dist #5 1988-; Poll Mgr of Voting Dist Martin Township; Sunday Sch Teacher; Vacation Bible Sch Teacher; Elem Sci Leadership Prgm; *home:* Rt 5 Box 105 Sunnyside Farm Anderson SC 29621

HAWKINS, PATRICIA AVERA, English 2nd Language Teacher; *b:* Schofield Barracks, HI; *m:* Billy W.; *c:* Stephen, Hope Roberts, David, Matthew, Faith Christopher, Thuan Nguyen, Dung Nguyen; *ed:* (BS) Scndry Ed, Bob Jones Univ 1955; WV Univ, Penn St Univ, Univ of GA, HACC, Clarion Univ; *cr:* 8th Grade Substitute Teacher Hollis Jr HS 1955-56; Phys Ed Teacher La Fayette Jr HS 1956-57; Sci/Rdng/Religion Teacher St Johns HS 1968-72; Sci/Eng as 2nd Lang Teacher Harrisburg HS 1972-; *ai:* Exch Trip with Hungarians; All Ethnic Celebrations for Foreign Stu; Amer Red Cross Instr 1978-83, Teacher of Yr 1980; Harrisburg HS Teacher of Yr 1987; Cmptrs in Classroom Grants; Exch Prgm in Hungary D/A Grant 1990; *office:* Harrisburg HS 2451 King Blvd King, Jr Blvd Harrisburg PA 17103

HAWKINS, PAULA COVINGTON, Spanish/Language Art Teacher; *b:* Martin, TN; *m:* Bill; *c:* Anita K., William P.; *cr:* Teacher Westview HS 1970-72, West HS 1972-74, Briarwood Sch 1975-; *ai:* BCEA, TEA, NEA.

HAWKINS, PHIL, English Teacher; *b:* Effingham, IL; *m:* Rosemary Nix; *c:* Scott, Kent; *ed:* (AS) Poly Sci, Olney Cntrl Coll 1973; (BA) Eng, 1975, (MA) Lit, 1979 E IL Univ 1979; US Navy 1969-72 IL Natl Guard 1986-88; *cr:* Eng Instr Effingham HS 1975-, Lit Instr Lakeland Jr Coll 1977-; *ai:* Soph Class, Jr Class, Jr Variety Show Spon; Key Club Adv; NEA, IL Ed Assn Treas 1988-89; IL Eng Teachers Assn 1975-88; BSA Scoutmaster 1974-; Fine Art of Effingham Cty Play Dir 1978; *office:* Effingham HS 600 Henrietta Effingham IL 62401

HAWKINS, ROB, Social Studies/History Teacher; *b:* Charleston, IL; *m:* Cynthia Lentz; *c:* Kyle; *ed:* (BA) His, Eastern IL Univ 1977; (MA) Cnslr Ed, Southern IL Univ Edwardsville 1980; *cr:* Teacher 1977-87, Cnslr 1989, Teacher 1989 Freeburg Dist 70; *ai:* 7th Grade Bsktbl Coach; Stu Cncl Spon; IEA/NEA 1977-; Freeburg Elem Teachers Assn Pres 1982; Freeburg Optimist 1990; *office:* Freeburg Sch Dist #70 408 S Belleville St Freeburg IL 62243

HAWKINS, ROBERT NEIL, Asst Principal/Science Teacher; *b:* Elkin, NC; *m:* Ashley A. Harding; *ed:* (BS) Bio Ed, Wingate Coll 1988; *cr:* Sci Teacher 1988-89, Asst Prin/Sci Teacher 1989- Tabernacle Chrstn Sch; *ai:* Honor Society & Beta Club Spon; HS Fine Art & Sch Sci Fair Coord; Sandy Ridge Baptist Church Organist 1987-; *home:* 109 S Stewart St Wingate NC 28174

HAWKINS, STELLA LOUISE SMITH, Fourth Grade Teacher; *b:* Brookhaven, MS; *m:* Johnny Lee; *c:* Jonathan, Jarrette, Candria; *ed:* (BA) Elem Ed/Spec Ed, Jackson St Univ 1972; Cmptr Trng, Advanced Sci Courses; Working Towards Masters Elem Ed; *cr:* Spec Ed Teacher 1972-73, Sci Teacher 1973-74 Wesson Elem Sch; 4th Grade Teacher Wesson Attendance Center 1974-; *ai:* Scout Troop 698; Redmond Day Care Summer Prgm Staff Mem; Elks Financial Secy 1983-87; STAR Teacher; *office:* Wesson Attendance Center 532 Grove St Wesson MS 39191

HAWKINS, THELMA TAYLOR, 8th Grade History Teacher; *b:* Greer, SC; *m:* William E. Jr.; *c:* Mark W.; *ed:* (BA) Poly Sci, Furman Univ 1965; Grad Stud; *cr:* Teacher Greenville Jr HS/Mid Sch 1965-; *ai:* Yrbk Adv; Greenville Cty Cncl for Soc Stud 1975-; SC Cncl for Soc Stud, NCSS 1986-; Delta Kappa Gamma 1984-; Teacher of Yr Greenville Mid Sch 1990; *office:* Greenville Mid Sch 339 Lowndes Ave Greenville SC 29607

HAWKINS, YOLANDA WILLIAMS, Kindergarten Teacher; *b:* Montgomery, AL; *m:* Otis W.; *c:* Keesha, Sylvie, Bridgette; *ed:* (BS) Early Chlhd Ed, Tuskegee Inst 1979; Elem Sch Counseling Prgm, AL St Univ; *cr:* Recep/Secy WQTY-WFMI Radio Station 1976-77, Wallace & Wallace Construction Co 1978-; Sales Clerk Parisian 1978-79; Receptionist WHHY-Y-102 1979-80; Substitute Teacher 1980-81, 1st/2nd & 2nd/3rd Grade Teacher 1981-84, Kndgrtn Teacher 1984- Montgomery Cty Public Sch; *ai:* Mem Courtesy Comm; Service Unit Y; Tutor Project Bootstrap; PTA Advisory Comm; Inservice Sub-Comm, Elem Spotlight on Achievement Mem; MCEA 1981-; NEA 1981-; Brownie Troop 295 Co-Leader 1989-; Residential Cmnty Pres 1987-88; United Way 1981-; PTA Advisory Comm; Publicity Chairperson Bellingrath May Festival 1989; *home:* 671 W Jefferson Davis Ave Montgomery AL 36108

HAWKS, GARY R., 4th Grade Teacher; *b:* Warsaw, NY; *m:* Mary Brandt North; *c:* Brandt, Whitney; *ed:* (BA) Elem, 1974, (MS) Elem, 1979, Rdng, 1982 Murray St; *cr:* 5th Grade Teacher 1974-87, 3rd Grade Teacher 1987-89, 4th Grade Teacher 1989- Trigg Cty Elem; *ai:* Chess & Newspaper Club; IRA, TCEA, KEA, NEA, PN Team 1974-.

HAWKS, KATHY JUNE, 5th Grade Teacher; *b:* Princeton, WV; *m:* Jerry Wayne; *c:* Russell Wayne, Jody Scott, Kayla Renee; *ed:* (BA) Elem Ed, Bluefield St Coll 1979; (MS) Comm, WV Univ 1987; *cr:* 3rd Grade Teacher 1979-85, 5th Grade 1985-Glenwood Elem; *ai:* Yrbk Comm; Interpret for Deaf During Church Act & Svcs; Johnston Chapel Church 1972-; Mini Grant for Trail of Fitness; *office:* Glenwood Elem Sch Rt 1 Box 460 Princeton WV 24740

HAWLEY, JERRY WAYNE, Science Teacher; *b:* Dexter, MO; *m:* Oralea Hudson; *c:* Karen, Michael; *ed:* (BS) Bio, 1967, (MS) Admin, 1979 Southeast MO St Univ; EMT US Army 1970-71; *cr:* Sci Teacher Bloomfield Sr HS 1967-69; Officer US Army 1969-74; Sci Teacher Bernie Sr HS 1974-; *ai:* 8th Grade Class Spon; Bernie Sch Improvement Comm; HS Sftbl Official; MO St Teachers Assn 1974-; Bernie Classroom Teachers Assn 1974-; Summer League Bsbl/Sftbl Coach; Bernie CTA VP/Pres/Legislative Officer/Executive Comm; MO St Teachers Assn Delegate; *office:* Bernie R-13 Schls PO Box 470 Bernie MO 63822

HAWLEY, WILLIAM DONALD, Asst Prin/8th Grade Teacher; *b:* Jacksonville, IL; *m:* Cynthia Ann Seay; *c:* Joshua; *ed:* (BS) Soc Sci, Concordia Coll 1986; *cr:* Teacher/Frosh Cnslr Martin Luther HS 1986-88; Asst Prin Christ Cmmty Lutheran Sch 1988-; *ai:* Stu Advisory Bd Spon; Girls & B Team Boys Bsktbl & Track Coach; ASCD 1988-; Lutheran Ed Assn 1986-; Concordia Jr Youth Bd 1988-; *office:* Christ Comm Lutheran Sch 110 W Woodbine Kirkwood MO 63122

HAWN, RONALD DALE, Biology Teacher; *b:* Seymour, IN; *m:* Sue Stingley; *c:* Brad; *ed:* (BS) Bio, Oakland City Coll 1976; (MS) Scndry Ed, IN Univ 1985; *cr:* Jr HS Sci/Phys Ed Carroll Jr-Sr HS 1977-86; Bio/General Sci Jeffersonville HS 1986-; *ai:* Boys & Girls Golf Coach; Boys Jr Var Bsktbl Coach; *office:* Jeffersonville HS 2315 Allison Ln Jeffersonville IN 47130

HAWORTH, CINDY HEISLER, Math Teacher; *b:* Houston, TX; *c:* Shawn, Justin; *ed:* (BS) Math Teacher Ed, Univ of Houston 1971; *cr:* Teacher Albuquerque Public Sch 1971-75, Manzans Chrtn Acad 1982, Spring Branch Sch 1985, Belen Sch 1988-; *ai:* Class of 90 Spon; Class of 93 Spon; Echo Spon; Stu Asst Team; Belen Sch Health Comm; Natl Honor Society Screening Comm; Policy Comm; Valencia Cty Safety Comm Mem 1989-; *home:* PO Box 1610 Belen NM 87002

HAWORTH, DENICE KAY, 4th Grade Sci & Math Teacher; *b:* OKeene, OK; *m:* Michael Dean; *c:* Christopher, Timothy; *ed:* (BS) Elem Ed, OK St Univ 1974; *cr:* 5th/6th Grade Teacher Yale Public Schls 1974-75; 4th Grade Teacher Fairview Public Schls 1975-; *ai:* Cornelsen Invention Fair Organizer; Fairview Ed Assn (VP 1988-89, Treas 1989-), Teacher of Yr 1989; Fairview Recycling Task Force; St Anns Study Club; MADD Mem; Bicentenniel Ed Grant 1989; *office:* Cornelsen Elem Sch 1400 E Elm Fairview OK 73737

HAWORTH, JEANNE CIARAMELLI, Physical Education Teacher; *b:* Mt Vernon, NY; *m:* James Jeffrey; *c:* James C.; *ed:* (BA) Phys Ed/Health, Montclair St Coll 1970; Family Living Seminars; *cr:* Phys Ed/Health Teacher Middletown HS N 1970-; *ai:* NEA, Middletown Ed Assn; *office:* Middletown HS North 63 Tindall Rd Middletown NJ 07748

HAWS, KAYLE E., Math Teacher; *b:* Eagar, AZ; *m:* Annette Whetten; *c:* Jeremy, Kellen, Deveney, Jesse, Annessa; *ed:* (BAE) Math, 1977, (MAE) Math, 1980 AZ St Univ; *cr:* Math Teacher Fremont Jr HS 1977-78, Mountain View HS 1978-; *ai:* Var Ftbl & Track Asst; *office:* Mountain View HS 2700 E Brown Rd Mesa AZ 85203

HAWTHORNE, LINDA DOUGLAS, Student Services Director; *b:* Wichita, KS; *m:* Charles E.; *c:* Lantz, Douglas; *ed:* (BA) Speech Therapy, S Meth Univ 1963; (MA) Educl Admin, NM St Univ 1986; Working Toward Masters Counseling; *cr:* Speech Therapist Lubbock Ind Schls 1963-64, Galena Park Ind Sch Dist 1964-68; Teacher of Hearing Impaired Fairbanks Ind Sch Dist 1968-69, Lubbock Ind Sch Dist 1970-73; Speech Therapist San Angelo Ind Sch Dist 1973-78; Spec Ed Teacher Ruidoso Municipal Schls 1978-; *ai:* Drug Free Schls & Cmmtys Advisory Cncl; Native Amer Task Force; Title V Indian Ed Secy; Spon Peer Assistance League & Indian Club; Academic Booster Club; Ruidoso Ed Assn Pres 1981-82; NEA, CEC Past Mem; Families in Action Publicity Chairperson 1987-89; 1st Chrstn Church Elder 1984-87; Childrens Choir Coord 1980-84; Co-Developed Ruidoso Impact Drug Prevention Prgm; Founded Peer Assistance League; Nomination Comm, Ruidoso Mid Sch Best in NM 1989; *office:* Ruidoso Mid Sch 200 Horton Cir Ruidoso NM 88345

HAXTON, JUDITH ANN, Fifth/Sixth Grade Teacher; *b:* Downey, CA; *m:* Paul Richard; *c:* Geoffrey, Christopher; *ed:* (BS) Elem Ed, Univ of Sci & Arts of OK 1975; *cr:* Elem Teacher Empire Elem 1975-; *ai:* 4-H Spon 1988-89; Empire Educators (Pres 1983-84, Mem) 1983-; OK Ed Assn 1975-; Teacher of Yr Empire Public Schls 1987; *office:* Empire Elem Sch Rt 1 Box 155 Duncan OK 73533

HAY, BARBARA BARKER, First Grade Teacher; *b:* Garden City, KS; *m:* Robert; *c:* Kimberly, Christopher, Douglas; *ed:* (BA) Ed, KS Wesleyan Univ 1972; Working Toward Masters, KS St; *cr:* 1st Grade Teacher Wellsville Elem 1956-57, Lincoln Elem 1957-58; 2nd Grade Teacher 1972-73, 1st Grade Teacher 1974- Franklin Sch; *ai:* Uniserv #114 Bd of Dir 1986-; Salina NEA Comm Chairperson 1989-.

HAY, NANCY ANN (LANDIS), Girls Physical Ed Teacher; *b:* Meyersdale, PA; *m:* Randy J.; *c:* Jennifer, Christy; *ed:* (BS) Health/Phys Ed, 1971, (MS) Health/Phys Ed, 1974 Slippery Rock St Coll; Cert Admin/Scndry Prin, California Univ of PA 1986; *cr:* Health/Phys Ed Teacher Gateway HS 1971-74; Asst HS Prin 1987-88, Health/Phys Ed Teacher 1974- Somerset HS; *ai:* Sftbl Coach; Maple Princess Adv; Cafeteria & Intramural Supvr; Sftbl Clinic; Camp Dir; Health Curr Comm Mem; Delta Kappa Gamma 1987-; PIAA (Sftbl Ofcls, Pres Somerset Cty) 1978-89; Trinity Evangelical Luth Church (Sunday Sch Teacher, Previous Bible Sch Dir, Mem); Woman of Yr Somerset Cty 1987; Ed Articles; Developed Various Sports Prgms; *office:* Somerset Area Sr HS S Columbia Ave Somerset PA 15501

HAY, PATRICE HILTON, Kindergarten Teacher; *b:* Ruston, LA; *m:* Thomas Fredrick; *c:* Heather L., Hilton T., Holly K., Haley P.; *ed:* (BA) Elem Ed, 1974, (MA) Elem Ed, 1977 LA Tech Univ; Grad Stud; *cr:* 5th Grade Teacher 1974-75, 4th Grade Teacher 1975-85, 1st Grade Teacher 1985-86, 4th Grade Teacher 1986-89, Kndgtn Teacher 1989- Hillcrest Elem; *ai:* Yrbk Comm Chm; Kappa Kappa Iota (Pres 1975-76, 1988-, Mem 1975-); Delta Kappa Gamma 1989-; First Baptist Church (Childrens Worship Leader 1989-, Sanctuary Choir 1971-, Property & Space Comm, Leader of Baptist Women Group 1989-, Dir Girls in Action 1988-); *office:* Hillcrest Elem Sch Kentucky Ave Ruston LA 71270

HAY, SANDEE GILLETTI, Special Programs Director; *b:* Walsenburg, CO; *m:* J. W.; *c:* Quinn M.; *ed:* (BA) Scndry Ed/HPER, 1970, (MA) Elem Ed, 1971 Adams St Coll; Type D Elem/Scndry, Univ of N CO 1989; *cr:* Elem/Scndry Teacher Moffat Public Schls 1968-70; Elem Sch Teacher 1970-89; Teacher/Diagnostician/Prin Summer Migrant Sch SLV BOCS 1972-; Spec Prgms Dir/GT/ELPA/Chapter I/Chapter II/Dist Testing Alamosa Public Schls 1989-; *ai:* Dist Accountability & Dist Rdng Lang Art Comm; SLVBOCS Staff Dev Team; Odyssey of Mind Adv; Natl Assn Migrant Ed Charter Mem; NEA, CEA, AEA (Mem 1970-, Negotiations 1986-); Phi Delta Kappa (Secy 1986-89, VP 1989-); ASCD Mem 1987-; Sacred Hearth Cath Church 1965-; Outstanding Young Educator Jaycees; Master Teacher St of CO Migrant Ed (Elem 1987-88 & Scndry 1988-89); Chairperson Natl Migrant Scndry Educators; Consultant Western & Cntrl Streams Migrant Ed; *office:* Alamosa Public Schls 209 Victoria Ave Alamosa CO 81101

HAYASHI, ALAN T., Mathematics Teacher; *b:* Honolulu, HI; *ed:* (BA/BS) Math/Liberal Stud, 1975, Teaching Credential Math/Ed, 1976 Univ of CA Riverside; Advance Stud in Math, Ed, Cmptrs at Numerous Coll & Univ; Working towards Masters in Math, OH St Univ; *cr:* Math Teacher Jurupa Jr HS 1976-79, Channel Islands HS 1979-83; Teaching Asst OH St Univ 1983-84; Math Teacher Channel Islands HS 1984-; Math Instr Oxnard Coll 1989-; *ai:* Track & Bsktbl Coach; Journalism, Asian-Amer Club, Math Club Adv; Gifted/Talented Ed Comm Mem; Academic Decathalon Team & Knowledge Bowl Team Coach & Adv; NCTM 1976-; Math Assn of America 1984-; Natl Assn of Educators 1976-; Intnl Relations Cncl of Riverside Publicity Coord 1975-76; CA Schlsp Fed Teacher of Yr Channel Islands HS 1989; CA St Dept of Ed Math Analysis Textbook Reviewer; Channel Islands HS Teacher of Yr 1983; Natl Sci Fnd Fellow 1981-82; CA St Dept of Ed Textbook Adoption, Evaluation & Review Mem; *office:* Channel Islands HS 1400 E Raiders Way Oxnard CA 93033

HAYDEN, CONNIE PLACKE, Sixth Grade Teacher; *b:* Batesville, IN; *m:* Richard Kimbel; *c:* Patrick, Brandon; *ed:* (BS) Elem Ed, Ball St Univ 1972; (MS) Elem Ed, IN Univ 1979; *cr:* 4th Grade Teacher 1972-81, 6th Grade Teacher 1981-85 Sunman/Dearborn Schls; 6th Grade Teacher Greensburg Cmmty Schls 1985-; *ai:* ISTA, NEA; GTA Secy 1989-; Kappa Kappa Kappa Inc (Secy 1986-87, VP 1988-89, Pres 1989-); *home:* 9 Lakeshore Dr Greensburg IN 47240

HAYDEN, HELENA, Teacher; *b:* Roscommon, Ireland; *ed:* (BA) His, St Mary Univ 1961; (MED) Admin & Supervision, Our Lady of the Lake Univ 1969; Math Wkshp TX Ed Agency; the Greater Dallas Cncl of Math Teachers 1974-75; *cr:* Teacher TX-MS & LA Cath Schls 1961-88; *ai:* Food Mgmt & Dietary Supervision in a Religious Institution San Antonio TX; *home:* 301 Yucca St San Antonio TX 78203

HAYDEN, JUDITH HILLMAN, Fifth Grade Teacher; *b:* Kingsport, TN; *m:* James H.; *ed:* (BS) Elem Ed, E TN St Univ 1966; *cr:* 5th Grade Teacher Richlands Elem Sch 1966-; *ai:* United Meth Women Local Pres 1986-; *office:* Richlands Elem Sch Rt 460 Richlands VA 24641

HAYDEN, JUDITH MARSHALL, 1st/2nd Grade Teacher; *b:* Lexington, KY; *m:* Gerald Alan; *c:* Benjamin R., Emily K.; *ed:* (BS) Ed 1973, (MA) Ed, 1974, (Rank I) Ed, 1981 W KY Univ; Accounting; *cr:* Teacher Utica Elem 1974-77, Calhoun Elem 1977-78; 1st/2nd Grade Teacher Utica Elem 1978-; *ai:* Comm & Rdng Comms; Effective Schls Prgm; Calhoun Baptist Church Comm Memberships 1974-; *home:* 7650 Hwy 1046 Calhoun KY 42327

HAYDEN, KENT KANE, Amer Govt/His HS Teacher; *b:* Inglewood, CA; *m:* Patricia F. Perkins; *c:* Kurt, Mitch, Kathy Omdahl, Michelle, Laura; *ed:* (BA) Sociology, 1953, (MA) Ed, 1962 Univ of Redlands; *cr:* Soc Stud Teacher/Coach Beaumont HS 1956-58; Var Bsktbl Coach 1958-86, Soc Stud/Governmnet/Ec/His Teacher 1958- Yucaipa HS; *ai:* Sr Class Adv; Yucaipa Educators Assn Rep; Univ of Redlands Alumni Outstanding Alumnus 1982; Teacher of Yr Yucaipa HS 1969; Homecoming Grand Marshall Yucaipa HS 1969, 1980; Sunkist League Bskbl Coach of Yr 1989; Yucaipa HS Commencement Speaker 1989; Yucaipa HS Sr Class Most Inspirational Teacher 1989-; *home:* 1304 Farview Ln Redlands CA 92374

HAYDOCK, SHERWOOD IORWETH, Business Teacher; *b:* Greenfield, IN; *m:* Cindy Ann Brooks; *c:* Jacqueline, Ashley; *ed:* (BS) Bus Ed, IN Cntrl Univ 1982; (MS) Scndry Ed IUPUI 1990; *cr:* Bus Ed Teacher S Decatur HS 1982-83, Franklin Cmmty HS 1983-86, Richmond HS 1986-88, Whiting HS 1988-; *ai:* Bsbl & Head Ftbl Coach; IN Ftbl Coaches Assn 1982-; *office:* Whiting HS 1751 Oliver St Whiting IN 46394

HAYES, ANNIKA ELLEN, Mathematics-Art Teacher; *b:* Degerfors, Sweden; *m:* John R.; *c:* Kerry; *ed:* Stu Examen Math/Physics, Asplundskolan Sweden 1967; (BA) Fine Art, Macalester Coll 1970; *cr:* Teacher Arickaree Sch 1974-; *ai:* Art Prgm, Art Shows; 4-H Horse Judge; Teacher of Yr; *office:* Arickaree Sch 12155 Rd NN Anton CO 80801

HAYES, BARBARA MYERS, Bio Teacher; *b:* Philadelphia, PA; *m:* Kim C.; *c:* Brian P., Sean M.; *ed:* (BS) Bio, NM St 1974; Advanced Ed Cmptrs, Physiology, Kinesiology; *cr:* Bio Teacher Las Cruces HS 1974-88, Onate HS 1988-; *ai:* Sch Improvement & North Cntrl Comm; Jr Class Spon; City Athletic Comm 1989; *office:* Onate HS 1700 E Spruce Las Cruces NM 88001

HAYES, BILLY, Science Teacher; *b:* Blakely, GA; *m:* Phyllis M. Dameron; *c:* Lynn, William, J. Alan; *ed:* (BS) Bio, 1959, (MED) Sci, 1988 Valdosta St Coll; Brick Masonry; Small Bus Management; Pursuing Educl Specialists Degree; *cr:* Teacher Lowndes Cty HS 1960-63; Cnslr Rehabilitation St Dept Human Resources 1963-71; Teacher Lowndes HS 1972-; *ai:* Sci Club Spon 1973-78; Little League Bsbl Coach 1983-84; NEA 1961-63; Natl Rehabilitation Assn 1964-71; Pi Kappa Phi Pres 1957-58; Lowndes Educl Assn Pres 1961-62; Building & Maintenance Comm Chm Lowndes HS 1987-88; *home:* Rt 10 Box 10 Valdosta GA 31601

HAYES, DARRELL RAYFEAL, Graphic Art Teacher; *b:* Atlanta, GA; *ed:* (BA) Studio Art, Troy St Univ 1984; Art Inst of Atlanta; T&I Ed, GA St Univ; *cr:* Graphic Art Teacher Harper HS 1985-; *ai:* Head Coach Cross Cntry, 8th Grade Boys Track & Asst Var Boys Bsktbl Coach; Natl Voc Tech Honor Society Chartering Spon; Key Club Adv; Artistic Stu; Natl Assn for Trade & Industrial Educator 1989-; GA Voc Assn, AVA 1986; GA Assn of Graphic Art Educator 1989-; Trade & Industrial Educator of GA 1986-; Elected W Cntrl Dist Adv; Voc Industrial Clubs of America; Academic Achievement Incentive Awd Winner; Atlanta Public Schl System Voc Ed; *office:* Charles L Harper HS 3399 Collier Dr Atlanta GA 30331

HAYES, DONALD PAUL, Calculus/Physics Teacher; *b:* Cleveland, OH; *m:* Linda Lou Bricker; *c:* Donny L.; *ed:* (BA) Geophysics, CA St Univ 1969; (MBA) Bus Admin, Univ of UT 1974; Teaching Certificate Univ of AR 1980; *cr:* HS Sci Teacher Santa Cruz Cooperative Sch 1981-82; Jr HS Math Teacher Sam Walton Jr HS 1982-84; HS Physics/Math Teacher Bentonville HS 1984-; *ai:* O M Team Coach; Radio/Electronics Organization Spon; AR Sci Teachers Assn; Walnut Grove Presbyn Church Elder 1989-; Dist Teacher of Yr 1987; AR Rep to Air Force Acad Sci Seminar 1986; Article Published 1990; *office:* Bentonville HS 402 Tiger Blvd Bentonville AR 72712

HAYES, DUANE COLE, 4th Grade Teacher; *b:* Woodstock, ME; *m:* Avis Marie Farr; *c:* Scot, Loanne, Joanne, Austin; *ed:* (BS) Ed, Gorham St Teachers Coll 1962; (MS) Public Sch Admin, Univ of ME Portland-Gorham 1972; Expressive Writing, Inst of Childrens Lit; *cr:* 6th Grade Teacher West Elem 1962-65; Prin Jackson Elem 1965-67, Guy E Rowe Elem 1967-70; 5th Grade Teacher Franklin St Sch 1970-74; 4th Grade Teacher Virginia Elem 1974-; *ai:* Core Curr & Sci Curr Comms; NEA, MTA 1962-; Local Assn Prof Rights/Responsibility 1962-; BSA Scout Master 1976-84; W Paris Athletic Assn Pres 1979-83, Citizenship 1983; W Paris Colt League Head Coach 1979-81; *office:* Virginia Elem Sch Forest Ave Rumford ME 04276

HAYES, FREIDA ROCHELLE, English/Home Economics Teacher; *b:* Jackson, MS; *c:* Deborah Ozborn, Dianne Smith, Catherine; *ed:* (BA) Eng, Millsaps Coll 1957; Grad Stud MS Coll, MS Southern, MS St Univ; *cr:* Eng/Home Ec Teacher Canton Acad 1970-; *ai:* 9th Grade Annual Jr Trip to WA Spon; MS Private Sch Assn Dist Chm 1970-; *office:* Canton Acad PO Box Canton MS 39046

HAYES, JERRY WAYNE, Amer His Teacher/Coach; *b:* Columbia, TN; *m:* Grace Schiro; *c:* Adam, Alex; *ed:* (BS) His, Union Univ 1972; (MEA) Admin, Memphis St 1977; *cr:* Teacher/Coach North Side HS 1974-81, Riverside HS 1981-84, Peabody HS 1984-85, South Side HS 1985-; *ai:* Head Ftbl; Chm His Dept; Spon Fellowship Chrstn Athletes; Inservice His Comm: Jr Class Adv; Madison Cty Ed Assn, TN Ed Assn, NEA; TRTV Tip Top Awd Cmmty Service 1988; Dist Coach of Yr 1981; W TN Coach of Yr 1985; Dist & TACA Coach of Yr 1988.

HAYES, KRISTY DENISE (JASEK), Choral Director; *b:* Abilene, TX; *m:* Van Lee; *ed:* (BM) Music Ed, 1979, (MM) Conducting, 1985 Hardin-Simmons Univ; *cr:* Grad Asst Hardin-Simmons Univ 1979-81; Asst Choral Dir Permian HS 1981-85; Choral Dir Big Spring HS 1985-; *ai:* Choral Dept Spon; TX Choral Dirs Assn; TX Music Educators Assn; Assn of Teachers & Prof Educators; Big Spring Jr Womens Club; 1st United Meth Church Pianist 1989-; Region VI Vocal Division TX Music Educators Assn Vocal Chm; *home:* 103 Lincoln Ave Big Spring TX 79720

HAYES, LINDA ANN (BATTISTA), Social Studies Teacher; *b:* Boston, MA; *m:* William L.; *c:* Amy, Matthew; *ed:* (BA) Government, Univ of MA Amherst 1971; (MED) Ed/Admin, Fitchburg St Coll 1978; *cr:* Soc Stud Teacher Shawsheen Tech HS 1971-79; Alternative/HS Teacher Raymond Jr/Sr HS 1981-82; Coord/Alternative HS Teacher Pelham HS 1982-85; Soc Stud Teacher Wilmington HS 1985-; *ai:* Model Congress Adv; NHS Faculty Adv; MA HS Teachers Assn; NCSS; St Francis Parish Cncl, Campbell Sch PTO Exec Bd 1989-; Teacher of Yr 1989-; *home:* 32 Wilshire Cir Dracut MA 01826

HAYES, LINDA KAYS, Language Arts Department Chair; *b:* Lebanon, KY; *c:* Brent, Lara; *ed:* (BA) Eng, Campbellsville Coll 1969; (MA) Eng Ed, 1977, (Rank I) Scndry Ed, 1986 W KY Univ; *cr:* Eng/Journalism/Speech Teacher Washington Cty HS 1969-73; Eng Teacher W Hardin HS 1973-76; Teacher of Gifted Ed/Lang Art Teacher Hardin Cntrl Mid 1976-; *ai:* Lang Art Dept Head; Academic Coach; KY Cncl Teachers of Eng 1976-; Intnl Rdng Assn KY St Cncl 1977-; KY Assn of Gifted Ed 1978-; KY Mid Sch Assn 1987-; Democratic Womens Club (Pres 1989, 1st VP 1988); *office:* Hardin Cntrl Mid Sch 3040 Leitchfield Rd Cecilia KY 42724

HAYES, MARVIN U., Craft Instructor; *b:* Meeker, CO; *m:* Opal Gail Forrester; *c:* Kimberly, Douglas; *ed:* (BA) Art, Univ of OR 1962; (MS) Interdiscplinary, S OR St 1984; *cr:* Art/Craft Teacher Crater HS 1962-; Craft Teacher Scenic Jr HS 1990; *ai:* Jr Class Adv; OEA 1962-; Concrete Sculpture Awd of Excl 1984.

HAYES, MARY ANN, Sixth Grade Teacher; *b:* Syracuse, NY; *m:* John Kevin; *c:* Jeffrey K., Emily A., Stacey M.; *ed:* (BA) Ed, St Univ of NY Cortland 1974; *cr:* Teacher Asst W Genesee Sch Dist 1975-78; Elem Teacher Holy Family Sch 1980-89; *office:* Holy Family Sch 130 Chapel Dr Syracuse NY 13219

HAYES, MYRA DUNLAP, Chapter I Home/School Teacher; *b:* Baltimore, MD; *m:* Earl L.; *c:* Jennifer; *ed:* (BA) Elem Ed, Winston-Salem St Univ 1966; (MA) Early Chldhd Ed, Bowie St Univ 1974; Certified Early Chldhd Elem & Mid Sch; *cr:* 1st Grade Teacher Lakeland Elem 1966-68; 1st-6th Grade Teacher Berkshire Elem 1968-84; Chapter I Home/Sch Teacher Yorktown Center 1984-; *ai:* 1st Baptist Church of Suitland (Mem, Sunday Sch Teacher); Advance Trng Courses Parent Involvement, Single Parenting, Working With Latch Key Children Trinity Coll; *home:* 1908 Porter Ave Suitland MD 20746

HAYES, PATRICIA SILVA, Foreign Lang Dept Chair; *b:* Providence, RI; *m:* David B.; *c:* Susan Hayes Barber, David B. Jr., Amy E., Kate E.; *ed:* (BA) Fr, Salve Regina Coll 1962; (MA) Fr, RI Coll 1986; Study at Universite De Paris VIII; *cr:* Fr/Span Teacher Medway Jr/Sr HS 1964-65; Dir Eng as Second Lang Portsmouth Abbey Summer Sch 1986-88; Foreign Lang Dept Chairperson Saint Raphael Acad 1979-; Adjunct Faculty RI Coll 1983-; *ai:* Jr Alliance Francaise & Societe Honoraire de Francais Adv; Soph Class Moderator; AATF Bd of Dir 1986-88; RI Foreign Lang Assn, Amer Assn of Teachers of Span & Portuguese; Preservation Society of Newport Cty, Portsmouth Lib Assn; Rockefeller Fellowship 1988; Schlsp of Fr Cultural Services 1987; *office:* St Raphael Acad 123 Walcott St Pawtucket RI 02860

HAYES, PEGGY ANN, 6th Grade Teacher; *b:* Springfield, IL; *m:* William J.; *ed:* (AA) Elem Ed, Springfield Coll 1967; (BS) Elem Ed, IL St Univ 1969; (MS) Elem Ed, E IL Univ 1981; *cr:* 2nd-6th Grade Teacher Oak Grove Elem Sch 1969-; *ai:* Delta Kappa Gamma 1985-; NEA, IL Ed Assn, Decatur Ed Assn 1969-; PEO (VP, Secy, Treas) 1974-; *home:* 3665 Woodridge Dr Decatur IL 62526

HAYES, PRESTON T., Chemistry Teacher; *b:* Greeneville, TN; *m:* Judith A.; *c:* Brian C., Kristin A.; *ed:* (BS) Chem, Univ of TN 1964; MAT Prgm Northwestern Univ; NSF Inst IL Inst of Technology; *cr:* Peace Corps Volunteer Peace Corps Philippines US St Dept 1964-67; Chem Teacher Von Steuben Metro Sci Center 1967-88, Phillips Acad 1979-89, Glenbrook South HS 1988-; *ai:* Sci Competition; Chemical Industries Cncl, Grove PB Stud, Chemcon Coord; ACS Advanced Exam Comm Mem; Judging Comm Chm; IACT, ISTA; Chemical Manufacturers Catalyst Awd 1984; Our Lady of Perpetual Help Baptism Comm 1977-84; NSF IIT 1971; Chicago Sci Fair Incorporated 1973-86; Vice-Chm CPSSF Incorporated 1984-85; *office:* Glenbrook South HS 4000 W Lake Ave Glenview IL 60025

HAYES, SADIE L., Second Grade Teacher; *b:* Marshfield, AL; *m:* O. G.; *c:* Randall N.; *ed:* (AA) Snead Jr Coll 1962; (BS) Elem Ed, 1964, (MS) Elem Ed, 1976 Jacksonville ST Univ; (AA) Elem Ed, Univ of AL 1978; *cr:* 2nd Grade Teacher Mc Cord Ave Elem 1964-83; Big Spring Lake Elem 1983-; *ai:* Sci Textbook Comm & Chairperson; 2nd Grade Chairperson; NEA; AEA; Albertville City Assn; *home:* Rt 3 Box 98 Albertville AL 35950

HAYES, SHARON (BIRD), Fifth Grade Teacher; *b:* Meadville, PA; *m:* Harold M.; *c:* James Bradley, Kathryn Bradley, Patrick Bradley, Douglas Bradley, Kevin, Linette; *ed:* (BS) Elem Ed, 1966, (MED) Elem Ed, 1977 Edinboro St Coll; Continuing Ed; *cr:* Teacher Townville Elem Sch 1973-81, Cussewago Elem Sch 1981-; *ai:* PSEA, NEA Building Rep 1988-; *office:* Cussewago Elem Sch RD 3 Saegertown PA 16433

HAYES, SHARON MILLER, Third Grade Teacher; *b:* Cambridge, OH; *m:* Thomas L.; *c:* Robyn, Bryan, Brady; *ed:* (BS) Ed, OH St Univ 1972; OH St Univ, Ashland Univ; *cr:* Substitute Teacher Columbus & Westerville & Worthington & West Jefferson 1972-73; Kndgtn Teacher 1973-77, 3rd Grade Teacher 1978- West Jefferson; *ai:* Elem Yrbk Adv & Ed; Just Say No Club; NEA, OH Ed Assn, W Jefferson Ed Assn 1972-; Spec Olympics Parent Advisory Cncl 1988-89; Perry Highlands Civic Assn 1987-; Natl Trust for Hispanic Preservation 1989-; Presenter at Madison Cty Volunteer Inservice 1987.

HAYES, WAYNE IVAN, Business Education Teacher; *b:* Sedro Woolley, WA; *m:* Pamela Margaret Green; *c:* Cheri Mc Call, Larry, Robbie, Michelle, Jerry, Tyson, Julio; *ed:* (BA) Bus Ed, 1968, (MS) Bus Ed, 1972 Cntrl WA Univ; Post Masters Stud Bus; *cr:* Teacher/Coach R A Long HS 1968-; *ai:* Head Coach Boys & Girls Tennis, Boys & Girls Bsktbl; W WA Bus Ed Assn Treas 1975; WA St Bus Ed Assn; *office:* R A Long HS 2903 Nichols Blvd Longview WA 98632

HAYES, WENDY SUKOW, First Grade Teacher; *b:* Merrill, WI; *m:* Steven A.; *c:* Todd, Tristan, Teagan; *ed:* (BS) Early Chldhd Ed, Univ of WI Milwaukee 1975; (MS) Rdng Ed, Univ of WI Oshkosh 1986; *cr:* 1st Grade Teacher Franklin Sch 1975-77, Elmwood Sch 1978-; *home:* W 5448 Campbell Rd Fond du Lac WI 54935

HAYES, WILLIE LEWIS, Mathematics Teacher; *b:* Mendenhall, MS; *m:* Ruby; *c:* Chadrick, Willis; *ed:* (BS) Elem Ed, 1974, (MS) Elem Ed, 1977 MS Valley St; Grad Stus Math Curr; *cr:* 5th-8th Grade Math Teacher Amanda Elzy Jr HS; *ai:* NEA, MS Ed Assn Mem 1974-; BSA Leader 1975-, Scout Master of Yr 1987; Masonic Masons Mem; US Army Reserves Recruiter 1989; Teacher of Yr 1987; *office:* Amanda Elzy Elem Sch Rt 4 Box 100 Greenwood MS 38930

HAYMAN, MAMIE (DOVE), English Teacher; *b:* Pine Bluff, AR; *m:* Madison; *c:* Alphia M., Cedric L.; *ed:* (BA) Speech/Drama, Univ of AR Pine Bluff 1968; (MA) Ed, Univ of MO Kansas City 1978; *cr:* Eng Teacher Martin Luther King Jr Jr HS 1968-70, Hilltop Sch for Girls 1973-80, Southwest HS 1983-; *ai:* NCTE 1975-; Poem Published; Selected to Attend Teacher Appreciation Dinner Univ of MO Columbia; Nom for Whos Who in Amer Ed; *home:* 10202 Bellaire Kansas City MO 64134

HAYNER, GEORGE WILLIAM, Fourth Grade Teacher; *b:* Berwyn, IL; *m:* Carol Coons; *c:* Matt, Doug, Mike; *ed:* (BSED) Geography, IL St Univ 1967; (MSED) Curr and Instruction, Natl Coll of Ed 1989; Northern IL Univ/Governors St Univ/Univ of WI Superior/IL St Univ; *cr:* 8th Grade Earth Sci Teacher Oswego Jr HS 1967-72; 6th Grade Teacher 1972-75, 4th Grade Teacher 1975-78, 5th Grade Teacher 1978-88, 4th Grade Teacher 1988- Eastview Elem; *ai:* Ftbl Scoreboard Operator; Bsktbl Scorer-Soph/Var; Patrol Spon; Soc Stud Curr Comm; Natl Cncl of Geographic Ed 1967-70; Oswego Ed Assn; IL Ed Assn; NEA 1967-; Home & Sch Assn 1984-; PTA 1967-84; Life Membership IL PTA 1980; Oswego Ed Assn VP 1970; *office:* Eastview Elem Sch Rt 71 Oswego IL 60543

HAYNES, ALAN KEITH, Assistant Principal; *b:* San Antonio, TX; *ed:* (BA) Poly Sci, 1979, (MA) Ed, 1987 San Antonio; *cr:* Teacher Robert E Lee HS 1980-89; Asst Prin Ed White Mid Sch 1989-; *ai:* Cross-Examination Debate, Speech 1982-89; Acad Decathlon 1985-85; Acad Pentathlon, Mid Sch Debate 1989-; NEA, TSTA 1980-; NASSP, ASCD 1989-; Natl Champion Debate Coach Supt Bd of Trustees Awd 1989; Natl Debate Champions NFL & NCFL Coach 1989; TX Forensic Assn Champions Coach 1988; *home:* 12222 Blanco #1604 San Antonio TX 78216

HAYNES, HEIDI SMITH, English/French Teacher; *b:* Cullman, AL; *m:* Roger D.; *cr:* 7th-11th Grade Eng/Fr Teacher Vinemont HS 1986-; *ai:* Pep Club, Fr Club Spon; AL Ed Assn, NEA 1986-; Vinemont Nom Jacksonville St Teacher Hall of Fame; *office:* Vinemont HS P O Box 189 Vinemont AL 35179

HAYNES, JAMES WALTER, Band Director/Arts Dept Chair; *b:* Pickens, SC; *m:* Stephanie Boiter; *ed:* (BA) Music Ed, Furman Univ 1980; *cr:* Band Dir Palmetto Mid Sch & HS 1980-86, Stratford HS 1986-; *ai:* Marching Band; MENC 1980-; ASBDA 1989-; *office:* Stratford HS Crowfield Blvd Goose Creek SC 29445

HAYNES, LILLIAN FAE, Fourth Grade Teacher; *b:* Durham, NC; *m:* James Robert; *c:* Susan L., James L.; *cr:* Elem Teacher Northside Elem Sch 1985-; *home:* 507 Pine Hill Dr Henderson TX 75652

HAYNES, LUISA PERERA, Spanish Teacher; *b:* Havana, Cuba; *m:* William Allison; *c:* Joshua P., Titus A.; *ed:* (BRE) Bible/Ed, Piedmont Bible Coll 1975; (BA) Span, Salem Coll 1976; Grad Stud Clemson Univ, NC St Univ; *cr:* Span Teacher Woodland Sch 1974, Reynolds HS, Hilton Head HS 1984-87, Southern HS 1987-; *ai:* Chairperson Intnl Festival Facilities 1987-, Entertainment Comm 1987-; Stu Cncl & Span Club Spon; Project Graduation Steering Comm 1987-; Foreign Lang Alliance of NC, Foreign Lang Alliance, Natl Assn of Sncdry Schls 1987-; NC Assn of Stu Cncls 1987; Trinity Baptist; Ag Cert Clemson Univ Grant 1989; VFW Citizenship Awd 1990; Participant NCCAT 1989; Featured on TV News & Educl Spec 1990; *office:* Southern HS 1818 Ellis Rd Durham NC 27703

HAYNES, LYNDA MORGAN, Math & Computer Teacher; *b:* Portales, NM; *m:* Richard L.; *c:* Jill, Susan, Kelly; *ed:* (BS) Math, E NM Univ 1966; Cmptr Sci, Applications; *cr:* Math Teacher Moriarty Schls 1966-69, Fort Sumner Schls 1969-72; Math Teacher/Cmptr Applications Fort Sumner Schls 1980-; *ai:* Sr Class Spon 1990; Chrldr Spon 1966-72; Fort Sumner Ed Assn VP 1985-86; 1st Baptist Church Treas 1979-; Teacher of Yr Moriarty Schls 1969; *home:* PO Box 35 Fort Sumner NM 88119

HAYNES, OSCAR, History/Government Teacher; *b:* Jayess, MS; *m:* Lenora Ashley; *c:* Charyce, Charae; *ed:* (BA) Soc Sci, Fresno St 1970; *cr:* Teacher Addams Jr HS 1971-75; Teacher/Coach Sequoia Jr HS 1975-78, Edison HS 1978-; *ai:* Track, Girls Bsktbl, Cross Cntry Coach; Sr Class Spon; Jr HS Activity Dir; FTA, NEA 1971-; AASS; Masonic; YMCA; *home:* 1596 S Bush Fresno CA 93727

HAYNES, PAULA CLOTFELTER, Gifted Language Arts Teacher; *b:* Harlan, KY; *m:* Danny Hardin; *c:* Jennings Burrell, Matthew Hardin; *ed:* (BA) Eng, Georgetown Coll 1969; (MA) Rdng Specialist, Univ of KY Lexington 1980; Rank I E KY Univ 1983; Gifted Cert Univ of KY 1989; *cr:* Eng Teacher/Drama Coach Crawford Jr HS 1969-71; Spec Ed Teacher Cummins 1971-72; Rdng Teacher Floyd Jr HS 1972-73; CORE Teacher West McDowell Jr HS 1973-74; Instr/Learning Lab Coord Mc Dowell Tech Inst 1974-75; Veterans Coord Lexington Tech Inst 1975; Eng Teacher Mortonsville Elem 1976-79, Woodford Cty HS 1979-80; Eng/Rdng Teacher 1984-86, Teacher of Gifted Eng 1986- Woodford Mid Sch; *ai:* Teacher Internship & Process Writing Trainer; Gifted, Rdng, PHilosophy, Lang Art Comm; KY Mid Sch Assn, NCTE, KY Assn for Gifted Ed, Intl Rdng Assn; DAR 1971-73; Womans Club 1971-75; Versailles Baptist Church Teacher 1983-; Olah H Miller Schlsp 1988-; Speaker Natl Assn of Gifted Children 1989; NCTL Center of Excl Applicant 1989; Southern Assn Evaluation Team 1990; KY Accreditation Classroom of Excl Nom 1989; *office:* Woodford Cty Mid Sch Maple St Versailles KY 40383

HAYNES, SHERI LEE, Basketball Coach; *b:* Mc Lean, TX; *ed:* (BS) Phys Ed, Wayland Baptist Coll 1979; *cr:* Teacher/Coach Lockney HS 1979-82; Sports Information Coach TX Tech Univ 1982-83; Teacher/Coach Roosevelt Ind Sch Dist 1983; *ai:* Fellowship of Chrstn Athletes Spon; Var Bsktbl Coach; 7th-9th Grade Asst & Jr Var Bsktbl Coach; Golf Coach; TX Assn of Bsktbl Coaches Mem 1979-89; TX Girls Coaches Assn; Lakeridge Meth Church; *office:* Roosevelt Ind Sch Dist Rt 1 Box 402 Lubbock TX 79401

HAYNES, THENA BYRD, 2nd Grade Teacher; *b:* Gallatin, TN; *m:* Glen E.; *c:* Edd, Scott, Amy; *ed:* (BA) Elem Ed, 1974, (MS) Elem Ed, 1982 TN Tech Univ; *cr:* Resource Teacher 1974-77, 1st Grade Teacher 1977-79, 2nd Grade Teacher 1979- Trousdale Cty Elem Sch; *ai:* Trousdale Cty Ed Assn, TN Ed Assn, TN Rdng Assn; Hartsville Church of Christ; *office:* Trousdale Co Elem Sch Lock 6 Rd Hartsville TN 37074

HAYNIE, JAMES ROY, Economics Teacher; *b:* Cleveland, TN; *m:* Sandra Kaye; *c:* Cami; *ed:* (AS) Ed, Cleveland St Comm Coll 1977; (BS) Sci, Lee Coll 1979; (MED) Scndry Ed, Univ of SW LA 1980; *cr:* Sci Teacher Vermilion Cath HS 1980-81; Phys Ed Teacher Riceville Elem 1981-82; Ec Teacher Mc Minn Cty HS 1982-; *ai:* Golf & Girls Sftbl Coach; Key Club Spon; Fund Raising Comm; Univ of SW LA Fellowship; *office:* Mc Minn County HS 2215 Congress Pkwy Athens TN 37303

HAYNIE, VERA FOSTER, First Grade Teacher; *b:* Hazelhurst, MS; *m:* Lonnie Jr.; *c:* Sandres M. Williams, Sonya R.; *ed:* (AA) General Ed, Utica Jr Coll 1960; (BA) Elem Ed, MS Valley St Univ 1966; (MS) Early Chldhd Ed, Jackson St Iniv 1976; MS Teacher Assessment Instruments Evaluation Certificate, MS Dept of Ed; *cr:* Teacher T Y Fleming Sch 1966-68; K-3rd Grade Teacher Hazelhurst Elem 1968-; *ai:* Faculty Membership Rep MAE/NEA Local; Chairperson & Asst Chairperson First Grade Hazelhurst Elem; MAE, NEA Faculty Rep 1968- Pin; Herion of Jerico 1985-.

HAYNSWORTH, SUSAN B., English Teacher; *b:* Spartanburg, SC; *ed:* (BA) Eng, Wofford Coll 1978; (MED) Eng, Converse Coll 1980; *cr:* Eng Teacher Jonesville HS 1980-83; La Grange Boys Jr HS 1985-87; Middleton HS 1987-; *ai:* Yrbk Adv.

HAYS, BETSY BAUER, GT Teacher/Coordinator; *b:* Russellville, AR; *m:* Dwight G.; *c:* Bryan, Rachael; *ed:* (BA) Eng, 1973; (ME) Gifted & Talented, 1989 AR Tech Univ; *cr:* Scndry Eng Teacher Wonderview HS 1973-80; Atkins H S 1980-88; Gifted & Talented Teacher Atkins Elem Sch 1988-; *ai:* Quiz Bowl Coach; Coord Mathathon for St Jude's Hospital; Coord for Cty-Wide Spelling Bee; Past Mem of Arch Ford Coop Teacher Ctr Comm; AR for Gifted & Talented Ed; Received Grant for AR Writing Project at AR Tech Univ; *office:* Atkins Elem 302 NW 5th Atkins AR 72823

HAYS, DEBRA LYNN ENGLAND, English Teacher; *b:* Norton, KS; *m:* William M.; *ed:* (BA) Eng, Kearney St Coll 1977; Eng Ed; *cr:* Eng Teacher Wauneta HS 1977-79; Art Teacher Hendley Public Sch 1980-82; Wilsonville Public Sch 1982-84; Eng Teacher Sargent HS 1984-; *ai:* Annual Staff Adv; Sargent Teachers Assn Pres 1988-89; Wauneta Teachers Assn Pres 1978-79; GSA Leader 1984-89; *office:* Sargent HS Box 366 Sargent NE 68874

HAYS, ELLEN DEE DEE GORDON, Mathematics Teacher; *b:* Pittsburgh, PA; *m:* Joseph; *ed:* (BS) Math Ed, Penn St Univ 1975; (MA) Math Ed, Univ of KY 1983; *cr:* Math Teacher Twin Lakes HS 1975-81, Henry Clay HS 1981-; Assoc Faculty Mem Univ of KY 1988-; *ai:* Sch Improvement Comm; Supervising Teacher for Stu Teachers Univ of KY; NCTM, KY Cncl Teachers of Math, Lexington Cncl Teachers of Math; Holmes Group Mem 1988-; Part Time Instr Lexington Comm Coll; IBM & Transylvania Univ Developed ACT & SAT Prep Course; Instructional Designer Current Nationwide Cable Channel Prgm; Lead Numerous Inservice Act St & Local Level; *office:* Henry Clay HS 2100 Fontaine Rd Lexington KY 40502

HAYS, MICHAEL ALAN, Sixth Grade Teacher; *b:* Fairmont, WV; *m:* Cheri L. Metz; *c:* M. Dustin, M. Daran; *ed:* (ABED) Elem Ed/Soc Stud, Fairmont St Coll 1976; (MS) Phys Ed, WV Univ 1983; Various Ed Classes, EMT Trng, Advanced First Aid Instr, Lifesaving Card; *cr:* Teacher Dunbar Elem Sch 1977-79, Mannington Mid Sch 1979-; *ai:* Ftbl & Wrestling Coach; Mat-Maid Adv; Yrbk Adv & Ed; Partners in Ed Comm; Mannington Parks & Recreation Commission (Secy, Treas) 1985-88; *office:* Mannington Mid Sch 113 Clarksburg St Mannington WV 26582

HAYS, PAMELA VERNER, Spanish/English/Drama Teacher; *b:* Dallas, TX; *m:* Donnie Wayne; *c:* Jennifer, Brian; *ed:* (AA) Ed, Paris Jr Coll 1975; (BA) Span/Eng, E TX St Univ 1977; Berlitz Sch of Lang Dallas 1976; *cr:* Secy/Receptionist Red River Cty Farm Bureau Ins Co 1977-83; Medical Asst Dermatology Clinic 1985-87; Teacher Rivercrest HS 1987-; *ai:* Span Club, Drama Club, Class Spon; One Act Play Dir; Assn of TX Prof Educators Local Treas 1988-89; ATPE Mem 1987-; Amer Assn Teachers Span; TX Assn Gifted & Talented Mem 1989-; Portugese AATSP 1987; *home:* Rt 1 Box 73 Detroit TX 75436

HAYSE, ANNA J., 4th Grade Teacher; *b:* Clarkson, KY; *ed:* (BA) Elem Ed, Campbellsville 1954; Philosophy of Ed; *cr:* 3rd Grade Teacher Clarkson Elem 1947-53; 4th Grade Teacher Lynnvale Elem 1954-; *ai:* Chrldr Spon; Ed Comm-Chairperson; KEA; NEA; FDEA; Teacher of Quarter Lynndale Sch; Rep Lynnvale 4th Dist Louisville.

HAYSLETTE, AMY RANDALL, Mathematics Teacher/Dept Chair; *b:* Astoria, NY; *m:* Robert Clayton; *c:* Steven, Sandra; *ed:* (BA) Math, Mary Washington Coll 1963; Cmptrs Stud; *cr:* Math Teacher Lexington HS 1963-66, 1967-68; Math Teacher/Dept Chairperson Natural Bridge HS 1974-; *ai:* SADD; *office:* Natural Bridge HS Natural Bridge Stn VA 24579

HAYWARD, KARLENE GALE, Business Teacher; *b:* Richland, WA; *c:* Kristine, James M.; *ed:* (BA) Broad Area Bus Educl/ Admin Office Management, Cntrl WA Univ 1979; (MA) Admin/ Curr Dev, Gonzaga Univ 1989; *cr:* Teacher Kettle Falls HS 1979-; *ai:* FBLA, Associated Stu Body, Safety Adv; WSBEA, WEA, NEA, Delta Kappa Gamma; WSSAC 1989-; Bus Lab Curr Issue of Resources in Ed Catalog 1983; *office:* Kettle Falls HS 1275 Juniper St Kettle Falls WA 99141

HAYWARD, SAMUEL L., Band Director; *b:* Midway, FL; *m:* Carrie B. Wilson; *c:* Roderick, Franz, Errol, Jada D. Davis, Montrae; *ed:* (BA) Music Ed, Lincoln Univ 1955; (MA) Music Ed, Univ of S FL 1973; *cr:* Band Dir Pinellas HS 1955-68, Clearwater Comprehensive Jr HS 1968-73, Seminole HS 1973-79, Countryside HS 1979-; *ai:* Co-Spon Tri-M; Chm Music Comm; Dept Head Clearwater Comprehensive/Seminole HS; PCMEA, FMEA, NEA, FABD, FBA 1955-; Phi Delta Kappa 1969-73; Kiwanis 1969-73; Clearwater Comprehensive Teacher of Yr 1971; Countryside HS Teacher of Yr 1981; *office:* Countryside HS 3000 State Rd 580 Clearwater FL 34619

HAYWOOD, DOROTHY CARSWELL, Eighth Grade Lang Arts Teacher; *b:* Brunswick, GA; *m:* James Stanley; *c:* Darryl L., Terrance C.; *ed:* (BA) Soc Sci, Benedict Coll 1968; Advanced Trng GA Southern Coll, Armstrong St Coll, Brunswick Coll; *cr:* Soc Stud Teacher Blanche Ely HS 1968-70; Elem Teacher Eulonia Primary Sch & Todd-Grant Elem 1970-78; Lang Art Teacher Mc Intosh Cty Acad 1978-80; 8th Grade Lang Art Teacher Jane Macon Mid Sch 1980-; *ai:* Peer Coach Glynn Ctys Model Effective Teaching; Lang Art Dept Chm Jane Macon Mid Sch; Intnl Rdng Assn Corresponding Secy 1984-86, Rdng Teacher of Yr 1985; NEA, GAE 1980-; PTSA Jane Macon Mid Sch Exec Bd Mem; Alpha Kappa Alpha Inc Grammateus 1986-; Bethel Evangel Temple Choir Dir 1988-; Jane Macon Mid Sch Teacher of Yr 1987, Positive Parent of Yr 1990; *office:* Jane Macon Mid Sch 3885 Atlanta Ave Brunswick GA 31520

HAYWOOD, IDA T., Science Teacher; *b:* Hickory Grove, SC; *m:* Lawrence F.; *c:* Eric, Bruce, Sharon, Lawrence F. II; *ed:* (BS) Bio, Claflin Coll 1965; (MED) Scndry Admin, The Citadel 1981; SC St Coll Orangeburg & Univ of FL Gainesville; *cr:* Sci Teacher Orangeburg Dist 5 Schls 1965-71, Charleston Cty Schls 1973-83, Manning HS 1983-84, Bennett Mid Sch 1984-; *ai:* Cluster Leader; Teacher Evaluator; Sci Club Adv; Volunteer Coord 1984-88; SACS Steering Comm; NEA, SCEA 1965-; NSTA 1990; SC2 1987-; N Orangeburg United Meth Church Secy 1967-; Amer Bus Womens Assn 1987-88; Moultrie Mid Sch 1978 & Bennett Mid Sch 1987 Teacher of Yr; Teacher Incentive Awd 1989; *office:* Bennett Mid Sch 919 Bennett Ave Orangeburg SC 29115

HAZARD, DONALD MAURICE, Fifth Grade Teacher/Adm Aide; *b:* Gorman, TX; *m:* Carolyn Mae Bassett; *c:* Lisa, Lauren; *ed:* (BBA) Mrktg, 1965, (MBA) Management, 1966 E TX St Univ; Grad Work E TX St & Our Lady of Lake Univs; *cr:* Teacher Morrill Elem 1967-; *ai:* Morrill Elem Safety Patrol Spon; Safety Comm Chm; Lang Proficiency Assessment Comm Chm; PTA 1967-90, Life Mem 1977; Harlandale Teachers Assn, TX St Teachers Assn, NEA; Nom Alamo Dist Cncl of Teachers of Math Exemplary Teacher Awd 1989-.

HAZELTON, ALEX, Social Studies Teacher; *b:* Brooklyn, NY; *m:* Karen Osmund; *c:* Alex, Jennifer; *ed:* (BA) Ed, SUNY New Paltz 1969; (MA) Ed, SUNY Stony Brook 1971; Grad Stud Ed; *cr:* Soc Stud Teacher Copiague Jr HS 1969-; *ai:* NYSSC 1978-; *office:* Copiague Jr HS 2650 Great Neck Rd Copiague NY 11726

HAZELTON, CAROLYN EASLEY, Fifth Grade Teacher; *b:* Hazlehurst, GA; *m:* John Jr.; *c:* Thandie, John III; *ed:* (BS) Elem Ed, Albany St Coll 1969; (MS) Elem Ed, Ft Valley St Coll 1973; Grad Stud Nova Univ; *cr:* Teacher Hazlehurst Elem & HS 1969-70, Sylvania Height Elem 1970-71, Everglades Elem 1973-75, Benjamin Franklin Cmmty Sch 1975-; *ai:* 4th/5th Grade Group Chairperson; Human Growth & Dev & AIDS Resource Person; Black His & Biracial Triethnic Comm; United Teachers of Dade, Miami Bd of Realtors; Jack & Jill of America Incorporated; Natl Cncl of Negro Women; Miami Alumni Chapter Albany St Coll Pres 1985-.

HAZELWOOD, FRANCES WALTHALL, English Teacher; *b:* Farmville, VA; *c:* Sandra R. Clements; *ed:* (BS) Eng/Speech, Longwood Coll 1974; *cr:* Eng Teacher Mecklenburg Acad 1971-73, Blackstone Jr HS 1974-77, Prince Edward Acad 1978-; *ai:* Coaching Forensics; Soph Class Spon; Teaching Writing Wkshps; Assn of VA Academics Exec Bd Mem 1989-; Prince Edward Fnd Ed Assn Pres 1985-88; *office:* Prince Edward Acad Catlin St Farmville VA 23901

HAZELWOOD, LINDA MARTIN, Kindergarten Teacher; *b:* Rock Camp, WV; *ed:* (BS) Elem Ed/Early Chldhd, Concord Coll 1973; (MS) Early Chldhd, Radford Univ 1981; WV Coll; *cr:* Head Start Teacher Petersown Union Elem 1973-80; Kndgtn/2nd Grade Teacher Union Elem 1973-74; Kndgtn Teacher Peterstown Elem 1974-; *ai:* WVEA 1973-; United Meth Women Secy 1973-; *home:* PO Box 26 Lindside WV 24951

HAZEN, ELIZABETH FRANCES MC DOWELL, 6th Grade Learning Disab; *b:* Lamar, CO; *c:* H. R., Bobby D., Anita Iezza, Gloria Gill; *ed:* (AA) Ed, Lamar Jr Coll 1946; (BSED) Elem Ed, 1967, (MED) Rdng Specialist, 1969 OK Southwestern Univ; Rank I Learning/Behavioral Disabilities, Eastern KY Univ 1983; *cr:* Speech/Hearing Therapist Maconaquah Public Schls 1970-72; Rdng Specialist Myers Mid Sch 1972-76; 7th Grade Core Westport Jr HS 1976-79; Learning Disabilities Teacher Westport Mid Sch 1979-; *ai:* Chairperson Exceptional Chldhd Ed; Bd Mem Parent/Teacher/Stu Assn; Jefferson Cty Teachers Assn, KY Teachers Assn, NEA; Hikes Point Church of The Nazarene (Dir of Vacation Bible Sch 1976) 1972-; Grade Teachers Magazine Awd Outstanding Teacher of Disadvantaged 1969; *office:* Westport Middle School 8100 Westport Rd Louisville KY 40242

HAZEN, RITA ANN, Mathematics Department Chair; *ed:* (BA) Math, Geneva Coll 1969; Grad Courses in Eng, Youngstown St Univ; *cr:* Teacher Ellwood City Cath Sch 1969-74, Ellwood City Area Sch Dist 1975-; *ai:* Math Dept Chairperson; Tri St Math Network; Educl Leadership & NHS Faculty Comms; NEA, PSEA, EAEA; Parish Cncl VP 1987-; *office:* Lincoln HS 501 Crescent Ave Ellwood City PA 16117

HAZLERIG, BONNIE SHELLEY, English/French Teacher; *b:* Covington, TN; *m:* Bill; *c:* Bret, Bryan; *ed:* (BS) Ed, Memphis St 1972; Grad Courses Guidance & Counseling; *cr:* Teacher Brighton Elem 1969-72, Brighton HS 1972-80, Covington HS 1980-; *ai:* Fr Club Spon; Faculty Sunshine & In-Service Comm; TCEA, TEA, NEA (Fac Rep, Election Comm) 1969-; Alpha Delta Kappa (Secy, Pledge Chm) 1985-; Tipton Fine Arts Comm 1980-; *office:* Covington HS 803 S College St Covington TN 38019

HAZLETT, BUD F., History Teacher; *b:* Borger, TX; *m:* Kimberley Kaye Arrington; *c:* Krista, Trudy; *ed:* (AA) Arts, Frank Phillips Jr Coll 1976; (BS) Soc Stud/Health/Phys Ed, W TX St Univ 1979; Advanced Trng Economics, TX A&M Univ; *cr:* 7th/ 8th Grade His Teacher Sunray Ind Sch Dist 1979-; *ai:* Coach Ftbl, Bsktbl, Track; Curr, Teacher Appraisal, Teachers Insurance Comm; Soc Stud Dept Chm; TX HS Coaches Assn 1979-; *office:* Sunray Mid Sch 700 E 7th PO Box 240 Sunray TX 79086

HAZLEWOOD, KATHY EDWARDS, 3rd Grade Teacher; *b:* Fulton, KY; *m:* David; *c:* Jill; *ed:* (BA) Elem Ed, 1971, (MA) Elem Ed, 1976 Murray St Univ; *cr:* Teacher Hickman Cty Elem Sch 1971-; *ai:* Hickman Cty Ed Assn; KY Ed Assn; NEA; *office:* Hickman County Elem Sch E Clay St Clinton KY 42031

HAZY, MARK, Industrial Technology Teacher; *b:* Charleroi, PA; *m:* Nancy Blake; *c:* Karen, Michael, Joseph, Carly; *ed:* (BS) Industrial Art Ed, CA Univ 1981; Grad Prgm Guidance & Counseling, Slippery Rock Univ; *cr:* Teacher Grove City Sr HS 1986-; *ai:* Asst Athletic Dir; Technology Ed Assn of PA; *home:* 1031 Liberty St Grove City PA 16127

HEACKER, THELMA WEAKS, Fourth Grade Teacher; *b:* Lakeland, FL; *w:* Howard Victor (dec); *c:* Victor H., Patricia Kitchin, Paula H. Mayorga, Jonathan, Johannah Thompson; *ed:* (BA) His/Ed, Carson-Newman Coll 1949; (MA) Elem Ed/Curr/ Instruction, TN Tech Univ 1980; Cmptr, Curr, New Trends; *cr:* 2nd/3rd Grade Teacher Alpha Elem 1949; HS Teacher Oliver Springs HS 1949-71; 3rd/4th Grade Teacher Orchard View 1952-53; Span Teacher Coalfield HS 1986-87; 4th/5th Grade Teacher Petros-Joyner Elem 1975-; *ai:* NEA; TN Ed Assn Teacher of Yr 1986; E TN Ed Assn; Morgan Cty Ed Assn 1975-, Teacher of Local 1986; Beta Sigma Phi (Pres, VP, Secy, City Cncl Rep) 1978-, Woman of Yr 1988; Whos Who Amer Ed 1989-; *office:* Petro-Joyner Elem Sch Rt 1 Box 110-A Oliver Springs TN 37840

HEAD, DERAL DEAN, Mathematics Teacher; *b:* Burnet, TX; *ed:* (BS) Math, Southwest TX St Univ 1970; Ed, Sul Ross St Univ; Math, Univ of MO; Ed, UTPB; Sci, Univ of Houston; *cr:* Math Teacher Rankin Ind Sch Dist 1970-74, South San Antonio Ind Sch Dist 1974-75, Brady Ind Sch Dist 1975-77, Rankin Ind Sch Dist 1977-; *ai:* Soph Spon; Math Dept Head; Number Sense Coach; Gifted & Talented Comm Mem; NCTM 1978-; TSTA Local Pres 1973; Rankin Cntry Club VP 1990; Nom Outstanding Math Teacher UT Ex-Stu Assn; *home:* Box 251 Rankin TX 79778

HEADWELL, ROBERT, JR., Dept Chair Technology; *b:* Ft Bragg, NC; *m:* Cynthia Ann; *c:* Sean, Robert, Laurel, Jeffrey; *ed:* (BS) Industrial Engineering, SUNY Cobleskill 1982; (BS) Industrial Art, 1984, (MS) Technology, 1986 SUNY Oswego; Apple Microcomputer Interfacing & Control; *cr:* Technology Dept Chm Keene Valley Cntrl 1984-85; Ceramics Instr SUNY Oswego Technology Dept 1985-86; Summer Instr NY St Ed Dept 1986; Technology Dept Chm Fonda-Fultonville Cntrl 1986-; *ai:* Var Wrestling Coach; US Swimming Ofcl; Phi Delta Kappa 1983-; Epsilon Pi Tau (Secy 1984) 1983-; US Swimming 1989-; William S Barnes Schlsp Awd 1986; *office:* Fonda-Fultonville Cntrl Sch Educational Plaza Fonda NY 12068

HEAGY, PAULA JO, First Grade Teacher; *b:* Springfield, IL; *m:* Robert D.; *c:* R. Dana, D. Mark, Melissa J. Beckler, J Nelson; *ed:* (BA) Elem Ed, Eastern IL Univ 1976; *cr:* 4th Grade Teacher 1962; 1st Grade Teacher 1963- Hamilton Elem Sch; *ai:* Hamilton Ed Assn 1970-; AFT; DAR 1969-; *home:* P O Box 51 Elvaston IL 62334

HEAL, HELEN ORTEGA, English Teacher; *b:* Kelly, NM; *m:* James A.; *c:* Mark, MaryAnne; *ed:* (BSED) Elem Ed/Eng, N AZ Univ 1962; Eng as 2nd Lang Endorsement; *cr:* 4th Grade Teacher Washington Elem Sch 1962-63; 5th/6th Grade Teacher Marshall Elem Sch 1963-72; 7th-9th Grade Eng Teacher E Flagstaff Jr HS 1973-89; Eng/Span Teacher Sinagra HS 1989-; *ai:* Span Club Spon; Philosophy & Goals Comm Sinagua HS; Cardinal Key Treas 1961-62, NEA Continuing Mem 1962-; Alpha Delta Kappa 1967-80; St Marys Regional Sch Bd Mem 1982-83, 1989-; *office:* Sinagua HS 3950 E Butler Ave Flagstaff AZ 86004

HEALD, CAMERON R., HS Driver Education Teacher; *b:* Sacramento, CA; *m:* Jean Gideon; *ed:* (AA) Ed, Chaffey Coll 1971; (BS) Phys Ed, CA St Univ Fullerton 1975; CA Driver Ed Credential Pepperdine Univ 1975; CA Woodworking Credential CA St Univ 1980; *cr:* Substitute Teacher Chaffey HS Dist 1975-76; Woodshop Teacher Montclair HS 1978-81; Woodshop Teacher 1981-87, Driver Ed Teacher Ontario HS 1987-; *ai:* Var Soccer 1986, Ftbl 1984-, SFtbl 1976-80, 1983- Coach; Peer Counseling Club Adv 1986-; NEA, CA Teachers Assn 1978-; CA Assn for Safety Educators 1975-; CA Peer Counseling Assn 1986-; *office:* Ontario HS 901 W Francis St Ontario CA 91762

HEALY, DENNIS F., Social Studies/PE Teacher; *b:* Bronx, NY; *m:* Jane Ann Garaas; *c:* Maureen, Dennis, John, Jennifer, Mechelle, Jana, Sara; *ed:* (BS) Soc Stud, Minot St Univ 1973; (MS) Soc Stud, Univ of MT 1981; *cr:* Teacher/Coach/Athletic Dir Alamo HS 1974-77; Teacher/Coach Ray HS 1977-78, Willston Jr HS 1978-; *ai:* Varsity Ftbl & 7th Grade Bsktbl Coach; Philosophy & Goals Comm; North Cntrl Accreditation Visitation Team Mem; ND HS Coaches Assn, NEA, NDEA, WEA, ND Officials Assn; Elks; Amer Legion; Chamber of Commerce Sports Comm; Coyote Athletic Booster Club; WDA Conference Ftbl Champs 1986/1988; State Runner Up Legion Bsbl 1977/1982; Vietam Veteran; *office:* Williston Jr H S 612 1st Ave W Williston ND 58801

HEALY, JACQUELINE ANN, 2nd Grade Teacher; *b:* Dixon, IL; *m:* Michael; *c:* Dan, Michelle; *ed:* (BA) Elem Ed, 1972, (MS) Elem Ed, 1986 N IL Univ; *cr:* 3rd Grade Teacher 1972-84, 2nd Grade Teacher 1984- Washington; *ai:* Cooperating Teacher for Stu Teachers; Public Relations, Amer Ed Week, WA Instructional Improvement Comm; Young Authors, Lang Art Comm; Rdng Comm; Ed Sch Keys; Curr Cncl; IL Ed Assn, NEA 1972-; IL Lang Experience Cncl 1984-88; Sauk Valley Rdng Cncl, IL Rdng Cncl 1980-; Home & Sch Assn Treas 1987-88; Mentor Teacher; Article Published; Class Sent Big Book to Barbara Bush Received Personal Response; *office:* Washington Sch 703 E Morgan Dixon IL 61021

HEALY, WILLIAM JOSEPH, English Teacher; *b:* Lynwood, CA; *m:* Nancy Howard; *c:* Sarah, Daniel, Matthew; *ed:* (BA) Eng, Loyola Mary Mount Univ 1974; (MA) Eng Ed, Santa Clara Univ 1982; *cr:* Eng Teacher Bellarmine Coll Prep 1974-; *ai:* Speech & Debate Team; Schls Writing Contest Coord; San Jose Univ Dorothy Wright Awd Outstanding HS Eng Teacher 1989; *office:* Bellarmine Coll Prep 850 Elm St San Jose CA 95126

HEARD, FELDA C., 9th Grade English Teacher; *b:* Jacksonville, TX; *m:* Dan H.; *c:* Joy, Amy; *ed:* (BA) Eng, Stephen F Austin 1958; Grad Stud E TX St, SMU; *cr:* Eng Teacher Port Arthur Ind Sch Dist 1958-59, Dallas Ind Sch Dist 1959-65, Richardson Ind Sch Dist 1976-; *ai:* Assn of TX Prof Educators, Dallas Cncl of Eng Teachers, Richardson Educl Assn 1989-; *office:* Lake Highlands Jr HS 10301 Kingsley Rd Dallas TX 75238

HEARD, FREDERICK RONALD, Mathematics/Science Teacher; *b:* Gueydan, LA; *m:* Mary L. Baker; *c:* Lori H. Guidry, Dean, Connie; *ed:* (BS) Math/Sci Ed, Mc Neese St Univ 1960; Math, Sci, Univ of SW LA; Ed Mc Neese St Univ; *cr:* Math/Sci Teacher Anacoco HS 1962-63, Gueydan HS 1963-; *ai:* Soph Spon; Math & Sci Comm; NEA, Vermilion Assn of Educators; Free & Accepted Masons 1969-; Woodmen of the World 1964-; Beta Club Spon Awd for Service; Commercial Ag Pilot; Flight Instr; *home:* PO Box 112 Gueydan LA 70542

HEARD, MARY COMBS, 5th Grade Mathematics Teacher; *b:* Lafayette, AL; *m:* John Talmadge; *c:* Traco, Ingram; *ed:* (AA) Art/Sci, S Union Jr Coll 1976; (BA) Elem Ed, Auburn Univ 1980; (MS) Elem Ed, Troy St Univ 1986; *cr:* Teacher Southside Elem Sch 1981-82, Fairfax Elem Sch 1983-; *ai:* NEA, Chamber Cty Ed Assn, Amer Ed Assn 1981-; Tulip Garden Club Treas 1986-87; *home:* 721 1st St SE Lafayette AL 36862

HEARLE, DEANNA ROSE, Earth Sci/Bio/Chem Teacher; *b:* Passaic, NJ; *m:* Robert James; *c:* Tami; *ed:* (BA) Bio, 1965, (MA) Bio/Chem, 1969 Montclair Coll; Bio/Chem, Purdue Univ, Johns Hopkins, Howard Univ, Univ of MD; *cr:* Teacher Pequannock HS 1965-66; Grad Asst Purdue Univ 1966-67; Bio/Botany Teacher James Caldwell HS 1967-70; Life Sci/Phys Sci/Health/AP Bio Teacher Greenbelt Jr HS 1970-81; Earth Sci/Bio/Chem/AP Chem Teacher Parkdale HS 1981-; *ai:* Sci Clubs, Future Scientists of America Clubs Spon Jr & HS; Supervised Stu Teachers Jr Sr HS; MSTA; Sigma Eta Sigma Mem Montclair St Coll; Participated NSF Inst Phys Sci, Geology, Astronomy, Earth Sci, Chem; Prince Georges Cty Sickle-Cell Anemia Wkshp; NSF Inst for Chemical Ed Prgm 1986; Advanced Placement Chem Wkshp 1988; Taught Bio 101 Howard Comm Coll; *office:* Parkdale HS 6001 Good Luck Rd Riverdale MD 20737

HEARN, JERRY B., Physical Science Teacher; *b:* Greenwood, AR; *m:* Launa R. Dunn; *c:* D. De Lynn Holleman, J. Keaton; *ed:* (BS) Bio, AR Polytechnic Coll 1960; (MED) Phys Sci, AR Tech Univ 1984; Numerous Univs; *cr:* Gen Sci/Sr Phys Ed Teacher Newport Jr/Sr HS 1961-63; Bio/Physics/Gen Sci Teacher Bradford Public Schls 1963-64; 7th Grade Gen Sci Teacher Osceola Jr HS 1964-68;Dept Chm/9th Grade Phys Sci Teacher Bryant Jr HS 1968-; *ai:* Various Sch & Dist Comm; Dept Chm; AEA Parliamentarian Rep to Convention 1961-76; NEA 1961-70; First Baptist Church Deacon 1983-; AR Nature Conservancy; Bryant Band Booster Club Pres 1978-83; Natl Sci Fnd Grant

Northwestern Univ 1966; Natl Sci Fnd Grant Univ of AR 1973; *office:* Bryant Jr HS 200 NW 4th St Bryant AR 72022

HEASLEY, WILLIAM W., Elementary Principal; *b:* Tarentum, PA; *m:* Virginia S. Howard; *c:* Rebecca, Jennifer, William; *ed:* (BS) Elem, IN Univ of PA 1972; (MED) Elem, PA St Univ 1978; (MCE) Guidance, Univ of Pittsburgh 1979; Lions Quest Skills for Adolescence Prgm; *cr:* 6th Grade Teacher Riverview Elem 1972-73; 5th Grade Teacher Wood St Elem 1973-84; Grade Level 5 Chairperson Highlands Sch Dist 1978-86; 5th Grade Teacher 1984-86; Prin 1986- Grandview Elem; *ai:* Scorekeeper-Boys Varsity Bsktbl; Sci Textbook Comm Chairperson; Academic Awds Comm; ESEA Comm; Teacher/Admin Advisory Cncl; PSEA/HEA Treas 1977-78; NAESP 1986-; PAESP 1986-; ASCD 1986-; Optimist Club of Alle Kiski Valley 1978-84; Knights of Columbus Insurance Rep 1984-; Blessed Sacrament Church Man of Yr 1985; Allegheny Intermediate Unit Ed Assn Prin of Month April 1987; *office:* Grandview Elem Sch East 9th Ave & Ross St Tarentum PA 15084

HEASTON, RUSSELL, Seventh Grade Science Teacher; *b:* Covington, TN; *m:* Sharon Jackson; *c:* Ashton; *ed:* (BS) Journalism/Mass Comm, Univ of TN Martin 1982; *cr:* 7th Grade Sci Teacher Covington Crestview Jr HS 1983-; *ai:* Newspaper Staff Spon; Boys Track Team Coach; Spon & Organizer of Crestview Gents Dance Group; Selection Comm for Gifted Stus; Alpha Phi Alpha; NEA, Tipton Cty Ed Assn; Tipton Cty Power of Positive Stus Teacher of Month 1988, 1989; *home:* 3604 Chantrey W 6 Memphis TN 38128

HEATER, SUZAN RIDDLEMOSER, First Grade Teacher; *b:* Hastings, NE; *m:* Rodney A.; *c:* Ann, Bradley; *ed:* (BA) Elem Ed, Coll of ID 1956; NW Nazarene Coll, Boise St Univ, Coll of ID; *cr:* 4th Grade Teacher Lakeview 1956-57; 3rd Grade Teacher Brookwood 1957-61; 1st Grade Teacher New Plymouth Elem 1961-62, Fruitland Elem 1962-66, Eastside Primary 1972-; *ai:* Career Ladder, Public Relation, & Inservice Comms; Chairperson Prof Dev Comm; OR Rdng Assn, Malhew Cty Rdng Assn, Intnl Rdng Assn 1987-; PEO Sisterhood (All Offices, Pres Pres) 1971-; ID Optometric Assn Womans Auxiliary to Pres 1963, 1978; *office:* Eastside Primary 1315 Center Ave Payette ID 83661

HEATH, BRENT EDWARD, Social Studies Dept Chair; *b:* Redlands, CA; *m:* Carol Mae Moshier; *c:* Justin B.; *ed:* (AA) Soc Sci, Highline Cmmty Coll 1973; (BA) His, Seattle Pacific Univ 1975; Poly Sci, San Jose St Univ 1977; (MA) Scndry Ed, CA St Univ Northridge 1981; Admin Trng Center Instr San Bernardino Schls Office 1988-; Natl Endowment for Hum Fellow 1985; Taft Inst Government Fellow 1977; *cr:* Soc Stud Teacher Christian Center Schls 1975-77, Los Primeros Sch 1977-79, Cabrillo Jr HS 1979-80; Soc Stud Chm De Anza Jr HS 1980-; *ai:* Chm Self Study Comm His/Soc Sci; Law Day Making Choices Conference CA St Univ San Bernardino; Sports & Law Prgm Constitutional Rights Fnd; Bicentennial Competition on US Constitution; NCSS 1975-; ASCD 1977-; Baldy Vista Soc Stud Cncl (Secy, VP) 1983-87; CA Cncl for Soc Stud 1975-; S CA Soc Sci Assn 1977-; Natl Trust for Historic Preservation 1988-; Colonial Williamsburg Fnd Fellowship 1985; Book 1984; Harvard Grad Sch of Ed Inst on Civic Ed 1990; City of Ontario Proclamation for Academic & Prof Distinction; Ontario Montclair Sch Dist Certificate of Gratitude 1989; James Madison Fellowship Project 1987-88; Gold Fellow Greater Ontario Leadership Dev 1987; *office:* De Anza Jr HS 1450 S Sultana Ontario CA 91761

HEATH, BRUCE WILLIAMS, 6th Grade Science Teacher; *b:* Niles, MI; *m:* Mary M. Quick; *ed:* (BA) Bus Admin Graceland Coll 1967; (MS) Elem Ed in Univ 1974; General Electric Programming S Ch 1967; Air Force Acad Space Wrkshp 1986; *cr:* Sales Liaison Clark Equipment Company 1967-68; Teacher West Cntrl Elem 1968-; *ai:* Outdoor Lab Coord; Outdoor Camping Experience Dir; NSTA 1980-; NEA 1968-; IN St Teacher Assn 1968-; Hoosier Assn of Sci Teachers 1985-; Lions Club Sec Governors Cabinet 1969-1985; Perfect Attendance Growth Award; Cty Recycling Commission 1990; Outstanding Elem Teachers of Amer 1975; Semi-Finalist in Teacher of Yr 1985; West Cntrls Teacher of Yr 1985; *home:* 7676 W 800 S Union Mills IN 46382

HEATH, CHARLEY MACK, SR., Principal; *b:* Smyrna, TN; *m:* Sandra Kaye Milligan; *c:* Lisa King, Charley Jr.; *ed:* (BS) Soc Stud, MTSU 1980; Minister, Free Meth Church N America; *cr:* Minister Free Meth Church 1973-86; 7th/8th Grade Teacher Woodbury Grammar 1980-88; Prin Woodland Sch 1989-; *ai:* Girls Bsktbl Coach; Spon Fellowship Chrstn Athletes 1980-; Chm Suspension Hearing Authority 1986-.

HEATH, DOROTHY MOORE, Full-Time Graduate Student; *b:* Big Rapids, MI; *m:* Jack A.; *c:* J. Christopher, Donald E., Jeffrey A.; *ed:* (BA) Eng/Ed, SUNY Geneseo 1972; (MED) Educl/Admin, Univ NC Greensboro 1990; Eng & Ed, SUNY Brockport 1973-77; *cr:* Scndry Eng Teacher Batavia Sr HS 1972-77, Newfane Cntrl Schls 1978-80, Medina Cntrl Schls 1980-87, Oak Ridge Military Acad 1987-89; *ai:* Creative Writing Club, Drama Club, Yrbk Asst Adv; Southern Assn Comm Mem & Chairperson; Mentor Teacher; Teacher In-Service Trng; Phi Delta Kappa 1990; NYSTA 1972-; United Meth Women; *home:* 8024 Fogleman Rd Oak Ridge NC 27310

HEATH, OLIVER N., JR., Mathematics/Science Teacher; *b:* Atlanta, GA; *m:* Mary Louise Thompson; *c:* M. Ezra, Micah D., Lydia M., Timothy A.; *ed:* (BS) Bio, Auburn Univ 1966; (MDIV) Theology, Golden Gate Seminary 1970; Grad Stud Mobile Coll; *cr:* Elder Covenant Church 1977-; Teacher Covenant Sch 1986-; *ai:* NSTA Mem 1988-; *office:* Convenant Sch 7150 Hitt Rd Mobile AL 36695

HEATHERLY, CHARLOTTE JASPER, Health Occupations Ed Teacher; *b:* Copia Cty, MS; *m:* Jerry R.; *c:* Amy K.; *ed:* Registered Nurse, Johns Hopkins Hospital Sch of Nursing 1967; Type I Day Trade Cert Voc Ed, Univ of AL Birmingham 1980; Advanced Cardiac Life Support; *cr:* General Duty/Inservice Ed Hardy Wilson Memorial Hospital 1968-74; LPN Instr Copiah-Lincoln Jr Coll 1974-79; Sch Nurse Cullman Cty Spec Ed 1979-81; Health Occupations Teacher Cullman Cty Voc Center 1981-; *ai:* Health Occupations Stu of America Club, Cullman Cty Chapter of Natl Voc Honor Society Adv; NEA, AVA; Delta Kappa Gamma Pres 1988-; *office:* Cullman Cty Area Voc Center Rt 15 Box 1790 Cullman AL 35055

HEATHINGTON, LINDA SUSAN, Spanish Teacher; *b:* Lubbock, TX; *m:* Marion L.; *c:* Dana, Jason; *ed:* (BA) Eng/Span, TX Tech Univ 1977; *cr:* Eng/Span Teacher Lubbock-Cooper Ind Sch Dist 1977-81, Slaton Ind Sch Dist 1981-; *ai:* UIL Spelling Spon; Kappa Kappa Iota 1982-; *office:* Slaton HS 300 S 9th St Slaton TX 79364

HEATLY, LYNDA KILLINGSWORTH, 1st Grade Teacher; *b:* Rotan, TX; *m:* Johnny Lee; *c:* Leigh Lowe, John T.; *ed:* (BS) Elem Ed, N TX St Univ 1962; Super Sounder, Panhandle St; Teacher of Apple; Assertive Discipline; *cr:* 1st Grade Teacher Trent Elem 1962-69; Kndgtn Teacher 1970-74, 1st Grade Teacher 1974- Albany Ind Sch Dist; *ai:* UIL; TX St Teachers Assn 1962-; DelTa Kappa Gamma 1981-; TX Dept of Kndgtn 1972; *home:* 820 Rose Box 932 Albany TX 76430

HEATON, KENNETH ROBERT, 6th Grade Teacher; *b:* Philadelphia, PA; *m:* Lynn Engel; *c:* Allison, Courtney; *ed:* (BS) Elem Ed, West Chester 1973; (MS) Intergrated Ed, Marywood 1978; Grad Stud Elem Ed; *cr:* 6th Grade Teacher Hatboro-Horsham Sch Dist 1974-; *ai:* Keith Valley Sporting Equipment Mgr & Asst Athletic Dir; NEA, PA St Ed Assn, Hatboro-Horsham Ed Assn Rep 1975-; Nom Champion of Learning Awd 1984-85; *office:* Keith Valley Mid Sch 411 Babylon Rd Horsham PA 19044

HEATON, ROBERT MAIN, American Studies Teacher; *b:* Oakland, CA; *m:* Catherine Laurick; *c:* Laura E., Jane A.; *ed:* (BS) Ed, Univ of CO 1971; Law Related Ed, Talented & Gifted Ed Seminars & Classes; *cr:* US/World His Teacher Castle Rock Jr HS 1971-80; Amer Stud/TAG Teacher Joseph Lane Jr HS 1980-; *ai:* Vlybl Coach 1980-; Onward to Excl Leadership; Ed Assn Building Rep; City of Roseburg Budget Comm Mem 1987-89; OR Law Related Ed Teacher of Yr 1988; Roseburg Downtown Dev Bd Public Service Awd 1985; *office:* Joseph Lane Jr HS 2153 NE Vine St Roseburg OR 97470

HEBB, BETTY ANN CASTO, Second Grade Teacher; *b:* Bridgeport, WV; *m:* Douglas L.; *c:* Jenny P. A. Hebb-Bolyard, Dianna L. Hebb-Barnosky; *ed:* (BS) Kndgtn/Elem Ed, Wright St Univ 1972; *cr:* Kndgtn Teacher Edison & Irving Elem 1972-73, Miami Chapel Elem 1973-74; 2nd Grade Teacher Louise Troy Elem 1974-; *ai:* Ec Sch Leader; Trng in British Primary Schls; *home:* 2230 S Patterson Blvd Dayton OH 45409

HEBB, CATHY MARKHAM, 6th-8th Grade Math Teacher; *b:* Silver Creek, NY; *m:* Robert James; *c:* Clare E., James A.; *ed:* (BS) Elem Ed, 1976, (MA) Comm Stud, 1980 WV Univ; Tucker Cty Teachers Acad 1990; *cr:* 3rd Grade Teacher Petersburg Elem Sch 1976-77; 7th-9th Grade Math Teacher Elkins Jr HS 1977-79; 4th Grade Teacher 1979-82, 6th-8th Grade Math Teacher 1982- Parsons Elem & Mid Sch; *ai:* Parsons Elem & Mid Sch Mathcounts Team Coach; REACT Team; Staff Dev Cncl; Sch Calender Comm; WV Ed Assn 1976-; Tucker Cty Ed Assn 1979-; 1st United Meth Church Mem 1980-; Daughters of Amer Revolution Mem 1989-; Parsons Elem & Mid Sch PTO Treas; 1st Place Regional Mathcounts Team Coach 1985, 1988; *office:* Parsons Elem & Mid Sch 501 Chestnut St Parsons WV 26287

HEBDON, STEPHANIE, Third Grade Teacher; *b:* Belfast, Nrthn Ireland; *m:* Matthew; *ed:* His/Elem Ed, Univ of Lees-Trinity & All Saints Teacher Training Coll Great Britain 1973; *cr:* 1st Grade Teacher St Joseph Infant Sch 1973-75, Sacred Heart Infant Sch 1975-77; 3rd Grade Teacher Frank Porter Graham Elem Sch 1978-; *ai:* Mentor Teacher & Rewards Incentives Comm for Chapel Hill; NCAE; Natl Travel Grant Chapel Hill Public Sch Fnd; *office:* Frank Porter Graham Hwy 54 Bypass 15-501 Chapel Hill NC 27514

HEBERT, BILLIE STREET, Fourth Grade Teacher; *b:* Port Arthur, TX; *m:* Horace John; *c:* Pamela K. Hebert Brown, Michael I., Penny M. Herbert Woodrow; *ed:* (BS) Elem Ed, Lamar St Coll of Technology 1964; AAT; *cr:* 5th Grade Teacher Winnie Ind Sch Dist 1964-69; 4th Grade Teacher Hamshire-Fannett Ind Sch Dist 1969-; *ai:* Math UIL Spon; CTA Winnie Pres 1966-67; CTA Hamshire-Fannett Pres 1975-76; PTA Pres 1960-61; *office:* Hamshire-Fannett I S D Rt 2 Box 302 Beaumont TX 77705

HEBERT, JAMES CLINT, Poly Sci/Ec/US His Teacher; *b:* Houston, TX; *m:* Kathy; *c:* Mallory; *ed:* (BS) Soc Stud, Lamar Univ 1974; *cr:* Loan Officer First Savings Assn 1977-80; Teacher Hamshire-Fannett HS 1980-83; Prin/Teacher Believers Chrstn Sch 1983-87; Teacher Warren HS 1987-; *ai:* Stu Cncl & Class Spon; Debate Coach; *office:* Warren HS PO Box 190 Warren TX 77664

HEBERT, WANDA ANN, 5th Grade Teacher; *b:* Plaquemine, LA; *ed:* (BS) Phys Ed, Nicholls St Univ 1982; *cr:* 5th/6th Grade Teacher Village East 1982-; *ai:* Sch Building Level & Assertive Discipline Comms; 4-H Club; LA Assn of Educators; *office:* Village E Sch 315 La Fayette Woods Blvd Houma LA 70363

HECK, JANIS LORRAINE (FRANCE), English/Home Ec Teacher; *b:* Huntington, WV; *m:* Timothy W.; *c:* Jaclyn L., Natalie L.; *ed:* (BA) Eng, Western IL Univ 1970; Lib Sci/Rdng; *cr:* Eng Teacher North Jr HS 1971-74; Lakeview Jr Hs 1974-77; El Paso HS 1979-82; Eng/Home Ec Teacher Toluca HS 1982-; *ai:* Natl Honor Society Adv; Roanoke Womens Club (Secy 1986-88 Pres 1989-); Distinguished Teaching Awd Western IL Univ 1986; *home:* 712 Randolph St Roanoke IL 61561

HECK, PATRICIA OGILVIE, PACE Cor/Teacher; *b:* Fresno, CA; *m:* Harry William; *c:* Mary B., Trudy Heck Mills, Matthew; *ed:* (BA) Elem Ed, Univ of CA San Jose 1960; Grad Stud; *cr:* 4th Grade Teacher Visalia Unified Sch; *ai:* 7th/8th Grade Stu Problem Solving Convocation; CCEA, NEA 1982-; St Patricks (Parish Cncl 1990, CDS 1985-, LVHA Secy 1985-89); *office:* Churchill Cty Sch Dist 545 E Richards St Fallon NV 89406

HECKENLIVLEY, REX J., Math Teacher; *b:* Hastings, NE; *m:* Jeanette Marie Jochum; *c:* Timothy James, Randy Lee, Rick Allen; *ed:* (BS) Math, 1966, (MA) Math, 1974 Univ of NE; *cr:* Math Teacher Sutherland Public Schls 1966-75, Chase Cty HS 1975-; *ai:* Asst Ftbl Coach; Asst Boys Track Coach; NE Math Teachers Assn 1986-; NE Coaches Assn 1966-; NE Teachers Assn 1966-; NE Math Scholars Prgm Sr Scholar; Asst Coach Western NE All Star Ftbl Game; *office:* Chase County H S 1000 Wellington Imperial NE 69033

HECKMAN, PAULINE BARTLEMAN, 8th Grade Mathematics Teacher; *b:* Philadelphia, PA; *m:* Willard T.; *c:* David, Catherine Pavlock, Judy Linder, Lisa; *ed:* (BS) Math/Soc Stud Ed, West Chester Univ 1953; Grad Stud; *cr:* Math Teacher Amerikan Kiz Lisesi Istanbul Turkey 1953-54, Wakefield HS 1954-56; Substitute Teacher Cntrl Bucks Sch Dist 1966-67; Substitute Teacher 1968-72, Math Teacher 1972- Abington Heights Sch Dist; *ai:* Future Teachers of America Spon; Stu Support Team; Team Leader; Jr Mothers TEA for Vespers; NE PA Cncl Math Teachers 1988-; Abington Heights Ed Assn, PA Ed Assn, NEA 1972-; GSA Leader 1967-72; Church Sch Teacher 1967-; Woman Club Bd; Amer Assn Univ Women Bd 1966-67; *home:* 110 Sunset Dr Rd 1 Dalton PA 18414

HECTOR, DONALD, 5th Grade Teacher; *b:* Monroe, GA; *m:* Mary Louise Hillman; *c:* Patrice, Patrick; *ed:* (BS) Elem Ed, Albany St Coll 1965; Univ of GA Athens 1970-72; GA St Univ Atlanta 1977-78; *cr:* Teacher Carver Elem Sch 1965-68, Monroe Elem Sch 1968-77; Asst Prin Carver Jr HS 1977-80; Teacher Loganville Mid Sch 1980-83, Monroe Elem Sch 1983-; *ai:* Co-Founder Interdenominational Sftbl League; Coached Little League Bsbl & Sftbl 1982-84; GA Assn of Educators (Pres Local Assn 1976, 1982-83, 1989-), Spec Recognition 1984; Natl Assn of Educators 1968-; Spring Hill AME Zion Church Pres Layman Society 1983-; GMBA Grand Lodge Pres 1989-; Campton Choir Pres 1965-, Leadership 1979; Best Teacher 1973; Outstanding Elem Teachers of America 1972; Human Relations Awd 1984; Prin Awd 1986.

HEDGEPATH, DORIS S., English Department Chair; *b:* Conway, SC; *c:* William F. II, Catherine M.; *ed:* (BA) Eng, Winthrop Coll 1965; (MED) Ed, Univ of SC 1980; *cr:* Teacher Dentsville HS 1965-66, Myrtle Beach HS 1966-67, Conway HS 1967-69, 1971-74, Winyah Acad 1975-76, Conway HS 1976-; *ai:* Sch Improvement Report Ed; Drama Club, Chrldr, Jr Class Spon; Winthrop Alumnae Assn Pres 1967; Delta Kappa Gamma 2nd VP 1977-; SC Cncl Teachers of Eng 1966-; Palmetto St Teachers Organization 1977-88; SCEA, NEA 1965-79; Ivy Garden Club 1968-88; March of Dimes Area Chairperson 1969; Amer Heart Assn Area Chairperson 1970; 1st United Meth Church Mem 1966-; Natl Inst on Ed Minimum Competency Testing Hearings Rep; *home:* 1508 Elm St Conway SC 29526

HEDGES, MOLLIE PETERS, Fourth Grade Teacher; *b:* Columbus, OH; *m:* Charles Richard; *c:* Christopher, Ben, Colin; *ed:* (BS) Elem Ed, Kent St Univ 1974; (MA) Ed/Guidance/Counseling, OH St Univ 1979; *cr:* Substitute Teacher Columbus Public Schls 1974-76; 5th Grade Teacher 1976-77, 4th Grade Teacher 1977- Circleville City Schls; *ai:* OH St Univ Alumni Schlsp Selection Comm Mem; AAUW 1985-; Presbyn Church Deacon 1990; *office:* Atwater Elem Sch 870 W Atwater Ave Circleville OH 43113

HEDGES, SARA FRAKER, English Teacher; *b:* Lancaster, OH; *m:* Lawrence Keith; *c:* Amy Henderly, Ginny Henderly; *ed:* (BS) Eng/Speech, OH St Univ 1972; Univ of Dayton; Univ Lancaster Branch; *cr:* Eng Teacher Stanbery Frosh Sch 1973-77, Lancaster HS 1978-; *ai:* Honors Eng 10 Selection Comm; NCTE 1987-; 6th Ave United Meth Church Sunday Sch Supt 1986-87; Female Teacher of Yr Lancaster HS 1984/85/87/88; Stu Cncls Teacher of Month 1986; *office:* Lancaster H S 1312 Granville Pike Lancaster OH 43130

HEDGESPETH, CATHE MC GINNIS, Mathematics Teacher; *b:* Versailles, KY; *m:* Alan Coleman; *c:* Garrett, Virginia, Halline R.; *ed:* (BA) Math Ed, Univ of KY 1972; (MS) Math Ed, Univ of Evansville; *cr:* Teacher Henderson City Schls 1972-76, Henderson Cty Schls 1976-; *ai:* Sch Day Restructuring, Math Textbook Adoption Comms; NCTM Mem 1989-; NEA Mem 1972-73; KY Ed Assn; United Meth Women (Group Pres 1988, 1990, Secy 1989, Bd Mem 1987-89); *office:* South Jr HS 800 S Alves Henderson KY 42420

HEDMAN, AUDREY JEAN, Third Grade Teacher; *b:* East Aurora, NY; *m:* Cleave Vern; *ed:* (BA) Foods/Nutrition, 1954, (BA) Ed, 1955 E WA Univ; *cr:* 2nd/3rd Grade Teacher Edison Elem 1955-59; 5th-6th Grade Teacher Harrison Grade Sch 1955-60; 3rd Grade Teacher Tekoa Elem 1960-63; 3rd/4th Grade

Teacher J A Wendt Elem 1971-; *ai:* WEA; Cathlamet Congregational Church (Choir Mem, Church Sch Teacher); GSA Leader 1970-80.

HEDRICK, JEANETTE FARMER, Fifth Grade Teacher; *b:* Dalton, GA; *m:* James Cecil; *c:* Laura Tyrelle; *ed:* (BS) Home Ec, 1970, (MA) Mid Grade/Lang Art/Sci 1980, Intermediate Mid Grades/Lang Art, 1990 Western Carolina Univ; Curr Teaching, UNC Greenboro; Curr Supervision/Admin 1989; Writing Project Fellow, UNC Asheville 1989; European Study Abroad 1988; *cr:* Teacher Hiwassee Dam Sch 1972-; Night Class Teacher Tri-Cty Comm Coll 987-; *ai:* Jr Beta Club Spon; Civic Oration Sch & Dist Coord; Senate Bill Cty Steering Comm; Hiwassee Dam Differentiated Pay & Sch Improvement Comm; Textbook Selection/Staff Dev Cncl; Health Dept Family Stability & Planning Cncl; 4-H Youth Advisory & Home Ec Cncl; PTA (Treas, Prgm Chm 1972-) Outstanding Teacher 1984; NEA, NCAE (Local VP 1972-); Macedonia Baptist Church Sunday Sch Teacher 1970-; WMU Pres 1975-: Guardian Ad Litem for Abused Youth 1975-; Governors Awd for Teaching 1988; NC Region 8 Lang Art Excl Teaching Awd 1988; Cherokee Cty Teacher of Yr 1987; Daughters of Amer Revolution Outstanding Teacher 1988; Graduate Acad Study Grant 1988-89; Christa Ma Cauliffe Awd St Semifinalist; *home:* Rt 4 Box 512 Bear Paw Murphy NC 28906

HEFFERNAN, LINDA MARASCIO, Language Arts Teacher; *b:* Indianapolis, IN; *m:* Edward; *c:* Michael, Erin; *ed:* (BS) Elem Ed, Monmouth Coll 1971; *cr:* 1st Grade Teacher Broad St Sch 1971-72; 2nd Grade Teacher Court Street Sch 1972-73; Kndgtn Teacher Toms River Nursery Sch 1979-82; 6th Grade Teacher Silver Bay Elem 1982-88; Lang Art/Lit Teacher Beachwood Elem 1988-; *ai:* Silver Bay Elem Cheerleading Coach & Yrbk Coord 1986-88; Beachwood Elem Cheerleading Coach 1988-; Pine Beach Elem Cmptr Coord 1988-; Toms River Schls Dist Writing Comm 1985-88; Toms River Schls Intergenerational Prgm 1984-86; NJ Ed Assn 1971-; Toms River Ed Assn 1982-; Ocean Cty Early Ed Assn Secy 1980-81; Who Whos Amer Colls & Univs 1970-71; Dover Township Beautification Awds 1982-88; *office:* Beachwood Elem Sch Berkeley Ave Beachwood NJ 08722

HEFLIN, DOUGLAS MILLER, Director of Vocal Music; *b:* Cincinnati, OH; *m:* Lisa Kuhn; *c:* Faith N.; *ed:* (BA) Music Ed, Coll of Music 1985; Univ of Rio Grande; *cr:* Dir of Vocal Music Jackson HS 1985-; *ai:* Responsible for 6 Choirs, Piano Studio; Band Asst; Asst Play Dir for Musical; Phi Mu Alpha Secy 1982-; Alpha Lambda Delta 1982-; OH Music Ed, NEA 1985-; Christ United Meth Church (Music Prgm, Youth Prgm) Michiani Brass Quintet Mem; *office:* Jackson HS Tropic & Vaughn Jackson OH 45640

HEFNER, RORY PRUETTE, Math Teacher; *b:* Toluca, NC; *m:* Ricky Lynn; *c:* Jason R., Aimee L.; *ed:* (BS) Math Ed, NC St Univ 1980; Working on MS Math, Appalachian St Univ; *cr:* 10th-12th Grade Math Teacher Freedom HS 1981-83, East Burke HS 1983-; *ai:* Teacher Recruiter; Spon Future Teachers of America Club; NC Cncl Teachers of Math 1983-; *home:* 113 33rd St NW Hickory NC 28601

HEFT, EDWARD A., JR., 4th Grade Teacher; *b:* Detroit, MI; *m:* Margaret Ann; *c:* Kristi, Michael, Tom; *ed:* (BS) Economics Bus, 1959, (BA) Elem Ed, 1961, (MA) Ed Admin, 1965 E MI; Drivers Ed; *cr:* 5th-6th Grade Teacher St Dennis 1961-63; 5th Grade Teacher Clawson Sch System 1964-65, Holland Elem 1965-78; 4th Grade Teacher Angus Elem 1980-; *ai:* Boat Club Pres; Coach Bsbl & Hockey; Pres Sch Bd, VP of Assn; WEA, MEA, NEA; Pine Lake Manor Assn; Pine Lake Boat Club; W Bloomfield Recreation Volunteer.

HEFTE, ARTHUR WILLIAM, Third/Fourth Grade Teacher; *b:* Caledonia, MN; *m:* Beverly Ione Brendsel; *c:* Scott, Todd; *ed:* (BA) Elem Ed, Luther Coll 1967; *cr:* 3rd-5th Grade Teacher Harley Hopkins Elem 1967-80; 4th Grade Teacher Burwell Elem 1980-81; 3rd-4th Grade Teacher Meadowbrook Elem 1981-; *ai:* Bus Safety Supvr; Team Leader; Cub Scouts Cub Master 1989-; Church Cncl Bd Mem 1984-87; Westonka Day Care Pres of Bd 1988-; *office:* Meadowbrook-Hopkins Elem Sch 5430 Glenwood Ave Golden Valley MN 55422

HEGAN, DONNA JANE, Jr HS Mathematics Teacher; *b:* Lynn, MA; *ed:* (BS) Bus Ed, Salem St Coll 1972; (MA) Ed, Suffolk Univ 1977; Grad Work Math, Eng, Ed, Salem St Coll; *cr:* 7th-9th Grade Soc Stud/Math/Eng/Typing Teacher Eastern Jr HS 1972-84; 7th/8th Grade Math Teacher Pickering Jr HS 1984-; *ai:* Math Team Adv 1986-88; Cheerleading Coach 1985-86, 1989-; Lynn Teachers Union 1972-; Elected Teacher of Month 1988; Building Based Support Team Funded Grant for St of MA Mem; *office:* Pickering Jr HS 70 Conomo Ave Lynn MA 01904

HEGARTY, DOROTHY LEPORE, Orchestra Director; *b:* Providence, RI; *w:* Gerald R. (dec); *c:* Robert L., Steven D.; *ed:* (BMUSED) Music Ed, Boston Univ 1958; String Instrument Ed, Hartt Coll, Univ MA; Historic Dance, Amherst Coll, Berea Coll; *cr:* String Instrument Instr Springfield Public Schls 1958-62; Orch Dir/String Instrument Instr Agawam Public Schls 1971-; *ai:* Mid Sch, Jr HS, Chorus, Plays, Soloists Piano Accompanist; Amer String Teacher Assn, Music Educators Natl Conference, Sigma Alpha Iota; Natl Organization for Women, Cntry Dance & Song Society; W Dist Jr Orch Mgr.

HEHR, LA RAE KAY (SCHULZ), 4th-6th Grade Teacher/Prin; *b:* Edgeley, ND; *m:* Darwin E.; *c:* Kimberly; *ed:* (BS) Elem Ed/Eng, Valley City St Coll 1970; Working towards Cert; *cr:* Kndgtn Teacher Monango Public Sch 1971; Teacher/Prin Kennison Dist Nortonville 1981-; Combination Teacher Public Sch; *ai:* Town & Cntry Homemakers 1970-75; *home:* 310 6th Ave E Box 594 Edgeley ND 58433

HEIBY, EDWARD C., Chemistry Instructor; *b:* Bowling Green, OH; *m:* Phyllis Jean Loomis; *c:* Leslie J. Clough, Allyson I. Heiby Isabelle, Rex C.; *ed:* (BBA) Bus Admin, General Motors Inst 1957; (BS) Phys Sci/Math, MI St Univ 1961; (MS) Chem, Univ of MO 1969; Advanced Sci & Math, Univ of WI Madison, CA Berkeley, CO Sch of Mines, Univ of CO, CO St Univ; *cr:* Sci/Math Teacher Mason Public Schls 1961-65, Greenville Public Sch 1965-71, Portage Public Schls 1971-76, Brighton Schls Dist 275 1976-78, Sci/Math Teacher St Urain Valley Sch Dist 1978-; *ai:* Former Head Ftbl Coach; Head Track Coach; Sci Dept Chm; Dist Athletic Dir; NHS Adv; Var Club Spon; Amer Chemical Society; Cntrl Pres Church Elder; *office:* Skyline HS 600 E Mt View Ave Longmont CO 80501

HEID, SHARON REECE, 8th Grade Health Teacher; *b:* Louisville, KY; *m:* Chester E.; *c:* Scott, Tim, Matthew; *ed:* (BA) Elem Ed, 1968, (MA) Elem Ed, 1972 Morehead St Univ; *cr:* 5th Grade Teacher Star Elem Sch 1968-70; 6th Grade Teacher Worthington Elem Sch 1970-72, Portland Chrstn Sch 1982-85; 8th Grade Sci Teacher 1985-89, 8th Grade Health Teacher 1989- S Oldham Mid Sch; *ai:* Red Cross Volunteer Coord; Kappa Delta Pi 1966-68; *office:* S Oldham Mid Sch 6403 W Hwy 146 Crestwood KY 40014

HEIDBRINK, BETTY PATTERSON, Science Teacher; *b:* Midland, TX; *m:* Lawrence J.; *c:* Joey, Tommy, Randy; *ed:* (BA) Ed, Hastings Coll 1974; (MED) Ed, Univ of SW LA 1978; Grad Stud Univ of SW LA 1982; *cr:* Rdng/Lang Teacher Paul Breaux Elem 1975-80; Sci Teacher Carencro Mid Sch 1980-; *ai:* Stu Cncl Spon; NEA, LAE, LPTA 1978-; PEO 1978-.

HEIDEL, CHARLES FRANKLIN, 4th Grade Teacher; *b:* Mount Union, PA; *ed:* (BS) Bio, Shippensburg Univ 1962; (MS) Bio, MI St Univ 1966; Parasitology, Oceanography, Amer Univ; Poleantology, Physiological Genetics, Cell Physiology, Valparaiso Univ; Cmptr Sci, Juniata Coll; Radiological Stud, PA St Univ; *cr:* Bio Teacher High Point HS 1963-1967; Sci Teacher Chief Logan HS 1967-74; Bio Teacher Mt Union HS 1971-72; Chem Teacher 1974-80, 4th/6th Grade Elem Teacher 1980- Tyrone Area HS; *ai:* PA St Ed Assn, NEA 1967-; NABT 1964-67; Tyrone Area Ed Assn 1974-; NSTA Elem Sci & Bio Cert 1988; STEP-PIES Grant-Sci Methods Course, PA St Univ 1987; *office:* Tyrone Area Sch Dist 1317 Lincoln Ave Tyrone PA 16686

HEIDLOFF, DALE R., Jr HS Teacher/Sci Dept Chair; *b:* Seymour, IN; *m:* Lori Borg; *c:* Sarah, Kristin; *ed:* (BA) Physics/Chem, Concordia Univ River Forest 1981; *cr:* Sci Teacher Luth HS 1981-83, Grace Luth Sch 1983-; *ai:* Boys Bsktbl Coach; Boys & Girls Track Coach; Yrbk Adv; NSTA 1981-; Luth Ed Assn 1983-; *office:* Grace Lutheran Sch 7300 W Division River Forest IL 60305

HEIM, WILLIAM A., Fourth Grade Teacher; *b:* Colby, KS; *ed:* (BS) Elem Ed, 1970, (MS) Elem Ed, 1973 Ft Hays Univ; Grad Stud; *cr:* 4th Grade Teacher Cntrl Sch 1970-75, Ashland Grade Sch 1976, Hoxie Grade Sch 1976-; *ai:* Prof Dev Cncl Mem; Stamp & Chess Clubs Adv; All Sch Fairs Comm; NEA, KS Ed Assn 1970-; Phi Delta Kappa 1981-; KS Assn Teachers of Sci 1971-; Elks 1977-; Knights of Columbus 1966-; Meals on Wheels Prgm; *office:* Hoxie Grade Sch 1117 Royal Ave Hoxie KS 67740

HEIMANN, SUSAN JAN, Second Grade Teacher; *b:* Dallas, TX; *m:* Vincent Robert; *ed:* (BS) Elem Ed, North TX St Univ 1978; *cr:* 2nd Grade Teacher Florence Hill 1979-81, Dickinson Elem 1981-; *ai:* Gifted Ed Teacher 1982-; *office:* Dickinson Elem Sch 1902 Palmer Grand Prairie TX 75052

HEIMBACH, ARNOLD MARK, Fifth Grade Teacher; *b:* Portland, OR; *m:* Virginia Margaret Malen; *c:* Kurt E., Shelby K.; *ed:* Elem Ed 1955, (BS) Elem Ed, 1959 OR Coll of Ed; (MS) Ed, Linfield Coll 1965; Portland St Univ; Univ of ID; *cr:* Elem Teacher Dayton Public Schls 1955-; *ai:* Child Dev Comm; Stu Teacher & Supervising Teacher; Dayton Ed Assn Pres, OR Ed Assn, NEA; BPO Elks, Riverwood Mens Club Pres Golfer of Yr 1985; Dayton Educl Citizen of Yr; *home:* 1025 SW Red Hills Dr Dundee OR 97115

HEIMEL, HELEN MILLER, Mathematics Teacher; *b:* Monocacy Station, PA; *m:* Kenneth E.; *c:* Andrew, Jeanette; *ed:* (BS) Scndry Ed, Kutztown St Teachers Coll 1954; Penn St Univ; Lebanon Valley Coll; *cr:* Math Teacher Annville Cleona HS 1954-58; Teacher/Dept Head Owen J Roberts HS 1958-61; Daniel Boone Area HS 1968-; *ai:* Advisory Cncl; Natl Honor Society; Supts Advisory Cncl; PSEA; DBEA; NEA; Eastern Star; *home:* 109 Yocum Rd Douglasville PA 19518

HEIMSOTH, ELROY LESLIE, Administrator; *b:* Cole Camp, MO; *m:* Paula Lorna; *c:* Corlis Williams, Daniel, Susan O Brien, Christine Mansfield; *ed:* (BS) Elem Ed, Concordia Coll 1953; Southeast MO St Univ; *cr:* Teacher Trinity Luth Sch 1953-56; Teacher-Prin St Johns Luth Sch 1956-58; Teacher Immanuel Luth Sch 1958-65; Teacher-Prin Zion Luth Sch 1965-; *ai:* Intnl Luth Laymens League Zone Sec/Zone Pres/Dist VP/ 1988-; *home:* R 5 Box 261PP Poplar Bluff MO 63901

HEINRICH, JOAQUENIA SHAW, Sixth Grade Teacher; *b:* Minneapolis, MN; *m:* Klaus Karl; *ed:* (BS) Elem Ed/Hum, Univ of MN 1968; (MED) Curr/Instruction, Seattle Univ 1986; TESA Trainer; *cr:* Title I Teacher 1968, 5th Grade Teacher 1969-84, 6th Grade Teacher 1985- Whitefish Public Schls; *ai:* Supt Search & Sci Fair Comms; Talent Show Coach; Whitefish Ed Assn Pres 1987-89; Phi Delta Kappa, ASCD; Expanding Your Horizons Treas 1989-; Dist Sabbatical; Governors Regional Ed Meeting Facilitator; *home:* 610 Monegan Rd Whitefish MT 59937

HEINRICH, SHARRON LYNNE, US History Teacher; *b:* Alhambra, CA; *m:* Paul J.; *c:* Terence F., Kevin J.; *ed:* (BA) His, Univ of CA Los Angeles 1982; Ryan Credential Soc Sci, CA St Univ Los Angeles 1984; Participated Amer Principles of Democracy Inst & Constitutional Rights Fnd Seminars; *cr:* Teacher Mark Keppel HS 1984-; *ai:* Girls League & Crown & Sceptre Adv; Debate Coach; Pi Lamda Theta, Delta Kappa Phi 1984-; Alhambra Teacher Assn Rep; Reader for Advance Placement US His Examinations 1990; *office:* Mark Keppel H S 501 E Hellman Ave Alhambra CA 91801

HEINS, SUE CULBERTSON, Third Grade Teacher; *b:* Kingsport, TN; *m:* Albert Gordon Jr.; *c:* Gordon, Carrie, Douglass, James Heins Jones; *ed:* (BS) Spec Ed, 1971; (MS) Remedial Rdng, 1973 Univ of TN; *cr:* 3rd Grade Teacher Brickey Sch 1973-; *ai:* Phi Kappa Phi, KCEA, TEA, NEA 1973-; Univ of TN Pres Club; Appalachian Zoology Society Life Membership; PTA Life Mem; Akima Club; *office:* Brickey Elem Sch Dry Gap Pike Knoxville TN 37918

HEINTZ, KAREN ANN, Jr HS Science Teacher; *b:* Chicago, IL; *ed:* (BS) Bio, N IL Univ 1979; Grad Stud Guidance & Counseling; *cr:* Jr HS Sci Teacher Holy Angels Sch 1979-; *ai:* Local Sci Fair Coord; Regional Sci Fair Judge; Co-Chairperson Area Sci Curr Dev Comm 1986-87; NCEA, NABT, IL Jr Acad Sci 1979-; Natl Arbor Day Fnd 1990; Smithsonian Natl Assn 1990; Charles Montgomery Awd 1979.

HEINTZ, SUSAN M., 8th Grade English Teacher; *b:* Philadelphia, PA; *ed:* (BS) Soc Sci, Neumann Coll 1974; St Joseph Univ Masters Prgm in Rdng; *cr:* 2nd Grade Teacher St Callistus 1971-73; 5th Grade Teacher Our Lady of Mt Carmel 1973-75; 7th-8th Grade Teacher St Charles Borremeo 1975-81; K-8th Grade Teacher READS Remedial Math/read 1981-82; 7th Grade Teacher St Bernards 1982-84; 8th Grade Teacher St Timothys 1984-; *ai:* Sch Newspaper & Spirit Day Moderator; Rdng, & Eng Coord; Discipline Comm; IRA 1985-; PA Writing Project 1984-85.

HEINZ, GERALD F., English Department Head; *b:* Salinas, CA; *m:* Theresa E. Hernandez; *c:* Javier, Joaquin; *ed:* (BS) Eng, Univ of San Francisco 1957; (MA) Creative Writing, San Francisco St Univ 1965; Scndry Teaching, Univ of HI 1959; *cr:* Teacher Washington Intermediate 1959-60, Mission HS 1960-63, Wilson HS 1963-72, Mission HS 1972-; *ai:* Sr Adv; NCTE; St Dunstan Athletic Bd Secy 1988-; Fullbright Teaching Grant 1966-67; Scholastic Teacher Article Awd & Film Reviews 1969-74; Bay Area Writing Project Fellowship 1975; Cmptr Cadre Project Mem; *office:* Mission HS 3750 18th St San Francisco CA 94114

HEISER, JAMES SCOTT, High School Principal; *b:* Midland, MI; *m:* Sandra R Perera; *c:* Cecily K., Brooke A.; *ed:* (BSED) Health/Phys Ed, 1970, (MED) Scndry Sch Admin, 1976 Miami Univ Oxford OH; *cr:* Health/Phys Ed Teacher New Miami Jr Sch 1974-87; Prin New Miami HS 1987-; *ai:* Scndry Personnel Dir; Butler Cty Consortium for Entry Level Teachers; Project Partnership & SW OH Cmptr Assn Advisory Cncl; Var Bsktbl Coach; New Miami Ed Assn (VP 1982, Pres 1983); Mason; *office:* New Miami HS 600 Seven Mile Ave Hamilton OH 45011

HEIST, DEBRA (ZUBOK), First Grade Teacher; *b:* Dearborn, MI; *m:* David C.; *c:* Bradford, Karie; *ed:* (BA) Elem Ed, MI St Univ 1974; Grad Work E MI Univ; *cr:* Primary Grade Teacher Northville Public Schls 1973-; *ai:* K-2nd Grade AIMS Sci Building Rep; Developmental 1st Grade Study Comm Mem; Essential Elements of Effective Instruction Certificate; MI Model Health Prgm Certificate; *office:* Silver Springs Elem Sch 19801 Silver Springs Dr Northville MI 48167

HEIST, KEITH DOUGLAS, Mathematics Teacher; *b:* Canton, OH; *m:* Melanie Rose Saracina; *c:* Jonathan, Emily; *ed:* (BS) Ec, Ashland Univ 1977; (BA) Math, Akron Univ 1978; (MA) Curr/Instruction, Ashland Univ 1984; *cr:* Math Teacher Perry HS 1978-; *ai:* Asst Bsktbl Coach; *office:* Perry Local HS 3737 13th St SW Massillon OH 44646

HEITBRINK, MARGARET WENNING, High School Science Teacher; *b:* Greenville, OH; *m:* John; *c:* Jessica, Jeanna; *ed:* (BS) Bio/General Sci/Comprehensive Sci, OH Univ 1972; Working Towards Masters In Sci Ed Wright St; *cr:* Jr HS Teacher Dixie Sch System 1972-77; HS Teacher Botkins Sch 1977-; *office:* Hotkins HS 208 N Sycamore Ave Botkins OH 45306

HEITING, JOAN KATHERINE (JELINSKI), Elementary Principal; *b:* Fond Du Lac, WI; *m:* Leo Norbert; *c:* David, Kathy Elkins, Michael; *ed:* (BS) Marquette Univ; (MA) Educl Admin, TX Womans Univ 1982; Grad Stud Plano Ind Sch Dist, Univ of N TX; Prof Conferences, Wkshps & Seminars; *cr:* 4th/5th/7th Grade Teacher Private Schls 1958-61; 5th Grade Teacher Plano Ind Sch Dist Schls 1975-83; K-5th Grade Prin Saigling Elem Sch 1984-87; K-6th Grade Prin Brinker Elem Sch 1988-; *ai:* Various Sch Dist Comms; Plano Prin Goals Comm Chairperson; Judge Extracurricular Academic Act; Intnl Rdng Assn Pres 1986; Alpha Delta Gamma Pres 1990; TX Elem Prin & Supvrs Assn; ASCD Mem; Heritage Farmstead Docent 1990; Natl PTA Honorary Life Membership 1989, Nom Phoebe Apperson Heart 1990; Outstanding Educator Awd 1990; Guest Speaker SMU Rdng Conference 1987; Inservice Presentation Plano Ind Sch Dist; St Commendation Saigling 1987-88; Saigling Teacher of Yr 1977-78; TX St Bd of Ed Cert of Exceptional Achievement 1988-89; *office:* Brinker Elem Sch 3800 John Clark Pkwy Plano TX 75093

HEIZER, CAROL GOODMAN, Substitute Teacher; *b:* East Liverpool, OH; *m:* J. David; *c:* Sarah E., James M.; *ed:* (BA) Speech/Drama, Asbury Coll 1967; (MED) Eng, Univ of Louisville 1989; *cr:* 7th Grade Eng Teacher Westgate Jr HS 1967-72; Mid Sch Eng/Amer His Teacher Alliance Chrstn Acad 1983-86; HS Eng Teacher Highview Baptist Sch 1986-89; Substitute Teacher Jefferson & Bullitt Ctys 1989-; *ai:* Textbook Selection Comm Mem; Curr Dev Comm; World Clown Assn Newspaper; ACSI 1984-; Public Sch Bd Mem 1974-76; Chrstn Sch Bd Mem 1980-83; Natl Right to Life Mem Cty Bd of Dir 1972; Good News Gospel Clowns (Founder, Mem) 1984-86; Author of Published Articles; *home:* 6513 Downs Branch Rd Louisville KY 40228

HEJL, JAMES GEORGE, Director of Bands; *b:* Caldwell, TX; *m:* Patsy A. Drury; *c:* Sandra, Janice, David; *ed:* (BM) Music Ed, Univ of TX 1962; (MM) Music Ed, Univ of MI 1968; Admin Cert IA St Univ; Univ of Houston; *cr:* Band Dir Wm B Travis HS 1962-68; Music Supv Eanes Ind Sch Dist 1969-70;asst Dir of Bands Univ of TX 1970-75; Dir of Bands Buena Vista Coll 1975-78; MS St Univ 1978-83; Angleton Sr HS 1983-; *ai:* Phi Beta Mu; Phi Mu Alpha Sinfonia; Pi Kappa Lambda; TX Bandmasters Assn; Kappa Kappa PSI; TX Music Educators Assn; Kiwanis Club 1975-78; Angelton Chamber of Commerce 1983-; Experienced Teacher Fellowship Univ of MI 1968; Who's Who in Midwest 1978; Who's Who in South & Southwest 1988; Outstanding Young Men of Amer 1976; Articles Published the Instrumentalist Magazine; Band Judge & Conductor TX/MS/AL/OH/TN/IA/MO/LA; *home:* 701 Milton Angleton TX 77515

HEKMAT, SUSAN RUSTIGE, English/Speech Teacher; *b:* St Louis, MO; *m:* Firooz; *ed:* (BSED) Speech/Theatre, SW MO St Univ 1977; (MSED) Speech/Eng, SE MO St Univ 1985; *cr:* 7th-9th Grade Eng Teacher RockWood Sch Dist 1978-83; 9th-12th Grade Eng Teacher Meadow Heights 1984-86; 10th-12th Grade Eng/Speech Teacher Cape Girardeau Public Sch 1986-; *ai:* Speech/Debate Coach 1988-; Drama Coach 1980-83; Wellness Comm 1989-; Natl Forensic League Spon 1988-; Extra Service Salary; Natl Forensic League 1988-; MO St Teachers Assn 1989-; Speech & Theatre Assn of MO 1980-; Speech & Debate Team Stus Qualified for St Level Competition; Eating Awareness Comm Started HS Level; *office:* Cape Central HS 205 Caruthers Cape Girardeau MO 63701

HELD, DENNIS LOUIS, First Grade Teacher; *b:* Oildale, CA; *m:* Karen Marie; *c:* Vicky, Kelly; *ed:* (BA) Eng/His, CA St Univ Northridge 1968; *cr:* Teacher Fred Williams Elem 1973-; *ai:* Chess Tournament Spon; Honorary Service Achievement Awd; *office:* Fred L Williams Sch 4300 Anchorage St Oxnard CA 93033

HELD, DONNA TECLAW, Gifted Coordinator; *b:* Milwaukee, WI; *m:* Robert C.; *ed:* (BA) Elem/Spec Ed, Univ of WI Whitewater 1978; (MS) Prof Dev/Gifted Ed, Cardinal Stritch 1988; *cr:* 4th/5th Grade Teacher Cty Line Sch & Mac Arthur Sch 1978-80; 7th Grade Rdng Teacher Kennedy Mid Sch 1980-85; Gifted Prgm Coord/Teacher Germantown Schls 1985-89;Temporary-Admin Asst Curr & Instruction 1989-; *ai:* Odyssey of the Mind Dist Coord; Facilitate a Parent Support Group for Gifted & Wkshps for other Dists on Gifted Ed; Differentiating Curr/Learning Centers; WI Cncl for Gifted and Talented 1985-; *home:* N27 W27166 Woodland Ave Pewaukee WI 53072

HELDERS, DIXIE LEE, 5th Grade Teacher; *b:* River Falls, WI; *m:* David W.; *c:* Rodney D., Stacey J.; *ed:* (BS) Elem Ed, Univ of WI River Falls 1964; Grad Stud Univ of WI River Falls, De Paul Univ, Hamiline Univ; *cr:* 2nd Grade Teacher Baldwin Woodville Schls 1964-65, San Bernardino Public Schls 1965-66; 1st-3rd/5th Grade Teacher St Croix Cntrl Schls 1966-; *ai:* Elem Play Dir; SCCEA Secy 1967-70; WEA, NEA; Church Chrstn Ed Bd 1984-; PTO Nom WI Teacher of Yr 1985; *office:* St Croix Cntrl Schls Roberts WI 54023

HELDRETH, CYNTHIA HOLT, Mathematics Department Chair; *b:* Hampton, VA; *m:* Thomas R.; *c:* Bryan; *ed:* (BS) Math Ed, 1974, (MS) Math Ed, 1979 Old Dominion Univ; *cr:* Math Teacher/Dept Chairperson Bethel HS 1974-; *ai:* Dial-A-Teacher; VA Peninsula Cncl of Math 1975-; Norfolk Ronald Mc Donald House Bd of Dirs 1987-; *office:* Bethel HS 1067 Big Bethel Rd Hampton VA 23666

HELDRETH, JACKIE BROOKS, Computer Laboratory Instructor; *b:* Point Marion, PA; *c:* Russell Jr., Mark, Gregory, David, Deborah Hapney; *ed:* (BS) Art/Home Ec, WV Univ 1965; Post Grad Work Elem Ed, Gifted Stu Ed, Microcomputers, Thinking Skills; *cr:* 2nd Grade Teacher A Lane Chrstn Sch 1973-74; Art/Home Ec/Pregnant Minors Teacher Cntrl HS 1975-76; 4th-6th Grade Teacher Lenwood Elem 1980-83; 5th/6th Grade Teacher 1983-86, Cmptr Lab Instr 1986- Adelanto Elem Sch; *ai:* Girls & Boys Bsktbl; Cheerleading, Stu Cncl, Sci Fair Adv; Adelanto Dist Teachers Assn VP 1984-86; Master Teacher for Stu Teacher; *office:* Adelanto Elem Sch 17931 Johnathan Ave Adelanto CA 92301

HELF, LINDA L., Fourth Grade Teacher; *b:* Oshkosh, WI; *ed:* (MS) Rdng, Univ of WI-Oshkosh 1969-74; *cr:* 4th Grade Teacher 1969-85; Unit Leader Grades 3-4 1970-85 Andrew Jackson Sch; 4th Grade Teacher James Monroe Sch 1985-; *ai:* Writing Across the Curr Comm; Mentor Prgm; WI Ed Assn Bd of Dir 1988-; Manitowoc Cncl Ed Assn Pres 1980 Outstnding Service 1981; Kettle Moraine Uniserv Cncl Pres 1983-85 Distinguished Service Awd 1978; United Way of Manitowoc (Bd of Dir 1978-89/Chm of Personnel Comm 1988-89); Marco Inc Bd of Dir 1987-89; Teacher of Yr Manitowoc Public Schls 1978; Outstnding Young Woman of Amer 1984; *home:* 1711 Meadowbrook #204 Manitowoc WI 54220

HELFRICH, KATHRINE HALE, 6th Grade Teacher; *b:* Ackley, IA; *c:* Steve, Gene, Patty Helfrich Hall, Mary; *ed:* (BS) Elem Ed, IA St Univ 1978; Music Ed, Oberlin Conservatory Music; Ed, Trinity Coll; Math/Cmptr Ed/Remedial Math, IA St Univ; Learning Styles/Whole Lang, Drake Univ; Math/Monoprints, NE MO; *cr:* 6th Grade Teacher, 4th-6th Grade Math Teacher, 3rd Grade Teacher, Spec Ed Remedial Teacher Newton Cmmty Schls; 4th-8th Grade Music Teacher St Norberts Church Sch; *ai:* Math Curr Comm; IA St Univ Advisory Comm Elem Ed Profile System; Adult Ed Calligraphy; IA Cncl of Math Teachers 1979-, Finalist Awd for Excl Elem Math 1985-86; NCTM 1979-; Kappa Delta Pi 1978-79; Newton Tennis Assn Publicity 1985; Church Organist; Outstanding 1st Yr Teacher Awd IA St Univ 1979; *office:* Woodrow Wilson Elem Sch 801 S 8th Ave W Newton IA 50208

HELGATH, NANCY L. (WILSON), English/Literature Teacher; *b:* Hollywood, CA; *m:* C. Neil; *c:* Randy, Karen Holton; *ed:* (BA) Speech, W WA Univ 1970; *cr:* 5th Grade Teacher 1970-76, 6th Grade Teacher 1976-82, 7th-8th Grade Teacher 1982- Cntrl Sch; *ai:* Speech & Debate Team Coach; NCTE, Northwest Rdng Cncl, AGATE; Directed Ed Television; *home:* 1700 W Lakeshore Dr Box 996 Whitefish MT 59937

HELGERT, MARK JAMES, Director of Bands; *b:* Waukesha, WI; *m:* Gwenda L. Noah; *ed:* (BA) Music Ed, Carroll Coll 1977; *cr:* Band Dir Butler Mid Sch 1977-; *ai:* Dir Butler Jazz I; Conductor Chamber Ensembles; Public Schls of Waukesha Scndry Employee of Month 1987; Waukesha Area Jazz Ensemble Conductor 1980-; Judged Woody Herman Schlsp Contest 1977-88, 1989; Jazz Coordinator Summer Music Clinic Univ of Pacific; *office:* Butler Mid Sch 310 N Hine Ave Waukesha WI 53188

HELINSKI, DAVID ALLEN, Secondary English Teacher; *b:* Carlisle, PA; *m:* Maureen Jansante; *ed:* (BA) Eng, Washington & Jefferson Coll 1984; (MED) Educl Admin, PA St Univ 1990; *cr:* Teacher Altoona Area HS 1986-; *ai:* Head Ftbl Coach D S Keith Jr HS; Saturday Dentention Coord Altoona Area HS; Stu Chapter PA St Ed Assn Pres 1984; Alpha Tau Omega Secy 1980-84; *home:* RD 4 Box 208 Duncansville PA 16635

HELLER, BEVERLY BUXBAUM, Sixth Grade Teacher; *b:* Brooklyn, NY; *m:* David; *c:* Aimee-Kim, Mandee-Jo, Cheree-Su; *ed:* (BBA) Merchandising & Sales, City Univ 1964; (MS) Ed, Hunter Univ 1969; Supervision/Admin Prgm, Nova Univ; *cr:* Teacher PS 168 K & 63Q 1963-70; Teacher/Adm Beth Sholom 1977-; Teacher Ida Fisher Elem 1987-; *ai:* MBJCC VP/Secy; Jewish Family Service-Exec Bd; M B Feeder Pattern Rep; MBSH Gifted Rep; DC Acad Advisory Comm VP; DC Oversight Comm; City Coll Alumni Society; Hunter Alumni; MBSH Curr Comm Co-Chm; Kappa Delta Pi 1969-; Phi Delta Kappa 1987-; Pals & Flag 1980-; DC PTSA Region VP 1984-86/1988-; DCAC Area/Rep 1986-; DC Magnet Adv Chirperson 1988-89; DC Gifted Assn Co-Chm 1987-; Natl Womens Amer Ort Chaired Telecare/Probe; *office:* Fisher Elem Sch 1424 Drexel Ave Miami Beach FL 33139

HELLER, DANIEL ALAN, English Department Chairman; *b:* Paterson, NJ; *m:* Nina Rovinelli; *c:* Benjamin; *ed:* (BA) Eng, Middlebury Coll 1975; (MED) Curr/Instruction, Keene St Coll 1980; (MA) Eng Lit, Bread Loaf Sch of Eng 1985; Educl Admin & Planning Univ of VT 1990; *cr:* Eng Teacher 1977-89, Eng Dept Chm 1989- Brattleboro Union HS; *ai:* Stu Lit Magazine Ed; ASCD, CSSEDC 1987-; NEA 1977-; NCTE (Peer Evaluation Comm Mem) 1978-; Article Published; Local/Natl Speaker Peer Teacher Supervision; *office:* Brattleboro Union HS Fairground Rd Brattleboro VT 05301

HELLER, JAMES MICHAEL, 4th-8th Grade Lit Teacher; *b:* Chicago, IL; *m:* Joanne Canyon; *c:* Zoe E.; *ed:* (BA) Poly Sci, 1968, (MED) Ed, 1970 Loyola Univ; Gifted Wkshp, Great Books Trng, Educl Admin; *cr:* Teacher Raymond Sch 1970-79, Burbank Sch 1979-; *ai:* Natl Beta Club Spon; IL Math & Sci Acad Awd of Excl 1989; *office:* Luther Burbank Sch 2035 N Mobile Ave Chicago IL 60639

HELLIER, AUDREY LEWIS, Third Grade Teacher; *b:* St Augustine, FL; *m:* George G.; *c:* Linda H. Kinlaw, Jane G. Hellier, Laurie H. Janz; *ed:* (BA) Span, Univ of FL 1953; Elem Ed; *cr:* 3rd Grade Teacher Lafayette Sch 1972-73; 6th Grade Teacher Webster 6th Grade Ctr 1973-79; 5th/6th Grade Teacher Mill Creek Elem 1979-83; 3rd Grade Teacher R B Hunt Elem 1983-; *ai:* Grade Level Chairperson; Alpha Delta Kappa Pres 1978-80; Alpha Delta Kappa Sec 1987-88; SJEA/NEA; Pilot Club (VP 1980-81 & Sec 1977-78); Blood Bank Bd; Girl Scouts.

HELLING, NANCY TAYLOR, First Grade Teacher; *b:* Moorhead, MN; *m:* Kenneth R.; *ed:* (BS) Early Chldhd/Elem Ed, Univ of ND 1972; (MS) Elem Ed/Curr/Instruction, St Cloud St Univ 1990; *cr:* Elem Teacher Karlstad Public Sch 1974-78; Elem Field/Resource Coord ND St Univ 1978-80; 1st/5th/6th Grade Teacher Avon Elem Sch 1980-; *ai:* Albany Fed of Teachers, ASCD; Avon PTA; Kimball Cmmty Club; Bethlehem Luth Church; MN PTA/PTSA Distinguished Service Awd 1985.

HELLRUNG, JOSEPH E., Teacher of Gifted & Talented; *b:* Alton, IL; *m:* Sarah Erbse; *ed:* (BA) Government/His, S IL Univ 1975; (MA) Eng, Ball St Univ 1980; Gifted & Talented Cert Ball St Univ; *cr:* Eng/Soc Stud Teacher Boston Jr HS 1976-81; 8th Grade Eng Teacher Test Jr HS 1981-83, Hibberd Mid Sch 1983-87; Resource Teacher of Gifted & Talented Test Mid Sch 1987-; *ai:* Richmond HS Asst Ftbl Coach; Bsktbl & Track Coach; Academic Team Spon; Natl Assn Gifted Children 1988-; NEA, ISTA; Richmond Assn Classroom Teachers VP 1985-86; IN Ftbl Hall of Fame Bd Mem 1985-; Tau Kappa Epsilon; Richmond Comm Schls Outstanding Educator Awd 1986; *office:* Test Mid Sch 33 S 22nd St Richmond IN 47374

HELM, BEVERLY J., 4th Grade Teacher; *b:* Bonne Terre, MO; *m:* William B.; *c:* Melody; *ed:* (BS) Ed, SEMO 1975, (MS) Ed, Webster 1989; *cr:* 4th Grade Teacher Belgrade 1975-76; Cntrl R-III 1976-; *ai:* MSTA; PTA; *office:* Central Elementary Sch 403 W Fite Elvins MO 63601

HELM, DIANNE M., Physical Science Teacher; *b:* Shelby, NC; *m:* James Shuttleworth; *c:* Eric, Dawn, Brian; *ed:* (BA) Bio, Gardner Webb 1962; (BS) Bio, Greensboro Coll 1964; Academically Gift Cert Courses; Cooperative Learning Support Group; Numerous Wkshps; UNCC Renewed Certificate 1982; *cr:* Sci Teacher George Washington HS 1964, Page Sr HS 1965-68; Therapist Dr W H Straughn 1975-82; Sci Teacher Smith Jr HS 1983-; *ai:* Var Bsktbl Games Ran Clock; Faculty Advisory Cncl; Career & Staff Dev Coord; 9th Grade Class Day; PTSA 9th Grade Rep; Career Dev Participant Career Status Level 2; *office:* Smith Jr HS 1600 Tyvola Rd Charlotte NC 28210

HELM, MICHAEL W., English/Psychology Teacher; *ed:* (BS) Ed/Psych/Eng, Univ of TX El Paso 1976; *cr:* Eng Teacher Parkland Jr HS 1977-80;Psych/Eng Teacher Parkland HS 1981 -; *ai:* Acad Decathlon Team Spon; Young Scholars Team Spon; High Q Team Spon; *home:* 4705 Tumbleweed El Paso TX 79924

HELM, MICHELLE I., Science Teacher; *b:* Las Vegas, NV; *m:* John D.; *c:* Amy, Daniel; *ed:* (BA) Scndry Ed, 1983, (MA) Admin, 1989 ASU; Working Towards PhD; *cr:* Teacher Connolly Mid Sch 1984-; *ai:* Stu Cncl Spon; Graduation, Human Dev, Retention Comm; Sci Textbook Selection; Sci Inservice Teacher Dist Curr & Say No Drug Comm; Tempe Elem Ed Assn Rep 1984-; General Fed of Women Clubs Tempe Jrs Pres 1980-81, Outstanding Pres 1981; Tempe Elem Dist Impact Awd 1990; Tempe Outstanding Young Women, Cmmty Leaders of America 1983; Accent AZ Sci & Math Publication 1987; *office:* Connolly Mid Sch 2002 E Concorda Tempe AZ 85282

HELM, NANCY SCHIEFELBEIN, 5th Grade Teacher; *b:* Milbank, SD; *c:* Sarah, Nathan; *ed:* (BA) Elem Ed, Sioux Falls Coll 1974; *cr:* 6th Grade Teacher 1974-75, 5th Grade Teacher 1975- Brandon Elem Sch; *ai:* NEA, SDEA, IRA; Brandon Luth Church Deacon 1988-; Friendship of Ed; Nom Teachers Who Make A Difference; *office:* Brandon Elem Sch 501 Holly Blvd Brandon SD 57005

HELMINK, C. NOEL, Mathematics & Computer Teacher; *b:* Durham, NC; *m:* Randolph; *ed:* (BS) Botany, Butler Univ 1965; (MS) Ed, IN Univ 1970; *cr:* Teacher Indianapolis Public Schls 1965-67, Speedway Jr HS 1967-; *ai:* NCTM, IN Cncl Teachers of Math; Speedway Classroom Teachers Assn Treas 1980-; *office:* Speedway Jr HS 5151 W 14th St Speedway IN 46224

HELMS, CHARLINE RIGNEY, Seventh Grade Teacher; *b:* Ft Worth, TX; *m:* Charles David; *c:* Clay, Ted; *ed:* (BS) Elem Ed, Abilene Chrstn Coll 1955; (MED) ELem Ed, GA St Univ 1976; *cr:* 1st Grade Teacher George C Clarke Elem 1955-61; 2nd Grade Teacher David Sellars Elem 1967-69; 2nd/3rd Grade Teacher Rainbow Elem 1973-78; 4th Grade Teacher Bonne E Cole Elem 1979; Title I Remedial Rdng Teacher St Tammany Jr HS 1979-80; 3rd Grade Teacher Bonne E Cole ELem 1980-82; 7th/8th Grade Teacher Loganville Mid Sch 1983-; *ai:* Media & Sunshine Comms; Grade Chm; Prof Assn of GA Educators 1983-; Loganville Mid Sch Teacher of Yr 1987; *office:* Loganville Mid Sch Loganville GA 30249

HELMS, DAVID CRAIG, Chemistry/Computer Teacher; *b:* Connellsville, PA; *ed:* Scndry Ed, Penn St Univ 1971-73; (BS) Chem Ed, CA Univ of PA 1987; *cr:* Asst Chief Chemist Duraloy BlaW-Knox 1974-83; Chemist MacKintosh-Hemphill 1982; Chemist Tech Graphics Control Corp 1984; Teacher Uniontown Area Sch Dist 1987-; *ai:* PSEA/NEA 1985-; Spectroscopy Society of Pittsbugh 1985-; Society of Analytical Chemists of Pittsburgh 1985-; BSA Scoutmaster 1983-; Internship Bureau of Mines US Dept of Interior 1987; Article in Journal of Steel Founders Society of America 1980; *office:* Uniontown Area HS 146 E Fayette St Uniontown PA 15401

HELMS, DEBRA RENE, Industrial Arts Teacher; *b:* Charlotte, NC; *ed:* (BS) Industrial Ed, 1976; (MED) Industrial Ed, 1981 Clemson Univ; *cr:* Industrial Arts Teacher Lakeview Mid Sch 1980-82; Bryson Mid Sch 1982-; *ai:* Chm-Related Arts Dept; Chm-Vocational Ed Dept-Building CoMm; Co-Chm-School Auction Comm; Mem-SACS Steering CoMm; Mem-Mission Statement Comm; SCIAEA 1980-; SCEA 1980-; Proposed Grant for Industrial Tech Ed for Bryson Mid Sch.

HELMS, ERMA B., Fifth Grade Teacher; *b:* Louisville, AL; *c:* Ronald; *ed:* (BS) Elem Ed, 1972, (MS) Elem Rdng, 1974, (AA) Elem/Rdng, 1978 Troy St Univ; *cr:* 5th Grade Teacher Louisville ELem 1974-; *ai:* Prof Dev Coord; 4-H Club Spon; Delta Kappa Gamma 1st VP 1978-; Kappa Delta Pi 1974-; Phi Delta Kappa 1978-; Public Lib Bd 1989; Rdng St Textbook Comm 1988-89; 4-H Club Certificate of Appreciation; *home:* PO Box 176 Louisville AL 36048

HELMS, JACK E., Science Teacher; *b:* Bloomfield, IN; *m:* Donna S. Dove; *c:* Aaron, Lisa; *ed:* (BS) Life Sci, 1958; (MS) Life Sci/Phys Ed, 1969 IN St Univ; *cr:* Sci Teacher Jasonville HS 1958-59; Life Sci Teacher Kankakee Valley Sch Corp 1959-; *ai:* Coached Ftbl & Bsktbl 1959-76; Coached Bsbl 1968-80; Spon Stu Cncl 8 Yrs; Little Leag Bsbl 1965-71; IN St Teachers Assn Treas

1973-78; NSTA 1980-88; Sons of Legion 1988-; *home:* RR 1 Box 13 Wheatfield IN 46392

HELMS, JEANNENE ASKEN, Third Grade Teacher; *b:* Center, TX; *m:* Thomas Marshall; *c:* Mark, Lori; *ed:* (AA) Panola Jr Coll 1970; (BS) Elem Ed, Stephen F Austin St Univ 1972; Working Towards Masters Elem Ed; *cr:* Eng Teacher Shelbyville Jr HS 1972-73; 3rd Grade Self-Contained Teacher S W Carter Elem 1973-; *ai:* UIL Storytelling Coach; Campus Planning Comm Past Mem; Assn of TX Prof Educators Mem 1990; PTO Mem; *office:* S W Carter Elem Sch Box 325 Shelbyville TX 75973

HELMS, NELLIE SUE, English Department Chairman; *b:* Brundidge, AL; *m:* W. Ray; *c:* Susan H. Harper, Alan, Glen; *ed:* (BA) Eng Ed, Troy St Univ 1962; Working Towards Masters; *cr:* Teacher Dothan HS 1963-64; Teacher/Eng Dept Chm Pike Cty HS 1978-89; *ai:* Journalism Club, Pierides Literary Club, Class Day Spon; Delta Kappa Gamma 2nd VP 1988-89; Sigma Tau Delta 1989-; First United Meth Church (Choir, Teacher) 1970-; Wiregrass Writing Project Fellowship; Gulf Coast Writing Convention Presenter 1988; *office:* Pike Cty HS S Main St Brundidge AL 36010

HELMUS, DONALD LEE, Foreign Language Chairperson; *b:* Muskegon, MI; *m:* Doris Renee Zahrt; *c:* Renee, Hans; *ed:* (BA) His/Fr/Ger, Western MI Univ 1969; Fr, MI St; Span, Calvin Coll; *cr:* Teacher Mona Shores Schls 1969-70; Reeths-Puffer HS 1970-; *ai:* Fr Club Adv; Bethany Chrstn Reformed Church Deacon 1985-87; Teacher of Yr 1985.

HELSEL, BYRON LEE, 5th/6th Grade Teacher; *b:* Mc Connellsburg, PA; *m:* Martha Gorman; *c:* Mary Jane Rena, Constance Lynn; *ed:* (BS) Elem Ed, York Coll of PA 1974; Elem Ed; *cr:* 4th/5th/6th Grade Teacher 1974- Forbes Road Elem; *ai:* Act 178 Staff Dev Comm; Intermediate Unit In-Service Comm; PA Assn 1974-; NEA 1974-; Forbes Road Ed Assn Pres 1974-; *office:* Forbes Road Elem Sch HCO 1 Box 222 Waterfall PA 16689

HELSLEY, MARTIN JACOB, JR., 8th Grade Math/Science Teacher; *b:* Winchester, VA; *m:* Dawn Foote; *c:* Todd W. Forrester; *ed:* (BS) Dairy Sci, VA Tech 1973; St Teachers Certificate, VA Tech 1974; *cr:* Teacher Cntrl HS 1976-81, Woodstock Mid Sch 1981-; *ai:* Ofcl Bsktbl Piedmont/Shenandoah Offcls Assn; Hamburg Ruritan Club 1976-; St Luke Lutheran Ch Treas 1986-; Supvr Shenandoah Cty Bd OF Supvrs 1979-83; Trustee Shanandoah Cty Public Lib 1984-88; *home:* Rt 3 Box 208 Edinburg VA 22824

HELTON, BRONNIE LOYD, TX History Teacher; *b:* Corsicana, TX; *m:* Judy Kay; *c:* Jeremy, Trevor; *ed:* (BA) Eng, 1974, (MED) Rdng, N TX St; Driver Ed; *cr:* Alternative Ed Teacher Newman Smith HS 1978-80; TX His Teacher Dewitt Perry Jr HS 1980-86; TX His/Dept Chm Charles Blalack Jr HS 1986-; *ai:* His Club Spon; Thinking Comm Carrollton/Farmers Branch Ind Sch Dist; Assn of TX Prof Educators (VP 1979-80, Pres 1980-81); TX Assn for Gifted & Talented 1989-; ATPE Schlsp 1979; James Butler Bonham Daughters of Republic of TX Outstanding TX His Teacher 1985; Carrollton/Farmers Branch Ind Sch Dist VIP Awd 1988; *home:* 3102 James St Sachse TX 75048

HELTON, KENNETH RAY, Principal; *b:* Morristown, TN; *m:* Teresa Reneau; *c:* Lance, Erica; *ed:* (BS) Elem Ed, 1974, (MS) Educl Admin, 1979 Univ of TN; Post Masters Stud; *cr:* 4th Grade Teacher Fairview 1974-76; 5th Grade Teacher Manley Elem 1976-81; Prin Witt Elem 1981-; *ai:* Elem Bsktbl Coach; NEA; Gideons; Cntrl Baptist Church Teacher; *office:* Witt Elem Sch 4650 S Davy Crockett Pkwy Morristown TN 37813

HELTON, RONALD L., Chemistry/Physics Teacher; *b:* Leon, IA; *m:* Roberta F. Henderson; *c:* Robert L.; *ed:* (BA) Bio/Chem, Graceland Coll 1969; (MS) Sci Ed, Drake Univ 1988; Univ of Mankato MN; Univ of N IA; *cr:* Chem/Physics Teacher Cntrl Decatur HS 1969-; *ai:* Prins Advisory Comm; NHS Selection Comm; Prins Comm on Sch Handbook Revision; Natl Sci Fnd Schlsp Grant to Univ of Mankato & Univ of N IA; *office:* Cntrl Decatur HS 1201 NE Poplar Leon IA 50144

HELTSLEY, GUYLA BETHEL, Fifth Grade Teacher; *b:* Fairfield, IL; *m:* Jeff; *c:* Robin, Kelly, Kerry; *ed:* (BA) Psych, 1973, (MAED) Elem Ed, 1984 W KY Univ; *cr:* 5th Grade Teacher Greenville Elem Sch 1982-; *ai:* KY Ed Assn, Muhlenberg Cty Ed Assn; 2nd Baptist Church; GSA Co-Leader 1984-86; *office:* Greenville Elem Sch 120 College St Greenville KY 42345

HELVEY, SUSAN KIMBERLEE, Freshmen Science Teacher; *b:* Smithville, MO; *ed:* (BS) Ed, Univ MO Columbia 1978; (MA) Ed/Curr/Instruction/Sci, Univ of MO Kansas City 1988; *cr:* Sci Teacher Pierson Jr HS 1978-; *ai:* Frosh Vlybl Coach; Sci Olympiad; Recycling Prgm Spon; NSTA, KS Natl Ed Assn, KS Assn Teachers of Sci; Natl Fed Interscholastic Coaches Assn, Wilderness Society, ASCD; Outstanding Jr HS Sci Teacher Sigma Xi Kansas City 1982; Excl in Teaching Nom Kansas City Learning Exch 1985, 1987, 1990; *office:* Pierson Jr HS 1800 S 55th St Kansas City KS 66106

HELVICK, LINDA A., Phys Ed Teacher/Dept Chairman; *b:* Sacramento, CA; *c:* Dana L.; *ed:* (BA) Phys Ed, Chico St 1969; Addl Studies Early Chldhd Ed; *cr:* Spec Ed Teacher 1976-78; Phys Ed Teacher 1977 Woodland Sch Dist; *ai:* Coaching Bsktbl 9th Grade Girls; Dept Chm Phys Ed Dept; CTA; NEA; CA Girls St 1960; Press Room City Cnslr; Chief Counslr 1988-; Teacher of Yr Dist Wide 1980; Teacher of Yr Church of Jesus Christ of Latter Day Saints 1989; *office:* Lee Jr H S 520 West St Woodland CA 95695

HELWICK, VIRGINIA DARE, Fourth Grade Teacher; *b:* Oak Creek, CO; *c:* Jamie, Christopher; *ed:* (BA) Elem Ed, Univ of N CO 1967; Math Instruction; Whole Lang Writing Process; Working Toward Masters Rdng; Critical Thinking Skills; *cr:* 5th/6th Grade Teacher Clayton Elem 1967-70; 3rd-5th Grade Teacher Brentwood Elem 1970-75; 6th/7th Grade Teacher Brentwood Mid Sch 1975-77; 4th/5th Grade Teacher Cameron Elem 1977-; *ai:* Sci Textbook Selection Comm; Thinking Skills Curr Dev; Reprioritize Dist Math Outcomes Comm; Delta Kappa Gamma 1977-; Alpha Delta Kappa 1974-88; PEO Guard 1978-; Greeley Chrstn Church (Pianist, Organist) 1970-; *home:* 2703 61st Ave Greeley CO 80634

HEMBY, SARAH DICKENS, 8th Gr Math/Pre-Algbra Teacher; *b:* Monroe, NC; *m:* Timothy A.; *c:* Meredith, Jessica; *ed:* Elem Ed, ASU 1973-74; Intermediate Ed, UNC Charlotte 1975; *cr:* Teacher East Union Mid Sch 1973-80, Sun Valley Mid Sch 1980-; *ai:* 8th Grade Chairperson; Sch Volunteer Prgm Coor; NCTM Outstanding Math Teacher Union Cty 1989; Teacher of Yr Sun Valley Mid; Jaycee Outstanding Young Ed Awd; *office:* Sun Valley Mid Sch 1409 Wesley Chapel Rd Matthews NC 28105

HEMER, NANCY PEARSON, 4th Grade Teacher; *b:* Greenville, OH; *m:* Peter Fremont; *c:* Jeffrey, Pam Walpole, David, Christopher; *ed:* (BA) Elem Ed, Wright St Univ 1976; Numerous Courses Lang Art, Problem Solving, Behavior Management; *cr:* 4th Grade Teacher Ansonia Elem 1976-; *ai:* Young Authors; Task Force; Spelling Bee; Lang Art; Rdng & Testing Comm; NCA; Phi Delta Kappa 1989-; NEA, WOEA 1976-; Anthony Wayne MR-DD Bd Mem 1990; Martha Holding Jennings Scholar; *home:* 236 Oakwood Greenville OH 45331

HEMLER, DEBRA A., Science Department Chair; *b:* Gettysburg, PA; *m:* Dale W. Wilson Jr.; *ed:* (BS) Bio, Northland Coll 1981; (MS) Wildlife Management, WV Univ 1989; Grad Stud Teaching Cert; *cr:* Teacher/Sci Dept Chairperson Bruceton HS 1987-; *ai:* Sr Spon; Sci Fair Coord; Wildlife Society; WV Teachers Assn; Wildlife Management Inst; Article Published 1983; *office:* Bruceton HS PO Box 106 Bruceton Mills WV 26525

HEMMERICH, CAROL JEAN, 7th/8th Grade English Teacher; *b:* St Henry, OH; *m:* Gary; *c:* Kevin, Krisann; *ed:* (BS) Elem Ed, Univ of Dayton 1966; *cr:* 4th Grade Teacher St Christopher 1963-64; 5th Grade Teacher Queen of Angels 1964-65; 6th Grade Teacher St James 1965-66; 2nd/3rd Grade Teacher Coldwater 1966-71; 6th-8th Grade Lang Art Teacher Ansonia Local 1971-; *ai:* Stu Cncl Adv; Staff Dev Comm; OH Ed Assn; Beta Sigma Phi (VP 1979-80, Pres 1980-81), Mem of Yr 1981; *home:* 9974 St Rt 118 Ansonia OH 45303

HEMMERLY, AUDREY SWITZER, Language Arts Teacher; *b:* Forest, OH; *m:* Henry Ohlin; *c:* Jona E. Hemmerly Kleman, Todd Switzer; *ed:* (BS) Elem Ed, OH Northern Univ 1964; (MS) Ed, Bowling Green St Univ 1976; *cr:* Jr HS Lang Art Teacher Riverdale Local Schls 1960-; *ai:* NEA, OH Ed Assn 1960-; Riverdale Ed Assn Pres 1984-85; Delta Kappa Gamma 1977-; Progress Literary Club (Pres 1976-77) 1971-; Riverdale Teacher of Yr 1979-80; *home:* 508 S Patterson St FOREST OH 45843

HEMOND, DIANE ROBITAILLE, Social Studies Chair; *b:* Woonsocket, RI; *m:* Dennis Gerard; *c:* Joni A., Elizabeth D., Katherine L.; *ed:* (BA) Soc Sci/Scndry Ed, RI Coll 1975; Law Related Classes, Taft Inst & Univ of UT 1989; Alcohol, Tobacco & Drug Prevention Class, Brigham Young Univ; *cr:* Soc Stud Teacher Blackstone-Millville Regional Jr/Sr HS 1978-81; Soc Stud Teacher/Dept Chairperson Orem HS 1981-; *ai:* Yrbk Adv 1982-; Mock Congressional Hearings on the Constitution Coach 1987-; AAUW 1986-; PTSA (Teacher, VP) 1982-; 1st Place Awd for Yrbk, Columbia Scholastic Press Assn 1988-89, 1st Place St Competition of Natl Competition on Constitution & The Bill of Rights, Will Compete at Natl Level in Washington, DC 1990.

HEMPEL, JAMES A., Latin Teacher; *b:* Cincinnati, OH; *ed:* (BA) Classics, Univ of Cincinnati 1960; Grad Stud Guidance & Counseling, Rdng, Psych Summers 1963-67, 1973, 1986; *cr:* Latin/Eng Teacher Oregon HS 1963-65; Latin Teacher Butler HS 1965-; *ai:* OH Classical Conference Cncl (Mem 1979-81) 1970-; Amer Classical League 1970-; Vergilian Society 1975-; Hildesheim Vase Awd by OH Clascical Conference for Outstanding Latin Prgm 1978; Stipend Latin Wkshp to Dev Rdng Materials OSU 1970; Montgomery Cty Excl Teaching Awd Finalist 1988; Delivered Paper at OH Classical Conference 1979; *office:* Butler HS 600 S Dixie Dr Vandalia OH 45377

HEMPEL, JUDITH GILMORE, Second Grade Teacher; *b:* Painesville, OH; *m:* Henry Max Sr.; *ed:* (BS) Elem Ed, Kent St Univ 1966; *cr:* 6th Grade Teacher Harvard Elem 1968-69; 1st/4th Grade Teacher Campbell Elem 1969-82; 1st/2nd Grade Teacher Bradenton Acad 1985-88; 2nd Grade Teacher Osborne Elem 1990; *ai:* Sandusky Ed Assn 1969-82; OH Ed Assn, NEA 1966-73; Delta Kappa Gamma 1978-82; Coll Womens Club 1972-82; Providence Womens Assn 1977-82; Womens Civic Club 1975-82; *home:* 214 46th St Sandusky OH 44870

HEMPSTEAD, LINDA R., French Teacher; *b:* Salem, OH; *ed:* (BA) Fr, Mt Union Coll 1970; (MS) Scndry Admin, Youngstown St Univ 1980; Univ DE Bordeaux France, Fr Summer Inst, Univ of N IA; Course Work At Kent St Univ, Coll of Mt St Joseph, John Carroll Univ; *cr:* Fr Teacher Beaver Local Schls 1970-71, Marlington Local Schls 1972-; *ai:* Adv to Fr Club; Teacher Cnslr to Amer Cncl Intnl Stud; Mem Stark Cty Foreign Lang Comm; Phi Delta Kappa; Delta Kappa Gamma Secy 1988-; OH Foreign Lang Teachers; Rotary Club of Sebring RI; Jennings Scholar 1982; Finalist Stark Cty Teacher of Yr 1988; Marlington HS Teacher of Yr 1989; Rotary Fnd Grad Fellowship 1971; Fr Canadian Inst for Lang & Culture 1989; Leona Glenn Awd 1990; *office:* Marlington HS 10450 Moulini Ave NE Alliance OH 44601

HEMSCHIK, TERRY KAHLERT, Reading Teacher/G T Coord; *b:* Scarsdale, NY; *m:* Wolfgang R. W.; *c:* Robert A., Holly K.; *ed:* (BS) Elem Ed, Kent St Univ 1968; (MS) Ed/Rdng, Univ of WI Whitewater 1980; Grad Stud; *cr:* 6th Grade Teacher Riverside Elem 1968-69, Concord Elem 1969-72; Rdng Teacher/Gifted Talented Coord Kettle Moraine Mid Sch 1977-; *ai:* Forensic Team Coach; Stu Senate Adv; Phi Delta Kappa 1990; Amer Field Service (Pres 1981-83) 1979-88; Church Cncl Secy 1988-; *office:* Kettle Moraine Mid Sch 301 E Ottawa Ave Dousman WI 53118

HENARD, JOHN C., Social Studies Teacher; *b:* Rockford, IL; *m:* Francine R.; *c:* Kristin, Kevin; *ed:* (BA) His, 1959, (MSE) Ed/Admin 1965 N IL Univ; Sch Admin, North IL Univ; Univ of TX Dallas; *cr:* 7th Grade Teacher Kinnikinnick Elem 1959-63; His Teacher Marsh Schl 1963-67; Supt Manchester Elem Dist 1967-68; Asst Regional Supt Boone Cty Regional Office of Ed 1968-75; Winnebago Cty Regional Office of Ed 1975-81; Soc Stud/His Teacher Longfellow Acad 1984-; *ai:* Phi Delta Kappa Pres Local Chapter 1975-76; Classroom Teachers of Dallas Poly Action Chm; Natl Endowment Hum Fellowship US Constitution 1987; Mentor Teacher Dallas Ind Sch Dist 1990; *home:* 5310 Keller Springs Rd 122 Dallas TX 75248

HENCKEL, GEORGE LEE, Reading/Language Arts Teacher; *b:* Elkton, MD; *m:* Wanda Lee Moore; *c:* Tami L. Henckel Goes, Travis L.; *ed:* (BA) Eng Lit, Washington Coll 1971; (MED) Admin/Supervision, W MD Coll 1976; Span, Human Dynamics, Univ of MD, Washington Coll; *cr:* Teacher Queen Annes Cty 1978-82; 7th/8th Grade Rdng/Eng/Soc Sci Teacher Sudlersville Mid Sch 1971-; Head Night Teacher Migrant Prgm 1983-; *ai:* Queen Annes Cty HS Ftbl Coach 1975-79; Sudlersville Mid Sch Budget Comm Chairperson; Sudlersville Mid Sch Prins Advisory, Outdoor Ed, Gifted-Talented Comms; MD Sch Performance Project Basic Key Teacher Cty Comm; Queen Annes Cty Ed Assn (2nd VP 1988-, Pres 1990); Sudlersville PTA Exec Comm Life Membership 1981; Queens Annes Cty Dept of Recreation & Parks (Teacher, Volunteer) 1971-; *office:* Sudlersville Mid Sch Church St Sudlersville MD 21668

HENCKEL, NANCY IRENE, Spanish Teacher; *b:* Salt Lake City, UT; *c:* Elissa; *ed:* (MA) Ed/Curr/Instruction, Boise St Univ 1990; *cr:* Span Teacher Lakeside HS 1970-72; Span/Eng Teacher Meridian Jr HS 1979-81; Span Teacher Meridian HS 1981-87, Centennial HS 1987-; *ai:* Centennial HS Intnl Club Spon; Amer Assn Teachers of Span & Portuguese 1975-89; *office:* Centennial HS 4600 E Mc Millian Rd Meridian ID 83642

HENDEL, MARC E., Mathematics Teacher; *b:* New London, CT; *m:* Linda Mae Fink; *ed:* (BA) Math, IA St Univ 1987; Working Towards Masters Math; Grad Level Dist Cmptr Seminar; *cr:* Math Teacher Valley HS 1988-; *ai:* Valley HS SADD Spon; CORE Intervention Team Mem; Teacher Group Asst Stu with Problems or Spec Needs Volunteer; Homecoming Act Comm; *office:* Valley HS 1140 35th St West Des Moines IA 50265

HENDERLY, ELAINE ANN, Jr HS Reading Teacher; *b:* Lancaster, OH; *m:* Terrence P. Daniels; *c:* Leah Henderly Daniels; *ed:* (BS) Elem Ed, OH St Univ 1980; Grad Work OH St Univ; *cr:* Eng/Lang Art Teacher 1980-84, Rdng Teacher 1984- Amanda-Clearcreek Local Sch System; *ai:* NEA, OH Ed Assn Mem 1980-; OH St Rdng Grant 1981; *office:* Amanda-Clearcreek Sch System 9096 Walnut St Stoutsville OH 43154

HENDERSON, BUCKNER L., Third Grade Teacher; *b:* Paris, KY; *m:* Cassandra Wright; *c:* Buckner II, Sebastian; *ed:* (BS) Early Chldhd Ed, 1977, (MS) Educl Admin, 1989 NC A&T St Univ; Air Data Cmptr Trng; Hotel & Motel Management Trng; NC Insurance Trng; *cr:* Asst Principal 1983-84, Teacher 1977- Elon Coll Elem; *ai:* Bsktbl Coaching; Stu Cncl & 5th Grade Boys Club Adv; PTA Pres 1988-89; Eng St Church of Christ Trustee 1980-; One Faith Musical Group 1985-, Mc Donald Carolina Gospel Fest 1st Place Winners 1990; Finalist Cty Teacher of Yr 1985; *office:* Elon Coll Elem Sch 510 E Haggard Ave Elon College NC 27244

HENDERSON, CANDEE FERRERA, Mathematics Teacher; *b:* Brooklyn, NY; *m:* Robert L. Sr.; *c:* Kristen, Robert Jr.; *ed:* (BA) Elem Ed, FL Atlantic Univ 1969; *cr:* 7th Grade Math Teacher Plantation Mid Sch 1969-73, 1976-77; 7th/8th Grade Math Teacher Douglass Mid Sch 1984-; *ai:* NEA 1969-73, 1985-; NCTM 1969-73, 1988-.

HENDERSON, CARL M., Business Ed/English Teacher; *b:* Franklin, PA; *m:* Florence Shotwell; *c:* Dianne Hicks, Brent; *ed:* (BS) Bus Ed, Anderson Univ 1957; (MED) Bus Ed, IN Univ of PA 1969; *cr:* Bank Teller Exchange Bank 1950-53; Bus Ed/Eng Teacher Garden City Schls 1956-57; Bus Ed Teacher Rocky Grove HS 1957-; *ai:* Drama Dir; Stage Mgr; FBLA Spon; NEA, PSEA; VGEA (Treas, Pres, Mem) 1956-; *office:* Rocky Grove HS 403 Rocky Grove Ave Franklin PA 16323

HENDERSON, CAROL JANE ROBERTS, Marketing Ed Instr/Coord; *b:* Harrison, AR; *m:* Steve L.; *c:* Cindy Redding, Tonya K., Mark S., Jon C.; *ed:* (BS) Voc Home Ec, 1958, (MBA) Real Estate/Mrktg, 1981 E NM Univ; Grad Stud Emphasis Cmptr Ed; Grad Realtor Inst; *cr:* Eng/Bus Instr ENMU-R 1968-70, 1979-83; Real Estate Broker Reliable Realtors 1973-; Eng Instr 1981-82, Implemented & Taught Voc Core 1982-83,

Mrktg Ed Instr Coord 1983- Goddard HS; *ai:* DECA Adv; Stu to St & Natl Career Dev Conferences Spon; NEA 1981-; Mrktg Ed, Voc Ed Assn 1983-; Local, St, Natl Assn of Realtors Ed Chairperson 1973-; Roswell Cmmty League Ways & Means Chairperson 1971-; Delta Kappa Gamma 1983-; 1st Chrstn Church Many Offices 1956-; Child Garden Kndgtn Chairperson Bd of Ed 1970-; *office:* Robert H Goodard HS 701 E Country Club Rd Roswell NM 88201

HENDERSON, FLORENCE BROWN, Teacher; *b:* New York, NY; *c:* Leslie D., Robert L.; *ed:* (BS) Health/Phys Ed, Fayetteville St Univ 1964; (MS) Phys Ed, N Central Univ 1970; (BA) Criminal Justice, Shaw Univ 1981; Soc Stud, Campbell Univ; *cr:* Teacher Johnsonville Sch 1964-65; Harnett HS 1965-70; Erwin HS 1970-75; Erwin Mid Sch 1975-; *ai:* NC Ed Assn; NEA; *office:* Erwin Mid Sch 301 S 10th St Erwin NC 28339

HENDERSON, JANET LOIS, Kindergarten Teacher; *b:* Limon, CO; *m:* Cloyce D.; *c:* Bradley D., Brenda L.; *ed:* (BA) Elem Ed, Univ of N CO 1964; (MA) Rdng, Univ of Colorado Springs 1989; Admin of Gesell Dev Screening; *cr:* 1st Grade Teacher Franklin Dist #11 1964-67; Kndgtn Teacher Ellicott Dist #22 1977-; *ai:* Designed Sch Readiness & Developmental Placement Prgm/All Day-Every Day Kndgtn Ellicott; Teach Super Saturday 6 Week Prgm Gifted Stu Univ of CO; Delta Kappa Gamma (Schlsp Comm 1978-87, Secy 1984-87); Ellicott Fire Dist (Pres 1988-, VP 1985-87); Galley Road Baptist 1970-; 4-H Project Leader 1977-85; Nom Governor of CO Excl in Ed Awd 1986; Presentor CO Assn Sch Bds Convention 1987, 1989; Ellicott Elem Perfect Attendance Awd; Article Published; *office:* Ellicott Elem Sch R R 2 Calhan CO 80808

HENDERSON, JOHN FRANKLIN, English Teacher; *b:* Terre Haute, IN; *m:* Ann Siebenmorgen; *c:* Adrianne, John, Allegra; *ed:* (BA) Eng, 1979, (MS) Ed, 1982 IN St Univ; *cr:* Teacher Gibault Sch for Boys 1979-80, N Vermillion HS 1979-; *ai:* Poetry & Travel Club; Gifted Comm; IN St Assn of Poets VP 1988-, Poet Awd 1989; Poetry Awds; Published Articles; St Recognition of Teaching Skills; *office:* N Vermillion HS RR 1 Cayuga IN 47928

HENDERSON, JOSIE RATLIFF, Jr HS Math & Reading Teacher; *b:* Lucedale, MS; *c:* Robert, Paul; *ed:* (BA) Elem Ed, Univ of MS 1958; MS St Univ, Spring Hill Coll, Auburn Univ, William Carey Coll; *cr:* Teacher Lake Charles LA 1958-59, Jonesboro AR 1968-70, Little Rock AR 1973-80, George Cty MS 1980-; *ai:* Stu Cncl & Chrldr Spon; Agricola Elem Sch 1980-, Teacher of Yr 1986-87; St Lucy Cath Church (Parish Cncl Secy 1986-89, CYU Adv 1986-89, For God & Youth 1988); *office:* Agricola Elem Sch P O Box 12 Lucedale MS 39452

HENDERSON, KAY EWING, Fourth Grade Teacher; *b:* Cincinnati, OH; *m:* Jesse Canter; *ed:* (AB) Elem Ed, Transylvania Un iv 1964; (MA) Elem Ed, Xavier Univ 1980; (Rank I) Supervision of Instruction; *cr:* Teacher Pendleton Cty Bd of Ed 1959-60, 1963-; *ai:* Curr Planning Comm; PTA; Pend Cty Ed Assn Pres; Alex Church of Christ Pres 1986-89, Lady of Yr 1989; *home:* RR 2 410 Johns Rd Butler KY 41006

HENDERSON, LINDA LEE (TURNER), 8th Grade Language Art Teacher; *b:* Streator, IL; *m:* James D.; *c:* Robert, Jaime; *ed:* (BA) Eng, Simpson Coll 1971; IA Writing Project, Cooperative Learning Cadre; *cr:* 7th Grade Eng Techer Clinch Cty Jr HS 1971-72; 8th Grade Lang Art Teacher 1972-79, 1982- Shenandoah Mid Sch; *ai:* IA Teachers of Eng Western Region (Secy, Treas) 1989-; IA Cncl Teachers of Eng; Northboro IA Centennial Comm Chairperson 1979-81; *office:* Shenandoah Mid Sch Center & Univerisity Shenandoah IA 51601

HENDERSON, MARY PUGH, Third Grade Teacher; *b:* Volney, VA; *m:* Breece Jessie; *c:* Lynn Burcham, Debra Caudell, Julia Combs; *ed:* (BS) Elem Ed, Radford Univ 1974, (Ms) Elem Ed, Radford Univ; *cr:* Teacher Grayson Cty Schls 1974-; *ai:* Grayson Cty Ed Assn 1980-; Blue Ridge Chapel; Baptist Church Teacher 1987-; *home:* Rt 3 Box 427 Galax VA 24333

HENDERSON, NANCY CHILTON, Home Economics Dept Chair; *b:* Harlingen, TX; *m:* Jefferson S. II; *c:* Jeff S. III, Alice Henderson Hall; *ed:* (BS) Home Ec, Univ of TX 1954; Grad Stud VA Tech, Univ of Va, James Madison Univ; *cr:* Home Ec Teacher Bandera HS 1954-56, Fulmore Jr HS 1956-59, West Spring HS 1967-71; Home Ec Dept Chairperson Robinson Scndry 1971-; *ai:* Stu Government, FHA Spon; Natl Bd of Dir Chairperson; AKT, BA Pres 1980-82; AVA, VVA, VHETA, NEA, VEA, FEA, AHEA, VHEA; FCHTA Pres 1976; Meth Church (Chairperson Local Cncl & Dist Cncl, Conference Youth Cncl); *office:* Robinson Scndry Sch 5035 Sideburn Road Fairfax VA 22032

HENDERSON, NELL AULTMAN, 5th Grade Teacher; *b:* Hattiesburg, MS; *m:* Frank; *c:* Kristi, Kerri, Matthew; *ed:* (BS) Eng/Elem Ed, Univ of S MS 1976; (MS) Elem Ed, William Care Coll 1981; *cr:* Teacher Sumrall Elem Sch 1976-; *ai:* Staff Dev Comm; Delta Kappa Gamma Secy 1988-; MS Assn Educators Building Rep 1985-; Teacher of Yr 1988.

HENDERSON, PATRICK M., Agriculture Teacher; *b:* Memphis, TN; *m:* Mary Jane; *c:* Beth, Joy; *ed:* (BS) Agriculture Ec, 1968, (MA) 1973 Agriculture Ed, Univ of KY; (Rank I) Voc Admin, W KY Univ 1980; *cr:* Voc Ag Teacher Hart Cty HS 1969-72, Breckinridge Cty HS 1972-; *ai:* FFA Adv; KY Voc Ag Teachers Assn (Secy 1974-75, Treas 1988-, Mem 1972-), Outstanding Young Teacher 1972, Outstanding Prog 1987; KVA; KY Assn Cons Dist Local Chm St Bd; Democrat Exec Comm Chm, Breck Cty Fair Livestock Chm; *office:* Breckenridge Cty HS R 1 Box 130 Harned KY 40144

HENDERSON, RICHARD SCOTT, Interim Assistant Principal; *b:* Baltimore, MD; *m:* Deborah Ann Haines; *c:* Jessica L., Brendon H.; *ed:* (BED) Ed/Bio, Univ of Miami 1978; (MS) Sci/Educl Leadership, Nova Univ 1990; Certified as Sun Coast Area Teacher Trng Honors Prgm; Clinical Teacher Univ of S FL 1987; *cr:* Sci Teacher 1980-, Sci Dept Chm 1988-, Interim Asst Prin/Advanced Technologies Magnet Prgm Instr 1990 Lakewood Sr HS; *ai:* Chairperson Tardy/Attendance Comm; Participant in Dist Stu Research Pilot Prgm; Pinellas Cty Sci Teachers Assn (Mem 1980-, Pres Elect 1989-, Pres 1990), Outstanding Sci Educator of Yr 1988; Pinellas Classroom Teachers Assn Dist V Dir 1987-89; NEA Mem 1981-; ASCD, FL Assn of Sci Teachers Mem 1989-; NSTA Mem 1990; Article Published FL Conservation News 1986; Co-Authored Bio Laboratory Safety Curr Pinellas Cty 1988; *office:* Lakewood Sr HS 1400 54th Ave S Saint Petersburg FL 33705

HENDERSON, ROBERT F., French/English Teacher; *b:* Columbus, OH; *m:* Pamela Watkins; *c:* Brian, Katy; *ed:* (BSC) Fr Ed, 1967, (MA) Fr Ed, 1969 OH St Univ; Fr, NDEA Lang Inst; Guidance/Counseling, OH St; Cert Cooperative Learning Seminar; *cr:* Fr/Eng Teacher Amanda-Clear Creek HS 1967-70, W Muskingum HS 1970-; *ai:* Asst Ftbl Coach; Stu Cncl Adv; Effective Schls Comm; Phi Delta Kappa 1987-; ASCD 1989-; OH Modern Lang Teachers Assn 1972-; Effective Schls Grant OH Dept of Ed; Advanced Trng Cooperative Learning; *office:* W Muskingum HS 200 Kimes Rd Zanesville OH 43701

HENDERSON, ROBERT G., Science Teacher; *b:* Butte, MT; *m:* Julia J.; *c:* Jenny, Anna, Bobby, Josh; *ed:* (BA) General Sci, WMC 1981; U M Missoulia MT; MT Tech Butte; *cr:* Sci Teacher Lincoln Cty HS 1981-; *ai:* Head Wrestling & Asst Ftbl Coach; *home:* 532 Spring St Eureka MT 59917

HENDERSON, RONALD W., Chemistry Teacher; *b:* De Ridder, LA; *m:* Lynne C.; *c:* Chad E., Brent L.; *ed:* (BS) Bio Ed, 1970, (MED) Admin Scndry Schls, 1974 Northwestern St Univ; *cr:* Teacher Southwood HS 1971-; *ai:* Sci Chm; Chemquest Spon; APEL; LA Acad of Sci; Amer Legion; *office:* Southwood HS 9000 Walker Rd Shreveport LA 71118

HENDERSON, RUSSELL GENE, Social Studies Teacher; *b:* Oxford, England; *m:* Janie Marcum; *c:* Brian, Megan; *ed:* (BSED) Soc Sci, Columbus Coll 1983; *cr:* Soc Stud Teacher Harris Cty HS 1985-; *ai:* Asst Var Bsbl, Head Jr Var, Jr Var Ftbl Coach; NEA, GA Athletic Coaches Assn 1987-.

HENDERSON, SHIRLEY COMUS, English Department Chairman; *b:* Baltimore, MD; *m:* James D. Jr.; *ed:* (BA) Eng, Univ of AL Huntsville 1970; (MA) Eng/Scndry Ed, AL A&M Univ 1988; *cr:* English/Advanced Placement Eng Teacher Lee HS 1970-; Instr Calhoun Comm Coll 1988-; *ai:* Academic Coach Scholars Bowl Team; NHS Spon; NCTE, NEA, ASCD, AL Ed Assn, Huntsville Ed Assn, AL Scholastic Competition Assn; Alpha Delta Kappa Corresponding Secy 1978-; Freedom Fnd of Valley Forge Natl Awd for Excl in Ed George Washington Awd; Nom Hunstville City Schls AL Teacher Hall of Fame 1986, 1988; *office:* Lee HS 606 Forrest Cir Huntsville AL 35811

HENDERSON, STEVEN BRENT, Biology Teacher; *b:* Oklahoma City, OK; *m:* Julie Irene; *ed:* (BS) Biomedical Sci, 1984, (MS) Curr/Instruction Ed, 1984 OK St Univ; *cr:* Lab/Botany Instr 1985, Lab/Zoology Instr, 1987 OK St Univ; Bio Teacher Wichita Falls HS 1987-88, S H Rider HS 1988-; *ai:* Key Club Spon; UIL Sci Tutor; TX Prof Educators Assn 1987-; Explorer Post 1957 Adv 1988-; Outstanding Young Men of America 1989; *office:* S H Rider HS 4611 Cypress Ave Wichita Falls TX 76310

HENDERSON, WANDA (PHILLIPS), 2nd Grade Teacher; *b:* Los Angeles, CA; *m:* Mark Edward; *c:* Teresa, Valerie, Maranda; *ed:* (BA) Eng, CA St Northridge 1982; Grad Stud Rehabiliation Cnslr & Peer Cnslr; *cr:* Cnslr Dept of Rehabilitation 1982-83; EDD Initial Claims Adj St of CA Employment Dev Dept 1983-86; Teacher Normandie Chrstn Sch 1986-; *ai:* Convalescent Homes Comm Mem; Athletic Coach & Spon of Low Income Stus; Electrical Contractor Union & License Owner 1987-; Church of Christ (Sunday Sch, Wednesday Sch, 3-5 Yr Old Bible Class Teacher); *home:* 5302 St Andrews Pl Los Angeles CA 90062

HENDERSON, WILLIAM RON, Teacher; *b:* Atlanta, GA; *c:* Abbie, Beth; *ed:* (BA) His, 1968, (MA) Mid Grades, 1975 N GA Coll; Sociology, Univ of TN 1968-70; *cr:* 8th Grade Teacher Oak Grove Elem 1970-72, Free Home Elem 1972-86, Dean Rusk Mid Sch 1986-88; *ai:* Bsktbl, Ftbl, Track Coach; Honor Club, Stu Cncl Spon; Comm Head Various PTA Function; Cty Sch Supt Advisory Comm; PTA Pres 1984-85; GA Assn of Educators 1975-83; Prof Assn of GA Educators 1983-88; Kiwanis Club of Canton 1987-89; Holbrook Campground Volunteer Fire Dept 1980-85; Dean Rusk Mid Sch Teacher of Yr 1987-88; *office:*

HENDRICKS, ANNA BELLE HASLEY, Eighth Grade English Teacher; *b:* Ignacio, CO; *c:* Sharron Torres, Gail Umbenhour, Weldon; *ed:* (BA) Hum, Ft Lewis Coll 1970; Eng/Spec Ed, Western Univ; Spec Ed, Adams St; Eng, Univ of CO; Journalism, Univ of KS; *cr:* 6th-8th Grade Eng/Soc Stud/Lang Art Teacher Shiprock Jr HS 1970-78; 6th-9th Grade Eng/Creative Writing Teacher Tse Bit ai Jr HS 1979-; *ai:* Stu Cncl Adv; Knowledge Bowl Spon; Scripts Howard Spelling Bee Coord; Illustrated Booklet of Stu Writing Cooperation with Art Dept; CCEA, NEA Treas 1974-82, 5 Yr Awds 1976, 1981, 1986; NM Soc Stud 1977-; NM Teachers of Eng 1973-; Phi Sigma Alpha (Treas 1964-70, Pres 1970-75), Woman of Yr 1971-73; Natl Teachers of Eng Convention Eng Teachers Spokesperson 1977; *office:* Tse Bit ai Mid Sch P O Box 1873 Shiprock NM 87420

HENDRICKS, BILL L., Math Teacher/Chairperson; *b:* Gary, IN; *m:* Sue; *c:* William, Marc, Michael; *ed:* (BA) Scndry Ed, 1966, (MA) Scndry Ed, 1967 W NM Univ; Continuing Ed, CO St Univ; *cr:* Lab Sch Asst Prin W NM Univ 1967-69; Math Teacher Ft Lupton HS 1972-75, John Dewey Jr HS 1976-; *ai:* Bsktbl Coach; Math Chairperson 1976-; NCTM 1976-; CO Cncl Teachers of Math 1972-; Mapleton Sch Dist Teacher of Yr Awd 1985; *office:* John Dewey Jr HS 7480 Conifer Rd Denver CO 80221

HENDRICKS, CORA LEE, 1st Grade Teacher; *b:* Pocatello, ID; *m:* Brian James; *c:* Brian J. II, Todd J., Berk J.; *ed:* (BA) Elem Ed, ID St Univ 1970; *cr:* 1st Grade Teacher Washington Elem 1970-71; 3rd Grade Teacher Bonneville Elem 1971-73; Kndgtn Teacher 1978-87, 1st Grade Teacher 1987- Thurkill Elem; *ai:* Cub Scout Leader; Young Womans Teacher; IEA, NEA 1970-; SSEA Building Rep 1988-89; PTO Comm Rep; Church (Teacher, Womans & Primary Presidencies); Easter Seals Drive Rep; Pocatello Teacher of Yr 1972; *office:* Thirkill Elem Sch 60 E 4th S Soda Springs ID 83276

HENDRICKS, ELLEN JEAN, 6th-8th Grade Art Teacher; *b:* Bloomington, IL; *m:* Byron Wayne; *ed:* (BS) Art Ed, NE MO St Univ 1967; (MA) Studio Batik, Lindenwood IV 1980; Art His, Fiber Art, Ed; *cr:* 7th-9th Grade Teacher Ferguson-Florissant Sch Dist 1967-68, 1970-74; 4th-8th Grade Teacher Wentzville R-IV Sch Dist 1974-80; *ai:* Just Say No Co-Spon; MO St Teachers Assn 1988-; MO Mid Sch Assn 1985-; MO Mid Sch Conference Comm 1986-88; Wentzville Mid Sch Teacher of Yr 1987 & 1988; *office:* Wentzville Mid Sch 600 Campus Dr Wentzville MO 63385

HENDRICKS, LOUANN DE WELL, Spanish/French Teacher; *b:* Gary, IN; *m:* Steven L.; *ed:* (BS) Span/Fr, De Pauw Univ 1971; (MA) Span, Purdue Univ 1983; Grad Stud Fr, Purdue Univ 1985, 1986, Univ of Angers France 1987, 1988; *cr:* Span/Fr Teacher Northfield HS 1971-73, Oakhill HS 1984-; *ai:* Span & Fr Clubs; Amer Assn Teachers of Span & Portuguese 1971-; AATF 1984-; Amer Mensa 1981-; Natl Endowment for Hum Fr Grant 1985; *office:* Oak Hill HS 7756 W Delphi Pike 27 Converse IN 46919

HENDRICKS, NINA TURMAN, English Teacher; *b:* Atlantic City, NJ; *m:* Wayne; *c:* Erinn, Kyle; *ed:* (BA) Eng Ed, Trenton St Coll 1972; Grad Stud Career Ed, Curr & Classroom Management; *cr:* Substitute Teacher Woodbine Elem Sch 1971; Eng Teacher Bridgeton Jr HS 1972-80, Bridgeton Sr HS 1980-; *ai:* Faculty Advisory, Stu Review Assessment, Black His Comm; Gifted & Talented Teacher Prgm; Cognetics Asst Coach; Mentor Teacher & Cert Comm Mem for Alternate Route Cert; Bridgeton Ed Assn Exec Comm Mem 1976-83; NJ Ed Assn (Uni-Serv Mem 1975-77) 1972-; NJ Assn of Black Educators 1986-; Millville PTA 1983-; Governors Recognition Awd 1988; *office:* Bridgeton HS West Ave Bridgeton NJ 08302

HENDRICKS, WILLIS AILEEN FARMER, Fifth Grade Teacher; *b:* Charleston, MO; *m:* Charles A.; *c:* C. Theodore, Randall E., Peggy Mossbarger, Scott A., Nathan B.; *ed:* (BS) Elem Ed, Miami Univ of OH 1971; Grad Stud; *cr:* 5th Grade Teacher Hopewell Elem 1971-; *ai:* NEA, OEA, LEA 1971-; Crestview Presbyn Church (Elder, Deacon, Teacher); Martha Holden Jennings Awd; *home:* 8336 Darlene Dr West Chester OH 45069

HENDRICKSON, CURTIS LOUIE, Third Grade Teacher; *b:* Quiring Twnshp, MN; *m:* Elizabeth A. Fuglestad; *c:* Micah, Josiah; *ed:* (AA) Gen Ed, Rainy River Jr Coll 1970; (BS) Elem Ed, Bemidji ST Univ 1976; Addl Studies Forestry Technician Univ of MN Forestry Technician Station 1974; *cr:* Substitute Teacher Intnl Falls, Littlefork and Indus Sch 1976-78; 3rd Grade Teacher Kelliher Public Sch Dist #36 1978-; *ai:* Bemidji Karate Club 1981-85, Black Belt 1984; First Baptist Church Sunday Sch Superintendent/Teacher 1976-; Writer for Complete Math Curr for Grades K-12 at Kelliher Public Sch; *office:* Kelliher Public Sch Dist 36 P O Box 259 Kelliher MN 56650

HENDRICKSON, JEAN PARTO, English & Reading Teacher; *b:* Fairmont, WV; *c:* Sandra; *ed:* (BS) Eng/Span, WV Univ 1962; Rdng Courses; *cr:* Span/Eng Teacher Ashland Jr/Sr HS 1962-64, Western Reserve HS 1964-70; Eng Teacher Lucas Schls 1970-; *ai:* Academic Challenge Coach; NEA, OH Educl Assn 1970-; LTA Building Rep 1986-.

HENDRICKSON, LYNNE NICHOLS, 2nd Grade Teacher; *b:* St Paul, MN; *m:* Dale A.; *c:* Mary Beth, Robert, Laurie; *ed:* (BA) His, Elem Ed, Mac Alester Coll 67; (MED) Elem Ed, Univ of MN 1986; *cr:* 2nd Grade Teacher Hale Elem Sch 86-; 3rd/4th Grade Teacher Hiawatha Elem Sch 1967-82; 4th Grade Teacher Hans C Andersen Elem Sch 1982-84; *ai:* Lang Art Comm Rep 1986-88; Bldg Advisory Cncl Co-Chm; MN Ed EffectiveNess Prgm Team Mem; Health Ed Learner Outcome Comm St Dept of MN; Health Ed Spring Health Conference Planning Comm St Dept of Ed; MFT/AFT 1970-; City of Mpls Ed Assn Bldg Rep 1967-70; PTA Teacher Rep 1967-; Minnehaha United Church of Christ (Sunday Sch Teacher 1980-89; Moderator 1983-85; Financial Secy 85-); Dir of Community Ed Prgrm Hiawatha Sch 1972-74; *office:* Hale Elem Sch 1220 E 54 St Minneapolis MN 55417

HENDRICKSON, PATRICIA (ROACH), English Teacher; *b:* Tahlequah, OK; *m:* Henry C.; *c:* Amber; *ed:* (BA) Eng/Speech, NE OK St Univ 1976; Curr Dev & Journalism; *cr:* 7th/8th Grade Eng Teacher Baxter Springs Public Schls 1976-77; 10th-12th Grade Eng Teacher Chilocco Indian Sch 1977-80; 9th-12th Grade Eng/Journalism Teacher Sherman Indian Sch 1980-86; 9th-10th Grade Eng Teacher Meeker Public Schls 1986-; *ai:* Jr & Sr Class Spon; Sigma Tau Delta (Pres, Mem) 1974-76; Whos Who in Amer Coll & Univ 1976; *office:* Meeker HS 214 E Main St PO Box 68 Meeker OK 74855

HENDRICKSON, ROBERT DEAN, Science Teacher; *b:* Tulare, CA; *m:* Jenean A.; *c:* Hilary, Kelsey; *ed:* (AS) Sci, Rogers St Coll 1982; (BS) Bio, Northeastern St Univ 1985; *cr:* Teacher Foyil Public Schls 1985-; *ai:* Academic Coach; Gifted Comm; Sci Dept Chm; OEA Mem 1985-; NEA Mem 1985-; Fact VP 1986-87; Teacher of Year 1988; *office:* Foyil Sch PO Box 49 Foyil OK 74031

HENDRIX, BEASEY SAMUEL, III, Developmental Guidance; *b:* Tuscaloosa, AL; *ed:* (BA) Comm, Univ of AL 1982; (MA) Psych, W GA Coll 1989; Lions Quest Skills for Adolescence; USA Wrestling Silver & Bronze Level Coaching Cert; *cr:* 8th Grade His Teacher Troup Jr HS 1982-86; His/Enrichment Teacher 1986-89, Developmental Guidance Teacher 1989- Whitesville Road Mid Sch; *ai:* Head Coach Troup Cty HS, Whatesville Road Mid Sch Cross Cntry, Mid Sch Wrestling; Asst Coach HS Wrestling; Troup Cty Human Resource, Media Comm Mem; GA Athletic Coaches Assn, GA HS Assn 1982-; USA Wrestling (AL St Chm 1980-81) 1975-88; MENSA 1986-; Natl Asst Wrestling Coach of Yr 1986; GA Coaches Region Coach of Yr Boys Cross Cntry 1986-89, Girls Cross Cntry 1988-89; Articles Published in Magazines; Edited & Produced Video; *home:* P O Box 3003 La Grange GA 30241

HENDRIX, MARGO WARD, Principal; *b:* Chester, MT; *m:* Roland M.; *c:* Nicole Bronec, Luke; *ed:* (BS) Elem Ed, W MT Coll; (MED) Ed Ad/Higher Ed, Univ of NV Reno 1981; *cr:* Teacher Outlook Elem 1960-62, Libby Elem 1962-63, Myrtle Creek Elem 1963-64, North Star Sch 1964-66; Teacher 1966-86, Prof Staff Trainer 1986-89 Humboldt Cty Schls; *ai:* Humboldt Cty Teachers Assn Pres 1978-79, Teacher of Yr 1986; Natl Staff Dev Cncl, Assn for Staff & Curr Dev 1986-; *office:* Grass Valley Sch 6465 Grass Valley Winnemucca NV 89445

HENDRIX, SALLY SLUSHER, Art Teacher; *b:* Radford, VA; *m:* Philip Taylor; *c:* Heidi; *ed:* (BS) Art, 1971, (MS) Art Ed, 1972 Radford Coll; *cr:* Art Teacher Dublin HS 1972-74, Radford HS 1974-; *ai:* Art Club Spon; Phi Delta Kappa 1975-; VA Commission for Arts (Advisory Comm Chm 1981-83) 1979-84; *office:* Radford HS 50 Dalton Dr Radford VA 24141

HENDRYX, PHYLLIS J. (ROTH), 2nd Grade Teacher; *b:* Cleveland, OH; *m:* Wilbur H.; *c:* Louise Walton, David R., Norma Polansky, Bruce D., Paula V.; *ed:* (BSED) Geography/Elem Ed, Flora Stone Mather Coll & Western Reserve Univ 1950; (MS) Elem Admin, Youngstown St Univ 1970; *cr:* Teacher Cleveland Elem Schls 1950-52, US Dependent Schls Germany 1952-53, Cleveland Elem Schls 1953-59, Joseph Badger Schls 1966-; *ai:* Badger Ed Assn (Treas, Pres, Building Rep, Mem 1968-); NE OH Ed Assn Consumer Affairs Comm Mem; Bus & Prof Women 1969-; *office:* Hartford Elem Sch St Rt 7 & 305 Hartford OH 44424

HENDRYX, WENDY GLASSNER, Guidance Counselor; *b:* Racine, WI; *c:* Katelyn; *ed:* (BS) Psych/Sociology, IN Univ of PA 1974; (MED) Counseling Psych, Boston Univ 1978; *cr:* Drug Treatment Spec Dir Cambridge Hospital/Somerville Mental Health 1979-81; Psychotherapist Lakes Region Family Services 1981-86; Mental Health Consultant Headstart 1982-86; Guidance Cnslr Spaulding HS 1986-; Lecturer Psych Lecturer Plymouth St Coll 1987-; *ai:* Substance Abuse Counseling; Coll & Financial Aid Seminars; Schlsp Comm; Child Abuse Team; New Stu Orientation; NH Assn for Counseling & Dev 1987-; *home:* RFD 1 Box 1837 Stone Rd Gilmanton I W NH 03837

HENGELFELT, DELORES HARLESS, Third Grade Teacher; *b:* Stromsburg, NE; *m:* Laird L.; *c:* Rodney, June; *ed:* (BS) Elem Ed, Midland Luth Coll 1966; (MA) Classroom Teaching, Concordia Teachers Coll 1974; Post Masters Stud; *cr:* Teacher Rural Polk Cty Schls 1947-54, Stromsburg Public Schls 1954-; *ai:* NE St Ed Assn 1965-; NEA 1990; Stromsburg Ed Assn; *home:* 903 E 7th St Stromsburg NE 68666

HENIKMAN, ROBERT HAROLD, Jr High Art Teacher; *b:* Cleveland, OH; *m:* Mary T. Laudick; *c:* Kelley, Robert Jr., John; *ed:* (BS) Scndry Ed/Art, Bowling Green Univ 1972; (MA) Scndry Supervision, 1982, (MA) Scndry Admin, 1985 Ashland Coll; Drug/Alcohol Abuse Prgm Cmmty Interaction Gifted Ed; *cr:* Stu Teacher Mentor HS 1971; Project-Interaction Teacher Toledo Scott HS 1971; Art Educator Ashland Jr HS 1972-; *ai:* Head Coed Swimming & Diving, Head Jr HS Girls Track Coach; Ashland City Teacher Assn 1972-; OH Ed Assn 1972-; Ashland YMCA Bd Mem 1985-87; Curr Writing 7th-8th Grade Art Prgm Speaker for Art Gifted Wkshps; *office:* Ashland Jr H S 345 Cottage St Ashland OH 44805

HENK, MARY TIDWELL, 7th Grade Lang Art Teacher; *b:* Austin, TX; *m:* Wilfred; *c:* David, John, Jimmy, Ron; *ed:* (BS) Journalism/Ed, 1951, (MS) Elem Ed, 1961 SW TX St Univ; *cr:* Spec Ed Teacher San Marcos Ind Sch Dist 1956-60; 6th Grade Teacher Kyle Ind Sch Dist 1962-64, Seguin Ind Sch Dist 1964-69; 7th Grade Lang Art Teacher San Marcos Ind Sch Dist 1969-; *ai:* Conservation Teacher of Yr San Marcos Ind Sch Dist 1980; *home:* Rt 1 Box 26 San Marcos TX 78666

HENKE, KENNETH EDWARD, Assistant Principal; *b:* Waynesville, NC; *m:* Nikki Smith; *c:* Dean, Len; *ed:* (BA) Ed, 1972; (MS) Ed, 1976; (EDS) Admin 1982; Western Carolina Univ; *cr:* 6th Grade Teacher Balfour Elem 1968-72; 7th-9th Grade Teacher Rugby Jr HS 1972-77; 8th Grade Teacher 1977-86; Asst Prin 1986- Fairview Elem; *ai:* Coach Girls Bsktbl 7th and 8th; Tarheel Assn of Prin and Asst Prin Mem 1986- ; Jackson Cty Youth Sports Bd Mem 1984-87; Lakeview Nazarene Church Trustee 1980-; *home:* PO Box 193 Sylva NC 28779

HENKEL, ANN MARIE V., Speech Communications Teacher; *b:* Kaukauna, WI; *m:* Brian David; *c:* Nathan, Meghan; *ed:* (BS) Scndry Ed, Univ of WI Oshkosh 1983; Working Towards Masters Counseling; *cr:* Lang Art/Speech/Eng Teacher West Bend West HS 1984-; *ai:* Forensics; *office:* West Bend West HS 1305 E Decorah Rd West Bend WI 53095

HENKEL, JANICE MAYFIELD, Business Teacher; *b:* Deepwater, MO; *m:* Lyle; *c:* Mark K., Tami Khoury, Tierney, Michelle; *ed:* (BS) Bus Ed, Cntrl MO St Univ 1959; (MS) Bus Ed, Univ of IL 1972; *cr:* Bus/Eng Teacher Trico Cmmty HS 1959-60; Bus Teacher Belleville Township HS West 1963-65; Bus Teacher Belleville Area Coll 1965-78; Bus Teacher Mascoutah HS 1978-; *ai:* Soph Class Spon; Law Contest Coach Adv; Sick Leave Bank Comm; Southwest Bus Educ Assn, NEA, Kappa Delta Pi; St of IL VIP Grant 1987; *office:* Mascoutah HS 1313 W Main St Mascoutah IL 62258

HENKEL, SUSAN DIANE, English Teacher; *b:* Los Angeles, CA; *ed:* (BA) Comm, Long Beach St Univ 1984; Teaching Credential Ed Dept, Long Beach St Univ 1985; Peer Counseling Trng, Los Angeles Inified Sch Dist 1988; *cr:* K-6th Grade Teachers Aide Burnett Elem Sch 1982; 6th Grade Teacher Aide Grant Elem Sch 1983; K-9th Grade Arts/Crafts Dir Tucker Elem 1983-84; 7th-9th Grade Remedial Rdng/Writing Laboratories Teacher Aide Hamilton Jr HS 1984; Stu Teacher Gardena HS 1985; Eng/Comm Educator San Pedro HS 1985-; *ai:* Natl Forensic League Speech Team Coach; Peer Counseling Coord & Adv; Delta Kappa Gamma 1989-, Outstanding Educator 1989-; San Pedro Lady Booster Club 1985-, Teacher of Yr 1988-89; Natl Forensic League Mem 1977-79, 1985-; Outreach for Christ Intnl Singer 1987-88; Western Bay Forensic League Secy 1989-; Delta Kappa Gamma Mem 1990-; Natl Fulbright Teacher Exch Finalist 1988-89; Jaycees Redondo Beach Outstanding Young Educator Finalist 1987-88; CA Teacher of Yr San Pedro HS 1986-87; Nom Los Angeles Apple Awd 1987-88; *office:* San Pedro HS 1001 W 15th St San Pedro CA 90731

HENLEY, MARY HELEN HUGHES, 5th Grade Teacher; *b:* Newland, NC; *m:* Isaac P.; *c:* Terri H. Herman, Patti H. Payne, Michael P.; *ed:* (AA) Elem Ed, Lees-McRae Coll 1955; (BA) Elem Ed, Mars-Hill Coll 1972; *cr:* Teacher Pisgah Elem Sch 1968-88; Vance Elem Sch 1988-; *ai:* Yrbk Adv; Textbook Comm; NC Assn for Ed 1968-88; Prof Ed of NC 1988-; NC Cncl of Teachers of M Th 1980-; West Asheville Baptist Church Choir (Pres 1989-90 VP 1988-89); Health Ed Grant 1980-81; *home:* 4 Sedgefield Dr Candler NC 28715

HENLEY, SHERYL BERGSTROM, 9th-12th Grade French Teacher; *b:* Pocatello, ID; *m:* Randy; *c:* Craig, Scott, Aimee; *ed:* (BA) Fr, Univ of ID 1970; One Yr Study Aix-en-Provence France; Various Classes & Wkshps in Eng & Foreign Lang Ed; *cr:* Eng/Speech Teacher Hennessey HS 1970-71; Eng Teacher Dysart HS 1971-72, Kaiserslautern Amer HS 1972-73; Eng/Fr Teacher Lowell Scott Mid Sch 1983-88; Fr Teacher Meridian HS 1988-; *ai:* Fr Club Asst Adv; ICTFL, AATF; *office:* Meridian HS 1900 W Pine Meridian ID 83642

HENNE, BETTY M., English Teacher/Chair; *b:* Essexville, MI; *m:* William M.; *c:* Sean, Tim, Paul; *ed:* (BS) Eng, 1965, (MA) Lib Sci, 1981 Cntrl MI Univ; *cr:* Eng Teacher Clarkston Mid Sch 1965-66, Marley-Stanwood HS 1966-68, Charlevoix HS 1970-; *ai:* Eng Dept Chairperson; Sr Class Spon; NEA, MEA, CEA, AAUW, NCTE, MCTE; Little Traverse Civic Theater, Little Traverse Conservancy, WATCH; Poetry Published Wkshp Publication; Best Teaching Idea Wkshp Publication; *office:* Charlevoix HS E Garfield Charlevoix MI 49720

HENNEN, BARB ANN, Business Education Teacher; *b:* Marshall, MN; *ed:* (BS) Bus Ed, Mankato St Univ 1988; Bus Ed Mankato St Univ; *cr:* Clerical Clear with Cmptrs 1987-88; Instr Rush City HS 1988-; *ai:* BPA Adv; 9th Grade Vlybl Coach; Supt Adv Bd; C E Jacobson Schlsp Comm; Mem Jaycee; Pi Omega Pi VP 1986-88 Bus Ed Schlsp 1988; Delta Psi Epsilon 1989-; Jaycees; *office:* Rush City HS 275 S Eliot Ave P O Box 566 Rush City MN 55069

HENNESSEY, CLARE, Fourth Grade Teacher; *b:* Whitefield, NH; *ed:* (BA) Ed, Mt St Mary 1966; (ME) Ed, Keene St 1977; *cr:* Teacher Various Parochial Schls; Prin Cath Berlin Sch 1969-74; Teacher St John Regional 1975-; *office:* St John Regional Sch 61 South St Concord NH 03301

HENNESSEY, DONNA GLEASON, Third Grade Teacher; *b:* Chicago, IL; *m:* Frank William; *ed:* (BS) Elem Type 3 Kndgtn-9th Grade, Univ of IL Champaign 1960; (MA) Guidance Counseling, Northeastern Univ 197 Learning Disabilities, Cmptr Sci/Gifted; *cr:* 3rd Grade Teacher South Sch Des Plaines Dist 62 1960-; Kndgtn-8th Grade Teacher Summer Sch Dist 62 1963-89; *ai:* Master Plan/Criterion Refernce Tests Gifted, Math, Lang Arts, Prof Concerns PTA; Inst Inservice Cmptrs Goals Soc Citizenship/Staff Dev Schl Comms; Cooperating Teacher for 20 Stu from 10 Univ Inservice Sessions Creative Teaching, Math, Lang Arts, Cmptrs; Educl Travel; NEA, IL Ed Assn 1960-; Des Plaines Ed Assn Chairperson of Soc Comm 1960-; PTA (Honorary Lifetime Mem VP/Teacher Rep) 1960-; IL Staff Dev Cncl; Advisory Bd of Des Plaines Historical Society 1986-88; Northwestern Univ Sci Consortium 1986-; Northern IL Univ Advisory Comm Composed of Deans/Admin/IL Teachers; IL Master Teacher Governors Master Teacher Prgm; Golden Apple Fnd for Excl Teaching Finalist; Outstanding Teacher of Yr; Northwest Chicago Suburbs; Nom for Natl PTA Phoebe Apperson Hearst Outstanding Educator Awd; Articles Published in Intnl Newspapers; *office:* South School District 62 1535 Everett Ave Des Plaines IL 60018

HENNESSEY, RADCLIFFE WILLIAM, 10th Grade Global Stud Teacher; *b:* Long Branch, NJ; *m:* Gail Ellen Skroback; *ed:* (BA) His, Hartwick Coll 1971; (MST) Soc Stud, SUNY Binghamton 1980; *cr:* Soc Stud Teacher Harpursville Cntrl Sch 1972-; *ai:* GED Prgm Adult Ed Teacher; Ski Club & 10th Grade Class Adv; Southern Tier Cncl for Soc Stud; NYSUT; *office:* Harpursville Cntrl Sch Main St Harpursville NY 13787

HENNIGAN, ALEXANDRIA, 5th Grade Eng/Lang Art Teacher; *b:* Scranton, PA; *m:* Paul J.; *c:* Shana, Kara; *ed:* (BS) Elem Ed, E Stroudsburg Univ 1973; Working toward Masters; *cr:* 2nd Grade Elem Teacher St Francis Cabrini Sch 1973-74, St Patricks Elem Sch 1974-75; 5th Grade Elem Teacher N Pocono Mid Sch 1975-; *ai:* Newspaper Adv; *home:* RD 7 Box 7346 Moscow PA 18444

HENNING, KENT S., Upper School Principal; *b:* St Paul, MN; *m:* Barbara K.; *c:* Joseph Rogers, Anne Dunlap; *ed:* (BA) Eng, Univ of the South 1959; (MA) Liberal Art, TX Chrstn Univ 1979; *cr:* Teacher Sewanee Acad 1959-63; Teacher/Admin Trinity Valley Sch 1963-76; Admin/Teacher All Saints Episcopal Sch 1976-; *ai:* Dir of Dev; TX Assn Scndry Sch Prins 1980-; ASCD 1986-; Tx Assn of Coll Admissions Cnslr, Natl Assn of Coll AdmissionS CNSr 1986; Natl Society of Fund Raising Execs 1989-; Sertoma Club VP 1964-70; Sr Citizens Inc Bd Mem 1972-76; Bd of Trustees, Univ of S Sewaanee TN; SW Assn of Episcopal Schls Pres; TX Assn of Non-Public Schls Chm; Commission on Episcopal Schls Fort Worth; Hill Schl Bd; *office:* All Saints Episcopal Sch 8200 Tumbleweed Trl Fort Worth TX 76108

HENNON, JOYCE ANN, HS Hearing Impaired Teacher; *b:* Ann Arbor, MI; *ed:* (BS) Spec Ed/Hearing Impaired, Eastern MI Univ 1966; Use of Graphing Calculators, Writing Curr Use in Math Classrooms 1990; *cr:* Teacher MI Sch for Deaf 1966-; *ai:* Cheerleading, Bsktbl, Track Coach; Sr Spon; Produced Several Plays; Produced Books in Eng; MI Cncl Teachers of Math; MI Assn for Cmptr Users in Learning; Matthaei Botanical Gardens Volunteer; Saline Cmnty Hospital, St Josephs Hospital Ann Arbor Volunteer Interpreter for Deaf; MI St Employees Assn Secy, Treas; United Auto Workers Local Health & Safety Rep; *office:* Michigan Sch For The Deaf Corner Court St/Miller Rd Flint MI 48502

HENRE, B. VAURI, English Instructor; *b:* Lawrence, KS; *ed:* (BA) Eng/Poly Sci, Stephen F Austin St Univ 1974; (MAE) Eng, Kearney St Coll 1990; Grad Stud Eng; *cr:* Eng Instr Arapahoe HS 1976-78, Norfolk Sr HS 1978-; *ai:* Jr Class Spon; Eng Curr Dev, Gifted Ed, Writing Project Comm; NCTE Mem 1978-; NEA Mem 1976-; United Meth Church Mem Chrstn Ed Comm 1987-; Amer Legion Outstanding Teacher Awd 1985; Staff Mem of Month 1989; Past Chm Prof Growth Comm Norfolk Public Sch Dist; *office:* Norfolk Sr HS 801 Riverside Blvd Norfolk NE 68701

HENRICHS, MARTIN WILLIAM, Social Studies Teacher; *b:* Iola, KS; *m:* Judy M. Mc Kean; *c:* Marlise K. Jones, Starla Vibeke; *ed:* (BA) His, Valparaiso Univ 1959; (MS) Ed, IN Univ 1963; Robert Taft Inst on Govt, Freedoms Fnd Valley Forge; Pacific Acad Advanced Stud ECS; *cr:* Eng Teacher Calumet Jr HS 1959-60; Soc Stud Teacher Roosevelt HS 1961-; *ai:* Acad Hoosier Bowl Soc Stud Coach; Martin Luther King Jr Adult Evening Sch Teacher; IN Prof Ed 1981-; Leadership Cncls of Amer Inc Founder/Pres 1987-89; The Leader Editor 1981-83; Amer Sentry Editor 1987-; Listed Under "Ed and Welfare" in Heritage Fnd Publication on Public Policy Experts; *home:* 392 S 200 W Valparaiso IN 46383

HENRICKS, JANE WHITE, English Teacher; *b:* Sharon, PA; *m:* Todd Chapman; *ed:* (BA) Span, Muskingum Coll 1983; *cr:* Span Teacher Buckeye Trail HS 1983-86; Eng Teacher Bethany HS 1986-; Span Teacher Bement HS 1990; *ai:* Jr Class Spon; Girls Var Track Coach; ASCD 1988-89; Jr Womans Club Secy 1988-; *home:* 111 E Hunt St PO Box 725 Cerro Gordo IL 61818

HENRICKSON, MAJEL PINNEY, Chorus Teacher; *b:* Sturgeon Bay, WI; *m:* Philip R.; *c:* Nicole; *ed:* (BA) Music Ed, UW Stevens Point 1977; *cr:* Mid Sch Vocal Instr Sturgeon Bay Mid Sch 1977-81; Elem/Jr HS Vocal and General Music Instr Jackson Elem Sch/Wilson Jr HS 1984-89; Jr HS Vocal and General Music Instr Wilson Jr HS 1989-; *ai:* Dir Stage Crew; Dir Crescendo Jr HS Extra Curr Swing Choir; Church Organist 1970-80; Wesley United Meth Church Organist/Choir Dir/Youth Dir 1982-88 Dir of Music Staff/Choir Dir 1989-; *office:* Woodrow Wilson Jr H S 1201 N 11th St Manitowoc WI 54220

HENRIKSEN, PENELOPE PEARSON, First Grade Teacher; *b:* Fremont, NE; *m:* Allen G.; *ed:* (BA) Elem Ed/Human Dev/The Family, Univ of NE 1976; Grad Stud Univ of NE Lincoln & Wayne St Coll; *cr:* 1st Grade Teacher Norfolk Public Schls 1976-; *ai:* Teaching Gifted Omnibus Unit Theater Arts; Self Esteem Comm; NE St Ed Assn 1976-; Beta Sigma Phi Pres 1984; PEO 1988-; *home:* 1901 N 17th St Norfolk NE 68701

HENRY, ANN CONNOR, Grad Assistant; *b:* Omaha, NE; *m:* John Kenneth; *ed:* (BSED) Elem Ed, Cntrl MO St Univ 1980; Working Towards MSE Curr, Instruction, Specializing Sci Ed; Basic Cert of Cathechists Center of Pastoral Life & Paul VI Inst; *cr:* 3rd/4th Grade Teacher Holy Rosary Cath Sch 1980-85; 2nd Grade Teacher St George Cath Sch 1985-86; Dir of Religius Ed/Catechist Holy Rosary Cath Sch 1986-89; *ai:* Mem Geology Club; Geology Tutor & Sci Fair Judge Cntrl MO St Univ; Substitute Teacher Clinton Public Schls; Tutor HS Stu Local Alcohol & Drug Center; NSTA 1990; GFWC Jr Progressives (1st VP, Historian) 7986-, Designed ST Winning Scrapbrook 1988; Local Church (Vocalist, Musican) 1980-; Artesian Priaire Players; Henry

Cty Soil & Water Conservation Schlsp; Composed Spec Services for Children & Articles.

HENRY, AUDREY PORTER, Kindergarten Teacher; *b:* Woodville, MS; *m:* Albert; *c:* Joey, Lance; *ed:* (BS) Elem Ed, Alcorn St Univ 1967; *cr:* 5th Grade Teacher Lidell Elem Sch 1967-68, Brumfield Elem Sch 1968-69; 4th Grade Teacher Wilkinson Cty Elem 1969-73; Kndgtn Teacher Enterprise HS 1973-; *ai:* Catahoula Assn of Educators Sch Building Rep 1977-; LA Assn of Educators Mem 1973-; Good Samaritan Lodge Secy 1975-; Edna Anderson Chapter Order of Eastern Stars Mem 1972-.

HENRY, BETTY GAUTHREAUX, Retired Teacher; *b:* New Orleans, LA; *c:* Kim C. Castenell, Sonia J. Walter; *ed:* (BA) Bus Admin, 1953, Elem Ed, 1956 Dillard Univ; *cr:* 3rd Grade Teacher 1957-70, Ranking Teacher 1965-66, 1st Grade Teacher 1970-73 Mc Donough 40 Elem Sch; 1st Grade Teacher Ray Abrams Elem Sch 1973-86; *ai:* Intnl Rdng Assn 1975-86; LA Ed Assn 1957-86; LA Retired Teachers Assn 1987-; Delta Sigma Theta 1951-; Amer Red Cross Sch Spon 1958-65, 5 Yrs 1963; GSA Troop Leader 1957-67; United Fund Sch Rep 1960-65; *home:* 5115 St Ferdinand Dr New Orleans LA 70126

HENRY, BILLIE DOUGLASS, Home Ec Teacher-Coordinator; *b:* Tulsa, OK; *m:* Sam Dennard; *c:* Vicki, Denise Henry Rachal; *ed:* (BS) Home Ec, 1973, (MS) Home Ec, 1985 Lamar Univ; *cr:* Instr Lamar Univ 1974-75; Teacher/Coord Thomas Jefferson HS 1977-; *ai:* FHA; Home Ec Related Occupations, Sr Coronation, Stu European Trips Spon; Supt Advisory, Schlsp, Monticello Guardian Awd Comm; Amer Home Ec Assn, TX Home Ec Assn, Sabine Area Home Ec Assn; Port Arthur Service League (Treas 1966-68) 1958-; Amer Cancer Society (Pres 1962-63, Mem 1962-), 25 Yr Service Awd 1988; Travis Elem PTA Pres 1966-68, TX Life Membership 1967; Port Arthur City PTA Pres 1968-69; Mrs S Jefferson Cty 1959; *home:* 3724 Boulder Ave Port Acres TX 77640

HENRY, CAROLYN HAHN, 2nd/3rd Grade Teacher; *b:* Delaware, OH; *m:* George H.; *c:* Susan Butler, George A.; *ed:* (BS) Elem Ed, OH St Univ 1965; Service Credential, Univ Ca 1979; (MS) Counseling, Ca St Univ 1983; Teacher Trng Inst for Project Read; *cr:* Teacher Health Sch System OH 1966-67; Santa Ana Unified Sch Dist Ca 1967-68; San Joaquin Sch Dist Ca 1969-77; Irvine Unified Sch Dist 1977-; *ai:* Schl Rep to ITA; PTO Greentree; Sch Site Cncl Greentree; Irvine Teachers Assn; Ca Teachers Assn; Natl Assn for Adv of Humane Ed; Saddleback Exchangettes 1974-76; Delta Gamma Soc Chm Pledge Class 1960-61; Teacher of Yr 1989-; *home:* 24401 Macedo Dr Mission Viego CA 92691

HENRY, CAROLYN SCHACHT, Sixth Grade Teacher; *b:* Johnson Cty, NE; *m:* Robert Marcus; *c:* Ann Henry Stough, Mark, Kirk; *ed:* (BSE) Elem Ed, Peru St Coll 1958; (MSE) Elem Ed, NW MO St Univ 1972; Grad Work; *cr:* K-8th Grade Teacher Rural Johnson Cty 1954-55; 5th-8th Grade Teacher Cook Public Schls 1956-57; 6th Grade Teacher Auburn Public Schls 1958-59; 6th Grade Teacher Kenwick 1959-60; 4th/5th Grade Teacher Schwegler 1964-65; 6th Grade Teacher Washington Mid Sch 1973-; *ai:* Juvenile Justice Comm; 5th/6th Grade Variety Show Co-Chairperson; Cmmty Teachers Assn (VP 1986-87, Pres 1987-88); MO St Teachers Assn 1973-; Delta Kappa Gamma 1983-; PEO Pres 1975-77; Order of Eastern Star 1964-; Alpha Omicron Pi 1953-; *office:* Washington Mid Sch 1st And Vine Maryville MO 64468

HENRY, CHARLES D., Mathematics Teacher; *b:* New Orleans, LA; *m:* Joyce M. Allen; *c:* Monica, Tomica; *ed:* (BS) Health Safety/Phys Ed, Grambling Coll 1969; (MS) Health Safety/Phys Ed/Math, Southern Univ 1985; Prof Prgm Trng Southern Univ 1983-84; Supvr Stu Teaching Math 1985; *cr:* Math Teacher 1969-87, Math/Health Safety/Phys Ed Teacher 1987- St Helena HS; *ai:* 9th Grade Class Spon; NEA; LEA, LAE 1970-; St Mary Baptist Church (Supt Sunday Sch, Deacon Bd); St Helena Police Jury Advisory Comm Hazardous Waste; *home:* PO Box 569 Greensburg LA 70441

HENRY, CLEVELAND, Planning Specialist; *b:* New Albany, MS; *m:* Snowrene Mitchell; *c:* Tony, Michell, Dartanya, Tamika, Tamira; *ed:* Criminal Justice, MI St Univ 1962; Surgical Technician, Mercy Hospital 1964; Psychologist, Syracuse Univ 1980; Positive Peer Culture, Guided Group Interaction Behaviorial Change Counseling; *cr:* Supvr Guided Group Interaction Prgm 1973-89, Planning Specialist 1990 Lansing Sch Dist; *ai:* Cmmty Coalition Against Drugs, Gangs, Violence; Dev of Prgms & Strategies; Ingham Cty Comprehensive Substance Abuse Treatment Prgm; Advisory Cncl; Handbook Published; Sch Bd Chm; Guided Group Interaction Counseling Service Owner; *office:* Lansing Sch Dist 500 W Lenawee St Lansing MI 48933

HENRY, CONNIE, Latin & English Teacher; *b:* Kansas City, KS; *m:* Steven K.; *c:* Jacob; *ed:* (BSE) Scndry Ed/Latin/Eng, 1980; (MA) Scndry Ed/Latin, 1988 Univ of KS; *cr:* Latin Teacher Salina South HS 1980-81; Latin/Eng Teacher Bonner Springs HS 1981-; *ai:* Jr Classical League Spon 1980-; NCTE 1989-; KS Ed Assn Building Rep 1980-; Amer Classical League 1980-; Foreign Lang Dept Chm 1985-86; *office:* Bonner Springs HS 100 Mc Danield Bonner Springs KS 66012

HENRY, DIANE LAZZELLE, Instructional Coach; *b:* Morgantown, WV; *c:* Karoline L.; *ed:* (BS) Elem Ed, WV Univ 1958-; (MS) Elem Ed, SUNY Fredonia 1987; Will Complete Advanced Certificate in Admin, SUNY Fredonia 1990; *cr:* Teacher Pittsburgh City Schls 1962-63, Rochester City Schls 1963-67, Hamburg Cntrl 1967-69, 1973-88, Coach/Teacher Hamburg Cntrl Schls 1988-; *ai:* Dist Strategic Planning; Co-Chm VPES Staff Dev; Mem PDM Team; ASCD 1987-; Sweet Adelines Various Offices 1969-; League of Women Voters Voter Service Chairperson 1988-; Republican Comm Person 1987-; Co-Authored Black His Elem Textbooks; Teach Cooperative Learning Course; Coord Fredonia-Hamburg Internship Prgm; *home:* 4284 Twilight Ln Hamburg NY 14075

HENRY, ISADORA WILLIAMS, Language Arts Teacher; *b:* Yonges Island, SC; *m:* George C. Jr.; *c:* Genyne, India; *ed:* (BA) Eng, Bendict Coll 1966; *cr:* Teacher WA HS 1966-68, Griffin Mid Sch 1974-; *ai:* Booster Spon; Godby Track Team; Leon Cty Teachers Assn; Teacher of Yr Griffin Mid Sch 1984.

HENRY, JO ANN SARAH, Retired 4th Grade Teacher; *b:* New Kensington, PA; *m:* Thomas Patrick; *c:* Thomas P. Jr., Timothy J.; *ed:* (BA) Speech/Drama, Carlow Coll 1968; (MED) Elem Ed, OH Univ 1976; Grad Stud Elem Ed; *cr:* 4th Grade Teacher Tiffin Elem 1968-75, Allen Elem 1975-77; Teacher of Academically Talented Worthington Elem 1977-79; 4th Grade Teacher Allen Elem 1979-; *ai:* Amer Assn of Univ Women Treas 1968-70; New Century Club Secy 1969-70; PTO 1968-; OH Retired Teachers Assn 1990; NEA, OH Ed Assn, Chillicothe Ed Assn 1968-; Jennings Scholar 1976-77; *home:* 33 Timberlane Dr Chillicothe OH 45601

HENRY, KATHRYN ANN (MARSH), Chapter I Reading; *b:* Greenville, OH; *m:* Burl Hamen; *c:* Don, Steve, Sheryl Riddle, Suzanne, Dale A. Copeland (dec); *ed:* (BS) Elem Ed, Urbana Coll 1973; (MA) Elem Ed, Wright St Univ 1989; *cr:* 1st Grade Teacher Ansonia Sch 1954-55; 3rd Grade Teacher Hubbard Sch 1955-57; 1st Grade Teacher 1966-78, 4th Grade Teacher 1978-85, Chapter I Rdng Teacher 1985- Lakeview Elem Sch; *ai:* Building Rep for Career Ed; Served on Comm Writing Sch Policy on our Philosophy; Indian Lake Ed Assn, OH Ed Assn, NEA; Kappa Delta Pi Honor Society in Ed; Presenter at Writing Conference 1989; Teachers Sharing With Teachers; Teacher Leader Networking Lang Arts St of OH; *home:* 504 E Sandusky Ave Bellefontaine OH 43311

HENRY, KILA ANN, Science Instructor; *b:* Bethany, MO; *ed:* (BS) Bio/Lib Sci, 1972, (MS) Bio, 1981 NW MO St Univ; Grad Stud NW MO St Univ 1982-; Rdng in Astronomy Cosmos, Univ of IA 1981; Telecourse Project Universe, Univ of IA 1982; *cr:* 7th-12th Grade Sci Instr S Nodaway R-IV 1974-80, NE Nodaway R-V 1980-; *ai:* 7th Grade Sci Club Spon; Jr & Sr HS Sci Olympiad Team Coach; Chem Educators Assn Pres 1987-; MO Sci Olympiad Exec Bd 1988-; Cmmty Teachers Assn Pres 1982-83, Teacher of Yr 1987; PTO 1980-; Wrote & Received Incentive Grant; See What Sci is All About Trainer; Sci Teachers of MO HS Sci Ed; *office:* NE Nodaway R-V Sch 126 High School Ave Ravenwood MO 64479

HENRY, LANETTE ALLISON, Secondary Business Teacher; *b:* Carmel, CA; *m:* LeRoy Fredrick; *c:* Lynsey A., Roy L. (dec); *ed:* (BS) Bus/Eng, Clarendon Coll 1969-71; (BS) Bus/Eng, Wayland Baptist Univ 1971-73; Bus, Wayland Baptist Univ; *cr:* Eng/Rdng/Phys Ed Teacher 1975-76, Bus Teacher 1976-78, 1982- Hart HS; *ai:* Sr Class & NHS Spon; PTA 1983-; Hart HS Teacher of Yr; *office:* Hart HS Box 490 Hart TX 79043

HENRY, LOIS E., Spanish Teacher; *b:* Punxsutawney, PA; *m:* Charles A. L.; *c:* C. Lynn, Pamela, Jennifer; *ed:* (BA) Fr/Eng/Span, Indiana Univ of PA 1953; Grad Stud Ed, Eng, Ger 1956-58; *cr:* Eng/Span/Fr Teacher Murraysville HS 1953-55; Fr/Eng Teacher Du Bois HS 1958-60; Span/Fr/Eng Teacher Punxsutawney Jr HS 1960-70, Punxsutawney Sr HS 1970-; *ai:* Span Club Co-Spon; MLA; *home:* 603 Union St Big Run PA 15715

HENRY, LOUISE ELVIRA (SEIBEL), Spanish Teacher; *b:* North Braddock, PA; *m:* Terry A; *ed:* (BSED) Span/Art, Edinboro St Univ 1975; Working Towards Masters Span, Indiana Univ of PA; *cr:* Art/Spanish Teacher Our Lady of Mercy Acad 1975-79, Serra Cath HS 1980-85; Span Teacher Hempfield Area Sr HS 1985-; *ai:* Venezuelan Exch Prgm Coord 1986-89; Span Club Moderator; Appalachian Lang Educators Society (Exec Bd Mem, Secy 1989-) 1987-; Natl Organization of Teachers of Span & Portuguese Newsletter Ed 1989-; Amer Family Inst Positive Teaching Awd 1986; Nom Outstanding Young Women in America 1987; *home:* RD 11 Box 354 Greensburg PA 15601

HENRY, MARIE DODSON, Mathematics Teacher; *b:* Arlington, VA; *m:* James Edward; *c:* Jacqueline, James E. IV; *ed:* (BS) Math, James Madison Univ 1971; *cr:* Math Teacher Martinsville City Schls 1971-72, Prince Georges Cty 1972-79; Mathematician Natl Oceanic & Atmospheric Admin 1986; Math Teacher Charles Cty Bd of Ed 1982-; *ai:* Math Team, Engineering Club Spon; NHS Adv; MD Cncl Teacher of Math Mem 1989-; Broadview Baptist Church Mem; Article Published; *office:* Lackey HS Rt 224 Indian Head MD 20640

HENRY, MICHAEL SCOTT, International Studies Coord; *b:* Mt Vernon, IL; *m:* Ann Howard; *c:* Kimberly; *ed:* (BA) Ed, 1968, (MA) Ed, 1971, (MA) His, 1977, (PHD) Ed, 1985 Univ of MD; *cr:* Teacher Parkdale HS 1968-89; Coord Cntrl HS 1989-; *ai:* NCSS 1968-, Honorable Mention Exemplary Dissertation 1985; Published 6 Articles; *office:* Central HS 200 Cabin Branch Rd Capitol Heights MD 20743

HENRY, MIXON LEE, Third Grade Teacher; *b:* Greenville, TX; *m:* Kathleen Clark; *ed:* (AA) Eastfield Jr Coll 1974; (BSED) Elem Ed, 1978, (MSED) Spec Ed, 1984 Univ TX Austin; *cr:* Cnslr Salesmanship Club Boys Camp 1974-76; Cnslr/Supvr Hope Center Boys Camp 1976-77; 3rd Grade Teacher Cedar Creek Elem Sch 1978-80, Valley View Elem Sch 1980-; *ai:* Track Coach Winston HS; Year-End Class Campout; Assn of TX Prof Educators, Tx Outdoor Ed Assn; Published Article; Fulbright Teacher Exch Prgm Canada; *office:* Cedar Creek Elem Sch 3301 Pinnacle Rd Austin TX 78746

HENRY, STEVEN R., Sixth Grade Teacher; *b:* Malta, MT; *m:* Judy Kay Bridgewater; *c:* Heidi, Heather; *ed:* (BS) Elem Ed, MT St Univ 1970; (MS) Elem Ed/General Curr, Eastern MT Coll 1975; Admin Endorsment, MT St Univ; Thomas Alva Edison Sci Institute 1982; *cr:* 5th Grade Teacher Rimrock Sch 1970-72, Bitterroot Sch 1972-76; 5th-6th Grade Teacher Rose Park Sch 1976-88; 6th Grade Teacher Central Heights Sch 1988; *ai:* Dist Insurance & Supt Search Comm; MT Assn of Supervision & Curr Dev Pres 1983-84; MT Ed Assn Bd of Dirs 1987-; Billings Ed Assn Pres 1990 Pres awd 1985/1988; Yellowstone Teachers Credit Union Supervisory Comm 1984-; Walsh Park Dev Comm Co-chm 1978-81 City Cncl Certificate of Recognition 1981; Atonement Luth Church Congregation Pres 1985; Eastern MT Coll Forum for Excl-Certificate of Recognition; Rocky Mountain Coll Teacher Ed Review Team; *home:* 1145 Toole Ct Billings MT 59105

HENRY, TERESA M., CSJ, Mathematics Teacher; *b:* New Britain, CT; *ed:* (BA) Ed, St Joseph Coll 1968; (MA) Math, Willanova 1981; Math Cmptrs, Cntrl CT St Univ, Univ New Haven; Math Wkshps; *cr:* 2nd Grade Teacher St Joseph 1968-69; 5th-8th Grade Teacher St Mary 1969-70; 6th/7th Grade Teacher St Augustine 1970-72; 7th/8th Grade Teacher St Joseph 1972-73;9th-12th Grade Math Teacher St Paul HS 1973-77; 7th/8th Grade Teacher St James 1977-79; 9th-12th Grade Math Teacher St Joseph HS 1979-; *ai:* Sch Drama Ticket Sales Chairperson; Walk-A-Thon Steering Comm; NCEA Mem 1979-; CT Assn Math Teachers Mem 1988-; SC Ed Assn Supplementary Materials Chairperson; Sisters of St Joseph of Chambery Mem 1963-; St Joseph HS Poetry Pusblished Annually; *office:* St Joseph HS 2320 Huntington Trnpke Trumbull CT 06611

HENRY, TINA GENEVA, Physical Science Teacher; *b:* Easton, MD; *m:* Clyde A.; *c:* Clydale, Jared; *ed:* (BS) Health Ed, DE St Coll 1984; *cr:* Phys Sci Teacher Colonel Richardson HS 1984-; *ai:* Athletic Dir; Girls Bsktbl Coach; Natl Teachers Assn, Caroline Cty Teachers Assn; *office:* Colonel Richardson HS Rt 2 Box 340 Federalsburg MD 21632

HENSARLING, NANCY GARLAND, 8th Grade English Teacher; *b:* Jackson, MS; *m:* Robert W. Sr.; *c:* Robynne L., Robb; *ed:* (BS) Elem Ed, William Carey Coll 1961; (MED) Elem Ed, 1973; (MED) Admin & Supvn, 1977 Southeastern LA Univ; *cr:* 2nd Grade Teacher Fulwiler 1961-62; Marshall 1962-63; Elem/Jr HS Eng Teacher Mc Comb Jr HS 1963-; *ai:* Chrldr Spon; Chm Eng Dept; Chm Writing Sch Dist; Mc Comb Assn of Ed Pres 1975-76; MS Prof Educators 1989-; NCTE 1983-; Pike Cty Arts Cncl VP 1980; Delta Kappa Gamma VP 1986; Kappa Delta Phi 1978-80; Mc Combs Outstanding Young Educator 1975 & 1976.

HENSCHEL, SANDI, Teacher of English; *b:* Brooklyn, NY; *c:* Lisa Grubert-Piccione, Rachel Piccione, Sarah Piccione; *ed:* (BS) Ed, 1960, (MS) Eng/Speech/Drama, 1966 SUNY Potsdam; (MA) Creative Writing, SUNY Brockport 1984; *cr:* 7th Grade Eng Teacher Potsdam Cntrl Sch 1960-61; 8th Grade Eng Teacher Norwood-Norfolk Cntrl Sch 1962-63; 7th Grade Eng Teacher Scotia-Glenville Jr HS 1965-68; Supervision of Stu Teachers of Eng Northern IL Univ De Kalb 1968-69; Writing Specialist SUNY Brockport 1973-74; 10th-12th Grade Eng Teacher Kendall HS 1974-; Teaching Asst 1978-79, Adjunct In Eng 1980- SUNY Brockport; *ai:* Drama Club Dir Kendall HS 1974-84; Class Adv 1978, 1987, 1991; Sr NHS Adv Kendall HS 1979-; Liaison/Coord Boces Adept Prgm Arts Cncl 1984-86; Teacher-Cnslr London England Trip 1986; Summer Curr Work Kendall HS; NEH Fellowship Natl Endowment for Humanities Seminar 1986; Awd for Excellence IN Scndry Sch Teaching Univ of Rochester 1986; Published Poetry in Magazines & Periodicals; Poetry Chapbooks; Extensive Theatrical Performance Experience in Non-Equity Prof & Cmmty Theatres & Companies; Dir & Tech Theatrical Experience HS Cmmty & Non-Equity Prof Levels; NDEA Arts & Hum Fellowship-Theatre Univ of CA Santa Barbara 1967; Prof Acting Trng 1965-66; Schlsp to Dramatic Wkshp 1955-56; *office:* Kendall HS Roosevelt Hwy Kendall NY 14476

HENSCHEN, RUTH L., 5th Grade/Gifted/Cmptr Teacher; *b:* New Knoxville, OH; *m:* Lester; *c:* Jeff, Mark, Kevin; *ed:* (BA) Elem Ed, 1971, (ME) Elem Ed/Media, 1981 Wright St Univ; Cert Trng for Cmptr & Gifted; *cr:* Teacher New Knoxville Local 1969-; *ai:* Recycling Co-Adv 1990; 5th-6th Grade Scholastic Bowl Adv 1987-89; Delta Kappa Gamma (Schlsp Chm 1988-) 1986-; OH Assn of Gifted Children 1984-; Friends of Lib 1989-; Range Athletic Boosters 1989-; New Knoxville Area Cmmty Fnd 1990; 4-H Adv 1984-; Jennings Scholar 1988-89.

HENSLER, SUSAN JEAN, Principal; *b:* Terre Haute, IN; *m:* Hans Heinrich; *c:* Gretchen Henseler Murphy, Hans E.; *ed:* (BS) Elem Ed, 1963, (MS) Elem Ed, 1969 IN St Univ; Counseling & Educl Admin; *cr:* Teacher Fairbanks Elem 1963-70, Fugua Elem 1971-79, Southeast Elem 1979-87; Prin Johns Hill Magnet 1987-; *ai:* Stu Assesment & Choice Schls Comms; Phi Delta Kappa, Nation Mid Sch Assn, ASCD; *office:* Johns Hill Magnet Sch 1025 E Johns Decatur IL 62521

HENSLEY, VICKY MOYER, English Teacher; *b:* Columbia, SC; *m:* Curtis Allen Sr.; *c:* William C. Jr., Mason; *ed:* (BA) Eng, Lander Coll 1985; *cr:* Eng Teacher Long Cane Acad 1988-; *ai:* Stu Government, Var Chrldr, Pep Club Adv; Piedmont Cncl of Eng Teachers; Natl Cncl of Eng Teachers; Yellow Jassamine Garden Club Chm of Conservation Comm 1977-83; Mu Rho Sigma Pres 1984-85; *office:* Long Cane Acad Schl 1317 Overbrook Rd Mc Cormick SC 29835

HENSON, BONNIE ANDERSON, Second Grade Teacher; *b:* Holcomb, MO; *m:* Kenneth M.; *c:* Scottie S.; *ed:* (BSE) Elem Ed, 1971, (MSE) Elem Ed, 1974 AR St Univ; *cr:* Bookkeeper Deering Gin & Mercantile Company 1950-56; Dispatcher Malden Air Base 1956-60; Postal Clerk Holcomb Post Office 1965-68; Teacher Holcomb Elem 1971-; *ai:* CTA VP; Profession Dev Comm Mem; Beginning Teachers Mentor; MSTA; CTA Pres 1985-88; *home:* PO Box 66 Holcomb MO 63852

HENSON, BUD, Art Teacher; *b:* Denver, CO; *m:* Cynthia Darling; *ed:* (BFA) Art, 1985, Art/Eng, 1986, Graceland Coll; *cr:* Art/Eng Teacher Centaurus HS 1986-; *ai:* Boys Jr Var Bsktbl; Girls Asst Track Coach; Dist Curr Comm Mem; *office:* Centaurus HS 10300 South Boulder Rd Lafayette CO 80026

HENSON, EARLENE VIOLA (OVLETREA), Jr HS Special Ed Teacher; *b:* Orlando, FL; *m:* David B.; *c:* Charles D., Mary P. Masi; *ed:* (BS) His, FL A&M Univ 1962; (MED) Scndry Ed/Soc Stud, Tuskegee Inst 1968; Clinical Trng Cedarhurst Sch & YPI of Yale Univ 1980-85; Further Stud Curr & Instruction, Cath Univ of America 1974-76; Grad Work Spec Ed & Rdng, FL Atlantic Univ 1985-86; Coursework Child Abuse & Neglect, CO St Univ 1990; *cr:* 7th-12th Grade Teacher/10th-12th Grade Group/Soc Stud Dept Chairperson Charles R Drew Jr/Sr HS 1962-66; Grad/Curr Lab Asst Tuskegee Inst 1966-68; 10th-12th Grade Soc Stud Teacher Maynard Evens Sr HS 1968-69; Head-Start Head Teacher Hawkeye Cmmty Assn 1969-70; MDTA Supvr/Instr Kirkwood Comm Coll 1969-72; Teacher IA Security Penal Facility 1971; Head Teacher Yale Univ Cedarhurst Sch 1980-85; 6th-8th Grade Teacher of Emotionally Handicapped Boca Raton Mid Sch 1985-88; 7th-9th Grade Teacher of Emotionally Handicapped/9th Grade Soc Stud Teacher Centennial Jr HS 1988-; Scndry Voc Teacher Boulder Valley Tech Ed Center 1989-; *ai:* Cosmetology Dept Advisory, Retention Intervention Comm Boulder Valley Tech Ed Center; Child Resource Team Centennial Jr HS Spec Ed Dept; Orange Cty FL Soc Stud Teachers Chairperson 1965-66; NCTE, NEA; Alpha Kappa Alpha (Pledge Dean 1960-62) 1959-; Nicheren Shoshu of America Group Leader 1988-; NSA WD Orch 1st Clarinet 1989-; Kappa Delta Pi 1968-; AKA Schlsp FL A&M 1958; Teacher of Yr C R Drew 1966; Fellowship for Outstanding Inservice Teachers Tuskegee Inst 1966-68; Cath Univ of America Fellowship & Grad Assistantship 1974-76; Teacher of Yr Cedarhurst Sch of Yale Univ 1985; Adult HS Outstanding Service Awd 1985; Service Awd Boca Raton Mid Sch 1988; *office:* Centennial Jr HS 2205 Norwood Ave Boulder CO 80304

HENSON, EXIE WILDE, Third Grade Teacher; *b:* Brevard, NC; *m:* Gene; *c:* Melody Fifer, Rebecca Dobson, Scott; *ed:* (BS) Elem Ed, TX Wesleyan Coll 1958; Portugese Lang Sch, Campinas Sao Paulo Brazil; *cr:* 5th Grade Teacher South Fort Worth Elem 1958-59; 7th Grade Teacher Duncan Chapel Elem 1961-63/1967-70; Prin Lake Park Baptist Sch 1974-77; 3rd Grade Teacher Rosman Elem 1979-; *ai:* Chairperson Senate Bill 2 & Writing a Grant Proposal RJR-Nabisco; Comm Sch Improvement & Accountability; NEA 1979-; NCEA 1979-; TCEA 1979-; Alumnus Mountain Area Writing Project & NC Center for Advancement of Teaching Western Caroline Univ; *home:* 211 Heathcote Rd Hendersonville NC 28739

HENSON, FRANKLIN DELANO, K-12th Grade Counselor; *b:* Little Rock, AR; *m:* Louise D. Havener; *c:* Stephen, Nathan; *ed:* (BSE) Bus Ed/Soc Stud, Harding Coll 1976; (MSE) Ed, Harding Univ 1982; Cert Counseling, UCA Conway 1989; *cr:* Bus Ed Instr Foothills-Voc-Tech Sch 1983-87; Cnslr/Teacher Griffithville Schls 1987-; *ai:* FBLA Co-Adv; HS Beta Club Adv; Just Say No Organization Spon; Local Teachers Organization Chm; AR Bus Ed Teachers Assn 1987-; AR Assn of Sch Cnslrs 1988-; AR Voc Guidance Organization 1988-; AR Fire Fighters Assn 1987-; Calvary Baptist Assn (Exec Bd 1977-, Assn Clerk 1984-); City of Griffithville (Alderman, Mayor); Volunteer Income Tax Assistance Prgm Coord-Worker; Masonic Lodge Volunteer of Yr Awd; *home:* PO Box 101 Griffithville AR 72060

HENSON, GLENDA GAYLE, 8th Grade English/Lit Teacher; *b:* Corsicana, TX; *m:* James Richard; *c:* Shane, Casey; *ed:* (BA) Elem Ed, Sam Houston St Univ 1973; (MA) Med Scndry Ed, Stephen F Austin St Univ 1981; Dunn & Dunn NYC SS 1987; *cr:* 4th Grade Teacher Kerens Ind Sch Dist 1973-79; 6th Grade Teacher 1979-89, 8th Grade Teacher Corsicana Ind Sch Dist 1990-; *ai:* Lead Teacher Lit Dept Drane Mid Sch; Curr Dev Lit Dept; Textbook Comm/Presentator; TAIR Rdng Conf Baylor Univ ; UIL Spon/Coach-Picture Money; Oral Rd g; Dictionary Skills; TX St Teachers Assn; NEA 1973-; Corsicana Educators Assn 1979-; TX Assn for Gifted & Talented 1988-89; Delta KAppa Gamma/Phi Delta Kappa 1990; Northside Baptist Church; Teacher of Yr 1980-88; Washington DC Trip Spon; *office:* Collins Mid Sch 1500 Dobbins Rd Corsicana TX 75110

HENSON, KIM ALLEN, Social Studies Teacher; *b:* Hagersstown, MD; *m:* Lora L. Gouff; *c:* Jared, Emily; *ed:* (AA) General Stud, Hagerstown Jr Coll 1971; (BA) Psych/Ed, 1973, (MED) Guidance/Counseling, 1979 Frostburg St Coll; Substance Abuse Counseling, MD St Dept of Health & Mental Hygene; *cr:* Soc Stud Teacher Flintstone Sch 1973-82; Substance Abuse Cnslr Allegany Cty Health Dept 1983-85; Soc Stud Teacher Oldtown HS 1989-; *ai:* Jr Class, Prom, Stu Helping Other People Adv; Allegany Cty Teachers Assn (Sch Rep 1975-77, Exec Bd 1977-80); St Paul Luth Church Vestry Mem 1986-; Allegany Cty Childrens Cncl Cmmty Service Awd; *office:* Oldtown HS Main St Oldtown MD 21511

HENSON, LENNA PERCEFUL, English/Language Art Teacher; *b:* Roland, OK; *m:* Herbert; *c:* Michael, Larry, Barry; *ed:* (BA) Eng/Elem, NEOSU Tahlequah 1971; Teaching HS Speech, W AR Coll Ft Smith; *cr:* 5th Grade Elem Teacher Muldrow HS 1971-78; Eng/Speech Teacher Roland HS 1978-; *ai:* Chrldrs, Drill Team, Speech & Drama Spon; Staff Dev, Lang Art Chm; NEO, OEA; RCTA Classroom Rep 1988-89; A L Auxiliary Pres 1971-73; Volunteer RS VP 1985-; *office:* Roland HS Ranger Blvd Roland OK 74954

HENSON, PHILIP GERALD, 6th Grade Science Teacher; *b:* Greenville, AL; *m:* Ruth Karene Childress; *c:* Wesley P.; *ed:* (BS) Elem Ed, Troy St Univ 1976; (MS) Elem Ed, Lagrange Coll 1978; (AAED) Elem Ed, Jacksonville St Univ 1985; Re-Cert Admin/Superlvision N-12 on Masters & AA Level Completed 1989; *cr:* 6th Grade Sci Teacher 1976-, Designated Asst Prin 1989- Handley Mid Sch; *ai:* Stu Cncl Spon; Key Club Laison Roanoke Kiwanis Club; Faculty Rep Local Ed Assn; NEA 1976-; AL Ed Assn 1976-; Roanoke Ed Assn Pres 1978-79; Roanoke Kiwanis Club Secy 1986-; Multi-Disciplinary Team Randolph Cty Child Abuse 1986-; 1982 Most Outstanding Teacher 6th Grade Handley Mid; *office:* Handley Mid Sch 207 West Point St Roanoke AL 36274

HENSON, REBECCA ANN (MC CLAW), Business/Computer Teacher; *b:* Many, LA; *m:* Charles Ray; *c:* Trell, Charris; *ed:* (BS) Bus Ed, Grambling St Univ 1969; (ME) Scndry Ed, Stephen F Austin 1988; Eng as a Second Lang, Mid Management, Curr; *cr:* Secy/Bookkeeper St Johns Cath Church Sch 1969-73; Supvr Clerks Vancouver Plywood Company 1973-81; Teacher Brookeland Ind Sch Dist 1983-; *ai:* Chm Curr Comm, Co Chm Gifted & Talented Comm, 8th Grade Graduation Spon, Absentee Comm; Phi Delta Kappa 1987; TSTA Pres 1988-; Teacher of Yr 1984-87; *office:* Brookeland Ind Sch Dist P O Box 8 Brookeland TX 75931

HENSON, RHONDA HARDEN, Mathematics Teacher; *b:* Waco, TX; *m:* Bobby Glenn; *c:* Elizabeth A., Margaret D., Cynthia L., Kristine R.; *ed:* (BAT) Physics/Math, Sam Houston St Univ 1977; Grad Work Physics, Chem, Univ of TX; Advanced Trng Algebra, Geometry Modules; *cr:* Teacher Dulles HS 1977-78, Marlin Mid Sch 1978-79, Marlin HS 1979-81, Academy HS 1981-; *ai:* Schlsp & Attendance Comm; Frosh Class Spon; Assn of TX Prof Educators 1987-89; *office:* Academy HS P O Box 548 Little River TX 76554

HENTGES, RAY CHARLES, Science/Religion Teacher; *b:* Jefferson City, MO; *m:* Marilyn Hoffmeyer; *c:* Le Ann Hentges Hoth, Chris, Susan, Janie, Michael; *ed:* (BS) Ed, Lincoln Univ 1961; (MA) Bio, WI St Univ La Crosse 1971; *cr:* Teacher/Coach Sch of The Osage 1961-64; Teacher/Coach/Athletic Dir Helias 1964-; *ai:* Ftbl & Golf Head Coach; Athletic Dir; MO Interscholastic Athletic Admin Assn 1978-; *office:* Helias HS 1305 Swifts Hwy Jefferson City MO 65109

HENTHORN, JOYCE BROCK, Art/Home Economics Teacher; *b:* Princeton, WV; *m:* Harry William; *c:* Karen Henthorn Rose, Rick A.; *ed:* (BS) Ed, Concord Coll 1964; Working on Degree in Health; *cr:* Home Ec Teacher Dowdell Jr HS 1964-65; Substitute Teacher Dublin Elem & Jr HS 1974-82; Home Ec/Art Teacher Rocky Gap Combined 1982-; *ai:* FHA & Natl Art Honor Society Spon; Natl Art Ed Assn 1985-; Beta Sigma Phi (VP, Secy) 1973-; Bland Cty Voc Comm 1989-; Ladies Auxiliary; VFW; Recognition of Promotion of Patriotic Art Contest 1987-; *office:* Rocky Gap Combined HS PO Box 10 Rocky Gap VA 24366

HENTZ, EMMA KAY, Eighth Grade History Teacher; *b:* Memphis, TN; *ed:* (BA) His, Delta St Univ 1969; Grad Courses Soc Sci, Univ of MS; *cr:* His Teacher Batesville Jr HS 1970-; *ai:* Mem Stu Asst Prgm to Help Stus with Drug, Alcohol, Emotional Problems; YMCA of MS Youth Legislature Adv 1983; Daughters of Amer Revolution Speaker 1979-84, Outstanding Teacher Dist I 1980; Panola Historical & Genealogical Society 1990; *home:* 221 Perkins Ln Batesville MS 38606

HEPPLER, LINDA JOYCE, French Teacher; *b:* Freeport, NY; *m:* Tracey Miles; *c:* Brett M., Jesse C.,; *ed:* (BA) Fr Ed, St Univ of NY Fredonia 1969; Grad Stud Elem & Scndry Ed; *cr:* Fr/Eng Teacher Sherman Cntrl Sch 1970-71; Fr Teacher Clymer Cntrl Sch 1971-75, Southwestern Cntrl Sch 1976-; *ai:* Fr Club Adv; NY St Assn of Foreign Lang Teachers; W NY St Assn of Foreign Lang Teachers, Chautauqua Cty Foreign Lang Teachers, NEA, NYEA, Southwestern Teachers Assn; NY St Fr Grant 1989; *office:* Southwestern Cntrl Sch 600 Hunt Rd Jamestown NY 14701

HEPSLEY, BONNIE K., Second Grade Teacher; *b:* Lakewood, NJ; *ed:* (BS) Elem Ed, 1971, (MED) Elem Ed, 1983 Trenton St Coll; *cr:* 2nd Grade Teacher 1971-72, 1st Grade Teacher 1972-82, Remedial Rdng Teacher 1983, 1st Grade Teacher 1983-89, 2nd Grade Teacher 1989- Washington Street Sch; *ai:* PTO Exec Bd Teachers Rep; Sunshine Club Treas; Kappa Delta Pi Mem; NEA; Governors Teacher Recognition Awd 1990; *office:* Washington Street Sch W Earl Ct Toms River NJ 08753

HEPTING, KAREN BYRAM, 9th-11th Grade English Teacher; *b:* Phoenix, AZ; *m:* James; *ed:* (BA) Eng Ed, AZ St Univ 1979; *cr:* Eng Teacher Agua Fria Union HS 1979-87, Barry Goldwater HS 1987-; *ai:* Literary Magazine Spon; Outstanding Teacher Awd Agua Falls HS 1986; *office:* Barry Goldwater HS 2820 W Rose Garden Ln Phoenix AZ 85027

HERALD, IMOGENE, Social Studies Teacher; *b:* Jackson, KY; *ed:* (BA) His/Fr, 1974, (MA) His, 1975 Eastern KY Univ; Grad Stud His, Field Stud, In Eastern US & Canada; *cr:* Substitute Teacher 1975-76, Soc Stud Teacher 1976- Bethel-Tate; *ai:* NHS Co-Spon; Public Relations; OEA, NEA; Bethel-Tate Teachers Assn (Secy, Building Rep); *office:* Bethel-Tate HS Hwy 125 Bethel OH 45106

HERB, MARK RAY, 7th Grade Science Teacher; *b:* Pottsville, PA; *m:* Rebecca Ann Sellani; *c:* Marisa R., Lauren A.; *ed:* (BS) Elem Ed/Spec Ed, 1975, (MS) Elem Ed, 1980 Millersville Univ; Mastery Teaching Madeline Hunter; Peer Ed Trainee; *cr:* 9th-12th Grade Spec Ed Teacher Blue Mountain HS 1975-76; 4th Grade Teacher Auburn Elem Sch 1976-81; 6th-8th Grade Teacher Blue Mountain Mid Sch 1982-; *ai:* Girls Var Bsktbl & Mens Var Track Coach; Mid Sch Peer Ed Adv; Blue Mountain Educators Assn, PA St Educators Assn, NEA 1975-; PTSO 1987-; Teacher of Yr Awd 1982-83; *office:* Blue Mountain Mid Sch Red Dale Rd Orwigsburg PA 17961

HERBEK, MELBA ELLEN, 4th Grade Teacher; *b:* Hillman, MI; *m:* Carl Ernest; *c:* Randy, Larry, Shari Herbek Mc Lennan; *ed:* (BS) Eng, Cntrl MI Univ 1971; *cr:* K-8th Grade Teacher Kolleen Sch 1955-57, Deerfield Sch 1957-58; Title I Teacher 1961-69, 4th Grade Teacher 1969- Hillman Cmmty Sch; *ai:* Delta Kappa Gamma Prof Affairs Comm Chairperson 1988-; *home:* Rt 1 Box 198 Hillman MI 49746

HERBEL, LE ANNA RODIE, 1st-3rd Grade Teacher; *b:* La Crosse, KS; *m:* Ray E.; *c:* Kathy L., Brent D.; *ed:* (BS) Elem Ed, 1978; (MAT) Rdng, 1988 Andrews Univ; *cr:* 1st-8th Grade Teacher Shaffer 7th Day Adventist Sch 1952-54; 8th-8th Grade Teacher Hutchinson 7th Day Adventist Sch 1954-56; 5th-6th Grade Teacher Wichita 7th Day Adventist Sch 1956-57; 1st-4th Grade Teacher Tri-City Jr Acad 1966-70; 7th-8th Grade Teacher Gobles Jr Acad 1970-77; 4th-5th Grade Teacher 1978-82; 1st-3rd Grade Teacher 1982- Niles 7th Day Adventist Sch; *ai:* Curr Comm MI Conference of 7th Day Adventists; Evaluation Comm; *office:* Niles 7th Day Adv Sch 110 N Fairview Niles MI 49120

HERBERT, CORNELIA MC LEOD, English Teacher/Academic Coach; *b:* Philadelphia, PA; *m:* David Joseph; *c:* Robert D; *ed:* (BA) His, Mary Baldwin Coll 1968; (MS) Eng, IN Univ 1979; Wkshp Advanced Coll Project, IN Univ; *cr:* Elem Ed Teacher Trent Acad 1968; Elem Music Teacher Escambia Cty Schls 1969; Elem Ed Teacher Ingleside Elem 1970-71; Elem/Rdng Teacher Sylvan Elem 1971-72; Scndry Rdng Teacher Boteler Jr HS 1972-74; Scndry Eng Teacher Mitchell HS 1974-85, Wabash HS 1985-; *ai:* Acad Competition Team Apache Aces Coach; NCTE 1985-; Presenter Fall Lang Art Conf Integrating Composition Scndry Classroom IN Univ 1984; *office:* Wabash HS 580 N Miami St Wabash IN 46992

HERBERT, DIANE HOLMES, Foreign Lang Dept Chair; *b:* Huntsville, AL; *m:* Brian A.; *c:* Brian Jr., Martina, Patrick; *ed:* (BSED) Eng/Span, Auburn Univ 1964; *cr:* Span/Eng Teacher Chapman Jr HS 1964-65; Span Teacher Lakeshore HS 1965-67; Eng Teacher Landon Jr HS 1967-68; Span Teacher Bishop Kenny HS 1979-; *ai:* Natl Span Honor Society Chapter, Span Club, Span Conference Spon; Amer Assn of Teachers of Span & Portuguese 1980-, FL Assn Teachers of Span & Portuguese 1980-; FL Foreign Lang Assn 1989-; Cath Jr Womans Club (Pres 1977-78) 1967-80; Delta Delta Delta 1987-; Parish Ministry Comm 1989-; *office:* Bishop Kenny HS 1055 Kingman Ave P O Box 5544 Jacksonville FL 32247

HERBERT, KAREN GRIGSBY, Social Studies Dept Chair; *b:* New Orleans, LA; *m:* William J. Jr.; *c:* Billy; *ed:* (BS) Soc Stud/Scndry Ed, Univ of S MS 1973; *cr:* Teacher/Soc Stud Dept Chairperson St John HS 1973-; *ai:* NHS Co-Spon; Management Cncl; Fun Day Chairperson; Academic Awds Prgm Chairperson 7th-11th Grade; MS Cncl for Soc Stud 1984-86; Receive His Teacher Publication; St Teacher 1989; *office:* St John HS 620 Pass Rd Gulfport MS 39501

HERBERT, MICHAEL K., Mathematics Teacher; *b:* Toledo, OH; *c:* Jean-Paul, Suzanne, Spencer; *ed:* (BA) Psych, Univ of CA Berkeley 1965; (MIM) Intnl Mgmt, Amer Grad Sch of Intnl Management 1971; *cr:* Math Teacher Corona Del Mar HS 1968-70, Miguel Hills Jr HS 1975-78, Shorecliffs Jr HS 1978-82, Fred L Newhart Jr HS 1982-; *ai:* Little League Bsbl Coach; Soccer, Ftbl, & Bsbl Officiate; *office:* Fred L Newhart Jr HS 25001 Oso Viejo Mission Viejo CA 92692

HERBIN, SHIRLEY TABORN, Business Teacher/Dept Chair; *b:* Apex, NC; *m:* Shelton C. Jr.; *c:* Shelvette Herbin Adderly, Sharnia; *ed:* (BS) Bus, 1962, (MS) Bus Ed, 1972 NC Cntrl Univ; *cr:* Admin Asst IBM Corp 1965-67; Bus Teacher/Dept Chairperson Hillside HS 1967-; *ai:* NHS Faculty Adv; Homecoming Adv; Bus Dept Chairperson; Advisory Comm Vice-Chairperson; NEA, NC Assn of Educators, Durham City Assn of Educators 1968-; Delta Sigma Theta Secy; St Josephs Church (Sarah Allen Missionary Circle, Stewardess) 1987-; Satterfield-Davis Club Secy 1980-; Durham City Schls Teacher of Yr Candidate 1987-88; Women of Achievement Awd 1988; *office:* Hillside HS 1900 Concord St Durham NC 27707

HERBISON, NANCY RAE (JOHNSON), Guidance Counselor; *b:* Baldwin, WI; *m:* Clare Leroy; *c:* Scott E., Kari J., James H.; *ed:* (BS) His, 1974, (MSE) Guidance/Counseling, 1975 Univ of WI River Falls; Active Parenting Leadership Trng, Trng to Administer GATB; *cr:* Guidance Counselor Tomahawk Jr/Sr HS 1975-; *ai:* Forensics Dir; Class Adv; Human Growth & Development, Emergency Nursing Service, At-Risk Stu, Local Schlsp Comms; Coord Teenage Parent Prgm; Co-Chairperson of Youth Issue Comm; Amer Assn of Counseling & Dev, WI Assn of Counseling & Dev 1982-; NEA 1975-; 4-H Club Adult Leader 1976-; Kinship Secy-Treas 1986-; Tomahawk Wellness Comm 1978-89; *office:* Tomahawk Sch Dist 1048 E Kings Rd Tomahawk WI 54487

HERBOLD, JUDITH HODOWAY, English/Speech Teacher; *b:* Hawarden, IA; *m:* Donald Dean; *c:* Anne Strempke, Amy Jolivette, Cheryl; *ed:* (BA) Speech/Eng, Wayne St 1961; (MA) Eng, Univ SD 1989; *cr:* Eng Teacher Washington HS 1961-63; Eng/Speech Teacher Lawton-Bronson HS 1977-; *ai:* Speech Club, Sch Newspaper & Prom Spon; Indiv Speech Coach; Alpha Delta Kappa Treas 1990; NCTE, IA Cncl Teachers of Eng, Amer Assn of Univ Women; Good Life Singers 1981-; Grant Natl Endorsment for Hum 1985; Ind Study Grant 1989; *home:* 2849 S Palmetto Sioux City IA 51106

HERBST, DAVID L., 7th-8th Grade Teacher; *b:* Brighton, MI; *m:* Cathy Hershberger; *ed:* (BA) Math, Univ of MI 1968; (MS) Phys Sci, 1971, (MA) Admin Degree, 1975 E MI Univ; *cr:* Math/Physics Teacher Dearborn Sch Dist 8 1968-69, Brighton Area Schls 1969-70; US Army 1970-72; Teacher Mid Sch 1972-; *ai:* MI Sci Teachers Assn; MI Cncl of Teachers of Math; *office:* Scranton Mid Sch 125 S Church St Brighton MI 48116

HERBST, HELEN GERTRUDE, Music/Liturgy Coordinator; *b:* Lakewood, OH; *ed:* (BME) Music Ed, Otterbein Coll 1973; Introduction Music Therapy, Cleveland St Univ 1981; Organ 1977-82; Vocal 1980-82, 1987-89; Liturgical Music Trng Various Wkshps; *cr:* 6th-9th Grade Instrumental Music/8th Grade General Music Teacher/Asst HS Band Dir Madison Local 1973-74; Instrumental Music/Childrens Liturgy Coord St Bernadette Sch 1974-79; Asst Band Dir Avon HS 1982-85; Instrumental Music/Parish Music Coord Holy Trinity Sch & Church 1984-; *ai:* Cath Hunger Center Volunteer; OH Music Educators Assn 1970-79; Natl Cath Band Dir Assn 1975-79; Natl Pastoral Musicians 1978-; Musicians Union Local 146 1972-80; Holy Trinity Church (Literary & Welcoming Comm, Cantor, Organist, Sick & Elderly & Youth Music Ministries, Eucharistic Minister, Ministry of Lecturers) Coord; *home:* 34660 Detroit Rd Avon OH 44011

HERBST, RICHARD ALAN, Technology Education Instr; *b:* Milwaukee, WI; *m:* Mary Lou Lungwitz; *c:* Jason, Peter, Travis; *ed:* (BS) Industrial Arts Ed, UW Stout 1976; Amer Industry; Cmptr & Guidance, UW Stout & UW Whitewater; *cr:* Industrial Arts Instr 1976-86; Technology Ed Instr 1986- Jefferson Mid Sch; *ai:* 7th & 8th Boys Bkstbl & Wrestling; 7th & 8th Girls Track; 7th & 8th Cross Cntry; Bsbl Card Club Adv; Sch Dist Cmptr Comm Mem; Sch Dist Safety Comm Mem; WI Career Information System Advisory Bd Mem 1985-; WI Career Information System Teacher 1985- Excl Awd 1987; Cmptr Learning Fnd Teacher Published Lesson Plan 1988; *office:* Jefferson Mid Sch 201 S Copeland Ave Jefferson WI 53549

HERBSTER, PHYLLIS FOSTER, Retired Elementary Teacher; *b:* Union Star, MO; *m:* Harlan D.; *c:* Deborah S. Herbster Jennings; *ed:* (BS) Elem Ed, NW MO St Coll 1967; *cr:* 1st-8th Grade Elem Teacher Clanton Sch 1950-51; 1st-4th Grade Teacher Castle Sch 1951-54; 1st Grade South Park Sch 1959-62, King City R-I 1963-84; *ai:* MO St Teachers Assn 1963-84, Retired Teachers Assn of MO 1985-; Beta Sigma Phi Pres 1968-69; General Federated Womens Club Star Culture Society Pres 1956-57; *home:* 407 Havre King City MO 64463

HERCHER, WENDI SMITH, Science Teacher; *b:* Richland, WA; *m:* John Douglas; *ed:* (BS) Earth Sci/Geology 1985, (BA) Ed, 1986 OR St Univ Corvallis; *cr:* Sci Teacher Parrish Mid Sch 1986-; *ai:* Chairperson Onward to Excl Comm; Vlybl Coach; Aeronautics Club Adv; Discipline Comm; Salem Ed Assn SEA Rep 1988-89; *office:* Parrish Mid Sch 802 Capitol St Salem OR 97301

HERD, DOROTHY PARKS, 3rd & 4th Grade Teacher; *b:* Altoona, PA; *m:* Charles Blount; *c:* Charles T., Benjamin P.; *ed:* (BS) Elem Ed, Lee Coll 1973; (MAED) Elem Ed, Tusculum Coll 1989; *cr:* Teacher Fairview Elem 1972-73, Ten Mile Elem 1973-; *ai:* 8th Grade Washington DC Trip Spon; Meigs Cty Spelling Bee Coord; 4-H Spon; Meigs Cty Assn VP 1974-75; East TN Ed Assn 1972-; NEA 1972-; PTA (Secy 1976-77, Pres 1977-79); TN Governor Career Ladder III Status; *office:* Ten Mile Elem Sch Rt 2 Box 5 Ten Mile TN 37880

HERDES, MARIE (PICKENS), Biology Teacher; *b:* Effingham, IL; *m:* Robert L.; *c:* Heather, Kevin, Dirk; *ed:* (BSED) Bio, E IL Univ 1968; Grad Level Ed Classes, E IL Univ; Summer Sci Wkshps 1987, 1989; Sci Grant Wkshp 1990; *cr:* Phys Ed Teacher Onarga Sch System 1968-69; Life Sci Teacher Windsor Jr HS 1969-86; Bio Teacher Windsor HS 1986-; *ai:* Adv for Windsor HS Stu Cncl & Class of 1992; Teacher Asst Team Comm for Windsor HS Faculty; NEA, IEA, Windsor Ed Assn, IL Sci Teachers Assn; Holy Cross Luth Church; Beta Sigma Phi Pres 1986-87, Girl of Yr 1987; *office:* Windsor Jr/Sr HS 1424 Minnesota St Windsor IL 61957

HEREFORD, GERALDINE C., Third Grade Teacher; *b:* Sylacauga, AL; *m:* Alfred Lee; *c:* Committer L. Booker, Margie O. Ramsey, Barbara J. Garner, Debra D. Booker; *ed:* (BS) Elem Ed, A&M Univ; Working Towards Masters in Early Chldhd Ed; *ai:* 3rd Grade Leader; AL Ed Assn, Cty Ed Assn, NEA; Intnl Chrstn Ed Assn; Licensed Evangelist; Sunday Sch Supt; Delta Sigma Theta; *home:* 3104 Patrick Huntsville AL 35810

HEREFORD, LOUNITA MAY LUCKETT, Third Grade Teacher; *b:* English, KY; *m:* Larry Andrew; *c:* Lance E.; *ed:* (BA) Music, Univ of Louisville 1967; (MS) Elem Ed, Georgetown Coll 1976; Elem Music Ed; *cr:* Eng/Lit Teacher 1968, Spec Ed Teacher 1968-69 Trimble Cty HS; Music Teacher Trimble Cty Mid Sch & Milton Elem 1969-72; 3rd Grade Teacher Milton Elem Sch 1972-; *home:* Rt 2 Box 243 Milton KY 40045

HERENS, DENISE CLARK, Mathematics Teacher; *b:* Philadelphia, PA; *m:* Edward M.; *c:* Heather, Kathryn; *ed:* (BS) Elem Ed, Gwynedd Mercy Coll 1986; Crisis Intervention; *cr:* Teacher St Aloysius 1969-73, Our Lady of Calvary 1978-; *ai:* Stu Government Moderator; Yrbk; Math Coord; Graduation Comm; NCEA; Elem Sch Math Curr Comm Distinguished Teacher Awd 1988; *office:* Our Lady of Calvary Sch 11023 Kipling Ln Philadelphia PA 19154

HERGESHEIMER, JOHN H., Social Science Dept Chair; *b:* Hollywood, CA; *m:* Elizabeth A.; *c:* Mark, Peter, Ruth Northrop; *ed:* (BA) Music/Soc Stud, Whittier Coll 1954; (MA) Music, CA St Univ Long Beach 1961; Course Work Univ of S CA; Whittier Coll; CA St Univ Long Beach; *cr:* Teacher Norwalk HS 1957-; *ai:* NCSS (Ad Hoc Comm Co-Chm, Annual Meeting Co-Chm 1990); CA Cncl for Soc Stud (Pres 1984-85, Newsletter Ed) 1984-85; S Whittier Sch Dist Sch Bd 1973-85; Whittier Area Admin Distinguished Service Awd 1986; Many Prof Articles; CA Model Curr Stans Co-Chm; Malone Fellowship Saudi Arabia Bahrain 1990; Keizai Koho Fellowship Japan 1983; *home:* 11603 Breckenridge Dr Whittier CA 90604

HERI, BARBARA A., 6th Grade Teacher; *b:* Youngstown, OH; *m:* Frank J.; *c:* James, Christine Heri Piligian; *ed:* (BSE) Elem Ed, 1961, (ME) Ed. 1973 Youngstown St; *cr:* Teacher Covington Elem 1961-68, Paul C Bun Elem 1968-77, Roosevelt Elem 1977-89, Kirkmere Elem 1989-; *ai:* Youngstown Ed Assn 1961-; NEA 1961-; OH Educl Assn 1961-; *home:* 530 Neoka Dr Campbell OH 44405

HERING, CAROL WILL, Retired 3rd Grade Teacher; *b:* Milwaukee, WI; *m:* Lee; *c:* Nancy Treul, Susan, Sandra, Karen; *ed:* (BS) Elem Ed, Univ of WI Oshkosh 1970; *cr:* 1st Grade Teacher 1970-73, 3rd Grade Teacher 1973-87 Black Creek Grade Sch; *home:* 1436 E Frances St Appleton WI 54911

HERITY, K. JOAN KELLY, Social Studies Teacher; *b:* New York, NY; *m:* Richard J.; *c:* Kathleen, Mary, Deirdre, Michael, Eileen, Joan; *ed:* (BA) His/Ed - Magna Cum Laude, Coll of MT St Vincent 1976; (MS) Ed/His, W CT St Univ 1983; Coll of New Rochelle, Bridgeport Univ, Long Island Univ; *cr:* 5th-8th Grade Soc Stud/6th Grade Homeroom Teacher Christ The King Sch 1977-78; 9th-12th Grade Teacher Somers HS 1978-; *ai:* AFS Adv 1981-84; Jr Var Sftbl Coach; NYSCSS 1989-; Somers Faculty Assn Secy 1986-; *office:* Somers HS Rt 139 Lincolndale NY 10540

HERLIHY, THOMAS M., Music Teacher; *b:* Rockville Centre, NY; *m:* Anne Marie Yetter; *ed:* (BM) Music Ed, 1973, (MM) Music Ed, 1989 SUC Fredonia; Guildhall Sch of Music & Drama London England; Coll of New Rochelle, Long Island Univ; *cr:* Trumpet Teacher/HS Youth Band Asst Conductor Chautauqua Inst 1980; Music Camp Dir Camp Pioneer Music Camp 1981-84; Music Teacher Lake Shore Cntrl Schls 1973-; *ai:* Jazz Ensemble; Marching Band; Asst Var Wrestling; MENC, NYSSMA, United Fed of Musicians #92, #649; Erie Cty Wind Ensembles VP; *office:* Lake Shore Cntrl Mid Sch 8855 Erie Rd Angola NY 14006

HERMAN, CHRISTINE, Fifth Grade Teacher; *b:* Palmerton, PA; *ed:* (AA) Assumpton Coll 1973; (BA) Elem Ed, Felician Coll 1977; *cr:* 2nd/4th/5th Grade Teacher Nativity BVM Sch 1979-; *ai:* Sci, Music, Sch Testing Coord; NCEA Teacher Assoc 1979-; *office:* Nativity BVM Sch Belgrade & Madison Sts Philadelphia PA 19134

HERMAN, LINDA SUE, Art Teacher/Dept Chair; *b:* Pittsburgh, PA; *ed:* (BA) Art Ed, 1967, (MA) Art Ed, 1969 Indiana Univ of PA; *cr:* Art Teacher Dobbin Area Voc HS 1969-70; Art Teacher/Dept Chairperson Massena Jr HS 1971-; *office:* J W Leary Jr HS School St Massena NY 13662

HERMAN, MARIONE JACKSON, Fr, Span Teacher/Dept Chair; *b:* Kings Mountain, NC; *m:* Harry T.; *c:* Todd; *ed:* (BA) Fr, NC Coll 1963; (MA) Fr, NC Cntrl Univ 1971; Fr & Span, NDEA Lang Inst; Fr, Immersion Prgm; Fr Art; *cr:* Teacher R L Vann HS 1963-70, Ahoskie HS 1970-88, Hartford Cty HS 1988-; *ai:* SGA, Quiz Bowl, Span Club Spon; Chairperson Discipline Comm; Foreign Lang Dept Teacher Recruiter; Teacher Advisory, Schlsp, Awds, Senate Bill Two Comm; NCEA, NEA Local Secy; AATSP, Paul Claudel Society; Delta Sigma Theta Secy Silver Anniversary 1989; New Ahoskie Baptist Church S S Supt; Governors Lang Inst; NC Writers Wkshp; NC Center for Advancement of Teaching; Hertford Cty Leadership Team; *office:* Hertford Cty HS 1st St Ext Ahoskie NC 27910

HERMAN, SALLY AUBUCHON, Jr HS Vocal Music Teacher; *b:* St Louis, MO; *m:* James; *c:* Scott Johnson, Lynette Johnson; *ed:* (BA) Music, AZ St Univ 1967; (MM) Music, Webster Univ 1985; *cr:* Music Teacher Athena R-8 Elem 1964-67, Fox Jr HS 1967-; Choir Dir/Adjunct Professor 1988-89; *ai:* Amer Choral Dir Assn, MO Music Educators Assn, Music Educators Natl Conference; Luther T Spayde Awd; Guest Conductor/Clinician several Univ; Eastman Sch of Music Conductor of Natl Jr HS Honor Choir 1989; Articles in Natl Magazines; Outstanding Educator Veiled Prophet Fair; Music & Book Published; *home:* 1418 Cedar Crest Barnhart MO 63012

HERMANSON, DIANE BRATLIE, Second Grade Teacher; *b:* Detroit Lakes, MN; *m:* Jim; *c:* Jesse, Randy; *ed:* (BS) Elem Ed, Concordia Coll 1971; *cr:* 5th Grade Teacher 1971-83, Title 1 Teacher 1983-84, 2nd Grade Teacher 1984- Henning Elem Sch; *ai:* Soc Stud Curr Comm; MEA, NEA, HEA 1971-; Henning Ed Assn Membership Chairperson 1973-76, 1989-; Good Shepherd Luth Church Bd of Ed 1978-81; Oakwood Ladies Golf League (Pres 1978, Mem) 1975-; *office:* Henning Elem Sch School Ave Henning MN 56551

HERMIE, MARIE ANN, English Department Chair; *b:* Chicago, IL; *m:* Jack Thomas; *c:* Jarie A., Jacquelene M., Jon T.; *ed:* (BS) Eng, W IL Univ 1959; Grad Stud Marycrest Coll, W IL Univ, Upper IA, N IA; *cr:* Eng Teacher Davenport HS 1959-60, West HS 1960-63, Blackhawk Jr Coll 1964-66, Sudlow Jr HS 1973-; *ai:* Dept Chairperson; Spelling Bee Coord; Anthology Adv; Curr Comm; IA Cncl Teachers of Eng 1976-; NCTE 1978-; Delta Kappa Gamma Membership Chairperson 1983-; *office:* Sudlow Jr HS 1414 E Locust St Davenport IA 52803

HERNANDEZ, DIANE, ESL/Soc Stud/Mentor Teacher; *b:* Los Angeles, CA; *m:* Sergio J.; *c:* Corina, Natalie, Jenna; *ed:* (BA) Chicano Stud, CSUN 1974; Bi-ling & Bi-Cultural Certificate of Competence; *cr:* Teacher 1976-78, Dean of Stu 1978-79, Bi-ling Coord/Cnslr 1979-84, Teacher 1984-86, Project Socrates Coord/Mentor Teacher 1986-88, 1990 San Fernando HS; *ai:* Asst MECHA Adv; Faculty Rep Sch Leadership Comm; Assn of Mexican Amer Educators 1976-; GSA Leader 1986-88; Guest & Keynote Speaker for Ed Classes at CA St Univ, N Valley Occupational Center Graduation; Various Chicano Youth Leadership Conferences Presenter; *office:* San Fernando HS 11133 O Melveny St San Fernando CA 91340

HERNANDEZ, DOLORES CADENA, Business Education Teacher; *b:* El Paso, TX; *m:* Dolores Cadena; *c:* Adrian, Ruben Andres; *ed:* (BS) Bus Ed, UTEP 1968; (MED) Cmptrs in Ed, Lesley 1990; Numerous Courses; *cr:* Teacher El Paso Public Schls 1970-; Instr Tech Voc Center 1975-76, El Paso Comm Coll 1974-80, 1989-; *ai:* Faculty Communications Comm; Sr Spon 1987-88; UIL Typing Coach; TBEA 1984-, Bus Teacher of Yr 1989-; TCTA 1984-; *office:* Burges HS 7800 Edgemere El Paso TX 79925

HERNANDEZ, ELIZABETH EZRA, 2nd Grade Teacher; *b:* Chicago, IL; *c:* James M.; *ed:* (BS) Elem Ed/Bi-ling, Angelo St Univ 1979; *cr:* 2nd/3rd Grade Teacher Grade Teacher Ft Concho Elem; *ai:* TX Classroom Teachers 1980-; Alpha Delta Kappa Secy 1985-89; TX St Teachers Assn; Ft Concho PTA Bd Mem; *office:* Ft Concho Elem Sch 310 E Washington San Angelo TX 76903

HERNANDEZ, FLORENCE THEURER, English Teacher; *b:* Ventura, CA; *c:* Marisa, Pilar, Guillermo, Carmen, Ana; *ed:* (BA) Humanistic Stud, St Marys Coll 1963; (MA) Ed, NM Highlands Univ 1984; Anthropology, Univ of KS 1972-75; *cr:* Eng Teacher Robertson HS 1984-; *ai:* Mock Trial Coach; NHS Spon; *office:* Robertson HS 5th St & Freadman Ave Las Vegas NM 87701

HERNANDEZ, GILBERT MENDEZ, Spanish Teacher; *b:* San Jose, CA; *m:* Fior Ballesteros; *c:* Hannah, Matilda, David; *ed:* (BA) Theology, Linda Vista Coll & Seminary 1988; Working Towards Masters Theology/Counseling; Music/Piano; *cr:* A D Teacher Keystone Chrstn Sch 1984-85; Teacher/Coach Victory Chrstn HS 1987-88, Chrstn HS 1989-; Dir Ebenez er Baptist Inst 1990; *ai:* Grade Adv; Jr Var Bsbl Coach; Music-Writing-Recording; Phi Kappa Pres 1978-79; Chaplin Pensacola Coll 1977-78; *home:* 1815 Greenfield Dr El Cajon CA 92021

HERNANDEZ, GUADALUPE R., 6th-8th Grade Math Teacher; *b:* Benavides, TX; *m:* Louisa G.; *c:* Cynthia Ann Solis, Julissa Lamar; *ed:* (BA) Ed, TX a & I Univ 1970; Addl Studies Administration; *cr:* Math/Hist Harlingen ISD 1970-73; Math West OSO 1973-74; Driscoll ISD 1974-; *ai:* UIL Number Sense Coach; Math Count Coach; Career Ladder Comm; Amer Math Competitions; TSTA 1970-; Lions Club; Career Ladder Three; *home:* P O Box 155 Driscoll TX 78351

HERNANDEZ, IRENE PINEDA, Jr High Language Art Teacher; *b:* Marfa, TX; *m:* Frank L.; *c:* Pauline R.; *ed:* (BA) Eng/Span, Sul Ross St Univ 1964; Elem, Bi-ling Certificates Sul Ross St Univ 1970 & 1982; *cr:* Span Teacher Balmorhea Ind Sch Dist 1962-63; HS Eng Teacher Marfa Ind Sch Dist 1963-64; 1st Grade Teacher St Marys Sch 1964-65; HS Span Teacher 1965-66, Pre-Sch/Kndgtn Teacher 1967-69 Terrell Cty Ind Sch Dist; Jr/Sr HS Eng Teacher Ft Davis Ind Sch Dist 1969-75; 3rd Grade Teacher Carlsbad Municipal Sch 1975-78; HS Cnslr 1977-78, 2nd Grade Teacher 1978-81, 6th Grade Teacher 1981-82, 4th Grade Teacher 1982-89, 7th-8th Grade Lang Art Teacher 1989- Presidio Ind Sch Dist; *ai:* Discipline & Textbook Comms; TX St Teachers VP 1988-89; Natl Teachers Assn, TX Assn for Improvement Rdng; Friend of Presidio Public Lib Pres Petite Friends 1988-89, Appreciation Plaque 1988-89; Elem Art Dept Chairperson 1977-78; Started Pre-Sch Prgm 1976-77; Cultural Fed Grant Historical Quilt Project 1976-77; Schlsp Elem Cert Terrell Cty Sch; *office:* Presidio Jr HS Box S Presidio TX 79845

HERNDON, RICHARD L., Mathematics Dept Chairman; *b:* Columbus, IN; *m:* Elizabeth B.; *c:* Carter A.; *ed:* (BA) Math, Franklin Coll 1967; (MA) Math/Ed, Ball St Univ 1973; Problem Solving Seminar Purdue Univ; Calculus Seminar IN Univ; Statistics Seminar Rose-Hulman; Schl Law, Admin Public Relations, Ball St Univ; *cr:* Teacher Franklin Jr HS 1967-69; Math Teacher/Dept Chm Elwood Cmmty HS 1969-78; Teacher Tipton Cmmty HS 1982-83; Math Teacher/Dept Chm Hamilton Heights HS 1984-; *ai:* Math Club; Sch Improvement, In-Service Team; IN Cncl of Teachers of Math 1967-; NCTM 1967-; IN St Teachers, NEA 1967-; Elwood Sch Bd Pres 1982-83; Elwood Zoning Bd Pres 1976-78; Elks; Elwood Cntry Club; IN Teacher of Yr 1988; Candidate Presidential Awds for Excl; Natl Sci Fnd 1987-88, 1990; *home:* 1609 S Anderson St Elwood IN 46036

HERNEISEN, CURTIS LEE, Second Grade Teacher; *b:* Lancaster, PA; *m:* Marjorie Diane Young; *ed:* (BS) Elem Ed, 1973, (MED) Elem Ed, 1976 Millersville Univ; Educl Admin, Temple Univ 1984; Wildlife Bio, UT St Univ 1968-70; Early Chldhd, Millersville Univ 1990; *cr:* 4th Grade Teacher Lindley Murray Elem 1973-76; 3rd Grade Teacher 1976-83, 4th-6th Grade Teacher 1983-86, 2nd Grade Teacher 1986-, Admin Aide 1985- Northwest Elem; *ai:* Wrestling Coach Lebanon 1973-76, Elco HS 1977-80; Northwest Elem Sch Admin Aide 1985-; Lebanon HS Athletic Trainer 1974-75; Early Chldhd Study Team; Eng, Sci, Soc Stud, Curr Comms; Lancaster Cty Wrestling Officials Pres 1983-84, 1990-; NEA, PSEA, Lebanon Ed Assn; Lebanon Cty Educl Honor Society; Marquis Whos Who in East.

HERNQUIST, DOROTHY BAUM, Lang Art Specialist Teacher; *b:* Chicago, IL; *m:* Robert Samuel; *ed:* (BE) Lib Art/Ed, Chicago Teachers Coll 1956; (MA) Teaching of Eng, Univ of MN 1974; Amer & Eng Lit, Northwestern Univ; *cr:* 5th-7th Grade Teacher Shakespeare Sch 1956-60, Madison Sch 1960-64; 3rd-8th Grade Teacher 1964-72, Lit/Composition Teacher 1974- Newberry Acad; *ai:* Pen & Paper Stu Publication; Young Authors Conference; NCTE; Partners of the Americas Sao Paulo/IL Partners Governing Bd 1987-; *office:* Newberry Math & Sci Acad 700 W Willow St Chicago IL 60614

HERON, JULIE ANNE, Spanish Teacher; *b:* Nashua, NH; *ed:* (BA) Scndry Ed/Span/Eng, TX Tech Univ 1987; *cr:* Span I Teacher 1987-88, Span I & III Teacher 1988-89, Span I & II Teacher 1989- C E Ellison HS; *ai:* Foreign Lang Club & Chrldr Spon; Textbook Adoption Comm; ASCD Mem 1990; Amer Cncl Teaching Foreign Lang Mem 1987-88; *office:* C E Ellison HS 909 Elms Rd Killeen TX 76542

HERR, ARTHUR LYNN, Physics Teacher; *b:* Lancaster, PA; *m:* Maryjon Hardin; *c:* Wayne Armstrong, Mark, Allan Armstrong, Andrew, Martha, Barry Armstrong, Tyler Armstrong; *ed:* (BS) Animal Husbandry, Rutgers Univ 1954; (BSE) General Sci, 1977, (MED) Adult Ed, 1978 Memphis St Univ; Numerous Trng, Management Courses; Advanced Field Career Physics, Astronomy; Aviatioin Courses; Licensed Commercial Pilot; *cr:* Naval Aviator US Navy 1954-75; Trng Dir Memphis St Univ 1975-76; Asst Dir Center for Nuclear Stud 1976-77; Curr Services Dir Tech Services 1978-80; Teacher Germantown HS 1980-; *ai:* Key Club Spon; Chairperson Sci Advisory Comm; Physics Club Spon; Communications Comm Chm; NSTA, Amer Physics Society 1985-; Old Antarctic Explorers 1964-; Assn of Naval Aviators 1954-; Lakeland Civic Club Pres 1985, Service Awd 1986; Lions Club Prgm Chm 1984-86; Delta Upsilon VP 1950-54; Explorer Club Fellow, Amer Polar Society Fellow 1964-; Adult Ed Grant; Published Curr Dev Articles; ECO Manual Author; Nom British Polar Society; Intnl Geographic Society Named Mountain; *office:* Germantown HS 7653 Old Poplar Pike Germantown TN 38138

HERR, GERRY, 3rd Grade Teacher; *b:* Libertyville, IL; *ed:* (BA) Elem Ed, Mundelein Coll 1955; (MA) Elem Ed Supervisory Certificate, IL Univ 1967; *cr:* 3rd Grade Teacher Kipling Sch 1957-; *ai:* PTA 1957-67; PTO 1967-; *office:* Kipling Sch Kipling Pl Deerfield IL 60015

HERR, JUDITH ANN (GORNDT), Elementary Teacher of Gifted; *b:* Elmhurst, IL; *m:* Richard Z.; *c:* David M., Daniel J., Douglas W.; *ed:* (BS) Elem Ed, Purdue Univ 1961; (MS) Educl Strategies/Dev, Wilkes Univ 1990; Courses at Millersville Univ, Shippensburg Univ, Lincoln Intermediate Units 12 & 13; Staff Dev Trng; Critical Thinking Trng; *cr:* 1st Grade Teacher Glen Ellyn Sch System 1961-63; Elem Teacher of Gifted Waynesboro Area Sch Dist 1978-; *ai:* Staff Dev Co-Chm; Gifted Dist Comm; Waynesboro Area Ed Assn 1980-;PA Assn of Gifted Ed 1980-, Gifted Teacher of Yr Finalist 1986; PA Assn of Supervision Curr Dev 1986-; Waynesboro Coll Club (Secy, Soc Chm) 1975-; Waynesboro Hospital Auxiliary 1975-; United Way Bd of Dir 1990; Newcomers Club (Pres 1974-75) 1973-76; Wkshp Presentation PASCD Conference Harrisburg PA; Inservice Wkshp Presentations Waynesboro Sch Dist; Wrote Pamphlet for Dist; *office:* Waynesboro Area Sch Dist 210 Clayton Ave Waynesboro PA 17268

HERREMA, KATHY ALLEN, Spanish/Geography Instructor; *b:* Clarinda, IA; *m:* Dennis J.; *c:* Jennifer, David; *ed:* (BA) Span/ Geography, Cntrl Coll 1969; *cr:* Span Instr/Geography Teacher Prairie City/Monroe HS 1971-; *ai:* Phase III Comm; Stus Trip to Mexico; Amer Assn of Teacher of Span & Portuguese, NCSS; Fulbright 6 Weeks in Mexico 1989; *office:* Prairie City/Monroe HS Hwy 163 Monroe IA 50170

HERRICK, ALBERTA ELAINE (LUGANO), English Teacher; *b:* Steubenville, OH; *m:* Michael P.; *c:* Danielle, Nicole, Michael R.; *ed:* (BA) Eng/Speech, W Liberty St 1968; Admin, Counseling Courses Dayton Univ, Steubenville Univ; *cr:* Title II Prgm Teacher Grant Sch 1967-68; 8th/9th Grade Eng Teacher Buchanan Jr HS 1968-; *ai:* Teacher Advisory Cncl; Eng Curr Dev Comm; Buchanan Teachers Writing Process Wkshp Presenter; NEA, OH Ed Assn, Indian Creek Ed Assn, Alpha Phi Sigma, St Agnes Home & Sch Assn, Beta Sigma Phi; Mingo Boosters & Indian Mothers Athletic Clubs; St Agnes Church Lector; *office:* Buchanan Jr HS 100 Park Dr Wintersville OH 43952

HERRING, PATRICIA WILSON, Third Grade Teacher; *b:* Clinton, NC; *m:* Charles D.; *c:* Charles Jr., Heather; *ed:* (BA) Elem Ed, 1967, (MS) Guidance/Counseling, 1989 Campbell Univ; *cr:* 3rd Grade Teacher Loch Lomond Elem 1967-70; 5th Grade Teacher Hargrove Elem 1971-77; 3rd Grade Teacher Hobbton Elem 1980-; *ai:* Senate Bill 2 & Sch Based Comm; Counseling Consultant; NEA, NCEA 1980-; Womans Club Pres 1983-85; PTO Treas; Nom Teacher of Yr 1989-; *home:* Rt 2 Box 36-A5 Newton Grove NC 28366

HERRING, PHILLIP DAVID, General Cooperative Ed Coord; *b:* Monticello, AR; *ed:* (BA) His/Poly Sci, Univ of AR Monticello 1977; (MS) Voc Ed, Univ of AR Fayetteville 1981; *cr:* GCE Coord Dermott Public Schls 1978-; *ai:* Class & GCE Club Spon; AVA 1980-; AR Ed Assn, NEA 1978-; Sigma Tau Gamma Treas 1977-; Cooperative Ed Coord of AR Pres 1978-; *office:* Dermott HS Hwy 35 E Dermott AR 71638

HERRINGTON, CAROLYN PETERSON, 7th & 8th Grade Band Director; *b:* Lincoln, NE; *m:* James G.; *c:* James B, Timothy M; *ed:* (BME) Music Ed K-12, Univ of Southern MS 1981; Univ of Southern MS; McNeese St Univ; *cr:* 6th Grade Band Dir East Side Elem 1982-84; 8th Grade Band Dir De Ridder Jr HS 1984-89; *ai:* Consulting Teacher 1988-; Club Spon High Notes; Counted Cross Stitch; Career Club; Church Youth Choir; Dist V Band Dir (VP 86-87/Sec 87); Dist Band Dir of Yr 1989-; Beta Sigma Phi 1984-89; Young Womens Leag 1989-; De Ridder Jr HS Teacher of Yr 1986-87; Beauregard Parish Teacher of Yr 1986-87; De Ridder Optimist Club Teacher of Yr 1988-89; *office:* De Ridder Jr HS 415 N Frusha Dr De Ridder LA 70634

HERRINGTON, DIANA L. (SLATER), Mathematics Teacher; *b:* Salinas, CA; *m:* Kenneth E.; *c:* Kendia; *ed:* (BS) Math, 1973, (MA) Math, 1974 CA Poly St Univ; *cr:* Teacher Riverview 1975-76, Green Acres Jr HS 1976-78, Kings River Comm Coll 1979-83, Clovis HS 1983-; *ai:* Sci Fair & Math Club Adv; Math Team & JETS Coach; Yr-Round Sch Comm; IB Math Coord; NCTM 1973-; Math Assn of America 1984-; CA Math Cncl 1988-; CA Math Project Mem; Articles Published in CMC Communicator; Clovis HS Teacher of Yr 1987-88; Leading Math Ed into the 21st Century Team Mem; *office:* Clovis HS 1055 Fowler Ave Clovis CA 93612

HERRINGTON, DON ALAN, Industrial Technology Chair; *b:* Edinburg, TX; *m:* Gayla Diann Bowerman; *c:* Gregory, Christopher; *ed:* (BSED) Industrial Art, Abilene Chrstn Univ 1980; Wkshps; *cr:* Ind Tech Instr Lincoln Mid Sch 1980-; *ai:* Industrial Tech Club Spon; Mens Sftbl; Ftbl & Track Coach; W Cntrl Tx Industrial Arts Assn (Secy, Treas) 1980-; Assn of TX Technology Educators 1980-; TIASA (Mem, Former Secy, Treas, VP Nominee); Assn of Teachers Prof Educator Building Rep 1982-85; TX St Teachers Assn 1980-82; Breakfast Optimist 1981-87; Whos Who Outstanding Young Men of America 1986; *office:* Lincoln Mid Sch 1699 S 1st St Abilene TX 79602

HERRINGTON, UMBRENDA, Fourth Grade Teacher; *b:* Philadelphia, PA; *ed:* (BA) Elem Ed, OH Wesleyan Univ 1974; Grad Work Bowie St Univ; Governors Acad for Math, Sci & Technology; *cr:* Teacher Laurel Elem Sch 1974-81, Bond Mill Elem Sch 1981-; *ai:* Math-A-Thon Coord; Grade Level Chm; Staff Dev Coord; Mentoring Team Mem; Sch Improvement Team Mem; PTA Exec Bd Faculty Rep; Problem Solving Team Mem; Soc Comm Chm; MD St Teachers Assn 1974-; NEA 1974-; Prince Georges Cty Educators Assn 1974-; Birch Run Homeowners Assn (Treas 1987-89, VP 1989-); Outstanding Young Woman of America 1984; Bond Mills Outstanding Educator 1985; Governors Acad for Math, Sci & Technology 1989; MD Governors Citation 1989; *office:* Bond Mill Elem Sch 16001 Sherwood Ave Laurel MD 20707

HERRMANN, GARY LEE, Sixth Grade Teacher; *b:* Mound City, KS; *m:* Jo C.; *c:* Susan, Garth; *ed:* (BS) Phys Ed, 1970, (MS) Elem Ed, 1978 PSU; *cr:* Jr HS Sci Teacher Jasper R-5 1970-75; 6th Grade Teacher Uniontown Unified Sch Dist 235 1976-; *ai:* Math Olympiad Spon; UTA, NEA; *office:* West Bourbon Elem Sch Rt 1 Uniontown KS 66779

HERROLD, JACQUELINE S., Journalism/English Teacher; *b:* Pattonville, TX; *m:* Ralph H.; *c:* Jack, Deidra; *ed:* (BA) Eng, Abilene Chrstn Univ 1963; (MED) Scndry Ed, Wichita St Univ 1986; *cr:* Eng Teacher Hart Jr HS 1963-64; Eng/Fr Teacher Plainview HS 1964-68; Teacher of Gifted/Eng/Journalism Hesston HS 1976-; *ai:* Newspaper, Literary, Quill & Scroll Adv; Scholars Bowl Coach; Delta Kappa Gamma 1983-88; NEA 1979-; Wichita St Univ KS Writing Project Mem & Grant; *office:* Hesston HS 200 N Ridge Rd Hesston KS 67062

HERRON, ELIZABETH L. ENGLAND, 7th/8th Grade English Teacher; *b:* Middlesboro, KY; *m:* Darryl F.; *ed:* (BA) Elem Ed/Kndgtn, Lincoln Mem Univ 1977; *cr:* Kndgtn Teacher Tazewell-New Tazewell Primary 1977-79; Elem Teacher La Follette Mid Sch 1979-; *ai:* Yrbk Spon 1981-85; Jr Varsity Chrldrs 1981; AFT 1982-; Apple Awd 1987; Local Awds; Yrbk Dedication; Schl Yrbk; *office:* La Follette Mid Sch Middlesboro Hwy La Follette TN 37766

HERRON, GAIL SONDERGARD, Science & Health Teacher; *b:* Los Angeles, CA; *m:* Jack Larry; *ed:* (AA) Biological Sci, El Camino Jr Coll 1963; (BA) Biological Sci, CA St Univ Long Beach 1965; Grad Work Phys Sci, Univ of CA Irving; Health Sci/ Counseling, CA St Univ Fullerton, CA St Univ Long Beach; *cr:* Sci Teacher La Puente HS 1966-; *ai:* Sigma Club Adv; Dist Health Consultant; Delta Kappa Gamma 1979-; CA Assn of Sch Health Educators 1984-; CA Teachers Assn, NEA 1966-; Amer Red Cross (Safety Services Comm 1978-83, Cardio Pulmonary Resuscitation Instr 1976-85); La Puente HS Staff Mem of Yr 1980; *office:* La Puente HS 15615 E Nelson Ave La Puente CA 91744

HERRON, JANE ELLEN LAWTON, Teacher/Department Head; *b:* Charleston, SC; *m:* Michael E.; *c:* Nicholas; *ed:* (BA) Arts/Letters, Univ of SC 1973; (MAT) Eng, The Citadel 1977; *cr:* 5th-8th Grade Teacher Sacred Heart Sch 1973-75; 6th-8th Grade Lang Art/Soc Stud/Religion Teacher/Eng Dept Coord Christ Our King-Stella Maris Sch 1975-; *ai:* Eng Dept & 6th-8th Grade Upper Sch Coord; Publicity Chairperson; Sch Newspaper Ed; NCEA; Christ Our King-Stella Maris Sch Bd 1981-; Comparative Ed Study Tour Moscow & Leningrad 1988; *office:* Christ Our King-Stella Maris 1183 Russell Dr Mount Pleasant SC 29464

HERRY, D. MARK, 6th Grade Teacher; *b:* Medina, NY; *m:* Deborah Mary Burrows; *c:* Caleb, Carissa; *ed:* (BA) Scndry Ed/ Math, Univ of Edinboro 1976; (MS) Elem Ed, Suny Geneseo 1980; Classroom Management, Elements of Inst, Talents Unlimited; *cr:* 7th/8th Grade Math Teacher Clifton Mid Sch 1976-77; 6th Grade Teacher 1977-85, 4th Grade Teacher 1985-86 Clifton Elem Sch; 6th Grade Teacher Midlakes Mid Sch 1986-; *ai:* Pico Math Olympiads; Organized Fund Drive for Starving in Ethiopia; *office:* Midlakes Mid Sch W Main St Phelps NY 14532

HERSBERGER-GRAY, DENISE ANNE, Math Teacher; *b:* Noblesville, IN; *m:* Robin L.; *c:* Ian, Lorean, Elliot; *ed:* (BA) Math, 1977; (BS) Math, 1977 Anderson Univ; (MS) Math, Ball St Univ 1981; *cr:* Jr Sr HS Math Teacher Lapel HS 1978-; *office:* Lapel Jr Sr HS P O Box 518 Lapel IN 46051

HERSEY, JUDITH TRACY, Sixth Grade Teacher; *b:* Lowell, MA; *m:* William R.; *c:* Kathleen, Thomas, Lynne, Justine; *ed:* (BSED) Elem Ed, Univ of Lowell 1961; *cr:* 5th Grade Teacher Chelmsford Public Schls 1961-62; 4th Grade Teacher Haverhill Public Schls 1962-63; Substitute Teacher Dracut Public Schls 1967-70; 6th Grade Teacher Franco Amer Sch 1970-71, 1979-; *ai:* NEA; Univ of Lowell Alumni (Secy 1977-78, Bd of Dir).

HERSH, JOHN, Third Grade Teacher; *b:* York, PA; *m:* Lynn Casselberry; *c:* Nathaniel, Nicholas; *ed:* (BS) Elem, Millersville Univ 1971; *cr:* 3rd-5th Grade Teacher Methacton Sch Dist 1972-; *ai:* Thinking Skills Comm; NEA/PSEA/MEA Membership Chm 1987-; BSA (Cubmaster 1987-/Chm 1989-); Nom PA Teacher of Yr 1990; *office:* Arrowhead Elem Sch 232 Level Rd Collegeville PA 19426

HERSHENSON, MARTHA BRADFORD, 5th Grade Teacher; *b:* Chicago, IL; *m:* Loren V.; *c:* Holly A. Boes; *ed:* (BS) His, Lake Forest Coll 1966; (MED) Ed, Natl Coll of Ed 1971; Grad Work Psych; *cr:* 6th Grade Teacher Deerfield, Gages Lake, Highland Park 1966-71; 4th/5th/6th Grade Teacher Highland Park Dist 108 1971-; *ai:* Rdng Writing Comm; Teacher Center Comm; Soc Comm Treas; Supvr of Practice Teachers 1983-84/1989-; Highland Park Ed Assn Rep for Sherwood Sch 1989-; IL Fed of Teachers Various Local & St Comm Memberships 1975-87; North Shore Help Live Volunteer; Reed Zone Center Suicide Line Volunteer; Mentor Prgm Lake Forest Coll; *home:* 700 Green Bay Rd Highland Park IL 60035

HERSHMAN, ALAN R., Teacher of Gifted & Talented; *b:* Philadelphia, PA; *ed:* (BA) Poly Sci, 1969, (MED) Ed, 1972, (MBA) Cmptr/Informational Sci, 1984 Temple Univ; Specialized Courses in Gifted Ed; Advanced Work with Cmptrs; *cr:* Teacher 1969-75, Gifted Teacher 1975- Sch Dist of Philadelphia; Adjunct Instr/Cmptr Sci Teacher Bucks Cty Comm Coll 1986-; *ai:* Sch Safety Patrol Spon; Building Rep for Teachers; Staff Dev Leader; Telecommunications; Faculty System Operator; City-Wide Telecommunications Network for Gifted Stus; PA Assn for Gifted Ed Mem 1984-; Assn for Computing Machinery Mem 1985-; Beta Gamma Sigma Mem 1984-; Nom for Rose Lindenbaum Awd; Nom as Gifted Teacher of Yr in PA; Nom as Cmptr Teacher of Yr; *office:* Greenberg Elem Schl Sharon & Alicia Sts Philadelphia PA 19115

HERT, THERESA MARIE, Mathematics Teacher; *b:* Fontana, CA; *m:* Paul Jeffrey; *ed:* (BA) Math, CA St San Bernardino 1985; Working Towards Certificate Microcomputers for Educators, Univ of CA Riverside Extension; *cr:* Engineering Analyst S CA Edison 1985-86; Math Teacher Norte Vista HS 1987-; *ai:* Stu Study Team; Stu of Month Comm; Disaster Preparedness Comm; *office:* Norte Vista HS 6585 Crest Ave Riverside CA 92503

HERTEL, ANNETTE JANE BERGER, 4th-5th Grade Fine Arts/Health; *b:* Weimar, TX; *M:* Earl; *ed:* (BS) Music Ed, TX Lutheran Coll 1962; (MED) Elem Ed, Sam Houston ST Univ 1975; Post Masters Studies Gen Elem Teaching Certificate & Gen Music Certificate; *cr:* Jr Hi Band & Choir Dir Calhoun Co ISD 1962-65; Aransas Co ISD 1965-67; Randolph Air Force Base ISD 1967-69; Beeville ISD 1969-71; 1st Thru 4th Grade Classrooms Teacher and 4th/5th Grade Fine Arts & Health Teacher Schulenburg ISD 1971-; *ai:* UTL Music Memory Spon 5th & 6th Grade; Faculty Rep for Schulenburg Teachers Assn; Campus Action Comm Mem, 4th & 5th Grade Club Coordin "Just Say No"; TX Classroom Teachers Assn; TX Music ED Assn; TX Choral Dir Assn; Schulenburg Comm Choir Dir; Adjucator for UTL & Other Music Contests; *office:* Schulenburg I S D 104 N Lyons Schulenburg TX 78956

HERTWECK, GERARD ANTHONY, Spanish Teacher; *b:* Lynn, MA; *m:* Rosalba A. Di Stasio; *ed:* (BA) Span, Iona Coll 1970; (MA) Liberal Stud, St Univ of NY Brockport 1980; Drivers Ed, NY St; Cmmty Intervention Adolescents, Drugs & Alcohol; *cr:* Span Teacher Cardinal Mooney HS 1970-89; Drivers Ed Cardinal Mooney HS & Aquinas HS 1978-; Span Teacher Pittsford Sutherland HS 1989-; *ai:* Cardinal Mooney Coach Bowling & Track; SADD Moderator; Campus Ministry Team & Bd of Discipline Core Team Mem; Dean of Men; Rochester Against Intoxicated Driving 1984-86; Teacher With Impact on Intellectual

Dev of Stus Univ of Rochesters Scholar Recognition Day 1986; *home:* 46 Andiron Ln Rochester NY 14612

HERTZ, PEGGY LADNER, Home Ec Teacher; *b:* Gulfport, MS; *m:* Warren R. Jr.; *c:* Wendy R., Warren R. III; *ed:* (BS) Home Ec, 1974, (MS) Home Ec, 1978 Univ of Southern MS; *cr:* Home Ec Teacher, Immaculata HS 1974-76; Gulfport Sch Dist 1976-; *ai:* Club Adv FHA; Alpha Delta Kappa 1988-; Amer Vocational Assn 1987-; FHA 1986-; *office:* Bayou View Jr HS 212 43rd St Gulfport MS 39507

HERTZOG, JUDITH ANN (TOBIAS), English Teacher; *b:* Reading, PA; *ed:* (BS) Scndry Eng 1971, (ME) Scndry Engl, 1977 Kutztown Univ; Word Processing; Group Dynamics; PA Writing Process; Anatomy, Psych, Breathwork & Acupressure to Prepare for Bus of Massage Therapist & Rebirther; *cr:* Eng Teacher Hamburg Area Jr/Sr HS 1971-; *ai:* Dir Plays; Chrldr Coach; Spon Tri-Hi-Y; Chaperoned Dances & Classtrips; Chaired Comm that Wrote Form & Style Handbook for Writing Research; PSEA 1971-; NEA 1971-; Church Mem Choir 1958-85; Nom for Thanks to Teachers; *office:* Hamburg Area Jr-Sr HS Windsor St Hamburg PA 19526

HERZER, CHARLENE BEEN, Second Grade Teacher; *b:* Okmulgee, OK; *m:* Joe; *c:* Scott, Brian; *ed:* (BS) Ed, NE OK St Univ Tahlequah 1972; Post Grad Work NW OK St Univ; Panhandle St Univ; *cr:* 1st/2nd Grade Teacher 1972-76, 1st Grade Teacher 1976-79 Schulter Public Schls; 2nd Grade Teacher Vici Public Schls 1979-; *ai:* Roman Nose Rdng Cncl Pres 1988-89; Dewey Cty OK Ed Assn Pres 1989-; Elm Street Baptist Church (Sunday Sch Teacher, Church Clerk) 1988-; Vici Sch Teacher of Yr; *home:* 1210 E Hanks Trl Woodward OK 73801

HERZINS, FRANK JAMES, JR., Social Studies Teacher; *b:* New York City, NY; *m:* Charlene Mason; *ed:* (APC) Soc Stud, Salisbury St Coll 1973; (BA) Soc Stud, Hiram Scott Coll 1969; *cr:* Teacher Washington HS; *ai:* Stu Cncl 1972-89; St Convention Adv 1979-80, 1986; E Shore Assn of Stu Cnslrs MD Regional Adv 1977-87; Natl Assn of Stu Cncls Exec Bd Mem 1983-86; Salisbury Jaycees Dir 1979-81, Outstanding Young Man 1979; Foreign Study League Summer Study/Tours European Stu Coord 1973-79; NY Liason Officer Pacific Amer Inst Summer Study Tours for European Stu 1980; *office:* Washington HS PO Box 189 Princess Anne MD 21853

HESPENHIDE, RODNEY T., English Teacher; *b:* Newport News, VA; *m:* Melissa T. Trevallion; *ed:* (BA) Eng, Christopher Newport Coll 1975; Working Towards Masters in Admin, Old Dominion Univ; *cr:* Eng Teacher George W Carver Jr HS 1976-81, H L Ferguson HS 1981-; *ai:* After-Sch Detention; At Risk Stu Comm & Commission; Comm Forum Rep; Debate Coach; VATE, BATE 1987-; ASCD 1990; North End Preservation Assn (Pres, VP) 1986-, Outstanding Civic Assn 1987-88; Newport News Land Use Task Force 1988-; Nom Sch Level Teacher of Yr; *home:* 316 60th St Newport News VA 23607

HESS, ADANA CREEL, Bio/Environmental Sci Teacher; *b:* Beaumont, TX; *m:* Willie F. Jr.; *c:* Steven J.; *ed:* (BS) Phys Ed/Bio, TX A&M Univ 1982; Cert in Phys Ed, Cmptr Literacy & Stu Teacher Supervision Courses; *cr:* Teacher/Coach A&M Consolidated HS 1983-; *ai:* Bsktbl & Track Coach; Jr Class Spon; Sci Curr Dev Comm; TX Assn Bsktbl Coaches Mem 1983-; TX Girls Coaches Assn (Mem, Jr Rep, Rep 1989) 1983-; Nom Coll Station Teacher of Yr 1989; TX Teacher of Yr 1989-; *office:* A&M Consolidated HS 701 W Loop College Station TX 77840

HESS, ANNE HEUSINGER, Music/Speech Teacher; *b:* Norfolk, NE; *m:* Arin L.; *c:* Sarah, Catherine, Jonathan; *ed:* (BS) Elem Ed, Bob Jones Univ 1977; *cr:* 1st Grade Teacher Bob Jones Elem 1977-79; K-6th Grade Teacher 1979-82, 1st-9th Grade Fine Arts Teacher 1982- Park Avenue Chrstn; *ai:* Prgm Dir; Speech Drama Coach; Band & Piano Instr; Cmmty Bible Church (Pianist & Youth Spon 1979-, Sunday Sch Teacher 1988-); *office:* Park Avenue Chrstn Sch 401 E Park Ave Norfolk NE 68701

HESS, DONNA MALONEY, Second Grade Teacher; *b:* Fond du Lac, WI; *m:* Robert M.; *c:* Barbara Watkins, Diane Kennedy, Brenda; *ed:* (BS) Elem, Mansfield St Univ 1970; *cr:* 2nd Grade Teacher W R Croman 1970-71; 2nd/3rd Grade Teacher Troy Elem Center East 1971-; *ai:* PA St Ed Assn 1970-; 4-H Club Photography Adv 1980-83; Friends of Lib Officer 1975-80; Grant for Installation of Classical Music Listening Prgm Troy Elem Center East Sch; *office:* Troy Elem Center E Sch RD 2 Troy PA 16947

HESS, JOAN C., Second Grade Teacher; *b:* New York Mills, MN; *m:* Douglas Lee; *c:* Leann, Bill, Mark, Kristi, Sandra, Wayne; *ed:* Provisional Elem, St Cloud St Coll 1953; (BA) Elem, Bemidji St Coll 1961; *cr:* 4th Grade Teacher Park Rapids Elem Sch; *ai:* Various Committees; MEA; *home:* Rt 3 Box 51 D Verndale MN 56481

HESS, JOHN LAWRENCE, Chemistry Teacher; *b:* Tucson, AZ; *m:* Carol Ann Yeoman; *c:* Kristin, Andrew; *ed:* (BS) Chem, 1970, (BS) Ed, 1970, (MSED) Scndry Ed, 1975 Univ of AZ; *cr:* Teacher/Coach 1970-86, Teacher/Dept Chm 1987-88, Teacher 1970- Pueblo HS; *ai:* NHS Spon; Coached Ftbl, Bsbl, Sftbl; ASCD 1990; Sci Teacher of Yr Awd by AZ Cnncl of Engineering & Scientific Assn 1990; *office:* Pueblo HS 3500 S 12th Ave Tucson AZ 85713

HESS, JUDY FRYE, Third Grade Teacher; *b:* Mc Cradys Gap, VA; *m:* Thomas Andrew; *c:* Tommy, Tammy Hess Gillespie, Terry J.; *ed:* (BA) Elem Ed, Emory & Henry 1970; (MS) Univ of VA 1980; *cr:* 2nd Grade Teacher Allison Gap Elem 1960-62; Title I Teacher Rich Valley Elem 1966-69; 2nd Grade Teacher Chilhowie Elem 1980-83, Rich Valley Elem 1983-; *ai:* Child Study Comm; SCEA Elem Chm 1982-83; VEA, NEA 1984-89; Delta Kappa Gamma; Smyth Cty Shelter Home; *home:* Rt 1 Box 42 Saltville VA 24370

HESS, MARK STEVEN, English Teacher; *b:* Yuma, CO; *m:* Melissa Rizzolo; *ed:* (BA) Eng Lit, CO Univ 1988; *cr:* Teacher Brush HS 1988-; *ai:* Head Track & Forensics Coach; Kappa Delta Pi Exec Cncl 1988-; Published Short Stores; *office:* Brush HS 400 West Brush CO 80723

HESS, MICHAEL HENRY, Physics Teacher/Sci Dept Chm; *b:* Lawrence, KS; *m:* Dana Lyn Alford; *c:* Abby, Chandler, Jordan; *ed:* (BS) Sci Ed, KS St 1979; Working Towards Masters Sci, Univ of KS; *cr:* Physics Teacher Emporia HS 1979-80; Sci Teacher Landon Mid Sch 1983-85, Capital City HS 1985-86; Physics Teacher Lawrence HS 1986-; *ai:* Textbook Selection Comm Chm; Prof Educators Assn of KS Treas 1987-; St Johns Church Lay Minister 1980-; Lawrence HS Teacher of Yr 1988, 1989; *office:* Lawrence HS 1901 Louisiana Lawrence KS 66046

HESSE, THOMAS RIED, Mathematics Department Chair; *b:* Dayton, OH; *m:* Julie; *c:* Anastasia; *ed:* (BA) Phys Ed, Capital Univ 1974; Health Ed, Continuing Math Ed, OH St Univ; *cr:* Teacher Columbus Diocese 1975-78, Bishop Flaget HS 1978-79; Math Instr Olentangy Schls 1981-; *ai:* Sr Class Adv; K-12 Grade Math Dept Chm; NEA, OEA, OTA 1981-.

HESSLER, DAVID ROBERT, Art Department Teacher/Head; *b:* Elyria, OH; *ed:* (BBA) Art/Bus Admin, Western MI Univ 1961; Commercial Art/Illustration, Famous Artist Sch 1965; (MA) Art/Painting/Ed, MI St Univ 1966; Guest Art, Cntrl MI Univ 1965; Various Wkshps Chicago Inst of Art; *cr:* Adult Ed Teacher Jackson Comm Coll 1966-84; Part-Time Art Ed Teacher Spring Arbor Coll 1972-73; Art Instr Concord HS 1966-; *ai:* JCEA Cty Art Fair Comm Mem; Cmmty & Various Art Clubs Guest Artist; Demonstrate Painting; MI Art Ed Assn Liasion Officer 1972-82; MI Watercolor Society, MEA, NEA; Natl Watercolor Society, Midwest Watercolor Society; Won Numerous Painting Awds; Demonstrated Watercolor for MAEA; Whos Who in the Arts; *office:* Concord Cmmty Schls 219 Monroe St Concord MI 49237

HESSONG, GREG ALAN, Biology Teacher; *b:* Indianapolis, IN; *m:* Jayne Ellen Siders; *c:* Sheri, Scott; *ed:* (BA) Sci Ed, IN Univ 1971; (MS) Scndry Ed, 1976 IN Univ Purdue 1976; *cr:* 8th Grade Sci/Bio Teacher South Wayne Jr HS 1971-81; 9th Grade Bio Teacher Ben Davis Jr HS 1981-; *ai:* 9th Grade Tennis Coach; Wayne Township Unified Teachers Assn VP 1977-78; IN St Teachers Assn, NEA 1971-; De Molay Advisory Chm 1989-; Sr Choice Awd; *office:* Ben Davis Jr HS 1155 S High School Rd Indianapolis IN 46241

HESTER, BARBARA OLSZEWSKI, Pre-Kindergarten Teacher; *b:* Brooklyn, NY; *m:* Patrick J.; *c:* Sean P., Justin T.; *ed:* (BS) Elem Ed, St Johns Univ 1964; *cr:* 2nd Grade Teacher PS 48 1964-66; 1st Grade Teacher Audubon Elem 1966-79; 1st Grade Intensive Basic Prgm Class 1979-86, Pre Kndgtn Teacher 1986- Francis X Hegarty; *ai:* Employee Assistance Prgm Sch Rep; Chairperson for Sunshine Comm; Mem of Curr Writing Comm; Island Park Teachers Assn 1966-; NY St Teachers Assn 1966-; Amer Fed of Teachers 1966-; Confraternity of Chrstn Doctrine from St Agnes Cathedral Teacher 1986-88; *office:* Francis X Hegarty Sch Radcliff Rd Island Park NY 11558

HESTER, BLONDY JEAN BURRIS, Business Education Teacher; *b:* Detroit, MI; *m:* Odis; *c:* Vernard O., Roselyn J., Patrick D.; *ed:* Diploma Secretarial Sci, Detroit Bus Inst 1965; (AS) Liberal Arts, Wayne Cty Cmmty Coll 1976; (BS) Bus/Voc Ed, Wayne St Univ 1987; *cr:* Secy Mumford HS 1967-76; Head Secy Renanissance HS 1976-85; Bus Ed Teacher Western HS 1987-; *ai:* Co-Chairperson Sch Improvement Team; Jr Class Spon; N Cntrl Assn Steering Comm; Exec Bd MI Bus Bd Ed Assn (Rep Det Bus Teachers Club) 1987-; MI Occupational Ed Assn 1989-; MI Bus Ed Assn, Outanding Stu Bus Educator Wayne St Univ 1987 Natl Assn for Advancement of Colored People Womens Comm 1986-; Natl Coalition 100 Black Women Bd Mem 1987-, Outstanding Mem 1990; New Prospect Baptist Church (Usher Bd, Sunday Sch Teacher 1976); *office:* Western HS 1500 Scotten Detroit MI 48209

HESTER, SUZANNE HOOTON, First Grade Teacher; *b:* Bessemer, AL; *m:* Frederick William; *c:* Kyle F., Andrew C., Bryan G.; *ed:* (BS) Early Chldhd, 1976, (MS) Early Chldhd, 1979 Auburn Univ; *cr:* 1st Grade Teacher Carver Primary 1976-; *ai:* Jaycettes Secy 1979-83; Opelika Arts Assn Childrens Festival 1989; Chi Omega Alumni Assn 1978-.

HETHERINGTON, DAVID A., Biology Teacher/Sci Dept Chm; *b:* Minneapolis, MN; *m:* Sheila F. Gilbert; *c:* Terri L. Alexander; *ed:* (BA) Zoology, Univ of MN 1968; (MS) Philosophy, E MI Univ 1974; Teacher Cert Human Reproduction, Growth & Dev, E MI Univ & Wayne St; *cr:* Bio/Sci Teacher Holly Sr HS 1968-; *ai:* Sci Dept Chm; Sci Curr; NHS Credentials Comm; NEA 1968-; Linden Faith Baptist Church Deacon Bd Chm 1984-86, 1990; *home:* 16449 Geneva Blvd Linden MI 48451

HETHERINGTON, JOHN SCOTT, Assistant Principal/Coach; *b:* Burlington, IA; *m:* Patricia Dyane Ladd; *c:* Scott, Dyane, Kara, Tara; *ed:* (BA) Soc Stud, Graceland Coll 1967; (MS) Phys Ed, Cntrl MO St 1974; Cert in Admin, Cntrl MO St; *cr:* Teacher/Coach S Harrison HS 1972-77; HS Teacher/Coach King City R-3 HS 1982-84; Teacher/Coach/Prin Miami Amoret HS 1984-87; Asst Prin/Coach Logan-Rogersville HS 1987-; *ai:* Girls Bsktbl Coach; Phi Delta Kappa, Natl Assn Scndry Sch Prin, Natl Fed Interscholastic Coaches Assn, MO Assn of Scndry Sch Prin; Natl HS Coaching Bronze Awd 1987; Outstanding Elem Teachers of America 1974; *office:* Logan-Rogersville HS Rt 4 Box 75 Rogersville MO 65742

HETRICK, MARY HURRELBRINK, First Grade Teacher; *b:* Pemberville-Woodvl, OH; *m:* William; *c:* Cynthia Fackler, Anne Nock, Lisa Stumpf, Mark; *ed:* (BSED) Elem Ed, Capital Univ 1958; *cr:* Kndgtn Teacher Columbus Public Schls 1958-60, Fremont City Schls 1960-62; Kndgtn Teacher 1970-76, 1st Grade Teacher 1976- Van Wert City Schls; *ai:* Van Wert Cty Governance Bd for Mentors; Van Wert City Schlsp Comm Chm; AFT 1980-; NEA, OH Ed Assn 1958-80; Van Wert City Ed Assn Secy; Amer Assn of Univ Women (Pres 1969-71, Treas 1967-69), 1960-; Action for Better Cmmty Dev; Outstanding Young Woman of OH Candidate 1968; *home:* 1015 E Ervin Rd Van Wert OH 45891

HETTLINGER, PATRICIA CALLICOAT, Spanish Teacher; *b:* Huntington, WV; *m:* Michael; *c:* Marc, Craig; *ed:* (BA) Eng/Span Ed, 1968, (MA) Span Ed, 1971 Marshall Univ; *cr:* Teacher Barboursville HS 1968-; *ai:* Spon Project Lead; WV Ed Assn 1970-; UNICEF Comm of Greater Huntington Secy 1987-; *home:* 5940 Mahood Dr Huntington WV 25705

HETZEL, NANCY K., German Teacher; *b:* New York, NY; *m:* David M.; *c:* Roderick D., Eric E.; *ed:* (BA) Eng, Amer Intnl Coll; (MA) Span, Cntrl CT St Univ; Ed, St Josephs Coll; *cr:* Dir of Public Relations Bay Path Jr Coll; Ger/Eng Teacher Germantown Luth Acad; Ger Teacher Mark T Sheehan HS; *ai:* Ger Club & NHS Adv; Faculty Senate; AATG, CT Cncl of Lang Teachers; Statewide Foreign Lang Comm; CT Dept of Ed St Teacher Assessor, Beginning Ed Support & Trng Prgms, Trainer & Content Test Comm; *home:* 7 High St Yalesville CT 06492

HEUKE, MARTHA PIERCE, First Grade Teacher; *b:* Frankfort, KY; *m:* Harold Jerome; *c:* Aaron, April; *ed:* (BS) Elem Ed, Campbellsville Coll 1976; Early Chldhd, Univ of Louisville 1987; *cr:* 1st Grade Teacher Kerrick Elem 1977-78, Wellington Elem 1978-; *ai:* Jefferson Cty Teachers Assn 1977-; *office:* Wellington Elem Sch 4800 Kaufman Lane Louisville KY 40216

HEUMAN, JANA SULLIVAN, Office Education Teacher; *b:* Monahans, TX; *c:* Jame, Carlee; *ed:* (BBA) Bus Admin, 1972, (MA) Bus Admin, 1973 Sul Ross St Univ; *cr:* Dept of Human Resources TX 1974-76; Office Ed Teacher Monahans HS 1987-; *ai:* Bus Prof of America Spon; ATPE, VOTAT; 1st Baptist Church Mem; *office:* Monahans HS 809 S Betty Ave Monahans TX 79756

HEWER, BARBARA ELLEN, 3rd Grade Teacher; *b:* Massillon, OH; *ed:* (BS) Elem Ed, Kent St Univ 1973; Grad Courses toward Masters; *cr:* 1st Grade Teacher 1974-77, 3rd Grade Teacher 1977- Genoa Sch; *office:* Genoa Sch 519 Genoa Rd SW Massillon OH 44646

HEWITT, BARBARA YAKLE, Jr HS Language Arts Teacher; *b:* Burlington, IA; *m:* Loyal Delaine; *c:* Kim; *ed:* (BA) Elem Ed, IA Wesleyan Coll 1963; *cr:* Jr HS Lang Arts Teacher Mediapolis Cmmty Sch 1963-67, Morning Sun Cmmty Sch 1967-; 6th Grade Teacher Morning Sun Cmmty Sch 1990; *ai:* 7th Grade Class Spon; *home:* PO Box 98 Morning Sun IA 52640

HEWITT, JANET STEINKE, Third & Fourth Grade Teacher; *b:* Boston, MA; *m:* Martin Alexander; *c:* Timothy, Julie Hewitt Drew, Laura; *ed:* (BSED) Elem Ed, Valparaiso Univ 1962; Gifted/Art/Reading, Whitworth Coll 1982; Problem Solving Natl Sci Fnd, Gonsaga Univ 1982; *cr:* 4th Grade Teacher Airport Rd Sch 1962-63; Elem Substitute Teacher Clayton Public Schls 1974-75; Private Pre-k Teacher/Dir St Pauls Sch 1975-78; 3rd/4th Grade Teacher Spokane Luth Sch 1978-; *ai:* Music Dir; Primary Chorus/Music; SLS Choir; Yearly Musical; Christmas Prgm; Violinist; Asst Concert Master Gonsaga Univ Symphony; Fesvital of MO Women in Arts Awd 1974; Article Published in Arithmetic Magazine 1981; *office:* Spokane Lutheran Sch W 4001 Fremont Rd Spokane WA 99204

HEWITT, MICHAEL DENNIS, 6th/7th/8th Grade Teacher; *b:* E St Louis, IL; *m:* Mary Ann Wagner; *c:* Patrick, Michael; *ed:* (BS) Phys Ed, E IL Univ 1974; Grad Stud Various Coll & Univs; *cr:* Rifleman US Marine Corps 1966-69; Teacher/Coach Fisher Grade Sch 1974-75, Broadwell Grade Sch 1975-; *ai:* Boys Bsbl, Bsktbl, Track & Girls Track Coach; IL Bsktbl Coaches Assn 1986-; Logan Cty Coaches Assn 1975-; IEA, NEA 1979-; Broadwell Chrstn Church Deacon 1977-; Broadwell Siltennial 1980; Cmmty Lincoln HS Bsbl Boosters Officer 1989-; IL Bsktbl Coaches Assn Dist Coach of Yr 1986-87; Lincoln Jaycees Logan Cty Outstanding Young Educator 1985-86; *office:* Broadwell Grade Sch Box 39 Broadwell IL 62623

HEWITT, PAT A., Phys Ed Dept Chair; *b:* Hartsville, SC; *m:* Robert Levan; *c:* Wayne J., Brandie L.; *ed:* (BS) Phys Ed, Coker Coll 1969; (MAT) Phys Ed, Univ of SC 1973; Doctoral Prgm, US Sports Acad; *cr:* Teacher/Coach Hartsville HS 1969-; *ai:* Var Girls Bsktbl Coach; Fellowship of Chrstn Athletes; SC Bsktbl Coaches Assn (VP, Pres) 1986-88, Coach of Yr 1986, AP of Yr 1990; Coaches Assn of Womens Sports VP 1989-, Leadership 1989; SC Assn of Health, Phys Ed & Recreation; 1st Church of the

Nazarenes Church Bd 1985-; Coker Coll Bd of Visitor 1990; *office:* Hartsville HS Clyburn Cir Hartsville SC 29550

HEYLER, CONSTANCE COLLUM, 6th Grade Teacher; *b:* Elmira, NY; *m:* Daniel; *c:* Gwen, Allen; *ed:* (BS) Elem, 1974, (MS) Elem, 1977 Mansfield Univ; *cr:* 6th Grade Teacher Westfield Area Elem 1974-; *ai:* PA St Ed Assn, NEA, N Tioga Ed Assn; Lecercle Moderne Book Club (Treas 1987-89, Pres 1989-); Westfield United Meth Church Sunday Sch Supt 1990; *home:* 704 E Main St Westfield PA 16950

HEYMES, SHIRLEY, Teacher; *b:* Detroit, MI; *ed:* (PHB) Eng, Siena Hieghts Coll 1953; (MED) Elem Ed, Univ of FL 1959; Ed & Admin Univ of Barry; UW Marquette Univ; *cr:* Teacher St Jude Sch 1964-66; Admin St Mary Sch 1966-71; Teacher Our Lady of Perpetual Help 1971-72, St Peter MI 1972-; *ai:* Conducted Wkshps Parents Preschoolers; Conducted Title III Wkshp; Lang Arts Coord-Coord Speech Fest Coord Spelling Bees; *office:* St Peter Sch 19800 Anita Harper Woods MI 48225

HIATT, ROCHELLE LYNN, Third Grade Teacher; *b:* Maryville, MO; *m:* Kevin Paul; *c:* Brock, Jordan; *ed:* (BS) Elem Ed/Learning Disability/EMH, NW MO St Univ 1981; *cr:* 3rd Grade Teacher Worth Cty R-3 Elem 1981-; *ai:* Prof Dev Comm Chairperson; Cmmty Teachers Assn (VP 1986-87, Pres 1990-91); *home:* PO Box 127 Grant City MO 64456

HIATT, VERNETTA NESS, Science Teacher; *b:* Dawson, MN; *m:* Thomas A.; *c:* Erik, Britt; *ed:* (BA) Sci Ed, W WA Univ 1988; Sci Ed, Environmental Stud; *cr:* Art/Sci Teacher Skykomish Jr/Sr HS 1988-; *ai:* Recycle Prgm & Art/Sci Festival Dir; Evening Class Coord; NSTA 1988-; Art Teachers Assn 1988-; Home Owners Assn Secy 1985-88; Luth Women Pres/Treas 1985-86; Poly Party Cty Comm Women 1983; PTSO Secy 1988; *office:* Skykomish Jr/Sr HS P O Box 325 Skykomish WA 98288

HIBBARD, JEANNETTE MARIE, Mathematics/Religion Teacher; *b:* Yonkers, NY; *ed:* (BS) Ed, Fordham Univ 1968; *cr:* 4th-6th Grade Teacher Albany Diocese 1960-63; 5th-8th Grade Teacher NY Archdiocese 1963-67, NY Archdiocese St Marys 1967-; *ai:* Math Coord; Run Mathathon St Jude Childrens Hospital Annually; Dance Marathon Fund Raiser for Field Trips; Sch Dance Coord; Kappa Delta Pi; NCEA; Article Published; *office:* St Marys Sch 15 St Marys St Yonkers NY 10701

HIBBARD, MAX ALBERT, JR., English Teacher; *b:* Wauseon, OH; *m:* Donna Lynne Stocker; *c:* Joshua, Aaron; *ed:* (BS) Eng/Scndry, 1970, (MS) Scndry Ed, 1982 Bowling Green St Univ; Directing Musicals, Vander Cook Coll of Music-Chicago; Assertive Discipline Video Course, Drake Univ; Theatre Educators Assn Seminar-Cincinnati; *cr:* Eng Teacher Bradford Ex Village Schls 1970-74, Gorham-Fayette Local Schls 1974-76; 8th Grade Eng Teacher Paulding Ex Village Schls 1976-; *ai:* Drama Dept Head; Dist Curr Dev Rep; Paulding Mid Sch Building Rep; NEA, OEA 1970-; NCTE 1989-; First Chrstn Church Deacon 1990; Paulding Lions Club 1st VP 1989-; The St Bd of OH Thespian Society; *home:* 333 W Jackson St Paulding OH 45879

HIBBERD, GRANVILLE HAINES, Social Studies Teacher; *b:* Baltimore, MD; *m:* Joyce May Abbey; *c:* David G., Shannon A.; *ed:* (BA) Philosophy, Washington Coll 1969; (MA) Philosophy, Univ of DE 1974; Admin, Counseling, Math, Ec, W MD Coll; *cr:* 5th Grade Teacher Mid Sch 1969-70; 4th Grade Teacher Tatnall Sch 1971-74; 6th Grade Teacher Manchester 1974-75; 4th Grade Teacher Elmer Wolfe 1975-87; Teacher Francis Scott Key HS 1987-; *ai:* Var Soccer Coach; Safety Comm; SGA Alternate Adv; NEA, MD Assn Soccer Coaches, NASSP; New Windsor Bicentennial Comm Treas 1976; Hard Lodging Comm 1988-; 2 Var Soccer St Championships; Develop Awd Winning Elem Sci Prgm 1980-83; 9th Graders J A Applied Ed 1990; *home:* 3314 Mill Dale Ln New Windsor MD 21776

HICKAM, JEFFREY BROWN, 7th Grade Tennessee History; *b:* Kingsport, TN; *m:* Margaret Sams; *c:* Eric, Stephanie; *ed:* (BS) His, East TN St Univ 1976; *cr:* 7th-8th Grade Teacher/Coach Sullivan West HS 1977-79; Teacher/Coach Ketron Mid 1980-89; *ai:* Head Ftbl & Boys Track Coach; TN Ed Assn 1977-; Sullivan Cty Ed Assn 1977-; *office:* Ketron Mid Sch 3301 Bloomingdale Pike Kingsport TN 37660

HICKEN, BARON B., Physics Teacher; *b:* Sanford, ME; *c:* Mark; *ed:* (BS) Sci Ed, Univ of ME 1963; (MS) Basic Sci, Clarkson 1970; Sci Curr, Univ of VA 1983; *cr:* Teacher Plainfield HS 1963-64, S Plainfield HS 1964-70; Physics Teacher Bridgewater-Raritan HS West 1970-; *ai:* Girls Track Coach; NJAAPT; Recipient NJBISEC Internship 1985; *office:* Bridgewater-Raritan HS West PO Box 97 Raritan NJ 08869

HICKENLOOPER, LINDA LEE, Third Grade Teacher; *b:* Melrose, FL; *m:* Harrison Thomas Jr.; *c:* Harrison T. III, James R.; *ed:* (BA) Elem Ed, 1979, (MS) Elem Ed/Rdng, 1985 Univ of N FL; *cr:* 5th Grade Teacher 1979, 2nd Grade Teacher 1979-80, 3rd Grade Teacher 1980- Kelley Smith; *ai:* Grade Chairperson; Kelley Smith Elem Advisory Bd; Delta Kappa Gamma 1986-; Rdng Cncl 1989-; PTO Pres 1966-67; Childrens Home Society 1966-; Alumni, Delta Delta Delta, Cotillion Club, Circus FL St Univ 1952-54; Panhellenic Assn; 1st Presbyn Church (Ed Comm, Choir Mem, Sunday Sch Teacher); *home:* Rt 3 Box 1822 Palatka FL 32177

HICKEY, ELIZABETH ANNE (SWEENEY), 4th Grade Teacher; *b:* New York, NY; *m:* William Lawrence; *c:* Brendan M., William P.; *ed:* (BS) Elem Ed, St Johns Univ 1967; (MA) Liberal Stud, St Univ Stony Brook 1979; Permanent Cert St of NY; *cr:* 6th Grade Teacher St Anastasia Cath Sch 1967; 4th Grade Teacher George Washington Sch 1967-68, Floral Park Bellerose Sch 1968-69, Patchogue Regional Cath Sch 1977-; *ai:* Health Coord Patchogue Regional Cath Sch; Ed Fair Comm; Heritage Day Dev & Coord; *office:* Patchogue Regional Cath Sch Divsion St Patchogue NY 11772

HICKEY, GEORGIANA HAYES, 7th/8th Grade Science Teacher; *b:* Brooklyn, NY; *m:* Joseph F.; *c:* Joseph III, Robert, George, Eileen; *ed:* (BA) Ed/Math, 1978, (MA) Ed/Sci, 1986 Brooklyn Coll; Advance Cert in Religious Ed; *cr:* Language Arts/Rdng Teacher St Francis De Chantel 1977-78; Soc Stud/Religion/Sci Teacher Our Lady of Guadalupe Sch 1978-; *ai:* Stu Cncl Moderator; Organizer of Sch Talent Show; *office:* Our Lady of Guadalupe Sch 1518 73rd St Brooklyn NY 11228

HICKEY, JEAN WESLEY, 6th Grade Teacher; *b:* Lexington, KY; *m:* Paul M.; *c:* Gregory, Ryan; *ed:* (BS) Elem Ed, E KY Univ 1965; (MS) Ed, IN Univ 1974; *cr:* 7th/8th Grade Eng/Soc Stud Teacher Kit Carson Sch 1965-66; 3rd-5th Grade Teacher Sandcreek Elem Sch 1966-77; 4th-6th Grade Teacher 1977-88, 6th Grade Teacher 1989 S Decatur Elem; *ai:* Performance Base Accreditation; Sch Awds Comm; Lang Art Book Adoption Decatur Cty; NEA Mem 1965-; ISTA Building Rep 1966-; Decatur Cty Ed Assn Discussion Leader 1966-; PTA; *home:* 702 E Gatewood Dr Westport IN 47283

HICKEY, LOIS MAY, 4th Grade Teacher; *b:* Chicago, IL; *m:* Dennis M.; *c:* Kathleen, Marianne; *ed:* (BS) Elem Ed, N IL Univ 1971; Grad Stud; *cr:* Teacher Forest View Elem 1971-80, Evergreen 1987, Forest View Elem 1987-; *ai:* Art Resource Person; IL Ed Assn, NEA 1971-; *office:* Forest View Elem Dist 59 1901 Estates Dr Mount Prospect IL 60056

HICKEY, MARY ALICE CIMMONS, 5th Grade Teacher; *b:* Athens, PA; *m:* John M.; *c:* John, Ann; *ed:* (BA) Elem Ed, PA St Univ 1961; Grad Stud PA St Univ, Temple Univ & Walsh Coll; *cr:* 3rd Grade Teacher Elmer Ave 1961-62; Acc 5th Grade Teacher Highland 1962-65; 5th Grade Teacher Avondale 1965-66; Kndgtn/Math Teacher Country Day 1975; 5th Grade Teacher St Michael 1975-; *ai:* Drug Awareness Chm; Teacher Rep Sch Comm; Lang Art, Sci Text Selection Comm; Artist Redidence Prgm; DARE Prgm; Guidance Comm Chm; OH Conservation & Outdoor Assn 1989-; OH Cath Ed Assn 1980-; United Way 1988-; Cath Youth Cncl 1985-; St Michael Parish Cncl 1982-86; Coll Club Garden Club Founder & Past Pres; Canton Art Inst Fund Raising Comm; New Neighbors Club Pres; Founding Comm Canton Montessouri Sch; *office:* St Michael Sch 3501 St Michael Dr NW Canton OH 44718

HICKEY, MICHELE SCHULTZ, Third Grade Teacher; *b:* Newport, KY; *m:* James G. Jr.; *c:* Lauren, Mark; *ed:* (BA) Elem/Kndgtn Ed, 1978, (MS) Elem Certificate/Kndgtn Teaching, 1982 N KY Univ; Resource Teacher for 1st Yr Teachers; *cr:* 1st Grade Teacher St Cecilia Sch 1978-80; 3rd Grade Teacher Northern Elem Sch 1980-; *ai:* KY Ed Assn 1980-; *office:* Northern Elem Sch Rt 1 Butler KY 41006

HICKINBOTHAM, DAVID LEE, 7th/8th Grade Math Teacher; *b:* Springfield, OH; *m:* Shirley O. Moshier Ake; *c:* Charles W. Ake III, James J. Ake; *ed:* (BS) Bus Admin/Accounting, Wittenberg Univ 1962; (MED) Elem Admin, Wright St Univ 1970; USAF Extension Courses, Command & Staff Coll; USAF Air Univ 1970; *cr:* 7th-8th Grade Math/OH His/Geography/First Aid/CPR Teacher Northridge Mid Sch 1970-; *ai:* Natl Jr Honor Society Co-Adv; Math Curr Comms Dist 1978-, Cty 1984-; OH Cncl Teachers of Math, NEA; Moorefield Township Fire Dept Pres Outstanding Firefighter of Yr 1979; Civil Air Patrol 1953-; Clark Cty Excl Math Teaching Awd 1984; *home:* 1405 Student Ave Springfield OH 45503

HICKMAN, BELLE SHELTON, Business Education Teacher; *b:* Vicksburg, MS; *m:* Lee Morris Sr.; *c:* Lee M. Jr., Alisa K.; *ed:* (BS) Bus Ed, 1980, (MS) Bus Ed, 1981 MS St Univ; Working Towards Cert in Rdng & Cmptr Ed 1990; *cr:* Examination Technician MS St Univ 1981-85; Bus Ed Teacher New Hope HS 1985-; *ai:* FBLA & Bible Club Spon; 5 Yr Planning Comm Co-Secy; New Hope HS Stu Support Team Mem; MS Assn of Educators (Mem 1986-, Secy 1986-89); *home:* 64 Lynn Cir Columbus MS 39702

HICKMAN, DORITA DODD, American History Teacher; *b:* Dumas, AR; *m:* Albert Lloyd; *ed:* (BS) Phys Ed, TX Wesleyan Coll 1980; Phys Ed & Amer His Curr; *cr:* Teacher/Coach Euless Jr HS 1982-; *ai:* Frosh, Vlybl, 8th Grade Bsktbl, Track Coach; Fellowship of Chrstn Athletes 1987-88, Most Outstanding Female Spon; Assn of Teachers, Prof Educators 1982-; TX Cncl Soc Stud 1984-; Mid-Cities Cncl Soc Stud 1984-; *office:* Euless Jr HS 306 W Airport Frwy Euless TX 76039

HICKMAN, JOAN SHEPPARD, 7th/8th Grade Language Teacher; *b:* Millville, NJ; *m:* George M.; *c:* Thomas, Jane; *ed:* (BA) Elem, Glassboro St Coll 1962; *cr:* 3rd Grade Teacher Dane Barse-Vineland 1962-69; 7th/8th Grade Lang Teacher Cumberland Chrstn Sch 1974-; *ai:* Yrbk Adv; *office:* Cumberland Chrstn Sch 1100 Sherman Ave Vineland NJ 08360

HICKOK, ALICE MARIE, Reading Specialist; *b:* Green Bay, WI; *ed:* (BA) Latin, Silver Lake Coll 1969; (MA) Elem Ed, Clarke Coll 1970; Ed Courses Rdng Working Towards St Endorsement (MA) Eng/Second Lang Northern AZ Univ; *cr:* 1st-5th Grade Teacher St James Schl 1961-63; 2nd-5th Grade Teacher Indian Mission Schls AZ 1963-69; Reading Spec Indian Oasis Dist #40 1970-74; 3rd Grade Teacher Cathedral Sch 1974-81, St Francis Sch 1983-85; Rdng Spec Immaculate Conception 1983-85; *ai:* Cub Reporter Adv; Creative Writing Comm; Intnl Rdng Assn 1970-; HI St Rdng Bd of Dir 1975-81; Yuma Local Rdng Correspond Secy 1984-; HI Right-To-Read Adv Cncl 1978-79; Experienced Teacher Fellowship Prgm NDEA 1969-70; Natl Endowment for Hum Grant Summer 1987; Field Based Bi-Ling Ed Trng Project 1989.

HICKS, ANNIE MAE, Fifth Grade Teacher; *b:* Kittrell, NC; *ed:* (BS) Elem Ed, Winston-Salem St Univ 1960; NC Ag & Tech St Univ; *cr:* 4th Grade Teacher R B Dean Sch 1960-82; 4th Grade Teacher 1982-88; 5th Grade Teacher 1988- Pembroke Elem Sch; *ai:* Sch Newspaper Chm; Sch Improvement Team Senate Bill 2; Sch Pageant Comm; Tutorial Prgrm Chm; Adult Ed Instr; Assault on Illiteracy Local Chairperson; NC Assn of Educators Bldg Rep 1983- Distinguish Svc 1986/87; NEA; Natl Assn of Univ Women; Natl Assn of Univ Women Pres 1985-89 Woman of Year 1987; Southeast Section Natl Assn of Univ Women (Corresponding Sec 1984-1986 Recording Sec 1986-); Outstanding Svc 1986; Delta Sigma Theta Inc; Bd of Trustees-Gilbert-Patterson Memorial Lib-Maxton; Robeson Tech Coll Adult Ed Advisory Cncl; *home:* 286 E Saunders St Maxton NC 28364

HICKS, BARBARA JEAN, Fifth Grade Teacher; *b:* Pomona, MO; *w:* Frank David (dec); *c:* David C., Garold D.; *ed:* (BS) Bus, 1976, (MED) Ed, 1989 Drury Coll; *cr:* 5th Grade Teacher Mountain View Elem 1964-71, Willow Springs RIV 1977-; *ai:* MCMT Contest Spon; Dist Volunteer Comm Chm; Career Ladder Comm Secy; Rdng, Christmas Parade, Cmmty/Sch Drug Abuse Comm; Willow Spring HS Schlsp Comm Mem 1988-; Kappa Delta Pi 1989; Alpha Phi Pres 1956-57; *home:* 201 W High Willow Springs MO 65793

HICKS, BARBARA MILEUR, Kindergarten Teacher; *b:* Lawton, OK; *m:* Aaron Lee; *c:* Bradford L., Joseph A.; *ed:* (BSED) Early Chldhd Ed, Appalachian St Univ 1969; Grad Courses USCA; *cr:* Chapter One Teacher C S Brown Elem 1979; 1st Grade Teacher Gloverville Elem 1979-84; 2nd Grade Teacher 1984-85, Kndgtn Teacher 1985- Clearwater Elem; *ai:* Just Say No Club Spon; PTA Bd & Teacher Rep; NEA 1969-; NCAE 1969-79; SCEA 1979-; Jaycees Secy 1988; Teacher of Yr Oak Summit Elem 1974; Teacher of Yr Clearwater Elem 1986-87; Teacher Incentive Awd 1989; *office:* Clearwater Elem Sch P O Box 397 Clearwater SC 29822

HICKS, BERDA WHITEHEAD, Third Grade Teacher; *b:* Americus, GA; *c:* Gerald, Stephanie; *ed:* (BS) Bus Admin, Ft Valley St 1966; (MS) Elem Ed, GA Southwestern 1977; Staff Dev & Recertification Educl Courses; *cr:* Teacher Sumter Cty Sch System 1972-; *ai:* 3rd Grade Lead Teacher; GA Data Collector; GAE, NEA; Ladies Comm Action Club Treas 1984-; GWF Phillip Temple #1020, Friendship Baptist Church; *home:* 902 Magnolia St Americus GA 31709

HICKS, BERNICE RAUCH, German Teacher; *b:* Allentown, PA; *m:* Robert R; *c:* Jo Anne L Givler; Robert R Jr; *ed:* (B) Ger, Millersville STC 1959; (MS) Ger, Kutztown St Coll 1968; Hofstra Univ 1962; Stanford Univ Germany 1963; Cedar Crest Coll 1980-81; Muhlenberg Coll 1982-83 Span; *cr:* Ger & Fr Teacher 1958-80, Ger Teacher 1980 Northern Lehigh Sch Dist; *ai:* Ger Club Adv; NLEA 1958-; PSEA 1958-; NEA 1958-; AATG 1958-; Pastorius Home Assn Membership Sec 1983-.

HICKS, BOBBIE CONLEY, 2nd Grade Teacher; *b:* Austin, TX; *m:* Merritt Lorenzo Jr.; *c:* Merritt III, Jacqueline, Gwendolyn; *ed:* (BS) Phys Ed, Huston-Tillotson 1945; Rdng Methods, Early Chld, Lang Art at Loyola, Chicago Teachers Coll, Chicago St Univ; *cr:* K-1st Grade Teacher Drake-Doolittle Public Sch 1950-53, St Elizabeth Cath Sch 1953-56, St James Cath Sch 1956-57, St Procopius Cath Sch 1960-68, Resurrection Cath Sch 1968-; *ai:* Religion Comm Chm; Black Cath Toltan Achievement Awd 1988; Westside Cluster Awd 1985; Chicago Archdiocese 1st Black Lay Teacher; 20 Yrs at Resurrection Cath Sch Awd 1988; *home:* 5122 W Quincy St Chicago IL 60644

HICKS, DIANE TROTTER, Fourth Grade Teacher; *b:* Athens, TN; *m:* Kenneth Gary; *ed:* (BA) Ed, TN Wesleyan 1974; (MS) Ed, Univ of TN 1983; *cr:* Teacher Idlewild Elem 1974-83, City Park Elem 1983-; *ai:* Coord Sch Based Adopt-A-Sch Prgm; Athens Adopt-A-Sch Cncl Chm 1988-; *office:* City Park Elem Sch 203 Keith Ln Athens TN 37303

HICKS, DON R., CAD/CAM Instructor; *b:* Eastland, TX; *m:* Cheryl L. Nicholson; *c:* Christie, Ron, Kris; *ed:* (BS) Indus Tech, North TX St Univ 1964; (MA) Indus Tech, Univ of NM 1972; *cr:* Teacher Highland HS 1964-87; Del Norte HS 1987-; *ai:* Voc Clubs of Amer Spon; Intnl Tech Assn NM Teacher of Yr 1989; NM Tech Assn; Sandia Natl Labs Summer Teacher Enrichment Prgm; *office:* Del Norte HS 5323 Montgomery Blvd Ne Albuquerque NM 87109

HICKS, GLORIA PREVOST, Kindergarten Teacher; *b:* Slidell, LA; *m:* Alex A. III; *c:* Sonovia M.; *ed:* (BA) Elem Ed, Southern Univ 1977; Early Chldhd Ed, Awareness Component; *cr:* 6th Grade Teacher Phillis Wheatly Elem 1977-78; Kndgtn Teacher Medard h Nelson Elem 1978-; *ai:* Lower Grade & Grade Chairperson; Jr GSA Leader; S U Cookie Dir; Chairperson Awd Comm; AFT Black Caucus 1990; UTNO; Pastor Aid Bd Secy 1989-; Sch America 1990; *home:* 213 S Gayoso St New Orleans LA 70119

HICKS, JANICE POINDEXTER, Language Art Teacher; *b:* Winston-Salem, NC; *m:* Archie B. Jr.; *c:* Bo; *ed:* (BS) Speech Ed, 1972, (MA) Mid Grades Ed, 1987 Appalachian St Univ; *cr:* 5th/6th Grade Teacher 1973-74, 6th-8th Grade Lang Art Teacher 1974- Fall Creek Sch; *ai:* Public Speaking Coach; Yrbk Spon; Southern Assn Accreditation Steering Comm Chairperson; NC Assn of Educators (Local Pres 1988-89, Secy 1983-85, Treas 1985-87, VP 1987-88, Government Relations Commission 1989-, Dist VP 1989-); Delta Kappa Gamma 1990; Teacher of Yr 1980-81, 1983-84, 1987-88; Yadkin Cty Sch Systems Teacher of Yr 1987-88; *office:* Fall Creek Sch Rt 1 Box 416A East Bend NC 27018

HICKS, LA DAWN ANN, Third Grade Teacher; *b:* Thomas, OK; *ed:* (BS) Elem Ed, SW OK St Univ 1978; *cr:* 1st Grade Teacher 1978-79, 4th Grade Teacher 1979-84, 3rd Grade Teacher 1984- Woodward Public Schls; *ai:* Woodward Ed Assn Building Rep 1974-; OK Ed Assn, NEA 1974-; First Assembly of God (Bus Captain 1979-87, Bus Coord 1989-, Mem 1979-, Choir Mem 1978-89); NW OK Genealogical Society Mem 1989-; *office:* Woodward Public Schls PO Box 592 Woodward OK 73802

HICKS, ROBERT ALLEN, Math & Computer Teacher; *b:* Spangler, PA; *m:* Margaret Painter; *c:* Dana, James, Craig; *ed:* (BS) Math, 1968, (MED) Math, 1973 IUP; Continuing Cmptr Ed; *cr:* Teacher Cambria Heights 1968-; *ai:* Presbyn Church (Elder, Trustee, Treas) 1977-; Cmmty Org Dir 1970-; *office:* Cambria Heights Jr HS 4th & Beaver Hastings PA 16646

HICKS, STEVEN PAUL, English/Computer Teacher; *b:* Joliet, IL; *m:* Roberta Egle; *c:* Jarred, Kerri, Jordan; *ed:* (BA) Eng Ed, 1976, (MS) Ed, 1981 IL St Univ; *cr:* Eng Teacher Mendota HS 1977-79; Eng/His Teacher Etuyre Mid Sch 1979-83; Admin/Teacher Bethel Chrstn HS 1983-87; HS Eng/Cmptr Lit/Yrbk Teacher Keswick Chrstn Sch 1987-; *ai:* Varsity Girls Sftbl Coach; Prayer, Fellowship Spon; *office:* Keswick Christian Sch 10101 54th Ave N Saint Petersburg FL 33708

HICKS, VIRGINIA WAGGONER, 1st Grade Teacher; *b:* Morton, MS; *m:* Mack O.; *c:* Jessia E., Dana H. Chapman; *ed:* (BS) Elem Ed, Univ of Southern MS 1972; *cr:* 1st Grade Teacher Glendale Elem 1964-68; Semmes Elem 1968-; *ai:* Kappa Kappa Iota (Treas 1978- 85 Pres 1986-87); Semmes Womens Club Treas/Pres.

HIEMANN, SHARON BLANKS, 3rd Grade Teacher; *b:* Dallas, TX; *c:* John Bernhard IV; *ed:* (BS) Ed, N TX St Univ 1965; Working Towards Masters N TX St Univ; Exemplary Center for Rdng Instruction 1987; Rdng Wkshps 1988-; *cr:* 3rd Grade Teacher Rosemont Elem Sch 1965-77; 4th Grade Teacher Martha Turner Reilly Elem 1977-84; 3rd Grade Teacher Hexter Elem Sch 1984-; *ai:* Tag Screening, Faculty Advisory, Pupil Assistance Services, Pupil-Personnel Comms; Winter Festival Prgms Chm; PTA Exec Bd Legislative Chm & Cultural Art Co-Chm; Delta Kappa Gamma Recording Secy 1985-; Zion Luth PTA 1974-77; Forestridge Elem PTA 1978-82; Liberty Jr HS PTA 1983-84; Berkner HS PTA 1985-87; Hexter Elem Teacher of Yr 1987; 100 Percent Club Outstanding TEAMS 1987-89; *office:* Hexter Elem Sch 9720 Waterview Rd Dallas TX 75218

HIERHOLZER, PERNINA CAPANNA, Kindergarten Teacher; *b:* Washington Mills, NY; *m:* Robert J.; *c:* Mary A. Di Giovanna, John R.; *ed:* (BS) Elem Ed Oswego St Teachers Coll 1954; (MA) Elem Ed, Rdng, Math, Syracuse Univ 1959; Whole Lang 1987-89; *cr:* Kndgtn Teacher Oriskany Cntrl Sch 1954-61; Holland Patent Cntrl Sch 1961-; *ai:* PTG Teacher Rep; Kndgtn Teachers Group of Our Area Organizer 1987; Teachers Applying Whole Language (TAWL); Kndgtn Pre-Schl or Kndgtn Screening Team; NYS Teachers Assn 1954-; Holland Patent Teachers Assn Bldg Rep 1970-71: (TAWL) 1989-; Talented and Gifted (Self) 1980-87; St Stephen Church (Trustee 1980-; Pres of Church Cncl 1984-); Parent Teacher Group Teacher Rep 1970-88; Parent Teacher Group for Service to Group and Students 1989; *office:* Holland Patent Cntrl Sch Rt 365 Holland Patent NY 13354

HIERMAN, SALLY ANN, 5th Grade Teacher; *b:* Granite City, IL; *m:* Kenneth P.; *c:* Cass, Holly; *ed:* (BS) Elem Ed, S IL Univ Edwards 1971; *cr:* 5th Grade Teacher 1983-85; 4th Grade Teacher 1985-86; 6th Grade Teacher 1986-89 Lincoln Sch; 5th Grade Teacher Washington Sch 1989-; *ai:* Delta Kappa Gamma 1989-; BSA (Cub Master 1983-85, Comm Mem 1985-86); East Alton Lib Trustee 1989-; East Alton United Meth Church; *office:* Washington Sch Smith East Alton IL 62024

HIESTAND, LARRY D., Jr HS & High School Teacher; *b:* Warren, OH; *m:* Karen E. Wiswell; *c:* Amy, Bryan, Matthew; *ed:* (BA) Psych, Youngstown St 1974; *cr:* Teacher Windham Schls 1974-79, Bristol Schls 1980-; *ai:* Bsktbl Coach; OH Ed Assn; *office:* Bristol HS 1872 Greenville Rd Bristolville OH 44402

HIGGINBOTHAM, ALFRED J., JR., 7th Grade Soc Stud Teacher; *b:* Camden, NJ; *m:* Helene Quinn; *c:* Alfred III, James; *ed:* (BA) Scndry Soc Stud, Glassboro St 1972; *cr:* 7th Grade Soc Stud Teacher Gloucester City HS 1974-89; *ai:* World Affairs Cncl of Philadelphia & Jr HS Stu Cncl Adv; *office:* Gloucester City Jr/Sr HS Rt 130 & Market St Gloucester City NJ 08030

HIGGINS, ALICE F., 6th/8th Grade Science Teacher; *b:* Sunbury, PA; *m:* Thomas J.; *c:* Cheryl Dorman, Tammy Meckley; *ed:* (BS) Elem Ed, Bloomsburg St Univ 1955; *cr:* Teacher Williamsport Sch Dist 1955-56; Teacher 1956-58, 1964- Millersburg Area Sch Dist; *ai:* Mid Sch Stu Cncl Adv; Prof Dev & Curr Guideline Comm; Millersburg Area Ed Assn (Pres, Secy, 1969-70), 1964-; PA St Ed Assn, NEA 1964-; St Pauls Luth Church Cncl Pres 1984-86; Order of Eastern Star Amaranth; *home:* 905 Meadow Ln Millersburg PA 17061

HIGGINS, DAN J., Principal/Athletic Director; *b:* Miami, FL; *m:* Linda Sue Hesskew; *c:* Kelly M.; *ed:* (BA) Eng, SW TX St Univ 1972; (MA) Ed Admin, Univ of TX San Antonio 1975; Doctorate in Ed Admin TX A&M Univ; *cr:* Eng/Government Teacher/Var Bsktbl Coach/Athletic Dir 1979-87; Eng/Government Teacher/Var Bsktbl/Tennis Coach/Athletic Dir/Prin 1987- St Anthony HS Seminary; *ai:* Dist Chairperson TX Chrstn Interscholastic League; TX Chrstn Interscholastic League (St Exec Bd Mem 1986-, Dist Chairperson 1985-); Phi Delta Kappa 1977-; TX Chrstn Interscholastic League AAA St Tennis Coach of Yr 1983; San Antonio Sub-5A Runner Up Bsktbl Coach of Yr 1977-78; Recipient of Piper Fnd Grant Recognizing Outstanding HS Eng Teachers 1984; *office:* St Anthony HS Seminary 3200 Mc Cullough Ave San Antonio TX 78284

HIGGINS, DONA SLOBOZIEN, Reading/Literature Teacher; *b:* Johnstown, PA; *m:* Patrick; *c:* Samantha, Jennifer, Joshua; *ed:* (BA) Eng Lit, Univ of Pittsburgh 1984; Cmptr Sci; *cr:* Rdng Teacher St Benedict Sch 1979-; *ai:* Sch Yrbk; ITEC I & II Microcmptrs Ed Course Grants; *office:* St Benedict Sch 2306 Bedford St Johnstown PA 15904

HIGGINS, DOROTHEA BUSCHE, 2nd Grade Teacher; *b:* Erie, PA; *w:* William H. (dec); *c:* Susan Higgins Packard, Christine Higgins Smith; *ed:* (BS) Elem Ed, Edinboro St Coll 1968; Grad Stud; *cr:* 6th Grade Teacher 1968-70, 2nd Grade Teacher 1970- Cambridge Springs Elem; *ai:* PA St Ed Assn 1968-; Shadbush Service Club Pres 1968, 1978; Alpha Delta Kappa Treas 1979-; Town & Cntry Garden Club Secy 1979-80; 1st Presbyn Church Elder 1989-; *office:* Cambridge Springs Elem Sch Steele St Cambridge Springs PA 16403

HIGGINS, GORDON WESLEY, English Teacher; *b:* Atlanta, GA; *m:* Anne Barre; *c:* Daryl, Jennifer, Jeffrey; *ed:* (BA) Journalism, Univ of GA 1970; (MED) Ed, GA St Univ 1978; *cr:* Teacher/Coach SW De Kalb HS 1972-79, Newton Cty HS 1979-80, Johnson HS 1980-; *ai:* Var Bsbl Head Coach; System-Wide Literary Magazine General Ed; GAE, NEA; Johnson Teacher of Yr 1988; Hall Cty Teacher of Yr 1989; Region 8AAA Coach of Yr 1989.

HIGGINS, JOANNE MAGUIRE, Spanish Teacher; *b:* Jersey City, NJ; *m:* Robert L.; *c:* Thais Fairlie, Joyce, Alison Torres, Jeanne Cook, Robert Jr.; *ed:* (BS) Scndry Ed/Span, Fordham Univ 1952; Italian Courses, Rutgers; *cr:* Span Teacher Madison Cntrl HS 1973-; *ai:* Span Club & Asian Unity Club Adv; FLE, NJ; Lions Club of Laurence Harbor 1st VP 1989-; League of Women Voters (Pres, VP) 1965-67; *home:* 62 Ocean Blvd Cliffwood Beach NJ 07735

HIGGINS, JOHN FRANKLIN, Mathematics Teacher; *b:* Seattle, WA; *m:* Claudia Kay North; *c:* Sarah, Mitchell, Laura; *ed:* (BS) Technology, W WA St Univ 1973; Cmptrs in Ed; *cr:* Industrial Art Teacher Mountlake Terrace Jr HS 1973-75, Madrona 1975-76; Math Teacher Kamiakin Jr HS 1976-; *ai:* Cmptr Coord; *office:* Kamiakin Jr HS 14111 132nd Ave NE Kirkland WA 98034

HIGGINS, JOHN MICHAEL, Latin Teacher; *b:* Norwich, CT; *m:* Ann Margaret Doody; *c:* Eoin, Deirdre, Colm; *ed:* (BA) Classical Lang, Fordham Univ 1975; (MLITT) Classics/Latin, Trinity Coll 1984; Prof Courses in Ed St Joseph Coll 1981-82; *cr:* Lexicographical Asst Royal Irish Acad 1978-79; Philosophy Lecturer NW CT Comm Coll 1982-83; Latin Teacher Gilbert Sch 1980-; *ai:* Faculty Adv Jr Classical League; Classical Assn of CT, Classical Assn of New England, Amer Classical League, Pioneer Valley Classical Assn; Monterey Public Lib Trustee 1986-; Monterey Democratic Town Comm (Secy 1990) 1989-; NEH Cncl for Basic Ed Fellow For Ind Hum Stud 1989; Published Articles 1985, 1990; *office:* The Gilbert Sch Williams Ave Winsted CT 06098

HIGGINS, JUDITH GIRARD, 8th Grade Math/Algebra Teacher; *b:* Teaneck, NJ; *m:* Roger G.; *c:* Victoria; *ed:* (BS) Merchandising, Carnegie Inst of Technology 1964; Expect to Complete Masters Walsh Coll 1991; *cr:* 5th Grade Teacher 1977-82, 8th Grade Math Teacher 1982- Jackson Mid Sch; *ai:* Mathcounts Coach; OCTM, GCCTM; *office:* Jackson Mid Sch 7355 Mudbrook StNW Massillon OH 44646

HIGGINS, MAR, 4th Grade Teacher; *b:* Grand Rapids, MI; *m:* Thomas; *c:* Molly; *ed:* (BA) Fine Art/Soc Sci, 1974, (MA) Rdng Instruction, 1978 MI St Univ; Madeline Hunter ITIP Trng; Numerous Courses Gifted & Talented Ed; Cmptr Sci, Grand Rapids Jr Coll; *cr:* 4th Grade Teacher Englishville Sch 1974-82; 7th/8th Grade Soc Stud/Lang Art/Research Teacher 1984-85; 4th Grade Teacher Sparta Mid Sch 1985-; *ai:* 4th-12th Grade Drama Coach; Voigt House Museum Ed Dir 1989-; Park Church Drama Dir 1986-; *office:* Sparta Mid Sch 240 Glenn Sparta MI 49345

HIGGINS, MAUREEN THERESE, Mathematics/French Teacher; *b:* Toms River, NJ; *ed:* (BA) Math Ed, 1985, (MA) Curr/Instruction, 1989 Univ of MO Kansas City; *cr:* Math Teacher Oak Park 1985-; *ai:* Fr Club & Frosh Class Spon: NES, NCTM.

HIGGINS, PAUL ROBERT, Econ/Contemp America Teacher; *b:* Weirton, WV; *m:* Diane Whittaker; *c:* Lesli, Robert; *ed:* (BA) Soc Stud/Phys Ed, W Liberty St Coll 1967; Various Grad Courses at WV Univ; *cr:* Teacher Wellsburg HS 1967-69, Brooke HS 1969-; *ai:* Hi-Y Club Adv; Conduct Supervised Study Sessions; Brooke Cty Ed Assn Pres 1972-76; WV Ed Assn Exec Comm 1973-76; NEA, WV Cncl of Soc Stud, NCSS; Jefferson Sch PTA Pres 1975-76; Trinity Luth Church Asst Treas 1978; Candidate in Democratic Primary Election for House of Delegates in WV; *home:* 128 Bonnie Prince Dr Follansbee WV 26037

HIGGINS, SABINE M., Assistant Production Mgr; *b:* Scranton, PA; *ed:* (BA) Elem Ed, 1954, (MS) Elem Ed, 1968 Marywood Coll; Numerous Courses Admin, Lehigh Univ & Loyola Univ; Span Conversation, Cath Univ; *cr:* 6th-8th Grade Math Teacher 1945-68, Prin 1968-80 Parish Schls; 5th/6th Grade Math Teacher St Mary of Mt Carmel Sch 1980-88; Asst Production Mgr IHM Art Studio 1988-; *home:* 2300 Adams Ave Scranton PA 18509

HIGGINS, SUSAN STANLEY, 4th Grade Teacher; *b:* Hagerstown, MD; *m:* Raymond Wilson; *c:* Levi R., Andrea R.; *ed:* (AA) Elem Ed, Hagerstown Jr Coll 1969; (BA) Elem Ed - Magna Cum Laude, Frostburg St Coll 1972; Masters Equivalency Elem Ed, W MD Coll, Shippensburg St Coll; *cr:* 3rd Grade Teacher Winter Street Elem Sch 1972-78; 4th Grade Teacher Hancock Elem Sch 1981-; *ai:* Sch Improvement Team Comm; Battle of Books of Washington Cty; Cub Scouts 1987-89, Appreciation Awd 1989; GSA 1990; *office:* Hancock Elem Sch 290 W Main St Hancock MD 21750

HIGGINS, THOMAS JOSEPH, Jr HS American History Teacher; *b:* Chicago, IL; *m:* Kathleen Sweeney; *c:* Bridget, Joseph, Molly; *ed:* (BA) Amer His, De Paul Univ 1965; De Paul Univ; Amer His/Cmptr Course, Moraine Valley Cmmty Coll; *cr:* 6th Grade Teacher 1965-76, 8th Grade Teacher 1976-89, 7th/8th Grade Teacher 1989- St Denis Grade Sch; *ai:* Southwest Archdiocesean Singles (Founder, 1st VP); Holy Redeemer Cath Church (Lector, Eucharistic Minister); *office:* St Denis Grade Sch 8300 S St Louis Chicago IL 60652

HIGH, BARBARA JEAN, English/Journalism Teacher; *b:* Nash Cty, NC; *ed:* (BA) Religious Ed, Campbell Univ 1972; (MDiv) Religious Ed, SE Theological Seminary 1976; Numerous Univs; *cr:* Minister Youth/Ed 1st Baptist Church 1970-73; Instr Nash Comm Coll 1974-77; Asst Dir Nash Cty Extended Day Prgm 1977-79; Dept Chm Weldon HS 1979-83; Sales New York Life 1983-86; Teacher NW Halifax HS 1986-; *ai:* Yrbk & Class Adv; NC Assn of Educators Local Pres 1989-; Bus & Prof Women St Pres 1985-86, St Career Woman of Yr Runner Up 1980; Natl Assn of Speakers Mem 1990; Region L Cncl of Government (Chm, Bd of Dirs) 1988-90; Red Oak Town Cncl Commissioner 1981-; Nashville Bus & Prof Women of Yr 1985; Enhancement of Women Leadership Awd 1988; Weldon HS Outstanding Educator 1980; Weldon City Schls Teacher of Yr 1981; *office:* NW Halifax HS Rt 2 Box 274 Littleton NC 27850

HIGH, DOROTHY JEAN, 5th Grade Teacher; *b:* Zebulon, NC; *ed:* (BA) Eng/Elem Ed, Spelman Coll 1956; Atlanta Univ; Shaw Univ; East Carolina Univ; *cr:* 5th Grade Teacher Washington Elem Sch 1958-59; 6th Grade Teacher Adkin Sch 1963-68; R H Lewis Sch 1969-; *ai:* 4H Extended Day Prgm; NCAE; NEA; *home:* 804 Fields St Kinston NC 28501

HIGH, JUDSON VIPPERMAN, 8th Grade History Teacher; *b:* Gastonia, NC; *m:* Deborah Hudson; *c:* Jennifer Thompson, Jill Thompson, Jodie Thompson, Joni Thompson; *ed:* (BS) Intermediate Ed/His, Gardner Webb Coll 1977; *cr:* 8th Grade Teacher Sacred Heart Grade Sch 1978-81; 5th Grade Teacher 1981-87, 8th Grade His Teacher 1987- Harris Sch; *ai:* Boys Bsktbl Head Coach; Stu Cncl Adv; Assertive Discipline & Variety Show Comms; *home:* 807 E Main St Forest City NC 28043

HIGHFIELD, THOMAS FRANK, 8th Grade Science Teacher; *b:* Fort Payne, AL; *m:* Carol Ann Whitehead; *ed:* (MS) General Sci/Scndry Ed, AL A&M Univ 1988; (BS) General Sci Scndry Ed, Univ of AL 1985; (AS) General Sci, NE AL St Jr Coll 1982; Sea Lab Teachers Marine Sci Course, Teachers Space Acad; *cr:* Teacher Riverton Sch 1985-; *ai:* Soccer Coach; Math Team Spon; Sci Fair Comm & Sci Dept Chm; AL Ed Assn 1985-; AL Sci Teachers Assn 1986-; PTA 1985-; Riverton Sch Teacher of Yr 1989-; *office:* Riverton Sch 2615 Winchester Rd Huntsville AL 35811

HIGHSMITH, JAMIE JONES, Counselor; *b:* Amarillo, TX; *m:* Harley W.; *c:* Sheli; *ed:* (BA) Eng, 1982, (MED) Ed, 1986 Angelo St Univ; Working Toward Masters in Eng; *cr:* Eng Teacher Paint Rock Ind Sch Dist 1982-87; Cnslr San Angelo Ind Sch Dist 1987-; *ai:* Bobcats Against Drugs & Drinking Spon; Support Group for Pregnant Girls Facilitator; Effective Schls Team Mem; Phi Delta Kappa 1986-; Three Rivers Assn for Counseling & Dev Secy 1987-; First Baptist Church (Schlsp Comm 1988-89, Handbell Choir 1989-) 1961-; *office:* Central HS 100 Cottonwood San Angelo TX 76901

HIGHSMITH, STEPHEN W., 6th Grade Teacher; *b:* Terre Haute, IN; *m:* Carol Zmich; *c:* Sean M.; *ed:* (BA) Elem Ed, 1971, (MS) Sci, 1975 IN St Univ; Advanced Cmptr Ed; Impact Trng; Quest Trng; *cr:* 5th Grade Teacher Attica Consolidated Schls 1971-73; 6th Grade Teacher Hanover Mid Sch 1973-77; 7th-8th Grade Teacher Brookwood Jr HS 1977-79; 6th Grade Teacher Crown Point Cmmty Schls 1979-; *ai:* High Technology Comm Mem; Book Adoption Comm; ISTA/NEA (Local VP, Dist Cncl Chm) 1983-84; St Johns UCC Choir Dir 1989-; Chorus of the Dunes Show Chm 1983-84; Electronic Learning Magazine Honorable Mention Educator of Yr 1983; Dist Dir Gifted & Talented 1979; *office:* Solon-Robinson Sch Wells & Pettibone Crown Point IN 46307

HIGHSTREET, JOHN L., Social Studies Teacher; *b:* Mt Clemens, MI; *m:* Brenda L. Kaatz; *c:* Jacob J.; *ed:* (AA) Soc Stud, MI Chrstn Coll 1977; (BSE) Soc Stud Composition, Lubbock Chrstn Coll 1980; *cr:* Soc Stud Teacher/Coach Atlantic Chrstn HS 1980-82; Soc Stud Teacher Algonac Learning Center 1982-83; Soc Stud Teacher/Coach/A D Pembroke Chrstn HS 1983-84; Soc Stud Teacher/Coach Plantation HS 1986-; *ai:* Head Girls Bsktbl & Jr Var Ftbl Coach; Youth in Government Club; *office:* Plantation HS 6901 NW 16th St Plantation FL 33313

HIGHT, BETTY MC LANE, Second Grade Teacher; *b:* Raytown, MO; *m:* Donald W.; *c:* Stephen D., Sheryl J. Hight Madden; *ed:* (BS) Ed, Pittsburgh St Univ 1967; *cr:* 2nd Grade Teacher Maple Street Sch 1967-68, Westside Unified Sch Dist 250 1968-; *ai:* Delta Kappa Gamma (2nd VP 1990), Secy 1976-77; Kappa Kappa Iota Pres 1988-; KS Ed Assn 1967-; Nom Master Teacher Unified Sch Dist 250 1988; *office:* Westside Elem Sch 430 W 5th Pittsburg KS 66762

HIGHTOWER, ERNESTINE ROLLINS, Third-Fourth Grade Teacher; *b:* Lawton, OK; *w:* Ted L. (dec); *c:* Steven, Neal, Clinton, Karin Godfrey; *ed:* (BS) Elem Ed, Cameron Univ 1970; Elem Sci, Univ of HI; *cr:* Teacher Whittier Elem Sch 1970-; *ai:* Spon Young Astronauts Club; Chm Lawton Dist Sci Curr Guide; Team Coord Intermediate; Gifted & Talented Summer Teacher Camp Goddard; Staff Dev Co-Chairperson 1987-; Assn of Classroom Teachers Pres 1976-77, Best TV Ed Prgm 1977; Prof Management & Planning Co-Chairperson 1980-81; Beta Sigma Phi (Pres, VP) 1985, 1990, Woman of Yr 1986; Kappa Kappa Iota Pres 1980, 1986; Alpha Delta Kappa 1983-; Distinguished Achievement Awd Elem 1988-89; 1st Runner Up Teacher of Yr 1988-89; Greenhouse Project Lawton Dist Conservation Awd; *office:* Whittier Elem Sch 1115 NW Laird Lawton OK 73507

HIGHTOWER, SHARRON YARBROUGH, Health Occupations Teacher; *b:* Memphis, TN; *m:* Fred J.; *c:* Korron; *ed:* Assoc Nursing, Shelby St Comm Coll 1981; (BS) Nursing, Memphis St Univ 1984; (MS) Ed, Univ of TN Knoxville 1990; Instr in Cardiopulmonary Resuscitation; *cr:* Staff Nurse The Medical RegionaL Center 1981-84; Industrial Nurse TN Valley Authority 1985-87; Health Occupations Teacher East HS 1986-; *ai:* Adv To Natl Youth Organization; Health Occupations Stus of America Guidance & Secme Comm; Phi Kappa Phi Mem 1990; NEA Mem; Alpha Kappa Alpha Mem 1984-; Amer Nurse Assn Mem 1982-; Amer Voc Assn 1989-; Certificate of Appreciation HOSA 1987-; RQ Venson Center for Elderly Spotlight 1982; *home:* 4827 Airways Memphis TN 38116

HIKES, BARBARA LUCKENBILL, Remedial Reading Teacher; *b:* Pottsville, PA; *m:* Stephen J.; *c:* Elizabeth, Rachel; *ed:* (BS) Elem Ed, 1976, (MED) Rdng, 1983 Shippensburg Univ; *cr:* 5th Grade Sci/Health/Remedial Rdng Teacher Pine Grove Area Mid Sch 1977-78; 2nd Grade Teacher Pine Grove Area Elem Sch 1978-88; Chapter I/Remedial Rdng Teacher Tremont Elem Sch & Pine Grove Area Mid Sch 1989-; *ai:* Lead Teacher; Grading Task Force Mem; Curr, Transitional Class, Building & Facilities Comm; Peer Coach; PA St Ed Assn, NEA 1978-; PA Assn of Federal Prgm Coord 1990; Pine Grove Cmmty Band Conductor 1983-; *office:* Pine Grove Area Sch Dist School St Pine Grove PA 17963

HILBERT, JEAN ANN, 4th Grade Teacher; *b:* Lancaster, OH; *m:* Larry L.; *c:* Jennifer, Courtney; *ed:* (BS) Ed, OH St Univ 1966; Grad Work; *cr:* 1st/2nd Grade Teacher Kent Elem 1966-70; 1st Grade Teacher Glendening Elem 1977-79; 3rd-5th Grade Teacher Groveport Elem 1979-; *ai:* HS Reserve Girls Tennis Coach; Groveport Elem Stu Cncl Adv; Right to Read Comm; Former Dist Food Drive Coord; NEA, OH Ed Assn, Groveport Madison Ed Assn, Cntrl OH Teachers Assn 1966-; Groveport Alumni (Exec Bd 1978-, Pres 1988); Groveport Hall of Fame Comm Mem 1982-; Groveport United Meth (Trustee 1989-, Chancel Choir Mem 1977-); Lifetime Alumni OH St Univ 1967; *office:* Groveport Elem Sch 715 Main St Groveport OH 43125

HILDEBRAND, LOU ANN PATTERSON, Mathematics Teacher; *b:* Meridian, TX; *m:* Donald Russ; *c:* Jeffery M., Kristen M.; *ed:* (AA) Ed, Hill Jr Coll 1970; (BS) Ed, SW TX St Univ 1972; Advanced Trng; Grad Work; *cr:* 3rd/4th Grade Teacher Adam Hill Elem 1972-74; Math Teacher Pease Mid Sch 1974-76; Chldhd Ed Dir 1st Baptist Church 1982-83; Math Teacher Coke Stevenson Mid Sch 1983-; *ai:* Math Coach Calculator Team; Academic Pentathlon Coach; Natl Jr Honor Society Adv; Assn of TX Prof Educators, Natl Cncl Teachers for Advancement of Math, TX Cncl Teachers for Advancement of Math, Alamo Dist Cncl Teachers for Advancement of Math 1982-; 1st Baptist Church (Childrens Coord 1980-81, 1983-89, Ed Comm Chm 1980-81, 1983-88, 1st Grade Teacher 1972-); Given Campus, Dist & St Level Wkshps; *office:* Coke Stevenson Mid Sch 8403 Tezel Rd San Antonio TX 78250

HILDERBRAN, BETTY FRANTZEN, Mathematics Dept Chairperson; *b:* Fredericksburg, TX; *m:* Victor; *c:* Sarah, Roy; *ed:* (BA) Math, SW TX Univ 1971; *cr:* Teacher Uvalde HS 1971-72, Coahoma HS 1972-73, Uvalde HS 1973-; *ai:* Math Club Spon; NCTM, TCTM, MAA, ADCTM; Delta Kappa Gamma, AAUW, Cub Scout Den Mother; *office:* Uvalde HS 1 Coyote Trl Uvalde TX 78801

HILDRETH, BARBARA PASCHAL, 7th Grade English/Rdng Teacher; *b:* Hot Springs, AR; *c:* Charlton, Kim Hildreth-Lee; *ed:* (BA) Eng, Univ of AR Pine Bluff 1961; Henderson St Univ; *cr:* Teacher Southwest Jr HS 1970-87, Hot Springs Mid Sch 1987-; *ai:* Phi-Teen Spon; AR Ed Assn, NEA; Gamma Phi Delta (VP, Charter Mem 1970), Mother of Yr 1984; Natl Assn for Advancement of Colored People; March of Dime Mothers March.

HILEMAN, BETH ANN, Drama Teacher; *b:* Peru, IN; *ed:* (BA) Theatre Ed, Brigham Young Univ 1986; *cr:* Drama Teacher Cedar City HS 1987-; *ai:* Thespian Spon; Tech Dir for Auditorium; UT Theatre Assn Secy 1988-; ITS (St Dir 1990) 1987-; Educl Theatre Assn 1989-; Best Play UT 3A Drama Competition 1989; Outstanding Stu in Scndry Ed Brigham Young Univ 1986; *office:* Cedar City HS 703 W 600 S Cedar City UT 84720

HILFINGER, JANYNE HLADIS, Teacher; *b:* Chicago, IL; *m:* Lawrence W.; *c:* Michael, Julie, Mark; *ed:* (BA) Sociology/Soc Work, Coll of St Theresa 1967; (MA) Soc Sci, E MI 1988; *cr:* Substitute Teacher Northville HS 1979-85; Soc Stud Teacher Plymouth-Canton HS 1985-; *ai:* NCSS, MI Ed Assn 1985-; Northville Mothers Club 1988-; Taft Inst Wkshp Loyola Univ of Chicago 1988; *home:* 43885 Galway Dr Northville MI 48167

HILGERS, STEVEN FRANCIS, Mathematics Teacher/Dept Chair; *b:* Moorhead, MN; *m:* Sharon Jo Kunze; *c:* Sarah J., Natalie J.; *ed:* (BS) Math, Moorhead St Univ 1974; Working Towards Masters; *cr:* Math Teacher Park HS 1974-75, Edenhope HS 1976-79, Barnesville HS 1979-; *ai:* Mathcounts Adv; Head Girls Vlybl & 9th Grade Boys Bsktbl Coach; MEA, BEA Pres 1988-; MN HS Coaches Assn 1980-, Dist Coach of Yr 1989; Knights of Columbus 1987-; Taught in Victoria Australia 1976-79; *office:* Barnesville HS 302-324 3rd St SE Barnesville MN 56514

HILL, AMY P., Fourth Grade Teacher; *b:* Brooklyn, NY; *w:* Roger L. (dec); *c:* Karen A. (dec), Roger L., Kathy M., Howard C.; *ed:* (BA) Eng, Howard Univ 1951; (MED) Counseling/ Personnel Services, Maryland Univ 1980; Grad Stud Coll of Preachers, Natl Cathedral 1974-77; *cr:* Teacher Maude Price Nursery Sch 1947-51, DC Public Schls 1958-67; Sch Psychologist Howard Cty 1975-78; Teacher St Gabriel Sch 1978-; *ai:* Accreditation Mid Sts & Lang Art Chairperson; Dev Comm Mem; NCEA 1987-89; Prof & Bus Women Inc 1975-80; League of Women Voters 1969-75; Episcopal Church Womens Awd 1976; Certified Civil Defense Volunteer 1968; Fellowship MD Univ 1975; *office:* St Gabriel Sch 510 Webster St NW Washington DC 20011

HILL, ARTHUR R., Mathematics/Science Supervisor; *b:* Woodbury, NJ; *m:* Andrea N. Curry; *c:* Todd, Drew; *ed:* (BA) Jr HS Sci/Scndry, 1968, (MA) Secy Sch Admin 1982 Glassboro St Coll; Natl Cncl Teachers of Math Standards; Hazardous Materials Trng; *cr:* Teacher Steinhauer Jr HS 1968-72; Teacher 1972-85, Math Supvr/Sci Teacher 1985- Maple Shade HS; *ai:* Staff Dev Cncl Mem; Curr Cncl; Testing & Stu Review Comm; Burl Cty Assn of Sch Admin, NJ Assn of Sch Admin Mem 1985-; NJ Ed Assn Mem 1968-85; *office:* Maple Shade HS Frederick & Clinton Aves Maple Shade NJ 08052

HILL, BARBARA KOPACK, Gifted & Talented Coordinator; *b:* Chicago, IL; *m:* Edward; *c:* Ted, Jeffrey; *ed:* (MED) Ed, National Coll 1987; (BA) Ed, Coll of Racine 1974; Working Towards Masters Admin Leadership Univ of WI Milwaukee, Gifted & Talented Univ of WI Whitewater; *cr:* Classroom Teacher Racine Unified Schls 1974-77; Classroom Teacher 1977-82, Gifted & Talented Coord 1982-89 Lighthouse Sch; Gifted & Talented Coord Burlington Area Schls 1989-; *ai:* Dist Wide Dev of Gifted & Talented Prgm; Dist Concerns Comm Mem; Cmmty Ed Advisory Cncl Chairperson; WI Assn of Educators for Gifted & Talented (St Dir 1989-) 1980-; ASCD 1985-; PDK 1989-; PTA 1974-, Citizen of Yr 1986; Artist in Residence Grant Writing 1985-86, 1988-89, 1990; *office:* Burlington Area Schls 100 N Kane St Burlington WI 53201

HILL, BETTIE SUE, 8th Grade Lang Arts Teacher; *b:* Quebeck, TN; *m:* George W.; *c:* Kevin, Kimberly Star Bridges; *ed:* (BS) Ed/ Psych/Eng, Union Univ 1972; (MS) Guidance, UTM 1982; *cr:* Teacher Huntingdon Jr HS 1972-; *ai:* Huntingdon Ed Assn Pres; Delta Kappa Gamma Comm Chm; AB Club Spon; Delta Kappa Gamma (Personal Growth Comm 1987-89, Comm Chm 1989-); *office:* Huntingdon Jr H S 223 Browning Ave Huntingdon TN 38344

HILL, BEVERLY ARNOLD, Teacher/Science Dept Chair; *b:* Savannah, GA; *c:* Brian, Gordon; *ed:* (BS) Bio/Ag, Berry Coll 1966; (MST) Sci Ed, 1977, (EDS) Sci Ed, 1985 GA Southern; *cr:* Teacher Brooks Cty Jr HS 1967-68, Lowndes Cty Jr HS 1968-71, Reidsville HS 1971-; *ai:* Sci Club Spon; NEA STAR Teacher 1978; NSTA Star Teacher 1988; Beta Sigma Phi 1972-; Meth Women 1987-; Dist Sci Teacher of Yr 1986.

HILL, BONNIE J., WA State/US History Teacher; *b:* Renton, WA; *m:* Robert E.; *c:* Sam, Peter; *ed:* (BA) Ed/Fine Art, Cntrl WA Univ 1969; Grad Stud; *cr:* 2nd Grade Teacher Ellensburg Public Schls 1969-72; Elem Teacher Lewiston ID & Clarkston WA 1972-77; Teacher Walla Walla Comm Coll 1977-79; 7th/8th Grade Teacher Clarkston Public Schls 1979-; *ai:* Rdng & His Curr Comm; Afterschool Behavior Class; Delta Kappa Gamma Pres 1980-82, 1990; PEO (Secy, Chaplain) 1983, 1984; Wesleyan Fellowship; Church Schlshp Comm Chm 1980-; NW Regional Natl Cncl Teachers of Eng Presentor 1988; Teaching Historical Fiction Books Mini Grant 1989; Schlshp WA Cncl Intnl Trade Seminar 1984-; *office:* Lincoln Mid Sch 1945 4th Ave Clarkston WA 99403

HILL, BRENDA BURGESS, Retired Second Grade Teacher; *b:* Kalamazoo, MI; *m:* Roy; *c:* Scott, Todd, Lori Reynolds; *ed:* (AA) Early Chldhd, Stephens Coll 1949; (BA) Elem Ed, MI St Univ 1952; Grad Stud W MI; *cr:* Elem Teacher Marshall Public Schls 1952-54; K-6th Grade Substitute Teacher 1956-65, Elem Teacher 1966-89 Galesburg-Augusta; *ai:* MI Educl Assn, NEA 1952-89; Galesburg Augusta Educl Assn 1966-89.

HILL, BRENDA G., Voc Business Teacher/Cnslr; *b:* Russellville, AR; *m:* Kenneth; *c:* Christina, Michael; *ed:* (BSE) Voc Bus Ed, AR Tech Univ 1981; Counseling & Voc Ed; *ai:* FBLA & Sr Class Spon; Sch Equity Officer; AR Bus Ed Assn, Southern Region Bus Ed Assn, NBEA; *office:* Fourche Valley HS HC 69 Box 138 Briggsville AR 72828

HILL, CAROL ANN, Home Economics Teacher; *b:* Hazleton, PA; *m:* Robert P.; *ed:* (BS) Home Ec Ed, Indiana Univ of PA 1972; (MS) Early Chldhd Ed, Marywood Coll 1986; Instr Lions Quest Prgm for Drug Alcohol Prevention; *cr:* Nutrition Asst Penn St Extension Service 1972-73; Food Preparation Instr Carbon Cty Voc Tech Sch 1973-74; Home Ec Teacher Weatherly Area Sch Dist 1974-; *ai:* Drama Club & Stand Tall Prgm, AIDS Peer Ed Team Adv; Queen of Hearts Dance, 8th Grade Picnic & Talent Show Spon; NEA, Amer Home Ec Assn; Western Pocono Home Ec Assn Secy 1989-; Weatherly Cmmty Chest 1986-; Weatherly Area PTA Legislative Chairperson 1986-88; Save Our Local Environment II; FHA Honorary Degree Awd 1975; Weatherly Elem Mid Sch Teacher of Yr 1986; *office:* Weatherly Area Mid Sch Evergreen Ave Weatherly PA 18255

HILL, CAROLYN COLE, 5th Grade Teacher; *b:* Stephenville, TX; *m:* Danny Joe; *c:* Tammy, Angela; *ed:* (BS) Home Ec Ed, TX Tech Univ 1967; (BS) Elem Ed, Tarleton St Univ 1974; *cr:* Teacher Ferris Elem 1967-77, Northside Elem 1977-; *ai:* SSC Pilot Prgm Participant; 5th Grade Level & Sci Fair Chairperson; Sch Curr Comm Advisory Cncl Rep; TX St Teachers Assn, NEA 1987-89; TX Prof Educators Assn Lifetime; WISD Northside Campus Teacher of Month & Yr 1987-88.

HILL, CAROLYN HALE, Science Teacher; *b:* Haletown, AR; *m:* Thomas J. Jr.; *c:* Roy, Wade, Mike, Pat, Scott; *ed:* (BSE) Sci & Phys Ed, Univ of AR 1967; AR Tech Univ; *cr:* 6th Grade Phys Ed Teacher Waldron Elem Sch 1967-68; 8th Grade Sci Teacher 1984-, 7th Grade Health Teacher 1989- Waldron Mid Sch; *ai:* Cheer Spon; 4-H Club Leader; Lib Bd Cty 1980-89; 4-H Cncl Cty 1977-; Sunday Sch Staff Teacher 1978-.

HILL, CHARLIE GAINES, Metal Trades Instructor; *b:* Charlston, MS; *m:* Barbara Fay Ford; *c:* Kimberly, Ann-Michelle; *ed:* Industrial Ed, NW MS Comm Coll 1961; Voc Ed, MS St Univ; Univ of S MS & William Carey Coll; *cr:* Production Control Supvr Mc Quay Incorporated 1961-68; Voc Metal Trades Instr Biloxi HS 1968-; *ai:* Prin Advisory Cncl; Teacher of Yr Selection Comm; AVA 1971-, Runner-Up Natl Teacher of Yr 1985, Candidate Region IV Teacher of Yr 1985; MS Assn of Voc Educators 1971-, Teacher of Yr 1985; MS St Cert Commission 1984-89; Coast Area Chamber of Commerce HS Teacher of Yr 1988-89; *office:* Biloxi Public Schls 1424 Father Ryan Ave Biloxi MS 39530

HILL, DAN ALLEN, Science Teacher; *b:* Dover, OH; *ed:* (BS) Elem Ed, Kent St Univ 1980; Grad Stud Univ of Houston; Natl Sci Fnd Honors Inst TX A&M Univ; *cr:* 5th/6th Grade Teacher New Philadelphia City Schls 1980-82; 6th Grade Sci Teacher Sugar Land Jr HS 1982-85, First Colony Mid Sch 1985-; *ai:* 6th Grade Sci Club Spon, Dist Teacher Advisory Comm, 6th Grade Sci Team Leader; FBEA Parliamentarian 1986-89; NEA Mem 1980-; TSTA Mem 1982-; STAT Mem 1983-; TAMU NSF Top 20 Elem Sci Teachers in St of TX; Building Teacher of Yr 1988-89; *office:* First Colony Mid Sch 3225 Austin Pkwy Sugar Land TX 77479

HILL, DELORES ANN, Second Grade Teacher; *b:* Olcott, WV; *m:* Robert Leon; *ed:* (BS) Elem Ed, WV St Coll 1964; (MA) Elem Ed, WV Univ 1972; Educl Seminars; Elem Ed, WV Coll of Grad Stud 1986; Boone Cty Rdng Cncl; 1st Responders Emergency Organization; *cr:* 1st-8th Grade Teacher Gillispie Sch 1960-67; 1st/2nd Grade Teacher Ashford-Rumble Grade Sch 1968-; *ai:* Boone Cty Assn of Ed Building Rep; Lang Art Textbook Comm Mem; Take-A-Kid-to-Dinner; PTA Comm Mem; WV Univ Alumni Life Mem 1984-; WV PTA 1975, Pin Life Mem; Boone Cty Rdng Cncl 1983-; NEA, WVEA Mem 1970-; Alum Creek Lioness Club; Lioness-Lions Club (Pres, Lioness Chairperson Dist 29-O) 1976-86, Perfect Attendance; Aid for Appalachian Youth Secy 1965-70; Emmons WV Cmmty Jay Rockefeller Coord; WV Sight Fnd; Co-Authored Cookbook; *home:* Rt 7 Box 282-A South Charleston WV 25309

HILL, DIANE LUSARA, 1st/2nd Grade Teacher; *b:* Los Angeles, CA; *ed:* (BA) Phys Ed/Elem/NTE, CA St Univ 1976; *cr:* Kndgtn Teacher Piute Mountain Sch 1985-86; 3rd Grade Teacher N Beardsley Sch 1987-88; K/1st Grade Teacher 1988-89, 1st/2nd Grade Teacher 1989- Piute Mountain Sch; *ai:* Just Say No To Drugs Club Adv; Kern Cty Rdng Assn 1989-; *office:* Piute Mountain Sch Star Rt Box 64-B Caliente CA 93518

HILL, DIANNE MANGUM, 6th Grade Teacher; *b:* Durham, NC; *m:* David E.; *c:* Jonathan, Brian; *ed:* (BA) Elem Ed, Univ of NC 1971; Grad Work Gifted Children Univ of NC; 1979-81; *cr:* 4th Grade Teacher Bragtown Sch 1971-73; 6th Grade Teacher Bragtown 6th Grade Ctr 1974-; *ai:* Comm Review Organizational Plans of Cty-Wide Acad Gifted Prgm; NEA 1971-; NC Assn of Ed 1971-; Assn of Classroom Teachers 1971-87; NCTE 1989-; Delta Kappa Gamma 1977- 2nd VP 1980-82; Bragtown Bapt Church Sr Adult Cncl Chm 1988-; Bragtown Bapt Church Pianist 1970-; Fnlst DUrham Cty Teacher of Yr 1980; Rep 5th Annual St Awareness Conf 1980; 1st Annual Triangle Consortium 1985; Nom By PTA Phoebe Apperson Hearst Outstanding Ed Awd 1987; Durham Cty Sch Nom Outstanding Lang Arts Teacher NC Awds Prgm 1988; *office:* Bragtown 6th Grade Ctr 320 Belvin Ave Durham NC 27704

HILL, FANNIE WILSON, Fourth Grade Teacher; *b:* Birmingham, AL; *m:* Winston Douglas; *c:* Winston II, Windall, Whitney; *ed:* (BA) Elem Ed, AL A&M Univ 1967; Cert Wayne St Univ; *cr:* Teacher Sch Two 1967-68; 1st Grade Teacher 1969-75, 3rd Grade Teacher 1976-81, 4th Grade Teacher/Gifted/Talented Teacher 1981- Priest Elem; *ai:* Creative Writing Comm; Chairwoman Sch Flower Comm; Teacher Etiquette Great Expectatiions Prgm; Detroit Fed; Awd for Excl Teaching Contributions Cluster Teacher MET Prgm 1987; *home:* 17615 Adrian Rd Southfield MI 48075

HILL, FRANCES FRENCH, Kindergarten Teacher; *b:* Alcoa, TN; *m:* Norman G.; *c:* Andrea H. Scott, David N., Angela M.; *ed:* (BS) Elem Ed, Univ of TN 1963; (MS) Curr/Instruction, Lincoln Memorial Univ 1988; *cr:* 3rd-8th Grade/HS Eng/Bible/Math/Psych/Drivers Ed Teacher/Prin Friendsville Acad 1953-71; Kndgtn Teacher Rockford Elem 1971-; *ai:* Delta Kappa Gamma (Corresponding Secy, Exec Bd Mem 1988-) 1978-; *home:* Rt 2 Box 611 Friendsville TN 37737

HILL, FRANCES JONES, Language Arts Teacher; *b:* Shreveport, LA; *w:* Hiram T. (dec); *c:* Corradina Develle Jones, Ianva Yvette Bickham; *ed:* (BS) Eng, Grambling St Univ 1970; Northeast LA Univ; *cr:* Teacher/Librarian Wesley Ray HS 1970-71; Teacher All Saints HS 1971-72, Transylvania Jr HS 1972; *ai:* 4-H Club Leader; SAPE Leader; LEA/NEA Faculty Rep 1970-; East Carroll Youth Spon Secy 1981-; CULP Coord 1982; Foster Parent Assn 1986- Foster Parent of Yr 1989; Teacher of Yr 1986; *home:* Rt 1 Box 203 B Sondheimer LA 71276

HILL, FRANK P., English Teacher; *b:* Chicago, IL; *m:* Terry Sharpe; *c:* Carla; *ed:* (BA) Eng, IL St Univ 1972; (MS) Eng, Northeastern 1979; Journalism; *cr:* Eng Teacher Proviso West HS 1972-78, Hoffman Estates HS 1978-; *ai:* Yrbk Adv; Journalism Ed Assn 1989-; Northern IL Press Assn Dir 1982-, Golden Eagle 1986-; Columbia Scholastic Assn 1982-, Silver Crown 1989; Schaumburg Athletic Assn Coach 1987-; Speaker IN Scholastic Press Assn Convention; Teacher IN SPA Summer Prgm; Teacher Rockford Coll Summer Prgm; *office:* Hoffman Estates HS 1100 W Higgins Rd Hoffman Estates IL 60195

HILL, FRED ALLEN, Science Teacher; *b:* Caldwell, ID; *m:* Connie J.; *c:* Cindy Rogers, Cheryl, Candi, Cary; *ed:* (BA) Bio, Northwest Nazarene Coll 1964; Acad Yr NC St Univ; *cr:* Sci Teacher Middleton Sch Dist 134 1963-66; Marsing Sch Dist 363 1966-67; Vallivue Sch Dist 139 1968-76; Nampa Sch Dist 131 1977-; *ai:* Nampa HS Sci Club Adv; Nampa Soph Class Adv; Natural His Class Teacher; Middleton Ed Assn Pres 1964-65; Marsing Ed Assn VP 1966-67; NABT 1980-; ID Outstanding Bio Teacher 1983-; Deer Flat Free Meth Church VP Corp/Chm Church Bd 1986-; Lizard Butte Sunrise Assn Corp Pres 1982-90; NSF Acad Yr 1966-67; ID Society of Energy/Env Ed Bd of Dir; Amer Bio Teacher Artilce 1986; Univ of ID Teaching Excl Awd 1988; Northwest Nazarene Coll Alumni Assn Excl Teaching Recognition 1988; Nom Pres Excl Awd 1989; *office:* Nampa Sr H S 203 Lake Lowell Ave Nampa ID 83686

HILL, GLEN ROY, Chemistry Teacher; *b:* Corbin, KY; *m:* Marcia L. Shaner; *c:* Steven S., Jennifer, Christopher; *ed:* (AB) Pre-Medical, Transylvania Univ 1962; Dental Sch, Univ of Louisville 1962-63; *cr:* Physics/Chem Teacher Pendleton Cty HS 1963-64; Chem/Sci Teacher Southwest Jr HS 1964-69; Bio/Anatomy/Physiology Teacher Okeechobee HS 1977-80; Oceanography Teacher Hallendale HS 1981-82; Chem Teacher Southeast HS 1982-; *ai:* Migrant Tutoring; Sch Improvement Planning Comm; STAR Group Cnslr; Amer Chemical Society 1987-; FL Assn of Sci Teachers 1977-80, 1983-86; Kiwanis Club 1982-88; Key Club Adv of Yr 1986; Natl Sci Fnd Grant to FL Inst of Technology; *office:* Southeast HS 1200 37th Ave E Bradenton FL 34208

HILL, JANE ELAINE, Jr HS Teacher; *b:* Marion, OH; *ed:* (BS) Elem, Olivet Nazarene Univ 1970; (MA) Elem/Pre Sch, Governors St Univ 1981; Cmptr Ed, Governors St Univ 1987-88; *cr:* 5th Grade Teacher Limestone 1970-88, Jr HS Teacher Limestone/Herscher Jr HS 1988-; *ai:* Accompanist Vocal & Emsemble Music Contests/Band-Orch-Chorus Contests & Competition; Work Bsktbl Games; NEA/IEA/HEA Secy 1972-73; NFT/IFT/U2CT Building Rep/Negotiations; 1st Church of Nazarene Church Bd/Sunday Sch Teacher/Choir/Pianist/Sub Under Shepherd; Life Membership PTA Awd; Crista Mc Auliffe Schlsp; *office:* Limestone Grade Sch RR 4 Box 242A Kankakee IL 60901

HILL, JEAN CAROLYN, First Grade Teacher; *b:* Lenoir County, NC; *m:* Richard Lee; *c:* Robert J.; *ed:* (BA) Elem Ed, NC Cntrl Univ 1976; (MS) Elem Ed, E Carolina Univ 1987; *cr:* 1st Grade Teacher Contentnea Elem 1976-; *ai:* NCAE Outstanding Educator 1989; Zeta Phi Beta Outstanding Young Educator 1989; Teacher of Yr Contentnea Elem Schl 1980; Teacher of Yr Lenoir Cty Schls 1989-; *home:* 1302-B W Washington Ave Kinston NC 28501

HILL, JEFF W., Mathematics Teacher; *b:* Dover, NH; *m:* Julie Ann Christ; *ed:* (BS) Psych, 1984, (MED) Scndry Ed, 1985 Tufts Univ; Grad Courses Math, Boston Univ; Fipse Geometry Wkshps for Teachers, Univ of NH; *cr:* Math Teacher Newport HS 1986-87, Timberlane Regional HS 1987-; *ai:* Math Team Co-Adv; Celebration of Learning & Communication for Excl Comm; *office:* Timberlane Regional HS 36 Greenough Rd Plaistow NH 03826

HILL, JERELYN R., Physical Education Teacher; *b:* Driggs, ID; *m:* Joe; *c:* Billy J., Robert J., Tori; *ed:* (BA) Phys Ed, Ricks Coll 1960; (BA) Phys Ed, ID St Univ 1972; *cr:* Phys Ed Teacher Teton HS 1967-83, Teton Mid Sch 1983-; *ai:* Cmmty Against Drug & Alcohol Abuse; ID Ed Assn 1967-; Outstanding Young Woman 1973; *home:* PO Box 81 Tetonia ID 83452

HILL, JOHN BRUCE, 9th-10th Grade History Teacher; *b:* Idabel, OK; *m:* Terri Lynn Burgess; *c:* Bradlee H., Joe B.; *ed:* Assoc His, Carl Albert Jr Coll 1976; (BA) His/Phys Ed/Driver Ed, SE OK St Univ 1978; *cr:* Teacher/Coach Ft Worth Brewer HS 1978-79, Idabel HS 1980-; *ai:* Head Bsbl & Asst Ftbl Coach; OK Bsbl Coaches Assn (Region Coach Yr 1981-84, All St Coach 1985) 1980-; Morning Lions Club 1986-88; *home:* 106 Hastings Ct Idabel OK 74745

HILL, JOYCE BLANTON, Educational Diagnostician; *b:* Roswell, NM; *m:* David D.; *c:* Cinnamon, Colleen; *ed:* (BA) Elem Ed, 1973, (MA) Curr, 1973 NM St Univ; Licensure Educl Diagnostics 1989; *cr:* Art Teacher Holloman Jr HS 1973-75; 4th Grade Teacher Holloman Intermediate Sch 1975-82; 6th Grade Teacher Sierra Elem Sch 1982-87; 5th Grade Teacher Buena Vista Elem Sch 1987-89; Educl Diagnostician Alamogordo Public Schls 1989-; *ai:* Dist Remediation Comm Mem; Tularosa Basin Sci Fair Bd Mem; Alamogordo Cncl 2nd VP 1988-89; Intnl Rdng Assn; NEA 1973-; Delta Kappa Gamma 1987-; Kappa Kappa Iota 1990; Alamogordo Kiwanis Intnl 1989-; *office:* Alamogordo Public Schls 301 Texas Ave Alamogordo NM 88310

HILL, JOYCE HOLT, 7th Grade Soc Stud/Eng Teacher; *b:* Eatonton, GA; *m:* Willie Sr.; *c:* Willie Jr., Tekeshia; *ed:* (BS) Soc Stud Ed, Savannah ST Coll 1977; (MA) Soc Stud Ed, GA ST Coll 1988; *cr:* Teacher Putnam Cty Mid Sch 1977-; *ai:* Organizer & Spon Putnam Mid Sch Cmmty Helper Club; GA Assn Educators 1977-; *office:* Putnam County Mid Sch 314 S Washington Ave Eatonton GA 31024

HILL, KAREN GAIL, Kindergarten Teacher; *b:* Glen Ridge, NJ; *m:* James; *ed:* (BA) Liberal Stud, CA St Univ Long Beach 1977; (MS) Educl Admin, CA St Univ Fullerton 1985; *cr:* Kndgtn Teacher Geddes Elem 1978-; *ai:* Kndgtn Chm; Sch-Wide Effectiveness Prgm Review Chm; *office:* Geddes Elem Sch 14600 Cavette Pl Baldwin Park CA 91706

HILL, KENNETH DUANE, Theatre/Fine Art Chair; *b:* Eureka, CA; *m:* Anne Marie Guglielmina; *c:* Bethany, Charlotte; *ed:* (BA) Eng - Summa Cum Laude, Bethany Bible Coll 1986; Working Towards Masters Theatre Art, San Francisco St Univ; Seminar Courses Drama, Film, Lit; *cr:* Sr Mgr Longs Drug Stores 1980-83; Secy Rev Rick Howard 1985-86, Dr Dwight Wilson 1984-86; Chaplain/Teacher/Dir/Chm Valley Chrstn Schls 1986-; *ai:* Seminar & Wkshp LEader; Theatre; Producer & Dir VCHS/VI Productions; Spec Events Speaker; Breakaway Awds Speaker; Light of Life/ELCA (Mem, Youth Adv) 1987-; Delta Epsilon Chi Mem; Santa Cruz Cty Actors Former Bd Mem; San Lorenzo Valley Youth Cncl Dir; Ind Film Producer; Theatrical Consultant; CAL Grant; Pell Grant; Alumni Assn & BBC Multiple Schlsp Awds; Whos Who Among Stu in Amer Univ & Colls 1985-86; B of A Achievement Awd; Published Author; *office:* Valley Chrstn HS 1 W Campbell Ave Campbell CA 95008

HILL, LARRY THOMAS, Mathematics Teacher; *b:* Reidsville, NC; *c:* Landon, Laura; *ed:* (BA) Health/Phys Ed, Atlanta Chrstn 1971; (MS) Safety/Driver Ed, NC A&T St 1990; *cr:* Teacher/Coach Bethany Sch 1971-; *ai:* Bsktbl Coach; NC Coaches Assn 1971-; NC Math Teachers Assn 1975-; NC Summer Math Inst; *office:* Bethany Elem & Jr HS Rt 4 Box 351 Reidsville NC 27320

HILL, LINDA LOU, History Department Chair; *b:* Livingston, TX; *ed:* (BA) Eng/His, Baylor Univ 1966; Various Univs; *cr:* Teacher Rice C Ind Sch Dist 1966-70; Dept Chairperson/Teacher Lamar C Ind Sch Dist 1970-; *ai:* Natl Jr Honor Society Spon; Stu Cncl; His Fair; Coach Academic Contest IN His; Bluebonnet Cncl for Soc Stud Treas 1983-; TX Cncl for Soc Stud Membership Comm 1987-; TX St Teachers Assn, NEA; Delta Kappa Gamma Correspondence Secy 1985-87; Order of Eastern Star Organist 1989-; Ft Bend Cty Museum, St Mar KS Episcopal Church Lay Reader; Full Fellowship From Jewish LaBor Comm & Houston Survivors Of HolocausT Study Israel 1989; *office:* George Jr HS 4601 Airport Rd Rosenberg TX 77471

HILL, LINDA WEST, Science Dept Chm/Chemistry; *b:* Mobile, AL; *c:* Kimberly Nicole; *ed:* (BA) Bio, Dillard Univ 1970; (MED) Bio, Univ South AL 1984; *cr:* Lab Asst Dillard Univ 1967-70; Teacher Mary G Montgomery HS 1970-; Cmmty Ed 1981-83; Instr S D Bishop Jr Coll 1987-; *ai:* Adv Natl Honor Society; Adv Scholars Bowl Sunday Sch Supt; Youth Adv Church; Alpha Kappa Alpha 1968-; Sickel Cell Anemia 1982-; NAACP 1986-87; NSF Fellowship 1972; Teacher of Yr 1980; Intnl Paper Co Grant 1978; Proposal in Earth Sci.

HILL, LORRAINE THERESA, 7th/8th Grade Math/Eng Teacher; *b:* Hartford, CT; *m:* Jeffrey; *c:* Jennifer, Audrey; *ed:* (BA) Eng, CSUN Northridge 1971; Grad Stud CA Luth Univ; *cr:* 5th Grade Teacher 1981-86, 7th/8th Grade Teacher 1986- St Rose of Lima Sch; *ai:* Stu Cncl Moderator; NCEA 1981-; *office:* St Rose of Lima Sch 1325 Royal Ave Simi Valley CA 93065

HILL, MARGARET LOUISE, First Grade Teacher; *b:* Gunnison, CO; *m:* Charles W.; *c:* Charles F., Thomas K., Julie A. Sherburne; *ed:* (BA) Ed Western St Coll 1959; Hearing Aid Dispensing License, Cerritos Coll; Solutions to Comm Span Course; Esl Trng; US Hist 1920-, Pepperdine; Educ, Both Halves of Brain, Univ of CA; *cr:* Teacher Pine Street Sch 1957-58; 1st Grade Teacher, Ynez Sch 1960-76; Granada Sch 1976-; *ai:* Sch Improvement Coord 12 Yrs; Dist Curr Com 2 Yrs; PTA Life Membership 1987; CA Teachers Assn 1960-; Alhambra Teachers Assn 1960-; *office:* Granada Sch 100 S Granada Ave Alhambra CA 91801

HILL, MARTHA E. (MATTILA), Second Grade Teacher; *b:* Humboldt, MI; *m:* Arthur J.; *c:* Vicki Usitalo, Rebecca Blomquist, Paula; *ed:* (BS) Fine Art/Soc Stud, 1972, (MA) Rdng Ed, 1980 N MI Univ; Secretarial Trng, Suomi Coll 1955-57; Gifted & Talented Wkshps & Seminars; *cr:* Teacher Chassell Twp Schls 1973-; *ai:* Sch Improvement Comm; Intnl Rdng Assn 1988-; Copper Country Camp of Auxiliary Gideons Intnl (Secy, Treas) 1982-; Copper Cty Chorale Soloist 1963-; *office:* Chassell Twp Schls PO Box 140 Chassell MI 49916

HILL, MAUDELLA M., Second Grade Teacher; *b:* Corinth, MS; *c:* Julian B. Jr., Ginny Hill Jones; *ed:* (BAE) Elem Ed, Univ of MS 1950; Grad Stud Univ of MS; *cr:* 5th Grade Math Teacher Corinth Sch System 1974-75; 2nd Grade Teacher Glendale Elem Sch 1975-; *ai:* Kappa Delta Pi 1949-50; GSA Leader 1966-70; BSA Den Mother 1959-61; *office:* Glendale Elem Sch Rt 1 PO Box 69 Glen MS 38846

HILL, MELVIN J., Life Science Teacher; *b:* Chester, MD; *m:* Ora Lee Bailey; *c:* Robin Thompson, Melvin Jr., Kendra M.; *ed:* (BS) Health/Phys Ed/Biological Sci, MD St Coll 1963; Grad Stud Trenton St Coll; *cr:* Sci Teacher Sampson G Smith Sch 1966-; *ai:* Homework Club Spon; Faculty Advisory Comm Mem; Franklin Teachers Building Coord 1979-; NJ Sci Teachers; NEA 1966-; Coll Alumni VP 1988-; Church Youth Comm Chairperson 1989-; Geology Inst Princeton Univ 1985; *office:* Sampson G Smith Sch 1649 Amwell Rd Somerset NJ 08873

HILL, NANCY SCHEAR, French Teacher; *b:* Mobile, AL; *m:* Richard William; *c:* Bryan C., Christine M.; *ed:* (BA) Span/Fr, Univ of TX Austin 1973; Rdng Specialist; *cr:* Span Teacher Weis Mid Sch 1974-80; Fr Teacher Theodore HS 1982-; *ai:* Fr Club & NHS Spon; Supt & Peer Advisory Review Cncl; Academic Letter Comm; NEA 1974-; AL Ed Assn, Mobile Ed Assn 1982-; Delta Kappa Gamma 1979-; Natl Cncl of Jewish Women 1974-.

HILL, NOLA HEDGES, Retired Teacher; *b:* Drummond, OK; *m:* Duane; *c:* Rick, Jan; *ed:* (BS) Commercial Ed/Elem Ed, Phillips Univ 1953; *cr:* 3rd-5th Grade Teacher Meno Grade Sch 1953-55; 5th/6th Grade Teacher 1955-58, 4th Grade Teacher 1970-89 Drummond Grade Sch; *ai:* Drummond Teacher Assn, OK Ed Assn, NEA 1970-89; Drummond Teacher of Yr 1982-83; *home:* Box 215 Drummond OK 73735

HILL, OPHELIA WEST, Retired Teacher; *b:* Hopkinsville, KY; *m:* Dennis Gilmer; *c:* Steven, Thomas, Alan; *ed:* (BS) Elem Ed, Austin Peay Univ 1958; *cr:* 1st-8th Grade Teacher Shiloh Elem 1943-46; 3rd/4th Grade Teacher 1946-55, 1st-2nd Grade Teacher 1956-64, 2nd Grade Teacher 1965-89 Sinking Fork Elem; *ai:* Alpha Delta Kappa Chaplain 1986-88; *home:* 3520 Quisenberry Ln Hopkinsville KY 42240

HILL, PATRICK LEWIS, Soc Sci Teacher/Dept Chair; *b:* Los Angeles, CA; *ed:* (AA) His, Los Angeles Valley Coll 1973; (BA) His/Philosophy, CA St Northridge 1976; Teaching Credential, CA Luth Univ; *cr:* Long Term Substitute Teacher Agoura HS 1981-82, Hughes Jr HS 1983, Calabasas HS & Linero Cyn Mid Sch 1984; Teacher/Chm Lindero Cyn Mid Sch 1985-; *ai:* Soc Sci Area Los Virgenes Unified Partnership in Schls Comm; S CA Geneological Society 1985; CA St Society Daughters of Amer Revolution Outstanding Teacher Awd 1990; Participation in His Day LA Act 1986-; Published Article 1989; *office:* Lindero Canyon Mid Sch 5844 Larboard Ln Agoura Hills CA 91301

HILL, PHYLIS DAVIS, 5th Grade Teacher; *b:* Knoxville, TN; *m:* James H. Jr.; *c:* John W., Pamela Sparks; *ed:* (BS) Elem Ed, Univ of TN 1961; *cr:* 4/5/6th Grade Teacher Mooreland Heights Elem 1961-64; Flenniken Elem 1964-89; 5th Grade Teacher Flenniken Elem 1989-90; *ai:* 1989-90 Knox Cty Ed Assn Rep; 1982-83 Knoxville Ed Assn Rep; 1987-88 Conducted Wrkshp on Math Manipulatives; 1984-90 Sci Coord; PTA Prgm Chm 1986; TN Ed Assn; Natl Teachers Assn; 1989-90 Mini Grant in Soc Stud; 1990 Nom for "Teacher of the Year 1991"; *home:* Rule Dr Rt 1 Box 374 Rockford TN 37853

HILL, PHYLLIS M., Retired English/Span Teacher; *b:* Grove City, PA; *ed:* (BA) His/Poly Sci, Grove City Coll 1948; Masters Equivalent Span, Natl Univ of Mexico 1964; Summer Sch Natl Univ of Mexico 1960, 1962, 1966, 1971; Mangold Lang Inst Spain 1972; *cr:* 8th Grade Teacher Corry Area HS 1948-86; *ai:* Adult Literacy Tutor 1987-.

HILL, ROBERT KERMIT, Social Studies Teacher; *b:* Las Vegas, NM; *m:* Wendy Joan Hummel; *c:* Shannon, Ryan; *ed:* (BA) His 1964, (MA) His 1969 Univ of NM; NM Highlands Univ; *cr:* HS His Govern/Coach Consolidated Schls 1965-66; Soc Stud Coach Harrington Jr HS Capshaw Jr HS 1966-; Soc Sci Instr Coll of Santa Fe NM/Penitentiary Coll 1972-83; His Instr Santa Fe Comm Coll 1983-; *ai:* Currently Team Leader of New Mid Sch Interdiscipline Team Family in Relearning Project & Coalition of Essential Schls Project; NEA 1965-; 3 Times Selected By Santa Fe HS Super Scholars One of Most Influential Teachers; Published 2 Articles in Southwest Heritage/REA Enchantment Magazine; *office:* Capshaw Mid Sch 351 E Zia Rd Santa Fe NM 87505

HILL, ROBERTA A., Chemistry Department Chair; *b:* Cookeville, TN; *m:* Ewing Kelly; *c:* Doyle R., Kelley A.; *ed:* (BS) Chem, 1959, (MA) Chem, 1961 TN Technological Univ; Ed, TN Technological Univ 1967-68; Ed, Univ of AL Tuscaloosa 1967-; Ed, Univ AL Huntsville 1970-71; *cr:* Chem Instr TN Technological Univ 1959-61, Springhill Coll 1961-64; Chem

Teacher Univ AL Huntsville 1965 & 1969, Huntsville City Public Schls 1965-; *ai:* Dept Chairperson; Chem Contest Coach; Help Coach Olympiads & Contest; HEA, NEA, AEA, 1969-; Natl Sci Teachers Assn; Huntsville Cncl Sci Teachers (Pres 1978-80, Secy 1987); Amer Red Cross Hospital Volunteer 1987-88; Church (Admin Bd, Schlsp Comm, Treas of Groups 1988-) 1985-; Summer Apprenticeship Army (Redstone Arsenal) 1984-86; Received Acknowledgement Publications; *office:* Grissom HS 7901 Bailey Cove Rd Huntsville AL 35802

HILL, SHARON REED, Second Grade Teacher; *b:* Charleston, WV; *m:* Donald A.; *c:* Brian J., Kevin J.; *ed:* (BS) Elem Ed, WV St Coll 1966; Grad Work Cmptr Trng 1989-; *cr:* Teacher Watts Elem 1966-69; Substitute Teacher Kanawha Cty Schls 1972-77; Teacher/Acting Prin 1983-87, Teacher 1977- J E Robins Elem; *ai:* PAC Comm; Art Chairperson; CASE Coord; WV Ed Assn, KTA, CTA Mem 1966-84; St Pauls Luth Church 1956-; Edgewood Pool Incorporated Bd Mem 1985-88; Wilson Booster Club Mem 1982-87; Stonewall Jackson Booster Club Mem 1986-88; Trained for St Accreditation Team; Helped Write & Rewrite Prgm Stud of Art for Kanawha Cty; Co-Authored Supplemental Text for Rdng; Graduated High Scholastic Achievement Awd; *office:* J E Robins Elem Sch 915 Beech Ave Charleston WV 25302

HILL, SHIRLEY BUTLER, Mathematics Teacher; *b:* Baltimore, MD; *m:* Alton Sr.; *c:* Saeed, Alton Jr.; *ed:* (BS) Early Chldhd/Math, Howard Univ 1973; (MS) Math, Morgan St Univ 1981; Word Processing, Cmptr Programming; *cr:* Elem Sch Teacher Elmer A Henderson #101 1974-80; Math Teacher Lombard Mid Sch 1980-; *ai:* GED Pgrm Tutor; Northwood Little League Bsbl Scorekeeper; Northwood PTA Secy; Omi Cri Nu 1973-; Fair Lanes Service Awds 1986-; St of MD Math Project Cert 1986; Northwood Day Camp Service Awd; Governors Citation for Outstanding Service Rendered to Northwood Elem Sch 1988-89.

HILL, TERESA ELLEN, 12th Grade English Teacher; *b:* Binghamton, NY; *m:* Michael H.; *c:* James Crandell, Colleen Crandell, Rebecca Crandell; *ed:* (BA) Eng/Fr Lit, 1966, (MA) Eng Lit, 1972, (PHD) Comparative Lit, 1978 SUNY Binghamton; Grad Courses Ed & Eng Scndry Methodology, Scranton Univ 1967, 1968; *cr:* 7th Grade Eng Teacher West Jr HS 1967-68; Part Time Eng Instr SUNY Binghamton & Broome Comm Coll 1970-75; 10th Grade Eng/Rdng Teacher North HS 1975-77; Head of Adult Voc Trng & Testing Binghamton Psyciatric Center 1978-79; 9th/10th Grade Teacher Johnson City HS 1979-; Tech Writing/Aerospace Spec Translation Singer/Link Binghamton 1985-; *ai:* Format Methodology Facilitator 1985-; In Service Summer Wkshps Whole Lang Curr Dev 1988-; Teacher Consultant Mastery Learning & Instructional Process 1987-; Summer Curr Dev 1980-; S Tier Inst for Performing Arts Active Rep 1985-; *home:* 11 Indiana St Binghamton NY 13903

HILL, VESPER LEE, Middle School Math Teacher; *b:* Princeton, IN; *m:* Carolyn Davidson; *c:* Brent; *ed:* (BS) Phy Ed/ Math, Oakland City Coll 1960; (MS) Math, IN St Univ 1967; Prin Cert, IN St Univ 1978-81; *cr:* Teacher/Coach Ft Branch HS 1960-64, Tecumseh HS 1964-69, Petersburg HS 1969-74; MS Prin/Ath Dir 1974-81, Teacher 1981- Pike Cntrl Mid HS; *ai:* Athletic Dir of Yr Dist 5 1979; Natl Sci Grant Carlton Coll 1963, Marquette Univ 1966, Univ of Evansville 1968; *home:* RR #1 Box 230 Hazleton IN 47640

HILL, VICKI L., Sixth Grade Teacher; *b:* Harrisburg, IL; *ed:* (BS) Elem Ed, 1973, (MS) Elem Ed, 1978, (PHD) Ed, 1988 S IL Univ; *cr:* Prin/Asst Supt/Athletic Dir Carrollton Unit Sch 1989; Teacher Fairfield Public Sch #112 1974-; Coll Instr Frontier Comm Coll 1988-; *ai:* IEA, NEA Pres 1987-; IPA 1987-89; Pi Lamda Theta 1988-89; B&PW Secy 1976-86; Beta Eta 1977-82; Beginning 1st Yr Teachers Perceptions of Characteristics of Effective Teaching; *home:* 410 Darr Fairfield IL 62837

HILL, WANA BRYANT, Retired Teacher; *b:* Wewoka, OK; *m:* Lonnie C.; *c:* Gail Jowers, Linda Bengs; *ed:* (AA) General, Wetumka Jr Coll 1942; (BS) Elem Ed/Bus Ed, E Cntrl St Univ & Univ of OK 1949; (MED) Bus Ed, OK Univ 1956; Consumer Ed, Univ of OK; *cr:* Bus Teacher Fairview HS 1942-49; Bus Teacher Wetumka HS 1950-71, 1977-80; 4th Grade Teacher Cntrl Grade Sch 1975-77, 1980-82; *ai:* NEA, OK Ed Assn 1950-71, 1974-82; Hughes Cty Retired Teachers Assn Pres 1986-88; *home:* 617 E Frisco Wetumka OK 74883

HILL, WILLIAM FRANK, History Teacher; *b:* E Liverpool, OH; *ed:* (BSED) Amer Stud, Bowling Green St Univ 1969; Amer Studs, Bowling Green Univ; *cr:* 8th Grade Teacher Mc Cord Jr HS 1969-77; His Teacher Southview HS 1977-; *ai:* Class of 1993 Adv; Cousa Review Dir; Building Advisory Comm; Sylvania Ed Assn VP 1973-74; OH Ed Assn, NW OH Ed Assn, NEA 1969-; NW Cncl for Soc Stud VP; Personal Rights Organization of Toledo Bd of Dirs 1987-; *office:* Southview HS 7225 Sylvania Ave Sylvania OH 43560

HILL, WILLIE D., JR., Social Studies Teacher; *b:* Birmingham, AL; *c:* Tonya R., Adrian D.; *ed:* (BS) Mid Sch Ed, AL St Univ; Mercer Univ, GA Coll Milledgeville, Emory Univ, Univ of GA Athens; *cr:* Teacher Maggie Califf HS 1969-70, Burghard Elem 1970-84, Appling Mid Sch 1984-; *ai:* Macon Recreation Leader; Bibb Cty Bd of Ed Teacher Recruiter 1979-84, Magnet Prgm, Global Geography, Accreditation Comm, Organized Elem Stu Cncl; Bibb Assn of Ed, GA Assn of Ed, NEA 1971-; Mid GA Soc Stud Cncl 1976-; Bibb Assn of Mid Sch Ed; PTA Pres 1977; St Luke Baptist Church (Deacon Bd Chm, Hymm Trng Teacher, Asst Adult Teacher, Male Chorus Mem, Gospel Ensemble, Finance Chm); Mc Kibbens Lane Awd Excl in Teaching 1978; Implemented Ec TV Prgm for Bibb Cty Univ of GA; *office:* Appling Mid Sch 1210 Shurling Dr Macon GA 31211

HILLARD, SAMUEL MARC, 7th/8th Grade Soc Stud Teacher; *b:* Jamestown, NY; *ed:* (BSED) Soc Stud/Geography, 1961, (MSED) Soc Stud, 1965 Edinboro St Coll; *cr:* Teacher Westmont Hilltop Jr HS & Mid Sch 1961-; *ai:* Jr HS Wrestling Coach 1976-80; Equipment Mgr Jr HS 1970; Mid Sch Advisory Comm; In Charge of Stu Ushers, Announcements, Daily Flag Raising; NEA, PA Ed Assn, Johnstown Ed Assn 1961-; NCSS, PA Cncl for Soc Stud 1961-; Natl Cncl for Geographic Ed; PA Cncl for Geographic Ed 1961-, Outstanding Teacher 1979; Johnstown Jaycees 1965-69; Westmont Fire Company (Fire & Police Chief) 1981-86; Certificate of Merit Run for Liberty Prgm 1986; *home:* 762 Sunset Ave Johnstown PA 15905

HILLEGAS, DONALD LEE, Social Studies Teacher; *b:* Lansdale, PA; *m:* Nancy Metz; *c:* Michael, Aimee; *ed:* (BS) Comp Soc Stud, 1972, (MA) Soc Stud/Ed, 1982 West Chester Univ; *cr:* 7th-9th Grade Soc Stud Teacher Methacton Sch Dist 1972-; *ai:* Adv Debate Club; Ping Pong Club; NEA; PA St Ed Assn; Methacton Ed Assn Building Rep 1984-; *office:* Arcola Intermediate Sch Eagleville Rd Norristown PA 19403

HILLEGASS, CYNTHIA REICHARD, Social Studies Teacher; *b:* Reading, PA; *m:* Richard D.; *c:* Kyle; *ed:* (BS) Soc Stud, Kutztown Univ 1972; Grad Stud; *cr:* Teacher Brandywine Heights HS 1974-; *ai:* Jr Class Adv; Consortium, Mentor Teacher HS In-Service Comm; Mem of Stu Asst Team Beacon; Brandywine Heights Ed Assn Pres 1984-85; US Cheerleading Assn Camp Dir 1980; Redeemer Luth Church (Church Cncl, Sunday Sch Teacher, Vacation Bible Sch Teacher) 1989-; E PA Cheerleading Invitational Judging Coord 1987; *home:* 2034 Custer St Allentown PA 18104

HILLER, MARLA STRICKLAND, Dance Teacher/Drill Team Dir; *b:* Austin, TX; *m:* Jay Darrell; *ed:* (BS) Ed, Univ of TX Austin 1985; Teaching Fields Phys Ed, Dance as Fine Art, Eng; *cr:* Substitute Dance Instr Tinkas Dance & Gymnastics 1980-85; Asst Choreographer & Captain Austin Aqua Festival Beauty Pageant 1982-85; Drill Team Dir A N Mc Callum HS 1984-85; Drill Team Dir/Dance Teacher L C Anderson HS 1985-; *ai:* Dance/Drill Team Dir; Faculty Courtesy Comm; Drill Team Dir of America 1985-; TX Dance/Drill Team Dir Assn 1989-; Assn of TX Prof Educators, Parent Teacher Stu Assn 1985-; Longhorn Phys Ed Assn 1983-85, Dr Lynn Mc Craw Awd of Excl 1984; *office:* L C Anderson HS 8403 Mesa Dr Austin TX 78759

HILLEY, MARY MARTHA SAWAYA, English Teacher; *b:* Ocala, FL; *m:* Daniel Nathan; *c:* Jennifer L., Karen E., Daniel J.; *ed:* (BA) Eng Lit, St Marys Coll 1964; (MAT) Eng, Rollins Coll 1983; *cr:* Teacher Winter Park HS 1964-71, Maynard Evans HS 1982-; *ai:* Sr Class Spon; Stu Assistance Prgm Cnslr; FL Teaching Profession, NEA 1964-71, 1982-; Orange Cty Classroom Teachers Assn 1983-; Orange Cty Cncl Teachers of Eng, FL Cncl Teachers of Eng 1964-71, 1982-; *office:* Maynard Evans HS 4949 Silver Star Rd Orlando FL 32808

HILLIARD, BARBARA THOMPSON, English/Journalism Teacher; *b:* Florence, MS; *m:* George Jr.; *c:* George III; *ed:* (BA) Eng, Tougaloo Coll 1962; (MA) Eng, Jackson St 1978; Univ of WI, MS St, Univ of TN, TN St; *cr:* Eng Teacher Brinkley Jr/Sr HS 1962-65; Eng/Fr Teacher Powel Jr HS 1965-69, Blackburn Jr HS 1969-85; Eng/Journalism Teacher Jim Hill HS 1985-; *ai:* Newspaper & 10th Grade Class Spon; JAE Dist Dir 1987-; MAE, NEA, MASCD; Alpha Kappa Alpha Grad Adv 1987-; TCNAA Pres Elect 1989-, Alumnus of Yr 1986; Links Journalist 1988-; STAR Teacher 1988-89, 1989-; City Wide Eng Dept Chairperson; St Liaison Leader NCTE Excl in Writing 1982-84; *home:* 2310 Queensroad Ave Jackson MS 39213

HILLIARD, BETTY CANTRELL, 1st Grade Teacher; *b:* Greenwood, MS; *m:* Willie D. Sr.; *c:* Alice E. Clemons, Cassandra Brown, Willie Jr., Fonda H. Dowl; *ed:* (AS) Secretarial Sci, Henderson Bus Coll 1951; (BS) Elem Ed, MS Valley St Univ 1965; (MA) Elem Ed, Univ of MS 1973; *cr:* Teacher Greenwood Bus Sch for Vets 1950-52; 1st Grade Teacher L S Rogers Elem Sch 1965-; *ai:* PET Presenter/Moderator for Scholastic Bowl; 1st Grade Chairperson; Youth Leader; PTA Sec; Mem Publicity Comm PTA Membership Comm;Mem Natl Cncl Negro Women; Church Clerk Announcer; NEA; MS Assn Ed; Leflore Cty Assn Ed Fin Teacher Yr 1989; Phi Delta Kappa; Delta Sigma Theta (Sec Chm Arts 1977- Letters Prgm Comm Mem) Cert Out Standing 1988; Les Douze Femme Elite (Pres/Sec/VP/Prgm Chm) Outstanding Mem 1980-89; Teacher of Yr Awd 1988-89/ 1977-78; *home:* PO Box 451 213 McKinley Itta Bena MS 38941

HILLIGOSS, ELIZABETH WELCH, 1st Grade Teacher; *b:* Shelbyville, IL; *m:* Darrell; *c:* Mitchell, Lindsey; *ed:* (BA) Elem Ed, E IL Univ 1976; *cr:* Kndgtn Teacher Shelbyville Cmmty Sch 1976-77; 2nd Grade Teacher 1977-83, 1st Grade Teacher 1986- Windsor Elem Sch; *ai:* Teacher Assistance Team Leader; IL Ed Assn, NEA; Jr Womens Club; *office:* Windsor Elem Sch 808 Wisconsin Windsor IL 61957

HILLMAN, JOHN M., Social Studies Teacher; *b:* Corning, NY; *m:* Linda M. Bevacqua; *c:* John Jr., Frank B.; *ed:* (AA) Liberal Art, Corning Comm Coll 1963; (BS) Scndry Ed/Soc Stud/Eng, SUNY Fredonia 1967; (MS) Scndry Ed, Elmira Coll 1971; *cr:* Teacher Ernie Davis Jr HS 1967-; *ai:* Davis Jr HS Boys Bsktbl Coach 1967-72; Elmira Free Acad Boys Bsktbl Coach 1973-80 & Boys Var Swimming Coach 1984-87; Jr HS Textbook Selection Comm; NY St Cncl for Soc Stud Mem; *office:* Ernie Davis Jr HS Lake St Elmira NY 14901

HILLMAN, SUE ANN (ELLIOTT), Math Teacher/GATE Teacher; *b:* Flint, MI; *m:* Scot Tyler; *c:* Jeff, Mallory; *ed:* (BA) Elem Ed/Soc Sci/Lang Arts, MI St Univ 1980; (MA) Ed/Math, Fresno Pacific 1989; *cr:* 7th & 8th Grade Teacher Cherry Avenue Jr HS 1980-85; 5th Teacher Cypress Elem 1985-87; 8th Grade Teacher Mulcahy Jr HS 1987-89; 8th Grade Teacher Live Oak Mid Sch 1989-90; *ai:* Cheerleading Adv; Staff Dev Comm; Phi Kappa Phi; AAUW Secy 1987-; *office:* Live Oak Mid Sch 980 N Laspina Tulare CA 93274

HILLS, KATHLEEN VINCENT, 4th Grade Teacher; *b:* Gary, IN; *m:* Edward; *c:* Cinda Hills Haney, Mike, Mark; *ed:* (BS) Rural Life & Ed/Elem Ed, Western MI Univ 1970; *cr:* 1st Grade Teacher 1967-82, 2nd Grade Teacher 1979-80 Bangor Elem; 4th Grade Teacher Bangor Mid Sch 1982-; *ai:* NEA; MI Ed Assn; Bangor Ed Assn (Secy, VBCEA Rep); MI Rdng Assn; Amer Scandinavian Stu Exch Prgm Host; *home:* 10121 60th St South Haven MI 49090

HILLYER, MARTHA FLYNN, Science Teacher/Dept Chair; *b:* Asheville, NC; *m:* Gerard C.; *c:* Kimberly D., Craig W.; *ed:* (BA) Bio/Chem/Phys Ed, Milligan Coll 1971; (MAED) Sci, W Carolina Univ 1983; Mentor Trng; Effective Schls Trng Advanced Placement Wkshps; *cr:* Phys Ed Teacher Ira B Jones Elem 1971-72; Life Sci Teacher Hill Street Mid Sch 1972-74; Bio Teacher Asheville HS 1975-; *ai:* Awds Comm Chairperson; Sci Dept Chairperson; Mentor Teacher; Sci Fair Coord; Senate Bill Rep; Cooperating Teacher with Univ of NC Asheville for Stu Teachers; Effective Schls Rep; NC Assn of Ed Pres 1971-; Delta Kappa Gamma 1985-; NSTA, NC Sci Teachers Assn 1977-; NABT NC Bio Teacher of Yr 1986; Red Cross Volunteer 1986; Bee Tree Chrstn (Sunday Sch Supt 1988-, Sunday Sch Teacher 1983-); Schlsp for Continuing Ed; Teacher of Yr 1988-89; Received Trip to Convention Seattle WA; *office:* Asheville HS 419 Mc Dowell St Asheville NC 28803

HILMES, CHARLES EDWARD, Jr High Teacher; *b:* Breese, IL; *m:* Dianne C. Usselmann; *c:* Jonathan, Phillip, Ashley; *ed:* (BA) Soc Stud, S IL Univ Carbondale 1972; Grad & Undergraduate Work; Natl Geographic Wkshp; *cr:* Cook Wil-Char Restaurant 1966-72; Teacher St Dominic Grade Sch 1972-78, Dist #12 1978-; *ai:* Bsktbl Coach; Park Comm Chm; His Club Adv; Little League Coach; IL Ed Assn 1978-; Breese Chamber of Commerce 1980-; Jaycees VP 1972-80, Jaycee of Yr 1975; Optimist Intnl Dir 1984-; City Cncl Aldermann 1987-; St Dominic & Augustine Curr Comm 1989; Breese Sommerfest Chm 1981-86; Whos Who Outstanding Young Men 1987, 1988; *office:* Dist 12 Schls Louis St Beckemeyer IL 62219

HILSABECK, MARCIA STEWMAN, English Teacher; *b:* Quanah, TX; *m:* Jimmy G.; *c:* Mary H. Wright, James, Guy, Michael; *ed:* (BA) Eng 1967, (MA) Eng, 1973 Univ of TX; Ed Supervision, Southwest TX St Univ; *cr:* Teacher Round Rock HS 1967-; Cntrl TX Coll 1974-75; Austin Commty Coll 1975-; *ai:* Coord Competitive Acad Act; Lit Criticism Coach; Sr Class Spon; NCTE; Publ Ctrl Tx Cncl of Teachers of Eng Newsletter; *office:* Round Rock H S 300 Lake Creek Dr Round Rock TX 78681

HILTON, FRANCIS KING, Science Dept Chair/Bio Teacher; *b:* Manning, SC; *w:* Charles (dec); *c:* Karen, Neilson, Kenya; *ed:* (BS) Bio, 1964, (MS) Ed/bio, 1979 SC St Coll; AP Bio, APT, PET, NSF, Cmptr Wkshps, Marine Stud; *cr:* Sci Teacher Lane Elem Sch 1964-66, St Mark HS 1966-67; Sci Teacher/Dept Chairperson C E Murray HS 1967-; *ai:* Sr Class Activity Coord; Honor Society, Sci Club Adv; Sch Improvement Cncl; Acad Team Judge Chairperson; SCJA Consultant; Sci Fair Coord; NSTA 1986-; SC Ed 1970-; NEA 1970-; Delta Sigma Theta Chaplin 1988-89; Natl Sci Fnd Grant; Co-Exec Secy SCANHS; Sea Sampler Publication Participant; Silver Tray, Hugo Volunteer; *home:* Rt 2 Box 257 Greeleyville SC 29056

HILZENDEGER, MAGGIE, Third Grade Teacher; *b:* Napoleon, ND; *m:* Valentine; *c:* Tina Tweeter, Rhonda Hartung, Doreen, Gregory, Kevin, Delaine, Thomas, Bruce; *ed:* (BA) Elem Ed, Univ Mary Bismarck 1979; *cr:* Teacher Rural Schls Logan Cty 1945-47; Cty Deputy Treas Logan Cty 1947-56; Teacher Rural Schls Logan Cty 1958-68; 3rd Grade Teacher Napoleon Public Sch 1970-; *ai:* NEA; NDEA (Secy, Treas); Legion Auxiliary (Secy, VP, Girl St Chm); Homemakers (Pres, Secy); Legion Auxiliary Membership Go Getters Awd; *home:* 122 E 4th St Napoleon ND 58561

HIMBERG, GLEN R., Science Teacher; *b:* Berkeley, CA; *ed:* (BA) Bio, San Francisco St Coll 1966; *cr:* Sci Teacher San Francisco Unified Sch Dist 1969-; *office:* Herbert Hoover Mid Sch 2290 14th Ave San Francisco CA 94116

HIME, SCOTT A., Social Studies Teacher; *b:* Greensburg, IN; *m:* Vicky Ann Martin; *c:* Courtney M.; *ed:* (BA) His, De Pauw Univ 1980; (MS) Ed, IN Univ 1986; *home:* 231 E Washington Greensburg IN 47240

HIMSTEDT, TILLIE, Mathematics Department Chair; *b:* Wichita Falls, TX; *ed:* (BA) Math/Chem, Hardin-Simmons Univ 1960; (MS) Math, Midwestern St Univ 1969; *cr:* Classroom Teacher Hirschi Jr HS 1962-64, Bear Creek Jr-Sr HS 1964, Barwise Jr HS 1965, S H Rider HS 1965-; *ai:* Math Team & Mu Alpha Theta Spon; NCTM, Math Assn of America, TX Cncl Teachers of Math; Delta Kappa Gamma; West Fnd Awds Meritorious Teaching; *office:* S H Rider HS 4611 Cypress Ave Wichita Falls TX 76310

HINCHBERGER, TERRY DALE, Sixth Grade Teacher; *b:* Butler, PA; *m:* Cynthia J. Miller; *c:* Bradley, Douglas; *ed:* (AA) Elem Ed, Butler Comm Coll 1973; (BS) Ed, Slippery Rock Univ 1975; Masters in Ed Slippery Rock Univ, Westminster Coll 1978; *cr:* 4th Grade Teacher 1975-79, 5th Grade Teacher Clearfield Elem 1979-80; 2nd Grade Teacher Emily Brittain Elem 1985-86; 6th Grade Teacher Clearfield Elem 1980-; *ai:* S Butler Little League Bsbl Coach; Numerous Curr Comm Butler Area Sch Dist; Butler Ed Assn, PA St Ed Assn, NEA; Service Youth Awd Butler YMCA 1980; Nom PA Teacher of Yr 1989; *office:* Clearfield Elem Sch 621 Clearfield Rd Fenelton PA 16034

HINCHEN, THOMAS M., 6th Grade Jr High Teacher; *b:* Springfield, MA; *m:* Libera Avitabile; *c:* Naomi; *ed:* (BA) Eng, St Josephs Univ 1973; (MS) Ed Rdng, Fordham Univ 1990; *cr:* 8th Grade Teacher St Veronica Sch 1973-79; Lay Missioner Maryknoll 1980-82; Jr HS Teacher St Catherine of Genoa Sch 1983-; *ai:* Math League Adv; NCEA 1983-; Cath Youth Organization Adult Adv 1974-79; *office:* St Catherine Of Genoa Sch 870 Albany Ave Brooklyn NY 11203

HINCHMAN, MYRON CRAIG, Chemistry Teacher; *b:* Erie, PA; *m:* Marjorie Sanger; *c:* Christopher; *ed:* (BS) Zoology, 1967, (MED) Sci, 1976 Penn St; NSF Grant on Environment, Gannon Univ 1975; *cr:* Sci Teacher Sheffield HS 1968-72; Sci/Chem Teacher Millcreek Sch Dist 1973-; *ai:* PJAS Spon; Sci Advisory Comm; MEA, PSEA, NEA Building Rep 1984-89; Children Services Foster Parent 1988-.

HINDEMAN, DONALD FRANK, Science Department Chairman; *b:* Brookville, PA; *m:* Margaret Runk; *c:* Daniel, Christopher; *ed:* (BS) Scndry Ed/Bio/Sci, Lock Haven Univ 1967; (MED) Scndry Ed, Shippensburg Univ 1971; *cr:* Sci Teacher Huntingdon Area Mid Sch 1967-; *ai:* PSEA, NEA, PSTA; *office:* Huntingdon Area Mid Sch 2500 Cassady Ave Huntingdon PA 16652

HINDMAN, NELLIE WAYLAND, Counselor; *b:* Newport, AR; *m:* Robert Donald; *c:* Robbie, Lisa Mongomery, Randall; *ed:* (BSE) Bus Ed, 1965, (MSE) Guidance/Counseling, 1968 AR St Univ; Univ of AR, Univ of Cntrl AR, Ar St Univ, Peabody Coll, Ouachita Univ; *cr:* Cnslr/Teacher Grubb Sch Dist 1966-69; Cnslr Pulaski Cty Spec Sch Dist 1969-; *ai:* Guidance Dept Head; Care Comm Spon; Sch Based Team; Sch Equity, Faculty Advisory, N Cntrl Accreditation Assn Steering Comm; Support Group Leader; Stu & Adult Trips to Europe Leader & Organizer; Parent Teacher Stu Assn 1975-; Pulaski Cty Counselors (Secy 1976-77, Treas 1980-81); NEA Life Mem 1967-; Pulaski Assn of Classroom Teachers Building Rep 1967-; Greater Little Rock Pres 1990, Alumnae Service 1987; Phi Mu Alumnae Chapter Treas 1987-89; Article Published; *office:* Sylvan Hills Jr HS 401 Forest Ridge Rd Sherwood AR 72120

HINDMAN, PAUL D., Mathematics Teacher; *b:* Casa Grande, AZ; *m:* Marsha; *c:* Misha, Preston; *ed:* (BA) Elem Ed, AZ St Univ 1976; *cr:* 8th Grade Math/Algebra Teacher Casa Grande Jr HS 1979-; *ai:* Chm Discipline & Mem Steering Comm; Natl Assn Math Teachers 1985-; Jaycees (Pres 1979-, Cty Rep 1990); AZ Assn for Learning About the Environment; *office:* Casa Grande Jr HS 300 W Mc Murray Blvd Casa Grande AZ 85222

HINDS, ANNE HUTCHINSON, 7th Grade Science Teacher; *b:* Cambridge City, IN; *m:* J. C. (dec); *c:* James R.; *ed:* (BA) Elem Ed, IN Univ 1960; (MA) Elem Ed, Ball St Univ 1965; Admin, Western KY Univ 1972; *cr:* Teacher Western Wayne Schls 1960-62, Muncie Cmmty Schls 1962-69, Jefferson Cty Schls 1969-; *ai:* Psi Iota Xi Philanthropic Speech & Hearing Pres 1960-89; Nom Teacher of Yr Muncie IN; *office:* Jefferson Cty Trad Mid Sch 1418 Morton Ave Louisville KY 40204

HINE, LINDA KAY (COOK), Social Studies Teacher; *b:* Westernport, MD; *m:* Charles H.; *c:* Valerie K. Frye, Kevin M., Darren M., April B.; *ed:* (BA) Elem Ed/Soc Stud/Eng, Shepherd Coll 1962; Working Towards Masters Supervision; *cr:* 3rd Grade Teacher Jefferson Cty Schls 1962-65, Winchester City Schls 1965-66; 3rd-6th Grade Teacher Jefferson Cty 1967-77; 6th Grade Teacher Frederick Cty 1979-81; 8th Grade Soc Stud Teacher Jefferson Cty 1982-; *ai:* Soc Stud Dept Head; Yrbk & Just Say No Club Adv; Soc Stud Fair Coord; Curr & Textbook Committees; Golden Horseshoe Test Coach; NEA, WVEA, JCEA; NCCS; Womans Club Cncl of Ministries Admin Bd Chm-Role & Status of Women 1988; Jefferson Cty Teacher of Yr Nom 1988; Outstanding Educator Nom 1988; *home:* 214 W Liberty St Charles Town WV 25425

HINEBAUGH, DEBRA KAY, Fifth Grade Teacher; *b:* Dola, WV; *ed:* (BS) Elem Ed, 1975, (MS) Ed, 1983 Frostburg St Univ; *cr:* 1st Grade Teacher Tunnelton Elem Sch 1976-79; Spec Ed Teacher 1979-80, 2nd/5th Grade Teacher 1980-82 Dennett Road Elem Sch; 5th Grade Teacher Broad Ford Elem Sch 1982-; *ai:* MSTA, NEA, GCTA Rep 1988-89; *office:* Broad Ford Elem Sch 905 Broad Ford Rd Oakland MD 21550

HINEGARDNER, BARBARA HARTMAN, Home Economics Teacher; *b:* Camden, NJ; *m:* Jack R.; *c:* Steve, Mike; *ed:* (BS) Home Ec, Bridgewater Coll 1960; *cr:* Home Ec Teacher Bel Air Jr HS 1960-64, Ridge Sch 1971-77, Westwood Jr HS 1977-83, Auburndale Sr HS 1983-; *ai:* FL Voc Assn 1985-; NEA 1977-; FL Home Ec Assn 1980-; *office:* Auburndale Sr HS 1 Bloodhound Trl Auburndale FL 33823

HINES, ANTHONY ALAN, Social Studies Dept Chairman; *b:* ASHEVILLE, NC; *m:* Loreece A. Harb; *c:* Melissa L.; *ed:* (BA) His, 1974; (MAED) Ed/His, 1976 Morehead ST Univ; *cr:* Teacher Dayton Public Sch 1976-82; Teacher/Cnslr Brevard Correctional Institute; Teacher Cocoa HS 1985-86; Teacher/Dept Chm Rockledge HS 1986-; *ai:* Boys' Golf Coach, Spon Future Educators of Amer; Spon Class of '90, Citizen Bee; Theta Chi Chaplain 1974, Pledge Marshall 1975; Outstanding Young Man of Amer 1981; Soc Stud Teacher of Yr Nominee 1986 & 1989; *home:* 959 Beechfern Lane Rockledge FL 32955

HINES, BEATRICE KAYE WILLIAMS, English Dept Chair; *b:* Princeton, WV; *c:* Daniel J.; *ed:* (BS) Psych/Eng, VA Polytechnic Inst & SU 1972; (MS) Psych/Spec Ed, Radford Univ 1975; *cr:* Spec Ed Teacher Peterstown Elem Sch 1972-80; Eng Teacher Peterstown HS 1980-; *home:* Star Rt 2 Box 56A Peterstown WV 24963

HINES, BETTY BURNHAM, Fifth Grade Teacher; *b:* Hanceville, AL; *m:* Robert Hugh Sr.; *c:* Robert Jr., Reid, Richard; *ed:* (BA) Early Chldhd/Elem Ed, 1976, (ME) Ed Leadership/Elem, 1989 Univ of W FL; *cr:* Teacher T R Jackson Elem 1976-78, Pace Elem & S S Dixon Elem 1978-; *ai:* Teacher Educl Cncl; 5th Grade Chairperson; St Rep Planning & Health Ed Comm; Sch & Cty Adv Bd; Phi Kappa Phi 1977-; Kappa Delta Pi 1989-; Delta Kappa Gamma 1990; Santa Rosa Prof Ed Dist Rep 1982-83; Teacher Ed Cncl Chairperson 1982-88; United Meth Bd Comm Parsons 1983; Univ of W FL Ec & Mrktg Awd; Teaching of Ec Excl 1985; Pace Elem & Santa Rosa Cty Teacher of Yr; *office:* S S Dixon Elem 401 Pace Rd Pace FL 32571

HINES, BONNIE L., Second Grade Teacher; *b:* Moorefield, WV; *m:* Richard C. Sr.; *c:* Richard Jr., Jonathan; *ed:* (BA) Elem Ed, Shepherd Coll 1965; (MA) Classroom Teacher, WV Univ 1970; WV Univ; Teachers Acad; *cr:* 2nd Grade Teacher Moorefield Graded Sch 1963-1969/1974-72; 1st-3rd Grade Teacher Rig Sch 1972-73; 2nd Grade Teacher Moorfield Elem 1973-; *ai:* VP Mc Coy Players; WVEA; WV Teachers Acad 1989-; Cultural Grant; *office:* Moorefield Elem Sch 400 N Main St Moorefield WV 26836

HINES, KATHLEEN CARSON, Math Dept Chair/Teacher; *b:* Culver City, CA; *m:* Rodney R.; *c:* John, David, Kenneth, Kevin; *ed:* (BA) Ed, Univ of Pacific 1963; Addl Studies/Psyc/Math & Instrct Technques/Strategies; *cr:* 1st/2nd/3rd/4th/6th Grade Teacher Stockton Unified Sch Dist 1963-83; Instrtnl Spec Taylor Elem Sch 1980-81; 7th/8th Grade Teacher 1983-; Math Dept Chr/7th-8th Grade Teacher 1985- Marshall Mid Sch; *ai:* Sch Adv Cncl; Sch Leadership Team; Math Dept Chr; STA/CTA/NEA 1963-; Assn for Sipvn & Curr Dev 1989-; Phi Kappa Phi Mem 1963-; *office:* Marshall Mid Sch 1141 Lever Blvd Stockton CA 95206

HINES, LARRY THEODORE, Mathematics Teacher/Dept Chair; *b:* Faith, SD; *m:* Diane Kaye Cassell; *c:* Kelli, Carmen; *ed:* (BA) Math, Black Hills St Univ 1964; (MS) Physics/Math, Univ of WY 1969; *cr:* Math Teacher Broadus HS 1964-67, Klamath Falls 1967-68; Math/Physics Teacher Sturgis HS 1969-; *ai:* Boys Jr HS Bsbl Coach 1969-84; Girls Var Bsbl Coach 1979-; NCTM, SD Ed Assn, Meade Ed Assn 1969-; SD Math Teacher of Yr 1984; Meade 46-1 Teacher of Yr 1976, 1985; SD Sch of Mines HS Math Teacher of Yr 1976; *home:* 3108 Greenwood Tr Sturgis SD 57785

HINES, PATRICIA PARKER, Third Grade Teacher; *b:* Utica, NY; *m:* Carl A.; *c:* Karen A., Kevin A., Mark A.; *ed:* (BA) Elem Ed, Cortland NY 1962; Assured Readiness for Learning & Math Problem Solving Seminars; *cr:* 2nd Grade Teacher Marathon Cntrl Sch 1962-63; 3rd Grade Teacher Appleby Elem 1980-; *ai:* Bible Baptist Church Cortland NY; *home:* RD 1 Box 396A Marathon NY 13803

HINKLE, BARBARA STONEKING, First Grade Teacher; *b:* Logansport, IN; *m:* Luther Edward; *c:* Lucas E.; *ed:* (BA) Elem Ed, 1971, (MS) Elem Ed, 1974 Ball St Univ; *cr:* 1st Grade Teacher Washington Elem 1971-; *ai:* Media Services; Sch Spirit Chm; Delta Kappa Gamma Pres 1984-86; Pi Lambda Theta; YWCA (Bd of Dir, Pres) 1980; Intnl Rdng Assn; *office:* Kokomo Center Township Sch 100 W Lincoln Rd Kokomo IN 46902

HINKLE, RUSSELL RAY, SR., Principal/Chapter I Teacher; *b:* Louisville, KY; *m:* Diana Ford; *c:* Russell Jr.; *ed:* (BA) Elem Ed, Univ of KY 1977; (MS) Rdng Instruction, 1982, (Rank I) Admin, 1984 Univ of KY Louisville; *cr:* Teacher Ekron Elem 1977-84; Teacher 1984-88, Prin/Chapter I Teacher 1988- Muldraugh Elem; *ai:* 5th/6th Grade Boys Bsktbl Coach 1983-88; Teacher Evaluation Comm 1986; KY Ed Assn, NEA 1977-88; KY Assn of Sch Admins 1988-; Muldraugh Lions Club 1st VP 1989-; Ekron PTO Pres 1984; Muldraugh PTO Pres 1985-87; *home:* 12017 Beechland Rd Louisville KY 40229

HINKLEY, GREGORY C., Elementary Teacher; *b:* Mount Kisco, NY; *m:* Rosalyn; *c:* Vanessa, Gabriel, Travis, Shanyn; *ed:* (BA) His/Poly Sci, 1971, (MA) Ed, SUNY Potsdam; Adjunct Prof of Ed Potsdam St 1974-76; *cr:* 4th-6th Grade Teacher Norwood-Norfolk Cntrl 1972-; *ai:* Nature Club Adv; Tri-Town Little League All Stars & Norfolk Hockey Team Coach; NNTA VP 1980-86; Audubon Society, Nature Conservancy Mem 1989-; Village of Norwood Dir of Summer Youth 1972-85; St Lawrence Cty Curr Writer Solid Waste Disposal Agency 1989; NY St 4th Grade Sci Curr Grant Writer.

HINMAN, BARBARA JEAN, Language Arts Dept Chairperson; *b:* Oakland, CA; *m:* Joseph C. Jr.; *c:* Lise, Leslie J. Stauber, Mark C.; *ed:* (BA) Eng/Speech, Univ of Pacific 1951; (MA) Hum, CA St Univ Dominquez Hills 1985; CA Lit Project 1986; *cr:* Speech Therapist Sacramento City Sch Dist 1956-57; Teacher/Eng Dept Head/Mentor Teacher Lyman Gilmore Sch 1973-; *ai:* CA Lit Project Acad Mem; CA Assn for Gifted 1983-; CA Teachers Assn 1973-; *office:* Lyman Gilmore Intermediate 10837 Rough & Ready Hwy Grass Valley CA 95945

HINMAN, DONALD REX, Social Studies Teacher; *b:* Michigan City, IN; *m:* Joni M. De Bell; *c:* Christopher, Corey; *ed:* (BA) Poly Sci, W MI Univ 1973; Working toward Masters in Guidance & Counseling, E MI Univ; *cr:* Teacher Camden-Frontier Sch 1973-; *ai:* Camden-Frontier Opposed to Pollution of Environment & Jr Class Adv; Stus at Risk, Big Brother-Big Sister, Stus Assisted by Team, CFEA Schlsp Comm Mem; MI Ed Assn, NEA; Buckskin Horse Assn of MI Pres 1985-86; Amer Buckskin Registry Assn Reserve Natl Champion Halter Horse 1981; Camden-Frontier Teacher of Yr 1980; FFA Honorary Mem 1983; *home:* 12483 Hogan Rd Clinton MI 49236

HINNANT, SHERIN COOK, Resource Teacher of Gifted; *b:* Trenton, NJ; *m:* Tony; *c:* Erin; *ed:* (BA) Eng, 1972, (MED) Eng, 1978 GA Coll; Gifted Endorsement 1979-80; *cr:* Classroom Teacher Warner Robins HS 1972-79; Resource Teacher of Gifted/Eng Teacher Warner Robins HS 1979-83, Northside HS & Warner Robins Jr HS 1983-85, Rumble Jr HS & Warner Robins Jr HS 1985-86, Rumble Jr HS 1986-; *ai:* Teacher Empowerment Comm; Poetry & Scenario Writing Contest Coach; GA Supporters of Gifted, NCTE, GA Assn of Supvrs & Curr Dirs, Phi Kappa Phi; Cntrl Baptist Church (Jr Womans Club, Church Music & Personnel Comm, Adult Choir Alto Section Leader) 1988-; STAR Teacher Warner Robins HS 1983, Northside HS 1987; Outstanding Young Women of America; *home:* 112 S Oaks Ln Warner Robins GA 31088

HINOJOSA, DORA, English Teacher/Dept Chair; *b:* Edinburg, TX; *m:* Frank R.; *c:* Cristina; *ed:* (BA) Eng, UT Pan Am 1970; Grad Stud NJ Magic Valley Writing Project; *cr:* 9th/10th Grade Teacher Edcouch Elsa HS 1970-73; 7th/8th Grade Eng Teacher Edinburg North Jr HS 1973-80; 8th/9th Grade Eng Teacher Edinburg Jr HS 1980-85; Eng Teacher Edinburg Frosh HS 1985-; *ai:* Eng Dept Chairperson Edinburg Jr HS 1980-85 & Edinburg Frosh Sch 1985-; Natl Jr Honor Society Club Adv; TX Classroom Teachers Assn; *home:* 3013 Goldcrest Mc Allen TX 78504

HINOJOSA, TOM, Science/Mathematics Teacher; *b:* Burbank, CA; *m:* Jill M. Francis; *c:* Emily F., Lionel L.; *ed:* (BA) Human Bio, Stanford Univ 1980; Working Toward Master in Bio, San Jose St Univ; *cr:* Sci Teacher/Coach St Francis HS 1980-83; Bio Instr/Researcher San Jose St Univ 1983-86; Sci/Math Teacher/Coach Mariposa Cty HS 1986-; *ai:* Pep Squad & Ski Club Adv; Extra Curricular Participation Comm Faculty Rep; NSTA 1981-; CA Sci Teacher ASSN, NEA, CA Teacher Assn 1989-; MCHS Boosters Club 1986-; Assn of Supervision & Curr Dev 1989-; MCHS Teacher of Yr 1988; *home:* 5935 Evergreen Ln Mariposa CA 95338

HINRICHS, LINDA CLAIRE, Coordinator; *b:* Springfield, IL; *ed:* (BSED) Elem Ed, IL St Univ 1969; (MS) Ed Admin, W IL Univ 1987; *cr:* Kndgtn Teacher 1969-80, 4th Grade Teacher CUSD 205 1980-84; 2nd Grade Teacher Leicester England 1984-85; 3rd Grade Teacher CUSD 205 1985-88; Coord Knox Cty Optional Ed 1988-; *ai:* Personal & Prof Growth Comm Mem CUSD 205; Mem IL Fulbright Interview Comm 1985-; Phi Delta Kappa VP Membership 1989, Gold Awd 1989; NEA 1969-; IL Alternative Ed Assn 1988-; PEO Corresponding Secy 1990; 1st United Presbyn Church Trustee 1989-; Fulbright Exchange Teacher for US Government Leicester England 1984-85; Grant From St Bd of Ed At Risk Youth Prgm for Knox Cty; *home:* 775 S West St Galesburg IL 61401

HINSHAW, KATHY KITTRELL, Third Grade Teacher; *b:* Laurel, MS; *m:* Donald E. Jr.; *c:* Hope, Corey; *ed:* (AA) Jones Cty Jr Coll 1969; (BS) Elem Ed, Univ of S MS 1971; *cr:* 3rd Grade Teacher Ellisville Elem Sch 1973-; *ai:* NEA, Jones Cty Ed Assn 1973-; Alpha Delta Kappa 1988-; Laurel Jones Cty Rdng Assn 1989-; *home:* 3029 Audubon Dr Laurel MS 39440

HINSON, NORMA ELAINE SMITH, 6th Grade Teacher; *b:* Elwood, NE; *m:* Jimmie L.; *c:* Elaine Joines, Beverly Brust, Jim, Jeff; *ed:* (BS) Elem Ed, MO Southern St Coll 1971; Grad Classes MO Univ, SW MO St Univ, Pittsburg St; *cr:* K-8th Grade Teacher Little Red Schoolhouse 1951-53; 6th Grade Teacher Columbian Elem 1971-; *ai:* Carthage Cmmty Teachers Assn Parliamentarian 1971-, Outstanding Mem 1989; MO St Teachers Assn 1971-; Alpha Delta Kappa (VP 1984-86, Chaplain 1990); *home:* Rt 4 Box 389 Carthage MO 64836

HINSON, PEGGY MILDRED, English Department Head; *b:* Thomaston, GA; *ed:* (BS) Ed, Auburn Univ 1954-58; (MED) Admin/Supervision, GA St Univ 1976; Several Univs; *cr:* 6th-8th Grade Eng Chairperson Faith Sch 1959-61; 6th-8th Grade Eng Chairperson/Faculty Chairperson/Intern Asst Prin Daniel Jr HS 1961-63; 6th-8th Grade Eng Chairperson 1967-75, 7th/8th Grade Eng Chairperson 1976- Rothschild Jr HS; *ai:* System Wide Steering Comm Chairperson Fort Benning GA 1960; Lang Art Textbook Selection Chairperson 1961; Rothschild Yrbk Adv 1969; Columbus Coll Curr Steering Comm 1982; Christmas Activity Class Project Dir 1986; Gifted Stus Advisory Comm 1980; Data Collector 1980; Eng Ed Comm 1982; Lady Faculty Bsktbl Team Coach 1986; Alpha Delta Kappa (VP, Prgm Chairperson, Sergeant-At-Arms) 1974-; Phi Delta Kappa 1983-; NCTE, GA Cncl of Eng Teachers, Page 1987; STAR Teacher 1975;

Commendation from US Pres 1976, US Congress 1977; Nom GA St Classroom Teacher of yr 1984; Muscogee Cty Hospital Authority Recognition 1985; GCTE Teacher of Yr 1988; Commendation Muscogee Cty Sch Dist Sch Bd 1988; Proclamation Columbus Consolidated Government 1988; Commendation US Senator Wyche Fowler 1989; *office:* Rothschild Jr HS 1136 Hunt Ave Columbus GA 31907

HINTON, EVELYN S., Coordinating/Resource Teacher; *b:* Evergreen, AL; *m:* Douglas Daniel; *c:* Jonathan D., Sharon S.; *ed:* (MA) Spec Ed/Visually Impaired; (MA) Elem Ed; *cr:* Teacher AL Sch for the Blind, Talladega Cty Sch Bd; Coordinating/ Resource Teacher Jonesview Sch; *ai:* 4-H Club Adv; PTA Mem; Textbook Comms; Lincoln Lib Bd Mem 1982-; Lincoln Garden Club Pres 1990; Civic Action Comm Mem 1970-73; Teacher of Yr 1986, 1988; *home:* 344 4th Ave Lincoln AL 35096

HINTON, INA HENDERSON, Fifth Grade Teacher; *b:* Jackson, MS; *m:* Cecil O.; *c:* Cecil D.; *ed:* (BS) Elem Ed, 1974, (MED) Elem Ed, 1983 William Carey Coll; *cr:* 1st Grade Teacher 1975-76, 3rd Grade Teacher 1976-78, 5th Grade Teacher 1978- Beaumont Elem Sch; *ai:* Local Sch & Dist Spelling Bee Coord; Staff Dev Chairperson; Dist Task Force Comm Mem; MS Assn of Educators 1976-82; *home:* 45 Vardaman Hinton Rd New Augusta MS 39462

HINTON, JANICE M., First Grade Teacher; *b:* Seattle, WA; *m:* Thomas D.; *c:* Robert, Robin; *ed:* (BA) Elem Ed, Metropolitan St Coll 1975; (MA) Elem Ed Univ of Northern CO 1979; Grad Work CO St Univ, CO Christian Univ, Univ of LaVerne, Regis Coll, Adams St Coll & Rockmont Coll; *cr:* 1st Grade Teacher Foster Elem Sch 1975-; *ai:* PTO Publicity Chairperson; Budget, Liason & Sch Improvement Process Comm; Phi Delta Kappa 1979-; Jefferson Cty Ed Assn 1975-; Order of Elks 1988-; Grad Summa Cum Laude Metropolitan St Coll; Curr Writing Team Field Testing Primary Integrated Curr; Revision Team Rdng Comprehension Testing Prgm; Develop Spelling Component of Lang Arts Guide; *office:* Foster Elem Sch 5300 Saulsbury Ct Arvada CO 80002

HINTON, LINDA COURTNAY, First Grade Teacher; *b:* Guthrie, OK; *m:* Dean P.; *c:* Matthew, Adam; *ed:* (BS) Elem Ed, OK St Univ 1978; (MED) Guidance/Counseling, Cntrl St Univ 1982; Grad Stud, Math; *cr:* Teacher Soldier Creek Elem 1978-; *ai:* Dist Rdng Curr Comm 1988-; Site-Soc Comm; Yr of Young Reader Comm 1989-; Former Asst Girls Bsktbl, Vlybl, Track Coach 1982-83; Talent Show Coord 1983-; OK Ed Assn, Mid-Del Assn of Classroom Teachers 1978-; Friends of the Lib 1988-; Site-Selected Teacher of Yr 1988-; *office:* Soldier Creek Elem Sch 9021 SE 15th St Midwest City OK 73130

HINTZ, MARLENE JOAN, Fourth Grade Teacher; *b:* Hurley, SD; *m:* Darold E.; *c:* Monty E., Robert J.; *ed:* (BA) Elem Ed, Yankton Coll 1970; Grad Courses in Elem Ed; *cr:* Teacher Country Schls Turner Co 1952-69, Parker Schls 1969-; *ai:* Elem Declam Chm; Americaism & Flag Chm; PEP; Amer Legion Auxiliary Pres 1985-88; Legionette of Yr 1983; Harmony Pres Church Trustee; Star Masons Electa; *home:* Rr 1 Box 100 Hurley SD 57036

HINZ, PAUL L., History/Lang Arts Teacher; *b:* Williston, ND; *m:* Carrie; *c:* Michael, Michele Reibsamen; *ed:* (BS) Ed, Univ of NV Reno 1965; Univ of CO Boulder, St Teachers Coll Minot ND, UCLA, Coll of Ed Monmouth OR; *cr:* Teacher Flaxton ND 1957-58, Bainville MT 1958-59; US Army 1959-60; Teacher Churchill Cty Fallon NV 1961-; *ai:* PR Comm; Churchill Cty Ed Assn Pres 1970-74; NV St Ed Distinguished Service Awd; Churchill Cty Ed Comm Service Awd, Teacher of Yr Awd 1987; Fallon Swim Team (Bd of Dirs, Pres) 1977; Fallon Booster Club (Bd of Dirs, Pres) 1979; *office:* Churchill Cty Jr HS 650 S Maine Fallon NV 89406

HIPP, KENNETH T., 4th Grade Teacher; *b:* New Milford, CT; *m:* Josephine Testani; *c:* Lawrence, Wendy; *ed:* (AS) Accounting/ Bus Admin, Post Jr Coll 1967; (BS) Accounting/Bus Admin, Quinnipiac Coll 1969; (MS) Elem Ed, W CT St Univ 1971; Elem Math & Sci/Process Writing, CT Inst for Teacher Learning; Cooperating & Mentor Teacher Prgm; *cr:* 4th Grade Teacher 1969-, 5th Grade Teacher 1972 Shelter Rock Sch; *ai:* Union Carbide Teacher of Yr Shelter Rock Sch 1988; News Times Carrier Hall of Fame Charter Mem; *office:* Shelter Rock Sch Shelter Rock Rd Danbury CT 06810

HIPP, MARYNETTE MYERS, Second Grade Teacher; *b:* Swanton, OH; *m:* James D.; *c:* David C., Susan K.; *ed:* (BSED) Elem Ed, Miami Univ OH 1955; (MED) Elem Ed/Rdng, 1966, Ed Specialist Elem Ed/Curr, 1976 Univ of Toledo; *cr:* 1st Grade Teacher Lincoln Sch 1955-57; 2nd Grade Teacher Horace Mann Sch 1957-61; Rdng Coord Washington Local Schls 1967; Elem Teacher Glendale Sch; *ai:* Glendale-Feilbach Sch Audio-Visual Coord; Delta Kappa Gamma Pres 1978-80; *home:* 2044 Heatherwood Dr Toledo OH 43614

HIPP, SARAH OLMERT, 3rd Grade Teacher; *b:* Bishopville, SC; *m:* Eddie R.; *c:* Bradley, Eve, Catherine; *ed:* (BS) Spec Ed/ EMH/Elem Ed, Presbyn Coll 1973; (MS) Early Chldhd, Univ of SC 1978; *cr:* Teacher Mossy Oaks Elem 1973-; *ai:* Grade Level Chm; Sci Resource Person; Sch Improvement Cncl; SC Sci Curr, ASCD; 1st Presbyn Church Deacon 1990; Mossy Oaks Elem Teacher of Yr 1990; *office:* Mossy Oaks Elem Sch Mossy Oaks Rd Beaufort SC 29902

HIRAI, EDEAN LEIGH, Third Grade Teacher; *b:* Honolulu, HI; *m:* Wallace T.; *c:* Matthew; *ed:* (BED) Elem Ed, 1971, (MED) Elem Ed, 1977 Univ of HI; *cr:* 6th Grade Teacher 1971-87, Teacher of Gifted & Talented Math/Lang Art Enrichment Teacher 1987-88 Waialua Elem; 2nd/3rd Grade Teacher 1988-89, 3rd Grade Teacher 1989- Salt Lake Elem; *office:* Salt Lake Elem Sch 1131 Ala Lilikoi St Honolulu HI 96818

HIRDLER, KENNETH EDWARD, Social Studies Dept Chair; *b:* Chicago, IL; *m:* Linda Pickett; *c:* Elizabeth, Katherine, William; *ed:* (BA) His, Univ of IL 1968; (MED) Curr, DePaul Univ 1981; Ag Ed Endorsement Univ of IL; *cr:* Teacher Tuley HS 1969-71, Harlan HS 1971-74; Teacher/Dept Chm Corliss HS 1974-86, Chicago HS for Ag Sci 1986-; *ai:* Yrbk, Heritage Club, Intramural Sftbl Spon; North Cntrl Evaluation Team & Planning Comm; Grad & Attendance Coord; Prof Problems Comm Chm; Chicago Teachers Union Delegate 1988-; IL Assn of Voc Ag Teachers 1986-; Chicago Cncl for Soc Stud 1968-; Natl Arbor Society 1988-; Kate Maremont Awd Nom; Chicago Metro His Fair Certificate; North Cntrl Assn Certificate; *office:* Chicago HS for Ag Sci 3807 W 111th St Chicago IL 60655

HIRSCH, JANET, Business Teacher; *b:* Ft Wayne, IN; *ed:* (MS) Ed, IN Univ 1983; (BA) Bus Ed, Anderson Univ 1979; (AS) Secretarial Cincinnati Bible Coll 1976; Midwest Travel Acad; *cr:* Bus Teacher Oregon-Davis HS 1979-81, Union City Cmmty HS 1981-; *ai:* Bus Prof of America Adv.

HIRSCHFELD, MARGARET ABT, 5th-8th Grade Lang Art Teacher; *b:* Cleveland, OH; *m:* Seth; *c:* Sara, Adam; *ed:* (BA) Eng, Univ of MI 1971; (MA) Rdng, NY Univ 1972; Additional Stud John Carroll Univ; *cr:* Rdng Teacher Euclid HS 1973-74, Mayfield HS 1979-83; Lang Art Teacher Agnon Sch 1983-; *ai:* Faculty Rep Planning & Ed Comm; *office:* The Agnon Sch 26500 Shaker Blvd Beachwood OH 44122

HIRSCHI, CLARK HUGH, Fifth Grade Teacher; *b:* Hurrican, UT; *m:* Ann Marie Dover; *c:* Teri A. Rigby, Mark C., Susan M. Snell, David, Linda Russell; *ed:* (BS) Scndry Ed, 1956, (MS) Ed, 1969 UT St Univ; *cr:* 4th Grade Teacher Blanding Elem 1958-62; 5th/6th Grade Teacher Sunset Elem 1963-80, Holt Elem 1981-; *ai:* Davis Ed Assn Exec Bd 1978-79; UT Ed Assn, NEA Mem 1958-.

HIRSCHY, RUSSEL PHILIP, Mathematics/Computer Teacher; *b:* St Louis, MO; *m:* Harriet Dowdy; *c:* Gretchen, Marthe; *ed:* (BSED) Math/Chem/Physics, Ball St Teachers 1964; (MA) Math, Ball St Univ 1966; Seminar Calculator, Cmptrs Math Problem Solving; *cr:* Math Instr N MI Univ 1966-67; Teacher Lyons Township HS 1967-71, Markesan HS 1971-; *ai:* Curr & Lead Comm; Math Dept Revolving Chm; Timer Ftbl, Bsktbl, Track, Cross Cntry; Cmptrs Co-Coord; NCTM, WI Math Cncl, Kappa Delta Pi, Phi Delta Kappa, NEA; United Meth Church Treas; Ripon Harmony Kings SPEBQSA 1980-88; SEC Math Evaluation Team; *office:* Markesan HS 100 Vista Blvd Markesan WI 53946

HIRSH, KATHY, Music Dept Chairperson; *b:* Syracuse, NY; *ed:* (BM) Music Ed, Crane Sch of Music 1975; (MS) Ed, Elmira Coll 1980; *cr:* Instrumental Music VVS HS 1975-83; Instrumental Music VVS Mid Sch 1984-; Music Dept Chm VVS Cntrl Sch 1988-; *ai:* Marching Band; Regional Prgm for Excl; Sch Improvement Prgm; NY St Sch of Music Assn 1975-; Music Educators Assn 1975-; NY St Band Dir Assn 1989-; Brass Adjudicator for NY St Sch of Music Assn; *office:* Vernon-Verona Sherrill Cntrl Rt 31 Verona NY 13478

HIRST, HELEN CARTER, 4th Grade Teacher; *b:* Omak, WA; *m:* Darryl D.; *c:* Christine K. Hirst Goins, Ann A. Hirst Goode; *ed:* (BA) Eng, E WA Univ 1980; Post Grad Credits in Ed; *cr:* 1st-7th Grade Teacher Index Elem Sch 1981-87; 1st Grade Teacher 1987-88, 4th-5th Grade Teacher 1988-89, 4th Grade Teacher 1989- Sultan Elem Sch; *office:* Sultan Elem Sch 501 Date St Sultan WA 98294

HIRST, RICHARD LEE, Vocal Music Director; *b:* St Louis, MO; *ed:* (BME) Vocal Music, SE MO St Univ 1975; (ME) Scndry Admin, Univ of MO St Louis 1986; Grad Stud NE MO St Univ; *cr:* Vocal Music Dir Ritenour HS 1977-; *ai:* Spring Musical, Concert Choir, Girls Chorus, Glee Club Dir; Soccer Coach; Cheerleading Spon; AFT 1979-; MMEA 1977-.

HISER, MARK CHARLES, English/Humanities Teacher; *b:* Columbus, OH; *ed:* (BS) Ed/Eng, 1978, (MA) Ed/Curr, 1982 OH St Univ; *cr:* Teacher Westerville South HS 1978-83, Columbus Tech Inst 1983-84, Westerville South HS 1984-; *ai:* Career Ed; ASCD; *home:* 1701 Schrock Rd Columbus OH 43229

HISLE, CLAUDIA PARKER, Science/Computer Teacher; *b:* Sherman, TX; *m:* Roland E. III; *c:* Wade, Amy; *ed:* (BA) Eng/Bio, E TX St Univ 1970; (MED) Eng, E Cntrl Univ 1976; *cr:* Eng/ Speech Teacher Denison Public Schls 1970-73; Sci/Cmptr Teacher Ada Public Schls 1973-; Adjunct Professor E Cntrl St Univ 1989-; *ai:* Honor Society, 8th Grade Class, Academic Bowl Spon; Scholastic Meet Coord; NEA, OEA, AEA 1973-; Kappa Kappa Iota Pres 1985-; Phi Delta Kappa 1990; OK Teacher of Yr Semifinalist 1987; Ada Sch Teacher of Yr 1987; Ada Teacher of Excl Awd 1984-87; *office:* Ada Mid Sch 223 W 18th Ada OK 74820

HITCHCOCK, PATRICIA RUTH, First Grade Teacher; *b:* Flint, MI; *ed:* (BSED) Child Dev, Cntrl MI Univ 1972; Wkshps, Seminars in Cmptr Sci, Health, Creative Writing, Gifted & Talented; *cr:* 1st Grade Teacher Montrose Cmmty Schls 1972-; *ai:* Young Authors Conference; Comm for Volunteers Tea; Mem of Emergency Team; MEA Building Rep 1976-77; United Meth Women Chrstn Personhood 1988-; Jobs Daughters Honored Queen 1968-; United Way Summer Recreation Prgm (Arts & Crafts Leader, Asst Sftbl Coach); Nom for Teacher of Yr 1986; *office:* Montrose Cmmty Schls 301 Nanita Dr Montrose MI 48457

HITCHINGS, LINDA (FLEBOTTE), 6th Grade Teacher; *b:* Springfield, MA; *m:* Matthew; *c:* Patrick; *ed:* (BA) Bio/Chem, 1979, (BA) Elem Ed, 1981, (MS) Elem Ed, 1982 IN Univ Bloomington; Gifted & Talented; *cr:* 6th Grade Teacher Owen Valley Mid Sch 1981-87, 1989-; 8th-9th Grade Teacher Private Teacher Gifted Prgm 1987-89; *ai:* Soc Stud Coord; Grade 6 OVMS; Soc Stud Adoption Spon; MGAP Comm Mem; NEA, ISTA; Fellowship to Visit Japan; *office:* Owen Valley Mid Sch State Hwy 46 W Spencer IN 47460

HITOMI, JENNIFER M., Kindergarten Teacher; *b:* Sacramento, CA; *ed:* (BA) Elem Ed, Sacramento St Coll 1959; *cr:* Teacher Winterstein Sch & Cottage Sch; *ai:* Cottage Sch PTA Teacher Liason; Winterstein Sch PTA; Buddhist Church Coord; Honorary Service Achievement Awd; *home:* 1161 Brownwyk Dr Sacramento CA 95822

HITT, DEBORRAH WOOD, English Teacher; *b:* Dallas, TX; *m:* Gil H.; *c:* Christianne, Erin; *ed:* (BA) Eng, Univ of Houston 1972; Grad Stud Univ TX Tyler; *cr:* Rdng Teacher Thomas Jr HS 1972-75; Eng Teacher Stewart Jr HS 1975-86, R E Lee HS 1986-; *ai:* 10th Grade Eng Lead Teacher; Sr Class Spon; Assn of TX Prof Educators Pres 1984-85; Delta Kappa Gamma; Nom Outstanding Scndry Educator to Univ TX; *office:* Robert E Lee HS 411 E Loop 323 Tyler TX 75703

HITT, MARTY THOMAS, Fifth Grade Teacher; *b:* Columbia, MS; *m:* Nancy Sumrall; *ed:* (BA) Elem Ed, Univ Southern MS 1975; *cr:* Classroom Teacher Bassfield Elem 1975-; *ai:* JDCAFT Pres 1989-; MAFT 1988-; MS Track Club 1988-; Gulf Coast Running Club 1989-; Road Runner Club Amer 1988-; *office:* Bassfield Elem Sch P O Box 8 Bassfield MS 39421

HITTLE, SUSAN HAESLY, Homemaking Teacher; *b:* San Angelo, TX; *m:* George M.; *c:* Jason K.; *ed:* (BS) Home Ec, TCU 1964; *cr:* Home Economist Lone Star Gas Co 1965-72; Homemaking Teacher N Oaks Jr HS 1973-89, Richland HS 1989-; *ai:* FAA & Jr Class Spon; Textbook Comm; Assn Teacher Prof Organization 1983-; *office:* Richland HS 5201 Holiday Ln E Fort Worth TX 76180

HITZ, BARBARA J., 3rd/4th Grade Algebra Teacher; *b:* Anderson, IN; *ed:* (BA) Fr/Math, 1975, (MS) Ed/Scndry Fr & Math, 1982 Butler Univ; *cr:* 7th/8th Grade Math Teacher Immaculate Heart of Mary 1975-81; 9th/12th Grade Math/Fr Teacher Anderson Highland HS 1981-; *ai:* Frosh & Jr Class Spon, Honor Society Faculty Advisory Bd; Stu Cncl Adv; Convo Comm; Kappa Kappa Kappa Service Organization 1982-87; Kappa Alpha Theta Alumni Club 1982-; First Presbyn Church 1968-; *office:* Highland HS 2108 E 200 N Anderson IN 46012

HITZFELDER, ELAINE WILLMANN, Advanced Placement Eng Teacher; *b:* San Antonio, TX; *m:* Gary M.; *c:* Kelley M., Glenn M., Jill K.; *ed:* (BA) Eng, SW TX St 1973; (MA) Higher Ed, Univ of TX San Antonio 1978; Supervision & Instruction, Cooperative Learning; *cr:* Eng Teacher Breckenridge & Wheatley HS 1974-80, Mac Arthur HS 1981-; *ai:* Pep Squad & Flag Team Guard Spon; Ready Writing Coach; Discipline Management Team; Thinking, Learning, Communicating Through Writing Team; NCTE, TX Joint Cncl Teachers of Eng 1980-; TX St Teachers Assn Rep 1989-; Hollywood Park Swim Team Treas 1989; TX Joint Cncl Teachers Eng Journal Work Published 1989; Coll Bd Grant 1984; NE Teacher Assn Schlsp; *office:* Douglas Mac Arthur HS 2923 Bitters Rd San Antonio TX 78217

HIX, SANDRA ELAINE, Third Grade Teacher; *b:* Fort Hood, TX; *m:* Gayle; *c:* Tracie, Mike, Randy; *ed:* (BS) Elem Ed, 1974, (MS) Rdng, 1976 Northeastern St; Grad Stud Counseling; *cr:* Grad Asst Northeastern St 1974-75; 1st Grade Teacher Salina OK 1975-77; 3rd Grade Teacher Leach OK 1977-; *ai:* Staff Dev Comm Mem; Delaware Cty OEA (Schlsp Comm, Secy) 1988-89; Rdng Activity Article Published St Dept Pamphlet; Teacher of Yr 1989; *home:* Box 128 Rose OK 74364

HIXON, BETTY DICKINSON, History Teacher; *b:* Brundidge, AL; *m:* William Owen; *c:* Kimberly Wise, Elizabeth Collier, William; *ed:* (BS) Elem Ed, Troy St Univ 1957; *cr:* Teacher Highland Avenue 1957, Inverness 1957-61, Pike Cty 1965-70, Pike Liberal Arts 1970-; *ai:* Sr Class & Nike Spon; Asst Headmaster; Kappa Delta Pi 1956-57; Alpha Delta Kappa Treas 1990; Brundidge Study Club Pres 1971, 1983; AL Cattlewomens Assn 1971-72; Banks United Meth Women Secy 1988-; Daughters of Amer Revolution His Teacher Awd 1989; *home:* Rt 2 Box 38 Banks AL 36005

HIXON, WILLIAM ROY, 4th Grade Teacher; *b:* Natick, MA; *m:* Grace Sebastiao; *c:* Jeffrey, Adrienne; *ed:* (BA) Elem Ed, Yankton Coll 1971; Spec Ed, Univ of SD Vermillion; Coll Courses Quinsigamond Comm Coll; *cr:* 6th Grade Teacher Sacred Heart Sch 1971-75; 4th Grade Teacher Denmark Elem Sch 1975-76, Whitefield Elem Sch 1976-80; 3rd/4th Grade Teacher Bethlehem Elem Sch 1980-; *ai:* Chm Math Curr Comm & BES Sunshine Fund; NEA Pres 1985-86; Outstanding Young Men of America 1975; *office:* Bethlehem Elem Sch Main St Bethlehem NH 03574

HJERMSTAD, ROSLYN (FLATEN), Sixth Grade Teacher; *b:* Faribault, MN; *m:* Robert A.; *c:* Marina L., Raelyn Priem, Rosalee Priem; *ed:* (BS) Elem Ed, Mankato St Univ 1969; (MA) Curr/Instruction, St Thomas Coll 1988; *cr:* 6th Grade Teacher Cannon Falls Sch Dist 252 1970-; *ai:* Sci/Health Dept Chairperson; MN Ed Assn 1970; MN Historical Society 1988-; Vasa Luth Church Sunday Sch Teacher 1985-; Writing for Publication; *office:* Cannon Falls Area Elem Sch 1020 E Minnesota St Cannon Falls MN 55009

HLAVACEK, PAULA J., Mathematics/Science Teacher; *b:* Chicago, IL; *m:* Dennis; *ed:* (BSED) Elem Ed, 1973, (MSED) Elem Ed, 1981 N IL Univ; Ed Admin, Vanderbilt Univ; *cr:* Teacher St Raphael Sch 1974-76, Agnes Hefty Jr HS 1976-; *ai:* Math/Sci Curr Comm; Effective Sch & Advisory Comm; Kappa Delta Pi 1980-; ASCD, IL Cncl Teachers of Math, NCTM; Assn for Women in Math 1990; Whos Who in Amer Ed 1989-; Teacher Ed Schlsp 1969-73; *office:* Agnes Hefty Jr HS 2220 Haddow Downers Grove IL 60515

HNATH, KATHLEEN MARIE, English/Journalism Teacher; *b:* Ashland, WI; *ed:* (BA) Eng/Physics, Northland Coll 1969; Physics Natl Sci Fnd Summer Inst; Comparative Ed, Soviet-Amer Seminar; Univ of WI Superior, Madison, Stevens Point; *cr:* Eng/Phys Sci Teacher Northland Pines HS 1969-76; Eng/Journalism Teacher Hayward Sr HS 1976-; *ai:* NHS Faculty Comm Rep; Hayward Cmmty Schls Outstanding Educator Excl Ed Awd 1988, 1990; *office:* Hayard Sr HS Greenwood Ln Hayward WI 54843

HO, ROBERT K. F., Physical Education Teacher; *b:* Honolulu, HI; *m:* Evelyn Frances Ching; *c:* Byron J. M., Candise S. Y.; *ed:* (AA) Art/Sci, Modesto Jr Coll 1955; (BS) Sociology, Brigham Young Univ 1957; *cr:* Military Enlistment US Army Reserve 1958; Banker Amer Security Bank 1959-68; Teacher Liliuokalani Elem 1970, Manana Elem 1970-75, Nuuanu Elem 1975-76, Kauluwela Elem 1976-; *ai:* Kauluwela Elem Schls Math Praise Math Team Coach 1988, 1989, Jump for Heart Coord 1990, Mem of Audio Visual & Phys Ed Comm; Kaimuki Bus & Prof Assn 1959-66; Kalihi Bus & Prof Assn 1967-68; HI St Teachers Assn 1972-; HI Fed of Teachers 1972-; Stevenson Intermediate Band Boosters Club Treas 1965-67; Leadership Trng Inst Cert 1962; *home:* 2929 Ala Ilima St Apt 904 Honolulu HI 96818

HOAG, RONALD GEORGE, Science Teacher; *b:* Perrysburg, OH; *m:* Vicki S. Erbskorn; *c:* Jennifer L., Patrick M., John R.; *ed:* (BA) Bio, Adrian Coll 1970; (MS) Scndry Ed, Univ of Toledo 1978; *cr:* Phys Sci Teacher Calvin M Woodward HS 1970-; *ai:* Toledo Fed of Teachers, Amer Fed of Teachers 1970-; Maumee Little League (Manager 1986-) City Champs 1986, 1989; *office:* Calvin M Woodward 600 E Streicher St Toledo OH 43608

HOBART, MICHAEL JAMES, Instrumental Music Teacher; *b:* Watertown, NY; *m:* Eleanor B.; *c:* Cynthia A., Michele D.; *ed:* (BS) Music Ed, 1965, (MS) Music Ed, 1971 St Univ Fredonia; *cr:* Instrumental Music Teacher Cleveland Hill Schls 1965-67, Williamsville Cntrl Schls 1967-71, Hamburg Cntrl Schls 1971-; *ai:* AF of M, MENC, ASTA, ECMEA, NYSTA, HTA, NSOA; Orchard Park Symphony Personnel Mgr 1976-; Clarence Summer Orchestra Contractor 1985-; Prof Violinist; Church Choir; *home:* 68 Euclid Ave Hamburg NY 14075

HOBBS, DEBRA CATHEY, Program Liaison; *b:* Philadelphia, PA; *ed:* (BA) Eng, 1988, Instructional I Scndry Ed/Fr/Eng, 1988, Certificate Fr, 1988 St Josephs Univ; *cr:* 9th Grade Eng/10th Grade Fr Teacher Bodine HS for Intnl Affairs 1988-; Prgm Liaison World Affairs Cncl 1990; *ai:* Grace Baptist Church of Germantown Chrstn Cmmty Center Bd Mem; *office:* Bodine HS for Intl Affairs 4th & George Sts Philadelphia PA 19123

HOBBS, EDITH MC CREAVY, 2nd Grade Teacher; *b:* Durant, OK; *m:* Thomas Dale; *c:* Douglas, Gregory; *ed:* (BS) Elem Ed, Coll of the SW 1969; (MA) Elem Ed, ENMU 1971; *cr:* Clerical C D Smith Wholesale Drugist 1950-52; Office Manager Lea Cty Credit Bureau 1953-56; Teacher Coronado Elem 1969-72, Broadmoor Elem 1972-; *ai:* Rdng Test & Delta Kappa Gamma COmmunications Comms; Classroom Teachers Assn; NM Ed Assn Building Rep 1974-76; *home:* 233 N Brazos Dr Hobbs NM 88240

HOBBS, KIMBERLY KEEN, Elementary School Librarian; *b:* Richlands, VA; *m:* John R.; *c:* Katelyn, Logan; *ed:* (BA) Elem Ed, Emory & Henry Coll 1979; (MED) Elem Ed, Univ of VA 1986; *cr:* 5th Grade Teacher 1979-89, Librarian 1989- Whitewood Elem Sch; *ai:* NEA, VA Ed Assn, Buchanan Ed Assn; *office:* Whitewood Elem Sch Gen Del Whitewood VA 24657

HOBBS, LUCILLE BLAKE, 6th Grade Teacher; *b:* Memphis, TN; *m:* Artice Lee; *c:* Mechelle, Renelle, Arlene, Artice II; *ed:* (BS) Ed, Amer Intnl Coll 1970; (MA) Ed, Wright ST Univ 1982; *cr:* Teacher Tapley Sch 1970-73, Olivehill Sch 1973-; *ai:* Head Teacher Intermediate Dept Unit Leader; Grant for Nutritional Ed Prgm in Sch Dist; Grant USC Diabetes Awareness-Jennings Lectures Scholar; *office:* Olivehill Elem Sch 1250 Olive Rd Dayton OH 45426

HOBBS, NINA MARION, Math Teacher; *b:* Carlsbad, NM; *c:* Brenda Powell, James K.; *ed:* (BS) Scndry Ed/Math, Coll of Southwest 1979; (MED) Scndry Ed, E NM Univ 1985; *cr:* Math Teacher Highland Jr HS 1979-; *ai:* Math Club Spon; NM Classroom Teachers Assn; Alpha Delta Kappa VP 1988-; *office:* Highland Jr HS 2500 N Jefferson Hobbs NM 88240

HOBBS, REBEKAH, 5th Grade Teacher; *b:* Alliance, OH; *m:* Frederick A.; *c:* Benjamin; *ed:* (BA) Elem Ed, Mount Union Coll 1979; (MA) Rdng Specialist, Kent St Univ 1985; *cr:* Learning Disability Tutor 1979-80; 2nd Grade Teacher 1980-85, 5th GradE Teacher 1985 West Branch Local Sch Dist; *ai:* Intnl Rdng Assn; Teachers Applying Whole Lang; OEA; West Branch Ed Assn; NEA; *office:* Knox Elem Sch 2900 Knox School Alliance OH 44601

HOBBY, DOUGLAS A., History Teacher; *b:* Montgomery, AL; *m:* Lynn; *c:* Jason, Weston, Adam; *ed:* (BAE) Soc Stud Ed, Univ of FL 1971; (MED) Curr/Instruction, Univ of W FL 1988; *cr:* Teacher FL St Prison 1971-72, Oak Hall Privte Sch 1972-74, Alachua Cty Schls 1974-75, Okaloosa Cty Schls 1985-; *ai:* Interact Club, Sr Class, Youth in Government Club Spon; *office:* Niceville HS 800 E John Simms Pkwy Niceville FL 32578

HOBBY, LINDA H., Kindergarten Teacher; *b:* Bimrmingham, AL; *m:* Paul L.; *c:* Carol, Patti Vines, Nancy Pless; *ed:* (BS) Early Chldhd 1976, (MA) Early Chldhd, 1978 Univ of AL Birmingham; *cr:* Dir/Coach Hilldale Kndgtn 1961-75; Teacher Tarrant Elem 1976-; *office:* Tarrant Elem Sch 1269 Portland St Tarrant AL 35212

HOBGOOD, GALE WILSON, 1st Grade Teacher; *b:* Madisonville, KY; *m:* Morris W.; *c:* Dirk D.; *ed:* (BS) Elem Ed, W KY Univ 1974; (MA) Elem Ed, Murray St Univ 1978; *cr:* 1st Grade Teacher Grapevine Elem 1974-; *ai:* Sch Guidance Comm; KY Ed Assn, Hopkins Cty Ed Assn, NEA 1974-; *home:* 3250 Rose Creek Rd Madisonville KY 42431

HOBICK, LAUREL D., Phys Ed/Driver Ed/Coach; *b:* Fithian, IL; *m:* Donna J. Coons; *c:* Michael, Steven; *ed:* (BA) Phys Ed/Soc Stud, William Jewel Coll 1954; (MA) Phys Ed Univ of AZ 1964; *cr:* Coach-Teacher Oakwood Twp HS 1957-60; Kofa HS 1960-64; Truman HS 1964-72; Cass-Midway RI 1972-81; Piper HS 1981-; *ai:* Head Coach Ftbl & Track; Spon Freshman Class; Curr Comm; Middle Sch Faculty Adv Comm; Lettermen Club Spon; National Fed of Coaches 1957-; 30 Yr Awd 1989; Mo St Teachers Assn 1972-81; Effective Teaching Wkshp 1981-; Coach of Yr 1976-78; Track-Ftbl Advisory Bd; Lecturer at Various Coaching Clinics; Teacher of Yr Truman HS; this is Your Life Presentation Yuma AZ; Whos Who in Am Colls & Univs Athlete of Yr; *office:* Piper HS 4400 N 107th St Kansas City KS 66109

HOBSON, FREDDIE CATHERINE, 10th Grade English Teacher; *b:* Elkin, NC; *ed:* (BA) Eng, Wake Forest Univ 1973; *cr:* 7th Grade Teacher East Bend Elem Sch 1973-74; 9th-12th Grade Eng Teacher Starmount HS 1974-; *ai:* NHS Adv; NCAE; Golden Eagle.

HOCEVAR, ELIZABETH ANN, French Teacher; *b:* Elkhart, IN; *m:* Robert Allen; *ed:* (BA) Fr, 1975, (MALS) Eng, 1981 Valparaiso Univ; *cr:* Teacher Valparaiso Cmmty Schls 1976-85, White Pigeon Cmmty Schls 1985-; *ai:* Fr & Ski Club; MALFP 1990; ACTFL, AATF 1975; *office:* White Pigeon HS 410 E Prairie Ave White Pigeon MI 49099

HOCH, MARGARET EWING, Fifth Grade Teacher; *b:* Lubbock, TX; *m:* Frank B. Jr.; *c:* Diana Malek, Frank Jr.; *ed:* (BS) Home Ec, 1951, (ME) Elem Ed, SW Tx 1962; *cr:* Home Ec Blanco Public Sch 1972-73; 3rd-5th Grade Elem Teacher San Marcos Consolidated Ind Sch Dist 1973-; *ai:* Travis Elem Sci Coord; Unit Leader; NEA 1970-; Classroom Teacher Assn, TX St Teacher Assn 1952-; Detta Zeta CCD 1970-74; Alpha Detta Kappa Secy 1988-; Outstanding Teacher 1988; *office:* Travis Elem Sch PO Box 2340 San Marcos TX 78666

HOCKING, MELANIE E., Chemistry Teacher; *b:* Martins Ferry, OH; *ed:* (BS) Chem, Marietta Coll 1973; (MS) Counseling, Univ of Dayton 1976; (JD) Law, Duquesne Univ 1986; (LLM) Oceans Law & Policy, Univ of VA 1987; Grad Fellowship Chem, OH Univ 1973; Grad Courses Ed, Univ of N CO Greeley 1973-74 & Univ of Dayton 1976-78; *cr:* Chem Teacher Wintersville HS 1975-; *ai:* Co-Dir Indian Creek Elem Talented & Gifted Sci Act & 3rd Grade Sci Enrichment Prgm; OH Academic Competition NE Regional, Jefferson Cty Sch Dist Sci Course of Study, NHS Faculty Comm; Winterville HS Faculty Cncl; NEA, OH Ed Assn 1975-; Indian Creek Ed Assn (Secy 1980-82) 1975-; PA Bar Assn 1986-; Upper OH Valley Adult Literacy Cncl Bd of Dir 1988-; Spectroscopy Society of Pittsburgh HS Equipment Grant 1988-89, Educl Prgm Support Grant 1990; Jefferson Cty Sch Dist Grant 1988, 1990; Most Influential Teacher Gold Key Honor Stu 1989, 1990; *office:* Wintersville HS 200 Park Dr Wintersville OH 43952

HOCOTT, JERRY DALE, Mathematics Department Chair; *b:* Greenwood, AR; *c:* Keith, Eric; *ed:* (BS) Math, AR Tech Univ 1965; *cr:* Math Teacher Gentry HS 1965-66; US Army 1966-68; Math Teacher Gentry HS 1968-72, Booneville HS 1972-; *ai:* Future Teachers Assn & Frosh Class Spon; BEA Pres 1988-; *office:* Booneville HS 835 E 8th St Booneville AR 72927

HODAPP, LEO JOHN, 7th & 8th Grade Teacher/Prin; *b:* Carlyle, IL; *m:* Karen Wehmueller; *c:* Ryan, Brad; *ed:* (BS) Ed, 1973, (MS) Ed Admin, 1987 Southern IL U-Carbondale; IL Prin Acad on Teacher Observation & Evaluation; *cr:* 5th/6th Grade Teacher 1974-87, 7th/8th Grade Teacher 1987-, Teaching Prin 1987- St Augustine; *ai:* Speech Coach; Field Day Chm; Sch Newspaper Moderator; Sci Fair, Fundr Aiser, Art Fair, Poster Contst Chm; Cath Sch Week Chm of Math-A-Thon Raises Money for Chldhd Cancers; Assn of Elem Prin 1985-; St Dominic Savia Club Moderator 1974-80 Unit Leader of Yr 1980; Waterloo Khoury League Mgr 2nd Place 1989; Waterloo Soccer Asst Coach 1st Pl 1989; Columbia/Red Bud Assn of Elem Prin Sec; Sec 1985-87/Chm 1986-87/1989-; *home:* 417 Sunset Ln Waterloo IL 62298

HODGE, CAROLYN LEOLA, Spanish Teacher; *b:* St Thomas, VI; *ed:* (BA) Scndry Span Ed, Univ of VI 1978; Grad Stud Univ of MN 1989; *cr:* 7th/8th Grade Span Teacher ADdelita Cancryn Jr HS 1978-; *ai:* Span Club Chairperson; United Negro Coll Fund Certificate of Appreciation 1988; King Juan Carlos I Fellowship & Summer Prgm 1989; *home:* PO Box 9903 Saint Thomas VI 00801

HODGE, CYNTHIA BROWN-WOODSON, English Teacher; *b:* Mullins, SC; *c:* Kevin, Marcus; *ed:* (BS) Eng, TN St Univ 1970; (MA) Comm Radio/Television, Univ of SC 1975; Working Towards Masters in Religion; *cr:* Eng Teacher Murfreesboro HS 1972-73, Bennettsville HS 1973-76; News Reporter WBTW TV 13 1976-77; Eng/Phys Ed Teacher Mullins HS 1977-; *ai:* Anti Drug Club; Jr/Sr Prom Comm; Sr Class Adv; Delta Sigma Theta 1967-; NEA, SCEA 1989-; St Mary AME Church Pastor 1988-; *home:* Rt 3 Box 410-U Mullins SC 29574

HODGE, IRIS DAVIS, Social Studies Teacher; *b:* Louisville, KY; *m:* Gerald; *c:* Kris, Jerrod; *ed:* (BS) His/Government, 1969, (MA) His Ed, 1974, (Rank I) Counseling, 1979 W KY Univ; *cr:* Teacher/Dept Chairperson N Hardin HS; Part Time Instr Elizabethtown Comm Coll; *ai:* Historical Society Spon; Numerous Cty Ed Comms; KEA, NEA, HCEA; Eastern Star; Outstanding Young Woman; Outstanding Soc Stud Teacher; *home:* 3023 S Wilson Elizabethtown KY 42701

HODGE, KAY BLAIR, Counselor; *b:* Ashland, AL; *m:* Donald Terry; *c:* Jessica B.; *ed:* (BS) Scndry Ed/Eng, Auburn Univ 1977; (MS) Guidance/Counseling, Jacksonville St Univ 1978; (AA) Cert Guidance/Counseling, 1982, (MS) Educl Admin, 1988 Auburn Univ; Approved Psychometrist; Certified to Administer General Aptitude Test Battery; *cr:* Cnslr/Librarian/Eng Teacher Bibb Graves HS 1977-80; Cnslr Alexander City St Jr Coll 1980-81, Coosa Cty HS 1981-88, Cntrl HS 1988-; *ai:* Stu Action for Ed Spon; Delta Kappa Gamma VP 1990; Phi Delta Kappa 1978-; *office:* Cntrl HS Rt 2 Box 62 Rockford AL 35136

HODGE, LINDA GAIL, English Teacher; *b:* Oklahoma City, OK; *m:* Kenneth Wayne; *c:* Dana Hodge Parker, Marianne; *ed:* (BA) Eng, 1963, (MA) Ed, 1967 Cntrl St Univ; Drug Trng to Work with Stus at Risk; *cr:* Eng Teacher Del Crest Jr HS 1964-67; Eng Teacher/Adjunct Instr Rose St Coll 1981-82; Eng Teacher Carl Albert Jr HS 1971-; *ai:* Mem Stu Assistance Comm 1988-; Teacher of 7th Grade Gifted & Talented; Pep Club & Honor Society Spon; Faculty Advisory Comm Mem 1988-; OK Ed Assn, NEA, Assn of Classroom Teachers 1964-; Wickline United Meth Church Mem; Good News Singers Gospel Singing Mem 1984-; Writing Project Grant 1990.

HODGE, LINDA S., History Teacher; *b:* Inyokern, CA; *m:* Richard; *c:* Matt Fox; *ed:* (BS) His 1970, (MED) Ed, 1990 GA Southwestern Coll; Teacher Monroe HS 1970-74 Ballard Hudson Jr HS 1974-77, Monroe HS 1977-79, Westover HS 1979-; *ai:* Yrbk Bus Staff; Tri-Hi-Y YMCA; Sr Class Spon; Voter Registrar; Prof Assn of GA Educators; Delta Gappa Gamma; Albany Musuem of Art; STAR Teacher 1974; *office:* Westover HS 2600 Patridge Dr Albany GA 31707

HODGE, LISA CHANCEY, Mathematics/Reading Teacher; *b:* Douglas, GA; *m:* James Corbitt; *c:* Jessica L.; *ed:* (AS) Cmptr Sci, S GA Coll 1980; (BS) Bus Ed, 1983, (MED) Mid Chldhd Ed, 1985 Valdosta St Coll; *cr:* 4th-6th Grade Teacher Satilla Elem 1983-; *ai:* Stu Study Team Comm Mem; Satilla Bulldogs Stu Handbook Comm Chairperson; 4th-6th Grade Math Manipulatives Comm Chairperson; PAGE; Eastside Baptist Church Childrens Dept Sunday Sch Teacher 1979-; Teacher of Month; *office:* Satilla Elem Sch Axon Hwy Douglas GA 31533

HODGE, YVONNE LA PLACE, Fourth Grade Teacher; *b:* St Kitts, British W Indie; *m:* Joseph E. Sr.; *c:* Valissa, Joseph Jr., James; *ed:* Diploma Ed, Teachers Trng Coll Univ of West Indies 1971; (BA) Elem Ed, Univ of Virgin IS 1984; (MS) Admin Supv, Nova Univ 1986; *cr:* Eng Teacher-Sandy Point HS 1971-79; 4th Grade Teacher-Lutheran Parish Sch 1980-84; Edith Williams Sch 1984-; *ai:* Licensed Evangelist & Church Leader in Church of God of Prophecy; *home:* Contant 7B PO Box 3427 VDA St Thomas VI 00803

HODGES, CHERYL ROBERTSON, English Teacher; *b:* Paducah, KY; *m:* Kerry D.; *c:* Kelly, Ryan; *ed:* (BA) Journalism, 1982, (MA) Scndry Ed, 1985 Murray St Univ; *cr:* Teacher Smithland Elem, Livingston Cty Mid Sch, Livingston Cntrl HS; *ai:* Cheerleading Coach 1989-; Speech Coach; Media Dir; United Meth Youth Fellowship Leader 1989-; Writing Consultant KY Dept of Ed Writing Projects.

HODGES, DENISE S., Business Teacher; *b:* Montpelier, ID; *m:* Jeffery D.; *ed:* (AS) Bus, Brigham Young Univ 1978; (BS) Bus, UT St Univ 1982; Grad Stud Bus Information Systems; *cr:* Bus Teacher Cottonwood HS 1982-; *ai:* Chrldr Adv; UBEA; Wrote & Designed Granite Dist Cmmty Ed Word Processing Curr; *office:* Cottonwood HS 5715 South 1300 East Salt Lake City UT 84121

HODGES, GENE, Biology/Anatomy Teacher; *b:* Temple, TX; *m:* Sarah Renee Roberts; *c:* Charlie, Matthew; *ed:* (BS) Health/Phys Ed, 1972, (MED) Health/Phys Ed, 1973 TX A&M Univ; (MED) Ed Admin, Sul Ross St Univ 1980; Honors Summer Course; Honors Wkshps; *cr:* Bio Teacher Kermit HS 1973-84; Sci Coord/Teacher Kermit Ind Sch Dist 1987-86; Teacher L D Bell HS 1986-; *ai:* Academic Quiz League Spon; TX Prof Educators Assn 1980-; NABT 1985-; TX Assn of Bio Teacher 1988-; Gideons

Intnl Chapter Pres 1985-86; Series of Articles for Sci Teachers; Nom for Outstanding Bio Teacher of TX Awd; Nom for Presidential Awd of Sci Teaching 1985, 1990; *office:* L D Bell HS 1600 Brown Trl Hurst TX 76054

HODGES, JAMES MELVIN, Guidance Counselor; *b:* Crescent City, CA; *c:* Pamela; *ed:* (BS) Biological Ed, OR St Univ 1955; (MED) Sci Ed, TX A&M Univ 1965; Counseling/Psych, Univ of OR; *cr:* Sci Teacher Wilson Jr HS 1957-63; Cnslr Whiteaker Elem Sch 1965-80, Jefferson Jr HS 1980-83, N Eugene HS 1983-; *ai:* Several Committees Dealing With Ed & Meeting Needs of Stu At Risk; Eugene Ed Assn Sch Rep 1959-64; OPGA Regional Dir 1966-68; OEA, NEA Mem 1957-; Elks 1965-; Governmental Grant TX A&M Univ 1963-65.

HODGES, JANET KENNEDY, 6th Grade Math Teacher; *b:* Washington, DC; *m:* Richard Warren; *c:* Warren H., Kathleen J.; *ed:* (BS) Elem Ed, Salisbury St Coll 1966; (MS) Elem Ed, Towson St Coll 1972; Math Cert Mid Sch; *cr:* 5th Grade Teacher Joppatowne Elem 1966-83; 6th Grade Math Teacher Magnolia Mid Sch 1983-; *ai:* Youth Soccer, Bsktbl, Sftbl, Jr Var Sftbl Coach; Youth Bsbl Scorekeeper; NEA, MSTA, NTM; *office:* Magnolia Mid Sch Fort Hoyle Rd Joppa MD 21085

HODGES, MARCELLA VALDEZ, 5th Grade Classroom Teacher; *b:* Dallas, TX; *m:* Bruce Robin; *ed:* (BFA) Music/Voice Applied, Stephen F Austin St Univ 1976; (MED) Elem Ed, 1979, (EDD) Elem Ed/Admin, 1986 E TX St Univ; *cr:* Music Teacher 1976-83, 5th Grade Teacher 1983- Edith Beaver Elem; *ai:* Rockwall Cty Lib Bd; TEAMS to TAAS Comm; PTA (1st VP 1988-89, Historian 1989-); Dissertation Miscues of Childrens Rdng.

HODGES, MARY H., Mathematics Teacher; *b:* Marion, KY; *m:* Reginald L.; *ed:* (BS) Math, 1972, (MA) Elem Ed, 1975 Murray St Univ; *cr:* Spec Ed Teacher Fohs Hall Elem Sch 1972-73; Math Teacher Crittenden Cty HS 1973-; Part Time Math Teacher Madisonville Comm Coll 1988-; *ai:* KY Cncl Teachers of Math, NCTM, KY Ed Assn, NEA; Marion Baptist Church Active in Music Department; *office:* Crittenden Cty HS PO Box 311 Marion KY 42064

HODGES, MARY NAPIER, Third Grade Teacher; *b:* Baldwin County, GA; *m:* Robert E.; *c:* Kay H. Wallace, Michael R., Mark L.; *ed:* (BA) Elem Ed, GA Coll 1951; (MA) Elem Ed, 1979, (AA) Elem Ed, 1982 Troy St; *cr:* 3rd Grade Teacher Longino Sch 1951-52; 6th Grade Teacher Parker-Mathis 1957-58; 3rd Grade Teacher Pine Grove 1958-60, Parker Elem 1961-66, Floyd Elem 1966-68, Seth Johnson 1970-73; 3rd-6th Grade Teacher Dalraida Elem 1973-; *ai:* Club Spon & Adv; Stu Cncl; Cmptr Comm; NEA, AEA, MCEA 1966-, Teacher of Yr 1982; PDK Treas 1982-; *office:* Dalraida Elem 440 Dalraida Rd Montgomery AL 36109

HODGES, SUE CARR, Fourth Grade Teacher; *b:* Marietta, OH; *m:* Walter Robin Sr.; *c:* Walter Jr., David; *ed:* (BS) Elem Ed, Cntrl St Univ 1960; (MED) Curr/Supervision, 1969, (MED) Admin 1989- Wright St Univ; *cr:* Teacher Dayton Bd of Ed 1964-; *ai:* OH Teacher Ed Loan Reviewer; Paul Douglas Teacher Schlsp Loan; NEA, OEA, DEA; Presenter of Effective Teacher Prgm 1987-88; *home:* 5962 Derby Rd Dayton OH 45418

HODGES, WALTER O., 4th Grade Head Teacher; *b:* Hartford, CT; *c:* Kristin K.; *ed:* (BA) 1967; Univ CT, Univ Hartford, Cntrl CT St Univ; *cr:* 4th Grade Teacher 1967-, Head Teacher 1977- Mary M Hooker Elem Sch; *ai:* Kappa Alpha Psi, NAACP; Hartford Fed of Teachers 1967-; Prince Hall Masons #17 F&AM; Shiloh Baptist Church (Supt Church Sch, Music & Choir Dir, Quartet Singer, Saxophone Soloist), Father of Yr, Man of Yr; Mary Hooker Sch & PTO Teacher of Yr Awds; Cmmty Awd for Outstanding Service; *office:* Mary M Hooker Sch 200 Sherbrooke Ave Hartford CT 06106

HODGINS, ALEC TERENCE, French/Ceramics Teacher; *b:* Red Deer AB, Canada; *m:* Christine Marent; *ed:* (BA) French/Ceramics, CA St Univ Sacramento 1983; *cr:* Eng Teacher Lycee Hotelier Toulouse France 1983-84, Nanjing Teachers Univ Nahjing China 1985-86; Eng/Fr Teacher Eerson Jr HS 1986-88; Fr/Ceramics Teacher Rio Americano HS 1988-; *ai:* Faculty Adv Class of 1992; Fr Club Adv; CA Teachers Assn; Distinguished Alumni CA St Univ 1988; Co-Authored Eng Lang Textbook; *office:* Rio Americano HS 4540 American River Dr Sacramento CA 95864

HODGKINS, JOHN W., Science Department Chairman; *b:* Bangor, ME; *m:* Sheila Jean Forrest; *c:* Ian, Gavin; *ed:* (BS) Bio, Univ of ME Orono 1976; (MS) Bio, 1983, (MS) Engineering, 1983 Univ of Lowell; *cr:* Environmental Ed Instr US Forest Service 1976-77; Water Treatment Plant Operator Digital Equipment Corporation 1981; Engineering Aid Dept of Environmental Quality Engrs 1982; Sci Teacher Burlington HS 1983; Sci Dept Head/Teacher Alvirne HS 1976-80, 1983-; *ai:* Boys Tennis Coach; Health Club Adv; Drivers Ed Instr; Ski Club Chaperone; St John USUI Natl Park Field Trip Coord; NSTA, NABT, NH Sci Teachers Assn 1983-; Amer Red Cross CPR Instr 1974-; Church of Good Shepherd Sunday Sch Teacher 1990; Actor Singers Chorus Singer 1976-80; *office:* Alvirne HS Derry Rd Hudson NH 03051

HODGKINS, PATRICIA MARION, Foreign Language Dept Chair; *b:* Temple, ME; *ed:* (BE) Fr/Latin/Eng, Keene St Coll 1961; (MS) Fr, Cntrl CT St Coll 1968; *cr:* Fr/Latin Teacher Wooster Jr HS 1961-63; Fr Teacher Weston HS & Mid Sch 1961-72, West Rocks Jr HS 1963-69; Fr Teacher/Dept Head Timberlane Regional HS 1974-; *ai:* Standardized Testing Coord; Eligibility & NHS Comm; Timberlane Regional HS Foreign Lang Curr; AATF; NH Assn Teachers of Fr (Pres Elect 1977-78, Pres 1978-79); NDEA Inst Levels I, II in CT & Lyon France 1964-65; ESL Prgm Sch Dist; Individualized Instruction Syllabus; *office:* Timberlane Regional HS 36 Greenoug Rd Plaistow NH 03865

HODGSON, GORDON B., HS Social Studies Teacher; *b:* Bayshore, NY; *m:* Janice Maria Rossi; *c:* Danielle, Edward; *ed:* (BS) Elem Ed/Soc Stud, St Univ of NY Cortland 1976; (MA) Educl Admin, Univ of SD Vermillion 1979; Counseling, Univ of Bridgeport; Cmptr, Dowling Coll; General Stud St Univ of NY Stonybrook; Internship N Adams St; Various Coaching Courses; *cr:* Elem Teacher Winner Schls 1976-78; Jr HS Soc Stud Teacher Rapid City Schls 1978-81; Scndry Soc Stud Teacher W Islip Schls 1981-; *ai:* Asst Var Ftbl & Var Bowling Coach; Bethpage HS Head Var La Crosse Coach; Academic Excl Awd Comm; Phi Delta Kappa 1979-, 10 Yr Service Awd 1989; NCSS, ASCD; W Islip Athletic Booster Club (Pres 1988-), 1981-; Bethpage Dads Club 1981-; Hassau Cty La Crosse Coaches Assn Pres 1989-; La Crosse League Coach of Yr 1988; *office:* West Islip HS Lions Path West Islip NY 11795

HODGSON, JANICE MARIAROSSI, Mathematics Teacher; *b:* West Islip, NY; *m:* Gordon Bruce; *c:* Danielle, Edward; *ed:* (BS) Scndry Ed/Math, E Stroudsburg St Coll 1981; (MA) Admin of Human Resources, SUNY Stony Brook 1986; *cr:* Summer Sch Math Teacher 1982-87, Substitute Teacher/Jr Var Vlybl Coach 1982 W Islip Public Schls; Substitute Teacher Babylon Public Schls 1982; Jr Var Field Hockey/Jr HS Vlybl Coach Locust Valley 1982-83; Jr Var Sftbl Coach 1982-88, Jr/Sr HS Math Teacher 1982- Locust Valley Cntrl Schls; *ai:* Stu Attitudes & Achievement Commitees; 7th Grade Advisorship; AFT 1982-; W Islip Booster Club 1984-.

HODGSON, NITA PARCEL, Teacher; *b:* Green Bay, WI; *m:* Jon G.; *ed:* (BA) Sociology, Univ of WI Milwaukee 1976; (MS) Curr & Instruction, Univ of WI Madison 1981; Teacher Cert Cardinal Stritch Coll 1979; *cr:* Research Asst Univ of WI Madison 1981; Teacher New Caney Mid Sch 1981-85; Dir Rdng Center 1985-86; Teacher Riverside Univ HS 1986-; *ai:* Young Educators Society Club Adv; Chrldrs Adv; Staff Soc Act Coord; Milwaukee Area Rdng Cncl 1988-; Milwaukee Teachers Educl Assn 1986-; Multicultural Ed; Analysis of Instruction; Cooperative Learning; Critical Thinking Skills; Cmptrs in Classroom; Tutor ESL Adults Milwaukee Achiever Prgm; *office:* Riverside Univ HS 1615 E Locust Milwaukee WI 53211

HODGSON, RANDY LLOYD, Physical Education Teacher; *b:* Boulder, CO; *m:* Holly Ion; *c:* Scott, Laura; *ed:* (BA) Phys Ed, Univ of Northern CO 1979; *cr:* K-12th Grade Phys Ed Teacher North Park Sch Dist 1981-; 7th-12th Phys Ed Teacher Clear Creek Scndry Sch 1979-81; *ai:* HS Girls Vlybl & Bsktbl; Elem Bsktbl; CHSAA 1988-; *office:* Northpark Jr HS PO Box 798 Walden CO 80480

HODNEFIELD, ELAINE MARIE, Third Grade Teacher; *b:* Jackson, MN; *ed:* (BS) Elem Ed, Mankato St Univ 1970; Grad Work Univ of SD Vermillion, Drake Univ; *cr:* 3rd Grade Teacher Paullina Cmmty Sch 1970-72; 4th Grade Teacher 1972-73, 5th Grade Teacher 1973-82, 3rd Grade Teacher 1982- Kingsley-Pierson Cmmty Sch; *ai:* NEA, IA St Ed Assn, Kingsley-Pierson Ed Assn, IA Rdng Assn, Cherry Plywood Rdng Assn; Worked with 4-H Prgm in MN; Received 4-H Alumni Awd; *office:* Kingsley-Pierson Cmmty Sch 90 Valley Dr Kingsley IA 51028

HODOR, FRANCES R., 3rd Grade Teacher; *b:* East Chicago, IN; *m:* Joseph J.; *c:* David, Joni Newborn, Joseph Jr., George, Jayne Willis, Jo Ann Harris; *ed:* (BS) Elem Ed, St Josephs 1968; (MS) Elem Ed, IN Univ Northwest 1971; *cr:* 3rd Grade Teacher Beiriger Sch; *ai:* Flower Comm Head; Amer Legion Auxiliary, PTA, AFT; Calumet Area Handwriting Analysts Treas 1988-; *home:* 222 N Ernest St Griffith IN 46319

HODOUS, KIMBERLY TUCKER, History Teacher; *b:* New Smyrna Beach, FL; *m:* Robert George; *c:* Lindsey, Alexandra; *ed:* (BA) Jr High-Mid Sch Ed, Ball St Univ 1985; *cr:* 7th Grade Teacher Kayenta Mid Sch 1985-86; Teacher Mingus Union HS 1987-; *ai:* Yrbk Adv; *office:* Mingus Union H S 1801 E Fir St Cottonwood AZ 86326

HODUM, ELLEN CLIBURN, First Grade Teacher; *b:* Magee, MS; *m:* John Hollis; *c:* Sarah; *ed:* (BS) Elem Ed, Univ of S MS 1970; (MS) Elem Ed, (AAA) Specialist Elem Ed, William Carey Coll; *cr:* Jr HS Eng Teacher Simpson Cty Acad 1970-77; 1st Grade Teacher Magee Elem 1977-; *home:* Rt 1 Box 91A Mendenhall MS 39114

HOECKER, RICHARD VINCENT, Elementary Teacher; *b:* St Joseph, MO; *m:* Patricia Lee Raymond; *c:* Shawn P., Kelly B.; *ed:* (BS) Scndry Ed/Psych/Health/Drlvers Ed, NW MO St Univ 1971; (BS) Elem Ed, MO Western St Coll 1973; (MS) Elem Admin/Supervision, NW MO St Univ 1976; Grad Stud, NW MO St Univ; *cr:* 3rd/6th Grade Teacher Lake Contrary Elem 1973-78; 6th Grade Teacher Linbergh Elem 1978-80, Hosea Elem 1980-; *ai:* Sci Fair; Safety Patrol Co-Spon; Dist Salary Comm; MO St Teachers Assn 1973-; NSTA 1987-; St Joseph Teachers Assn 1973-, Finalist Teacher of Yr 1989; King Hill Baptist Church (Sunday Sch Dir 1988-, Deacon 1980-, Sunday Sch Teacher 1975-); Wrote Supts Grant 1988-89; *office:* Hosea Elem Sch 10th & Felix Sts Saint Joseph MO 64501

HOEFER, SHARON M., 7th-8th/Social Studies Teacher; *b:* Higginsville, MO; *ed:* (BS) Soc Stud, 1971, (MS) Guidance/Counseling, 1977 Cntrl MO St Univ; *cr:* HS Soc Stud Teacher R-VII Sch Dist 1973-75; HS Teacher Lincoln Cty R-I Sch Dist 1975-77; 7th-12th Grade Cnslr 1977-83, 7th-9th Grade Teacher 1983- New Franklin R-I Sch Dist; *ai:* Class Spon; New Franklin CTA Treas 1977-; MSTA 1973-; MO & NCSS 1983-; Inservice, Univ of MO Fall Writing Confernece Presenter; *home:* PO Box 227 New Franklin MO 65274

HOEFLING, JUDY ELAINE, 4th Grade Teacher; *b:* Saginaw, MI; *ed:* (BA) Elem Ed/Eng, 1968, (MA) Guidance/Counseling, 1969 Cntrl MI Univ; Instructional Theory Practice Trng; Various Wkshps; *cr:* 2nd Grade Teacher 1969-74, 3rd Grade Teacher 1975-78, 4th Grade Teacher 1979 Owosso Cntrl Sch; *ai:* Health, Lib, Communications, Soc Stud Comm; Cooperating Teacher with MI St Univ; Owosso Ed Assn, MI Ed Assn; Whos Who in Amer Ed 1988; Whos Who of Amer Women 1990; *office:* Central Sch-Owasso Public Sch 600 W Oliver St Owosso MI 48867

HOEHN, SHARON GILLUM, Fourth Grade Teacher; *b:* Hannibal, MO; *m:* Robert P.; *c:* Robert E., Bethany A.; *ed:* (BS) Ed, Univ of MO 1964; *cr:* 6th Grade Teacher 1964-75, 4th Grade Teacher 1975- Van-Far Elem; *ai:* Local Teachers Assn Comm Groups; Sick Leave Pool; New Hartford Baptist Church (Organist, Teacher) 1974-; *home:* 1105 S Monroe Vandalia MO 63382

HOEKEMA, BONNIE LOU, Social Science Teacher; *b:* Bellingham, WA; *ed:* (BRE) Biblical Stud, Reformed Bible Coll 1977; (BA) Soc Sci, Seattle Pacific Univ 1979; Lang Art, W WA Univ 1985; Career Counseling Trng; *cr:* Bus/Home Ec Teacher Noatak Sch 1979-80; Soc Sci/Lang Art Teacher Everett Chrstn Sch 1980-85; Soc Sci Teacher Seattle Chrstn HS 1987-; *ai:* Sr Class Adv 1987-; Cheer Coach 1988-; Girls Club Adv 1987-89; Stu Government & Jr HS Yrbk 1980-85; WORD 1981-85; Occupational Cncl 1988-; *office:* Seattle Chrstn HS 19639 28th Ave S Seattle WA 98148

HOELSCHER, JUDITH C. (BAX), 4th-6th Grade Science Teacher; *b:* Jefferson City, MO; *m:* Leonard R.; *c:* Jennifer, Steven; *ed:* (BS) Ed/Sci, Lincoln Univ 1974; Grad Stud Sci; *cr:* 7th-8th Grade Teacher Visitation Sch 1974; 2nd-6th Grade Teacher Blair Oaks Elem 1974-87; 4th-6th Grade Teacher Belair Elem 1988-; *ai:* Sci Curr Comm for Belair; CTA (Secy, VP & Pres) 1982-85; MSTA 1974-87; MNEA 1987-; CCD Educator 1978-; 4-H Leader 1994-; *office:* Belair Elem Sch 701 Belair Jefferson City MO 65102

HOEPER, CONNIE KAY, Fifth Grade Teacher; *b:* W Palm Beach, FL; *c:* Rebecca Hoeper Taylor, William F.; *ed:* (BSE) Ed, 1964, (MSE) Elem Sch Admin, 1971 Cntrl MO St Univ; Grad Stud Specialist Ed; *cr:* Classroom Teacher Consolidated Dist #4 1964-; *ai:* Grandview Natl Ed Assn Pres 1984-86; PTA.

HOERAUF, KENNETH A., Counselor; *b:* Royal Oak, MI; *m:* Jacqueline J.; *c:* Geoffrey, Beth; *ed:* (BA) Soc Stud/Math, Alma Coll 1958; (MA) Counseling, Wayne St Univ 1967; *cr:* Teacher Royal Oak Sch Dist 1958-61, Clawson Sch Dist 1961-62; Teacher/Cnslr Roseville Sch Dist 1962-; *ai:* Track Coach 1979-84; 7th Grade Girls Bsktbl 1984; Frosh Sftbl 1990; Natl Jr Honor Society 1976-; MCACD 1988-; St Dennis Sch Bd (Pres 1976) 1970-76; Bishop Foley HS Dads Club Asst Dir of Admission 1978-, Dad of Month 1979.

HOERSTEN, THOMAS J., 6th Grade Teacher; *b:* Lima, OH; *m:* Mary Ann; *c:* Chad, Renee; *ed:* (BSED) Bio, Univ of Dayton 1969; (MSED) Elem Ed/Sci, St Francis Coll 1974; Elem Admin, Univ of Dayton; *cr:* Teacher Ottoville Local Schls 1971-; *ai:* Cmptr Dir; Ottoville Local Ed Assn Pres 1976-86, 1989; Martha Holden Jennings Scholar; *office:* Ottoville Local Schls Box 248 Ottoville OH 45876

HOESLY, CLARENCE L., Science-Health-Algebra Teacher; *b:* Rock County, WI; *m:* Nancy Ann Woodbury; *c:* Jill M., Kurt D., Mark A., Jane L.; *ed:* (BE) Sci, Univ WI Whitewater 1962; (MED) Sci, TX A&M 1968; Health, Univ WI Superior; *cr:* General Sci/Chem/Physics Teacher Mineral Point HS 1962-63; Math/Sci/Chem/Physics Teacher Hazel Green Union HS 1963-67; Math/Earth Sci Teacher Barron Mid Sch 1968-69; Math/Phys Sci Teacher Ladysmith HS 1969-70; Math/Life Sci/Health Teacher Ladysmith Mid Sch 1970-; *ai:* Health Class Concessions for MD & Special Olympics; Asst Prin; Ftbl Coach 1963-70; Track Coach 1963-67; Bsktbl Coach 1963-65, 1969-70, 1972-73; Ladysmith Ed Assn (VP 1971-72, Pres 1972-74); Church of Christ (Deacon, Treas) 1969-; Teacher of Yr 1983; *office:* Ladysmith Mid Sch 115 E 6th St S Ladysmith WI 54848

HOFFEE, BETTY C., Teacher/Department Chairperson; *b:* Bonne Terre, MO; *m:* Andrew; *ed:* (BBA) Bus Admin, Memphis St Univ 1965; *cr:* Accounting/Bus Law Teacher De Soto Sr HS 1965-; *office:* De Soto Sr HS 731 Amvets Dr De Soto MO 63020

HOFFENBACHER, SUSAN E. (BEARDSLEY), Business Education Teacher; *b:* Dearborn, MI; *m:* David Duane; *c:* Kristin N.; *ed:* (BA) Bus Ad/Phys Ed, Spring Arbor Coll 1984; Bus Ed, E MI Univ; *cr:* Accounting Mgr Palmer Moving & Storage 1984-87; Bus Ed Teacher Southfield Chrstn HS 1987-; *ai:* Girls Var Bsktbl & Jr Var SftbL Coach; Bus Ed Dept Head; MI Bus Ed Assn Mem 1988-; *office:* Southfield Chrstn HS 28650 Lahser Rd Southfield MI 48034

HOFFER, HOWARD WILLIAM, Science/Mathematics Teacher; *b:* Culver City, CA; *m:* Sandra Lee; *c:* Aaron, Amanda; *ed:* (AA) Soc Sci, Santa Monica City Coll 1961; (BA) Liberal Arts/Sci, 1964, (MA) Ind Arts Ed, 1966 CA St Univ Chico; *cr:* Machine Shop Teacher Marshfield HS 1965-78; VP/Work Experience Coord M HS 1972-78; Sci/Math Teacher Millicoma Mid Sch 1979-; *ai:* OR Ed Assn Bd of Dir 1981-83; Coos Bay City Budget Comm 1988-; Public Safety Comm 1988-; *office:* Millicoma Mid Sch PO Box 509 Coos Bay OR 97420

HOFFERT, FRANK, Social Studies Department Chm; *b:* Cleveland, OH; *m:* Geraldine J. Siat; *c:* Stephen, Susan, Paul; *ed:* (BA) His, 1959; (MA) His, 1964 Case W Reserve Univ; Inst of Rome Society of Dante Alighieri; NDEA Inst European Intellectual His Williams Coll; Cleveland St Univ; John Carroll Univ; Univ of CO; Westminster Coll; *cr:* Soc Stud Teacher 1959-, Soc Stud Dept Chm 1969- Euclid HS; *ai:* Stu Cncl,Hum Club,Academic Decathlon, Citizen Bee Spon; Running Jr Achievements Applied Ec Prgm; Greater Cleveland Cncl for Soc Stud Pres 1969-70; OH Cncl for Soc Stud Exec Bd 1968-70; NCSS Delegate to House of Delegates 1968-70; Winner Charles R Keller Awd 1967; Euclids Outstanding Young Educator Awd Euclid Jr Chamber of Commerce 1970; Jennings Scholar; Outstanding Hs Teacher Awd Univ of Chicago; *office:* Euclid HS 711 E 222nd St Euclid OH 44123

HOFFMAN, ANNETTE RAPER, Fourth Grade Teacher; *b:* Fallon, NV; *m:* Dale Francis; *c:* Trevor J., Spencer J.; *ed:* Elem Ed, IA St Univ; (BA) Elem Ed, Univ of SC 1980; *cr:* 4th Grade Teacher Everett Elem 1980-81, Burnett Elem 1981-84; *ai:* Clear Lake Bible Church Awana Cubbies Dir; *home:* 407 Hedgecroft Seabrook TX 77586

HOFFMAN, CHRISTINA LOUISE, Fourth Grade Teacher; *b:* Pasco, WA; *ed:* (BA) Ed, Gonzaga Univ 1968; *cr:* 3rd Grade Teacher Federal Way Sch Dist 1968-70; 4th Grade Teacher East Lyme Sch Dist 1970-74; 4th-6th Grade Teacher Auburn Sch Dist 1974-.

HOFFMAN, ELIZABETH ANNE, Music Director; *b:* San Mateo, CA; *ed:* (BM) Music, San Francisco St Univ 1977; *cr:* Dean of Girls Mendocino Music Camp 1978; Music Teacher 1979-85, Music Dir 1986- Sugarloaf Fine Arts Camp; Music Dir Pollock Pines Sch Dist 1978-; *ai:* Dist Liason Comm for Selection of New Dist Supt; Music Educators Natl Conference, CA Music Educators Assn 1978-; Sierra Symphony (Bd Mem 1988-, Participating Mem 1986-).

HOFFMAN, GERALD VICTOR, Third Grade Teacher; *b:* New Brunswick, NJ; *m:* Nancy Jane Cotter; *c:* Drew C., Dane C.; *ed:* (BS) Elem Ed, Indiana Univ of PA 1974; Masters Equivalency; *cr:* 4th-6th Grade Sci Teacher Sonestown Elem 1974-77; 3rd Grade Teacher 1978, 4th Grade Teacher 1979, 4th-6th Grade Teacher 1979-85, 2nd Grade Teacher 1985-89, 2nd Grade Teacher 1985-89, 3rd Grade Teacher 1989- Sullivan Cty; *ai:* Head Bsktbl Coach Sullivan Cty HS; Elem Bsktbl Coach Sullivan Cty Elem Schls; PSEA; Lions Club 1990, Eagles Mere Athletic Assn 1983-, Theta XI; Eagles Mere Boro Zoning Officer 1983-; *home:* Box 236 Eagles Mere PA 17731

HOFFMAN, JEROME MICHAEL, Math & Foreign Lang Teacher; *b:* South Bend, IN; *m:* Norma Jean Bikowski; *c:* Lorilynn, Lisa; *ed:* (BS) Math/Sci, Notre Dame Univ 1957; (MA) Russian Lang/Lit, IN Univ 1960; Post Grad Work Soviet Area Stud, Notre Dame; Fullbright Fellow, Warsaw Poland Univ; Summer Inst Moscow USSR Univ; *cr:* Teacher N Liberty HS 1957-59, South Bend Cmmty Sch Corporation 1961-; *ai:* Head Cross Cntry & Asst Track Coach; Sch Bd Mem; ICTM 1957-; IATCCC 1989-, Coach of Yr 1989; Achievement Forum Bd Mem 1960-, Achiever of Yr 1983; People to People 1989-; *home:* 52239 Tally Ho Dr N South Bend IN 46635

HOFFMAN, KAREN A., 7th/8th Grade Reading Teacher; *b:* Refugio, TX; *ed:* (AAS) Bus, Bee Cty Coll 1977; (BS) Elem Ed, Corpus Christi St Univ 1981; Teacher Expectations Stu Awareness; *cr:* 6th Grade Teacher Ingleside Ind Sch Dist 1981-85; 7th/8th Grade Teacher Beeville Ind Sch Dist 1985-; *ai:* UIL Oral Rdng Mgr; Effective Schls Building Leadership Team Mem; Assn of Prof Educators Pres 1983-85; TX St Teachers Assn 1988-; *office:* Thomas Jefferson Jr HS 701 E Hays Beeville TX 78102

HOFFMAN, LILLIAN E. KUBALA, Third Grade Teacher; *b:* Chicago, IL; *m:* George N.; *c:* George, Lois Richter, Marybeth A.; *ed:* (BA) Ed, St Xavier Coll 1977; *cr:* K-8th Grade Substitute Teacher 1967-76, 3rd Grade Teacher 1976- St Gall Sch; *office:* St Gall Sch 5515 S Sawyer Ave Chicago IL 60629

HOFFMAN, MARTA S., Chemistry/Science Teacher; *b:* Havana, Cuba; *c:* Jessica, Bettie; *ed:* (BS) Chem, 1964, (PHD) Biochemistry, 1968 Univ of FL; Post Doctoral Fellow Univ of TX Dallas 1968-70, 1977-80; *cr:* Chem/Bio Teacher Coronado HS 1982-83; Chem/Physics Teacher Woodland Park HS 1984-; *ai:* Sci Olympiad & TEAM Coach; Class Spon; Phi Delta Kappa, Phi Beta Kappa, CO Chem Teachers Assn, NSTA; NIH Grant; NIH & Welch Fellowship; *office:* Woodland Park HS PO Box 6820 Woodland Park CO 80866

HOFFMAN, NORMA JEAN, English Teacher; *b:* South Bend, IN; *m:* Jerome Michael; *c:* Lorilynn, Lisa; *ed:* (BA) Eng, 1969, (MA) Ed, 1974 Ball St Univ; Bay Area Writing Project; Individualized Lang Art Prgm; *cr:* Eng Teacher Washington HS 1969-79, John Adams HS 1979-; *ai:* St Joseph HS Cross Cntry Asst Coach; Girls Athletic Bd Mem; Cross Cntry Spon; NCTE; NEA; St Anthony Parish Eucharistic Minister; *office:* John Adams HS 808 S Twyckenham Dr South Bend IN 46615

HOFFMAN, SHARON KILE, Jr. HS English Teacher; *b:* Terre Haute, IN; *m:* Steelman Lee; *ed:* (AS) General Stud, Lincoln Trail Coll 1984; (BS) Jr HS Ed, Eastern IL Univ 1986; *cr:* Jr HS Eng Villa Grove Schls 1986-; *ai:* HS Girls Vlybl Coach Head Var; Villa Grove Ed Assn 1987-; IEA 1987-; NEA 1987-; *office:* Villa Grove Jr H S Rt 130 N Villa Grove IL 61956

HOFFMAN, VALERIE JEAN (BRADLEY), Eng/Span/Lang Dept Chair; *b:* Los Angeles, CA; *m:* Robert Louis; *ed:* (BA) Eng, 1964, (MA) Eng, 1965 CA St Univ Long Beach; Univ of CA Irvine, Univ of La Verne; *cr:* Eng/Span Teacher Jefferson Jr HS 1965-68, Long Beach Polytechnic HS 1968-73; ESL Dept Chairperson/Span Teacher Woodrow Wilson HS 1973-; *ai:* Club Spon, Zygomas, Girls Tennis, Badminton, Coach of Girls Var Tennis; Jr Var Badminton Co-Ed; Cnslr for Long Beach Sch for Adults; Phi Kappa Phi VP 1964-65; Long Beach Teachers Assn, CTA, NEA 1965-; CATESOL 1980-88; Ladies of Net Tennis Team 1988-; Volvo Tennis 1986-87; Multi-Cultural Grant 1987; Mentor Teacher 1985-88; Faculty (Pres 1979-81, Cnslr 1986-89); AFS Spon 1975-81; *office:* Woodrow Wilson HS 4400 E 10th St Long Beach CA 90804

HOFFMANN, CARMELITA LANGUIT, 2nd Grade Teacher; *b:* Schofield Barracks, HI; *m:* Robert J.; *c:* Roberto, Timothy, Shannon; *ed:* (BS) Ed, Univ of HI 1961; (MA) Cmptrs in Ed, Lesley Coll 1984; *cr:* K-2nd Grade Teacher Venetucci Elem 1963-87; 2nd Grade Teacher French Elem 1987-; *ai:* Cmptr Resource Team; Widefield Ed Assn, NEA, Intnl Rdng Assn; *office:* Candace A French Elem Sch 5225 Alturas Dr Security CO 80911

HOFFMANN, JOAN ELLEN, Guidance Counselor; *b:* St Louis, MO; *m:* Gerald C.; *c:* Jill, Catherine; *ed:* (BA) Elem Ed, Harris-Stowe St Coll 1966; (MED) Scndry Counseling, Univ MO St Louis 1981; Psychometrist Cert 1982; Doctoral Candidate St Louis Univ; *cr:* Elem Teacher Ritenour Sch Dist 1966-71; Psychologist Consultant Behavioral & Psychological Assocs 1982-85; Self Employed SAT Preparation Service 1985-88; HS Cnslr Parkway Sch Dist 1988-; *ai:* PTO; Athletes at Risk; Project Reach; Sr Yr Transition Comm; Cntrl Advancement Team; Cntrl Coalition; Counseling Advisory Comm; Amer Assn Counseling & Dev 1981-; Pi Lamda Theta 1990; MO Assn Coll Admissions Cnslrs 1988-; Green Trails Parent Organization Pres 1976-87 Recognition Awd 1983-84; Parkway Cntrl Jr HS Parent Organization Treas 1983-89 Recognition Awd 1989; Parkway Cntrl HS Parent Organization Pres 1985- Recognition Awd 1987; Sr Yr Cmmty Service Comm; PTO VP & Various Comms Chairperson; Parkway Parent Support Group; Parkway Citizens Advisory Comm; Parkway Strategic Planning Comm; *office:* Parkway Central H S 369 N Woods Mill Rd Chesterfield MO 63017

HOFFMANN, RICHARD DANIEL, Social Studies Teacher; *b:* Milwaukee, WI; *m:* Le Ann Kay Saunder; *c:* Kurt R., Kari L.; *ed:* (BS) His, 1979, (MED) Ed/Soc Stud, 1986 Univ of WI Platteville; Coach Concentration Univ of WI Platteville 1979; Broadfield Cert Univ of WI Green Bay 1981; *cr:* Stu Supvr Glenview Commons Food Service 1973-79; Soc Stud Teacher/Coach Shawano-Gresham Sch Dist 1979-; *ai:* Head Coed Track Coach; Chess Coach; Faculty Extracurricular Act Head; St of WI Soc Stud Comm Mem; WI Cncl Soc Stud 1979-; US Chess Fed 1988-; WI HS Track Coaches Assn 1982-; WI Ed Assn Cncl (Pres 1987-88, VP 1986-87); WI Interscholastic Athletic Assn Bsktbl Ofcl; Jaycees Pres 1982-87, Jaycee of Yr 1983-84; WI PTA Pres 1984-; Shawano Area Ofcls Assn (Pres 1986-87) 1983-; City of Shawano Voter Registrar 1989-; Taft Inst 2-Party Government 1987; WI Global Stud Inst 1980; *office:* Shawano HS 1050 S Union Shawano WI 54166

HOFFMANN, ROBERT LOUIS, History Teacher; *b:* St Louis, MO; *m:* Jean Kozeny; *c:* Bill, Linda, Jeff; *ed:* (BA) His, 1961, (MA) Amer His, 1962 St Louis Univ; WA Univ, Univ of MO St Louis, S MO St Univ, Stanford Univ; *cr:* His Teacher Vianney HS 1961-; *ai:* Chess & Soccer Coach; Sch Bd of Dir; Coe Fellowship Stanford Univ 1989; *office:* Vianney HS 1311 S Kirkwood Rd Kirkwood MO 63122

HOFFMEISTER, WESLEY KEITH, Science Teacher; *b:* Louisville, KY; *m:* Phyllis Proctor; *c:* Brent, Beth; *ed:* (BA) Bio, Univ of Louisville 1962; (MS) Scndry Ed, IN Univ 1965; *cr:* General Sci Teacher Hazelwood Jr HS 1962-; *ai:* New Albany Floyd Cty Sch Corp K-12th Grade Sci Curr Chm; NEA, IN St Teacher Assn, Floyd Cty Teacher Assn 1962-; PTO 1962-; Talks With Governor Team; *office:* Hazelwood Jr HS Hazelwood Ave New Albany IN 47150

HOFFMEYER, THOMPSON PRICE, JR., Mathematics Teacher; *b:* Florence, SC; *ed:* (BS) Scndry Ed, 1976, (MAT) Math, 1981 Univ of SC; *cr:* Math Teacher S Florence HS 1977-84, Socastee HS 1984-85, Spring Valley HS 1985-; *ai:* Asst Var Ftbl & Boys Tennis Coach; SC Athletic Coaches Assn 1977-; SC Tennis Coaches Assn 1985-, St Coach of Yr 1988; *home:* 229 Windsor Pt Rd Unit 7F Columbia SC 29223

HOFFPAUIR, FRANCES MILLER, First Grade Teacher; *b:* Many, LA; *m:* Jessie L. Jr.; *c:* Jason, Brent; *ed:* (BA) Elem Ed, NW LA St Univ 1969; *cr:* 2nd Grade Teacher E Feleciana Parish Sch Bd 1969-71; 1st/5th/6th Grade Teacher Natchitoches Parish Sch Bd 1971-; *ai:* Delta Kappa Gamma (Pres 1989-, Treas 1986-88, Secy 1984-86); Los Adais Fnd; Robeline First Baptist Church; *home:* PO Box 327 Robeline LA 71469

HOGAN, DURLEY HOWARD, Spanish Teacher; *b:* Stuart, FL; *m:* Phillip L.; *c:* Todd A., Kelleye D., Tracy D.; *ed:* (BA) Eng/ Span Ed, Palm Beach Atlantic Coll 1985; *cr:* Teacher Stuart Mid Sch 1985-87, Martin Cty HS 1987-; *ai:* Coord for Schls Partnerships; Intnl Span Exch Prgm; Sch Discipline Comm; Private Tutoring at Rehabilitation Hospital; Natl Amer Pen Women Membership Nom 1990; Amer Assn for Teachers of Span & Portuguese, FL Assn for Teachers of Span 1985-; Chrstn Womens Club Pres 1976; *office:* Martin Cty HS 2801 S Kanner Hwy Stuart FL 34994

HOGAN, ERNESTINE DEARING, Mathematics Teacher; *b:* Atlanta, GA; *m:* Marshall; *ed:* (BA) Math, Spelman Coll 1968; (MED) Math/Ed, GA St Univ 1974; Supervision of Instruction IS-5 Cert, GA St Univ; *cr:* Math Teacher Smith HS 1968-85, Southside HS 1986-; *ai:* NHS Adv; Homecoming Act Coord; Math Club & Andover-Dartmouth Math Competition Team Spon; AFT, NCTM 1968-; Atlanta Public Schls Teacher of Yr 1989-; Featured in Book; Star Teacher 1974; City of Atlanta Incentive Math Teacher Awd 1988-89; *office:* Southside Comprehensive HS 801 Glenwood Ave Atlanta GA 30312

HOGAN, GORDON C., Mathematics Teacher; *b:* Bancroft, ID; *m:* Linnea C.; *c:* Josh, Audrene; *ed:* (BS) Phys Ed/Math, UT St Univ 1967; *cr:* Math Teacher/Head Ftbl/Bsktbl/Track Coach/ Athletic Dir Hansen HS 1967-75; Math Teacher/Head Ftbl Coach Kimberly HS 1975-; *ai:* Natl Fed of Interscholastic Coaches 1982-; ID Coaches Assn (VP, Pres) 1967-, Ftbl Coach of Yr 1971-75; 4th Dist Coaches Assn Pres 1967-, Ftbl Coach of Yr 1971, 1975, 1980-82, 1985; *office:* Kimberly HS P O Box 0 Kimberly ID 83341

HOGAN, KATHERINE LOUISE (VUKOVICH), English Teacher; *b:* Globe, AZ; *c:* Darcy L. Hogan Walker, Timothy M. Jr., John W.; *ed:* (BA) Eng, AZ St Univ 1958; (MA) Ed, Univ of San Francisco 1978; *cr:* Eng Dept Chairperson Rincon Valley Jr HS 1979-89; Eng Mentor Santa Rosa City Schls 1986-87; Eng Teacher Rincon Valley Jr HS 1966-; *ai:* Honor Society Club Spon; Dist Eng Curr, GATE, 9th Grade Transition to HS Comms; NEA, CTA 1968-; SRTA (Membership Chairperson 1980-87, Grievance Rep 1989-); Order of Eastern Star, Order of Rainbow for Girls (Grand officer, Mother Adv), Daughters of the Nile, AAUW, Phi Delta Kappa; Santa Rosa City Sch Teacher of Yr; Santa Rosa Chamber of Commerce Jr HS Teacher of Yr; Sonoma Cty Teacher of Yr; *office:* Rincon Valley Jr HS 950 Middle Rincon Rd Santa Rosa CA 95409

HOGAN, MARIE GLORIA (PHILLIP), Third Grade Teacher; *b:* Brooklyn, NY; *m:* William H. Sr.; *c:* Nancy, Ellen Hogan Cormack, William H. Jr., Paul W.; *ed:* (BA) Sociology, Marymount NY 1950; (MA) Ed, Paterson St 1971; *cr:* 4th Grade Teacher Convent of Sacred Heart 1950-54; 3rd Grade Teacher Wyckoff Bd of Ed 1971-; *ai:* Curr Cncl & Grant Comm of Wyckoff; NJEA, Wyckoff Ed Assn, NEA; NJ Rdng Assn 1976-89; Teacher of Yr Coolidge Sch 1989; *office:* Coolidge Sch 420 Grandview Ave Wyckoff NJ 07481

HOGAN, SHEILA MAUREEN (KROTZ), Biology Teacher; *b:* Lincoln, IL; *m:* Phillip Joseph; *c:* Celia, Nicole; *ed:* LPN Nursing, Decatur AVC 1979; (AS) Bio, Richland Comm Coll 1983; (BS) Bio/Ed, Millikin Univ 1985; Russian Stud Eastern WA Univ; *cr:* Office Nurse Dr C T Johnson MD 1979-83; Charge Nurse Cmmty Center 1981-84; Lab Asst Millikin Univ 1983-85; Bio Teacher Mt Zion HS 1985-; *ai:* Medics Club, Sci Olympiad Adv; IL Health Occupations Assn Comm Chm 1987-; Il Health Occupations Stus of America St Rep 1987-; IL Coordinating Cncl of Voc Organizations Vice-Chm 1987-; IL Voc Assn; IL Sci Teachers Assn 1985-; NSTA 1985-; NABT 1985-; Phi Theta Kappa Mem; People to People Youth Sci Exch USSR Delegation Leader 1990; *office:* Mt Zion H S 305 S Henderson Mount Zion IL 62549

HOGAN, SHIRLEY A. VAN AELST, Sixth Grade Teacher; *b:* Manistee, MI; *m:* Homer A.; *c:* Terry L. Hogan Hrincius; *ed:* (BS) Elem Ed/Soc Sci/Ag, Cntrl MI Univ Mt Pleasant 1962; Grad Sch; *cr:* 5th/6th Grade Teacher Cty Line Elem Sch 1955-76, Warren Consolidated Schls 1955-, Gordon J Warner Elem Schl 1976-; *ai:* Building Planning Comm; Cty Line PTA (Teacher, VP) 1955-58; *office:* Gordon J Warner Elem Sch 2791 Kaper Sterling Heights MI 48310

HOGE, MICHAEL E., Band Director; *b:* St Joseph, MI; *m:* Julie A.; *ed:* (BA) Music Ed, Bethel Coll 1983; *cr:* Band Dir Bangor Public Schls 1983-88; Berrien Springs Public Schls 1988-; *ai:* Pep Band; Marching Band; Southwest MI Band/Orch Assn Treas 1988-; *office:* Berrien Springs H S One Sylvester Ave Berrien Springs MI 49103

HOGE, SUSAN MARIE, Spanish Teacher/Dept Coord; *b:* Topeka, KS; *m:* Kenneth F.; *c:* Justin, Lauren, Evan; *ed:* (BA) Span, Washburn Univ 1979; *cr:* Teacher Highland Park HS 1981-; *ai:* Span Club Spon; Public Image Comm; KS Foreign Lang Assn; Awarded Schlsp from Pittsburg St Univ 1988; *office:* Highland Park HS 2424 California Topeka KS 66605

HOGENSON, THOMAS E., Guidance Counselor; *b:* Decorah, IA; *m:* Sara J. Morley; *c:* Matthew; *ed:* (BA) Sociology Ed, Univ of N IA 1978; (MA) Guidance & Counseling, NE MO St Univ 1988; *cr:* Mid Sch Teacher Belmond Cmmty Schls 1978-82; Jr HS Teacher Sheridan Cmmty Schls 1982-83; Scndry Sci Teacher Eddyville Cmmty Schls 1983-89; Scndry Guidance Cnslr Eddyville Sr HS 1989-; *ai:* Ftbl Coach; Stu Cncl Adv; Talented & Gifted, Stu At Risk Comm; Crisis Intervention Team Mem; NEA, ISEA 1978-; IACD 1990; Eddyville Ed Assn VP 1988-; Upward Bound Instr 1985; *office:* Eddyville HS Rt 1 Eddyville IA 52553

HOGER, GRACE KATHRYN, Vocal Music Teacher; *b:* Crawfordsville, IN; *ed:* (BS) Music Ed, Concordia Coll 1986; (MS) Music Ed, W CT St Univ 1991; *cr:* Vocal Music Teacher Rhinebeck Cntrl Schls 1986-89, Valley Stream N HS 1989-; *ai:* Swing Choir; MENC 1986-; *home:* 80 Molyneaux Rd Valley Stream NY 11580

HOGG, FARRELL F., Mathematics Teacher; *b:* Lamesa, TX; *m:* Ulma Grace Alexander; *c:* Theresa Dickey, Kenneth, Kevin, Kerek; *ed:* (BA) His, 1948, (MED) Ed, 1954 TX Tech Univ; NDEA Inst Geography Univ SW LA, Speech Arts, WA St Univ, Eng, W WA St Univ; EPDA Inst Geography KS Univ; Amer Heritage, Abilene Chrstn Univ; *cr:* Elem Prin/Teacher Loop Ind Sch Dist 1948-49; Teacher Dawson HS 1949-50, 1952-53; Sargent US Army 1950-52; Teacher Crane HS 1953-59, Abilene Ind Sch Dist 1959-; *ai:* Mathcounts Club; NEA, TX St Teachers Assn 1948-; Abilene Educators Assn Treas 1959-; Phi Delta Kappa 1976-; TX Classroom Teachers Assn St Bd Mem 1976-80; Abilene Teachers (Pres 1988-89, Sick Leave Bd VP 1987-88) 1984-89; Freedoms Fnd Valley Forge Teacher Medal Awd; *home:* 802 Harwell Abilene TX 79601

HOGLIN, JAY VAUGHN, Math/Computer Dept Head; *b:* Drayton, ND; *ed:* (BS) Math, Univ of ND 1973; Math/Cmptr Sci, Bemidji St Univ; Math, St Cloud St Univ; *cr:* Math/Cmptr Teacher St Michael Mid Sch 1976-; *ai:* Math Club Coach; Walleye Math Competition Supvr; St Cloud Math Contest Supvr; NCTM; *office:* Little Falls Mid Sch 1000 1st Ave NE Little Falls MN 56345

HOHMANN, DARRELL R., Science Computer; *b:* Elk City, OK; *m:* Sherry Stewart; *c:* Terrie, Darrin, Jarrod; *ed:* (BA) Sci, OK Univ 1962; Cmptr Ed; *cr:* Teacher West Jr HS 1962-68, Lone Wolf 1968-; *ai:* Ger Club Coach; Stu Cncl & Sr Spon; Co; Lions Club Pres 1974-75; *office:* Lone Wolf HS Box 158 Lone Wolf OK 73655

HOHNBAUM, DANIEL LAWRENCE, Science Teacher; *b:* Des Moines, IA; *m:* Keri Curtis; *ed:* (BS) Bio, IA St Univ 1979; (MAT) Teaching in Sci, Univ of TX Dallas 1986; *cr:* Sci Teacher Osage Cmmty Sch 1980-83, Plano Ind Sch Dist 1984-89, Fort Bend Ind Sch Dist 1989-; *ai:* Cobblestone Homeowners Assn Pres 1988-89; Plano Ind Sch Dist Strategic Planning Process Action Team Mem 1987; Shepton HS Teacher of Yr 1986; 4th Place St of IA Physics Olympics 1983; 2nd Place St of IA Physics Olympics 1982; *office:* I H Kempner HS PO Box 1004 Sugar Land TX 77487

HOKE, ARDEEN DENISE, Kindergarten Teacher; *b:* Chicago, IL; *m:* Wayne R.; *c:* Jamie, Andrew; *ed:* (BAED) Elem Ed, Northern IL Univ 1974; (MSED) Curr Instruction, Chicago Univ 1982; Admin Certificate; *cr:* Instructional Aide 1974-76, 5th/6th Grade Teacher 1976-81, Kndgtn Teacher 1981- Sch Dist 124; *ai:* Kndgtn Dist Comm; Head Teacher; Chairperson Dist Ed Comm; ASCD 1989-; IFT Local 943 Secy 1987-; IFT Cncl 1250 (Pres 1985-87, VP 1979-80) 1985-; Kirby PTO 1985-; PTA 1974-; Tinley Park Athletic Club 1989-; Honary Life Membership IL Congress of Parents & Teachers; Nom for Kohl Intnl Awd; Outstanding Young Women in Amer 1985.

HOLAK, THOMAS, Social Studies Teacher; *b:* Hillsboro, WI; *m:* Mary C.; *c:* Stacey, Cindy; *ed:* (BA) Soc Stud, Univ of WI Platteville 1964; (MS) Guidance/Counseling, N IL Univ 1970; Learning Disabilities, Natl Coll of Ed 1976; Ec; *cr:* Teacher Jefferson Jr HS 1964-67, Lincoln Jr HS 1967-68, Jefferson Jr HS 1968-70; Cnslr 1970-72, Teacher 1972- Washington Jr HS; *ai:* Chess Club; Ftbl & Bowling Coach; Learner Outcome Comm; NEA, IEA, AEA Sch Rep; Amer Legion; Church Work.

HOLBERT, MARY LOU COLLINS, Retired Teacher; *b:* Waleska, GA; *w:* Gary Lamar (dec); *ed:* (BS) Elem Ed, GA St Coll for Women 1959; (MA) Elem Ed, Atlanta Univ 1972; *cr:* Teacher Glen Haven Elem 1959-64, Atherton Elem 1964-89; *ai:* De Kalb Assn of Educators 1959-89; GA Assn of Educators, NEA 1959-64; *home:* 1477 Montevallo Cir Decatur GA 30033

HOLBROOK, CHARLES D., Mathematics Teacher; *b:* Billings, MT; *m:* Vicki Farrell; *c:* Kyle, Linsey; *ed:* (BA) Ed, Univ of MT 1978; *cr:* Math Teacher Browning Mid Sch 1978-; *ai:* Yrbk Adv; Math Curr Comm; NCTM 1983-; *office:* Browning Mid Sch Box 610 Browning MT 59417

HOLBROOK, HELEN ANDREWS, Mathematics Teacher; *b:* Magnolia, MI; *m:* Adolph A.; *c:* Andre A., Anson A.; *ed:* (BS) Math, Alcorn St Univ 1970; (MS) Math, Univ of S MS 1976; Math & Cmptr Sci Fellowship, FL A&M Univ 1972; M-Teach & M-Reach Project, Univ of S MS 1981, 1985; *cr:* Math Teacher South Pike HS 1970-80; Math Instr Alcorn St Univ 1981-82; Math Teacher South Pike HS 1981-; *ai:* South Pike HS Math Bowl Team Coach; Mu Alpha Theta Spon; Math & Cmptr Sci Fellowship 1972; STAR Teacher 1974, 1984.

HOLBROOK, MARY LOU COFFEY, Coordinator of Gifted/Talented; *b:* Westerly, RI; *m:* Charles P.; *c:* Marc, Allyson; *ed:* (BS) Ed, Cntrl CT St Univ 1960; (MA) Ed, Univ of CT 1963; Wesleyan Univ, Bridgewater St Teachers Coll; *cr:* 5th Grade Teacher Stonington CT; 1st/5th Grade Teacher, 5th-8th Grade Teacher of Gifted & Talented/Visual Art, K-12th Grade Teacher/Coord of Gifted & Talented Thomaston Schls; *ai:* Interdistrict Arts Comm; CT Ed Assn, NEA, Cape Cod Art Assn; Watertown Art League Exec Bd; Thomaston Womens Club (Pres, VP) 1966-67; Thomaston Lib Bd; CT St Celebration of Excl Advisory Bd 1988-, Awd 1988; Outstanding Elem Teachers of America 1974; Exemplary Mid Sch Projects 1990; *home:* 335 Hickory Hill Thomaston CT 06787

HOLBROOK, SHEILA MARY, Jr HS Teacher; *b:* Chicago, IL; *m:* James J. Jr.; *c:* Joy M.; *ed:* (BA) Art, Alverno Coll 1964; *cr:* Art Teacher St Patrick Acad 1964-67; Art Teacher 1971-85, Jr HS Teacher 1985- St Pascal Sch; *ai:* Safety Patrol Supvr; Religious Ed Comm; *office:* St Pascal Sch 6143 W Irving Park Rd Chicago IL 60634

HOLCOMB, ELIZABETH TURNER, English Teacher; *b:* Jackson, MS; *m:* Robert William; *c:* Lisa; *ed:* (BA) Eng, 1966, (MED) Eng, 1990 MS Coll; Real Estate License; Classes in AP Eng & Gifted Ed; *cr:* Teacher Cobb Cty GA 1966-70; Adult Ed Teacher 1977-80; Teacher Cobb Cty GA 1981-88, Jackson Public Schls 1988-; *ai:* Teacher of Advanced Placement Stu; Class Spon; Alpha Delta Kappa (Secy 1980-82, Treas 1983-85); Symphony League; Mellon Grant Advanced Placement Teaching Eng; Outstanding Young Women of America 1979; *home:* 699 Spring Lake Dr Jackson MS 39208

HOLCOMB, KATHY MARIE, Fifth Grade Teacher; *b:* Fremont, OH; *ed:* (BS) Elem Ed, Bowling Green St Univ 1974; Great Books Leader; Counseling Gifted & Talented; *cr:* Teacher St Joseph Elem Sch 1976-; *ai:* Cross Cntry Coach; Quizbowl Moderator; Talent Show & Christmas Play Dir; Art Fair Coord; *office:* St Joseph Elem Sch 716 Croghan St Fremont OH 43420

HOLCOMB, SUE CAGLE, 6th Grade Teacher; *b:* Ozark, AR; *m:* Ron; *c:* Jennifer, Kathryn; *ed:* (AA) Elem Ed, Westark Comm Coll 1980; (BS) Elem Ed, Univ of AR Fayetteville 1982; *cr:* 5th/6th Grade Sci Teacher, 6th Grade Teacher Mountainburg; *ai:* Odyssey of Mind Head Judge; Gifted & Talented Advisory Comm; AR Ed Assn, Natl Teachers Assn 1982-85; Kappa Kappa Iota Secy 1986-; *office:* Mountainburg Elem Sch P O Box 15 Mountainburg AR 72946

HOLDEN, CYNTHIA ANNE, Social Studies Teacher; *b:* Birch Tree, MO; *ed:* (MS) Scndry Admin, Cntrl MO St Univ; *cr:* Teacher Santa Fe HS 1986-; *ai:* Var Ftbl Statistician; 5th/6th Grade Girls Bsktbl Coach; Newspaper, Stu Cncl, Jr HS Cheerleading, Sr Class Spon; NCSS, MO St Teacher Assn 1986-; ASCD 1990; Todays Women of Alma (Secy, Treas) 1986-88; PTO Finance Comm 1986-89; MO Democratic Party 1984-; Little League Coach 1988-89; Learning Facilitator for Constitutional Grant at MO Valley Coll; Participant in US Constitution Seminar & Wkshp; Project STAR Participant; *office:* Santa Fe R-10 HS 108 N Mitchell Alma MO 64001

HOLDEN, NANCY BYRUM, Third Grade Teacher; *b:* Wheeling, WV; *m:* David B. Jr.; *c:* Robert T., Molly E.; *ed:* (BS) Early Chldhd Ed, Davis & Elkins Coll 1979; Grad Work WV Univ; TESA Trng, Project Charlie Trng; *cr:* 4th Grade Teacher Ritchie Elem Sch 1979-81; 4th Grade Teacher 1981-83, 3rd Grade Teacher Bethlehem Primary Sch 1983-; *ai:* Dept Chairperson Bethlehem Primary Sch 1987-; Organize & Participate in Schls Friday Night Prime Time Rdng Celebration; Bethlehem PTA Comm Chairperson 1986-; *office:* Bethlehem Primary Sch 22 Chapel Rd Wheeling WV 26003

HOLDEN, PATSY TUCKER, 6th Grade Teacher; *b:* Dallas, TX; *m:* Robert Lee; *c:* Patrick, Michael, Christopher, Shawn; *ed:* (BS) Elem Ed, 1969, (MAT) Elem Ed, 1974, (MED) Sch Admin 1978 Angelo St Univ; *cr:* 1st Grade Teacher 1969-82, 6th Grade Teacher 1982 Santa Rita Elem Sch ; *ai:* TX St Teachers Assn Campus Rep 1978-79/1981-82; TX St Teachers Assn Bd of Dir 1979-80; NEA Delegate Natl Convention 1980; Fresh Womens Honor Society 1967; Beta Beta Beta 1968; Alpha Chi-1968; Kappa Delta Pi-1968; Whos Who in Amer Coll-1969; Presidential Awd-ASU-1969; Grad Summa Cum Laude 1969; *office:* Santa Rita Elem Sch 615 S Madison San Angelo TX 76901

HOLDEN-MC QUERTER, DANA, 7th & 8th Grade Math Teacher; *b:* Springfield, MO; *m:* James L. Mc Querter; *c:* Wendy, Jennifer; *ed:* (BSED) Elem Ed, SW MO St Univ 1983; Psych & Math Ed; *cr:* Math Teacher Pleasant View Jr HS 1983-; *ai:* Math Club Spon; Mathcounts Coach; Intramural Sports Spon; Textbook Selection Comm for Math, Pre-Algebra, Algebra I; MO St Teachers Assn Prof Rights & Responsibilites Comm; MO St Teachers Assn, Springfield Assn Building Rep 1988-; NEA, NCTM 1989-; *office:* Pleasant View Jr HS Rt 1 Box 401 Springfield MO 65803

HOLDER, AMELIA BABETTE, Bio I/Anatomy Teacher; *b:* Galax, VA; *ed:* (AS) Sci, Lees-Mc Rae Coll 1984; (BA) Bio Ed, Emory & Henny Coll 1987; *cr:* Bio I/II Teacher Grayson Cty HS 1987-; *ai:* SADD, Jr Class, Assoc Thespian Spon; MACC Head; All Around Coach, Athletic Trainer; Southwest VA Assn of Sci Teachers Secy 1988-; VA Assn of Sci Teachers; Grayson Cty Ed Assn.

HOLDER, CAROLYN ADCOCK, Science Research Teacher; *b:* Baltimore, MD; *m:* Duane Milo; *c:* Stefanie; *ed:* (BS) General Sci/His, Univ of Baltimore 1965; (MS) General Sci, FL Inst of Technological 1978; Gifted Sci & His; Peer & Alternative Ed; *cr:* Teacher Cntrl Jr HS 1971-88; Research/Gifted Teacher Southwest Jr HS 1988-; *ai:* Natl Jr Honor Society & Sci Club Spon; FL Assn of Gifted, FL Assn of Sci Teachers; COPE; *office:* Southwest Jr HS 451 Eldron Blvd SE Palm Bay FL 32909

HOLDER, ELAINE THORNTON, 7th Grade Lang Arts Teacher; *b:* Russell Springs, KY; *m:* Huey C.; *ed:* (BS) Eng, Campbellsville Coll 1964; Lib Sci, Eastern KY Univ 1981; *cr:* Eng Teacher Lee Cty HS 1964-65; Bus Teacher Ferguson HS 1965-68; Eng Teacher Ferguson Elem 1968-78, Nancy HS 1978-81, Nancy Jr. HS 1981-87; Lang Arts Teacher Northern Jr. HS 1987-; *ai:* NEA 1964-; KEA 1964-; Pulaski Cty Teachers Assn 1968-; Sunday Sch Chldrns Div Teacher Yr 1983-84; Campbellsville Coll Outstanding Service to Ed Awd 1987; *office:* Northern Jr H S 350 Oak Leaf Ln Somerset KY 42501

HOLDER, LISA DOZIER, Language Arts Instructor; *b:* Mc Alester, OK; *m:* John Todd; *c:* Adam J., Andrew J.; *ed:* (BA) Eng, 1984, (MED) Ed, 1989 NW OK St Univ; Numerous Seminars Various Fields; *cr:* Eng Teacher Sharon-Mutual HS 1984-85, Alva HS 1986-; *ai:* Sch Newspaper & Stu Cncl Spon; Past Girls Tennis Coach; Handbook, Drop Everything, Read Comm; Academic Team Scorekeeper; Alva Classroom Teachers Building Rep 1988-; OEA, NEA 1984-; PEO Chaplain 1986-87; Delta Zeta Alumnae 1984-; N Cntrl Evaluation Team; Alva HS Teacher of Yr 1989-; Stu Cncl Teacher of Month; Channel 5 OK Best Honor Roll; Journalism Class Alva HS Originator 1990; *office:* Alva HS 14th & Flynn Alva OK 73717

HOLDERBAUM, SUZANNE BARTLEY, 4th Grade Teacher; *b:* Akron, OH; *m:* John Henry; *c:* Emily A.; *ed:* (BS) Elem Ed, Akron Univ 1972; Addl Stud Sci Ed, Cmptr Sci Ed, Lib Sci, Kent St Univ; *cr:* 4th Grade Teacher 1972-73, 5th Grade Teacher 1973-74, 6th Grade Teacher 1974-80, 7th/8th Grade Sci/Math/Cmptr Sci Teacher 1980-88 Farmington Local Sch; 4th Grade Teacher Farmington Elem 1988-; *ai:* Cheerleading & Sch Sci Fair Adv; OH Conservation Outdoor Ed, Sci Ed Cncl of OH 1986-; Medina Cty Herb Club Pres 1979-; PTA, PTO; Martha Holden Jennings Scholar; *office:* Farmington Elem Sch 121 N 2nd St West Farmington OH 44491

HOLDERIEATH, EVELYN STONER, Business Teacher; *b:* Marceline, MO; *m:* Harry Jr.; *c:* Alicia, Jason; *ed:* (BSED) Bus Ed, NE MO St Univ 1970; (MSED) Bus Ed, Univ of MO 1977; *cr:* Bus Teacher Northwestern R-1 Sch 1970-; *ai:* NHS Adv; MO St Teachers Assn, MO Voc Assn, MO Bus Ed Assn 1970-; 4-H Club Lucky Star Leader 1987-89, Chariton Cty Family of Yr 1989; *office:* Northwestern R-1 Sch PO Box 43 Mendon MO 64660

HOLDREN, ROBERT EARL, Music Teacher/Department Chair; *b:* Cambridge, MD; *m:* Nancy Parker; *c:* Justin, Ryan; *ed:* (BA) Sacred Music, TN Temple Univ 1976; Grad Stud Pensacola Chrstn Coll; *cr:* Music Teacher Elkton Chrstn Sch 1976-77, Timberlake Chrstn Sch 1977-78, Elkton Chrstn Sch 1978-82; Elem Teacher Odenton Chrstn Sch 1982-84; Music/Eng Teacher Alamance Chrstn Sch 1984-; *ai:* Yrbk Adv; NC Chrstn Act Assn All St Band Chm 1988, 1990; NC Chrstn Educators Assn Convention Wkshp Speaker; *office:* Alamance Chrstn Sch PO Box 838 Town Branch Rd Graham NC 27253

HOLDSHIP, CANDICE KAY (GOLDING), Sixth Grade Teacher; *b:* Bad Axe, MI; *m:* Richard Paul; *c:* Lisa A.; *ed:* (BS) Music/Geography/Phys Ed, Cntrl MI Univ 1971; Grad Stud General Ed; *cr:* 5th Grade Teacher Bad Axe Intermediate Sch 1967; HS Phys Ed Teacher Ubly HS 1968-69; Elem Music/Phys Ed Teacher 1969-71, Elem Grade Teacher 1974- Ubly Elem Sch; *ai:* Safety Patrol Adv; Gifted & Talented Teacher; Academic Track Coach; Piano Player for Sch Prgms; MEA, NEA; Lioness 1989-; Child Study Club 1972-76; *home:* 1900 Mc Taggart Ubly MI 48475

HOLIAN, JACK FRANCIS, Math Teacher; *b:* Waterbury, CT; *m:* Elizabeth; *c:* Kathleen, Robert; *ed:* (BA) Ec, Univ of CT 1969; (MS) Ed, Central CT St Univ 1974; 6th Yr Cert Admin & Supv Southern CT St Univ 1989; *cr:* 6th Grade Teacher 1969-1978, 8th Grade Math Teacher 1979- Lincoln Mid Sch; *ai:* Assn Teachers Math Ct; AFT; Waterbury BPOE Elks Club 1976-.

HOLIDAY, DELORISE REESE, Mathematics Teacher; *b:* Albany, GA; *m:* George; *c:* Jessica M., George A.; *ed:* (BA) Math, 1971, (BS) Math Ed, 1973, (MED) Math Ed, 1987 Albany St Coll; Grad Stud Univ of AL; *cr:* Teacher Tift Cty Bd of Ed 1971-72, Dooly Cty Bd of Ed 1972-73, Dougherty Cty Bd of Ed 1974-; *ai:* Mathcounts Regional Coach 1988-89; NEA, GA Assn of Educators, Dougherty Cty Assn of Educators; 1st Bethesda Baptist Church Primary Class Sunday Sch Asst Teacher 1988-; *home:* 2514 Calvary Rd Albany GA 31707

HOLIDAY, VIVIAN WHISNANT, English Teacher/Dept Chair; *b:* Sumter, SC; *m:* Duncan D. Jr.; *c:* Jason D., Philip H.; *ed:* (BA) Eng, Lander Coll 1971; *cr:* Teacher Ware Shoals HS 1971-72, Jefferson Davis Acad 1976-78; Teacher/Dept Chairperson Barnwell HS 1978-; *ai:* SCEA, NEA; *office:* Barnwell HS Jackson St Barnwell SC 29812

HOLIFIELD, TERRY LYNN, Biology Teacher; *b:* Laurel, MS; *m:* Sylvia Flowers; *c:* Shelley, Kelsey; *ed:* (BS) Bio, 1969, (MS) Sci Ed, 1976 Univ of Southern MS; *cr:* Teacher West Jones HS 1969-74, Laurel City Schls 1974-78, NE Jones HS 1982-; *home:* Rt 1 Box 225 A Ellisville MS 39437

HOLLADAY, ANNE BOUKNIGHT, Social Studies Dept Chair; *b:* Memphis, TN; *m:* Charles H. Jr.; *c:* James S., Erin M.; *ed:* (BA) Theater/Speech, Columbia Coll 1970; Admin & Supervision, Winthrop Coll; *cr:* Latin/Drama Teacher Hughes Jr HS 1970-71; Soc Stud Teacher 1971-73, Teacher/His Dept Chairperson 1973-79 Bennettsville HS; Drama/His Teacher S Florence HS 1979-83; Psych Teacher Lancaster HS 1983; Drama/His Teacher Great Falls Mid Sch 1983-; *ai:* Sch Yrbk Adv; 8th Grade & Drama Club Spon; Homecoming Coord; Faculty Cncl Chm; NEA, SCEA, CCEA 1984-; Soc Stud Cncl 1988-; SC Theater Assn Bd Mem 1984-89; Palmetto Dramatic Assn (VP, Adjudicator) 1978, 1986; Outstanding Teacher of Yr 1985, 1990;

Jaycees Outstanding Young Educator 1971; Outstanding Young Women of America 1975; *office:* Great Falls Mid Sch 850 Chester Hwy Great Falls SC 29055

HOLLADAY, BETTY PHILLIPS, Kindergarten Teacher; *b:* Haskell, TX; *m:* Grover Cleveland Jr.; *c:* Freddie Holladay Duree, Joe, Kerry, Thomas; *ed:* (BS) Phys Ed, Hardin Simmons 1953; Kndgtn Cert 1970; *cr:* HS Sci Teacher 1953-54, 1963-64, 3rd Grade Teacher 1964-69, 1st Grade Teacher 1969-74, Kndgtn Teacher 1974- Buena Vista Ind Sch Dist; *ai:* HS Girls Vlybl 1953-54 & Jr HS Vlybl 1966-67 Coach; TSTA Pres 1968-69; ATEP VP 1989-; *home:* Box 281 Imperial TX 79743

HOLLAN, SHERRY ANN, 8th Grade Math/Sci/Eng Teacher; *b:* Poteau, OK; *m:* Jeffrey Allen; *c:* Rocky A., Tara A.; *ed:* (BA) Lang Art/Elem Ed, Southeastern St Univ 1973; Working Towards Masters; *cr:* Teacher Howe Public Sch 1973-74, Wister Public Sch 1974-; *ai:* 8th Grade Mathcounts Team; Staff Dev Comm; OK Ed Assn, NEA, CTA; *office:* Wister Public Schls Box 489 Wister OK 74966

HOLLAND, CAROLYN CERNOSEK, 1st Grade Teacher; *b:* Shiner, TX; *m:* Homer M.; *c:* Keith Jacobs, Justin Jacobs; *ed:* (BA) Elem Ed, TX A&I Univ 1963; (MS) Rdng Speclst, Pan Amer Univ 1983; Gifted Ed Univ of TX; *cr:* 3rd Grade Teacher Flato Elem Sch 1963-65; Robert E Lee Elem Sch 1966-70; 2nd Grade Teacher 1965-66; Kndgtn Teacher 1971-72 Lamar Elem; 1st Grade Teacher Austin Elem 1976-; *ai:* UIL Elem Coach; Hospitality Comm; Harlingen Proud Sch Comm; TX St Teachers Assn 1963-; Intnl Rdng Assn 1989-; Kappa Delta Pi 1983-; TX Assn Gifted/Talented 1984-; PTA (Historian/V Pres/Secy 1963-); Beta Sigma Phi (Pres/V Pres/Secy/Treas 1965-); Sweetheart Girl of Yr; Quarterback Club Bd of Dir 1986-89; *office:* Austin Elem Sch 700 E Austin St Harlingen TX 78550

HOLLAND, CONNIE ENYART, Social Studies Dept Chair; *b:* Pryor, OK; *m:* Dick J.; *c:* Chad; *ed:* (BA) His, Northeastern St Univ 1973; Art Criminal Justice Juvenile, Impart Chemical Abuse Counseling & Prevention, Teachers Rights, Negotiating, Sch Finance; *cr:* His/Art Teacher Chouteau-Mazie Mid Sch 1973-85; His Teacher 1985-88, Soc Stud Dept Chairperson/His Teacher 1988- Chouteau-Mazie HS; *ai:* Sr Class & St Honor Society Spon; Impact-Drug Awareness Counseling; Soc Stud Dept Chairperson; OK Ed Assn Legislative Contact 1989-; NEA, Chouteau Mazie Ed Assn, OK Cncl for Ec; Phi Alpha Theta, Amer Quarter Horse Assn, Alaskan Malamute Club of America; Whos Who in Amer Women Nom; *office:* Chouteau-Mazie HS P O Box 969 Chouteau OK 74337

HOLLAND, DAVID JOSEPH, Assistant Manager; *b:* Perryville, MO; *ed:* (BS) Elem Ed, Semo St Univ 1976; *cr:* Learning Disabilities Instr 1977-78, 1st Grade Teacher 1978-89 Washington Sch Dist; *home:* PO Box 24 Saint Marys MO 63673

HOLLAND, ELIZABETH GRIFFIN, Retired Teacher; *b:* Chilocco, OK; *m:* James M.; *c:* James Jr., Thomas W., Mary Holland Carpenter; *ed:* (BS) His/Span, Coll of Charleston 1949; (MED) Elem Admin, Univ of SC 1975; *cr:* Teacher Aiken Cty Sch Dist 1970-89; *home:* 1915 Pisgah Rd North Augusta SC 29841

HOLLAND, GEOFFREY CRAIG, History Department Chairman; *b:* Carlinville, IL; *m:* Amelia Allen; *c:* Jennifer, Diane; *ed:* (BA) His, 1967, (MAED) His, 1968 AZ St Univ; *cr:* 7th/8th Grade Teacher San Benito Cty Office of Ed 1968; Frosh His Teacher Gavilan Jr Coll 1968-69; 8th Grade US His Teacher Hollister Sch Dist 1968-; *ai:* His Dept Chm; Mem Dist Soc Stud Comm; CTA Head Negotiator; CA Teachers Assn (Pres, Negotiator) 1970-, We Honor Ours Awd 1981; Hollister Elem Teacher Assn (Pres, Negoiator) 1968-69; BPOE Elks (Pres, Trustee 1983-89, Dist Youth Act Chm 1988-), Ritual Winner 1987; San Benito Republicans Mem Cent Comm 1970-76; San Benito Cty Soc Stud Cncl Mem 1988-89, Framework Conf Coord 1988-89; CA Directory Instrs of Gifted Studs; *office:* Rancho San Justo Mid Sch 1201 Rancho Dr Hollister CA 95023

HOLLAND, JAN CRUMP, 4th Grade Teacher; *b:* Toccoa, GA; *m:* Roy Edwin; *c:* Eddie, Chuck, Walt; *ed:* Music Ed, Young Harris Coll 1973; (BM) Music Ed, Univ of GA 1976, (MED) Elem Ed 1977, (EDS) Early Chldhd Ed Univ of GA; *cr:* Teacher Lavonia Elem 1977-90; *ai:* Church Organist-1st Baptist Church; Delta Kappa Gamma 1988-; Page 1982-; PTO Pres 1988-89; *office:* Lavonia Elem Sch Hartwell Rd Lavonia GA 30553

HOLLAND, JAN IVES, Biology Teacher; *b:* Dallas, TX; *m:* Jimmy; *ed:* (AS) Health/Phys Ed, Navarro Coll 1977; (BS) Health/Phys Ed, TX A&M Univ 1979; Graduate Courses, East TX St Univ; *cr:* Phys Ed Teacher Ehrhardt Elem 1979-80; Life Sci/Athletics Teacher Agnew Mid Sch 1980-81; Phys Ed Teacher Episcopal Day Sch 1981-82; Bio Teacher Rockwall HS 1982-; *ai:* Chrldr & Natural Helpers Spon; Girls Athletic Coach; ATPE Mem; *office:* Rockwall H S 1201 High School Rd Rockwall TX 75087

HOLLAND, JEFFREY DEAN, Spanish Teacher; *b:* Winston-Salem, NC; *ed:* (BA) Eng, Campbell Univ 1979; Span Courses; Grad Stud Journalism, CBN Univ; *cr:* Eng/Span Teacher James Wood HS 1980-81, Temple Chrstn Sch 1987-; *ai:* Annual Adv 1987-; *home:* 717 Dogwood Ln Rockingham NC 28379

HOLLAND, KAREN LYNN, History Teacher; *b:* Jonesboro, AR; *ed:* (BA) Poly Sci, 1973, (MAT) His, 1974 Harding Univ; Advanced Academic Trng Region X Ed Service Center; *cr:* Eng/His Teacher Dallas Chrstn HS 1975-; His Teacher Sunnyvale Ind Sch Dist 1980-; *ai:* Vlybl Coach 1984-; Sunnyvale Ed Assn (VP 1989-, Treas 1984-85, Concessions 1990); Bible Credit Teachers Assn 1986-88; Level 3/Career Ladder for Outstanding TX Teachers; *office:* Sunnyvale Ind Sch Dist 417 Tripp Rd Sunnyvale TX 75182

HOLLAND, LINDA WESTFALL, Sixth Grade Teacher; *b:* Tryon, OK; *m:* Lonnie D.; *c:* Gregory; *ed:* (BS) Elem Ed, Cntrl St Univ 1974; Advanced Skills Adolescence Quest Intnl; *cr:* Nursery Sch Teacher DOD Sch System 1975-77; 5th Grade Teacher 1978-85, 6th Grade Teacher 1986- Choctaw Elem Sch; *ai:* Daily OK Pee Wee Spelling Bee, 5th & 6th Grade Spelling Bee, Choctaw Elem Sci Fair Coord; Skills for Adolescence Teacher; Delta Kappa Gamma Initiation Chm 1986-; Choctaw/NP ACT Building Rep; *office:* Choctaw Elem Sch 14667 N E 3rd Choctaw OK 73020

HOLLAND, MARK ROBERT, Mathematics Teacher; *b:* Long Beach, CA; *m:* Gita Satyendra; *ed:* (BA) Psych, Chapman Coll 1975; *cr:* Teacher Paramount HS 1979-; *ai:* CA Quality Educator 1987; *office:* Paramount HS 14429 S Downey Ave Paramount CA 90723

HOLLARS, ANN MOODY, Media Librarian; *b:* Hattiesburg, MS; *m:* Roger G.; *c:* Sam, Amanda H.; *ed:* (BS) Elem Ed/Eng, Cumberland Coll 1966; (MA) Elem Ed/Rdng, E KY Univ; (Rank I) Elem Ed, W KY Univ; *cr:* Remedial Rdng Teacher 1966-72, 2nd Grade Teacher 1974-88 Burnside Elem Media Librarian Northern Pulaski Jr HS 1989-; *ai:* 9th Grade Academic Team Coach; Sch PR Person; PCEA, KEA, NEA 1966-; IRA 1966-72; KSMA, KLA, ALA, AALl 1989; *office:* Northern Pulaski Jr HS 350 Oak Leaf Ln Somerset KY 42501

HOLLARS, ROGER G., School Counselor; *b:* Tateville, KY; *m:* Ann Moody; *c:* Sam, Amanda; *ed:* (BS) Elem Ed, Cumberland Coll 1966; (MA) Guidance/Counseling, E KY Univ 1968; (Rank I) Guidance/Counseling, W KY Univ 1978; *cr:* Teacher Pulaski Cty HS 1966-68; Cnslr Burnside HS 1968-87, Pulaski Southern Jr HS 1987-; *ai:* Girls Bsktbl Coach; KY Assn of Counseling Dev; Mid-Cumberland Assn of Counseling Dev Pres Elect 1990-91; Burnside Meth Church (Trustee, Chm of Church Bd); Burnside Municipal Waterworks Bd Mem.

HOLLDORF, CHERYLL NOVOTNY, Fifth Grade; *b:* Rice Lake, WI; *m:* Merwyn; *c:* Jeffrey, Carrie; *ed:* (BS) Elem Ed, Univ of WI River Falls 1973; *cr:* Elem Teacher Omaha Cath Schls 1964-67, Glenwood City Public Schls 1967-; *ai:* Elem Yrbk Adv; NEA, WI Ed Assn 1967-; West Cntrl Ed Assn Building Rep 1990; *office:* Glenwood City Elem Sch 3rd & Oak Glenwood City WI 54013

HOLLENBECK, BONNIE MORRIS, Language Art Teacher; *b:* Carlsbad, NM; *c:* Heather, Kathryn; *ed:* (BA) Elem Ed, Cntrl CT St Univ 1967; *cr:* 5th Grade Teacher Carl Ben Eilson 1967-68; Rdng Specialist Ben Franklin 1969-70; Supvr Stu Teachers Univ of ND Grand Forks 1976-78; 5th/6th Grade Lang Art Teacher Convent of Visitation 1978-; *ai:* Network; MO Schls E2 Officio Mem Visitation Bd of Dir & Finance Comm; Faculty Negotiation & Educl Equity Diversity Comm; Intnl Rdng Assn; Jr League of St Paul Exec Bd 1974-80; House of Hope Presbyn Church Deacon 1976-; Teacher Rep Christopher Columbus Celebration Natl Comm; Nom Ashland Oil Teacher Awd; *office:* Convent of Visitation 2455 Visitation Dr Mendota Heights MN 55120

HOLLENBECK, JAN K., Jr High Math Teacher; *b:* Battle Creek, MI; *ed:* (BS) Elem Ed, Western MI Univ 1965; Drivers Ed; *cr:* 6th Grade Teacher Mendon Elem 1965-75; 7th-8th Grade Math Teacher Mendon Jr/Sr HS 1975-; *ai:* 7th-12th Grade Class Spon; X Cntry, Girls Sftbl, JV Bsbl, 7th-9th Bsktbl Coach; Ski Club Spon; Vicksburg Fire Dept Treas 1965- 20 Yr Awd 1985; *home:* 112 S Michigan Ave Vicksburg MI 49097

HOLLEY, MARY SHAW, English Department Chair; *b:* Gulfport, MS; *m:* E. Joseph; *c:* Andrea; *ed:* (BS) Eng, 1971, (MS) Eng/Amer Lit, 1974 Univ of S MS; Inst for Advanced Placement, Millsaps Coll; MS Teacher Assessment Instruments Evaluator; *cr:* Eng Teacher Harrison Cntrl HS 1971-; Eng/Adjunct Teacher/Faculty MS Gulf Coast Comm Coll 1974-; *ai:* Self Study Exec Steering Comm; MA Cncl of Eng Teachers 1989-; Eastern Star 1969-; *office:* Harrison Cntrl HS 15600 School Rd Gulfport MS 39503

HOLLEY, MILDRED NORRIS, High School Teacher; *b:* Heflin, LA; *w:* Merrel T. (dec); *c:* Merrel T. Jr., Verna M.; *ed:* (BS) Health/Phys Ed, Northwestern St Univ 1941; (MS) Health/Phys Ed, LA St Univ 1948; Numerous Courses; *cr:* Teacher/Coach Cross Roads Jr HS 1941-43, Cotton Valley HS 1943-57; Teacher Bossier HS 1958-61, Berwick Elem Sch 1962-70; Asst Prin Bayou Vista Elem Sch 1970-76;Teacher Berwick HS 1976-77, Holy Cross Elem 1977-83; Teacher/Asst Admin Immanuel Chrstn Sch 1984-; *ai:* HS Admin; Guidance Cnslr; HS & Jr HS Coord; Prof Teachers Organizations (Mem, Parish Pres, St Chairmanships); Kappa Delta Pi 1939-; Epsilon Sigma Alpha (Pres, Various Offices 1974-76, 1984-87, Secy 1988-), Girl of Yr 1979, 5 Yr Perfect Attendance 1979; AARP; 1st Baptist Church Berwick Sunday Sch Teacher 1960; Everett Berry Lighthouse Museum Comm Secy 1988-; Various Newsletter Publications; Assortment Poetry Contest Awds; Ford Fnd Grant 1948; *home:* 11 Carolyn St Morgan City LA 70380

HOLLIDAY, BARBARA GAYLE OVERBY, 5th Grade Teacher; *b:* Sumter, SC; *M:* Louis A.; *c:* Louis A. III; Jeffrey L. Overby; *ed:* (BA) Health/Phys/Recreation/Bio, Lander Coll 1961; Univ of SC; *cr:* Teacher Alice Drive Jr HS 1961-62; Willou Gray Opportunity Sch 1962-69; Shell Point Elem Sch 1969-70; BriadRriver Elem Sch 1970-; *ai:* Academic Challenge Coach 1985-; Supt Cabinet 1989-; Oratory Contest Spon; Low Ctry Rdng Cncl 1987-; S Edng Assn 1987-; Intl Rdng Assn 1987-; Alpha Delta Kappa Treas 1969-; Rdng Teacher of Yr 1988; Teacher of Yr Broad River Elem 1988-89; *home:* 13005 Melton St Burton SC 29902

HOLLIDAY, DIANE JONES, English Teacher; *b:* Philadelphia, PA; *m:* Charles A.; *c:* Sheantai A. R., Charles T. Q.; *ed:* (BA) Eng/Span, Tuskegee Univ 1973; *cr:* Teacher Sch Dist of Philadelphia 1974-; *ai:* Var Cheerleading Coach; 9th Grade Yrbk & Club UNO Spon; 9th Grade & HS Renewal Comm; Philadelphia Bus Acad Team & 8th Grade Baccalaureate Comm Mem; Black Womens Educl Alliance 1983-; Swing Phi Swing Pres 1988-; Twigs Incorporated; ARCO Excl & Achievement in Teaching; Semi-Finalist Teacher of Yr 1988-.

HOLLIDAY, ROBERT DOC, World History/Cultures Teacher; *b:* Houston, TX; *c:* Heather, Michael; *ed:* (AA) Liberal Art/Theology, Concordia Coll 1958; (BS) Scndry Ed/Soc Sci, WA Univ 1966; (MS) Scndry Ed & Admin Curr, Univ S CA 1969; *cr:* Elem Teacher Markus & Bethesda 1960-66; Soc Sci Teacher Intnl Sch Hong Kong 1970-72, Lutheran HS 1966-70, 1972-79, Lutheran HS South 1979-; *ai:* Boys Ftbl, Bsktbl, Bsbl Coach; Stu Mock Trials Competition, World His Quiz Bowl Spon; Traveled 27 Countries; *office:* Lutheran HS South 9515 Tesson Ferry Dr Saint Louis MO 63123

HOLLIMAN, SHERRY RAINEY, K-12th Grade Resource Teacher; *b:* Chicago, IL; *m:* Gary Lynn; *c:* Jerem G. Rainey; *ed:* (BSE) Elem, 1977, (MSE) Elem/Rdng Specialist, 1989 ATU Russellville; Spec Ed, UCA; *cr:* 3rd/4th Combined Grade Teacher Perry-Casa Public Schls 1977-; *ai:* 10th Grade Spon; AEA, NEA; Casa Baptist Church; *home:* Rt 1 Box 183 Casa AR 72025

HOLLINGER, CURTIS L., Director of Bands; *b:* Blakely, GA; *m:* Earlene Walker; *c:* Curtis Jr.; *ed:* (Bs) Music Ed, AL St Univ 1966; (MMED) Music Ed, Vander Cook Coll of Music 1972; *cr:* Dir of Bands Lamar Cty HS 1966-72, George Washington Carver HS 1972-; *ai:* Dir of Marching/Symphonic Bands; AL Ed Assoc; NEA; Music Ed Natl Conference; AL Bandmasters Assn; Montgomery Co Educators Assoc; Montgomery Sym Orch Prin Clarinet 1984-; Omega Psi Phi; Pi Kappa Lambda; Kappa Kappa Ksi.

HOLLINGER, MARTHA REESE, Mathematics Teacher; *b:* Hatcher, GA; *m:* Alfred; *ed:* (BA) Eng/Math, FL A&M Univ 1964; (MA) Curr/Instruction, Univ of N CO 1972; *cr:* Math Teacher/Chairperson Edison Mid Sch 1967-72; Math TSA North Cntrl Area Office 1972-73; Math Teacher Norland Mid Sch 1973-; *ai:* Dade Cty Teacher of Math Bd Mem 1984-85; FL Teacher of Math; NC Teachers of Math; Dade Cty & St of FL Author of Sample Tests of Basic Skills & Stans of Excl; *office:* Norland Mid Sch 1235 NW 192 Terr Miami FL 33169

HOLLINGSHEAD, BRUCE LEROY, Social Studies Teacher; *b:* Hagerstown, MD; *m:* Elizabeth Anne Hall; *c:* Wendy E.; *ed:* (BA) His/Poly Sci, Bridgewater Coll 1976; *cr:* Soc Stud Teacher Buffalo Gap HS 1976-84; Asst Pastor/Teacher Trinity Chrstn Schls 1984-87; Soc Stud Teacher Buffalo Gap HS 1987-; *ai:* Asst Ftbl, Jr Var Ftbl & Track Coach; Trinity Church (Asst Pastor, Minister 1986) License to Preach; Word Ministries Magazine Ed 1989; *home:* 204 Broad St Bridgewater VA 22812

HOLLINGSHEAD, CHERYL RODGERS, Sci Dept Chairperson-Teacher; *b:* Fort Smith, AR; *c:* Jess, Jackie; *ed:* (BS) Bio/Math, Ouachita Baptist Univ 1966; (MSE) Bio/Ed, Henderson St Univ 1979; (EDD) Ed/Sci, East TX St Univ 1992; P E T; Natl US Forest Service Facilitator Trng; Co-operative Learning; Wild Facilitator & Learning Tree Facilitator Trng; Assertive Discipline; *cr:* Sci/Math Teacher & Dept Chairperson Lake Hamilton Jr HS 1972-; Consultant on Text Books Silver Burdette & Addison-Wesley 1987-; Gen Bio/A&P Instr 1988-89, Fundamental Math Instr 1990 Garland Cty Comm Coll; *ai:* Chairperson Regional Sci Fair; Bd Dir AR St Sci Fair; AR St Curr Standards Comm; Dist Textbook Adoption Comm; NSTA 1980-Newmast Pres Awd 1987; AR Sci Teacher Assn 1980- Excl Math, Sci 1990; AFT; ASCD; Soil Conservation Service Volunteer 1986- Volunteer of Yr 1989; Ouachita Childrens Center 1985-87 Volunteer of Yr 1986; Audubon Society Eagle Watch Volunteer 1986-89 Special Awd Eagle Awareness 1987; U S Soil Conservation Service Top 5 Env Ed Prgm; 1st Natl Bank Math & Sci Cmptr Network; Southwestern Bell Math & Sci Cmptr Bulletin Bd; AR Math & Sci Leadership Conference Presenter; Natl Sci Teacher Assn; Astronomy Workbook Elem & Jr HS Teachers; *office:* Lake Hamilton Jr H S 105 N Wolf Dr Pearcy AR 71964

HOLLINGSWORTH, DORIS WALKER, 5th Grade Teacher; *b:* Montgomery, LA; *m:* Millard; *c:* Malcolm T., Marvin D.; *ed:* (BA) Elem Ed, Grambling Coll 1961; Northwestern St Univ & LA Tech Univ; *cr:* Teacher New Enterprise Sch 1961-78, Atlanta HS 1979-89; *ai:* Pleasant Hill BC Financial Coord; LA Ed Assn, NEA; Teacher of Yr Atlanta Elem 1986, 1988; Dean of Ed Baptist Assn Grant.

HOLLIS, JIMMIE ANNETTE HICKS, Second Grade Teacher; *b:* Madisonville, TX; *m:* William Darrell; *c:* Kathryn D. Scamardo, Lori L. Brandes; *ed:* (BS) Elem Ed, Univ of Houston 1960; *cr:* 2nd Grade Teacher Pasadena Ind Sch Dist 1960-75, Sealy Ind Sch Dist 1975-; *ai:* Assn of TX Prof Educators; Delta Kappa Gamma Society Intnl; First Baptist Church Mem 1975-; *office:* Selman Elem Sch 1741 Hwy 90 W Sealy TX 77474

HOLLIS, JOYCE EILEEN, English Teacher; *b:* Council Bluffs, IA; *m:* Ronald L.; *c:* Jason, Jeff; *ed:* (BS) Eng, Univ of NE Lincoln 1967; (MA) Scndry Ed, 1982, (MA) Elem Ed, 1985 N AZ Univ; Natl Endowment for Inst in Hum, N AZ Univ, 1984 & 1988; Teacher Residency Pilot Prgm, N AZ Univ; *cr:* Eng Teacher Lincoln East HS 1967-69, Univ of NE Extension 1969-70, Mohave Comm Coll 1974-76, Lake Havasu HS 1976-; *ai:* Stu Government Adv; Dist #1 Needs Analysis Task Force Dept Chairperson; Phi Kappa Phi 1982-; Phi Delta Kappa Delegate 1988-; Alpha Delta Kappa Pres 1990-; NCTE; Beta Sigma Phi City Cncl Pres 1989-; Lake Havasu Dist #1 Teacher of Yr 1988; Lake Havasu HS Teacher Of Yr 1979; *home:* 2550 Calypso Dr Lake Havasu City AZ 86403

HOLLIS, JUNE DAVIDSON, Social Studies Dept Chair; *b:* Jackson, MS; *m:* L. Wendell Jr.; *c:* Scott, Mark, Drew; *ed:* (BS) His/Eng, Univ of S MS 1965; (MED) Ed/His, MS St Univ 1979; Grad Work Geography; *cr:* Teacher Florence Jr HS 1965-68, Chastain Jr HS 1968-73, Pearl Jr HS 1980-82, Brandon HS 1982-; *ai:* Soc Stud Chm; Faculty Fund Comm; Jr Historical Society Spon; MS Prof Educators; MS Cncl of Soc Stud Dist Contact Person; NCSS; MS & AL Geography Alliances Teacher Consultant; Crossgates Baptist Church; MS Rep AL Geography Inst; AL Geography Alliance, Natl Geographic Society Teacher Consultant; Whos Who in MS; MS Rep Natl Geography Inst; *office:* Brandon HS 408 S College St Brandon MS 39042

HOLLIS, PEGGY D., Principal; *b:* Thomaston, GA; *m:* Charles B. IV; *c:* Randy Moody Jr., Josh Moody; *ed:* (BA) ECE, Wesleyan Coll 1979; (MED) ECE, GA Coll 1984; (EDS) Admin/Supervision, Univ of GA 1989; Data Collector; *cr:* K-4 Teacher 1979-86, Asst Prin 1983-86 W B Redding Sch; Asst Prin Union Elem Sch 1986-88; Prin Taylor Sch 1988-; *ai:* Delta Kappa Gamma 1988; ASCD; Phi Kappa Phi; Phi Delta Kappa; Outstanding Young Teacher of Yr 1986; *office:* Rosa Taylor Elem Sch 2976 Crestline Dr Macon GA 31204

HOLLOMAN, ANNA RUTH MINTER, Mathematics/Science Teacher; *b:* Charleston, WV; *m:* Richard M.; *c:* Richard M. (dec), Beverly L.; *ed:* (BS) Bus Admin, WV ST Coll 1951; *cr:* Teacher Bishop Healy Sch, De Porres Sch, St Roses Sch, Visitation Sch; *ai:* Math League Coach.

HOLLOMAN, MARY ALICE JACKSON, Mathematics Dept Chairman; *b:* Ripley, MS; *w:* John H. (dec); *c:* Myna; *ed:* (BA) Math, 1945, (MA) Math, 1970 MUW; *cr:* Teacher Jonesboro AR 1946-48, Amory HS 1951-53, S D Lee HS 1953-58; Math Chm/Teacher S D Lee HS 1971-; *ai:* MO Alpha Theta; Math Team Spon; NEA, MAE, CEA; Columbus Jr Auxiliary Pres 1967-68; Columbus Chamber of Commerce, Woman of Yr 1967; STAR Teacher 1988-; *office:* S D Lee HS 1815 Military Rd Columbus MS 39701

HOLLON, DOROTHY MARIE (KEARNS), Third Grade Teacher; *b:* Brookfield, MO; *m:* Floyd Curtis; *c:* Tony C., Joyce A. Blattner, Marilyn M. Olmstead, Kevin G., Lisa K. Hilsabeck, Verl R., Floyd C. Jr.; *ed:* (BS) Voc Home Ec/Phys Ed/Elem Grades, NE MO St Univ 1957, 1976; *cr:* Voc Home Ec Teacher Denmark HS 1957-58; Phys Ed/Home Ec Teacher Northwestern HS 1961-63; Home Ec Teacher Linneus HS 1964-65; Voc Home Ec Teacher Putnam Cty R-1 1966-67; 3rd Grade Elem Teacher Milan C-2 Sch 1975-; *ai:* Alpha Phi Sigma Master Mem, Colhecon, Womans Athletic Assn, Future Teachers of America 1953-57; Alpha Delta Kappa 1988; Pi Kappa Sigma (Secy, Treas) 1953-57; 4 1st Place Table Tennis Trophies; 1st Place Sftbl Pitching Awd; *home:* RR 2 Milan MO 63556

HOLLOWAY, AMARYLLIS BARBER, Retired Elem Music Teacher; *b:* Lincoln, NE; *d:* Roy; *c:* Jane Garfield, Peggy Hoyvocks, Steve; *ed:* (BM) Applied Music/Voice, NE Weslyan 1948; (MM) Music Ed, Univ of NE Lincoln 1970; Numerous Wkshps in Ed Through Music; *cr:* Music/Eng Teacher Fairbury Jr HS 1948-51; Elem Music Teacher Fairbury Grade Schls 1957-60; Vocal Music Teacher Fairbury Jr HS 1966-70; Elem Music Teacher Fairbury Grade Schls 1970-89; *ai:* 6th Grade Ensembles; PTA Life Membership; NE St Music Educators, Natl Music Educators Assn, NEA; Fairbury Area Cmmty Theater; Daughters of Amer Revolution; Order of Eastern Star; Delta Kappa Gamma; Church Choir (Chrstn Dir 1950-75, Presbyn Dir 1978-89).

HOLLOWAY, JANE CROW, Language Arts Teacher; *b:* Macon, GA; *m:* Watson L.; *c:* Ian, David, Noel, Shane, Sarah; *ed:* (BA) Eng, Mercer Univ 1970; *cr:* Lang Art Teacher Glynn Mid Sch 1984-; *office:* Glynn Cty Mid Sch 901 George St Brunswick GA 31520

HOLLOWAY, JUNE FRENCH, Fifth Grade Teacher; *b:* Holdenville, OK; *m:* Philip L.; *ed:* (BA) Ed, OK City Univ 1962; *cr:* 4th-6th Grade Teacher OK City Sch System 1962-72; 5th Grade Teacher Heritage Hall Sch 1972-; *ai:* Alpha Delta Kappa 1965-; *office:* Heritage Hall Sch 1401 N W 115th St Oklahoma City OK 73114

HOLLOWAY, LINDA MORGAN, Math/Computer Teacher; *b:* Whittier, CA; *m:* Gary Cook; *c:* Theresa, Kenneth; *cr:* Math Teacher Amador HS 1963-65; Math/Comp Dublin HS 1976-; *ai:* Sch Site Cncl; CA Schlrsp Fed Adv; Teacher Assn Rep; Natl Comp Cont Est Coach; CA Math Cncl 1976-; Cmptr UserEducators; Valley Teachers Assn; CA Teacher Assn 1976-; Teacher Leader for Supercomputers Honors Prgm at Lawrence Livermore Natl Lab; *office:* Dublin H S 8151 Village Pkwy Dublin CA 94568

HOLLOWAY, RAMONA CARLOCK, Mathematics Teacher; *b:* Little Rock, AR; *m:* Paul Ernest; *c:* Justin, Jerrod; *ed:* (BA) Math, Hendrix Coll 1968; Cmptrs, AR St Univ & Cntrl St Univ; *cr:* Math Teacher Keiser HS 1969-70, Harrisburg HS 1970-73, Humphrey HS 1973-74, De Valls Bluff HS 1984-87, Des Arc HS 1987-; *ai:* Sr Class Spon; Personnel Policy Comm Mem; AR Ed Assn 1989-; Des Arc Ed Assn 1988; Teacher of Yr Des Arc HS 1988; *home:* Rt 1 Box 102 Des Arc AR 72040

HOLLOWAY, SHARON SOSSAMON, Vocational Business Teacher; *b:* Fort Smith, AR; *m:* David; *ed:* (MS) Bus Ed/Jr Coll Teaching, 1987, (BS) Bus Ed, 1980 Northeastern St Univ; Shorthand & Cmptr Courses Tulsa Jr Coll; *cr:* Voc Bus Teacher Pawhuska HS 1982-; *ai:* FBLA Adv; Chrldr Spon; Bus Dept Curr Chairperson; OK Ed Assn 1982-; Ok Voc Assn 1982-; Pawhuska Ed Assn 1982-; Delta Zeta Alumnus 1980-; Tau Beta Sigma Alumnus 1980-; Helped Asst Supvr in Writing Cmptr Grants for Sch; *office:* Pawhuska H S 1505 Lynn Pawhuska OK 74056

HOLLOWAY, WILLIE MAE (SMITH), Government/History Teacher; *b:* Natchez, MS; *m:* Robert Allen; *ed:* (BS) Poly Sci, Alcorn St Univ 1970; (MS) Psych, Our Lady of Lake Univ 1989; Counseling; *cr:* Teacher Central HS 1970-71, Holmes HS 1977-; *ai:* Spon Afro-Amer Club; Government Textbook Comm; Self-Help, At-Risk & Cmmty Groups; ATPE 1987-; Earth Day Spon 1990; Youth Group Leader 1988-; At-Risk Spon 1988-; Univ of TX Outstanding HS 1989; Wrote Paper on AT-Risk Stus Ins & Outs; *home:* 2510 Fairburn San Antonio TX 78228

HOLLOWAY, WOMACK, Social Studies Dept Chair; *b:* Fayetteville, TN; *m:* Fred O.; *c:* Justin, Aaron; *ed:* (BS) Scndry Ed/Psych/His, Univ of TN Knoxville 1978; (MA) Admin/Supervision, TN St Univ 1982; *cr:* 6th Grade Teacher Flintville Elem 1978-79; 7th Grade His Teacher Cntrl Jr HS 1979-81; 9th Grade Civics/World Geography Teacher Cntrl Jr HS 1982-; *ai:* Annual, Homecoming, 9th Grade Spon; Mem Sch Improvement Comm; Lincoln Cty Ed Assn 1979-; Lincoln CoEd Assn Rep 1983-84; TN Ed Assn 1979-; Served on Soc Stud Curr Cncl of TN 1989-; *office:* Cntrl Jr HS 900 S Main Ave Fayetteville TN 37334

HOLLOWELL, ELAINE F., 6th Grade English Teacher; *b:* Bound Brook, NJ; *m:* Herbert G.; *c:* Merrill H. Hutchinson, H. Gordon, Matthew S.; *ed:* (BA) Eng, MI St Univ 1957; Cert Ed Courses Scndry Ed, Rutgers Univ 1958; *cr:* 9th/10th Grade Eng Teacher Bound Brook HS 1958-59; 7th-8th Grade Eng Teacher Middlesex HS 1959-61; 8th Grade Eng Teacher 1983-89, 6th Grade Eng Teacher 1989- Readington Mid Sch; *ai:* End of Yr Act Class Trip & Dinner Dance Class Adv; Parent Conference Evaluation Comm; Home Sch Assn Rep; NJ Ed Assn 1958-61, 1983-; Readington Ed Assn 1984-; E German Shorthair Pointer Club Incorporated (VP, Field Trial Secy, Bd of Dirs 1970-); Hunterdon Hills Kennel Club Bd of Dirs 1980-; *office:* Readington Mid Sch Readington Rd Readington NJ 08870

HOLLWEDEL, ROBERT MARK, Teacher/Department Chair; *b:* Buffalo, NY; *m:* Barbara J. Allen; *c:* David; *ed:* (AAS) Criminal Justice, Genesee Comm Coll 1979; (BS) Industrial Arts, 1981, (MS) Industrial Arts, 1984 St Univ Coll Buffalo; Elements of Instruction Trng 1981; Classroom Management Instruction 1989; *cr:* Intern Monroe Cty Sheriffs Dept 1978; Asst Photography Prof Genesee Comm Coll 1979; 10th-12th Grade Teacher Fairport Cntrl Sch 1982; 7th-12th Grade Teacher Alexander Cntrl Sch 1982-; *ai:* Safety Comm Technology Rep; Occupational Ed Dept Chm; Batavia Jaycees; Amer Industrial Arts Assn, NY St Industrial Arts Assn Mem 1982-85; Genesee Orleans Industrial Arts Assn 1982-; ASCD 1989; Campground Owners of NY Bd of Dir 1983-85; Indian Falls Fire Dept Incorporated Asst Chief 1989-; *office:* Alexander Cntrl Sch 3314 Buffalo St Alexander NY 14005

HOLM, DALE WILLIAM, Sixth Grade Teacher; *b:* Milwaukee, WI; *ed:* (BS) Elem Ed, Northland Coll 1962; *cr:* 3rd/5th Grade Teacher Ashland City Schls 1962-67; Outdoor Ed/Home/Sch Liaison 1968-70, 5th/6th Grade Teacher 1970- Canton City Schls; *ai:* Employee Suggestion Plan Comm Mem & Elem Rep Canton City Sch 1987-; 6th Grade Outdoor Ed Comm 1968-70, 1989; Elem Report Card Comm 1985-88; AIDS Policy & Ed Comm 1987-88; Canton Prof Educators Assn (Exec Bd, Mem) 1986-, OH Membership Pacesetter 1988-89; OH Ed Assn, NEA 1967-; Loyal Order of Moose (Past Governor, Past Dist VP, N Legion Moose, St Bd Mem, Delegate Natl Convention) 1967-, Pilgrim Degree of Merit 1988; Fraternal Order of Eagles, Veterans of Foreign Wars Volunteer 1970-; Army-Navy Union Volunteer 1982-; Tuscaraws Valley Pioneer Power Assn Volunteer 1976-; Canton YMCA Camper Exchange Leader to Europe 1967; VFW Voice of Democracy Judge Indian Valley Schls 1988-89; *office:* Canton City Schls 2339 17th St S W Canton OH 44706

HOLM, PHILLIP DONALD, Music Director; *b:* Minneapolis, MN; *ed:* (BS) Music Ed, Univ of MN 1987; *cr:* Edina Jazz Ensemble Dir Edina Public Schls 1984-86; Music Dir Cntrl Public Schls 1987-; *ai:* Pep & Marching Band; Sr HS Jazz Ensemble; Music Dept Chairperson; Cntrl Ed Assn Secy 1989; Natl Tour Musical Comedy; *office:* Central Public Schls 4605 Gilford Dr Edina MN 55435

HOLMAN, CHRISTINE (KEEFER), English Teacher; *b:* Oil City, PA; *m:* Tom M.; *c:* Matthew, Elizabeth; *ed:* (BA) Eng, Grove City Coll 1971; Masters Equivalency Certificate; *cr:* Eng Teacher Butler Jr HS 1971- *ai:* CORE Team; Butler Ed Assn Building Rep 1984-86; PSEA, NEA; *office:* Butler Jr HS E North St Butler PA 16001

HOLMAN, COLE ALBERT, 6th Grade Science Teacher; *b:* Sumter, SC; *m:* Alice Ann Domingos; *c:* Mary A., Robert; *ed:* (BA) Psych/Ed, Furman Univ 1974; (MA) Learning Disabilities, Univ NC Chapel Hill 1975; USC Spartanburg 1990; Project Scope, Project Learning Tree, Center of Excl in Sci Teaching; *cr:* Learning Disabilities Teacher Sirrine Elem 1975-79; 6th Grade Teacher Hillcrest Mid 1979-; *ai:* Co-Spon Sci Club; Discipline Comm; CEC Pres 1978-79; Phi Beta Kappa; Teacher of Yr 1985; Finalist Greenville Cty Teacher of Yr 1985; Southern Bell Grant for Creative Teaching 1989; *office:* Hillcrest Mid Sch 510 Garrison Rd Simpsonville SC 29681

HOLMAN, GAY LOUISE, Business Department Instructor; *b:* Centerville, IA; *m:* Larry Kenneth; *c:* Ashlynn; *ed:* (BSE) Bus Ed, NE MO St Univ 1972; (MSE) Bus Ed, Cntrl MO St Univ 1984; Univ of MO Columbia; *cr:* Bus Instr Schuyler R-1 HS 1972-74; Bank Teller/Bookkeeper Bank of Odessa 1974-75; Bus Instr Odessa R-7 HS 1975-; *ai:* NHS, FBLA, Class Spon; Weighted Class Comm; Academic Letter Prgm Coord; Pep Club & Stu Cncl Spon; Cntrl Bus Educators Assn Mem 1975-; NBEA Mem 1978-; Cmmty Teachers Assn Mem 1975-; MO Voc Assn; Odessa Youth Fair Treas 1977-79; Odessa Cmmty Betterment Bd 1978; Pi Upsilon Beta Sigma Phi Ways & Means Pres; Chrstn Church Womens Fellowship (Pres, Secy); Initiated, Promoted, Adopted Odessa Academic Letter Prgm; *office:* Odessa R-7 HS 713 S 3rd St Odessa MO 64076

HOLMAN, HARRY STUART, Social Studies Chairman; *b:* Chambersburg, PA; *m:* Linda Sue Bracey; *c:* Mary S.; *ed:* (BA) His, Elizabethtown Coll 1971; (MA) His, Old Dominion Univ 1973; Teachers Cert Shippensburg St Univ 1975; *cr:* Instr Brunswick Acad 1976-; *ai:* Spon NHS; Brunswick Cty Historical Society Pres 1978-86; Hicksford Chapter Sons of the Amer Revolution Pres 1979-81; Society of Cincinnati 1971-; Amer of Royal Descent 1984-; Va St Academic Schlsp 1971; Published Books; *home:* 706 Windsor Ave Lawrenceville VA 23868

HOLMAN, HELEN H., First Grade Teacher; *b:* Idaho Falls, ID; *m:* Gerald W.; *c:* Sandra L., Ryan; *ed:* (AS) Elem Ed, Ricks Coll 1959; (BS) Elem Ed, Brigham Young Univ 1961; Grad Study, UT St Univ, ID St Univ, Brigham Young Univ; *cr:* Elem Teacher Salt Lake City Sch Dist 1962-63, Idaho Falls Dist 191 & 93 1963-67, Rigby Elem Sch 1976-79, Ririe Elem Sch 1979-; *ai:* Spelling Bees; Sch Musical Production; NEA, Ririe Ed Assn; Hospital Volunteer, Meals on heels; Latter Day Saints Church Pres Various Organizations 1960-; *home:* 288 N 4500 E Rigby ID 83442

HOLMAN, LARRY KENNETH, Health/Physical Ed Teacher; *b:* Keokuk, IA; *m:* Gay Anderson; *c:* Ashlynn Suzanne, Nichelle Leanne Miller; *ed:* (BSE) Phys Ed, Northeast MO St Univ 1968; (MSE) Safety Ed, Central MO St Univ 1972; *cr:* Teacher/Coach Vit HS 1968-69; Cuba HS 1969-70, Schuyler R-I HS 1972-74, Odessa R-VII Jr HS 1974-; *ai:* Prof Dev Comm; Cadre Techer Improvement Grant; Cmmty Drug Ed Prgm; AADTSE 1986-; MAREHD 1974-; Christian Church Deacon 1981-86; *home:* 708 Ozark Short Line Odessa MO 64076

HOLMAN, PATRICIA HAYES, English Dept Chair/Teacher; *b:* Newport News, VA; *c:* Sylvia, Evalle; *ed:* (BA) Eng, Hampton Univ 1958; (MA) Eng, Columbia Univ 1964; Advanced Composition, Univ of CT; Modern Grammar, Univ of VA; *cr:* Teacher Huntington HS 1958-71; Eng Dept Chairperson Warwick HS 1971-; *ai:* Advanced Placement Coord; Rdng Cncl Coll Bd Adv; Tutorial Staff; Advisory & Sch Cmmty Relations Comm; NCTE, VA Assn of Teachers of Eng; Phi Beta Sigma Educator of Yr 1980; Cosmotology Sch Martam Daniels Educator of Yr 1987; Boys Club Bd of Dir (Asst Secy, Chairperson Finance Comm) 1983-; Bd of Trustees for the Lib 1985-; *office:* Warwick HS 51 Copeland Ln Newport News VA 23607

HOLMES, DAVID ASA, Secondary Mathematics Teacher; *b:* Malone, NY; *m:* Nora Haberly; *c:* Jeff, Carol; *ed:* (AAS) Electrical Technology, Mohawk Valley Comm Coll 1964; (BA) Scndry Math Ed, 1967, (MS) Ed, 1971 St Univ NY Potsdam; *cr:* Scndry Math Teacher Brushton-Moira Cntrl Sch 1967-; *ai:* Academic Letters Awd Comm; NY St United Teachers; *office:* Brushton-Moira Cntrl Sch Gale Rd Brushton NY 12916

HOLMES, DELIGHT (ANDERSON), Kindergarten Teacher; *b:* Pomona, CA; *c:* Holly, John; *ed:* (AA) Pre-Teaching, San Bernardino Valley Coll 1954; (BA) Psych/Home Ec/Ed, Whittier Coll 1956; Univ of CA Riverside, Univ of La Verne, Claremont Grad Sch, Chapman Coll, Univ of Redlands; *cr:* Teacher Alice Birney Sch 1956-72, Paul J Rogers 1972-73, Gerald A Smith 1973-77, Mary B Lewis 1977-; *ai:* Safety Comm; Curr Cncl; Sch Chorus Accompanist; NEA, CTA; ACE Corresponding Secy 1958-59; Reach to Recovery, Probation Dept Volunteer; Amer Cancer Society (Leadership Comm 1988) 1984-; *office:* Mary B Lewis Sch 18040 San Bernardino Ave Bloomington CA 92316

HOLMES, DIANE WARD, 1st Grade Teacher; *b:* Troy, NY; *m:* Gregory; *c:* Mac Kenzie, Colin; *ed:* (BA) Ed, SUNY Oswego 1975; Graduate Prgm, SUNY Albany; *cr:* Kndgtn Teacher Hoosic Valley Elem Sch 1976-85; 1st Grade Teacher Mechanicville Elem Sch 1985-; *ai:* Young Authors Comm; Lang Art & Writing; Curr Developer for Neighboring Sch Dist; Whole Lang Speaker; *home:* 17 Walden Glen Ballston Lake NY 12019

HOLMES, GERRY A., US History Teacher; *b:* Grants Pass, OR; *m:* Judith Greenberg; *c:* Mark A., Christopher R.; *ed:* (BS) US His, S OR St 1966; Pepperdine Univ, UCLA, Univ of Pacific, Univ of CA Berkeley, Univ of OR, S OR St Univ; *cr:* World His Teacher Roosevelt Jr HS 1966-72; US His Teacher 1972-, Mentor Teacher 1985- F C Beyer HS; *ai:* Wrestling Coach 1972-79; Bsbl Coach 1972-74; New Teacher Mentor Teacher 1987-89; CA Teachers

Assn, Modesto Teachers Assn 1966-; Phi Delta Kappa Historian 1969-75; North Villas Homeowners Assn (Bd Mem 1979-81, Pres 1981); Robert A Taft Fellowship Univ of OR 1982; Teamsters Fellowship Univ of CA Berkeley 1988; Econimics Ed Fellowship Univ of the Pacific 1981; Ec Consultant Stanislaus St Univ 1988-; Figgie Fellowship UCLA 1981; *office:* Fred C Beyer HS 1717 Sylvan Ave Modesto CA 95355

HOLMES, JAMES ROBERT, Social Studies Teacher; *b:* Erie, PA; *m:* Sherlyn S. Loyd; *c:* Jennifer L., Amy C.; *ed:* (BS) Scndry Ed, Edinboro St Univ 1965; (MED) Ed, Xavier Univ 1980; Univ of IL Psych; OH St Univ Theory & Practice/Multi-Cultural Ethnic; *cr:* Teacher Danville Jr/Sr HS 1965-; Summer Sch Prgm Teacher Mount Vernon HS; *ai:* Yrbk Adv; Photo Adv; Sr Class Adv; Frosh Class Adv; Danville Volunteer Fire Dept Firefighter 1977-; Danville Volunteer Emerg Squad Adv EMT-AE 1980-; COE Fellowship Amer Stud OH Northern Univ 1968; *office:* Danville Local Sch Rambo St PO Box 30 Danville OH 43014

HOLMES, JOSEPHINE SARA, Mathematics Teacher; *b:* Bridgeton, NJ; *ed:* (BA) Math, Trenton St 1962; (MA) Math Ed, Kean Coll 1972; *cr:* Math Teacher Union HS 1962-; *ai:* Class Adv 1966, 1969; Twirling Adv 1962-72; Union Teachers Assn Rep 1962-; NEA, NJ Ed Assn, NJ Math Teachers Assn 1962; *office:* Union HS N 3rd St Union NJ 07083

HOLMES, KATHY ANN, First Grade Teacher; *b:* Lebanon, IN; *m:* Bruce L.; *c:* Abby, Katie; *ed:* (MS) Elem Ed/Early Chldhd Ed, IN Univ 1978; *cr:* 1st Grade Teacher Harris Elem 1976-; *ai:* Lang Art Curr Comm 1983-; IN Rdng Assn 1982-84; Tri Kappa 1983-; *home:* 20 Fairlane Dr Brownsburg IN 46112

HOLMES, LINDA K., Science Teacher; *b:* Scranton, PA; *m:* Terrence; *c:* Terrence; *ed:* (BS) Chem, Marywood Coll 1971; Working towards Masters General Sci; *cr:* Sci Teacher Scranton Sch Dist 1971-; *ai:* PA Jr Acad of Sci Spon; *office:* W Scranton Intermediate Sch Fellows & Parrott Ave Scranton PA 18504

HOLMES, PATRICIA PALMER, Peer Counseling Teacher; *b:* Live Oak, FL; *m:* Myron; *c:* Corey, Jaret; *ed:* (BS) Eng Ed, 1972, (MS) Counseling/Human Systems, 1981 FL St Univ; *cr:* Teacher/Librarian Brooks Cty Elem Schls 1973-74; Peer Counseling Teacher Suwannee HS 1985-; *ai:* Chairperson Faculty Advisory & Mem of Drug Free Schls Comm; Adv/Spon Suwannees Pride-Youth Team of Americas Pride; Delta Kappa Gamma 1990; Live Oak Jr Womans Club Chairperson Ed Dept 1984-89; *office:* Suwannee HS 1314 Pine St Live Oak FL 32060

HOLMES, RUTH RICHARDSON, Teacher; *b:* Tuskegee, AL; *m:* Cephas Daniel; *c:* Loretta A. Stockling, Angela O. Merritt, Dierdre R. Motley, Liticia M. Nock, Cephas D. Jr.; *ed:* (BS) Home Ec Ed, Tuskegee Inst 1969; Additional Study in Ed, Rdng, Elem & Early Chldhd Ed; *cr:* 1st Grade Teacher, 5th/6th Grade Teacher, 4th Grade Teacher Deborah Cannon Wolfe; *ai:* NEA, AL Ed Assn, Macon Cty Ed Assn 1969-; Cncl for Soc Stud & Eng; Greenwood Missionary Baptist Church Nursery Chm 1972-88; Democratic Club.

HOLMES, VAL G., Physical Education Teacher; *b:* Springfield, MO; *ed:* (BS) Phys Ed, Southwest MO St Univ 1975; (MS) Mid Management, Prairie View A&M Univ 1990; *cr:* Phys Ed Teacher/Coach Norwood Schls 1975-78, Cabool Mid Sch 1978-80; James S Hogg Mid Sch 1981-; *ai:* Coach Vlybl, Swimming, Track; Co Spon Stu Hall Monitors; Chrstn Church Mem; *office:* James S Hogg Mid Sch 1100 Merrill Houston TX 77009

HOLMES, WILLIAM H., Choral Director; *b:* Harrisonburg, VA; *ed:* (BA) Music Ed, Rutgers Univ 1978; *cr:* Choral Dir Watchung Hills Regional HS 1980-; *ai:* Boys, Girls, Mixed Ensembles; Drama Club Musical Dir; MENC, NJMEA, NEA; *office:* Watchung Hills Regional HS 108 Stirling Rd Warren NJ 07060

HOLOVACS, MARY CONNORS, Special Needs Teacher; *b:* Hoboken, NJ; *m:* Thomas N.; *c:* Mary, Tom, Tim; *ed:* (BA) Eng, Montclair St Coll 1964; (MEd) Spec Ed, William Paterson 1980; *cr:* Teacher Hoboken Bd of Ed 1963-64, Union City Bd of Ed 1964-65, Engle Sch 1972-76, Sussex Cty Voc Tech Sch 1976-; *ai:* Spec Olympics Coach; NJEA Spec Ed Rep 1987-; Cultural Affairs Comm 1981-87; NJ Spec Ed Grant; Nom Spec Ed Teacher of Yr Sussex Cty Voc Tech; *office:* Sussex Cty Voc Tech Sch 105 N Church Rd Sparta NJ 07871

HOLSAPPLE, LOUISE HERNANDEZ, Kindergarten Teacher; *b:* Hollister, CA; *m:* Dan E.; *c:* Christina, Bradley; *ed:* (AA) Soc Sci, Gavilan Jr Coll 1969; (BS) Soc Sci, CA Poly San Luis Obispo 1971; Credential San Jose St 1972; *cr:* Kndgtn Teacher Sunnyslope Sch 1971-72; 5th/6th Grade Teacher Warner Springs Sch 1973-74; Kndgtn Teacher Sunnyslope Sch 1976-; *ai:* Mexican Amer Comm on Ed; San Benito Cty Rdng Cncl (Pres 1984, Secy 1982); Asilomar Regional Rdng Conference Bd of Dir 1985-88; CA Rdng Assn; 4-H Projects Leader 1985-; GSA Asst Leader 1981-84; Little League Team Mom 1988-89; Amer Field Service (Secy 1987-88, VP 1988-89); Mentor Teacher 1985; *office:* Sunnyslope Sch 1475 Memorial Dr Hollister CA 95023

HOLSINGER, DEE (LYNN), Middle Sch Gen Music Teacher; *b:* Scottsbluff, NE; *m:* Tom; *ed:* (BM) Hastings Coll 1969; (MS) Mid Sch Ed, St Cloud St Univ 1985; *cr:* 7th/8th Grade Music Teacher Barrigada Jr HS 1970-72; Kndgtn-6th Grade Music Teacher Pinewood Elem 1973-75; 7th-12th Grade Music/Choir Teacher Rocori Area Schls 1977-; *ai:* Comprehensive Arts Planning Prgm Co-Chairperson; MMEA 1977-; Teacher of Yr Candidate; *office:* Rocori Area Schls Cold Spring MN 56320

HOLSTE, DANIEL PAUL, Physics/Chemistry Teacher; *b:* Goodland, KS; *m:* Jean Louise Wagstaff; *c:* Diane, Ellen; *ed:* (BA) Physics/Math, Wartburg Coll 1968; (MA) Sci Ed, Fisk Univ 1971; *cr:* Sci Teacher Alta Cmmty Sch Dist 1968-70, Eddyville Cmmty Sch Dist 1971-74, Humboldt Cmmty Sch Dist 1974-; *ai:* Academic Co-Coord JETS-TEAMS Competition, Physics Olympics, Natl Sci Olympiad, Physics Bowl, Knowledge Master Open; IA Acad of Sci Life Mem, IA Sci Teachers Section of IA Acad of Sci; NEa 1968-; IA St Ed Assn 1968-; Humboldt Ed Assn (Pres 1980-81, 1989-) 1974-; IA St Ed Assn (Uniserv Unit 10, Exec Bd 1983-); Chemical Ed Divsion of Amer Chemical Society; Natl Earth Sci Teachers Assn, IA Earth Sci Teachers Assn; Okoboji Luth Bible Camp Exec Bd 1977-83; Humboldt Luth Church (Mem, Pres) 1976-; Oskaloosa Luth Church Finance & Constitution Comm Chm 1973-74; IA Dist Fort Dodge Conference Luth (Mem, Treas) 1986-87; W IA Synod Conference 7 Luth (Mem, Bd Mem) 1988-, Mission Task Force Comm 1989-; Kiwanis Key Club Past Adv; Local Emergency Planning Comm 1989-; Los Alamos Scientific Laboratories Co-Authored Paper 1971; Oak Ridge Associated Universities 1971; US Dept of Ag 1966; Arrowhead Area Ed Agency 1977, 1978, 1985; *office:* Humboldt Cmmty Sch Dist 1500 Wildcat Rd Humboldt IA 50548

HOLSTE, ROBERT W., Eighth Grade Teacher; *b:* Ludell, KS; *m:* Betty Jean Prange; *c:* Kathy Johnson, Scott, Richard, Timothy; *ed:* (BA) Elem Ed, Concordia Teachers Coll 1954; (MA) Elem Ed, Univ of Evansville 1970; *cr:* 1st-6th Grade Teacher Trinity Luth Sch 1952-53; 5th/6th Grade Teacher St John Luth Sch Stuttgart 1954-57; 7th Grade Teacher St John Luth Sch Chester IL 1957-67; Prin/8th Grade Teacher Trinity Luth Sch 1967-71; 8th Grade Teacher Evansville Luth Sch 1971-; *ai:* Coaching; Athletic Dir; Yrbk Spon; Luth Ed Assn 1973-; Trinity Luth Church (VP 1974-76, Bd of Ed Chm 1984-86, 1988-); Natl Sci Fnd Grant 1966, 1967; *home:* 1262 Sheffield Dr Evansville IN 47710

HOLSTEAD, CHARLES, US History Teacher; *b:* Shreveport, LA; *m:* Dianne C.; *c:* Travis, David; *ed:* (BA) Sociology, Univ of GA 1972; (MAT) Ed, Winthrop Coll 1974; *cr:* Teacher Sullivan Jr HS 1973-77, Oakway HS 1977-81, Mc Duffie HS 1981-85, D W Daniel 1985-; *ai:* Girls Var Bsktbl Coach.

HOLT, BRENDA BOTTOM, Chapter Math Teacher; *b:* Russell Springs, KY; *m:* Jerry Wayne; *ed:* (AA) Elem Ed, Lindsey Wilson Coll 1966; (BS) Elem Ed, Campbellsville Coll 1968; (Rank II) Univ KY 1973; (Rank I) Western KY Univ 1974; *cr:* Spec Ed Teacher Russell Springs Elem 1968-70; 2nd Grade Teacher Hogue Elem 1970-74; 3rd Grade Teacher Russell Springs Elem 1974-88; Chapter Math Teacher Russell Cty Jr HS 1988-; *ai:* Champions Against Drugs Spon 1988-89; Russell Cty Teacher Assn Past Bd Dir; KY Ed Assn, Natl Ed Assn; Kappa Kappa Iota-Gamma (Past Treas, St Secy 1990-); *home:* Rt 2 Box 41 Russell Springs KY 42642

HOLT, CARYLA SHADDEN, Kindergarten Teacher; *b:* Sherman, TX; *m:* Charles E.; *c:* Crista, Cayla; *ed:* (AS) Grayson Coll 1973; (BS) Elem Ed/Math/Kndgtn, TX Wesleyan Coll 1976; Intnl Inst of Literacy Learning, The Bill Martin Literacy Conference; *cr:* 1st Grade Teacher Hardeman Elem 1976-78; 4th Grade Teacher Whitesboro Elem 1978-81; 5th-8th Grade Math Lab Teacher 1983-87, 1st Grade Teacher 1987-88, 2nd Grade Teacher 1988-89, Kndgtn Teacher 1989- Honey Grove Elem; *ai:* UIL Coach 4th-6th Grade Number Sense, 6th-8th Grade Calculator Applications; Honey Grove Prof Educators Pres 1984-86; PTO Secy 1983-84; TX Cmmty Schls; 1st Baptist Church Teacher of Youth 1982-; Gospel Heirs Singer 1988-; *office:* Honey Grove Elem Sch 601 10th St Honey Grove TX 75446

HOLT, DOROTHY HOLLAND, English Teacher; *b:* Houston, TX; *m:* Orren A.; *c:* Joan Holland Helton, James, John, Jerry, Jean L. Willingham; *ed:* (BA) Fr/Eng, Rice Univ 1942; *cr:* Fr/Eng Teacher Dickinson Ind Sch Dist 1962-65; Eng Teacher TX City HS 1965-; *ai:* Prin Rdng Comm; TCTA 1987-; Alpha Delta Kappa 1988-; Smithsonian, Audubon, World Wildlife, Cousteau Societies; *home:* 2705 Crockett Dr S La Marque TX 77568

HOLT, GERALDINE FAY (GROTH), Challenge Class Teacher; *b:* Cooperton, OK; *m:* Arvil Ewell; *c:* Beverly J. Holt Stewart, Dale L., Darbie G. Holt Whiting, Brian E.; *ed:* (BS) Scndry Ed/Eng, Howard Payne Coll 1954; (MED) Elem Ed, SW TX St Teachers Coll 1959; Wkshps, Seminars, Conferences; Philosophy of Ed, ASCI; Bible Course Columbia Bible Coll; *cr:* 1st Grade Teacher Price Elem 1953-54, Coronado Elem 1954-55; 5th Grade Teacher Grimes Elem 1955-56; 2nd/3rd Grade Teacher Lakeview Baptist Elem 1957-58, 1963-66; 2nd-12th Grade Teacher Curtist Baptist Elem HS 1966-; *ai:* Fall Festival, Family Day, Curr Comms; Girls Club of America Bible Teacher 1966-, Volunteer of Yr 1987; Master Teacher Awd; *office:* Curtis Baptist Elem Sch 1326 Broad St Augusta GA 30910

HOLT, KENNETH A., Sci Dept Chair/Chem Teacher; *b:* Montpelier, VT; *m:* Nancy Hartman; *c:* Timothy, Kristin; *ed:* (AA) Ed, Polk Jr Coll 1967; (BS) Chem Ed, 1970, (MS) Sci Ed, 1973 FL St Univ; *cr:* Teacher Boone HS 1970; Teacher 1970-, Sci Dept Chm 1982- Colonial HS; *ai:* Sci Dept Chm; Colonial HS Enrichment Prgm Steering Comm; NEA, UTP, CTA 1970-; Natl Educators Fellowship (Treas, Local Pres) 1973-76; FL Assn of Sci Teachers 1988-; Developed Chem II Individualized Instruction 1973; Assoc Master Teacher for St of Fl 1985-86; *office:* Colonial HS 6100 Oleander Dr Orlando FL 32807

HOLT, SHARA WIGGINTON, Eng Teacher/Dual Enrollment; *b:* Forrest City, AR; *m:* Jeff Clark; *ed:* (BSE) Eng, Univ of Cntrl AR 1973; (MED) Eng, MS Coll 1986; Univ of London; *cr:* 10th/12th Grade Eng Teacher Canton Acad 1979-83; 12th Grade Eng/Psych Teacher Mc Cluer Acad 1983-85; 9th/12th Grade Eng Teacher Brandon Acad 1985-86; 12th Grade Eng/Comp I & II Teacher St Augustine HS 1986-; *ai:* Attendance Comm Mem; FL Cncl Teachers of Eng, Phi Delta Kappa, Sigma Tau Delta; Stu-Teacher Achievement Recognition 1983, 1986; *office:* Saint Augustine HS 3205 Varella Ave Saint Augustine FL 32084

HOLTAN, DONNA CHARLSON, Third Grade Teacher; *b:* Forest City, IA; *m:* Jerry; *c:* Jason; *ed:* (BS) Elem Ed, Mankato St Univ 1970; Drake Univ, IA St Univ, Univ N IA; *cr:* 3rd Grade Teacher Gilbert Elem Sch 1971-85; 5th Grade/Pre-1st Transition Teacher Manheim Township Sch 1985-87; 3rd Grade Teacher Roland Story Elem Sch 1987-88; 3rd Grade Teacher Gilbert Elem Sch 1988-; *ai:* Cmptr Technology Ed, Gifted & Talented Identification, Sci & Health Comm; NEA 1971-; IA St Ed Assn UNISERV Unit 5 Pres Cncl 1971-85, 1987-; Gilbert Ed Assn (Pres, VP, Secy, Treas) 1971-; Delta Kappa Gamma 1988-; PEO Guard 1980-; Gilbert Luth Church of Evangelism; Outstanding Young Women of America 1982; Adopt-A-Teacher Awd 1989; *home:* Rt 4 Ames IA 50010

HOLTZMILLER, DAN R., Chemistry Teacher; *b:* Reedsburg, WI; *m:* Connie Marie Petesch; *c:* Katie, Kara; *ed:* (BS) Phys Ed/Natural Sci Ed, Univ of WI Madison 1973; Working Toward Masters Cmptrs; *cr:* Bio Teacher New Berlin West HS 1976; Bio/Chem/Nat Sci Teacher Oconomowoc Sr HS 1976-; Anatomy-Physiology Lab Teacher Madison Area Technical Coll 1989-; *ai:* Girls Gymnastics, Girls Track, Wrestling, Boys Golf Coach; *home:* 1011 Green Meadow Dr Oconomowoc WI 53066

HOLY, JO ALICE CRENSHAW, 6th Grade Teacher; *b:* Montgomery, AL; *c:* Douglas W., Muriel Holy Brown; *ed:* (BA) Elem Ed, AL St Univ 1964; *cr:* Teacher Waren Elem, Bond Hill Chldhd Dev Center, Cincinnati Public Schls; *ai:* Stu Cncl; Spelling Bee; Awd Prgms; Discipline Comm; Young Authors; *home:* 7670 Clovernook Ave Cincinnati OH 45231

HOMER, WILLIE, Gifted/Talented Teacher; *b:* Medera, CA; *ed:* (BS) Phys Ed, 1974, (MS) Ed, 1976 SE OK St Univ; Earth Sci, Physics, Chem; *cr:* Grad Asst Southeastern OK St Univ 1975-76; Gifted/Talented Sci Teacher/Coach Hughes Jr HS 1976-79, Sulphur HS 1979-81, Shawnee Public Schls 1981-; *ai:* HS Ftbl, Wrestling & Soccer Coach; Sci Fair Spon; NSTA 1985-; Natl Strength & Conditioning Assn 1989-; OK Coaches Assn 1979-; Wrestling USA Magazine Honorable Mention Asst Coach of Yr 1989; Nom Teacher of Yr 1989-; *office:* Shawnee Jr HS 501 N Union Shawnee OK 74801

HOMILIUS, LOUISE ANN, Third Grade Teacher; *b:* Comfort, TX; *m:* Jimmie; *c:* Elizabeth Pyka, Thomas R.; *ed:* (BS) Elem Ed, Univ of TX Austin 1968; *cr:* 3rd Grade Teacher St Johns Elem 1968-71, Tivy Elem 1971-87, Nimitz Elem 1987-; *ai:* Grade Chairperson; Kerrville Teachers Assn Pres 1973-74; Assn TX Prof Educators Building Rep 1988-; Delta Kappa Gamma Intnl (Corresponding Secy 1978 80, Membership Chm 1980-82, 1988); *office:* Nimitz Elem Sch 100 Valley View Dr Kerrville TX 78028

HOMSEY, THOMAS, Phys Ed/Drivers Ed Teacher; *b:* Bismarck, ND; *m:* Kathleen Ann Dormanen; *ed:* (BS) Phys Ed, Valley City St Coll 1971; *cr:* Teacher Wachter Jr HS 1972, Warwick HS 1973-75, Tolna HS 1976-78, Surrey HS 1979-; *ai:* 5th-8th Grade Girls Bsktbl Coach; 9th Grade Class Adv; Drivers Ed Assn Pres 1981-83, Teacher of Yr 1980; *office:* Surrey Public Sch 200 SE 2nd Surrey ND 58785

HON, DIANNE HESS, Home Economics Instructor; *b:* Butler, MO; *m:* Steven W.; *c:* William E.; *ed:* (BSE) Voc Home Ed, Cntrl MO St Univ 1981; *cr:* Voc Home Ec Instr/Head Vlybl Coach Cass Midway R-I HS 1981-84, 1985-88; Voc Home Ec Instr Sherwood Cass R-VIII HS 1988-; *ai:* FHA Adv; *office:* Sherwood Cass RV-III HS P O Box 98 Creighton MO 64739

HON, TIMOTHY DANE, Science Teacher; *b:* Indianapolis, IN; *m:* Debbie L.; *c:* Phillip, Laurie; *ed:* (BS) Ed, 1970, (MS) Ed, 1975 Butler Univ; *cr:* Sci Teacher Westlane Mid Sch 1971-; *ai:* Coaching Cross Cntry, Bsktbl, Track; Kiwanas Builders Club Spon; Optomist Club Intnl 1989-; Town Cncl Trustee 1988-91; *office:* Westlane Mid Sch 1301 W 73rd St Indianapolis IN 46260

HONDA, ROBERT K., Counselor/Coach; *b:* Lihue, HI; *m:* Joyce Fujii; *c:* Daryl, Wesley, Kristl; *ed:* (BA) Phys Ed/Math, 1961, (MA) Ed, 1972 CA St Univ Sacramento; *cr:* Teacher SCUSD 1963-78: Cnslr Mc Clatchy & Kennedy 1978-79, Sacramento HS 1979-; *ai:* Head Var Mens Bsktbl; Block S Society; SCPPA; Hawaiian Athletic Assn Treas; Univ of IL Natl Sci Fnd Grant 1969; *office:* Sacramento HS 2315 34th St Sacramento CA 95817

HONECKER, DAVID WARREN, Social Studies Teacher; *b:* Pittsburgh, PA; *m:* Sandra Jean Cook; *c:* Christopher J., Adam E.; *ed:* (BSED) Soc Stud, Indiana Univ of PA 1975; (MED) Admin/Supervision/Curr, Univ of MD 1981; *cr:* Soc Stud Teacher G Gardner Shugart Jr HS 1975-81; Tag/Tineront Teacher 5 Schls in PG Cty 1981-82; 7th-8th Grade Teacher Greenbelt Mid Sch 1982-84; Civics/Geography/His/Anthropology/Foreign Policy Teacher Du Val HS 1984-; *ai:* Stu Government Assn; Mock Trial Team & Jr Var Bsbl Coach; Faculty Advisory Cmmty Sch Based Management Cncl; Christ Episcopal Church (Mem, Co-Author of Church His Booklet); *office:* Du Val HS 9880 Goodluck Rd Lanham Seabrook MD 20706

HONEY, JOHN H., Biology Teacher; *b:* New York City, NY; *m:* Judith Spencer Ferguson; *ed:* (BS) Bio, W CT St Univ 1966; (MS) Bio, Univ of Bridgeport 1972; Drug Inst S CT St Univ 1978; *cr:* Bio Teacher Andrew Warde HS 1966-87, Fairfield HS 1987-; *ai:* Boys Tennis Coach 1974-; Fairfield Ed Assn, CT Ed Assn 1966-;

NEA; Town of Fairfield Youth Commission Adv 1990; Natl Sci Fnd Grant Bowdoin Coll Marine Bio 1972; *office:* Fairfield HS Melville Ave Fairfield CT 06430

HONEYCUTT, AVA KELLEY, Kindergarten Teacher; *b:* Chester, MD; *m:* Lathern N.; *c:* Dale H. Wheatley, Kimberly M.; *ed:* (AA) Chesapeake Coll 1973; (BA) Eng/Early Chldhd, Univ of MD Coll 1974; (MED) Early Chldhd, Towson St Univ 1978; *cr:* Kndgtn Teacher Grasonville Elem 1966-678 Kent Island Elem 1967-; *ai:* Kndgtn Chairperson Educl Management Team; Bd of Ed Comm; Queen Annes Cty Ed Assn, MSTA, NEA, PTA Honorary Life Membership 1986; Chesterwye Inc Chairperson of Bd 1986-88; Kent Island United Meth Church (Sunday Sch Teacher 1944-84, Childrens Church 1987-), Service Awd 1984; *office:* Kent Island Elem Sch Stevensville MD 21666

HONEYCUTT, JAMES ALLEN, Biology Teacher/Football Coach; *b:* Madison, TN; *m:* Dawn Marie Brady; *ed:* (BS) Health/Phys Ed, TN St Univ 1984; *cr:* Phys Ed Teacher Portland HS 1985; Teacher/Coach Westmoreland HS 1985-; *ai:* Var Ftbl Coach 1985-; Var Bsbl Coach 1986-88; Southern Assn of Schls Admin Comm; TN Ed Assn, NEA, TN Athletic Assn, Natl Fed Interscholastic Coaches Assn 1985-; Cty Bsbl Coach of Yr 1987; *office:* Westmoreland HS PO Box 119 Old Scottsville Hwy Westmoreland TN 37186

HONISH, RICHARD A., Professor of Music; *b:* Newark, NJ; *m:* Marcia Hutchison; *c:* Richard C., Kristin K.; *ed:* (BME) Music, Coll of Emporia 1966; (MME) Music, Ft Hays St 1975; Advance Conducting Robert Winslow, William Revellie; *cr:* Dir of Bands Paradise Valley Schls 1975-78; Instr Coord Unified Sch Dist 480 1978-89; Prof of Music Dodge City Comm Coll 1989-; *ai:* Phi Mu Alpa Music; Willow Tree Golf Club Advisory Bd; Russian Government Cultural Exch Prgm; *home:* 611 N Tulane Liberal KS 67901

HOOD, FERGENIA HARRISON, English Teacher/Dept Chair; *b:* Duckhill, MS; *m:* Henry T.; *c:* Gary Hannah, Paigelyn Hannah; *ed:* (AA) Eng, Univ of MS; (BA) Eng, Rust College 1970; (MS) Rdng, Univ of MS 1975; *cr:* Broadstreet HS 1970-73; Henry Jr HS 1973-75; Holly Springs Intermediate 1975-; *ai:* Stu Cncl Adv; Oratorical Coach; MAE; Rdng Assn; Zeta Phi Beta VP 1978-80; *home:* 605 Swaney Rd Holly Springs MS 38635

HOOD, FRANK RICHARD, Phys Ed/Soc Stud Teacher; *b:* Minneapolis, MN; *m:* Deborah Dawn Rosenthal; *ed:* (BBA) Ec, Wake Forest Univ 1969; (BA) Phys Ed, 1972, (MED) Ed, 1974 William & Mary; *cr:* Phys Ed/Soc Stud Teacher St Clare Walker Mid Sch 1969-71; K-12th Grade/Phys Ed Teacher Surry Cty Acad 1974; 7th-9th Grade Phys Ed/Soc Stud Teacher Irving Jr HS 1975-; *ai:* 9th Grade Boys Bsktbl Coach; Prevention Team; Outdoor Ed; River Trip Captain; Intramurals Talent Show; Biddy Bsktbl Supvr 1979-; Green Mountain Falls Centennial Comm 1989-; Dist Curr & Athletic Handbook Comms; Bsktbl Chairperson; NEA, CEA, CSEA 1975-; *home:* 7145 Iona St Green Mntn Flls CO 80819

HOOD, MARYANN CAVENDER, Middle School English Teacher; *b:* Cleburne Cty, AL; *m:* Curtis L.; *c:* Joseph M., Rebecca J. Hood Rung Sang, James S., Laura A. Hood Nichols; *ed:* (BS) Elem Ed, 1951, (MS) Elem Ed, 1966, (AA) Certification, 1974, (EDS) Elem Ed, 1989 Jacksonville St Univ; Natl Writing Project Jacksonville St Univ 1987; *cr:* 3rd Grade Teacher Fort Payne City Schls 1951-52; 4th Grade Teacher Gadsden City System 1952-53; Teacher of Missionary Children Bolivian Jungle 1977-78; 2nd-6th Grade Teacher Etowah Cty System 1964-; *ai:* Speech Class; Sch Math Bee & Ben Franklin Stamp Club Leader; Disaster Comm; PTA Cultural Arts 1964-89, Life Mem; AEA (Building Rep, Delegate); NEA, Etowah Cty Ed Assn, EEA; Cntrl United Meth Church Chm of Commission on Missions 1988-89; Natl Writing Project 1987; Wrote Book of Illustrated Poetry; *office:* Highland Sch Rt 8 Box 125 Gadsden AL 35901

HOOD, ROSEMARY GRENNAN, English Teacher; *b:* Decatur, IL; *m:* John; *c:* Michael, Christopher, David; *ed:* (BS) Eng, E IL Univ 1961; (MS) Instructional Tech, N IL 1976; Grad Classes at Univ of IL; Governors St IL Inst of Technology & Rosary Coll; *cr:* Eng Teacher Lakeview HS 1961-62, Westerville HS 1962-63, Larkin HS 1963-65, 1976-; *ai:* Class Spon; Sch Dept Comm Pres, Rdng Evaluation Comm; NCTE; Cath Charities Bd of Dir; AAUW 1970-80; *office:* Larkin HS 1475 Larkin Ave Elgin IL 60123

HOOD, SHEILA CHISHOLM, Eighth Grade Teacher; *b:* Pampa, TX; *m:* Jack; *ed:* (BA) Soc Stu/Eng, Benedictine Hts Coll 1960; *cr:* 8th Grade Teacher Pampa Jr HS 1960-66; 6th Grade Teacher St Annes Sch 1968-70; 8th Grade Teacher St Cecilia Sch 1972-; *ai:* Stu Cncl Moderator; WCEA Self-Study Comm Lang Arts Extracurricular; NCEA 1972-; Curr Comm for Eng Archdiocese San Francisco; Staff Leadership Trng Assn Cath Stu Cncls; WCEA Visitation Team 1989; *office:* St Cecilia Sch 660 Vicente St San Francisco CA 94116

HOOK, ELISE A., English Teacher/Gifted Program; *b:* Deer Lodge, TN; *m:* John Windsor; *ed:* (BA) Eng/Ed, TN Wesleyan Coll 1962; (MED) Rdng, LA St Univ 1984; Academically Talented Cert LA St Univ; Advanced Placement Seminars LA St Univ; *cr:* Eng Teacher Jefferson City Elem 1962-63, Clewiston HS 1963-65; 4th Grade Teacher Creel Elem 1965-66; Rdng Teacher Rockledge HS 1966-80; Eng Teacher Mc Kinley Sr HS 1980-; *ai:* Academic Quiz Bowl Team Coach; Gifted & Honors Eng Curr Comm 1990; EBRPC Eng Teachers, LA Cncl of Eng Teachers, NCTE, PTA 1989-; Delta Kappa Gamma 1979; Rockledge HS Teacher of Yr 1979; Mc Kinley Sr HS Teacher of Yr 1985; Top Finalist E Baton Rouge Parish HS Teacher of Yr 1985; *home:* 12334 Gawain Ave Baton Rouge LA 70816

HOOK, ELIZABETH ANN (PRICE), First Grade Teacher; *b:* Defiance, OH; *m:* Edward L.; *c:* Steven C., Devera A. Harter, Bruce E.; *ed:* (MS) Spec Ed, Bowling Green St Univ 1983; *cr:* Eng Teacher Payne HS 1965-66; 2nd Grade Teacher Paulding Exemped Village 1966-67; 1st Grade Teacher Payne Elem 1967-; *ai:* Phi Dela Kappa Mem; *office:* Payne Elem Sch Box 12 RR 2 Payne OH 45880

HOOK, ELLEN SMITH, Mathematics Teacher; *b:* Norfolk, VA; *m:* Eugene Wayne; *c:* Michael R., Christine C.; *ed:* (BS) Math, Mary Washington Coll 1969; (MA) Math, Glassboro St Coll 1978; George Washington Univ 1992; Math Ed, OH St Univ 1990; *cr:* Math Teacher Thomas Eaton Jr HS 1969-73; Adjunct Professor Glassboro St Coll 1975-78; Math Teacher W Deptford HS 1973-78; Adjunct Professor Tidewater Comm Coll 1978-; Math Teacher Granby HS 1978-; *ai:* SCA Spon; Frosh & Soph Class Adv; NCTM 1988-; VA Cncl Teachers of Math Exec Bd 1989-; Tidewater Cncl Teachers of Math 1988-; Delta Kappa Gamma 1986-; Sch Bell Awd 1988; Teacher of Yr Granby HS 1990; Tandy Scholar Awd 1990; *office:* Granby HS 7101 Granby St Norfolk VA 23505

HOOK, TRACY WILLIAM, 7th-12th Grade Teacher; *b:* Creston, IA; *m:* Janice L. Miller; *c:* Summer T.; *ed:* (BA) Industrial Technology, Wm Penn 1982; (MA) Scndry Admin, NW MO St 1990; *cr:* Industrial Art Dunlap HS 1982-86, Corning HS 1986-; *ai:* Asst Ftbl Coach; Head Bsktbl Coach; ISEA Building Rep 1989-; Tall Corn Conference Coach of Yr 1987-88; *home:* RR 4 Box 33A Creston IA 50801

HOOKER, CAROLYN SUSIE, Ag Language Arts Teacher; *b:* Asheville, NC; *c:* Clayton; *ed:* (BA) Lit, Univ of NC Asheville 1969; Currently Working on Master of Arts in Ed Mid Grades Lang Arts at Western Carolina Univ Cullowhee NC; *cr:* 9th-12th Grade Eng Teacher Asheville Cath HS 1971-72; 8th Grade Lang Arts Waynesville Jr HS 1972-; *ai:* Stu Cncl Spon & Literary Magazine Spon; Sch Improvement Comm; NC Assn Of Educators (Dist 1 Pres 1989-91, Haywood Cty Pres 1987-89); NC Assn of Gifted & Talented 1987-; Haywood Cty Schls Fnd 1987-89; Democratic Women 1987-; Keep NC Clean & Beautiful St Teacher Awd 1989-; *office:* Waynesville Jr H S 507 Brown Ave Waynesville NC 28786

HOOKER, GEORGE E., Bio/Health Teacher/Sci Chair; *b:* Rutland, UT; *m:* Cheryl Mazzariello; *c:* Sam, Molly, Emily, T. J.; *ed:* (BS) Bio/Ed, Castleton St Coll 1973; Grad Stud Bio, Health, Ed; *cr:* Sci/Health Teacher Rutland HS 1973-; *ai:* Dept Chm; Sci Club Adv; NSTA; BSA Leader 1989-; Fulbright Teacher Exch to England 1990; Outstanding Teacher Awd Univ of VT 1989; *office:* Rutland HS Library Ave Rutland VT 05701

HOOKER, LINDA M., Mathematics Teacher; *b:* E St Louis, IL; *m:* Larry D.; *c:* Jason Putz, Gigi, Michael, Larry W.; *ed:* (BA) Math, Benedictine Coll 1973; Grad Stud Math, Cmptrs, Accounting; *cr:* Math Teacher Spring Garden Mid Sch 1973-75, Hazelwood West HS 1975-77, O Fallon Township HS 1977-78, Marie Schaefer Jr HS 1978-; *ai:* ICTM, AFT, IFT; PTA; Stu Success Trophies Chapter, St, Natl Mathcounts Competitions; *office:* Marie Schaefer Jr HS 505 S Cherry O'Fallon IL 62269

HOOKS, CLAUDIA MOORE, Social Studies Dept Chair; *b:* Eustis, FL; *m:* James Edward; *c:* James Jr., Adrian; *ed:* (BS) Elem Ed, FL A&M Univ 1973; Spec Ed; *cr:* Soc/Eng Teacher Cypress Lake Mid 1973-76; Soc Stud Teacher Eustis Mid Sch 1976-; *ai:* Stu Cncl; Guidance & SACS Comm; TEC FAcilitator; Peer Teacher; Soc Stud Dept Head; Team Leader; Criterion Club Outstanding Teacher 1990; Youth Choir Spon 1976-86, 10 Yr Service 1986; Reach-Out Spon 1988, Tutorial 1989-; Red Apple Awds; Teacher Appreciation Awd; Eustis Mid Sch Soc Stud Teacher of Yr; *office:* Eustis Mid Sch 1801 E Bates Ave Eustis FL 32726

HOOKS, JAMES BYRON, JR., English Literature Teacher; *b:* Birmingham, AL; *m:* Marcell Elizabeth Forbes; *c:* Angelique, James B. III, Kimberly, Jamal, Joffrey, Keisha; *ed:* (BS) Eng/Music, IN Univ 1955; (MA) Admin, Roosevelt Univ 1969; (PHD) Admin, Northwestern Univ 1975; *cr:* Eng/Music Teacher 1959-70, Asst Prin 1971-75 Chicago Bd of Ed; Prin Evanston Bd of Ed 1975-78; Eng Teacher Chicago Bd of Ed 1978-; *ai:* Attendance Dean Comm; Patience A Hill Benevolence Fund; Bryn Mawr Multi Age Gifted Group; NASSP, ASCD 1969-78; Natl Alliance of Black Sch Educators 1975-78; PAHBF Pres 1974-80, Service 1978; BMMAG Pres 1972-78, Civic 1979; Federal Grant Study Desegregation of Evanston Public Sch; *office:* Whitney Young HS 211 S Laflin St Chicago IL 60607

HOOKS, WILLIE HUGH, Mathematics Department Chair; *b:* Prescott, AR; *m:* Carolyn Sue Lewallen; *c:* Tammy Scoggins, Cindy Webb; *ed:* (BSE) Math, Henderson St 1959; (MSE) Math, E TX St 1962; *cr:* Math Teacher Altheimer HS 1959-69, Lakeside HS 1969-; *ai:* Sr Class Spon; Baptist Church; Natl Sci Fnd Grant; *office:* Lakeside HS 4429 Malvern Hot Spgs Natl Pk AR 71901

HOOPER, CHARLOTTE E. INMAN, Teacher/Assistant Principal; *b:* Centre, AL; *m:* Claude C. Jr.; *c:* Happy, Heather; *ed:* (BA) Phys Ed, 1971, (MS) Phys Ed, 1984 Jacksonville St Univ; Admin Cert Admin, Univ of AL 1990; *cr:* Eng/Hy/Phys Ed Teacher/Coach 1972-88, Hy/Phys Ed Teacher/Coach/Asst Prin 1988- Sand Rock HS; *ai:* Jr & Var Cheerleading Spon; Homecoming Dir; Calendar Club Coord; Sftbl Coach; AL Ed Assn, NEA 1971-; AL Cncl for Sch Admin & Supervision, AL Cncl for Elem Admin 1989-; Al St Assn for Health, Phys Ed, Recreation, Dance 1971-; Cherokee Cty Teachers Assn 1971-; Cherokee Cty System Teacher of Yr 1987; Amer Red Cross Heart Assn Certificate of Appreciation 1980-84; *office:* Sand Rock HS Rt 1 Leesburg AL 35983

HOOPER, MARVIN RAY, Assistant Band Director; *b:* Austin, TX; *m:* Aliah; *c:* Tressie; *ed:* (BM) Music, Prairie View A&M Univ 1978; TX A&I Univ; *cr:* Band Dir Dwight Mid Sch 1981-87; Asst Band Dir S San Antonio HS 1987-; *ai:* Responsible for Marching Band, Concert Band, Stage Band, Show Choir, Colorguard; TMEA, TBA Mem 1981-; TSCGA Mem 1988-; *office:* S San Antonio HS 2515 Navajo San Antonio TX 78224

HOOPER, NANCY WELLS, Social Studies Teacher; *b:* National City, CA; *m:* Earl Raymond; *ed:* (BA) His, 1963, (MED) Ed, 1969 Whittier Coll; *cr:* 7th Grade Soc Stud Teacher Hillview Intermediate Sch 1964-68, Margate Intermediate Sch 1968-76, N Kitsap Mid Sch 1977-; *ai:* Soc Stud Dept Chairperson; Dist Soc Stud Curr Comm Rep; N Kitsap Ed Assn, WA Ed Assn 1977-; NCSS 1986-; Unity Church Bainbridge Island 1984-; *office:* N Kitsap Mid Sch 2003 NE Hostmark Poulsbo WA 98370

HOOPES, JEWEL EDWARDS, Coord/Facilitator Gifted Prgm; *b:* Twin Falls, ID; *m:* Tim A.; *c:* Adam, Jaimen, Andra-Sha; *ed:* (BS) Elem Ed, Brigham Young Univ 1970; (MED) Elem Ed/Gifted, UT St Univ 1990; Ed Trng; *cr:* 6th Grade Teacher Grants Sch Dist 1970-71; 1st Grade Teacher Clark Cty Sch Dist 1971-72; 6th Grade Teacher 1972-87, Gifted/Talented Facilitator 1987-88, Prgm Coord 1988- Bonneville Sch Dist #93; *ai:* Future Problem Solving Coach; Phi Kappa Phi Initiated 1990; NEA, ID Ed Assn; Bonneville Cty Centennial Comm 1989-; ID Career Ed Grant; Co-Author of Bonneville Sch Dist Career Ladder; *office:* Bonneville Sch Dist #93 3497 N Ammon Rd Idaho Falls ID 83401

HOOPS, JUDITH ANN, Third Grade Teacher; *b:* Spring Valley, WI; *m:* Marvin W.; *c:* David, Michael; *ed:* (BA) Elem Ed/Art Bethel Coll 1975; *cr:* K-4th Grade Substitute Teacher Glencoe Public Schls 1975-77; K/1st Grade Substitute Teacher Brownton Public Sch 1975-77; 3rd Grade Teacher 1978, 3rd/4th Grade Combination Teacher 1978-79, 4th Grade Teacher 1979-80, 3rd/4th Grade Combination Teacher 1980- Green Isle Public; *ai:* Delta Kappa Gamma Society Intnl Mem 1987-; Good Shepherd Luth Church (Sr Youth Cnslr, Sunday Sch Teacher, Vacation Bible Sch Teacher) 1985-; 4-H Leader 1978-80; Luth Assn of Pastors & Pilots Dist Rep 1985-; *home:* Rt 1 Box 66 Glencoe MN 55336

HOOPS, YVONNE HELENE (SEYBOLD), First/Second Grade Teacher; *b:* Concordia, KS; *m:* Michael Ray; *c:* Sarah M., Joshua M., Kate D.; *ed:* (AA) Cloud Cty Comm Jr Coll 1972; (BS) Elem Ed, KS St Univ Manhattan 1974; (MS) Ed, KS St Univ 1978; *cr:* 2nd Grade Teacher Jefferson Elem 1974-75, Washington Elem 1975-76, Jefferson Elem 1976-80; 3rd-4th Grade Teacher 1981-86, 1st-2nd Grade Teacher 1986- Byron Elem; *ai:* NEA 1974-; *office:* Byron Grade Sch Box 115 Byron NE 68325

HOOTEN, NORMA WHITTON, Middle School Science Teacher; *b:* Richmond, VA; *m:* William S. Jr.; *ed:* (BA) Health & Phys Ed, Lynchburg Coll 1972; Mid Sch Counseling Courses Toward Med, Lynchburg Coll; *cr:* Phys Ed Teacher Seven HS for Girls 1972-74; Teacher Lancaster Chrstn Acad 1979-81; Sci & Phys Ed Teacher Timberlake Chrstn HS 1981-83; Sci & Learning Center Teacher Lynchburg Chrstn Acad 1983-89; Mid Sch/Sci Teacher Landmark Chrstn HS 1989-; *ai:* Class Spon 1987-; Natl Jr Honor Society 1983-86; Var Sftbl Coach 1981-; Jr/Sr Spon 1989; *office:* Landmark Chrstn HS 120 Johnson Ave Fayetteville GA 24503

HOOTMAN, DANIEL WINFIELD, Teacher; *b:* Sewickley, PA; *c:* Julie S., Vicki L.; *ed:* (BS) Bio Ed, 1975, (MED) Bio, 1982 Edinboro Univ of PA; Prin Certificate, Edinboro Univ of PA 1987; *cr:* Teacher Meadville Jr HS 1976-81, Meadville Sr HS 1981-; *ai:* Meadville Sr HS Audio-Visual Dir; Township Supvr Vice Chm 1988-; *home:* RD 2 Tanglewood Dr Linesville PA 16424

HOOVEN, SANDRA J., English Teacher; *b:* Waterloo, IA; *m:* Patrick J.; *c:* Dan Zaretsky, Diane Zaretsky, Mike, Dave, Matt, Cathy Seckington; *ed:* (BA) Eng, Wayne Coll 1962; (MA) CA St Los Angeles; (MA) CA Poly Pomina; *cr:* Teacher Wayne HS 1962-64, Chino HS 1965-69, Glendora HS 1980-; *ai:* Lit Club Adv; Co-Coach Academic Decathlon Team; Peer Assistance Teacher; Hughes Mini Grant 1988-89; Article on Cmptrs-Lang Arts Curr Published by NCTE; *office:* Glendora H S 1600 E Foothill Blvd Glendora CA 91740

HOOVER, BEVERLY MARIE (KIRK), 6th Grade Teacher; *b:* Logan, WV; *m:* Paul Clinton; *c:* Wendy J.; *ed:* (BS) Elem Ed, Kent St Univ 1972; (MA) Remedial Rdng Specialist, Baldwin Wallace Coll 1981; Grad Stud Music; *cr:* 5th Grade Teacher Crestwood Elem Sch 1972-73; 4th Grade Teacher Mc Kinley & Crestwood Elems 1973-83; Chapter I Rdng Teacher Crestwood Elem 1983-87; 6th Grade Teacher Elyria & Crestwood Elem 1987-; *ai:* Honor Roll Comm; Kappa Delta Phi; Lake Ridge Sweet Adelines (Pres, 1985-, Asst Dir 1985-); Church Teen Spon; *home:* 41815 W Rambler Ave Elyria OH 44035

HOOVER, CLARKE HUTCHISON, Senior English Teacher; *b:* Fairfax, SD; *m:* Gayle; *c:* Kathryn Fujan, Robin Kansanback, Nancy Kunz; *ed:* (BA) Eng, Sioux Falls Coll 1958; Grad Stud Univ of SD Vermillion; Several Wkshps; *cr:* Eng Teacher/Librarian Parker HS 1959-; *ai:* Oral Interpretation Coach; NHS Adv; SD Lib Assn, NCTE; Order of Eastern Star, 1st Baptist Church; KDLT TV Plaque for Teacher Who Made Difference; *office:* Parker HS Box 517 Parker SD 57053

HOOVER, DIANE ERVINE, 1st Grade Teacher; *b:* Cherry Grove, WV; *m:* Dewey T.; *ed:* (AB) Elem Ed, Marshall Univ 1972; *cr:* 3rd Grade Teacher 1972-74; 1st Grade Teacher 1974 Green Bank Elem Sch; *ai:* Sch Advisory Comm; Teacher of Yr Green Bank Elem Sch 1987-88; *home:* PO Box 35 Sheets Rd Green Bank WV 24944

HOOVER, LYNN A., Math Teacher/Math Dept Chair; *b:* Rochester, PA; *m:* Robert C.; *ed:* (BS) Ed, Edinboro 1970; (MS) Math, Clarion Univ 1976; Grad Courses in Cmptr Sci; *cr:* Teacher Hopewell Area Sch Dist 1970-76; Math Teacher Cntrl Greene Sch Dist 1977-; *ai:* Cntrl Green Sch Dist Curr Cncl; Math Dept Chairperson; NCTM Mem 1978-; Math Cncl of W PA Mem 1978-; Math Assn Amer Mem 1990; PA St Ed Assn Mem 1970-; NEA Mem 1970-; *office:* Margaret Bell Miller Mid Sch 126 E Lincoln St Waynesburg PA 15370

HOOVER, NORMA THARP, English/Literature Teacher; *b:* Norwood, MO; *m:* Rolland; *c:* Diane Hoover-Sweeney, Kathy Sexauer; *ed:* (BS) Phys Ed/Health Ed/Bus Ed, Ball St Univ 1956; (MED) Elem Ed, Univ of AZ 1966; Studies Coll of William & Mary; Loyola of Chicago; Boise St Univ; Southern or St Coll; Univ of OR; Univ of Portland; Rogue Cmty Coll; *cr:* PE Specialist 1-3 Niles Public Sch Dist 1956-57; HS PE/Health/Bus Ed Salem Twp Daleville 1957-58; 5th Grade Teacher Sinclair Sch 1959-61, Anderson Elem Sch 1966-68, Williams Elem Sch JCSD 1978-87; Ungraded 6th Yr Seaford & Dare Elem Schls 1968-70; PE/Health Jr HS Wagner Mid Sch 1971-72; Learn Diff/TA 1973-74, PE Specialist K-3 1974-76 Base Primary Sch 1974-76; Eng/Lit Mid Sch Fleming Mid Sch JCSD 1987-; *ai:* NEA/OEA/JCES; *office:* Fleming Mid Sch 6001 Monument Dr Grants Pass OR 97526

HOOVER, PATRICIA ZERBEE, 1st Grade Teacher; *b:* Spangler, PA; *m:* Donald L.; *c:* Nichole, Martina, Lindsey; *ed:* (MA) Psych, IN Univ of PA; Grad Courses Lead Teacher Center; *cr:* 3rd Grade Teacher 1973-80, 2nd Grade Teacher 1981-83, Kndgtn Teacher 1983-87, 1st Grade Teacher 1988- Cambria Heights Sch; *office:* Cambria Heights Sch 510 Beech Ave Patton PA 16668

HOOVER, SARAH LYNDA, Vocal Music HS Teacher; *b:* Gonzales, TX; *ed:* (BMUSED) Vocal Music, E TX St Univ 1979; (MS) Choral Conducting, Eastmon Sch of Music 1985; *cr:* Asst Choir Dir A&M Consolidated HS 1980-84; Vocal Music Dir Choctraw HS 1985-; *ai:* Show Choir Dir; OK Music Educators Assn, OK Choral Dirs Assn, Amer Choral Dirs Assn Membership 1990; Edmond Cmmty Chorale 1988-; Rochester Cmmty Chorus Asst Dir 1984-85; Bev Henson Chorale Soloist 1981-83.

HOOVER, SHARON POPE, Sixth Grade Teacher; *b:* Jacksonville, NC; *m:* Ronald Lee Sr.; *ed:* (BS) Elem Ed, 1973, (MS) Elem Ed, 1977 GA Southwestern Coll; *cr:* 3rd/5th Grade Teacher Claxton Elem 1973-75; Title I Rdng Lab Teacher Isabella Elem 1975-82; 6th Grade Teacher Morningside Elem 1982-85, Radium Springs Mid Sch 1985-; *ai:* Beta Club Spon; Prof Assn of GA Educators 1982-; *office:* Radium Springs Mid Sch 2600 Radium Springs Rd Albany GA 31705

HOOVLER, LEE W., Chemistry Teacher; *b:* Butler, PA; *m:* Mary Ann Novak; *c:* David, Carole; *ed:* (BS) Chem/Math, Muskingum Coll 1960; (MST) Chem, Univ of NH 1967; NSF Summer Insts Muskingum Coll 1968, Hope Coll 1972; *cr:* Math Teacher Zanesville HS 1961-62; Math/Chem Teacher 1962-, Sci Dept Chm 1968- Knoch HS; *ai:* NEA, PA St Ed Assn; Meridian UP Church Elder 1966-; *office:* Knoch HS Dinnerbell Rd Saxonburg PA 16056

HOPEN, DIANNE BROWN, French Teacher/Intnl Specialty; *b:* Saint Paul, MN; *ed:* (BSC) Fr/His Ed, 1969, (MA) Second Lang Ed/Psych, 1980 Univ of MN Minneapolis; Working on PhD Second Lang Ed/Psych, Univ of MN; Honors Certificate Univ D Angers France 1978; Certificate Univ De Nantes France 1985; *cr:* Fr Teacher St Paul Public Schls 1969-; Dean/French Village 1972-84, Leader/Biking in France 1975- Concordia Coll; Consultant/Fr Materials DC Heath Co 1985-; Consultant/Writer/Fr Materials EMC Corporation 1985-; Intnl Planner St Paul Public Schls 1987-; *ai:* Fr, Ski, Intnl Clubs Adv; World Lang Dept Chairperson; Principals Advisory Bd Mem; Curr Steering & Multicultural Comm Mem; AATF Regional Rep 1981-87; MN Ed Assn 1978, 1989, Honor Roll Teacher; MN Bus Fnd 1984, Teacher of Excl; St Paul Rotary Club 1989, Educator of Yr; Intnl Inst of MN Bd Mem 1989-; Fulbright Teacher Exchange 1985; Guest of Fr Ministry of Ed Paris 1986; Guest of Fr Ministry of Ed Burgundy 1987; Ecolab Excl in Ed Grant 1988; Author Fr Materials for Concordia Coll Lang Villages & EMC Corporation; *office:* Humboldt Scndry Complex Sch 30 E Baker St Saint Paul MN 55107

HOPES, NANCY JEAN, Fourth Grade Teacher; *b:* Ft Benning, GA; *c:* Cassandra; *ed:* (BA) Elem Ed/His, Huston Tillotson Coll 1967; Cooperative Learning; Whole Lang Intergrating All Subjects; Heres Looking at You Drug Awareness Prgm, Prof Groth, Several CA Insts; *cr:* Headstart Educator/Rdng Specialsit Blackshear Elem Sch 1967-69; Educator T A Brown Elem Sch 1970-73, Northwood Elem Sch 1974-76, Summerdale Elem Sch 1976-; *ai:* Safety Patrol Coord; Cmptr Comm; CTA Human Rights Secy 1975-; NEA 1975-; *office:* Sumerdale Elem Sch 1100 Summerdale Dr San Jose CA 95132

HOPKINS, ADA R. YOUNG, 1st Grade Teacher; *b:* Gadsden, SC; *w:* Oliver (dec); *c:* Oliver J. Jr., Anthony B.; *ed:* (BA) Elem Ed, Benedict Coll 1953; SC St Coll; Univ of SC; the Citadel; Winthrop Coll; *cr:* Teacher Elloree Elem Sch 1967-.

HOPKINS, BONNIE CLAPPER, Sixth Grade Teacher; *b:* Morgantown, WV; *m:* John Franklin; *c:* John Jr., Derek D., Scott C.; *ed:* (BA) Elem Ed, Rivier Coll 1980; *cr:* Substitute Teacher Salem Sch Dist 1978-80; 3rd Grade Teacher Underhill Sch 1981; 5th-6th Grade Eng Teacher St Annes 1982-87; 6th Grade Teacher Holy Family 1987-88, Kingston Elem 1988-; *ai:* Faculty Advisory Comm 1989-; Health Curr Dev Comm; Horace Mann Grant Recipient 1989-; Parts of Speech Mastery; Golden Apple Awd 1988; Rainbows For All Gods Children Facilitator; *home:* 52 Old Washington St Pembroke MA 02359

HOPKINS, DEBORAH L., Science Teacher; *b:* Kittery Naval Base, ME; *ed:* (BS) Sci Teaching, Clemson Univ 1988; *cr:* Sci Teacher Walhalla HS 1988-; *ai:* Sci Club Spon; Sci Olympiad Coach; Faculty Relations Management Comm; NSTA 1988-; SC Sci Cncl 1989-; *office:* Walhalla HS Razorback Ln Walhalla SC 29691

HOPKINS, GARY A., 6th Grade Teacher; *b:* Brookville, PA; *m:* Vickie Lynn Zimmerman; *c:* Matthew, Courtney; *ed:* (BS) Elem Ed, 1973, (MED) Ed, 1978, (ACSA) Sch of Admin, 1981 Edinboro Univ; *cr:* Teacher Corry Area Sch Dist 1975-84; Prin Grand Valley Mid Sch 1984-85; Teacher Corry Area Sch Dist 1985-; *ai:* Little League Soccer & Golf; NEA, PSEA, PASCD, CAEA; Zam Zam Shrine 1988-; Oasis Lodge #416 Jr Master of Ceremonies 1984-; Influencial Teacher with Graduating Honor Stu; *office:* Spartansburg Elem Sch Water St Spartansburg PA 16434

HOPKINS, GEORGE EDWARD, JR., Principal/Dist Fed Prgms Dir; *b:* Herrin, IL; *m:* Tina Marie Webster; *c:* Austin, Dustin; *ed:* (AA) John A Logan Coll 1971; (BA) Poly Sci/Speech, Murray St Univ 1973; (MS) Educl Leadership, S IL Univ 1984; Ed Admin & Higher Ed, Doctoral Prgm S IL Univ; *cr:* 7th/8th Grade Teacher Pinckneyville Cmmty Consolidated Dist 212 1974-76; Eng/His Teacher Cntrl Jr HS 1978-86: Asst Prin Frankfort Cmmty HS 1986-87; Curr Dir Frankfort Commty Unit Dist 168 1987-89; *ai:* Jr HS Bsbl Coach; Regional Elem Prin Networking Group Coord; Phi Delta Kappa 1983-; ASCD 1987-89; Sch Masters Club 1986-; W Frankfort Recreation Assn 1989-; W Frankfort Arts Cncl 1985-; *office:* Denning Elem Sch 1401 W 6th West Frankfort IL 62896

HOPKINS, JACKIE JONES, Instructional Computer Coord; *b:* Trenton, TN; *m:* Charles Emmett; *c:* Will, Sherry, Jenny, Hank; *ed:* (BS) Ed, Memphis St Univ 1961; Grad Stud W GA Coll; *cr:* Elem Teacher Canton Elem 1961-68; Math Teacher Hickory Flat Elem 1968-88; Cmptr Coord Cherokee Cty Bd of Ed 1988-; *ai:* Staff Dev Instr; Delta Kappa Gamma 1981-; PAGE 1985-; Jaycees Outstanding Young Educator 1973; *office:* Cherokee Cty Bd of Ed 110 Academy St Canton GA 30114

HOPKINS, JODY JAHNA, Phys Ed Teacher/Coach; *b:* Silver City, NM; *ed:* (BA) Phys Ed, W NM 1983; *cr:* Phys Ed Teacher/Coach Ruidoso Mid Sch 1984-87, Ruidoso HS 1987-; *ai:* Vlybl & Bsktbl Coach; *office:* Ruidoso HS 200 Horton Ruidoso NM 88345

HOPKINS, KAREN PAYNE, Math Teacher; *b:* Lynchburg, VA; *m:* J. W. Jr.; *c:* Julia D.; *ed:* (BS) Math/Physics, Longwood Coll 1975; (MED) Admin, Lynchburg Coll 1981; *cr:* Math Teacher 1975-82; Math Dept Chairperson 1979-82 Linkhorne Mid Sch; Math Teacher Heritage HS 1987-; *ai:* Sr Class Spon; Lynch Public Schls News Team; Teacher Recognition Comm; NCTM 1989-; *office:* Heritage H S 3020 Wards Ferry Rd Lynchburg VA 24502

HOPKINS, KATHRYN HARMON, Science Teacher; *b:* Houston, TX; *m:* Mark Alan; *c:* Paula, Jennifer, Laura; *ed:* (BA) Bio, 1975, (MSED) Ed, 1982 Baylor Univ; Wkshp Prgm, M D Anderson U T Cancer Center 1989; *cr:* Eng/Sci Teacher Mart HS 1976-77, Aquilla HS 1977-83; Eng Teacher HubbaRd HS 1983-84; Sci Teacher Robinson HS 1985-; *ai:* Sci Fair, UIL Sci; NSTA, NABT 1985-; Robinson Classroom Teachers Assn (Pres 1988-89) 1985- Schlsp 1988, 1989; Camp Fire Leader 1986-87; Alpha Delta Kappa Mem 1989-; Gifted & Talented Ed Grant 1990; TX Joint Cncl of Eng Teachers 1st Place Essay 1979; *office:* Robinson HS 500 W Lyndale Waco TX 76706

HOPKINS, LINDA HOLT, Computer Literacy Teacher; *b:* Richmond, VA; *m:* Zenas Warren Jr.; *c:* Natalie; *ed:* (BA) Math, Univ of Richmond 1972; Working Towards Masters Ed, Old Dominion Univ; *cr:* Math Teacher Craddock HS 1972-73, Maggie L Walker 1973-76, Azalea Garden Jr HS 1976-79, Deep Creek Jr HS 1979-87; Cmptr Literacy Teacher Deep Creek HS 1987-; *ai:* Stu Cooperative Assn Spon; Responsible for Academic Assembly & Banquet; Chesapeake Ed Assn, VA Ed Assn, NEA, Tidewater Cncl Teachers of Math; PTA (VP 1989-, Bd Mem 1988-89), Life Membership 1988-89; Deep Creek Jr HS Teacher of Yr 1988-89; *office:* Deep Creek Jr HS 1955 Deal Dr Chesapeake VA 23323

HOPKINS, MICHELLE LEE, English Teacher; *b:* Muncy, PA; *ed:* (BS) Eng, Bloomsburg Univ 1979; *cr:* Eng/Long Term Substitute Teacher 1979-89, Eng Teacher 1989- Montoursville HS; *ai:* Jr HS Girls Bsktbl Coach; Warriorette Dancers Adv; Organization of Montoursville Educators; *office:* Montoursville HS 100 N Arch St Montoursville PA 17754

HOPKINS, PAMELA LEE, English Teacher; *b:* Kosciusko, MS; *ed:* (BA) Eng, MS St Univ 1973; (MA) Ed Psych, Univ of AZ 1978; Course Work in Various Field; *cr:* Eng Teacher Starkville HS 1973-74; Teacher of Gifted/Eng Sunnyside HS 1978-86; Eng Teacher Desert View HS 1986-; *ai:* Girls Bsktbl & Academic Decathlon Coach; Planet Outreach & Ocean Outreach Spon; EEI Facilitator; Earth Day Coord; Career Ladder Mentor; NCTE 1973-; NEA 1978-; AZ Eng Assn 1976-; Academic Decathlon 1984; Ideals Corporation Grant 1990; *office:* Desert View HS 4101 E Valencia Tucson AZ 85706

HOPPE, SUSAN HANSON, Third Grade Teacher; *b:* Tomahawk, WI; *m:* Richard; *c:* Laura; *ed:* (BS) Elem Ed, Univ of WI Stevens Point 1978; *cr:* Mid Sch Teacher 1978-87, 3rd Grade Teacher 1987- Winneconne Cntrl Sch; *ai:* NCTE 1986-87; *office:* Winneconne Cntrl Mid Sch 233 S 3rd Ave Winneconne WI 54986

HOPPENJANS, DIANE GOGEL, 5th/6th Grade Math Teacher; *b:* Huntingburg, IN; *m:* Alvin; *ed:* (BA) Elem Ed, 1976, (MS) Elem Ed, 1978 IN St Univ; Cmptr Trng, IN St Univ; Math & Rdng Achivevement Wkshps; Cmptr Software In-Services; TTT, TESA, Madeline Hunter Trng; *cr:* 4th Grade Teacher 1976-78, 1st/2nd Grade Teacher of Gifted 1978-79 Holy Family Sch; 5th/6th Grade Math Teacher Ferdinand Elem 1979-; *ai:* Cmptr & Math Facts Hall of Fame Coord; Technology, Slide Shw, Talent Show, REAP Grant, Hoosier Sch Awd Comms; IN Rdng Assn; NEA, ISTA 1976-; PTO Bd 1979-81; Book Published; Ind Colls & Univs of IN Incorporated Grant; *office:* Ferdinand Elem Sch 930 Maryland Ferdinand IN 47532

HOPPENRATH, PATRICIA J., Physical Ed Teacher/Coach; *b:* Hinsdale, IL; *ed:* (BSED) Phys Ed/Bus Admin, 1982, (MSED) Adapted Phys Ed, 1984 N IL Univ; Water Safety & Lifeguard Instr; First Aid, CPR; *cr:* Head Lifeguard/Pool Mgr Emerald Green Rec Assn 1976-; Phys Ed Teacher/Coach Naperville Cntrl HS 1984-; Athletic Camp Dir Naperville Park Dist 1989-; *ai:* Girls Bsktbl & Sftbl Coach; Athletic Supvr; Amer Alliance for Health, Phys Ed, Recreation, Dance; IL Alliance for Health, Phys Ed, Recreation, Dance; CEC; IL Coalition of Univ Prgms in Adapted Phys Ed; Nom Kohl Intnl Teaching Awd 1990; Nom IL Teacher of Yr Awd 1990; *office:* Naperville Cntrl HS 440 W Aurora Ave Naperville IL 60540

HOPPER, BARBRA ANNE, Advanced Learning Teacher; *b:* Middletown, NY; *m:* Charles Hugh; *c:* Charles S., Christina L.; *ed:* (BA) His, Emory Univ 1969; (MED) Ed, GA SW 1977; Grad Stud Sci, Gifted; *cr:* Scndry Teacher Londiani Scndry Sch 1970-71; Soc Stud/Teacher of Gifted Perry HS 1972-79; Soc Stud Teacher Cobb Cty 1975-79; Teacher of Gifted Walton HS 1975-; *ai:* Academic Bowl Spon Jr Var Team; Stu for Promotion of Environmental Awareness; *office:* Walton HS 1590 Bill Murdock Rd Marietta GA 30062

HOPPER, ELLEN REAL, Third Grade Teacher; *b:* Sallisaw, OK; *m:* David D.; *c:* Jeani A.; *ed:* (BA) Elem Ed, 1969, (ME) Elem Ed 1974 Northeastern St Univ; *cr:* Teacher Spiro Elem Sch; *ai:* NEA 1975-; OEA 1969-; OK Rdng Assn 1986-88/1990; Internal Rdng Assn 198-89/1990; *home:* HC 61 Box 248 Sallisaw OK 74955

HOPPER, MARTHA KETCHUM, 5th Grade Reading Teacher; *b:* Dyersburg, TN; *m:* Collie Bill; *ed:* (BA) His, Union Univ 1971; (ME) Rdng, Memphis St Univ; Grad Stud Univ of TN Martin; *cr:* 6th Grade Teacher Lauderdale Cty Schls 1971-72; 5th Grade Rdng Teacher 1972-76, 3rd Grade Teacher 1976-86 Cntrl Elem; 5th Grade Rdng Teacher Dyersburg Intermediate Sch 1986-; *ai:* Dyersburg Ed Assn (Mem, Soc Comm Mem) 1980-82; TN Ed Assn; Hawthorne Baptist Church Clerk 1980-84; Hawthorne Acteens Leader 1983-85; *home:* PO Box 671 Welch Rd Dyersburg TN 38025

HOPPER, MARTY LUKE, Eighth Grade Teacher; *b:* Rutherford, NC; *m:* Shelia Melton; *c:* Lukas; *ed:* (BS) Intermediate Ed, Wingate 1984; *cr:* 6th-8th Grade Sci Teacher Bostic Elem 1984-; *ai:* Boys & Girls Bsktbl & Boys Sftbl.

HOPPER, PEGGY MC PHERSON, Art/Reading/Spelling Teacher; *b:* Enterprice, AL; *c:* Jonna L.; *ed:* (MS) Elem Ed, 1987, (BA) Ed, 1977 Souhtwestern OK St Univ; Lions Quest Skills for Adolescents Facilitator; *cr:* Art Teacher Vici & Sharon Mutual 1978-80; Art/Rdng/Spelling & Lions Quest Teacher Sharon Mutual 1980-85, Vici Sch 1985-; *ai:* Class Spon for 1990 Seniors; Continuing Ed Comm; Lions Quest Facilitator; Lioness VP 1988; Wrote a Grant for Lions Quest Skills for Growing; *home:* 701 Canterbury Altus OK 73521

HORA, LINDA BEATON, Sixth Grade Teacher; *b:* Waterloo, IA; *m:* Charles E. (Ted) II; *c:* Natalie, Amber; *ed:* (BA) Elem Ed, Univ of N IA 1968; Grad Stud IA St Univ; *cr:* 1st Grade Teacher Dubuque Schls 1968; 6th Grade Teacher Franklin Elem 1983-; *ai:* Sch Improvement Model Stakeholder; Performance Base Pay Participant; Art Vertical, Level Comm Chm; Boone Ed Assn Secy 1985-87; IA St Ed Assn, NEA 1982-; N Cntrl IA Presbyn Sewing & Supplies Chairperson 1978-81; *office:* Franklin Elem Sch 1924 Crawford St Boone IA 50036

HORACK, LARRY, 5th Grade Teacher; *b:* Bakersfield, CA; *m:* Donna Overstreet; *c:* Mike, Brad; *ed:* (BA) Ed, Fresno St Univ 1962; *cr:* 6th Grade Teacher Highland Elem 1962-64; 7th/8th Grade Teacher Math/Span/Construction/Mechanical Drawing/Metal Shop/Wood Shop Stan Jr HS 1965-79; Fencing Contractor Self Employed 1979-81; 4th Grade Teacher Stan Elem 1981-83; 7th/8th Grade Teacher Wood Shop/Metal Shop/ Stan Jr HS 1984-89; 5th Grade Teacher Highland Elem 1989-; *ai:* CEC; CTA Salary Chm 1964; NEA; CTA CEC 1989-; NSF Grant Univ CA Berkeley; *home:* 6905 Kimberly Ave Bakersfield CA 93308

HORAN, MARTHA ANN, French Teacher; *b:* Delano, PA; *m:* John; *c:* David, Karen; *ed:* (BS) Fr/Scndry Ed, Bloomsburg Univ 1970; *cr:* Fr/Eng Teacher Mahanoy Area HS 1970-; *ai:* Fr Club

Adv; NEA, PSEA, MAEA, AATF; *office:* Mahanoy Area HS 800 W South St Mahanoy City PA 17948

HORD, CHERYL SNAPP, Fourth Grade Teacher; *b:* Willard, OH; *m:* Randy Lee; *c:* Arielle R.; *ed:* (BS) Elem Ed, OH St Univ 1980; Ethics in America, Cleveland St Univ; *cr:* Substitute Teacher Mansfield City Schls 1980; 4th Grade Teacher S Cntrl Local Schls 1980-; *ai:* Pilot Prgm Character Ed; Course Study for Sci, Rdng, Assessment Team Comm; *office:* S Cntrl Local Schls New St Greenwich OH 44837

HORD, RANDY LEE, Bio/Life Science Teacher; *b:* Willard, OH; *m:* Cheryl A. Snapp; *c:* Arielle R.; *ed:* (BS) Elem Ed, OH St Univ 1979; Addl Studies Univ of WA; Heidelberg Coll; Ashland Univ; OH St Univ; *cr:* Elem Phys Ed Jr HS Health Teacher 1979-80; Jr HS Eng Teacher 1980-81 Mansfield St Peters; Elem Teacher Buckeye Central 1981-85; Jr HS 9th Grade Sci Teacher 1985-89 Buckeye Central; Bio/Life Sci Teacher Norwalk HS 1989-; *ai:* Varsity Ftbl Asst Coach; North Cntrl Conference Pres 1988-89; *home:* 1039 Townline Rd 12 Willard OH 44890

HORIN, LEON W., Mathematics Teacher; *b:* Millvile, NJ; *m:* Angela Tammaro; *c:* Michele, Leon W. Jr., Jeffrey, Brian; *ed:* (BS) Accounting/Finance, Villanova Univ 1960; *cr:* 5th Grade Teacher Port Norris 1963-64, Park & East Sch 1964-65; 7th-9th Grade Math & JBT Teacher Memorial Sch 1965-74; 7th Grade Math Teacher Landis Sch 1974-; *ai:* Shop-Rite Apple Cmptr Give Away Prgm; NJ Mid Sch Math Contest; NEA, NJ Ed Assn, Cumberland Cty Ed Assn 1963-; Vineland Ed Assn 1964-; St John Bosco Church; Knights of Columbus; *office:* Landis Mid Sch 61 W Landis Ave Vineland NJ 08360

HORN, GAYLE PATRICIA, Peer Teacher/Counselor; *b:* Bonne Terre, MO; *m:* Kenneth Wayne; *c:* Angela G., Adam W.; *ed:* (BS) Eng, SE MO St Univ 1965; (MED) Guidance/Counseling, Univ of MO St Louis 1980; Licensed Prof Cnslr 1989; *cr:* 10th/12th Grade Teacher Ritenour HS 1965-67; 7th/9th Grade Teacher Hardin Jr HS 1968-80; 9th-12th Grade Teacher 1980-82, 9th-12th Grade Cnslr 1982- St Charles HS; *ai:* Co-Teach Peer Facilitator Class; HS Taught Elem Prgm Spon; Pirate Pals; Choices Group; Ambassadors Club; Adv Sr Class; Mentors for At Risk Stu Dir; NHS Asst; Amer Assn of Counseling & Dev 1988-; NEA 1970-; MO Peer Helpers Assn Bd Mem 1989-; Mid Rivers Assn for Counseling & Dev 1983-, Service 1987; Intnl Assn for Marriage & Family Counseling 1989-; Achievement Awd Peer Facilitator; Impact Awd; Service Awd St Charles Sch Dist; Natl Peer Helpers Assn Presenter; *office:* St Charles HS Kings Hwy & Waverly Saint Charles MO 63301

HORN, JEANETTE REED, Second Grade Teacher; *b:* Hawthorne, CA; *m:* Robert Alan; *ed:* (BA) Liberal Stud, CA St Univ Fullerton 1977; Grad Stud; *cr:* 2nd Grade Teacher Friends Chrstn Sch 1977-; *ai:* Lead Teacher; Amer Riding Club for Handicapped Equitation Trainer 1980-; *office:* Friends Chrstn Sch 5211 Lakeview Yorba Linda CA 92686

HORNADAY, THERESA (WILSON), Fourth Grade Teacher; *b:* New Castle, IN; *m:* James D.; *c:* Jason, Ryan; *ed:* (BS) Elem 1979, (MA) Elem, 1983 Ball St Univ; *cr:* 4th Grade Teacher Sulphur Springs Elem 1979-; *ai:* Henry Cty Rdng Cncl; ISTA; *office:* Sulphur Springs Elem Sch Box 38 Sulphur Springs IN 47388

HORNBECK, JANEL MONIQUE, Mathematics Department Chair; *b:* Chico, CA; *m:* Parker Britten; *c:* Britt, Juli, Jennifer, Jill; *ed:* (BA) Liberal Stud, CA St San Francisco 1982; (MA) Ed, St Marys-Moraga 1986; Enrolled in Admin Staff Dev Credential Prgm; *cr:* Teacher/Dept Chairperson Charlotte Wood Sch 1984-; Math Task Force Chairperson San Ramon Valley Unified Sch Dist 1986-; *ai:* CJSF Spon; Math Advisory Comm Mem; Mentor Teacher; Testing & Staff Dev Comm; NCTM 1985-; Amer Red Cross (First Aid Instr 1970-, CPR 1972-); Natl Ski Patrol (Winter First Aid Instr 1972-, Secy 1988-); *office:* Charlotte Wood Sch 566 S Hartz Ave Danville CA 94526

HORNBERGER, PATRICIA ORR, Kindergarten Teacher; *b:* Crown City, OH; *m:* D. William; *c:* Cherie Smith, Mark D., Jennifer Phipps; *ed:* (BSC) Elem Ed, OH St Univ 1953; 5th Yr Elem Ed, Cntrl WA Univ 1981; *cr:* Kndgtn Teacher Mc Guffey Elem Sch 1954-55; Dir Cross Age Tutoring Christ United Meth Church 1969-70; Teachers Aide Park Mid Sch 1975-77; Kndgtn Teacher Westgate Elem Sch 1977-; *ai:* Delta Kappa Gamma Hospitality Co-Chm 1988-; WORD 1987-; Cub Scouts Den Mother ; *office:* Westgate Elem 2515 W 4th Kennewick WA 99336

HORNE, BRUCE ARTHUR, Fifth Grade Teacher; *b:* Ridley Park, PA; *m:* Nancy C. Clune; *c:* Eric, Laurie; *ed:* (BS) Elem Ed, West Chester St Univ 1974; (MS) Rdng, Temple; *cr:* 2nd Grade Teacher 1975-82, 4th Grade Teacher 1982-87, 6th Grade Teacher 1987-88, 5th Grade Teacher 1988- Eddystone Elem; *ai:* Safety Prgm Dir; 4-H Leader; Intramural Leader; Co-Ed Newspaper; Video Leader; Fall Fair Chm; NEA 1975-; Home & Sch Teacher Rep 1987-, Appreciation Awd 1989; *office:* Eddystone Elem Sch 9th & Simpson Sts Eddydstone PA 19013

HORNE, DON CLAYTON, Social Studies Teacher; *b:* Wood, VA; *m:* Virginia Caplinger; *c:* Justin K.; *ed:* (BS) His/Government, OH St Univ 1968; (MS) Ed, East Cntrl OK St Univ 1978; *cr:* Teacher Checotah OK 1970-71, Mc Alester OK 1971-; *ai:* Textbook Comm; OK Curr Soc Stud; Assn of Classroom Teachers Chief Negotiator 1978-79; Rural Water Bd (Secy, Treas) 1989-; US Army Captain 1968-70; Influencial Teacher Univ of Chicago; Freedoms Fnd Schlsp; *home:* Rt 1 Box 129 Stuart OK 74570

HORNE, JAMES D., World History Instructor; *b:* Salt Lake City, UT; *m:* Lynne Carman; *c:* Matthew, Allison; *ed:* (BS) Scndry Ed, Univ of WY 1982; *cr:* Educator/Coach Dean Morgan Jr HS 1982-84; Kelly Walsh HS 1989-; *ai:* Ftbl Coach; Fellowship of Chrstn Athletes Huddle Spon; Spec Budget Comm Mem; NCSS Mem 1986; Natrona Cty Teachers Assn 1982-83; *office:* Kelly Walsh HS 3500 E 12th St Casper WY 82609

HORNE, LINDA ARDIS (PITZEN), Teacher of Gifted; *b:* Roseburg, OR; *ed:* (BS) Bio, Whitworth Coll 1967; (MED) Curr/Instruction/Learning Styles/Brain Research/Gifted, Seattle Pacific Univ 1990; Grad Stud Various Courses; *cr:* Elem Teacher Huntington Beach 1967-69, Highline Schls Dist 1969-71, Chimacum Elem 1971-72, Grass Lake 1972-78; Teacher of Gifted Ridgewood Elem 1978-; *ai:* Staff Dev & Prof Growth Instr; Sch Based Management Team Leader; Master Teacher; Planning Comm Mem; Sci Curr Writer; PTSA, WA Assn for Ed of Talented & Gifted, NW Gifted Child Assn, ASCD, NSTA 1989-; Greenpeace, World Wildlife Organization, Natl Humane Society; WORD & WAETAG Presentor Awds; UPS Schlsp; Gifted Ind Stud Writers Grant; *home:* PO Box 58371 Renton WA 98058

HORNER, CAROL ELIZABETH, Mathematics Teacher; *b:* Bedford, PA; *m:* Randy W.; *ed:* (BA) Health/Phys Ed/Recreation, Lock Haven Univ 1983; Stud Intnl Sch of Theology San Bernardino CA & GA St Univ; *cr:* Staff Mem Campus Crusade for Christ Intnl 1984-86; Substitute Teacher/Coach Chestnut Ridge Sch Dist 1986-87; Math Teacher/Coach De Kalb Chrstn Acad 1987-; *ai:* Var Asst Coach Girls Sftbl 1988-89, Bsktbl 1987-; Math Team Spon 1989-; GA Cncl of Teachers of Math 1989-; Phi Kappa Phi 1983-; Kappa Delta Pi 1981-; Trinity Evangelical Presbyn Church 1989-; *home:* 1452 Derby Downs Dr Lawrenceville GA 30243

HORNER, ELAINE CARMICHAEL, Math & Algebra Teacher; *b:* Portales, NM; *m:* Bill G. Sr.; *c:* Billy G. Jr., Frances Horner Moreau, Aaron J.; *ed:* (BA) Elem Ed, 1973, (MS) Scndry Ed, 1978 ENMU; Elem & Scndry Courses, ENMU, ENMU-R, NMSU-C; *cr:* Math Teacher Park Jr HS 1973-; *ai:* Artesia Educl Assn VP 1988-89; Delta Kappa Gamma Treas 1988-; NCTM, NCTM-NM; *home:* 2406 N Haldeman Rd Artesia NM 88210

HORNER, KAREN MATHEWS, First Grade Teacher; *b:* Miami, OK; *m:* Jimmie Warren; *c:* Warren K., Michael T.; *ed:* (BS) Elem Ed, 1969, (MED) Rdng, 1980 W TX St Univ; *cr:* 1st Grade Teacher Hamlet Elem 1969-70; Kndgtn Teacher Humphreys Highland Elem 1971-74; 1st Grade Teacher Sunrise Elem 1976-; *ai:* Mem of Supts Teacher Communication Comm 1989-; NEA, TX St Teachers Assn, Amarillo Classroom Teacher Assn 1976-; PTA 1976-; Sunrise Elem Teacher of Yr 1989-; *office:* Sunrise Elem Sch 5123 E 14th Amarillo TX 79104

HORNER, TANYA EVON (FEDORA), Mathematics Teacher; *b:* Brownwood, TX; *m:* Thomas R.; *c:* Brant, Brinn; *ed:* (BA) Math, Howard Payne Univ 1968; (MST) Math, Tarleton St Univ 1980; *cr:* Math Teacher Brownwood Jr HS 1968-83, Brownwood HS 1984-; *ai:* Key Club Adv; Just Say No & Ftbl Spirit Ribbon Sales Coord; Jr HS Occupational Investigation Advisory Cncl; TX St Teachers Assn Pres 1984-85; TX Cncl Teachers of Math, TX Assn for Continuing Adult Ed; Lions Mothers Club Scrapbook Chairperson 1984-85; Kiwanis; Cntrl TX Cooperative Teacher Center Secy 1985-88; Brownwood HS Teacher of Yr 1988-89; Brownwood Ind Sch Dist Cmmty Ed Advisory Cncl Secy; Brownwood Beautification Comm; *office:* Brownwood HS 2100 Slayden Brownwood TX 76801

HORNER, TONYA EVON (FEDORA), Mathematics Teacher; *b:* Brownwood, TX; *m:* Thomas R.; *c:* Brant, Brinn; *ed:* (BA) Math, Howard Payne Univ 1968; (MST) Math, Tarleton St Univ 1980; *cr:* Math Teacher Brownwood Jr HS 1968-83, Brownwood HS 1984-; *ai:* Key Club Adv; Just Say No & Ftbl Spirit Ribbon Sales Coord; TX St Teachers Assn Local Pres 1984-85; TX Cncl Teachers of Math, TX Assn for Contunuing Adult Ed; Lions Mothers Club Scrapbook Chairperson 1984-85; Kiwanis; Cntrl TX Cooperative Teacher Center Secy 1985-88; TX-OK Key Club Faculty Adv of Yr 1989-; Brownwood HS Teacher of Yr 1988-89; Jr HS Occupational Investigation Advisory Cncl; Brownwood Ind Sch Dist Cmmty Ed Advisory Cncl; Brownwood Beautification Comm; *office:* Brownwood HS 2100 Slayden Brownwood TX 76801

HORNER, WILLIAM ALVIE, 6th Grade Science Teacher; *b:* Bridgeport, OH; *ed:* (BS) Elem Ed, Salisbury St Univ 1954; (MED) Elem Ed, Appalachian St Univ 1966; *cr:* 6th Grade Elem Teacher Havre de Grace Elem 1954-66; 6th Grade Mid Sch Sci Teacher Havre de Grace 1967-; *ai:* Sci & Bsktbl Clubs; Taught Chorus; Bi-Centennial Organizer for Schls 1975; Woodworking; Harford Cty Ed Assn, MD St Teachers Assn, NEA; Elk Lodge, BSA; Harford Cty Outstanding Educator 1985; *home:* 101 Deaver St Havre De Grace MD 21078

HORNEY, ROBERT R., Elem Music/Mid Sch Chorus; *b:* Plymouth, IN; *m:* Marianne Ward; *c:* Marc, Kevin; *ed:* (BS) Elem Ed, Manchester Coll 1960; (MS) Elem Ed/Sch Admin, IN Univ 1965; Admin & Ed; *cr:* 5th Grade Teacher Maple Park Elem Sch 1960-64, Valley View Elem Sch 1964-68; Elem Music Teacher Valley View/Palm View Elem Schls 1968-72; Elem Prin Palm View Elem Sch 1972-76, San Jacinto Elem Sch 1976-83; Elem Music/Mid Sch Chorus Teacher Monte Vista Mid Sch 1983-; *ai:* Chorus Club Adv; Coachella Teachers Assn Pres 1968; San Jacinto Teachers Assn (Pres 1986-88, Chief Negotiator 1986, 1989); Amer Youth Soccer Organization Registration; Hyatt Elem Sch Teacher of Yr 1985-86; *home:* 42060 Acacia Ave Hemet CA 92344

HORNICK, JERI LYN, 3rd Grade Teacher; *b:* Ark City, KS; *m:* Herbert; *c:* Jon, James; *ed:* (BS) Elem Ed, OK St Univ 1974; Gesell Examiner Advncd Trng; *cr:* Libn Ponca City Sch 1974-75; Kndgtn Teacher 1975-85; 3rd Grade Teacher 1987- Duncan Schls; *ai:* Delta Kappa Gamma 1985-; *office:* Horace Mann Elem Sch 1201 Whisenaut Duncan OK 73533

HORNS, DAVID H., 6th Grade Teacher; *b:* Willmar, MN; *m:* Jane Colton; *c:* Sarah, Steven; *ed:* (AA) Elem Ed, Willmar Jr Coll 1967; (BS) Elem Ed, 1969, (MS) Elem Ed, 1975 St Cloud St; *cr:* 6th Grade Teacher Kenneth Hall Elem 1969; *ai:* Grade Level Rep; TAT; Mem of Comm on Reporting and Evaluation; Mem Comm on Retention & Promotion Comm on Students at Risk; Spring Lake Park Elem 1984-; Fed of Teachers VP; *office:* Kenneth Hall Elem Sch 8089 Able St Ne Spring Lake Park MN 55432

HORNSBY, JUDITH BENNETT, Teacher Visually Handicapped; *b:* Xenia, OH; *m:* Orson; *c:* Jeffrey W., Mary K.; *ed:* (BSED) Music Ed, OH Univ 1964; (MA) Spec Ed, OH St Univ 1966; Rdng Teachers Certificate & Educable Mentally Retarded Certificate Univ of Cincinnati; *cr:* Teacher of Visually Handicapped Cincinnati Public Schls 1964-70; Rdng Teacher Cincinnati Cntry Day Sch 1972-75; Pre-Sch Teacher of Visually Handicapped Cincinnati Public Schls 1975-80; Teacher of Visually Handicapped Hamilton City Schls 1981-; *ai:* Visually Handicapped Stus Camping Experiences Organizer; Arranged HS Stus to Attend Congressional Youth Leadership Cncl; Alpha Delta Kappa (Historian 1982-86, Chaplain 1986-88, Corresponding Secy 1988-); Intnl Rdng Assn; Natl Assn Educators & Rehabilitation Workers; OH Assn Educators & Rehabilitation Workers Bd Mem 1988-; Natl Braille Assn, Sigma Alpha Iota; SW OH Spec Ed Regional Resource Center Outstanding Spec Ed Teacher; Helped Revise Booklet for Visually Handicapped; *office:* Hamilton City Schls 332 Dayton ST PO Box 627 Hamilton OH 45012

HORNSBY, NANCY GARY, Elementary Teacher; *b:* Lake Charles, LA; *m:* Larry Dale; *c:* Jonathan P., Jennifer L., Megan N.; *ed:* (BA) Elem Ed, Mc Neese 1979; Grad Stud 1980-83; *cr:* 6th Grade Teacher St Margarets 1979-80; Teacher South Beauregard Elem 1980-; *home:* Rt 1 Box 81 Ragley LA 70657

HOROWICZ, RICHARD EDMUND, History Teacher; *b:* Mc Keesport, PA; *m:* Robbye Barrow; *c:* Neysa L., Christopher, Benjamin, Joshua; *ed:* (BS) Intnl Affairs, Georgetown Univ 1961; (MS) Ed, Johns Hopkins 1969; *cr:* Dept Head/Instr US Army Intelligence Sch 1967-69; Teacher Northern HS 1969-75, Talmudical Acad 1971-; Teacher/Dept Head Northwestern HS 1975-; *ai:* MO Cncl for Soc Stud, Mid St Cncl for Soc Stud, NCSS; Hamdel Choir of Baltimore 1985-; MD & Natl His Day Fair Judge; *office:* Talmudical Acad 4445 Old Court Rd Baltimore MD 21215

HOROWITZ, EVELYN, English Teacher; *b:* Boston, MA; *m:* Michael Malinowitz; *ed:* (BS) Theatre, Emerson Coll 1968; Grad Stud Cinema, NY Univ; *cr:* Eng Teacher Susan E Wagner HS 1968-86, Norman Thomas HS 1986-; *ai:* Poets House, Outstanding Teacher of Poetry 1986; Fellowship Bennington Coll 1979; Poetry Published; *office:* Norman Thomas HS 111 E 33rd St New York NY 10453

HOROWITZ, STEVEN ABRAHAM, 4th Grade Instructor; *b:* Grand Rapids, MI; *c:* Ludington; *ed:* (BS) Group Sci, W MI Univ 1971; *cr:* 5th Grade Teacher 1972-82, 4th Grade Teacher 1982- Hilltop Elem; *ai:* Cedar Springs Historical Society Pres 1989-; Mackinac Assocs Mem 1989-; Horowitzsonian Inst Dir; Hilltop Sch Teacher of Yr 1989; Historical Video; *home:* 423 S Main St Cedar Springs MI 49319

HORSEY, GERALDINE E. WARREN, Teacher; *b:* Indian Head, MD; *m:* Franklin; *ed:* (BA) Elem Ed, Bowie St Univ 1968; (APC) Elem Ed, George Washington Univ 1978; Several Wkshps, Univ of MD; Energy Wkshp, Charles Cty Comm Coll; *cr:* Teacher Nanjemoy Elem Sch 1968-70, Walter J Elem Sch 1970-; *ai:* Sci Fair Chairperson 1990; Ed Assn Charles Cty Membership; Person for Walter J Mitchell 1990; Charles Cty Ed Assn Membership 1988-; Walter J Mitchell Membership 1988; AAUW Membership 1984-86 Outstanding Educator 1985; Math Advisory Bd Mem 1980-85; Nom for Agnes Meyer Awd Wash Post 1988; Named Exemplary Teacher Charles Cty 1986; Participated Video Tape Production Guidelines for Charles Cty Teachers; *home:* PO Box 66 Pomfret MD 20675

HORST, BRENETTA DUKES, Instrumental Music Teacher; *b:* Highland Park, MI; *m:* Walter Osband; *c:* Armand O., Ramone K.; *ed:* (BA) Music Ed, Olivet Coll 1974; Working Towards Masters Educl Admin, Wayne St Univ; *cr:* Instrumental Music Teacher Ann Arbor Trail Mid Sch 1977-; *ai:* Word of Faith Chrstn Center Orch Asst Dir; MI St Band Orch Assn Mem; *office:* Ann Arbor Trail Mid Sch 7635 Chatham Detroit MI 48239

HORST, JOHN RUSSELL, Latin & Classics Teacher; *b:* Denver, CO; *m:* Kathryn Marie Girardo; *c:* Amy, John, Stephen; *ed:* (BA) Classical Lang 1969, (MA) Latin, 1971, (PHD) Classics, Univ of CO Boulder 1987; Inservices & Wkshps on Classics/Methodology of Teaching Latin; Trip Greece & Spain; Writer of Latin Curr Writer; *cr:* Eng Teacher 1971-72, Latin/Classical Teacher 1972-, His/Eng Teacher 1972- St Dominics; *ai:* Latin Club Adv & Spon 1972-; NHS Spon 1983-85; Former Mem Articulation Comm; Foreign Lang Dept Chm; Second Langs Coord 1984, 1985; CO Classics Assn 1988-; CO Teacher of Yr 1985; Pamphlets Writer & Developer; Guest Speaker; *office:* Arvada Sr/Golden Sr 7951 W 65th Ave Arvada CO 80004

HORSTMAN, JO ANN ELIZABETH, 6th Grade Teacher; *b:* Watkins, MN; *m:* John William; *c:* Jody, Jay; *ed:* (BA) Elem Ed, 1974; (MA) Elem Ed, 1986 St Cloud St Univ; *cr:* Teacher S/D 881 Maple Lake Elem 1974-; *ai:* Teacher Assisting Teachers; Centennial Playground; Chess Club; *home:* 9247 Zinnia Ln Maple Grove MN 55369

HORSTMANN, JUDY BENTON, Fourth Grade Teacher; *b:* Greenville, OH; *m:* Kenneth E.; *c:* Autumn J.; *ed:* (BS) Eng/Lib Sci, Bowling Green St Univ 1965; (BS) Elem Ed, Wright St 1973; *cr:* 9th-12th Grade Eng Teacher Bethel HS 1965-68; 4th Grade Teacher Westlake Elem 1969-; *office:* Westlake Elem Sch 621 Walsh Dr New Carlisle OH 45344

HORTERT, RUTH ELLEN, Fifth Grade Teacher; *b:* Butler, PA; *ed:* (BS) Elem Ed, Clarion St Teachers Coll 1967; Working Towards Masters in Cmptr Ed; *cr:* Art Supvr Chartiers Houston 1967, Redbank Valley 1967-69; Intermediate Grades Teacher Pinewood Elem 1969-; *ai:* Art, Cmptr Software, Soc Comm; BFT Rep; Advisory Comm Rep; Delta Kappa Gamma 1982-; PTO Rep; *home:* 22 E Towne Pl Titusville FL 32796

HORTON, BARBARA TAYLOR, 4th Grade Teacher; *b:* Monroe, LA; *m:* Lawrence O.; *c:* Glenn, Lawrence; *ed:* (BA) Spec Ed/Elem Ed, Grambling St Univ 1976; (MS) Elem Ed, OK City Univ 1987; *cr:* Intermediate Teacher Martin Luther King Sch 1977-78, Polk Elem Sch 1978-; *ai:* Sci Fair Coord; Hospitality Comm Mem; Vlybl Coach; Rdng Cncl 1988-; Chosen Most Outstanding Grad Stu OK City Univ 1987; Nom Educators Excellent Teacher by Jr League of OK City; *office:* Polk Elem Sch 3806 N Prospect Oklahoma City OK 73111

HORTON, ELAINE AUSTIN, First Grade Teacher/Admin Asst; *b:* Greenwood, SC; *m:* Paul Mackey; *c:* Alison; *ed:* (BS) Elem Ed, Lander Coll 1965; (MED) Elem Ed, Clemson Univ 1977; *cr:* Teacher Sch Dist of Pickens Cty 1965-; Admin Asst Morrison Elem Sch 1989-; *ai:* Chairperson of Adopt Morrison & Dist Elem Lang Art Curr Comm; Mem Sch Improvement Cncl; Phi Delta Kappa Local Pres 1985-86, Distinguished Service in Elem & Scndry Ed 1982; Pickens Cty Ed Assn Pres 1978-79, Friend of Ed 1978; Alpha Delta Kappa Publicity Chairperson; PTO VP; Clemson Child Dev Center Bd Mem 1989-; Voices for Children; Citizens Task Force on Ed; SC St Dept of Ed Teacher Grants; SC Arts Commission Lang Art Through Art Grant; Pickens Cty Career Woman of Yr 1987-88; *home:* 102 Valley View Ct Clemson SC 29631

HORTON, GARRY CURNINZA, Mathematics Teacher; *b:* Griffin, GA; *m:* Elsena Mae Shields; *c:* Sienna, Andre, Andreana; *ed:* (BS) Math/Chem, Albany St Coll 1970; (MS) Math, Univ of WA 1974; *cr:* Math Teacher Vienna HS 1970-71; Math Prof Eagle River Comm Coll 1973-74; Math Teacher Romig Jr HS 1974-76, Abbott Loop Chrstn Sch 1976-80; Math Prof/Teacher Univ of AK 1980-; *ai:* Coach Girls Bsktbl 1988- & Wrestling 1974-76; *office:* Jane Mears Mid Sch 2700 W 100th Ave Anchorage AK 99515

HORTON, HAZEL BOWMAN, Kindergarten Teacher; *b:* Laurel Fork, VA; *m:* William N.; *c:* Jean H. Nobblitt, Lisa H. Smith *ed:* (BA) Eng, King Coll 1954; Cert Elem Ed Radford Univ; Extension Classes Univ of VA, VA Polytechnic, St Univ Wytherville Cmmty; *cr:* 3rd Grade Teacher 1954-56, 1st Grade Teacher 1956-83, Kndgtn Teacher 1983- Hillsville Elem Sch; *ai:* Southern Assn Self Study Steering Comm Mem; Kndgtn Comm Curr Dev; NEA, VA Ed Assn, Carroll Ed Assn 1954-; Delta Kappa Gamma 1969-; Fair View Presbyn Church (Youth Adv, Sunday Sch Teacher) 1974-88; Outstanding Young Educator of Carroll Cty 1968; *home:* Rt 2 Box 735 Hillsville VA 24343

HORTON, JUDY RECTOR, Fifth Grade Teacher; *b:* Waynesburg, KY; *m:* Larry Denton; *c:* Artie R., Chelsea L.; *ed:* (BS) Elem Ed, Campbellsville Coll 1973; Elem Ed, E KY Univ 1976; *cr:* 1st Grade Teacher Waynesburg Elem 1973-75; 5th Grade Teacher Kings Mountain Memorial Elem 1975-; *home:* 135 Oak Dr Waynesburg KY 40489

HORTON, LIBBY MARTIN, Second Grade Teacher; *b:* Waycross, GA; *m:* Robert Thomas; *c:* Robby, Amy, Holly; *ed:* (BS) Elem Ed, GA Southern 1956; *cr:* 1st Grade Teacher Sidney Lanier Elem 1956-63, Ballard Elem 1965-66; 1st Grade Teacher 1970-83, 2nd Grade Teacher 1983- Frederica Acad; *ai:* Faculty Forum; Sunshine Comm; GA Cncl of Teachers of Eng, GA Cncl of Ec Ed; Pine Ridge Baptist Church Young Adult Bible Teacher 1964-; AARP; *office:* Frederica Acad 200 Hamilton Rd Saint Simons Isl GA 31522

HORTON, LINDA JEAN, Business Teacher/Chairman; *b:* Indianapolis, IN; *ed:* (BS) Behavioral Sci, Grace Coll 1981; Working Towards Masters Biblical Counseling; *cr:* Teacher/Athletic Dir/Girls Coach Lakeland Chrstn Acad 1981-; *ai:* Atletic Dir; Girls Vlybl, Bsktbl, Sftbl Coach; Class Spon; IN Chrstn Athletic Assn Secy 1988-89; Franklin Life Insurance Natl Coaching Awds Vlybl 1987, Bsktbl 1988; *office:* Lakeland Chrstn Acad Rt 8 Box 226 Wooster Rd Warsaw IN 46580

HORTON, MABEL MARIE RICHMOND, 4th Grade Teacher; *b:* Boissevain, VA; *M:* John W.; *c:* Tina M., Lisa R, Helen E.; *ed:* (BS) Eng, Soc Stud, Elem Ed, Bluefield St Coll 1967; Univ of VA; *cr:* 4th Grade Teacher Abbs Valley Boissevain Elem 1967-; *ai:* Adv Schl Newspaper; Chairperson Staff Dev Comm Classroom Mgmt; PTA Secy 1968-69 Life Mem 1985; Nom Teacher of Yr 1987; Alpha Kappa Alpha 1964-; *home:* Box 324 Boissevain VA 24606

HORTON, SARAH BURKS, First Grade Teacher; *b:* Fort Payne, AL; *m:* Bobby J.; *c:* Brad, Elizabeth Fleming, Brian; *ed:* (BS) Elem Ed/Eng, Jacksonville 1969; (ME) Elem Ed/Spec Ed, AL A&M 1974; (AA) Elem Ed, Univ of AL 1979; *cr:* Teacher Henagar Sch 1970-72; 1St Grade Teacher Plainview Sch 1973-; *ai:* NEA, AEA, DEA 1970-; Alpha Delta Kappa (Historian, Correspondence Secy 1973-); PTA, PTO VP 1970-; Mt Hermon Baptist Church (VP, Clerk, Teacher); Childrens Story Published in Turtle Magazine; Ideas Published in Mailbox & Instr-Ed Magazine; *home:* Rt 3 Box 999 Fort Payne AL 35967

HORTON, THOMAS J., Physical Ed/Health Teacher; *b:* Long Beach, CA; *m:* Melodee Ann Boxell; *c:* Shane, Sarah; *ed:* (AA) Liberal Art, Ventura Coll 1969; (BA) His/Phys Ed, CA St Univ Northridge 1970; Teacher Trng, Univ of CA Santa Barbara; Various Univs; *cr:* Teacher/Coach St Thomas Aquinas Sch 1970-72, Chaparral HS 1972-74, Prescott HS 1987-89; Teacher/Admin Bayfield HS 1989-; *office:* Bayfield HS PO Box 258 Bayfield CO 81122

HORTON, V. MARIE KNIGHT, 7th Grade Language Art Teacher; *b:* Grand Saline, TX; *c:* Kenneth D., John F. Williams JR.; *ed:* (BA) His, S Nazarene Univ 1951; (MS) Lib Sci, E TX St Univ 1965; *cr:* 4th Grade Teacher KS Sch System 1951-52; 3rd-5th Grade Teacher Hickman Mills MO Sch 1952-54; Teacher/Librarian Grand Saline Ind Sch Dist 1959-65; 4th/6th Grade Teacher Midland TX Ind Sch Dist 1965-; 6th Grade Soc Stud Teacher Owasso Schls 1972-75; 7th Grade Lang Art Teacher Grand Saline Ind Sch Dist 1975-; *ai:* Grand Saline Sch Teepee Times, Dallas News, Spelling Bee, Univ Scholastic League Spelling & Dictionary Skills Spon; TX St Teacher Assn Pres 1961-64; TX Classroom Teacher Assn Secy 1975-76; Athena Club 1960-64; *home:* 310 N Oleander Grand Saline TX 75140

HORVAT-LELLING, ARLENE FOGELSON, 1st Grade Teacher; *b:* Dover, NJ; *m:* Bernard Lelling; *c:* Debra Gardner, D Andrea, Robin G. Hardman, Scott Gardner, Nicole; *ed:* (BS) Ed, Cedar Crest COll 1958; Marywood Coll; *cr:* Kndgtn Teacher 1967-86; 1st Grade Teacher 1986- Hopatcong-Bono; *ai:* NJ Ed Assn; Hopatoons Ed Assn Rep Cncl 1987-88; Sussex Cty Ed Assn; Cmmty Soup Kitchen Active Mem; *office:* Durban Avenue Sch Durban Ave Hopatcong NJ 07843

HORVATH, KATHRYN COREY, German Teacher; *b:* Olivia, MN; *m:* William J.; *c:* Erika, Naomi; *ed:* (BA) Ger, St Olaf Coll 1969; (MAR) Ger/Ed, Yale Univ 1970; Addl Stud Various Univ; *cr:* Ger Teacher/Dept Chairperson Cranbrook Educl Cmmty 1970-76; Ger Instr San Antonio Coll 1977-78; Ger Teacher Ti-In Network 1985-; *ai:* AATG; Jr League; *home:* 218 Canterbury Hill San Antonio TX 78209

HOSACK, WILLIAM DALE, Mid Sch Industrial Art Teacher; *b:* Hastings, NE; *m:* Carmen P. Anderson; *c:* Katherine, Thomas, David; *ed:* (BS) Industrial Art, Peru St Univ 1976; Grad Stud Kearney St Univ, Drake Univ, IA St Univ, NW MO St Univ, Univ of NE; *cr:* Industrial Art Teacher Tecumseh HS 1977-78; Industrial Art/Phys Ed Teacher Harlan Cmmty Schls 1978-; *ai:* Asst Var Ftbl & Track Coach; 8th Grade Girls Bsktbl Coach; Pheasants Forever Bd Mem 1987-89; *office:* Harlan Cmmty Mid Sch 2102 Durant Hayes SD 57537

HOSBEIN, ANN BUSS, Dir Religious Education; *b:* Carroll, IA; *m:* Michael L.; *c:* William, Katherine; *ed:* (BA) Psych, Briar Cliff Coll 1979; Spec Ed Coursework, IA St Univ; Activity Coord Cert From IA; *cr:* 3rd-4th Grade Teacher St Joseph Sch 1979-82; Activity Coord Hilltop Cave Center 1982-85; Dir of Religious Ed Immaculate Conception Parish Cherokee 1985-86, Immaculate Conception Parish Deer Lodge 1987-88, Sacred Heart Parish 1989-; *ai:* Parich Cncl Secy 1988-; CCW (Treas 1989-, VP 1986-); *home:* 1221 N 5th St Miles City MT 59301

HOSENFELD, MARTHA WATT, English Teacher; *b:* Dansville, NY; *m:* Walter R.; *c:* Jeffrey, Donald; *ed:* (AB) Classics, 1965, (MS) Latin Ed, 1967 Syracuse Univ; Cert in Eng SUNY Geneseo; *cr:* Latin Teacher Churchville-Chili Jr HS 1966-72, Eng Teacher Churchville-Chili Sr HS 1974-; *ai:* Several Dist Comms; NCTE; Churchville-Chili Teacher of Excl Awd 1987; *home:* 137 Hillary Dr Rochester NY 14624

HOSFORD, SHELBY A., English & Spanish Teacher; *b:* Seattle, WA; *m:* Grant A. III; *c:* Grant IV, Andrew; *ed:* (BA) Eng, Univ of OR 1966; Eng, Span Univ of WA; *cr:* Teacher Pleasant Hill HS 1966-69, Totem Jr HS 1975-78, Amer Intnl Sch Nigeria 1978-80, Lakota Jr HS 1980-85, Decatur HS 1985-; *ai:* Soph Class Adv; Supts Long Range Planning Comm; Global Stud & Care Team; FWEA, WEA, NEA, WA Foreign Lang Teachers, WA Assn for Gifted & Talented; NCTE Natl Conference Presenter 1990; NEH Asian Inst 1989; *office:* Decatur HS 2800 SW 320th Federal Way WA 98023

HOSKEN, MELBA PRATOR, First Grade Teacher; *b:* Anchorage, AK; *m:* Howard Harrison; *c:* Brian, Terri; *ed:* (BED) Elem Ed, Univ of AK Fairbanks 1963; Univ of AK Anchorage; AK Pacific Univ; Portland St Univ; *cr:* Teacher Rabbit Creek Sch 1963-65; Piano Teacher 1965-72; Pre-Sch Teacher St Marys Episcopal 1972-73; Teacher Rabbit Creek Sch 1973-84, Bear Valley Elem 1984-; *ai:* Delta Kappa Gamma 1980-; *office:* Bear Valley Elem Sch 15001 Mountain Air Dr Anchorage AK 99516

HOSKINS, CHARLOTTE THOMPSON, Math Teacher; *b:* Newport News, VA; *m:* Larry Wayne Sr.; *c:* Larry W. Jr., Stacey L.; *ed:* (BS) Math, Campbell Univ 1969; (MS) Math Ed, Old Dominion Univ; *cr:* Math Teacher Denbish HS 1969-72, Bozier Intermediate Sch 1977-78, Menchville HS 1978-79, Warwick HS 1979-81, Tabb HS 1981-; *ai:* Var Chrldr Coach; Youth Ed Assn; NEA; Kappa Delta Phi Honor Society; Grafton Bethel PTA Treas 1990-; Windy Point Pool Bd Dir Secy 1991- Treas 1988-; Bethel Baptist Church (Womans Missionary Group Treas 1986-88/ Sunday Sch Dir 1986-89); *office:* Tabb H S 4431 Big Bethel Rd Tabb VA 23602

HOSKINS, EURADELL EPPS, Third Grade Teacher; *b:* Shreveport, LA; *m:* Elve; *c:* Elyssa D.; *ed:* (BS) Early Chldhd Ed, Grambling Univ 1968; (MS) Curr, Natl Coll of Ed 1989; *cr:* Teacher Caddo Parish Sch Bd 1968-71, Racine Unified Sch Dist 1971-; *ai:* Gifford Concerns & Positive Action Guidance Comm; Phi Delta Kappa (Secy 1976-77, Prince Hall Asst Secy 1980-81); Order of Eastern Star Ester 1981-82; *home:* 5514 Alburg Ave Racine WI 53406

HOSKINS, KAREN BOESEL, Soc Stud Teacher/Dept Chair; *b:* Schuylkill, PA; *m:* John D.; *c:* David G., Jordan P.; *ed:* (BS) Ed/Soc Stud, 1977, (MA) Ed/Curr/Instruction, 1984 NM St Univ; *cr:* Teacher Heights Jr HS 1980-; *ai:* Vlybl Coach 1980-83; Soc Stud Dept Chairperson 1984-; Dist Calendar Comm 1989-; Heights Budget Comm 1987-; Sick Leave Bank Chairperson 1987-89; NEA Building Rep 1987-; *office:* Heights Jr HS 3700 College Blvd Farmington NM 87401

HOSKINS, LOY MAC, Second Grade Teacher; *b:* Cyril, OK; *m:* Rhonda Kay Dillard; *c:* Jimmy, Mickey; *ed:* (BSED) Elem Ed, 1984, (MED) Elem Ed, 1987 SW OK St Univ; Sch Admin Courses, SW OK St Univ; *cr:* 2nd Grade Teacher Thomas Public Sch 1984-; *ai:* Girls Sftbl Fastpitch Asst HS Coach; Bsktbl Official Timer; Fellowship of Chrstn Athletes Huddle, Summer League Bsktbl Coach; Academic Bowl Regional Judge; Sr Class Spon; Substitute Bus Driver; OK Ed Assn Delegate 1984-; Thomas Ed Assn Pres/Legislative Contact 1984-; Roman Nose Rdng Cncl Bd of Dir 1984-86; BSA Cubmaster 1986-; Cubmaster Awd 1990; First Chrstn Church Elder 1984-; Doctoral Intern Teaching Assoc Awd NM St Univ 1990; Outstanding Elem Ed Stu SW OK St Univ 1984; SW OK St Univ Ed Assn Mem Of Yr 1983; *office:* Thomas Public Sch 900 N Main St Thomas OK 73669

HOSKINSON, MARJORIE LEAH, Collaborating Teacher; *b:* Elizabethtown, KY; *m:* Alan Drury; *c:* Cloda L. Best, Kathy, Albert; *ed:* (BS) Elem Ed, 1951, (MA) Elem Ed, 1976 Western KY Univ; *cr:* Teacher Ft Knox 1948-51; Teacher Elizabethtown Ind 1963-55, 1965-; *ai:* Jr Womans Club St Pres 1950-51; Elizabethtown Ed Assn 1966-67; *home:* 301 Rosedale Dr Elizabethtown KY 42701

HOSSLEY, HENRY FIELDING, Middle Ed Learning Specialist; *b:* Vicksburg, MS; *ed:* (BA) Music Theory/Literature, LA St Univ 1968; (AA) Applied Music, Hinds Jr Coll 1985; FL Tech Univ; Rollins Coll; Univ FL; *cr:* Music Teacher Saturn Elem Schl 1968; Teacher/Specialist Madison Mid Sch 1971-; *ai:* Lang Arts Dept Chm; Science Research Adv; Spon Natl Jr Honor Society; Restructuring Comm; Guidance Comm; Curr Comm; Admin Team; FL Natl Cncl Teachers of Eng 1976-; ASCD 1989-; Phi Delta Kappa 1981-; Phi Mu Alpha Sinfonia 1965-; Teacher of Yr Madison Mid Sch 1975/1980/1981; Teacher of Yr North Area Brevard Cty-1975-80; Challenger Awd Madison Mid Sch-1989; *office:* Madison Mid Sch 3375 Dairy Rd Titusville FL 32796

HOSTETLER, HERALD EDWARD, III, Mathematics Teacher; *b:* Plymouth, IN; *m:* Karen Jean Kornell; *c:* Katherine; *ed:* (BA) Fr Ed/Math Ed, Ball St Univ 1980; (MSE) Ed/Math, Purdue Univ 1985; *cr:* Fr/Math Teacher Cntrl Cath HS 1980-86; Math Teacher Kankakee Valley HS 1986-; *ai:* Soph Class Spon; AAFT 1981-83; *home:* 2554 Domke Ct Valparaiso IN 46383

HOSTETLER, STANLEY B., Biology Teacher; *b:* Woodburn, IN; *m:* Karen R. Hostetler Ehle; *c:* Pamella S. Hostetter Thorp, Heath B.; *ed:* (BS) Phys Ed/Health, Purdue Univ 1963; (MS) Ed, St Francis Coll 1968; Advanced Schooling Life Insurance & Annuities License; *cr:* Teacher/Coach East Allen Cty Public Schls 1963-86; Teacher New Haven HS 1963-; *ai:* Jr Class Spon; New Haven Wrestlers Club Originator & Spon; Sci Fair Coord 1963-89; 9th Grade Track Coach 1963-72; Var Ftbl Asst Coach & 9th Grade Head Reserve Team 1963-72; Var Wrestling Head Coach 1964-86; East Allen Ed Assn, IN St Teachers Assn 1963-; NEA 1963-, Life Member 1968; NSTA, IN St HS Ofcls Assn, IN HS Athletic Assn 1968-; IN HS Wrestling Coaches Assn 1963-87, Elected into Hall of Fame 1986; NE IN Ofcls Assn, Natl Fed of HS Assn 1986-; St Peters Luth Mens Club 1964-79; New Haven Adult Wrestling Booster Clkub Dir 1971-; Dedication Service Awd 1986; Article Published 1974; New Haven Age Group Wrestling Tournament Dir 1971-89; *home:* 16829 Shadyview Dr Woodburn IN 46797

HOSTETTER, KATHERINE BALSLEY, English Teacher; *b:* Pittsburgh, PA; *m:* Harold H.; *ed:* (BS) Eng, Bowling Green St Univ 1966; St Johns Univ, Lake Erie Coll, Ursuline Coll; *cr:* Eng Teacher Willowick Jr HS 1966-75, North HS 1976-; *ai:* Faculty Sunshine Comm Chm; Class, NHS, Cheerleading, Newspaper Adv; N Cntrl Steering, Evaluation, Dist Writers Comm Mem; NE OH Ed Assn, OH Ed Assn, NEA 1966-; St Williams Womens Guild; Helped Write Teachers Manual; Elected Teacher of Yr for 14 Yrs; Written Curr Guides for Sch Dist; *office:* North HS 34041 Stevens Blvd Eastlake OH 44095

HOTT, KAREN SUE, Teaching Principal; *b:* Winchester, VA; *m:* Allen; *c:* Jon T., Melanie J.; *ed:* (BA) Elem Ed, Shepherd Coll 1972; (MS) Educl Admin, VA Tech 1986; *cr:* 1st/2nd Grade Teacher 1972-84, Prin 1975-, 3rd/4th Grade Teacher 1985- Grassy Lick Elem; *ai:* NEASP, Phi Kappa Phi; Amer Legion Auxiliary.

HOTTLE, NANETTE SEYBOLD, Fifth Grade Teacher; *b:* Troy, OH; *m:* Steven J.; *c:* Megan, John; *ed:* (BA) Elem Ed, Wright St Univ 1979; OH Writing Project Miami Univ 1986; *cr:* Elem Teacher Tri Village Intermediate 1979-; *ai:* Martha Jennings Scholar 1983-84; OH Ed Assn 1979-; Eastern STAR 1983-; Delta Zeta 1978-; Evangelical United Meth Mem 1984-; *home:* 204 Meeker Ave Greenville OH 45331

HOTTOVY, THOMAS R., Mathematics/Computer Teacher; *b:* David City, NE; *m:* Susan E. Matthies; *c:* Sara E., Melissa L.; *ed:* (BS) Math/Phys Ed, 1973, (MS) Math/Cmptrs, 1991 Univ of NE Lincoln; *cr:* Teacher Adams HS 1973-; *ai:* HS/Jr Hs Athletic Coach; Class Spon; NE 8-Man Ftbl Coaches Assn (Secy, Treas) 1979-82; NE Coaches Assn; NE Educl Technology Assn; NMTA; *office:* Adams Public Sch 415 8th St Adams NE 68301

HOTZ, CAROL POE, Junior HS Sci/Cmptr Teacher; *m:* Frederick Albert; *c:* Michael F., Cathy A.; *ed:* (BS) Bio, Southern IL Univ Carbondale 1964; *ai:* Beta Club Honor Society; Sci Fair Spon; 8th Grade Spon; Il Sci Teachers; Nsta; Natl TeAchers Assn; IL Teachers Assn; Millstadt Civic Club Pres 1990-91; Zion United Church of Christ Secy Church Cncl 1982-85; Excl in Teaching Awd 1987; Southern IL Univ Edwardville Sci Teachers Awd; *office:* Millstadt Conslidated Schl 211 W Mill Millstadt IL 62260

HOUCK, BARBARA KAYE, Life Science Teacher; *b:* Glen Rogers, WV; *m:* Terry; *c:* Michael; *ed:* (BS) Bio/General Sci, Concord Coll 1972; (MA) Speech Comm, WV Univ 1983; Wkshp Seminar to Teach Advanced Placement Bio; *cr:* Life Sci Teacher Herndon HS 1973-83, Mullens HS 1983-; *ai:* Jr, Prom, Honor Society, Honor Formal Spon; In Charge of Raising Money for Prom; Awds Day; Comm on Cty Level for Weighing Classes; NEA, WVEA; Methodist Church; *office:* Mullens HS 801 Moran Ave Mullens WV 25882

HOUCK, C. BRUCE, Business Education Teacher; *b:* Altoona, PA; *m:* Anne Tate; *c:* Laura A., Lynne M., Adam B. Tate; *ed:* (BS) Bus Ed, 1971, (MS) Voc Industrial Ed, 1975 The PA St Univ; *cr:* Bus Ed Teacher 1971-, Bus Ed Teacher/Dept Chair 1982- Bald Eagle Area Jr/Sr HS; *ai:* Steering Comm Mem; Chairperson Tells Grant Comm & Bus Ed Dept; *office:* Bald Eagle Area Jr/Sr HS Box 4 Wingate PA 16880

HOUDE, JANET LYNNE, 8th Grade Soc Stud Teacher; *b:* Clarksville, TN; *ed:* (MA) Admin/Supervision, 1983, (BS) Bus Ed, 1979 Austin Peay St Univ; *cr:* Bus Teacher Northeast HS 1981-84; 2nd Grade Teacher Byrns Darden Elem Sch 1985-86; Soc Stud Teacher New Providence Mid Sch 1986-, Northeast Mid Sch 1990; *ai:* NEA, TN Ed Assn 1981-; Amer Assn of Univ Women; Gamma Beta Phi; Kappa Delta Phi; Natl Bus Ed Assn Awd 1979; Outstanding Young Women of America; Whos Who Amoung Stus in Univs & Colls; *office:* New Providence Mid Sch 146 Cunningham Ln Clarksville TN 37042

HOUDEK, ALLEN J., US His/Span/Psych Teacher; *b:* Chicago, IL; *c:* Amanda; *ed:* (BS) Span/Soc Stud, 1972 Bemidji St Univ; (MS) Counseling/Human Dev, Moorhead St Univ 1985; *cr:* Instr Frazee HS 1972-; Adjunct Instr Fergus Falls Comm Coll 1980-; *ai:* Jr Class, Prom Banquet, Jr Class Magazine Drive, Span Club Adv; Developed Coll Credit Prgm for HS Stu; *office:* Frazee HS P O Box 186 Frazee MN 56544

HOUFEK, GARY WILLIAM, United States History Teacher; *b:* Appleton, WI; *ed:* (BS) Poly Sci/US His, Univ of WI Madison 1976; *cr:* Substitute Teacher Madison Metro Sch Dist 1977-86; US His Teacher Los Alamos Public Schls 1986-; *ai:* Mock Trial Adv; Asst Ftbl, Track Coach; NM Law Related Ed, NM Soc Stud Cncl Mem; Madison Substitute Union Pres 1983-86; *office:* Los Alamos HS 1300 Diamond Dr Los Alamos NM 87544

HOUGARDY, DANIEL ALLEN, Science Education Specialist; *b:* Henryetta, OK; *c:* Mark D.; *ed:* (BA) Ed, Tulsa Univ 1973; (ME) Sci Ed, 1976, (ME) Biological Sci, & Cont Ed, 1980 Northeastern OK Univ; (EDD) Adult/Continuing Ed, OK St Univ 1990; *cr:* Teacher Oologah Sch System 1973-, Tulsa Jr Coll 1988-; *ai:* Aids Ed Cncl, Alert Prgm; Outdoor Ed Wrkshps; Dist Sci Fairs; OK Jr Acad of Sci; BSA; Curr Design Tulsa Jr Coll; Phi Delta Kappa Mem 1989-; OK Acad of Sci Mem 1980-; OK Sci Teachers Assn Mem 1973-; OK Teacher of Yr Semi-Finalist 1989-; *home:* Rt 5 Box 281 Claremore OK 74017

HOUGH, CHERYL MOORE, Fine Arts Teacher; *b:* Nueilly-Sur-Seine, France; *m:* John Allan; *c:* Erin B.; *ed:* (BA) Fine Arts Studio/Ed, Kean Coll 1976; Grad Stud Montclair St Coll 1977-79; Ceramics Studio, Acad of Applied Arts 1978-79; Ceramics, Peters Valley Crafts Center 1976, 1978, 1980, 1988; *cr:* Ceramics Teacher Hunterdon Cty Adult Ed 1976-77, Warren Cty Adult Ed 1981-85; Art Dept Teacher N Warren Regional HS 1979-; *ai:* N Warren Regional HS Sch Musical & Sr Play Productions Art & Set Dir 1979-85; NJ Art Educators 1981-; NJ Designer Craftsman 1978-; Peters Valley Crafts 1976-; Metropolitan Museum of Art Mem 1979-; Cousteau Society 1978-; Natl Audubon Society 1982-88; Montclair St Coll Alumni Assn Grant 1978; *office:* N Warren Regional HS PO Box 410 Lambert Rd Blairstown NJ 07825

HOUGH, FRANCIS MADISON, JR., English Dept Chairman; *b:* Lancaster, SC; *ed:* (BA) Eng - Cum Laude, Presbyn Coll 1971; (MA) Eng, Winthrop Coll 1974; Grad Stud in Film, Univ SC; *cr:* 7th-9th Grade Eng Teacher South Jr HS 1971-; *ai:* Sch Newspaper Faculty Adv; Sch Spelling Bee Coord; Dept Chm; Faculty Advisory & Sch Improvement Cncls; NCTE 1971-80; NEA, SCEA, LCEA Cty Rep 1972-74; Phi Kappa Phi 1974-; Natl Bd of Review 1975-87; Articles Published; Freelance Film Critic; *home:* 3000 Selwyn Ave Charlotte NC 28209

HOUGH, JOHN T., 6th Grade Teacher; *b:* Lehighton, PA; *m:* Diane Messinger; *c:* Jessica, John; *ed:* (BA) Elem Ed, Kutztown Univ 1973; Grad Stud PA St Univ, E Stroudsburg Univ, Wilkes Coll; *cr:* 6th Grade Teacher Weisenberg Elem 1973-75, Northwestern Elem 1975-; *ai:* Sci Fair Coord; Sci Comm; Slatington Borough Pres; *office:* Northwestern Elem Sch RD 2 Box 66 New Tripoli PA 18066

HOUGHLAND, DEBBIE JOHNSON, Math/Cmptr Sci Teacher; *b:* Greenville, KY; *m:* John Lynn; *c:* Stephen, Sarah; *ed:* (BA) Eng, 1971, (MA) Eng, 1979 W KY Univ; Post Grad Stud Cmptr Sci; *cr:* Teacher Greenville HS 1971-72, Drakesboro HS 1978-; *ai:* Math Club, Academic Team Ofcl, KEST, Teacher Evaluation, Textbook Adoption Comm; NCTM 1983-; KLCTM 1987-; KS Ed Assn, MCEA, NEA 1978-; RCT Thomas Awd 1971; *home:* PO Box 34 Beechmont KY 42323

HOUGHTEN, DOUG W., Eng Dept Chm/Coord Testing; *b:* Antioch, CA; *m:* Evelynne Fullmer; *c:* Marylynne Graff, Karen Carly, Suanne, James, Diane; *ed:* (BS) Ed, Brigham Young Univ 1971; Addl Studies Admin BYU; Recertification Classes UT St Univ; *cr:* Teacher 1971-89; Teacher/Coord 1989- Payson Mid; *ai:* Yrbk Coord; Lang Arts Comm; Profl Rights & Responsibilities Comm; Dist Ins Comm; Dist Rng Comm; Nebo Ed Assn Pres 1976-77; Bonneville Uniserv Bd of Dir 1975-77; UT Ed Assn Delegate 1975-77; Boy Scouts Scoutmaster 1967-70; Boys Bsbl Coach 1977-84; Boys Bsktbl Coach 1977-84; Nebo Sch Dist Teacher of Yr 1987-88; Nebo Dist Teacher of Month - Sept 1989; *office:* Payson Mid Sch 250 S Main Payson UT 84651

HOULTON, JANET HANNON, 7th-8th Grade English Teacher; *b:* Selma, AL; *m:* Roy Hinton Jr.; *c:* Lauren H., Roy H. III, Allyson H.; *ed:* (BS) Eng/His, Auburn Univ 1976; (MS) Rdng, AL St Univ 1980; *cr:* Rndg Teacher Houston Hill Jr HS 1977-80; Eng Teacher Montgomery Cty HS 1981-; *ai:* Yrbk Adv 1989-; Inservice Chairperson 1985-; NEA, AL Ed Assn, Montgomery Cty Ed Assn 1977-; *office:* Montgomery Cty HS Rt 1 Box 1 Ramer AL 36069

HOUNCHELL, MONTE SLATER, Tenth Grade History Teacher; *b:* Manchester, KY; *m:* Lola Roberts; *c:* Avril Easter, Monica M. Baker; *ed:* (BS) Soc Stud, Cumberland Coll 1963; (MA) Ed/Geography, E KY Univ 1972; Scndry Principalship, E KY Univ; *cr:* 3rd-8th Grade Teacher Chop Bottom Elem 1960-61, Otter Creek Elem 1962-64, Beech Creek Elem 1964-65; 7th Grade Teacher Goose Rock Elem 1965-67; His Teacher Clay Cty HS 1967-; *ai:* Bible Club Spon; KEA, NEA.

HOUNSHELL, JANET BANKS, 6-8th Grade Teacher; *b:* Independence, KY; *m:* Ancil R.; *c:* Robert V.; *ed:* (BS) Elem Ed, 1968; (MA) Ed, Spec in Rdng, 1975 Eastern KY Univ; *cr:* 6th-8th Grade Teacher Rousseau Elem 1968-70; 6th Grade Teacher 1971-81; Rdng Teacher 1981-83; 5th Grade Teacher 1984-88 LBJ Elem; 6th-8th Grade Teacher Rousseau Elem 1988-; *ai:* 4-H Club Leader; Trainer In-Service Prgm; Mem Book Selection Comm; BCEA; KEA; NEA; 4-H Cncl (Cty Pres 1988- J M Fettner Awd 1988 Delegate to Area & State 1981- Leadership Awd 1981); Extension Cncl Mem of Bd 1989-90; 1989 Outstanding Citizen in Ed By Breathitt Cty Honey Festival Comm; *home:* Box 36-D Hwy 30 E Noctor KY 41357

HOUPT, DIANE LEE, English/Journalism Teacher; *b:* Erie, PA; *ed:* (BA) Eng, 1966, (MA) Eng, 1976, (MS) Admin, 1981 St Univ of NY Albany; *cr:* Eng Teacher/Publications Adv Deer Valley HS 1984-, Rensselaer HS 1966-83; *ai:* Newspaper, Yrbk, Literary Magazine Adv; Sr Class Spon; N Cntrl Steering Comm; AZ Interscholastic Press Assn St Convention Coord 1986-; Journalism Ed Assn 1986-; NEA, AZ Ed Assn, Deer Valley Ed Assn 1984-; Deer Valley HS Teacher of Yr 1988-89; *office:* Deer Valley HS 18424 N 51st Ave Glendale AZ 85308

HOURIGAN, DON T., HS Mathematics Teacher; *b:* San Francisco, CA; *m:* J. Suzanne Judd; *c:* Michael; *ed:* (BS) Ec/Math, Univ of San Francisco 1960; General Scndry Credential; *cr:* Teacher/Dept Chm Davidson Mid Sch 1962-79; Teacher/Athletic Dir San Rafael HS 1979-; *ai:* Sr Class Adv 1990; Asst Var Ftbl, San Rafael Pop Warner Ftbl Coach 1965-74; Jr/Sr Var Ftbl Coach 1975-83; San Marin Pop Warner Coach 1989; NEA Mem 1962-; Athletic Dir 1978-80; Novato Youth Soccer Coach 1984-88, Coach of Yr 1988; Novato Little League Bd Mem 1990; *office:* San Rafael HS 185 Mission Ave San Rafael CA 94901

HOUSE, ALMA F., Third Grade Teacher; *b:* Oneida, KY; *ed:* (BS) His/Poly Sci, 1973, (BS) Elem Ed, 1979 Cumberland Coll; Grad Stud E KY Univ & Union Coll 1983; *cr:* Social Worker Dept of Human Resources 1974-79; Teacher Goose Rock Elem & Manchester Grade Sch 1979-; *office:* Manchester Elem Sch Rt 7 Box 42 Manchester KY 40962

HOUSE, FRANK CHARLES, Principal; *b:* Central Square, NY; *m:* Cheryl Fuller; *c:* Melissa, Trista, Vanessa, Edson; *ed:* (BA) His, Univ NV 1969; (MS) Admin, SUNY Oswego 1980; (CAS) Admin, SUNY Oswego 1980; *cr:* Teacher 1970-75, Dept Chm 1975, VP 1980-88, Prin 1988- Pulaski Jr Sr HS; *ai:* Cooperative Extension VP; Suprvr Town of Parish; Phi Delta Kappa 1987-; Lions Club 1988-; *office:* Pulaski Jr-Sr HS 7250 Salina St Pulaski NY 13142

HOUSE, KAY MARIE TUTTLE, History/English Teacher; *b:* Glendale, CA; *m:* Stanley; *ed:* (BA) Poly Sci, CA St Univ San Diego 1968; *cr:* Teacher Southwest Jr HS 1970-71, Montgomery Jr HS 1971-; *ai:* GATE Classes; Spelling & Geography Bee; Golden Bell CA US His & Rdng Curr Runner-Up; *office:* Montgomery Jr HS 1051 Picador San Diego CA 92154

HOUSE, LEON HAROLD, Science Teacher; *b:* Mandan, ND; *m:* Jeanne; *c:* Kevin, Keith, Sharyl, Jeff, Kari, Kami; *ed:* (BA) Bio/Phys Ed, Dickinson St 1965; ND St Univ, Minot St Coll, Univ of ND; *cr:* Teacher/Coach St Marys HS 1965-67, Watford City HS 1967-74, Ft Yates HS 1974-75; Teacher/Coach Mandan Jr HS 1975-; *ai:* HS Cross Cntry & Jr HS Track Coach; Mandan Ed Assn 1990; NEA, ND Ed Assn 1965-; Mandan Track Club Dir 1981-, AAU Dir of Yr 1986; Eagles Club 1984-; Cross Cntry Coach of Yr 1981, 1986; Sci Grant NC & Yankton Coll; *home:* 900 4th Ave NW Mandan ND 58554

HOUSEHOLDER, BRENDA JANE, Health Occupations Instructor; *b:* Cincinnati, OH; *m:* Melvin Kenneth Jr.; *c:* Perry; *ed:* Registered Nurse Deaconess Hospital Sch of Nursing 1962; *cr:* Operating Room Nurse Prince George Cty Hospital 1962-67, Memorial Hospital 1967-71, Peninsula General Hospital; Sch Nurse Wicomico Cty Bd of Ed 1974-85; Health Occupational Instr Wicomico Applied Technology Center 1985-; *ai:* Voc Industrial Clubs of America Adv; MD St Teachers Assn, Wicomico Cty Ed Assn; *office:* Wicomico Applied Technology 607 Morris St Salisbury MD 21801

HOUSEMAN, TERRY E., Fifth Grade Teacher; *b:* Medina, NY; *m:* Margaret Nowak; *c:* Andrew E.; *ed:* (BS) Ed/Soc Stud, St Univ NY Brockport 1967; Working Towards Masters in Admin; *cr:* 5th Grade Teacher Barker Cntrl Sch 1967-70, Lyndonville Cntrl Sch 1970-; *ai:* Adv Elem Stu Cncl; Lyndonville Teachers Assn (Advisory Cncl, Building Rep, Pres 1977-89); NY St United Teacher, AFT 1967-; Masons Jr Warden 1988-89; Orleans Cty 4-H Pres 1988-; United Meth Church Admin Bd Chm 1987-89; Northeast Regional Center Drug & Alcohol Free Schls Particpant & Team Leader; *home:* 2346 Swett Rd Lyndonville NY 14098

HOUSER, JACALYN CAROL, Third Grade Teacher; *b:* Johnstown, PA; *m:* David Edward; *c:* Rebecca; *ed:* (BS) Elem, Slippery Rock St Coll 1972; *cr:* 1st Grade Teacher 1972-75, 3rd Grade Teacher 1975- W Branch Elem Sch; *ai:* Cntrl Intermediate Unit Inservice Cncl Rep; Staff Dev, Combined Inservice Comm; Cooperative Learning Trng Group; *home:* RD Box 433A West Decatur PA 16878

HOUSER, RAYMOND E., Social Science/Reading Teacher; *b:* Leon, KS; *m:* Donna L. Snyder; *c:* Laura, Darla; *ed:* (BAED) Soc Stud, Wichita St Univ 1962; (MS) US His, Emporia St Univ 1971; *cr:* His/Government Teacher Lamar HS 1962-63; His Teacher El Dorado Jr HS 1963-66, Iola HS 1966-74; Soc Sci/Rdng Teacher Iola Jr HS 1974-; *ai:* Athletic Dir; Frosh Girls Bsktbl; Discipline Comm Mem; *office:* Iola Jr HS 600 East St Iola KS 66749

HOUSER, STEVEN DOUGLAS, Social Studies Teacher; *b:* Suffern, NY; *m:* Patricia Anne Mc Mahon; *c:* Christopher, Meghan; *ed:* (BS) European His/Soc Sci Ed, SUNY Oneonta 1979; (MS) European His, NY Univ 1984; His, Art His, Philosophy, Poly Sci, Columbia Univ; *cr:* Soc Stud Teacher Edmeston Cntrl Sch 1977-79, Horace Greeley HS 1979-; *ai:* Track, Cross Cntry, Sftbl Coach; Juggling, Current Events, Debate Club Adv; Faculty Advisory Cncl; NCSS, NY St Teachers Union; West Chester Poly Action Comm, Presbyn Church of Brewster; *home:* 57 Lakeview Rd Carmel NY 10512

HOUSEWRIGHT, ROY L., Texas History Teacher; *b:* Fort Worth, TX; *m:* Nancy L. Patterson; *c:* Steven L., Guy A.; *ed:* (BS) Integrated Soc Stud, N TX St Univ 1965; Certified Prgm Dir YMCA; Court Stenographer St of TX; *cr:* Teacher Gold-Burg HS 1966-68, Southwest HS 1968-71; Court Reporter Metroplex Court Reporters 1971-75; Teacher Meadowbrook Mid Sch 1975-; *ai:* Natl Jr Honor Society, Meadowbrook Buffalo Yrbk Spon; Whiz Quiz Coach; Assn of TX Prof Educators Ft Worth Chapter Pres 1987-88; Trinity Chrstn Church (Elder, Minister of Music) 1990; Nom Gold-Burg Ind Sch Dist Teacher of Yr 1970; *office:* Meadowbrook Mid Sch 2001 Ederville Rd Fort Worth TX 76103

HOUSKA, MARY KAY (KELLEY), 7th Grade English Teacher; *b:* Rapid City, SD; *m:* John C.; *c:* Mitzi, Shane; *ed:* (BS) Eng/Lit, Black Hills St Univ 1966; SD Cert Teaching Talented & Gifted; *cr:* Sr HS Eng Teacher Gregory HS 1966-69; Spec Prgm Girls/Boys in Need Huron HS 1970-76; 7th Grade Eng Teacher South & North Jr HS 1976-; *ai:* Resource Teacher Academically Gifted; Facilitator for Sci Club/Knowledge Bowl/Cmptr Class; Delta Kappa Gamma 1987-; South Park UCC (Christian Ed Chm 1980/Mem 1976/Diaconate Sec); Placerville Church Camp Asst Dean 1988-; Eng Curr Continuum Comm 7th-9th Grades 1978-79.

HOUSTON, DAVID GEORGE, 7th Grade Science Teacher; *b:* Long Beach, CA; *ed:* (BS) Bio/Biochemistry, 1975, Credential Ryan Multiple Subject, 1976 Univ of CA Irvine; (MA) Ed, Pepperdine Univ 1980; Credential Ryan Single Subject, Univ of CA Irvine 1985; *cr:* 4th-6th Grade Teacher San Juan Elem 1976-80; 5th/6th Grade Teacher Fred L Newhart Elem 1980-84; 8th Grade Math Teacher 1984-85, Math/Sci Teacher 1985-86, 7th Grade Sci Teacher 1986- Fred L Newhart Jr HS; *ai:* 7th-12th Grade Sci Fair & Dist Sci Curr Steering Comm; Orange Cty Sci Fair Sch Site Rep; Elem Sci Fair Comm 1984-87; Jr HS Academic Pentathlon Coach 1984-88; CTIIP Jr HS Competition & Elem Sci Lab Coord 1984-85; Elem Sci Resource Mentor Teacher 1984-86; Mentor Teacher 1988-89; BSA (Summer Camp Staff 1968-, Asst Scoutmaster 1971-74, Eagle W/Palm 1970); Kiwanis Club of

Mission Viejo Outstanding Achievement 1986; *office:* Fred L Newhart Jr HS 25001 Oso Viejo Mission Viejo CA 92692

HOUSTON, RODNEY DEAN, Math Department Chairman; *b:* Quincy, IL; *m:* Cathy Sue Watson; *c:* Mark A., Ryan D.; *ed:* (AS) Phys Ed, Spoon River Jr Coll 1976; (BS) Phys Ed, W IL Univ 1978; Grad Stud W IL Univ 1985; *cr:* Teacher/Coach Monmouth HS 1978-80, Cntrl HS 1980-; *ai:* Head Var Ftbl & Wrestling Coach; *home:* RR 1 Box 62 A Golden IL 62339

HOUT, JAY W., 5th Grade Teacher; *b:* Steubenville, OH; *m:* Rita Kay Converse; *c:* Judah; *ed:* (BA) Theatre, OH St Univ 1974; Bible, Ft Wayne Bible Coll; *cr:* 4th Grade Teacher College Heights Chrstn Schls & Mesilla Valley Chrstn Sch 1982-88; 4th/5th Grade Teacher 1988-89, 5th Grade Teacher 1989- Mesilla Valley Chrstn Schls; *ai:* Drama Production Asst; Chapel Accompaniest; ASCI 1982-; NM Wildlife Fed 1987-; *office:* Mesilla Valley Chrstn Schls 2010 Wisconsin Ave Las Cruces NM 88001

HOUTCHENS, KARL J., Social Studies Teacher; *b:* Peoria, IL; *ed:* (BS) His/Phys Ed, Univ WI La Crosse 1977; *cr:* Phys Ed/His Teacher Walker HS 1977-78; Soc Stud Teacher Boscobel HS 1978-; *ai:* Var Girls Bsktbl & Bsbl Coach; Athletic Dir; FCA Adv; NEA, Boscobel Ed Assn, WI Bsktbl Coaches Assn, Womens Bsktbl Coaches Assn, Nation Phys Ed & Health Assn; Boscobel Jaycees (VP 1986, Treas 1987, Secy 1988, St Dir 1989); Chuck Yahn Memorial Awd Outstanding Contribution Boscobel Athletics; SWAL Coach of Yr; Dist Coach of Yr; Nom St Coach of Yr; *office:* Boscobel HS 300 Brindley St Boscobel WI 53805

HOUTZ, CURTIS LYNN, World Cultures/US His Teacher; *b:* Lewistown, PA; *m:* Judy Ann Page; *c:* Derek, Nicole; *ed:* (BS) His, Shippensburg Univ 1972; Post Grad Stud PA St Univ & Shippensburg Univ; *cr:* World His/US His Teacher Tuscarora Jr HS 1974-80; World Cultures/US His Teacher Juniata HS 1980-; *ai:* Jr Class, Vlybl Club, Auto Racing Club Adv; NEA, PA St Ed Assn, Juniata Cty Ed Assn 1976-; St Stephens Luth Church 1950-; *home:* RD 3 Box 1015 Mifflintown PA 17059

HOVEKAMP, ROBERT NEIL, Guidance Counselor; *b:* Paducah, KY; *c:* Emily; *ed:* (BS) Industrial Art Ed, Western KY Univ 1975; (MA) Scndry Guidance, 1983, (MA) Scndry Admin, 1988 Murray St Univ; *cr:* Industrial Art Teacher Heath Mid Sch 1977-85; Regional Cnslr Region I Voc Ed 1985-86; Guidance Cnslr Lone Oak Mid Sch 1986-; *ai:* Mc Cracken Cty Drug Steering & Cmmty-Parent Advisory Comm; W KY Assn of Counseling & Dev 1985-; KY Assn of Counseling & Dev 1985-; *home:* 310 Tudor Blvd Paducah KY 42003

HOVERTER, CHARLENE MOKOS, 7th/8th Grade Teacher; *b:* Chicago, IL; *M:* Robert T.; *c:* Michael, Terence, Brandy; *ed:* (BS) Sociology, Ed, St Louis Univ 1968; Admin, Georgian Court Coll; *cr:* 5th-8th Grade Teacher Belmar Elem Sch 1970-, *ai:* Prof Peer Coach; Inservice Consultant-Staff Dev; Mentor Teacher for Alternate Teacher Prgm; Secy 1974-76; VP 1978-80/1984-88 Belmar Techers Assn; Neptune Soccer Assn (Mem 1979-; Coach 1988-); NJ Teacher Recognition Awd 1986-87; Instructional Theory Into Practice Trng; *office:* Belmar Elem Sch 1101 Main St Belmar NJ 07719

HOVEY, ALFRED ALLAN, JR., Science Teacher Coordinator; *b:* Muscatine, IA; *m:* Gail Fiedler; *c:* Gwen Ellen, Carrie Jane; *ed:* (BS) Elem Ed, Lakeland Coll 1966; (MS) Earth Sci, Northern AZ Univ 1972; Portland St Univ/WV Univ; *cr:* Sci Coord & Teacher Shawano-Gresham 1966-; Co-Dir Sci World WI DPI 1986-; *ai:* Sci Olympiad; Radio Club; WI Society Sci Teachers Past Pres Regional Excl Awd 1989; Natl Assn Geology Teachers Past Pres 1976-89, Outstanding Earth Sci Teacher 1987; Natl Earth Sci Teacher Assn; AAAS; WEST; WESTA; Sigma XI Awd 1989; 4-H Past Pres 1954-89 Outstanding WI Alumni Awd 1988; Farm Progress Days Youth Chm 1989; Mount St Helens Wkshp PSU 1986; Radio Astronomy Wkshp WVU 1989; NASA Pilot Prgm CRAF/CASSINI JPL 1989; Dedicated Teacher Awd 1986; *home:* 314 Fairview Way Shawano WI 54166

HOWARD, ALBERT R., Civics Teacher; *b:* Winchester, VA; *ed:* (BA) Poly Sci, Lincoln Univ 1970; (MED) Sch Admin, George Mason Univ 1977; Grad Stud Urban Ed, Brooklyn Coll; *cr:* 5th Grade Teacher PS 26K Brooklyn 1970-71; Resource Coord PS 208M NY 1973-75; 5th Grade Teacher Douglass Elem Sch 1975-76; 7th Grade Teacher J L Simpson Mid Sch 1976-77; 8th Grade Civics Teacher Seneca Ridge Mid Sch 1977-; *ai:* NEA 1975-; VA Ed Assn Bd of Dir 1987-; Loudoun Ed Assn Local Pres 1986-; VA Statewide Systems Change Advisory Bd; Governors Educl Block Grant Advisory Bd; *home:* PO Box 1705 Middleburg VA 22117

HOWARD, ALICE AUD, Second Grade Teacher; *b:* Whitesville, KY; *m:* Charles F.; *c:* David A., Rachel M.; *ed:* (BA) Elem Ed, Brescia Coll 1969; (MA) Elem Ed, W KY Univ 1977; *cr:* 3rd Grade Teacher Precious Blood Grade Sch 1964-65; 2nd Grade Teacher 1965-66, 4th Grade Teacher 1968-69 Mary Carrico Grade Sch; 2nd Grade Teacher Pleasant Ridge Grade Sch 1969-70, St Marys Grade Sch 1970-; *ai:* Faculty Service Comm; Coord of Lenten, May Act, Christmas Eve Mass, Sacramental Prgm; Vacation Bible Sch Teacher; NCEA; Certificate Recognition Service/Teaching Follow Through Prgm 1971-80 GA St Univ; *home:* 10385 Main Cross St Whitesville KY 42378

HOWARD, ANN R., Biology Teacher; *b:* Columbia, SC; *m:* Edwin M.; *c:* Angela, Amy, Jeremy, Joshua; *ed:* (BA) Bio, UNC-Charlotte 1974; ASCP Registered Medical Technologist; *cr:* Bio Teacher Heritage Chrstn Schl 1982-86, Wilson Chrstn Acad 1987-; *ai:* Chrldr Adv; Quiz Bowl Coach; *office:* Wilson Christian Acad P O Box 3818 Wilson NC 27895

HOWARD, BOBBIE JEAN (THOMAS), Second Grade Teacher; *b:* Golinda, TX; *w:* Horace Jr. (dec); *ed:* (BS) Ed, Paul Quinn Coll 1965; (MS) Ed, Praire View Univ 1972; Higher Ed Inservice/Wkshps Baylor Univ; *cr:* 1st Grade Teacher Rosenthal Elem 1967-68; 2nd Grade Teacher Robinson Ind Sch Dist 1968-; *ai:* Gifted & Talented Planning Comm; Robinson Classroom Teachers (Pres 1978-79, Treas 1981-82) Gold Personalized Pen Set 1979; Mc Lennan Cty TSTA (Treas 1982-83), TSTA, NEA; Church Ushers VP 1984-; Jr Ushers Supvr 1986-; Lodge Jr Matron 1979-83; BSA (Den Leader, Comm); Robinson Teacher of Month; *home:* 2108 Broadway Waco TX 76704

HOWARD, CAPRIECE COLE, 4th Grade Teacher; *b:* Shady Valley, TN; *m:* Earl Butler; *c:* Earl B. Jr., Jeffrey C.; *ed:* (BS) Elem Ed, E TN St Univ 1971; *cr:* Teacher 1962-86, Chapter I Rdng/Math Teacher 1986-89, Classroom Teacher 1989- Shady Valley Elem Sch.

HOWARD, CHARLES RONALD, HS Mathematics Teacher; *b:* Shelby, NC; *m:* Phyllis L.; *c:* Adriane, Jessica; *ed:* (BS) Math, Lenoir-Rhyne Coll 1979; (MAED) Scndry Math, W Carolina Univ 1989; *cr:* Teacher Tuscola HS 1979-; *ai:* MAO-Math Club Adv; Sch Cmptr Coord; NCAE 1986-; NCCTM 1980-; NC Teachers Schlsp 1986-87; Tuscola HS Teacher of Month June 1989; *office:* Tuscola HS 350 Tuscola School Rd Waynesville NC 28786

HOWARD, CONSTANCE ROSE DAVANE, 8th Grade Teacher; *b:* N Versailles, PA; *m:* John P.; *c:* Johnette, Mark, Lisa, Connie; *ed:* (BS) Elem Ed, Carlow Coll 1964; (MS) Elem Ed, Duquesne Univ 1970; Certificate Religion Diocese of Pittsburgh; *cr:* Elem Teacher E Allegheny Schls 1964-68; 8th Grade Teacher St Robert Bellarmine 1970-; *ai:* 8th Grade Serra Club Essay Contest, 6th-8th Grade Spelling Bee Contests Pittsburgh Press & Cath War Veterans Spon & Adv; *office:* St Robert Bellarmine Sch 1301 5th Ave East McKeesport PA 15035

HOWARD, CORKY, Computer Coordinator; *b:* Harrison, AR; *m:* Lisa Boles; *c:* Stephanie, Jonathan, Joshua, Ashley; *ed:* (BSE) Phys Ed, AR Tech Univ 1977; IMPAC Trng; Near Completion on Masters in Admin; *cr:* Boys Coach/Health Caddo Hills HS 1977-79; Girls Coach/Asst Ftbl Vilonia HS 1979-81; Boys Coach/Sci Teacher Blue Eye HS 1982-83; Girls Coach/Sci/Cmptr Teacher Bergman HS 1983-; *ai:* Cmptr Coord; Word Processing, Data Base, Sci Teacher; Girls BB, Boys BB, Track, Bsbl, Sftbl Coach; 7th Grade Spon; AVA Mem 1990; Dist Coach of Yr 1980; *office:* Bergman HS Hwy 7 North Bergman AR 72615

HOWARD, CURT S., 6th Grade Teacher; *b:* Sumner, IA; *m:* Nancy Luebbers; *ed:* (BA) Elem Ed, Wartburg Coll 1978; (MA) Elem Ed, Univ Northern IA 1987; *cr:* 6th Grade Teacher Irving Elem Sch 1978-.

HOWARD, EDWARD FRANK, Elem Instrumentl Music Teacher; *b:* Cleves, OH; *m:* Dona Jeannine Spronk; *c:* Linda Yoder, Carolyn O Shaughnessy, Donald E.; *ed:* (BS) Music Ed, 1959, (MMus) Theory & Composition, 1962 Miami Univ of OH; *cr:* 9th-12th Grade Inst Music Teacher Three Rivers Local Schls 1962-65; 7th/8th Grade General Music/7th-12th Grade Inst Music Teacher Wyoming Schls 1965-67; Elem General Music Teacher 1967-70, Elem Inst Music Teacher 1970- Three Rivers Local Schls; *ai:* Music Educators Natl Conference 25 Yr Mem Awd 1988; Free & Accepted Masons 1968-; York Rite Masonic Bodies 1973-, Knight York Cross of Honour 1985; Scottish Rite Masonic Bodies Most Wise Master 1969-, 33rd Degree 1990; Cincinnati Civic Orch 1989-; Educator of Yr 1989 Miami Heights Elem Sch PTA, Three Rivers Local Schls PTA, Hamilton Cty Cncl of PTA; Composed & Arranbged Music.

HOWARD, FLORASTINE WILLIAMS, Math Department Chairman; *b:* Atmore, AL; *m:* Willie C.; *ed:* (BS) Math, AL A&M Univ 1969; (MED) Admin, AL St Univ 1975; Math, FL A&M Univ 1972 & LA St Univ 1973; *cr:* Math Teacher Frisco City HS 1969-; *ai:* Frisco City HS Stu Cncl Spon; Math Dept Chairperson; NEA, AEA, MEA; Delta Sigma Theta 1967-; Church of God Temple 1984-; *home:* Rt 3 Box 195A Atmore AL 36502

HOWARD, GARY WAYNE, Social Studies Dept Chairman; *b:* Bellows Falls, VT; *m:* Karin Sylvia Hacker; *c:* Jennifer A., Neil A., Hannah M., Julia K.; *ed:* (BED) Soc Sci, Univ of NH 1968; (MDIV) Theology, General Theological Seminary NYC 1971; US Army Officer Basic Trng; US Army Advanced Trng Course; Clinical Pastoral Ed Psych; *cr:* Soc Stud Teacher/Dept Chm Wells Cntrl Sch 1986-; *ai:* Stu Cncl Adv Wells Cntrl Sch; US Army Reserve (Chaplain, Captain) 1987-; Army Phys Fitness Awd 1989; Army Achievement Medal Awd 1989; Research for Book Entitled Earths Shifting Crust by Charles Hapgood; *home:* Box 158 Lake Pleasant NY 12108

HOWARD, GLADYS MEIER, Reading Teacher; *b:* Medford, WI; *c:* John D. P.; *ed:* (BS) Ed, Univ of WI Eau Claire 1962; (MS) Remedial Rdng, Univ of WI Milwaukee 1968; Post Grad Stud; Mastery Teaching Grad; *cr:* 1st Grade Teacher Phillips Public Sch 1955-61, West Allis Public Sch 1962-70; 7th Grade Teacher West Allis Public Sch 1970-; *ai:* Horace Mann Sch Newspaper; *home:* 4886 N Mohawk Glendale WI 53217

HOWARD, JANE ELIZABETH (GOINS), Third Grade Teacher; *b:* Paragould, AR; *m:* Jearl F.; *c:* Carie L., Samuel, Timothy L.; *ed:* (BA) Elem Ed, Harding Univ 1962; *cr:* 2nd Grade Teacher Perryville Public Schls 1960-61; 4th Grade Teacher Paragould Public Schls 1961-66; 3rd Grade Teacher Crowleys Ridge Acad 1975-; *ai:* Alpha Delta Kappa (Pres, Treas, VP, Corresponding Secy, Recording Secy) 1962-; Women for Crowleys Ridge Coll Pres; Parents Teachers & Friends Assn; AR Chrstn Teachers Assn; Paragould Classroom Teachers Assn Pres; *office:* Crowleys Ridge Acad 626 Academy Dr Paragould AR 72450

HOWARD, JIMMY BRUCE, Science Department Chair; *b:* Lubbock, TX; *m:* Gwynne Gale; *c:* Rachel G., Samuel B., Rebekah J., Stephen M.; *ed:* (BS) Bio Ed, KS St Univ 1978; (MRE) Religious Ed, SW Baptist Seminary 1980; Ed, Biochem, Univ N TX; *cr:* Teacher/Sci Dept Chm Lake Cty Chrstn Sch 1980-; *ai:* ACSI Regional Conventions Seminar Instr; Sch & ACSI Upper Level Regional Sci Fair Dir; Lake Cntry Chrstn Sch Soccer & Head Bsktbl Coach; Taps Dist IX Pres 1986-88, Coach of Yr 1986-88; CSAF Pres 1984-86; Outstanding Young Men of America 1987; *office:* Lake Cntry Chrstn Sch 7050 Lake Country Dr Fort Worth TX 76179

HOWARD, JOHN WHITNEY, SR., Science Teacher; *b:* Schenectady, NY; *m:* Ethel Villeneuve; *c:* John Jr.; *ed:* (BS) Bio-Chem, Rensselaer Polytechnic Inst 1950; (MS) Ed, Siena Coll 1960; Chem Study Prgm, MI St Univ 1962; NSF Research Prgm, Rensselaer Polytechnic Inst 1960; *cr:* Pharmacologist Sterling-Winthrop Research Inst 1950-57; Chem/Bio Teacher Amsterdam Public Schls 1957-58; Chem Teacher Schenectady Public Schls 1958-; *ai:* Teach Chem Evenings at Schenectady Cty Comm Coll; Tuition Waivers Comm; Delta Epsilon Sigma 1960-; Schenectady Fed of Teachers VP 1970-; ASCD 1989-; Hoffmans Volunteer Fire Dept 1955-80; Knights of Columbus 1957-65; Outstanding Sci Teacher by Assn of Schenectady Engrs 1960; GE Fnd Prgm Star 1987; CASDA Comm for Excl in Ed 1989; Nom for Presidential Awds for Excl 1989; *home:* RD 4 Box 524 Schenectady NY 12302

HOWARD, KEN R. Z., Kindergarten Teacher; *b:* Washington, PA; *m:* Louisa Zuccaro; *c:* Sarah, Katie; *ed:* (BA) Early Chldhd Elem, IN Univ of PA 1974; *cr:* Kndgtn Teacher Burg Area Sch Dist 1974-89; *ai:* HS Bsktbl/Tennis 1975-89; *home:* 220 Sharon Dr Weirton WV 26062

HOWARD, LUPITA SALAZAR, Mathematics Department Chair; *b:* Laredo, TX; *m:* Emmett Lee Jr.; *ed:* (BS) Math/His, 1964, (MS) His/Supervision, 1968 TX A&I Univ; Math, Laredo St Univ; Advanced Courses Towards Cert Teaching the Gifted; *cr:* Teacher Lamar Jr HS 1964-71; Teacher/Dept Head Martin HS 1983-; *ai:* Martin HS NHS 1975-83; Lamar Jr Natl Honor Society 1964-71; Schlsp & Inservice Comms; Assn of TX Prof Educators (Secy 1985, Membership Chairperson 1988-); ASCD 1980; NCTM 1983-; Amer Assn of Univ Women (Secy, Treas, Mem) 1975-; NSF Grant 1969; Local Inservice Meetings Presider & Presentor; Southern Assn Accreditation Team Mem; Local Textbook Adoption Comm Mem; *office:* Martin HS 2002 San Bernardo Laredo TX 78040

HOWARD, MARGARET BURCH, Vice Prin/5th Grade Teacher; *b:* Washington, DC; *m:* George Wilbur; *c:* John G., Marc C.; *ed:* (BA) Elem Ed, Coll of Notre Dame 1969; Towson St, Loyola Coll; *cr:* 1st Grade Teacher Christ the King 1964-67; 2nd Grade Teacher St Marys 1967-68; 1st Grade Teacher St Peters 1968-69; 2nd Grade Teacher Padonia Elem 1969-70; 3rd Grade Teacher St Marys 1970-71; Vice Prin/Teacher Archbishop Neale Sch 1979-; *ai:* Sacred Heart Parish Cncl Mem; St Marys Ryken HS Parents Cncl Mem; *home:* PO Box 447 Waldorf MD 20604

HOWARD, MARVIN JEROME, Teacher; *b:* Montezuma, GA; *m:* Susie A. Mc Rae; *c:* Marvin Jr.; *ed:* (BS) Mid Grades Ed, Albany St 1983; *cr:* Teacher Cntrl Elem 1983-88; Coach Telfair Cty HS 1983-; Teacher Telfair Cty Mid Sch 1989-; *ai:* Girls Bsktbl, Sftbl, Girls/Boys Track Head Coach; Prof Assn GA Educators 1989-; GA Athletic Coaches Assn 1989-; Wheeler Cty BOE Vice Chm 1988-89; Earnest Chaper 17 Order of Eastern Star Worthy Patron 1985-; Phi Beta Sigma Pres 1983; Master Mason Jr Warden 1985; Published Several Articles; Outstanding Citizen Awd; Wheeler Cty NAACP Pres; Outstanding Young Men of America; *home:* PO Box 32 Alamo GA 30411

HOWARD, MARY KATHLEEN, 4th/5th Grade Teacher; *b:* San Francisco, CA; *ed:* (BA) His, California Baptist Coll 1968; *cr:* 4th Grade Teacher Live Oak 1969; 5th Grade Teacher Andrew H Wilson 1969-72; 4th/5th Grade Teacher Bridge City 1972-; *ai:* Natl Academic Games Spon; Jefferson Parish Natl Academic Games Treas; Soc Stu Fair Judge; Jefferson Fed of Teachers Mem; Bridge City Teacher of Yr 1987-88; *office:* Bridge City Elem Sch 1805 Bridge City Ave Bridge City LA 70094

HOWARD, NANCY CAROLE (ARNOLD), Fifth Grade Teacher; *b:* Santa Ana, CA; *c:* Tommy, Tricia; *ed:* (BA) Ed, NE St Univ Tahlequah 1965; Cert K-8th Grade Elem, K-12th Grade Art, Jr HS 7th-8th Grade Lang Art; *cr:* Art Teacher Sullivan HS 1964-65, South Jr HS 1965-67; 1st Grade Teacher Claremont Elem 1967-69, Westside Elem 1977-78; 1st Grade Remedial Math Giddings Elem 1979-82; 5th Grade Teacher Lone Wolf Elem 1983-; *ai:* Art, Archaeology & Pep Club Spon; NEA, OEA; *home:* PO Box 505 Lone Wolf OK 73655

HOWARD, PEGYY MOORE, English Teacher; *b:* Jackson, MS; *m:* Frederick Leon Sr.; *c:* Frederick II *ed:* (BS) Eng, 1971, (MAT) Eng, 1979 Jackson St Univ; *cr:* Eng Teacher Simmons HS 1971-79, Jackson Public Schls 1979-; *ai:* Yrbk Adv; Jackson Assn of Educators, MS Assn of Educators 1979-; ASCD 1990: Delta Sigma Theta 1968-; STAR Teacher 1976, 1987; Teacher of Yr 1988; MTAI Evaluator; Dist Chairperson Jr HS Eng Dept 1989-; *home:* 249 Rowland Ave Jackson MS 39209

HOWARD, SANDRA REID, 8th Grade Mathematics Teacher; *b:* Paris, KY; *m:* Gary; *c:* Pamela, Mark, Jeremy; *ed:* (BS) Math, 1976, (MS) Math, Morehead St Univ 1979; *cr:* Math Teacher Harrison Cty HS 1976-82; 8th Grade Math Teacher Harrison Cty Mid Sch 1982-; *ai:* Stu Awds Comm; Plexing Problems Math Club; NEA, KY Ed Assn, NTCM 1977-; *office:* Harrison Cty Mid Sch 149 Education Dr Cynthiana KY 41031

HOWARD, SARAH LEE FLOWERS, Sixth Grade Teacher; *b:* Wilmington, NC; *m:* John Wallace; *c:* Kimberly M., John W. II, Richard L., Steven W., Lisa B.; *ed:* (BS) Elem Ed, Brigham Young Univ 1966; Grad Stud Univ of UT & UT St Univ; *cr:* 6th Grade Teacher West Jordan Elem Sch 1966-67, J C Roe Elem Sch 1967-68, Central Elem Sch 1982-; *ai:* Spec Prgms Coord-Spelling Bee, Sci & Fine Arts Fair; Rdng Lead Teacher for Several Yrs; Sch Accrediation Comm; Tutor Rdng & Math; Teacher Coord Maturation Prgm; Select Dist Teacher of Yr Comm; NEA, UT Ed Assn, Tooele Ed Assn 1982-; Nominee for Dist Teacher of Yr 1990; Heart Assn, Cancer Society, MS Fund, March of Dimes, Childrens Hospital, Church; *office:* Cntrl Elem Sch 55 N 1st W Tooele UT 84074

HOWARD, SERETHA SIBLEY, Counselor; *b:* Gary, IN; *m:* Rapheal Curtis; *c:* Kromeklia Bryant, Angelo; *ed:* (BA) Elem Ed, Lane Coll 1970; (MA) Elem Ed/Guidance Counseling, IN Univ 1978; Grad Stud Gifted & Talented; *cr:* Teacher Evansville-Vanderburgh Sch Corporation 1972-76; Cnslr Gary Manpower 1977-78; Teacher Hammond City Schls 1979-86; Adv/Part-Time Cnslr Purdue Univ 1985-; Cnslr Hammond City Schls 1986-; *ai:* Academic Decathlon, Hoosier Super Bowl, Spell Bowl, Sci Coach; Cheerleading Spon; Phi Delta Kappa 1990; Zeta Phi Beta 1969; BSA 1988-; NAACP; Amer Cancer Society 1973-74; TN St Univ Nashville Fellowship; Sewing Awd; Counseling Publication; *office:* George Rogers Clark Sch 1921 Davis St Whiting IN 46394

HOWARD, STEVEN PHILLIP, Mathematics Teacher; *b:* Columbus, OH; *m:* Sharron Johnson; *ed:* (BME) Music Ed, Amer Univ 1974; (MME) Music Ed, IN Univ 1978; Math, Numerous Univs & Colls; *cr:* Music Teacher Indianapolis Public Schls 1978-80; Math Teacher Acad of Notre Dame 1982-83, Paterson Bd of Ed 1983-85, Rialto Unified Sch Dist 1985-; *ai:* Home Visitations; Extra Parent Meetings; PTA; Math Tutor; Black Stu Union Spon; Census Registration; Contributor & Organizer Sch Assemblies; CAP Test Prerparation Cmptr Prgm Writer; NCTM, Music Educators Natl Conf Mem; Eastside HS Perfect Attendance Awd 1985, Teacher of Month; *home:* PO Box 41 Bryn Mawr CA 92318

HOWARD, SUSAN CHEYNE, Third Grade Teacher; *b:* Anniston, AL; *m:* Michael Gray; *ed:* (BS) Elem Ed, 1973, (MS) Elem Ed, 1976 Jacksonville St Univ; *cr:* 2nd Grade Teacher Calhoun Cty Trng Sch 1973-79; Adult Basic Ed Teacher Calhoun, Cherokee, Cleburne Cty Bds of Ed 1982-84; 3rd Grade Teacher Bynum Elem Sch 1979-; *ai:* Screening, Cty Continuum of Basic Skills Elem Teachers Writing, Supts Elem Advisory Comm; Calhoun Cty Ed Assn (Exec Bd 1988-, Legislative & Poly Action Comm Chairperson) 1973-; AL Ed Assn Legislative Contact Team 1973-; NEA 1973-; Natl Reference Inst Whos Who in Amer Ed 1987-88; *office:* Brynum Elem Sch P O Box 338 Bynum AL 36253

HOWARD, WILLIAM CAMERON, English Teacher; *b:* Tucson, AZ; *m:* Karen Lee Lanza; *c:* Rachel, Emily; *ed:* (BA) Eng, 1977, (MA) Eng, 1980 CA St Univ Fullerton; *cr:* Eng Teacher Judson Sch 1980-86, Rio Salado Jr Coll 1986, Sylmar HS 1986-, Pasadena City Coll 1987-; *ai:* Sylmar Storytellers, Stu Teachers Educl Partnership Spon; Intnl Festival Comm; Claremont Folk Festival (Presentor, Stage Mgr) 1987-; La Basin Storytelling Festival (Presentor, Staff) 1989; Presentor CA Rdng Assn Convention 1979; Word Weaving Trainer of Trainers; *office:* Sylmar HS 13050 Borden Ave Sylmar CA 91342

HOWARTH, DOUGLAS, Counselor; *b:* National City, CA; *m:* Michele R.; *c:* Kate N., Gwendolyn F.; *ed:* (BA Sociology, Univ of CA Berkeley 1973; (MA) Ed, Point Loma Coll 1980; US Intnl Univ 1974; Point Loma Coll 1980; *cr:* Teacher Castle Park Mid Sch 1974-80; Teacher Southwest Jr HS 1980-86; Cnslr Chula Vista Jr HS 1986-88; Cnslr Bonita Vista HS 1988-; *ai:* At Risk Stu Spon; Boys Wrestling/Girls Track Coach; Grad Class Adv; Bible Club Adv; CA Teacher Assn Mem 1987-; Dept of Ed Mem 1975-Project Wild 1984; Wilderness Society Mem 1973-; Natl Wildlife Fed 1973-; Natl Parks/Conservation Assn 1976-; Bonita Weslyan Church of Valley Mem 1989-; CA Dept of Ed GATE Cert 84; Sch Improvement Grant Winner 85; Participant CA Dept Fish/Game Coop Dept of Ed; Participant NH Coll Consortium; *office:* Bonita Vista HS 751 Otay Lakes Rd Chula Vista CA 92013

HOWAT, JANET MICHELLE, Fifth Grade Teacher; *b:* Morgantown, WV; *c:* James C., David S.; *ed:* (BS) Fr/Art Scndry Ed, WV Univ 1965; (MA) Elem Ed/Art Specialty 1978; Grad Stud Elem Ed; *cr:* 6th Grade Teacher Stoney Brook Elem 1965-68; Art Teacher Adamsville Mid Sch 1968-70; 5th/6th Grade Teacher Star City Elem 1978-80; 5th Grade Teacher North Elem 1980-; *ai:* Phi Delta Kappa; Tutoring Grant for At Risk Stus.

HOWAT, SANDRA WILSON, Second Grade Teacher; *b:* Baton Rouge, LA; *m:* Wade E.; *c:* Cheri, Vicki; *ed:* (BS) Elem Ed, LA St Univ 1963; Working Toward Masters Univ S MS 1990; *cr:* 3rd Grade Teacher Orleans Parish Schls 1963-67; 2nd Grade Teacher S Bay Union Schls 1967-69; 1st/2nd Grade Teacher Jackson Cty Schls 1973-; *ai:* Dist Insurance Comm; NEA, MS Assn of Educators (Building Rep 1985-) 1980-; MS Coast Kennel Club 1988-; *office:* St Martin North Elem Sch 16300 Le Moyne Blvd Biloxi MS 39532

HOWE, BRUCE VINCENT DE PAUL, Human Anatomy Instructor; *b:* Oklahoma City, OK; *ed:* (BS) Chem/Bio/Latin/His, 1971, (BSE) Sci Ed, 1972 Cntrl St Univ; (MS) Human Bio, OK Coll of Osteo Med 1981; Medical Ed, Moscow Univ 1990; Working on Athletic Trainers Certificate, Washburn Univ; Working on Masters in Jr Coll Ed, Cntrl St Univ; *cr:* Sci/Wrestling Teacher Douglass HS 1972-73; Sci/Wrestling/Tennis Teacher NW Classen HS 1973-74; Anatomy/Physiology/Tennis Teacher Heritage Hall Upper Sch 1974-77; Human Anatomy with Dissect Teacher Bishop Mc Guinness HS 1982-; *ai:* Tae Kwon Do Championships Mens Blackbelt Sr Division 1st Place US Open, 3rd Place US Intnl 1988; Oklahoma City Arts Cncl Asst to Dir of Oklahoma City Festival 1977-80; Vietnam Veterans Assn General Mem 1984-; USAF SSgt Pararescue 1964-70, Multiple Awds 1964-68; Univ of TX Seminar on Sci Ed 1989; *office:* Bishop Mc Guinness HS 801 NW 50th Oklahoma City OK 73118

HOWE, ROBERT W., Mathematics Teacher/Coach; *b:* Greensburg, IN; *m:* Judy A. Helm; *c:* Erin N., Deanna B.; *ed:* Math/Phys Ed, TN Tech Univ; (BS) Math/Phys Ed, In Cntrl Coll 1971; (MS) Ed/Math/Phys Ed, Purdue Univ 1981; *cr:* Math Teacher Indian Creek HS 1971; Math Teacher/Coach Jeffersonville 1971-73, Floyd Cntrl 73-75, Jennings Cty 1975-; *ai:* Girls Bsktbl 4 Yrs; Bsbl 10 Yrs; ISTA; IHBCA/ABCA; HBCA Coach Of Yr 1988; IBCA; Publish ABCA Coaching Notebook; *home:* RR 5 North Vernon IN 47265

HOWELL, ANN PRIDGEN, Eng Teacher/Guidance Counselor; *b:* Florence, SC; *m:* Sam L.; *c:* Jennifer D.; *ed:* (BA) Eng, Columbia Coll 1974; (MED) Guidance, Winthrop Coll 1976; Citadel, Bread Loaf Sch of Eng, Wofford Coll, Converse Coll; *cr:* Eng Teacher Airport HS 1974-75; Eng/Psych Teacher/Guidance Rock Hill HS 1976-80; Part-Time Instr York Tech Coll 1979; Adjunct Instr Presbyn Coll 1986-; Eng Teacher/Guidance Laurens Dist 55 HS 1980-; *ai:* NHS Adv; Natural Helper; Prom Invitation & Ticket Comm Coord; Faculty Interaction Comm, Honor Cncl Chm; NEA, SC Ed Assn 1982-83, 1989-; NCTE, SC Cncl Teachers of Eng 1982-; Laurens Mental Health Assn 1989-; Alpha Delta Kappa (VP, Pres) 1986-; Piedmont Tech Coll Bd of Visitors; Bread Loaf Sch of Eng Schlshp; Coll Bds Mellon Fnd Stipend Winner; *office:* Laurens Dist 55 HS P O Box 309 Princeton Rd Laurens SC 29360

HOWELL, BARBARA BROWN, Sixth Grade Teacher; *b:* Plainfield, NJ; *m:* Robert C.; *ed:* (BS) Elem Ed, Boston Univ 1957; *cr:* 6th Grade Teacher 1957-72, 5th Grade Teacher 1973-77, 6th Grade Teacher 1978- Washington Sch; *ai:* Academic Achievement Recognition & Improvement of Self-Esteem Act Spon; NCTM; Delta Sigma Theta; Natl Assn of Univ Women 2nd VP 1989-; Frontiers Intnl Excl in Ed Awd 1989; NJ Governors Teacher Recognition Prgm 1989.

HOWELL, BEVERLY SALMANS, Grammar & Art Teacher; *b:* Houston, TX; *m:* Galen; *c:* Kathy J. Howell De Werff, Tracy L. Howell Thomsen; *ed:* (BS) Art Ed, Ft Hays St Univ 1969; Schls without Failure Facilitator; Teacher Expectations & Stu Achievement Coord; *cr:* Art Teacher 1969-79, Lang Art Teacher 1979- Dist #495; *ai:* NEA, KS Ed Assn, Ft Larned Ed Assn 1972-; Prairie Arts Unlimited; PEO Sisterhood 1989-; Barton Cty Comm Coll Art Teacher; Inservice Teacher; *home:* 916 West 5 Larned KS 67550

HOWELL, DONALD RICK, Social Studies Teacher; *b:* Celina, OH; *m:* Jeri Ruth Butdorf; *c:* Kristin, Melissa, Julie, Jeff; *ed:* (BA) Soc Stud Comp, Wright St Univ 1975; (MS) Sch Cnslr Ed, Univ of Dayton 1986; *cr:* Infantry US Army Vietnam 1969-71; Teacher/Coach Fremont Jr HS 1975-80; Teacher/Wrestling Coach Rio Grand Coll 1985-87; Teacher/Coach Gallia Acad 1981-; *ai:* Sr Class & OH Mock Trial Adv; Ftbl & Wrestling Coach; OEA, SEOEA 1975-; GEA VP 1989-; OH Cncl for Soc Stud 1975-80, 1989-; Kiwanis Club (VP, Pres, Dist Pres 1987) 1984-; Lions Club Secy 1975-80; Big Brother/Big Sisters Bd of Dir 1986-; Amer Cancer Society Chm; Jenning Scholar 1980; Outstanding Young Men of America 1980; Bicentennial Comm 1990; *home:* 9 Willow Dr Gallipolis OH 45631

HOWELL, FAITHE BOATNER, English/Speech Teacher; *b:* Jackson, MS; *m:* Eric Lee; *c:* Kevin C., Tristan S.; *ed:* (BA) Ed/Speech, Univ of MS 1969; *cr:* 5th Grade Teacher West Hills Elem 1971; Eng/Speech Teacher Leake Acad 1982-; *ai:* Drill Team, Jr Class, Drama Club Spon; MS Private Sch Dist Assn 1982-; STAR Teacher 1990; *office:* Leake Acad 1 Rebel Dr Madden MS 39109

HOWELL, FAYE JOYNER, Sixth Grade Teacher; *b:* Suffolk, VA; *m:* Gary; *c:* Kevin; *ed:* (BS) Elem Ed, James Madison Univ 1975; *cr:* 6th Grade Rdng Teacher Southwestern Intermediate Sch 1975-; *ai:* Club Spon; Stu Cncl Assn; VA Ed Assn; Ed Assn of Suffolk Pres 1980-81; NEA, Suffolk Rdng Cncl, Poly Action Comm; Chesapeake Bay Ed Assn; Tidewater Uniserv Chm 1983-84; VA St Rdng Cncl; Bus & Prof Womens Club 1978-80; Jr Volunteer Service Corp 1981-; *office:* Southwestern Intermediate Sch 9301 Southwestern Blvd Suffolk VA 23437

HOWELL, JACK MARION, Fifth Grade Teacher; *b:* Haleyville, AL; *m:* Linda Finney; *c:* Julia R.; *ed:* (BS) Elem Ed, 1963, (MA) Elem Ed, 1974 Florence St; *cr:* 5th/6th Grade Elem Teacher Riverton Sch 1963-65; Case Worker AL Dept of Pen & Security 1966-72; 5th Grade Teacher Haleyville City Schls 1972-; *ai:* Various Sch Comms; Sch Bd of Dirs Chm; Evaluation Comm; HEA, NEA, AEA 1972-; Friends of Lib Charter Mem 1985-; Lib Bd 1988-; 4-H Club Local Leader 1972-, Leadership Awd 1984; *home:* 2810 18th Ct Haleyville AL 35565

HOWELL, JANIE LLOYD, 8th Grade Lang Art Teacher; *b:* Hartsville, SC; *m:* Willie James; *c:* Steven, Susan; *ed:* (BA) Elem Ed, Francis Marion Coll 1980; Elem Ed, Univ SC Sumter Branch; *cr:* 7th/8th Grade Lang Art Teacher Lamar HS 1980-83; 8th Grade Lang Art Teacher Spaulding Jr HS 1983-; *ai:* Beta Club, 8th Grade Prom & Graduation Spon; Intnl Rdng Assn, NEA, SC Ed Assn, Delta Kappa Gamma 1990; Sch Teacher of Yr 1985-86, 1989-; Individual Incentive Teacher 1988-89; SC BSAP II Writing Comm Mem; Lieutenant Governors Dist Teacher 8th Grade Writing Awd 1987-; *home:* Rt 1 Box 283-A Lamar SC 29069

HOWELL, JULIE BELLE HUDSON, Elementary Teacher Retired; *b:* New Hartford, MO; *m:* J.B. (dec); *ed:* (AE) Elem Ed, Hannibal-LaGrange 1946; (BS) Elem Ed Culver-Stockton 1954; *cr:* Teacher Rural Sch Pike Cty 1943-51; Teacher Olney 1-4 Elem Lincoln Co 1951-53; Teacher Warrenton Seventh Grade 1953-59; Teacher Bowling Green Elem 1959-83; *ai:* Pike Co Area Retired Teachers Treas 1985-; Hopke Christian Church 1963.

HOWELL, KATHERINE COLLINS, Second Grade Teacher; *b:* Leon, IA; *m:* Gail E.; *c:* Sean, Tifany, Jeremiah; *ed:* (BA) Elem Ed, Univ of N IA 1971; (MSE) Ed, Drake Univ 1988; *cr:* Title Rdng Teacher 1971-73, 3rd Grade Teacher 1980-81, 1st Grade Teacher 1987-88, 2nd Grade Teacher 1973- Cntrl Decatur; *ai:* Soc Stud Curr Comm Mem; HIV/AIDS Teacher Trainer; NEA, IA St Ed Assn, Cntrl Decatur Ed Assn 1971-; Girl Scouts Leader 1984-; *office:* South Elem Sch 201 SE 6th Leon IA 50144

HOWELL, LAURA COOLEY, Math Teacher; *b:* Travis AFB, CA; *m:* James Edward III; *ed:* (BS) Scndry Ed/Math, Old Dominion Univ 1985; Peer Assistance Group; Hampton Instructional Improvement Model; *cr:* Math Teacher Kecoughtan HS 1985-; *ai:* Chrldr Coach 1986-; Suicide Prevention Crisis Team Mem 1988-; SCA Advisory Comm 1988-; PTA 1987-; Order of Eastern Star 1984-; *office:* Kecoughtan HS 522 Woodland Rd Hampton VA 23669

HOWELL, LINDA CREEKMUR, Biology Teacher; *b:* Norfolk, VA; *m:* Coy L. Jr.; *c:* Paula G., Elizabeth A.; *ed:* (BSMT) Medical Technology, 1966, (MSED) Scndry Ed, 1985 Old Dominion Univ; Working on EDs in Admin & Supervision, George Washington Univ; *cr:* Bio Teacher Great Bridge HS 1982-; *ai:* Doria Tri Hi Y Adv; Substance Abuse, All Night Prom Party, Study Skills Dev 10th Grade Stu Comm; Alpha Delta Kappa 1987-; NEA 1982-; VA Educators Assn, Chesapeake Educators Assn, VA Assn of Sci Teachers, Tide Water Assn of Sci Teachers, NABT; St YMCA Service to Youth Awd 1988; Nom Presidential Awd Excl in Sci & Math 1986, 1989; *office:* Great Bridge HS 301 W Hanbury Rd Chesapeake VA 23320

HOWELL, MYRTLE ELIZABETH (HANNA), Fourth Grade Teacher; *b:* Altha, FL; *m:* Corbett Raymond; *c:* Seth, Scott, Steven; *ed:* (BS) Elem Ed, FL St Univ 1962; Grad Work, Sci; *cr:* Lucille Moore Elem 1962-63; Grenada MS Welfare Dept 1964-65; Blountstown HS 1966-68; Port St Joe HS 1976-77; Highland View Elem 1978-; *ai:* Calendar/Inservice Comms; SACS Study Team; GCTA, FTP, NEA; Delta Kappa Gamma 1986-; FL Cncl Elem Ed Study Team Chm 1982-; Teacher of Yr 1982-83 & 1989-90; *home:* 259 Marshall Rd PO Box 802 Port Saint Joe FL 32456

HOWELL, NANCY IRENE, Latin Teacher; *b:* Nashville, TN; *ed:* (BA) Classics, SW at Memphis 1973; Grad Courses, Memphis St Univ, TN St Univ & Kent St Univ; *cr:* Latin Teacher Lausanne Sch 1973-74; Latin/Math Teacher C H Spurgeon Acad 1974-75; Latin Teacher Brentwood Acad 1975-76; Latin/Math Teacher Franklin Road Acad 1976-; *ai:* Jr Classical League; Quiz Bowl Team; Boys & Girls Golf Coach; Frosh Class Spon; NHS Adv; Amer Classical League; TN Foreign Lang Teaching Assn Bd Mem 1985-88; TN Classical Assn, Classical Assn of Mid West & South; TN Athletic Coaches Assn Boys Dist Golf Coach of Yr 1989; Fellowship to New England Classical Inst at Tufts Univ 1990-91; *office:* Franklin Road Acad 4700 Franklin Rd Nashville TN 37220

HOWELL, NANCY WARD, Teacher of Gifted; *b:* Cincinnati, OH; *m:* Kent Parks; *c:* Michael, Laura; *ed:* (BS) Elem Ed, Benedictine Coll 1976; (MED) Mid Sch, GA St Univ 1988; Grad Stud Gifted & Human Relations; *cr:* Teacher Shaefer Sch 1978, Fairfax Cty Schls 1978-81, Cherokee Cty Schls 1981-82; Teacher of Gifted Cobb Cty Schls 1982-; *ai:* Faculty Advisory Comm Chairperson; Cty Comm of 100 Sch Rep; Stu Cncl Spon; Interdisciplinary Comm Mem; Natl Mid Sch Assn, America Society for Trng & Dev; March of Dimes Sch Chairperson 1987-; Presenter Natl Mid Sch Assn Conference Toronto 1989; *home:* 816 Hillwood Dr Marietta GA 30068

HOWELL, SARAH SAWYER, Social Studies Teacher; *b:* Enterprise, AL; *m:* Shepherd L.; *c:* Laura, Sawyer; *ed:* (BA) His/Sociology, Samford Univ 1979; *cr:* Soc Stud Teacher Cass Mid Sch 1980-81, Adairsville Mid Sch 1981-83, Cass HS 1983-; *ai:* Bartow Cty Sch Climate Steering Comm Mem; Kappa Delta; *office:* Cass HS 738 Grassdale Rd Cartersville GA 30120

HOWELLS, ELLEN SCOFIELD, 7th Grade Mathematics Teacher; *b:* Birmingham, AL; *m:* Byron Jr.; *ed:* (BS) Elem Ed, 1978, (MS) Elem Ed, 1980 Sanford Univ; Admin/Supervision; *cr:* 6th/7th Grade Teacher Cherokee Bend Elem Sch 1978-80; 7th Grade Teacher Griffin Mid Sch 1981-; *ai:* Team Leader; Sch Math Coord; PTSA 1981-; *office:* Griffin Mid Sch 4010 King Springs Rd Smyrna GA 30080

HOWETH, JOHN TRAVIS, Science Teacher; *b:* Wittman, MD; *m:* Linda Anne; *c:* Tony, Travis, Michelle, Beth, Joe, Chris, Michael, Geoffrey; *ed:* (BS) Forest Resources, Univ of GA 1970, (MED) Sci Ed 1984, (EDS) Sci Ed, 1988 Univ of GA; Several

Wkshps; *cr:* Teacher Oglethorpe Cty Mid Sch 1975-76, Oglethorpe Cty HS 1976-78, Cedar Shoals HS 1979-83, Oglethorpe Cty HS 1983-; *ai:* Beta Club Spon; Sr Class Spon; Vice-Chm Exec Cncl; Chm Southern Assn Accredidation Comm; Prof Assn of GA Educators Building Rep 1984-; GA Sci Teachers Assn (Dist Level, St Level) 1982-; Amer Cancer Society Health & Safety 1989; Oglethorpe Cty Foster Parents Assn 1985; GA Secy of St Good Citizenship Awd 1988; Star Teacher 1978/1983/1990; Oglethorpe Cty Teacher of Yr 1985; Presidential Awd Finalist 1985-86; Dupont Awd 1982; Published Several Articles The GA Sci Teacher; Several Wrkshps; *office:* Oglethorpe County H S Highway 78 Lexington GA 30648

HOWIE, MARY SUE, 6th Grade Lang Art Teacher; *b:* Eau Claire, WI; *c:* David A., Jill Howie Rickey, Charles C., Richard A.; *ed:* (BS) Elem Ed, Bradley Univ 1962; *cr:* 6th Grade Teacher 1961-62, 5th Grade Teacher 1962-63 Highland Elem Sch; 5th Grade Teacher Kalayaan Elem Sch 1963-64; Eng Conversation Teacher Chinese Military Inst 1978-79; TESOL Teacher Pearl City HS 1980-81; 6th Grade Teacher Bellview Mid Sch 1981-; *ai:* NHS Co-Spon; 6th Grade Eng Co-Chm; Escambia Cty Cncl Teachers of Eng 1989-; Featured on Local Television Station 1986; *office:* Bellview Mid Sch 6201 Mobile Highway Pensacola FL 32506

HOY, HAROLD ARTHUR, Wood Shop Teacher; *b:* Tillamook, OR; *m:* Carolyn Sue Beecher; *c:* Allan, David, April, Lorallan; *ed:* (BS) Elem Ed, 1958, (MS) Elem Ed, 1964 OR Coll of Ed; *cr:* 6th Grade Teacher 1958-60, 5th Grade Teacher 1960-62 Blossom Gulch Elem; 5th Grade Teacher Milner Crest Elem 1962-64; 8th Grade His Teacher 1964-75, Wood Shop Teacher 1975- Millicoma Mid Sch; *ai:* Mid Sch Athletic Dir & Ftbl Coach; Marshfield HS Var Bsktbl Asst; Eastside City Cncl Councilman 1971-74; *office:* Millicoma Mid Sch 2nd Ave Coos Bay OR 97420

HOY, STEVEN WAYNE, English/Reading Teacher; *b:* Halifax, PA; *m:* Laura Lynn Olsen; *c:* Jacob, Matthew, Alyssa; *ed:* (BA) Eng, Cedarville Coll 1978; *cr:* Jr HS Eng Teacher Evangel Chrstn Sch 1980-83; Jr HS Eng/Rdng Teacher 1st Baptist Chrstn Sch 1983-; *ai:* AV Coord; Bsktbl & Soccer Coach.

HOYE, PRESENTATION, CSJ, Jr HS Teacher; *b:* Derby, CT; *ed:* (BS) Ed, Diocesan Sisters Coll 1954; (BS) Music Ed, Nazareth Coll 1966; (MS) Music Ed, Univ of Bridgeport 1973; *cr:* Teacher/Prin St Lawrence Sch 1954-; *ai:* Librarian; NCEA; *home:* 233 Main St West Haven CT 06516

HOYME, DEBORAH J., Sixth Grade Teacher; *b:* Canby, MN; *m:* Curtis H.; *c:* Derek, Daniel, Marit; *ed:* (BS) Elem Ed, Moorhead St Univ 1972; *cr:* Title I Teacher Canby Elem Sch 1972-73, Ivanhoe Elem Sch 1973-75; Title I Teacher 1978-83, Jr HS Math Teacher 1983-85 Canby HS; 6th Grade Teacher Canby Elem Sch 1986-; *ai:* Christmas & Spring Musicals Co-Adv; NEA, MEA 1979-; CEA (Secy, Membership) 1979-; Canby Area Chamber of Commerce Dir 1987-89; Lacqui Parle-Yellow Bank Watershed Dist Secy 1985-; Our Saviours Luth Handbell Choir (Mem, Soloist) 1979-.

HREN, DIANE COPELTON, Science Department Chair; *b:* Paterson, NJ; *m:* Benedict J.; *ed:* (BA) Bio/Psych, Hiram Coll 1982; *cr:* Bio Teacher Warren Cty HS 1985-87; Bio Teacher/Dept Chairperson S S Peter & Paul HS 1988-; *ai:* Jr Class Adv; MD Assn of Outdoor & Environmental Educators Mem 1987-; NABT Mem 1986-; The Wildfowl Trust of North America Ed Bd Mem 1986-; *office:* S S Peter & Paul HS 900 High St Easton MD 21601

HRNICEK, NOREEN THERESE, Chemistry Teacher; *b:* David City, NE; *cr:* Chem Teacher Pius X HS 1986-; *ai:* Soph Class Spon; *office:* Pius X HS 6000 A Street Lincoln NE 68510

HRONEC, SUZANNE KOVALCHIK, Reading Teacher; *b:* Zanesville, OH; *c:* Aaron; *ed:* (BS) Elem Ed, OH Univ 1973; (MA) Elem Ed, Coll of Mt St Joseph 1987; Data Processing; *cr:* 5th-6th Grade Teacher Noble Local Sch Dist 1973-76; 1st/5th Grade/Chaper I Teacher Rolling Hills Sch Dist 1977-; *ai:* Stu Cncl Adv; Project KARE; Dist Sci Fair Judge; Lang, Soc Stud, Rdng Curr Dev Comms; Teacher for Prime Time Rdng; Delta Kappa Gamma, Intnl Rdng Assn, ASCD, OH Ed Assn, NEA; Campfire Bd Dirs, Guernsey Memorial Hospital Auxiliary, Home & Sch Assn, Orthodox Church in America Delegate to All Amer Cncl; Fed Russian Orthodox Clubs; Church (Cncl Mem, Choir Mem Sunday Sch Teacher); OH Dist FROC (Convention, Oratorical, Bowling Tournament Chairperson); *home:* 220-2 S 4th St Byesville OH 43723

HROVATIC, NATALIE STANSFIELD, Fourth Grade Teacher; *b:* Falls Mills, VA; *m:* Carl De Wayne; *c:* Mark, Terri H. Herald; *ed:* (AA) Liberal Arts, Bluefield Coll 1951; (BS) Elem Ed, Bluefield St Coll 1971; Grad Sch of Univ of VA; *cr:* Teacher 1955-64, Rdng Specialist 1964-74 Abbsvalley Elem Sch; Teacher Tazewell Elem 1974-; *ai:* 4th Grade 4-H Leader; Prin Advisory Comm; NEA 1955-; VA Ed Assn 1955-; Tazewell Ed Assn 1955-; PTA 1955-; VA St Rdng Assn Bd of Dir 1971-74; Tazewell Cty Rdng Assn Pres 1972-74; VA Fed of Garden Clubs Bd of Dir 1974-77; VA Coll Bd Comm 1981-89 Secy 1981-85; Southwest VA Cmmty Coll Bd (Treas 1984-85, Vice Chm 1985-86/Chm 1986-87); Tazewell Cty Bd of Supvrs Certificate for Outstanding Service 1986; *home:* 806 Fincastle Dr Bluefield VA 24605

HRUBY, DALE, Vocational Agriculture Instr; *b:* Wilton, ND; *m:* Karla Eckroth; *ed:* (BS) Ag Ed, ND St Univ 1977; *cr:* Voc-Ag Instr Mc Clusky Public Sch 1977-78, Center Public Sch 1978-79, Bismarck Public Schls 1979-; *ai:* FFA Adv; NEA, AVA, NDVATA; Elks; *office:* Bismarck Voc Center 1500 Edwards Ave Bismarck ND 58501

HRUSKA, CECILIA ANNE, First Grade Teacher; *b:* Houston, TX; *ed:* (BA) Elem Ed, St Thomas Univ 1965, (MED) Elem Ed, Univ of Houston 1969; *cr:* 2nd Grade Teacher St Annes Sch 1965-68; 3rd Grade Teacher Sherman Elem 1968-71, Crawford Elem 1971-72; 1st Grade Teacher St Francis de Sales Sch 1972-; *ai:* 2nd Grade Teacher for Continuing Chrstn Ed Prgm; Greater Houston Area Rdng Cncl 1987-; NCEA 1988-; Early Chldhd Assn 1989-; St Francis de Sales Church Parish Cncl; *office:* St Francis de Sales Sch 8100 Roos Rd Houston TX 77036

HSUE, BETTY LOCKE, English/Reading/Math Teacher; *b:* Liuchow, China; *m:* Harry; *c:* Gunther, Heidi; *ed:* (BA) Span, San Francisco St Univ 1965; Completed Eng Endorsement; Working on Bus Endorsement; *cr:* 7th-9th Grade Eng as 2nd Lang Teacher Marina Jr HS 1971-75; 7th-10th Grade Eng/Rdng/8th Grade Rdng/Math/9th Grade Cmptr Literacy Teacher San Francisco Jr Acad 1975-; *ai:* Church Young Adults Class Sabbath Sch Teacher; Project STAR Awd 1990; *office:* San Francisco Jr Acad 66 Geneva San Francisco CA 94112

HUBBARD, BEVERLY FLACK, Third Grade Teacher; *b:* Kansas City, MO; *m:* J. Roger; *c:* James, Lori; *ed:* (BS) Elem Ed, Univ of NE 1959; Grad Stud Elem Ed; *cr:* 5th Grade Teacher Omaha Public Schls 1959-63; 3rd Grade Teacher S Sioux Cmmty Schls 1968-; *ai:* PTA Rep 1969-, Life Mem 1976; NEA, NSEA, SSCEA Rep 1968-; *home:* Rt 1 Box 339 Dakota City NE 68731

HUBBARD, BILL M., 8th Grade Mathematics Teacher; *b:* Scot AFB, IL; *m:* Janet Bowers; *c:* Karen, Andy; *ed:* (BSED) Math, Univ of MO Columbia 1974; (MS) Guidance, Univ of MO St Louis 1987; *cr:* Math Teacher Mexico Sr HS 1974-76, Fort Zumwalt Cntrl Jr HS 1976-79, Pacific Sr HS 1979-85, Mehlville Washington Jr HS 1985-; *ai:* Math Club Spon; MO Cncl Teachers of Math; *office:* Washington Jr HS 5165 Ambs Rd Saint Louis MO 63128

HUBBARD, CARLA INGALLS, Social Studies Teacher; *b:* Ft Lewis, Washington; *m:* Mac F.; *c:* Andrea, Jarred; *ed:* (BS) Soc Stud, 1978, (MS) Soc Stud, 1989 Columbus Coll; *cr:* Teacher Richards Jr HS 1978-79, Morgan Cty Schls 1979-83, Harris Cty Mid Sch 1983-; *ai:* GA His Bowl Team; Talent Show Emcee; Soc Stud Fair Coord; Soc Stud Dept Chairperson; Chrldr Spon; Prof Assn of GA Ed 1989-; GA Cncl Soc Sci 1986-; Geography Ed Prgm of GA 1986-; Journal Column; Articles Published; *home:* PO Box 22 Hwy 116 Shiloh GA 31826

HUBBARD, CONNIE HARLESS, Science Teacher/Sci Dept Chair; *b:* Charleston, WV; *m:* Charles Edward; *c:* Melinda G.; *ed:* (BA) Bio/Chem, Malone Coll 1975; (MED) Curr/Instruction, Ashland Coll 1983; Cmptrs, Interfacing, Micro Chem; *cr:* Bio/Chem/Physics Teacher 1979-80, Chem/Physics Teacher 1978-, Sci Dept Chairperson 1985- Minerva HS; *ai:* Sci Fair & Sci Day Spec Awds Chairperson; Project Redesign the Instruction of Sci & Math; Doing Chem & Physics; Teach to Learn; NSTA, Sci Ed of OH 1985-; OH Acad of Sci (Secy, Jr Section Acad Acker 1989, Krecker 1990) 1985-; NEA, OH Ed Assn, Minerva Local Ed Assn; Minerva Athletic Boosters Club 1981-; Jennings Scholar; Battelle Awd for Prof Dev; Governors Awd for Excl in Sci Ed; Newmast; *office:* Minerva HS 501 Almeda Ave Minerva OH 44657

HUBBARD, EMMA MACK, Business Teacher; *b:* Orangeburg, SC; *m:* Hiram Jr.; *c:* Samuel B. Glover Jr., Brian G; *ed:* (BS) Bus Ed, SC St Coll 1974, (MED) Bus Admin, SC St Coll 1977; Univ of SC; Winthrop Coll; Midlands Tech Coll; Orangeburg-Calhoun Tech Coll; *cr:* Bus Teacher Holly Hill HS 1977-80, St Matthews HS 1980-82; Elem Teacher Guinyard Elem Sch 1982-83; Bus Teacher Calhoun Cty HS 1983-; *ai:* Adv FBLA Club; Adv Cncl Calhoun Cty HS Bus Dept; Adv Cncl Calhoun/Orangeburg Voc Ctr; SC St Coll Sec 1976-80 2 Yr Awd 1979; Alumni Assn; CCEA Membership Comm 1980- Service 1984; SCEA 1980-; PBAa/Phi Beta Lambda Inc Adv 1980- Service 1985; St Luke Presbyn Church Treas 1983-; NEA 1980-; Edisto Federal Credit Union Adv Comm 1989-; Presidential Schls 1970-74/77; Mem Realtors Assn 1984-86.

HUBBARD, LEON DAVID, JR., 1st-5th Grade Phys Ed Teacher; *b:* Lamar, CO; *m:* Geraldine P. Bach; *c:* Kimberly, Davina; *ed:* (AA) Phys Ed, Lamar Jr Coll 1967; (BS) Phys Ed, 1969, (MS) Phys Ed, 1970 Chadron St Coll; Grad Studs, Chadron St Coll; *cr:* Elem Phys Ed Instr 1970-, Driver Ed Summers 1975, 1977-79, 1981 Alliance City Schls; Adjunct Faculty Mem Chadron St Coll 1976, 1979, 1980; *ai:* AAHPER 1970-; AEA, NSEA, NEA 1989-; NE Prof Practices Commission Peer Reviewer Appointed 1987; *home:* 424 Potash Ave Alliance NE 69301

HUBBARD, MICHAEL LANE, Remediation Teacher; *b:* Barbourville, KY; *m:* Phyllis Jeanette; *c:* Michael E., Heather M.; *ed:* (BA) Elem Ed, 1973, (MA) Ed, 1976, (Rank I) Admin, 1978 Union Coll; Drafting Trng, Knox Voc Sch 1968-69; *cr:* Teacher/Coach Barbourville City Schls 1973-74; Agent Metropolitan Life Insurance 1974; Teacher/Coach Dewitt Elem Sch 1974-; *ai:* KY Ed Assn Building Rep 1987-; NEA Mem 1973-; Knox Public Lib Bd Vice Chm 1986-; Activity Books Published; KY Dept of Ed Spec Certificate; *home:* PO Box 35 Bimble KY 40915

HUBBARD, TERESA SIMPSON, Teacher of Gifted & Talented; *b:* Gadsden, AL; *m:* David Burr; *c:* John, Paul; *ed:* (BSE) His/Eng, Jacksonville St Univ 1971; (MA) His, Univ of AL Huntsville 1986; (MA) Gifted Ed, Univ of AL Birmingham 1986; Cert Endorsement; *cr:* His/Eng Teacher Athens City Schls 1971-73; Teacher of Gifted & Talented Limestone Cty Schls 1983-86, Decatur City Schls 1985-86, Madison Cty Schls 1986-87, Limestone Cty Schls 1987-; *ai:* Duke Univ Talent Identification Prgm Coord; Phi Alpha Theta 1984-; Kappa Delta Pi 1986-; AL Ed Assn 1971-73, 1983-; NEA 1971, 1983-; Bus & Prof Womens Club 1973-74; Honors Schlar; Outstanding Young Women of America 1986; Whos Who in Amer Ed 1989; *home:* 111 Missy Leigh Ln Athens AL 35611

HUBBS, TIMOTHY L., Religion Teacher/Chaplain; *b:* Newark, NJ; *ed:* (BA) Philosophy. Univ of Scranton 1980; (MDIV) Theology, St Johns Seminary 1984; Grad Work Marywood Coll & St Charles Seminary; Officers Basic, US Army Reserve; *cr:* 7th Grade Teacher Honesdale Cath 1984-86; Religious Formation Dir Bishop O'Reilly HS 1986-89; Chaplain/Religion Teacher Wildwood Cath HS 1989-; *office:* Wildwood Cath HS 15th & Central Ave Wildwood NJ 08260

HUBER, BARRY ROBERT, Choral Music Teacher; *b:* Philadelphia, PA; *m:* Caroleen Faust; *c:* Bradlee F., Courtney L., Brandon C.; *ed:* (BME) Music, 1969, (MME) Music, 1978 Temple Univ; Masters Plus 30 Status 1989; *cr:* Music Teacher Widener Memorial Sch for Orthopedically Handicapped 1969-78; Vocal Music Teacher Martin Luther King HS 1978-88; Dir Choral Acts Cntrl HS 1988-; *ai:* All Philadelphia Sr HS Choir Asst Dir 1978-; Mens Chorale Dir 1984-; Amer Choral Dirs Assn Mem 1988; Church of Ephipany Choir Mem 1981-; Philadelphia Boys Choir & Mens Chorale Asst Dir 1970-82; Acad of Music Philadelphia Piano Accompanist; *office:* Cntrl HS Ogontz & Olney Ave Philadelphia PA 19141

HUBER, GEORGE RICHARD, Mathematics Department Chair; *b:* Charleston, IL; *m:* Carol Jean Krupa; *ed:* (BS) HPER, 1963, (MS) Phys Ed/Ed, 1967, (EDS) Admin/Supervision, 1983 IN St Univ; *cr:* Teacher/Coach Bowling Green HS 1963-64, Clark HS 1964-65; Teacher Morton HS 1968-; *office:* Morton HS 6915 Grand Ave Hammond IN 46323

HUBER, JUDY S., English Teacher; *b:* Mt Sterling, KY; *m:* Charles D.; *c:* Cherylynne; *ed:* (AB) Eng/Soc Stud, Morehead St Univ 1964; *cr:* Soc Stud/Eng Teacher Manchester HS 1964-68; Eng Teacher Bath Cty HS 1968-; *ai:* Majorettes; Sr Play; Yrbk; Jr-Sr Prom; Bath Cty Ed Assn Building Rep 1968-; KY Ed Assn, NEA 1968-; Owingsville Womans Club Treas 1969-71; Bath Cty Band Boosters Secy 1982-86.

HUBER, LOUIS ANTHONY, Social Studies Teacher; *b:* Passaic, NJ; *m:* Alice Jean Voorman; *c:* Denise Jordan, Daniel, Laura Alden; *ed:* (BAED) Soc Sci, William Paterson Univ 1961; (MAED) His, W WA Univ 1976; Ec & Law Related Ed; *cr:* Investigator US PHS 1962-64; Elem Teacher Wharton Public Schls 1964-67; Jr HS/Elem Teacher Port Angeles Public Schls 1967-86; Teacher Port Angeles HS 1986-; *ai:* Knowledge Bowl Coach; SADD; Rough Riders Against Drugs & Drunk Driving; Port Angeles Ed Assn Building Rep 1967-75; WEA Rep Assembly Delegate 1970-; Clallam Cty Sheriffs Dept Crime Prevention Deputy Sheriff 1967-; Natl Rifle Assn Instr 1985-; DWL Task Force Awd 1988; WA St Soc Stud Guidelines Writing Comm; Amer Bar Assn Law Related Ed Conference Fellows; *office:* Port Angeles HS 304 E Park Port Angeles WA 98362

HUBER, NORMAN C., Biology Teacher; *b:* Crestline, OH; *m:* Sharon Lynn; *c:* Lynnette, Cindi, Andrew, Carrie; *ed:* (BA) Soc Sci/Bio, OH St 1971; (MA) Bio Sci, Ashland; Grad Stud Quest, Impact; *cr:* General Sci/Bio Teacher River Valley HS 1971-77; Bio Teacher Col Crawford 1979-; *ai:* Bio Club; OEA, HEA, SECO; Lions Club Pres; 4-H Club; Consistory; *office:* Col Crawford HS St Rt 602 North Robinson OH 44856

HUBERT, KATHLEEN ANNE (MITCHELL), Third Grade Teacher; *b:* Harrisburg, PA; *m:* David R.; *c:* Jeffrey T., Glenn S., Douglas A., Kyle J.; *ed:* (BS) Ed/Early Chldhd, SUC Plattsburgh 1964; Grad Courses SUC Plattsburgh; *cr:* Kndgtn Teacher Glens Falls Sch System 1964-69; 1st/2nd Grade Teacher 1979, 1987, 3rd Grade Teacher 1980-86, 1988- Warrensburgh Cntrl Sch; *ai:* Prof Advancement & Observation/Evaluation Comm; Prin Selection Comm Chairperson; BOCES Conference on Adriondacks Planning Comm; Odyssey of Mind Judge; Warrensburg Teachers Assn Building Rep 1982-; West Point Parents Club 1986-; Mastersingers (Bd of Dirs, Librarian) 1987-; Christ Church United Meth (Music Comm 1984-, Chancel & Handbell Choirs 1975-); Glens Falls Fresh Air Fund (Comm 1966-76, Chairperson 1970-74); Glens Falls Operetta Club 1970-80; *office:* Warrensburg Cntrl Sch 1 James St Warrensburg NY 12885

HUCK, BARBARA RALPH, Comm Disorder Specialist; *b:* Vernal, UT; *m:* William Lao; *c:* Todd; *ed:* (BS) Speech Pathology, 1974, (MS) Comm Disorders, 1976 UT St Univ; Comm Disorders/Gen Ed, UT St Univ/Boise St Univ/ID St Univ/Coll of ID/ID Land Dev Acad; *cr:* Speech Pathologist Billings MT Public Schls 1975-78; Comm Disorders Specialist Weiser Public Schls 1978-, Private Practice 1980-; *ai:* Facilitator for Sign Lang Study Groups; Cub Scout Leader; Co-Organizer Weiser Lib Summer Rdng Prgm; Amer Speech/Lang/Hearing Assn 1975-; ID Speech/Lang/Hearing Assn 1979-; Natl ID Ed Assn 1988-; Delta Kappa Gamma 1989-; Pioneer Elem Teacher of Yr 1983; Snake River Spec Services Co-Op Exemplary Service Awd 1987; *office:* Weiser Park Sch 624 Pioneer Rd Weiser ID 83672

HUCK, LINDA A., Assistant Band Director; *b:* Perryville, MO; *m:* Keith M.; *c:* Claire; *ed:* (BME) Instrumental Music, 1982, (BM) Performance, 1982, (MME) Music Ed, 1986 SE MO St Univ; *cr:* Asst Band Dir Farmington R-7 Schls 1983-; *ai:* Color Guard; Jr/Sr HS Solo & Ensembles; HS Woodwind Choir; MO Music Educators Dist Jr HS VP 1983-; Cmmty Assn Teachers Assn, MO St Teachers Assn, Intnl Double Reed Society 1983-;

BSA Merit Badge Cnslr 1986-; Guest Conductor of SE MO Jr HS Honors Band 1990; Guest Clinician SE MO Jr HS Band Festival 1990; *office:* Farmington R-7 Schls 506 S Fleming Ave Farmington MO 63640

HUCKABAY, PAULA, English Teacher; *b:* Shreveport, LA; *ed:* (BS) Eng, TX Tech Univ 1977; Working Toward Masters in Counseling, Univ of TX; *cr:* Teacher Robert E Lee HS 1978-89; *ai:* Lee HS Literary Magazine Spon; TX Joint Cncl Teachers of Eng Mem 1988-; Recipient PTA Super Teacher Awd 1990; *office:* Robert E Lee HS 3500 Neely Midland TX 79705

HUCKABEE, GLORIA D., English Teacher; *b:* Linden, AL; *m:* Larry K.; *ed:* (BS) Eng/Bus Ed, 1977, (MS) Eng/Scndry Ed, 1981 Livingston Univ; Bio-Prep Trng for Advanced Placement of Advanced Stus Univ of AL Tuscaloosa; *cr:* Eng Teacher Austin Jr HS 1980-; *ai:* Delta Kappa Gamma (Secy 1988-, VP 1990); *home:* Rt 1 Box 902 Linden AL 36748

HUCKABY, SCOTT ALLAN, Science Dept Chair/Asst Prin; *b:* Metarie, LA; *m:* Glenda Nease; *ed:* (BS) Geology, GA St Univ 1983; Post Grad Work Geology, GA St Univ; *cr:* Asst Teacher GA St Univ 1985-86; 7th-12th Grade Teacher 1986-, HS Asst Prin 1989- Harvester Acad; *ai:* Sci Club & Stu Cncl Adv; Geological Society of America 1980-89; BSA Scoutmaster 1984-; *office:* Harvester Acad 4650 Flat Shoals Pkwy Decatur GA 30034

HUCKSTEP, ALICE DAMIN, Art/Humanities Teacher; *b:* Tell City, IN; *m:* David B.; *ed:* (BS) Art Ed, IN St Univ 1974; Early Chldhd Dev, Cmptr Sci Ed; *cr:* Teacher Staunton & Clay City Elem 1974-75; Teacher/Dir Private 1980-84; Teacher Newberry Jr/Sr HS 1983-84; Owner/Dir Alices Gingerbread House Child Care/Pre-Sch 1983-; Teacher Santa Fe HS 1984-; *ai:* Art Club Spon; T-Ball & Minor League Bsbl Sponsorship; N FL Art Educators Assn; Natl Fed of Ind Bus; Alachua Cty Child Care Bd 1981; Alachua City Chamber of Commerce 1984-; Alumni Alpha Chi Omega; *office:* Santa Fe HS U S 441 Alachua FL 32615

HUDAK, ALICE IDE, Elementary Teacher; *b:* Kingston, PA; *m:* John J.; *c:* Suzanne Hudak-Rismondo, John J. Jr.; *ed:* (BS) Elem Ed, Coll Misericordia 1959; Masters Equivalency Marywood Coll, Portland Univ, Univ of Southern CA, Penn St; *cr:* Elem Teacher Tunkhannock Area Schls 1959-; *ai:* Elem Cncl Mem; NEA, PA St Ed Assn, Tunkhannock Area Ed Assn 1959-; Lake Lehman Band Spons Pres 1982; Delta Kappa Gamma Society Intnl 1990; Harveys Lake Womans Service Club Pres 1982; Monroe Township & Evans Falls PTA (Secy, VP) 1978; St Therese Church (CCD Teacher 1970-75, Eucharistic Minister 1989); *home:* RR 4 Box 238 Dallas PA 18612

HUDAK, JOAN KRISTENAK, Chapter 1 Reading; *b:* Lakeside, OH; *ed:* (BA) Elem Ed, 1966, (MA) Ed, 1976 Bowling Green St Univ; Siena Heights Coll Adrian MI; *cr:* Elem Ed/Music Teacher Cath Schls in IL/MI 1959-63; Elem Ed Teacher 19 4-85, Chapter 1 Rdng Teacher 1985 Port Clinton City Schls; *ai:* Rdng Textbook Comm; Chairperson for Right To Read Week; Assisted In Music Ed; Ottawa Cty Women of Yr Awds; Ottawa Cty Hospice; Immaculate Conception Church Lay Ministry; Martha Holden Jennings Scholar; Delta Kappa Gamma Intnl Ed Society For Women; NCEA; OH & Amer Fed of Teachers; *home:* 280 E Bayview Dr Port Clinton OH 43452

HUDDLESTON, CHARLES RAY, Science Teacher; *b:* Burkesville, KY; *m:* Audry Adams; *c:* Beverly, Heather; *ed:* (BS) Elem Ed, 1980, (MA) Elem Ed, 1986 Western KY Univ; *cr:* 7th/8th Grade Rdng Teacher 1980-82, 6th Grade Self Contained Class Burkesville Elem 1983; 7th Grade Self Contained Class Kettle Elem Sch 1984-86; 6th-8th Grade Sci Teacher Cumberland Cty Mid Sch 1987-; *ai:* Head Boys Bsktbl Coach; *office:* Cumberland Cty Mid Sch P O Box 70 Burkesville KY 42717

HUDDLESTON, RUTH MOORE, Second Grade Teacher; *b:* Jackson, MS; *m:* Thomas Jefferson III; *c:* Dwayne E. H.; *ed:* (BS) Elem Ed, Jackson St Univ 1965; Working Toward Masters Degree in Admin, Early Childhd Ed; Teaching in Multi-Cultural Situation, Teaching HandiCapped-Mainstreaming in Classroom, Classroom Management, Cmptr Literacy, Introduction to Word Processing & Introduction to DOS; Prgm for Effective Teaching; *cr:* Spec Rdng Teacher/Title I Coord Madison Cty Schls 1966-70; Rdng Facilitator Madison Cty Schls Jr/Sr HS 1970-73; Lang Art Teacher Madison Cty Schls Intermediate & Jr HS 1973-78; Title I Math Teacher 1978-79, Elem Teacher 1979- Yazoo City Schls; *ai:* Private Tutorial Services; Quality Ed Project; Drug Awareness, Advisory, Children at Risk Comm; March of Dimes; United Negro Coll Fund Telethon; MS Rdng Assn, MS Assn of Educators, Intnl Rdng Assn, MS Staff Dev Assn; Natl Friends of Amistad (Bd of Dir, Parlimentarian) 1987-; Educators United for Global Awareness; MS St Fed of Colored Womens Clubs Incorporation, Dist Pres 1988-; Zeta Phi Beta Zeta Woman of Yr Awd 1980; Natl Black Media Coalition, Storks Nest, Bench & Bar Assn; Youth Court Volunteer Cnslr; Federal Marshal Asst; Transport Prisoners; PTA Mem; Natl Endowment of Hum; MS Culture Seminar Fellowship; Adopt-A-Family Public Service Awd; Functional Literacy Project Participant; Assertive Discipline Team Leader, Conference Grant Univ of St Thomas; Star Teacher Awd, Cmptr Literacy Certificates; Perfect Attendance Awds; Humanitarian Letter; Teaching Rdng in Content Areas Consultant; Whos Who Among Young Women of America Awd; *home:* 720 Webster Ave Yazoo City MS 39194

HUDDLESTON, WAYNE SCOTT, Math Teacher/Football Coach; *b:* Seymour, IN; *M:* Pamela S. Dunigan Huddleston; *c:* Ryan, Brad; *ed:* (BS) Phys Ed & Health 1975, (MA) Phys Ed & Health 1978 Ball St Univ; Mid Sch License 1989; *cr:* Math/Health Teacher South Putnam Schs 1975-76; Math Teacher MississineWA HS 1976-79; Health/Math Teacher Seymour Mid Sch 1979-; *ai:* Coaching Mid Sch Ftbl and Girls Track; Math Counts & Math Academic Competions Spons; Math Club Spons; NCTM 1986-; ICTM 1986-; IN St Teachers Assn 1975-; Seymour Chrstn Church Elder 1986-; Jackson Cty Chrstn Mens Fellowship Treas 1981-; Jesus and Me Founder 1989-; Semifinalist ICTM Teacher of Yr Awd 1988-89; Speaker Regional NCTM 1986; *home:* 2121 Marl Twain Ave Seymour IN 47274

HUDDLESTONE, ROBERT THOMAS, Youth in Custody Dept Head; *b:* Detroit, MI; *ed:* (BA) Eng, E MI Univ 1977; *cr:* Dept Head Hillcrest HS 1981-; *ai:* Mens & Womens Swimming & Diving Head Coach; Soc Comm Treas; Asst Strength Coach; *office:* Hillcrest HS 7350 S 9th E Midvale UT 84047

HUDGINS, CAROLYN SUE BREWER, 1st Grade Teacher; *b:* Mangum, OK; *m:* Edwin Earl; *c:* Amanda S.; *ed:* (BA) Elem Ed, Wayland Baptist Univ 1971; (MSM) Human Resource Management, Houston Baptist Univ 1982; (BA) Principles of Accounting, Wayland Baptist Univ; Bi-ling Ed, Sage Gifted & Talented Trng; Trng Through Ed Service Center in Spec Ed, Nutrition, & Ec; Speech, Creative Dramatics, Phys Ed, Kinesiology, Wayland Baptist Univ; Ed, Help Relationship, Clsr MH, Human Relation Wkshp, W TX Univ; Educl Service Center; Bi-ling Inst; Monoling Inst; *cr:* Remedial Math Teacher Eastland Elem 1971; 1st Grade Teacher Highland Elem 1971-86, Casey Elem 1986-; *ai:* Local Textbook Comm; Assn of TX Prof Educators; *home:* 1 Bennett Cir Wolfforth TX 79382

HUDGINS, LYNN, 4th-6th Grade English Teacher; *b:* Birmingham, AL; *ed:* (BA) Elem Ed, 1974, (MS) Elem Ed, 1976 Univ of AL Birmingham; *cr:* 5th/6th Grade Eng Teacher 1974-76, 3rd Grade Teacher 1976-77, 5th/6th Grade Soc Stud Teacher 1977-82, 4th-6th Grade Eng Teacher 1982- Mt Olive Elem; *ai:* Annual Spon; Track Coach; Art Chm; Gymnastics Rep; Tutorial Club Spon; Festival of Arts Co-Chm; Second Mile Teacher; 4-H Spon; NEA 1974-; AEA, JCEA Sch Rep 1974-; ADK 1988-; Accreditation Team Mem; Textbook Comm; Cty Calendar of Events Comm Mem; Author of Patriotism Units for All Cty Schls; *home:* Rt 2 Box 284 A Empire AL 35063

HUDGINS, REBECCA, Business Teacher; *b:* Loraine, TX; *ed:* (BBA) Bus Ed, 1975, (MA) Ed, 1981 TX Tech Univ; *cr:* Bus Teacher Crowell Ind Sch Dist 1975-81, Ira Ind Sch Dist 1981-; *ai:* Annual & Class Spon; Gifted & Talented Coord; NBEA, TX Bus Ed Assn, TX Classroom Teachers Assn; *office:* Ira Ind Sch Dist Box 240 Ira TX 79527

HUDSON, ANDREW D., Guidance Counselor; *b:* Knoxville, TN; *ed:* (BS) Educl/Counseling Psych, Berry Coll 1975; (MS) Educl/Counseling Psych, Univ of TN 1987; *cr:* Guidance Cnslr Pigeon Forge Mid Sch 1986-87, Mc Minn Cty HS 1987-; *ai:* Spec Hearing, Tennis Comm; Faculty Adv; NHS; Bsbl Coach; TN Sch Cnslrs Assn 1986-; TN Ed Assn, NEA; Stokely Fellowship Univ of TN 1987; *office:* Mc Minn Cty HS 2215 Congress Pkwy Athens TN 37303

HUDSON, ANITA KAY (SANDERS), Language/Spelling Teacher; *b:* Paris, IN; *m:* Larry Dale; *c:* Haley A., Kayla E.; *ed:* (BS) Elem Ed, Univ of TN Martin 1980; *cr:* Teacher Gleason Sch 1980-; *ai:* Part Time Work Family Owned Bus 1968-; Cheerleading & G Club Spon; Homecoming Coord; SACS Steering Comm; True Colors & Marginal Learner Sch Rep; Phi Kappa Phi 1979-; TEA, NEA, WCEA, Gleason Sch Assn 1980-; Aunt Maude Circle, Gleason Booster Club 1980-; Church (Choir Dir 1984-89, Youth Cnslr 1982-85); Univ of TN Martin Outstanding Teacher Awd 1989; Outstanding Young Woman of America 1981; *office:* Gleason HS 101 Front St Gleason TN 38229

HUDSON, BEVERLY SLEDGE, 4th Grade Teacher; *b:* Mobile, AL; *m:* Richard Lee; *c:* Christina, Jennifer, Todd; *ed:* (BS) Home Ec, Univ of Montevallo 1973; (MA) Elem Ed, MS Univ for Women 1977; *cr:* 6th Grade Elem Teacher 1974-75; 4th Grade Teacher 1975- Vernon Elem Sch; *ai:* Easter Seal Spellathon Sch Coord, Cty Wide Math Prgm Dev; Taught Cmmty Ed Prgms; NEA 1974-; AEA Convention Delegate 1974-.

HUDSON, CAROLYN FEDER, Soc Stud Teacher/Dept Chair; *b:* Conway, SC; *m:* Alphie M.; *ed:* (BA) His, Limestone Coll 1969; Grad Work at The Citadel & Univ of SC; *cr:* Teacher Andrews Elem 1969-70, St Helena Jr HS 1970-76, Ruffin HS 1976-; *ai:* Jr Class, Staff Dev, Soc Stud Dept Chm; SC Ed Assn, NEA 1976-; Colleton Cty Ed Assn (Treas 1977-78, Rep 1988-, Chairperson Human Relations Comm 1989-) 1976-; Daughters of The Amer Revolution, Amer His Teacher of Yr Colleton Cty 1988; *home:* Rt 2 Box 426 Ruffin SC 29475

HUDSON, CHRISTINE, Social Studies Teacher; *b:* Yazoo City, MS; *c:* Cassondra F.; *ed:* (BA) Elem Ed, Northeastern IL Univ 1975; Chicago St Univ; Natl Teachers Coll; *cr:* K-8th Grade Teacher Ella Flagg Young; Doo Little West; Zeno Coleman; 6th-8th Grade Teacher John Fiske Elem Sch; *ai:* John Fiske Elem Sch-8th Grade Spon; New Philadelphia Church Baptist Secy Sunday Sch; Past Supt Sunday Sch; Jr Sunday Sch Teacher; Private Tutoring; Wedding Coord; Choir Mem; John Fiske Sch Teacher of Yr Awd 1988; Teacher of Yr Teaching Techniques 1982; New Philadelphia Church Teacher of Yr Sunday Schl 1981; Cert of Appreciation Chicago St Univ 1987; *home:* 7414 S Indiana Ave Chicago IL 60619

HUDSON, ELIZABTH GRAYER, Third Grade Teacher; *b:* Macon, GA; *c:* Cynthia C. Pitts, Earnestine C. Montgomery, Leroy Jr., Willie Jr.; *ed:* (BS) Elem Ed, 1963-67, (MA) Elem Ed, 1970-72 Ft Valley St Coll; Motivational Strategies for Exceptional Child, Staff Dev, Instructional Strategies for Learning Disabled, Staff Dev; *cr:* 7th Grade Teacher Bellevue Elem Sch 1967-71; 2nd-4th Grade Teacher Florence Bernd Elem Sch 1972-; *ai:* Sunshine, Bulletin Bd, Planning, Lib Comm; Spec Sch Acts Asst Art Coord; Iota Phi Lambda; Bernd Elem Stu Support Team Chairperson; Bibb Educl Assn Mem, GA Educl Assn Mem 1967-; New Hope Baptist Church Secy of Sunday Sch 1950-51; GA St Univ Atlanta Test Writer 1983-84; Criterion Reference Test Comm; Nom Florence Bernd Elem Sch Teacher of Yr 1980; *home:* 2049 Fairway Dr Macon GA 31201

HUDSON, GEORGE WALKER, JR., Social Studies Dept Chair; *b:* Ft Benning, GA; *m:* Sherry Williams; *c:* George K., Amy L.; *ed:* (BA) His, Wofford Coll 1966; *cr:* Teacher/Coach Cleveland Jr HS 1966-70, College Park HS 1970-73; Teacher/Coach/Dept Chm Lakeshore HS 1973-88, Westlake HS 1988-; *ai:* Head Var Boys Bsktbl Coach; Asst Ftbl Coach; World of Difference Prgm Instr; GA Athletic Coaches Assn 1970-, St Coach of Yr 1980, 1987, Region Coach of Yr 1978, 1981, 1984, 1986-87, 1990; NCSS 1974-; Atlanta Tipoff Club 1970-, Coach of Yr 1980, 1987; Exch Club 1987-; STAR Teacher Lakeshore HS 1980, 1986; Teacher of Yr Westlake HS 1990; Published Articles; *office:* Westlake HS 2370 Union Rd Atlanta GA 30331

HUDSON, GWENDOLYN ELEASE, Earth Science Teacher; *b:* Sumter, SC; *ed:* (BS) Phys Ed, Benedict Coll 1976; (MED) Cnslr Ed, SC St Coll 1978; Pursuing Doctoral Degree Ed Admin, Univ of SC; *cr:* Phys Ed/General Sci/Psych Teacher Scotts Branch HS 1976-77; Gymnastics Instr 1986, Sci Asst 1987, Resident Camp Dir 1988 Hofstra Univ; Earth Sci Teacher Manning Mid Sch 1978-; *ai:* Track Coach; Aerobics Club Adv; Outstanding Young Women of America 1981, 1983; Presidential Awd Excl in Sci & Math Teaching Nom 1989-; Assisted in Producing Book for Earth Sci Teachers; *home:* Rt 1 Box 1405 Alcolu SC 29001

HUDSON, HAZEL (ECKLES), HS Mathematics Teacher; *b:* Sedalia, MO; *ed:* (BS) Elem Ed, Cntrl MO St Coll 1967; (MS) Math, Cntrl MO St Univ 1974; *cr:* 4th-6th Grade Teacher Bonner Springs KS 1967-68; 5th Grade Teacher Shelby NC 1968-69; 7th-9th Grade Teacher 1969-80, 9th-12th Grade Teacher 1980- Smithton R-VI Sch; Tech Math II Teacher St Fair Comm Coll 1990; *ai:* Math Club & Frosh Class Spon; *office:* Smithton R-VI Box 97 Myrtle St Smithton MO 65350

HUDSON, JANICE BRITT, Fourth Grade Teacher; *b:* Newton Grove, NC; *m:* Robert Sutton; *c:* Robin Whitman, Lisa Tart; *ed:* (BS) Elem Ed/Soc Stud, Campbell Univ 1978; *cr:* 4th Grade Teacher Butler Avenue 1979-; *ai:* Sci Club Teacher & Adv; Publicity & Public Relations, Hospitality & Sch Beautification Comm; St Paul Baptist Church Pianist 1975-; Article Published 1983; *office:* Butler Avenue Sch 301 Butler Ave Clinton NC 28328

HUDSON, JO ELLEN THORNE, Fourth Grade Teacher; *b:* Anderson, AL; *m:* Reginald D.; *c:* Ross A., Joandra D.; *ed:* (BS) Elem Ed, 1971, (MA) Elem Ed, 1974 Univ of N AL; *cr:* 1st-3rd Grade Teacher Rhodesville Elem 1971-72; 5th-6th Grade Teacher Underwood Elem 1972-86; 4th Grade Teacher Cntrl Elem 1986-; *ai:* 4-H 4th Grade Spon; NEA, AL Ed Assn, Lauderdale Cty Ed Assn 1972-; *office:* Cntrl Elem Sch Rt 4 Box 241 Florence AL 35633

HUDSON, JOAN LEHMAN, 7th/8th Grade Teacher; *b:* Decatur, IN; *m:* Mark Kevin; *c:* Jason M.; *ed:* (BA) Elem Ed, Bluffton Coll 1979; (MS) Elem Ed/Rdng Concentration, Wright St Univ 1984; *cr:* Mid Sch Lang Art Teacher Covington Exempted Village Schls 1979-; *ai:* Mid Sch St Cty Adv 1980-88; OH Ed Assn, NEA, Covington Ed Assn 1979-; *office:* Covington Exempted Village Sch 25 Grant St Covington OH 45318

HUDSON, JULIA TREECE, Mathematics Teacher; *b:* Concord, NC; *m:* Coy L.; *c:* Rodney, Scott, Wesley; *ed:* (BA) Math Ed, Elon Coll 1969; (MED) Math Ed, NC St 1973; *cr:* Math Teacher Surry Cntrl HS 1969-71, Cary Elem 1971-72, Broughton HS 1980-81, Millbrook HS 1981-82, St Stephens HS 1984-; *ai:* Math Club Spon; Math Comprehensive Team Coach; NCTM, NTM, NCAE; *office:* St Stephens HS Rt 2 Box 150 Hickory NC 28601

HUDSON, LAURA LORENE, 8th Grade Science Teacher; *b:* Salina, KS; *m:* Christopher; *c:* Damon M., Deborah Hudson Frazey, Daniel; *ed:* (BS) Botany, OK Univ 1969; Grad Courses AZ St Univ & Univ of AZ; *cr:* 7th/8th Grade Sci Teacher Coolidge Jr HS 1969-71; 9th Grade Sci/Bio Teacher Gerard HS 1972-76; 8th Grade Sci Teacher Sierra Vista Mid Sch 1976-; *ai:* Sierra Vista CTA Secy 1979-81; NSTA 1985-; *home:* 5223 Sioux Ave Sierra Vista AZ 85635

HUDSON, MABLE MARGARET TODD, Third Grade Teacher; *b:* Bryan, TX; *m:* R. L.; *c:* Caron A. Hudson Tippitt, Debra K.; *ed:* Elem Ed - Cum Laude, 1978, (MS) Elem Ed, 1980 TX A&M Univ; Currently Working on Elem Princs Cert; *cr:* 3rd Grade Teacher Blackshear Elem 1976-; *ai:* Stu Teachers Supvr TX A&M Univ; TSTA Treas 1977-78; TX Cncl of Admin Spec Ed Regular Educator of Yr 1985; Phi Delta Kappa 1980-; Kappa Delta Phi 1979-; Whos Who in Amer Ed 1988-89; *office:* Blackshear Elem Sch 1401 W 3rd Hearne TX 77859

HUDSON, MAGGIE JUMPER, Fourth Grade Teacher; *b:* Phenix City, AL; *w:* George Jr. (dec); *ed:* (BS) Elem Ed, AL St Univ 1959; (MS) Elem Ed, Troy St Univ 1980; Curr Wkshps, Inservice Prgms; *cr:* 4th Grade Teacher S Girard Elem 1960-68, Meadowlane Elem 1968-70, Westview Elem 1970-; *ai:* Flag Patrol Adv; Adopt-A-Sch Comm Mem; NEA, AL Ed Assn, Ed Assn of Phenix City; Phenix-Russell Boys Club (Secy, Bd of Dirs) 1983-,

Bronze Keystone 1990; Amer Legion Auxiliary Post 331 Pres 1976-78; *home:* 3803 Ukraine Dr Columbus GA 31906

HUDSON, MARIAN SMITH, Kindergarten Teacher; *b:* Whiteville, NC; *m:* Donald Ray; *c:* Jennifer, Jonathan, Joshua; *ed:* (BS) Early Chldhd Ed, Campbell Coll 1971; (MA) Early Chldhd Ed, Campbell Univ 1979; *cr:* K/1st Grade Teacher Gentry Primary Sch 1971-; *ai:* Soc Stud & Grade Level Lead Teacher; Intnl Rdng Assn (Treas 1983-84, 1986-88, Mem 1980-); NEA, NCAE Mem 1971-; Delta Kappa Gamma Mem 1984-; Order of the Eastern Star Organist 1982-; Dunn Adv Chrstn Church (Organist, Choir Dir) 1973-; Soc Stud Curr Conference Presenter 1983; NC St Dept of Ed Participant Soc Stud Curr Design; *home:* 500 E Cumberland St Dunn NC 28334

HUDSON, MICHELLE TERLAU, English Teacher; *b:* Cincinnati, OH; *m:* Robert Linn; *c:* Rachel, Matthew, Michael; *ed:* (BA) Span, Univ of KY 1975; (MA) Ed, N KY Univ 1979; *cr:* Span/Eng Teacher Conner Jr HS 1975-; *ai:* KY Ed Assn, Boone Cty Ed Assn 1975-; *office:* Conner Jr HS 3300 Cougar Path Hebron KY 41048

HUDSON, ORA HOLLIS, Elementary Teacher; *b:* Chalybeate, MS; *m:* J. Graham; *c:* Amy L. Hudson Burks; *ed:* (BA) Elem Ed, Blue Mountain Coll 1952; (MED) Elem Ed, Ole Miss 1971; *cr:* Teacher Walnut Elem Sch 1950-51, Houston Elem Sch 1952, Walnut Elem Sch 1952-62, Ripley Elem Sch 1965-68, Walnut Elem Sch 1968-; *ai:* Sci Fair Presentations; Annual Adv; Spon Music Prgms, Numerous Field Trips St Capitol & AL Space Center; Kappa Kappa Iota; MS Prof Educators; PTO; Blue Mountain Coll Natl Alumnae Assn; Womans Club; Chalybeate Baptist Church (Mem, Music Dir): *home:* Rt 2 Box 12 Walnut MS 38683

HUDSON, PENNIE DIANNE, Fifth Grade Teacher; *b:* Waterbury, CT; *m:* Herbert Allen; *c:* Michael, Christopher; *ed:* (BA) His/Ed, Sacred Heart Univ 1971; (MA) Ed, Cntrl CT St Univ 1975; *cr:* 3rd Grade Teacher Merriman Sch 1971-74; 4th Grade Teacher Wendell Cross Sch 1974-79; 5th Grade Teacher Walsh Sch 1980-87, Wendell Cross Sch 1987-; *ai:* Curr Advisory Cncl; CEU Comm; Waterbury Teachers Assn, Ct Ed Assn, NEA; ZBC Schlsp Comm; *office:* Wendell Cross Sch 1255 Hamilton Ave Waterbury CT 06706

HUDSON, RICHARD LEE, Math Teacher; *b:* Clifton Springs, NY; *m:* Elizabeth Ann Toher; *c:* Richard Todd; *ed:* (BS) Ed, St Univ Coll Brockport 1967; *cr:* Math Teacher Rush Henrietta Cntrl Schls 1967-69, Geneva City Schls 1969-; *ai:* Geneva Teachers Assn 1969-; NYEA 1969-; NEA 1969-; *office:* Geneva Mid Sch 63 Pulteney St Geneva NY 14456

HUDSON, RITA GILLILAND, 2nd Grade Teacher; *b:* Harrodsburg, KY; *m:* Michael T.; *c:* Michelle L., Richard G.; *ed:* (BS) Elem Ed, Campbellsville Coll 1971; Rank II Elem Ed, E KY Univ; *cr:* 1st Grade Teacher 1972-78, 2nd Grade Teacher 1979-Mercer Cty Elem; *office:* Mercer Cty Elem Sch Rt 5 Tapp Rd Harrodsburg KY 40330

HUDSON, TRUDY CASTRUP, Math/Language Art Teacher; *b:* Evansville, IN; *m:* Melvin Eugene Sr.; *c:* Mel Jr., David S.; *ed:* (BA) Ed/Math, 1972, (MA) Ed/Lib Sci, 1976 Univ of Evansville; CA St Univ Fullerton; *cr:* Teacher Henderson Cty Sch Corporation 1973-80; 7th/8th Math/Lang Art Teacher Placentia Unified Sch Corporation 1981-; *ai:* Sch Improvement Plan Coord; Curr Comm Mid Sch; CA League of Mid Schls, NCTM, ASCD, NEA, CA Teachers Assn, WHO Awd; Placentia Unified Ed Assn Negotiator; PTA Honorary Service Awd; *office:* Bernardo Yorba Jr HS 5350 Fairmond Blvd Yorba Linda CA 92686

HUDSPETH, JANET (MAUCK), Language Arts Teacher; *b:* Denver, CO; *m:* Thomas M. III; *c:* Whitney A. Clouthier; *ed:* (BA) Elem Ed, Univ of Northern CO 1964; (MA) Curr/Instruction, Lesley Coll 1985; Lang Art, NDEA Inst; Individualized Rdng & Lang Art Instructions, Loretto Heights Seminars; Jr Great Books Leadership Trng; *cr:* Lang Art Teacher Kullerstrand Elem 1964-71; Rdng Specialist 1971-84, Lang Arts Teacher Arvada Jr HS 1984-; *ai:* Odyssey of Mind Coach; Jr Great Books, North Cntrl Assn Steering Comm; North Cntrl Assn Visiting Team; Liason Comm; Jefferson Cty Curr Guides; NEA, Jefferson Cty Ed Assn 1964-; Intnl Rdng Assn Outstanding Rdng Teacher of CO; CO Lang Arts Society 1971; CO Ed Assn Master Teacher 1964-; Pi Lambda Theta, Kappa Delta Pi; Published Articles in Prof Journals; Conducted St Dept Ed Wkshp for WY; *office:* Arvada Jr HS 5751 Balsam St Arvada CO 80002

HUEGEL, DARLENE MARIE, German Teacher; *b:* Erie, PA; *ed:* (BA) Ger, Thiel Coll 1967; (MED) Scndry Sch Guidance Cnslr Cert, Gannon Coll 1971; Numerous In-Service Prgms; *cr:* German Teacher Mc Dowell HS 1967-; *ai:* Mc Dowell HS Mixed Boys & Girls Bowling League Club Coach; Mc Dowell HS Club Adv; PA St Ed Assn, NEA, Millcreek Ed Assn; Amer Legion Ladies 1967-; Lawrence Park Ladies Bowling League, Ladies Golf League; Ger Prgm Mc Dowell 1967; *office:* Mc Dowell HS 3580 W 38th St Erie PA 16506

HUENEMANN, LINDA NICHOLAS, Senior English Instructor; *b:* Ottawa, KS; *c:* Heidi Ann, Mary Kirsten; *ed:* (BSE) Secy Eng Ed, Northeast MO St U 1976; (MA) Eng, Central MO St U 1987; *cr:* Mgr Dairy Queen Brazier 1972-74; Supervisor/Trnr Mansfields IGA Groceries 1974-77, Wal-Mart 1979-; Sr Eng Instr Benton Cty R-II 1980-; *ai:* Adv Cardinal Yrbk; Photographer for Sch; Adv Cardinal Quotes News Magazine; Prof Dev Comm; Sch Publicist Part-Time; NCTE 1986-; Comm Teacher Assn Sec/VP 1982-84 Outstanding Teacher 1988; MSTA 1987-88 Outstanding Dist Teacher; Station KMOS-TV PBS Adv 1986-; Faith Luth Church Supt of Ed 1987-; Guest Speaker for The MO Assn of Sch Lib Twice; Named Outstanding Graduate Stu for Cntral MO St Univ Coll of Arts Benton Cty R-II; Awarded Graduate Schlsp CMSU; *home:* RR 1 Box 327 Lincoln MO 65338

HUERTA, JUAN M., Language Arts Teacher; *b:* Donna, TX; *ed:* (BA) Scndry Eng, Univ of TX 1971; TX Womens Univ; *cr:* Coll Eng Teacher Durham Bus Coll 1971-73; Eng/Speech Teacher LA Feria HS 1973-74; St Mary Diocesan HS 1977-78; Eng/Lang Arts Teacher Dallas ISD 1978- ; *ai:* Coached All UIL Events Including One-Act Play at La Feria HS; Spon Two Stu to Dist Competition of Optomists Club Intnl; Dallas Joint Cncl Eng Teachers 1989-; United Teachers of Dallas 1989-; Served on Dallas ISD Textbook Adoption Sub-Comm 1989; *office:* Greiner Mid Sch 625 S Edgefield St Dallas TX 75208

HUEY, CAROLYN COOK, 7th Grade Math Teacher; *b:* Lansing, MI; *m:* Donald Max; *c:* Lee R., Stewart H.; *ed:* (BS) Elem Ed, Univ of S MS 1969; (ME) Elem Ed, William Carey Coll 1975; *cr:* 6th Grade Teacher Petal Jr HS 1969-79; 5th Grade Teacher W L Smith Elem 1980-85; 7th Grade Teacher Petal Mid Sch 1985-; *ai:* Chrldr Spon; Stu Cncl Adv; Petal Assn Educators Pres 1980-81; Alpha Delta Kappa (Chaplain 1988-, Pres 1990); Magnolia Home & Garden Club Pres 1974-76; Petal Cosmopolitan Club VP 1986-; Amer Cancer Society Residential Chm 1985-88; MS Republican Party Forrest Cty Comm Mem 1985-88; MS Power Fnd Grant Teacher Expectations & Stu Achievement; *home:* PO Box 314 Petal MS 39465

HUFF, C. MICHAEL, Social Studies Teacher; *b:* Columbus, OH; *m:* Beverly Reilly; *ed:* (BS) Scndry Soc Stud, OH St Univ 1976; *cr:* Teacher St Mary Mid Sch 1976-81, St Michael Sch 1981-87, Bishop Watterson HS 1987-; *ai:* Girls Jr Var Bsktbl Coach; Var Sftbl Co-Coach; Hi-Y Club Adv; Knights of Columbus 1990, 1st Degree 1990; Marietta Jaycees 1978-81, Outstanding Young Educator 1980; *office:* Bishop Watterson HS 99 E Cooke Rd Columbus OH 43214

HUFF, CHARLES CARLTON, Soc Stud Dept Chair/Teacher; *b:* Ridgely, MD; *m:* Shirley M. Baynard; *c:* Barry, Shane, Charles II; *ed:* (BA) Soc Sci, Univ MD 1969; (MA) Comm, Norfolk St Univ 1978; Grad Courses Temple Univ; *cr:* Supvr/Cnslr Ferris Sch for Boys 1970-72; Teacher Wilmington Public Schls 1972-78, Christina Sch Dist 1979-; *ai:* His Club, Peer Cnslrs Club Adv; Drama Club & Home Ec Club Co-Adv; Cmmty of Caring; Boys Bsktbl Coach; Bsktbl Camp Coord Del-Tech & Comm Coll; Dept Chairperson; Liaison Comm Mem; NCSS, Mid Sts Cncl Soc Stud 1980; DE Geographic Alliance, ASCD 1988; Kappa Alpha Psi 1968; Jr Achievement of DE Inc 1980, Outstanding Service Awd; DuPont Company Mini-Grant Awd; *home:* Rt 3 Box 56B Denton MD 21629

HUFF, DENISE HORAD, Second Grade Teacher; *b:* Boston, MA; *c:* Erika K., Jonathan M.; *ed:* (BA) Ed, American Univ 1971; (MS) Early Chldhd Ed, Youngstown St Univ 1982; Univ of Geneva 1966; *cr:* 3rd Grade Teacher Shephard Elem 1971-73; Adult Basic Ed Teacher Youngstown Public Sch 1984-86; 2nd Grade Teacher Sheridan Elem 1973-; *ai:* Jr Civic League 1987-; Jack & Jill Interest Group VP 1988-.

HUFF, DONALD DEAN, II, Physical Education Teacher; *b:* Columbia, MO; *m:* Christa Rawson; *c:* Jennifer Lynn, Keith Michael; *ed:* (BS) Phys Ed/Driver Ed, Univ MO 1980; Grad Courses Southeast MO St Univ; *cr:* Teacher/Coach Fredericktown R-1 1980- *ai:* Varsity Vlbl Coach; Mid Sch Bsktbl Coach; Varsity Golf Coach; MSTA 1980-; Cmmty Teachers Assn 1980-; Natl Fed Interscholastic Coaches Assn 1982-; Masonic Lodge 1990-; PTA 1987-.

HUFF, JETTIE CLENNEY, Fourth Grade Teacher; *b:* Sardis, TN; *m:* Jerry Lynn; *ed:* (BS) Scndry Ed/Sci, 1970, (MS) Elem Ed/Curr/Instruction, 1978 Univ of TN Martin; *cr:* Math Teacher Clarksburg HS 1970-71; 5th-8th Grade Math/Rdng Teacher Dixie Sch 1972-73; Teacher Hornbeak Elem Sch 1973-85; 4th Grade Teacher Black Oak Elem Sch 1985-; *ai:* Obion Cty Ed Assn Faculty Rep 1986-88; PTA, Natl Teachers Ed Assn 1972-; GSA Troop Leader 1984-87; Ladies Auxiliary United Rubber Workers 1989-; First Apostolic (Christmas Prgm, Church Pianist, Gospel Singing Group Pianist); *office:* Black Oak Elem Sch PO Box 31 Hornbeak TN 38232

HUFF, PATSY JO HERNANDEZ, Fourth Grade Teacher; *b:* Prescott, AZ; *m:* John Stewart; *c:* Sarah; *ed:* (AA) Ed, Yavapai Coll 1973; (BA) Elem Ed, AZ St Univ 1975; (MA) Curr & Instruction, N AZ Univ 1982; *cr:* Elem Teacher Prescott Public Schls 1975-79, South Sioux City Cmmty Schls 1979-; *ai:* NEA 1980-; Loess Hills Audubon Society Ed Chairperson 1986; PTA 1975-, Founders Day Awd 1986; *home:* 519 E 31st South Sioux City NE 68776

HUFF, SHERRY LYNN (BRUEGGEMAN), 4th Grade Teacher; *b:* Wood River, IL; *m:* Arthur Joseph; *c:* Brett; *ed:* (BS) Elem Ed; *cr:* 4th Grade Elem Teacher Bethalto East Grade Sch 1971-; *ai:* Selection of New Lang Series Comm; NEA, IEA 1971-; VFW Womens Auxiliary 1975-; Teacher of Yr Bethalto Dist 8 1982; *home:* 1006 Rhondell East Alton IL 62024

HUFFERD, DORCAS A., English Teacher; *b:* Rushville, IN; *m:* John Lowell; *c:* John, Kevin, Linda, Joseph; *ed:* (BA) Eng/Journalism, Ball St Univ 1958; Eng & Ed; *cr:* Eng/Journalism Teacher Royerton 1959-60, Yorktown HS 1960-62, Brea Jr HS 1966-84, Brea HS 1984-; *ai:* Dist Curr Cncl, Dist Continuum Cncl Dept Chm 1983-84; Newspaper Adv; Brea-Olinda Teachers Assn (Secy 1978-80, Pres 1980-81) WHO Awd 1984; CA Teachers Assn St Cncl Rep 1981-87; Brea-Olinda Bargaining Team; Journalism Ed Assn & Natl Journalism Ed Assn 1985-; *home:* 4121 Denver Yorba Linda CA 92686

HUFFMAN, BETTY L. LAURSEN, Mathematics Teacher; *b:* Alliance, NE; *m:* Ronald W.; *c:* Bret Corbin, Lori Corbin; *ed:* (BS) Phys Sci Ed, Kearney St 1961; (MAT) Math Ed, CO Coll 1967; Grad Stud Various CO Colls; *cr:* Rural Teacher Box Butte Cty Schls 1956-59; Math/Sci Teacher Pierce HS 1961-62; Math Teacher Kearney Jr HS 1963-64; Math/Sci Teacher Aurora Public SchlS 1964-; *ai:* Mu Alpha Theta Math Club Spon; CO Ed Assn 1964-; NEA, NCTM 1964-; CO Dept of Ed Grant to Write a Math Problem Solving Course 1985; *office:* Gateway HS 1300 S Sable Blvd Aurora CO 80012

HUFFMAN, CALVIN D., Chem/Physics/Sci Teacher; *b:* Creston, IA; *m:* Dianne Young; *c:* Todd, Troy; *ed:* (BS) Bio, NW MO Univ 1964; (MS) Chem, Tuskegee Inst Univ 1969; *cr:* Chem/ Phys Sci Teacher Omaha Public Schls 1964-65; HS Sci Teacher Mound City Sch Dist 1965-68; Chem/Phys Sci Teacher Dist #37 1969-; *ai:* 8th Grade Spon; Greater NE Sci Teachers, Natl Biological Teachers, NE Ed Assn, NEA; BSA Leader 1964-65; Cub Scout Leader 1969-76; Outstanding Young Educator; City Councilman; *office:* District #37 Sch 810 Central Ave Humboldt NE 68376

HUFFMAN, CAROLE BARDEN, 4th Grade Teacher; *b:* Petoskey, MI; *m:* Stanley Ray; *c:* Charlene N., Eric W., Derek B.; *ed:* (BA) His, MI St Univ 1968; Working Towards Masters Elem Curr Dev, Lib Sci; *cr:* 7th/8th Grade Teacher Grand Ledge Public Sch 1968-74; 3rd/4th Grade Teacher Harbor Springs Public Sch 1974-; *ai:* NEA, MI Ed Assn 1968-; *office:* Harbor Springs Public Sch 146 Lake Rd Harbor Springs MI 49740

HUFFMAN, JERRY ALVIN, Business Education Teacher; *b:* Christiansburg, VA; *m:* Trudy Turner; *c:* Jerry Jr., Heather D.; *ed:* (BS) Bus Admin, VPI & SU 1968; Bus Ed Cert, VPI & SU 1983-84; Lotus 1 2 3 Course, New River Comm Coll 1988; Motivation & Classroom ManagementCourse, U of VA 1988; *cr:* Inventory Management Specialist USAF 1967-72; Asst Mgr Leggett 1972-83; Teacher Pulaski Cty HS 1984-; *ai:* FBLA; Pulaski Cty Ed Assn, VA Ed Assn, NEA 1988-; Amer Legion Commander 1980-; 1st Chrstn Church Deacon; Town Councilman; Little League Ftbl Coach; *home:* 207 Holston St Narrows VA 24124

HUFFMAN, ROBERT K., III, 7th Grade Mathematics Teacher; *b:* Staunton, VA; *m:* Cynthia Marie Ballew; *c:* Katie N., Robert W.; *ed:* (BA) Elem Ed, Bridgewater Coll 1976; *cr:* Phys Ed/Health Teacher Verona Elem 1976-77; Phys Ed/Health/Soc Stud Teacher New Hope Elem 1977-80; 7th Grade Math Teacher Stewart Mid Sch 1980-; *ai:* Fort Defiance Girls Var Vlybl 1980-, Jr Var Girls Bsktbl 79-, Girls Var Sftbl 1985-; VHSCA 1979-, Vlybl Coach of Yr 1987, 1988; VHSL AA St Vlybl Champions 1986-; *home:* Rt 2 Box 822 Greenville VA 24440

HUFFMAN, SHARON MESMER, 5th Grade Teacher; *b:* Spokane, WA; *m:* Terry A.; *c:* Lisa Shipman, Paul A.; *ed:* (BA) Eng, Fort Wright Coll 1968; Grad Stud, Eastern WA Univ; *cr:* 3rd Grade Teacher Opportunity Elem 1968-71; 2nd/6th/5th Grade Teacher Medical Lake Elem 1975-; *ai:* NEA 1968-; ASCD 1984-; WA Org Rdng Dev; *office:* Medical Lake Elem Sch P O Box 128 Medical Lake WA 99022

HUFFMAN, SUSAN E., Language Art Teacher; *b:* Riverton, WY; *m:* Buzz Bowman; *ed:* (BA) Phys Ed/Health, Univ of MT 1978; (MA) Phys Ed/Art/Ed, W OR St Coll 1984; *cr:* Phys Ed/ Lang Art Teacher Sheridan HS 1978-79; Lang Art Teacher Mc Minnville HS 1980-81, North Marion HS 1982-; *ai:* Var Vlybl Coach; Soph Class Head Adv; Impact-Core Team Mem; Natural Helper; Wellness Team Mem; United North Marion Educators Pres 1988-; NEA 1978-79, 1980-81, 1982-; OR Coaches Assn 1978-; OR Ed Assn Goal I Comm Mem 1989-, Apple Awd 1989; *home:* 20936 SW Winema Dr Tualatin OR 97062

HUFFSTUTLER, PHYLLIS LEWIS, Principal; *b:* Barboursville, WV; *m:* Barry A.; *c:* Douglas, Donah; *ed:* (AB) Elem Ed, 1963, (MA) Elem Ed, 1968 Marshall Univ; *cr:* 3rd Grade Teacher Herbert H Mills Elem 1964-65, Cox Landing Elem 1965-69; 4th Grade Teacher Simms Elem 1968-69; 2nd-4th Grade Teacher Milton Elem 1969-79; Gifted Teacher Multi Schls 1979-81; 2nd-4th Grade Teacher 1981-85; Rdng Specialist Milton Elem 1988-89; Asst Prin 1988-89 Milton Elem; Prin Geneva Kent Elem 1989-; *ai:* WV Ed Assn; WV Assn Elem Sch Prin; NAESP; NEA; Intnl Rdng Assn; Milton Womens Club Rec Secy 1979-81; *home:* Rt 2 Box 616 Milton WV 25541

HUFSTEDLER, SHIRLEY LEWELLEN, Social Studies Teacher; *b:* Pineville, KY; *c:* Amy Spencer; *ed:* (AB) Sociology, 1957, (MA) Ed/His, 1971 Union Coll; (Rank 1) Supvr/Scndry Principalship, E KY Univ 1979; *cr:* Soc Stud Teacher Bell Cty HS 1957-; *ai:* Sr Class Spon; Bell Cty Ed Assn, Upper Cumberland Ed Assn, KY Ed Assn, NEA 1957-; *office:* Bell Cty HS Rt 1 Box 88 Pineville KY 40977

HUFTEL, MONICA ROSE, Kindergarten Teacher; *b:* Menomonie, WI; *ed:* (BS) Early Chldhd Ed, Univ of WI Stout 1986; Elem Cert Univ of River Falls; *cr:* Kndgtn Teacher Clintonville Public Schls 1986-; *ai:* Pom Pon Squad Coach; Choregraph Routines for Super Singers Chorus; WI Kndgtn Assn 1987-; Started Clintonvilles 1st Pom Pon Squad; Participated in Clintonvilles Staff Dev Prgm.

HUGGET, ANN MOORE, 4th Grade Lang Art Teacher; *b:* Daytona Beach, FL; *w:* Ernest E. (dec); *ed:* (BA) Elem Ed, FL St Univ 1954; *cr:* 5th Grade Teacher Highlands Elem 1954-55, Spring Park Elem 1955-57; 6th Grade Teacher Atlantic Beach Elem 1957-63, 1965-68; Jacksonville Beach Elem 1970-71; 4th Grade Teacher Seabreeze Elem 1969-70, 1971-; *ai:* Duval Cty Rdng Cncl Membership Chm 1984-86; Faculty Forum Rep 1981; Beach United Meth Church Sunday Sch Teacher 1973-75; *office:* Seabreeze Elem Sch 1400 Seabreeze Ave Jacksonville FL 32250

HUGGINS, ALBERTA PETRIE, Teacher/Reading Specialist; *b:* Huntington, WV; *m:* William C.; *c:* Virginia H. Garvin, Constance H. Knuth, William D.; *ed:* (BA) Elem Ed, W Liberty St Coll 1972; (MA) Rdng/Rdng Specialist, WV Univ 1978; 15 Addl Stud Guidance & Counseling; *cr:* Teacher/Rdng Dir Wheeling Cntry Day Sch 1968-76; Teacher/Rdng Specialist The Linsly Sch 1976-; *ai:* Adv & Cnslrs; Lower Sch Newspaper Adv; Publicity Dir All Sch Annual Extravaganza; Intramural Spon; Lower Sch Declamation Adv; Delta Kappa Gamma Society Intnl (Chapter Past Pres 1986-88, St Dir 1989-91); Delta Kappa Gamma Univ of TX Austin 1990; Leadership/Management Seminar 1990; Delta Kappa Gamma Society Intnl Alpha Phi St Organization Offices (Comm Chairman 1987-89, St Regional Dir 1989-91); Delta Kappa Gamma Epsilon Chapter Offices (Treas 1980-84, 1st VP 1984-86, Pres 1986-88); *office:* Linsly Sch Knox Ln Wheeling WV 26003

HUGGINS, BETTY FORD, 8th Grade Mathematics Teacher; *b:* Marion, SC; *m:* Garvin L. Jr.; *c:* Lann, Mark, Chad; *ed:* (BA) Elem Ed, 1975, (MED) Elem Ed, 1986 USCC; Cert Mid Sch Math, Lang Art, Sci, Soc Stud; *cr:* Resource Teacher 1976-77, 6th Grade Math/Sci Teacher 1977-83, 8th Grade Math Teacher 1983- Conway Mid Sch; *ai:* Math Counts, Brain Blitz Coach; Math Dept, Southern Assn of Colls & Schls Chairperson; NEA, SCEA; Math Advancement Cncl VP Mid Schls 1987-89; Alpha Delta Kappa 1988-; Intnl Honary For Women Educators; Conway Mid Sch Individual Teacher Incentive Pay 1987-88; SC Palmettos Finest Awd 1989-; *office:* Conway Mid Sch 1104 Elm St Conway SC 29526

HUGGINS, CARLA ADAMS, Language Arts Teacher; *b:* Lumberton, NC; *m:* Johnny Lee; *c:* Leigh, Holly; *ed:* (BS) Elem Ed, 1978, (MA) Elem Ed, 1981 Pembroke St Univ; *cr:* Teacher Red Springs Mid Sch 1978-; *ai:* Stu Cncl Spon; NEA, NCAE Mem 1979-; Robeson Assn of Educators Faculty Rep 1988-; Lumberton Jaycettes Dir 1979-80; Lumberton Jr Womans Club 1984-85; Godwin Heights Baptist Young Women (Pres, Secy) 1979-; Served on Accreditation Comm as Chairperson for Communication Skills; Nom for Teacher of Yr; Conducted in Service Wkshps for Fellow Teachers; Served on Teacher of Yr Selection Comm; *office:* Red Springs Mid Sch 302 W 2nd Ave Red Springs NC 28377

HUGGINS, CHARLES WADE, III, 6th Grade Math Dept Chairman; *b:* Bucyrus, OH; *m:* Julia Donnenwirth; *c:* Chuck IV, Neil; *ed:* (BA) Elem Ed, Bluffton Coll 1978; Working Towards Masters Admin, Ashland Univ; *cr:* 5th Grade Teacher Roosevelt Elem 1978-81; 6th Grade Teacher Colonel Crawford & Sulphur Springs Elem 1981-84, Colonel Crawford Intermediate Sch 1984-; *ai:* Colonel Crawford Girls Bsktbl & Sftbl Prgm Head Coach; Asst Athletic Dir; 6th Grade Class Adv Chm; *office:* Col Crawford Intermediate Sch State Rt 602 North Robinson OH 44856

HUGH, DONNA S., 4th Grade Teacher; *b:* Chicago, IL; *ed:* (AA) Liberal Arts, 1962, (BA) Ed, 1964 William Woods Coll; (MED) Curr & Instruction, Natl Coll of Ed 1987; Grad Stud Educl Field; *cr:* 4th Grade/4th-6th Grade Girls Phys Ed/4th-6th Grade Span Teacher Corona Unified Sch Dist 1964-65; 5th Grade Teacher 1965-72, 4th Grade Teacher 1972-74, 6th Grade Teacher 1974-85, 4th Grade Teacher 1985- Deerfield Public Sch; *ai:* Cmptr Curr Comm 1988-; DEA, IEA, NEA 1986-; *office:* South Park Elem Sch 1421 Hackberry Rd Deerfield IL 60015

HUGHES, ANITA ANDERSON, Social Studies/English Teacher; *b:* Enid, OK; *m:* James Mc Cain; *c:* Adam, Drew; *ed:* (BS) Ed, 1974, (MS) Higher Ed, 1975 OK St Univ; *cr:* Eng/Soc Stud Teacher Drummond Public Schls 1976-; *ai:* Soph Class & Play Spon; Gifted & Talented Coord; Soc Stud Improvement Plan; Academic Coach; Staff Dev Comm; Drummond Teachers Assn Building Rep 1975-, Teacher of Yr 1989-; OK Ed Assn, NEA 1975-; OK Scndry Schls Assn Coaches Organization 1989-; OK Academic Team Coaches Awd 1989-; Outstanding Teacher Awd; Charter Mem Distinguished Stu of America; *home:* PO Box 1485 Enid OK 73702

HUGHES, BARBARA HUTCHINSON, Home Economics Instructor; *b:* Charleston, WV; *m:* Richard; *c:* Rick, Mike, Craig, Greg; *ed:* (BS) Hm Econ, 1962; (MS) Hm Ec/Nutrition, 1969 Marshall Univ; Post Masters Studies Bowling Green 1974; *cr:* Voc Home Ec, Ravenswood WV 1963-68; Paulding HS 1968-; *ai:* FHA Spon; HOT; OHEA 1968-; AVA 1968-; OEA 1968-; CHE; Grant-OH St 1989; *office:* Paulding Exempted H S 405 N Water Paulding OH 45879

HUGHES, BETTY JEAN, Latin Teacher; *b:* Biloxi, MS; *m:* Kenneth R. Sr.; *c:* Kenny, Dow, Damian; *ed:* (BA) Eng/Latin, MS St Coll for Women 1960; Grad Stud; *cr:* Eng/His/Latin Teacher Cntrl Jr HS 1960-70; Eng Teacher Nichols Jr HS 1970-84; Latin Teacher Biloxi HS 1984-; *ai:* Jr Classical League Spon; Teacher Advisory Comm; Class Spon 1984-87; MS Ed Assn Bd of Dir 1967-73; MS Assn of Educators Mem 1973-; Alpha Delta Kappa Pres 1968; Biloxi Teachers Federal Credit Union (Treas, Mgr) 1966-; Gulf Coast Chapter Credit Unions Pres 1984; Star Teacher 1985; Beverly Briscoe Awd Outstanding Teacher 1989; Biloxi Jaycees Outstanding Young Educator 1971; *office:* Biloxi HS 1424 Father Ryan Ave Biloxi MS 39530

HUGHES, CAROLE A. HURLEY, English Department Chair; *b:* Staten Island, NY; *c:* Lisa A., Douglas A.; *ed:* (BS) Eng/Ed, 1961, (MS) Adult Ed, 1977 Univ of ID; Grad Stud Eng & Ed; *cr:* 6th Grade Lang Art/Soc Stud Teacher Forest Road Sch Dist 102 1962-63; 11th/12th Grade Eng Teacher Coeur d Alene HS 1964-65; 9th Grade Eng Teacher Burbank Jr HS 1967-68; Adult Teacher All Subjects Lewis-Clark St Coll 1973-79; Speech/Yrbk Teacher 1977-86, Eng Teacher 1977- Moscow HS; *ai:* Moscow HS Eng Dept Chairperson; Dept Chairs Comm; Pleiades Poetry Contest Coord; NEA, ID Ed Assn 1977-; Moscow Ed Assn (Secy, VP, Rep Cncl, Delegate Assembly) 1977-; Idahonian Cmmty Bd of Dirs 1988-; Latah Cty Democratic Party Delegate to ID St Convention 1988, 1990; Democratic Natl Convention 1988; Veterans of Foreign Wars Voice of Democracy Speech Coord Appreciation Awd 1987-; N ID Writing Project; Whittenberger/ID Summer Writing Project; Columbia Scholastic Press Silver Medal Awds Yrbk 1984, 1985, 1986; Univ of ID Teaching Excl Awd 1985; Moscow HS Stu Cncl Appreciation Awd 1985; *home:* 1224 Nearing Loop Moscow ID 83843

HUGHES, CECILLIA ANN SMITH, 6th Grade Teacher; *b:* Detroit, MI; *m:* Thomas Rex; *c:* Leslye A. Wilmont; *ed:* (BS) Elem Ed/Eng, OH Univ 1969; (MS) Elem Ed, E MI Univ 1973; Specialist Elem Ed, MI St Oakland, Cntrl MI Univ 1983-87; Grad Stud Ed in Comm & Lang Art; *cr:* 2nd Grade Teacher/5th Grade Headstart Teacher Washington Local Sch Dist 1967-69; Owner/Operator Cake & Candy Supply Store 1975-83; 4th-8th Grade Teacher Mt Morris Sch Dist 1969-; *ai:* Mt Morris Ed Assn (Secy, Treas, St Rep); MI Ed Assn (Secy, NEA Rep, Teacher); Developed & Coord 1st Headstart Prgm Scioto Cty OH 1967-69; *office:* Cntrl Elem Sch 1000 Genesee Mount Morris MI 48458

HUGHES, CHARLES EVANS, JR., HS Mathematics Teacher; *b:* Sapulpa, OK; *m:* Lola Maxine Gann; *c:* David P., Tim C., Stacey A.; *ed:* (BSED) Math Ed, 1964, (MSED) Math Ed, 1972 NSU; *cr:* Math Teacher Bates HS 1964-65, Okay Public Sch 1965-; *ai:* Jr Spon; Upward Bound Tutor; HS Bsbl Coach; 8th-9th Grade & Jr-Sr Spon; Classroom Negotiating Comm; Indian Prgm Tutor; OEA, NEA 1966-; Masonic Lodge #12 1980-; Summer League Bsbl Coach 1966-82; Local & Cty Teacher of Yr 1980-81; St Textbook Comm 1981-83, 1987-89; *home:* P O Box 88 Okay OK 74446

HUGHES, CHARLES LEON, Biology Teacher; *b:* Tams, WV; *m:* Valerie Jean Conwell; *ed:* (AA) Beckley Coll 1968; (BS) Ed/Biological/General Sci, WV St Coll 1971; (MA) Ed/Admin/Supervision, WV Coll of Grad Stud 1975; Cogs & Marsall Univ 1976-88; AP Trng in Bio Concord Coll 1988; *cr:* Life Sci Teacher Stoco Jr HS 1971-76; Sci Camp Teacher Fayette Cty 1974; Bio Teacher Independence HS 1976-; *ai:* Independence HS Chapter of Natl Beta Club Spon; Raleigh Cty Ed Assn, WV Ed Assn, NEA; Faith Temple Church (Trustee, Deacon); Finalist Raleigh Cty Teacher of Yr 1987; Nom for Presidential Awd for Excl in Sci & Math Teaching; *office:* Independence HS PO Drawer A A Coal City WV 25823

HUGHES, DEBBIE A., 7th Grade Rdng/Soc Std Teacher; *b:* Akron, OH; *c:* Jeremy; *ed:* (BS) Sociology/Elem Ed, Marietta Coll 1976; Cmptr Programming; Word Processing; *cr:* 6th Grade Teacher 1976-78; Talented/Gifted 1978-83; 7th Grade Teacher 1983- Belpre City Schs; *ai:* 7th/8th Grade Stu Cncl Adv; Partners in Ed; In-Service Comm; Rdng Course Study Comm; Delta Kappa Gamma Society 1989-; NEA 1976-; OH Ed Assn 1976-; Belpre Ed Assn Pres 1983-89; Outstanding Young Ed-Belpre Jaycees; Featured Teacher Marietta Times; Ed-Share Comm Chairperson of Negotiations; *office:* Belpre City Schls Stone Rd Belpre OH 45714

HUGHES, DONNA BEVERLY, Fifth Grade Teacher; *b:* Nashville, TN; *m:* Robert Wallace; *c:* Elizabeth, Robert, Kenneth; *ed:* (BA) Elem Ed, Univ of KY 1970; Rank II; *cr:* 2nd Grade Teacher 1970-80, 5th Grade Teacher 1980- Tates Creek Elem; *ai:* DAR, Jr Womans Club, Beta Sigma Phi; *office:* Tates Creek Elem Centre Pkwy Lexington KY 40517

HUGHES, GLINDER FLOWERS, Sixth Grade Teacher; *b:* Collins, MS; *m:* Charles E. Patterson; *c:* Maurice; *ed:* (BS) Bus Ed, Southern Univ 1972; (MSED) Elem Ed, William Carey Coll 1990; *cr:* Teacher Seminary Attendance Center 1973-; *ai:* Key Teacher Comm; CCTA 1985-; Covington Cty Democratic Exec Comm Secy 1988-; *home:* Rt 1 Box 21 Collins MS 39428

HUGHES, IRENE MARY, English Dept Chair; *b:* Ford City, PA; *m:* Harry; *c:* Stephen, Harry J.; *ed:* (BBA) Ec/Bus Admin, Westminster Coll 1949; (BS) Eng, IN Univ of PA; (MA) Rdng, Frostburg 1971-72; Penn St 1965, Frostburg 1972, IUP 1965; *cr:* Private Secy Ringold Corporation 1948; 5th/6th Grade Elem Teacher Cadogan PA 1950; 9th Grade Eng Teacher Kittanning PA 1959; 7th-11th Alt Grade Eng/Rdng Teacher Mt Savage MD 1970-; *ai:* Basic Skills, Writing, Extra Curr Pay, May Day Comm; Gifted & Talented; Spelling Bee; Eng Dept Chm; Head Start Teacher; MSTA, ACTA, NEA, Armstrong Ed Assn; Conference Chrstn Mothers Pres 1966; Holy Trinity Sch Bd of Ed, St Ambrose Church Bd of Ed, AAUW; Cub Scout Den Mother; Parish Rep; Jr Womens Club Secy; Sacred Heart Hosp Auxiliary; Article Published; *home:* 200 N Belair Dr Cumberland MD 21502

HUGHES, JACK HOBART, Retired Mid Sch Teacher; *b:* Coweta, OK; *c:* Cindy Miller, Craig, Melony Gravener, Marsha Wiseman; *ed:* (BA) Soc Stud, OK Univ Norman 1950; (MS) Ed, Northeastern St 1984; Sergeant US Paratroops World War II 1943-46; *cr:* Teacher Fay HS 1950-52, Wagoner HS 1952-54, Okmulgee HS 1954-57; Braggs HS 1966-77, Duncan Jr HS 1981-87; *ai:* OEA, NEA, DEA; *home:* 1008 1/2 Pecan Duncan OK 73533

HUGHES, JEANINE BENTON, 3rd Grade Teacher; *b:* Thomaston, GA; *m:* Clyde Reginald; *c:* Thomas Alan, Timothy Mark, Carolyn Sawyer; *ed:* (AA) Ed, Mars Hill 1956; (BS) Ed, Old Dominion Univ 1974; *cr:* 3rd Grade Teacher Francis Asbury Sch 1956-57; 4th Grade Teacher Central Christian 1971-73; 5th Grade Teacher Robert E Lee 1974-79; 3rd Grade Teacher Barron 1979-; *ai:* HEA 1974-; VEA 1974-; NEA 1974-; *office:* Barron Fundamental Elem Schl 45 Fox Hill Rd Hampton VA 23669

HUGHES, JOYCE ELLEN, English Teacher; *b:* Danville, IL; *m:* James Allen; *ed:* (BS) Eng, IN St Univ 1973; Grad Stud IN Univ; *cr:* Teacher 1st Baptist Chrstn Sch 1983-86; Learning Disabilities Aide 1986-87, Teacher 1987- Covington Mid HS; *ai:* Frosh Class Spon; Covington HS Jr/Sr Plays Dir & Coach; Eng Textbook Adoption Chm 1990; Delta Kappa Gamma; N Cntrl Cert (Chm, Comm Mem); *office:* Covington HS 515 Commercial St Covington IN 47932

HUGHES, KATHY ANN, Science Teacher; *b:* Dutton, AL; *m:* Ralph Edward Edmonds; *c:* Laurel S. Edmonds; *ed:* (BS) Health/Phys Ed, 1975, (MED) Health/Phys Ed, 1976 Auburn Univ; *cr:* Health/Phys Ed Teacher/Coach Lafayette HS 1976-79; Teacher/Coach St Petersburg Chrstn HS 1979-80; Health/Phys Ed Teacher The Canterbury Sch 1980-81; Health/Phys Ed Teacher/Coach Northeast HS 1981-83; Sci Teacher/Asst Prin Section HS 1983-; *ai:* Head Girls Bsktbl Coach; Alpha Delta Kappa Pres 1990; Kappa Delta Pi Pres 1976-77; Civitan Intnl 1986-88; *office:* Section HS PO Box A Section AL 35771

HUGHES, LARRY M., Industrial Art Dept Chair; *b:* Hoopeston, IL; *m:* Phyllis K. Clem; *c:* Lorna K. Scholtus; *ed:* (BS) Industrial Ed, 1963, (MS) Industrial Ed, 1966 IN St Univ; *cr:* Teacher/Dept Chm Frankfort Sr HS 1963-; *ai:* Division of Adult Ed Dir; *office:* Frankfort Sr HS 1 Maish Rd Frankfort IN 46041

HUGHES, LEE THOMAS, Director of Bands & Orchestra; *b:* Trenton, NJ; *m:* April Lane; *c:* Natalie M., Lauren E., Lee T. Jr., Edward K.; *ed:* (BA) Applied Music, FL Intnl Univ 1975; Grad Work FL Intnl Univ; *cr:* Music Teacher Milam Elem Sch 1979-80; Band Dir Carol City Mid Sch 1980-82, Thomas Jefferson Jr HS 1982-84; Band/Orch Dir Miami Sunset Sr HS 1984-; *ai:* Theatre Orch Dir; Annual Musical Production Music Dir; Spon Marching Band Color Guard; Various Comms Sch Base Management; FL Bandmaster Assn 1979-; Music Educators Natl Conference 1979-; Phi Mu Alpha 1971-; Free & Accepted Masons Jr Deacon 1989-; Kiwanis 1977-80; FL Intnl Univ Band Camp; Orange Bowl Classic Half Time Show; Mem Various Local Philharmonic Symphonies & Cmmty Bands; *office:* Miami Sunset Sr HS 13125 S W 72nd St Miami FL 33183

HUGHES, MARIE BELONGIE, Middle Level Teacher; *b:* Escanaba, MI; *ed:* (BA) Elem Ed, Univ of WI Oshkosh 1975; *cr:* Jr HS Teacher St Mary Grade Sch 1975-89; Mid Level Teacher Seton Cath Mid Sch 1989-; *ai:* Stu Cncl Moderator 1986-88; *office:* Seton Cath Mid Sch 312 Nicolet Blvd Menasha WI 54952

HUGHES, MARIE GRACE, Science Teacher; *b:* Greenville, SC; *ed:* (BS) Bio, Carson Newman 1975; (MED) Mid Sch Ed, Clemson Univ 1978; Environmental Ed/Math & Calculators; Chemical Sci; *cr:* Sci Teacher Northwood Mid Sch 1975-; *ai:* Sci Fair; Stu Cncl; Sci Dept Comm; 5 Yr Study Comm; Walking for Your Health Class; Sci Teachers Assn; Beta Sigma Phi All Offices 1977-; Alpha Omega 1982; Beta Sigma Phi Girl of Yr 1983-85; Teacher of Yr 1981; *office:* Northwood Mid Sch 710 Ikes Rd Taylors SC 29687

HUGHES, MARJORIE LEANNA, Fifth Grade Teacher; *b:* Muskogee, OK; *m:* Lindal Jack; *c:* Angie, Chris; *ed:* (BA) Elem, 1976, (MS) Rdng, 1980 NE St Univ Tahlequah; *cr:* 1st/2nd Grade Teacher Gregory Sch 1976-77; 5th Grade Teacher Ellington Elem 1977-78, Cntrl Elem 1978-; *ai:* Supt Advisory Comm; Wagoner Classroom Teachers Assn 1977-; NEA, OK Ed Assn 1976-; *home:* 1001 S E 12th Wagoner OK 74467

HUGHES, O. KEITH, Technology Education Teacher; *b:* Bellefonte, PA; *m:* Jean Nehls; *c:* Marcella, Andrew; *ed:* (BS) Ind Art/Technology Ed, California Univ of PA 1978; California Univ of PA, Penn St Univ Du Bois, Wilkes Coll, Indiana Univ of Pa; *cr:* Teacher Purchase Line Jr-Sr HS 1979-82, Punxsutawney Area HS 1982-; *ai:* Technology Stu Assn Adv; Jr HS Wrestling Coach 1982-85; Track & Field Coach 1982-; Technology Ed Assn of PA 1985-; Intnl Technology Ed Assn, NEA, Punxsutawney Area Ed Assn, PA St Ed Assn; Punxsutawney Presbyn Church (Deacon 1985-87, Elder 1988-); *office:* Punxsutawney Area HS N Findley St Punxsutawney PA 15767

HUGHES, OPHELIA ANN, Assistant Principal; *b:* Anniston, AL; *ed:* (BS) Elem Ed, Jacksonville St Univ 1966; (MED) Elem Ed, West GA Coll 1973; Sci/Gifted Ed/Admin/Supvsn; *cr:* Teacher Grades 3/4 Fruithurst Jr HS 1966-67; Teacher Grades 4/5 Buchanan Jr HS 1967-73; Teacher Gifted Ed Haralson Cty Schls 1973-77; Teacher Grades 5/6 1977-88Asst Prin 1988- H a Jones Elem; *ai:* Stu Cncl Spon; Sch Pride Chairperson; 4-H Ed Adv; Coord 5th Grade Washington/Williamsburg Study Grp; NEA 1966-; ASCD 1986-; GACIS 1984-; GSTA 1988-; 4-H (Vol Leader/Sr Dist Chairperson 1980-82/Jr Exec Bd 1985-87/GA Rep 1984); Sorosis Sec 1986-88; Curr Adv K-12; Staff Dev Coord; *office:* H A Jones Elem Sch 206 Lakeview Dr Bremen GA 30110

HUGHES, PAUL BUCKNER, Biology Teacher; *b:* Jackson, MS; *m:* Cathy Keen; *c:* Stacy D.; *ed:* (BS) Bio, 1979, (BA) His, 1979, (MED) Ed/His, 1983 William Carey Coll; Univ of S MS, William Carey Coll; *cr:* GED Sci/Math Instr Hattiesburg Public Schls 1983-84, 1985-86; General Bio/Zoology/His Adjunct Teacher William Carey 1983-85, 1987-89; Sci Instr Hattiesburg Public Schls 1981-; *ai:* Ecology & Video Club Spon; Sch Improvement, Discipline, Natl Jr Honor Society, Public Relations Comms; Hattiesburg Prof Educators (VP 1984-85, Pres 1986-87); MS Acad of Sci MS Sci Teachers Assn, MS Assn of Biologists; Hawkins Jr HS PTA 1981-83; Lillie Burney Jr HS PTA 1983-87; Rowan Jr HS PTA 1988-; Lillie Burney Teacher of Yr 1984-85, 1986-87; Hardin Fnd Fellowship Earthwatch 1986; Hattiesburg Jaycees Outstanding Young Educator 1987; EESA Title II Exemplary Funds Grant 1987-88; *office:* Rowan Jr HS 1500 Martin Luther King Dr Hattiesburg MS 39401

HUGHES, ROBERT D., Mathematics Teacher; *b:* Portales, KS; *m:* Martha L. Simms; *c:* Deena Kline, Brian, Joe; *ed:* (BS) Ed/Phys Sci/Math, KSTC Emporia 1961; (MS) Ed/Math, E NM Univ 1982; *cr:* Jr HS Math Teacher Hoisington Public Schls 1961-64; Math Teacher Partridge HS 1964-66, Mayetta HS 1966-69, Silver Lake Schls 1969-76, Vaugh Municipal Schls 1977-78, Ft Sumner HS 1978-; *ai:* Jr Class Spon; Natl Sci Fnd Summer Inst 1966 & Grant 1967; Outstanding Scndry Educators of America 1974; *office:* Ft Sumner HS P O Box 387 Fort Sumner NM 88119

HUGHES, ROBERT EDWARD, 5th Grade Teacher; *b:* Lynn, MA; *m:* Susan M. Strang; *c:* Lisa Bendickson, Jayme, Shawna; *ed:* (BA) Elem Ed, 1970; (MA) Elem Ed, 1974 AZ St Univ; *cr:* Teacher Madison Rose Lane Sch 1970-78; Teacher Madison No 1 Sch 1978-; *ai:* Coaching & Ofctng 7th & 8th Grade Sports; Fed Madison Teachers (VP 1975-78/Pres 1978-79); *office:* Madison Number One School 5525 N 16th St Phoenix AZ 85016

HUGHES, RONALD D., 8th Grade English Teacher; *b:* Hays, KS; *m:* Kathleen Johnson; *c:* Chris, Kelly; *ed:* (BA) His, Western St Coll 1971; *cr:* Librarian Carbondale Elem/Carbondale Mid 1976-78; Rdng/Eng Teacher Carbondale Mid Sch 1978-; *ai:* Coach Girls Bsktbl; Spon Stu Cncl; Dir Stu Recognition; Disc Jockey Sch Dances; Admin Asst; at Risk Kids Comm; Stu Recognition Comm; 8th Grade Continuation; NCTE; CO Cncl Intnl Rdng Assn Rdng Educator of Yr 1988; Carbondale Mid Sch Teacher of Yr 1986 & 1988; RE-1 Sch Dist Teacher of Yr 1987-1988; *office:* Carbondale Mid Sch 455 S 3rd St Carbondale CO 81623

HUGHES, RONDA L., First Grade Teacher; *b:* Alger, OH; *m:* Conrad W.; *c:* Conrad M., Susan E. Lupfer, Gregory L., Angela D. Pifer; *ed:* (BS) Elem Ed, OH Northern Univ 1967; *cr:* 1st Grade Teacher Upper Scioto Valley Sch Dist 1967-70; Kenton City Sch Dist 1970-; *home:* 15845 Beverly Dr Kenton OH 43326

HUGHES, SANDRA JORDAN, Teacher; *b:* Charleston, WV; *m:* Samuel Thomas; *c:* Chris; *ed:* (BA) Scndry Ed, Marshall Univ 1975; *cr:* Teacher Huntington Chrstn Acad, Grace Chrstn Sch; *ai:* Sr Spon; Vlybl Coach; Admin Asst; *office:* Grace Chrstn Sch 1111 Adams Ave Huntington WV 25704

HUGHES, SHARYN BURGESS, First Grade Teacher; *b:* American Fork, UT; *m:* Arthur Lavell; *c:* Paula L., Suzette, Thomas A., John C., Coralie; *ed:* (BA) Elem Ed, Brigham Young Univ 1967; *cr:* 2nd Grade Teacher 1967-68, 3rd Grade Teacher 1968-69 W Kearns Elem; 2nd Grade Teacher 1977-80, 1st Grade Teacher 1985- Book Cliff Elem; *ai:* Book Cliff Elem Teacher of Yr 1988-89; Wrote Sch Stu Handbook 1989-; *office:* Book Cliff Elem Sch Box 485 Green River UT 84525

HUGHES, SUSAN BREMER, Fourth Grade Teacher; *b:* Topeka, KS; *m:* Charles A.; *c:* Courtney S.; *ed:* (BS) Ed, Emporia St Univ 1978; *cr:* 4th/5th Grade Teacher Unified Sch Dist #365 1978-; *ai:* Unified Sch Dist #365 Facilities Comm; Beta Sigma Phi 1978-82; *office:* Unified Sch Dist #365 E 3rd St Garnett KS 66032

HUGHES, W. HERBERT, English Teacher; *b:* Washington, PA; *m:* Ellen M. Wirth; *c:* Mark, Clare, Paul, Justin; *ed:* (BA) Eng, Washington & Jefferson Coll 1963; (MED) Scndry Admin, Duquesne Univ 1969; Doctoral Studs, Univ of Pittsburgh; *cr:* 12th Grade Eng Teacher 1963-69, Asst HS Prin 1970-79 Mc Guffy HS; 8th Grade Eng Teacher Mc Guffey Mid Sch 1980-; *ai:* NEA, PA St Ed Assn, Mc Guffey Ed Assn, NCTE; Fairhill Manor Chrstn Church; WA Lodge #164 F&AM; Syria Shrine Temple; *office:* Mc Guffey Mid Sch RD 1 Box 219 Claysville PA 15323

HUGHES, WRELDA VIRGINIA, US History Teacher; *b:* Longview, TX; *m:* Chauncey Reedy; *c:* David, Malaisha, Nathalie; *ed:* (BA) Span, 1972, (BA) Pan-African Stud, 1973 CA St Los Angeles; Advancement Candidacy Doctoral Prgm 1976; *cr:* Instr CA St Univ Los Angeles 1974-76; Teacher Monroe Jr HS 1978-, La Tijera Sch 1982-; *ai:* Stu Cncl Adv; GSA Leader 1980-89; BSA Institutional Coord 1976-79; Atlantis Swim Team Corr Secy 1976-80; Chamber of Commerce Teacher ofYr 1986; Natl Fellowship Fnd; Zeitlin & Ver Brugge Book Awd; Articles Journal of the Black Experience & Rdng in Black Dialect; *office:* La Tijera Elem/Jr HS 1415 N La Tijera Ave Inglewood CA 90302

HUGHEY, WILLIAM WALKER, Fifth Grade Teacher; *b:* Waverly, TN; *m:* Marge Loretta Wekemann; *c:* Patricia Pozciwinski, William Jr.; *ed:* (BS) Elem Ed, 1959, (MS) Elem Admin, 1962 Buffalo St Teachers; Grad Courses Niagara Univ; *cr:* 4th-6th Grade Teacher Niagara-Wheatfield Sch Dist 1959-; *ai:* Niagara-Wheatfield Teachers Assn VP; Colonial Village Presbyn Church Elder 1987-; Colonial Village Fire Hall Fireman 1962-.

HUGHS, NANCY GRACEY, 2nd Grade Teacher; *b:* Dallas, TX; *m:* Glenn R.; *c:* Amy E., Charles R.; *ed:* (BS) Elem Ed, Univ of TX 1976; (MED) Elem Ed, Univ of N TX 1980; Grad Stud Sci, Multi-Sensory Approach to Lang Art, Advanced LOGO, BASIC, Brookhaven Coll; *cr:* 1st Grade Teacher O Brown Elem 1976-82; Logo Teacher Irvine Ind Sch Dist 1983-85; 2nd Grade Teacher O Brown Elem 1983-; *ai:* Cmptr Comm Prgm Adv; Lang Art Textbook Comm Sub-Comm; Phi Delta Kappa 1980-; Alpha Chi Omega 1973-; The 500 Incorporated 1980-85; Mortar Bd Alumnae 1976-; PTA Local Exec Bd Mem 1976-; Wrote Curr & Set-Up Cmptr Lab 1984-89; Commodore Cmptr Grant; *office:* Otis Brown Elem Sch 2501 W 10th Irving TX 75060

HUGO, JUDY A., Guidance Counselor; *b:* Gloversville, NY; *m:* Donald F.; *c:* Amanda; *ed:* (MSED) Stu Personnel/Counseling, 1971, (BS) Elem Ed, 1969 St Univ Coll Buffalo; TESA, Drug & Alcohol Awareness; *cr:* 1st Grade Teacher Buffalo Schls 1969-70; Guidance Cnslr Mid Cntry Cntrl Sch Dist 1972-79; Teacher of Gifted & Talented/Sub Services Coord Tri Cty BOCES 1979-85,Teacher of Gifted & Talented Tri Cty BOCES 1985-56; Guidance Cnslr Mayfield Cntrl Sch 1985-; *ai:* SADD, Take Charge, Key Club, Project TEACH Adv; NY St Sch of Excl & Mid Sch Prgm Comm; Effective Schls Building Level Team; Stu At Risk Prgm; NY St Sch Cnslrs Assn 1989-; Tri Cty Cnslr Assn (Secy 1989-, VP 1987-89, Mem 1986); PTA, Parent Teacher Stu Organization 1982-; GSA Leader 1985-; NY St Teacher Center Grant; *office:* Mayfield Cntrl Sch School St Mayfield NY 12117

HUGULEY, ELSIE WANDA, AP English Teacher/Counselor; *b:* Lanier Hosp Valley, AL; *m:* George Washington; *c:* Bryant; *ed:* (BA) Eng, Talladega Coll 1974; (MED) Eng Ed, Auburn Univ 1981; Masters Cert Cnslr Ed, Auburn Univ 1990; *cr:* Rdng Teacher Shawmut Elem Sch 1976-78; Eng Teacher 1978-89, Cnslr 1989- Valley HS; *ai:* Honor Society Spon; Chambers Cty Ed Assn (Treas 1979-80, Pres 1981-82); Alpha Kappa Alpha 1974-; NAACP 1980-; *office:* Valley HS Hwy 29 Valley AL 36854

HUIE, ROLAND EUGENE, JR., Band Director; *b:* Mobile, AL; *m:* Melody Ann Collins; *c:* Roland E. III, Patrick L.; *ed:* (BM) Music Ed, 1978, (MM) Music Ed, 1979 Univ of S MS; Grad Stud Loyola Univ, Univ of New Orleans, SE LA Univ, Holy Cross Coll; *cr:* Band Dir St Bernard HS 1979-82; Band Dir/Music Dept Chm Chalmette HS 1982-; *ai:* Marching, Concert, Jazz Band; Guitar; LA Music Ed Assn (Marching Festival Co-Chm 1982-88) 1982-; LA Bandmasters Assn 1982-; NEA, LA Assn of Educators 1979-; Sigma Phi Epsilon Alumni Bd Pres 1982-84, Alumni of Yr 1985; St Tammary Parish Ensemble Festival Judge 1989; Dist VI Honor Band Competition Judge 1982-86; *home:* 2204 Munster Blvd Meraux LA 70075

HUISMAN, PEGGY JANE, 2nd Grade Teacher; *b:* Eldora, IA; *ed:* (BA) Elem Ed, Univ of N IA 1971; Grad Stud Drake Univ, Mary Crest, Univ of N IA, Leslsey Coll; *cr:* 4th Grade Teacher 1971-86, 2nd Grade Teacher 1986- Rudd Rockford Marble Rock Cmmty Sch; *ai:* NEA, IA St Ed Assn 1971-; Literary Leaders 1985-; *home:* 809 2nd Ave SE Rockford IA 50468

HUKARI, KAREN (HANSEN), English Teacher; *b:* Bremerton, WA; *m:* William A.; *c:* Jonathan, Jeffrey; *ed:* (AA) Eng, Everett Comm Coll 1965; (BA) Eng Ed, Univ of WA 1967; Post Grad Stud Univ of WA & Univ of OR; *cr:* Eng Teacher Ingraham HS 1967-72, Pleasant Hill HS 1972-74, Kentridge HS 1977-; *ai:* NHS; Commencement Speaker; Sr Class Adv; WA St Cncl Teachers of Eng, NCTE; Greenpeace; Beta Sigma Phi 1965-; *office:* Kentridge HS 12430 SE 208th Kent WA 98031

HULBERT, LU ANN, Social Studies Teacher; *b:* Hicksville, OH; *m:* Steven; *c:* Brittany, Landon; *ed:* (BS) Elem/Spec Ed, Kent St 1978; (MS) Admin/Supervision, Bowling Green 1985; *cr:* Teacher Edgerton Mid Sch 1978-; *ai:* Alpha Delta Kappa; *office:* Edgerton Mid Sch East River Edgerton OH 43517

HULGAN, CHARLES HAROLD, Band Director; *b:* Tenbrook, AL; *m:* Janice Cherry; *c:* Teri L.; *ed:* (BA) Music, 1958, (MA) Music, 1961 Univ of AL Tuscaloosa; *cr:* Band Dir Pittman Jr HS 1958-; *ai:* Music Combo Leader & Owner; NEA 1962-; Music Educators Natl Conference 1958-; Pleasant Ridge Baptist Church Choral Dir 1979, 1984; Delta Tau Delta House Mgr 1956-58; Music Clinician; Honors Band Dir; 18 Superior & 9 Excellent Ratings St Contest; *home:* 1565 Oak Ln Hueytown AL 35023

HULL, HELEN LESTER, Mathematics/Geometry Teacher; *b:* Fort Worth, TX; *m:* Don M.; *c:* Steven, Amy Hull Chazarreta, Brooks; *ed:* (BS) Scndry Ed, TX Chrstn Univ 1964; Grad Stud OK St Univ, TX Wesleyan Univ; *cr:* Math Teacher Euless Jr HS 1964-65, Carter-Riverside HS 1968-69, Ponca City-East Jr HS 1980-84, Crowley HS 1984-; *ai:* Var Chrldr Spon; TX PTA Lifetime Membership 1989; Teacher of Yr Crowley HS 1985; *office:* Crowley HS 1005 W Main Crowley TX 76036

HULL, LINDA DU PUIS, Art Teacher; *b:* Vancouver, WA; *m:* Lowell C.; *c:* John, Jim; *ed:* (AA) Art, Clark Jr Coll 1963; (BA) Art/Elem Ed, Univ of WA 1965; Edge Learning Inst; Lions Quest; Dynamic Image Color Analysis Trainer & Consultant; *cr:* Art Teacher Denali Elem & Univ Park Elem 1965-66, Instructional Television Elem 1966-68; 3rd Grade Teacher North Pole Elem 1968-69; Art Teacher Main Jr HS 1969-75, Tanana Jr HS 1975-; *ai:* Tanana Eagle Printers; Natl St Teachers of Yr; NAEA Outstanding Art Teacher 1980; Fairbanks Ed Assn, AK Ed Assn Teacher of Yr 1985-86; NEA; West Valley Wrestling Boosters (Pres 1986-87, Treas 1989-); Natl Rifle Assn Sharpshooter 1982; Burger King Fnd Honor of Excl in Ed 1986; *home:* 2181 Twin Flower Dr Fairbanks AK 99709

HULL, STANLEY W., 6th Grade Teacher; *b:* Harrisburg, IL; *m:* Judith Ann Cheek; *c:* Stacy, Eric Adams; *ed:* (BS) Ed/His/Eng 1970, (MS) Spec Ed/BD, 1980 S IL Univ; Grad Stud Educ Admin, S IL Univ 1988; *cr:* 6th Grad Teacher/Asst Prin Baylis Elem Sch 1970-80; 6th Grade Teacher East Side Elem Sch 1980-; *ai:* Teacher-Admin Comm Adv; Dare Facilitator; Regional Advisory Comm; Sch Photographer; NEA, IL Ed Assn 1970-; Harrisburg Ed Assn (Treas 1972) 1970-; Phi Delta Kappa 1988-; Outstanding Teacher Awd 1983-84; Article Published Regional Newletter; *home:* 721 S Mc Kinley Harrisburg IL 62946

HULLETT, ARTHUR JOSEPH, III, Social Studies Teacher; *b:* Baltimore, MD; *m:* Catherine Ford; *c:* Stacy E., Arthur J. IV; *ed:* (BS) Soc Stud, James Madison Univ 1967; Amer His, World His, Black His, Numerous Scndry Ed Courses, James Madison Univ, Univ of VA; *cr:* His/Civics Kate Collins Jr HS 1967-77; VA Gifted Stud Prgm Coord Natl Geographic Society 1977-81; Amer His/Applied Ec Teacher Waynesboro HS 1981-; *ai:* Beta Club Spon 1984-; SADD & PADD Mem; NEA, VEA 1985-; Applied Ec Cncl Mem 1989-; Masonic Lodge 1970-86; SPCA Bd Mem 1988-; PTA Mem 1983-; Jr Achievement Mem; Waynesboro Credit Union (Adv, Rep 1989-); *home:* 2125 Pickett Rd Waynesboro VA 22980

HULSE, RAYMOND BURRELL, Chemistry Teacher; *b:* River Rouge, MI; *m:* Elizabeth Dolente; *c:* Raymond B., Donald A., Peter D.; *ed:* (BS) Chem, Baker Univ 1965; Environmental Sci, WA Univ; Bus Admin, Lindenwood Coll; Cmptr Sci, West Chester Univ; *cr:* Chem Teacher Orchard Farm HS 1964-68; Environ Chem Envirdoyne Incorported 1967-80; Dir of Labs Wapora Incorporated 1980-82; Chem Teacher Haverford HS 1983-; *ai:* Faculty Advisory & Act Comm; Scotts Hi-Q Academic Team Coach; HS Ski Club Spon; HS Chess Club Adv; Asst Tennis, Cross Cntry, Sci Olympiad; NEA, PSTA, HTEA, US Chess Fed 1983-; Amer Chemical Society 1968-80; BSA Den Leader; Meth Church Comm Mem; Co-Patented Several Designs in Environmental Research; Co-Edited Many Articles on Environmental Dev; Coord Many Environmental Research Projects; Teacher of Yr 1987.

HULSEY, DOROTHY LEE, Fourth Grade Teacher; *b:* Gainesville, GA; *m:* Ben J.; *c:* Ben, Allison, Holly, Stephanie; *ed:* (AS) Biological Sci, Gainesville Coll 1967; (BS) Elem Ed, Brenau Coll 1979; (MED) Early Chldhd Ed, 1972, (EDS) Learning Disabilities, 1974 Univ of GA; *cr:* Teacher Lanier Sch 1969-72; Learning Disabilities Resource Teacher Hall Cty System Wide 1972-77; Bd Teacher Pioneer CESA 1977-79; Teacher Lakeview Acad 1979-; *ai:* Lower Sch Stu Cncl Adv; Article Published; *office:* Lakeview Acad 796 Lakeview Dr Gainesville GA 30505

HULSEY, JERRI ODELL, English Teacher; *b:* Albertville, AL; *m:* John Thomas; *c:* Jeremy; *ed:* (BS) Bus Ed, 1973, (MS) Scndry Ed, 1976 Jacksonville St Univ; Grad Work Ed Specialist Degree; Certified Voc Ed; *cr:* Secy Jacksonville St Univ 1972-73; Teacher Weaver HS 1974-83, Pleasant Valley Sch 1983-; *ai:* Jr Class & Prom Spon; Calhoun Cty Rep 1986, Nom Teacher Hall of Fame; Angel Fire Dept Secy 1988-89; PTO Treas 1990; Angel Grove Church Class Pres 1989-; *office:* Pleasant Valley HS 4141 Pleasant Valley Rd Jacksonville AL 36265

HULTSLANDER, JO A., Spanish Teacher; *b:* Stefano Quisquina, Italy; *m:* Bruce; *c:* Brent, Kimberlee; *ed:* (BS) Span, Buffalo St Coll 1978; (MA) Latin Amer Stud, G W Univ; Cert Italian, L Univ Di Siena; Cert Span, Univ De Facultad Y Letras; *cr:* Eng Teacher 1979-80, Span Teacher Williamsport HS 1979-; Span Instr Frederick Comm Coll 1988-; *ai:* Sch Improvement Team; Stu Incentives Chairperson; Pilot Final Exams; Span Club; Soc Comm Chairperson, Cmptr Comm; WMFLTA Treas 1989-; MFLA Bd of Dirs 1989-; *office:* Williamsport HS 5 S Clifton Dr Williamsport MD 21795

HUMBERTSON, BONNIE R., 8th Grade Reading Specialist; *b:* Cumberland, MD; *m:* G. Raymond; *ed:* (BS) Poly Sci, Frostburg St Coll 1969; (MED) Rdng, Frostburg St Univ 1973; *cr:* Rdng Specialist WA Mid Sch 1969-; *ai:* Adult Basic Ed Instr; MSTA, NEA; *office:* Washington Mid Sch 200 N Mass Ave Cumberland MD 21502

HUMBLE, CATHERINE S., 3rd Grade Teacher; *b:* Bluejacket, OK; *m:* Wm. Harlow; *c:* Tony M., Todd W.; *ed:* (BS) Elem Ed, Northeastern St Univ 1973; *cr:* 4th Grade Teacher Bluejacket Public Schls 1973-75; 3rd Grade Teacher Vinita Public Schls 1975-; *ai:* Delta Kappa Gamma Corresponding Secy/2nd VP/Prgm Chm; NEA; Vinita Classroom Teachers Assn; 1st Bapt Church Children I Dept Dir 1963-; Teacher of Yr Vinita Sch Sys 1983; *office:* Hall Halsell Elem Sch 402 W Clyde Vinita OK 74301

HUMBLE, SUSAN LORRAINE, 7th Grade Teacher; *b:* Pasadena, CA; *m:* Robert A.; *c:* Thomas, Megan; *ed:* (BA) Liberal Stud, 1978, (MA) Ed, 1984 CA Polytechnic Univ Pomona; (AA) Liberal Stud, Saddleback Jr Coll; *cr:* Teacher Baldwin Park Unified Sch Dist 1979-; *office:* Olive Jr HS 3701 Olive St Baldwin Park CA 91706

HUME, MARIAN RUBY, Fifth Grade Teacher; *b:* Marshall, MO; *ed:* (AE) Ed, SW Baptist Coll 1944; (BA) Math/Ed, Baylor Univ 1949; (MRE) Religious Ed, 1951, (DRE) His of Religious Ed, 1964 New Orleans Baptist Theological Seminary; (CAS) Intermediate Ed, Univ of NC Charlotte 1986; Working Towards Masters in Math Ed, Univ of MO Columbia & Baylor Univ; *cr:* Elem Teacher Saline Cty Rural Schls 1942-48; Music/HS Math/Eng Teacher Pilot Grove Sch 1956-58; Pre-Sch Laboratory Sch Supvr New Orleans Baptist Theological Seminary 1962-64; Math Assoc Professor Wingate Coll 1964-70; 5th Grade Teacher Wingate Elem Sch 1970-; *ai:* SACS Self-Stud Steering Comm; Prof Advisory Cncl Mem; Sch Planning Team; NC Assn of Educators (Sch Rep) 1970-; NEA 1970-; NCTM 1964-; NC Cncl

Teachers of Math 1971-, Union Cty Schls Outstanding Elem Math Teacher 1985; MO St Teachers Assn 1956-58; Wingate Womans Club (dept Chm 1965-69, Treas 1985-); Womans Missionary Union Dir 1974-; Union Baptist Assn; Daughters of Amer Revolution 1966-; Wingate Elem Sch Teacher of Yr 1977-78; NC Governors Bus Awd Outstanding Math Teacher 1990; Taft Inst Grant 1982; *home:* 410 N Main St PO Box 443 Wingate NC 28174

HUMES, GLORIA PERRY, Home Ec Dept Chairperson; *b:* Vienna, GA; *m:* Anthony Eugene; *c:* Charissa; *ed:* (AA) Pre-Home Ec Miami-Dade Comm Coll 1971; (BS) Home Ec, 1978, (MS) Home Ec, 1981 FL Intnl Univ; Certificate in Voc Ed for Handicapped 1978; HRS Child Care Trainer Certificate 1986; *cr:* Lang Art Teacher Miami Edison Mid Sch 1979; Home Ec Teacher Sunland Trng Center 1982-84, American HS 1979-; *ai:* FHA & Home Ec Club Adv; Occupations FHA/HERO Stu Organization; Sch Based Management Planning Comm; Dade Cty Home & Family Assn Pres 1984-85; Amer Home Ec Assn, FL Home Ec Assn, Dade Voc Assn 1979-; Womens Growth Inst Group Leader 1987-; PTA 1987-; Certified Home Economists; *office:* American HS 18350 NW 67th Ave Hialeah FL 33015

HUMMASTI, NEIL W., English Teacher; *b:* Astoria, OR; *ed:* (BA) Eng/His Portland St Univ 1973; Overseas Prgm, Hebrew Univ Jeruslaem Israel, Oxford Univ, Oxford England; *cr:* Eng Teacher Warrenton HS 1973-74, Molalla HS 1977-82, Jewell HS 1982-; *ai:* Drama; Bsbl Coach; Molalla HS Teacher of Yr 1981-82; Publication of Articles, Short Stories, Poetry; *office:* Jewell Sch Elsie Rt Box 1280 Seaside OR 97138

HUMMEL, CAROLE DEVLIN, Health/Physical Ed Teacher; *b:* Phoenixville, PA; *m:* John W.; *c:* Kathleen Adams, Courtnee L.; *ed:* (BS) Health/Phys Ed, W Chester St 1965; Driver Ed Cert Glassboro St; *cr:* Teacher Penns Grove HS 1965-; *ai:* Field Hockey; Sr Class Spon; CORE Team Mem; Faculty Substance Abuse Cnslr; NJEA 1965-; USFHA 1965-75, 1988; NASSP 1988-; Amer Alliance for Health, Phys Ed, Recreation, Dance; *office:* Penns Grove HS Harding Hwy Carneys Point NJ 08069

HUMMEL, CHERYL ANN, Business Education Teacher; *b:* Huntingdon, PA; *m:* David Lee; *c:* Matthew J., Michael P.; *ed:* (BS) Bus Ed, Shippensburg St Coll 1981; Instructional II Prof Cert Bus Ed, Accounting, Typewriting, Secretarial, St of PA 1986; *cr:* Substitute Teacher Tyrone Area HS 1981-82; Adult Ed Teacher Huntingdon Cty Voc Schls 1982-85; Bus Ed Teacher Forbes Road HS 1982-88, S Huntingdon Cty HS 1988-; *ai:* Sr Class Adv; Bus Dept Head; PA St Ed Assn 1988-; PA Bus Ed Assn 1982-; St Luth Church; *office:* S Huntingdon Cty HS P.O. Box 68 Orbisonia PA 17243

HUMMEL, DANIEL, School Counselor; *b:* Oak Park, IL; *m:* Dixie Livingston; *c:* Julia, Chad; *ed:* (BS) Accounting, Lewis Univ 1967; (MS) Guidance/Counseling, IL St Univ 1971; Univ of WI Milwaukee; *cr:* Math Teacher E M Walsh Sch 1967-72; Cnslr Shorewood Intermediate Sch 1974-76; Guidance Dir Ashland Public Schls 1976-78; Cnslr Woodbury Sch 1978-; *ai:* Steering Comm; Woodbury Comprehensive Guidance & Counseling; Salem & NH CG&C; Woodbury Skills for Adolescence; Salem Schls Strategic Planning Action Team; NH Sch Counseling 1978-; NE Assn of Schls & Colls Visiting Comm 1979, 1988; NH League of Craftsman Exec Comm 1989-; NH Composite Guidance & Counseling Co-Author; *office:* Woodbury Sch 289 Main St Salem NH 03079

HUMMEL, PAMELA BIERY, Forensics Director; *b:* Temple, TX; *m:* Gregory; *c:* Danielle; *ed:* (BA) Speech/Eng, Trinity Univ 1979; IA Debate Inst 1988, 1989; Writing Inst of Northside 1986; *cr:* Teacher John Jay HS 1979-85; Teacher/Forensics Dir W H Taft HS 1985-; *ai:* Debate & Oral Interpretation Coach; Univ Interscholastic League Coord; Natl Ftbl League Club; TX Forensic Assn, Natl Forensic League, Amer Forensic Assn; Whisper Creek Homeowners Assn Pres 1985-86; Natl Endowment Hum Research Asst Dartmouth Debate Inst; *office:* William Howard Taft HS 11600 Fm 471 W San Antonio TX 78253

HUMMEL, SUZANNE DEFORREST, Ninth Grade English Teacher; *b:* Washington, DC; *m:* Keith Alan; *ed:* (BS) Eng, E Stroudsburg Univ 1979; Working Toward Masters Shippensburg Univ; *cr:* Eng Teacher Tuscarora Jr HS 1979-89, Juniata HS 1989-; *ai:* Class Play Dir; Masque & Gavel Club Adv; *home:* Box 1 Devon Court Rd Selinsgrove PA 17870

HUMMER, GEORGE BARTON, A P English Teacher/Dept Chair; *b:* Madera, CA; *m:* Pamela Margaret Johnson; *c:* Joseph G., Benjamin E.; *ed:* (BA) Poly Sci, Univ of CA Berkeley 1947; (MA) Eng, Univ of CA Los Angeles 1953; Shakespeare Inst, Univ of Birmingham England at Stratford-Upon-Avon; *cr:* Lecturer Univ of MD Overseas 1955-56; Ed Officer US Air Force 1956-61; Writer/Dir US Air Force Information Directorate 1961-69; Teacher Dept of Defense Dependent Schls 1970-; *ai:* Drama Coach; Newspaper & Literary Magazine Spon; Mem Regional Accrediation Teams; Articles, Poems, Stories, Plays Published; *office:* Croughton Amer HS RAF Croughton APO New York NY 09378

HUMPHREY, BARBARA JONES, Vocational Home Ec Teacher; *b:* Mt Vernon, OH; *m:* Dan Eugene; *c:* David, Mark, Aaron; *ed:* (BA) Home Ec/Eng, Otterbein Coll 1970; *cr:* Voc Home Ec Teacher Mc Comb HS 1970-72; Domestic Sci Teacher Leona Scndry 1972-74; Voc Home Ec Holgate HS 1974-75, Mt Vernon HS 1987-; *ai:* FHA, HERO; OH Ed Assn, NEA, OH Voc Assn, OH Home Ec Assn; 4-H Club Adv 1985-; Fredricktown United Meth Church; *office:* Mt Vernon HS Martinsburg Rd Mount Vernon OH 43050

HUMPHREY, BRENDA LAE ADAIR, Teacher; *b:* Chicago, IL; *m:* Ralph; *c:* Tiffany; *ed:* (BA) Elem Ed, Chicago St Univ 1972; (MA) Educl Admin, NE IL Univ 1986; Local Site Coord Educl Research & Dissemination Prgm 1987-; CTU Sch Leadership Trainer; *cr:* Clerk/Typist United Insurance Company 1968-69, Continental Bank 1969-70; Teacher Aide 1970-72, Teacher 1972- Bd of Ed Chicago; *ai:* Chrldr Coach & Spon; Bsktbl Teacher & Spon; Art Club Spon; Prof Problems Advisory Comm Chairperson; Chicago Teachers Union Sch Leadership Trainer 1990; *office:* Jacob A Riis Sch 1018 S Lytle Chicago IL 60607

HUMPHREY, CHARLES EDWARD, Science Teacher; *b:* Pine Bluff, AR; *ed:* (BS) Bio, AM&N 1971; (MSED) EDucl Admin, Univ of AR 1978; *cr:* Bio/Phys Sci Teacher Jacksonville HS 1971-75; Alternative Sch Teacher N Pulaski HS 1975-80; Phys Sci Teacher Northwood Jr HS 1980-; *ai:* Sch Planning Comm; Pulaski Assn of Classroom Teachers, AEA, NEA 1971-; AR Sci Teachers 1980-; Big Brothers/Big Sisters 1988-; *home:* 1919 Vaugine Pine Bluff AR 71601

HUMPHREY, EDWARD JOHN, 7th Grade Geography Teacher; *b:* Jersey City, NJ; *m:* Karen M. Meyer; *c:* Paul L., Audra L., Heather A.; *ed:* (BA) His, E NM Univ 1964 ; Grad Work Univ of TX El Paso & Univ of NM; *cr:* 7th Grade Teacher Anthony Gadsden Jr HS 1964-66; 6th Grade Teacher Mesa Elem Sch 1966-67; His Teacher Los Alamos HS; Soc Stud Dept Head/ 7th Grade Soc Sci Teacher Cumbres Jr HS & Los Alamos Mid Sch 1966-; *ai:* Head Ftbl, Bsktbl, Sftbl Coach Cumbres Jr HS & Los Alamos HS 1972-; Head Coach 7th Grade Ftbl Cumbres Jr HS 1972-78; Asst Ftbl Coach & Defensive Coord Los Alamos HS 1984-87; Head Coach 8th/9th Grade Ftbl, 8th Grade Bsktbl, 9th Grade Sftbl Cumbres Jr HS; Head Coach Frosh Ftbl Los Alamos HS 1985-86; Head Coach Jr Var Ftbl Los Alamos HS 1985-87; Asst Coach Girls Sftbl Los Alamos HS 1984-87; Soc Stud Dept Head; NM Teachers Fed; Trails End Ranch Head Wrangler 1966; Bradbury Sci Museum Guide 1967-68; YMCA Summer Camp Dir 1970-71; Barranca Mesa Pool Mgr 1974; Canyon Vista Pool Mgr 1976-77; Sports Writer & Play By Play Announcer Radio Station KRSN; Electronics Technician Los Alamos Scientific Laboratory 1960-64; *office:* Los Alamos Mid Sch 2101 Cumbres Dr Los Alamos NM 87544

HUMPHREY, EILEEN ROSS, 4th Grade Teacher; *b:* Warren, PA; *m:* Harry L.; *c:* Heather, Daniel; *ed:* (BS) Elem Ed, Edinboro Univ of PA 1969; Rdng, SUNY Fredonia; *cr:* Teacher Cattaraugus Elem Sch 1969-; *ai:* Cattaraugus Teachers Assn; Free Meth Church; *office:* Cattaraugus Cntrl Sch Jefferson St Cattaraugus NY 14719

HUMPHREY, GAYLE CORLEY, 8th Grade Soc Stud Teacher; *b:* Lincoln, AL; *m:* Huey Penton; *c:* Robert H., Michael H., Joseph H.; *ed:* (BA) His/Eng, Birmingham Southern Coll; (MS) Scndry Ed/Soc Sci, Troy St Univ 1980; *cr:* 7th Grade Soc Stud/Eng Teacher Baker Jr HS; 6th Grade Teacher Alexander City Elem Jr HS; 4th/5th Grade Math Teacher Jim Pearson Sch; 9th Grade AL His/Civics Teacher Alexander City Jr HS; 8th Grade Soc Stud Teacher Alexander City Mid Sch; *ai:* Alexander City Ed Assn (Pres, VP, Secy) Advisory Cncl (Pres, Secy) 1986-88; NEA Delegate; AEA Legislative Commission 1987-, Spec Awd; Zeta Tau Alpha Life Mem; Kappa Delta Epsilon, Kappa Delta Phi; Alpha Delta Kappa Secy; Alexander City Dixie Bsbl/Sftbl Assn (Secy, Bd of Dir); First United Meth Church (Admin Bd, Ministries Cncl, Race Relations Chm, United Meth Women Exec Bd, Global Concerns Chairperson); Sponsorship Jr Achievement Awd; 20 Yr Teaching Service Pin; Criminal Justice Grant; *office:* Alexander City Mid Sch PO Box 817 Alexander City AL 35010

HUMPHREY, JANET RAE (KIMBRELL), 4th Grade Teacher; *b:* Ada, OK; *m:* Terry Lynn; *c:* Kaleb Wade; *ed:* (BS) Elem, E Cntrl St Univ 1953; (MA) Instructional Media, Cntrl St 1989; *cr:* 4th Grade Teacher Wellston Elem 1983-; *ai:* Wellston Ed Assn Pres 1986-87; Kiwanianne Club Pres 1988-89, Kiwanianne of Yr; *home:* Rt 1 Box 443-R Wellston OK 74881

HUMPHREY, JANICE BRENNAN, Mathematics Teacher; *b:* E St Louis, IL; *m:* Steve; *c:* Jennifer, Michael; *ed:* (BS) Elem Ed, 1967, (MS) Elem Ed, 1968 S IL Univ Carbondale; Working Towards Math Cert; *cr:* 5th Grade Teacher Carterville Elem 1968-70; Kndgtn/1st Grade Teacher CCSD #15 1970-81; Math Teacher Linn Mid Sch 1981-; *ai:* LCTA (Treas 1985-86, VP 1990-); NEA, IEA, MNEA 1968-; Elem Ed Fellowship 1967-68; *office:* Linn Mid Sch 1212 E Main St Linn MO 65051

HUMPHREY, LINDA KAY COLE, Physics Teacher; *b:* Kerrville, TX; *m:* Gerald D.; *c:* Wesley, Tera; *ed:* (BS) Math, SW TX St Univ 1971; Univ of Houston & Prairieview A&M Univ; *cr:* 6th Grade Teacher Eanes Ind Sch Dist 1972; 7th Grade Math Teacher Spring Wood Jr HS 1973; Physics Teacher Spring Woods HS 1973-77, Klein Oak HS 1987-; *ai:* Jr Engineering Tech Society Spon; TX St Teachers Assn 1972-77, Awd 1987-; NEA, Klein Ed Assn 1987-; Kathy Shearer Awd for Outstanding Jets Faculty Spon St of TX 1989-; *office:* Klein Oak HS 22603 Northcrest Spring TX 77388

HUMPHREY, MARY SUE F., Teacher of the Deaf; *b:* Kinston, NC; *m:* Clen W. Jr.; *c:* Thomas C., Michael B.; *ed:* (BS) Elem Ed, Atlantic Chrstn Coll 1962; Ed of Hearing Impaired 1972; (MAED) Learning Disabilites, E Carolina Univ 1980; *cr:* 2nd Grade Teacher Southwood Sch 1962-63; Special Ed Teacher N Edgecombe Sch 1963-64; 1st Grade Teacher Wilson City Sch 1964-67; 2nd Grade Teacher Wilson Cty Sch 1967-70; Teacher of the Deaf E NC Sch for Deaf 1970-; *ai:* Sci Club for Primary Grades; NC Assn of Educators, St Employees Assn of NC 1989-; Beta Sigma Phi Treas 1988-, Alpha-Omega Awd 1975; *home:* 706 Anson St Wilson NC 27893

HUMPHREYS, BETTY FARRIS, Teacher of Gifted & Talented; *b:* Morrilton, AR; *m:* Bob; *c:* Gregory, Bradley; *ed:* (BSE) Elem Ed, AR Tech Univ 1967; Grad Stud Elem Ed, Gifted/ Talented, ATU Russellville; *cr:* 3rd Grade Teacher A R Hederick Elem 1967-68; 5th Grade Teacher Ben Cravens Elem 1968-71; 3rd Grade Teacher Plumerville Elem 1973-80; 3rd Grade Teacher 1980-85, Teacher of Gifted & Talented 1985- Reynolds Elem; *ai:* Conway Cty Youth Talent Comm 1989-; Delta Kappa Gamma Secy 1986-88; NEA 1973-82; AR Ed Assn Membership Chairperson 1967-82; Intnl Rdng Assn SW Regional Conference Host; AR Gifted & Talented Ed 1985-; S Conway Cty Teacher of Yr Awd 1982-83; *home:* 110 Cedar Crest Morrilton AR 72110

HUMPHREYS, LA FUAN E., ECO/Enriched US His Teacher; *b:* Lubbock, TX; *m:* Ted O.; *c:* Lori Schultz, Ted II; *ed:* (BSED) Government, TX Tech Univ; Numerous Courses & Schls; *cr:* US His/World His Teacher/Dept Head O L Slaton Jr HS 1960-79; US His/Ec/Civics/Law/Government Teacher Eldorado HS 1979-83; US His/Civics Teacher Del Norte HS 1983-85; Enriched US His/US His/Ec/Government Teacher Eldorado HS 1985-; *ai:* Eldorado HS Teacher Advisory Comm Supt Rep 1989-; Eldorado TAC Rep 1987-89; SASS Spon 1987-89; Sch Improvement Team 1981-85; Prin Advisory 1980-81; Del Norte HS N Area TAC Rep 1984-85; Co-Spon BSU 1984-85; Attendance, Stu & Cmmty Morale, Excalibur, Selection & Prins Advisory Comm Mem 1984-85; Coordination of Ec in Soc Stud & Bus Marketing Courses Comm Co-Chairperson 1988; Instructional Services & Support Advisory Bd; St of NM Soc Stud Teacher of Yr Runnerup 1989-; Endowment for Hum 1987; Dev of Ec Curr Guide for APS Consultant 1987-88; Presented Various Seminars; NM Chambers of Commerce Convention Guest Speaker 1979; Lubbock Ind Sch Dist Inservice Presentor & Facilitator; West Publishing Company Textbook Reviewer; Dist Ec Curr Video Tape Reviewer.

HUMPHREYS, STEPHEN W., Instrumental Music Teacher; *b:* Jasonville, IN; *m:* Donna C. Moore; *ed:* (BA) Music, IN St Univ 1959; (MA) Music, Ball St Univ 1968; *cr:* Instrumental Music Teacher Indianapolis Public Schls 1960-; *ai:* Staff Mem; Indianapolis All/City Jr HS Band; Music Educators Natl Conference, IN St Teachers Assn, NEA, Indianapolis Ed Assn; IN Sch Music Assn; IN Music Assn Contests 1st Division Awds; *office:* Forest Manor Sch 4501 E 32nd St Indianapolis IN 46218

HUMPHRIES, GOLDA VANDYGRIFF, Principal; *b:* Roxton, TX; *m:* George M.; *c:* Brian, Kyle; *ed:* (AA) Elem Ed, Paris Jr Coll 1961; (BS) Elem Ed, 1974, (MED) Elem Ed, 1984 E TX St Univ; Ed Admin; *cr:* 5th Grade Teacher 1974-78, Elem Prin/3rd Grade Teacher 1978-87, K-12th Grade Prin 1987 Roxton Ind Sch Dist; *ai:* UIL, PEIMS, At-Risk, Drug Awareness Coord; TX Elem Prin Assn 1987-; ASCD Dir 1987-; TX Assn of Scndry Sch Prins 1987-89; FHA Regional, St Membership 1988-89; FFA Regional Honorary Membership 1989-; Leadership Lamar Cty Chamber of Commerce 1989-; *office:* Roxton Ind Sch Dist PO Box 307 Roxton TX 75477

HUMPHRIES, JAMES HUNTER, 5th Grade Soc Stud Teacher; *b:* La Grange, GA; *m:* Kay Thompson; *c:* Betsey L.; *ed:* (BA) Eng, Huntingdon Coll 1975; (MED) Mid Grades Ed, W GA Coll 1985; *cr:* 4-H Cty Coord Univ of GA Extension Service 1976-80; 5th Grade Teacher Rosemont Elem Sch 1980-; *ai:* Rosemont 5th Grade 4-H Club Coord; Certified Data Collector; Various Curr & Book Adoption Comms; Troup Cty 4-H Clubs Teacher/Club Adv of Yr 1989; *office:* Rosemont Elem Sch 4679 Hamilton Rd La Grange GA 30240

HUMPHRIES, LA DONNIA V. BOUTWELL, Jr HS Math Teacher; *b:* Pelham, GA; *m:* T. M. Jr.; *c:* C. Todd, Nive R. Humphries Moore; *ed:* (AS) Ed, Thomas Cty Comm Coll 1977; (BS) Elem/Mid Ed, Valdosta St Coll 1979; Mid Sch Math, Valdosta St Coll; *cr:* Jr HS Math Teacher Shiver Sch 1979-; *ai:* Beta Club Spon 1979-; Teacher of Yr, Shiver PTO Carnival Funds, SACS Steering Comm Mem; Stu Support Team Mem 1987-; Mathcounts, Math-A-Thon Adv; GA Assn of Ed Pres 1989-, Membership Honor Roll 1990, Outstanding Leadership 1989-; NCTM Mem; Harmony Club BYW (Pres 1970-71, Secy 1973-74); Several Poems Published; *home:* Rt 2 Box 126 Pelham GA 31779

HUMSTON, SANDRA JEAN (JEVONS), Kindergarten Teacher; *b:* Emporia, KS; *m:* Edward A. Jr.; *c:* Kristi; *ed:* (BSE) Elem Ed, Emporia St Univ 1966; Grad Stud Ed; *cr:* Kndgtn Teacher Rochester Elem Sch 1966-; *ai:* SPEAK (VP, Secy, Chm); PTA (Pres, Treas) 1970; 4-H Leader 1980; GSA Brownies; Rochester Sch Teacher of Yr 1983, 1987.

HUNDLEY, RUBY LEE ELLIS, Second Grade Teacher; *b:* Meaford ON, Canada; *m:* John Paul; *c:* Lucille, Paul, Lori, Philippe; *ed:* (BA) Speech/Eng, Harding Coll 1953; Ed, Wichita St 1968; Spec Stud Fr, Univ of Lausanne Switzerland 1969; *cr:* 2nd Grade Teacher Memphis Chrstn Sch 1953-56, Warwick Public Schls 1956-57; Kndgtn/1st Grade Teacher Dallas Chrstn Schls 1959-61; 4th Grade Teacher Wichita KS 1967-68; 5th Grade Teacher Cresent Sch 1973-75; 2nd Grade Teacher Sonrise CA 1975-79, Hackett AR 1979-; *ai:* WEA 1974-75; *home:* 7608 Euper Ln Fort Smith AR 72903

HUNER, RITA A., Home Economics Dept Chair; *b:* Napoleon, OH; *ed:* (MHE) Home Ed/Clothing/Textiles, Bowling Green St Univ 1988; *cr:* Voc Home Ec Teacher/Chairperson Edgerton Local Schls 1972-; *ai:* FHA; Mat Maids; Amer Home Ec Assn 1986-; OVA, AVA 1987-; OEA, NEA 1980-; NW OH Ec Assn 1975-; Delta Kappa Gamma 1984-; Williams Cty Panhellenic 1978-; Planning Comm for all OH Voc Conference 1990; *office:* Edgerton Local Schls 324 N Michigan Edgerton OH 43517

HUNGERFORD, RICHARD RAY, Teacher/Coach; *b:* Stuart, NE; *m:* Sydney A.; *c:* Kim, Richard, Greg, Pam, Gary; *ed:* (BS) Phys Ed, 1952, (MA) Sch Admin/Phys Ed, 1962 Univ of NE; *cr:* Teacher/Coach Cortland HS 1958-59, Bishop Mc Guinness HS 1959-60, Farmersville Elem Sch 1960-61, Redwood HS 1961-; *ai:* Golf Coach 1966-; VUTA, CTA, NEA; Lions; USMCR Lt Col; *office:* Redwood HS 1001 W Main Visalia CA 93291

HUNKELER, MARGARET LOUISE, Third Grade Teacher; *b:* Brookfield, IL; *ed:* (BS) Ed - Cum Laude, 1966, (MA) Elem Ed, 1969 St Marys Coll; Grad Stud Admin/Ed; *cr:* 3rd Grade Teacher St Michaels Sch 1955-57; 5th Grade Teacher St Raymond Cathedral 1957-59; 5th-6th Grade Teacher St Louis of France Sch 1959-61; 5th Grade Teacher St Marys Sch 1961-62; 5th-7th Grade Teacher St John Baptist Sch 1961-67; 3rd/6th Grade Teacher Corpus Christi Sch 1967-76; 2nd-6th Grade Teacher Holy Family Sch 1976-; *ai:* 3rd Grade Catechist Teacher; Diocese of Ft Wayne & South Bend Catechist 1962-82, 1985-, Prof I Certificate 1979.

HUNNICUT, WARREN, IV, Biology Teacher; *b:* St Petersburg, FL; *c:* Phillip D.; *ed:* (AA) General, St Petersburg Jr Coll 1969; (BS) Zoology, FL Southern Coll 1972; (MA) Spec Ed/Gifted, Univ of S FL 1983; Working Towards PhD Marine Vertebrate Zoology; Various Wkshps, Inst, Seminars; *cr:* Dept Chair St Pauls Sch 1977-81; Teacher of Gifted Morgan Fitzgerald Mid Sch 1981-82; Teacher Gibbs HS 1982-85, St Petersburg HS 1985-; Adjunct Prof St Petersburg Jr Coll 1985-; *ai:* St Petersburg HS Intnl Baccalaureate prgm Teacher; Academic Coaching & Research Paper Supervisorship; Speaker Marine Bio & Environment; NSTA, NEA, FL Assn of Sci Teachers, FL Marine Sci Educators Assn; AIDS Coalition Pinellas Ed 1989-; Dali Musem Docent 1985-87; Various Wildlife Conservation, Environmental Organizations; Delegation Leader Youth to Youth Sci Exch Between USSR & US Marine Biology; Articles Published; *office:* Saint Petersburg HS 2501 Fifth Ave N Saint Petersburg FL 33713

HUNNICUTT, ANNABELLE, Administrative Assistant; *b:* Battle Ground, WA; *m:* Richard L.; *c:* Steven S Nelson, Susan Fultz, Judy Domke, Karen Snelson, Mary Smith, Holly Jessee, Marlene Pruden, Lolena Clark, Orie; *ed:* (BA) Ed, Portland St Univ 1972; (MAT) Ed, Lewis & Clark Coll 1975; Prin Cert Ed, Eastern WA Univ 1984; *cr:* Teacher Battle Ground Sch Dist 1973-79, Northport Sch Dist 1981-88; Teacher/Admin Northport Sch Dist 1988; *ai:* N Club Adv; *office:* Northport Elem Sch P O Box 180 Northport WA 99157

HUNNICUTT, NETTIE O'DONLEY, Reading/Math Lab Teacher; *b:* Utica, OK; *m:* Edward Waller; *c:* Amy D.; *ed:* (BSED) Elem Ed, 1978, (MS) Rdng Specialist, 1983 SE OK St Univ; Prins Cert; *cr:* 4th Grade Teacher 1979-81, Rdng Lab Teacher 1981-83, 4th Grade Teacher 1983-88, Rdng Lab Teacher 1988- NW Heights; *ai:* Kappa Delta Pi Secy 1976-77; Delta Kappa Gamma 1st VP 1988-; Durant Ed Assn Building Rep 1985-87; *office:* Northwest Heights Sch 1601 University St Durant OK 74701

HUNSAID, ANN BERG (NAGEL), Language Art Teacher; *b:* Minot, ND; *m:* Irvin F.; *c:* Jacquelin Nagel Hurst, Paul F.; *ed:* (BS) Eng, N MT Coll 1968; ND St Univ, Univ of ND, Minot St Univ; *cr:* Lang Art Teacher Minot Public Schls 1969-; *ai:* Essay Contest Writing Coach; NEA, NDEA, MEA 1969-; PDK Secy; Delta Kappa Gamma Treas 1990; Federated Womens Club, PTA; Mayors Comm Hire Handicapped Outstanding Educator 1988, Optimist Club Outstanding Educator Awd 1988; *office:* Minot Public Schls Magic City 1100 11th Ave SW Minot ND 58701

HUNSDON, LINDA BOSHEARS, Mathematics Teacher & Coord; *b:* Medford, OR; *m:* Scott H.; *ed:* (BS) Psych, Willamette Univ 1983; *cr:* Math Teacher Sellwood Mid Sch 1983-; *ai:* Math Coord; *office:* Sellwood Mid Sch 8300 SE 15th Ave Portland OR 97202

HUNSUCKER, CLARA BROYHILL, 4th Grade Teacher; *b:* Charlotte, NC; *m:* Julian C.; *c:* Catherine H. Tuggle, Sharon H. Du Rant, Bob C.; *ed:* (BS) Elem Ed, TX Tech Univ 1958; (MS) Elem Ed, Clemson Univ 1976; *cr:* 4th Grade Teacher Northside Elem 1968-73; 4th Grade Teacher 1973-89, 5th Grade Teacher 1989- Ravenel Elem; *ai:* Rdng, Math & Book Comm; Tennis Team Captain; Study Club (Pres, Treas); Bridge Club; SCEA, NEA; *office:* Ravenel Elem Sch 1700 Davis Creek Rd Seneca SC 29678

HUNT, BARBARA J., English Teacher; *b:* Grundy, VA; *m:* Clell Jr.; *c:* Christina, Kelly; *ed:* (BS) Eng, Pikeville Coll 1973; (MA) Ed, Morehead St; Rank I; *cr:* Teacher Fedscreek HS 1973-; *ai:* Sch Newspaper & Sr Spon; Faculty Handbook Chairperson; *home:* Box 33 Fedscreek KY 41524

HUNT, DENNIS CHARLES, History Teacher; *b:* New Haven, CT; *m:* Karen Spargo; *c:* Jennifer, Matthew; *ed:* (BA) Ed, Fairfield Univ 1967; (MA) His, S CT St Coll 1968; *cr:* His Teacher Amity Regional Sr HS 1968-; *ai:* Youth & Government Club Adv; Amity Ed Assn VP; CEA, NEA; Church Garden Group Organizer 1986-; YMCA Youth & Government (Legislative Process Chairperson 1986-, Adv 1980-), Recognition 1987, 1989, Man of Yr 1986; Yrbk Dedication; PTSA Teacher of Yr; Gold Pen Awd; Bd of Ed Teacher of Yr Awd; *office:* Amity Regional Sr HS Newton Rd Woodbridge CT 06525

HUNT, DONNA MONKS, Sixth Grade English Teacher; *b:* Tahona, OK; *m:* Melvin Ronald; *c:* David R., Melvin B.; *ed:* (BA) Ed, NE St Univ Tahlequah 1969; *cr:* 2nd Grade Classroom Teacher 1969-72, 3rd Grade Classroom Teacher 1974-76, 6th Grade Classroom Teacher 1981- Hartshorne Public Sch; *ai:* NEA, OK Ed Assn 1969-; Hartshorne Ed Assn (Curr Chairperson 1987-89) 1971-; *office:* Hartshorne Public Sch 821 Arapaho Hartshorne OK 74547

HUNT, EMILIE WINIFRED, French Teacher/Dept Chair; *b:* Philadelphia, PA; *ed:* (BA) Fr, Dunbarton Coll of Holy Cross 1972; (MA) Ed, Univ of MD Coll Park 1983; Proficiency Inst 1986; *cr:* Fr Teacher 1972-, Dept Chairperson 1978- St Vincent Pallotti HS; *ai:* Alumni Relations & Foreign Lang Honor Societies Coord; Fr Club Moderator; AATF, Greater WA Assn for Teachers of Fr; *office:* St Vincent Pallotti HS 113 8th St Laurel MD 20707

HUNT, JOYCE ARLENE (OLNEY), Retired Teacher; *b:* Owasso, MI; *m:* Woodrow; *c:* Sharon, Lorna, Gary, Gail; *ed:* (BA) Soc Sci, CMU 1963; Rdng; *cr:* K-3rd Grade Teacher Swan Creek Sch 1956-58, Zigler Sch 1958-59, Chesaning Public Schls 1960-62; 1st/2nd Grede Teacher St Charles Public Sch 1962-82; *ai:* MEA, NEA; Sunday Sch Teacher 1945-68; 4-H Club Leader 1949-60; Church Womans Club Pres 1980-81; *home:* 616 Baltic St Saint Charles MI 48655

HUNT, LAURA ERICKSON, Art Instructor; *b:* Bridgeport, CT; *ed:* (BS) Elem Ed, Cntrl CT St Coll 1973; (MS) Rdng, Univ of Bridgeport 1979; Fine Arts at Sacred Heart Univ, Yale, Cntrl CT St Univ, Housatonic Comm Coll; *cr:* 2nd Grade Teacher 1973-77, 4th Grade Teacher 1977-89, Art Teacher 1989- Daniels Farm Sch; *ai:* Amer Heart Assn Local Jump Rope for Heart Coord 1988-; NEA, CEA, TEA 1973-; Rdng Instruction Article Published; General Electric Fnd & Bridgeport Area Fnd Math Grant 1986-87; *office:* Daniels Farm Sch 710 Daniels Farm Rd Trumbull CT 06611

HUNT, M. ELIZABETH MURRAY, English Teacher; *b:* Cohoes, NY; *m:* Frank; *c:* Kathleen Hunt Carpenter, John J., Daniel L.; *ed:* (BA) Ed/Soc Stud, 1956, (MA) Ed/Eng 1962 NYS Coll for Teachers Albany; Advanced Courses Eng & Rdng, Russell Sage Coll, Oneonta Coll; *cr:* 7th/8th Eng/Soc Stud Teacher Cntrl Park Jr HS 1956-63; Substitute Teacher Fonda-Fultonville Cntrl Sch/Canajoharie Cntrl Sch 1971-81; Eng Teacher Fort Plain Cntrl Sch 1981-; *ai:* Co-Adv Jr HS Stu Cncl; Building Team Mem Effective Schls Prgm; Cath Family & Cmmty Services (Bd of Dir 1982, VP 1987-); Colonial Club of Canajoharie (Prgm Dir 1987, VP 1986); Eng Teacher of Excl NYS Eng Cncl Fort Plain Nom 1990; *office:* Fort Plain Cntrl Sch High St Fort Plain NY 13339

HUNT, MIYUKI TYLER, 4th Grade Teacher; *b:* Kisarazu, Japan; *m:* John Henry; *c:* Kimi L.; *ed:* (MA) Ed/Cmptrs, CA Poly Univ 1985; (BA) Liberal Stud, CA St Univ Fullerton 1979; Marilyn Capenter Whole Lang Seminar 1989; Wkshp Center for Sci & Math Ed 1990; *cr:* Rdng/Math Teacher Richman Elem 1980-81; 2nd/4th Grade Teacher Los Serranos Elem 1981-87; 4th/6th Grade Teacher G F Litel Elem 1987-; *ai:* Classroom Teacher Instructional Improvement Prgm Grant Co-Author *office:* G F Litel Elem Sch 3425 Eucalyptus Chino CA 91709

HUNT, PATRICIA ANN, Bio/Chem/Physics Teacher; *b:* Sweetwater, TN; *ed:* (BS) Bio, TN Wesleyan 1983; Masters Stud Curr & Instr, Sci Ed, Univ of TN Knoxville; *cr:* Teacher Meigs Cty HS 1983-; *ai:* Sci Club & Jr Class Spon; Needs Assessment Advisory Bd Extended Contract Act; Comprehensive Career Dev Steering Comm; *office:* Meigs Cty HS PO Box 128 Decatur TN 37322

HUNT, RODERICK JOSEPH, Biology Teacher; *b:* Farmington, NM; *m:* Patrice Barton; *c:* Denzel, Jaimi, Brandon, Kristy J., Amelia; *ed:* (BS) Zoology, 1979, (MS) Zoology, 1985 Brigham Young Univ; *cr:* Bio Teacher Whitehorse HS 1981-84, Dixie HS 1985-; *ai:* Sci Fair, Sci Club, NHS, Soph Class Adv; Sci Dept Head; NABT; *home:* PO Box 418 Santa Clara UT 84765

HUNT, SANDRA LEE (CIOTTI), Spanish/French/German Teacher; *b:* Salem, OH; *m:* John V. Jr.; *c:* Amy L.; *ed:* (BSED) Span, Kent St Univ 1970; Fr/Italian, 1978, Ger, 1980 Coll of Du Page; *cr:* Span Teacher Nordonia Hills HS 1971-76; Span/Italian Teacher Rolling Meadows HS 1976-80; Span Teacher Charlotte Sch Dist 1981-87; Span/Fr Teacher Georgetown HS 1987-; *ai:* Foreign Lang Dist Wkshp Coord; SC Teacher Forum; Academic Competition Team Coach; Natl Span Honor Society, Natl Fr Honor Society Adv; Academic Seminar; Fr Club Adv; Knowledge Masters Open Coach; Prin Incentive Prgm; Substitute Teacher Manual Task Force; Amer Assn of Teachers of Span & Portuguese 1975-; AATF 1987-; Amer Assn of Teachers of Italian 1980; Delta Kappa Gamma 1990; Georgetown Cty Sch Dist Teacher of Yr, Georgetown HS Teacher of Yr, Blue Ribbon Teacher 1989-; Cadet Pet Teacher 1988-; Role Model Teacher for Prgm for Effective Teaching; Named to SC Dept of Ed Evaluation Team of Coll & Univ 1988-; Jennings Scholar 1975; Magazine Articles Published; *office:* Georgetown HS 2500 North St Georgetown SC 29440

HUNT, SHARON (MYERS), English/Speech Teacher; *b:* Alton, IL; *m:* Dennis D.; *c:* Daron; *ed:* (BS) Speech, S IL Edwardsville 1963; *cr:* Eng/Speech Teacher Roxana Jr HS 1963-; *ai:* Rdng Comm; NEA, IEA, Roxana Ed Assn; *home:* 157 Rosewood Ln East Alton IL 62024

HUNT, SHIRLEY, Spanish Teacher; *b:* Newark, NJ; *m:* Theodore; *c:* Janice, Theodore Jr.; *ed:* (BA) Span, Rutgers Univ Coll 1976; Grad Prgm, Kean Coll NJ; Public Sch Supvr/Admin; *cr:* Teacher of Span Orange HS 1978-; Adult Ed Coord Ministry of Ed 1984-86; Producer of Educl Radio Prgm Peace Corps 1985-86; *ai:* Frosh, Soph, Jr, Sr Class Adv 1980-84; Intnl Club Adv 1989; Pres Black Peace Corps Volunteers 1984-85; Black Returned Peace Corps Volunteers Assn Mem; Alpha Sigma Lambda-Beta Zeta Chapter Mem-Rutgers Univ 1976-; *office:* Orange H S 400 Lincoln Ave Orange NJ 07050

HUNT, SUSAN CONWAY, English Teacher; *b:* Cincinnati, OH; *m:* Anthony; *c:* Julianne, Christopher; *ed:* (BA) Fr/His, Univ of Toronto 1963; (MA) Guidance/Counseling, Univ of NM 1968; (MA) Linguistics, San Diego St Univ 1980; *cr:* Teacher US Peace Corps Nigeria 1963-65; Dist Dir Campfire Girls Albuquerque 1966-68; Teacher Waterville Jr HS 1969-72, Univ of Wroclaw Poland 1975-76; Fulbright Lecturer Univ of Osijek Yugoslavia 1986-87; Teacher SESO 1973-; *ai:* Eng Drama Club; Model United Nations Moderator; Spelling Bee & 7th-12th Grade Eng Curr Coord; NCTE 1988-; TESOL PR 1987-; Coll Eng Assn 1986-; Natl NEH Endowment for Hum 1984-88; Fulbright Jr Lectureship Yugoslavia 1986-87; Articles Published; *office:* SESO P O Box 40 Mayaguez PR 00709

HUNTE, RUTH ALICE, Science Dept Chairperson; *b:* Greenville, OH; *m:* Havelock E.; *c:* Esther J., Jonathan L.; *ed:* (BS) Elem Ed, Manchester Coll 1962; (MA) Sch Admin, Roosevelt Univ 1972; Physics, Cleveland St Univ & Case Western Univ; Admin, Kent St Univ & Syracuse Univ; Sci, Cleveland St Univ; *cr:* 3rd Grade Teacher Meadowwood Sch 1962-63; K-8th Grade Teacher Chicago Bd of Ed 1965-72; 8th Grade Teacher Channahon Sch 1973-74; 7th-9th Grade Sci Teacher Cleveland Public Schls 1979-; *ai:* Sch Newspaper, Academic Action Team, Spelling Bee, Sci Fair, Cmptr Club, Black His Team, Sci Olympiad Team, Math Club Adv; NSTA 1985-; Regional Sci Teachers 1983-; Sci Olympiad Regional Dir 1986-; GSA (Leader, Adv) 1983-89; Foster Parent 1975-79; League of Women Voters 1975-80; PTA Treas 1972; Cleveland Ed Fnd Awd 1989-; Teacher Cadre 1982-85; *office:* Empire Jr HS 9113 Parmalee Ave Cleveland OH 44108

HUNTER, CHARLOTTE WILLIAMS, 1st Grade Teacher; *b:* Pasadena, CA; *m:* Jack L. II; *c:* Brandon; *ed:* (BA) Eng/Speech, Occidental Coll 1968; Univ Laverne 1971; *cr:* 4th Grade Teacher Palm View Sch 1973-74; 1st-2nd Grade Teacher Washington Sch 1974-78; 1st-2nd Castle Rock Elem Sch 1978-79; 1st-2nd Maple Hill Sch 1979-; *ai:* Disater Comm Chm; SIP Ldrsp Team; Webb Affiliates Assemblies Chm 1988-89; Cinders 1979-; Presbyn Church Elder/Deacon 1973-77; Teacher of Yr 1989; Article Publ CA St Text; *office:* Maple Hill Elem Sch 1350 S Maple Hill Rd Diamond Bar CA 91765

HUNTER, CYNTHIA LEE, Home Economics Teacher; *b:* Minneapolis, MN; *m:* John Luther; *c:* Sarah, Jenny; *ed:* (BS) Home Ec Ed, Univ of MN St Paul 1978; *cr:* Home Ec Teacher Mounds View Sr HS 1978-79, Maple Lake Sr HS 1979-80, Valley Mid Sch 1980-85, Rosemount Sr HS 1985-; *ai:* Home Ec Curr Comm; Rosemount Ed Assn (Rep Cncl 1986-, Grievance Comm Chairperson 1990-); MN Cncl of Family Relations, Amer Home Ec Assn, MN Home Ec Assn 1990; *office:* Rosemount HS 3335 142nd St W Rosemount MN 55068

HUNTER, FRANCES RAMSEY, Science Teacher; *b:* Madisonville, VA; *m:* William Allen Sr.; *c:* William Jr., Martha E., Charlotte L.; *ed:* (BS) Bio/Chem, 1952, (MS) Supervision, 1983 Longwood Coll; *cr:* Teacher Randolph-Henry HS 1961-65, Charlotte Elem Sch 1971-79, Central Mid Sch 1979-; *ai:* Coaching Girls Bsktbl Team; Chrldr & SCA Spon; Charlotte Cty Ed Assn Treas 1962-64; Presbyn Church Teacher; Red Cross Treas; Amer Legion Auxilliary 1987-; *home:* Rt 1 Box 471 Appomattox VA 24522

HUNTER, FRANK A., Speech Teacher & Theater Dir; *b:* Torrington, WY; *ed:* (BA) Tech Theater, Hastings Coll 1958; (MA) Speech Ed, Univ of NE 1962; *cr:* Teacher Gering HS 1958-61, Sterling HS 1965-; *ai:* Dept Coord; Theater Dir; CO Assn for Rural Ed, Theatre Ed Assn; BPOE, Master Mason, Amer Legion; Lions Secy; *office:* Sterling HS W Broadway Sterling CO 80751

HUNTER, JANE GRAY, 4th Grade Lang Arts Teacher; *b:* Allendale, SC; *m:* Richard E. Jr.; *c:* Richard E. III, Sallie Gray; *ed:* (BA) Elem Ed, Univ SC 1972; *cr:* Sci Teacher E L Wright Mid Sch 1972-73; Rdng Teacher Wagener Mid Sch 1973-74; Lang Arts Teacher Barnwell Elem Sch 1974-76; Eng Teacher Guinyard Butler Mid Sch 1977-78; Lang Arts Teacher Barnwell Elem Sch 1978-; *ai:* Evaluation/Placement Team Mem; Talented & Gifted Academic Prgm; Promotion/Retention Policy Comm Mem; Wildwood Garden Club (Pres & Secy); Winton Assembly; Natl Society Magna Charta Dames; *office:* Barnwell Elem Sch Marlbaro Ave Barnwell SC 29812

HUNTER, JON ROBERT, Social Studies Teacher; *b:* Detroit, MI; *m:* Mary Louise; *c:* Jordan D.; *ed:* (BA) Poly Sci, Wayne St Univ 1970; Grad Stud His & Philosophy of Ed; *cr:* Soc Stud Teacher Ferndale HS 1971, Troy HS 1971-74, Athens HS 1975-82; Sci Teacher Smith Mid Sch 1983-85; Soc Stud Teacher Athens HS 1985-; *ai:* Soc Stud Club, Citizen Bee, Sesquicentenniel Sch, Ecology Club & Nursing Home Visitation Spon; *office:* Athens HS 4333 John R Troy MI 48098

HUNTER, MARILYN ENYARD, Fourth Grade Teacher; *b:* Glasgow, MO; *c:* Tyrone; *ed:* (BA) Elem Ed, Lincoln Univ of MO 1965; (MA) Vocational Tech Ed, Univ of IL 1980; Career Guidance Inservice Trng/Resources/Materials; *cr:* Primary Teacher Thomas Edison Elem Sch 1965-67; Primary/Intermediate Teacher Ludwig Van Beethoven Elem Sch 1967-77; Intermediate Teacher Mary Lyon Elem Sch 1977-; *ai:* Prof Problems Comm; Soc Comm; Instructional Materials Comm Chairperson; 4th Grade Majorette Instr; Summer Sch Music Production; Chicago Teachers Union 1967-; Black Teachers Caucus 1977-; AFT 1967-; Alpha Kappa Alpha; Pilot Teacher-Holt Basic Rdng System; Commendation for Stu Performace-WBEZ Radio Chicago; Gold Apple Awd-Dist 4 Mary Lyon Sch; *home:* 6020 S Stony Island #2s Chicago IL 60637

HUNTER, NANCY CROCKER, English Teacher; *b:* Pueblo, CO; *m:* Randy L.; *c:* Diana, Christie; *ed:* (BA) Eng Ed, Univ of N CO 1980; (MA) Guidance & Counseling, Adams St Coll 1990; *cr:* Fr/Eng Teacher Montezuma-Cortez HS 1980-85, Fruita Monument HS 1985-; *ai:* CO Congress Foreign Lang Teachers 1980-; NCTE 1980-.

HUNTER, NANCY SUE, Math Department Chairperson; *b:* Lake City, FL; *ed:* (AA) Young Harris Coll 1956; (BS) Ed, FL Southern 1958; (MED) Math Ed , MS Univ 1979; *cr:* Eng & Math Teacher Lake City Jr HS 1959-70; Cmptr Prog Columbia Cty Schls 1970-73; Math Teacher Richardson 9th Grade Ctr 1973-75; Columbia HS 1975-; *ai:* Math Dept Chm; Columbia Teachers Assn Secy 1969; FL Teaching Prof; NEA; Awarded Methodist Schlsp 1956-57; *office:* Columbia HS P O Box 1869 Us 441 S Lake City FL 32056

HUNTER, ROBERT CHARLES, Art Teacher; *b:* Oakland, CA; *m:* Linda Spencer; *c:* Joel S.; *ed:* (BA) Art Ed, 1979, Art Ed, 1984 W WA Univ; Working Toward MED in Studio Art/Art Ed, W WA Univ; *cr:* Art Teacher Hopkins Jr HS 1979-80, Weatherwax HS 1980-; *ai:* Art Club Adv; Dept Head; WA Ed Assn 1979-; WA Art Ed Assn 1980-; Rhode Island Sch of Design Schlsp 1986; Childrens Mural Comm Co-Chm 1989 & Governors Certificate; Nom WA St Awd for Teaching Excl Christa Mc Auliffe Awd 1987, 1989-; *office:* Weatherwax HS 414 North I St Aberdeen WA 98520

HUNTLEY, ANONA SAVAGE, Science Teacher; *b:* Jackson, TN; *m:* Floyd; *c:* Sheri, Christopher, Ashlei; *ed:* (BS) Bio, Lambuth Coll 1969; (MA) Ed, Montclair St Coll 1983; *cr:* Sci Teacher Seventh Ave Jr HS 1969-78, Barringer Prep 1978-; *ai:* Stu Cncl & Stu Leaders Adv; Soc & Welfare Comm Chairperson; NJ Sci Teachers, NSTA, Newark Teachers Union, AFT; *office:* Barringer Prep 63 Webster St Newark NJ 07104

HUNTLEY, JAMES BRYAN, Social Studies Teacher; *b:* Waynesburg, PA; *m:* Jamie Snyder; *c:* James, Jill, Jason, Jessica; *ed:* (BA) Soc Sci, IN Univ of PA 1970; (MA) His, Bloomsburg Univ of PA 1980; *cr:* Instr Columbia-Montour AVTS 1970-; *ai:* Head Girls Var Bsktbl & Boys Var Bsbl; *office:* Columbia-Montour Voc-Tech RD 5 Bloomsburg PA 17815

HUNTSINGER, JO ANNETTE, Teacher/Coach; *b:* El Dorado, KS; *ed:* (BSE) Health Ed/Bio/Phys Ed, KS Univ 1982; *cr:* Teacher/Coach Lawrence HS 1984-; *ai:* Jr Var Vlybl Coach; SADD Spon; NABT 1989; Outstanding SADD Chapter in KS 1989.

HUNTZINGER, JUNE CLIFFORD, Second Grade Teacher; *b:* Ashland, KY; *m:* Earl Junior; *c:* Diane Jane; *ed:* (AA) Elem Ed, Ashland Jr Coll 1957; (BS) Elem Ed, Anderson Univ 1962; (MA) Elem Ed, Morehead St Univ 1989; *cr:* 1st Grade Teacher Summit Elem 1957-59, Coll Corner Elem 1961-64; 3rd Grade Teacher Star Elem 1964; 1st Grade Teacher Summit Elem 1964-68; 2nd Grade Teacher Ironville Elem 1968-71, Summit Elem 1975-; *ai:* Elem Bsktbl Prgm-Official Scorekeeper/Official Timekeeper; Boyd Ed Assn Recording Secy 1965-66; KEA; NEA; Church of God (Sunday Sch Teacher, Supt, Music Dir, Soloist, Womens Society Pres, St Spiritual Life Dir, Youth Dir) 1954-; 1st VP of PTA 83-86; Pres of PTA 86-87; *home:* 4626 Roberts Dr Ashland KY 41101

HUNTZINGER, PENNEY MARIA (DIOLORDI), Language Art Dept Chair; *b:* Detroit, MI; *m:* Jonathan David; *ed:* (BA) Comm/Eng, Oral Roberts Univ 1984; *cr:* Eng/Speech Teacher Jenks HS 1984-85; Eng/Speech/Drama Teacher 1986-88, Lang Art Dept Chairperson 1988- Victory Chrstn Sch; *ai:* Theater Dir; Speech & Debate Coach; Sr Class & Stu Missions Spon; Staff Dev Comm; NCTE 1989-; Whos Who Among Amer Univ Stus 1984; Outstanding Teacher of Yr 1987-89; *office:* Victory Chrstn Sch 7700 S Lewis Tulsa OK 74163

HUPPENBAUER, PATRICIA BREUER, Home Economics Teacher; *b:* Burlington, IA; *m:* Thomas R.; *c:* Sarah, Annie, Ellen; *ed:* (AA) SE IA Comm Coll 1971; (BSE) Home Ec, NE MO St Univ 1973; *cr:* Home Ec Teacher James Madison Mid Sch 1978-; Part Time Sci Teacher Apollo 1975-78; Substitute Teacher Burlington Sch Dist 1974-75; *ai:* Crisis Team; Stu at Risk; Mid Sch Subcomm; Burlington Ed Assn, NEA 1977-; *office:* James Madison Mid Sch 2132 Madison Ave Burlington IA 52601

HURBEAN, JEAN MARY, Second Grade Teacher; *b:* Barberton, OH; *ed:* (BS) Elem Ed, 1971, (MS) Elem Admin, 1984 Univ of Akron; *cr:* 2nd Grade Teacher Hazelwood Elem 1973-80, Portage Elem 1980-; *ai:* Elem Asst Prin; Safety Patrol Adv; Delta Kappa Gamma (Corresponding Secy 1986-88, Recording Secy 1990); Phi Lamda Theta, Phi Delta Kappa; Magic City Kiwanis 1989-.

HURCKES, DORENE ALLEN, Principal; *b:* Chicago, IL; *m:* Michal F.; *c:* Alexandra, Jennifer; *ed:* (BSED) Elem Ed, De Paul Univ 1971; (MA) Supervision/Adm, Saint Xavier Coll 1988; Grad Stud Rdng; *cr:* 1st Grade Teacher 1971-73, Kndgtn Teacher 1974-89, Prin 1988- St Barbara Elem; *ai:* Archdiocese of Chicago Prins Planning Comm for the Regionalization of Cath Schls; Sch Evaluation Team Mem; Archdiocese of Chicago Confirmation Team Mem St Barbara Parish; NCEA 1971-; ASCD 1986-; RASC Swim Club Pres 1986-89; RAF Swim Club Publicity 1989-; IL St Grant 1968-71; Outstanding Young Woman in America 1983; Mayor Daley Schlsp 1968; Sisters of Mercy Schlsp 1986-88; Natl Deans List Natl Collegiate Awd 1988; *office:* Saint Barbara Elem Sch 2867 S Throop St Chicago IL 60608

HURD, BARBARA STEVENS, Mathematics Teacher/Dept Chair; *b:* Corning, NY; *m:* Richard C.; *c:* Paul R., Erin J., Amy E.; *ed:* (BS) Scndry Math, SUNY Brockport 1970; Grad Stud Scndry Math, SUNY Brockport; *cr:* 9th Grade Math Teacher Gates Chili Cntrl Sch 1970; 7th-8th Grade Math Teacher Albion Cntrl Sch 1970-79; 10th-12th Grade Math Teacher 1979-, Dept Chairperson 1986- Addison Jr/Sr HS; *ai:* Key Club Adv; GED Adult Ed Prgm Instr; APEX Sch Improvement Comm; BSA (Comm Chairperson, Commissioner) 1983-89; GSA Asst Leader 1987-; 4-H Club (Asst Leader, Leader) 1984-; Church Choir 1985-; *office:* Addison Jr Sr HS 1 Colwell St Addison NY 14801

HURD, MICHAEL DON, US History Teacher; *b:* Superior, NE; *m:* Rita Marlene; *c:* Jeremy, Jarrod; *ed:* (AA) General Ed, Cloud Cty Comm Jr Coll 1970; (BS) Scndry Ed, TN Temple Coll 1979; (MA) Scndry Admin, Univ of MO Kansas City 1987; *cr:* Jr/Sr HS Sci Teacher Tri-City Chrstn Schls 1979-; *ai:* HS Discipline Coord; Transportation Dir; Asst Var Bsktbl Coach; *office:* Tri-City Chrstn Schls 4500 S Selsa Rd Blue Springs MO 64015

HURDLE, JAMES WALTER, 7th Grade English Teacher; *b:* Waterbury, CT; *m:* Sheila Ann Sockwell; *c:* James C., Matthew D., Mark A.; *ed:* (BS) Elem Ed, 1974, (MS) Rdng, 1980 Cntrl CT St Univ; Alliance Theological Seminary, Nyack Coll; *cr:* 3rd/4th Grade Teacher Walsh Elem 1974-76; 8th Grade Sci Teacher Maplewood Elem 1976-81; 6th/8th Grade Sci Teacher Blackham Elem & Wilbur Cross 1981-83; 3rd/5th Grade Teacher E Farms Elem & Hopeville Elem 1983-85; 7th Grade Eng Teacher North End Mid Sch 1985-; *ai:* Waterbury Teachers Assn 1974-76, CT Ed Assn 1983-; Zion Baptist Church Deacon 1982-, Man of Yr 1984; Gideons Intnl Living Memorial Bible Plan Co-Chm 1989; North End Cmmty Tutorial Prgm 1989-, Outstanding Dedication & Service Role Model 1990; *office:* North End Mid Sch 460 Bucks Hill Rd Waterbury CT 06704

HURLBERT, MICHAEL RAY, Soc Stud/English/Rdng Teacher; *b:* Mt Vernon, WA; *m:* Sally J.; *c:* Lisa R.; *ed:* (BA) Ed/Music, Western WA SC 1972; Prof Ed Certificate 1977; *cr:* Music Teacher Port Gardner Mid Sch 1973-80, North Mid Sch 1980-81, Eisenhower Mid Sch 1981-88; Block Teacher Eisenhower Mid 1988-; *ai:* Ftbl Coach 1972-; Wrstlng Coach 1983-; Stu Cncl Adv 1989-; EEA 1973-; *office:* Eisenhower Mid Sch 2500 100th Se Everett WA 98208

HURLBURT, RUTH HASS, 7th/8th Language Arts Teacher; *b:* La Crosse, WI; *m:* Wesley Winsor; *c:* Ann M.; *ed:* (BS) Eng/Music, Univ of WI La Crosse 1965; Lang Art, Drug & Alcohol Trng; Mid Level Ed; *cr:* 7th-9th Grade Eng/Music Teacher Dr S G Knight Public 1965-67; 7th-9th Grade Music/10th Grade Eng Teacher Onalaska Jr/Sr HS 1967-70; K-6th Grade Music Teacher Fauver Hill Elem 1970-71; 7th-9th Grade Eng/Music Teacher Onalaska Jr/Sr HS 1971-72; 7th/8th Grade Eng Teacher Onalaska Mid Sch 1972-; *ai:* Solo-Ensemble Contest Accompanist; NCTE 1980-89; NEA 1965-; WI Ed Assn 1967-; WI Assn for Mid Level Educators 1985-; Delta Kappa Gamma Pres 1990; Order of Eastern Star Worthy Matron 1972-73; Youth for Understanding Intnl Exch Area Rep 1989-; WAMLE Convention Presenter 1989; Midwest WI Rdng Cncl Presenter 1989, 1990; Poetry Published; *office:* Onalaska Mid Sch 711 Quincy St Onalaska WI 54650

HURLEY, CAROL ANN (HELLER), First Grade Teacher; *b:* White Plains, NY; *m:* William L. Jr.; *c:* Andrew, Jonathan; *ed:* (AA) Early Chldhd Ed, S Seminary Jr Coll 1972; (BA) Early Chldhd Ed, Lynchburg Coll 1975; *cr:* 2nd Grade Teacher 1975-76, 1980-81, 1st Grade Teacher 1981-82, 1986-87, 2nd Grade Teacher 1987-88, 1st Grade Teacher 1988-, Otter River Elem; *ai:* Effective Sch Comm; NEA 1975-; Bedford Cty Ed Assn Alternate Rep 1987-88.

HURLEY, CAROL PROVOST, Business Education Teacher; *b:* Sault Ste Marie, MI; *m:* John W.; *c:* W. M., John Jr.; *ed:* Assoc Bus Management, Katharine Gibbs Sch 1962; (BS) Bus Management/Ed, Notre Dame 1980; *cr:* Asst to VP HD Nottingham Assn 1962-64; Bus Educator Trinity HS 1980-; *ai:* Trinity HS Adv; NHS & FBLA Trinity HS Faculty Cncl; NH Bus Ed Assn, NE Bus Ed Assn, Eastern Bus Ed Assn, NBEA; Fund Cmptrs for Bus Ed Local Grant; *office:* Trinity HS 581 Bridge St Manchester NH 03104

HURLEY, DIANA HUNT, 6th Grade Teacher; *b:* Salt Lake City, UT; *m:* Gerald Gordon; *c:* Blaine L., Shawn E., Teresa, Corinne Johnson; *ed:* (BS) Elem Ed, Brigham Young Univ 1957; *cr:* 5th Grade Teacher Glendale Park Elem 1957-59, W Kearns Elem 1959-62; Music Specialist/Teacher David Gourley Elem 1969-75; 5th/6th Grade Teacher S Kearns, Western Hills, Beehive 1980-; *ai:* Building Comm, Grade Level Chm; Career Incentive Teacher; Delta Kappa Gamma 1982-; *office:* Beehive Elem Sch 5655 S 5220 W Kearns UT 84118

HURLEY, ELLEN MARIE, 4th Grade Teacher; *b:* Springfield, MA; *ed:* (BA) Sociology, Elms Coll 1974; Working Towards Masters Educl Admin; *cr:* Chapter I Teacher 1975-76, 4th Grade Teacher 1976- Brightwood Sch; *ai:* Brightside Corporator; ASCD 1989-; MA Teachers Assn 1975-; *office:* Brightwood Sch 471 Plainfield St Springfield MA 01107

HURLEY, INA WORTH, Fifth Grade Teacher; *b:* Jefferson, NC; *m:* Benjamin Gale Sr.; *c:* Benjamin Gale Jr. *ed:* (BS) Elem Ed, Appalachian St Teachers Coll 1956; (MA) Mid Sch Appalachian St Univ 1977; *cr:* 7th Grade Teacher Fleetwood Elem Sch 1956-59; 3rd Grade Teacher 1959-63, 5th Grade Teacher 1969- Jefferson Elem Sch; *ai:* Sch Newspaper Co-Editor; Media Comm; Stu Teacher Supervisor; NCAE Treas 1957-58; NCAE, NEA; Jeffersons Jr Womens VP; Ladies Golf Club Assn Pres; United Meth Women Pres; *office:* Jefferson Elem Sch W Main St Jefferson NC 28640

HURLEY, JAMES RAY, Chemistry/Physics Teacher; *b:* Boone, IA; *m:* Janet Kaye Carlson; *c:* Timothy J., Staci L.; *ed:* (BSE) Physics, Drake Univ 1972; (MA) Ed, Univ of N IA 1982; Grad Stud Chemical Ed, Wartburg Coll; *cr:* Teacher Waverly-Shell Rock HS 1973-; Asst Professor Univ of N IA 1988-; *ai:* Performance Based Pay Comm; IA Acad of Sci 1988-, Physics Teacher of Yr 1989; AAPT IA VP 1973-; NEA, IA St Ed Assn 1973-; IA Physics Task Force Curr Dev; *office:* Waverly-Shell Rock HS 4th Ave SW Waverly IA 50677

HURLEY, MARTHA CAROL, English Teacher; *b:* Douglas, GA; *ed:* (BA) Eng, La Grange Coll 1980; (MED) Sec Ed/Eng, Valdosta St Coll 1989; *cr:* Teacher Jeff Davis HS 1980-; *ai:* United Meth Women VP 1982-; *office:* Jeff Davis H S Broxton Rd Hazlehurst GA 31539

HURM, JUDY (PAYNE), Fourth Grade Teacher; *b:* Owensboro, KY; *m:* Roger Dale; *c:* Christopher, Darrell; *ed:* (BA) Elem Ed, Brescia Coll 1973; (MS) Elem Ed, W KY Univ 1979; *cr:* 4th/5th Grade Teacher Grayson Cty Schls 1973-74; 3rd/4th Grade Teacher St Alphonsus Sch 1974-80; 5th Grade Teacher St Stephens Sch 1980-81; 4th Grade Teacher St Mary of the Woods 1981-; *ai:* Stu Cncl Spon; *office:* St Mary of the Woods Sch 10521 Franklin St Whitesville KY 42378

HURST, LARRY WADE, 8th Grade English Teacher; *b:* Hamblen Cty, TN; *m:* Letha; *c:* Jennifer, Amy; *ed:* (BS) Eng, Univ of TN 1975; (MA) Elem Ed, Union Coll KY 1986; *cr:* Teacher Hillcrest Elem; Teacher/Coach Lincoln Mid Sch & West View Mid Sch; *ai:* Bsktbl Coach; MEA, TEA, NTEA; *home:* 722 Barbara Dr Talbott TN 37877

HURST, MARSHA OWINGS, Third Grade Teacher; *b:* St Louis, MO; *m:* Ronald Dean; *c:* Jill Christine, Amy Lynn; *ed:* (BS) Elem Ed, Northwest MO St Univ 1970; *cr:* 2nd Grade Teacher Amazonia Elem 1970-71; 1st/5th Grade Teacher Potosi Elem 1971-73; 1st Grade Teacher 1974-76; 2nd/3rd Grade Teacher 1978- SM Rissler Elem; *ai:* Co-Chm Rissler Staff Fund; Trenton Teachers Assn 1978-; PTO VP 1978-; Chapter MN PEO Corresponding Secy 1987-; *home:* 210 Town & Co Ln Trenton MO 64683

HURST, SUSAN HEINRICH, 6th Grade Rdng/English Teacher; *b:* Saint Louis, MO; *m:* William Floyd; *c:* Scott, Kelly; *ed:* (BA) Elem Ed, 1965, (MED) Elem Admin, 1979 Drury; *cr:* Teacher Ozark Elem Sch 1964-69, Logan Rogersville Mid Sch 1969-72/1975-89; *ai:* MSTA Secy 1965-89; PTA 1965-89; *office:* Logan-Rogersville Mid Sch 208 212 Mill St Rogersville MO 65742

HUSBAND, CLAUDINE CLARK, Science Teacher; *b:* Laurel, MS; *ed:* (BS) Bio, MS Valley St Univ 1968; (MS) Geology, Univ of Houston 1971; Addl Stud, Jackson St Univ, Alcorn A&M St Univ, Cleveland St Univ; *cr:* Sci Teacher MS Sch Systems 1968-70, E Cleveland Bd of Ed 1971-73, Warrensville Bd of Ed 1973-74, Cleveland Bd of Ed 1974-81; United St Army Reserve 1975-77; Sci Teacher Cleveland Bd of Ed 1988-; *ai:* Marathon Holding Jenning 1976; *home:* 3286 E 143rd St Cleveland OH 44120

HUSER, BILLIE, Fifth Grade Teacher; *b:* Tolu, KY; *m:* John R.; *c:* Lori Hoff, Eric; *ed:* (BS) Elem Ed, 1970, (MS) Elem Ed, 1974 Bradley Univ; Grad Work Elem Ed; *cr:* Kndgtn Teacher Germantown Hills 1957-58; 7th Grade Teacher Oak Grove W 1970; Jr HS Teacher 1970-80, Elem Teacher 1980- District 50; *home:* 209 Regal Ln East Peoria IL 61611

HUSHEK, JOSEPH CHARLES, Math/Science Div Chairperson; *b:* Milwaukee, WI; *m:* Kathleen Louise Mc Fall; *ed:* (BA) Chem, Occidental Coll 1976; *cr:* Teacher 1977-, Dept Chm 1984-, Mentor Teacher 1985, Division Chm 1986- Selma HS; *ai:* Academic Decathalon Coach; Jr Class & CSF Adv; CA Sci Teachers Assn, Cntrl CA Sci Teachers Assn; Mentor Teacher; Division Chairperson for Math, Sci; *office:* Selma HS 3125 Wright Selma CA 93662

HUSKINS, CATHERINE JOAN, English Teacher; *b:* Toledo, OH; *ed:* (BE) Int Comm, 1982, (ME) Scndry Ed, 1988 Univ of Toledo; *cr:* Teacher Evergreen HS 1983-; P/T Faculty Univ of Toledo Comm & Tech Coll 1989-; *ai:* Adv Newspaper; Jennings Scholar; *office:* Evergreen HS 14544 Co Rd 6 Metamora OH 43540

HUSMANN, LU ANN FINK, Second Grade Teacher; *b:* Grundy Center, IA; *m:* James A.; *c:* Annika, Mitchell; *ed:* (BA) Elem Ed/Rdng, Univ of N IA 1977; *cr:* Remedial Rdng Teacher Lien Elem Sch 1978-79; 6th Grade Teacher 1979-84, 2nd Grade Teacher 1984- Lincoln Sch; *ai:* CFEA, ISEA, NEA; *office:* Lincoln Sch 7th And Franklin Sts Cedar Falls IA 50613

HUSON, JIM E., Freshman US History Teacher; *b:* Eugene, OR; *m:* Dawn L.; *c:* Chelsea; *ed:* (BS) Phys Ed/Soc Stud, Evangel Coll 1983; Working Towards Masters Phys Ed, Drury Coll; *cr:* Grad Asst Univ of OR 1983-84; Teacher/Coach Republic HS 1985-; *ai:* Var Asst, Jr Var Head Coach Ftbl.

HUSS, JOHANNA C., Mathematics Teacher; *b:* St Bartholomeh, Yugoslavia; *c:* Edward J. Jr., Joan Huss Davis; *ed:* (BS) Math, SUNY Coll Buffalo 1963; Grad Stud Buffalo St, Nova Univ, Univ S FL; *cr:* Math Teacher Cleveland Hill HS1963-64, Genesee-Humboldt Jr HS 1964-67, Clewiston HS 1977-; *ai:* Math

Club & Mu Alpha Theta Spon; NCTM; FL Cncl Teachers of Math; Delta Kappa Gamma 2nd VP 1990; Actors Cmmty Theatre; *office:* Clewiston HS 1501 S Francisco St Clewiston FL 33440

HUSS, SALLY HUTCHINSON, Jr HS Mathematics Teacher; *b:* Huntington, WV; *m:* Charles; *c:* Jane A., Sara; *ed:* (AB) Elem Ed, 1972, (MA) Elem Ed, 1977 Marshall Univ; *cr:* Math Teacher Ceredo Kenova HS 1972-76; Grad Asst Marshall Univ 1976-77; Math Teacher Maysville Jr HS 1982-; *ai:* Mathcounts Team Coach; Jr HS Stu Cncl Spon; MEA, KEA, NEA; Trinity Luth Church; *home:* Rt 5 Box 374A Maysville KY 41056

HUSSA, EDWIN F., Mathematics Department Teacher; *b:* Bryn Mawr, PA; *m:* Sarah Reese; *c:* Emily, Ben; *ed:* (BA) Math/Ec, Cornell Univ 1970; (MA) Math Ed, SUNY Albany 1972; *cr:* Math Teacher Warwick HS 1972-74, Kaiserslautern HS 1974-76; Math Teacher/Dept Head Glens Falls HS 1976-; *ai:* Tennis Coach; Math & Quiz Team Adv; NY Assn of Math Teachers 1976-; *office:* Glens Falls HS Quade St Glens Falls NY 12801

HUSTO, DIANN JANE WILLIAMSON, High School Art Teacher; *b:* Columbus, OH; *m:* Paul Edward; *c:* Clarissa J., Amber D.; *ed:* (BA) Art Ed, Harding Univ 1970; (MAED) Teaching Competency, Coll of Mt St Joseph 1988; Fine Art, Capital Univ; Art Ed, OH St Univ; *cr:* Eng/Art Teacher Reynoldsburg Mid Sch 1970-72; Art Teacher Reynoldsburg HS 1972-; *ai:* Art Club Adv; Spon Travel Ed Trip To NYC; Mem Sch Curr Cncl; Prin Advisory Comm; Effective Schls Team; REA 1970-, Teacher of Yr 1988; OEA, COTA, NEA 1970-; OAEA 1970-, Nom OH Art Teacher of Yr 1983, Outstanding Art Teacher 1990; GSA Troop Leader 1987-; Grove City Cruisers 1988-; Alkire Road Church of Christ Comms Chairperson 1980-; Ft Hill Chrstn Youth Camp Craft Dir 1987-, Ft Hills Finest Awd 1989; *home:* 3434 Park Ridge Dr Grove City OH 43123

HUTAFF, FLORA GILBERT, Teacher; *b:* Erwin, NC; *w:* Charles D. III (dec); *c:* Chuck, Tom, Marc; *ed:* (BA) Early Chldhd, Elon Coll 1953; *cr:* Part-Time Remedial Rdng Teacher Mary Stewart 1971; 2nd Grade Teacher Magnolia Sch 1972-85, Harnett Primary 1985; *home:* 410 S General Lee Ave Dunn NC 28334

HUTCHENS, MIKE, 8th Grade English Teacher; *b:* Billings, MT; *m:* Janice; *c:* Emily, Rachel; *ed:* (BS) Eng, Univ of TX Austin 1974; *cr:* Teacher/Coach Kenmare HS 1975-76, Evans Jr HS 1977-; *ai:* 8th Grade Ftbl & Track Coach; *office:* Evans Jr HS 4211 58th St Lubbock TX 79413

HUTCHENS, PATRICIA W., Biology Teacher; *b:* Gadsden, AL; *m:* Wesley E.; *c:* Kristie L., Joshua; *ed:* (BS) Bio/Phys Ed, 1970, (MS) Ed, 1974 Jacksonville St Univ; Sea Lab; Prof Dev Act; Travel; *cr:* Anatomy/Bio/AP Bio Teacher Etowah HS 1971-; *ai:* Gymnastics Coach; Prom, Homecoming & Sch Clubs; Work with Natl Competition Cheerleading; NEA, AEA, EEA, PAAE, Gadsden Art Assn; AL Watercolor Society Membership 1989; Kappa Delta Epsilon; John Croyles Boys Ranch Supporter; Heart Assn, Cystic Fibrosis, Cmmty Ed Prgm, PTA; - Nom Presidential Awd for Excl in Sci 1984-86; Nom Attalla City Teacher of Yr; James B Allen Outstanding Coll Stu; *office:* Etowah HS 316 Jones St Attalla AL 35954

HUTCHESON, KIRK STEVEN, Science Teacher; *b:* Lewiston, ID; *c:* Ryan, Lisa; *ed:* (BS) Zoology, Univ of ID 1975; *cr:* Sci Teacher Gooding HS 1975-76; 7th Grade Life Sci/8th Grade Phys Sci Teacher Sacajawea Jr HS 1977-; *ai:* Lewis-Clark Regional Sci & Engineering Fair Bd of Dir 1980-; 9th Grade Girls Vlybl Coach; ID Educl Assn, NEA, Lewiston Educl Assn 1979-; *office:* Sacajawea Jr HS 3610 12th St Lewiston ID 83501

HUTCHINGS, DONALOU NELSON, Scndry Eng/Rdng Teacher; *b:* Fergus Falls, MN; *m:* Robert L.; *c:* Kris Larson, Timothy, Larry, Ricky, Michael; *ed:* (BA) Eng/Speech Scndry Ed, Univ of MN Morris 1974, 1975; Grad & Undergraduate Level Courses in Writing & Related Areas *cr:* Eng/Rdng Lit Teacher Evansville Public HS 1975-; *ai:* Teaching Writing & Research Skills Preparing Stus for Coll; Presbyn Church Active Mem; *office:* Evansville HS 123 2nd Ave Evansville MN 56326

HUTCHINGS, FAYE MARIE, Kindergarten Teacher; *b:* Chappell, NE; *m:* Roger H.; *c:* Gregory, Nancy, Brent; *ed:* (BA) Elem Ed, NE Wesleyan Univ 1956; *cr:* Kndgtn Asst Park Elem 1954-56; Kndgtn Teacher Westgate Sch 1956-60, Kirkland Elem 1960-61, Wilson Elem 1979-; *ai:* Endowment Comm Chairperson; Wilson Sch Sch-Bus Partner Comm Mem; Medford Ed Assn (Communications Comm Chairperson 1985-87) 1979-; Citizen of Month 1988; Delta Kappa Gamma 1986-; PEO (Secy, Chaplain) 1968-; Dist Feasibility Study (Kndgtn Comm Chairperson 1973-74, Artists in Sch Comm 1970-73); Curr Cncl (Chairperson 1983-84, Secy) 1980-86; United Way Chairperson 1980-81.

HUTCHINS, CAROL E., Third Grade Teacher; *b:* Rochester, NY; *ed:* (BA) Math/Ed, 1961, (MS) Ed, 1966 SUC Brockport; Staff Dev; *cr:* Kndgtn/3rd-4th Grade Teacher/Team Leader W Ridge Sch & Greece Cntrl 1961-80; 3rd Grade Teacher/Team Leader Holmes Road Sch 1980-87, Buckman Heights Sch 1987-; *ai:* 3rd Grade Unit Facilitator; Staff Dev Mgr; NEA Elem Soc Stud Teacher of Yr 1989; NYSTA; GTA Recording Secy 1970; Natl Geog Society, Seneca Zoological Society; Rochester Museum Sci Center; *office:* Buckman Heights Sch 550 Buckman Rd Rochester NY 14615

HUTCHINS, TERA L., Science Teacher; *b:* Columbus, OH; *ed:* (BS) Sci Ed, OH St Univ 1985; *cr:* Instr Covington HS 1987-; *ai:* Sci Olympiad & 7th Grade Girls Bsktbl Coach; Sci Club & Class Adv; Instructional Cncl; Intervention Assistance Team; NSTA 1988-; Guest Speaker Optimists Club; *office:* Covington HS 807 Chestnut St Covington OH 45318

HUTCHINSON, CAROLYN BURNEY, Third Grade Teacher; *b:* Palatka, FL; *m:* William R.; *c:* Dru Dehart, William, Janel; *ed:* (BS) Elem, Tift Coll 1958; *cr:* 2nd Grade Teacher Fairlawn Elem 1958-60; 3rd Grade Teacher Ft Pierce Elem 1963; Lawnwood Elem 1963-; *ai:* St Luice Cty Classroom Teachers 1958-; Kappa Kappa Iota Zeta (Pres 1967-68 Mem 1964-70); St Lucie Cattlewomen Pres 1982-83; St Lucie Cty Fair (Womans World Chairperson 1986-88 Bd of Dir 1981-82); Order of Eastern Stars 1973-; Parkview Bapt Church 1948-; *office:* Lawnwood Elem Sch 1900 S 23rd St Fort Pierce FL 34950

HUTCHINSON, GRETCHEN HUDSON, History/Spanish Teacher; *b:* Newport News, VA; *m:* Rod; *c:* Holly, Heather; *ed:* (BS) Ed/Soc Stud, Appalachian St Univ 1973; Span, Univ of AL Birmingham; *cr:* 9th-12th Grade His Teacher Avery Cty HS 1973-75; 7th/8th Grade His/Sci Teacher Newland Elem 1975-76; 6th-8th Grade His/Sci/Math Teacher Arden Cahill Acad 1978-80; 9th-12th Grade His/Span Teacher Cathedral Chrstn Sch 1980-; *ai:* Sr Class, SGA, Span Club Spon; Air Force Recruiting Service Certificate of Appreciation; Yrbk Dedication 1985; *office:* Cathedral Chrstn Sch 1401 Huffman Rd Birmingham AL 35215

HUTCHINSON, JOHN STEVE, 5th Grade Teacher; *b:* Alhambra, CA; *m:* Edith Laura Hughes; *c:* John S., Craig A.; *ed:* (AA) Ed, Palomar Coll 1956; (BA) Ed, San Diego St Univ 1958; (MA) Ed, US Intnl Univ 1975; Clinical Teaching Coach Cognitive Level Teaching Strategies; Ethics; Holestics Lang Art; Human Behavior; Assertive Disipline; Outdoor Ed; His; Yearound Operational Courses; Conservation; *cr:* 5th Grade Teacher Cntrl Sch 1958, Felicita Sch 1966; 6th Grade Team Leader Miller Sch 1971; 2nd/3rd Grade Combination Teacher 1980, 5th/6th Grade Combination Teacher/5th Grade Teacher 1980- Oak Hill Sch; *ai:* Summer Sch Head Teacher; Playground Supvr City Parks & Recreation; Youth Bsbl Umpire; Scoutmaster; Merit Badge Cncl; Eagle Scout & Explorer Adv; Headmaster of Private Sch; Escondido Elem Educators Finance Comm, Teacher of Yr 1972, 1977; CA T eachers Assn 1958-; Phi Delta Kappa 1957; Alpha Gamma Sigma, Mason; Whos Who in the West 17th Edition 1978; Outstanding Service to Scouting 1976; Outstanding Teacher from Palomar Resource Conservation Dist 1976; *office:* Oak Hill 980 N Ash Escondido CA 92027

HUTCHINSON, MARILYN E., English Dept Chair/Teacher; *b:* Canonsburg, PA; *m:* Jack C. Johnson; *c:* Matthew M., Shane Johnson; *ed:* (BA) Hum, Penn St 1966; (MS) Elem Ed, MI St 1972; *cr:* Teacher Lansing Sch Dist 1967-; *ai:* Curr Steering Comm; Lansing Bsbl Secy 1987-; Eng Dept Chairperson; Nom Teacher of Yr 1984; *office:* Gardner Mid Sch 333 Dahlia Rd Lansing MI 48911

HUTCHINSON, MARY CHRISTENE DEAN, Kindergarten Teacher; *b:* Huntsville, TX; *m:* Ernest Francis Jr.; *c:* Ernest F. III, Richard T.; *ed:* (BA) Elem Ed, 1955, (MA) Elem Ed, 1956 TX Southern Univ; Early Chldhd Ed 1975-85; *cr:* Kndgtn Teacher DOD Tokyo Japan 1958-60; 3rd Grade Teacher Gage Elem 1962-64; Kndgtn Teacher Hapgood Elem 1964-; *ai:* Lang Art Book Selection & Kndgtn Task Force Comm; Delta Sigma Theta Mem At-Large 1952-; Beta Pi Sigma Financial Grammateus 1988-; Classroom Teacher Instructional Improvement Cmptr Prgm Grant; *office:* Arthur Hapgood Elem Sch 324 South A Street Lompoc CA 93436

HUTCHINSON, SUSAN THOMAS, Math Dept & Cmptr Sci Chair; *b:* Indianola, MS; *m:* Bill; *c:* Andrea, Suzanne; *ed:* (AA) Math, MDJC 1968; (BSE) Math, Delta St Univ 1971; (MED) Math, Delta St Univ 1980; Cmptr Sci, Northeast LA Univ 1981-84; *cr:* Math Dept Chm Deer Creek Sch 1971-82; Math & Comp Sci Dept Chm Indianola Acad 1982-; *ai:* Coach Math Team; Delta Kappa Gamma, Phi Delta Kappa; NCTM, MS Cncl of Teac Ath, MS Educl Computing Assn; Presidential Awd for Excl in Math Teaching; Star Teacher 1982, 1987 & 1990; *office:* Indianola Academy Sch Dorsett Dr Indianola MS 38751

HUTCHISON, ADELIA CAIRNS, Social Studies Chairman; *b:* Sugar Creek, MO; *M:* James P.; *c:* Brad J., Dee Ann L. Aull, Jamie H. Mc Devitt, Dana; *ed:* (BA) Elem Ed, San Jose St Univ 1959; *cr:* Elem Teacher Versailles Schls 1952-56; Elem & Jr HS Teacher Monterey Public Schls 1956-64; HS Teacher 1968-82; Mid Schl Teacher 1982- Morgan Cty R-II; *ai:* Advisory Cncl; Natl Honor Soc Spon; Drill Team Spon; MO Mid Sch Assn 1988-; MO Geographic Alliance 1986-; Soc Stud Assn 1969-; Baptist Church 1954-; Amer Legion Aux 1980-; Outstanding Educator Cntrl Dist Mo; Grade Level Chm Monterey Public Schls; *office:* Morgan Cty R II Schls Hwy 52 W Versailles MO 65084

HUTCHISON, PAMELA JEAN, English And Spanish Teacher; *b:* Minneapolis, MN; *m:* Dennis; *c:* Brent, Brock, Brett; *ed:* (BA) His/Poly Sci, Bethany Coll 1969; KS St Univ; Eng/Span Cert, Ft Hays St Univ; *cr:* 7th/8th Grade Soc Stud/Eng/Rdng Teacher Scandia Elem 1969-72; Pre-Sch Teacher Smith Center Nursery Sch 1977-85; Eng/Soc Stud/Psych/Current Events/Span Teacher Osborne HS 1985-; *ai:* Sr Class Spon; NEA, KS Ed Assn 1969-72, 1985-; Osborne Ed Assn Building Rep 1985-; NCTE 1986-; Young Mothers Club 1973-77; Beta Sigma Phi 1977-82; Foreign Lang Study Grant St of KS; *home:* 513 N Washington Smith Center KS 66967

HUTH, FREDERICK LLOYD, JR., Bible Teacher; *b:* Polk, PA; *m:* Jewell Lena Bell; *c:* Joyce F. Munro, F. L. III, Grace A. Suiter; *ed:* (BABE) Bible Ed, Columbia Bible Coll 1956; Educl Work Univ of MD College Park; Spec Math & Electrical Theory US Navy; *cr:* 6th Grade Teacher Seat Pleasant Elem 1958-62; HS Teacher Johnstown Mennonite Sch 1963-65, Salem Schls 1967-71; Sumter Chrstn HS 1978-; *ai:* Ind Fundamental Churches of America Secy 1964-; Dixie Ind Church Mission Dir 1967-; Numerous Magazine Articles in Several Natl Periodicals; *office:* Sumter Chrstn Sch P0 Box 1855 Sumter SC 29150

HUTSHINSON, JULIE SMITH, Teacher; *b:* Macomb, IL; *m:* Michael Dean; *ed:* (BSE) Eng Ed, NE MO St Univ 1982; Masters Prgm Univ of MO Columbia; *cr:* Eng Teacher Milan C-II Sch Dist 1982-85; Eng/Speech Teacher Sturgeon R-V Sch Dist 1985-; *ai:* Spon Jr Class & Thespian Club; Secy Career Ladder Reviewing Comm; Salary Comm Chm; Quiz Bowl Moderator; NCTE 1986-; Cmmty Teachers Assn Standing Comm Chm 1985-; MO St Teachers Assn 1982-; MO Most Influential Teachers 1988-89; Mentor Teacher 1989-; *home:* 3617 Sugar Tree Ln Columbia MO 65201

HUTSON, CARRIE M. (SIMPERS), Mathematics Teacher; *b:* Wilmington, DE; *ed:* (BS) Phys Ed, Hampton Inst 1960; Cert Elem Ed, Univ of DE 1973; (ME) Widener Univ 1989; Several Wkshps; *cr:* Health Teacher Englewood Jr HS 1960-65; Prgm Dir YWCA 1967-69; Elem Teacher Charles B Lore 1969-78, Baltz Elem Sch 1978-86; Teacher 1986-87, Chapter I Math Teacher 1987- Conrad Mid Sch; *ai:* Natl Assn of Univ Women Schlsp Comm Chairperson Recognition Awd; Natl Assn of Phi Delta Kappa Incorporated Commission Civil Rights in Ed; NCTM; Red Clay Ed Assn Negotiating Team Mem; DE St Ed Assn, NEA, Delta Sigma Theta; NAACP (Life Mem, Golden Heritage Mem, General Membership Chairperson, 3rd VP, Secy Admin Branch, Secy Labor & Industry Comm, Chairperson Housing Comm); Forum to Advance Minorities in Engineering Past Bd Mem; Eastside Citizens Incorporated (Past Bd Mem, Housing Chm); Dr Martin Luther King Jr Woman of Yr Awd Organization of Minority Women Incorporated 1988; Recognition of Notable Accomplishments 1989; Recognition Generous Support United Negro Coll Fund 1989; Certificate of Appreciation Participating Delta Internal Dev Wkshp DE St Cncl Delta Sigma Theta.

HUTTON, GARY KENT, 8th Grade English Teacher; *b:* Sumner, IL; *m:* Marilyn Ann Buchko; *c:* Timothy, Dawn Nichting; *ed:* (BA) Bible/Eng, Bob Jones Univ 1960; (MA) Scndry Ed, Bradley Univ 1969; Writing, Cmptrs, Teaching Methods; *cr:* 6th-8th Grade Eng Teacher Dunlap Grade Sch 1962-68, Princeville Grade Sch 1969-70; 7th/8th Grade Eng/Lit Teacher Pioneer Jr HS 1972-; *ai:* Boys Bsktbl, Ftbl, Track, Soccer & Girls Bsktbl, Track Coach; 8th Grade Adv; Dunlap Ed Assn, IL Ed Assn, NEA; Grace Presbyn Church; *home:* RR 1 Dunlap IL 61525

HUTTON, JO ANNE WOLF, 8th Grade Eng/Math Coop Coord; *b:* Mt Clemens, MI; *m:* Robert W.;; *c:* Cherie Bignell, Suzanne Torp, Jodie K. Land; *ed:* (BS) Bus Ed, Wayne St Univ 1982; (MA) Bus Ed, E MI Univ 1987; *cr:* Teacher L Anse Creuse Adult & Cmmty Ed 1982-83, Macomb Comm Coll 1983-88, Harper Woods Scndry Sch 1982-; *ai:* Eng, Lang Art Curr Study Chairperson 1988-; New Definition Rdng Comm Mem; MI Educl Assessment Prgm Comm; Delta Pi Epsilon Outstanding Grad Stu 1987; MI Rdng Assn, Effective Instruction Consortium 1990; MI Bus Ed Assn (Divisional Rep 1986-89, Conventions Speaker 1984-85, Fall Conference Chairperson 1983) 1980-; Pi Lambda Theta 1982-; Golden Key NHS 1982; Survey on Cmptr Use in Bus Ed Macomb & Oakland Ctys 1986; *office:* Harper Woods Scndry Sch 20225 Beaconsfield Harper Woods MI 48225

HUX, BARBARA SMITH, Business Education Teacher; *b:* Mc Comb, MS; *m:* Jimmy M.; *c:* Lisa Hux Copeland, Daniel C.; *ed:* (AA) Bus, Southwest Comm Coll 1959; (BS) Bus/Eng, Univ S MS 1961; *cr:* Bus Teacher Carters Creek HS 1961, Meadville HS 1961-62; Jr HS Eng Teacher Enterprise Sch 1962-64; Bus/Eng Teacher Bogue Chitto HS 1964-; *ai:* Sr Class & Yrbk Adv; Journalism Teacher; Yrbk Publication Dir; Delta Kappa Gamma 1970-; PTA 1960-; Natl Society Daughters Amer Revolution Schlsp 1970-; STAR Teacher; Teacher of Yr; *office:* Bogue Chitto HS P O Box 128 Bogue Chitto MS 39629

HUXFORD, PAMELA WILSON, Compensatory Reading Teacher; *b:* Moncks Corner, SC; *m:* William Wilkes Jr.; *c:* Meggan C., Erin E., William W. III; *ed:* (BA) Early Chldhd, Univ of SC 1979; (MED) Rdng, The Citadel 1986; Amer Sign Lang; *cr:* 2nd Grade Teacher St Stephens Elem 1979-81; 3rd Grade Teacher 1981-89, Rdng Teacher 1989- Berkeley Elem; *ai:* Kappa Kappa Iota 1990; NEA 1979-81; Berkeley Rdng Cncl 1989-; Edna Jones Circle 1980-83; 1st Chrstn Church 1962-; *office:* Berkeley Elem Sch 107 E Main St Moncks Corner SC 29461

HYATT, DONNA FOWLER, Chemistry/Physics Teacher; *b:* Waynesville, NC; *m:* Roger Douglas; *ed:* (BS) Chem, 1987, (BS) Sci Ed, 1987 W Carolina Univ; *cr:* Chem/Physics Teacher Forest Hills HS 1987-; *ai:* Sci Fair Chairperson; Sci Olympiad, Fellowship of Chrstn Athletes Spon; Honor Society Cncl Mem; Schlsp & Remembrance, Senate Bill II Comm Mem; Cty Sci Fair; NCAE Mem; Forest Hills HS Teacher of Yr 1989-; *home:* 108 Deese Rd Monroe NC 28110

HYDE, BONNIE FOREHAND, Sixth Grade Teacher; *b:* Nashville, TN; *m:* Paul Gillespie; *ed:* (BS) Soc Sci, 1971, (MAT) Sociology, 1975 Mid TN St Univ; Ed, TN St Univ 1978; *cr:* 6th Grade Teacher Carter-Lawrence 1972-77, Mc Kissack 1977-79; 5th/6th Grade Teacher Haywood 1979-83; 5th Grade Teacher Wade 1983-84; 6th Grade Teacher Eakin Elem 1984-; *ai:* Nashville Inst of Arts, Environmental Ed Trips, PTO Faculty Rep,

Excel & Lang Art Comm; Phi Delta Kappa 1987-; Intnl Rdng Assn Exec Bd 1989-; NEA, TN Ed Assn, Metropolitan Nashville Ed Assn 1971-; Teacher of Yr; Mini Grant Metropolitan Nashville Public Ed Fnd 1989.

HYDE, CONSTANCE DEANE CRIMMINGS, English Instructor; *b:* Boston, MA; *m:* Randy Bruce; *c:* Alexander Crimmings; *ed:* (BA) Eng, Howard Payne Univ 1970; (MA) Eng, Univ of N TX 1973; John Robert Powers Sch of Modeling 1978; *cr:* Producer/Talk Show Hostess/News Anchor KXTX TV-39 1979-85; Adjunt Eng Instr/Speech Comm Teacher Dallas Cty Comm Coll Dist 1984-; Eng Instr William Mid Sch 1985-; *ai:* Univ Interscholastic League Coach One Act Play, Public Speaking, Writing; Speakers Bureau Dallas Cty Comm Coll Dist; Assn TX Prof Ed; Amer Assn Univ Women; March of Dimes Collector 1989-; Buckner Orphanage Fellowship of Caring 1979-; Howard Payne Univ Alumni Assn 1982-85; Personalities of South 1976; S Baptist Convention Chrstn Single Contributing Writer; Lamar Cty Big Brothers/Big Sisters Guest Star Appearance; Progressive Citizens League Grand Marshall; Outstanding Young Women of America 1981-.

HYDE, DONNA THROWER, Business Teacher; *b:* Okmulgee, OK; *c:* Matthew; *ed:* (BS) Bus Ed, Northeastern St Univ 1973; Grad Stud Northeastern St Univ; *cr:* Bus Ed Teacher Morris Public Schls 1973-76, Muskogee HS 1976-; *ai:* NEA, OK Ed Assn, Muskogee Ed Assn 1976-; *home:* Rt 1 Box 3008 Fort Gibson OK 74434

HYDE, HARRYETTE BURDEN, Language Arts Teacher; *b:* Dallas, TX; *m:* Glenn W.; *c:* Richard; *ed:* (BA) His/Eng, Stephen F Austin St Univ 1974; Univ of TX Arlington, E TX St Univ; *cr:* Gifted/Talented Lang Art Teacher 1975-; *ai:* Sch Newspaper & Local Spelling Bee Spon; Jr Highlights; Co-Spon Sch Yrbk; Lion Tracks; Assn TX Prof Educators; Featured in Magazine 1989; Author Workbook 1990; *office:* Ennis Jr HS 501 N Gaines St Ennis TX 75119

HYDE, KAREN M., 6th Grade Science Teacher; *b:* Morgantown, WV; *m:* John F.; *c:* Elizabeth, Emily; *ed:* (BS) Elem Ed, WV Univ 1965; Elem Ed; *cr:* 3rd/4th Grade Teacher Bruceton Elem Sch 1965-67; 4th/5th Grade Teacher 1972-80, 6th Grade Sci Teacher 1980 Philippi Mid Sch; *ai:* Sci Dept Chairperson; North Central Accrededation Comm Co-Chairperson; Ecology Field Day; Delta Kappa Gamma; PEO Sisterhood; Barbour Cty Teachers Center Awds; WV St Mini Grant Awd; *office:* Philippi Mid Sch Rt 3 Box 40 Philippi WV 26416

HYDE, KATHLEEN SCULLY, Health Education Teacher; *b:* Astoria, NY; *ed:* (BSED) Health/Phys Ed, St Univ Coll Brockport 1968; Grad Stud Health Ed, Brockport NY; Guidance & Counseling, Bowie St Univ; *cr:* 7th-12th Grade Teacher Churchville-Chili Cntrl Schls 1968-74; 9th-12th Grade Teacher Penn Yan Acad 1974-76; Nutrition Ed Specialist Prince Georges Public Schls 1982; 7th-9th Grade Teacher Glenridge Jr HS 1976-; 9th-12th Grade Teacher Duval HS & Douglass HS 1976-; *ai:* Var Sftbl Coach; SADD, Stu Helping Other People Adv; Crisis Intervention Team Comm; MD Assn of Health, Phys Ed, Recreation & Dance; Frederick Douglass HS Booster Club; P G Cty Sftbl Coach of Yr 1985; *office:* Frederick Douglass HS 8000 Croom Rd Upper Marlboro MD 20772

HYDE, MARY ANGEL, Retired 5th/6th Grade Teacher; *b:* Jacksonville, AL; *m:* James Carl; *c:* Kay Hyde Griffin, Lea; *ed:* (BS) Elem Ed, Jacksonville St Coll 1950; (MS) Elem Ed, Jacksonville St Univ 1977; *cr:* 3rd Grade Teacher Calhoun Cty Bd of Ed 1950-60; 5th Grade Teacher Okoloosa Cty Fl 1961-62, Calhoun Cty Bd of Ed 1962-86; 5th-6th Grade Teacher Faith Temple Chrstn Acad 1986-; *ai:* Chrldr & Math Club Spon; 4-H Club Adv; NEA, AEA; Church Sunday Sch Teacher; Cmmty Affairs; Fire Dept Mem; *home:* 914 Angel Dr S Jacksonville AL 36265

HYDER, EDNA RUTH, History Teacher; *b:* Johnson City, TN; *ed:* (BA) His, Carson-Newman Coll 1950; Univ of TN, S IL Univ, Penn St; *cr:* Jr HS Teacher Baptist Childrens Home 1950-61; His Teacher Harrison Chilhowee Baptist Acad 1961-; *ai:* Sr Class, TN Tomorrow Political Club Spon; Foothills Cncl; TN Cncl for Soc Stud; Mellon Fellow Grants 1986, 1988, 1989; Storley Fellow 1985; Natl Endowment for Hum 1984; HS Subject Selection Comm; NEH Natl Comm; *office:* Harrison Chilhowee Baptist Sch 202 Smothers Rd Seymour TN 37865

HYKE, DOUGLAS DWAYNE, Sci Dept Chm/Bio Teacher; *b:* Bowman, ND; *ed:* (BS) Bio/Soc Stud/Phys Ed, Dickinson St Univ 1951; (ME) Ed, Univ of MT 1958; Sci, Univ of NE & WA St Univ; *cr:* Lemmon HS 1954-58; Valley City HS 1958-59; Havre HS 1959-; *ai:* Coached Ftbl, Bsktbl, Track, Cross Cntry, Wrestling & Bsbl; Spon Sci Clubs; Class Adv; MT Sci Teachers Assn, MT Ed Assn, NEA; NSTA Mem; MT Coaching Assn Track Coach of Yr; Dickinson St Univ Track Hall of Fame Mem, Athlete of 50s Decade; NSF Grant Univ of MT & WA St Univ; Track Coaching Book Co-Author; Articles Published in Coaching Magazines.

HYLAND, MARIE GARGARELLA, Language Arts Teacher; *b:* Fairmont, WV; *m:* Richard J.; *c:* Christopher, Shelley; *ed:* (BA) Bus, Fairmont St Coll 1962; (MA) Scndry Ed, WV Univ 1970; *cr:* Teacher Gen Burnie HS 1962-63, Holy Rosary Jr HS 1972-75, Sacred Heart Jr HS 1976-85, Thornton HS 1986-; *ai:* Forensics Coach; Impact Team; Inservice Comm; CO Lang Art Society, NEA 1986-; Phi Delta Kappa 1988-; *office:* Thornton HS 9351 Washington St Thornton CO 80229

HYLTON, NANCY NYE, Mathematics Teacher; *b:* Nassawadox, VA; *c:* Mary Ann Hylton Kramer, Richard Jr., David W.; *ed:* (BS) Math/Chem, Mary Washington Coll 1955; Univ of VA, George Mason Univ; *cr:* 7th Grade Teacher Fort Belvoir Dependent Sch 1955-56; Math Teacher Francis C Hammond HS 1956-58, Groveton HS 1961-66, Minnie Howard Mid Sch 1969-80; Math Dept Chairperson 1981-88, Math Teacher 1980- Francis C Hammond Jr HS; *ai:* Saturday Sch Tutorial Prgm 1983-86; City-Wide Dept Chairperson Study; Phi Delta Kappa 1986-; NEA, VA Ed Assn, Alexandria Ed Assn 1969-; George Washington Univ Outstanding Educator 1984; *office:* F C Hammond Jr HS 4646 Seminary Rd Alexandria VA 22304

HYMAN, LUANNE K., 9th/10th Grade English Teacher; *b:* Seattle, WA; *m:* Andy Jr.; *c:* Cameron, Trish; *ed:* (BA) Eng, Troy St Univ 1980; (MA) Ed, Livingston Univ 1987; Contining Ed Courses; Working Towards AA Cert; *cr:* Eng Teacher Stokes Acad 1980-84, Sweet Water HS 1984-; *ai:* Capital City Spelling Bee, Birmingham Post-Herald Spelling Bee, Speech Club, Foxfire Presentation, Writing Act Spon; Judging Bridge Submission Advisory Comm Mem; Univ of AL Bio-Prep Mem; NEA, AEA 1986-; NEH Grant Univ of AL 1987-89 & Livingston Univ; Poem Published 1989; *office:* Sweet Water HS PO Box 127 Sweet Water AL 36782

HYNES, CYNDY, Physical Education Teacher; *b:* Buffalo, NY; *m:* Michael J.; *c:* Colin, Erin; *ed:* (AS) Phys Ed, Genesee Comm Coll 1976; (BS) Phys Ed, Ithaca Coll 1978; (MS) Elem Ed, Elmira Coll 1982; *cr:* Phys Ed Teacher Candor Cntrl 1978-; *ai:* Jr HS, Var Girls & Boys Vlybl, Jr Var Sftbl Coach; NY St Health, Phys Ed, Recreation, Dance 1977-; PTA Mem 1988-; Candor Facility Assn Mem 1978-; Candor Youth Commission Mem 1984-86; St Francis Parish Cncl Mem 1989-; US Vlybl Assn Mem; Amer Legion Auxillary; St Francis Religious Ed Comm Mem; Scholastic Bronze Medal Coaching Awd 1988; *office:* Candor Central Sch Box 145 Academy St Candor NY 13743

I

IACHETTI, ROSE MARIA ANNE, Fourth Grade Teacher; *b:* Watervliet, NY; *ed:* (BS) Elem Ed, Coll of St Rose 1961; (MED) Elem Ed, Univ of AZ 1969; Noviate Sisters of Mercy 1949-66; Normal Sch Certificate, Maria Coll 1949-51; *cr:* 1st-4th Grade Teacher Albany Diocese 1952-66; Fine Art Dept Teacher Watervliet Jr-Sr HS 1966-67; 2nd Grade Teacher Mother of Sorrows 1967-68, Walter J Meyer Elem 1968-71; 2nd/3rd Grade Teacher Colonel Johnston Sch 1971-78; 3rd-5th Grade Gifted Prgm Teacher Myer Sch 1978-89; *ai:* Tombstone Cmmty Health Services Pres 1978-80; Tombstone Democratic Club; Lecturer & Mem of Intnl Platform Assn; Tombstone Bus & Prof Women; Amer Legion Auxiliary; Tombstone Assn of Arts; AZ Ed Assn S Regional Dir 1971-73; Pi Lambda Theta Mem 1969-; Delta Kappa Gamma Pres 1982-84; Phi Delta Kappa (Charter Mem 1979, Historian 1979-82, 2nd VP 1982-83); Tombstone Dist #1 Educators Assn Pres 1969-71; Bicentennial Commission for AZ 1972-76; Tombstone Centennial Commission Chm of Centennial Ball 1979-80; Tombstone City Cncl 1982-84; Tombstone Sch Bd 1971-80; Gifted & Talented Prgm 1981-85; SE AZ Health Ed Cncl Pres 1989-; Cmmty Leaders & Noteworthy Amers Awd Bicentennial Ed 1976-77; Notable Amers of Bicentennial Era 1976; Inner Senatorial Circle Mem 1989-; Amer Women 1975; The World 1984-; Whos Who in the West 1980-; *office:* Myer Elem Sch Drawer Q Fort Huachuca AZ 85613

IACOBUCCI, NANCY BEARD, English Teacher; *b:* Mc Keesport, PA; *m:* Walter C.; *c:* Joanne Tovissi; *ed:* (BA) Eng, Carlow Coll, Univ of Pittsburgh, Penn St Univ 1952; *cr:* Eng Teacher Elizabeth Forward HS 1957-59, Quaker Valley Jr HS 1965-; *ai:* Quaker Valley Jr HS Steering Comm; Delta Kappa Gamma Pres 1983-85; Bus & Prof Women 1983-87; Penn St Eng Teachers Consortium 1983-; Mc Intyre Civic Assn 1981-; Martin Luther King Recognition Awd; *office:* Quaker Valley Jr HS Harbaugh St Sewickley PA 15143

IAGULLI, THOMAS LOUIS, 8th Grade English Teacher; *b:* Youngstown, OH; *m:* Susan Mary Weller; *c:* Jonathan J., Jill A., Jeffrey T.; *ed:* (BA) Speech/Eng, Salem Coll 1970; *cr:* Scndry Eng Teacher Liberty HS 1970-72, Chestnut Ridge HS 1972-81; 8th Grade Eng Teacher Chestnut Ridge Mid Sch 1981-; *ai:* Var Ftbl, Lead Teacher & Skills for Adolescence Instr; Teachers Assisting Teachers Team Mem; NEA 1970-; PA St Ed Assn, Chestnut Ridge Ed Assn 1972-; Alum Bank United Meth Lay Leader 1987-; Inter-Media Unit 08 Lead Teacher Facilitator 1989-; Yrbk Dedications; Jr Natl Honor Society Teacher of Yr.

IANZANO, ARLENE MARONE, Second Level Teacher; *b:* Hackensack, NJ; *m:* Peter; *c:* Lisa Ianzano Gazzo, Peter Jr.; *ed:* (BA) Elem Ed - Magna Cum Laude, William Paterson Coll 1976; Grad Stud Rdng, Montclair St, William Paterson, Jersey City St Coll; *cr:* 2nd Grade Teacher 1977-78, Kndgtn Teacher 1978-80, 3rd Grade Teacher 1980-82, 2nd Grade Teacher 1982- Washington Park Sch; *ai:* Co-Author Soc Stud Curr Washington Park Sch; NJEA, Totowa Ed Assn 1977-; Intnl Rdng Assn 1984-; Pi Lambda Theta 1976-78; Philosophy for Children Lecturer Stockton St Coll Lehigh Univ; Interviewed & Article Published Natl Magazine; *office:* Washington Park Sch 10 Crews St Totowa NJ 07512

IATESTA, SUSAN FRISK, Band Director; *b:* Meadville, PA; *m:* John; *c:* Catherine; *ed:* (BME) Music, Wittenberg Univ 1972; (MA) Rutgers Univ 1982; *cr:* Band Dir Salt Brook Mid Sch 1972-; *ai:* Stage Band Dir; All Sch Band Dir; Music Educators Natl Conference 1972-; *office:* Salt Brook Sch 40 Maple St New Providence NJ 07974

IAZZETTA, JOHN H., Earth Science Teacher; *b:* Jersey City, NJ; *m:* Kathleen Kinyon; *c:* Christopher, Kerry, Jaime; *ed:* (MS) Earth Sci, N AZ Univ 1973; Geology, SD Sch of Mines; Physics, NJ Inst of Technology; Paleontology, Rutgers Univ; *cr:* Physics Teacher Oratory Prep Sch 1965-67; 7th/8th Grade Sci/Math Teacher Hillside Sch 1967-; *ai:* Cross Cntry, Swimming, Soccer, Track Coach; Coord Washington Trip; Spon Radio Controlled Car Club; NEA, NJ Ed Assn, Somerset Cty Ed Assn, Bridgewater-Raritan Ed Assn 1966-; Hunterdon Cty YMCA Commissioner 1984-; Round Valley Radio Control Club Secy 1980-; Natl Sci Fnd Grants NJ Inst of Technology, SD Sch of Mines & Technology, N AZ Univ, Rutgers Univ; Golden Apple Awd Bridgewater-Raritan Regional Sch Dist; *office:* Hillside Sch 844 Brown Rd Bridgewater NJ 08807

IBEZIM, HEDY SMITH, 8th Grade Science Teacher; *b:* Huntsville, AL; *m:* Mike Chidi; *ed:* (BS) Home Ec/Music, AL a & M Univ 1964, (MS) Early Chldhd Ed a & M 1974, Elem Ed a & M Univ 1979; *cr:* Teacher Madison Cty Bd of Ed 1964-89; *ai:* Prgm Spon Veterans Day/Xmas Prgm/8th Grade Sch Closing Prog; AEA; MCEA; NEA; Delta Sigma Theta Mem 1963-; *home:* 5115 Ortega Cir NW Huntsville AL 35810

ICHIKAWA, DOROTHY SEKI, French Teacher; *b:* Imperial City, CA; *c:* Jeri S. Whitten, Colin M.; *ed:* (BA) Fr, CSU Dominguez Hills 1970; (MA) Ed/Soc Sci, Azusa Pacific Univ 1977; *cr:* Fr Teacher 1973-78, Rdng ESL 1978-81, Span Teacher 1982-86 Dominguez HS; GATE/Fr Teacher Compton HS 1987-; *ai:* Fr Club, Jr Class, Travel Club Adv; Foreign Lang & Bi-ling Dept Chairperson; AATF 1973-78; AFT, CA Fed of Teachers 1973-; Japanese Amer Citizens League 1986-; CA Cty Constructive Discipline Prgm; Region 8 Alcohol & Drug Prevention Prgm.

IDEKER, JOAN FENSTERMAN, English Teacher; *b:* Sioux Falls, SD; *m:* Ray H.; *c:* Jason H.; *ed:* (BS) Eng, SD St Univ 1965; Advanced Placement Wkshps, W Carolina Univ; *cr:* Eng Teacher/Drama Coach Clinton HS 1965-67; Eng Teacher 1968-78, 1986-Brevard HS; *ai:* Drama & Stu Cncl Spon; SAT & Schlsp Comms; NCTE 1987-; NEA, NCAE, TCAE 1965-, Transylvania Cty Teacher of Yr 1976; Delta Kappa Gamma; Book & Plate Club Pres 1989; NC Fed of Womens Clubs Poetry Awd.

IDEKER, SUSAN JARVIS, Vocal Director; *b:* Joplin, MO; *m:* Darrell L.; *c:* Joseph, Amy, Jaxon; *ed:* (BSE) Voice/Piano, MO Southern St Coll 1975; *cr:* K-12th Grade Vocal Music Teacher Seneca Sch Dist R-7 1975-76; 1st-6th Grade Vocal Music Teacher Carl Junction Sch Dist R-1 1976-77, Martin Luther Elem 1977-78, Carl Junction Sch Dist R-1 1983-84; 8th-12th Grade Vocal Music Teacher Joplin Sch Dist R-8 1984-; 8th-12th Grade Vocal Music Teacher Joplin Sch Dist R-8 1984-; *ai:* Solo & Ensemble Club Spon; Sch Musical Production Musical Dir; Discipline Task Force; Sch Effectiveness Comm; MO St Teachers Assn Building Rep 1975-; SW MO Music Educators Assn, MO Music Educators Assn Natl Music Educators Assn 1983-; Immanuel Luth Church Choir Dir 1974-; BSA Day Camp Dir 1986-88; Nom Golden Apple Awd 1986; *office:* Joplin HS 2102 Indiana Joplin MO 64804

IERY, ROBERT LEROY, 7th Grade Lang Arts Teacher; *b:* Vanceburg, KY; *m:* Susan Lee Webb; *ed:* (AS) General Stud, Maysville Coll 1975, (BA) Elem Ed, 1977; (MA) Elem Ed, 1981 Morehead St Univ; *cr:* 7th/8th Grade Math/Rdng/Lang Arts Teacher Mason Co Bd of Ed 1977-; *ai:* 7th Grade Girls Bsktbl Coach; Mid Sch Basbl Coach; Aberdeen Baptist Church Deacon1987-; Aberdeen Baptist Church Sunday Sch Dir 1988-; *home:* Rt 3 Box 371B Maysville KY 41056

IGNICO, BONNIE LYNN, Teacher of Gifted; *b:* Mineola, NY; *m:* Vincent Anthony Jr.; *ed:* (BA) Art Ed, Univ of S FL 1974; Grad Stud Gifted Ed, Univ of S FL 1986; *cr:* Substitute Teacher Broward Cty Sch System 1974-77; 5th-8th Grade Art Teacher Inverness Mid Sch 1977-86; Teacher of Gifted Ed Citrus HS 1986-; *ai:* Jr Class Spon 1987-; Day Care Personnel Trng Course CFCC Extended Prgm Instr 1987-89; FL Assn for Gifted 1987-; Zeta Theta Pres 1989-, Perfect Attendance 1988-; Beta Sigma Phi Recording Secy 1989-; St Selected Art & Gifted Ed Exams Writer; Inverness Mid Sch Teacher of Yr 1982; Outstanding Young Women of America 1982; *office:* Citrus HS 600 W Highland Blvd Inverness FL 32652

IIJIMA, MIKE, Biology & Anatomy Teacher; *b:* Chicago, IL; *m:* Betty Maria Fong; *c:* Matthew L., Richard C.; *ed:* (BS) Bio/Sci, CA St Univ 1968; Medical US Army; *cr:* Sci Teacher Woodrow Wilson Jr HS 1970, Dublin HS 1971-; *ai:* Girls Var Bsktbl Coach; North Coast Athletic Section Comm 1988-; CA Teachers Assn 1971-; *office:* Dublin HS 8151 Village Pkwy Dublin CA 94568

IKEMOTO, ATSUSHI, Social Science Teacher; *b:* Tule Lake, CA; *ed:* (BA) Phys Ed, 1967, (BA) Soc Sci, 1970 CA St Univ Sacramento; (MA) Sch Admin, Chapman Coll 1977; (MS) Sch Counseling, Univ of Laverne 1986; Grad Stud Soc Sci, 1971; Coaches, Referee Judo Cert; *cr:* Ftbl/Judo Coach Immaculate Conception Sch 1966-70; Teacher/Coach Sacramento HS

1971-76; Rdng Teacher Stanford Opportunity Jr HS 1976-77; Teacher/Coach John F Kennedy HS 1977-; *ai:* Wrestling Coach; Judo Club; AFT 1972-; Assn of CA Sch Admin 1977-; CA Teachers Assn 1985-; Exch Club 1988-; Footprinters 1986-; Team Sacramento Sr Instr 1986-; Coached Judo Champions; *home:* 716 Roundtree Ct Sacramento CA 95831

IKER, JOAN WHITE, Mathematics Teacher; *b:* Durant, OK; *m:* Steve; *c:* Holly, Brandon, Natalie; *ed:* (BSED) Math, 1973, (ME) Math, 1985 SE OK St Univ; *cr:* Math Teacher Antlers Jr HS 1974; Temporary Part-Time Math Instr SE OK St Univ 1980, 1982; Math Teacher Bokchito HS 1982-; *ai:* Jr Class, Prom & Fundraisers Spon; NHS, Cmmty Project & Cultural Trip Adv; SOSU Curr Chm; Silo Extension Homemakers Pres 1981-82, Homemaker of Yr 1982; Durant HS Band Boosters Secy Elect 1990; *office:* Bokchito HS PO Box 161 Bokchito OK 74726

ILLICK, MARILYN ANITA, Elementary Music Teacher; *b:* Paso Robles, CA; *m:* Frederick S.; *c:* James, Mark, Timothy, Maria Joy; *ed:* (BS) Elem Ed, Concordia Teachers Coll 1958; (MS) Human Dev, Univ of MD 1981; Structuring Musical Experiences for Elem Stud 1988; *cr:* 4th/6th Grade Teacher St PaulsLuth Sch 1958-60; Yoder Sch 1978-79; 8th/5th Grade Teacher Friendsville Elem 1979-84; 3rd/5th Grade Teacher JC Parks Elem 1986-88;Music Teacher Dr Mudd Elem 1988-; *ai:* Organist at Grace Luth Church Music Educators 1988-; Natl Conf; NEA/MSTA 1978-84; *home:* P O Box 476 La Plata MD 20646

IMBRIACO, DIANNA ROSE, Business Teacher; *b:* Providence, RI; *m:* Stephen E. Savoie; *c:* Jeffrey, Jennifer, Christopher; *ed:* (MS) Bus Teacher Ed/Accounting, Bryant Coll 1970; Masters Degree Univ of RI; *cr:* Bus Teacher Plainfield HS 1970-; *ai:* Attendance Comm; CT Bus Ed of America 1970-; *office:* Plainfield HS 87 Putnam Rd Plainfield CT 06332

IMHOFF, CALVIN PAUL, Math/Phys Ed/Health Teacher; *b:* Hamilton, OH; *m:* Karen Sue Mort; *c:* Heather A., Gretchen A., Emily A. (dec); *ed:* (BS) Phys Ed/Health/Bible, Grace Coll 1977; (MS) Phys Ed/Health/Scndry Ed, St Francis Coll 1980; Math, Grace Coll 1985; Teaching Endorsement Math, IN Univ, Purdue Univ 1989; *cr:* Teacher Whitley Cty Schls 1978-80; Instr Grace Coll 1972-73, 1975-77, 1985-; Teacher Ft Wayne Chrstn Schls 1984-; *ai:* Gymnastics Coach 1977-; 9th-12th Grade Class Spon Ft Wayne Chrstn Sch 1984-; Church Sunday Sch Office 1980-; US Gymnastics Fed Coach 1985-; Natl Fed of St HS Assn Ofcl 1975-; YMCA (IN St Gymnastics Bd 1978-80, 1986-) 1977-; Cmmty Grace Brethren Church (Secy, Sunday Sch) 1989-; *office:* Ft Wayne Chrstn Schls 1800 Laverne Ave PO Box 11120 Fort Wayne IN 46855

IMLER, MARY ELIZABETH, Science Department Chairperson; *b:* Fort Wayne, IN; *ed:* (BS) Chem/Physics/Scndry Ed, Notre Dame Univ 1975; (MS) Chem/Physics, IN Univ 1980; Natl Inst OSHA for Safety Cert; NSF Summer Inst Chem; Laser/Hologram Stud Cert; *cr:* Research & Dev Chemist Uniroyal 1975-76; Physics Dept Chair Con Jesu Acad 1976-80; Sci Dept Chm St Joseph HS 1980-84; Bishop Luers HS 1985-; *ai:* Sci Club Moderator; Inter-Club Cncl Faculty Adv; Stu Congress Co-Spon; NCE Team Curr Comm; Amer Chem Soc 1974; Outst Teacher Nom 1988-89; Hoosier Assn Sci Teachers in Dist Rep 1979; Published Art 1981; Sci Central Diocesan Rep 1988; Key Club/Kiwanis 1987-89; Outstanding Fac Adv 1988; Ed Adv Bd (Pres & VP); Regional Site Recycling Proj Pres 1989-; IN & MI Energy Grant; Excellence in Ed Awd; Sci Scndry Teacher of Yr; Phi Delta Kappa Outstanding Teacher of Scndry Sci; Presidential Awds for Excl Nom 1989; *home:* 11417 Old US 27 South Fort Wayne IN 46816

IMMEL, CHERYL ANN PENDELL, 5th Grade Teacher; *b:* Springfield, OH; *m:* Ivan Lorin; *c:* John L., Kathelyn T.; *ed:* (BA) Lang Art/Elem Ed, MI St Univ 1965; *cr:* Speech/Theater Teacher Okemos Public Sch 1966; Eng/Speech Teacher Coronna Public Sch 1966-67; 4th Grade Teacher Manchester Public Sch 1967-68, Salem City Schls 1968-69, United Local Schls 1971-72; K/1st/5th Grade Teacher Preble Shawnee Public Schls 1973-; *ai:* Career Ed Spon; PSLEA Building Rep; Preble Shawnee Local Ed Assn; Living Word Church Deaconess; Significant Teacher 1989; *office:* West Elkton Elem Sch PO Box 97 West Elkton OH 45070

IMPAGLIATELLI, LEONARD N., Sixth Grade Teacher; *b:* Plainfield, NJ; *m:* Patricia Ann Holzapfel; *ed:* (BA) Elem Ed, 1966, (MA) Elem Ed/Advanced Specialization, 1968 Kean Coll; *cr:* 6th Grade Teacher John F Kennedy Sch 1966-70; 7th Grade Teacher Sayreville Jr HS 1970-71; 6th Grade Teacher Quibbletown Sch 1971-; *ai:* Piscataway Ed Assn Sr Rep 1975-; NJEA, NEA Mem 1966-; Middlesex Ed Assn Rep 1966-; *office:* Quibbletown Mid Sch Washington Ave & Academy St Piscataway NJ 08854

IMUNDI, JANICE BONANNO, Assistant Principal; *b:* New York, NY; *m:* Ronald; *c:* Lauren, Andrea; *ed:* (BA) His/Sociology, Hunter Coll 1969; (MA) His/Government, Herbert H Lehman Coll 1972; Prof Diploma Admin/Supervision, Fordham Univ 1977; Spec Ed, Coll of New Rochelle 1982; *cr:* Teacher John Philip Sousa Jr HS 1969-77, Dist 11 Funded Prgms 1977-84, Teacher 1984-88, Asst Prin 1988- Frank D Whalen Jr HS; *ai:* GSA Co-Leader Pelham Cncl of Westchester Putnam Cty; Cncl of Suprvr & Admin, Manhattan Rdng Cncl 1988-; NY City Assn of Teachers of Eng, NAASP 1989-; NY City Dept of Aging 1982-84, Certicate of Appreciation 1982; NY St Senate Recognition 1985; *office:* Frank D Whalen Jr HS 2441 Wallace Ave Bronx NY 10467

INCE, SUSAN M., English Teacher; *b:* Bryn Mawr, PA; *ed:* (BA) Eng Lit, 1970, Teaching Credential Ed, 1971 CA Western Univ; (MA) Fine Art, St Johns Coll 1987; *cr:* Eng/Span Teacher Lone Pine HS 1972-74; Eng Teacher Beit Sephr Betih Ehinuch 1975-78, Santa Fe Springs HS 1979-80, Elsinore Jr HS 1980-85, Elsinore HS 1985-; *ai:* Sr Class Adv; *home:* 15-301 El Contento Dr Elsinore CA 92330

INDERHEES, CAROL LOUISE, RSM, Jr HS English Teacher; *b:* Cincinnati, OH; *ed:* (BA) His, Edgecliff Coll 1969; (MA) Ed, Spalding Univ 1987; Lib Sci Classes, Cert Librarian 1987-; *cr:* 4th/5th Grade Teacher St Teresa Sch 1969, 1971-74; 4th Grade Teacher St Mary Sch 1974-78; Teacher/Asst Prin StAthanasius Sch 1978-82; 3rd/4th Grade Teacher St Basil Sch 1982-83; 7th/8th Grade Teacher St Polycarp Sch 1983-; *ai:* Stu Cncl Moderator; NCTE, Mercy Elem Ed Network 1988-; *office:* St Polycarp Sch 7724 Columbine Dr Louisville KY 40258

INDIVIGLIO, KAYE GOULD, Orchestra Director; *b:* New York, NY; *c:* David; *ed:* (BA) Ed, Fairleigh Dickinson Univ 1976; (MS) Scndry Ed/Music, Hofstra Univ 1979; *cr:* String Specialist W Hempstead UFSD 1977-; Orch Dir W Hempstead Mid/HS 1984-; *ai:* All Dist Orch, HS String Ensemble Adv & Dir; Mid Sch Drama Club Dir; Ramittes HS Kickline Adv; Nassau Music Educators Assn (Secy 1986-87, Orch Chm 1984-85, Exec Bd 1987), Service Awd 1979-87; Long Island String Festival Assn Secy 1982-84; Music Educators Natl Conference; Massapegna Philharmonic 1984-; New Classical Consort 1980-86; Nassau Cty Citation for Excl in Teaching 1980; *office:* W Hemstead Mid-HS 400 Nassau Blvd West Hempstead NY 11552

ING, TERRY LEE, Second/Third Grade Teacher; *b:* Chicago, IL; *m:* Franklin Deep; *c:* Alexander; *ed:* (BA) Elem Ed, Univ of IL Chicago Circle 1975; *cr:* Primary Teacher James Ward Elem 1975-; *ai:* Art Fair, Rdng/Lit, Sch Spelling Fair, Sch Climate Comms; Childrens Expressways Museum; Outstanding Teacher of Yr & Perfect Attendance Awds 1978; *office:* James Ward Elem Sch 2701 S Shields Chicago IL 60616

INGE, GREGORY E., History Teacher; *b:* New Brighton, PA; *m:* Christine Ann Jasper; *c:* Jeb S.; *ed:* (BS) Scndry Ed/Soc Stud, Edinboro Univ 1979; (MA) His, Indiana Univ ofPA 1982; Confederate & Civil War His Seminars; *cr:* His Teacher Blairsville Sr HS 1979-; *ai:* Founder & Adv Blairsville Civil War Club; Asst Var Wrestling Coach 1982-89; Mock Trial Team Coach; Blairsville Saltsburg Ed Assn, PA St Ed Assn 1979-; WPXI-TV Pittsburgh PA 1982, Unsung HCVO Awd; *home:* 4 W Chestnut St Blairsville PA 15717

INGRAHAM, PAUL ANDERSON, English Teacher; *b:* Winchester, MA; *m:* Lynne Beth Touissant; *c:* Laurel B.; Carolyn Taylor; *ed:* (BA) Eng Lit, Hawthorne Coll 1970, (MED) Scndry Eng Ed, Northeastern Univ 1973; Doctoral Prgm Ed Admin, Rutgers Univ; *cr:* Eng Teacher Intermed Sch 1974-76, Muzzey Jr HS 1976-79; Sci/Eng Teacher Peck Sch 1979-82; Eng Teacher Shore Cty Day Sch 1982-84; Soc Stud/Eng Teacher Park Sch 1984-87; Eng Teacher St Sebastians CDS 1987-; *ai:* Debate Team Coach: Literary Magazine Adv; Former Coach Soccer, Hockey, Track & Drama Team; NCTE Mem 1977-; Lexington Theatre Company Former Mem; Anthology of Poetry Currently Prepared for Publication; *home:* 14 Heather Dr Cohasset MA 02025

INGRAM, ADRIENNE ELAINE, State Pre-Kindergarten Teacher; *b:* Chicago, IL; *c:* Bria; *ed:* (BA) Elem Ed, 1974, (MS) Early Chlhd Ed, 1975 N IL Univ; *office:* Van Vlissingen Elem Sch 137 W 108th Pl Chicago IL 60628

INGRAM, DENISE GUPTON, Kindergarten Teacher; *b:* Wharton, TX; *m:* Bobby E. Jr.; *c:* Rikki D., Lorey L.; *ed:* (BS) Elem Ed, Stephen F Austin St Univ 1975; *cr:* Kndgtn Teacher Smithville Ind Sch Dist 1975-; *ai:* Campus Improvement Plan & TextBook Comm; Brown Primary Textbook Coord; *office:* Brown Primary Sch 4th & Harris St Smithville TX 78957

INGRAM, GAIL LOGGINS, English Teacher; *b:* Gainesville, GA; *m:* Colvin W.; *c:* Kevin B., Kerry L.; *ed:* (BA) Eng, N GA Coll 1969; (MED) Eng Ed, 1976, Ed Specialist/Eng Ed, 1986 Univ of GA; *cr:* Eng Teacher E Hall HS 1969-70, 1971-72, Johnson HS 1972-78, Gainesville HS 1978-; *ai:* Dir of Forensics, Debate & Competitive Speaking; Sch Newspaper, Literary Magazine & Video Yrbk Spon; Gainesville Assn of Educators (Treas 1985-87, Pres 1988-89), Early Bird Membership Awd 1989; Phi Delta Kappa; NCTE, GA Cncl of Teachers of Eng; GA Assn of Educators (9th Dist Pres 1988-89) Outstanding Leadership 1989; League of Women Voters Bd of Dir 1989-91; Lanierland Amateur Radio Club (VP 1987-89, Pres 1989-); Lanier Educl Fnd 3 Grants for Innovative Teaching; Gainesville Boosters Club 2 Grants for Teaching Ideas; *office:* Gainesville HS 1120 Rainey St Gainesville GA 30505

INGRAM, KATHY DURDEN, History Teacher; *b:* Portsmouth, VA; *m:* Michael J.; *c:* Lisa, Cameron; *ed:* (BA) Soc Stud Ed, 1971, (MAT) Soc Stud Ed, 1979 Univ of NC Chapel Hill; *cr:* Teacher J S Waters Sch 1972-74, Horton Mid Sch 1974-75, Northwood HS 1975-86; Regional Teacher Recruiter SDPI 1986-87; Teacher Lee Sr HS 1987-; *ai:* Prom Comm Chm; NCAE, NEA, NC Cncl for Soc Stud; Northwood HS Teacher of Yr 1983, 1986; Chatham Cty Teacher of Yr 1986; Nom Governors Awd for Excl Teaching 1989; *home:* 326 Mayflower Cir Sanford NC 27330

INGRAM, MARIE HORTON, Math Teacher; *b:* Aberdeen, NC; *m:* Matthew; *c:* William, Brenda I. Donaldson; *ed:* (BS) Math, Livingstone Coll 1954; Benedict Coll; Clemson Univ; Univ of SC; Winthrop Coll; *cr:* Math Teacher Harnet Cty HS 1954-55; Math/Sci Teacher Roswneals HS 1955-56; Soc Stud Teacher C a Johnson HS 1963-66; Math/Sci Teacher Lexington Rosenwald 1966-68; Fairfield Cntrl HS 1968-; *ai:* Senior Class Adv; Chm Math Dept; BETA Club Spon; Band Spon; Evaluation Comm Chairperson; Mem Steering Comm; Fairfield Cty Ed Assn 1968-; SC Ed Assn 1968-; NEA 1968-; Math Teachers Assn 1985-; Red Cross 1985-; Volunteer Cancer Chairperson 1984; Volunteer Heart Fund 1985-; NAACP 1968-; 10 & 15 Yr Svc Awd; Benedict Coll Upward Bound Prgm; *office:* Fairfield Central H S Rt 5 Box 60 Winnsboro SC 29180

INGRAM, MARJORIE MARY, Counselor; *b:* Philadelphia, PA; *m:* Jeff; *ed:* (BA) Soc Sci/Anthropology, CO St Univ 1967; (MA) Counseling/Guidance, 1972, (EDS) Counseling/Organizational Dev, 1980 Univ of CO.

INGRAM, MARSHA COX, Eighth Grade Teacher; *b:* Ida Grove, IA; *m:* Michael L.; *c:* Melanie, Matthew; *ed:* (BA) Elem Ed, Buena Vista Coll 1982; *cr:* Tag/Chapter I Teacher Lake View-Auburn Cmmty Sch 1985-89; 8th Grade Teacher Storm Lake Cmmty Sch 1989-; *ai:* Jr HS Stu Cncl; Lang Art Comm; IA Talented Gifted Assn 1986-; Intnl Rdng, IA Rdng Assn 1982-89; *home:* 107 Hudson Storm Lake IA 50588

INGRAM, PEGGY WEISS, Science Teacher/Dept Chair; *b:* Wichita Falls, TX; *m:* Darwin Keith; *c:* Lindsey; *ed:* (BS) Bio, W TX St Univ 1966; (MNS) Natural Sci, Univ of OK 1972; E NM Univ; NASA NEWMAST Wkshp 1990; *cr:* Teacher Palo Duro HS 1966-72; Texico HS 1972-73, E NM Univ Clovis 1981-82; Teacher/Dept Chairperson Clovis HS 1973-; *ai:* ROTC Field Trip Spon; Sci Fair & Sci Curr Comm; Delta Kappa Gamma 1st VP 1986-; Clovis Ed Assn Faculty Rep 1974-; NEA, NM Ed Assn; NSTA, NMSTA, NM Acad of Sci; Clovis HS Excl in Teaching Awd 1989; *home:* 2501 Williams Clovis NM 88101

INGRAM, SUSAN PATTON, Science Teacher; *b:* Tuscaloosa, AL; *m:* Darren W.; *c:* Melanie, Molly; *ed:* (BS) Bio, Samford Univ 1975; (MED) Scndry General Sci, Univ of Montecello 1986; Registered Medical Technologist Baptist Medical Centers; *cr:* Teacher B B Comer 1986-; *ai:* Chrstn Life Club Spon; *office:* B B Comer HS 8th & Seminole Sylacauga AL 35150

INGRAM, TOMISENE MC ALISTER, Vocational Home Ec Teacher; *b:* Oklahoma City, OK; *m:* Francis W.; *c:* Desiree Luster, Wesley, Leisa Weintraub, Michael; *ed:* (BS) Voc Home Ec, OK St Univ 1960; (MED) Elem, Univ of AZ 1972; Admin Trng; *cr:* Home Ec Teacher Eagle Butte HS 1963-64; Home Ec Teacher SD St Extension Service 1964-68, Rice Elem 1968-74; Voc Home Ec Teacher Oney HS 1976-; *ai:* FHA & Young Homemakers of OK Adv; St Textbook Adoption & Career Ed Comm; Dist FHA Cnslr; Caddo Cty OEA Pres 1989-; OVA VP 1988-89; AVA, OAOHET; United Meth Church Trustees 1990; Local OEA Teacher of Yr 1986-87; *office:* Oney Sch Box 128 Albert OK 73001

INMAN, CAROLYN, 7th Grade Language Art Teacher; *b:* Hahira, GA; *c:* Sharon Thomas, Pamela Thomas; *ed:* (BS) Home Ec Ed, Ft Valley St Coll 1965; GA Cert Elem & Mid Grades, GA Southern Coll; *cr:* Lang Art Teacher Cntrl Mid Sch 1965-; *ai:* Y Club Adv; Grade Lead Teacher; GA Assn of Educators, Natl Teachers Assn; Pride of Screven, Order of Eastern Star; GSA Leader; Whole Lang Approach Wkshps, In-Services, Conventions Participant; *office:* Central Mid Sch 501 Pine St Sylvania GA 30467

INMAN, JOHN GEORGE, English Teacher; *b:* Altoona, PA; *m:* Anita Krumenaker; *c:* Juliana, Jaime; *ed:* (BS) Scndry Soc Sci, Lock Haven Univ 1972; *cr:* Eng Teacher Penn Cambria Sch Dist 1974-; GED Teacher Altoona Area Sch Dist 1980-; Eng Teacher Cntrl Cambria Sch Dist 1987, 1989-; *ai:* Asst Forensics Speech Team Coach; Penn Cambria Long Range Planning & Curr Advisory Comm; Penn Cambria Educl Union Exec Comm; PA St Ed Assn, NEA 1974-; PA Adult Continuing Ed 1980-; Altoona Continuing Ed Center Dir N Cambria Cty 1980-, Achievement 1986; Published Article 1987; *office:* Penn Cambria Intermediate Sch Jefferson Heights Gallitzin PA 16641

INMAN, PAULA KAY (HICKEY), Third Grade Teacher; *b:* Morristown, TN; *c:* James, Ralph; *ed:* (BS) Elem Ed, Carson-Newman Coll 1964; Walter St Comm Coll, Univ of TN, E TN St Univ, Carson-Newman Coll; *cr:* 3rd Grade Teacher 1964-68, 4th Grade Teacher 1968-70, 3rd Grade Teacher 1971-75, 1977- Hillcrest Elem Sch; *ai:* Amer Ed Week Comm Hillcrest Elem Sch 1989-; Soc Stud Textbook Adoption Comm Morristown City Schls 1983-84; Rdng Textbook Adoption Comm Hamblen Cty Schls 1988-89; NEA, TN Ed Assn, Hamblen Cty Ed Assn; PTA 1964-88; *office:* Hillcrest Elem Sch 407 S Liberty Hill Rd Morristown TN 37813

INMAN, SANDRA HILLARD, 7th Grade Language Art Teacher; *b:* Newport, TN; *m:* Tom W.; *c:* Cierra, Mc Kenzie; *ed:* (BA) Eng, Carson Newman Coll 1983; (MED) Rdng, E TN St Univ 1988; *cr:* 7th Grade Lang Art Teacher Newport Grammar Sch 1983-; *ai:* NGS Players Spon; Gifted & Talented Comm 1988-; BASF Exemplary Status Comm 1987-88; Homecoming Comm 1985-; West End Baptist Church Organist 1974-; *office:* Newport Grammar Sch 202 College St Newport TN 37821

INMAN, THOMAS CHARLES, Physical Education Teacher; *b:* Highland Park, IL; *m:* Marcia Diane Curby; *c:* Michelle, Richard; *ed:* (BS) Phys Ed, Western IL Univ 1967; (MS) Phys Ed, 1978, Phys Ed, 1981 Northern IL Univ; *cr:* Phys Ed Teacher Sandburg Jr HS 1967-; *ai:* Boys & Girls Bsktbl Coach; IL Bsktbl Coaches Assn 1973-; Dist 5 Jr HS Coach of Yr 1987 & 1988; *office:* Sandburg Jr H S 345 E St Charles Rd Elmhurst IL 60126

INMAN, TRACY FORD, English Teacher; *b:* Louisville, KY; *m:* John B. II; *ed:* (BA) Eng, W KY Univ 1986; Working Towards Masters in Eng, Scndry Ed Minor; Natl Endowment for Hum, Dante Inst; *cr:* Eng Teacher Warren Cntrl HS 1988-; Mythology Teacher W KY Univ 1990; *ai:* Literary Club Spon/Founder; NCTE, KY Cncl of Teacher of EnG 1987-; Intl Rdng Assn 1989-; Phi Kappa Phi, Omicron Delta Kappa 1986-; Natl Endowment for Hum Dante Inst; Warren Central Outstanding Young Educator; KY Cncl of Teachers of Eng St Conf; *office:* Warren Cntrl HS 559 Morgantown Rd Bowling Green KY 42101

INMAN, VERNON KERRY, English Teacher; *b:* Old Town, ME; *m:* Irene L. Richards; *c:* Rebekah, Johanna, Sarah; *ed:* (BA) Eng, Univ of ME 1968; (MDIV) Divinity, 1974, (THM) Old Testament, 1979 Westminster Theological Seminary; (MA) Biblical Stud, Dropsie Univ 1983; *cr:* Officer US Marine Corps 1968-71; Coord PA Sch for the Deaf 1974-77; Dean Pinebrook Jr Coll 1980-83; Eng Teacher Philmont Chrstn Acad 1987-; *ai:* Advisory Comm for Gifted & Talented Ed Abington-Rockledge Sch Dist 1988-; Articles in Westminster Theological Journal, New Horizons; *home:* 1040 Arbuta Rd Abington PA 19001

INNIGER, CINDY (ZEIGLER), School Counselor; *b:* Hartford City, IN; *m:* Don; *c:* Erika, Ashlea; *ed:* (BA) Span/Scndry Ed, Ball St Univ 1974; (MS) Ed, IN Univ 1978; *cr:* Span/Fr Teacher 1974-78, Sch Cnslr 1978-80, 1982- Adams Cntrl Sch; *ai:* Peer Facilitator Group; Delta Kappa Gamma Schlsp Chairperson 1988-; IN Assn for Counseling & Dev 1978-; Adams Cntrl Schlsp Fnd 1978-80, 1982-; Barbara Walters Cole Awd for Sch Counseling 1986; *office:* Adams Cntrl HS 222 W Washington St Monroe IN 46772

INOUYE, JUDITH SHIZUE, Science Teacher; *b:* Honolulu, HI; *m:* Herbert Susumu; *c:* Michael S., Kara E.; *ed:* (BA) Biological Sci, Univ of CA Berkeley 1962; Prof Cert Scndry Ed, Univ of HI 1963; Grad Stud Univ of HI & Univ of AL Huntsville; *cr:* Sci Teacher Fairfax HS 1963-65, Niu Valley Intermediate Sch 1967-70, Mc Kinley HS 1980-81, Kawananakoa Intermediate Sch 1981-; *ai:* Kawananakoa Space Camp Field Trip Coord; Aerospace Ed Advisory Comm, Office of Space Industry BBED; HI St Teacher Assn, HI Sci Teacher Assn 1980-; ECIA Channel 2 Dev Grant; *office:* Kawananakoa Intermediate Sch 49 Funchal St Honolulu HI 96813

INTRAVAIA, JAMES A., Sixth Grade Teacher; *b:* Plymouth, WI; *m:* Annette Dekker; *c:* Anthony, Patrick; *ed:* (BS) Elem Ed, WSU Oshkosh 1965; (MS) Educl Admin/Supervision, Univ of Milwaukee 1973; *cr:* 5th Grade Teacher Johnson Elem Sch 1965-71; 6th Grade Teacher Pershing Elem Sch 1971-; *ai:* Vice Prin; Safety Cadet Patrol Adv.

IRISH, ALICE MC CLOUD, Science/Gifted Teacher; *b:* Perrysburg, OH; *m:* Terrance D.; *c:* Erin Irish Szymkowiak, Neil, Dale, Colleen; *ed:* (BS) Geology, Bowling Green St Univ 1957; *cr:* Sci Teacher U L Light Mid Sch 1973-; *office:* U L Light Mid Sch 292 E Robinson Ave Barberton OH 44203

IRISH, NANCY HATTER, Lang Arts Teacher/Coordinator; *b:* New Brunswick, NJ; *m:* Donald; *c:* Kevin, Shannon Irish Hirsch; *ed:* (BS) Eng, Trenton St Coll 1958; Numerous Prgms & Wkshps, NJ Regional Curr Services Unit; *cr:* Eng Teacher Linwood Jr HS 1958-60; Language Arts Teacher Jonas Salk Mid Sch 1970-; *ai:* Lang Arts Coord; Dist-Wide Curr Evaluation Comm; NCTE; Alpha Delta Kappa; Jaycee-ettes (VP, Pres) 1960; *office:* Jonas Salk Mid Sch W Greystone Rd Old Bridge NJ 08857

IRLE-KELLY, LISA, Speech/Drama/Lang Art Teacher; *b:* Warrensburg, MO; *m:* Thomas; *c:* Shawn T.; *ed:* (BA) Speech/Theatre/Eng, Mc Pherson Coll 1982; (MED) Eng Ed, Univ of MO Columbia 1986; *cr:* Teacher Plattsburg Jr HS & HS 1987-; *ai:* Drama Club & Soph Class Spon; NCTE, MO St Teachers Assn 1986-; *office:* Plattsburg HS 800 Frost St Plattsburg MO 64477

IRVIN, CONNIE ADAMS, Kindergarten Teacher; *b:* Clarinda, IA; *m:* Michael Allen; *ed:* (BA) Elem Ed, Univ of N IA 1971; Grad Stud; *cr:* Kndgtn Teacher S Page Cmmty Schls 1971-; *ai:* S Page Advisory Comm; Early Chldhd Cadre Mem; S Page Ed Assn, IA St Ed Assn, NEA 1971-; United Meth Church (Bd of Trustees 1987-89, Parish Relations Pastor 1985-87); *home:* Box 143 Coin IA 51636

IRVIN, DIANN F., Reading Teacher of Migrants; *b:* West Columbia, TX; *m:* Harold; *c:* Melissa Irvin Blaschke; *ed:* (BA) Elem Ed/Psych, Univ of Houston; Working Toward MA in Admin; *cr:* Teacher Pe Hus Elem 1972-79, Yorktown Elem 1979-; *ai:* Effective Sch Comm; Teacher of Gifted & Talented; TSTA (Pres 1985-, Secy & Treas 1984-85); Literacy Cncl Choir Parmentar 1989; *office:* Yorktown Elem Sch P O Box 487 Yorktown TX 78164

IRVIN, LEAH CLARK, Sixth Grade Teacher; *b:* New Orleans, LA; *c:* Monique P.; *ed:* (BA) Elem Ed, Xavier Univ 1961; Prof Improvement Courses, Loyola Univ; *cr:* Financial Secy Gloryland Mt Gillion Baptist Church 1976-; *ai:* PIP & Stu Act Coord; Chairperson Departmental Upper Division, 6th Grade, Budget & Finance; Drill Team & Marching Unit Dir; Credit Comm Co-Chairperson Credit Union; Intnl Rdng Assn; LA Rdng Assn Recording Secy 1990; LA Assn Public Continuing Ed 1963-; Hardin Sch Teacher of Yr 1987; *home:* 2110 Dumaine St New Orleans LA 70116

IRVIN, MARINA BADGETT, English Teacher; *b:* Mt Vernon, IL; *m:* Donald Louis; *c:* Marc, Douglas, Kathleen Irvin Agnew; *ed:* (BA) Speech/Eng, Univ of IL 1952; (MTA) Eng, Jackson St Univ 1986; *cr:* Sch Newspaper Spon 1981-87, Eng Teacher 1969- Chastain Jr HS; *ai:* Co-Spon Yrbk; Spon Sequoya Literary Magazine; Supts Advisory Cncl; Public Relations Comm; MS Cncl Teachers of Eng, NCTE 1975-89; *home:* 1012 Briarfield Rd Jackson MS 39211

IRVINE, MARGIE YESKE, 4th Grade Teacher; *b:* Hillsboro, IL; *m:* Jeffrey W.; *c:* Jason; *ed:* (BS) Elem Ed, Eastern IL Univ 1972; *cr:* 4th Grade Teacher Witt Unit Sch Dist #66 1975-; *ai:* Chairperson Teacher Consultation Team; Supervising Teacher Stu Intern-Practicum Experience; AFT Pres 1988-89; NEA Pres 1978-79; Lioness Pres 1988-89 Club of Yr Region I-L 1989; *office:* Witt Public Sch 220 N Third Witt IL 62094

IRVING, DIANA WILLIAMSON, 5th Grade Teacher; *b:* Mooreland, OK; *m:* Clyde Everett; *c:* Emmy E.; *ed:* (BS) Elem Ed, E NM Univ 1971; Grad Stud; *cr:* 5th Grade Teacher Woodward Public Schls 1971-; *ai:* Woodward Cty Spelling Bee Dir; NEA 1976-; OK Ed Assn 1971-; Woodward Ed Assn (Building Rep 1973) 1971-; Kappa Kappa Iota (Voting Convention Delegate 1990, Pres 1977) 1972-; Disciples of Christ Church St of OK Dist I, Chrstn Womens Fellowship Treas; *office:* Woodward Public Schls 9th & Maple Woodward OK 73801

IRVING, JOHN HENRY, History Teacher; *b:* Binghamton, NY; *m:* Sanrdalyn Fay Gifford; *c:* Sheri L.; *ed:* (BS) Ed, 1961, (MS) Ed, 1970 SUNY Oneonta; (CAS) Sch Admin/Supervision, SUNY Cortland; *cr:* Scndry Teacher Johnson City Schls 1961-63; Elem Teacher Binghamton City Schls 1966; Scndry Teacher Bethlehem Cntrl Schls 1966-67, Binghamton City Schls 1967-; *ai:* Stu Government Adv; Frosh Ftbl Coach; Kelly Swim Fund for Pediatric Brain Tumor Research Pres 1983-; *office:* Binghamton HS 31 Main St Binghamton NY 13905

IRWIN, DENISE HIEBERT, Gifted Education Teacher; *b:* Sedan, KS; *m:* Rex Lee; *c:* Jacqueline A.; *ed:* (BS) Theatre, Emporia St Univ 1975; (MS) Educl Psych, Wichita St Univ 1983; Mastery Teaching Trng 1987-; *cr:* Prgm Dir Terramara Incorporated 1975-77; Behavioral Disorders Teacher Unified Sch Dist 402 1977-79; Gifted Ed Teacher Unified Sch Dist 490 1981-; *ai:* KS Ed Assn 1977-; Natl Assn Teachers of Eng 1987-; Trinity Episcopal Church Vestryperson 1987-91; KS Spec Olympics Area 6 Dir 1976-78, Distinguised Service Awd 1978; Trinity Players Youth Musical Theatre Dir 1989-; Written & Produced Musical Plays for Youth 1988, 1990; *office:* Skelly Elem Sch 1420 W Towanda Eldorado KS 67042

IRWIN, EVELYN MARIE, Retired Elementary Teacher; *b:* Bronaugh, MO; *m:* Robert Donald; *c:* Lyndon, Gary; *ed:* (BS) Elem, PSU 1962; *cr:* Elem Teacher Bronaugh R-7 1945-47, 1958-88; *ai:* Bronaugh CTA, MSTA; *home:* Rt 1 Box 64 Bronaugh MO 64728

IRWIN, ROBERT MOWRY, History/Drivers Ed Instructor; *b:* Oakland, CA; *m:* Susan; *c:* Megan, Holly, Brendan, Emily; *ed:* (BA) Geography, CA St Univ 1973; (MA) Admin, St Marys Coll 1985; *cr:* Teacher/Coach S Tahoe HS 1975-79; Dept Chm/Coach/Teacher St Patrick HS 1979-84; Substitute Teacher Chico/Los Molinos Unified Sch Dist 1975-; Teacher/Coach 1984-, Athletic Dir/Summer Sch Prin 1989- California HS; *ai:* PTA (Bd Mem 1987-, Pres 1987-88); CTA, NEA, San Ramon Valley Ed, N Coast Athletic Dirs, CA St Athletic Dirs; Church; *office:* California HS 9870 Broadmoor Dr San Ramon CA 94583

IRWIN, THOMAS JOSEPH, Instructor; *b:* Johnstown, PA; *ed:* (BA) Latin/Math, Coll of St Thomas 1970; *cr:* Jr HS Instr Sacred Heart 1970-71, Holy Family 1972-73; Math Instr St Andrew Schl 1973-; *ai:* IL Cncl Teachers of Math 1971-; Headstart Will Cty Bd of Dirs Pres 1981-86; Will Cty Span Center Bd Mem 1987-88; Agencies United Mem 1985-89; *home:* 538 Tonelli Trl Lockport IL 60441

IRWIN, VICTORIA DEL VECCHIO, 6th Grade Teacher; *b:* Ashland, KY; *m:* Harry Carroll; *c:* Jason A.; *ed:* (BS) Elem Ed, 1972, (MA) Rdng, 1974 E KY Univ; *cr:* 5th/6th Grade Eng/Soc Stud Teacher 1972-83, 5th/6th Grade Eng Teacher 1983-88, 5th/6th Grade Soc Stud Teacher 1988-89, 6th Grade Self Contained Teacher 1989- Kirksville Elem; *ai:* KY Ed Assn, NEA, Madison Cty Ed Assn 1972-; Fine Arts Mini Grant.

ISAAC, MARVIN D., Principal; *b:* Meade, KS; *m:* Edna Mays; *c:* Tony, Steven; *ed:* (BA) Natural Sci/Bible, Tabor Coll 1962; (MS) Natural Sci, OK St Univ 1972; (MED) Scndry Sch Admin, Northeastern St Univ 1985; Fr Lang, Brussels Belgium 1967-68; *cr:* Teacher Nyanga Sch 1969-71; Teacher 1972-, Prin 1980- Markoma Bible Acad; *ai:* Stu Life Comm VP; Vineyard Cmmty Church Pastor 1985-; *office:* Markoma Bible Acad Rt 6 Box 237 Tahlequah OK 74464

ISAACSON, MATTHEW OKE, Sixth Grade Teacher; *b:* Jamestown, NY; *ed:* (BS) Ed, St Univ Coll of NY Brockport 1976; Grad Stud St Univ Coll of NY Fredonia; *cr:* Headstart Aide Jamestown Public Schls 1975; 5th Grade Teacher 1977-80, 6th Grade Teacher 1980- Bemus Point Elem Sch; *ai:* Play Dir; Spelling Bee Coord; Textbook Selection Comm; NEA, NYEA, Bemus Point Faculty Assn 1977-; Bemus Point Public Lib (Trustee, Pres 1989-) 1987-; Town of Ellery Youth Recreation Prgm Commissioner 1988-; Bemus Point PTA Teacher Liaison 1983-89, Honorary Life Mem; Apples for Teachers WJTN Radio Awd 1987; *office:* Bemus Point Elem Sch Liberty St Bemus Point NY 14712

ISBELL, DAVID WHITNEY, Mathematics/Science Teacher; *b:* San Francisco, CA; *m:* Linda Kay; *c:* Diane, Valiere, Lila; *ed:* (BA) Ed, 1951, (MA) Ed, 1956 Stanford Univ; Summer Inst Numerous Univs; *cr:* Teacher Ione Union HS 1952-56, Greenville HS 1956-69, Burney HS 1969-; *ai:* 7th Grade Adv; NSTA 1956-; NCTM 1975-; AAPT 1980-; General Electric Fellowship Syracuse Univ 1956; Natl Sci Fnd Grants Univ of ID 1957, WA St Univ 1958-60, Univ of Santa Clara 1965; *office:* Burney HS P O Box 950 Burney CA 96013

ISBELL, VIVIAN ANN BOGART, 5th Grade Teacher; *b:* Stockton, CA; *m:* Robert Reid; *c:* Christie Isbell Southard, Allison A.; Steven Bogart; *ed:* (BS) Elem Ed, Univ of TX Austin 1968; (MS) Elem Ed, Stephen F Austin Univ; *cr:* 1st Grade Teacher Dallas Ind Sch Dist 1968-69, Bryan Ind Sch Dist 1970-71; Kndgtn Teacher Marvin United Meth Church 1971-72, 1st Baptist Church 1980-82; 5th Grade Teacher Mildred Ind Sch Dist 1982-; *ai:* UIL Spon; Mildred HS Drill Team Dir; Mildred Ind Sch Dist Missions & Textbook Comm; Alpha Delta Kappa 1989-; Mildred Classroom Teachers Assn (Pres, Secy, Treas) 1981-; TX Utilities Grant Ec, Energy & Environment Seminar; TX PTA Schlsp Awd; *home:* Rt 1 Box 147 Corsicana TX 75110

ISEMINGER, ROBERT FLETCHER, Teacher of Gifted/Talented; *b:* Roanoke, VA; *ed:* (BS) Elem Ed/Math, Elizabethtown Coll 1971; Grad Course Work in Gifted Ed , Univ of VA; *cr:* 6th Grade Teacher Lincoln Terrace Sch 1971-80, Fishburn Park Sch 1980-82; 4th-9th Grade Teacher Roanoke City Schls 1979-82; 4th-6th Grade Teacher Fishburn Park Sch 1982-; *ai:* Plato Center Team Leader; Instructional Cncl Mem; Plato Prgm Field Trip Coord; REA, VEA, NEA, NCTM, VA Assn for Ed of Gifted; Cntrl Church of Brethren (Bd Mem, Trustee) 1978-; Leadership Roanoke Valley City Schls Rep 1985-86; Outstanding Young Educator Roanoke Jaycees 1979; Selected Outstanding Young Man of Amer 1985; Roanoke City Teacher of Yr 1985-86; Competed for VA Teacher of Yr.

ISENBERG, OLIVIA LASSITER, Assistant Principal; *b:* Nashville, TN; *c:* Mary F., Jonathan; *ed:* (BS) Bio, Mid TN St 1977; (MED) Admin/Supervision TN St 1983; *cr:* 7th Grade Life Sci Teacher 1977-83, Asst Prin 1983- T W Hunter Mid Sch; *ai:* T W Hunter Mid Sch Curr Coord; Prgm Improvement Comm Co-Chairperson; Assertive Discipline Comm Chairperson; Inservice Planning Comm; Sumner Cty Ed Assn (Pres Elect 1982-83, Pres 1983-84, Past Pres 1984-85, Mem 1977-), Awd of Distinction 1986, Certificate of Appreciation 1984; NEA, TN Ed Assn Mem 1977-; TN Assn of Mid Schls Mem 1980-; PTA Mem 1973-; Career Ladder Level III Admin 1988; *office:* T W Hunter Mid Sch 3140 Long Hollow Pike Hendersonville TN 37075

ISHEE, RHONDA WILSON, English Teacher; *b:* Brookhaven, MS; *m:* Ray; *c:* Brad, Marci; *ed:* (BSE) Eng, 1971, (MLS) Media/Lib Sci, 1979 Delta St Univ; Grad Stud Cmptr Sci & Cmptr LIteracy; *cr:* 6th Grade Teacher Nailor Elem 1971-72; 11th Grade Eng Teacher Greenwood HS 1976-78; Librarian 1979-85, Eng Teacher 1985- Wesson HS; *ai:* Wesson HS Tennis Coach; Stu Lib Asst of MS Spon; Faculty Advisory Comm; Delta Kappa Gamma Mem 1984-; Society Intnl Chm of World Fellowship Comm 1988-; Wesson PTA Secy 1986-87; Wesson Garden Club Mem 1985-88; *office:* Wesson HS 532 Grove St Wesson MS 39191

ISHERRANEN ABELE, MARIE ALENA MAUNULA, Language Art Teacher; *b:* Haapajarvi, Finland; *m:* Harris Dean; *c:* David T., Mikel D.; *ed:* (BS) Eng/Ger Bemidji St 1966; Lang Art, Germ Finnish, Eng as 2nd Lang, Media; *cr:* Jr HS Eng/Ger Teacher 1966-76, 9th-12th Grade Eng Teacher 1976-, Dept Chairperson/Eng Teacher 1985-, Summer Sch Lead Teacher/Prin 1985-, Honors II Eng Teacher 1987- Richfield; *ai:* Danceline Adv/Coach 1981; NHS Adv 1982-; Graduation Speakers Adv 1983-; Writing Contests Coord; MCTE, NCTE; BSA Comm Chairperson; Translations of Patient Handbooks Eng, Finnish; NHS Staff Mem of Yr 1989-; *office:* Richfield Sr HS 7001 Harriet Ave S Richfield MN 55423

ISHIBASHI, ANDREW WAYNE, Music Director; *b:* Los Angeles, CA; *ed:* (BA) Music, Loyola Marymount Univ 1985; Grad Division Loyola Marymount Univ; *cr:* Music Dir Hawthorne HS 1987-; *ai:* Band & Stage Band Dir; Discipline Comm; Assessment Planning Intervention Adv; CA Teachers Assn 1987; Phi Sigma Kappa Pres 1984-85, Outstanding Pres 1985; LMU Grad Grant 1985-86; Centinela Valley Union HSD Outstanding Achievement Awd & Nom Sallie Mae Teacher Awd; *office:* Hawthorne HS 4859 W El Segundo Blvd Hawthorne CA 90250

ISHUM, MARCELLA LUCKETT, 6th Grade Teacher; *b:* Kansas City, KS; *m:* Lawrence E. Jr.; *c:* Laura A., David L.; *ed:* (BS) Elem Ed, St Mary Coll 1969; (MS) Master Teacher/Elem, Emporia St Univ 1987; *cr:* 6th Grade Teacher Bethal Elem Sch 1969-70; 7th Grade Teacher St Agnes Sch 1970-75; 3rd-5th Grade Teacher Morris Elem Sch 1975-89; 6th Grade Teacher Highland Mid Sch 1989-; *ai:* KS NEA 1977-; *office:* Highland Mid Sch 3101 S 51st St Kansas City KS 66106

ISKRA, DONALD, Counselor; *b:* Detroit, MI; *m:* Miriam Fsadni; *c:* David, Thomas, James; *ed:* (BSED) Math/Amer His, 1964, (MED) Guidance/Counseling, 1967 Wayne St Univ; Post Masters Stud Guidance & Counseling, Wayne St Univ; *cr:* Math Teacher Cadillac Jr HS 1964-66, Levey Jr HS 1966-67; Punt Teacher Fuhrmann Jr HS 1967-70; Punt Coord 1970-71, Adult Ed Teacher 1967-74, Cmmty Ed Cnslr 1974- Warren Consolidated Schls; Cnslr Melby Jr HS 1971-81, Fuhrmann Jr HS 1981-; *ai:* Future Problem Solving Coach; Curr Dev for Prgm Underdeveloped Natural Talent 1967-71; Adult Basic Ed Grant Writer 1974-83; Future Problem Solving Teams QUalified for St Championship

1985-89, Intnl Finalists 1988; *office:* Fuhrmann Mid Sch 5155 14 Mile Rd Sterling Heights MI 48310

ISLER, WILLIAM CONRAD, Science Teacher; *b:* Warren, OH; *m:* Ruth Ann Mizner; *c:* Bill, Gregg; *ed:* (BA) Sci/Phys Ed, Hiram Coll 1963; (MED) Guidance/Counseling, Kent St Univ 1968; Natl Sci Fnd Physics Grant, John Carroll; NSF Chem Grant, SW OK; Natl Endowment Hum Seminar Cornell IA; *cr:* Sci Teacher Twinsburg Chamberlin HS 1963-68, Hudson Mid Sch 1969-; *ai:* Summer Sci Enrichment Prgm; OH Ed Assn Ideal Classroom Task Force 1989-; *office:* Hudson Mid Sch 120 N Hayden Pkwy Hudson OH 44236

ISMAIL, ABED M., Teacher; *b:* Arrabah, Jordan; *m:* Adalat Shi Naser; *c:* Randa, Reem, Roshad; *ed:* (BA) His/Psych, Covenant Coll 1967; (BS) His/Psych/Sociology, 1970, (MS) Soc Sci, 1970 Bemidji St Univ; Certificate of Advanced Study in Amer Politics; Served on Staff of Dothan Archaeological Expeditions; Critical Thinking & Clinical Teaching 1960-62/1964; *cr:* Lecturer Near East Sch of Archaeology 1967; Teacher Nevis HS 1967-69, Larkin HS 1970-; Part Time Lecturer Judson Coll; *ai:* Mem Scndry Soc Stud Advisory Comm; Mem Soc Stud & Soc Sci Writing Team LAP; Mem Amer Security Cncl Natl Advisory Bd 1976; Elgin Teachers Assn (Rep 1975-78/1986-87 Mem 1970-); IL Ed Assn, NEA 1970-; Faculty Senate Pres 1975-76; Republican Party Sustaining Mem 1977-; Assn of Arab Amer Univ Grads 1970-; Outstanding New Citizen of Yr 1975; Republican Campaign Victory Certificate 1982; Schlsp from Robert A Taft Inst of Government; Seminars to Study Amer Politics 1969; *home:* 1681 Kimberly Ave Elgin IL 60123

ISOM, GEORGE HEMINGWAY, 8th/9th Grade English Teacher; *b:* St Louis, MO; *m:* Jeanne Frances Boehmer; *ed:* (BA) His/Soc Sci, 1965, (MA) His/Soc Sci, 1971 City Coll of NY; (EDM) Educl Admin, T C Columbia Univ 1972; (PHD) Scndry Curr, Univ of IA 1980; *cr:* Dir Afro-Amer/Hispanic His & Culture Prgm New York City Sch Dist 7; Mgr ESEA Title I Field Office NY St Ed Dept 1973-74; Scndry Ed Teacher Univ of IA 1978-80; Teacher of Gifted/Talented Satellite East Jr HS 1981-; *ai:* Phi Delta Kappa 1979-81; ASCD 1978-80; Martin Luther King Jr Schlsp Columbia Univ; *office:* Satellite East Jr HS 50 Jefferson Ave Brooklyn NY 11216

ISON, CAROL FIELDS, Middle School English Teacher; *b:* Dongola, KY; *m:* Kendall R.; *c:* Marshall D., Valerie Horn; *ed:* (BA) Elem Ed, Pikeville Coll 1970; (MA) Elem Ed, Morehead Univ 1984; (Rank I) Guidance/Counseling; *cr:* Cty Coord Rural Child Care Project 1966-73; Clinic Administratrix Mountain Comp Health Corp 1973-79; Classroom Teacher Martha Jane Potter Elem 1979-; *ai:* 4-H Leader; Letcher Cty Teachers Organization, KY Ed Assn 1980-; Letcher Cty Clean Cmmty Prgm Chairperson 1985-, Woman of Yr 1985; *office:* Martha Jane Potter Elem Sch Kona KY 41829

ISON, LOUIS CHARLES, Chemistry/Physics Teacher; *b:* Lexington, KY; *m:* Robin Singer; *c:* Stewart, Nan, Laura, Zack; *ed:* (BS) Chem/Physics, 1967, (MA) Ed, 1979 Georgetown Coll; Univ of TN; *cr:* Physics/Chem Teacher Jessamine Cty HS 1969-; *ai:* Substance Abuse Stu Assistance Prgm; NEA, KY Ed Assn 1969-; Jessamine Cty Ed Assn Pres 1975.

ISON, WALTER S., Soc Stud/Phys Ed Teacher; *b:* Columbus, GA; *m:* Patricia Allene Pursselley; *c:* Marcell R. Ison Phillips; *ed:* (BS) Elem Ed, Columbus Coll 1972; (MS) Ed Admin/Supervision, 1975, (EDS) Ed Admin/Supervision, 1978 GA St Univ; *cr:* 6th Grade Teacher Mathews Elem 1972-75; 5th/6th Grade Teacher St Marys Elem 1975-87; 4th Grade Teacher Britt David Elem 1987-; *ai:* Prof Assn of GA Educators; PTA Outstanding Teacher of YR 1983-85; St Marys Elem Teacher of Yr 1984.

ISRAEL, MARCIA SOLON, Reading Specialist; *b:* New York, NY; *m:* Allen; *c:* Jeffrey, David, Robert; *ed:* (BS) Elem Ed/Spec Ed, C W Post Long Island Univ 1973; (MED) Rdng, Boston St Coll 1978; Grad Stud Bridgewatr St Coll; *cr:* Teacher M E Young Sch 1973-81; Rdng Specialist John F Kennedy Jr HS 1982-86; Devine Sch 1987-; *ai:* Intnl Rdng Assn South Shore Cncl; MA Teachers Assn, NEA; Womens Amer Ort; Hadassah VP 1987-; Donovan Sch PTO 1988-.

ISSA, ASWAD HASHIM ASIM, Social Studies Teacher; *b:* Detroit, MI; *m:* Diane Christine Gray; *c:* Jamila B. S., Bomani A. O., Akilah S. N.; *ed:* (BS) Soc Stud/Ed, 1971, (ME) Scndry Soc Stud, 1977 Wayne St Univ; (MDiv) Biblical Historical Investigation, Interdenominational TheologicaL Center Morehouse 1981; IBM Cmptr Concept Prgm, IBM Extension 1984; Enhancing Pastoral Care Skills, Samaritan Hospital 1986; Growing Up Gifted, Wayne St Univ 1987; Alcohol & Drug Abuse Prevention, US Dept of Ed Concordia Coll 1990; *cr:* Staff Asst Wayne St Univ 1968-71; Instr/Supvr WSU Summer Youth Sports Prgm 1971-78; Asst Supvr Detroit Summer Youth Employment Prgm 1979-81; Contract Worker Detroit Sr Citizens Dept 1982; Teacher Detroit Public Schls 1971-; *ai:* Osborn HS African Amer Cultural Festivities & Detroit Fed of Teachers Election Comm Chm; Osborn HS United Negro Coll Fund & Urban Leagues Distinguished Warriors Youth Seminars Adv; African His Pilot Prgm Mem 1989-; Kappa Alpha Psi Mem 1970-; MI Young Lawyers PSA Project Mem 1987; NAACP Mem 1985-; Cncl of Baptist Pastor Mem 1987-; Progressive Natl Baptist Conv Instr 1986-; WQBH AM 1400 Detroit Radio Commentator 1988; Detroit Public Schls Pursuit of Excl Awd 1986, 1988, Teacher of Yr Awd 1984-85; Detroit City Cncl Testimonial Resolution 1987; Wayne Cty Commission Certificate of Appreciation 1987; St of MI 84th Legislature Spec Tribute 1987; *office:* Osborn HS 11600 E Seven Mile Rd Detroit MI 48205

ISTRE, GAYNELL SATTERFIELD, 5th Grade Teacher; *b:* Jennings, LA; *m:* James R. Satterfield; *c:* Jeffery A., James B.; *ed:* (BA) Elem Ed, 1973, (MA) Elem Ed, 1976; *cr:* 5th Grade Teacher Borden Elem 1973-; *ai:* 4th-5th Grade Drama; West Clark Teachers Assn, IN St Teachers Assn, NEA 1973-; Phi Lambda Theta 1986-.

ITO, TERUYO SHIRAKI, English Teacher; *b:* Kurtistown, HI; *m:* George H.; *c:* Dean A., Reid T., Colleen A., David L., Brian C.; *ed:* (BED) Eng, Univ of HI 1955; MI St Univ; *cr:* Eng Teacher Cntrl Jr HS 1957-58, Walter French Jr HS 1959-60, Pinole Valley HS 1980-81, Harry Ells HS 1981-82, Downer Jr HS 1982-83, Crespi Jr HS 1983-85, Pinole Jr HS 1985-; *ai:* Sch Site Cncl; Care Team Mem; Natl PTA Life Membership 1970-; *office:* Pinole Jr HS 1575 Mann Dr Pinole CA 94564

IVENS, DEBORAH RUSSELL, Chemistry-Physics Teacher; *b:* Athens, TN; *m:* John; *ed:* (BA) Bio, Carson-Newman Coll 1984; *cr:* Teacher Chattanooga Cntrl HS 1986-87, Soddy-Daisy HS 1987-88, Mc Minn Cty HS 1988-; *ai:* Engineering Team, Sci Club, Jr Class Spon; TN Teacher, Industry, Environment Conference; *office:* Mc Minn Cty HS 2215 Congress Pkwy Athens TN 37303

IVERSON, FRANCES SIMPSON, Fifth Grade Teacher; *b:* Roanoke, AL; *m:* Roy; *c:* Timothy; *ed:* (BS) Elem Ed, Jacksonville St 1965; *cr:* Teacher Folsom Jr HS 1965-67; 4th Grade Teacher Ball Ground Elem 1967-68, Canton Elem 1968-69, 1971-72, Sand Hill Elem 1972-78; 4th-5th Grade Teacher Roopville Elem 1978-; *ai:* Media Comm Roopville Elem Sch; Southern Assn of Educators (Steering Comm, Chairperson Philosophy & Objectives Dev); Roopville Elem Sch Teacher of Yr 1986-87; *office:* Roopville Elem Sch 60 Old Carrollton Rd Roopville GA 30170

IVERSON, JON R., Chemistry Instructor; *b:* Omaha, NE; *m:* Carolyn J. Parde; *c:* Kathy, Joan, Tom; *ed:* (BS) Phys Sci, Peru St Coll 1962; (MS) Chem, Univ of MO Rolla 1969; Grad Stud Univ of NE Omaha, IA St Univ, Univ of IA; *cr:* Chem Instr Missouri Valley HS 1962-79; Phys Sci/Physics/Quant Analysis Teacher Sioux City West HS 1979-; *ai:* Publicity Dir West HS; NHS & Quiz Bowl Team Adv; NEA, IA St Ed Assn 1962-; Sioux City Ed Assn 1979-; Kiwanis Intnl Local Pres 1962-79; Connie Belin Fellowship for Gifted Ed 1986; *office:* West HS 2001 Casselman Sioux City IA 51103

IVES, JUDITH C., Fifth Grade Teacher; *b:* Sidney, NY; *m:* Albert G.; *c:* Gail, Andrew, Alex; *ed:* (BS) Elem Ed, 1966, (MS) Elem Ed, 1990 SUC Oneonta; *cr:* 3rd Grade Teacher 1966-67, 6th Grade Teacher 1970-71, 1972-74, 3rd Grade Teacher 1976-78, 5th Grade Teacher 1978- Baingbridge-Guilford; *ai:* Dist Leadership Team for Effective Schls; Guilford Center Presbyn Church (Elder 1985-, Organist 1958-); Catskill Choral Society; *office:* Bainbridge-Guilford Cntrl Sch Greenlawn Ave Bainbridge NY 13733

IVEY, LEON ENLO, Chemistry Teacher; *b:* Decaturville, TN; *m:* Susan Kinzer; *c:* Eric, Stephen, Melissa; *ed:* (BS) Chem, TN Tech 1962; (MBA) Bus Management, GA St Univ 1972; 6th Year Stud Mid TN St 1975-78; *cr:* Sr Research Engr Lockheed Aircraft Corp 1962-69; Math Teacher Hickman Cty Jr HS 1970-73; Math/Sci Teacher Hampshire HS 1973-74; Chem/Math/Ec Teacher Cntrl HS 1974-; *ai:* Stu Extracurricular Research Adv; Maury Cty Ed Assn Pres 1977, Teacher of Yr 1986; *office:* Cntrl HS 721 Experiment Station Ln Columbia TN 38401

IVINS, GEORGE ANTHONY, English Teacher; *b:* Salt Lake City, UT; *m:* Barbara E. Dubuy; *c:* Elizabeth A., Margaret E.; *ed:* (BA) Eng, Univ of NC 1967; (MA) Ed, Univ of NC 1970; Course Work Gifted Ed; *cr:* Teacher Eng Williston Sr HS 1 967-68; New Hanover HS 1968-69; Casa Grande Union HS 1969-; *ai:* Jr Class Spon; Cmptr Dev Comm; NEA 1985-87; AZ Ed Assn Delegate 1970-; Casa Grande Ed Assn Pres 1986-87; Kiwanis Intnl 1970-76; Citizens Planning Comm 1986-88; Citizens for Better Government 1988-; Univ of Chicago Outstanding Teacher Awd 1988-89; Finalist-Teacher-of Year-Partners in Ed 1989; *office:* Casa Grande Union H S 420 E Florence Blvd Casa Grande AZ 85222

IVNIK, KATHRYN (DAVISSON), Physical Education Teacher; *b:* East St Louis, IL; *m:* Richard L.; *c:* Richard A., Paul D.; *ed:* (BS) Phy Ed, S IL Univ Edwardsville 1977; (MA) Educl Admin & Supervision, Governors St Univ 1989; *cr:* Phys Ed Teacher Northview Elem Sch 1981, R C Hill & Valley View & Oakview Elem Schls 1981-82; Phys Ed Teacher Hubert H Humphrey Mid Sch 1982-; *ai:* Phys Ed Mid Sch Curr Dev Comm; *office:* Hubert H Humphrey Mid Sch 777 Falcon Ridge Way Bolingbrook IL 60439

IYER, MALINI K., Mathematics Dept Chair; *b:* Mayuram, India; *m:* Krishna; *c:* Balaji K.; *ed:* (BS) Math, Madras Univ 1965; TX Teacher Certificate Math, Pan Amer Univ 1984; (MSIS) Math, Univ of TX Pan Amer 1987; Grad Stud Doctoral Prgm Univ of Houston; Coll Bd Wkshp on Advanced Placement Calculus Prgm; Math, UT Pan Amer Univ 1987; *cr:* Math Teacher Red Mount Grammar Sch Orissa India 1967-69, Shaaban Robert Scndry Sch Dar es Salaam Tanzania 1970-76, Expatriates Study Group Tanzania 1979, Intnl Sch of Tanganyika 1980-82, Univ Preparatory Sch 1982-83, Cummings Jr HS 1985-86; Adjunct Professor Univ of TX Pan Amer 1987-; Advanced Placement Teacher Course on Sundays & Holidays 1989-; Math Teacher/Dept Chairperson Gladys Porter HS 1989-; *ai:* Stu for Advanced Placement Prgm in Calculus Coach; Parent Teacher Stu Assn Awd; Nom Presidential Awd for Excl in Teaching Math 1990; Nom Rotary Club Awd for Excl in Teaching Math 1990; Mellon Fnd Schlsp; E Africa Publication Company Review & Author Math Textbooks; Recognized for Teaching Excl British System; EXCET Tests Math Tutor St Level; *home:* 74 Ray Ave Brownsville TX 78521

IZZARD, MARILYN JONES, Kindergarten Teacher; *b:* Lancaster Cty, SC; *m:* Odell; *c:* Terrence S., Kyle O.; *ed:* (BA) Early Chldhd, 1979, (MS) Early Chldhd, 1988 Univ of SC Columbia; Spec Ed Prgm Winthrop Coll; *cr:* Teachers Aide Kershaw Elem & Mid Sch 1971-78; Grad Asst 1979-80, Assoc Teacher 1980 Univ of SC Columbia; Kndgtn/2nd Grade Teacher Kershaw Primary 1980-; Consultant Winthrop Coll 1989-; *ai:* All Star Club Spon; Cmptr Club; Various Sch Act; SC Assn for Children Under Six (Presenter, Consultant) 1989-; Kershaw Arts Cncl Pres; Cultural Visions; Sand Hill Baptist Church Club Advs Coord; Univ of SC Early Chldhd Dept Fellowship Awd; *home:* Rt 3 Box 208 Kershaw SC 29067

J

JACAK, JUDITH LAVARDA, English/Geography Teacher; *b:* Brownsville, WI; *m:* Clem; *c:* Craig, Carey, Cameron, Jama; *ed:* (BS) Scndry Ed/Eng, Univ of WI Milwaukee 1973; (ME) Ed, Natl Coll of Ed 1987; *cr:* Eng/Geography Teacher Mayville HS 1973-78, Kewaskum HS 1978-; *ai:* Asst Dir Musical Production; Asst Adv Forensics; St Anthonys Parish Cncl Secy 1984-86; *office:* Kewaskum HS 1510 Bilgo Ln Kewaskum WI 53040

JACK, REBECCA G., French/Spanish Teacher; *b:* Oklahoma City, OK; *c:* Aaron, Adrianne; *ed:* (BA) Fr/Span, Univ of OK 1982; Univ of Geneva 1968, Univ of Nice 1971-72, OK St Univ 1982; *cr:* Fr Teacher Ponca City HS 1983-84; Fr/Span Teacher Union Jr HS 1984-; *ai:* Fr Competition; Mardi Gras Spon; After-Sch Elem Fr Teacher; Foreign Lang Dept Head; OK Ed Assn, NEA, OK Foreign Lang Teachers Assn 1990; Union Sch Dist Teacher of Month 1988; OK St Univ Span Summer Immersion Grant; NACEL Chaperone; *office:* Union Jr HS 7616 S Garnett Broken Arrow OK 74012

JACK, WINIFRED BOOKHOUT, Social Studies Dept Chair; *b:* Dallas, TX; *c:* William G.; *ed:* (BA) Soc Sci, Susquehanna Univ 1974; *cr:* 8th Grade Soc Stud Teacher Woodlawn Jr 1974-77; 8th/9th Grade Soc Stud Teacher Deep Creek Jr/Mid 1977-; Dept Chm/6th/-8th Grade Teacher Dudalk Mid 1984-; *ai:* Values Comm Chm; Dr Martin L King Co-Chm Dundalk Mid Sch; Team Leader Soc Stud; Helped Write 6th-8th Grades Soc Stud Curr Baltimore Cty Public Schls; *office:* Dundalk Mid Sch 7400 Wunmlnway Baltimore MD 21222

JACKSON, ALICIA ANNETTE (WALKER), Spanish/English Teacher; *b:* Garnett, KS; *m:* Dale W.; *c:* Gretchen A., Meaghan A.; *ed:* (BSE) Eng/Span, 1975, (MA) Eng, 1977 Emporia St Univ; *cr:* Eng Instr Emporia St Univ 1975-76; Eng Adjunct Instr Fort Scott Comm Coll 1986-; Eng/Span Instr Uniontown HS 1976-; *ai:* Organize & Spon Stu Trips; Span Club & Soph Class Spon; Cooperating Teacher; In-service Presenter; Dist Curr Comm Chm; Dist Study Comm Secy; NEA, KS Ed Assn 1976-; Uniontown Teachers Assn (Pres, VP, Secy, Coordinating Cncl, Negotiations Chm) 1976-, Golden Apple 1986, Dist KS Teacher 1989, Master Teacher 1989; Alpha Delta Kappa (Secy, Chaplain) 1983-; AATSP, KS Foreign Lang Assn 1984-; KS Assn Teachers of Eng 1988-; United Meth Women VP 1977-; Uniontown United Meth Church (Pianist, Sunday Sch Teacher, Bible Sch Teacher, Asst Supt) 1977-; 4-H Judge 1978-; Society of Mayflower Descendants 1981-; Eng Grad Assistantship 1975; Presidential Assistantship 1975; Outstanding Young Women of America 1984; KS Teacher of Yr Finalist 1989; KS Master Teacher Nominee 1989; Baker Univ Outstanding Teacher Awd 1989; Unified Sch Dist 235 Philosophy & Performance Teaching Commendation 1988; NCATE Bd of Examiners KS Ed Assn Observer; *office:* Uniontown HS Box 70 Uniontown KS 66779

JACKSON, ALMA ROSE, 5th Grade Teacher; *b:* Wilmet, AR; *m:* James E.; *c:* Sonja, Jennifer; *ed:* (BA) Elem Ed, Amin Coll 1969; UCA; UALR; UAPB; *cr:* Teacher Albion Public Sch 1969-70; Pine Bluff Public Sch 1972-; *ai:* Sci Comm; Dist Wide Curr Comm; AR Ed Assn; Pine Ed Assn Chairperson/Human Rets 1989-; Outstanding Sci Teacher 1988-89; *home:* 1519 Olive St Pine Bluff AR 71601

JACKSON, ANGELA NEDA, 6th Grade Teacher; *b:* Tallahassee, FL; *ed:* (BS) Elem Ed, FL A&M Univ 1980; *cr:* 2nd Lieutenant US Army Field Artillery 1980; Teacher CETA FL A&M Univ 1983; 6th Grade Math Teacher R Frank Nims Mid Sch 1984-; *ai:* Yrbk Spon; Girls Sftbl Coach; Saturday Sch Prgm Act Leader; NEA, Leon Cty Teacher Assn 1985; Natl Assn of Univ Women 1986; Order of Eastern Star 1985-; Sigma Gamma Rho 1982-; *office:* R Frank Nims Mid Sch 723 W Orange Ave Tallahassee FL 32310

JACKSON, ANJEANETTE BENEFIELD, Social Studies Teacher; *b:* Detroit, MI; *c:* Anthony; *ed:* (AB) Ec, 1970, (MS) Scndry Ed, 1974 IN Univ Bloomington; Ed, Soc Stud & Microcomputers, N IL Univ, NE IL Univ & Aurora Univ; *cr:* Educator/8th-9th Grade Soc Stud Teacher Hanley Jr HS 1974-77; Basic Skills Instr Main Baptist Church 1986; Microcomputer Instr

CETA Prgm 1987, Waubonsee Comm Coll 1988; Educator Jefferson Mid Sch 1977-; *ai:* Soc Stud Dept Team Leader; 7th & 8th Grade Soc Stud Amer His & Geography; 7th Grade Girls Track, Cheerleading & Pom-Pomr Squad Coach;Extended Learning Prgm; Sch Building Leadership Team; Cmptr Planning & Policy Comm; IL Ed Assn, NEA; Aurora Ed Assn W Building Rep; IL Geographical Society; Delta Sigma Theta; Big Brothers-Big Sisters; City of Aurora Today Outstanding Teaching Awd; Aurora Actionnaires Awd for Outstanding Teaching & Cmmty Service; Natl Geographic Society Prgm Participation for Outstanding Geography Teachers; Wkshp Presenter on Cmptrs for Teachers; *office:* Thomas Jefferson Mid Sch 1151 Plum St Aurora IL 60506

JACKSON, BARBARA HOWARD, English Teacher; *b:* Tensaw, AL; *m:* J. Malcolm; *c:* Traci; *ed:* (BA) Eng, AL St Univ 1974; (MS) Eng, Troy St Univ 1977; *cr:* Teacher Bay Minette Mid Sch 1974-; *ai:* Eng Dept Chairperson; Natl Jr Honor Society Chapter Adv; NEA, AL Ed Assn 1974-; BCEA Bd of Dir 1986-; *office:* Bay Minette Mid Sch 1000 Track St Bay Minette AL 36507

JACKSON, BESSIE ANDERSON, English Teacher; *b:* Carrollton, MS; *m:* William Arthur; *c:* Dexter A., Stephen N.; *ed:* (BS) Eng, MS Valley St Univ 1965; (MS) Theater/Comm Arts, Memphis St Univ 1979; Admin/Supervision, Memphis St Univ; Media Research; Free Lance Writer; *cr:* Eng Teacher Gentry HS 1966-67, Wonder HS 1967-68, Memphis City Schls 1968-; Overton HS of Creative Performing Arts 1989-; *ai:* Overton HS Eng Dept Chm 1987-88; NCTE, Intl Rdng Assn, TN Ed Assn, Shelby Memphis Cncl of Teachers of Eng; Church Youth Cncl 1980-; Article Published.

JACKSON, CAROLYN DENISE (JACKSON), Mathematics/ Reading Teacher; *b:* Ocilla, GA; *m:* Thomas Timothy; *c:* Tina K.; *ed:* (BBA) Bus/Mrktg, Valdosta St Coll 1985; *cr:* Teacher Coffee Jr HS 1985-; *ai:* Sch Pep Club Adv; Mem Schls Video Production & Stu at Risk Comms Mem; Intnl Rdng Assn Mem 1989-; Yuppies of Tomorrow Pres 1986-; *office:* Coffee Jr HS Drawer 999 S Gaskin Ave Douglas GA 31533

JACKSON, CAROLYN WALLIS, English Teacher; *b:* Booneville, MS; *m:* Calvin G.; *c:* Tommy Green, Rose A. Green, Leigh C.; *ed:* (BSE) Soc Sci/Eng, Delta St Univ 1956; Grad Work MS St Univ & Univ of MS; *cr:* Teacher Lambert 1956-57; Eng Teacher Falkner 1957-60, Rienzi 1960-61, Jumpertown 1961-73, Bouneville HS 1973-; *ai:* Anchor Club & Class Spon; Home Room; Kappa Kappa Iota Pres; Pilot Pres-Elect; Kappa Kappa Iota (Pres, Secy) 1978; Pilot (Anchor Chm, Pres-Elect) 1987-89, Perfect Attendance Awd 1990; First United Meth Church Life Membership; Teacher of Yr; STAR Teacher; *home:* 610 9th St Booneville MS 38829

JACKSON, CHARLES BORDEN, History Teacher; *b:* Alton, IL; *m:* Ellen Fischer; *c:* Matthew, Jane, David; *ed:* (BA) His, 1976, (BS) His, 1977 S IL Univ Edwardsville; *cr:* Teacher Fenton HS 1977-78, Triad HS 1978-; *ai:* Coached Bsktbl, Tennis, Golf; Spon Camera Club, Investment Club; Tour Guide Stu Tours of Europe; NCSS 1987-89; Teacher of Yr Triad HS 1979-80, 1985-86; *office:* Triad HS R R 1 Saint Jacob IL 62281

JACKSON, CLARENCE, JR., In-Sch Suspension Supervisor; *b:* Mobile, AL; *m:* Evelyn Delores Lyons; *c:* Craig, Wayne, Ryan, Britt; *ed:* (BS) Music/Soc Stud, AL St Univ 1957; (MED) Admin/Supervision, Univ of GA 1976; Data Collector Teacher Evaluation; *cr:* Soc Stud Teacher 1987-89, In-Sch Suspension Prgm Supvr 1989- West Laurens HS; *ai:* Prom, Public Relations, Staff Dev Comm; Laurens Assn of Educators Legislative Chairperson 1987-89, Certificate 1987-89; Black Festival Comm 1987-89, Certificate 1987-89; Black Man of Yr 1985; *office:* West Laurens HS Rt 5 I-16 441 S Dublin GA 31021

JACKSON, CYNTHIA CHILDERS, Biology Teacher; *b:* Columbia, SC; *m:* John Morgan Jr.; *ed:* (BS) Bio, Auburn Univ 1983; *cr:* Bio/Health Teacher Jones Valley Magnet HS 1984-87; Bio Teacher La Grange HS 1987-; *ai:* SADD & NHS Adv; NEA, GA Ed Assn; La Grange Jr Womens Club Ways & Means Chm 1988-; Laurel Garden Club 1990; Troup Cty Historical Society 1988-; *office:* La Grange HS 516 N Greenwood St La Grange GA 30240

JACKSON, CYNTHIA THOMAS, First Grade Teacher; *b:* Philadelphia, PA; *m:* Larry T.; *c:* Kelley; *ed:* (BS) Elem Ed, Cntrl St Univ 1971; *cr:* Group Cnslr South Phila Cmmty Center 1971-72; Prgm Coord AFNA 1972-73; Teacher Stephen Girard Elem Sch 1973-; *ai:* Sch Newspaper Editor; Bldg Rep; Bldg Comm; Grade Chairperson; *office:* Stephen Girard Elem Sch 18th Snyder Ave Philadelphia PA 19145

JACKSON, DAN ADRIAN, English Teacher; *b:* Clarksdale, MS; *ed:* (BA) Eng, Ottawa Univ 1989; *cr:* Chemist Great Lakes Chemical Company 1974-83; Teacher Eureka 1989-; *ai:* Journalism & Yrbk; Sr Class Spon; KNEA 1985-; *home:* 401 N Oak Eureka KS 67045

JACKSON, DEBBIE HOFFMAN, Third Grade Teacher; *b:* Lubbock, TX; *m:* Robert; *c:* Meredith, Vanessa; *ed:* (BS) Elem Ed, TX Tech Univ 1976; *cr:* 3rd Grade Teacher Christ The King 1976-; *ai:* Confirmation & Eucharist Class Instr; *office:* Christ The King Sch 4011 54th St Lubbock TX 79413

JACKSON, DELORES LYON, Remedial Education Teacher; *b:* Avondale, GA; *m:* Bryan H.; *c:* Bryan Jr., Len, David; *ed:* (BS) Scndry Ed/His, Univ of TN 1982; (MED) Mid Grades, W GA Coll 1987; *cr:* Spec Ed Teacher La Fayette Jr HS 1982-84; Eng Teacher Rossville Jr HS 1984-85; His/Government Teacher 1985-89, Remedial Math/Rdng Dept Chm 1989- La Fayette HS; *ai:* Stu Government Spon; Stus Staying Straight Team Mem; Library Comm; *home:* 1012 Sizemore St P O Box 703 La Fayette GA 30728

JACKSON, DENNIS MURL, 8th Grade History Teacher; *b:* Murray, KY; *m:* Patricia Ann Brandon; *c:* Brandon; *ed:* (BS) His/ Phys Ed, 1966, (MA) Ed, 1971, Ed, 1976 Murray St; Individualized Ed 1972; Drug Ed Univ of Miami Sch of Medicine 1975; YCC Cnslr 1978; *cr:* Teacher Trigg Cty KY Bd of Ed 1966-67, Benton Harbor MI Bd of Ed 1967-68; Teacher/Coach Paducah City Bd of Ed 1968-; *ai:* Pep Comm; Social Study Curr Comm Vice Chm; Athletic Comm; Mem Paducah Mid Sch Comm; KEA; NEA; PEA; Paducah Human Rights Comm Chm Budget Comm 1985-; Murray St Univ Alumni Assn Ex-Cncl Chm Schlsp Comm 1988-; KY St Cncl on Higher Ed Task Force on Minority Stu Ed; *office:* Paducah Mid Sch 342 Lone Oak Rd Paducah KY 42001

JACKSON, DONALD RAY, Physics/Mathematics Teacher; *b:* Rayville, LA; *ed:* (BS) Physics/Math, Grambling St Univ 1979; Certificate Physics/Phys Sci/Math, Univ of TX Dallas 1983; Numerous Courses; *cr:* Engr Gearhart Owens 1979-80; Exec Asst Diamond Shamrock Corp 1980-82; Telemarketing Supvr Marc Inc 1981-86; Math/Sci Teacher Richardson Ind Sch Dist 1983-; *ai:* Natl Jr Hs Society Spon 1989-; Boys Tennis Court 1989-; Site Base Management Mem Academics; Math & Sci Textbook Adoption Comm; Explorer Club; Greater Dallas Math Teacher Assn, Assn of TX Educators, N TX Sci Teachers Assn, Richardson Educators Assn 1983-; Explorer Club Exec Adv 1986-87; Kappa Alpha Psi Historian 1989-; TX Utilities Grant Sci Principles & Energy Ed Instruction Univ of TX Arlington 1988; *home:* 3015 Valley Meadow Dr Dallas TX 75220

JACKSON, DONNA HOPKINS, English/Business Teacher; *b:* Bramwell, WV; *m:* Taylor; *c:* Tonya, Taneesa, William; *ed:* (BS) Bus Ed/Eng, Bluefield St 1971; Grad Stud, WV Coll; *cr:* Typing Teacher Elkhorn Jr HS 1971-75; Eng Teacher Northfork HS 1978-85; Key/Eng Teacher Elkhorn Jr HS 1986-; *ai:* Co Spon of Jr Honor Society Elkhorn Jr HS; WVEA, NEA 1978-; *home:* Box 25 Worth WV 24897

JACKSON, DORIS DE VANEY, Mathematics Teacher; *b:* Russellville, AL; *m:* Luther A.; *c:* Michael G.; *ed:* (BS) Elem Ed 1967, (MA) Elem Ed, 1968 Florence St; (EDS) Elem Ed, Univ of AL 1974; Rdng Specialist; *cr:* 6th Grade Teacher Howell & Graves 1968-69; 6th Grade Teacher 1969-74, Title I Rdng Teacher 1974-81, 7th Grade Math Teacher 1981-82, 6th Grade Teacher 1982- Avalon Mid Sch; *ai:* Natl Math League, Mathematical Olympiads Elem Schls, AL LA Miss Math League, St Judes Math-A-Thon Spon; Media Center, Sch & Cmmty, Math Curr, Cmptr Curr Comm; Muscle Shoals Prof Organiations Secy 1976-78; NEA, AEA, MSEA 1968-76; *home:* Rt 7 Box 334 Sky Park Rd Florence AL 35630

JACKSON, DORIS HOPE, Science Teacher; *b:* Gary, IN; *m:* Troy II; *c:* Tramell, Dontrell; *ed:* (BA) Natural Sci, George Williams Coll 1974; Teachers Certificate, IN Univ NW 1977; Working Toward Masters Educl Admin, Chicago St Univ 1990; *cr:* Teacher Gary Sch Corp 1974-77, Harvey Public Schls Dist 152 1977-; *ai:* Stu Asst Core Team; Curr, Textbook Selection Comm; HEA, NEA; Nom for IL Golden Apple Awd 1989-; YMCA Service Awd 1989; Outstanding Women America Awd 1979; *office:* Brooks Jr HS 14741 Wallace Ave Harvey IL 60426

JACKSON, FLO WHITFIELD, Science Department Head; *b:* Jasper, GA; *m:* Reginald V.; *c:* Melodie; *ed:* (BS) Chem, Univ of GA 1959; (MRE) Youth Work, S Baptist Seminary 1962; (MED) Sci Ed, GA Southern 1983; *cr:* Math/Sci Teacher Oglethorpe Chrstn Acad 1979-81, Brunswick Chrstn Acad 1981-82; Sci Teacher Mc Intosh Cty Acad 1982-; *ai:* Beta Club Spon; Var Cheerleading Coach; Chm In-Sch Schlsp Fund for Outstanding Sr; NSTA, GA Educators Assn 1989-; GA Sci Teachers Assn 1988-; Mc Intosh Star Teacher; *home:* PO Box 575 Jackson St Darien GA 31305

JACKSON, GARRY DALE, Assistant Principal; *b:* Louisville, KY; *m:* Nancy A.; *c:* Brandon, Jeffrey; *ed:* (BA) Elem Ed, Morehead St Univ 1976; (MED) Admin, 1978, (Rank I) Admin, 1980 Xavier Univ; *cr:* Teacher Lincoln Elem 1976-77, Caywood Elem 1977-86; Prin Ryland Elem 1986-89; Asst Prin Scott HS 1989-; *ai:* Phi Delta Kappa 1979-, 10 Yr Awd 1989; Soc Stud Innovative Grant 1985; *home:* 3035 Winding Trails Dr Edgewood KY 41017

JACKSON, GINGER KAY (JACKSON), Kindergarten Teacher; *b:* Union City, IN; *m:* Melvin Dean; *c:* Joni K. Steveson, Aimee N. Simmons; *ed:* (BS) Elem Ed, 1967, (MA) Elem Ed, 1972 Ball St Univ; Kndgtn Endorsement; *cr:* 1st Grade Teacher 1967-68, Kndgtn Teacher 1969-70, Kndgtn Teacher 1972- Monroe Cntrl Elem; *ai:* NEA, IN St Teachers Assn, Monroe Cntrl Teachers Assn 1967-; *office:* Monroe Cntrl Elem Sch RR 1 Parker City IN 47368

JACKSON, GLENDA SERITA, 5th Grade Teacher; *b:* Gadsden, AL; *ed:* (BS) Elem Ed, Jacksonville St Univ 1977; (MS) Elem Ed, Univ of AL Birmingham 1980; *cr:* Spec Ed Teacher Thompson Elem 1978-81; 3rd-6th Grade Teacher Constantine Elem Sch 1981-86; Alternative Teacher 1986-87, 5th Grade Teacher 1987- Johnston Elem Sch; *ai:* Coach Boys Bsktbl Team; Minister; Just Say No Club Coord; Jail Ministry; Phi Delta Kappa, NEA, AL Ed Assn; Agency for Substance Abuse, Sav-A-Life Bd of Dir; *home:* 725 Crestview Dr Gadsden AL 35901

JACKSON, H. KENNETH, JR., 5th/6th Grade Soc Stud Teacher; *b:* Pennsboro, WV; *m:* Nancy S. Markland; *c:* Kathy A., Brian T., Judy L.; *ed:* (BA) Elem Ed, Math, Soc Stud, 1980; *cr:* 6th Grade Teacher Murphytown WV 1980-83; 5th-8th Grade Soc Stud/Math Teacher Ellenboro WV 1983-86; Soc Stud/Math Teacher Pennsboro WV 1985-; *home:* Rt 1 Box 162 Pennsboro WV 26415

JACKSON, HENRY HOYT, Counselor; *b:* Mountain Park, OK; *m:* Sharon; *ed:* (BSE) Math/Ed, 1967, (MS) Math/Counseling, 1970 Midwestern St Univ; Counseling, Midwestern St Univ St Cert 1971; Sch Admin, SW TX St Univ St Cert 1977; Counseling, Univ of TX 1973; *cr:* Math Teacher Wichita Falls HS 1967-71, Crockett HS 1971-73; Psychometrist Corinth Admin Annex 1973-74; Cnslr Lamar Mid Sch 1974-; *ai:* TACD, TSCA, CTACD, NEA, TSTA, AAT; Cntrl Assembly of God Church (Sunday Sch Teacher, Church Governing Bd); Mobilization & Placement Service; H & Q Fitness Center; St Cnslrs Convention 1987; Prgm Presenter 1987; *office:* Lamar Mid Sch 6201 Wynona Austin TX 78757

JACKSON, J. DONALD, 9th Grade Teacher; *b:* York, PA; *m:* Barbara S.; *c:* Mitchell, Matthew, Mark; *ed:* (BSED) Soc Stud, Millersville Univ 1965-; Masters Equivalency Temple Univ, & W MD; *cr:* Amer His Teacher Spring Grove Jr HS 1966-; *ai:* Golf Club Adv; PSEA, NEA, SGEA 1966-; *home:* 774 Baltimore St Hanover PA 17331

JACKSON, JACK DEAN, 7th Grade Teacher; *b:* Storm Lake, IA; *m:* Mary Ann Stockey; *c:* Julie, Jill; *ed:* (BA) Psych, Univ IA 1968; (MA) Counseling, NE MO St Univ 1980; *cr:* Mrktng Rep Mobil Oil Corporation 1969-70; Teacher Indian Trail Jr HS 1971-73, Taft Mid Sch 1973-; *ai:* 7th Grade Block Leader, Track Coach; Phi Delta Kappa 1981-; Natl Mid Sch Assn 1987-; CREA, TSEA, NEA 1971-; *office:* Taft Mid Sch 5200 E Ave NW Cedar Rapids IA 52405

JACKSON, JAYNE RUSSELL, 5th Grade Teacher; *b:* Nashville, TN; *m:* Darryl Douglas; *c:* Kristin, David, Joshua; *ed:* (BS) Art/Elem Ed, 1970, Career Ladder I Elem Ed, 1984 Middle TN St Univ; *cr:* 7th Grade Teacher Kingston Jr HS 1970-72; 4th-7th Grade Teacher Midtown Sch 1976-; Teacher Roane St Comm Coll 1979; *ai:* Sci Chairperson Just Say No Club Co-Chairperson 1989-; Academic Comm Chairperson; PTAC; RCEA 1970-; TN Ed Assn 1970-; Natl Ed Assn 1970-; Career Ladder I Certificate Qwd of Recognition Roane Cty Sch Bd 1984; Pottery Exhibition Oak Ridge Museum 1979; *office:* Midtown Elem Sch Rt 8 Box 188 Harriman TN 37748

JACKSON, JEANETTE HENRY, Soc Studies Teacher/ Counselor; *b:* Cheyenne, WY; *m:* Donald M.; *c:* Donalynn Sloan, Carleen Robinson; *ed:* (BS) His/Eng, 1966, (MS) Teaching His/ Eng, 1972 Univ of OR; Counseling Trng Univ of OR; *cr:* His/Eng Teacher 1966-80, Cnslr/His Teacher 1980- Pleasant Hill Jr HS; *ai:* Drug Abuse Response & Stu Assistance Team Leaders; Peer Cnslr Trainer/Adv; Phys Ed Assn Schlsp Comm; Pleasant Hill Ed Assn Building Rep 1977-78, 1980-81; OR Ed Assn, NEA; *office:* Pleasant Hill Jr HS 36386 Hwy 58 Pleasant Hill OR 97455

JACKSON, JEFFREY MAXWELL, Computer Teacher; *b:* Cumberland, MD; *c:* Jerilyn; *ed:* (BA) Bio, W MD Coll 1979; (MED) Admin/Supervision, Frostburg St Univ 1985; *cr:* Sci Teacher 1979-88, Cmptr Teacher 1989- Northern Mid Sch; *ai:* Golf Coach 1980-83, Northern HS; MD St Teachers Assn, Garrett Cty Teachers Assn, NEA; Maplehurst Cntry Club, BPOE Elks, Presbyn Church; Articles/Features Published Golf Shop Operations Magazine; W MD Golf Owner; *office:* Northern Mid Sch Rt 2 Box 5 Accident MD 21520

JACKSON, JOHN CHARLES, Ohio & US History Teacher; *b:* Columbus, OH; *m:* Carol N. Tiggelbeck; *ed:* (BS) Ed, Soc Stud, Ohio St Univ 1961; Addl Studies Eng Cert Oh St; Drug & Alcohol Ed Oh St; His; *cr:* 7th-12th Grade Teacher Buckeye Local Schls 1961-62; 7th/8th Grade Teacher Grandview Heights City Schls 1962-; *ai:* Cooperating Teacher-Project Bus Jr Achievement 8th Grade Stu 1984-88; Grandview Teacher Assn Pres 1967-68; 1962-; Ohio Ed Assn 1961-; NEA 1961-; Univ Lodge 631 F&AM 1969-; Scottish Rite 1974-; Aladdin Temple Shrine 1974-; Whos Who in the Midwest 1990-91 Edition; Scholar-Martha Holden Jennings Fnd 1968-69; *home:* 5741 Aspendale Dr Columbus OH 43235

JACKSON, JOYCE ELLEN, School Counselor; *b:* Washington, PA; *ed:* (AB) Elem Ed, Glenville St Coll 1963; (MED) Scndry Sch Counseling, OH Univ 1970; Eng, Counseling Psych, WV Univ; *cr:* 1st Grade Teacher Fairplains Elem 1963-64; Eng Teacher Lewis Cty HS 1964-69; Cnslr Morgantown HS 1970-; *ai:* WVACD, WVSCA; Mountaineer Kennel Club Bd of Dir; Back Fork Books Publishing Editorial Adv; WV St Dept of Ed Outstanding Stu Support Service Awd 1986; WV Hum Fnd Fellowship; *office:* Morgantown HS 109 Wilson Ave Morgantown WV 26505

JACKSON, KEITH D., Sixth Grade Teacher; *b:* Ottawa On, Canada; *m:* Ofelia O. Alaira; *c:* Heidi J. Jackson Severtson, Todd D.; *ed:* (BA) Anthropology/Soc Sci, Nyack Coll 1963; (MDIV) Theology & Counseling, Fuller Theological Seminary 1968; Ed, Monterey Inst of Intnl Stud; *cr:* Instr Seminario Biblico Alianza 1965-66; Asst Pastor Union Presbyn Church 1967-69, Carmel Presbyn Church 1970-71; 7th/8th Grade Teacher Mango Jr HS 1972; 8th Grade Math Teacher J W Fair Jr HS 1972-73; 4th/5th Grade Teacher Seven Trees Elem Sch 1973-79; 6th Grade Teacher

Hillsdale Elem Sch 1979-; *ai:* Lang Art Comm Hillsdale Sch; Franklin Mc Kinley Ed Assn Treas 1981-83, 1985-86, Negotiator; CA Teachers Assn St Cncl Rep 1986-; NEA St Rep to Rep Assembly 1989-; Hillsdale Teacher of Yr 1985-86; Deans List Monterey Inst of Intnl Stud 1971; Distinguished Service Awd 1968; Extensive World Travel; *office:* Hillsdale Year Round Sch 3200 Water St San Jose CA 95111

JACKSON, KENNETH AUBREY, 8th Grade English Teacher; *b:* Tulsa, OK; *m:* Doretta Spielbusch; *c:* Brian, Matthew, Lisa; *ed:* (BA) Eng, 1972, (MS) Admin, 1983 OK St Univ; *cr:* Teacher/Coach Drumright HS 1972-76, Newkirk HS 1976-83, East Jr HS 1983-; *ai:* 7th Grade Ftbl, Jr HS Wrestling, Boys & Girls Golf Coach; *home:* 619 S 10th St Ponca City OK 74601

JACKSON, LA ROSE BLACKMAN, 9th Grade English Teacher; *b:* Goldsboro, NC; *m:* William Allen Jr.; *c:* William A. III, Jason T.; *ed:* (BS) Lang Art, Atlantic Chrstn Coll 1982; (MS) Ed Admin, E Carolina Univ 1986; *cr:* Teacher Grantham Sch 1982-; *ai:* Eng, Jr HS Chairperson; Yrbk Adv; Teacher Assistance Team & Sch Advisory Comm; Media Center Comm Mentor Teacher; Presidential Schlsp; Scholastic Awds; Graduated Summa Cum Laude Chief Marshall Coll; *office:* Grantham Sch Rt 1 Box 221 Goldsboro NC 27530

JACKSON, LINDA L., American Literature Teacher; *b:* Clara City, MN; *ed:* (AA) Eng/Scndry Ed, Trinidad St Jr Coll 1962; (BA) Eng/Scndry Ed, Adams St Coll 1964; Grad Stud; *cr:* Teacher Raton Public HS 1964-; *ai:* Rodeo Club, Frosh Class Spon; Raton Rodeo Assn Secy 1981-88; *office:* Raton HS S 4th Tiger Dr Raton NM 87740

JACKSON, LOREN E., JR., 8th Grade Soc Stud Teacher; *b:* Tucson, AZ; *m:* Paula J.; *c:* Jeffrey, Christopher, Joe Merideth, Danica Merideth, Erin Merideth; *ed:* (BA) Scndry Ed/Soc Stud, Univ of AZ 1970; (MA) Psych/Counseling/Guidance, Univ of N CO 1974; *cr:* 8th Grade Soc Stud Teacher Chaparral Jr HS 1975-; *ai:* NEA Pres 1986-87; Alamogordo Music Theater (Historian 1986-, VP 1990); *office:* Chaparral Jr HS 1401 College Ave Alamogordo NM 88310

JACKSON, LYNN MC CLURE, 3rd Grade Teacher; *b:* Crescent City, CA; *m:* James Dennis; *c:* Casey M., Erin L., Scott M.; *ed:* (BA) Sociology, Chico St Univ 1970; CSUC 1972-73; *cr:* 6th Grade Teacher Holy Angel Sch 1970-71; 1st-4th Grade Teacher of Educationally Handicapped 1973-76, 2nd-4th Grade Teacher 1976- Luther Sch; *ai:* Dist Wide Curr Comm Mem; CTA, NEA Treas; AAUW Corresponding Secy 1987-89; *office:* Luther Sch 10123 Connecticut Ave Live Oak CA 95953

JACKSON, MALDONIA, English Teacher; *b:* White Hall, AL; *c:* Nancy, Arthur; *ed:* (BS) Eng/Ed, Tuskegee Univ 1968; (ME) Eng/Ed, Auburn Univ 1979; Grad Course Teaching Eng as Second Lang; *cr:* Eng Teacher Westside Jr HS 1968-73, 1975-84, IAI Girls Sch Japan 1973-75, Selma HS 1984-; *ai:* SEA, AEA, NEA; *home:* 745 Jackson Rd Hayneville AL 36040

JACKSON, MARJORIE TANCIMORE, Fifth Grade Teacher; *b:* Mt Dora, FL; *w:* Fred R. (dec); *c:* Arthur D., Yvette S. Williams; *ed:* (BA) Elem Ed, FL A&M Univ 1954; Certified Early Chldhd Ed, Rollins Coll; *cr:* Teacher Roseborough Elem 1987-; *ai:* Chairperson Sch Cmmty Relations Comm; 5th Grade Level Chairperson; Lake Cty Teachers Assn, NEA 1987-; NE Plus Ultra Civic Club Bus Mgr 1982-; Briley Singers Bus Mgr 1990; Gamma Phi Delta Treas 1985-87; Teacher of Yr 1988; Peer Teacher for Beginning Teachers; *home:* 1465 Highland St Mount Dora FL 32757

JACKSON, MICHAEL BRYANT, Industrial Arts Teacher; *b:* Augusta, ME; *m:* Suzanne L. Pinkham; *c:* Todd, Scott; *ed:* (BA) Industrial Art, Univ of S ME 1969; Cmptr Programming, Ed; Real Estate Law; First Aid & CPR Cert; *cr:* Graphic Art Teacher Reading Memorial HS 1969-70; Industrial Art Teacher Winslow Jr HS 1970-73; Drafting/Woodworking Teacher Cony HS 1973-76; Industrial Art Teacher Buker Jr HS 1976-; *ai:* Set Up Prgms for Functionally Handicapped Stus & Cmptr Curr; St of ME Industrial Art Curr Comm Mem; Manchester Sch Building Comm Chm; ME Assn Industrial Educators Pres 1971-73; Augusta Teachers Assn, ME Teachers Assn, NEA Mem; NE Teachers Convention St Coord 1974; Shrine Circus Chm 1988-91; Little League (Mgr, Coach) 1987-; Town of Manchester Selectman; *office:* Buker Jr HS Armory St Augusta ME 04330

JACKSON, MICKEY STEVEN, Elementary Counselor; *b:* Johnson City, TN; *m:* Vicki Diane Bowman; *c:* Beth; *ed:* (BS) Sci Ed/Bio, 1973, (MA) Sci Ed/Bio, 1978 E TN St Univ; Supvervision/Counseling; *cr:* 7th/8th Grade Sci Teacher Unicoi Elem Sch 1973-86; Bio Instr Unicoi Cty HS 1986-88; Elem Cnslr Unicoi Cty Schls 1988-; *ai:* Unicol Cty HS Asst Bsbl Coach 1980-; Amer Assn for Counseling & Dev 1988-; ASCD 1989-; TN Ed Assn, NEA 1973; Unincoi Cty Drug Free Alliance Pres 1988-; PTA Lifetime Membership 1986; Unicol Elem Sch Teacher of Yr 3 Times; Unicoi Cty Conservation Ed Teacher of Yr 1983; *office:* Unicoi County Schls 600 N Elm Erwin TN 37650

JACKSON, OSCAR R., Director of Bands; *b:* Shaw, MS; *c:* Monica Warren Gray; *ed:* (BS) Music Ed, Knoxville Coll 1964; (MS) Elem/Music Ed, Fiore Valley St Coll 1975; Univ of GA; Columbus Coll; Berklee Coll of Music; TN St Univ; Univ of TN; *cr:* Band Dir Lucy Addison HS 1964-65, Washington Jr HS 1964-65, Appling Jr/Sr HS 1966-70, Southwest Jr/Sr HS 1970-; *ai:* Judge Music Festivals; Omega Phi Delta Band Honor Society Adv; GMEA Instrumental Chm 1980-81; MENC; IAJE; *office:* Southwest H S 1730 Canterbury Rd Macon GA 31206

JACKSON, REGINA B., 9th Grade English Teacher; *b:* Washington, DC; *m:* Laurence A.; *c:* Shawn R.; *ed:* (BA) Eng/His, DC Teachers Coll 1955; (MS) Urban Learning, George Washington Univ 1979; Grad Work Trinity Coll; Summer Wkshps Univ of ME 1970; *cr:* Teacher Hine Jr HS 1955-; *ai:* Incentive Awd Comm; Sch Newspaper Spon; Schlsp Comm; Adv Creative Writing Project; DC Cncl of Eng 1989-; Natl Cncl of Negro Women Life Membership; Sigma Gamma Rho; Distinguished Service Awd Cardozo HS Alumni; Outstanding Teacher Awd; DC Rdng Cncl of Intnl Rdng Assn; Pilot Folger Lib DC Public Schls Project; Dept of Transportation Partners-In-Ed Service Awd; *office:* Hine Jr HS 8th & Pennsylvania Ave SE Washington DC 20003

JACKSON, RICHIE, Civics/Free Enterprise Teacher; *b:* Shreveport, LA; *m:* Teri Jean; *c:* Patrick, Sandi, Somer, Darek; *ed:* (BS) Health/Phys Ed, Northwestern St 1967; *cr:* Teacher/Coach Bossier HS; *ai:* Fellowship Chrstn Athletes Spon; Bossier HS Intra-Club Cncl Head; Bossier City Parks & Recreation Bd Mem 1989; Bossier HS Teacher of Yr 1974; *office:* Bossier HS 700 Coleman St Bossier City LA 71111

JACKSON, RITA EILEEN HAMILTON, Fifth Grade Teacher; *b:* Miami, FL; *m:* Hugh Jr.; *c:* Robert, Jabari; *ed:* (BA) Psych, Chicago St Univ 1970; (MS) Ed, De Paul Univ 1978; Grad Work in Rdng, Governor St Univ; *cr:* Elem Teacher Holy Angles 1970-76, St Martin 1976-77, Dist 147 1977-; *ai:* Report Card Comm; Gifted Ed Teacher; Cmmty Tutor; Black His Prgm Adv; KY St Alumni Chm 1980-; Quettes Organization Adopt-A-Stu Fund Raiser Schlsps 1985-; Neighborhood Tutor Pres 1984-; New Faith Baptist Church Mem 1983-; Rosa Parks Sch My Hero Awd 1987; Harvey Cmmty First Awd 1989; Newspaper Interview IL Young Authors Contest; *office:* Martin Luther King Elem Sch 14600 Seeley West Harvey IL 60426

JACKSON, ROBERT WALTER, English Teacher; *b:* New York, NY; *m:* Evelyn Stein; *c:* Laura, Kerry, Brendan; *ed:* (BA) Eng Lit, Williams Coll 1962; (BA) Eng Lang/Lit, Oxford Univ 1964; (MA) Eng Lit, Harvard Univ 1965; (MAT) Ed, Harvard GSE 1966; *cr:* Eng Intern Teacher Brookline HS 1965-66; Hum Coord Upward Bound Tougaloo Coll 1966; Eng Teacher Ardsley HS 1966-; *ai:* Amnesty Intnl Adv; Ardsley Congress of Teachers (Building VP 1989-, Building Rep 1987-89); NYSUT; Phi Beta Kappa; *office:* Ardsley HS 300 Farm Rd Ardsley NY 10502

JACKSON, RUDELLE WILLIAMS, Third Grade Teacher; *b:* Timmonsville, SC; *m:* Rufus T.; *c:* Kevin P., Rufus, Reynelda; *ed:* (BS) Elem Ed, Claflin Coll 1974; (MA) Ed, Francis Marion Coll 1988; *cr:* Teacher Brockington Elem Sch 1975-; *ai:* SC Ed Assn; NEA; BSA Den Mother 1987-88; Law Assn Grant 1989-; *office:* Brockington Elem Sch 401 N Brockington St Timmonsville SC 29161

JACKSON, SANDRA COBB, Sci Teacher/Sci Dept Chairman; *b:* Idabel, OK; *m:* Bruce; *c:* Thomas; *ed:* (BS) Chem, SE OK St Univ 1976; (MS) Ed, E TX St 1984; *cr:* 7th Grade Sci Teacher De Queen Mid Sch 1981; Spec Ed Teacher 1981-85, Sci/Chem/Physics/Bio Teacher 1985- Lockesburg HS; *ai:* Chrldr, Jr Class, Sr Class Spon; Chm Personnel Policies Comm; Staff Dev Coord; Certified Personnel Evaluation & Sch Policy Comms; Delta Kappa Gamma (Expansion Comm 1989-, VP 1987-88, Pres 1988-); United Meth Women (Pres, Secy, Treas 1982-84, Secy 1984-86, Treas 1986-, Dist Treas 1986-88); Garden Club (PreS 1988-89, VP 1989-); NASA Seeds Project 1990; *office:* Lockesburg HS P O Box 88 Lockesburg AR 71846

JACKSON, SHARON POWERS, Teacher of Gifted & Talented; *b:* Jackson, MI; *c:* Sarah, Rich, Shelley; *ed:* (BA) Ed, 1965, (MA) Gifted & Talented, 1967 Western; *cr:* LEAP Coord 1974-78, 5th/6th Grade LEAP Teacher 1979- Jackson Public Schls; *ai:* MI Assn Academically Talented Pres 1980-82; *office:* Jackson Public Schls 1227 S Wisner Jackson MI 49201

JACKSON, SUSAN BAILEY, Fouth Grade Teacher; *b:* Chillicothe, MO; *m:* Donald Edward; *c:* Christy, Katie, Jordan; *ed:* (BS) Elem Ed, NW MO St Univ 1974; Grad Courses NW MO St Univ, Univ of MO Columbia; *cr:* 2nd Grade Teacher Dewey Elem 1979-80; Kndgtn Teacher Dabney Garrison 1980-81; 4th Grade Teacher Field Schls & Cntrl Schls 1981-; *ai:* Classroom Size Comm; CTA, MSTA 1979-; YMCA Bd 1989-; Cray Fnd Awd.

JACKSON, TERON D., Science Teacher/Coach; *b:* Dade City, FL; *c:* William C., Jamie L.; *ed:* (BS) Ag & Ext Ed Entomology/Nematology, 1980; (MA) Ag & Ext Ed, 1983 Univ of FL; Project Wild; Project Learning Tree; *cr:* Vo-Ag Teacher Zephyrhills Jr HS 1980-81; Vo-Ag Teacher George C Miller Mid Sch 1983-84; Sci Teacher Moore-Mickens Mid Sch 1986-87; Pasco Mid Sch 1987-; *ai:* Asst Coach Ftbl; 7th Grade Boys Bsktbl Coach; Head Coach Boys Track; Leag of Environmental Educators in FL 1988-; NSTA 1988-89; United Sch Employees of Pasco 1990; Trilby Masonic Lodge 141 Sr Warden 1990; *office:* Pasco Mid Sch 505 S 14th St Dade City FL 33525

JACKSON, THOMAS ROLAND, JR., Computer Science Teacher; *b:* Hickory, NC; *m:* Patsy Earp; *c:* Thomas III, Kristen, Amy, Lori; *ed:* (BS) Cmptr Sci, NC St Univ 1972; Ed Course E Carolina Univ & Atlantic Chrstn Coll; *cr:* Math Teacher S Johnston HS 1972-84; Part Time Instr Johnston Tech Coll 1982-86; Cmptr Sci Teacher Smithfield-Selma HS 1984-; *ai:* Sr Spon; Chm of Unit Senate Bill 2 Steering & for Cmptr Programming Adv Comm, Johnston Tech Coll; Cmptr Sci Club Adv Rep for Cty Senate Bill 2 Comm; NC Cncl for Teachers of Math 1988-; Kenly Masonic Lodge Past Master 1980-; Kenly Lions Club VP 1978-86; *office:* Smithfield-Selma HS Booker Dairy Rd Smithfield NC 27577

JACKSON, TIMOTHY, Biology Teacher; *b:* Grand Bayou, LA; *m:* Lorine Avery; *c:* Kendrix B., Kelvin B., Karen B.; *ed:* (BS) Bio, Jarvis Chrstn Coll 1959; (MS) Bio, AL A&M Coll 1964; Southern Univ 1960; San Houston St Univ 1966; Dillard Univ 1968; Mc Neese St Univ 1980-84; *cr:* Sci Teacher Vinton Northside HS 1959-69; Bio Teacher W O Boston HS 1969-70; Sulphur HS 1970-; *ai:* Announcer Bsktbl Games; NEA 1959-; Calcasie Assn of Educators 1959-; LA Assn of Educators 1959-; Natl Sci Teacher Assn 1988-; Mens Social & Civil Clubs VP 1975- Outstanding Mem 1982; Grants Natl Sci Fnd 1963-64, 1966, 1968; *home:* 1200 Mill St Vinton LA 70668

JACKSON, VALETTA BYRDSONG, 1st Grade ESL Teacher; *b:* Carthage, TX; *c:* Lavordye Ervin, Reliford Jones, Nathan Jones, Ivan P. Jones, Marcus W. Jones, Marcelyn Cunningham; *ed:* (BA) Elem Ed, Wiley Coll 1957; (MA) Rdng, TX Women Univ 1968; Career Ladder Level III 1984-85; *cr:* Teacher Ft Worth Ind Sch Dist; *ai:* NEA, TSTA Life Mem; Ft Worth CTA Faculty Rep 1983-85; Phi Delta Kappa Mem; PTA Pres 1960-62; WSCS W TX Conference Pres 1967-69; Thompson Chapel United Meth Church (United Meth Women Pres, Sunday Sch Teacher, Worship Comm Chairperson); Cntrl TX Conference Lay Speaker; *home:* 2830 Prospect Fort Worth TX 76106

JACOB, ELIZABETH ANN, Fifth Grade Math Teacher; *b:* Highland Park, MI; *ed:* (BS) Later Elem, E MI Univ 1972; (MA) Elem Ed/Math, Cntrl MI Univ 1976; *cr:* 5th Grade Math Teacher Tawas City Elem 1972-; *ai:* NCTM, MI Cncl Teachers of Math 1972-; Amer Red Cross Water Safety Instr 1979-; Zion Luth Church (Sunday Sch Teacher 1976-89, Bd of Ed 1990); *office:* Tawas City Elem 825 2nd St Tawas City MI 48763

JACOB, NANCY L., English Teacher; *b:* Brooklyn, IA; *m:* Daniel; *ed:* (BA) Eng, Univ of IA Cedar Falls 1966; *cr:* Teacher Logan Jr HS 1966-80, East HS 1980-; *ai:* The Wooden Horse Literary Publication; Academic Letters; Honor Roll; Olympiad Club; Stu Assistance Team; Phase III Cadre; At-Risk Comm; Waterloo Ed Assn, ISEA, NEA, IA Cncl Teachers of Eng; Friends of Lib, Allen Hospital Auxiliary; *office:* East HS 214 High St Waterloo IA 50703

JACOBI, ALLEN LEE, Driver Education Teacher; *b:* Milwaukee, WI; *m:* Deanna L. Ohman; *c:* Ben; *ed:* (BA) EMR, 1971, (MA) LD, 1976, Traffic Safety, 1971 Univ of WI Whitewater; Drug, Alcohol & Safety Ed; *cr:* Teacher Waukesha Public Schls 1971-; *ai:* SADD Adv; WDTSEA Mem 1981-; ADTSEA Mem 988-; *office:* Waukesha North HS 2222 Michiganave Waukesha WI 53188

JACOBS, BRUCE RICHARD, English Teacher; *b:* Bronx, NY; *m:* Miriam Frenkel; *c:* Matthew, Paul; *ed:* (BA) Eng, CCNY 1971; (MA) Eng, Boston Univ 1972; (PHD) Eng, Fordham Univ 1988, *cr:* Eng Teacher HS of Art & Design 1972-; *ai:* Phi Beta Kappa Mem 1971-; Fellowship Boston Univ; Dissertation Fordham Univ; *office:* HS of Art & Design 1075 2nd Ave New York NY 10022

JACOBS, CARLA M., 6th Grade Science Teacher; *b:* Salina, KS; *m:* Steven L.; *c:* Tim, Jason; *ed:* (BA) Elem Ed, 1973, (MA) Ed, 1980 Wichita St Univ; Elem Ed/Sci Ed; *cr:* 5th Grade Teacher Ingalls Elem 1973-89; 6th Grade Sci Teacher Coleman Mid Sch 1989-; *ai:* Spon Performing Ensemble Intermurals; Environmental Club Adv; Wichita Fed of Teachers 1980-; GSA Camping Services/Outdoor Ed 1988-; *office:* Coleman Mid Sch 1544 N Governeour Wichita KS 67206

JACOBS, DONIS L. HEIDER, Business Teacher; *b:* Denver, CO; *m:* Duane D.; *c:* Shandra L.; *ed:* (BS) Phys Ed/Bus, Eastern NM Univ 1973; Cmptr Sci, Voc Ed; *cr:* Teacher Sanford-Fritch HS 1974-; *ai:* Effective Schls Leadership Panel Lecturer; Chrldr, HS & Mid Sch Annual, Jr & Sr Class Spon; Tennis Coach; TX Classroom Teacher Assn (St, Local Campus Rep) 1974-; TX Bus Ed Assn 1986-; Drug Free Graduation Party Co-Chm 1990; Outstanding Young Women of America 1975; Rookie of Yr Annual Awd 1982; Teacher of Month; *office:* Sanford-Fritch HS 538 Eagle Blvd Fritch TX 79036

JACOBS, ELSIE LEE, Fifth Grade Teacher; *b:* Caswell Cty, NC; *ed:* (BA) Elem Ed, Bennett Coll 1965; (EMT) Emergency Medical Technician, 1981, (EMT) Emergency Medical Technician , 1983 St of NC; Effective Teacher Trng 1988-89; *cr:* 5th Grade Teacher Parkview Elem Sch 1965-69; 6th Grade Teacher Univ of NC Greensboro Elem Lake Sch 1969-70; Asst Dir United Way Summer Prgm 1971-73, David D Jones Union Memorial 1971-72; Dir of Site Claremont 1973; *ai:* NEA, ACT, NCAE 1970-; Cone PTA 1970-, Nom Drug Prevention Awd 1990; New Light Baptist Church Fellowship (Chairperson, VP) 1987-89; New Light Baptist Church Nurse Cncl Coord 1981-83; Nocho Cmmty Club Pres 1985-88; Eta Phi Beta Charter Mem; C H Brown Fellowship VP 1987-89, Charter Mem 1986; Choir Cone PTA Awd 1987, Cone Teacher 1987; Sickle Cell Agency Volunteer 1988-89; Cone Sch Teacher of Yr 1973-74; Outstanding Elem Teacher of America 1973; Visiting Team To Charlotte for Eng as Second Lang Prgm 1987-88; *office:* Ceasar Cone Elem Sch 2501 Church St Greensboro NC 27405

JACOBS, PAT KEMPTER, 6th Grade Teacher; *b:* Lansing, MI; *m:* Richard D.; *c:* William, Carrie; *ed:* (BA) Eng, MI St Univ 1973; *cr:* 8th Grade Eng Teacher 1975-85, 6th Grade Teacher 1985 Reed City Mid Sch; *ai:* Mid Sch Yrbk Adv; Gifted & Talented Comm; *office:* Reed City Mid Sch 238 W Lincoln Ave Reed City MI 49677

JACOBS, REBA I., English/Psychology Teacher; *b:* Fayette, AL; *m:* Charles F.; *c:* Mark, Shannon; *ed:* (BS) Scndry Ed/Eng, Livingston Univ 1971; (MA) Scndry Ed/Soc Stud, 1975, (AA) 1979 Univ of AL; *cr:* Eng/Psych/Soc Stud Teacher Fayette Cty HS 1971-; *ai:* Sr HS NHS Adv; Scholars Bowl Coach; Eng Dept Chm; Alpha Delta Kappa (Treas 1984-86, Corresponding Secy 1988-); *office:* Fayette Cty HS 418 3rd Ave NE Fayette AL 35555

JACOBS, TERESA HORTON, English Teacher; *b:* Clovis, NM; *m:* J.R.; *c:* Abbye, John, Brandon; *ed:* (BS) Comm/Speech, 1977 (ME) Scndry Ed, 1984 Eastern NM Univ; *cr:* Eng Teacher Clovis HS 1980-; *ai:* Adv of HS Newspaper the Purple Press 1980-87; Key Club Adv 1987-89; Jr Class Adv & Coord of Jr-Sr Prom 1988-; NCTE 1988-; Spon Youth Awd from Kiwanis Intl 1987-88; *office:* Clovis H S 1900 Thorton Clovis NM 88101

JACOBS, TROY MAX, Secondary Social Sci Teacher; *b:* Alexander City, AL; *m:* Glenda Avery; *c:* Mark, Monica, Butch; *ed:* (BS) Soc Sci, Auburn Univ 1967; Law & Courts Seminar Univ of AL 1982; Consumer Ec, Univ of AL Birmingham 1989; *cr:* Soc Sci Teacher J D Thompson HS 1967-70, Coosa Cty HS 1970-88, Cntrl HS 1988-; *ai:* Stu Cncl Adv; Scope & Sequence Soc Sci Comm Chm; Coosa Cty Soc Sci Textbook Comm Mem; Coosa Cty Ed Assn, AL Ed Assn, NEA; 1st United Meth Church (Mens Club Past Pres, Chancel Choir Past Pres, Mem); 4-H Club Leader Pearl Clover Awd, Gold Clover Awd; Workbook Published.

JACOBS, WILLIAM MICHAEL, Head Teacher; *b:* Boston, MA; *m:* Mary A. Green; *c:* William J., Michael K.; *ed:* (BS) Elem Ed, 1968, (MS) Ed, 1972 Boston St; Grad Stud Admin & Guidance; *cr:* Eng/Phys Ed Teacher Newman HS 1968-69; 5th Grade Teacher Norwood Public Schls 1969-; *ai:* Report Card Revision Comm 3rd-5th Grade; Textbook Adoption Comm Soc Stud, Rdng, Eng; Prin & Supts Advisory Comms; Norwood Teachers Assn Asst Faculty Rep 1980-88; MTA, NEA, ASCD Master Teacher; Norwood Elks 1977; MA Bsbl Coaches Assn, Norwood Babe Ruth, Norwood Little League, Norwood HS Boosters Assn; PTA Faculty Rep; Awarded Horace Mann Math Grant 1989; *office:* F A Cleveland Elem Sch Nichols St Norwood MA 02062

JACOBSEN, SUSAN KAY (NESS), 5th Grade Teacher; *b:* Minot, ND; *m:* Dale R.; *c:* Tiffany, Amber; *ed:* (BS) Elem Ed, Minot St Univ 1979; Grad Stud; *cr:* 5th Grade Teacher Jefferson Elem 1979-; *ai:* Supts Advisory Comm Mem; Prof Growth & Curr Mem; Dickinson Public Schls Math Textbook Selection Comm; Badlands Rdng Cncl Pres 1989-, Honor Cncl 1990; ND Rdng Assn Mem-At-Large 1989-; Intnl Rdng Assn; Dickinson Ed Assn Building Rep 1983; NEA 1979-; Our Saviours Luth Church (HS Youth Adv, Sunday Sch Inservice Instr) 1987-; *office:* Thomas Jefferson Elem Sch PO Box 1057 Dickinson ND 58601

JACOBSON, DIANA R., English Teacher; *b:* Los Angeles, CA; *m:* Richard L.; *c:* Mark, Scott, Steve, Mike, Roger, Lisa, Patrick; *ed:* (BA) His, Univ of CA Los Angeles 1965; Grad Stud Loyola Marymount; *cr:* Eng Teacher Aviation HS 1973-82; Eng Teacher/Dept Chairperson Mira Costa HS 1982-; *ai:* Mentor Teacher; Rep to Mira Costa PTA; Mentor Teacher Selection Comm; NCTE 1980-; NEA, CTA 1973-; UCLA Alumni Schlsp Comm 1975-78; Teacher of Yr Aviation HS 1974-; Mentor Teacher 1988-; *office:* Mira Costa HS 701 S Peck Ave Manhattan Beach CA 90266

JACOBSON, GREGORY DOUGLAS, Language Arts Instructor; *b:* St Paul, MN; *ed:* (BA) Eng, Augsburg Coll 1970; (MA) Eng Ed, Coll of St Thomas 1971; Trng Seminar 1987-, Human Relations Trng Seminar 1974 Univ of MN; *cr:* Instr Stillwater HS 1970-71, Mounds View HS 1971-; Instr/Lecturer Univ of MN 1987-; *ai:* Planning & Dev Comm; Former Ftbl & Bsbl Coach; NEA, MN Ed Assn, Mounds View Ed Assn 1971-; Univ of MN Coll in Schls Modern Fiction Core Mem; NEH Summer Seminar Scndry Teachers 1986; MN St Bsbl Tournament Recognition Awd 1979; *office:* Mounds View HS 1900 W Cunty Rd F Saint Paul MN 55112

JACOBSON, JULIE JOHNSON, Middle School Teacher; *b:* Anderson, IN; *m:* Michael; *ed:* (BA) Elem Ed, Edgewood Coll 1980; Grad Stud Soc Stud, Methods, Sci; *cr:* 4th Grade Teacher St Joseph Sch 1980; 5th/6th Grade Teacher St Matthews Sch 1980-81; 4th-6th Grade Teacher Blessed Sacrament 1981-87; 5th-8th Grade Teacher Deerfield Cmmty Schls 1988-; *ai:* Cheer Coach Jr Var & Var Ftbl & Bsktbl Squads; Building Concerns Team Mem; Sch Evaluation Consortium Sci & Foreign Lang, Competency Based Testing Comm Mem; WI Elem Sci Teachers, WI Society of Sci Teachers 1989-; WI Assn of Cheer & Pom Coaches 1988-; Neighborhood House Child Care Supervisory Bd 1983-86; Sci World 1989; Sci Technology & Society Wkshp 1990; WI Energy Ed Wkshp 1987; *office:* Deerfield Mid Sch 300 Simonson Blvd Deerfield WI 53531

JACOBSON, ROBERT PAUL, Chemistry Teacher; *b:* Marquette, MI; *m:* Alyce June Krause; *c:* Robert Jr., Barbara; *ed:* (BS) Chem/Bio, 1967, (MA) Biochemistry, 1969 N MI Univ; (MAT) Scndry Admin, Saginaw Valley Coll 1985; *cr:* Night Mgr Univ Center 1967-68, Grad Asst 1968-69 N MI Univ; Teacher Lakeview HS 1970-80, Chippewa Valley HS 1980-; *ai:* HS Sci Olympiad Team Coach; K-12th Grade Sci Olympiad Prgms Coord; K-12th Grade Sci Curr Cncl; MI Sci Teachers Assn, NSTA 1975-; Metropolitan Detroit Sci Teachers Assn; Textbook Reviewer 1987; Macomb Cty Outstanding Sci Teacher 1989; *office:* Chippewa Valley HS 18300 19 Mile Rd Mount Clemens MI 48044

JACOBY, CHARLINE, 8th Grade Math/Cmptr Teacher; *b:* Lexington, KY; *c:* Gwen Sharb, Rodney G.; Joseph G. II; *ed:* (BS) Ed, Dallas Baptist Univ 1974; (MED) Rdng, 1976, Admin, 1978 TX Womans Univ; Supervision, St Cmptr Cert; *cr:* Teacher Waxachachie Ind Sch Dist 1974-; *ai:* Yrbk & Stu Cncl Spon; Local Church; NCTM, TX Conference Teachers of Math 1974-; League of Women Voters; BSA Den Mother; GSA Leader; TX St Parent Teacher Life Membership 1965; Amer Assn of Univ Women; Amer Bus Women Assn; Waxahachie Gingerbread Trail Comm Chm 1984; George Washington Honor Medal Awd 1965; *office:* Waxahachie Ind Sch Dist 411 Gibson St Waxahachie TX 75165

JACQUES, TALMADGE MOLETT, US History Teacher; *b:* Dallas, TX; *m:* William Bernard; *c:* Wendy B., William B. Jr.; *ed:* (BS) Government, North TX St Univ 1968; (MS) His, East TX St Univ 1976; *cr:* His Teacher L G Pinkston HS 1968-71, Bryan Adam HS 1971-81, W H Gaston Mid Sch 1981-; *ai:* Chairperson W H Gaston Soc Stud Dept; Mem Attendance Comm; African-Amer His Month Chairperson; Classroom Teachers of Dallas, TX St Teachers Assn, NEA 1968-; Adelle Turner PTA Pres 1988- Life Mem 1989; Iota Philamboda Inc Regional Secy 1982-86 Soror of Yr 1977-; GSA Brownie Leader 1985- Green Angel 1985; W H Gaston Mid Sch Teacher of Yr 1987-88; *home:* 922 Stillmeadow Rd Dallas TX 75232

JACQUES, VERLINE JAMISON, Pre-Kindergarten Teacher; *b:* Rowesville, SC; *m:* Lasalle; *c:* Denise Nikita-Lasalle, Kenneth Kentrell; *ed:* (BS) Elem Ed, 1972, (MS) Spec Ed, 1973, IS Specialist Early Chldhd, 1986 SC St Coll; Prgm for Effective Teaching, Assessments of Performance in Teaching, Promoting SC Future ECE; *cr:* 4th Grade Teacher 1972-77, 5th Grade Teacher 1977-81, 2nd Grade Teacher 1981-82 Felton Laboratory Sch; 4th Grade Teacher 1982-86, Pre-K Teacher 1986- Marshall Elem Sch; *ai:* At Risk Prevention Comm; APT Observer; Sch America Comm; Orangeburg Wilkinson PTSA; Delta Theta Incorporated; Felton Laboratory PTA; Spec Ed Fellowship; *home:* P O Box 2064 Orangeburg SC 29116

JADIN, RITA, Fifth Grade Teacher; *b:* Luxemburg, WI; *ed:* (BA) Eng, Alverno Coll 1968; (MA) Rdng, Clarke Coll 1976; Botany, Geology, Univ of Dubuque; Teacher Effectiveness Trng, Prof Refinements Developing Effectiveness, Card nal Stritch Coll; *cr:* 1st/2nd Grade Teacher St John Baptist 1968-69; 1st/2nd/6th-8th Grade Teacher Holy Spirit 1969-80; 7th Grade Eng/His/7th-8th Grade Sci/Math Teacher 1981-88, 5th Grade Teacher 1988- St Matthias; *ai:* Sci Curr & Art Comms; Parochial Sch Comm Alternate Rep; Tutor Elem Grades; Chrstn Women Treas; CCD Coord 1971-78; Sch Sisters of St Francis Cmmty Area Coord 1989-91; Census Worker New Orleans 1984; *office:* Saint Matthias Sch 9300 W Beloit Rd Milwaukee WI 53227

JAEGER, BONNIE LONGMORE, Second Grade Teacher; *b:* Grand Rapids, MN; *w:* Ernest A. (dec); *c:* Kenneth, Randy, Daniel; *ed:* (BS) Elem Ed, Pan Amer Univ 1978; Span Lang; *cr:* Lib Aide 1968-78, Teacher 1978- Zavala Elem 1978-; *ai:* Univ Interscholastic League Coach; Tutor Literacy Centers of Amer; *home:* 2018 Theresa HARLINGEN TX 78550

JAEGER, JEAN VANDEMARK, 1st Grade Teacher; *b:* Passaic, NJ; *m:* Philip; *c:* David; *ed:* (BA) Elem Ed, William Paterson Coll 1961; (MA) Personnel & Guidance, Montclair St Coll 1971; *cr:* 5th Grade Teacher 1961-63, 6th Grade Teacher 1963-64 Westmoreland Sch; Substitute Teacher Irvington Public Schls 1964-69; 2nd Grade Teacher 1971-83, 1st Grade Teacher 1983- Ridge Road Sch; *ai:* Reorganization Comm; Health Curr Comm; NEA 1971-; NJ Ed Assn 1971-; Cedar Grove Ed Assn Secy/Rep 1971-; NJ Governors Teacher Recognition Prgm; *home:* 9 Bradford Way Cedar Grove NJ 07009

JAEGER, JULIE D., Math/Language/Rdng Teacher; *b:* Fargo, ND; *m:* Curtis; *c:* Sarah, Matthew; *ed:* (BS) Elem Ed, 1977, (BS) Speech Pathology, 1977 Minot St Coll; Grad Stud in Speech Pathology, Elem Ed, Math; *cr:* Speech Therapist Wells Cty of ND 1977-79; Elem Teacher/Mid Sch Math/Sci/Lang Art Teacher S Prairie Elem 1979-; *ai:* 8th Grade, Pom-Pon, Yrbk Adv; Dir of Sch Plays; Math Curr Coord; Coach for Math Track & Mathcounts Teams; Coord of Cty Sch Math Track Meet; NDEA 1977-; SPEA (Pres, Negotiator) 1979-, Teacher of Yr 1982; Lutheran Brotherhood Jr Luther League (Branch Pres, Adv, Coord) 1990; Nom Outstanding Math & Sci Teacher St of ND; Nom ND Teacher of Yr; *home:* 1015 1st St NE Minot ND 58701

JAEHNE, JULIE SIMON, Business/Office Ed Teacher; *b:* Fort Worth, TX; *m:* Keith C.; *c:* Brandon; *ed:* (BBA) Bus, Baylor 1980; (MS) Occupational Ed, Univ of Houston 1985; *cr:* Eng Teacher Arnold Jr HS 1981-84; Bus Dept Chairperson 1984-88, Office Ed Coord 1988- Langham Creek HS; *ai:* FBLA Head Spon; Bus Profs of Amer; Natl Voc Tech Honor Society; NBEA, AVA, TX Cmptrs Ed Assn, NEA; Zeta Tau Alpha Alumni; Houston Baylor Womens Assn; *home:* 9029 Kenilworth Houston TX 77024

JAFFE, CARREN GERB, Art Teacher; *b:* Brooklyn, NY; *m:* Stuart; *c:* Lian, Samara, Eric; *ed:* (BA) Fine Art, Brooklyn Coll 1970; (MS) Guidance/Counseling Long Island Univ 1975; Grad Stud Nassau Comm Coll, Telaviv Univ, NY Univ; *cr:* Art Teacher Ind Sch 223K 1970-75, Ind Sch 201K 1975-; *office:* Dyker Heights Jr HS 8010 12th Ave Brooklyn NY 11228

JAGOW, BEVERLY SIEVERT, Computer Teacher; *b:* South Gate, CA; *w:* Herbert A. (dec); *ed:* (BS) Phys Ed, Univ of Redlands 1950; (MA) Counseling, San Francisco St; Cmptr Courses, Stanford & San Diego St; *cr:* Teacher Walter Colton Jr HS 1950-52, Lake Arrowhead Elem 1952-53, Dugway HS 1955-58, Santa Venetia 1958-59, Dependent Schls 1959-66; Dir Army Ed Center 1960-63;Teacher Lincoln Elem 1963-64; Teacher/Cnslr Hill Jr HS 1964-83; Teacher Marin Comm Coll 1985-86, Sinaloa Mid Sch 1983-; *ai:* Sch Cmptr Coord; Cmptr Lab Supvr; Intnl Society for Teaching in Ed 1985-; Cmptr Using Ed 1983-; Buck Research in Aging Fnd Interviewer 1989-; Novato Cmptr Task Force; *office:* Sinaloa Mid Sch 2045 Vineyard Rd Novato CA 94947

JAHAN-TIGH, BATUL LAVON, 11th Eng Honors/GT & Advanced; *b:* Clay City, IL; *m:* Geoffrey; *c:* Reza, Alicia, Lavonne, Geneva; *ed:* (BA) Sociology, Eastern IL Univ 1970; (MED) Scndry Ed Pan Amer Univ 1981; *cr:* Scndry Teacher Faulk Intermediate Sch 1980-84, Homer Hanna HS 1984-; Adjunct Professor TX Southmost Coll 1985-; *ai:* Spon Natl Honor Society 1985-; *office:* Homer Hanna HS 2615 Price Rd Brownsville TX 78521

JAHDE, TOM, Physical Education Teacher; *b:* Carroll, IA; *m:* Patricia Heires; *c:* Tracy, Gregory; *ed:* (AA) Phys Ed, IA Cntrl Comm Coll 1971; (BA) Phys Ed, Buena Vista Coll 1973; (MA) Phys Ed, Kearney St Coll 1987; *cr:* Resident Cnslr Jerry Rabiner Boys Ranch 1973-77; Phys Ed Teacher/Coach Bellwood 3-R Sch 1977-; *ai:* Vlybl, Girls & Boys Bsktbl & Track Coach; Bellwood Faculty Assn Pres 1987-88; NE St Ed Assn; NE Coaches Assn; NE Assn for Health, Phys Ed, Recreation & Dance; Bellwood Bsbl Assn Pres 1990; Bellwood Jaycees Outstanding Young Educator 1981; *home:* Box 125 Bellwood NE 68624

JAHN, DIANE SUE, Language Arts Teacher; *b:* Jasper, IN; *ed:* (BS) Elem Ed, 1968, (MS) Elem Ed/Eng, 1971 IN Univ; Cmptr Basic Programming & Word Processing; *cr:* 6th Grade Teacher Loogootee Elem 1968-69; Eng Teacher Loogootee Jr HS 1969-; *ai:* Jr Division Spell Bowl, Eng, Soc Stud Academic Bowl Coach; Martin Cty Spelling Bee Coord; Jr HS Newspaper & Yrbk Spon; NEA, IN St Teachers Assn, Loogootee Educl Assn; Academic Coaches Assn Advisory Bd 1989-; *office:* Loogootee Jr HS 201 Brooks Ave Loogootee IN 47553

JAHNKE, SUSAN ALICE, First Grade Teacher; *b:* Hartford, CT; *ed:* (BS) Early Chldhd Ed, 1974; (MS) Early Chldhd Ed, 1977 Southern Ct St Univ; Post Masters Studies Kindermusik Teacher Cert; Celebrate New World of Music Ideas & Solutions for Elem Music Teacher Westminster Choir Coll; *cr:* 1st Grade Teacher John F. Kennedy Sch 1974-; *ai:* Cooperating Teacher Comm 1987-; Wrote & Dir Musical Comedy for Children 1978; Right to Read Task Force 1980; Delegate to Governor's Leadership Symposium on Career Ed 1980; Adv NJHS 1982; Faculty Rep Red Cross 1982-86; Ct Ed Assn Convention 1984-85; PA Teacher of the Yr 1984-85; Numerous City, Sch & Ed Comm 1978-89; Kappa Delta Epsilon Pres of Undergrad & Alumnae Chapters 1973-75; Outstanding Young Educator 1984; Public Relations Chairperson for Milford Ed Assn; Editor MEA Communique 1983-85; Editor Burning the Midnight Oil 1984-85; Voted Best Cmmty Newsletter at 1985 CEA Convention; *office:* John F Kennedy Elem Sch 100 W Ave Milford CT 06460

JAMBOR, GLENN JOHN, English Teacher/Chair; *b:* Cleveland, OH; *m:* Susan Anne Stazyk; *c:* Owen, Alison, Kevin, Robert; *ed:* (BSED) Eng, OH Univ 1973; (MED) Curr/Instruction, Cleveland St Univ 1987; *cr:* Teacher Garfield Heights HS 1973-; *ai:* Eng Dept Chm; Yrbk, Newspaper, Quill & Scroll Adv; NEA, OEA Pres 1973-, Service Awd 1984; NCTE 1973-; Jennings Scholar; Educator of Yr; Teacher of Month; *home:* 4345 Elmhurst Dr Stow OH 44224

JAMELL, VIRGINIA SHEPPARD, Third Grade Teacher; *b:* New Orleans, LA; *m:* Kassen; *c:* Kamell S. Jamell Putnam, Kassen A.; *ed:* (BS) Ed, Mc Neese St Univ 1962; Post Grad Courses; *cr:* Teacher S Conway Cty Sch System 1981-; *ai:* NTA; *home:* PO Box 261 Atkins AR 72823

JAMEN, DONNA LEE LORETTA (MARTIN), 6th & 7th Grade Teacher; *b:* Chicago, IL; *m:* Joseph; *c:* Erin M.; *ed:* (BA) Ed/Math, Chicago St Univ ; *cr:* 6th-7th Grade Math Teacher St John of God Sch; 7th-8th Grade Math/Sci Teacher St Jerome Sch; 6th-7th Grade Math Teacher St Maurice Sch; *ai:* Rainbow Facilitator 1987-; Chicago Boys & Girls Club Commitment to Quality Bd 1989-; *office:* St Maurice Sch 3625 S Hoyne Chicago IL 60609

JAMES, ANITA MARIE YOUNG, 8th Grade English/Rdng Teacher; *b:* Zanesville, OH; *m:* Donald Earl; *c:* Donald E., Dana E., Amy J.; *ed:* (BSED) Elem Ed, OH Univ 1967; *cr:* 4th-5th Grade Teacher S Zanesville Elem 1964-80; Rdng Teacher 1980-89, Rdng/Eng Teacher 1989- Maysville Jr HS; *ai:* Stu Cncl Adv 1988-; Cheerleading Adv 1986-87; Course of Study Cty Comm 1985-86; OEA, MEA, NEA 1989-; UMW Pres 1989-; Sweet Adelines (Pres, VP, Secy, Asst Dir, Choir Dir, Lay Speaker, Ed Chm) 1967-; S Zanesville United Meth Church; Currently Enrolled at Garrett Evangelical Seminary in Evanston Preparing for Ministry as Certified Candidate; *home:* 32 Juanita Dr Sonora OH 43701

JAMES, BETTY ANN WINTERS, Third Grade Teacher; *b:* Lead, SD; *m:* William Rogers; *c:* Bruce C., Dennis R., William A.; *ed:* (BS) Elem Ed, W MI Univ 1972; Grad Courses MI St Univ, W MI Univ; *cr:* Substitute Teacher Branch Cty Schls 1929-72; 3rd Grade Teacher Bronson Cmmty Schls 1972-; *ai:* Sch Improvement & Sci Comm; Bronson Ed Assn Soc Chm 1982-84; MI Ed Assn, NEA; Amer Womens Bus Assn (VP, Pres), Woman of Yr 1976; Riverview Meth Church Pres 1959; Riverview Garden Club Pres 1962; Rebekah Lodge #186 1989; Chrstn Womens Assn 1973-74; Cub Scout Den Mothers Awd; Meth Chrstn Awd for Work in UNICEF United Nations Organization 1967; *office:* Ryan Elem Sch 465 Rudd St Bronson MI 49028

JAMES, CAROL A., Home & Career Skills Teacher; *b:* Beaver Meadows, PA; *m:* John W.; *ed:* (BS) Home Economics, PA State 1965; NYU; Hofstra; C W Post; Long Island Univ; *cr:* H&C Skills Teacher 1965-, H&C Coord 1970- Bethpage NY; *ai:* NY St Home Economics Teachers Assn; Amer Home Economics Assn; NY St United Teachers; Participated Field Test Teacher NY St Home & Career Skills Curr; *office:* John F Kennedy Jr H S Broadway Bethpage NY 11714

JAMES, CARRIE MARSHALL, Home Economics Teacher; *b:* Columbia, MS; *m:* Roscoe; *c:* Lonell Brown-James, Mitchell, Irvin (dec); *ed:* (BS) Home Ec Ed, Alcorn St Univ 1951; Tuskegee Inst, Univ of S MS; MS St Univ; *cr:* Sci Teacher Friendship Voc HS 1951-54; Home Ec Teacher Lampton Voc HS 1954-59, Marion Cntrl HS 1959-70, E Marion HS 1970-; *ai:* FHA Adv; Sr Class Spon; Natl Teachers Assn; Natl Assn of Educators; Progressive Arts Federated Club; MS Rural Center (Pres 1972-75, Bd of Dirs); Heroines of Jericho Court 205 Sr Matron; *home:* Rt 2 Box 360 Columbia MS 39429

JAMES, CORA GILFORD, Mathematics Teacher; *b:* New Waverly, TX; *ed:* (BS) Math, 1961, (MED) Scndry Ed, 1968 TX Southern Univ; *cr:* Sci Teacher A R Turner HS 1961-63; Math Teacher Sam Houston HS 1963-69; Life Sci Teacher Huntsville Intermediate Sch 1969-79; Life Sci Teacher 1979-84, Math Teacher 1984- Mance Park Jr HS; *ai:* HISD Stipend Review, Mance Park Jr HS Attendance Comm; TX St Teachers Assn, NEA, NCTM; Natl Cncl of Negro Women; Wesley Fnd; Mance Park Jr HS PTA; Natl Sci Fnd Grants to Study Math Summer Insts TX Southern Univ 1964, West TX St Univ 1966; *home:* PO Box 841 Huntsville TX 77342

JAMES, DANA CLIFTON, Mathematics Teacher; *b:* Opelika, AL; *m:* Sheila Maria Jackson; *c:* Daniel, Andrew; *ed:* (AS) Math, Young Harris Coll 1979; (BSED) Math Ed, 1981, (MED) Math Ed, 1986 Univ of GA; *cr:* Teacher/Coach Oconee Cty HS 1981-; *ai:* Girls Var Bsktbl Coach; Fellowship of Chrstn Athletes Spon; GA Athletic Coaches Assn 1981-; *office:* Oconee Cty HS PO Box 534 Watkinsville GA 30677

JAMES, DANIEL DOUGLAS, World Cultures Teacher; *b:* Parkersburg, WV; *m:* Nancy Ann Crowley; *c:* Lorrie, Pam; *ed:* (BA) Soc Stud,Phys Ed, Marshall Univ 1961; (MA) Ed, Salem Coll 1980; Work Lean Appointment Shell Chemical; *cr:* Teacher/Coach Jackson Jr HS 1961-63, Parkersburg HS 1963-; *ai:* Head Ftbl Coach; St Ftbl Comm; NEA, WV Ed Assn, Wood Cty Teachers Assn 1961-; Natl Coaches Assn, WV Coaches Assn St Ftbl Comm, Wood Cty Coaches Assn 1963-; Written Articles; Europe & Communism Study Grants; *office:* Parkersburg HS 2101 Dudley Ave Parkersburg WV 26101

JAMES, DIANE MARIE, 2nd Grade Teacher; *b:* Sharon, PA; *ed:* (BS) Elem Ed, Edinboro St Coll 1971; Grad Work Elem Ed, Penn St; *cr:* Remedial Rdng Eckles Elem 1971-72; 2nd Grade Teacher 1972-74; 1st Grade Teacher 1974-80; 2nd Grade Teacher 1980- St Josephs; *ai:* NEA; *office:* St Joseph Sch 760 E State St Sharon PA 16146

JAMES, GWENDOLYN RAINES, Early Childhood Teacher; *b:* Buffalo, NY; *m:* J. C.; *c:* Lisa, Jason; *ed:* (BS) Elem/Early Chldhd, Cntrl St Univ 1970; (MED) Learning Disability/Ec Ed, John Carroll Univ 1986; Conflict Mediation, Ursuline Coll; Ec Ed, John Carroll Univ; Whole Lang, Baldwin-Wallace Coll; *cr:* Kndgtn Teacher Harvey Rice 1974-75, Euclid Park 1975-78; Early Chldhd Teacher Charles Orr 1978-83, Charles H Lake 1983-; *ai:* Charles H Lake Staff Lead Team & Volunteer Tutor; Cleveland Young Children Ed Assn, Metro CABSE Comm Committee 1986-; Natl Assn Negro Bus Prof Women 1989-; GSA (Leader, Troop Adv); Urban League; Cory United Meth Church Volunteer; Cleveland Educl Fund Grant; *office:* Charles H Lake Sch 9201 Hillock Ave Cleveland OH 44108

JAMES, JEANETTE LOVE, Retired 4th Grade Teacher; *b:* Cottonwood, AL; *m:* Bill M.; *c:* Jennifer J. Cutchens; *ed:* (BS) Elem Ed, Troy St Univ 1957; *cr:* 4th Grade Teacher Cedar Grove Elem 1958-59; 4th-6th Grade Phys Ed Teacher Northwood Elem 1959-88; *ai:* Delta Kappa Gamma Chairperson Research Comm 1988-; FL Retired Educators Assn, Okaloosa Retired Educators Assn; Amer Legion Auxiliary Secy 1982-; Teacher of Yr Northwood Elem 1984-85; *home:* 1540 Texas Pkwy Crestview FL 32536

JAMES, KAREN LAVENS, English IV Teacher; *b:* Wendell, ID; *m:* Jerry C.; *c:* Jon, Justin, Julee; *ed:* (BS) Speech/Comm, UT St Univ 1965; Eng, ID St Univ; *cr:* Eng/Speech Teacher Filer HS 1965-66; Eng/Journalism Jerome HS 1966-; *ai:* Speech Club; Advanced Speech; Rodeo Club Coach; ACA-DECA Asst; IEA & NEA 1975-; Miss Rodeo America Inc Dir 1980; Teacher of Yr 1988; *office:* Jerome H S 04 North 100 East Jerome ID 83338

JAMES, LAMARR, Mathematics Instructor; *b:* Vancouver, WA; *ed:* (BS) Math, Univ of OR 1970-73, 1982-85; (MS) Ed/Math, S OR St Coll 1986-; *cr:* Math Teacher Upward Bound Pacific Univ 1985, Eagle Point HS 1986-; *ai:* SAT Adv & Coach; *office:* Eagle Point HS P O Box 198 Eagle Point OR 97524

JAMES, LILLIE MARIE EVERSON, Lead Science Teacher; *b:* Sylvester, GA; *m:* Jackie; *c:* Kevin D., Justin D., Travis D., Jeremy R.; *ed:* (BS) 7-12 Sci Ed/Bio Emphasic, Albany St Coll 1972; (MS) 7-12 Sci Ed/Bio Ed, GA St 1979; (MS) Mid Grades Ed, Add ON 1989; *cr:* Teacher Northside Mid Sch 1972-; *ai:* Advisory Comm; Lead Teacher Mid Sch Team; Page 1974-; *home:* 105 Galahad Dr Warner Robins GA 31093

JAMES, LILLIE PEARL, Seventh Grade Teacher; *b:* Washington, GA; *m:* Kinsley; *c:* Michelle Davis, Jerald Davis; *ed:* (BS) Elem Ed, 1970, (MS) Rdng 1983 Chicago St Univ; Security Licensed Selling Mutual Funds; Music Trng Piano; *cr:* Teacher Cook Elem 1970-71, Alcott Elem 1971-78, Lincoln Elem 1978-82, Mary Lyon Elem 1982-; *office:* Mary Lyon Elem Sch 2941 N Mc Vicker Chicago IL 60634

JAMES, LISA HANDWERGER, Math/Computer Teacher; *b:* Manhattan, NY; *m:* Gary Leonard; *ed:* (BS) Ed, Univ of Hartford 1978; Working Towards MEd in Admin; *cr:* Teacher N Kingstown Sch Dist 1981-84, Merrimack HS 1984-; *ai:* HS Rep for Dist Prgm Evaluation Review Comm; Chairperson for Math Accreditation Comm; Intramural Vlybl; Dir of Summer Sch Merrimack HS; *office:* Merrimack HS 38 Mc Elwain St Merrimack NH 03054

JAMES, OLIVIA ELLIS, Sch Dev Teacher Consultant; *b:* Marks, MS; *m:* Benson Roger; *c:* Cynthia, Olivia, Aaron; *ed:* (BA) Eng, 1973, (MA) Ed Leadership, 1989 W MI Univ; Essential Elements of Effective Instructions; Cooperative Learning; Peer Counseling; Admin Intern Sch Dev Facilitator Trng; *cr:* Teacher 1973-89, Sch Dev Prgm Teacher Consultant 1989- Benton Harbor HS; *ai:* Prof Dev Consortium; Class of 1982 & 1987 Class Sponsorship; Pep Club Spon; Textbook Selection & 9th-11th Grade Curr Comm; Peer Cnslr; Partnership Eng Instr; EEEI Coach; In-Dist Inservices 1973-89; ASCD; Alpha Kappa Alpha 1973-; Co-Authored Partnership Eng Handbook; *home:* 449 Eloise Benton Harbor MI 49022

JAMES, REBEKAH MARKEE, Phys Ed Teacher/Coach; *b:* Dallas, TX; *ed:* (BS) Phys Ed, Mc Murry Coll 1982; (MS) Phys Ed, W TX St Univ 1985; Model for Effective Teaching, Supervision Trng; *cr:* Teacher/Coach Canyon Jr HS & HS 1982-88, Randall HS 1988-; *ai:* Jr Var Girls Bsktbl Coach; Var Girls Track Head Coach; TX Girls Coaches Assn, Assn of TX Prof Educators 1982-; PTA 1988-; *home:* 6725 Michelle Amarillo TX 79109

JAMES, RENNY, Art/Chemistry Teacher; *b:* Denver, CO; *m:* Lynn L. Clark; *ed:* (BA) Art Ed, Univ of CO 1985; *cr:* 7th-12th Grade Eng Teacher Liberty HS 1986; 7th-12th Grade Sci Teacher Pritchett HS 1987-88; Art/Chem/Yrbk Teacher Mc Clave Schls 1988-; *ai:* Yrbk; Photography; Sci Fair Dir; Concession Stand; Sr Class NEA; Human Anatomy & Physiology Teacher Lamar Comm Coll; *office:* Mc Clave HS 308 Lincoln Ave Mc Clave CO 81057

JAMES, ROSEMARY W., Language Arts Teacher; *b:* Axson, GA; *m:* John Walter; *c:* Tamra Alexander, Cynthia Davidson, Sandra Inwright, John W. Jr.; *ed:* (AB) Eng, GA Coll Milledgeville 1957; Working Toward Masters Valdosta St Coll; *cr:* Eng Teacher Atkinson Cty HS 1956-57, Avondale Estates HS 1957, Georgetown HS 1970-71; Lang Art Teacher Atkinson Cty Jr HS 1971-80, Atkinson Cty HS 1981-; *ai:* Adv Omega Tri-Hi-Y Club; NEA, GAE 1971-, Habitat for Humanity; Carver Baptist Church; *office:* Atkinson Cty HS P O Box 248 Pearson GA 31642

JAMES, RUTH ANDERSON, 1st Grade Teacher; *b:* Wink, TX; *m:* Donald M.; *c:* Pat M., Donna Bruner, Michele Logan; *ed:* (BS) Elem Ed, Sul Ross Univ 1957; Career Ladder Kermit 1989; *cr:* 1st Grade Teacher Kermit Ind Sch Dist 1959-; *ai:* ATPE.

JAMES, SANDRA BELLER, French Teacher; *b:* Charleston, WV; *m:* Robert Ray; *c:* Jodi R.; *ed:* (BS) Scndry Ed/Fr/Eng, WV St Coll 1967; (MA) Scndry Ed/Fr/Eng, WV Coll of Grad Stud 1975; Teacher Expectations Stu Achievement; Impact Youth Empowering Systems; Peer Counseling Kreig Model; *cr:* Fr/Eng Teacher Dunbar Jr HS 1967-84; Fr Teacher John Adams Jr HS 1984-; *ai:* Sch Newspaper & Majorette Spon; Alpha Delta Kappa (Secy, Chaplain, Historian) 1973-; WVEA Area Rep 1967-; Dunbar Lib Bd Mem 1980-; Dunbar 1st Baptist Church (Sunday Sch Teacher 1968-; Church Bd of Chrstn Ed Mem 1984-Deaconess 1980-86); Selected for an Inst Teaching the Bible as Lit Univ of IN 1971; *home:* 128 Greenbrier Ln Dunbar WV 25064

JAMES, SHARON J. SUE, Business Teacher; *b:* Amsterdam, NY; *m:* Michael J.; *c:* Michelle L., Marc A.; *ed:* (AAS) Secretarial Sci, SUNY Cobleskill 1975; (AAS) Bus Admin, Fulton-Montgomery Comm Coll 1978; (BS) Bus/Distributive Ed, SUC Buffalo 1980; (MS) Advanced Classroom Teaching, SUNY Albany 1985; *cr:* Bus Teacher Sharon Springs Cntrl 1980-81, Stratford Cntrl 1982-84, Dolgeville Cntrl 1984-; *ai:* HS Day Cobleskill Adv; Bus Teacher Assn 1980-; Order of Eastern Star 1977-; *office:* Dolgeville Cntrl Sch Slawson St Dolgeville NY 13329

JAMES, SUE MILLER, First Grade Teacher; *b:* Hanover, PA; *m:* Wayne N.; *c:* Eric, Nathan; *ed:* (BS) Elem Ed, Kutztown St Coll 1971; (MA) Guidance & Cnslg, Western MD Coll 1975; Classroom Management; Prcp Stud; *cr:* 3rd Grade Teacher 1971-82; Kndgtn Teacher 1982-85; 1st Grade Teacher 1986-Littlestown Sch Dist; *ai:* PTO Adv; DSEA/NEA/LEA Faculty Rep 1982-84; *office:* Littlestown Sch Dist 150 E Myrtle St Littlestown PA 17340

JAMES, TYRONE, Chemistry Teacher/Sci Chair; *b:* Amory, MS; *m:* Debra Smith; *c:* Amber; *ed:* (BS) Bio/Chem, Lane Coll 1974; *cr:* Teacher Amory Mid Sch 1975-82, Amory HS 1982-; *ai:* MAE, NEA, AEA; PTO Pres 1989-; SWEEPS (Mem, E911 VP); *office:* Amory HS PO Box 330 Amory MS 38821

JAMES, WILLIAM, JR., 6th/7th Grade Phys Ed Teacher; *b:* Vidalia, GA; *m:* Phyllis Smith; *c:* William Hunter, Wendi Blair; *ed:* (AA) Health/Phys Ed, Brewton-Parker Jr Coll 1971; (BS) Health/Phys Ed, GA Southern 1974; *cr:* Athletic Dir Vidalia Recreation Dept 1970-; Teacher/Coach Lyons Jr HS 1974-78, J R Trippe Mid Sch 1978-; *ai:* Bsbl, Bsktbl, Ftbl Coach; GA HS Assn 1978-; Natl Fed Ofcls 1980-; Mt Vernon Ofcl Assn (Pres, VP) 1978-; Jaycees 1985-; GA Recreation Parks Society 1970-; 1st United Meth Church Admin Bd; Sam Galloway Memorial Schlsp Awd; Teacher of Yr Toombs Cty 1977; *office:* J R Trippe Mid Sch 302 W 2nd St Vidalia GA 30474

JAMESON, PHYLLIS MORROW, 2nd Grade English Teacher; *b:* Belle Vernon, PA; *m:* Frederick B.; *ed:* (BS) Eng Comm Ed, Indiana Univ of PA 1977; Working Towards Masters Eng Ed, Univ of MD; *cr:* Eng/Scndry Ed Teacher La Plata HS 1977-; *ai:* La Plata HS Var Chrldr Squad & Class of 1990 Spon; NCTE 1989-; NEA, MD St Teachers Assn 1979-; *office:* La Plata HS PO Box 790 La Plata MD 20646

JAMKA, MERCEDES HENRY, Jr High Science Teacher; *b:* Chicago, IL; *c:* Loriann, Gregory; *ed:* (BA) Latin, Siena Heights Coll 1963; (MA) Sci Ed, Colgate Univ 1970; Geology, Univ of CA Berkeley; *cr:* Jr HS Sci Teacher Queen of Apostles 1968-70; Earth Sci Teacher Regina HS 1970-71; Sci/Bio Teacher Aquinas HS 1971-73; Jr HS Sci Teacher Sharon Cmmty Sch 1980-; *ai:* Big Foot Area Schls Curr Comm; Outdoor Ed & Quest Coord; NEA, WSST, NSTA, SLUE; Opera House Volunteer Usher; NSTA Study Grants 1970-89; *office:* Sharon Cmmty Sch 104 School St Sharon WI 53585

JAMROCK, MAUREEN S., Science Department Chair; *b:* Evergreen Park, IL; *m:* Leonard P.; *c:* Melissa; *ed:* (BS) Biological Sci, IL St Univ 1971; (MSED) Elem Ed, Purdue Univ 1975; PHD Stu Univ of IL Chicago 1991; *cr:* Sci Teacher Coolidge Jr HS 1971-; *ai:* Sci Olympiad Team Coach; 8th Grade Class Adv; Sci Seminar Spon; ASCD Mem 1986-; IL Sci Teachers Assn (Bd of Dir 1989-, Mem) 1981-; NSTA Mem 1985-; Cncl for Elem Sci Intnl Mem 1986-; Natl TTT Society 1983-; GSA Troop Leader 1986-; Published Article; Outstanding Sci Teacher in IL Jointly Presented by IL Sci Teachers Assn & NSTA 1985-88; Sch Dist 151 Bd of Ed Merit Awd 1983, 1985; *office:* Coolidge Jr HS 155th St & 7th Ave Phoenix IL 60426

JANAK, BONNIE LOWE, Math Teacher; *b:* Ann Arbor, MI; *m:* Larry F.; *c:* Craig, Karen; *ed:* (BS) Elem Ed, 1977, (BS) Scndry Math, 1984 Univ of Houston; *cr:* Teacher True Cross 1977-79, Alvin Jr HS 1979-80, Mayde Creek Jr HS 1980-83, Mayde Creek HS 1983-; *ai:* NHS Cncl; Class of 89 Spon; TX Cncl Teachers of Math; NCTM; *office:* Mayde Creek H S 19202 Groschke Rd Houston TX 77084

JANES, ALLEN L., Mathematics Teacher; *b:* Bismarck, ND; *ed:* (BS) Math, Dickinson St Coll 1975; (MS) Ed, Univ of ND 1982; Advanced Placement Calculus Trng Several Natl Wkshps; *cr:* Math Teacher Washburn HS 1975-76; Math/Ger Teacher Watford City HS 1976-79; Math Teacher Red River HS 1979-; *ai:* Math Track Team Co-Adv; Grand Forks Scndry Math Teachers Co-Chm; Jr Class Adv; NHS Adv; Intramural Bsktbl Adv; ND Cncl Teachers of Math Bd Mem 1986-88; NSTUY Mem 1980-87; ND Teacher of Yr 1986; NCTM 1985-; Grand Forks Chrstn Singles (VP 1981-82, Treas 1988-); Holy Family Cath Church 1979-; Math Curr Improvement Title II Grant 1990; *office:* Red River HS 2211 17th Ave S Grand Forks ND 58201

JANEWAY, WANDA BROWN, Sixth Grade Teacher; *b:* Hartselle, AL; *m:* Alton Nathaniel; *c:* Alton Jr.; *ed:* (BS) His, Mid TN St Univ 1970; (MED) Mid Grades Ed, West GA Coll 1989; Elem Ed, Univ of TN Chattanooga 1980; *cr:* Teacher Cloud Springs Sch 1970-71, North Rossville Elem 1980-89, Rossville Mid 1989-; *ai:* Chm of Dept Rossville Mid Sch; Walker Cty Assn of Educators (Newsletter Staff 1980) 1987-88; GA Assn of Educators 1980-; Pi Gamma Mu 1968-; Kappa Delta Pi, Tau Omicron, Phi Alpha Theta 1969-; Listed in Outstanding Coll Stus of America 1988-89; Teacher of Yr N Rossville Elem 1989; *office:* Rossville Mid Sch Bryan St Rossville GA 30741

JANOTA, CHRISTINE ANNE, Band Director; *b:* Chicago Heights, IL; *ed:* (BM) Music Ed, 1973, (MS) Music Ed, 1974, (MS) Conducting, 1978 E IL Univ; *cr:* Band/Music Dir Divernon Schls 1975-78, Martinsville Schls 1978-80, Atwood-Hammond Schls 1980-86; Chorus/Band Dir Altamont Cmmty Schls 1986-; *ai:* Dance Team; Flag Corps; NEA; Music Educators Natl Conference Dist V Chm; Natl Band Assn, Women Band Dirs Assn; Sigma Alpha Iota, Tau Beta Sigma, Alpha Delta Kappa; Effingham Cty Cmmty Concert Assn Bd of Dirs; Outstanding Young Women of America; Cmmty Service Awd Altamont Chamber of Commerce; Great Teacher Awd E IL Univ; *home:* 1105 Holly Dr Apt E Effingham IL 62401

JANOVIC, SUSAN GILLETTE, Third Grade Teacher; *b:* Hartford, CT; *m:* Robert John; *c:* Melissa; *ed:* (BS) Elem Ed, Univ of CT 1970; (MS) Lang Art/Ed, Cntrl CT St Coll 1975; Teacher Effectiveness Stu Achievement Talents Unlimited, Jr Great Books; *cr:* 3rd Grade Teacher 1970-71, 2nd Grade Teacher 1971-84, 3rd Grade Teacher 1984- Harwinton Consolidated Sch; *ai:* Staff Dev Comm; Lead Teacher; Regional Ed Assn Dist 10 (VP 1974-75, Treas 1973-74); *office:* Harwinton Consolidated Sch E Litchfield Rd Harwinton CT 06791

JANSEN, EULOGIA, 1st/2nd Grade Teacher/Prin; *b:* Albers, IL; *ed:* (BS) His, 1955, (MED) Ed, 1962 St Louis Univ; Grad Stud; Several Wkshps; *cr:* Principalship/Teacher 1955-; Elem Teacher 1942-; Supvr Diocesan Schls Belleville Diocese 1969-80; Regional Coord Archdiocesan Sch 1988-89; *ai:* Chrstn Formation

Parish Bd of Ed Chairperson; Adult Ed Prgm Active Mem; Parish Organist; NCEA 1942-; Articles Published; *home:* RR 1 Box 115 Red Bud IL 62278

JANSEN, GEORGE F., Band Director; *b:* Houston, TX; *m:* Barbara Ann Boutwell; *ed:* (BA) Music Ed, Southwestern Univ 1968; (MS) Music, Univ of TX 1980; *cr:* Band Dir Pearsall Jr HS 1969-73, C D Fulkes Mid Sch 1973-; *ai:* TX Bandmasters Assn, TX Music Educators Assn; TX Army Natl Guard Band 1968-74; Jr HS Region Band Chm 1979-82; Sweep Stakes Awd Winning Band; *office:* C D Fulkes Mid Sch 300 W Anderson Round Rock TX 78664

JANSEN, JOYCE AKERS, Home & Family Life Teacher; *b:* Tacoma, WA; *m:* George T.; *c:* Jeffrey, Julie, Joel; *ed:* (BS) Home Ec Ed, Univ Of Puget Sound 1971; Grad Stud Home Ec & Health; *cr:* Home & Family Life Teacher Puyallup HS 1971-; *ai:* Dept Chairperson, Centennial &Finance Comm; PEA, WEA 1971-; Puget Sound Home Ec Assn Secy 1971-; *office:* Puyallup HS 105 7th St SW Puyallup WA 98371

JANSEN, MICHAEL MARION, Business Teacher; *b:* Elmira, NY; *w:* Betsy (dec); *c:* Christopher; *ed:* (MS) Ed, Elmira Coll 1987; (BS) Bus/Distributive Ed, SUNY Coll of Tech 1984; *cr:* Bus Teacher SCT BOCED Elmira NY 1984, Horseheads HS 1985, Haverling Cntrl Sch 1985-; *ai:* Class Adv; Track Coach; Hammondson & Nursery Sch Fund Raising Chm 1989-; *office:* Haverling Cntrl Sch 2K Ellas Ave Bath NY 14810

JANSSEN, ELAINE WHITMORE, Fourth Grade Teacher; *b:* Garden City, KS; *m:* Charles A.; *ed:* (BA) Elem Ed, Baylor Univ 1970; *cr:* 3rd Grade Teacher Waco Ind Sch Dist 1970-71, S Cayuga Schls 1971-73; 4th Grade Teacher Freehold Borough Schls 1975-; *ai:* NJEA, NEA 1976-; *home:* 12 Summit Ave Manalapan NJ 07726

JANSSEN, ROBERT E., Sixth Grade Teacher; *b:* Oregon, IL; *m:* Eleanor A.; *c:* Gregory R., Cynthia E.; *ed:* (BS) Ec, IL Wesleyan Univ 1963; (MS) Rdng Scndry Level, N IL Univ 1970; Univ WI Whitewater, N IL Univ; *cr:* 7th/8th Grade Math/Sci Teacher 1965-71, 5th/6th Grade Teacher 1971-89, 6th Grade Teacher 1990 New Milford Sch; *ai:* Designated Teacher; Safety Patrol Helper; Rockford Ed Assn (Dir, Exec Bd) 1979-; Phi Delta Kappa 1988-; Church Cncl VP 1983-85, 1987-; Winnebago Fans Club 1979-89; BSA Asst Scoutmaster 1982-84; *home:* 311 N Benton Box 497 Winnebago IL 61088

JANTOLAK, LAURA JEAN, 6th Grade Teacher; *b:* Cokato, MN; *ed:* (BS) Elem Ed, Univ of AZ 1968; His Grad Stud, St Univ Fullerton & Univ of CA Irvine; *cr:* 5th Grade Teacher Raymond Temple Elem 1968-75; 5th/6th Grade Combination Teacher Coyotes Elem 1975-; *ai:* Chairperson of Los Coyotes Bicentennial Comm; Geography Bee Coord & Moderator; Sch Key Planner; Dist Soc Sci & Educl Technology Comms; NEA, CA Teachers Assn, CEA 1968-, Teacher of Yr 1981; Phi Kappa Phi 1968; Phi Alpha Theta 1973-74, Achievement 1985, 1989; Centralia Sch Bd Appreciation 1981; Wrote Lessons Tests & Rules for Eng Grammar Series 1988-; *office:* Los Coyotes Elem Sch 8122 Moody St La Palma CA 90623

JAQUIS, MAURINE WHITE, Second Grade Teacher; *b:* Dumont, IA; *m:* Gordon Max; *c:* Juline Blanford, Elise Howe; *ed:* Elem Ed, 1952, (BA) Elem Ed, 1972 Univ of N IA; Educl Theory/Lesson Design; Thinking Skills/Learning Channels & Integrative Accelerated Learning, Drake Univ & IA St Univ; Cooperative Learning, Univ of IA; *cr:* 4th Grade Teacher 1952-56, Kndgtn-8th Grade Substitute Teacher 1956-64, Jr HS Eng/Rdng Teacher 1964-65, 3rd Grade Teacher 1965-66, 4th Grade Teacher 1966-67, 2nd Grade Teacher 1967-73, 1st Grade Teacher 1973-74, 2nd Grade Teacher 1974- New Hartford Cmmty Sch; *ai:* Staff Dev, Prins Advisory Comm; Drug Free Schls Team; Phase III Evaluation Comm; Thinking Skills Coord/Teacher Inservice; New Hartford Ed Assn 1965-; IA Ed Assn 1970-; NEA Life Mem; Cty Mem IA Conservation Ed Cncl Founding Mem 1989-; United Meth Church 1944-; Unit II Instructional Prof Dev 1988-; *home:* RR 1 Parkersburg IA 50665

JARABA, MARTHA DONALDSON, ESOL Teacher; *b:* San Pedro Sula, Honduras; *m:* Jaime Isaac; *c:* Janine, Jimmy; *ed:* (BA) Fr, LA St Univ 1972; Grad Work Ed; *cr:* Fr/Span Teacher Marjorie Walters Sch for Gifted & Talented 1974-76; Fr/Eng Teacher United Intermediate 1977-79; ESOL Teacher El Paso HS 1980-; *ai:* LPAC; Modern Lang Poetry Spon & Coach; TESOL Intnl, Textesol I, NEA, TX St Teachers Assn; Teacher of Yr El Paso Ind Sch Dist; Comm of Examiners NTE ESL ETS; Published Achieving Eng Proficiency; *office:* El Paso HS 800 E Schuster El Paso TX 79902

JARAMILLO, MARILYN, Third Grade Teacher; *b:* Taos, NM; *ed:* (AA) Early Chldhd Ed, (BA) Elem Ed, 1978 NM Highlands Univ; *cr:* 1st Grade Teacher Taos Elem Sch 1978-79; 2nd Grade Teacher 1979-81, 3rd Grade Teacher 1981- Questa Elem Sch; *ai:* 3rd-5th Grade Head Teacher Questa Elem Sch; Phi Kappa Phi Honor Society 1976-; *home:* 2376 Kiowa Rd PO Box 80 Questa NM 87556

JARBOE, SHARMAN (MULZER), Art Teacher; *b:* Tell City, IN; *m:* Harold M.; *ed:* (BA) Art Ed, 1974, (MA) Art Ed, 1977 Univ of Evansville; Teacher Expectation/Stu Achievement Prgm; *cr:* Art Teacher S Spencer Sch Corp 1974-80; Sub Teacher Troy-Tell City Sch Corp 1980-85; Art Teacher Cannelton City Schls 1985-; *ai:* Jr Class Spon; Help Coord & Present Annual Haunted House; NEA; IN St Teachers Assn; Troy Cmmty Assn Secy 1986-; Pres Cannelton Classroom Teachers Assn; *office:* Cannelton Jr Sr HS 3rd & Taylor Sts Cannelton IN 47520

JARELL, STANLEY MC CLURE, Assistant Principal; *b:* Tullahoma, TN; *m:* Lynne Zachry; *c:* Ashley, Allison, Zachry; *ed:* (BS) Health/Phys Ed, Univ of TN Chattanooga 1977; Admin & Supvr; *cr:* Teacher/Ftbl Coach Cntrl HS 1977-80, Westwood Jr HS 1980-84; Teacher/Coach 1984-86, Asst Prin/Coach 1986- Coffee Cty HS; *ai:* Coffee Cty Jr HS Ftbl Coach & Ath Dir; TEA, NEA; *office:* Coffee Cty Jr HS Mc Minnville Hwy Manchester TN 37355

JAREMBA, MARC ALLEN, Principal; *b:* Saginaw, MI; *m:* Sherri Woodrow; *c:* Jason, Jamie, Matthew; *ed:* (BA) Elem, 1981, (MA) Elem Admin, 1990 Saginaw Valley St Univ; *cr:* Pre-K Teacher 1981-83, 4th Grade Teacher 1983-85, 5th-8th Grade Sci/Soc Stud/Religion/Rdng Teacher 1985-89 Donovan Mayotte; Prin St Elizabeth Cath Sch 1989-; *ai:* Athletic Dir; MI Assn of Non-Public Schls (Planning Comm Mem 1989-, Mem): Natl Chrstn Ed Assn Mem; *home:* 714 Stoker Saginaw MI 48604

JARMA, DONNA MARIE, English/Spanish Teacher; *b:* Portsmouth, VA; *ed:* (AA) Eng, Temple Jr Coll 1969; (BA) Eng, Mary Hardon Baylor 1971, (MA) Eng, TX Womans Univ 1990; Several Seminars; Spec Trng Sessions; *cr:* Eng/Span Teacher Troy HS 1971-77, Howe HS 1977-; *ai:* UIL Poetry, Prose, Journalism & Ready Writing; Vlybl & Tennis Coach; Class & Span Club Spon; TX Classroom Teachers Assn, TX Educl Prof Assn; St Marys Cath Church PTA; FHA & FFA Honorary Mem; Various Plaques & Certificates; Poems & Articles Various Magazines & Newspapers; *home:* 416 W Dexter Sherman TX 75090

JARMOLA, CHRISTINE, Spanish Teacher; *b:* Nowata, OK; *m:* Dariusz; *ed:* (BA) Span Ed, OK Baptist Univ 1984; *cr:* Eng 2nd Lang Instr RBTS Switzerland 198577Span Teacher Carroll Cty HS 1988; *ai:* Span & Key Club Spon; *office:* Carroll Cty HS 1706 Highland Ave Carrollton KY 41008

JAROS, SHERRY (GREEN), Second Grade Teacher; *b:* Port Hueneme, CA; *m:* James Richard; *c:* Jennifer; *ed:* (BS) Elem Ed, Univ of NE Lincoln 1976; Grad Stud; *cr:* 2nd Grade Teacher Fort Crook Elem 1976-; *ai:* Team Leader Primary Grades; *office:* Fort Crook Elem Sch 12500 S 25th St Omaha NE 68123

JARRELL, MARGARET ANN, Teacher of Oral Expression; *b:* Detroit, MI; *m:* Dwight; *c:* Kathy Madigan; *ed:* (PHB) His/Eng, Siena Heights Coll 1950; Many Courses in Art, Drama, Speech; *cr:* 1st Grade Teacher Ann Arbor Trail Elem 1950-57; 3rd Grade Teacher Custer Elem 1957-58; 4th Grade Teacher Higgenbotham Elem 1958-65; Auditorium/4th Grade Teacher Fitzgerald Elem 1965-; *ai:* Drama Club; Audio Visual Supvr; *office:* Fitzgerald Elem Sch 8145 Puritan Ave Detroit MI 48238

JARRETT, GLORIA BARKSDALE, Business Teacher; *b:* Drakes Branch, VA; *m:* Arthur Lewis Jr.; *c:* Arthur L. III, Jerard B.; *ed:* (BS) Bus Ed/Stenography, St Pauls Coll 1982; (MS) Scndry Curr/Instruction, Longwood Coll 1990; Certificate for Writing Childrens Stories, Inst of Childrens Lit 1990; *cr:* Bus Teacher/FBLA Adv Cntrl of Lunenburg 1982-84; Bus Instr Southside VA Comm Coll 1982-86; Ed/Typesetter Brunswick Publishing Corporation 1984-86; Bus Teacher James S Russell Jr HS 1984-; *ai:* Jr Optimist Club Adv; Homecoming Comm; Cmptr Lab Chairperson; Sch Policies Task Force; Cooperating Teacher for Teacher Ed Prgm; Homebound Instr; Talented & Gifted Wkshp Instr; Brunswick Ed Assn (Building Rep 1985-88, VP 1986-87, Secy 1987-88, Pres 1988-); Alpha Kappa Alpha 1982-; BSA 1989, Service Awd Certificate; Spec Olympics 1985-89, Serivce Awd Certificate; Check Excl in Voc Ed 1989-, 1st Place Regional Awd; *home:* Rt 1 Box 228-01 Lawrenceville VA 23868

JARRIN, MARIANO, Spanish Teacher; *b:* Salamanca, Spain; *m:* Barbara Molina; *c:* Elisa L.; *ed:* (BS) Modern Lang, Univ of Salamanca 1974; (MS) Span, Appalachian St Univ 1981; *cr:* Span Teacher Buckinghamshire Coll of Higher Ed England 1976-77; Asst Span/Foreign Lang Teacher/Hall Coord Appalachian St Univ 1977-79; Eng Teacher Monfort HS Spain 1979-80; Span Teacher W Henderson HS 1981-; *ai:* Span Club Spon; Sch Foreign Exch Prgm Coord; NEA, NCAE; Grad Fellowship Appalachian St Univ; Intnl Study Fellowship Buckinghamshire Coll England; *office:* W Henderson HS 3600 Haywood Rd Hendersonville NC 28739

JARVIS, EDNA B., Fifth Grade Teacher; *b:* Hava De Grasse, MD; *ed:* (Ba) Ed, Old Dominion Univ 1965; Graduate Work in Psych/Cmptr Sci; *cr:* 5th Grade Teacher Mary Calcott Elem 1965-70; 4th Grade Teacher Exmore Willis Wharf Elem 1971-82; 5th Grade Teacher Norfolk Acad 1983-; *ai:* Spon Stu Cncl Lower Sch; Craft Club Spon Lower Sch; Chm Sunshine Comm Lower Sch; Tidewater Cncl of Teachers of Math 1983-89; NEA 1965-83; VEA 1965-83; St Andrews Episcopal Church 1983-; Eng Speaking Union 1983-88; Town-N-Gown 1984-89; Norfolk Society of Arts 1985; VA Symphony League 1985; *office:* Norfolk Acad 1585 Wesleyan Dr Norfolk VA 23502

JARVIS, REBECCA MAIKRANZ, Fourth Grade Teacher; *b:* Youngstown, OH; *ed:* (BA) Elem Ed, Youngstown St Univ 1979; (MS) Counseling, OH Univ 1988; *cr:* 7th/8th Grade Teacher 1979-89, 4th Grade Teacher 1989- Pennsville Elem; *ai:* Bsktbl Coach; Class Adv; Track, Cheerleading, Sci Fair Coord; Career Dev Comm; Textbook Comm; Sigma Chi Iota; PTO Pres; MLEA Rep; Delta Zeta; *home:* Rt 3 St Rt 377 Malta OH 43758

JARZAB, ARLENE ROBERTA, ATP Humanities Teacher; *b:* Chicago, IL; *m:* August A. Porreca; *ed:* (BA) Comm/Eng, NE IL Univ 1972; (MED) Ed/Admin, Univ of IL Chicago 1983; Gifted Ed, Natl Coll of Ed; *cr:* Faculty Asst NE IL Univ 1972-73; Teacher Immaculate Heart of Mary HS 1973-83; Lecturer Rosary Coll 1975-77; ATP Teacher Roosevelt Sch 1983-; *ai:* IL Future Problem Solving; River Forest Ed Assn (VP 1985, Pres 1986, Chief Negotiator 1986-89); IL Cncl for Gifted; *office:* Roosevelt Sch 7560 Oak St River Forest IL 60305

JASEN, ELIZABETH GRACE, Fourth Grade Teacher; *b:* St Louis, MO; *m:* Frank S.; *c:* Frank S. Jr., William G., Olivia A.; *ed:* (BA) Eng, Webster Coll 1950; Various Univs; *cr:* 4th Grade Teacher Riverview Gardens 1951-52, Dayton HS 1954-56, Lompoc HS 1974-77, Mountain Home 1978-; *ai:* Delta Kappa Gamma Society Intnl Mem; Veterans Foreign Wars Auxiliary, US Power Squadrons, Disabled Amer Veterans Auxiliary Mem; *office:* Guy Berry Intermediate Sch 1001 Main St Mountain Home AR 72653

JASLOW, BARBARA FECHTER, Language Art Teacher; *b:* New York, NY; *m:* Howard; *c:* Eric, Kenneth; *ed:* (BA) Ed/Home Ec, Hunter Coll 1966; Coll of New Rochelle, Coll of St Rose; *cr:* 3rd Grade Teacher Thiells Elem Sch 1975-80; Home Ec Teacher James A Farley Mid Sch 1980-81, Emerson Sch 1981-82, Nyack Jr HS 1982-83; 7th Grade Lang Art Teacher James A Farley Mid Sch 1983-; *ai:* N Rockland Peer Coaching Prgm Coach; Yr of the Reader Comm; Participant-Improving Writing Eng Conference 1988-; NYS Rdng Assn; Rockland Cty Rdng Cncl 1987-; N Rockland Jewish Center; NRJC Youth Group (Founder, Past Dir), Service Awd; BSA Merit Badge Cnslr; *home:* 171 Lakeview Dr Tomkins Cove NY 10986

JASMER, ALICE GUYTON, Mathematics Teacher; *b:* Alexandria, LA; *m:* David Lloyd; *c:* William T. Levie, Alice M. Levie; *ed:* (BA) Ed, NE LA Univ 1960; Grad Work AZ St Univ & NE LA Univ; *cr:* 6th Grade Teacher Monroe City Schls 1960-64; Librarian Lowndes Cty Lib System 1964-66; 5th Grade Teacher Mt Salus Day Sch 1975-78; Scndry Math Teacher Window Rock Sch Dist 1981-; *ai:* Academic Coaching; Dist Peer Evaluator; NCTM, ASCD, AFT; Alpha Delta Kappa; Window Rock Teacher of Yr 1986; *office:* Window Rock HS Box 559 Fort Defiance AZ 86504

JASON, ERNST W., Science Dept Chairman; *b:* Berlin, Germany; *m:* Johanna S. Jewett; *c:* Sandy; *ed:* (AAS) Liberal Arts/Bio, Broome Comm Coll 1967; (BS) Scndry Ed/Bio, St Univ of NY Oswego 1970; Cmptr Programming, Mid Level Ed, Child Psych, Animal Behavior, Sex Ed; *cr:* 7th Grade Sci Teacher/Dept Chair/Ftbl Coach/Ski Club Adv African Rd Jr HS 1969-; *ai:* Ski Club Adv; Mid Level Ed, Building Renovation, St Ed, RCT Liaison, Life Sci Curr Advisory Comm; African Rd Jr High Teachers Action Cncl Dept Rep 1969-84; NY Ed Assn 1969-; Vestal Teachers Assn Building Rep 1971-78; St Pauls Church Cncl (Councilman 1989-, Usher 1989-); Audobon Society FL Spon; Lifetime Achievement Awd Greek Peak Ski Area; 20 Yr Service Awd Vestal Cntrl Schls; *office:* African Road Jr HS S Benita Blvd Vestal NY 13850

JASPERSON, J. DAN, English Teacher; *b:* Afton, WY; *m:* Lori Luckert; *c:* Clint, Dane; *ed:* (BA) Eng, Univ of WY 1972; (MED) Gifted/Talented Curr, Lesley Coll 1988; Hotel Mgmt, RMI 1 1979; Personnel Relations, RMI 1981; Gifted/Talented Ed, Univ of WY Laramie 1986; *cr:* Eng Teacher Cheyenne East HS 1972-76; VP Luxury Villa Inc & DDP Motels Inc 1976-82; Adjunct Instr Laramie Cty Cmmty Coll 1982-86; Eng/G/T Teacher Johnson Jr HS 1983-; *ai:* Adv Congressional Awd Prgm; Yrbk Spon; Gifted/Talented Building Representative; NCTE 1972-; Cheyenne Sheriffs Rose (Pres) 1979- Mem of Yr Awd 1982; William Robertson Coe Fellowship 1975; *office:* Johnson Jr H S 1236 W Allison Rd Cheyenne WY 82007

JASSO, ANGELA CARDENAS, Office Education Teacher; *b:* North Laredo, TX; *m:* Alfredo Jr.; *c:* Alfredo III, Rodolfo; *ed:* (BS) Bus Ed, Laredo St Univ 1978; *cr:* Teacher J W Nixon HS 1979-83, Dr Leo G Cigarroa HS 1983-; *ai:* TX Classroom Teachers Assn 1988-; Bus Prof of Amer Club Adv; *office:* Dr Leo G Cigarroa HS 2600 Zacatecas Laredo TX 78043

JAVORSKY, RONALD JOSEPH, Social Studies Teacher; *b:* Steubenville, OH; *m:* Cathy Clark; *c:* Aaron J., Angela J., Annette J., Anthony J.; *ed:* (BA) Soc Stud, W Liberty St Coll 1972; Grad Stud; *cr:* 7th Grade Soc Stud Teacher 1973-88, 8th Grade Soc Stud Teacher 1988- Wellsburg Mid Sch; *ai:* Boys & Girls Bsktbl & Track; Little League Coach Mgr 1966-85; *office:* Wellsburg Mid Sch Main St Wellsburg WV 26070

JAVUREK, JEFFREY J., Mathematics Teacher; *b:* Chicago, IL; *m:* Deborah A. Petz; *c:* Jaclyn A., Jason J.; *ed:* (BA) Math Ed, Univ of IL 1972; (MA) Cnslr Ed, N IL Univ 1978; *cr:* Math Dept Chm 1977-78, Math Teacher 1972-, Team Leader 1979- Thomas Jr HS; *ai:* 8th Grade Girls Bsktbl Coach 1986-; Mathletes Coach 1987-; NEA, IL Ed Assn; Arlington Teachers Assn Pres 1984-; IL PTA 1972-, Honorary Lifetime Membership 1990; YMCA Indian Princesses 1988-; *office:* Thomas Jr HS 303 E Thomas St Arlington Heights IL 60004

JAYE, PAMELA YOUMANS, 6TH Grade Eng/Soc Stud Teacher; *b:* Anchorage, AK; *m:* David R. III; *c:* Molly, Joshua; *ed:* (BA) Elem Ed/Eng, Augsburg 1976; Working Towards Masters Ed, St Marys Coll; *cr:* Eng Teacher Fairbault Immaculate Conception 1976-79; Eng/Soc Stud Teacher Rosemount Mid Sch 1979-; *ai:* Girls Vlybl & Sftbl Coach; AFT; Rosemount Fed of Teachers; Church Sunday Sch Asst Supt 1983-85; Cmmty Vlybl & Sftbl Teams; Article Published *office:* Rosemount Mid Sch 3333 143rd St W Rosemount MN 55068

JEAN, JACK ALLEN, English Teacher; *b:* Fayetteville, TN; *ed:* (BA) Eng Ed, David Lipscomb Coll 1983; Post-Grad Stud, Mid Tn St Univ; Grad Space Acad Teacher Prgm, Huntsville Al; Grad, Tn Instructional Module Prgm; *cr:* Stu Asst Teacher David Lipscomb Coll 1981-83; Teacher Lincoln Cty HS 1984-; *ai:* Scholastic Team Coach; Beta Club Spon; Literary Magazine Spon; Teacher of Advanced Placement Prgm; In-Service Comm; Lib Comm; NCTE 1983-; NEA 1984-; Tn Ed Assn 1984-; Lincoln Cty Ed Assn 1984-; Church of Christ Mem/Part-TimeMinister 1979-; World Wildlife Fund Mem 1988-; *office:* Lincoln Cnty H S 1233 Huntsville Hwy Fayetteville TN 37334

JEANES, LOVELYN TOMPKINS, Science Teacher; *b:* Houston, TX; *c:* Eb, Don P.; *ed:* (BAT) Phys Ed/Eng/Sci/Health, 1972, (MED) Ed/Phys Ed, 1979 SHSU; Grad Stud Alcohol & Drug Abuse Trng; *cr:* Teacher Humble Ind Sch Dist 1973-76, Corrigan-Camden 1979-87, Humble Ind Sch Dist 1987-; *ai:* Cmmty PTO; Needs Assessment Comm; Cncl on Ministers Church & Society 1989-; Sunday Sch Teacher 1987-; At-Risk Stu Core Team Mem 1988-89; *office:* Humble Mid Sch P O Box 2000 Humble TX 77347

JEFFERS, HENRY BYRON, Physical Education Teacher; *b:* Lyons, GA; *m:* Cathy Knight; *c:* Seth, Tyrus, Jencey; *ed:* (AA) Phys Ed, ABAC 1970; (BA) Phys Ed, Univ of GA 1972; (MED) Phys Ed, GA Southern Coll 1985; Data Collector Certified St of GA; *cr:* Teacher/B-Team Coach Terrell Cty HS 1973-74; Lyons HS 1974-75; Teacher/Jr HS Coach Tattnall Elem Sch 1977-; *ai:* Sport & Phys Ed Coord; 7-8th Grade Ftbl Coach; 7-8th Grade Girls Bsktbl Coach; Amer Assn of Health/Phys Ed/recreation/ Dance; GA Assn of Health/Phys Ed/Recreation/Dance; NEA; *home:* Rt 4 Box 60-A Lyons GA 30436

JEFFERS, MARTHA GAYNELLE (NEASE), Fourth Grade Teacher; *b:* Pomeroy, OH; *m:* Donald Ray; *ed:* (BA) Elem Ed, Fairmont St 1974; Grad Work WV Univ, Salem Coll; *cr:* 3rd Grade Teacher Parsons Grade Sch 1975; 4th Grade Teacher Simpson Elem Sch 1975-; *ai:* Stamp Club Adv 1976-77; Arbor Day Chm; Amer Ed Week, Ed Fair, Sch of Excl, Spelling Bee, Textbook Adoption Harrison Cty Rdng Comm; Intermediate Lunch Supvr; WV Ed Assn, Harrison Cty Ed Assn, 1975-; Alpha Delta Kappa 1988-; Bridgeport Jr Womens Club Treas 1990-92; Sigma Kappa (Membership Officer 1972, Corresponding Secy 1973); *home:* PO Box 391 Bridgeport WV 26330

JEFFERSON, FRANCES MALONE, 2nd Grade Teacher; *b:* Albany, GA; *c:* Kenneth I. Malone; *ed:* (BS) Ed, Albany St Coll 1962; (BA) Music, 1964; *cr:* Teacher Flintside Elem 1965-66, Roseville Avenue 1968-85, Dr E Alma Flagg 1985-; *ai:* Jr Choir Abyssian Baptist Church; Sandalwood Fed Club; Alpha Kappa Alpha Chaplain 1983-; *home:* 205 Eastern Pkwy Newark NJ 07106

JEFFERSON, HAZEL, Language Art Teacher; *b:* Opelousas, LA; *ed:* (BS) Scndry Ed, Grambling St 1965; (MED) Supversion/ Admin, USL Lafayette 1973; Prof Improvement Prgm; *cr:* Home Ec Teacher Adams HS; Lang Art Teacher Oberlin HS; Teacher Holy Ghost Cath Sch 1965, Headstart Teacher 1966, 1968; *ai:* Adams HS Sr & Jr Class Spon; Home Ec Club; Spon Thanksgiving Prgm Oberlin Elem; Adult Ed Sewing Teacher; NEA (Covention Delegate 1986) 1965-; Allen Parish Assn of Ed 1970-; Sch Building Rep 1985-; Allen Parish Grambling Alumni 1980-89; Little Zion Church (Mem, Celestial Choir Mem 1966, Sunday Sch Teacher r Class, Sr Usher Bd Mem, Building Fund Comm Chm, Jr Red Circle Girls Dir, Calendar Comm Chm, Matrons Jr Mission Pres, Sr Mission Mem); 7th Dist Usher Dept Baptist Assn (Secy, Instr, Co-Chm); LA St Usher Dept of LA Baptist Convention Bd Mem; Baptist Youth Emcampment at Grambling St Univ & S Univ Instr; Zeta Phi Beta Grambling St Univ Mem 1963; *home:* 435 Avenue A Opelousas LA 70570

JEFFERSON, MAUDINE, 6th/7th Grade Reading Teacher; *b:* Dublin, GA; *ed:* (BS) Elem Ed, Savannah St Coll 1972; (MED) Elem Ed, Savannah St & Armstrong St Coll 1978; *cr:* 4th Grade Teacher 1972-73, 1st Grade Teacher 1973-74, 4th Grade Teacher 1974-78 E Laurens Primary; 6th-7th Grade Teacher E Laurens Elem 1978-; *ai:* Instructional Prof & Dev Comm Chairperson; GA Assn of Educators; Heart of GA Rdng Cncl; Dublin-Laurens Cty Black Festival Comm Chairperson 1983-84, Distinguished Service Plaque; S Chrstn Leadership Conference Bd Chairperson 1987, Certificate of Recognition 1987; Natl Assn Advancement of Colored People Fund Raiser Chairperson 1989-, Among Most Influential Black Women Mid GA 1989; Assistantship Awd Rdng Ed Univ of GA; Certificate of Recognition 1989-; Black Woman of Yr 1989; E Laurens Elem Teacher of Yr 1989; *home:* 713 Soperton Ave Dublin GA 31021

JEFFERSON, WILLIE L., Social Studies Teacher; *b:* Waco, TX; *m:* Shirley A. Reese; *c:* Evelyn M., Michael W., Marlana P., Tracy L.; *ed:* (BS) Poly Sci, Univ of NE 1970; (MS) Management & Human Relations, Webster Coll 1974; (ED Spec) Ed, Wichita St Univ 1982; *cr:* Teacher Air Force Comm Service Acad 1970-75, Wichita Public Schls 1976-; *ai:* Feed Our Children Under Starvation Club Adv; Kappa Alpha Psi News Reporter; Mid Schls of KS, NEA Vice-Chm Minority Affairs, KS Assn Multi-Cultural Dev 1990; KanLead Fellowship 1990.

JEFFERY, MARYETTA M. LOFTUS, Guidance Counselor; *b:* Chicago, IL; *m:* Thomas P. Sr.; *c:* Thomas Jr., Stephen, Daniel; *ed:* (BA) Elem/Early Ed, 1979, (MA) Cnslr Ed, 1985 Univ of S FL; *cr:* Elem Teacher 1979-85, Guidance Cnslr 1985- Riverview Elem; *ai:* Spec Services Team Chairperson; Peer Group Spon; Delta Kappa Pi 1979-85; Phi Delta Kappa 1990; PTA VP 1986-87; Citizens Against River Pollution 1985-; ECIA Grant 1990; *office:* Riverview Elem Sch 10809 Hannaway Dr Riverview FL 33569

JEFFERYS, GLENN WILLIAM, 5th Grade Teacher; *b:* Elizabeth, NJ; *m:* Janice; *c:* Dane; *ed:* (BA) Elem Ed, Univ of N FL 1977; *cr:* 5th Grade Teacher Atlantic Beach Elem 1977-81, Neptune Beach Elem 1981-; *office:* Neptune Beach Elem Sch 1515 Florida Blvd Neptune Beach FL 32233

JEFFORDS, CYNTHIA MAE, Third Grade Teacher; *b:* Huntington, WV; *ed:* (BA) Soc Stud/Scndry Ed, Marshall Univ 1972, 1974; Post Masters Stud Soc Sci; *cr:* 4th Grade Teacher Culloden Elem 1973-74; 4th Grade Teacher 1974-79, 6th Grade Teacher 1979-84, 3rd Grade Teacher 1984- Barboursville Elem; *ai:* Sch Planning Team Chairperson 1989-; Liason between Sch & Dropout Prevention Prgm Bd; Cabell Cty Rdng Cncl Annual Mem; 5th Avenue Baptist Church Leadership Ed Comm (Vice-Chairperson 1988-, Chairperson 1990); Taft Fellowship 1976; *office:* Barboursville Elem Sch 718 Central Ave Barboursville WV 25504

JEFFREY, RICHARD JAMES, History Teacher; *b:* Inglewood, CA; *m:* Julie Beth Gustafson; *c:* Kristin J., Andrew J., Tiffany D.; *ed:* (BA) His, Long Beach St Univ 1967; (MA) Ed, Kearney St Coll 1982; *cr:* Teacher/Coach Inglewood HS 1968-74, Mammoth HS 1974-79, Cambridge HS 1979-81, Kearney St Coll 1981-82, Holdrege HS Mid Sch 1982-; *ai:* Boys & Girls Cross Cntry & Boys Track Head Coach; Natl Coaches Assn, NE Coaches Assn 1979-; Church Youth Spon 1988-; Coaching Clinics Presenter; *office:* Holdrege Mid Sch 6th & Burlington Holdrege NE 68949

JEFFRIES, ELIZABETH WARREN, Mathematics Teacher; *b:* Lake Charles, LA; *m:* James David Sr.; *c:* James D. Jr., John W.; *ed:* (BS) Math, LA Tech Univ 1963; *ai:* Geometry Team; Graduation Comm; *office:* Murphy HS 100 Carlen St Mobile AL 36605

JEFFRYES-ROSE, BILLIE SCOTT, 5/6 Grade Teacher; *b:* Great Bend, KS; *m:* Alan Lee; *c:* Scott Jeffryes, Chris Jeffryes; *ed:* (BS) Bus Ed, KS St Univ 1958; Grad Stud Elem Ed & Spec Trng in Slingerland; *cr:* Bus Ed Teacher Herington HS 1958-60; Phys Ed Teacher Estelle Kampineyei & Marie Schafer Elem 1970-71, Orion Elem 1975-76; 5th/6th Grade Slingerland Teacher Orion Elem 1976-; *ai:* Sci Fair Chairperson 1985-; 5th Grade Math Derby 1988-; 6th Grade Battle of Books 1990; Curr Writing Earth Sci & Phys Sci; ASTA; AK Sci Teachers Assn Treas 1986-87; AK Ed Assn 1975-; NEA; Anchorage Sch Dist Sci Comm 1985-; Anchor Park Meth Church 1990; Teacher in Space Prgm Candidate; *office:* Mt Spurr Elem Sch 7-500 I Street Elmendorf AFB AK 99506

JEGGE, THOMAS C., Social Studies Teacher; *b:* Paterson, NJ; *ed:* (BA) Mid Sch Soc Stud/Eng, William Paterson Coll 1977; St Peters Coll; Jersey City St Coll; E Stroudsburg Univ; *cr:* Chief of Security Great Amer Recreational Assn 1980-84; Teacher Roxbury Township 1977-; *ai:* Little League Coach; Prof Ski Instrs Alliance of America 1982-; Canadian Ski Instrs Alliance 1976-.

JELLE, BERNIECE JEANETTE, 6th Grade Teacher; *b:* Fosston, MN; *m:* Walter; *c:* Brenda Albaugh, Bruce, Michelle; *ed:* (BS) Elem Ed, 1972, (MS) Elem Ed, 1981 Bemidji St Univ; Several Wkshps MN Dept of Ed; *cr:* Intermediate Elem Teacher 1950-52, Intermediate Elem/Part Time Elem Music Teacher 1953-59, Elem Music Teacher 1963-69, 1971-74, Intermediate Lang Art/Music Teacher 1975- Grygla Sch Dist #447; *ai:* Dist Sch Patrol Adv; Planning Evaluation Reporting & Assurance Of Mastery Comms;mn Educl Effectiveness Prgm Dist Team Mem; MN Spelling Bee Dist Coord; Rdng, Lang Art, Music Curr & Textbook Selection Comms; MN Ed Assn Local Pres 1980-81, Citation of Merit 1981; Natl Fed of Music Clubs Mem 1989-; Grace Luth Church (organist 1960-, Praise Singers 1982-); Delta Kappa Gamma Society Intnl 1989-; Basic Skills Comm Writing Dir Grygla Sch Bd & Admin; Chm of Comm Developing Procedural Manual for Writing Grygla Sch K-12; Grygla Sch Dist #447 Teacher of Yr 1989; *home:* 6th Ave Box 83 Grygla MN 56727

JEMISON, LINDA JOY (OGLE), 5th-6th Grade Teacher; *b:* Coleman, OK; *m:* Thomas M.; *c:* James; *ed:* (BS) Elem Ed, 1970, (MS) Elem Ed, 1983 SOSU; *cr:* Teacher Coleman 1970-; *ai:* Coach 5th-6th Grade Girls; NEA/OEA 1970-89; 4-H Leader VP 1989-, Leader of Yr 1988-89; *office:* Coleman Box 218 Coleman OK 73432

JEMO, DAVID NICHOLAS, Social Studies Chairman; *b:* Hazleton, PA; *m:* Linda Younker; *c:* Nicholas, David Jr.; *ed:* (BS) Soc Stud, Penn St 1969; Ed, Marywood Coll; *cr:* Teacher Weatherly HS 1970-; *ai:* Var Golf 1972-, Var Bsbl Coach; Video Club Adv 1986-; Town Councilman; *office:* Weatherly HS Spring St Weatherly PA 18255

JENDRO, LINDA COWSER, Business Education Teacher; *b:* Canton, IL; *m:* Alexander; *c:* Jennifer A., Daniel P., Kristen E.; *ed:* (BS) Bus Ed, 1974, (MS) Bus Ed, 1977 N IL Univ; Numerous Cmptr Classes; *cr:* Bus Teacher Glenbard S HS 1974-79, Millbrook Sr HS 1985-86, Hale HS 1988-; *ai:* Jr Class & Prom Adv; BSA Tiger Cub Organizer 1989-; GSA Troop Leader 1987-89; Sunday Sch Teacher 1981-89; *office:* Hale HS 3400 White Oak Rd Raleigh NC 27609

JENKINS, DAVID GERARD, English Department Head; *b:* Cambridge, MA; *m:* Ruth Begley; *c:* Pamela, Karen, Edmund, Matthew; *ed:* (BS) Ed, Boston St Coll 1970; (MSED) Eng, Bridgewater St Coll 1974; Certificate in Cmptr Basic, Norwood Public Schls; *cr:* Eng Teacher 1970-88, Eng Dept Head 1988- Norwood Jr HS; *ai:* Audio-Visual Coord; Norwood Teachers Assn, Norfolk Cty Teacher Assn, NEA 1970-; Tucker Sch PTO VP 1980-81; *home:* 37 Concord Ave Milton MA 02186

JENKINS, DEANN S., 7th-8th Grade Math Teacher; *b:* Clare, MI; *m:* John C.; *ed:* (BSED) Math, Cntrl MI Univ 1977; Grad Courses Math, Math Ed; *cr:* 7th-8th Grade Teacher Birch Run Area Schls 1978-; *ai:* Academic Track Coach; NCTM, MI Cncl Teachers of Math; Dist Curr Cncl Mem 1986-88; Natl Ski Patrol System; Amer Red Cross CPR & Standard 1st Aid Instr; Honors Algebra Wkshp Funded by Natl Sci Fnd 1987-88; NASA Educl Wkshp for Math & Sci Teachers 1990; MCTM Guest Speaker Annual Conference 1989; *office:* Marshall Greene Mid Sch 8225 Main St Birch Run MI 48415

JENKINS, DORRIS HAMBY, Retired 3rd Grade Teacher; *b:* Harrisburg, IL; *m:* George Douglas; *c:* Laura D. Limberg, Georgianna Richey; *ed:* (BS) Elem Ed, S IL Univ Carbondale 1962; Teaching the Gifted, Spec Ed; *cr:* 1st Grade Teacher New Diggings Sch 1962-63, Marshall Sch 1963-65, Mitchell Sch 1965-67; Eng/Rdng/Girls Phys Ed/Health Teacher Carterville Jr HS 1967-68; 1st Grade Teacher 1968-75, 3rd Grade Teacher 1975-87 Jefferson Sch; *ai:* Ed Sch Newspaper; Spon Gifted Groups; NEA, IL Ed Assn; United Meth Church (Ministers Wife, Sunday Sch Teacher, Youth Groups, Womens Groups); *home:* 1204 Election Dr Benton IL 62812

JENKINS, EDNA SELMAN, 6th Grade Teacher; *b:* Portales, NM; *m:* J. J.; *c:* Patsy Mohon, Nancy Haney, Jayna Wellman, Meri Reinhart; *ed:* Grad Work E NM Univ & TX Tech Univ; *cr:* 3rd Grade Teacher Lorenzo Elem 1953-54, Westside Elem 1956-57; 2nd Grade Teacher Smyer TX 1957-58; Piano Teacher Morton TX 1959-65; 5th-6th Grade Teacher Monterrey 1968-85, Military Heights 1985-; *ai:* Military Heights 6th Grade All City Chorus Mem Spon; Stu Assistance Comm; Fantastic Arts Fair Co-Dir; NEA, NMEA, REA 1968-; Delta Kappa Gamma (1st VP, 2nd VP) 1972-; Cmmty Concert Assn Bd Mem 1985-87; First Baptist Church (Sunday Sch 1982-, Pianist 1978-82); *home:* 2703 N Orchard Roswell NM 88201

JENKINS, ELIZABETH MC DANIEL, Mathematics Teacher; *b:* Maxton, NC; *m:* James Edward; *ed:* (BS) Math, Livingstone Coll 1960; Hunter Coll; *cr:* Math Teacher Scott Memorial HS 1960-62, Mary M Bethune HS 1962-70, John W Dodd Jr HS 1970-76, Woodbridge Sr HS 1976-82, Milton Jr HS 1982-; *ai:* Math League Coach; NEA, DSEA, NCTM; *home:* 711 Collins Ave Seaford DE 19973

JENKINS, KEVIN A., Mathematics Teacher; *b:* Camden, ME; *m:* Kathleen D'Amboise; *c:* Andrew, Eileen, Emily, Brian; *ed:* (BA) Math, Univ of S ME 1980; Working Toward Masters Educl Leadership; *cr:* Math Teacher Old Orchard Beach HS 1980-81, Gorham HS 1981-; *ai:* Var Bsktbl Coach; ME Assn Bsktbl Coaches (Secy 1987-89, Pres 1989-); *office:* Gorham HS 41 Morrill Ave Gorham ME 04038

JENKINS, LEILA DON, Fourth Grade Teacher; *b:* Mc Gregor, TX; *m:* Michael Ray; *c:* Michael S.; *ed:* (BS) Elem Ed, N TX St Univ 1959; (MS) Ed, Baylor Univ 1963; *cr:* 5th Grade Teacher Mc Gregor Ind Sch Dist 1959-60; 4th Grade Teacher Temple Ind Sch Dist 1960-61; 1st-5th Grade Teacher Corsicana Ind Sch Dist 1963-; *ai:* Consultation Comm 1970-74, 1987-91, Chairperson 1973-74, Secy 1972-73; TSTA, NEA 1959-; Corsicana Educators (Pres 1973-74, VP 1972-73, Secy, Faculty Rep 1971-72, 1985-86); Northside Baptist Church Sunday Sch Teacher 1963-; Delta Kappa Gamma (Pres 1976-78, Secy 1974-76); *home:* 1421 Bowie Cir Corsicana TX 75110

JENKINS, LINDA H., 5th Grade Mathematics Teacher; *b:* Birmingham, AL; *m:* Charles W.; *c:* C. Wesley, Jonathan S.; *ed:* (BS) Elem Ed, 1972 (MS) Mid Grades Ed/Math, 1982 Columbus Coll; Leadership Endorsement, Troy St Univ; Problem Solving Grant, Columbus Coll; *cr:* Teacher Mathews Elem 1972-74, Eastway Elem 1974-; *ai:* Math Team Spon; Teacher Cert Test Consultant; Chattahoochee Cncl Teachers of Math Treas 1986-; Muscogee Assn of Educators Secy 1977; Little League Bsbl Asst Dist Admin 1976-, Service to Youth Awd 1979; GA Cncl Teachers of Math Speaker 1988-89; Arithmetic Teacher Article 1987; Southern Assn of Colls & Schls Visiting Comm Mem 1988; *office:* Eastway Elem Sch 4601 Buena Vista Rd Columbus GA 31907

JENKINS, LON W., English Teacher; *b:* Union City, PA; *ed:* (BA) Eng, Gannon Univ 1984; Eng, Gannon Univ; *cr:* Eng Teacher Garwood Mid Sch 1985-86, General Mc Lane HS 1986-; *ai:* Drama Club Adv; Stu Support Prgm Mem; Fellow of the Northwestern PA Writing Project; *office:* General Mc Lane H S 11761 Edinboro Rd Edinboro PA 16412

JENKINS, LOWELL PARKER, 6th Grade Teacher; *b:* Macomb, NY; *m:* Anita Florence Brunell; *c:* Bradley L., Todd H.; *ed:* (BS) Elem Ed, 1955, (MS) Elem Ed, 1961 Plattsburgh St; Grad Stud; *cr:* 7th/8th Grade Teacher Union Free Sch #9 1955-56; 5th Grade Teacher Moreau Elem 1958-62; 4th/5th Grade Teacher Wilton Elem 1963-64; 6th Grade Techer Spring Street 1965-67, Tanglewood Elem 1967-; *ai:* HS Cross Cntry & Track Teams Coach; S Glen Falls Faculty Assn Pres 1966-67; *home:* 7658 Jackson Rd South Glens Falls NY 12803

JENKINS, MARY LOUISE BARNETT, Second Grade Teacher; *b:* Harrodsburg, KY; *m:* Leslie Graham Jr.; *c:* Graham, Beth; *ed:* (BA) Elem Ed, Georgetown Coll 1957; (Ma) Elem Ed, Univ of KY 1963; Elem Ed, Western KY Univ 1981; *cr:* 2nd & 3rd Grade Teacher Goldsmith Sch 1957-68; 2nd Grade Teacher Cntrl Elem 1968-86, J R Allen Elem 1986-; *ai:* Alpha Delta Kappa Chapter Pres 1962-; Delta Kappa Gamma Chapter Pres 1980-;

Meade Cty Homemakers Club Pres 1988-; Teacher of Yr Buechel Jaycees 1967; *home:* 222 Lawrence St Box 546 Brandenburg KY 40108

JENKINS, RHONDA LYNNE, Language Art Teacher; *b:* Morgantown, WV; *m:* Ralph D.; *c:* Ashley, Alex; *ed:* (AB) Ed, Fairmont St Coll 1974; Working Towards Masters in Ed & Lib Sci; *cr:* Teacher Newburg HS 1974-77, Newburg Jr HS 1977-87, Valley Jr HS 1987-; *ai:* Lib Sci Club Spon; Discipline & Staff Relations Comm; WV Ed Assn (Secy 1988-89) 1974-; Newburg Jr HS Teacher of Yr 1982-83; Valley Jr HS Teacher of Yr 1988-89; *home:* Rt 1 Box 57 Newburg WV 26410

JENKINS, ROBERT, English Teacher; *b:* Henderson, KY; *m:* Vicki Ann; *c:* Amy, Wes; *ed:* (BS) Eng, 1971, (MA) Scndry Ed, 1978, (Rank I) Guidance/Counseling 1981 Murray St Univ; *cr:* Eng Teacher Owensboro HS 1971, Henderson City HS 1971-76, South Jr HS 1976-; *ai:* Natl Aububon Society VP 1989-; Murray St Alumni Assn 1978-; League of KY Sportsman 1985-; Henderson City HS Teacher of Yr 1975; *home:* 717 Harris Dr Henderson KY 42420

JENKINS, SUSAN, 8th Grade Teacher; *b:* Holtville, CA; *ed:* (BA) Elem Ed, San Diego St Univ 1964; (MA) Educl Psych, San Diego Univ 1970; Admin Credential 1974; *cr:* 6th Grade Teacher Hedrick Sch 1964-66; 4th Grade Teacher Westview Elem 1966-68; 8th Grade Teacher Wilson Mid Sch 1968-86, 1989; Guidance Teacher Eisenhower Elem 1986-89; *ai:* 8th Grade & Annual Adv; After Sch Sports; DSTA VP 1975-80; Phi Delta Kappa Treas 1986-.

JENKINS, SYLVIA L., Third Grade Teacher; *b:* Winston-salem, NC; *c:* Shawn; *ed:* (BS) Early Chldhd Ed, Winston-Salem St Univ 1969; *cr:* 2nd Grade Teacher Pittsylvania Cty Schls 1970-72, Surry Cty Schls 1972-76; 3rd Grade Teacher Winston-Salem/Forsyth Cty Schls 1976-; *ai:* Forsyth Assn of Classroom Teachers, NC Assn of Educators, NEA; Alpha Kappa Alpha; 1st Baptist Church; *office:* Winston-Salem/Forsyth Cty 4332 Country Club Rd Winston-Salem NC 27103

JENKINS, THELMA MILLER, Home Economics Teacher; *b:* Kinston, NC; *c:* Trista; *ed:* (BS) Home Ec, NC CU 1960; Vocational Ed General; *cr:* Home Ec Teacher Hilly Branch HS 1960-62, Cntrl HS 1962-66; Pre Voc Teacher Woodington Sch 1966-; *ai:* FHA/Hero Adv; CECNC Adv; 8th Grade Adv; Hospitality Comm; Vocational Ed Dept Head & Cty Lead Teacher; NC Teachers Assn Publicity Chm 1985-89 Certificate 1986; *home:* Rt 1 Box 254A Kinston NC 28501

JENNER, JAMES LOWELL, Retired Social Studies Teacher; *b:* Pipestone, MN; *m:* Marlene M. Wrege; *c:* Jonatha L. Kalayjian, Jayme L. Osborne; *ed:* (BS) Phys Ed/Soc Stud, Bemidji St Univ 1957; (MS) Soc Sci/Scndry Ed, Los Angeles St Univ 1959; Sci, Health, Safety Ed, Drivers Ed, Recreation; Ford Fnd & Claremont Grad Sch Team Teaching; *cr:* Soc Stud Teacher Azusa HS 1957-61, Costa Mesa HS 1961-66; Soc Stud/Gifted/Honors World His Teacher Estancia HS 1966-89; *ai:* Azusa HS Bsktbl & Tennis Coach; Pep Squad Adv; Team Teaching Leader; Costa Mesa HS Bsktbl & Tennis Coach; Pep Squad Adv; Estancia HS Tennis Coach; Pep Squad, Frosh Class Adv; Dist Curr Comm, Soc Stud Consultant; Coastline Comm Coll Tennis Prgm Teacher 1979-89; CA Teachers Assn, NEA 1957-66; Presbyn Church (Deacon, Elder) 1963-67, 1981-85, 1988-89; Share Ourselves; S CA Top Tennis Prgm Recognition; Estancia HS Teacher of Yr 1979-80, 1988-89; Tennis Camps Prof Teacher & Dir; PTSA Excl Teaching Awd 1986; *office:*

JENNERJOHN, MARILYN RINKER, English Teacher; *b:* Easton, PA; *m:* Frederick A.; *c:* D. Gregory Witmer, Stephanie R. Witmer; *ed:* (AB) Eng, Lebanon Valley Coll 1962; (MA) Journalism, Penn St Univ 1976; Grad Course in Learning Disabilities; *cr:* Eng Teacher Manheim Township HS 1962-66; Adjunct Eng Instr York Coll of PA 1977-78; Eng Teacher Spring Grove Sr HS 1978-; *ai:* NEA, PA St Ed Assn 1983-; NCTE 1986-; Spring Grove Ed Assn (Negotiations Comm, Negotiations Team) 1983-; Amer Assn of Univ Women (Lancaster Publicity Chm 1969-70, York Co-Founder 1972, Pres 1973-75); Womens Assn of York Symphony Newsletter Ed 1970-72; York Cmmty Access TV Publicity Chm 1976-77; Bel Canto Singers of York 1982-84; Church (Choir Soloist 1972-, Worship Comm 1990); Kappa Tau Alpha 1976; *home:* 370 Old Garden Ln York PA 17403

JENNINGS, DEBORAH CRAWFORD, Math/Computer Teacher; *b:* Johnson City, TN; *m:* Charles Hampton; *c:* Charles R., Jessica B.; *ed:* (BS) Math, 1981, (MED) Scndry Ed/Math, 1990 E TN St Univ; *cr:* 7th/8th Grade Math Teacher Vance Jr HS 1981-85; Math/Cmptr Teacher Bristol TN HS 1985-; *ai:* Stu Cncl Adv; Class Coord; Bristol TN Ed Assn Building Rep 1988-; NEA, NCTM 1981-; Upper E TN Cncl Teachers of Math 1985-; Natl Sci Fnd Grant 1986-87; *office:* Bristol TN HS 1112 Edgemont Ave Bristol TN 37620

JENNINGS, JEANNE CARLSON, Third Grade Teacher; *b:* Omaha, NE; *c:* Belinda J. Johns, James, Jon; *ed:* (BA) Eng Lit, CA St Univ Long Beach 1972; (MA) Educl Admin, Azusa Pacific Univ 1983; Structure of Intellect Trainer, Consultant; *cr:* 6th/8th Grade Art Teacher 1972, 5th Grade Teacher 1972-74, 4th/5th Grade Teacher 1975-89 Harbour View Sch; CA St Sci Mentor Teacher Ocean View Sch Dist 1984-; 3rd Grade Teacher Harbour View Sch 1989-; *ai:* Univ CA Irvine Summer Sci Inst Consultant 1987; NSTA 1984-; CA Sci Teachers Assn 1989-; Cmptr Using Educators 1987; W Orange Cty Teachers Center Policy Bd Mem 1984-; *office:* Harbour View Sch 4343 Pickwick Cir Huntington Beach CA 92649

JENNINGS, K. ALFONSO, Phys Ed/XC/Track Coach; *b:* Suffolk, VA; *m:* Gwendolyn S.; *c:* Kohlilaha; *ed:* (BS) Phy Ed, MD St 1969; (MAT) Urban Ed, Montclair St 1971; (MS) Phy Ee, Trenton St 1972; *cr:* Teacher/Track Coach 1970-; XC Coach Trenton Cntrl 1974-; *ai:* Coach Trenton Track Club; NJEA 1971-; NEA 1971-; Kappa Alpha Psi 1967; *office:* Trenton Central HS Chambers & Greenwood Ave Trenton NJ 08609

JENNINGS, PATRICIA SUE, 7th/8th Grade Math Teacher; *b:* Abilene, TX; *m:* G. Gregory Jr.; *c:* Ryan Maxfield, John Maxfield, Danielle Maxfield; *ed:* (BMED) Music, 1969, (MED) 1973 TX Tech; *cr:* 2nd Grade Teacher Roosevelt Sch 1969-70; 4th-6th Grade Teacher Guadalupe Sch 1970-73; 4th-8th Grade Teacher Crockett Sch 1973-; *ai:* Tutor for Enriched Math; Supervising Teacher for Stu Teachers; Career Ladder Level 3 Master Teacher; *home:* 513 Crown Point El Paso TX 79912

JENNINGS, WANDA DOUGLAS, Social Studies Dept Chairman; *c:* Jim, Jennifer; *ed:* (AA) Admin of Justice, Santa Ana Coll 1975; (BS) Criminal Justice CA St Univ Long Beach 1977; Teaching Credential Soc Stud Univ of CA Riverside; *cr:* 8th Grade Soc Stud Teacher Elsinore Jr HS 1987-; *ai:* Yrbk Adv; Counseling Group Facilitator; Natl Cncl of Soc Stud; CA Teachers Assn; Outstanding Stu Teacher 1987 Delta Kappa Gamma; *office:* Elsinore Jr H S 1203 W Graham Ave Lake Elsinore CA 92330

JENRETTE, DALE WILLIAM, Fourth Grade Teacher; *b:* Akron, OH; *m:* Carol Semchuck; *c:* Taryn, Kyle; *ed:* (BS) Ed, Univ of Akron 1975; Working Towards Masters Educl Leadership, Univ of S FL; *cr:* Teacher Pfeiffer Mid Sch 1976-79, Bauder Elem Sch 1979-; *ai:* Bauders Sci Coord; Math Monitoring Comm; Instructional Technology Rep; FL Assn of Sci Teachers 1983-; Ec Fair 1st Place Awd; Mainstream Teacher of Yr Finalist; *office:* Bauder Elem Sch 12755 86th Ave N Seminole FL 34646

JENSEN, CAROLYN, English Teacher; *b:* Galveston, TX; *m:* Ronald L.; *c:* Ronnamarie; *ed:* (BS) Music Ed, Union Coll 1968; Eng, Comm, Univ of Cincinnati, Wright St Univ; *cr:* Music/Eng Teacher Oregon Conference of 7th Day Adv 1974-76; Asst Girls Dean Mt Vernon Acad 1978-81; Private Music Studio 1981-85; Eng Teacher Spring Valley Acad 1985-; *ai:* Stu Cncl Spon; Curr, Honor Society, Lib Comms; NCTE 1985-; *office:* Spring Valley Acad 1461 E Spring Valley Rd Centerville OH 45458

JENSEN, JALAINE P., 2nd Grade Teacher; *b:* Smithfield, UT; *m:* Paul H.; *c:* Paula J. J. Goodfellow; *ed:* (BS) Elem Ed/Child Dev, 1967, (MS) Child Dev, 1969 UT St Univ; Lang Art, Sci, Gifted Ed; *cr:* Laboratory Head/Teacher UT St Univ 1968; 3rd Grade Teacher 1969, 2nd Grade Teacher 1970- Summit Elem; *ai:* 2nd Grade Faculty Rep; Cache Cty Lang Art Comm; Intnl Rdng Assn 1988-; Cache Cty Rdng Assn 1988-, Promoting Literacy Awd 1990; PTA Pres 1966-68; Cache Cty Lib Bd Mem 1986-; Cache Cty Sch Bd Teacher Recognition Awd; Article Published; *office:* Summit Elem Sch 80 W Center Smithfield UT 84335

JENSEN, JAMES H., Science Teacher; *b:* Wausau, WI; *m:* Linda M. Garski; *c:* Eric, Kristin; *ed:* (BS) Bio/Ed/General Sci, Univ of WI Stevens Point 1973; Working Towards Masters Cardinal Stritch Coll; *cr:* Sci Teacher Cambria-Friesland Sch Dist 1975-76; Pharmaceutical Sales Wallace Labs 1976-80; Sci Teacher Appleton & Neenah & Menasha Dists 1980-83, Oconomowoc Sr HS 1983-; *ai:* Oconomowoc Ed Assn (Union Rep 1989-, Mem) 1983-; NEA, WI Ed Assn 1983-; Univ of WI Madison Natl Sci Fnd Fellowship 1985; *office:* Oconomowoc Sr HS 641 E Forest Oconomowoc WI 53066

JENSEN, JAY W., Drama Director/Teacher; *b:* Irvington, NJ; *ed:* (AA) Speech/Drama Ed, St Petersburg Jr Coll 1952; (BED) Speech Ed, 1954, (MED) Admin/Curr/Supervision, 1960 Univ of Miami Coral Gables; Univ of Americas Mexico City 1967; *cr:* Speech/Drama Teacher Little River Jr HS 1954-55, Miami Springs Jr HS 1955-57, Filer Jr HS 1957-59, Miami Beach Sr HS 1959-; *ai:* Drama & Officer Mc Gruff Youth Crime Watch Dir; Thespian Spon; Cmmty Theatre Spon & Dir; FL Theatre Conference Mem 1956-; Dade Cty Speech Teachers Pres 1959-60; Thespians Region 15 Dir 1970-79; Univ of Miami Friends of Theatre 1985-; Univ of Americas Alumni 1975-; Univ of Miami Alumni 1970-; Teacher of Yr 1972, 1988; Nom Univ of Miami Teacher of Yr 1975; City of Miami Beach Outstanding Citizen; ITS Thespian Awd 1974; *office:* Miami Beach Sr HS 2231 Prairie Ave Miami FL 33139

JENSEN, JOCELYN REID, Fine Arts Dept Chairman; *b:* Las Vegas, NV; *m:* Ronald B.; *c:* Rustin; *ed:* (MED) Music Ed, Univ of NV Reno 1964; (MM) Music Ed, UT St Univ 1972; (EDD) Post Scndry Ed, Univ of NV Las Vegas 1982; *cr:* Speech/Drama/ Vocal Music/Eng Teacher J C Fremont Jr HS 1959-62, 1963-64; Teacher J D Smith Jr HS 1965-66, Valley HS 1966-69, Orr Jr HS 1970-73; Teacher/Dept Chm Eldorado HS 1973-; *ai:* Pop Ensemble; Mixed, Mens & Ladies Choir; Madrigals; Allied Arts Cncl, Music Educators Natl Conference, Amer Choral Dirs Assn, S CA Vocal Assn; Latter Day Saints Church (Compassionate Service Leader 1984-, Organist 1985-); Clark Cty Honor Choir Chm; Case Study Rural Schls Univ N Las Vegas Lib; *home:* 767 N Los Feliz Las Vegas NV 89110

JENSEN, JOHN A., US History Teacher; *b:* Jackson, MN; *m:* Elizabeth Hansen; *c:* Laura, Mary, Nicklas; *ed:* (BA) His/Eng, 1966, Teaching Credential, 1983 Augustana Coll; CA St Fresno & Fresno Pacific Coll; *cr:* Teacher Tulare Union HS 1983-; *ai:* Articles Published; *office:* Tulare Union HS 755 E Tulare Ave Tulare CA 93274

JENSEN, JON CHRISTIAN, Principal; *b:* Jackson, MI; *m:* Sue Dible; *c:* Kristen, Ryan; *ed:* (BS) His, Central MI Univ 1968; (MA) Ed, MI St Univ 1972; *cr:* His Teacher/Coach Litchfield Public Schls 1968-72, Wayland Union Public Schls 1972-81; Earth Sci Teacher/Coach Wayland Jr HS 1981-85; His & Soc Teacher/ Coach Wayland HS 1985-89; Prin Wayland Jr HS 1990; *ai:* Coaching-Track Cross Cntry; Wayland Union Ed Assn Pres/Chief Negotiator Grievance Chairperson; MI Elem & Mid Sch Principals Assn; Teacher of Year-Wayland Schls 1988-89; *office:* Wayland Jr H S 203 Pine Wayland MI 49348

JENSEN, LUCY, English Teacher; *b:* Salt Lake City, UT; *ed:* (BA) Eng, 1966, (BA) Anthropology, 1966, (MA) Eng, 1977, (PHD) Eng, 1984 Univ of UT; *cr:* Teacher St Marys Acad 1966-69; Teaching Fellow Univ of UT 1970-75; Teacher Brighton HS 1979-; *ai:* Adv for Honor Stu Society; UEA, JEA, NCTE, NEA 1987-89; *office:* Brighton HS 2220 E 7600 S Salt Lake City UT 84121

JENSEN, PATRICIA A., Sixth Grade Teacher; *b:* Champaign, IL; *m:* Richard George; *c:* Carson, Carrie; *ed:* (BS) Elem Ed, 1976, (MS) Elem Ed, 1980 IN Univ & Purdue Univ; Rdng Endorsement & Cert Gifted & Talented, Purdue Univ & IN Univ; *cr:* 6th Grade Teacher NW Hendricks Sch Corp & N Salem Elem 1976-; *ai:* 5th/6th Grade Cheerleading Spon; K-6th Grade Newspaper Ed & Spon; Alpha Delta Kappa (Treas, Past Mem); Intnl Rdng Assn Past Mem; ISTA (Mem, Treas) 1989-; *office:* N Salem Sch SR 75 PO Box 69 North Salem IN 46165

JENSEN, RHINER CHRISTEN, Social Studies Teacher; *b:* Los Angeles, CA; *m:* Nancy Ann;; *c:* Jon M., Kristina E. Notar; *ed:* (BA) His, Pepperdine Univ 1951; (MA) His, Univ of S CA 1958; *cr:* Teacher Los Angeles Unified Sch Dist 1953-54, US Army 1954-56, Los Angeles Unified Sch Dist 1956-; *ai:* Leadership Spon; Los Angeles Unified Sch Dist Area D Teacher of Yr 1976, 1986; *office:* Daniel Webster Jr HS 11330 W Graham Pl Los Angeles CA 90064

JENSEN, SARA O., Second Grade Teacher; *b:* Manchester, IA; *m:* John C.; *c:* Kelly Dusenberry, Tony Dusenberry, Suzanne Nisely; *ed:* (AA) Liberal Art, Glendale Comm Coll 1972; (BA) Elem Ed, AZ St Univ 1974; Grad Stud Educl & Sch Psych, AZ St Univ; *cr:* 3rd Grade Teacher Barcelona Elem Sch 1974-79; Gifted Ed Teacher Barcelona/Catalina/Sevilla Schls 1979-86; 2nd Grade Teacher Barcelona Elem Sch 1986-; *ai:* Sch Literary Magazine Ed; Parent Booster Club Faculty Rep; Phi Delta Kappa 1980-; NEA, AZ Ed Assn 1974-; Alhambra Dist Assn Classroom Teachers VP 1981; BSA Den Mother 1968-70; GSA Brownie Leader 1970-71; AZ Assn Gifted & Talented Chairperson 1980-82; AZ Teacher of Yr Finalist; Greater Phoenix Writing Project Charter Mem; Phi Theata Kappa, Phi Beta Kappa & Phi Kappa Phi; *office:* Barcelona Elem Sch 4432 W Maryland Ave Glendale AZ 85301

JENSEN, STEVEN H., Teacher; *b:* Gridley, CA; *m:* La Ree Adams; *c:* Bradley, Robert, Wendy Jensen Hansen; *ed:* (BA) Math, Chico St Coll 1959; *cr:* Teacher Wheatland HS 1961-62, Gridley Union HS 1962-; *ai:* Academic Decathlon Coach; Sr Class Adv; Gridley Teachers Assn Pres 1974-75, 1980-81, 1987-88; CA Teachers Assn, NEA; BSA Dist Commissioner 1985-; LDS Church (Young Men Leader, Pres) 1985-; Mentor Teacher 1984-88; Outstanding Teacher 1987-88; *office:* Gridley Union HS 300 E Spruce St Gridley CA 95948

JENSEN, SUZI M., CP English & Dance Teacher; *b:* Ogden, UT; *m:* Kevin A.; *c:* Kolten B., Jasey; *ed:* (BS) Eng, Weber St Coll; *cr:* Eng Teacher 1982-, Eng/Dance Teacher 1990 Roy HS; *ai:* Dance & Drill Team Adv; UHSAA Dance & Drill, AAHPERD; Dance & Drill Team Region, St, Natl Champions 1982-; *office:* Roy HS 2150 W 4800 S Roy UT 84067

JENSON, JAMES CURTIS, Physical Education Teacher; *b:* Spokane, WA; *m:* Dianna Lynn Dunford; *c:* Tiffany L., Tracee B.; *ed:* (BA) Ed, E WA Univ 1968; (MA) Counseling/Guidance, Whitworth Coll 1974; *cr:* Soc Stud/US His/Phys Ed Teacher Chief Moses Jr HS 1968-70; Phys Ed Teacher Farwell Elem 1970-71, Mead Mid Sch 1971-81, Northwood Jr HS 1981-; *ai:* Head 8th Grade Ftbl Coach; Head 7th Girls Vlybl & Bsktbl, 8th Grade Girls Bsktbl, 7th & 8th Boys Track; Fed of Chrstn Athletes; *home:* N 21415 Panorama Rd Colbert WA 99005

JENSON, JANE ELIZAZBETH, Third Grade Teacher; *b:* Rockford, IL; *ed:* (BA) Elem Ed/Natl Sci, Augustana Coll 1976; Numerous Wkshps, Inservices, Extensive Traveling; *cr:* Teacher Barbara Olson Sch of Hope 1976-77; Substitute Teacher Rockford Public Schls 1977-78; Teacher Keith County Day Sch 1978-; *ai:* Independent Sch Assn of Greater Chicago Sch Rep; 5th-6th Grade Vlybl COach; Sch Comm Participation; Church Cncl Secy 1980-81; Rockford Pro Am 1987-; *office:* Keith Country Day Sch 1 Jacoby Dr Rockford IL 61107

JENTES, RALPH EMERSON, Social Studies Teacher; *b:* Canton, OH; *ed:* (BA) His/Comprehensive Soc Stud, Mt Union Coll 1977; (MA) Scndry Sch Admin, Kent St Univ 1980; Educl Admin, Speech, Debate Coaching Wkshps; *cr:* 8th Grade US His/ 9th Grade Civics/World His Teacher Louisville Jr HS 1977-; *ai:* Competitive Forensics, Speech, Debate Coach; Louisville Jr HS Jr NHS Faculty Cncl; Natl Forensic League 1970-; Louisville Ed Assn, OH Ed Assn, NEA 1977-; OH HS Speech League Canton Dist Comm 1977-78, 1986-87; Louisville City Cncl Excl in Coaching Forensics 1983; *office:* Louisville Jr HS 300 E Gorgas St Louisville OH 44641

JEPSEN, KATHLEEN HAGERTY, 7th-8th Grade Eng Teacher; *b:* Philadelphia, PA; *m:* William George Jr.; *c:* Erika, Haakon, Britta; *ed:* (BA) Speech/Drama, Cath Univ 1969; Working Towards Masters in Liberal Arts, Johns Hopkins Univ; Gifted & Talented Trng Wkshp, Anne Arundel Cty; *cr:* 7th-8th Grade Eng Teacher George Fox Mid Sch 1983-87; 8th Grade Eng Teacher/Drama Coach Northeast HS 1987-89; 7th-8th Grade Eng Teacher George Fox Mid 1989-; *ai:* Materials of Instruction, 7th & 8th Grade Curr Writing Comm Anne Arundel Cty; Gifted & Talented Comm; Amer Cancer Society (Pres 1980-82, Anne Arundel Cty Bd of Dir 1980-82, Residential Campaign Chairperson 1982-83, Daffodil Day Comm, Volunteer 1984-); Nom Anne Arundel Cty Teacher of Yr Awd & Eugene Meyer Awd 1989; *office:* George Fox Mid Sch Outing Ave Pasadena MD 21122

JEPSON, MARY JO MEYERS, Secondary English Teacher; *b:* Martins Ferry, OH; *m:* Edwin C. III; *ed:* (BA) Eng, Wheeling Jesuit Coll 1970; Lib Sci, OH Dominican Coll; Marketing, W Liberty St Coll; Ed, OH St Univ; Comm Stud Prgm, WV Univ; *cr:* Teacher Buckeye Local Sch Dist 1970-72, Diocese of Columbus 1972-86; Mrktg Rep Wheeling Dollar Bank 1987; Teacher Bellaire City Schls 1987-; *ai:* Stu Cncl & NHS Adv; Diocesan Lang Art Curr Comm; OH Cncl of Lang Art Teachers; Bellaire Ed Assn, OH Ed Assn, NEA Mem 1987-; Wheeling Symphony & Hospital Auxiliary 1989-; *home:* 2 Hazlett Ct Wheeling WV 26003

JERCINOVIC, EUGENE, Teacher Mid Sch Honors Seminar; *b:* Los Alamos, NM; *m:* Elizabeth Griffin; *c:* Jason, Jessica; *ed:* (BS) Physics, 1969, (MS) Physics, 1972 NM Tech; *cr:* Teacher Garfield Jr HS & Mid Sch 1973-79, Mid Sch Honors Seminar in Math 1979-; *ai:* Article Published 1983; NCTM Regional Conferences Speaker; Nom Univ of NM Distinguished Teacher; Nom NM Tech Alumni Assn Presidential Awd; Distinguished Achievement Awd; *office:* Albuquerque Public Schls 725 University SE P O Box 25704 Albuquerque NM 87125

JERRIS, CAROL ANN (ROUSSEAU), Third Grade Teacher; *b:* Winchendon, MA; *m:* B. Alan; *c:* Robyn, Randon; *ed:* (BS) Elem Ed, Fitchburg St Coll 1966; *cr:* Head Start Teacher Town of Athol 1966; 2nd Grade Teacher Sanders Street Sch 1966-67, Bennett Hemenway Sch 1967-68; 2nd Grade Teacher 1979, 4th Grade Teacher 1980-85, 3rd Grade Teacher 1987- St Joseph Sch; *ai:* Mission Coord; Mid St Evaluation Study Team; NCEA 1980-85, 1987-; *home:* 16 Twin Park Dr PO Box 388 Brookside NJ 07926

JESPERSON, KIM MARIE (CARNEGLIA), Mathematics Teacher; *b:* New Brunswick, NJ; *m:* John Edward; *c:* Erik; *ed:* (BA) Scndry Ed/Math/Earth Sci, Glassboro St Coll 1980; *cr:* Math Teacher Sterling Regional HS 1980-81, Cumberland Regional HS 1981-87, Ocean City HS 1987-; *ai:* Jr Class Adv; NJ Math Teachers Assn; *office:* Ocean City HS 5th & Atlantic Sts Ocean City NJ 08226

JESSAMINE, VICKI LEE, English Teacher; *b:* Phillipsburg, NJ; *ed:* (BA) Eng, Cedar Crest Coll 1980; (MED) Scndry Ed/ Eng, Kutztown Univ 1984; Admin, Lehigh Univ; Psych, Harvard Univ; *cr:* 3rd Grade Teacher Notre Dame of Bethlehem 1981-83; Eng Teacher Colonial Northampton IU 20 1984-85, Easton Area Sch Dist 1985-86, Northampton Area Sch Dist 1986-; *ai:* Soph Class Adv; Graduation & Act Advisory Comm; Stu Support Prgm; NCTE; Grad Asst Kutztown Univ 1983-84; Whos Who in American Ed 1989-; Article Published Morning Call Allentown PA; *office:* Northampton Sr HS 1619 Laubach Ave Northampton PA 18067

JESSEN, JANE SMITH, Fifth Grade Teacher; *b:* North Platte, NE; *m:* Wade; *c:* Christopher, Sara; *ed:* (BA) Elem Ed, Kearney St 1977; Kearney St, Wayne St Coll; *cr:* 2nd Grade Teacher North Platte Public Schls 1977-79; 5th Grade Teacher Norfolk Cath Schls 1984-; *ai:* Alpha Delta Kappa VP 1986-; Cath Daughters Monitor 1986-; Outstanding Teacher of Yr 1988; *home:* 511 Opal Ln Norfolk NE 68701

JESWALD, MARCIA A., 7th Grade Reading Teacher; *b:* Youngstown, OH; *m:* Joseph R.; *ed:* (BS) Elem Ed, 1976, (MS) Curr, 1980 Youngstown St Univ; Cert Gifted & Talented; *cr:* Teacher Austintown Mid Sch 1976-; *ai:* OEA 1977-; *office:* Austintown Mid Sch 5800 Mahoning Ave Youngstown OH 44515

JETT, SHARON ADAMS, 6th Grade History Teacher; *b:* Hooker, OK; *m:* Ted; *c:* Clay, Marla; *ed:* (BS) Elem Ed, Panhandle St Univ 1966; Grad Courses OK St Univ; *cr:* Teacher Guymon Jr HS 1974-81, Pampa Mid Sch 1981-; *ai:* TX Classroom Teacher Assn Faculty Rep 1984-86; TX Cncl for Soc Stud 1988-; *home:* 2325 Fir Pampa TX 79065

JETT, WILLIS WARREN, III, Science/Mathematics Teacher; *b:* Houma, LA; *m:* Tommie Lee Prisk; *c:* Warren, Kathleen; *ed:* Industrial Chem, LA St Univ; Second Man & Bus Dir, Beth Haven Bus Dir Sch; *cr:* Sr Asst Chemist Dow Chemical Company 1960-70; Assoc Pastor Bible Baptist Church 1973-; Teacher Hendersonville Chrstn Acad 1987-; *office:* Hendersonville Chrstn Acad 355 Old Shackle Island Rd Hendersonville TN 37075

JETTE, BETH HUNTER, Mathematics Teacher; *b:* Burlington, VT; *m:* Andre M.; *c:* Jessica, Andrea; *ed:* (BS) Scndry Math Ed, Castleton St Coll 1973; (MED) Curr/Instruction, Univ of VT 1988; *cr:* Math Teacher 1973-, Dir of Summer Ed 1981-85, 7th Grade Team Leader 1980- Missisquoi Valley Union HS; *ai:* VT ASCD 1987-; NCTM, NEA 1973-; VT Mid Sch Assn 1986-; Swanton Jaycee Women VP 1984; Dev Gifted & Talented Summer Prgm 1983-; ATMNE Conference 1987; Natl ASCD Mid Sch Consortium Presider 1986-88; Presenter Effective Teaching Mastery Learning Conference 1984; Dist Curr Steering Comm 1987-; 8th Grade Graduation, Math Challenge League, Parent Group in Support of Excl in Jr HS, Rewarding Excl in Math Grants; *office:* Missisquoi Valley Union HS Rt 78 Swanton VT 05488

JEWEL, BETH ANN, Biology Teacher; *b:* Toledo, OH; *ed:* (BA) Earth Sci Ed, Bowling Green St Univ 1983; (MS) Soc Fnd of Ed, Univ of VA 1989; *cr:* Teacher Prince William Cty Schls 1984-86, Fairfax Cty Schls 1986-88, W Springfield HS 1988-; *ai:* Cheerleading; Rdng Writing Comm; Environmental & Partners Club; AFT 1986-; Fairfax Cty Teacher Recognition Awd; *office:* W Springfield HS 6100 Rolling Rd Springfield VA 22152

JEWETT, EVERELL W., Biology Teacher; *b:* Hornell, NY; *m:* Virginia Mc Laughlin; *c:* Molly; *ed:* (BA) Bio Ed, Alma Coll 1966; (MS) Bio Ed, Buffalo St Univ 1972; Grad Stud; *cr:* Bio/General Sci Teacher Wilson Cntrl HS 1967-69; Regents/AP Bio Teacher Grand Island HS 1969-; *ai:* Class Adv 1976, 1981, 1986, 1989; Graduation Coord; Coach Track & 9th Grade Bsktbl; NABT 1987-; US Powers Squadron Ed Officer 1978-, Krawl Awd 1984; Youngstown Yacht Club Head Sailing Instr 1979-; Amer Chemical Society W NY Teacher of Yr 1982.

JILKA, KEVIN JOE, 7th & 8th Grade Math Teacher; *b:* Logan, KS; *m:* Janet M. Johnson; *ed:* (BA) Colby Comm Jr Coll 1975; (BS) Phy Ed, Fort Hays St Univ 1977; *cr:* Math Teacher Norton Jr HS 1978-; *ai:* Asst HS Ftbl; Head HS Girls Bsktbl; Head Jr HS Girls Track; KS Bsktbl Coaches Rep 1988-; *home:* 701 N Jones Norton KS 67654

JIMENEZ, BENJAMIN SOTO, Mathematics Teacher; *b:* Los Angeles, CA; *m:* Sara; *c:* Daniel, Rachael; *ed:* (BA) Math, San Diego St Univ 1974; *cr:* Math Teacher Garfield HS 1975-; *ai:* NCTM; Hispanic Urban Center Teacher Awd 1990; CA Educator Awd 1989; Los Angeles Unified Certificate of Recognition 1989; Amigo de MAES 1989; Chicanos for Creative Medicine Educator Awd 1988; CA Schlsp Fnd Outstanding Teacher Awd 1985; *office:* Garfield HS 5105 E 6th St Los Angeles CA 90022

JIMENEZ, JOHN FRED, Sixth Grade Teacher; *b:* Clayton, NM; *m:* Joyce Lopez; *c:* John F.; *ed:* (AA) Ed, Trinidad Jr Coll 1963; (BA) Elem Ed, Adams St Coll 1965; (MA) Elem Ed, Highlands Univ 1971; *cr:* 6th Grade Teacher Kearny Elem Sch 1965-66, Acequia Elem Sch 1966-; *ai:* Acequia Madre Sch Art Instr; Acequia Mardre Elem Sch Drug Coord; Classroom Teachers Assn, NM Ed Assn, NEA 1965-; Garcia Street Club Bd Mem 1983-85; Theater of Music Bd Mem 1987-; Span Colonial Society Mem 1976-; Mayors Art Recognition Awd 1988; Outstanding Elem Teachers of America 1972; Nom Century Federal Great Teachers Awd 1990; *home:* PO Box 403 Santa Fe NM 87504

JIMENEZ, OLIVIA M. T. G., Eng/Span/Jrnlsm Teacher; *b:* Prescott, AR; *m:* Edward J.; *c:* Mia, Granillo; *ed:* (BA) Eng, AZ St Univ 1972; *cr:* Teacher Apollo HS 1972-73; 9th Grade Eng/Span/ Journalism Teacher McKemy Jr HS 1973-; *ai:* Pom & Chrldr Spon 1981-84 & 1987-88; Champions Chrldr 1982 & 1988; Yrbk Spon 1989-; TEFT; Class Produces Sch Yrbk & Sch Newspaper; *office:* McKemy Intermediate 2250 S College Ave Tempe AZ 85282

JIMENEZ, SANDRA KAY, History Teacher; *b:* Victoria, TX; *ed:* (BS) Phys Ed/Health, TX A&I Univ 1979; His, Univ of Houston 1986; *cr:* Teacher/Coach Crain Intermediate Sch 1982-85, Victoria HS 1985-87, Bloomington HS 1987-; *ai:* Girls Vlybl, Bsktbl & Track Head Coach; Honor Society Selection Comm; TX Classroom Teachers Assn, TX Girls Coaches Assn, TX Assn of Bsktbl Coaches, Natl Fed Interscholastic Coaches Assn.

JIMINEZ, FELIPE DE JESUS, JR., English Teacher; *b:* Laredo, TX; *m:* Mary Esther Reyes; *ed:* (BS) Eng/His, TX A&I Univ Laredo 1977; Grad Stud; *cr:* 7th/8th Grade Rdng Teacher M B Lamar Jr HS 1977-83; 8th Grade His Teacher Dr Joaquin G Cigarroa Mid Sch 1983-84; 9th-12th Grade ESL/CLA Teacher Dr Leo G Cigarroa HS 1984-; *ai:* Law Enforcement Club Spon; TX St Teachers Assn 1977-83; Amer Fed of Teachers Rep 1983-85; TX Classroom Teachers Assn Rep 1986-88; Evening Lions Club (Secy, Treas) 1978-83; Border Olympic Tennis 1983-85; Laredo Police Dept Explorer Post Adv 1989-, Recognition 1990; *office:* Dr Leo G Cigarroa HS 2600 Zacatecas St Laredo TX 78043

JOACHIM, JOHN RICHARD, Biological Science Teacher; *b:* Cincinnati, OH; *m:* Carol Jean; *c:* John K., Kimberly K. Hamann; *ed:* (BS) Bio/Health Ed, 1965, (MED) Curr, 1972 Univ of Cincinnati; Miami Univ, VA Polytechnical Inst, Xavier Univ; Natl Sci Fnd Leadership Specialist Wkshp MI St Univ 1974; *cr:* Sci Instr Greenhills-Forest Park City Sch 1965-69, Princeton City Schls 1970-; *ai:* Sci Curr; Phi Delta Kappa 1970-; NEA, OH Ed Assn 1965-; NSTA, NASSP, Princeton Ed Assn; Natl Sci Fnd Fellowship Miami Univ In-Service 1965-66, Miami Univ Summer 1967, Univ of Cincinnati Population Dynamics 1972; Jennings Scholar Awd 1975; Enrichment Stud Awd Martha Holden Jennings Fnd 1973 & Greater Cincinnati Fnd 1974; OH Teacher of Yr Awd 1976; Hamilton Cty Environmental Teacher of Yr 1978-80; Dept of Energy Summer Fellowship VA Polytechnical Inst 1979; OH Bd of Regents Geology Summer Fellowship 1989; BP America Excl Awd 1989; Bus Week Awd 1990; *office:* Princeton Jr HS 11157 Chester Rd Cincinnati OH 45246

JOB, PATRICIA FORREST, English Teacher; *b:* Jersey Ci[...] NJ; *ed:* (BA) Eng, Fairleigh Dickinson 1966; British Lit, Advanc[...] Placement Inst 1986; *cr:* 7th Grade Eng Teacher Parsippaany Hi[...] HS 1967-; *ai:* Graduation Advisement; Essay Writing Adv; NCT[...] 1967-; Parsippany Tauy Hills Ed Assn Bd of Ed Liason 1975-[...] Alpha Delta Kappa Schlsp Chairperson 1985-86; Morris Cty St[...] Leader Ed of 1988; Rotary Outstanding Educator 1988; *offi[...]* Parsippany Hills H S 20 Rita Dr Parsippany NJ 07054

JOB, VALERIE Y'LLISE, Spanish Teacher; *b:* Lubbock, TX; [...] (BA) Elem Ed/Bi-ling Span & Eng, 1981, Scndry Ed - Cu[...] Laude, Wayland Baptist Univ; Grad Level Psych & Span; [...] Bi-ling Kndgtn Teacher Olton Ind Sch Dist 1981-83; Bi-ling 2[...] Grade Teacher Seminole Ind Sch Dist 1983-86; Grad As[...] Wayland Baptist Univ 1986-87; Span Teacher Plainview Ind S[...] Dist 1987-; *ai:* Span Club Spon; Region 17 Service Center Med[...] Advisory Comm; Continuing Ed Prgm Span Teachers; TX Foreig[...] Lang Assn, Amer Assn Teachers of Span & Portuguese 1989; T[...] Classroom Teachers Assn 1987; Wayland Baptist Univ Dea[...] Honor Roll; Wayland Baptist Univ Peer Teaching; *offi[...]* Plainfield HS 1501 N Quincy Plainview TX 79072

JOBE, DONNA JAREE, 6th Grade Teacher; *b:* Macomb, IL; [...] (BA) Music Ed, W IL Univ 1983; Cert Elem Ed, IL St Univ 198[...] Grad Courses Elem Teaching, IL St Univ; *cr:* Pre Kndgtn Teach[...] 1984, 5th Grade Teacher 1984-85, 5th-6th Grade Split Cla[...] Teacher 1985-86, 6th Grade Teacher 1986- Peoria Chrstn Sch; [...] ACSI Speech Meet Co-Asst Chm; Mu Phi Epsilon Chaplai[...] 1980-83; *office:* Peoria Chrstn Sch 3506 N California Peoria I[...] 61603

JOCK, SUE MERCURIO, Sixth Grade Teacher; *b:* Rome, N[...] *c:* Katie, Kristin; *ed:* (AA) Liberal Arts, Mater Dei 1971; (BA[...] Elem Ed/Sociology, 1973, (MS) Ed/Learning Disabilities 198[...] SUNY Potsdam; ESPET Trng; Cmptrs Classroom; *cr:* 4th Gra[...] Teacher 1973-87, 3rd Grade Teacher 1987-88 Twin Rivers Elem[...] 4th Grade Teacher 1988-89, 6th Grade Teacher 1989- Nightenga[...] Elem; *ai:* Aids Advisory Cncl; STANYS 1989-; NCCIR[...] 1978-88; Coll Club 1975-78; Curr Writing Massena Cntrl Schl[...] Wrote Childrens Book about AIDS; Sexual Abuse Awarene[...] Educators; Sci Curr & Media Coordination; *office:* Nightenga[...] Elem 290 Main St Massena NY 13662

JOERS, CAROL LIPPHARDT, 6th Grade Teacher; [...] Plainfield, NJ; *m:* John A.; *c:* Jodi L Bovre, Sheri L Donahu[...] Scott A., Jill M. Reimann, Craig E. Thomas C. Isabell, Kristin C[...] Daniel J.; *ed:* (Ba) Elem Ed, Carroll Coll 1966; (MEPD) Psyc[...] Univ of WI Whitewater 1985; Quest Trng; AODA Trng; *cr:* 2n[...] Grade Teacher Superior Public Schls 1966-67; 3rd Grade Teach[...] Elmbrook Public Schls 1967-69; 6th Grade Teacher Mukwonag[...] Public Schls 1979-; *ai:* SAP Building Coord; Cncl Me[...] Mukwonago Area Cncl Opposed to Alcohol & Drugs; Soc Stu[...] Content Area Team; Beha Vorial Comm; Delta Kappa Gamm[...] 1985-88; Church Vestry 1990; *home:* S 56 W 29597 Roanoke D[...] Waukesha WI 53188

JOFTIS, FRANK JAY, 8th Grade Teacher; *b:* Philadelphia, PA[...] *m:* Bess Fall; *c:* Cara; *ed:* (BA) Temple Univ Coll of Liberal Ar[...] 1969; (MED) Curr/Instruction/Rdng, Temple Univ Grad Sch o[...] Ed 1972; Cert PA Permanent Teacher; Ed, Temple Univ, Gra[...] Sch of Ed 1973-75; PA Prin Certificate Univ of PA 1977-78; *c[...]* Phys Ed Teacher 1969, 6th Grade Teacher 1969-74 M H Stanto[...] Elem Sch; Summery Sch Instr Wordsworth Acad 1973-74; K-6t[...] Grade Lang Art Teacher M H Stanton Elem Sch 1974-75[...] Demonstration Teacher John Hancock Demonstration Sc[...] 1975-78; 4th-6th Grade Teacher Martha Washington Elem Sc[...] 1979; 8th Grade Teacher Fitler Academics Plus 1979-; *a[...]* Warrington Athletic Assn; Girls & Boys Bsktbl & Sftbl Coac[...] 1982-; Var Bsktbl Coach Fitler Academic Plus 1985-; Colleagu[...] Mentor 1989; Union Rep 1975-88; Yrbk Spon 1979-; Planning[...] Comm for Graduation Chairperson 1980-; Safety Patrol Spo[...] 1980-; Sch Human Relations, Sch Curr & Instruction Comm Mem[...] 1979-; De Valley Assn for Supervision Speaker; Speaker &[...] Panelist Middle Sts Regional Meeting of Coll Bd Strategies fo[...] Change 1982; Dir of Swim Club 1972-73; Bnai Brith Educator[...] Lodge 1970-; Warrington Athletic Assn 1973-86; *office:* Fitle[...] Academics Plus Sch Seymour & Knox Sts Philadelphia PA 1914[...]

JOHANSEN, WILLIAM CARL, English Dept Chairman; *b[...]* Grantsville, UT; *m:* Ila Anderson; *c:* Carl B., Rebecca Johanso[...] Van Dyke, Pamela Johanson Mills, Terri, Paul T., Ann, Boyd R., William R., James M., Jeffrey A., Barbara, Jeanne; *ed:* (BS) His/ Scndry Ed, UT St Univ 1966; Eng, UT St Univ; Latin & Greek, Brigham Young Univ; Other Classes Weber St Coll & Univ of NV Las Vegas; *cr:* Eng/His Teacher Box Elder Jr HS 1966-67; Eng Teacher Grantsville HS 1967-75, Latin/Classical Civilizations Instr Brigham Young Univ 1975-77; His/Eng Teacher Garside Jr HS 1978-79; Eng Teacher Orem HS 1979-80, Mountain View HS 1980-85, Canyon View Jr HS 1985-; *ai:* Chess Club Adv; Tooele Educl Assn (Bd of Dir 1969-73, Pres 1973-74); UT Educl Assn House of Delegates 1969-74, NEA Convention Delegate 1973; Bonneville Uniserv (Bd of Dir 1972-74, Bd Pres 1973-74); Delta Sigma Phi (Charter Mem, Treas, Asst House Mgr) 1959-66; Intercollegiate Knights Mem 1959-60; Lindon City Cncl Councilor 1982-86; Republican Party Dist Chm; Cty, St Delegate; Consultant for Mc Millan Publishing Company; *office:* Canyon View Jr HS 655 E 950 N Orem UT 84057

JOHN, ILA MARLENE, Home Economics Teacher; *b:* Malad, ID; *ed:* (BS) Home Ec, 1974, (MS) Home Ec Ed, 1983 UT St Univ; *cr:* Teacher North Rich Sch 1974-76; Coord Adult Home Ec Bridgerland Area Voc Center 1976-79; Teacher North Ogden Jr HS 1979-82, South Ogden Jr HS 1982-; *ai:* Weber Ed Assn Building Rep; Asst Coach Vlybl; Head Track Coach; Weber Ed

Assn (Faculty Rep 1981-82, Building Rep 1989-); *home:* 1732 N 400 E #7 Ogden UT 84414

JOHNS, FERN (LEFFEL), Retired First Grade Teacher; *b:* Buckland, OH; *m:* Ned E.; *c:* Faye Bartlett, Luanne Davakos, Jodi Goens, Gary, Kathy Frankenberg; *ed:* (BA) Elem Ed, OH Northern Univ 1968; (MS) Classroom Teacher, Wright St Univ 1972; *cr:* 1st/2nd Grade Teacher Noble Elem Sch 1948-49; 1st Grade Teacher East Elem Sch 1949-53, West Elem Sch 1961-87; *ai:* Dist Mgr World Book Incorporated; Intntl Rdng Assn Auglaize Cncl (Pres, Charter Mem); Delta Kappa Gamma Pres 1976-78; St Pauls United Church of Christ (Supt, Chm, Sch Teacher); Womens Guild Pres; *home:* 1103 Neil Ave Saint Marys OH 45885

JOHNS, MARGARET RIGGS, 3rd Grade Teacher; *b:* Owosso, MI; *m:* Dale V.; *c:* Thomas, Heidi Weston; *ed:* (A) Psych, Asbury Coll 1951; (BA) Eng/Sci, 1967 (MA) Elem Ed 1972 MI St Univ; *cr:* Sec General Telephone Co Hq 1953-58; Teacher Bennett Cntry Sch 1963-64; Teacher Corunna Public Schls 1965-; *ai:* Curr Cncl Ofcr Corunna; Ed Assn Dept Head 3rd Grade; Cmmty Ed Cmptr Trnr; Corunna Ed Assn Sec 1968-75; 25 Yr Tchg Awd 1989; *home:* 606 Crestview Dr Corunna MI 48817

JOHNS, RICHARD A., 3rd Grade Teacher/Tennis Coach; *b:* Glens Falls, NY; *m:* Karen S.; *c:* Nicole A.; *ed:* (BA) Elem Ed, St Univ Coll Potsdam 1972; Graduate Work Ed, Russell Sage Coll; *cr:* Teacher Saratoga Springs City Sch Dist; 3rd/5th Grade Teacher Saratoga Springs NY 1972-; *ai:* Varsity Girls Tennis Coach Saratoga Springs City Schls; NYS Public HS Athletic Assn Comm Mem 1985-89; St Tennis Comm; United States Tennis Assn Mem; Eastern Tennis Assn Coach of Yr 1985; NYSPHSAA Tennis Coord 1985-89; YMCA Bd of Dir 1989-; Articles World Tennis Magazine Published;Potsdam St Sports Hall of Fame; *office:* Geyser Road Elem Sch Geyser Rd Saratoga Springs NY 12866

JOHNS, RITA MAE, OSU, Jr HS Math/Science Teacher; *b:* Toledo, OH; *ed:* (BA) Chem, Mary Manse Coll 1973; (MA) Ed, Univ of Dayton 1983; *cr:* 2nd Grade Teacher St Joseph 1967-69; Jr HS Math/Sci Teacher St Patrick 1969-71, St Angela Hall 1971-74, St Joseph 1974-; *ai:* Soar & Gifted Math Prgm; Sci Fair Adv; Chrldr Coach; Toledo Diocesan Teacher of Yr 1979; *home:* 162 Ann Tiffin OH 44883

JOHNSEN, MARILYN THORNBY (SNELLING), Teacher; *b:* Omaha, NE; *m:* Stanley E.; *c:* Kathryn Weidmaier, Shari Snelling, Trisha Snelling, Heidi Snelling; *ed:* (AA) Liberl Arts, 1956, (BS) Ed, 1969 William Woods Coll; (MED) Sch Admin, Lincoln Univ 1987; Prof Classes Univ of MO & Lincoln Univ; *cr:* Teacher Omaha Public Schls 1966-67, Teacher Jefferson City Public Schls 1969-; *ai:* Elem Girls Sftbl Coach; St Soc Stud Curr Comm; Just Say No Spon; MSTA 1970-88; NEA 1989-; Cncl for Drug Free Youth 1989-; Prof Dev Comm Chm; *office:* Belair Sch 701 Belair Jefferson City MO 65101

JOHNSEN, PEGGY MAC GOWN, 6th Grade Teacher; *b:* Spokane, WA; *m:* Jerrold P.; *c:* Erik, Peter; *ed:* (BA) Music, Univ of WA 1964; (MA) Rdng & Learning Disabilities, CA St Univ 1971; Lang/Rdng Acquisition; *cr:* Teacher Issaquah Schls 1964-66, Wiseburn/Santa Monica Schls 1966-72; Asst Professor Whitworth Coll 1975-79; Teacher Mead Sch Dist 1979-; *ai:* Chrprsn Soc Stud Comm K-6 1979-84; Co-Chrprsn Learning Across the Curr K-12 1984-; Comm Rep Rdng Comm 1979-; in Service Instr for Dist 1979-; Intnl Rdng Assn 1979-; *office:* Colbert Elem Sch E 4526 Greenbluff Rd Colbert WA 99005

JOHNSON, ALICE FAE, Vocational Home Ec Teacher; *b:* Hays, KS; *m:* Garold W.; *c:* Alicia M. Hollingsworth, Mark W.; *ed:* (BS) Home Ec, TX Womans Univ 1980; Grad Stud Consumer Ec, TX Womans Univ; At Risk Trng Potential Dropout Stus Univ of N TX; *cr:* Voc Home Ec Teacher Garland HS 1980-; *ai:* Garland HS Key Club Faculty Adv; FHA Spon; Amer Home Ec Assn, TX Home Ec Assn 1980-; Amer Assn of Univ Women 1981-88; Ki-Wani-Annes 1976-; Chrstn Church Disciple of Christ Comm Chairperson 1974-; *home:* PO Box 201 Rowlett TX 75088

JOHNSON, ALLENE P., English Department Chair; *b:* Johnson Cty, GA; *m:* Herbert; *c:* Dawn H. Tripp, Shari Hobby; *ed:* (MS) Eng, GA SW 1974; *cr:* Eng Dept Chairperson Albany HS; *ai:* Coll Bowl Adv; Literary Coord; Page; Alan Review; Star Teacher; *office:* Albany HS 801 N Residence Ave Albany GA 31701

JOHNSON, AMY BALLANTYNE, 7th Grade Geography Teacher; *b:* Flint, MI; *m:* Edwin Harold; *c:* Lori, Matthew, Meredith; *ed:* (BA) Soc Stud Ed, FL St Univ 1968; Gifted Cert 1988; *cr:* Teacher Satellite HS 1969-71, Wymore Voc Tech Sch 1973-75, S Seminole Mid Sch 1983-; *ai:* Stu Cncl Co-Spon; Maitland Soccer Club Pres 1984; Cntrl FL Youth Soccer League Secy 1982-84.

JOHNSON, ANGELA SHARPE, English Department Chair; *b:* Fayetteville, NC; *m:* Alison Blount; *ed:* (BS) Eng, E Carolina Univ 1974; (MED) Gifted & Talented, Univ of NC Greensboro 1983; *cr:* Eng Teacher 1976-, Debate/Speech Teacher 1987- SE Guilford HS; *ai:* Debate/Speech Coach; Dept Chairperson; Alpha Delta Kappa 1989-; *office:* SE Guilford HS 4530 Se School Rd Greensboro NC 27406

JOHNSON, ARLENE BROWN, Physical Science/Chem Teacher; *b:* Holly Hill, SC; *m:* Larry D. Sr.; *c:* Larry Jr.; *ed:* (BS) Chem, Claflin Coll 1984; Critical Needs Cert Prgm; *cr:* Sci Teacher T E Mullins HS 1984-; *ai:* Var Cheerleading Coach; Color Guard Dir; SC Assn of Chem Teachers, SC Sci Cncl, SC Chrldrs Coaches Assn, NSTA; *office:* Mullins HS Rt 3 Box 451 Mullins SC 29574

JOHNSON, BARBARA BERGER, Retired 3rd/4th Grade Teacher; *b:* Nebraska City, NE; *c:* John Nekich, Sally A. Nekich O'Dell; *ed:* (BA) Bio/Soc Stud, NE St Coll Peru 1948; Elem Ed, Omaha Univ 1956; Elem Ed, Univ of NE Lincoln 1948, 1968, 1972; *cr:* 3rd Grade Teacher Valley Public Schls 1952-53; 3rd-6th Grade Teacher Pershing Elem Sch 1956-88; *ai:* Kappa Kappa Iota Pres 1985-86; NEA, NSEA, LEA; Bus & Prof Women (Recording Secy, Treas) 1983, 1985; Team Leader 1978-80.

JOHNSON, BARBARA D. KILGORE, Language Arts Chair; *b:* Clarendon, TX; *c:* James M., Michael D., D. Shawn, Holly D. J. Gettle; *ed:* (BA) Elem Ed/Eng, West TX St Univ 1972; (MED) Scndry/Lang Art Comp, Eastern NM Univ 1980; Grad Stud Drivers Ed; *cr:* Lang Arts Teacher Deming Jr HS 1972-73, Mineral Wells Jr HS 1973-74, Tucumcari Jr HS 1975-; *ai:* Journalism Newspaper, Annual; Stu Cncl; Drill Team; NM NEA (VP 1979-80, Pres 1980-81); NCTE; Delta Kappa Gamma 1975-; BPW Schlsp Chairperson 1987-; *home:* 1115 S 4th St Tucumcari NM 88401

JOHNSON, BARBARA LOUISE (STRAUDER), 9th Grade English Teacher; *b:* Xenia, OH; *m:* Robert Louis Sr.; *c:* Robert L. Jr.; *ed:* (BS) Eng, Cntrl St Univ 1975; Re-Cert Diagnostic/Developmental Rdng K-12, Cleveland St Univ 1984; *cr:* Eng Teacher Glenville HS 1975-77, James Ford Rhodes HS 1977-79, Collinwood HS 1979-81; Rdng/Eng Teacher Wilbur Wright Jr HS 1981-86; Eng Teacher John Hay HS 1986-; *ai:* CORE Teacher Thematic Prgm; Right-to-Read Comm Mem; Eng Helper for Gifted & Talented Stus; Greater Cleveland Teachers of Eng Mem 1988-; Churchs Young Peoples Auxiliary Treas 1988-; *office:* John Hay HS 2075 E 107 St Cleveland OH 45102

JOHNSON, BARBARA MANESS, 5th Grade Teacher; *b:* Jackson, TN; *m:* George R.; *c:* Tammy Lynn Johnson Neely; *ed:* (BA) Elem Ed, Lambuth Coll 1963; Memphis St; Cert, Jackson St Comm Coll; *cr:* Classroom Teacher Beech Bluff Sch 1963-64, Brice OH 1964-65, Beech Bluff Sch 1966-; *ai:* 4-H Club; MCEA 1966-; TEA 1966-; NEA 1966-; Grace Presbyn Church Chm of WIC 1987-88; Madison Cty Democratic Executive Comm Secy 1984-; Southwest-Madison Cty Ruritan Chm Public Relations 1986-89; Outstanding Elem Teacher in Amer; Chm F Madison Cty In-Service Prgm 5th Grade; Chm of Soc Stud Textbook Comm; Mem of Evaluation Comm for Madison Cty; Faculty Rep.

JOHNSON, BERTHA HICKMAN, 2nd Grade Teacher; *b:* Chattonooga, TN; *c:* Reginald J. Hargis; *ed:* (BA) Music Ed, Fisk Univ 1947; (MA) Elem Ed, Univ of KY 1972; *cr:* Music Instr Lincoln Cty HS 1947-48, Blind, Deaf & Orphan Sch 1948-50; Management Aide Chattanooga Housing 1952-56; Elem Teacher Fayette Cty Schls 1956-79, Atlanta Public Schls 1980-; *ai:* NEA, Atlanta Assn of Educators; Alpha Kappa Alpha, Links Incorporated; *office:* Minnie S Howell Sch 399 Macedonia Rd SE Atlanta GA 30354

JOHNSON, BETTY LLOYD, Middle School Teacher; *b:* White Lake, SD; *m:* Dale Edward; *c:* Linda K. Anderson, Lois J. Rogers, Wayne E.; *ed:* (BS) Ed/Soc Sci, Southern State Teachers Coll 1954; WI St Univ, Univ of SD; *cr:* 1st-8th Grade Teacher Sunnyside Sch 1944-45; 7th-8th Grade Teacher Trent Public Schls 1945-46, Winner Jr HS 1955-, Winner Mid Sch; *ai:* BSA Cnslr; Lib Improvement Planning Comm; SD Ed Assn Delegate to St Convention 1944-76; Winner Ed Assn (Pres, Secy, Treas); Alpha Delta Kappa; Veterans of Foreign War Auxiliary Secy 1985-89; Amer Legion Auxiliary Historian; Bus & Prof Women; Cath Daughters of the Americas VP 1986-; Women of Yr Bus & Prof Women 1987; Diana Awd Epsilon Sigma Alpha 1988; *home:* 930 E 10th Winner SD 57580

JOHNSON, BEVERLY ANNISE BUTLER, Reading Teacher; *b:* Akron, OH; *m:* Robert E.; *c:* Monique A.; *ed:* (BA) Elem Ed, Fayetteville St Univ 1971; Rdng Recovery Prgm, OH St Univ; *cr:* 3rd Grade Teacher 1971-79; 2nd Grade Teacher Portage Path 1988; Chapter I Rdng Teacher Crosby Elem 1988-; *ai:* Teacher Faculty Comm; Intnl Rdng Assn; Natl Assn of Black Educators 1988-; Alpha Kappa Alpha; Church Choir; *home:* 2158 Drury Ave Akron OH 44305

JOHNSON, CAROLE JO, Fifth Grade Teacher; *b:* Chicago, IL; *m:* Jerry R.; *c:* Tammy, Jerry; *ed:* (BA) Ed, Chicago St 1962; (MS) Ed, Univ of WI Whitewater 1979; Grad Stud Univ of WI Whitewater; *cr:* 6th Grade Teacher Christ The King 1967-68, St Dennis 1968-69; 5th Grade Teacher Purdy Elem 1969-; *ai:* Textbook Selection; Lang Art; Artist in Residence; Pal Day; Phi Kappa Phi Mem 1980-; FEA, NEA, SWEO Mem 1969-; *home:* 1016 Heth Fort Atkinson WI 53538

JOHNSON, CAROLYN CRAWFORD, Teacher; *b:* Chicago, IL; *m:* Henry Jr.; *c:* Henry J. II, Christopher, Chaun; *ed:* (BA) Ed, 1976, (MA) Ed, 1987; Northeastern IL Univ; Drug Ed Cert; Inner City Stud; *cr:* Clerk/Typist Dr Joseph F Parrili Optometrist 1969-71; Teacher Chicago Bd of Ed 1976-78; Our Lady of Lourdes Chicago Archdioces 1978- ; *ai:* Sch Music Dept Choir Dir; Tutoring; Prgm Organizer; Sch Rep; Leadership Comm; Fellowship Church Choir Dir 1980-; 800 North Kedvale Block Club 1988-; John Crawford Ensemble Bus Mgr 1989-; *office:* Our Lady of Lourdes 1449 South Keeler Ave Chicago IL 60623

JOHNSON, CATHERINE M., Chairperson of English Dept; *b:* Jackson, TN; *m:* Jeffery; *c:* Kenneth B; *ed:* (BA) Eng, Lane Coll 1954; (MA) Eng, Univ TN 1980; *cr:* Teacher Hamilton HS, J L Campbell Sch of Religion; *ai:* Pre-AP Honors Eng Teacher; Harry T Cash Capter of the NHS Spon; Liasion Teacher HHS & Bd of Ed MCS; Coord Largest Homework Center in TN; Hamilton HS Mentor; Coord HHS Southern Assn of Coll & Schls Evaluation; Grad HS Tracking Coord; Chairperson Eng Dept; Parliamentary Law Consultant LeMoyne Coll; HHS Retirement & Courtesy Comm; Prin Advisory Bd; Parent Teacher Stu Assn Spokesman; NEA, TEA, WTEA 1954-80; MEA 1954-80 Teacher of Yr 1988; NAACP 1985-; HHS 1985- Teacher of Yr 1985; St John Baptist Church Chrstn Woman of Yr 1988; Pat Carter Pontiac Teacher of Month Awd 1987; *office:* Hamilton H S 1363 Person Ave Memphis TN 38114

JOHNSON, CELESTE C. (NICHOLSON), 12th Grade Teacher; *b:* Philadelphia, PA; *c:* Coleen R.; *ed:* (BS) Eng, Cheyney Univ 1968; *cr:* Teacher Harding Jr HS 1968-70, Cooke Jr HS 1970-73, Wagner Jr HS 1974-85, Germantown/Lankenau HS 1985-; *ai:* 9th Grade, Stu Government, Yrbk, Jr/Sr Class Spon; Sftbl Coach; Assembly Organizer Chairperson; Renewal Team Mem; Stu Act Liaison; Women in Ed 1987-; Educators Roundtable 1989-; Optimist 1989-; *home:* 212 Grist Mill Ct Ambler PA 19002

JOHNSON, CHARLES, Band Director; *b:* Sweetwater, TX; *ed:* (BME) Music Ed, W TX St Univ 1979; *cr:* Private Woodwind Instr Pampa Ind Sch Dist 1979-80; Asst Band Dir 1980-82, Head Dir 1982- Pampa HS; *ai:* TX Bandmasters, TX Music Ed Assn; Fellowship of Chrstn Musicians.

JOHNSON, CHARLES ANDREW, Art Teacher; *b:* Quantico, MD; *m:* Mary Hill; *ed:* (BS) Art Ed, Morgan St Univ 1960; (MS) Gen Prof, St Univ NY 1972; *cr:* Art Teacher Elizabethtown/Lewis Central Sch 196-63; Saratoga Springs Sch Dist 1965-; *ai:* NSTA 1960-; Elizabethtown Teacher Assn Pres 1962-63; YMCA Bd Mem 1964; *home:* 326 Gurn Sprngs Rd Gansevourt NY 12831

JOHNSON, CHERYL ANN, 8th Grade English Teacher; *b:* Spokane, WA; *m:* Robert E.; *c:* Christopher, Alicia; *ed:* (BA) Eng, E WA St Univ 1972; (MA) Guidance/Counseling, Whitworth Coll 1989; *cr:* 7th-9th Grade Eng/His/Phys Ed Teacher Park Jr HS 1972-86; 8th Grade Eng/Phys Ed/Health Teacher Argonne Jr HS 1986-89, Centennial Mid Sch 1989-; *ai:* Girls Vlybl & Bsktbl Coach; NEA, WA Ed Assn Mem 1972-; West Valley Ed Assn Mem/Rep 1972- Teacher of Yr Nominee 1985; *office:* Centennial Mid Sch N 915 Ella Spokane WA 99212

JOHNSON, CHRISTENE EARNEST, Third Grade Teacher; *b:* Holly Grove, AR; *m:* Willie James Sr.; *c:* Shanell, Sharell, Willena, Willie Jr., Shalawn; *cr:* Teacher Clarendon Elem Sch 1974-; *ai:* Pew Wee Bsbl Coach; NEA, AEA, CEA Mem 1974-.

JOHNSON, CHRISTINE H., Counselor; *b:* Chicago, IL; *m:* Richard; *ed:* (BA) Eng/Sncdry Ed, NE IL Univ 1978; Guidance & Counseling; *cr:* Guidance Cnslr Leland HS 1987-; *ai:* SADD; *office:* Leland HS 370 N Main St Leland IL 60531

JOHNSON, CLIFFORD F., Science Department Chair; *b:* Montobello, CA; *m:* Susan J.; *c:* Julie, Justin, Marie, Joy; *ed:* (BA) Bio, CA St San Bernardino 1972; (MAT) Ed, AK Pacific Univ 1990; *cr:* Bio Teacher Chugiak HS; Sci Teacher Gruening Mid Sch; *ai:* Wrestling Coach; Sci Club; Phi Delta Kappa 1989-; NASTA 1989-; AK St Promising Practices Awd 1987; AK Merit Awds Inventors Fair, Mouse Trap 1989; *office:* Gruening Mid Sch 9601 Lee St Eagle River AK 99577

JOHNSON, CORY JORDAN, Phys Ed Teacher/Coach; *b:* Duluth, MN; *ed:* (BS) Phys Ed, Univ of MN Duluth 1982; Driver Ed Certificate, St Cloud St 1984; Quest Skills Adolescents Driver Ed; *cr:* Phys Ed Teacher 1983-, Ftbl Coach 1983-88, Bsbl Coach 1983-, Girls Bsktbl Coach 1983- Floodwood Sch; *ai:* Head Bsbl & Girls Bsktbl; MN Coaches Assn 1983-; *office:* Floodwood Sch Hwy 73 Floodwood MN 55736

JOHNSON, DANNY JAMES, Algebra I & II Teacher; *b:* Inman, SC; *m:* Kathy Blackwell; *c:* Amy M., Matthew C.; *ed:* (BS) Math, Limestone Coll 1972; (MED) Math, Converse Coll 1987; SC Prgm for Effective Teaching; *cr:* Math Teacher Boiling Springs HS 1972-79; Algebra Teacher Boiling Springs Jr HS 1979-; *ai:* Dist Math Curr & Sch Curr Dev Comm; Sch Improvement Cncl; NEA, SCEA 1977-; *office:* Boiling Springs Jr HS 3655 Boiling Springs Rd Spartanburg SC 29303

JOHNSON, DAVID LEE, Business Teacher; *b:* Milbank, SD; *ed:* (BS) Bus Ed, 1987, (BS) Bus Admin, 1987 Dakota St Coll; *cr:* Stu Teacher Howard HS 1987; Bus Teacher Hitchcock HS 1988-; *ai:* Head Boys Bsktbl, Asst Girls Bsktbl, Elem & Jr HS Boys Bsktbl Coach; NBEA 1988-89 Awd of Merit 1988; Outstanding Sr Bus Ed Stu; Kinship Coord 1986-87; *home:* 323 Cherry St Box 53 Hitchcock SD 57348

JOHNSON, DAWN RENEE, Math/Computer Dept Chair; *b:* Watford City, ND; *ed:* (AS) Cmptr Programming, ND St Coll of Sci 1983; (BS) Math, Minot St Univ 1986; *cr:* Math/Cmptr Dept Chairperson Balta Public Sch 1986-; *ai:* Dir of Drama; Yrbk Adv; NCTM 1986-; *office:* Balta Public Sch PO Box 398 Balta ND 58313

JOHNSON, DEBBIE CAROL (ABEL), Junior High & HS Art Teacher; *b:* Bedford, IN; *m:* Robert K.; *c:* Sebastian; *ed:* (BS) Art Ed, IN Univ 1982; *cr:* Jr HS/HS Art Instr Bloomfield HS 1985-; *ai:* Jr HS/HS Art Club Spon; Gifted & Talented Art Instr; NCEA 1990; *office:* Bloomfield Jr H Sch PO Box 266 West Spring St Bloomfield IN 47424

JOHNSON, DEBORAH LESLIE, Eighth Grade English Teacher; *b:* Kansas City, MO; *ed:* (BS) Elem Ed, Univ of KS 1967; (MS) Scndry Ed, The Wichita St Univ 1988; *cr:* 5th-6th Grade Teacher 1968-71, 3rd-4th Grade Teacher Abrams Elem 1979-82; 7th-8th Grade Teacher Trinity HS 1982-84; 8th Grade Eng/Comm Liberty Mid Sch 1984-; *ai:* NCTE 1987-; Finalist Educator of Yr Awd 1983; *office:* Liberty Mid Sch 200 W 14th Hutchinson KS 67501

JOHNSON, DEBRA ANITA, Language Art Teacher; *b:* Lincoln, NC; *c:* Corey; *ed:* (BA) Eng, Winston-Salem St Univ 1976; Learning Disabilities, Univ of NC Charlotte 1979; *cr:* Lang Art Teacher Lincolnton Jr HS 1976-79, N Surry HS 1979-81; Exceptional Childrens Lang Art Teacher Northeast Jr HS 1981-; *ai:* Vlybl Coach; Boys Track Asst Coach; Comprehensive Sch Plan Comm Chairperson; *office:* Northeast Jr HS 5960 Brickston Dr Charlotte NC 28227

JOHNSON, DELORES ANN (AMOSS), Kindergarten Teacher; *b:* Albia, IA; *m:* Michael Andrew; *c:* William , Brian; *ed:* (BS) Elem Ed, Drake Univ 1977; Madeline Hunter Trng; Outcome Based Ed; Chapter Rdng Endorsement; *cr:* Chapter I Rdng Teacher Monroe HS 1984-85; Kndgtn Teacher Monroe Elem Sch 1985-; *ai:* Early Chldhd & Rdng Comm; Kappa Delta Pi 1977; Monroe BSA Treas; Kids-Kickers Square Dance Treas; *office:* Monroe Elem Sch 400 N Jasper PO Box 394 Monroe IA 50170

JOHNSON, DENISE CLARY, Fourth Grade Teacher; *b:* Winter Haven, FL; *m:* Gary Stephen; *ed:* (AA) Elem Ed, Polk Comm Coll 1972; (BA) Elem Ed, Univ of S FL 1974; *cr:* 5th Grade Teacher 1974-89, 4th Grade Teacher 1989- Lena Vista Elem Sch; *ai:* Cypress Cathedral Supt of Childrens Dept 1979-; Candidate for Teacher of Yr 1984-85; Excl in Ed Awd 1990; *office:* Lena Vista Elem Sch 208 S Berkley Rd Auburndale FL 33823

JOHNSON, DENNIS ALAN, Band Director; *b:* Atlanta, GA; *ed:* (BA) Music Ed, Auburn Univ 1983; Grad Work Troy St Univ; *cr:* Band Dir Capitol Heights Jr HS 1983-86, Lee HS 1987-; *ai:* Music Appreciation Club Spon; MENC; Dist VI Vice Chm 1986; *office:* Robert E Lee HS 225 Ann St Montgomery AL 36107

JOHNSON, DENNIS D., Science Department Chair; *b:* Stanley, WI; *ed:* (BS) Bio, Univ of WI Stevens Point 1970; (MS) Sci Ed, Univ of WI Eau Claire 1990; *cr:* Sci Chm White Lake HS 1970-76, New Auburn HS 1976-; *ai:* Yrbk & Class Adv; Bsktbl & Bsbl Coach; Schlsp, Calender, Bus Driver, Curr Comm; Judo Instr; Natl Bio Teachers Assn 1970-; Jaycees (Dir, VP) 1976-78; BSA Scout Master 1970-80; Chippewa Bowhunters Dir 1988-; *home:* 316 W Elm St Box 19 New Auburn WI 54757

JOHNSON, DIANE LOUISE, 7th/8th Grade Math Teacher; *b:* Butte, MT; *m:* James L.; *c:* Thomas O'Neill, Christine O'Neill, Robert O'Neill, Kelley O'Neill; *ed:* (BA) Math, Univ of MT 1971; Working Toward Masters Elem Ed; *cr:* Math Teacher Hellgate HS 1972-73, Math Teacher Cntrl Jr HS 1984-; *ai:* Mathcounts Adv; Expanding Your Horizons Panel Mem; Chamber of Commerce 1987-89, Nom Golden Apple 1986-89; Recipient of Natl Sci Fnd Grant 1971, 1987-88; *office:* Central Jr HS 400 W Park St Butte MT 59701

JOHNSON, DONNA LEE, Kindergarten Teacher; *b:* Winston-Salem, NC; *m:* Mark; *ed:* (BA) Elem Ed, Sam Houston St Univ 1973; Advanced Coll Hours Early Chldhd, Art, Math, Rdng Ed; *cr:* Kndgtn Teacher Alvin Primary 1973-75, Webster Primary 1975-76, P H Greene Elem 1976-79, C D Landolt Elem 1979-; *ai:* TX St Teachers Assn, Clear Creek Educators Assn; *office:* C D Landolt Elem Sch 2104 Pilgrims Point Friendswood TX 77546

JOHNSON, DONNIS KAY, Math Department Chairman; *b:* Forest City, NC; *ed:* (BA) Math, UNC-Greensboro 1971; *cr:* Teacher 1971-76, Math Dept Chairperson 1976- Chase HS; *ai:* Yrbk & Keywanettes Adv; Cty Textbook & Cty Curr Comm; Nc Assn of Educators (Dist Pres, Secy Cty Pres, Treas) 1971-; NCC Teachers of Math 1980-; *office:* Chase H S Rt 5 Forest City NC 28043

JOHNSON, DORIS (LARSON), Retired Third Grade Teacher; *b:* Watertown, SD; *m:* Robert Burton; *c:* Laurie, Robert II; *ed:* (BS) Elem Ed, Bob Jones Univ 1956; *cr:* 4th Grade Teacher Webster Elem 1956-57; 5th Grade Teacher San Souci Elem 1957-58; 4th Grade Teacher Reedurban Elem 1959-60; 3rd Grade Teacher Heritage Chrstn 1978-87; *ai:* Canton Baptist Temple (Adult Bible Study Leader 1990, Choir Mem 1958-, Childrens Dir 1963-78); *home:* 4015 Bel Air Dr NW Canton OH 44718

JOHNSON, DORIS LUELLA (WALKER), First Grade Teacher; *b:* Ft Smith, AR; *m:* Howard Jerry; *c:* Barrett A.; *ed:* (BSED) Bus, 1954, (MED) Elem, 1972 Northeastern St Coll; *cr:* Secretary OK St Capitol 1954-58; Bus/Soc Stud Teacher Central HS 1968-69; 1st Grade Teacher Sallisaw Public Schls 1969-; *ai:* OK Ed Assn, NEA 1969-; Sallisaw Assn of Classroom Teachers Teacher of Yr 1983; PTO; Amer Legion Aux; First Baptist Church (Sunday Sch Teacher, Choir Mem); Outstanding Elem Teachers of Amer 1974; Alpha Sigma Alpha Beta Gamma Chapter Sweetheart 1952.

JOHNSON, DORIS MARIE, 3rd Grade Elementary Teacher; *b:* Jackson, MS; *m:* Robert Lee; *c:* Jeffrey K., Kevin D.; *ed:* (BS) Elem Ed, Jackson St 1967; (MS) Elem Ed, 1977 MI St Univ; Elem Ed; *cr:* Teacher Westside Elem 1967-68, Frost Elem 1971-; *ai:* Natl Assn of Univ Women Pres 1981-85; Natl Alliance of Black Sch Educators; Natl Deans List 1988-.

JOHNSON, DWIGHT HARVEY, Teacher of Special Education; *b:* San Diego, CA; : Sylvia Arlene Mehaffey; *c:* Jeremiah, Gabriel, Victoria, Jesse; *ed:* (AS) Sci, Lees Mc Rae Coll 1973; (BS) Bio, Appalachian St Univ 1976; Behavioral Emotional Handicapped, Appalachian St Univ; Laubach Literacy Tutor Cert Behaviorally Emotionaly Handicapped Inst; *cr:* Teacher of Spec Ed Micaville Elem Sch 1976-86, East Yancey Mid Sch 1986-; *ai:* Mayland Amateur Radio Club; Cncl of Exceptional Children, Cncl for Children with Behavioral Disorders 1989-; Soil & Water Conservation Yancy Cty Supvr 1987-; *office:* East Yancy Mid Sch Rt 6 Box 87 Burnsville NC 28714

JOHNSON, EDWARD MATTHEW, Fifth Grade Teacher; *b:* Anaconda, MT; *m:* Eileen Edwards; *c:* Mark, Bart, Simone, Luke; *ed:* (BA) Ed, Univ of MT 1961; Grad Stud MT Univ; *cr:* Teacher Lowell Sch 1961-62, Anderson Sch 1962-63, Lowell Sch 1963-69, Federal Prgms Coord Missoula Elem 1969-72, Teacher Emma Dickinson Sch 1972-; *ai:* Missoula Sch Dist 1 Health Comm Rep; NEA; MT Ed Assn Regional Cncl Rep; Missoula Elem Ed Assn 2nd VP 1988-; Missoula City Band 1986-; Univ of MT Alumni Band 1989-; *office:* Emma Dickinson Sch 310 S Curtis Missoula MT 59801

JOHNSON, ELAINE SIMPSON, English Teacher; *b:* Gadsden, AL; *c:* Joseph D.; *ed:* (BS) Eng/Hist, Jacksonville St Univ 1976; (MA) Eng, UAB 1982; *cr:* Eng Teacher Fairview HS 1979-; *ai:* Spelling Bee Spon; Scholars Bowl Spon; Chrldr Spon; Jr Honor Society Spon; Cullman Cty Ed Assn 1979-; AL Ed Assn 1979-; NEA 1979-; *office:* Fairview H S Rt 7 Box 1905 Cullman AL 35055

JOHNSON, ELEANOR HARTMAN, Second Grade Teacher; *b:* Ft Wayne, IN; *m:* William Rowe; *c:* Bradley A. Bucher, Melissa S. Bucher Stein; *ed:* (BS) Elem Ed, 1961, (MS) Elem Ed, 1969 Ball St Teachers Coll; *cr:* Kndgtn Teacher Ft Wayne City Schls 1961-62; 1st Grade Teacher Leach Sch 1962-63, S Madison Sch Corporation 1968-70; Kndgtn Teacher 1970-74, 2nd Grade Teacher 1974- Franklin Elem & Anderson City Sch; *ai:* Various Sch Related Comms; Kappa Delta Pi 1959-61; Phi Beta Psi Pres 1963-70; Pendleton Baptist Church Clerk 1980-; *office:* Franklin Elem Sch 2200 E 38th St Anderson IN 46013

JOHNSON, ELEANOR TAYLOR, Retired Fifth Grade Teacher; *b:* Cincinnati, OH; *m:* Richard Eugene (dec); *c:* William R., James T., Marianne Johnson Harden, Jeffery B.; *ed:* (BA) Elem Ed, WV St 1961; (MA) Elem Ed, Marshall Univ; *cr:* 6th Grade Teacher Point Harmony Elem 1961-70; 5th Grade Teacher 1970-85, Substitute Teacher 1985- Mc Dowell Elem; *ai:* WV Ed Assn 1961-70; Russell Ed Assn, NEA 1970-85; *home:* 1701 Clay St Flatwoods KY 41139

JOHNSON, ELIZABETH A., French Teacher/Dept Chair; *b:* Newark, NJ; *ed:* (BA) Fr, Univ of CA Berkeley 1956; (MA) Fr, Middlebury Coll 1970; Sarbonne Paris, Univ of Guadalajara, Univ Laval Quebec; *cr:* Eng Teacher Lycee Blois France 1962-63; Fr Teacher Las Lomas HS 1957-; *ai:* Fr & Intnl Club; AATF (Bd Mem 1986-88, Mem 1972-), Schlsp 1984; Natl Endowment for Hum; Ind Study Grant France 1983; Quebec Government Schlsp 1984; *office:* Las Lomas HS 1460 S Main St Walnut Creek CA 94596

JOHNSON, ERLING ROGER, Guidance Counselor; *b:* Perley, MN; *ed:* (BS) Elem Ed, Moorhead St Univ 1966; (MS) Ed Admin, ND St Univ 1974; *cr:* 6th Grade Teacher Moorhead Dist 152 1966-76; Guidance Cnslr Wilton HS 1981-; *ai:* NDVGA Pres 1985-86, ND Guidance Cnslr of Yr 1984; *home:* 1200 Meadowbrook Dr B210 Washburn ND 58577

JOHNSON, ERNESTINE LETICE, Foreign Language Dept Chair; *b:* Quitman, GA; *m:* Edward Eugene; *c:* Edward E. Jr.; *ed:* (BA) Fr, Clark-Atlanta Univ 1966; Matriculated at Univ of GA and W GA Coll in Eng; *cr:* Classroom Teacher Fountain HS 1966-69, Morrow HS 1970-; *ai:* Spon Fr Club; AATF, NEA, FLAG; Rotary Club Star Teacher 1985; Star Teacher; Crystal Apple Awd; Most Unique Teacher 1978-79; *office:* Morrow Sr H S 2299 Old Rex Morrow Rd Morrow GA 30260

JOHNSON, FLOYD WILLIAM, Life Science Teacher; *b:* Pryor, OK; *m:* Mary Joan Mernders; *c:* Jennifer A., Kristin R., Grant R.; *ed:* (BS) Animal Sci, CO St Univ 1970; (BS) General Sci, NEO 1972; (MS) Ed, 1982, (MS) Admin, 1984 ECU; *cr:* General Sci Teacher 1972-75, Chem Teacher 1975-76, CUET Sci Teacher 1977-79, Physics Teacher 1979-81, Life SciTeacher 1981-; *ai:* Asst Athletic Dir; Wrestling Coach; Kiwanis (Mem, Key Club Adv) 1974-; Elks Bd Mem 1976-; *office:* Pauls Valley Mid Sch Lee Mid Sch Pauls Valley OK 73075

JOHNSON, GAIL ANNA, English/Journalism Teacher; *b:* Midland, MI; *m:* Gary L.; *c:* Allison, Jennifer, Darren; *ed:* (BS) Ed/Eng/Journalism/His, W MI Univ 1970; Teaching & Comm, Webster Univ; *cr:* Eng Teacher Oakville Sr HS 1986-; *ai:* Yrbk Spon; NCTE, Natl Scholastic Press Assn, Columbia Press Assn 1989-; MO Interscholastic Press Assn 1989-, 1st Honors Yrbk 1989; *office:* Oakville Sr HS 5557 Milburn Rd Saint Louis MO 63129

JOHNSON, GAIL MARGARET (FLAIG), 3rd Grade Teacher; *b:* Isabel, SD; *m:* Robert Ward; *c:* Susan Bowles, Darla Peterson; *ed:* (BS) Elem Ed, Black Hills Teachers St 1970; ID St Univ, Boise St Coll; *cr:* 3rd Grade Teacher Riverton WY 1955-56; 1st Grade Teacher Glenns Ferry 1958-62, Hepner OR 1962-63, Glenns Ferry 1964-68; 3rd Grade Teacher Aberdeen 1968-; *ai:* Aberdeen Ed Assn (Pres 1985-86, Secy 1989-); PTA VP; Delta Kappa Gamma (VP, Secy, Research Comm); Jobs Daughters Cncl 1976-84; Bus Week Cnslr 1987; Young Peoples Group Adv 1962-63.

JOHNSON, GAILE D., Spanish Teacher; *b:* Grand Rapids, MI; *m:* Owen C.; *c:* Erik, Craig; *ed:* (BA) Span, Univ of IL 1983; Teaching Cert Univ of IL Chicago; Univ of Madrid; *cr:* Span Teacher Butler Jr HS 1984-85; Downers Grove South HS 1985-; *ai:* Span Club Adv; AATSP 1983-; ICTFL Charter Mem 1987-; ACTFL 1985-; Art Inst of Chicago; Mexican Line Arts Center; Porsche Club of America; *office:* Downers Grove South HS 1436 Norfolk Downers Grove IL 60516

JOHNSON, GALE PEIRCE, 6th Grade Teacher; *b:* Placerville, CA; *m:* Michael; *c:* Lavonne T., Sheryll C., Marlane; *ed:* (BA) Ed, CSUS 1977; *cr:* 4th-7th Grade Elem Teacher 1979-86, Sci Resource Teacher 1986-89, 6th Grade Teacher 1989- Pleasant Grove; *ai:* Active in Strauss Waltz Festival 1986-.

JOHNSON, GARY LEONARD, Science Department Chairman; *b:* Minneapolis, MN; *m:* Linda Sofia; *c:* Micah, Jeshua; *ed:* (BS) Biological Sci, Univ of MN 1970; Biblical Stud, Oak Hills Bible Inst; *cr:* Sci Teacher Bayfield HS 1969-71, Lincoln Jr HS 1971-72; Sci Teacher/Chm Aurora Chrstn Sch 1978-; *ai:* Adv of Sci Club; Dir of Aurora Chrstn Clearinghouse for Sci Materials; *office:* Aurora Chrstn Sch 14 Blackhawk Aurora IL 60506

JOHNSON, GAYLA ANN, 12th Grade English Teacher; *b:* Dallas, TX; *m:* Gregory Wade; *c:* Ron Gregory, Jonathan Wade; *ed:* (BA) Eng/His, Stephen F Austin St Univ 1970; Ok His & Ed Exceptional Child; *cr:* 10th-12th Grade Eng Teacher S Grand Prairie HS 1970-74; Sr Eng Teacher Wagoner HS 1988-; *ai:* Jr Class & Chrldr Spon; OK Cncl Techers of Eng 1989-; Bd of Wagoner Chamber of Commerce 1980; Beta Sigma Phi Civic 1975-82; Auxiliary Amer Dental Assn (Pres St Auxiliary & Trustee Natl Auxiliary); *office:* Wagoner HS 300 N Ward Wagoner OK 74467

JOHNSON, GAYNELL, 1st & 2nd Grade Teacher; *b:* Bowling Green, KY; *ed:* (BA) Elem Ed 1973, (MA) Elem Ed 1977; *cr:* 1st Grade Teacher 1973-88, 2nd Grade Teacher 1988- White Plains; *ai:* Hopkins Cty Human Relation Comm; KEA; NEA; Alpha Delta Kappa Corresponding Secy 1988-.

JOHNSON, GLENDA L. FARRER, Kindergarten Teacher; *b:* Ashiya Air Base, Japan; *m:* Stephen James; *ed:* (BA) Liberal Stu, CA St Univ Sacramento 1975; Ed 1976-88; *cr:* Substitute Teacher Fairfield-Suisun Unified Sch Dist 1976-77; Primary Teacher Cleo Gordon Sch 1977-86; Kndgtn Teacher K I Jones Sch 1986-; *ai:* Soc Comm K I Jones Sch; CA Kndgtn Assn 1989-; *home:* 2548 Vista Grande Fairfield CA 94533

JOHNSON, GREGORY O., Speech/English Teacher; *b:* Linton, IN; *m:* Carolyn; *c:* Erin F.; *ed:* (BS) Eng/Speech, 1970, (MS) Eng/Speech, 1973 IN St; *cr:* Teacher Loogootee HS 1970-; *ai:* Lit Academic Coach; Jr Class Spon; Loogootee Schlsp Comm; NEA.

JOHNSON, GRETCHEN VAN BIBER, German Teacher; *b:* Portland, OR; *c:* Rachel, Matthew, Benjamin; *ed:* (BA) Ger, Pacific Luth Univ 1973; Grad Stud Pacific Luth Univ 1982; *cr:* Ger Teacher Washington HS 1973-77; Ger/Elem Teacher of Gifted Collins 1979-81; Ger Teacher Washington HS 1981-; *ai:* Parent Involvement 4-H & Church Act; Delta Kappa Gamma 1984-89; Stipend Awd 1984.

JOHNSON, GWENDOLYN ANN, Math/Sci/ESL Teacher; *b:* San Francisco, CA; *ed:* (BA) Diversified Liberal Stud, Westmont Coll 1979; Lang Dev Cert for Teaching Eng as Second Lang, San Francisco; *cr:* Soc Stud/Teacher of Gifted & Talented Ed 1986-87, Newcomers/Self-Contained Teacher 1987-88, 6th Grade Math/Sci Teacher 1988-89, Eng as Second Lang/Math/Sci Teacher 1989- Presidio Mid Sch; *ai:* Yosemite Club; *office:* Presidio Mid Sch 450 30th Ave San Francisco CA 94121

JOHNSON, H. WADE, Band Director; *b:* Washington, DC; *m:* Deborah F.; *c:* Adrena Shantae, Ryan T., Justin W., Kari Z. Enri; *ed:* (BS) Instrumental Music, 1979, (MED) Scndry Counseling, 1989 SC St Coll; *cr:* Grad Asst SC St Coll 1980-82; Band Dir Lucy C Laney HS 1982-83, Edisto Schls 1983-; *ai:* Mem Sch Improvement Cncl; Assist Bsktbl Coach; Counsel Music Stu; Music Educators Natl Conference 1979-; SC Band Dir Assn 1980-; SC Ed Assn 1982-; Kappa Kappa Psi Natl Band 1977-; Most Outstanding Bandsman 1975-79; Thomas A Dorsey Conductors Awd 1982; Jazz Band Hall of Famer 1979; Performed with Nationally Known Musicians & Composers; *office:* Edisto Schls 500 R N Foster Dr Cordova SC 29039

JOHNSON, HAROLD G., 5th Grade Teacher; *b:* Jamaica, West Indies; *ed:* (BS) Elem Ed, 1972, (MS) Ed of Disadvantage, 1974 KS St Univ; *cr:* 4th-5th Grade Teacher Oakdale Elem Sch 1972-74; 5th Grade Teacher K L Rutherford Elem 1974-; *ai:* HS Ski Coach 1974-80; Elem Ski Adv 1988-; Sci Mentor 1983-88; Holiday Mtn Ski Club 1980, Harris Gordon 1989; *office:* K L Rutherford Elem Sch 9 Patricia Ln Monticello NY 12701

JOHNSON, HELEN C., First Grade Teacher; *b:* Ogden, UT; *m:* Ray; *c:* Kelly, Kirk, Kory, Kristen; *ed:* (BS) Elem Ed/Early Chldhd, UT St Univ 1959; *cr:* 2nd Grade Teacher Plain City Elem 1959-60, 1961-62, North Ogden Elem 1967-69; 1st Grade Teacher Plain City Elem 1977-90; *ai:* 1st Grade Chm; Weber Sch Dist Spelling Pilot Prgm; UT Ed Assn 1977-; Weber Ed Assn 1977-; Scouting Commissioner 1984-87, Dist Awd of Merit 1987; Nom Teacher of Yr 1989; Nom Thanks to Teachers Excl Awd 1990; *home:* 1012 W Pleasant View Dr Ogden UT 84414

JOHNSON, HENRY EUGENE, III, Mathematics Dept Chairperson; *b:* Hopewell, VA; *m:* Debra Montague Hutchison; *c:* Catherine Hirst Cerna, Lara Webster, Sarah E.; *ed:* (MED) Educl Leadership, 1979, (EDS) Educl Leadership, 1982, (EDD) Educl Leadership, 1988 FL Atlantic Univ; *cr:* Asst Prin Deerfield Mid Sch 1985; Supvr of Testing FL Atlantic Univ 1982-; Math Dept Chm Deerfield Beach Mid Sch 1983-; Ed Consultant 1985-; *ai:* Curr Cncl & Teachers Ed Center Chm; Sports Referee; ASCD 1988-; Natl Staff Dev Cncl 1989-; NCTM 1983-; Phi Delta Kappa 1988-; FL Cncl Teachers of Math, Broward Cty Cncl Teachers of Math; BSA Eagle Scout; Articles Published; Nom Math Teacher of Yr; Pres Awd Excl Teaching; *home:* 2201 NW 41st Terr Coconut Creek FL 33066

JOHNSON, HUGH JAMES, JR., Band Teacher; *b:* Clarksville, TX; *w:* Gloria D. (dec); *ed:* (BA) Music Ed, Wiley Coll 1963; (MED) Music Ed, N TX Univ 1974; *cr:* Band/Chorus Teacher Cntrl HS Springfield 1963-67, Cntrl HS Mc Rae 1968-69, West Hardeville HS 1969-70; Band Teacher Hubert Mid Sch 1971-; *ai:* Chorus & Band Dir; Music Consultant; GA Music Educators Assn, Natl Music Educators Assn, NEA 1970-; Omega Psi Chaplain 1961-; *home:* 7108 Hialeah Cir Savannah GA 31406

JOHNSON, IVONNE M., 1st Grade Bilingual Teacher; *b:* Colon, Panama; *m:* Eugene A.; *c:* Monica King, Gina, Eugenio, Danilo; *ed:* Elem Ed, Escuela Normal JDA 1956; (BA) Eng, Univ of Panama 1972; *cr:* 2nd Grade Teacher Almirante-Bocas Del Toro 1956-57; Elem Eng Teacher Pan Amer Institute 1957-60, Instituto Pedagogico 1970-80; *ai:* Extended Day Summer Sch; Houston Fed of Teachers 1983; Houston Area Assn for Bi-Ling Teachers-Distingushed Teacher 1989; *office:* James Davis Ryan Elem Sch 4001 Hardy St Houston TX 77009

JOHNSON, IVRIA, JR., Science Teacher; *b:* Brinkley, AR; *m:* Brenda (Baltimore); *c:* Cecily, Ivria III, Crystal; *ed:* (BA) Psych, 1978; (BS) Bio, 1977 Philander Smith Coll; UCA; UALK; *cr:* Lab Asst/Gen Bio Philander Smith Coll; Gen Sci Teacher Lonoke Jr HS 1977-84; Mann Arts & Sci Magnet Jr HS 1984-; *ai:* Young Astronauts; NEA; AR Ed Assn; Naval Reserve (Career Cnslg 1980-86 Dept Chief 1988-89); Public Svc Awd; *office:* Mann Arts & Sci Magnet Jr HS 1000 E Roosevelt Rd Little Rock AR 72202

JOHNSON, JANET JO LOCKHART, 6th Grade Language Art Teacher; *b:* Rock Island, IL; *m:* Julious James; *c:* Justin J., Joshua J.; *ed:* (BA) His, Tougaloo Coll 1971; Level 1 & 2 Trng Inst Gifted Ed; Great Books Leader Trng; *cr:* 4th Grade Teacher Lincoln Elem 1971-73; 6th Grade Teacher Longfellow Elem 1974-; *ai:* Longfellow Safety Patrol; Cultural Art Chairperson PTA; Variety Show Spon; Gifted & WA Jr HS NOW Comm; IL Ed Assn, Rock Island Ed Assn 1971-; Ethnic Minority Rep Region 18 1989-91; Quad City Negro Heritage Society Secy; Zeta Phi Beta Inc; Longfellow PTA Life Membership 1985; Adah Chapter 10 Order of Eastern Star Past Matron; Quad Cities United Way Allocation Comm; Tri-Cities Assembly 53 Order of Golden Circle Loyal Lady Ruter; Masgat Court 167 Daughters of Isis 1st Lieutenant Commandress; 2nd Baptist Church Sr Choir Mem Morning Star Club; Sr Citizen Club Martin Luther King Center Volunteer; Prof Elected Ethnic Minority Rep; *home:* 4509 24th Ave Rock Island IL 61201

JOHNSON, JANICE, Jr HS Teacher; *b:* Chicago, IL; *ed:* (BA) Chrstn Ed, Westmont Coll 1971; *cr:* 5th Grade/JR HS Teacher Hesperia Chrstn Sch 1971-; *ai:* CA JR Schlsp Fed Adv.

JOHNSON, JANICE WARWICK, 5th Grade Teacher; *b:* Monte Vista, CO; *m:* Howard D.; *c:* Elizabeth Johnson Fulce, Karen Johnson Mc Kearan, Jennifer, Jared; *ed:* (BS) Elem Ed, Sam Houston St Univ 1963; *cr:* Teacher Lufkin Ind Sch Dist 1964-66, Port Neches Groves Ind Sch Dist 1966-70, Denison Ind Sch Dist 1970-; *ai:* PTA Life Mem; Delta Kappa Gamma; Epsilon Sigma Alpha Chaplin; Parkside Baptist Church; *office:* Hyde Park Elem Sch 1701 Hyde Park Denison TX 75020

JOHNSON, JAY M., 6th Grade Mathematics Teacher; *b:* Philadelphia, PA; *m:* Linda S.; *c:* Jennifer, Emily; *ed:* (BMUSED) Vocal Music, Temple Univ 1972; (MMUSED) Vocal Music, Trenton St Coll 1977; Elem Ed, Beaver Coll 1981-86, Temple Univ 1977-80; *cr:* Vocal Music Teacher Armstrong Mid Sch 1972-77, Struble Elem Sch 1977-80; 5th Grade Teacher Valley Elem Sch 1980-87; 6th Grade Math Teacher Snyder Mid Sch 1987-; *office:* Cecelia Snyder Mid Sch 3330 Holmeville Rd Bensalem PA 19020

JOHNSON, JAYNE ANN, 7th-8th Grade Soc Stud Teacher; *b:* Sarcoxie, MO; *m:* Kenneth M.; *ed:* (BS) Soc Stud/Ed, Univ of MO 1964; (MA) His/Soc Sci, Highlands Univ 1971; *cr:* 10th/11th Grade His Teacher Hickman HS 1964-67; Soc Stud Teacher Memorial Mid Sch 1970-75; 7th-8th Grade Soc Stud Teacher Alameda Jr HS 1977-; *ai:* NEA Treas 1985-87; Pi Lambda Theta, Pi Gamma Mu; *home:* Rt 19 Box 90-16 Santa Fe NM 87505

JOHNSON, JEANNIE S., Mathematics Teacher; *b:* Lowell, MA; *ed:* (BA) Math, St Anselm Coll 1983; *cr:* Math Teacher Pembroke Acad 1983-; *ai:* NHS & Yrbk Adv; Math Curr Comm Chairperson & Current Guide; NCTM 1987-; *office:* Pembroke Acad 209 Academy Rd Pembroke NH 03275

JOHNSON, JEFFREY SCOTT, Social Studies Teacher; *b:* Ridgway, PA; *m:* H. Pamela Baieroski; *c:* J. Scott; *ed:* (BSED) Intnl Stud, Indiana Univ of PA 1978; *cr:* Armor Officer US Army Europe 1978-82; 8th Grade Teacher Caesar Rodney Jr HS 1983-; *ai:* Head Wrestling Coach; Honor Society Adv; Steering Comm; NEA, DE St Ed Assn, Caesar Rodney Ed Assn 1983-; Read Aloud Adv 1987-; Kappa Sigma Alumni Assn 1979-; Natl Assn Stu Activity Advs 1987-; Teacher of Yr Caesar Rodney Jr HS 1988-89; Re-Learning Project 1989-; *office:* Caesar Rodney Jr HS 25 E Camden-Wyoming Ave Camden-Wyoming DE 19934

JOHNSON, JERE, Phys Ed/Athletic Director; *b:* Ft Wayne, IN; *ed:* (BS) Phys Ed/Health, Taylor Univ; *cr:* Sci Teacher/Coach R J Baskett 1987; Phys Ed Teacher/Coach/A D Lakeview Chrstn Sch 1987-; *ai:* Var Bsktbl Coach 1985-; Sr Class Adv 1989-; Vlybl 1989; Stu Govt Adv 1987-88; Golf 1988; Midland Athletic Conf Secy 1988-89; IN Bsktbl Coaches Assn 1989-; Church Youth Spon 1989-; South Bend IN ACSI Convention Seminar Bsktbl Speaker; *office:* Lakeview Christian Sch 5316 S Western Ave Marion IN 46952

JOHNSON, JIMMIE YOUNG, 4th Grade Teacher; *b:* Kenedy, TX; *m:* Warren G. Sr.; *c:* Anna L. Hicks, Warren G. Jr.; *ed:* (BS) Elem Ed, Southwest TX 1965; Gifted Prgm St Thomas Univ; *cr:* 6th Grade Teacher 1957-70; GED Teacher 1969 Kenedy Jr HS; 4th Grade Teacher Mae Smythe Elem 1970-; *ai:* 4th Grade Gifted Prgm; Asst Prin; Dist Comm Comm Alternate; PTA Lifetime Mem; Kenedy Jr HS Cncl Spon 1965-70; Kenedy Cub Yrbk Dedicated to Me 1967-68; *office:* Mae Smythe Elem Sch 2202 Pasadena Blvd Pasadena TX 77502

JOHNSON, JO ANNE PADGETT, Art Teacher; *b:* Selma, AL; *m:* Willie Thomas Jr.; *c:* Michael A.; *ed:* (BS) Elem Ed, SW TX St Univ 1980; Cmptr Ed Trng; *cr:* 2nd/3rd Grade Teacher Forest Hills Elem 1981-83; Pre-Sch Teacher Pathway Pre-Sch 1983-86; 4th Grade Teacher Forest Hills Elem 1986-88; Art Teacher Westwood Terrace & John Glenn Elem 1988-; *ai:* Art Club Spon1989-; Soc Stud Textbook Adoption Comm 1987-88; Vlybl Captain Sch 1989- & YMCA Intermediate League 1988-; TSTA 1981-83; ATPE 1986-88; *office:* Westwood Terrace Elem 7615 Bronco Ln San Antonio TX 78227

JOHNSON, JOHN C., 6th-8th Grade Teacher/Coach; *b:* Forest, MS; *m:* Sonda Floy Tarver; *c:* Jana Floy; *ed:* (BAE) Elem Ed, Univ of MS 1980; (MA) Elem Ed, 1984, (MA) Admin Supervision, 1988, (EDS) Elem Ed, 1988 MS Coll; *cr:* Teacher Cedar Elem 1980-81; Teacher/Coach Morton Mid Sch 1981-85; Teacher Raines Elem 1985-86, Rosa Scott Mid Sch 1986-89, Morton Mid Sch 1989-; *ai:* 7th/8th Boys Bsktbl, Asst Ftbl Coach; Van Winkle Baptist Church 1985-; *office:* Morton Mid Sch Drawer L Morton MS 39117

JOHNSON, JOHN W., JR., Mathematics Dept Chairman; *b:* Wadesboro, NC; *m:* Shirley Brooks; *c:* John W. III, Reginald J., Kimberly M.; *ed:* (BS) Math, Shaw Univ 1969; (MED) Math, SC St Coll 1985; Math Wkshp Univ of SC 1986; Advanced Placement Calculus Trng Francis Marion Coll 1989; Guidance, Univ of SC Salkehatchie 1973-77; *cr:* Specialist 4 US Army 1969-71; Math Teacher 1971-, Math Dept Chm 1979- Estill HS; *ai:* Adv Jr Class, Chess Club, Newspaper 1971-81; Curr Comm Mem; Coach Girls Sftbl 1979-81, Bsbl 1983-89; Beta Club 1985-87; NEA, SCEA, HCEA 1971-; 1st Estill Baptist Church (Deacon 1976-, Sunday Sch Supt 1979-); Westinghouse STAR Teacher Awd 1980, 1985, 1989); *home:* 13 Nix St Hampton SC 29924

JOHNSON, JON W., 4th Grade Teacher; *b:* Bozeman, MT; *m:* Janet; *c:* Brandi, Stacee; *ed:* (BA) Phys Ed, 1970, Elem Ed, 1973 MT St Univ; Grad Stud Math & Curr, MT St Univ; *cr:* 4th Grade Teacher 1973-; *ai:* Intramural Sports Coach; Asst HS Wrestling; Army; NEA, MT Ed Assn 1973-; Math Ideas Prgm Trng; MT Math

JOHNSON, JOYCE TATE, 5th Grade Teacher; *b:* Memphis, TN; *c:* John A. III; *ed:* (BS) Bio, Philander Smith 1960; (MED) Elem Ed, Memphis St Univ 1969; Elem Ed, Admin, Sci; *cr:* 6th Grade Teacher Shannon Elem 1961-69, Gragg Jr HS 1969-72; Methods Instr Lemoyne Owen Coll 1979-82; 5th Grade Teacher Cummings Elem 1977-; *ai:* Sci & Spelling Bee Coord; Cubmaster; Childrens Pianist; Treas Cmmty Service Organization; Sunday Sch Teacher; Memphis Ed Assn Faculty Rep 1980-89, Leadership Diploma 1989; Unified Teachers Assn; Intnl Rdng Assoc 1980-; Alpha Kappa Alpha Treas 1988-, Soror of Yr 1989; BSA Leader 1978-, Dist Awd of Merit 1987; United Meth Women (Pres, VP, Secy, Treas) 1960-; Career Ladder III, Sci Fellowships; Prin Awd; Grade & Sac Effective Schls Chairperson; *home:* 1130 Esplanade Memphis TN 38106

JOHNSON, JOYCE YANCEY, English Teacher/Eng Dept Chair; *b:* Clarksville, VA; *c:* David, Holly; *ed:* (BA) Eng, Elon Coll 1959; Eng, Univ of Toledo, Coll of William & Mary, Bowling Green St Univ; *cr:* Eng Teacher Great Bridge HS 1959-61, Frank Cox HS 1961-63, Colonel Crawford HS 1963-; *ai:* Jennings Scholar; *office:* Colonel Crawford HS 2303 S R 602 North Robinson OH 44856

JOHNSON, JUDITH HILL, Language Art Teacher; *b:* Clarksville, GA; *m:* Troy Alan; *c:* Mary E., Logan A., Troy K.; *ed:* (AA) Eng, Truett Mc Connell Coll 1978; (BSED) Speech/Eng Ed, Univ of GA 1981; (MED) Eng Ed, Univ of Ga Grad Sch 1987; *cr:* Teacher Loganville Mid Sch 1981-82, Newton Cty HS 1987-; *ai:* Interact Club Spon; NCTE 1981-; 1st Baptist Church; Whos Who Among Amer Educators; *office:* Newton Cty HS 140 Ram Dr Covington GA 30209

JOHNSON, JUNE THURSTON, First Grade Teacher; *b:* Middlesex, VA; *m:* Timothy; *c:* Timothy; *ed:* (BS) Elem Ed, VA St Univ 1964; (MED) Ed, Beaver Coll 1977; PA St Univ, Temple Univ, St Josephs Univ; *cr:* Teacher Portsmouth Sch Dist 1964-65, Camden Sch Dist 1965-68, Philadelphia Sch Dist 1969-; *ai:* 1st Grade Chairperson; Loesche Sch Calligraphy Club Spon; Rdng & Math Tutor; NEA 1964-65; NJEA 1965-68; AFT 1969-; Alpha Kappa Alpha 1963-; Inst Elem Sci Federal Grant Division of Sci Ed 1989; *office:* Wm H Loesche Elem Sch Bustleton Ave & Tomlinson Rd Philadelphia PA 19116

JOHNSON, KAREN ARLENE (GATES), Former Teacher; *b:* El Dorado, KS; *m:* Gregory W.; *c:* Joel, Ryan, Seth; *ed:* (BA) Elem Ed, Denver Baptist Bible Coll 1980; *cr:* 3rd/4th Grade Teacher Bennett Baptist Sch 1981-84.

JOHNSON, KAREN BOLDT, Fourth Grade Teacher; *b:* Prairie Du Chien, WI; *m:* Brad Lee; *ed:* (BS) Elem Ed, Univ of WI 1978; *cr:* 5th-6th Grade Teacher Harding Elem 1978-81; 7th Grade Teacher John Adams Mid Sch 1981-82; 4th Grade Teacher Harding Elem 1982-; *ai:* Harding Elem Building Leadership Team, Rdng Comm Mem; Mason City Ed Assn (Building Rep 1981-82, Publicity Comm 1988-89, Co-Chairperson); Organized IA Wildlife Project; *office:* Hardin Elem Schl 1239 N Rhode Island Mason City IA 50401

JOHNSON, KARLEEN MARTIN, Kindergarten Teacher; *b:* St Regis Falls, NY; *m:* Gene I.; *c:* Heidi, Kary Mulverhill, Dawna, Genek, Noel; *ed:* (BA) Elem Ed, St Univ Coll Potsdam 1970; *cr:* Kndgtn Techer St Regis Falls Cntrl 1970-; *ai:* Mentor for Psychologist Resource Room Teacher; Teacher Liasion Comm of Spec Ed; Kndgtn Screening, Sick Pool, Class Size Comm; Executive Comm of SRFTA; Cmmty Playground Comm 1987-89; St Regis Falls Teachers Assn Secy 1983-; Order of Eastern Stars Matron 1963-64; Cub Scouts Den Leader 1984; Early Saturday Nite Mixed Bowling League Secy; *home:* Blue Mt Rd Saint Regis Falls NY 12980

JOHNSON, KELLEY SUE, 1st Grade Teacher; *b:* Penn Yan, NY; *m:* Timothy E.; *ed:* (BS) Elem Ed, Keuka Coll 1988; Ed, Elmira Coll; *cr:* 1st Grade Teacher Penn Yan Elem 1988-; *ai:* 7th-8th Grade Modified Vlybl & Var Cheerleading Coach; Developmental Philosophy Comm; Intnl Rdng Assn 1988-; Team Teaching in a Congruency Situation; *office:* Penn Yan Elem Sch Maple St Penn Yan NY 14527

JOHNSON, KELLY KIRKES, Business & Office Instructor; *b:* Wilburton, OK; *m:* Anthony E.; *ed:* (BS) Bus Ed, Southeastern OK St Univ 1987; *cr:* Evening Boe Instr Kiamichi Area Vo-Tech 1987-88; Cmptr Teacher Dustin Publis Schls 1988-89; Boe Instr Kiamichi Area Vo-Tech 1989-; *ai:* FBLA & PBL Adv; Class Spon; Red Oak Alumni Assn VP 1989-; OK Bus Ed Assn Cty Rep 1988-89; VBOE, NBEA, OEA, AVA, NEA Mem 1989-; Hartshorne Booster Club Chairperson 1989-; Hartshorne Young Farmers Cmmty Service Mem Projects 1989-; *office:* Kiamichi Vo-Tech PO Box 308 Mc Alester OK 74502

JOHNSON, KEN L., English Teacher; *b:* Madison, WI; *m:* Cynthia J. Vogel; *c:* Jessica D., Joshua J., Jennifer B., Jillian A.; *ed:* (BS) Eng Ed, Univ of WI Whitewater 1972; Cardinal Stritch Coll & Univ of WI Madison; *cr:* Eng Teacher Johnson Creek HS 1972-; *ai:* Head Bsktbl & Drama Coach; Athletic Dir; Class Adv; Teacher of Yr 1989-; E Suburban Conference Coach of Yr 1989-; *office:* Johnson Creek HS 111 South St Johnson Creek WI 53038

JOHNSON, KERMIT WEBB, Teacher; *b:* Evansville, IN; *ed:* (BS) Eng/Soc Stud, Oakland City Coll 1958; (MA) Eng/Soc Stud, Univ of Evansville 1968; *cr:* Teacher Bicknell HS 1958-59, Francisco HS 1959-60, Owensville HS 1961-74, Owensville Mid Sch 1975-; *ai:* Academic Bowl Spon; NEA, IN St Teachers Assn, S Gibson Teacher Assn 1958-; Owensville Lib Bd; Mu Tau Kappa Scholastic.

JOHNSON, KEVIN LEE, 7th Grade Science Teacher; *b:* Burlington, IA; *ed:* (BS) Phys Ed, IN St Univ 1982; (MS) Ed, IN Univ 1988; *cr:* 7th Grade Sci Teacher Lake Station Edison Jr/Sr HS 1982-; *ai:* Jr Var Boys Bsktbl & Asst Jr HS Ftbl Coach; IN Bsktbl Coaches Assn; *office:* Lake Station Edison Jr/Sr HS 3304 Parkside Ave Lake Station IN 46405

JOHNSON, LAURENCE THOMAS, Jr HS Band Director; *b:* Lemmon, SD; *m:* Mary Jo Clausen; *c:* Christopher T., Thomas M.; *ed:* (BFA) Music Ed, Univ of SD 1973; *cr:* Band Dir Menno Public Sch 1973-75, Clark Public Sch 1976-77, Pierre Public Sch 1978-; *ai:* Jr HS Musical Dir; SD Bandmasters Assn; NEA, SDEA, PEA; Pierre Players Bd of Dir 1980-89; SS Peter & Paul Folk Group Choir Dir 1981-; Black Hills Playhouse Musical Dir 1989; *home:* 1204 E Franklin Pierre SD 57501

JOHNSON, LAURENCE WELDON, Upper Grade Science Teacher; *b:* Chicago, IL; *ed:* (AA) Liberal Arts, Southeast Jr Coll 1964; (BS) Ed, IL Teachers Coll 1966; Phys & Biological Sci; Group Dynamics Educl Leadership Inst; Educl Methodology Lazanov Usakning Inst; *cr:* 4th Grade Teacher Wentworth Elem 1967; Upper Grade Teacher Parker Elem 1968-82; Upper Grade Sci Teacher Parker Cmmty Acad 1982-; *ai:* Sci Fair Coord; Spec Events Music Coord; Union Rep; Drug Ed Comm; Prof Problems Comm; Chicago Area Rdng Assn 1989; Chicago Area Round Dance Leader Society 1984-; Roundalab 1989-; Center for New Schls Outstanding Teacher 1981; General Supt Quest for Quality Awd 1979; Advisory Bd Teacher Prof Dev Project St Xavier Coll 1987-88; *office:* Parker Community Academy 6800 S Stewart Ave Chicago IL 60621

JOHNSON, LINDA BAYLISS, Social Studies Teacher; *b:* Oakland, CA; *m:* Stanley E.; *ed:* (BA) Poly Sci, Wittenberg Univ 1968; (MED) Curr/Supervision, Miami Univ 1975; Grad Stud OH Univ & OH St Univ; *cr:* 6th Grade Teacher Amanda-Clearcreek Local Sch Dist 1970-74; 5th Grade Teacher 1975-76, 4th Grade Teacher 1976-83, Soc Stud Teacher 1983- Heath City Schls; *ai:* Soph Class Adv; Soc Stud Textbook Selection Comm; Heath Ed Assn Treas 1988-; Cntrl OH Cncl for Soc Stud, OH Cncl for Soc

Stud, Delta Kappa Gamma; Marabar Heights Garden Club VP 1989-; Broad Street Presbyn Church; Martha Holden Jennings Teacher Scholar 1971-72, 1986-87; Heath HS & Dow Chemical Company Outstanding Teacher Awd 1988; *office:* Heath HS 300 Licking View Dr Heath OH 43056

JOHNSON, LINDA DAVIS, Fifth Grade Teacher; *b:* Mc Minnville, TN; *m:* Reggie Herman; *c:* Jeffery B., Kristin A.; *ed:* (BS) Elem Ed, 1976, (MED) Curr/Instruction, 1985 Mid TN St Univ; *cr:* 4th Grade Teacher 1976-77, 4th-5th Grade Teacher 1977-84, 5th-6th Grade Sci/Soc Stud Teacher 1984-85, 5th Grade Teacher 1985- Hillsboro Elem; *ai:* Cheerleading, Just Say No, 4-H Spon; Soc Stud & Math Textbook Comms; 5th Grade Chairperson; NEA, TN Ed Assn, Coffee Cty Ed Assn 1976-88; Coffee Cty Task Force Advisory Comm 1988-89; Coffee Cty Beautification 1988-89; Career Level I; Article Published; *office:* Hillsboro Elem Sch Rt 2 Hwy 127 Hillsboro TN 37342

JOHNSON, LINDA L., 5/6th Grade Sci/Eng Teacher; *b:* Gordon, NE; *m:* Edwin; *c:* Megan; *ed:* (BA) Elem Ed, Co Womens Coll 1968; Sci, Univ of North CO & CO St Univ; *cr:* 6th Grade Teacher Jefferson Cty Schls, Kilgore Elem, Dept of Defense Schls West Germany; *ai:* Outdoor Ed Spon & Dir of All Activities Grade 6; Outdoor Ed Trip to the Co Rockies; NEA 1975-; CEA 1975-; Weld Cntrl Teachers Assn Pres 1975-; Elem Sci Curr Dir; Wrote and Developed Current Sci Prgm; Developed Inservices for Teachers Grant; Univ of Northern Co Sci & Math Wkshp; *office:* Keenesburg & Prospct Vly Elem 33318 Colorado Hwy 52 Keenesburg CO 80643

JOHNSON, LINDA T., Math/Science/History Teacher; *b:* Rutland, UT; *m:* Chris A.; *ed:* (BS) Math/Sci, Castleton St Coll 1966; (MED) Elem Ed/His, Coll of St Joseph 1978; Ed, His Courses; *cr:* Jr HS Teacher Otter Valley Unified HS 1966-72; Jr HS Sci Teacher 12th Street Jr HS 1972-73; Teacher West Rutland HS 1973-; *ai:* Class of 1992 Adv; West Rutland HS Inservice Comm Chairperson; Teachers Union Negotiating & PSA Chairperson; VT St Sci Teacher 1986-; VEA, NEA 1979-; Rutland Town Fire Auxiliary (Pres, VP) 1972-78, 1980-85; *office:* West Rutland HS Main St West Rutland VT 05777

JOHNSON, LORRIE, 4th Grade Teacher; *b:* Latrobe, PA; *ed:* (BS) Elem Ed, Salem Coll 1972; Writing Project, PA Dept of Ed; *cr:* Teacher Salts Elem Sch 1973-; *ai:* Treas SES Soc Comm; Supervising Teacher Affiliation Indiana Univ of PA; PA Health Ed Assessment Advisory Comm; Chrstn Fellowship Acad Sch Bd Secy 1990-; *home:* 415 A Point St Saltsburg PA 15681

JOHNSON, LOUIS B., 7th-10th Grade Teacher; *b:* Fayetteville, OH; *m:* Dolores Molitor; *c:* Louis Jr., Sandra Lesterburger; *ed:* (BA) His/Poly Sci, Wilmington OH 1975; Certificate Univ of Xavier; *cr:* Teacher Fayetteville Perry Local 1975-; *ai:* Class Spon; Jr HS Bsktbl, Var Bsktbl & Bsbl Coach; Knothole Bsbl Pres 1977-85; Responsible for Raising Money to Develop Bsbl Fields at Sch.

JOHNSON, LOUIS HOWARD, Mathematics/Physics Teacher; *b:* Newport News, VA; *m:* Terry Holder; *c:* Ann, Howard III, Katie; *ed:* (BA) Math/physics, Elon 1966; *cr:* Teacher Liberty Mid Sch 1966-76, E Randolph HS 1976-; *ai:* Ftbl & Bsktbl Coach 1966-77; NCAE; *office:* E Randolph HS Box 180 Ramseur NC 27298

JOHNSON, LYNETTE EILEEN (GEIZLER), Fourth Grade Teacher; *b:* Bottineau, ND; *m:* Brian C.; *c:* Chad, Jason; *ed:* (BS) Elem Ed, Minot St Univ 1973; Advanced Study at Various ND Universities; *cr:* 1st/2nd Combination Room Kramer Public Sch 1973-75; 6th Grade Teacher 1976-77, 4th Grade Teacher 1977- Bottineau Public Schls; *ai:* Bottineau Ed Assn; ND Ed Assn; *home:* 416 Spruce St Bottineau ND 58318

JOHNSON, MADELINE STUBBLEFIELD, Second Grade Teacher; *m:* Gene R.; *c:* Teena L.Jordan, Penny J. Little, Anita K. Reno; *ed:* (BS) Elem Ed, Western KY Univ 1971; Elem Ed, Murray St Univ 1978; *cr:* 1st Grade Teacher Longest Elem 1971-76; 2nd Grade Teacher Graham Elem 1978-; *ai:* Textbook Comm; NEA/KEA/MCA 1971-; KY Colonel 1971; Woman Club 1962-65 KEA Delg to St Organization; *home:* 217 Twin Hill Dr Greenville KY 42345

JOHNSON, MARIAN RUTH, 3rd Grade Teacher; *b:* Jackson, TN; *ed:* (BA) Elem Ed, Lane Coll 1965; Cert Early Dev Univ of OK; Addl Studies Northeast MO St Univ; *cr:* 1st Grade Teacher Booneville Elem Sch 1955-56; Dawson and Obannon Elem Schs 1956-68; Central Elem Sch 1968-69 2nd Grade Teacher 1969-87; 3rd Grade Teacher 1987 Becky-David Elem Sch; *ai:* Francis Howell Ed Assn 1968-; MO Ntnl Ed Assn 1975-; *office:* Becky David Elem Sch 1155 Jungs Station Rd Saint Charles MO 63303

JOHNSON, MARION CRIST, Mathematics Teacher; *b:* Piqua, OH; *m:* Alfred T.; *ed:* (BS) Math, Wittenberg Univ 1967; (MAT) Math/Ed, Johns Hopkins Univ 1968; *cr:* 5th/6th Grade Math/Sci Teacher Urbana Local Intermediate 1968-70; Math Teacher Urbana HS 1970-; *ai:* Gifted & Talented Curr Cncl & Competency Based Ed Comm; Urbana Assn of Classroom Teachers (Secy, Pres) 1968-; OH Ed Assn 1970-; OH Cncl Teachers of Math, NCTM 1970-75, 1985-: Order of Eastern Star (Deputy Grand Matron, Worthy Matron) 1968-; Garden Club (Secy, VP, Pres) 1970-; United Meth Church 1968-; Outstanding Teacher Urbana City Schls 1979, 1989; *home:* 4373 Bump Rd Cable OH 43009

JOHNSON, MARY BONDS, English Teacher; *b:* Madison Cty, TN; *c:* Marcellaus; *ed:* (BS) Bus ED, Lane Coll 1966; (MS) Scndry Ed, Emporia St Univ 1979; Ottawa Univ; *cr:* Eng/ Journalism Teacher Northeast Jr HS 1969-74; Eng Teacher Rosedale Mid Sch 1974-; Teacher 1984-, Dean of Stus 1988- Dickinson Bus Sch; *ai:* Rosedale Eng Dept Chairperson; NBEA 1987-; KS NEA 1970-; Acad of Amer Educators 1973-74; KS Cncl Teachers of Eng 1980-; *office:* Rosedale Mid Sch 3600 Springfield Kansas City KS 66103

JOHNSON, MARY ETTA, 4th Grade Teacher; *b:* Louisville, KY; *m:* Gregory; *c:* Brittney; *ed:* (BA) Elem Ed, Eastern KY 1974; (MA) Ed, Univ of Louisville 1977; *cr:* 2nd Grade Teacher Jacob Elem 1974-79; K-5 Rdng Specialist Fern Creek & Klondike Elem 1979-80; 2nd Grade Teacher 1980-83, 3rd Grade Teacher 1983-85; 4th Grade Teacher 1985- Carter Traditional Elem; *ai:* Sci Fair Coord; Jefferson Cty Teachers Assn; Alpha Kappa Alpha; Asbury Chapel Church Steward/Youth Supervisor 1988-; *home:* 1806 Allston Ave Louisville KY 40210

JOHNSON, MARY SERRANO, Teacher; *b:* Hawthorne, NV; *m:* Robert W.; *c:* Gabe, Carly; *ed:* (BA) Span, Univ NV Reno 1974; Eng & Bi-ling Ed Minor; *cr:* Adult Ed Teacher Fairfax Cty Sch Dist; Teacher Garrett Jr HS 1980-; *ai:* Drama Club Spon; Talent Show Dir; Speech/Drama Festival; Sch Plays Dir; Dance Club, E F Ed Tour Spon; Teacher Sunshine Comm; Teachers Foreign Lang Assn of NV; Jr HS Sunday Sch Teacher; Master Teacher; *office:* Garrett Jr HS 1200 Avenue G Boulder City NV 89005

JOHNSON, MELBA J., Fifth Grade Teacher; *m:* Oliver S.; *ed:* Assoc of Ed Elem Ed, Waldorf Coll 1945; Luth Bible Sch 1949; Escuela de Idiomas 1957; (BA) Elem Ed, Univ of N IA 1965; *cr:* 6th/7th Grade Teacher Swea Public Sch 1945-48; 4th-6th Grade Teacher Missionary Sch 1949-51; 6th Grade Teacher Swea City Public Sch 1953-56, 1961-67; 5th Grade Teacher Cokato Elem Sch 1969-; *ai:* NEA 1945-48, 1953-56, 1961-67, 1969-; IEA, MEA Membership 1945-48, 1953-56, 1961-67, 1969-; Dassel-Cokato Ed Assn (Treas 1981-85) 1969-; Luth Church Women (Bible Teacher 1967-, Church Cncl, Chairperson 1986-88); Candidate Teacher of Yr 1980; Teachers of Excl; Amer Legion Awd Meritorious Service 1980; *home:* Rt 2 Box 245 Cohato MN 55321

JOHNSON, MELODY WALLACE, Elementary Phys Ed Teacher; *b:* Tampa, FL; *m:* James Dale; *c:* Jayme D., Zachary L.; *ed:* (BS) Phys Ed, S IL Univ 1975-79; Suncoast Area Teacher Trng, Clinical Teachers, Univ of S FL; Supervising Interns Elem Phys Ed Univ of S FL; *cr:* Elem Phys Educator Richey Fundamental Sch 1981-; *ai:* News & Scheduling Comm Chm; Organize/Choreograph Kids in Motion; Organize Field Days & Stu Faculty Sftbl Games; Creator of Richey Tiger Spirit; FL Assn for Health, Phys Ed, Recreation, Dance, Drivers Ed 1980-; W Pasco Girls Sftbl Assn Team Mgr 1990, GSA (Brownie Asst Leader 1989-, Daisy Asst Leader 1988-89); Developed Report Card Phys Ed; Nom Teacher of Yr 1986-89; *office:* Richey Fundamental Elem Sch 6807 Madison St New Port Richey FL 34652

JOHNSON, MILLER JONES, Biology Teacher; *b:* Thomaston, AL; *m:* Edwin Van; *c:* Lisa R., Kwon K.; *ed:* (MA) Bio, Miles Coll 1963; (MA) Scndry Ed, 1975, Supvrs Certificate, 1976, Advanced Certificate of Ed, 1977 Univ of AL; *cr:* Teacher Eliza Miller Jr HS 1963-65, W A Bell Jr HS 1965-68; JCCEO Coord JCCEO; Interviewer Iris Parker Interviewing Company 1979; *ai:* Bio Club Spon; AEA, NEA, JCEA, Delta Sigma Theta; Crumbey Bethel Baptist Church /Primitive Secy; Short Term Schlsp Essay Contest Tuskegee Inst; *home:* 11th Ct N #9 Birmingham AL 35204

JOHNSON, MYRA LA COMBE, English Teacher; *b:* De Quincy, LA; *m:* Larry D.; *c:* Lori, Lana, Brad; *ed:* (BA) Scndry Ed, Mc Neese St Univ 1987; Lsue; *cr:* Eng Teacher Vinton HS 1987-; *ai:* Pep Squad Spon; SAPE & SACS Steering Comm; Eng Contact Teacher; LA Cncl Teachers of Eng 1989-; LA Ed Assn 1987-89; Calcasieu Assn of Ed 1987-89; *office:* Vinton HS 1603 Grace Ave Vinton LA 70668

JOHNSON, MYRTLE REASONS, Social Studies Teacher; *b:* Wilson County, NC; *m:* Ralph Luclair; *c:* Shannon L.; *ed:* (BA) Eng/Soc Stud, Atlantic Chrstn Coll 1961; (MA) Eng/Soc Stud, E Carolin Univ 1964; *cr:* Teacher Wilson Cty Schls 1961-64, Raleigh City Schls 1964-74, New Hanover Cty Schls 1974-; *ai:* Spirit Club; Hoggard Advisory Comm; NC Soc Stud Cncl 1985-; *office:* John T Hoggard HS 4305 Shipyard Blvd Wilmington NC 28403

JOHNSON, NANCY O., Second Grade Teacher; *b:* Mc Minnville, TN; *m:* Russell K.; *c:* Keith, Kyle; *ed:* (BA) Elem Ed, 1976, (MED) Elem Ed, 1983 Trenton St Coll; Eng/Lang Art Ed, Rutgers; *cr:* 1st/3rd Grade Teacher W Windsor-Plainsboro Regional Schls 1976-88; 2nd Grade Teacher Riverside Sch 1988-; *ai:* Kappa Delta Pi; NJ Cncl Teachers of Eng; NJ Governors Teacher Grant 1988-; NCTE Researcher Awd 1989-; Speaker NJ Assn of Supts 1990; Published Article NJCTE Focus; Whos Who in Amer Ed 1989; *office:* Riverside Sch 58 Riverside Dr Princeton NJ 08540

JOHNSON, NEDD JAMES, Guidance Counselor; *b:* Daytona Beach, FL; *m:* Mary Lena Carter; *ed:* (BA) His/Ed, 1982; (MA) Stu Personnel Services, 1989 Glassboro St; *cr:* Soc Stud Teacher A P Schalick HS 1983-88; Guidance Cnslr Pittsgrove Township Schls 1988-; *ai:* Asst Boys Cross Cntry & Track; Frosh Boys Bsktbl; Black Cultural League; Affirmative Action Comm; NJ Ed Assn 1983-; Salem Cty Cnslrs 1988-; NJ Assn of Sch Cnslrs 1988-; King Acad Bd Mem 1984- Mem of Yr 1987; NJ Assn Black Educators 1983-; *office:* Pittsgrove Township Sch RD 1 Box 312 Elmer NJ 08318

JOHNSON, NELDA BURROUGHS, Third Grade Teacher; *b:* Gadsden, AL; *m:* Herman Lee Jr.; *c:* Dwayne, Lisa K. Johnson Isbill; *ed:* (BS) Elem Ed, Jacksonville St Univ 1958; Elem Ed, Univ of AL 1976; *cr:* 4th Grade Teacher C A Donehoo 1958-59; Full Time Substitute Teacher Fort Smith AR 1959-60; 3rd Grade Teacher Ben Milam Elem 1960-61; 4th Grade Teacher Dawnville Elem 1962-69; 5th Grade Teacher Jesup Jr HS & Northside Mid Sch 1969-72; 5th Grade Teacher 1973-76, Chapter 1 Rdng Teacher 1972-, 3rd Grade Teacher 1976- Evans Elem; *ai:* Class Chm; Albertville Classroom Teachers Assn 1972-; AEA, NEA; *home:* 403 Forestdale Ave Albertville AL 35950

JOHNSON, PATRICIA FELKINS, Music Specialist; *b:* Stillwater, OK; *m:* Donald Earl; *c:* Gary D., Stephen W.; *ed:* (BA) Music, OK St Univ 1968; Orff Cert; Numerous Univs; *cr:* Substitute Teacher Denver CO Public Schls 1968-69; K-6th Grade Music Specialist Rosendale Elem 1969-73; 7th/8th Grade Music Specialist Gove Jr HS 1973-74; K-6th Grade Music Specialist Shady Oaks Elem 1974-79, Walter Hall Elem 1979-; *ai:* Hall Elem 5th & 6th Grade Choir; Clear Creek Ind Sch Dist Curr Writer; Hall Elem Sch Climate Comm; Alpha Delta Kappa Pres 1988-; Sigma Alpha Iota VP 1989-; Gulf Coast Orff Secy 1990-92; TX Music Ed Region 19 Chm 1989-; PTA Life Membership, Service Pin; Clear Lake Baptist (Youth Choir Dir, Organist); Outstanding Young Women of America 1972; Accompanist for Clear Creek Theatre; TX St Teachers Assn Music Ed Natl Conference; *office:* Walter Hall Elem Sch 5931 Meadowside Dr League City TX 77573

JOHNSON, PATRICIA TURNER, Social Studies Teacher; *b:* Roscoe, TX; *m:* W. C.; *c:* Deborah Holt, Amelia Mc Owen; *ed:* (BA) Elem Ed, Wayland Baptist Univ 1967; (ME) Elem Ed, TX Tech Univ 1972; *cr:* 3rd Grade Teacher 1967-70, 5th Grade Teacher Hillcrest 1970-75, 6th Grade Teacher Ash 1975-90; *ai:* Assn of TX Prof Educators 1976-; PTA TX Life Membership; Teacher of Week 1989-; Teacher of Month 1973-.

JOHNSON, PATSY JUNE, Fourth Grade Teacher; *b:* Brush, CO; *ed:* (AA) Liberal Arts, Northeastern Jr Coll 1963; (BA) Elem Ed, Univ of N CO 1965; UNC Greeley, CSU Ft Collins, Univ of UT; *cr:* 5th Grade Teacher 1965-67, Kndgtn Teacher 1967-70, 4th Grade Teacher 1970- Buffalo RE4J; *ai:* Jr HS Pep Club Spon 1967-72; Class Plays 1970-; Merino Ed (Pres, VP, Secy-Treas) 1965-; CEA (Delegate 1967, 1975-76, Mem 1965-); NEA (Delegate 1975, Mem 1965-); Delta Kappa Gamma (Pres 1986-88, VP 1984-86, Secy 1982-84, Mem 1976-); United Presbyn Church 1974-; Evangelical Free Church Sunday Sch Teacher 1960-70; Dem Cty (Comm Person 1975-88, Delegate to Cty 1975-); Willarno (Pres, VP, Secy, Mem) 1965-; Friendship (Pres 1976-82, Mem 1970-); Merino Centennial Treas 1972-76; Merino Bicentennial Treas 1976-79; Padroni Conservation Dist Schlsp 1967; Outstanding Young Women of Amer Awd 1967; Performed Cmmty Plays Centennial 1972, BiCentennial 1976, Book Promo 1985; *office:* Merino Elem Sch Box 198 Lee St Merino CO 80741

JOHNSON, PATTI L., Science Instructor; *b:* Devils Lake, ND; *m:* Vern; *c:* Carrie; *ed:* (BSED) Bio/Psych, Univ of ND 1980; Bemidji St Univ; *cr:* Management Aide Grygla Public Sch 1981-82; Sci Instr Goodridge Public Sch 1982-; *ai:* Head Girls Bsktbl & Vlybl Coach 1982-87; Jr, Sr, Yrbk, Stu Cncl Adv; MN Ed Effective Prgm Leadership Team; Schlshp Comm; MN Sci Teachers Assn 1989-; MN Ed Assn 1982-; Kramer Brown Uniserve VP 1985-; MN Women of Today (Dir 1989, Pres 1990) Presidential Medalion 1990; MN Jaycees (ID VP 1989, Secy 1990); Goodridge Teacher of Yr 1988; *office:* Goodridge H S P O Box 195 Goodridge MN 56725

JOHNSON, PAUL DOUGLAS, Electronics Teacher; *b:* Kingsford, MI; *m:* Nancy Shier; *c:* Anna, Jeff, Paul, Don; *ed:* (BS) Industrial Ed, 1966, (MA) Scndry Ed, 1967 N Mi Univ; Grad Stud; *cr:* Grad Asst N MI Univ 1966-67; Teacher Port Huron Northern HS 1967-; *ai:* Voc Industrial Clubs of America Adv; *office:* Port Huron Area Schls 1799 Krafft Rd Port Huron MI 48060

JOHNSON, PAUL EMANUEL, Spanish Teacher; *b:* Seattle, WA; *c:* Melissa, Robert, Heather; *ed:* (BA) Span, Univ of WA 1973; *cr:* Math Teacher Grand Coulee Dam Jr HS 1973-75, Montesano Jr HS 1975-76; Span Teacher Stanwood HS 1976; *ai:* Head Coach Boys & Girls Cross Cntry, Boys Bsktbl, Boys & Girls Track; *office:* Stanwood HS 7400 272nd NW Stanwood WA 98292

JOHNSON, PAULA LARSEN, Third Grade Teacher; *b:* Omaha, NE; *m:* Gary Lynn; *c:* Kevin, Kelli A.; *ed:* (BS) Elem Ed, GA St Univ 1977; Grad Work Univ of NE Omaha; *cr:* Title I Rdng Teacher Irvington Elem 1977-80; 3rd Grade Teacher Minne Lusa Elem 1980-; *office:* Minne Lusa Elem Sch 6905 N 28th Ave Omaha NE 68112

JOHNSON, PAULA LAUER, 2nd Grade Teacher; *b:* Bluffton, IN; *m:* Walter D.; *c:* Jeremiah, Jessica; *ed:* (BS) Elem Ed, Manchester Coll 1973; (MS) Elem Ed, IN Univ 1977; Maintaining Teacher Effectiveness Maas; *cr:* 2nd Grade Teacher Pierceton Elem Sch 1973-74; 2nd/3rd Grade Teacher Lincoln Elem 1974-76; 2nd Grade Teacher S Peru Elem 1976-; *ai:* Sigma Delta Pi 1979-; NEA, IN St Teachers Assn 1973-; *home:* 35 Whippoorwill Dr Peru IN 46970

JOHNSON, PAULA PARKER, 3rd Grade Teacher; *b:* Fairfield, AL; *m:* Jay R.; *c:* Josh; *ed:* (BA) Elem Ed, Univ of AL Birmingham 1975; *cr:* 1st Grade Teacher 1976-81, 2nd/3rd Grade Teacher 1982-85, 3rd Grade Teacher 1985- Pleasant Grove Elem; *ai:* Pleasant Grove Jr HS Chrldrs Spon; AEA 1975-; Bethel Baptist, Pleasant Grove Athletic Assn, Pleasant Grove Soccer Assn; *home:* 1022 12th Ave Pleasant Grove AL 35127

JOHNSON, PEGGY JOHNSON, Third Grade Teacher; *b:* Malvern, AR; *m:* Billy Michael; *ed:* (BSE) Elem Ed, Southern St 1975; Elem Ed, AR St Univ Jonesboro 1977; Elem Ed/Sci, S AR Univ-Tech E Camden 1988; Elem Ed/Ec, Henderson St 1990; *cr:* 4th-6th Rdng/Math Teacher Bradley Elem 1975; Kndgtn Teacher Harrisburg Elem 1975-81; 3rd/4th Grade Teacher First Baptist Sch 1981-84; Individualized Instr AR Baptist Sch 1985; 3rd/5th/6th Grade Teacher Harmony Grove Elem 1986-; *ai:* Camden Pro-Family Advocates Pres 1989-; *office:* Harmony Grove Elem Sch Rt 3 Box 644 Camden AR 71701

JOHNSON, PEGGY SHARON, Kindergarten/1st Grade Teacher; *b:* Banner Elk, NC; *ed:* (BS) Primary, Appalachian St Univ 1964; Lees Mc Rae/MD Tech Coll/Appalachian St Univ; *cr:* Teacher Valmead Elem Sch 1964-66, Elk Park Elem Sch 1966-68; Beech Mountain Elem Sch 1968-; *ai:* Asst with Bsktbll; Senate Bill 2-Steering Comm; Mentor-Support Team; Round Table Rep; Past Comms Textbook/Calendar/NCAE/NEA; Newland Church Chrstn; *home:* P O Box 123 Minneapolis NC 28652

JOHNSON, PHILIP ROY, American History Teacher; *b:* Detroit, MI; *m:* Cornelia Delaney; *c:* John C., William; *ed:* (BA) Ed, Univ of KY 1969; (MS) Ed, Elmira Coll 1988; *cr:* Teacher North Rose 1969-70, Geneva Public Schls 1973-; *ai:* Ftbl Coach; Ski Club Adv; Sch Improvement Team Chairperson; Geneva Teachers Assn Pres 1978-82, 1986-89; NY Ed Assn; Univ Rochester Excl in Scndry Teaching 1986; *home:* 4333 Rt 96A Geneva NY 14456

JOHNSON, PHILLIP LEE, 7th Grade Soc Stud Teacher; *b:* Canton, OH; *m:* Melynda S. Masters; *ed:* (BS) Ed, Kent St 1970; (MSED) Elem Ed, Univ of Akron 1976; *cr:* Dist Exec BSA 1970-72; Teacher Canton City Schls 1972-73, Lake Local Schls 1973-; *ai:* 7th-9th Grade/Var Ftbl, 7th/Var Asst Boys Bsktbl, 8th/Var Girls Bsktbl Coach; Lake Local Ed Assn, OH Ed Assn, NEA 1973-; CYC Girls Bsktbl All Star Coach; *office:* Lake Mid Sch 12001 Market Ave Hartville OH 44632

JOHNSON, RANDY SCOTT, His/Psychology Teacher/Coach; *b:* Norfolk, NE; *m:* La Donna D. Janzen; *c:* Levi, Seth; *ed:* (BS) His, W TX St Univ 1985; *cr:* His Teacher Canyon Jr HS 1986; His/Psych Teacher Dalhart HS 1986-; *ai:* Var Vlybl, Bsktbl, Track Asst Coach; TX Classroom Teachers Assn, Daalhart Classroom Teachers Assn Mem 1986-; TX Assn Bsktbl Coaches, TX Girls Coaches Assn Mem 1988-; *office:* Dalhart HS 1802 E 16th Dalhart TX 79022

JOHNSON, RICHARD LEWIS, Sixth Grade Teacher; *b:* Rockford, IL; *m:* Joan E. Frykman; *c:* Cindi A., Susan E.; *ed:* (BS) His, WI St Platteville Univ 1968; (MS) Educ Admin, Northern IL Univ De Kalb 1978; *cr:* Teacher Kishwaukee Elem 1968-73, Beyer Elem 1974-79, Bloom Elem 1979-; *ai:* Instr Outdoor Dd; Cmptr Instr Rock Valley Coll; NEA 1968-; *home:* 420 29th St Rockford IL 61108

JOHNSON, RICHARD ORLAND, Language Arts Teacher; *b:* Mc Leansboro, IL; *c:* Greg, Tom; *ed:* (BA) Ed/Eng/Music/Speech, E NM Univ 1965; (MA) Comm Ed, Univ of CO DenVer 1974; (PHD) Comm, Univ of CO Boulder 1990; *cr:* Instr Red Rocks Comm Coll 1987-89; Adjunct Faculty Instr Univ of Denver 1989; Teacher/Advanced Placement Coord Lakewood HS 1969-; *ai:* Advanced Placement Coord; NHS & Natl Forensic League Spon; Speech Team Coach; Liason, Accountability Comm; Former Dept Chairperson; Leadership Team Teacher; Past Dist Speech Dir; CO Speech Comm Assn Oral Interpretation/Instructional Leader 1986-; NEA 1965-; Phi Delta Kappa Fnd Dir 1987-89; NCTE; Speech Comm Assn 1969-; Western Sts Comm Assn 1969-; CO Lang Art Society; Choral Dir Various Churches; Various Publications & Presentations to Numerous Organizations; Commencement Speech Presentor Various Occasions; Sch Rep for Teacher of Yr Candidate; *office:* Lakewood HS 9700 W 8th Ave Lakewood CO 80215

JOHNSON, RICK JOE, 6th Grade Teacher; *b:* Woodward, OK; *m:* Joyce Davis; *c:* Brent, Melissa; *ed:* (BS) Elem Ed, NW OK St Univ 1985; *cr:* 6th Grade Teacher Fargo Public Sch 1985-; *ai:* Sr Class Spon; Staff Dev Comm Mem; OK Ed Assn, NEA 1985-; Fargo Teacher of Yr 1989; *home:* 124 NW 2nd Buffalo OK 73834

JOHNSON, ROBERT ARTHUR, Literature & Geography Teacher; *b:* Boston, MA; *m:* Mary Ann Forrest; *ed:* (BA) Poly Sci, Univ of MA Amherst 1972; (MED) Rdng Ed, Fitchburg St Coll 1975; Bridgewater St Coll; *cr:* Sociology Teacher Littleton HS 1974-75; Rdng Teacher Cushing Academy 1975-77; Rockland HS 1977-81; Literature, His & Geography Teacher East Bridgewater Mid Sch 1983-; *ai:* Sch Improvement Cncl; after Sch Bsktbl; East Bridgewater Ed Assn 1983-; MA Teachers Assn 1974-; NEA 1974-; *home:* 68 Maple Ave Hanover MA 02339

JOHNSON, ROBERT BRUCE, Reading/Writing Teacher; *b:* Colorado Springs, CO; *m:* Carol L. Coffey; *c:* Katheryn; *ed:* (BA) Lit, 1972, (MAT) Scndry Teaching, 1979 CO Coll; *cr:* Tutor Rampart Boys Home 1976; Teacher Park Mid Sch 1976-; *ai:* Swim Coach; Stu Cncl Spon; Lang Art Curr Comm; Policy Comm Dist; Estes Park Ed Assn 1976-; Phi Delta Kappa 1988-; Amer Swim Coaches Assn 1984-; Estes Park Masters Coach 1989-; Park Sch Dist Tommy Thompson Teacher of Yr Awd 1984; *office:* Park Mid Sch Box 1140 Estes Park CO 80517

JOHNSON, ROBERT WAYNE, Science/Reading Teacher; *b:* Chicago, IL; *m:* Judy Lyons; *c:* Christine, Lynn; *ed:* (BA) Chem, IA St Univ 1965; (MA) Chem, Univ of Northern IA 1970; *cr:* Sci Teacher Klemul HS 1966-69; Sci Dept Chm Ben Franklin Jr HS 1971-72; Sci Teacher Monroe Jr HS 1972-85; Sci/Rdng Teacher Adams Mid Sch 1985-; *ai:* Girls Ftbl/Bsktbl Coach; Amer Sci Teacher Assn Pres 1982-84, Yungclas Awd 1985; Republican Party Cty Chm 1986-88, Bush Awd 1987; Sci Clubs of America Drobny Trophy; *home:* 3 Fair Meadow Ct Mason City IA 50401

JOHNSON, ROGER, 7th/8th Grade Teacher; *b:* Martin, KY; *m:* Brenda S.; *c:* Matthew Kreigh; *ed:* Phys Ed, Morehead St Univ 1982; *cr:* Phys Ed/Health Teacher Allen Cntrl HS 1977; 7th Grade Teacher Wayland Elem 1978-80; 7th & 8th Grade Teacher Dr W D Osborne Elem 1981-; *ai:* Wheelwright HS Ftbl Coach; *home:* PO Box 31 Bevinsville KY 41606

JOHNSON, RONDA PARKER, English Teacher; *b:* Atlanta, GA; *m:* Robert H. Jr.; *c:* Kevin, Kristi; *ed:* (BSED) Eng, Univ of GA 1972; *cr:* Jr/Sr Eng Teacher 1972-77, Soph Eng Teacher 1985- Calvary Baptist HS; *ai:* Yrbk Spon 1979-77; NHS Spon 1985-; Eng Dept Head; Poetry Society of GA Mem; STAR Teacher Awd 1989; *office:* Calvary Baptist HS 4625 Waters Ave Savannah GA 31404

JOHNSON, ROSAIRE REGINA, 8th Grade Homeroom Teacher; *b:* Montclair, NJ; *ed:* (BA) Ed/Soc Stud, 1978, (MS) Ed/Foundations & Teaching, 1989, (MS) Ed/Sch Cnslr, 1990 Niagara Univ; *cr:* Grad Asst Niagara Univ 1978-80; 6th Grade Teacher 1980-83, 8th Grade Teacher/Vice Prin 1983-84 St Peter Sch; Travel Consultant Niagara Frontier Travel Service 1984-85; 8th Grade Teacher Sacred Heart Sch 1985-; *ai:* 8th Grade Class Trip Moderator; Niagara Univ Learning Partnership Prgm 1989; Girls Bsktbl Coach 1981-89; Girls Asst Sftbl Coach 1982; St Peter Sch Home & Sch Rep 1981-83; Amer Assn For Counseling & Dev, Amer Sch Cnslr Assn 1990; Niagara Frontier Ofcls Assn 1984-86; Amer Sch Cnslr Assn Umpire 1984-86; Cath Girls Bsktbl League Pres 1983-84; *home:* 2210 Woodlawn Ave Niagara Falls NY 14301

JOHNSON, ROSE MARIE STORM, 3rd Grade Teacher/Elem Prin; *b:* St Louis, MO; *w:* Willard R. Jr. (dec); *c:* David, Michael, Stephen, Martha, Susan, Andrew, Sarah; *ed:* (BS) Chem, Fontbonne Coll 1948; Grad Work Memphis St Univ & Union Univ; *cr:* 5th Grade Teacher Polk Cty Schls 1968-69; 2nd/3rd Grade Teacher 1970-88, 3rd Grade Teacher/prin Elem Sch 1988- Rossville Acad; *ai:* Spon GSA & Brownies; Delta Kappa Gamma VP 1990; Literacy Cncl 1987-; MS Private Sch Assn Teacher of Yr Nom 1990; *office:* Rossville Acad 29 High St Rossville TN 38066

JOHNSON, RUTH ANN (TILLEY), Guidance Counselor; *b:* Lebanon, MO; *m:* James Andy; *c:* Jay A., Jana D.; *ed:* (BSED) Bus Ed, SW MO St 1965; (MEED) Guidance/Counseling, Univ of MO 1969; Several Voc Bus Wkshps, SW MO St Univ; *cr:* Elem Phys Ed Teacher Waynesville Sch System 1965-66; Guidance Cnslr/Elem Phys Ed Teacher Plato Sch 1966-71; Bus Teacher Plato HS 1977-89; Guidance Cnslr Strafford HS 1989-; *ai:* Strafford Care & Cmmty Action, Child Study, Career Ladder Comm Assessment Teams; Cmmty Teachers Assn VP 1974-; MO St Teachers Assn 1975-; MO Sch Cnslrs Assn 1989-; Muscular Dystrophy Assn 1978-89, Hall of Fame 1987; Salute Univ of MO Columbia Most Influential Teacher 1989; Voted Teacher of Yr 1987-88; *office:* Strafford HS Mc Cabe St Strafford MO 65757

JOHNSON, RUTH B., English/Great Lit Teacher; *b:* Salt Lake City, UT; *w:* Clyde L. (dec); *c:* Lorie, Leslie J. Weber, Kathy J. Stewart, Carrie J. Bench, Wendy J. Asay, Christy; *ed:* (BA) Eng/His - Magna Cum Laude, Univ of UT 1952; Inservice Ed Classes; Several Wkshps; *cr:* Eng/His Teacher Olympus Jr HS 1952-56; Research & Editorial Consultant 1963-76; Gifted Prgm Teacher Specialist Mt Diablo Sch Dist 1967-69; Eng Teacher Timpview HS 1977-78; Eng/Great Lit Teacher 1978-, Dept Chairperson 1987-88 Dixon Mid Sch; *ai:* Dixon Mid Sch Curr Comm 1989-; Provo Sch Dist Critical Thinking Task Force 1987-88, Scndry Lang Art Comm 1983-87; NEA, UT Ed Assn, Provo Ed Assn; Dixon PTA 1977-, Outstanding Educator 1987-88; Auerbachs Youth Advisory Cncl 1973-76; Phi Kappa Phi; Phi Alpha Theta; Alpha Lambda Delta; Golden Apple Awd; Daughters of Amer Revolution Oratory & Lit Awd; *office:* Dixon Mid Sch 750 W 200 N Provo UT 84601

JOHNSON, RUTH ELAINE, Social Studies Dept Chairman; *b:* Cape Girardeau, MO; *ed:* (BA) His/Sociology, OK City Univ 1973; (MA) His, Univ of Tulsa 1976; *cr:* His Teacher/Dean of Women Moody Chrstn Acad 1976-85; His Teacher Tulsa Chrstn Schls 1985-; *ai:* His Club; His Dept Chm; *office:* Tulsa Chrstn Schls 3434 S Garnett Rd Tulsa OK 74146

JOHNSON, RUTH FLOYD, Social Studies Teacher; *b:* Plateau, AL; *c:* Anthony, Walter, Camille; *ed:* Tuskegee Inst 1951-53; (BS) His, Bowie St Coll 1970; (MEDEQ) Counseling/Personnel Services, Univ of MD 1977; (PHD) Human Services Admin, Univ for Humanistic Stud 1982; *cr:* Numerous Posts Federal Government; Radio Personality WMOZ; Owner/Dir Azalea Sch of Dance; Teacher/Admin PublicSchls of Prince Georges Cty; Teaching Counselor Dunbar STAY Sch; Instr Univ of MD Child & Youth Study Div; Teacher Los Angeles Unified Sch Dist; Chief Exec Officer Diametron Corp; Teacher Pasadena Unified Sch Dist, Rialto Unified Sch Dist; *ai:* Adv Eisenhower HS Pep Squads Coach; Eisenhower HS Decathalon Team Mem; Eisenhower Cncl; Zeta Phi Beta, Gamma Phi Delta, Natl Assn of Univ Women, Natl Cncl of Negro Women, NEA, CA Cncl for Soc Stud; Held Offices in Several PTAS; Local, St, Natl Delegate to PTA Congresses 1965-77; Mem Organizing Comm; Peppermill Village Civic Assn 1966; Volunteer BSA 1968-72; Volunteer Sr Citizen 1974-76; Mem Bd of Dir Mill Point Improvement Assn 1975-78; Mem Bdof Dirs Combined Cmmtys in Action 1976-78; Nom for Bd Mem Prince Georges Cty Public Schls 1977; Appointed Commissioner Prince Georges Cty Hospital Commission 1978; Outstanding Service to Children & Youth MD Congress PTA 1969; Services to BSA 1969; Services to Sr Citizens 1975; Personalities of W & Midwest 1978; Sixth Edition Dictionary of Intnl Biography 1980 Vol 16; Zeta Service Awd 1980; Zeta of Yr 1981; NCNW Cmmty Service Awd 1981; Facets of CA Finest 1983; Nom Gamma Far W Region Woman of Yr 1984; Co-Author Government/Contemporary Issues a Curr Guid 1976; Author Redediating Mass Poverty Dev of a Model Prgm 1982; Currently in Process of Writing Novel; Currently Writes Bi-Monthly Column for Westside Story Newspaper, San Bernardino, CA; *home:* PO Box 1946 Rialto CA 92377

JOHNSON, RUTH REBECCA SEABORN, Fourth Grade Teacher; *b:* Ozona, TX; *m:* Cecil Jr.; *c:* Seth P., Reed H.; *ed:* (BA) Elem Ed, 1976, (MS) Ed/Guidance/Counseling, 1982 Angelo St Univ; *cr:* 4th-5th Grade Teacher 1976-86, 4th Grade Teacher 1986- Veribest Ind Sch Dist; *ai:* Effective Schls Comm; TX Classroom Teachers Assn 1986-; *home:* 122 N Bishop San Angelo TX 76901

JOHNSON, SADIE ROBINSON, 2nd Grade Teacher; *b:* Montgomery, AL; *m:* Wade; *c:* Lolita; *ed:* (BS) Elem Ed, AL St Univ 1963; Supervision & Admin; *cr:* 3rd Grade Teacher Masses Mill Elem Sch 1964-65, Fleetwood Elem Sch 1965-66; 3rd/5th Grade Teacher 1971-78, 2nd Grade Teacher 1978- Our Lady of Lourdes Sch; *ai:* New Covenant Missionay Baptist Church Cnslr, Choir Mem, Sunday Sch Teacher; Cmptr Coord; NCEA Mem; Priscilla Circle Bible Teacher 1984-; Cath Television Network of Chgo Coord 1980-89; Eastern Star Chapter 611 1963-; Teacher of Month Awd Oct 1988; *home:* 1136 E 82nd Pl Chicago IL 60619

JOHNSON, SANDRA B., Social Studies Chair; *b:* Norman, OK; *m:* Dale C.; *c:* Kresta Bowman, Kerry V.; *ed:* (BS) Elem Ed, Soc Stud, OK St 1961; Grad Stud OK St; *cr:* 4th Grade Teacher Sapulpa Public Schls 1961-69; 6th Grade Teacher 1969-70, 7th Grade Teacher 1970-83, 8th Grade Teacher 1983- Owasso Public Schls; *ai:* Jr HS Stu Cncl Spon; Drug Ed Needs Assessment Cncl; Jr HS Career Planning Comm; Jr HS Soc Stud Dept Chairperson; NEA, OEA Dist Rep 1966-67; Owasso Ed Assn (Secy 1967-69, VP 1970-71); OK Cncl Soc Stud; Kappa Kappa Iota (Secy, VP, Pres) 1966-69; Rotary Anns; Historical Society; Chamber of Commerce; ESA-Philanthropicc (Secy, VP) 1975-80; Young People Trainer; Comm Adv; Sch Cmmty Red Ribbon Drug Cncl; Drug Grant Prgm Dev Comm.

JOHNSON, SHARON DENTON, French & Spanish Teacher; *b:* Pensacola, FL; *m:* Robert J.; *c:* Casey, Leigh; *ed:* (BA) Fr, Lake Forest Coll 1969; (MA) Fr, WA Univ 1971; *cr:* Fr/Span Teacher Cowing Jr HS 1974-77; Fr Teacher St Annes 1984, John Battle HS 1985-89; Fr/Span Teacher Virginia Jr/Sr HS 1989-; *ai:* Span Club Adv; Holston Lang Assn; Phi Beta Kappa 1969; *office:* Virginia Jr/Sr HS 501 Piedmont Bristol VA 24201

JOHNSON, STANLEY EUGENE, 9th Grade Phys Science Teacher; *b:* Jerome, ID; *m:* Kenna Gaye Ellis; *c:* Benjamin, Courtney, Hannah; *ed:* (BSE) General Sci/Bio, AR St Univ 1985; *cr:* 9th Grade Teacher Mountain Home Jr HS 1985-; *ai:* Church of Christ Deacon 1988-; *office:* Mountain Home Jr HS Rodeo Dr Mountain Home AR 72653

JOHNSON, STANLEY FRANCIS, ESL Span Teacher/Frn Lang Chm; *b:* Columbus, OH; *ed:* (BA) Poly Sci 1979; (BS) Ed-His, 1980 OH St Univ; *cr:* Recreation Leader Cols Recreation & Parks 1975-80; Teacher DCPS 1980-; *ai:* Fundraising Chair; Keyperson DC One Fund; Dance Team Spon; Fellowship-Georgetown Univ 1984-85; *office:* Abraham Lincoln Jr HS 16th & Irving St N W Washington DC 20010

JOHNSON, STEVE, English Teacher; *b:* Cloquet, MN; *ed:* (BA) Eng, 1971, (MA) Rdng, 1979 George Mason Univ; *cr:* Eng Teacher Bishop Denis J O Connell HS 1972-; *ai:* Forensics, Sr Class, Summer Sch Prgm Moderator; Prins Advisory Comm Mem; VA Assn Teachers of Eng, NCEA 1980-; NCTE 1981-86; *office:* Bishop Denis J O Connell Sch 6600 Little Falls Rd Arlington VA 22213

JOHNSON, SUSAN ANDERSON, Behavior Learning Teacher; *b:* Minneapolis, MN; *m:* Royce R.; *c:* Dana, Nicholas; *ed:* (BA) Elem Ed, Coll of St Benedict 1976; (MS) Elem Ed, Univ of MN Duluth 1988; Educl & Behavioral Disorders Licensure St Cloud St Univ; *cr:* 4th Grade Teacher St Peter & Paul Sch 1976-78; 6th Grade Teacher Edgewood Elem 1978-79; 4th Grade Teacher 1979-89, Behavior Learning Center Teacher 1989- Sandstone Elem; *ai:* Sandstone Fed of Teachers Secy 1985-.

JOHNSON, SUSAN RYKERT, Science Teacher; *b:* Vallejo, CA; *m:* Rod; *c:* Julia Koester, Andrew, Laura; *ed:* (BA) Math/Sci, Stanislaus St Univ 1963; *cr:* 4th/6th Grade Teacher Orange Unified Sch Dist 1963-67; 1st/3rd Grade Teacher John Muir 1975-83; 7th/8th Grade Teacher La Loma Jr HS 1984-; *ai:* Curr Comm for Sci; CTA; NEA; *office:* Laloma Jr H S 1800 Encina Ave Modesto CA 95354

JOHNSON, TERRI BERNHARDT, Mathematics Dept Chairperson; *b:* Binghamton, NY; *m:* Philip C.; *c:* Gretchen, Matthew; *ed:* (BS) Math Ed, SUNY Brockport 1969; (MS) Math Ed, SUNY Cortland 1972; Grad Stud SUNY Binghamton; *cr:* Teacher Chenango Forks Cntrl Sch 1968-70, Voorheesville Cntrl Schls 1970-72, Vestal Cntrl Schls 1972-; *ai:* NCTM, AMTNYS, NY Ed Assn, NEA; *office:* Vestal Cntrl Schls Main St Vestal NY 13850

JOHNSON, TERRY GRANT, 7th Grade Soc Stud Teacher; *b:* Hattiewburg, MS; *ed:* (BS) Soc Stud, Univ of Southern MS 1979; *cr:* HS/Jr HS Soc Stud Teacher Oak Grove Mid Sch & HS 1981-; *ai:* Asst Spon Fellowship Chrstn Athletes; NEA 1982-; MS Assn of

Educators 1982-; Purvis Masonic Lodge #434 Mem 1980-Worshipful Master 1985; Purvis Lions Club VP 1988-; Purvis First Baptist Church Deacon 1985-; *home:* PO Box 186 Purvis MS 39475

JOHNSON, THOMAS ERNEST, 7th Grade Life Sci Teacher; *b:* Portsmouth, VA; *m:* Barbara K. Duck; *c:* Jennifer; *ed:* (AS) Teacher Ed, Tidewater Comm Coll 1970; (BS) Ed/Bio, E TN St Univ 1973; (MSED) Scndry Ed/Bio, Old Dominion Univ 1985; *cr:* Life Sci Teacher Western Branch Jr HS 1973-; *ai:* Stu Cooperative Assn; Wrestling Coach; Natl Jr Honor Society, Bruin Adv Comm, Marshalls, Sci Club Spon; Mid Sch, Curr & Textbook Comms; Gifted & Talented Instr; Chesapeake Ed Assn, VA Ed Assn, NEA 1973-; NSTA 1984-; PTA 1973-, Lifetime Mem 1978; Western Branch Athletic Club 1975-80; Western Branch Jr HS Teacher of Yr 1982; *office:* Western Branch Jr HS 4201 Hawksley Dr Chesapeake VA 23321

JOHNSON, THOMAS WILLIAM, Mathematics Teacher-Dept Chm; *b:* Ottumwa, IA; *m:* Sandra Kay Swanson; *c:* Eric Reed, Brian; *ed:* (AA) Math, Centerville Comm Coll 1968; (BA) Math, Parsons Coll 1971; (MA) Math, Northeast MO St Univ 1987; *cr:* 8th-12th Grade Math Teacher Fremont Cmmty Schls 1972-77; 9th Grade Math Teacher Oskaloosa Cmmty Schls 1978-; *ai:* 7th/8th Grade Wrestling Coach; 9th Grade Math Team Coach; NCTM, IA Cncl Teachers of Math 1986-; Amer Legion 1975-; *home:* RR 3 Box 126 A Oskaloosa IA 52577

JOHNSON, TOMIE L., Business Teacher; *b:* Golden, TX; *c:* Craig, Clint; *ed:* (BS) Bus Ed, E TX St Univ 1959; Ec & Finance Wkshp E TX St Univ; Cmptr Trng Tyler Jr Coll; *cr:* Bus Teacher Quitman HS 1965-; *ai:* UIL Typing & Shorthand Coach 1989-; Delta Kappa Gamma Treas 1978-79, TBEA 1988-89, Quitman Classroom Teachers Assn; *home:* Box 205 Quitman TX 75783

JOHNSON, VALERIE K., Biology/Physiology Teacher; *b:* Toledo, OH; *m:* William C.; *ed:* (BS) Bio, Hillsdale Coll 1980; *cr:* Bio/Honors Bio/Physiology Teacher Anthony Wayne HS 1981-; *ai:* Stu Cncl Adv; NSTA, OH Ed Assn 1981-; *office:* Anthony Wayne HS 5967 Finzel Rd Whitehouse OH 43571

JOHNSON, VERTA NORRIS, First Grade Teacher; *b:* Albany, KY; *m:* Aubrey; *c:* Rodney; *ed:* (BA) Elem Ed, Union Coll 1952; (MS) Elem Ed, W KY Univ 1962; *cr:* Teacher Jamestown Elem 1952-70, Union Chapel Elem 1971-74, Jamestown Elem 1975-; *ai:* Russell Cty Teachers Organization VP 1972-73; KY Ed Assn, NEA; Jamestown PTO, Russell Cty Athletic Booster Club, Jamestown Meth Church Mem; Outstanding Service Awd for Excl in Teaching Campbellsville Coll; *home:* RR 2 Box 217 Jamestown KY 42629

JOHNSON, WALTER BRUCE, Spanish Teacher; *b:* Wadsworth, OH; *m:* Alma E. Miller; *c:* James D., Naomi R., Debra M., Timothy A.; *ed:* (AB) Eng/Bible/Missions, Gods Bible Sch & Coll 1975; (MED) Curr/Instruction, Univ of Cincinnati 1976; Span Lang Trng, Santa Cruz Inst 1980-81; *cr:* Prin Union Bible Seminary Acad 1978-80; Dir Friends Bible Inst 1982-86, St Pauls Seminary 1985-86; Pres Carolina Chrstn Acad & Coll 1986-88; Span Teacher N Davidson Sr HS 1988-; *ai:* NC Foreign Lang Assn Mem 1988-; Amer Teachers Foreign Lang Conference Mem 1989-; *office:* N Davidson Sr HS Rt 10 Box 1685 Lexington NC 27292

JOHNSON, WANDA ANDREWS, Math Dept/Computer Teacher; *b:* Coy, AL; *m:* Carlton S. Sr.; *c:* Candace C. Russell, Carlton S. Jr.; *ed:* (AA) Cmptr Sci, Pensacola Jr Coll 1977; (BS) System Sci, Univ of W FL 1979; *cr:* Cmptr/Math Teacher St Jude HS 1987-; *ai:* Operate Math Dept Bookstore; *home:* 847 Corbett St Montgomery AL 36108

JOHNSON, WANDA FAE, Remedial Reading Teacher; *b:* Bulan, KY; *M:* Patrick; *c:* Regina C., Patrick D.; *ed:* (BS) Bus Ed, Eastern KY Univ 1968; (MA) Elem Ed, Univ of Cincinnati 1978; *cr:* Elem Teacher Grants Lick Elem 1964-65; AD Owens Elem 1966-69; Scndry Teacher Newport HS 1969-70; Elem Teacher 1971-85; Remedial Rdng 1985- AD Owens Elem; *ai:* Sch Calendar Comm; Sch Newspaper Comm; Delta Kappa Gamma Finance Comm 1987-; Intl Rdng Assn 1986-; Newport Teachers Assn Pres 1982-83; Academic Schlsp; Lifetime Membership AD Owens PTA; Helped Structuring Rank I Prgm Northern KY Univ; Nom KY Teacher of Yr 1981; *home:* 750 Dry Creek Ct Villa Hills KY 41017

JOHNSON, WAYNE KEITH, HS Biology Teacher; *b:* Palestine, IL; *m:* Karen Twigg; *c:* Kimberly, Kyle; *ed:* (BS) Zoology, E IL Univ 1974; *cr:* 6th-8th Grade Sci Teacher Green Valley Grade Sch 1974-84; Bio Teacher Robinson HS 1985-; *ai:* Girls HS Bsktbl & Track Coach; IL Ed Assn, NEA; *office:* Cmmty Unit #2 2000 N Cross Robinson IL 62454

JOHNSON, WILLIAM RICHARD, English/Social Studies Teacher; *b:* Warren, OH; *m:* Patricia Poponak; *c:* Meghan, Zachary; *ed:* (BA) Eng, Univ of N CO 1981; (MA) Eng, Case Western Reserve Univ 1987; *cr:* Teacher Univ Sch 1984-; *ai:* Cmmty Service Comm; Davey Fellows Tutor; Head Track Coach; Literary Magazine Spon; NCTE; Native Seeds 1987-89; Poets League of Greater Cleveland 1987-; Poetry & Criticism Published; *office:* Univ Sch 20701 Brantley Rd Shaker Heights OH 44122

JOHNSON, WINNIE SCOTT, 7th Grade Mathematics Teacher; *b:* Adel, GA; *m:* Eddie L.; *ed:* (BA) Music, Fort Valley St 1951; (MA) Math, GA St Univ 1980; Fr, Atlanta Univ; Music, Cath Univ; Math Curr Wkshp, MI St Univ; *cr:* Music Teacher Elm Street HS 1951-55; 6th Grade Teacher E Rivers Elem 1955-60; 6th/7th Grade Math Teacher Sutton Mid Sch 1960-; *ai:* Math & Cmptr Project Emory Univ; NEA, GAE, AAE 1951-; NAACP 1960-; March of Dimes 1965-; AUCC 1976-; Andover-Dartmouth Math Teachers Inst; MCTM Prof Dev Wkshp; Sutton Mid Sch Teacher of Yr 1986; *home:* 7275 Roswell Rd NE 498-19 Atlanta GA 30328

JOHNSON, YVONNE A., 5th Grade Teacher; *b:* De Kalb, IL; *ed:* (BSED) Home Ec, N IL St Teachers 1951; (MSED) Elem Ed, N IL Univ 1960; Various Univ; *cr:* 1st-8th Grade Teacher Love 1951-53; 6th Grade Teacher 1953-55, 5th Grade Teacher 1955-Sycamore C Unified Sch Dist; *ai:* Faculty Adv; ISTA, ASCD, SEA, NSTA, IEA, CESI; NEA Life Mem; Sycamore Public Lib Bd Pres 1984-; First Luth Church Cncl/Congregational Secy 1974-79; Sycamore BPW Pres; NSF Grants 1961-62, 1985-87; IL Honors Sci Teacher; Conservation Teacher De Kalb Cty; NEWEST 1988, 1990; *office:* Sycamore C Unified Sch Dist W 240 Fair St Sycamore IL 60178

JOHNSON-LOWE, DELORES KATHLEEN, Home Ec Teacher; *b:* Berea, KY; *m:* Thirston; *c:* Michael Johnson, Mark Johnson; *ed:* (BS) Home Ec, KY St Coll 1955; (MS) Home Ec Clothing, Wayne St Univ 1962; *cr:* Teacher Campbellsville KY Hs 1954-55, Boysville 1980-82, Pelham Mid Sch 1956-; *ai:* Spon/Dir Fashion Shows in CmmtY Centers & Churches; Delta Sigma Theta 1948; Natl Assn for Colored People; Marian Park Block Club; *office:* Pelham Mid Sch 2001 M L King Blvd Detroit MI 48208

JOHNSON-RUSSELL, JANE MARGARET, Spanish Teacher/Dept Chairman; *b:* Fort Worth, TX; *m:* Frank; *c:* Larry, Jeff, Stacy; *ed:* (AA) Liberal Stud, Fresno City Coll 1978; (BA) Span, CA ST Univ 1979; *cr:* Personnel Technician ST of CA/ Corrections & Health Svcs 1972-77; Admin Asst ST of CA/ Health Service Dept 1977-79; Span/Eng Teacher Merced HS 1981-86; Foreign Lang Dept Head Span I/III/IV Teacher Atwater HS 1986-; *ai:* CA Teachers Assn 1985-; Dist Teachers Assn 1985-; Merced Track Club 1977- Runner of Yr 1983-84; Teacher of Month Atwater HS 1986; *office:* Atwater HS 2201 Fruitland Ave Atwater CA 95301

JOHNSTN, BRION D., Band Director; *b:* St Louis, MO; *m:* Lisa Charlene; *ed:* (BA) Instrumental Music, AZ St Univ 1979; Grad Stud Ed Amin, E NM Univ: *cr:* Band Dir Los Lunas Mid Sch/ Daniel Fernandez Mid-Elem Sch 1979-87, Portales Schls 1988-; *ai:* Leadership Comm Portales Jr Hs; Portales HS Asst Band Dir; Music Educators Natl Conference, NM Music Educators Assn 1979-; Phi Beta Mu, Amer Sch Band Dirs Assn 1986-.

JOHNSTON, ARNOLD WAYNE, Mathematics Dept Chair/ Teacher; *b:* Palestine, TX; *m:* Nanette Arnold; *c:* Donna J. Chaffin, Joanne J. Moore, Russell; *ed:* (BS) Math/Chem, Stephen F Austin St Univ 1961; NSF Summer Inst in Modern Algebra, SFASU 1968; NSF Summer Inst in Astronomy, SHSU 1970; *cr:* Chemist Signal Oil Company 1961-63; Math/Sci Teacher Westwood HS 1963-66; Math Teacher Palestine HS 1966-; *ai:* Number Sense Mental Math Spon; Faculty Advisory & NHS Selection Comms; TX Classroom Teachers Assn 1990; PTA Schlsp 1967; Slocum Baptist Church Deacon 1980-; MENSA 1987-; GTE Gift Fellow 1986-87; Teacher of Month 1984; TX Teachers Career Ladder Level III 1987; *office:* Palestine HS Loop 256 E Palestine TX 75801

JOHNSTON, BARBARA DESSLER, Substitute Teacher; *b:* Sewickley, PA; *m:* Dwight; *c:* Dwight, Erica, Joseph; *ed:* (BS) Elem Ed, 1970, (MED) Elem Ed, 1974 PA St Univ; *cr:* Elem Teacher Juniata Cty Sch Dist 1970-89; Substitute Teacher York Suburban-Red Lion-Dallastown 1990; *home:* 345 Pulaski Pl Dallastown PA 17313

JOHNSTON, CATHERIE BYRD, 8th Grade Science Teacher; *b:* Vander, NC; *m:* Robert W.; *c:* Robert Jr., Reginald, Lynn B., Katrina; *ed:* (BS) Elem Ed, Fayetteville St Univ 1965; (ME) Math, Coll of Notre Dame 1972; Math, Sci, Government, Poly His; *cr:* 7th Grade Teacher E A Armstrong 1965-66; 6th Grade Teacher VA St Sch 1966-67; 5th Grade Teacher Mannheim Amer Elem Sch 1968-72, Churchville Elem Sch 1972-75, El Paso Schls 1975-79; 8th/9th Grade Teacher Reid Ross Jr HS 1980-; *ai:* Dir of Sci Club; Stu Cncl Adv; Writing Consultant ACES Fayetteville St Univ; NC Teachers of Math 1981-; NC Sci Teachers Assn 1984-; NEA 1970- Life-Time Membership; NC Ed Assn 1980-; Mt Olive Hospitality VP 1988-89; Field Enterprises Mem 1973-74 Top Achievement 1974; Mt Olive Ed Dept Mem 1988-; Fayetteville Tech Comm Coll Staff Mem; Robert A Taft Fellowship; Math Grant; Whos Who Among Stu in Amer Coll & Univ; NC Writing Fellowship; *office:* Reid Ross Jr HS 3200 Ramsey St Fayetteville NC 28302

JOHNSTON, CHERYL CURRY, Mathematics Teacher; *b:* Portsmouth, VA; *m:* David T.; *c:* Sarah, Eric; *ed:* (BSED) Math, 1977, (MS) Math, 1981 N AZ Univ; Cmptr Sci Certificate AZ Western Coll; *cr:* Sci Teacher Shadow Mountain HS 1978; Math Teacher Yuma HS 1978-88, Cibola HS 1988-; *ai:* Academic Decathlon Math Coach; AZ St Math Contest Admin Cibola HS Coord; CTA Negotiations Team Mem; Effective Schls Comm Chairperson; NCTM, AZ Assn Teachers of Math 1980-; NEA, AZ Ed Assn 1978-; AZ Classroom Teachers Assn Secy 1978-; Pride of Yuma Awd Outstanding Service Yuma Union HS Dist 1989; Nom Cibola HS Teacher of Yr 1990; *office:* Cibola HS 4100 W 20th St Yuma AZ 85364

JOHNSTON, CYNTHIA FAITH, Fourth Grade Teacher; *b:* Willard, OH; *ed:* (BS) Elem Ed, Bowling Green St Univ 1976; *cr:* 4th Grade Teacher Nankin Elem 1976-86, Polk Elem 1986-; *ai:* Mapleton Teacher Assn, NEA, OEA 1976-; Omega Phi Alpha 1976-; *office:* Polk Elem Sch E Congress St Polk OH 44866

JOHNSTON, DARRELL L., Physical Ed/AL History Teacher; *b:* Tallassee, AL; *m:* Jeri Maria Fowler; *ed:* (BSED) Phys Ed, Troy St Univ 1973; (MS) Jacksonville St Univ 1989; *cr:* Teacher/Coach Liberty Cty HS 1973-75, Lincoln HS 1975-76, Notasulga HS 1976-77, AL Sch for Deaf 1977-79, Lincoln HS 1979-; *ai:* Ftbl, Bsktbl, Track Coach; AEA, NEA 1975-; AAHPERD; PTA 1975-; Cty Track Coach of Yr 1978-79, 1989; *office:* Lincoln HS P O Box 197 Lincoln AL 35096

JOHNSTON, DEBORAH ROPER, 4th Grade Teacher; *b:* Rome, GA; *m:* Richard D.; *ed:* (BA) Elem Ed, Shorter Coll 1972; (MED) Elem Ed, Berry Coll 1974; *cr:* 1st Grade Teacher Krannert Elem 1972-75; Educl Therapist NW GA Evaluation & Service Ctr 1975; 5th/6th Grade Teacher Midway Elem 1976-79; 1st/4th/5th Grade Teacher Johnson Elem 1979-; *ai:* Stu Support Team Chairperson; Bus Ed Partnership Rep; FCAE Rep; Floyd Cty Assn of Ed 1972-89; GA Assn of Ed 1972-89; Natl Assn of Ed 1972-89; *office:* Johson Elem Sch 1910 Morrison Campground Rd NE Rome GA 30161

JOHNSTON, DORIS CLARK, Language Art Teacher; *b:* Wynnewood, OK; *m:* Allen Franklin; *c:* Laura A., Jay A., Roy D.; *ed:* (BAED) Eng Ed, 1970, (MA) Eng, 1985 East Cntrl St Univ; ACT Trainer Wkshp OK St Univ; March of Dimes Parenting, Planned Parenthood, DARE to Be You Seminar Presenter; *cr:* 10th/11th Grade Eng Teacher Henryetta HS 1970-72; 5th-8th Grade Remedial Ed Teacher Bearden Elem Sch 1972-73; Lang Art/Rdng Teacher Okemah Noble Mid Sch 1973, 1982-; *ai:* Teen Pregnancy Prevention Prgm Presenter; Supervising Teacher; Staff Dev Comm Mem; Teacher Advisory Comm Secy; Okemah Sch ACT Trainer/AIDS Prevention Educator; Okemah Ed Assn Secy 1973, 1982-, Teacher of Yr 1988-89; Okfuskee Cty Ed Assn 1972-73, 1982-; OK Ed Assn (Youth at Risk Cadre Mem 1970-73, 1982-, AIDS Prevention Trainee, Teen Pregnancy Prevention Educator); Okemah Extension Homemakers (Pres, Secy) 1974-, Homemaker of Yr 1980; Okfuskee Cty Historical Society Charter Mem; OK Extension Homemakers St Membership Comm Chm 1982-83, Great Amer Family 1985; Teacher of Yr 1988-89.

JOHNSTON, ELIZABETH J., Home Economics Teacher; *b:* Benonia, MS; *m:* Steve A.; *c:* Deanna L., Lacinda J., Stephane R.; *ed:* (BSE) Home Ec, Univ of Cntrl AR 1965; Grad Stud; *cr:* Home Ec Teacher Lepanto Public Schls 1965-66, Little Rock Public Schls 1966-69, Cooperative Extension Service 1969-74; 3rd Grade Teacher Snowlake Public Schls 1978-79; Home Ec Teacher Marland Public Schls 1980-89, Frontier Public Schls 1989-; *ai:* NHS; Academic Team Coach; NEA, OK Ed Assn, Frontier Ed Assn; Teacher of Yr 1983; Staff Dev Chm 1983-85; *home:* 1604 NE Woodland Ponca City OK 74604

JOHNSTON, F. JOAN STEWART, 7th Grade English/Art Teacher; *b:* Malad, ID; *c:* Ellen E. J. Gwynn, Ann Stewart; *ed:* (BS) Art/Interior Decorating/Eng, UT St Univ 1951; Teaching Cert Scndry Ed, Brigham Young Univ 1962; Various Courses & Wkshps; *cr:* Interior Decorator Jeffs & Jones Company 1951-53; Asst Claim Mgr Spec Agents Mutual Benefit Assn 1953-57; Asst Auditor Sears Roebuck & Company 1960-61; Scndry Teacher Bountiful Jr HS 1962-; *ai:* 7th Grade Class Adv; Chm Art Advertising & Soc Comm; Textbook Selection Comm; UT Art Ed Assn St Secy 1982-84; Delta Kappa Gamma (Corresponding Secy 1984-86, Chapter Pres 1982-84); Davis Ed Assn Sch Rep; UT Ed Assn, NEA 1962-; Republican Dist (Chm 1985-87, Asst Chm 1988-); Daughters of Amer Revolution Society 1989-; Sch Joint Study Staff Comm & Spring Festival Asst Chairperson; *home:* 1853 S Jeri Dr Bountiful UT 84010

JOHNSTON, JERI BOULWARE, Speech Department Chairperson; *b:* Wichita Falls, TX; *m:* Robert Wilson; *c:* Robert, Brent; *ed:* (BA) Speech/Drama, TX Wesleyan Univ 1967; Theater, E TX St Univ 1986; *cr:* Eng Teacher T C Williams HS 1967-68; Speech/Theater Teacher Richardson Jr HS 1982-87; Speech/Debate Teacher/Speech Dept Chairperson Berkner HS 1987-; *ai:* Berkner Speech Club, Natl Forensic League, KRAM Announcers Spon; Speech Tournament Squad & Debate Team Coach; TX Forensic Assn 1983-; Natl Forensic League 1989-; Dallas Childrens Theater (Bd of Trustees 1985-88, Bd of Advs 1988-); *office:* Berkner HS 1600 E Spring Valley Rd Richardson TX 75081

JOHNSTON, JOHNNY BEN, Social Studies Chairman; *b:* Oklahoma City, OK; *m:* Joann Robbins; *c:* Paul; *ed:* (AA) Soc Stud, Oscar Rose 1972; (BA) Soc Stud, Cntrl St Univ 1975; (MS) Scndry Admin, Fort Hays St Univ 1989; *cr:* Teacher/Coach Wichita Cty Jr HS 1975-; *ai:* Jr HS Ftbl Coach; Jr Wrestling Coach; Jr Track Coach; NFICA Mem 1975-; *office:* Wichita Cty Jr HS PO Drawer 908 Leoti KS 67861

JOHNSTON, JULIE ANN, Mathematics Teacher; *b:* Minneapolis, MN; *ed:* (BA) Math, SW St Univ MN 1973; (MED) Math, Univ of MN 1981; PhD Candidate Univ of NM; *cr:* Teacher/Coach Chippewa Mid Sch 1973-82, Los Alamos Mid Sch 1982-; *ai:* NM Athletic Assn Vlybl Ofcl; NM Mathcounts Team Coach for Natls 1985, 1986, 1988; NM Cncl Teacher of Math VP 1989-; ASCD 1988-; Math Publications; Los Alamos Natl Laboratory Affiliate; Presidential Awd Excl in Math/Sci Ed St Level Awardee 1988, 1989; *office:* Los Alamos Mid Sch 2101 Cumbres Dr Los Alamos NM 87544

JOHNSTON, MARSHA GREGG, Second Grade Teacher; *b:* Borger, TX; *m:* Billy Joe; *c:* Jeff, Jarrett; *ed:* (BS) Elem Ed/Eng, Frank Phillips Jr Coll; (BS) Elem Ed, W TX St Univ 1970; Kndgtn Endorsement Early Chldhd, E TX St Univ 1975; *cr:* 1st

Grade Teacher 1970-73, Kndgtn Teacher 1973-75 H P Webb Elem; 2nd Grade Teacher Fritch Elem 1978-80, Cntrl Elem 1980-81, Gateway Elem 1981-; *ai:* Grade Level Chairperson; Friday Night Prime Time Coord; TX St Teachers Assn 1970-; TX Classroom Teachers Assn (Faculty Building Rep 1990) 1970-; Delta Kappa Gamma 1988-; Beta Sigma Phi Treas 1977-79; Math Book Adv & Reviewer; *office:* Gateway Elem Sch 1403 Sterling Borger TX 79007

JOHNSTON, MARY H., English Teacher; *b:* Ogden, UT; *m:* Greg; *c:* Brian, Michael, Stuart, Jennifer; *ed:* (BS) Eng, Weber St Coll 1985; Pursuing Masters Ed & Admin; *cr:* Eng Teacher Sand Ridge Jr HS 1985-89, Bonneville HS 1989-; *ai:* Chrldr & Drill Team Adv; Drama Teacher; Dept Head; UEA; WEA Rep 1987-88; BSA Cncl Rep 1984-85; Weber St Alliance Prgm Co-Dir; *office:* Bonneville HS 251 E Laker Way Ogden UT 84405

JOHNSTON, MILDRED SCHRIMSHER, Kindergarten Teacher; *b:* Athens, AL; *m:* Thomas Sidney; *c:* Nancy C., Susan Sidney, Albert Sidney; *ed:* (BA) Elem Ed, Athens St Coll 1957; (MA) Early Chldhd, Al A&M 1980; Post Grad Work Early Chldhd Athens St Coll 1975; Grant GA St Early Chldhd Curr; *cr:* 2nd Grade Teacher Athens Elem Sch 1958-60; Kndgtn Teacher Cowart Elem Sch 1975-; *ai:* Supts Forum; AL Ed Assn 1975-; NEA 1975-; Athens Readiness Center Bd Mem 1986-; Athena League Assn Mem 1971-80; Nom James L Cowart Teacher of Yr 1990; *office:* James L Cowart Elem Sch 1701 W Hobbs Athens AL 35611

JOHNSTON, PAMELA WARNER, English Teacher; *b:* Salina, KS; *m:* Steven Douglas; *c:* Shannon D., Steven D. Jr., Mattthew D.; *ed:* (BA) Eng Ed, Bethany Coll 1971; Various Univ; *cr:* Eng Teacher Manhattan HS 1980-81; Highland HS 1981-85; Landon Mid Sch 1985-86; French Mid Sch 1986-; *ai:* Overbrook Lib Bd 1990; *office:* French Mid Sch 5257 W 33rd Topeka KS 66614

JOHNSTON, SANDI RAE, Assistant Principal; *b:* Springboro, PA; *ed:* (BS) General Sci, 1975, (MS) Sch Admin, 1981 Edinboro Univ; *cr:* Teacher 1977-, Asst Prin 1990 Northwestern Sch Dist; *ai:* Phi Delta Kappa 1989; Northwestern Ed Assn Membership 1987-; Springboro Boro Cncl Councilman 1986-89; *office:* Northwestern Sr HS 1 Harthan Way Albion PA 16401

JOHNSTON, SHELIA POWELL, Special Education Teacher; *b:* Haleyville, AL; *m:* Mac Anthony; *c:* Sara, Tara, Olivia; *ed:* (BA) Spec Ed, Univ of N AL 1979; *cr:* Spec Ed Phillips Elem Sch 1979-81, Brilliant HS 1983-; *ai:* Textbook Comm; NEA, AL Ed Assn 1983-; PTO 1983-.

JOHNSTON, STAN W., English Teacher; *b:* Los Alamos, NM; *m:* Pamela S. Herron; *c:* Bradley S.; *ed:* (BS) Eng Ed, ENMU 1972; *cr:* Eng Teacher Eunice Municipal Schls 1972-73; Eng/Drama Teacher Los Alamos Public Schls 1973-; Public Liaison Los Alamos Natl Laboratories 1981-; *ai:* Yrbk Adv; Sch Management Team Mem; Phi Kappa Phi Honors Society Mem 1972-; La Natl Laboratory 1988, Oppenheimer Fellowship Schlsp; People-to-People HS Stu Ambassador Prgm, Area Coord 1982; Las Cumbres Learning Services Pres of Bd 1980-82; Oppenheimer Fellowship Schlsp Recipient 1988; *home:* 913 Capulin Rd Los Alamos NM 87544

JOHNSTON, TIMOTHY JAMES, Fifth Grade Teacher; *b:* Barstow, CA; *m:* Rebecca Joy Gledhill; *c:* Kasey, Korey, Makay, Mc Kenzie; *ed:* (AA) Bi-ling Ed, Palomar Jr Coll 1980; (BS) Elem Ed, Brigham Young Univ 1982; Working Towards Masters in Ed; *cr:* Teacher Brookside Elem 1982-; *ai:* Dist Prof Improvement Comm 1987; Career Ladder Comm 1989; Teacher Leader 1986-87; Outdoor Ed Camp Dir 1983-86; NEA 1984; UT Ed Assn Mem Cncl of Local Pres 1988-; NEBO Ed Assn Pres 1988-; Church of Jesus Christ of Latter Day Saints (St Pres of Local Area Sunday Schls 1988-, Local Missionary Pres 1986-88); Outstanding Young Men of America 1990; *home:* 1755 S 350 E Springville UT 84663

JOHNSTON, VIRGINIA MONTGOMERY, 6th Grade Teacher; *b:* Philadelphia, PA; *c:* Elizabeth M.; *ed:* (BS) Elem Ed, Univ of Chattanooga 1962; Courses in Gifted Ed; *cr:* Teacher McBrien Elem 1962-63, Sts Peter & Paul Elem 1965-66, Fairyland Elem 1966-; *ai:* Coord of CCD Prgm; Building Rep on Lang Art; Curr Comm; Team Leader for Math Project; Prof Assn of GA Educators, NCTE, Intnl Rdng Assn; Jr League of Chattanooga; Chosen to Write a Project on How Children Think & Learn; *home:* 315 W Brow Rd Lookout Mountain TN 37350

JOHNSTONE, MARY K., 3rd/4th Grade Teacher; *b:* Anchorage, AK; *m:* Stowell; *c:* Matt P.; *ed:* (BA) Psych, Seattle Univ 1969; (MED) Rdng, Univ of AK Anchorage; Cert Prgm in Public Sch Admin, Univ of AK Anchorage; *cr:* Asst Registrar SW Univ of Sch of Law 1971-72; Teacher Ocean View Elem Sch 1975-78, Abbott Loop Elem Sch 1978-; *ai:* Phi Delta Kappa 1988-; ASCD 1985-; Intnl Rdng Assn 1980-; Anchorage Mental Health Assn 1985-; *home:* 4822 Loretta Ln Anchorage AK 99507

JOHSON, BRETT ALAN, Band Director; *b:* Lake Charles, LA; *m:* Cynthia Woods; *c:* Jacob; *ed:* Grad Stud W TX St Univ; *cr:* Dir Leesville HS 1982-85; Asst Dir Mccullough HS 1985-87; Dir Robert E Lee HS 1987-; *ai:* TMEA, TBA 1985-; *office:* Robert E Lee HS 411 Loop 323 Tyler TX 75701

JOINER, CAROLINE B., Social Studies Teacher; *b:* Clarksdale, MS; *c:* Sara; *ed:* (BA) His, Rice Univ 1963; St Thomas Univ, Univ of CO, SE WA St Univ, Trinity Univ, TX A&M Coll Station; *cr:* Soc Stud Teacher Freeport Jr HS 1963-69; Brazosport HS 1969-78; Moulton Jr/Sr HS 1978-; *ai:* UIL Literary Contest & 1 Act Play Coach; Sr Class Spon; NEA; TX St Teachers Assn; Lavaca Cty TSTA Unit Pres 1988-; TX Cncl for Soc Stud; Lavaca Cty Democrats Club 1988-, St Convention Delegate 1988; Brazosport Ind Sch Dist Merit Teacher; Moulton Ind Sch Dist Career Ladder Awd; NDEA Inst; Petroleum Inst; Taft Inst; *office:* Moulton Jr/Sr HS PO Drawer C Moulton TX 77975

JOINER, JO WILLIAMSON, Science Teacher; *b:* Albany, GA; *m:* Danny; *c:* Lisa M., Daniel G. II; *ed:* Sci, Darton Coll; (BS) Math, 1975, (MED) Sci, 1976 GA Southwestern; *cr:* Teacher Albany HS 1976-; *ai:* Fellowship Chrstn Athletes, PRIDE, Sci Olympiad Co-Spon; Swimming Asst Coach; 5 Yr Planning Comm Chm; Ga Sci Teachers, Local Amer Chemical Society 1990; Dougherty Cty Assn of Educators, NEA 1976-; Avalon United Meth Church 1973-; Lights of Love 1980-; Albany Little Theatre 1986-; Albany HS Teacher of Yr 1988-89; ChemCom Wkshp 1988-89; Sci Teacher of Yr Nom 1989-; SECME Teacher; *office:* Albany HS 801 Residence Ave Albany GA 31707

JOINER, LANA FAYE (BAGEN), Language Art/5th Grade Teacher; *b:* Wharton, TX; *m:* Cecil O.; *c:* Rachel, Kristine; *ed:* (BS) Elem Ed, Sam Houston St 1967; Advanced Trng; *cr:* 4th Grade Teacher Tomball Elem 1967; Spec Ed Teacher Anderson Elem 1967-70 Lang Art Teacher Crockett Inter & Jr HS 1970-78, Reaves Intermediate 1978-; *ai:* Odyssey of Mind Coach; Howdy Corporation Spon; Assn of TX Educators Building Rep; 1st Baptist Church; Beta Sigma Phi; Reaves PTR; Conroe Ind Sch Dist Band Boosters; Golden Girls Boosters; Spec Ed Schlsp Grant Sr Yr Coll 1966-67; Master Teacher Acad Region VI Huntsville TX 1990; *office:* Reaves Intermediate Sch 1717 Loop 336 W Conroe TX 77304

JOINER, MARION FOWLER, English Teacher; *b:* Lawrenceburg, TN; *m:* Charles David Sr.; *c:* Charles, Willie, Kristina; *ed:* (BS) Home Ec, 1974, (BS) Eng, 1975, (MA) Ed, 1982 Univ of N AL; Ed, TN St Univ; *cr:* 12th Grade Eng Teacher Lawrence Cty HS 1975-; *ai:* Fellowship of Chrstn Athletes Spon; Advisory Cncl of Lawrence Cty Mem; Lawrence Cty Ed Assn, TN Educl Assn, NEA 1976-; NCTE 1980-; Delta Kappa Gamma 1987-; Kappa Omicron Phi 1976-; Lawrence Cty Study Club 1984-; *home:* Rt 1 Box 168 Five Points TN 38457

JOINER, SHARON MARIE, Language Arts Teacher; *b:* East St Louis, IL; *c:* Jessica, Michael, Mark; *ed:* (BS) Eng Ed, 1969, (MS) Eng Ed, 1979 Southern IL Univ; *cr:* Lang Art Teacher East St Louis Sr HS 1969-; Part Time Eng Teacher Belleville Area Coll 1987-89; *ai:* Graduation Coord; Prin Advisory Comm; NCTE; IL Assn Teachers of Eng; Kappa Delta Pi; ASCD; NAACP; Awd By Bd Ed Achievement In Teaching Writing Skills 1989; VFW Awd Voice of Democracy; Eng Teacher of Yr Natl Honor Society of East St Louis Sr HS; *office:* East St Louis Sr HS 4901 State St East Saint Louis IL 62205

JOLLEY, ALTON ROGER, Social Studies Dept Chairman; *b:* Mooresboro, NC; *m:* Nancy Ruth Harp; *c:* Terry, Cynthia, Darrell, David; *ed:* (AA) His, Gardner Webb 1960; (BA) His, Carson Newman 1962; (MAT) His, Mid TN St 1970; Univ of TN Chattanooga & Univ of the South; *cr:* Teacher Jefferson Elem Sch 1962-64, Franklin Cty HS 1964-, Motlow St Comm Coll 1978-; Sales Clerk Walmart 1982-; *ai:* Jr Class Steering Comm Chm; Little League Sftbl Coach; NEA, TN Ed Assn 1962-; Franklin Cty Ed Assn Pres 1978-80; Southern Assn of Schls Evaluator; Jr Civitan Spon 1973-77, Man of Yr 1975-76; Gideons Intnl Treas 1980-85; Distinguished Classroom Teacher Awd 1980-81; Aerospace Ed Grant 1964; His Wkshp Grant 1968; City of Decherd Alderman 1971, 1974, 1977, 1980, 1986; *home:* 400 Main St Decherd TN 37324

JOLLEY, BETHANY ELLEN, Second Grade Teacher; *b:* Sharon, PA; *ed:* (BS) Elem Ed, IN Univ of PA 1967; *cr:* 3rd Grade Teacher Lorah Park Elem 1967-68, Orchard Villa Elem 1968-79; Kndgtn-1st Grade Teacher Ben Franklin Elem 1980-87; 3rd Grade Teacher Palm Springs N Elem 1987-88; 2nd Grade Teacher Joella Good Elem 1989-; *ai:* Future Educators of America Spon; Soc Comm & Grade Group Chairperson; Phi Delta Kappa (Fnds Rep 1987-89, Historian 1989-); *office:* Joella Good Elem Sch 17615 NW 82nd Ave Hialeah FL 33015

JOLLY, DONALD T., 6th Grade Teacher; *b:* Streator, IL; *m:* Nancy Mersinger; *c:* Michael, Kathryn; *ed:* (BA) Ger Stud, MacAlester Coll 1966; (MA) Ger Lang/Lit, Case Western Reserve Univ 1968; Rdng/Ed Admin Grad Work Sangamon St Univ; Univ of IL, N IL Univ, W IL Univ; *cr:* Instr Case Western Reserve Univ 1967-68; HS Teacher Kamakwee Scndry Sch 1969-71; Peace Corps Volunteer Sierra Leone W Africa; *ai:* Elem Teacher Jefferson Elem Sch 1973-; 6th Grade Chicago Trip Leader; Steering Comm; Accelerated Sch Project; Jacksonville Ed Assn, IEA, NEA, Cntrl IL Rdng Conference; Morgan Cty Big Brother/Big Sister Assn, Big Brother of Yr 1974; Presbyn Church Day Care Ctr Bd Mem; 1st Presbyn Church of Deacons Moderator; *office:* Jefferson Elem Sch 733 N Clay Jacksonville IL 62650

JOLLY, DONNA MARIE SKIPPER, 6th Grade Teacher/Chairperson; *b:* Lake Charles, LA; *m:* Willard; *c:* Michael, Monica R.; *ed:* (BA) Elem Ed, Bishop Coll 1967; (MS) Elem Ed, Prairie View 1978; Advanced Trng in Math; *cr:* 6th Grade Teacher 1972-, 6th Grade Team Leader 1983- T G Terry; *ai:* Boys & Girls After Sch Sports, Track & Sftbl; 6th Grade Team Leader; Math Olympiad Spon; CTD Mem 1972-85; Dallas Fed Mem 1989-; ETA Phi Delta Mem 1987; PTA Life Membership; *home:* 25418 Arcady Ln Lancaster TX 75146

JOLMA, BARBARA HEIDEGGER, First Grade Teacher; *b:* Kettle Falls, WA; *m:* Clarence W.; *c:* Collen Charlson, Thelma Rosenlund, Aaron, Twila Joyce Munger, Eric, Jennifer, Marcia; *ed:* (BA) Ed, Cntrl WA Coll 1953; Standard General Cert Ed, Cntrl WA St Coll 1964; *cr:* K-8th Grade Teacher Various Schls 1953-76; 1st-4th Grade Teacher Camas Prairie Sch 1976-80; 1st Grade Teacher Hot Springs Elem 1980-; *ai:* NEA, MT Ed Assn; Hot Springs Ed Assn Pres 1985-86; Delta Kappa Gamma 1986-88; *home:* 2237 Hwy 28 Hot Springs MT 59845

JONAS, JEFFREY STEPHEN, Science Teacher & Coach; *b:* Berkeley, CA; *c:* (BA) Phys Ed, San Francisco St Univ 1987; *ed:* Single Subject Credential, Natl Univ 1988; *cr:* Stu Teacher De Anza HS 1988; Sci Teacher Benicia HS 1988-89, De Anza HS 1989-; Ftbl/Bsktbl/Sftbl Coach De Anza HS 1982-; *ai:* Womens Var Sftbl, Var Asst Ftbl, Var Asst Bsktbl Coach; *office:* De Anza HS 5000 Valleyview Rd Richmond CA 94803

JONAS, KAREN ELAINE, 4th-6th Grade Gifted Teacher; *b:* Dallas, TX; *m:* David Gene; *c:* Rebecca; *ed:* (BSED) Speech Pathology, Stephen F Austin St Univ 1974; (MED) Elem Ed, E TX St Univ 1979; Gifted Ed, Univ of TX Dallas; Mid-Management Cert, TX Womens Univ; *cr:* Resource Teacher 1974-79, 3rd Grade Teacher 1979-87, 1st Grade Teacher 1987-88 Terrace Elem; Gifted 4th-6th Grade Teacher R I S E Acad 1988-; *ai:* Curr Writing Team Gifted Prgms; Odyssey of Mind-Spontaneous Problem Captain Local; Assn of TX Prof Educators, TX Assn of Gifted & Talented, ASCD, Richardson Ed Assn; Delta Kappa Gamma; Appointed Mem R I S E Teacher Cadre; *office:* R I S E Acad 13630 Coit Road Dallas TX 75240

JONASSEN, LARS ERIC, 7th Grade Teacher; *b:* Waterville, ME; *m:* Sandra Clark; *c:* Kelly A., Keith E.; *ed:* (BS) Math, Univ of S ME 1975; Working on Masters in Gifted & Talented Ed, Bowdoin Inst for Gifted & Talented; *cr:* 3rd Grade Teacher Benton Elem Sch 1975-78; 7th Grade Teacher 1979-83, Prin 1983-85, 7th Grade Teacher 1985- Lawrence Jr HS; *ai:* Jr HS Girls Field Hockey, 8th Grade Bsktbl Coach; Jr HS Drama Set Dir; Jr HS Stu Cncl Co-Adv; Albion Lions Club (Secy, VP) 1989-; SAD 49 Bd of Dir Certificate of Excl Lawrence Jr HS; *office:* Lawrence Jr HS School St Fairfield ME 04937

JONASSEN, LINDA JEAN, 6th Grade Teacher; *b:* Amityville, NY; *ed:* (BS) Elem Ed, the Kings Coll 1973; (MED) Rdng, Towson St Univ 1978; *cr:* Nursery Sch Teacher the Little Sch 1973-74; 4th/5th/6th Grade Teacher Arlington Baptist Sch 1974-80; 6th Grade Teacher Chrstn Heritage Sch 1980-; *ai:* ACSI Cert 1983-; Seminar Leader Teachers Conventions Public Speaker for Church Groups & Other Schls; *office:* Christian Heritage Sch 575 White Plains Rd Trumbull CT 06611

JONES, AL CHARLES, 4th-5th Grade Teacher; *b:* St Paul, MN; *m:* Mary Elleson;; *c:* Alexandra, Preston; *ed:* (MA) Curr & Instr, Coll of St Thomas 1983; (BA) Elem Ed, Beth Coll 1978; *cr:* 4th Grade Teacher Kenneth Hall Elem 1978-79; 4th-5th Grade Teacher North Branch Elem 1979-86; Exch Teacher Euxton Primary Sch-England 1986-87; 4th-5th Grade Teacher North Branch Elem 1987-; *ai:* Coach-North Branch Runners Club; North Branch Pres 1987-88; Ed Assn 1989-; Fulbright Exch Teacher to England 1986-87; *office:* North Branch Elem Sch 1108 1st Ave North Branch MN 55056

JONES, ALICIA DAVILA, Two-Way Bilingual Prgm Coord; *b:* San Antonio, TX; *m:* Kenneth Leon; *c:* Lee, Debbie Teal, Michael Boerschig, Bruce, Ruth Marsh, Brian, Gregory A. Boerschig, Gary C., Tim Boerschig, Peter Boerschig; *ed:* (BA) Span Ed - Magna Cum Laude, 1972, (MA) Foreign Lang Ed, 1978 St Univ of NY Buffalo; Elem Ed, Bi-ling Ed, SUNY Buffalo; Admin Prgm, St Univ Coll Buffalo; Multifunctional Resource Prgm, Hunter Coll; *cr:* Span/Foreign Lang Teacher Riverside HS 1972-78; Bi-ling Elem Teacher Herman Badillo Bi-ling Acad 1979-88; 1st/2nd Grade Prgm Coord/3rd/4th Grade Two-Way Bi-ling Prgm ECC #36 & HBBA #76 1989-; *ai:* Span Lang Art Curr & ESL Curr Comm; Stu Government Club Adv; Parent & Cmmty Involvement Comm Chairperson; Buffalo Teacher Fed Building Rep 1979-88; ASCD Mem 1986-; TESOL Mem 1990; St Assn of Bi-ling Ed Mem 1979-; W NY Hispanics & Friends Civic Assn Mem 1990; Puerto Rican & Chicano Comm (Bd VP 1974-79, Building Rep); Wrote City Span Lang Art Curr Sch Dist; *office:* Public Schls #76 & #36 10 Days Pk Buffalo NY 14201

JONES, ALMA WYATT, Social Studies Teacher; *b:* Montgomery, AL; *m:* Melvin O.; *ed:* (BS) Soc Stud, 1959, (MED) Scndry Ed, 1966 AL St Univ Montgomery; Purdue Univ, E KY Univ, Univ of AL; *cr:* Soc Stud Teacher Druid HS 1959-68, Westlawn Jr HS 1968-78, Cental HS W 1978-; *ai:* Honor Society Faculty Cncl; Spec Ed Comm; Prof Educators of Tuscaloosa Exec Bd 1968-; AL Ed Assn, NEA 1959-; Zeta Phi Beta Former Basileus 1957; Mc Donald Hughes Cmmty Center Bd of Dirs 1989; St Paul AME Church 1st Woman Steward 1990; Central HS W Teacher of Yr 1989-; *home:* 1605 Montrose Dr Tuscaloosa AL 35405

JONES, ANGELA DENISE, History Teacher; *b:* Birmingham, AL; *ed:* (BA) His, Carleton Coll 1979; (MA) His, St Univ of NY Binghamton 1982; *cr:* Prgm Secy 1982, Prgm Coord 1983 Broome Cty Urban League; Part Time Librarian Asst, Teacher 1983- Westminster Schls; *ai:* Mentor Westminster & GA St Univ Intern Prgm; Asst Track Coach; Co-Spon Service Cncl; Chaparone 1989 Close-Up Fnd Trip to Washington DC; Delta Sigma Theta; Participant AL Geography Alliance 1990; Panel Discussion GA Ind Sch Assn 1987; Alumni Admissions Rep Carleton Coll; *office:* Westminster Schls 1424 W Paces Ferry Rd NW Atlanta GA 30327

JONES, ANN ELIZABETH GIBLIN, Junior High English Teacher; *b:* Philadelphia, PA; *m:* Vernon E. Jr.; *c:* Aimee, Jennifer, Vernon III, Daniel; *ed:* (BS) Elem Ed, E Stroudsburg St Univ 1966; Glassboro St Univ, St Charles Barromeo Sch of Religious Stud, St Leos Coll, Univ of S Fl; *cr:* Stu Teacher Stroud Township Schls 1964-65, Wind Gap Elem Sch 1965-66; 3rd Grade Teacher Holy Name Sch 1966-67; 4th Grade Teacher St Matthew Sch 1979-80; Substitute Teacher Gloucester Township Schls 1980-82; Eng Teacher Most Holy Redeemer Interparochial Sch 1984-; *ai:* Chairperson Eng Dept; Sci Fair Coord; Spon/Coach Spelling Bees, Essay & Oratorical Competition; Spon Safety Patrol; Jr HS Chairperson Awds Ceremony; Beginning Teacher Prgm Peer Teacher; ACEI (Secy 1962-63, VP 1963-65, Pres 1965-66); Assn for Children with Learning Disabilities Auxiliary (Treas 1972-73, VP 1973-74); Assn for Children with Learning Disabilities Prof Assoc 1975-; Natl Cncl of Cath Educators 1978-; NCTE, FL Cncl Teachers of Eng; Jr Womans Club St Coll 1968-70; Jr Womans Club Haddonfield Secy 1972; GSA Troop Leader 1970-78; BSA 1970-; Confeternity of Chrstn Doctrine Prgms (Pre-Sch Coord 1973-82, Instr 1983-); Parent Involvement Prgm Tampa Cath HS 1982-; *office:* Most Holy Redeemer Interparoch 302 E Linebaugh Ave Tampa FL 33612

JONES, ANNA HECKEL, Second Grade Teacher; *b:* Litchfield, Hungary; *m:* Billy A.; *c:* Karen A.; *ed:* (BS) Elem Ed, Akron Univ 1973; *cr:* 1st Grade Teacher 1974-80, Pre 1st Grade Teacher 1980-84, 2nd Grade Teacher 1984- Greenwood Schls; *ai:* Parents as Partners Chairperson; Soc Stud Course of Study Rep; Greenwood Ed Assn, OH Ed Assn, NEA; Martha Holden Jennings Awd; *office:* Greenwood Elem Sch 2250 Graybill Rd Uniontown OH 44685

JONES, ANNADA ELLIOTT, 7th-8th Grade Hnrs Eng Teacher; *b:* Sulphur Springs, TX; *m:* James F.; *ed:* (BS) Bus Ed, 1962, (MED) Elem Ed, 1971 E TX St Univ; *cr:* Art Teacher 1975-77, Experienced Based Career Ed Pilot Prgm Teacher 1977-80, Eng Teacher 1968- Sulphur Springs Mid Sch; *ai:* Sulphur Springs Mid Sch Yrbk Adv; TX St Teachers Assn 1968-77; TX Prof Educators 1977-80; Assn of TX Prof Educators 1980-; *home:* 122 Sherry Ln Sulphur Springs TX 75482

JONES, ANNE W., Retired English Teacher; *b:* Mousie, KY; *m:* Linvel; *c:* Regina; *ed:* (BA) Eng, Pikeville Coll 1962; *cr:* Teacher Four Mile Elem 1956-62; Eng Teacher Hindman HS 1962-73, Belmont Jr HS 1973-88; *ai:* Faculty Adv; Schls Academic Team Coach; KY Retired Teachers Assn 1988-; NEA, KEA, CCEA Natl/St/Local Mem; Mended Hearts Support Group Heart Patients 1984-; St Joseph Hospital Volunteer; Proofreader Jerrico Incorporated; *home:* 3489 Bathurst Ct Lexington KY 40503

JONES, ANNIE WALTON, Business Education Instructor; *b:* Marshall, TX; *c:* Ardis D. Walton, Kristie E.; *ed:* (BA) Office Admin Ed, Wiley Coll 1976, 1981; (MED) Guidance/Counseling, Prairie View A&M 1984; Occupational Investigation Cert N TX 1985; Licensed Cosmetologist 1972; *cr:* Respiratory Therapy Technician Marshall Memorial Hospital 1972-76; Dev Admin Asst Wiley Coll 1979-81; Jr HS Classroom Teacher 1982-89, Sr HS Classroom Teacher 1989- Marshall Ind Sch Dist; *ai:* Marshall Womens Sftbl League; Greater Oak Grove Young Adult Choir Mem; TX St Teachers Assn, NEA, Delta Sigma Theta, TX Alliance of Black Sch Ed; St John Baptist Church Inspirational Choir Mem; *office:* Marshall Sr HS 1900 Maverick Dr Marshall TX 75670

JONES, BARBARA PIERCE, Chemistry Teacher; *b:* Jacksonville, FL; *c:* William M.; *ed:* (BS) Sci, Edward Waters Coll 1966; (MS) Chem, Univ of N FL 1980; Numerous Colls; *cr:* Algebra/Physics/Bio Teacher Douglas Anderson Jr-Sr HS 1966-68; Teacher/Dept Chm Esperanza Mid Sch 1968-69, Ilima Intermediate Sch 1969-74; Chem Teacher Sandalwood Sr HS 1974-81, Coconut Creek Sr HS 1981-; *ai:* Free Sci Tutoring; Zeta Phi Beta Cmmty Service Awd 1986; Pop Warner Ftbl Black Youths Organizing Asst; Mentor Francine Genn Sci Westinghouse Sci Awd Honor Group 1985; Broward Cty Sch Bd Recognition Certificate 1985; Spec Teacher Recognition Awd 1985; *office:* Coconut Creek HS 1400 NW 44th Ave Coconut Creek FL 33066

JONES, BEATRYCE LEWIS, Retired Second Grade Teacher; *b:* Bloomington, IN; *m:* John I.; *c:* Elaine Marshall, William, Faith Byrd, Timothy; *ed:* (BA) Span/Eng, IN Univ 1942; (MA) Elem Ed, Oneonta St 1958; In-Service Courses; Rdng, Sci,Cmptr, William Glasser; *cr:* Clerical Checker General Electric Company 1942-45; Typist Schenectady Cty Dept Soc Services 1945-47; Elem Teacher Schenectady City Sch Dist 1956-59; Soc Worker Schenectady Cty Dept Soc Services 1962-67; Elem Teacher Schenectady City Sch Dist 1968-87; *ai:* Soc Stud; Bd of Deacons, Elder & Sunday Sch Teacher; AAUW League Women Voters, YWCA Mem.

JONES, BERNITA MOIR, Social Studies Teacher; *b:* Blytheville, AR; *m:* James W. Jr.; *c:* Webb, Wesley, Derek; *ed:* (BS) His/Poly Sci, Memphis St Univ 1967; Grad Stud, Univ of S FL; *cr:* Soc Stud Teacher Judson B Walker Jr HS 1968-72, Plant City HS 1983-; *ai:* Soc Stud Club, Soc Stud Academic Team, Citizen Bee Competition, WA Close-Up & Bicentennial Constitution Contest Spon; Hillsborough Cty Cncl for Soc Stud; Outstanding Soc Stud Teacher Awd 1990; *office:* Plant City HS 1 Raider Pl Plant City FL 33566

JONES, BETTY WADE BLANTON, Science Department Chair; *b:* Victoria, VA; *m:* Jerry Hall; *c:* Sara E. Hall, J. Hall Jr., W. Blanton; *ed:* (BS) Chem, Westhampton Coll Univ of Richmond 1961; (MTS) Physics/Math, Coll of William & Mary 1966; Grad Stud Univ of Richmond, Univ of VA, VA Commonwealth Univ; *cr:* Sci Teacher Richmond VA Public Schls 1961-65, Petersburg VA Public Schls 1965-67, Prince George Cty Public Schls 1977-; *ai:* Natl Assn of Geology Teachers St Cnclr 1990; Geological Society of America Ed Comm 1987-; VA Acad of Sci (Ed Selection Chairperson, Vice Chairperson, Secy) 1980-86; Covenant Presbyn Church Elder 1987-; Peer Reviewer Natl Sci Fnd 1985, 1987-88; Presidential Awd for Excl in Sci Teaching VA 1984; Article Published 1985; Scott Foresman Publishers Reviewer 1986; *office:* N B Clements Jr HS 7800 Prince George Dr Prince George VA 23875

JONES, BEVERLY BROWN, 8th Grade Science Teacher; *b:* Springfield, MO; *M:* Clinton E.; *c:* Julie, Dean, Maggie, Cass; *ed:* (BS) Voc Home Ec Ed, Univ OF MO Columbia 1972; Ed; *cr:* 7th-12th Grade Home Economics Teacher Harrisburg R-VIII Sch 1973-74; 10th-12th Grade Home Economics Teacher 1974-76, 7th-9th Grade Home Economics Teacher 1980-88, 8th Grade Sci Teacher 1988- Salem Jr HS; *ai:* Stu Cncl Spon; 8th Grade Class Spon; Chm R-80 Prof Dev Comm; MSTA 1980-; Tri-C 1982-; Bonebrack MC Murtrey Fnd 1988-; *office:* Salem R-80 Jr HS W 3rd St Salem MO 65560

JONES, BILLIE PORTER, Fifth Grade Teacher; *b:* Haskell, OK; *c:* Scott, Lance; *ed:* (BS) Elem Ed, Sul Ross 1958; (MS) Rdng, Univ of TX Permian Basin 1989; *cr:* Classroom Teacher Andrews Ind Sch Dist 1958-.

JONES, BOB LLOYD, Director of Forensics; *b:* Sacramento, CA; *m:* Anne Louise Holweger; *ed:* Speech, Lindfield Coll 1967; (BS) Eng/Ed, OR Coll of Ed 1968; (MA) Speech Ed, W OR St Coll 1980; *cr:* Eng Teacher Bell Gardens Jr HS 1968-70; Speech/Eng Teacher Sherwood HS 1970-71; Head Teacher OR St Hospital Sch 1973-80; Dir of Forensics Brooking Harbor HS 1980-84, Canby Union HS 1984-; *ai:* Coaching Speech & Debate; Canby Comm Strategy Group; OR Ed Assn Uni-Serve Pres 1987-89, Presidential Citation for Poly Action 1990; OR Speech Coaches Assn Pres 1989-; Natl Forensic League Extemp Topic Comm Chm 1986-, Distinguished Servi e Awd 1989; Toastmasters Educl VP 1988-, CTM 1987, Toastmaster of Yr 1989; Nom Citizen of Yr 1988; Canby Union HS Teacher of Yr 1989-; *office:* Canby Union HS 721 SW 4th Canby OR 97013

JONES, BRENDA YARBROUGH, English Teacher; *b:* Athens, AL; *c:* George III, Margaret; *ed:* (BS) Eng, AL A&M Univ 1967; (MA) Ed Management, Univ of TX San Antonio 1980; *cr:* Elem Teacher Owens Jr HS 1967-68; Eng Teacher Edison HS 1968-69; His/Eng Teacher Wagner HS 1969-71, Sam Houston HS 1971-75; Eng Teacher Jefferson HS 1976-80, Wheatley-Brackenridge HS 1980-89, Branckenridge HS 1989-; *ai:* 10th Grade Lead Teacher; Curr Design Comm; Clearly Outstanding Teacher Ratings Career Ladder; Sr Class Spon Awd 1969-71; Outstanding TEAMS Coach Awd TX Assessment of Basic Skills; *office:* Brackenridge HS 400 Temple San Antonio TX 78210

JONES, CALVIN MILTON, Soc Sci Teacher; *b:* Los Angeles, CA; *m:* Bernice; *c:* Valencia, Shawnse, Shannon, Canisha; *ed:* (AA) His, Componton & Laney Coll 1974-; (BA) Poly Sci, Southern Univ & CA St Dominguez 1977; (MS) Sch Management, Pepperdine Univ 1984; UCLA; Effective Sch; Team Power; Pepperdine Univ; *cr:* Teacher Compton Coll Migrate Prgm 1977, St Albert the Great 1978, Willowbrook Jr HS 1979, Clearwater Intermediate 1980; *ai:* 7th Grade Spon; Honor Society Comm Chm; Tour Dir Washington DC; Bsktbl & Golf Coach; Chm Discipline Comm 1984 & Curr Comm 1987; Teacher Assn Sch Rep 1981-83, Sch Quality 1987; Teacher of Yr Candidate; Nom Chm Disaster Comm; Outstanding Leadership in Ed Awd; *home:* 607 Holborn Dr Carson CA 90746

JONES, CAROL CRANFORD, Home Economics Teacher; *b:* El Dorado, AR; *m:* Stephen Wayne; *c:* Angela, Chad; *ed:* (BA) Voc Home Ec Ed, Univ of W FL 1986; *cr:* Home Ec Teacher King Mid Sch 1986-; *ai:* Stu Cncl Spon; *home:* 6192 Jays Way Milton FL 32570

JONES, CATHERINE GLOCKNER, Junior High School Teacher; *b:* Covington, KY; *m:* Robert Bradley; *ed:* (BA) Scndry Eng, N KY Univ 1984; Grad Stud N KY Univ; *cr:* Teacher Holy Trinity Sch 1984-88, St Mary Sch 1988-89, Holy Trinity Sch 1989-; *ai:* Academic Team Coach Mid Sch Level; Trinity Tribune Sch Newspaper Spon; Sch Advisory Comm Mem; NCTE 1984-; NCEA 1987-89; *office:* Holy Trinity Sch Hwy 421 S Harlan KY 40831

JONES, CHARLES, English Teacher; *b:* Oklahoma City, OK; *m:* Karen Q.; *c:* Ethan, Arthur; *ed:* (BS) Ed, N TX St Univ 1964; (MED) General Curr, 1968, (EDD) Educl Admin, 1976 Univ of WA; *cr:* Teacher Taft HS 1964-66; Instr Summer Drama Inst 1966; Teacher 1966-, Eng Dept Chm 1974-77 Lake Washington HS; *ai:* Phi Delta Kappa; ASCAP; Fellowship Natl Endowment for Humanities 1986; *office:* Lake Washington HS 12033 NE 80th Kirkland WA 98033

JONES, CHARLES ALAN, US Government/Econ Teacher; *b:* Cameron, TX; *m:* Debra Lynn Delulio; *c:* Megan N.; *ed:* (BS) Poly Sci, Univ of Mary Hardin-Baylor 1979; (MA) Poly Sci, Univ of TX Arlington 1990; *cr:* US Government/Ec Teacher Copperas Cove Sr HS 1980-81, Everman Sr HS 1986-; *ai:* NHS & Sr Class Spon; Assn TX Prof Educators 1986-; Alpha Chi Natl Collegiate Honor Society Pres 1979-; Pi Sigma Alpha Natl Poly Sci Honor Society 1987-; Frances Letitia Hailes Memorial Schlsp 1976-79; *home:* 400 Palo Duro Cir Saginaw TX 76179

JONES, CHARLES T., 5th Grade Teacher; *b:* Dallas, TX; *m:* Pamela Wilson; *c:* Bethany, Jon M.; *ed:* (BA) Elem Ed, W TX St Univ 1979; *cr:* Substitute Teacher 1979, Bus Driver 1979-89, 5th Grade Teacher 1979- Canyon TX Ind Sch Dist; *ai:* Vice Chm; Dist Instructional Advisory Comm; Safety Patrol Spon; Assn of TX Prof Educators 1981-; TX PTA Life Membership 1989; Party Precinct Chm 1989, 1990; *home:* 6820 Daniel Amarillo TX 79109

JONES, CHRISTOPHER ARLEN, Science Teacher; *b:* Detroit, MI; *m:* Lynn Susan Klear; *c:* Sean C., Stephanie L.; *ed:* (BS) Zoology, Univ of MI 1965; (MSE) Scndry Ed, Univ of PA 1969; (EDD) Scndry Sci Ed, Boston Univ 1978; Peace Corps Trng, Syracuse Univ 1965; Post Doctoral Brandeis Univ 1981; *cr:* Sci Teacher Amoud Scndry Sch Somalia East Africa 1965-67, Penn Treaty Jr HS 1967-69; Adjunct Professor Boston Coll 1982-85; Sci Teacher Newton North HS 1969-; *ai:* Head Coach Mens Swim Team; Asst Coach Womens Swim Team; Human Rights Comm Newton North HS; Pi Lambda Theta 1978-, Key 1978; BSA Asst Scoutmaster Comm 1980-, Eagle 1956; PTO Westwood HS 1989-; World Organization Study Club Pres 1987-88; Assistantship Boston Univ 1977; Doctoral Thesis on Outward Bound; *office:* Newton North HS 360 Lowell Ave Newtonville MA 02160

JONES, CHRISTOPHER MICHAEL THOMAS, English Teacher; *b:* Richmond, VA; *m:* Cindy Mae Kilgore; *ed:* (BA) Eng, Elon Coll 1980; (MED) Counseling, VA Commonwealth Univ 1987; *cr:* Teacher/Coach Bollingbrook Sch 1981-83, Chincoteague HS 1985-88, Nandua HS 1988-; *ai:* Drama & Forensics Coach; Cty Eng Div Chm; NEA, VA Ed Assn, Accomack Ed Assn 1985-; Petersburg Kiwanis 1981-83; *office:* Nandua HS PO Box 489 Onley VA 23418

JONES, CORA LEE, Jr HS English Teacher; *b:* Vardaman, MS; *m:* Jimmy Dell; *c:* Roderick, Terez, Kenneth, Jeffrey, Kelton, Michelle, Jimmy; *ed:* (BS) Eng, MS Valley St Coll 1968; Grad Stud Univ of MS, Ms St Univ; *cr:* Eng Teacher Calhoun Cty Schls 1967-78, W Clay HS 1982-; *ai:* Stu Government Assn Adv; Sch Improvement Team Mem; NEA 1984-; Clay Cty Assn of Educators Pres 1987-88; MS Assn of Educators 1984-; *home:* Rt 2 Box 69AA Houston MS 38851

JONES, CORA M., 5th Grade Teacher; *b:* Bernice, LA; *c:* Teno, Olanda, Donyea, Coyunna; *ed:* (BS) Elem Ed, Grambling St Univ 1960; Grad Stud MI St, Wayne St Univ; *cr:* Teacher Grambling St Univ 1960, Buena Vista Sch Dist 1969-; *ai:* Organized & Spon Save Our Girls Club; 4-H Club & Church Youth Adv; Phi Delta Kappa Dean of Pledgees; Saginaw Ed Assn, Buena Vista Educl Assn; Saginaw Employee Credit Union; Advancement of Colored People Natl Awd; Public Service Awd.

JONES, CORRINE B., Social Studies Teacher; *b:* Chicago, IL; *m:* Gardner L.; *c:* Jerry, Jeannie Beck, Tim, Cathy Brown; *ed:* (BS) Philosophy, Loyola Univ 1954; Music, Roosevelt Univ 1955-57; Ed, Univ of S FL 1975-78; *cr:* 2nd Grade Teacher St Walters Elem Sch 1967-68, Ontarioville Sch 1968-72; 1st/2nd/5th Grade Teacher Venice Elem Sch 1973-82; Soc Stud Teacher Venice Area Mid Sch 1982-; *ai:* Run Annual Ec Unit Christmas Bazaar; Amer Assn of Univ Women 1987-89; Venice Art League 1983; Articles Published 1985-87; *office:* Venice Area Mid Sch 1900 Center Rd Venice FL 34292

JONES, CYNTHIA LOU KUNDRAT, Second Grade Teacher; *b:* Weirton, WV; *m:* Ronald E.; *ed:* (BA) Early Chldhd, 1975; (MA) Elem Ed, Marshall Univ 1982; *cr:* 2nd & Third Grade Teacher Dingess Elem 1977-80; 2nd Grade Teacher Hamlin Elem 1980-; *home:* 522 Lower Terrace Huntington WV 25705

JONES, DAVID L., Third Grade Teacher; *b:* Bennetsville, SC; *m:* Patsy Littleton; *c:* Kara, Cameron; *ed:* (BS) Elem Ed, E MT Coll 1972; (MA) Early Chldhd Ed, 1986, (MA) Sch Counseling, 1989 W Carolina Univ; *cr:* 5th Grade Teacher Broadus Elem 1972-73; 6th Grade Teacher Edneyville Union Sch 1973-74; 4th Grade Teacher 1974-81, 3rd Grade Teacher 1981- Edneyville Elem; *ai:* Soccer Referee; Youth Wrestling & Track Coach; Bus Driver; Amer Sch Cnslr Assn, NC Sch Cnslr Assn 1989-; NC Ed Assn, NEA 1974-78; *office:* Edneyville Elem Sch Rt 9 Box 448 Hendersonville NC 28739

JONES, DAVID MARCUS, SR., World History Teacher; *b:* Jacksonville, FL; *m:* Lois Christine Shipman; *c:* Lorna C., Taylor, Cynthia D. Maulden, David M. Jr., Cheryl D. Stone; *ed:* (BA) His, 1970, (MA) His, 1971 Mid TN St Univ; Grad Stud Ed; *cr:* Teacher Hendersonville HS 1971-; *ai:* NEA, TEA, SCEA, MTEA 1971-; BSA Summer Camp Cnslr 1974; Knox Doss Teacher of Yr Awd 1980; *home:* 2505 Western Hills Dr Nashville TN 37214

JONES, DELORES M., Kindergarten Teacher; *b:* Warren Cty, IA; *m:* Howard E.; *c:* Roger, Rosemary Ralston, Russell; *ed:* (BA) Eng, Drake Univ 1968; Elem Ed; *cr:* 4th/5th Grade Classroom Teacher Harlford Consolidated 1947-49; Kndgtn Teacher De Sota Cmmty 1961-63, Van Meter Cmmty 1963-; *ai:* K-6th Grade Elem Annual; Building Comm; IA St Ed Assn, NEA 1963-; Van Meter Ed Assn Secy 1977-80; Friends Church Missions Chm 1989-; PTA Mem 1988-; United Society of Friends Women Secy 1958-60; Cub Scout Den Mother 1957-60, 1961-64; *home:* Rt 1 Box 27 Earlham IA 50072

JONES, DENNIS LEE, American History Teacher; *b:* Elk City, OK; *m:* Nana L. Ormand; *c:* Brian L., Lance R.; *ed:* (BA) Teacher Ed/His, Southwestern St Coll 1969; (MA) Spec Ed, Univ of CO Colorado Springs 1979; Cadre I Increasing Teacher Effectiveness; Trng Application of Clinical Teaching & Supervision; Peer Observation; *cr:* Teacher/Coach Nickerson Elem 1969-70, Panorama Jr HS 1977-84, Panorama Mid Sch 1984-; Coach Sierra

HS 1984-87; *ai:* Dist & Building Accountability Comm; ASCD Consortium Rep; Harrison Ed Assn, NEA Mem 1975-81; YMCA Bsktbl Coach 1984-88; Panorama Mid Sch Teacher of Yr 1985-86; Panorama Mid Sch Horizon Excl in Teaching Awd 1984-85; Team Publications in CO 1989-; *office:* Panorama Mid Sch 2145 S Chelton Dr Colorado Springs CO 80916

JONES, DIANE GARCIA, 5th Grade Teacher; *b:* Weslaco, TX; *m:* Mark Lathian; *c:* Natalie, Derek, Trent, Lindsey; *ed:* (BA) Elem Ed, TX Womans Univ 1974; Grad Stud Discipline, Management, Piagel, Kamii, TX Womans Univ 1985; Problems in Teaching Rdng, TX Womens Univ 1986; *cr:* Conversational Span Teacher Adult Ed 1974-77; 5th Grade Teacher Robert E Elem 1974-87; 5th Grade Teacher Newton Rayzor Elem 1987-; *ai:* 5th Grade Level Chairperson Newton Rayzor; Denton Classroom Teachers Assn (Public Relations 1976-77) 1974-; TX St Teachers Assn, NEA 1974-.

JONES, DORIS ANDREWS, Second Grade Teacher; *b:* Troy, TN; *m:* Kenneth Howard; *c:* John K.; *ed:* (BS) Elem Ed, Univ of TN Knoxville 1964; *cr:* Special Ed Obion Cty Bd of Ed 1964-65; 3rd Grade Teacher Ft Campbell KY 1965-66; 5th Grade Teacher Tullahoma TN 1966-67; K-2nd Grade Teacher Troy Elem 1973-87; 2nd Grade Teacher Hillcrest Elem 1987-; *ai:* Delta Kappa Gamma; TN Ed Assn, NEA, Obion Cty Ed Assn 1973-; Troy Womens Club; 1st Baptist church of Troy Youth Dept Secy; TN Career Ladder Level I; *home:* Rt 1 Chestnut St Troy TN 38260

JONES, DOROTHY HELLEN, Second Grade Teacher; *b:* Hope, AR; *c:* Wendell, Shenita; *ed:* (BA) Home Ec, Langston Univ 1955; *ai:* Calendar, Audio Aide, Health, Nutrition Comms; ACTA, NEA, OEA; ACTA Building Rep, Service Pin 1988; Lang Art Inst Grant; *home:* 626 E Main Ardmore OK 73401

JONES, DUKE GREG, Music Instructor; *b:* Wilkes Barre, PA; *m:* Elizabeth A.; *ed:* (BA) K-12th Music Ed, Berklee Coll of Music 1981; *cr:* Music Instr Pembroke Hill Sch 1982-85, Pembroke Acad 1982-, Pembroke High Street Sch 1985-; *ai:* Pembroke Acad Pep & Jazz Band; Music Educators Natl Conference, NEA; *office:* Pembroke Acad/High Street Sch 209 Academy Rd Suncook NH 03301

JONES, EDITH HOPKINS, Sixth Grade Teacher; *b:* Wayland, KY; *m:* William Gerald; *c:* Carolyn Jayne; *ed:* (AA) Alice Lloyd Coll 1963; (BA) Elem Ed, 1965, Elem Ed, 1984 Morehead St Univ; Mid Sch Trng; *cr:* Rdng Teacher Mc Dowell Elem 1966-68; Spec Ed Teacher 1969-71, 6th Grade Teacher 1971- Clark Elem; *ai:* NEA 1966-; KY Ed Assn 1966-; Natl Mid Sch Assn 1989-; KY Mid Sch Assn 1989-; KY Assn for Progress in Sci 1990; *home:* 1122 Cardinal Dr Box 1236 Prestonsburg KY 41653

JONES, ELIZABETH SCHULZE, English Coordinator; *b:* Woodward, TX; *m:* Bobbie Frank; *c:* Louis F., Robert C., Julia A. Gerhards; *ed:* (BS) Eng, TX A&I Univ Kingsville 1960; Various Wkshps, Seminars & Writing Prgms; *cr:* K-12th Grade Rdng Specialist Taft Ind Sch Dist 1960-70; 7th-8th Grade Rdng Coord 1970-73, 7th-8th Grade Rdng/Lang Arts Teacher 1973-76, 7th-12th Grade Eng Coord 1976- Cotulla Ind Sch Dist; *ai:* Los Jefes NHS Spon; ASCD 1988-; TX Joint Cncl Teachers of Eng 1980-; TX Assn of Gifted/Talented 1988-; NCTE 1980-; Delta Kappa Gamma VP 1980-; La Salle Cty Livestock & Cty Show 1967-; United Meth Women (Pres, VP, Secy) 1967-; GSA Leader 1967-69; Cub Scout Leader 1965-67; Teacher Comm; Taught TECAT Sessions for Fellow Teachers; Wkshps for Teachers Current Trends in Ed; *office:* Cotulla HS Box 699 Hwy 97 E Cotulla TX 78014

JONES, EVELYN ROJEAN, English Teacher/Dir of Theatre; *b:* Albuquerque, NM; *ed:* (BA) Psych/Human Relations, Lubbock Chrstn Coll 1975; (MA) Theatre Managment, Angelo St Univ 1980; *cr:* Managing Dir Angelo Civic Theatre 1978-80; Teacher/Dir Monahams HS 1980-; *ai:* Drama Club Spon; UIL Prose & Poetry Coach; UIL Extemporaneous Speaking Coach; TFA Duet Acting Coach; TFA Dra Matic Interp; TFA Humorous Interp-Coach; Assn of TX Prof Educators 1980-; Ward Cty Act Cncl Advisory Bd 1985-; Intnl Youth in Achievement 1981; Young Cmmty Leaders of Amer; Ward Cty Act Cncl Sch Friend Awd 1989; *home:* 812 S Bruce Monahans TX 79756

JONES, FLOYD B., Teacher; *b:* Ashland, AL; *m:* Thelma Kilgore; *ed:* (BA) Mid Grades, Brenau 1983; Working on Masters Ed; *cr:* Comm US Navy 1953-75; 4th-6th Grade Math Teacher Eton Elem 1983-84; 8th Grade Math Teacher Murray Cty Mid Sch 1984-89, Bagley Mid Sch 1989-; *ai:* Tutoring Students Who Need Help; Chatsworth Masonic Lodge 1975-; Order of Eastern Star; *office:* Bagley Mid Sch PO Box 40 Chatsworth GA 30705

JONES, FRANK, Physical Education Teacher; *b:* Bonne Terre, MO; *c:* Aubrey E.; *ed:* (BSED) Phys Ed, SE MO St Univ 1976; *cr:* Phys Ed Teacher/Coach Cntrl Mid Sch 1976-; *ai:* Cntrl Mid Sch 8th Grade Girls Bsktbl & 7th/8th Grade Girls Track Coach; MSTA 1988-89; *home:* R 1 Box 358 Elvins MO 63601

JONES, FRED L., Fifth Grade Teacher; *b:* Harlan, KY; *m:* Janice E. Mills; *c:* Eva Lorie; *ed:* (BA) His, Lincoln Mem Univ 1963; Univ of GA; Lincoln Mem Univ; *cr:* Teacher Whitfield Cty 1963-68; Welfare Work Whitfield Cty & Hancock Cty 1969-79; Self Employed Grocery Store 1980-83; Teacher Hancock Cty 1983; *ai:* Girls Bsktbl Coach; NEA 1983-89; TEA 1983-89; HCEA 1983-89; Natl Arts Acad Grant; Elem Prin; Bsktbl Coach; *home:* Rt 2 Box 287 Sneedville TN 37869

JONES, FREDA IKNER, Jr HS Mathematics Teacher; *b:* Evergreen, AL; *m:* Jerry L.; *c:* Justin L., Jeremy L., Jessica L.; *ed:* (BA) Math/Phys Ed, Troy St Univ 1979; *cr:* Teacher/Dept Head Enterprise Jr HS 1979-; *ai:* Math Club, Mathcounts, Annual Spon; HS Vlybl Ofcl; NCTM, ACTM 1983-; AHSAA Vlybl Ofcl 1986-; Goodman Baptist Church (Pianist 1975-, Teacher 1975-, Youth & Music Leader 1980-); *office:* Enterprise Jr HS 401 W College Enterprise AL 36330

JONES, GAI LAING, Theatre Instructor; *b:* Chickasha, OK; *m:* Wendell H.; *c:* Karyn Laing, Marcie; *ed:* (BA) Speech/Drama, OK Coll for Women 1964; (MA) Theatre, CA St Univ Fullerton 1968; Extension Classes, UCLA & USC; Commercial Classes, Weist-Barron-Hill & Tepper-Gallegos; *cr:* Camp Cnslr GSA 1960-64; Lifeguard/WSI Instr YMCA 1960-64; Eng/Drama Teacher Fullerton Union & Wilshire Jr HS 1964-68; Drama Teacher El Dorado HS 1968-; *ai:* Dir HS Theatre; Adv Drama Club, Troupe 199 ITS; S CA Educl Theatre Assn Wkshp Leader 1980; Theatre Educators Assn, Amer Assn Theatre Educators, CA Educl Theatre Assn, Drama Teachers of S CA, Zeta Phi Eta; Placentia Unified Ed Assn, NEA, CA Teachers Assn, PTSA; Los Altos HS Swim Bd Treas 1986-; COAST Swim Bd 1989; Church Bd Mem 1984; Asst Room Mother 1977-81; Asst Brownie Leader 1979; Soccer Team Mother 1981; Placentia Unified Outstanding Young Teacher 1970; Outstanding Young Women of America 1965; Leader Scndry Ed 1972; 30 Yr Mem GSA 1979; Nom OCW Hall of Fame 1979;Wkshp Leader CA St Thespian Conference 1980-; Dir All St Thespian Shows 1980-; CA St Bd Mem 1980-; CA St Thespian Dir 1990; PTSA Honorary Sevice Awd 1989; *office:* El Dorado HS 1651 N Valencia Ave Placentia CA 92670

JONES, GARA FRENCH, English Teacher; *b:* Akron, OH; *m:* James Evan; *c:* Robert K., James W.; *ed:* (BA) Eng, Mt Union Coll 1967; Elem Certificate Akron Univ; *cr:* Teacher Coventry Jr HS 1967-68, Masson Jr HS 1968-; *ai:* Eng Curr & Good Conduct for Stu Comm; OEA, NEA, LEA, NEOTA, NEOEA; Vermilion Intermediate Sch PTO Secy 1989-.

JONES, HARVEY WAYNE, Science Department Chair; *b:* Winston-Salem, NC; *m:* Alice Fern Janssen; *c:* Anita, Lynnette; *ed:* (BS) Ed/Scndry, 1970, (MS) Ed/Admin, 1983 Bob Jones Univ; Math Ed, Clemson Univ; *cr:* Math Teacher Bob Jones Acad 1970-71, 1973-78; Prin Landmark Chrstn Acad 1978-86; Math/Sci Teacher Colonial Chrstn Sch 1986-; *ai:* Yrbk Spon; Amer Assn of Chrstn Schls 1978-; IN Assn of Chrstn Schls 1986-; *office:* Colonial Chrstn Sch 8140 Union Chapel Rd Indianapolis IN 46240

JONES, HELEN KANE, Fourth Grade Teacher; *b:* Bellaire, OH; *w:* Dale M. (dec); *c:* Dalene Heaton, Kitty Lewis, Stephanie J.; *ed:* (BS) Elem Ed, OH Univ 1969; (MS) Educl Admin, Univ of Dayton 1983; *cr:* 1st Grade Teacher Powhatan York Elem 1967-69; 3rd-5th Grade Teacher Shadyside Local Sch Dist 1969-; *ai:* Curr Comm; NEA, OH Ed Assn 1967-; Shadyside Ed Assn (Secy, Pres 1969-, Negotiations Comm 1970-89); Shadyside Willow Twig 1987-; Delta Kappa Gamma 1988-; Martha Holden Jennings Scholar; *home:* 236 W 43rd Shadyside OH 43947

JONES, IREAN V. BUCKLEY, Third Grade Teacher; *b:* Simpson Cty, MS; *w:* Willie A. (dec); *ed:* (BS) Elem Ed, MS Ind Coll 1962; (MS) Elem Ed, Univ of MD 1975; Cosmotology Certificate 1984; *cr:* Teacher Simpson Cty MS 1954-65, Charles Cty MD 1965-; *ai:* MD Teachers Assn, Charles Cty Teachers Assn, NEA 1965-; PTO 1965-; Ushers Assn VP 1967-; Intnl Ushers Organizations 1967-; *home:* 4032 Martin L King Jr Ave Washington DC 20032

JONES, JEAN MARIE (NAYDOCK), Middle School Art Teacher; *b:* Wilmington, DE; *m:* Richard N.; *c:* Lindsey M.; *ed:* (BS) Art Ed, Kutztown Univ 1977; Scndry Counseling, Kutztown Univ; *cr:* HS/Mid Sch Art Teacher 1977-79, Mid Sch Art Teacher 1979- Brandywine; *ai:* Art Enrichment Prgm; Festival of Arts & Crafts Dir; Yrbk Adv; PA St Ed Assn, NEA 1977-; NAEA 1990; Outstanding Young Educator Awd 1986-87; *office:* Brandywine Heights Sch Dist 200 Weiss St Topton PA 19562

JONES, JERRY I., Mathematics Teacher; *b:* Evansville, IN; *m:* Brenda Somogie; *c:* Jeffrey I.; *ed:* (BA) Math Endorsement Elem Ed, 1970, (MS) Elem Ed/Math, 1974 Univ of Evansville; *cr:* 5th-8th Grade Math Teacher Wheeler Elem Sch 1970-72; 5th/6th Grade Math Teacher Mc Gary Elem Sch 1972-84; 6th-8th Grade Math Teacher Mc Gary Mid Sch 1984-; *ai:* Math Coach 1984-89; Evansville Teachers Assn Building Rep 1970-80; NEA 1970-, Life Mem; SW IN Cncl Teachers of Math 1988-; IN St Teachers Assn 1970-; Natl Rifle Assn 1980-; Ducks Unlimited 1970-; *home:* 2253 Cherry Ln Evansville IN 47711

JONES, JESSIE WALKER, 6th Grade Teacher; *b:* Yazoo City, MS; *m:* Clifton L.; *c:* Marlana Claree; *ed:* (BS) Elem Ed, MS Valley St 1971; (MS) Elem Ed, Jackson St Univ 1973; Spec Ed, MS Coll; Effective Teaching & Assertive Teaching Wkshps; *cr:* 4th/5th Grade Teacher 1972-77, 6th Grade Teacher 1977- Woolfolk Elem Sch; *ai:* Adv Stu Cncl; 6th Grade Team Leader; Mem Team Pupil-Teacher Intervention; Natl Teachers Assn Building Rep 1972-; GSA Leader 1976- 11 Yr Service Pin; NAACP 1980-; *home:* 201 E 3rd St Yazoo City MS 39194

JONES, JOHN PAUL, 9th Grade Science Teacher; *b:* Jackson, MI; *m:* Connie Renee Mc Clure; *c:* John D., Derek R.; *ed:* (BS) Bio/Chem, 1985, (MS) Bio, 1990 Morehead St Univ; *cr:* Teacher Introduction Chem/Physics Johnson Cntrl HS; *ai:* Cntrl Elem Grade Sch Bsktbl & Ftbl Coach 1987-89; *office:* Johnson Cntrl HS Rt 276 Box 202 Paintsville KY 41240

JONES, JONI GILLILAND, Second Grade Teacher; *b:* Chillicothe, MO; *m:* David Duane; *c:* Quentin C., Jaryn L.; *ed:* (BS) Elem Ed, MO Western St Coll 1978; Grad Stud Univ of MO, NW MO St Univ; *cr:* 2nd Grade Teacher Braymer C-4 Sch 1978-; *ai:* Prof Dev & Curr Comm; Cmmty Teacher Assn 1978-; Ludlow Cmmty Church (Pianist, Youth Puppet Ministry Coord); *office:* Braymer C-4 Sch 1 Bobcat Ave Braymer MO 64624

JONES, JOSEPH ALAN, English Teacher; *b:* Oak Hill, OH; *m:* Teresa Hope Crabtree; *c:* Erin S.; *ed:* (BS) Ed, Rio Grande Coll 1971; (MA) Eng/Hum Ed, OH St Univ 1977; *cr:* Teacher Operation Head Start 1969-73; Instr Amer Inst of Banking 1974-82; Teacher Fulton Mid Sch 1971-838 Heath HS 1983-; *ai:* Dramatics Coach; Frosh Class Adv; Thespian Society; Footlighters; Soliloquy Lit Magazine; Heath Ed Assn Pres 1979-80; OEA, NEA, 1st Meth Church; Denison Univ Teacher Ed Advisory Cncl; Licking Cty Educator Awd; Jennings Scholar; Dow Educator Awd; Key Club Teacher of Yr; *office:* Heath HS 300 Licking View Dr Heath OH 43056

JONES, JOYCE M., 5th Grade Teacher; *b:* Clovis, NM; *m:* Walter; *c:* Beverly Potter Bennett, Terry Potter Turner, Rick Potter; *ed:* (BS) Elem Ed, E NM Univ 1982; *cr:* 5th Grade Teacher Floyd Sch 1983-; *home:* Rt 2 Box 228 Portales NM 88130

JONES, JUDY ANN, 5th Grade Teacher; *b:* Flint, MI; *ed:* (BA) His/Elem Ed, Western MI Univ 1971; *cr:* 6th Grade Teacher 1971-76; 5th Grade Teacher 1976-77; 3rd Grade Teacher 1977-81; 5th Grade Teacher 1981- Dowagiac Union Schls; *ai:* Dowagiac Bus & Prof Women Secy; Beta Mu (Secy/Pres).

JONES, JUDY BROWN, Mathematics Teacher; *b:* Milledgeville, GA; *m:* Tullie C. Jr.; *c:* Tricia, Lisa, Leslie; *ed:* (BS) Math, GA Coll 1969; *cr:* Teacher GA Military Sch 1979-; *ai:* NHS; *home:* 413 Browns Crossing Rd Milledgeville GA 31061

JONES, JUDY KAY, Business Education Teacher; *b:* Ardmore, OK; *m:* James E.; *c:* Jennifer K.; *ed:* Assoc Ed, E OK St Coll 1971; (BSED) Elem Ed/Bus Ed, NE St Univ 1973; (MA) Elem Ed, SE St Univ 1983; *cr:* 4th Grade Teacher Whitesboro Public Sch 1975-77; 6th Grade Math Teacher Plaza Towers Elem 1977-79; 4th Grade Techer Red Oak Public Sch 1979-80; Bus Ed Teacher Panola Public Sch 1980-; *ai:* Sch Yrbk & Newspaper Adv; Sr Class Spon; OK Ed Assn Cty Delegate; Latimer Cty Ed Assn Pres 1981-82; Panola Teachers Assn VP 1989-; Panola Baptist Church (Sunday Sch Teacher 1985-87, Bible Sch Art Dir 1988-89); EOCS Tole Painting Instr 1989; *office:* Panola HS Box 6 Panola OK 74559

JONES, KAREN MAE, Vocational Home Ec Teacher; *b:* Hutchinson, KS; *ed:* (BS) Home Ec Ed, S Nazarene Univ 1959; (MS) Voc Home Ec, KS St Univ 1981; *cr:* Jr HS Teacher Chisholm Jr HS 1959-74; Mid Sch Teacher Chisholm Mid Sch 1974-; *ai:* Boys Jr HS Cooking Skill Club; NEA (Soc Chm 1962-74) 1959-; KS Ed Assn (Newton Soc Chm 1962-74) 1959-, 1st Runner Up Awd 1985; KHEA Dist G (Treas 1975-77, Pres Elect 1989-, Pres 1990); KVHET Mid Sch Prep Ex Bd 1988-; Delta Kappa Gamma 1975-; Harvey Cty Home Ec Assn 1969-; Amer Voc Home Ec Assn 1965-; AVA, Ks Voc Home Ec Teachers 1975-; Harvey Cty Home Ec Assn Pres 1985-86; Carl Perkins Grant Self-Esteem 1987-88, Human Sexuality 1989-; KS Ed Assn Teacher of Yr 1985; *home:* PO Box 2 Newton KS 67114

JONES, KATIE MAE, Language Arts Teacher; *b:* Bartow, FL; *ed:* (BS) Lang Art, FL Memorial Coll 1969; (MS) Admin/Supervision, Nova Univ 1976; *cr:* Lang Art Teacher Dade Cty Public Schls 1969-; *ai:* Lang Art Dept Chairperson 1979-84; Lake Stevens Mid Sch Team Leader 1987-; United Teachers of Dade; Zeta Phi Beta Charter Mem 1972; New Hope Primitive Baptist Church Mem; Lake Stevens Mid Sch Person of Month 1990 & Mother of Yr 1981-82; *office:* Lake Stevens Mid Sch 18484 NW 48th Pl Miami FL 33055

JONES, KENNETH EARL, Seventh Grade English Teacher; *b:* Roswell, NM; *ed:* (BS) Elem Ed/Eng, Univ of TX El Paso 1969; (MRE) Religious/Ed Admin, SW Baptist Theological Seminary 1974; Basic Youth Conflicts Seminars 1972; *cr:* Missionary Teacher Foreign Mission Bd 1969-71; 6th Grade Teacher Mesa Vista Elem Sch 1971-73; 5th/6th Grade Teacher Thomas Manor Elem 1974-80; 7th Grade Eng Teacher Eastwood Mid Sch 1980-; *ai:* TX Classroom Teachers Assn 1984-; Intnl Rdng Assn 1986-; Paso Del Norte Cncl Teachers of Eng 1985-; Eastwood Mid Sch Teacher of Yr 1981; Outstanding Men of America; Thomas Manor Elem Teacher of Yr 1977; *office:* Eastwood Mid Sch 2612 Chaswood Dr El Paso TX 79935

JONES, LAWRENCE ARTHUR, Mathematics Teacher; *b:* Somerset, PA; *m:* Linda Sue Jackson; *c:* Eric, Michael; *ed:* (BS) Math Ed, 1968, Master Equivalence Math Ed, 1975 Indiana Univ of PA; Cmptr Classes, PA St Univ; Ed Bus Needs; *cr:* Part Time Math Teacher Comm Coll of Allegheny Cty 1984-85; Robert Morris Coll 1985-; Math Teacher Carlynton Sch Dist 1968-; *ai:* NCTM 1980-; Sharon Cmmty Presbyn Church Elder 1987-; *office:* Carlynton Jr/Sr HS 435 Kings Hwy Carnegie PA 15106

JONES, LORETTA HALL, Fifth Grade Teacher; *b:* Tuscaloosa, AL; *m:* Joe Eddie; *c:* Tamara, La Chelle; *ed:* (BS) Elem, AL A&M Univ 1972; (MS) Curr Instruction, Ashland Coll 1989; Supervision/Admin Cert; *cr:* 4th Grade Teacher Maulton Elem 1972-73, Charleston Sch 1975-76; 6th Grade Teacher Jane Lindsay Elem Sch 1976-77, Hawthorne Boone Sch 1977-86; 5th Grade Teacher Fairhome Acad 1986-; *ai:* Hawthorne Jr HS Track Coach 1984-85; Lorain Intnl Comm 1987-89; Stu Cncl Adv 1984-86; Anti-Drug Campaign Coord; Concerned Parent

Commission Chaperone; Stu Recognition Prgms; Adopt-A-Sch Prgms Drug Wkshp Operator; OH Ed Assn Delegate 1986-, 1988, Human Relations Awd 1988; Lorain Cty Alliance of Black Sch Educators Secy 1989-; Alpha Kappa Alpha 1988; Lorain City PTA Cncl 1st VP 1988-, Outstanding Educator of Yr 1990; Lorain YWCA Bd of Trustees (Secy 1989, 2nd VP 1990); Outstanding Safety Patrol Adv 1977-80; Martha Holden Jennings Scholar 1985; Outstanding Bible Sunday Sch Teacher; Natl Sch Public Relations Awd 1986; Employee of Yr 1986; Cmmty Grants; *home:* 125 Potomac Elyria OH 44035

JONES, LORRAINE SNYDER, Elementary Gifted Teacher; *b:* West Reading, PA; *m:* Donald E.; *c:* Douglas T., Cathy L.; *ed:* (BS) Elem Ed, Kutztown Univ 1956; Villanova Univ, Temple Univ; *cr:* Teacher Tredyffrin-Easttown Sch Dist 1956-57, Wyomissing Area Sch Dist 1957-58, Schuylkill Haven Sch Dist 1958-61, Blue Mountain Sch Dist 1970-; *ai:* PSEA, NEA; St Johns UCC Consistory Pres 1986-87; GSA Leader; Sunday Sch Teacher; Bd of Chrstn Ed Pres 1975-76; Taught Classes In Systematic Trng for Effective Parenting & Teaching; Taught Inservice Prgms for Teachers on Writing; Involved in Temple Univ Law Ed Prgm; *office:* Blue Mountain Elem Sch Reddale Rd Orwigsburg PA 17961

JONES, LOUISE LINNEMEIER (CUBBLER), 8th/9th Grade English Teacher; *b:* Reading, PA; *m:* Paul Leonard; *c:* Andrew Linnemeier Cubbler (dec), Matthew J. Cubbler; *ed:* (BS) Eng, Shippensburg Univ 1965; Grad Stud Eng, Middlebury Breadloaf Sch of Lang, West Chester Univ; *cr:* 9th Grade Eng Teacher Boyertown Area HS 1965-67; 10th Grade Eng Teacher Lower Merion Sr HS 1967-68; 6th/7th Grade Eng Teacher 1979-89, 8th/9th Grade Eng Teacher 1989- Tredyffrin Easttown Intermediate; *ai:* Co-Adv Literary Magazine; 9th Grade Creative Writing Teacher; Writing Across Curr Dev Comm; TEEA, PSEA 1979-; Poems Published Local Poetry Newsletter, World of Poetry Press 1989; Sch Rep with Prin Natl Excl in Ed Awd 1987; *office:* Tredyffrin Easttown Sch 840 Old Lancaster Rd Berwyn PA 19312

JONES, MARCELINE YVONNE, Mathematics Teacher; *b:* Detroit, MI; *c:* Charles E. Jr., Calli E.; *ed:* (BED) Elem Ed, 1975, (MED) Math, 1980 Wayne St Univ; Various Wkshps Lewis Research Center; Mem Success Leadership Trng Prgm; *cr:* Relief Teacher, 1st Grade Homeroom Teacher Burns Elem; 1st/2nd Grade Homeroom Teacher J R King Elem; 3rd Grade Homeroom Teacher; 5th Grade Math Teacher; 3rd/5th/6th Grade Math Teacher; 5th Grade Homeroom Teacher; *ai:* Spon Sch Skating Parties; NCTM, MI Cncl Teachers of Math 1989-; NASA, NSTA, NEWEST Mem, Outstanding Teacher 1989; Sch Teacher of Yr 1989; *office:* J R King Elem Sch 16800 Cheyenne Detroit MI 48219

JONES, MARY ANN DEITRICK, Fourth Grade Teacher; *b:* Defiance, OH; *m:* Gregory A.; *c:* Kelly, Kara, Kirk; *ed:* (BS) Elem Ed, Defiance Coll 1974; *cr:* 1st Grade Teacher St Mary's 1974-81; 4th Thru 6th Math Teacher 1982-83, First Grade Teacher 1984-88, 4th Thru 6th Grade Soc Stud Teacher 1988- St Mary's Sch; *ai:* Religious Coordin; Natl Catholic Ed Assn; Girl Scouts 1990; Participated in Dev & Writing of the Toledo Diocesean Rdng Curr Guidelines

JONES, MARY FRANCIS, Sixth Grade Teacher; *b:* Springfield, MO; *m:* Morris R.; *c:* Russ, Beth; *ed:* (BS) Elem/Scndry Ed, Memphis St Univ 1970; *cr:* Teacher Holmes Elem Sch 1976-82, Tabernacle Elem Sch 1970-76, Crestview Elem Sch 1982-; *ai:* NEA, TEA Mem 1970-; Career Level I Teacher; Career Teacher; *home:* Rt 2 Box 319 Covington TN 38019

JONES, MARY LONGORIA, Third Grade Teacher; *b:* Galveston, TX; *m:* Gary Allen; *c:* Taylor A.; *ed:* (BA) Elem Ed, Univ of AZ 1979; (MA) Eng, Northern AZ Univ 1989; Using Lit to Motivate Rdng & Writing Across Curr, Whole Lang in Classroom; *cr:* 3rd Grade Teacher A J Mitchell Elem 1979-; *ai:* Drama Coach & Choreography; Soc Stud Curr & Textbook Adoption Comm; AZ Ed Assn, NEA, Prof Educators of Nogales Mem 1979-; AZ Assn Learning about Environment Mem 1988-; AZ Nature Conservancy Mem 1987-; *office:* A J Mitchell Sch 222 Plum St Nogales AZ 85621

JONES, MICKEY TUBBS, Second Grade Teacher; *b:* Dyersburg, TN; *m:* Donald Rube; *c:* Jamey D., Jenney R.; *ed:* (BS) Elem Ed, Austin Peay St Univ 1974; (MS) Curr/Instruction/Rdng, Univ of TN Martin 1979; *cr:* Teacher Dyersburg Primary Sch 1974-; *ai:* Dyersburg Ed Assn Assembly Rep; W TN Teacher Center Policy Bd Pres; Apple Chorus Singer; Delta Kappa Gamma Corresponding Secy 1987-; Dyersburg Ed Assn (Past Treas 1988-89) 1974-; GSA Leader 1984-, 20 Yr Pin 1989; Hillcrest Ensemble Singer 1987-; Dyersburg City Schls Teacher of Yr 1986-87; Dyersburg St Comm Coll Distinguished Alumni; *office:* Dyersburg Primary Sch Lewis St Dyersburg TN 38024

JONES, NEDRA GOOD, Retired 1st Grade Teacher; *b:* Great Falls, MT; *c:* Robert, Nancy Peck, Mary Asher; *ed:* (BSED) Elem Ed, MSSC Joplin 1971; Grad Stud Pittsburg St Univ; *cr:* 1st Grade Teacher Liberty Elem 1971-88; *home:* 330 Garfield Box 104 Baxter Springs KS 66713

JONES, NINA CLARE, Spanish Teacher/Dept Chairman; *b:* Fort Mc Clellan, AL; *ed:* (BA) Span, Augusta Coll 1978; (MA) Ed, Austin Peay 1987; *cr:* Span Teacher Glenn Hills HS 1978-81; Testing Coord US Army Ed Center 1982-85; Span Teacher Northeast HS 1986-; *ai:* Wrestling Chrldr Spon; Intnl Club Co-Spon; Dept Chairperson; NEA, TEA; *office:* Northeast H S 3701 Trenton Rd Clarksville TN 37040

JONES, NORMAN HOOPER, Eng as Second Lang Teacher; *b:* Nashville, TN; *m:* Jean Waits; *c:* Brittany J.; *ed:* (BA) Eng, George Peabody Coll 1960; (MS) Curr & Instruction, Univ of TN 1971; (EDD) Ed Admin & Supervision, Vanderbilt Univ 1981; Peabody Coll Japan 1980, WV Univ, TN St Univ, Mid TN St Univ; *cr:* Teacher Red Bank Jr HS 1959-66, Nashville North HS/Du Pont Jr HS/Cameron Mid Sch 1966-; *ai:* NEA Life Mem 1950-; TN Ed Assn 1959-; Metropolitan Nashville Ed Assn Dist Dir 1966-; TN Foreign Lang Teachers Assn Life Mem; TN Teachers Study Cncl Dist Chm 1985-; Childrens Intnl Educl Comm 1985-; Mason/Shriner 1959-; Nashville Area World Coin Club 1978-; Career Ladder III Teacher 10 Yr Cert; *office:* Cameron Mid Sch 1034 1st Ave S Nashville TN 37210

JONES, PATRICIA A., 6th Grade Mathematics Teacher; *b:* Bainbridge, GA; *d:* Junior L. Robinson; *c:* Patrina F. Robinson; *ed:* (BA) Ed, 1978, (MA) Ed, 1981 MI St Univ; Math, Univ of Detroit; Math Educl Trng Wkshps; Essential Elements of Effective Instructions 1988; *cr:* Asst Supvr Marine Midland Bank & Trust 1965-71; Math Teacher Detroit Bd of Ed 1978-; *ai:* Math Club Gifted Talent; Union Rep; AFT Delegate 1983-89; Zeta Phi Beta 1989; ASCD 1985-; Metropolitan Detroit Rdng Cncl 1989-; MI Teachers Convention Delegate 1983-; PTA Election Comm 1990; Spirit of Detroit Awd City Cncl of Detroit 1988; *home:* 22150 Pembroke Detroit MI 48219

JONES, PATRICIA ANN, Eng & Teacher of at Risk Stu; *b:* Lebanon, IN; *m:* Robert D.; *c:* Anna, Jack, Amy, April, Joel; *ed:* (BA) Elem Ed, Univ of CO 1967; (MA) Ed-Rdng, Univ of Portland 1985; *cr:* Lib/Teachers Aide 1965-67; Upper Elem 1967-69 CO Springs Public Sch; Ed Dir First United Meth Church 1982-85; Eng Teacher of At Risk Stu Ridgefield Sch Dist 1985-; *ai:* Yrbk Adv; Stu Lit Mag Adv; Sch 21st Century Plan Co-Chm; NEA; WA Ed Assn 1985-; Ridgefield Ed Assn Treas/Secy 1987-; NCTE 1985-; Ridgefield Food Bank Founder Co 1981-85; Ridgefield Cmmty Ctr Founder Coord 1983-85; Institute Developmental Sci-Chm of Bd 1985-88; Natl Endowment for Humanities Grant; Ridgefield Schls Good News Awd; WA Sch Bd Assn Teacher Yr Honarable Mention; WA St Teacher Excl Nom; Clark Cty Woman of His; *home:* 1285 SW 84th Ave Portland OR 97225

JONES, PATRICIA LINLEY, English Teacher/Chair; *b:* Norfolk, VA; *m:* B. J.; *c:* Bill, Paula, Elizabeth; *ed:* (AA) Jr Coll of Broward Cty 1963; (BS) Eng/His, Baylor Univ 1975; Working Towards Masters Eng, Baylor Univ; *cr:* 8th Grade Eng Teacher Hearne Jr HS; 12th Grade Eng Teacher Hearne HS; *ai:* UIL Prose, Poetry, Spelling; orosh Class Spon; TJCET; Bremond PTA Pres 1976-78; *office:* Hearne HS 1210 Hackberry Hearne TX 77859

JONES, PATRICIA WARREN, Kindergarten Teacher; *b:* Indiana, PA; *m:* Mark Richard; *c:* Heidi L., Laura B.; *ed:* (BS) Elem Ed, 1972, (MS) Early Chldhd, 1976 Indiana Univ of PA; *cr:* Classroom Teacher Marion Center Area Schls 1973-; *ai:* Creekside Washington Head Teacher; MCAEA, PSEA, NEA 1973-; Wee Angels Pre-sch Chairperson 1985-; Barbara Freund Peace Awd 1990; *office:* Creekside Washington Elem Sch RD 1 Box 199 Creekside PA 15732

JONES, PATSY LEE, English/Physical Ed Teacher; *b:* Beckley, WV; *ed:* (BSED) Ed/Eng/Phys Ed, Concord Coll 1966; (MSED) Ed, George Mason Univ 1980; *cr:* Phys Ed Teacher Fairfax HS 1966-68; Eng/Phys Ed Teacher Herndon HS 1968-75, Falls Church HS 1975-80, Cabrillo Mid Sch 1981-; *ai:* Var & Jr Var Field Hockey, Bsktbl, Sftbl Coach; Herndon HS Forensics; Girls Athletic Assn, Soph Class Spon Herndon HS; First Aid Taks Force Ventura Unified; NEA 1966-; CA Teachers Assn, Ventura Ed Assn 1981-; NCTE 1988-; VA Ed Assn, Fairfax Ed Assn 1966-80; *office:* Cabrillo Mid Sch 1426 E Santa Clara Ventura CA 93001

JONES, PAULA LARAINE, Science Teacher; *b:* Hobbs, NM; *ed:* (BA) Russian, 1967, (MA) Guidance Counseling, 1971 AZ St Univ; *cr:* Sci Teacher Sierra Vista Elem 1967-73, Kennedy Mid Sch 1973-81; 7th/8th Grade Teacher Greenfield Elem 1981-85; Sci Teacher M O Bush Elem 1985-; *ai:* Girls Bsktbl Team Coach; Drama Club Spon; AZ Sci Teachers, NSTA 1988-; NEA, AEA 1967-; M O Bush Teacher of Yr; *office:* Maxine O Bush Elem Sch 602 E Siesta Way Phoenix AZ 85040

JONES, RETA MORTON, Fifth Grade Teacher; *b:* Caryville, TN; *m:* J. W.; *c:* Nancy Pierce, J. W. II, Ken M.; *ed:* (BA) Elem Ed, Univ of TN 1974; (MS) Elem Ed, TN Tech Univ 1987; *cr:* Teachers Aide 1967-68; 3rd Grade Teacher 1968-89; Girls Bsktbl Coach 1974-78; 5th Grade Teacher 1989- Eaton Elem; *ai:* Young Astronauts Spon; 4-H Club Spon; Loudon Cty Ed Assn 1968-Teacher of Yr 1984-85; East TN Ed Assn 1968-; TN Ed Assn 1968-; NEA 1968; Bradbury United Meth Church Teacher, Yth Cnslr, & Asst Lay Leader 1966-; *home:* Rt 1 Woodlawn Rd Lenoir City TN 37771

JONES, RHONDA FULGHUM, First Grade Teacher; *b:* Dublin, GA; *m:* Kermit Elwood Sr.; *c:* J. Michelle, Kermit E. Jr.; *ed:* (BA) Elem Ed, 1978, (MS) Rdng, 1980 Longwood Coll; *cr:* Kndgtn Teacher 1978-79, 1st Grade Teacher 1979-80 Banco Dist Elem Sch; 3rd Grade Teacher 1980, 1st Grade Teacher 1980-85 Central Elem Sch; 1st Grade Teacher Eureka Elem Sch 1985-; *ai:* Child Study & Self Study Comm; Lang Art & Music; Mt Tirzah Baptist Church (Teacher, Youth Choir Dir, Acteens Leader, Activator Leader) 1989-; Charlotte Cty Leaders Against Litter Chm 1988-; VA Governors Merit & Excl Awd 1989; *home:* PO Box 408 Charltte Ct Hse VA 23923

JONES, RICKY ELWIN, Eighth Grade Science Teacher; *b:* Loretto, TN; *m:* Martha Ann Evers; *c:* Amy S., Christopher E.; *ed:* (BS) Psych, Florence St Univ 1973; (MED) Admin/Supervision, TN St Uni 1984; *cr:* 5th/6th Grade Teacher Sacred Heart Elem 1973-74; 7th/8th Grade Teacher St Joseph Elem Sch 1974-85; South Lawrence Elem Sch 1985-; *ai:* Boys Bsktbl Coach; Southern Assn of Elem Schls Steering Comm Mem; Lawrence Cty Ed Assn 1974-; TN Ed Assn 1974-; NEA 1974-; *office:* South Lawrence Elem Sch 707 2nd Ave S Loretto TN 38469

JONES, ROBERT ALLEN, History Teacher; *b:* Salt Lake City, UT; *m:* Vera Coleen Glass; *c:* Christopher, Clark, Channing, Adam, Cydnie; *ed:* (BA) His, Brigham Young Univ 1967; (MS) His, Univ of UT 1986; *cr:* Teacher Cyprus HS 1967-; *ai:* Chess Team, Quiz Team, Model United Nations, NHS, His Fair Adv; Stu Schlsps; UT HS Chess Assn Pres 1977, 1981, 1984, 1989; Stratford Fellowship Recipient; Teacher of Yr Cyprus HS 1983-84; Reader Advanced Placement Amer His Exams; Co-Author; *home:* 3358 S 7730 W Magna UT 84044

JONES, ROBERT CLAIR, Social Studies Teacher; *b:* Norfolk, VA; *m:* Geri Lee Siebels; *c:* Adam, Matt, Aaron, Lee; *ed:* (BS) Ed, 1971, (MS) Scndry Ed, 1981 Old Dominion Univ; *cr:* Teacher VA Beach Jr HS 1971-73, Kempsville Jr HS 1973-; *ai:* Chm K Jr HS In-Service Comm; Mem Faculty Advisory Comm; Va Beach Soc Studies Curr Comm 1989-91; Elect Mem VA Beach Pgm Dev Comm; Intensive Assistance Team; Ad Hoc Soc Stud Comm for Mid Schls; Soc Stud 8 Curr Dev Comm; VA Beach Ed Assn; VA Cncl of Soc Stud Tidewater Regional Teacher of Yr 1986; VA Cncl of Soc Stud VA Teacher of Yr 1986; Daughters of Amer Revolution- Outstanding Teacher of Amer History Lynhaven Chapter 1985; Old Dominion Univ Outstanding Soc Stud Educator 1981; Mem VA Beach Instructional Strategies Team 1990; Taught Staff Dev Course, Improving Stu Achievement Soc Stud 1989/1990; Conducted Numerous St & City Inservice Prgms & Conference Sessions; *office:* Kempsville Jr H S 860 Churchill Dr Virginia Beach VA 23464

JONES, ROBERT EDWARD, Teacher; *b:* Oak Hill, OH; *m:* Betty L. Fuller; *c:* Kathy L., Pamela L.; *ed:* (BS) Scndry Ed, Rio Grande Coll 1966; (MA) Math, LA St Univ 1969; *cr:* Math Teacher Fairborn City Schls 1965-; *ai:* Fairborn HS Sports Dept Videographer & Intramural Dir; OH Cncl Math 1966-; City of Fairborn Parks Bd 1978-82; Natl Sci Math Grant 1968-69; Fairborn City Schls Teacher of Yr 1986-87; *office:* Fairborn HS 900 E Dayton-Yellowsprings Rd Fairborn OH 45324

JONES, RONALD A., Jr HS Science/Health Teacher; *b:* Akron, OH; *m:* Carmen M. Ortiz; *c:* Scott, Jennifer, Jonathan; *ed:* (BS) Elem Ed, Malone Coll 1971; US Navy Pharmacy Tech; Akron Univ; Kent St Univ; Youngstown St Univ; *cr:* Pharmacy/Tech US Navy 1961-66; Teacher Sebring McKinley HS 1971-; *ai:* NEA/OEA; Quest Intnl; SLEA Pres; Friends Disaster Service 1987-; Prison Fellowship Ministries 1988-; Alliance Right to Life 1989-; Vietnam Vet 1965-66; *home:* 329 W High St Alliance OH 44601

JONES, RONALD E., Student Activities Director; *b:* Antioch, CA; *m:* Mary Ann Kyle; *c:* Craig, Michael, Deborah; *ed:* (BMUS) Music Ed, Univ of the Pacific 1963; *cr:* Teacher 1963- Stu Act Dir 1987- Del Oro HS; *ai:* Stu Act Dir; Stu Cncl Adv; CA Teachers Assn, NEA, CA Music Educators Assn, Music Educators Natl Conference, N CA Band Dir Assn, CA Band Dir Assn, S CA Sch Band & Orch Assn, CA Assn of Dirs of Act; N Sacramento Valley Music Festival Assn (Organizing Chm, 1st Pres); N CA Band Dirs Assn (Secy/Treas 1972-74, Pres 1974-76, 1986-87, Immediate Past Pres 1976-77, 1987-89); CA Music Educators Assn (Band Rep 1976-78, Honor Band Site Audition Chm 1984-85, Pres Elec/Treas 1986-88; Placer Cty Teacher of Yr 1987; N CA Band Dir of Yr 1988; Rocklin Rotary Club Cmmty Service Awd 1988; CA Band Dirs Assn Distinguished Service Awd 1989; Del Oro HS Mentor Teacher 1988-; *office:* Del Oro HS 3301 Taylor Rd Loomis CA 95650

JONES, ROSA SCOTT, Assistant Principal; *b:* Melder, LA; *m:* Melford; *c:* Melonie D. Jones Blanco; *ed:* (BA) Elem Grades, Southern Univ 1959; (MA) Admin/Supervision, Northwestern St Univ 1980; LA Teacher Evaluation Prgm Assessor; *cr:* Teacher 1959-77, Asst Prin 1978-79 Lincoln Williams Elem Sch; Asst Prin Lecompte Elem Sch 1979-80, Carter C Raymond Jr HS 1980-; *ai:* Supervision of Bsktbl Games & Night Act; PTA; LA Assn of Ed 1959-; RFT 1979-; NASSP, LA Assn of Sch Exec 1980-; Lecompte Voters League Asst Secy 1980-; Zeta Phi Beta VP 1978-, Zeta of Yr 1989; Order of Eastern Star 1965, Outstanding Service 1975; Daughters of Isis Deputy of Oasis 1980-84; Rapides Assn of Prin & Asst Prin; *home:* 1508 Maple St PO Box 1007 Lecompte LA 71346

JONES, ROSIE DUNN, Third Grade Teacher; *b:* Gould, AR; *m:* Johnny James; *c:* Cedric R., Cindy R. Jones Luckett; *ed:* (BS) Elem Ed, AM&N Univ AR Pine Bluff 1962; *cr:* 3rd Grade Teacher Gould Elem Sch 1962-64; 3rd Grade Teacher 1964-71, 4th Grade Teacher 1971-77 Star City Elem Sch; 3rd Grade Teacher Carver Elem Sch 1977-; *ai:* NEA, AR Ed Assn, Pine Bluff Ed Assn; Faith Presbyn Church, Delta Sigma Theta; Awd for Dedicated Service & Support of Stu Teaching Prgm 1989, 1990; Teacher of Month 1986.

JONES, S. DIANE HODGE, 6th Science Teacher; *b:* Chattanooga, TN; *m:* Chris; *c:* Kip, Whitney; *ed:* (BS) Carson Newman Coll 1963, (MS) Union Coll 1975; Grad Stud Union Coll 1977; *cr:* Teacher Spalding Jr HS 1963-65, Oglethorpe Elem 1968-70, Jefferson Elem 1971-85, Jefferson Mid Sch 1985-; *ai:* Young Astronaut & Sci Fair Club; Working With Young People in Church & Sunday Sch Teacher; NEA, JCEA; *office:* Jefferson Mid Sch Andrew Johnson Hwy Jefferson City TN 37760

JONES, SARAH A., Sixth Grade Teacher; *b:* Washington, GA; *ed:* (BS) Bus Admin, Paine Coll 1981; Mid Grades Cert, Augusta Coll; Grad Work Elem Ed, Univ of SC; *cr:* 6th Grade Teacher Washington-Wilkes Mid 1981-82; Data-Entry Clerk Plant Vogtle 1983-85; 6th Grade Teacher Morgan Road Mid 1985-; *ai:* Sci Bowl Comm Spon; GA Assn of Educators, Richmond Cty Assn of Educators, NEA.

JONES, SHARON GAYE, Spanish & French Teacher; *b:* Ft Worth, TX; *ed:* (BA) Span, Univ of TX Arlington 1983; Working Towards Masters TX Chrstn Univ; Intermediate & Advanced Span, Malaga Spain; *cr:* Span/Fr Teacher Everman HS 1983-; *ai:* Everman HS Foreign Lang Club; Amer Assn Teachers of Span & Portuguese, AATF, TX Foreign Lang Assn; Fr Amer Inst for Intnl Stud; Phi Sigma Iota Pres 1982-83; Amer Cncl for Teachers of Foreign Lang; Rockefeller Fnd Fellowship for HS Foreign Lang Teachers 1989; Shirley Gibson Chapman Schlsp TX Chrstn Univ 1989; *office:* Everman HS 1000 S Race Everman TX 76140

JONES, SHERRY BOYLES, Social Studies Teacher; *b:* Tallulah, LA; *m:* Henry Ronald; *c:* Rick; *ed:* (BA) Scndry Ed, NE LA Univ 1970; (MED) Admin & Supervison, Nicholls St Univ 1989; Admin Internship, LA St Univ 1989; *cr:* Teacher La Salle HS 1970-77, Winnsboro Jr HS 1977-80, Ellender Memorial Sch 1980-82, Houma Jr HS 1982-; *ai:* Positive Attitude Club & Responsibly Educated Adolescents Can Help Adv; Assn Prof Educator of LA, Terrebonne Prof Educators 1989-; Parish Employee Comm Rep 1990; La Salle Parish Outstanding Young Educator 1972; Teacher of Yr Houma Jr, Terrebonne Parish & Region VI of LA Mid Sch/Jr HS 1989-; Master Teacher 1990-; *office:* Houma Jr HS 200 St Charles St Houma LA 70360

JONES, STANLEY ALAN, Social Studies Teacher; *b:* Austell, GA; *m:* Carolin; *c:* Alicia, Anthony; *ed:* (BA) His, 1969, (MED) Scndry Ed, 1977 W GA Coll; *cr:* Teacher Lindley Jr HS 1969-71, N Cobb HS 1972-74, Nash Mid Sch 1976-; Cntrl Alternative HS 1990; *office:* Cntrl Alternative HS Ward St Smyrna GA 30080

JONES, SUSAN, 7th Grade English Teacher; *b:* Logan, WV; *ed:* (BS) Home Ec/Eng, Univ of MS 1961; *cr:* Home Ec Teacher Appalachian Power Company 1961-63; Eng Teacher Sharples HS 1963; Eng Teacher/Dean of Girls Man Jr HS 1963-73; Eng Teacher Logan Cntrl Jr HS 1973-; *ai:* Builders Club Co-Spon; Effective Schls Comm Chm; St & Cnty Textbook Comm; Writing Assessment Scorer; Aracoma Story Inc (VP 1988-, Bd of Dir 1985-, Cosrumer Summer Productions 1984-); 1st Presbyn Church Mem; Sunday Woman of Week Logan Banner St Comm for Evaluation of Lang Art Test; *office:* Logan Cntrl Jr HS Kanada St Logan WV 25601

JONES, SUSAN CLAUNCH, 2nd Grade Teacher; *b:* Sheffield, AL; *m:* Robert Lynn; *c:* Seth T., Christian L.; *ed:* (BS) Accounting, MS St Univ 1975; (MS) Elem Ed, Trevecca Nazarene Coll 1986; *cr:* Accountant Jones CPA 1976; Teacher Pickwick Southside Sch 1976-; *ai:* NEA, TEA; Lions Club; *home:* Rt 2 Box 262 Michie TN 38357

JONES, SUSAN HILL, French Teacher; *b:* Ellwood City, PA; *m:* John W. Jr.; *c:* Jodie, Wade, Tracey; *ed:* (BA) Fr, Thiel Coll 1963; *cr:* Fr Teacher Fort Chiswell HS & George Wythe HS 1985-; *ai:* Fr Club Spon; *office:* Fort Chiswell HS Rt 3 Box 255 Max Meadows VA 24360

JONES, SUZANNE GRILLO, 2nd Grade Teacher; *b:* Akron, OH; *m:* Edwin F. III; *c:* Jennifer, Christopher; *ed:* (BS) Elem Ed, OH St Univ Columbus 1974; *cr:* 2nd/3rd Grade Split Class Teacher Scioto Elem 1974; Kndgtn Teacher 1974-86, 2nd Grade Teacher 1986- Kinnison Elem; *ai:* Jackson City Ed Assn, OH Ed Assn 1974-; *home:* 69 David Ave Jackson OH 45640

JONES, SUZANNE RYALS, Science Teacher; *b:* St Petersburg, FL; *ed:* (BA) Bio Ed, Cntrl Wesley Coll 1982; Natural Sci Ed, Clemson Univ; *cr:* Math/Sci Teacher Ben Hagood Elem Sch 1984; Sci Teacher Pickens Sr HS 1984-; *ai:* Cheerleading Spon; Sci Club Co-Spon; Awds Comm; SC Sci Cncl 1986-.

JONES, THEODORE RICHARD, JR., Assistant Principal; *b:* Chatham, VA; *m:* Rosalind Amelia Johnson; *c:* Theodore III, Kiva S.; *ed:* (BS) General Bus, St Pauls Coll 1967; (CPC) Ed, Richmond 1968; (MED) Admin, Univ of VA 1982; Stratford Coll, Lynchburg Coll, Danville Comm Coll; *cr:* Teacher/Coach Gretna Elem Sch & Jr HS 1971-88; Cnslr/Coach Gretna Jr HS 1985-87; Teacher/Coach Gretna Mid Sch & HS 1988-89; Asst Prin Gretna Elem Sch 1989-; *ai:* Gretna Jr HS Bsktbl, HS Ftbl & Bsktbl, Mid Sch Bsbl, Little League Bsbl & Ftbl Coach; Cmmty Ed Advisory, Supt Advisory Comm; Phys Ed Curr Comm Chm; Prins Assn (Mem, Delegate); Pittsylvania Ed Assn Pres; VA Ed Assn (Delegate, Mem); NBEA Teacher; PTO Pres 1986-87, Outstanding Achievement Key Man 1988; Jaycees VP 1980-89, Numerous Plaques 1981-; Gretna Youth Sports (Pres, Commissioner) 1980-; Cmmty Ed Tax Inst; Cmmty Youth Action Prgm Bd Mem 1989-; Pittsylvania Cty Chamber of Commerce Mem; Mental Health Assn; HS Coaches Assn Credit Union Rep; Developed Articles of Incorporation & By-Laws; *home:* PO Box 844 Gretna VA 24557

JONES, THOMAS EDWARD, 7th Grade Life Science Teacher; *b:* Cleveland, OH; *m:* Gretchen Ann Corp; *c:* Emily M., Peter T., Alex E.; *ed:* (BS) Phys Ed, Cleveland St 1978; General Sci, Adaptive Phys Ed, Health; *cr:* Phys Ed Teacher Harding Mid Sch 1979-81; 7th Life Sci Teacher Hoarce Mann Mid Sch 1981-; *ai:* Stu Cncl & Sci Olympiad Adv; 7th Grade Team Leader; 9th Grade Boys Bsktbl Coach; Sci Cncl Rep; Sci Fair Coord; OH Mid Sch, Lakewood Teachers Assn Mem; Chart Big Brothers 1983-84; Lakewood Mid Sch Teacher of Yr 1986; Christa Mc Auliffe Fellowship Runnerup; *office:* Horace Mann Mid Sch 1215 W Clifton Lakewood OH 44107

JONES, TOM, Social Science Teacher; *b:* Indianapolis, IN; *m:* Pamela J. Mallett; *c:* Mollie; *ed:* (MA) Phys Ed, 1972, (BA) Phys Ed/His, 1970 Univ of Pacific; *cr:* Soc Sci Teacher Turlock Union HS 1972-73, Amos Alonzo Stagg HS 1973-74; Math Teacher Daniel Webster Mid Sch 1974-75; Soc Sci Teacher Thomas A Edison HS 1975-; *ai:* Little League Coach 1989-; City of Stockton Tennis Tournament Referee 1979-89; *office:* Edison HS 1425 S Center St Stockton CA 95206

JONES, VANESSA ANN (DILLAHUNT), Teacher of Gifted & Talented; *b:* Kinston, NC; *c:* Clarence L. IV; *ed:* (BS) Elem Ed, Winston-Salem St Univ 1974; Working Towards Masters Cmptrs in Ed, Columbia Univ Teachers Coll; *cr:* Teacher Columbian Elem Sch 1975-; T S A Staff Dev E Orange Bd of Ed 1990; *ai:* Young Leaders Against Drugs Prgm; YMCA E Orange Cnslr; Apples for Stus Campaign Coord; Career Awareness Chairleader; TALC & EOEA Staff Reps; Gifted & Talented Sch, Dist Liason; NJ Ed Assn 1975-; E Orange Ed Assn Building Rep 1989-; NJ Gifted & Talented Assn 1989-; Delta Sigma Theta 1974-; New Hope Baptist Church 1987-; Teacher of Yr 1990; Exemplary Sch Prgm Awd 1988-89; Parent Involvement Awd 1987; *home:* 678 Eagle Rock Ave West Orange NJ 07052

JONES, VERNA M., Sixth Grade Teacher; *b:* Suffolk, VA; *m:* Thomas W.; *c:* Candice J., James R.; *ed:* (BS) Elem Ed, Radford Univ 1972; (MS) Admin/Supervision, Old Dominion 1981; *cr:* 2nd Grade Teacher Knightdale Sch 1972-73; 3rd/4th/6th Grade Teacher Windsor & Carrsville Elem 1973-; *ai:* PTA Secy 1987-89; Phi Kappa Phi; *office:* Windsor Elem Box 287 Windsor VA 23487

JONES, VICKI GALLOWAY, English Teacher; *b:* Livingston, TX; *m:* Corry Howard; *c:* Elizabeth; *ed:* (GBA) Bus, Sam Houston St 1981; Working Towards MED Sam Houston St Univ; *cr:* Eng Teacher Corrigan-Camden Ind Sch Dist 1985-89, Leggett Ind Sch Dist 1989-; *ai:* 6th & 10th Grade Spon; *office:* Leggett JR/SR HS PO Box 68 Leggett TX 77350

JONES, WANDA DONELL, Kindergarten Teacher; *b:* Gainesboro, TN; *ed:* (BS) Elem Ed, TN Techological Univ 1973; (MA) Rdng, 1974, (MA) Elem Ed, 1976 Mid TN St Univ; *cr:* 1st Grade Teacher 1974-75, Kndgtn Teacher 1975-76 Smyrna Primary; Kndgtn Teacher Smyrna West 1976-77, John Coleman 1977-78, Smyrna Primary 1978-81, David Youree 1981-86, Smyrna West 1986-89; *ai:* Attendance Chm 1988-; REA Rep 1976-77; TEA; Educator of Week 1989-; *home:* 224 Eastland Murfreesboro TN 37130

JONES, WILLIAM ARTHUR, Science Teacher/Coach; *b:* Ft Hall Indian Res, ID; *m:* Pauline Rae Cox; *c:* Randy A., Renee L., *ed:* (AA) Phys Ed, Boise Jr Coll 1959; (BA) Ed/Sci, Boise Coll 1968; (MS) Ed/HPER, UT St Univ 1974; Grad Stud Admin/ Principalship, Univ of ID; *cr:* Athletic Trainer Boise Jr Coll 1965-74; Trainer/Coach Boise Coll 1974-76; Ed Asst Professor Boise St Univ 1976-80; Teacher/Coach Meridian Dist 1982-; *ai:* Ski Coach; Athletic Trainer; Swimming/Vlybl Coach to Europe Good Will Games 1986; IAHPE&R Vice Chm 1959-62; NSTA Textbook Comm 1987; Natl Ski Patrol Pres 1966; Toboggan Handling NSPS 1968; Textbooks & Articles Published; *office:* Lowell Scott Mid Sch 3400 E Mc Millan Rd Meridian ID 83642

JONES, WILLIAM H., Biology Teacher; *b:* Craigsville, PA; *m:* Sally J. Porter; *c:* Sherry J. Patton, William Jr., Eric J., Susan J. Nemes, Sheila J.; *ed:* (BS) Bio, Geneva Coll 1962; (MED) Bio, Slippery Rock Univ 1974; *cr:* Bio/Gen Sci Teacher Northwestern Beaver Cty Schls 1962-66, Mohawk Area Schls 1966-; *ai:* 9th Grade Class Adv; Mohawk Ed Assn VP/Building Rep 1970; PA Ed Assn 1962-; NEA 1962-; Wampam U P Church Elder/Deacon 1966-78; Big Beaver Grange Asst Stewart; *home:* R D 2 Box 2457 Wampam PA 16157

JONGEKRIJG, ALLEN J., Teacher; *b:* Zeeland, MI; *m:* Rosalie J. Bergman; *c:* Todd, Scott; *ed:* (BA) Elem Ed, Calvin Coll 1971; (MA) Ed Leadership, W MI Univ 1974; *cr:* Teacher Kentwood Public Schls 1972-; *ai:* Ski Club Spon; Tennis Coach; Jr Achievement Project Bus Educator of Yr 1990; City of Kentwood Citizines Comm 1990; Brookside Chrstn Reformed Church Cncl 1978-81, 1986-89; NEA, MI Ed Assn, Kentwood Ed Assn; *home:* 5421 Londonderry SE Kentwood MI 49508

JONKER, JEAN E. (BOROWSKI), English Teacher; *b:* Holyoke, MA; *ed:* (BA) Eng, Elms Coll 1973; *cr:* Cmptr Consultant/Instr Holyoke HS 1985-86; Cmptr Instr MA Migrant Ed Prgm 1986; Eng Teacher Holyoke HS 1973-; *ai:* Holyoke HS Hall of Fame Founder & Chairperson; Holyoke HS Philosophy Comm Co-Chm; Holyoke HS Scndry Level Homeowrk Policy Comm; NCTE 1985-; Holyoke Teachers Assn Public Relations 1985-89; MTA, NEA 1973-89; Holyoke Elms Alumnae Pres 1979-83; Holyoke HS Women Teachers Club Treas 1975-77; Horace Mann Grant 1987, 1988; *office:* Holyoke HS 500 Beech St Holyoke MA 01040

JONTE, ELIZABETH ODOM, Language Art Teacher; *b:* Kingstree, SC; *m:* Robert Welles Jr.; *c:* Robert W. III, Thomas S.; *ed:* (BA) Eng, Columbia Coll 1974; Grad Work PET Trng; *cr:* Teacher C E Murray HS 1974-75, Clarendon Hall Acad 1975-78; Teller Bank of Greeleyville 1978-79; Teacher Williamsburg Acad 1979-80, C E Murray HS 1980-; *ai:* Jr Beta Club Spon; Local Advisory Cncl Honor Society Mem, Sch Improvement Cncl; Bus Ed Contact Person; Academic Challenge Team Coach; Sch Meetings Recorder; NEA, Williamsburg Cty Ed Assn 1988-89; Greeleyville United Meth Church Admin Bd; Daughters of the Amer Revolution; Sch Teacher of Month; *home:* PO Box 65 Greeleyville SC 29056

JOOS, JANET WESTRA, English Instructor; *b:* N Tonawanda, NY; *m:* Gregory David; *c:* Jordan, Troy; *ed:* (BS) Eng/Scndry Ed, St Univ of NY Buffalo 1982; Prof Resume Writer; *cr:* Eng Teacher Holy Family Sch 1984-87; Eng Instr IL Cntrl Coll 1987-; *ai:* Coll for Kids; Stu Cncl Adv 1984-87; Peoria Area Cmmty Events Volunteer; Published Articles & Poems; *office:* IL Cntrl Coll East Peoria IL 61635

JOPP, HARLAN V., Science/Agricultural Teacher; *b:* Watertown, MN; *m:* Louann Barbara Berg; *c:* Karrie, Erik; *ed:* (BS) Ag Ed, 1964, (MA) Ag Ed, 1970 Univ of MN; Grad Stud at Coll & Univ in MN; *cr:* Ag/Sci Teacher Cosmos Public Schls 1964-66, St Cloud Public Schls 1966-; *ai:* FFA Adv; MN Voc Ag Teachers Assn St Secy 1970-71, Sound Officer for Ag 1981; Chamber of Commerce Ag Division Chm 1979-81; Apppointed Stearns Cty Adjustment Bd & Served as Vice Chm; Elected St Augusta Township Clerk; *office:* Technical HS 233 12th Ave S Saint Cloud MN 56301

JORDAHL, GINA MARIE, Spanish Teacher; *b:* Minneapolis, MN; *m:* Clinton D.; *c:* Joann, Paul; *ed:* (BS) Span, St Cloud St Univ 1982; Teachers of Span Summer Inst St Cloud St Univ 1985; *cr:* Span Teacher Humboldt Scndry 1982-84, Howard Lake-Waverly HS 1984-87, Dassel-Cokato HS 1984-87, St Michael-Albertville HS 1987-; *ai:* Adv Span Club Trip; AATSP, MCTFL 1987-; *home:* 16183 231st Ave Big Lake MN 55309

JORDAL, DAVID L., Biology/Chemistry Teacher; *b:* Rochelle, IL; *m:* Carol J. Trumpour; *c:* Loreen White, Mark; *ed:* (BS) Bio, 1961, (MS) Bio, 1968 N IL Univ; E IL Univ, IL St Univ, W IL Univ, Univ of WI; *cr:* Sci Teacher Mendota Township HS 1961-69; Bio/Chem Teacher La Salle-Peru Township HS 1969-; *ai:* IL Sci Teachers Assn, IL Assn of Chem Teachers, NSTA; BPOE; *office:* La Salle-Peru Township HS 541 Chartres St La Salle IL 61301

JORDAN, ANDREW LEE, Business Education Instructor; *b:* Greenwood, MS; *m:* Arella Love; *c:* Bernice, Rosa M., Mary E., Velma L., Evonne; *ed:* (BS) Bus Ed, MS Valley St Univ 1960; (MS) Bus Admin/Supervision, Bowling St Univ 1978; Athletic Management, OH St Univ; Advanced Study European His, Univ of Toledo; *cr:* HS Teacher Perry Cty Trng Sch 1960, Purvis Trng Sch 1961, Spencer Sharples HS 1965-80, Bowsher HS 1980-; *ai:* OH Army Natl Guard Supply Specialist & Staff Sergeant; TFT Bd of Dir 1968-; BEA 1970-; NEA 1985-; Nubia, Red Cross 1980-; NAACP 1960-; Southwestern Publishing Company Certificate of Professionalism; Radio Shack & OH Athletic Management Inst Certificate of Accomplishment; *home:* 5 S King Rd Holland OH 43528

JORDAN, BRUCE ALAN, High School Principal; *b:* Sioux Falls, SD; *m:* Sandy K. Sullivan; *c:* Nicholas, Ryan; *ed:* (BA) Music/Industrial Arts, Dakota St Univ 1975; (MA) Public Sch Admin, SD St Univ 1983; Working Towards Educl Specialists Degree Univ of SD; *cr:* 5th-8th Grade Instrumental Music Teacher West Cntrl Schls 1977-84; 7th-12th Grade Prin Lemmon Public Schls 1985-86; 9th-12th Grade Prin Hill City HS 1987-; *ai:* Stu Cncl; N Cntrl Assn Reviewer; SD Band Masters 1977-84; SD Assn of Scndry Sch Prin (Rep 1985-, Pres Elect) 5 Yr Membership Awd 1990; SD Curr Coalition Bd Mem 1988-; Hill City Lions Club 1st VP 1989-; Hill City Park Bd VP 1989-; Cub Scout Pack Leader 1988-; Hartford Area Jaycees Outstanding Young Educator Awd & Outstanding Young Religious Leader; *office:* Hill City HS PO Box 659 Hill City SD 57745

JORDAN, CAROL MORGAN, Choral Director; *b:* Dayton, OH; *m:* Todd H.; *c:* Andrew, Aaron; *ed:* (BA) Music Ed, Univ of GA Athens 1975; (MA) Music, GA St Univ Atlanta 1979; Educl Admin, Advanced Conducting; *cr:* 1st-7th Grade Music Teacher Evansdale Elem 1976; 1st-6th Grade Music Teacher Riverdale Elem 1976-78; 10th-12thGrade Choral Dir Riverdale Sr HS 1978-82; 6th-8th Grade Choral Dir Duluth Mid Sch 1982-; *ai:* Asst Supt Instructional Improvement Cncl 1988-91; Chorus & Drama; GA Music Educators Assn (Stu Secy 1973-75, Convention Session 1990), Superior Ratings Festivals; Music Educators Natl Conference; Amer Choral Dir Assn; Pilgrimage Presbyn Church Music Dir 1985-; Presbyn Organization of Musicians; Duluth Mid Sch Teacher of Yr 1986; 9th Dist Honor Chorus Dir 1986; *office:* Duluth Mid Sch 3057 N Peachtree St Duluth GA 30136

JORDAN, DENNIS R., Social Studies Teacher; *b:* Stanley, WI; *m:* Mary Stopple; *c:* Daniel, Rebecca, Thomas; *ed:* (BS) Ecs, Univ of WI Milwaukee 1963; (MAT) Broad Field Soc Stud, Univ of WI Eau Claire 1968; *cr:* Teacher Dist 50 Harvard Schls 1968-; *ai:* IL Ed Assn Bd of Dir 1970-71, 1980-83.

JORDAN, EDWARD HILL, Mathematics/Science Teacher; *b:* Pittsburgh, PA; *m:* Laura Dundon; *c:* Brian Thomas, Edward, Jennifer; *ed:* (BS) Bio, Marietta Coll 1968; (PHD) Botany, Syracuse Univ 1973; Microbiology, Upstate Medical Center; *cr:* Adjunct Faculty Onondaga Comm Coll 1975-77; Petroleum Engr N L Industries Incorporated 1977-81; Farmer SG&S Farms Incorporated 1981-86; Teacher Cato-Meridian HS 1986-; *ai:* Calculus Club Adv; Sci Teachers Assn of NY 1987-; Math Teachers Assn of NY 1988-; Published Articles; NPEA Title IV Fellowship Syracuse Univ; NSF Physics Fellowship Ithaca Coll; *office:* Cato-Meridian HS Rt 370 Box 100 Cato NY 13033

JORDAN, FRED, Director of Bands; *b:* San Diego, CA; *m:* Margaret Cavenagh; *c:* John T., Cheryl C.; *ed:* (BMED) Music Ed, 1980, (MMED) Music Ed, 1981 E TX St Univ; (EDD) Music Ed, Univ of Houston; *cr:* Asst Band Dir E TX St Univ 1980-81, La Marque HS 1981-82; Asst Band Dir 1982-84, Band Dir 1984- S Houston HS; *ai:* Dir Mighty Trojan Marching Band, So Ho Jazz, Wind Ensemble, Concert Chamber Ensemble; Organizer Band Act Region & St & 1989 Region XIX Band Competition; Instrumental Chm S Houston HS Fine Arts Dept; Trojan Band Adv; TX Music Educators Assn (Panel Mem, Regional Contest Chm 1989-) 1980-; TX Bandmasters Assn 1981-; Music Educators Natl Conference 1986-; Trojan Band Booster Club Adv 1984-; Friendswood Dev Corporation Adv 1985-; Courtesy Club Fine Arts Rep 1987-; Grant Univ of Houston Teachers Dev Comm; Dissertation Abstract Approved & Published; Articles Published; *office:* S Houston HS 3820 S Shaver South Houston TX 77587

JORDAN, GERALD EUGENE, English Teacher; *b:* Trinidad, CO; *m:* Cynthia L. Sheppard; *c:* Lauri R., Zoe, Ryan; *ed:* (BA) Scndry Ed/Phys Ed, 1966 (MA) Scndry Ed/Phys Ed, 1969 Adams St Coll; Admin; *cr:* Teacher/Coach Pagosa Springs Schls 1965-66, Monte Vista Sch Dist 1966-74; Teacher/Coach/Ad Brighton Public Schls 1975-77; Teacher/Coach Jefferson Cty Schls 1977-; *ai:* Monte Vista Ed Assn Pres 1970-74; San Luis Valley Pres Cncl Chairperson 1973-74; Southern Peaks Act Assn Secy-Treas 1972-74; Co Ed Assn 1966-; Jefferson Cty Ed Assn 1977-; Monte Vista Old Timers Boys Bsbl Bd Mem; CO Old Timers Boys Bsbl Southwest Regional Dir; Natl Fed of Interscholastic Officials Assn 1981-; Intl Assn of Approved Bsktbl Officials 1981-; CO Bd Four of Approved Bsktbl Officials 1981-; Officiated Dist Playoffs 1989; Officiated Girls St Bsktbl Tournament A-11; CO HS Umpires Assn 1987-; (St Exec Comm Mem, Area Dir 1987-, St Secy-Treas 1989-, St Pres Elect); Outstanding Young Educator-Monte Vista Jaycees.

JORDAN, KATHY FOSHEE, Junior High Math Teacher; *b:* Natchitoches, LA; *m:* Robin D.; *c:* Tyler; *ed:* (BA) Elem Ed, Northwestern of LA 1982; (MED) Supervision & Admin, NSU of LA 1987; *cr:* 6th Grade Teacher Provencal Elem 1982-84; 5th Grade Teacher NSU Laboratory Sch 1984-87; 6th/7th/8th Grade Math Teacher Marthaville Jr HS 1987-; *ai:* Math Counts Team Spon; Math Club Spon; Pepsquad Spon; Girls Sftbl Coach; Faculty Improvement Comm Chm; Alpha Delta Kappa Pres 1988-; Phi Delta Kappa Mem 1987-; Phi Kappa Phi Mem 1982-; Beta Sigma Phi Mem 1987-; 1989- Natchitoches Parish Jr HS Teacher of Yr; 1989- Jaycees Outstanding Young Educator; *office:* Marthaville Jr H S P O Box 148 Marthaville LA 71450

JORDAN, LINDA COLBY, Math Resource Specialist; *b:* Newport, RI; *m:* Frederick C.; *ed:* (BSED) Elem Ed, 1974, (MED) Ed, 1982 Bridgewater St Coll; Cmptr Ed Basic Logo, Diagnosis & Remediation of Learning Problems in Math, Math Their Way, Math a Way of Thining; *cr:* 2nd Grade Teacher Brockton Public Schls Downey 1974-83; 6th Grade Teacher Brockton Public Schls Hancock 1983-87; 1st-6th Grade Math Specialist Brockton Public Schls Paine 1987-; *ai:* Brockton Ed Assn Rep 1987-; Gladys L Allen Schlsp; Horace Mann Educator 1987-89; Curr Guide Teaching Math with Manipulatives; *office:* Brockton Sch 43 Crescent St Brockton MA 02402

JORDAN, LINDA GOLDEN, Fifth Grade Teacher; *b:* Denver, CO; *m:* Robert L.; *c:* Allison Jordan McCord, Jennifer Ashley; *ed:* (BAE) Scndry Eng/Soc Stud, Univ MS 1962; (MED) Elem, MS St Univ 1967; *cr:* Eng Teacher Canton HS 1963-65; 7th Grade Eng/Soc Stud Teacher Starkville Jr HS 1965-67; 5th Grade Teacher Oxford Elem Sch 1969-; *ai:* Delta Delta Delta Alumni; NEA/MAE/OAE Treas/Bldg Rep 1969-; Phi Delta Kappa 1986-; PTA 1969-; 1st Presbyn Church Elder 1989-; Sunday Sch Teacher 1986-89; Oxford Elem Sch Teacher of Yr 1985-86; Elem Sch Educator Awd 1986; NSBSAP Item Review Comm 1985-; *office:* Oxford Elem Sch Hwy 30 E Oxford MS 38655

JORDAN, MARGARET TAYLOR, 7th/8th Grade Math Teacher; *b:* Unadilla, GA; *m:* Jack; *c:* Linda; *ed:* (BS) Elem Ed, 1959, (MS) Elem Ed, 1960 Fort Valley St Coll; Specialist Mid Grades, GA SW 1983; *cr:* Teacher Dooly Cty Sch System; *ai:* Dooly Cty Assn Ed Pres 1988-89; GAE, NEA 1989-; Church Clerk 1990; *office:* Dooly Cty Mid Sch Hwy 41 N Vienna GA 31092

JORDAN, MARY ELLEN HAUPT, Fourth Grade Teacher; *b:* Cincinnati, OH; *m:* Donald S.; *c:* Julie, Janie, Michael; *ed:* (BS) Ed, Miami Univ Oxford 1960; *cr:* 4th Grade Teacher Mt Healthy Sch Dist 1960-67, 1978-; *ai:* Building, Dist, Parent Advisory Cncl; NEA, OH Ed Assn, Mt Healthy Ed Assn, SW OH Ed Assn 1960-67, 1978-; Delta Kappa Gamma Intnl 1967-; *home:* 2056 Persimmon Ct Cincinnati OH 45231

JORDAN, MERCEDES KRONFELD, 7th/8th Grade Jr HS Teacher; *b:* Woodland, CA; *m:* Scott C.; *ed:* (BA) Ger Lit/Lang, Univ of PA 1982; (MA) Ger Lit/Lang, Univ of CA Irvine 1984; *cr:* Lang Instr/Eng/Ger Teacher Inlingua 1979-80; Ger Teacher Univ of CA Irvine 1982-84; Head of Intensive Summer Prgm in Ger Univ Extension Univ of CA Irvine 1984; Ger Instr Long Beach City Coll 1985-87; 6th-8th Grade Jr HS Teacher Carden 1986-; *office:* Carden of Huntington Beach 721 Utica Huntington Beach CA 92648

JORDAN, NANCY YOUNGBLOOD, 3rd Grade Teacher; *b:* Charleston, SC; *m:* William Capers; *c:* Capers, Gray, Meghan, Elise; *ed:* (BA) Spec Ed, Columbia Coll 1967; (MED) Rdng, The Citadel 1981; Various Wkshps & Seminars; Grad Courses; *cr:* Prin Hope Kndgtn for Retarded Children 1969-70; Teacher Martinsburg Elem 1971; Resource Teacher Riverland Terrace Elem 1971-72; Self Contained Teacher of Learning Disabilites Stiles Pt Elem 1972-76; 3rd Grade Teacher Porter Gaud Sch 1976-; *ai:* 3rd Grade Curr Coord; Sunshine Comm; NCTM, Intnl Rdng Assn; Grace Church (Altar Guild, Wedding Comm Chm); Began Class for Learning Disabilities Stus James Island Sch Dist.

JORDAN, NELLIE L. HOWARD, Gifted Education Teacher; *b:* Fort Worth, TX; *m:* James H. Sr.; *c:* James H. Jr., Susan L.; *ed:* (BS) Elem Ed, Bishop Coll 1967; (MED) Elem Ed, Prairie View A&M Univ 1975; Endorsement Gifted Ed, Univ of TX; *cr:* Teacher John Neely Bryan Elem 1967-; *ai:* Pupil Assistance Support System; NEA, TX St Teachers Assn, Classroom Teachers of Dallas 1967-; Tx Assn for Gifted & Talented 1970-; Natl Assn for Gifted Children 1988-; IBPO Elks of World 1970-; Alpha Kappa Alpha 1966-; Teacher of Yr 1979-80, 1986-87; Chairperson Young Peoples Univ 1985-87; *office:* John Neely Bryan Elem Sch 2001 Deer Path Dallas TX 75216

JORDAN, RUTH WILLIAMS, English Teacher; *b:* Florence, SC; *m:* Boykin Bristow; *c:* Boykin B. Jr., Valerie V. Jordan Williams, Llewellyn L.; *ed:* (BA) Music/Eng, Claflin Coll 1958; (MA) Ed, Francis Marion Coll 1982; Univ of N FL, Univ of SC; *cr:* Teacher Johnson HS 1958-63, 1969-70, Dept of Defense Philippines 1970-72, Timmonsville HS 1976-; *ai:* Beta Club, Soph Class Spon; Chorus Dir; Dist SAT Verbal Coord; SCEA, NEA, IRA; Delta Sigma Theta 2nd VP 1983-85; Order of Eastern Star Worthy Matron 1979-, Service Awd 1987, 1989; United Tents Leader 1987-; Order Golden Circle LL Ruler 1989; *office:* Timmonsville HS 605 W Market St Ext Timmonsville SC 29161

JORDAN, SUE ALLEN, 5th Grade Teacher; *b:* Conway, SC; *m:* Arthur B.; *c:* Arthur Bennett III; *ed:* (BS) Elem Ed, Winthrop Coll 1970; Grad Stud Univ of SC; *cr:* 3rd Grade Teacher Meadowfield Sch 1970-72; 1st-3rd Grade Combination Teacher Turbeville Elem 1972-73; 5th Grade Teacher Alcolu Elem 1973-; *ai:* 5th Grade Sci Coord; Conservation Comm Chm; Planning Comm for Dist Outdoor Environmental Classroom; SC Sci Cncl; Palmetta St Teachers Assn; Environmental Ed Assn; Intnl Rdng Assn; Azalea Garden Club Pres 1987-88; Manning United Meth Church Sunday Sch Teacher; Clarendon Dist Teacher of Yr 1980; Conservation Teacher of Yr 1988; Sch Awarded Conservation Sch of Yr Clarendon Cty 1988; Alcolu Teacher of Yr 1990; Pee Dee Ed Fnd Mini Grant; *home:* Rt 3 Box 537 Manning SC 29001

JORDAN, SUNDRA SYKES, Earth Science Teacher; *b:* New York, NY; *m:* James; *c:* James M., Joel M., Ursula M., Barbara M., Jeremy P., Jennifer L.; *ed:* (BA) His, Univ of San Diego 1968; Ed/Cert, Prairie View A&M; Earth Sci Symposium, Univ of TX San Antonio 1989; NASA Aerospace Inst Univ of Houston; *cr:* Teacher St Charles Sch 1967-68, Oak Harbor Jr HS 1968-71, George Jr H S 1981-; *ai:* Stu Against Drugs, Sci Olympiad Team, Sci Club Spon; Gifted & Talented Curr, Teacher Expectation-Stu Achievement, Prin Advisory, Supt Advisory Comm; TX Classroom Teachers Assn 1981-; Lamar Classroom Teachers Assn Legislative Comm Chairperson 1989-; TX Earth Sci Teachers Assn 1987-; NSTA 1989-; *office:* George Jr HS 4201 Airport Rosenberg TX 77471

JORDAN, THOMAS ADAM, Physics Teacher; *b:* Burlington, VT; *m:* Andrea Sawyers; *ed:* (BS) Ed, Univ of S FL 1987; Working Toward Masters Astronomy, Univ of AZ; Assoc Natl Radio Astronomy Observatory Green Bank WV; *cr:* Phys Sci Teacher Madison Jr HS 1987-88; Physics/Astronomy Teacher Bloomingdale Sr HS 1988-89; Physics Teacher Chamberlain Sr HS 1989-; *ai:* Sci Academic Society & Photography Club Spon; Sci Brain Bowl Team & Jr Engineering Team Coach; Amer Assn of Physics Teachers, Suncoast Physics Teachers 1987-; Seminole Heights Preservation Society 1987-; Presenter NSTA Conventions Phoenix 1989 & Atlanta 1990; Fellowship Univ of AZ Grad Sch; Fellowship Natl Radio Astronomy Observatory 1989; *office:* Chamberlain Sr HS 9401 N Boulevard Tampa FL 33612

JORDAN, VASHTI, Teacher; *b:* Galloway, TN; *c:* Ricky L.; *ed:* (BS) Health/Phys Ed, Lane Coll 1963; (MS) Supervision/Admin, Trevecca 1989; *cr:* Teacher Fayette Ware HS; *ai:* Beta Club & Teens No Team Spon; Health & Phys Ed Chairperson; AHEC & HBP Chairperson & Drug Liaison For Fayette Ware; NEA, TEA, FCEA Mem 1965-; Teacher of Yr 8 Yrs at Fayette Ware; *home:* Box 132 Center Pt Dr Gallaway TN 38036

JORDAN, VIVIAN DU-BOSE, Retired/Substitute Teacher; *b:* Marshallville, GA; *ed:* (BS) Music/Elem Ed, Western Reserve Univ 1943; *cr:* Music Teacher Marion/Woodland Hills 1943-47, Kinsman Sch 1947-66; Elem Teacher Dike & Chestnut Schls 1966-81; Teacher of Gifted/Talented Gracemount Elem 1981-87; Substitute Teacher Cleveland Public Schls 1987-; *ai:* Childrens Christian Bible Soc Spon 1953-; Sharing our Faith Radio Broadcast Speaker 1953-; Alias Santa for Cleveland 1958; Choir Invited to Sing in Washington DC 1977; OH Christian Ashrams Youth Dir; *home:* 3641 Martin Luther King Dr Cleveland OH 44105

JORDI, REBECCA HADDOCK, Jr/Sr High School Teacher; *b:* Jacksonville, FL; *m:* Douglas Keith; *c:* Benjamin, John M., Nathan; *ed:* (AA) General Coll, FL Comm Coll 1974; (BS) Soc Stud, FL St Univ 1976; Working Towards Masters in Bio; Seminars on Teacher Trng & Supervisory Positions; *cr:* 9th Grade His Teacher Northwestern Jr HS 1978; Reservationist Delta Airlines 1979-82; Jr/Sr Teacher Word of Life Schls 1983-; *ai:* Yrbk Spon; Math Competitions; *office:* Word of Life Schls 8855 Sanchez Rd Jacksonville FL 32217

JORGENSON, PAT S., Fifth Grade Teacher; *b:* Powers Lake, ND; *m:* Jerry; *c:* Jeff, Jon; *ed:* (BA) Elem/Spec Ed, Univ of ND 1970; Grad Work at Minot St Univ; *cr:* Classroom Teacher Minot Public Schls 1971-; *ai:* ND Ed Assn Bd Dir 1981-89; Delta Kappa Gamma 1989-; Phi Delta Kappa 1985-; Minot Ed Assn VP 1989; Minot Ed Assn Teacher of Yr 1988; *home:* 205 8th St SE Minot ND 58701

JORSTAD, PRISCILLA KMIECIK, 6th-8th Lang Arts/Rdng Teacher; *b:* Chicago, IL; *m:* Kenneth; *c:* Brett, Kendra, Kara; *ed:* (BSED) Elem Ed, IL St Univ 1972; *cr:* 6th-8th Grade Remedial Rdng/Math Teacher Coal City Mid Sch 1972-75; 6th Grade Lang Art/Math Teacher Yorkville Cmmty Unit 1975-76; 5th Grade Teacher 1976-77, 6th-8th Grade Lang Art/Rdng Teacher 1987- Lisbon Grade Sch; *ai:* Stu Cncl Adv; Literary Contest Coach; PTO Treas 1987-89; *office:* Lisbon Grade Sch RR 1 Box 62 Canal St Newark IL 60541

JOSEPH, AUDREY JENKINS, Second Grade Teacher; *b.* Huntington, WV; *m:* William A. Jr.; *c:* Julia A.; *ed:* (BA) Elem Ed 1973, (MA) Elem/Gifted Ed, 1980 Marshall Univ; Grad Stud Gifted Ed, WV Coll, Wright St Univ 1985-87; Grad Level Coursework Cmptr Technology, OH Univ; *cr:* 2nd Grade Teacher Fairland East Elem 1973-86; Gifted Prgms Coord Lawrence Cty Bd of Ed 1986-88; 2nd Grade Teacher Fairland East Elem 1988-; *ai:* NEA, OEA Mem 1973-; OAGC, NAGC, Phi Delta Kappa Mem 1986-; Friends of the Lib; United Meth Women Officer; River Cities Cultural Cncl 1986-; GFWC Proctorville Womens Club 2nd VP 1989-; Outstanding Young Women of America 1987; Martha Holden Jennings Schlr 1983; *home:* Rt 4 Box 388 Gardner Terr Proctorville OH 45669

JOSEPH, BETTY PARKER, English/Reading Teacher; *b:* Prince Georges Cty, MD; *m:* Ronald L.; *ed:* (BA) Eng, Bowie St Univ 1973; Grad Stud; *cr:* Teacher Robert Goddard Mid Sch 1973-; *ai:* Doing Something Right Comm Spon; Sch Based Management Comm Mem; Effective Schls; Team Leader; MSTA, PGCEA, NT of Eng 1973-; Cath YAC VP 1984; Prince Georges NCNW (Parliamentarian, Co-Founder) 1982-87; Voted Favorite Teacher; Best Liked Teacher 1989; *office:* Robert Goddard Mid Sch 9850 Goodluck Rd Seabrook MD 20706

JOSEPH, RELLA MARIE, 6th Grade Elem Teacher; *b:* Ville Platte, LA; *c:* Savitri D.; *ed:* (BS) Elem Ed, Grambling St Univ 1976; (MED) Elem Ed, Southern Univ 1979; Univ of S LA & LA St Univ; *cr:* Adult Ed Teacher James Stephens HS 1966-69; 2nd Grade Teacher Carver Elem 1969-71; Spec Ed Teacher Basile HS 1971-73; 6th Grade Teacher Bayou Chicot HS 1973-; *ai:* Beta Club Spon; Supervisory Comm Chairperson; Sch Building Level Comm; Substance Abuse Team Co-Chairperson; Comm of Educators; Evangeline Assn of Educators Treas 1987-; LA Assn of Educators Mem 1988-89, Plaque; NEA Mem 1989-, Plaque; Church (Financial Secy 1988-, Sunday Sch Supt, Lafayette Dist Fine Art Prgm, Spelling Bee Chairperson); Nom Teacher of Yr 1987-88; *office:* Bayou Chicot HS Rural Sta Rt 3 Ville Platte LA 70586

JOSEPH, RICHARD HENRY, Biology/Physics Teacher; *b:* Springfield, MA; *m:* Maggie Newman; *c:* Ashlie; *ed:* (BS) General Sci, Westfield St Coll 1968; (MST) General Sci, Amer Intntl Coll 1972; Biological Scis, Univ of MA 1984; Cmptr Scis, Springfield Tech Comm Coll 1988-; *cr:* Teacher Duggan Jr HS 1968-70, Holyoke Comm Coll 1984-85, Agawam HS 1970-; *ai:* NHS Faculty Comm; Bio & Ski Club Adv; MA Teachers Assn, NEA 1968-; Agawam Ed Assn Schlsp Comm Chairperson 1988-; Natl Sci Fnd Grant Masters Study 1971-72; *office:* Agawam HS 760 Cooper St Agawam MA 01001

JOSEPH, ROSE MARIE, Fifth Grade Teacher; *b:* Windsor, NC; *ed:* (BA) Ed, Univ of NC Greensboro 1962; (MED) Ed, George Mason Univ 1973-; Post Grad Work Univ of VA, Univ of Dayton, Univ of MD; *cr:* 4th-6th Grade Teacher 1962-82; Jermantown Elem 1962-82; 5th/6th Grade Teacher Fairfax Villa 1982-; *ai:* Bus Sch Partnership Liaison; Fairfax Cty Fed of Teachers Bldg Rep 1988-; Soroptimist Intnl of Fairfax Cty (VP 1983-84, 1986-87, Secy 1988-, Bd of Dir 1985); Hospice (Volunteer 1988-, Benefit Project Chairperson 1986); Classroom Management Publication; Teacher Evaluation Prgm Consulting Teacher; *office:* Fairfax Villa Elem Sch 10900 Santa Clara Dr Fairfax VA 22030

JOSEPH-PERNAMBUCO, LYNETTE BARBARA, Chairperson Science Dept; *b:* Georgetown, Guyana; *m:* Dionisio; *c:* Andrew, Tekakwitha Wise, Adele, Moira, Mona; *ed:* (BA) Ed, Univ of Guyana 1979; Ed, Brooklyn Coll; *cr:* Guidance Cnslr Christ Church HS Guyana 1977-79; Soc Stud Chm 1981-85; Sci Chm 1985-; Guidance Placement 1985- St Catharine; *ai:* Brooklyn Diocese Ed Dept for Sci Comm 1989; Sci Curr 1989; R C Diocese Brooklyn Teacher 1980-85 Svc 1985; *home:* 955 E 58th St Brooklyn NY 11234

JOSEPHSEN, STEVEN ARTHUR, Director of Gifted Education; *b:* W Palm Beach, FL; *m:* Brenda Jean Hall; *c:* Beth, Brian, Mark; *ed:* (BS) Elem Ed, Nyack Coll 1977; (MED) Ed of Gifted, Univ of VA 1985; *cr:* 2nd Grade Teacher 1977-79, Dir Gifted Ed 1979- Norfolk Chrstn Schls; *ai:* Compose Praise & Worship Music; Music Team for Church; *office:* Norfolk Chrstn Schls 255 Thole St Norfolk VA 23505

JOSEY, JANEEN (CURL), Instructional Supervisor; *b:* Swainsboro, GA; *m:* C. Ray; *c:* Emily, Mark; *ed:* (BS) Bus Ed, GA Southern Coll 1967; (MED) Bus Ed, W GA Col; 1975; *cr:* Bus Ed Teacher Armuchee HS 1967-68, Cedartown HS 1968-71, Fairmount HS 1971-75, Pepperell HS 1975-77, Valdosta HS 1980-89; Instructional Supvr Valdosta City Schls Supt Office 1989-; *ai:* INTERACT & FBLA Spon; GA Bus Ed Assn (Secy, Dir Elect, Dir) 1967-, Bus Ed Teacher of Yr 1983; GA Sch Public Relations Assn Mem 1989-; Valdosta Rotary Club (Honarary, INTERACT Spon), Paul Harris Fellow 1989; Trinity Presbyn Church (Charter Mem, Adult Choir, Youth Leader); Valdosta Bar ssn Liberty Bell Awd 1986; Teacher GA Governors Honors Pgm 984; Teacher of Yr Fairmont HS & Valdosta HS 1989; System eacher of Yr Valdosta City System 1984; *office:* Valdosta City ch System PO Box 5407 Valdosta GA 31603

OSLIN, JOYCE ANN, Fr/Eng as Second Lang Teacher; *b:* roy, NY; *ed:* (BA) Fr, S Meth Univ 1961; (MA) Fr, Middlebury oll 1972; *cr:* Fr/Ger Instr Lake Highlands HS 1966-72, Jesuit oll Prep of Dallas 1972-74; Fr/Eng as Second Lang Teacher imitz HS 1975-; *ai:* Nimitz Fr Club Spon; N TX AATF (VP 977-78, Pres 1978-79); AATG 1969-79; Dallas Cty Heritage ociety 1980-83; Ger Government Travel Study Grant 1969; N TX ATF Travel Study Grant 1988; *office:* Nimitz HS 100 W akdale Irving TX 75060

OUAS, LINDA MAZZOLA, French/Spanish Teacher; *b:* Port hester, NY; *m:* Jean Pierre; *c:* Jean-Christophe, Jean-Philippe; *d:* (BA) Fr, Univ of Hartford 1974; (MA) Fr, Middlebury Coll 975; Master Stud Licence d Anglais, Univ de Coen France 1981; *r:* Eng as Second Lang Rockland Cmmty Coll 1983-85; Fr eacher Scarsdale HS 1985-86; Fr/Span Teacher Bronxville HS 986-; *ai:* Club Adv; AFS Intnl Club; Group Coord & Leader of xchange Pgrm France; NYSAFLT 1986-; AATF 1988-; alisades Cmmty Center Treas 1984-; Palisades Swim Club Swim eam Parent Coord 1986-; *office:* Bronxville HS Pondfield Rd ronxville NY 10708

OURET, CAROLYN SKELTON, Language Arts/English eacher; *b:* Brooklyn, NY; *m:* Edward E.; *c:* Michael, David erlach, Stefan, Evangela Gerlach; *ed:* (BA) Eng, Wagner Coll 965; Various Photography Wkshps; *cr:* Lang Art Teacher Meadowlawn Mid Sch 1981-83; Yrbk Adv/Lang Art Teacher Riviera Mid Sch 1983-; *ai:* Numerous Prizes in Photography; *office:* Riviera Mid Sch 501 62nd Ave NE Saint Petersburg FL 33704

JOY, HENRY FRANCIS, III, Language Art Teacher; *b:* Johnson City, TN; *m:* Flora Crowe; *ed:* (BS) Eng/Poly Sci, 1966, (MA) Rdng, 1975 E TN St Univ; *cr:* Eng Teacher Greenville HS 1966-73; Rdng Teacher West Side Sch 1974-75; 5th Grade Teacher King Springs Elem 1976-88; Lang Art Teacher Liberty Bell Mid Sch 1988-; *ai:* Team Leader 6A Liberty Bell; Little League Bsbl Coach; Johnson City Ed Assn Pres 1984-85; Intnl Rdng Assn Treas 1976-77; Johnson City Little League Incorporated Bd of Dir 1986-, Coach of Yr 1983; *office:* Liberty Bell Mid Sch Liberty Bell Blvd Johnson City TN 37601

JOY, JAMES RUSSELL, Supvr Certificated Personnel; *b:* Memphis, TN; *m:* Brenta Joyce Bowen; *c:* Whitney, Lindsey; *ed:* (BA) His, Chrstn Brothers Coll 1976; (MED) Educl Admin/ Supervision, Memphis St Univ 1987; *cr:* Tutorial Coord Shelby St Comm Coll 1976-77; 6th/7th/8th Grade Teacher 1977-86, Curr Coord/Asst Prin 1986- Collierville Mid Sch; Supervisor/ Certificated Personnel Shelby Cty Bd of Ed 1990; *ai:* Soc Stud Dept, Act Comm Chm; Say No to Drugs Spon; Stu Assistance Prgm Admin Mem; Shelby Cty Ed Assn Faculty Rep 1977-78; West TN Ed Assn VP West Dist 1986-87; TN Cncl of Soc Stud Teachers 1977-; Teacher of Yr Collierville Mid Sch; Outstanding Teacher Awd By Chrstn Brothers Coll; Saturday Cnslr Memphis Partners Inc; Cnslr Father Love; *office:* Shelby Cty Schls 160 S Hollywood St Memphis TN 38112

JOYCE, DARLENE R., English Teacher/Dept Chair; *b:* Littlefield, TX; *m:* Richard B.; *c:* David R., Anthony B.; *ed:* (BBA) General Bus, TX A&I 1968; (MED) Guidance/Counseling, Univ of Houston-Victoria; Teacher Expectations & Stu Achievement; *cr:* Elem Teacher 1969-70, Scndry Teacher Devine Ind Sch Dist 1970-76, Ganado Ind Sch Dist 1976-77; Scndry Teacher/Eng Dept Head Palacios Jr/Sr HS 1977-; *ai:* TX Ed Agency TASA Review, Gifted & Talented Comms; TX Academic Decathlon Coach; NHS Spon; UIL Coach & Spon; TX Joint Cncl of Teachers of Eng 1980-; Alapha Club (Secy 1985-86, Pres 1989-); TX Excl Awd for Outstanding Teachers 1987; Outstanding Teacher of Graduating Honor Stu 1986, 1988-89; *home:* 510 Green Ave Palacios TX 77465

JOYCE, GLENDA SHELTON, Fifth Grade Teacher; *b:* Martinsville, VA; *m:* James Randolph Jr.; *ed:* (BS) Elem Ed, Radford Univ 1972; (MA) Ed, Univ of VA 1986; *cr:* 7th Grade Teacher Mary Hunter Elem Sch 1972-73; 7th Grade Teacher 1973-78, 5th Grade Teacher 1978- Fieldale Elem Sch; *ai:* Self Study Steering Comm; Newspaper Staff; Delta Kappa Gamma 1989-; NEA, VEA Rep; Collinsville Jr Womans Club; PTO Exec Comm; *home:* PO Box 67 Rangeley Rd Fieldale VA 24089

JOYCE, JANET M., Language Arts Teacher/Chair; *b:* High Point, NC; *m:* Billy J.; *c:* Joseph A., Annette Langhorne, Allison, Amber; *ed:* (BA) Elem Ed, High Point Coll 1963; Lib Sci, Univ of NC Greensboro 1966; *cr:* 3rd Grade Teacher Danbury Elem Sch 1960-62; 5th Grade Teacher Lawsonville Elem Sch 1962-64; 8th Grade Teacher/Librarian King Elem Sch 1964-74; 7th/8th Grade Teacher/Lang Art Dept Chairperson Chestnut Grove Jr HS 1974-; *ai:* Jr Beta Club; Annual; *office:* Chestnut Grove Jr HS Rt 4 Box 185 King NC 27021

JOYCE, JERALD L., 5th Grade Teacher; *b:* St Louis, MO; *m:* Barbara L. Craddock; *c:* Sarah, Brandi, Jerry; *ed:* (BA) Ed, Harris-Stone Coll 1978; Sports Management, US Sports Acad; *cr:* Substitute Teacher Fox C-6 Sch Dist 1975-78; 5th Grade Teacher Seckman Elem 1978-; *ai:* Asst Ftbl Coach Fox C-6 Sch Dist; Head Bsktbl Coach Jefferson Coll; NJCAA Coaches Assn 1986-; MO Foster Parents 1987-; Meramec Elks 1983-; *office:* Seckman Elem Sch 2824 Seckman Rd Imperial MO 63052

JOYCE, PATRICK FRANCIS, Language Art Teacher; *b:* Pittston, PA; *m:* Ann Iannuzzo; *c:* Ryan, Shawn; *ed:* (BA) Span, Kings Coll 1974; (MS) Eng, Univ of Scranton 1983; Grad Stud Scndry Admin; *cr:* Lang Art Teacher 1978-, Dir of Public Relations 1988- Riverside Jr-Sr HS; *ai:* Yrbk Staff Adv 1978-; Ski Club Adv 1988-; Newspaper Staff Adv 1989-; Homework Policy Comm Chairperson; NEA 1979-; NE PA Writing Cncl 1983-; NCTE 1985-; Riverside Ed Assn Contract Negotiating Team; PA Writing Assessment Advisory Comm Mem Harrisburg; Riverside Jr-Sr HS Developed Successful Public Relations & Process Writing Curr; Northeast Educl Intermediate Unit Sch Visitation Team; Mid St Visitation Team; *home:* 812 Grace Ln Moosic PA 18507

JOYE, LARRY G., Biology Teacher; *b:* Lake City, FL; *m:* Tscharna Hartsfield; *c:* Jacob, Bradford; *ed:* (BS) Zoology, 1970, (MS) Entomology/Nematology, 1976 Univ of FL; Specialist Degree Educl Leadership, Univ of FL; Summer Inservice Advanced Marine Bio Trng 1987-89; *cr:* Math/Bio Teacher Lake City Jr HS 1970-74; Bio Teacher Lake City Jr HS West 1976-83, Lake City Jr HS East 1983-; *ai:* Stu Aides Supvr; Past Youth Cncl Spon; Past Natl Jr Honor Society Spon; NSTA; Lions Club (VP 1987-89, Pres 1990), Lion of Yr 1986-87; Ducks Unlimited Area Chm 1983-85; Natl Wild Turkey Fed Secy 1987-89; Lake City Jr HS East Campus Teacher of Yr 1983-84; *office:* Columbia HS PO Box 1178 Lake City FL 32055

JOYNER, LEA W., Bus Data Processing Dept Chair; *b:* Charlotte, NC; *c:* Donna Burgess; *ed:* (BS) Ed, 1968, (MS) Ed, 1972 Memphis St Univ; IBM & Hewlett Packard Systems & Programming Classes; Shelly-Cashman COBOL Wkshp; *cr:* Teacher 1968-71, Area Specialist 1971-75, Supvr 1975-78, Instr in EDP Bus Data Proc/Cmptr Programming 1978- Memphis City Schls; *ai:* Bus Prof of Amer Spon; Data Processing Mgrs Assn 1980-86; NEA, TN Ed Assn, Memphis Ed Assn 1968-; Telecommunications Regulatory Bd City of Memphis 1975-78; Educl Technology Magazine 1971; Co-Worker on Paper Presented before Southeast Psychological Assn 1971; Served as Project Dir & Wrote Final Reports for Title-III, ESEA CAI Project 1969-71; *office:* Trezevant Voc Tech 3224 Range Line Rd Memphis TN 38127

JOYNER, PATRICIA FENNESSEY, Counselor; *b:* Boston, MA; *m:* R. S.; *c:* Ryan, Meredith; *ed:* (BS) Health/Phys Ed, E Carolina Univ 1969; (BS) Sci Ed, Univ of NC Wilmington 1978; (MAED) Counseling, E Carolina Univ 1986; *cr:* Phys Ed Teacher J T Barber 1969-71, Pensacola HS 1972-74; Sci Teacher Pinetops HS 1974-75; Stu Loan Officer Univ of NC Chapel Hill 1975-78; 4th Grade Teacher St Marys 1978-82; Teacher 1982-86, Cnslr 1986- New Bern Schls; *ai:* Teacher Liaison; Public Information Officer; Sch Assistance Team Chairperson; NCSCA 1986-; Project Graduation Co-Chairperson; St Paul Sch Bd Mem; *office:* Roger Bell Elem Sch 500 Hwy 101 Havelock NC 28532

JOYNT, MARILYN C., Second Grade Teacher; *b:* Fall River, MA; *m:* Gerald D.; *c:* Melissa, David; *ed:* (BA) Psych, SE MA Univ 1971; *cr:* 2nd Grade Teacher 1971-80, 4th Grade Teacher 1980-83, 3rd Grade Teacher 1983-85, 2nd Grade Teacher 1985-89 Chace St Sch; 2nd Grade Teacher Wilbur Sch 1989-; *ai:* Sci Comm; *office:* Wilbur Sch Brayton Pt Rd Somerset MA 02726

JUAREZ, PAMELA RODRIGUEZ, Science Teacher; *b:* Laredo, TX; *m:* Benito D.; *c:* Anissa, Benito J.; *ed:* (BS) EDCI/ Bio/Composite Sci, TX A&M Univ 1977; (MS) Bi-ling/Bicultural Ed, TX A&I Univ 1980; Mid-Management Admin; Writing Throughout the Curr & Critical Thinking Skills Advanced Trng; *cr:* Teacher Martin HS 1977-78, Meyer Elem 1978-80, Eagle Pass HS 1981-83, Sul Ross Univ 1981, J W Nixon HS 1984-; *ai:* Sch Dist Sci Fair Coord; Spon 1st Annual Physics Day; Campus Teacher Trainer; TX St Teachers Assn 1984-; Sci Teachers Assn of TX 1975-; Kappa Delta Pi 1977; Newman Elem PTA 1989-; St John Neuman Parish Mem 1983-; TX A&M Assn of Former Students 1977-; TX A&I Alumni; Presentor for Prof Growth Inservices on Discipline & Related Topics; Campus Advanced Trng Rep; Clearly Outstanding Evaluations Yearly; *home:* 900 Samlon Dr Laredo TX 78041

JUARROS, ELAINE PADILLA, 3rd Grade Teacher; *b:* Mora, NM; *m:* Dennis M.; *c:* Charles J.; *ed:* (BA) Art/Elem Ed, NM Highlands Univ 1972; Grad Work NM St Univ; Bi-ling Ed Endorsement, Univ of NM; *cr:* 1st/2nd Grade Teacher 1972-73, 3rd Grade Teacher 1973-75 E Las Vegas Public Schls; 4th Grade Teacher 1975-76, 1st Grade Teacher 1976-78 Truth or Consequences Municipal Sch; 6th Grade Teacher Espanola Public Schls 1980-82; 3rd/6th Grade Teacher Santa Fe Public Schls 1982-; *ai:* Honor Roll; Lang Art, Stu of Month, Art Rep; Chrldr Spon; Little League Coach; NEA Rep 1972-88; Delta Kappa Gamma 1986-87; Coll Park Homeowners Assn Secy 1985-; Santa Fe Ind Youth League 1979-84; Santa Fe Public Schls Teacher of Yr 1986; Nom NM & Natl Teacher of Yr 1986; Voted Santa Fe Who Made a Difference 1987; *home:* Rt 10 Box 87J Santa Fe NM 87501

JUDD, EDWARD EMIL, Business Education Teacher; *b:* New Britain, CT; *c:* Reid D., Ross E.; *ed:* (BS) Industrial Admin, Univ of CT 1958; (MS) Bus Ed, Cntrl CT St Univ 1969; Univ of Hartford; *cr:* Accounting Teacher Newburgh Free Acad 1959-63; Bus Teacher Valley Regional HS 1963-; *ai:* CT Bus Educators Assn, NEA, CT Ed Assn; *office:* Valley Regional HS Kelsey Hill Rd Deep River CT 06417

JUDD, MARILYN DOROTHY, First and Second Grade Teacher; *b:* Flint, MI; *ed:* (BA) Elem Ed, Alma Coll 1974; (MA) Recreation & Park Admin, Cntrl MI Univ 1980; Counseling & Personal Dev, CMU 1990; *cr:* Teacher Montabella Cmmty Schls 1975-; *ai:* Sex, Health Ed, Soc Stud, Fine Arts Ed Curr Sub-Comm; Amer Humane Soc; Alumni Bd Alma Coll 1978-81; *office:* Blanchard Elem Sch 405 S 4th St Blanchard MI 49310

JUDD, RANDAL GLEN, Social Studies Dept Teacher; *b:* Connersville, IN; *m:* Julie Anne Burch; *c:* Clayton; *ed:* (BA) Soc Stud, Earlham Coll 1984; (MA) Soc Stud, Ball St Univ 1987; *cr:* Teacher Connersville HS 1984-; *office:* Connersville HS 1100 Spartan Dr Connersville IN 47331

JUDE, CASSANDRA JOY, Elementary Music Teacher; *b:* Ashland, KY; *m:* Lowell Edward; *c:* Joshua C.; *ed:* (BME) Music, Morehead St Univ 1976; Music, E KY Univ 1979; *cr:* Elem Music Teacher Providence, Trapp & Fannie Bush Elem Schls 1976-; *ai:* KEA, NEA; Leader of Music Makers Church Choir; Church Sanctuary Choir & Ladies Trio Mem; Church Soloist; Clark Cty Sch System Teacher of Month; *office:* Fannie Bush Elem Sch Lexington Rd Winchester KY 40391

JUDE, GRETCHEN WOLFE, High School English Teacher; *b:* Lancaster, WI; *m:* John David; *ed:* (BS) Eng Ed - Summa Cum Laude, Univ of WI Platteville 1986; *cr:* Eng Teacher Mc Farland HS 1986, Kofa HS 1986-87, Tempe HS 1987-; *ai:* Forensics Coach 1987-; Natl Forensics League Adv 1989-; Soph Eng Chairperson Tempe HS 1989-; South Cntrl Dist Forensics Rep 1990; Phi Kappa Phi Membership 1986-; Univ of WI Platteville Senator Coll Stu Senate of Ed 1985-86; Univ of WI Platteville Excl Awd 1982; Margorie Huginin Teaching Excl Awd 1986; *office:* Tempe HS 1730 S Mill Ave Tempe AZ 85282

JUDICE, ANTHONY DOMINIC, English & Computer Teacher; *b:* Johnsonburg, PA; *m:* Janet Lee Oesterling; *c:* Anthony Jr.; *ed:* (BS) Eng Ed, Penn St Univ 1973; Grad Stud Ed, Bloomsburg Univ; Cmptr, Penn ST; *cr:* Eng Teacher 1973-88, Cmptr Teacher/Coord 1989- Richboro Jr HS; *ai:* Athletic Dir Richboro Jr HS; Cncl Rock Dist Cmptr Comm; Ivyland Boro (Councilman 1982-84, Park & Rec Bd 1980-); *office:* Richboro Jr HS Upper Holland Rd Richboro PA 18954

JUDIE, FLORINE WADDLETON, 6th Grade Teacher; *b:* Winnsboro, TX; *m:* Charlie Lee; *c:* Derek; *ed:* (BS) Bus Ed, 1960, (MS) Elem Ed, 1967 Prairie View A&M Univ; Wkshps; *cr:* Secy/ Teacher Boling Voc Sch 1960-65; 5th Grade Teacher 1966-86, 6th Grade Teacher 1987- Blackshear Sch; *ai:* UIL Poetry Spon; TSTA, NEA 1960-; Bethel AME Church Bookkeeper 1975-; *office:* Blackshear Sch 1401 W 3rd St Hearne TX 77859

JUDY, BEVERLY G., Middle School Gifted Program; *b:* Cynthiana, KY; *m:* John Mitchell Jr.; *c:* Thad, Lora; *ed:* (BA) Elem Ed, Univ of KY 1971; (MS) Elem Ed, Georgetown Coll 1978, Elem Ed, Georgetown Coll 1987; *cr:* Rdng Teacher Harrison Cty HS 1972-73; 4th Grade Teacher Eastside Elem Sch 1973-88; Gifted Ed Teacher Harrison Cty Mid Sch 1988-; *ai:* Beta Sigma Phi Corresponding Secy 1988-89; Helping Hands Circle Past Pres 1985-86; Indian Creek Chrstn Church Mem; *home:* 132 N Elmarch Ave Cynthiana KY 41031

JUDY, LOIS JEAN, 6th Grade English Teacher; *b:* Greenville, OH; *m:* Paul E.; *c:* Cindy, Deborah, Becky, Steven; *ed:* (BS) Elem Ed, Miami Univ 1968; *cr:* 4th/5th Grade Teacher Arcanum-Butler Elem Sch 1958-62; 6th/7th Grade Teacher Arcanum-Butler Mid Sch 1966-; *ai:* Stu Cncl Adv; Arcanum-Butler Classroom Teachers Assn, OEA; PTO Rep; Outstanding Leaders in Elem & Scndry Ed Achievement Awd 1976; *home:* 6999 Ott-Ithaca Rd Arcanum OH 45304

JUERS, DOUGLAS H., Mathematics/Science Teacher; *b:* Portland, ME; *ed:* (BA) Physics, Cornell Univ 1987; *cr:* Crew Coach Cornell Univ 1987-88; Teacher Carrabassett Valley Acad 1988-; *ai:* Cycling Coach; Dorm Parent; Outing Club; *office:* Carrabassett Valley Acad RR 1 Box 2240 Kingfield ME 04947

JUILLARD, EDWARD DAVID, Religious Studies Teacher; *b:* Chicago, IL; *ed:* (BA) Theology, Loyola Univ 1977; Grad Stud St Mary of the Lake Seminary, Mundelein Coll; *cr:* Teacher/Dept Chm Mother Mc Auley Lib Arts HS 1978-87; Religious Stud Teacher/Tutoring Moderator St Ignatius Coll Prep 1987-; *ai:* Moderator Cmmty Tutoring Alliance; 2 Time Recipient Univ of Chicago Outstanding Teacher Awd.

JUKES, MARGUERITE A. V. ESPOSITO, Third Grade Teacher; *b:* New York City, NY; *m:* Thomas Hughes; *c:* Kenneth, Caroline Knueppel, Dorothy M. Jukes Hudson; *ed:* (BA) Chem/ Physics/Bio/Eng, Hunter Coll 1941; (MA) Chem/Physics/Bio/ Eng, Montclair Univ 1950; Life Cred Univ of CA Berkeley 1965; *cr:* Teacher Clarkstown Cntrl Sch Dist 1952-59, Skillman NJ 1962, Berkeley Unified Sch Dist 1966-; *ai:* Berkeley Teachers Center Advisory Bd; Berkeley Teachers Union Building Rep; Amer Assn of Univ Women, Delta Kappa Gamma, Pi Lambda Theta, CA Teachers Assn, Berkeley Teachers Assn, NEA, Berkeley Fed of Teachers; Martin Luther King Awd 1980.

JUKURI, ELDRED W., Seventh Grade Teacher; *b:* Mohawk, MI; *m:* V. Juanita Murray; *c:* David, Steven, Daniel; *ed:* (BA) Bible/Theology, Cntrl Bible Inst & Seminary 1955; (BS) Eng/Soc Sci, 1963, (MA) Elem Ed, 1969 E MI Univ; *cr:* Teacher Cheboygan MI 1957-58, Flat Rock MI 1958-60, S Rockwood MI 1960-62, Monroe MI 1962-; *ai:* Bsktbl Officiating; Monroe City Ed Assn, MI Ed Assn, NEA; MI Amateur Hockey Assn; *home:* 735 N Roessler Monroe MI 48161

JULIAN, CAROLANN SIMPSON, Third Grade Teacher; *b:* Rural Comanche Cty, OK; *m:* Jimmy Lee; *c:* Audrey D., Dan C.; *ed:* (BS) Elem Ed, Cameron Univ 1980; *cr:* 4th Grade Teacher Marlow Elem Sch 1981-84; 5th Grade Teacher Marlow Mid Sch 1984-85; 3rd Grade Teacher Marlow Elem Sch 1985-; *ai:* Marlow ACT Building Rep; Ok Ed Assn, NEA; *home:* 913 W Choctaw St Marlow OK 73055

JULIAN, THELMA RAY, Spanish Teacher; *b:* Christopher, IL; *m:* Thomas Eugene; *c:* Andrew C., Aaron R.; *ed:* (BS) Scndry Ed/Span/Sociolgy/Eng, SIU Carbondale 1973; Counseling Prgm Dept of Educl Psych; *cr:* Teacher Johnston City HS 1973-78; Supvr/Teacher Benton Chrstn Sch 1978-80; Teacher Hamilton Cty Unit 10 Schls 1983-; *ai:* Delta Kappa Gamma 1986-89; Amer Assn of Counseling & Dev 1990; Heights Church of God (Parliamentarian, Pianist, Sunday Sch Supt/Teacher, St Bd of Chrstn Ed); Educl Service Region Certificate of Recognition.

JULY, FELICIA LA JEAN (WILLIAMS), 6th Grade Soc Stud Teacher; *b:* Gallatin, TX; *m:* Travis; *c:* Ferlich R., Travon M.; *ed:* (BA) Music, 1962, (MS) Elem Ed, 1965 Prairie View; Certificate Elem Supvr, Prairie View & Stephen F Austin 1968; Certificate Mentally Retarded, Stephen F Austin 1971; AAT Wkshps, Region VII Ed Service Center; *cr:* Music Teacher 1962-72, Music/Spec Ed Teacher 1969-73, Soc Stud Teacher 1974- Jacksonville Mid Sch; *ai:* Tutor After Sch; Music Dir for Benson Memorial CME Youth Choir; TSTA (Local Mem, Life Time Mem); Spec Ed Music Teacher 1970-75, Certificate for Service Rendered 1971; Career Ladder Teacher.

JUNE, DEANA, First Grade Teacher; *b:* Greeleyville, SC; *ed:* (BS) Elem Ed, SC St Coll 1973; Montgomery Cty Public Schls; *cr:* 4th Grade Teacher Williamsburg Cty Public Schls 1973-74; 1st Grade Teacher Montgomery Cty Public Schls 1974-; *ai:* Discipline Comm; 1st Grade Chairperson; Human Relations Comm; Mont Co Ed Assn 1974-; NEA 1974-; MD St Teachers Assn 1974-; New Pilot Prgm Improve Achievement for Black & Hispanic Stu; *office:* Wyngate Elem Sch 9300 Wadsworth Dr Bethesda MD 20817

JUNGBLUTH, SHIRLEY ANNE, Teacher of the Gifted; *b:* Dalhart, TX; *m:* Sam Glen; *c:* Steven G., Stanley D.; *ed:* (BS) Scndry Ed, Univ of NM 1963; Grad Stud Gifted Ed; Great Books Leadership Trng Courses; *cr:* Eng Teacher Pampa HS 1963-66; Piano Teacher for Adults 1960-75; Teacher of Gifted Highland HS 1984-; *ai:* Local Teachers Against Substance Abuse, Chrstn Stu Club, In-Charge Teacher Chrstn Fellowship Teacher Group Spon; At Risk Stu Comm Mem; Society of Gifted & Talented 1982-88; CEC 1986-88; Public Service Awd for Work with Homeless of Albuquerque 1986; Albuquerque Prof Businesswomens Club Schlsp Awd 1984; Published Articles on Underachieving Gifted Stus; *office:* Highland HS 4700 Coal Ave SE Albuquerque NM 87108

JUNKER, CONSTANCE WILLIAMS, Librarian/Media Director; *b:* Cable, WI; *m:* James John; *c:* James John Jr. *ed:* (BA) Eng/Speech/Drama, Northland Coll 1957; Library, Media; *cr:* Eng Teacher Park Falls HS 1957-58; Eng/Civics/Dir Cable HS 1959-67; Librarian 1967-, Media Teacher 1987- Ashland HS; *ai:* Ashland HS Stu Cncl & Amer Field Service Adv; AFT; Ashland Teachers Secy 1974; Federal Grand Jury (Mem, Asst Foreman) 1975; NW WI Lib System Pres 1972-75; Indianhead Lib System Pres 1973; *home:* 1420 11th Ave W Ashland WI 54806

JUREK, KENNETH J., English Department Chairman; *b:* San Antonio, TX; *m:* Judy Sonderburg; *c:* Melody, Warren; *ed:* (BA) Eng, Sam Houston St Univ 1971; Univ of Houston Clear Lake; *cr:* Teacher Windham Sch Dist 1971-81; Dept of Eng Chm Danbury HS 1981-; Teacher Brazosport Coll 1986-; *ai:* Speech & Debate Society; Academic Excl, Principals Advisory, Campus Planning Comm; Natl Forensic League; NHS; Univ Interscholastic League Dist Literary & Academic Coord; Toastmasters Intnl Area Governor; Natl Endowment for Hum Duquesne Univ; Grad Fellowship; Greater Houston Area Writing Project Univ of Houston Clear Lake; *office:* Danbury HS 5611 Panther Dr Danbury TX 77534

JURMAN, LARRY H., 5th/6th Grade Teacher; *b:* Los Angeles, CA; *ed:* (BA) His/Poly Sci, San Francisco St 1968; (MA) Ed, Oakland Univ 1970; *cr:* Teacher/Intern Detroit MI 1968-70; Teacher Glen Alta Elem 1970-81, Oxnard Street Elem 1981-; *ai:* Stu Cncl Leader; Co-Chm Leadership Cncl; Faculty Chm; UTLA House of Rep 1970-; *home:* 15911 Joseph Ct Sylmar CA 91342

JURS, BARBARA MENDES, Visiting Spanish Professor; *b:* Columbia, SC; *m:* Dennis Gregg; *c:* Jason R.; *ed:* (BA) Span, Furman Univ 1976; (MA) Span, Appalachian St Univ 1983; Various Courses Prof Growth, The Citadel, Coll of Charleston, Univ of Richmond, VA Commonwealth Univ, E TN St Univ 1977-82; *cr:* Span/Eng Teacher N Charleston HS 1977-78, Chester Mid Sch 1978-81; Grad Teaching Asst Appalachian St Univ 1982-83; Span Teacher John S Battle HS 1984-89; Visiting Span Professor King Coll 1989-; *ai:* Span Club Spon; Intnl Dinner Comm Chm; Span Competitions Fine Art Coach; Foreign Lang Dept Chm; Cty Curr & Writing Comm for Foreign Lang Chm; Textbook Adoption Comm Co-Chm; FLAVA 1988-89; Sigma Delta Pi VP 1982-83; ACTFL 1988-; VEA, NEA, WCEA 1984-; Holston Lang Assn Pres 1986-87; Jr Womans Club of Abingdon (Secy 1984, Membership Chm 1985, Health Chm 1990), Outstanding Jr 1986; Big Brothers/Big Sisters Bd Mem 1985-88; Washington Cty Outstanding HS Teacher of Yr 1989; Nom Distinguished St Foreign Lang Teacher of Yr 1988; Selection Comm Outstanding Teacher Bristol Schls 1986-; Outstanding Young Women of America 1983; Governors Span Acad Selection Comm Chm 1986-; Tazewell Cty Schls Southern Assn Accreditation Visiting Team Mem for Evaluation.

JURY, MARGARET TELLER, Third Grade Teacher; *b:* Bellingham, WA; *m:* Robert M.; *c:* Scott, Lori Jury Walker, Jennifer; *ed:* (BA) Elem Ed, W WA Coll 1953; *cr:* 2nd Grade Teacher Esperance Sch 1953-54, Mt Home 1954-55, Esperance Sch 1955-56; 3rd Grade Teacher Alder Elem 1965-; *office:* Reynolds Alder Sch 17200 SE Alder St Portland OR 97233

JUSTH, DARREL R., Music Teacher; *b:* Lewisberry, PA; *m:* Mary Gray; *c:* Darrel Jr., Amy, Katie; *ed:* (BS) Music Ed, Mansfield Univ 1967; Wilks Coll; Penn St; Lancaster Seminary; *cr:* Band Dir Dover Jr/Sr HS 1967-85; General Music & Vocal Music Teacher 1985-Dover Intermediate; *ai:* Dir of Show Choir; Dover Area Ed Assn 1967-; Hayshire UCC Minister of Music 1989-; *office:* Dover Intermediate Sch Intermediate Ave Dover PA 17315

JUSTICE, LARAINE CASS, 7th Grade Math Teacher; *b:* Forth Worth, TX; *m:* Wayne A.; *c:* Starlet Darden, Donna, Waynette, Felicia, Daryl; *ed:* (BA) Math, Huston-Tillotson Coll 1970; Graduate Classes, TX Chrstn Univ/TX Womans Univ; *cr:* Math Teacher Forest Oak Mid Sch 1970, Meacham Mid Sch 1970-74, Dunbar Mid Sch 1974-90; *ai:* 7th Grade Homeroom Adv/Campus Coord Comm; Natl Jr Honor Society Spon; Math Club Spon; the Working Connection; 7th Grade Inter Disiplinarian Team Mem; NEA 1970-; TSTA 1970-; Outstanding Teacher Math Plaque 1974; Ft Worth Classroom Teachers Assn; Bethelem Center Worker Cert 1976-77; Fellows for The Advancement of Math; St Andrews United Meth Church Sunday Sch Teacher; *office:* Dunbar Middle School 1209 Stalcup Fort Worth TX 76105

JUSTICE, PENELOPE HARPLEY, 4th Grade Teacher; *b:* Fostoria, OH; *m:* Thomas R.; *c:* Jason, Joel; *ed:* (BS) Elem Ed, Bowling Green St Univ 1968; *cr:* Kndgtn Teacher Bettsville Elem Sch 1968-69; 2nd Grade Teacher 1969-70, 1st Grade Teacher 1970-87, 4th Grade Teacher 1987- Longfellow Elem Sch; *ai:* Fostoria Ed Assn 1969-; OH Ed Assn, NEA 1968-; Kappa Delta Pi; *office:* Longfellow Sch 619 Sandusky St Fostoria OH 44830

JUSTIN, MARY ANNE BANIA, Sixth Grade Teacher; *b:* Rutland City, VT; *c:* Brian Jr., Andrea; *ed:* (BS) Elem Ed, Castleton St 1963; (ME) Ed, St Joseph Coll 1978; Advanced Educl Ed; *cr:* 5th Grade Teacher Northeast Supervisory 1963-64; 5th-6th Grade Teacher Rutland City 1966-; *ai:* Adelphia Univ Drug Abuse Project Team; Hulbert Outboard Center for Outdoor & Self Esteem; IHM Church Secy 1990; Outstanding Young Woman & Teacher of America 1972; *office:* Northwest Sch Pierpoint Ave Rutland VT 05701

JZYK, LINDA ZONFRILLO, Biology Teacher; *b:* Providence, RI; *m:* John E.; *c:* Nicholas, Alexander, Peter; *ed:* (BA) Biological/Medical Sci, Brown Univ 1974; (MBA) Public Management, Bryant Coll 1986; Sci, Univ of RI, Providence Coll, RI Coll; *cr:* Life Sci Teacher Woonsocket Jr HS 1974-87; Bio Teacher Woonsocket Sr HS 1987-; *ai:* Alternatives to Alcohol & Drugs Coord; SADD Adv; In-Service Comm Woonsocket Sr HS; RI Sci Teachers Assn 1977-; Brown Univ (Class of 1974 VP 1989-, Reunion Comm 1984, 1989); Dept of Energy Residential Energy Management Inst 1979; Providence Coll Bio Coord & Laboratories & Demonstrations Forum 1987; Woonsocket Sr HS Commencement Speaker 1989; RI Invent America Delegate 1987; *office:* Woonsocket Sr HS 777 Cass Ave Woonsocket RI 02895

K

KABATZNICK, JOEL MAX, English Teacher; *b:* Middletown, CT; *m:* Aurelie Jacquelyne Bald; *c:* Paul; *ed:* (BA) Math, Amherst Coll 1962; (MAT) Eng, Harvard Univ 1963; *cr:* Eng Teacher Wellesley Sr HS 1963-70, Private Amer Schls Overseas 1970-82, Wasilla HS 1982-; *ai:* NEA Life Membership 1970-; Sacred Heart Church Parish Cncl 1985; Table Leader Coll Bd Rdngs; Published Eng Journal 1970; Participant in Natl Endowment for Hum; Sponsored Summer Seminars for Sch Teachers 1988; *home:* PO Box 871924 Wasilla AK 99687

KABLE, JANICE HOLPE, Instructional Specialist; *b:* Filbert, WV; *m:* Gary Marshall; *c:* Carolyn M., Angela Kirkpatrick, Stephanie Stoneberger; *ed:* (BS) Spec Ed/Eng, 1968, (MA) Speech Communication, 1980 WV Univ; *cr:* Eng Teacher Charles Town HS 1968-72, Jefferson HS 1972-89; Instructional Specialist Jefferson Cty Schls 1989-; *ai:* Cty Coord WV Challenge; Coord of Scndry Sci Fairs Cty Level; Staff Dev Cncl Cty Level; WVEA, JCEA, NEA 1968-; WV Rdng Cncl 1968-72; WV Soc Stud 1989-; Cty Teacher of Yr Finalist; Jefferson HS Teacher of Month; *office:* Jefferson Cty Schls PO Box 987 Charles Town WV 25414

KACHEL, BETH JOHNSEN, Mathematics Teacher; *b:* St Paul, MN; *m:* Thomas; *c:* Karen, Matthew; *ed:* (BA) Math, Hamline Univ 1982; *cr:* Teacher St Agnes HS 1982-84, Parkview Mid Sch 1984-85, Hill-Murray HS 1985-; *ai:* Mathcounts Coach; Curr Review Comm OBE; MN Cncl Teachers of Math; MN Math Mobilization; *home:* 6886 Crystal Ct Lino Lakes MN 55014

KACHUR, BETTY RAE, 1st Grade Teacher; *b:* Lorain, OH; *ed:* (BS) Ed, Kent St Univ 1963; (MA) Rdng, Univ of AZ 1971; *cr:* Teacher Lorain City Sch System 1961-; *ai:* Intnl Rdng Assn (Treas, Local Cncl) 1986-.

KACHURIK, ELIZABETH M., Business Education Teacher; *b:* Wheeling, WV; *d:* Philip; *c:* Renee; *ed:* (BA) Bus Ed, W Liberty St Coll 1968; Working on Masters in Speech Comm, W VA Univ; *cr:* Bus Teacher John Marshall HS 1968-69, Triadelphia HS 1970-76, Wheeling Park HS 1976-; *ai:* FBLA, Future Secretaries Assn; Cheering Coach; OH Cty Ed Assn, WV Ed Assn, NEA 1976-; Amer Vocation Assn 1980-85; Alpha Delta Kappa Recording Secy 1985-; Bus Dept Chairperson; HS Drug Abuse Facilitator; Blue Ribbon Comm; *office:* Wheeling Park HS Park View Rd Wheeling WV 26003

KACZOR, CHARLES S., 8th Grade History Teacher; *b:* Yonkers, NY; *m:* Mary S. Oliver; *c:* Mark A., Brian C., Dennis J.; *ed:* (BA) His, St Anslem Coll 1950; Grad Stud Univ IN 1965 & Univ of CT 1967-69; *cr:* Retired Major/Pilot USAF 1942-67; Commanding Officer Atlas F Cuban Missle Crisis 1962; 8th Grade His Teacher Dr Charles E Murphy Jr HS; *ai:* Boys Cross Cntry Coach; Sunday Sch Teacher; New England Assn of Soc Stud; BSA Comm Chm 1972-76; Waterford Tax Payors Assn Treas 1976-78; Montville Teacher of Yr 1989-; Nom St Teacher of Yr.

KADANI, LINDA HAE, Educator-English Teacher; *b:* Monterey, CA; *ed:* (BA) Eng, Stanislaus St Univ 1974; *cr:* Teacher Mark Twain JR HS 1975-81, Roosevelt JR HS 1981-; *ai:* CA JR Scholastic Fed Adv; CA Assn Gifted; Modesto Teachers Assn; CA Teacher Assn ; Childrens Home Society; *office:* Roosevelt Jr HS 1330 College Ave Modesto CA 95350

KADE, DEBORAH ANN (KALENTEK), 4th Grade Teacher; *b:* Ware, MA; *m:* Michael J.; *ed:* (BS) Elem Ed, Keene St Coll 1973; (MED) Admin, Springfield Coll 1978; *cr:* 4th Grade Teacher Ware Elem Sch 1973-89; *ai:* NEA; MTA; WTA; Parent Teachers Club; *home:* 9424 N 105th St Scottsdale AZ 85258

KAECH, JOE, JR., Sixth Grade Teacher; *b:* Frances, WA; *ed:* (BA) Soc Stud, Cntrl WA Univ 1964; Univ of WA, Univ of Puget Sound, Cntrl WA Univ; *cr:* 5th Grade Teacher Raymond Elem 1964-67; 4th Grade Teacher Overseas Dependent Schls 1968-70; 5th-8th Grade Teacher Fairview Mid Sch 1971-76; 6th Grade Teacher Woodlands Elem 1979-; *ai:* Building Management Team; After Sch Study Session for Stus; Dist 5th & 6th Curr Review Comm; NEA, WA Ed Assn, CKEA (Assoc VP 1965-66, Chief Negotiator 1977-77), Teacher of Yr 1978; PTA 1964-89 Nom Outstanding Educator Awd 1988; Lewis-Pacific Swiss Society 1960-; *office:* Woodlands Elem Sch 7420 Central Valley Rd NE Bremerton WA 98310

KAELIN, JOHN MICHAEL, Fifth Grade Teacher; *b:* Tacoma, WA; *m:* Susan Twardoski; *c:* Micala, Jeffrey, Kraig, Bradley; *ed:* (AA) General, Green River Comm Coll 1973; (BA) Elem Ed, Cntrl WA 1975; *cr:* 6th Grade Teacher 1976-88, 7th Grade Teacher 1983-84 White River Mid Sch; 5th Grade Teacher Foothills Elem 1988-; *ai:* WREA 1976-; Swiss Sportsmens Club 1973-.

KAEMPFER, LEE MAGILL, Mathematics Department Chair; *b:* Cape Girardeau, MO; *m:* William; *c:* Paul, Karen; *ed:* (BS) Math, SE MO St Univ 1945; *cr:* Teacher Sikeston HS 1945-47, Amarillo Jr HS 1949-51, Roosevelt Military Acad 1962-70, Aledo HS 1975-; *ai:* Academic Bowl Coach; AEA Schlsp Comm; IEA, NEA, MSTA; *office:* Aledo HS S College Ave Aledo IL 61231

KAEPERNICK, KENNETH LEE, Math/Computer Science Teacher; *b:* Fond Du Lac, WI; *m:* Kathlyn Sanford; *c:* Kristine; *ed:* (BS) Elem Ed, Math, 1967; (MS) 1975 UW Oshkosh; Post Masters Studies Cmptr Sci; *cr:* Teacher/Prin Lebanon Pub Sch 1956-57 Wyocena Pub Sch 1957-58; Teacher Thiensville Mequon Sch Dist 1958-61; Instr/Instr Trainer US Army Signal Sch 1962-64; Math Teacher 1964-; Computer Sci Teacher 1982 Mayville Pub Sch; *ai:* Organizer Sch Safety Patrol; Designer Organizer of Cmpter Lab/Comptr Courses; NEA 1956-; WI Ed Assn 1956-; Mayville Ed Assn Negotiator 1964-; St Pauls Luth Church Congregation Secy 1985-; *home:* W 3899 Hwy S Iron Ridge WI 53035

KAESER, ROMELLE, Jr HS Teacher; *b:* Crab Orchard, IL; *m:* John L.; *c:* Diane Lazorchak, Steven D., David J.; *ed:* (BS) Ed, S IL Univ Carbondale 1978; Problems & Characteristics of Gifted, SIU-E 1979; Gifted Ed, Summer Inst 1979-80, 1982; *cr:* 1st Grade Teacher 1978-79, 5th Grade Teacher 1979 Goreville Grade Sch; Teacher Goreville Jr HS 1979-; *ai:* Coord & Teacher Gifted Prgm; Scholar Bowl Coach; Scheduling Comm; NCTE; Pi Lambda Theta 1977-; Beta Sigma Phi 1958-; Marion Hospital Auxiliary Life Mem; Zion United Church of Christ 1958-; *office:* Goreville Cmmty Unit #1 Collins St Goreville IL 62939

KAETHER, WILLIAM OWEN, JR., English Teacher; *b:* Madison, WI; *m:* Cynthia L.; *c:* Jeffrey; *ed:* (BS) Comm Art, 1970, (MS) Ed/Admin, 1985 Univ of WI Madison; *cr:* 7th-8th Grade Lang Art Teacher Palmyra Jr HS 1971-74; 8th Grade Eng Teacher Winnequah Mid Sch 1974-; *ai:* Stu Cncl & Sport Club Adv; 8th Grade Girls Bsktbl Coach; Dist Lang Art Comm; MGEA, WEA, NEA; Beta Theta Pi, Spec Olympics; USTA WI #1 Boys 1966; Univ of WI Madison Practincum Teachers Trng Prgm; *office:* Winnequah Mid Sch 800 Greenway Rd Monona WI 53716

KAFER, CATHERINE RAMHARTER, 1st Grade Teacher; *b:* Chippewa Falls, WI; *m:* Joseph A.; *c:* Sean, Rachel; *ed:* (BS) Elem Ed, Univ of WI River Falls 1972; (MA) Ed, Viterbo Coll 1990; *cr:* 1st Grade Teacher New London Public Schls 1972-; *ai:* NEA, New London Ed Assn 1972-; GSA Brownies Co-Leader 1989-; *home:* 636 Martin St New London WI 54961

KAHN, CAMILLE MINNICINO, Basic Skills Teacher; *b:* Irvington, NJ; *c:* Michelle Dougherty, Sean Dougherty; *ed:* (BA) Eng, Wayne St Univ 1971; (MALS) Eng Literature, Kean Coll 1982; NH Writing Project Rutgers Univ; Eng Literature Courses Kean Coll; Crises Mgmt Trng; *cr:* 6th Grade Self Cont Mc Kinley 1974-76; 6th Grade Self Cont McKinley Sch 1973-74; Elm St Sch 1974-76; 4th Grade Self Cont Franklin Sch 1975-76; Washington Sch 1977-78; Eng Teacher Roosevelt Int Sch 1978-89; Basic Skills Mc Kinley Sch 1989-; *ai:* Westfield Ed Assn (Treas 1985-86 Public Rel Chairperson 1982-85); Published Bus Ed Guide; *home:* 900 Harding St Westfield NJ 07090

KAHN, MARGUERITE K., Librarian; *b:* Lafayette, LA; *ed:* (BA) Eng Ed/Lib Sci, Univ of SW LA 1974; (MED) Admin/Supervision LA St Univ 1981; *cr:* Librarian Armstrong Mid Sch 1974-; *ai:* Lib Club Spon; Chrldr Co-Spon 1989-; Sci & Soc Stud Fair, Sch Policy Advisory Comm; Acadia Parish Librarians Assn (Secy, Treas) 1990; *office:* Armstrong Mid Sch 700 M L King Dr Rayne LA 70578

KAHN, STEVEN P., Physical Education Teacher; *b:* Michigan City, IN; *m:* Linda Sue Harris; *c:* Mark, Holly; *ed:* (BS) Phys Ed, Ball St Univ 1974; (MS) Scndry Ed, IN Univ 1982; *cr:* Phys Ed Teacher Elston Jr HS 1975-77, Krueger Jr HS 1977-; *ai:* Asst Var Ftbl Coach; Discipline Comm; Sch Cabinet; Krueger Stand; AFT, IN Ftbl Coaches Assn; *office:* Krueger Jr HS 2001 Springland Ave Michigan City IN 46360

KAHRL, SUSAN THOMPSON, 6th Grade Teacher; *b:* Mt Vernon, OH; *m:* Timothy; *c:* Andrew, Allison; *ed:* (BS) Elem Ed, Edinboro St Univ 1970; Grad Work OH St Univ; *cr:* 6th Grade Teacher Mt Vernon Mid Sch 1970-; *ai:* Mid Sch Talent Show Dir; World Culture Day Coord; Curr Cncl Mem; Natl Geographic Geography Bee Coord; Mt Vernon Ed Assn Corresponding Secy 1973-74; Mt Vernon Players Pres 1986-89, Distinguished Service Awd 1989; Amer Assn Univ Women (Pres 1978-80, 1981-83), Service Awd 1982; Academic Challenge Participant OH St Univ; *home:* 601 E High St Mount Vernon OH 43050

KAIGLER, ANQUANITA MADDEN, 6th Grade Reading Teacher; *b:* Cushing, OK; *m:* Kevin C.; *c:* Shamone, Wesley; *ed:* (BA) Elem Ed, Cameron Univ 1974; (BA) Elem Ed, OK 1976; *cr:* Elem Teacher Carriage Hills Elem 1974-; *ai:* Mem Martin Luther King Planning Comm of Lawton; Soccer Team Coach 1989-; Textbook Selection Comm; Team Leader Carriage House Hills Intermediate; Amer Classroom Teacher Rep; Lawton Area Rdng Cncl 1987-; NEA, OK Ed Assn, Prof Educators of Lawton 1974-; Delta Sigma Theta Soc-Action Chairperson 1989-91; *office:* Carriage Hills Elem Sch 215 SE Warwick Way Lawton OK 73507

KAIL, SHERRY FREEMAN, Fifth Grade Teacher; *b:* Humboldt, TN; *m:* Jere M.; *c:* Jenny, Mack, Shiloh; *ed:* (BS) Elem Ed, Lambuth Coll 1969; (MED) Educl Admin/Supervision, Memphis St Univ 1989; *cr:* 5th Grade Teacher Glenview Elem 1969-70, Crockett Cty Elem 1970-72, Bells Elem 1983-; *ai:* Honor Club Adv; Delta Kappa Gamma 1985-; TN Ed Assn, NEA 1988-; Crockett Cty Chamber of Commerce Leadership Dev Task Force 1990; TN Chrstn Womens Fellowship Dist 5 Dir 1989-.

KAISER, LOUISE M., 4th Grade Teacher; *b:* Anderson, SC; *m:* Paul III; *c:* Chip, Ashley; *ed:* (BA) Elem Ed, Clemson Univ 1976; Grad Stud Rdng Clemson Univ; *cr:* Math Teacher Mc Cants Mid Sch 1977-79; 3rd Grade Teacher 1980-84, 4th Grade Teacher 1984- S Fant Elem Sch; *ai:* Advisory Sch Cncl; Bus-Sch Partnership; Awds Day; Spelling Bee Chairperson; Sch Dept Head; Tactics Comm Mem; NEA 1975-, Teacher of Yr 1987-88; DAR Chairperson 1985-, Good Citizen of Yr Dist 5 1988; *home:* 203 Wren Way Anderson SC 29625

KAISER, MARY DONNA LINTON, Biology/Chemistry Teacher; *b:* Cullman, AL; *m:* Edward John; *c:* Kathryn, Susan, Bradley; *ed:* (BS) Ed, Auburn Univ 1964; (MAT) Bio, The Citadel 1972; Ed Spec Sci, GA Southern Univ; *cr:* Bio/Phys Sci Teacher Summerville Intermediate HS 1974-76; Bio/Chem Teacher Summerville HS 1979-83; Chem Instr Baptist Coll Charleston 1985-86; Bio/Chem Teacher Camden Cty HS 1987-; *ai:* NHS Adv; Frosh Class Spon; CCHS Substitute Orientation & Safety Comm; Tpai Mentor Teacher; Prof Assn of GA Educators 1987-; NSTA 1987-; GA Sci Teachers Assn 1987-; Delta Kappa Gamma Society Intnl 1990; GA Wildlife Fed 1990; Camden Cty HS Teacher of Yr & Teacher of Yr 1989; Certificate of Recognition Key Club Intnl; *home:* 1208 Live Oak Ln Saint Marys GA 31558

KAKACEK, STEVEN JACOB, Band Director; *b:* Waterloo, IA; *m:* Kathleen Annette Riley; *c:* Janet, Beth; *ed:* (BA) Music, Univ of CA Riverside 1973; Teaching Credential Music, ID St Univ 1975; Ed & Math Classes; *cr:* Band Dir Selmer Corporation 1973-74, Sch Dist #91 1975-; *ai:* Jazz Band; ID Music Educators Assn 1980-; Music Club 1988-; Cmmty Bd (Co-Founder, Dir) 1983-; Church Choir Dir 1986-; *office:* Claire E Gale Jr HS 955 Garfield Idaho Falls ID 83401

KAKUGAWA, FRANCES H., Third Grade Teacher; *b:* Kapoho, HI; *ed:* (BED) Elem Ed, 1958, Elem Ed, 1959 Univ of HI; *cr:* Curr Writer St Dept of Ed 1972-79; 6th Grade Teacher Nimitz 1979-84; Lecturer Univ of HI 1980-84; Writing Resource Teacher Nimitz 1984-85; 3rd Grade Teacher Hahaione Sch 1985-; Kndgtn-1st Grade Teacher Waiakea Elem; *ai:* Natl Teachers Org; Books of Poetry; Published Poetry, Articles, Short Stories in Eng Journal; *home:* 531 Hahaione St 2-2C Honolulu HI 96825

KALCIC, LYNN ANN DWIEL, Mathematics/Computer Teacher; *b:* Pensacola, FL; *m:* Brian W.; *c:* Christine, Andy; *ed:* (BS) Physics/Math, IL Benedictine Coll 1974; Environmental Eng, IL Inst of Technology; Teacher Cert NE IL Univ 1976-77; Cmptr Courses, WA Univ; *cr:* Math Teacher Orchard Farm Sch Dist 1977-79; Math/Sci/Cmptr Teacher Mary Inst 1979-; *ai:* Soph Class Spon; Grant & Schlsp Comm; Tandy Technological Scholar Mary Inst 1990; Semi-Finalist Thanks to Teachers Campaign 1990; *office:* Mary Inst 101 N Warson Saint Louis MO 63124

KALDAHL, JEAN CLARK, 3rd Grade Teacher; *b:* Berwick, IA; *m:* Charles L.; *c:* David; *ed:* (BA) Soc Sci, St Univ Northern IA 1950; (MA) Diversified/Elem Ed, San Francisco St Univ 1968; Univ of S CA Ext; Lone Mtn; St Marys; Univ of Phoenix; *cr:* 9-12th Grade Teacher Harlan HS 1950-53; 7th/8th Grade Teacher Okmulgee Jr HS 1953-54; 8th Grade Teacher Dexter Sch 1954-55; 1-6th Grade Teacher Pleasant Valley Sch 1960-62; 7th & 8th Grade Teacher Ben Franklin Jr HS 1962-77; 3rd/5th/6th Grade Teacher T Edison Elem Sch 1977-; *ai:* Safety Patrol; Stu Cncl; Class Prgms; Latin Club; Pep Club; Jr-Sr Banquet Planning; NEA Mem 1950-; CA Teachers Assn St Cncl Mem We Honor Ours Awd 1986; CA Assn Chldhd Ed Honorary Mem 1985; Amer Assn Univ Women 1954-55; Bus & Prof Women 1950-53; Mentor Teacher 1985-87; Wrote Unpublished Book Teaching of Research Schls to Upper Grade Students; Demonstration Teacher; Project Write.

KALEHUAWEHE, CATHERINE BISHOP, Kindergarten Teacher; *b:* White Plains, NY; *m:* Angel N.; *c:* Chad, Christy, Caan; *ed:* (BA) Elem Ed/Phys Ed, Western St Coll 1970; Prof Certificate; *cr:* K/1st/4th/6th Grade Teacher Makawao Elem 1970-75; 2nd/3rd Grade Teacher Pukalani Elem 1975-88; Kndgtn Teacher Wailuku Elem 1988-; *ai:* NAEYC, MCEYC VP 1989-; PTA Secy 1989-; Alpha Delta Kappa (Historian 1986-88, Teacher); *home:* 656 Anela Pl Wailuku HI 96793

KALER, MARGIE WOOLCOCK, English Teacher; *b:* Millville, PA; *m:* Richard Dale; *c:* R. Alan, Kimberly A; *ed:* Eng, Dickinson Coll; (BA) Eng, Lycoming Coll 1975; *cr:* Eng Teacher Bloomsburg HS 1978-79, Benton Area HS 1979-80, Waubonsie Valley HS 1982-; *ai:* Drama Asst Dir; *office:* Waubonsie Valley HS 2590 Ogden Rt 34 Aurora IL 60504

KALEY, REANN ALLYN, Social Studies Teacher; *b:* Chicago, IL; *ed:* (BSED) Scndry Soc Stud, Univ of MO Columbia 1986; *cr:* Teacher Pattonville HS 1986-; *ai:* Youth Assn for Retarded Citizens Spon; Amer His Curr & Hall of Fame Selection Comm; Strategic Planning Comm Cmmty Relations; NEA Stu Teacher of Yr 1986; Supts Advisory Cncl 1990; Pattonville Ed Assn Building Rep; Jr League of MO; Kappa Kappa Gamma Night Owl Secy 1986-; *office:* Pattonville HS 2497 Creve Coeur Mill Rd Maryland Heights MO 63044

KALIADES, DEBRA KIMMISH, Second Grade Teacher; *b:* Jersey City, NJ; *m:* Paul J.; *c:* Alexis, Stephanie, Charles; *ed:* Elem Ed, St Peters Coll 1972; *cr:* 4th Grade Teacher PS 14 1972-75; 2nd/3rd/7th Grade Teacher PS 28 1975-; *ai:* Jersey City Ed Assn Dir 1985-87; Working Parents Assn of Longfellow Sch Co-Pres 1988-; *office:* No 28 School 139 Hancock Ave Jersey City NJ 07666

KALINKEWICZ, DENISE FILION, English Teacher; *b:* Ballston Spa, NY; *m:* John J.; *ed:* (BA) Eng Ed, SUC Plattsburgh 1974; Working Towards Rdng Specialist, Russel Sage Coll 1976; *cr:* Eng Teacher Galway HS 1974-; *ai:* Class, Stu Senate, Mock Trial, Drama Adv; Soccer Coach; NCTE; Big Brothers-Big Sisters; *office:* Galway HS Rt 147 Galway Galway NY 12074

KALINOWSKI, JACQUELINE IMPERO, English/Drama Teacher; *b:* Binghamton, NY; *m:* Thomas J.; *c:* Elisa; *ed:* (BA) Eng, St Univ of NY Albany 1973; Grad Courses Plattsburgh St Coll, Pottsdam St Coll; *cr:* Teacher Saranac Lake HS 1973-; *ai:* Sr Play Dir; Homework & Testing Comm Chairperson; Saranac Lake Teachers Assn Secy 1978-80; *office:* Saranac Lake HS Lapan Hwy Saranac Lake NY 12983

KALLUS, FRANK THEODORE, Science Teacher; *b:* La Grange, TX; *c:* Jennifer A., Angela M.; *ed:* (MD) Medicine, Southwestern Medical Sch 1961; (BS) Zoology, TX A&M Coll 1966; (PHD) Physiology, Southwestern Medical Sch 1970; Meth Hospital of Dallas 1961-62; Sch of Aerospace Medicine 1962; Residency Anesthesiology, Parkland Memorial Hospital 1964-66; *cr:* Physiology/Biophysics Asst Professor LSU Sch Med 1970-72; Anesthesiology Asst Professor Southwestern Medical Sch 1972-84; Anesthesiology Asst Professor Southwestern Medical Sch 1972-84; Physiology Adjunct Assn Professor Baylor Coll of Denistry 1983-86; *ai:* Amer Chemical Society 1982-; Amer Physiological Society 1970-86; Amer Medical Assn 1972-84; Park Cities YMCA Bd of Dir 1973-75; USPHS Physiology Spec Fellow 1966-70; Amer Society of Anesthesiologists Refresher Course Lecturer 1983; Published Chapter in Book; Refresher Courses in Anesthesiology 1983; Numerous Articles Published; *office:* The Episcopal Sch of Dallas 4100 Merrell Rd Dallas TX 75229

KALLUS, SYBIL MARKS, Retired Fourth Grade Teacher; *b:* Prescott, AR; *w:* Raymond F. (dec); *c:* Ray, Kay Kallus Weathers, Sally Kallus Medlin, Suzy Kallus Bland; *ed:* (BS) Ed, 1964, (MED) Spec Ed, 1965 E TX St Univ; *cr:* Spec Ed Teacher William B Travis 1965-70; 4th Grade Teacher Sam Houston Elem 1970-85; *ai:* Building Rep; Supts Communication Comm; TX St Teachers Assn 1964-85; 1st Rung-Career Ladder 1985; *home:* 705 W Knox St Ennis TX 75119

KALMAN, RICHARD, Math Teacher; *b:* New York, NY; *m:* Hermine Toplitzky; *c:* Wendy Tohar, Douglas; *ed:* (BA) Liberal Arts/Math, Brooklyn Coll 1960; Grad Stud Brooklyn Coll, NY Univ, Long Island Univ, Hebrew Union Coll; *cr:* 7th-9th Grade Math Teacher George Gershwin Jr HS 1960-68; 10th-12th Grade Math Teacher 1968- Wantagh HS; *ai:* Wantagh HS Math Team Coach; Nassau Cty Math League Pres; Prins Advisory Cncl; Driver Ed Summer Sch Coord; NCIML (Pres 1986-91, VP 1984-86), All-Star Coach 1984-86; NCMTA Mem 1968-, Top Teacher 1985; NYSMTA Mem 1968-; NCTM; NY St Math League Bd of Dirs 1985-87; Amer Regions Math League Bd of Dirs 1990; Wantagh United Teachers (Newsletter Editor 1969-72, Treas 1972-80, Negotiator 1972-80); Bellmore-Merrick Bsbl League (Co-Founder, VP 1976-81), Service 1978; Religious, Cmmty Memberships; NCIML Author/Editor 9 Books; ARML Newsletter Ed 1990; Nassau Math Tourney Founder & Dir 1984-86; *office:* Wantagh HS Beltagh Ave Wantagh NY 1193

KALOCAY, BERNARD ANDREW, Elementary School Principal; *b:* Mc Keesport, PA; *m:* Mary Lee; *c:* Michael, Jennifer, Jacqueline; *ed:* (BS) Elem Ed, 1965, (MED) Elem Ed, 1982 CA St Coll; Elem Prin, Duquesne Univ 1985; Certified St & Coll Bsktbl, Bsbl Ofcl; *cr:* 4th Grade Teacher 1965-67, 6th Grade Instr 1967-72 Port Vue Elem; Head/6th Grade Teacher 2nd Ward Elem 1972-78, 3rd Ward Elem 1979-81; Elem Prin Port Vue Elem & Manor Elem 1988-; *ai:* Chess Club Spon Port Vue & Manor Elem Schls; Fund Raising for Childrens Hospital; ASCD 1988-; Port Vue PTA, Manor PTA 1988-; Liberty Boro Veterans Assn 1987-; Glassport Sons of Italy 1986-; *home:* 398 Winfred Manor Dr Bethel Park PA 15102

KALOCAY, MARY LEE, Science Teacher; *b:* Pittsburg, PA; *m:* Bernard A.; *c:* Michael, Jennifer, Jacqueline; *ed:* (BS) Ed, California Univ of PA 1965; Masters Equivalency Degree in Ed Sci; Currently Enrolled at Carlow Coll Working Toward Prin Cert; *cr:* Sci Teacher Glassport Jr HS 1966-67; Jr HS Sci Teacher St Valentine Sch 1978-; *ai:* PA Jr Acad Sci Competitions Stu Spon; Awd Chairperson Region 7 PA Jr Acad of Sci; Co-Chairperson St Valentines Sci Fair; Extracurricular Sci Act Spon; PA Jr Acad of Sci Awd Chairperson 1979-; PA Acad of Sci 1988-; Society of Analytical Chemists 1987- Teachers Awd 1984; NCEA 1979-; Nom Thanks to Teachers Excl Recgonition 1990; *office:* St Valentine Sch 2709 Mesta St Bethel Park PA 15102

KALTREIDER, CAROLYN ANN, 8th Grade English Teacher; *b:* York, PA; *ed:* (BA) Eng-Cum Laude, Amer Univ 1969; Fr, Grenoble Univ France; Shippensburg Coll; Univ Northern CO; *cr:* 8th Grade Eng Teacher Dover Intermediate Sch 1970-; *ai:* NEA/PSEA/DAEA 1970-; *office:* Dover Intermediate Sch 4500 Intermediate Ave Dover PA 17315

KAMERER, RICHARD DANIEL, JR., Mathematics/Physics Teacher; *b:* Glasgow AFB, MT; *m:* Lori Margaret Vandervert; *c:* Justin, Jaren; *ed:* (BA) Math, Whitworth Coll 1987; Grad Stud Gifted Ed; *cr:* Math/Sci Teacher Douglas Cty Chrstn 1988-; *ai:* 7th & 8th Grade Bsktbl Asst Coach; *office:* Douglas Cnty Chrstn Sch 2079 NW Witherspoon Roseburg OR 97470

KAMERLANDER, RICHARD LEE, Social Studies/US His Teacher; *b:* Oak Park, IL; *c:* Karma, Kyle, Kaila; *ed:* (BA) Psych, 1970, (BS) Ed, 1970 N IL Univ; (MA) Clinical Psych, Univ of AZ Rockwell 1981; Working Toward PhD in Clinical Psych, Univ of AZ Rockwell 1990; *cr:* Teacher/Group Therapist IL Dept of Corrections Valley View 1970-71; Mental Health Therapist Alexian Brothers Medical Center 1970-73; 6th Grade Teacher Woodland Heights Sch 1971-74, Cntrl Sch 1974-76, Heritage Elem 1976-81; 7th/8th Grade Soc Stud Teacher Canton Mid Sch 1981-; Mental Health Worker/Therapist Alexian Brothers Medical Center 1989-; *ai:* NEA, IL Ed Assn, Elgin Teachers Assn 1979-; Kiwanis Intnl Prgm Chm 1972-77; Little League Bsbl VP 1987-89; Presenter Natl Mid Sch Conference; *office:* Canton Mid Sch 1100 Sunset Cir Streamwood IL 60107

KAMINSKI, ALLEN WAYNE, Agriculture Teacher; *b:* Bellville, TX; *m:* Sandra Stehling; *ed:* (AA) Ag, Blinn Coll 1983; (BS) Ag Ed, 1985, (MS) Animal Sci, 1988 Sam Houston St; Hunting Instr; AI cert; Phy Sci Teacher; *cr:* Grad Asst Sam Houston St 1985-86; Ag Teacher Sealy HS 1986-; *ai:* FFA Adv; VATA, SHSU Alumni 1986-; Farm Bureau 1987-; Lions 1986-; Grad Asst; 4th Place Hoards Dairyman Contest; Honorary Lone St Farmer; *office:* Sealy HS 939 West St Sealy TX 77474

KAMINSKI, GLORIA LEBEL, 6th Grade Teacher; *b:* Salem, MA; *m:* Bernard; *c:* Kathryn, Karyn; *ed:* (BS) Ed Elem, N Adams St 1953; *cr:* 6th Grade Teacher Lynnfield Jr HS 1953-54; 7th Grade Teacher Brooklyn Park Jr/Sr HS 1954-55; 4th Grade Teacher Amherst MA 1956-58, Springfield MA 1962-63; 7th/8th Grade Teacher Holliston Jr/Sr HS 1963-66; 6th Grade Teacher Jaffrey Graole & Mid Sch 1966-; *ai:* Staff Dev, Vice-Chairperson Sci Curr, 75th Building Anniversary Comms; NELMS 1989-; NEA; Team Leader; *office:* Jaffrey-Rindge Mid Sch 109 Stratton Rd Jaffrey NH 03452

KAMMAN, SUE ELLEN, Second Grade Teacher; *b:* Conroe, TX; *m:* Eldred Keith; *c:* Robin Cochran, Wendi, Bradley; *ed:* (BA) Elem Ed, Sam Houston St Univ 1977; Grad Work St Thomas Univ; *cr:* 2nd Grade Teacher Runyan Elem 1977-78; 3rd Grade Teacher 1978-84, 2nd Grade Teacher 1984- Rice Elem; *ai:* Gifted/Talented & Odyssey of Mind Coach; TX St Teachers Assn 1987-88, Teacher of Yr 1988; *office:* B B Rice Elem Sch 904 Gladstell Conroe TX 77304

KANADY, FREEDA MAE, Fifth Grade Teacher; *b:* Ripley, MS; *m:* Dale Eugene; *c:* J'ne D. Amber G.; *ed:* (BA) Eng Lit, Sangamon St Univ 1971; (MS) Elem Ed, S IL Univ Carbondale 1980; *cr:* 5th Grade Teacher Chrstn Elem Sch 1971-72; Jr HS Rdng/Eng Teacher 1974-82, 5th Grade Teacher 1982- Jasper Grade Sch; *ai:* Colt Backers Club & Enrichment Comm; Rdng Cncl 1979-85; New Life Word Church Song Leader 1986-; Assembly of God Sunday Sch Supt 1980-86, Appreciation; PTO; Outstanding Teacher Awd 1979; S IL Instructional Television Assn Awd 1985; *home:* 400 N 1st Fairfield IL 62837

KANDLER, DOROTHEA HELEN, 2nd Grade Teacher; *b:* Saint Paul, MN; *ed:* (BS) Elem Ed, MacAlester Coll 1957; Univ of MN; Mankato Univ; St Cloud Univ; Hamline Univ; St Thomas Coll; *cr:* 2nd Grade Teacher Field & Minnehaha Schls 1957-65; 4th Grade Teacher Minnehaha & Morris Park Schls 1965-81; Coord/K-3rd Grade Teacher Gifted Prgm 1981-88, Chapter I 1981-88, 2nd Grade Teacher New Life Chrstn Sch 1988-; *ai:* United Way; Bldg Rep MEA; MEA 1957-88; NEA 1957-88; Sunday Sch Teacher; Mission Cncl Rep Church; *office:* New Life Chrstn Sch 6758 Bailey Rd Woodbury MN 55125

KANDROS, SANDRA L. (JONES), 10th-12th Grade Art Teacher; *b:* Washington, PA; *m:* Larry E.; *c:* Chad, Micah, Ashley, Kerri; *ed:* (BA) Art Ed, W Liberty St Coll 1970; PA St Univ, TN St Univ, Vol St Comm Coll; *cr:* 7th-9th Grade Art Teacher Beth Center Jr HS 1970-71, Hankins Jr HS 1971-87; 10th-12th Grade Teacher Hendersonville HS 1988-; *ai:* Spon for Hendersonville Natl Art Honor Society; Prom & Homecoming Comm; Fine Arts Chm; TEA, NEA 1971-; NAEA 1986-; Hendersonville Arts Cncl Gallery Comm; Sumner Cty Teacher of Yr 1987; *office:* Hendersonville HS 201 E Main St Hendersonville TN 37075

KANE, CYNTHIA ANN, First Grade Teacher; *b:* Pittsburgh, PA; *m:* Jeffrey Joseph; *c:* Amanda, Anthony; *ed:* (BS) Elem Ed, Clarion Univ 1975; Working Towards Masters Shippensburg Univ; *cr:* 1st Grade Teacher Arendtsville Elem 1976-; *ai:* Private Piano Teacher; READ Comm Chairperson; Progress Teacher Trainer Dist Prgm on Staff Dev; PSEA, NEA Faculty Rep 1987-; ASCD 1989-; Kappa Delta Pi 1975-80; Soroptimist Club 1990; Live Stock Teacher of Yr 1986-87; Outstanding Young Woman of America 1987; Written, Produced & Directed 5 Childrens Plays; Working on Getting Childrens Book Published; *office:* Arendtsville Elem Sch 136 Fohl St Arendtsville PA 17303

KANE, DOLORES SOLAN, 1st Grade Teacher; *b:* Bayonne, NJ; *w:* George E. (dec); *c:* George E. Jr., Kathleen Simon, Thomas M., Elizabeth Gulino, James J.; *ed:* (BS) Sci, (BA) Ed, St Peters Coll; Drug & Alcohol Wkshp; *cr:* Teacher St Andrew Sch 1967-; *ai:* NCEA; *office:* St Andrew Sch 126 Broadway Bayonne NJ 07002

KANE, MARY KERWICK, Third Grade Teacher; *b:* Emmetsburg, IA; *m:* Joseph M.; *c:* David J.; *ed:* (BA) Elem Ed, Westmar Coll 1963; Addl Stud Elem Lib Sci; *cr:* Kndgtn Teacher 1961-62, 2nd Grade Teacher 1961-62, 3rd Grade Teacher 1962- Remsen-Union Cmmty Schls; *ai:* Advisory Comm; TSEA 1961-75; Remsen Public Lib Bd Mem 1983-; *office:* Remsen-Union Cmmty Schls 412 Fulton Remsen IA 51050

KANE, SYBIL K., Earth Science Teacher; *b:* Kane, PA; *ed:* (BA) Earth Sci, Edinboro Univ 1980; *cr:* Pres Mountain Gas Corp 1979-82; 7th-8th Grade Sci Teacher Meadville Jr HS 1981-; *ai:* Coach MJHS ECO Team; PSEA 1980-; *office:* Meadville Jr H S 847 N Main St Meadville PA 16335

KANEKO, KIMI YOKOYAMA, Elementary School Principal; *b:* Merced, CA; *m:* Yuji; *c:* Quinn, Shawn; *ed:* (BA) Ed, CA St Univ San Francisco 1965; *cr:* Elem Sch Teacher Elk Grove Unified Sch Dist 1965-68, 1983; Elem Sch Prin Elk Grove Unified Sch 1983-; *ai:* Elk Grove Unified Sch Dist Recruitment Team; Admin Trng Center; Mentor Teacher Selection Team; Affirmative Action Comm; Assn of CA Sch Admin 1983-89; Elk Grove Confidential & Admin Assn Pres 1988-89; *office:* Pleasant Grove Sch 10160 Pleasant Grove School Rd Elk Grove CA 95624

KANEY, LANOR ECCLESTON, 6th Grade Teacher; *b:* Anaconda, MT; *m:* James V.; *c:* Michelle, Zeke; *ed:* (BA) Elem Ed, Carroll Coll 1970; MT Agate Gifted & Talented Prgm; *cr:* 4th-6th Grade Sci Teacher W K Dwyer 1971-76; 4th-6th Grade Soc Stud Teacher 1978-81, 6th Grade Teacher 1981- Dwyer Intermediate Sch; *ai:* MT Teen Inst Parent Adv; Effective Parenting Leader; Anaconda Cath Cmmty Liturgy Commission; MT Fed of Teachers 1971-; Delta Kappa Gamma 1990; MT Assn Gifted/Talented 1973; PTA Adv; Anaconda PTA Teacher of Yr 1988-89; MT PTA Teacher of Yr Nominee 1989-; *home:* 1210 Elaine Dr Anaconda MT 59711

KANITRA, EDMUND ANDREW, Social Studies Teacher; *b:* California, PA; *m:* M. Dianne Underwood; *c:* Leah, Janis, Kira; *ed:* (BA) Composite Soc Stud, Geneva Coll 1965; Post Grad Courses Univ of Penn St; PA Dept of Ed Staff Dev; *cr:* Elem Teacher Hopewell Sch Dist 1965-66, E Palestine Sch Dist 1966-67; Soc Stud Teacher Hopewell Sch Dist 1967-; *ai:* Asst Ftbl Coach; Attendance Comm; Mock Trial Faculty Adv; New Teacher Staff Dev; Asst Athletic Dir; NCSS 1973-; NEA 1967-; PA St Ed Assn, Hopewell Ed Assn 1967-; Our Lady of Fatima Cath Church 1962-; *office:* Hopewell HS 1215 Longvue Ave Aliquippa PA 15001

KANNARD, SUSAN DIANE (MONK), Third Grade Teacher; *b:* Denver, CO; *m:* James Robert; *c:* Kristal, Mattie, Patrick; *ed:* (BA) Elem Ed, Ft Lewis Coll 1971; Post Grad Stud Numerous Univs; *cr:* Substitute K-12th Grade Teacher Farmington Municipal Schls 1978-79, 1982-83; Substitute K-6th Grade Teacher Gateway Borough Dist 1979-80; 1st/3rd/4th Grade Teacher Parochial Sch, Home Schooler 1981-82; 1st-8th Grade Teacher San Juan Chrstn Acad 1983-85; 3rd Grade Teacher Farmington Municipal Schls 1986-; *ai:* Core Team Chm; Sch Budget & Dist Calendar Comms; NM Cncl of Teachers of Eng Seminar Teacher Annual Conference 1989-; Cntrl Baptist Church (Choir, Youth) 1988-; 4-H Worker 1988-; San Juan Cty Election Judge 1990; *office:* Animas Elem Sch 1612 Hutton Farmington NM 87401

KANNING, MARIE TOEPFER, Kindergarten Teacher; *b:* Peru, IN; *m:* Gerald; *c:* Gwen, Gail; *ed:* (BS) Elem Ed, Valparaiso Univ 1963; (MS) Ed, IN Univ 1973; Early Chldhd Ed, St Francis Coll; *cr:* Teacher Ft Wayne Cmmty Sch 1963-65, Luth Sch System 1965-68, Chrstn Union Sch 1973-; *ai:* Curr Comm; Ft Wayne Pre-Sch Teachers Assn (Secy 1973-75) 1973-.

KANTOR, KAREN DIANE, 2nd Grade Teacher; *b:* Brooklyn, NY; *m:* Marvin P.; *c:* Amy, Scott; *ed:* (BA) Ed, Brooklyn Coll 1966; *cr:* 1st Grade Teacher Public Sch 29 1966-69; Cluster Teacher 1977-82, 3rd Grade Teacher 1982-83, 2nd Grade Teacher 1983- Public Sch 238; *office:* Anne Sullivan Sch 1633 E 8th St Brooklyn NY 11223

KANTRUD, LARRY HARLEY, Business Teacher; *b:* Fergus Falls, MN; *m:* Karen Rae Stigen; *c:* Kari K. Mobraten, Kelly S.; *ed:* (AA) Bus, Fergus Falls Comm Coll 1963; (BS) Bus Ed, Moorhead St Univ 1966; Various Insts; *cr:* MDTA Granite Falls Tech Coll 1966-67; Bus Teacher Henning Public Schls 1967-; *ai:* Bus Profs of Amer-Henning Chapter Adv; NEA 1966-; MN Ed Assn Western Division Bd of Dir 1968-; Bus Prof of America (Region Chm, Bd of Dir, Advisory Comm 1990) 1978-80; MN Bus Ed Western Division VP 1970-72; MEA (Western Division, Uniserv Western South Bd of Dir) 1968-80; Cert of Commendation from Governor Perpich of MN 1990; *office:* Henning Public Sch School Ave Henning MN 56551

KANY, RONALD E., Teacher; *b:* Auburn, NY; *ed:* (BA) Elem Ed, SUNY Brockport 1970; SUNY Cortland; *cr:* Lang Arts Teacher Blessed Trinity Sch 1970-; *ai:* Lang Arts/Rdng Coord; Mid Sch Coord; Stu Activity Adv; Yrbk Adv; Newspaper Adv; *office:* Blessed Trinity Sch 101 E Genesee St Auburn NY 13021

KANYID, ANN MARIE, Team Leader; *b:* Ontario, OR; *ed:* (BA) Ed/Eng/Art/Curr/Instruction, 1960, (MED) Ed/Eng/Curr/Instruction 1964 Cntrl WA St Univ; Elem Prim Credentials Cntrl WA St Univ 1973; *cr:* 4th/5th Grade Teacher Yakima Public Sch 1960-62; 3rd-8th Grade Teacher West Valley Public Sch 1962-73; 6th Grade Teacher Seaside Public Sch 1973-74; 8th Grade Teacher 1974-85, 8th Grade Team Leader 1985- Portland Public Sch; *ai:* Team Leaders 1968-73, 1976-85; Intermediate Sch Dist Comm Mem; Minimum Stans Comm; Whitaker Mid Sch Leadership Team Mem 1985-; WA Ed Assn Local Unit Pres 1960-73; OR Ed Assn 1973-; West Valley Ed Assn (Negotiating Team Mem 1967-71, Pres 1970-71); Northwest Regional Educl Laboratory (Bd of Dirs Mem 1966-70, User Review Panel Mem 1973); Title Spec Project Grant Mem 1966-70; Title II Spec Purpose Grant Elem Materials Coord 1969-73; *office:* Whitaker Mid Sch 5700 NE 39th Portland OR 97211

KAPES, CHARLES PETER, 5th Grade Teacher; *b:* Chicago, IL; *m:* Cheryl L.; *ed:* (AA) Liberal Arts/Sci, Morton Jr Coll 1967; (BA) Elem Ed, Roosevelt Univ 1970; (MED) Elem Ed, Natl Coll of Ed 1986; Grad Stud Various Insts; *cr:* 4th Grade Teacher Chicago Public Sch; 7th-8th Grade Sci/Math Teacher/Asst Prin St Leonard Sch; 5th Grade Teacher Waterbury Sch; *ai:* Nom Jaycee Teacher of Yr; *office:* Waterbury Elem Sch 355 S Rodenburg Rd Roselle IL 60192

KAPLAN, JO ANN, Elem/Substitute Teacher; *b:* Kansas City, MO; *m:* Gary E.; *c:* Sam; *ed:* (BA) Elem Ed, Univ of MO Kansas City 1971; *cr:* Teacher James Elem 1971-86.

KAPLAN, LORRAINE STEINER, Third Grade Teacher; *b:* New York City, NY; *c:* Stacey; *ed:* (BSED) Psych/Ed, City Coll of NY 1965; (MA) Elem Ed, Furman Univ 1990; *cr:* 6th Grade Teacher Public Sch 67 1965-66; 5th Grade Teacher Killeen TX Sch System 1967-68; 6th Grade Teacher Public Sch 67 1968-75; 4th Grade Teacher Public Sch 201 1975-77; 3rd Grade Teacher Mauldin Elem 1978-; *ai:* SACS Steering Comm Chairperson; Spon Cmptr Club; SIC Recording Secy; Sci Rep; Sci Olympiad Comm Mem; Math & Soc Stud Rep; NSTA, Math Teacher Assn; *office:* Mauldin Elem Sch 101 E Butler Rd Mauldin SC 29662

KAPLAN, PAUL WILLIAM, 5th Grade Teacher; *b:* Boston, MA; *m:* Cindy Mc Dermott; *ed:* (BS) Ec, Univ of PA 1964; (MA) Ed, Boston Coll 1974; Arts, Dartmouth Coll; *cr:* 5th Grade Teacher Cornwall Elem Sch 1970-85, Vail Mountain Sch 1985-86, Cornwall Elem Sch 1986-; *ai:* Ski Prgm; Nantucket Island Overnight Trip & Sch Flea Market Planner; VT Ed Assn; CO Environmental Coalition 1987-; Town of Goshen Planning Comm 1976-; West End House Boys Club 1976-; Dartmouth Coll Sexual Harrassment Comm Mem 1989-; Dartmouth Outing Club 1989-; VT Outstanding Teacher 1988-89; Various Grants; *office:* Cornwall Elem Sch RD 2 Middlebury VT 05753

KAPLAR, DENISE BALBI, Biology Teacher; *b:* Rockville Centre, NY; *m:* Gregory; *ed:* (BA) Bio/Ed, C W Post Long Island Univ 1983; (MALS) Natural Sci, St Univ of NY Stonybrook 1987; *cr:* Bio/Health Teacher Pitman HS 1983-84; Bio Teacher Wm Floyd HS 1984-85, Bay Shore HS 1985-; *ai:* Frosh Class Adv; Var Cheerleading Coach; Mid St Steering Comm; Womens Center Cmmty Service Awd; Parents & Friends of C W Post Cmmty Service Awd; *home:* 192 Thames St Port Jefferson Sta NY 11776

KAPLOWITZ, MARSHA LOIS, First Grade Teacher; *b:* Bronx, NY; *ed:* (BS) Elem Ed, Monmouth Coll 1969; (MA) Elem Ed, Adelphi Univ 1972; Grad Stud; *cr:* 1st Grade Teacher Babylon Elem Sch 1969-; *ai:* Lang Art Comm Appreciation Awd; Babylon Teachers Assn, AFT, PTA, NY St United Teachers; *office:* Babylon Elem Sch 171 Ralph Ave Babylon NY 11702

KAPORCH, MOYA REGINA, English Teacher/Lecturer; *b:* Bristol Township, PA; *ed:* (BA) Eng/Ed, Immaculata Coll 1981; (MA) Ed/Written Comm, Beaver Coll 1988; *cr:* Eng Teacher Nazareth Acad HS 1981-; Eng Lecturer Holy Family Coll 1989-; *ai:* Sch Literary Magazine, Jr Class Act, Quill & Scroll Society Adv; NCTE, NCEA; Parish Eucharistic Minister 1989-; Immaculata Coll Alumnae Assn Bd of Governors Mem 1986-87; *office:* Nazareth Acad HS Grant & Torresdale Ave Philadelphia PA 19114

KAPPELER, SHIRLEY SIMONS, Spanish Teacher; *b:* Blawnox, PA; *m:* Edward Richard; *c:* Edward, Faith; *ed:* (BA) Span, Univ of Pittsburgh 1956; Temple Univ; Hispanic Lang & Lit, Univ of Pittsburgh; *cr:* Span Teacher Taylor-Allderdice HS 1956; Span/His Teacher Plymouth-Whitmars HS 1956-58; Half-Time Span/Fr Teacher Mars HS 1968-71; Half-Time Span Teacher Seneca Valley Jr HS 1971-72; Full-Time Span Teacher Seneca Valley Sr HS 1972-; *ai:* PA St Modern Lang Assn; Seneca Valley Ed Assn Building Rep 1978-80; Travelers Pres 1988-; Amer Field Service Faculty Mason 1978-80; Indiana Univ of PA Oral Proficiency Wkshp Grant 1987; *office:* Seneca Valley HS RD 1 Harmony PA 16037

KAPPHAN, ELAINE DOWLING, Second Grade Teacher; *b:* Millville, NJ; *m:* William G.; *c:* Jody, Zachary; *ed:* (BA) Elem Ed, Salem Coll 1972; (MS) Elem Ed, WV Univ 1978; Kodaly Music; Project Charlie; Elem Ed, WV Univ 1983; *cr:* 3rd Grade Teacher East View Elem 1973-76; 3rd Grade Teacher 1976-88, 2nd Grade Teacher 1988- Harden Elem; *ai:* Soc Stud Fair Coord; Remediation/Acceleration Rdng Prgm; Lake Floyd Jr Club Adv; Textbook, Hospitality, Lake Floyd Swim & Beach Comm; WVEA, HCEA, NEA, Rdng Cncl; 1st Presbyn Church Clarksburg Sunday Sch Supt 1978-80; Lake Floyd Womens Club (Treas, VP) 1987-88; *office:* Harden Grade Sch E Main St Salem WV 26426

KAPSULIS, DULCIE J., Kindergarten Teacher; *b:* Youngstown, OH; *m:* George T.; *c:* Cathy, Christine; *ed:* (BSED) Elem Ed, Youngstown St 1961; *cr:* 1st Grade Teacher Harrison Sch 1961-66; Teacher Head Start Prgm 1966-67; Head Teacher Covington Sch 1966, Roosevelt Sch 1967, Jefferson Sch 1968; 1st Grade Teacher Marry Haddow 1966-70; Kndgtn Teacher Holy Trinity 1978-; *ai:* K-4th Grade Christmas Prgm; Right to Read, Liturgy, Parent Advisory Comm; YEA (Sch Rep 1967) 1961-70; OEA, NEOTA 1961-70; Youngstown Pan Hellenic Various Comm 1971-; Intl Rdng Assn 1980-; Nom Miriam Joseph Farrell Awd; Set Up Prgm for Pre-Screening Kndgtn Children; Set Up Parent Orientation Meeting for New Kndgtn Parents.

KAPUSINSKI, MARIANNE WALLS, Math/Physical Ed Teacher; *b:* Youngstown, OH; *m:* Edward E.; *ed:* (BSED) Elem Ed, 1973, (MSED) Rdng, 1978 Youngstown St Univ; *cr:* 7th/8th Grade Teacher Lincoln Jr HS 1973-80, North Jr HS 1980-; *ai:* Faculty Mgr of Athletics; *office:* North Jr HS 2724 Mariner Ave Youngstown OH 44505

KAPUSTA, OLGA (SKRENTA), Fifth Grade Teacher; *b:* Karlsruhe, Germany; *m:* Al Nick; *ed:* (BS) Ed, 1968, (MS) Ed, 1974 City Coll of NY; Grad Stud Spec Ed, Art, Math, Ecology; *cr:* 1st-2nd/5th Grade Teacher 1968-76, Early Chldhd Coord 1971-72, Teacher/Headstart Teacher 1968-70 P S 43 Bronx; 5th Grade Teacher P S 70 Queens 1976-; *ai:* Ukrainian Teachers Assn Pres 1988-; Outstanding Elem Teacher of America 1972-; *office:* P S 70 Queens 30-45 42nd St Astoria NY 11103

KARBAN, MARY FELTS, First Grade Teacher; *b:* East St Louis, IL; *m:* Alan L.; *c:* Kari, Kasey; *ed:* (BS) Elem Ed, S IL UNIV 1975; Working on Masters Degree Elem Ed; *cr:* 1st Grade Teacher St Augustine Sch 1975-88, Jefferson Sch 1988-; *ai:* Natl Congress of Parent & Teachers 1988-; *home:* 168 Forestview Dr Belleville IL 62220

KARDASH, PATRICIA ANN (CUNNINGHAM), Fifth Grade Teacher; *b:* Pittsburgh, PA; *m:* J. Roger; *ed:* (BS) Elem Ed, California Univ of PA 1962; *cr:* 1st-5th Grade Classroom Teacher Hempfield Area Sch Dist 1962-; *ai:* Hempfield Area Ed Assn (Secy, Rep); PA St Ed Assn, NEA Mem; Greensburg Coll Club (Secy, Treas); PTA Mem; Scndry Ed Publication 1971; Amer Family Inst Honoree 1986; *office:* Hempfield Area Sch Dist W Newton Rd Greensburg PA 15601

KARDON, KATHLEEN RICE, Teacher of Gifted & Talented; *b:* Ft Dix, NJ; *m:* Alan; *c:* Kristinn, Ryan, Jordan, Alana, Rachel; *ed:* (BS) Ed, SW TX St Univ 1981; Working on Masters in Gifted Ed; *cr:* Kndgtn/3rd Grade Teacher Royal Gate Elem 1981-83; Teacher/Dept Chairperson Shepard Mid Sch 1983-; *ai:* Gifted & Talented Class, Comm Art Prgm & All Star Prgm Spon; Campus Improvement & Communication Comm Mem; NCTE 1985-; Amer Amateur Karate Fed Instr 1988-; PTA 1981-; Teacher of Yr Sch Awd 1989; Published Poem 1989; *office:* Alan B Shepard Mid Sch 5558 Ray Ellison San Antonio TX 78242

KAREM, KENNY, Junior HS Teacher/Writer; *b:* Louisville, KY; *ed:* (BA) His, Notre Dame 1966; (MA) His/Span, Georgetown Univ 1971; Environmental Ed Specialist, Audubon Camp Sierra Club, Project Learning Tree; *cr:* Peace Corps Volunteer Chile 1966-68; 7th/8th Grade Teacher Holy Comforter Sch 1969-71; 5th/6th Grade Teacher St Francis Sch 1971-76; Museum

Educator Louisville Museum of His & Sci 1977-78; Writer Urban Environmental Educ 1978-; 7th/8th Grade Teacher KY Country Day Sch 1981-; *ai:* 7th & 8th Grade Environmental Ed Weeks; Bsktbl Coach; Hiking, Backpacking; Wilderness Jefferson Co (Chm 1990) 1975-; KY Assn of Environmental Ed 1980-, KY Dept of Ed Outstanding Contribution to Environmental Ed 1988; Louisville Historical League Bd 1980-; Louisville Sierra Club (Pres, Conservation Chm) 1975-, Natl Conservation Awd 1989; Falls of OH Nat Wildlife Conservation Bd 1975-; Published Book Discover Louisville 1988; St of KY Preservation Alliance Awd; KY Alternate to NASA Teacher in Space Shuttle 1986; Louisville Cmmty Fnd, Louisville Leadership & Eric Davis Outstanding Teacher Awds; Articles on Photos on Conservation, Environmental Ed in Magazines & Newspapers; *office:* Kentucky Country Day Sch 4100 Springdale Rd Louisville KY 40222

KARG, KATHLEEN ELIZABETH, 1st Grade Teacher/Asst Prin; *b:* Buffalo, NY; *ed:* (AA) Liberal Arts, Hilbert Coll 1972; (BS) Elem Ed, Daemen Coll 1974; (MS) Elem Ed/Rdng, Canisius Coll 1978; *cr:* Substitute Teacher 1974-77, Kndgtn Teacher 1976-77 Orchard Park Cntrl Schls; 1st Grade Teacher Immaculate Conception Sch 1978-; *ai:* Church Organist & Choir Dir; Writing Series of Lang Art Workbooks for Children; *home:* 6680 Cole Rd Orchard Park NY 14127

KARIAK, JUDY M., 8th Grade Earth Sci Teacher; *b:* New Haven, CT; *ed:* (MS) Ed/Earth Sci, Stephen F Austin St Univ 1983; Environmental Sci; *cr:* 8th Grade Earth Sci Teacher 1983-88, 8th Grade Earth Sci Teacher/Team Leader 1989- Schimelpfenig Mid Sch; *ai:* Chrldr Spon; Faculty Cncl & Earth Day Rep; Sci Club; Kids Against Drugs; Presidential Academic Fitness Awd Prgm; Trained Stu Teachers; TX Ed Assn Mem 1983-; TX Sci Teachers Assn Mem; Wilderness Society Mem 1988-; Sierra Club Mem 1986-; Amer Heart Assn Volunteer 1989-; Rookie Teacher of Yr 1983; Teacher of Month 1990; Team Leader 8th Grade Sci Dept; Newspaper Article Published; *home:* 18081 Midway #2825 Dallas TX 75287

KARL, ROBERT JOHN, Art Instructor; *b:* Long Branch, NJ; *ed:* (BS) Art Ed, 1971, (MAED) Art Ed, 1973 E Carolina Univ; Post Grad Stud Gifted Ed 1980; Fulbright-Hayes Schlsp for Study in Japan 1977; *cr:* Art Instr J H Rose HS 1971-72; Grad Teaching Fellow E Carolina Univ 1972-73; Art Instr/Dept Chm Aycock Jr HS 1973-80; Art Instr Norfolk Acad 1981-86, Old Donation Center for Gifted & Talented 1986-; Part-Time Art Instr VA Wesleyan Coll 1987-; *ai:* Old Donation Center Curr Evaluation Comm 1989-; NAEA 1973-; VA Art Ed Assn 1980-; Tidewater VA Art Ed Assn 1980-, Elem Art Educator of Yr 1990; Friends of Norfolk Juvenile Court 1983-, Outstanding Cmmty Service 1987; Outstanding Young Man of America Awd 1985; Old Donation Center for the Gifted & Talented Teacher of Yr 1987, 1990; Articles Published 1984, 1985; *office:* Old Donation Center/Gifted 1008 Ferry Plantation Rd Virginia Beach VA 23455

KARLIN, LARRY, Scndry Eng/Soc Stud Teacher; *b:* Hays, KS; *m:* Sharon; *c:* Michelle, Chris, Stephanie, Nathan, Shawn; *ed:* (BS) Soc Stud, OR Coll of Ed 1971; *cr:* Teacher Bonanza HS 1971-72, Scandia HS 1972-74, St Johns Grade & HS 1974-84, Sylvan Unified HS 1984-; *ai:* SADD Spon; Coaching; NCTE; Lions VP 1989-; *home:* Rt 1 Sylvan Grove KS 67481

KARLOVETZ, MARILYN WAYTHE, Business Teacher; *b:* Vernon, TX; *m:* Jim; *c:* Shelly; *ed:* (BA) Bus Admin, Tarleton St Univ 1970; Spec Ed, Midwestern St Univ; Cmptr Applications & Voc Courses, Loretta Heights Coll, CO St Univ; *cr:* Spec Ed Teacher 1977-80, Bus Ed Teacher 1980-81 Chillicothe HS; Bus Ed Teacher Agate HS 1981-85, Pawnee HS 1985-; *ai:* Yrbk Staff Adv; CO Educators For & About Bus 1981-; NBEA 1980-; NEA, CO Educators Assn 1981-; FBLA (Local Chapter Adv, Dist Adv); Chos Tae Kwon Do Acad 1988-, Black-Tip, Red Belt 1989; CO FBLA Adv of Yr 1990; Article Published in SPEAKS, Paper Published for CO St Univ Voc Class Guide; *office:* Pawnee HS Chatoga St Grover CO 80729

KARN, CHERRIE ANNETTE, 2nd Grade Teacher/Director; *b:* Wayne, OK; *m:* Hayden M.; *c:* Kip, Sean; *ed:* (BS) Elem Ed/Fine Arts, E Cntrl St Univ 1967; Various Stud & Univs; *cr:* 2nd Grade Teacher Moore Public Schls 1967-69, Norman Public Schls 1970-74; Adult Basic Ed Yukon Satellite 1975-85; 2nd Grade Teacher Yukon Public Schls 1974-; Dir Yukon Adult Learning Center 1985-; *ai:* Teachers Day Conference Comm 1988; Employment & Trng Task Group 1990; Advisory Comm Learning Resource Center Media Dept E OK Cty Area Voc Center; Workplace Literacy 1990; Amer Assn for Adult & Continuing Ed, OK Ed Assn, NEA, Yukon Prof Ed Assn, OK Adult Basic Ed Assn; Literacy Coalition, Kappa Kappa Iota; Delta Kappa Gamma Schlsp Comm; OK City Running Club; *office:* Yukon Public Schls 6th & Maple Yukon OK 73099

KARNEI, SHIRLEY ANN (GEFFERT), Journalism/English Teacher; *b:* Cuero, TX; *m:* Marvin Ray; *c:* Heather, Jarred; *ed:* (BS) Eng/His, TX A&I Univ 1971; NJ Writing Project; *cr:* Teacher Meyersville Ind Sch Dist 1972-73, Yorktown HS 1973-; *ai:* Wildcat Record Adv; UIL Journalism Coach; Communications Comm Rep; Sr Class Spon 1989-90; NCTE 1980-; Yorktown Historical Society Secy 1989-; Yorktown Athletic Booster Club Reporter 1984-; *home:* P O Box 5 Yorktown TX 78164

KARNER, ROBERT F., Senior Master; *b:* Saline, MI; *m:* Barbara Albert; *c:* Jesse, Chris; *ed:* (BS) Zoology, MI St 1975; (MS) Bio, Univ of MI 1979; *cr:* Teacher 1977-86; Sr Master 1987-; *ai:* NHS Adv; Academic Affairs Comm & Math/Sci Dept Chm; MI Sci Teachers Assn; Glenlake Church Elder 1986-; Giedeons Intnl 1990; Speaker & Guest Lecturer for Local Civic Organizations; *office:* Leelanau Sch 1 Old Homestead Rd Glen Arbor MI 49636

KARNES, PAT ANN (LEACH), 5th Grade Science Teacher; *b:* Robbs, IL; *m:* Robert Joe; *c:* Jeff, Jason, Jarrod; *ed:* (AS) Lang Arts, John a Logan Jr Coll 1978; (BS) Southern IL Univ 1980; SIU; *cr:* 3rd Grade Teacher Wheatley Elem Sch 1980-81; 4th Grade Teacher McKinley Sch 1981-82; 5th Grade Teacher J B Ward Sch 1982-; *office:* J B Ward Sch 120 E Spring Du Quoin IL 62832

KARNS, JEFFREY DEAN, Math, Physical Ed Teacher; *b:* Wabash, IN; *m:* Linda K. Hughes; *c:* Erin, Dean, Brandon; *ed:* (BS) Phys Ed, Grace Coll 1979; *cr:* Phys Ed Teacher Grace Chrstn Sch 1981-82, Sebring Chrstn Center 1982-84; Athletic Dir Arcadia Chrstn Center 1984-86; Math/Phys Ed Teacher Lakeland Chrstn Sch 1986-; *ai:* Var Athletic Trainer, Girls Bsktbl Coach; FL Athletic Coaches Assn 1987-; St of FL Bsktbl Final Four 1990; *home:* 1213 Marrick Cir Lakeland FL 33801

KARNS, MARY BUCKEY, 7th/11th Grade Eng Teacher; *b:* East Derry, NH; *m:* Harry Sr.; *c:* Harry Jr., Jeffrey, Adam; *ed:* (BS) Ed/Eng, Shippensburg Univ 1969; Grad Stud Shippensburg Univ; *cr:* Teacher Bedford HS 1969-71, Everett Area HS 1983-; *ai:* Literary Magazine Adv; Everett Stu Assistance Prgm Core Team Mem; Lead Teacher Facilitator; NCTE; *office:* Everett Area HS N River Ln Everett PA 15537

KARPENKO, JENNIFER PERRY, French Teacher; *b:* Versailles, France; *m:* Paul Daniel; *ed:* (BA) Fr/Intnl Stud, Univ of SC 1986; Jr Yr Abroad Mulhouse France 1984-85; *cr:* Fr Teacher Madison HS 1987-; *ai:* Fr Club; Var Chrldr Coach; Intervention Comm; NCAE, NAE; *office:* Madison HS Box 306 Marshall NC 28753

KARPINSKY, BO, Teacher; *b:* Hamtramck, MI; *m:* Sylvia; *c:* Nicholas, Joseph; *ed:* (BA) Soc/Ed, 1978; (MAT) Teaching, Wayne St Univ 1990; *cr:* Teacher Grayling Elem Sch 1978-79; Teacher 1979-84; Acting Asst Prin 1984 Dickinson Elem Sch; Teacher Kosciuszko Mid Sch 1990; *office:* Dickinson Elem Sch Burger Hamtramck MI 48212

KARPYK, PETE, Chemistry Teacher; *b:* Kettering, England; *m:* Nancy Jean; *ed:* (BA) Psych, 1974, (BA) Chem, 1977 Youngstown St Univ; (MS) Comm, WV Univ 1982; Grad Stud WV Univ 1989; *cr:* Tutor Howland Bd of Ed 1976-77; Substitute Teacher Trumball Cty & Youngstown Bd of Ed 1976-77; Chem Teacher Hancock Cty Bd of Ed 1977-; *ai:* Chem Club Spon; RESA Parenting Convention & Sch Improvement Comm; Readers Digest Finalist 1990; Amer Heroes in Ed; Hancock Cty Teacher of Yr 1989; HS Equipment Grant Spectroscopy Society of Pittsburgh 1986, 1990; *office:* Weir Sr HS Red Rider Rd Weirton WV 26062

KARR, ROSEMARY KENNY, Kindergarten Teacher; *b:* Akron, IA; *m:* Calvin Louis; *c:* Cynthia L. Skinner, Karen K. Mathews; *ed:* (BS) Elem Ed, Southwestern Univ 1952; (MS) Ed, TX A&I 1979; Human Dev Trng Inst; *cr:* 3rd Grade Teacher Oak Park 1952-53; 1st Grade Teacher Windsor Park 1953-55, Glorietta 1955-56; 1st Grade Teacher 1957-68, Kndgtn Teacher 1968- Welder Elem Sch; *ai:* Assn of TX Prof Educators (Pres 1987-88, Secy 1985-86); Beehive Daycare Center Bd of Dirs 1983-; TX Career Ladder III Teacher; *home:* 1117 Adeline Sinton TX 78387

KARRICK, BRANT GILMORE, Instrumental Music Teacher; *b:* Bowling Green, KY; *ed:* (BME) Music Ed, Univ of Louisville 1982; (MME) Music Ed, W KY Univ 1984; *cr:* Dir of Bands Beechwood Ind Sch 1984-86, Bowling Green HS 1986-; *ai:* Marching & Pep Band; Jazz Ensemble; Natl Band Assn 1986-, Marching Excl 1989; KY Bandmasters Assn Dist Rep 1985-; MENC 1984-; *home:* 1768-A Patrick Way Bowling Green KY 42104

KARST, TERI SUSAN, Fifth Grade Teacher; *b:* Brooklyn, NY; *m:* Raymond J.; *ed:* (BA) Ed, SUNY Stony Brook 1976; (MAT) Ed, Sacred Heart Univ 1986; Various Courses; *cr:* Sci Teacher Lindenhurst Jr HS 1977; 6th/7th Grade Sci Teacher Accompsett Intermediate 1977-79; 7th Grade Sci Teacher L P Wilson 1982-83; 8th Grade Sci Teacher Wooster Intermediate 1983-88; 5th Grade Elem Teacher Franklin Elem 1988-; *ai:* Safety Patrol Adv; Report Card Comm; NEA 1982-; NSTA 1982-88; Nom Teacher of Yr; Magna Cum Laude Grad & Undergraduate Work; *office:* Franklin Elem Sch 1895 Barnum Ave Stratford CT 06497

KARSTEDT, JULIE ANN GREENFIELD, Mathematics/ Science Dept Chair; *b:* Tacoma, WA; *m:* Michael Thomas; *c:* Brandi L.; *ed:* (BS) Math, 1979, (MS) Scndry/Post Scndry Voc, 1985 Univ of NV Las Vegas; *cr:* Teacher Brinley Jr HS 1979-81, Dell Robison Jr HS 1981-; *ai:* Ski Club; Flag Team; Hiking; Math Counts Competition; Sci Fair Adv; Mini Grant; *office:* Dell Robison Jr HS 825 N Marion Dr Las Vegas NV 89110

KARTAGINER, MARILYN, Mathematics Teacher; *b:* New York City, NY; *m:* Pinchas; *c:* Ruth, Abraham, Dov; *ed:* (BS) Math, Brooklyn Coll 1972; (MS) Math, Richmond Coll 1976; *cr:* Math Teacher Samuel J Tilden HS 1972-73, Erasmus Hall HS 1973-74, F D Roosevelt HS 1984-; *office:* F D Roosevelt HS 5800 20th Ave Brooklyn NY 11204

KARWACKI, MARGARET WOLSKI, First Grade Teacher; *b:* Baltimore, MD; *m:* Eugene J. Sr.; *c:* Eugene Jr., Joan Barnhart, Thomas, William; *ed:* (BS) Home Ec/Sci, St Joseph Coll 1951; Amer Dietetics Assn Jewish Hospital 1952; Masters Equivalency Early Chldhd Ed, Mt St Agnes Coll 1970, Essex Comm Coll 1971-73, Loyola Coll 1973-76; *cr:* Remedial Rdng Teacher St Clement Sch 1967-68, Our Lady of Hope 1968-70; 1st-2nd Grade Teacher St Clement Sch 1970-; *ai:* Chairperson Steering Comm; Mid St Evaluation Curr Coord; Mem Mid States Evaluating Team; Presenter Wkshp Leader NCEA Mini Convention; NCEA; Archdiocese of Baltimore Service Awd 1988; *home:* 3908 Eland Rd Phoenix MD 21131

KARWOSKI, JOSEPH PAUL, Computer Coordinator; *b:* Johnstown, PA; *ed:* (BS) Math/Sci, Univ of Pittsburgh Johnstown 1977; (MS) Math, PA St 1982; Class I Cmptr Technician; Lectured Cmptrs Austria, West Germany, England, Scotland & Whales; Doctorial Stu PA St; *cr:* Math/Sci Teacher Conemaugh Valley Jr/Sr HS 1982-83; Cmptr/Math Teacher Cntrl Cambria HS 1983-; Cmptr Instr Univ of Pittsburg Johnstown 1985-; Math/ Cmptr Instr Saint Francis Coll 1987-; *ai:* Cmptr Team & Club; Natl Honor Comm; PSEA, CCEA, NEA; Merrill Math Advisory Panel; ITEC Grants; Teacher of Yr Saint Francis; Nom Teacher of Yr 1990; Numerous Cmptr Programming Awds; *office:* Central Cambria H S Box 800 Rd 4 Rt 422 West Ebensburg PA 15931

KARY, LEON JAMES, Social Studies Teacher; *b:* Mandan, ND; *ed:* (BS) His, Mary Coll 1978; *cr:* Teacher/Coach/Admin Christ the King Sch 1978-; *ai:* Boys Bsktbl/Boys & Girls Track Coach; Stu Cncl Adv; Dean of Stu; ND Ofcls & Coaches Assn 1982- Milestone 1985; Natl Coaches & Ofcl Assn 1982-; Natl Cath Ed Assn 1978-; Mandan Jaycees 1988-; Mandan Eagles 1987-; Mandan Elks 1979-; Teacher of Yr Christ the King Sch 1989; *office:* Christ The King 1100 3rd St NW Mandan ND 58554

KASBERGER, KAY MARY, English Teacher; *b:* Chicago, IL; *ed:* (BS) Speech/Drama - Magna Cum Laude, Syracuse Univ 1953; (MA) Speech Ed, Columbia Teachers Coll 1957; *cr:* Speech/ Drama Teacher Sleepy Hollow HS 1957-63; Eng Teacher Nottingham HS 1963-; *ai:* Meadowbrook Art & Literary Magazine Adv; NCTE, Syracuse Teachers Assn 1970-; NY St Eng Cncl 1985-, Teacher of Ecxl Awd 1986; NY St United Teachers 1975-; Awd for Excl Teaching Syracuse Univ Sch of Ed 1984; Nottingham HS Outstanding Teacher & Faculty Awd 1989; *home:* 135B Croyden Ln Dewitt NY 13224

KASEMAN, RAY WILLIAM HENRY, Health Phys Ed Teacher; *b:* Shamokin, PA; *m:* Jane L.; *c:* Debra R. Bladlick, Kaseman Acosta, Scott; *ed:* (BS) Health/Phys Ed, East Stroudsburg 1955; *cr:* Teacher/Coach Greenpark Union HS 1957-65, West Perry Jr HS 1965-; *ai:* Head Jr HS Bsktbl Coach; NEA 1957-; PSEA 1957-; WPEA 1965-; Awarded Bsktbl Coach of Yr 1979-80; Commonwealth of PA Citation by House of Rep for Achievements in Bsktbl; Natl HS Coaching Awd; *home:* 103 N Carlisle St New Bloomfield PA 17068

KASHUBA, CYNTHIA TEATER, First Grade Teacher; *b:* Charleston, SC; *m:* Thomas Edward; *c:* Thomas Martin, Michelle Leigh; *ed:* (BA) Elem Ed, Towson St Univ 1965; Course Work Univ of MD Coll PArk Campus, Trinity Coll, Marywood Coll; Bowie St Coll; *cr:* 2nd Grade Teacher 1965-67; 6th Grade Teacher 1968-70 Berkshire Elem; Remedial Rdng Teacher Edison/Ft Augusta Elem 1971-72; 5th Grade & Head Teacher Rohrbach Elem 1973-75; 1st-5th Grade Gifted Instr Rohrbach & Maclay Elem 1978-82; 2nd Grade Teacher Maclay Elem 1982-86; 4th Grade Teacher 1986-87; 1st Grade Teacher 1987-Oaklyn Elem; *ai:* ACT 178; NEA; PSEA; SEA; Elected St Michaels Sch Bd; Co-Authored Teachers Manual & Developed MateRials; Presenter PSEA Convention Lanaser 1990; *home:* Box 395G Rd 2 Sunbury PA 17801

KASPAR, KENNETH WAYNE, American History Teacher; *b:* Corpus Christi, TX; *m:* Susan Weaver; *ed:* (BA) Phys Ed/His, TX A&I 1978; *cr:* Teacher/Coach Brazosport HS 1978-; *ai:* Head Var Bsktbl & Jr Var Girls Track Coach; TABC Mem 1987-; THSCA Mem 1978-; Coach of Yr 1987-88, 1989-; Brazosport Facts Coach of Yr; *office:* Brazosport HS PO Box Drawer Z Freeport TX 77541

KASPER, LINDA HALLER, Teacher; *b:* Cincinnati, OH; *m:* William G.; *c:* Jonathan, Emily; *ed:* (BSED) Spec Ed, Univ of Cincinnati 1975; (MED) Elem Ed, Xavier Univ 1978; *cr:* 2nd-8th Grade Lang Art/Rdng Teacher Resurrection Sch 1975-77; 5th-8th Grade Lang/Rdng Teacher St Catharine Sch 1977-79; 7th/8th Grade Lang/Rdng Teacher St Vivian Sch 1979-; *ai:* Adv Sch Newspaper; 3rd-6th Grade Enrichment Prgm St Vivian Sch 1979-; NCTE; Teachers Applying Whole Lang; *home:* 5060 Chantilly Dr Cincinnati OH 45238

KASPER, PHIL B., 5th/6th Grade Head Teacher; *b:* Oroville, CA; *m:* Shirley Jean Schmitt; *c:* Krystal, Traci; *ed:* (BA) Elem Ed, Southern UT St 1978; (MA) Elem Admin, Western St 1985; *cr:* 3rd/5th Grade Teacher Monroe Elem 1978-79; 4th Grade Teacher Mexican Hat Elem 1979-80; 5th/6th Grade Head Teacher Pleasant View Sch & Lewis Amiola Sch 1980-; *ai:* Sftbl, Bsktbl, Vlybl, Track Coach; Dist Steering & Accountability Comm; Dist Wide Sports Dir Prgm; Gideons Intnl VP 1988-; Montelores Baptist Church Deacon 1981-; *home:* 25920 CR P Dolores CO 81323

KASPROWSKI, JACQUELINE BOLLERHEY, English Department Chairperson; *b:* Cleveland, OH; *m:* Darryl L.; *c:* Gayle C., Darra L. Cover; *ed:* (BA) Eng, Coll of St Francis 1973; (MED) Curr/Cmptrs in Composition, Cleveland St Univ 1988; *cr:* Eng/ Math Teacher Bath HS 1973-74; Lorain Cath HS 1976-78; Math Instr Bishop Borgess HS 1974-78, Lima Cntrl Cath HS 1978-79; Eng/Math/Cmptr Instr Lorain Cath HS 1979-; *ai:* Eng Dept Chm; Secy of Curr Comm; Prin Advisory Bd; Chrldng Coord; Sr Class Moderator; NCTE 1977-; OH Cncl of Teachers of Math 1988-; Lake Erie Math Cncl Treas 1988-; Masters Thesis the Effects of the Use of Rhetorical Invention Software on the Writing of HS Seniors; *office:* Lorain Catholic H S 760 Tower Blvd Lorain OH 44052

KASSABIAN, NANCY BAZARIAN, Spanish/French Teacher; *b:* Watertown, MA; *m:* Krikor Vahridj; *c:* Lori, Gary, Debra, Michael; *ed:* (BA) Fr/Span, Simmons Coll 1968; (MAED) Ed, Tufts Univ 1989; *cr:* Foreign Lang Teacher Waltham Public Schls 1968-70; Eng Teacher Watertown Public Schls 1979-83; Fr/Bi-ling/ESL Teacher Medford 1984-85; Fr/Span/Exploratore F L Teacher Malden Public Schls 1985-; *ai:* Adv 8th Grade Class & Stu Cncl; Dir Sch Act-Fundraisers; Adv/Coach Academic Quiz Team; MA Assn of Forign Lang 1985-; St James Armenian Church; Horace Mann Grant Recipient 1986-88; Stu Support Team 1986-.

KASSENS, ZOLA I., Third Grade Teacher; *b:* Ottumwa, IA; *m:* Elmer; *c:* Dougals Dodson, Harold Dodson, Michael Dodson, Michael; *ed:* (BA) Elem Ed, 1968, (MA) Pupil Personnel/Counseling, 1972 Coll of ID; Creative Writing; Cmptr Trng; Impact Trng; *cr:* 3rd-5th Grade Teacher Butte View Elem 1968-; *ai:* Cmptr Room; Curr Writing; Needs Assessments; PTA; Boise St Univ Creative Writing Grant; Articles Published in Ed Magazines; Book Manuscript Purchased; *office:* Butte View Elem Sch 400 S Pine Ave Emmett ID 83617

KASSING, SHARON F., SL, 5th-8th Grade Science Teacher; *b:* St Louis, MO; *ed:* (MNS) Natural Sci/Earth Sci, Univ of OK 1976; Music Ministry Cert, Archdiocese St Louis 1989; *cr:* 2nd-8th Grade Sci Teacher Visitation-Holy Ghost Elem Sch 1967-74; 4th-8th Grade Sci Teacher St Pius V Elem Sch 1974-; *ai:* Church Musicians & Accompanist; Intnl Bonhoeffer Society 1976-; NCEA Exhibitor St Louis; *office:* St Pius V Elem Sch 3530 Utah Saint Louis MO 63118

KASTENS, DIANNA (HURST), 5th Grade Teacher; *b:* Atwood, KS; *m:* Gary; *c:* Susan, Zachary; *ed:* (BS) Elem Ed, Ft Hays St Univ 1973; Grad Stud; *cr:* 1st/2nd Grade Teacher 1975-81, 3rd/4th Grade Teacher 1981-87 Herndon Grade Sch; 5th Grade Teacher Atwood Grade Sch 1987-; *ai:* Prof Dev Cncl; KNEA; Trinity Luth Church; *home:* Rt 2 Box 81 Herndon KS 67739

KASTER, CINDI LOU (STAUFFER), Third Grade Teacher; *b:* Monroe, WI; *m:* Dean; *c:* Bradley, Scott; *ed:* (BS) Elem Ed, Univ of WI Platteville 1976; Grad Stud; *cr:* 4th Grade Teacher 1976-87, 3rd Grade Teacher 1987- South Wayne Elem; *ai:* Blackhawk Ed Assn Mem 1979-; SWEAC Mem 1979-; NEA Mem 1979-; Our Saviors Luth Church Cncl (Secy 1985-88, Mem 1985-); Browntown Firemens Auxiliary Co-Chm 1977; Our Saviors Luth Sunday Sch Teacher 1972-89; Black Hawk Elem Teacher of Yr 1984-85; Balckwhak Elem Nom Kohl Fnd Elem Teacher Awd 1990; *home:* N 1726 Co Trk M Browntown WI 53522

KASZUBA, JILL ELIZABETH (MONAGHAN), English Teacher; *b:* Trenton, NJ; *m:* George Gerald; *ed:* (BA) Eng Lit, 1976, (BA) Comm Sci/Disorders, 1976 Montclair St; *cr:* Eng Teacher Toms River HS North 1977-78, Toms River HS East 1978-; *ai:* NJ Ed Assn; *office:* Toms River HS East Raider Way Toms River NJ 08753

KATEEB, LINDA, Language Art Teacher; *b:* Chicago, IL; *ed:* (BA) Eng Ed, Univ of IL Chicago 1971; (MA) Rdng, NE IL 1976; Grad Work Assorted Disciplines; Master Stud In Linguistics; *cr:* Teacher River Grove Sch 1976-77; Acting Asst Prin 1989-, Teacher 1978- Mc Dade Classical Sch; *ai:* Literary Magazine Spon; Drama, Speech, Essay, Spelling Coach; Mem of Prof Personnel Advisory Comm; Pension Rep; Young Authors Liaison; Chicago Area Rdng Assn 1988-; Intnl Rdng Assn 1971-75, 1990; NCTE 1971-73, Literary Magazines Awd of Excl; United Holy Land Fund Local Secy 1975; Arab Amer Univ Grads Local Secy 1978; Columbia Scholastic Press Assn Awd; Teacher Appreciation Day Awd 1989-; Excl in Teaching Golden Apple Awd 1988; Nazareth Work Camp Participant 1981; Mid-East Travel & Study at IN Univ; *office:* Mc Dade Classical Sch 8801 S Indiana Ave Chicago IL 60619

KATHAN, GARY OTIS, Chemistry/Physics Teacher; *b:* Mitchell, SD; *m:* Rita Butler; *c:* Gregory, Jason, Britany; *ed:* (BS) Sci/Chem, Northern St Coll 1964; Working towards Masters Math, Sci, Ed Courses; *cr:* Sci Teacher Plankinton HS 1964-66, Chamberlain HS 1966-70, Rawlins HS 1970-; *ai:* NHS Spon; Carbon Cty Sch Dist #1 Teachers Ed Assn Pres 1989-; Nom for US W Outstanding Teacher Awd & Presidential Awd for Outstanding Teachers; *office:* Rawlins HS 1401 Colorado Rawlins WY 82301

KATTAU, EVA J., Speech/Theatre Teacher; *b:* Springfield, TN; *m:* Harold O. Jr.; *ed:* (BA) Phys Ed, 1962, (MA) Ed, 1975 Univ of Evansville; Numerous Theatre Stud; IN Univ Childrens Theatre; Tufts Univ Boston MA; Evansville Civic Theatre, Newburgh Theatre, Evansville Childrens Theatre; Evansville Museum; *cr:* Teacher Columbia Elem Sch 1962-64, Francis Joseph Reitz HS 1964-; *ai:* Play, Acotrs Wkshp, Childrens Puppet Theatre, Mime Troupe, Vlybl Dir; Pep Club; Teacher/Staff Recognition; Social Comm; Commencement Speakers; Commencement Mantle Pledge; NCTE, NEA, Fireside Theatre; Evansville Civic Theatre Bd of Dir 1969-70; Newburgh Theatre (Pres, VP) 1970-72; Univ of Evansville Pres 1966; Outstanding Sr in Theatre; Assistantship in Theatre; *office:* Francis Joseph Reitz HS Forest Hills Evansville IN 47712

KATZBECK, RAEANN GETTY, Teacher/Coordinator; *b:* Tarentum, PA; *m:* Lawrence; *c:* Laura, Kristin; *ed:* (BS) Bus Ed, Indiana Univ of PA 1971; Cnslr Ed, Indiana Univ of PA; Cmptr Sci, Anne Arundel Comm Coll, Howard Comm Coll; *cr:* Bus Teacher Clairton Sch Dist 1971-73, Penncrest Sch Dist 1973-76; Bus Ed/Coord Anne Arundel Cty Schls 1976-; *ai:* FBLA Adv; MD Voc Assn; MD Bus Ed Assn; Mayfield Ave Cmmty Assn Bd of Dir 1987-; *home:* 8117 Green Tree Dr Baltimore MD 21227

KAUFER, LARINDA DYSON, First Grade Teacher; *b:* Meshoppen, PA; *m:* Neil H.; *c:* Seth, Adam, Aaron; *ed:* (BA) Elem Ed, 1975, (MS) Elem Ed, 1989 Wilkes Coll; *cr:* Kndgtn Teacher 1975-76, 1st Grade Teacher 1976-78 Mill City Elem Sch; 1st Grade Teacher 1978-83, Kndgtn Teacher 1984-86, 1st Grade Teacher 1986- Evans Falls Elem; *ai:* Tunkhannock Area Ed Assn (Building Rep 1986) 1975-; Evans Falls PTA (VP 1985, Treas 1986) 1978-; Luzerne Cty Rdng Cncl, Keystone St Rdng Assn 1987-; Jewish Cmmty Center of WY Valley Bd of Dirs 1989-; Temple Israel; Kingston Little League Team Mother 1990; Excl in Teaching Awd 1987; *home:* 322 Reynolds St Kingston PA 18704

KAUFFMAN, CAROL ANNUZZI, First Grade Teacher; *b:* Warren, OH; *m:* William R.; *ed:* (BS) Early Chldhd/Art Ed, Youngstown St Univ 1969; Writing to Read IBM 1985; Whole Lang Dev Society for Developmental Ed 1990; Working Towards Masters Rdng Youngstown St Univ; *cr:* 1st Grade Teacher Jefferson Sch 1969-80, Washington Sch 1980-; *ai:* Creative Writing Coach; Writing to Read Adv; Jr Red Cross Comm Adv; Niles Classroom Teachers Assn, NE OH Ed Assn, OH Ed Assn, NEA 1969-; Natl Wildlife Fed 1970-; Niles Historical Society 1973-; Amer Indian Heritage Fnd 1969-; The Smithsonian Assocs 1988-; Trumbull Area Red Cross Disaster Team 1985-86; *home:* 329 Illinois Ave Mc Donald OH 44437

KAUFFMAN, ELLEN GANFIELD, Mathematics/Physics Teacher; *b:* Osceola, MO; *m:* Robert C.; *ed:* (BSED) Math, 1967, (MA) Math, 1970 Cntrl MO St Univ; *cr:* Teacher Pittman Jr HS 1967-68, Clinton Jr HS 1968-69, Plattsburg HS 1970-72, Ritenour HS 1972-76, Winona HS 1977-78, Alton HS 1978-; *ai:* Beta & Quiz Bowl Spon; Alton Ed Assn Pres 1988-; MO Ed Assn (Collective Bargaining Chairperson, PAC Cncl) 1988-; NEA Congressional Contact 1986-; OR Cty Lib Bd Secy 1983-88; OR Cty Unit Amer Cancer Society Bd Mem 1988-; Amer Civil Liberties Union Mem.

KAUFFMAN, LINDA SELLERS, Sixth Grade Teacher; *b:* Greenfield, OH; *m:* William Joseph Sr.; *c:* William J. Jr., Douglas B.; *ed:* (AB) Elem Ed, Pikeville Coll 1963; Spec Ed, AL A&M; *cr:* 1st Grade Teacher Pike Cty 1963-64; 1st Grade Teacher 1965-68, 6th Grade Teacher 1974- Huntsville City Schls; *ai:* Huntsville Ed Assn; *home:* 1817 Haynes Ave Huntsville AL 35811

KAUFFMAN, PATRICIA WOLFE, 6th Grade Teacher; *b:* Anchorage, AK; *m:* Craig S.; *c:* Debra Wilson, Rebecca Duda, Michelle; *ed:* Med Tech, 1959; (BA) Gen Sci, 1970 Univ of IA; (MED) Rdng Ed, Univ of AK 1976; *cr:* Teacher Rogers Park Sch 1973-; *ai:* Sci Coord of Sci Fair; Delta Kappa Gamma Treas; Pioneers of AK; Eastern Star; Attended Sci & Tech for Children Elem Sci Matls Dev Wkshp 1987.

KAUFMAN, BRIAN RUSSELL, Fifth Grade Teacher; *b:* St Clair, MI; *m:* Lou Anne; *c:* Craig, Rebecca, Kristin; *ed:* (BA) Speech Correction, Cntrl MI 1973; (MA) Elem Ed, MI St 1982; *cr:* Elem Teacher E China Schls 1973-; *ai:* Coaching Intramurals; Sci Olympiad Organizer; Gifted & Sch Improvement Comm; Singing Barbershop Group Mem 1974-, St Champs 1979, 1982, 1987; *home:* 524 Connecticut Marysville MI 48040

KAUFMAN, CYNTHIA BAGWELL, Spanish/English Teacher; *b:* Monroe, LA; *m:* James V.; *c:* Joel C., Brian K. Galyean, Carey D. Galyean; *ed:* (BS) Scndry Ed, 1969, (MED) Scndry Ed, 1989 NE LA Univ; *cr:* Eng Teacher Lake Providence HS 1969; Span/Eng Teacher Neville HS 1969-72, 1982-85, Eng Teacher Martin HS 1985-86; Span/Eng Teacher Montgomery HS 1987-; *ai:* Chldr & Yrbk Sponl Span Club Adv; LA Ed Assn 1969-72; LA Assn of Prof Educators 1982-85, 1987-89; NCTE, Amer Cncl of Foreign Lang Teachers 1990; USL Prgm Costa Rica Exch Teacher; *home:* 64 Big Hill LA Natchitoches LA 71457

KAUFMAN, JEAN GARLOCK, Sixth Grade Teacher; *b:* Salem, OH; *m:* George Albert; *c:* Douglas A., Scott, Diane; *ed:* (BS) Elem Ed, Kent St Univ 1971; 6th Grade Teacher Buckeye Elem 1971-78, Prospect Elem 1978-; *ai:* Kent St Univ Martha Holden Jennings Scholar Awd 1978-79; Mt Union Coll Teacher Ed Advisory Cncl; *home:* 750 Adams Salem OH 44460

KAUFMAN, JON MICHAEL, Math & Phys Ed Dept Chair; *b:* Toledo, OH; *ed:* (AA) Accounting, Citrus Jr Coll 1971; (BS) Phys Ed, Cal Poly San Luis Obispo 1975; *cr:* Teachers Aide/Phys Ed Teacher Nipomo Elem Sch 1977-78; Math/Phys Ed Teacher/Athletic Dir Old Mission Sch 1979-; *ai:* Boys & Girls Athletic Dir; Soccer, Bsktbl, Sftbl Coach; NCEA Mem 1979-; Dedicated Service Educator Awd Presented by Supt Diocese of Monterey 1989; Outstanding Leadership in Youth Sports Awd San Luis Obispo Recreation Dept 1986; *office:* Old Mission Elem Sch 761 Broad St San Luis Obispo CA 93401

KAUFMAN, JOSEPH ROBERT, Biology Teacher; *b:* Menominee, MI; *m:* Diane L; *c:* Brandon, Bryan; *ed:* (BA) Bio, 1972, (MA) Bio Ed, 1978 N MI Univ; *cr:* Teacher Stephenson Area Public Schls 1972-; Instr Stephenson Cmmty Schls 1977-80; *ai:* Dept Chairperson; Soph Adv; Sci Fair Judge; P2M Seaberg Center NMU 1988-; NEA, MEA, SEA (VP, Secy, Treas) 1976-85; Menominee Cty Ind Sch Dist Math Sci Policy Bd 1990; Daggett Volunteer Fire Dept (Secy, Treas 1978-88), Course 1985; Mid Cty Little League Coach 1986-; MI Dept Natl Resources Hunter Safety Instr 1974; Nom NABT Outstanding Bio Teacher 1980; Nom Presidential Awd for Excl 1990; *office:* Stephenson HS Bartell St Stephenson MI 49887

KAUFMAN, ROSANNE, Thinking Skills Coordinator; *b:* Brooklyn, NY; *ed:* (BS) Ed, Long Island Univ 1969; (MA) Ed, NY Univ 1973; Extra Courses Gifted Ed & Art, Various Univs; *cr:* Teacher Public Sch 114 1969-85; Asst Dir of Gifted Prgms 1985-86, Thinking Skills Coord 1986- Cmmty Sch Dist 18; *ai:* Project Dir Reasoning & Thinking Skills in Math; New York Assn Teachers of Math; Advocacy for Gifted & Talented Ed; Natl Cncl of Teachers of Mathematics; Assn for Supervision & Curr Dev; Received Gubinatorial Citation for Citizenship 1984; *office:* Cmmty Sch Dist 18 755 E 100th St Brooklyn NY 11236

KAUFMAN, SUSAN BLAND, 6th Grade Teacher; *b:* Medicine Lodge, KS; *m:* Alan K.; *c:* Kristen Leigh; *ed:* (BA) Elem Ed, Bethany Coll 1983; (MS) Gifted Ed, KS St Univ 1984; Various Seminars; *cr:* Teacher of Gifted Valley Center Public Schls 1984-88; 6th Grade Teacher Maize Intermediate Sch 1988-; *ai:* 7th/8th Grade Girls Vlybl & Chrldrs; 4th-6th Grade Young Astronauts; Stock Market Club; Photography Interest Group; Scholars Bowl Team; NEA (Stu VP 1982-83, Stu Pres 1983-84, Natl Resolutions Comm 1983-84, Local Pres 1985-88); KS Assn of Gifted & Talented, KS Assn of Mid Schls Mem; 4-H (Pres, VP, Secy) 1968-79, Key 1979; Outstanding Young Women 1983, 1985; Whos Who Among Colls & Univs 1983; *office:* Maize Intermediate Sch 304 W Central Maize KS 67101

KAUL, TIM HERMAN, Business Teacher/Co-Op Dir; *b:* Saginaw, MI; *m:* Carleen Beth Bickel; *c:* Kyle, Katrina; *ed:* (AB) Delta Coll 1970; (BS) Bus Ed, 1972, (MA) Voc Ed, 1979 Cntrl MI Univ; *cr:* Coop Dir/Bus Teacher Buena Vista HS 1973-; *ai:* Homecoming, Calendar, Graduation, Spring Carnival Comms; Newspaper Adv; Sch Improvement Team; SVRACC, MVCA, MOEA 1975-; Trinity Luth Sch Bd of Ed Secy 1989-; *office:* Buena Vista HS 3945 Holland Rd Saginaw MI 48601

KAULS, GUIDO PERCY, Ger Teacher/World Lang Chair; *b:* Riga, Latria; *m:* Ann Franklin; *c:* Alex, Gregory; *ed:* (BA) Ger/His, 1957, (BS) Ger/His, 1959, (MA) Foreign Lang Ed, 1970 Univ of MN; *cr:* Ger/His Teacher/Soccer/Track Coach Minnehaha Acad 1957-; *ai:* Boys Soccer & Track; Ger Club; Ed Comm; Jr Class Adv; AATG 1965-; AATGM (VP 1979-81, Pres 1981-83); Bethlehem Cov Church 1957-; Brackett Park Bd Soccer 1977-82; Organized 1st HS Boys Soccer League MN 1962; Started 1 of 3 Girls Soccer Teams MN 1977; Regional & Midwest Soccer Coach of Yr 1982; MN Soccer Coach of Yr 1981-82; *office:* Minnehaha Acad 3107 47th Ave S Minneapolis MN 55406

KAUTZ, ROBERT DUANE, Crafts Teacher; *b:* Gering, NE; *m:* M. Susan Witschy; *c:* Jeffrey, Robin Yamani, Douglas; *ed:* (AA) Liberal Arts, Scottsbluff Jr Coll 1960; (BS) Industrial Arts, Chadron St Teacher Coll 1962; (MS) Elem Ed, Western St Coll 1971; *cr:* K-8th Grade Teacher/Prin/Coach Gering Valley Sch 1963-66; Prin/Teacher/Coach Merino Elem Sch 1966-69; Teacher/Coach Stevens Elem Sch 1969-86, Sterling Jr HS 1986-; *ai:* Boys Ftbl, Boys & Girls Bsktbl Coach; NEA & CEA; South Platte Ed Assn Chm of Teacher Welfare; BPOE #1336; *home:* 105 Delaware Dr Sterling CO 80751

KAUTZ, VIOLA E., Counselor; *b:* Lovell, WY; *m:* Leroy; *c:* Toby, Jeff, Millie Duffy; *ed:* (BA) Elem Ed, Panhandle St Univ 1973; Endorsement Eng Second Lang, W TX St 1974; (MS) Cnslr, SW OK St 1983; *cr:* Kndgtn Teacher Stratford Ind Sch Dist 1973-81; Instr Frank Phillips Coll 1985-86, W TX St Univ 1990; Cnslr Stratford Ind Sch Dist 1981-; *ai:* Gamma Xi Delta Kappa Gamma Prof Affairs Chm 1982-; TX Assn Counseling & Dev; TX St Teachers Assn Chm; 4-H Youth Cncl Chm; Sherman Cty Child Welfare Chm; Moore Cty Teachers Credit Union Bd Mem; St Josephs Finance Comm 1987; Cath Family Service Volunteer 1987-; Honorable Mention Seven Who Care.

KAUZA, BEVERLY, 8th Grade Teacher; *b:* Detroit, MI; *m:* Thomas; *c:* Jacqueline K.; *ed:* (BED) Elem Ed, Univ of AK 1973; (MA) Eng Lang/Lit, Univ of MI 1979; *cr:* Teacher St Marys Parish Sch 1976-; *ai:* Drama Group Dir; NCEA; *office:* St Marys Parish Sch 151 N Monroe St Monroe MI 48161

KAVANAUGH, DAVID BERNARD, Mathematics Chairman; *b:* Washington, IN; *m:* Cleta Helen Edmondson; *c:* David A., Karalyn J., Kristine M., Kayla R.; *ed:* (MA) Math, Vincennes Univ 1968; (BS) Math, 1970, (MS) Ed, 1972 IN St Univ; *cr:* Teacher Loogootee Cmmty Schls 1970-; *ai:* Timekeeper Bsktbl Games; Chaperone Jr HS Games & Dances; Officiate for HS Vlybl, Bsbl & Girls & Boys Bsktbl; Loogootee Ed Assn Treas 1970-; IN St Teachers Assn, NEA 1970-; Montgomery Ruritan Club (Treas, Secy) 1972-; *home:* RR 1 Box 33 Montgomery IN 47558

KAVETT, PAULA D., Sixth Grade Teacher; *b:* New York, NY; *m:* Nat; *c:* Mark, Wendy Kavett Brodsky; *ed:* (BA) TV/Radio, NY Univ 1949; (MS) Ed, Yeshiva Univ 1959; Adelphi Univ, Coll of New Rochelle, Hofstra Univ, C W Post Univ; *cr:* Teacher East Meadow Schls 1959-; *ai:* Mid Level Ed, Supt Day, Nuclear Ed Comm; Newsday Spelling Bee Coord; Policy Bd Teacher Center; EMTA Union VP; Grade Level Chairperson; NYSUT, EMTA (Pres, VP) 1988-; Various Books & Articles Published; *home:* 11 Craig St Jericho NY 11753

KAWAGUCHI, THELMA ODA, Fifth Grade Teacher; *b:* Honolulu, HI; *m:* George Jitsuro; *c:* Guy T., Eric H.; *ed:* (BED) Elem Ed, 1961, Certificate Elem Ed, 1962 Univ of HI; *cr:* Teacher Waianae Elem Sch 1962-65, Sagamihara Elem Sch 1965-66, Palisades Elem Sch 1966-; *ai:* Track Coach; Pi Lambda Theta

1960-; HI St Teachers Assn 1962-; *office:* Palisades Elem Sch 2306 Auhuhu St Pearl City HI 96782

KAWALEC, WALTER M., JR., English Teacher; *b:* S Amboy, NJ; *m:* Constance Kulczynski; *c:* Laura Schubert, Donna Cardaneo, Joseph; *ed:* (BA) Foreign Lang, Seton Hall Univ 1961; (MA) Personnel Services, Trenton St Coll 1973; *cr:* Teacher Middlesex HS 1961-62, Sayreville War Memorial HS 1962-68, Sayreville Jr Mid Sch 1968-; *ai:* Latin Club; Foreign Lang Festival; Adult Sch Dir; Sayreville Girls Sftbl Coach 1979-80; *office:* Sayreville Mid Sch 800 Washington Rd Parlin NJ 08859

KAWAMOTO-COMBES, BARBARA KIKUE, Health/Guidance J H Teacher; *b:* Honolulu, HI; *m:* Gary Paul Combes; *ed:* (AA) Soc Sci, Foothill Jr Coll 1975; (BA) Sociology, Univ of CA Santa Barbara 1977; Prgm Quality Review Certificate of Trng 1989; *cr:* 5th/6th Grade Teacher Templeton Unified Sch Dist 1979-81, Almond Elem 1982-83; 6th Grade Teacher Loyola Elem 1983-89; 7th/8th Grade Health Teacher/Guidance Black Intermediate 1989-; 7th Grade Eng Teacher.

KAY, CHERYL, Former Teacher; *b:* Garden City, KS; *ed:* (BA) Elem Ed, Baptist Bible Coll of Denver 1973; (MS) Admin, TN Temple Univ 1980; *cr:* Elem Teacher Bethany Baptist Sch 1976-79; Elem Teacher Silver St Baptist Sch 1976-79.

KAY, HARVEY PETER, Lang Arts Teacher/Librarian; *b:* Brooklyn, NY; *m:* Joan Ellen; *c:* Scott M., Lorin R.; *ed:* (BBA) Bus Admin, 1969, (MS) Ed, 1975 Hofstra Univ; Post Grad Stud Sch Admin, Hofstra Univ; *cr:* Lang Art Teacher 1970-83, Teacher Trainer 1983-89, Lib Coord 1988- Margaret S Douglas Intermediate Sch; *ai:* Sr Adv; Comprehensive Sch Improvement Prgm; Pupil Personnel Comm; NY Regents Action Plan; Society of Childrens Book Writers 1987-; Phi Delta Kappa 1990-; Author of Articles; Co-Author Study Guides; *office:* Intermediate Sch 292 300 Wyona St Brooklyn NY 11207

KAY, NANCY, 5th Grade Teacher; *b:* Kingsville, TX; *ed:* (BS) Elem Ed, TX A&I 1977; Mid-Management-Masters Prgm in Progress; *cr:* 3rd-6th Grade Teacher Corpus Christi Chrstn Sch 1977-83; 5th Grade Teacher Sinton Ind Sch Dist 1983-; *ai:* ATPE 1984-; *home:* 4209 D Acushnet Corpus Christi TX 78413

KAYE, STEPHANIE ROMANISCON, Spanish Teacher; *b:* Shenandoah, PA; *ed:* (BS) Span, Lock Haven Univ 1973; Bloomsburg Univ, Alvernia Coll, Penn St Univ; *cr:* Span Teacher Mahanoy Area HS 1973-; *ai:* Span Club & Sch Newspaper Adv; Mahanoy Area Ed Assn Secy 1985-89; NEA, PA St Ed Assn; Ladies of Elks 1533; *office:* Mahanoy Area HS 800 W South Mahanoy City PA 17948

KAYLOR, MARTHA BULLMAN, Kindergarten Teacher; *b:* Spartanburg, SC; *m:* Thomas H.; *ed:* (AA) Eng, Anderson Coll 1964; (BS) Elem Ed, 1966, (BS) Elem Ed, 1974 Carson-Newman Coll; TN Early Chldhd East TN St Univ; *cr:* 2nd Grade Teacher Norton Park Elem 1966-67, Rose Elem 1967-75; Kndgtn Teacher West Elem 1975-; *ai:* PTO; Alpha Delta Kappa (Corresponding Sec 1982-84 Treas 1984-88 Pres Elect 1988-); Amer Outstanding Elem Teacher 1974; *office:* West Elem Sch 235 W Converse St Morristown TN 37814

KAYNE, STEPHEN G., Eighth Grade Teacher; *b:* Paterson, NJ; *m:* Arlene Lipari; *c:* Jeffrey, Lisa; *ed:* (BA) Soc Sci/Scndry Ed, William Paterson Coll 1969; *cr:* 6th-8th Grade Teacher Public Sch 20 1970-78; Math Resource Teacher 1982-88, 8th Grade Teacher 1982- Public Sch 2; *ai:* Paterson Ed Assn, NJEA, NEA; Sparta Soccer Club VP 1988; Sparta Girls Sftbl Coach 1989; Governors Outstanding Teachers Awd 1986; *office:* Public Sch 2 Passaic Near Mill St Paterson NJ 07504

KAYS, JOHN BELDON, Math Teacher/Department Chm; *b:* Mabton, WA; *m:* Darlene Lodenna Cox; *c:* Jason Mc Kenzie, Marie A.; *ed:* (BA) Math Ed, Univ of WA 1956; (MS) Math Ed, Univ of OR 1964; Single/Multi-Engine Pilot Trng, Randolph Field & Reese AFB; Officer Trng USAF; Grad Stud, Univ of MT; WA Ed Assn Leadership Trng; *cr:* Airforce Officer/Pilot USAF 1949-53; Math Teacher 1956-; Math Dept Chm Port Angeles HS; Immigration Inspector USINS 1966-; *ai:* Knowledge Bowl Coach; Math Team Adv; WA Ed Assn Bd Dir 1970-74; Port Angeles Ed Assn (Pres, Various Comm Chm) 1956-; NEA Life Mem; NCTM Membership 1956-86; Natl Sci Fnd Schlsp Awd; Air Medal USAF; Coach/2nd Place St Awd Knowledge Bow 1983-84; *office:* Port Angeles Sr HS 304 E Park Ave Port Angeles WA 98362

KEA, SUZIE BREWER, English Instructor; *b:* Mc Comb, MS; *m:* Richard B.; *c:* Jessica, Lerin; *ed:* (AA) Eng Ed, SW MS Jr Coll 1976; (BS) Eng Ed, LA St Univ 1978; (MED) Eng Ed, Univ of S MS 1980; *cr:* Eng Teacher N Pike Mid Sch 1976-87, N Pike HS 1987-89; Eng Instr Univ of N AL 1989-; *home:* 204 Woodstock Dr Florence AL 35630

KEAIRNES, WILLIAM PAUL, 5th Grade Teacher; *b:* Omaha, NE; *m:* Anita Ball; *ed:* (BA) Elem Ed, 1980, (MS) Ed Admin, 1990 Univ of Las Vegas; *cr:* 4th/5th Grade Teacher Pat Diskin Elem 1980-85; Jr Var Bsktbl Coach Western HS 1985, Univ of UT 1985-86; 5th Grade Teacher Diskin Elem 1986- Eisenburg Elem; *ai:* Cmptr & Woodworking Club; Boys & Girls Bsktbl; Lunchtime Act Coord; Boys & Girls Club; *office:* Pat Diskin Elem Sch 4220 S Ravenwood Las Vegas NV 89117

KEAN, BETH, Elementary School Counselor; *b:* Austin, TX; *m:* Roy Carroll Bowen; *ed:* (BS) Elem Ed, TX Wesleyan Coll 1972; (MED) Counseling, TX Chrstn Univ 1981; Art, TX Tech Univ; Grad Work in Art Therapy; British Ed Wkshp, Richmond Coll; *cr:* Teacher 1972-85, Cnslr 1985-88 Ft Worth Ind Sch Dist; Art Therapist Psychiatric Inst 1987-; Cnslr Hurst Euless Bedford 1988-; *ai:* Parent Ed Chairperson Bell Manor; Delta Kappa Gamma 1985-; PTA 1989-, Life Membership Awd 1988; Art Ed Assn VP 1982-84; TX Art Therapy Assn (VP, Treas) 1982-84; TX Assn of Counseling & Dev 1985-; N TX Assn of Counseling & Dev 1988-; Stress Management Curr 1988-; Metro Mc Gee Assn; Art Curr Ft Worth Ind Sch Dist 1983-85; *office:* Hurst Euless Bedford Ind Sch 1300 Winchester Way Bedford TX 76022

KEANE, JOHN PATRICK, Eighth Grade Teacher; *b:* Jacksonville, FL; *w:* Carol Henderson (dec); *c:* Sean, Bryan, Kristen; *ed:* (BA) His, Marquette Univ 1969; *cr:* Teacher St Matthews Sch 1969-; Summer Bsbl Prgm Coord Oak Creek Dept Parks & Recreation 1987-; *ai:* Intramural Sports Dir; Bsktbl Coach 1986-89; 8th Grade Fundraiser Mardi Gras Coord; St Matthews Annual Field Day Coord; NCEA 1969-; Certificate of Appreciation OuTstanding Teacher Awd; League of Home & Sch Assns Archdiocese of Milwaukee 1972; *office:* St Matthews Sch 9329 S Chicago Rd Oak Creek WI 53154

KEARNS, J. TIMOTHY, History/Geography Teacher; *b:* Lynn, MA; *ed:* (BA) His, Salem St Coll 1975; *cr:* Teacher Winthrop HS 1976-77, Suitland HS 1986-; *ai:* Faculty Advisement Comm 1989-; PGCEA Union Building Rep 1989-; Delegate to St Teachers Convention 1988-89; Var Bsbl Head Coach 1988-; Ancient Order of Hibernians DiV 10 1975-; St Johns The Baptist Choir 1988-; Co-Authored Amer Civilization Curr for Cty Univ HS Prgm; *office:* Suitland Sr H S 5200 Silver Hill Rd Forestville MD 20747

KEARNS, JOHNETTA GEOGHEGAN, 7th Grade Science Teacher; *b:* Cynthiana, KY; *m:* John Michael; *c:* John M. II, Shelby L.; *ed:* (BA) Phys Ed, E KY Univ 1973; (MS) Scndry Ed, Georgetown Coll 1976; *cr:* Phys Ed Teacher Westside Elem 1974-79; Migrant Teacher Harrison Cty Jr HS 1979-81; Sci Teacher Harrison Cty Mid Sch 1981-; *ai:* Sch Spirit Chm; After Sch Act Helper; Indian Creek Chrstn Church (Sunday Sch Secy, Sunday Sch Treas).

KEARNS, MICHAEL PATRICK, Eng/Photo Journalism Teacher; *b:* Pittsburgh, PA; *m:* Shanda Rae Baker; *c:* Kelsey N.; *ed:* (BA) Journalism/Eng/His, OH Univ 1982; *cr:* Laborer Droz Steel Corp 1976-78; Sportswriter The Baytown TX Sun 1983-87; Eng I/Photo Journalism Cypress Fairbanks HS 1988-; *ai:* Honorable Mention All TX Spot Sportswriting 1983.

KEATING, MARY MALAN, 6th Grade Teacher, Team Leader; *b:* Camden, NJ; *m:* Richard R.; *ed:* (BA) Elem Ed, FL St Univ 1975; *cr:* 6th Grade Teacher Glen Landing Mid Sch 1975-; *ai:* Team Leader 1984-; 6th Grade Dist Rep; Track Coach; *home:* 423 Barton Run Blvd Marlton NJ 08053

KECK, ROBERT F., Honors Biology Teacher; *b:* Chicago, IL; *m:* Ann L.; *c:* Sabrina, Katelynn; *ed:* (AA) Liberal Art, Harper Coll 1979; (BS) Botany/Zoology, 1982, (MS) Biological Sci Ed, 1988 E IL Univ; *cr:* 8th Grade Earth Sci Teacher 1982-83, 7th Grade General Sci Teacher 1983-85 Tafft Mid Sch; Bio/Phys Sci Teacher 1985-86, Honors Bio Teacher 1986- Streamwood HS; *ai:* Sci Bowl Scholastics Team Adv; Class of 1991 Spon; Sch Dept Comm 1985-86; Elgin Teachers Assn Dept Rep 1986-87; NEA Assoc Mem; IL Sci Teachers Assn Assoc Mem 1985-; Amer Museum of Natural His Assoc Mem 1982-; Participated US & China Scientific Educl Exch 1984; *office:* Streamwood HS 701 W Schaumburg Rd Streamwood IL 60107

KEDERSHA, LUCILLE R., English Teacher; *b:* Nanticoke, PA; *m:* Thomas J.; *c:* Janna, Jaki, Jarrod; *ed:* (BA) Speech/Theatre/Eng, 1970, (MED) Stu Personnel Services, 1983 Trenton St Coll; *cr:* Eng Teacher Centennial Sch Dist 1970-; *ai:* 9th Grade Play Dir; Sunshine Club Chm; Rdng & Lang Art Task Force; Faculty Chorus; Kappa Delta Pi 1984-; *office:* E Klinger Jr HS Second St Pike Southampton PA 18966

KEDZIORA, HELENE J., 4th Grade Teacher; *b:* Philadelphia, PA; *ed:* (BS) Elem/Psych, Westchester Univ 1966; Grad Work Towson, Univ of DE; Spec Ed Cert, Loyola; *cr:* 3rd Grade Teacher Chesapeake City Elem 1966-67; 4th Grade Teacher Elkton Elem 1967-70; Spec Ed Teacher Perryville/Holly Hall 1970-80; 2nd/4th-6th Grade Teacher Cecilton Elem 1980-; *ai:* Sci Coord; Curr Dev, Environment Curr Dev, Arbor Day, Earth Day Chairperson Comm; Project Wild Teacher; MSTA (Delegate, Rep) 1978-86; NEA; Cecil Cty Classroom Teachers Organization PAC Chairperson Rep; League of WV Energy Chairperson; Energy Grants; *office:* Cecilton Elem Sch 251 W Main St Cecilton MD 21913

KEE, LISA LANGE, English Teacher/Academic Coach; *b:* Corning, NY; *m:* Jimmy Wayne; *c:* Kevin Lange, Laura K., Marisa E., Jared R.; *ed:* (BA) Eng, AZ St Univ 1967; (MAT) Eng, Memphis St Univ 1969; Eng Classes; Advanced Placement Wrkshps & Seminars; *cr:* Eng Teacher, Trezevant HS; Lang Art Teacher, Travis AFB Schls, Solano Chrstn Acad; Eng/Speech/Hum Teacher Jackson Chrstn Sch; *ai:* Natl Honor Society Spon; Class Spon; United States Academic Decathalon Coach; Academic Banquet Annual Spon; Joagthon Coord Annually Fundraiser; Academic Cncl Mem; Bowl Team Spon; Bradford Eng Competition Spon; West TN Cncl Teachers of Eng Treas 1988-, Secy 1989-); NCTE 1980- Speaker Spring Convention 1990; Pro Family Forum; JCS Eagle Club Secy 1981-82; TN Medical Auxiliary; Mid-South Youth Camp Bd Mem 1990; Natl Assn Stu Activity Adv; TN HS Speech/Drama League Mem; Speaker TN Cncl Teachers of Eng Annual Conventions 1987-89; NCTE Spring Convention; Colorado Springs CO 1990; West TN Cncl Teachers of Eng 1990; Memphis City Schls System; Teacher In-Service 1989; Governing Bd Mem of TN Academic Decathalon; Alpha Delta Kappa; Governing Bd of USAD TN; Outstanding Young Woman of America 1981; Plaques/Certificates for Organizing Annual Jogathon at JCS; Plaques for Coaching USAD Tea at JCS; JCS Annual Dedication; Whos Who in West 1980; Whos Who Among Women Executives in America 1990; Dictionary of Intnl Biography; St Dept of Ed Certificate of Appreciation 1990; Annual Awards Appreciation Banquet Jackson Chrstn Sch 1989-; *office:* Jackson Christian Schl 832 Country Club Ln Jackson TN 38305

KEE, MARY V., 7-8th Grade Teacher; *b:* Akron, OH; *m:* James; *ed:* (BS) Elem Ed, Univ of Akron 1975; Cmptr Sci; *cr:* Teacher Christ The King Sch 1976-; *ai:* Spelling Bee & Yrbk Adv; Cmptr Coord; Integrating Cmptrs into Curr Instr Cleveland Diocese 1986-88; Excl in Ed Awd 1988; *office:* Christ The King Sch 1558 Creighton Ave Akron OH 44310

KEECH, TANYA MENDENHALL, Science Teacher; *b:* Olney, IL; *m:* Stephen D.; *c:* Andrea, Laura; *ed:* (BS) Jr HS Ed, E IL Univ 1976; (MS) Scndry Ed, N IL Univ 1984; *cr:* Sci Teacher Seneca Grade Sch 1976-; *ai:* Seneca Ed Assn (VP 1981, Pres 1982); *home:* 1012 Lakewood Dr Morris IL 60450

KEEHN, KEVIN B., 8th Grade Science Teacher; *b:* Milwaukee, WI; *m:* Mary; *c:* Emily; *ed:* (BSED) Elem Ed/Sci/Math, N IL Univ 1978; *cr:* 3rd Grade Teacher Pleasant Hill Elem Sch 1979; 8th Grade Sci Teacher Walter R Sundling Jr HS 1979-; *ai:* Staff Dev Chm; ISTA, NSTA Mem 1980-; IJAS Region 6 Chm 1987, 1989; IL Jr Acad of Sci Bd of Dir; Created Sch Advisory Prgm; *office:* Walter R Sundling Jr HS 1100 N Smith Rd Palatine IL 60067

KEELING, BRENDA WALKER, 6th Grade Teacher; *b:* Harmony, NC; *m:* C. D. Jr.; *c:* Emily, Amanda; *ed:* (BS) Elem Ed, Western Carolina Univ 1969; (MS) Elem Ed, Winthrop Coll 1979; *cr:* 4th-5th Grade Teacher Montlieu Ave Elem 1969-76; 6th Grade Teacher Oakdale Elem 1976-77; 5th-6th Grade Teacher Ebinport Elem 1977-; *ai:* Adv Stu Cncl; Soc Stud Comm Ebinport Sch; Mid Sch Math Comm Rock Hill Dist 3; Sch Improvement Cncl; NEA 1969-; SC Ed Assn 1976-; Rock Hill Ed Assn Faculty Rep 1976-; NC Ed Assn 1969-76; Wild Flower Garden Club 1975-76; Dir Vacation Bible Sch 1974; Church Chior; Sunday Sch Teacher; Teacher of Yr-Montlieu Ave Elem Sch 1975; Teach of Yr-Ebinport Elem Sch 1985 & 88; Finalist-Teacher of Yr Rock-Hill Sch Dist 3 1988; *office:* Ebinport Elem Sch 2142 India Hook Rd Rock Hill SC 29732

KEELING, WANDA ENSEY, Kindergarten Teacher; *b:* Coleman, TX; *m:* John A.; *c:* Peter, Michael Guild; *ed:* (AA) Elem Ed, San Jacinto Coll 1973; (BS) Elem Ed, 1975, (MS) Elem Ed, 1981 Univ of Houston; Educl Concepts Seminars & Wkshps; *cr:* Kndgtn Teacher Fisher Elem 1975-; *ai:* Preparation Wkshps; Wrote & Direct Kndgtn Play; NEA, TX St Teachers Assn, Pasadena Ed Assn 1975-; TX PTA Lifetime Mem; Golden Apple Awd; Houston Bus Comm Mini-Grant; *office:* Fisher Elem Sch 2220 Grunewald Pasadena TX 77502

KEELY, MICHAEL LANE, Science Teacher; *b:* Oil City, PA; *m:* Carolyn Esther; *c:* Joshua; *ed:* (BS) Ed, 1972, (MED) Sci Ed, 1988 Clarion Univ; Grad Work Quest Trained, Penn St Univ; *cr:* Sci Teacher Curwensville HS 1973-; *ai:* Stu Cncl Faculty Adv; Stu Assistance Prgm Team Mem; Act 178 Mentor Teacher; PA Sci Teachers Assn; GTE Growth Initiatives Teachers Fellow 1990; *office:* Curwensville HS Beech St Curwensville PA 16833

KEENE, JANICE WHEAT, Chemistry/Physics Teacher; *b:* Columbia, KY; *c:* Jennifer C.; *ed:* (BS) Chem, Campbellsville Coll 1975; (MS) Ed, Western KY Univ 1978; Rank I Scndry Ed; *cr:* Chem/Physics Teacher Casey Cty HS 1975-85, Russell Cty HS 1985-88, Russell Cty Jr Hs 1988-; *ai:* Attendance Policy Comm; Curr & Scope & Sequence Review Comm; Russell Cty Ed Assn Bd of Dir 1985-; KY Ed Assn 1975-; Russell Cty Deer Club 1989- Top Shooter of Yr 1989; *office:* Russell County Jr H S R R 7 Box 230 Russell Springs KY 42642

KEENE, LUCY M., Counselor; *b:* Forest, MS; *m:* Lindsey; *c:* Russell; *ed:* (BS) Ed, 1975, (MS) Ed, 1980, (EDS) Counseling, 1989 MS St Univ; *cr:* Elem Teacher SE Lauderdale Elem 1977-84; Math Teacher SE Lauderdale Jr HS 1985-87; Cnslr SE Lauderdale HS & Jr HS 1987-; *ai:* Instructional Management Comm; Chi Sigma Iota Mem 1990; MCA Mem 1987-; *office:* SE Lauderdale HS Rt 7 Box 477 Meridian MS 39301

KEENER, DEBORAH ANN (ROSEMAN), Mathematics Teacher; *b:* York, PA; *m:* Stephen Todd; *c:* Krysten, Brooks; *ed:* (BS) Elem/Early Chldhd Ed, 1979, (MS) Elem/Early Chldhd Ed, 1982 Millersville Univ; (BS) Scndry Math, Towson 1985; Essential Elements of Instruction; *cr:* 1st Grade Teacher Canadochly Elem Sch 1979-80; Math/Science Teacher Clearview Mid Sch 1980-83, Red Lion Jr HS 1983-84; 3rd Grade Teacher Edgar Moore Elem Sch 1984-85; Math Teacher Red Lion Area Jr HS 1985-87, Red Lion Area Sr HS 1987-; *ai:* Curr Cncl; Cheerleading Adv; Cheerleading Club; Moore Elem Sch PTO Bd; Talent Show Coord; Mid States Sch & Cmmty, Mid States Hospitality, Mid States Music; Graduation Comml Frosh Class Adv; Church Choir; Jr Church Leader; Bible Sch Music Coord; Red Lion Womens Club 1986-89; Bus & Prof Womens Club 1983-85; Bethany U M Church Adult Work Cncl Coord 1990; SICO Fnd Schlsp; Teacher of Yr Brogue Jaycees; Cora Catherine Bitner Music Awd; *home:* 60 Curtis Dr Red Lion PA 17356

KEENEY, ARLENE ANN, Chapter I Teacher; *b:* Scotch Plains, NJ; *m:* James John; *c:* John; *ed:* (BS) Elem Ed, WV Univ 1969; (MS) Elem Ed, FL Intnl Univ 1982; *cr:* 4th Grade Teacher Mt Horab Elem Sch 1969-70; 2nd/3rd Grade Teacher D O D Schls West Germany 1970-73; 5th/6th Grade Teacher 1974-89, 3rd/4th Grade/Chapter I Teacher 1989- Stanley Switlik Elem; *ai:* Walking Field Trips Spon; Drug Abuse Awareness Comm; Alpha Delta Kappa Treas 1984-88; Garden Club Mem 1980-; *home:* 1020 E 75th St Ocean Marathon FL 33050

KEENNON, CAROL COLLEEN, 5th & 6th Grade Teacher; *b:* Sioux City, IA; *c:* Michael, Michelle, Kimberly Keennon Jones; *ed:* (BA) Sociology/Speech, CA St Univ Stanislaus 1966; Grad Stud Various Univs 1966-; Techniques for Supervising Stu Teachers, CA St Univ Stanislaus 1985; *cr:* Kndgtn Teacher Mountain View Elem Sch 1963-67; Headstart Teacher Stanislaus Cty Schls 1964-71; Elem Teacher Chatom Elem Sch 1972-; *ai:* Quality Prgm Reviewer for Supt Office Stanislaus Cty; Chatom Sch Stu Cncl Adv & Gifted Stu Comm; Stanislaus Cnty & Chatom Sch Self-Esteem Comm; Chatom Union Educators Assn Pres 1981-82; Alpha Delta Kappa Beta Phi Pres 1980-81; Amer Assn of Univ Women (VP 1972, Secy 1973); Stanislaus Cty Task Force for Self-Esteem 1988-; Cntrl Valley Ballet Co Bd Dir 1975-79; Teacher of Yr 1975, Mentor Teacher Chatom Sch 1985-87; CA Soc Stud Curr Book 1980-82; *home:* 1979 Mira Flores Turlock CA 95380

KEEVER, PATRICIA ROUZER, 8th Grade Teacher Lang Arts; *b:* Charlotte, NC; *m:* John F. Jr.; *c:* Jennifer, Elizabeth; *ed:* (AB) Elem Ed, Duke Univ 1969; (MAED) Early Chldhd Ed, W Carolina Univ 1979; *cr:* 7th-8th Grade Teacher Carrington Jr HS 1981-82; 8th Grade Teacher Valley Springs Mid 1982-83, Venable Elem 1983-86, Enka Mid Sch 1986-; *ai:* Sch Newspaper Adv; NCAE, NEA (Local Pres 1987-89, Dist Pres 1988-89, IPD Chairperson/VP/Pace Chairperson 1983-89); League of Women Voters (Local Pres, Voter Service Chairperson) 1977-79; Outstanding Young Woman of Yr Asheville Jaycees 1977.

KEGERREIS, PHYLLIS KNUDSEN, First Grade Teacher; *b:* Philadelphia, PA; *m:* George Deatrick; *c:* Harold K., George D. Jr., Christopher D.; *ed:* (BS) Elem Ed, Lebanon Valley Coll 1973; Various Courses; *cr:* 1st Grade Teacher Fishing Creek Valley Elem 1973-; *ai:* Progress Elem PTA Pres 1967-70; Fishing Creek Valley PTA (Recording Secy 1979-80, VP 1987-88); Order of Eastern Star Worthy Matron 1982-83; Cub Scouts Den Mother 1967-75; *office:* Fishing Creek Valley Elem Sch 1524 Pine Tree Ave Harrisburg PA 17112

KEGLEY, SANDRA ANN (PETTIT), Third Grade Teacher; *b:* Ottumwa, IA; *m:* Richard Dwight; *c:* Helen, Rickie A., Linda; *ed:* (BA) Ed, San Jose St Univ 1962; Post Grad Work San Jose St Univ 1962; *cr:* Teacher Cambrian Sch Dist 1962-79; Rdng Specialist Concord City Schls 1979-81; Teacher Cambrian Sch Dist 1981-; *ai:* Sch Leadership Team; Math Mentor Teacher 1987-89; CA Teachers Assn 1962-; Cambrian Dist Educators Assn (Ed, Building Rep 1962-); Natl Teachers Assn 1962-; NCTM 1988-89; NC Teachers Assn 1979-81; GSA Leader 20 Year Pin; Childrens Play House of San Jose Bd Mem 1989-91; ACE Consortium Writing Team for Seven Math Strand Binders for K-3rd Grade; *office:* Sartorette Elem Sch 3850 Woodford Dr San Jose CA 95124

KEGLOVITS, MICHAEL J., History Teacher; *b:* Allentown, PA; *m:* Pamela Hoffner; *c:* Michael Jr., Marion; *ed:* (BS) Poly Sci, IN St Univ 1975; Masters Equivalency Eng, Lehigh Univ 1989; West Chester Writing Project, Kutztown Univ, Wiles Univ; *cr:* Teacher Northampton Jr HS 1975-; *ai:* Lehigh Valley Faculty Partnership; 8th Grade Gifted Prgm; PA Cncl for Soc Stud, NCSS; Northampton Jaycees Pres 1980-82; *office:* Northampton Area Sch Dist 1617 Laubach Ave Northampton PA 18067

KEHLENBECK, ANTHONY PAUL, English Teacher; *b:* Fresno, CA; *ed:* (BA) Eng, CA St Univ 1975; Spec in Ed & Poetry Writing; *cr:* Teacher Sequoia Jr HS 1976-78, Kings Canyon Mid Sch 1978-86, Mc Lane HS 1986-; *ai:* Class of 1992 Spon; Sch Site Cncl; Sch Building Comm; NEA, CTA, FTA; Fresno Tree People; Poems Published.

KEHLER, JOYCE ANN, 3rd Grade Teacher; *b:* Holton, KS; *ed:* (AA) Elem Ed, Highland Comm Jr Coll 1976; (BSE) Elem Ed, Emporia St Univ 1978; *cr:* Classroom Teacher USD 454 1978-; *ai:* Dist Staff Dev Comm; All Sch Musical Asst Dir; Burlingame Teachers Assn; KS Natl Ed Assn; NEA; *office:* USD 454 303 S Dacotah Burlingame KS 66413

KEHOE, COLEEN RICE, 6th Grade Science Teacher; *b:* Borger, TX; *w:* Jack Howard (dec); *c:* Anna M. Kehoe Murphy, Gregory C.; *ed:* Certificate Piano, S Nazrene Univ 1952; (BSED) Eng - Cum Laude, Corpus Christi St Univ 1979; *cr:* Substitute Teacher Corpus Christi Ind Sch Dist 1974-79; Elem Teacher Shaw Elem 1979-84, Allen Elem 1984-87; Sci Teacher Driscoll Mid Sch 1987-; *ai:* Co-Spon Driscoll Sci Fair; Spelling Bee, Choir Dir, Newspaper Spon; Citizenship Wkshp Presenter; Amer Assn of Univ Women 1979; Kappa Delta Pi 1981; Church (Organist, Pianist, Teacher); Most Prominent Educators of TX 1983; Academic Schlsp 1979; NHS & Bethany Nazarene Coll Honor Cheerleading Letter; *home:* 428 Ohio Corpus Christi TX 78404

KEHOE, STEVEN EDWARD, Agriculture Education Teacher; *b:* Fort Dodge, IA; *ed:* (BS) Ag Ed, NW MO St Univ 1982; *cr:* Ag Ed Teacher Charter Oak-Ute HS 1983-86, West Bend Cmmty HS 1986-; *ai:* FFA Adv; 8th Grade Class Spon; Asst Vlybl Coach; WBEA (VP, Pres) 1989, 1990; IvATA 1983-; Lions Club 1988-; Farm Bureau Assn 1983-; Outstanding Young Teacher Awd IVATA SW IA 1984; N Cntrl Dist FFA Adv Elected 1988-; IA FFA Bd of Dir 1989-; *office:* West Bend Cmmty HS Box 247 West Bend IA 50597

KEHRES, DONNA GIRARD, 5th & 6th Grade Teacher; *b:* St Louis, MO; *m:* William L.; *c:* Will, Steve; *ed:* (BA) Elem Ed, Fontbonne Coll 1969; (MED) Elem Ed, Univ of MO St Louis 1989; *cr:* 5th Grade Teacher Pattonville Sch Dist 1969-71, St Joan of Arc 1976-81; 5th/6th Grade Teacher Our Lady of Lourdes 1981-; *ai:* Math & Intermediate Grade Coord; Steering & Chairperson Math Curr Comm; MO Cncl Teachers of Math; Math Educators of Greater St Louis; Phi Kappa Phi Honor Society; *home:* 5643 Pernod Ave Saint Louis MO 63139

KEIFER, LINDA LEHR, First Grade Teacher; *b:* Sunbury, PA; *ed:* (BA) Elem Ed, Wilmington Coll 1969; *cr:* 1st Grade Teacher Gregory Sch 1969-70; William H Blount 1970-; *ai:* Staff Volunteer Coord; Intl Rdng Assn Sch Rep 1987-; NC Cncl Teachers; Beta Sigma Phi Pres 1989-; Mini-Grant Recipient Wilmington Chamber of Commerce; *office:* William H Blount Sch 3702 Princess Place Dr Wilmington NC 28405

KEIL, CHINESE AMELIA, 6th Grade Teacher; *b:* Bogalusa, LA; *ed:* (BA) Upper Elem Ed, Southern Univ 1962; Grad Stud Southeastern Univ 1987; *ai:* Bogalusa Federal Teachers Assn 1987-89; Natl Advancement of Colored People; *home:* 391-B Torrence Rd Bogalusa LA 70427

KEILL, JOHN HENRY, 9th World Geography Teacher; *b:* Lincoln, NE; *m:* Terry U. Thorpe; *c:* Lindsey, Jonathan; *ed:* (BS) Soc Sci/His, Winona St Univ 1976; (MA) Ed/Admin, SD St Univ 1988; *cr:* 8th Grade Black Teacher 1977-85, 9th Grade W Geography Teacher 1985 Edison Jr HS; *ai:* Coaching Track 1977-82, Wrestling/Ftbl 1977- , Wrestling 1981/1989-; SFEA, SDEA, & NEA (Faculty Rep 1977-79, Sekota Uniserv 1979-80); Current Nom for Outstanding Young Men of America; *home:* 1515 S Glendale Sioux Falls SD 57105

KEILTY, CARLA LEE, Fourth Grade Teacher; *b:* Twin Falls, ID; *m:* William B.; *c:* Jacqueline, Meghan; *ed:* (BA) Elem Ed, 1974, (MA) Elem Ed/Curr Dev, Boise St Univ; On-Going Wkshps; *cr:* 6th Grade Teacher Maple Grove Elem 1974-75; Kndgtn Teacher Navajo Reservation 1975-77; Elem Teacher Mc Millan Elem 1977-; *ai:* Staff Dev, Centennial Week Comm; Meridian Ed Assn Rep 1988-89; Delta Kappa Gamma 1988; Mc Millan Teacher of Yr 1987; *office:* Mc Millan Elem 10901 Mc Millan Rd Boise ID 83704

KEIM, MARGRET AUGHBAUGH, 5th Grade Lang Art Teacher; *b:* Troy, OH; *m:* Edward E.; *c:* Paul, Margaret A. Keim Roth, Joel; *ed:* (BSED) Elem Ed, Capital Univ 1952; (MSED) Elem Ed, Univ of Toledo 1979; *cr:* 2nd/3rd Grade Teacher Lostcreek Public Sch 1944-46; 2nd Grade Teacher Columbus Public Sch 1946-48, Green Bay Public Sch 1948-49; 3rd Grade Teacher Columbus Public Sch 1950-53; 5th Grade Teacher Botkins Schls 1963-65, Archbold Area Schls 1968-; *home:* 405 S Defiance St Archbold OH 43502

KEIME, AL, Social Studies Teacher; *b:* Sterling, CO; *m:* Judy Rogers; *c:* Amy, Mandy, Christopher, Carrie Haley; *ed:* (BA) His, Brigham Young Univ 1971; (MED) Soc Stud Curr, UT St Univ 1979; Gifted & Talented Ed, Ec & Free Enterprise Trng; Taft Government Inst; *cr:* Teacher Millcreek Jr HS 1973-74, North Layton Jr HS 1974-79, Clearfield HS 1979-80, North Davis Jr HS 1980-; *ai:* Soc Stud Dept Chairperson; Standards & Joint Staff Study Comm Mem; Mentor Teacher; NEA, UT Ed Assn, Davis Ed Assn Mem 1973-; *office:* North Davis Jr HS 835 S State Clearfield UT 84015

KEITER, WILLIAM J., World Geography Teacher; *b:* Parsons, KS; *m:* Carol Lee Palmer; *c:* Jason, Drew; *ed:* (BA) Poly Sci/Ed, 1968, (MS) Scndry Sch Ed, 1972 KS Univ; Grad Stud Various Institutions; *cr:* Teacher Milburn Jr HS 1968-86, Shawnee Mission West HS 1986-; *ai:* Issues Prgm; Amnesty Intnl; Cooperative Learning Comm; Soc Stud Task Force; NEA 1968-; Nom Teacher of Excl; *office:* Shawnee Mission West HS 8500 Antioch Overland Park KS 66212

KEITH, ARLYN DALE, Science Teacher; *b:* Minot, ND; *m:* Nora; *c:* Andrew, Marcella, Alicia; *ed:* (BS) Bio, Minot St Univ 1973; *cr:* Teacher Glen Ullin HS 1973, Sherwood HS 1974-; *ai:* Sci Club & Soph Class Adv; NDEA 1973-; Church Bd Pres 1986-89; Rural Water Bd 1988-; Rural Fire Bd Pres 1982-88; *home:* RR 2 Box 87 Sherwood ND 58782

KEITH, DAN K., Science Department Chairman; *b:* Gregory, SD; *m:* Joyce A. Osnes; *c:* Kelly, Brit; *ed:* (BSE) Bio, Univ of SD 1969; (BSE) Phys Ed, Univ of SD 1969; Univ of WY; Univ of SD; SD ST Univ; *cr:* Sci Alpena HS; Delmont HS; Wall HS; Twin Spruce Jr HS; *ai:* Sci & Music Instr; Bsktbl Coach Boys & Girls; NSTA 1970-; Boy Scout Leader 1970-75; Campbell Cty Sch Dist Teacher of Yr 1989-; *home:* 7200 Robin Gilette WY 82716

KEITH, EFFIE MELTON, Curriculum Director; *b:* Mobile, AL; *m:* Gert; *ed:* (BS) Eng Ed, FL St Univ 1972; (MED) Ed/Eng, 1988, (MED) Admin/Supervision, 1989 Valdosta St Coll; Working Towards Ed Specialist Degree; *cr:* Teacher Godby HS 1973-76, Brooks Cty Jr HS 1976-84, Brooks Cty HS 1984-88; Curr Dir Brooks Cty Bd of Ed 1988-; *ai:* St Textbook Adoption Comm Chairperson 1990; Governors Honors Comm Arts Interviewer; NCTE, GA Cncl Teachers of Eng, ASCD, GA Assn Supervision & Curr Dev, Natl Staff Dev Cncl; Phi Delta Kappa; Articles Published; GA Dept of Ed GA Runner-Up Teacher of Yr 1988; Brooks Cty STAR Teacher 1989; Comparative Ed Trip Soviet Union 1987; *office:* Brooks Cty Bd of Ed 704 N Talloaks Rd Quitman GA 31643

KEITH, JANICE DICKEY, 6th-8th Grade Teacher; *b:* Helena, MT; *m:* Roger; *ed:* (BS) Elem Ed, N MT Coll 1970; Grad Work Elem Ed, Cmptr Sci; *cr:* 6th Grade Teacher Conrad Schls 1970-71; 6th-8th Grade Teacher Brady Schls 1971-; *ai:* Jr HS Class Adv; 6th-8th Grade Sci Fair Coord; MT Ed Assn, NEA Mem 1970-; Nom Outstanding Young Educator Awd 1976; *office:* Brady Sch Box 166 Brady MT 59416

KEITHLEY, ILA MAY, Fifth Grade Elem Teacher; *b:* Palisade, CO; *m:* William Allen; *c:* Thomas R. Graham, Mathew A.; *ed:* (AB) Soc Sci, Univ of Denver 1949; Univ of N CO, Western St Coll, Univ of CO, CO St Univ, Univ of CA Los Angeles; *cr:* Asst St Educl Dir Rocky Mountain Farmers Union 1947-52; CO St Home & Trng Sch for Mentally Handicapped 1952-54; Prin/3rd-6th Grade Teacher La Sal UT 1954-55; 5th Grade Teacher Mesa CO 1955-56; Teacher Uravan CO 1956-59; 3rd Grade Teacher 1959-63, Kndgtn/Homebound Teacher 1963-64, Elem Teacher 1964- Sch Dist 51; *ai:* Dist Building Rep for Soc Sci Curr Dev; Family Math Instr; Teaching Gifted Summer Sch; CEA, NEA, PVEA, MVEA, LVEA Building Rep 1953-85; Phi Delta Kappa 1988-89; Broadway PTA; Rocky Mountain Farmers Union Asst Educl Dir 1948-52, Torch Bearer 1947; Redlands Cmmty Church Charter Mem; Mesa Cty Historical Society 1978-; Outstanding Teacher Awd Grand Junction Chamber of Commerce 1990; Nom Outstanding Teacher St of CO 1975; Nom Bd of Dir Teachers Credit Union 1990; *home:* 2211 Broadway Grand Junction CO 81503

KEJNER, MARTA, Spanish Teacher/Chair; *b:* Tucuman, Argentina; *ed:* (MS) Span Lang/Lit, Cordoba Univ 1956; Certificate Span/Eng, St Marys Univ 1980; Certified Advanced Placement Coll Instr, Trinity Univ 1983; *cr:* Span Teacher IPET No 10 1956-77; Span Teacher 1981-, Chairperson/Foreign Lang Dept 1983- Incarnate Word HS; *ai:* Span Contest Adv 1982-; Curr Comm Mem; Coll Bd of Ed Schlsp 1983; *office:* Incarnate Word HS 727 E Hildebrand San Antonio TX 78284

KELBLY, NORMA KAY, Teacher; *b:* Wooster, OH; *ed:* (BS) Health, TX A&M Univ 1983; Scndry Ed, Univ of N TX; *cr:* 6th/7th Grade Sci Teacher Bowie Jr HS 1984-; *office:* Bowie Jr HS 600 E 6th St Irving TX 75060

KELEMEN, ELIZABETH, Mathematics Department Teacher; *b:* Cumberland, KY; *ed:* (BA) Elem Ed, Thomas More Coll 1953; (MED) Elem Ed, Xavier Univ 1955; *cr:* Teacher St Vincent de Paul Sch 1946-48, St Thomas 1948-62, Christ the King 1962-67, St John the Baptist 1979-; *ai:* Youth Mininster; Stu Cncl & Field Trips Moderator; Math Coord; Cnslr; BSA God & Cntry Awd Preparation Teaching Coord 1974-76, St George 1975; Hands Across America Organized Group 1986; *home:* 5351 Dry Ridge Rd Cincinnati OH 45252

KELLAR, DIANNA DAVIS, English Teacher; *b:* Conway, AR; *m:* Johnny S.; *c:* Tony, Nolan; *ed:* (BSE) Soc Stud/Eng 1974, (MSE) Eng, 1979 Univ of Cntrl AR; *cr:* Eng Teacher Mena Public Schls 1974-79, Greenbrier Public Schls 1979-; *ai:* Delta Kappa Gamma; *office:* Greenbrier Public Sch School Dr Greenbrier AR 72058

KELLAR, TRACY PRATHER, English/Language Arts Teacher; *b:* Rockwall, TX; *m:* Bryan Leslie; *c:* Tara, Katie; *ed:* (AA) Elem Ed, Pearl River Jr Coll 1979; (BS) Elem Ed, MS St Univ 1981; In Service Trng Staff Dev; *cr:* 2nd Grade Teacher 1982, 5th Grade Teacher 1982- Pearl River Cntrl Mid Sch; *ai:* Discipline & Stu Cncl Comm; MS Assn of Educators Mem 1982-; PTO Teacher 1982-, Outstanding Teacher; 1st Baptist Church of Nicholson Personnel Graduation 1978-; *office:* Pearl River Cntrl Mid Sch PO Box 430 Mc Neill MS 39457

KELLER, CARMEN JOAN, Third Grade Teacher; *b:* San Antonio, TX; *m:* Gary W.; *c:* David, Traci; *ed:* (BS) Elem Ed, SW TX Univ 1961; *cr:* 1st Grade Teacher Westwood Terrace Elem 1961-66; 2nd/3rd Grade Teacher Thunderbird Hills Elem 1966-; *ai:* Grade Level Chairperson; Hospitality, Positively T-Bird, Paper-Work Comm; Sci Facilitator; Faculty Forum Rep; *office:* Thunderbird Hills Elem Sch 6003 Thunder Dr San Antonio TX 78228

KELLER, CAROL SKIERKOWSKI, Middle School Teacher; *b:* Michigan City, IN; *m:* Darrell; *c:* Todd, Scott, Jason; *ed:* (BS) Speech Therapy/Deaf Ed, Ball St Univ 1965; (MS) Deaf Ed, Butler 1973; *cr:* Teacher IN Sch for Deaf 1965-68, 1975-; *ai:* Rdng Core Comm; *office:* IN Sch for Deaf 1200 E 42nd St Indianapolis IN 46205

KELLER, CHRISTINA HARRIS, First Grade Teacher; *b:* Morganton, NC; *m:* Roy Westley; *c:* Jason W., Julie C.; *ed:* (BS) Elem Ed, Bob Jones Univ 1974; *cr:* 1st Grade Teacher Tabernacle Chrstn Sch 1974-; *office:* Tabernacle Chrstn Sch 201 Tabernacle Rd Morganton NC 28655

KELLER, CORINNE CONLON, English Teacher; *b:* Sacramento, CA; *m:* Richard Paul; *c:* Emily; *ed:* (BA) Eng, 1969, (MED) Eng Ed, 1988 Univ of FL; *cr:* Eng Teacher Conway Jr HS 1970-71, T W Pyle Jr HS 1971-79, N Marion Mid Sch 1981-85, Ft Clarke Mid Sch 1985-; *ai:* 8th Grade Asst Team Leader; Kappa Delta Pi, Alachua Cty Teachers Union; *office:* Fort Clarke Mid Sch 9301 NW 23rd Ave Gainesville FL 32601

KELLER, ELLEN FREEDKIN, English Teacher; *b:* Brooklyn, NY; *m:* Harvey; *c:* Robert Sheps, Nancy Sheps; *ed:* (BA) Eng, 1964, (MA) Eng/Ed, 1968 Brooklyn Coll; Rdng Brooklyn Coll; Womens Lit; Aesthetic Ed, Lincoln Center; *cr:* Teacher Winthrop Jr HS 1964-68; Teacher Canarsie HS 1968-70, 1977-; *ai:* Literary Magazine; SAT Tutoring; United Fed of Teachers Exec Bd 1984-; Frequent Letter to Editor; Mentor Teacher; *office:* Canarsie HS 1600 Rockaway Pkwy Brooklyn NY 11236

KELLER, GEORGE RAY, Phys Ed/Social Studies Teacher; *b:* Colorado Springs, CO; *m:* Christina Lyn Hammerstrom; *c:* Shae L.; *ed:* (BA) Phys Ed, Univ of S CO St Coll 1971; Spec Classes & Trng in Health Ed; *cr:* Admin Asst 1980-84, Acting Supt 1981-82, Teacher 1971- Miami Yoder Sch; *ai:* Miami Yoder Mid Sch & Stu Cncl Spon; Mid Sch Boys Bstkbl & Track Coach; All Star Girls Bsktbl Team Coach 1987; CO Traffic & Safety Ed Assn 1976-; CO Assn for Health, Phys Ed 1987-; Recreation & Dance; United Meth Church 1980-; Buffaloe Booster Club 1988-; CO Master Teacher Awd 1986; Nom for Cmmty Educl Leader Awd 1987-; All Star Girls Bsktbl Team Coach 1987; Veterans of Foreign Wars Voice of Democracy Awd 1984; *office:* Miami Yoder Sch Rt 1 Rush CO 80833

KELLER, JANIE CUMBERFORD, 5th Grade Teacher; *b:* Monterey Park, CA; *m:* Ed; *ed:* (BA) Liberal Stud, CA St Univ Bakersfield 1975; *cr:* 4th Grade Teacher Morrison Acad 1975-77; 6th Grade Teacher Norris Elem Sch 1977-89; 5th Grade Teacher Olive Drive Elem 1989-; *ai:* Active in Church Act; Leadership Comm; Olive Drive Staff; CA Teachers Assn 1977-; Fruitvale Cmmty Church & Sunday Sch Teachers 1977-79; Staff Awd for Outstanding Parent Comm in Dist; *office:* Olive Drive Elem Sch 7800 Darrin Bakersfield CA 93308

KELLER, MARY, English Teacher; *b:* Mobile, AL; *m:* Mark Dana; *c:* Ashley; *ed:* (BA) Eng, AL Coll of Liberal Arts 1969; *cr:* Eng Teacher River East Sch Dist 1971-74, Rossville HS 1984-; *ai:* Yrbk Adv; *office:* Rossville HS 800 S Main Rossville KS 66533

KELLER, SHARON KAY (DUKATZ), Fifth Grade Teacher; *b:* Minneapolis, MN; *m:* Gary Neil; *c:* Christopher, Melissa; *ed:* (BS) Elem Ed, Univ of MN 1968; (MS) Curr/Instruction, Coll of St Thomas 1984; *cr:* 3rd Grade Teacher Madison Elem 1968-70; 5th Grade Teacher Grandview Elem 1970-71, Delano Mid Sch 1971-; *ai:* Teacher Adv Comm; MAMLE 1988-; NEA, MEA 1971-.

KELLER, VIRGINIA DORITY, Fifth Grade Classroom Teacher; *b:* Greeley, CO; *m:* Randy; *ed:* (BA) Elem Ed/Early Chldhd, Univ of N CO 1980; *cr:* 4th Grade Teacher Fruita Elem 1980-81; 5th Grade Teacher Shelledy Elem 1981-; *office:* Shelledy Elem Sch 353 N Mesa Fruita CO 81521

KELLER, WILLIAM J., Elementary School Teacher; *b:* Hoboken, NJ; *m:* Mary Porter Ballard; *c:* Joe R., Kieran; *ed:* (BA) Eng Lit, St Peter Coll 1967; (MA) Anglo Irish Lit, Univ Coll Dublin Ireland 1973; *cr:* Adjunct Instr St Peters Coll 1968-69, 1972, 1975; Eng Teacher Hoboken HS 1977; Teacher Joseph F Brandt Elem Sch 1978-; *ai:* Hoboken Elks Lodge #74 Irishman of Yr 1987; Poetry Published; Monthly Bulletin Column; *office:* Joseph F Brandt Elem Sch 9th & Garden Sts Hoboken NJ 07030

KELLERS, ANNE O'NEILL, English Teacher; *b:* Hackensack, NJ; *m:* Jay Morgan; *ed:* (BA) Eng, Coll of St Elizabeth 1965; (MA) Eng, NY Univ 1971; *cr:* 1st Grade Teacher 1961-64, 7th Grade Teacher 1964-67 St Aloysius Elem Sch; Eng Teacher St Marys HS 1967-71, College of St Elizabeth 1970, Lincoln HS 1971-; *ai:* Contest Coord; NHS Adv; NEA, NJEA, JCEA; NJ Governors Teacher Recognition Awd 1986; Lincoln HS Hall of Fame 1981.

KELLEY, BEVERLY CASHUL, Reading/World History Teacher; *b:* Buffalo, NY; *m:* M. David; *c:* Kristopher; *ed:* (BS) Scndry Soc Stud, FL Atlantic Univ 1968; (MED) Educl Leadership Univ of W FL 1980; (EDSP) Admin/Supervision, NOVA 1985; *cr:* 5th Grade Teacher Eastpoint Elem Sch 1968-69; 7th/8th Grade Soc Stud Teacher Chapman Jr HS 1969-70; Title I Rdng Teacher Chapman Elem Sch 1972-80; Rdng/Soc Stud Teacher Apalachicola HS 1980-; *ai:* Frosh, Jr, Sr Class Spon; ECTA, NEA Mem 1968-; Delta Kappa Gamma Pres 1986-88; Philaco Womans Club Pres 1984-86; FL Fed of Womans Clubs (Dist Dir 1984-86, St Chm 1986-88); Stella Mara Guild Mem 1980-; Abstract Published; *home:* PO Box 405 26th St Apalachicola FL 32320

KELLEY, FRED JONATHAN, Science Teacher; *b:* Orlando, FL; *m:* Rita Mc Collough; *c:* Amy, Allison; *ed:* (BS) Bio/Sci, 1984, (MS) Phys Ed, 1989 Troy St; *cr:* Sci Teacher Red Level HS 1984-; *ai:* Var Boys & Girls Bsktbl, Var Girls Sftbl, Asst Ftbl Coach; Natl Fed of Coll Coaches, AL HS Athletic Assn, NEA, AL Ed Assn 1984-; Nom Red Level Teacher of Yr 1985-86; *office:* Red Level HS Brooklyn Rd Draw D Red Level AL 36474

KELLEY, GARY STEWART, Mathematics Teacher; *b:* Bay City, MI; *m:* Marian T. Wozneak; *c:* Ray, Colleen, Scott, Eileen, Andrew; *ed:* (BS) Math Ed, MI St 1969; (MS) Ed, Canisius Coll 1974; *cr:* Teacher Kenmore East HS 1970-71; 7th-9th Grade Math Teacher Hoover Mid Sch 1972-; *ai:* Extramural Boys/Girls Tennis, Boys Vlybl Coach; Mem Sch Planning Team, Faculty Cncl, Teacher Selection Comm; NY St United Teachers 1970-; Amherest Hockey Assn (Coach, Mgr) 1978-; Indian Y Guides Tribal Chief 1978-88; Finalist United Way Thanks to Teachers Awd 1990; Nom Erie Cty PTA Teacher of Yr; Hoover Mid Sch Teacher of Yr 1989-; Kenmore Teacher Center Grant; *office:* Hoover Mid Sch 249 Thorncliff Rd Kenmore NY 14150

KELLEY, GWENDOLYN JULIA, Second Grade Teacher; *b:* Indianapolis, IN; *m:* Woodrow Jr.; *c:* Natalie, Nichole; *ed:* (BS) Elem Ed, 1967, (MS) Elem Ed, 1972 IN St Univ; Grad Stud Rdng, Lang Art, Purdue Univ; *cr:* Kndgtn Teacher/2nd/3rd Grade Indianapolis Public Schls; *ai:* Effective Schls Steering Comm; Grade Level Chm; Instructional Focus Comm Chairperson; Supervising Stu Teacher; Indianapolis Ed Assn, IN St Teachers Assn, NEA 1967-; Alpha Kappa Alpha 1964-; 4-H Co-Leader 1984-; Love Chrstn Fellowship Church (Vacation Bible Sch Dir, Sunday Sch Bd Mem, Sunday Sch Teacher); Sch #67 Teacher of Yr 1990; Henrietta West Grant; Marva Collins Natl Teacher Trng Inst Grant 1990; Outstanding Young Women in America 1973; Outstanding Elem Teachers of America 1972; *home:* 2727 Orlando St Indianapolis IN 46208

KELLEY, HOUSTON DALE, Assistant Principal; *b:* Enterprise, AL; *m:* Faye Kilcrease; *c:* Brandon, Lindsey; *ed:* (BS) Elem Ed, 1979, (MS) Admin, 1981 Troy St Univ; *cr:* Airman USAF 1973-77; Teacher Ashford Elem 1979-87; Ashford HS 1987-89, Asst Prin Ashford HS 1989-; *ai:* Ftbl & Bsktbl Assn; Fellowship Chrstn Athletes; Cmptr Club Spon; Steering Comm AL Sch Accreditation; *office:* Ashford Elem Sch PO Drawer 5 Ashford AL 36312

KELLEY, KAREN MILLER, Sixth Grade Teacher; *b:* Rochester, NY; *m:* Larry D.; *c:* Kevin, Timothy; *ed:* (BA) K-6th Grade Ed/7th-9th Grade Eng, 1969, (MS) K-6th Grade Ed/ 7th-9th Grade Eng, 1971 SUNY Potsdam; *cr:* 4th Grade Teacher Madison Elem Sch 1969-70; 3rd/4th/6th Grade Teacher Chateaugay Cntrl Sch 1970-73; 6th Grade Teacher York Cntrl Sch 1979-; *ai:* Project Intervention Team; Mid Sch Comm; Faculty & Admin Liasion Comm; St Marys Church Jr HS Teacher 1982-88; Kiwanis Youth Hockey (Secy 1986, Pres 1987); *office:* York Cntrl Sch Rt 63 Retsof NY 14539

KELLNER, LAURA WARD, Algebra Teacher; *b:* San Benito, TX; *m:* Milton Frank; *c:* Martin W., Leslie D.; *ed:* (BS) Math/ Bus/Ed, TX A&I Univ 1967; (MS) Guidance/Counseling, Prairie View A&M 1975; *cr:* Math Teacher Thomas Edison Jr HS 1967-69, Sterling HS 1969-, Lee Coll 1974-; *ai:* Future Teachers of America, SADD Spon; Ed Advisory Cncl; NEA, TX St Teachers Assn, TX Classroom Teachers Assn 1967-; Houston Coaches Wives Pres 1976-84; Delta Kappa Gamma 1988-; Lady Ranger Booster Club Treas 1987-; Baytown Teacher of Yr 1988; Houston Chanel 13 Teachers Make a Difference 1989; Whos Who of Amer Women; *home:* 3020 Terry Ln Baytown TX 77521

KELLOGG, LORENA M., 5th Grade Teacher; *b:* Gove, KS; *m:* Wilmer; *cr:* 2nd Grade Teacher Plainville KS; 3rd Grade Teacher Palco KS; 2nd Grade Teacher Salina KS; 5th/6th Grade TeacheR Hays KS; *ai:* Alpha Delta Kappa VP, Chm; *home:* 201 Castillian Gardens Hays KS 67601

KELLY, AMY ADDISON, Science Teacher/Team Leader; *b:* Greensboro, NC; *m:* R. Fred Jr.; *ed:* (BA) Sociology, NC St Univ 1982; Teaching Certificate Ed/Sci, Meredith Coll 1983; FAST Teacher Trng I/II; *cr:* 6th/8th Grade Sci Teacher 1983-, Team Leader 1989- West Millbrook Mid Sch; *ai:* Sci Club 1988-89; NCAE, NEA Membership 1983-; Prof Dev Plan Awd 1987-89; *office:* West Millbrook Mid Sch 8115 Strickland Rd Raleigh NC 27615

KELLY, ANNE M., Fifth Grade Teacher; *b:* Mt Pleasant, PA; *ed:* (BS) Eng/Scndry, 1974, (MED) Rdng Specialist, 1977 CA St Coll; Grad Stud Elem Ed; *cr:* Teacher Briar Mid Sch 1974-77, Perkins HS 1976-77, Mt Pleasant Area Sch Dist 1977-; *ai:* PSEA 1977-; Womans Club of West Newton Pres 1986-88; *office:* Ramsay Elem Eagle St Mount Pleasant PA 15666

KELLY, BOBBY LEJUENE, SR., Science Department Chairperson; *b:* Birmingham, AL; *m:* Sarah A. Johnson; *c:* Roberta, Renita, Bobby Jr., Renaldo; *ed:* (BS) Bio, AL A&M Univ 1968; Cold Spring Harbor DNA Literacy Wkshp, Macys Bio Prep Wkshp, Phys Sci Wkshp, Univ of AL; *cr:* Teacher Greensboro Public East 1968-; *ai:* Sch Exec Comm Person; Temporary Band Dir; Sci Fair, Past Jr Class, Stu Cncl, Sci Club Spon; NSTA, NEA, AL Ed Assn 1968-; Hale Cty Teachers Assn 1968-; *office:* Greensboro Public Sch East PO Box 460 Greensboro AL 36744

KELLY, CAROL J. BIGG, Kindergarten Teacher; *b:* Ottumwa, IA; *m:* Kevin A.; *ed:* (BA) Elem Ed, WM Penn Coll 1976; *cr:* Kndgtn Teacher Pekin Elem Sch 1976-; *ai:* Phase III Planning Comm; Early Chldhd Comm; NEA, IA St Ed Assn 1976-; Pekin Ed Assn Treas 1988-; TTT Camp Chm 1984-86; *office:* Pekin Elem Sch RR Packwood IA 52580

KELLY, CHERYL SAWYER, First Grade Teacher; *b:* Atmore, AL; *m:* James C.; *c:* Wesley, Will; *ed:* (BS) Elem Ed, 1971, (MS) Elem Ed, 1979 Troy St Univ; *cr:* 6th Grade Teacher Monroeville Mid Sch 1971-74; Kndgtn Teacher 1974-78, 1st Grade Teacher 1978- Monroeville Elem Sch; *ai:* NEA, AL Ed Assn 1971-; Delta Kappa Gamma Secy 1988-; Monroeville Little League 1987-; 1st Baptist Church of Monroeville Sunday Sch Teacher; Belles Lettres Study Club Jr Club Spon 1984-86; Cub Scouts Den Mother 1985-86; *office:* Monroeville Elem Sch 410 S Mt Pleasant Ave Monroeville AL 36460

KELLY, DARLENE WARREN, 3rd-4th Grade Teacher; *b:* Eskridge, KS; *m:* Billy C.; *c:* Karl James, Kay Lynn Usrey, Janet Elaine; *ed:* (BA) Music Ed, 1953; (MS) Elem Ed, 1969 Emporia St Univ; Univ of HI; KS St Univ; Washburn Univ; *cr:* Elem Instrumental Music Teacher Wellington KS 1953-56; Music/ Math Teacher Pahala HI 1956-58; Math/Govt Teacher Lewisville Jr HS 1959-60; Music Teacher Eskridge HS 1967-69; 3rd & 4th Grade Teacher Stout Elem 1969-; *ai:* Math Club & Contest Spon Stout Intermediate Grades; NEA/KNEA 1969-85; GSA Ldr 1972-74; BSA Volunteer 1969-75; *home:* 2530 Valley Glen Ct Topeka KS 66614

KELLY, FLORA M., Kindergarten Principal; *b:* Brookhaven, MS; *m:* Phillip Earl Sr.; *c:* Louwlynn V., Phillip Earl III; *ed:* (BS) Elem Ed, 1963, (MS) Rdng 1974, (MS) Admin, 1984 Jackson St; *cr:* Teacher Mullins Elem Sch 1963-70; Asst Prin Mamie Martin Elem Sch 1970-86; Prin Brookhaven Kndgtn 1986-; *ai:* Brookhaven Staff Dev Comm; Adult Ed Tutor 1989-; ASCD Mem 1970-; Phi Delta Kappa Mem 1974-; For Youth Dev Mem 1987-; Jackson St Univ Alumni Assn VP 1989-; Fellowship Jackson St Univ 1968; Brookhaven Schls Teachers Appreciation Grant 1974; *home:* 2433 Brignal Rd Brookhaven MS 39601

KELLY, GLADYS BERNICE (WEBER), Second Grade Teacher; *b:* Ashley, ND; *m:* Thomas Harold; *c:* Cynthia L. Heupel, Charlotte L. Andersson, Juliet I. Parten; *ed:* Undergrad Valley City St Teachers Coll 1955-56; (BS) Elem Ed, Ellendale Coll 1967; (MS) Supvr Elem Classroom, Northern St Univ 1974; Portland St Univ, St Univ of OR, Univ of OR, Univ of La Verne; *cr:* Teacher Kisslingberry No 30 1952-53, Beresinia No 23 1953-56, Richland No 37 1956-57, Savo No 3 1957-58, Coos Bay Public Sch No 9 1960-; *ai:* Report Cards, Textbooks, Classroom Comm; Art, Music, Math, Sci, Phys Ed Wkshps; Creative Writing; Onward to Excl Comm Mem; NEA 1952-, OR Ed Assn, Coos Bay Ed Assn, SD Ed Assn, ND Ed Assn; Leaders of Amer Elem & Scndry 1971; Outstanding Teachers Awd 1971; *office:* Milner Crest Sch 13th & Hemlock Coos Bay OR 97420

KELLY, HAZEL E., Jr HS Math Teacher; *b:* Jamaica, NY; *ed:* (BA) Math, St Johns Univ 1976; Advanced Stud Lang Art, Fnds in Rdng II, Diagnosing Pupil Learning Needs; *cr:* 6th Grade Rdng/Lang Art Teacher 1976-77, 5th/6th Grade Lang Art Teacher 1977-79, 6th Grade Math/Sci/Health/Religion Teacher 1979-83, 6th Grade Teacher 1983-84, 6th-8th Grade Math Teacher 1984- Sacred Heart Sch; *ai:* Math Club & Math Tutoring 1979-; Elem Math Cncl 1984-; NCEA 1976-; Awd of Merit Office of Cath Ed 1986; *office:* Sacred Heart Sch 115-50 221 St Cambria Heights NY 11411

KELLY, JOE B., English Teacher; *b:* Los Angeles, CA; *m:* Cynthia; *c:* Erin, Cammie; *ed:* (BA) Eng, 1967, (MA) Ed, 1968 CA St Univ Long Beach; Grad Stud; *cr:* Eng Teacher Palos Verdes HS 1968-; *ai:* Cross Cntry Coach, CA St Champions Division I 1987-89; Track Coach; CA Coaches Assn, CA Coach of Yr 1988; Natl HS Athletic Coaches Assn, Western US Coach of Yr 1988; CA Interscholastic Fed, S Section, Service Awd 1989; Article Published; *office:* Palos Verdes HS 600 Cloyden Rd Palos Verdes Pnsla CA 90274

KELLY, JOLIE ANNE, Seventh Grade Teacher; *b:* Atlanta, GA; *ed:* (BSED) Elem Ed, 1973, (MED) Elem Ed, 1980 GA St Univ; Data Collector Trng; Numerous Staff Dev Mid Sch Courses Cmptrs, Lang, Math; *cr:* 6th/7th Grade Teacher Grayson Elem 1973-74; 6th Grade Teacher 1974-82, 7th Grade Teacher 1982- Snellville Mid Sch 1982-; *ai:* Team Leader; Rock Eagle, Discipline, Awds Day, Talent Show, Motivation/Academic Improvement Comms; Jr Beta Club, Stu Cncl Spon; Assist Band & Dances; Coach Stu Drill Team; Coord for Needy Families; Organizer Craft/Projects for Cmmty; Tutoring Sessions; Gwinnet Cty Ed Assn, GA Ed Assn, NEA, PTA 1973-; Kappa Delta Pi 1980-; Jaycette Mem; Teacher of Yr Snellville Mid Sch; Judge Natl Baton Twirling Assn; *office:* Snellville Mid Sch 3155 E Pate Rd Snellville GA 30278

KELLY, LAURA JEAN, Jr HS Mathematics Teacher; *b:* Florence, AL; *ed:* (BS) Industrial Chem/Math, Univ of N AL 1984; *cr:* Math/Physics Teacher Marshill Bible Sch 1986-88; Math Teacher Avalon Mid Sch 1988-; *ai:* Math Team & Sci Olympiad Coach; Annual & Honor Day Comms; NCTM 1988-; *office:* Avalon Mid Sch 1400 E Avalon Ave Muscle Shoals AL 35661

KELLY, LILLIE BROWN, Science Teacher; *b:* Birmingham, AL; *m:* Joseph Edward Jr.; *c:* Catherine, John, Peter; *ed:* (BS) Bio, Judson Coll 1975; (MAED) Ed, Univ of AL Birmingham 1978; Medical Technology, Baptist Medical Centers Sch of Medical Technology 1976; Auburn Univ, SE Bible Coll; *cr:* Health Occupations Intern Cullman Cty Area Voc Center 1976-78; Health Occupations Teacher Lamar Cty Area Voc Sch 1978-79; Teacher Auburn HS 1979-82, Okaloosa Chrstn Acad 1983-84, Shades Mtn Chrstn Sch 1987-; *ai:* Sci Club Adv; AL Jr Acad of Sci Adv to St Pres; Church Choir 1970-; Merrill Teachers Advisory Cncl; Charles E Merill Publishing Prof Consultant in Teacher Ed; AL St Dept of Ed 1978-82; Teacher Intern; Teacher Corps; US Dept of Ed 1976-78; *office:* Shades Mtn Chrstn Sch 2281 Old Tyler Rd Birmingham AL 35226

KELLY, MARTHA JEAN (MC COY), Science Teacher; *b:* Olive Hill, KY; *c:* Victoria, Rachel; *ed:* (BS) Bio/Cmptr Sci, 1973, (MA) Scndry Ed, 1980 Morehead St Univ; Chem & Physics; *cr:* Teacher West Carter Cty HS 1973-85, Arcanum HS 1985-; *ai:* SADD Club Adv; Arcanum-Butler Classroom Teachers Assn Pres; PTO Talent Show Chairperson; Summer Youth Girls Sftbl Team Mgr; KEA, NEA 1973-85; ABCTA, OEA, NEA (Pres 1989-) 1985-; OH Sci Teachers Assn 1988-; Eastern Star Chaplin Star Point 1980-; OH Highway Safety Awd to SADD Club & Adv 1989-; *office:* Arcanum HS 310 N Main St Arcanum OH 45304

KELLY, MARY BILLE, Second Grade Teacher; *b:* Casper, WY; *ed:* (BA) Elem Ed, Univ of WY 1972; (MBM) Bus Management, Lesley Coll 1976; *cr:* 5th Grade Teacher 1972-74, Chapter I Lang Teacher 1974-75 Cole Elem Sch; 2nd Grade Teacher Baggs Elem

Sch 1975-; *ai:* Curr Cncl Gifted & Talented Comm; Cheyenne Teachers Assn, WY Ed Assn 1972-; Delta Kappa Gamma (1st VP, Pres) 1976-; Laramie Cty United Way Rural Division 1988-; SE WY Mental Health Bd Mem 1989-; Airport His Comm Public Relations 1990; Corral of Westerners Secy 1974-; Civil Air Patrol 1989-; *office:* Baggs Elem Sch 3705 Cheyenne Cheyenne WY 82001

KELLY, MARY LOU, Science Teacher; *b:* Moyers, WV; *m:* Forrest R.; *c:* Michael, Mark; *ed:* (BS) Bio, Capital Univ 1952; Towson St, Univ of MD, Azusa Pacific; *cr:* Phys Ed/Sci Teacher Clarksville Jr HS 1952-58; Sci Teacher Glenelg HS 1958-59; Sci/Soc Stud Teacher Clarksville Mid Sch 1967; Sci Teacher Glenwood Mid Sch 1967-; *ai:* HCEA, MSTA, NEA; PTA Teacher Rep 1988-.

KELLY, NANCY SUE (PIERSON), English/Media Teacher; *b:* Tuscola, IL; *m:* Terry L.; *c:* Jeff, Jami; *ed:* (BS) Eng, 1970, (BS) Elem, 1983 E IL Univ; K-12th Grade Media Prof Departmentalized Elem & Jr HS Lang Art & Soc Stud; *cr:* Unit Librarian Sherrard HS 1969-70; HS Eng/Media Teacher KS Unit #3 1971-; *ai:* Yrbk, Drama Club, Sch Play, Lib Club, Class Spon; Rdng is Fundamental; Gifted Prgm; IL Teachers of Eng, IL Ed Assn, NEA; *office:* Kansas HS Front St Kansas IL 61933

KELLY, NICHOLAS JUSTIN, Fifth Grade Teacher; *b:* Little Falls, NY; *m:* Jean Long; *c:* Jane Guzewich, Nicholas, William, David; *ed:* (BS) Public Relations/Journalism, Utica Coll 1958; (MS) Elem Ed, SUNY Oneonta 1962; Prin Cert, NY St 1965; *cr:* 6th Grade Teacher Old Forge NY 1958-60; 6th Grade Teacher 1960-80, 5th Grade Teacher 1980- Clinton NY; *office:* Clinton Cntrl Sch 75 Chenango Ave Clinton NY 13323

KELLY, PAULA RAMSEY, Biology Teacher; *b:* Hamilton, OH; *ed:* (BA) Sci/Psych, 1962, Teaching Cert Sci, 1969 TX Chrstn Univ; (MA) Sci Ed, W GA Coll 1986; Various Post Masters Courses; *cr:* Bacteriologist City of Ft Worth 1964-71; General Phys Sci/Life Sci/Anatomy/Physiology/Bio/Health Ed Teacher Ft Worth Ind Sch Dist 1972-85; Gen Phys Sci/Chem/Bio III Levels Teacher Griffin Spalding Sch Dist 1985; *ai:* Griffin HS Hospital & Homebound Instr; Griffin HS Environmental Club Adv; NSTA, GA Sci Teachers, NABT, AFT, Griffin Spalding Sci Teachers; Kappa Delta Province Pres 1966-71; *office:* Griffin HS 1617 W Poplar St Griffin GA 30223

KELLY, R. MAXINE, Fifth Grade Teacher; *b:* Johnstown, PA; *m:* Tom; *c:* Laura A.; *ed:* (BS) Elem Ed, IN Univ of PA 1964; Grad Stud Univ of Pittsburgh, Shippensburg Univ, IN Univ of PA, Penn St Univ; *cr:* 2nd/3rd Grade Remedial Rdng Teacher Ligonier Valley Sch Dist 1964-66, 1967-71; Remedial Rdng Teacher Hempfield Area Sch Dist 1971-72; Remedial Rdng Teacher 1972-76, 3rd-5th Grade Teacher 1976- Ligonier Valley Sch Dist; *ai:* PSEA, NEA, LVEA 1964-; Ligonier Valley AFS Intnl/Intercultural Prgms (Pres 1985-87, Secy 1987-); *office:* Laurel Valley Elem Sch Ligonier Valley Sch Dist R D 1 New Florence PA 15944

KELLY, RUBYE M., French/Eng Teacher of Gifted; *b:* Albuquerque, NM; *m:* James Elvis; *c:* Kristopher A., Austin B.; *ed:* (BA) Eng, Hardin-Simmons Univ 1970; (MS) Counseling Psych, Amer Technological Univ 1985; *cr:* Eng Teacher Cooper HS 1971-73; Eng Teacher/Dept Chm J L Williams Jr HS 1980-85; Fr Teacher 1986-, Eng Teacher of Gifted & Talented 1989- Copperas Cove HS; *ai:* Fr Club & Jr Class Spon; Supts Advisory, Campus Planning, Mastery Learning Inservice Comms; Copperas Cove Chamber of Commerce Mem; Exch Club Educator of Month 1984; *office:* Copperas Cove HS PO Box 580 Copperas Cove TX 76522

KELLY, SHIRLEY TATRO, Mathematics Teacher; *b:* Postville, IA; *m:* John; *c:* Cynthia, Kyle; *ed:* (BA) Math/Lib Sci, Univ N IA 1970; Working Towards Masters Edu cl Admin; *cr:* Math Teacher Charles City HS 1970-; *ai:* NHS Spon; Instructional & Prof Dev Assn Comm; Charles City Ed Assn Pres 1980-81, 1987-88; NCTM, IA Cncl Teachers of Math, IA Ed Assn, NEA; Alpha Delta Kappa Treas 1990-; ASCD; Charles City Cmmty Grant Prgm Excl in Ed Awd 1987-88; *office:* Charles City Sr HS Salsbury Dr Charles City IA 50616

KELLY, STEPHAN A., Ind Arts/Technology Teacher; *b:* Cincinnati, OH; *m:* Susan Louise Smith; *c:* Elissa, Patrick, Theresa, Tammi, Andrew; *ed:* (BSED) Industrial Ed, 1971, (MED) Industrial Ed, 1972 Miami Univ OH; (PhD) Industrial Ed, MI St Univ 1986; Robotics, S OH Coll Cincinnati; Autocad-Inacomp Troy MI; Cmptrs Admin Internship, EEEL Battle Creek Public Schls; Technology Ed, St Dept of MI Kalamazoo; *cr:* Ind Arts/Tech Ed Teacher Battle Creek Public Schls 1972-; *ai:* Tech Ed Comm Chm; Sch Improvement Comm Chm; Battle Creek Public Schls Dist Sch Improvement Comm; W K Kellogg Jr HS Sch Improvement Comm Chm; MEA, NEA, BCEA Bldg Rep 1973-75; AIAA, ITEA MI Teacher of Yr 1985; PDK; EPT; Parish Cncl Pres 1984-86; Teacher Incentive Awd 1986; PhD Dissertation; Design Copyright; *office:* W K Kellogg Jr HS 60 W Van Buren Battle Creek MI 49017

KELLY, SUSAN MARIE, 5th-8th Grade Science Teacher; *b:* Peoria, IL; *ed:* (BS) Elem Ed, 1980, (MS) Elem Ed, 1982 Bradley Univ; Sci, Gifted Ed, Admin; *cr:* 3rd/4th Grade Teacher Monroe Avenue Sch 1979; 4th Grade Teacher St Mark Grade Sch 1980-89; 3rd/4th Grade Teacher Bradley Univ Gifted Inst 1984-; 5th-8th Grade Sci Teacher St Mark Grade Sch 1989-; Teacher Participant Lakeview Museum of Arts & Sci 1990; *ai:* 5th-8th Grade Sci Fair Spon; NCEA Mem; Energy Unit Published 1982; *office:* St Mark Grade Sch 711 N Underhill Peoria IL 61606

KELLY, TERESA BAKER, English Teacher; *b:* Tallassee, AL; *m:* John W. III; *c:* J. Wesley IV, Ryan; *ed:* (BS) Eng/Lib Sci, Univ of AL 1971; (MA) Eng, Livingston 1987; Humanities Institute; Cambrid Ge England Summer 1985; Amer Helenie Univ Athens Greece Summer 1987; *cr:* Librarian Wallace Comm Coll 1974-75; Teacher/Newspaper Adv Westside Mid Sch 1975-; *ai:* Newspaper Adv; Spon-Natl Jr Honor Society; Eng Dept Chairperson; Selma Ed Assn, NEA, AL Ed Assn, NCTE, AL Cncl Eng Teachers; Participant NEH Summer Seminar His & Literature Prejudice 1965; *office:* Westside Middle School 1701 Summerfield Rd Selma AL 36701

KELLY, WILLIAM DAVID, JR., Social Studies Teacher; *b:* Philadelphia, PA; *ed:* (BS) Soc Sci, 1968, (MS) Soc Sci, 1978 Temple Univ; Music/Choral Trng, Westminster Choir Coll Princeton; *cr:* Teacher Overbrook HS 1968-69, Phoenixville Jr HS 1969-; *ai:* 7th-9th Grade Pep Club, Stu Cncl Moderator; Producer Annual Spring Musical Show; Philadelphia Art Alliance Artist Mem 1972-; Christ Church Music Comm 1970-; Univ of PA Glee Club Honorary Mem 1987-; Musical Fund Society Philadelphia Bd of Dirs 1980-88; Teachers Medal Freedoms Fnd Valley Forge 1976; Spirit of Philadelphia Awd by WCAV-TV 1984.

KELSCH, BRAD JAMES, 4th Grade Teacher; *b:* Idaho Falls, ID; *m:* Marlene; *c:* Kelli, Cortney; *ed:* (BA) Elem Ed, ID St Univ 1975; (MS) General Ed, Gonzaga Univ 1979; Cmptrs, His, Gifted Ed, Sci, Psych, Math; *cr:* 6th Grade Teacher Johnson Elem 1975-76; 5th Grade Teacher 1976-85, 6th Grade Teacher 1985-87, 4th Grade Teacher 1987- Plummer Elem; *ai:* Elem Cmptr Coord; 5th Grade Girls & Boys Bsktbl Coach; NEA Delegate 1975-; Libby Little League Coach 1990; Kiwanis Coach 1980-81; *office:* Plummer Sch 247 Indian Head Rd Libby MT 59923

KELSHAW, RONALD H., Guidance Counselor; *b:* Hazleton, PA; *m:* Lisa Stoudt; *c:* Lauren; *ed:* (BA) Sociology, Moravian Coll 1974; (MED) Scndry Sch Counseling, Kutztown Univ 1977; Elem Sch Counseling Cert Lehigh Univ 1981; Grad Work Penn St Univ; *cr:* Sch Cnslr Bloomsburg Mid Sch 1977-85, Bloomsburg Memorial Elem Sch 1985-87, Weatherly Area HS 1987-; *ai:* Stu Assistance Comm Chm; HS Envirothon Team Adv; Public Relations Comm; PA Sch Cnslrs Assn, PA St Ed Assn 1977-; Cntrl Susquehanna Cnslrs Assn 1977-85; Save Our Local Environment II 1987-; Zion Evangelical Luth Church Choir 1983-; Helped Develop Alternative Ed Prgm Potential Dropouts; Served Multidisciplinary Team for Prevention & Management of Child Abuse; Helped Develop Stu Assistance Prgm; *office:* Weatherly Area HS Spring & E Main Sts Weatherly PA 18255

KELSO, SANDRA EDWARDS, HS Mathematics Teacher; *b:* Creston, IA; *m:* William; *c:* Brent W., Derrek R.; *ed:* (BS) Math, 1968, (MS) Guidance/Counseling, 1972 IA St Univ; Grad Stud Cmptr Usage, Cmptr Programming, Thinking Skills, Talented & Gifted; *cr:* HS Math Teacher/Counselor Murray Cmmty Sch 1969-71; Jr/Sr HS Math Teacher Clarke Cmmty Schls 1975-; *ai:* Jr & Frosh Class Spon; Clarke Cmmty Ed Assn, IA St Ed Assn, NEA 1975-; United Meth Church (Ed Comm 1983-86, 1987-) 1955-; *office:* Clarke Cmmty Schls 800 N Jackson Osceola IA 50213

KELTNER, BARBARA LISS, Third Grade Teacher; *b:* New York, NY; : Gerrold Burney; *c:* Micahl J.; *ed:* (BA) Ed/Lit, Univ of CO Boulder 1965; (MS) Curr Design, Cal Poly Tech Univ 1976; Cmptr Sci, Cal Poly Tech Univ 1981; *cr:* Cmptr Sci Instr Univ of La Verne CA Elem Sch 1983-88; 1st/3rd Grade Teacher Camino Grove Sch 1965-; *ai:* Stu Cncl Adv Spon; CTA, NEA 1965-; Honorary Service Camino Grove PTA 1986; Wrote Book 1986; *office:* Camino Grove Sch 700 Camino Grove Arcadia CA 91006

KELTNER, MARC E., Mathematics Department Teacher; *b:* Indianapolis, IN; *m:* Sarah Dolliver; *ed:* (BA) Physics/Math, Hanover Coll 1968; (MS) Physics, 1970, (MS) Math, 1974 SD Mines; Geophysics/Geology, Univ of Tulsa; Scndry Ed, Metro St Coll; *cr:* Math Dept Teacher Westridge Mid Sch 1988, Judson HS 1988-; *ai:* Math Lab Supvr; NEA, TX St Teachers Assn, Judson Teacher Assn 1988; Argonne Natl Lab Fellowship 1969; Articles Published Argonne Natl Lab; Whos Who in South & Southwest 1985; *office:* Judson HS 9142 FM 78 Converse TX 78109

KELTS, DAVID WILLIAM, Fifth Grade Teacher; *b:* Beaumont, CA; *ed:* (BA) His, Claremont Mc Kenna Coll 1970; Teaching Cert/Internship Claremont Graduate Sch 1970-72; Sci, Univ of CO; Cmptr, Fresno Pacific Coll; *cr:* 3rd Grade Teacher Lajes Elem Sch 1978-79, M C Perry Elem Sch 1979-80; 5th Grade Teacher Mc Perry Elem Sch 1980-88, Sollars Elem Sch 1988-; *ai:* Educators Day Comm; Star Lab Comm; Sch Advisory Comm; Cmptr Club; North East Asia Teachers Assn Faculty Rep Spokesperson 1980-87 & 1990; PTO (VP 1989-, Treas 1986-88); Chapel Cncl Pres 1986-88; Around-Japan Youth Boat Trip Spon 1980-88; Sustained Superior Teaching Awd 1985-83/1985-88; Special Service Awd 1988-89; *home:* Box 7702 APO San Francisco CA 96519

KEMMER, JACQUELYN J., Language Arts Teacher; *b:* Ottumwa, IA; *m:* Lawrence M.; *c:* David, Martha Kemmer-Contreras, Jane A.; *ed:* (BA) Eng/Speech/Drama, Wm Penn Coll 1961; Drake Univ, CO St Univ, Univ of N CO, Univ of Denver; *cr:* Eng Teacher Maxwell HS 1961-62; Lang Art Teacher Nathan Weeks Jr HS 1962-63; Eng/Drama Teacher Des Moines Tech HS 1965-77; Lang Art/Drama Teacher Estes Park Mid Sch 1977-; *ai:* Mid Sch Drama Coach; 6th Grade Team Leader; Lang Art Curr Comm; Dist Staff Recognition Comm Chm; Delta Kappa Gamma, CO Lang Art Society, NCTE; Museum of NM, Museum of N AZ; CLAS Spring Conference Presenter 1987; W Regional Mid Sch Conference Presenter 1990.

KEMMERLIN, STEPHEN KEARSE, Driver Education Teacher; *b:* Bamberg, SC; *ed:* (BS) Phys Ed, Univ of SC 1978; (MS) Cnslr Ed, SC St Coll 1983; *cr:* Teacher/Coach Hunter-Kinard-Tyler HS 1978-85, Wade Hampton HS 1985-; *ai:* Head Var Bsbl & Asst Var Ftbl Coach; Palmetto Teacher Assn 1986-; SC Coaching Assn 1978-; Natl Fed of Coaches 1980-; Methodist Mens Club 1990; All Star Bsbl Coach 1989; *home:* 407 Everett St Hampton SC 29924

KEMP, KATHLEEN BERNADETTE, Social Studies/Art Teacher; *b:* Minneapolis, MN; *ed:* (BA) His, Mt St Marys Coll 1955; Additional Trng & Ed, Univ of CA Los Angeles, Pepperdine, Loyola Univ Los Angeles, Reiss-Davis Clinic; *cr:* 2nd-6th Grade Teacher Archdioceses of Los Angeles 1955-60; 4th-6th Grade Nongraded Team Teacher El Mirino 1960-74; K-12th Grade Eng Teacher/Prin New Era K-12th Grade Sch Addis Ababa Ethiopia 1974-75; 6th-8th Grade His/Art Teacher Culver City Mid Sch 1974-; *ai:* Culver City Teachers Assn (Secy 1988-, Pres 1979-84), Who Awd 1980, 1983; Westside Teachers United (Pres, Chairperson) 1980-; Raintree Condominiums Assn (Pres, Bd Mem) 1977-88; Fulbright Hayes Fellowship Univ of CA Los Angeles 1972; Wrote Many Articles on Team Teaching & Cooperative Learning 1968-74; *office:* Culver City Mid Sch 4601 Elenda St Culver City CA 90230

KEMP, MARY ANN, Sixth Grade Math Teacher; *b:* Sylvania, GA; *ed:* (BS) Elem Ed, GA Southern Coll 1957; Numerous Courses; *cr:* 6th Grade Teacher Sidney Lanier 1957-75, Risley Mid Sch 1975-; *ai:* Team Leader Interdisciplinary Teaching Team; Math Curr Revision, Staff Dev, Teacher of Yr Comm; Tutorial Prgm; Stu Cncl Adv; Glynn Cty Assn of Educators; GA Assn of Educators; NEA, Kappa Delta Pi; 1st Presbyn Church (Elder 1985-88, Clerk of Session 1985-87); Amer Red Cross; Meth Home for Children & Youth Auxiliary Membership; Mental Health Assn; The Salvation Army; Parent Teacher Student Assn; Risley Mid Teacher of Yr 1981-82; Contribution to GA Congress of Parents & Teachers Given by Risley Mid in Honor of Mary Ann Kemp 1983; Awd of Dedication Risley Mid Stu Cncl 1986-87; Non Presidential Awds Excl in Math Teaching 1990; *home:* 202 Norman St Brunswick GA 31520

KEMP, PATRICIA, Language Arts Teacher; *b:* Baltimore, MD; *ed:* (BA) Ed, 1968, (MED) Ed, 1975 Salisbury St Coll; Post Grad Stud Western MD Coll; *cr:* Teacher Westminster Jr HS 1968-71, Westminster East Mid Sch 1971-; *ai:* Discipline Comm; Mission Statement Comm; Carroll Cty Ed Assn; MD St Teacher Assn; NEA; Team Leader; *office:* East Mid Sch Longwell Ave Westminster MD 21157

KEMP, PATRICIA MARY, Second Grade Teacher; *b:* Milwaukee, WI; *m:* Croydon L.; *ed:* Russian, Univ of Moscow 1966; (BA) Elem Ed/Russian, MI St Univ 1967; (MA) Rdng, Cardinal Stritch Coll 1977; Various Courses & Wkshps Rdng, General Ed, Cmptrs; *cr:* 5th Grade Teacher 1967-68, 2nd Grade Teacher 1969- Greendale Sch Dist; *ai:* Unit Leader Highland View Sch; GEA Exec Bd; *office:* Greendale Sch Dist 5900 S 51st St Greendale WI 53129

KEMPKER, LORI ANN, Business Education Teacher; *b:* Jefferson City, MO; *m:* Michael Lee; *c:* Aaron, Brooke; *ed:* (BA) Bus Ed, 1984, (MS) Bus Ed, 1988 Univ of MO Columbia; *cr:* Bus Teacher Blair Oaks HS 1984-; *ai:* FBLA, Stu Cncl, Sr Class Spon; Faculty Advisory Comm Mem; MO Bus Ed Assn, MO Voc Assn 1985-; Delta Pi Epsilon 1988-; Cmmty Teachers Assn Mem; *office:* Blair Oaks HS 6124 Falcon Ln Jefferson City MO 65101

KEMPSON, G. TIM, Science Teacher; *b:* Elizabeth, NJ; *m:* Susan G. Long; *c:* Sibyl, Timothy, Meredith; *ed:* (BA) Soc Sci, Elon Coll 1966; (MA) Environmental Stud, Montclair St Coll 1975; *cr:* Sci Teacher Bloomingdale Public Schls 1966-69, Butler Public Schls 1969-; *ai:* Stu Cncl Adv; DC Trip Teacher; Fairview Lake Environmental Ed Teacher; Phi Delta Kappa Mem 1976-; NEA Local Grievance Chm 1980-; Vernon Township Environmental Commission Mem 1990-; *office:* Richard Butler Sch Pearl Pl Butler NJ 07405

KENDALL, ARNOLD VAN, 8th Grade Science Teacher; *b:* Chicago, IL; *m:* Vanessa Lamar; *c:* Gerald, Ahmand, Aiyana, Nyia, Arnold; *ed:* (BA) Ed, Univ of MA 1972; (MA) Ed, Univ of IL 1981; Real Estate Salesmanship License Awd; *cr:* 8th Grade Teacher Mary Lyon 1975-82; 7th/8th Grade Teacher Parker Acad 1982-89; 8th Grade Teacher Shakespeare 1989-; *ai:* Bsktbl Asst Coach, Bsbl Coach Parker Acad; N Kenwood Cmmty Cncl Bd of Dir 1984-; Local Sch Cncl Shakespeare Teacher Rep; *home:* 4551 S Ellis Chicago IL 60653

KENDALL, JAMES E., English Teacher; *b:* Aberdeen, SD; *m:* Carol Redlin; *c:* Thomas, Jim, David; *ed:* (BS) Eng/Psych, Dickinson St Univ 1972; Grad Stud Eng & Ed, ND St Univ, Univ of ND, Minot St Univ, Valley City St Univ; *cr:* USAF 1966-70; Lang Art Instr Oakes Public HS 1972-73; Employment Mgr Field Enterprises Educl Corporation 1973-78; Lang Art Instr Oakes Public HS 1978-; *ai:* Asst Girls Var Bsktbl & 9th Grade Girls Bsktbl Coach; At-Risk Eng Curr Developer; N Cntrl Accreditation Comm Mem; HS Eng Curr Dev Comm; NHS, Amer Legion Oratorical Contest, VFW Voice of Democracy Adv; NCTE, Oakes Educl Assn, ND Educl Assn, NEA 1978-; Grace Luth Church Congregation Pres 1987; Amer Legion 1972-; ND Ofcls Assn 1988-; *home:* 909 Dogwood Ave Oakes ND 58474

KENDALL, MARIA PERICO, Spanish Instructor; *b:* Bogota, Colombia; *m:* Bernard H.; *c:* Begona M., Cinthia A., John A.; *ed:* (BAED) Span, Wichita St Univ 1974; Span Lit; Travelled with Students Numerous Countries for Further Ed; *cr:* Span Instr Billings West HS 1974; *ai:* Span Club Spon; AFS Club Active

Adv; MALT, MEA Building Rep; GSA Leader 1970-79; Church Org; Three Foreign Lang Grants to Develop Foreign Lang Festival; Key Club Outstanding Teacher West HS 1988-89; *office:* Billings West HS 2201 St Johns Ave Billings MT 59102

KENDALL, SARAH BROOKS, Third Grade Teacher; *b:* Shelbyville, KY; *c:* Gordona, Tonja, Shelby; *ed:* Grad Stud Univ of Louisville; *cr:* Rdng Instructional Coord 1981-87, 3rd Grade Teacher 1966- Southside Elem; *ai:* 3rd Grade Christmas Play Dir; Curr Writing, Safety Patrol, Guidance, Textbook Adoption Comm; Grade Group Coord; Shelbyville Ed Assn VP 1968; Shelby Cty Ed Assn, KY Ed Assn, Northside Southside PTA Secy; Highland Baptist Church (Sunday Sch Teacher, Homebound Dir, Church Trng Dir, Mission Organizations, Youth Leader); Order of Eastern Star; Nom Southside Schls Teacher of Yr; Southside KY Teacher Recognition Banquet Rep; *office:* Southside Elem Sch 800 8th St Shelbyville KY 40065

KENDALL, SUSAN SHINNICK, English Teacher; *b:* Dixon, IL; *m:* Prescott James III; *c:* Sean, Ryan, Michael; *ed:* Grad Stu Univ CA Berkeley; *cr:* 7th Grade Teacher St Joseph Sch 1978-80; 8th Grade Teacher St Thomas Apostle 1980-81; 7th-8th Grade Eng Teacher Santa Catalina Sch 1981-; *ai:* Literary Magazine Ed; Stu Adv; Univ of CA Berkeley 1977-78, Grad Fellowship 1977; Amer Assn of Univ Women 1983-85; Jr League of Monterey Cty 1988-; *office:* Santa Catalina Sch Mark Tomas Dr Monterey CA 93940

KENDERES, GEORGE STEVEN, German/History Teacher; *b:* Pittsburgh, PA; *ed:* (BA) Ger/His, Grove City Coll 1976; (MA) His, Duquesne Univ 1978; *cr:* Teacher North Hills Sch Dist 1979; Teacher Butler Area Sch Dist 1980-; *ai:* Adv Sch Newspaper; Ger Club; Fulbrights Scholar Holland 1984; *office:* Butler Intermediate H S 151 Fairground Hill Rd Butler PA 16001

KENDRICK, DOROTHY JEAN, Fifth Grade Teacher; *b:* Springfield, MO; *m:* Steven L.; *c:* Derek Laney, Lovena, Jennifer Laney, Steve; *ed:* (BS) Elem Ed, SW MO St Univ 1976; Working Towards Masters; *cr:* 5th Grade Teacher Republic RIII Sch Dist 1976-; *ai:* Sch Historical Prgms Dir & Dance Coord; Local Debate & Speech Tournaments Judge; MSTA (Rep, Treas 1984-85, Building Rep 1988-); Kappa Delta Phi; PTA Mem; *office:* Republic RIII Mid Sch 518 N Hampton Republic MO 65738

KENDRICK, EARLENE WATKINS, Communication Arts/ Unit Leader; *b:* Drew, MS; *c:* Clairce Collins, Carlene Millerton; *ed:* (BA) Ed, Chicago Teachers Coll 1963; (MS) Admin, Univ of Dayton 1987; *cr:* 8th Grade Teacher Coleman Sch 1964-69, Emerson 1969-74, Mc Guffey 1974-76; Math Teacher Wogaman 1977-81; Lang Art Teacher Fairport 1981-; *ai:* Soccer, Vlybl, Bsktbl, Track Coach; Phi Delta Kappa 1989; DEA, OEA, NEA 1969-; Dayton Teachers Guild Pres 1978-81; Amer League Womens Auxiliary 1st VP 1989-; Delta Sigma Theta 1984-; Natl Teacher of Yr Finalist 1974; *office:* Fairport Intermediate Sch 1952 Fairport Ave Dayton OH 45406

KENDRICK, JORETTA BREWTON, Seventh Grade Teacher; *b:* Ocala, FL; *c:* Tracy D. Brewton, Edwin N. III; *ed:* (BA) Public Admin/Criminal Justice Univ of Cntrl FL 1981; *cr:* Lab Technician Munroe Memorial Hospital 1974-75; Para Prof Belleview Elem Sch 1975-81; Teacher Alyce D Mc Pherson Youth Dev Sch 1981-83, S R Dinkins Elem Sch 1984-85, Morgan Road Mid Sch 1985-; *ai:* Future Teachers of America Club Spon; GAE, NEA 1984-; Ministry of Helps Coord 1990; *home:* 205 Pineview Dr Augusta GA 30906

KENDRICK, JOSEPH ROBERT, Mathematics Teacher; *b:* Flinton, PA; *m:* Sherry Mae Morton; *c:* Joseph, Janeen, Jamie, Jeremy; *ed:* (BS) Scndry Math, Ashland Univ of OH 1974; Masters Equivalency Cleveland St Univ; *cr:* Math Teacher Brunswick City Schls 1974-80, Curwensville Area Schls 1980-; *ai:* Ski Club, Stu Cncl, Frosh Class, Outdoormen Club Adv; Jr HS Ftbl Coach; PSEA, NEA; *office:* Curwensville Area Sch 650 Beech St Curwensville PA 16833

KENDRICK, KAY WILSON, English/History Teacher; *b:* Knoxville, TN; *m:* Edward Jr.; *c:* Amanda C.; *ed:* (BA) Eng, Mid TN St Univ 1971; (MED) Curr, Univ of S FL 1976; Working Towards Prin Cert; *cr:* Eng Teacher Sea Breeze HS 1972, Winter Haven HS 1973-76, Albany Jr Coll 1977-79, Germantown HS 1979-87, Glencliff HS 1987-; *ai:* Glencliff HS Stu Cncl Spon; Field Coord for Presidential Classroom; Glencliff Future Teachers of Amer Spon; Shelby Memphis Cncl Teachers of Eng Pres 1986-87; NEA 1979-; TN Assn of Stu Cncl Exec Secy; Knights of Columbus Auxiliary 1989-; Teacher Survival Kits Published; Teacher of Yr 1986; *office:* Glencliff HS 160 Antioch Pike Nashville TN 37211

KENDRICK, MARGARET BUXTON, Chemistry Teacher/ Science Dept; *b:* New Augusta, MS; *m:* Charles Leon; *c:* Dana M., Tracy L.; *ed:* (BS) Bio/Chem, Univ of S MS 1965; *cr:* Medical Technologist Pathology Laboratory 1966-75; Chem Teacher Petal HS 1976-; *ai:* Prom Spon; *office:* Petal HS 1145 Hwy 42 Petal MS 39465

KENDRICK, PATRICIA G., First Grade Teacher; *b:* Waynesboro, MS; *m:* Hubert T.; *c:* Kelly, Holly; *ed:* (BS) Elem Ed, Univ of So MS 195; MS Teacher Assessment Instruments Evaluator 1988; Job Trng Partnership Act; MS Writing/Thinking Inst; *cr:* Remedial Rdng Teacher Quitman Consolated Sch System 1965; 1st Grade Teacher 1965-67, 5th Grade 1967-68, 1st Grade Teacher 1969, 1st Grade Teacher 1969- Waynesboro Elem; *ai:* Mem Various Comm PTA; Mem of Calvary Baptist; Teacher of JTPA Prgm; Teacher of Adult Rdng Ed; City Auditorium Comm Mem 1989; *home:* 116 Miss Dr Waynesboro MS 39367

KENNARD, BERNICE VIEAU, 6th Grade Teacher/Math Coord; *b:* Rochester, NY; *m:* Philip R.; *c:* Philip Jr., Randy, Jennifer, Samantha; *ed:* (BA) Math, Assumption Univ 1963; Cmptr, Eng Courses; *cr:* 5th Grade Teacher Our Lady of Mercy 1963-67; 8th Grade Teacher Sacred Heart 1967-71; 3-4 Year Old Teacher Wesley Pre Sch 1976-80; 6th Grade Teacher St John the Evangelist 1981-; *ai:* Math Coord; Vice Prin; Rochester Area Rdng Cncl, NY St Rdng Assn 1988-; Maverick Soccer Club Registrar 1976-80; Sacred Heart Sch Bd (Pres 1980) 1977-80.

KENNARD, FRANCES LEWIS, Third Grade Teacher; *b:* Cameron, Milam; *m:* Daniel Jr.; *c:* Priscilla, Sharon, Daniel, Crystal, Kristopher; *ed:* (BA) Elem Ed, Paul Quinn Coll 1969; *ai:* Stu Cncl & Drill Team Spon; NEA, TSTA 1974-; AFT 1985-; Sigma Gamma; *office:* Prescott Elem Sch 1945 Gollihar Corpus Christi TX 78416

KENNEDY, ALAN L., Chemistry Teacher; *b:* Bay City, MI; *ed:* (BS) Sci Ed, Ferris St Univ 1971; (MS) Cmptr Ed, Nova Univ 1987; *cr:* 1st Lieutenant USAF 1971-74; Sci Teacher Whittemore Prescott HS 1974-79; Chem Teacher Riverdale HS 1982-; *ai:* Chem Competition Team Coach; Lee Cty Textbook Review Comm; *office:* Riverdale HS 2815 Buckingham Rd SE Fort Myers FL 33905

KENNEDY, ALBERTA THOMAS, 4th Grade Teacher; *b:* Franklinton, LA; *m:* Harvey Ellis; *c:* Richard Ellis, Suzanne; *ed:* (BS) Home Ec, 1955, (ME) Elem Ed, 1963 LA St Univ; Cert Gifted Ed Delta St Univ 1979; *cr:* Home Ec Teacher Mandeville HS; Elem Teacher Gonzales HS; East Baton Rouge Parish; Leland Consolidated Sch Dist; Leland Acad; Indianola Acad; *ai:* MPSEA; *home:* 302 Seymour Dr Indianola MS 38751

KENNEDY, ALICE LOUISE (FREESE), Music Teacher; *b:* Lexington, MO; *m:* Paul Evan; *ed:* (BME) Music Ed, Cntrl Meth Coll 1980; *cr:* Music Teacher Odessa MO R-7 Schls 1980-82; Piano Teacher Private Homes 1980-; Music Teacher Francis Howell Schls 1982-; *ai:* MO Music Educators Assn, Music Educators Natl Conference, MO St Teachers Assn 1980-; St John UCC (Chancel Choir 1988-, Adult Handbell Choir 1986-); O Fallon Cmmty Band 1988.

KENNEDY, ANNIE RUTH, 4th Grade Teacher; *b:* Greenville, NC; *m:* Samuel; *c:* Le Roy D., Ruth D.; *ed:* (BS) Elem, Barber-Scotia Coll 1964; NC Cntrl Univ, Furman Univ; *cr:* Teacher Greenville Cty Schls 1964-; *ai:* Sci Coord; NEA, GCEA; *home:* 217 Libby Ln Mauldin SC 29662

KENNEDY, CAROLYN BARR, Biology Teacher; *b:* Columbia, SC; *m:* Isaac; *c:* Kim Mc Kinley, Paul, Carmen; *ed:* (BS) Biological Sci, Benedict Coll 1963; (MA) Ed, Cleveland St Univ 1978; Internships & Wkshps; *cr:* Teacher Addison Jr HS 1966-69, John Adams HS 1970-; *ai:* United Way Fund Raiser; Cleveland Regional Cncl of Sci Teachers; *office:* John Adams HS 3817 Martin Luther King Jr Dr Cleveland OH 44105

KENNEDY, CATHAL HALLORAN, Kindergarten Teacher; *m:* Joseph F.; *c:* Shawn, Cribari, Mark, Daniel, Michael; *ed:* (BA) Eng, NY St Coll for Teachers 1949; (MS) Elem Ed, Oneonta St Teachers Coll 1952; *cr:* 2nd/3rd Grade Teacher Cohoes Elem Schls 1950-54; Supvr Stu Teachers Coll of St Rose 1962-64; Kndgtn Teacher Lansingburgh Public Schls 1970-; *ai:* Arts in Ed Comm; NAEYC; Lansingburgh Historical Society (VP 1964-66, Bd of Trustees 1990); RPES PTA VP 1988-; Rens Cty Cncl on Arts 1966-; *office:* Rensselaer Park Elem Sch 110th St & 8th Ave North Troy NY 12182

KENNEDY, DANIEL COFFEY, English Teacher; *b:* Norman, OK; *m:* Denise Holland; *c:* Jennifer, Joshua, Jamie, Caleb; *ed:* (BS) Lang Art Ed, Univ of OK 1978; *cr:* Eng Teacher Tuttle HS 1978-83; Eng/Soc Stud Teacher Chandler HS 1984-89; Eng Teacher Sperry Mid Sch 1989-; *ai:* Head Womens Bsktbl & Track Coach; OK Coaches Assn 1978-; OEA, NEA Local VP 1979-80; Teacher of Yr Chandler OK 1988-89; *office:* Sperry Mid Sch PO Box 610 Sperry OK 74073

KENNEDY, EILEEN NEVINS, English Teacher; *b:* New York, NY; *m:* James P.; *c:* James, Deirdre; *ed:* (BA) Eng, Coll of Mt St Vincent 1969; (MA) Eng, Fordham Univ 1971; *cr:* Eng Teacher Sacred Heart HS 1970-75; Substitute Teacher Rockville Centre Diocese 1980-86; Eng/SAT Tutor CERTA Learning Center 1989-; Eng Teacher Sacred Heart Acad 1986-; *ai:* Contest Coord; *home:* 48 Collins Ave Williston Park NY 11596

KENNEDY, ERNEST JAMES, Spec Ed Resource Specialist; *b:* Brooklyn, NY; *ed:* (BS) Behavioral Sci, St Univ New Paltz 1966; (MA) Ed/Psych, NY Univ 1969; Eng Second Lang Queretaro Mexico; Courses at Univ CA Berkeley, Univ CA Hayward; Sabatical Teaching in Mexico; *cr:* Spec Ed Teacher BOCES 1966-67; Teacher New York City Bd of Ed 1967-68, Peru South America 1968-69; Spec Ed Teacher Richnond CA 1969-; *ai:* Spec Ed Chairperson Helms Jr HS; CTA/NEA Mem 1988-; Rich Fed Teachers 1969-72; Neighborhood House Tutor 1969-70; US Navy Honorable Discharge 1967; NY St Grant Spec Ed; CETIP Chairperson Elected By Teachers in RUSD & Comm Mem; *office:* Helms Jr H S 2500 Rd 20 San Pablo CA 94806

KENNEDY, JAMES E., JR., 11th Grade Eng Paideia Teacher; *b:* Raleigh, NC; *ed:* (AB) Eng/Fr, 1978, (MED) Eng, 1983 Campbell Univ; Paideia Inst Natl Paideia Fnd ; *cr:* Math/Rdng Teacher N Edgecombe HS 1978-79; Tutor Coord Wayne Comm Coll 1979-84; Fr Teacher Coastal Carolina Comm Coll 1984-85; 9th-11th Grade Eng/11th Grade Paideia Teacher Millbrook HS 1985-; *ai:* SADD, Debate Club, Soph, Jr & Sr Class Adv; SAT Improvement Scores, Talking With Educators & Eng Curr Writing Committees; Modern Lang Assn, Fr Teachers of America, NEA, NC Assn of Educators; *office:* Millbrook HS 2201 Spring Forest Rd Raleigh NC 27615

KENNEDY, JAN HARRIS, 4th Grade Teacher; *b:* Albany, GA; *m:* Augustus B. III; *c:* Courtney, Tripp Macolly, CarsoN Macolly; *ed:* (BA) Early Chldhd Ed, GA SW Coll 1978; *cr:* 4th Grade Teacher Mamie Brasnan Elem 1980-81, Mock Road Elem 1981-; *ai:* 4th Grade Chairperson; Dougherty Cty Sci Textbook Comm; Sci Quality CORE Curr Writing Comm 1987-88; *office:* Mock Road Elem Sch 2237 Cutts Dr Albany GA 31707

KENNEDY, JEAN BOYD, English Department Chairperson; *b:* Granite Quarry, NC; *M:* Royal L.; *c:* Jennifer, Sharon, Joy; *ed:* (BA) Eng, Livingstone Coll 1967; *cr:* Eng Teacher, Dunbar HS 1967-68; North Rowan HS 1968-; *ai:* Jr Class; Future Teachers of America; Mentor; Teacher Recruiter; Guidance Comm; Planning/ Schlsp Comm; School Improvement Comm; Ira; Pres/Secy/Treas NCEA/NEA /NCTE/NCETA; Alpha Kappa Alpha Sorority (Pres, VP) Outstanding Soror 1985; Salibury-Rowan Families in Action; Dow Jonesw Newspaper Fellow 86; Rowan-Salisbury Schls Personnel Comm; 1st Runner-Up Rowan Salisbury Teacher Yr 1989; *office:* North Rowan H S 300 Whitehead Ave Spencer NC 28159

KENNEDY, LINDA GULMIRE, Second Grade Teacher; *b:* Reedsburgh, WI; *m:* Terrance; *c:* Kelley Harris, Sherry; *ed:* Elem Ed, Juneau Cty Teachers Coll 1962; (BA) Elem Ed, Univ of WI Oshkosh 1971; Alcohol & Drug Abuse Facilitator; Protective Behaviors for Children Instr; *cr:* 1st/2nd Grade Teacher Adell Elem Sch 1962-63; 1st-4th Grade Teacher Eldorado Sch 1963-74; 2nd Grade Teacher Rosendale Elem Sch 1974-; *ai:* Dist Public Relations Chairperson, Advisory Counciling Comm Elem Rep, Chemical Awareness Comm; Rosendale-Brandon Ed Assn (Pres 1983-84, Public Relations Chairperson 1984-85); WI Ed Assn, Northeastern Ed Assn, NEA; Oshkosh Chamber of Commerce Womens Div Bd of Dir 1985-88; Miss WI Schlsp Pageant Hostess 1976-84; Miss Oshkosh Schlsp Pageant Reception 1987-89; Experimental Aircraft Assn Convention Local Information Chm 1988-; St Public Relations Outreach Awd; *home:* 55 Lake Rest Ave Oshkosh WI 54901

KENNEDY, LINDA HAVENS, Secondary Math Teacher; *b:* Albany, NY; *m:* Brian F.; *ed:* (BS) Math, 1974, (MS) Advanced Classroom Teaching/Scndry Sch Math, 1982 SUNY Albany; *cr:* Math Teacher Vincentian Inst 1974-77, NY St Job Corps 1977-78, Cath Cntrl HS 1978-84, Rensselaer Mid Sch 1984-; *ai:* Math Club, Jr Class 1987, Sr Class 1988 Adv; Discipline, Inter Disciplinary Comms; Seminar on Excl in Ed Mem 1988; NYSUT 1984-; NY Assn of Math Teachers, NCTM 1985-; AFT 1984-; Delta Kappa Gamma 1988-; *office:* Rensselaer Mid HS 555 Broadway Rensselaer NY 12144

KENNEDY, LYNDA HERNDON, Traveling Mathematics Teacher; *b:* Humboldt, TN; *m:* Eldredge J.; *c:* Marilyn, Ruth A., Rachel; *ed:* (BS) Eng, 1959, (MS) Math Ed, 1964 Univ of TN; Grad Work Recertification; NCTM & Univ of TN Professors Wkshps; *cr:* HS Teacher Knoxville City Schls 1959-62; Kndgtn Teacher 1979-80, Mid Sch Teacher 1980-89, Traveling Math Teacher 1989- Knox Cty Schls; *ai:* Knox Cty Mid Schls PICO Math Olympiad; Knox Cty Math & Natl Society of Prof Engrs Adopt-a-Sch; Dist Teachers Study Cncl Secy; Phi Delta Kappa; Smoky Mountain Math Educators Assn (Secy, Treas 1989-) Mem 1982-; TN Math Teachers Assn; NCTM, NEA, TN Educators Assn, Knox Cty Ed Assn 1980-; TN Assn of Mid Schls 1985-; Knoxville Nativity Pageant, Dogwood Arts Festival; Chamber of Commerce 1st Class of Leadership Ed; TN Career Ladder III; Knox Cty Teachers Center Advisory Bd; *home:* 1101 Venice Rd Knoxville TN 37923

KENNEDY, MICHAEL JOHN, Science Teacher; *b:* Rantoul, IL; *m:* Anne F. Fitzgerald; *c:* Jill, Lisa, Sean; *ed:* (BS) Bio, Santa Clara Univ 1972; (MPH) Health Ed, 1975, Teaching Credential Ed, 1984 San Jose St Univ; *cr:* Project Coord 1976-77; Health Educator Washje Cty Health Dept 1977-79, Monterey Cty Health Dept 1979-83; Sci Teacher Modesto City Schls 1984-; *ai:* Coached Girls Bsktbl, Tennis, Soccer, Sftbl; Friday Night Live Club Adv; NSTA Mem 1984-; Salinas Sunrise Toastmasters Club Pres 1978-79; *office:* Fred C Beyer HS 1717 Sylvan Ave Modesto CA 95355

KENNEDY, MICHELLE PITTS, Biology Teacher; *b:* Oceanside, CA; *m:* Marvin; *c:* Alan, Brian, Christina; *ed:* (BS) Scndry Ed/Bio, 1973, (MS) Scndry Ed/Bio, 1988 Valdosta St Coll; *cr:* Bio Teacher Tucker HS 1973-75, Tift Area Acad 1975-76, Tift Cty HS 1976-80, Turner Cty HS 1985-; *ai:* Sci Club Spon; Sci Dept Chm; GA Sci Teacher Assn 1985-; Prof Assn of GA Educators 1985-; *office:* Turner Cty HS 601 E Madison St Ashburn GA 31714

KENNEDY, MIGUELINA ROURA, Spanish Teacher; *b:* New York, NY; *m:* John; *c:* Matthew, Michelle; *ed:* (BA) Span, Hunter Coll 1963; *cr:* 5th Grade Teacher PS 19 1963-64; 2nd Grade Teacher Eltingville Luth Sch 1964-65, PS 20 1965-66; 6th-8th Grade Span/Eng Teacher Eltingville Luth Sch 1968-69; 1st-2nd Grade Teacher New York City Schls 1971-73; 1st Grade/Span Teacher Timothy Chrstn Sch 1974-76, 1981-; *ai:* Hospitality & Lang Dept Comm; Local Church (Deaconess, Sunday Sch Teacher, Extended Session Teacher); *home:* 27 Racoon Dr Hazlet NJ 07730

KENNEDY, PATRICIA E., Director of Choral Activities; *b:* Columbus, OH; *m:* Jefferson L.; *c:* Kristen M. Turner; *ed:* (BS) Music Ed/Piano, Otterbein Coll 1968; (MS) Music Ed, 1971, (MM) Choral Conducting, 1973 Univ of IL; Aspen Sch of Music, IN Univ, Roosevelt Univ; *cr:* Teacher Vocal Cmmty Schls Unit 3 1968-73; Asst Professor of Music Univ of KY 1975-79; Assoc Faculty IN Univ & Purdue Univ Ft Wayne 1980-84; Dir of Choral Act Wayne HS 1987-; *ai:* Dir Jazz Choir & Elizabethan Madrigal Singers; Amer Choral Dir Assn; 1st Wayne St United Meth Church; Fellowship Aspen Festival Music Chamber Choir; Prof Choir Santa Fe Desert Choral 1987-; *office:* Wayne HS 9100 Winchester Rd Fort Wayne IN 46819

KENNEDY, ROSLYNE (DIXON), Mathematics Teacher; *b:* Houston, TX; *c:* Amanda E.; *ed:* (BA) Math, N TX St Univ 1973; (MED) Math, TX Southern Univ 1978; *cr:* Math Teacher Marshall Mid Sch 1974-86, Barbara Jordan HS for Careers 1986-; *ai:* Barbara Jordan HS for Careers Discipline & Schlsp Comm; ATPE 1988-; San Jacinto GSA 1986-; *office:* Barbara Jordan HS for Careers 5800 Eastex Freeway Houston TX 77026

KENNEDY, SANDRA HUGHES, Honors Eng Teacher; *b:* Wheeling, WV; *m:* Robert R.; *c:* Alicia L., Kerry D.; *ed:* (BA) Eng/Speech, West Liberty St Coll 1965; (MA) Drama, WV Univ 1970; Cert Gifted Ed, WV Coll of Grad Stud 1981; Grad Courses Poly Sci & Educl Admin; Trng to Teach Advanced Placement Eng Lit & Composition, Eng Lang & Composition; *cr:* Teacher 1966-68, 1971-72, Substitute Teacher 1973-80, Teacher 1980- Marshall Cty Bd of Ed; *ai:* JETS Adv; Educl Enrichment Trips & Prgms; Cty Grading Policy & Advanced Placement Comm; NEA, WV Ed Assn, Marshall Cty Ed Assn; Delf Norona Museum Bd of Dir; City of Cameron Cncl Councilwomen 1986-; Cameron Little Theater (Pres, Dir) 1976-78; Cameron Emergency Medical Technician; Bill Geer Minigrants; WV Ed Minigrant; Nom Teacher of Yr; Leaders of Learning Conference Speaker 1988; *home:* RD 3 Box 3 Cameron WV 26033

KENNEDY, TERRANCE E., Social Studies/Geo Teacher; *b:* New Lisbon, WI; *m:* Linda Rae; *c:* Kelley J. Harris, Sherry L.; *ed:* (BS) Elem Ed/His, Univ of WI Oshkosh 1967; Increasing Teaching Effectiveness; Teachers Expectations & Stu Achievement Instr; Lee Canters Assertive Discipline Phase II; *cr:* Teacher Hustisford Public Sch 1962-63, Rosendale Brandon Sch System 1967-; *ai:* 8th Grade Class Adv; Rosendale Brandon Teachers Assn Pres 1982-83; Saw Dust Days Incorporated Pres 1975-76; Van Dyne Sportsman Club VP 1985-87; DNR Safety Instr 1975-88; *office:* Rosendale Mid Sch Hwy 26 Rosendale WI 54974

KENNEDY, TERRY R. MC MILLAN, Science Teacher/Dept Head; *b:* Bamburg, SC; *m:* Robert R. Jr.; *c:* Charlotte, Katy, Robert R.; *ed:* (BS) Sci Teaching, Clemson Univ 1976; (MED) Sci Teaching, Univ of GA 1982; *cr:* Sci Teacher Salponte HS 1976-78, Fairfax Elem 1978-79, Oconee Cty HS 1979-83, Dublin HS 1983-; *ai:* Sr Class Adv; GA Sci Teachers Assn 1979-89; Teacher of Yr; STAR Teacher; *office:* Dublin HS Stadium Rd Dublin GA 31021

KENNEY, CLIFFORD ORRIN, 4th Grade Teacher; *b:* Leominster, MA; *m:* Nancy C. Ryerson; *c:* Heather; *ed:* (BS) Ed, 1970; (MED) Edlem Guidance, 1976 Fitchburg St Coll; Post Masters Studies Univ of CO; Anna Maria Coll; Fitchburg St Coll; Fitchburg MA; *cr:* Elem Teacher Johnny Appleseed Elem 1972-90; *ai:* After Sch Ski Prgm Coord; Sch Cmptr Specialist; Grade 4 Newspaper Coord; Workshop Presenter-Teachers Conf; MA Teachers Assn 1972-90; NEA 1972-90; Leominster Teachers Assn 1972-90; Natl Space Fnd 1989-90; First Baptist Church Mem Officer, Trustee, Deacon 1980-90; Awarded 2 Horace Mann Grants to Dev Outdoor Classroom Indoor Grow Lab Unit; *office:* Johnny Appleseed Elem Sch 845 Main St Leominster MA 01453

KENNEY, MICHELLE D. ST. HILAIRE, Social Studies Teacher; *b:* Manchester, NH; *m:* W. Bruce; *ed:* (BA) His, Notre Dame Coll 1974; Educating the Exceptional Learner, Educating the Emotionally Disturbed Stu, Paralegal Stud; NH His; *cr:* Soc Stud Teacher 1977-, Curr Coord 1981-82 Southside Jr HS; *ai:* Academic Awds Comm Adv; Dist/Local Staff Dev Comm Mem; Participation in Sch Spon Spirit Club Act; NH & Manchester Historical Society 1987-; Natl & NH Cncl Soc Stud 1981-; ASCD 1982-; NEA, MEA Rep 1977-79; Staff Dev Comm Mem 1985-88/ 1989-; NEA, St, Local MEA Instructional & Prof Dev Comm; MEA Assembly Rep South Side Jr HS Curr Coord; Law Related EdPrgm; St Local Accountability Comm; Initiated Interdisciplinary Teaching Prgm; Dev Jr HS Orientation Prgm Study Survival Skills; *office:* Southside Jr H S 140 S Jewett St Manchester NH 03103

KENNEY, VALERIE DENISE, Social Studies Teacher; *b:* Chester, PA; *c:* Shannon; *ed:* (BA) His, Christopher Newport Coll 1979; Prgm for Effective Teaching Ed, NNPS 1982; Substance Use Univ of VA 1989; Teacher Effectiveness Trng Lynchburg Coll 1989; *cr:* Soc Stud Teacher Windsor HS 1980, 1981- Menchville HS; *ai:* Soph Class & Hugh O Brian Leadership Awd Spon; Odyssey of Mind Coach; Mid Sch Articulation Comm 1987-89; Soc Stud Curr Dev 1986; Participant Menchville Bridge Prgm; *office:* Menchville HS 275 Menchville Rd Newport News VA 23602

KENNEY, W. BRUCE F., Science Teacher; *b:* Franklin, NH; *m:* Michelle D. St Hilaire; *ed:* (BED) Bio, Keene St Coll 1968; *cr:* Sci Teacher Southside Jr HS 1968-; *ai:* STADCOM Chm; Jr HS Sci Curr Comm; NEA Life Mem, Manchester Ed Assn, NH Ed Assn 1969-; NH Sci Teachers Assn 1989-; Instructional Prof Dev Comm 1980-81; Curr Developer Southside Jr HS 1981-82; Adelphi Drug Prevention Team 1977-78; *office:* Southside Jr HS 140 S Jewett Manchester NH 03103

KENNEY-FRANZESE, LAURETTE DIANE, English Dept Chair; *b:* Miami, FL; *c:* Arielle Levine, Amanda Levine; *ed:* (BA) Eng, FL St Univ 1965; (MLA) Hum, Oklahoma City Univ 1983; *cr:* Teacher Pierce Sch 1965-66, Lynnville HS 1966-69, Ward-Melville HS 1970-71; Teacher/Chairperson Bishop Mc Guinness HS 1979-; *ai:* Faculty Spon; Literary Artistic Magazine; Advanced Placement Coord; Hum Fellowship Independent Study; Adult Inst in Arts Schlsp; Cornell Univ Master Teacher Awd; *office:* Bishop Mc Guinness HS 801 NW 50th St Oklahoma City OK 73118

KENNISTON, MICHAEL ROBERT, Science Teacher; *b:* Tupper Lake, NY; *m:* Susan Elizabeth Mac Donald; *c:* Korey, Laura; *ed:* (BS) Ed, Plattsburg St Univ 1976; Grad Ed Plattsburg St Univ, Potsdam St Univ; *cr:* Sci Teacher Tupper Lake Jr-Sr HS 1977-; *ai:* Bsktbl, Bsbl Coach; ASCD Mem 1990; *office:* Tupper Lake Jr-Sr HS 25 Chaney Ave Tupper Lake NY 12986

KENNY, JOANNE PATRICE, English Teacher; *b:* Jersey City, NJ; *ed:* (BA) Eng, 1968, (MA) Eng, 1978 Jersey City St Coll; *cr:* Prin St Marys Grammar Sch 1985-87; Eng/Comm Art Teacher James J Ferris HS 1968-; *ai:* Adv Newspaper 1972-76, Yrbk 1977-; Cnslr Time Out Prgm; Co-Chairperson FHS/SPC Partnership Comm; Co-Commissioner Jersey City Scholastic Bowl; Eng/Comm Arts Curr Leader; NCTE, Columbia Scholastic Press Assn, NEA, NJ Ed Assn; Jersey City Ed Assn (Exec Bd Mem 1972-89, Communications Comm Chairperson, Anne Fasciano Schlsp Comm Chairperson, Newletter Ed 1976-89); Phi Delta Kappa 1989; St James Church (Family Youth Mass Dir 1985-88, Youth Group Leader 1986-); Confraternity of Chrstn Doctrine Teacher 1985-; Jersey Journal Woman of Achievement 1973; Outstanding Young Women of America 1974; Bus & Prof Womens Club Cty Rep 1975; Governors Teacher Recognition Awd 1986; Jersey City St Coll Outstanding Alumnea 1986; *home:* 64 Sherwood Rd Springfield NJ 07081

KENSETH, TED L., 7th Grade Lang Arts/Math/Rdng; *b:* Edgerton, WI; *m:* Beth Ann; *ed:* (BS) Elem Ed, UW River Falls 1979; Athletic Coaching; Ed; *cr:* 7th/8th Grade Teacher River Falls Jr HS 1979-87; 8th Grade Math/Lang Arts/Rdng Teacher 1988-89, 7th Grade Math/Lang Arts/Rdng Teacher River Falls Mid Sch 1990; *ai:* 8th Grade Boys Bsktbl Coach; NCTE; *office:* River Falls Mid Sch 211 N Fremont River Falls WI 54022

KENSINGER, GRACE WILLETTS, 6th Grade Quest Teacher; *b:* Bellefontaine, OH; *m:* Richard Glenn; *c:* Kimberley Tupps, Kristen Booher, Richard G. II, Robert Donn; *ed:* (MS) Music, Cedarville Coll 1959; Working Towards Masters Elem Counseling; *cr:* 7th-9th Grade Music/7th Grade Math Teacher Newhall Jr HS 1959-61; 2nd/3rd Grade Teacher Xenia City Schls 1961-62; 3rd Grade Teacher Crestview Elem Sch 1963-64; 7th-8th Grade Music/8th Grade Eng Albion Jr HS 1971-74; 6th-8th Grade Rdng/Quest/Health/Art Greenville Jr HS & North 1974-; *ai:* Greenville Jr HS Theater Wkshp; Phi Delta Kappa Research Chair 1988-; Greenville Advocate Cornerstone of Cmmty Awd 1990; North Sch Teacher of Yr 1988-89; Whos Who Amoung Mid-Western Women 1989; *office:* North Sch 211 W Main St Greenville OH 45331

KENT, LYDIA LAWLESS, Spanish Teacher; *b:* Martinsville, VA; *m:* Michael Archer; *c:* Benjamin A., Whitney G.; *ed:* (AS) Sci, VA Western Comm Coll 1978-79; (BA) Span Ed, Longwood Coll 1975; *cr:* Teacher Huguenot Acad 1979-85, Great Bridge HS 1985-; *ai:* Drama & Span Club; *office:* Great Bridge H S 301 W Hanbury Rd Chesapeake VA 23320

KENT, SUE KATHERINE WYATT, Learning Disabilities Resource; *b:* Beckley, WV; *m:* F. Gene; *c:* William F., Edward G., Richard L.; *ed:* (AAS) Teacher Aide Ed, Prarie ST Coll 1976; (BA) Elem Ed, Governors ST Univ 1978; (MED) Rdng & Learning Disabilities, DePaul Univ 1981; Post Masters Studies Sci of Teaching; Cmptrs; Performance Learning Systems Courses; *cr:* 1st Grade Teacher 1978-81; Master Teacher 1981-84 Hickory Elem; Learning Disabilities Resource Teacher Deer Creek Jr Hi 1984-88; Learning Disabilities Resource Teacher Crete-Monee Jr Hi 1988-; *ai:* Crete-Monee Ed Assn, Assn Rep 1985-; *office:* Crete-Monee Jr H S 1500 Sangamon Rt 1 & Monee Rd Crete IL 60417

KENT-WOHLRAB, JILL E., Gifted Consultant Teacher; *b:* Toronto, Canada; *m:* Charles; *c:* Kirsten, Kellie; *ed:* (BAE) Elem Ed, FL Atlantic Univ 1973; (MS) Gifted Stu Ed, 1985, (EDSP) Admin/Supervision, 1987 Nova Univ; *cr:* 2nd-5th Grade Teacher Broward Cty 1974-80; Teacher of Gifted 1980-88, Admin Asst 1988-89, Gifted Consultant Teacher 1989- Volusia Cty; *ai:* Young Astronaut Prgm; Fancy Steppers Dance Group; Current Events Bowl Coach; NEA, FL Assn for the Gifted 1980-; VISION Gifted Parent Support Group 1987-; Chisholm Teacher of Yr 1988; Volusia Cty Outstanding Sci Teacher 1987, Teacher of Yr Finalist 1988; UCF Excl in Economic Ed 1988; IBM Teacher of Yr Nom 1988; Published Outstanding Ed Improvement Projects 1987; *office:* Volusia Cty Schls 557 Ronnoc Ln New Smyrna Beach FL 32169

KENWORTHY, CHERYL LEE, 3rd Grade Teacher; *b:* Indianapolis, IN; *ed:* (BA) Elem Ed, 1978; (MS) Elem Ed, 1983 in Univ; *cr:* 3rd Grade Teacher 1979-80, 4th Grade Teacher 1980-84, 5th Grade Teacher 1984-87, 3rd Grade Teacher 1987- Decatur Township; *ai:* Sch Improvement Cncl; Decatur Ed Assn 1979-; *office:* Valley Mills Elem Sch 5101 S High School Rd Indianapolis IN 46241

KENYON, BOBBYE AKIN, Earth Science Teacher; *b:* Houston, TX; *c:* George N., Donald W., Carol N. Kenyon Milam; *ed:* (BS) Chem, Sam Houston Univ 1958; Numerous Inservice Wkshps; Grad Stud Chem, Univ of TX San Antonio 1975-81; Harvard Project Physics; Trinity Univ; Civil Defense; *cr:* Sci/Math Teacher Harris Jr HS 1960-61; Earth Sci/Phys Sci Teacher Page Jr HS 1962-68; Physics/Chem/Phys Sci Teacher Fox Tech HS 1969-79; Teacher/Adv Univ of TX San Antonio 1975; Physics Lab Instr San Antonio Coll 1975-76; Math/Earth Sci Teacher Irving Mid Sch 1979-; *ai:* Fox Tech HS Univ Interscholastic League Sci Coach 1970-79, Sci Club Co-Spon & Spon 1969-79, Radiation Safety Officer 1974-79, Jr Engineering Tech Society Spon 1977-79; Textbook Adoption Comm; Co-Author Physics/Chem Criterion Reference Test; San Antonio Teachers Cncl, TX St Teachers Assn, TX Classroom Teachers Assn, NEA, TX Selection Amer Assn of Physics Teachers, Alamo Area Physics Teachers Assn Treas 1970-72; PTA 1959-; United Meth Church Choirs 1951-; United Meth Women (Circle Chm 1989, Circle Treas 1990); Univ United Meth Church (Educl Cncl, Worship Cncl, Mission Cncl); Earth Sci Photography Target Grant 1990.

KEOSSEIAN, ELLEN JANE, English/Journalism Teacher; *b:* Wilmington, DE; *m:* John Mark; *ed:* (BA) Eng Ed, Univ of DE 1980; (MED) Scndry Ed, Bowie St Univ 1987; *cr:* Teacher Calvert HS 1980-; *ai:* Courier & Patapeake Adv; *office:* Calvert HS 600 Daves Beach Rd Prince Frederick MD 20678

KEOSSEIAN, JOHN MARK, Eng Teacher/Dir Mentor Prgm; *b:* Brooklyn, NY; *m:* Ellen Jane; *c:* Celene A.; *ed:* (BA) Eng, St Francis Coll 1971; (MS) Scndry Ed/Eng, Coll of Staten Island 1976; Grad Work Gifted Ed, Univ of MD 1981-83, Cert Admin & Supervision, Bowie St Univ 1988-; *cr:* Eng Teacher St John the Evangelist 1971-73, St Francis of Assissi 1973-75, St Saviour HS 1975-79; Eng Teacher/Dir Mentor Prgm Calvert HS 1979-; *ai:* Dir Cmmty Mentorship Prgm Academically Talented HS Stus; NCTE 1977-; NEA & MD St Teachers Assn 1979-; Odyssey of Mind 1983-85; Calvert Cty Public Schls Teacher of Yr 1988; St Marys Coll Exceptional Teacher Awd 1985; Created Cmmty Mentorship Prgm Calvert Cty Public Schls 1984; *office:* Calvert HS Dares Beach Rd Prince Frederick MD 20678

KEOUGH, KATHERINE NELSON, Fifth Grade Teacher; *b:* Laramie, WY; *m:* Edward H.; *c:* Caroline Harris, Sheryl Compton, Theresa Kuminski, Linda Heck; *ed:* (BSE) Elem Ed, 1965, (MSE) Rdng, 1976 Univ of Cntrl AR; Prgm for Effective Teaching; Teacher Expectation & Stu Achievement; Classroom Management; *cr:* Elem Teacher N Little Rock Spec Sch Dist 1965-; *ai:* 5th/6th Grade Civic Achievement Awd Prgm Coord; N Little Rock Classroom Teachers Pres 1980; Delta Kappa Gamma Secy 1981; Order of Eastern Star Worthey Matron 1976; Kappa Delta Alumni Pres 1977; St Lukes Episcopal Church (Vestry Mem 1984, Lay-Reader, Chalice Bearer 1978-); Grad Theological Ed by Extention Univ of South; *home:* 3131 Ridge Rd North Little Rock AR 72116

KEPHART, HELEN ORR, Mathematics Teacher; *b:* Sioux Falls, SD; *m:* Harold F.; *c:* Jo L., Ann M.; *ed:* (BA) Math, 1967, (MA) Scndry Ed, 1983 Univ of SD; *cr:* 7th/8th Grade Math Teacher Vermillion Mid Sch 1970-87; Math Teacher Vermillion HS 1987-; *ai:* Math Club Adv; Delta Kappa Gamma (Treas, VP) 1976-; NCTM 1970-; SDCTM Secy 1970-; Presidential Awd for Excl in Math SD 1989; *office:* Vermillion HS 1001 E Main St Vermillion SD 57069

KERBEL, CAROL SUSAN (LAUCK), Home Ec/Career Invst Teacher; *b:* Fort Morgan, CO; *m:* Larry; *c:* Gregory, Kevin; *ed:* (BS) Vocational Home Ec, CO StUniv 1964; East TX St Univ; *cr:* Homemaking Teacher Morrill HS 1964-66, Dallas Ind Schls 1968-80; Homemaking Teacher & Career Investigation Teacher Obanion Mid Sch 1980-; *ai:* Faculty Hospitality Comm; Y-Teens Spon; St & Dist Textbook Selection Comm; TX Vocational Guidance Assn 1989-; Garland Symphony League 1987-88; 1st Bapt Church-Hospitality Chm 1985-89; Church Choir Sec 1986-87; Selected for St & Dist Textbook Comm; Outstanding Young Women of Amer 1966; *home:* 1513 Merrimac Trl Garland TX 75043

KERINS, STEPHEN JOSEPH, Business Teacher; *b:* New York, NY; *w:* Eileen Ann Collins (dec); *c:* Tracie; *ed:* (BBA) Labor/Management, 1964, (MBA) Mrktg Manhattan Coll 1983; *cr:* Business Teacher Cardinal Hayes HS 1984-85, Cardinal Spellman HS 1985-; *ai:* Lay Faculty Assn, NCEA 1984-; Amer Society of Notaries Mem 1990; *office:* Cardinal Spellman HS 1991 Neeham Ave Bronx NY 10466

KERKENBUSH, ANN HANSMEIER, 8th Grade Language Art Teacher; *b:* Waukon, IA; *m:* Thomas H.; *c:* Lisa J. Fahlgren, Gregory T., Martin D.; *ed:* (BA) His/Eng, Viterbo Coll 1961; Grad Stud; *cr:* 8th Grade Lang Art/Soc Stud Teacher Carpentersville IL 1961-62; 8th Grade Lang Art Teacher Evansville WI 1965-; *ai:* Bus & Ed Partnership Comm; WEAC Poly Action; NEA, WI Ed Assn, Evansville Ed Assn; *office:* J C Mc Kenna Mid Sch 307 S 1st St Evansville WI 53536

KERL, THOMAS J., 5-6th Grade Reading Teacher; *b:* Carbondale, PA; *m:* Kathleen Foley; *c:* Elizabeth A., Mary K., Margaret R.; *ed:* (BS) Elem Ed, 1962, (MS) Elem Ed, 1969 Univ of Scranton; *cr:* 5th-6th Grade Teacher Frelinghuysen Sch 1963-64; 6th Grade Teacher Elk Lake Sch Dist 1964-66; 5th-6th Grade Teacher Forest City Regional Schls 1966-; *ai:* Sport Events Supervision; PSEA Local Treas 1974-; Volunteer Fireman 1964-; *office:* Forest City Regional Sch 100 S Susquehanna St Forest City PA 18421

KERLEY, RUTH DAVIS, Language Arts Teacher; *b:* Crossville, TN; *ed:* (BS) Elem Ed, TN Tech 1958; Graduate Work Ed, TN Tech; *cr:* 6th Grade Teacher Mayland 1954-55; 1st-4th Grade Teacher Hales Chapel 1955-57; Soc Sci Teacher Oak Dale HS 1957-59; 3rd Grade Teacher Emory Heights 1959-61; Prin/7th-8th Grade Teacher Lantana 1961-62; Supervising Prin Homestead 1962-64; 5th Grade Teacher Crossville Elem 1964-77, Cumberland Elem 1977-80; 7th/8th Grade Lang Arts Teacher South Cumberland Elem 1980-; *ai:* 4-H Club Honor Awd; Cumberland Cty Ed Assn 1961-89; TN Ed Assn 1961-89; NEA 1961-89; *office:* S Cumberland Elem Sch Rt 11 Box 316 D Lantana Rd Crossville TN 38555

KERN, DENNY LEE, 5th & 6th Grade Teacher; *b:* Saginaw, MI; *m:* Joan Marie Hildebrand; *c:* Nicole, Timothy, Christopher, Eric; *ed:* (AA) Teacher Ed, Concordia 1970; (BA) Soc Sci, Concordia 1972; (MA) Rdng, Eastern MI 1978; *cr:* Teacher Our Savior Lutheran Sch 1972-79; Christ Lutheran Sch 1979-; *ai:* Athletic Dir; Coach Bsktbk, Sftbl, Track; Yearbook Adv; VP of Congregation; Bd Mem of MI Dist Bd of Evangelism & Church Growth, Chm of Asbestos Comm; Phi Delta Kappa 1980-; LEA 1980-; MLSPEA 1976-; New North Flint Businessmen 1974-76; Prgm Chm NW Teachers Conerence 1983; *home:* 1159 Adams Drive St Joseph MI 49085

KERN, ELLEN CORNELL, Third Grade Teacher; *b:* Scranton, PA; *c:* Donald; *ed:* (BA) Fr, Coll of St Elizabeth 1961; Working Towards Masters Elem Ed, Seton Hall Univ; *cr:* 5th Grade Teacher St Vincents 1960-61; 6th Grade Teacher St Rose 1961-64; 8th Grade Teacher Holy Name 1964-67; 6th Grade Teacher Sts Peter & Paul 1967-70; 3rd Grade Teacher St Andrews 1974-; *ai:* St Andrews Jr Honor Society Adv; NCEA 1974-; *office:* St Andrews Cath Sch 3717 Stadium Dr Fort Worth TX 76109

KERN, RANDY L., History Teacher; *b:* Paris, AR; *m:* Debbie Spencer; *c:* David, Jamie, Matthew; *ed:* (BA) His/Poly Sci, AR Tech Univ 1982; *cr:* His Instr Southside HS 1983-; *ai:* Citizen Bee Spon; *office:* Southside HS 4100 Gary Fort Smith AR 72903

KERN, ROBERT F., Eighth Grade Teacher; *b:* Paterson, NJ; *m:* Janice Gornick; *c:* Daniel, Brian; *ed:* (BA) Scndry Ed/Soc Stud, Jersey City St Coll 1973; (MA) Comm Arts, William Paterson Coll 1981; Elem Ed Cert, Supvr & Prins Cert, William Paterson Coll; *cr:* Teacher Saddle Brook Public Schls 1974-77, Oxford Cntrl Sch 1977-; *ai:* Teacher-In-Charge; Chm Soc Stud Curr; 8th Grade Class Adv; Asst Sftbl Coach; Warren Cty Jr Athletic Conference Pres 1983-87; Lakeland Emergency Squad Incorporated (Chief 1987-88, Dept Chief 1984-86); Saddle Brook Volunteer Ambulance Corporation Life Mem 1973-; *office:* Oxford Cntrl Sch Kent St Oxford NJ 07863

KERN, SANDY G., Reading/Language Teacher; *b:* Chicago, IL; *m:* Greg; *c:* Alexis, Ashley; *ed:* (BA) Eng, Western IL Univ 1970; Gifted; IGE; *cr:* Teacher Twin Groves Sch 1970-; *ai:* Dist Ed Assn Rep; NCTE 1988-; Piana Dei Gracie Italian/Amer Organization 1990; *office:* Twin Groves Jr HS 1072 Ivy Hall Ln Buffalo Grove IL 60089

KERN, STEPHANIE PERRY, Computer Science Teacher; *b:* Brownsville, TX; *m:* Ronald P.; *c:* Stephanie R., Jayson P.; *ed:* (BS) Chem, Cntrl St Univ OK 1970; (MT) Scndry Ed, Univ of AZ 1978; TX Ed Agency Trng in Math, Calculator & Cmptr; *cr:* Math Teacher Luling HS 1973-74; Sci Teacher Samuel Clemens HS 1974-75; Chem/Physics Teacher Parker HS 1976-78, 1979-81; Sci Teacher Mt Valley Mid Sch 1978-79; Chem 2/Physics/Algebra 2 Teacher Permian HS 1981-85; Math Teacher Stevenson Mid Sch 1985; Math Chm Maypearl HS 1986-88; Cmptr Sci Teacher Princeton HS 1989-; *ai:* NHS; Academic Decathlon 1984-85; NCTM 1988-; Phi Delta Kappa, Sci Teachers Assn of TX 1974-; AMATYC 1990; Kappa Kappa Iota Pres Elect 1985; Distinguished Educators Awd; Natl Society of Microbiology; Tea Technology Super Trainer; TEA Math Module Trainer; Presented Paper STAT 1975; Notable Women of TX; Outstanding Young Women of America; NSF Research Physics Grant; TX Physics EXCET Test Chm; Certificate of Recognition Intnl Sci & Engineering Fair; *home:* Box 630 Allen TX 75002

KERN, TERESA N., Instructional Lead Teacher; *b:* Nestorville, WV; *m:* Roy M.; *c:* Matthew, Lori; *ed:* (BA) Bus Ed/Eng, Alderson-Broaddus Coll 1962; (MA) Mid Sch Ed, GA St Univ 1981; Leadership Certificate 1988; *cr:* Bus Ed Teacher Annapolis HS 1963-66; 6th Grade Teacher Forrest Hills Elem 1979-81; 6th Grade Teacher 1981-84, Remedial Math Teacher 1984-89 Dresden Elem; Instructional Lead Teacher Livsey Elem 1989-; *ai:* Math Counts Team Coach; De Kalb Assn of Educators, Kappa Delta Pi; *office:* Livsey Sch 4137 Livsey Rd Tucker GA 30084

KERNAGIS, RUTH, Teacher; *b:* Chicago Heights, IL; *m:* James; *c:* Kathleen, Wendelin Luekcke, Daniel; *ed:* (BA) Liberal Art, Cornell Coll 1960; (MA) Ed, Valparaiso Univ 1975; *cr:* Teacher Hubbard Trail Jr HS 1964-65, Crete-Monee HS 1966-68, Crown Point HS 1969-; *ai:* Jr Classical League Latin Club Spon; Delta Kappa Gamma; IN Latin Teacher of Yr 1981, 1987; Amer Legion Teacher of Yr 1989; FOE Teacher of Yr 1988; *home:* 357 NW Lakeshore Dr Crown Point IN 46307

KERNES, BEN O., Mathematics Teacher; *b:* Nebraska City, NE; *m:* Mary Beth Lavigne; *c:* Beth A., Juliet, Tom; *ed:* (BS) Ed/Math/Physics, Peru St 1964; Grad Stud Math/Pedagogy; Rural Ed/Math, Peru St; *cr:* HS Math Teacher Sterling Public Sch 1965-67; Scndry Math Teacher Nebraska City Public Sch 1967-69, Sidney Public Schls 1969-75, Nebraska City Public Sch 1979-; *ai:* NE St Ed Assn, NEA 1965-; NCTM 1984-; Julian Village Cncl (Chm 1970-75) 1969-; Julian Volunteer Fireman 1969-; Elks Lodge 1972-; *home:* 604 3rd Box 207 Julian NE 68379

KERNISH, EDWARD S., Speech & Theatre Teacher; *b:* Norristown, PA; *m:* Susan Margaret Dickey; *c:* Carlen; *ed:* (BA) Speech/Theatre/Eng, Calvin Coll 1968; (MA) Theatre, Penn St Univ 1975; Acting & Directing, Univ of MI Ann Arbor; Eng Lit & Sociology, Univ of Durham; *cr:* Teacher Orchard View HS 1968-70, State Coll HS 1973-83; Trainer Univ of MI 1985-86; Instr Baker Comm Coll 1986-87; *ai:* Theatre Arts; Forensics; Sch Improvement/High Expectations & Friends of Boehm Theatre Restoration Comm; Albion Civic Theatre Bd Mem & Artistic Dir; Amer Theatre Assn 1968-76; Amer Society for Trng & Dev 1984-86, Prgm Excl 1985; MI Speech Assn 1990; ASCD 1989; Daughters of Amer Revolution Amer His & Citizenship Awd 1963; Big Brothers 1969-71; Penn St Univ Theatre Arts Fellowship; Albion Bd of Ed Grant; MI Ed Assn Curr Dev Pilot Study; Experimental Theatre in HS Curr Submitted for Publication 1975; MI Interscholastic Forensic Assn 1st Place 1988, 2nd Place 1989; *office:* Albion Sr HS 225 Watson St Albion MI 49224

KERNS, YOLANDA CANDELARIA, 4th Grade Teacher; *b:* East Chicago, IN; *m:* James Thomas; *c:* Vanessa Y, Jennifer J.; *ed:* (BS) Elem Ed, St Joseph's Coll 1974; (MS) Elem Ed, IN Univ; *cr:* 3rd Grade Bi-Lingual Teacher Jefferson Elem 1974-75; 5th Grade Teacher John Vohr Elem 1975-76; 1st Grade Teacher 1976-81; 6th Grade Teacher 1981-82; 2nd Grade Teacher 1982-88; 4th Grade Teacher 1988- Aetna Elem; *ai:* Black History Mth Comm; Sch Accreditation Improvement Team; STAR Prgrm; Union Building Comm & Critical Thinkers Comm; Rdng Cncl 1981-; Soc Stud Cncl 1981-; PTA 1974-; *office:* Aetna Elem Sch 1327 Arizona St Gary IN 46403

KERR, DONALD L., French Teacher; *b:* Frankfort, OH; *ed:* (BA) Fr, Capital Univ 1961; (MA) Fr Ed, Miami Univ Oxford 1974; Teaching Certificate Capital Univ 1962-63; Soc Stud, OH St Univ 1966-67; *cr:* Fr Teacher Linden-Mc Kinley HS 1963-66; Fr/Eng/Soc Stud Teacher Fairview HS & Jr HS 1968-87; Fr/Soc Stud Teacher John H Patterson Career Center 1987-; *ai:* Dayton Ed Assn, NEA 1968-78, 1988-; Government Title III Trng Prgm Fr Instrs OH St Univ 1963; *office:* Patterson Career Center; 118 E 1st St Dayton OH 45402

KERR, HAROLD R., Social Studies Teacher; *b:* New Castle, PA; *m:* Sherry Williams; *c:* Brian, Ricky; *ed:* (BA) Soc Stud, Indiana Univ of PA 1966; (MS) Soc Stud, Slippery Rock Univ 1969; *cr:* Teacher Mohawk Area Schls 1966-; *ai:* PA St Ed Assn, NEA; *home:* 132 Hickory St Beaver PA 15009

KERR, JANIS GARRETT, Science Teacher; *b:* Oklahoma City, OK; *m:* William S. II; *c:* Jana Garrett Beihl, Roger Garrett; *ed:* (BA) Elem Ed, OK Univ 1967; Sci Seminar, OK City Univ; Project Wild; *cr:* 5th Grade Teacher Steed Elem Sch 1967-71; Pre-Sch Teacher Hillcrest Presbyn Church 1977-80; Math/Sci Teacher John Carroll Sch 1980-83; Sci Teacher Heritage Hall 1985-; *ai:* Sci Fair Spon; Co-Spon Sci Club; Faculty Advisory Comm; *office:* Heritage Hall Sch 1401 NW 115th St Oklahoma City OK 73114

KERR, LINDA BROWN, English/Mathematics Teacher; *b:* Bloomington, IL; *m:* John N.; *c:* Elizabeth, Michelle, Timothy, Jennifer; *ed:* (BA) Bible/Chrstn Ed, Maranatha Baptist Bible Coll 1970; *cr:* Substitute Teacher Dade Chrstn Sch 1971-72; Eng Teacher Maranatha Baptist Bible Coll 1972-85; Eng/Math Teacher Suburban Baptist Schls 1985-; *ai:* Suburban Baptist Church Sunday Sch Teacher 1985-, Mother of Yr 1987; *office:* Suburban Baptist Schls 722 E S County Line Rd Indianapolis IN 46227

KERSCHEN, LUCILLE RITA, ASC, Elementary Teacher; *b:* Garden Plain, KS; *ed:* (AA) KS Newman Coll 1947-51; (BS) Ed, Sacred Heart Coll 1952-58; (MA) Theology, St Johns Univ 1971-77; Grad Stud Latin & Ancient His, De Paul Univ 1959-60; Elem Supervision & Admin, Sacred Heart Coll 1961; Latin, Creighton Univ 1962-63; Elem Prin & Eng, Wichita St Univ 1964-65; Higher Ed, St Louis Univ 1966-68; *cr:* 2nd Grade Teacher Aide St Joseph 1945-46; 1st-4th Grade Teacher St Marys Kinsley KS 1948-50; 1st-3rd Grade Teacher St Marys Inner City Mc Alester OK 1950-51; 2nd Grade Teacher Christ the King 1951-52; 1st-8th Grade Teacher/Prin St Peter & Paul 1952-53; 3rd-5th Grade Teacher/Prin St Nicholas 1953-59; 3rd-5th Grade Teacher/Prin St Marys Inner City 1959-61; 5th-8th Grade Teacher St Francis of Assisi 1961-64; Ed Supvr Diocese of Wichita 1964-66; 7th-8th Grade Departmental Lang Art Teacher St Margaret Mary 1969-78; 6th 8th Grade Departmental/Lang Art/Religion Teacher St Anne 1980-85; 6th-8th Grade Lang Art/Religion Teacher St Joseph Mid Sch 1986-89; *ai:* 7th Grade Homeroom Spon; St Joseph Parish Ed Commission Chairperson; St Joseph Sch Bd Faculty Rep; Project Headstart Volunteer 1968; Civil Defense Shelter Management 1963; Ungraded Primary 1964; Inter-Faith Offender Concerns Comm 1975; Lang Art Textbook Adoption Comm 1988; NCTE Mem 1989; NCEA Mem 1990; BSA Cnslr 1976; KS Newman Coll Bd of Dir 1969-79; KS Cncl on Crime & Delinquency 1973-75; Title IV Fellowship St Louis Univ 1966-68; Nom Teacher of Yr 1979; Human Potential Dev Sex Respect 1987; KS Sch Team Trng for Substance Abuse Prevention 1986; *office:* St Joseph Sch 139 S Millwood Wichita KS 67213

KERSEY, L. WILBUR, Principal; *b:* Richmond, VA; *m:* Katharine Clark Kersey; *c:* Barbara, David, Marc; *ed:* (BA) Sociology, Univ of Richmond 1956; (MDIV) Ministry 1959, (DMIN) Ministry, 1975 Southeastern Baptist Theological Seminary; Guidance/Cnslng Old Dominion Univ 1971; *cr:* Pastor Reedy Creek/Dolphin Baptist Churches 1956-59; Pastor Court Street Baptist Church 1960-; Prin Court Street Acad 1965-; *office:* Court Street Acad Court & Queen St Portsmouth VA 23703

KERSEY, MICHELE L., Teacher; *b:* Ogden, UT; *m:* Steve; *c:* Brandy L., Jami Uragami; *ed:* (BS) Eng/Poly Sci, Weber St Univ 1984; Working Towards Level III Math Endorsement; *cr:* Teacher T N Bell Jr HS 1984-; *ai:* Spirit Builder 8th Grade Adv; Stu Government; Dist Champions in Krypko 1988-89; *office:* T H Bell Jr HS 165 W 5100 S Ogden UT 84405

KERSH, TANYA JONES, Reading Teacher, Chair & Coord; *b:* Dallas, TX; *m:* Steven Eugene; *c:* Joseph, Steven, Lauren; *ed:* (BA) Eng/His, Dallas Baptist Univ 1974; (MS) Spec Ed, Univ of TX Dallas 1981; Specialist Rdng, Univ of N TX 1983; Advanced Rdng Skills Instr; Edmar Dyslexia Instr; *cr:* Eng Teacher Duncanville HS 1974-77; Rdng Teacher 1981-, Rdng Dept Head/Dist Coord 1985-, Technology Coord 1989- Lancaster HS; *ai:* Dept Chairperson; Testing, Ability Grouping, Dist Improvement Plan, Dyslexia, Textbook Adoption Comms; Dist Rdng Comm Chairperson; TX St Rdng Assn; Ellis Cty Rdng Assn; Intnl Rdng Assn; Alpha Delta Kappa 1990; Co-Authored Project Pass; *office:* Lancaster Ind Sch Dist 1105 Westridge Lancaster TX 75146

KERSHAW, JOHN DARREN, Jr High/High School Teacher; *b:* Silver Creek, NE; *m:* Joyce Ann Runge; *c:* Joshua, Jordan; *ed:* (BA) Soc Sci, Kearney St Coll 1983; Grad Work Kearney St Coll; *cr:* Math/His/Phys Ed Jr HS Teacher Culbertson Schls 1983-; *ai:* Jr HS Girls Vlybl, Head Bsktbk, Track, Asst Ftbl Coach; FCA Spon; NHS & Schlsp Comm; Culbertson Ed Assn, NE Ed Assn, NEA 1983-; *office:* Culbertson Schls 702 Arizona Culbertson NE 69024

KERSHNER, CAREN DONCASTER, Science Teacher; *b:* Dayton, OH; *c:* Avery Runner, Carey B.; *ed:* (BS) Bio/Environmental Sci, Adams St Coll 1988; Several Wkshps; *cr:* Teacher Moffat HS 1988-; *ai:* Knowledge Bowl Coach; Cheerleading & Class Spon; Sci Fair & Health Promotion Team Coord; Democratic Party Co-Chairperson 1987-; *office:* Moffat HS 501 Garfield Ave Moffat CO 81143

KERSHNER, PAUL RUSSELL, HS Physical Education Teacher; *b:* Pottsville, PA; *m:* Judy Angier; *c:* Mark, Lynn, Steven, Matthew; *ed:* (BS) Phys Ed, 1960, (MED) Scndry Ed, 1964 Univ of AZ; *cr:* Permanent Substitute Phys Ed Teacher Tucson Unified Sch Dist 1960-61; Phys Ed/Health Teacher/Swim Coach Rincon HS 1961-72; Swin Coach/Dept Chm/Phys Ed/Health/Driver Ed Teacher 1972-89, Swim Coach/Phys Ed/Driver Ed Teacher 1989- Sabino HS; *ai:* Swim Coach; After-Sch Driver Ed Behind-the-Wheel Instr; Natl Interscholastic Swim Coaches (VP, St Delegate) 1970-88, Outstanding Service Awd 1988; NEA, AEA, TEA 1961-89; Natl Fed of Athletic Coaches Dist 7 Swim Coach of Yr 1985; AZ Interscholastic Assn Swim Rep 1965-82, 1989-; Safari Club (Bd of Dirs, Ed Rep) 1984-; Tucson Unified Sch Dist Supt Awd 1988; Amer Wilderness Leadership Sch Grant; *home:* 841 N Corinth Tucson AZ 85710

KERVICK, IRENE THERESE, 8th Grade Teacher; *b:* Bristol, PA; *ed:* (BA) Ed, Immaculata Coll 1971; (MA) His, Villanova Univ 1978; La Salle Univ, Trenton St; *cr:* 4th-5th/8th Grade Teacher Saint Matthew Demonstration Sch 1960-68; 8th Grade Teacher Saint Agnes Demonstration Sch 1968-72, Sts Simon & Jude 1972-76; St William 1976-80, St Matthew 1980-83, Blessed Virgin Mary 1983-88, St Andrew 1988-; *ai:* Lang Art Comm for Archdiocese of Philadelphia; Writing Examinations For Archdiocese; St Simon & Jude Girls Bsktbl, Sftbl Coach; Lang Art Comm Co Chairperson, Mem 1962-80; Involved in Speaking on Effects of Shock Rock Lyrics on Teens; *home:* 131 S Sycamore St Newtown PA 18940

KERVIN, SHIRLEY DIETER, 5th Grade Teacher; *b:* Bradford, PA; *m:* Jerry H.; *c:* Christopher, Peter; *ed:* (BS) Elem Ed, St Bonaventure Univ 1974; Grad Stud Dyke & Spencerian Coll of Commerce; *cr:* Secy Oil Company & Insurance Adjuster & Attorney 1948-60; 2nd-5th Grade Teacher Bradford Area Sch Dist 1974-; *ai:* Soc Stud Textbook Adoption Comm; Bradford Area Ed Assn Building Rep 1989-.

KERVITSKY, CAROL DIANE, English Teacher; *b:* New York, NY; *ed:* (BA) Eng, Pace Univ 1968; (MED) Eng/Ed, Trenton St Coll 1977; *cr:* Substitute Teacher JHS 1969; Eng Teacher John F Kennedy HS 1970-; *ai:* Yrbk Adv; NJEA 1970-; *office:* John F Kennedy Jr HS Kennedy Way Willingboro NJ 08046

KERWIN, BARBARA MARY, First Grade Teacher; *b:* St Paul, MN; *m:* Paul John; *c:* Mary Partington, Kathy Hahn, Trish Scorpio, Sheila; *ed:* (BA) Eng/Scndry Ed, Coll of St Catherine 1958; Cert Elem 1st-6th Grades 1976; *cr:* 3rd Grade Teacher Holy Family Sch 1958-59; 1st Grade Teacher St Pascals Sch 1977-; *ai:* Staff Dev Comm; NCEA 1978-; Teacher of Yr Service Awd 1988-89; *office:* Saint Pascal Baylon Sch 1770 E 3rd St Saint Paul MN 55106

KESLER, SUE POTTER, Business Education Teacher; *b:* Winder, GA; *m:* James Royce Sr.; *c:* James R. Jr.; *ed:* (BBA) Secretarial Sci, Univ of GA 1954; (MBE) Bus Ed, GA St Univ 1980; Typing Wkshp Florence/Darlington Tech Coll 1988; *cr:* Bus Teacher Braselton HS 1954-57, Douglas Cty HS 1959-62; Career Ed Teacher Cousins Mid Sch 1975-81; Bus Teacher Newton Cty HS 1981-; Accounting Teacher Gordon Jr Coll 1986; Keyboarding Teacher DeKalb Tech Coll 1989-; *ai:* FBLA Co-Spon; NBEA, SBEA 1981-88; Appointed GA Textbook Advisory Comm 1987; Appointed Governors Safety Cncl 1983-; *home:* 1501 West End Dr Hartwell GA 30643

KESSEL, CATHERINE HEATH, 3rd Grade Teacher; *b:* Moline, IL; *c:* Christine, Kurt; *ed:* (AA) Ger, Blackhawk Coll 1964; (BA) Ger, Augustana Coll 1966; Grad Credits Related Ed Courses; *cr:* 5th Grade Teacher Ericson Elem 1966-67, Bainbridge Island 1967-68; 3rd Grade Teacher 1971-, Art/Span Teacher 1988- C R Hanna; *ai:* Staff Improvement & Dev Comm; NEA, IEA 1971-; Orion Ed Assn Membership Chm 1980-84; Orion Booster Club; *office:* C R Hanna Elem Sch 900 14th Ave Orion IL 61273

KESSIE, ALAN I., Business Ed & Computer Teacher; *b:* Waukegan, IL; *m:* Lyn Machemeta; *c:* Cami Myers, Brad, Amy Canty, Audrey; *ed:* (BS) Bus Admin, Roosevelt Univ 1962; John Marshall Law Sch; N IL Univ; Univ of NC Greensboro; *cr:* Management Sears Roebuck & Co 1967-71; Owner Prestige Porsche Audi 1971-74; General Mgr Yeresi Chevrolet Olds 1975-81, Owner Showcase Gallery of Art 1981-82; Teacher Richmond Burton HS 1982-85, Olympic HS 1985-; *ai:* Asst Var Ftbl & Wrestling Coach Adv Cmptr Club, FBLA, Human Relations; Sch Cmptr Resource Person; NC Bus Ed Assn 1986-; NEA 1983-; IL Eng Teachers Assn 1983-85; Chevrolet & Oldsmobile Divisions of General Motors Natl Sales Mgmt Awds; *office:* Olympic HS 4301 Sandy Porter Rd Charlotte NC 28217

KESSINGER, KIMBERLEY DAWN, Reading/English Teacher; *b:* Christiansburg, VA; *ed:* (BS) Early Chilhd Ed, VPI & SU 1986; *cr:* 7th Grade Teacher Brownsburg Mid Sch 1986-; *ai:* Yrbk Adv; 7th Grade Team Leader; Arts Dept Chairperson; Delta Kappa Gamma; NMSA; VPI Alumni Soc Chairperson 1987-89; 1st Brethern Church Drama Coach 1988-89; *office:* Brownsburg Mid Sch Main St Brownsburg VA 24415

KESSLER, MARCIA FIELD, Adjunct Faculty; *b:* Boston, MA; *m:* Robert Alan; *c:* Jerzy A.; *ed:* (BS) Spec Ed, Fitchburg St Coll 1977; (EDM) Interactive Technology, Howard Univ 1985; Designing Software Trng; *cr:* Title I Teacher Georgetown Public Schls 1977-78; Asst Professor North Essex Comm Coll 1978-79; 4th Grade/Spec Ed Teacher Weathersfield Public Schls 1979-84; Trng Mgr Polaroid Corporation 1985-89; Adjundt Faculty Lesley Coll 1988-; *ai:* Lesley Coll Mentor Teacher; Consultant to Apple Cmptr Dealer; Amer Society of Trng & Dev 1985-; Rochester Womens Club 1989-; Literary Volunteers of America 1977-; Teaching Fellow Harvard Univ; Human Resource System Personnal Convention Trng Prgm Guest Speaker; Article Published; *home:* 571 Neck Rd Rochester MA 02770

KESSLER, VIRGINIA ANNE, Second Grade Teacher; *b:* Peoria, IL; *c:* Kellee L. Kessler Sullivan; *ed:* (BS) Elem Ed, W IL Univ 1964; Grad Course 1968-89; Educl Admin; *cr:* 4th Grade Teacher Industry Cmmty Sch Dist 1964-65; Kdngtn Teacher Macomb Cmmty Unit Dist 1965-; *ai:* Elem Teacher Rep on Dist Behavior Comm; Phi Delta Kappa Chairperson Awds 1989-; W IL Rdng Cncl 1985-; W IL Whole Lang Support Group 1988-; Macomb Ed Assn Pres; Wesley United Meth Church (Litergist 1989-, Sunday Sch Teacher) 1975-84; *home:* 1131 Bobby Ave Macomb IL 61455

KESTER, PAULA WATSON, Fifth Grade Teacher; *b:* Cassville, MO; *m:* Dennis; *c:* Jeff, Jason; *ed:* (BA) Elem Ed, Southwest Baptist Univ 1969; (MS) Elem Ed, Drury Coll 1973; *cr:* 3rd-4th Grade Teacher Ritter Elem/Springfield R-12 1968-; 5th Grade Teacher Jeffries 1980-; *ai:* PTA Finance Comm; SEA/MSTA Chm of Election Comm 1974-75 1968-88; NEA/SNEA 1989-; Kickapoo Band Boosters Membership Chm 1982-83; Kickapoo Bsktbl Boosters 1989; *office:* Jeffries Elem/Springfield R-12 4051 S Scenic Springfield MO 65807

KESTERSON, CHARLES E., Social Studies Teacher; *b:* Belpre, OH; *m:* Louise Long; *c:* Robin Scheffert, John, Charles F.; *ed:* (BA) His, Olivet Nazarene Coll 1964; (MA) His Ed, NE MO St Univ 1980; *cr:* Teacher Cullom HS 1964-66, Anson Jr HS 1966-86, Marshalltown HS 1986-; *ai:* NEA 1966-; IA St Ed Assn Exec Bd Mem 1984-85; Marshalltown Ed Assn Building Rep 1989-; IA Cncl for Soc Stud 1987-; *home:* 119 S 10th St Marshalltown IA 50158

KETCHAM, THOMAS JOHNSON, 7th Grade Lead Teacher; *b:* Rutland, VT; *m:* Sandra Whitescaver; *c:* Pamela, Michael, Matthew, Jody; *ed:* (BA) Soc Sci, Parsons Coll 1968; Grad Stud Univ of VT, Castleton St Coll, Lesley Coll, St Joseph Coll; *cr:* Summer Youth Employment Prgm VT Dept of Ed 1977-; Teacher Otter Valley Union HS 1968-; *ai:* Geo-Bee Club Spon & Adv Coach; NCSS, NEA, VT Ed Assn 1968-; ASCD 1988-; Town Selectman Chm 1980-; St Thomas Grace Church (Vestryman, Clerk) 1989; Town Republican Party Vice Chm 1976-; VT St Dept of Ed Youth Employment Prgm Awd 1978-; Town of Whiting Certificate of Appreciation for Lib Work 1983; Outstanding Service to Stu Body Merit Awd 1984; Crystal Apple Faculty Awd 1988; *office:* Otter Valley Union HS Rt 7 S Brandon VT 05733

KETCHER, RONALD LORENZ, 8th Grade Teacher; *b:* Watertown, MN; *m:* Susan Cora Dunker; *c:* Joshua, Lindsay; *ed:* (BA) Elem Ed/K-12th Grade Phys Ed, Concordia Coll 1983; *cr:* 7th Grade Teacher Immanuel 1983-85; 4th Grade Teacher 1985-86, 8th Grade Teacher 1986- Holy Cross Luth; *ai:* Kansas City Luth Athletic League Secy; Athletic Dir; Soccer, Track, Bsktbl & Cmmty Wrestling Coach.

KETCHUM, NELLINE DELHOUSAY, Second Grade Teacher; *b:* Bell, CA; *m:* Donald L. Jr.; *c:* Donelle, David; *ed:* (BA) Elem Ed, Long Beach St Coll 1965; *cr:* 2nd Grade Teacher Pomona Elem 1965-68; Kndgtn Teacher Northside Elem 1968-69; 1st Grade Teacher Edison Elem 1969-70; 2nd Grade Teacher Anderson Elem 1975-80, Grace Chrstn 1980-; *ai:* Co-Authored Math Book for Kndgtn Teachers 1969; *home:* 5216 Monlaco Rd Long Beach CA 90808

KETCHUM, WANDA MARIE MORROW, Fourth Grade Teacher; *b:* Uncas, OK; *m:* Jimmie Gene; *c:* Gary, Melinda, Rick, Bryan; *ed:* (BS) Elem, OK St Univ 1961; *cr:* 3rd Grade Teacher Riverside Elem 1962-64; Kndgtn Teacher 1969-70, 4th/6th Grade Teacher 1972-73 Hearst Elem; 4th Grade Teacher C E Gray Elem 1973-; *ai:* NEA, OK Ed Assn, Bixby Ed Assn; Free Will Baptist Church (Mem, Childrens Church Leader, HS Sunday Sch Teacher); *home:* 8300 E 181st S Bixby OK 74008

KETRON, CARRIE OGDEN, Teacher; *b:* Clifton, TX; *m:* N. M.; *c:* John, Bobby; *ed:* (BAAS) Ed, Univ of N TX 1990; Voc Cosmetology Instr License; *cr:* Hairstylist Keller Beauty Salon 1970-78; Cosmetology Instr Renees Cosmetology Center 1978 83; Teacher Duncanville HS 1983-; *ai:* Amer Voc Assn Membership 1984-; Voc Industrial Clubs of America Adv 1983-; TX Voc Teacher Assn 1984-; Alpha Chi (Natl Convention 1990) 1989-; Iota Lambda Sigma (New Mem Initiation Team Chm, Natl Convention Delegate 1989) 1979-; ASCD 1989-; Golden Key Natl Honor Society (Cmmty Chairperson 1990) 1989-; TX Industrial Voc Assn (Procter St Teachers In-Service 1989, Advisory Comm 1988) 1983-; Phi Theta Kappa Natl Convention Delegate 1987, Schlsp Awd 1988; World Vision Spon 1989; Adopt A Highway 1989; Spec Olympics 1989; Child Abuse Campaign 1989; Cmmty Food Basket Project 1989; House of Rep Certificate of Citation 1988; Muscular Dystrophy Assn Money Raiser 1987, Citation of Merit 1988; Duncanville-Cedar Hill Nursing Home Volunteer 1987; On Task Force That Developed VICA Prof Dev Prgm & Club Standards Prgm; Several Publications; *office:* Duncanville HS 900 W Camp Wisdom Rd Duncanville TX 75116

KETRON, MILDRED F., Science Teacher; *b:* Toughkennamon, PA; *m:* Robert G.; *c:* Kathryn K. Bull, Martha K. Kaminsky, Laura K. Hughston; *ed:* (BS) Sci Ed, E TN St Coll 1954; (MS) Sci Ed, Univ of TN 1981; *cr:* Sci Teacher Doyle HS 1973-; *ai:* Spon Sci Club; Teacher Evening Alternative Sch; Mem Advisory Comm; Tutor Adult Literacy Prgm Knox City; KCEA, TEA, NEA, NSTA, Phi Delta Kappa; Stokely Fellow Univ of TN; Knoxville Leadership Ed 1989-; *office:* Doyle H S 2020 Tipton Station Rd Knoxville TN 37920

KETTERING, DONALD R., 6th Grade Teacher; *b:* Ashland, OH; *m:* Unie Draper; *c:* Brian, Jessica; *ed:* (AS) Ed, OH St Univ 1970; (MS) Curr Dev, Ashland Univ 1987; *cr:* 6th Grade Teacher Shelby City Schls 1970-; *ai:* Ashland Soil & Water Conservation Dist Supvr 1987-; 4-H Adv; OH Ed Comm Mem 1989; OH Soil Conservation Dist; OH Cncl on Ec Ed Outstanding Conservation Farmer of Yr; Whos Who in Ag 1989.

KETTON, GLORIA LAWRENCE, K-6th Grade At-Risk Teacher; *b:* Tyler, AL; *m:* Henry Wallace; *c:* Alesia, Leslie, Janique; *ed:* (BS) Elem Ed, 1970, (MS) Elem Ed, 1976- AL St Univ; *ai:* Chairperson Local Sch In-Service & Soc Comm; NEA, AL Ed Assn, Dallas Cty Prof Ed Assn; Venusette Civic Club Parliamentarian 1987-; *office:* Southside Elem Sch 3104 Old Montgomery Hwy Selma AL 36701

KETZ, JOSEPH PATRICK, A P Chem & Chem I Teacher; *b:* Beckley, WV; *m:* Stephanie Lee; *ed:* (BS) Scndry Ed, 1980, (MS) Comm, 1986 WV Univ; Grad Stud; *cr:* Teacher Woodrow Wilson HS 1980-; *ai:* Tennis Coach; Faculty Soc Comm; NEA; *office:* Woodrow Wilson HS 410 Stanaford Rd Beckley WV 25801

KEY, CONNIE WILKINS, English Teacher; *b:* Reidsville, NC; *m:* Denny Sr.; *c:* Denny Jr., Amanda; *ed:* (BA) Eng, Winthrop Coll 1972; (MA) Mid Grades Ed, ASU 1987; *cr:* 8th Grade Rdng Teacher York Mid Sch 1972-74; Rdng Lab Teacher N Surry HS 1974-75; Teacher of Learning Disabilities/Eng Teacher Starmount HS 1975-79, 1983-84; Eng Teacher of Learning Disabilities Forbush HS 1979-80; Teacher of Academically Gifted Yadkinville Elem 1984-89; Eng Teacher Starmount HS 1989-; *ai:* Sch Wide Assistance Team; NC Academically Gifted Teachers 1988-89, Yadkin Cty Outstanding Teacher; *home:* 7641 Rolling Oak Ct Clemmons NC 27012

KEY, DEBORAH GALLOWAY, Elem/Family Life Skills Coord; *b:* Henderson, KY; *m:* Bev Ray; *c:* Mandy, Ashley, Casey; *ed:* (BA) Elem Ed, 1971, (MS) Elem Guidance Counseling, 1974; Rank I Elem Ed, Murray 1981; Endorsement Elem Principalship/ Supervision, W KY 1989; *cr:* 4th-6th Grade Teacher Cairo Elem 1971-; 5th Grade Teacher 7th St Elem 1984-; Drug/Alcohol & Family Life Skills Coord Henderson Cty Schls 1989-; *ai:* Fine Arts Performance Fund Comm Chairperson; In Service/Calendar Comm; Delta Kappa Gamma Mem 1990; KEA Mem 1971-; Henderson Arts Cncl Bd Mem 1988-; Delta Kappa Gamma Mem 1990; Democratic Womens League of Voters Mem 1988-; Published Learning Disabilities Booklet; KET Grant for Creative Writing in Classroom; Dist & St Historical Map Contest Winners; *home:* 1021 N Main Henderson KY 42420

KEY, HELEN ELAINE, Business Education Teacher; *b:* Cleveland, OH; *ed:* (BS) Comprehensive Bus Ed, WV St Coll 1968; (MA) Higher Ed Admin, Cleveland St Univ 1977; Completed Advanced Courses in Admin, Kent St 1989; *cr:* Secy Standard Oil of OH 1964-68; Adult Instructional Employee Cleveland Heights Univ 1975-76; Instr Dyke Coll 1978-88; Instr Cuyahoga Comm Coll 1686- Instructional Employee Cleveland Bd of Ed 1968-; *ai:* Stu Leadership & Trng Organization Adv; Career Dev Building Rep; Sch Based Mangement & Anti Substance Abuse on TASC Comm Mem; Cleveland Teachers Union Asst Building Rep 1985-88; Cleveland Area Bus Teachers Assn, AFT, NEA 1969-; Alpha Kappa Alpha (Secy, Treas) 1974-; Eloquent Pearls Club of Intnl Trng in Comm Pres 1986-87, Speech Contest Winner 1988; GBC Credit Union Treas 198-; Pi Lambda Theta Charter Mem; Notary Public; *home:* 564 Wilkes Ln Richmond Heights OH 44143

KEY, MARVELLIA MC FADDEN, Kindergarten Teacher; *b:* Marianna, AR; *m:* Kennis; *c:* Kimberlyn Mc Fadden, Nina, Kennis B.; *ed:* (BA) Early Chldhd Ed, Philander Smith Coll 1975; Early Chldhd Ed, Univ of AR; Educl Wkshps; *cr:* 2nd Grade Teacher Nunnally Elem 1975-76; Kndgtn Teacher Whitten Elem 1976-; *ai:* Kndgtn Dept Secy Whitten Elem; AR Ed Assn 1975-; LCEA; Eastern Star Chapter #22 Assn Mem 1976-; New Jerusalem Cogic Active Mem; *home:* 253 Bryants Ln Marianna AR 72360

KEYES, MARY PALCICH, English Teacher; *b:* Hibbing, MN; *m:* Joe; *ed:* (BA) Eng/Comm/Theatre, Coll of St Catherine 1979; Classes in Writing, His, Lit; Trng in Appleworks Microsoftword Cmptr Software Prgms; *cr:* Eng Teacher Hill-Murray HS 1979-84, 1985-; *ai:* Speech Coach/Judge; NHS Selection, Campus Ministry, Curr Comms; Hill-Murray Faculty Senate, Elected Mem 1987-88; Speech Assn of MN Treas 1981-85; Speech Assn of MN Co-Ed Newsletter 1982-83; MN Cncl Teachers of Eng Mem; Speech Assn of MN Mem; Presentation of Mary Parish, Liturgy Comm 1982-86; Yugoslav-Amer Society 1985-; Natl Endowment for Hum Grant Selected for Seminar in Classical Greek Lit 1989-; Lesson of Excl Teaching Awd 1988; Speech Assn of MN Outstanding New Mem in field; *home:* 2657 Granite Cir N Oakdale MN 55128

KEYTE, NANCY MADISON, 3rd Grade Teacher; *b:* Canonsburg, PA; *m:* Joel; *ed:* (BA) Elem Ed, CA St Los Angeles 1965; (MA) Admin Services, CA Polytechnic San Luis Obispo 1982; *cr:* Teacher Vincent Elem Sch 1965-72, Atherwood Elem Sch 1972-76, Oceano Elem Sch 1977-84, Grover City Elem Sch 1 84-; *ai:* Assn Of CA Sch Admins 1981-; Lioness (Pres, Secy) 1982-87, Lioness Of Yr 1984, 1986; Lions Dir 1987-; Quota (Pres, Dist Governor) 1983-; Math Grant; *office:* Grover City Elem Sch 365 S 10th St Grover City CA 93433

KHAN, MARIAMA JOSHUA, Mathematics Teacher; *b:* Lahore, Pakistan; *m:* Frank Habibullah; *c:* Michael Dilshev, Sarah, Ribka; *ed:* (BA) Eng/Math, Kinnaird Coll 1958; (MA) Eng, Punjab Univ 1960; (MA) Classroom Teaching, MI St Univ 1987; *cr:* Lecturer Kinnaird Coll 1960-66; Instr Government Polytechnic Inst 1966-79; Teacher Union HS 1983-.

KHOURY, ANTHONY JOHN, Social Studies Teacher; *b:* Geneva, NY; *m:* Clare Cerza; *c:* Julie Ghaffary, Kim Berger, Claire A. Gavin; *ed:* (BA) Ec/Math, Hobart Coll 1950; Post Grad Stud Ed; *cr:* Bus Owner Super Market 1950-71; Teacher Geneva Schls 1971-; *ai:* Var Bowling Coach; Assn of Soc Stud Teachers; Free & Accepted Masons (Dist Deputy, Grand Master) 1979-; *home:* 400 Hamilton St Geneva NY 14456

KHOURY, CAROL G., Fifth Grade Teacher; *b:* Engelwood, NJ; *ed:* (BA) Sociology, Wagner Coll 1978; (MSED) Rdng, St Johns Univ 1980; *cr:* Rdng Teacher The Cmmty Sch 1980-81; 7th Grade Teacher 1982-88, 5th Grade Teacher 1988- Our Lady of Sorrows Sch; *office:* Our Lady of Sorrows Sch 30 Madonna Pl Garfield NJ 07026

KIBILDIS, JOHN FRANCIS, Social Studies Teacher; *b:* Brooklyn, NY; *m:* Dianna June Haggerty; *c:* John; *ed:* (BA) Soc Stud, Montclair St 1968; (MA) Ed Admin/Supervision, William Paterson 1978; Municipal Finance Certificates, Rutgers Univ; Working Towards Masters Montclair St Coll & William Paterson Colll; *cr:* 4th Grade Teacher 1968-70, 6th Grade Math/Sci Teacher 1970-71 Hardyston Elem Sch; 7th/8th Grade Soc Sci Teacher Ogdensburg Public Sch 1971-; *ai:* Stu Cncl, Yrbk Adv; Girls Bsktbl Coach; Core Team Mem for At-Risk-Stus; Co-Ed Vlybl Coord; Ogdensburg Steering Comm Mem; NEA, NJEA 1968-; Ogdensburg Historical (Project Dir, Trustee) 1987-, Life Mem 1989; Ogdensburg Fire Dept Honorary Mem 1987, Service Plaque 1986; Ogdensburg Historical Society Service Plaque 1987; Ogdenburg Mayor Service Plaque 1989; Appointed Ogdensburg Borough (Cncl 1978-81, Cncl Pres 1979-82, Mayor 1982, Chm Planning Bd 1989-90); *office:* Ogdensburg Public Sch Main St Ogdensburg NJ 07439

KICK, STEPHEN P., American History Teacher; *b:* Akron, OH; *m:* Kay Ellen Schlessman; *c:* Ellen, Phillip, Andrew; *ed:* (BSED) Poly Sci/His, Capital Univ 1964; (MED) Guidance, Bowling Green St Univ 1968; Transportation Wkshp OH Univ; Course Work Univ of Dayton; *cr:* Teacher/Coach Riverdale HS 1964-65; Teacher/Coach/Cnslr Upper Scioto Valley HS 1965-69; Teacher/ Coach/Cnslr/Transportation Supvr Patrick Henry HS 1969-76; Teacher/Coach Kenton HS 1976-83, Ridgedale HS 1983-88, Loudonville HS 1988-; *ai:* Head Boys Bsktbl, Jr Var Boys Bsbl Coach; HS Rep Supt Advisory Comm; OH HS Bsktbl Coaches Assn (Pres 1987-88, Mem) 1964-; OH Ed Assn, NEA 1964-; Church Cncl (Pres 1981-84) 1968-69, 1974-75, 1979-85, 1989-; City Recreation Bd 1978-83; Outstanding Teachers of America 1975; Coach of Yr 1968, 1969, 1973, 1974, 1984; *office:* Loudonville HS 421 Campus Ave Loudonville OH 44842

KIDD, CAROL (WINSTON), French Teacher; *b:* London, England; *m:* Kenneth R.; *ed:* (BA) Fr/Scndry Ed, Frostburg St Coll 1968; (MED) Foreign Lang Ed, Univ of MD 1974; Grad Courses Univ of MD; Inst for Canadian Study for US Fr Teachers SUNY Plattsburgh 1989; The Child in Lit ofCanada & Africa NEH 1988; Various Wkshps & In-Service Courses; *cr:* Teacher Laurel Jr HS 1968-69; Teacher/Dept Chairperson D D Eisenhower Jr HS 1969-81, Laurel HS 1981-; *ai:* Natl Fr Honor Society; Ski Club; Class Spon; Stu European Travel Trip Leader; AFT 1975-; AATF 1980-; MD Foreign Lang Assn 1985-; Ski Club 1987-; Co-Author of 2 Curr Guides for Foreign Lang, Organized

& Chairperson Fr Total Immersion Project Prince Georges Cty; *office:* Laurel HS 8000 Cherry Ln Laurel MD 20707

KIDD, GALE RICKETTS, Chemistry Teacher; *b:* Danville, VA; *ed:* (BS) Bio/Chem, Averett Coll 1982; (MAED) Curr/Instruction/Sci, VPI-SU 1989; Nursing; Respiratory Therapy; *cr:* Teacher Halifax Cty Public Schls 1983-85, Pittsylvania Cty Public Sch 1985-; *ai:* Sftbl & Bsktbl Coach; Yrbk Spon; Church Youth Leadership Coord; Danville Comm Coll Public Speaking Instr; NSTA; Toastmasters (Area Governor 1988-, Pres 1987), Area Gov of Yr 1990; Commonwealth of VA Grant; *home:* Rt 8 Box 574 Danville VA 24540

KIDD, JOHN EDWARD, Teacher/Department Chairman; *b:* Brooklyn, NY; *m:* Sally Ruth Openhym; *c:* Tammy Kidd Weber, Scott E., Lorene Kidd Nolan; *ed:* (MED) Soc Stud, William Paterson Coll 1974; Grad Work Hamline Univ & Union Coll; *cr:* Teacher/Dept Head Cntrl Mid Sch 1961-; *ai:* Bsbl Coach; NEA, NJEA, PTHEA; NJ Cncl Soc Stud 1961-; NCSS; Boro of Ogdensburg (Boro Clerk 1963-67, Mem Common Cncl 1968-72); Fellowship Hamline Univ 1967, Union Coll 1968; Prof Book Reviews; Book Ed; *home:* 18 Madison Dr Ogdensburg NJ 07439

KIDD, KIMBERLY SCOTT, Mathematics Teacher; *b:* Chicago, IL; *c:* Kristyn; *ed:* (BA) Ed, Natl Coll of Ed 1977; Working Towards Masters Cmptr Ed; *cr:* Teacher Sandburg Elem Sch 1977-81, Gwendolyn Brooks Jr HS 1981-; *ai:* Pom Pon Spon; Comm to Improve Sch Environment; Alpha Kappa Alpha; *home:* 1204 Williamsburg Country Club Hills IL 60478

KIDD, LOIS ELLIS, Language Teacher; *b:* Menard, TX; *c:* Stan, Suzanne Corso, Clay, Katharine Lindsey; *ed:* (BA) His, Eng, Pan American Univ 1971; Univ of TX Permian Basin Western St Coll Gunnison Co; *cr:* Teacher Donna HS 1971-76, Iraan HS 1976-79, Lathan Walker Jr HS 1980-; *ai:* Stu Cncl Spon; Ready Writing UIL; TSTA St Del 1971-74; TCTA 1977-; TSTE 1980-; *home:* 1301 S Gary Monahans TX 79756

KIDD, MARY GRACE, Graphic Arts Instructor; *b:* Douglas, GA; *m:* Alan; *c:* Cliff Dix, Cathy Dix, Michelle Satterfield, David, Shannon; *ed:* (BA) Voc Ed, Valdosta St Coll; Graphic Art Instr at Graphic Arts Tech Institution 1989; *cr:* Co-Owner/Operator Insta Print Copy Center Incorporated 1974-; Instr Lee Cty HS 1988-; *ai:* Project Success Team Mem CVAE; Graphic Arts Tech Fnd, PAGE Mem 1989-; Recognized By Natl Assn Quick Printers 1987; *office:* Lee Cty HS 439 Firetower Rd Leesburg GA 31763

KIDD, SHARON ELAINE, Soc Stud Dept Chair & Teacher; *b:* Cookeville, TN; *m:* Randy; *c:* Caleb; *ed:* (BS) Scndry Ed/Soc Stud, 1977, (MA) Scndry Counseling 1987 TN Tech; *cr:* Teacher White Cty Mid Sch 1978-; *ai:* His Club Adv; 5-8 Grades Teacher of Yr; *office:* White County Jr H S 217 High School Sparta TN 38583

KIDD, STEPHANIE FOSTER, Mathematics Teacher; *b:* Salem, MA; *m:* R. Thomas; *c:* S. Chandler, Benjamin A., Elizabeth F.; *ed:* (BS) Math, 1964, (MA) Math/Ed, 1966 Murray St Univ; *cr:* Math Teacher South Marshall HS 1964-66, Huntington Cty Sch 1966-67, Fairfield Jr HS 1967-71, Homestead HS 1982-; *ai:* Class Spon; NEA 1964-87; KY Teachers Assn 1964-66; IN St Teachers Assn 1982-87; Aboite Lake Estates Bd Secy 1989-; *home:* 4413 Aboite Lake Dr Fort Wayne IN 46804

KIDDER, JEWELL LANDRY, 7th-8th Grade English Teacher; *b:* Lafayette, LA; *m:* Antoine C.; *c:* Aimee, Allison; *ed:* (BA) Fr/Liberal Arts, 1976, (BA) Eng Ed, 1977 Univ of Southwestern LA; LA Prof Improvement Plan; *cr:* 8th Grade Teacher Little Flower Elem 1975-76; 7th/8th Grade Teacher St Ignatius Elem 1978; 9th Grade Eng Teacher St Martinville Jr HS 1978-81; 7th/8th Grade Eng Teacher Cecilia Jr HS 1981-; *ai:* Awds Assembly Coord; Comm Rep; Limited Eng Proficient Stu; AFT 1988-; *office:* Cecilia Jr H S P O Box 129 Cecilia LA 70521

KIDNEIGH, JANE LISBETH, Language Arts Teacher; *b:* Sturgis, SD; *c:* Justin; *ed:* (BA) Eng Ed, Univ of WY 1964; Models of Teaching; Talents Unlimited; *cr:* 8th Grade Rdng Teacher Dean Morgan Jr HS 1966-76; 9th-12th Grade Eng Teacher Dubois HS 1979-84; 6th Grade Eng/Soc Stud Teacher 1984-86, 6th Grade Comm Skills Teacher 1986-87, 8th Grade Eng Teacher 1987- Powell Mid Sch; *ai:* Lang Art Dist Curr Comm Chm; Asst HS Speech Team Coach; Powell Ed Assn, WY Ed Assn, NEA 1984-; Beta Sigma Phi Secy 1990; WY Teacher of Yr Nominee; Appointed NCA Visitation Teams; WY Teachers Consultant; *home:* Box 786 Powell WY 82435

KIDWELL, RODNEY EUGENE, 10th/11th Grade Eng Teacher; *b:* Crossett, AR; *m:* Debra Mae Carl; *c:* Savannah C.; *ed:* (BA) Eng, Univ of AR Monticello 1974; (MA) Eng, Univ of MS 1981; *cr:* Eng Teacher Mc Crory HS 1978-; Part-Time Adjunct Eng Instr AR St Univ Beebe 1985-; *ai:* 9th Grade Class Spon; Gifted & Talented Selection Comm; *home:* 304 N Wade Mc Crory AR 72101

KIDWILER, BETTY ENGLE, 6th Grade Teacher; *b:* Engle, WV; *m:* Charles J.; *ed:* (BA) Elem, Shepherd Coll 1955; *cr:* Teacher C W Shipley Elem 1955-; *ai:* Shipley Ed Assn; Jefferson County Ed Assn Treas 1957-58; Keller Chapel United Meth Church (Sunday Sch Treas 1950-89, Pianist 1948-89); Charles Town Amer Legion Schlsp; *office:* C W Shipley Elem Sch Rt 3 Box 270 Harpers Ferry WV 25425

KIEC, PATRICIA MC CARTHY, First Grade Teacher; *b:* Buffalo, NY; *m:* Rodney F.; *c:* Lisa; *ed:* (BA) Elem Ed, Canisius Coll 1976; (MS) Elem Ed/Rdng, SUC Buffalo 1981; Essential Elements of Ed, Early Literacy Inservice Course; *cr:* 6th Grade Teacher Holland Cntrl Sch Dist 1976-77; 1st/2nd Grade Teacher Pioneer Cntrl Sch Dist 1977-; *ai:* Peer Partnering Comm; Grade Level Chairmanship; Mentorship Prgm; *office:* Delevan Elem Sch School St Delevan NY 14042

KIEFER, PATRICIA (MAY), First Grade Teacher; *b:* Canton, OH; *m:* Gregory L.; *c:* Gregory S., Todd L.; *ed:* (BS) Elem Ed, Malone Coll 1966; Completing MED Degree Curr & Instruction Ashland Univ; *cr:* 3rd Grade Teacher Garfield Elem Sch 1966-67; 1st/2nd Grade Teacher Mc Gregory Elem Sch 1979-; *ai:* Co-Operating Teacher 1987-89; Completed Mentor Teacher Trng; Mentor Teacher; OH Ed Assn 1979-; Canton Prof Ed Assn 1979-; Amer Cancer Inst Volunteer 1984; Malone Coll Alumni Assn 1970; *home:* 356 Linwood Ave NW Canton OH 44708

KIEFER, SHEILA DIANE, Second Grade Teacher; *b:* Wabash, IN; *m:* Arnold C.; *c:* Douglas, Mark, Mary B.; *ed:* (BS) Ed, 1973, (MS) Ed, 1977 IN & Purdue & Ft Wayne; Cert Advance Study in Sci; Project 2000 Drug & Alcohol Prevention; *cr:* 1st Grade Elem Teacher Ft Wayne Cmmty Schls 1973; 1st/2nd Grade Elem Teacher NW Allen Schls 1974-; *ai:* Chairperson of Comm to Further Study of Sci in Elem Ed; Discussables Comm; Delta Kappa Gamma Recording Secy; Pi Lambda Theta Corresponding Secy; IN MI Electrical Company Teachers Advisory Panel 1986-; Textbook Adoption for Sci at St Level; *office:* Perry Hill Elem Sch 13121 Coldwater Rd Fort Wayne IN 46845

KIEFER, YVONNE BAKER, First Grade Teacher; *b:* West Frankfort, IL; *m:* Noel George; *c:* Micheal, Cassandra Kiefer Herman, Tina Kiefer Burns; *ed:* (BS) Elem Ed, 1976, (MA) Elem Ed, 1981 USM; *cr:* Librarian/Teacher 1969-73, 1st Grade Teacher 1974- Nativity BVM; *ai:* Volunteer Elderly Care Center; USM Alumni; NCEA; Our Lady of Fatima Church (Cantor, Lector, Eucharistic Minister); Todays Cath Teacher Natl Awd of Excl 1988; *office:* Nativity BVM 1046 Beach Blvd Biloxi MS 39531

KIEHL, JAMES ROBERT, Reading Specialist; *b:* Milwaukee, WI; *m:* Ann Marie Carroll; *c:* Kelly, Heidi, Kevin; *ed:* (BS) Upper Elem & Intermediate Ed, WI St Univ Stevens Point 1969; (MA) Supervision of Rdng Instruction K-12, Cardinal Stritch Coll Milwaukee 1974; *cr:* Phys Ed Teacher 1969-71; Rdng Resource Teacher Milwaukee Public Schls 1969-78; Sales 1978-84; Rdng Teacher WI Heights Public Schls Black Earth Elem 1984-; *ai:* Jr HS Bsktbl Coach; K-6 Soccer Coach; *home:* 10 Harwood Cir S Madison WI 53717

KIEL, ALICE, English Teacher; *b:* Newark, NJ; *ed:* (BA) Eng, Kean Coll 1970; *cr:* Eng Teacher East Orange HS 1970-77, Toms River HS North 1977-; *ai:* Jr Var Cheerleading Coach; NEA 1977-; NJ Ed Assn 1990; Toms River Ed Assn; *office:* Toms River HS North Old Freehold Rd Toms River NJ 08753

KIENER, SHARON JUNE (BURNS), English Teacher; *b:* Mc Alester, OK; *c:* Amanda, Jordan; *ed:* (BA) Lang Art, Cntrl St Univ 1977; Northeastern St Univ; *cr:* Eng Teacher Eufaula Public Schls 1977-; *ai:* Acad Team Spon, Coach; ECTA, OEA, NEA; Eastern Star; *home:* 610 Grand Ave Eufaula OK 74432

KIENOW, EVELYN ANGERHOFER, 5th Grade Teacher; *b:* Aberdeen, SD; *m:* Henry; *c:* Kimberly; *ed:* (BS) Elem Ed, Northern St Univ 1970; *cr:* 5th Grade Teacher Leola SD 1970-73, Lincoln Elem Sch 1973-; *ai:* Math & Standardized Testing Comm; Sch Patrol, Lunchroom Stu Volunteer Workers, Jump Rope For Heart Teacher Adv; NEA 1973-; SD Ed Assn 1970-; Intnl Rdng Assn 1988-; PTA 1970-; Aberdeen SD Teacher of Yr; *office:* Lincoln Elem Sch 414 S 10th St Aberdeen SD 57401

KIER, JOELLE ANDERSON, Kindergarten Teacher; *b:* Storm Lake, IA; *m:* Timothy; *c:* Alex, Kalee; *ed:* (BA) Elem Ed, Buena Vista Coll 1973; Numerous Courses; *cr:* Kndgtn Teacher Newell-Providence Sch 1973-; *ai:* IA St Ed Assn, NEA; 1st Congregational Church (Bd of Ed, 1986-88, Sunday Sch Teacher); Newell Lib Bd Secy 1987-; *home:* 426 W Jensen Newell IA 50568

KIER, VERNICE E., Mathematics Teacher; *b:* Capron, VA; *c:* Mika R.; *ed:* (BS) Math Ed, VA St Univ 1973; *cr:* Math Teacher Dinwiddie Cty Jr HS 1973-76, John Lewis Jr HS 1976-80, Dinwiddie Cty Jr HS 1980-83, Great Neck Jr HS 1983-; *ai:* Co-Spon Mathcounts; Pep Club Spon; Tutor; Stu at Risk Comm; Virginia Beach Ed Assn, NEA, VA Ed Assn; *office:* Great Neck Jr HS 1848 Great Neck Rd Virginia Beach VA 23454

KIERNEY, ROBERT JAMES, Social Studies Teacher; *b:* Jersey City, NJ; *m:* Patricia; *c:* Sean, Meagan; *ed:* (BA) His, Jersey City St 1974; (MA) Admin/Supervision, Montclair St 19 *cr:* Teacher Belleville Mid Sch 1975; *ai:* Mid Sch Audio/Visual Coord; Union Rep; Phi Alpha Theta 1973-; N Arlington Soccer Dir 1985-; N Arlington Little League Coach 1988-; NJ Governors Teacher Recognition Awd 1986; *office:* Belleville Mid Sch 279 Washington Ave Belleville NJ 07109

KIESZ, MARGARET (SWENSON), Retired Teacher; *b:* Halliday, ND; *m:* Harold Christian; *c:* Karen, Harold Jr., Carol Sailey, Robley, Lynelle, Dick, Bruce, Kim Brown; *ed:* (BS) Elem Ed, Mayville St 1974; Numerous Courses Bismarck St Coll 1977 & Univ of NE Lincoln 1980; EMT Ambulance Natl Registry 1977; *cr:* 1st-8th Grade Teacher Dunn 28 1938-39, Mercer 32 1939-41, Rolette 25 1940-42; 4th-6th Grade Teacher Dunn 8 1942-44; 1st-8th Grade Teacher Mercer 24 1947-50; 1st/2nd Grade Teacher Mercer 20 1951-57; 7th/8th Grade Teacher 1957-61, 5th/6th Grade Math/Soc Stud/Eng 1961-65, 5th/6th Grade Math/Eng Teacher 1965-68, 6th Grade Math/Eng Teacher 1968-71 Stanton Sch Dist 22; 6th Grade Rdng/Eng/Spelling Teacher 1971-77, 5th/6th Grade Soc Stud Teacher 1977-85 Napoleon Sch Dist; *ai:* ND Ed Assn 1939-85; NEA Rdng Cncl 1971-85; Napoleon Ambulance Service 1974-84, Cmmty Service Awd 1984, Dedicated Ambulance Service 1986; Eagle Auxiliary 2328; Amer Legion Auxiliary Pres 1953-89; AARP Acting Secy 1989; Delegate to Legislature Logan Cty 1988-87 & Cass Cty SHA 1990; *home:* 1564 27th Ave S Fargo ND 58103

KIGER, JUDY CALHOUN, 5th Grade Teacher; *b:* Thomasville, NC; *m:* James Clinton; *c:* Rance, Mindi; *ed:* (BA) Elem Ed, Appalachian St Univ 1973; Math Academically Gifted, Catawba Coll 1987; *cr:* 4th/5th Grade Teacher Fair Grove Elem 1973-; *ai:* Local Sch Budget Comm; Textbook Adoption Comm; Co-Spon Sch Sci Fair; NC Math Assn 1987-; Thomasville Furniture Industries Mini-Grant Nature Sci Center & Weather Observation; Selected Mentor Trng; Presider NC Math Convention; Teaching Children Best They Can Be; *home:* 210 Game Trl Thomasville NC 27360

KIGHT, LAURIE ANN, Soc Stud Dept Chairperson; *b:* Pittsfield, MA; *c:* Kyanne, Kyle, Kasey; *ed:* (BA) Sociology, E Carolina Univ 1968; Grad Courses Univ NC Chapel Hill, Ec Univ, Columbia Univ; *cr:* Teacher Harnett Cty Schls 1968-69, Cumberland Cty Schls 1969-70, White Oak HS 1970-71, Chapel Hill HS 1971-73, Rocky Mt SC 1973-77, West Carteret HS 1981-; *ai:* Future Teachers of America, Human Relations & World Peace Club Adv; Academic Achievement Awds, Senate Bill 2 Comm; SACS Steering Dept Chairperson; System Leadership Team; Advanced Placement Coord; NC Soc Stud Mem 1988-; Sunday Sch Pres 1987-88; Helpline Pres of Bd 1988-; Gull Harbor Homeowners Pres of Bd 1983-84; *office:* West Carteret HS Rt 2 Box 390 Country Club Dr Morehead City NC 28557

KIJEWSKI, EDWARD JOHN, JR., Social Science Teacher; *b:* Philadelphia, PA; *m:* Elaine A. Benedetto; *ed:* (BA) His/Poly Sci, Widener Univ 1967; (MED) Scndry Elem Ed, West Chester Univ 1970; Japan & China Asian Stud; St Consultant for Japan 1979; Foreign Policy Wkshps; *cr:* 6th Grade Elem Teacher O W Holmes 1967-70; Scndry Soc Sci Teacher Upper Darby HS 1970-84; 5th Grade Elem Teacher Highland Park 1984-86; Scndry Soc Sci Teacher Upper Darby HS 1986-; *ai:* Intramural Spon Swimming & Water Polo; Prin Advisory Comm; *office:* Upper Darby HS Lansdowne Ave & School Ln Upper Darby PA 19082

KIKER, RUTH BLAYLOCK, Teacher; *b:* Jefferson Cty, AL; *m:* John D.; *c:* Brenda K. Hudson, Michael; *ed:* (BS) Elem Ed, Jacksonville St 1958; (MA) Elem Ed, 1968, (AA) Admin, 1978 Univ of AL Tuscaloosa; *ai:* NEA, AEA, PTA, WCCA; *office:* Valley Jr HS Rt 12 Box 81-B Jasper AL 35501

KILBY, JOE H., Physical Education/Sci Teacher; *b:* Tacoma, WA; *m:* Jill Karlene Cochrane; *ed:* (BED) Elem Ed/Phys Ed, Univ of Puget Sound 1983; Univ of Puget Sound 1978; FAST Sci Trng; Cntrl WA St, WA St Univ, W WA St; *cr:* 4th/6th Grade Teacher Federal Way Sch Dist 1974-77; 5th-6th Grade Teacher Orting Elem Sch 1977-85; Mid Sch Core/Math/Sci Teacher Orting Mid Sch 1985-88; Phys Ed/Sci/Math Teacher Orting Mid Sch/Sr HS 1987-; *ai:* Field Trip Chm; Head Coach HS Girls Sftbl; Head Mid Sch Ftbl Coach; 5th-6th Grade Boys & Girls Bsktbl Coach; Outdoor Ed; Asst Bsbl Coach Univ of Puget Sound; NEA 1974-; WA St Coaches Assn; Lions Club 1985-; Moose Club 1989-; Nisqually League Coach of Yr 1986, 1989; *office:* Orting Mid Sch P O Box 460 Orting WA 98360

KILDAY, CONNIE CARDWELL, Mathematics Department Chair; *b:* Jacksonville, FL; *m:* John Kevin; *c:* Kathleen N., Kristin M., Sean K.; *ed:* (BA) Psych, Univ of Dallas 1975-76; Grad Stud Univ of Dallas, E TX St Univ; Academic Trng, TESA; *cr:* Math Teacher Gunn Jr HS 1976-80; Math Teacher 1980-86, Math Dept Chairperson/Teacher 1986- Nimitz HS; *ai:* Textbook & Goals Comm; Curr Writing; Assn of TX Prof Educators (Building Rep 1980-85, 1987-89, Pres Elect 1989-, Pres 1990), Nimitz Teacher of Yr Nominee 1986; NCTM 1980-; Kappa Delta Pi (VP 1977-78, Pres 1978-79); PTA 1976-; *office:* Nimitz HS 100 W Oakdale Irving TX 75060

KILE, CAROL A., Business Teacher; *b:* Beatrice, NE; *ed:* (BA) Ec/Bus, Marymount Coll 1959; (MED) Bus/Office, CO St Univ 1971; *cr:* Bus Teacher Girls Cath HS 1959-61; Secy Martin-Marietta Corporation 1961-62; Bus Teacher South HS 1962-74, John F Kennedy 1974-; *ai:* Accounting Ed for the Forum; Building Comm; CO Educators For/About Bus Pres 1980-81; Delta Pi Epsilon Pres 1985-87; Mountain Plains Bus Ed Assn Panel Mem 1981; Admin Management Society Bd of Dir 1979-80; *office:* John F Kennedy HS 2855 S Lamar Denver CO 80227

KILE, DIANA LYNNE, Kindergarten Teacher; *b:* Ft Meade, MD; *m:* Gregory G.; *c:* Justin, Courtney, Kelly; *ed:* (BS) N-K-3, Bloomsburg St Coll 1978; Working Toward Permanent Cert Elem Ed; *cr:* 3rd Grade Teacher St Josephs Sch 1979-86; 1st Grade Teacher 1986-87, Kndgtn Teacher 1987- Holy Family Sch; *ai:* Sci Fair Coord; Bloomsburg Univ Alumni Assn 1979-; NCEA Mem 1979-; Cub Scout Den Mother 1989-; *office:* Holy Family Sch 728 Washington St Berwick PA 18603

KILE, DOUGLAS L., English Teacher; *b:* Glendale, OH; *m:* Carolyn S. Wells; *c:* Melinda K., Michael D.; *ed:* (BS) Eng/Ec, Univ of TX 1975; *cr:* Eng Teacher Harding Frosh Sch 1975-83, Harding HS 1983-; *ai:* Stu Cncl Adv; Lang Art Curr Comm; Portfolio Writing Prgm.

KILGO, JACQUELYN JARVIS, Mathematics Teacher; *b:* Dallas, TX; *m:* Charles Wayne; *c:* Lyn Campbell, Bill Campbell, Gary, Steve; *ed:* (BA) Elem Ed, Southern Meth Univ 1968; Math, E TX St; *cr:* 5th Grade Teacher White Rock Elem 1969; 6th/7th Grade Teacher Spring Branch Jr HS 1970-71; 5th-8th Grade

Teacher Hubbard Ind Sch Dist 1972-; *ai:* Jr HS Stu Cncl Spon; UIL Literary Coach; Number Sense Calculator; Delta Kappa Gamma 1977-78; Hubbard Garden Club 1975-76; PTO; TX Math Modules Trainer; Certified Teacher Appraiser; *home:* 115 Powell Dr Hubbard TX 76648

KILIAN, ANNE E., Third Grade Teacher; *b:* Dunkirk, NY; *m:* Adrian J.; *cr:* 3rd Grade Teacher Gowanda Elem 1966-; *office:* Gowanda Elem Sch School St Gowanda NY 14070

KILLAM, GEORGE ROBERT, History Teacher/Coach; *b:* Lufkin, TX; *m:* Scottie Dione; *c:* Dustin, Meagan; *ed:* (BA) His, 1984, (MA) His, 1988 Stephen F Austin; *cr:* Coach/Teacher Hudson Ind Sch Dist 1984-85, 1985-87; Teacher Hudson Ind Sch Dist 1987-89, Angelina Jr Coll 1988-; Coach/Teacher Douglass Ind Sch Dist 1988-; *ai:* Jr HS Boys Bsktbl, Cross Cntry, Track, HS Bsktbl, Bsbl, Cross Cntry, Track Coach; Class Spon; Sunday Sch Teacher; TABC 1989-; Moffett UFD Pres 1987-88, Service 1988; Angelina Cty Firefighter Pres 1984, Service 1984; Eagle Scout; Kiwanas 1981-84.

KILLEBREW, CATHERINE DENISE ANDERSON, Kindergarten Teacher; *b:* Greensboro, NC; *m:* James A. II; *c:* Jason A., Jordan A.; *ed:* (BS) Early Chldhd, Loma Linda Univ 1977; *cr:* Kndgtn Teacher San Gabriel Acad Elem 1978-; *ai:* K-10 Curr Comm; Violet & Thomas Zapara Teacher of Yr Awd 1990; *home:* PO Box 1477 Monrovia CA 91017

KILLEBREW, LOREE SIMPSON, Second Grade Teacher; *b:* Goodman, MS; *m:* William O.; *c:* Craig, Ronald, Murray, Gloria Phillips; *ed:* (BS) Elem Ed, Univ of So MS 1975; (MED) Elem Ed, Wm Carey Coll 1977; *cr:* Teacher Beauvoir Elem Sch 1975-; *ai:* BEA, MEA, NEA; *home:* 1722 James Madison Dr Biloxi MS 39531

KILLGORE, CONNIE BOWLING, Journalism/English Teacher; *b:* Wharton, TX; *c:* Laurel C.; *ed:* (BJ) Journalism, Univ of MO Columbia 1969; Cert Scndry Eng Ed, 1987, Scndry Ed Journalism, 1990 Southwest MO Univ; Grad Stud Numerous Universities; *cr:* Journalism/Eng Teacher Mtn Grove HS 1987-; *ai:* Sch Newspaper, Yrbk Adv; NCTE 1987-; MO Interscholastic Press Assn 1987-; Journalism Ed Assn 1987-; Ozarks Publications Advs 1989-; PTA 1989-; GSA Co-Leader 1989 ; Teacher of Month 1988-; *office:* Mountain Grove H S 420 N Main Mountain Grove MO 65711

KILLIAN, BONNIE BEAN, Learning Lab Instructor; *b:* Palmeton, PA; *m:* John E.; *c:* Jessica Killian Brodman, Amy M.; *ed:* (BS) Elem Ed, Kutztown Univ 1966; Diagnostic Prescriptive Math Trng; *cr:* 3rd/4th Grade Teacher Riverview Park Elem Sch 1966-84; Learning Lab Elem Cole Intermediate Sch 1984-; Gifted Elem Instr Muhlenberg Primary Sch, Cole Intnl Schl, Muhlenberg Mid Schl 1990; *ai:* Conducted Parent Make & Take Sessions; Taught Courses Berks Cty Inter Unit; Conduct In-Service Prgm Rdng & Math; NEA; PA Ed Assn; Muhlenberg Ed Assn Dir 1988-; Keystone Rdng Assn; PA Sch Bd Assn; Calvary Baptist Church Choir; Schuylkill Valley Sch Bd 1989-; PASCD, NCTM, PA Cncl of Teachers of Math & Keystone St Rdng Conference; *home:* RD 2 Box 2597 Reading PA 19605

KILLIAN, ELLEN GLENN, Fourth Grade Teacher; *b:* Rigby, ID; *m:* Duane; *c:* Vikki Ricks, Jeanie Briggs, Dana, Terri Criddle, Bret, Wendy Davis; *ed:* (BA) Ed, 1974, (MA) Counseling, 1985 Brigham Young Univ; *cr:* 5th Grade Teacher 1974-75, 4th Grade Teacher 1975- Bonneville Sch Dist ; *ai:* Fairview Elem Prof Dev Comm Chm; Dist Prof Dev Organization Comm Mem; E ID Rdng Cncl (Secy 1978-79, Young Authors Chm 1988-89); BSA Dist & Local Leader 1951-72, Silver Fawn Awd 1972; Nom Teacher of Yr 1979; *office:* Fairview Elem Sch 979 E 97 N Idaho Falls ID 83401

KILLIAN, RONALD VERNON, History Teacher; *b:* Great Falls, SC; *m:* Martha Brenda Gulley; *c:* Marty R., Ronald J.; *ed:* (BA) Philosophy, Univ of SC 1959; (MA) Soc Sci, Auburn Univ 1966; Advanced Cert Soc Sci; *cr:* His Teacher Pleasant Hill HS 1962-67, Paul M Dorman HS 1967-; *ai:* Sch Lockers; Saturday Sch; NEA, SC Ed Assn; *office:* Paul M Dorman HS 1491 Ezell Blvd Spartanburg SC 29301

KILLIAN, WILLIAM CLARENCE, 5th Grade Teacher; *b:* Altoona, PA; *m:* Kathy Jane Ruggles; *ed:* (AA) Bus Admin, Altoona Sch of Commerce 1972; (BS) Elem Ed, Penn St 1976; (MED) Ed, St Francis Coll 1980; *cr:* 5th Grade Teacher 1976-; 6th Grade Teacher Altoona Area Sch Dist 1976-; *ai:* Track Coach; Various Comm; Phi Delta Kappa 1976-.

KILMER, BRUCE NORBERT, Science Teacher/Content Ldr; *b:* Oconto Falls, WI; *m:* Rita; *c:* Barrett, Bridget, Jeffrey, Christopher; *ed:* (BS) Bio, UW Oshkosh 1964; (MS) Sci Ed, Univ of UT 1968; Natl Sci Fnd Summer Institute, AZ St; Edinboro Univ in PA; Univ of WI; *cr:* Teacher Richland Center HS 1964-65; Sun Prairie Jr HS 1965-67; Washington Jr HS 1968-70; Edison Mid Sch 1970-; *ai:* Group of Stud 100 Mile Bicycle Camp; NEA; WEAC; NSTA; WSST; WESTA; Natl Sci Fnd Grants Univ of UT-AZ St/Univ of WI Green Bay-Univ of WI Oshkosh Resulting MS Degree; *office:* Edison Mid Sch 442 Alpine Dr Green Bay WI 54302

KILMER, EDDIE J., English Teacher/Coach; *b:* Clovis, NM; *m:* Lesie Ann Romero; *c:* Dean, Kevin C.; *ed:* (BA) Phys Ed, West TX St Univ 1975; (MS) Ed, E NM Univ 1980; *cr:* Teacher/Coach Alamogordo HS 1975-76, Marshall Jr HS 1976-79, Clovis HS 1979-; *ai:* Ftbl & Golf Coach; Soph Class Spon; *office:* Clovis HS 1900 Thornton Clovis NM 88101

KILMER-GARRIDO, CAROL LOUISE, Spanish Teacher; *b:* Buffalo, NY; *m:* Antonio; *ed:* (BA) Span, St Univ Coll Brockport 1976; (MA) Span, Middlebury Coll 1979; Universided De Sevilla Spain; Course Work for BA Inst Intnl Madrid Spain; Course Work for MA; *cr:* Eng Teacher Harlow Acad 1978-80, Private Classes Madrid Spain 1980-81; Span Teacher Saint Francis HS 1988-; *ai:* Jr Class Moderator; Mem Discipline Bd; Amer Cncl Teaching Foreign Lang, Foreign Lang Assn Santa Clara, Foreign Lang Assn N CA.

KILPATRICK, SANDRA F., Biology/A P Biology Teacher; *b:* Pine Bluff, AR; *m:* Steve; *ed:* (BA) Bio, Hendrix Coll 1969; Grad Stud Phys Sci, Univ of MO Kansas City; Geology, KS St Univ; PET, Henderson Univ; *cr:* Sci Teacher Darby Jr HS 1970-71, Center Jr HS 1971-75, Newport Jr HS 1977-79; Bio/Chem/Physics Teacher Lavaca hs 1979-80; Bio Teacher Southside HS 1980-; *ai:* NSTA; Delta Kappa Gamma, Natl Sci Fnd Grant Geology; Marine Resource Fnd Grant Marine Bio.

KILTS, CLAIR THEODORE, Social Studies Chairperson; *b:* Ogden, UT; *m:* Liliane Lucie Burgat; *c:* Jeffery, Timothy, Mark, Rebecca, Matthew; *ed:* (AS) Sociology, Weber Coll 1950; (BA) His, 1957, (MA) His, 1959 Brigham Young Univ; Univ of UT, UT St Univ; *cr:* Teacher Mt Ogden Jr HS 1959-81, Mt Ogden Mid Sch 1981-; *ai:* Law Related Ed; Ogden Ed Assn (Pres 1974, 1980, 1985) Awd of Honor 1980; NEA; UT Ed Assn; Phi Delta Kappa; BSA Scoutmaster 1962-, Silver Beaver Awd 1969; UT Historical Society Outstanding Teacher Awd 1978; Hooper Water Conservation Dist Trustee 1968-88, Awd of Merit 1988; Night Class Instr Weber St Coll, Brigham Young Univ; Liberty Bell Awd 1980; *home:* 6008 W 5500 S Hooper UT 84315

KIM, EDWARD, AP Physics Teacher; *b:* Brooklyn, NY; *ed:* (AB) Chem/Environmental Sci, Dartmouth 1986; *cr:* Teacher/Coach Delbarton Sch 1986-87; Jr Moderator/Admissions Delbarton Sch 1989-; *ai:* Var Ftbl Defensive Coord; Head Var Bsbl; Admissions Comm; Jr Class Moderator Adv; Amer Chemical Society 1989-; AAPT 1987-; US Army Summer Associateship 1987; *office:* Delbarton Sch 270 Mendham Rd Morristown NJ 07960

KIM, ELIZABETH ANN (ALLEN), Kindergarten Teacher; *b:* Dawn, MO; *m:* J. H.; *ed:* (AA) Elem Ed, Southwest Baptist Coll 1957; (BA) Elem Ed, William Jewe Ll Coll 1959; (MA) Elem Ed, Univ of MO 1981-; UMKC; *cr:* Kndgtn Teacher 1959-60; 3rd Grade Teacher 1960-62; Kndgtn Teacher 1962- Randall Elem; *ai:* ACEI Early Chldhd Chairperson 1959-80; MO St Teachers Assn 1959-; IRA Bldg Rep 1988-; 1st Baptist Church SS Teacher Adult Choir 1959-68; 1st Presbyn Church Adult Choir/Childrens Choir/Deacon/SS Teacher 1968-; *office:* Randall Elem Sch 509 Jennings Rd Independence MO 64056

KIM, KANDICE KAY, Third Grade Teacher; *b:* Des Moines, IA; *m:* J. Lynne; *c:* Amanda, Sarah; *ed:* (BS) Elem Ed, Portland St Univ 1979; (MS) Curr/Instruction, Univ of OR 1981; *cr:* 3rd Grade Teacher 1980-82, 2nd Grade Teacher 1982-84, 1st Grade Teacher 1984-85, 3rd Grade Teacher 1985- Hall Elem; *ai:* Art Coord; Art Teacher Trng; Summer Art Inst; TAG Activity & Family Math Classes; *office:* Hall Elem Sch 2505 NE 23rd Gresham OR 97030

KIMBAL, RICHARD ALLEN, JR., Academic Supervisor; *b:* Jamestown, NY; *m:* Martha Lowder; *c:* Laura, Richard, David; *ed:* (BA) His, SUNY Albany 1965; (MS) Educl Admin, St Bonaventure 1980; Grad Stus His & Ed, SUNY Fredonia 1969-70; *cr:* His Teacher 1965-77, Academic Supvr 1977- Jamestown Public Schls; *ai:* Golf Coach 1968-; Class Adv 1971-74; NYCSS (Bd of Dir 1989-) 1965-; NY St Soc Stud Supvrs Assn 1977-; City of Jamestown Councilman 1978-; Boys & Girls Club Secy 1982-; Fenton Historical Society Bd of Trustees 1977-; *office:* Jamestown Public Schls 350 E 2nd St Jamestown NY 14701

KIMBERLAIN, CAROL BOSLEY, Language Arts Teacher; *b:* Lebanon, KY; *m:* Larry E.; *c:* Jon, Rob; *ed:* (BA) Eng, Univ of KY 1968; (MA) Counseling, 1978, (Rank I) Scndry Ed, 1986 W KY Univ; *cr:* Lang Art Teacher John F Kennedy Jr HS 1968-72, Lincoln Trail Elem 1974-76, Hardin Cntrl Mid Sch 1976-; *ai:* Current Events Bowl Spon; Calligraphy Writer; Counseling Advisory Comm; KY Assn for Gifted Ed 1985-89; KY Mid Sch Assn 1987-; *office:* Hardin Cntrl Mid Sch 3040 Leitchfield Rd Cecilia KY 42724

KIMBERLY, RENEE GEIGER, Choral Director; *b:* Macon, GA; *c:* Bradley E.; *ed:* (AA) Music, Macon Jr Coll 1978; (BME) Music Ed, GA Coll 1980; (MMU) Music, 1984, (EDS) Music, 1990 GA St Univ; *cr:* Music Specialist Kaiserslautern Elem Sch 1981-82; Choral Dir Ballard-B Mid Sch 1982-86, Southwest HS 1986-; *ai:* Music Educators Natl Conference, GA Music Educators Assn 1983-; Amer Choral Dir Assn 1985-.

KIMBLE, BETTY CROCKETT, 8th Grade Lang Art Teacher; *b:* Wilmington, DE; *m:* Philip N.; *ed:* (BS) Scndry Eng, West Chester Univ 1968; Grad Stud, Rdng, Spec Ed, Physch; *cr:* Lang Art Teacher/Team Leader Interboro Sch Dist Jr HS 1972-80; Eng/Rdng/Lang Art Teacher Interboro Sch Dist 1968-; Lang Arts Interboro Sch Dist Mid Schls 1982-; *ai:* Stu Cncl Adv; Spelling Bee Spon; Graduation & Fund Raising Coord; IEA, PSEA, NEA 1968-; *office:* Glenolden Sch Mac Dade Blvd Glenolden PA 19036

KIMBLE, DOTTIE MARTIN, Third Grade Teacher; *b:* Philadelphia, PA; *m:* Dan M.; *c:* Coreen, Jennifer; *ed:* (BA) Elem, 1963, (MA) Elem, 1967 CA St Univ Long Beach; Gesell Wkshp; *cr:* Teacher Los Alamitos Sch Dist 1963-69, Placentia Unified Sch Dist 1974-; *ai:* Mentor; Inservices Math, Lang Art; CTA, NEA, PVEA; CTIIP Grant Math 1985, Rdng 1986; *office:* Wagner Elem Sch 717 Yorba Linda Blvd Placentia CA 92670

KIMBLE, LARRY L., Jr HS Science Instructor; *b:* Mount Ayr, IA; *m:* Mary E. James; *c:* Vickie Harris, Kurtis; *ed:* (BS) Sci Ed, Northwest MO St Univ 1961; (MS) Sci Ed, Univ of IA 1990; Summer Inst Winona St Univ; CA Graduate Classes Northwest MO St Univ; *cr:* JR HS Sci Inst Mount Ayr Commty Sch 1961-; *ai:* NEA 1961-; NSTA 1986-; Lead Teacher Univ IA Chateaqua Prgm 1983-; Summer Inst Natl Univ CA Berkeley; Presenter Natl Convention NSTA 1987; *office:* Mt Ayr Community HS E Lincoln Mount Ayr IA 50854

KIMBLE, RITA BROUSSARD, 1st Grade Teacher; *b:* Opelousas, LA; *m:* Douglas; *c:* Deirdre, Douglas A.; *ed:* (BA) Elem Ed, Grambling St 1967; (MED) Admin/Supervision, Southern Univ 1983; *home:* Rt 6 Box 452 Opelousas LA 70570

KIMBRELL, CHARLOTTE WADE, Fifth Grade Teacher; *b:* Demorest, GA; *m:* Sanford; *c:* Tom, Joe; *ed:* (BA) Elem Ed, Piedmont Coll 1981; (MS) Mid Grades Ed, Brenau 1985; *cr:* 5th Grade Teacher Baldwin Elem 1981-; Educator Piedmont Coll 1988; *ai:* VBS Dir; Church & Wm Secy; PTA Prgm Chm 1986-87; HAE, GAE, NEA 1982-; Piedmont Coll Torch Club (Pres 1987-89, Secy 1983-85); Bd of Dir Alumni Assn Piedmont Coll; Baldwin Elem Teacher of Yr 1986-87; Woman of Yr 1990 Cornelia Church.

KIMBREW, PAUL RICHARD, Technology Teacher; *b:* Fairmont, WV; *m:* Donna Ellen Vangilder; *c:* Stacey A., Lauren A.; *ed:* (BA) Industrial Art, Fairmont St Coll 1975; *cr:* CPL USMC 1966-70; Teacher Sabraton Jr HS 1975-80, South Jr HS 1980-; *ai:* Technology Stu Assn Adv; WV Technology Ed Assn (Secy, Treas 1980-84, Exec Bd Mem 1989-); Epsilon Pi Tau Honorary 1974; WV Outstanding Technology Prgm of Yr 1986; WV Technology Teacher of Yr 1990; *office:* South Jr HS 500 E Parkway St Morgantown WV 26505

KIMBROUGH, VALINDA CARTER, Mathematics Teacher; *b:* Whiteville, NC; *c:* Steven; *ed:* (BS) Math, Fayetteville St 1974; A & T St Univ; Appalachian St Univ; *cr:* Math Teacher Cntrl Jr HS 1974-78, Career Center HS 1978-81, Paisley HS 1981-84, R J Reynolds HS 1984-; *ai:* Soph Class Spon; Sch Improvement Comm; NC Ed Assn Sch Rep 1987-89; R J Reynolds Tobacco Co R J R Schlsp 1980; NAACP Sat Dir 1989-; Volunteer Math Tutor First Baptist Church 1988-; *office:* R J Reynolds HS Hawthorne Rd Winston-Salem NC 27105

KIMERY, ROSEANNA CLARK, 8th Grade US History Teacher; *b:* Shelbyville, TN; *m:* Joe Frank; *c:* Lindsey, Jessica; *ed:* (BS) Soc Sci, 1975, (MS) His, 1981 Mid TN St Univ; *cr:* 7th Grade TN His/Civics Teacher Cntrl Jr HS 1975-79; 8th Grade US His Teacher Harris Mid Sch 1980-; *ai:* Soc Stud Dept Harris Mid Sch; Southern Assn Steering Comm Mem; Bedford Cty Ed Assn, Delta Kappa Gamma; 8th Grade Annual Trip Washington DC; *office:* Harris Mid Sch 400 Elm St Shelbyville TN 37160

KIMSEY, VIRGINIA WISNOM, Business Education Teacher; *b:* Dothan, AL; *m:* Phillip David; *c:* Krista L.; *ed:* (BS) Bus/Scndry Ed, Kennesaw St Coll 1987; Working Towards Masters W GA Coll; *cr:* Secy Bartow Cty Health Dept 1979-81, State Farm Insurance Claims Office 1984-86; Teacher Cass Comprehensive HS 1987-; *ai:* SADD Club, FBLA Club Spon; Cass HS Effective Comm Task Force Mem; *office:* Cass Comprehensive HS 738 Grassdale Rd Cartersville GA 30120

KINARD, CAROLE WRIGHT, Fourth Grade Teacher; *b:* Latrobe, PA; *m:* Byron N.; *c:* Scott; *ed:* (BA) Elem Ed, WV Wesleyan Coll 1975; Grad Stud Salem-Teikyo Univ; *cr:* Asst Group Therapist Latrobe Area Hospital Mental Health Clinic 1975-; 3rd Grade Teacher 1977-78, 4th Grade Teacher 1978 Simpson Elem; *ai:* Monthly Recycling Prgm; Bridgeport Jr Womans Club (Historian, St Project 1986-88), Best Overall GFWC-WVFWC WV Beautiful St Project 1988.

KINCAID, GINGER LEE, Physical Education Dept Chair; *b:* Baltimore, MD; *m:* Richard Alan; *c:* Kristina, Michael; *ed:* (BS) Health/Phys Ed, Madison Coll 1975; (MED) Scndry Ed, Towson St Univ 1985; *cr:* Teacher Glenelg HS 1978-; *ai:* Var Field Hockey & Var Lacrosse Coach; AAHPERD 1975-, MAHPERD 1975-, Merit Teacher Awd 1989; Delta Kappa Gamma 1989-; *office:* Glenelg HS 14025 Burnt Woods Rd Glenelg MD 21737

KINCAID, LORI TUCK, Social Studies Teacher; *b:* Durham, NC; *m:* Michael L.; *ed:* (BA) Ed, Elon Coll 1983; Soc Stud, NC St Univ 1990; *cr:* 6th Grade Teacher Woodland Elem Sch 1984-85; 9th Grade Eng Teacher 1985-86, 8th/9th Grade Soc Stud Teacher 1986 Southern Jr HS; *ai:* CO Club Adv NC Jr Historian Club; Media Advisory Cncl; NC Council for Soc Stud; Roxboro Jr Service League (ME) at Large 1986-1987 Treas 1987-1988); Long Memorial United Methodist Women (Circle 8) Southern Jr HS Teacher of Yr Nom 1987-1988; *office:* Southern Jr H S P O Box 642 Roxboro NC 27573

KINCAID, VERLINDA BRADLEY, Physical Education Teacher; *b:* Marks, MS; *m:* Mose Edward; *c:* Curtis; *ed:* (BS) Health/Phys Ed, Univ of MS 1974; (MS) Guidance/Counseling, Chicago St Univ 1989; *cr:* Teacher Quitman Cty Sch System 1975-76; Substitute Teacher Chicago Public Sch System 1976-78; K-8th Grade Phys Ed Teacher Irving & Portage Pk Schls 1978-80, La Salle Lang Acad 1980-; *ai:* Vlybl Coach; Guidance Group, Safety Patrol, Cheerleading Spon; Tutoring Co-Spon; Graduation Comm; Amer Assn for Counseling & Dev, IL Assn for Health &

Phys Ed 1988-; Kate Mae Mont Aware Nominee; *home:* 12015 S Laflin Chicago IL 60614

KINCH, KATHLEEN ANN (GOLOMBEK), Secondary EMI Teacher; *b:* Jackson, MI; *m:* Robert J.; *c:* Christopher, Alexis; *ed:* (BS) Ed of Mentally Handicapped, Cntrl MI Univ 1973; (MA) Guidance/Counseling, Eastern MI Univ 1976; Accounting, Cmptr/Data Processing & Art; *cr:* Scndry EMI Teacher Vandercook Lake Schls 1973-74, MI Center Schls 1975-77/1982-85; K-2nd Grade Elem Teacher 1977-82/1985-87, Scndry Emi Teacher 1987- MI Center Schls; *ai:* Tutoring Non-Spec Ed Stus; 9th Grade Class Adv; Mem of CORE Team for Stu Assistance Prgm; NEA, MEA, JCEA 1973-; MCEA (Treas 1977-78) 1973-; CEC 1973-74; Cub Scouts Treas 1986-; Created Summer Skills Booklets for K & 2nd Grade Classes; Developed A Citizenship Behavior Prgm to Share With Colleagues; *office:* MI Center H S 400 S State St Michigan Center MI 49254

KINDCHY, ERROL ROY, Middle School Teacher; *b:* Galesville, WI; *ed:* (BA) Soc Stud, Univ of Denver 1959; (MA) Ed, Univ of WI La Crosse 1972; *cr:* HS Soc Stud Teacher West Salem Area Schls 1956-64; Mid Sch Soc Stud Teacher Air Force Schls DOD 1964-66, West Salem Area Schls 1966-; *ai:* Annual; Amer Heritage; Jr Historical Society; Jr Stu Cncl; Soc Stud Curr Chm; WI Cncl Soc Stud, Natl WI Cncl Soc Stud; WI St Historical Society Bd of Curators 1987-; West Salem Historical Society Pres 1988-; Our Saviors Luth Church; West Salem Lions Club Bovay Awd 1986; WI Republican Party; His of West Salem Published 1981; Univ of WI La Crosse Educator of Yr 1988-89; West Salem Lions Citizen of Yr 1983; Valley Forge Teachers Medal 1973; *office:* West Salem Mid Sch 450 N Mark West Salem WI 54669

KINDER, MARY KATHLEEN, Reading Teacher; *b:* Dallas, TX; *m:* Joe Ed; *c:* Mary K.; *ed:* (BA) Elem Ed, TX Tech Univ 1983; (MA) Rdng/Ed, Univ of TX Permian Basin 1988; *cr:* Rdng Teacher San Jacinto Jr HS 1984-; *ai:* Stu Cncl Spon; Core Team Chm; Classroom Teachers Assn, PTA 1984-; Natl Rdng Assn 1988-; *office:* San Jacinto Jr HS 1103 North N Street Midland TX 79701

KINDLON, TIMOTHY MARK, 5th-6th Grade Teacher/Adm Asst; *b:* Chicago, IL; *m:* Lucinda; *c:* Tanya, Sean, Trevor; *ed:* (BA) Elem Ed, North Cntrl Coll1977; (MSE) Supervision & Admin, Natl Coll of Ed 1988; *cr:* 5th Grade Teacher Mark Delay Ssh 1977-86; 5th-6th Grade Teacher/Admin Asst Marion Hills Sch 1986-; *ai:* Ftbl, Sftbl, Bsktbl Coach; Cncl for Elem Sci Intnl; *office:* Marion Hills 133 Plainfield Rd Darien IL 60559

KINDRICK, MILTON E., Biology/Spanish Teacher; *b:* 0itzimons, CO; *m:* Deanna Jo Comstock; *c:* Joel; *ed:* (BA) Soc Sci, San Francisco St Univ 1965; (MA) Bio, Pacific Union Coll 1975; (MA) Span, CA St Univ Sacramento 1989; Advanced Trng Bio-Geology, Univ of WY; *cr:* Teacher Pleasant Hills Jr Acad 1966-71; Prin Pine Hills Jr Acad 1971-76; Teacher Sacramento Adv Acad 1983-; *ai:* Span Club, Backpack Club, Jr Class Spon; Span His & Lit Stud Fellowship 1982-83; Univ of Calgary Curr Dev Stud Fellowship; *office:* Sacramento Adv Acad 5601 Winding Way Carmichael CA 95608

KING, BARBARA A. DEMBSKI, 6th Grade English Teacher; *b:* Holyoke, MA; *m:* William R.; *ed:* (BS) Elem Ed/Eng, Worcester MA 1973; Grad Stud; *cr:* 6th Grad Soc Stud Teacher 1986-89, 5th-6th Grade Eng Teacher 1973, North Brookfield Elem; *ai:* Pen Pal Stu Letters to Russian Stu 1989-; Contract Negotiations Served on Bargaining Comm 1978-80; Published Sch Newspaper; Directed Holiday Plays 1973-82; Published Stu Newspaper 1974-75; NCT 1990-; MA Teachers Assn 1973-; NEA 1973-; Local Union NBTA 1973-; West Brookfield Democratic Comm 1975-85; Green Peace, Wildlife, PETA 1984-; *office:* North Brookfield Elem Sch New School Dr North Brookfield MA 01535

KING, CRIS, 7th/8th Grade Soc Stud Teacher; *b:* Columbus, OH; *m:* Le Ann Botimer; *c:* Jeremy C., Cristen L.; *ed:* (BS) Soc Stud Comp, OH Univ 1969; Private Pilot & Commercial License; *cr:* 7th/8th Grade Soc Stud Teacher/HS Coach 1970- Mt Gilead Exempted Village Schls; *ai:* Var Asst Ftbl Coach 19 Yrs; OH Ed Assn 1970-; Natl Muzzle Loader Assn 1982-85; *home:* 4955 SR 61 S Mount Gilead OH 43338

KING, DEBORAH (BOOKHEIMER), HS English Teacher; *b:* Mc Connellsburg, PA; *m:* Thomas S.; *ed:* (ASB) Legal Asst, Cntrl PA Bus Sch 1985; (BS) Eng, Shippensburg Univ 1988; M S Ed Prgm Shippinsburg Univ; *cr:* Legal Secy James Schall Attorney 1984-87, Fulton Cty Dist Attys Office 1985-86; HS Eng Teacher Forbes Road SchDist 1988-; *ai:* Sch Newspaper, Press Club, Frosh Class Adv; Forbes Road SD Teacher of Month 1989; Fort Littleton UM Church (Mem, Church Pianist, Choir Dir); *office:* Forbes Roah H S HCO 1 Box 222 Waterfall PA 16689

KING, DIANE, Third Grade Teacher; *b:* Yazoo City, MS; *ed:* (BME) Music Ed, 1974, (MM) Music Ed, 1977 Delta St Univ; (ME) Elem Ed, MS St Univ 1983; *cr:* Music Teacher Kemper Acad 1974-80; 3rd Grade Teacher Clarkdale Sch 1981-; *ai:* Meth Church Organist 1989-; Music Club Supvr 1989-; DEBS Adv 1985-86; *office:* Clarkdale Attendance Center Rt 1 Box 217 Meridian MS 39301

KING, DIANE DUVALL, History Teacher; *b:* Savannah, GA; *m:* James Meyers; *c:* Mara E., James R.; *ed:* (BA) Eng, 1968, (MED) Mid Sch, 1981 Armstrong St Coll; *cr:* Teacher Mercer Mid Sch 1968-69, Windsor Forest HS 1969-73, Blessed Sacrament Elem 1973-81, Calvary Baptist Day Sch 1981-85, Savannah Chrstn Preparatory 1985-; *ai:* Anchor Club, Jr Class, Stu Cncl & Beta Club Adv; Prof Assn of GA Educators; Chrstn Womens Club 1989-; Savannah Jaycettes Secy 1969-77; United Meth Women 1986-; *office:* Savannah Chrstn Prep Sch 2415 E Derenne Ave Savannah GA 31406

KING, DONNA FOSTER, 5th Grade Chairperson; *b:* New Orleans, LA; *c:* Meleka, Alvin Jr.; *ed:* (BA) Elem Ed, Southern Univ 1974; Tulane Univ Masters Prgm; Pip Prof Improvement Prgm; *cr:* 6th Grade Teacher Laurel Elem Sch 1974-84; 5th Grade Teacher 1985-88, 4th/5th Grade Teacher 1989- H W Allen Fundamental Sch; *ai:* Stu Cncl Adv; 4-H Club Leader United Teachers of New Orleans, LEA; Austerlitz Church Steering Comm 1990; Outstanding PTA Teacher; *office:* H W Allen Fundamental Sch Loyola Ave New Orleans LA 70115

KING, EDDIE, English/Journalism Instructors; *b:* Wagon Mound, NM; *m:* Katherine Martinez; *c:* Krystle; *ed:* (BA) Eng/Span/Journalism/Scndry Ed, 1976, (MA) Span, 1980 NM Highlands Univ; Post Grad Work Ed, NM Highlands Univ; *cr:* Instr Luna Voc-Tech Inst 1979-83; Visiting Instr NM Highlands Univ 1979-; Instr Memorial Mid Sch 1980-; *ai:* Yrbk & Newspaper Adv; Lang Festival Chairperson; Domestic Stu Exch Prgm Coord; Phi Kappa Phi, Phi Sigma Iota; NM Cncl of Teachers of Eng, Las Vegas Cncl Rdng, Intnl Rdng Assn; Portrait of America Educator Prgm Spon by Turner Educl Services Incorporated; Teaching Excl Golden Apple Awd IL Excl in Teaching; Natl Teacher of Yr Nom; *office:* Memorial Mid Sch 901 Douglas Ave Las Vegas NM 87701

KING, ELAINE MARIE, Third Grade Teacher; *b:* Peoria, IL; *ed:* Assoc Elem Ed, IL Cntrl Coll 1973; (BS) Elem Ed, W IL Univ 1975; (MS) Ed Admin, Univ of WY 1984; Grad Stud Curr/Instruction, Counseling, Spec Ed; *cr:* Teacher J J Mc Nally Grade Sch 1976-78, Sunnyside Elem Sch 1978-; *ai:* Young Authors Writing Contest; Lang Art Curr Comm; Sunnyside Elem Books & Beyond Rdng Prgm; WY Ed Assn 1978-; NEA 1976-; Intnl Rdng Assn 1978-; ASCD 1986-; Delta Kappa Gamma VP 1990; *home:* 238 11th St Rawlins WY 82301

KING, GRACIE M., Junior High English Teacher; *b:* Pickens, AR; *ed:* (BA) Eng, Univ of AR Pine Bluff 1978; *cr:* Jr HS Eng Teacher Cotton Plant HS 1978-85, Delta HS 1985-; *office:* Univ of AR Pine Bluff P O Box 41 Rohwer AR 71666

KING, HELEN, Retired Third Grade Teacher; *b:* Vancouver, Canada; *c:* John Dallain, Paul Dallain, Cathy Morris, Susan Colarossi; *ed:* (BED) Elem/Scndry, Univ of Alberta 1945; Kndgtn, Univ Alberta; Rdng & Writing, Univ Pittsburgh; Lang, Comm; *cr:* 1st-8th Grade Teacher Crossfield Alta 1945; Arrowwood Alta 1946-47; Kndgtn Teacher Calgary Alta 1947-48; Prin Small Sch Pq 1957-59; 3rd Grade Teacher Shawbridge ST Bruno Pq 1959-60; 5th-8th Grade Teacher Yeshiv Achitimmin 1960-63; 5th Grade Teacher St Augustines 1963-64; 3rd Grade Teacher Sewickley Acad 1965-88.

KING, JANET MARCIA, First Grade Teacher; *b:* Albany, NY; *ed:* (BS) Elem Ed, St Rose 1964; Permanent Cert, NY St 1973; *cr:* 1st Grade Teacher St Paul the Apostle 1953-58, Sacred Heart 1958-61; 2nd Grade Teacher St Patricks-Ravena 1961-66; Maria Coll 1966-67; Kndgtn Teacher St Margaret Marys 1967-69; 1st Grade Teacher St Theresa of Avile 1969-81, Holy Cross 1981-.

KING, JANICE MORTON, Chairman of Music Department; *b:* Birmingham, AL; *c:* Elisabeth L., John F., Mari C.; *ed:* (BME) Music Ed, Univ of Montevallo 1971; *cr:* Music Dept Chm Shades Mountain Chrstn Schls 1985-; *ai:* Vocal Coach; Piano Teacher; Brandon HS Music Hall of Fame 1967; Phi Alpha Mu 1971; Shades Mountain Ind Church Interim Minister of Music; Latin & Fr Foreign Lang Awd 1967; *office:* Shades Mountain Chrstn Schls 2281 Old Tyler Rd Birmingham AL 35226

KING, JOAN BLACK, Third Grade Teacher; *b:* Guntersville, AL; *m:* Tommy Clifton; *c:* Tanya L., Bradley C., Ashleigh R.; *ed:* (BS) Elem Ed, S Benedictine 1972; (MED) Rdng Spec, AL A&M 1978; Rdng, Univ of AL; *cr:* 1st Grade Teacher 1972-75, 2nd Grade Teacher 1975-76 City Sch; 1st Grade Teacher Arab Primary 1976-87; 3rd Grade Teacher Arab Elem 1987-; *ai:* Textbook, Insurance, Advisory Comm; Arab Teachers Assn (VP 1979-80, Pres 1980-81); AEA Dist Secy 1980-81; Teachers Assn Sch Rep; MOM Club Pres 1979-80; *home:* 1406 Martha Ln Rt 4 Arab AL 35016

KING, JOAN DEAN, Reading Resource Teacher; *b:* St Louis, MO; *m:* Alfred James M.; *c:* Penny Harney, Marj Tidd, Stephen; *ed:* (BS) Ed, MO Univ Kirksville 1954; Elem Ed, Rollins Coll 1971; *cr:* Chapter I Rdng Resource Teacher Cypress Park Elem Sch 1988-; *ai:* Ed Lobbyist; Legislative Comm; Classroom Teachers Assn of Orange Cty; Fringe Benefits Comm Orange Cty Schls; Orange Cty Classroom Teachers Assn Pres 1978-80; Natl Cncl of Urban Ed Assn (Secy, Treas) 1981-85; Parent Resource Center Bd Mem 1981-83; Additions Sch Volunteers Bd of Dir 1978-80; Selection Comm Japanese Amer Schlsp Prgm Lauton Chiles Senator 1982; Natl PTA Phoebe Apperson Hearst Outstanding Educator Awd Nominee 1984.

KING, JOAN EDWARDS, Biology Teacher; *b:* Portsmouth, VA; *m:* Al; *c:* Jeff, Ginger; *ed:* (BS) Home Ec/Sci, W Carolina Univ 1961; In-Service Wkshps; *cr:* Phys Sci/Bio Teacher E Rutherford HS 1962-67; Life Sci Teacher New Hope Mid Sch 1976-86; Bio Teacher Rutherford-Spindale Cntrl HS 1986-; *ai:* NCSAS Adv Sci & Pres Adult Booster Club; Drama Coach; Delta Kappa Gamma; Lamar Stringfield Music Club Pres; Laymans Teacher of Yr; Rutherford Cty Teacher of Yr; Selected to Attend NC Center Advancement Teaching; *office:* Rutherfordton Spindale Sch Laurel Dr Rutherfordton NC 28139

KING, JULIA CONNIE JAMES, L D Resource Teacher; *b:* Bristol, TN; *m:* Johnny Fredrick; *c:* Kevin, Jamie; *ed:* (BS) Phys Ed/Health Ed, E TN St Univ 1966; Endorsement To Teach Learning Disabilities Classes, ETSU & VA Tech; *cr:* Phys Ed Instr Patrick Henry HS 1966-69, John S Battle HS 1973-74; Learning Disabilities Instr High Point Elem Sch 1979-; *ai:* NEA, VA Ed Assn, Washington Cty Ed Assn Mem; *home:* 100 Pine Hill Rd Bristol VA 24201

KING, JULIE DEAN, His Teacher/Asst Dir Admission; *b:* Cambridge, MA; *m:* James G. III; *ed:* (BA) His, Williams Coll 1984; Working toward Masters in His, NY Univ; *cr:* Eng/Dance Teacher/Asst to Dir of Dev The Harvey Sch 1985-86; His Teacher 1986-89, His Teacher/Asst Dir of Admissions 1989- Hackley Sch; *ai:* Stu Newspaper & Stu Literary Magazine Adv; Writer for Hackley Review; Sr Yrbk Dedication Awd 1989; *office:* Hackley Sch 293 Benedict Ave Tarrytown NY 10591

KING, KAREN BUFF, Speech/Drama Instructor; *b:* Charlotte, NC; *m:* Peter; *ed:* (BS) Speech/Theatre, Moorhead St Univ 1969; Intnl Inst of Readers Theatre, Univ of AK, Univ Puget Sound, San Diego St Univ, Univ Cntrl FL; *cr:* Teacher AK Bus Coll 1970-71, Service Hanshew Scndry Sch 1971-78, Pine Lake Mid Sch 1980-81, Tolt Mid & HS 1981-; *ai:* Dramatic Act Coach; Natural Helpers; NEA, NCTE 1970-; WEA 1980-; Natl Readers Theatre Inst 1975-; WA St Legislative Comm for Ed; W WA Univ Awd for Prof Excl 1987-88, WA Awd for Excl in Ed Christa Mc Auliffe Awd 1988-89; Honorable Mention Natl Christa Mc Auliffe Fellowship Prgm 1990; *office:* Tolt Mid HS 3740 Tolt Ave Carnation WA 98014

KING, KATIE JOHNSON, School Counselor; *b:* Paris, AR; *m:* Stevie Preston; *c:* Stephanie K., Kimberly F.; *ed:* (BS) Phys Ed/Health, AR Tech Univ 1974; (ME) Spec Ed, 1980, Ed Specialist Counseling, 1989 Univ of AR; Gifted Ed, Trng in TESA, Investments in Excl, IMPACT, LIFT, Career Orientation Voc Ed; *cr:* 7th/8th Grade Sci/Sr HS Health Teacher Magazine Sch Dist 1974-75; Scndry Spec Ed Teacher 1975-79, Sch Cnslr 1983- Mulberry Sch Dist; *ai:* Sr Class Spon; Crawford Cty Park Bd Mem; AR Valley Voc Tech for GED/ADE Prgm Advisory Bd Chairperson; Assist Crawford Cty Queens Contest; AR Ed Assn 1986-; NW AR Sch Cnslrs Assn 1980-, Nom Cnslr of Yr 1990; AR Sch Cnslr Assn 1980-; Delta Kappa Gamma 1988-; Beta Sigma Phi Pres 1980-; Woman of Yr 1982-84; Nom Career Orientation Teacher of Yr; *office:* Mulberry Public Schls Drawer D Mulberry AR 72947

KING, KITTYE BARNES, Mathematics Teacher; *b:* Beaver Dam, KY; *m:* Bruce E.; *c:* Liessell A. Vice, Kari R. Vice; *ed:* (BS) Math, KY Southern Coll 1967; *cr:* Math Teacher Jarman Jr HS 1969-72, Carl Albert Jr HS 1973-75, Ohio Cty Mid Sch 1982-84, Ohio Cty HS 1985-; *ai:* Beta Club Co-Spon; Ohio Cty Golf Coach; Teacher Evaluation Revision & Ohio Cty Voc Agriculture Comms; OK Ed Assn 1969-75; Ohio Cty Ed Assn, KY Ed Assn 1982-; NEA 1969-75, 1982-; *home:* Rt 3 Box 367 Beaver Dam KY 42320

KING, LINDA MARIE, French/Spanish/English Teacher; *b:* Rutland, VT; *ed:* (BA) Modern Foreign Lang/Fr/Span, the Kings Coll 1975; Diplome Annuel La Sorbonne Univ Paris 1973; *cr:* Substitute Prof the Kings Coll 1974-75; Teacher Camp Springs Chrstn Schls 1975-76; Substitute Teacher Prince Georges Cty Schls 1976-77; Teacher/Admin Capital Luth HS 1977-90; *ai:* Homeroom Adv 12th Grade; Sftbl Coach; Alumni Adv; Yrbk Adv; Tutoring Hotline; NCTE 1985-87; Greater WA Assn of Foreign Lang Teachers 1984-87; Neighborhood Watch 1990; Evangel Assembly of God 1978-; Master Teacher Awd Capital Luth HS 1987; 10 Yr Service Awd Capital Luth HS 1987; 10 Yr Service Awd Luth Church Southeastern Dist; Teachers Conference 1986; *home:* 2712 29th St SE Washington DC 20020

KING, LOIS ELLEN, Kindergarten Teacher; *b:* San Francisco, CA; *m:* James F.; *c:* Stephanie, Michael; *ed:* (BA) Elem Ed, CA St Univ San Francisco 1964; *cr:* 5th Grade Teacher Centennial Elem 1964-66; Kndgtn Teacher Bell Hill 1975-; *ai:* NAEYC; CA Kndgtn Assn; Music in Mountains 1979-; *home:* 302 Gethsemane St Nevada City CA 95959

KING, LOREN DENNIS, Math Department Chairman; *b:* Cortez, CO; *m:* Nancy Rossi; *c:* Christopher; *ed:* (BA) Soc Sci, Univ CA Chico 1971; *cr:* Teacher Fairview Mid Sch 1971-; *ai:* Mentor Teacher; Math Dept Head; Dir of Cmptr Lab; Dev Cmptr Lab; Network Apple II Developed; *office:* Fairview Mid Sch Drawer G Gonzales CA 93926

KING, MARTIN W., Band Director; *b:* Wichita, KS; *m:* Jamie C. Ned; *c:* Kyle; *ed:* (BME) Music Ed, 1976; (MME) Music Ed, 1979 Central St Univ; *cr:* Band Dir Western Oaks Jr HS 1976-82; Band/Orch Dir Putnam City North HS 1982-84; Band Dir Putnam City Cntrl Jr HS 1984-; *ai:* 7th Grade Concert & Symph Bands; Cntrl OK Dir Assn Pres 1976-; Phi Beta Mu 1980-; Natl Assn Jazz 1976; Teacher Yr 1981; Teacher Yr 1990; Guest Clinican Northeast OK All Region Band 1987; Guest Clinician North Cntrl OK All Region Band 1988.

KING, MARY ALICE, English Teacher; *b:* Buena Vista, GA; *c:* Toni L., Antwan M.; *ed:* (BS) Scndry Eng, Fort Valley St Coll 1974; Rdng, Valdosta St Coll; Rdng/Ed, Fort Valley St Coll, GA Southwester Coll, Troy St Univ; *cr:* Rdng Teacher Stewart Cty HS 1974-76; Eng Techer Cntrl HS 1976-; *ai:* Literary Coach; Dramatics Club Adv; Sr Class Adv; Talbot Cty Assn of Ed/GAE/NEA 1974-; Brown Chapel Ame Secy 1976-; Sunday Sch (Asst Supt, Teacher; 1989-; STAR Teacher 1980; *office:* Central Elem/HS P O Box 308 Talbotton GA 31827

KING, MARY KAY, Business Law Teacher; *b:* Winchester, TN; *m:* Ted; *c:* Kathryn, Robert; *ed:* (BS) Bus Admin, TN Tech 1964; Grad Stud; *cr:* Teacher W End HS 1964-66; Instr St Voc Sch 1967-69; Teacher Dickson Cty Sr HS 1976-; *ai:* FBLA Spon; Mock Trial Adv; Pathfinders Coach; TN Ed Assn 1976-; Delta Kappa Gamma 1985-; Pi Omega Pi 1963-64; Kappa Delta Pi 1962-; Dickson Cty Ed Assn Faculty Rep; Career Level III; Governors Acad for Teachers of Writing; St Textbook Adoption Comm; *office:* Dickson Cty Sr HS Henslee Dr Dickson TN 37055

KING, MARY S., Third Grade Teacher; *b:* Chippewa Falls, WI; *m:* Ronald P.; *ed:* (BA) Scndry Ed/Eng/Fr, UW Green Bay 1973; (BS) Elem Ed, UW Eau Clair 1984; *cr:* Jr HS Teacher Horicon Jr HS 1976; 7th & 8th Grade Eng Teacher Holy Ghost 1976-79, 3rd Grade Teacher Holy Ghost Elem 1979-; *ai:* Liturgy Comm; Curr Comm; NCTE; NCEA; *office:* Holy Ghost Elem Sch 436 S Main St Chippewa Falls WI 54729

KING, MICHAEL DANA, 8th Grade Soc Stud Teacher; *b:* Decatur, GA; *ed:* (BSE) Soc Stud, GA St Univ 1985; *cr:* Jeweler Cohen Company 1980-82; Travel Agent Northlake Travel 1982-85; Teacher Pinckneyville Mid Sch 1985-; *ai:* Var Ftbl Coach Dacula HS; Asst Bsktbl Coach Pinckneyville Mid Sch; Game Club Spon Pinckneyville Mid Sch; Stu Govt Spon; PAGE Mem 1985-87; GHSA Mem 1985-; GCAE Mem 1987-; 1st Baptist Church Mem 1970-; Berkmar HS Reunion Comm Mem 1980-; Guinnett Co Staff Dev Cncl; *office:* Pinckneyville Mid Sch 5440 W Jone Bridge Rd NW Norcross GA 30072

KING, MORRIS WAYNE, Science Teacher; *b:* Reidsville, NC; *m:* Hattie May Noland; *c:* Timothy W., Belynnda M. Metzler, John E. (dec); *ed:* (BA) Art, CA St Univ Fresno 1970; Cmptr Sci, Sci, Math, Natl Sci Fnd AIMS Project; Mentally Gifted Prgm, Univ of San Francisco; US Navy Aviation; *cr:* Adj US Navy 1956-63; Office Mgr Allis Chalmers Manufacturing Company 1963-67; Teacher Clovis Unified Sch Dist 1970-72, Lemoore Union Elem Sch Dist 1972-; *ai:* Outdoor Classroom Dir; Elem Advisory Comm Mem; Kappa Delta Pi, NEA Mem 1971-; Lemoore Elem Teachers Assn Arbitrator 1971-; CA Teachers Assn 1971-; Glad Tidings Church; Co-Author Published Project AIMS Series Books 1981; Sci/Math Schlsp Mentally Gifted Minor Chm; Letters of Commendations from St of CA, Sch Dists, Pres US of America John F Kennedy, Distinguished Sch of CA; *home:* 951 W Yosemite Dr Hanford CA 93230

KING, NANCY KAY, Coord Health Occupations Instr; *b:* Twin Valley, MN; *m:* Robert D.; *c:* Darcy King Schauer, Darin; *ed:* Practical Nursing, ND St Sch of Sci 1959; Registered Nursing, St Lukes Hosp Nursing 1976; Ed, Valley City St Univ/ Moorhead St Coll; *cr:* LPN New Rockford Cmmty Hosp 1960-65, Mercy Hospital 1965-68; Clinical Instr for LPNS Mercy Hospital 1968-76; Health Occupations Instr Valley City Vocational Center 1977-; *ai:* VICA Adv; VICA Exec Comm ST ND; Trade/Tech/ Ind Health Instr Pres 1980-84; Outstanding Educator 1980; Health Occ Inst Assn Pres 1981-82; VICA Advisory Comm Mem 1976 Outstanding VICA Adv; Trade Tech Ind & Health Assn Mem 1976-; Service Awd 1985; Health Occ Curriculum Comm Chm 1989-; Competency Based Ed Comm Mem 1980-86 Service Awd 86; Ex Comm of ND Amer Heart Assn Mem 1988-; United Way of Barnes Cty Mem 988-; *home:* 221 14th St NE Valley City ND 58072

KING, NINA MARRS, 3rd Grade Teacher; *b:* Birmingham, AL; *m:* Daniel B. Sr.; *c:* Daniel Jr.; *ed:* (BS) Elem Ed, 1976; (MS) Early Chldhd Ed, 1980 Jacksonville St Univ; *cr:* 1st Grade Teacher Wagner Elem Sch 1976-77; 1st Grade Teacher 1977-83; 3rd Grade Teacher 1983-89 Floyd Elem Sch; *ai:* AL Ed Assn 1976-89; NEA 1976-79; Poly Action for Gadsden Educators 1976-89; Gadsden Service Guild 90; PTA Outstanding Educator 1983; *home:* 300 Azalea Dr Gadsden AL 35901

KING, NORMA LASURE, Business Education Teacher; *b:* New Martinsville, WV; *m:* Richard Lee; *c:* Christine De Sea, Alan; *ed:* (BA) Bus Principles, Fairmont St Coll 1965; Pre-Voc Cert Marshall Univ; Teaching Cert WV St Coll; Various Cmptr Ed, WV Coll of Grad Stud; Teaching Teachers How to Teach Cmptrs Univ of Berkeley; *cr:* Math Teacher Hayes Jr HS 1965-67; Substitute Teacher Kanawha Cty Schls 1975-77; Bus Teacher Nitro HS 1977-; *ai:* Soph Class, NHS Spon; FBLA Co-Spon; Sch Newsletter Co-Editor; Alpha Delta Kappa Secy 1988-; Kanawha Cty Bus Teachers; WV Bus Ed Assn; St Andrew United Meth Church (Admin Bd Chm 1985, Ed Commission Chm 1990); Kanawha Cty Teacher of Month 1989, Teacher of Yr 1989-; *office:* Nitro HS 21st St Nitro WV 25143

KING, PAT BRIAN, Phys Ed-Sports Development; *b:* Kelso, WA; *m:* Debbie Lanshutz; *c:* Patrick G., Jennifer L.; *ed:* (AA) Phys Ed, Lower Columbia Coll 1973; (BS) Health/Phys Ed, 1975, (MAT) Health/Phys Ed, 1980 Lewis Clark Coll; First Aid/CPR Instr; *cr:* Head Wrestling Coach Lewis Clark Coll 1975-77; Health Teacher/Asst Wrestling Coach Oregon City HS 1978-79; Health/ Phys Ed Teacher/Asst Ftbl Coach Evergreen HS 1979-81; Phys Ed Coach/Asst Ftbl Coach/Head Wrestling Coach Mountain View HS 1981-; *ai:* Asst Ftbl Coach; Head Wrestling Coach; Evergreen Coaches Assn Pres 1985-; WA St Coaches Assn 1984-; *office:* Mountain View HS 1500 SE Blairmont Dr Vancouver WA 98684

KING, PATRICIA EVERETTE, Reading Lab Teacher; *b:* Greensboro, NC; *m:* Kenneth D.; *c:* Allison; *ed:* (BA) Elem Ed, 1977, (MS) Mid Grades Ed, 1989 Univ of NC Greensboro; *cr:* 4th-6th Grade Sci/Soc Stud Teacher 1985-87, Rdng Lab Teacher 1988-89 Bethany Elem Sch; *ai:* Chrldr Coach; Mid Grades Task Force; Gradespan Chairperson; Sci Fair Coord; NC Assn of Educators, NEA, NC Sci Teachers Assn, Intnl Rdng Assn; Bethany Sch Teacher of Yr 1986-87; Greensboro Area Math & Sci Ed Center-Sci Fellowship; *home:* Rt 2 Box 548 Reidsville NC 27320

KING, REBECCA COLLIER, English Department Teacher; *b:* Brownwood, TX; *m:* Charles R.; *ed:* (BA) Eng, Southern Meth Univ 1977; *cr:* Teacher Brownwood Jr HS 1978-83, Brownwood Sr HS 1983-; *ai:* Sr Class Spon; Parent/Teacher Advisory Cncl; Classroom Teachers 1978-; Cmmty Cultural Affairs Dance Panel Chm 1988-; *office:* Brownwood Sr HS 2100 Slayden & 10th St Brownwood TX 76801

KING, RHONDA MICHELE, 7th/8th Grade English Teacher; *b:* Harlem, NY; *ed:* (BA) Eng, 1976, (MS) Ed in Rdng, 1982 Coll of New Rochelle; Apple Works II 1986; Educl Research & Dissemination I & II; Apple Works/Beagle Brothers 1989; *cr:* Eng Teacher Mt Vernon HS 1979-80, Nichols Mid Sch 1980-; *ai:* Chaperone Nichols Skating Party 1981-82; Girls Leadership Club 1984-86; Top Class Teachers Singing Group 1985-86; Sch 1st Annual Dance 1986 & Bowling Trip Chaperine 1989; Afro-Amer Wkshp (Mem, Volunteer) 1982-83; The Dreamers (Volunteer Tutor, Teacher) 1988-; Mount Vernon Day Care Center (Entertainment, Rappin Teacher) 1987; African-Amer Family Day (Participant, Rappin Ms K/Teacher MC) 1989; PTA (Mmem 1981-, Talent Show Participant 1987); *office:* Nichols Mid Sch 455 N High St Mount Vernon NY 10550

KING, RICHARD WILLIAM, JR., 12th Grade English Teacher; *b:* Pittsburgh, PA; *m:* Brenda H.; *c:* Richard, John; *ed:* (BS) Ed/Eng, Cheyney St Coll 1971; (MED) Ed/Eng, Trenton St Coll 1979; Rutgers Univ, Glassboro St Coll, Temple Univ; *cr:* Eng Teacher Trenton Jr HS 1971-77, Camden HS 1977-; *ai:* Frosh Boys Bsktbl Coach 1985-; Var Boys Bsktbl Statistician 1979-84; Kappa Alpha Psi 1977-, Distinguished Service 1979; Whos Who Among Stu in Amer Colls & Univs 1971; *office:* Camden HS Baird & Park Blvd Camden NJ 08105

KING, ROSALIE C., Retired Third Grade Teacher; *b:* Leeds, SC; *c:* Michael D., Richard B.; *ed:* (BA) Ed, Erskine Coll 1956; (MA) Elem Ed, Clemson Univ 1975; *cr:* 1st Grade Teacher Kelton Elem 1935-36, Lockhart Elem 1937-40, Chicora Elem 1944-45; 1st-3rd Grade Teacher Pine Grove Elem 1946-51; 3rd Grade Townville Elem 1952-63, Pine St Elem 1964-68; 1st Grade Teacher Fairplay Elem 1969-80; 1st-6th Grade Teachers Ahuas 1981; *ai:* Delta Kappa Gamma VP 1971-73; Seneca Womens Club; Hospital Auxiliary Pres 1987-88; Oconee Art Assn; Pinnacle Care Coord 1989-; Fairplay SC Teacher of Yr 1977; *home:* 3 Grace Apts 5 Fairplay St Seneca SC 29678

KING, ROSEMARY, Fourth Grade Teacher; *b:* Philadelphia, PA; *ed:* (BA) Soc Sci, Temple Univ 1974; ITEC Microcomputers Temple Univ 1986; 2000 Energy Prgm, Penn St Univ 1989; *cr:* Aide Delarc Dev Ctr 1975-76; Teacher Norwood Fontebonne Acad 1976-77; St Edmond Sch 1977-; *ai:* Sci Coord; Cmptr Coord; CAC Chairperson 1989-; KEEN; 1985-86 NASA Teacher Space Prgm; *office:* Saint Edmonds Sch 1919 S 23rd St Philadelphia PA 19145

KING, SHIRLEY DEBERRY, Primary Reading Teacher/Asst; *b:* Red Springs, NC; *c:* Brenda, Sandra, Deborah, Annette; *ed:* (AS) Applied Sci, Rubeson Tech Univ 1978; R & I General Office Technology, Bus Admin, Teacher Assn; *cr:* Primary Rdng Teacher S Lumberton Elem Sch 1978-87; Kndgtn Asst Teacher W H Knuckles Elem Sch 1987-; *ai:* Reinforcement All Acts; NTA, NCAE; *office:* W H Knuckles Elem Sch Martin L King Jr Dr Lumberton NC 28358

KING, STANLEY EWIN, Science Department Chair; *b:* Casper, WY; *m:* Margaret Fetter; *c:* Carissa A.; *ed:* (AS) Pre Med, Casper Coll 1969; (BA) Scndry Ed/Biological Sci Univ of WY 1971; Numerous Univs & Wrkshps; *cr:* Teacher Dubois Sch 1972-73, East Jr HS 1973-86; Teacher/Dept Chm Centennial Jr HS 1986-; *ai:* Chm Verticle Sci Curr, Textbook Selection, Sci Process Skills, Building Faculty Advisory Comms; Sci Club; NSTA; WY Sci Teachers Assn, NEA, WEA, Natrona Cty Classroom Teachers Assn; *office:* Centennial Jr HS 1421 S Waterford St Casper WY 82601

KING, THOMAS C., Teacher of Gifted; *b:* Columbus, OH; *m:* Karen S. Walser; *c:* Andrew T., Peter A.; *ed:* (BS) Elem Ed, OH St Univ 1969; (MA) Supervision, Ashland Univ 1987; *cr:* 5th Grade Teacher 1969-71, 4th Grade Teacher 1971-72, 1st Grade Teacher 1972- Hamilton Local Schls; 2nd Grade Teacher 1980-85, 4th/5th Grade Teacher of Gifted 1985- Bexley City Schls; *ai:* Adjunct Instr Ashland Univ; Soc Comm Chairperson Maryland Avenue Sch Soc Comm Chairperson; Conferences on Gifted Presenter; Kappa Delta Pi 1989; Phi Delta Kappa 1986; OH Ed Assn; NEA; OH Assn for Gifted Children Mem, Certificate of Merit 1987; Bexley Celebrations Assn (Pres Elec 1989-, Essay Chairperson 1987-89); Bexley Schls Facilities Task Force 1989-; OH St Univ Cooperating Teacher Awd 1984-85; Bexley Jaycees Educator of Yr 1988-89; Martha Holden Jennings Scholar 1980-81; *office:* Bexley City Schls S Cassingham Bexley OH 43209

KING, THOMAS FOLGER, 7th/8th Social Studies Teacher; *b:* Columbus, IN; *m:* Julia Ann Mc Cray; *c:* Sarah N.; *ed:* (BA) Poly Sci, Hanover Coll 1981; Studs in World His & Sociology; USAF Officer Trng Sch; *cr:* Teacher Cntrl Mid Sch 1983-; *ai:* Var Ftbl Asst Coach, Boys & Girls Track Coach Columbus North HS; Intramural Boys Bsktbl Spon Cntrl Mid Sch; IN Ftbl Coaches Assn 1989-; *office:* Cntrl Mid Sch 725 7th St Columbus IN 47201

KING, TIMOTHY BRENT, Sixth Grade Teacher; *b:* Virginia, MN; *m:* Laurie Essler; *c:* Tyler; *ed:* (BS) Elem Ed, Bemidji St Univ 1981; (MED) Elem Ed, Univ of MN 1988; *cr:* 4th Grade Teacher 1981-82, 6th Grade Teacher 1982- Orchard Lake Elem; *ai:* Head Cross Cntry Run Coach; Gifted & Talented Task Force Rep; TELE Building Rep; Stu Cncl Adv; *office:* Orchard Lake Elem 16531 Klamath Trl Lakeville MN 55044

KING, WANDA (BAILEY), Fourth Grade Teacher; *b:* Birmingham, AL; *m:* James S.; *ed:* (BS) Elem Ed, Livingston Univ 1970; Admin & Supervision; *cr:* Teacher Brooksville Elem 1970-72, Spring Hill Elem 1972-73, Eisenhower Elem 1973-; *ai:* Officer Friendly Coord; Pinellas Cty Teachers Assn Rep 1975-78; 2nd Place Natl Awd Ec Project; *office:* Eisenhower Elem Sch 2800 Drew St Clearwater FL 34619

KING, WANDA DAWN, 6th Grade Teacher; *b:* Coatesville, PA; *ed:* (BS) Elem Ed, Westchester Univ 1984; *cr:* 7th Grade Math Teacher 1984-85, Asst Prin 1989, 6th Grade Teacher 1986- Octorara Intermediate Sch; *ai:* 5th-8th Grade Stu Cncl Adv; 9th-12th Grade Stage Adv; Spring Variety Show Dir; PTO Newsletter Comm; Octorara Area Ed Assn, PA St Ed Assn 1985-; Cochranville Fire Company 1988-; *office:* Octorara Area Intermediate Sch RD 1 Box 65 Atglen PA 19310

KING, WAYNE H., Mathematics Teacher; *b:* Darby, PA; *ed:* (BA) Math Ed, Glassboro St 1974; Pine Algebra Project; AP Calculus Seminars, St Johnsbury VT; *cr:* Teacher/Coach Gloucester Cath HS 1973-74; Teacher/Admin/Coach Camden Cath HS 1974-85; Teacher/Coach Delsea Regional HS 1985-; *ai:* DEA Ed, Discipline Review, Awds Selection Comm; Schls of Excl; Tandy Technology Scholars Outstanding Teacher Awd 1989-; *office:* Delsea Regional HS Blackwoodtown Rd Franklinville NJ 08322

KING, WILLIAM FRANCIS, Industrial Arts Teacher; *b:* Scranton, PA; *ed:* (BS) Industrial Art Ed, Millersville Univ 1985; Working Toward Masters Scndry Sch Admin, Univ of Scranton; *cr:* Industrial Art Teacher W Scranton HS 1986-; *ai:* Stu Cncl Moderator; Cross Cntry Head Coach; Industrial Art Dept, Sch Facility Comm for Evaluation Head; Scranton Cntrl HS Asst Var Boys Track & Field Coach; Scranton Organization of Area Runners Bd Mem 1990; *office:* W Scranton HS 1201 Luzrene St Scranton PA 18504

KING, WILLIAM RIGBY, III, English Teacher; *b:* Johnson City, TN; *m:* Mimi Kathryn Price; *c:* Kathryn C., Mimi C.; *ed:* (BS) Eng/Bio, 1976, (MED) Supervision/Admin, 1987, (EDS) Admin, 1990 E TN St Univ; *cr:* Eng Teacher 1976-77, 1979, 1981, 1982-, Alternative Sch 1977-78, Bio/Ecology Teacher 1982 Tennessee HS; *ai:* Academic Decathlon; Big Brothers & Big Sisters; Scholars Bowl; NEA, TN Ed Assn 1976-; Bristol TN Ed Assn (Pres 1989-) 1976-; ASCD; NCTE; TN Cncl Teachers of Eng; Phi Delta Kappa; Danforth Fellow 1989; Rotary Club Outstanding Teacher of Yr 1987; System Teacher of Yr 1988; Papers Presented at Amer Educl Research Assn; Natl Cncl of States on Inservice Ed; *home:* 425 Dartmouth Dr Bristol TN 37620

KINGERY, ELIZABETH MARIE, English Teacher/Dept Chair; *b:* Rantoul, IL; *m:* Alan W.; *c:* Alex, Matthew, Sarah; *ed:* (BA) Scndry Ed, Morris Harvey Coll 1974; Working Towards Masters Rdng; *cr:* Teacher Teays Valley Chrstn Sch 1981-; *ai:* Forensic Coach; Annual Statewide Speech Tournament Coord; Literary Review Spon; *office:* Teays Valley Chrstn Sch P.O. Box 168 Scott Depot WV 25560

KINGSBURY, VICKI COSE, English & Speech Teacher; *b:* Ida Grove, IA; *m:* Donald Bradford; *ed:* (BA) His/Eng, Morningside Coll 1975; (MS) Ed, Drake Univ 1988; *cr:* 7th/9th/10th Grade Teacher West Monona Cmmty Sch 1975-; *ai:* Cheerleading, Stu Cncl, AFS, Spelling Bee Spon; WMEA Membership Chairperson 1985-; AFS Selection Comm 1971-72; Order of Eastern Star Mem 1975-; Poetry Published; AFS Schlsp; *home:* 151 Main Blencoe IA 51523

KINGSLEY, JOAN B., Kindergarten Teacher; *b:* Auburn, NY; *m:* David K.; *c:* David M., Daniel M.; *ed:* (BA) Elem Ed, SUNY Oswego 1958; Elem Ed, SUNY Oswego & Potsdam 1961-65; *cr:* Kndgtn Teacher West Hill Sch 1958-61, East Side Sch 1961-67, Fowler Elem 1973-; *ai:* Fowler Elem Sch Parents as Rdng Partners Coord; NEA; Fowler Schls Parent-Teacher Group; *home:* RD 3 Box 277 Gouverneur NY 13642

KINGSLEY, LINDA C., English Teacher; *b:* Dayton, OH; *m:* Douglas F.; *c:* Steven, Scott; *ed:* (BA) Eng, KY Wesleyan Coll 1962; (MS) Ed, W KY Univ 1988; *cr:* Eng/Speech Teacher Owensboro HS 1962-67; Bus Eng Instr Owensboro Bus Coll 1966-68; Eng Teacher Owensboro Jr HS 1983-; *ai:* Young Republicans Club; Guidance Comm; Owensboro Educl Assn, KY Educal Assn, NEA 1962-67, 1983-; Owensboro Panhellenic Assn Pres 1970-71; Daviess Cty Homemakers Assn 1967-; Whos Who Among Outstanding Women; *home:* 2603 Dartmouth Dr Owensboro KY 42301

KINGSTON, DEE ANN STICE, Third Grade Teacher; *b:* Jacksonville, IL; *m:* Joseph Raymond; *c:* Patrick, Alaisa; *ed:* (BA) Elem Ed, Mac Murray Coll 1965; *cr:* 2nd Grade Teacher Chatham IL 1966-67; 2nd-6th Grade Teacher Franklin-Alexander CUSD 1 1965-; *ai:* IEA, NEA 1965-; IL Math Cncl; Eastern Star; *office:* Alexander Grade Sch 110 State St Alexander IL 62601

KINKEAD, MILLARD CLAY, JR., Social Studies Teacher; *b:* Jefferson City, MO; *ed:* (MSED) Educl Admin, SW MO St Univ 1987; (BSED) Scndry Ed/Soc Stud, Univ of MO Columbia 1984; Ed Specialist Univ of MO Columbia; *cr:* Teacher Lebanon HS 1984-; *ai:* Stu Cncl Adv; Lebanon Youth-At-Risk Task Force; Teacher/Admin Bd Comm Mem; MO St Teachers Assn Mem 1989-; Lebanon Educl Assn Bd Rep 1988-; NASSP 1984-; *office:* Lebanon HS 777 Brice Lebanon MO 65536

KINKEL, MERLYN RILEY, Biology Teacher; *b:* Longville, MN; *m:* Patricia Anne Holmquist; *c:* Gary, Jane, Linda, Katie; *ed:* (BA) Health/Phys Ed, Hamline Univ 1955; (MA) Sci Ed, St Thomas Coll 1969; Grad Stud Univ of MN & Macalester Coll; *cr:* Teacher/Coach NY Mills HS 1955-58, Chaska HS 1958-; *ai:* Chaska Ed Assn (Pres 1962, Building Rep 1983-84); MN Ed Assn, NEA; Moravian Church (Elder 1981-87, Trustee 1975-81); Chaska Sch Dist Teacher of Yr 1972, 1977, 1983; *home:* 7090 Redman Ln Chanhassen MN 55317

KINMAN, RICHARD JAMES, 7th/8th Grade Science Teacher; *b:* Keokuk, IA; *m:* Denise Kay; *c:* Dorian D., Travis J., Cortney E., Marnie L.; *ed:* (BS) Phys Ed/Health, Culver Stockton Coll 1970; (MS) Ed/Sci, W IL Univ 1980; *cr:* Teacher Hamilton Mid Sch 1971-; *ai:* Ftbl & Bsktbl Coach; Bsbl 1976-86; Sci Teachers Assn 1988-; IL Ftbl Coaches Assn; Hamilton Ed Assn Pres 1986-87; *home:* 310 N 10th Hamilton IL 62341

KINNEY, CLAIRE MULLEN, Guidance Counselor; *b:* Columbia, SC; *m:* Ronald W.; *c:* Julia, Timothy; *ed:* (BA) Elem Ed, Columbia Coll 1973; (MED) Elem Guidance, Univ of SC 1976; *cr:* Teacher Fairwald Annex 1973-75; St Andrews Elem 1975-76; Hyatt Park Elem 1976-77; St Andrews Elem 1977-89; Guidance Cnslr H B Rhame Elem 1989-; *ai:* Rdng Area Cncl 1985-89; PTO; SC Sch Cnslrs Assn 1989-; Columbia Coll Afternoon Alumnae Club 1980- Pres 1989-; Coll Place United Meth Church Youth Coord; *office:* H B Rhame Elem Sch 1300 Arrowwod Rd Columbia SC 29210

KINNEY, CORDELIA ROSE, First Grade Teacher; *b:* Los Angeles, CA; *ed:* (BA) Sociology, Immaculate Heart Coll 1970; Sch of X-Ray Technology Queen of Angeles Hospital 1960-62; *cr:* Chief Technician St Marys Hospital 1962-65; 3rd Grade Teacher Sacred Heart 1966-67; 1st Grade Teacher St Adelaides 1967-68; 2nd Grade Teacher St Aloysius 1970-74; 1st Grade Teacher St Pius X 1974-76, Our Lady of Guadalupe 1976-; *ai:* Girls Bsktbl Coach; Athletic, WTR Coord; Eucharistic Minister; NCEA 1970-; Amer Registry of Radiological Tech 1960-; Cath Youth Organization 1970-76, Dist Coach of Yr 1976; Los Angeles Archdiocese 19 Yr Teaching Certificate 1989, 20 Yr Teaching Medal 1990; *office:* Our Lady of Guadalupe Sch 530 N Juanita Ave Oxnard CA 93030

KINNEY, ELYRIA OAKLEY, Fourth Grade Teacher; *b:* Cleo Springs, OK; *m:* John; *c:* Richard Mosher, Jennie L. Mosher Marx; *ed:* (BS) Elem, 1973, (MS) Rdng, 1978 TX Womans Univ; Working Toward Phd in Scndry Ed & Curr; *cr:* Spec Ed Teacher 1973-76, 4th Grade Teacher 1976- Bowie Elem; *ai:* Odyssey of Mind Bldg & Cmptr Contact Person; Sight Based Management; Core & Teacher Legislative Comm Mem; Natl Teachers Assn, TX St Teachers Assn 1973-; Richardson Ed Assn, N TX Rdng Assn, Phi Delta Kappa, ASCD.

KINNEY, MICHAEL WALTON, Social Studies Teacher; *b:* Sonora, KY; *m:* Karen Denise Sammons; *c:* Mark, Leslie; *ed:* (BA) His, 1969 (MA) Scndry Ed, 1973, (Rank I) Sch Admin, 1980 W KY Univ; *cr:* 8th Grade Teacher Rineyville Elem Sch 1969-74; Part Time His Instr Elizabeth Comm Coll; Soc Stud Teacher E Hardin HS 1974-; *ai:* KY Youth Assembly Spon; Hardin Cty Ed Assn (Pres 1981-82) 1969-; KEA & NEA Delgate 1969-; Rineyville Optimist Club 1973-77; Glendale Lions Club 1976-81; Outstanding Young Men of Amer Awd; *office:* E Hardin HS 129 College St Glendale KY 42740

KINSEL, GLORIA ANN, First Grade Teacher; *b:* Rehoboth, NM; *ed:* (BA) Psych, NM Highlands Univ 1971; (MS) Elem Ed, Univ of NM 1979; Elem Ed, Bi-ling Ed Teacher Cert, Univ of NM 1974; *cr:* Soc Service Assoc BIA-Gallup Branch Soc Services 1970; Educl Technician Wingate HS 1972-75; Prgm Specialist II Univ of NM 1975-76; Educl Career Specialist Navajo Division of Ed Univ of NM 1976-77; Teacher Gallup Mc Kinley Cty Schls 1977-; *ai:* Festival of Arts & Sci Coord; Cmptr, Sch Design, Indian Act Comm; Developed Navajo Lang Primary Component Curr Sanostee Bi-ling Prgm; Navajo Tribal Schlsps; Nom Mc Kinley Cty Teacher of Yr 1988; Natl Distinguished Achievement Awds, College of Teacher Ed Trng Prgm & Certificate of Achievement; Bi-ling Ed Navajo Teacher Ed Dev Prgm; *home:* PO Box 2333 Gallup NM 87305

KINSER, JENNIFER BOWMAN, 4th Grade Teacher; *b:* New Castle, IN; *m:* Dennis L.; *c:* Stephanie, Christopher; *ed:* (BA) Elem Ed, 77;(MA) Elem Ed, 1981 Ball St Univ; *cr:* 3rd Grade Teacher 1978-79;5th Grade Teacher 1982-84;4th Grade Teacher 1984- Spiceland/Tri Elem; *ai:* ISTA Bldg Rep; Contract Negotiator 1985-; Delta Kappa Gamma 1984-; *home:* 419 Christopher Dr New Castle IN 47362

KINSEY, JOYCE ARCHAMBAULT, Primary Kindergarten Teacher; *b:* Clare, MI; *m:* Roy; *c:* Colette Bender, Colene Brock, Connie Hahn, Cathi Kushion; *ed:* (BA) Elem Ed, Alma Coll 1972; Grad Classes Cntrl MI Univ & Oakland Univ; *cr:* 2nd Grade Teacher 1972-82, Kndgtn Teacher 1982- Chesaning Union Sch; *office:* Chesaning-Brady Elem 17295 S Hemlock Rd Oakley MI 48649

KINSINGER, H. LEE, Reading Specialist; *b:* Confluence, PA; *m:* Kathleen Arriell; *c:* Joshua, Matthew; *ed:* (BA) Elem Ed, Marshall Univ 1972; (MA) Rdng, Frostburg Univ 1980; *cr:* 4th Grade Teacher Wood Cty Schls 1973-78; Rdng Specialist 1978-88; Athletic Dir 1988-89; Rdng Specialist 1989-Merersdale Area; *ai:* Strength Coach-Parent Coord; PSEA/NEA 1978-80; Benevolent Order of Elks 1988-; PA St Athletic Dir Assn 1988-; *office:* Meyersdale Area H S RD 3 Meyersdale PA 15552

KINSOLVING, BARBARA (WILLS), Science Teacher; *b:* Charleston, WV; *c:* Holly A., Ashleigh A.; *ed:* (BS) Bio/Gen Sci, WVIT Montgomery 1978; Additional Endorsement in Voc Ed, Marshall Univ; *cr:* Teacher Kanawha Chrstn Acad 1978-79, Cedar Grove Cmmty Sch 1979-; *ai:* Sci Dept Chm; Sci Fair Coord; SBAT Voc Club Spon; *home:* Box 678 Cedar Grove WV 25039

KINZER, CAROL VARNER, Spanish Teacher; *b:* Akron, OH; *m:* Harold James; *c:* Jeffery A., Gregory S.; *ed:* (BA) Span, Otterbein Coll 1965; (MA) Span, Kent St Univ; Mid Sch Cert UT St Univ; *cr:* Teacher Mt Logan Mid Sch 1982-; *ai:* Span Club Adv; Logan Ed Assn Assoc Rep 1989-, Teacher of Month 1990; UT Foreign Lang Assn; Amer Assn Teachers of Span & Portuguese; Co-Author Lang Course; *home:* 1963 N 1000 E North Logan UT 84321

KINZER, MARY GRISE FORESTER, Theatre/English Teacher; *b:* Bowling Green, KY; *ed:* (AB) Eng, W KY Univ 1960; (MA) Theatre/Drama, IN Univ 1968; *cr:* Teacher Elizabethtown HS 1960-61, Pleasure Ridge Park HS 1961-63, Bloomington HS S 1963-; *ai:* Dir Theatre South; IN St Textbook Rdng Comm; NEA 1965-; IN St Teachers Assn, Monroe Cty Ed Assn 1963-; IN Theatre Assn (Founder, VP, Pres); Amer Theatre Assn; Natl Society of Arts & Letters Treas; 1st United Meth Church; Monroe Cty Democratic Women; Natl Society for Arts & Letters Spec Certificate for Contributions to Theatre; NDEA Univ of VA; NEH OH Wesleyan; *office:* Bloomington HS S 1965 S Walnut Bloomington IN 47401

KIOLBASSA, ELIZABETH RISING, Chem Teacher, Sci Dept Chair; *b:* El Paso, TX; *m:* Rick J.; *c:* Courtney A., Allison K.; *ed:* (BS) Medical Technology, CCSU 1979; Ed Courses, CCSU 1986-87; *cr:* Phys Sci Teacher 1987-89, Bio Teacher 1988-89, Chem Teacher 1989 Incarnate Work Acad; *ai:* Sci Club & Soph Class Head Spon; Tri Beta, NSTA, TX Sci Teachers Assn; *office:* Incarnate Word Acad HS 2910 S Alameda Corpus Christi TX 78404

KIPER, NANCY COOPER, Gifted Mathematics Teacher; *b:* Monroe, LA; *c:* Melissa L.; *ed:* (BS) Math Ed, 1977, (MED) Scndry Ed/Math, 1981 NE LA Univ; Grad Stud; *cr:* Math Teacher Riverfield Acad 1977-78, Carroll HS 1978-79, Riser Jr HS 1979-83, W Monroe HS 1983-; *ai:* Stu Cncl Adv; APEL 1989-; NCTM; Alpha Delta Kappa (Recording Secy 1986-88, 1989-, Historian 1990-); Ridge Avenue Baptist Church (Sunday Sch Teacher, Church Trng & Girls in Action Leader, Vacation Bible Sch Teacher); *office:* W Monroe HS 201 Riggs Rd West Monroe LA 71291

KIRALY, BARBARA JEAN (MRAZEK), Third Grade Teacher; *b:* Masontown, PA; *m:* Edmund William; *c:* Susan B. Moser, William E., Wendy J.; *ed:* (BSED) Elem/Mentally Retarded, CA St Coll PA 1963; *cr:* Spec Ed Teacher Uniontown Schls 1963-64; 3rd Grade Teacher Porter Tower Union 1964-65; Kndgtn/1st-4th Grade Elem Teacher Williams Valley Sch Dist 1971-; *ai:* PTO Elem Yrbk Staff; Textbook, Curr, Advisory Comm; PCRP II Writing Wkshps; NEA 1963-65, 1971-; PA St Ed Assn, Williams Valley Educators Assn (VP 1976-77) 1971-; Sigma Sigma Sigma 1961-; *office:* Williams Valley Sch Dist Rt 209 Tower City PA 17980

KIRALY, KATHLEEN MC DONOUGH, Health/Physical Ed Teacher; *b:* Pittsburgh, PA; *m:* Timothy; *ed:* (BS) Health/Phys Ed, Kent St Univ 1970; Health, Phys Ed, Guidance, Counseling; *cr:* Teacher Brentwood HS 1970-71, Saline Mid Sch 1972-; *ai:* Reproductive Health Comm; Substance Abuse Crisis Team; Stu Cncl; MAHPERD, MAMSE 1985-; Most Outstanding Teacher Mid Sch Level 1985; *office:* Saline Mid Sch 7265 Saline-Ann Arbor Rd Saline MI 48176

KIRBY, CARRIE HUTCHINSON, Media Coordinator; *b:* Darlington, SC; *m:* Michael L.; *c:* Katherine; *ed:* (BS) Bus Ed, Winthrop Coll 1965; (MAED) Rdng Ed, W Carolina Univ 1988; Working Towards EDS in Educl Media, Appalachian St Univ; *cr:* 6th Grade Teacher N Augusta Elem 1965-66; Bus Ed Teacher W Henderson HS 1967-69, Brevard HS 1969-70; 5th Grade Teacher Brevard Elem 1976-88; Media Coord T C Henderson Elem 1988-; *ai:* Transylvania Cty Arts Cncl; Natl Teachers Assn, NC Assn of Educators, TCAE; Kappa Delta Pi.

KIRBY, GLORIA, Reading Teacher; *b:* Shreveport, LA; *m:* Riley; *c:* Ronn A., Stella L.; *ed:* (BA) Elem Ed, Grambling St Univ 1961; Grad Courses Rndg, Univ of TX San Antonio; *cr:* 4th Grade Teacher Oberlin Elem 1963-64; 8th Grade Teacher Oberlin HS 1971-72; 6th/7th Grade Teacher Madison HS 1978-81, John H Wood 1981-; *ai:* Alamo Rdng Cncl, Intnl Rdng Cncl, NEA, TX St Teacher Assn; *office:* John H Wood Mid Sch 14800 Judson Rd San Antonio TX 78233

KIRBY, JIMMY RAY, Mathematics Teacher; *b:* Altus, AR; *m:* Patricia; *c:* Angela, Meredith, Chris; *ed:* (BS) Elem Ed, Univ of Ozarks 1974; Berkley Health, Hunter Ed Instr; *cr:* Teacher Pleasant View Elem 1974-75, County Line Elem 1977-; *ai:* 5th Grade Hunter Ed Course Teacher; *office:* County Line Elem Schl Rt 1 Box 105 Branch AR 72928

KIRBY, JOSEPH FRANCIS, Aquatic Director; *b:* Bryn Mawr, PA; *m:* Barbara Edna Hyneman; *c:* Joseph F. Jr., Richard A., Pamela L.; *ed:* (BS) Health/Phys Ed/Eng/Gen Sci, 1961, (MS) Health/Phys Ed, 1966 West Chester Univ; Trenton St Coll, Bloomsburg Univ, PA St Univ; Water Safety Instr & Lifeguard Instr Trainer; Amer Red Cross CPR First Aid Instr; *cr:* Phys Ed/Sci Dept Chairperson Conshohocken HS 1961-64; Sci/Phys Ed Teacher Neshaminy HS 1965-69; Phys Ed/Continuing Ed/Grad Level Instr PA St Univ 1968-73; Aquatic Dir Bensalem Township Sch Dist 1969-; *ai:* Boys HS Swim Coach; Intramural Swim Dir; Yr Round Cmmty Swim Prgm Dir; NEA (Mem 1961-, Denver Convention St Delegate 1962, VP) Local Ed Assn Mem 1961-; US Swimming Assn Mem 1988-; Amer Red Cross Health Services Chairperson 1975-83;Amer Heart Assn Assn Mem 1971-74; Coached St Championship Class C Bsktbl Team 1963-64; Philadelphgia Inquirers & Maxwell Club Coach of Yr; Bucks Cty Courier Times 3 Time Swimming Coach of Yr; Mid-Atlantic St Evaluation Team; *office:* Bensalem Township Sch Dist 4319 Hulmeville Rd Bensalem PA 19020

KIRBY, KIMBERLY COBB, English Teacher; *b:* Paris, TN; *m:* Timothy W.; *ed:* (BA) Eng/Ed, Univ of NC Chapel Hill 1985; Teaching Creative Writing; *cr:* Teacher Ridgeway HS 1985-; *ai:* Jr HS Stu Cncl Spon; HS Var Track, Wordsmith Coach; Jr HS Awds Prgm Chairperson; Memphis-Shelby Cty Teachers of Eng; Natl Assn of Stu Cncls; Episcopal Church Women; *office:* Ridgeway HS 2009 Ridgeway Rd Memphis TN 38119

KIRBY, KIT CHADWICK, Math Teacher; *b:* Parks, AZ; *m:* Ruth M.; *c:* Lisa Gilbert, Keri Adickes, Melanie; *ed:* (BA) Music, 1958, (MA) Ed, 1962 NAU Flagstaff; Math; *cr:* Music Teacher WA Elem Dist 1958-63; Band 6th Grade Teacher Chino Valley Sch Dist 1963-67; Instrumental Music Prescott Unified Sch Dist 1967-76; Music/Math Cottonwood/Oakcreek Sch Dist 1979-; *ai:* ASCD 1988-; ADODA 1958-86; *office:* Cottonwood Jr H S 6th and Mingus Cottonwood AZ 86326

KIRBY, OZETTA, Third Grade Teacher; *b:* Sebree, KY; *m:* Prentiss L.; *c:* Leslie Still, Latanya Price, Kenneth P., Prentice R., Kent M.; *ed:* (BA) Elem Ed, Dominican Coll 1974; (MS) Educl Psych, Univ WI Milwaukee 1976; Grad Stud Educl Admin; *cr:* Teacher Asst 1970-74, Teacher 1974- Racine Unified Sch Dist; *ai:* Dist Concerns Comm; Dr Jones EPIC Comm; Chaperone Minority Leadership Prgm; Chm Racine Black Teachers Caucus Schlsp Comm; WI Ed Assn (Minority Affairs Chm, Public Relations Comm) 1985-88; The Links Inc Co-Chm Natl Trends 1988-89; Wayman Church Sunday Sch Supt; Natl Assn Advancement of Colored People Ticket Chm 1989; Bd of Chrstn Ed Mem; J W Wilkerson Schlsp Fund Chm 1990; Mem Onsite Review Team Teacher Preparation Prgm Univ WI; Univ of WI Women of Distinction Awd 1989; Park HS Ha Ll of Fame 1988; Nom Racine Women of Yr 1985, 1988, 1989; *home:* 1500 Oxford Ln Racine WI 53406

KIRBY, ROSEMARY ESTRADA, English Teacher; *b:* Las Cruces, NM; *c:* Melanie, Kelly; *ed:* (BS) Scndry Ed/Eng, 1970, (BS) Scndry Ed/Math 1979, (MA) Spec Ed/Gifted/Talented, NM St Univ; *cr:* Co-op Stu NM St Univ Ed Prgm 1966-70; Kndgtn Teacher Little Playmates Child Care 1970-71; Math/Span Teacher USA Action/Peace Corps 1971-73; Teacher Alameda Jr HS & Sierra Jr HS & Onate HS 1977-; *ai:* NHS Chapter Spon; Sr Class Spon; KARE Drug Free Sch Promotions Club Spon; NEA Mem 1977-85; Las Cruces Assn Classroom Teachers Mem 1977-, Teacher of Yr 1988-89; Publication of Articles; Alameda Jr HS Teacher of Yr 1980-81; Co-Authored Gifted & Talented Prgm 1981; *office:* Onate HS 1700 E Spruce Ave Las Cruces NM 88005

KIRBY, RUBY STILTNER, Assistant Principal; *b:* Grundy, VA; *c:* Cynthia K. Farmer, Jeffrey M.; *ed:* (AB) Sci, King Coll 1963; (MS) Supervision/Admin Radford Univ 1982; VA Polytechnic Inst, St Univ, Univ of VA; *cr:* Quality Control Analyst US Borax/Chemical Corporation 1961-62; Bio Teacher Grundy Jr HS 1962-64; Chem/Physics Teacher/Sci Dept Chm Grundy Sr HS 1964-89; Girls Bsktbl Coach Grundy Sr HS 1973-75; Adjunct Faculty/Bio Teacher SW VA Comm Coll 1982-85; Asst Principal Garden HS 1989-; *ai:* Gamma Gifted Comm; AAPT 1985-89; VA Assn of Sci Teachers 1973-89; NEA, VA Ed Assn, Buchanan Ed Assn 1980-; Region V Governors Sch for Sci & Technology Prgm Dir 1985-88; Varina Fellow Varina HS; Governors Center for Educl Innovation & Technology 1985; Designed & Dir Sci Seminar for Sr Gifted Stu Grundy Sr HS 1982-89; *office:* Garden HS PO Box GHS Oakwood VA 24631

KIRBY, SANDY SWIFT, 8th Grade Teacher; *b:* Elkin, NC; *m:* Randy; *c:* Brandy, Joseph; *ed:* (BS) Bus Ed, Gardner Webb Coll 1973; Francis Marion Coll; Univ of SC; *cr:* 4th Grade Remedial Rdng Teacher Lake City Elem 1973-79; 8th Grade Teacher Lang Arts Copeland Elem Sch 1979-; *ai:* Lead Teacher 1989-; Beta Sigma Phi President 1984-85 Girl of Yr 1985; Surry Cty Rdng Assn 1989-; Surry Cty Teacher of Yr 1984; *home:* Rt 1 Box 19 Forest Dr State Road NC 28676

KIRBY-BECKER, MAUREEN THERESE (KIBRY), Biology Teacher; *b:* Cleveland, OH; *m:* Brian Joseph; *c:* Kirby; *ed:* (BSED) Biological Sci, Univ of Dayton 1979; Phys Ed; Chemical Dependency, Glenbeigh Hospital; *cr:* Bio Teacher St Joseph HS 1979-83; Earth Sci Teacher Villa Angela Acad 1982-83; Bio/Chem Teacher Beaumont Sch 1983-84; Bio Teacher Regina HS 1985-; *ai:* Intramurals Dir; Fund Raising Comm; Jr Var & Var Womens Tennis, Bsktbl & Sftbl Coach; Cheerleading, Ski, Fencing Club Moderator; Sch Photographer; Sr Class Adv;Chemical Dependency & NHS Comm Mem; NABT 1985-; Cath Youth Organization Coach 1979-84; BMW Sports Campus Co-Dir 1984-88; City of Solon Recreation (Summer Camp Co-Dir, Cnslr) 1979-87; Greater Cleveland Cath Conference Coaching

Awds; Sftbl Coach of Yr 1984; Bsktbl Sectional Champions & Dist Runners Up 1989; NE OH Regional Slowpitch Sftbl Tournament Runners Up 1989; *office:* Regina HS 1857 S Green Rd South Euclid OH 44121

KIRCHMAN, MARY KASAL, Language Art Teacher; *b:* Kewaunee, WI; *m:* Harold L.; *c:* David, Jo Ann, Carol L., Robert, Mary B. Jerovetz, James; *ed:* (BS) Ed/His/Eng, Univ of WI O hkosh 1952; Univ of WI-Green Bay, Univ of WI-Milwaukee, Univ of Mn; *cr:* Teacher Pulaski HS 1952-55, E De Pere HS 1957-58, W De Pere HS 1962-; *ai:* One Act Forensic Play Dir; Forensics Head; All Sch Play Dir; Drama Club Adv; W DePere Ed Assn (Pres, PR Chairperson) 1988-89; WI Cncl of Eng Teachers Dist Chairperson 1988-; Outstanding Master Teacher St Norbert Coll 1988; Outstanding Scndry Teacher of Dist 1987; Outstanding Educator of Univ Women 1988; Outstanding Dir Awd St Contest 1989; *office:* W De Pere HS 665 Grant St De Pere WI 54115

KIRCHNER, GENE, Guidance Counselor; *b:* Louisville, KY; *m:* Susan Wilson; *ed:* (BA) His, 1981, (MA) Scndry Guidance, 1985 E KY Univ; Working on Cert Xavier Univ; *cr:* 7th Grade Soc Stud Teacher Verity Mid Sch 1982-84; His Teacher/Boys Bsktbl Coach W Hardin HS 1985-86, Simon Kenton HS 1986-89; Guidance Dixie Heights HS 1989-; *ai:* Chm Dixie Heights Stu Assistance Team; NEA; KY Ed Assn 1989-; Phi Delta Kappa 1988-; *office:* Dixie Heights HS 3010 Dixie Hwy Fort Mitchell KY 41017

KIRELAWICH, MARGARET REBER, Math Teacher & Dept Chairman; *b:* Pottsville, PA; *m:* William; *c:* Miki, William, Jacob; *ed:* (BS) Math, PA St Univ 1972; (BS) Eng, Bloomsburg Univ 1982; Math & Eng Courses; *cr:* Teacher Pottsville Area Sch 1972-81, Monongalia Cty Schls 1982-; *ai:* Math Dept Chairperson; WV Math Teachers, NEA, WVEA; *home:* 5001 Lake Lynn Dr Morgantown WV 26505

KIRK, DIANNA MARIE, High School English Teacher; *b:* Peekskill, NY; *m:* Lawrence S.; *c:* Scott; *ed:* (BA) Eng/Scndry Ed, SUNY New Paltz 1971; (MS) Eng/Scndry Ed, W CT St 1976; *cr:* 9th-12th Grade Eng Teacher Carmel HS 1971-; *ai:* Frosh & JV Cheerleading Coach; Adult & Summer Adult Ed; NEA, NY St United Teachers, NCTE Mem 1971-; Summer Curr Wkshp; *office:* Carmel HS 30 Fair St Carmel NY 10512

KIRK, DWIGHT DAVID, 5th Grade Teacher; *b:* Pennington Gap, VA; *m:* Kristie Rebecca Neeley; *c:* Leah, Thomas, Anna, Joel; *ed:* (BS) Elem Ed, 1974, (MA) Admin/Supervision, 1981 E TN St Univ; *cr:* 5th Grade Teacher 1974-75, 4th Grade Teacher 1975-76, 6th Grade Teacher 1977-80, 5th Grade Teacher 1980-81, 3rd Grade Teacher 1981-82, 5th Grade Teacher 1982- Washington-Lee Elem; *ai:* Bristol VA Sch System Communications Comm 1978-80; Keep Bristol Beautiful 1985-87; Washington-Lee Elem Self Study Comm; 1st Baptist Church Sunday Sch Dir 1985-, Church Service Awd 1987; *office:* Washington-Lee Elem Sch Washington Lee Dr Bristol VA 24201

KIRK, JAN BAECHLER, Biology Teacher; *b:* Milford, DE; *m:* Vernon A.; *c:* Erin A.; *ed:* (BA) Bio, Univ of DE 1970; Ed, Univ of DE; Coulter Immunology Summer Lab Trng, Miami; *cr:* Bio Teacher Dover HS 1970-; *ai:* Lib Faculty Comm Book Selection; NHS Faculty Bd; Building Rep St Teacher Center; NEA, DE St Ed Assn; Capital Ed Assn Secy 1978-85; DE Teachers of Sci, NSTA; Youth Conservation Corps (Environmental Specialist 1972-81, Camp Dir 1982-85); GSA Troop Leader 1988-; DE Bio Teacher of Yr 1976; Dover HS Teacher of Yr 1985; Natl Youth Conservation Corps Trng Cadre 1976-79; Dist Teacher Effectiveness Trng Team 1986-88; *office:* Dover HS 625 Walker Rd Dover DE 19901

KIRK, KATHLEEN ANNETTE, Biology Teacher; *b:* Dallas, TX; *m:* James W. Mc Robbie; *c:* Mary Mc Robbie, Bill Mc Robbie; *ed:* (BS) Phys Ed/Fr, TX Chrstn Univ 1979; (MS) Phys Ed/Ed Admin, 1980, (MS) Bio, 1984 E TX St Univ; Doctoral Stud Baylor Coll of Dentistry; *cr:* Phys Ed Teacher Hickman ELem & Davis Elem & Warren Elem & Shorehaven Elem; Bio Teacher North Garland HS 1979-; *ai:* Garland Assn of TX Prof Educators 1979-; *office:* North Garland HS 2109 Buckingham Garland TX 75042

KIRK, KEVIN EDWARD, Teacher/English Dept Chair; *b:* Worcester, MA; *c:* James, Brianna; *ed:* (BA) Eng, Assumption Coll 1976; Grad Stud Eng, Worcester St Coll; *cr:* Teacher St Peter-Marian 1977-; *ai:* Head Coach Boys & Girls Cross Cntry Prgms; Yrbk & Sr Class Adv; Diocese of Worcester Distinguished Teacher of Yr 1988; *office:* St Peter-Marian CCHS 781 Grove St Worcester MA 01605

KIRK, PATRICIA EDWARDS, First Grade Teacher; *b:* Wilkes-Barre, PA; *m:* Kenneth G.; *c:* Gayle A. Kirk Cobb, K. G.; *ed:* (BS) Elem, Bloomsburg Univ 1954; Grad Studies; *cr:* Primary Teacher 44 PA Dist 1954-61; 1st Grade Teacher Dallas PA Dist 1970-; *ai:* Curr Comm Mem; NEA 1954-61/1970-; PA St Ed Assn 1954-61/1970-; Dallas Ed Assn 1970-; PTO 1954-61/1966-; United Meth Women Circle Chairperson; Excl in Staff Dev Awd; Certificate of Attainment Wilkes Univ Substance Abuse & Young; *home:* 12 Windsor Dr Dallas PA 18612

KIRK, RICHARD KENNETH, 7th & 8th Grade Sci Teacher; *b:* Flushing, NY; *m:* Cynthia Weeks; *ed:* (BS) Bio/Ed, Univ of Scranton 1981; Post Grad Sci Courses, Rutgers Univ & Georgian Court Coll; Masters Degree Admin/Ed, Georgian Court Coll; *cr:* Earth Sci/Bio Teacher St Peters HS 1981-84; 7th/8th Grade Sci Teacher Manasquan Elem Sch 1984-; *ai:* Boys Bsktbl Asst Coach; Dist Core Team Stu Assistance Comm Mem; NSTA, NJ Sci Teachers Assn 1982-; NJ Bio Teachers Assn 1989-; NJ Ed Assn, NEA 1984-; Planetary Society 1985-; Manasquan Elem Sch Teacher of Yr 1987-88; *office:* Manasquan Elem Sch Broad St Manasquan NJ 08736

KIRK, ROBERT FRED, Science Teacher; *b:* Oklahoma City, OK; *m:* Vicki Johnson; *c:* Timothy, Mark; *ed:* (BS) Bio/Ed, 1966, (MS) Ed, 1972, (PHD) His & Phil of Ed/Admin, 1977 OK Univ; Numerous Courses & Wkshps Several Univs; *cr:* Scndry Teacher Moore Public Schls 1966-67; Pilot USAF 1967-72; Teacher/Asst Prin Norman Public Schls 1972-74; Teaching Asst OK Univ 1974-77; Asst Professor OK Baptist Univ 1977-81, SW OK St Univ 1981-85; *ai:* Prin Advisory & Staff Dev Comm; Authors of Several Grants; Several Prof Articles; Published Viet Nam Book; Cmptr Software Evaluation/Learning Objectives Book; *office:* Hesperia HS 9898 Maple Ave Hesperia CA 92345

KIRK, ROSA WHISENHUNT, Mathematics Teacher; *b:* Coeburn, VA; *m:* John Robert; *c:* Robert, Elizabeth; *ed:* (BA) Math, Berea Coll 1975; (MA) Math/Ed, E KY Univ 1976; *cr:* Math Teacher Sheldon Clark HS 1976-77, Ervinton HS 1982-; *ai:* NHS Spon; NEA 1983-; Received Fellowship to Complete Masters Prgm; *office:* Ervinton HS Nora VA 24272

KIRK, SARAH ELAINE, English Teacher; *b:* Cheverly, MD; *m:* Jim; *ed:* (BA) Eng Ed, AZ St Univ 1985; Various Wkshps; *cr:* Eng Teacher Flowing Wells HS 1985-; *ai:* Academic Decathlon Coach; New Teacher Coord; Train with Cross Cntry Team; Track Meet Worker; AZ Fed Teachers Mem 1988-; NEA Mem 1985-88; Vineyard Chrstn Church HS Youth Leader 1985-; *office:* Flowing Wells HS 3725 N Flowing Wells Rd Tucson AZ 85705

KIRK, SILVYA A., History Department Chair; *b:* Woodridge, NY; *m:* Precel D.; *c:* Dana, Shoan, Rhyan; *ed:* (AAS) Bus, SUNY Sullivans; (BS) His/Eng, Tuskegee Inst; (MS) Public Admin, Univ of OK; Rdng Specialist Trng, Realtor, TV Production Instr; Post Grad Stud Univ of W FL; *cr:* Teacher Fallsburg Cntrl HS 1973-74; Teacher/Cnslr Mosley HS 1975-77; Teacher Biloxi HS 1978-79; Teacher/Cnslr Republic of Philippines 1980-82; S Dade Sr HS 1984-87; Teacher/Dept Chairperson Carl Albea Sr HS 1988-; *ai:* Yrbk, Worlds Fair, Heritage Club, Talent Show Spon; Alpha Kappa Alpha Heritage Chairperson 1971-; NEA, OEA 1988-; Phi Delta Kappa 1976-; Teacher of Yr 1984, 1989; Mid-Del Finalist Teacher of Yr 1990; OK Black Family of Yr 1989; *home:* 11618 Mark St Midwest City OK 73130

KIRKBY, HELEN SMITH, 5th Grade Teacher; *b:* Mobile, AL; *m:* Robert K.; *c:* Will; *ed:* (BS) Elem Ed, 1969; (MS) Elem Ed, 1985 Troy St Univ; *cr:* 3rd Grade Teacher Headland Prmary Sch 1967-75; 5th Grade Teacher Abbeville Chrstn Acad 1984-; *home:* 801 Westgate Pkwy Dothon AL 36303

KIRKHAM, BETTY JANE, 8th Grade Literature Teacher; *b:* Alcoa, TN; *m:* David R. Jr.; *c:* Nathan, Sam, Luke; *ed:* (BS) Elem Ed, TN Tech Univ 1972; Working Towards Masters in Admin 1991; *cr:* 3rd Grade Teacher Elizabeth Sch 1972-73; 3rd/4th Grade Teacher Rhea Cty Schls 1973-76; 8th Grade Rdng Teacher Rockwood Jr HS 1979-; *ai:* Jr HS Girls Bsktbl Coach; Rdng Textbook Comm; Phi Kappa Phi; Rockwood Jr HS Teacher of Yr 1981.

KIRKHAM, MILDRED JONES, Mathematics Teacher; *b:* Marengo County, AL; *m:* Jack Bruce; *c:* Jane K. Seanor, Camille, Carmen, Carrla; *ed:* (BS) His, Livingston Univ 1951; (MA) Scndry Ed/Math, Univ of AL 1965; *cr:* Math/Soc Stud Teacher Millery HS 1951-53, Thomasville HS 1953-55; Math Teacher Japan & England Dependent Schls 1955-59, Linden City Sch 1960-68, Morgan Acad 1969-71, Marengo Acad 1971-; *ai:* NHS Spon; *home:* Rt 2 Box 245 Sweetwater AL 36782

KIRKINDOLL, BETTY FENNEL, Fifth Grade Teacher; *b:* Bonham, TX; *m:* Charles Rex; *ed:* (BS) Elem Ed/Eng, 1961, (ME) Elem Ed, 1965 E TX St Univ; Supervision, Guidance, His, Linguistics; *cr:* Scndry Supt Schls Winnsboro Ind Sch Dist 1951-54; 6th Grade Teacher Mesquite Ind Sch Dist Cntrl 1961-62, Hanby Elem 1962-63, Florence Black Elem 1963-67; 5th/6th Grade Teacher Range Elem Sch 1967-; *ai:* Bus & Prof Womens Club Secy 1952; TX St Teachers Assn 1973; Assn of TX Prof Educators, Mesquite Ed Assn 1961-; 1st Baptist Church (General Secy 1980-, Mem) 1961-; PTA Life Membership 1985; *home:* 420 W Grubb Dr Mesquite TX 75149

KIRKLAND, CATHY TRIGG, English Teacher; *b:* Columbus, GA; *m:* James Michael; *c:* Cathleen; *ed:* (BS) Scndry Eng Ed, 1976, (MS) Scndry Eng Ed, 1979 Columbus Coll 1979; *cr:* Eng Teacher Carver HS 1979-; *ai:* Muscogee Cty Sch Dist Public Relations Comm; Beta Club Spon; GA Power Adapt-A-Sch Prgm, Carver Media Comm Mem , Honors Night Comm Mem; Sch Mentor; NCTE 1980-; GA Cncl Intnl Rdng Assn, Prof Assn of GA Educators 1985-; GA Cncl Teacher of Eng 1990; Beta Sigma Phi 1986-; Trinity Episcopal Church (Mem, 3rd Grade Church Sch Teacher).

KIRKLAND, DOROTHY YATER, Business Dept Chair; *b:* Indianapolis, IN; *m:* Hoyt Wesley Sr.; *c:* H. Wesley Jr.; *ed:* (BA) Bus Ed/Office Admin, Univ of TN 1956; Voc Cert; *cr:* Bus Teacher Pi Beta Phi Settlement Sch 1956-58, Holston HS 1958-61; Bus Teacher 1962-70, Bus Teacher/Dept Chairperson 1970- Farragut HS; *ai:* Sch Bookstore Mgr; Annual Financial, FBLA Adv; Sr Class Spon; Bus Advisory Comm; ETEA, TEA, NEA 1956-; NBEA 1975-; *office:* Farragut HS 11237 Kingston Pike Knoxville TN 37922

KIRKLAND, GERALDINE, Kindergarten Teacher; *b:* Jasper, TX; *m:* Joseph L.; *c:* Thomas G. Hood, Theresa M. Hood Myers; *ed:* (BS) Ed, Lamar Univ 1977; Working Toward Masters Rdng, Early Chldhd; *cr:* Kndgtn Teacher Hardin-Jefferson Ind Sch Dist 1977-; *ai:* Tutor Before Sch; Write Guidelines for Math Prgm; Hardin-Jefferson Ed Assn (Secy, Treas, Membership Gov) 1981-88, Appreciation 1988; Kndgtn Teachers of TX 1984-; Assn TX Prof Educators 1989-; Jefferson Cty 4-H Adult Leaders Secy 1984; Wesley United Meth (Past Pres, Secy) 1987-; *office:* China Elem Sch P O Box 398 China TX 77613

KIRKLAND, KAREN ELIZABETH, First Grade Teacher; *b:* Rock Hill, SC; *ed:* (BS) Early Chldhd Ed, 1975, (MED) Elem Ed, 1977 Winthrop Coll; *cr:* Grad Asst York Teacher Corps Project 1975-76; 1st Grade Teacher Finley Road Elem Sch 1976-; *ai:* BSAP Math, Soc Stud & Cmptr Comms; Stu Ed Assn VP 1973-76; Rock Hill Ed Assn, SC Ed Assn, NEA 1976-; Palmetto Rdng Cncl 1987-; ASCD 1989-; Northside Baptist Church Sunday Sch Teacher 1986-; SC St Grant; October Teacher of Month 1988 Finley Road Sch; Teacher of Yr 1989- Finley Road Sch; Grade Level Chairperson 1987-89; Cmptr Inservice Presentations;Math Textbook Selection Comm 1987-88; *office:* Finley Road Elem Sch 1089 Finley Rd Rock Hill SC 29730

KIRKLAND, KATHI HENRY, 8th Grade Teacher; *b:* New Albany, MS; *m:* John Stephen; *c:* Russell, John Hardeman; *ed:* (BAE) Eng/Speech, 1972, (MAE) Eng 1975, (AAA) Cert Eng/ Scndry Ed 1977 Univ of MS; Ms Teacher Assessment Instr Evaluation for The Cert of Teachers in The St of MS Awared Certificate in 1988; Grad Level Course Work Univ of MS; *cr:* 9th-12th Grade Eng/Speech Teacher Amory HS 1972-73; Remedial Rdng Teacher 1973-74, 7th Grade Eng Teacher 1974-85 New Albany Mid Sch; 9th Grade Eng Teacher 1978-79, 11th Grade Eng Teacher 1978-80 W P Daniel HS; 8th Gradt Eng Teacher New Albany Mid Sch 1974-; *ai:* Yrbk Spon 1976; Chairperson of Scndry Eng/Lang Art Curr Re-Organization Dept; Edcul Priorities Comm; Chairperson of Curr & Goals Comm New Albany Mid Sch; Chairperson of Stu Act Comm; Phi Delta Kappa Mem 1977, Teacher of Yr New Albany; Phi Kappa Phi Mem 1977; MS Cncl of Teachers of Eng; Pres Elect of New Albany Ed Assn; 1st United Meth Church Mem 1973-; New Albany Garden Club Mem 1978-80; *office:* New Albany Mid Sch 400 Apple St New Albany MS 38652

KIRKLAND, MICHAEL WAYNE, Life Science Teacher; *b:* Atlanta, GA; *ed:* (BSED) Soc Sci Ed, Univ of GA 1985; (MSED) Mid Grades Ed, W GA Coll 1990; *cr:* Soc Sci Teacher Oconee Cty Intermediate Sch 1985-86; Life Sci/Soc Sci Teacher J C Booth Mid Sch 1986-; *ai:* Sci Club, Sci Olympiad Team Spon; Mid Grades, Media Comms; NSTA, GA Sci Teachers Assn; NEA, GA Ed Assn; Masons; *office:* J C Booth Mid Sch 250 Peachtree Pkwy Peachtree City GA 30269

KIRKLAND, VIRGINIA FAYE, Third Grade Teacher; *b:* Carbon Hill, AL; *m:* Jack K.; *c:* Barry T., Vicki L. Howard; *ed:* (BA) Elem Ed, 1981, (MS) Elem Ed, 1987 Univ of AL Birmingham; *cr:* Teacher Carbon Hill Jr HS 1981-; *ai:* Club Spon; Carbon Hill Ed Assn (VP, Pres); Carbon Hill PTA (Secy, VP); *office:* Carbon Hill Jr HS PO Box 609 Carbon Hill AL 35549

KIRKMAN, CAROL JONES, Math Teacher/Dept Chairperson; *b:* Madison, TN; *m:* Paul D.; *c:* Pamela Laine, Randal Todd, James Bradley; *ed:* (BS) Health/Phys Ed, 1975, (MA) Math/Ed/Health Ed, 1984 Austin Peay St Univ; TESA Trng; *cr:* 7th/8th Grade Math Teacher Elkton Elem Sch 1975-88; 8th Grade Math Teacher Todd Cty Mid Sch 1988; *ai:* Academic Team Coach; Leadership Team Mem; KY Mid Sch Assn 1987-90; NCTM; NEA/KEA 1975-; 4-H Leadership Cncl; *home:* 2380 Allensville Rd Elkton KY 42220

KIRKMAN, JEFF, 5th Grade Teacher; *b:* Fall River, MA; *m:* Barbara; *c:* Erin, Megan, Cailyn; *ed:* (BA) Bus Mrktg, Bryant Coll 1973; Ed, Southeastern Univ MA 1975; *cr:* Teacher St Louis 1975-; Teacher in Charge St Louis 1982-; *ai:* Intramural Coed Sports Prgm 1987-; Sch Improvement Cncls; Project Succeed; Sch Booster Club; MTA 1975-; NEA; Swansea Little League Coach 1975-86; Swansea Girls Sftbl Mgr 1987-.

KIRKMAN, JOSEPH ROY, Teacher of Academically Gifted; *b:* Winston-Salem, NC; *ed:* (BA) His, Wake Forest Univ 1973; *ai:* Teacher Franklin Elem 1973-; NC Assn of Educators, NEA 1973-; *office:* Franklin Elem Sch 727 So Franklin Rd Mount Airy NC 27030

KIRKMAN, KAREN KIRKLAND, Biology Teacher/Sci Dept Chair; *b:* Andalusia, AL; *m:* Ted; *ed:* (BA) Bio, Univ of NC 1974; Grad Stud, George Mason Univ & Univ of VA; *cr:* Teacher Garinger HS 1975-79, Thomas Jefferson HS 1980-81; Teacher/ Dept Chairperson James Madison HS 1982-; *ai:* Faculty Advisory Comm 1987-89; NABT 1983-; *office:* James Madison H S 2500 James Madison Dr Vienna VA 22181

KIRKWOOD, JANET MARION, 7th/8th Grade Science Teacher; *b:* Pinebluff, AR; *m:* Jeffri L.; *c:* Austin, Jordan, Kalin; *ed:* (BS) Home Economics, Univ of Southern MS 1980; *cr:* Sci Teacher Sadre V Thompsom Jr HS 1980-83; Mc Lauren Sch 1983-89; Natchez Mid Sch 1989-; *ai:* Yrbk Spon 4 Yrs; Natl Mid Sch Assn 1990; Pilgrimage Garden Club 1983-; Published Article Sci & Children 1984; Evaluator Natl Sci Teachers Convention 1984; Applicant NASA Teacher Space Prgm 1985; Chamber of Commerce Ed Comm 1988; *home:* 216 Linton Ave Natchez MS 39120

KIRKWOOD, RICHARD M., 5th Grade Teacher; *b:* Syracuse, NY; *m:* Zara Zelesnik; *c:* Christopher, Kevin; *ed:* (BA) Elem Ed, SUNY Potsdam 1973; Rdng; *cr:* Elem Teacher East Syracuse Minoa Sch Dist 1973-; Park Hill Elem Sch 1973-79; Kinne St Elem Sch 1979-; *ai:* Frosh Coach Soccer 1974-, Bskbl 1975-, Bsbl 1974-89, Lacrosse 1990; East Syracuse Minoa United Teachers Assn 1973-; *office:* Kinne St Elem Sch 230 Kinne St East Syracuse NY 13057

KIRSCH, LAURA JEAN MC ANULTY, First Grade Teacher; *b:* Barnesboro, PA; *m:* Vinceant; *ed:* (BS) Elem, Indiana Univ of PA 1965; PA St Univ, Ball St Univ, Carlow Coll; *cr:* 1st Grade Teacher Northern Cambria 1965-; *ai:* NEA, PA St Ed Assn; Northern Cambria Ed Assn PTA Life Membership; *office:* Northern Cambria Sch 600 Joseph St Barnesboro PA 15714

KIRSCH, PATRICIA ANN PICKERING, Kindergarten Teacher; *b:* Centerville, IA; *m:* Russell Miner; *c:* Tia M., Devin B.; *ed:* (BSE) Elem Ed, Northeast MO St Univ 1974; Early Chldhd Ed, Child Abuse Trng, Supervisory Skills Trng, Drug Awareness Trng, Environmental Ed; *cr:* Spec Ed Aide Kooskia Elem Sch 1974; Johnson OMalley Tutor Kamiah Elem Sch 1974; 2nd/3rd Grade Teacher Elk City Schl 1974-75; K Teacher Kamiah Elem Schl 1975-; Summer Latch Key Teacher Orofino City Park 1990; *ai:* Summer Girls Sftbl Coach; Summer Bible Sch Teacher; Kamiah Ed Assn (Treas 1982, Delegate Assembly 1977/1984/1987); Kamiah Chamber of Commerce (Kidie Parade Organizer 1985/1986/1987, MudWrestling Tournament Organizer 1982/1983/1984, Wine Tasting Festival 1987); Helped set up Pre-Schls, Donating Learning Materials & Labor; Working Towards Spec Ed Early Chldhd Degree; *home:* PO Box 222 Kamiah ID 83536

KIRSCHNER, PATRICIA GRAY, Chemistry Teacher; *b:* Galveston, TX; *m:* Gordyn S.; *c:* Valerie Martin, James K. Martin, Michael B. Martin; *ed:* (BA) Zoology, Univ of TX Austin 1952; (MS) Chem, Univ of Houston 1972; Chem, NSF Inst & Brown Univ 1964; Math, Univ of RI 1965-66; *cr:* Math Teacher Norview HS 1959-61; Chem Teacher Rogers HS 1964-67, Stu Act Dir 1970-89, Chem Teacher 1967- Ball HS; *ai:* Ball HS Sci Club Spon; Galveston Youth Leadership Awd Prgm; TX Learning Technology Group; Chem Curr Dev; NEA 1959-; TX St Teachers Assn, Galveston Ed Assn 1967-; Amer Chemical Society 1987-; Sci Teachers Assn of TX 1985-; Natl Assn of Wkshp Dirs 1975-89; Natl Assn of Stu Act Advs 1970-89; TX Assn of Stu Cncls Leadership Consultant; Leadership Consultant Wkshps for HS Stus 1974-; Pat Kirschners Leadership Awd 1986; Educator of Yr Young Lawyers Assn of Galveston 1989; Ball HS Wall of Honor 1988; *office:* Ball HS 4115 Ave O Galveston TX 77550

KIRTON, CHARLOTTE MARIE, Life Science Teacher; *b:* Jacksonville, FL; *ed:* (BA) Bio/Chem, Cocker Coll 1961; (MS) Bio/Ed, N GA Coll 1985; *cr:* Teacher Southside Jr HS 1965-68; Chemist FL Dept of Health 1968-73; Trainer Exten Farm 1973-79; Teacher Dawson Cty Mid Sch 1979-; *ai:* Sci Club Spon; After Sch Detention; Dawson Cty Fed of Teacher Pres 1980-; AFT 1980-; GA Cocker Spaniel Club Bd of Dir 1988-; Teacher of Yr Dawson Cty Mid Sch 1987; Advanced Technology Dev Center Teacher Awd 1989-; *office:* Dawson Cty Mid Sch PO Box 688 Dawsonville GA 30534

KIRTON, TIMOTHY LEE, English Department Chair; *b:* Orlando, FL; *m:* Jennifer Carol Myers; *c:* T.J., Andrea, Andrew; *ed:* (BA) Eng, Vanderbilt Univ 1967; (MAT) Eng, Rollins Coll 1970; Peer Teacher Observation Trng; *cr:* Eng Teacher Apopka Memorial Mid Sch 1967-; *ai:* Chm Eng Dept, Faculty Advisory Comm; Team Leader Achievers Team; Orange Cty Evaluation Comm; Peer Teacher; 1st Baptist Church Recreation Comm 1990, Coach of Sftbl Champions 1990; Teacher of Yr Nom 1984; *office:* Apopka Memorial Mid Sch 425 N Park Ave Apopka FL 32712

KISER, BERNAL ALLEN, JR., Chemistry Department Chair; *b:* Huron, SD; *ed:* (BA) Chem, Huron Coll 1963; (MS) Ed, SD St Univ 1966; St Norbert Coll, Univ WI Green Bay, IL Sch of Ed, Marion Coll; *cr:* Physics Teacher Lane HS 1963-64; Chem Teacher Holy Reedemer HS 1966-67, La Crosse Cntrl 1967-69; Naval Intelligence Kamiseya Japan 1969-71; Chem Teacher Premontre HS 1971-; *ai:* Premontre HS Fundraising; Asst Ski & Sci Academic Team Coach; Journal of Chemical Ed Contributor; Premontre Teacher of Yr 1986.

KISER, GLENDA WALTERS, Teacher/Principal; *b:* Beach, ND; *m:* Keith; *ed:* (BS) Elem Ed, Dickinson St 1975; Grad Stud Univ of Mary & Univ of ND Grand Fork; *cr:* Teacher Lemmon Public Schls 1975-76, Plainview Sch 1976-79; Teacher/Dir Childs Eye View 1980-82; Teacher/Prin Menoken Sch 1982-; *ai:* Young Citizens League Adv; Academic Competition Coach; ND Ed Assn 1982-; Delta Kappa Gamma 1st VP 1987-; *office:* Menoken Sch Box D Menoken ND 58558

KISH, CHARLES NICHOLAS, Science Teacher; *b:* Warren, OH; *m:* Randi Martin; *c:* Rachel, Robin, James; *ed:* (BA) Bio, Kent St Univ 1976; (MST) Sci Ed, Union Coll 1980; *cr:* 8th/10th Grade Sci Teacher Tupper Lake Jr/Sr HS 1976-77; 7th/8th Grade Sci Teacher Saratoga Springs Jr HS 1977-; *ai:* Sci Club; Technology Advisory & Dist Wide Cmptr Ed Comm; Sci Teachers Assn of NY St 1986-; Optical Society of America Outstanding Sci Teachers NY St 1987; Schuylerville Cntrl Sch Bd of Ed Bd Mem 1987-; Church of St Peter Contemporary Music Group Dir 1983-; NY St Ed Dept Consultant Mid Jr HS; Harcourt Brace Jovanovich Publishing Sr Editorial Adv; General Sci Text 1989; Writer Cross Disciplinary Act; *office:* Saratoga Springs Jr HS 5 Wells St Saratoga Springs NY 12866

KISOR, MARGARET AYRES, Social Studies Teacher; *b:* Binghamton, NY; *m:* Manown Jr.; *c:* Anne, Judith, William; *ed:* (BA) Pysch, Mount Holyoke Coll 1959; Elem Ed, Kean Coll 1975; (MAT) Rdng, Oakland Univ 1982; *cr:* 5th Grade Teacher 1978-81, Soc Stud Teacher/Scndry Sch Adv 1981- Kingsbury Sch; *ai:* Yrbk Adv; Steering Comm; Group Leader 6th-8th Grade Teachers; NCSS 1981-; Sch Evaluator Ind Schls Assn of Cntrl Sts; *home:* Rt 1 Box 215-C Mount Solon VA 22843

KISSELMAN, KENNETH L., 4th Grade Teacher; *b:* Windsor, CO; *ed:* (BA) Elem Ed, 1961, (MA) Elem Admin 1966 Univ of Northern CO; *cr:* Elem Teacher Johnstown Co Dist RE 5J 1961-71; Elem/Head Teacher Windsor Co Dist RE 4 1971-; *ai:* Benjamin Franklin Stamp Club Spon; CCTM; Faith United Meth Church of Christ Dir Bible Sch 1988; Natl Sci Fnd Grant Study Elem Math; Nom by Peers CO St Teacher of Yr; Nom Jaycee Oustanding Young Educator.

KISSLER, JODENE (BARTOLO), Mathematics Teacher; *b:* Pueblo, CO; *m:* Kirk D.; *c:* Mark; *ed:* (BS) Math, Univ of S CO 1977; (MA) Math, Univ of N CO 1981; Working Toward PhD in Math Ed, Univ of Denver; Woodrow Wilson Inst on Math Modeling, Princeton Univ 1987; Clinical Supervision/Models of Teaching, Douglas Cty Schls 1987; Word Processing in Ed, Rockmont Coll 1985; Cmptr Applications in Math, Univ of CO Denver 1984; Chem/Electronics, Univ of N CO 1983; Micromanagement in Classroom, Rockmont Coll 1983; Pascal for Educators, CO St Univ 1983; Increasing Your Motivation to Teach, CO Dept of Ed 1983; *cr:* Scndry Math Teacher Harrison Sch Dist 1977, Pueblo Sch Dist 70 1977; Dept Chair Douglas Cty Sch Dist 1981-87; Various Adult Courses Teacher SE Metropolitan Bd of Cooperative Services 1982; Mentor Teacher 1987-89, Scndry Math Teacher 1977-, Math Supv 1989- Douglas Cty Sch Dist; *ai:* Graduation Comm; Soph Girls Bsktbl Coach; Math Club Spon; NCTM 1975-; CO Cncl Teachers of Math (Secy, Treas 1985-89) 1976-, Service Awd 1989; Natl Cncl Supvrs of Math 1988-; Math Assn of America 1986-; Metro St Coll Advisory Math Ed Comm 1986-87; CO Fed of Teachers; Church Volunteer Groups; Amer Assn of Univ Women; Presidential Awd for Math Teaching St Level 1985; Woodrow Wison Fellowship Princeton Univ 1987; CO Teacher Awd for Ed & Civic Achievement 1984; KCNC Teacher Who Makes a Difference 1989; Nova Awd for Creative Teaching Douglas Cty Schls 1988; 3 Grants for Materials Scndry Math; *home:* 510 Vista Dr Castle Rock CO 80104

KITCHEN, KATHRYN HUNT, Mathematics Teacher; *b:* Hartford, CT; *m:* David Brent Sr.; *c:* David Jr., Melody L.; *ed:* (BS) Math, Anderson Univ 1983; *cr:* Math Teacher Madison Nazarene Chrstn Acad 1984-86, Mt Juliet Chrstn Acad 1986-; *ai:* Cheerleading Spon; *office:* Mount Juliet Chrstn Acad PO Box 397 Mount Juliet Rd Mount Juliet TN 37122

KITCHENS, WILEY H. (CUBY), Retired Teacher; *b:* Paducah, TX; *m:* Bobbie Ford; *c:* Keith, Karen Kitchens Marsh, Kelly; *ed:* (BA) Phys Ed, 1951, (MS) Ed, 1956 W TX St Univ; *cr:* Teacher/Coach White Deer Ind Sch Dist 1951-52; US Navy 1952-54; Teacher/Coach Groom Ind Sch Dist 1954-55, Hereford Ind Sch Dist 1955-83; Jr HS Prin Hereford Ind Sch Dist 1983-89; *ai:* TSTA, NEA; TASP 1983-89; THSCA 1954-83; *home:* 319 Stadium Dr Hereford TX 79045

KITCHINGS, VIRGINIA JOAN HUDSON, Social Studies Chairperson; *b:* Wagener, SC; *m:* Perrie; *c:* Brian O Neal; *ed:* Bus Transfer Curr, Voorhees Coll 1963; (BS) Bus, Allen Univ 1965; *cr:* Teacher Hunter-Kinard-Tyler HS 1965-74, A L Corbett Mid Sch 1974-; *ai:* Head Coach Boys Bsktbl; Co-Spon Jr Beta Club; Chrldr Coach & Adv; Asst Coach Girls Bsktbl; Orangeburg Ed Assn 1965-74; Aiken Cty Ed Assn 1974-; SCEA, NEA 1965-; Omicron Epsilon Society (Grand Secy 1977-86, Worthy Matron 1976-), Star of Yr 1980, Natl Star of Yr 1981; *home:* Box 551 Center St Wagener SC 29164

KITE, DON BRADFORD, Jr High Language Arts Teacher; *b:* Petersburg, WV; *ed:* (BA) Eng/Soc Stud, Fairmont St Coll 1969; *cr:* Soldier US Army 1970-71; Learning Disabilities/Remedial Rdng Aide Petersburg HS 1974-78; TEFL Instr Tarsus Amer Sch Turkey 1980; Lang Art Instr Petersburg HS 1980-; *ai:* VFW Post 6454, Amer Legion Post 78; Sold Short Story; Published Book 1978; Honorable Mention World of Poetry Contest 1988; *home:* 210 N Main St Petersburg WV 26847

KITOVER, MARY JANE MC GARRY, Eng as Second Lang Teacher; *b:* New York, NY; *m:* David; *ed:* (BA) Sociology Ed, 1958, (MA) Sociology Ed, 1962 Hunter Coll; Natl Univ Mexico 1963-65; Fordham Univ 1973; Univ CA 1972; *cr:* CB Teacher PS 7 1958-66; CB Teacher 1966-75, Eng as Second Lang Teacher 1975- PS 170; *ai:* Sch Staff Relations Comm; UFT Chapter Chairperson; Cath Teachers Assn, Emerald Society NYC Bd of Ed.

KITTENBRINK, LANA JO BEABER, 1st/2nd Grade Teacher; *b:* Detroit, MI; *m:* Kenneth Jay; *c:* Leah Kittenbrink Bromen, Jenneth; *ed:* Elem Grad Prgm, N KY Univ; *cr:* Teacher Ball Elem 1970-71, Williams Avenue 1973-74, St Paul Luth 1976-; *ai:* OH Dist Mission Bd Teacher Rep; Lutheran Ed Assn 1978-; Dept of Early Chldhd Ed 1980-; OH Cncl Teachers of Math 1987-; NCTM 1987-; *home:* 5258 Bell Ave Cincinnati OH 45242

KITTINGER, THOMAS WILLIAM, Vocal Music Instructor; *b:* Gettysburg, PA; *m:* Denise Ann Nagle; *c:* Thomas Jr., Gina R., Kristy L.; *ed:* (BA) Music Ed, Anderson Univ 1969; (MM) Music Ed, Towson St Univ 1978; *cr:* Teacher Littlestown Area Sch Dist 1969-; *ai:* Dir 7/8 Grade Chorus/Show Choir/Frosh Chorus/Concert Choir/Centenary U Meth Sr Choir; ACMEA Pres 1971-72; PMEA; MENC; ACDA PA St Chair Jazz/Show Choir Comm; UCP of PA VP 1985 Plaque 1989; Jaycees Outstanding Young Men of Amer 1978; *home:* 11 Mummert Dr Littlestown PA 17340

KITTLEBERGER, FREDERICK WILLIAM, Mathematics Teacher/Dept Chm; *b:* Mt Vernon, OH; *m:* Mary Lou Evans; *c:* Eric, Jason; *ed:* (BS) Civil Engineering, Case Inst of Technology 1959; (MS) Sci Ed, UniV of UT 1968; *cr:* Math Teacher Scharf Jr HS 1963-65; Math Teacher/Dept Chm Hillside Jr HS 1965-; *ai:* Prepare Stu for OH Test of Scholastic Achievement; NEA, OH Ed Assn, Parma Ed Assn, NE OH Teacher Assn 1963-; Univ of UT Masters Degree Prgm Academic Yr Inst 1967-68; *office:* Hillside Jr HS 1320 Education Park Dr Seven Hills OH 44131

KITTLER, WILLIAM H., Junior Science Teacher; *b:* Carlisle, AR; *ed:* (BS) Bio, Ouachita Baptist Univ 1962; *cr:* Jr HS Sci Teacher Carlisle HS 1989-; *ai:* Jr Class Spon; AR Ed Assn; Local Ed Assn Past Pres; Lions Club, Masonic Lodge, Meth Church; *home:* Rt 2 Box 71 Carlisle AR 72024

KITTRELL, PAMELA ANN, Special Education Teacher; *b:* Detroit, MI; *m:* Sydney David; *c:* Brittney; *ed:* (BS) Spec Ed, 1980, (MS) Pre Sch, 1986 Wayne St Univ; *cr:* Level K Teacher Mooris Child Dev 1980-81; ESRP Teacher Butzel Mid Sch 1981-82; Spec Ed Teacher Farwell Mid Sch 1982-; *ai:* Alpha Kappa Alpha Mem 1978-; NAACP Mem 1980-; *home:* 15490 Warwick Detroit MI 48223

KITTS, JAMES WILLIAM, History Teacher; *b:* Cass City, MI; *m:* Sandra Beth Boley; *ed:* (BSED) Soc Sci, Cntrl MI Univ 1981; *cr:* Resident Schls Field Rep De Vry Inst of Technology 1983-85; Sales Rep Thorn Apple Valley Inc 1985-87; Teacher Montrose Cmmty Schls 1987-; *ai:* Var Club Spon & Adv; Var Head Track & Asst Ftbl Coach; Witner Track Club Adv; Natl Strength & Conditioning Assn, MI Historical Society Mem 1988-; Project Grow Policy Bd Mem 1989-; United Way Chairperson for HS 1989-; Intermediate Sch Dist Educl Grant 1990; *office:* Montrose Hill-Mc Cloy HS 301 Nanita Dr Montrose MI 48457

KIVLON, BARBARA O' TOOLE, Staff Development Trainer; *b:* Jersey City, NJ; *m:* Michael Donald Joseph; *ed:* (BS) Elem Ed - Magna Cum Laude, 1979, (MA) Admin/Supervision, 1986 Seton Hall Univ; Candidate Doctoral Prgm Admin/Supervision, Seton Hall Univ 1990; *cr:* W Orange Bd of Ed 1979-80; 5th Grade Teacher Washington Sch 1980-89; Staff Dev Trainer W Orange Bd of Ed 1989-; Admin Intern St Cloud Sch 1989-; *ai:* Stu Cncl; Building Management, Math Acceleration & Grouping, Elem Sci & Math, Evaluation, Environmental Ed, Soc Stud Evaluation Team, Alignment with Basic Skills, Citizenship Ed, Eng as Second Lang, Study Skills & Manual Curr Comm; Kappa Delta Pi 1978-; Natl Staff Dev Cncl 1989-; NJ Staff Dev Cncl; Washington Sch PTA Treas; NJ Teacher of Yr Awd 1988; Outstanding Young Woman of America; Whos Who in Amer Ed; Governor Kean Ed Conference Teacher Rep; Whos Who Amoung Amer Colls & Univs; *home:* 43 3rd St C6 Clifton NJ 07011

KIZEWIC, RICHARD DONALD, United States History Teacher; *b:* Racine, WI; *m:* Shirley M. Chapek; *c:* Richard S., Joan Rediske; *ed:* (BA) US His, Univ WI Parkside 1972; Phys Ed, Univ WI Milwaukee 1975; Grad Stud Carthage Coll, Univ WI Parkside; *cr:* Soc Stud Teacher Washington Park HS 1973-; *ai:* Bsktbl Coach & Scout; Old Timers Lettermans Club Coord Adv 1982-.

KJENDALEN, DIANNE MARIE (MIERKIEWICZ), Computer Coordinator/Teacher; *b:* Milwaukee, WI; *m:* Curt; *ed:* (BS) Math, Univ of WI Oshkosh 1974; Miscellaneous Cmptr Related Courses; *cr:* Ad Hoc Staff Fox Valley Tech Coll 1981-84; Cmptr Sci/Math Teacher Marion HS 1975-; Ad Hoc Staff Univ of WI Stevens Point 1990; Cmptr Coord Marion HS 1989-; *ai:* Class Adv; License Review Comm & Fund Raising Comms; Marion Ed Assn Secy 1989-; Marion Lioness Club (Charter Secy 1984-86, Pres 1986-87); Lioness Dist 27 B2 (Charter Secy 1985-86, VP 1986-87, Pres 1987-88; Hillshire Recognition of Excl Awd Scndry Teacher of Yr 1989; CESA 8 Scndry Ed Rep to WI St Teachers Forum 1988; Orgaizational Comm Mem CESA 8 Teachers Forum 1989; *office:* Marion HS 105 School St Marion WI 54950

KJOS, DOUG GLEN, Science/Computer Sci Teacher; *b:* Minot, ND; *m:* Sue Kathryn Spain; *c:* Sarah, Molly, Anne; *ed:* (BA) Bio, Minot St Univ 1973; Physics, Chem, Cmptr Sci, Bio, Earth Sci, Univ of ND & MO St Univ; *cr:* Teacher Plaza Public Sch 1974-; *ai:* Annual & Class Adv; Scorekeeper; Plaza Ed Assn, Amer Assn for Advancement of Sci 1974-89; Programmed Educl Chem & Bio Systems; *home:* PO Box 54 Plaza ND 58771

KLAHN, NORMA JEAN, Social Studies Teacher; *b:* Springville, NY; *ed:* (BS) Scndry Ed, St Univ Fredonia NY 1960; (MS) Scndry Ed, St Univ Buffalo NY 1966; *cr:* 7th/8th Grade Soc Stud Teacher 1960-65, 7th/8th Grade Eng Teacher 1966-67, 8th Grade Soc Stud Teacher 1968-88, 7th/8th Grade Soc Stud Teacher 1988- Holland Cntrl Sch; *ai:* Yearly Talent Show Producer & Dir; Plan & Execute Spec Prgm; 8th Grade Class Adv 1968-78; NY Ed Assn, NEA, Holland Teachers Assn 1960-.

KLAPPER, MARGERY MAHLER, English/Journalism Teacher; *b:* Bogota, South America; *c:* Elizabeth C; *ed:* (BA) Ger, PA St Univ 1969; (MEd) Ger, Temple Univ 1974; Cert Eng, Univ of MD/Prince Georges Comm Coll; *cr:* Ger Teacher Abraham Lincoln HS 1969-73; Eng/Journalism/Ger Teacher Bladensburg HS 1973-; *ai:* Newspaper Adv; Literary Magazine Adv; Drama Club Co-Spon; Scoring Team Mem; Publication Comm Chairperson; Talented & Gifted Comm Mem; Article in Die

Unterrichtspraxis 1973; *office:* Bladensburg Sr H S 5610 Tilden Rd Bladensburg MD 20710

KLAPPERICH, MARGARET R., Art Teacher; *b:* Marytown, WI; *ed:* (BS) Art Ed, 1960, (MS) Art Ed, 1971 Univ of WI Milwaukee; *cr:* Art Teacher Ripon Sr HS 1960-, Moraine Park Tech Inst 1960-84, Ripon Coll 1988-; *ai:* Drama Costume Designing & Construction; Chemical Abuse Awareness Prgm Facilitator; Gifted & Talented Prgm; NEA 1970-; WI Ed Assn, Ripon Teachers Ed Assn 1960-; *home:* 410 E Sullivan Ripon WI 54971

KLASSEN, JAMES REED, Mathematics Teacher/Dept Chair; *b:* Newton, KS; *m:* Ly Thi Tran; *ed:* (BA) Math, Bethel Coll 1969; (MDIV) Bible, Mennonite Biblical Seminary 1972; *cr:* Bible/Eng Teacher Mennonite Stu Center 1973-76; Math/Forensics Instr Part-Time Bethel Coll 1977-79, 1982; Vietnamese Lang Instr Wichita St Univ 1980; Eng as Second Lang Teacher Associated Cath Charities 1984-85; HS Math Teacher Tulsa Chrstn Sch 1986-; *ai:* Math Club & Sr Class Spon; Vietnamese Mission Church Deacon 1987-; Mennonite Cntrl Comm Vietnamese Lang Consultant 1979-82; Bethel Coll Young Alumnus Awd 1976; Book Published 1986; Articles & Poems Published.

KLAUS, RICHARD RALPH, Retired Fifth Grade Teacher; *b:* Benton Harbor, MI; *m:* Donna J. Bishop; *c:* Paul R., Phillip J.; *ed:* (BS) Ed Four Minors, E MI Univ 1965; Advanced Elem Ed; *cr:* 5th/8th Grade Teacher Sanilac Cty 1956-68; 6th Grade Teacher Sarasota 1968-71; 5th Grade Teacher Yale Public Schls 1971-86; *ai:* MEA 1956-68, 1971-86; NEA 1971-86; MARSP 1986-; AAL Branch 7369 Pres 1988-; Port Sanilac Choral Club 1958-88; *home:* 6096 Deckerville Rd Deckerville MI 48427

KLAVERKAMP, DIANE M., 4th Grade Teacher; *b:* St Cloud, MN; *ed:* (AA) Secretarial Sci, 1970, (BS) Elem Ed, 1976 St Cloud St Univ; *cr:* 2nd Grade Teacher 1976-80, 4th Grade Teacher 1980-SS Peter & Paul; *ai:* Ben Franklin Stamp Club Adv; Dist Consultant for Total Rdng Prgm; MN Rdng Assn 1986-; *office:* SS Peter & Paul Sch 111 Central Ave N Richmond MN 56368

KLAYBOR, STANLEY J., Retired Biology Teacher; *b:* South Bend, IN; *m:* Mary Jane Dobbelaere; *c:* Kathy, Dan, Jeff, Kelly; *ed:* (BS) Phys Ed/Bio, Hanover Coll 1953; (MS) Ed, IN Univ 1958; Purdue Univ; SE MO St; OK Univ; W MI; Bio Stud, NSF Inst; *cr:* Bio Teacher Washington 1955-65, LaSalle 1965-70, Washington 1970-88; *ai:* Class Spon 1961, 1965, 1987; Izaak Walton HS Club Spon; Head Ftbl & Track Coach; Asst Ftbl; Soc Comm; Starter for in Girls St Track Meet 1989; Referee St Track Meet 1990; AFT 1955-85; NEA 1985-88; Izaak Walton League Prgm Chm 1962-, Walton of Yr 1987; St John The Baptist Cath Parish Church Usher 1955-; Natl Sci Fnd Schlsps 1961, 1965, 1968; Teacher of Yr Washington HS; Audubon Schlsp 1988; *home:* 1609 N Iowa St South Bend IN 46628

KLEBSCH, SHIRLEY GOLDSMITH, Fourth Grade Teacher; *b:* Highmore, SD; *m:* Kenneth Chancey; *c:* Susan, Michael, Rodney; *ed:* (BS) Elem Ed/Art & Lib Sci, Northern St Univ 1971; Advanced Trng Cmptr Sci; *cr:* Swimming Instr Highmore Municipal Pool 1960-62; Elem Rural Teacher Hyde Cty 1960-63; 4th/5th Grade Combination Teacher Highmore Elem 1963-67; 4th Grade Teacher Hyde Cty Ind Sch Dist 1968-; *ai:* Jr Cath Daughters Leaders 1978-82; SDEA, NEA 1959-; HCEA Secy 1959-; NCTM 1980-; SDCTM 1984-; Red Cross Water Safety Chm 1963-; Cath Daughters (St Cmmty 1988-, Dist Deputy 1984-88, Pres); Outstanding Young Woman of Highmore 1968; *home:* 309 1st St Highmore SD 57345

KLECKLEY, PATRICIA JOHNSON, Fourth Grade Teacher; *b:* Asheboro, NC; *c:* Stephanie; *ed:* (BA) Elem Ed, Columia Coll 1976; (MS) Elem Ed, Univ of SC 1987; *cr:* 3rd 4th & 5th Grade Teacher Colonial Chrstn Sch 1979-81; 6th Grade Teacher Ridge Monetta Elem 1981-84; 2nd-4th Grade Teacher John P Thomas Elem Sch 1984-88; 6th Grade Teacher Swansea Intermediate Sch 1988-89; 4th Grade Teacher Frances F Mack Elem Sch 1989-.

KLECKLEY, RAYNA WAITES, 8th Grade Soc Studies Teacher; *b:* Columbia, SC; *m:* Russell Thomas; *ed:* (BA) Elem Ed, Columbia Coll 1986; His/Guidance, USC; Mid Sch, Columbia Coll, Cmptrs in Ed, USC; Quest Trained Teacher; *cr:* 8th Grade Teacher Lexington Mid Sch 1987-; *office:* Lexington Mid Sch 702 N Lake Dr Lexington SC 29072

KLECKNER, ROGER EUGENE, Mathematics Teacher; *b:* Sandusky, OH; *m:* Deanna S. Weaver; *c:* Laura; *ed:* (BSED) Math, 1969, (MBA) Math, 1980 Bowling Green St Univ; Various Conferences Advanced Placement Calculus 1989; *cr:* 7th Grade Teacher Huron Mid Sch 1969-72; Teacher Margaretta HS 1973-81; Asst Prof of Applied Sci Teacher Firelands Coll 1981-84; Teacher Margaretta HS 1984-; Visiting Asst Professor Firelands Coll 1989-; *ai:* Coll Test Preparation Coord; NEA, OEA 1972-; Margaretta Teachers Assn 1972-89; Phi Delta Kappa 1989-; Margaretta NHS Honorary Mem Teacher 1988; Outstanding HS Teacher Erie Cty 1989; Outstanding Young Men of America 1972; Whos Who in Amer Politics 1971; *office:* Margaretta HS 209 Lowell St Castalia OH 44824

KLEE, KATHLEEN M., Math Dept Chair/Cmptr Coord; *b:* Syracuse, NY; *m:* Karl J.; *ed:* (BS) Math, St Bonaventure Univ 1970; (MA) Math, SUNY Geneseo 1975; NCEI Summer Inst on Microcomputer Applications Cntrl St Univ OK; Advanced Placement Calculus Inst Alleghany Coll; Cmptr Sci Courses, SUNY Fredonia & Jamestown Comm Coll; *cr:* Math Teacher Red Jacket Cntrl Sch 1970-77, Randolph Cntrl Sch 1977-; *ai:* Acad Quiz Team Adv; K-12th Grade Cmptr Coord; Math Dept Head; Yrbk & Class Adv; NY St Assn of Math Teachers, NCTM, Assn of Computing Machinery 1977-; NY St Cmptr & Technology Ed 1980-; People-To-People Delegation of Cmptr Sci Educators to Bulgaria & Soviet Union 1989; *office:* Randolph Central Schl Main St Randolph NY 14772

KLEEMAN, RUTH S., Counselor; *b:* Rome, GA; *m:* Peter; *c:* Michael, Kimberly; *ed:* (BS) Home Ec, Berry Coll 1970; (MED) Home Ec, Univ of GA 1976; Cert Guidance & Counseling, W GA Coll 1989; *cr:* Home Ec Teacher Trion HS 1970-71, N Whitfield HS 1971-72, Red Bud HS 1972-89; Cnslr Red Bud Jr/Sr HS 1989-; *ai:* Literary, Sr, Homecoming Coord; Delta Kappa Gamma (Treas 1990-92) 1982-; GA Assn Educators, NEA 1987-; GA Vocation Assn 1970-89; GA Cnslrs Assn 1989-; Cherokee Capital Fair Assn Bd of Dir 1985-; St Clements Cath Church Choir 1980-; Winners Club Tutoring 1985-; Red Bud HS STAR Teacher 1978, 1983-85, 1990 & Teacher of Yr 1980-84; Gordon Cty STAR Teacher 1985 & Teacher of Yr 1984; Nominee Cty Voc Teacher of Yr 1987; *home:* 233 Kleeman Rd Calhoun GA 30701

KLEIER, CATHERINE BOONE, Mathematics Teacher; *b:* Howardstown, KY; *m:* Daniel Anthony; *c:* Heidi A., Curt K.; *ed:* (BA) Math, Bellarmine Coll 1967; (MS) Math, Univ of Notre Dame 1972; Cmptr Sci, Union Coll; Advanced Placement Pascal, Univ of San Francisco; *cr:* Math Teacher Sacred Heart Acad 1967-68, Brandywine HS 1968-70, BollingBrook Day 1970-71, Hopewell HS 1971-72, Matignon HS 1972-73, Acton-Boxboro HS 1973-75, Los Alamos HS 1979-80, St Joseph Cntrl HS 1980-81; Math Chairperson/Teacher Cntrl Cath HS 1982-86; Math Teacher St Marks HS 1986-; *ai:* Model UN Moderator; Math League Coach; NCTM 1980-; NSF Grants 1968-72; *office:* St Marks HS Pike Creek Rd Wilmington DE 19808

KLEIMAN, JOHN REEVE, English Teacher; *b:* San Angelo, TX; *m:* Jillaine Campbell; *c:* Heather, Nathan; *ed:* (BA) Eng/Speech, Dallas Baptist Univ 1978; (MA) Ed Admin, Univ of TX-San Antonio 1984; Teacher Appraisal Trng & Admin Trng; *cr:* Teacher San Marcos Baptist Acad 1978, San Antonio Acad 1979-81, W W Jackson Mid Sch 1981-86; Asst Prin Nimitz Mid Sch 1986-88; Teacher W W Jackson Mid Sch 1988-; *ai:* Natl Jr Honor Society Spon; Pal-Comm Mem; at Risk-Comm Mem; Phi Delta Kappa; Shearer Hills Baptist Church Teacher; Certificate of Recognition Battered Womens Shelter; *office:* W W Jackson Mid Sch 4538 Vance Jackson San Antonio TX 78230

KLEIN, DAVID JOSEPH, Soc Sci/Jr H S/H S Teacher; *b:* Platteville, WI; *m:* Constance Anne Cummins; *c:* Wyatt, Rachel, Noelle; *ed:* (BA) Bus/Economics, 1970, (BA) Scndry Ed/Soc Sci/His, 1973 Univ WI Platteville; Scndry Ed Admin, Loras Coll; *cr:* Soc Sci Instr Shullsburg Public Schls 1975-; *ai:* Asst Dir Musical Production; Comm Mem Drug & Alcohol Abuse; Schlsp Comm Mem; Shullsburg Ed Assn Negotiator Mem 1987; WI Ed Assn; NEA; Elk Grove Township Supvr 1987-; Cuba City 4-H Leader 1989-; Dist Teacher of Yr Awd 1981; *home:* 28201 Back Rd Cuba City WI 53807

KLEIN, DORRIS AHRENHOLTZ, Kindergarten Teacher; *b:* Crawford City, IA; *m:* Clifford J.; *c:* Curtiss, Lucinda Klein Lombardo, Nicolette, Timothy, Mary E., Jodine Holloway; *ed:* (BS) Elem Ed, Dana Coll 1975; Addl Stud Continuing Ed; *cr:* Teacher Crawford Cty Rural Schls 1947-49, Shelby Cty Rural Schls 1955-65, St Peter & Paul Parochial Sch 1965-66; Kndgtn Teacher Harlan Cmmty Schls 1966-; *ai:* Amer Assn of Univ Women 1976-; NEA Lifetime Mem; ISEA, HEA Locals 1966-; Amer Legion Auxiliary Local Pres 1960-62; Harlan Chamber of Commerce Teacher Recognition Awd 1988; Spec Recognition Coll of St Mary Omaha 1989; *home:* 1202 Durant Harlan IA 51537

KLEIN, RHONDA MARY, Teacher; *b:* Northfield, MN; *m:* William Robert; *c:* Joseph, Robert, Kathryn; *ed:* (AA) Ed, Anoka-Ramsey Jr Coll 1969; (BA) Elem Ed, Univ of MN Minneapolis 1971; Hamline, Univ of MN, River Falls; *cr:* 5th Grade Teacher Battle Creek Elem 1971-76, 5th Grade Teacher 1976-89, Chapter I Teacher 1989- Cherokee Hts Elem; *ai:* 4th-6th Grade Stu Expections; Soc Comm; MN Ed Assn 1971-76; AFT 1976-; PTA 1971-; Republican Party Delegate 1980-; MCCL 1984-; Concerned Women of America 1984-; *office:* Cherokee Heights Elem Sch 694 Charlton St Saint Paul MN 55107

KLEINHENZ, EMMA AMERSON, Mathematics/Physics Teacher; *b:* Lexington, KY; *m:* Paul Joseph; *c:* Paul, Aaron; *ed:* (BS) Chem, 1972-73, (MA) Ed, 1980-81 Georgetown Coll; *cr:* Teacher Georgetown Hs 1973-75, Georgetown Mid Sch 1975-77, Scott Cty HS 1978-; *ai:* Sci Club & Chrldr Spon; Math Academic Coach; Team Leader Scott Cty HS; NSTA 1980-; *office:* Scott Cty HS 1036 Long Lick Pike Georgetown KY 40324

KLEINSCMIDT, MARLENE (COLICHO), First Grade Teacher; *b:* Fort Wayne, IN; *m:* Don W.; *c:* Donald M., Donna M.; *ed:* (BS) Ed, Concordia Teachers Coll 1960; (MS) Ed, Purdue Univ Ft Wayne 1981; Assertive Discipline Hands on Sci; *cr:* 3rd-4th Grade Teacher Trinity/Green Park St Louis, MO 1960-62; 2nd Grade Teacher Concordia Peoria, IL 1962-63; 5th Grade Teacher Zion Ferguson, MO 1963-64; Pre-Sch Teacher 1975-77, 1st Grade Teacher 1977-80 St Paul Ft Wayne, IN; 1st Grade Teacher Concordia Ft Wayne, IN 1980-; *ai:* Y-Teen Club Adv; Intnl Rdng Assn 1990-; Luth Ed Assn 1977-; IN Rdng Assn 1981-; Church Handbell Choir; *office:* Concordia Luth Sch 4245 Lake Ave Fort Wayne IN 46815

KLEINSTUBER, MARGARET MASON, 2nd Grade Teacher; *b:* Glens Falls, NY; *m:* David H.; *c:* Erik Bullard; *ed:* (BS) Elem Ed, SUNY Plattsburgh 1969; Cmptr Literary; Drug/Alcohol Abuse Awareness; Whole Lang Approach to Rdng; *cr:* Elem Teacher Malone Cntrl Sch Dist 1969-77; Sheburne Earlville Cntrl Sch Dist 1978-; *ai:* Adv Cncl; Teacher-Child Asst Team; Sherburne-Earlville VP/Pres 1982-85; Poly Action Chm 1985-87; NEA St Delegate 1982-; Chenango Valley Rdng Cncl 1988-; NYS Rdng Cncl 1988-; YMCA Swim Parents Booster Org; Chenango Cnty Chamber Commerce; Broad Street Meth Church; *office:* Sherburne Earlville Cntrl Sch Utica Rd Sherburne NY 13460

KLEPADLO, SHIRLEY J., Chemistry Teacher; *b:* Montaque, MA; *ed:* (BA) Chem, Anna Maria Coll 1966; (MS) Radiological Health, Rutgers Univ 1967; (CA) Accountancy, Bentley Coll 1982; Ed Courses, Univ of MA; Bio, Framingham St Coll; *cr:* Research Asst Worcester Fnd Exper Bio 1967-68; Chem Teacher Marlborough HS 1968-71, Maynard HS 1971-; *ai:* Cheerleading Coach 1969-74; SADD Adv 1987-88; Maynard Teachers Assn Secy 1971-; MA Assn Sci Teachers 1975-; NEA 1968-; Marlborough Girls Club 1981-84; Amer Heart Assn Volunteer 1989-; US Public Health Service Fellowship 1966-67; Bentley Coll Excl in Teaching HS 1987; NE Section Amer Chemical Society Excl in Teaching Chem 1988; *office:* Maynard HS Great Rd Maynard MA 01754

KLESATH, JULIE KAY, Chemistry/Physics Teacher; *b:* Mason City, IA; *ed:* (AA) General Stud, N IA Comm Coll 1986; (BA) Chem Ed, Univ of N IA 1988; *cr:* Chem/Physics Teacher Boscobel HS 1988-; *ai:* Soph Class, Yrbk, Photo Club Adv; Head Cross Cntry Coach; WI Cross Cntry Coaches Assn 1989-, 2nd Place Sectional Team 1989; *office:* Boscobel HS 300 Brindley St Boscobel WI 53805

KLETT, KATHRYN V., Mathematics Teacher; *b:* Syracuse, NY; *m:* John E.; *c:* J. Paul, James W.; *ed:* (BA) Math, Marymount Coll 1964; (MA) Math Ed, Syracuse 1968; *cr:* Teacher Syracuse Public Schls 1964-72, Martin Cty Schls 1974-; *ai:* Math Club; Past Math Dept Chm; FL Academic Tournament Spon; NCTM; St Josephs Church Eucharistic Minister; Outstanding FL Math Teacher 1984; *home:* 8831 SW 17th Ave Stuart FL 34997

KLIMEK, PATRICIA EVERETT, Spanish Teacher; *b:* Urbana, IL; *m:* James Henry; *ed:* (BA) Span, 1972, (MSED) Admin, 1987 Univ Of IL Urbana Champaign; *cr:* Span Teacher/Dept Head Jefferson Jr HS 1974-77; Span Teacher Cntrl HS 1977-84, Centennial HS 1984-; *ai:* Span Club Adv; Class Spon; Chairperson Comm on Stu Success; Peer Mentor; Phi Delta Kappa; Cherry Hills Homeowners Assn Secy 1988-; Grant from Champaign-Urbana Fnd; *office:* Centennial HS 913 S Crescent Dr Champaign IL 61821

KLINAR, ANN ELIZABETH, Fifth Grade Teacher; *b:* Newport News, VA; *ed:* (BS) Elem Ed, Sam Houston St Univ 1968; Grad Work Univ of TX 1972, Univ of Houston 1974; Numerous Wkshps in Lit & Art; *cr:* 5th/6th Grade Teacher Beverly Hills Intermediate 1968-71; 6th Grade Teacher Meador Elem 1971-72; 5th/7th Grade Teacher George Thompson Intermediate 1972-75; 5th Grade Teacher Richey Elem 1975-; *ai:* Coach Powder Puff Team; Safety Patrol Spon; Wrote, Directed, Choreographed 6 Musical Productions 1975-79, 1982, 1984; Pasadena Ind Sch Dist Music Festivals Choreograph Dance Numbers 1978, 1982, 1988; PTA Cultural Arts 1987-88, Lifetime Membership 1981; Zeta Tau Alpha Alumnae Assn 1987-; Zeta Tau Alpha (Alumna Adv, Soc Prgm 1987-89, Alumna Adv, Gen Adv 1989-); Career Ladder Level III; *office:* Richey Elem Sch 610 S Richey Pasadena TX 77506

KLINE, ARTHUR HAROLD, Science Teacher; *b:* Huntington, IN; *m:* Joanna Kay Bingham; *c:* Komeh, Adam; *ed:* (BA) Psych, Purdue Univ 1975; (BS) Sci Ed, Univ of New Orleans 1985; (MS) Bio/Chem/Ind Ed, IN Univ 1989; Commerical Diving Center; Air/Mixed Gas Diving 1977; *cr:* Commerical Diver Taylor Diving 1977-85; Sci Teacher Jefferson Parish Schls 1985-86, Huntington Cty Cmmty Sch &Huntington N HS 1986-; *ai:* Class Spon; Soccer Asst Coach; *office:* Huntington North HS 450 Mc Gahn St Huntington IN 46750

KLINE, PATRICIA FLETCHER, Middle School Teacher; *b:* St Louis, MO; *m:* Steven Louis; *c:* Timothy, Stephanie, Alisha; *ed:* (BS) Elem Ed, Univ of OK 1968; *cr:* Classroom Teacher Putnam City Schls 1977-80, Jones Public Schls 1980-; *ai:* Honor Society & Chrldr Spon; Sch Talent Show, Sch Play, Interscholastic Competition Adv; Voc Tech Liaison; OEA Building Rep 1980-, Teacher of Yr 1985; Jones Ed Assn, OK Ed Assn; PTA VP 1987-88; Team Leader-Coordination of 10 Teachers; *office:* Jones Public Schls Rt 1 Box 670 Jones OK 73049

KLINE, VICKI SULLINS, 9th Grade English Teacher; *b:* Cartersville, GA; *c:* Patricia L., David S.; *ed:* (AA) Ed, Brewton-Parker Jr Coll 1964; (BS) Ed/Eng, Valdosta St Coll 1966; (MED) Ed/Eng, GA Southern Coll 1976; Various Seminars; *cr:* Eng/Civics Teacher Clinch Cty HS 1966-67; Eng Jane Macon Jr HS 1967-69; Eng/His Mc Intosh Acad 1972; Eng Teacher Glynn Acad 1976-; *ai:* Textbook Adoption Comm; GA Cncl Teachers of Eng, NTE 1988-; 1st Baptist Church Sunday Sch Teacher 1985-; Passage Writer For 10th Grade GA Basic Skills Test; *office:* Glynn Acad PO Box 1678 Brunswick GA 31520

KLING, ANN ROUSH, Kindergarten Teacher; *b:* Lock Haven, PA; *m:* Robert E.; *c:* Craig R., Kurt E.; *ed:* (BS) Elem, Lock Haven Univ 1957; *cr:* Kndgtn Teacher Keystone Cntrl Sch Dist 1957-; *ai:* PA St Ed Assn, NEA, Delta Kappa Gamma Society, Lock Haven Univ Alumni; *office:* Woodward Sch RD 1 Lock Haven PA 17745

KLINGLESMITH, KENDRA COLWELL, English/Spanish Teacher; *b:* Union City, IN; *m:* Shawn; *ed:* (BA) Eng, Cumberland Coll 1988; *cr:* Teacher Dilce Combs Memorial HS 1988-; *ai:* Span

Club Spon; Bible Club & Anti-Drug Organization Co-Spon; *office:* Dilce Combs Memorial HS Box 159 Jeff KY 41751

KLINK, MARLENE GROENER, 7th Grade English/Sci Teacher; *b:* Oak Park, IL; *w:* Karl Albert (dec); *c:* Charles, William, Kate; *ed:* (BS) Phys Ed/Sci, IA St Univ 1967; Northwestern Coll; *cr:* Scndry Teacher Mt St Mary Acad on the Fox 1967; Scndry Teacher 1967-71, Mid Sch Teacher 1987- Primghar Comm Schls; *ai:* Class Supvr; P Club Adv; Woolverine Reporter Adv; Guidance Advisory Comm; Primghar Advisory Comm; NW IA Eng Teachers Assn; Primghar Ed Assn Pres 1988-89; Primghar Womens Club Chair Book Club 1986; IA St Univ Alumni 1978-80; Primghar Bd of Ed Dir/Pres/VP 1971-86, Service Awd 1986; Area 4 Ed Bd Dir 1980-83, Service Awd 1983; United Church of Primghar Financial Fund Raiser; I Have Written Articles for a Voc Ag Book Published By Data Transmission Network; These Articles Deal with Marketing in Ag; *office:* Primghar Community Schl Primghar IA 51245

KLIPSCH, KAREN TRELINSKI, Second Grade Teacher; *b:* Jonesboro, AR; *m:* Robert C.; *c:* Emily L.; *ed:* (BS) Elem Ed, IN Univ 1973; (MS) Elem Ed, Univ of Evansville 1976; *cr:* 6th Grade Teacher Owatonna Sch Corp 1973-74; Homebound Instr Henderson Cty KY; Spec Ed Instr Vanderburg Sch Corp; 2nd Grade Teacher Pike Cty Sch Corp; *ai:* Chapter Advisory, Gifted Talented Advisory, Rdng Book Adoption Comm; ISTA, NEA 1976-; *home:* RR 1 E Main Petersburg IN 47567

KLISIAK, JANICE GESCHEIDLER, First Grade Teacher; *b:* Hammond, IN; *m:* Stanley; *ed:* (BS) Ed, 1971, (MS) Ed, 1975 IN Univ; *cr:* 2nd-3rd Grade Teacher Irving Elem 1973-74; 1st Grade Teacher Franklin Elem 1975-76, Harding Elem 1979-; *ai:* Adv Comm for Hammond Leadership & Prgm Devel Acad; City Report Card Devel Comm; Chairperson Sch Faculty Adv Team; Hammond Area Rdng Cncl; *office:* Warren G Harding Elem Sch 3211 165th St Hammond IN 46323

KLIZA, NANCY G., English Teacher; *b:* Detroit, MI; *m:* Gary A.; *ed:* (BS) Eng Lit/Lang, Eastern MI Univ 1970; (JD) Law, Detroit Coll of Law 1975; Admin Courses, Wayne St Univ 1978-82; *cr:* Soc Stud Teacher Wayne-Westland Cmmty Schls 1970-77; Asst Prin Wayne Memorial HS 1977-78; Grants Coord Wayne-Westland Cmmty Schls 1978-81; Eng Teacher John Marshall Jr HS 1981-; *ai:* Natl Jr Honor Society Adv 1983-; MI Ed Assn 1970-; MI Cncl Women in Educl Admin (Exec Bd 1979-82, Treas 1980-81); Women Lawyers Assn of MI 1977-82; Macomb Cty Comm Coll Displaced Homemakers Project Advisory Bd 1979-81; MI Employment Trng Inst Consultant 1979-81; N Cntrl Evaluation Team 1974-80; *office:* John Marshall Jr HS 35100 Bayview Westland MI 48185

KLOC, SHEILA SCHWEITZER, Second Grade Teacher; *b:* Sandusky, OH; *m:* Norbert F.; *c:* Laura, Jacqueline, Christopher; *ed:* (BA) Eng, Notre Dame Coll 1962; Elem Cert Bowling Green St Univ; Cmptr Cert John Carroll Univ; Teaching Drug Abuse Prevention Courses; *cr:* 1st Grade Teacher Madison Sch 1963-64, Walton Sch 1964-65; Teacher St Joseph Sch 1980-; *ai:* Coord Rainbows Prgm; Teacher Quest Prgm; Teacher Sacramental Prgms; *home:* 32688 Surrey Ln Avon Lake OH 44012

KLOCK, FRANK C., Religion Dept Chairperson; *b:* Chicago, IL; *m:* Mary C. Mc Gowan; *ed:* (BA) Eng, Niles Coll of Loyola Univ 1973; (MRE) Ed, Loyola Univ Inst of Pastorial Stud 1983; *cr:* Teacher St Joseph HS 1976-77; Teacher/Dept Chm Lourdes HS 1977-; *ai:* Kairos Retreat Bd of Dir; NHS Cncl; Curr Comm Spon for Ecology; Peace Movement; Cncl for Basic Ed 1986-; Religious Ed Assn 1987-; Partners ACT Big Brother 1989-; Natl Fellowship 1986; Cncl for Basic Ed; Ind Hum Stud; Chicago Cath Youth Office; Youth Ministry Awd 1988; Theatrical Lighting Design Consultant; *office:* Lourdes HS 4034 W 56th St Chicago IL 60629

KLOECK, VERA, SR., Religion/Math/Reading Teacher; *b:* St Meinrad, IN; *ed:* (BS) Elem Ed, St Benedict Coll 1963; (MED) Ed/Psych, Spalding Univ 1970; Catechist Cert; *cr:* 1st Grade Teacher St Joseph 1953-60; 1st-2nd Grade Teacher St Clement 1960-61; 1st/6th-8th Grade Teacher St Benedict 1961-67; 4th/5th Grade Teacher Ireland Public 1967-69; Prin Nativity 1969-71; 3rd/5th/6th Grade Teacher Ferdinand Public 1971-80; 5th-8th Grade Teacher St Philip 1980-; *ai:* Religion Prgm Coord; Eucharistic Minister/Lecturer; NCEA, Evansville Area Rdng Cncl; Benedictine Sister of Ferdinand; Diocesan Sisters Senate; Article Published; *office:* St Philip Sch 3420 S St Philip Rd Mount Vernon IN 47620

KLOPP, WILLIAM A., JR., Teacher/Mathematics Dept Chair; *b:* Cincinnati, OH; *m:* Judy Fosdick; *c:* Brian Silz, LeeAnne, Billy, Aaron, Emily; *ed:* (BS) Math/Physics, Morehead St Univ 1970; (MED) Ed, Xavier Univ 1973; Grad Work N KY Univ; *cr:* Teacher/Coach Campbell Cty HS 1970-72, Newport HS 1972-73, Walton Verona HS 1973-75, Bellevue HS 1975-; *ai:* Girls Bsktbl Coach; Principals Advisory Comm; KY Assn of Physics Teachers; KY HS Coaches Assn, Natl HS Coaches Assn 1972-; N KY Ofcls Assn 1980-; Nalt Golf Fnd, Assn of Golf Educators; Ft Thomas 1st Baptist Church Deacon 1988-; Golden Apple Teacher of Yr 1990; Finalist Advanced Placement Albright Awd; *office:* Bellevue HS 201 Center St Bellevue KY 41073

KLOSE, JANICE KAYE, Fourth Grade Teacher; *b:* Lampasas, TX; *ed:* (BS) Elem Ed, 1976, (MED) Elem Ed, 1979 Tarleton St Univ; Working on Admin Cert; *cr:* 4th Grade Teacher Kline Whitis Elem; *ai:* Church Youth & Ed Comms; Delta Kappa Gamma 1st VP 1986-, Perfect Attendance 1990; TSTA Building Chm; 4-H Adult Leader 1984-86, Outstanding Adult Leader 1984, Excellent Leadership 1986; Cow Cntry Cloggers (Chm, Treas); Whos Who Among Stus in Amer Univs & Colls 1975-76; Outstanding Educator Agriculture 1989; Outstanding Young Women of America 1987; *home:* Rt 1 Box 39 Lampasas TX 76550

KLOSTERBUER, MARY SUE, Fourth Grade Teacher; *b:* Luverne, MN; *ed:* (BS) Elem Ed, Dakato St Coll 1969; (MS) Elem Ed, Mankato St Univ 1979; Project Charlie Trainer; *cr:* 4th Grade Teacher Windom Public Schls 1969-; *ai:* Elem Cmptr Coord; Staff Dev & Technology Comms; Windom Ed Assn 1969-, Teacher of Yr 1982; SW MN Rdng Cncl (Membership, Chairperson 1983-84) 1969-; 1st Presbyn Church Elder 1990; Outstanding Young Women of America 1979; Outstanding Leaders in Elem & Scndry Ed 1976; MN Dept of Ed Curr Writing 1987.

KLOZOTSKY, ROBERT JOHN, Language Art Teacher; *b:* Oconto, WI; *m:* Jane Moody; *c:* Michael, Elizabeth; *ed:* (BS) Eng, 1970, (MS) Eng/Amer Lit 1979 Univ of WI Oshkosh; Alcohol & Drug Abuse Prevention Courses in Lang Art & Writing; Tranescent Seminar Univ of WI Platteville; *cr:* Lang Art Teacher Little Chute Mid Sch 1970-; *ai:* Drama Dir; Head Forensics Coach; Newspaper & Yrbk Adv; Stu Asst Prgm Staff Mem; K-12 Lang Art Comm; 6th-8th Grade Unit Leadedr; NEA, WI Ed Assn, Little Chute Ed Assn 1970-; WI Assn of Mid Level Educators 1985-; NE WI Ed Assn 1987-; WI Forensics Assn Mem 1979-; Jr Division Advisory Comm; 1st United Meth Church Mem 1970-; Oconto Cty Historical Society Mem 1969-; Kaukauna Cmmty Players (VP, Ed, Bd of Dir, Mem) 1987-; Little Chute Ed Assn Mid Sch Teacher of Yr 1984; *office:* Little Chute Mid Sch 329 Grand Ave Little Chute WI 54140

KLUBENSPIES, CLAUDE SALERNO, Third Grade Teacher; *b:* Oujda, Morocco; *m:* Joseph H.; *c:* John, Alex; *ed:* (BS) Experimental Sci, Bordeaux Univ 1956; (BA) Ed, Newark St Coll 1968; (MA) Early Chldhd, Kean Coll 1981; *cr:* 3rd/4th Grade Teacher Casablanca Morocco 1958-59; Elem Grades Teacher Woodbridge Sch System 1968-; *ai:* Health Spa Instr; Therapeutic Massage Therapist; NEA, NJ Ed Assn 1968-; Amer Massage Therapy Assn 1989-; *office:* Lafayette Estates Sch Ford Ave Fords NJ 08863

KLUKAS, MYRT BLASEY, Spanish and Debate Teacher; *b:* Crookston, MN; *m:* Richard W.; *c:* Tom, Tim; *ed:* (BS) Foods/ Journalism, Univ of MN 1963; (BA) Lang Art/Comm, Dakota Wesleyan 1983; SD St Univ; *cr:* Span/Debate Teacher Hot Springs HS 1979-; *ai:* Debate & Oral Interpretation Coach; Hot Springs Ed Assn Pres 1985-88; SD Ed Assn; SD Forensics Coaches Assn; SD Speech Coaches Assn; NEA; Natl Fed Interscholastic Debate Assn; Phi Delta Kappa; SD Foreign Lang Teachers Assn; Natl Organization for Women St Pres 1980-83; Natl Womens Political Caucus; Hum Grants 1985, 1988; *office:* Hot Springs HS 1609 University Hot Springs SD 57747

KLUNDER, FRANCINE M., Business Education Teacher; *b:* Elizabeth, NJ; *ed:* (BA) Bus, Trenton St 1965; Supervision Keane Coll; Cmptr Sci Union Cty Tech; *cr:* Bus Ed Teacher Linden HS 1965-; *ai:* Class Adv 1977-; FBLA Adv; Home Instr Tutorial Prgm; NEA; NJ Bus Ed Assn; Linden Ed Assn; Teacher of Yr Nom 1989; *office:* Linden HS 1275 St Georges Ave Linden NJ 07036

KNAGG, KATHRYN LYNN, World History Teacher; *b:* Denison, TX; *ed:* (BA) His, Univ of TX Arlington 1981; *cr:* Teacher 1981-, Soc Stud Dept Chairperson 1984- Cedar Hill HS; *ai:* Jr Class Spon; Natural Helpers; NCSS 1989-; TX Soc Stud Supvrs Assn 1990; *office:* Cedar Hill HS P O Box 248 Cedar Hill TX 75104

KNAPP, BRENDA S., Performing Arts Teacher; *b:* Bowdon, GA; *c:* Brady, Brian; *ed:* (BS) Music, 1971, (MS) Music, 1972- Auburn; Drama Cert/Voice West GA Coll; *cr:* Teacher Auburn HS, Notasula HS, Carrollton HS & Jr HS; *ai:* Private Voice, Literary Events Coach; Trio, Quartet, Oral Int & Soloist; Church Organist; MENC/GEMA; GTC; GAE; GMTA; Teacher of Yr AL.

KNAPP, DONALD E., Social Science/Drama Teacher; *b:* Caldwell, ID; *m:* Barbara J.; *c:* Lise S. Longwell, Frank M. II; *ed:* (BA) Sociology, Boise St Univ 1969; (MA) Sch Admin, Univ of AK Juneau 1985; *cr:* Teacher Caldwell HS 1966-69, Schoenbar Jr HS 1970-; *ai:* Stu Cncl Adv; HS & Jr HS Track, Bsktbl, Drama Coach; Play Dir; Jr HS Many Building & Dist Comms Chm & Mem; Phi Delta Kappa 1985-; Ketchikan Children Home Pres 1975-87; Numerous Wkshps & Spec Meetings for Dist Sch & Dept; *home:* 2603 4th Ave Lower Ketchikan AK 99901

KNAPP, DONALD LEE, Earth Sci/Astronomy Teacher; *b:* Springfield, MO; *m:* Joyce Anne Mayfield; *c:* Abigail L., Stephanie A., Emily D.; *ed:* (BSEd) Phys Ed, SW MO St Univ 1973; (MS) Scndry Ed, Drury Coll 1980; Coaching Cert TAC Level I, II; FAA Pilot Trng Licensed 1985; *cr:* Sci Teacher/Coach Lebanon HS 1974-79; Phys Ed Teacher/Coach Willow Springs HS 1980-81; Sci Teacher/Coach Rolla HS 1982-; *ai:* FCA Spon; Boys & Girls Cross Cntry, Track & Field Coach; 9th-12th Grade Wrestling, 7th-8th Grade Bsktbl, 7th-8th Grade Ftbl Coach; MO St Teachers Assn 1974-; Articles Published; *home:* 606 Fox Creek Rolla MO 65401

KNAPP, GLORIA MAURICE (BUCHFINK), Health/Ch Dev Teacher; *b:* Beulah, ND; *m:* Steven Ward; *c:* Jennifer, Joseph; *ed:* (BS) Health/Phys Ed, 1971, (MA) Ed, 1975 OR St Univ; *cr:* Health/Phys Ed Teacher 1972-75, Phys Ed/Health Teacher/Dept Head 1975-76, Health Dept Head Teacher 1976-80, Health/Ch Dev Teacher 1981- Lebanon Union HS; *ai:* Co-Facilitator Teen Parent Group; Stu Assistant Team; Alcohol & Drug Advisory, Behavior Management Steering, Staff Dev Comm; 20-20 Teacher Management Team; NEA, OR Ed Assn, Lebanon Ed Assn; Finalist Teacher of Yr 1987-89, 1980-81; *office:* Lebanon Union HS 1700 S 5th Lebanon OR 97355

KNAPP, HELEN M., Reading Specialist; *b:* Flushing, NY; *m:* John F.; *c:* Jane Scott, Andrea, John, James; *ed:* (BA) His/Poly Sci, Adelphi Univ 1951; Diploma of Teaching Rdng, Sturt Coll 1975; (MA) Rdng, Wm Patterson Coll 1979; *cr:* Elem Teacher Gardiners Ave Sch 1951-55; HS Rdng Specialist Port AdelaiDe HS 1974-75; Rdng Specialist/Learning Disability Teacher 1984-86, Rdng Specialist 1986- Eisenhower Mid Sch; *ai:* Intnl Rdng Assn 1975-; NJ Ed Assn 1975-; NEA 1975-; Bergen Cty Ed Assn 1975-.

KNAPP, JOHN DAWAIN, Math & Social Science Teacher; *b:* Rapid City, SD; *m:* Kristin Kay; *c:* Christopher, Nicholas; *ed:* (BA) His, Black Hills St Univ 1979; *cr:* Teacher South Jr HS 1979-80, Hill City Mid Sch 1980-; *ai:* Jr HS Ftbl, Bsktbl, Track; HS Letter Club & Fellowship of Chrstn Athletes Adv; Jr HS Althletic Dir; Hill City Teacher Organization Pres 1988-; Hill City Lions Club (Pres 1987-88) 1983-88 Lion of Yr 1987; Cmmty Luth Church Cncl Pres 1987-89; *office:* Hill City Sch Dist 51-2 Box 659 Hill City SD 57745

KNAPP, JOHN P., 4th Grade Teacher; *b:* Rockville Centre, NY; *m:* Marie Raso; *c:* John M.; *ed:* (BA) Elem Ed, 1973, (MALS) 1978 SUNY Stony Brook; Admin Internship, C W Post NY; *cr:* Teacher Chippewa Sch 1975-; *ai:* Bsktbl Team; Safety Patrol; *office:* Chippewa Elem Sch 1 David Mello Dr Holtsville NY 11742

KNAPP, LINDA SINGLEY, English/Spanish Teacher; *b:* Delhi, LA; *m:* James Edward; *ed:* (BA) Eng, 1969, (MA) Eng, 1979 NE LA Univ; *cr:* Eng Teacher Fair Park HS 1969-75; Eng Grad Asst NE LA Univ 1975-76; Eng Teacher Fair Park HS 1976-77; Eng/ Span Teacher Riverfield Acad 1977-79, Mangham HS 1979-; *ai:* Sr Spon; ATPEL; Fellowship Grad Assistantship NLU 1975-76; Mangham HS Teacher of Yr 1988; *office:* Mangham HS P O Box 348 Mangham LA 71259

KNAPP, PATRICIA ANNE, Activities Dir/Bus Teacher; *b:* Big Rapids, MI; *ed:* (BS) Bus Ed, Ferris St Univ 1969; Scndry Admin Wayne St; Rdng; *cr:* Bus Teacher 1970-; Stu Act Dir 1989- Port Huron Northern HS; *ai:* Class of 1989 Adv; Stu Act Dir; Bus Prof Amer Adv; Curr Comm Voc Ed/Bus Math; Port Huron Ed Assn Treas 1970-74; Bldg Procedures Cncl Secy 1977-; MI Bus Ed Assn; Leag Women Voters Treas 1982; Delta Kappa Gamma 1981-82; Co-Author OFC Voc Pgm 1977; *office:* Port Huron Northern Sch 1799 Kraft Rd Port Huron MI 48060

KNAPP, RICHARD LAURENCE, 2nd Grade Teacher; *b:* Bloomington, IL; *m:* Leigh Ann Roznowski; *c:* Matthew, Gretchen, Lindsey; *ed:* (BS) Elem Ed, IL St Univ 1974; (MS) Elem Ed, N IL Univ 1979; *cr:* 2nd/3rd Grade Teacher 1974-, Admin Asst 1989- Algonquin Road Sch; *ai:* Admin Asst; Recycling Chm; *home:* 74 Mc Henry Ave Crystal Lake IL 60014

KNAPPER, PATRICIA TARRANT, Teacher; *b:* Fairfield, AL; *c:* Veronica N.; *ed:* (BA) Eng, AL A&M Univ 1971; (MS) Ed, Beaver Coll 1977; Univ of PA, Temple Univ, Marywood Coll, Coll of The Performing Arts; *cr:* Teacher Get Set Day Care 1971-72, Austin Meehan Mid Sch 1972-; *ai:* Graduation Comm Secy; Chm Awds Comm for Teachers; Natl Jr Honor Society, Drama Club, Annual Holiday Show Spon; Delta Sigma Theta; Sydenham Block Organization Secy; Philadelphia Bd of Ed Teacher of Excl 1987-88; Celebration of Excl Awd; *office:* Austin Meehan Mid Sch 3001 Ryan Ave Philadelphia PA 19152

KNAUS, BETTY KOSE, Third Grade Teacher; *b:* Chicago, IL; *m:* Bobby Lee; *c:* Jeffrey M., Mark A.; *ed:* (BA) Elem, 1967, (MS) Elem 1970 Ball St Univ; *cr:* 2nd Grade Teacher Jefferson Elem 1967-69, Chesterfield Elem 1969-74; 3rd Grade Teacher Killbuck Elem 1974-; *ai:* Enrichment Comm; AARC Rdng Cncl; Cntrl IN Wkshp Way Ed; Intnl Assn of Wkshp Way Ed; Recepient Prof Dev Grant Lilly Endowment; *home:* 2304 Meadow Way Anderson IN 46012

KNECHTEL, VICTORIA LYNN (ASHE), Chemistry/Physics Teacher; *b:* Butler, PA; *m:* Karl Anthony; *c:* Kara M.; *ed:* (BS) Scndry Ed, PA St Univ 1985; Working towards Cert in Physics; *cr:* Teacher Butler Area Sr HS 1985-; *ai:* Prom Co-Chairperson; NEA, PSEA, BEA 1986-; BSA Explorer Post Adv 1984-; *office:* Butler Area Sr HS 167 New Castle Rd Butler PA 16001

KNEPPER, KATHLEEN ALLWEIN, 8th Grade Mathematics Teacher; *b:* Lebanon, PA; *m:* Richard L.; *ed:* (BSED) Math/Ger, Shippensburg St Coll 1980; Grad Stud; *cr:* 8th Grade Math Teacher Lewistown Mid Sch 1980-83, New Cumberland Mid Sch 1983-; *ai:* Math Curr Comm; Teacher Induction & Preparation Service Mentor Prgm; PSEA, NEA 1980-; *office:* New Cumberland Mid Sch 331 8th St New Cumberland PA 17070

KNETEN, DOROTHY SMITH, K-4th Music/4th Grade Teacher; *b:* Waco, TX; *m:* Garland James; *c:* Kristin, Karen; *ed:* (BS) Music, TX Luth Coll 1962; *cr:* 1st-8th Grade Music Teacher Muskego-Norway Consolidated Schls 1963-64; 4th-6th Grade Rdng Teacher 1975-80, 4th-6th Grade Music/Math/Sci Teacher 1980-82 Bartlett Ind Sch Dist; 4th Grade Teacher 1984-88, K-4th Grade Music/4th Grade Teacher 1988- Holland Ind Sch Dist; *ai:* UIL Coach Picture Memory Team; TSTA, NEA; Delta Kappa Gamma Music Chm 1986-; Church Choir 1962-; Luth Church Women Pres 1988-89.

KNETZER, KATHLEEN HOPPER, Mathematics Teacher; *b:* Litchfield, IL; *m:* James W.; *c:* Kristofer, Kara; *ed:* (BA) Math, Blackburn Coll 1972; (MS) Educl Admin, St IL Univ Edwardsville 1977; *cr:* Math Teacher Carlinville HS 1972-74; 6th Grade Teacher Carlinville West Sch 1974-77; Elem Curr Dir Carlinville Sch Dist 1977-81; Math Teacher Carlinville HS 1981-; *ai:* Scholastic Team Coach; Jr Class Spon; Carlinville Ed Assn Secy 1985-87; *office:* Carlinville HS 829 W Main St Carlinville IL 62626

KNICKEL, KAREN LENORA, Fourth Grade Teacher; *b:* Celina, OH; *m:* Deverre B.; *c:* Ben C.; *ed:* (BA) Elem Ed, 1964, (MA) Ed/Elem Guidance, 1969 OH St Univ; Grad Courses Elem Ed; Jr Great Books Leadership Trng; *cr:* 4th/5th Grade Teacher Main St Elem 1964-67; 4th Grade Teacher Wilson Hill Elem 1967-72, Ridgewood Elem 1974-; *ai:* K-12th Math Curr Comm; Intervention Assistance Team; OH Ed Assn, NEA 1964-; United Way Rep; Develop Math Minimum Competency Objectives & Tests; *office:* Ridgewood Elem Sch 4237 Dublin Rd Hilliard OH 43026

KNIES, WILLIAM STANTON, Principal/Teacher; *b:* Greeley, CO; *m:* Wilma J.; *c:* David, Richard, Kara; *ed:* (BS) Bus Ed, Univ of CO 1955; (MA) Ed, Univ of N CO 1965; *office:* Prospect Valley Elem Sch 33318 Hwy 52 Keenesburg CO 80643

KNIFONG, DYLE DEAN, Counselor/Athletic Dir; *b:* Kirksville, MO; *m:* Debbie Ann De Vore; *c:* Brian D., Brad A., Aaron M.; *ed:* (BSE) Health/Phys Ed, 1971, (MA) Guidance/Counseling, 1980 NMSU; *cr:* Phys Ed Coach Bucklin R-2 Sch 1974-77; AD/Phys Ed Coach Wellsville-Middletown R-1 Sch 1975-77; Cnslr/AD/Coach Linn Cty R-1 Sch 1977-; *ai:* HS Boys Track, 7th/8th Grade Boys Track, 7th-9th Grade Girls Bsktbl Coach; Athletic Dir; MO St Teachers Assn, N Cntrl Cnslr Group 1989-; *office:* Linn Cty R-1 Sch Rt KK Box 130 Purdin MO 64674

KNIGHT, CAROL BUCY, Teacher/Principal; *b:* Paragould, AR; *m:* Robert Darrell; *c:* Robert A., Jonathan D.; *ed:* (BS) Voc Home Ec, 1974, (MED) Elem, 1977 Harding Coll; *cr:* 1st Grade Teacher Memphis City Schls 1974-75; 1st Grade Teacher 1975-79, 1984-89, Teacher/Prin 1989 Harding Acad; *office:* Harding Acad Wooddale 1100 Cherry Rd Memphis TN 38117

KNIGHT, DIANA SMITH, 4th Grade Teacher; *b:* Mc Keesport, PA; *c:* Briana; *ed:* (BS) Elem Ed, CA St Univ 1972; *cr:* Jr 1st Grade Teacher Whiteley Elem Sch 1972-75, S Ward Sch 1975-76; Jr 1st Grade Teacher 1976-79, 4th Grade Teacher 1979- E Franklin Elem; *ai:* CGSD Employees Wellness Prgm Coord; 20th Century Club.

KNIGHT, DIANE DYER, Spanish Teacher; *b:* Lakeville, KY; *m:* Michael; *c:* Jessica; *ed:* (BA) Span, Morehead St Univ 1975; (MS) Scndry Ed, IN Univ 1987; *cr:* Eng Teacher Briam Inst 1975-76; Span Teacher Green HS 1976-83, Stonybrook Jr HS 1985-86, Scecina Memorial HS 1988-; *ai:* Span Club Co-Spon; Kappa Delta Pi 1986-; ACTFL 1985-; *office:* Scecina Memorial HS 5000 Nowland Ave Indianapolis IN 46201

KNIGHT, JIMMY, 11th Grade Amer His Teacher; *b:* Tuskegee, AL; *m:* Linda Hadrie; *c:* Tamika, Christopher; *ed:* (BS) Scndry Ed, Auburn Univ 1973; SE Regional Mid E Islamic Stud Seminar, Emory Univ 1982; Auburn Univ Ec Inst; AP Amer His Seminar, Univ of AL; *cr:* Amer His Teacher Buckhorn HS 1973-; *ai:* Sigma Delta Omega Spon; Asst Ftbl Coach; Sr Spon Buckhorn HS; Madison Cty Ed Assn (Building Rep, Bd of Dir) 1973-; AL Ed Assn, Amer Ed Assn 1973-; NAACP 1985-88; AL Cncl of Soc Stud 1987-; S Historical Assn 1990; Teacher of Yr 1988, 1985, 1980, 1984; Madison Cty His Textbook Comm Chm 1976, Co-Chm 1986; Madison Cty Ed Assn Building Rep & Bd of Dir.

KNIGHT, JOSEPHINE MORRISON, French Teacher; *b:* Glasgow, Scotland; *c:* Anne M. Hepp. David J. Mosley, Carol E. Taussig; *ed:* (BA) Fr, Univ of CO 1969; Working Towards Masters Fr; *cr:* Fr Teacher Broomfield HS 1969; *ai:* Foreign Lang Dept Head; Fr Club Spon; Ed Assn Building Rep; CO Mountain Club 1971; *office:* Broomfield Hs 1000 Daphne St Broomfield CO 80020

KNIGHT, KATHY HUMPHREY, 4th Grade Teacher; *b:* Meadville, MS; *m:* James Irby Sr.; *c:* Jennifer, James, Amanda, Benjamin; *ed:* (BS) Elem Ed, MS St Univ 1973; *cr:* 7th-8th Grade Eng Teacher Franklin Jr HS 1973; 1st Grade Teacher 1974-75, 2nd Grade Teacher 1974-75, Franklin Elem Sch; 1st Grade Teacher 1975-76, 4th Grade Teacher 1976-77 Denhamtown Elem; 4th Grade Teacher Pleasant Hill Elem 1977-; *ai:* Parent Volunteer Comm Chm; LAE, NEA; Teacher Of Yr Pleasant Hill Sch 1986, 1988; *office:* Pleasant Hill Elem Sch 725 Avenue C Bogalusa LA 70427

KNIGHT, MARY ANN (PHILLIPS), Kindergarten/Elem Principal; *b:* Caddo, OK; *m:* Larry J.; *c:* Clint, Braley; *ed:* (BS) Bus Ed, 1974, (MS) Elem Ed, 1977 SOSU; Elem Prin Cert; *cr:* Kndgtn 1975-, Elem Prin 1982- Bennington Public Sch; *ai:* 4-H Leader; COSA; *office:* Bennington Public Sch Box 10 Bennington OK 74723

KNIGHT, MICHAEL W., Fourth Grade Teacher; *b:* Evansville, IN; *m:* Kathryn Ellen Overdorf; *c:* Ann E., Whitney J.; *ed:* (BA) Elem Ed, 1970, (MA) Elem Ed, 1973 Univ of Evansville; *cr:* 4th/6th Grade Teacher Lynnville Elem 1970-; *ai:* Credit Union Building Rep; Faculty Advisory Comm; ISTA, NEA 1970-; WCTA 1970-, Building Rep; Cancer Society Pres 1985; Kiwanis Admin Bd 1985; PTO Treas 1983-84; IN St Comm for Dev of IN St Test.

KNIGHT, PAM, Language Arts Teacher; *b:* Sweetwater, TX; *m:* Flint Levi; *c:* Mandi L., Lauren L.; *ed:* (BSED) Phys Ed/Eng, SW TX St Univ 1981; *cr:* 8th Grade Lang Art Teacher/Coach/9th Grade Communication Skills Teacher Heizer Jr HS 1981-; *ai:* Girls Bsktbl Coach; Stu Cncl Spon; Hobbs Assn of Classroom Teachers; *office:* Heizer Jr HS 101 E Stanolind Rd Hobbs NM 88240

KNIGHT, ROY THOMAS, ROTC Instructor; *b:* Moss Point, MS; *m:* Juanita Fay Wilson; *c:* Allen, Lisa Gray, Rebecca Ortgies, Kathy, Scott Williams; *ed:* US Army Retired; *cr:* Instr 1965-68, 1971-72, Recruiter 1972-84 US Army; *ai:* ROTC Drill Team Spon & Coach; Natl Rifle Assn Mem 1977-; Houston Teachers Fed Mem 1986-; TX Hunters Safety Instr 1985-, Top Dist Instr 1987; Banana Bend Civic Club Mem 1989-; *office:* Barbara Jordan HS for Careers 5800 Eastex Frwy Houston TX 77026

KNIGHT, SHOWALTER ALTON, Classics Teacher; *b:* Bogalusa, LA; *ed:* (BA) Classics/Fr, 1970, (MA) Classics, 1977 Tulane Univ; *cr:* Cnslr New Orleans Skills Trng Center 1971-75; Teacher Ursuline Acad 1978-79, Jesuit HS 1979-; *ai:* Jr Classical League; Classical Assn of the Midwest & South, NCTE; Natl Endowment for Hum Fellowship 1983, Dir of Directed Grant 1985; *office:* Jesuit HS 4133 Banks St New Orleans LA 70119

KNIGHT, TERRY LYNN, Art Teacher; *b:* Macon, GA; *m:* Margaret W.; *c:* Justin T.; *ed:* (BS) Art, Berry Coll 1976; *cr:* Art Instr Gordon Cntrl Complex 1985-; *ai:* Art Club Spon; Tech Adv all Acts; Art Instr Continuing Ed Dalton Coll; Elected Positive Personnel 1989; *office:* Gordon Cntrl HS 335 Warrior Path Calhoun GA 30701

KNITTEL, MARETTA WHEELER, Language Arts Teacher; *b:* Knoxville, TN; *m:* Thomas Sr.; *c:* Paul N., Kathleen G., Elizabeth R.; *ed:* (BA) Eng/Psych, Univ of TN 1965; (MALS) Ed, Hollins 1973; Governors Acad of Writing Univ of TN 1986; *cr:* Teacher Carter HS 1965-69, E Vinton 1969-76, Sullivan Cntrl 1985-86, Cosby 1986-; *ai:* 8th Grade Spon; VA PTA Life Membership; NEA Life Membership 1965-; TN Ed Assn Local VP; VA Ed Assn Local VP; Clear Sp Math Church (Chairperson Worship Service, Pianist) 1985-; Vinton PTA 1965-, Teacher of Yr 1974; *office:* Cosby Sch Rt 1 Cosby TN 37722

KNOBLAUCH, SUSAN EVANS, Speech Teacher; *b:* St Louis, MO; *m:* Herb T.; *c:* Evan; *ed:* (BA) Speech Comm, IL St Univ 1987; Masters Work in Speech Comm; *cr:* Scndry Speech/Drama Teacher Morton HS 1987-; *ai:* Cheerleading, Speech Team, Drama Coach; MEA, NEA, IEA, ISCCA 1987-; *office:* Morton HS 350 E Illinois Ave Morton IL 61550

KNOEPFEL, SELMA ESNEAULT, 7th Grade Life Science Teacher; *b:* Lutcher, LA; *m:* Gerald; *ed:* (BS) Chem/Bio/Ed/Soc Stud, Univ oF SW LA 1951; (MEPD) Ed, Univ of WI-Stevens Point 1981; Ed, Univ WI Stevens Point; *cr:* Chem/Bio/Soc Stud Teacher Lutcher HS 1951-57; Chem/Bio Teacher Dept Defense 1957-65; Life Sci Teacher Waupaca Mid Sch 1965-; *ai:* Waupaca Teachers Assn Pres 1980-81; WI Ed Assn; NEA; Fine Arts Festival Historian 1965-; Amer Assn Univ Women; Grant Environmental Field Stud; *office:* Waupaca Mid Sch 407 School St Waupaca WI 54981

KNOEPKE, ROBIN MC COMES, English Teacher; *b:* Denver, CO; *m:* Jeffrey; *c:* Christopher, Sam; *ed:* (BA) Eng, 1973, (MA) Teaching, 1980 The CO Coll; *cr:* Eng/Drama Teacher North Jr HS 1973-76; Eng Teacher Doherty HS 1976-; *ai:* Forensics Coach; Extra-curricular Drama Dir; Phi Delta Kappa 1987-; Amer Assn of Univ Women 1986; Honorable Mention CO Teacher of Yr 1985; *office:* Thomas B Doherty H S 4515 Barnes Rd Colorado Springs CO 80917

KNOLL, MALVA ANN, Chemistry Teacher; *b:* Walsenburg, CO; *m:* Michael G.; *c:* Jessica, Gary; *ed:* (BS) Bio/Chem, Univ SC 1974; (MA) Scndry & Adult Teacher Ed/Sci, Univ NM 1982; *cr:* Student Teacher Berkeley HS 1974-75; Scndry Sci Teacher Albuquerque Public Schls 1975-; *ai:* Spon Drill Team & Chrldrs 1975-77; Spon Contemporary Issues in Sci Forum 1982-83; Spon Expanding Your Horizons/Network of Women in Sci & Engineering 1983-; Spon Northwest Regional & NM St Sci Fairs 1983-; Spon Amer Chemical Soc Chem Olympiad 1986-; Spon Intnl Sci/Engineering Fair 1987-88 & Teacher Awd 1986; Spon Space 89 Conf BDM Corp 1988-; NM Women in Engineering Prgm 1988-89; Choate Young Sci Scholars Prgm 1989-; NSTA; NM Sci Teachers Assn; Albuquerque Sci Teachers Assn (VP 1985-86 Pres 1986-87); NM Acad Sci Amer Assn for Advancement of Sci Secy 1988-; Spec Awds Judge NW Reg Sci Fair 1972; Albuquerque Public Schls Dist Inservice Presentation 1985; ASTAR Contributor Editorials & Essays; Teacher Awd; Contributor to Sci Fair Handbook Scndry Schls, Textbook Adoption Comm 1987 & Instr Serv & Support Presenter Sci Fair 1989; Albuquerque Sci Teachers Review Conbributor Editorials & Essays 1985-87; NM St Textbook Adoption Comm 1986; *home:* 13613 Rebonito Ct NE Albuquerque NM 87111

KNOOP, FAYE BREWER, Third Grade Teacher; *b:* Louisville, KY; *m:* Walter K.; *c:* Kristina, Marie; *ed:* (BA) Elem Ed, 1962, (MS) Elem Ed, 1965 IN Univ; *cr:* 2nd Grade Teacher Eastlawn Greatr Clark Schls 1962-75; 2nd-3rd Grade Teacher Northaven Greater Clark Schls 1975-; *ai:* Mentor Comm for Greater Clark Schls; Grade Level Chairperson of Building; Rdng Comm on Selecting Textbooks Chairperson; ISTA, IRA Building Rep 1989-; Mem of Mentors in Greater Clark Pilot Group First 1987-89; Wall Street Meth Church Children & Youth Groups, Missionary Circle 1981-; *home:* 3310 Royal Oaks Jeffersonville IN 47130

KNOPF, DONALD HENRY, Third Grade Teacher; *b:* Rogers City, MI; *m:* Linda Anne Rahdert; *c:* Timothy, Alison; *ed:* (AA) Pre Theology, Concordia Jr Coll 1955-57; (BA) Foreign Lang, Concordia Sr Coll 1957-59; (BS) Elem Ed, Concordia Teachers Coll 1959-62; (MS) Elem Ed, St Francis Coll 1967-69; *cr:* 4th Grade Teacher Evergreen Luth Sch 1959-60; Prin Teacher Emmanuel Luth Sch 1960-69; 4th Grade Teacher Hoagland Sch 1969-; *ai:* Natl Geographic Society Mem 1989; Elem Geography Network of IN 1989; Allen Cty Historical Society Ed Chm 1974-79; Historic Ft Wayne INcorporated (Interpretor 1976-) Bear the Bell 1988; IN Jr Historical Society Mem 1970-; Published Recipe Cookbooks; *home:* 5234 W Arlington Pk Blvd Fort Wayne IN 46835

KNOTT, MARK A., Sch Counselor/Business Teacher; *b:* Lima, OH; *m:* Mary Jo Beining; *ed:* (BS) Comp Bus Ed, Defiance Coll 1979; (MS) Sch Counseling, Univ of Dayton 1988; *cr:* Bus Teacher 1979-, Guidance Cnslr 1987- Ottoville Local HS; *ai:* Stu Cncl Adv; Var Bsbl, Var Bsktbl, Frosh Bsktbl, Reserve Bsktbl Coach; NEA, OH Ed Assn 1979-; OLEA (Pres Elect 1990) 1979-; *office:* Ottoville Local HS Box 248 Ottoville OH 45876

KNOTTS, EDITH PRIESTLEY, Third Grade Teacher; *b:* Flushing, NY; *m:* Kenneth D.; *c:* Keith D., Karen Knotts Swartz, Jill Knotts Walters, Kathryn Knotts Pepper; *ed:* (BS) Home Ec, 1956, (MS) Ed, 1972 Univ of DE; Grad Stud; *cr:* 4th Grade Teacher Leasure Lower Sch 1969-76; 5th Grade Teacher 1976-85, 3rd Grade Teacher 1985- Smyrna Elem Sch; *ai:* Delta Kappa Gamma Corresponding Secy 1986-; Smyrna Ed Assn 1976-; NEA, DE Ed Assn 1969-; Asbury United Meth Church (VP 1990, United Meth Women Pres 1976, Lay Leader 1987-); Article Published; *office:* Smyrna Elem Sch School Ln Smyrna DE 19971

KNOTTS, LINDA MARIE (KING), Kindergarten Teacher; *b:* Grafton, WV; *m:* Edward F.; *c:* Jonas, Brianna; *ed:* (BA) Elem Ed, Fairmont St 1974; (MS) Elem Ed, WV Univ Morgantown 1979; Teaching Through Learning Channels Trng; *cr:* Kndgtn Teacher Newburg Elem 1974-; *ai:* WVEA, NEA 1974-; WV Rdng Cncl, Preston Cty Rdng Cncl 1986-; PTO Pres 1988-; Fellowsville Lib Comm 1990; Mini-Grant Awd; *office:* Newburg Elem Sch PO Box 247 Newburg WV 26410

KNOWLES, BEATRICE MILLIKEN, Fourth Grade Teacher; *b:* Brockton, MA; *m:* Beryl B. Jr.; *c:* David, Jon; *ed:* (BS) Ed, Bridgewater St Coll 1963; Grad Courses Framingham St Coll & SE MA Univ; *cr:* 5th Grade Teacher Fisher Sch 1963-66; 4th Grade Math Teacher Park Row Sch 1968-72, Robinson Sch 1972-84; 4th Grade Math/Sci/Soc Stud Teacher Robinson Sch 1984-; *ai:* Math Comm to Develop Objectives & Curr; Mansfield Educators Assn Chairperson Public Relations 1988-; MA Teachers Ed Assn (Building Rep, Mem); NEA; St Marys Bowling League 1st Place Team 1989-; MA Teachers Assn Convention Delegate 1990; MTA Leadership Conference Williamstown MA 1989; *office:* Everett W Robinson Elem Sch 250 East St Mansfield MA 02048

KNOWLES, CLIFTON D., Science Department Chair; *b:* Wallace, NC; *m:* Nancy Pendleton; *c:* Sandi, Beth, Kirk; *ed:* (BS) Sci/Phys Ed, 1958, (MA) Scndry Ed, 1960 Appalachian St Univ; CA St Coll Los Angeles, Univ of CA Los Angeles, Ca St Long Beach, Ca St Fullerton; *cr:* Teacher 1962-, Sci Dept Chm 1983- Mark Keppel HS; *office:* Mark Keppel HS 501 E Hellman Ave Alhambra CA 91801

KNOWLES, DANNY LEE, Life/Earth Science Teacher; *b:* Union, MS; *m:* Phyllis Ann King; *c:* Christopher, Lee; *ed:* (BA) Sci, Lamar Univ 1978; *cr:* Math/phys Ed Teacher Beaumont Charlton-Pollard HS 1979-81; Sci Teacher Stephen F Austin Mid/HS 1981-; *ai:* Mid Sch Ftbl & Bsktbl Coach; ATPE; *office:* Stephen F Austin Mid/HS 2441 61st St Port Arthur TX 77640

KNOWLES, LINDA K., Mathematics Teacher; *b:* Higgins, TX; *m:* Jerry D; *c:* Jeffrey, Denise, Lance; *ed:* (BS) Phys Ed, NW OK St Univ 1966; Classes & Grad Work; *cr:* Math Instr Higgins Ind Sch 1966-75, Arnett Ind Sch 1975-; *ai:* Chrldrs & Math Club Spon; EOEA (Pres 1977-78, Building Rep 1985-); Teacher of Yr 1986; *office:* Arnett Ind Sch P O Box 317 Arnett OK 73832

KNOX, BARBARA A., Mathematics Teacher; *b:* Scotland Cty, NC; *c:* Karl, Karen, Stephanie; *ed:* (BS) Math, Shaw Univ 1965; (MA) Admin/Supervision Higher Ed, Univ of DC 1983; George Washington Univ 1969-72; Georgetown Univ 1988; *cr:* Math Teacher Eastern Sr HS 1969-72, Kelly-Miller Jr HS 1972-73, Francis Jr HS 1973-; *ai:* Cmptr Club; Tutor Chapter I; Building Coord DC Teachers Convention; Sch Chapter Advisory Comm Mem; NCTM 1980-; *office:* Francis Jr HS 24th & N Street NW Washington DC 20037

KNOX, LUCINDA SUSAN, Mathematics Teacher; *b:* Rochelle, IL; *m:* John David; *c:* Robert; *ed:* (BA) Math, Monmouth Coll 1982; Math, TX A&M Univ; *cr:* 6th Grade Math Teacher Andrews Mid Sch 1983-85; Math Teacher Andrews HS 1985-86, Hillsboro HS 1986-; *ai:* Assn of Tx Prof Educators Local Treas 1988-; *office:* Hillsboro HS 210 E Walnut Hillsboro TX 76645

KNUDSEN, MARYANNE ACKLEY, Spanish Teacher; *b:* Bridgeton, NJ; *m:* Arthur E.; *c:* Melanie, Margaret; *ed:* (BA) Span, Rutgers 1971; *cr:* Teacher Bridgeton HS 1979, A P Schalick HS 1979-; *ai:* Sr Co-Adv; Exch Stu Spon & Placement Person; Liaison Comm; Jr Class Adv; Stu Cncl Teacher of Month 1990; St Teresa of Avila (Liturgical Pres 1989-, Choir Mem 1970-, Parish Cncl Mem 1989-); *office:* A P Schalick HS R D #1 Elmer-Centerton Rd Elmer NJ 08318

KNUDSON, JOHNETTE WALKER, 2nd Grade Teacher; *b:* Hico, TX; *m:* Ole Carroll; *c:* Jeffrey, Tiffany; *ed:* (BS) Elem Ed, Tarleton St Univ 1973; Methods for Effective Teaching, Tarleton St Univ; AAT Courses Career Ladder Level III; *cr:* Secy TX Dept of Agriculture 1975-83; 2nd Grade Teacher Halstead Elem 1983-86, Lampasas Ind Sch Dist 1986-; *ai:* 4-H Foods Group Project Leader; Grade Level Chm 1987-88, 1988-89; Assn TX Prof Educators (Treas 1988-89, Secy 1989-); Beta Mu Philanthropic Chairperson 1989-; Career Ladder 1988-89; *office:* Kline Whitis Elem Sch 500 S Willis Lampasas TX 76550

KNUEPPE, SHARON L., 7th/8th Grade Art Teacher; *b:* Mattoon, IL; *m:* Arthur E.; *c:* Chad; *ed:* (BS) Art Ed, Southern IL Univ 1967; (MAT) Art Ed, Webster Univ 1983; Personality Fitness Trng; Impact-Drug Prevention Trng; Lindbergh Cmmty Baseline Trng; *cr:* Art Teacher 1967-71; 1975- Lindbergh Sch Dist; *ai:* In Charge of Drug-Prevention Weekend Retreat SCAT; Sperreng Transition Comm Chm; LNEA Building Rep 1985-87; Lindbergh Cmmty Star Prgm; Cmmty Task Force; Lindbergh Leader Awd 1987; Teacher of Month; *office:* Sperreng Mid Sch 12111 Tesson Ferry Rd Saint Louis MO 63128

KNURR, ALLEN D., Chemistry/Physics Instructor; *b:* Waukesha, WI; *m:* Judith S.; *c:* Rick, Kim Heckmann, Timothy, Kurt, Christopher; *ed:* (BS) Sci, Univ of WI Whitewater 1959; (MED) Chem, Penn St 1963; Bowling Green St Univ, Univ of WI Oshkosh; *cr:* Chem Instr Antioch HS 1959-62; Chem/Physics Instr Omro HS 1963-; *ai:* NHS Adv; Phi Delta Kappa; NSF Acad Grant 1962, Summer Grant 1967, 1970; WI Society of Prof Engrs Sci Teacher of Yr 1979; *office:* Omro HS 455 Leach St Omro WI 54963

KOBA, STANLEY J., Social Studies Teacher; *b:* Middletown, CT; *m:* Linda Herbster; *c:* Stacey, Lauren, Nancy; *ed:* (BS) His, Cntrl CT St Univ 1973; (MA) Supervision/Curr, Georgian Court Coll 1984; *cr:* Soc Stud Teacher Freehold Boro HS 1973-; *ai:* Jr Class Adv; Coord Life Discussion Peer Counseling 1985-89; Article Published in Soc Stud Newsletter of NJ 1989; *office:* Freehold Boro HS Robertsville Rd Freehold NJ 07728

KOBES, BETTY J., First Grade Instructor; *b:* Eldora, IA; *m:* David A.; *c:* Jason C., Shelby D.; *ed:* (GBS) Elem Ed - Cum Laude, Upper IA Univ 1979; Grad Stud Marycrest Coll; *cr:* 3rd/4th Grade Teacher Ocheyedan Chrstn Sch 1969-71; Kndgtn Teacher 1979-89, 1st Grade Teacher 1989- Kanawha Elem; *ai:* Staff Dev; Math Articulation; Kanawha Ed Assn, NEA 1987-; Belmond Reformed Church (Sunday Sch, Vacation Bible Sch, Catechism Teacher); Chrstn Reformed Church Kanawha (Catechism, Sunday Sch, Bible Sch Teacher); Cmmty Act Prgm Cnslr 1973; Friendship House Volunteer 1965; Guiding Light Mission Volunteer; Le Mars Chrstn Reformed Church; St Johns Chrstn Reformed Church; Numerous Magazine Articles Published; *office:* Kanawha Elem Sch 423 E 5th St Kanawha IA 50447

KOBLE, CAROL F., Fifth Grade Teacher; *b:* Findlay, OH; *m:* Carroll L.; *c:* Mark A., D. Craig, Stephan W.; *ed:* (BA) Elem Ed, Goshen Coll 1972; (MA) Elem Ed, IUPU 1974; Courses in Cmptr Sci & Gifted /Talented Ed; *cr:* 4th Grade Teacher N Webster Elem 1972-73; 4th Grade Teacher 1973-78, Kndgtn Techer 1978-82, 5th Grade Teacher 1982- Syracuse Elem; *ai:* Curr Selection Comm Lang Arts; PBA Sch Comm-Accrediting Comm for St a Credidation; WCEA 1972-; First Church of God; Womens Bible Fellowship 1990; Syracuse Town Bd 1988; Liason Officer to Park Bd; *office:* Syracuse Elem Schl 201 E Brooklyn St Syracuse IN 46567

KOCH, HELMUT JOHN, Chemistry Teacher; *b:* Concord, NE; *ed:* (MA) Scndry Admin, Wayne St Coll 1977; (MNS) Chem, Univ of SD 1969; (BA) Phys Sci, Wayne St Coll 1960; Physics Optics, Univ of SD; Harvard Project Physics; Environmental Chem; Phys Sci, Drake Univ Ed; *cr:* Chem/Physics Teacher Snyder Public Schls 1960-63; Physics/Math Teacher Hartley Cmmty 1964-65; Chem/Physics Pender Public Schls 1965-67, S Sioux City Cmmty 1969-; *ai:* NE St Ed Assn Dist III (Treas, Pace Dir); NSTA; Lions Club Pres 1961-62; Veterans of Foreign Wars Commander 1987-89; Academic Yr Inst, Univ of SD Vermillion 1968-69; *home:* 324 W 19th St South Sioux City NE 68776

KOCH, JANET (GOFF), French Teacher; *b:* Indianapolis, IN; *m:* Donald L.; *c:* Kimberly A.; *ed:* (BA) Fr, 1969, (MA) Fr, 1974 Ball St Univ; *cr:* Fr Teacher Pendleton Heights HS 1969; *ai:* Fr Club; AATF 1984-90; *office:* Pendleton Heights HS RR 3 Jct 67 & 38 Pendleton IN 46064

KOCH, JUDITH MILLER, Mathematics Teacher; *b:* Downey, CA; *m:* Cyril Arnold; *c:* Jonathan; *ed:* (BA) His, 1967, (MA) Ed, 1981 Azusa Pacific Univ; Math Credential; *cr:* 6th Grade Teacher Geddes Elem 1967-68; 7th-8th Grade Teacher Landis Mid Sch 1968-69, Charles D Jones Mid Sch 1969-77; 9th-12th Grade Teacher Sierra Vista HS 1977-; *ai:* Service Club Big & Little Sisters; Supt Advisory Comm; NCTM 1989-.

KOCH, LINDA OUIMETTE, Eighth Grade Teacher; *b:* Washington, DC; *m:* Frank Henry; *c:* Frank Jr., Richard, Jacqueline; *ed:* (BA) Elem Ed, Barry Univ 1969-70, 1973-74; Univ of W Australia 1971; (MAT) Mid Grades Ed, Emory Univ 1980-81; (MA) Mid Grades Ed, Oglethorpe Univ 1985; *cr:* 7th Grade Teacher Woodward Elem 1978-81; 6th/7th Grade Teacher Sweetwater Mid Sch 1981-85; 9th-12th Grade Math Teacher Lockridge Sr HS 1986; 8th Grade Teacher Sweetwater Mid Sch 1986-; *ai:* Mathcounts & Oddysey of Mind Coach; Sch System Curr & Cnty Test Developer; Sch of Excl Comm; Mini-Worlds Fair Developer & Coord; Supporters of Gifted Sch Rep 1989-; GA Assn of Educators Vital Link Rep 1976-82; Natl Alpha Chi 1976-; Gwinnett Swim League Pres 1978-85, Service Awd 1985; PACT (Pres, Chm) 1984-86; Cty Soc Sci Fair Judge 1987-; Outstanding Contributor to Gifted Prgm Awd 1989; Teacher Advisory Cncl Mem 1987-; Peer Helper 1988; SACS Chairperson SS 1989; Teacher of Yr 1985, 1987; Mathcounts GA Coaches Awd 1990; *office:* Sweetwater Mid 3500 Cruse Rd Lawrenceville GA 30244

KOCH, SHERYL JARZE, 7th Grade English Teacher; *b:* Sioux Falls, SD; *m:* Dennis D.; *c:* Christopher; *ed:* (BA) Eng, Univ of SD 1971; *cr:* 7th-9th Grade Eng Teacher Bloomer Jr HS 1971-73; 7th Grade Eng Teacher Kirn Jr HS 1973-; *ai:* CBEA; ISEA; NEA; ICTE; Sarah Circle Salem Methodist Church 1989-; *home:* 151 Charles Park Dr Council Bluffs IA 51503

KOCHAR, KARLEN BERNET, Mathematics Teacher; *b:* Pittsburgh, PA; *m:* William Thomas; *ed:* (BS) Physics, Stetson Univ 1969; (MRE) Missions, Canadian Theological Coll 1974; *cr:* Math Teacher Shelburne Falls HS 1971-73, Oak Ridge HS 1978-; *ai:* Teacher of Yr Oak Ridge HS 1986, 1988; *office:* Oak Ridge HS 6000 Winegard Rd Orlando FL 32809

KOCHENSPARGER, KEVIN PHILIP, Mathematics Teacher/Dept Chair; *b:* Zanesville, OH; *ed:* (BS) Math Ed, Miami Univ of OH 1983; *cr:* Math Teacher Eaton HS 1983-; *ai:* Var Womens Bsktbl Coach; Eaton Classroom Teachers Assn Treas 1987-; OH Cncl Teachers of Math 1989-; *office:* Eaton HS 307 N Cherry St Eaton OH 45320

KOCHER, STEPHEN L., Arts & Crafts Instructor; *b:* Olney, IL; *m:* Ruth Robinson; *c:* Stephanie A. Kocher Dickinson, Stephen P.; *ed:* General Stud, Olney Cntrl Coll 1970; (BS) Art Ed, E IL Univ 1972; NE Univ, Kearney St Coll, Flagstaff Coll, Phoenix Univ; *cr:* Art Teacher Sidney Elem 1980-83; Arts/Crafts Teacher Kingman Jr HS 1983-86; Act Dir Fishermans Retreat 1986-88; Art/Crafts Teacher Kingman Jr HS 1988-; *office:* Kingman Jr HS 1969 Detroit Ave Kingman AZ 86401

KOCHINSKY, ROBERT JOHN, History/Civics Teacher; *b:* Spangler, PA; *ed:* (BA) His, IN Univ 1971; (MS) Penn St Univ 1976; *cr:* Teacher Cambria Heights Mid Sch 1971-; *ai:* Cambria Heights Ed Assn Pres 1984-85; PSEA, NEA Faculty Rep 1972-; Political Action Comm Ed Chm 1976-89; Carrolltown Volunteer Fire Company, Ambulance Assn 1971-73; *office:* Cambria Heights Mid Sch Beaver St Hastings PA 16646

KOCSIS, DANIEL JOHN, English Teacher; *b:* Passaic, NJ; *m:* Nancy Schmidt; *ed:* (BA) Sociology, 1969, (MAT) Scndry Ed, 1971 Seton Hall Univ; Elem Ed Certificate 1977; *cr:* 4th Grade Teacher Montclair Kimberley Acad 1974-78, Washington Cntrl Sch 1978-79; 8th Grade Eng Teacher Kearsarge Reg Mid Sch 1980-; *ai:* Bsktbl Coach; Drama Dir; Sch Newsletter; Eng Dept Head 1987-89; Article Published; *office:* Kearsarge Regional Mid Sch Main St New London NH 03257

KODISH, NANCY WHITESIDE, Health/Physical Ed Teacher; *b:* Philadelphia, PA; *m:* Raymond S.; *c:* Stephen, Scott; *ed:* (BS) Health/Phys Ed, 1975, (MED) Health/Phys Ed, 1981 West Chester Univ; NATA Certified Athletic Trainer/CPR Instr; *cr:* Athletic Trainer/Teacher Spring-Ford HS 1976-81; Health/Phys Ed Teacher Spring-Ford Mid Sch 1981-; *ai:* NEA, PA St Ed Assn, Spring-Ford Ed Assn, PATS 1975-; *home:* 19 Blossom Ln Schwenksville PA 19473

KOEBERL, MARY MARIE KRANAWETTER, First Grade Teacher; *b:* Uniontown, MD; *m:* Leonard H.; *c:* Andrew, Alaina; *ed:* (BS) Voc Home Ec, 1969, Elem Certificate, 1971 SE MO St; Grad Stud Elem Ed; *cr:* Voc Home Ec Teacher Wentzville HS 1969-70, Chaffee HS 1971; 3rd Grade Teacher 1971-87, 4th Grade Teacher 1987-89, 1st Grade Teacher 1989- Oak Ridge R-6 Elem; *ai:* Cmmty Teachers Assn, MO St Teachers Assn; *home:* Rt 1 Box 312 Jackson MO 63755

KOEHLER, JANET HURSEY, Business Education Teacher; *b:* Somerset, OH; *m:* David L.; *ed:* (BS) Bus Ed, Capital Univ 1964; (MS) Voc Ed, OH Univ 1983; Additional Courses Wright St, OH St Univ, Univ of Akron; *cr:* Bus Ed Teacher Sheridan HS 1964-67, Utica HS 1967-68, Sheridan HS 1968-; Adult Ed Teacher Sheridan HS 1977-79; *ai:* Bus Prof of America Club Adv; Delta Pi Epsilon Treas 1984-; Delta Kappa Gamma (Pres 1980, VP 1976, Exec Bd 1985-87) 1970-; OH Bus Teachers Assn Exec Bd Mem 1984-88; Office Ed Assn (St & Natl Offices, St Advisory Bds), Super Adv Awd, Scholar Merit 1986, Life Mem; OH Voc Assn Life Mem; NEA, AVA Mem; Olivet Church of the Brethren (Deacon 1989-, Bd Clerk 1990, Bd Chm 1988); Martha Jennings Scholar 1985-86; *office:* Sheridan HS 8660 Sheridan Rd N W Thornville OH 43076

KOEHLER, MICHAEL H., Math Teacher/Dept Chairperson; *b:* Brookfield, MO; *c:* Mike; *ed:* (BS) Math, 1969, (MA) Scndry Math, 1972, Curr & Instruction Math, 1987 Univ of MO Kansas City; *cr:* Teacher Southeast Jr HS 1969-70, Southwest HS 1970-82; Teacher/Dept Chm Blue Valley HS 1982-86, Blue Valley North HS 1986-; *ai:* NHS Spon; Math Team Spon; NCTM; Kansas City Area Teachers of Math HS Dir 1986-; Mathematical Assn of America; Phi Delta Kappa; NEA; Univ of MO Kansas City Sch of Ed Alumni Assn Bd of Dir Treas 1987-; Interscholastic League Athletic Dir of Yr 1979; Excl in Ed Awd Blue Valley USD #229 1986; Univ of KS HS Teacher Recognition Awd 1986 & 1989; Presidential Awd Excl in Sci & Math Teaching KS Final Three 1988; *office:* Blue Valley North H S 12200 Lamar Overland Park KS 66209

KOEHN, KAREN LEIGH, High School Counselor; *b:* Liberal, KS; *m:* Byron L.; *ed:* (BS) Elem Ed, 1980, (ME) Guidance/Counseling, 1985 NW OK St Univ; *cr:* 4th Grade Teacher Tonkawa Public Schls 1980-82; K-12th Grade Sch Cnslr Cherokee Public Schls 1982-85; 9th-12th Grade Cnslr Alva HS 1985-; *ai:* NHS & Alva HS Stu Cncl Spon; Alva Classroom Teachers Mem 1985-; OK Ed Assn Mem 1980-; NW OK St Univ Alumni Assn (Bd of Dir 1980-, Pres 1983-85); NEA; OK Assn for Counseling & Dev; Amer Assn for Counseling & Dev; Alva Public Schls (Staff Dev Chairperson 1987-88, Comm Mem 1986-87); NW OK Area Health Ed Center Bd of Dir; Alumnae Chapter VP 1990-; NW Family Services (Bd Dir 1986-, Pres Elect 1987-88, Pres 1989-91); Wesley Fnd/United Meth Coll Youth Organization Bd Dir 1984-; Special Recognition Outstanding Women of America 1984-85; Teacher of Month Alva HS 1989; Certificate of Appreciation USAF, Veterans of Foreign Wars, Ladies Auxiliary; *office:* Alva HS 14th & Barnes Alva OK 73717

KOEHN, KATHY B., 7th Grade English Teacher; *b:* San Angelo, TX; *m:* J. D.; *c:* Courtney; *ed:* (BA) Eng, Angelo St Univ 1976; Advanced Trng 1985; *cr:* Teacher Lee Jr HS 1978-; *ai:* Honors Eng Teacher; Stu Cncl Spon; Dist Supt Advisory Comm; Support Group Leader; TX St Teachers Assn Mem 1978-87; TX Classroom Teacher Assn Mem 1988-; Beta Sigma Phi Corresponding Secy 1985-86; Eng Honor Society 1972-76; Teacher of Yr Contest Campus Rep; Dist Teacher Comms Team; *home:* 407 S Tyler San Angelo TX 76901

KOEHN, RONALD H., HS Social Studies Teacher; *b:* Joliet, IL; *m:* Constance Hardman; *ed:* (BSED) His, 1973, (MS) His, 1982 IL St Univ; Grad Stud W IL Univ; *cr:* Teachers Aide Peotone HS 1973-74; Soc Stud Teacher Fulton HS 1974-; *ai:* Fulton HS Scholastic Bowl Team Faculty Spon; Fulton HS Closeup Prgm Teacher-Coord; Prins Cabinet Mem; NCSS, IL Cncl for Soc Stud, NEA, IL Ed Assn, River Bend Ed Assn; Fulton Presbyn Church (Ruling Elder 1982-84, 1987-, Clerk of Session 1989-); Schmaling Memorial Lib Bd of Fulton Trustee 1990; *office:* Fulton HS 1207 12th St Fulton IL 61252

KOELLING, SHIRLEY (JOHNSON), Mathematics Dept Chair; *b:* Sycamore, IL; *m:* Vern; *c:* Kristin, Erik; *ed:* (BA) Math, Augustana Coll 1971; (MA) Math Ed, De Paul Univ 1990; *cr:* Math Teacher Fairmont Sch 1971-72, Channahon Elem 1972-75; Math Teacher/Dept Chairperson Grant Park HS 1975-; *ai:* Math Team & ICTM St Math Contest Coach 1981-82; NCTM, IL Cncl of Teachers of Math, Math Assn of America; NEA, IEA LocaL Treas 1978-80; Lioness Club (Bd of Dirs 1982-83) 1980-; Altar Guild, Church Choir; GSA Leader 1987-88; *office:* Grant Park HS 421 W Hambleton St Grant Park IL 60940

KOENIGSBERGER, THOMAS G., Science Teacher Dept Chair; *b:* Chicago, IL; *m:* Lynne Koetz; *c:* Karl, Kurt; *ed:* (BS) Zoology, 1969, (MS) Bio, 1976 N IL Univ; *cr:* Sci Teacher Roosevelt Jr HS 1969-72; Sci Teacher 1973-86, Sci Dept Chm 1987- Jefferson HS; *ai:* Jr Engineering Technology Society & Intnl Chem Olympiad Coach; Phi Sigma Society 1970-; Amer Chemical Society 1986-; Audubon Society Ed Chm; Forward Rockford Comm Co-Chm 1972; Stephen Minister 1980-; Rockford Public Schls HS Teacher of Yr 1985-86, IL St Finalist 1986; IL Distinguished Educator Awd 1988; *office:* Jefferson HS 4145 Samuelson Rd Rockford IL 61109

KOEPPL, GRETCHEN LOUISA SCHERZER, 8th Grade Reading Teacher; *b:* Vincennes, IN; *m:* Ronald Frank; *c:* Todd C., Scott F.; *ed:* (BA) Eng/Speech/Dramatic Arts, Elmhurst Coll 1961; Courses in Rdng Specialist, Natl Coll of Ed & Univ of IL Chicago; IL Writing Project, Advanced IWP, Roosevelt Univ; Directing Project, IL St Univ; *cr:* Speech/Amer Lit/Grammar/Composition Teacher St Charles HS 1961-64; Lay Reader Teacher St Charles Sch Dist #303 1964-74; Title I Rdng Teacher 1974-77, 8th Grade Rdng Teacher 1977- Haines Jr HS; *ai:* Creative Writing Magazine Spon 1986-; Theatre Vocal Music Dir 1984-89; Lang Art, Rdng Curr, Childrens Theatre Prgm Comms; Scndry Rdng League, IL Rdng Assn; IEA, NEA, SCEA 1961-; St Charles Ed Assn (Exec Comm 1989-, In Touch Negotiations Comm 1989-); NCA Theatre Company (Musical Dir 1988, Vocal Dir 1990) 1988-; Playmakers Leading Roles; Congregational United Church of St Charles Mem 1961-; Amer Assn of Univ Women (Charter Mem, Pres), Gift Honor 1988; Vocal Music Dir IL St HS Theatre Festival; Outstanding Young Women of America 1970; *office:* Haines Jr HS 9th & Oak Sts Saint Charles IL 60174

KOERNER, KAREN SUE, 6th Grade Teacher; *b:* Excelsior Springs, MO; *m:* Daniel Paul; *c:* Nicole, Jill, Kevin; *ed:* (BS) Elem Ed, 1980, (MS) Curr/Instruction, 1985 Cntrl MO St Univ; Working Towards Specialist Degree; *cr:* 6th Grade Teacher Orrick Elem 1981-; *home:* Box 207 Orrick MO 64077

KOESTER, CAROLE (MOON), English-Speech Teacher; *b:* Galena, IL; *m:* Cletus L.; *ed:* (BS) Eng, Univ of WI Platteville 1959; Grad Stud Various Insts of Learning; *cr:* Jr-Sr HS Lang Art Teacher Elizabeth Schls 1959-61; 5th Grade Teacher Galena Mid Sch 1961-85; Eng/Speech Teacher Galena HS 1985-; *ai:* Speech Team Coach; Drama Club & Class Adv; Dir of Drama Club Fall & Spring Play; IL HS Theater Festival; NEA, IL Ed Assn, Galena Ed Assn 1959-88; IL Fed of Teachers, Galena Fed of Teachers 1989-; IL Speech & Theater Assn 1987-; NCTE, Intnl Thespian Society; Galena Art Theatre 1960-; Galena Choral Society Secy 1965-; Save Turner Hall Fund Inc (Secy, VP, Fund Raising Chm) 1968-; St Michael Church Choir & Liturgy Commission; *office:* Galena HS 1206 N Franklin St Galena IL 61036

KOESTER, IRENE SCHMIDT, Band Director; *b:* Effingham, IL; *m:* Dennis J.; *c:* Bradley, Bruce, Anthony, Ben; *ed:* (BSED) Music, E IL Univ 1973; *cr:* Private Teacher 1976-84; Band Dir St Anthony HS 1984-; *ai:* Spring Musical, Choral Dir; Frosh Class Moderator; Church Organist; Natl Cath Band Dir Assn 1985-; IL Music Educators Assn 1989-; Sigma Alpha Iota 1971-; St Annes Sodality 1975-; 4-H 1984-; *office:* St Anthony HS Roadway Ave Effingham IL 62401

KOFSKY, JACQUELYN GOLDMAN, Teacher of Gifted; *b:* St Louis, MO; *m:* Alan W.; *c:* Martin, Shelley; *ed:* (BA) Elem Ed, Harris Teachers Coll 1971; (MED) Remedial Rdng, Univ of MO St Louis 1974; *cr:* Remedial Rdng Teacher 1971-73, 3rd Grade Teacher 1973-87, Teacher of Gifted 1987- Ritenour Sch Dist; *ai:* Staff Dev 1989; Sci Fair Building, Dist, Regional 1988-; AFT, MO St Teachers Assn 1971-; St Louis Assn of Gifted Educators (Corresponding Secy 1989) 1988-; Jewish Cmmty Center Assn (Chairperson Childrens Comm 1986-89, Teen Comm Mem 1989); *office:* Ritenour Sch Dist 1836 Dyer Ave Overland MO 63114

KOGER, JANET M. (FRAZIER), First Grade Teacher; *b:* New Castle, IN; *m:* Lyle R.; *c:* Leesa Koger Meyers, Kent A.; *ed:* (BS) Elem Ed, 1955, (MA) Elem Ed, 1961 Ball St Univ; *cr:* 2nd Grade Teacher Parker Elem Sch 1955-56; 3rd Grade Teacher 1956-59, 1st Grade Teacher 1961-63, 1965- Greenstreet Elem Sch; *ai:* IN St Teachers Assn, NEA 1955-; ACEI Secy 1953-; New Castle Educl Assn Bd Rep; United Meth Women Assn 1960-; Bus & Prof Women Assn 1956-60; Joseph Greenstreet Awd Service & Dedication in Ed.

KOGER, JEFFREY PAUL, Fifth Grade Teacher; *b:* Muncie, IN; *m:* Karen Lynn Papenhause; *c:* Matthew; *ed:* (AS) Elem Ed, Wabash Valley Coll 1980; (BA) Elem Ed, E IL Univ 1982; *cr:* 5th Grade Teacher Divernon Jr HS 1982-85, Riverton Mid Sch 1985-; *ai:* Stu Cncl; Jr HS Sftbl; HS Bsktbl Coach; *office:* Riverton Mid Sch 1710 Lincoln Riverton IL 62561

KOGER, KAY JO, Mathematics Teacher; *b:* Richmond, IN; *m:* Stephen C.; *c:* Aaron; *ed:* (BA) Phys Ed, IN St 1977; (MST) Phys Ed, Univ of IL 1981; Professionalized Math Minor; *cr:* Phy Ed Teacher Shawano HS 1977-80; Math Teacher Northeastern Jr/Sr HS 1981-84, Richmond HS 1984-; *ai:* Gymnastics Coach; Class Spon; *office:* Richmond HS 380 Hub Etchisn Pkwy Richmond IN 47374

KOHARIK, WILOMENE MOLE, Retired Jr HS Math Teacher; *b:* Grafton, OH; *c:* John R. (dec), Penny L. Koharik Nemitz; *ed:* (BA) Ed, Kent St Univ 1972; (MS) Ed Admin, Bowling Green St Univ 1982; Cmptr Trng for Educators, Math Seminars, Cmptr Programming, Classes for Teaching Gifted & Talented; *cr:* 5th/6th Grade Teacher Wellington Township Sch 1938-40, Grafton Township Sch 1940-46, Eaton Township Sch 1948-49; 7th/8th Grade Teacher Grafton Township Sch 1949-51; 5th/6th Grade Teacher 1951-54, 7th/8th Grade Math Teacher 1955-86 Columbia Local Sch; *ai:* Textbook Comm; Cheerleading & Stu Cncl Adv; Math Competitions Chairperson; After Sch Tutoring; PTA Secy; Columbia Local Ed Assn (Pres, VP, Treas); OH Ed Assn, NEA, NE OH Teachers Assn, OH Teachers of Math Assn; Amer Bus Womens Assn Chairperson for Schlsp Awds 1984-86; Elyria Womens Club; Midview Womens Club Schlsp Comm; Kappa Delta Pi; Awd for Excl Math Teacher; Master Teacher Awd; OH St Bd of Ed Awd; *home:* 34695 Grafton E Rd Grafton OH 44044

KOHEL, RHONDA MARTHENA (GROOMS), Home Economics Teacher; *b:* Valentine, NE; *m:* Edward Arlen; *c:* Scott, Kimberly; *ed:* (BS) Scndry Ed/Home Ec/Speech/Drama, Chadron St Coll 1986; *cr:* Home Ec/Speech/Drama Teacher Harding Cty HS 1986-87; Home Ec/Speech Teacher Bennett Cty HS 1987-; *ai:* FHA Adv; Oral Interpretation & One-Act Play Coach; All-Sch Musical Dir; Amer Home Ec Assn, Amer Voc Assn 1987-; Epsilon Sigma Alpha Ed Leader 1990-91; Extension Club (Secy, Treas) 1988-1989; *home:* Box 697 Martin SD 57551

KOHL, GORDON, SR., Mathematics Department Supvr; *b:* Lebanon, PA; *m:* Gayle Lucinda Conner; *c:* Ellen L., Gordon Jr.; *ed:* (BS) Math, Millersville St Coll 1962; Math, Cath Univ of America 1966-69; (MED) Math, Millersville Univ 1974; Supvr of Math; Grad Courses Univ of PA; Cmptr Grad Courses Millersville Univ; *cr:* Teacher E Lebanon Cty HS 1962-63; Teacher 1963-73, Supvr 1973- Lebanon HS; *ai:* TELLS Asst HS Level; NCTM, PCTM 1984-; MAA, PCSM 1985-; ASCD, PSCD 1974-; Cath Univ Natl Sci Fnd Grant 1966-69; Pre-Algebra Book Review; Merrill Publishing Advisory Cncl & Co-Mem; PSEA Friend of Ed Awd; *home:* 218 Karinch St Lebanon PA 17042

KOHL, VIRGINIA NESTOR, Speech/Drama/Yearbook Teacher; *b:* Covington, KY; *m:* Harold Douglas; *c:* David E.; *ed:* (AB) Eng/Speech & Drama, Univ of KY 1964; *cr:* Eng/Speech/Drama Teacher Lloyd HS 1964-68, Ockerman Jr HS 1974-83; Boone Cty HS 1983-; *ai:* Forensic Team, Yrbk, Spotlighters, Sch Play Spon; KY HS Speech League St Bd 1989-; KY Intersholastic Speech & Drama Assn Mem 1989-; Natl Forensic League 1989-; N KY Univ Comm Bd 1988-; Daughters of Amer Revolution 1964-; Magna Carta Dames; SADD Chapter at Boone Cty HS; No 3 Forensic Team Coach in St; Boones Rep Golden Apple Awd; Lib Bd Boone Cty; *office:* Boone County HS 7056 Burlington Pike Florence KY 41042

KOHLER, DANIEL RICHARD, Chemistry/Physics Teacher; *b:* Lakeview, MI; *m:* Betsy Floro; *ed:* (BS) Bio/Phys Sci, MI St Univ 1987; *cr:* Teacher/Coach White Pigeon HS 1987-; *ai:* Jr Var Ftbl & Sci Olympiad Coach; Prof Cncl; NEA 1987-; MHSFCA Mem 1989-; Teacher of Month; 2nd Place Sci Olympiad Coach 1987-88; MI Sci Teacher of Yr Nominee 1988; *home:* 63416 W Fish Lake Sturgis MI 49091

KOHLER, JAKI, English Department Chair; *b:* Canton, IL; *m:* J. Charles; *c:* John C., Christine A.; *ed:* (BS) Eng, 1966, (MS) Eng, 1971, (EDS) Admin, 1988 E IL Univ; *cr:* Teacher Lewistown HS 1966-67, Spoon River Coll 1969-72, Canton HS 1967-; *ai:* Prin Advisory Comm; Curr Cncl; Phi Delta Kappan, IL Assn Curr Dev, Phi Kappa Phi, NEA, IEA, CEA; *office:* Canton HS 1001 N Main Canton IL 61520

KOHLHOFF, CARLENE (BURMEISTER), Kindergarten Teacher; *b:* Cedar Rapids, IA; *m:* Joel Ray; *c:* Zach; *ed:* (BA) Elem Ed, Univ of N IA 1971; Grad Stud; *cr:* 1st Grade Teacher 1971-79, Kndgtn Teacher 1979- Corning Cmmty Schls; *ai:* NEA, ISEA, CCEA 1971-; IAEYC 1989-; *office:* Corning Cmmty Sch 1012 Loomis St Corning IA 50841

KOKES, MARK D., Vocational Agriculture Teacher; *b:* Sidney, NE; *m:* Peggy Ann Saylor; *c:* Cameron D.; *ed:* (BA) Ag Ed, CO St Univ 1984; Working Towards Masters Ag Ed; *cr:* Ag Instr Hi-Plains HS 1984-86, Fort Morgan HS 1986-; Young Farmer Instr Morgan Comm Coll 1986-; *ai:* Young Farmer & FFA Adv; FFA St Executive Comm; Co Voc Teachers Assn Public Relations Chm; CO Voc Ag Teachers Assn 1989-, Outstanding Young Mem Awd 1989; Natl Voc Ag Teachers Assn; Fort Morgan HS Faculty Pres 1987-88; *office:* Fort Morgan HS 709 E Riverview Ave Fort Morgan CO 80701

KOLB, MARY L., Mathematics Dept Chairperson; *b:* Baltimore, MD; *m:* T. Ronald; *c:* Adam T., Brian J.; *ed:* (BA) Math/Ed, Mt St Agnes Coll 1970; Grad Courses Loyola Coll of MD; *cr:* Math Teacher Northern HS 1970-81; Math Dept Chairperson Our Lady of Pompei HS 1982-; *ai:* Class Adv; *office:* Our Lady of Pompei HS 201 S Conkling St Baltimore MD 21224

KOLB, PAUL STEPHEN, Social Studies Teacher; *b:* Atlantic, IA; *m:* Janice Matthiesen; *c:* Kristin, Scott; *ed:* (AA) Wentworth Military Acad 1966; (BS) Soc Sci, Dana Coll 1972; (MS) Scndry Ed Soc Sci, Univ of NE at Omaha 1978; Counseling Classes, Univ of NE; Physiological Psych/Counseling Classes, Creighton Univ; *cr:* Soc Stud Teacher Macy Public Sch 1973, Blair Cmmty Schls 1973-; *ai:* HS Stu Cncl Adv; Soc Stud Curr, Teacher/Adv, Hum Comm; NCSS; Blair Ed Assn (Pres-Elect 1983-84, Pres 1984-85); NEA, NE St Ed Assn; *office:* Blair Jr-Sr HS 440 N 10th Blair NE 68008

KOLB, SHEILA S., Physics Teacher; *b:* Athol, KS; *ed:* (BS) Chem, KS St Univ 1970; (MA) Counseling, 1975, (MAT) Chem, 1983 Cntrl MI Univ; Chem Teachers NSF Summer Project 1978; HS Chem Dreyfus Summer Inst 1982; AP Physics, TX A & M 1986; Cmptr Conference Physics Instruction 1988; *cr:* Research Chemist Dow Corning Corp 1970-71; Chem/Physics Teacher Cass City Public Schls 1971-75, Shepherd Public Schls 1976-83; Physics Teacher Plano Sr HS 1983-; *ai:* Academic Decathlon Coach; NSTA 1970-; AAPT 1983-; Phi Kappa Phi, Phi Lambda Upsilon Mem; Amer Chemical Society Midland Section Outstanding Chem Teacher 1981; Nom for Excl in HS Teaching; *office:* Plano Sr HS 2200 Independence Pkwy Plano TX 75075

KOLENDRIANOS, CAROL ATHANS, Physical Science Teacher; *b:* Sacramento, CA; *m:* Harry T.; *c:* Elizabeth, Stacy; *ed:* (AA) Bio, Amer River Coll 1969; (BS) Biological Sci, Univ of Southern CA 1971; *cr:* Earth Sci Teacher Robert E Lee Jr HS 1971-72; Phys/Earth Sci Teacher Blairs Jr HS 1972-73; Phys Sci Teacher John M Langston Jr HS 1983-; *ai:* Natl Jr Honor Society & Sci Club Spon; Photography Comm Chm; Staff Dev Comm; Sch Chm & Division Rep; Phi Delta Kappa 1988-; Amer Assn of Univ Women Pres 1981-83, Name Grant Honoree 1981; VA Assn of Sci Teachers; Academic Booster Club 1984-; PTA 1979-; Church Ladies Society Secy 1971-; Teacher of Yr 1986; Leadership Awd 1987; Career Teacher Rank Danville City Schls 1988-; *office:* John M Langston Jr HS 228 Cleveland St Danville VA 24541

KOLIS, JEANNE EILEEN, Science Dept Chairperson; *b:* Sterling, IL; *m:* Michael Walter; *c:* Stefan, Benjamin; *ed:* (BS) Bio, N IL Univ 1984; TEACH, PRIDE, IDEAS; *cr:* Sci Chairperson Tampico HS 1985-; *ai:* Jr Class Spon; Adv Earth Week Celebrations; Good Shepherd Womens Society Secy 1988-; *office:* Tampico HS 306 E Kimball St Tampico IL 61283

KOLLARS, CATHERINE ANNE, 8th Grade Teacher; *b:* Oceanside, CA; *m:* Randy H.; *ed:* (BA) US His, CA St Univ Sacramento 1980; Audited Regis Coll Masters Prgm Adult Chrstn Cmmty Dev 1988-89; *cr:* 6th Grade Teacher Presentation of the Blessed Virgin Mary 1983-84; 7th/8th Grade Teacher St Piux X Sch 1984-88, St Joseph Cathedral Sch 1988-; *ai:* Bellarmine Speech League Regional Coord; Stu Offering Support Sch Spon; NCEA 1985-; *office:* St Joseph Cathedral Sch 2303 W Main Jefferson City MO 65109

KOLLEN, VICKI L. (SIMMS), Spanish/French Teacher; *b:* South Bend, IN; *m:* Richard P.; *c:* Jonathan Shaller; *ed:* (BA) Fr, Kalamazoo Coll 1971; (MA) Fr, Simmons Coll 1975; *cr:* Fr Teacher Malden HS 1971-80; Fr/Span Teacher 1980-87, Lang Dept Coord 1987-88 Lexington Public Schls; Asst Prin Diamond Mid Sch 1988-; *ai:* Spon Sch Newspaper; Organize Foreign Exch Trips to Venezuela, Mexico, France, Canada, Washington DC; ASCD 1987-; Kappan 1989-; *office:* Diamond Mid Sch Massachusetts Ave Lexington MA 02173

KOLLER, CATHERINE A., Social Studies Dept Chair; *b:* Omaha, NE; *m:* Stephen J.; *ed:* (BA) Speech, 1968, (MA) His, 1970 Creighton Univ; *cr:* His Teacher Benson HS 1970-73, Singapore Amer Sch 1981-83, Karachi Amer Sch 1983-86; Dept Chairperson Marymount Sch of NY 1986-; *ai:* Sr Homeroom & Model United Nations Adv; Mock Trial Coach; Assn of Teachers in Ind Schls 1986-; Cncl for Soc Stud 1989-; *office:* Marymount Sch of NY 1026 5th Ave New York NY 10028

KOLLER, CATHERINE MARY, Seventh Grade Teacher; *b:* Kibbie, MI; *ed:* (BA) Sci, Coll of St Francis 1952; Franciscan Theology, Rdng Disabilities, Lib Courses; *ai:* Religious Ed Stus in Public Schls; Amer Red Cross Classroom Instr; Foreign Study in Mexico; *home:* 3108 W 24th St Chicago IL 60623

KOLLER, JOHN ALBERT, Elementary Phys Ed Teacher; *b:* Mc Keesport, PA; *m:* Rose Marie Kovacs; *c:* Marguerite A., Sara E.; *ed:* (BS) Health/Phys Ed, PA St Univ 1969; (MED) Health/Phys Ed, Univ of Pittsburgh 1976; *cr:* 1st-6th Grade Phys Ed Teacher Moss Side Sch 1970-83; K-4th Grade Phys Ed Teacher Ramsey Sch 1983; *ai:* Elem Intramurals/Phys Ed Curr Comm; Gateway Ed Comm; Consultant to Allegheny Cty Intermediate Unit for Mainstreamed Spec Ed Stu; NEA 1970-; PA St Assn for Health/Phys Ed; PA St Ed Assn 1970-; PA Army; Natl Guard Platoon Sergeant 1972-; Research Study Published Research Quarterly 1977; Nom PA Teacher of Yr 1983; Certified Trainer PA St Military Acad; *office:* Ramsey School Gateway Sch Dist 2200 Ramsey Rd Monroeville PA 15146

KOLLING, NOLA RAE, Kindergarten Teacher; *b:* Wray, CO; *m:* William Scott; *ed:* (AA) Northeastern Jr Coll 1966; (BA) Elem Ed/Arts/Sci, Univ of N CO 1968; Grad Stud; *cr:* Primary Teacher Migrant Sch 1969-70; Kndgtn Teacher Wray Elem Sch 1968-; *ai:* Accountability Comm; Wray Elem Sch Rep; NEA, CO Ed Assn; E Yuma Cty Ed Assn Secy; Bus & Prof Womens Club Young Career Woman 1970; Home Extension Club; Wray Meth Church Active Mem; *office:* Wray Elem Sch 30204 Cty Rd 35 Wray CO 80758

KOLLMAN, JAMES PETER, Chemistry/Biology Teacher; *b:* Iowa Falls, IA; *m:* Deborah Midland Judson; *c:* Liz Judson, Nate Judson; *ed:* (BA) Sci, Univ of N IA 1987; Sci Ed, Univ of IA; *cr:* Chem/Bio Teacher Denison HS 1987-; *ai:* Mock Trial Coach; Pride Club Adv; Technology Comm & Tabs Team Mem; NSTA 1985-; Amer Chemical Society 1989-; Knights of Columbus 1975-; Eisenhower Grant; Dept of Natural Resources IA Grant; *office:* Denison HS N 16th St Denison IA 51442

KOLOSZAR, JAN LEE, Gifted Ed Resource Teacher; *b:* Kokomo, IN; *m:* Michael Joseph; *c:* Grant R.; *ed:* (BS) Elem Ed, IN Univ Bloomington 1976; (MS) Elem Ed, IUPUI 1981; Endorsement Gifted Ed, Purdue Univ West Lafayette; *cr:* 3rd Grade Teacher Ervin Elem 1976-80; 3rd/5th Grade Teacher 1980-88, Gifted & Talented Research Teacher 1988- Northwestern Elem; *ai:* Geography Bee, Young Authors Comm; 1st Chrstn Church Sunday Sch Teacher 1988-; *office:* Northwestern Elem Sch 4223 W 350 N Kokomo IN 46901

KOLPAS, SIDNEY J., Mathematics Teacher; *b:* Chicago, IL; *m:* Laurie Ann Puhn; *c:* Allison, Jamie; *ed:* (BA) Math, 1969, (MS) Math, 1971 CA St Univ Northridge; (EDD) Math Curr/Instruction, Univ of S CA 1979; NASA Educators Wkshp; Woodrow Wilson Natl Fellowship Master Teacher Inst; Trng with Tandy Corporation; *cr:* Teacher Burbank Unified Sch Dist 1970-; Tutor/Consultant Contractor Many Companies 1970-; Teacher Tandy Corporation 1979-85, Coll of Canyons 1985-; *ai:* Sr Class Adv; Mentor Teacher; NCTM 1970-; CA Math Cncl Southern Section Evaluations Chm 1970-, Nom Presidential Awd 1985-89; Phi Delta Kappa 1977-; Foothill Math Cncl Pres; Marshall Mc Luhan Distinguished Teaching Awd 1985; Whos Who in the West 1982-83; Woodrow Wilson Awd 1988; NASA Honors Teachers Awd 1987; Kiwanis Teacher of Yr Burbank 1985; *home:* 12001 Salem Dr Granada Hills CA 91344

KOLSKY, HELEN PAULA, English Teacher; *b:* Boston, MA; *m:* Wesley Michel; *c:* Sara J., Michel; *ed:* (BA) Eng/Amer Lit, Brandeis Univ 1963; (MFA) Comm, New Sch for Soc Research 1983; *cr:* Art Buyer Ketchum Mac Leod & Grove; Art/Photo Rep Magnum Photos 1963-70; Teacher Washington Irving HS 1971-75, Haaren HS 1976-78; Teacher/Sr Adv Park West HS 1978-; *ai:* Gathering Intnl Families Together (VP 1982-84, Pres 1984-86); Now NARAL 1975-; Sr Coord Combined with Teaching; Instituted an Awds Night, Sr Day, Sr Trip; Expanded Prom & Financial Aid for Sr Dues; *office:* Park West HS 525 W 50th St New York NY 10019

KOLZOW, DAVID ALAN, Phys Ed/Health Teacher; *b:* Aurora, IL; *m:* Kelli Lynn Mc Cown; *ed:* (BA) Phys Ed, Aurora Univ 1987; *cr:* Phys Ed/Health/1st Aid Teacher/Head Boys Athletics Community R-VI HS 1987-; *ai:* Head Boys Bsktbl/Bsbl; Jr HS Boys Bsktbl Coach; NEA 1987-; MO Bsbl Coaches Assn 1990; *home:* Rt 4 Box 198 Mexico MO 65265

KOMANAPALLI, SAM BOB, Science Teacher; *b:* Chivatam, India; *m:* Prema Leela Vangalapudi; *c:* Lalita, Julia, Christopher, Joyce, Esther; *ed:* (BA) Bio, S CA Coll 1970; (MA) Ed, Chapman Coll 1973; *cr:* Teacher Stacey Intermediate Sch 1972; *ai:* Sci Club Adv; Teacher of Yr 1990 Westminster Sch Dist; *office:* Stacey Intermediate Sch 6311 Larchwood Dr Huntington Beach CA 92646

KOMANDOSKY, SUSAN WHITE, Journalism Teacher; *b:* Houston, TX; *m:* Edmond S.; *ed:* (BS) Journalism, SW TX St Univ 1968; (MS) Journalism, Univ of N TX 1981; *cr:* Journalism Teacher Austin HS 1970-75; Eng/Journalism Teacher Taylor HS 1975-83; Journalism Teacher Round Rock HS 1983-; *ai:* Yrbk & Newspaper Adv; Stu Cncl Spon; TX Assn of Journalism Educators Secy 1989-; Journalism Ed Assn St Dir 1986-88; Columbia Scholastic Press Advs Assn (St Dir, Treas); Amer Heart Assn Secy 1986-; Taylor Lib Bd (Secy, Pres); Friends of the Moody Museum (Pres, VP); Edith Fox King Awd Interscholastic League Press Conference 1982; Outstanding Young Women in America 1982; Nom Round Rock HS UT Exes Teacher of Yr 1990; *office:* Round Rock HS 300 Lake Creek Dr Round Rock TX 78681

KOMAREK, ANN L., Business Teacher; *b:* Phillipsburg, NJ; *ed:* (BS) Bus Ed, 1957, (MA) Bus Ed, 1962 Rider Coll; *cr:* Teacher Ramsey HS 1957-59, DE Valley Regional HS 1959-61, Bridgewater-Raritan HS 1962-; *ai:* NEA, NJ Bus Ed Assn, Bridgewater Ed Assn; *office:* Bridgewater-Raritan HS West PO Box 97 Raritan NJ 08809

KOMATZ, PENNY R., Mathematics Teacher; *b:* Milwaukee, WI; *ed:* (BS) Math/Speech Ed, Univ of WI Oshkosh 1983; (ME) Prof Dev, Cardinal Stritch 1989; *cr:* Math Teacher Sussex Hamilton HS 1983-; *ai:* Forensics Coach; Ed Schlsp Comm; WI Math Cncl 1986-; Natl Forensic League 1979-; Published Articles; *office:* Sussex Hamilton HS W220 N6151 Town Line Rd Sussex WI 53089

KOMENDA, ALISON B., Mathematics Teacher; *b:* Springfield, MA; *m:* John; *c:* Erich; *ed:* (BA) Liberal Art, Univ of VT 1967; (MA) Math, Bowdoin Coll 1971; Grad Courses at Assumption Coll & Anna Maria Coll; *cr:* Math Teacher Essex Junction HS 1967-70, Wachusett Regional HS 1971-; *ai:* Sr Class Adv Class of 1990; NHS Advisory Bd; Wachusett Regional Teachers Assn, MA Teachers Assn, NEA; Natl Sci Fnd Grant for Advanced Study; *office:* Wachusett Regional HS 1401 Main St Holden MA 01520

KONCAR, GEORGE ALAN, Mathematics Teacher; *b:* Kenton, OH; *m:* Jody Ann Kasler; *c:* Glenda A., Jessica R.; *ed:* (BA) Math Ed, Capital Univ 1972; (MS) Math, Oh Univ 1988; *cr:* 7th Grade Math Teacher Hilliard Jr HS 1972-73; 10th-12th Grade Math Teacher Maysville HS 1973-; *ai:* Co-Dir of All Sch play; Asst Marching Band & Flag Corps Dir; OH Cncl Teachers of Math 1972-; NCTM 1982-85; Kiwanis Key Club Adv 1975-85, Outstanding Service 1984; Muskingum Cty Math Course of Study Comm 1979, 1984, 1989; *home:* 112 Juanita Dr South Zanesville OH 43701

KONDRATOWICZ, NINETTE WALDO, Science/Health Teacher; *b:* Troy, NY; *m:* Michael; *ed:* (BA) Elem Ed, Anna Maria Coll 1973; (MS) Health Ed, Russell Sage Coll 1980; Grad Stud Admin; *cr:* Kndgtn Teacher Venerini Acad 1971-72; 1st Grade Teacher St Anthony Sch 1973-75; Sci Teacher Holy Cross Sch 1976-; *ai:* Organize Act Skating Parties, Holy Cross Marathon, Craft Clubs; NCEA 1976-; *office:* Holy Cross Grammar Schl 10 Rosemont St Albany NY 12203

KONEMANN, SHONDA LAYNE, English/Spanish Teacher; *b:* Ardmore, OK; *m:* Charles; *c:* Nathaniel, Nachel; *ed:* (BAED) Eng/Span/Librarian, Northeastern St Univ 1984; *cr:* Librarian 1984-88, Eng Teacher/Journalism 1986-88 Braggs HS; Eng/Span Teacher Vian HS 1988-; *ai:* Academic Team Coach; Span Club, Sr Class, Interscholastic Team Spon; NCTE, OK Ed Assn, NEA 1984-; Braggs Ed Assn Secy 1987-88; Sequoyah Cty Ed Assn (Secy, Treas) 1989-; Served Homecoming Comm for Vian During St-Wide Homecoming Yr Long Events 1990; *home:* Rt 1 Box 95-1 Braggs OK 74423

KONNIE, JAMES GERARD, Physics Instructor; *b:* Detroit, MI; *ed:* (BS) Geophysics, W MI Univ 1983; (MAT) Scndry Sci Ed, Wayne St Univ 1989; *cr:* Physics/Math Teacher Utica HS; *ai:* Sci Olympiad, Asst Wrestling, Girls Sftbl Coach; IM Bsktbl; MEA, UEA, NEA; *office:* Utica Sr HS 47255 Shelby Rd Utica MI 48087

KONYAK, DANIEL MICHAEL, Social Studies Teacher; *b:* Uniontown, PA; *ed:* (BA) Scndry Ed/Soc Stud, Glassboro St Coll 1981; *ai:* Soviet Union Tour Coord 1990; Boys & Girls Tennis Coach; NCSS; Natl Geographic Society Geographic Summer Inst 1989; *office:* West Deptford HS Old Crown Point Rd Westville NJ 08093

KOOI, WARREN JAMES, Biology/Computer Teacher; *b:* Oakland, CA; *m:* Barbara Ann Detz; *c:* Katie, Jaclyn; *ed:* (BS) Bio, E KY Univ 1970; (MA) Technology Ed, WV Univ 1979; Energy Ed, Miami Univ of OH; Sci Ed, Duquesne Univ; *cr:* Sci/Math Teacher Mid Township HS 1974-80; Bio Teacher Comm Coll of Beaver Cty 1989; Sci/Cmptrs Teacher Moon Sr HS 1980-; *ai:* Bio Club Spon; Bermuda Biological Station for Research Field Trip Spon; NABT, PA Assn Bio Teachers; Organic vs Chemical Gardening Mini-Grant; Association Works; *office:* Moon Sr HS 904 Beaver Grade Rd Coraopolis PA 15108

KOON, ANNE MITCHELL, English Teacher/Dept Chair; *b:* Lumberton, NC; *m:* Thomas Lewis; *c:* James D. Grimes, Sarah G.; *ed:* EZng, NC St Univ 1973-76; (BA) Comm Art, 1977, (MA) Eng Ed, 1986 Pembroke St Univ; *cr:* Eng Teacher Latta HS 1978-79, Flora Mc Donald Acad 1979-81, Lumberton HS 1983-84; Eng Dept Chm St Pauls HS 1984-; Composition Instr Pembroke St Univ 1986-; *ai:* Dept Chairperson; Mentor Teacher Recruiter Coord; Teacher Cadet Prgm Adv; Future Teachers of Amer Comm of Eight; Sch Improvement Act; Phi Delta Kappa 1988-; NCAE, NEA 1989-; St Pauls HS Teacher of Yr 1988-89; *home:* Rt 1 Box 65G Saint Pauls NC 28384

KOONCE, PATRICIA BAGLEY, Chapter 1 Reading Teacher; *b:* Amarillo, TX; *m:* Ronald Scott; *c:* Amy, Ashley; *ed:* (BA) Elem, Tarleton St Univ 1979; Renee Herman Reverse Rdng Failure; Dyslexia; Fnds of Rdng; *cr:* 3rd Grade Teacher Halstead Elem 1979-80; 6th Grade Teacher 1980-86, Chapter Rdng Teacher 1987- De Leon Elem; *ai:* UIL 5th Grade Spelling Coach; Assoc of TX Prof Educators Treas 1981-86; *home:* Rt 2 Box 88 De Leon TX 76444

KOONCE, VONNIE YEAGER, 8th Gr Sci/Cmptr Sci Teacher; *b:* Charlotte, NC; *m:* John Shackelford III; *c:* Matthew, Melissa; *ed:* (BA) Inter Ed, UNC-Wilmington 1973; Cmptr Sci, UNC Wilmington; NASA Langley Research Center Affiliated with OK St Univ; *cr:* 5th Grade Teacher Peabody Sch 1973-76; 4th & 5th Grade Teacher John J Blair Elem Sch 1976-84; 7th & 8th Math/Sci Teacher MCS Noble Jr HS 1984-88; 8th Grade Sci/Cmptr Sci Teacher MCS Noble Mid Sch 1988-; *ai:* Adv Young Astronaut Club & Sch Newspaper; 8th Grade Coord; Instr of Cmptr Literacy Wkshp for Teachers; NC Sci Teachers Assn 1984; NEA/NC Educl Assn 1973-89 Cty Finalist in Teacher Yr 1987 & 1989; Alpha Delta Kappa Ed Corresponding Secy 1986-; Natl Space Society 1987-; Myrtle Grove Presbyn Church Nursery Chm 1975-; Dwight Eisenhower Math/Sci Grant/Fellowship to NASA Educl Wkshp for Math & Sci Teachers; Newmast Reader for a Sci Textbook Co; Nom for Presidential Awd for Excl in Teaching Sci & Math; Compiled 3 Manuals Sci Fairs/Lab Act/Stu Thinking Skills; *office:* M C S Noble Mid Schl 6520 Market St Wilmington NC 28405

KOONS, PAULA JENYK, 6th Grade Teacher; *b:* Columbus, OH; *ed:* (BS) Ed, OH Univ 1966; *cr:* 1st/4th Grade Teacher Smith Road Sch; 5th/6th Grade Teacher Weinland Park Sch; 6th/7th Grade Teacher Linmoor Mid Sch; Teacher of Developmentally Handicapped Weinland Park Sch; 6th Grade Teacher Dominion Mid Sch; *ai:* Teach Rdng Improvement at Columbus St Comm Coll; Columbus Cncl PTA Educator of Yr 1988-89; North Area Real Estate Assn Creating a Nation of Neighbors 1989; *office:* Dominion Mid Sch 330 E Dominion Blvd Columbus OH 43214

KOONTZ, PATRICIA SHAEFFER, 8th Grade Lang Arts Teacher; *b:* St Louis, MO; *m:* Gary E.; *c:* Dana, Derek, Darren; *ed:* (BS) Eng, 1966, (MS) Elem Ed, 1972 S IL Univ; *cr:* Teacher Washington Sch 1966-; *ai:* Honor Club & Cheerleading Spon; Spelling Bee Coord; Cty Advisory Bd; Scholar Bowl & Knowledge Master Coach; IL Ed Assn, S IL Teachers of Eng, Johnston City Ed Assn, S IL Univ Alumni, NEA 1990; Church Cncl Bd of Chrstn Ed 1990; *office:* Washington Jr HS 100-200 E Adams Johnston City IL 62951

KOONTZ, RONALD DOUGLAS, History Teacher; *b:* Ft Campbell, KY; *m:* Rita Shimasaki; *ed:* (BS) Scndry Ed/His, Austin Peay St 1979; (MS) Scndry Ed, Univ of Louisville; *cr:* Calvary Officer US Army 1979-84; Teacher Hardin Cty Bd of Ed 1984-; *ai:* Ftbl, Wrestling, Weightlifting Coach; Soph Class Spon; IN Wishbone Assn 1989-; Bluegrass Military Collectors Club Treas 1983-; KY Historical Society 1985-; Custer Battlefield Historical & Museum Assn 1985-; *office:* North Hardin HS N Logdson Radcliff KY 40160

KOOS, P. KAY THOMAS, First Grade Teacher; *b:* Sidney, NE; *m:* David E.; *c:* Thomas, Todd; *ed:* (BA) Elem Ed, CO St Coll & Univ N CO 1961; *cr:* 2nd Grade Teacher Albia Cmmty Schls 1961-62; 1st Grade Teacher Bridgewater-Fontanelle 1962-63; Rdng Instr Simpson Coll 1971-75; Child Care Instr IA Western Comm Coll 1977-78; 1st Grade Remedial Rdng Teacher Harlan Cmmty Schls 1979-; *ai:* Harlan Ed Assn (Secy 1987-89, Assembly Delegate 1990); Amer Assn of Univ Women (Membership Chairperson 1988-, ISE VP 1980-82, Pres 1982-84); Federated Womens Progessio Club (Pres 1986-88, Treas 1990); *home:* 1406 Southridge Dr Harlan IA 51537

KOPCHO, CHRISTINE A., Biology Teacher/Science Chair; *b:* Pittston, PA; *m:* John J.; *c:* Jonelle; *ed:* (BS) Bio, Coll Misericordia 1970; (MS) Bio Ed, Wilkes Univ 1976; Temple Univ, Penn St Univ, Pocono Environmental Center; *cr:* Earth/Sp Teacher Pittston Area HS 1976; Bio Teacher/Sci Dept Chairperson 1980-Lake Lehman Sr HS; *ai:* NEA, PSEA, LLEA Secy 1974-75; N Bio Teachers of America; Coll Misericordia Teaching Awd 1983; Wilks Coll Univ Teaching Awd 1989.

KOPFLER, JUDITH HALL, Director/Founder; *b:* Syracuse, NY; *c:* Thomas Jr., Jane L., Katherine; *ed:* (BS) Elem Ed, SUNY Oswego 1967; (MED) Spec Ed, SE LA Univ 1979; (PHD) Psych, Columbia Pacific Univ 1985; Grad Stud; *cr:* Teacher Liverpool Mid Sch 1967-68; Teacher/Team Leader Skyline Elem 1968-71; Spec Ed Teacher K-Bar-B Residential Treatment Center 1976-79; Teacher of Severe & Profound Ed Bd SE LA Hospital 1979-81; Founder/Dir/Teacher Emerson Acad 1983-; *ai:* Admin Teacher Trng Counseling, Stu Adv, Teacher of Psych & His, Fundraising Dir, Public Relations, Elem Adv Consultant to Area Psychiatric Hospitals; ASCD, Assn for Mental Health Counselors of America, Amer Assn for Counseling & Dev, LA Assn for Counseling & Dev 1988-; Rosicrucian Order, AMORC 1986-; NY Acad of Sci 1987-; Directory of Distinguished Amer, Wrote Article for Book; Whos Who in Amer Ed; *office:* Emerson Acad 1050 Old River Rd Slidell LA 70461

KOPIL, JOAN DAMMS, First Grade Teacher; *b:* Ellenville, NY; *m:* Stephen J.; *c:* Mary E. Jordan, Melissa; *ed:* (BS) E Stroudsburg 1961; *office:* Bridgewater-Raritan Sch Dist Hamilton Sch Hamilton Rd Bridgewater NJ 08807

KOPP, CHARLES F., Civics Teacher; *b:* Buffalo, NY; *c:* Brennan, Kevin, Melissa; *ed:* (BS) Ed, St Univ of NY Coll Buffalo 1967; (MAED) Scndry Ed, W Carolina Univ 1975; Learn To Learn Wkshp; *cr:* 7th-8th Grade Soc Stud Teacher Starpoint Cntrl Sch 1967-68; 9th-12th Grade Soc Stud/US His/Geography/World His/Civics Teacher Enka HS 1968-; *ai:* His Club; NC Closeup Raleigh; Homework Hotline Buncombe Cty; NC Assn of Educators 1968-; Classroom Teacher Assn Secy 1973-74; NCSS 1990; N Buncombe Optimist Club 1979-88; Volunteer Work Asheville Buncombe Cooperative Chrstn Ministry Homeless Shelter; Participant Natl Regional Constitution Wkshps; Sch Rep Buncombe Cty Bicentennial Commission; *office:* Enka HS New Enka Lake Rd PO Box 579 Enka NC 28728

KOPP, SANDY GLAVIN, Social Studies Teacher; *b:* Atchison, KS; *c:* George, Debby, Amy, Christy; *ed:* (BA) Poly Sci, Univ of MO Kansas City 1967; Grad Stud Educl Admin; Environmental Teaching NSF Grant; *cr:* 7th/8th Grade Teacher St Peters Sch 1983-86; 7th/8th Grade Teacher/Vice Prin Visitation Sch 1986-88; Soc Stud Teacher Belton HS 1988-; *ai:* 9th Grade Vlybl Coach; Stu Cncl Asst & Spon; Sr Class Spon; Amnesty Intnl Co-Spon; PAC Comm Mem; NEA 1988-; Phi Delta Kappa, ASCD 1986-; K C Consensus; Soc Stud & Sci Teacher Teams NSF Grant; Nom for K C Star, Learning Exch Excl in Teaching 1985-86, 1988-89; *office:* Belton HS Sunrise & Colbern Belton MO 64012

KOPRA, GREGORY THOMAS, Religion Teacher/Retreat Dir; *b:* Portland, OR; *m:* Maria Therese Natta; *c:* Timothy; *ed:* (BA) Eng/Psych, Gonzaga Univ 1979; (MED) Religious Ed, Univ of Portland 1988; *cr:* Eng Teacher/Stu Ministries Coord St Mary of the Valley HS 1979-80; Eng Teacher Gonzaga Preparatory Sch 1980-81; Seminarian Society of Jesus OR Province 1981-83;Religion Teacher/Retreat Dir/Coll Cnslr Cntrl Cath HS 1983-; *ai:* Pacific NW Assn of Coll Admissions Cnslrs 1989-; *office:* Cntrl Cath HS 2401 S E Stark Portland OR 97214

KOPRAL, IRENE KUNTUPIS, 5th Grade Teacher; *b:* Steubenville, OH; *m:* James; *c:* Jay, Leanne; *ed:* (BA) Elem Ed, West Liberty St 1966; Coll of Steubenville; Univ of Steubenville; *cr:* Kndgtn Dillonvale Elem 1966-68; 7th & 8th Grade Teacher Brilliant Jr HS 1968-72; 5th Grade Teacher Brilliant Elem 1972-84; Yorkville Elem 1984-; *ai:* Young Buckeyes Midget Ftbl Adv Cheering 1987-89; *home:* 610 Buckeye St Tiltonsville OH 43963

KOPRESKI, KATHLEEN J. ROCHETTI, Mathematics Teacher; *b:* Vineland, NJ; *m:* Donald L.; *c:* Kara L., Alison P.; *ed:* (BA) Math, Douglass Coll 1972; Grad Work Curr Dev & Career Ed, Glassboro St Coll; *cr:* Pre-Sch Teacher Port Norris Summer Sch Migrant Prgm 1967-72; Scndry Math Teacher Vineland HS S 1972-; *ai:* Assn of Math Teachers of NJ Annual Math Contest, Amer HS Math Exam Contest Mgr; Vineland Math Curr Review Comm; Assn Math Teachers of NJ (Pres-Elect, Former VP, Treas) 1990; NCTM (NE Regional Prgm Comm, Chairperson 1989), 1974-; NJ Ed Assn Math Section Convention 1972-; Alpha Delta Kappa 1985-; Nominee Presidential Awd Excl Math Teaching 1983-84; NSF Grant; NJ St Math Coalition of Mathematical Sci Ed Bd 1990; Speaker & Wkshp Leader Math Numerous AMTNJ, NCTM & NJEA Conventions; *office:* Vineland HS South 2880 E Chestnut Ave Vineland NJ 08360

KORCHNAK, KAREN H., Business Teacher; *b:* New Kensington, PA; *m:* Lawrence C.; *c:* Lawrence D.; *ed:* (BS/BA) Bus Ed, 1983, (MS) Bus Ed, 1988 Robert Morris Coll; *cr:* Bus Teacher W Allegheny HS 1984-85, Robert Morris Coll 1984-85, Comm Coll Beaver Cty 1984-, Fort Cherry Jr/Sr HS 1985-; *ai:* Afro-Amer Club Co-Spon; Tri-St Bus Ed Assn 1983-; Robert Morris Coll Bus Ed Advisory Comm 1989-; *office:* Fort Cherry Jr/Sr HS RD 4 Box 145 Mc Donald PA 15057

KORDEK, CHARLOTTE CRAWFORD, Biology Teacher; *b:* Wilkes-Barre, PA; *m:* Edward Peter Jr.; *c:* Abby, Amy; *ed:* (BS) Bio/General Sci, Kings Coll 1973; (MS) Ed, Wilkes Coll 1983; Grad Cmptr Sci, Wilkes Coll; *cr:* General Sci Teacher 1973-88, Bio Teacher Wilkes Barre Area School Dist 1983-; *ai:* Sci Club Adv; PSEE, NEA 1973-; Luzerne Cty Sci Teacher 1975-; Amer Diabetes Assn Bd Mem 1989; *office:* Plains Jr HS 33 W Carey St Plains PA 18705

KORF, LONA DELL CONLEY, Science Teacher; *b:* Beaver, OK; *m:* Lawrence Dean; *c:* Lyle; *ed:* (BS) Bio, 1966, (MS) Bio, 1969 Ft Hays St Univ; Certified 7th-12th Grade Counseling; *cr:* Sci Teacher Stockton HS 1966-67, Sharon Springs HS 1967-68, Dighton HS 1968-69; Soc Worker La Cross Soc Services 1969-70; Sci Professor KS St Univ 1988-89; Sci Teacher Kinsley HS 1970-; *ai:* Class Spon; KS Assn of Teachers of Sci, KS Assn for Supervision & Curr Dev, KS Alliance of Sci Teachers 1988-; Beta Sigma Phi 1976-80; *office:* Kinsley HS 716 Colony St Kinsley KS 67547

KORN, J. DAVID, English/Latin/History Teacher; *b:* Zanesville, OH; *ed:* (BA) Philosophy, John Carroll Univ 1962; (MA) Eng, ID St Univ 1968; (EDD) Curr/Supervision, 1978, (MA) Libarianship, 1983 Univ of Denver; *cr:* Eng Teacher Elyria HS 1964-65, Zanesville HS 1965-66; Eng Instr ID St Univ 1966-68; Teacher/Admin/Librarian Thornton HS 1969-; *ai:* Knowledge Bowl Team; Advanced Placement, Gifted & Talented Prgm Coord; NEA, ASCD; NCTE Natl Affiliate Chm 1982-83; Pdk 1975, Univ of Denver Awd; CO Teacher of Yr Honorable Mention 1984; *office:* Thornton HS 9351 Washington St Thornton CO 80229

KORNEMANN, ANNE CHANDLER, Fourth Grade Teacher; *b:* Ruffin, NC; *m:* Herb; *ed:* (BA) Ed, Univ of NC 1963; *cr:* 3rd Grade Teacher VA Beach Schls 1963-64, Burlington City Schls 1964-67; 4th-6th Grade Teacher Raleigh City Schls 1968-77; 3rd-4th Grade Teacher Wake Cty Schls 1978-; *ai:* Grade Level Chm 1986-87; Staff Dev Chm; Lang Art & Faculty Rep; Act Rep 1974-76; Wake Cty Intnl Rdng Assn Chm 1989-; NEA Mem 1964-; First Presbyn Church Mem 1970-; Assn Classroom Teachers 1968-; *home:* 105 Govan Ln Cary NC 27511

KORTH, JEFFREY GILBERT, Teacher/Athletic Dir/Vice Prin; *b:* Beaver Dam, WI; *m:* Sheryl Ann Fehrman; *ed:* (BS) Elem Ed, Doctor Martin Luther Coll 1971; *cr:* Prin/Teacher/Coach Emanuel Luth 1971-16, Zion Luth 1976-86; Vice Prin/Teacher/Athletic Dir St Lucas Luth 1986-; *ai:* Boys Bsktbl & Sftbl Coach; Girls Bsktbl Coach; WI Coaches Fed; *home:* 5751 S Merrill Ave Cudahy WI 53110

KORTHALS, TAMERA RUHTER, Transitional 1st Grade Teacher; *b:* Cheyenne, WY; *m:* Thomas Eugene; *c:* William; *ed:* (BA) Elem Ed, 1973, (MA) Curr/Instructional, 1981 Univ of WY; Certified Gesell Screener; Consultant Lang Arts Leir Encyclopedia Brittanica; *cr:* 5th Grade Teacher Fincher Elem 1973-74; 4th Grade Teacher Alta Vista Elem 1974-75; 3rd Grade Teacher 1975-81, 4th Grade Teacher 1981-82, 1st Grade Teacher 1982-87, Transitional 1st Grade Teacher 1987- Bain Elem; *ai:* Staff Dev, Dist Transitional First, Centennial, Playground Improvement Comm; Dist Faculty Adv; Phi Delta Kappa, Kappa Delta Gamma; PEO Sisterhood; Standards of Excl Lang Arts Co-Author; Lecturer Dev Ed, Intnl Rdng Assn Lang Experience St Level; *home:* 3418 Central Ave Cheyenne WY 82001

KORTYKA, DENNIS L., Art Teacher; *b:* Ashatabula, OH; *m:* Donna L.; *c:* Dedra, Darrin; *ed:* (BS) Art Ed, OH Univ 1970; (MED) Studio Painting, Edinboro St Coll; *cr:* Art Teacher N Kingsville Elem 1970-71, Wallace H Braden Jr HS 1971-81, Edgewood HS 1981-; *ai:* Sr Class & Art Club Adv; Buckeye Ed Assn, OH Ed Assn, NEA 1970-; N Kingsville Fire Dept (Chief 1988-89, Lieutenant Captian/Asst Chief 1983-88, Fire Fighter) 1972; OH St Fire Chiefs Assn 1988-89; Ashtabula Cty Fire Chiefs Assn 1988-89; *office:* Edgewood Sr HS 2428 Blake Rd Ashtabula OH 44004

KORUS, PAULA SAWYER, History Teacher; *b:* Stephensville Cros, CA; *m:* Joseph C.; *ed:* (BA) Soc Stud, MT St 1986; *cr:* Teacher Crystal Lake South HS 1987-89; *ai:* Coached Girls Vlybl/Track/Field.

KORVNE, ERIK P., Academic Advisor; *b:* Buffalo, NY; *ed:* (BA) Eng, St Bonaventure Univ 1987; Coll Counseling/Stu Personnel Admin, SUNY Buffalo 1991; *cr:* Substitute Teacher Allegany Cntrl Sch 1986-87; HS Eng Teacher Bolivar Cntrl Sch 1987-89; Academic Adv SUNY Buffalo 1989-.

KORYTOSKI, WANDA JOYCE BROGDON, English/GA History Teacher; *b:* Fort Benning, GA; *M:* James P.; *c:* Jameson R., Kalie P.; *ed:* (BS) Scndry Ed, Eng, Columbus Coll 1977; (MA) Scndry Ed, Lang Arts, Troy St Univ 1987; Troy St Univ; *cr:* Eng Teacher Harris Cnty Mid Sch 1977-82, Woodbury HS 1982-84, Hogansville Elem 1984-87, Hogansville HS 1987-89, Lees Crossing Mid Sch 1989-; *ai:* Spon Eng Club;Spon Beta Club Hogansville; NCTE Page 1977-; Pilot Club 1985-87; *office:* Lees Crossing Mid Sch 80 N Kight Dr La Grange GA 30240

KOSEK, JOHN K., Art Teacher/Observatory Dir; *b:* Scranton, PA; *m:* Theresa R. Foy; *c:* Christopher; *ed:* (BA) Art Ed, Wilkes Coll 1972; (MA) Ed, PA Dept of Ed 1983; *cr:* Teacher Riverside Jr/Sr HS 1973-; *ai:* Art & Astronomy Club; Astronomical Observatory Dir; NEIU #19 In-Service Cncl; Steering Comm for Mid States Evaluation Co-Chair; PA St Ed Assn Instructinal Prof Dev Comm Chm 1975-80, PSEA Awd For Innovative Dev 1978, 1980; St Catherine of Siena Parish Confraternity of Chrstn Doctrine Teacher 1982-86; Solicited Federal Funding to Construct & Equip Astronomical Observatory 1975-78; Nom by Dist PA Teacher of Yr 1979; Taught Numerous In-Service Courses Art & Astronomy 1978-; *home:* PO Box 176 Moscow PA 18444

KOSHGARIAN, EILEEN MC CORMICK, Elementary School Principal; *b:* Providence, RI; *m:* Robert; *ed:* (BA) Psych, Roger Williams Coll 1971; (MED) Remedial Rdng, RI Coll 1974; Spec Ed, Sch Admin; *cr:* Elem Teacher Nathan Bishop Mid Sch 1971-85; Asst Elem Prin George J West 1985-87; Elem Sch Prin R F Kennedy 1987-; *ai:* Natl Assn Sch Admin 1985-; RI Assn Elem Sch Prin; Assn of Sch Asmin Recording Secy; RI Lieutenant Governors Teenage Suicide Task Force 1985-; *office:* Robert F Kennedy Sch 195 Nelson St Providence RI 02908

KOSIAK, KEVIN JON, Vocal Music Instructor; *b:* Richfield, MN; *m:* Rita K. Sheppard; *c:* Sarah; *ed:* (BM) Music Ed, Univ of ND 1984; Music Ed, Mankato St Univ; *cr:* Vocal Music Teacher Springfield Public Sch 1984-; *ai:* Madrigal & Mens Choir; Sch Musical; Amer Choral Dir Assn 1986-; Music Ed Natl Conference 1984-; Lions Club 1985-87; 1st Place Trophy Choir Six Flaggs Music Festival; 2nd Place Trophy Choir All Amer Music Festival; MN Music Educators Assn Convention Guest Performance 1990; *office:* Springfield Public Sch 12 S Burns Springfield MN 56087

KOSKI, BARBARA ANN, Teacher/Coord of Gifted; *b:* Warren, OH; *m:* Charles E.; *c:* Charles E. II; *ed:* (BS) Elem Ed/Eng, BGSU 1970; (MA) Elem Admin, Westminster Coll 1976; Various Univs; *cr:* 2nd Grade Teacher 1970-75, 6th Grade Teacher 1976-78, 4th Grade Teacher 1979-80, 4th-6th Grade Teacher/Coord 1981- Champion Local Schls; *ai:* Stu Cncl & Vindicator Spelling Bee Adv; Awards Tea & Cmptr Sci Coord; Building Rep; Supts Advisory Cncl; Prin Advisory Cncl; Apple-Users Cmptr Club; Childrens Olympics Coord & Adv; Champion Ed Assn Soc Dir; Trumbull Ed Assn Soc Dir; OH Ed Assn; NEA; NEOTA; OH Assn Gifted Children Coord, Natl Assn for Gifted Children; Kappa Delta Pi; Appella Choir; PTO Rep; Teen Inst Prevention of Alcoholism & Chemical Dependency Teacher & Adv; Industrial Inst Outstanding Cmmty Teacher Interest & Involvement; Spec Recognition Right to Read Week; Spec Recognition for Advancement of Technology Clarkson Coll; Stu Ed Assn Stu Teacher of Yr Amer Cncl Exceptional Children; *home:* 9330 Sunview NE Warren OH 44484

KOSSMANN, JOHN CHARLES, Math Teacher; *b:* Hackensack, NJ; *m:* Patti Jo Mc Curdy; *c:* Kristen, Louis; *ed:* (BA) Math Ed, 1976, (MA) Math, 1984 Trenton St Coll; *cr:* HS Geometry Teacher St Anthonys HS 1976-77; Gen Math/Alg I Teacher Trenton Jr HS #1 1977-78; 8th Grade Math/Algebra I Teacher Carl W Goetz Mid Sch 1978-; *ai:* Math Club Coach & Spon; *office:* Carl W Goetz Mid Sch Patterson Rd Jackson NJ 08527

KOSTECKA, JOE M., Mathematics Teacher; *b:* Spokane, WA; *m:* Tami Lee Arkills; *c:* Jessica, Tara; *ed:* (BA) Math/Ed, E WA Univ 1982; Cooperative Learning Classes & Wkshps; *cr:* Teacher Nooksack Valley HS 1982-84, University HS 1984-; *ai:* Asst Ftbl & Head Track Coach; *office:* University HS E 10212 9th Ave Spokane WA 99206

KOSTRABA, PATRICIA FERKO, English Teacher; *b:* Warren, OH; *m:* Andrew L.; *c:* Andrew J., Steven M.; *ed:* (BA) Eng/sociology, Kent St Univ 1971; (MA) Ed, Coll of Mount St Joseph 1988; *cr:* Eng Teacher Warren G Harding HS 1971-74, Warren Western Reserve HS 1984-85, Maplewood HS 1985-; *ai:* NEA 1971-74/1985-; OH Ed Assn 1971-74/1985-; Maplewood Ed Assn 1985-; Garfield PTO (VP 1982-83, Pres 1983-84); Waren Parent Teacher Cncl Rep 1982-83; Maplewood HS Chapter NHS Honorary Mem 1988, Honored Teacher Awd; Maplewood Sr Class Favorite Teacher Awd 1989-; *office:* Maplewood H S 2414 Greenville Rd N E Cortland OH 44410

KOTAL, EDITH MARIE, Second Grade Teacher; *b:* Ventura, CA; *m:* Edward L.; *c:* Michael E., John H.; *ed:* (AA) Elem Ed, Ventura Jr Coll 1959; (BA) Elem Ed, Univ of the Pacific 1961; Trng in CPR through Amer Heart Assn Denver; *cr:* 2nd/4th Grade Teacher Stockton Unified Sch Dist 1961-63; 1st Grade Teacher Long Beach Unified Sch Dist 1963-64; 1st/2nd/5th Grade Teacher Las Virgenes Unified Sch Dist 1981-; *ai:* Sustainer Jr League of Los Angeles; Kappa Alpha Theata Alumni; CTA, NEA 1981-; *office:* Willow Elem Sch Laro Dr Agoura Hills CA 91301

KOTARA, DOROTHY MOY, Science Teacher; *b:* Floresville, TX; *m:* Alan P.; *c:* Jason, David, Amanda; *ed:* (BA) Bio/Chem, Incarnate Word Coll 1977; (MA) Scndry Ed, Southwest St Univ 1987; *cr:* Sci Teacher Falls City ISD 1978-; *ai:* Soph Spon; UIL Spon Spelling & Sci; Attendance Comm; NHS Comm; GT Comm; *home:* Rt 2 Box 86 Stockdale TX 78160

KOTOFSKIE, JAMES W., English/Humanities Teacher; *b:* Monterey, CA; *m:* Sheila; *ed:* (BS) 1964, (MA) Oriental Stud, 1980 Univ of AZ; *cr:* Teacher Catalina HS 1971-; *ai:* NHS Spon; Soph Class Adv; Tucson Ed Assn 1971-; *office:* Catalina HS 3645 E Pima Tucson AZ 85716

KOTRLIK, HELEN G., Mathematics Teacher/Dept Chair; *b:* Sacramento, CA; *m:* Patrick; *c:* Michael L.; *ed:* (BA) Math/Ger, CA St Univ Sacramento 1964; Math & Ed Courses Summer Inst Klausenhof Lang Acad Germany; *cr:* Teacher Mills Jr HS 1964-66; Teacher 1966-, Dept Chm Cordova HS 1990; *ai:* CA Schlsp Fed Spon; Natural Helper Peer Cnslr; Ger Club Asst Adv; Folsom-Cordova Ed Assn Site Secy 1970-71; NEA, CTA, Sacramento Area Math Educators; BSA Cub Master 1982-85; Loomis Youth Soccer Coach 1984-87; Presidential Awd for Excl in Sci & Math Teaching Nominee 1989; *office:* Cordova HS 2239 Chase Dr Rancho Cordova CA 95670

KOTSOVOS, JERRY FRANK, Social Studies Teacher; *b:* Portland, OR; *m:* Sharon Irene; *c:* Darren W., Laura E.; *ed:* (BS) Poly Sci, Univ of OR 1968; (MS) Poly Sci, S OR St Coll 1971; Grad Stud Univ of VA, Univ of Portland; *cr:* Amer His/Government/Economics Teacher Marshfield HS; *ai:* NEA, OR Ed Assn, Coos Bay Ed Assn; Advanced Placement Amer His Test Grader; St of OR Presidential Classroom Participant Washington DC 1974; *office:* Marshfield HS 7th & Ingersoll Coos Bay OR 97420

KOTTKAMP, G. MICHAEL, Jr HS Mathematics Teacher; *b:* Centralia, IL; *m:* Joyce; *c:* Tony Cluck, Kelly Cluck, Eddie Cluck; *ed:* (BA) Math Ed, S IL Univ Carbondale 1969; (MS) Math Ed, S IL Univ Edwardsville 1972; *cr:* Jr HS Math Teacher Lebanon Grade Sch 1969-; *ai:* 8th Grade Class, Natl Jr Honor Society, Safety Patrol Spon; Mathcounts Coach; *home:* Box 222 Irvington IL 62848

KOTTKE, CARLYLE MARVIN, Fifth Grade Teacher; *b:* Lena, WI; *m:* Sandra J. Gruenwald; *c:* Raymond A., Marcia K.; *ed:* Elem Ed, Marinette Cty Teachers Coll 1952; (BA) Elem Ed, UW Oshkosh 1964; (BA) Elem Ed, St Marys Coll 1988; *cr:* Elem Prin Coleman Public Sch 1956-58; Elem Prin Elkhorn/West Side Sch 1958-61; Gifted Ed/Dir Kaukauna Public Sch 1961-64; Elem/Teacher 5th Grade Waupaca Centralsch 1964-; *ai:* 5th Grade Stamp Club; Coin Club; Class Play Dir; Art Show Chm; Soc Stud Dept-Dept Head; Waupaca Ed Assn VP/Pres 1968-71; WI Cncl for Soc Stud Presenter 1984-; *home:* E 2101 S Westgate Acres Rd Waupaca WI 54981

KOTTMEYER, GEORGINE, 1st/2nd Grade Teacher; *b:* Centralia, IL; *m:* Roger; *c:* Matthew, Michael; *ed:* (BS) Elem Ed, Murray St Univ 1969; *cr:* 1st/2nd/5th Grade Teacher Elem Dist 12 1969-; *office:* Elem Dist 12 1100 N 7th St Breese IL 62230

KOUBA, SHARON SHACHTER, Fifth Grade Teacher; *b:* Chicago, IL; *ed:* (BA) Sociology, 1965, (MS) Ed, 1979 N IL Univ; Grad Work Beyond MS; *cr:* 5th Grade Teacher Cntrl Elem Sch 1968-82, North Elem Sch 1982-; *ai:* Lang Arts Comm 1987-; Sycamore Ed Assn 1968-; Delta Kappa Gamma Intnl 1976-; NEA, IL Ed Assn 1968-.

KOUNS, HARRIETT SUSIE, Lang Art/Hlth/Phys Ed Teacher; *b:* Grayson, KY; *ed:* (BA) Phys Ed/Health, 1976, (Rank II) Ed, 1979, (Rank I) Ed, 1983 Morehead St Univ; *cr:* Teacher Homebound 1976-77, Hitchins Elem 1977-; *ai:* 8th Grade Spon; Cheerleading A & B Teams Spon 1977-81; Girls Sftbl Coach 1977-81; Academic Co-Spon 1987-89; Carter Cty Ed Assn; *home:* PO Box 168 Hitchins KY 41146

KOURTALIS, BEATRICE, Teacher of Gifted & Talented; *b:* Vineland, NJ; *ed:* (BA) General Elem, Glassboro St Coll 1968; *cr:* Teacher Main Road Sch 1968-; *ai:* Textbook Selection, Curr Dev, Math, Gifted & Talented Comms; Franklin Township Teachers Assn (Pres 1972-73, 1978-79, 1989-); Order of Eastern Star Matron 1982-83; *home:* 1910 S Main Rd Vineland NJ 08360

KOUTSOUMPAS, HARRIET, CSJ, Science Dept Chairperson; *b:* St Louis, MO; *ed:* (BS) Chem, Fontbonne Coll 1949; (MS) Chem, St Louis Univ 1957; Chem, Univ of NC; Theology Univ of Notre Dame, Creighton Univ, Marquette Univ; *cr:* Elem Teacher St Louis St Trng Sch 1949-50; 5th Grade Teacher St Leos Sch 1952-53; Scndry Math/Chem Teacher St Josephs Acad 1953-54; 5th Grade Teacher St Margarets Sch 1954-55, St Anthonys Sch 1955-56; Chem Instr Coll of St Teresa 1957-; Scndry Chem/Physics Teacher St Josephs Acad 1962-68; Asst Prof of Chem Anita Coll 1968-72; Scndry Math/Physics/Chem Teacher St Teresas Acad 1980-; *ai:* Chairperson Sci Dept; Ofcl Soccer Statistician for Vlybl/Bsktbl Teams; North Cntrl Comm Sch Philosophy Mem; Pi Mu Epsilon Schlsp; Teacher Advisory Cncl Mem; Natl Sci Fnd Grant.

KOVACH, SANDRA MARY, Health Occupations Instructor; *b:* Chicago, IL; *m:* Emil P.; *c:* Kenneth; *ed:* (MS) Psychiatric Nursing - Summa Cum Laude, MD Univ Baltimore 1974; (BS) Industrial Ed - Summa Cum Laude, MD Univ College Park 1973; RN Nursing, Sibley Memorial Hospital 1959; *cr:* Supvr In & Out Surgery, Head Nurse-Emergency Room/Staff Nurse-Medical Floor, 1960-61 Prince Georges General Hospital; Office of Drs Mayers, Comeau & Cameron 1961-66; Health Occupations Instr Bladensburg HS 1966-; *ai:* Dept Chairperson; Sch Management Team; NEA 1966-; MD Voc Assn (Health Occupations Chairperson 1979, Dir 1966-); Sigma Theta Tau Nursing NHS 1974-; Phi Kappa Phi 1973-; Rotary Club Outstanding Teacher 1970; Iota Lambda Sigma 1973; Outstanding Scndry Educators of America Awd 1975; Health Career Club Spon; In Service & Awds Comms; Sch Management Team; In Sch Writing Improvement Team; Occupational Skills Dept Chairperson; Sigma Theta Tau Nursing NHS 1990; MD Grant; St of MD Distinguished Prgm Awd 1985; *office:* Bladensburg HS 5610 Tilden Rd Bladensburg MD 20710

KOVAR, RITA (ANDERSEN), Sixth Grade Teacher; *b:* Freeport, NY; *m:* Antonin; *c:* Antonin E.; *ed:* (BS) Elem Ed, SUNY Oswego 1962; (MS) Elem Ed, C W Post Long Island Univ 1986; Grad Stud; *cr:* 4th-6th Grade Teacher Westbrook Sch 1962-70, 1972-; *ai:* Math & Geography Contests; Academic Fitness Awds; West Islip Teachers Assn (Secy, Building Rep, Various Comm); Westbrook Sch PTA Treas Honorary Life Membership; West Islip Chamber of Commerce; *office:* Westbrook Sch Higbie Ln West Islip NY 11795

KOVATS, ELIZABETH A., 4th Grade Teacher; *b:* Zalaegerszeg, Hungary; *m:* Bela; *c:* Peter; *ed:* (BS) Ed, St John Coll Cleveland 1966; *cr:* 3rd/4th Grade Teacher St John Greek Cath Sch 1963-65, St Margaret of Hungary 1966-77; 4th Grade Teacher St Louis Sch 1977-; *ai:* #1 Club Diocese of Cleveland Excl in Teaching 1989; *office:* St Louis Elem Sch 2463 N Taylor Rd Cleveland OH 44118

KOVREG, MARIE ANN, Principal; *b:* New York, NY; *ed:* (BSED) Ed, OH Dominican 1968; (MED) Ed/Admin, Xavier Univ 1980; Instruction & Service Specialist; *cr:* Teacher 1966-84, Prin 1984-88 St Francis de Sales; Prin Sacred Heart 1988-; *ai:* Amer Bus Womens Assn (Pres, Treas) 1970-85, Woman of Yr 1974; NCEA, Prin Assn Cath Elem Schls; Valley Forge Teachers Seminar Freedoms Fnd Schlsp 1974; Sertuma Clubs Local & Dist Service to Mankind Awd 1976; *home:* 707 W Church St Newark OH 43055

KOWALCZYK, JOANNE GRACE, Third Grade Teacher; *b:* New Bedford, MA; *m:* Robert E.; *ed:* (BS) Ed, Framingham St Univ 1968; *cr:* 3rd Grade Teacher Acushnet Sch System 1968-; *ai:* Delta Kapa Gamma (Recording Secy 1988-, VP 1990-); Horace Mann Grant 1986-87; *office:* Acushnet Elem Sch 800 Middle Rd Acushnet MA 02743

KOWALCZYK, STEPHANIE JACQUELINE, Kindergarten Teacher; *b:* Somerset, PA; *ed:* (BS) Elem Ed 1972, (MED) Elem Ed 1975, Univ of Pittsburgh; *cr:* 1st Grade Teacher 1972-74, Kndgtn Teacher 1974-78, 1st Grade Teacher 1978-80, Kndgtn Teacher 1980- North Star Sch Dist; *ai:* PA Kndgtn Identification

& Developmental Screening Project; Sci in Kndgtn Curr Dev Comm; PA St Ed Assn Mem 1972-; NEA Mem 1972-; North Star Ed Assn Mem 1972-; St Stanislaus Cath Church K-6th Grade Religious Ed Coord 1976-82; *home:* 212 Susquehanna St Boswell PA 15531

KOWALSKI, MARSHA MARIE, English Teacher; *b:* Wausau, WI; *m:* Michael S.; *c:* Cassondra; *ed:* (BS) Elem Ed, Univ of WI STevens Point 1984; Grad Stud Eng, Bio, Discipline; *cr:* Eng Teacher St Pauls Sch 1984-; *office:* St Pauls Sch 404 High St Mosinee WI 54455

KOWALSKI, NELLIE LAMAS, English Teacher; *b:* Mc Allen, TX; *m:* Joseph Lawrence; *ed:* (BA) Inter-American Stud, 1978, (MA) Eng, 1983 Pan Amer Univ; *cr:* Jr HS Eng Teacher Travis Jr HS 1978-79; HS Eng Teacher Mc Allen HS 1979-88; Eng Teacher/CLA Coord Mc Allen HS 1988-; *ai:* TX St Teachers Assn 1978-84; Assn of TX Prof Educators 1984-; *office:* Mc Allen HS 2021 La Vista Mc Allen TX 78501

KOZA, BURT T., 7th/8th Grade Soc Stud Teacher; *b:* Amityville, NY; *m:* Margaret; *c:* Jason; *ed:* (BA) His, Marist Coll 1968; (MA) Liberal Stud, St Univ of Stony Brook 1978; *cr:* 8th Grade Soc Stud Teacher St Josephs Sch 1968-72; Asst Prin 1972-73, 7th/8th Grade Soc Stud Teacher/Soc Stud Coord 1972- Our Lady of Perpetual Help Sch; *ai:* Stu Cncl Founder & Adv Our Lady of Perpetual Help Sch; Owl Teacher Resource & Cmptr Trng Center Policy Bd Asst Treas 1985-; NCSS 1980-; Copiague Youth Cncl Bd Mem 1989-; Babylon Town Historical Commission Mem 1990; Town Of Babylon Consumer Protection Bd Chm, Dir; Cmmty Service Awd 1986; Stu Government Founder; *home:* 600 Pinelawn Ave Copiague NY 11726

KOZAK, CARL EUGENE, Technology Education Teacher; *b:* Milwaukee, WI; *m:* Sylvia; *c:* Benjamin, Meredith, Jessica, Sarah, Gretchen, Peter; *ed:* (BS) Ag Ed, Univ of WI River Falls 1967; (MS) Technology Ed, Univ of WI Stout 1974; *cr:* Voc Ed Teacher West Bend WI 1968-72, Hayward WI 1972-; *ai:* VICA & Frosh Adv; Dept Head; NEA, WEAC; NUE Unit Dir 1980-82; Knights of Columbus 1975-; Town of Hayward Fire Dept Asst Chief 1990; City of Hayward Variance Bd Chairperson 1987-; *office:* Hayward Cmmty Schls 515 W 5th St Hayward WI 54843

KOZLEN, DIANA LATO, Spanish Teacher; *b:* St Louis, MO; *m:* Keith D.; *c:* Kevin, Kelly; *ed:* (BA) Span, Univ of MO Columbia 1972; (MSED) Scndry Ed/Span, Univ of MO St Louis 1975; Cert Bus Ed 1977; *cr:* Span Teacher Fox Sr HS 1972-; *ai:* Span Club Spon; Project Graduation Participant; St Louis Foreign Lang Teachers Assn, MO Foreign Lang Teachers Assn 1975-; C-6 Ed Assn Grievance Comm Chm 1987-; MO Ed Assn, NEA 1983-; Natl Assn Teachers of Span & Portugese 1979-; BSA (Den Leader, Comm Chairperson) 1982-85; GSA Asst Troop Leader 1986; St Louis Archdiocese Cvc Sports Prgms (Lay Dir, Divisional Coord) 1987-; Immaculate Conception Athletic Assn (Mgr, Exec Bd Mem) 1983-; *office:* Fox Sr HS 745 Jeffco Blvd Arnold MO 63010

KOZLEUCHAR, BARBARA E., Jr High School Teacher; *b:* Milwaukee, WI; *ed:* (BA) Sociology, Quincy Coll 1965; (MS) Ed Admin, Univ WI Milwaukee 1988; *cr:* Teacher St James Sch 1968-70, Holy Name Sch 1970-77, St Mary Sch 1977-83, Holy Name Sch 1983-; *ai:* Stu Cncl Adv.

KOZLOWSKI, DAVID, Asst Principal; *b:* Detroit, MI; *m:* Barbara Ann Charnley; *c:* Kristy, Bridget, Ellen, Mark; *ed:* (BA) Eng, Univ of Detroit 1970; (MA) Math Ed, Univ of MI 1976; *cr:* 7th/8th Grade Teacher Epiphany Sch 1970-73; Math Teacher 1973-75, Disciplinarian 1975-86, Math Teacher 1986-88, Asst Prin 1988- Brother Rice HS; *ai:* Past Jr Var & Var Asst Bsbl Coach; Jr Var Golf Coach; NCEA; *office:* Brother Rice HS 7101 Lahser Rd Birmingham MI 48010

KOZUCK, JOHN, Physical Education Teacher; *b:* Brooklyn, NY; *m:* Helen Haight; *c:* Amanda, Jeremy; *ed:* (BA) Health/Phys Ed, Hunter Coll 1971; (BS) Health Ed, Brooklyn Coll 1975; Certificate Supervision/Admin, Queens Coll 1980; Certified CPR Instr 1988; *cr:* Health/Phys Educator IS 162 1971-86, Truman HS 1986-; *ai:* Boys Cross Cntry Track & Wrestling Coach; NY Wrestling Ofcls Assn, Long Island Wrestling Ofcls Assn 1981-; CUNY Wrestling Coaches Assn 1971-77, Coach of Yr 1975; City Univ NY Wrestling Coach of Yr; NY Alliance Teacher of Yr; Truman HS Teacher of Yr 1988-89; *office:* Harry S Truman HS 750 Baychester Ave Bronx NY 10475

KRAEMER, KRISTI, Eng Teacher/Stu Teacher Supvr; *b:* Los Angeles, CA; *m:* Joseph O'Hagan; *c:* John O'Hagan; *ed:* (AB) Eng/Sociology, Univ of CA Davis 1972; (MA) Lang/Literacy/ Writing, Univ of CA Berkeley 1984; Standard Scndry Teaching Credential, Univ of CA Davis 1973; Natl Writing Project 1978; *cr:* Eng Teacher El Camino HS 1977-84; Area III Writing Project Dir 1985-87, Lecturer/Supvr 1985- Univ of CA Davis; Eng Teacher Davis HS 1987-; *ai:* Area III Writing Project Open Prgm Instr Univ of CA Davis; CA Assn Teachers of Eng Mem at Large 1984-; Natl Writing Project Local Acting Dir 1985-87; Distinguished Teaching Awd San Juan Unified Sch Dist 1983, Univ of CA Davis Continuing Ed Extension 1989; *office:* Davis Sr HS Univ of CA Davis Division of Ed Davis CA 95616

KRAETSCH, CAROLYN JONES, Teacher of Gifted & Talented; *b:* Evanston, IL; *m:* Ralph B.; *c:* Edmund, Katherine Strelkoff, John, Ellen Brown; *ed:* (BS) Eng Lit, Northwestern Univ 1950; *cr:* Teacher Bakersfield Sch Dist 1965-71; Teacher 1971-87, Teacher of Gifted & Talented 1987- Mt Diablo Sch Dist; *ai:* Docent Lindsay Museum & Heather Farms Garden Center; Kids on the Block Chm Assistance League of Diablo Valley; Teacher Enrichment & Gifted/Talented Prgms in Creative Dramatics for Mt Diablo & Pleasanton Sch Dist; Bay Area Theater; *home:* 88 Karen Ln Walnut Creek CA 94598

KRAFT, JUDY A., English Teacher; *b:* Bismarck, ND; *m:* Michael D.; *c:* Michael J., Matthew J., Anne J.; *ed:* (BS) Eng, Univ of Mary 1977; Advanced Placement Wkshp Classes; Grad Work Univ of ND; Ind Study Grad Work Univ of MN; *cr:* 7th-12th Grade Eng Teacher Solen HS 1977-78; 9th/10th Grade Eng Teacher Minot Cntrl Campus 1978-81; 9th/12th Grade Eng Teacher Williston HS 1983-; *ai:* Jr Class Prom & Banquet, Sch Newspaper, Frosh Class Adv; Asst Coach; Debate Team; NDCE, NCTE 1978-; NDEA 1978-82, 1989-; AAUW 1982-83; Chrstn Women 1981-; Chamber of Commerce Ed Comm 1979-81; Minot Schls NCA Evaluation Co-Chairperson & Visiting Teams; In-Service Coordinating Team; *home:* 840 Park Pl Williston ND 58801

KRAFT, MARSHA LEANN, Kindergarten Teacher; *b:* Kansas City, KS; *ed:* (AA) Crowder Coll 1974; (BSE) Elem Ed, MO Southern St Coll 1977; (MED) Elem Ed, Univ of MO Columbia 1978; *cr:* Kndgtn Teacher/Elem Librarian Westview Elem 1978-79; Kndgtn Teacher Goodman Elem 1979-81, Benton Elem 1981-, Field Elem 1990; *ai:* Phi Delta Kappa, MO St Teachers Assn, MO Assn of Elem Sch Prin; *office:* Field Elem Sch N High St Neosho MO 64850

KRAHN, ANN CHRISTIANSEN, English Teacher; *b:* Harrisonburg, LA; *m:* Rick D.; *c:* Christopher F.; *ed:* (BSE) Eng, Delta St Univ 1975; (ME) Eng, 1980, Specialist Eng, 1988 Univ of S MS; *cr:* Eng Teacher Block HS 1976-; *ai:* 4-H Club Spon; Catahoula Writing Comm Chairperson; Eng Dept Head; NEA 1980-; LA Assn of Educators; Catahoula Assn of Educators Faculty Rep; Jonesville Womens Club 1987-; Teacher of Yr Catahoula Parish HS 1986 & Block HS 1989; *office:* Block HS 300 Division St Jonesville LA 71343

KRAISINGER, KAREN STONER, Fourth Grade Teacher; *b:* Mt Pleasant, PA; *m:* Frank J.; *c:* Jessica, Kelly; *ed:* (BS) Elem Ed, PA St Univ 1973; (MA) Elem Ed, WV Univ 1976; *cr:* 2nd Grade Teacher 1973-78, 4th Grade Teacher 1978- Southmoreland Sch Dist; *ai:* Act 178 Comm St Rep; NEA; PA St Ed Assn Intergroup Relations Commission 1979; Southmoreland Ed Assn (VP 1983-86, Political Action Comm for Ed Chairperson 1988-); Pi Lambda Theta Inducted 1973; Christ United Meth Church Choir 1979-; Westmoreland Cty Democratic Comm 1986-89; PTO 1986-; *office:* Alverton Elem Sch Box C Alverton PA 15612

KRAISINGER, MARGARET BELLER, Business Teacher; *b:* Garden City, KS; *m:* Gary Lee; *c:* Kurt, Eric, Kristi J.; *ed:* (BA) Eng, Fort Hays Univ 1964; (MS) Bus Ed, Emporia St Univ 1967; Grad Stud Numerous Colls; *cr:* Eng/Bus Teacher Dighton HS 1964-67, Wichita USD 259 1978-79; Bus Teacher Halstead HS 1980-; *ai:* Soph Class Spon; MCREL Team Mem; Kayette Club Head Spon; Various Comms; Meth Church Wkshp Chairperson 1986-89; *home:* 822 W 4th Halstead KS 67056

KRAJCIK, JACKIE HARTER, Guidance Counselor; *b:* Wooster, OH; *m:* Anthony Shelby; *c:* Daniel A.; *ed:* (BS) Scndry Ed/Eng, OH St Univ 1982; (MS) Scndry Ed/Guidance, Univ of Akron 1986; *cr:* Eng Teacher 1982-88, Guidance Cnslr 1987-, Northwestern Local Schls; *ai:* Teen Inst Drug Prevention Group; OH Sch Cnslr Assn 1988-; *office:* Northwestern HS 7569 N Elyria Rd West Salem OH 44287

KRAJEWSKI, JOAN F., English Department Chair; *b:* Chicago, IL; *ed:* (BA) His, Barat Coll 1966; (MA) Eng, De Paul Univ 1969; Ger, Bus, St Xavier & Moraine Valley Comm Coll; *cr:* Eng Teacher Mother Mc Auley HS 1966-68, Simeon Voc HS 1969-72, Moraine Valley Comm Coll 1979-82, Morgan Park HS 1972-; *ai:* IL Assn Teachers of Eng; St Francis Hosp, Beverly Art Center Volunteer; Fry Fnd Fellowship Grant; St of IL Real Estate Sales License; *office:* Morgan Park HS 1744 W Pryor Chicago IL 60643

KRAL, ELMER A., English Instructor; *b:* Wilber, NE; *ed:* (BS) Span/Soc Stud, 1960; (MED) Eng/Scndry Ed, 1965 Univ of NE; Post Masters Studies Natl Univ of Mexico 1961; NE Writing Project Univ of NE 1978; Models of Reasoning Inst CA ST Univ at Fullerton 1981, Portland ST Univ 1983, AZ ST Univ 1984; *cr:* Spanish Teacher Irving Jr High 1960-63; Livingston HS 1963-64; Eng Teacher Grand Island Sr HS 1965-; *ai:* Creative Writing Adv 1968-71; Dev of Reasoning Researcher 1980-; NE Mod Lang Assn Pres 1962-63; NEA Mem 1965-; ASCD Thinking Skills Net Mem 1985-; NE Cncl Teacher Ed Mem 1979-81; CSICOP Ed Co-Chm 1979-81; NE ST Hist Society Consultant 1990-; Donor NE Para Coll 1985/Para Tele Serv 1987 at Univ of NE Med Ctr; Donor Kral Photo Coll at NE ST Hist Society 1985; Author of Articles in Educational Forum 1985, the Skeptical Inquirer 1979 & 1984, Omaha World Herald 1983, Research Papers the Modern Way 1989; Finalist UNL Freda Battey Dist Ed Awd 1987; *home:* Box 356 Wilber NE 68465

KRAL, GERALD DAVID, Science Department Chair; *b:* Sleepy Eye, MN; *m:* Lynell M. Zwieg; *c:* Joni, Jason, Kelly; *ed:* (BA) Phys Ed, St Cloud St Univ 1970; (BA) Biological Sci, Mankato St Univ 1979; Biotechnology Wkshp, Mankato St 1985; *cr:* Phys Ed/Bio Teacher Cedar Mt HS 1971-; *ai:* Sci Fair Coord; Asst Ftbl & Head Wrestling Coach; Boys Sports Rep; MN Coaches Assn 1971-; MN Sci Teachers Assn, MN Wrestling Coaches Assn; VFW 1970-; Natl Sci Fnd Grant Biotechnology; Region 3A Wrestling Coach of Yr 1982; *office:* Cedar Mt HS Box 188 Morgan MN 56266

KRAL, MICHAEL EMIL, Science/Mathematics Teacher; *b:* Hinsdale, IL; *m:* Elisabeth Pedersen; *c:* Kirsten, Anne, Katherine; *ed:* (BS) Bio, Univ of IL Chicago 1972; Rank II Univ of Louisville; *cr:* Teacher Howevalley Sch 1975-; *ai:* Governors Cup & Math Counts Coach; Math Bowl Coach 1977-; Sci Comm Cty; Sci Fair Chm 1976-86; Jr Beta Club Spon 1988-; KY St Sci Teachers Bd of Dir 1987-; KEA, HCEA, NSTA Local Pres 1989-; Teacher of Quarter Hardin Cty Bd of Ed 1981, 1982; *office:* Howevalley Sch 8450 Hardinsburg Rd Cecilia KY 42724

KRALOSKEY, GEORGE MICHAEL, English Teacher; *b:* Saginaw, MI; *m:* Lynn Lesnau; *ed:* Eng, Delta Coll 1970; (BS) Eng, Cntrl MI Univ 1973; Ed, Cntrl MI Univ; Government, Univ of Houston; *cr:* Eng Teacher Our Lady of Perpetual Help 1973-76, Swan Valley HS 1976-81, Elsik HS 1981-; *ai:* TX Joint Cncl Teachers of Eng Mem; Pioneer Alief Cmptr Writing Lab; NEA Awd for Excl 1989; *office:* Elsik HS P O Box 68 Alief TX 77411

KRAMER, CONNIE NOBLIN, Seventh Grade Teacher; *b:* Jacksonville, FL; *m:* Robert Roy; *c:* Robert K., Beaman K.; *ed:* (BS) Elem Ed, MS St Coll for Women 1967; *cr:* Teacher Mars Hill Elem; *ai:* Madison Cty NC Assn of Educators Pres; His Club Spon; NCAE (VP 1988-89, Pres 1989-); Mars Hill United Meth Church (Sunday Sch Teacher 1968-84, Pres Meth Women 1987-88); Sing With Group Trillium Mountain Folk Music 1973-; *office:* Mars Hill Elem Sch 176 Bailey St Mars Hill NC 28754

KRAMER, JANE, Third Grade Teacher; *b:* Hackensack, NJ; *c:* Christina; *ed:* (BA) His, Cath Univ 1968; (MED) Elem Ed, Clemson Univ 1983; *office:* Ellen Woodside Elem Sch 9130 Augusta Rd Pelzer SC 29669

KRAMER, JANE B. (HARTSFIELD), Social Studies Teacher; *b:* Pleasant Point, TN; *m:* James W.; *c:* Kimala C. Bond, James II; *ed:* (BA) Soc Stud/Vocal Music, USM Hattiesburg 1975; *cr:* Teacher St Rose of Lima 1965, St Johns 1966-70, Mc Caughan Elem 1975-86, Long Beach Mid Sch 1986-; *ai:* NCBE 1988-; Amer Family Assoc 1989-; Concerned Women of Amer 1989-; MS Rep to Statue of Liberty; Vocal Ensemble 1986.

KRAMER, JOSEPH JOHN, Business Teacher; *b:* Dayton, OH; *m:* Ann Conway; *c:* Ryan J.; *ed:* (BA) Phys Ed, 1977, (MS) Scndry Admin, 1979 Miami Univ; *cr:* Bus Teacher Chaminade-Julienne HS 1977-78; Asst Bsbl Coach Miami Univ 1978-79; Bus Teacher Valley View HS 1979-83; Asst Bsbl Coach Univ of Dayton 1983-84; Bus Teacher West Union HS 1984-; *ai:* Bsbl Coach; Adv Stock Market Team & Chess Club; M Club 1977-; Holy Trinity Cath Church Instr of HS CCD Class 1989-; Knothole Little League Coach 1990; OH Teacher Forum 1986; *office:* West Union HS 201 W South St West Union OH 45693

KRAMER, LISA BREWER, Science Teacher; *b:* Garland, TX; *m:* Evan; *ed:* (BA) Bio, Rice Univ 1987; *cr:* Sci Teacher Christ The King Cathedral 1987-; *ai:* Sci Fair Dir; 9th Grade Class & Stu Cncl Spon; *office:* Christ The King Cathedral Sch 4011 54th St Lubbock TX 79413

KRAMER, MARLA J., 8th Grade Science Teacher; *b:* Cincinnati, OH; *ed:* (BS) Environmental Sci, Lehigh Univ 1985; Cert Scndry Sci, Morarian Coll 1986; *cr:* 8th Grade Sci Teacher Stroudsburg Mid Sch 1986-; *ai:* Cross-Cntry Running, Hiking, Sci Olympiad Team Spon; Stu Recognition Comm; NSTA, PA Sci Teachers Assn 1986-; *office:* Stroudsburg Mid Sch Chipperfield Dr Stroudsburg PA 18360

KRAMER, NANCY KAUFFMAN, English Teacher; *b:* Hamburg, PA; *m:* Eugene D.; *c:* Patricia Kramer Greene, E. David Jr., Laurette; *ed:* (BS) Eng, 1967, (MA) Eng, 1982 Kutztown Univ; *cr:* Teacher Hamburg Area Sch Dist 1967-; *ai:* Sch Newspaper Adv; NEA, PSEA, PA Cncl Teachers of Eng; *home:* 105 W 9th Box 1914 Shoemakersville PA 19555

KRAMER, SUSIE, Physical Education Coach; *b:* Brenham, TX; *ed:* (AA) Phys Ed, Temple Jr Coll 1979; (BS) Phys Ed, OK St Univ 1981; (MA) Behavioral Sci/Outdoor Ed, Univ of Houston 1985; *cr:* Teacher/Coach Baker Jr HS 1982-86, Lomax Jr HS 1986-; *ai:* Girls Bsktbl & Track Coach; TX Girls Coaches Assn, TX Assn for Health, Phys Ed, Recreation, Dance; *office:* Lomax Jr HS 9801 N Avenue L La Porte TX 77571

KRAMLICH, CAROLYN WALZ, Middle School English Teacher; *b:* Atlanta, GA; *m:* Kenneth R.; *ed:* (BA) Chrstn Ed, Atlanta Chrstn Coll 1976; (MED) Mid Sch Ed, GA St Univ 1981; *cr:* Teacher Pathway Chrstn Sch 1978-83; Eng Teacher Woodward Acad 1983-; *ai:* Adv Mid Sch Newspaper; Articles Published 1983-85; Musical Published 1985; *office:* Woodward Acad 1662 Rugby Ave College Park GA 30337

KRAMME, THEODORE W., Math Teacher; *b:* Washington, MO; *m:* Patsy L. Stahlman; *c:* Michele L.; *ed:* (BSED) Math, S IL Univ 1963; (MA) Math, Univ of IL Urbana 1968; St Louis Univ, NE MO St Kirksville, S IL Univ Edwardsville, Maryville Coll; *cr:* Math Teacher St Clair HS 1963-67, Niles N HS 1968-69, Pattonville HS 1969-; *ai:* Pattonville Ed Assn Exec Bd 1973-; NCTM 1964-; Math Educators of Greater St Louis 1988-; St John United Church of Christ (Treas, Church Cncl) 1974-; NSF Academic Yr Inst Univ of IL Urbana & Fellowship S IL Univ Edwardsville; Pattonville Sch Dist Employee of Yr Awd 1989; *office:* Pattonville HS 2497 Creve Coeur Mill Rd Maryland Heights MO 63043

KRANEDONK, HENRY A., Math/Computer Science Teacher; *b:* Oostburg, WI; *m:* Jean Freiman; *c:* Laura, Kristin, Abbey; *ed:* (BS) Math, Carroll Coll 1971; (MS) Math, Marquette Univ 1980; *cr:* Math Teacher West Division HS 1971-74; Math Specialist 1974-78, Asst Dir of Upward Bound 1978-80 Marquette Univ; Math/Cmptr Sci Teacher Rufus King HS 1980-; *ai:* Intnl Baccalaureate Computing Stud Subject Comm & Asst Examiner; Cmptr Club Adv; Milwaukee Area Math Cncl Pres 1985-87; WI Math Cncl 1978-; Milwaukee Ed Computing Assn 1984-; Advocates for Retarded Citizens 1985-; Milwaukee Fnd Math Profile & Counseling Prgm Grant; *office:* Rufus King For College Bound S 1801 W Olive St Milwaukee WI 53209

KRANZLER, LINDA TERVEEN, 3rd Grade Teacher; *b:* Mitchell, SD; *m:* Steven B.; *c:* Christopher, Kara; *ed:* (BS) Elem Ed, Sioux Falls Coll 1969; SD St Univ/Augustana Coll; *cr:* 1st Grade Teacher Jane Addams Elem 1969-80; 3rd Grade Teacher Lincoln Elem 1981-; *ai:* SDEA 1969-; NEA 1969-; *home:* 401 E 29th Sioux Falls SD 57105

KRASTEK, ROBERT ANTHONY, Social Studies Teacher; *b:* Altoona, PA; *m:* Leila Regina Mc Guire; *c:* Eric, Caroline; *ed:* (BA) Poly Sci, Duquesne Univ 1971; (MAT) Soc Stud Ed, Trenton St Coll 1975; Penn St, Glassboro St; *cr:* Soc Stud Teacher St Joan of Arc 1971-73; Adjunct Instr Burlington Cty Coll 1977-81; Soc Stud Teacher Holy Cross HS 1973-; *ai:* Soccer & Bsbl Coach; NCSS, Natl Soccer Coaches Assn of America, United Nations Assn US of America; Riverside Pal (VP 1983, Little League Dir 1981-82); Duquesne Alumni Recruitment Team; Taft Poly Inst Seminar Schlsp; Chm Mid Sts Comm Soc Stud; Public Affairs Seminar Univ of PA; *office:* Holy Cross HS Rt 130 Delran NJ 08075

KRATZ, JANIE ADAMS, Principal; *b:* Okeene, OK; *m:* Ron L. Swank; *c:* Paul; *ed:* (BA) Elem, Southwestern Univ 1964; (MA) Elem Ed, Adams St Coll 1985; Admin Cert, Western St Gunnison Cty 1987; *cr:* 4th Grade Teacher Putnam City Sch Dist; 3rd Grade Teacher Chinle Elem; Librarian Window Rock Sch Dist; 3rd/6th Grades Teacher Prin Dolores REHA; *office:* Dolores Elem Sch Box 757 12th & Hillside Dolores CO 81323

KRATZER, DOROTHY JOHNSON, Second Grade Teacher; *b:* Stamford, NE; *c:* Kathleen Schulz, Carol Sykes, Kent Wolf; *ed:* (BA) Elem Ed, CO St Coll 1969; (MA) Elem Ed, Univ of N CO 1980; Grad Stud in Ed; *cr:* Teacher 1944-45, Stamford Sch 1945-47, Pete Mirich Elem 1969-; *ai:* 4-H Leader 1959-62; *home:* 1130 24th Ave Ct Greeley CO 80631

KRAUS, COLETTE, Third Grade Teacher; *b:* San Antonio, TX; *ed:* (BA) Ed, Univ of Dallas 1972; (MRS) Religious Stud, Incarnate Word Coll 1989; *cr:* 5th Grade Teacher St Marys Sch 1971-73; 2nd Grade Teacher Immaculate Conception Sch 1973-79; 1st/3rd Grade Teacher Our Lady of Perpetual Help Sch 1979-; *office:* Our Lady of Perpetual Help Sch 7625 Cortland Dallas TX 75235

KRAUS, PATRICIA BRENDA (BORN), Language Arts Teacher; *b:* Spokane, WA; *ed:* (BA) His, Eng Gonzaga Univ 1960; *cr:* Teacher Muroc Unified Sch Dist 1960-63; Coeur Daleen Jr HS 1963-82; Coeur Dalene HS 1974-82; Canfield Mid Sch 1982-; *ai:* NEA 1963-; IEA 1963-; CEA 1963-.

KRAUS, PATRICK J., Industrial Arts Teacher; *b:* N Platte, NE; *m:* Joan; *c:* Angela, Mathew, Nicole; *ed:* (MS) Industrial Art, Chadron St 1977; *cr:* Teacher Mc Pherson Cty HS 1977; Teacher/Coach Maxwell Public Sch 1978- *ai:* HS & Jr HS Ftbl, Bsktbl, Track Coach; NE Eight Man Ftbl Coaches Assn VP 1987-89; *office:* Maxwell Public Sch P O Box 188 Maxwell NE 69151

KRAUS, ROBERTA M., First Grade Teacher; *b:* Bronx, NY; *m:* Robert L.; *c:* Elizabeth Kraus Sher, Jonathan E.; *ed:* (BS) Early Chldhd/Elem Ed, Wilson Teachers Coll 1950; Working Towards Masters; *cr:* Elem Teacher Bunker Hill Sch 1950-51, Eugene Field Sch 1951-58, John F. Kennedy Sch 1967-; *ai:* Wayne Schls Elem Rep Cafeteria Comm; Kappa Delta Pi; PTO Teacher Liaison; Wayne Ed Organization Sch Rep 1983-89; Concerned Eductors of Wayne 1988-; NJ Governors Teacher Recognition Awd 1987-88; Comprehensive Lesson Unit for Soc Stud Curr; Updated Curr Guide for 1st Grade; *office:* John F. Kennedy Elem Sch 1310 Ratzer Rd Wayne NJ 07470

KRAUSE, JAN GEIST, English Teacher/Dept Chair; *b:* Washington, DC; *m:* Harold Benjamin Jr.; *c:* Halby, Jeremy, Karl, Neil, John; *ed:* (BA) Eng, Boston Coll 1970; *cr:* Eng Teacher Stoughton HS 1971-75; Night Copy Ed 1986, Columnist 1987- Middlesex News; Eng Teacher 1987-, Eng Dept Chairperson 1988- Hopkinton Jr/Sr HS; *ai:* Reach Prgm Comm Gifted & Talented; Hopkinton Teachers Assn Schlsp Comm; NCTE 1988-; MA Teachers Assn, NEA 1987-; Weekly Column in Middlesex News; *office:* Hopkinton Jr-Sr HS Hayden Rowe Hopkinton MA 01748

KRAUSE, LINDA JONES, Fifth Grade Science Teacher; *b:* Stamford, TX; *m:* Carl E.; *c:* Kelly H.; *ed:* (BS) Elem Ed/Spec Ed, East TX St Univ 1976; *cr:* Spec Ed Teacher 1976-80, 5th Grade Teacher 1980-81 Central Elem, Highland Village Elem 1981-; *ai:* Stu Cncl Spon; Campus General Chairperson; Camp Goddard Coord; NEA 1976-; TX St Teachers Assn 1976-; Lewisville Ed Assn (Teacher Rep, Secy) 1976-; Sci Teachers Assn of TX 1989-; TX Cncl for Elem Sci 1989-; TX Terrific Teacher 1984; TX & Highland Village Elem PTA Life Membership 1985; Highland Village Elem Teacher of Yr 1983-84; *home:* 800 Waite Dr Copper Canyon TX 75067

KRAUSE, VALETA, Chapter I & Migrant Aide; *b:* Norman, OK; *m:* Herbert R.; *c:* Herbert R. Jr.; *ed:* Microcomputer, Math Manipulation, Rdng, Eng Wkshps; *cr:* Child Care Yorktown TX 1973-81; Aide Yorktown Ind Sch Dist 1981-; *ai:* Migrant & Chapter I Tutorials; St Paul Luth (Teacher 1969-81, Luth League Spon 1978-84); *office:* Yorktown Ind Sch Dist P O Box 487 Yorktown TX 78164

KRAUSE, WILLIAM EDWARD, Drafting Instructor; *b:* Oakland City, IN; *m:* Devara C. Hughes; *c:* Timothy S. Fears; *ed:* (BS) Industrial Arts Ed, Mid TN St Univ 1972; (MS) Industrial Arts Ed, 1977, (EDS) Sch Admin, 1985 IN St Univ; Cmptr Aided Drafting, Vincennes Univ 1985; *cr:* Teacher Cobb Cty 1973, Brevard Cty 1974, Teacher 1975, Asst Prin 1981, Teacher 1983- Pike Cty; *ai:* Industrial Arts Club; Odessey of Mind Structure Team; Industrial Ed Assn 1977- Meriterous Teacher 1988; F&AM Jr Warden 1966; AASR 1966; Hadi Shrine Pres 1981; BSA 1953- Buffalo 1980; Versa CAD Natl Champions 1987 & 89; IN Industrial Ed; Assn St Champions CAD 1987 & 89; Assn St Champions Adv Mechnical Drafting; Architectural St Champions 1979-80 & 85; *office:* Pike Cntrl Mid-HS Rt 3 Petersburg IN 47567

KRAVITZ, MERRYL LESLIE, Language Arts Teacher; *b:* New York, NY; *ed:* (BA) Anthropology/Linguistics, St Univ of NY Binghamton 1974; (MA) Anthropology, 1976, (PHD) Educl Fnds/ Linguidistics, 1985 Univ of NM; *cr:* Teaching Asst Univ of NM 1974-77; Teacher Los Alamitos Mid Sch 1979-81; Teacher Harrison Mid Sch 1982-; Instr Albuquerque Tech Voc Inst 1983-; *ai:* Harrison Mid Sch Connect Team & Sch Support Team Chairperson; Linguistic Society of America 1975, Summer Fellowship 1976; Operation Rescue Chairperson 1987; Mensa 1983-; Connect Team Grant At-Risk Stus 1989-; Alternative Prgm Awd 1989; Regents Schlsp & Incentive 1970-74; *office:* Harrison Mid Sch 3912 Isleta Blvd SW Albuquerque NM 87105

KRAY, PATRICIA PAULY, Computer Teacher; *b:* Dubuque, IA; *m:* Vaughn; *c:* Erin, Steven; *ed:* (BA) Eng, Clarke Coll 1974; Working Toward Masters Degree in ED; Clarke Coll; Trng in Substance Abuse Intervention, Great Books Leader Trng Course, Human Relations; *cr:* 3rd Grade Teacher 1974-76, 5th Grade Teacher 1977-79 Nativity Sch; 6th Grade Teacher Balltown-Sherrill Cath Sch 1982-83; Jr HS Teacher 1983-85, Learning Center Teacher 1985-86, Cmptr Teacher 1986- Nativity Sch; *ai:* Sch Newspaper Adv; Visions & Values Comm & Cmptr Curr Chairperson; Great Books Leader; Kappa Gamma Pi 1974-; Intnl Society for Technology in Ed 1986-; Hospice of Dubuque Volunteer 1987-; Sr Mary Edward Dolan Grad Schlsp; *office:* Nativity Sch 1001 Alta Vista St Dubuque IA 52001

KRAYCSIR, ANDREW, JR., Sixth Grade Teacher; *b:* Bay City, MI; *m:* Barbara; *c:* Tim, Andy, Erin; *ed:* (BS) Sci, 1972, (MA) Educl Admin, 1978 Cntrl MI Univ; *cr:* 6th Grade Teacher 1972-75, 7th Grade Teacher 1976-79, 6th Grade Teacher 1980- Freeland; *ai:* Freeland Ed Assn Pres 1988-; MEA, NEA; *home:* 3760 Wheeler Rd Bay City MI 48706

KRAYENVENGER, DAVE E., 6th Grade Teacher; *b:* Buffalo, NY; *c:* Daren, Traci, Jeff; *ed:* (BS) Elem Ed, St Univ of NY Geneseo 1972; Grad Stud St Univ of NY Potsdam; Effective Teaching; Teaching of Rdng in Content Areas; Self-Esteem Trng; *cr:* 4th-6th Grade Teacher H T Wiley Elem 1972-; *ai:* Sci-Tech Center Mem; Elem Mem at Large, Watertown Ed Assn; Mem Crisis Comm Watertown Ed Assn; Tri Cty Credit Union Pres 1985; Alumni Conifer Park 1990; *office:* H T Wiley Sch 1351 Washington St Watertown NY 13601

KRAYER, WILLIAM REED, Science Teacher; *b:* Philadelphia, PA; *m:* Wendy Chernikoff; *c:* Beth, Joel; *ed:* (BS) Meteorology, Rutgers Univ 1969; (MED) Earth Sci, PA St Univ 1971; Natl Sci Fnd Summer Inst, CO Sch of Mines 1975; *cr:* Sci Teacher Toms River HS North 1972-74, Takoma Park Jr HS 1974-79, Gaithersburg HS 1979-; *ai:* Sci Cmptr Evaluation Comm Montgomery Cty Public Schls; NSTA, Natl Earth Sci Teachers Assn, Natl Weather Assn; Gaithersburg Lib Advisory Comm Chm 1988-; Natl Space Club Intern Goddard Space Flight Center 1987; Presidential Awd Excl Sci Teaching 1989; *office:* Gaithersburg HS 314 S Frederick Ave Gaithersburg MD 20877

KRBLICH, EDITH LEVERING, Fifth Grade Teacher; *b:* St Petersburg, FL; *m:* Charles A.; *c:* Charles A., Linda L. Begley; *ed:* (BS) Elem Ed, FL St Univ 1956; (ME) Ed, Natl Coll of Ed 1988; Ed, Brevard Jr Coll 1965, Rollins Coll, Winter Park 1969, FL Tech Univ 1970; *cr:* 4th Grade Teacher Roser Park Elem Sch 1956-57; 7th Grade Teacher Lakehurst Elem Sch 1957-58; 2nd Grade Teacher Cross Bayou Elem Sch 1959-60; 6th Grade Teacher Sabal Elem Sch 1965; 4th Grade Teacher Fairmount Park Elem Sch 1965-67; 4th/5th Grade Teacher Sabal Elem Sch 1967-72; 7th/8th Grade Teacher Auburndale Sch 1973-75; 5th Grade Teacher Berclair Elem Sch 1975-77, Brownsville Elem Sch 1977-78; 4th/ 5th Grade Teacher Irene H King Elem Sch 1979-; *ai:* Sch Dist Rdng, PTO, Math, Staff Dev Comm; Stu Teacher Instr & Cnslr; NEA; *office:* Irene H King Elem Sch 301 Eaton Romeoville IL 60441

KREAIS, MARY L., Math/Cmptr Science Teacher; *b:* Tiffin, OH; *ed:* (BA) Math, OH Northern 1981; Grad Stud Ashland Univ; *cr:* Teacher South Cntrl Sch 1981-; *ai:* Stu Cncl Adv; NCTM; Delta Kappa Gamma Newsletter Ed 1988-; 20th Century Rdng Circle; Nom Ashland Oil Schlsp; *home:* 11 S Kniffin St Greenwich OH 44837

KREBS, MARY SCHAEFFER, Fifth Grade Teacher; *b:* St Louis, MO; *m:* Charles; *c:* Mary Hopfinger, Glennon, Paul, Anne, Thomas; *ed:* (BA) Elem Ed, Webster Coll 1951; Paul VI Inst of Catechetical & Pastoral Stud; *cr:* 2nd Grade Teacher Hyde Park Sch 1951-52, Wyman 1952-53; 1st/4th/5th Grade Teacher St Catherine Laboure 1974-; *ai:* Spelling Bee Moderator; NCEA, Intnl Rdng Assn; *office:* St Catherine Laboure Sch 9750 Sappington Rd Sappington MO 63128

KREFT, BONNIE RAE (BELLVILLE), High School English Teacher; *b:* Elyria, OH; *m:* Timothy R.; *c:* Amy M. Bradley; *ed:* (BS) Ed Eng/Journalism, Bowling Green St Univ 1969; Scndry Sch Curr, Univ of Toledo OH 1991; *cr:* Teacher/Dept Chairperson Macomber HS 1969-73; Teacher St Hyacinth Elem 1980-81, Mc Auley HS 1981-82, Bedford HS 1986-; *ai:* MI Ed Assn, Bedford Ed Assn 1986-; Toledo Fed of Teachers 1969-73; OH Fed of Teachers; Grace United Meth Church (Advisory Cncl 1989-, Sunday Sch Teacher 1989-) St Pauls Episcopal Church Sunday Sch Teacher; *home:* 336 Southwood Perrysburg OH 43551

KREIDLER, KATHLEEN RIDGES, Chemistry Teacher; *b:* Chicago, IL; *m:* Thomas F.; *c:* Susan M., Joseph T., William T., Paul T.; *ed:* (BA) Elem Ed, 1979, (MS) Analytical Chem, 1989 Governors St Univ; *cr:* Jr HS Math/Sci Teacher St Victor Sch 1980-83; Phy Sci Teacher Thornwood HS 1983-84; Phys Sci/ Chem Teacher Thornridge HS 1984-; *ai:* Publicity Coord; IL Sci Teachers Assn, NSTA, IL Assn of Chem Teachers, Amer Chemical Society Assn, NEA, IL Ed Assn; *office:* Thornridge HS Sibley & Cottage Grove Dolton IL 60419

KREIGER, FREDERICK DONALD, JR., Govt Teacher/ Coach; *b:* Cumberland, MD; *m:* Susan Shipley Kreiger; *c:* Frederick D. Kreiger III; *ed:* (BA) Soc Sci, 1977; (MS) Ed, 1980 Frostburg St Univ; *cr:* Teacher/Coach Allegany HS 1978-81; South Hagerstown HS 1981-85; Boonsboro HS 1985-89; South Hagerstown HS 1990; *ai:* Head Bsbl Coach; Chm Bsbl Monolacy Valley Athletic League; Prof Bsbl Chicago Cubs Organization; MD Cncl Soc Stud 1985-; Amer Bsbl Coachers Assn 1978-; Protective Order of Elks 1987-; Loyal Order of Moose 1981-; Clinician CA Ripken Bsbl Sch; Clinician GA Tech Bsbl Camp.

KREINBERG, TIMOTHY LEE, History Teacher; *b:* Quincy, IL; *m:* Mary Ann Aspeotis; *ed:* (BA) His, W IL Univ 1979; Grad Stud W IL Univ 1982-83; *cr:* Educl Consultant World Federalists Assn 1979-80; Teacher/Coach Quincy HS 1980-82; Grad Assistantship W IL Univ 1982-83; Teacher/Coach Unity HS 1983-; *ai:* Europe & Mexico Foreign Travel Spon 1988-; Ftbl, Bsktbl, Bsbl Asst Coach; Odyssey Travel Club Spon; Amer Legion Bsbl Coach 1980-82; Camp Ojibwa Cnslr 1984-86; IL Fed of Teachers Local VP 1990; E F Educl Tours Foreign Travel Spon Awd; *home:* 811 S 23rd Quincy IL 62301

KREINER, SANDRA BECKWITH, Social Studies Teacher; *b:* Akron, OH; *c:* J. Kraig; *ed:* (BA) Psych/Finance/Comprehensive Soc Stud, Univ of Akron 1973; Psych, Univ of Akron; *cr:* Soc Stud Teacher Cuyahoga Falls HS 1975-; *ai:* NHS Adv; NEA, OH Cncl Soc Stud 1973-; Amer Psychological Assn 1985-; Republican Party Committeeman; *office:* Cuyahoga Falls HS 2300 4th St Cuyahoga Falls OH 44221

KREINER, SHERYL LYNN, Social Studies Teacher; *b:* Yale, MI; *ed:* (BA) His/Scndry Teacher, Univ of MI Flint 1985; Dev in Ed; Grad Work in Counseling, Oakland Univ; *cr:* Soc Sci Teacher Brown City HS 1985-; *ai:* 7th Grade Spon; SADD Adv; Amer Assn for Counseling & Dev 1988-; Amer Sch Counseling Assn 1989-; *office:* Brown City HS 4290 2nd St Brown City MI 48416

KREITZ, CAROL JANE (SMITH), Fourth Grade Teacher; *b:* Allentown, PA; *m:* William Charles; *ed:* (BS) Elem Ed, 1968, (MED) Elem Guidance/Counseling, 1972 Kutztown St Coll; *cr:* 4th/6th Grade Teacher Boyertown Area Sch Dist 1968-74; Homebound Instr 1974-77, 2nd/4th Grade Teacher 1977- Bethlehem Area Sch Dist; *ai:* Cooperating Teacher for Stu Teachers; NEA, PA St Ed Assn, Bethlehem Ed Assn.

KREKE, LORETTA MARIE, Fifth-Sixth Grade Teacher; *b:* Breese, IL; *ed:* (BS) Elem Ed, 1972, (MS) Elem Ed, 1978 Southern IL Univ Edwardsville; *cr:* Teacher Elem Dist #12 1972-; *office:* Beckemeyer Grade Sch PO Box 307 Beckemeyer IL 62219

KRELL, SUSAN BECKER, English Teacher; *b:* Newark, NJ; *m:* Arthur; *ed:* (BA) Eng, Univ of CT 1969; (MAT) Eng, Farleigh Dickenson 1970; Grad Stud; *cr:* Urban Intern Essex Cty Coll 1969-70; Eng Teacher Rahway HS 1970-78, Farmingdale HS 1980-; *ai:* Future Teachers of America Adv; St Judge NCTE Writing Awds; Nom NYS Eng Cncl Teacher of Excl; Teacher of CLEP Course; *office:* Farmingdale HS Lincoln St Farmingdale NY 11735

KREMER, GREGORY LAWRENCE, Social Science Teacher/ Coach; *b:* Saginaw, MI; *m:* Connie; *c:* Michael Mellow, Siobhan Mellow, Heather Wakeman, Claire; *ed:* (BA) Sociology - Cum Laude, John Carroll Univ 1974; (MA) Sociolgy, Univ of Akron 1978; Enrichment Soc Sci, Purdue Univ, FL Keys Comm Coll; World Hunger Seminar Washinton Univ St Louis; *cr:* Teacher/ Coach Akron Hoban HS 1975-77, Cathedral HS 1977-78, Lafayette Cntrl Cath HS 1978-81, Lorain Cath HS 1984-88, Key West HS 1988-; *ai:* Ftbl Asst Coach Dist & Regional Champ 1988, Dist Regional Champ St Finalist 1989; Deans List; Grad Assistantship; Lorain Cty All Stars Bsbl Coach 1984; Lorain Cty All Star Ftbl Coach 1987; Runner Up Teacher of Yr 1989-; *office:* Key West HS 2100 Flagler Ave Key West FL 33040

KREMPASKY, MATTHEW FRANCIS, Music Teacher; *b:* Pompton Plains, NJ; *ed:* (BS) Music Ed, Gettysburg Coll 1982; *cr:* Music Teacher Columbia HS 1985-, Roxbury HS 1982-85; *ai:* Marching, Symphonic, Frosh Band Dir; Jazz, Brass, Percussion, Woodwind, Synthesizer Ensemble; Music Educators Natl Conference, NJ Ed Assn 1982-; Intnl Assn of Jazz Educators 1985-; Class Act Music Arranging Service Co-Founder 1987-; Various Music Wkshps; Write Music for Bands, Drum, Bugle Corps; *office:* Columbis HS 17 Parker Ave Maplewood NJ 07040

KREMPIN, L. JEAN STANLEY, Computer/Geometry Teacher; *b:* Oakland, CA; *m:* Charles Leroy; *c:* Carrie, Tony; *ed:* (BS) Chem, 1979, (MS) Math, 1982 Tarleton St Univ; *cr:* Classroom Teacher Hamilton HS 1980-; *ai:* Drill, UIL Number Sense, UIL Calculator Team; Flag Corps; Chrldrs; TX St Teachers Assn Local Pres 1987-89; TX Cncl Teachers of Math 1984-; *home:* Rt 1 Box 281 Hamilton TX 76531

KRESGE, WILLIAM EUGENE, 8th Grade Physical Sci Teacher; *b:* East Stroudsburg, PA; *ed:* (BA) Bio, 1971, (BS) Bio/ Scndry Ed 1974 E Stroudsburg Univ; Plant Pathology, PA St Univ 1972-73; Physics & Bio, E Stroudsburg Univ 1988-89; *cr:* 7th/8th Grade Sci Teacher Pleasant Valley Jr/Sr HS 1974-75; 8th Grade Phys Sci John C Mills Mid Sch 1975-89, Pleasant Valley Mid Sch 1989-; *ai:* Stock Market Game & Chess Club Adv; Model Rocket Club Spon; Pleasant Valley & PA St Ed Assn 1975-; NSTA 1985-; AIBS 1969-72; West End Little League (Secy, VP) 1967-85; PA St Univ Plant Pathology Research Fellowship 1972-73.

KRESSE, MARGARET FLETCHER, Guidance Counselor; *b:* Memphis, TN; *c:* Eric F.; *ed:* (BM) Music, N TX St Univ 1959; (MED) Guidance/Counseling, Univ of MS 1963; Univ of GA, Cnslr Inst, Univ of SW LA; Trained in Drug Prevention & Addiction Vail CO 1977; Coll Credit Trinity Univ; Johnston Inst Trng on Drug & Alcoholic Addiction 1983; Trng Wkshp at CDU of Arcadiana on Chemical Dependency 1985; Licensed Prof Cnslr by LA Prof Cnslr Bd of Examiners License Number 777; *cr:* Teacher Star City HS 1959-60, Grady HS 1960-61; Teacher/ Cnslr Murray Cty HS 1961-69; Cnslr Lafayette HS 1970-; *ai:* AA Support Group for Stus Returning from Treatment Centers 1970-; Children of Alcoholic Support Group; Children of Divorced & Separated Parents; Group Therapy for Depressed & Suicidal Stus; Self-Esteem Support Group; Lafayette Parish Cnslrs Assn Pres 1984-85; Cajun Raod Runners Club Mem, St Bernard Club of America; Amer Assn for Counseling Dev, LA Assn for Counseling Dev, Lafayette Parish Cnslrs Assn; Lafayette Ulster Project Cath Coord 1983-84; St Pius X Cath Church & Holy Cross Cath Church Song Leader & CCD Teacher; GA Jaycees STAR Teacher Awd 1968; Speaker on Depression & Suicide; Three St Key Club Convention Lafayette LA 1986, LA St Stu Cncl Convention Alexandria 1986, New Iberia 1987; Organized First Chapter of SADD Club in LA at Lafayette HS 1984; Directed & Produced Musical The Wizard of Oz Chatsworth 1967, The Sound of Music Chatsworth 1968; *office:* Lafayette HS 3000 W Congress St Lafayette LA 70506

KRETZLER, MARY JANE HUNTER, 5th Grade Math/ Science Teacher; *b:* Albany, NY; *ed:* Karen, Tom, Nancy; (BS) Elem Ed, SUNY Cortland 1960; (MS) Guidance, SUNY Albany 1969; *cr:* 5th/6th Grade Teacher 1960-65, Remedial Rdng Teacher 1966-67 Sch 17; 4th/5th Grade Teacher Sch 19 1970-; *ai:* PTA Life Membership Awd 1963; *office:* Public Sch 19 369 New Scotland Ave Albany NY 12208

KRIBELL, FLORENCE EDITH, Retired Teacher; *b:* Beresford, SD; *ed:* (BA) Soc Sci/Eng, Mt Marty Coll 1954; (ME) Elem/ Scndry Ed/His, Univ of SD 1959; Grad Stud Univ of SD Vermillion; *cr:* Teacher SD 1 Room Schls 1937-44; 6th-8th Grade Teacher Inwood Public Sch 1944-53; 7th/8th Grade Teacher Yankton Public Sch 1953-87; *ai:* SD Ed Assn Helpmobile 1937-44, 1953-87; NEA 1937-87; IA Educl Assn 1944-53; Delta Kappa Gamma Secy 1956-; NRTA 1987-; SD Teacher of Yr 1974; Valley Forge Teachers Medal 1973; Outstanding Soc Stud Teacher 1973; Certificate Leadership in Ed Mt Marty Coll 1988; Teacher Who Makes a Difference KDLT-TV 1987; Spec Recognition for Contribution in Athletics Youth Ed 1986-87; *home:* 706 Broadway #3 Yankton SD 57078

KRICK, PAUL BRIAN, Health Teacher; *b:* El Monte, CA; *ed:* (BA) His, Loras Coll 1984; Phys Ed, Driver Ed, Health Ed; *cr:* Phys Ed/World His Teacher Forreston HS 1984-85; Health/ DED/Phys Ed Teacher Bradford HS 1987-89; Health Teacher Rock Island HS 1989-; *ai:* Boys Var Bsktbl & Tennis Asst; Fellowship of Chrstn Athletes Coach 1989-.

KRIEDER, HARRY MOYER, Biology Teacher/Sci Dept Chm; *b:* Hershey, PA; *m:* Ruth J.; *c:* Marc A., Wayne E.; *ed:* (BS) General Sci, Millersville Univ 1963; (MST) Bio/Chem, Univ of ND 1968; Plant Sci Wkshp; Cmptr Assisted Instruction Bio; DE Nature Center Wildflowers & Amphibians; DuPont Company & Univ of DE Seminars; *cr:* Teacher/Dept Chm Forwood Jr HS 1963-71, Talley Jr HS 1972-81, Claymont HS 1982-; Teacher Concord HS 1990; *ai:* Sci Dept Chm; NHS Co-Adv; NEA 1965-; Brandywine Ed Assn 1982-; DE Assn Bio Teachers 1986-; Natl Sci Fnd Academic Yr Grant 1966; DE Presidential Excl Sci Awd 1988; Univ of DE Summer Coll Teaching Fellow 1989; *home:* 1105 Maplefield Rd Newark DE 19713

KRIEG, BARBARA NICELY, Gifted Education Teacher; *b:* Indianapolis, IN; *c:* Robin; *ed:* (BA) Elem Ed, Purdue Univ 1973; (MED) Gifted Ed, Coll of Mt St Joseph 1985; *cr:* 6th Grade Teacher Delshire Elem 1974-85; 4th-6th Grade Teacher of Gifted/ Talented Oak Hills Sch Dist 1985-; *ai:* Cmptr Club; Coach Intramural Bsktbl; Sci Curr Comm; Instr Super Saturday Prgm for Gifted; NSTA 1980-; OH Assn for Gifted Children 1987-; NEA 1976-; Cincinnati Historical Society Ed Advisory Comm 1989-; Delshire Elem Educator of Yr 1984; Sch Bd Recognition 1990; Presenter OAGC St Conference 1990; Miami Univ Math & Sci Grants; *office:* Oak Hills Sch Dist Delshire 4402 Glenhaven Rd Cincinnati OH 45238

KRIEG, JOHN MARK, Chemistry Teacher; *b:* North Manchester, IN; *m:* Beverly Marriott; *c:* John B., Julie A.; *ed:* (BS) Bio, Purdue Univ 1972; (MAT) Sci Ed, De Pauw Univ 1978; *cr:* Bio/Chem Teacher Oregon-Davis HS 1972-74; Sci Teacher Southwood Mid Sch 1974-75; Chem Teacher Sullivan HS 1977-90; *ai:* Asst Ftbl Coach 1981-; Varsity Track Coach 1977-88; Asst Varsity Bsktbl 1989; Jr HS Bsktbl 1977-81; Key Club Spon; IN Tournament of Academic Competition Coach 1978-; IN Assn of Chem Teachers 1988-; IN St Teachers Assn 1977-; Methodist Mens Organization 1989; Elks 1984-89; Kiwanas Club 1978-82; Jr Sci & Hum Symposium Awd 1988; Conf Coach of Yr Track 1978-88 1988; Amer Chem Society Awd 1987-88; Cert of Merit in Acad All Stars 1988; *office:* Sullivan H S 902 N Section St Sullivan IN 47882

KRIEGER, MORTON IRWIN, Math Teacher; *b:* Norwich, CT; *m:* Roslyn Sybil Becker; *c:* Lori, Beth; *ed:* (BS) Math, Univ of CT 1958; (MS) Ed, Eastern CT St Univ 1967; *cr:* Teacher Elizabeth St Sch 1961-62; Asst Prin 1970-71, Math Teacher 1962- Kelly Jr HS; *ai:* Dir & Color Guard PRIDE: Norwich Teach Lg (VP, Treas) 1961- Nom Teacher of Yr 1987; Norwich Mid Ft Lg (Founder, Bd of Dir) 1964- Founders Awd 1989; *office:* Kelly Jr H S Mahan Dr Norwich CT 06360

KRIENER, ROBERT PETER, Jr HS Mathematics Teacher; *b:* Fort Atkinson, IA; *m:* Susan Mary Mahoney; *c:* Michael, Christopher (dec); *ed:* (BA) Elem Ed/His, Upper IA 1970; (BA) Math, Univ of IA 1988; Phys Ed & Coaching; *cr:* 6th Grade Teacher/Coach Nashua Cmmty Schls 1970-76; 5th/6th Grade Teacher/Coach Olin Cmmty Schls 1976-79; 7th/8th Grade Math Teacher/Coach BGM Cmmty Schls 1979-; *ai:* HS Bsbl, Jr HS Math Teach Coach; Negotiations & Performance Base Pay Chm; BGM Ed Assn Pres 1980-81, 1983-84; Nashua Ed Assn Pres 1874-75; Olin Ed Assn Pres 1977-78; Nashua Cmmty Bsbl Assn Adv 1973; Brooklyn Deer Club Treas 1989; IA Bsbl Coaches Assn All-Dist Comm 1989-; Wapsi Conference Girls Bsktbl Coach of Yr 1978-79; S IA Cedar League Bsbl Coach of Yr 1980, 1983, 1986; Area Ed Assn Jr HS Math Teacher of Yr 1987, 1990; *home:* Box 342 Holiday Lake Brooklyn IA 52211

KRIENS, JILL ANNE CHURCHILL, 4th-8th Grade Teacher; *b:* Park Rapids, MN; *m:* Michael L.; *c:* Raquel; *ed:* (BS) Soc Stud, 1973, Spec Ed Cert/Learning Disabilities, 1977 Bemidji St Univ; *cr:* 7th-12th Grade Soc Stud Teacher Cleveland Public Schls, Sheyenne Public Schls; 7th-12th Grade Spec Ed/Learning Disabilities Teacher Menahga Public Schls; K-12th Grade Spec Ed Teacher Savoonga Bering Straits Sch Dist, Bristol Bay Borough Sch Dist; 4th-8th Grade Teacher Kena Borough Sch Dist; *ai:* Stu Government, Close Up; AFT; *home:* Box 8066 English Bay AK 99603

KRINER, LEON DALE, Data Processing Teacher; *b:* Du Bois, PA; *m:* Hazel Delp; *c:* Dale, Amy; *ed:* (BS) Bus Admin, 1957, (MS) Bus Ed, 1972 Penn St Univ; *cr:* Teacher Clearfield Cty Voc Tech 1970-73; Admin Du Bois Area Schls 1973-78; Teacher Jeff Tech 1978-; *ai:* Vica Opening & Closing Ceremonial Team Adv; JCDAVT Ed Assn Treas 1985-; Outstanding Voc Instr Awd PA Coll of Technology-1988; *office:* Jeff Tech Sch 100 Jeff Tech Dr Reynoldsville PA 15851`

KRISS, PHYLLIS S., Third Grade Teacher; *b:* Brooklyn, NY; *m:* Charles N.; *c:* David, Jaime; *ed:* (BA) Elem Ed, Brooklyn Coll 1962; (MS) Rdng/Spec Ed, Adelphi Univ 1986; *cr:* 2nd/3rd Grade Teacher 1962-67, Rdng Teacher Public Sch 288; Division Leader Summer Camps; Nursery Teacher Sum mer Camps; 2nd-4th Grade Teacher Public Sch 123 1977-; *ai:* Rdng Tutor; NYC Rdng Teachers, NYC Teachers of Eng; Kappa Delta Pi Mem 1962, Ed Honor Society; *office:* Public Sch 123K 100 Irving Ave Brooklyn NY 11237

KRIST, BETTY JANE, Assoc Professor Mathematics; *b:* Buffalo, NY; *ed:* (BS) Math, 1968, (MS) Math Ed, 1971, (EDD) Math Ed, 1980 SUNY Buffalo; Numerous Univs; *cr:* Math Teacher W Seneca Cntrl Sch 1968-76, 1977-81; Math/Cmptr Sci Assoc Prof D'Youville Coll 1981-87; Gifted Math Prgm Co-Dir SUNY Buffalo 1980-; Math Assoc Prof SUC Buffalo 1987-; *ai:* Grad Math Faculty Chairperson; SUC Buffalo Math Dir; NY St Summer Inst in Math, Sci Consultant; Niagara Frontier Math League Project Admin; EESA, DDE Title II Grant; NCTM Chairperson Editorial Panel 1987-88; Sci Service Advisory Cncl 1987-; Math Assn of America; Amer Assn for Advancement of Sci; Assn of Supervision, Curr Dev; W Seneca Teacher Center Bd of Dirs 1988-; W Seneca Teacher of Yr 1976; Co-Author 4 Books; Author 4 Book Chapters, 6 Articles; Speaker, Numerous Wkshps, Conferences; *office:* St Univ Coll 1300 Elmwood Ave Buffalo NY 14222

KRIST, CATHERINE A., Second Grade Teacher; *b:* E Pittsburgh, PA; *m:* Ernest A.; *c:* Tonette Krist Pels, Kathryn Krist Brunson, Pamela Krist Cook, Lawrence P.; *ed:* (BS) Psych, Duquesne Univ & Univ of Pittsburgh 1951; Ed Cert, Penn St & Seton Hill; Post Grad Work Elem Ed; *cr:* Substitute Teacher Imaculate Conception Church 1968-70; 2nd Grade Teacher St Agnes Sch 1970-; *ai:* Tutoring Ill in Hospital; Cath Teacher 1974; Newcomers Club of Irwin Pres 1957-58; Larimer PTA Pres 1975-76, Presidents Pin; Founders Day Chm 1959-69; Norwin Cncl of PTA Schls; *office:* St Agnes Sch 11400 St Agnes Ln North Huntingdon PA 15642

KRISTAN, LINDA ANDERSON, Enrichment Coordinator; *b:* Boston, MA; *m:* John; *ed:* (BA) Psych, William Smith Coll 1961; (MA) Government, Boston Univ 1963; Grad Stud, Univ of Penn, Temple Univ, Univ of VT, Johnson St Coll; *cr:* Teacher Vaux HS, Edison HS, Overbrook HS 1966-72, Teacher/Enrichment Coord Peoples Acad 1972-; *ai:* Drama; Scholars Bowl; Literary Magazine Adv; VT ASCD 1987-; ASCD; *office:* Peoples Acad Copley Ave Morrisville VT 05661

KRISTENSEN, SANDY JACOBS, Voc Home Economics Teacher; *b:* Atlantic, IA; *m:* Donald E.; *c:* Toni, Vicki Shaver, Clay, Dean, Kari; *ed:* (BSED) Voc Home Ec/Bus, NW MO St Univ 1967; Grad Stud; *cr:* Voc Home Ec Teacher Unified Sch Dist 430 1966-71, Audubon Cmmty Schls 1971-; *ai:* FHA; Sr Class Adv; Curr, Human Growth & Dev, Phase III Steering Comm; Cmptr Instr; NEA; ISA (Uniserv Pres 1974) 1967-; AHEA; IHEA Various Comm 1967-; Patterns Dist Chairperson 1980-; Embroiders Guild Comm Chairperson 1986-89; 4-H (Leader 1989-, Judge 1980-); Curr Writing for St Dept; Single Parenting Project Grant; Nutrition Project Grant; *office:* Audubon Cmmty Schls 3rd Ave Audubon IA 50025

KRITZ, IRENE BEDFORD, 7th/8th Grade Math/His Teacher; *b:* Pasadena, CA; *m:* Leroy Lawrence; *c:* LeAnn, Jamie, Kyle; *ed:* (BS) Ag Bus Management, Cal Poly Pomona 1967; *cr:* 2nd Grade Teacher Pomona Unified Elem 1968-69; 1st/2nd/4th-8th Grade Teacher Lo-Inyo Elem & Olancha Elem 1969-; *ai:* Reviewer of Prgm Quality Review; Pottery Teacher; His Day Coord; His, Soc Sci, Curr Dev; S Inyo Teachers Assn (Pres 1986-87, VP 1989-); 4-H Leader 1969-74, 1987-; Red Cross Instr 1985-89; Selected Mentor Teacher for 1990; *office:* Lo-Inyo Elem Sch Locust St Lone Pine CA 93545

KRIVAK, JOHN A., Religion Teacher; *b:* Allentown, PA; *ed:* (BA) Philosophy, Univ Scranton 1978, (MDIV) Theology, 1981, (THM) Theology, 1985 Mary Immaculate Seminary; (MED) Admin, Lehigh Univ 1988; Grad Stud Teacher Ed Lehigh Univ; *cr:* Teacher Notre Dame HS 1982-83, Reading Cntrl Cath HS 1983-86, Allentown Cntrl Cath HS 1986-; *ai:* NCEA 1983-; Lehigh Univ Assn of Sch Admin 1989-; *office:* Allentown Cntrl Cath HS 4th And Chew St Allentown PA 18102

KRIVOKUCHA, ELIZABETH W., Vocal Music/Art Instructor; *b:* Rochester, MN; *m:* Michael; *ed:* (BS) Voice/ Keyboard, Northern St Coll 1968; (MM) Music Ed, Univ of SD Vermillion 1974; *cr:* Vocal Instr Flandreau Indian Sch 1968-69, Pierre Jr HS 1969-76; Vocal/Art Instr Wilson Jr HS 1976-; *ai:* Swing Choir; Choreography; Vocal Ensembles; IA Choral Dir Assn St Bd 1981-87; Music Educators Natl Conference; Natl Fed Interscholastic Music Assn; Opera/Omaha Chorus Mem 1979-86; Voices of Mel Olson Chorus Mem 1976-79; Kanesville Cmmty Chorus 1987-89; *home:* 2519 7th Ave Council Bluffs IA 51501

KROEGER, JANET GARRIS, Guidance Director; *b:* Latrobe, PA; *m:* Gary H.; *c:* Mike; *ed:* (BA) Home Ec, WV Univ 1963; (MSED) Guidance, FL Atlantic Univ 1973; Grad Stud Guidance/ Admin & Supervision; *cr:* Home Ec Teacher McArthur HS 1963-65; Home Ec Teacher 1966-73, Guidance Cnslr 1974-79, Guidance Dir 1980- Sunrise Mid Sch; *ai:* Cheerleading Spon 1984-; Yrbk Adv 1983-86; WSMS Anchor Crew Adv 1982-; Child Abuse Designee; Disney World Trip Spon; BR Cty Counseling Assn; PTSA Sunrise Mid & Ft Lauderdale HS Equal Access Coord; Cyesis Prgm Designee; Mid Sch Guidance Dir Exec Comm 1988-; New River Optomist Club 1988; PTSA Service Awd (Sunrise 1981-85, Ft Lauderdale HS 1984); *home:* 2221 NE 19th St Fort Lauderdale FL 33305

KROELLS, SANDRA L., Kindergarten & ECSE Teacher; *b:* Glencoe, MN; *ed:* (BS) Elem Ed, Mankato St Univ 1975; *cr:* Classroom Aide 1975-77, Chapter I Teacher 1977-78, Kndgtn Teacher 1978- Central Elem; *ai:* Sci Comm & Fair; MN Kndgtn Assn, NAEYC 1978-; *office:* Central Elem Sch 210 W 7th St Norwood MN 55368

KROGNESS, MARY MERCER, English/Language Arts Teacher; *b:* Cleveland, OH; *m:* John M.; *ed:* (BA) Eng, 1961, (BS) Elem Ed, 1961 OH St Univ; (MA) Ed, John Carroll Univ 1974; Bread Loaf Sch of Eng Middlebury Coll; Writing Course, Lincoln Coll & Oxford Univ England 1986; Drama Wkshp Northwestern Univ 1973; Dialect Differences 1988; *cr:* K-6th Grade Teacher Columbus Public Schls 1961-62, Shaker Heights Schls 1962-66, Cleveland & Washington Schls 1966-68; Visiting Instr/ Preparation Teacher Cleveland St Univ 1986-87; Teacher of Gifted & Talented/Lang Art Teacher Shaker Heights City Schls 1971-; Eng/Lang Art Teacher Shaker Heights Mid Sch 1987-; *ai:* Sch-Wide & Lang Art Dept Publication Ed; Curr Comm, North Cntrl Evaluation, Lang Art Curr Guide, Young Authors Conference, Poetry Awd Selection Comm ChairpersonDebate Team Coach; Elem Section Comm Mem; Notable Books Comm; Task Force on Centers of Excl; Directed Plays; Lang Art Editorial Bd; NCTE 1978-, Writing Awd; Commission on Lit; Eng Speaking Union Awd Excl in Eng Teaching 1989; Articles Published; Martha Holden Jennings Fnd Master Teacher Awd; Salem HS Alumnae Awd; Eng Coalition Conference; *office:* Shaker Heights Mid Sch 20600 Shaker Blvd Shaker Heights OH 44122

KROKROSKIA, KAREN LEE, 7th/8th Grade Soc Stud Teacher; *b:* Picher, OK; *m:* Gary Lee; *c:* Sean L., Shanon Krokroskia Graham; *ed:* (BA) Elem Ed, 1980, (MS) Elem Admin, 1987 Pittsburg St Univ; *cr:* 7th/8th Grade World Geography/ Amer His/8th Grade Math Teacher Baxter Springs Mid Sch 1980-; *ai:* Drawing & Girl Talk Club; Coin Collecting; PSU Outstanding Stu Teacher 1980; KAMLE 1987-; House of Prayer Church (Sunday Sch Teacher, Youth Leader) 1987-; *office:* Baxter Springs Mid Sch 1520 Cleveland Baxter Springs KS 66713

KROLL, GREGORY EDWARD, 7th-12th Grade Phys Ed Teacher; *b:* Chicago, IL; *m:* Helen M. Witort; *c:* Kevin, Bridget, Paul; *ed:* (BA) Phys Ed/Health/Recreation, Aurora Univ 1972; Learning Disabilities, De Paul Univ; Phys Ed & Athletics Admin, Teachers Coll Columbia Univ; *cr:* Phys Ed Teacher Batavia Jr HS 1973-76, Mendham Twp Mid Sch 1976-77; Phys Ed/Health/Athletic Dir Morris Plains Mid Sch 1977-85; Phys Ed/Health Teacher/Phys Ed Dept Chm Morristown-Beard Sch 1985-; Dir Randolph Day Camp 1989-; *ai:* Head Var Bsbl, Asst Var Ftbl, Mid Sch Bsktbl Coach; Athletic Procedures, Curr Review, Faculty Concerns & Educl Policies, Sr Project Comms; Greater Morris Cty Jr Sch Coaches Assn (Pres 1983-85) 1977-85; US Bsbl Fed, Amer Bsbl Coaches Assn, NJ Bsbl Coaches Assn 1985-; Aurora Municipal Bsbl League 1973-76; Morris Cty Majors Bsbl League 1977-79; NJ Over 30 Bsbl League 1985-87, MVP 1985; *office:* Morristown-Beard Sch PO Box 1999 Morristown NJ 07962

KROMPASKY, RENATE MARIA, Principal; *b:* Hardheim, Germany; *ed:* (BA) Elem Ed, 1973, (MED) Rdng, 1976, (MED) Educl Admin, 1985 Univ of AZ; Several Wkshps; *cr:* 3rd Grade Teacher Prescott Dist 1973-74; 1st/3rd Grade Rdng Teacher Laguna Elem 1974-85; Asst Prin 1985-86, Prin 1986- Richardson Elem; *ai:* AASA 1989-; ASCD, NAESP, AZ Assn of Admins 1986-; Delta Kappa Gamma; Optimist Club (Secy, Treas) 1988-; Ed Alumni Cncl (VP 1988-89, Secy 1989-); *home:* 3943 E Paseo Dorado Tucson AZ 85711

KRON, REBECCA ANN, 5th Grade Teacher; *b:* Eau Claire, WI; *m:* James Alan; *ed:* (BS) Elem Ed, Il St Univ 1975; *cr:* Sub Teacher Moline Sch Sys 1976-77; 5th Grade Teacher C R Hanna Elem Sch 1977-; *ai:* Ed Comm; Orion Ed Assn (Assn Rep) 1985-9; IL Ed Assn; NEA; *office:* C R Hanna Elem Sch 900 14th Ave Orion IL 61273

KRONCKE, THOMAS JOHN, 3rd Grade Teacher; *b:* Hackensack, NJ; *m:* Sara Peatick; *ed:* (BA) Elem Ed, Paterson St Coll 1973; (MA) Cnclg, W Paterson Coll 1976; *cr:* 4th Grade Teacher Robert Erskine Sch 1973-1976; 5th Grade Teacher E G Hewitt Schl 1976-1981; 3rd Grade Teacher Peter Cooper Sch 1981-1989; *ai:* Through & Efficent Ed Comm; Teacher Evaluation Comm; Sci Curr Revision Comm; NEA 1973-; NJ Assn 1973-; Ringwood Ed Assn Pres 1980-82; Nutrition Grant; *office:* Peter Cooper Sch Fountain Dr Ringwood NJ 07456

KRONE, JAMES LAWRENCE, Social Studies Teacher; *b:* Beloit, KS; *m:* Sharon Lou Shamburg; *c:* Jason, Shannon; *ed:* (BS) Ed, KS St Univ 1974; *cr:* Soc Stud Teacher St Xavier HS 1974-76, Maur Hill Preparatory Sch 1976-83, Atchison Jr HS 1983-; *ai:* Bsktbl & Track Coach; *office:* Atchison Jr HS 301 N 5th St Atchison KS 66002

KRONENWETTER, SALOME MARIE LION, Third Grade Teacher; *b:* St Marys, PA; *w:* Roy R. (dec); *c:* Michael (dec), David, John, James; *cr:* Teacher Queen of the World Sch 1955-; *ai:* Cub Scouts Den Mother 1950-55; Elk Cty Concert Assn (Worker 1949-70, Bd of Dir 1965-70).

KROOS, JUDITH TRUELL, Asst Principal of Academics; *b:* Omaha, NE; *m:* Robert Joseph; *c:* Jennifer L., Sarah A.; *ed:* (BA) Eng/His, Univ of NE 1960; (MED) Curr, Univ of NV Las Vegas 1977; (MED) Scndry Admin, Coll of ID 1981; *cr:* Ed Cnslr Mountain Home AFB 1977-79; Asst Prin of Academics & Counseling Bishop Kelly HS 1979-; Grad Sch Faculty Coll of ID 1988-; *ai:* Sr Class Adv; NASSP, ASCD, ID Cnslrs Assn, NW Women in Ed Admin; Soroptimists; Boise Futures Fnd; Hugh O Brien Planning Task Force; Univ of ID Parents Advisory Cncl Pres; Boise St Univ Coll of Ed Advisory Bd; *home:* 8250 Crestwood Dr Boise ID 83704

KROPOG, SUSAN RESOR, Assistant Principal; *b:* New Orleans, LA; *m:* Olin L.; *c:* Troy M.; *ed:* (BA) Ed, SE LA Univ 1979; (MED) Spec Ed, Univ of New Orleans 1983; Grad Stud Admin & Supervision; *cr:* Teacher Estelle Elem Sch 1979-80, St Ann Sch 1980-83; Spec Ed Teacher St Ann Sch 1983-88; Part-Time Instr Univ of New Orleans 1984-87; Asst Prin St Ann Sch 1988-; *ai:* Drug Free Schls Sch Chm; Sch Building Level Comm Mem; NEA 1980-; Phi Kappa Phi 1978-80; Chapelle HS Distinguished Alumni Honor; Presidential Awd for Academic Excl SE LA Univ 1979.

KROPP, JOHN FREDERICK, 5th Grade Teacher; *b:* Chicago, IL; *m:* Liga; *c:* Tanya, John; *ed:* (BS) Elem Ed, Roosevelt Univ 1967; Outdoor Ed Norther Il Univ; *cr:* 6th Grade Teacher 1967-85; 5th Grade Teacher 1985-Dist #54; *office:* Adlai Stevenson III Elem Sch 1414 Armstrong Ln Elk Grove Village IL 60007

KROUSE, ANN WOLK, High School English Teacher; *b:* Chicago, IL; *m:* George; *c:* Kerry, Melissa; *ed:* (BA) Eng, Univ of IL 1977; Northwestern Univ; *cr:* Eng Teacher, Thomas Dewey H S 1978-82; Eng Teacher, Ben Franklin H S 1983-; *ai:* Fine Arts Club Adv; Fclty Senate; Phi Delta Kappa; Lions Club, Stu Speech Cntst Coord 1986-; *office:* Ben Franklin H S 1200 Green Bay Rd Lake Forest IL 60045

KRUDWIG, GERALDINE ZACHRY, English/French/Speech Teacher; *b:* De Queen, AR; *m:* Larry S.; *c:* Ashlie; *ed:* (BA) Eng/Fr, Ouachita Baptist Univ 1987; *cr:* Teacher Blevins Public Schls 1987-; *home:* Rt 1 Box 132 Mc Caskill AR 71847

KRUEGEL, LINDA A., Chemistry Teacher; *b:* Hackensack, NJ; *m:* Reinhard; *c:* Michele L., Brian R.; *ed:* (BS) Chem, Univ of RI 1971; (MAT) Sci Ed, Fairleigh Dickinson 1977; *cr:* Chemist Fritzche Dodge Olcott 1973-74; Chem Teacher Immaculate Heart Acad 1974-75, Paterson Cath 1975-76, Allentown HS 1977-80, Princeton HS 1980-; *ai:* Stu Cncl Adv; ETS Chem Achievement Comm; ETS AP Chem Reader; Mid Sts Evaluator; NJEA, NEA; *office:* Princeton HS 151 Moore St Princeton NJ 08540

KRUEGER, ALBERT R., IV, Science Teacher/Team Leader; *b:* Stuart, FL; *ed:* (AA) Bio, Brevard Comm Coll 1977; (BA) Biological Sci, 1979, (MA) Microbiology, 1981 CA St Univ Sacramento; (EDS) Educl Leadership, FL Atlantic Univ 1989; *cr:* Sci Teacher 1985-, Sci Team Leader 1989- South Fork HS; *ai:* Class Spon 1985-88; Tennis Coaach 1986-89; Golf Coach 1990; Phi Theta Kappa 1976; Kappa Delta Pi 1990; South Fork HS Teacher of Yr 1989-; *office:* South Fork HS 10205 SW Pratt & Whitney Rd Stuart FL 34997

KRUEGER, BARBRA K. (SELLERS), Phys Ed Teacher/Coach; *b:* Dallas, TX; *m:* Curtis Karl; *c:* Garrett, Mike T., Jason; *ed:* (BS) Eng/Phys Ed, E TX St Univ 1968; (MS) Mid-Management/Admin, TX A&I Univ 1988; *cr:* Phys Ed Teacher/Coach Bryan Adams HS 1968-70, Lincoln HS 1970-71, Jackson Mid Sch 1971-73, Rayburn Mid Sch 1975-85, Rudder Mid Sch 1985-; *ai:* Head Womens, Vlybl & Track Coach; Soc Comm, Publicity, Mid Sch Curr Comm Chm; TSTA, NEA, TAHPERD; NW Little League Bd 1979-83; *office:* Rudder Mid Sch 6558 Horn Blvd San Antonio TX 78240

KRUEGER, DANIEL WILLIAM, Vocal Music Director; *b:* Louisville, KY; *m:* Margaret Ann Wolf; *c:* David O., Stacy M.; *ed:* (BME) Music, E KY 1975; (MMED) Music Ed, Vandercook Coll 1980; *cr:* Jr HS Band Dir Glen Este Mid Sch 1975-85; Vocal Music Dir Glen Este HS 1975-; *ai:* Music Dir & Producer Musicals at Glen Este; Ye Olde Traditional Christmas Feaste Producer; Glen Este HS Choral Dir; OH Music Ed Assn 1975-; Amer Choral Dir Assn 1980-; Clermont Cty Choral Dir Assn 1985-; *office:* Glen Este HS 4342 Glen Este Withamsville Rd Cincinnati OH 45245

KRUEGER, JOAN CAROL (WHALEN), Fifth Grade Teacher; *b:* Austin, MN; *m:* Charles Robert; *c:* Barbara, Karla, Rhonda; *ed:* (BA) Elem Ed/Phys Ed, Trinity Coll 1978; (MA) Elem Ed, Natl Coll of Ed 1990; *cr:* 4th Grade Teacher 1978-79, 4th-5th Grade Teacher 1979-80, 4th Grade Teacher 1980-82 Douglas Elem; 5th Grade Teacher Carl Sandburg 1982-; *ai:* Upper Elem Sch Detention Prgm Coord; NEA, IEA 1979-; Excl in Teaching Awd 1989; *home:* 1157 W Pleasant Free Port IL 61032

KRUEGER, JOANNE NOVAK, 2nd Grade Teacher; *b:* Antigo, WI; *m:* James C.; *c:* Jeffrey, Jamie Brooks; *ed:* 2 Yr Cert Elem Ed, Langlade Cty Normal Sch 1952; (BS) Elem Ed, Univ of WI Oshkosh; Various Ed Courses; *cr:* 1st-8th Grade Teacher Antigo Area Rural Schls 1952-54, 1957-62; Primary Grades Teacher Winneconne Cmmty Sch 1963-; *ai:* Rdng Curr Comm; WI Ed Assn, NEA, Winneconne Ed Assn; *office:* Winneconne Elem Sch 233 S 3rd Ave Winneconne WI 54986

KRUEGER, JOYCE M., English Teacher; *b:* Trenton, MI; *m:* Herbert G.; *ed:* (AA) Sci and Arts, Monroe Cty Comm Coll 1973; (BS) Early Elem Ed, 1975, (MA) Elem Ed, 1979, (MA) Guidance & COunseling, 1988 Eastern MI Univ; Doctoral Prgm - Educl, Psych, Gifted & Talented, Univ Toledo; *cr:* 6th Grade Teacher Waterloo Elem 1975-81; Alternative Ed Teacher Orchard Alternative 1981-84; 8th Grade Eng Teacher Monroe Jr HS 1984-; Coord Scndry Enrichment Prgm/Monroe Public Schls; *ai:* Coord of Jr HS Enrichment Program TAG; Facilitator Cnslr Stud Support Groups; Monroe Cty Stu Assistance Prgm Comm; Phi Delta Kappa Mem; ASCD Mem; Kiwanis Monroe Breakfast; Recipient of Presidents Schlsp to EMU 1973; Phi Theta Kappa 1975; Mortarboard 1975.

KRUEGER, NANCY L., Business Education Dept Chair; *b:* Oconomowoc, WI; *ed:* (BSED) Bus Ed, 1970, (MST) Bus Ed, 1982 Univ of WI Whitewater; Grad Stud; *cr:* Bus Ed Teacher 1970-, Bus Ed Teacher/Dept Chair 1982- Milwaukee Luth HS; *ai:* Sch Evaluation Consortium; Steering Comm Chairperson; Phi Kappa Phi 1983-; Delta Pi Epsilon (Corresponding Secy 1983-85, VP 1985-87, Pres 1987-89, Past Pres 1989-) 1981-; NBEA, WI Bus Ed Assn 1970-; Milwaukee Area Bus Ed Assn 1971-; Luth High Founders 1983-; Mt Olive Luth Church Bd of Parish Ed 1990; Nom Milwaukee Area Bus Educator of Yr Awd; Spoke to Assn of Luth Scndry Sch Prin & Supts at Annual Conference on Bus Ed & Cmptr Ed in Luth Scndry Schls 1987; *office:* Milwaukee Luth HS 9700 W Grantosa Dr Milwaukee WI 53222

KRUG, BRENDA ILLENE (OHM), 5th Grade Teacher; *b:* Phoenix, AZ; *m:* Knox Edward; *c:* Katy, Kimberley; *ed:* (BA) Soc Sci, San Diego St Univ 1967; (MA) Ed, Pepperdine Univ 1975; *cr:* 4th Grade Teacher Hawthorne Elem 1968-70; 5th Grade Teacher 1970-74, 4th-6th Grade Teacher of Gifted & Talented 1975-80, 5th Grade Teacher of Gifted & Talented 1981- Leif Ericson Elem; *ai:* Alpha Kappa Delta 1979-; Girl Scout & Brownies Co-Leader; CA Congress of Parents, Teachers & Stus Incorporated Honorary Service Awd 1981; *office:* Leif Ericson Elem Sch 11174 Westonhill Dr San Diego CA 92126

KRUG, DON LEE, Jr High Band Director; *b:* Crawfordville, IN; *m:* Diana; *c:* Darren, Dyna; *ed:* (BA) Music Ed, IN St Univ 1966; (MA) Music Ed, Ball St Univ 1973; *cr:* Asst HS Band Dir 1969-71, Lewis Cass Jr/Sr HS 1971-; *ai:* Marching Band; Track Judge; Jr Natl Honor Society Comm Mem; Curr Comm Chm; At Risk Prgm; *home:* Box 271 107 W Grace Walton IN 46994

KRUG, JUNE, Teacher/Student Activities Dir; *b:* Indianapolis, IN; *ed:* (BS) Phys Ed, IN Univ 1963; (MA) Sch Admin/Supervision, CA St Univ Hayward 1983; (MA) Educl Leadership, St Marys Coll 1989; Additional Upper Division Coursework Art San Ramon Valley HS 1967-; *ai:* Stu Cncl Act Adv; Dist Curr Cncl; Renaissance Excl Coord; Bay Area Regional Administrative Trng Center Prgm; Class Adv 1978-81; Girls Athletic Assn Adv 1963-75; East Bay Athletic League Girls Tennis 1976-78, Swim Team 1967-78 Coach; Contra Costa Sports Assn Bd (Secy Treas, Ed) 1967-74; Fresno City/Cty & San Joaquin Valley Girls Swim Team Coach 1967; Fresno City Girls Phys Ed Curr Comm Secy 1963-67; CA Act Dir Assn 1986-; NASSP Div Stud Act 1988-; Natl Assn Wkshp Dir 1989-; Assn of CA Sch Admin Mem 1988-; Santa Ramon Valley Ed Assn (Mem 1967, Faculty Rep 1967-69); Prof Growth Advisory Bd 1967-73; Prof Rights & Responsibilities Advisory Bd 1969-72; Stained Glass Assn of Amer Mem 1974-; CA Art Educators Mem 1975-; CA Teachers Assn Mem 1963-; Walnut Creek Civic Arts Assn Bd of Dir 1983-88, Service 1987; Walnut Creek Parks & Rec Commission Chairperson 1983-88; Oakland Tribune Advisory Bd 1984-88; San Ramon Valley HS Staff Service Awd 1990; Women in Design San Francisco Bd Mem 1980-82; CA Work Experience Educators Assn Cty Rep 1982-83; Fresno Opera Assn (BD, Costume Designer, Wardrobe Mistress) 1964-68; West Accreditation Schls, Coll Accreditation, Quality Review Team Mem 1986-; WASC Accreditation Sch Self Study Chairperson 1987-88; San Ramon Valley HS WASC Accreditation Report 1988; San Ramon Valley Cmmty Resource Directory 1988; San Ramon Valley Ed Fnd Grant 1988; *office:* San Ramon Valley HS 140 Love Ln Danville CA 94526

KRUGER, GARY L., Teacher of Behavior Disorders; *b:* Kansas City, MO; *m:* Mary; *c:* Matthew, Jacob, Joseph; *ed:* (BS) Ed, Cntrl MO 1974; (MA) Counseling, Univ of MO Kansas City 1979; Cert Behavior Disorders, Univ of KS 1982; *cr:* Teacher/Shop Foreman Work Experience Prgm Tmr Kansas City Public Schls 1974-76; Teacher St Peters Cath Sch 1976-77; Group Home Mgr Div Youth Services St of MO 1979-80; Cnslr Cmmty Mental Health Center 1980-83; Teacher Indian Trail Jr HS 1983-89; Teacher Frontier Trail Jr HS 1989-; *ai:* Asst Cross Cntry Coach Olathe South HS; Indian Trail Jr HS Asst Track Coach; Girls Bsktbl & Boys Track Head Coach Frontier Trail Jr HS 1989-90; Kappa Delta Pi NHS Ed 1974; St Peters Cath Church Youth Minister 1983-; *office:* Frontier Trail Jr HS 15300 W 143rd St Olathe KS 66062

KRUGLE, MAX E., Civics/Psychology Teacher; *b:* New Kensington, PA; *m:* Barbara E. Wilson; *c:* Lindsay, Brian; *ed:* (BA) Comprehensive Soc Sci, Findlay Univ 1972; Indiana Univ of PA, Univ of Pittsburgh, Penn St Univ; *cr:* Teacher Burrell Sch Dist 1972-77, Charles Cty Sch Dist 1978-80, Freeport Area Sch Dist 1980-; *ai:* 9th Grade Asst Ftbl Coach; Freeport Area Core Team; PA Cncl for Soc Stud 1986-; *office:* Freeport Sr HS P O Drawer H Freeport PA 16229

KRUMMEL, BETTY SANDERS, High School English Teacher; *b:* Trousdale, OK; *m:* Clay Alex; *c:* Cassandra J. Krummel Golden, Melissa K.; *ed:* (BA) Eng, OK Baptist Univ 1955; (MRE) Religious Ed, SW Baptist Theological Seminary 1958; Albany St Coll; *cr:* Kndgtn Teacher First Baptist 1960-61; Mid Sch Eng Teacher First Baptist Schls 1972-76; Kndgtn Teacher Cmmty Chrstn Sch 1978-80; HS Eng Teacher Byne Memorial Baptist Sch 1983-; *home:* 404 5th Ave Albany GA 31701

KRUPA, CAROL CONNERY, Junior High Unit Chairman; *b:* Chicago, IL; *m:* Thomas W.; *c:* Karen, Thomas, Peter, Robert; *cr:* 7th-8th Grade Teacher St James Sch 1972-74, St Colette Sch 1974-76, St Raymond Sch 1983-; *ai:* Stu Cncl Spon; Stu To Save A Valuable Environment; NCEA; Nominee for Excl in Teaching 1988; *office:* St Raymond Sch 300 S Elmhurst Ave Mount Prospect IL 60056

KRUPNIK, THOMAS EDWARD, 5th/6th Grade Science Teacher; *b:* Shadyside, OH; *m:* Vicky Lynn Wade; *c:* Jennifer, Mark, Nikki; *ed:* (BSED) Elem Ed, OH Univ 1978; (MSED) Ed/Admin, Univ of Dayton 1984; Various Yearly Educl Wkshps; *cr:* 2nd Grade Teacher St Francis Xavier 1978-79; 4th Grade Soc Stud Teacher North Sch 1979-81; 5th/6th Grade Sci Teacher Steeple Valley Sch 1981-; *ai:* Sci Curr Comm; Past Girls Track Coach; *office:* Steeple Valley Sch 3105 Colerain Pike Martins Ferry OH 43935

KRUSE, DONNA MAE (HASSE), Second Grade Teacher; *b:* Nashua, MN; *m:* Arthur; *c:* Jill, Joel, Kimberly; *ed:* (BA) Elem Ed, Concordia Coll 1960; *cr:* 1st-4th Grade Teacher St Pauls Luth Sch 1953-54; 1st-2nd Grade Teacher Immanuel Luth Sch 1954-60; 2nd Grade Teacher St John Luth Sch 1983-; *ai:* 2nd-4th Grade Cherub Choir Dir; Asst Organist; Vacation Bible Sch Teacher & Dir; Sunday Sch Adult Study Leader; Luth Ed Assn 1983-; *office:* St John Luth Sch 305 Circle Ave Forest Park IL 60130

KRUSE, LINDA HUMPHREY, Third Grade Teacher; *b:* Los Angeles, CA; *m:* John Richard; *c:* Shawn R., Adam N.; *ed:* (AA) El Camino Jr Coll 1968; (BA) His/Elem Ed, 1970, Teaching Credential 1971 CA Univ Long Beach; Numerous Courses; *cr:* Legal Secy Superior Court Inglewood Ca 1964-69; Medical Secy Harbor Gen Hospital 1969-71; 3rd/4th Grade Teacher Eucalyptus Elem Sch 1971-75; 2nd/3rd Grade Teacher Jefferson Elem Sch 1975-; *ai:* El Segundo HS Booster Club; Selection of New Textbook, Lottery, Film, United Way, Chm Grant, Media, Soc, Yr Round Dist Cmmty, Calendar, Curr, Time Scheduling Comms; Eucalyptus PTA 1971-75, Teacher Awd 1974; Jefferson Elem PTA 1975-, Continuous Life Service Teacher Awd 1986; Math Ed CA Cncl Membership 1989 & 1990; Inglewood YMCA Camp Prgm (Ysmenettes, Camp Conrad Counseling) 1963-; Babe Ruth Bsbl Team Mom 1990; 1st Presbyn Church (Deacon, Elder, Sunday Sch Teacher, Youth Spon, Walk for Hunger Prgm); Hrs of Service & Yrs Dedication to Youth Recognition; Hawthorne Ed Teachers Assn Union Rep 1990; Volunteer Service to Youth & S

Bay Legal Secretaries Assn Awds; *office:* Jefferson Elem Sch 4091 W 139th St Hawthorne CA 90250

KRUSE, RICHARD AUGUST, Head Music Dept/Band Director; *b:* Schenectady, NY; *ed:* (BA) Music Ed 1964, (MA) Music/Wind Instruments 1965 Univ of MI; Musical Arts 1966; Cmptr Networking 1989; *cr:* Teaching Fellow Univ of MI 1964-66; Band Dir Romulus Jr HS 1966-; Mus Ic Dept Head Romulus Schls 1974-; Music Consultant Wayne Cty Intermediate Schls 1989-; *ai:* Chm for Dist & St Band Festival Sites; Clinican for Music Wayne Cnty; MI Sch Band & Orchestra Assn 1966- Lansing Performance 1983-85; Elem Wkshps 1986-; Washtenaw Cntry Club 1972-; Adjudictaor MSBOA Festivals 1982-; Teacher of Yr 1983 Romulus Schls; Finalist for Wayne Cty Teacher Yr 1989; Runner-Up Person of Yr Associated Newspapers; *office:* Romulus Sch 37300 Wick Rd Romulus MI 48174

KRUSE, THOMAS R., Director of Instrumental Music; *b:* Aurelia, IA; *m:* Judy Thompson; *c:* Scott, Stacy; *ed:* (BA) Music Ed, 1962, (MA) Music Ed, 1966 Univ of SD; *cr:* Instrumental Music Teacher Boyden-Hull Cmmty Schls 1962-69; Instrumental Music/Music Theory Teacher IA Cntrl Comm Coll 1969-74; Instrumental Music Teacher Cherokee Cmmty Schls 1974-; *ai:* Pep, Jazz, Marching, Concert Bands; IA HS Music Assn (Bd Mem, Adjudicator) 1984-87; NW IA Band Dir Assn Pres 1976; IA Bandmasters Assn Mem 1962; Guest Conducted Several IA Festivals; *home:* 540 Bailey Ct Cherokee IA 51012

KRUSEN, HANK E., JR., Science Department Teacher; *b:* Bryn Mawr, PA; *m:* Elisabeth A.;; *c:* Lindsey E.; *ed:* (BA) Bio, Ottawa Univ 1970; (MLA) Psych, SMU Baker Univ 1980; *cr:* Phys Sci Teacher Washington HS 1970-72, Eisenhower Jr HS 1972-73; Bio Teacher F L Schlagle HS 1973-81; General Bio/CP Bio Teacher Olathe North HS 1981-; *ai:* KATS 1988-; NSTA 1989-; Presenter KATS, NSTA 1989; *home:* 4707 W 77th St Prairie Village KS 66208

KRUSER, EDWARD, Social Studies Teacher; *b:* Staten Island, NY; *m:* Jeanne Stannard; *c:* Garrett, Derrick; *ed:* (BA) Ed, Soc Cci, 1971, (MS) Ed, His, 1980 St Univ Oneonta; *cr:* Soc Stud DE Acad 1971-; *home:* RD 1 Box 3B Franklin NY 13775

KRUSHENSKI, BARBARA GOUGE, Second Grade Teacher; *b:* Washington, DC; *m:* Kenneth Raymond; *c:* Kevin, Kurt, Karl; *ed:* (BS) Elem Ed, E Carolina Univ 1972; (MS) Curr/Rdng, Univ of TN 1975; *cr:* 4th Grade Teacher Berkeley Manor Elem Sch 1972-73; 4th/6th Grade Math Teacher Cntry Day Sch 1973-74; Grad Stu Univ of TN 1974-75; 2nd/3rd Grade Teacher Woodland Elem Sch 1975-; *ai:* Oak Ridge Ed Assn, TN Ed Assn, NEA 1975-; Intnl Rdng Assn 1988-; Anderson Cty Bar Auxiliary (Co-Pres 1985-86, Treas 1981-82, 84-85); Univ of TN Non-Service Fellowship; *office:* Woodland Elem Sch 168 Manhattan Ave Oak Ridge TN 37830

KRUTSCHEWSKI, PENELOPE L., 4th Grade Teacher; *b:* Ferndale, MI; *ed:* (BA) Ed, 1967, (MA) Environmental Ed, 1971 MI St Univ; *cr:* 4th Grade Teacher Lansing Sch Dist 1969-; Adjunct Instr MSU 1985-; *ai:* Budget Comm; Ski Club; *office:* Forest View Elem Sch 3119 Stoneleigh Dr Lansing MI 48910

KRUVCZUK, SANDRA DEWOLFF, English/Reading Teacher; *b:* Philadelphia, PA; *m:* Robert; *c:* Nicole, Heather, Michelle; *ed:* (BS) Ed, 1972, (MED) Rdng Specialist, 1979 Temple; Wkshp & Grad Course in Appleworks; *cr:* Rdng Teacher John Wanamaker Jr HS 1973-74; Eng Teacher Wm Tennent Intermediate HS 1974-76; Rdng/Eng Teacher Redeemer Luth Sch 1981-; *ai:* Sch Literary Magazine Spon; Keystone St Rdng Assn 1988-; Redeemer Youth Group Dir 1985-89; GSA Cookie Coord 1983, 1987-88; Co-Authored 7th & 8th Grade Stu Plays; Articles Published; Co-Established a Nursery & Kndgtn at Good Shepherd Church; *office:* Redmeemer Lutheran Schl 3212 Ryan Ave Philadelphia PA 19136

KUBAL, CYNTHIA CANLAS, English Teacher; *b:* New Orleans, LA; *c:* Ursula; *ed:* (BA) Eng, CA St Univ 1969; *cr:* Eng Teacher Mark Keppel 1981-; *ai:* CSF Adv; Sec 1985-87; Pres 1987-89; Sec 1989- MKHS Faculty Assn; Voted Most Appreciated Teacher 1987; *office:* Mark Keppel H S 501 E Hellman Ave Alhambra CA 91801

KUBERA, MARY BETH, English Teacher/Hum Chair; *b:* La Salle, IL; *ed:* (BA) Eng, Walsh Coll 1977; (MED) Ed, Loyola Univ 1987; *cr:* Jr HS Teacher Our Lady of Peace Sch 1974-76; Eng Teacher Marillac HS 1976-; *ai:* Yrbk, Frosh Class, Service Club Moderator; NCTE, IL Cncl Teachers of Eng; *office:* St Louise De Marillac HS 315 Waukegan Rd Northfield IL 60093

KUBINA, BEVERLY POWELL, Mathematics Teacher; *b:* Pensacola, FL; *m:* Gary; *ed:* (BS) Math Ed, Troy St Univ 1978; (MED) Scndry Math, Univ of S AL 1986; *cr:* Math/Psych Teacher Sparta Acad 1978-79; Math Teacher K J Clark Mid Sch 1979-81, Citronelle Mid Sch 1981-; *ai:* Math Team & Break-Time Tutoring Spon; Supts Advisory Cncl; Citronelle Mid Sch Cmmty Relations Comm Mem; Mobile Cty Ed Assn, AL Ed Assn, NEA 1979-; St Pauls Evangelical Luth Church 1988-; Outstanding Grad Stu Awd; Youth & Adult Ed Univ of S AL 1986; Teacher of Yr Citronelle Mid Sch 1987-88.

KUBLBECK, JANE ANN, Home Economics Teacher; *b:* Worcester, MA; *m:* David P.; *ed:* (BS) Scndry Home Ec Ed, Framingham St Coll 1981; (MBA) Bus, NH Coll 1986; *cr:* Teacher Salem HS 1981-; *ai:* FHA 1981-; Home Ec Adv 1981-; Class Adv 1986-; Steering Comm Comprehensive Guidance 1989-; Fashion Show Adv 1985-; Adv Prin 1987-88; NH Home Ec Assn Rockingham Dist Co Chairperson 1983-84; *office:* Salem HS 44 Geremonty Dr Salem NH 03079

KUCHAR, ALEX N., Sixth Grade Teacher; *b:* Jersey City, NJ; *m:* Kathy Kane; *c:* Christine, Alex, Kevin, Kaitlin; *ed:* (BA) Elem Ed, Jersey City St Coll 1969; *cr:* 5th Grade Teacher Englewood Cliffs 1969-70; 7th Grade Teacher Hanover Township 1970-71; 5th Grade Teacher Huber St Sch 1971-; 6th Grade Teacher Clarendon Sch 1971-; *ai:* Sci Trip Elem Coord; Audio-Visual Coord Clarendon; Asst Cross Cntry & Girls Bsktbl Coach Secaucus HS; *office:* Clarendon Sch 685 5th St Secaucus NJ 07094

KUCHTA, LINDA ZACCARI, Sixth Grade Teacher; *b:* Baltimore, MD; *m:* Steven Thomas; *c:* Steven T., Heather L.; *ed:* (BS) Elem Ed/Psych, Univ of MD 1972; (MS) Ed/Rdng, John Hopkins Univ 1977; *cr:* 6th Grade Teacher Our Lady of Perpetual Help 1972-79, John Paul Regional 1979-; *ai:* Mid St Evaluation, Teacher Fundraiser, Math Curr, Math-A-Thon Chairperson; Sensa Team Leader; *office:* John Paul Regional Sch 6946 Dogwood Rd Baltimore MD 21207

KUCHYNKA, RANDALL G., World His/US His Teacher; *b:* Lawton, OK; *ed:* (BA) His, Cameron Univ 1981; Grad Trng, Midwestern St Univ, OK St Univ; *cr:* Adjunct Instr Cameron Univ 1988-; Classroom Teacher Eisenhower Sr HS 1983-; *ai:* Academic Team Volunteer Coach; Young Democrats Adv; Prof Ed Assn of Lawton (Treas 988-, VP 1990); OK Ed Assn St Delegate 1988-; NEA Natl Delegate 1990; OK Historical Assn 1979-; NCSS 1983-; *office:* Eisenhower Sr HS 52nd W Gore BLvd Lawton OK 73505

KUCZYNSKI, EVELYN KATHLEEN, Mathematics Teacher; *b:* Blakely, GA; *c:* Joseph E. Griffin; *ed:* (AA) Ed, Wallace Coll 1978; (BS) Elem Ed, 1979, (MS) Mid Chldhd, 1982 Troy St; Working Toward Masters; *cr:* Teacher Early Cty Mid Sch 1979-; *ai:* Beta Club & Chrldr Spon; Steering Comm; GA Assn of Ed; Early Cty Assn of Ed Past Treas; NEA, ASCO 1990; ECAE, GAE, NEA, ASCD, Kappa Delta Pi; Gamma Sigma Pi; Pilot Club Past Mem; ECAE Past Treas; First Baptist Church (Youth Sunday Sch Teacher, Mem of Choir); *office:* Early Cty Mid Sch Columbia St Blakely GA 31723

KUDO, MAE T., 5th Grade Teacher; *b:* Honolulu, HI; *m:* Tsukasa; *c:* Kimberley, Leslie; *ed:* (BA) Ed, 1965, Elem Ed, 1979 Univ of HI; *cr:* Teacher Lincoln Sch, Queca Kaahuwanu Elem Sch; *office:* Kaahumanu Elem Sch 1141 Kinau St Honolulu HI 96814

KUEBLER, KAREN L., Science Teacher; *b:* Milwaukee, WI; *c:* Lisa Schmick, Ernst Schmick; *ed:* (BED) Sci Ed, Univ of Miami 1966; (MS) Sci Ed, FL Intnl Univ 1978; Ed Research & Dev Teacher; *cr:* Sci Teacher Miami Killian Sr HS 1967-69, Facilitator Drug Intervention Counseling 1987; Sci Teacher Miami Palmetto Sr HS 1969-; *ai:* SADD Spon; IOF; Social Forum VP 1982-85; *office:* Miami Palmetto Sr HS 7460 SW 118th St Miami FL 33156

KUEHLWEIN, ROBERT ELVIR, Social Studies Teacher; *b:* Chicago, IL; *m:* Teresa Hall; *c:* Michael, Kevin, Shannon; *ed:* (BA) Poly Sci, Ripon Coll 1960; (MED) Soc Sci, Univ of DE 1972; Various Soc Stud Courses; Military Intelligence Trng US Army 1960-68; *cr:* Teacher William Penn HS 1969-; *ai:* NHS Selection Comm; CEA, DEA, NEA Rep 1969-; DE Cncl for Soc Stud 1988-; Episcopal Cathedral Church of St John (Jr Warden 1989-, Vestry Mem 1984-); Pepper Ridge Civic Assn Rep 1987-; Various Animal Rights & Environmental Organizations Activist; DE Sch Dist Teacher of Yr 1972; Natl Cncl for Geographic Ed Meritorious Teaching Awd 1971; William Penn HS Teacher of Yr 1987; *office:* William Penn HS Basin Rd New Castle DE 19720

KUEHN, ALICE ASPLUND, Third Grade Teacher; *b:* Commonwealth, WI; *m:* Francis W.; *c:* Kathryn, Richard W., Laurie Kuehn Gelhar; *ed:* (BS) Kndgtn Primary Ed, Univ WI Oshkosh 1955; Grad Stud; *cr:* 2nd Grade Teacher Elem Sch 1956-57; 1st-8th Grade Teacher Osborn Sch 1957-59; 3rd-4th Grade Teacher 1959-61, 3rd Grade Teacher 1973- Markesan Dist Schls; *ai:* Rock River Rdng Cncl 1988-; WI St Rdng Assn 1989-; *office:* Markesan Dist Schls 100 Vista Blvd Manchester WI 53945

KUEHN, REMAE L., Bus/Office Education Teacher; *b:* Elgin, ND; *ed:* (AA/AAS) Legal Secy, Bismarck Jr Coll 1974; (BS) Bus & Office Ed, Dickinson St Coll 1976; *cr:* Bus & Office Ed Center HS 1976-; *ai:* FBLA Adv; Center Ed Assn (VP 1989-, Secy 1986-88); ND Bus & Office Ed Assn Secy 1987-88; Named Miss Future Bus Teacher 1976, Competed Nationally in Washington DC; *office:* Center HS Box 248 Center ND 58530

KUH, ELAINE E. (OTTO), Teacher; *b:* Chicago, IL; *m:* Robert; *c:* Robert, Diane, Jonathan; *ed:* (BA) Elem Ed, Concordia Univ 1959; Various Seminars & Wkshps in Early Chldhd Ed, Rdng; *cr:* 3rd-5th Grade Teacher St Johns Luth Sch 1959-60; 4th Grade Teacher Marengo Zion Luth 1960-64; 1st-4th Grade Teacher Chicago Zion Luth 1961-64, 1969-72; Teacher Chicago Public Schls 1964-68, Salem Luth 1972-; *ai:* Spelling Bee Coord; Choir Dir; Asst Prin; Luth Ed Assn 1986-; *home:* 837 Overlook Ct E Frankfort IL 60423

KUHLES, BILLIE LOUISE, 5th Grade Teacher; *b:* Yuma, AZ; *ed:* (BA) Elem Ed, 1968, (MA) Ed/Admin, 1979 Univ of NV Reno; *cr:* 3rd Grade Teacher 1968-72, 4th Grade Teacher 1972-79, 5th Grade Teacher 1979- Lincoln Park Elem Sch; *ai:* NEA 1968-; NV St Ed Assn 1968-; Washoe Cty Teachers Assn Rep 1986-; NV Humane Society 1980-; Animal Protection Inst Greenpeace Lifetime Mem 1980-; Washoe Cty Teachers Dedicated Service Awd 1988.

KUHLMEIER, SANDRA GELLERT, 4th Grade Teacher; *b:* Cincinnati, OH; *m:* Raymond J. Jr.; *c:* Kassie, Adam; *ed:* (BS) Elem Ed, Ball St Univ 1970; *cr:* 1st Grade Teacher Longview Elem 1970-71; 5th Grade Teacher 1972; 3rd Grade Teacher 1972-73 George Cannon Sch; 4th/5th Grade Teacher Baton Rouge Prep Sch 1983-89; 4th Grade Teacher Episcopal HS 1989-; *office:* Episcopal H S 3200 Woodland Ridge Blvd Baton Rouge LA 70816

KUHN, BERNARD MICHAEL, United States History Teacher; *b:* Bennington, VT; *m:* Jan Gallant; *c:* Amy, Sara; *ed:* (BA) Scndry Ed, Johnson St Coll 1971; Numerous Courses Johnson St 1971; *cr:* Soc Stud Teacher Bellows Free Acad 1972-; *ai:* 5th-8th Grade Stu Cncl Adv; VT Ed Assn, NEA; Knights of Columbus Trustee 1988-; *office:* Bellows Free Acad Hunt St Fairfax VT 05454

KUHN, DANIEL FRANKLIN, Social Studies Teacher; *b:* Warsaw, IN; *m:* Julie H; *c:* Emily Jayne; *ed:* (BS) Soc Stud, 1971, (BA) Soc Stud 1976 IN Univ; *cr:* Teacher Warsaw Cmmty HS 1977-; *ai:* TESA/Teacher Trng Model Co-Dir; Natl Assn of Soc Stud 1990; *office:* Warsaw Cmmty HS 1 Tiger Ln Warsaw IN 46580

KUHN, DEANNA JENKINSON, Third Grade Teacher; *b:* Spokane, WA; *c:* Kelly A.; *ed:* (BA) Lit/Eng, Gonzaga 1959; Univ of S CA, Univ of CA Los Angeles, Univ of San Diego; *cr:* 3rd Grade Teacher Jesuit Mission Sch 1959-60; 5th Grade Teacher Elmendorf AFB 1961-64; 2nd-5th Grade Teacher Los Angeles City Schls 1965-; *ai:* Soc Comm 1978-84; Sci Fair Comm 1980-; United Teachers of Los Angeles (Chairperson 1980-, House of Rep 1986-, Bd of Dir 1988-); CTA, NEA; Fullbright Teacher Exch to England 1976-77; *home:* 419 N Larchmont Blvd #189 Los Angeles CA 90004

KUHN, KATHRYN ERNA, Highly Able Special Enrichment; *b:* Hanover, NH; *ed:* (BS) Elem Ed, Towson St 1972; (MS) Elem Ed, Salisbury St/Loyola 1982; Several Wkshps; *cr:* 3rd-5th Grade Teacher 1972-85; 1st-5th G/T Lab Teacher 1985- Buckingham Elem; *ai:* Film Festival Spon; after Sch Calligraphy Teacher; Yrbk Spon; Sci Fair Coord; Art Teacher for 45 Min Daily; Gifted & Talented Act Coord; Elem Rep on Worcester Cty Cultural Arts Comm; Coord for Artist in Residence Prgm; Public Relations Rep; TESA Ldshp Conf-TESA Teacher to Local Cty Teachers 1985; Buckinghams Teacher of Yr 1989; Mini-Grant from Delmarva Power & Light to Expand Ecology Unit 1987; St Film Festival Winner 1988; Outward Bound Chesapeake Prgm for Educators-Summer 1988; Cty Sci Fair Winner 1987 & 1989; *office:* Buckingham Elem Sch 100 Buckingham Rd Berlin MD 21811

KUHN, VICKI SUE (AKERS), Mathematics Teacher; *b:* Dayton, OH; *m:* Edward A. Jr.; *ed:* (BS) Elem Ed, Cumberland Coll 1972; (MED) Teacher Leader in Curr/Supervision, Wright St Univ 1983; Data Processing, Project IMPACT, Mathematical Problem Solving in Mid Sch; *cr:* Teacher Clearcreek Local Schls 1972-; *ai:* Cheerleading & Newspaper Adv; CEA, NEA, OCTM; Centerville Cmmty Band; *office:* Springboro Jr HS 705 S Main St Springboro OH 45066

KUKES, PATRICK J., Orchestra Director; *b:* Laurel, MT; *c:* Kiara, Kelly; *ed:* (BA) Music Ed, MT St Univ 1974; Grad Work; *cr:* Orch Dir C R Anderson Mid Sch & Capital HS 1974-; *ai:* Music Dept Chm; Staff Dev Comm; Track & Bsktbl Coach; 4-H Adv; Helena Ed Assn Exec Bd 1976, 1981-83, 1988; MT String Teachers Assn VP 1980-81; Civitan Club Pres 1980-81; Composer; Published Articles; Artist & Studio Musician; *office:* Capital HS 100 Valley Dr Helena MT 59601

KUKIS, GARY, Mathematics Instructor; *b:* Cleveland, OH; *ed:* (AA) Soc Sci, Amer River Coll 1970; (BA) Math, CA St Univ 1973; (MED) Scndry Ed, Stephen E Austin Univ 1980; Grad Stud Math, Univ of Houston & Sam Houston St Univ; *cr:* Math Instr San Juan Unified Sch Dist 1974-78, Humble HS 1978-, North Harris Cty Coll 1980-; *ai:* TX St Teachers Assn Mem 1985-; Church Mem 1979-; Level III Math Instr; *home:* 20507 Spoonwood Humble TX 77346

KUKOWSKI, ELIZABETH ANN (BILLO), 5th Grade Teacher; *b:* Milwaukee, WI; *m:* Ronald Lambert; *c:* Kristyn, Laura, Jacklyn; *ed:* (BS) Ed, Cardinal Stritch Coll 1967; Post Grad Stud Alverno Coll; *cr:* 5th Grade Teacher St Bernard Sch 1967-68; 1st Grade Teacher A E Burdick 1968-70; All Grades Substitute Teaching 1970-76; 5th Grade Teacher St Veronica Sch 1976-; *ai:* Vlybl, Sftbl Coach; Girl Scout Leader; Cooperating Teacher Stu Teachers Alverno Coll; Religious Ed Teacher; NCEA 1975-; WI Cncl for Soc Stud 1986-; Archdiocesan Evaluating Team Prof Dev 1981; St Veronicas Sch Ed Comm Chairperson 1980 Awd of Excl 1980; Certificate of Appreciation Outstanding Service Archdioces of Milwaukee & Catholic Home & Sch; *office:* St Veronica Schl 341 E Norwich St Milwaukee WI 53207

KUKULICA, ANN PERREIRA, Teacher/Curriculum Leader; *b:* Oakland, CA; *m:* Nicholas; *ed:* (AA) General Ed, Chabot Jr Coll 1968; (BS) Phys Ed, CA St Hayward 1969-70; *cr:* Teacher New Haven Unified 1970-; *ai:* Athletic League Secy; *office:* New Haven Mid Sch 2801 Hop Ranch Rd Union City CA 94587

KULA, MURRAY ROBERT, Health/Phys Ed Teacher; *b:* Springfield, MO; *m:* Cheryl; *c:* Brian, Lindsey, Brigg; *ed:* (BA) Phys Ed, 1971, (MA) Phys Ed, 1976 Univ Northern Co; *cr:* Teacher/Coach Highland HS 1971-72, San Juan HS 1972-74, Park HS 1974-75, Windsor HS 1984-; *ai:* Var Ftbl & Track;

Lettermans CLub; Natl Strength & Conditioning Assn 1985-; NEA 1984-; Dev Contemporary Health Curr, Soc Issues Currently Used in Dist; *office:* Windsor HS 110 W Main St Windsor CO 80550

KULACK, ROBERT JOHN, Social Studies Dept Chair; *b:* Winnipeg MB, Canada; *m:* Lynn Stewart; *c:* Mark, Christopher, Katie; *ed:* (BA) Geography, 1968, (MED) Geography, 1971, Admin, 1985 Univ of ND; *cr:* 7th/9th Grade Teacher Schroeder Jr HS 1969-; *ai:* Ftbl & Track Coach; Natl Cncl for Geographic Ed Outstanding Teacher of Geography 1975, 1980; Grand Forks Ed Assn Pres 1985-86; ND Cncl for Soc Stud Pres 1973-74, 1981-82; Assn of ND Geographers; North Cntrl Grand AM Bsktbl Tournement Mgr 1988-; ND Adv & Responder Natl Commission on Soc Stud; Outstanding Educator Awd Center for Teaching & Learning Univ of ND 1986; *office:* Schroeder Jr HS 800 32nd Ave S Grand Forks ND 58201

KULAGE, RICHARD HENRY, Science Teacher; *b:* St Louis, MO; *m:* Joyce Marie Mihalovich; *c:* Allison, Melissa; *ed:* (BS) Bio, 1968, (BS) Ed, 1968, (MA) Bio, 1972 NE MO St Univ; Grad Stud Scndry Admin; *cr:* 9th Grade Bio Teacher Kirby Jr HS 1969-74; Sr Life Sci Teacher Hazelwood East HS 1974-78; Bio/Sci Teacher Francis Howell 1978-; *ai:* Scndry Sci Fair Spon; Francis Howell Steering Comm; Francis Howell Ed Assn VP 1989-; NEA 1970-; Francis Howell Band Boosters VP 1988-89; Natl Sci Fnd Grant; *office:* Francis Howell North HS 2549 Hackman Rd Saint Charles MO 63303

KULHANEK, JEFFERY MORGAN, Science Teacher/Dept Head; *b:* Saginaw, MI; *m:* Karen Gilmour; *ed:* (BS) His/Bio, N MI 1982; (MS) Ed Admin/Supervision, E Carolina; Numerous Courses; *cr:* Sci Teacher/Dept Head 1982-, Asst Admin 1988- Knapp Jr HS; *ai:* Bsktbl & Bsbl Coach; Sci Club & Albemarle Pamlico Esturine Study Adv; ASCD 1989-; Natl Wildlife Fed 1982-89; Developed Integrated Math/Sci Curr; Nom Governors Awd of Excl; Spoke at Natl Mid Schls Conference Toronto Canada 1989; NC Math Conference Speaker 1990; *office:* J P Knapp Jr HS Star Rt Box 2 Curriluck NC 27929

KULL, KENNETH K., Band Director; *b:* Chicago, IL; *m:* Mary Margaret E. Lamberton; *c:* Damien Blackwell, Mark Blackwell, Leslie; *ed:* (BME) Music Ed, Benedictine 1966; (MME) Music Ed, NE at Lincoln 1973; (EDSPEC) Admin, NE at Lincoln 1984; (MS) Scndry Counseling, NE Omaha 1990; *cr:* K-12th Grade Music Teacher Unifed Sch Dist 221 Haddam 1966-67; 5th-12th Grade Music Teacher Aquinas HS 1967-74, SENC Stella 1974-77; 6th-12th Grade Band Teacher Plattsmouth Cmmty Schls 1977-; *ai:* Band; Friends Against Drugs; NSBA Secy 1983-84; MENC, NMEA, NEA, NSEA, PEA; *home:* 3816 Cypress Ct Plattsmouth NE 68048

KULLE, CARLTON DAVID, JR., Third Grade Teacher; *b:* Waukegan, IL; *m:* Pauline Margaret Olson; *c:* Kimberly R. Ness, Karen M. Buckley; *ed:* (BAED) Ed, Seattle Pacific Univ 1961; (MED) Counseling/Guidance, Univ of Miami 1969; *cr:* Teacher Alki Elem 1961-78; Spelling Consultant Seattle Public Schls 1976; Teacher Cascade Elem 1978-; *ai:* Dist General Instruction Comm; Safety Patrol & Intern Supvr; NEA, WA Ed Assn 1961-; Renton Ed Assn 1978-; PTA Golden Acorn, Meritorious Service to Children; NDEA Eng Fellowship Univ WA 1965, Fellowship Cnslr/Guidance Univ Miami 1968-69; Renton Elem Sch Teacher of Yr 1988-89.

KULT, DEBORAH LONG, Vocal Music Director; *b:* Carroll, IA; *m:* Jerald Allen; *c:* Jennifer L., Keegan J.; *ed:* (BFAE) Instrumental Music, Wayne St Coll 1975; Grad Work Wayne St Coll, Drake Univ; *cr:* Asst Band/Elem Music Teacher Eldora Cmmty Sch 1976-77; K-12th Grade Band/Vocal Teacher Bayard Cmmty Sch 1978-86; 6th-12th Grade Vocal Asst Instrumental Teacher Coon Rapids-Bayard Cmmty 1986-; *ai:* Flag Corp Dir; Cheerleading Coach; Music Ed Natl Conference, IA Choral Dir Assn, IA Ed Assn 1985-; CU TTT (Camp Chm 1988, Chm 1990); Cath Ladies Guild 1977-; Cath Choir Dir 1980-; Head of Music Dept 1989-; Coon Rapid-Bayard Cmmty Sch; *office:* Coon Rapids Bayard HS 905 North Box 297 Coon Rapids IA 50058

KUMM, KATHRYN JANE, Biology Teacher; *b:* Osmond, NE; *ed:* (BA) Bio, Gustavus Adolphus Coll 1987; *cr:* Teacher Harlan Cmmty HS 1987-; *ai:* Cheerleading, Pom Pon, Yrbk Spon; IA St Ed Assn, NEA 1987-; Harlan Ed Assn Building Rep 1989-; Amer Assn of Univ Women 1987-; IA Cheerleading Coaches Assn 1988-; *office:* Harlan Cmmty HS 2102 Durant St Harlan IA 51537

KUMMER, REBECCA DINWIDDIE, Retired Substitute Teacher; *b:* Franklin, KY; *w:* Arnold (dec); *ed:* (BS) Elem Ed, W KY Univ 1966; *cr:* 1st-8th Grade Teacher Independence 1934-37; 3rd Grade Teacher Round Pond 1938-39; 1st-8th Grade Teacher Bethel Grove 1940-41; 1st Grade Teacher Barnes Sch 1944-62, Franklin Elem 1962-82; *ai:* Active in Ag Act; KEA, NEA; Retired Teachers 1930-82; First Baptist Church (Mem, Adult Choir, Choir VP 1980-, Sunday Sch Class Pres 1987-); Music Club (Secy 1942-43, VP 1989-); Homemakers Club, Womens Missionary Union; Jr & Young People Choir (Dir, Leader); Flutophone Band Dir; 4-H Judging Comm; *home:* 403 E Madison Franklin KY 42134

KUNIYASU, KEITH KAZUMI, Comm Technology Facilitator; *b:* Honolulu, HI; *ed:* (AA/AS) Liberal Arts/Graphic Arts, Univ of HI 1978; (BS) Industrial Arts Ed/Comm, W WA Univ 1982; (MED) Technology Ed, OK St Univ 1987; *cr:* Comm Facilitator Oak Harbor HS 1982; Spec Ed Facilitator Highlands Intermediate Sch 1983-84; Instrumental Music Facilitator AIEA Intermediate Sch 1983-88; Comm Technology Facilitator 1984-; *ai:* Voc Industrial Clubs of America Adv; St of WA Supt of Public Instruction Curr Study, Rewrite, Competency Validation Comm Bainbridge HS; Accreditation Study Team 1988-89; WA Assn of Graphics Instrs; Graphic Arts Tech Fnd; Intnl Technology Ed Assn WA Affiliate Rep 1990; WA Technology Ed Assn Newsletter Ed 1985-87; AVA; Intnl Graphic Arts Ed Assn; Article Published 1987; Booklet Series, Brochures; St of WA Voc Admin Prgm Intern; *office:* N Kitsap HS 18360 Caldart Ave NE Poulsbo WA 98370

KUNKA, JAMES CHARLES, 8th Grade Math Dept Chair; *b:* Minot, ND; *m:* Sharon Eleanor Lee; *c:* Robert, Joseph, Michael, Steven; *ed:* (BS) Math, Minot St Coll 1960; (MNS) Math, Univ of ID 1968; *cr:* Math Teacher Lemmon HS 1960-63; Math/Sci Teacher Plaza HS 1963-64; Math Teacher Bonners Ferry HS 1964-68; 8th Grade Math Teacher East Mid Sch 1968-; *ai:* 7th Grade Ftbl & Bsktbl Coach; NSF Univ of ID 1965-68; NSF Univ of IL 1975; Jr Chamber of Commerce 1963; *office:* East Mid Sch 4040 Central Ave Great Falls MT 59401

KUNKEL, DONALD RAY, Science Department Chair; *b:* St Louis, MO; *m:* Anna Jo Lee; *ed:* (BS) Bio, AR Coll 1984; Cert Univ of AR; *cr:* Sci Teacher Ola Jr/Sr HS 1987-; *ai:* Quiz Bowl Coach; FFA Advisory Comm; Class Spon; AR Sci Teachers Assn 1987-; Tau Kappa Epsilon 1981-; *office:* Ola Jr/Sr HS Hill St Ola AR 72853

KUNKEL, MARCIA LEE, Fifth Grade Teacher; *b:* Knox City, TX; *m:* Jerome Paul; *c:* Keith L., Kevin P.; *ed:* (BS) Ed, 1968, (MS) Ed, 1972 N TX St Univ; *cr:* Teacher Birdville Ind Sch Dist 1968-, Granbury Ind Sch Dist 1978-; *ai:* Tri-Cty Humane Society Volunteer; TSTA 1978-; *home:* Rt 8 Box 95 Granbury TX 76048

KUNTZ, KAREN F. (MERTH), Junior Kindergarten Teacher; *b:* Amery, WI; *m:* James E.; *c:* Sara J., Kelli; *ed:* (BS) Elem Ed, Univ WI River Falls 1974; *cr:* 5th Grade Teacher Albany Elem Sch 1974-76; 2nd Grade Teacher 1976-85, Jr Kndgtn Teacher 1986- Clayton Elem Sch; *ai:* Gifted & Talented Comm; Insurance Comm; Kndgtn Stan Comm; Faculty Schlsp Participant; St Croix Valley Rdng Cncl 1976-; Clayton Prof Educators (Treas 1978-80) 1978-; WI Fed of Teachers 1978-; AFT 1978-; Miss Clayton Coronation Comm 1987-; St Ann Altar Society 1976-; St Isadore Circle 1978-; Bd of Dirs Preschool Playhouse Treas 1988-89; Wrote & Presented Jr Kndgtn Curr to WI St Sch Bd Convention Milwaukee 1990; *home:* Rt 1 Box 3 Clayton WI 54004

KUNZ, DIANNE PATRICIA (OHL), 5th Grade Teacher; *b:* Belleville, IL; *m:* Walter Julius; *c:* Nikolas W., Jackey L.; *ed:* (BA) Phys Ed/Elem/Scndry - Cum Laude, Mc Kendree Coll 1973; Elem Ed 1976; *cr:* Phys Ed Teacher 1973-75, HS Vlybl Coach 1973-77, 5th Grade Elem Ed Teacher 1975- Wesclin Sch Dist 3; *ai:* NEA, WEA; PTA Active Mem 1984-; *home:* RR 2 Box 63 Trenton IL 62293

KUNZ, MELANIE ROUNDY, 4th/5th Grade Teacher; *b:* Provo, UT; *m:* Klay Morgan; *c:* Morgan, Rozalyn, Jacob, Seth; *ed:* (BA) Elem Ed, Brigham Young Univ HI 1979; (MS) Elem Ed, Weber St Univ 1987; *cr:* Medical Receptionist Dr Tanner MD 1980-82; 5th Grade Teacher West Point Elem 1982-86; 4th Grade Teacher Morgan Elem 1986-; *ai:* Davis Ed Assn, UT Ed Assn, NEA 1982-; *home:* 1115 W 550 S Layton UT 84041

KUNZ, NADINE MASH, Fifth Grade Teacher; *b:* Washington, DC; *m:* Marlon E.; *c:* Paula Calton, Ronald E., Claudia Kenyon, Kelly Runyon; *ed:* (BA) Child Dev/Elem Ed, UT St Univ 1965; *cr:* 2nd Grade Teacher Sandy Elem & Oakdale Elem & Majestic Elem 1965-78; 1st Grade Teacher 1978-81, 4th Grade Teacher 1981-83, 3rd Grade Teacher 1983-87, 5th Grade Teacher 1987- Sprucewood Elem; *ai:* Sch After-Sch Chorus; Gifted/Talented, Sandy Pride, Cmptr Technology, Career Ladder Screening Comm; Textbook Adoption; UT Ed Assn, Jordan Ed Assn, NEA 1965-; UT St Bd of Ed Assn Outstanding Teacher of Yr 1990; *office:* Sprucewood Elem Sch 12025 S 1000 E Sandy UT 84092

KUNZ, PAMELA, 2nd Grade Teacher; *b:* Casa Grande, AZ; *c:* Tiffany, Alyse; *ed:* (BA) Elem Ed, AZ St Univ 1969; Grad Courses Sacramento St Univ, Univ of CA Davis, AZ St Univ; *cr:* 2nd Grade Teacher Sacramento Unified Sch Dist 1969-73; Pre 1st/1st/2nd Grade Teacher Stanfield Elem Sch 1973-; *ai:* Chairman Academic Excl Comm; Soc Stud Adoption Comm; Delta Kamma Gamma (Pres 1982-) 1984-86; Beta Sigma Phi (Pres, VP, Secy, Treas) 1979-, Woman of Yr 1989.

KUPKA, JANICE HOULAHAN, Second Grade Teacher; *b:* Manchester, IA; *m:* Charles R.; *c:* Joseph Houlahan, Erin Houlahan, Travis, Alyssa; *ed:* (BA) Elem Ed, Upper IA Univ 1967; Ed of Gifted Stu; At-Rish Stu Prgm Dev; Children of Alcoholics/Chemical Dependency; Thinking Skills; *cr:* 1st Grade Teacher Freeport IL 1967-68; 1st-3rd Teacher Linn-Mar Cmmty Schls 1968-; *ai:* Building Growth Cadre Leader; Staff Dev Instr; Dist Planning Comm for Prgm; LMEA, ISEA, NEA 1989-; Drug Free Schls Consortium 1988-; Wellington Heights Assn 1989-; Merit Pay Awd; Performance Pay Awd; *office:* Linn-Mar Cmmty Schls 3333 N 10th St Marion IA 52302

KUPSIS, DAVID C., 5th Grade Teacher; *ed:* (BS) Elem, 1963, (MED) Educl Media, West Chester Univ; Elem Sch Principalship, Villanova Univ; *cr:* Teacher West Chester Sch Dist 1963-; *ai:* Sci Advocate; West Chester Ed Assn; Brookhaven Jets; Brookhaven Babe Ruth League Secy; Brookhaven Biddy Bsktbl League; CCD Class Pope Pius X Medal for Service; *office:* Penn Wood Elem Schl 1470 Johnny's Way West Chester PA 19382

KURACKA, LORRAINE BANKS, First Grade Teacher; *b:* Isom, KY; *m:* Metry Jr.; *c:* Derrick; *ed:* (BS) Elem Ed, Pikeville Coll 1962; (MA) Elem Ed, Morehead St Univ 1979; *cr:* 2nd Grade Teacher Colson Elem 1962-76; 1st Grade Teacher 1976-86, Chapter I Rdng Teacher 1986-87, 1st Grade Teacher 1987- Beckham Bates Elem; *ai:* KY Ed Assn; Letcher Cty Teachers Organization Treas 1979-; PTO Treas 1988-; Presbyn Church (Elder 1985-, Clerk of Session 1986-).

KURCZ, MARY ANN HERHAL, 5th-8th Grade Science Teacher; *b:* Hazleton, PA; *m:* Robert; *c:* Nathan; *ed:* (AA) Elem Ed, Lehigh Cty Comm Coll 1974; (BS) Elem Ed/Sci, Bloomsburg Univ 1977; Temple Univ, Allentown Coll, Berks Cty Intermediate Unit, Marywood Coll; *cr:* 5th-8th Grade Sci Teacher Most Blessed Sacrament 1977-; *ai:* Sci Coord; Drama Act Dir; Crisis Intervention Sch Rep; NEAA 1977-; Folk-Contemporary Choir Dir 1970-89; Sch Evaluation for Mid Sts Cert; *home:* 7 Haaf Cir Fogelsville PA 18051

KURILLA, JOAN HEURANG, 5th/6th Grade Teacher; *b:* Avon, MN; *m:* Steve; *c:* David, Christopher; *ed:* (BS) Elem Ed, St Cloud St Univ 1960; Masters Prgm St Cloud St Univ; *cr:* 3rd Grade Teacher Moundsview Sch Dist 1960-64; Title I Teacher 1971-80, 5th/6th Grade Teacher 1980- Avon Elem; *ai:* Building Supvr; Albany Fed of Teachers, Natl Fed of Teachers; PTA.

KURNS, BRENDA SALOWITZ, Science Teacher; *b:* New Britain, CT; *m:* Irwin B.; *c:* Amy, David; *ed:* (BA) Bio, C W Post Coll 1965; (MS) Biological Ed, Cntrl CT St Univ 1971; *cr:* Research Technician Grad Research Center of SW 1965-66; Research Technician SW Medical Sch 1966-67; Bio/Phys Sci Teacher Hamden HS 1967-68, Bristol Eastern HS 1968-72, Madison Township HS 1972-74, Silas Deane Mid Sch 1984-85; Ed Dept Sci Museum of CT 1985-86; Teacher Wethersfield HS 1986-87, Dr James H Naylor Sch 1987-; *ai:* Stu Cncl Adv; Ad Hoc Comm on Quality Ed; Alpha Delta Kappa 1989-; Celebration of Excl 1989; *office:* Dr James H Naylor Sch 639 Franklin Ave Hartford CT 06114

KURPGEWEIT, JOLINE (SMITH), Fifth Grade Teacher; *b:* Clearwater, NE; *m:* Richard; *c:* Karen Funk, Kevin; *ed:* (BS) Elem Ed, Dana Coll 1972; *cr:* K-8th Grade Teacher Holt Cty Rural Schls & Antelope Cty Rural Schls 1951-77; 5th Grade Teacher Ewing Public Schl 1977-; *ai:* NSEA, NEA, ETA; *home:* HC 62 Box 104 Ewing NE 68735

KURSEWICZ, LYNN MARIE, Second Grade Teacher; *b:* Nashua, NH; *m:* Paul; *ed:* (BA) Elem Ed, Rivier Coll 1970-74; Elem Level Educl Seminars, Wkshps & Courses; *cr:* Nursery Sch Teacher/Kndgtn Aide 1974-75, Kndgtn Teacher 1975-76 Winnie the Pooh Sch; Substitute Teacher Nashua Sch System 1976-77; 2nd Grade Teacher Auburn Village Sch 1977-; *ai:* Rdng Comm Mem; Lang Arts, Soc Stud, Discipline & Cafeteria Noise Comm; Safety Discipline Prgm Chairperson & Co-Chairperson; Auburn Ed Assn, (Pres, VP, Secy, Negotiations, Membership) 1977-; NH Ed Assn 1977-; PTA Secy; Spring Fair Chairperson; Natl Arbor Day Fnd 1990.

KURTIAK, CARL ALLAN, History Teacher; *b:* Perth Amboy, NJ; *m:* Elizabeth J. Guiliano; *c:* David, Philip, Vanessa; *ed:* (BA) Ed, 1963, (MA) Ed, 1967 Trenton St Coll; Grad Courses Jersey City St Coll, Kean St Coll, Rutgers Univ, Farleigh Dickinson Univ; *cr:* 6th Grade Teacher James Madison Sch 1963-66; Soc Stud Teacher Herbert Hoover Jr HS 1966-79; His Teacher John P Stevens HS 1979-; *ai:* Sr Class Awds Chairperson; Class Adv; Frosh Bsbl Coach; NEA, NJ Ed Assn, Middlesex Ed Assn, Edison Township Ed Assn 1963-; Edison Township 1st Aid & Rescue Squad #1 Cadet Adv 1972-75; Franklin Township Civic Assn Chairperson 1985-; Franklin Township Comm (Committeeman 1987-, Mayor 1989); Quakertown Fire Company 1986-; Chosen as Governors Sch Teacher Scholar 1990; Have written the Course of Study for Advanced Placement Modern European His, Current World Issues, Sociology, US His II; *office:* John P Stevens HS Grove Ave Edison NJ 08820

KURTZ, CEDALIA LATHAM, Third Grade Teacher; *b:* Temple, TX; *m:* Weldon; *c:* Kevin, Karmen; *ed:* (BS) Elem Ed, Univ of Mary Hardin-Baylor 1978; *cr:* Migrant Teacher Tyler Elem 1978-80; Chapter I Math Teacher Belton Mid Sch 1980-82; 3rd Grade Teacher Cntrl Elem 1982-; *ai:* Writing Curr for Math; Annual Staff; Faculty Advisory Comm; TX St Teachers Assn, NEA 1978-; Holland Chamber of Commerce 1990; *home:* 608 Travis Holland TX 76534

KURTZ, CHRISTINE MARSHALL, Communication Arts Teacher; *b:* Monroe, MI; *m:* Rodney A.; *c:* Erika, Karlene, Jaclyn; *ed:* (BA) Eng, Univ of MI 1968; *cr:* Teacher Brien Mc Mahon HS 1968-69, Ishpeming HS 1969-72, Traverse City Sr HS 1985-; *ai:* Sch Newspaper, Sch Yrbk Adv; Journalism Ed Assn; Cmmty Lib Bd of Trustees VP 1985-; *office:* Traverse City Sr HS 1150 Milliken Dr Traverse City MI 49684

KURZ, JEROLD M., 6th Grade Teacher/Chairperson; *b:* Wadena, MN; *m:* Karen L. Franklin; *c:* Kyle, Alison; *ed:* (BA) Elem Ed, Univ of MN Morris 1969; St Thomas Coll, Mankato St Coll; *cr:* 6th Grade Elem Teacher Morris Public Schls 1969-72; Asst Ftbl Coach Univ of MN Morris 1960-70; Asst Ftbl Coach 1971, Asst Bsktbl/Track Coach 1970-72 Morris Public Schls; *ai:* Grade Level Chairperson; MN Ed Assn Building Rep 1982-83; MN Fed of Teachers; Church Choir 1982-87; *office:* John F Kennedy Elem Sch 21240 Holyoke Ave Lakeville MN 55044

KURZ, THOMAS E., Soc Stud Dept Chairman; *b:* Owensboro, KY; *m:* Mary Ann Johnson; *c:* Kevin, Stephanie, Mark; *ed:* (BS) Poly Sci, Brescia Coll 1968; (MA) Ed, W KY Univ 1974; *cr:* Teacher 1967-72, Teacher/Dept Chm 1973-, Teacher/Textbook Coord 1979- Owensboro HS; *ai:* Stu Cncl Spon 1969-; Hosted St Stu Cncl Convention 1988; Owensboro Ed Assn 1967-, Teacher of Yr 1989-; KEA, NEA 1967-; DSA 1988-; TX Gas Grad Schlsp 1973, 1974.

KURZON, PAUL W., Accounting Teacher; *b:* Brooklyn, NY; *m:* Norberta David; *c:* Matthew; *ed:* (BBA) Accounting, Pace Univ 1967; (MS) Guidance/Counseling, Long Island Univ 1974; Educl Supervision, CCNY 1975; *cr:* Teacher Berriman Jr HS 1967-75, Port Richmond HS 1975-; *ai:* Treas Port Richmond HS; Var Bsbl Head Coach 1982-88; *office:* Port Richmond HS Innis St And St Joseph Staten Island NY 10302

KUSH, DAVID JOHN, Fourth Grade Teacher; *b:* Johnstown, PA; *m:* Patricia Flowers; *c:* Michelle; *ed:* (BS) Elem Ed, 1972, (MED) Elem Ed, 1975, Elem Prin Cert 1977 Univ of Pittsburgh; *cr:* Elem Teacher Conemaugh Valley Sch Dist 1972-; *ai:* PSEA, NEA; *office:* Conemaugh Valley Sch Dist 1451 Frankstown Rd Johnstown PA 15902

KUSMAUL, GERALD JOSEPH, Biology Instructor; *b:* Ottawa, IL; *m:* Martha Jeanne Fugate; *c:* Wendy, Kristen, Katherine; *ed:* (BS) Ag, IL St Univ 1961; (MS) Bio, IL Wesleyan Univ 1967; Sci, Math; *cr:* Sci Teacher Chiddix Jr HS 1961-; *ai:* Unit 5 Sci Curr & Sci Textbook Adoption Comm; 8th Grade Washington DC Trip Spon; Church Choir/Percussionist 1982-; Habitat for Humanity 1986-88; Natl Sci Fnd Grant MS IL Wesleyan Univ 1965-67; NSF Grant Biotechnology 1990; *home:* 2930 Capen Dr Bloomington IL 61704

KUSNIERZ, ANNE DONNELLY, Fourth Grade Teacher; *b:* Holyoke, MA; *m:* Theodore Thomas; *c:* Todd, Katherine, Sarah Jane, Rebecca, Adele, Rachel; *ed:* (BA) Sociology, Univ of MA 1956; (MS) Ed, SUNY 1990; *cr:* 5th Grade Teacher Elmwood Sch 1956-58; 3rd Grade Teacher Harrison Ave Sch 1958-59; Kndgtn Teacher Lake George Cntrl 1959-60; 3rd Grade Teacher 1960-62, 4th Grade Teacher 1980- Warrensburg Cntrl; *ai:* NYS Teachers Assn 1989-; Warrensburg Cntrl Teachers Assn 1989-; Crandall Lib Trustee 1982-; Glens Falls Club of Coll Women 1979-; Moreal Town Bd Cncl Women 1990; *home:* Candy Cane Farm Moreau NY 12828

KUSS, KATHLEEN D. CLEMENTE, 6th Grade Science Dept Teacher; *b:* Buffalo, NY; *m:* Paul Francis; *c:* Nichole C.; *ed:* (BS) Elem Ed, Medaille 1974; (MA) Elem Ed, Buffalo St Univ 1977; *cr:* 5th Grade Teacher St Marys Elem 1974-80; 5th/6th Grade Teacher Our Lady Sacred Heart 1984-; *ai:* Nom Local Thanks to Teachers Campaign; Initiating 6th Grade Sch Recycling Prgm; *home:* 3686 Woodhaven Cir Hamburg NY 14075

KUSSEROW, JAMES VERNON, Band Director; *b:* Susanville, CA; *m:* Kellie Munger; *c:* Kaylan; *ed:* (BA) Music Ed, San Jose St Univ 1980; (MA) Sch Admin, CA St Univ Bakersfield 1990; *cr:* Band Dir Mulcahy Jr HS 1981-88; 5th Grade Teacher Garden Elem 1988-89; Band Dir Live Oak Mid Sch 1989-; *ai:* Tulare Cty Symphony Prin Trumpet; Live Oak Marching Band & Jazz Ensemble Dir; Sequoia Brass Performer; Tulare Cty Music Educator Assn (Pres 1985-86, Secy 1983-84); Music Educators Natl Conference 1981-; Tulare Jaycess 1981-84; Tulare Kiwanis 1987-89; Frank Howard Awd for Outstanding Music Ed 1984; *home:* 3102 W Howard Visalia CA 93274

KUST, JOAN KAY, K-12th Grade School Counselor; *b:* Oconto Falls, WI; *m:* Fred Burts; *ed:* (BS) Psych, Univ WI Stevens Point 1974; (MED) Guidance & Counseling, Univ WI Oshkosh 1976; Alcolol & Drugs, Art Therapy & Stress Management; *cr:* Supervisor Taylor Childrens Home 1976-77; Cnslr 1977, 1982-84, Asst Dir 1978-82 Waples Group Home; Career Cnslr Caddett Prgm 1984; Elem Cnslr Two Rivers Sch 1984-85; K-12th Grade Cnslr Hilbert Schls 1985-; *ai:* AOD Prgms; Advisory Comm Mem; CESA & AOD Consortium; Phi Delta Kappa 1988-; WI Sch Cnslr Assn; Amer Assn for Counseling & Dev 1986-; Cmmty AOD Comm 1985-; Women Reaching Women 1983-85; Alcohol & Drug Prgm Leadership Prgm Grants; Stu Asst Prgm; *office:* Hilbert Public Schls 11th & Milwaukee St Hilbert WI 54129

KUSTER, SYLVIA LEWIS, 4th Grade Teacher; *b:* New Bern, NC; *m:* Dewey III; *c:* Maria L., Sarah J.; *ed:* (BS) Elem Ed/ Geography, E CaroLina Univ 1969; (MA) Elem Ed/Geography, Georgetown Coll 1979; *cr:* 5th Grade Teacher Brinson Memorial 1969-70; 6th Grade Teacher Woodland Park Elem 1970-72; 7th Grade Eng/Soc Stud Teacher Havelock Jr HS 1973; 4th Grade Teacher 1973-76, 3rd Grade Teacher 1976-77 Westside Elem; 4th Grade Teacher Southside Elem 1977-; *ai:* Harrison HS Academic, Bsktbl, Cheerleading Booster Clubs; KY Ed Assn Mem; Beta Sigma Phi (Treas 1984-85, Soc Chm 1983-84, Historian 1982-83); Cynthiana Chrstn Church (Treas, Agape Sunday Sch Class); *home:* Rt 1 Box 129 Edgewater Pike Cynthiana KY 41031

KUTCH, FALMA ANNE, Third Grade Teacher; *b:* Gladewater, TX; *m:* Pat D.; *c:* Pat D. Jr., Lay L.; *ed:* (AA) Fine Art, Chrstn Coll 1950; (BA) Elem Ed, Pan Amer Coll 1965; Minor in Fine Arts & Fr Lang; *cr:* Classroom Teacher Mc Allen Ind Sch Dist; *ai:* ATPE; Phi Theta Kappa VP 1948-50; Phi Delta Delta, Sigma Phi Gamma 1948-50.

KUTZ, HARVEY J., 6th Grade Math/Reading Teacher; *b:* Brookville, PA; *m:* Melissa Pozza; *ed:* (BA) Elem Ed, Westminster Coll 1981; (MSED) Ed, Wilkes Univ 1990; *cr:* 5th Grade Math Teacher 1982-83, 6th Grade Teacher 1983-86, 6th Grade Math Teacher 1986- Middletown Sch Dist; *ai:* Jr HS Track Coach; Team Leader; Hunting & Fishing Club Adv; MAEA, PSEA 1982-; Annual Math Fair Grant; *office:* Middletown Sch Dist 214 Race St Middletown PA 17057

KUTZ, WILLIAM CRAIG, Social Studies Teacher; *b:* Brookville, PA; *m:* Linda Maxwell; *c:* Charles Maxwell; *cr:* (BA) Psych, Waynesburg Coll 1977; (BS) Soc Stud Ed, Clarion Univ 1985; Teacher Brookville Area HS 1985-; *ai:* Ftbl Coach 1977-; Track Coach 1985-; Stu Assistance Team; *office:* Brookville Area HS Jenks St Brookville PA 15825

KUVINKA, ERIC WILLIAM, Mathematics/Science Teacher; *b:* New Eagle, PA; *c:* Terri, Eric; *ed:* (BS) Ed, CA Univ of PA 1967; *home:* PO Box 748 Charleroi PA 15022

KUWADA, HAJIME, Band Teacher; *b:* Puunene, HI; *m:* Kiyoko Hada; *c:* Scott, Dana; *ed:* (BED) Music Ed, 1954, 5th Yr Diploma Music Ed, 1955 Univ of HI; *cr:* Music/Band/Chorus Teacher Lahainaluna HS 1955-62; Band Teacher Frankfurt Jr HS 1962-67; Band/Chorus/Soc Stud Teacher Zama Amer HS 1967-72; Band Teacher Aiea Intermediate Sch 1972-; *ai:* Amer Sch Band Dir Assn St Chm 1977-; MENC, HSTA, HMEA Secy 1984-88; Freedom Fnd Valley Forge Teachers Medal 1976; Outstanding Performance of Duty as Teacher USDESEA Frankfurt Jr HS 1967; *office:* Aiea Intermediate Sch 99-600 Kulawea St Aiea HI 96701

KUYKENDALL, PATRICIA WOGENSTAHL, 4th/5th Grade Teacher; *b:* Hamilton, OH; *m:* David V.; *c:* Jennifer L. Back; *ed:* (BS) Elem Ed, 1962, (MS) Aerospace Ed, 1976 Miami Univ; Intnl Visiting Teachers Prgm For Comparative Ed, St Thomas Coll; Comparative Ec, Univ of Cincinnati; Numerous Ed, Career Ed Wkshps, Univ Cincinnati, Butler Cty Career Ed Dept; *cr:* 4th Grade Teacher Ross Local Schls 1956-60; 5th Grade Teacher Fairfield Elem Sch 1964-66; 4th/5th Grade Teacher St Ann Sch 1968-71; 1st/4th/5th Grade Teacher New Miami Elem Sch 1976-; *ai:* Coordinating Cncl 1990; Test Selection Comm 1990; Career Coord 1986-88; Lang Art Comm Chm; Local Minimum Competencies Comm; NEA 1956-61; OEA Delegate 1964-66; SWOEA 1976-; New Miami Ed Assn 1976-; Faith UCC Deacon 1990; *office:* New Miami Elem Sch 600 N Riverside Dr Hamilton OH 45011

KUZIO, JANICE CHURCH, Home Economics/Science Teacher; *b:* Massillon, OH; *m:* Jeffrey; *ed:* (BS) Elem Ed, 1970, (MA) Elem Ed, 1987 OH Univ; *cr:* Kndgtn Teacher Centerville Elem Sch 1969-70; 3rd/4th Grade Teacher Washington Local Elem Sch 1971-76; Remedial Math Teacher 1976-77, Remedial Rdng Teacher 1977-79, Home Ec/Science Teacher 1979- Powhatan Elem Sch; *ai:* Young Authors Comm, Jr HS Model United Nations, Resident Outdoor Ed Adv; Sci Fair Adv & Dist Judge; Home Ec Curr Comm; OH Ed Assn, NEA 1969-; Switzerland of OH Ed Assn 1971-; 4-H Club Adv 1981-; Natl Wildlife Fed 1966-; Natl Audubon Society 1987-; *home:* 55021 Clover Ridge Rd Jacobsburg OH 43933

KUZMA, BARBARA A., Teacher; *b:* Youngstown, OH; *m:* Jerry; *c:* Mary K., Lori, Lynn, Mark, Matt; *ed:* (BS) Ed, 1976, (MS) Guidance/Counseling, 1985 Youngstown St Univ; *cr:* Teacher St Edward Sch 1976-78; Cnslr Jackson Milton Schls 1985-87; Teacher Jackson Milton Mid Sch 1979-; *ai:* Sch Newspaper; Youngstown St Eng Festival Rep & Judge; Prin Advisory Comm; OH Teachers of Lang Art 1980-; Jackson/Milton Ed Assn (VP 1987, Negotiator 1986-88); Published Article 1988; Project ARETE; *office:* Jackson Milton Mid Sch 14110 Mahoning Ave North Jackson OH 44451

KVAMME, MO LLOYD, Mathematics Department Chair; *b:* Mobridge, SD; *m:* Pat Hand; *c:* Nathaniel; *ed:* (BS) Scndry Ed, Northern St Coll SD 1971; (MA) Math, Univ of SD 1975; *cr:* Teacher Murdo HS 1971-74; Programmer/Analyst St of SD 1975-76; Teacher Murdo HS 1977-80, Windsor HS 1980-; *ai:* Asst Ftbl Coach; NCTM; Optimist Pres 1987.

KVAPIL, DONNA LEE TRUJILLO, Business Education Dept Chair; *b:* Monte Vista, CO; *m:* Edward Louis Jr.; *c:* George A.; *ed:* (BA) Admin Services, Univ of TX El Paso 1983; Career Ladder Level II 1986, Career Ladder Level III 1989; *cr:* Teachers Aide 1977-81, Bus Ed Teacher 1983- El Paso Ind Sch Dist; *ai:* Univ Interscholastic League Shorthand & Accounting; Andress HS FBLA Chapter Spon; TX Bus Ed Assn (St Reporter Historian, Dist Pres 1989) 1984-, Teacher of Yr 1987; NBEA 1986-; TX Cmptr Ed Assn 1987-; TX St Teachers Assn 1985-; Parent, Teachers & Stus Assn (1st VP, Schlsp Chairperson 1989-) 1986-; Effective Schls Project Action Planning Team Mem & Task Force Facilitator; Certificates of Appreciation 1985-; El Paso Ind Sch Dist Teacher of Yr, Certificate of Excl in Teaching 1987-88; Outstanding Faculty Mem 1988; Whos Who in Amer Ed 1987-88; *office:* Andress HS 5400 Sun Valley Dr El Paso TX 79924

KWIATKOWSKI, CHRISTINE A., Spanish Teacher; *b:* New Brunswick, NJ; *ed:* (BA) Span, Douglass Coll 1971; Ed, Rutgers Grad Sch; *cr:* Teacher Sayreville War Memorial HS 1971-; *ai:* Span Club Adv; Span Honor Society Adv; NEA, NJEA; Sayreville Ed Assn; Amer Assn Techers of Span & Portuguese; NJ Governors Teacher RecognitiOn Awd Recipient 1986; *office:* Sayreville War Memorial HS 820 Washington Rd Parlin NJ 08859

KYANKO, CAROLYN MARIE, Principal; *b:* Barton, OH; *m:* Raymond M.; *c:* Eric D. Kocsis, Erin J. Kocsis; *ed:* (BS) Elem Ed, OH Univ 1967; (MS) Ed Admin, Univ of Dayton 1983; ON TASC; *cr:* Teacher Columbus City Schls 1968, St Clairsville Schls 1968-69; Teacher 1969-72, 1974-89, Prin 1989- Bellaire City Schls; *ai:* Lang Art Comm Chairperson; Mid Sch Cheerleading & Newspaper Adv; OAESA, OEA, NEA Mem; BEA Pres; *home:* 54090 Colerain Pike Martins Ferry OH 43940

KYLE, MAXINE W., 4th Grade Teacher; *b:* Oneida, TN; *m:* Everette J.; *c:* Mary K. Sexton; *ed:* (BA) Elem Ed, 1959, (MS) Elem Ed, 1970, (EDS) Elem Ed/Rdng, 1974 TN Tech Univ; *cr:* Teller 1st Natl Bank Oneida 1946-52; 4th Grade Teacher Oneida Elem Sch 1958-; *ai:* Oneida Ed Assn (Pres 1968, Secy 1969-70); Delta Kappa Phi; Oneida Bus & Prof Womens Club (Pres 1974, Secy 1981-82); *home:* Rt 3 Box 781 Oneida TN 37841

KYLMANEN, RUTH HILMA, Retired Elementary Teacher; *b:* Ashtabula Harbor, OH; *ed:* (BA) Elem Ed, OH St Univ 1941; Elem Ed, Kent St Univ; *cr:* Teacher Geneva Sch Dist 1941-42, Fairport Harbor 1943-60, Perry Local Schls 1961-85; *ai:* Delta Kappa Gamma Corresponding Secy 1964-; Luth Church (Sunday Sch Teacher, Mem Womens Groups, Various Comms); Martha Holden Jennings Scholar 1966-; *home:* 3667 Laurel Dr Perry OH 44081

KYNAST, GREGORY JOSEPH, Spanish Teacher; *b:* Mt Vernon, NY; *m:* Lana Carol Wright; *c:* Kara N.; *ed:* (BA) Scndry Ed, Univ of FL 1980; (MA) Span, Univ of FL 1988; *cr:* Head Soceer Coach P K Yonge HS 1979-82; Bi-ling Educator Duval Elem 1980-82; Head Golf Coach 1985-86, Teacher/Head Soccer Coach 1982- Gainesville HS; *ai:* FL St Span Conference Spon 1990; Southern Assn of Colls & Schls Foreign Lang Comm Chm; Span Honor Society Spon; Amer Assn Teachers of Span & Portuguese, FL Assn Teachers of Span & Portuguese 1982-; Alachua Cty Ed Assn 2983-; Fellowship of Chrstn Athletes Spon 1980-; Westside Baptist Church Sunday Sch Teacher 1984-; FL Athletic Coaches Assn Area Rep 1986-; FL Athletic Coaches Assn of America 1986-; Key to City of Gainesville for Work with Young People 1988; *office:* Gainesville HS 1900 NW 13th St Gainesville FL 32609

KYNOCH, ANN OVERLY, 4th Grd Rdng/Lang Arts Teacher; *b:* San Jose, Costa Rica; *m:* Jeffrey P.; *c:* Carl E.; *ed:* (BS) Elem Ed, Fl St Univ 1971; *cr:* 5th Grade Teacher 1974-77; 6th Grade Teacher 1977-78 Washington Mid Sch; 4th Grade Teacher Whigham Public Sch 1978-; *ai:* Library Cncl; GAE 1978-; NEA 1978-; *office:* Whigham Public Sch Box 6 Whigham GA 31797

KYPER, NANCY VAUGHN, Mathematics Teacher; *b:* Huntingdon, PA; *m:* Bernard A.; *c:* Stephen J. Sergeant, Sandra S. Decker, Kimberley A. Sergeant; *ed:* (BS) Math, Juniata Coll 1954; Grad Stud Penn St, Shippensburg Univ, Lafayette Coll; *cr:* Teacher Huntingdon Area Schls 1954-61, N Penn Schls 1961-62, Juniata Valley Sch Dist 1962-; *ai:* Girls Cross Cntry Statistician; Var Girls Bsktbl Score Keeper; Girls Track Asst Coach; Mathcounts & Summer Track Coach; PA St Ed Assn 1954-; Juniata Valley Ed Assn 1962-; NEA 1954-; St James Luth Church 1949-; Friends of Lib Juniata Coll; J C Blair Hospital, Elks Auxiliary; Outstanding Teacher & Univ Lecturer S Cntrl PA Joint Cncl for Sch Improvement 1986-87; *office:* Juniata Valley HS RD Alexandria PA 16611

L

LAAKE, GARY EDWARD, Business Education Instr/Chair; *b:* Davenport, IA; *m:* Diane Marie Christensen; *c:* Andrew, Angela, Alyssa; *ed:* (AA) Bus, Palmer Jr Coll 1970; (BA) Phys Ed/Bus, St Ambrose Univ 1974; Grad Work Western IL Univ; *cr:* Bus Chm Assumption HS 1974-; *ai:* Coaching Girls Golf Sftbl; IBEA 1984-; *office:* Assumption HS 1020 W Central Park Ave Davenport IA 52804

LA BAR, WILLIAM D., Sixth Grade Teacher; *b:* Waupaca, WI; *m:* Vickie A Williquette; *c:* Brook L., Britney L., Brenda L., Brett W.; *ed:* (BS) Elem Ed/Growth/Dev, 1975, (MS) Environmental Sci, 1986 Univ of WI Green Bay; Grad Stud Viterbo Coll; *cr:* 4th Grade Teacher 1975-78, 4th-5th Grade Teacher 1978-80, 5th Grade Teacher 1981-83 Badger Sch; 4th Grade Teacher 1984-87, 6th Grade Teacher 1988- Franklin Sch; *ai:* Elem Soc Stud & Chairperson Inservice Comm; Safety Patrol Adv; Boys Intramurals Prgm Coord; NEA, WI Ed Assn Cncl, Appleton Ed Assn 1975-; Green Bay West Side Kiwanis Girls Sftbl Coach 1988-; Young Adult Bowling Alliance Coach 1987-; *office:* Franklin Elem Sch 2212 N Jarchow Appleton WI 54911

LA BELLE, MICHAEL MAURICE, 7th Grade Science Teacher; *b:* Biddeford, ME; *m:* Sue Ellen Mooney; *c:* Evan, Janet; *ed:* (BS) Bio/Chem, Univ of ME Orono 1973; (MS) Bio, Univ of NH 1978; Supervisory Certificate Sci 1985; *cr:* Bio/Earth Sci Teacher Stevens HS 1973-79; Phys Sci Teacher Mt Pleasant Mid Sch 1979-; *ai:* Girls Bsktbl Coach; Livingston Ed Assn, NJ Ed Assn, NEA 1979-; Writer for Silver Burdett & Ginn Elem Sci; Author Elem Sci Video Labs; *office:* Mt Pleasant Mid Sch 11 Broadlawn Dr Livingston NJ 07039

LA BERGE, MICHAEL IVAN, 6th/7th Grade Teacher; *b:* Longview, WA; *m:* Valerie Ann Leavitt; *c:* Jennifer A.; *ed:* (BA) Elem Ed, WA St Univ 1973; Grad Stud; *cr:* 6th Grade Teacher Robert Gray Elem 1973-81; 5th Grade Teacher Columbia Valley Gardens 1981-83; 6th-8th Grade Teacher Monticello Mid Sch 1983-; *ai:* Intramural Act for 6th Grade Stus; 8th Grade Girls & Boys Bsktbl Coach; Rdng Dept Chm; Longview Educl Assn Rep 1974-75; NEA; White Pass Ski Acad Bd of Dirs 1989-; *office:* Monticello Mid Sch 28th & Hemlock Longview WA 98632

LACER, ROBERT LEE, JR., Counselor; *b:* Evansville, IN; *m:* Vicki Katterhenry; *c:* Jamie L., Jana L.; *ed:* (BA) Speech/Drama/ Eng, KY Wesleyan Coll 1971; (MS) Ed, Univ of Evansville 1975; *cr:* Teacher 1971-87; 1988-89 Booneville HS; Cnslr Castle Jr HS 1990; *ai:* Tennis Coach; Stu Cncl Spon; Faculty Advisory Comm; Natl Honor Society Selection Comm; Warrick Cty Teachers Assn 1971-; IN St Teachers Assn 1971-; NEA 1971-; United Meth Mens Pres 1988-; Good Neighbor Awd; Outstanding Leader in Elem & Scndry Ed 1976; *home:* 2255 Fuquay Rd Newburgh IN 47630

LA CERRA, MARGARET L., 6th Grade Teacher; *b:* Brooklyn, NY; *w:* Joseph (dec); *c:* Charles, Robert, Mark, Timothy; *ed:* (BA) Poly Sci/His, St Joseph Coll 1951; Continuing Ed Fordham Univ 1952-53; *cr:* 4th/8th Grade Teacher Sacred Heart 1969-76; 8th Grade Teacher St Joseph 1976-80; 5th-6th Grade Teacher St Charles Borromeo 1981-; *ai:* Safety Patrol Moderator; Curr Comm; 4th-6th Grade Cath Schls Week Musicle; Grandparents Day; NCEA 1969-; Local Assistance Chairperson Bd Palmyra 1986-; Advisory Comm Palmyra 1988-89; Bd of Ed Palmyra 1969-72; Rep Committeewoman for 5th Dist Palmyra; *office:* St Charles Borromeo Sch Branch Pike & Pomona Rd Cinnaminson NJ 08077

LACEY, CRAIG TERHUNE, 4th Grade Teacher; *b:* Patterson, NJ; *m:* Linda Jo Worth; *c:* Terri, Kristi, Tiffani; *ed:* (BS) Elem Ed, Midwestern Coll 1969; Working towards Masters in Math & Sci; *cr:* 6th Grade Teacher Schleswig Cmmty Sch 1969-71, Jesup Cmmty Sch 1971-86; Jr HS Math/Sci Teacher 1986-89, 4th Grade Teacher 1989- Beardstown Unit 15 Sch; *ai:* 7th Grade Ftbl & Bsktbl, HS Girls Track Coach; BEA, NEA, IEA 1986-89; Beardstown Lions Club (Secy 1987-88, Bd Dir, Lion Tamer 1988-89); Buchannan Cty & NE IA Conservation Teacher of Yr 1977; NE IA Track Coaches Assn Asst Track Coach of Yr 1980-81; *home:* 806 Monroe Beardstown IL 62618

LACEY, DAVID STEVEN, Assistant Principal; *b:* San Diego, CA; *m:* Suzanne Smith; *c:* Erin, Steven, Daniel; *ed:* (AA) Psych, Palomar Jr Coll 1969; (BA) Sociology, Univ of CA San Diego 1971; (MA) Educl Admin, San Diego St Univ 1981; *cr:* 3rd-6th Grade Teacher Crestview Elem Sch 1972-84; 1st/2nd/4th Grade Teacher Grapevine Elem Sch 1984-87; Resource Teacher 1987-88, Dean/Asst Prin 1988- Bobier Elem; *ai:* Assn of CA Sch Admin Mem 1989-; *office:* Bobier Elem Sch 1234 Arcadia Ave Vista CA 92084

LACEY, REBECCA RUMBERGER, Teacher of Gifted; *b:* Harrisburg, PA; *m:* Kevin Robert; *ed:* (BS) Scndry Ed/Soc Stud, Millersville Univ 1977; (MED) His, Shippensburg Univ 1980; Intensive Intermediate Trng in Individualized Educl Programming for Gifted 1978-79; Ind Travel-Study Europe Through Goddard Coll; Grad Credits in Motivating Stus Through Wilkes Coll; *cr:* 7th Grade His Teacher 1977-78, 8th/9th Grade Teacher of Gifted 1978-81, 7th/8th Grade Gifted/7th Grade Learning Disabilities Soc Stud Teacher 1981- Mechanicsburg Sch Dist; *ai:* Co-Ed of Apprentice Sch Yrbk; Sch Natl Mathcounts Team & PA Math League Team Coach; Volunteer Club & Natl His Day Competition Spon; Photography Club Adv; Coach Scripps-Howard Spelling Bee Winner; Mechanicsburg Ed Assn (VP 1986-88, Newsletter Ed 1986-88); PA Assn of Gifted Ed; PA Historical Society; Amer Red Cross 1980-, Outstanding Volunteer 1989; The Volunteer Center 1980-, Recognition by PA Secy of Ed for Directing Young People to Volunteer 1987; Honored by Pres Reagan & PA Governor Dick Thornburgh for Coaching 1986; Scripps-Howard Natl Spelling Bee Champion; Shippensburg Univ His Day Teacher of Yr 1988;Recipient Mechanicsburg Sch Dist Service to Pupils Awd; Nom PA St Teacher of Yr Awd; Certificates Merit PA Historical Society St His Day 1987-89; Plaques For Successful Coaching Capital Region Mathcounts Team; Certificates of Merit from NCSS for Stus Winning St His Day 1987-89; *office:* Mechanicsburg Area Sch Dist 500 S Broad St Mechanicsburg PA 17055

LACEY, SUE, Counselor; *b:* Purdy, MO; *m:* Steve; *c:* Mike; *ed:* (BA) Elem Ed, MO Southern St Coll 1978; (MS) Guidance/ Counseling, S MO St Univ 1988; *cr:* 6th Grade Teacher 1978-88, Guidance Cnslr 1988- Wheaton R-III Sch; *ai:* Stu Cncl, SADD, Jr Class Spon; *office:* Wheaton HS PO Box 249 Wheaton MO 64874

LACEY, VICKY SHANKLIN, K-6th Grade Phys Ed Teacher; *b:* Charleston, WV; *m:* Virgil M.; *c:* Cynthia, Jennifer, Jamie; *ed:* (BA) Elem, Glenville St 1972; WV Univ; *cr:* Teacher Rayon Elem 1972-; *ai:* Textbook Adoption Comm; Phys Ed Curr Guide; Coach-Boys-Girls Track Teams; Coach-Double Dutch Treat Traveling Jump Rope Team; Spon Field Day Event; Bicycle Safety Prgm; May Day Ceremonie; WV Assn Health Phys Ed Rep & Dance VP 1987-89; Presidential Citation 1988; WV Ed Assn 1972-; Wood Cty Teachers Assn 1972-; Wood Cty Rdng Cncl 1972-; Womans Club (VP 1979, Sec 1980); Wood Cty PTA 1972-; Intnl Rope Skipping Assn 1984-; 4-H Cmmty Leader Volunteer 1986-87; Elizabeth United Meth VBS Recreational Leader; PEPE-Region Rep; *office:* Rayon Elem Sch 1508 Rayon Dr Parkersburg WV 26101

LA CHAT, ROBERT JOEL, Science Dept Chair; *b:* Highland Park, IL; *ed:* (BS) Scndry Ed/Earth Sci, 1980, (MA) Teaching Earth Sci, 1990 N AZ Univ; Grad Work AZ St Univ; *cr:* Sci Teacher Wellton Elem Sch 1980-81; Sci Chm Seligman HS 1981-; *ai:* Ftbl Head Coach 1983-; Jr HS Girls/Boys Bsktbl Coach 1980-; NSTA 1987-; NEA, AZ Ed Assn 1980-; Seligman Volunteer Fire Dept Building Officer 1984-; Natl Sch Public Relations Assn, Awd of Honor 1985; Conducted Research, Grand Canyon Natl Park; Compiled Reports, CO River Investigations; Volumes VI & VIII N AZ Univ; Visiting Asst Professorship N AZ Univ Scndry Sci Teacher Trng Project Awd 1990; *office:* Seligman HS 500 N Main St Seligman AZ 86337

LACHER, MARY SUE SADOWSKY, 2nd Grade Teacher; *b:* Dickinson, ND; *m:* Daniel M.; *c:* Sarah E., David J.; *ed:* (BS) Elem Ed, Coll of St Catherine 1974; *cr:* 1st Grade Teacher St John the Baptist Sch 1974-76, St Michaels Sch 1976-78, Christ the King Sch 1978-82, Lewis & Clark Sch 1982-84; 2nd Grade Teacher Roosevelt Sch 1984-; *ai:* Delta Kappa Gamma Chapter Pres 1985-; NEA, ND Ed Assn, Mandan Ed Assn 1982-; *home:* 220 N Anderson St Bismarck ND 58501

LACHES, ROBERT DUANE, Electronics Technology Instr; *b:* Elgin, ND; *ed:* (Diploma) Comm Systems Tech, 1973, (AAS) Comm Systems Tech, 1980 ND St Coll of Sci; *cr:* Technician KDIX-TV & Radio 1973-76; KBMR Music Systems Inc 1976-77; Electronic Tech Instr Bismark Public Schls 1977-; *ai:* Voc Industrial Clubs of Amer Adv; NDVA/AVA 1980-; *office:* Bismarck Public Schls 400 Avenue E East Bismarck ND 58501

LACKEY, PHILIP C., Science Teacher; *b:* Kingsville, TX; *m:* Cynthia W. Mc Gough; *c:* Pamela Nichole, Philip Leonard; *ed:* (BS) Ag Ed/Bio, TX A&M Univ 1975; *cr:* Ag Ed Teacher Martin HS 1975-76; Sci Teacher Freer HS 1976-78; San Diego HS 1984-85; *ai:* First Baptist Church Trng Union Dir 1987-89; Baptist Men 1988-; *home:* PO Box 1417 Freer TX 78357

LACKEY, SHERRY HARWELL, Third Grade Teacher; *b:* Statesville, NC; *m:* Stephen Dale; *c:* Kimberly, Kellye; *ed:* (BA) Elem Ed, Catawba Coll 1966; *cr:* 3rd Grade Teacher Mc Iver Sch 1966-67, Fred L Wilson Sch 1968-70; 2nd-4th/6th Grade Teacher Monticello Sch 1971-; *ai:* Staff Volunteer Coord 1987-88; Supt Advisory Comm 1989-; NEA, NCAE 1966-82; Glen Echo Ladies Club Secy 1984; Christ Boulevard United Meth Church (Admin Bd 1982-83, Pastor Parish Comm 1984-85, Trustees 1989-).

LACKEY, SUE ANDRA, Music Teacher/Advisor; *b:* Robinson, IL; *ed:* (BS) Music, 1966, (MA) Music, 1967 E IL Univ; (ACME) Music, Univ of IL 1972; *cr:* Teacher Milwaukee Schls 1967-68, Shorewood Public Schls 1968-70; Teacher/Adv Dist 300 Schls 1970-; *ai:* Dist 300 Vocal Festival; Essential Schls; Numerous Comms; MENC; *office:* Carpentersville Mid Sch 100 Cleveland St Carpentersville IL 60110

LA COUR, MICHAEL EDWARD, Band Director; *b:* St Petersburg, FL; *m:* Jill Justin-Bredthauer; *c:* Caia, Matthew; *ed:* (BME) Music, Baylor Univ 1976; *cr:* Asst Dir Round Rock HS 1977-79; Head Dir Round Rock 9th Grade Center 1979-891; Asst Dir Chisholm Trial Mid Sch 1981-84; Head Dir Canyon Vista Sch 1984-; *ai:* Band; TX Music Educators Assn, TX Bandmasters Assn 1977-; *office:* Canyon Vista Mid Sch 8455 Spicewood Springs Rd Austin TX 78759

LA CROCE, JULIANNE BAINBRIDGE, English Teacher/ Guidance Cnslr; *b:* Shamokin, PA; *m:* Eugene Anthony; *c:* Eugene A. Jr., Maria Pryor, Regina, Kathleen, James; *ed:* (BS) Eng Ed, Mt St Marys Coll 1977; (MA) Guidance, Hood Coll 1986; *cr:* 6th-8th Grade Eng/Lang Art Teacher Mother Seton Sch 1977-83; 7th/8th Grade Eng/Lang Art Teacher Middletown Mid Sch 1983-84; 9th-12th Grade Eng/Lang Art Teacher Walkersville HS 1984-86; 9th-12th Grade Eng Teacher/Guidance Counseling St Johns Prospect Hall HS 1986-; *ai:* Drama Club, Mock Trial Team, SADD Adv; *office:* St Johns Literary Inst 889 Butterfly Ln Frederick MD 21701

LACY, DARLA BAKER, Secondary Mathematics Teacher; *b:* Post, TX; *m:* Michael Craig; *c:* Andrea, Scott; *ed:* (BS) Ed, TX Tech Univ 1982; Working Towards Masters Ed, Math; *cr:* Math Teacher Seagraves HS 1983-; *ai:* Chrldr, Number Sense, Jr Class Spon; Tennis Coach; TCTA, TMSCA; 1st Baptist Church; *office:* Seagraves HS 1801 Avenue K Seagraves TX 79359

LACY, JANINE DAWN, Kindergarten Teacher; *b:* Manning, IA; *m:* Donald D.; *c:* Nathan, Kyle, Patrick; *ed:* (BS) Elem Ed, U of Mo Columbia 1976; *cr:* 1st Grade Teacher 1976-80; Kndgtn Teacher 1980- Southern Boone Cty Ri Schls; *ai:* Mo St Teachers Assn 1976-; Cmmty Teachers Assn Sec/Treas 1986-87; Peace United Church of Christ Trustee 1987-; *home:* Rt 1 1501 E Hwy MM Ashland MO 65010

LACY, MARTHA A., Science Teacher; *b:* Guthrie Center, IA; *ed:* (BS) Earth/Space Sci, 1984, (MA) Scndry Ed, 1988 Ball St Univ; *cr:* Earth/Space Sci Teacher Concord HS 1984-; *ai:* HASTI, NSTA.

LACY, MARY FRANCES LEWIS, Sixth Grade Teacher; *b:* Mobile, AL; *m:* William A.; *c:* Taryn K., Teisa K.; *ed:* (AA) Elem Ed, Mobile St Jr Coll 1967; (BS) Elem Ed, AL St Univ 1969; (MED) Educl Admin, Xavier Univ 1986; *cr:* Teacher Wilkes Cty 1969-70, Belle Haven Elem Sch 1971-; *ai:* Entry Yr Teacher Assistance Mentor Prgm; Cmmty Cncl; NEA, OEA, DEA 1971-; Lioness Club 1984; Alpha Kappa Alpha; Natl Cncl of Negro Women; Jack & Jill of America; *home:* 4130 Merryfield Ave Dayton OH 45416

LADA, JUDSON RAY, Guidance Counselor; *b:* Steubenville, OH; *m:* Carol Faye Weekly; *c:* Tawnya, Tiffany; *ed:* (BA) Eng, Univ of Steubenville 1976; (MS) Ed, Univ of Dayton 1983; CEU Composing Rdng & Writing, Univ of Akron; NACAC Sch Cnslr Inst; Drug Free OH Prgm, Bowling Green St Univ; Completed Sch Cnslr Inst Tools of Trade 1989; *cr:* Eng Teacher 1976-, Eng Teacher/Guidance Cnslr 1989-, Guidance Cnslr 1990 Conotton Valley HS; *ai:* Beta Club 1978-86, Frosh Class 1984-89, Stu Cncl Adv 1989-; Contton Valley Teachers Assn, OH Ed Assn, NEA 1976-; Natl OH Assn of Coll Admissions Cnslrs 1989-; Otterbein United Meth Church Sunday Sch Supt 1987-; Drug Free OH Cmmty Action Trng Prgm 1990; *office:* Conotton Valley HS 7205 Cumberland Rd SW Bowerston OH 44695

LADD, ANN NEWMAN, Math Department Chairperson; *b:* Eupora, MS; *m:* Albert J.; *c:* Deborah A. Ladd James *ed:* (BS) Math Mid TN St Univ 1968; (MS) Math Mid TN St Univ 1971; Post Masters Studies Adm & Supv Mid TN St Univ 1985; *cr:* Grad Teaching Asst Mid TN St Univ 1968-70; Math Teacher Mt Juliet HS 1970-; *ai:* Spon Keyette Club; Spon Acad Awd Banq for Honor Stud; Faclty Adv Comm (Bldg Level) Mem; Needs Assessment Comm (System Wide) Mem; Natl Cncl Teachers of Math 1969-; TN Math Teachers Assn 1980- ; NEA/TEA 1970-; Wilson Cty Ed Assn 1970- ; Pres 1984-85; *office:* Mt Juliet H S 216 Mt Juliet Rd Mount Juliet TN 37122

LADE, DIANE MORLEY, 5-8th Grade Math Teacher; *b:* Creston, IA; *m:* Robert Lee; *c:* Abbey, Dana, Robert; *ed:* (BA) Ed/ Bus Admin, Tarkio Coll 1977; *cr:* Health Teacher Pleasant Hill Schls 1978-80; 5th-8th Grade Math Teacher St Gregory Barbarigo 1980-; *ai:* 7 & 8 Spon; NCTM 1987-; NCEA 1981-.

LADE, J. W. DON, Counselor; *b:* Waco, TX; *c:* Donna F. Lade Mc Graw; *ed:* (BS) Art/Bio, Stephen F Austin 1955; (MA) Counseling/Psych, Univ of N TX 1975; Sam Houston St, TCU, Winona St Coll, Univ of OK, Univ of CA; *cr:* Art/Bio Teacher Poly HS 1955-68; Bio Teacher Trinity HS 1968-75; Cnslr Hurst Jr HS 1975-79, Reagan HS 1979-83, Sam Houston Jr HS 1983-; *ai:* Co-Spon Natl Jr Honor Society; Assn of TX Prof Educators 1985-; North Cntrl TX Prof Guidance Assn 1975-; TX St Awd for Outdoor Learning Center; Articles, Cartoons Published in Ft Worth Star Telegram, Mid-Cities Daily News; *office:* Sam Houston Jr HS 3033 Country Club Rd Irving TX 75038

LADIS, DEBORAH J., Speech Teacher/Debate Coach; *b:* Dallas, TX; *m:* Matthew; *c:* Justin B.; *ed:* (BS) Scndry Ed, N TX St Univ 1977; (MA) Theatre, TX Womens Univ 1984; Coursework towards Admin Cert; *cr:* Hughes Mid Sch 1978-79; Carpenter Mid Sch 1979-83; Vines HS 1983-; *ai:* Natl Forensic League Spon; Speech/Debate Team & Acad Octathlon Team Coach; TX Forensic Assn (Secy, Region Rep); Natl Forensic League 1983-, Diamond Key Coach 1988; Finalist for Plano Ind Sch Dist Teacher of Yr; AAUW Schlsp; *office:* Vines HS 1401 Highedge Plano TX 75075

LADNER, ANNE BROWN, Fifth Grade Teacher; *b:* Mobile, AL; *m:* Mike; *c:* Emily, Sarah; *ed:* (BS) Bus Ed, MS St Univ 1968; (MS) Elem Ed, Univ of Southern MS 1974; *cr:* Teacher North Bay Elem 1969-71, Quarles Elem 1972-; *ai:* Quarles Saints Jr Chrldrs Spon; 5th Grade Grad Coord; MEA & NEA 1969-80; AFT 1980-; Beta Sigma Phi 1972-76 Sweetheart Awd 1974; Newspapers in Ed Teacher of Wk; VP Quarles PTO; *home:* 20057 Pineville Rd Long Beach MS 39560

LA DUCA, FRANCIS, 6th Grade Teacher; *b:* Buffalo, NY; *m:* Anna Marie Bianchi; *c:* Anne La Duca Herman, Linda La Duca Domres, Francis S.; *ed:* (BA) Elem Ed, Buffalo St Coll 1953; Trained in Supervision of Reserve Officers in Army; *cr:* 4th Grade Teacher Niagara Street 1953-54; Army Instr US Army 5th Army Headquarters 1954-55; 6th Grade Teacher Niagara Falls Schls 1955-; *ai:* Building Leadership Comm; Little League Coach; *home:* 456 Campus Dr Snyder NY 14226

LA DUE, STUART R., Dean of Stus/Soc Stud Teacher; *b:* Amsterdam, NY; *c:* Karyn, Thomas, Robert; *ed:* (AA) Liberal Art, Fulton Montgomery Comm Coll 1966; (BS) Scndry Ed/Soc Stud, SUNY Oneonta 1968; (MS) Ed Admin, SUNY Albany 1989; *cr:* Teacher Endwell Jr HS 1968, Mayfield Jr-Sr HS 1968-; Dean of Stus 1987- Mayfield Jr-Sr HS; *ai:* Newspaper, Post Prom Party, Jr Class Adv; Natl Intercollegiate Soccer Ofcls Assn (VP, E KY Bd) 1979-, NCAA Playoffs 1987-89; E NY Approved Soccer Ofcls Assn 1975-, NY St Championship Class A Finals 1986; *office:* Mayfield Jr-Sr HS 1 School St Mayfield NY 12117

LA DUKE, RICHARD MARTIN, Physical Education Teacher; *b:* St Lawrence, NY; *m:* Kathryn Jean Wolf; *c:* Robert K., Dona K.; *ed:* (BS) Phys Ed, 1975, (MED) Ed, 1976 St Lawrence Univ; NJ Drivers Ed, Jersey City St Coll; *cr:* Phys Ed Teacher Clifton HS 1976-; *ai:* Defensive Coord Ftbl; Asst Ftbl, Head Girls Var Sftbl, Head Boys Ice Hockey, Head Girls Vlybl Coach; Ski Club Adv; Weight Lifting Club; Passaic Cty Coaches Assn 1976-, Sftbl Coach of Yr 1989; NFICA 1985-; NEA, NJEA, PCEA, CTA 1976-; Hardyston Township VFD House Comm 1989-; Sussex Cty Firemens Assn 1989-; Clifton Ice Hockey Booster Club Founder 1976-87, Man of Yr 1988; NRA 1988-; Sigma Pi Life Mem 1988-; Passaic-Bergen Umpire Sportsmanship Awd 1987; Clifton Coaches Assn Past Pres; *home:* 26 Maple Dr Stockholm NJ 07460

LADWIG, AGNES TEETER, Third Grade Teacher; *b:* Poynette, WI; *m:* Delano (dec); *c:* Jerry, Mike, Michelle Lange; *ed:* (BA) Elem Ed, 1974, (MA) Elem Ed, 1984 Univ of WI Whitewater; Comparative Ed, Australia 1989; *cr:* 3rd Grade Teacher Marshall Public Sch 1962-63; 3rd-4th Grade Teacher Lowell Public Sch 1965-66, Fall River Sch 1972-; *ai:* FREA Local Treas; Children at

Risk Comm; WEA, NEA; FREA Treas 1989-; *home:* 332 W Prairie St Columbus WI 53925

LAESCH, PHILLIP L., German Instructor; *b:* Bloomington, IL; *ed:* (BSED) Eng/Latin, IL St Normal Univ 1957; (MED) Ger, Univ of IL 1968; Summer Inst Study, Cologne Germany 1963; Innsbruck Austria 1972; Vienna Austria 1976; Middlebury Sch of Lang 1972; *cr:* Eng/Latin Teacher Flint Cntrl HS 1957-59, Flint Southwestern HS 1959-60, Buda Sr HS 1960-61; Latin Teacher 1961-65, Ger Teacher 1968- Princeton HS; *ai:* Fine Arts Productions Asst; IEA, NEA 1968-; *office:* Princeton HS 103 S Euclid St Princeton IL 61356

LA FAVE, RICHARD EDWARD, Mathematics Teacher; *b:* Forsyth, MI; *m:* Gloria J.; *c:* Louise Ingalls, Richard P.; *ed:* (BSEE) Electronic Engr, Univ of WY 1964; (MS) Engr Management, Renselaer Polytec Inst 1968; *cr:* Math Teacher Gwinn Area Cmmty Schls 1974-; *ai:* Class Adv; Grace Luth Church Chm 1974-86; Vets of Foreign Wars Dist Commander 1989-; Military Order of World Wars 1989-; *home:* Box 464 Gwinn MI 49841

LA FAVER, CAROL LEDBETTER, 6th Grade Teacher; *b:* Rosnell, NM; *c:* Amy, Jeremy; *ed:* (BA) Elem Ed, Univ of NM 1966; Addl Studies Univ of CA; Univ of MT; MT St Univ; *cr:* 4th Grade Teacher Riverside Sch Dist 1966-68; Teacher Trainer Peace Corps - Honduras 1968-70; 1st Grade Teacher Santa Fe Public Schls 1970-74; 5th - 6th Grade Teacher Helena Sch Dist No 1 1974-; *ai:* Math Curr Comm; Lang Arts Curr Comm; Collective Gaining Comm; GESA Facilitator-Staff Dev Project; NEA; NCTM; MT Assn; MT Cncl Soc Stud; Helena Ed Assn; Alpha Delta Kappa; Support of Helena Schls Comm; Leadership Helena; United Way; Childrens World Bd of Dir; Teacher of Yr 1989; State Teachers Convention Chm 1988; Taft Inst Fellow 1988; Dir Title IV Incentive Grant 1983; Womens Leadership Trng Cadre 1985-; *home:* 1073 Woodbridge Helena MT 59601

LAFFERTY, WILLIAM PATRICK, Social Studies Teacher; *b:* Amboy, IL; *m:* Sonje Alice Chamness; *c:* Mary-Kathleen, Karen J. Burress, Michael J.; *ed:* (BA) Ec/Bus Admin, Monmouth Coll 1955; (MA) Teaching Rockford Coll 1968; Univ of IL; N IL Univ; *cr:* Teacher/Coach Challand Jr HS 1960-70, Dixon HS 1970-; *ai:* NEA, IL Ed Assn 1960-; Dixon Ed Assn 1970-; Evening Lions 1975-80; Episcapal Mens Club Pres 1965; Consulting Teacher Prgm; Selected Jr Achievement Hall of Fame for Teacher of Applied Ec; *office:* Dixon HS Lincoln Statue Dr Dixon IL 61021

LAFFIE, LYNNE P., English Teacher; *b:* Lynn, MA; *c:* Robert, Steven; *ed:* (BA) Eng, Salem St 1968; Grad Courses Gifted & Talented Instruction; *cr:* Eng/Rdng Teacher Selden Jr HS 1968-69; Eng Teacher Reading HS 1969-73, Newburyport HS 1983-; *ai:* Stu Cncl Adv; Paideia Seminar Leader & Teacher; NEA, MA Teachers Assn 1983-; NCTE 1988-; Alliance of Parents & Teachers 1987-; Horace Mann Grants 1986-; Creative Writing Published 1987-; *office:* Newburyport HS 241 High St Newburyport MA 01950

LA FLAMME, PAMELA, English Teacher; *b:* Williamsport, PA; *m:* Lawrence; *ed:* (BA) Eng, Montclair St Coll 1968; *cr:* Eng Teacher Morris Hills HS 1968-; *ai:* Sch Literary Magazine Adv 1987-88; NEA, NJ Ed Assn 1968-; NCTE; Morris Hills Regional Dist Ed Assn Exec Cncl 1989; NJ Governors Teacher Recognition Awd 1990; *office:* Morris Hills HS 520 W Main St Rockaway NJ 07866

LA FLEUR, KRISTI JEAN, Physical Ed/Health/Sci Teacher; *m:* Dennis; *c:* Matthew, Michael; *ed:* (BS) Phys Ed, 1974, (MS) Health Ed, 1984 Cntrl MI Univ; *cr:* Teacher Bad Axe Public Schls 1975-76, Coleman Cmmty Schls 1977-82, Chippewa Hills Schls 1982-83, Coleman Cmmty Schls 1984-; *ai:* Dept Head Phys Ed & Health; Girls Var Track Coach; Sch Wellness Head; AAHPER; Alpha Sigma Tau Housing Corporation VP.

LA FONTAINE, MARY LOUIS, Teacher; *b:* Lafayette, LA; *m:* Herman; *c:* Kasandra A., Tammie; *ed:* (BA) Elem Ed, Southern Univ 1968; USL Sch Law; Cmptr; Sign Lang; *cr:* Teacher Paul Breaux 1968-69, S J Montgomery 1969-70, Houston Ind Sch Dist 1972-73, Acadian Elem 1973-83, Broussard Mid Sch 1984-; *ai:* Drama Day; NEA 1985-; Lafayette Parish Soc Stud Cncl Parliamentarian 1988-; *home:* 207 S Hamner Lafayette LA 70501

LA FONTAINE, PATRICIA JO, French Teacher; *b:* Decatur, IN; *ed:* (BA) Eng/Fr, 1969, (MS) Eng/Fr, 1972 St Francis Coll; Fr, Inst for Amer Univs Avignon France 1970, Quimper France 1982; Fr, Universite Laval 1979-80, 1983; *cr:* Fr/Eng Teacher Portage Mid Sch 1969-77; Fr Teacher North Side HS 1977-85; *ai:* AFS Foreign Lang Club Spon; AAFT, ACTFL, NEA, ISTA; *office:* North Side HS 475 E State St Fort Wayne IN 46805

LA FOUNTAINE, GLENN MICHEL, 5th Grade Teacher; *b:* New London, CT; *m:* Kathryn Mary Civitello; *c:* Michelle, Abby Cross; *ed:* (AA) Liberal Arts, RI Jr Coll 1977; (BA) Elem Ed, Univ of Cntrl FL 1980; *cr:* Dir Gerber Childrens Center 1980-81; 4th Grade Teacher 1981-85, 5th Grade Teacher 1985- Dr Phillips Elem; *ai:* Sci Coord Dr Phillips Elem; Young Astronauts 1985-87; Cousteau Society Mem 1990; Greenpeace Mem 1990; Sci Grant for Paper 1987; Teacher of Yr 1985-86; *office:* Dr Phillips Elem Sch 6909 Dr Phillips Blvd Orlando FL 32819

LAFRAMBOISE, JOAN C., Eighth Grade Teacher; *b:* Brooklyn, NY; *m:* Albert G.; *c:* Laura, Brian; *ed:* (BS) Soc Stud/Eng, Springfield Coll 1956; *cr:* Eng/Soc Stud Teacher Memorial Sch 1956-61; Eng Teacher Midland Park HS 1961-63; Soc Stud/Eng Teacher Luke Garrett Mid Sch 1983-; *ai:* NCSS; Knights of Lithuania (Pres Cncl 35 1975-76, New England Dist Pres 1976-77); *home:* 2891 Dara Dr NE Marietta GA 30066

LA FRANCE, ERNESTINE CHRISTINE GETTYS, Biology/Computer Teacher; *b:* Oklahoma City, OK; *m:* Gary; *c:* Terry M., Lori D., Stacie L.; *ed:* (BS) Naturas Sci, OK St Univ 1968; (MED) Bio, Northeastern St Univ 1973; Working Towards Doctorate; *cr:* Jr HS/Elem Sci Teacher Haworth Public Schls 1968-69; HS Math/Sci Teacher Tuttle Public Schls 1969-71; Jr HS Sci/Math Teacher Pryor Public Schls 1973-77; Jr HS/9th Grade Phys Sci Teacher Cleveland Public Schls 1977-80; HS Sci/Cmptr Teacher Drumright Public Schls 1980-; *ai:* Academic Team Coach; Cmptr Club & Sci Club Spon; OK Ed Assn, OK Sci Teachers Assn 1973-; Phi Delta Kappa 1985-; Bus & Prof Womens Club Pres 1985-86; Citizens for Environ Safety Steering Comm 1989-; St Albans Episcopal Church Vestay 1988-; Runner-Up Bio Teacher of Yr; *office:* Drumright HS 301 S Pennsylvania Drumright OK 74030

LA FRANCE, RAYMOND JOSEPH, Religious Studies Chairperson; *b:* Central Falls, RI; *m:* Rose Mary Muhovich; *c:* Michael J., Paul L., Mary A. La France Rawls, Jeannine La France Hodge, Steven R.; *ed:* (BGS) His/Poly Sci, Univ NE 1972; (MA) Theology, Providence Coll 1983; *cr:* Military Officer USAF/Army 1950-74; Real Estate Management De Felice Realtors 1972-82; Chm/Religious Stud Teacher Bishop Keough HS 1983-; *ai:* Campus Ministry; Counseling; Dev Fund; Natl Assn of Realtors (Grad Realtors Inst 1975, Certified Residential Specialist 1978); RI Assn of Realtors Sr Instr 1983; Knights of Columbus Grand Knight 1978-79, Columbian 1979; Rotary Intnl Dev 1981; US Navy Yacht Club Commodore 1981-82; Legion of Merit, Bronze Star, Meritorious Service Medal, Joint Services Commendation Medal, Army Commendation Medal US Military 1950-74; Knights of Columbus Family of Yr 1981; *home:* 60 Mark Dr North Kingstown RI 02852

LA GRAFF, JOHN MARTIN, English Teacher; *b:* Alpena, MI; *ed:* (BA) Eng, Cntrl MI Univ 1973; Scndry Guidance & Counseling; Certified Facalitator New Age Thinking Prgm; *cr:* 10th Grade Eng Teacher Mayville HS 1973-82; 7th Grade Eng Teacher Mayville Mid Sch 1982-84; 11th Grade Eng Teacher 1984-89, 11th/12th Grade Eng Teacher 1989- Mayville HS; *ai:* Mayville Ed Assn (Pres, VP); *office:* Mayville HS 6250 Fulton St Mayville MI 48744

LA GRANGE, SANDRA LANDRY, English Teacher; *b:* Lafayette, LA; *m:* Glenn J.; *c:* Brandon, Bryce; *ed:* (BA) Eng Ed/Bus Ed, Univ of S LA 1985; *cr:* Eng Teacher Teurlings Cath HS 1985-; *ai:* Jr-Sr Prom; Homecoming Court Act; NCEA 1985-; Teurling Cath HS Teacher of Yr 1989-; *home:* Rt 6 Box 1132 Breaux Bridge LA 70517

LAGUNA, BILLY N., Health Teacher; *b:* Yuma, AZ; *m:* Diane Peralta; *c:* Greg, Rocky; *ed:* (BA) Phys Ed, N AZ Univ 1980; Working Towards Masters Admin; *cr:* Phys Ed Teacher Crane Rancho Viejo Sch 1980-84; Sci Teacher 1984-87; Health Teacher 1988- Kofa HS; *ai:* Bsbl Var Asst Coach; Intramural Dir; NEA, AEA 1980-; Amer Bsbl Coaching Assn 1988-; Babe Ruth Bsbl Bd of Dir Secy 1987-; *office:* Kofa HS 3100 S Ave A Yuma AZ 85364

LAGUNA, ROLANDO A., Mathematics & Physics Teacher; *b:* Panama City, Panama; *m:* Tatiana Smaranda; *c:* Andrew R., Alexis A.; *ed:* (BS) Mechanical Engineer, Polytechnic Inst Romania 1985; *cr:* Adjunct Teacher Essex Cty Coll 1986-87; Teacher St Mary HS 1987-; *office:* St Mary HS 64 Chestnut St Rutherford NJ 07070

LAHMANN, JAMES VICTOR, Sixth Grade Teacher; *b:* Owosso, MI; *m:* Elizabeth Diane; *c:* Victoria, Rebekah, Jamie; *ed:* Grad Stud MI St; ITIP Trained; Gifted Talented Math; Stu Assistance; - *cr:* Teacher/Coach Beal City Public Schls 1967-69, Flushing Public Schls 1969-70, New Lothrop Public Schls 1970-; *ai:* Stu Support Groups; Var Ftbl Coach; Sftbl Coaches Assn 1982-88; Class C Coach of Yr 1982; MI HS Coaches Assn 1982-; Ftbl Coaches Assn 1985-; Village of New Lothrop Trustee 1984-; Village of New Lothrop Mayor 1990; Phi Kappa Tau Domain Dir 1970-, Phi Awd 1990; Grant to Study SE Asia at U of MI; Union Offices With NLEA; *home:* 9392 Maple Box 88 New Lothrop MI 48460

LAIDACKER, LARRY M., Fourth Grade Teacher; *b:* Williamsport, PA; *m:* Suzann L Spencer; *c:* Joshua, Jeremy, Jacey S.; *ed:* (BS) Elem Ed, Bloomsburg St Coll 1968; (MS) Ed, Bucknell Univ 1974; *cr:* 4th Grade Teacher Sullivan Cty Sch Dist 1968-; *ai:* Sullivan Cty Sch Dist Jr HS Wrestling Coach; NEA, PA St Ed Assn 1968-; BSA Comm Mem 1987-; *home:* RD 1 Box 11 Muncy Valley PA 17758

LAIL, VIOLA, Third Grade Teacher; *b:* Covington, KY; *ed:* (BA) Elem Ed, Univ of Cincinnati 1966; (MS) Elem Ed, N KY Univ 1982; *cr:* 1st Grade Teacher Lincoln Elem 1963-70, Grandview Elem 1970-; 3rd Grade Teacher Grandview Elem 1980-; *ai:* NEA 1963-; BEA 1970-; *home:* 439 Lafayette Ave Bellevue KY 41073

LAIN, DEBORAH REYNOLDS, JTPA Teacher; *b:* El Paso, TX; *m:* Roy L.; *c:* Danielle Niolet, Courtney Nicolet; *ed:* (BS) Home Ec Ed, MS St Univ 1973; *cr:* Home Ec Teacher Long Beach HS 1978-81; Home Ec Teacher 1981-, JTPA Teacher 1987- Hancock N Cntrl; *ai:* JTPA Pgrm Coord; Long Beach Amer Fed Treas 1979-81; *office:* Hancock N Cntrl HS 6122 Cuevas Town Rd Pass Christian MS 39571

LAINE, NANCYE ALLEN, 5th Grade Teacher; *b:* Farmville, VA; *m:* William E. Jr.; *c:* Jennifer L.; *ed:* (BS) Home Ec, Longwood Coll 1960; (BS) Elem Ed, Christopher Newport 1984; Latest Techniques in Math Course; *cr:* 7th Grade Teacher Chuckatuck; Home Ec Teacher John Yeates; 5th Grade Teacher Windsor Elem; *ai:* 4-H Club Sch Rep; Cmmty & Church Work.

LAIRD, BRENDA RATCLIFF, Biology Instructor; *b:* Providence, RI; *w:* John M. Jr. (dec); *c:* Cassie, Jolynne; *ed:* (BS) Bio/Eng, 1965, (MS) Bio, 1973, Specialist Bio, 1977 Univ of S MS; *cr:* Bio/Chem Teacher S Pike HS 1965-70; Part-Time Sci Instr Copiah-Lincoln Jr Coll 1976-84; Bio/Chem Franklin Cty HS 1970-; *ai:* MS Assn of Educators (Local Secy, Treas) 1985-89, Leadership Awd 1989; Delta Kappa Gamma Mem 1971-82; Univ S MS Bio Fellowship; Natl Sci Fnd Awd for Extended Study; Franklin Cty STAR Teacher; *office:* Franklin Cty HS P O Box 666 Meadville MS 39653

LAIRD, CONNIE CHRESTMAN, First Grade Department Chair; *b:* Lubbock, TX; *m:* Russell C.; *c:* Ryan; *ed:* (BS) Elem Ed, TX Tech Univ 1974; (MS) Rdng, Univ of Houston Clear Lake City 1980; Gifted/Talented; *cr:* 1st Grade Teacher Parkwood Elem Sch 1976-77; 1st Grade Teacher 1977-87, 1st Grade Dept Chairperson 1987- Dabbs Elem Sch; *ai:* Stu Cncl Spon; Assn of TX Prof Ed 1980-; *office:* J P Dobbs Elem Sch 302 Lambuth Deer Park TX 77536

LAIRD, SHIRLEY BARNES, Chapter 1 Lead Teacher; *b:* Mount Olive, MS; *m:* John O.; *c:* Gerald, Glenn; *ed:* (BA) Elem Ed, Tougaloo Coll 1964; (MS) Elem Ed, Jackson St Univ 1978; *cr:* 1st Grade Teacher Carver Elem 1964-68; 2nd Grade Teacher J E Johnson 1968-70; 3rd Grade Teacher Bassfield Elem 1970-74; 1st Grade Teacher 1974-89; Chapter 1 Lead Teacher 1989- Prentiss Elem; *ai:* Sunshine Comm Chairperson; Teacher Assisting Teachers Chairperson; MS Teachers Assessment Instrument Evaluator; MS Assn Dist Secy 1965-70; MS Assn of Ed 1970-Membership Awd 1981-82; Promotion Awd 1983; NEA 1970-; PTA (Secy 1982-86); Jeff/Davis Co Prentiss Optimist Club 1988; Jeff/Davis Co NAACP 1970; Chapter 1 Lead Teacher; Natl Sci Grant; *home:* PO Box 503 Prentiss MS 39474

LAIRD, VIRGINIA ORR, Mathematics Teacher; *b:* Winona, MS; *m:* David Edward; *c:* Shelley; *ed:* (BSE) Math, Delta St Univ 1971; Advanced Stud MS St Univ, MS Coll, TX A&M Univ, Woodrow Wilson Inst; *cr:* Teacher Cleveland HS 1971-72, Yazoo City Jr HS 1972-81, Katy Ind Schls 1981-; *ai:* Stu Cncl Co-Spon; Handbook Revision, Textbook Evaluation, Chairperson Tardy Policy Comm; NCTM, TX St Teachers Assn, NEA; Holy Covenant Meth Church; Governors Awd for Outstanding Volunteers 1976; Whos Who Among College Stu 1971; Outstanding Young Women of America 1980; *office:* Mayde Creek HS 19202 Groschke Rd Houston TX 77084

LAKE, ALBERT CLARK, JR., Science Teacher; *b:* Jacksonville, FL; *m:* Marion Whittier; *c:* Stephen, Jennifer; *ed:* (BED) Sci/Math, Keene St Coll 1964-; (MS) Chem, Purdue Univ 1969; Radio Chem, MT St Univ; Math & Physics, Univ of NH; *cr:* Teacher 1964-71, Sci Dept Head 1971-85, Teacher 1985- Salem HS; *ai:* Sch Dist Cmptr Assisted Instruction & Strategic Planning Comm; NEA 1985-; NH Ed Assn Regional Rep 1990; Salem Ed Assn Pres 1987-; Hampstead Fire Dept Volunteer Fireman 1970-; Hampstead Sch Bd Mem 1974-77; Hampstead Budget Comm Mem 1978-; Salem Ed Assn Teacher of Yr 1988; Teacher Idea & Information Exch Article Published 1989; Chm Local & St Instructional Convention 1989; *office:* Snook Sch Geremonty Dr Salem NH 03079

LAKE, DIANE KAY, Phys Ed & Health Teacher; *b:* Fort Wayne, IN; *m:* James Edward; *c:* Cory, Christopher; *ed:* (BA) Phys Ed/Health, Purdue 1972; (MS) Scndry Phys Ed, St Francis 1975; *cr:* 8th/9th Grade Phys Ed/Health Teacher New Haven HS 1973-74; 6th-8th Grade Phys Ed/Health Teacher New Haven Mid 1974-; *ai:* Bsktbl, Vlybl, Track & Gymnastics Coach; Chrldrs & GAA Spon; East Allen Educators Assn Building Rep 1983-83, 1985-87 & 1988-; Ft Wayne Area Cncl Intnl Rdng Assn; *office:* New Haven Mid Sch 900 Prospect Ave New Haven IN 46774

LAKE, FREDERICK NELSON, Third Grade Teacher; *b:* Spokane, WA; *m:* Linda Kay Blair; *c:* Willie, Samuel; *ed:* (BS) Phys Ed, Univ of ID 1974; Elem Ed; *cr:* 1st Grade Teacher 1974-76, 6th Grade Teacher 1976-80, 3rd Grade Teacher 1980- Fruitland Elem; *ai:* Var Track; *office:* Fruitland Elem Sch 401 Iowa St Fruitland ID 83619

LAKE, JOELLE BONHAM, Third Grade Teacher; *b:* Gardena, CA; *m:* David E.; *c:* Michael, Morgan; *ed:* (AA) Modesto Jr Coll 1977; (BA) Liberal Arts, CA St Univ Sacramento 1979; *cr:* 1st/2nd Grade Teacher 1979-81, 5th Grade Teacher 1981-86, 3rd Grade Teacher 1987- Pleasant Valley Sch; *ai:* Lang Art Coord & Chm; Mentor Teacher 1988-; CA Rdng Assn 1979-; Intnl Rdng Assn 1990; CA Teachers Assn 1979-; Pleasant Valley Sch Dist Golden Apple & Valuable Service Awd; *office:* Pleasant Valley Sch 14685 Pleasant Valley Rd Penn Valley CA 95946

LAKE, PETER JOHN, 6th Grade Mid Sch Teacher; *b:* Concord, NH; *m:* Judith Hopkins; *c:* Joshua S., Stephen P., Daniel B.; *ed:* (BS) Elem Ed, Gordon Coll 1982; (MS) Elem Admin, Villanova Univ 1990; *cr:* 7th/8th Grade Teacher N Shore Chrstn Sch 1982-83; 6th Grade Teacher/Team Leader Delaware Cty Chrstn Sch 1983-; *ai:* Designed & Taught Human Sexuality Course; Mid Sch Soccer, Bsktbl, Track & Field Coach; Cmptr Teacher; Covenant Fellowship Mid Sch Youth Leader 1989-; *office:* Delaware Cty Chrstn Sch Malin Rd Newtown Square PA 19073

LAKEFIELD, BRADLEY RONALD, Sci/Math/Computers Supervisor; *b:* Passaic, NJ; *c:* Scott; *ed:* (BA) Comprehensive Sci, 1968, (MA) Admin/Supervision, 1980 Montclair St Coll; Numerous Courses; *cr:* Sci Teacher Washington Sch & Franklin Sch 1968-84; Sci Dept Supvr Hawthorne Sch Dist 1984-87; Sci/Chem Teacher Fairlawn HS 1985-88; Sci Teacher Hawthorne HS 1984-; Math/Sci/Cmptrs Supvr Hawthorne Sch Dist 1987-; *ai:* NHS, Sci League Adv; NJ Sci Supvrs Assn, Assn Math Teachers of NJ, Prin & Supvrs Assn; Phi Kappa Phi 1979; Pi Lambda Theta 1987; Hawthorne Town Environmental Comm 1988-; High Grade Average all Grad Work; Several Inservice Prgms; *home:* 32 Summit Ave Hawthorne NJ 07506

LAKEY, GLENDA DE VORE, Second Grade Teacher; *b:* Ft Worth, TX; *m:* Harold Dean; *c:* Susan R., Sarah B.; *ed:* (BSED) Elem/Kndgtn Cert, 1973, (MSED) Early Chldhd, 1975 SE OK St Univ; Various Courses; *cr:* Kndgtn Teacher Hurst-Euless-Bedford Ind Sch Dist 1973-76; 2nd Grade Teacher 1976-77, Kndgtn Teacher 1977-82, 2nd Grade Teacher 1982- Denison Ind Sch Dist; *ai:* 2nd Grade Team Leader; TX Classroom Teachers Assn, Denison Ed Assn, Delta Kappa Gamma, Cardinal Key; Denison Drug Advisory Comm 1990; Layne PTO Cultural Art Chairperson; *home:* 2604 Biscayne Sherman TX 75090

LALA, CLARENCE MAX, Mathematics Teacher; *b:* Great Falls, MT; *m:* Donna Mae Miller; *c:* Michael L., Chad C., Jay D.; *ed:* (BA) Phys Ed, 1965, (BS) Math, 1971 E MT Coll; *cr:* Math Teacher Circle Public Sch 1965-; *ai:* Mathcounts Team & Mathletes Coach; MT Ed Assn (Local VP 1967, Local Pres 1968); *home:* Box 383 Circle MT 59215

LA LIBERTE, LOIS DE LA MATER, Fifth Grade Teacher; *b:* Troy, NY; *m:* Robert J.; *c:* Robert J. Jr.; *ed:* (BSED) Elem Ed, Coll of St Rose 1964; *cr:* 5th Grade Teacher Gardner Dickinson Sch 1964-; *ai:* NYS Teachers Assn 1964-; *office:* Gardner-Dickinson Sch PO Box 345 Wynantskill NY 12198

LALICKER, BEVERLY SUE SELLS, Kindergarten Teacher; *b:* Las Vegas, NV; *m:* Eric Lewis; *c:* Andrea L.; *ed:* (BS) Elem Ed/Soc Stud/Child Dev, Coll of S UT 1969; Word Weaving; Natl Inst of Child Dev; Math Their Way; *cr:* Kndgtn Teacher Cerritos Sch 1969-70; 1st-4th Grade Summer Sch Teacher El Dorado Sch & Monte Vista Sch 1971-76; 3rd Grade Teacher 1969-83, 2nd Grade Teacher 1983-87, Kndgtn Teacher 1987- El Dorado Sch; *ai:* Pres Teachers Bowling League; Dist Academic Comm; Human Relations Coord; Teachers Assn of Lancaster, NEA, CA Teachers Assn 1970-; NAEYC 1989-; Foster Parent 1987-; PTA El Dorado Honorary Service Awd Honorable Mention; *home:* 44626 2nd St E Lancaster CA 93535

LA LONDE, JANET ARNDT, Kindergarten Teacher; *b:* Detroit, MI; *m:* Ronald L.; *c:* Philip L., Carl W.; *ed:* (BA) Kndtn/Primary Ed, Capital Univ 1968; Gesell Tester; *cr:* Teacher B Beck Sch 1968-; *ai:* NEA; MI Ed Assn; Redford Union Ed Assn; Oak Branch Charter Chapter Amer Bus Womans Assn Woman of Yr 1978; *office:* B Beck Elementary School 27100 Bennett Redford MI 48240

LAMANSKY, CONSTANCE MARYANN, Fourth Grade Teacher; *b:* Milford, MA; *ed:* (BA) Ed, Anna Maria Coll 1972; (MA) Elem Ed, RI Coll 1976; Working Beyond Masters Cmptrs in Ed; *cr:* 6th Grade Teacher 1972-73, 4th Grade Teacher 1973-74 Citizens Memorial, Bernon Heights 1974-; *ai:* Greater Woonsocket Amer Assn of Univ Women Secy 1981-82; Delta Kappa Gamma Mem; Bernon Heights PTO 1976-77; Polish Subcommittee of RI Heritage Commission (Secy 1983-85, Vice Chm 1985-87, Chm 1987-89); *home:* 80 Napoleon St Woonsocket RI 02895

LAMAR, SUE BEAN, Mathematics Teacher; *b:* Lebanon, TN; *m:* Thomas G. Jr.; *c:* Sarah R., Martha G.; *ed:* (BS) Math, MTSU 1970; *cr:* 7th Grade Teacher Wharton Jr HS 1970-78; 7th/8th Grade Teacher West End Jr HS 1978-80; 5th/6th Grade Math Support Teacher Haynes Elem 1980-81; 7th/8th Grade Teacher Bellevue Mid Sch 1981-85; 9th-12th Grade Teacher Antioch HS 1985-; *ai:* NHS Spon; NEA, TEA, MTEA 1970-; *office:* Antioch HS 5050 Blue Hole Rd Antioch TN 37013

LAMATRICE, LOUIS F., Counselor; *b:* Steubenville, OH; *m:* Mary Elizabeth; *c:* L. Gregory, Elizabeth, Susan; *ed:* (BA) Soc Stud, 1967, (BS) Scndry Ed, 1967 OH St; (MS) Guidance, Univ of Dayton 1976; *cr:* Soc Stud Teacher Jefferson Union HS 1967-87; Cnslr Edison S HS 1987-; *ai:* NEA, OEA, OSCA; *office:* Edison S HS PO Box 308 Richmond OH 43944

LAMB, CAROLYN FISHER, Health/Physical Ed Teacher; *b:* Baton Rouge, LA; *m:* John; *c:* Paul, Greg, Janelle Marks, John Jr,; *ed:* (BS) Health/Phys Ed, Grambling St Univ 1970; (MSED) Admin/Supervision, Southern Univ 1983; Univ of AR Little Rock; *cr:* Phys Ed Teacher Behrman Martin HS 1970, Quachita Jr HS 1970-73; Phys Ed Teacher/Coach Glen Oaks Jr HS 1973-80;Phys Ed Teacher Capitol Mid Sch 1980-82, Robert E Lee HS 1982-83; Health/Phys Ed Teacher Philander Smith Coll 1983-84; *ai:* Care Comm Chairperson; BCC & Assessment Team Comm Mem; AEA Mem; Delta Sigma Theta; Baton Rouge Outstanding Teacher of Yr Awd 1975; *home:* 10813 Valiant Dr Little Rock AR 72209

LAMB, GEORGIA MORRIS, Teacher/Department Chair; *b:* Memphis, TN; *m:* Robert Hugh; *c:* Lynde; *ed:* (BS) Bio, TN Wesleyan 1967; (MS) Bio, TN Tech 1970; Teacher Madisonville HS 1968-69, West Point HS 1969-70, Mc Minn Cty HS 1970-; *ai:* Stu Cncl; J-Teens; Sci Club; MCEA Pres 1979; TEA, NEA; Jaycettes Pres 1974, St Speak-Up; Fellowship to Earthwatch; TN Outstanding Sci Teacher; Career Ladder Level III; *office:* Mc Minn Cty HS 2215 Congress Pkwy Athens TN 37303

LAMB, JIMMY G., History/Economics Teacher; *b:* Hopkinsville, KY; *m:* Joan Joiner; *c:* Joshua, Jody M.; *ed:* (BS) His/Geography, 1973, (MA) Ed/His, 1979 Austin Peay St Univ; *cr:* Teacher Robertson Cty Schls 1973-; *ai:* Chess Club; NEA, TN Ed Assn, Robertson Cty Ed Assn 1973-; Book Published 1979; *office:* East Robertson Sch E Robertson Rd Cross Plains TN 37049

LAMB, MAX SUEL, Educator; *b:* Logan, UT; *m:* Barbara Jo Hamilton; *c:* Michael, Gloria, Stephen, Brenda; *ed:* (BS) Elem Ed, UT St Univ 1970; Several Wkshps; *cr:* Teacher Lynn Elem 1969-; *ai:* Supts Advisory & Math Comm; Acting Prin; OEA, UEA, NEA Mem; BSA (Scoutmaster, Order of Arrow Adv), Silver Beaver Awd 1976, Vigal 1978; Little League (Pres, Coach); *office:* Lynn Elem Sch 605 Grant Ave Ogden UT 84404

LAMB, PATSY HOPKINS, Fourth Grade Teacher; *b:* Winfield, TX; *m:* Rex Jr.; *c:* Rex III, Amy; *ed:* (BS) Elem Ed, 1962, (MED) Elem Ed, 1967 E TX St Univ; *cr:* 2nd Grade Teacher San Jacinto Elem 1962-64, Ascher Silverstein 1964-65; 1st Grade Teacher S Franklin Elem 1965-67, Bowie Elem 1968-69; 1st/4th Grade Teacher Dobbs Elem 1976-.

LAMB, RUTH BOWEN, English Teacher; *b:* Birmingham, AL; *m:* Curtis Alan; *c:* Alan, Lana J. Lamb Miller; *ed:* (BS) Ed, IN Univ 1985; *cr:* Kndgtn Teacher Shirely Heights 1970-73; Eng Teacher Franklin Cty HS 1986-; *ai:* Future Problem Solvers Coach 1989-; Drama Club Spon 1987-89; Delta Kappa Gamma Alpha Beta Prof Teachers 1989-; Kappa Delta Pi Honor Society in Ed 1989-; IN Cncl of Teachers Eng 1985-; IN Rdng Specialists Cncl 1985-; IN Teachers of Writing 1985-; Margaret Mary Cmnty Hospital Guild Bd Pres 1975; *office:* Franklin County H S P O Box 1 Brookville IN 47012

LAMBERT, DEBBE KILBY, Physical Education Teacher; *b:* Indianapolis, IN; *m:* David; *c:* Jake, Josh; *ed:* (BS) Phys Ed, Manchester Coll 1983; (MS) Scndry Ed, IN Univ 1987; Adolescents Trng Wkshp, Dynamic Phys Ed Bob Pangrazi, Drug Awareness of Children with Alcoholic Parents; *cr:* Phys Ed Teacher Pierceton Mid/Elem Sch 1984; Health Teacher 1984-89, Phys Ed Teacher 1984- Marshall Mid Sch; *ai:* Girls Jr League Dir; Jr Athletic Assn Asst Dir; Girls & Boys Asst Track Coach; IN Prin Leadership Acad Participant; IN Dept of Ed Pilot Group for Creative Dance; *home:* R R 1 Barbee Lake Pierceton IN 46562

LAMBERT, EDWARD EUGENE, English/Social Studies Teacher; *b:* Dunlap, IA; *m:* Jolene A. Gonzales; *c:* Marc, Megan, Kristen, Jessica; *ed:* (BA) His, Univ of N CO; Liberal Arts, St Johns Coll; *cr:* Teacher Hanna Eli Mountain HS 1974-77, Salida HS 1977-; *ai:* Knowledge Bowl Team & Parliamentary Procedure Team Spon; Girls & Boys Tennis Coach; NEA 1974-; Salida Ed Assn (Co-Pres 1990) 1977-; CO Ed Assn 1977-; Salida Aspen Concert Series 1985-; Natl Environment for Hum Fellowships 1987-89; Attended St Johns Coll NEH Fellow; *office:* Salida HS PO Box 70 Salida CO 81201

LAMBERT, HAROLD SCOTT, JR., Band Director; *b:* Bristol, VA; *m:* Patti Dee Blackwell; *c:* Erica; *ed:* (BS) Music Ed, E TN St 1974; (MS) Music Ed, Radford Univ 1979; Additional Course Work VA Tech; *cr:* Band Dir John Battle HS 1974-; *ai:* Clinician & Adjudicator in 8 States; Arranged Music & Written Field Shows for over 20 Marching Bands in 5 Sts; Coda Software Division of Wenger Corporation & Total Show Computerized Show Design; Amer Sch Band Dir Assn, Natl Band Assn, Music Educators Natl Conference, Phi Mu Alpha Sinfonia; Phi Beta Mu Pres; VA Music Ed Assn Dist VII (Secy, Treas, Vice Chm, Chm); VA Band & Orch Dirs Assn Past Pres; Natl Band Assn Citation of Excl, Honored by VA Music Educators Assn; Amer Sch Band Dirs Assn Stanbury Awd 1983; Twice Honored by Bristol Jaycees for Cmmty Service; Selected to Outstanding Young Men of America; *office:* John Battle HS Rt 5 Lee Hwy Bristol VA 24201

LAMBERT, JIMMY D., Assistant Principal; *b:* Goodway, AL; *m:* Evelian Stacey; *c:* Michael, Patrick, Lee Anne; *ed:* (BS) Phys Sci/Math 1968, (MED) Admin, 1987 Livingston Univ; *cr:* Sci Teacher/Bsktbl Coach Union HS 1968-70; 7th Grade Math Teacher/Asst Prin Monroeville Mid Sch 1970-79; Sch Bus Driver 1970-; 8th Grade Math Teacher/Asst Prin Monroeville Jr HS 1979-; *ai:* Monroe Cty Teachers Assn, AL Ed Assn, NEA 1968-; J U Blacksher HS Athletic Club; *office:* Monroeville Jr HS 315 York St Monroeville AL 36502

LAMBERT, JUDITH BERGERON, Mathematics/French Teacher; *b:* Livonia, LA; *m:* Evans D.; *ed:* (BS) Math Ed, LA St Univ Baton Rouge 1971; *cr:* 7th/8th Grade Math Teacher Marksville Jr HS 1972-77; 7th-12th LA His/Math/Fr/Sci Teacher Hessmer HS 1977-89; 9th-12th Grade Math/Fr I/Fr II Teacher Bunkie HS 1989-; *ai:* Avoyelles Assn of Educators, LA Assn of Educators, NEA 1972-; *home:* PO Box 275 Hessmer LA 71341

LAMBERT, KATHERINE DAVIES, Religion & Mathematics Teacher; *b:* Pittston, PA; *m:* Greg; *c:* Jeff, Kate; *ed:* (BA) Music Ed, Barry Univ 1970; *cr:* Math/Music Teacher St Helen Sch 1964-66, St Jude Sch 1966-71; Music Teacher Orchard Villa Sch 1973-75; Religion/Math Teacher St Lawrence Sch 1981-; *ai:* Jr HS Coord; Stu Cncl Adv; Chrldr Spon; NCEA, FL Math League; *office:* St Lawrence Sch 5223 N Himes Tampa FL 33614

LAMBERT, OPAL KIMBRIEL, Science Teacher; *b:* Portsmouth, VA; *m:* T. J.; *c:* Tammy R., Rebekah A.; *ed:* (BS) Sci Interdisciplinary, Univ of W FL 1981; Cmptr Sci; *cr:* 8th Grade Sci Teacher Pace Mid Sch 1981-; *ai:* Direct Yearly Sci Fair; Teach Cmptr Eccological Summer Camp; Santa Rosa Cty Ecology Act Comm; NSTA, FAST; Berryhill Road Baptist Church Treas; Whos Who of the Gulf Coast; *office:* Pace Mid Sch 411 Norris Rd Pace FL 32571

LAMBERT, SHERYL DARLENE, HS Mathematics Teacher; *b:* Benson, AZ; *m:* Daniel Eugene; *c:* Cyndria L., Angela L.; *ed:* Assoc Math, Connors St Coll 1975; (BA) Scndry Ed Applied Sci, NSU 1982; *cr:* HS Math Teacher Wagoner Public Schls 1982-84, Crowder Public Sch 1984-; *ai:* Frosh Spon; Staff Dev Comm Mem; Taught Jr HS Stus Materials for Mathcount Competition; OK Ed Assn, NEA Mem 1982-; Crowder Ed Assn Mem 1984-; *office:* Crowder Public Sch Box B Crowder OK 74430

LAMBERT-SCRONCE, KATHERINE L., English Teacher; *b:* Newton, NC; *m:* Clifton E.; *c:* Rachel; *ed:* (AB) Eng, Lenoir-Rhyne Coll 1977; *cr:* Eng/Latin Teacher Statesville HS 1977-80; ESL Teacher Catawba Valley Comm Coll 1980-82; Eng Teacher St Stephens HS 1981-82, Hickory HS 1984-86, Fred T Foard HS 1986-; *ai:* Quiz Bowl Coach; NEA, NCAE; Teaching Portfolio Published by Cliffs Notes; *home:* 219 Fairway Dr Newton NC 28658

LAMBERTI, CARLO, Fifth Grade Homeroom Teacher; *b:* Detroit, MI; *m:* Gail Ann Karbowski; *c:* Carlo D., Gina M.; *ed:* (BSED) Geography, 1967, (MA) Elem Sch Admin, 1976 Cntrl MI Univ; Quest Trng 1989; *cr:* 7th Grade Teacher Ford Mid Sch 1967-71; 5th-6th Grade Teacher Linwood Elem Sch 1971-; *ai:* Girls & Boys Soccer & Girls Vlybl Coach; Referee of Bsktbl & Vlybl; MI Sesquicentennial Prgm Dir; 200th Anniversary Celebration of US Constitution Sch Dir; Mc Donalds Speech Contest Building Dir; MEA, NEA; Linwood Civic Improvement; Knights of Columbus; Elected Rep of Sch System at Jeffersonian Meeting 1988; *home:* 615 Handy Dr Bay City MI 48706

LAMBIE, ROBERT BROOKS, Head Ftbl Coach/Math Teacher; *b:* Phoenix, AZ; *m:* Sandra Cone; *ed:* (BA) Phys Ed, AZ St Univ 1980; *cr:* Math Teacher/Ftbl Coach Paradise Valley HS 1983-; *ai:* Head Ftbl Coach; AZ Coaches Assn 1987-; AZ St Alumni Assn 1980-; Region Coach of Yr 1989; *office:* Paradise Valley HS 3950 E Bell Rd Phoenix AZ 85032

LAMBING, MARGARET LOUISE, Kindergarten Teacher; *b:* New Kensington, PA; *ed:* (BS) Elem Ed, 1981, (MED) Elem Ed, 1982 IN Univ of PA; *cr:* 3rd Grade Teacher Hyde Park Elem 1982-83; 5th Grade Teacher North Vandergrift Elem 1983-84; 3rd Grade Teacher Paulton Elem 1984-85; 1st Grade Teacher Weinels Elem 1985-86; Kndgtn Teacher North Vandergrift/Wilson Elem 1986-87; 1st Grade Teacher North Washington Elem 1987-88, Weinels Elem 1988-89; Kndgtn Teacher Allegheny-Hyde Park Elem 1989-; *ai:* PA ST Ed Assn; NEA; Kiski Area Sch Dist Supts Perfect Attendance Awd 1988-89; *home:* 329 Kings Rd Apollo PA 15613

LAMBRIGHT, KEVIN DAVID, Social Studies Teacher; *b:* Oakdale, LA; *ed:* (BA) Soc Stud Ed, LA Coll 1985; *cr:* Teacher Pickering HS 1985-; *ai:* Bsbl & Asst Ftbl Coach; Sr 4-H Spon; *home:* PO Box 117 Pitkin LA 70656

LAMER, JOSEPH, US History/ESL His Teacher; *b:* Los Angeles, CA; *ed:* Eng/Ec, Loyola Univ; (BA) His/Eng AR St Univ 1971; *cr:* Teacher/Coach/Athletic Dir St Johns Indian Sch 1968-76, Judson Sch 1976-; *ai:* Bsbl Coach; League Bsbl Champions 1980-89, St Ind Bsbl Champions 1983,1984, 1985, 1987, 1988, 1989; *office:* Judson Sch 6704 N Mockingbird Ln Scottsdale AZ 85253

LAMERATO, JANET, Teacher; *b:* Hamtramck, MI; *ed:* (BA) His, Univ of Detroit 1963; (MED) Soc Stud, Wayne St Univ 1974; *cr:* Teacher Lincoln Park HS 1963-65, Lowrey Jr HS 1965-82, Fordson HS 1982-; *office:* Fordson HS 13800 Ford Rd Dearborn MI 48126

LAMLE, JACK DUANE, JROTC Instructor; *b:* Wiley, CO; *m:* Sheila Moorcroft; *c:* Mike, Frances Tedford, Catherine Werner, Patricia; *ed:* (BSC) Voc Ed/Ag, CO St Univ 1961; Adjutant General Army Officers Career Course; Public Admin, Univ of CO; *cr:* Voc Ag Teacher Bayard HS 1961-63, Schuyler HS 1963-64; Officer US Army 1964-79; Substitute Teacher Sch Dist 10, 49, 27 CO Springs 1981-84; US Army JROTC Instr A Lincoln HS 1984-; *ai:* FFA Spon 1961-64; Coach FFA BB Team, US Army Ordinance Ctr BB Team, A Lincoln JROTC Rifle Teams, Drill Teams; Sch Improvement/Accountability Comm; Alpha Tau Alpha 1961-; Retired Officers Assn 1979-; Knights of Columbus 1984-; Holy Trinity Church Choir 1976-; CO St Univ Deans List 1961; Mem Honorary Prof Ag Ed; Bronze Star; Joint Services Commendation Medal; Meritorious Service Medal; Army Commendation Medal; Good Conduct Medal; Vietnamese Cross of Gallantry with Palm; *home:* 4907 Crestwood Dr Colorado Spgs CO 80918

LAMMELA, ROBERT J., Chemistry Teacher; *b:* Fitzwilliam, NH; *m:* Barbara Jean Judd; *c:* Debra Pawlek, Michael; *ed:* (BED) Ed, 1962, (MED) Ed, 1975 Keene St Coll; *cr:* Teacher Walpole HS 1962-65, Marlboro HS 1965-67, Fall Mountain Regional HS 1967-74, Keene HS 1974-; *ai:* NEA, NHEA VP Local Ed Assn, NHSTA, NHEA Delegate 1989-; Lions Club Dir 1984-89; *office:* Keene HS Arch St Keene NH 03431

LAMMONS, LEISA SCOGGINS, Language Arts Teacher; *b:* East Point, GA; *m:* Richard; *ed:* Assoc Eng Ed, Young Harris 1984; (BA) Eng Ed, Mercer Univ 1986; *cr:* Lang Art Teacher Meadowcreek HS 1986-; *ai:* Var Cheerleading Spon 1987-; Co-Spon Stu Cncl 1987-89; Page; *office:* Meadowcreek HS 4455 Steve Reynolds Blvd Norcross GA 30093

LAMON, JANET GUNTER, Language Arts Teacher; *b:* Fitzgerald, GA; *m:* Eddie L.; *c:* James E., Joseph R.; *ed:* (BA) Eng, 1972, (MED) Rdng, 1980 Valdosta St Coll; *cr:* Lang Art Teacher Hahira Mid Sch 1974-; *ai:* Loundes Assn of Educators, GA Assn of Educators, NEA 1974-; *home:* 2208 Dogwood Dr Valdosta GA 31602

LA MONICA, FRANK ANTHONY, HS Mathematics Teacher; *b:* Raritan, NJ; *ed:* (MA) Math, Cntrl MI Univ 1973; (BA) Math, Trenton St Coll 1965; Numerous Univ; *cr:* Math Teacher Brick Township HS 1965-66, Saranac HS 1966-; *ai:* Honor Society & Sr Class Adv; NCTM, MI Cncl Teacher Math 1975-; Saranac Ed Assn Treas, MI Ed Assn, NEA 1966-; Natl Sci Fnd Grant to Kent St Univ 1990; Exch Stu to Sweden 1966; Experiment in Intnl Living; *home:* 1721 Millbrook SE Grand Rapids MI 49508

LAMORE, DAVID L., Jr High School History Teacher; *b:* Kankakee, IL; *m:* Margie De Martini; *c:* Kyle D.; *ed:* (BS) His, E IL Univ 1969; *cr:* Jr HS His Teacher A R Graiff Grade Sch 1969-; *ai:* Metro-East Journals Bi-Cty Coach of Yr 1975; Coach 1969-77; AFT 1986-; Olive Township Clerk 1985-; Williamson Volunteer Fire Dept Treas 1982-; Williamson Village Bd (Trustee, Mem) 1978-86; Nom For SIUE Excl in Teaching Awd 1988; Olive Fire Dept Bd of Review Mem 1984-; Livingston PTO Mem; Given Key to Village of Livingston 1977; *home:* PO Box 312 Livingston IL 62058

LAMOREAU, SUSAN BEVERLY, Business Teacher; *b:* Lewiston, ME; *ed:* (BS) Bus Teacher Ed/Office Management/ Secretarial Stud, Husson Coll 1987; *cr:* Bus Teacher 1987-, Adult Ed Teacher 1988- Sanford HS; *ai:* FBLA Adv 1987-; Distaff Yrbk Adv 1988-; Bus Ed Assn of ME 1986-; *office:* Sanford HS 2R Main St Sanford ME 04073

LAMOREAUX, FRANK C., English Teacher; *b:* Willard, OH; *m:* Kelly Anne Getz; *c:* Matthew; *ed:* (BA) Eng/HPE, Heidelberg Coll 1980; Bowling Green St Univ, Ashland Coll, Heidelberg Coll; *cr:* 7th-9th Grade Eng Teacher Garfield Heights City Schls 1980-82; 7th/8th Grade Eng/HPE Teacher Seneca East Jr HS 1982-85; Comm Teacher Pioneer Joint Voc Sch 1986; 10th-12th Grade Eng Teacher Seneca East HS 1986-; *ai:* Sr Class Adv; Asst Var Ftbl & Head Var Bsbl Coach; OH Ed Assn, NEA 1980-; Seneca East Ed Assn VP 1982-; Benevolent & Protective Order of Elks 1984-; Archaeological Society of OH 1985-; *office:* Seneca East HS Box 462 Seneca St Attica OH 44807

LAMOREE, BARBARA J., Fourth Grade Teacher; *b:* Stromsburg, NE; *m:* Robert K.; *c:* Douglas, David, Rebecca; *ed:* (BS) Elem Ed, Univ of NE 1963; Grad Stud Kearney St Coll, Univ of NE, Leslie Coll; *cr:* Classroom Teacher Stromsburg Public Sch 1960-62, Polk Public Sch 1963-64, Stromsburg Public Sch 1970-; *ai:* Swedish Festival Smorgasbord; Stromsburg Ed Assn Secy 1987-88; NEA, NE Ed Assn, N Cntrl NE St Rdng Assn; Salem Luth Church Sunday Sch Teacher; Stromsburg Cmmty Theatre; *home:* 18 Wall Stromsburg NE 68666

LAMPERELLI, ROBERT NICHOLAS, Social Studies Dept Chair; *b:* Norwich, CT; *m:* Barbara Lee De Carolis; *c:* Stacey; *ed:* (BA) Soc Sci, 1965, (MS) His, 1970 Cntrl Ct St Univ; Admin/ Supervision, S Ct St Univ 1981; Trng Hunter Methodology; Ct Copentencies in Teaching; *cr:* Teacher Silas Deane Jr HS 1965-66, Montville HS 1967-76; Asst Prin 1976-86, Prin 1983-87 Murphy Jr HS; Teacher/Dept Chm Montville HS 1987-; *ai:* Departmental Mems & Soc Stud Curr Supvr; Town of Montville Evaluation Comm Mem; Montville Little League Sr League Sftbl VP 1986-; *office:* Montville HS Old Colchester Rd Oakdale CT 06370

LAMPLEY, GORDON BROOKS, Middle Grades Teacher; *b:* Albemarle, NC; *m:* Madilyn Morton; *c:* Kelley Lampley Long, Brandon, Cameron; *ed:* (BA) Elem Ed, Pfeiffer Coll 1975; (MED) Mid Grade Sci, Univ of NC Charlotte 1978; Appalachian St Univ 1980; Univ NC Charlotte Summer Sci Inst 1983; Univ of NC/ Duke Power 1984; *cr:* Classroom Teacher Ridgecrest Sch 1975-89, Millingport Sch 1989-; *ai:* Stanly Cty Schls Sci Curr Comm; Higher Ed Commission; NCAE Local Pres 1987-89; Stanly Cty Teacher of Yr 1987; *home:* Rt 2 Box 485 Norwood NC 28128

LAMPROS, SANDY BREWER, Teacher of Academically Gifted; *b:* Grappenhall, England; *c:* Nicole; *ed:* (BA) Intermediate Ed, Elon Coll 1971; (MED) Admin, Campbell Univ 1990; Mentor Trng; Writing, Inst of Childrens Lit; *cr:* Teacher Lincoln Elem 1971-77, Greensboro City Schls 1977-79, Southern Pines Mid Sch 1982-87; Interim Dir Mid Schls Moore Cty Schls 1987-88; Ag Teacher Southern Pines Mid Sch 1988-; *ai:* Beta Club Spon; NC Assn of Educators, NEA 1971-; Jr Womens League 1980-82; Episcopal Day Sch Bd 1985-88; Youth Adv Emmanuel Church 1984-87; Appointed Sch Bd Episcopal Day Sch; *home:* 170 W Hedgelawn Way Southern Pines NC 28387

LAMPTON, C. DIANE, English & Writing Teacher; *b:* Kansas City, MO; *m:* Michael W.; *c:* Taylor; *ed:* (BS) Eng, Cntrl MO St Univ 1975; Grad Level Courses Ed & Kansas City Writing Project, Univ of MO Kansas City; *cr:* 7th Grade Eng Teacher 1975-, Dept Chairperson/Eng Teacher 1983-, 8th Grade Creative Writing Teacher 1985- Ervin Jr HS; *ai:* Young Authors Conference Coord Scndry Level; Stu Cncl Adv; Staff Morale Comm; United Teachers Assn (Building Rep 1983-85, Negotiations Team 1984-85); Nom Outstanding Young Educator St of MO 1986; Nom Excl in Teaching Awd 1985-88; Stus Literary Magazines Published; St of MO Mentor Prgm; Nom Dist Teacher of Yr 1987, 1988, 1989; *office:* Ervin Jr HS 10530 Greenwood Rd Kansas City MO 64134

LAMSON, ROBERTA TANISER, 7th Grade Math Teacher; *b:* Allentown, PA; *m:* Merritt R. Jr.; *ed:* (BA) Elem Ed, Marywood Coll 1963; Teacher of Handicapped Cert; *cr:* 2nd Grade Teacher Cleveland Sch 1963-64; 3rd/4th Grade Teacher Green Hill Sch 1964-65; 4th Grade Teacher Lincoln Sch 1965-67; 5th/6th Grade Teacher Freehold Township NJ 1967-65;5th/6th Grade Teacher/ Comp Ed/Compensatory Ed 1967-85; 7th Grade Math Teacher Conway Mid Sch 1985-; *ai:* Stu Cncl Adv; 7th Grade Team Chairperson; SACS Comm; Math Counts Asst Adv; NEA/SCEA/ HCEA; MAC; SC Mid Sch Assn Mem; Prof & Bus Womans Organization Grand Strand; Church Cantor; 1989-90 SC Palmettos Finest Awd Faculty Mem; Faculty Mem SC St Incentive Awd; *office:* Conway Mid Sch 1104 Elm St Conway SC 29526

LAMUNYON, KELLY BROUSSARD, Jr HS Home Economics Teacher; *b:* Morgan City, LA; *m:* William Robert Jr.; *c:* William III.; *ed:* (BS) Home Ec Ed, Nicholls St Univ 1985; Working on Masters Certified Home Ec; *cr:* Morgan City Jr HS 1985-; *ai:* FHA Club Adv; Amer Home Ec Assn 1982-; LA Home Ec Assn 1982, Young Achievers Awd 1990; SE Dist LA Home Ec Assn (Pres, VP, Reporter, Nominating Chm, Secy) 1982, Outstanding Young Prof Awd 1988; Curr Guides Project Asst; Helped Edit Text 1990; *office:* Morgan City Jr HS 911 Margurite St Morgan City LA 70380

LANCASTER, FRAN MITCHELL, 6th, 7th, 12th Grade Teacher; *b:* Forsyth, GA; *m:* William Eugene; *c:* Jill R., William P.; *ed:* (BS) Elem Ed, Univ of GA 1972; (MED) GA Coll 1978; *cr:* Teacher Hubbard Elem 1972-76, 1978-79; IMTS Instr Taylor Cty Voc Tech 1980-82; Teacher Hubbard Elem 1982-85, Mary Persons HS & Monroe Acad 1986-; *ai:* Jr Beta Club Spon; PAGE 1982-85; *home:* Rt 3 Blue Store Rd Forsyth GA 31029

LANCASTER, JUDY E., 1st Grade Teacher; *b:* Shreveport, LA; *m:* Jimmy Dee; *c:* Jimmy J., Joshua E.; *ed:* (BS) Elem Ed, Stephen F Austin St Univ 1972; Ed Courses Toward Masters Stephen F Austin St Univ, East TX St Univ; *cr:* 2nd-5th Grade Teacher Hughes Springs Elem 1973-78; 2nd Grade Teacher New Diana Elem 1978-80; 1st Grade Teacher Hughes Spring Elem 1980-86, New Diana Elem 1986-; *ai:* Spon New Diana Elem Chrldrs; Several Comms at Church; Delta Kappa Gamma 1985-; TX Classroom Teachers Assn (VP 1984-85, Pres 1985-86); PTA Parlimentarian 1990; *home:* PO Box 135 Diana TX 75640

LANCASTER, LANNY E., English Teacher; *b:* Gadsden, AL; *m:* Karen L Mc Donald; *c:* Kathryn; *ed:* (BS) Scndry Ed/Eng, 1975, (MS) Scndry Ed, 1979 Jacksonville St Univ; *cr:* Eng Teacher Ed White Mid Sch 1975-79, J O Johnson HS 1979-85, Gadsden HS 1985-; *ai:* Sch Yrbk Adv; Sr Class Spon; Supt Advisory Comm Sch Rep; Huntsville Ed Assn Pres 1984-85; AL Ed Assn St Comm Chm 1987-89; Gadsden Ed Assn Pres 1990-91; Imagination Places Childrens Museum Gadsden Advisory Comm 1989-; Gadsden Ed Assn Newsletter Ed 1987- Outstanding Newsletter 1989; Nom Huntsville Rdng Teacher of Yr 1979; Huntsville City Schls Nom Jacksonville St Univ Teacher Hall of Fame 1985; AL Career Incentive Prgm Working Comm 1986-88; Gadsden Comm Develop Local Personnel Evaluation Prgms; *office:* Gadsden HS 607 S 12th St Gadsden AL 35999

LANCLOS, PATSY FELT, Facilitator/Coord Instrl Tech; *b:* San Antonio, TX; *m:* Charles Allen; *c:* Jon C., Jene; *ed:* (BS) Sci Composite, Univ of Tx Austin 1959; (MED) Curr/Instruction, Univ of Houston 1984; Working on Admin Cert, Univ of Houston Clear Lake; *cr:* Science Teacher Whittier Jr HS 1959-60, Spring Branch Jr HS 1960-67; Cmptr/Math Teacher Spring Branch Sr HS 1985, Northbrook HS 1985-88; Lecturer Adjunct Univ of Houston Clear Lake 1987-; Scndry Technology Specialist Spring Branch Ind Sch Dist 1988-; Facilitator/Coord of Instructional Technology Spring Branch Ind Sch Dist 1990-; *ai:* Advisory Bd for Occupational & Technical Ed; Delta Kappa Gamma; TX Cmptr Ed Assn, Ed of Yr Finalist 1987; Assn for Supervision & Curr Dev; PTA (TX Life Mem 1978, Natl Life Mem 1982) Prgm Dev Cncl Pres 1987-88; Univ of TX Ex Stu Assn Outstanding Teacher 1986-87; Grand Prize Winner Cmptr Learning Month 1987; *office:* Sprng Branch Independent Sch 955 Campbell Rd Houston TX 77024

LAND, DEBRA LYNN POGUE, English/Speech Teacher; *b:* St Louis, MO; *m:* Ronnie; *c:* Jeremy Sullins, Dixie; *ed:* (BS) Eng/ Speech Ed, Southwest Baptist Coll 1976; (MD) Ed, LA St Univ Shreveport 1989; *cr:* Speech Teacher Raymore-Peculiar Mid Sch 1979-81; Eng Teacher Mansfield HS 1981-82; Eng/Speech Teacher 1982-83, Eng Teacher 1984-89, Eng/Speech Teacher 1989- Logansport HS; *ai:* Chrldr, Beta Club Spon; Eng Dept Chairperson for SAC Visit; Jr Class Spon for Jr Sr Prom; NEA, LA Ed Assn; De Soto Parish Assn of Ed Secy 1984-; Kappa Delta Phi; Steering Comm for Sch Tax Proposal; Teacher of Month 1988; Teacher of Yr 1988, 1989; Parish Rep St Teachers Convention; Parish HS Teacher of Yr 1989; *office:* Logansport HS P O Box 489 Logansport LA 71049

LAND, EXCELL, Fifth Grade Teacher; *b:* Jackson, MS; *c:* Carl; *ed:* (BS) Elem Ed, Jackson St Univ 1965; Soc Sci, Marquette Univ; San Diego St Univ; Univ of WI Milwaukee; *cr:* Head Teacher John F Kennedy Child Care Center 1966-67; Teacher Milwaukee Technical Coll 1966-68; Case-Worker Milwaukee Cty Welfare Dept 1967-68; Substitute Teacher San Diego City Schls 1974-76; Educl Dir Jackson St Univ Day Care Center 1978-79; Teacher Christ Missionary & Industrial Coll 1973-; *ai:* Courtesy & Discipline Comm; Sunday Sch Teacher; Mt Sinai Baptist Church Supt 1984-89; *office:* Christ Missionary/Indstrl Coll 3910 Main St Jackson MS 39213

LANDECK, DOREEN RAE, Language Art/Art Teacher; *b:* Berwyn, IL; *ed:* (BA) Soc Sci, Cntrl MI Univ 1970; Oakland Univ, E MI Univ, Univ of Detroit, Saginaw Valley Univ; *cr:* 1st Grade Teacher 1970-74, 3rd Grade Teacher 1974-77, 5th Grade Teacher 1977-78 Armada Elem Sch; 6th Grade Teacher 1978-88, 6th/7th Grade Teacher 1988- Armada Mid Sch; *ai:* Project Pride Spon; Chaperone Ski Club, Theater Outing Group; Lang Art Comm Building Chm; Leadership Sch Improvement Plan Comm; MI Assn of Mid Sch Educators 1988-.

LANDECK, JOE JOHN, Phys Ed & Drivers Ed Teacher; *b:* Oak Forest, IL; *m:* Sandra Borchardt; *c:* Lance, Joey L; *ed:* (BS) Phys Ed/Engl, 1969, (MS Phys Ed Prgm Management, 1973 Eastern IL Univ *cr:* Jr HS Sci/Math/Eng Teacher Cntry Club Hills 1968-70; 5th Grade Teacher 1970-80, Elem Phys Ed/His/Drivers Ed Teacher 1980- Villa Grove; *ai:* Intramural Dir Cntry Club Hills 1969-70; Ftbl 1970-76, Jr HS Bsktbl 1970-85, Jr HS Track 1975-81, HS Girls Bsktbl 1986-88, HS Sftbl 1987- Coach; Hockey Coach/Dir 1984-; Villa Grove Summa Recreation Pres 1986-89; Villa Grove Jaycees VP 1981, Jaycee of Yr 1980; *office:* Villa Grove Sch Dist #302 N Sycamore St Villa Grove IL 61956

LANDERS, BECKY LYNNE, Vocational Home Ec Teacher; *b:* Humansville, MO; *m:* Thomas F.; *c:* Jason Cunningham, Brandon; *ed:* (BS) Ed, Univ of MO 1981; *cr:* Learning Disabilities Lockwood HS 1982-83; Home Econ Greenfield HS 1983-; *ai:* Career Ladder Comm; FHA Adv; AVA 1987-; CTA VP 1989-; MO Home Econ Teachers Assn 1987-; MO St Teachers Assn 1982-; MO Voc Assn 1987-; PTO Sec 1988-; Dade Cty Extension Young Homemakers Awd 1986; *office:* Greenfield H S R-4 410 W College Greenfield MO 65661

LANDERS, NELL JOHNSON, Art Teacher; *b:* New Brighton, PA; *m:* Kenneth E. Sr.; *c:* Kenneth Jr.; *ed:* (BS) Art Ed/Home Ec, WV St Coll 1977; Classes Coll of Grad Stud Inst WV; *cr:* Interior Designer Ted Keiffer & Co 1968-73; Art Teacher Clendenin Jr HS 1980-85, Sissonville HS 1985-; *ai:* Yrbk; Honor Society & Soph Spon; Group Counseling Adv; Co-Spon Photo Club; Kanawha Cty Art Assn Pres 1989-; Sissonville Historical Awareness Chairperson 1986-; Aldersgate United Meth Church; Wrote Published Book; *office:* Sissonville HS 6100 Sissonville Dr Charleston WV 25312

LANDERS, R. MICHAEL, Mathematics Teacher; *b:* Athens, GA; *m:* Shirley J.; *c:* Ryan; *ed:* (BS) Elem Ed, Lee Coll 1978; (MS) Deaf Ed, Univ of TN Knoxville 1979; Ed Admin, W GA Coll; *cr:* 4th Grade Teacher Cleveland City Schls 1979-86; Sign Lang Instr Cleveland St Comm Coll 1979-86, Lee Coll 1978-86; Math Teacher Mt Paran Chrstn Sch 1986-; *ai:* Yrbk Spon; Math Curr Adoption Chairperson; GA Assn of Educators, NEA 1986-; TN Registry of Interpreters for the Deaf VP 1984-85; *office:* Mt Paran Christian Sch 1700 Allgood Rd Marietta GA 30062

LANDMAN, JANE SHEIMO, English Teacher; *b:* Mitchell, SD; *m:* Kirk R.; *ed:* (BS) Eng/His, SD St Univ 1963; Grad Work Eng, Ed, Several Univs; *cr:* Eng Teacher Tracy HS 1963-; *ai:* NEA, MEA, TEA Local Pres 1977-78.

LANDMAN, SHERI WATERS, English Department Chairperson; *b:* Dallas, TX; *m:* Michael; *ed:* (BA) Eng/Phys Ed, 1971, (MS) Scndry Ed/Counseling, 1974 East TX St Univ; *cr:* Eng/Rdng/Health/Phys Ed Teacher Wylie Mid Sch 1972-74; Elem Phys Ed Teacher Hanes Elem Sch 1974-76; Phys Ed/Coach 1976-78, 7th-8th Grade Eng Teacher Haggard Mid Sch 1978-; *ai:* Natl Jr Honor Society Spon; Dist Grading Comm; Faculty Cncl Dist; Summer Sch Headmaster; Delta Kappa Gamma 1987; NCTE; TX Joint Cncl Teachers of Eng; Greater Dallas Cncl Teachers of Eng; Teacher of Yr Nom 1985; Perot Awd Teacher of Yr Finalist 1985; *office:* Haggard Mid Sch 2401 Westside Dr Plano TX 75075

LANDREMAN, KRISTINE MARIE, 1st-6th Grade Art Specialist; *b:* Appleton, WI; *m:* Peter J. Bebeau; *c:* Joseph Landreman Bebeau; *ed:* (BA) Art Ed, St Norbert Coll 1975; Addl Studies, Art, Univ of MN; Univ of WI; *cr:* 1st-6th Grade Art Specialist West Depere Schl Dist 1975-; *ai:* Art Club; Grades 3-6-Schsp Spon Christmas Art Fair & Fundraiser; Artist in Residence Comm; Art Museum Annual Fieldtrips; Art Contest Coord Local & Natl; Sec Auditor; Art & Environment Ed Curr Comm; Amer Craft Cncl 1985-; NEA 1975-; WEA 1975-; PTO 1975-89; UNEA Public Relations Comm State Awd 1983; St Norbert Alumni Assn; Display Stu Work Each Spring Green Bay Public Lib; Corp Pres-Kristine Marie Jewelry Inc; Art Exhibits-St Norberts & St Cloud Univ Handmade Paper; *office:* West Depere Sch Dist 1155 Westwood St De Pere WI 54115

LANDRUM, ADA POWELL, 6th Grade Homeroom Teacher; *b:* Nashville, TN; *w:* William J. (dec); *c:* William J. Jr., Ronald, Francine Landrum Christian; *ed:* (BS) Ed, TN St Univ 1943; (MA) Ed, Wayne St Univ 1979; TN St Univ, Fisk Univ; *cr:* Teacher Hermitage Elem 1943-45, Providence Elem 1945-47, Haynes Elem 1947-56, Mc Kinstry Elem 1956-; *ai:* Mc Kinstry Home Relations Comm & Wayne St Alumni Effective Plan Chairperson; Pearl HS Club; TN St Alumni; Sch Spelling Bee Chairperson; Sch Union Comm; Teacher Helper Club Adv; Stu Teacher Spon; Detroit Teachers Union Rep; Booker T Washington Educators Achievement Awd.

LANDRY, BEVERLY A. (CLUFF), President/Kindergarten Teacher; *b:* Lowell, MA; *m:* Robert A.; *ed:* (BA) Ed, 1969, (MA) Religious Ed, 1976, (MED) Counseling, 1986 Rivier Coll; Marketing Cert NH Coll; Creative Art, Lesley Coll; *cr:* 5th/6th Grade Teacher St Louis Sch 1965-66; 1st Grade Teacher Lowell Public Schls 1966-68; 1st/3rd Grade Teacher Hudson Public Schls 1969-73; VP/Pres/Teacher Kinder World Incorporated 1973-; *ai:* Rivier Coll & Nashua Schls Early Chldhd Advisory Cncl; Early

Chldhd Craft Comm Aluirne HS; NH Assn of Readiness Teachers 1973-; NH Assn for Ed of Young Children 1973-; John Clough Genealogical Society 1984-; Hudson Fortnightly Secy 1988-; Rivier Alumni Assn Act Mem 1988-, Certificate 1989; NAEYC, NHAEYC, NHART, NHACD Mem; St Kathryn Church (Mem, Organist 1969-); Rivier Alumni Bd 1988-; Rivier Coll ECE Advisory Cncl Mem; Clough, Cluff, Clow Society Mem 1984-; Nashua Bd of Realtors Mem 1978-; Clowns of America Intnl, World Clown Assn, Clown Hall of Fame Mem; Kinder World Owner & Operator; *office:* Kinder World Incorporated 75 River Rd Hudson NH 03051

LANDRY, HANK, Social Studies Teacher/Coord; *b:* St Louis, MO; *m:* Linda C.; *ed:* (BS) Ed, 1975, (MED) Curr/Instruction, 1979 Univ of MO; Stratford Hall-Monticello Univ VA 1985; Effective Instruction Cadre Trng, Columbia Public Schls 1988-89; *cr:* GTA Univ of Mo 1982-89; Teacher 1975-, Dept Coord 1986-Hickman HS; *ai:* Mock Trial Coach; Hickman Academic Tournament Spon & Organizer; Franklin Club His & Poly Sci Spon; Former Tennis & Bsbl Coach; CPS Effective Instruction Cadre; Boone Cty Bar-Columbia Public Schls Partners-In-Ed Steering Comm; NCSS; MO Cncl for Soc Stud VP 1990; Phi Delta Kappa Pres 1986-88; Soc Stud Teacher of Yr 1989; Amer Cancer Society Boone Unit (Mem, Bd of Dirs) 1989-; Outstanding Grad Achievement Awd 1985, Outstanding Grad Teaching Awd 1990, Coll of Ed UMC; Outstanding HS Educator Columbia Public Schls 1989-; *office:* Hickman HS 1104 N Providence Rd Columbia MO 65203

LANDRY, LINDA DUGAS, Reading Lab Teacher; *b:* Thibodaux, LA; *m:* Ronald Paul; *c:* Ryan P.; *ed:* (BA) Kndgtn/Elem, 1972, (MED) Early Chldhd/Psych/Supervision, 1976 Nicholls St Univ; Grad Stud Prof Improvement Practices, Gesell Testing Inst; Diagnosis & Implementation of Learning Styles; *cr:* 1st Grade Teacher Gibson Elem 1972-74; Supvr of Stu Teachers Nicholls St Univ 1975-85; Kndgtn Teacher 1975-86, 3rd Grade Teacher 1987-88, Rdng Lab Teacher 1989- Schriever Elem; *ai:* Sch Building Level & Curr Dev Comm; Substance Abuse Prevention Ed; Phi Delta Kappa 1978-80; Terrebonne Assn of Educators, LA Assn of Educators, Natl Assn of Educators 1972-; Nicholls/LA Rdng Cncl 1988-; Jaycee/Jaynes 1976-78; Thibodaux Service League 1985-87; *office:* Schriever Elem Sch 1018 Hwy 24 Schriever LA 70395

LANDY, KAREN ANN, 6th Grade Teacher; *b:* Paterson, NJ; *m:* Richard Joseph; *ed:* (BA) Elem Ed, Paterson St 1969, (MA) Lang Art, William Paterson Coll 1978; *cr:* 6th Grade Teacher M J Ryerson 1969-; *ai:* Pi Lambda Theta Mem 1976-; *home:* 80 Scrivani Dr Wanaque NJ 07465

LANE, BARBARA T., English Teacher; *b:* Somerville, NJ; *ed:* (BA) Eng, Mount St Mary Coll of NH 1965; (MA) Eng, Villanova 1967; Grad Stud; *cr:* Asst Teacher Villanova 1967; Eng Teacher Bridgewater-raritan HS East 1967-; *ai:* Acad Team; Var Bsktbl Ofcl Scorer; Intramural Bowling Adv; NHS Selection Comm; Attendance Appeals; Stu Cncl Asst; Big Brothers/Big Sisters of Somerset (Secy 1970, Bd Mem); Bridgewater-Raritan HS East Teacher of Yr 1987; Governors Teacher Recognition Prgm; Published Childrens Book; *office:* Bridgewater-Raritan HS East PO Box 301 Martinsville NJ 08836

LANE, CAROLINE DENNEHY, Second Grade Teacher; *b:* Terrell, TX; *m:* Kenneth Earl; *c:* Joshua J.; *ed:* (BS) Elem Ed, E TX St Univ 1979; Counseling/Guidance 1990; *cr:* 3rd Grade Teacher W H Burnett Elem 1979-85; 2nd Grade Teacher Good Shepherd Episcopal Sch 1986-87, W H Burnett Elem 1987-; *ai:* Young Authors Extravaganza Adv; UIL Coach & Judge; Whole Lang Curr Chairperson; ATPE Building Rep 1989-; Beta Sigma Phi Secy 1982-85; Terrell Jaycees Secy 1989-; Terrell Ind Sch Dist Teacher of Month 1988; *home:* Rt 5 Box 228 Terrell TX 75160

LANE, CHERYL JOYCE, Third Grade Teacher; *b:* Sacramento, CA; *ed:* (BS) Elem Ed, Belmont Coll 1979; (MSED) Curr/Instruction, Mid TN St Univ 1987; *cr:* 5th Grade Teacher Walter Hill Elem Sch 1979-85; 7th/8th Grade Math Teacher 1985-88, 3rd Grade Teacher 1988- Walter Hill Elem Sch; *office:* Walter Hill Elem Sch Rt 3 Box 171 Murfreesboro TN 37129

LANE, DANIEL S., Chemistry Teacher; *b:* Havre De Grace, MD; *m:* Ruth Ann Loeffler; *ed:* (BA) Bio, WA Univ 1976; Cert as Medical Technologist; *cr:* Sci Teacher South Cty Tech Sch 1985-86; Chem Teacher Univ City HS 1986-; *ai:* Sci Olympiad Coach; NSTA 1987-; NEA 1985-; Amer Assn for Advancement of Sci 1989-; *office:* University City Sr HS 7401 Balson Ave University City MO 63130

LANE, DAVID MARLAND, Mathematics Dept Chm/Teacher; *b:* Fairmont, MN; *m:* Debra Dee Hansen; *c:* Matthew D., Katie E., Marcus J.; *ed:* (AA) General, Golden Valley Luth Coll 1973; (BA) Math/Phys Ed, Augsburg Coll 1976; Colloquy Trng, Concordia Coll, Concordia Univ, Mankato St Univ, Hamline Univ; *cr:* Teacher/Coach/Athletic Dir East Monona Cmmty Sch 1976-81; Teacher/Coach Luth HS 1981-; *ai:* Sr Class Adv; Head Bsbl; Asst Bsktbl; FCA Huddle Leader; Amer Bsbl Coaches Assn Mem 1985-, 100 Victories Club 1989; MN Bsbl Coaches Assn Dist Rep 1989-, Dist Coach of Yr 1985, 1988, 1989.

LANE, DEREK RAY, Speech/Drama/Debate Teacher; *b:* Torrington, WY; *m:* Janice Eileen; *ed:* (BS) Speech Comm, Chadron St Coll 1986; Ed/Theatre, (AA) Comm, E WY Coll 1983; Teaching Law in Classroom, Chadron St Coll 1988-; *cr:* Admissions Cnslr E WY Coll 1986-88; VP Torrington Office Products & Supplies 1983-; Teacher Scottsbluff HS 1988-; *ai:* Scottsbluff HS Forensics, Speech, Debate, Mock Trial Team Coach; Play Dir & Spon; NEA, NE Ed Assn, Scottsbluff Ed Assn 1988-; Outstanding Young Men of America 1988; *office:* Scottsbluff HS 313 E 27th Scottsbluff NE 69361

LANE, DONNA-MARIE M., Sixth Grade Teacher; *b:* Dayton, OH; *c:* Teri L. Brown; *ed:* (BS) Elem Ed, Cntrl St Univ 1972; (MED) Curriculum, Instr, Cleveland St Univ 1986; Elem Sch Math; Space Ed; *cr:* Teacher Aide Career Opportunities Prgm 1970-71; Teacher/Dayton Public Schls 1971-72; Cleveland Public Schls 1972-81; Shaker Hts City Sch Dist 1981-; *ai:* Math Comm Shaker Hts City Sch Dist; Adv Bd Cleveland Childrens Museum; Young Astronauts Chapter Adv; Natl Pi Lambda Theta Hnr & Prof Assn in Ed Chapter Secy 1985-; Metro Cleveland Alliance Of Black Sch Ed 1985-; Greater Cleveland Cncl Teachers of Math 1981-; Natl Space Socty 1987-; Planetary Socty 1982-; Natl Air & Space Smithsonian 1985-; Career Cnslng Videotape Cleveland St Univ; Cert Regntn Martha Holden Jennings Fnd; Cert of Regntn USAF Recruiting Svc; *office:* Woodbury Elem Sch 15400 South Woodland Rd Shaker Heights OH 44120

LANE, INA DUNGAN, English Teacher; *b:* Charleston, SC; *m:* Ervin Earl; *c:* Nathan, Adam, David; *ed:* (BS) Eng Ed, Elizabeth City St Univ 1985; *cr:* Eng Teacher/Guidance Cnslr Albemarle Acad 1985-; *ai:* Sftbl & Vlybl Coach 1987-; Sr Class Adv; Curr, Faculty, Bd Comm; Elizabeth City Jr Womens Club Teacher of Month 1988, Tarheel Ind Conference Coach of Yr Vlybl 1989; *office:* Albemarle Acad Rt 6 Box 178 Elizabeth City NC 27909

LANE, JANICE M., Chemistry Teacher; *b:* Hammond, IN; *m:* Jeremy; *c:* Kim, Jeremy Jr.; *ed:* (BA) Chem, Rosary Coll 1966; (MAT) Chem, Fairleigh Dickinson Univ 1971; Univ of MN, St Cloud St, Univ of CA Berkeley, Mankato St; *cr:* Chem Teacher Columbia HS 1966-69, Regina HS 1978-86, St Louis Park HS 1986-; *ai:* Sci Challenge Team Coach; Curr Advisory Cncl Faculty Rep; Scope & Sequence Sci Co-Chairperson; MN Sci Teachers Assn 1979-; NSTA, Twin Cities Chem Assn; Greenpeace 1985-; Natl Sci Fnd Grant Univ of CA Berkeley 1989; Nom MN Sci Teacher of Yr 1984-86, 1990; *office:* St Louis Park Sr HS 6425 W 33rd St Saint Louis Park MN 55426

LANE, JUDITH ANN, AP Hum/British Lit Teacher; *b:* Enid, OK; *ed:* (BFA) Theatre Art, Ithaca Coll 1966; (MA) Theatre Art, Univ of N CO 1972; Stud Abroad Cambridge England; *cr:* Prof Actress Actors Equity Assn 1967-; HS Teacher Poudre R1 Schls 1974-; Prgm Dir Hum Inst 1983-; *ai:* Choral & Solo Music Ministry; Dir Tri-High Musical Production Cmmty Arts Center; CO Speech & Drama Assn Pres 1979-80; Honorable Mention CO St Teacher of Yr Awd; *office:* Poudre HS 201 Impala Dr Fort Collins CO 80521

LANE, LA DONNA C. (GARTNER), 4th Grade Teacher; *b:* Vincennes, IN; *m:* Thomas H.; *c:* Ryan Thomas, Nathan Howard, Adam Benjamin; *ed:* (BS) Elem Ed, 1971, (MS) Elem Ed, 1974 IN St Univ; *cr:* Elem Teacher Harrison Sch 1971-75, Franklin Sch 1975-; *ai:* IN St Teachers Assn 1971-; Intnl Rdng Assn; *office:* Franklin Sch 2600 Wabash Ave Vincennes IN 47591

LANE, MARCELLA ANN, Eng/Advanced Placement Teacher; *b:* Akron, OH; *ed:* (BA) Scndry Ed, Univ of NV Las Vegas 1965; (MA) Eng Lit, Univ of NV Las Vegas 1970; Philosophy/Ethics Courses; *cr:* Eng Teacher Valley HS 1965-84, Las Vegas HS 1986-; *ai:* Var Quiz Coach; Kadettes Drill Team; Natl Honor Society Adv; SNTE 1966-75; NEA 1965-; CCTA 1965-; St Judes Auxiliary; Democratic Women, Univ Women; Intnl Baccalaureat Valley HS Rep; European Prgm Seminar Presenter; *office:* Las Vegas HS 315 S 7th St Las Vegas NV 89102

LANE, MARCY DICKSON, Mathematics Teacher; *b:* Waco, TX; *m:* David Paul; *c:* Katy, Kevin; *ed:* (BS) Math, Stephen F Austin St Univ 1978; *cr:* Math Teacher S Garland HS 1979-; *ai:* TX St Teachers Assn 1980-89; *office:* S Garland HS 600 Colonel Dr Garland TX 75043

LANE, MARY WINSTON, Teacher; *b:* Middlesboro, KY; *w:* Richard Alan (dec); *c:* Barbara A. Partin, John B.; *ed:* (BS) Chem/Math/Minor Physics, Eastern KY Univ 1944; (MST) Chem, Univ MO Rolla 1966; (Rank I) Ed, Union Coll 1979; Physics Update/Energy, OH St Univ; *cr:* Technician Oak Ridge Tn 1945-48, Donner Radiation Lab 1949-59; Teacher/Head of Dept Bell Cty Sch 1959-66; Teacher Porta HS 1967-68, Ottiville HS 1970-73, Bath HS 1973-78, Middlesboro HS 1978-; *ai:* Sci Club; Sci Olympaid Coach-St Winner Team; NSTA; KY Sci Teachers Assn Bd Mem; Delta Kappa Gamma 1976-; South East Sci Fair 1962-66; SMAPS EKU 1964; Most Outstanding Teacher South Eastern KY 1964; Natl Sci Olympiad.

LANE, MICHELE J. F., Chairwoman Language Dept; *b:* Paris, France; *ed:* (BA) Fr, 1965, (MA) Fr, 1967 Hunter Coll of CUNY; (MS) Counseling, Coll of Staten Island CUNY 1985; (PHD) Fr, Grad Center of City Univ of NY 1976; Grad Stud; *cr:* Lecturer St Univ at Stony Brook 1974-77; Acting Chairperson Allentown Coll 1977-79; Asst Prof of Fr 1980-88; Adjunct Asst Professor Languages York Coll 1965-75; Chairperson Lang Dept St Saviour HS 1979-; *ai:* St Savior HS Fr Club Moderator; Dir of Yearly Cultural Trips to France & Francophone; CUNY Alumni Assn (Bd of Dir 1980-82, 1985-, Treas 1982-84); Modern Lang Assn 1969-; AATF 1990; Womens Museum of Washington DC Honorary Mem 1988-; Monets Magic Garden Television Prgm; Paris Go Round Television Prgm; La Mise en Scene Dans L oeuvre de Chretien de Troyes 1976; City Univ of NY NDEA Dissertation Yr Fellowship 1972-73; *office:* St Saviour HS 588 6th St Brooklyn NY 11215

LANE, PRISCILLA A., Assistant Professor; *b:* Richmond, KY; *ed:* (BA) Music/Art, 1961, (MA) Ed, 1970 E KY Univ; *cr:* 5th Grade Teacher 1963-65, Vocal Music Teacher 1965-67 Lexington City Sch System; Elem Ed Teacher Model Laboratory Sch 1967-; *ai:* Governors Cup Academic Team Co-Spon & Coach; Alpha Delta Kappa (Dist & St Music Chm 1986-88, Pres 1984-86), Cleo Dawson Awd 1988, Co-Wrote St Song 1988; Phi Delta Kappa 1980-; Task Force for Latch-Key Children 1990; Commonwealth Inst for Teachers 1990; E KY Univ Centennial Excl in Teaching Awd 1974; Published Sci, Health, Drug Ed Textbook Series; *office:* Model Laboratory Sch E KY Univ Richmond KY 40475

LANE, SANDRA MULLIN, Vocational Teacher; *b:* Turkey, TX; *m:* Lawrence Leonard; *c:* Buster G. Fisher, S. Lori Richter, Scott E., Donna S. Smith, George K., Laurie D. Lowery; *ed:* Voc Cert SW TX St Univ 1979; Beyond Assertive Discipline, TX Wesleyan Coll 1987; Human Relations in Classroom & Classroom II, St Marys Univ 1984, 1985; *cr:* Teacher/CVAE-Bus Office Clerical Roosevelt HS; *ai:* Bus Prof of America Assoc Division; NEA, TX St Teachers Assn, AVA, Natl Assn of Classroom Educators in Bus Ed, Voc Office Ed Teachers Assn of TX; Voc Office Careers Clubs of America St Advisory Bd; TX St PTA, Honorary Life Membership 1989; *home:* 12715 Country Oaks San Antonio TX 78216

LANE, SYLVIA BRISTOW, Fifth Grade Teacher; *b:* Winston-Salem, NC; *m:* Herbert Benton; *c:* Jennifer L.; *ed:* (BFA) Art Ed, 1985, (MED) Mid Sch, 1989 Valdosta St; Data Collector 1989; *cr:* 5th Grade Teacher Quitman Elem; *ai:* United Daughters of Confederacy Mem 1980; Honors Day Comm 1986-89; Grade Coord 1986-; Fair Booth Comm 1987-89; Prof Assn of GA Educators Mem 1988; Stu Support Team 1987-; Art Show Coord 1988-89; Whos Who in Amer Ed 1989; *home:* Rt 3 Box 1120 Quitman GA 31643

LANEY, CHARLES AUSTIN, 5th Grade Teacher; *b:* Elizabeth, NJ; *m:* Mary Ann Ceremsak; *c:* Austin; *ed:* (BA) Elem Ed, Glassboro St Coll 1982; Project Write & Jr Great Books Trng; *cr:* 5th Grade Teacher Lillian M Dunfee Sch 1982-; *ai:* 5th/6th Grade Bsktbl Asst Coach; Little League Coach; Cnslr in Trng; Camp Lighthouse for Blind; Spec Olympics Tournament of Champions; *office:* Lillian M Dunfee Sch Barnegat Blvd Barnegat NJ 08005

LANEY, DOROTHY HOOVER, Fourth Grade Teacher; *b:* Blakely, GA; *w:* Joe Dean (dec); *c:* Joseph, Jeff, James; *ed:* (BS) Elem Ed, Troy St Univ 1969; Working Toward Masters Degree Troy St Univ; *cr:* 4th Grade Teacher Iron City Elem 1947-48, Jakin Georgia Elem 1948-50; 4th-6th Grade Teacher Midland City AL Elem 1963-67; 6th Grade Teacher Ariton Elem 1967-; *ai:* 4-H Club, Jr Beta Club Spon; NEA, AL Ed Assn 1963-; Dale Cty Teachers Assn (VP 1970-71, Membership Chm 1965-66, Faculty Rep 1970-82); Delta Kappa Gamma (VP, Secy); Matrons Study Club (Secy, Pres), Woman of Yr 1988; Sunday Sch Dir 1988-; Former Sunday Sch Teacher; Dale Cty Elem Teacher of Yr 1986-87; *home:* PO Box 136 Ariton AL 36311

LANEY, REGINA ANN TATUM, Kindergarten Teacher; *b:* Richlands, VA; *m:* Edward Lee; *c:* Drennon H., Crystal L. A.; *ed:* (BS) Elem Ed, E TN St Univ 1975; Grad Work; *cr:* 4th Grade Teacher 1975-77, 5th Grade Teacher 1977-86, 3rd Grade Teacher 1986-87, Kndgtn Teacher 1987- Tazewell Elem.

LANFREY, JAMES FREDERICK, Federal Programs Coordinator; *b:* Williamsport, PA; *m:* Judith Lee; *c:* Jill, Jody; *ed:* (BSED) Elem Ed, Lock Haven Univ 1963; (MSED) Elem Ed/Rdng Spec, Bloomsburg Univ 1968; (EDD) Rdng Ed, Univ of GA 1975; Grad Stud Penn St Univ, Univ of WI, Trenton St Coll; *cr:* Elem Teacher Loyalsock Township 1963-66; Rdng Specialist Cncl Rock Sch Dist 1967-74; Coll Professor Bucks Cty Comm Coll 1976-77, Bloomsburg Univ 1976-80; Federal Prgms Coord Cncl Rock Dist 1975-; Co-Owner/Dir Lanfrey Educl Clinic 1977-; *ai:* Bucks Cty Cncl IRA Pres 1971-72, 1985-86, Literacy Awd 1986; *office:* Cncl Rock Sch Dist 116 Newtown-Richboro Rd Newtown PA 18940

LANG, BARBARA ANN (KNOX), 5th Grade Teacher; *b:* Grand Rapids, MI; *m:* Farm; *c:* Lisa M. Lang Snyder, Amy M. Lang Stebbins; *ed:* (BA) Elem Ed, W MI 1965; Several Classes Calvin Coll, CMU Western; *cr:* 4th/5th Grade Teacher Kent City Schls 1965-.

LANG, BEVERLY SMITH, Science Teacher; *b:* Villa Rica, GA; *m:* Gary Wayne; *ed:* (BA) Bio, W GA Coll 1971; (MED) Sci Ed, GA St Univ 1978; (EDS) Sci Ed, W GA Coll 1989; *cr:* Sci Teacher, Sci Teacher/Dept Chairperson Newnan HS; *ai:* Newnan HS Sci Olympiad Team Dir; HS Sci Team Co Spon; Coweta Cty Sci Safety Comm Chm; GA Sci Teachers Assn 1984-, Dist Sci Teacher of Yr 1987; NSTA 1985-; Coweta Cty Assn of Educators, GA Assn of Educators, NEA; GA Presidential Awd for Excl in Sci & Math Teaching 1986; Teacher of Yr 1982, 1984, 1986; Runner Up Coweta Cty Teacher of Yr 1984, 1986; *office:* Newnan HS 190 La Grange St Newnan GA 30263

LANG, CHARLES RICHARD, Physics Teacher; *b:* Oakland, NE; *ed:* (BA) Physics, NE Wesleyan Univ 1960; (MED) Physics, Univ of MN 1969; (PHD) Curr/Instruction, KS St Univ 1975; Stanford Univ 1966; *cr:* Sci Teacher Stromsburg Public Sch 1960-62; Physics Teacher Westside Hs 1962-; *ai:* Developing HS Physics Video Discs; Phi Delta Kappa, AAPT 1966-; Paul Harris Fellow Rotary Intnl; Articles Published; *office:* Omaha Westside HS 87th & Pacific Omaha NE 68124

LANG, DEBBIE CARLSON, Home Economics Teacher; *b:* Moab, UT; *m:* Douglas Jay; *c:* Dixie, Denise, Dyan; *ed:* (BS) Home Ec Ed, Brigham Young Univ 1978; *cr:* Teacher Viewmont HS 1978-; *ai:* Home Ec Dept Chm; FHA & HERO Adv; *office:* Viewmont HS 120 W 1000 N Bountiful UT 84010

LANG, ELEANOR, Chemistry Teacher; *b:* Albany, NY; *m:* Donald B. Walter; *ed:* (BA) Chem, Montclair St Coll 1963; (MST) Chem, Cornell Univ 1968; Grad Stud Univ of WA & Seattle Pacific Univ; *cr:* Chem Teacher Governor Livingston Regional HS 1963-67; Research Chemist Univ of WA Medical Sch 1968-73; Chem Teacher Edmonds HS 1973-76; Math/Bio/Chem Teacher Interlake HS 1976-; *ai:* Stu Internship Prgm Coord; NSTA 1976-; WSTA 1973-; NEA 1963-67, 1973-; Orchst Island Fnd Treas 1984-; Ford Fellows Steering Comm; Van Hargon Task Force; *office:* Interlake HS 16245 NE 24th St Belleville WA 98008

LANG, JACKLYN HARRIS, French Teacher/Lang Dept Chm; *b:* Los Angeles, CA; *c:* Angela, Gavin; *ed:* (BA) Fr, Univ of CA Los Angeles 1970; Post Grad Work Fr; Bi-ling Cert Span; *cr:* Teacher 1971-81, Master Teacher 1973-81 Virgil Jr HS; Lecturer Univ of CA Los Angeles 1975-76; Teacher 1981-, Mentor Teacher 1987-, Dept Chairperson 1986- Belmont HS; *ai:* Fr Club Spon; Sr Act Lecturer; Psychological Crisis Team Mem; UTLA 1971-; *office:* Belmont HS 1575 W Second St Los Angeles CA 90026

LANG, JUDITH K., First Grade Teacher; *b:* Freeport, IL; *m:* Jerry Dean; *c:* Jennifer; *ed:* (AA) Freeport Comm Coll 1965; (BA) Elem Ed, 1967, (MA) Elem Ed, 1969 IL St Univ; Several Wkshps & Seminars, IL St Univ; Math Grant, IL St Univ & US Dept of Ed 1989-; *cr:* 1st Grade Teacher Lincoln Sch 1967-73, Sheridan Sch 1975-; *ai:* General Comm with Sch 1989-; BEA, IEA, NEA 1967-; Delta Kappa Gamma 1989-; PTA Lifetime Membership Awd; *home:* 2921 Capen Bloomington IL 61704

LANG, JULIE JONTZ, Fourth Grade Teacher; *b:* Marshalltown, IA; *m:* Steve; *c:* Josh, Joey, Brooke; *ed:* (BA) Elem Ed, 1971, (MA) Ed Admin, 1976 Univ of N IA; *cr:* 3rd/4th Grade Teacher Anson Elem 1971-; *ai:* MEA, ISEA, NEA; Up With Downs Support Group Chm 1986-88; PEO Secy 1986-88; Dist Elem Soc Stud Comm Chairperson 1987-89; Teacher Resource Specialist Unit C; AEA VI Parent Educator Connection; *office:* Anson Elem Sch S 3rd Ave Marshalltown IA 50158

LANG, MARLENE WEGEHOFT, 4th Grade Teacher; *b:* Indianapolis, IN; *m:* Larry; *c:* Jeffrey, Belinda; *ed:* (BS) Ed, Ball St Univ 1963; (MS) Ed, IN Univ 1967; *cr:* 4th Grade Teacher Glenns Valley Elem 1963-; *ai:* Lang Arts Adoption Comm; NEA; IN St Teachers Assn; Perry Ed Assn; *office:* Glenns Valley Elem Sch 8239 Morgantown Rd Indianapolis IN 46217

LANG, SHARON SMITH, Fourth Grade Teacher; *b:* Huntington, WV; *m:* David D.; *c:* Kathryn M., Jennifer F., Shelley R.; *ed:* (AB) Elem Ed, Marshall Univ 1965; Working Towards Masters OH Univ; *cr:* 4th Grade Teacher Chesapeake Union Exempted 1965-69, 1978-; *ai:* 4-H Adv 1976-; Career Ed Grant; *home:* Rt 1 Box 490 South Point OH 45680

LANGABEE, JOANNE MARIE, Physics Instructor; *b:* Des Moines, IA; *m:* Robert Edward; *c:* Vincent, Troy; *ed:* (BS) Chem/General Sci, Univ of NE Omaha 1972; (MS) Sci Ed, Creighton 1981; *cr:* Sci/Phys Sci/Chem Teacher Notre Dame Acad 1972-74; Teacher Papillion La Vista HS 1974-; *ai:* Sci Olympiad Coach; NE Assn Teachers of Sci (Bd Mem 1984-86, Secy, Treas 1986-); NSTA, AAPT; NE Amer Assn of Physics Teachers Pres Elect 1990; Cub Scouts Awds Chairperson 1985-88; Physics Teaching Resource Agent; Megger Awd; Educl Service Unit 3 Technology Grant; Article Published; *office:* Papillion La Vista HS 402 Centennial Rd Papillion NE 68046

LANGAGER, HARVEY JAMES, Business Education Teacher; *b:* Wolf Point, MT; *m:* Bonnie Jean Kautz; *c:* Gina M., Ross Norven; *ed:* (BS) Bus Admin, Rocky Mountain Coll 1973; Teaching Certificate E Mt Coll 1975; *cr:* Teacher/Coach Plentywood HS 1975-77, Shepherd HS 1978-80, Laurel HS 1981-; *ai:* Coached Ftbl, Bsktbl, Track & Bsbl; Class Adv; LEA, MEA, NEA 1975-; *home:* 3452 Windmill Cr Billings MT 59102

LANGAN, ROBERT MICHAEL, HS Social Studies Teacher; *b:* Pittston, PA; *m:* Jannette Morgan; *ed:* (BS) Ed, Bucknell Univ 1975; Working Towards Masters; *cr:* Substitute Teacher Wyoming Area HS 1975-84; Soc Stud Teacher Lake Lehman 1984-; *ai:* Asst Var Ftbl Coach; PA St Ed Assn, NEA; *home:* 13 North St West Pittston PA 18643

LANG BRANNEN, WILLIAM LANGLEY, Business Teacher; *b:* Savannah, GA; *m:* Tammy Lynn Turk; *ed:* (BBA) Mgmt, GA Southern Coll 1981; Teaching Cert Bus Ed, Armstrong St 1986; *cr:* Teacher/Coach Herschel V Jenkins HS 1986-; *ai:* Asst Ftbl Coach 1986-; Head Track Coach 1986, 1989; GA Bus Ed Assn 1989; *office:* Herschel V Jenkins HS 1800 E De Renne Ave Savannah GA 31406

LANGDON, EVERETTE WIMS, Fourth Grade Teacher; *b:* Blakely, GA; *m:* Elisha Jr.; *c:* Everette L.; *ed:* (BS) Elem Ed, Albany St GA 1953; (MED) Elem Ed, AL St 1976; Delta St Univ; *cr:* Teacher H M Nailor Elem Sch 1956-59, Ruleville Cntrl Elem Sch 1959-67, Washington Elem Sch 1967-68, Addison Mid Sch 1968-74, I T Montgomery Elem Sch 1974-; *ai:* Elem Spelling Bee; 4th Grade Chm; Elem Sci Fair, Lang Arts Comm; Bolivar Cty Educators Assn Pres 1989-91, Membership Awd 1990; MS Assn of Educators, NEA 1956-; Soloman Chapel Ame Church; Zeta Phi Beta Treas 1977-; Albany St Alumni Assn, AL St Alumni Assn; Natl Cncl of Negro Women Inc; Outstanding Elem Teachers of America 1975; SCIS Sci Inst NSF 1971; *home:* PO Box 373 Ruleville MS 38771

LANGDON, WILMA JOY, Biology Teacher/Vlybl Coach; *b:* Ralls, TX; *ed:* (BS) Ed/Bio/Phys Ed, West TX St Univ 1977; (ME) Ed, TX Tech Univ 1985; *cr:* Bio/Coaching Dexter HS 1977-85; Monterey HS 1985-; *ai:* Head Vlybl Coach; Asst Track; TX Girls Coaching Assn 1985-; Lubbock Ed Assn 1985-; TX Classroom Teachers Assn 1985-; NEA 1985-; *office:* Monterey H S 3211 47th St Lubbock TX 79413

LANGE, IRIS NELSON, Fourth Grade Teacher; *b:* Strandburg, SD; *m:* Henrick A.; *c:* Linda Nelson, Larry, Laurel Wathier; *ed:* (BS) Elem Ed, Dakota St Coll 1969; Grad Stud Elem Ed, Cmptrs, Photography; *cr:* Teacher Grant Cty Rural Schls 1947-52, Codington Cty Rural Schls 1960-66, Watertown Public Schls 1966-; *ai:* SD Ed Assn, NEA; Watertown Ed Assn Outstanding Service Awd 1989; Grace Luth Church Bd of Ed; IBM & Classroom Cmptr Learning Magazine SD Cmptr Teacher of Yr 1989; *home:* 109 10th Ave NW Watertown SD 57201

LANGE, LEON L., Biology Teacher/Dept Head; *b:* West Bend, WI; *m:* Kathleen Golla; *c:* Kit; *ed:* (BS) Bio, Univ of WI Stevens Point 1969; (MA) Ed, 1974, (EDS) Ed, 1981 Austin Peay St Univ; *cr:* US Army Fort Campbell KY 1969-71; Grad Asst Austin Peay St Univ 1971-73; Bio Teacher Fort Campbell HS 1973-; *ai:* Head Cross Cntry & Track Coach; Sci Club, Head Class, Academic Team Spon; Pupil Activity & Supt Discussion Comm; Fort Campbell Ed Assn VP 1974-75; BSA Dist Comm 1981-, Long Rifle 1987; Article Published; *office:* Fort Campbell HS Ohio Ave at Falcon Loop Fort Campbell KY 42223

LANGE, WILLIAM JOHN, History Teacher/USI Coord; *b:* Audubon, NJ; *m:* Kathryn Marchese; *c:* Bill, Mark; *ed:* (BS) His, St Josephs Univ 1970; Adv Degree Work Glassboro St; *cr:* Soc Stud Teacher/Minority Stud Coord Camden Cath HS 1970-72; Soc Stud Teacher Overbrook Sr HS 1972-89; Soc Stud Teacher/USI Coord Bishop Eustace Prep 1989-; *ai:* Boys Var Bsktbl Coach; NJ Educl Assn Union Pres 1980-89; NCEA 1989-; St Awd Innovative Law Course 1976; Nom S Jersey Coach of Yr 1978-; Won Continental Bsktbl Assn Natl Audition Commentator 1984-85; *office:* Bishop Eustace Preparatory Sch Rt 70 Pennsauken NJ 08109

LANGENDERFER, DUANE LEE, English Teacher; *b:* Toledo, OH; *ed:* (AA) Bus, Lincoln Coll 1959; (BS) Ec, Culver-Stockton Coll 1962; Grad Work Loyola Univ & Natl Coll of Ed; *cr:* Eng Teacher Fenwick HS 1965-; *ai:* Asst Moderator Writing Tutorial Service; NCEA; Consultant Frosh Level Lit Textbook; *office:* Fenwick HS 505 Washington Blvd Oak Park IL 60302

LANGENEGGER, FRANKIE HUGHES, Eighth Grade English Teacher; *b:* Abilene, KS; *m:* David L.; *c:* Roger A. Golden, Beverly Patterson, Pagan Grant, Brian Carricaburo; *ed:* (BA) Eng, San Bernardino St Univ 1976; *cr:* Eng Teacher Oakdale Jr HS 1977-80; Eng Teacher/Yrbk Spon Northwest HS 1980-81; Eng Teacher/Dept Chairperson Oakdale Jr HS 1981-; *office:* Oakdale Jr HS 511 N Dixieland Rogers AR 72756

LANGENFELD, THOMAS EDWARD, History & Government Teacher; *b:* Des Moines, IA; *m:* Ann Delores Mueggenberg; *ed:* (BA) His, IA St Univ 1975; (MA) His, Univ of IA 1984; Univ of N IA 1980 & 1982; Univ of Vienna 1985; Creighton Univ 1986; Coe Coll 1987; *cr:* Soc Stud Teacher Storm Lake HS 1975-; *ai:* Model United Nations & Washington Close-Up Spon; Track & Cross Cntry Asst Var Coach; NCSS; IA Cncl of Soc Stud Teachers; Amer Field Service Pres 1988-; Presidents Cncl on Academic Excl Awd; Distinguished Teacher 1989; *office:* Storm Lake HS 621 Tornado Dr Storm Lake IA 50588

LANGER, NORBERT J., III, German Teacher; *b:* Brooklyn, NY; *m:* Marian Cruger; *ed:* (BA) Philosophy/Ger, Fordham Univ 1971; (MA) Ger, Univ of MA Amherst 1973; FL & Teaching Courses, Goethe Inst NY & Germany, Fordham Univ, Montclair St Coll, Monmouth St Coll; Cmptr Courses, Iona Coll; *cr:* Part-Time Ger/Latin Teacher S Hadley HS 1973-74; Ger Teacher Park Ridge HS 1975-; *ai:* AFS Club Adv; Ger Amer Partnership Prgm Exch Coord; Faculty Cncl Mem; NJ Ger Heritage Festival Comm Stu Act Coord 1982-; Amer Assn of Teachers of Ger 1975-; Fulbright Study Grant 1979; NJ Governors Outstanding Teacher Awd, Park Ridge & Greater Montvale Bus Assn Distinguished Service Awds 1986; *office:* Park Ridge HS 2 Park Ave Park Ridge NJ 07656

LANGEVIN, PATTY THOMAS, English Teacher; *b:* Indianapolis, IN; *m:* Ronald Leon; *c:* Tina R., Tammy L.; *ed:* (BS) Eng/Scndry Ed, 1968, (MS) Ed/Eng, 1973 Ball St; Cmptr Class; Gifted Honors Wkshps; *cr:* 9th-12th Grade Teacher Crawfordsville HS 1968-70, Northwestern HS 1970-71, 1973, Haworth HS 1977, Kokomo HS 1979-85, Northwestern HS 1986-; *ai:* Mentor 1989-; Kokomo HS Speech Team; IUK of Kokomo Adjunct Teacher; Church Ed Comm Dir; *office:* Northwestern HS 3431 N Cty Rd 400 W Kokomo IN 46901

LANGFORD, BELINDA HALL, Kindergarten Teacher; *b:* Rison, AR; *m:* Harold Eugene; *c:* Meleah, Joshua, Jonathan; *ed:* (BA) Elem Ed, Univ of AR Monticello 1975; Graduate Work in Elem Ed, Univ of AR Fayetteville; Little Rock; Monticello; *cr:* Kndgtn Teacher Dewitt Public Schls 1975-78, Fordyce Public Schls 1978-; *ai:* NEA, AEA 1975-; SEACIS 1989-; Hebron Meth Church Sunday Sch Teacher 1971-; Lib Mem of Bd 1988-; *home:* Rt 1 Box 35 New Edinburg AR 71660

LANGFORD, JOY ANN, 8th Grade Mathematics Teacher; *b:* Gainesboro, TN; *ed:* (BS) Elem Ed, 1981, (MA) Admin/Supervision, 1988 TN Technological Univ; *cr:* Legal Secy Reneau & Reneau Attorneys 1975-79, Flatt & Jared Attorneys 1981-83; Prin/Teacher Maple Grove Sch 1984-86; 8th Grade Math Teacher Cntrl Mid Sch 1987-; *ai:* Macon Cty Alcohol-Drug Advisory Cncl Mem; TN Ed Assn 1983-; Phi Kappa Phi 1988-; Career Level I Teaching Certificate 1988; *home:* Rt 1 Box 44B Hilham TN 38568

LANGFORD, LIZZIE HOLT, Retired Teacher; *b:* Hilham, TN; *m:* William Minor; *c:* Douglas Bronstetter, Garry, Joy; *ed:* Permanent Prof Certificate Elem Ed, TN Technological Univ 1940; Prof Certificate *cr:* Teacher Clay Cty Schls 1940-54; Partner Holts Variety Store 1954-66; 1st-3rd Grade Teacher Maple Grove 1966-67; 5th Grade Teacher Celina Elem 1967-82; *ai:* Volunteer Work Plaque Maple Grove Sch Staff & Stu 1984-85; Tutor Stus in Adult Literacy Prgm 1982-; TN Ed Assn 1982; Clay Cty Retired Teachers Assn 1982-; Clay Cty Bd of Ed Volunteer Work 1984-85; Stu TN Ed Assn & Dr Pepper Bottling Company Volunteer Work Recognition 1985-86; *home:* Rt 1 Box 44B Hilham TN 38568

LANGFORD, MYRA A. (WILSON), Assistant Principal; *b:* New York, NY; *ed:* (BS) Ed, Fordham Univ 1963; (MS) Ed, Hunter Coll 1967; (EDM) Educl Admin, Teachers Coll Columbia Univ 1973; Course Work Teachers Coll Columbia Univ; Master Teacher Trng Prgm City Coll of CUNY; Probability & Statistics Stu Grades 5th-8th; Spec Ed & Bi-ling Spec Ed Stu; *cr:* Teacher Public Sch 145 Man 1963-87; Supv of Stu Teachers Teacher Coll Columbia Univ 1969; Interim Acting Asst Prin 1988, Teacher Trainer 1988-89, Asst Prin 1989- Public Sch 145 Man; *ai:* Comprehensive Sch Improvement Prgm Comm Mem; Parent Involvement Prgm; Coach Perspective Hunter HS Stu; Cncl of Supvrs & Admins 1989-; United Fed of Teachers 1963-89; Stu Ed Assn of NY St VP 1962-63; Alpha Kappa Alpha; Master Teacher Prgm City Coll Research Center; Teacher of Yr Dist 3 Teacher Recognition Day 1979; Article Published; Whos Who Among Amer Colls & Univs 1963; *office:* Public Sch 145 Man 150 W 105 St New York NY 10025

LANGFORD, STEPHEN RAY, Chemistry Teacher; *b:* Monett, MO; *m:* Penni Gene Gage; *c:* Justin; *ed:* (BS) Bio/Chem, Southwest Baptist Univ 1978; *cr:* Research Amoco Production Co 1978-80, Occidental Oil Co 1980-83; Teacher Jenks HS 1983-; *ai:* Head Var Coach Girls Bsktbl; JCTA/OEA/NEA 1983-; OK Coaches Assn 1983-; *office:* Jenks H S 1st And B St Jenks OK 74037

LANGLEY, CAROL BARKLEY, Guidance Counselor; *b:* Albertville, AL; *m:* Tommy; *c:* Mandy, Adam; *ed:* (BS) Scndry Ed, 1972, (MS) Guidance/Counseling, 1973 Jacksonville St Univ; *cr:* Teacher 1973-76, Cnslr 1976-79 Boaz Mid Sch; Teacher Corley Elem Sch 1979-82; Cnslr Boaz Hs 1982-; *ai:* Schlsp Comm; Schl Calendar Chairperson; Peer Cnslr Adv; AL Assn for Counseling & Dev, AL Sch Cnslr Assn 1980-; AL Ed Assn 1973-; AL Assn for Religious & Value Issues in Counseling 1987-; Ladies Tennis Assn VP 1988-; 1st Baptist Church (Sunday Sch Teacher 1979-, Asst Organist 1980-); *office:* Boaz HS Brown St Boaz AL 35957

LANGLEY, DENISE BLANK, Mathematics Department Head; *b:* Frostburg, MD; *m:* Thomas James; *c:* Tammi B., Jason T.; *ed:* (BS) Ed, Frostburg St 1984; Math Certificate; *cr:* Math/Cmptr Teacher Bishop Walsh HS 1985-86; Math/Algebra I Teacher Northern Mid Sch 1986-; *ai:* NCTM 1989-; MD St Teachers Assn 1986-; *home:* Rt 2 Box 239 Frostburg MD 21532

LANGLEY, DOROTHY FINCHER, Fifth Grade Teacher; *b:* Atlanta, GA; *m:* Donald A.; *c:* Donna Langley Duff, Joy S.; *ed:* (BA) Eng, Emory Univ 1960; (MED) Elem Ed, W GA Coll 1976; Classes at Univ of GA; *cr:* Office Worker D C Heath & Company 1960; 7th Grade Teacher Moreland Elem 1960-63; 6th Grade Teacher Mc Eachern Sch 1967-75, Tapp Mid Sch 1975-76; 5th Grade Teacher Compton Elem 1976-; *ai:* Staff Cncl; Sci Contact Person Compton Elem Sch; Grievance Comm; GA Assn of Educators Area Rep 1984-87; Cobb Cty Assn of Educators Building Rep 1984-, Bat Team Awd 1984; Alpha Delta Kappa Pres 1984-86; PTA; NEA; Eight O Clocks Pres 1970; Mc Eachern United Meth Church (Choir Mem, Pastor/Parish Relations Comm); Kappa Kappa Gamma; Cheatham Hill Cmmty Club; Comptons Sci Teacher of Yr 1988-; Nom for Ga Sci Teacher of Yr 1989; Whos Who in Ed 1989-; Teacher of Yr Compton Sch 1981; *office:* Compton Elem Sch 3450 New Macland Rd Powder Springs GA 30073

LANGLEY, KATRINA JUANNELL, Retired Teacher; *b:* Winchester, TN; *m:* George; *c:* Samantha; *ed:* (BS) Elem Ed, Trevecca 1975; *cr:* Teacher Liberty 1966-68, Sewanee 1968-77, Cowan Elem 1977-89; *ai:* Just Say No, 4-H Club; Franklin Cty Ed Assn, TN Ed Assn 1966-89; NEA 1975-89; Nazarene Church Teacher; Nom Teacher of Yr 1986; *home:* Rt 1 Belvidere TN 37306

LANGLEY, ROBERT E., JR., Biology Teacher; *b:* Cherrypoint, NC; *m:* Christine Marie Cutter; *c:* Robert III, Shannon, Gary, Matthew; *ed:* (AA) Riverside Comm Coll 1980; (BS) Bio, Univ CA Riverside 1983; *cr:* Bio Teacher Moreno Valley HS 1986-88; 8th Grade Sci Teacher Mountainview Mid Sch 1988-89; Bio Teacher 1989-, Co-Sci Dept Chm 1989- Valley View HS; *ai:* Asst Boys Track; Site & Dist Level Curr Cncls; *office:* Valley View HS 24551 Dracaea Ave Moreno Valley CA 92388

LANGLEY, SHEILA PILCHER, Marketing Coordinator; *b:* Ripley, TN; *m:* Kenneth; *c:* Douglas, Jason; *ed:* (AA) Mrktg, Dyersburg St Cmmty 1972; (BS) Ed, Memphis St 1974; *cr:* Mrktg Coord Ripley HS 1982-; Case Worker Dep Human Services

1981-82; Mrktg Coord 1977-81, Teacher 1975-77 Ripley HS; Mrktg Coord Halls HS 1974-75 *ai:* DECA Adv Mem/Mrktng Adv Cncl; SCA Adv; Sftbl Coach; TEA 1989-; NEA 1989-; NADET 1989-; Easter Seals Chairperson 1990; Sunday Sch Teacher 1985-; *home:* Rt 3 Ripley TN 38063

LANGLINAIS, JACQUELINE SMITH, Mathematics Department Chair; *b:* Abbeville, LA; *m:* Glenwood P.; *c:* Scott, Mark, Blake, Jenna; *ed:* (BA) Math, Univ of SW LA 1975; *cr:* Teacher Northwestern Mid Sch 1976-77, Abbeville HS 1977-79, 1985-; *ai:* Stu Cncl; NCTM 1977-; *office:* Abbeville HS 101305 Senior Dr Abbeville LA 70510

LANGLITZ, NANCY (HILL), Fifth Grade Teacher; *b:* Fort Dodge, IA; *m:* Harlan; *c:* Brooke, Lincoln; *ed:* (BA) Elem Ed, Univ of N IA 1972; Grad Work Elem Ed; *cr:* Upper Elem Teacher Meservey Thornton Cmmty Sch 1972-; *ai:* Advisory, Performance Based Pay, At-Risk, Global Ed Committees; Lib Bd 1979-; Reformed Church Women 1976-80; Meservey Improvement Club 1974-80; *home:* 640 4th St Meservey IA 50457

LANGMEYER, DOUGLAS FREDERICK, Biology/Science Teacher; *b:* Saline, MI; *ed:* (BA) Biological Sci, MI St Univ 1984; (MA) Educl Leadership, W MI Univ 1990; *cr:* Bio/General Sci Teacher Niles Sr HS 1984-; *ai:* Frosh Girls Bsktbl Coach; Soph Class Adv; Natl Sci Teachers Assn 1987-; Niles Sr HS Building Senator; *office:* Niles Sr HS 1441 Eagle St Niles MI 49120

LANGO, PAUL JOSEPH, Computer Science Teacher; *b:* Worcester, MA; *ed:* (AA) Liberal Arts, Worcester Jr Coll 1970; (BA) Elem Ed, 1973, (MS) Educl Leadership/Admin, 1977, (MS) Cmptr Sci, 1981 Worcester St Coll; *cr:* 5th Grade Teacher Webster Mid Sch 1973-84; Cmptr Sci Teacher Bartlett HS 1984-; Adjunct Faculty Nichols Coll 1987-, Quinsigamond Comm Coll 1981-; *ai:* Coach Boys Cross Cntry 1973-, Track 1979-; *home:* 2 Sunset Dr Webster MA 01570

LANGSTON, BARBARA RICE, 7th Grade Mathematics Teacher; *b:* Albany, GA; *m:* W. Jerry; *c:* Jean A. Langston Albritton, Clifton M.; *ed:* (BS) Elem Ed, GA Coll 1964; (MED) Mid Grades, 1981, (SED) Mid Grades/Math/His, 1988 GA Southwestern; Grad Stud Admin, Data Collecting; Working Towards Specialized Degree in Admin & Supervision; *cr:* Teacher Watson Elem 1964-65, Perry Jr HS 1965-66, Perry Elem 1966-70, Perry Mid 1974-; *ai:* 7th Grade Team Leader; Assn Supervision & Curr Dev, Prof Assn GA Educators, NCTM, GA Cncl Te achers of Math; Daughters of Amer Revolution (V Regent, Corresponding Secy) 1986-; Daughters of Amer Colonists Wolcott Society St VP 1980-; Magna Carta Dames; Houston Cty Leadership Inst 1989-; *office:* Perry Mid Sch Sunshine Ave Perry GA 31069

LANHAM, WILLIAM L., Social Studies Dept Chairman; *b:* Lebanon, KY; *m:* Brenda Hargrove; *c:* Carey J.; *ed:* (BA) His, Spalding Univ 1974; (MS) His, Northern Ky Univ 1982; KY Intern Teaching Prgm; *cr:* Teacher Newport HS 1974-; *ai:* Spon KY United Nations Assembly; Close-Up Fnd; Academic Team; Membership Comm for NHS; Trainer of Ftbl Team; KEA & NTA (Building Rep 1989-, KEA St Rep 1989-); Trainer for Effective Schls Comm; Mem of the Prin Advisory Bd; *office:* Newport H S 900 E 6th St Newport KY 41071

LANIER, CHERYL GAY, Teacher; *b:* Raleigh, NC; *m:* Robert A.; *c:* Inga G. Paxton, Robert; *ed:* (AB) Soc Stud, Atlantic Chrstn Coll 1969; *cr:* Teacher/Dept Chm Zebulon HS 1976-89; Teacher East Wake HS 1989-; *ai:* East Wake HS Schlsp; Zebulon Jr Womans Club 1976-1980; Jr Woman Yr 1978; Sunday Sch Teacher Zebulon Baptist Church 1974-84; Freedom Shine Documents for Zebulon HS; *home:* 3 Box 110 Zebulon NC 27597

LANIER, DOROTHY HILL, Sixth Grade Teacher; *b:* Monroe, LA; *m:* Glenn E.; *ed:* (BA) Elem Ed, Southern Univ 1952; Elem Ed, Counseling, Guidance, Chicago St Univ & Univ of Chicago; *cr:* Teacher Medill Primary 1960-64, Wacker Elem 1964-77, O A Thorp Elem 1977-78, William H Ray 1978-; *office:* William H Ray Sch 5631 S Kimbark Chicago IL 60637

LANIER, LOUISE BIRD, Fifth Grade Teacher; *b:* Metter, GA; *m:* James Clyde Jr.; *c:* Jimmy, Johnny, Janie L. Mc Cook, Jill; *ed:* (BS) Elem Ed, GA Southern Coll 1971; *cr:* 7th Grade 1971-74, 6th Grade Teacher 1974-78, 5th Grade Teacher 1978- Metter Mid Sch; *ai:* Local Spelling Bee Teacher & Spon; Eng Dept Chm; Honors Day Comm Mem; PAGE; Metter Mid Sch Teacher of Yr 1988; *home:* Rt 2 Box 131 Metter GA 30439

LANIER, MIKE GREGORY, Science Teacher/Coach; *b:* El Campo, TX; *c:* Alyson; *ed:* (BAT) Phys Ed/Bio, Sam Houston St Univ 1982; *cr:* Teacher/Coach George Jr HS 1982-; *ai:* Ftbl, Bsktbl, Track Coach; TX Classroom Teacher Assn; TX HS Coaches Assn; *office:* George Jr HS 4201 Airport Rd Rosenberg TX 77471

LANIER, WILLIE DELORIS CALHOUN, Fourth Grade Teacher; *b:* Mobile, AL; *m:* Willie Davis; *c:* Amie, Ramona; *ed:* (BS) Elem Ed, Univ of S AL 1981; (MED) Elem Ed, Livingston Univ 1987; *cr:* Secy/Bookkeeper Wilson Hall Sch 1965-81; Teacher Grove Hill Elem Sch 1981-; *ai:* Soc Stud, 4th Grade, Spelling Bee Chairperson; Soc Stud Fair Chairperson 1985 ; Design for Learning & Lang Arts Comm; Clarke Cty Ed Assn (Pres 1987-88, VP 1986-87, Secy 1984-86); Univ of AL SARIC Bd Mem 1985-; AL Ed Assn (Legislative Commission mem, Contact Legislative Team Mem) 1986 ; Pine Chapel Baptist Church Dir; GSA Leader; Womens Affairs Comm of Election Secy 1989-; Clarke Cty Teacher of Yr 1986-87; Nom to Jacksonville St Univ Teachers Hall of Fame 1986-87.

LANKFORD, CURTIS MITCHELL, Science Teacher; *b:* Dierks, AR; *m:* Ila Rae Tyler; *c:* Tiffny D., Candice R.; *ed:* (BS/BSE) Chem, Henderson St Univ 1970; *cr:* Insurance Agent Shelter Ins Company 1972-81; HS Teacher Mena Sch Dist 1981-; *ai:* Jr HS Class Spon to Conduct Prom Act, SADD, Fellowship of Chrstn Stu; Phi Delta Kappa 1987-; Mr PTA; Published Article Bogard Press Publications Magazine; *home:* 1213 Bert St Mena AR 71953

LANKFORD, JERRY DALE, 5th Grade Teacher; *b:* Neosho, MO; *ed:* (BS) Ag, 1967; (BS) Elem Ed, 1970 Mc Pherson Coll; Emporia St, Wichita St; *cr:* 5th Grade Teacher Mc Pherson 418 1970-; *ai:* NEA, KNEA 1970-; Mc Pherson Teachers Assn Constitution Comm 1970-; 1st United Meth Church (Trustee, 1982-86, Pastor-Parish 1989-, Admin Bd 1979-82, Pres 1975-76); Kiwanis Pres 1975-76; 4th Project Leader 1976-83, Alumni Awd 1981; *office:* Lincoln Sch 900 N Ash Mc Pherson KS 67460

LANKFORD, NANCY, Fourth Grade Teacher; *b:* Mangum, OK; *m:* Craig B.; *ed:* (BA) Elem Ed, 1974, (MAT) 1978 OK City Univ; Rdng Certificate; Assertive Discipline; Effective Elements of Instruction; *cr:* 6th Grade Teacher 1974-75, 3rd Grade Teacher 1975-80, 4th Grade Teacher 1980-, 4th-6th Grade Span Elem Foreign Lang Teacher 1985- Overholser Elem; *ai:* Curr & Multi-Cultural Comm; Putnam City Rdng Cncl (Pres 1981-82, VP 1980-81, Membership Chm 1988-); OK Rdng Assn, Intnl Rdng Assn, OK Ed Assn, NEA; Putnam City Assn of Classroom Teachers Building Rep 1976-78, 1989-; Alpha Delta Kappa, Kappa Phi; Overholser Teacher of Yr 1984; *home:* 4201 N Georgia Oklahoma City OK 73118

LANNINGHAM, KAREN KUENSTLER, Math Department Chairman; *b:* Austin, TX; *m:* Sammy Dee; *c:* Lisa, Julianne; *ed:* (BSE) Speech & Hearing Therapy, Abilene Chrstn Univ 1973; Math & Sci Cert, Univ TX Arlington 1983-90; *cr:* Teacher Fort Rucker Pre-Sch Assn 1970-72; Speech Therapist West TX Rehabilitation Center 1973-74; Speech Therapist/Teacher/Coord Pre-Sch Handicapped Class 1974-76; Math/Sci/Bible Teacher Southwest Chrstn Sch 1983-; *ai:* Yrbk Spon; Assn TX Prof Educators 1983-; *office:* Southwest Chrstn Sch 4600b Altamesa Blvd Fort Worth TX 76133

LANTZ, ALBERTA BUSBY, Fifth Grade Educator; *b:* Tacoma, WA; *m:* Jon Dale; *c:* Michael J.; *ed:* Teaching Certificate Elem Ed, Racine-Kenosha Teachers Coll 1962, (BA) Elem Ed, Univ of WI Whitewater 1972; Working Towards Masters Elem Ed, Viterbo Coll 1991; *cr:* 5th/7th Grade Teacher Prairie View Sch 1962-67; 2nd/3rd Grade Teacher Barstow & Whiterock 1967-69; 2nd-4th Grade Teacher Heyer & Bethesda 1972-87; 5th Grade Teacher Bethesda 1987-; *ai:* Bethesda Sch Climate, Math Comm, Sch Store Adv; Waukesha Lang Art Study Skills Comm; Ed Assn of Waukesha Building Rep 1967-69, 1972-; WI Ed Assn, NEA 1962-69, 1972-; Delta Kappa Gamma 1987-; Ascension Luth Altar Guild 1972-; Waukesha Employee Recognition 20 Yrs of Service 1990; *home:* 741 S Grandview Blvd Waukesha WI 53188

LANTZ, KAREN SUE, English Teacher; *b:* Parkersburg, WV; *m:* J. Mike; *c:* Michael; *ed:* (BSED) Eng, WV Univ 1967; *cr:* Teacher Vandevender Jr HS 1967-68, De Sales Heights Acad 1968-69, Mountain St Bus Coll 1969-70, Belpre Mid Sch 1970-71, Parkersburg HS 1975-; *ai:* Future 2000 Planning & Textbook Comm; NCTE 1988-; *office:* Parkersburg HS 2101 Dudley Ave Parkersburg WV 26101

LANTZ, MARY LOU FITTRO, Fifth Grade Teacher; *b:* Clarksburg, WV; *m:* Richard; *c:* Erik Allen, Sara Ann; *ed:* WV Univ 1975-80; *cr:* 1st/5th Grade Teacher Enterprise Sch 1972-; *ai:* Youth Church at Bapt Church: *office:* Enterprise Grade Sch P O Box 327 Enterprise WV 26568

LANZALACO, JOSEPH MICHAEL, Dean of Students; *b:* Rochester, NY; *ed:* (BA) Philosophy, St John Fisher Coll 1983; (MS) Divinity, St Michaels Univ; *cr:* Teacher 1985-86, Campus Ministry Teacher 1988-89, Dean of Students 1989- Andrean HS; *ai:* Var Girls Sftbl Head Coach; *office:* Andrean HS 5959 Broadway Merrillville IN 46410

LA PENNA, JAMES PAUL, Fifth Grade Teacher/Dept Chair; *b:* E Stroudsburg, PA; *m:* Susan Ann Urbandwicz; *ed:* (BS) Elem Ed, Kutztown Univ 1975; *cr:* Stu Teacher of 6th Grade Northampton Sch Dist; Stu Teacher of 4th Grade Parkland Sch Dist 1974; Substitue Teacher Allentown Sch Dist 1975-; *ai:* 5th Grade Teacher/Dept Head Everglades Elem 1978-; Allentown YMCA Mens Health Club, Public Library; Spring Hill Nurseries Garden Club; Okeechobee Cty Outstanding Soc Stud Teacher 1982; *office:* Everglades Elem Sch 3725 SE 8th St Okeechobee FL 34974

LA PERRIERE, PAUL FREDERICK, JR., 9-12th Grade Soc Stud Teacher; *b:* Winchendon, MA; *c:* Andrea, Amy; *ed:* (BE) Soc Stud, Keene St Coll 1967; Notre Dame, NH Voc Tech Coll, Eastern Coll; *cr:* Teacher Alvirne HS 1967-; *ai:* Hudson Teachers Assn Pres 1968-69; NH Army Natl Guard Staff Sargeant 1967-; Schlsp E Baptist Coll 1969; *office:* Alvirne HS 102 Derry Rd Hudson NH 03051

LAPIC, TERRY MARK, Mathematics Teacher; *b:* Faribault, MN; *ed:* (AA) General, Navarro Coll 1984; (BS) Math, Stephen F Austin St Univ 1987; *cr:* Math Teacher Ennis HS 1987-; *ai:* Stu Cncl Spon; Math Club; *office:* Ennis HS 1405 Lake Bardwell Dr Ennis TX 75119

LAPIN, GLORIA CODNER, First Grade Teacher; *b:* Pittsburgh, PA; *m:* Richard; *c:* Michelle, Sharon; *ed:* (BA) Art/Archeology, WA Univ 1969; (MED) Elem Ed, GA St Univ 1974; *cr:* 1st Grade Teacher Pierremont 1969-70; 1st/4th/5th Grade Teacher De Kalb Cty Schls 1970-; *ai:* PAGE Building Rep 1984-; NSTA 1989-; Evansdale Teacher of Yr 1974; Oakcliff Honor Teacher 1990; Published Article in GA Journal of Soc Sci & Soc Ed 1975; Freelance Writer for Worksheets Magazine & Primary Mailbox; Co-Illustrator for Aim for Increasing Mastery for Math; Jr League of De Kalb Cty Awd; *office:* Oakcliff Elem Sch 3150 Willow Oak Way Doraville GA 30340

LA PLANTE, CYNTHIA ANN, PM, 4th Grade Teacher; *b:* Coventry, RI; *ed:* (BA) Elem Sci, Rivier Coll 1974; (MA) Religious Stud, Providence Coll 1985; *cr:* 4th-6th Grade Teacher St Joseph 1963-67; 6th-8th Grade Teacher St Regis 1967-71; 5th-8th Grade Teacher Christ the King 1971-72, Presentation of Mary 1972-88; 4th Grade Teacher Notre Dame Regional 1988-.

LAPOINTE, KAREN MARGARET (ANDERSON), First Grade Teacher; *b:* Idaho Falls, ID; *m:* John Stephen; *c:* Laura; *ed:* (BS) Elem Ed, Bowling Green St Univ 1975; *cr:* 4th Grade Teacher Christ the King Sch 1975-76; 1st Grade Teacher St Brendan Sch 1976-; *ai:* Testing Coord; Adopt-a-Child Prgm for Head Start Children Spon; NCEA 1976-; Kappa Delta Pi; Palmetto Jrs 1984-87; Easter Seal Telethon 1985-86; Spec Olympics 1984-86; Nominee for Miriam Joseph Farrell Awd; Diocese of Orlandos Honored Teacher Awd; *home:* 1033 Parkwood Dr Ormond Beach FL 32174

LAPP, JESSICA W., English Teacher; *b:* Harrisonburg, VA; *ed:* (BA) Eng, Goshen Coll 1986; *cr:* Eng Teacher Lancaster Mennonite HS 1986-; *ai:* Yrbk Adv; Jubilee Campaign, Cmptr Study, Cultural Affairs Comm; NCTE 1988-; Sunset Published Poetry; Yrbk won Top Honors St & Natl Level Competitions; *office:* Lancaster Mennonite HS 2176 Lincoln Hwy E Lancaster PA 17602

LA PRESTO, AMY C., Theatre Arts Teacher; *b:* Augusta, GA; *ed:* (BFA) Theatre/Drama/Eng, Univ of TX Austin 1969; *cr:* Theatre Art/Eng Teacher Alamo Heights Ind Sch Dist 1969-70; Theatre Art/Spec Ed Teacher San Antonio Ind Sch Dist 1971-73; Spec Ed Teacher Pat Neff Mid Sch 1973-77, Northside Ind Sch Dist 1973-79; Theatre Art/Eng Teacher Northside Opportunity Center 1977-79; Cnslr/Admin/Teacher for Emotionally Disturbed Stu Glendale Unified Sch Dist 1979-80; Theatre Art/Spec Ed Teacher East Cntrl Sch Dist 1981-82; 6th-8th Grade Theatre Art Teacher Omar Bradley Mid Sch 1984-88; *ai:* Actors Equity Mem; Coordinate Annual Sch Musical; Drama/Speech Contests Coach; Direct Productions; Mem of Dee Marcus Improvisational Troupe; Taught Creative Dramatics; Head Start/Discovery Prgm; Head of Theatre Art Prgm Bradley Mid Sch; Adapted Many Fairy Tales Childrens Theatre; Wrote Mid Sch Theatre Art Curr Guide NE Sch Dist; TX Ed Theatre Assn 1987-; TX Educl Theatre Assn Mem; Actors Equity 1980-; Bradley PTA Outstanding Teacher 1988; *office:* Bradley Mid Sch Heimer Rd San Antonio TX 78232

LARAMEE, PAULA WEBBER, Teacher of Gifted/Talented; *b:* Fort Bragg, NC; *m:* Roger; *c:* Grace Lang, Michael, Lisa, Andrew; *ed:* (BED) Elem Ed, RI Coll 1963; Religious Ed Certificate Diocese Providence; Gifted & Talented Certificate RI Coll; *cr:* 2nd Grade Teacher Sacred Heart Sch 1963-64; 6th Grade Teacher Anna Mc Cabe Sch 1964-65; Nursery Sch Teacher Pied Piper Child Center 1977-81; Soc Stud/4th-6th Grade Eng/3rd-8th Grade Teacher of Gifted/Talented St Matthew Notre Dame 1983-; *ai:* Book Fair Chm; Week of Young Child Coord; NCEA 1983-; Kappa Delta Pi Mem; St Cecilias Womens Club VP 1988-; St Matthews Womans Club.

LARCOM, LULA FRANCES, Third Grade Teacher; *b:* Greenwood, MS; *m:* Charles Luther; *c:* Kip C.; *ed:* (BSE) Elem Ed, Delta St Univ 1965; (MED) Elem Ed, Armstrong St Coll 1976; Specialists Degree Courses & Cert Supervising Stu Teachers; Data Collection Courses Gifted Prgm; *cr:* 1st Grade Teacher Lockard Elem 1965-66; 5th Grade Teacher Riverside Elem 1966-67; 1st/3rd/5th Grade Teacher White Bluff Elem 1967-; *ai:* Steering Comm SACS; Delta Kappa Gama 1980-; PTA 1965-; Chatham Assn Educators 1967-74; GA Assn of Educators 1967-74; Amer Heart Assn Volunteer 1974-75; Supervised Stu Teachers; *office:* White Bluff EleM Sch 9902 White Bluff Rd Savannah GA 31406

LAREDO, DELFINO, 6th Grade Teacher; *b:* Rosita, TX; *m:* Anna; *c:* Delfino J.; *ed:* (BSED) Industrial Arts, TX A&M Univ 1959.

LARIMORE, DORA TRADER, Math Teacher; *b:* Salisbury, MD; *m:* Wm. L.; *c:* Kimberly Carey; *ed:* (BS) Elem Ed, (MS) Ed, 1978 Salisbury St Univ; Course-Role of the Vice Prin; Course-Role of Guidance Cnslr; *cr:* Math Teacher Berlin Mid Sch 1973-; *ai:* Math Club Enrichment Act Aftersch; Sch Climate Comm; Trinity United Meth Church 1960-; Nom for Presidential Awd for Excl Teaching Math; Nom for Teacher of Yrin Worcester Cty MD; *office:* Berlin Mid Sch 308 Franklin Ave Berlin MD 21811

LARIMORE, MARILYN MINIARD, 6th Grade Lang Arts Teacher; *b:* Stephenville, TX; *m:* James A.; *c:* Terri M. Nall, Sherry L. Curtis, Andrew; *ed:* (BS) Elem Ed, Midwestern Univ 1965; (MED) Elem Ed, East TX St Univ 1976; METS *cr:* 6th Grade Teacher Fain Elem 1965-66; 3rd Grade Teacher Travis Elem 1966-67; 6th Grade Teacher Chamberlin Elem 1969; Stephenville Mid Sch 1969; Stephenville Intermediate 1969-; *ai:* Univ Interscholastic Leag - Oral Rdng & Spelling Spon Grade 6; Textbook Comm; Chm Comm Higher Order Thinking Skills; TX Classroom Teachers Assn 1965-; TX St Teachers Assn; Stephenville Classroom Teachers Assn (Sec 1970-71 VP 1971-72

Pres 1972-73 Parliamentarian 1973-74); NEA; Phi Delta Kappa 1976-80; Delta Kappa Gamma 1985-88; *office:* Stephenville Intermediate Sch 950 N Dale Stephenville TX 76401

LARKEE, MARY LUCHTERHAND, 3rd Grade Teacher; *b:* Marshfield, WI; *m:* James; *c:* Daniel, Lisa; *ed:* (BA) Music, Dr Martin Luther Coll 1966; *cr:* 1st Grade Teacher 1960-63, 4th Grade Teacher 1963-64 St Peters Luth Sch; 3rd/4th Grade Teacher Zion Luth Sch 1964-66; 3rd/4th Grade Teacher Gloria Dei-Bethesda Luth 1966-67; 2nd/3rd Grade Teacher 1977-89, 3rd Grade Teacher 1989- Peace Luth Sch; *ai:* Cheerleading Coach; Lib Coord; WA Ozaukee Rdng Cncl 1990; *office:* Peace Luth Sch 1025 Peace Lutheran Dr Hartford WI 53027

LARKIN, ROSEMARY SUE TILLMAN, English Teacher; *b:* Dyersburg, TN; *c:* John T., Ellen; *ed:* (BA) Eng/Ed, Bethel Coll 1984; Working on Masters Eng; *cr:* Eng I/II/IV Teacher 1984-86, Speech/Eng IV/Writing Teacher 1986-89 Dyer Cty HS; Coord JPTA 1988-89; Adjunct Faculty Dyersburg St Comm Coll 1988-; Eng IV/Academic Stud Teacher Dyer Cty HS 1989-; *ai:* Coach Academic Decathlon; Sch Theater Dir; TEA, NEA Mem 1985-; DCEA Building Rep 1988-89; Stage Door Players Chm of Bd 1989, Bd Mem 1987-89; Newbern Womans Club Mem 1987-; United Meth Women (Mem, Cmmty Relations Rep) 1988-; Teacher of Writing Awd TN Writers Contest 1990; *office:* Dyer Cty HS Lanesferry Rd Newbern TN 38059

LARKIN, SUSAN M., 5th Grade Teacher; *ed:* (BA) Ed, Mercy Coll 1964; (MA) Guidance, Plattsburgh St 1970; *office:* Little Tor Elem Sch Gregory St New City NY 10956

LARNER, PATRICIA BLACK-LOCKS, Vocational Counselor; *b:* Brownwood, TX; *m:* Edward J.; *c:* Clint A. Locks; *ed:* (BS) Bus, Howard Payne Univ 1969; (MED) Ed/Guidance Cnslr, Tarleton St Univ 1986; Voc, E TX St Univ 1987; Reality Inst Therapy; *cr:* Teacher Cntrl TX Commercial Coll 1972-74, Brownwood Jr HS 1974-; Teacher/Cnslr Howard Payne Univ 1988-89; Voc Cnslr Brownwood Ind Sch Dist 1990; *ai:* Natl Jr Honor Society Spon; TX Curr Review Comm; Career Investigation Secy; TX Voc Guidance Assn 1984-, Outstanding Voc Teacher 1989; AVA; Beta Sigma Phi 1988-; Delta Kappa Gamma Secy; Brown Cty Youth Fair Secy 1975-76; Brown Cty 4-H Adult Spon 1975-88; Career Investigation, Cen-Tex Dinner Club Pres 1988-; Outstanding Voc Teacher St of TX; 15 Yr Service Awd Brownwood Ind Schls; *office:* Brownwood Jr/Sr HS 1200 Avenue D Brownwood TX 76801

LA ROCHELLE, DONNA SMITH, Student Adv/Lang Art Teacher; *b:* Brookfield, IL; *m:* Lyn Alan; *c:* Amy, Andrew; *ed:* (BA) Speech Comm, CA St Univ Long Beach 1971; (MS) Sch Admin, Azusa Pacific 1988; St Dept K-8th Grade Family Life Ed Trng; *cr:* Spec Ed Aide Hamilton Jr HS 1970-72; 1st/2nd Grade Teacher A A Mayo 1972-73; 4th-6th Grade Alta Loma Elem 1973-86; 2nd-8th Grade Teacher Alta Loma Jr HS 1986-; *ai:* Stu Adv; Alta Loma Jr HS Attendance Team, Liaison Dept Rep, Grad Comm Planner & Fund Raiser, Mission Statement & Goal Setting Team, Chapter 2 Mem, Cmmty Cncl Secy; Admin & Dist Mentor Teacher Selection Comm; Dist Curr Cncl Inservice Facilitator; Sch Site Cncl VP; Sch Improvement Coord; Site & Dist Chapter 1 Rep; Vineyard Jr HS Improvement Instructional Strategies Chm; CA Teachers of Eng; Alta Loma Educators Assn (Negotiator 1981-86, Membership Chairperson 1986-); Span Trails GSA Public Service Chairperson; PTA (VP, Auditor, Secy, Honorary Service Chm) 1979, Honorary Life Service Awd; CA St Univ SPURS Honor Society; AB 1470 Technology Grant Writer Team; CA St Univ San Bernardino Master Teacher; Outstanding Teacher of Yr; ALSD Dist Rep Good Teaching Conference; Azusa Pacific Univ Clinical Supervision Model Presenter; *office:* Alta Loma Jr HS 9000 Lemon Ave Alta Loma CA 91701

LA ROE, KATHERINE VAN STORY, English Department Chair; *b:* Memphis, TN; *m:* Joe; *c:* Kristi, Wendy; *ed:* (BA) Span, 1969, (MED) Public Sch Admin, 1987 Univ N TX; Several Wkshps; Cmptr Literacy Ed Trng; 8th Grade Lang Art; *cr:* Admin Secy US Army; Exec Secy General Portland Cement Co; Teacher Richardson Ind Sch Dist; *ai:* Faculty Advisory, Mid Sch Staff Dev Comm; Eng Dept Chairperson; Site Base Management Facilitator; Pi Kappa Delta 1987-; Kappa Kappa Gamma; Richardson Ind Sch Dist Spotlight Teacher of Month, Bar Pin Awd, Admin Intern Prgm; *office:* Parkhill Jr HS 16500 Shadybank Dallas TX 75248

LARRABEE, LUANN E., 7-8th Grade Teacher; *b:* Cedar Rapids, IA; *ed:* (BS) Phys Ed, Concordia Teachers Coll 1979; *cr:* 7th Grade Teacher St Johns Luth Sch 1979-87; 7th-8th Grade Teacher Shepherd of the Hills Chrstn Sch 1987-; *ai:* Coaching Vlybl-Bsktbl Sftbl; Track & Field Athletic Dir; *office:* Shepherd Of The Hills 7691 S University Blvd Littleton CO 80122

LARRIVY, JEAN MARIE SCOTT, 4th Grade Teacher; *b:* Mahnomen, MN; *m:* Edward E.; *c:* Maria, Katie, Brian; *ed:* (BS) Elem Ed, Bemidji St Univ 1975; (MS) Gifted Ed, Moorhead St Univ 1985; Grad Stud in Ed; *cr:* 2nd Grade Teacher Adams Sch 1975, 1977; 2nd Grade Teacher 1977-81, 3rd Grade Teacher 1981-85, 2nd Grade Teacher 1985-86, 4th Grade Teacher 1986- Cleveland Sch; *ai:* NEA, MEA; *office:* Cleveland Elem Sch 919 Northern Ave Fergus Falls MN 56537

LARSEN, DEBORAH S., Spanish Teacher; *b:* Granite City, IL; *m:* Steve; *c:* Mark, Matthew; *ed:* (BS) Span, E IL Univ 1974; (MS) Scndry Ed, N IL Univ 1989; Univ of Madrid Spain; *cr:* Span/Eng Teacher Rather Jr HS 1974-75, Sandwich Jr HS 1975-76; Span Teacher Delavan HS 1976-84, Sterling HS 1984-88, Granite City Sr HS 1988-; *ai:* Span Club Adv; IL Foreign Lang Teachers Assn 1974-.

LARSEN, LARRY DUANE, Futurism Teacher; *b:* Bismarck, ND; *ed:* (BS) Soc Sci, Dickinson St Coll 1965; Grad Stud-Univ of ND/ND St Univ/Mary Coll; *cr:* Teacher Williston HS 1965-; *ai:* WEA/NDEA/NEA; Dev of HS Futurism Curr; Drug Awareness Curr; HS AIDS Curr; *office:* Williston Sr H S 502 W Highland Dr Williston ND 58801

LARSON, ANNE BREINHOLT, Sixth Grade Teacher; *b:* Salt Lake City, UT; *m:* Larry O.; *c:* Suzanne, Stacy J., Barry O Neil, Blake C.; *ed:* (BS) Elem Ed, Brigham Young Univ 1968; Upper Division Classes, Brigham Young Univ; *cr:* 4th Grade Teacher 1968-72, 3rd Grade Teacher 1972-77, 6th Grade Teacher 1979- Provost Elem; *ai:* Building Soc Stud Dept Chm; NEA, UT Ed Assn, Provo Ed Assn 1968-; Delta Kappa Gamma 1990; Provo Freedom Festival Comm Historian 1989-; *office:* Provost Elem Sch 629 S 1000 E Provo UT 84606

LARSON, B. KAYE, Health/Phys Ed Teacher; *b:* Dennison, OH; *m:* John Roger; *c:* Timothy, Jeffrey; *ed:* (BS) Health/Phys Ed, Bowling Green St Univ 1964; Working Toward Masters Health Ed, S CT St Univ 1990; *cr:* Teacher Mt Lebanon Public Schls 1965-66, Fox Chapel Public Schls 1966-67, Gateway Public Schls 1967-68, Guilford Public Schls 1983-; *ai:* Stu Cncl Adv; Field Hockey & Intramural Coach; Faculty Cncl; Unified Arts Team Leader; Amer Assn of Health, Phys Ed, Recreation, Dance 1983-; CT Assn of Health, Phys Ed, Recreation, Dance 1983-, Teacher of Yr; Youth Service Bureau Cmmty Bd of Dir 1988-; Mobilization Team Mem 1988-; Pres Unitarian Universal Society; CT Scndry Phys Ed Teacher of Yr 1986; *home:* 289 Laurelbrook Dr Guilford CT 06437

LARSON, BILL MARTIN, 6th Grade Teacher; *b:* Duluth, MN; *m:* Karen L. Christophersen; *c:* Eric, Christy, Becky, Jackie, Betsy; *ed:* (BA) Phys Ed/Elem Ed, St Cloud 1967; *cr:* 6th Grade Teacher Sauk Rapids Elem 1968-70; Elem Phys Ed Teacher Sauk Rapid Dist 1970-71; Elem Phys Ed Teacher 1971-79, 6th Grade Teacher 1984- White Bear Lake; *ai:* HS Hockey Coach; MEA, NEA 1970-; Coaches Assn 1980-; *office:* Birch Lake Elem Sch 1616 Birch Lake Ave White Bear Lake MN 55110

LARSON, CAROL J., Second & Third Grade Teacher; *b:* Minot, ND; *m:* Wallace A.; *c:* John, Juli; *ed:* (BS) Elem Ed/Commerce, Minot St Teachers 1956; Continuing Ed, Univ of MT Missoula; *cr:* 4th Grade Teacher Watford City ND 1956-59; 2nd Grade Teacher Havre MT 1959-62, Missoula MT 1962-63, Conrad MT 1963-65; 2nd/3rd Grade Teacher Brady MT 1968-; *ai:* NEA, MEA 1968-; BEA Pres 1987-; Jaycees (Pres 1969, St Dir 1970); Outstanding Elem Teachers of America 1973.

LARSON, CHERISMA E. MYHERS, 6th Grade Teacher; *b:* Eau Claire, WI; *m:* Rodger C.; *c:* Beth Peterson, Mark; *ed:* (BS) Elem Ed, 1971; (MS) Elem Ed, 1976 Univ of WI; *cr:* 6th Grade Teacher Little Red Sch 1974-81; W R Manz Elem 1981-; *ai:* 6-8 Mid Sch Comm; Mid Sch Act Comm; Mid Sch Discipline Comm; Preparation for Mid Sch 1990-; NEA 1980-; Eau Claire Womens Chorus Pres 1986; Delta Kappa Gamma Society Intnl 1985-; Unit Leader - Manz Sch 1983-; *home:* 1525 Drury Ave Eau Claire WI 54703

LARSON, DAVID JON, Mid Sch Social Studies Teacher; *b:* Primghar, IA; *m:* Marjorie K. Kees; *c:* Jessica, Taylor, Jon; *ed:* (BS) Soc Sci, Dana Coll 1975; Grad Work Hist/Poly Sci, Univ of IA/Univ of Northern IA Cedar Falls; *cr:* Mid Sch S S 1975-77, Sr Government 1977-78 Eagle Grove Cmnty Schls; HS Soc Stud Primghar Cmnty Schls 1986-89; MS Soc Stud Paullina/Primghar 1989-; *ai:* Head Ftbl Coach South OBrien HS; Weight Club Spon; IA Ftbl Coaches Assn 1978-; ISEA, PEA VP 1989-; Northwest IA Coach of Yr; *home:* RR 2 Box 134 Primghar IA 51245

LARSON, ERIC A., JR., Band Director/Music Teacher; *b:* Poughkeepsie, NY; *m:* Catherine J. Healey; *c:* Patrick M., David A., John E.; *ed:* (BS) Music Ed, 1975, (MS) Music Ed, 1981 W CT St Univ; Admin/Supervision, S CT St Univ 1985-; *cr:* Music Teacher Stamford Cath HS 1975-77; Band Dir New Fairfield Jr/Sr HS 1977-80, E Ridge Mid Sch 1980-83; Music Teacher Ridgefield HS 1983-; *ai:* Marching Band, Color Guard, Jazz Band; Faculty Cncl Field Trip Comm Mem; Music Prgm Chm New England Assn of Schls & Colls Evaluation Music Comm Chair; CT Music Educators Assn (Regional Band Chm 1979-80, Regional Festival Chm 1982-83, Regional Band Chair 1989-); BSA Cub Pack #9 (Webelos Leader 1988-, Adult Trainer 1989-); Project Submitted S New England Telephones Committment to Excl Prgm; *home:* 26 Caye Rd Danbury CT 06811

LARSON, JAMES E., Social Studies Teacher; *b:* Portland, OR; *m:* Cora Leah; *ed:* (BS) Soc Sci, S OR St Coll 1968; (MS) Curr/Instruction/Disabled Youth Ed, 1972, (MS) Juvenile Corrections, 1976, (MS) Geography, 1978 Univ of OR; Taft Fellow Taft Inst for Two Party Government, Univ OR 1985; *cr:* Substitute Teacher Eugene Public Schls; Detached Worker Metro Branch YMCA; Instr Division of Continuing Ed Umpqua Comm Coll; Soc Stud Teacher Coffenberry Jr HS; *ai:* 6th-8th Grade Boys Intramural Bsktbl Prgm; Jr HS Coach & Prgm Coord; Assn of OR Geographers, NEA, OR Ed Assn; S Umpqua Ed Assn (Mem, Negotiation Comm Chairperson 1977-78, Pres Elect, VP 1979-80); Assn of Retarded Persons (Secy, Bd Mem) 1985-89; Douglas Cty Juvenile Services Commission (Mem, Secy Cmmty Action Comm Mem 1990) 1982-; Poetry Published; *office:* Coffenberry Jr HS 591 NE Rice St Myrtle Creek OR 97457

LARSON, KATHLEEN KARST, Teacher of Gifted & Talented; *b:* Milwaukee, WI; *m:* Roger Leigh; *c:* Todd, Tim; *ed:* (BA) Theatre/Drama, Lawrence Univ 1960; TX Cert & Gifted Ed, Univ of TX Pan Amer; *cr:* 3rd Grade Teacher John Marshall Sch 1960-63; 2nd Grade Teacher Carnahan Sch 1969-70; 5th Grade Teacher Eli Whitney 1971-72, David Crockett 1972-86, Christa Mc Auliffe 1986-; *ai:* Stu Cncl Spon; TCTA Faculty Rep 1974-; TAGAT; PTA (Secy 1974-76, Membership VP 1984-85); Mc Allen Leadership VI; Mc Allen Friends of Lib Pres 1973; Kappa Alpha Theta Rio Grande Valley Rush Chairperson; Joint Prof Consultation Comm Pres & Secy; *home:* 1416 Highland Dr Mc Allen TX 78501

LARSON, LINDA CHRISTIAN, Third Grade Teacher; *b:* Lindsborg, KS; *m:* Bruce N.; *c:* Syri; *ed:* (BA) Elem Ed/Phys Ed, Bethany Coll 1963; (MA) Elem Ed, WV Univ 1979; *cr:* 5th Grade Teacher Lowell Elem 1963-66; 3rd/5th Grade Teacher Binictican Elem 1967-68, Fort Gulick/Margarita 1968-71; Intinerant Learning Disabilities Teacher Hampshire Cty 1974-76; 2nd-4th Grade Teacher John J Cornwell Elem 1976-; *ai:* Acting Asst Prin 1980-; Textbook Adoption Comm; Teachers Advisory Cncl; WV Ed Assn; KS St Teachers Assn.

LARSON, LORNA MAY, Eighth Grade Teacher; *b:* Cambridge, MA; *ed:* (BSED) Elem Ed, 1962, (MA) Elem Ed, 1969 Boston St Coll; *cr:* 4th Grade Teacher Otis AFB 1962-63; 6th Grade Teacher 1963-65, 7th Grade Teacher 1965-80, 8th Grade Teacher 1980- Longfellow Sch; *ai:* Gifted & Talented Comm; Vlybl Coach; Cambridge Teachers Assn FacultY Rep 1963-, 25 Yrs Service Awd 1988; Horace Mann Grant; *office:* H W Longfellow Schl 359 Broadway Cambridge MA 02139

LARSON, LYNN J., 5th Grade Teacher; *b:* Glenbar, AZ; *m:* Lois Peel; *c:* Alana R., Vonda, Royce, Don, Robert, Laura, Bruce; *ed:* (AA) Pre-Pharmacy, Eastern AZ Coll 1959; (BA) Span, AZ St Univ 1966; Addl Studies, Brigham Young Univ; Univ of AZ; Northern AZ Univ; *cr:* Teacher Sanders HS 1966-67; Teacher/Coach Pima Unified Schls 1967-; *ai:* Pima HS Tennis Coach (2nd Year); Mem Pima Unified Schls Safety & Recreation Comm; Pima CTA VP 1984-85; a L Williams Dist Mgr 1987-; Summer Youth Employment Pgm Coord/Supv 1980-83 Outstanding Supv 1983; Boy Scouts of America Scoutmaster 1966-67 Certificate of Appreciation 1967; Adult Basic Ed Inst Eng Second Lang 1976-86; *home:* 151 W 2nd S Pima AZ 85543

LARSON, PAUL THEODORE, 6th Grade Teacher; *b:* Mankato, MN; *m:* Kay I. Kelly; *c:* Kristine, Kari; *ed:* (BS) Elem Ed, 1969, (MS) Elem Rdng, 1973 Mankato St Univ; Counseling & Audio-Visual Ed; *cr:* 6th Grade Teacher Albert Lea Public Schls 1969-; *ai:* Coach 6th Grade Girls Vlybl; 6th Grade Boys/Girls Track; Coord Rdng 6th Grade; Coord Soc Stud Curr; MEA 1969-; NEA REP; United Meth Church (Admin 1985-88/Bd Chm & Finance Dir 1983-85); Nom Teacher Yr 1985; Cert Appreciation Innovative Rdng Project 1989; *home:* 1606 Southview Ln Albert Lea MN 56007

LARSON, ROBERT WAYNE, Mathematics Teacher; *b:* Minneapolis, MN; *m:* Susan S.; *c:* Amy, Peter; *ed:* (BA) Math, Mankato St Univ 1974; (MED) Math Ed, Univ of MN 1981; *cr:* Math Teacher Osseo Jr HS 1974-; *ai:* Jr HS Golf & Swimming Coach; NCTM 1985-; MN Swimming Officials Assn VP 1986-87; *office:* Osseo Jr HS 10223 93rd Ave N Osseo MN 55369

LARSON, SHEILA FIFE, 1st Grade Teacher; *b:* Idaho Falls, ID; *m:* Eugene G.; *c:* Guy R., Christine D.; *ed:* (BS) Elem Ed, Brigham Young Univ 1968; Credits in Early Chldhd Ed; *cr:* 4th Grade Teacher Robert Sanders Mt Pleasant Dist 1968-69; 3rd Grade Teacher Whitney Sch 1969-72; Private Kndgtn Teacher Home Meridian ID 1974-75; 1st Grade Teacher Whitney 1977-78, Amity Elem 1978-; *ai:* Curr Writing Comm for Dist in Soc Stud & Substance Abuse Prevention; ASCD Mem 1984-; NAEYC Mem 1983-; BSA (Cub Scout Leader 1973-74, 1979-80, Den Mother 1980-83); 1st Grade Soc Stud Curr, Substance & Drug Abuse Prevention Curr Boise Sch Dist; Inservice Trainer for Curr; Writing Road to Rdng, Soc Stud, Substance & Drug Abuse Prevention; *home:* 4355 W Victory Rd Meridian ID 83642

LARTIQUE, CHAURICE RANSOM, 2nd Grade Teacher; *b:* Austin, TX; *m:* Jonal; *c:* Michon, Jeremy; *ed:* (BA) Sociology, CO Coll 1972; Teacher Cert Univ of CO Colorado Springs 1976; Working Toward Counseling Degree, UCCS 1982-83; *cr:* 1st/2nd/4th Grade Teacher Monterey Elem 1976-83; 2nd Grade Teacher Forest Oak Elem 1985-87; 2nd/4th Grade Teacher Oak Creek Elem 1987-; *ai:* NEA, HEA, CEA 1987-; Alpha Kappa Alpha 1976-; *home:* 7565 Dairy Ranch Rd Colorado Spgs CO 80919

LASATER, MARY JANE, 1st Grade Teacher; *b:* Van Buren, AR; *m:* William B.; *c:* Melinda, David; *ed:* (BS) Elem Ed, Murray St Univ 1964; (MA) IN Univ Bloomington 1970; *cr:* 1st Grade Teacher Van Voorhis; 1st/2nd Grade Teacher Jackson Sch; 1st Grade Teacher Brown Sch; *ai:* SEA, NEA; Tri Kappa Corresponding Secy 1972-73.

LA SCOLA, LINDA L., Pre-School Owner/Teacher; *b:* Meadville, PA; *m:* James C.; *c:* Amy, Beth; *ed:* (BS) Elem Ed, 1966, (MA) Elem Ed, 1969 Edinboro Univ of PA; *cr:* Kndgtn Teacher Cambridge Springs Elem Sch 1966-70; 2nd Grade Teacher 1978-79, 3rd Grade Teacher 1979-80 East End Elem Sch; Pre-Sch Owner/Teacher Sunshine Pre-Sch 1980-; *ai:* Jaycee-ettes Pres 1973; Jr Womans Club Ways & Means Officer 1979-81; GSA Troop Leader 1980-85; Medical Center Auxillary 1980-.

LASH, PAMELA PATTISON, English/Social Studies Teacher; *b:* Warren, OH; *m:* David W.; *c:* Jennifer L. (dec), Melissa A., Andrea N., Kimberly S.; *ed:* (BE) Eng/Soc Stud, Univ of Toledo 1971; Eng as 2nd Oral Lang, Family Research, GED Trng; *cr:* GED Teacher Defiance Coll 1972-74; Teacher Gorham-Fayette HS 1972-; *ai:* Eagle Hi-Life Yrbk & Scholastic Quiz Team Adv; Citizen Bee Coord; Gorham-Fayette Teachers Assn (Building Rep

1988-89) 1972-; NW OH Ed Assn, OH Ed Assn, NEA 1972-; Williams Cty Genealogical Society (VP 1980-81 & 1988-89, Newsletter Ed 1981-86); 1st Presbyn Church of Bryan; Phi Beta Psi; Bryan Swim Team; Natl Society of Daughters of Amer Revolution (Local Corresponding Secy 1988-) 1981-; Bryan Music Boosters; PTO; Author Newspaper Column; St of OH Dept of Ed Citizen Bee Public Service Awd 1988-; Williams Cty Genealogical, Historical Research Data Compiler; *office:* Gorham-Fayette HS N Eagle St Fayette OH 43521

LASHLEY, BARBARA REINER, 2nd Grade Teacher; *b:* Pottsville, PA; *m:* William H. Jr.; *ed:* (BSED) Ed/Eng, Millersville Univ 1970; (MED) Ed, Trenton St Coll 1978; Post Grad Work Critical Thinking, Villanova Univ 1985; *cr:* 1st Grade Teacher 1970-72, 2nd Grade Teacher 1972- Southard Sch; Teacher Step-Ahead Summer Prgm; *ai:* Staff Dev Comm Mem; Howell Township Ed Assn Recording Secy; Amer Assn of Univ Women Mem 1990; Delta Phi Eta Past Mem 1970-; *office:* Southard Sch Kent Rd & Lanes Mills Rd Howell NJ 07731

LASICH, VIVIAN E. (LAYNE), 8th Grade Eng Lang Teacher; *b:* Hopewell, PA; *m:* William G.; *c:* C. Laurence, Celeste M., Michelle R.; *ed:* (AB) Eng/Speech/Drama, Geneva Coll 1956; (MAED) Ed, N MI Univ 1970; Grad Stud Various Courses; *cr:* System Wide Dir of Drama/Scndry Eng Lit/Speech/Drama Teacher Freedom HS 1956-57; 5th Grade Teacher Gilbert Elem Sch 1967-69; 8th Grade Eng Lang Teacher Gwinn Mid Sch 1971-; *ai:* Voluntarily Conduct Writing Labs; Phi Delta Kappa; Marquette Cmmty Theatre (VP 1962-63, Bd 1963-74), Commitment to Excl 1965; Upper Peninsula Arts Coordinating Bd (Pres 1976-78, VP 1974-76, Bd 1978-84), Devotion to Arts Dev 1979; MI Assn Cmmty Arts Agencies Bd 1976-78; MI Cmmty Theatre Assn Bd 1966-68; MI Cmmty Arts Panel Bd 1975-79; MI Arts in Ed Panel Bd 1979-80; MI Arts Congress Cntrl (Bd, Organization Comm, VP, Chairperson) 1975-76; MI Dept of Ed; MI Arts Ed Bd Mem 1977-80.

LASKOWSKA, MARY LOYOLA, Clerical Assistant; *b:* Chicago, IL; *ed:* (BA) Ed, 1956, (MA) Latin, 1966 De Paul Univ; (MA) Religious Ed, Fordham Univ 1972; Northwestern Univ 1970-71; Lib Competency Course, Fordham Univ 1971; *cr:* 3rd Grade Teacher St Hedwig Sch 1944-48; 4th Grade Teacher St Michael Sch 1948-53; 6th Grade Teacher St Ann Sch 1953-55; Asst Dir of Novices 1955-56; 8th Grade Teacher St Camillus Sch 1956-59, Holy Family Acad 1959-77, Regina Dominican HS 1977-81, St Michael Jr HS 1981-87; Clerical Asst St Hyacinth Sch; *ai:* Preference Strength Profile 1977; Myers-Briggs Type Indicator Report Form; ENFP Results; IL Classical Latin Week Conference Chm 1967-77; Archdiocese of Chicago Service Ed Awd 1985; *home:* 3651 W George St Chicago IL 60618

LASKY, MARSHA SOMER, Social Studies Teacher; *b:* New York City, NY; *m:* Stanley; *c:* Sean, Brian; *ed:* (BA) His, 1963, (MA) His, 1966 Brooklyn Coll; *cr:* Soc Stud Teacher Ind Sch 14 1963-70, Long Island Sch for Gifted 1985-; *ai:* Hebrew Sch Teacher; Long Island Cncl for Soc Stud 1986-; NCSS 1985-; Organization of Amer Historians 1987-88; Womens Morning Out Pres 1974-80; *home:* 18 Downey Dr Huntington NY 11743

LASKY, PHYLLIS MC NAIR, Third Grade Teacher; *b:* Meteong, NJ; *w:* George (dec); *ed:* (BS) Elem Ed, Newark St Teachers Coll 1949; *cr:* 5th/6th Grade Teacher Mt Hope Elem 1949, Denville Elem 1949-50; 3rd Grade Teacher Rahway Elem 1950-52; 5th Grade Teacher Hopatcong Elem 1952-55; 3rd Grade Teacher Stanhope Elem 1965-; *office:* Stanhope Elem Sch Valley Rd Stanhope NJ 07874

LASNIK, JERRY L., Biology Teacher; *b:* Cleveland, OH; *m:* Pam Foster; *c:* Amanda, Adam; *ed:* (BA) Bio, 1966, (MS) Bio, 1969 CA St Univ Northridge; Teaching Credential CA St Univ Northridge 1969; *cr:* Teacher Agoura HS 1969-; *ai:* Ecology Club Faculty Adv; NEA 1969-; Natl Wildlife Fed; Cousteau Society; HS Teacher of Yr Sci Frat CA St Univ Northridge; Teacher of Month 1989; Newspaper, Magazine, TV, Radio Recognition of Cadaver Prgm 1981-; *office:* Agoura HS 28545 Driver Ave Agoura Hills CA 91301

LASOCKI, ANN LESLIE, First Grade Teacher; *b:* Neenah, WI; *ed:* (BA) Elem Ed, Univ of WI Eau Claire 1971; Comparative Ed, US & Britain; *cr:* Kndgtn/1st Grade Teacher Bloomer Public Schls 1972-; *ai:* Stu Assistance Prgm; Eau Claire Rdng Cncl 1988; Taught in Walls UK; *office:* Bloomer Public Schls 1715 Oak St Bloomer WI 54724

LA SOTA, GLORIA, Business Department Chairman; *b:* Buffalo, NY; *ed:* (AA) Liberal Art, Villa Maria Coll 1970; (BA) Bus Ed, Daemen Coll 1972; (MA) Occupational Ed, St Univ of NY Buffalo 1974; Doctoral Stud St Univ of NY Buffalo 1978-81; *cr:* Bus Teacher 1972-, Work Study Coord 1974-, Continuing Ed Dir 1988- Cheektowaga Cntrl HS; *ai:* Sr Class, Book Store, FBLA Adv; European Easter Trip with Stu; NY St United Teachers, NY St Bus Teachers Assn; NY St FBLA (Secy 1974-85, Bd Chm 1985-, Bd of Trustees Chm 1985- Natl Bd Dir 1988-); Millard Fillmore Suburban Hospital Volunteer; *office:* Cheektowaga Cntrl HS 3600 Union Rd Cheektowaga NY 14225

LASSITER, BOBBYE BURRIS, Business Ed Dept Chairman; *b:* Foreman, AR; *m:* Jerry Holland; *c:* Karen Lassiter Barber, Kay Lassiter Morris; *ed:* (BS) Bus Ed/His, E Tx St Univ 1951; (MED) Bus Ed, Univ of Ga 1977; *cr:* Bus Ed Instr Ingleside HS 1952-52; Graduate Asst Bus Ed Dept Univ of GA 1976-77; Bus Ed Instr Winder Barrow Comprehensive HS 1977-; *ai:* Supts Advisory, Accreditation Steering, First Attendance Appeals, Review Grade Reporting System, Select HS Teacher for Awd Atlanta Constitution Journal, Design Stu Detention Prgm, Design New

Method Computing GPA Comm; Academic Decathelon Judge; Womens Clinic Nancy Hill Health Center Volunteer Worker; Northwoods Homeowners Assn Co-Pres; First Chrstn Church Ofcl Bd Mem; Winder Womens Club Publicity Chm; North Springs Civic Club Secy; Garden Club Secy; Delta Phi Epsilon (Project Comm Chm, Service Comm Chm); St Semi-Finalist Teacher of Yr; GA Bus Ed Assn 9th Dist Runner Up Teacher Educator of Yr; Bus & Office St Vocational In-Service Conference Speaker; Intensive Office Procedures Coord St Chm; Outstanding Service Awd Bus & Office Ed; Develop St Scndry Bus Ed Competency-Based Curr Guide Comm; Minimum Competency Item Review Conference GA Teaching Field Criterion-Reference Test Bus Ed; On-Site Evaluation Team Fulton Cty Sch System; *home:* 109 Hickory Hollow Winder GA 30680

LASSITER, PATRICIA JONES, English Teacher; *b:* Murray, KY; *m:* Jerry Bailey; *c:* Jody A., Jared T.; *ed:* (BA) Eng/Speech, 1970, (MA) Scndry Ed, 1973 Murray St Univ; Post Master Studies Eng Murray St Univ 1977; *cr:* 8th Grade Teacher Almo Sch 1970-74, North Elem 1974-79, Calloway Mid Sch 1979-; *ai:* Coach Calloway Mid Speech & Drama Team; Dept Chm Eng Dept; KY HS Speech League Bd; NEA, KY Ed Assn, KY HS Speech League, Calloway Ed Assn, NCTE; United Meth Reporter 1989-; Women Independence Meth Church; *office:* Calloway County M S Box 2108-A Murray KY 42071

LASSWELL, JUANITA GLASPIE, Mathematics Teacher; *b:* Richmond, VA; *d:* Bruce E.; *c:* Megan; *ed:* (BS) Math, James Madison Univ 1970; *cr:* Math Teacher Falling Creek Jr HS 1970-72, Clover Hill HS 1972-; *ai:* NCTM 1972-; Natl Wildlife Fed Audubon Society; *office:* Clover Hill HS 13900 Hull St Rd Midlothian VA 23113

LATFORD, JAMES NELSON, Science Teacher; *b:* Ingersoll ON, Canada; *m:* Ann Roberta Pratt; *c:* Donald, Gwendolyn Ambrefe, James, Gordon; *ed:* (BS) Division of Math/Sci, Eastern Nazarene Coll 1958; (MS) Physics Ed, Temple Univ 1964; (AS) Electronic Technology, Northern Essex 1984; PSSC Physics; Harvard Project Physics; Aerospace Technology; Machine Shop Practice; Civil Defense; Nuclear Power; Atomic & Nuclear Conservation; Asbestos & Industrial Management; *cr:* Math/Sci Teacher Dover HS 1959-62; Physics Teacher/Dept Head Exeter HS 1962-85; Electronics/Physics Teacher Northern Essex Comm Coll 1983-85; Trainer AT&T 1985-87; Sci Teacher Willsboro Cntrl Sch 1987-; *ai:* Tri State Math League Secy 1961-62; Natl Sci & Woodrow Wilson Fnd Natl Defense; *office:* Willsboro Cntrl Sch School St Willsboro NY 12996

LATHAM, ANDREW J., Teacher/Coordinator; *b:* York, AL; *m:* Teresa Dale Huggins; *c:* Robert, Bo; *ed:* (BS) Bus Admin, Univ of AL Birmingham 1973; (MA) Mrktg Ed, Univ of AL Tuscaloosa 1978; M2 Voc Cert Ed Admin, Univ of A&M 1982; Management Trng Winn Dixie Supermarket; *cr:* Management Winn Dixie 1967-77; Co-Op Coord Brewer HS & Voc Tech 1977-; Night Mrktg/Management Instr Calhoun Comm Coll 1980-; *ai:* DECA Adv; HS & Coll Bsktbl Ofcl, Referee; AL Mrktg Educators Assn Pres 1982-83; MEDA; Morgan Cty Voc Assn Pres 1984-85; Meth Lay Person; Morgan Cty Industrial Comm Mem; *office:* Mrktg Co-Op Rt 2 Box 149 Somerville AL 35670

LATHAM, BILLY RANDALL, Industrial Arts & Art Teacher; *b:* Antlers, OK; *m:* Phyllis Gayle Thomas; *c:* Randall C.; *ed:* (BA) Industrial Arts Ed, SE OK St Univ 1978; Working Toward Masters in Sch Cnslng; *cr:* Industrial Arts Teacher Wewoka HS 1978-79; Industrial Arts/Art Teacher Obuch Jr HS 1979-; *ai:* 8th Grade Class Spon; SOSU Industrial Arts Fair Participant; Classroom Teacher Assn Mem 1989; Pusmataha Cty Sportsman Club (Pres 1984-85, 1988-, VP 1986-87) Pres Plaque 1984-85, 1989; 1st Baptist Church of Antlers Mem; Industrial Arts/Technology Ed Prof Leadership Awd 1986, 1989; *office:* Obuch Jr HS PO Drawer 627 Antlers OK 74523

LATHAM, PATRICIA ANN, Mathematics Teacher; *b:* Baltimore, MD; *ed:* (BS) Math, Westminster Coll 1968; (MA) Psych, Washington Coll 1982; Math, Univ of Md; *cr:* Math Teacher Severna Park Jr HS 1968-83, Severna Park HS 1983-; *ai:* Math Team Adv; Woods Memorial Presbyn Church (Ordained Elder, Choir Mem, Pianist) 1968-83; Christ Our Anchor Presbyn Church (Ordained Elder, Choir Mem, Pianist) 1983-.

LATHEM, SKIP J., Mathematics Teacher; *b:* Sebastopol, MS; *m:* Ruth Ann Mc Daniel; *ed:* (AA) Scndry Ed, E Cntrl Jr Coll 1980; (BS) Scndry Ed, 1982, (MED) Scndry Ed, 1987 MS St Univ; Grad Stud MS Coll; *cr:* Math Teacher Murphy HS 1982-83, Morton HS 1983-; Math Instr E Cntrl Comm Coll 1987-; *ai:* Math Team Adv; Math Tutor; Conduct ACT Wkshps; Soph Class Spon; Chm of Math Dept; Sch Cmptr Prgms; MS Cncl Teachers of Math Mem 1989-; E Cntrl Comm Coll Alumni Assn (Mem 1986-, VP 1990); STAR Teacher 1985-87, 1989-; Math Teacher Awd MS St Univ Sigma Chi 1990; *home:* PO Box 232 Morton MS 39117

LATHROP, JANICE KATHERINE, Third Grade Teacher; *b:* Portland, OR; *m:* William Allen;; *c:* Mark, Melinda Raffi, Matthew, Maria; *ed:* (BA) Ed/Psych, Chico Univ 1965; Working Toward Masters Ed; *cr:* 1st Grade Teacher Pleasant Hill Sch; 1st/2nd Grade Teacher Orland Sch Dist; 3rd Grade Teacher Notre Dame; *ai:* Notre Dame Testing Dir; Primary Grades Section Leader.

LATINI, JANE CAIRO, Vice Principal; *b:* Trenton, NJ; *m:* Joseph E.; *c:* Janeen M., Joseph J.; *ed:* (AA) Liberal Arts, Mercer Cty Coll 1968; (BA) Elem Ed, Trenton St Coll 1970; Grad Stud Supervision/Curr/Admin, Georgian Court Coll, Trenton St Coll; *cr:* Teacher Trenton Head Start Prgm 1970, Hamilton Township Public Schls 1970-73; Teacher 1981-89, Vice Prin 1989- St

Gregory the Great Sch; *ai:* Safety Patrol Adv; Renew Moderator; Eucharistic Minister; Religious Ed Teacher; Election Poll Monitor; Chairperson Mid St Steering Comm; Religious Stud & Chrstin Action Project Coord; Red Cross Teacher & Spon; Facilitator in Rainbow Prgm; Red Cross Advisory Bd 1984-, Service Awd 1989; ASCD 1989-; NCEA 1981-; NJ Pharmaceutical Assn Auxiliary; Mercer Cty Pharmacists Auxiliary Society; St Gregory Pastoral Care 1985-; Hibernian Soccer Club 1986-; Altar-Rosary Society; *home:* 1133 Estates Blvd Hamilton Square NJ 08690

LATRAGNA, SAM, Principal; *b:* St Louis, MO; *m:* Christine Kohlman; *c:* Christopher, Kimberly; *ed:* (BA) Eng, Univ of MO St Louis 1971; (MBA) Bus, Fontbonne 1990; *cr:* 7th/8th Grade Math Teacher St Ambrose 1971-73, St Josephs 1973-84; 5th-8th Grade Math Teacher 1984-85, Prin 1985- Immaculata; *office:* Immacolata Sch 8910 Clayton Rd Richmond Heights MO 63117

LATSON, JACQUELINE MORGAN, 2nd Grade Teacher; *b:* Memphis, TN; *m:* Raymond Douglas; *c:* Kris Stanback, Leslye Stanback; *ed:* (BA) Elem Ed, Lane Coll 1975; (MED) Ed, E TX St Univ Texarkana 1988; *cr:* 1st Grade Teacher Cairo Public Sch 1975-76; 1st/2nd Grade Teacher Foreman Public Sch 1976-; *ai:* Personnel Policy Comm 1988-89; Gifted & Talented Screening Comm 1989-; AR Ed Assn Mem 1976-; Classroom Teachers Assn VP 1989-; Order of Eastern Star (Worthy Matron 1987-, State Queen 1988); AR Grand Lodge Grand Conductress 1987-; Craig Chapel Church Pastors Aid Assn Pres 1987-; Zeta Phi Beta 1973-; Outstanding Woman in America 1987; Miss Saratoga Pageant Judge 1987; *office:* Foreman Lower Elem Sch P O Box 280 Foreman AR 71836

LAUBACH, ELIZABETH DE MARTE, English Department Chair; *b:* Harrisburg, PA; *c:* Lynne Goldman, Jeffrey; *ed:* (BS) Eng, Bloomsburg St 1960; (MS) Ed, Elmira Coll 1968; *cr:* Eng Teacher Corning Dist 1961-; *ai:* Sch Newspaper Adv; NCTE 1975-; NY St Teachers 1961-; *home:* 3133 Sing Sing Rd Horseheads NY 14845

LAUCHNOR, DEBORAH RUND, Second Grade Teacher; *b:* Palisades Park, NJ; *m:* Terrance; *c:* Meghan, Julie; *ed:* (BA) Elem Ed, Grove City Coll 1972; Elem Ed, Millersville Univ 1974; *cr:* Teacher Salisbury Elem 1972-; *ai:* Pequea Valley Sch Dist Wellness Comm; Salisbury Elem Soc Comm; NEA, PSEA 1972-; Keystone Rdng Assn 1989; Good Shepherd Church Ed Comm 1988-; *home:* 148 Edgewood Dr New Holland PA 17557

LAUDATI, EDMUND A., Mathematics Teacher; *b:* Waterbury, CT; *m:* Catherine Cronan; *c:* Dana; *ed:* (BA) Ed/Math, S CT St 1965; (MA) Ed/Math, Cntrl CT St 1969; Ed, St Joseph; *cr:* Teacher Mary Abbott 1965-78, N End Mid 1978-; *office:* North End Mid Sch Bucks Hill Rd Waterbury CT 06704

LAUDE, MAUREEN HANAFIN, Mathematics Teacher; *b:* Chicago, IL; *m:* Edward J.; *c:* Maribeth, Edward M., Kevin R., Margaret D., Stephen H.; *ed:* (BA) Math, Mundelein Coll 1963; (MS) Math, Chicago St Univ 1980; Univ of IL, IL St Univ, Lake Forest Coll, St Xavier Coll; *cr:* Math Teacher Acad of our Lady HS 1963-66, Mother of Sorrows HS 1977-79; Math Instr Moraine Valley Comm Coll 1980-88; Math Teacher Queen of Peace HS 1979-; *ai:* Sr Class Moderator; European Trip Chaperone; Math Teachers Assn Pres 1989-; MTA, IL Cncl Teachers of Math, NCTM 1977-; Woodrow Wilson Fellowship Fnd Fellowship Awd 1988; St Thomas More Home Sch Assn VP 1975-78; St Thomas More Sch Bd (Mem, Secy) 1988-; NEWMAST NASA Wkshp 1987; Honors Wkshp Discrete Math & Combinatorics 1985; Univ of IL Math Fellowships 1986, 1989; *office:* Queen of Peace HS 7659 S Linder Burbank IL 60459

LAUDERDALE, B. JO PUTT, English Teacher; *b:* Rensselaer, IN; *c:* Lowellette; *ed:* (BA) Latin, Milligan Coll 1965; Human Dev & Counseling, Sangamon St Univ; Teaching Gifted St of IL; *cr:* Latin Teacher Fort Carolina Jr HS 1965-67; Eng Teacher Eisenhower HS 1967-; *ai:* Clown Club & Sunshiners Chrst Club Spon; FTL 1989-; DEA 1988; Northwest Chrstn Church; *office:* Eisenhower HS 1200 S 16th St Decatur IL 62521

LAUDERDALE, RIONA SUE (STACY), Mathematics Teacher; *b:* Wichita Falls, TX; *m:* James Madison; *c:* Paul, Staci; *ed:* (AA) Math - Cum Laude, San Jacinto Coll 1978; (BA) Lit Univ of Houston Clear Lake 1983; *cr:* Math Teacher Galena Park HS 1984-; *ai:* Curr Comm; Phi Theta Kappa 1976-79; TSTEA Treas 1977-78; TSTA 1984-88; CTA 1989-; Northshore Area Chamber Of ComMerce 1989-; Galena Park Civic Club 1987-88; Deans List Univ of Houston Clear Lake 1984; Published in SE TX Historian & Webb Society Published 1977; *office:* Galena Park HS 1000 Keene St Galena Park TX 77547

LAUER, DAVID CHARLES, SR., 6th Grade Health Teacher; *b:* Phill, PA; *m:* Joanne Shoyer; *c:* David Jr., Maria; *ed:* (BS) Elem Ed, Kutztown 1980; *cr:* 6th Grade Math Teacher 1982-84, 5th Grade Math Teacher 1984-85, 7th-8th Grade Sci Teacher 1985-86, 6th Grade Health Teacher 1986- Selinsgrove Mid Sch; *ai:* Head Girls Track Coach Selinsgrove HS; Peer Leadership Coord; *office:* Selinsgrove Area Mid Sch N 18th St Selinsgrove PA 17870

LAUGHERY, GWEN MARIE, Third Grade Teacher; *b:* Stromsburg, NE; *m:* James W.; *c:* Anne M., Beth N.; *ed:* (BS) Elem Ed - Magna Cum Laude, SW MO St Univ 1974; Grad Work Univ of NE Omaha, SW MO St Univ; *cr:* 6th Grade Teacher Cntrl City Schls 1974-75, Blair Cntrl Sch 1975-85; 3rd Grade Teacher Blair N Sch 1985-; *ai:* Odyssey of Mind Coach; Jr HS Vlybl Coach; Gifted Ed, Technology, Skills for Growing Advisory Comm Mem; Blair Ed Assn (Building Rep Nomination Comm 1988-89,

1989-, Mem 1975-); NEA Mem 1974-; *home:* RR 2 Lakeland LL33 Blair NE 68008

LAUGHLIN, DEBRA J. (PUMMILL), Marketing Education Teacher; *b:* Dayton, OH; *m:* Michael G.; *c:* Sara A., Matthew S.; *ed:* (BS) Bus Ed, Bowling Green St Univ 1978; (MS) Sch Counseling, Univ of Dayton 1985; Mrktg, Wright St Univ; *cr:* Mrktg Ed Teacher Middletown HS 1979-83, Centerville HS 1983-; *ai:* DECA Adv; NEA 1983-; Amer Voc Assn, OH Mrktg Ed Assn 1988-; S Metro Optimists VP 1988-89; W OH Ed Assn & Univ of Daytons Teacher of Yr; *home:* 450 Roselake Dr Centerville OH 45458

LAUGHLIN, TERESA ANN, 7th Grade English Teacher/Chm; *b:* Lenoir City, TN; *ed:* (BS) Eng, 1970, (MAT) Eng, 1973 Mid TN St Univ; *cr:* Teacher Highland Park Sch 1970-78; 7th Grade Eng Teacher North Mid Sch 1978-; *ai:* Natl Jr Honor Society-Faculty Cncl; Grade Level & Subject Area Chm; Spon Duke Univ Talent Identification Prgm; Chm PTO Parent Vol Prgm; LCEA; TEA; NEA; Ruritan Club Outstanding Young Educator Loubon Cty System 1973; *office:* North Mid Sch Rt 1 Hickory Creek Rd Lenoir City TN 37771

LAUGISCH, HELEN PAGE, English Teacher; *b:* Salt Lake City, NC; *m:* Henry Carl; *c:* Frederick, Henry, Mark, Laurie; *ed:* (AA) Eng, Campbell Coll 1959; (AB) Eng, Flora Mac Donald-St Andrews 1961; (MSED) Ed, Univ of S CA 1977; Rdng/Ag Cert, E Carolina Univ; Writing, Pembroke St Univ; Intermediate Grades Cert, Campbell Univ; Advanced Placement Eng, Univ NC of Charlotte; Writing, Univ of NC Wilmington; *cr:* Eng Teacher Copperas Cove HS 1961-62; 2nd/7th Grade Teacher College Lakes Elem Sch 1966-70; 7th Grade Teacher Sherwood Park Elem 1972-74; Eng as Foreign Lang Teacher Berlin Ed Center 1975-77; 7th/9th Grade Teacher South View Jr HS 1977-85; 9th-12th Grade/Eng Dept Chm South Brunswick HS 1985-; *ai:* NC Regional Teacher Recruiter; Mentor Teacher; NC Teaching Fellows Selection Comm Regional; Regional Teacher of Yr & Prin of Yr Selection Comm; NC St Task Force for Excl in Scndry Ed Teacher Study Panel; Beautification Comm Chairperson 1983-85; NCAE, ASCD, NEA, Phi Delta Kappa, NCTE, NCETA; Democratic Party Precinct Comm 1984; Baptist Church (Sunday Sch Teacher, Prgm Chairperson) 1975-77; Runner-Up Intnl Disabled Prof Woman of Yr 1990; NC Disabled Prof Woman of Yr 1990; Intnl NC Region II Teacher of Yr 1989-; Brunswick Cty Teacher of Yr 1987-89; Brunswick Cty Woman of Achievement in Ed 1989; Writing Project Research Fellowship Great Britain 1989; NC Writing Project Fellowship 1980; Teacher of Yr Southview Jr HS 1983 & Sherwood Park Elem Sch 1974; Mid Grades Fellow FCDPI Wake Forest Univ 1979; Articles & Books Published 1988, 1989; *office:* South Brunswick HS Cougar Dr BSL Southport NC 28461

LAUKHUF, BETTY L., 4-6th Grade Tlnted/Gft Teacher; *b:* Hamlin, OH; *m:* Gerald G.; *c:* Lorrie, Amy L. Fitch; *ed:* (MED) Talented/Gifted Ed, Bowling Green St Univ; Bowling Green St Univ; *cr:* 6th Grade Teacher 1959-72; Jr HS Teacher 1972-85; 6th Grade Teacher 1979-85; 4th/5th/6th Grade Resource/Talented-Gifted Teacher 1985-89 Bowling Green City Schls; *ai:* Problem Capt Odyssey Mind; Mentor Bowling Green HS Madrigal; Singers Soviet Union 1990; Delta Kappa Gamma Ed Honorary Pres 1984-85; Local Ed Assn Human Relations Chm 1980-82; Japan Fnd Fellowship 1983; Jennings Schlr 1979-80; League of Women Voters United Nations Chm Voters Svc; Outstanding Young Women of Amer Awd Amer Assn of Univ Women 1969; Japan Fnd Fellowship Awd 1984; Excl Ed Grant Dev Sci Curr OH 1985; *office:* Bowling Green Jr H S 160 S Grove St Bowling Green OH 43402

LAUMBACH, BELINDA PACHECO, Fifth Grade Teacher; *b:* Las Vegas, NM; *m:* Greg E.; *c:* Hank, Greg M.; *ed:* (BA) Span, 1972, (MA) Elem Bi-ling Ed, 1982 NM Highlands Univ; *cr:* 5th/6th Grade Teacher Roy Municipal Schls 1972-79; Math/Span Teacher Mora HS 1979-80; 8th Grade Teacher Mora Jr HS 1980-89; 5th Grade Teacher Mora Elem 1989-; *ai:* NHS; NEA Pres 1986-88; Mora Valley Clinic Bd Chairperson 1981-83; Amigos de las Americas Volunteer 1979; Masters Bi-ling Ed Grant 1979-80; *home:* PO Box 27 Rainsville NM 87736

LAURENCE, ALLAN HARDEE, US History/Government Teacher; *b:* Corpus Christi, TX; *m:* Bonita Jo Johnson; *c:* Weldon, Travis, Curtis; *ed:* (BA) Phys Ed/Sci, TX Chrstn Univ 1960; (MA) Scndry Ed, Antioch of OH 1978; *cr:* Teacher/Coach Tuloso-Midway HS 1960-62, Victoria HS 1962-76, Mary Carroll HS 1977-78; Athletic Dir Bloomington HS 1978-80; Teacher Howell Jr HS 1980-; *ai:* TSTA Dir at Large 1980-84; AFT Campus Rep 1984-; Kiwanis Intl Key Club Spon 1972-76; Victoria HS Stu Cncl Teacher of Yr 1969, 1971; Victoria Local TSTA Teacher of Yr 1983-84; Victoria Ind Sch Dist Teacher of Yr 1988; *home:* 506 Bedivere Victoria TX 77904

LAURICELLA, MARY ANN SPALLINO, 6th Grade Teacher; *b:* Buffalo, NY; *c:* Anna M.; *ed:* (BS) Nursery-6th Grade Elem Ed, 1967, (MS) Elem Ed/Eng, 1971 St Univ Coll NY Buffalo; *cr:* 4th Grade Teacher Niagara Sch 1967-68; 6th Grade Teacher Eden Cntrl Sch 1968-; *ai:* NYSTA 1967-; Phi Dela Kappa 1989-; *office:* Eden Elem Sch Box 267 Eden NY 14057

LAUTERBACH, KAREN ELAINE (HOLLIDAY), Math/Chemistry Teacher; *b:* Peoria, IL; *m:* Robert L.; *c:* Scott, Andrea; *ed:* (BSED) Math, 1972, (MSED) Curr & Instruction, 1990 IL St Univ; *cr:* Math Teacher Elmwood HS 1972-74; Math/Chem Teacher Gardner South Wilmington HS 1981-; *ai:* Mathlete Coach; Class Spon; Math Club; NHS & Teacher Adv Comm; Delta Kappa Gamma 1988-; NCTM 1986-; IL Cncl Teacher of Math 1984-; ASCD 1989-; St Peters Luth Church (Church Cncl 1983-85, Financial Secy 1989-); W IL Univ Distinguished Teacher Awd 1987; Nom Presidential Awd Excl in Teaching Math; Educl Service Center Math Cadre Mem 1988-89; *home:* 119 Scott Dr Dwight IL 60420

LAUZON, SALLY, Science Department Chair; *b:* Malone, NY; *ed:* (BS) Ed/Bio, SUNY Plattsburg 1984; (MS) Rdng Ed, SUNY Oneonta 1990; *cr:* 7th-9th Grade Teacher Sharon Springs Cntrl 1985-; *ai:* Soph Class & Explorer Adv; Stu Cncl & NHS Co-Adv; Var Girls Sftbl Coach; NY St Coaches 1989-; Rescue Squad 1987-; BSA Honor Awd; Whos Who Among Amer Profs; *office:* Sharon Springs Cntrl Sch PO Box 218 Sharon Springs NY 13459

LAVALLEE, CAROL ANN, 1st Grade Teacher; *b:* St Johns NF, Canada; *ed:* (BS) Elem Ed, Keene St Coll 1974; (MED) Advanced Rdng, Notre Dame Coll 1982; *cr:* 1st Grade Teacher J Mastricola Elem Sch; *ai:* Math Curr Facilitator; Math Steering Comm Mem; Teacher Rep Parent-Teacher Group; Merrimack Teachers Assn Excl in Ed Awd, Parent Recognition 1988.

LAVALLEE, MARIE THERESA GUIMOND, Pre-Kindergarten Teacher; *b:* New Bedford, MA; *m:* Maurice; *c:* Donald, Diane, Marie, Robert, Maurice Jr.; *ed:* Elem Ed, Sacred Heart Coll 1962-63; Religious Ed Trng; *cr:* Kndgtn Teacher 1964-65; 1st Grade Teacher 1965-66; Kndgtn Teacher 1966-82; Pre Kngtn Teacher 1981- St Joseph; *ai:* Stu Craft Fair Coord & Instr; Co-Chm Grandparents Day; Co-Chm in Service Prgm. An OK Classroom; Anniversary Celebration for Diocese of Fall River Schl Comm; Outstanding Elem Teacher of Amer 1975; NCEA 1964-; Cath Scouting Den Leader Coach1960-75 Pelican 1970; Cath Women Pres 1979-83; AARP Cath Golden Age; Teacher of 1st Communion & Confirmation Classes; Eucharistic Minister; *office:* St Josephs Sch 35 Kearsarge St New Bedford MA 02745

LAVENDER, MARY MACHA, Sixth Grade Teacher; *b:* East Bernard, TX; *M:* Myron D.; *c:* Roderick, Randy; *ed:* (BA) Elem Ed, Sam Houston St Univ 1973; *cr:* 2nd-3rd Grade Teacher Iola ISD 1973-75; Rdng Teacher 1978-79, Kndgn Teacher 1979-80, 5th Grade Teacher 1979-80, 6th Grade Teacher 1981 Anderson Shiro CISD; *ai:* Textbook Comm; UIL Spon; Sci Fair Coord; 4-H Spon; ATPE; 4-H Spon; Short Stories Childrens Magazines; *office:* Anderson-Shiro CISD Sch P O Box 289 Anderson TX 77830

LAVERTY, LARRY LEE, Science Teacher; *b:* Isabella Cty, MI; *m:* Mignon Mogg; *c:* Jennifer, Allison, Steven; *ed:* (BS) Bio, 1964, (MA) Admin Ed, 1970 Cntrl MI Univ; Ferris St & Regions Drug Abuse Seminar; *cr:* Bio Teacher Farwell HS 1964-76; Sci Teacher Farwell Mid Sch 1976-; *ai:* MI Ed Assn, NEA 1964-; MI Sci Teachers Assn 1986-; Mi Assessors Assn 1988-; Surrey Township (Supvr 1988-, Lib Bd Chm 1985-88, Assessor, Township Trustee 1964-84); Central MI Cmmty Federal Credit Union Pres; Rotary Pres; Cub Scout Merit Badge Cnslr; *office:* Farwell Mid Sch 399 E Michigan Farwell MI 48622

LAVERY, MARY LOUISE JONES, English Teacher; *b:* Hopkinsville, KY; *m:* William D. Jr.; *c:* Daniel, Susannah; *ed:* (BS) Eng/Bio, W KY Univ 1966; (MA) Eng, Murray St Univ 1969; *cr:* Lang Arts Teacher Antioch HS 1966-67, Koffman Jr HS 1967-68; Bio Teacher Haddon Heights HS 1969-72; Writing Skills Teacher Camden Cty Coll 1982-87; Eng Teacher Haddon Heights HS 1987-; *ai:* Newspaper Spon; NJ Ed Assn 1969-72; NEA 1987-; Jr Womens Club Pres 1980-82; *office:* Haddon Heights HS 300 2nd Ave Haddon Heights NJ 08035

LA VIETES, ANNE SHERR, Spanish Teacher/Dept Liason; *b:* Allentown, PA; *c:* Rebecca, Debra, Stephen; *ed:* (BA) Span, Penn St 1966; Span/Ed, Penn St, OR St Univ, Lewis & Clark, Portland St; Several Wkshps; *cr:* Span Teacher Bellefonte HS 1967-68; Instr Penn St Univ 1968; Spec Prgms Coord Dabney S Lancaster Comm Coll 1978-84; Span Teacher Crescent Valley HS 1984-, Linn Benton Comm Coll 1985-; *ai:* Span Club Adv; Curr & Foreign Lang Comm; Corvallis Ed Assn Union Building Rep; Amer Assn of Teachers of Span & Portuguese (VP 1989-, Pres 1990); Confederation of OR Foreign Lang Teachers 1984-; Amer Cncl of Foreign Lang Teachers; Pacific NW Conference of Foreign Lang Teachers 1984; Rockbridge VA Childbirth Ed Assn (Founder, Teacher 1971-84); Distinguished Educator 1989; Linn Benton Comm Coll Outstanding Part-Time Instr 1990; Conference Wkshps Presenter; Reader & Grader ETS Advanced Placement Span Exam; *office:* Crescent Valley HS 4444 NW Highland Dr Corvallis OR 97330

LAVIGNE, DEBORAH MC DONALD, Junior High Science Teacher; *b:* Oakdale, LA; *m:* Joseph Andrew Jr.; *c:* Meredith, Laureen; *ed:* (BA) Phys Ed, 1974, (MA) Phys Ed, 1978 S LA Univ; Ed; *cr:* Grad Asst S LA Univ Lab Sch 1975; Math/Phys Ed Teacher Champ Cooper M id Sch 1975-77; Jr HS Teacher Nesom 1977-; *ai:* Yrbk Faculty Adv; Chrldr, Pep Squad Spon; Girls Athletic Coach; Southern Assn Comm Chairperson; Asst Prin; Awd Day Spon; Kappa Kappa Iota 1989-; PTO Cncl Officer 1988-; AOTT Alumnae; Textbook Adoption Comm Elem Scndry Sci; Teacher of Yr Faculty Awd 1988-89.

LAVINGHOUSEZ, WILLIAM EVAN, JR., Magnet Program Director; *b:* Mobile, AL; *m:* Camille Ricciardelli; *c:* Laura, Patricia, Tercia, William III, Chad; *ed:* (AA) Liberal Arts, St Thomas Seminary JC 1968; (BA) Scndry Sci Ed, 1970, (MED) Scndry Bio Ed, 1973 Univ of Cntrl FL; Molecular Bio & Environmental Sci, Summer Inst; Survey of Exceptionalities, Nova Univ; *cr:* Sci Teacher Melbourne HS 1970-; Adjunct Professor FL Inst of Technology 1984-; Magnet Prgm Dir Ronald Mc Nair Mid Sch 1990; *ai:* Parent Seminars; Sch Advisory & Sch Restructuring Comm; Phi Delta Kappa Treas 1990-; FL Assn Sci Teachers Teacher of Yr 1983; S Brev Chamber of Commerce Teacher of Yr 1979; Young Floridian Teacher of Yr 1988; Tandy Technology Scholars Top 100 Teachers 1990; Melbourne HS Teacher of Yr 1979, 1988; Numerous Sci Fair Awds; *office:* Ronald Mc Nair Mid Sch 501 Poinsett Dr Cocoa FL 32922

LAW, BARBARA DOYLE, Home Economics Teacher; *b:* Caro, MI; *m:* Jeffrey L.; *c:* Stephanie S.; *ed:* (AA) Home Ec, Potomac St Coll of WVU 1980; (AAS) Child Care/Dev, (BA) Voc Home Ec, Fairmont St Coll 1982; Grad Stud Towards Masters; *cr:* Teacher Kiddie Cntry Developmental Learning Center 1984-86; Asst Teacher Head Start Garrett Cty 1986-87; Teacher Northern Garrett Cty HS 1987-; *ai:* FHA & St Officer Adv; Curr Coordinating Team; Soc Comm; Restraint Team; NEA 1987-; GCTA, MTA; Garrett Cty Teen Pregnancy Comm 1987-; WISP Ski Club; *home:* Star Rt 1 Box 136 Mc Henry MD 21520

LAW, HATTIE WYNN, Guidance Counselor; *b:* Capeville, VA; *m:* James; *ed:* (BS) Office Management, VA St Univ 1969; (MA) Stu Personnel Services, Kean Coll 1978; *cr:* Elem Sch Teacher S 17th Street Sch 1970-82; Guidance Cnslr Weequahic HS 1982-; *ai:* NHS Asst Adv; Essex Cty Guidance & Personnel Assn 1984-; Newark Guidance Cnslrs Assn 1987-; Kappa Delta Pi 1978-; NJ Unit Natl Assn of Negro Bus; Prof Womens Club Inc Recording Secy 1987-; *office:* Weequahic HS 279 Chancellor Ave Newark NJ 07112

LAW, JEAN SMITH, 7th Grade Mathematics Teacher; *b:* Gallatin, TN; *m:* Larry Clay; *c:* Greg A.; *ed:* (BS) Elem Ed, TN St Univ 1980; *cr:* 6th Grade Teacher Westmoreland Elem 1980-81; 7th Grade Math Teacher Westmoreland Jr HS & Mid Sch 1982-; *ai:* Drama Teacher; Jr Honor Society Spon; 7th Grade Team Leader; TN Teachers Study Cncl 1987-; TN Jaycettes Awds Chm 1973-74, Lifetime Mem 1974; Westmoreland Jaycettes Pres 1971-72, Pres of Yr 1972; *office:* Westmoreland Mid Sch PO Box 69 Old 31E Westmoreland TN 37186

LAW, ROBERT THOMAS, Bible/Government Teacher; *b:* Leaksville, NC; *m:* Nancy Kay Fox; *c:* Jeremy R., Anna E.; *ed:* (THB) Theology/Bible, Piedmont Bible Coll 1979; (MDIV) Bible/New Testament Greek, Denver Baptist Theological Seminary 1984; *cr:* HS Teacher Denbigh Baptist Chrstn Sch 1985; *ai:* Asst Prin; Soph Spon; Bible Quiz Team Coach; HS His/Soc Stud Dept Head; Dandy Baptist Church Pastor 1987-; DBCS Sr Class Yrbk Dedication; *office:* Denbigh Baptist Chrstn Sch 13010 Mitchell Point Rd Newport News VA 23602

LAW, SUZANNE LOUISE, Junior High School Teacher; *b:* Tecumseh, MI; *m:* Michael D.; *c:* Amy, Micah, Zachary; *ed:* (AA) Ed/Eng, York Coll 1966; Grad Stud; *cr:* Volunteer Teacher Encinitas Chrstn Sch 1977-; *ai:* Chrldr Spon; Speech & Drama Coach; Direct Plays & Chapel; Chrstn Youth Theatre Bd of Dir 1985-86; Victory Chrstn HS Curr Comm 1989-; Encinitas Chrstn Advisory Comm 1987-.

LAWALIN, EDWARD ALAN, Fifth Grade Teacher; *b:* Tell City, IN; *m:* Bonnie Kay Powers; *c:* Derrick, Ben, Kristi; *ed:* (BS) Elem/Spec Ed, Brescia Coll 1976; (MA) Elem/Spec Ed, Univ of Evansville 1980; *cr:* 5th Grade Teacher 1976-88, 6th Grade Teacher 1988-89, 5th Grade Teacher 1989- Cannelton Elem Sch; *ai:* Jr HS Boys Bsktbl, Elem Girls Bsktbl, Elem Boys Bsktbl, Little League Coach; NEA, IN St Teachers Assn 1976-; Sunday Sch Teacher for Mentally Handicapped Adults; Human Rights Comm VP 1987-; *office:* Cannelton Elem Sch 6th & Taylor St Cannelton IN 47520

LAWLER, MARTHA LYNN, Science Teacher; *b:* Bowling Green, KY; *ed:* (BS) Phys Ed, Univ of N AL 1983; *cr:* Teacher/Coach Crestview Elem 1983-84, Covington HS 1984-; *ai:* Head Girls Bsktbl & Fast Pitch Sftbl Coach; Fellowship of Chrstn Athletes Spon; TN Athletic Coaches Assn Mem 1984-; TN Ed Assn & NEA Mem 1983-; Booster Club Mem 1984-; TN Sftbl Coach of Yr 1989; Power of Positive Stus Teacher of Month 1988; *office:* Covington HS 803 S College Covington TN 38019

LAWLER, MICHAEL JOSEPH, Sixth Grade Teacher; *b:* Lebanon, MO; *c:* Nicole; *ed:* (BA) Ec, 1966, (MS) ED, 1970 SUNY Buffalo 1970; *cr:* 4th Grade Teacher 1966-69, 5th Grade Teacher 1970-77 Public Sch 8; 5th Grade Teacher 1977-82, 6th Grade Teacher 1982- Public Sch 6; *ai:* HS Golf Coach; NEA, NYSTA, BTF 1966-; Univ Club of Buffalo Pres 1977-78; WNYPLGA Pres 1969-; *office:* Academic Challenge Center Hickory & S Division Buffalo NY 14204

LAWLER, TERRY LEE, English Department Co-Chair; *b:* Appleton, WI; *m:* Lorna Lee; *ed:* (BED) Eng, 1968, (MST) Eng, 1977 Univ of WI Whitewater; *cr:* Eng Teacher Tremper HS 1968-; *ai:* Sch Building Level Team; Dist Eng Task Force; Eng Dept Co-Chm; Christmas Feast Adv; Asst Swim Coach 1968-72; Drama Coach 1968-73; NEA 1968-; NCTE 1978-; Lakeside Players Past Pres 1973-, Lifetime Achievement Awd 1984; BPO Elks 1984-; Outstanding Instr Awd Univ of Chicago 1989; *office:* Treamper HS 8560 26th Ave Kenosha WI 53140

LAWLESS, JAMES RANDALL, Mathematics Teacher; *b:* Corbin, KY; *m:* Karen Huddleston; *ed:* (BS) Math, 1986, (MA) Math Ed, 1988 Cumberland Coll; *cr:* Math Teacher Whitley Cty HS 1986-; *ai:* HS Academic Events Reader; KEA, NEA, WCEA 1986-; *home:* Rt 1 Box 328 Williamsburg KY 40769

LAWLESS, SHERYL BOHN, 2nd Grade Teacher; *b:* Urbana, IL; *m:* Michael; *c:* Brett, Jason; *ed:* (BS) Elem Ed, E IL Univ Charleston 1967; Psych, IL St Univ; *cr:* 1st Grade Teacher Pleasant Acres 1967-68; 4th Grade Teacher Rogers Grade Sch 1968-69; 1st Grade Teacher Jefferson Grade Sch 1970-71; Kndgtn Teacher Homer Grade Sch 1972-78; Title I Teacher 1978-80, 2nd

Grade Teacher 1980-86, 2nd/3rd Grade Teacher 1986-88, 1st Grade Teacher 1988-89, 2nd Grade Teacher 1989- Newman Sch Dist; *ai:* Cheerleading Spon; Creative Thinking Class Teacher; Summer Sch Creative Writing; Illini Rdng Cncl 1985-; NEA, IEA 1977-; *home:* 516 N Coffin Newman IL 61942

LAWRANCE, ANN H., Mathematics Teacher; *b:* Raleigh, NC; *m:* John S.; *c:* Carter; *ed:* (BS) Math Ed, NC St Univ 1969; *cr:* Math Teacher Rosewood HS 1969-72, Millbrook HS 1972-73, E Millbrook Jr HS 1974-76, Erwin Mid Sch 1977, Enka HS 1977-; *ai:* Jr Class Spon, Sch Improvement Team Chairperson; NCEA, NEA Local VP 1990; NCTM, NCCTM; Harmony Incorporated; *office:* Enka HS 475 Enka Lake Rd Enka NC 28728

LAWRENCE, BARBRA JEAN (BITTO), Fourth Grade Teacher; *b:* Swoyersville, PA; *m:* Melvin M.; *ed:* (BS) Ed, Univ of MD 1971; Masters Equivalent Ed, W MD Coll 1977; Grad Stud W MD Coll; *cr:* Teacher Watkins Mill Elem Sch 1971-; *office:* Watkins Mill Elem Sch 19001 Watkins Mill Rd Gaithersburg MD 20879

LAWRENCE, BECKY RUSSELL, 1st Grade Teacher; *b:* Broken Bow, NE; *m:* Gary C.; *c:* Brian; *ed:* (BA) Elem Ed, 1974; (MS) Elem Ed, Chadron St Coll 1982; ECRI Trng Rdng Instructions; *cr:* K-3rd Grade Teacher Dist 42 1974-1975; 1st Grade Teacher Alliance City Schls 1975-; *ai:* Supervisor Cadet Teacher; Co-Supervisor Stu at Risk Prgm; Alliance Ed Assn Treas 1976; Alpha Delta Kappa Secy 1979; Jaycee Jills Pres 1982-83; Sparkette Key Woman 1981; Whos Who Amer Women 1980; *home:* 3011 Big Horn Alliance NE 69301

LAWRENCE, CHERYL LYNN, Fourth Grade Teacher; *b:* Lima, OH; *ed:* (BS) Elem Ed, OH St Univ 1975; Arts Unlimited, BGSU 1985-87; Private Voice Lessons 1986, 1988-89, 1990; *cr:* 5th Grade Teacher 1975-83, 4th Grade Teacher 1983-84 Irving Elem Sch; 4th Grade Teacher Whittier Arts Magnet 1984-; *ai:* Lima Ed Assn, OH Ed Assn, NEA 1975-; Friends of Whittier Arts Magnet Treas 1985-; Irving PTA 1975-85; Whittier PTA 1984-; Lima Area Concert Band 1975-85; Lima Baptist Temple (Choir 1980-, Orch 1981-, Beginner II Worker 1982-, Visionaires Worker, Missionary Outreach); Lima City Schls Lottery Grant Recipient 1987-89; Service Awd Whittier Sch 1986; Army Commendation 1974; *home:* 725 Mackenzie Dr Lima OH 45805

LAWRENCE, ERNEST JOSEPH, Physics Teacher/Sci Dept Coord; *b:* Oneida, NY; *m:* Sandra Caldwell; *c:* Amanda, Andrew; *cr:* Teacher Letchworth Cntrl Sch 1977-; Professor SUNY Geneseo 1979-; *ai:* Sci Dept Coord; Spec Ed Comm Mem; AFT, NEA; Geneseo Valley Teachers Assn Comm Mem Teacher of Yr 1985; Assn of Retarded Citizens.

LAWRENCE, JANET MARIE, Science Teacher; *b:* Tahlequah, OK; *m:* Mathew Willard; *c:* Charles; *ed:* (BS) Bio, Northeastern St Univ 1985; *cr:* Sci Teacher Sequoyah HS 1985-86; Adjunct Bio Teacher Bacone Coll 1987; Sci Teacher Tahlequah HS 1986-; *ai:* Bio Club & Spirit Club Spon; Mem of Staff Dev for Dist Chm of Four-Yr Dist Plan Sci Comm; NSTA 1988-; Co-Presenter of Wkshp at Natl Sci Teachers Assn; *office:* Tahlequah HS 625 Jones Ave Tahlequah OK 74464

LAWRENCE, KEITHA DENISE, High School History Teacher; *b:* Tarboro, NC; *ed:* (BA) His/Poly Sci, Univ of NC Greensboro 1982; (MPA) Public Admin, Univ of ND 1985; PhD Public Admin, FL Intnl 1992; *cr:* Soc Stud Teacher Miami Carol City Sr HS 1985-; Teacher/Soc Stud Coord Magnet Sch for Advanced Stud 1990; *ai:* Black His & Cultural Brain; Soc Stud Honor Society; Peer Teacher; Faculty Cncl; Natl Bicentennial Competition; Model United Nations; Law Advocacy Prgm for Elderly; Amer Society for Public Admin 1990; Alpha Kappa Alpha 1981-; Local Cncl for Soc Stud 1985-; Deloris Auzenne Fellowship; Outstanding Young Woman of America; Teacher of Month; *home:* 5665 W 20th Ave Apt 303 Miami FL 33012

LAWRENCE, KIM CHONTOSH, Math Department Chairperson; *b:* Massena, NY; *m:* Timothy John; *c:* Kendall Marie; *ed:* (BA) Math/Scndary Ed, SUNY Potsdam 1980; (MS) Scndary Ed, SUNY Oswego 1985; Cert of Admin; *cr:* Math Teacher 1980-88, Math Dept Chairperson 1989- Pulaski Acad/Central Sch; *ai:* Varsity Club Adv; Stu Outcomes Core Group; Girls Athletic Club Adv; Dist Advisory Cncl; AMTNYS 1980-; NCTM 1980-; ASCD 1989-; Mem of Regents Comm for Course I Regents Exam; *office:* Pulaski Acad/Central Sch 7250 Salina St Pulaski NY 13142

LAWRENCE, MARJORIE JULIE, 7th-8th Grade Eng-Lit Teacher; *b:* Hollywood, CA; *ed:* (BA) Theatre/Eng, Whittier Coll 1979; *cr:* Teacher Walter Dexter Jr HS 1981-; *ai:* Act Dir; Stu Cncl Adv; Graduation Speaker Coach; Phi Beta 1977-; Delta Sigma Chapter Delta Kappa Gamma Society Intnl 1987-; *office:* Walter Dexter Jr HS 11532 E Floral Dr Whittier CA 90601

LAWRENCE, PATRICIA, 1st/2nd Split Grade Teacher; *b:* Salt Lake City, UT; *ed:* (BS) Elem Ed, Univ of UT 1966; *cr:* 6th Grade Teacher Howard R Driggs Elem 1966-67; 5th Grade Teacher 1967-69, 1st-2nd Grade/2nd-4th Grade Teacher of Gifted 1969- Cottonwood Hts Elem; *ai:* PTA Teacher & Cmmty Cncl Rep; Name the Artist; Look Alike Master Art; Artist Monthly Bulletin Bd; Art Facts-Ideas & Spelling Bee Chm & Week of Arts Chm; Teacher of Month 1986; *office:* Cottonwood Hts Elem Sch 2415 E 7600 South Salt Lake City UT 84121

LAWRENCE, PEGGY L., English Department Teacher; *b:* Kinta, OK; *c:* Waynetta, Gailey, Laurie; *ed:* (BS) Elem Ed, 1973, (BA) Scndry Lang Art, 1973 SE OK St Univ 1973; Southeastern St Univ, East Cntrl Univ; *cr:* Eng Dept Head Talihina Public Schls 1974-88; Adjunct Eng Teacher E OK St Coll 1984-88; Job Developer Kiamichi Area Voc-Tech 1988-89; Eng Dept Chairperson Wilburton Public Schls 1989-; *ai:* Jr Class Spon; Interscholastic Contests; Future Teachers of America; Chapter II Philosophy & Goals; Steering & Curr Comms; Lang Art Dept; OEA, NEA 1974-; WEA 1989-; Bus Prof Women Finance Chairperson 1988-89; Amer Assn of Univ Women 1989; Delta Kappa Gamma Recording Secy 1990; *office:* Wilburton Public Schls 1201 W Blair Wilburton OK 74578

LAWRENCE, ROBERT KENT, English Department Chair; *b:* Pomona, CA; *m:* Diane Marie Parkinson; *c:* Matthew, Bret; *ed:* (BA) Eng, CA Poly Pomona 1971; (MA) Ed, Chapman 1990; *cr:* Eng Teacher Cabrillo HS 1972-; *ai:* Var Cabrillo Water Polo, Swimming Coach; Swin & Polo Club; Soph Class Adv; Lompoc Fed Teachers Mem 1975-; South Coast Writers Project; Cath Church Lector; Village Hills Bsktbl Bd Mem; YMCA Bd Mem; Little League Coach; *office:* Cabrillo HS 4350 Constellation Rd Lompoc CA 93436

LAWRENCE, SUSAN JANE (SHANKS), Business Education Teacher; *b:* Hinton, WV; *m:* Richard Thomas; *c:* Richard T. II; *ed:* (BS) Scndry Ed/Bus Ed/Lang Art, Concord Coll 1987; Working Towards Masters Counseling, Univ of WV; *cr:* Instr Natl Bus Coll 1987-88; Adjunct Faculty Concord Coll 1987-88; Teacher Hinton HS 1988-; *ai:* Hinton HS Tri-Hi-Y Adv; NBEA, Delta Kappa Gamma; 1st Baptist Church Treas 1986-; *home:* PO Box 116 Evergreen Cir Hinton WV 25951

LAWRENCE, VICKI LASS, Eng Teacher/Dept Chairperson; *b:* Moline, IL; *m:* John William; *c:* Joseph E., Millicent E.; *ed:* (BS) Eng/Ed, 1968, (MS) Ed, 1969 IN Univ; Grad Level Courses, Univ of S MS; *cr:* 7th/8th Grade Eng Teacher Binford Jr HS 1969-71; Eng Teacher/Yrbk Staff Bayou View Jr HS 1971-; *ai:* Annual & Newspaper Staff Spon; Teach Dramatics; NEA 1971-76; NCTE 1976-; Beta Sigma Phi (Pres 1973-74, 1987-, Secy 1975-87), Valentine Queen 1974, 1988, Girl of Yr 1973-74, 1988-89; Bethel Luth Church Cncl Secy 1990; Nom Outstanding Young Educator of Yr 1980, 1981; Outstanding Young Woman in America 1982; *home:* 30 45th St Gulfport MS 39507

LAWS, MARTHA FAIR, Third Grade Teacher; *b:* Elizabethton, TN; *m:* Dan Marion III; *c:* Wendy, Daniel IV; *ed:* (BS) Ed, Milligan Coll 1972; Grad Stud; *cr:* Teacher East Side Sch 1972-; *ai:* Areas of Learning Soc Stud Chairperson; Areas of Learning Sci; Text Book Rdng Comm; NEA, TN Ed Assn 1972-; Elizabethton Ed Assn Delegate 1972-, Delegate Awd; Immanuel Church Youth 1972-, Asst Dir Awd; Heart Fund Worker 1980-85; Cancer Society Worker 1982-87; Grant to CTSU Sci Grad Work; *office:* East Side Elem Sch Old Siam Rd Elizabethton TN 37643

LAWSON, ANNIE BROWNLEE, English Chair; *b:* Memphis, TN; *m:* Edgar W.; *ed:* (BSED) Ed, Memphis St Univ 1977; Grad Stud Curr, Memphis St, Trevecca Nazarene; *cr:* Teacher Northside HS 1982-85, Snowden Jr HS 1985-86; Eng Chairperson Manassas HS 1986-89, Northside Deregulated HS 1989-; *ai:* VP Local Sch Cncl; Sch Improvement Plan & Act Comm; Journalism Club; Memphis Ed Assn, TN Ed Assn 1977-; Church Choir Pres 1988-89; Organized Dept Effort Grant Proposal Funding Lang & Rdng Curr Laboratory; Career Ladder Master Teacher; *office:* Northside HS 1212 Vollentine Memphis TN 38107

LAWSON, BECKY J. (WILLIAMSON), First Grade Teacher; *b:* La Porte, IN; *m:* Douglas M.; *c:* Jeremy; *ed:* (BS) Elem Ed, Manchester Coll 1973; (MS) Elem Ed, Purdue Univ 1978; Cmptr Classes, Seminars Individualization Math, Center Act; Wkshp for Math Our Way; *cr:* 1st Grade Teacher N Newton Sch Corp 1973-; *ai:* Spelling Bee, Cmptr, Book Adoption, Talent Show, Funding, Report Card Committees; Taught Summer Sch; NNEA, NEA, ISTA 1973-; PTO Treas 1982; *office:* Lincoln Elem Sch PO Box 303 Roselawn IN 46372

LAWSON, CHARLOTTE PENNEBAKER, Art/Photography Teacher; *b:* Bardwell, KY; *m:* James Edgar; *c:* Frederica Bosemer, Teresa Boulos; *ed:* (BS) Art, Murray St Univ 1959; Grad Stud W KY Univ, Univ of Louisville; *cr:* Art Teacher Western HS 1962-68, Stuart HS 1969-81, Fairdale HS 1982-85, Fern Creek HS 1985-87, Fairdale HS 1988-; *ai:* Yrbk Spon; Jefferson Cty Ed Assn, KY Ed Assn, NEA; KY Water Color Society; Water Color Paintings Awds; *home:* 2207 High Pine Dr Louisville KY 40214

LAWSON, DICK, Third Grade Teacher; *b:* Dalhart, TX; *c:* Samuel, Benjamin; *ed:* (BA) Soc Stud, 1970, (MED) Elem Ed, 1970 West TX St Univ; *cr:* Teacher South Elem 1970-; *ai:* Coach-future Problem Solving; TX St Teachers Assn Pres 1981-82 & 1989-; Citizen of Yr-Levelland Chamber of Commerce; *home:* 500 A&M H-8 Levelland TX 79336

LAWSON, JAMES HENRY, Administrative Dean; *b:* Columbia, SC; *c:* James, John, David; *ed:* (BA) Eng, Benedict Coll 1977; (MS) Educl Leadership, Nova Univ 1989; Grad Stud Gifted Ed & Cmptrs; *cr:* Eng Teacher Boylan-Haven-Mather Acad 1977-80; Adult Ed Instr Army Ed Center 1981-83; ESOL/Admin Cntrl TX Coll 1983-84; Eng/Gifted Teacher Southwest Mid Sch 1984-86; Eng/Teacher of Gifted 1986-88, Admin Dean 1988- Oak Ridge HS; *ai:* Admin; NCTE, FL Cncl of Teachers of Eng; ASCD 1989-; Outstanding Teacher Boylan-Haven-Mather Acad; *office:* Oak Ridge HS 6000 Winegard Rd Orlando FL 32809

LAWSON, JEAN ELIZABETH, 7th Grade Earth Sci Teacher; *b:* Shreveport, LA; *m:* Terry Steven; *c:* Zachary, Stephen, Brittany, Elizabeth; *ed:* (BS) Ed, 1972, (MA) Guidance/Counseling, 1977 Miami Univ; Cmptr Sci, Xavier Univ 1989; *cr:* 3rd Grade Teacher Jonathan Wright Elem 1970-71; 6th Grade Teacher Clearcreek Elem 1971-84; 7th Grade Teacher Springboro Jr HS 1985-; *ai:* Sci Course Study Chairperson; Curr Guide Dev Comm; Behavioral/Academic Intervention Team; Good Citizenship Comm; OEA 1973-; CEA 1973-; NEA 1973-; Mu Alumni Assn 1972-; Warren Cty Innovative Teacher Grant; Tools for Discovery Exploring Nature with Microcomputer Based Laboratory Instruments; *office:* Springboro Jr H S 705 S Main St Springboro OH 45066

LAWSON, KATHY FLEEMAN, Kindergarten Teacher; *b:* Royston, GA; *m:* Bobby Wayne; *c:* Micah J., Krista J.; *ed:* (AA) General Ed, Emmanuel Coll 1973; (BS) Elem Ed, Univ of GA 1975; (MA) Ed, Brenau Coll 1979; GA Mountains Writing Project 1979; Crisis Intervention Techniques 1989; *cr:* Classroom Teacher Jones Elem 1975-77, Myers Elem 1977-; *ai:* T-Ball First Aid Mom; Youth Dept Secy for Cntrls SS; Soprano in Cntrls Adult Choir; GAE Building Rep; PAGE (Building Rep, Mem); Cntrl Baptist of Gainesville 1st-6th Grade Choir Dir; Baptist Young Women; Articles Published; *home:* 10 Cherrywood Dr Gainesville GA 30501

LAWSON, LOUDELIA SERENA, Second Grade Teacher; *b:* Durham, NC; *m:* Arthur Lee; *c:* Arthur L., Anthony L., Ardelia L.; *ed:* (BA) Elem Ed, Shaw Univ 1964; Grad Stud Toward Masters, Rdng Specialist; *cr:* Teacher A G Richardson Elem 1964-68, Sycamore Park Elem 1968-89; Rdng Teacher Ann Wingfield Sch 1972; Head Teacher Farmington Elem 1974; *ai:* NEA, VA Ed Assn, Culpeper Ed Assn; *home:* Rt 1 Box 288 Culpeper VA 22701

LAWSON, MARGARET ARIAIL, AP English/German Teacher; *b:* Florence, SC; *m:* Thomas Clay; *c:* Thomas S., James A.; *ed:* (BA) Eng/Music/Drama, Columbia Coll 1948; Grad Work Eng, Univ of NC Chapel Hill; Grad Work Ed, Samford Univ, Univ of AL Huntsville, AL A&M Univ; *cr:* Teacher Union HS 1948-50, Anderson Jr HS 1951-52, Jefferson Cty Schls 1953-54, Fairfield HS 1953-56, Lee HS 1973-; *ai:* Frosh Class & Ger Club Spon; Delta Kappa Gamma; NCTE, AL Assn Ger Teachers; PTA Blossomwood Sch 2nd VP; Huntsville Mid Sch PTA, Cosmopolitan Club, Huntsville Dental Auxiliary Pres; Huntsville Civic Club Cncl VP; Huntsville Cncl of PTA Secy; *office:* Lee HS 606 Forrest Cir Ne Huntsville AL 35811

LAWSON, MARIAN BOYD, 5th Grade Lang Art Teacher; *b:* Tuskegee, AL; *m:* Alonzo F. Jr.; *c:* Melanye, Deryck; *ed:* (BS) Health/Phys Ed, Tuskegee Univ 1952; (ME) Elem Ed, Wayne St Univ 1975; *cr:* Teacher Detroit Bd of Ed 1952-53, 1967-; *ai:* Sch Charities Chairperson; Black United Fnd & United Fnd; Sch Employees Comm; Good Fellow Inc; Natl Assn for the Advancement of Colored People; Creative Writing & Rdng Road Quiz Coord & Spon; Wayne St Univ Alumni Rep; Teacher Excl; Math & Sci Fair; Detroit Fed of Teachers, MI Fed of Teachers, Detroit Teachers Credit Union 1967-; Plymouth Congregational Church 1962-; Local Sch Cmmty Organization 1979-; Parent Teachers Neighborhood Organization 1969-; Perfect Attendance 15 Yrs; Detroit Public Ed Fund, Wayne Cty Intermediate Sch Dist Grants; The Detroit Center for Prof Growth & Dev; Bi-ling & Improving Ed in Diverse Classrooms Grants; *office:* Grayling Elem Sch 744 W Adeline Detroit MI 48203

LAWSON, PATRICIA B., English Teacher; *b:* Lebanon, KY; *m:* Glenn; *c:* Tim; *ed:* (BS) Eng, Campbellsville Coll 1969; (MA) Eng, E KY Univ 1976; Working on Rank I in Ed & Cert in Supervision; *cr:* Teacher Springfield Mid Sch 1969-80; Instr Campbellsville Coll 1983; Adjunct Instr St Catharine Coll 1985-89; Eng Teacher Washington Cty HS 1981-; *ai:* KY Resource Teacher; Inservice Planning, Parent Advisory, Curr Steering, Faculty Advisory Comm; NEA, KEA; Washington Cty Ed Assn (Secy 1986-88, Building Rep 1989-); *office:* Washington County HS Lincoln Park Rd Springfield KY 40069

LAWSON, RAMONA ASCOUGH, 6th Grade Teacher; *b:* Cumnock, NC; *w:* B. F. (dec); *c:* Jeffrey Z., Robin Hardy; *ed:* (BA) Eng/Fr, Wake Forest Univ/Flora Mac Donald Coll 1951; Addl Studies Elem Teacher Cert UNC; East Carolina Univ; *cr:* HS Eng/Fr Teacher Randolph Cty Schls 1951-53; 8th Grade Teacher Sanford City Sch 1953-56; 7th Grade Teacher Alamance HS 1956-57; Jr HS Eng/Soc Stud Greensboro City Schls 1957-59; 6th Grade Teacher Guilford Cty Schls 1964-66; Lee Cty Schls 1966-; *ai:* Sch Soc Stud Chairperson Southern Assn of Schls & Colleges; Foreign Lang Comm Lee Cty Basic Ed Plan; Alternate Comm Mem On-Site Based Curr Comm; Asst Coach Kiwanis Track Meet 1990; NEA 1951-90; Sec 1989-; Treas 1984-85 Certificate of Appreciation 1984-85; Plaque of Appreciation 1981-82; NC Assn of Educators; NC Cncl of Math 1989-; Pres 1981-82; VP 1980-81; Assn of Classroom Teachers; UM Church Recording Sec Chairperson 1989-; United Meth Church 1988- (Lay Leader 1989- Adult Sunday Sch Teacher 1970- Pianist 1970-); Delegate to St NCAE Convention 1979- ; Math Awd Outstanding Math Teacher 1987; NC Cncl of Teachers of Math; *office:* J R Ingram Jr Elem Sch 3309 Wicker St Sanford NC 27330

LAWTON, DIANE BIVES, Elementary Phys Ed Teacher; *b:* New Orleans, LA; *m:* Michael J.; *c:* Laura, Dana, Stacy; *ed:* (BA) Elem Ed, Mc Neese St Univ 1967; (MA) Elem Teaching, Northwestern St Univ 1981; Northwestern St Univ 1983; *cr:* 1st Grade Teacher San Jacinto Elem 1960-61; 6th Grade Teacher 1967-69, 1st Grade Teacher 1969-80, 3rd Grade Teacher 1980-82, 4th Grade Teacher 1985-89, Elem Phys Ed Teacher 1982-84/1989- Buckeye Elem; *ai:* Supts Forum Faculty Rep; Phi Delta

Kappa 1986; LA Sci Teachers 1986-; Republican Women (Secy 1989- VP 1990-).

LAWTON, NEIL EDWARD, History/Psychology Teacher; *b:* Hampton, IA; *m:* Denise R. Lenhart; *c:* Blair, Keely; *ed:* (BA) His, Wayne St Coll 1976; (MA) His, Univ Northern IA 1987; *cr:* Scndry Soc Stud Teacher West Lyon Cmmty Schls 1976-; *ai:* Jr Class Spon; Jr High Bsktbl; Delta Psi Omega Theatre; Kappa Delta Pi Ed; *office:* West Lyon H S Rr Inwood IA 51240

LAWYER, ARANKA VINCZE, English Teacher; *b:* New York, NY; *m:* Robert R.; *c:* Robert Jr., Jeffrey; *ed:* (BS) Elem Ed, 1958, (MS) Ed, 1964 St Univ of NY Oneonta; *cr:* Jr HS Eng Teacher 1957-64, 1966-, Jr HS/HS Eng Teacher 1987-, Richmondville Cntrl Sch; *ai:* 7th Grade Class Adv; Grievance Comm Chm; Delta Kappa Gamma (Secy 1978-80, Finance Chm 1988-); *home:* 12 Robert St Richmondville NY 12149

LAX, DONALD LIONEL, Industrial Arts Instructor; *b:* Buchanan, TN; *m:* Betty Ann Rowlett; *c:* Lionel D., Lisa A.; *ed:* (MA) Ed, 1958, (MA) 1961 Murray Univ; Grad Stud Industrial Technology; *cr:* Dept Head Woodland HS 1958-89; *ai:* Amer Industrial Arts Assn Life 1958-89, Outstanding Industrial Arts Teacher of Yr Awd 1968; Rotary (Pres 1969-, Mem 1960); AF&A, (Mem 1956, Worshipful Master 1976); Trowel Lodge 440; 1st Baptist Church Deacon; Industrial Art Handbook Author; *home:* Rt 2 Box 4A Lutesville MO 63762

LAY, DOROTHY HOEKMAN, Fifth Grade Teacher; *b:* Slayton, MN; *m:* Donald; *c:* Donna Foppe, Jill Brandsma, Derek, Jon; *ed:* (BA) Elem Ed, Southwest St Univ 1971; Additional Stud; *cr:* 5th Grade Teacher Westside 1970-71, Winfield 1971-72, Progress S Ft Zumwalt 1972-75; 6th Grade Teacher Cainsville Elem 1975-77; 5th/6th Grade Teacher Francis Howell Cntrl Elem 1977-; *office:* Francis Howell Cntrl Elem Sch 4525 Central School Rd Saint Charles MO 63303

LAYGO, TERESITO MARQUEZ, Mathematics Teacher; *b:* Malolos, Philippines; *m:* Andrea Catalan; *c:* Patrick, Christina, T. J.; *ed:* (BA) Ed, Ateneo de Manila Univ 1955; (MA) Math, Boston Coll 1964; Guidance & Counseling, Ateneo de Manila Univ; Sch Admin, Centro Escolar Univ; Multicultural Ed, Univ of San Francisco; *cr:* 6th Grade Teacher Ateneo de Manila Grade Sch 1955-60; HS Math Teacher Ateneo de Manila HS 1960-69; Math Assoc Prof Ateneo de Manila Univ 1969-75; Curr Specialist Asian Amer Bi-ling Center 1975-82; Math Teacher Lowell HS 1982-83, Jefferson HS 1983-85, Phillip & Sala Burton Academic HS 1985-; *ai:* Math Teachers Assn of Philippines Pres 1969-75; NCTM Mem 1962-; Knights of Columbus Grand Knight 1966-67; Natl Sci Fnd Academic Yr Inst Grant 1962-63; Books Published.

LAYMAN, CHARLES CLIFTON, JR., Communications Teacher; *b:* New Orleans, LA; *ed:* (BA) Speech Ed, 1980, (MED) Curr & Instrtn, 1984 Univ of New Orleans; *cr:* Teacher F W Gregory Jr HS 1980-83, S J Peters Mid Sch 1983-85, F C Williams Mid Sch 1985-87, F T Nicholls HS 1987-; *ai:* Publications Adv & Newspaper & Yrbk; Speech & Debate Team Coach; New Orleans Speech League Mem 1980-; Metro Area Comm Mini Grant; Univ of New Orleans Writing Fellowship; *office:* Nicholls HS 3820 St Claude Ave New Orleans LA 70117

LAYMAN, HATTIE CYNTHIA, Science Department Teacher; *b:* Roanoke, AL; *m:* W. C.; *c:* Christy Adams; *ed:* (BS) Sci/Math, 1967, (MS) Sci, 1970 Univ of TN; Auburn Univ; *cr:* Teacher Amer Dependant Sch 1968-69; Cntrl HS 1970-77, Randolph Cty Sch System 1978-; *ai:* 4-H Spon; NEA, AL Ed Assn, Randolph Ed Assn 1978-; Greens Chapel Church Mem 1952-; *office:* Woodland HS PO Box 157 Woodland AL 36280

LAYMAN, JIMMIE ESTES, 5th Grade Teacher; *b:* Lee Cty, MS; *m:* Richard G.; *c:* Susan Layman Cook, Mark, Jennifer; *ed:* (BA) Elem Ed, Blue Mountain Coll 1965; (MA) Elem Ed, Univ of AL Birmingham 1980; *cr:* 2nd Grade Teacher Moody Elem Sch 1964-66; 3rd Grade Teacher 1967-79, 4th/5th Grade Teacher 1979-81, 5th Grade Teacher 1981- St Clair Cty HS; *ai:* Band Booster Concessions; 4-H Club Spon; Mission Volunteer Coord; Band Booster Secy; Local, AEA, NEA 1965-; PTA Pres; *office:* St Clair Cty HS Burgess Dr Odenville AL 35120

LAYMAN, MARY JO FLETCHER, 6th Grade Teacher; *b:* Mt Vernon, OH; *m:* David E; *c:* Shannon, Bret; *ed:* (BS) Elem Ed/ Spec Ed, Bowling Green St Univ 1969; Oh St Univ, Ashland Univ; *cr:* Primary EMR Teacher Mt Vernon City Schls 1969-71; Jr HS Eng Teacher 1982-85, 6th Grade Teacher 1985- Northridge Local; *ai:* Skills for Adolescence; Prime Time Friday Night Rdng; Building Mentor; Mt Vernon Nazarene Coll Cooperating Teacher; NEA, OEA 1982-; NREA 1982-, Outstanding Teacher 1988; Homer PTO (Pres, VP, Treas) 1980-84; Highwater Congregational Church (Sunday Sch Teacher, VBS Dir); Whos Who Among Americas Young Women; Ashland Oil Nom; *home:* 2868 Lake Fork Rd Utica OH 43080

LAYMAN, SANDRA HALL, Business Department Chair; *b:* Rocky Mount, VA; *m:* Frank Benjamin III; *c:* Malinda, Benji; *ed:* (BS) Bus Ed, James Madison Univ 1975; *cr:* Teacher Franklin Cty HS 1975-; *ai:* FBLA Spon; Alpha Delta Kappa, PTO; Antioch Church of Brethren (Clerk, Sr/Jr HS Cnslr, Sunday Sch Teacher, Substitute Sunday Sch Teacher); *office:* Franklin Cty HS 506 Pell Ave Rocky Mount VA 24151

LAYN, SHENA COOPER, 9th Grade English Teacher; *b:* Duncan, OK; *m:* Joe Weldon; *c:* Zackary, Shiloh; *ed:* (BS) Health/ Phys Ed/Eng, Wayland Baptist Coll 1978; (MED) Phys Ed, W TX St Univ 1982; *cr:* Asst Coach/Player Dallas Diamonds 1979-80; Teacher/Coach Snyder HS 1980-82, Marlow HS 1982-; *ai:* Fellowship of Chrstn Athletes Spon; Marlow Assn of Classroom Teachers Soc Comm; Marlow Assn of Classroom Teachers (Mem, Building Rep) 1980-; OK Ed Assn, NEA Mem 1980-; Coaches Assn Dist Rep 1987-89; FCA Spon 1980-, OK HS Coach of Yr 1986; 1st Baptist Church (Sunday Sch Teacher, Youth Comm) 1980-; *home:* 908 S 7th Marlow OK 73055

LAYNE, ROBERT W., 8th Grade Mathematics Teacher; *b:* New York, NY; *m:* Hilah E. Vaughan; *c:* Amity, Tara, Luke; *ed:* (BS) Phys Ed/Math, Concord Coll 1971; (MA) Elem Admin, VA Tech 1988; *cr:* 1st-5th Grade Phys Ed Teacher Richlands Elem Sch 1972-78; 6th-8th Grade Math Teacher Richlands Mid Sch 1978-; *ai:* Art Club Co-Spon; Admin Evaluation Comm Chm; Tazewell Ed Assn (Pres 1974, Mem 1971-75, 1980-); VA Mid Sch Assn 1986-; Art & Soul Incorporated Pres 1989-; *office:* Richlands Mid Sch Rt 460 Richlands VA 24641

LAYNG, CONSTANCE TWIETMEYER, Business Education Teacher; *b:* Waterloo ON, Canada; *c:* Larry, Jeffrey, Lisa Carter, Kathryn, Daniel; *ed:* (BS) Bus Admin, Carthage Coll 1952; (MED) Voc Ed, Univ of IL 1981; *cr:* Bus Ed Teacher Leland HS 1952-53; 7th Grade Teacher Whig Hill Sch 1953-54; 7th/8th Grade Math Teacher Lincoln Mid Sch 1970-71; Bus Ed Teacher West HS 1971-89, Auburn HS 1989-; *ai:* Girls Tennis Team Coach; Voc Teachers Curr Comm; Delta Kappa Gamma Mem 1977-; Rockford Ed Assn; Gloria Dei Luth Church Choir 1979-; *office:* Auburn HS 5110 Auburn St Rockford IL 61101

LAYTON, CAROLYN HOLLINGSWORTH, Vocational Skills Instructor; *b:* Hattiesburg, MS; *m:* James L.; *c:* Joshua J.; *ed:* (BS) Home Ec Ed, 1975, (MS) Clothing/Textiles, 1980 Univ of S MS; *cr:* Teacher St Martin HS 1976-84, St Martin Jr HS 1984-; *ai:* FHA & Yrbk Adv; MAVE (By Laws Comm Chairperson 1988-89, Mem 1986-); AVE Mem 1986-; St Martin Youth Organization Secy 1986-88; Jackson Cty Schls Teacher of Yr 1989; *home:* 16004 Cherry Dr Biloxi MS 39532

LAYTON, JESSE J., English/History Teacher; *b:* Hastings, NE; *m:* Mary K. Gilbert; *c:* Russell, Brad; *ed:* (BA) His/Eng, Univ of NM 1970; Ed/Cmptr, Adams St & CO St Univ; *cr:* NCO Trng Officer USMCR 1970-76; 4th/5th Grade Soc Stud Teacher Manzano Day Sch 1973-76; Teacher Bayfield Mid Sch 1977-; *ai:* Head Ftbl Coach; Head Boys & Girls Bsktbl Coach; Nom for US West Teacher of Yr; *office:* Bayfield Mid Sch PO Box 258 Bayfield CO 81122

LEABO, BARBARA DICKESON, 6th Grade Tchr/Science Spclst; *b:* Independence, MO; *m:* Gary J.; *c:* Chad, Todd; *ed:* (BED) Elem Ed, Washburn Univ 1964; (MS) Scndry Ed, Univ MO Kansas City 1983; Sci Specialist Awarded By Natl Fnd of Sci & Univ MO Kansas City 1987; *cr:* 5th Grade Teacher Katherine Carpentar Sch 1964-65, Central Park Sch 1965-66, Marsha Bagby Sch 1966-67; Field Dir Girl Scout Cncl 1975-77; 6th Grade Teacher William Yates 1977-; *ai:* Sci Specialist for Blue Springs Sch Dist; Literature Club Spon; Safety Patrol Adv; Sci Fair Chm; Natl Sci Teachers 1987-; Comm Educators Assn Rep 1985-88; Greater Kansas City Sci Teachers 1987-; Jr Service League 1972-; Girl Scouts Trainer 1975-80; Outstanding Young Woman of Independence 1976; Whos Who Among Amer Women; Teacher of Yr Nom 1988; Employee of Month 1989; *office:* William Yates Elem Sch 3600 Davidson Independence MO 64055

LEACH, BARRY DOUGLAS, 5th Grade Teacher; *b:* Sumter, SC; *m:* Sharon Ceceilia Johnson; *ed:* (BS) Bio/Zoology, Clemson Univ 1968; (MED) Elem Admin, Univ of SC 1975; Ed Specialist Prgm, Univ of SC; *cr:* Capt/Trng Officer USAF 1968-72; Phys Ed Teacher 1972-73, 5th Grade Teacher 1973- Millwood Elem; *ai:* Sumter Dist 17 Elem Sci Comm Secy; Millwood Sch Prin Advisory Comm Faculty at Large Rep; SCEA, NEA 1985-89; St Elem Comm Mem Southern Assn of Colls & Schls; Received Awd from Winthrop Coll 1988-89; *office:* Millwood Elem Pinewood Rd Sumter SC 29150

LEACH, JUDY ANN, English Teacher; *b:* Union, MS; *m:* Alton Reagan; *c:* David A.; *ed:* (AA) Liberal Art, E Cntrl Jr Coll 1973; (BS) Eng/Scndry, Livingston Univ 1975; *cr:* Eng Teacher Beulah Hubbard HS 1975-; *ai:* Beta Club Spon; STAR Teacher 1989; *office:* Beulah Hubbard HS Rt 1 Box 108 Little Rock MS 39337

LEACH, LINDA SUE, English IV Teacher; *b:* Monroe, MI; *ed:* (BA) Eng, E KY Univ 1983; Grad Stud; *cr:* Eng IV/Journalism/ Speech/Drama Teacher Cumberland HS 1987-; *ai:* Speech & Drama Club Sr Spon; Newspaper; Annual; KEA, NEA; Dante Inst W KY Univ 1989; *office:* Cumberland HS Redskin Dr Cumberland KY 40823

LEACH, WILLIAM GORDON, JR., Vocational Electricity Teacher; *b:* Morristown, NJ; *m:* Jane A.; *c:* Cara A., Randolph W., Erin C.; *ed:* (BA) Industrial Technology, Trenton St Coll 1968; CIE Cert; Certified NJ Electrical Contractor; Auto Mechanics Cert; *cr:* Owner Colley Auto Body 1974-80; Gen Mgr Image Boat Comany 1980-85; Teacher Sussex Cty Voc Tech HS 1985-; *ai:* Voc Ed Assn of NJ 1985-; NJ Ed Assn Local VP 1986-; NJ Electricity Teacher of Yr 1989; *home:* 67 Ripplewood Dr Lake Hopatcong NJ 07849

LEADBETTER, LOLA M., Fifth Grade Teacher; *b:* Jacksonville, TX; *c:* James S., Roy A., Andy R., Robert G.; *ed:* (BS) Elem Ed, Stephen F Austin Univ 1965; *cr:* Teacher Calhoun Cty Ind Sch Dist 1965-; *ai:* Faculty Rep for Teacher Advisory Comm; TCTA Faculty Rep 1965-; Delta Kappa Gamma (2nd VP 1990, Treas 1986-).

LEADER, TIMOTHY MICHAEL, Fifth Grade Teacher; *b:* Madison, WI; *m:* Julia Turner; *c:* Chris, Scott, Jane, Jay; *ed:* (BS) Elem Ed, WI St Univ Oshkosh 1968; Grad Work Univ of Wi Milwaukee; FCC Amateur Radio Novice License; Technician License; Advanced License; Extra Class License; *cr:* 5th-8th Grade Teacher S Bryon Sch 1960-61; 7th-8th Grade Teacher Richfield Elem Sch 1961-65; 5th Grade Teacher Kewaskum Sch Dist 1965-; *ai:* Soc Stud Evaluation Comm Secy; NEA; WI Ed Assn Cncl; Kewaskum Ed Assn; Cedar Lake United Educators; Natl Assn of Radio & Telecommunications Engrs Inc; Amer Radio Relay League; Rock River Radio Club; Radio & Telecommunication Career; *office:* Kewaskum Elem Sch 1550 Reigle Dr Box 127 Kewaskum WI 53040

LEADER, VIRGINIA WRIGHT, 8th Grade English Teacher; *b:* Augusta, GA; *m:* Ronald David; *c:* Laurie M., Brandon T.; *ed:* (BS) Elem Ed, W GA Coll 1971; *cr:* 2nd Grade Teacher Lillie E Suder Elem 1971-74; 7th/8th Grade Teacher North Clayton Jr HS 1979-80; 8th Grade Eng Teacher Morrow Jr HS 1980-; *ai:* Media, Cmmty Partners in Ed, Cty Curr Comm; Team Leader; GCTE 1979-87; GA Rdng Assn 1980-85; Ann Weeks Schlsp Awd 1987-88; *office:* Morrow Mid Sch 5968 Maddox Rd Morrow GA 30260

LEAF, BUSTER CARL, Athletic Director; *b:* Artesia, NM; *m:* Becky Boyd; *c:* Brenda, Tommy, Monty, Keith; *ed:* (MED) Ed Admin, 1984, (BS) His, 1970 Sul Ross St Univ; Instructional Leadership Trng; Appraisal Trng for Evaluations; *cr:* Elem Phys Ed Teacher Stockton Ind Sch Dist; Jr HS His Teacher Lewisville Ind Sch Dist; HS His Teacher Midland Ind Sch Dist, Idalou Ind Sch Dist, New Deal Ind Sch Dist; Athletic Dir/HS Health Teacher Mc Camey Ind Sch Dist; *ai:* Head Ftbl Coach & Athletic Dir; TX HS Coaches Assn Regional Dir 1987-; Drug Awareness; *office:* Levelland Ind Sch Dist 1400 Hickory Levelland TX 79336

LEAGANS, WANDA KITCHINGS, Second Grade Teacher; *b:* Statesville, NC; *m:* Stephen G.; *c:* Susan M.; *ed:* (BA) Elem Ed, Lenoir Rhyne Coll 1968; *cr:* Teacher Raleigh City Schls 1968-76; Davie Cty Schls 1977-89; *ai:* Publicity Chairperson for Sch 1988; Whole Lang Support Group of Davie Cty Sch Mem; NC Assn of Educators, NEA; Sigma Kappa Coll & Alumnae, Clemmons Jaycettes, Adult I Sunday Sch Clemmons First Baptist; *office:* Mocksville Elem Sch 295 Cemetary School Mocksville NC 27028

LEAR, DOUGLAS GORDON, Instrumental Music Director; *b:* Columbus, OH; *m:* Cynthia Jean; *c:* Kristen, Andrew; *ed:* (BA) Music Ed, Capital Univ 1982; *cr:* Band Dir Teays Valley HS 1982-83, Pickerington HS 1984-85, Bloom Carroll HS 1985-; *ai:* Marching Band, Pep Band, Musical Orchestra Dir; OH Music Educators Assn, Music Educators Natl Conference, NEA 1982-; Performed with Guy Lombardos Royal Canadians; Played for Various Jazz Artists; *home:* 12102 Twin Creek Dr Pickerington OH 43147

LEARN, NELSON R., 8th Grade Math/Algebra Teacher; *b:* Berwick, PA; *m:* Bonnie J. Smith; *c:* Tenette Smith, Radel Gizenski, Timothy, Christopher; *ed:* (BS) Scndry Math, Bloomsburg Univ 1970; Grad Courses In Prgm Leading To Supervisory Certificate; *cr:* Teacher Berwick Area Sch Dist 1970-; *ai:* NEA 1970-; PA St Ed Assn 1970-; Berwick Area Ed Assn (Treas, VP); Berwick Area Ambulance Assn (Pres 1985, Treas 1988-, Emergency Medical Technician 1984-).

LEARY, CATHERINE WILSON, Third Grade Teacher; *b:* Mt Sterling, KY; *m:* Don W.; *c:* James; *ed:* (BS) Elem Ed, 1974, (MA) Elem Ed, 1976 E KY Univ; *cr:* 1st Grade Teacher 1974-76, 3rd Grade Teacher 1976- Odell Gross Elem; *ai:* Sch Guidance & Grant Review Comm; CLark Cty Ed Assn, KY Ed Assn, NEA; E KY Univ Alumni Assn, Chrstn Womens Fellowship, Odell Gross PTA; KY Dept Ed Grant for Guidance Prgm 1987; Clark Cty Elem Teacher of yr 1988; *office:* Odell Gross Elem Sch 150 Maryland Ave Winchester KY 40391

LEARY, EDWARD WILLIAM, Teacher; *b:* Rochester, NY; *c:* Kristen; *ed:* (BS) Ed, 1968, (MS) Ed, 1973 SUC Brockport; *cr:* Sci Teacher Rush Henrietta Cntrl Schls 1968-; *ai:* Tennis & Sftbl Coach; Ski Club Adv; NYSUT 1968-; NY St Retirement Rep 1987-; Yr Long Fellowship in Physics SUC Brockport 1986.

LEARY, JUDY LYNETTE, Fifth Grade Teacher; *b:* Elizabeth City, NC; *ed:* (AA) Coll of Albermarle 1976; (BS) Intermediate Ed, 1979, (MA) Elem Ed, 1989 E Carolina Univ; *cr:* 5th-7th Grade Teacher Camden Mid Sch 1979-; *ai:* Asst Girls Sftbl Coach; Grade Chairperson; Co-Chairperson Southern Assn Accredition Comm; Mem Faculty Advisory, Differential Pay, Critical Analysis Performance Evaluation Comm; NC Assn of Educators 1979-; Shiloh Baptist Church (Adult Choir 1970, Womens Missionary Union 1980, Carol Leigh Circle Pres 1980-82) 1967-; *home:* PO Box 87 Shiloh NC 27974

LEARY, LINDA HUGHES, English Teacher; *b:* Burlington, NC; *m:* Gerald Philip; *ed:* (BA) Eng, Univ NC Greensboro 1974; (MED) Eng, 1980, (EDS) Admin/Ed, 1985 Converse; *cr:* Eng Teacher Spartanburg HS 1975-; *ai:* Spon NHS; Knowledge Masters Open Team, Future Problem Solving, Odyssey of the Mind Coach; NEA, SCEA; Spartanburg Jaycees Young Educator of Yr Awd 1986; NEH Stipend-Homeric Seminar Northwestern Univ 1987; NEH Fellowship-Classical Stud Tufts Univ 1990-91; *home:* 420 Patch Dr Spartanburg SC 29302

LEAS, LOYAL STAPLETON, English Teacher; *b:* Springfield, MO; *m:* Terrence; *c:* Meredith D., Laura A.; *ed:* (BS) Eng Ed, FL St Univ 1972; (MED) Eng Ed, Valdosta St Coll 1981; *cr:* Eng Teacher Thomasville HS 1972-; *ai:* Prom; GA Assn of Educators,

NEA 1972-; Jr Girl & Brownie Troop Leader; *office:* Thomasville HS 315 S Hansell St Thomasville GA 31792

LEASOR, CHARLENE JANET, 6th-8th Grade Phys Ed Teacher; *b:* Gainesville, FL; *m:* Theodore W.; *c:* Jennifer, Ted Jr.; *ed:* (AA) General, FL Coll 1976; (BS) Phys Ed/Health/Recreation, Univ of FL Gainesville 1979; (MA) Admin, Nova Univ 1988; *cr:* Life Sci Teacher Dixie Cty HS 1980-82; Phys Ed Teacher Old Town Elem 1982-84; Phys Ed/Sci Teacher Mainland Sr HS 1984-85; Earth Sci/Phys Ed Teacher 1985-88, Phys Ed Teacher 1988- Deltona Mid Sch; *ai:* 6th-8th Grade Intramural Dir; Cty Recreation Girls Sftbl Coach; Volusia Teachers Organization; *office:* Deltona Mid Sch 250 Enterprise Rd Deltona FL 32725

LEATHERWOOD, MARY LEORA (MORRIS), 8th Grade Math/Team Leader; *b:* Dayton, OH; *c:* Vaughn L.; *ed:* (BSED) Elem Ed, OH Univ Athens 1960; Jr HS Math, Courses in Cmptr Sci; *cr:* 5th/6th Grade Teacher Longfellow Elem 1956-58, Edwins Elem 1968-71; 5th Grade Teacher Polk & Nicholson Elem 1971-73; 3rd/6th Grade Teacher Shalimar Elem 1973-80; 5th Grade Teacher Valparaiso Elem 1980-83; 6th-9th Grade Teacher Ruckel Mid Sch 1984-; *ai:* Coach Knowledge Master Team; Academic Bowl & Mathcounts Team Asst; Okaloosa Cncl of Teachers of Math (Secy, Charter Mem) 1987-89, Legislative 1989-; NCTM Delegate to Convention 1989; Okaloosa Cty Ed Assn Bldg Rep 1988-; Amer Assn of University Women Membership Veep 1987-; Valparaiso Elem Teacher of the Yr 1984; Ruckel Mid Sch Teacher of Yr 1989; *office:* Ruckel Mid Sch N Partin Dr Niceville FL 32578

LEAVELLE, MARTHA CAROLE (GRAYSON), Retired Teacher; *b:* Holdenville, OK; *m:* Royce F. Jr.; *c:* Lori C., Kaye E.; *ed:* (BA) Elem Ed, ID St Univ 1964; (ME) Ed, Stephen F Austin St Univ 1988; *cr:* 4th Grade Teacher J T Mc Williams Elem 1964-65; 7th Grade Eng/Soc Stud/Gifted Teacher College Park Jr HS 1966-68; 6th Grade Teacher Wayside Mid Sch 1972-74; 5th Grade Math/Sci/Soc Stud Teacher W D Wilkerson Intermediate 1979-89; Teacher of Gifted Conroe Ind Sch Dist 1988-89; *ai:* Team Leader; Master Teacher for Stu Teacher; NASA Sch Rep; In-Service Presentations Sch, Dist; Building Comm; Delta Kappa Gamma Society Intnl; TX Assn for Gifted & Talented, TSTA, NEA; Kiwanis; Peoples Scene, Person of Yr 1989; Wilkerson PTA Teacher of Yr 1989; Quest Excl Awd 1988; 5th Grade Teacher for David the Bubble Boy; Career Ladder III.

LEAVITT, LAUREL ELGART, Second Grade Teacher; *b:* Brookline, MA; *m:* Steve; *c:* Scott, Debbie; *ed:* (BA) Ed, Univ of MA 1969; Drug Awareness Prgm Heres Looking at You Too; Math Their Way Prgm; *cr:* 3rd Grade Teacher Pine Orchard Sch 1969-70; 1st-2nd Grade Teacher Monroe Center Sch 1970-75; 2nd/3rd Grade Teaacher Reeds Ferry Sch 1980-82; 2nd/5th Grade Teacher Thorntons Ferry Sch 1982-; *ai:* 2nd Grade Math Coord; Merrimack Teachers Assn, NEA 1980-; Derry Jr Womens Club Ed Chm 1982-83, Ed Awd 1983; Jewish Refugee Resettlement Comm Bd of Dir 1989-; Womens Amer Organization for Rehabilitation through Trng 1981-; S Range Sch PTA Recording Secy 1983; Jewish Refusnile Family get out of Soviet Union & Settled in NH; *office:* Thorntons Ferry Sch Camp Sargeant Rd Merrimack NH 03054

LEBARON, EDWIN IVAN, High School Teacher; *b:* Centralia, WA; *m:* Suzi Ritschard; *c:* Chelsea, Jadrian; *ed:* (BA) Industrial Technology, W WA Univ 1979; (MA) Industrial Technology Ed, OR St Univ 1986; Counseling, Portland St Univ; *cr:* Teacher/Coach/Act Dir Portland Public Schls 1979-; *ai:* Act Dir; Ftbl, Wrestling, Sftbl Coach; UICA Adv 1989-, 100% Club 1989; PIEA, OEA, NEA 1979-; GFCC Deacon 1990; *office:* Marshall HS 3905 SE 91st Portland OR 97266

LEBBY, GLORIA J., Fifth Grade Teacher; *b:* Raleigh, WV; *c:* Kevin, Kimberly; *ed:* (BA) Ed, 1967, (MS) Ed, 1972 Queens Coll; Cmptrs in Ed; *cr:* 5th Grade Teacher Grand Avenue Sch 1971-; *ai:* Grade Level Chairperson; A-V Coord; Natl Alliance of Black Sch Educators; Uniondale Teachers Assn Rep; Delta Sigma Theta 1961-; *office:* Grand Avenue Sch 711 School Dr North Baldwin NY 11510

LE BEAU, PAUL ANTHONY, Foreign Language Dept Head; *b:* Holyoke, MA; *m:* Madeline A.; *c:* Suzanne, Laurie, Rick, Tina; *ed:* (BA) Fr/His, 1963, (MA) Ed 1966 Elms Coll; (CAGS) Ed, Westfield St 1969; *cr:* 6th Grade Teacher Enfield CT 1963-65; 4th-8th Grade Fr Teacher 1966-68, Elem/Foreign Lang/Bi-ling Ed Supvr 1968-81, HS Foreign Lang Dept Head 1981- Chicopee MA; *ai:* Var Sftbl Coach 1985-; Class of 1991 Adv; Chicopee Comprehensive Evaluation Team Steering Comm Mem; ACTFL, Boston Museum of Fine Arts 1986-; Foreign Lang Teacher of W MA 1981-; St Rose de Lima Cncl Pres 1971-72; Joan of Arc Sch Bd Chm 1968-69, 1971; Mobile Home Commission Vice-Chm 1987-; Chicopee Bicentennial Comm Vice-Chm 1976; Chicopee Jaycees Nom Man of Yr 1972, 1973; Chicopee Boys Club Man of Yr 1987; *home:* 79 Trilby Ave Chicopee MA 01020

LEBIEDZINSKI, CAROL SUSAN, Science Teacher; *b:* Syracuse, NY; *ed:* (BS) Bio, 1971, (MS) Scndry Ed, 1981 St Univ of NY Oswego; *cr:* Sci Teacher Chittenango Cntrl Schls 1971-; *ai:* Explorer Scout & Conservation, Jr HS Cross Cntry Ski Club & Jr/Sr HS Ski Club Downhill Skiing Adv; Whale Watching Project Coord & Resource Person; Chitteango Teachers Assn Pres; NY St Outdoor Teachers Assn; CT Cetacean Society; NY St Teachers Assn; Our Future in Depth Marine Mammal Chairperson; Greenpeace; Whale Protection Fund; Oceanic Society; Guest Speaker Beaver Lake Nature Center, Natl Audubon Society, Rotary, Lions; *home:* 815 Leta St Chittenango NY 13037

LE BLANC, BARRY EDWARD, Music Teacher/Band Director; *b:* Portsmouth, VA; *m:* Cynthia M. Lotze; *c:* Joshua, Charity; *ed:* (BMUS) Music Ed, 1980, (MMUS) Music Ed, 1984 Univ of GA; Grad Stud Music Ed & Cmptr; *cr:* Teacher Clarke Cty Sch Dist 1980-; *ai:* Percussion Instr; Cedar Shoals HS Band; Music Educators Natl Conference 1990; 1st Assembly of God Music Dir 1985-; *office:* Hilsman Mid Sch 870 Gaines Schl Rd Athens GA 30605

LE BLANC, KATHERINE VENNARD, English Teacher; *b:* SHreveport, LA; *m:* Joseph Remi; *c:* Elizabeth Gray, William, James; *ed:* (BS) Eng Ed, Univ of IL 1953; (MA) Guidance/Counseling, Univ of CA Berkeley 1956; Grad Stud Northwestern Univ & San Francisco St; *cr:* Teacher Elmhurst Jr HS 1953-54, Spruce Sch 1954-55, Crane Sch 1956, Barstow Sch 1968-; *ai:* Adv Ed & Curr Comms; NCTE; Cunm Laude Society Secy 1985-; Friends of Art, Santa Fe Trail Historical Society; Barstow Sch Great Britain Study Grant; *office:* Barstow Sch 11511 State Line Rd Kansas City MO 64114

LE BLANC, LINDA MARIE, 4th & 5th Grade Math Teacher; *b:* New Orleans, LA; *c:* Sebastian K.; *ed:* (BA) Elem Ed/Spec Ed, 1971, (MS) Guidance/Counseling, 1976 Southern Univ Baton Rouge; Adult Ed, Chapter I & Summer Sch Teacher for Pre-Sch & Regular Sch; *cr:* Adult Ed Teacher 1976-; *ai:* La Tip/La Tep Prgm System for Teaching, Learning Assessment & Review; Math Facilitator; Textbook Curr & Pilot Comm; Leadership Camp; Southern Assn Comm Mem; Chairperson Math-A-Thon, Black His Essay/Poster Contest, Canned Food Drive; Chaperone Educl Trip To Baton Rouge St Capital; Womens Day Comm Secy & Mem; Church Anniversary & Josephette Comm Mem; AFT, Jefferson Fed of Teachers, LA Assn of Teachers of Math; Westwego Elem PTA Mem; Morning STAR Baptist Church (Choir Mem); 4-H (Leader, Advisory Comm Mem, Fundraiser); 4-H Metro Leadership Conference Officers Trng Meeting & Wkshp; *home:* 447 Saddler Rd Marrero LA 70072

LE BLANC, LOREE, English Teacher; *b:* New Orleans, LA; *ed:* (BA) His/Poly Sci/Writing, SE LA Univ 1974; (BA) Soc Stud/Eng Ed, LA St Univ 1976; (MED) Guidance/Counseling, Loyola Univ of South 1984; *cr:* Teacher Buras HS 1976-77, Ursuline Acad 1977-84, De La Salle HS 1984-85, St Marys Dominican HS 1985-; *ai:* Coordinated Classes & Act; NCEA 1980-; LA Assn of G G, Larvic 1988-; *office:* St Marys Dominican HS 7701 Walmsley Ave New Orleans LA 70125

LE BLANC, MARGARET JUMONVILLE, Director/Elementary School; *b:* New Orleans, LA; *m:* Sam; *c:* Tim O.; *ed:* (BA) Elem Ed, UNO 1969; (MED) Counseling Ed, Loyola 1989; *cr:* 5th Grade Teacher Orleans Parish Schls 1969-72; Dir/Teacher St Marks Cmmty Center 1973-75; Dir Woodridge Acad 1975-; *ai:* Counseling; Phi Beta Kappa 1988-; AASCD, LASCD, NAEYC 1986-; Alpha Sigma Nu, Chi Sigma Iota; Harvard Prin Wkshp; Founder Woodridge Acad; *office:* Woodridge Acad 40149 Crowe Landing Rd Pearl River LA 70452

LEBOLD, VIRGINIA ANN, English Teacher; *b:* Kansas City, MO; *ed:* (BA) Eng, Cntrl Meth Coll 1972; (MS) Library Sci, Cntrl MO St Univ 1982; Grad Fellow Rotary, Philips Univ Marburg West Germany; Eng Speaking Union Scholar Univ of London England; *cr:* Teacher Northumberland HS 1972-73; Lancaster HS 1974-77; Santa Fe HS 1977-; *ai:* Scorekeeping Bsktbl & Vlybl; ME Assn Teacher of Eng Budget Comm Store; NCTE; MO St Teachers Assn; CTA (Secy, Pres, Treas); SF Booster Club; United Meth Church.

LEBSOCK, RICHARD DALE, 7th Grade Teacher; *b:* Brush, CO; *m:* Ellen Cline; *c:* Michael, Ronald, James; *ed:* (BA) Fine Arts, Univ of N CO 1961; Grad Work Univ N CO & Fresno Pacific Coll; *cr:* 7th Grade Teacher John Muir Jr HS; Art/Drama/Adult Ed Art Instr Corcoran Jr HS 1962-65; Art/Drama Instr Corcoran HS 1966-70; Art Instr Sch Dist RE-2 Jr HS 1970-77; Art Teacher Morgan Comm Coll 1971-77; 6th-8th Grade Math/Sci Instr/8th Grade Home Room Teacher Visalia Chrstn Acad 1982-86; 7th Grade Instr Three Rivers Union Sch 1986-; *ai:* Sch Yrbk & Newspaper Adv; Adult Ed Art Prgm; Established Theater Group; Asst Jr HS Track & Golf Team Coach; Judo Instr; Art Prgm; Ftbl Coach; Sci Curr Chm; Art Dept Chm & Curr Writer; Owner Lebsocks Limited 1977-81; *office:* Three Rivers Union Sch 41932 Hwy 198 Three Rivers CA 93271

LECH, PATRICIA ELIZABETH, 4th Grade Teacher; *b:* Chicago, IL; *ed:* (BA) Elem Ed, Univ IL Circle Campus 1974; Grad Stud Rdng; *cr:* 2nd-4th Grade Teacher O Toole Schl 1975-80; 4th Grade Teacher Powell Sch 1980-; *office:* Adam Clayton Powell Jr H S 7530 S South Shore Dr Chicago IL 60649

LECHNER, MARGARET A., District Science Coordinator; *b:* St Louis, MO; *m:* Frank J.; *ed:* (BA) Theology/Ed, Notre Dame 1962; (MA) Comprehensive Sci, Northeast MO St 1985; (EDS) Sci Ed, Univ of MO Columbia 1987; *cr:* Teacher Pvt & Public Schls 1955-75; Jr HS Sci Coord Washington Jr HS 1980-86; Dist Sci Coord Mehlville Sch Dist 1986-; *ai:* NSTA; Sci Teachers of MO; Cncl of Elem Sci; MNEA Teacher of Yr 1982 & 1983; St Louis Areas Sci Teacher of Yr 1989; Presents 60 Wkshps Per Year; *office:* Mehlville Sch Dist 3120 Lemay Ferry Rd Saint Louis MO 63125

LE CLERC, DONALD ROBERT, Phys Ed/Cmptr Teacher; *b:* Salem, MA; *m:* Eileen Taylor; *c:* Katelyn, Daniel, Kyle; *ed:* (BS) Phys Ed/Health, Springfield Coll 1975; (MED) Admin, Salem St Coll 1980; Project Adventure Trng 1987-89; Cmptr Ed; *cr:* Teacher Middleton Public Schls 1975-76; Teacher/Coach Marblehead Public Schls 1977-; *ai:* Marblehead Curr Study Co-Chm 1989-; Salem St Coll Mens & Womens Head Swim Coach 1986-; Childrens Swim Camp Dir 1990; MA Assn of Health, Phys Ed, Recreation, Dance 1975-; ASCD 1989-; YMCA; Statewide Teacher Recognition Awd 1989-; *office:* Glover Sch 9 Maple St Marblehead MA 01945

LEDBETTER, PATRICIA NANN, Business Dept Chairperson; *b:* Booneville, MS; *ed:* (BS) Bus Ed, Blue Mountain Coll 1965; (MED) Office Admin, Memphis St Univ 1970; Office Admin, Memphis St Univ 1975; *cr:* Dir of Public Affairs Secy WREG Television & Radio 1965-66; Bus Teacher Frayser HS 1966-; *ai:* Bus Prof of America Spon; Memphis Bus Ed Assn, NEA, Memphis Ed Assn 1966-; Outstanding Teacher Awd, Mercy Coll.

LEDERER, EMMA CINCINNATO, Spanish/Italian Teacher; *b:* Bronx, NY; *m:* Neil; *c:* Laurie A.; *ed:* (BA) Span, St Johns Univ 1978; (MA) Liberal Stud, SUNY Stonybrook 1981; Educl Admin Long Island Univ; C W Post Coll; *cr:* Span/Italian Teacher Lindenhurst HS 1978-; *ai:* Class Adv Fresh, Soph, Jr, Sr; Italian Club Adv; NYSAFLT, AATI; *home:* 1405 Sara Cir Port Jefferson NY 11776

LEDFORD, GLENNA HELTON, Remedial Reading Teacher; *b:* Hammond, KY; *m:* Henry Clifton; *c:* Brian Keith, Jeffrey Cole; *ed:* (BS) Elem Ed, 1966, (MA) Elem Ed, 1969, Elem Ed, 1979 Union Coll; *cr:* 5-8th Grade Teacher Flat Lick Elem 1966-69; Spec Ed Teacher 1969-70; 7-8th Grade Math Teacher 1970-72; 7-8th Grade Sci Teacher 1972-76; 3rd Grade Teacher 1976-89; Remedial Rdng Teacher 1989- Dewitt Elem; *ai:* Curr & Learning Environment Comm; Responsible Pupil Conduct Comm; Spelling Bee Coach; KEA; NEA; Stinking Creek Teachers Assn Pres 1968-72; Knox Cty Teachers Assn; Coles Branch Baptist Church (Pianist 1968- /Youth Choir Dir 1980- /Sunday Sch Clerk 1986-); *office:* Dewitt Elem Sch Gen Delivery Dewitt KY 40930

LEDFORD, GWEN GREEN, Guidance Counselor; *b:* Morristown, TN; *m:* Robert; *ed:* (BS) Scndry Math, 1987, (MA) Educl Psych, 1988 TN Technological Univ; *cr:* Guidance Cnslr Rutledge HS 1987-; *ai:* Cheerleadng Coach; Peer Facilitator Spon; Drop Out Advisory Comm; NEA, TEA; Beta Sigma Phi Secy 1989-; 1st Baptist Church White Pine (Choir, Handbell Choir).

LEDFORD, TERESA ANN, Band/Choral Director; *b:* Nashville, TN; *ed:* (BME) Music Ed, Univ of MS 1976; (MA) Scndry Ed, 1985, (MA) Sch Counseling, 1986 W KY Univ; *cr:* Band Dir OH Cty Mid Sch 1978-86; Asst Band Dir OH Cty HS 1976-86; Band/Choral Dir Cannon Cty HS 1986-; *ai:* Cannon Cty Cmmty Chorus Dir 1990; Whos Who Among Amer Prof 1988; *office:* Cannon Cty HS 1 Lion Dr Woodbury TN 37190

LEDNUM, SHIRLEY LINEBERRY, Third Grade Teacher; *b:* Asheboro, NC; *c:* Charles, Maria; *ed:* (BA) Elem Ed, Cntrl Wesleyan Coll 1965; *cr:* Teacher Randleman Elem 1965-67, Franklin Sch 1967-; *ai:* Assistance Team, Media Center, Sci, Volunteer Sch Comms; Rand Cty Sci Fair Comm; NCAE, NEA; Franklinville Sch Distinguished Educator Awd 1985-86, Teacher of Yr 1985-86; *home:* Rt 4 Box 387 Liberty NC 27298

LE DOUX, RITA TATE, Math Teacher; *b:* Mamou, LA; *m:* Albert; *c:* Rachelle L. Guillotte, Johanna L. Perron; *ed:* (BA) Elem Ed, USL 1968; Cmptr Literacy; *cr:* Teacher L J Alleman Mid Sch 1968-70, Paul Breaux Mid Sch 1970-80, Youngsville Mid Sch 1980-; *ai:* Jr Beta Club Co-Spon; Math Counts Coach; Sch Photographer; St Jude Mathathon & Bike-A-Thon Chairman; NEA/LAE/LPAE Par Assn Rep 1988-; *home:* 141 La Rue Malaga Broussard LA 70518

LE DUC, ESTHER MARY, Clinical Social Worker; *b:* Detroit, MI; *ed:* (BA) Ed, Marygrove Coll 1971; (MED) Ed, Oakland Univ 1977; (MSW) Clinical Soc Work, Washington Univ 1985; *cr:* Kndgtn Teacher Gesu 1971-73; 1st-4th Grade Teacher St Regis 1973-76; 1st Grade Teacher St Gerard Majella 1973-83; Therapist Cath Family Services/Sisters IHM 1985-; *ai:* NASW 1983-; NEA 1971-83; *office:* Cath Family Serv Sisters 610 W Elm Monroe MI 48161

LEDWELL, VICTORIA LEE, Biology Teacher; *b:* Asheboro, NC; *ed:* (BS) Bio, Appalachian St Univ 1974; *cr:* Phys Sci Teacher Asheboro Jr HS 1974-86; Bio Teacher Asheboro HS 1986-; *ai:* Schlsp Comm; Senate Bill Comm; Homecoming Comm; Jr Class Adv; Mentor Teacher; St Accreditation Comm; Southern Assn Accreditation Steering Comm; NEA; NC Assn of Educators 1974-; Asheboro Assn of Educators; Prof Rights & Responsibilities (Chm 1987-89/Faculty Rep 1989-); St Certified Mentor Teacher; Outstanding Young Educator Asheboro HS 1989-; *office:* Asheboro H S 1221 S Park St Asheboro NC 27203

LEE, ALEXANDER H., 8th Grade Math Dept Chairman; *b:* Yazoo City, MS; *m:* Margaret Ainsworth; *ed:* (BS) Scndry Ed/Math, 1973, (MS) Scndry Ed/Math, 1975 MS St Univ; Problem Solving Wkshp, Univ S MS 1979; Career Ed, MS Coll 1981; *cr:* 9th Grade General Math Teacher Pearl Jr HS 1973-74; Coll Algebra Teacher MS St Univ 1974-75; 8th Grade General Math Teacher 1975-78, 8th Grade General Math/9th Grade Plane Geometry 1978-81, 8th Grade General Math/Algebra I/9th Grade Plane Geometry 1981-83, 8th Grade General Math/Algebra I 1983-89, Introduction to Cmptrs 1987- Pearl Jr HS; Elem/Intermediate Algebra Rankin/Hinds Comm Coll 1985-; *ai:* Jr HS Chess Club, Annual Staff Spon; Head Coach Girls HS Ftbl; Jr HS Math Dept Chm 1989-; MS Assn of Educators Treas; MS Prof Educators (Secy, Treas, Mem); NCTM Mem; MS Cncl of Teachers of Math Mem; Pearl Youth Assn (Girls Sftbl Coach, Bd of Dir, VP, Over-All Pres, Chm of Bd), 10 Yr Service Awd 1987; Mc Laurin Heights United Meth Church (Youth Dir, Single Again Group 1989-); Jackson Preparatory Sch Methods to Motivate Jr

HS Stus Wkshp 1975; WLBT Spirit of MS; Jr HS Annual Dedication 1989; HS Sftbl Coach of Yr; Teacher of Yr Pearl Jr HS 1988-89; *office:* Pearl Jr HS 200 Mary Ann Dr Pearl MS 39208

LEE, BARBARA JEAN ROBISON, Mathematics & Science Teacher; *b:* Nabb, IN; *m:* Norman K.; *c:* Michael, Bruce; *ed:* (BA) Chem, Vanderbilt Univ 1957; (MA) Sci, Ball St Univ 1963; Post Grad Stud Math & Cmptr Sci; *cr:* Sci Teacher Maplewood-Richmond Jr HS 1964-65, Desota Jr & Sr HS 1965-66, Southwestern HS 1966-68, Somerset Jr HS 1968-69; Sci/Math Teacher Monroe Cntrl HS 1969-; *ai:* Sci & Math Academic Team Coach;Schl Discipline Policy Comm Mem;Acting Sci Dept Chairperson; Monroe Cntrl Teachers Assn, IN St Teachers Assn, NEA (Pres, Chairperson of Bargaining Team) Mem 1969-; Hoosier Assn of Sci Teachers, NSTA 1986-; IN Cncl of Teachers of Math 1987-; Delta Kappa Gamma Society Intnl 1982-; Presbyn Church Trustee 1987-; 4-H Horse & Pony Leader 1975-76; Part Time Correspondent for Muncie Star Newspaper; Numerous Articles & Photography Works Published; *office:* Monroe Cntrl HS R R #1 Box 17 Parker City IN 47368

LEE, BARRON WILSON, History Teacher; *b:* Lincolnton, NC; *m:* Carolyn Kay Hargrave; *c:* Lauren, Whitney; *ed:* (BS) Phys Ed/Health/Soc Stud, Appalachian St 1963; Southeast Baptist Theological Seminary; *cr:* 7th Grade Teacher/Coach Newton-Conover Sch 1963-64; 8th Grade Teacher/Coach Balls Creek Sch 1964-65; Phys Ed/His Teacher/Coach Dallas HS 1966-71, His Teacher N Gaston HS 1971-; *ai:* Sr Class Adv; Southern Assn of Schls Local Chm; Jr Civitan Club Spon; NEA, NC Assn of Educators, 20 Yr Service 1984; Dallas Optomist Club Pres 1967, 1970; Dallas Baptist Church Deacon Chm 1975, 1981, 1986, 1990; Outstanding Young Men in America Awd; Bsbl & Vlybl Conference Coach of Yr Awds; *office:* N Gaston HS Rt 3 Ratchford Rd Dallas NC 28034

LEE, BETH L., English Teacher; *b:* Middlesboro, KY; *ed:* (BA) Eng, Centre Coll 1983; Grad Stud Eng, Univ of KY Lexington; *cr:* Grad Asst Univ of KY 1983-85; Eng Teacher Scott Cty HS 1985-; *ai:* Team Leader; Co-Teacher of Yr Scott Cty HS 1986-87; *office:* Scott Cty HS Long Lick Pike Georgetown KY 40324

LEE, BETTY JUNE (SWANSON), Mathematics Dept Chair; *b:* Lamar, CO; *c:* Sean W., Jennifer N.; *ed:* (AA) Biological Sci, 1966, (BS) Biological Sci, 1968, (MS) Teaching, 1974 S CO St Coll; Grad Stud Western St, Adams St, S CO Coll, DU, Mines; *cr:* 7th-8th Grade Math Teacher Freed Mid Sch 1968-; *ai:* Math Dept Head; Curr & Textbook Adoption Comm; NHS Advisory Bd & Helper 1986-88; Soc Comm 1986-87; Building Advisory 1984-88; Math Dept Chm 1983-; Climate Comm 1986-; Stu Cncl Spon 1975-77; Mathcounts 1984-85; Soccer & T-Ball Coach; CO Cncl Teachers of Math Outstanding Math Teacher Awd 1990; NCTM (Presider 1972) 1968-; CCSSP Participant 1971; CCTM, CEA, NEA, PEA 1968-; Delta Kappa Gamma 1974-79; *office:* Freed Mid Sch 725 W 20th Pueblo CO 81003

LEE, BEVERLY HANSON, Business Education Teacher; *b:* Durand, WI; *m:* D. Bruce; *c:* Stephen; *ed:* (BBA) Bus Ed, 1963, (MS) Bus Ed, 1975 Univ of WI Madison; Certified H&R Block Basic Tax Accounting Course 1988; *cr:* Bus Ed Teacher Oconomowoc HS 1963-69, 1971-; *ai:* FBLA Local Chapter Adv & Natl Leadership Conference; Challenge Prgm Advocacy Bd; NBEA, WI Bus Ed Assn 1963-; Delta Pi Epsilon (Current Asst Treas, Membership) 1967-; NEA, WI Ed Assn Cncl, S WI Educl Inservice Organization; Oconomowoc Ed Assn; Alpha Delta Kappa Current St Corresponding Secy 1978-; Lac La Belle Cntry Club 1966-; AT&T Investment Challenge Professor Division 7th Pl 1989-; Great Ideas for Tomorrow Prgm Presentor 1990; *home:* 5848 Farmwood Heights Oconomowoc WI 53066

LEE, BYRON, Teacher; *b:* Honolulu, HI; *m:* Harriet Aline Wilson; *c:* Shawn Lee, Jason Lee; *ed:* (BA) His, San Francisco St 1969; Ed, San Francisco St 1973; *cr:* Teacher Mission HS 1969-70; Teacher Loma Vista Intnl 1970-80; Teacher Oak Grove Mid 1980-; Learning Opportunity Teacher Oak Grove 1986-; *ai:* MDUSD Human Relations Commission; Contra Costa Cty Human Relative Commission; Family Ed Comm MDUSD; CA Teacher Assn; Mt Diablo Ed Assn; *office:* Oak Grove Mid Sch 2050 Minert Rd Concord CA 94518

LEE, CALVIN C., Teacher; *b:* Fort Wayne, IN; *m:* Donna J.; *c:* Kevin, Tim; *ed:* (BS) Biological Sci, Ball St Univ 1960; (MS) Elem Ed, St Francis Coll 1965; *cr:* Teacher Hoagland Elem Sch 1960-; *ai:* NEA, ISTA; Ball St Alumni Outstanding Alumni 1982; White House Conference on Youth & Children Ind Steering Comm; St Supts Comm Teacher Concerns; IN Teacher of Yr 1981; Sagamore of Wabash Awd; Amer Legion St Merit Awd; Good Housekeeping & Encylopedia Britannica Awd 1981; Midwest Whos Who in Amer 1989-; Outstanding Elem Teachers of America 1973-74; East Allen Teachers Assn Golden Apple Awd 1977, 1980; East Allen Cty Schls Teacher of Yr 1980; IN Instant Copy Excl in Ed Awd 1984; IN House & Senate Joint Resolution Honor 1981; *home:* 2708 Waynedale Blvd Fort Wayne IN 46809

LEE, CLARENCE A., Math/Science/Computer Teacher; *b:* Grove City, PA; *m:* Susan J. Wakeley; *ed:* (BRE) Elem Ed, Baptist Bible of PA 1978; (MED) Ed, Edinboro Univ of PA 1984; *cr:* Math/Sci Teacher 1978-, Cmptr Sci Teacher 1983-, Math Dept Chm 1989- Bethel Chrstn of Erie; *ai:* Soccer Coach 1978-80; Sftbl Coach 1978-80, 1985-88; Stu Cncl Adv 1978-; ACSI 1980-; *office:* Bethel Chrstn Sch of Erie 1781 W 38th St Erie PA 16508

LEE, DANIEL OWEN, Soc Stud Teacher/Dept Chair; *b:* Louisville, KY; *m:* Linda Akins; *c:* Jacob, Stephen; *ed:* (BS) His/Eng, Murray St Univ 1975; (MA) His, W KY Univ 1980; *cr:* Soc Stud/Eng Teacher Hardin Cntrl Mid Sch 1977-; *ai:* Soc Stud Dept Chair; Equal Ed Opportunity Comm; Orphan Brigade Kinfolk 1989-; Hardin Cty Historical Society 1985-; *office:* Hardin Cntrl Mid Sch 3040 Leitchfield Rd Cecilia KY 42724

LEE, DONALD H., Mathematics/Physics Teacher; *b:* Louisville, KY; *m:* Evelyn Diane Deweese; *c:* William D., Jason Deweese, Donna M., Diane E.; *ed:* (BS) Math/Physics, Murray St Univ 1969; (MA) Sci/Ed, W KY Univ 1975; *cr:* Math/Physics Teacher Leitchfield HS 1969-74, Grayson Cty HS 1975-; *ai:* Bsbl, Boys & Girls Cross Cntry Head Coach; Fellowship of Chrstn Athletes Spon; KEA, NEA, GEA; Natl Physics Inst Centre Coll 1989; *office:* Grayson Cty HS 240 High School Rd Leitchfield KY 42754

LEE, DOROTHY RICHARDSON, Fourth & Fifth Grade Teacher; *b:* Mt Pleasant, TN; *w:* Jack Lyndell (dec); *c:* Jana M.; *ed:* (BS) Elem Ed, Mid TN St Univ 1955; *cr:* 3rd-5th Grade Teacher Farmington Sch 1953-54; 4th Grade Teacher 1955-89, 4th/5th Grade Teacher 1990 Cornersville Sch; *ai:* Just Say No Club Spon 1987-88; Marshall Cty Ed Assn, TN Educl Assn, NEA; Ladies VFW Auxiliary Secy; Cornersville Garden Club Secy; Cornersville 1st Baptist Church Mem; Delta Kappa Gamma Mem; *home:* PO Box 84 Cornersville TN 37047

LEE, ESTHER WHITE, Seventh Grade Science Teacher; *b:* Little Rock, AR; *c:* Erika V.; *ed:* (BA) Bus Ed, Philander Smith Coll 1964; (MA) Cultural Stud/Black Stud, Governors St Univ 1975; *cr:* IL Dept of Public Aid Kenwood Office 1966-68; Teacher P Sheridan Elem Sch 1968-; *ai:* Local Sch Cncl Teacher Rep 1989-; Assoc Union Delegate for P Sheridan Sch; Alpha Kappa Alpha; *home:* 17686 Hillcrest Dr Country Club Hills IL 60478

LEE, FARRELYN MANKIN, Second Grade Teacher; *b:* Bonham, TX; *m:* James M.; *c:* Joshua J., Mankin J.; *ed:* (BS) Elem Ed, 1971, (MED) Early Chldhd Ed, 1976 E TX St Univ; *cr:* Remedial Rdng Teacher Savoy Ind Sch Dist 1971-72; Kndgtn-4th Grade Teacher Des Moines Municipal Schls 1972-74; Kdngtn-2nd Grade Teacher Mc Coy Elem, Aztee Municipal Schls 1974-; *office:* Mc Coy Elem Sch Mc Coy Ave Aztec NM 87410

LEE, GAIL B., Lead Reading Teacher; *b:* Fayetteville, NC; *m:* James Edward Jr.; *c:* Jennifer, James; *ed:* (BA) Ed, Univ of NC Chapel Hill 1970; (MA) Ed, Pembroke St Univ 1990; *cr:* 7th/8th Grade Lang Art/Soc Stud Teacher Cntrl Mid Sch 1974-79, Shaw Mid Sch 1979-84; 8th Grade NC His Teacher Sycamore Lane Mid Sch 1984-89; 7th Grade Rdng Teacher I Ellis Johnson Mid Sch 1989-; *ai:* Drama & Beta Club; Stu Cncl Intergrade Coord; Lead Teacher; NCAE (Secy 1976-77, PPR Chairperson 1988-89), Outstanding Young Educator 1976, Teacher of Yr 1978; St Luke United Meth Church United Meth Women Pres; *office:* I Ellis Johnson Mid Sch 815 Mc Girts Bridge Rd Laurinburg NC 28352

LEE, GERIANNE C., US History Teacher; *b:* Honolulu, HI; *ed:* (BA) His, San Jose St 1967; Teachers Certificate Univ of HI 1968; *cr:* Teacher St of HI 1968-; *ai:* Close-Up Teacher & Coord; Citizen Bee Coach; *office:* Kaimuki HS 2705 Kaimuki Ave Honolulu HI 96816

LEE, GREGORY ROBERT, English/Governments Teacher; *b:* Geneseo, IL; *m:* Nancy Wagle; *c:* Kevin, Melissa, Andrew; *ed:* (BA) Poly Sci/Econ, Lawrence Univ 1966; (MA) His, Univ of WI Oshkosh 1969; Variety of Courses In Eng, Comptrs, Ed; *cr:* Teacher Appleton Area Sch Dist 1966-; *ai:* Track Coach; Noon Hour Supervision; Professionalism Comm; Phi Kappa Tau Bd of Govenors 1982-; *office:* Roosevelt Jr HS 318 E Brewster St Appleton WI 54911

LEE, HARRY M., History/Geography Teacher; *b:* Camp Kilmer, NJ; *m:* Debra Baumeister; *c:* Ashley, Vincent, Travis, Jamie; *ed:* (AA) Art, Valencia Comm Coll 1973; (BA) Art, Univ of Cntrl Fl 1975; (MA) Soc Sci, Rollins Coll 1981; *cr:* His Teacher Bagonet Point Mid Sch 1982-84, Hudson Mid Sch 1984-; *ai:* Bsbl Club, Sch Newspaper, Save Our Springs, Fact Canoe Trip Spon; Boys Track Coach; ISS Comm Chm; FL Historical Society 1988-; Pasco Cty Soc Stud Society 1988-; Whos Who Among Stu Amer Jr Coll; UCF Volunteer, VCC Stu Achievement, Golden Poet Awd; Rollins Kappa Delta Phi Honor Society; *home:* 8108 Oriole Ave New Port Richey FL 34654

LEE, JANET HIEBERT, Bilingual Elem Teacher; *b:* Upland, CA; *m:* Scott; *c:* Nathan S., Kathryn I., Ryan S.; *ed:* (BA) His, 1971, Elem Ed, 1972 Univ of CA Hayward; Working Toward Masters in Marriage, Family & Child Counseling; *cr:* 1st Grade Teacher Mc Kevett Sch 1973-75; Kndgtn Teacher Sespe Sch 1978-82; K-2nd Grade Teacher San Cayetano Sch 1982-; *ai:* Young Authors Faire Comm Mem; Teacher Talent Show Chairperson; Fillmore Unified Teachers Assn (VP 1988-, Pres 1990); Fillmore Womens Service Club Pres 1977-79; BSA Den Leader 1983-87, Cubber of Yr 1985; *office:* San Cayetano Elem Sch 514 Mountain View Fillmore CA 93015

LEE, JANET KAY LEDFORD, Principal; *b:* Carnegie, OK; *m:* Ted Monroe; *c:* Jason T., Juli J.; *ed:* (BA) Elem Ed, Southwestern St Univ 1971; (MS) Early Chldhd, 1974; (MS) Admin, 1985, Cntrl St Univ; *cr:* Kndgtn Teacher Mc Loud Elem 1971-74; 4th Grade Teacher Ranchwood Elem 1974-82; Teacher of Gifted Ed 1982-85, Asst Prin/Remedial Math Teacher 1985-86, Prin 1986- Surrey Hills Elem; *ai:* Yukon-Mustang Schls Early Chldhd Comm; OK Assn of Elem Sch Prins Nom Comm; Delta Kappa Gamma Pres 1984-87; Rdng Cncl Pres 1978-79; OK Rdng Cncl Presenter; Kappa Kappa Iota Pres 1976-77; OK Assn of Gifted & Talented Presenter; PTO Treas 1973-74, 1976-77; 1st Baptist Church (Sunday Sch Teacher, Bible Sch Dir); Democrat Precinct Delegate 1980-81; Ranchwood Teacher of Yr 1980; Young Writers Conference Presenter; Leadership in Effective Admin Dev Presenter; *office:* Surrey Hills Elem Sch 10700 N Hastings Yukon OK 73099

LEE, JANICE BARTON, Latin Teacher; *b:* Norfolk, VA; *m:* Gregg L.; *c:* Michael, Stephen, Christopher; *ed:* (BA) Classical Stud, Coll of Charleston 1986; Addl Studies Ed, UNCC; *cr:* Latin Teacher 1st Bapt 1986; Wilson Hall 1986-87; West Meck 1988-; *ai:* Latin Club Adv; Eta Sigma Phi Pres 1985-86; Coll of Charleston Mourzor Class Stud Awd 1986; Amer Classical League 1988; Favorite Teacher of Yr Stu Selected Wilson Hall 86; *office:* W Mecklenburg Sr H S 7400 Tuckaslegee Rd Charlotte NC 28214

LEE, JAY W., Social Science Teacher; *b:* Chicago, IL; *m:* Amy Feun; *c:* Jared, Jeremy, Jamie; *ed:* (BA) His, Univ of IL 1971; Grad Courses Univ of IL; *cr:* Soc Stud Teacher Marla HS 1972-74; Teacher Haines Elem Sch 1974-75, Whitney Young HS 1975-; *ai:* Academic Olympics, Knowledge Master Coach; Economics Tutor Academic Decathelon Team; Bus Mgr for the Company Theater Group; Outstanding Teacher of Yr 1977; *office:* Whitney Young HS 211 S Laflin Chicago IL 60607

LEE, JENNIFER MORITA, Sixth Grade Teacher; *b:* Fairfield, CA; *m:* Kenneth Wilson; *c:* Jessica, Jordan; *ed:* (BA) Eng, UCLA 1971; *cr:* Teacher Grant Elem Sch 1973-81, Gates Street Elem 1981-85, Eastman Avenue Sch 1985-; *ai:* Earthquake Comm; Teacher of Gifted & Talented; Sci Adv; Cub Scouts Den Leader 1989-; *office:* Eastman Avenue Sch 4112 S Olympic Blvd Los Angeles CA 90023

LEE, JO ANN MOORE, Counselor; *b:* Gadsden, AL; *c:* John J. II, Joni C.; *ed:* (BS) Eng, Jacksonville St Univ 1960; (MA) Guidance/Counseling, Univ of AL Birmingham 1974; AA Cert Guidance/Counseling, Univ of AL Birmingham 1987; *cr:* Eng Teacher Walnut Grove HS 1960-61; Eng/Soc Stud Teacher 1961-62, Choral Dir 1962-64 Disque Jr HS; Eng Teacher Etowah HS 1970; Choral Dir 1971, Hum/Eng/Speech Teacher 1971-72, Eng Teacher 1972-73, Admin Asst 1973-74 Disque Jr HS; Cnslr Disque Jr HS/Mid Sch 1974-; *ai:* Stu Cncl, SADD, Reach Out America Spon; Delta Kappa Gamma-Alpha Iota 1973-; Kappa Delta Pi 1985-; Kappa Delta Epsilon, Chi Sigma Iota 1986; Prof Assn of Gadsden Educators, AL Ed Assn, NEA, Amer Assn of Univ Women, AL Personnel & Guidance Assn, AL Sch Cnslr Assn, AL Voc Guidance Assn, AL Mental Health Cnslrs, AL Cnslr Ed & Supervision; Gadsden Service Guild (Follies Chm 1969, Pres 1970-71, Bd of Dirs); Gadsdens Jr Singing Ambassadors Dir; Gadsdens Singing Ambassadors Chorus (Mem, Soloist); Gadsden Civic Music Chorus; 1st Baptist Church Gadsden (Mem, Soloist - Chancel Choir, Active in Sunday Sch, Trng Union, WMU, Spec Pgrms with Youth & Adults); Mental Health Schlsp Auburn Univ 1961; Converse Coll Literary Publication Short Story; *office:* Disque Mid Sch 612 Tracy St Gadsden AL 35901

LEE, JOANNE MAE (HOFFMAN), 2nd Grade Teacher; *b:* Lewiston, ID; *c:* Roy J. Thornton Jr., Aaron C. Thornton; *ed:* Elem Ed, Lewis & Clark St Coll 1960; (BSED) Elem Ed, Univ of ID 1972; Working Towards Masters Univ of ID; *cr:* 1st Grade Teacher Tualatin Elem 1960-61, Coos Bay Elem 1961-62; Kndgtn Teacher Reedsport Elem 1964-66; 2nd Grade Teacher Orofino Elem 1968-; *ai:* CEA, IEA, NEA 1970-; Democratic Party Precinct Comm Woman 1972-73; Church of God Regional Delegate 1986-89; Chairperson Assorted Comms; Region 2 Secy 1971-72, Region Delegate to St Meetings 1977-78, 1982, Local Delegate 1982-88; *home:* 1295 Michigan PO Box 1856 Orofino ID 83544

LEE, JOHN WESLEY, JR., Social Studies Teacher; *b:* Brunswick, GA; *m:* Ann M. Barnes; *c:* Cynthia, John III; *ed:* (BS) Soc Sci, Valdosta St Coll 1973; (MS) His, Armstrong St Coll 1980; Admin & Supervision, GA Southern Coll 1987; *cr:* Soc Stud Dept Chm Jane Macon Mid Sch 1976-; *ai:* NEA; Omega Psi Phi Chaplin 1976-, Service Awd 1988; *office:* Jane Macon Mid Sch 3885 Altama Ave Brunswick GA 31520

LEE, JOHN WOODIE, Fifth Grade Teacher; *b:* Delhi, LA; *m:* Marilyn Maxine Day; *c:* Renee, Gordon, Jennifer; *ed:* (BA) Elem Ed, Northeast LA Univ 1973; *cr:* Elem Teacher Ward III HS; *ai:* Jr 4-H Leader; *office:* Ward III HS Rt 1 Winnsboro LA 71295

LEE, LAURA A., Sixth Grade Teacher; *b:* St Louis, MI; *w:* Robert Lee (dec); *c:* Laureen K.; *ed:* St Limited Certificate Elem Ed, Cntrl MI Univ 1959; (BA) Soc Sci, W MI 1974; Working Towards Masters Aquinas Coll; *cr:* Teacher C A Frost Elem 1959-70, W Leonard Elem 1970-72, Oakleigh Elem 1972-76, Covell Elem 1976-; *ai:* Grand Rapids Public Schls Rdng, Math, Soc Stud Comms; Grand Rapids Ed Assn Building Rep 1961-86; Campfire Girls Leader 1960-63; After Sch Recreation Leader 1963-67; Presbyn Church (Sunday Sch Teacher, Supvr, Choir Mem, Bd Mem); Adult Ed Math/Rdng Instr; *home:* 957 Van Ess NW Grand Rapids MI 49504

LEE, MARY ANN ANN HICKMAN, Home Economics Teacher; *b:* Hattiesburg, MS; *m:* Darrell Victor; *c:* Darren V., Warren W.; *ed:* (BA) Home Ed, Univ of S MS 1972; *cr:* Teacher Earl Travillion Attendance Ctr 1977-81, South Forrest Attendance Ctr 1981-86; *ai:* FHA Adv; Graduating Comm Head; FHA; Woodrow Hickman Memorial Sch Trust Fund (VP 1989-, Bd Mem 1989-, Treas 1990, Mem 1990); *home:* Rt 1 Box 230 Lumberton MS 39455

LEE, MARY ANN HAMLIN, French Teacher/Lang Chairman; *b:* Paris, France; *m:* Ronald Scott; *c:* Elizabeth, Scott, Katherine; *ed:* (BA) Fr, SUNY New Paltz 1969; (MAT) Fr, Colgate Univ 1981; Certifat D Etudes Sorbonne Univ 1968; *cr:* Teaching Asst Univ of CT 1969-71; Fr Teacher 1971-, Lang Dept Chm 1974- Clinton Cntrl; *ai:* Stu Cncl, 10th Grade, Key Club, Fr Club Adv; Chaperone Trips to France; AATF (Chm Natl Fr Contest) 1979-; Foreign Lang of NY; Book Published; *office:* Clinton Cntrl Sch Chenango Ave Clinton NY 13323

LEE, MARY HARRISON, 6th Grade Math Teacher; *b:* Manila, Philippines; *m:* Gene L.; *c:* Gene L II, Daryl L., Angelique C.; *ed:* (BS) Elem Ed, Tougaloo Coll 1962; (MS) Educ Admin/Supverision, Jackson St Univ 1989; Univ of Kansas City; Math, KS St Univ; Individualized Instruction, Brigham Young Univ; *cr:* Elem Teacher Picayune Public Sch 1962-66; Kansas City Public Sch 1966-73; Dept of Defense Dependents Sch 1973-81; Jackson Public Sch 1982-; *ai:* Team Leader; Cmptr Contact Teacher; MS Teacher; Assessment Instruments Evaluator; Staff Dev Chm; Math Grade Level Chm; Dist, Local Textbook Selection Comm; Natl Math Assn 1986-88; Phi Kappa Phi 1989-; Neighborhood Assn Public Rel 1985-87; Natl Sci Fnd Fellowship Math; Ed Fnd Trust-Grants 1987-88; "Good Apple Awd" Staff Recognition Pgm 1986-87 & 1988-89; "Silver Apple Awd" Dist Recognition Prgm 1988-89; *home:* 752 Woodhill Rd Jackson MS 39206

LEE, MARY HONG, 3rd Grade Teacher; *b:* Kona, HI; *c:* Patrick, Douglas, Jeffrey; *ed:* (BA) Sociology, Univ of HI 1952; CSU Long Beach; *cr:* 4th Grade Teacher Cypress Elem Sch 1965-75; 6th Grade Teacher 1975-86; 3rd Grade Teacher 1986- Christine Swain Sch; *ai:* Cypress Sch Dist Budget & Finance Comm; Prof Growth Panel Mem; Swain Sch Sci Fair Chairperson; Assn of Cypress Teachers Pres 1985-87 Who Awd 1987; *office:* Christine Swain Elem Sch 5851 Newman Ave Cypress CA 90630

LEE, PATTI HAZZARD, English/History Teacher; *b:* Chicago, IL; *m:* Daniel R.; *c:* Courtney, Kevin, Tyler; *ed:* (BAED) Eng/His, 1977, (MAED) His, 1984 Kearney St Coll; *cr:* 7th-9th Grade His/Eng Teacher Wheatland Schls 1977-; *ai:* 7th & 8th Grade Class & Annual Staff Spon; Wheatland Ed Assn Treas 1977-; NE St Ed Assn 1977-; *office:* Wheatland Schls Box 38 Madrid NE 69150

LEE, RANDAL E., High School English Teacher; *b:* Placerville, CA; *ed:* (BA) Speech/Drama, Occidental Coll 1975; (MFA) Film/Television Writing, Univ of CA Los Angeles 1977; Working Towards Teaching Credential CA St Univ Dominguez Hills; *cr:* Teacher Gardena HS 1983-84, Carson HS 1984-87, Hamilton HS Acad of Music 1987-; *ai:* Boys & Girls Swim Team Head Coach; Academic Decathlon Team Asst Coach; United Teachers of Los Angeles, CA Teachers Assn, NEA 1984-; Pacific Chrstn Center Deacon 1987-; Natl Endowment for Hum Stipend; Summer Seminars Awds; Contributing Writer to Encyclopedia; *office:* Hamilton HS Acad of Music 2955 S Robertson Blvd Los Angeles CA 90034

LEE, RONALD HARRISON, Social Science Instr; *b:* North Bend, WA; *m:* Dorothy F. Snellgrove; *c:* Rhonda Hoyt Woodworth, Anette Lee Carlson, Brian H., Vicki Hoyt, Ronda A. Webb, Sharon L.; *ed:* (BA) Ed/His, Western WA Univ 1958; (MA) Poly Sci, Willamette Univ 19 65; AP European His Univ WA 1960; AP Amer His Pacific Luth Univ 1989; Univ WA Liberal Arts 1964-68; *cr:* Soc Sci Instr Edmonds Sr HS 1958-63; Soc Sci Inst/Dept Head Meadowdale Sr HS 1963-70, Lynnwood Sr HS 1970-; *ai:* Scott Paper Hi-Q, Ed Soc Dist 1989, Knowledge Bowl Co-Adv; Commencement Dir Building Diploma, Dist 15 Educl Specifications Comm; NCSS Mem 1967-; Edmonds Ed Assn Mem 1958-; NEA Life Mem 1958-; Elks Lodge #1604 Mem 1982-; COE Fellowship Willamette Univ 1965; NDEA His Fellowship Portland St 1968; Amer Legion WA St Teacher of Yr 1975; *office:* Lynnwood H S 3001 184th St SW Lynnwood WA 98036

LEE, RONDA F., Speech Teacher; *b:* Chattanooga, TN; *m:* William Edward; *c:* Deanah; *ed:* (MS) Speech/Dramatic Arts, Univ of Montevallo 1977; (BS) Speech/Ed, Auburn Univ 1969; *cr:* Instr Jefferson St Jr Coll 1972-75; Teacher Ramsay HS 1970-; Instr Samford Univ 1988-; *ai:* SGA & Speech Club Spon; Directed & Acted Various Plays; *office:* Ramsay HS 1800 13th Ave S Birmingham AL 35205

LEE, SANDRA ANN, English/Literature Teacher; *b:* Detroit, MI; *ed:* (BA) Lang Art, Oakland Univ 1981; Working Toward Masters ITIP Trng; Cert to Teach Health/Sex Ed; *cr:* Summer Sch Teacher Utica Cmmty Schls 1982; Intramural Sports Dir Surline Mid Sch 1982; Perm Sub Teacher/Track Coach Ogemaw Heights HS 1983; Eng/Lit Teacher Rose City Mid Sch 1983-; *ai:* Eng Curr Comm; MEA, NEA 1983-; *office:* Rose City Mid Sch 215 W Page Rose City MI 48654

LEE, SCOTT ARLAN, Fifth Grade Teacher; *b:* La Crosse, WI; *m:* Judy Daily; *c:* Carne, Mark; *ed:* (BA) Sociology/Psych, Luther Coll 1971; (BS) Elem Ed, Winona St Univ 1975; Various Courses; *cr:* Elem Teacher Trempealeau Elem Sch 1975-; *ai:* Ftbl, Bsktbl, Jr Var Golf Coach; Environmental Curr Comm Chm; NEA, WEA, GETEA 1975-; WI Assn of Env Ed 1983-, WI Environmental Teacher of Yr 1990; Conservation Ed Assn 1983-; Friends of Perrot St Park VP 1985-; Hiawatha Valley Audubon Bd of Dir 1984-; Town of Trempealeau Sanitary Dist Pres 1986-; Mount Trempealeau Corporation (Pres, VP) 1981-; Western WI Natural Resources Awd 1989; Trempealeau Citizen of Yr 1988; Top Volunteer Trempealeau Natl Wildlife Refuge; *office:* Trempealeau Elem Sch 4th & Grove Sts Trempealeau WI 54661

LEE, THEBA HODGES, Drama Teacher; *b:* Greensboro, AL; *m:* Drake K.; *c:* Scott Gibson, Sean L.; *ed:* (BA) Speech/Dance Ed, 1982, (MS) Theatre/Eng Ed, 1986 Univ of AL; Dan Netherland Sch of Ministry; *cr:* Eng/Multicultural Ed Instr Univ of AL 1983-89; HS Eng/Drama Teacher Tuscaloosa City Sch System 1988-; *ai:* Drama Club Spon Intl; Forensic Individaul Events Coach; PTSA Treas; Phi Delta Kappa; United Cerebral Palsy Fund Raising Comm 1988-89; Univ of AL Grad Teaching Asst 1982 Outstanding Performances Grad Stu 1982; *office:* Central H S East 905 15th St Tuscaloosa AL 35401

LEE, TIMOTHY RAYMOND, Social Studies Teacher; *b:* Zion, IL; *m:* Eva Gail Gaines; *c:* Christian, Scott, Jamie; *ed:* (BA) Poly Sci, Carthage Coll 1972; Northern IL Univ; Natl Coll OfEd; *cr:* 6th Grade Teacher West Elem Sch 1974-76, Ellis Sch 1976-77, West Elem Sch 1977-85; Soc Stud Teacher Cntrl Jr HS 1985-; *ai:* Soc Stud Learner Assessment Comm; Zion Ed Assn (Pres 1985-86) 1980-; NEA, IEA; *office:* Central Jr H S 1716 27th St Zion IL 60099

LEEK, PRISCILLA F., History/Soc Psychology Teacher; *b:* Los Angeles, CA; *m:* Roy; *c:* Joel Rushton; *ed:* (BA) His, Brigham Young Univ 1984; *cr:* His/Psych/Ec Teacher Springville HS 1984-85; His Teacher Springbranch Jr HS 1985-86, Springville Jr HS 1986-87; His/Psych/Ec Teacher Springville HS 1987-; *ai:* Citizen Bee Competition Adv; *office:* Springville HS 1205 E 900 S Springville UT 84663

LEEK, RICHARD JOHN, Orchestra Teacher; *b:* Little Falls, NY; *m:* Carol L. Thompson; *ed:* (BM) Music Ed, 1971, (MM) Music Ed, Univ of AZ; *cr:* Music Teacher Utterback Mid Sch 1971-74, Naylor Mid Sch 1980-; Musician Tucson Symphony Orch 1966-; *ai:* Serving on Tucson Unified Sch Dist Music Curr Review Comm; AZ Music Ed Assn VP Jr HS String 1987-; AZ String Teacher Assn Treas 1988-; Several Compositions for Orchestra Premiered By Jr HS Honor Orchestras; *office:* Naylor Mid Sch 1701 S Columbus Blvd Tucson AZ 85711

LEEKS, ALEXIS BRYANT, 6th Grade Teacher; *b:* Philadelphia, PA; *m:* David Leon; *c:* David A., Dion A.; *ed:* (BA) Elem Ed, Temple Univ 1974; (MS) Mid Grades Ed, Mercer Univ 1984; *cr:* 3rd Grade Teacher 1974-75, 1st Grade Teacher 1975-77, Kndgtn Teacher 1977-80 Robert Fulton Elem Sch; 4th Grade Teacher 1980-87, 6th Grade Teacher 1987- Cary Reynolds Elem Sch; *ai:* Teacher Forum Group & Soc Stud Sch Rep; Attendance Awd 1984-85; WPLO Teacher of Day 1980; *office:* Cary Reynolds Elem Sch 3498 Pine St Doraville GA 30340

LEEMAN, PEGGY ANN MOORE, English Department Chairman; *b:* Gober, TX; *m:* John H.; *c:* Debra L. *ed:* (BS) Bus/Eng, 1954, (MED) Admin Ed/Eng, 1957 E TX St Univ; TX Womens Univ; NE TX Writing/Bay Writing Project; Talented & Gifted, Univ of TX Austin; Advanced Placement Eng, S Meth Univ; AAT Trng; Advanced Placement Seminars; *cr:* Bus Dept Chm Ozona HS 1954-58; Eng Dept Chm Robert T Hill Jr HS 1958-76; Advanced Placement Eng Chm Bryan Adams HS 1976-; *ai:* NHS & Literary Society Adv; UIL Ready Writing Coach; TX Assn for Gifted & Talented; Delta Kappa Gamma Pres 1984-86, Achievement; Assn of Prof Educators Schlsp Chm 1986; ASCD, NCTE, Dallas Cncl Teachers of Eng; TX St Teachers Assn St Secy 1955; 1st Presbyn Church Elder 1960-; PTA 1954-, Life Membership 1985; Cabell Awd; Perot Awd; Jim Collins Awd; Teacher of Excl Awds; Meadows Fnd for Advanced Placement Grants SMU; Articles Published; *office:* Bryan Adams HS 2101 Millmar Dallas TX 75228

LEES, RICHARD LAWRENCE, Science Supervisor/Teacher; *b:* Jersey City, NJ; *m:* Irene Witer; *c:* Michael, Daniel, Jeremy; *ed:* (BA) Sci, 1963, (MA) Sci, 1966 Jersey City St Coll; (MA) Earth Sci, Franklin & Marshall Coll 1973; Earth Sci, Several Univs; *cr:* Teacher 1963-, Teacher/Supvr 1986- Lyndhurst HS; *ai:* Sci & Rocket Club Adv; Dist RTK Coord; Monitoring Comm; Natl Assn of Geology Teachers 1967-, Best Earth Sci Teacher 1977; Natl Sci Supvr Assn, NSTA, NJ Sci Supvr Assn, NJ Sci Teachers Assn; Readers Digest Books Earth Sci Consultant; Author Sci & Mankind; Newmast Honors Participant; NJ Govenors Awd; Finalist Princeton Dist Teacher; NSF Grants; Numorous St Grants; Exch Visit to China; *office:* Lyndhurst HS Weart Ave Lyndhurst NJ 07071

LEES, ROBERT MICHAEL, Mathematics Dept Instructor; *b:* Altus, OK; *m:* Judy Pate; *c:* Gregory, Russell; *ed:* (BS) Math, Southwestern OK St Univ 1968; *cr:* Math Instr Tucumcari HS 1968-89; *ai:* Jr Class Spon; NM NEA 1968-; Elks 1984-; *home:* HC 65 Box 107 Logan NM 88426

LEFEBER, DAVID D., Sixth Grade Teacher; *b:* St Joe, WI; *m:* Ruth Ann; *c:* Chad, Dana, Jeanna, Judd, RonnA, Wade; *ed:* (MS) Elem Ed, Univ of Platteville 1975; *cr:* Kndgtn Teacher Racine Public Schls 1968-69; 1st Grade Teacher 1969-77, 5th/6th Grade Teacher Potosi Public Sch; *ai:* Outdoor Ed Dir; Potosi Ed Assn Pres 1989-; BSA Scout Master Awd of Merit 1986; Masonic Lodge; *home:* 8648 Irish Ridge Rd Cassville WI 53806

LEFEVER, FRANCES H., 4th Grade Teacher; *b:* Lancaster, PA; *m:* Charles R.; *c:* Lynette Trout, Alexis V.; *ed:* (BS) Elem Ed, Millersville Univ 1971; Addl Studies Millersville Univ; PA St Univ; Shippensburg Univ *cr:* 6th Grade Teacher; 4th Grade Teacher Kreutz Creek Elem; 4th Grade Teacher Wrightsville Elem; *ai:* Owner-Mgr Country Club Kennel Inc; Interior Decorator & Seasonal Design Coord Oak Leaf Manor Personal Care Home; PSEA 1971-; EYEA 1971-; Order of the Eastern Star Worthy Matron 1989-; The Cousteau Society 1988-; *office:* Wrightsville Elem Sch 300-350 Chestnut St Wrightsville PA 17368

LEFEVER, HAROLD M., JR., Technology Education Teacher; *b:* Lancaster, PA; *ed:* (BS) Industrial Art, Millersville St Coll 1980; (MS) Technology Ed, Millersville Univ of PA 1987; *cr:* General Teacher Manheim Cntrl Sch Dist 1980-83; Electronics Teacher Lebanon HS 1983-85; Drafting/Electronics Teacher Warwick HS 1985-; *ai:* Wrestling & Weight Trng Coach; TSA Adv; Faculty Rep; LLTEA Pres 1988-; TEAP 1978-; ITEA 1984-; Jaycee Outstanding Young Educator Awd 1989; Article Published 1986; *office:* Warwick HS 301 W Orange St Lititz PA 17543

LE FEVER, LLOYD WILSON, Social Studies Teacher; *b:* Stockton, CA; *m:* Carla; *c:* Renee, Amy, Gina, Jason; *ed:* (BS) Park Admin, 1971, (MA) Ed, 1973 CA St Univ San Jose; Teacher Ed Prgm, Cnslr Ed Prgm Univ of CA Santa Cruz; *cr:* Cmmty Sch Dir 1971-74, Jr HS Teacher 1974-81 Oak Grove Sch Dist; Insurance Agent NY Life Oregon 1981-84; HS Teacher Crater HS 1984-; *ai:* Bsktbl Coach; Stu Government Adv; Soph/Jr/Sr Class Co-Adv; Natural Helprs Prgm Coord; Prom, Reach Adv; Faculty Advisory Comm; OR Ed Assn, NEA 1984-; Rogue Valley Life Underwriters 1981-84 Agent of Yr 1982; Southern OR Drug Awareness 1989-; *office:* Crater HS 4410 Rogue Valley Blvd Central Point OR 97502

LEFFEW, ROBERT JOE, Eng/Foreign Lang Teacher/Chair; *b:* Dayton, TN; *m:* Shirley Lue Kibler; *c:* Tanya; *ed:* (BA) Eng, TN Tech 1966; *cr:* Eng Teacher Adairsville HS 1966-68, Charleston HS 1968-76; Eng/Foreign Lang Teacher Trewhitt Jr HS 1976-; *ai:* Beta Club Spon; Textbook Comm; Academic Contests Coach; NEA, TEA, ETEA, BCEA; Local Ed Assn Teacher of Month; Bradley Cty Teacher of Yr; 1st Negotiations Team; *home:* Rt 7 Box 303 Cleveland TN 37311

LEGASSE, KENNETH J., Business Department Chair; *b:* Cohoes, NY; *m:* Marion C. Hicks; *c:* Kenneth S., Tarrayon; *ed:* (BS) Ec, Siena Coll 1966; Grad Work St Univ of NY Albany; *cr:* Teacher Tamarac HS 1966-; Adjunct Professor Hudson Valley Comm Coll 1986-; *ai:* Class, Bus Club Adv; Rep Stu Senate; Effective Schls Team Mem; Coaching; NY Coaches Assn 1985-; *home:* 4 Okemo Ct Clifton Park NY 12065

LEGER, BRADLEY A., Voc Agriculture Instructor; *b:* Crowley, LA; *ed:* (BS) Voc Ag Ed, 1979, (MS) Voc Ag Ed, 1982 LA St Univ Baton Rouge; Grad Stud LA St Univ & Univ of S LA; *cr:* Voc Ag Instr Midland HS 1979-; *ai:* FFA Adv; 4-H Club Spon; Stu Asst Team; LA Voc Ag Teachers Assn Pres 1988-89, St Outstanding Young Teacher 1983, St Outstanding Teacher 1988; LA Voc Assn Exec Bd 1979-; Natl Voc Ag Teachers Assn 1979-; AVA 1979-82, 1986-; Natl Assn of Conservation Dist & St Teacher of Yr 1989-; Knights of Columbus 1975-; Farm Bureau 1975-; FFA Honorary St Degree; *office:* Midland HS P O Box 66 Midland LA 70557

LEGG, WAYNE E., Mathematics Teacher; *b:* Milton, WV; *ed:* (BS) Math/Soc Stud, WV St Coll 1976; (MA) Scndry Ed, Marshall Univ 1981; Grad Stud Mid Chldhd Ed, Cmptr Ed, Curr/Instruction Grad Stud; *cr:* Math Teacher Lincoln Jr HS 1988-80, Ona Mid Sch 1980-; *ai:* WV Ed Assn, NEA; Amer Legion (Commander 1971-73), Life Membership 1989; Veterans of Foreign Wars Quartermaster 1987-; Cabell Ctuy Curr Cncl Math Sub-Comm; *office:* Ona Mid Sch 2300 Rt 60 Ona WV 25545

LEGGE, SHARON ANN, Fourth Grade Teacher; *b:* Corpus Christi, TX; *c:* Justin, Monica; *ed:* (BA) Religion/Eng, Southwestern Univ 1965; (MED) Counseling/Guidance, Pan Amer Univ 1983; Elem Ed, E TX St Univ, Sam Houston St Univ, TX A&M Univ; *cr:* Oral Lang Teacher Mission Consolidated Sch Dist 1975-76; 5th Grade Teacher Sharyland Ind Sch Dist 1976-85, Mission Consolidated Ind Sch Dist 1985-88; 4th Grade Teacher Sharyland Ind Sch Dist 1988-; *ai:* Univ Interscholastic League Literary Coach; Delta Kappa Gamma 1981-; Mission Service Project Coord 1984-; United Meth Church 1954-; *office:* Sharyland Ind Sch Dist 1106 N Shary Rd Mission TX 78572

LEGGETT, SHIRLEY BRASSELL, 5th Grade Teacher; *b:* Carthage, TX; *m:* Wilbur P.; *c:* Mark W., Mary L.; *ed:* (BA) Eng, Univ of TX; (MS) Elem Ed, Nova Univ 1980; *cr:* 6th Grade Teacher Kit Carson Center 1976-77; 3rd Grade Teacher 1977-79, 5th Grade Teacher 1977- Walter V Long Elem; *ai:* Drug Abuse Awareness Ed Coord; Grade Chm; *office:* Walter V Long Elem Sch 2000 S Walnut Rd Las Vegas NV 89104

LEGGETTE, PAULA BOUDREAUX, Bio Teacher/Sci Dept Chair; *b:* Abbeville, LA; *m:* Jack W.; *c:* Rebecca, Amy; *ed:* (BS) Bio/Math Ed, 1970, (MED) Sci/Admin Superv, 1980 Univ of SW LA; Prof Improvement Prgm; *cr:* Math/Sci Teacher Abbeville HS 1970-71; E Broussard HS 1972-76; Sci Teacher 1976- Sci Dept Chairperson 1988- Abbeville HS; *ai:* Abbeville HS Sci Fair Co-Dir; Sci Olympiad Team Co-Spon; Faculty Advisory Comm; Academic Awd Banquet Past Coord; NSTA 1987-; LA Sci Supvrs Organization 1990; NEA, LA Assn of Educators, Vermilion Assn of Educators 1984-; Vermilion Organization of Classroom Educators Pres 1984-85; USL Alumni Assn 1970-; Friends of LA Public Broadcasting 1984-; LA Wildlife Fed 1986-; MADD 1988-; Developed Curr for Honors Bio I 1989-, Zoology/Botany 1984-85; Nom NSTA Presidential Awd of Excl 1989-; Nom Abbeville HS Distinguished Teacher Awd 1989-; *office:* Abbeville HS 1305 Senior High Dr Abbeville LA 70510

LEGGIN, JULIA ANNE (YADACK), Eighth Grade Teacher; *b:* Mc Keesport, PA; *m:* Michael J.; *ed:* (BS) Scndry Ed, CA St Coll 1970; Post Grad Stud Duquesne Univ; *cr:* Teacher St Robert Bellarmine Sch 1970-79, Duquesne Cath Sch 1979-; *ai:* PA Jr Acad of Sci, Mon Yough Sci Fair, Serra Club Essay Contest Spon; *home:* 2700 Turkey Farm Rd North Huntington PA 15642

LEGGINS, CARL JOSEPH, Marine Biology Teacher; *b:* Miami, FL; *ed:* (AA) Forestry, Miami Dade Comm Coll 1982; (BS) Forest Resources/Conservation, Univ of FL 1984; Ed, Miami Dade Comm Coll & FL Intnl Univ; *cr:* Forester St Joe Paper Company 1984-85; Forestry Technician/Firefighter USDA Forest Service; Teacher Hialeah HS 1986-; *ai:* Boys & Girls Cross Cntry Coach; League of Environmental Educators of FL 1987-; FL Assn of Sci Teachers 1986-89; Univ of FL Sch of Forest Resources & Conservation, Stu Cncl Pres 1983-84, Presidential Recognition Awd 1984; Xi Sigma Pi Forestry Honor Society 1983-84; Gamma Sigma Delta 1983-84; *office:* Hialeah HS 251 E 47th St Hialeah FL 33013

LEH, RUTH (NELSON), First Grade Teacher; *b:* Haddonfield, NJ; *m:* Robert G.; *c:* Thomas F.; *ed:* (BS) Kndgtn/Primary Ed, Trenton St Coll 1953; Art Ed, Philadelphia PA Museum Sch of Art 1953-55; *cr:* 7th/8th Grade Sci/Math/Phys Ed Teacher DE Township Elem 1955; 3rd Grade Teacher Airport Height Elem 1955-57; 3rd/4th Grade Teacher DE Township Elem 1955-58; 5th/6th Grade Art Teacher Becht Elem 1961-63; Asst Dir/Montessori Pre-Sch Teacher Bloomington IL 1968-69; 1st Grade Teacher Oakdale Elem Unit 5 1969-; *ai:* Core I, III, IV Cooperating Teacher; ISU & IWU Stu Teacher; Phi Delta Kappa Mem 1984-; *office:* Oakdale Elem Sch 601 S Adelaide St Normal IL 61761

LEHMANN, PATRICIA ERNST, English Teacher; *b:* Dubuque, IA; *m:* Edward G.; *c:* Laura, Lindsey; *ed:* (BA) Eng, Loras Coll 1984; Stu Assistance Trng; Continuing Ed Courses; Yrbk Wkshps; *cr:* Eng Teacher Beckman HS 1984-; *ai:* Yrbk & Newspaper Adv; NHS Selection & Liturgy Comms; NCTE, IA Cncl Teachers of Eng Mem 1984-; Delta Kappa Gamma Mem; Farm Bureau 1986-; Cath Order of Foresters 1990; *home:* 21319 Springdale Durango IA 52039

LEHNING, E. JANE, Teacher Learning Disabilities; *b:* Ft Madison, IA; *m:* Harry P.; *c:* Kathleen Lorenzi, Ellen, Michael; *ed:* (BSED) Eng, W IL Univ 1954; *cr:* Eng Teacher Avon Sch Dist 1954-55; K-4th Grade Elem Ed Teacher 1967-77, Resource Teacher of Learning Disabilities/Jr HS Lang Art Teacher 1977-89, Resource Teacher of Learning Disabilities 1989- Ladd Cmmty Consolidated Sch 94; *ai:* IEA, NEA 1967-; CEC 1985-; *office:* Ladd Cmmty Consolidated Sch 232 E Cleveland Box 457 Ladd IL 61329

LEHTONEN, ROSEANN (BOND), Health Teacher/Dept Chair; *b:* Syracuse, NY; *m:* James; *ed:* (AAS) Recreation Supervision, Hudon Valley Comm Coll 1971; (BS) Health, Suny Brockport 1973; (MS) Health, OSWEGO-Suny 1980; Advanced Trng Wkshps on Aids, Alcohol, Substance Abuse & Family Life; *cr:* Health Teacher Shea Mid Sch, Fowler HS 1975-77, Edward Smith Elem 1977-78, Blodgett Mid Sch 1978-82, Henninger HS 1982-; *ai:* Extended Learning Day Prgm Coord; Health Dept Chairperson 1984-; NY St Fed of Prof Health Educators 1975-; Cmmty Intervention Inc, Helps Combat the Problems of Drug & Alcohol Abuse in our Schls & Cmmtys; *office:* Henninger HS 600 Robinson St Syracuse NY 13206

LEIER, JULIE M., Agriculture Education Teacher; *b:* Ford Ord, CA; *ed:* (AAS) Ag Bus, Bismarck Jr Coll 1977-80; (BS) Ag Ed, SD St Univ 1981-82; *cr:* Ag-Ed/Sci Instr Bowdle HS 1983-84, Highmore HS 1984-89; Ag-Ed Instr Wall HS 1989-; *ai:* Bowdle FFA, Jr Class; Highmore FFA; Soph Class; Cheerleading Adv; Wall FFA Jr Class; Asst Gymnastics Coach; SDVATA 1983-89, Exch of Ideas 1987; NVATA 1983-; Highmore Womens Golf League (2nd 1987) 1987-89; Church Bazaar Comm 1987-88; Highmore Womens Bowling League 1985-88; Highmore Jaycees Outstanding Young Teacher; *office:* Wall Sch Dist Box 414 Wall SD 57790

LEIGH, ANNA LEE (MAY), Fourth Grade Teacher; *b:* Waynesburg, KY; *m:* Gerald; *c:* Steve, Angela Leigh Smith; *ed:* (BS) Elem Ed, 1970, Ed, 1975 Eastern KY Univ; *cr:* 7th Grade Teacher Eubank Elem 1954-55; 5th Grade Teacher Goshen Elem 1956-57; 6th Grade Teacher Lebanon Junction 1958-59; 1st Grade Teacher 1970-73, 4th Grade Teacher 1973- Eubank Elem; *ai:* 4-H Club Leader; Work Childrens Church; PTA Treas 1972-73; Certificate of Appreciation Hal Roger Mem of Congress 5th Dist of KY 1987; *home:* 1501 Hillview Dr Science Hill KY 42553

LEIGH, GARY ANDRE, Math Teacher; *b:* Washington, DC; *ed:* (BS) Math, DC Teachers Coll 1971; (MA) Math, The Amer Univ 1973; *cr:* Math Teacher John Hanson Jr HS 1973-83; Math Dept Chm Stephen Decatur Mid Sch 1983-86; Math Teacher Bladensburg HS 1986-; *ai:* Chess Club Spon; Introductory Algebra Comm; Cmptr Math Comm; Math Assn Amer 1990-; US Chess Fed 1989-; Head of Advanced Math Comm Bladensburg 1986-; *office:* Bladensburg Sr HS 5610 Tilden Rd Bladensburg MD 20710

LEIGH, NATHAN A., Fifth Grade Teacher; *b:* Ontario, OR; *m:* Glenda Darlene Weygandt; *c:* Eric, Craig; *ed:* (AS) Mechanical Technology, Treasure Valley Coll 1966; (BA) Elem Ed, Boise St Univ 1977; (MED) Pupil Personnel Services, Coll of ID 1981; Trng Chemical Dependency, Substance Abuse Ed; Wildlife & Environmental Issues Ed; *cr:* 5th Grade Teacher Wilder Elem Sch 1977-79, Parma/Roswell Grade Sch 1979-81; 4th Grade Teacher Maxine Johnson Elem Sch 1981-87; 5th Grade Teacher Roswell Mid Sch 1987-; *ai:* Textbook Selection, Staff Dev Comm; Sci & Health Curr; ID Rdng Cncl 1980-85; Parma Ed Assn Building Rep 1985-; BSA (Scoutmaster 1970-80, Cubmaster 1985-); *office:* Roswell Mid Sch P O Box 246 Parma ID 83660

LEIGHTON, BILL DODGE MUNRO, Middle School Teacher; *b:* Chicago, IL; *m:* Judy Munro; *c:* Kristin, Colleen; *ed:* (BA) Sociology, Loyola Univ 1970; (MED) Ed, Univ of KY Lexington 1972; Educl Admin, Univ of Louisville 1985; *cr:* 1st-8th Grade Teacher Louisville/Jefferson Cty Public Schls 1970-; *ai:* Prof Dev & Participatory Leadership Comms; Youth for Peace; Inservice Comm; NEA 1986-; ASCD 1988-; Leadership Ed Alumni Assn Dir 1986-89; Peace Ed Prgm Bd of Dir Co-Chm 1988-; Highland Youth Recreation Coach 1985-; Co-Founder Portland Museum Louisville; Author 2 Childrens His Books; KY Teacher Intern/Resource Teacher; *home:* 1312 Willow Ave Louisville KY 40204

LEIMAN, RONALD LEE, Athletic Supervisor; *b:* Huntington, IN; *m:* Rosemary Navarro; *ed:* (BS) Phys Ed, Ball St Univ 1973; (MED) Phys Ed, Bowling Green St Univ 1978; (MS) Recreation, Univ of OR 1983; Doctoral Stud Socio-Psychological Aspects of Sports, Univ of OR 1981-83; *cr:* Teacher/Coach Blackhawk Jr HS 1973-77, Bassett Jr HS 1978-79, Parkland HS 1979-81, Hanks HS 1983-89; Athletic Supvr Ysleta Ind Sch Dist 1989-; *ai:* Ysleta Ind Sch Dist Mid Sch/HS Athletic Prgms; Natl Interscholastic Athletic Admin Assn, TX HS Athletic Dir Assn 1989-; Assn of TX Prof Educators 1979-81, 1983-; Sierra Club (Chm 1988, Newsletter Ed 1989-); *office:* Ysleta Ind Sch Dist 9600 Sims El Paso TX 79925

LEIMAN, ROSEMARY N., Student Activity Director; *b:* El Paso, TX; *m:* Ronald Lee; *ed:* (BS) Health/Phys Ed, Univ of TX El Paso 1974; (MS) Ed, Sul Ross St Univ 1986; *cr:* Phys Ed Teacher Burleson Elem 1975-76; Dance Teacher Austin HS 1976-80, Hanks HS 1981-86; Stu Act Dir Socorro HS 1986-; *ai:* Sr, Jr Class Stu Cncl; Silhouettes, Orchesis Dance Club; Just Say No, Partners in Ed Comm; B-Team Vllybl Coach; UIL Academics Coord; Natl Assn of Stu Act (Adv, Mem); TX Assn of Stu Cncls Mem; Trans-Pecos Health & Phys Ed Secy; Sierra Club.

LEIMBACH, JUDITH HANAGAN, Teacher of Gifted; *b:* Hammond, IN; *m:* Thomas W.; *c:* Kathleen S., Robert W.; *ed:* (BS) Elem Ed, Ball St Univ 1958; (ME) Ed/Gifted, Natl Coll of Ed 1982; *cr:* Kndgtn Teacher St John Luth 1966-67; 2nd Grade Teacher Schrum Sch 1967-72; Primary Teacher 1972-79, Teacher of Gifted 1979- Briar Glen Sch; *ai:* Gifted Comm; Teachers Assn VP; Phi Delta Kappa (Secy 1986-87, VP 1987-89), Educator of Yr 1986; St John Luth Expansion Comm 1989-; Authored & Co-Authored Articles; *office:* Briar Glen Sch 1800 Briarcliffe Blvd Wheaton IL 60187

LEINBACH, JAY P., Teacher; *b:* Reading, PA; *m:* Linda R. Holland; *c:* Lisa; *ed:* (BS) Elem Ed, West Chester St Univ 1969; (MED) Elem Ed, PA St Univ 1974; Grad Stud Various Inst; *cr:* Teacher Mt Penn Elem 1969-; *ai:* Video Dept; Photography; Elem Intramural Sports; Antiatam Ed Assn (Pres 1974) 1969-; Explorer Post 902 Adv 1985-; Published Photographer; *office:* Mt Penn Elem Sch 24 & Cumberland Ave Reading PA 19606

LEININGER, RALPH E., Social Studies Teacher; *b:* Reading, PA; *m:* Carol Levan; *ed:* (BS) Scndry Ed Soc Stud, Kutztown St Univ 1967; Grad Work Kutztown St Univ; *cr:* 7th-8th Grade His/Geography Teacher Tulpehocken Jr HS 1967-86; Civics/West Culture/Amer His Teacher Tulpehocken HS 1986; *ai:* Jr HS Bsktbl Coach 1968-69; Var Bsbl Coach 1969-75; NEA, PSEA, TEA 1967-; *office:* Tulpehocken HS R D 2 Bernville PA 19506

LEISE, MAUREEN WILKINSON, Teacher/Forensics Moderator; *b:* Philadelphia, PA; *ed:* (BA) Speech/Hearing, Temple Univ 1976; Grad Work in Theology, St Charles Seminary; *cr:* Teacher/Forensics Moderator Nazareth Acad 1982-; *ai:* Forensics Moderator & Coach; PA Speech & Debate Assn, Speech Comm Assn, NCEA 1982-; *office:* Nazareth Acad Grant & Torresdale Aves Philadelphia PA 19114

LEISETH, KEITH M., Science Teacher; *b:* Buffalo, MN; *m:* Patty A. Schutz; *c:* Krissy, Jon; *ed:* (BA) Bio/Health, Augsburg Coll 1961; (AMS) Mort Sci, Univ of MN 1967; Grad Stud; *cr:* Sci Teacher Camrose Luth Coll 1961-63, Richfield HS 1963-66; Teaching Asst Univ of MN 1966-67; Health Instr Augsburg 1969-71; Sci Teacher Maple Lake HS 1985-; *ai:* NHS Adv; MN Ed Assn, NEA; 4-H Adult Leader; Cty Extension Comm; *home:* Rt 2 Box 126 A Buffalo MN 55313

LEIST, DAVID P., Music/Drama Teacher; *b:* Circleville, OH; *ed:* (BME) Music Ed, Otterbein Coll 1973; *cr:* Music Teacher Springboro HS 1973-, Miamisburg City Schls 1982-83; Music/Drama Teacher Waynesville HS 1983-; *ai:* Jr HS & HS Choir; Drama Dir; Musical Production Producer & Dir; Theatre Ed Assn 1989-; Music Educators Natl Conference, OH Music Ed Assn 1973-; Mason Cmmty Players Treas 1984-, Acting Awd 1984; *home:* 1065 E Main St Lebanon OH 45036

LEITCH, CHRISTINA LEE, 7th Language Arts Teacher; *b:* Sheridan, MI; *m:* Martin; *c:* Season, Shane; *ed:* (BSED) Speech Comm, Cntrl MI Univ 1978; Working Towards MA Jr HS Ed; *cr:* Adult Ed Teacher Montabella HS & Chippewa Hills Sch Dist 1978-79; Lang Art Teacher Cntrl Montcalm Mid Sch 1979-; *ai:* Sch Improvement Plan, ODDM Chm; Poetry Contest Supvr; Nila Banton Rdng Cncl 1985-; MI Rdng Assn 1988-; NEA 1979-; St of MI Grant to Encourage Stu Writing 1987; *office:* Cntrl Montcalm Mid Sch 1480 S Sheridan Rd Stanton MI 48888

LEIVESTAD, CAROLYN MC GEE, Fifth Grade Teacher; *b:* Butte, MT; *ed:* (BA) Psych, W WA St Coll 1972; Working On Masters In Curr & Instruction, Lesley Coll 1990; *cr:* Spec Ed Teacher Cedar Valley Elem Sch 1973-75; 1st-3rd/5th Grade Teacher Lake Youngs Elem Sch 1975-; *ai:* CARE Team Founding Mem; Organized Sch Money Raising Project; PTA Golden Acorn Awd for Service to Children 1990; Grant to Raise Salmon in my Classroom.

LELAND, JEANNE CAROL, Community Education Director; *b:* Shawano, WI; *m:* Greg; *c:* Tyler, Caranda; *ed:* (BA) Elem Ed, UW River Falls 1978; (MS) Cmmty Ed St Thomas Coll 1982; *cr:* 4th/7th Grade Teacher Hudson Elem/Mid Schls 1978-79; 7th Grade Eng/6th Grade Speech/Drama Teacher North Branch Mid Sch 1979-88; Cmmty Ed Dir ISD 138 1987-; *ai:* ISD 138 Comm Coord; North Branch Celebrate MN 1990 Festivals Chairperson; NCEA/MCEA; MSPRA/NSPRA; North Branch Area Chamber of Commerce Bd of Dir Secy 1990-; Two Articles Published in Group Magazine; Presentor at Multi-St Cmmty Conference; Presentor at MN Mid Sch Conference; *office:* ISD #138 320 Main St North Branch MN 55056

LELAND, ROGER WAYNE, Soc Stud Teacher, Dept Chm; *b:* Plymouth, IN; *m:* Jane Anne Ives; *c:* Amanda; *ed:* (BA) Soc Stud Ed, Purdue Univ 1969; (MS) Ed, St Francis Coll Ft Wayne 1974; *cr:* Soc Stud Teacher Lincoln Jr HS 1969-; *ai:* PEA, ISTA, NEA 1969-; PEA Negotiations Comm 1987; Marshall Cty Historical Society Bd Dirs 1988-; Trinity United Meth Church His Comm 1989-; Marshall Cty Trail of Death Sesquicentennial Commemoration Chm 1988; Marshall Cty Historical Society Long-Term Planning Comm Chm 1989; *office:* Lincoln Jr H S 220 N Liberty St Plymouth IN 46563

LELM, STAN, English/Teacher of Gifted; *b:* Peoria, IL; *c:* Jennifer; *ed:* (AA) Commercial Art, S IL Univ 1968; (BA) Eng/Ed, W IL Univ 1974; Vietnam Veteran/US Army; Trained as Peer Facilitator; Completed Suncoast Area Teacher Trng; Took Courses to be Certified in Gifted; *cr:* Eng/Art Teacher Southeastern HS 1974-82; Eng/Teacher of Gifted King Sr HS 1982-87, Bloomingdale Sr HS 1987-; *ai:* Stu for Environmental & Soc Awareness Club Spon 1988-; Eng Academic Coach Hillsborough Cty Academic Team 1988-; Southeastern Ed Assn Pres 1980-81, Outstanding Teacher Awd 1981; Hillsborough Cty Teachers of Eng 1989-; Elected Cty Rep NEA St Convention IL 1980; Appeared on Local TV Talk Show 1988; Published in FL Project Mental Illness Non-Discrimination 1987; Teacher of Month Awd 1989; *office:* Bloomingdale Sr HS 1700 E Bloomingdale Ave Valrico FL 33594

LE MAIRE, ELIZABETH GRIFFIN, 6th-8th Grade Soc Stud Teacher; *b:* Brooklyn, NY; *m:* Asa C.; *c:* Brian, Lisa; *ed:* (BA) Scndry Ed, Our Lady of the Lake Univ 1970; *cr:* 3rd/4th Grade Rdng Teacher 1979-80, 3rd Grade Teacher 1980-89, 6th/8th Grade Soc Stud Teacher 1989- St Thomas More; *ai:* Soc Stud Coord; Primary Level Coord 1984-88.

LE MAIRE, ROSELYN, Sixth Grade Teacher; *b:* Abbeville, LA; *m:* Carroll; *c:* Errol B., Clay C.; *ed:* (BA) Elem Ed, Mc Neese Univ 1969; (MED) 1975; *cr:* 6th Grade Teacher Kaufman Elem 1969-70; 4th/5th Grade Teacher South Cameron Elem 1970-71; 6th/7th Grade Teacher 1971-75, 3rd Grade Teacher 1975-80 Cameron Elem;6th Grade Teacher Grand Lake HS 1980-; *ai:* Project Leader Elem 4-H Club; Chm Substance Abuse Prgm Ed; LAE, NEA 1969-; CAE 1970-; St Mary of Lake Cath Church Lector, Religion Teacher; Fund Raiser Trips For Underprivileged.

LEMANSKY, ARLENE GONDEK, 7th Grade Teacher; *b:* Allison, PA; *m:* Francis; *c:* Barton; *ed:* (BA) Soc Stud, Waynesburg Coll 1964; *cr:* Soc Stud Teacher Redstone HS 1964-66, Butler Area HS 1966-67; 7th Grade Teacher St John the Evangelist Sch 1967-; *ai:* Forensic Speech Moderator; Lang Art Chairperson; Awd for 20 Yrs of Ministry St John the Evangelist Sch; *office:* St John the Evangelist Sch 88 Pennsylvania Ave Uniontown PA 15401

LE MASTER, BETH ANN, Science Teacher; *b:* Lubbock, TX; *m:* Ronald Cris; *ed:* (BA) Microbiology, Univ of TX 1985; Certificate in Bio, Univ of TX 1989; *cr:* Sci Teacher Salado HS 1989-; *ai:* Jr Class Spon; UIL Sci Coord; *office:* Salado HS PO Box 98 Salado TX 76571

LE MASTER, LINDA DANTZLER, Choral Director; *b:* Walterboro, SC; *m:* Harley S.; *c:* David, Robert; *ed:* (BS) Music Ed/Choral, Winthrop Coll 1965; *cr:* Choral Dir Southside Mid Sch & S Florence HS 1986-; *ai:* S Florence Choraliers Show Choir & Sch Drama Production Dir; SC Music Educators Assn Sr HS Comm 1989-; Music Educators Natl Conference 1987-; Amer Choral Dirs Assn 1989-; *office:* S Florence HS 115 E Howe Springs Rd Florence SC 29501

LEMLEY, JOAN RAE, English Teacher; *b:* Charleston, WV; *m:* Rodney B.; *ed:* (BA) Lang Art, WV Inst of Tech 1975; (MA) Scndry Ed Admin, WV Univ 1983; *cr:* Eng Teacher Parkersburg HS 1975-; *ai:* AFT 1986-; Emmanuel Baptist Church 1986-; Eastern Star 1976-; *office:* Parkersburgh HS 2101 Dudley Ave Parkersburg WV 26101

LEMMON, GENE, Technology Education Instr; *b:* Shawnee, OK; *m:* Shirley Houston; *c:* Shannon, Tiffany; *ed:* (BA) Elem Ed, 1984, (BA) Industrial Art, 1985 NSU; Basic Electrician USMC 1972; MCI Basic Elec & Marine NCO 1973; *cr:* Ind Art Instr Vian Public Sch; *ai:* Class Spon; Outstanding Ind Art Achievement Awds 1985-88; *office:* Vian HS Box 434 Vian OK 74962

LEMMON, PATTI ELSE, Mathematics Department Teacher; *b:* Butte, MT; *m:* Steve; *c:* David, Rebecca, Theresa; *ed:* (BS) Math, WMC Dillon 1976; *cr:* Math Teacher Judith Gap Sch 1976-78, 1985-; *ai:* Stu Cncl; Class of 1988, 1989, 1993 Spon; MCTM, NCTM, MEA, NEA, JGEA (Sec, Treas) 1987-; Cmmty Club; OES (ADAH, Assoc Cond) 1983-; MT St Univ Most

Inspirational Teacher 1990; Judith Gap Teacher of Yr 1988; *office:* Judith Gap Sch Box 67 Judith Gap MT 59453

LEMOINE, VIRGINIA MARY, Second Grade Teacher; *b:* Marksville, LA; *m:* George R. Jr.; *c:* David, Jeanne Ryan; *ed:* Ed, Univ of SW LA; Religious Ed Wkshps; *cr:* 2nd Grade Teacher Fifth Ward HS 1946-48; 1st Grade Teacher St Gerard Majella Elem 1953-55; 2nd Grade Teacher St Anthony Sch 1968-85, St Gerard Majella Elem 1985-; *ai:* 1st Communion Class Coord; St Anthony Sch Asst Prin; NCEA; Rosary Altar Society, Cath Daughters of America, AARP; *home:* 3968 Beech St Baton Rouge LA 70805

LEMON, RUTH MARIE, German/Eng/Tutoring Teacher; *b:* Artesian, SD; *m:* Thyron Oakley; *c:* Bruce D., Diane M., Barbara R. Dowling, Craig M., Luellen L. Hampton, Loren J.; *ed:* (BA) Elem Ed, Huron Univ 1966; Numerous Courses; *cr:* Secy Civil Service Commission 1944-46; Teacher Iroquois Public Sch 1966-; *ai:* Ger & Pep Club Adv; SD Educl Assn 1966-; NEA; Iroquois Ed Assn Pres 1972-73, Teacher of Yr 1974-75; PTA Life Membership 1962; AAUW Outstanding Contribution to Ed 1988; Intnl Trng Comm Course & Accreditation Awd 1987; NDEA Inst Ger 1967; Stipend Mellon Inst 1988; *office:* Iroquois HS Box 98 Iroquois SD 57353

LEMON-ANDERSON, SHEILA E., Science Teacher; *b:* Chicago, IL; *m:* Del Anderson; *c:* Latina M. Lemon; *ed:* (BS) Spec Ed, Chicago St Univ 1977-; Sci Ed, Natl Lewis Coll of Ed; Cooperative Extension Courses Sci Ed, Univ of IL; *cr:* Teacher Chicago Public Schls 1978-; *ai:* Sci Fair Coord; Sci Club Spon; IL Sci Teachers Assn Mem 1987-; CEC Membership Chairperson 1975-77, Increased Membership Awd 1976; Chicago Police Beat Rep Volunteer 1986-; PTA; CSU Alumni Assn 1988-; Amoco Fellow 1985; *home:* 1533 S St Louis Chicago IL 60623

LE MONDS, JIM EDWARD, English Teacher/Dept Chairman; *b:* Longview, WA; *m:* Sherry Carter; *c:* Kimberly, Kami; *ed:* (BA) Eng/Soc Stud, W Wa Univ 1972; (MA) Ed, Lewis & Clark Coll 1978; *cr:* 7th Grade Soc Stud Eng Teacher Cascade Mid Sch 1972-80; Eng Teacher R A Long HS 1981-; *ai:* Asst Ftbl Coach; Eng Dept Chm; Cascade Mid Sch & R A Long HS Teacher of Yr Honors 1975, 1987; *office:* R A Long HS 2903 Nichols Blvd Longview WA 98632

LEMONS, DORIS BOWDEN, K-12th Grade Art Teacher; *b:* Cape Girardeau, MO; *m:* Robert N.; *c:* Robyn S. Albright; *ed:* (BSED) Art, SE MO St Univ 1972; Grad Courses Art & Learning Disabilities; *cr:* Art Teacher Oak Ridge Schls 1975-; *ai:* Yrbk Adv; Natl Art Honor Society & Class Spon; MO St Teachers Assn 1975-; NAEA 1980-; Cmmty Teachers Assn 1975-; *home:* 1545 Price Dr Cape Girardeau MO 63701

LENHARDT, KATHLEEN HANNEMANN, English & Speech Teacher; *b:* Wausau, WI; *m:* John; *c:* Amy, Kyle; *ed:* (BA) Comm Arts, CA Luth Univ 1977; Grad Prgm Speech Comm CA St Univ Fullerton; *cr:* Teacher De Anza HS 1979, Dana Jr HS 1979-; *ai:* Coach Forensics Team; Western Bay Forensic League Treas 1989-; CTIIP Grant to Start Video Lab.

LENIG, STEVEN DALE, General Science Teacher; *b:* Norfolk, VA; *m:* Cheryl L. Wideman; *c:* Justin; *ed:* (BS) Bio/Ed, Manchester Coll 1976; Grad Work Purdue Univ; *cr:* Teacher Highland Jr HS 1976-81; Outdoor Ed Coord Lake Cty Park Dept 1978-81; Teacher Wilmington Mid Sch 1981-85, Coal City Mid Sch 1985-; *ai:* Head Wrestling & Asst Track Coach; Dir Homeroom Act; IEA, NEA Local Dist Building Rep; Meth Church (Youth Group Spon, Chair Trustees) 1988-; BSA (Asst Scoutmaster 1976, Comm Chm 1989-); *office:* Coal City Mid Sch 305 E Division Coal City IL 60416

LENIGAN, HOWARD EDWARD, Principal; *b:* Berkley, MI; *m:* Jeannene Guard; *c:* Michael, Patrick, Carol Townsend, Daniel; *ed:* (BS) Elem Ed/Soc Stud, Andrews Univ 1976; (MED) Supervision/Admin, W MD Coll 1981; *cr:* Teacher MI, PA & NY 1961-75, Grest Lane Sch 1975-79, Greater Baltimore Jr Acad 1979-81; Prin Eastern Shore Acad 1981-; *ai:* Yrbk Spon; Photography Adv; ASCD 1980-; *office:* Eastern Shore Acad R R 1 Box 54-B Sudlersville MD 21668

LENNA, BRENDA WILLIAMS, 5th/6th Grade Teacher; *b:* Columbus, GA; *m:* Joseph Jr.; *c:* Nathan, Nicholas; *ed:* (BA) Elem Ed, Southeastern Coll975; (MS) Rdng Diagnosis, St Univ NY Albny 1989; Univ of S FL Tampa; *cr:* 5th Grade Teacher Eagle Lake Elem 1975-76; 2nd-4th Grade Teacher 1978-79, 4th/5th Grade Teacher 1979-80, 7th/8th Grade Teacher 1980-86 Pine Valley Chrstn Sch; 3rd-6th Grade Teacher Covenant Chrstn Day 1984-; *ai:* Pioneer Girls Spon Leader; Tutored Urban Children City Mission of Schenectady NY 1987-89; *office:* Covenant Chrstn Day Sch 1414 Cliffwood Dr Greensboro NC 27406

LENNON, THELMA GORDON, Supply Teacher; *b:* Charlotte, NC; *c:* Gregory D., Christopher C., Clarence E., Kevin B., David C.; *ed:* (BA) Elem Ed, Johnson C Smith Univ 1955; (MSED) Counseling/Guidance, Chicago St Univ 1978; *cr:* Teacher Charlotte Bd of Ed 1955, Bd of Ed Oxford 1957-58, Chicago Bd of Ed 1961-89; Supply Teacher Fulton Cty Schls 1989-.

LENNON, VICKIE DAVIS, English Teacher; *b:* Wilmington, NC; *m:* Randall Perry; *c:* Randall P. II; *ed:* (BA) Eng, Univ of NC Wilmington 1986; *cr:* Primary Rdng Aide Wrightsville Beach Elem 1978-80; Eng Teacher E A Laney HS 1986-; *ai:* Genealogy Club Adv; Diamond Girls for Boys Var Bsbl Mgr; Cape Fear & Natl Writing Project 1989-; NC Cncl Eng Teachers 1987-; NCTE 1986-; Published Poetry; *office:* E A Laney HS 2700 N College Rd Wilmington NC 28405

LENNOX, ANGELA JANE, Biology Teacher; *b:* Watford, United Kingdom; *m:* David P.; *ed:* (BS) Marine Sci/Botany, 1975, (PHD) Marine Sci, 1979 Univ Coll of N Wales; Grad Stud Univ of NH; *cr:* Research Asst Univ Coll of N Wales 1975-78; Asst Professor Merrimack Valley Coll 1980-81, St Anselms Coll 1981-82; Summer Sch Faculty Shoals Marine Laboratory 1983; Faculty Univ of NH 1984-85; Summer Sch Faculty Pine Manor Coll 1983-87; Sci Faculty Exeter Area HS 1985-; *ai:* Sci Club Adv; Advance Placement Bio Stus Coach; Sch Dist Spec Ed Comm Mem; NABT 1985-, NH Bio Teacher of Yr 1989; British Phycological Society 1975-; Amer Assn Advancement of Sci 1979-; NH Sci Teachers Assn 1985-; Amer Red Cross CPR Instr 1983-; Kensington Volunteer Fire Dept Rescue 1982-, Kensington Congregational Church 1982-; Sir Alfred Lewis Prize Univ Coll of N Wales 1975; *office:* Exeter Area HS 30 Linden St Exeter NH 03833

LE NOIR, JENNIFER TOMLIN, English Teacher; *b:* Las Cruces, NM; *m:* James U.; *c:* Joshua; *ed:* (BS) Scndry Ed, 1983, (MS) Ed Admin, 1989 NM St Univ; *cr:* Eng Teacher Andress HS 1984-85, Hatch Valley HS 1985-; *ai:* Class Spon; NEA Secy 1986; *office:* Hatch Valley HS PO Box 790 Hatch NM 87937

LENTZ, ANNE STONE, Fifth Grade Teacher; *b:* Statesville, NC; *m:* Wade Wesley; *c:* Laura A., Timothy W.; *ed:* (BA) Elem Ed, Lenior-Rhyne 1968; (MED) Elem, Univ of NC Charlotte 1971; *cr:* Teacher Monticello Sch 1968-; *ai:* Sch A-Team Chairperson; PTA Faculty Rep; NEA 1968-89; PACE; PTA VP 1987-88; *office:* Monticello Schl Rt 13 Box 134 Statesville NC 28677

LENTZ, BARBARA GERESSY, Science Teacher/Dept Chair; *b:* Youngstown, OH; *m:* John Robert Jr.; *c:* Ryan P., Jessica D.; *ed:* (BS) Bio - Cum Laude, Appalachian St Univ 1971; (MED) Scndry Sci, Clemson Univ 1978; *cr:* Bio Teacher Crest HS 1971-74; Earth Sci Teacher Hillcrest Mid Sch 1975-; *ai:* Sci Dept Chm; Natl Jr Beta Club & Citizen of Month Spon; Stu IncentiveS Coord; Greenville Cty Sci Teacher Assn, SC Sci Cncl, NSTA; Keep America Beautiful Comm; Teacher of Yr 1984-85; Sci Teacher of Yr 1987-87; NEWMAST Participant 1987; *office:* Hillcrest Mid Sch 510 Garrison Rd Simpsonville SC 29681

LENTZ, JERRY DUANE, English Department Chair; *b:* Minden, NV; *ed:* (BA) Eng Lit, Fresno St Coll 1969; A I Technician Univ of CA Davis 1979; MBA Work Univ of CA Riverside 1973; *cr:* Independent Study Inst 1988-; Cmptr Writing Lab 1988-, Advanced Placement Eng 1988-, Eng Dept Chm 1990 Victor Valley Sr HS; *ai:* Advanced Placement Eng Club & Yrbk Adv; Teachers Union Site Rep; High Teach Comm Mem; Victor Advisory Team; Teacher of Yr 1989; *office:* Victor Valley Sr HS 16500 Mojave Dr Victorville CA 92392

LENZI, LINDA JEAN, Teacher of Talented & Gifted; *b:* Monongahela, PA; *ed:* (BA) Elem Ed, Univ of Steubenville 1970; (MS) Sch Admin, Univ of Dayton 1974; Gifted Ed, St of OH Validation; *cr:* 5th-6th Grade Teacher Wintersville Elem 1970-82; 2nd-5th Grade Rdng Teacher Elizabeth Forward Sch Dist 1971; Elem Teacher of Gifted Indian Creek Local Sch Dist 1982-; *ai:* Indian Creek Policy Comm; Co-Dir Indian Creek Elem Talented & Gifted Sci Act Prgm, Indian Creek 3rd Grade Sci Enrichment Prgm; Indian Creek Talented & Gifted Parents Group; Jefferson Cty Sch Dist Gifted Ed Course of Study, Performing Arts Grants, OH Academic Competition NE Regional Comms; OH Assn for Gifted Children; NEA, OH Ed Assn; Indian Creek Ed Assn (Pres, Secy, Negotiations Team) 1980-84, 1988-; OH Valley Uni Serv Pres 1984-; Delta Kappa Gamma 1983-; OH Valley Labor Management Cncl 1989-; Jefferson Cty Democratic Party Exec Comm; Co-Author Jefferson Cty Sch Dist Grants 1988, 1989; Co-Author Care Packages Material for Gifted Stu; Indian Creek Scholar Stu Teacher Recognition Awd 1989; *home:* 2239 1/2 Cherry Ave Steubenville OH 43952

LEON, MARCIA (KRAUS), Pre-School Day Care Operator; *b:* Quinter, KS; *m:* Mickey Tony; *c:* Jennifer, Christopher, Cory, Jamie; *ed:* (BS) Elem Ed, Ft Hays KS St Univ 1976; Grad Stud at Ft Hays KS St Univ; *cr:* Spec Ed Skills Teacher Developmental Services of NW KS 1973-77; Stu Teacher Lincoln Elem Sch 1975; K-2nd Grade Elem Ed Teacher Unified Sch Dist 292 1977-81; Pre-Sch/Elem Ed Teacher 1981-; Elem Ed Teacher Unified Sch Dist 293 1990; *ai:* Cub Scouts; Religious Ed for Adults; Cancer Society Volunteer; KS Child Care Coalition; Gore Cty Food Prgm Chairperson; Designed Government Hospital Logo; Bible Sch Teacher; Cheerleading Spon; Ft Hays KS St Univ Mortarboard 1972-73; KS Ed Assn Stu Organization 1975-76; Stu Cncl (Secy, Treas) 1970-72, Outstanding Stu Awd; Amer Legion Awd at Graduation 1972; Academic Grants from Ft Hays KS St Univ Farm Bureau Schlsp; *home:* 214 Castle Rock Rd Quinter KS 67752

LEONARD, ANN BURDETT, High School English Teacher; *b:* San Bernardino, CA; *m:* Larry W.; *c:* Valerie; *ed:* (BA) Multiple Subject/Eng, 1973, (MA) Ed Admin, Univ of Redlands; *cr:* 4th-6th Grade GATE Sci Teacher Lincoln Elem 1973; 7th-9th Grade Math/Eng/Arts & Crafts Teacher Cope Jr HS 1973-79; 8th-9th Grade Eng/Math Teacher Moore Jr HS 1979-87; 10th-12th Grade Eng Teacher Redlands HS 1987-; *ai:* Peer Counseling Facilitator; Eng Curr Comm; CA Assn of Teachers of Eng; NCTA; CA Teachers Assn; Alpha Delta Kappa Secy; Alpha Theta Phi Alumnae Organization Pres; Panhellenic Alumnae Pres; *office:* Redlands HS 840 E Citrus Ave Redlands CA 92374

LEONARD, BARBARA BALLARD, Science Teacher; *b:* Opelousas, LA; *m:* David Walter Sr.; *c:* Joseph F. Richard III, Boroskie J. Richard; *ed:* (BS) Home Ec, Southern Univ 1960; (MAT) General Sci, IN Univ 1971; (MAT) Physics, Loyola & Cornell Univ 1973; Bio, Dillard Univ 1966; Astronomy, Univ of S MS 1978, Tulane Univ 1968-69; Cmptr, St Bernard Comm 1978; Nuclear Physics, LA St Univ 1969; Thermodynamics, Delgado Jr Coll 1983; Earth Sci, Nicholls St 1970; *cr:* Home Ec Teacher Paul L Dunbar HS 1960, Phyllis Wheatley HS 1962-63, J S Clark HS 1963-64; Phys/General Sci Teacher A J Bell Jr HS 1965-; *ai:* 4-H Club Spon; Orleans Parish 4-H Advisory Cncl & LA Cooperative Extension Service Chairperson; Textbook Adoption & Local/St Curr Guides Comm; NSTA 1969-; LA Sci Teachers Assn (Secy, Treas); United Teacher of New Orleans Teacher of Yr 1982; Alpha Kappa Alpha 1958-; Aviations Creative Educators of Sci 1989-; New Light Baptist Church Bible Teacher 1981-; Shell Merit Fellow Cornell Univ 1970; Articles Published; *home:* 2127 St Maurice Ave New Orleans LA 70117

LEONARD, CAROLE AUSTIN, Mathematics Teacher; *b:* Nanty Glo, PA; *m:* Daniel J. Jr.; *c:* Daniel III, Carole M., Rita, Maria, Neil; *ed:* (BS) Math, St Francis Coll 1959; *cr:* Math Teacher Saltsburg HS 1959-62, Blacklick Valley Jr/Sr HS 1978-; *ai:* NHS Advisory Bd; NEA, PSEA, BVEA 1987-; *office:* Blacklick Valley Jr/Sr HS 555 Birch St Nanty Glo PA 15943

LEONARD, CHERYL L., Mathematics Teacher; *b:* Weatherford, OK; *m:* Gary M.; *c:* Leslie, Cara, Stacey; *ed:* (BS) Math, 1974, (MED) 1988 SW Ok St Univ; *cr:* Math Teacher Washita Heights HS 1974-75; Adjunct Instr SW OK St Univ 1980, 1981, 1986, 1990; Math Teacher Weatherford HS 1987-; *ai:* Stu Cncl Adv; Illyria Club Recording Secy 1987-88; Weatherford HS Teacher of Yr 1988-89; *office:* Weatherford HS 1500 Washington Weatherford OK 73096

LEONARD, CYNTHIA CAIN, Fourth Grade Teacher; *b:* Fairmont, WV; *m:* Michael Allan; *c:* Amanda D., Adam M.; *ed:* (BA) Elem Ed, Fairmont St Coll 1980; (MA) Elem Ed, WV Univ 1983; Post Grad Stud Elem Ed WV Univ; *cr:* 4th/5th Grade Teacher Fleming Sch 1980-84; 4th Grade Teacher Watson Elem Sch 1984-; *ai:* Watson Sch Soc Stud Fair, Math Field Day Competition Comms; PTA, Marion Cty Rdng Assn, WV Ed Assn, NEA 1980-; United Meth Temple Church Mem 1958-; *office:* Watson Elem Sch Mary Lou Retton Dr Fairmont WV 26554

LEONARD, ELIZABETH V. ADAMS, Science Department Chairman; *b:* Anderson, IN; *c:* Hillary E., Trevor T., Tyler R.; *ed:* (BA) Bio Ed, Univ of Indpls 1977; (MS) Bio Ed, Butler Univ 1983; *cr:* Sci Teacher Woodview Jr Hs 1977-80; Sci Dept Chairperson Hamilton Southeastern HS 1980-; Ed Lecturer Marian Coll 1985-; *ai:* Sr Class Spon; Sci Dept Chairperson; Sci Club Spon; Coaching; North Cntrl Evaluation Sch & Cmmty Chairperson; Long Range Planning Facility Inventory Comm Chairperson; Curr Comm; Hoosier Assn of Sci Teachers 1980-; NEA 1977-; IN St Teachers Assn 1977-; GSA Mount Vernon Trails Service Units Nominating Comm 1989-91; Selected Teacher Study Various Teaching Methods in Bio Purdue Univ 1985; *home:* 618 Holiday Dr Fortville IN 46040

LEONARD, GAIL MC DANIEL, 2nd Grade Teacher; *b:* Middlesboro, KY; *m:* Stanley H.; *ed:* (BA) Eng, 1975; (BS) Elem Ed, 1978; (MS) Curr & Instruction, 1987 Lincoln Memorial Univ; *cr:* 2nd Grade Teacher TNT Primary Sch 1975-86; Sndry Eng Teacher Claiborne Cty HS 1986-87; 2nd Grade Teacher TNT Primary Sch 1987-; *ai:* Homework Hotline; Curr Dev in Rdng; Spon Child Brazil Chrstn Childrens Fund; Claiborne Cty Ed Assn 1975-; East TN Ed Assn 1975-; NEA 1975-; Natl Geographics Society Men 1985-; Green Peace Mem 1989-; Humane Society 1986-; Amer Cancer Society 1982-; Career Ladder Level III Status TN Career Ladder Prgm Highest Level Achievement; *home:* 415 Russell Rd S New Tazewell TN 37825

LEONARD, JANET EDINGER, Fifth Grade Teacher/Cmptr Chm; *b:* Lima, OH; *m:* Michael Jan; *c:* Pamela S.; *ed:* Elem Ed, Bluffton Coll 1965; Learning Styles, Cmptr Ed, Helping Children with Learning Differences, Counseling, Wright St Univ; *cr:* 4th/5th Grade Teacher Cory-Rawson Bd of Ed 1958-60; 4th Grade Teacher Port Clinton Bd of Ed 1960-65, Lima City Bd of Ed 1965-69; 4th-6th Grade Teacher Shawnee Bd of Ed 1969-; *ai:* Cmptr Camp Dir; Quiz Bowl Coach; Cmptr Curr Comm; OH Ed Assn, NEA 1959-; Shawnee Ed Assn (Negotiations Comm 1989-) 1970-; GSA Leader 1962-65, 1979-84; Luth Church (Sunday Sch Teacher 1965-, Luther League Leader 1988-); Martha Holden Jennings Scholar Awd 1984-85; *home:* 3827 Meadowview Dr Lima OH 45805

LEONARD, JEANNE EBELEIN, 6th Grade Teacher; *b:* Lexington, NC; *m:* C. Perry; *c:* Heather; *ed:* (BA) Span/His, Meredith Coll 1968; *cr:* Span Teacher East Davidson HS 1968-71; 6th Grade Teacher Pilot Elem 1971-79, E L Brown Mid Sch 1979-; *ai:* NC Cncl of Teachers of Math; Charity League 1987-; TFI Grant; *office:* E Lawson Brown Jr H S 1140 Kendall Mill Rd Thomasville NC 27360

LEONARD, JUDITH ESSEX, 6th Grade Teacher; *b:* Providence, RI; *m:* Gerry W.; *c:* Gerry, Julie Ann; *ed:* (BA) Eng, 1963, (MED) Ed, 1984 Univ of RI; Grad Stud; *cr:* 4th Grade Teacher N Kingstown Sch Dept 1963-65; 6th Grade Teacher 1973-, Elem Math Coord 1982- Narragansett Schls; *ai:* 5th/6th Grade Math Competitions; URI Comm; RI Math Teachers Elem Bd 1989-; NCTM 1989-; NEA NARRA Treas 1984-86; Town of N Kingstown Planning Bd 1984-89; Affordable Housing Comm N Kingstown 1989-; Southern RI Math Teacher of Yr 1990; K-3rd Grade Math Specialist Exxon Grant; NSF Sci Fellowship 1988-, 21st Century Math Project 1990; RIMTA Elem Math Appointee to Bd 1989-; *office:* Narragansett Schls 55 Mumford Rd Narragansett RI 02882

LEONARD, MARGARET JEAN, Business Teacher; *b:* Rolla, ND; *m:* Charles; *c:* Nicole R., James C.; *ed:* (BS) Eng/Bus Ed, Minot St Univ 1969; *cr:* Eng Teacher Belcourt HS 1969-73; Owner Leonards Accounting 1972-78; Bus Instr Turtle Mountain Comm Coll 1986-87; Bus Teacher Belcourt HS 1987-; *ai:* FBLA & Soph Class Adv; NBEA, NEA 1987-; Whos Who in Amer Coll & Univs; *office:* Belcout HS Box 440 Belcourt ND 58316

LEONARDO, MICHAEL JOSEPH, Mathematics Teacher; *b:* Syracuse, NY; *m:* Judith A.; *c:* Susan, Thomas, Michael, Andrew, Paul; *ed:* (BS) Physics, St Univ Oswego 1965; (MS) Math Ed, Syracuse Univ 1969; *cr:* Teacher 1966-76, Math Chm 1970-76 Bishop Ludden HS; Math Chm West Hill HS 1978-85; Instr Adjunct Onon Comm Coll 1970-; *ai:* HS Academic Decathlon Coach; NYSYT, OCMTA 1966-; NSF 1970; Outstanding Amer Educator 1972; *home:* 421 Ontario Ave Syracuse NY 13209

LEONG, ROSE LEE, Second Grade Chairman; *b:* Honolulu, HI; *c:* Karen J. Leong Faran, Ann-Marie M.; *ed:* (BS) Recreation, 1958, Certificate Elem Ed, 1960 Univ of HI; UCLA Grad Sch; *cr:* Teacher Ewa Beach Elem 1960-62, Mokapu Elem 1962-63, Lincoln Elem; *ai:* HI Fed of Teachers, HI St Teachers Assn 1972-; Moanalua Valley Assn 1963-80; Moanalua HS 1960-64.

LEONHARDT, ROSE MARIE LEONARDO, Drama Teacher; *b:* Brooklyn, NY; *m:* Walter; *c:* Erich; *ed:* (BS) Elem Ed, St Johns Univ 1964; Various In-Service Wkshps & Courses; *cr:* Title I Rdng/Math Teacher Elmont Schls 1976-80; Title I Rdng Teacher Barton Elem 1980-82; Rdng/Eng/Drop Out Prevention/Drama Teacher Crestwood Mid Sch 1982-; *ai:* Drama Club Spon & Coach; Morale & Adv Advisee Comm; Palm Beach Cty Rdng Cncl Recording Secy 1983-84; The Henry Morrison Flagler Museum Guides Assn (Life Mem, Charter Mem); Palm Beach Cty Cncl of Arts Mem; YMCA Repertory Theater 1975; Teacher of Month Crestwood Mid Sch 1988.

LEPAK, NORMA GRIFFITH, 5th Grade Teacher; *b:* Denver, CO; *c:* Marc Childs, Robin Childs, Kimberly Childs, Joe Childs; *ed:* (BA) Elem Ed, Amer Univ of Beirut 1959; (MA) Elem Ed, Univ of N CO Greeley 1967; Univ of AK; Univ of WA; AK Pac Univ; *cr:* Teacher Anchorage Sch Dist 1959-; *ai:* Cross Cntry Ski Club; Downhill Ski Prgm; Delta Kappa Gamma 1970-; PTA 1959-; IRA, ACTM 1970-75; Anchorage Writing Prgm 1987-; Nordic Ski Club 1971-81; Prospectors Club 1989; Graphics Art Project Co-Spon; *home:* Box 7700-10 Eagle River AK 99577

LEPORATI, DEBRA ANN, English Teacher; *b:* New York, NY; *ed:* (BS) Elem Ed/Eng Ed, St Univ of NY Oneonta 1985; (MS) Scndry Eng Ed, St Univ of NY New Paltz 1988; Various Conferences, Wkshps & Inservice Courses; *cr:* 7th/8th Grade Eng Teacher 1985-, House Leader 1987- Warwick Valley Mid Sch; SAT Prep Course Teacher Warwick Valley HS 1989-; *ai:* Cty Spelling Contest Scorer; Honors & Mid Sch Reorganization Comms; 7th/8th Grade Eng Honors & Spelling Contest Coord; WV Teachers Assn, NYS United Teachers, Amer Fed of Teachers 1985-; Warwick Valley PTA 1985-; *office:* Warwick Valley Mid Sch PO Drawer E Warwick NY 10990

LEPPALUOTO, MIKAEL EDWARD, 6th Grade Teacher; *b:* Berkeley, CA; *m:* Shirlee Jean Palesotti; *c:* Jason, Jessica; *ed:* (BA) Soc Sci/Eng, Pacific Luth Univ 1967; (MA) Ed, Northern MI Univ 1970; *cr:* 6th Grade Teacher Gilbert Elem Sch 1967-85; 7th Grade Math/Eng Teacher Gwinn Mid Sch 1985-86; 6th Grade Teacher Gilbert Elem Sch 1986-; *ai:* Head Coach-Varsity Tennis Gwinn HS; MI Educl Assn 1967-; Gwinn Educl Assn 1967-; Grace Lutheran Church; MI St Teacher of Yr Finalists 1981-82; *home:* 246 S River Dr Gwinn MI 49841

LE RAY, JUNE SMITH, Dept Chair of Languages; *b:* Hornell, NY; *m:* Donald B.; *ed:* (BA) Latin, Alfred Univ 1956; Grad Work Alfred Univ, St Bonaventure Univ, Ithaca Coll, Geneseo SUNY; *cr:* Latin/Eng Teacher Avoca Cntrl Sch 1956-62; Lang Chairperson/Latin Teacher Haverling Cntrl Sch 1962-; *ai:* Natl Jr Classical League Convention Adv, Chm 1985-87; Haverling Cntrl Sch Latin Club Adv; Mem NY St Latin Regents Testing Comm; Delta Kappa Gamma (Pres 1972-74) 1966-; Classical Assn of Empire St (Nominations Chairprson 1982-89) 1956-; NY St United Teachers Assn; Amer Classical League (Executive Cncl 1985-87) 1956-; Bath Country Club (Bd of Dir, Womens Assn Pres 1976-78) 1969-; Bath Womens Bowling Assn Pres 1956-; Full Tuition Schlsp Alfred Univ; Mem 5-87; Full Tuition Schlsp Alfred Univ; Item Writer Regents Examinations; NY St Jr Classical League Chm 1972-76; *office:* Haverling Cntrl Sch Ellas Ave Bath NY 14810

LE RETTE, JACQUELINE ANN (SCHMITT), Fourth Grade Teacher; *b:* Streator, IL; *m:* Dale A.; *c:* V. Shawn, Michael A., Melanie A.; *ed:* (BS) Elem Ed, IL St Univ 1974; *cr:* 1st Grade Teacher 1976-77, 5th Grade Teacher 1977-79, 2nd Grade Teacher 1979-80, 1st Grade Teacher 1980-83, 4th Grade Teacher 1983- Woodland Unit #5; *ai:* 5th-8th Grade Literary Coach; Discipline, Playground, Positive Reinforcement Comm; IEA, NEA 1976-; Woodland Teachers Assn Building Rep 1976-; *office:* Woodland Unit #5 Sch R R 2 Streator IL 61364

LESHER, ANN WINTER, Music Educator; *b:* Fairfield, IA; *m:* Robert R.; *c:* Robert R., Richard H., Ruth Lesher Walser; *ed:* (BA) Music, Univ of Houston 1966; (MA) Curr Construction, 1974, Admin Curr Construction, 1975 Concordia Univ; Working Towards Certificate Advance Stud/Counseling; *cr:* Choir Dir/ Organist Our Saviors Luth Church Tyler TX 1956-58; Choir Dir Faith Luth Church Evansville IN 1958-62; Music Teacher Houston Ind Sch Dist 1966-67; Music Educator Itasca Sch Dist #10 1967-; *ai:* Choral Dir Concert & Swing Choirs; Report Card, Curr, Teacher Evaluation Comm; Ed Assn of Itasca (Pres, Chief Negotiator); Sigma Alpha Iota Alumni Pres 1959-60; Reorganized Sigma Alpha Iota Music Univ of Houston; Honorary Teacher of Yr St of IL 1978.

LESHER, CURTIS ALAN, Guidance Counselor; *b:* Chicago, IL; *m:* Jane Harriet Hanover; *c:* Andrew, Jordan; *ed:* (BA) Psych, Grove City Coll 1974; (MS) Mental Health Counseling, Wright St Univ 1982; (MA) Pastoral Psych/Counseling, Ashland Theology Seminary 1984; *cr:* 7th/8th Grade Math Teacher New Carlisle-Bethel Local Schls 1976-82; Ind/Marriage/Family Cnslr Ashland Guidance Center 1983-84; Family Cnslr Richland Hospital 1984-86; Guidance Cnslr Ontario Local Schls; *ai:* Soph Class Adv; Substance Abuse Coord; Kappa Delta Pi 1986-87; OFT, AFT 1986-; Drug Free Schls Grant 1987-; *office:* Ontario HS 467 Shelby Ontario Rd Mansfield OH 44906

LESINSKI, JEROME CARL, Teacher; *b:* Buffalo, NY; *m:* Beverly Anne Scilingo; *c:* Nicole M., Mark C.; *ed:* (BA) Sociology, 1970, (MED) Soc Stud, 1972 St Univ of NY Buffalo; Grad Stud; *cr:* Teacher West Seneca Cntrl Schls 1970-; *ai:* West Seneca Cntrl Employees Federal Credit Union Pres 1984-; Soc Stud Dept Chm Allendale Jr HS 1981-87; *office:* West Seneca W Jr HS 395 Center Rd West Seneca NY 14224

LESKO, JOSEPH P., English Teacher; *b:* United, PA; *ed:* (BA) Sociology/Eng, St Vincent Coll 1962; (MA) Eng, VA Polytech Inst 1968; (MED) Spec Ed, IN Univ of PA 1982; ABD Status in Rhetoric IN Univ of PA; W PA Writing Project Fellow; *cr:* Teacher Mt Pleasant Area Schls 1962-; *ai:* NCTE, PCTE; Kappa Delta Pi; *office:* Mt Pleasant Area HS RD 4 Box 2222 Mount Pleasant PA 15666

LESLEY, SHARON KNIPSTEIN, Lang Art/Gifted Teacher; *b:* Lampasas, TX; *m:* Royce Gene; *c:* Alan B., Nathan E.; *ed:* (BS) Elem Ed, 1969, (MA) Ed, 1972 Tarleton St Univ; Advanced Trng; *cr:* 3rd Grade Teacher Paducah TX 1969-70; 1st-4th Grade Teacher Morgan Mill TX 1970-72; 6th Grade Teacher 1972-74, 7th/8th Grade Teacher 1974- De Leon TX; *ai:* Stu Teacher Supvr; Mentor Teacher; Stu Advisory Cncl Adv; TX St Teachers Assn (Secy, 1st VP); Delta Kappa Gamma (2nd VP, Pres); *office:* Perkins Mid Sch PO Box 256 De Leon TX 76444

LESLIE, ANGELA MC CLAIN, Migrant Education Teacher; *b:* Fort Payne, AL; *m:* Larry Marvin; *ed:* (BA) Northeast Jr Coll 1975; (BS) Phys Ed/Eng, Jacksonville Univ 1978; (MA) Phys Ed, Univ of AL Birmingham 1980; *cr:* Eng/Phys Ed Teacher Adamsburg Jr HS 1978-86; Migrant Ed Teacher Ruhama Jr HS 1986-; *ai:* Jr HS Girls Bsktbl Coach; Yrbk, Pageant, Jr Prom Spon; Alpha Delta Kappa ADK Week Media Chm 1988-; Cedar Bluff 1st United Meth Church Comm Dir 1989-; Summer Migrant Conference; Womens Intnl Honorary Teacher; *home:* Rt 2 Box 97 Cedar Bluff AL 35959

LESLIE, LEE K., Physical Education Teacher; *b:* Great Falls, MT; *:* Jill T.; *c:* Kenny, Jake; *ed:* (BA) Sociology/Phys Ed, S UT St 1985; *cr:* Head Swim Coach 1985-86, Head Bsbl Coach 1986-, Head Ftbl Coach 1987- Tooele HS; *ai:* UT AAA Region 6 Bsbl Rep 1989, Ftbl Rep 1988; UT AAA All Star Bsbl Head Coach 1990; Teacher of Month 1988; Nom Tooele Sch Dist Teacher of Yr 1988-; *home:* 433 Salton Tooele UT 84074

LESLIE, MARGARET MARY, HM, Mathematics Teacher; *b:* Youngstown, OH; *ed:* (BSED) Math/educl Media, Youngstown St Univ 1982; Working towards Masters in Bus Admin, John Carroll Univ; *cr:* 7th/8th Grade Teacher St Brendan 1982; Math Teacher Magnificat HS 1982-84; Financial Asst Rosemary Center 1986-87; Math Teacher Erieview Cath HS 1987-; *ai:* Stu Cncl Moderator; Asst Sftbl Coach; Mission Effectiveness Team, Campus Ministry Team & Faculty Soc Comm Mem; Greater Cleveland Assn of Math Teachers 1988-; *office:* Erieview Cath HS Villa Maria Community Center Villa Maria PA 16155

LESNAU, GARY STEPHEN, HS Social Studies Teacher; *b:* San Francisco, CA; *m:* Donna Irene Wyman; *c:* Thomas, Tracy; *ed:* (BA) His, Univ of MI Ann Arbor 1974; Eng, Univ of MI Dearborn 1976; Ec Schlsp, Albion Coll; Substance Abuse Cert for Assisting HS Stus With Dependencies; *cr:* 8th Grade Eng Lit Teacher Sts Peter & Paul Elem 1974-78; Soc Stud Teacher Divine Child HS 1978-; *ai:* Congressional Seminar Coord; Pocket Billiards Club Moderator; Faculty Rep Chm Fact Finding Comm; Intramurals & Capitalist Club Dir; Close Up Moderator; NCEA Membership 1974-; NCSS Membership 1984-; Smithsonian Assoc Club Membership 1986-; Dearborn Hts Precinct Delegate 1989-; Amer Assn of Individual Investors Mem 1989-; Mathias Club Mem 1986-; Amer Pool Players Assn 1984-; Moose Club 1979-, St Doubles Pool Champion 1989; Candidate for Sch Bd Crestwood Sch Dist 1989; *home:* 5651 Charlesworth Dearborn Hgts MI 48127

LESPIER, LEYINSKA, English Teacher; *b:* Caguas, PR; *m:* Ivan Torres Sosa; *c:* Ginky-Lee Torres, Ivan E. Torres, Armando Torres; *ed:* (BA) Eng, CAAM 1976; Microcomputers, Eng, Math Instruction Values Course; *cr:* 10th-12th Grade Bi-ling Eng Teacher 1979-82, 12th Grade Eng Teacher 1982-83, 10th Grade Eng Teacher 1983-84 Luis M Marin HS; 7th-9th Grade Teacher Pedro N Colberg Jr HS 1984-; *ai:* Lions Club.

LESSARD, LOIS P., Fifth Grade Teacher; *b:* Quincy, MA; *m:* Bruce; *c:* Lesa, Katherine Touafek; *ed:* (BA) Elem Sci, Bridgewater Coll 1970; Courses Lesley Coll; *cr:* 5th Grade Teacher Easton 1970-; *ai:* Mem of Team to Present Mid Sch Philosophy & Acad Structure for Parents; Gifted & Talented Stus Academic Prgm Mem 1987-89; Planning Bd Mem 1979-83; NESDEC Adv; *office:* Middle Sch Lincoln St North Easton MA 02375

LESSENBERRY, KAREN OXLEY, Social Studies Teacher; *b:* Pontiac, MI; *m:* Jack William Jr.; *ed:* (BA) European His, Oakland Univ 1964; (MA) European/Russian His, Cntrl MI Univ 1970; *cr:* Soc Stud Teacher Northeast Intermediate 1964-65, Jefferson Intermediate 1965-66, Groves HS 1966-; *ai:* Stu Government Adv; Comm Against Racial Exploitation Spon; Birmingham Ed Assn, MI Ed Assn 1966-; *office:* Wylie E Groves HS 20500 W 13 Mile Birmingham MI 48010

LESTER, BETTYE PLUMMER, Fourth Grade Teacher; *b:* Fort Worth, TX; *m:* Billy L.; *c:* Michael L., Terry K.; *ed:* (BS) Elem Ed, TX Womens Univ 1968; Audio Visual, Advanced Academic Trng; *cr:* Teacher Keller Ind Sch Dist 1968-; *ai:* TX St Teachers Assn 1968-75; Assn of TX Prof Educators 1976-; PTA Historian, Pin & Certificate 1960; Keller Garden Club (Reporter 1956-64); Keller Study Club 1958-64; TX PTA Honorary Life Membership 1988; Keller Ind Sch Dist Appreciation Awd 1988 & 50 10, 15, 20 Yr Service Awd; *office:* Florence Elem Sch 3095 Johnson Rd Southlake TX 76092

LESTER, J. DAVID, Mathematics Department Chair; *b:* Pikesville, KY; *m:* Judy Herron; *c:* Amanda; *ed:* (BS) Math, Pikesville Coll 1971; (MA) Scndry Ed 1981, (EDS) Ed Admin & Supervision, 1988 Morehead St Univ; *cr:* Adjunct Faculty Pikeville Coll 1982-83; Math Instr Belfry HS 1971-; ADjunct Faculty S WV Comm CoLL 1971-; NCTM 1985-; KASCD Field Rep 1988-; *office:* Belfry HS PO Box 160 Belfry KY 41514

LESTER, JOAN (NIKOLAI), Scndry Social Studies Teacher; *b:* Madison, MN; *m:* James Earl; *c:* Robert, Angela; *ed:* (BA) Fr/Soc Stud, Mt Mary Coll 1965; (MSW) Social Work, Univ of MN Minneapolis 1976; *cr:* Teacher Totino-Grace HS 1968-73; Disposition Adv Hennepin Cty Public Defender Office 1975-78; Sch Soc Work/Teacher De La Salle HS 1976-79; Soc Worker Bello Group Homes 1979-84; Teacher Bigfork HS 1984-; *ai:* Stu Cncl & Annual Staff Adv; Close-Up Club Coord; MN Cncl for Soc Stud 1986-89; ACLU 1980-; Project MN Leon 1984-; Greenpeace 1986-; Invented & Marketed Educl Game; *office:* Bigfork HS PO Box 228 Bigfork MN 56628

LESTER, LOU ANN (WIGHT), Fifth Grade Teacher; *b:* Glendale, CA; *m:* Douglas Warren; *c:* Robert, Melinda Cheetham, Jon, Karey, Dean; *ed:* (AA) Liberal Arts, Stephens Coll 1958; (BA) Elem Ed, Univ of MO 1960; Various Univs; *cr:* 2nd Grade Teacher 1970-71, 1st/2nd Grade Teacher 1971-72, 5th/6th Grade Teacher 1973-74, 4th Grade Teacher 1981-82, 3rd/4th Grade Teacher 1982-84, 1st Grade Teacher 1984-85 Ruth Brown Sch; 5th/6th Grade Teacher of Gifted & Talented 1985-86, 4th/5th Grade Teacher 1987-89, 5th Grade Teacher 1989- Margaret White Sch; *ai:* Supts Advisory Cncl; Chairperson CO Cntry Fair Writing Competition; St Prgm Quality Review Leadership Team; 5th Grade Chairperson; Palo Verde Unified Sch Dist Lang Art Comm; Delta Kappa Gamma 1988-; Palo Verde Valley 4-H Club Leader 1973-86; Teacher of Yr Ruth Brown Sch & Palo Verde Unified Sch Dist 1984; Riverside Cty Teacher of Yr Honorable Mention 1984; *office:* Margaret White Elem Sch 201 N 1st St Blythe CA 92225

LESTER, RODNEY GARNET, 7th Grade Teacher; *b:* Drill, VA; *m:* Marilyn Matherly; *c:* Scot; *ed:* (BA) Elem Ed, Clinch Valley Coll 1972; *cr:* 5th Grade Teacher 1972-73, 7th Grade Teacher 1973- Swords Creek Elem; *ai:* Little League Coach; NEA, VEA 1985-.

LESTER, VIRGINIA MASTERS, Fifth Grade Teacher; *b:* Livingston, MT; *m:* Von; *c:* Julie; *ed:* (BS) Elem Ed, Stephen F Austin Univ 1972; (ME) Rdng, Univ of TX Tyler 1979; Gifted & Talented Ed; *cr:* Upper Elem Teacher Bullard Elem Sch 1973-; *ai:* Stu Newsletter Supvr; Oral Rdng UIL Coach; *office:* Bullard Elem Sch PO Box 250 Bullard TX 75757

LETA, FRANCES BANAS, Asst Headmaster for Humanities; *b:* Norwich, CT; *m:* Louis P. Jr.;; *c:* L. Paul III, Maureen E.; *ed:* (BS) Eng, (MS) Eng, E CT St Coll; Intermediate Cert Univ of CT; Undergrad Stud Journalism, Univ of CT & Columbia; *cr:* Part-Time Eng Lecturer E CT St Coll 1980-82, Mohegan Comm Coll 1981-88; Eng/Soc Stud/Rdng Teacher Norwich Free Acad 1958-; *ai:* Teacher Supvr; Jr Class Admin Liaison; Writing Center, Sch Newspaper, Yrbk Consultant; NCTE, CT Cncl Teacher of Eng, NEA, CEA; NFA Ed Assn (Past Secy, Adivsory Committeewoman); Kappa Delta Pi, Delta Kappa Gamma (Recording Secy, VP); Bus & Prof Womens Club; Prof Bus Womens Assn Woman of Yr 1984; Norwich Hospital Auxiliary VP; Norwich Coll Club Past Pres; Norwich Rose Arts Bd of Dirs; CT Scholastic Press Assn Past Secy; Sacred Heart Guild Lay Minister; Sr League Girls Sftbl (Coach, Mgr); Columbia Scholastic Press Assn Former Pres; Whos Who Amoung Stus in Amer Coll 1958; Scholastic Magazine Outstanding Teacher of Writing; Ran Spelling Bee 1982-88; Wkshps Participant; *office:* Norwich Free Acad 305 Broadway Norwich CT 06360

LETCHER, GAIL EDWARD, Fifth Grade Teacher; *b:* Taylorville, IL; *m:* Darlene Ann Wiegard; *c:* Hilary, Andrea, Adam; *ed:* (BS) Ed, E IL Univ 1971; (MS) Ed, S IL Univ 1987; *cr:* 5th Grade Teacher Red Bud Elem Sch 1971-; *ai:* Sts Peter & Paul Sch Jr HS Girls Bsktbl Coach; Red Bud Ed Assn (Regional Cncl 1975-76, Legislative Chairperson 1981-); *office:* Red Bud Elem Sch 200 Field Dr Red Bud IL 62278

LETCHFORD, ROY L., Mathematics Teacher; *b:* Waterloo, IA; *m:* Sherry L. Carter; *c:* Joshua C.; *ed:* (BA) Math Teaching, Univ of N IA 1969; Various Stud; *cr:* Math Teacher Spirit Lake Cmmty Schls 1969-70, Camanche Cmmty Schls 1970-; *ai:* Wrestling Coach; Math Contest Spon; Staff Dev Comm; Park & Recreation Comm Chm 1986-88; *office:* Camanche Cmmty Sch 1400 9th St Camanche IA 52730

LETHERBY, FRANK EDWARD, 6th Grade Teacher; *b:* Traverse City, MI; *m:* Nancy; *c:* Mike, Frank, Cindy; *ed:* (BS) Elem Ed, Cntrl MI Univ 1960; (MA) Admin, Univ of MI 1963; (EDS) Admin/Personnel, MI St Univ 1968; *cr:* Teacher Monroe Public Schls 1960-1963; Teacher/Prin East Grand Rapids Public Schls 1964-; *ai:* Stu Cncl Intramural Spon; Mid Sch Bsktbl Coach; MI Ed Assn 1963-; NEA 1963-; MI Assn Mid Schl Educators 1983-; *office:* E Grand Rapids Mid Sch 2425 Lake Dr S E Grand Rapids MI 49506

LETHGO, LINDA DAYE, Fifth Grade Teacher; *b:* Ravenna, KY; *ed:* (BA) Ed, Berea Coll 1962; IN Univ; Brigham Young Univ; Miami Univ; Univ of Dayton; *cr:* 5th Grade Teacher Mayfield Elem 1962-; *ai:* Teacher Rep PTO; Proficiency Testing Comm Middletown Sch Sys; Middletown Teachers Assn; NEA; OH Ed Assn; Southwestern OH Ed Assn; Who's Who in Amer Ed 1988-89; Delta Kappa Gamma Mem; Phi Delta Kappa Mem; Middletown Teachers' Assn (Former Corresponding Sec 2 Terms; Former Bldg Rep; Former Mem Teachers Ed/Prof Standards, Former Chm Balloting Comm); *office:* Mayfield Elem Schl 3325 Burbank St Middletown OH 45044

LETNER, AL C., Art Teacher; *b:* Kileen, TX; *m:* Diane M. Blessant; *c:* Joshua, Ian; *ed:* (BS) Art Ed/His, Pittsburg St Univ 1976; *cr:* HS Soc Stud/Art Teacher Wheaton R-1 Schls 1976-77; HS Art Teacher Carl Junction R-1 Schls 1979-; *ai:* Campus Artists Spon; North Cntrl Assn HS Steering Comm Mem; SW Dist Art Teachers Assn Mem 1986-; Little Balkans Review Editorial Bd Mem 1989-; Ceramics & Sculpture Wkshps Presenter; Art Work Exhibits PAACA Gallery 1987, 1990; *office:* Carl Junction R-1 Schls Box 4 W Allen St Carl Junction MO 64834

LETT, ROSA STANTON, 6th Grade Teacher; *b:* Tunnel Springs, AL; *m:* Eddie Arnold; *c:* Eddie D., Tanya L., Candace Y.; *ed:* (BS) Elem Ed, AL St Univ 1972; *cr:* Kndgtn Teacher Millers Ferry HS 1972-75, Tates Chapel 1975-76; 6th/7th Grade Math/Rdng Teacher Frisco City HS 1976-78; 6th Grade Teacher Frisco Elem 1978-; *ai:* NEA, AEA, MCTA; *office:* Frisco City Elem Sch PO Box 160 Frisco City AL 36445

LETTIERRE, ANGELA VALENTE, Third Grade Teacher; *b:* Cervinara, Italy; *m:* Anthony Michael; *c:* John A., Joseph G.; *ed:* (BS) Elem Ed, 1973, (MS) Spec Ed/Elem Ed, 1979 Coll of St Joseph; Castleton St Coll; Group Leader Trng for Self Esteem Groups; *cr:* Teacher Clarendon Elem Sch 1973-; *ai:* NEA Negotiator 1987-; VT Educl Assn Pres; Christ the King Church Religious Ed Instruction Volunteer 1989-; Appointed to Cert Appeals Comm St of VT 1979-81; *home:* R D 1 Box 3900 Rutland VT 05781

LETTON, GERALDINE ASHTON, 2nd Grade Teacher; *b:* Louisville, KY; *m:* Robert W.; *c:* Robert W. Jr., William C.; *ed:* (BA) Elem Ed, Emory Univ 1963, (MA) Ed, Morehead St Univ 1977; *cr:* Kndgtn Teacher LONDON KY 1969 70; Teacher Mount Sterling Elem 1972-75/1976- Mapleton Elem 1975-76; *ai:* Kea 1977-; Womans Civic Club; Nom Ashland Oil Teacher of Yr; Served As Mem of Review Teams of Sov Assn of Schls & Coll; *home:* 414 Hollow Creek Rd Mt Sterling KY 40353

LETTS, CINDY J. (LAUE), 5th Grade Teacher; *b:* Vincennes, IN; *m:* George R.; *c:* Jonas R., Nathaniel V.; *ed:* (BS) Elem Ed, 1977, (MS) Elem Ed, 1982 IN St Univ; Elem Counseling; Maintaining Teacher Effectiveness Teacher Trainer; *cr:* Cnslr Vincennes Univ 1977-80; 5th Grade Teacher 1980-83, 6th Grade Teacher 1983-86, 5th Grade Teacher 1986- Franklin Elem; *ai:* Mem & Chairperson-Phi Delta; Coord Gifted/Talented Prgm; Comm for Curr Dev; Volunteer Classroom & Supervising Teacher for Initial Experience Stu; Phi Delta Kappa Prgm Comm/Publicity Chairperson 1989-; Knox Cty Rdng Cncl (Vp 1986-87 Pres 1987-88); Amer Bus Women Assn Pres 1978 -80; Public Service Grant 1987-88; Nom for Golden Apple Awd 1987-88; *office:* Franklin Elem Sch 2600 Wabash Ave Vincennes IN 47591

LEUCHS, JOHN JAMES, JR., Elementary Teacher-Gifted; *b:* Greenwich, CT; *ed:* (BA) Elem Ed, Kean Coll 1969; (ma) Curr/Teaching, 1974, (MED) Curr/Instr Practice, 1981 Teachers Coll Columbia Univ; *cr:* Elem Teacher Hudson St Sch 1969-71, South Mountain Sch 1971-82, Jefferson Sch 1982-85; Teacher Gifted South Orange 1985-; *ai:* Mem Dist Math & Dist Gifted/Talented Comm; Co-developer Dist Curr for Grades 3-5; Mem MENSA; Essex Cty Steering Comm Gifted/Talented NJ Ed Assn; NCTM; Coalition Unity South Orange/Maplewood Chm Poly Action Comm 1985-87; Coorganizer South Orange-Maplewood Harmony Day 1986; Mem Comm Schls Task Force Promote Racial Harmony; Amer Civil Liberties Union; Natl Organization Women; Amnesty Intnl; Spon Save the Children; Created & Published Bd Games Math; Established Creative Educl Materials Company NY 1975; *office:* South Orange/Maplewood 525 Academy St Maplewood NJ 07040

LEUENBERGER, ROBERT CHARLES, Sixth Grade Teacher; *b:* Canton, OH; *m:* Victoria Lynn Strasser; *c:* Anne, Matt, Curtis; *ed:* (BSED) Elem Ed, Bowling Green St Univ 1976; *cr:* 3rd/4th Grade Teacher 1977-87, 6th Grade Teacher 1988- Pleasant Grove Elem; *ai:* Intramural & Frosh Girls Bsktbl Coach; OH Ed Assn; Jennings Scholar 1984-85; *office:* Pleasant Grove Elem Sch 9955 Louisville St N E Louisville OH 44641

LEUTHOLD, CHRISTOPHER JOHN, Mathematics Dept Chairman; *b:* Wauseon, OH; *ed:* (BSED) Math, Ashland Univ 1974; (MED) Admin, Bowling Green St Univ 1978; *cr:* Teacher Cory-Rawson Local Sch 1974-; *ai:* Girls Var Vlybl & Boys Jr Var Bsktbl Coach; Sr Class Adv; Prin Selection Comm; OHSVCA Dist Rep 1986-88; OHSVCA Mem 1984-; Bethel Church of Christ Sunday Sch Teacher 1980-; Cory-Rawson Teacher of Yr 1985; BVC Vlybl Coach of Yr 1985; *office:* Cory-Rawson HS 3930 Cty Rd 26 Rawson OH 45881

LEVANT, CHARLENE SCHWARTZ, Primary Teacher of Gifted; *b:* Chicago, IL; *m:* Richard S.; *c:* Karen J. Goodman, Mark; *ed:* (BA) Ed, Roosevelt Univ 1956; (MA) Spec Ed/Teaching Gifted, NE IL Univ 1985; Lib Sci, Admin, Supervision; *cr:* Teacher Marshall Elem 1956-58, Bateman Elem 1958-59, Hibbard Elem 1962-63; Teacher Gale Elem 1963-65, 1967-79, Burbank Elem 1979-; *ai:* Chorus; Recorder Ensemble Group; Chicago Teachers Union Delegate 1984-89; IL Cncl for Gifted 1981-; *office:* Luther Burbank Elem Sch 2035 Mobile Chicago IL 60639

LE VAR, PEARL ANN (KING), 6th Grade Teacher/Librarian; *b:* Henderson Cty, NC; *m:* Willie Randall; *ed:* (AA) Gardner-Webb Coll 1956; (BS) Ed/Psych, Carson-Newman Coll 1958; (MA) Ed/Public Sch Media, W Carolina Univ 1984; *cr:* 6th Grade Teacher Edneyville Elem Sch 1958-62; Clerk Army Ed Center 1963-65; 3rd Grade Teacher Dana Elem Sch 1965-66; 5th/6th Grade Remedial Rdng Teacher Govalle Elem Sch 1967-68; 4th Grade Teacher 1969-70, 3rd Grade Teacher 1970-72 SHAPE Amer Elem Sch; Substitute/5th Grade Teacher Lake Worth Elem Sch 1973; 6th Grade Lang Art Teacher Lily Hill Mid Sch 1974-76; 1st-6th Grade Remedial Math Teacher Howard II Elem Sch 1976-79; 6th Grade Teacher/Sch Librarian Tuxedo Elem Sch 1980-; *ai:* Media Advisory Comm; NEA, NCAE, Hendersonville Cty Assn of Educators Membership Chm 1985-89; NC Assn of Sch Librarians 1989-; Refuge Baptist Church (Librarian 1986-, Organist 1989-, Sunday Sch Teacher 1982-); *home:* Rt 6 Box 281A Hendersonville NC 28792

LEVELL, SUE KING, Social Studies Teacher; *b:* Evansville, IN; *m:* Gene; *c:* Angelique Hill, Rebecca S. Britton; *ed:* (BA) Soc Stud, Long Beach St 1957; (MAT) Amer His, IN Univ 1967; *cr:* Soc Stud Teacher Martinsville HS 1967-; *ai:* Academic Decathalon Coach; NHS Spon; Jail Study Comm; Phi Delta Kappa, IN Historical Society; Tri Kappa (Pres, Secy) 1964-; Jail Building Corporation Pres.

LEVENTHAL, SHEILA SMITH, 4th Grade Teacher/Team Leader; *b:* Raymondville, TX; *m:* Ira Yale; *c:* Adam; *ed:* (BS) Elem Ed, 1963, (MED) Elem Ed, 1965 Univ of North TX; Post Grad, Univ of North TX, Nova Univ; Logo Cmptr Trng, MIT; *cr:* Elem Teacher Grapevine Ind Schls 1963-65, Lamplighter Sch 1965-; *ai:* Team Leader; Sch Prgm, Sci, Rdng, Cmptr Steering Comm; Cmptr Camp; Women of St Francis VP 1986-87; Sch of Spirituality (Table Leader 1981-86, Dir 1989-); Computing Publication 1984; Whos Who of Amer Women 1984, 1985, 1987, 1988, 1990; Whos Who in the World 1984; *office:* Lamplighter Sch 11611 Inwood Rd Dallas TX 75229

LEVERETTE, JANNIE LEE (SMITH), Mathematics Dept Chairman; *b:* Greenwood, MS; *m:* Walter Norman; *c:* Monica R., Ursula L.; *ed:* (BSE) Elem Ed/Rdng/Math/Eng, Jackson St Univ 1973; (MA) Ed, Atlanta Univ 1975; Numerous Wkshps & Educl Trng Point Loma Coll; *cr:* Substitute Teacher Atlanta Public Sch Dist 1974; 1st-6th Grade Title I Rdng Prgm Teacher Tyrone Elem Sch 1974-75; 3rd Grade Teacher Crystal Springs Elem Sch 1975-76; Remedial Rdng Teacher General Joseph Finegan Elem 1977-78; Substitute Teacher Oceanside Unified Sch Dist 1982; Math Skills Reinforcement Teacher 1983-84, 7th-9th Grade Math Teacher 1984-85 Alexander G Bell Jr HS; 7th/8th Grade Math/World His/Amer His/Phys Sci/Life Sci Teacher 1985-86, Math/Pre-Algebra/Algebra I Teacher 1986- Jefferson Jr HS; *ai:* Math Tutor; Sch Leadership Team; Sch Site Cncl; Cmptr Technology, High Risk Stu, Greater San Diego Math Comm; Prgm Quality Review; Family Math; Natl Teacher Assn, CA Teacher Assn; OTA Grievance Comm; United Meth Church Crusade Schlsp 1974.

LEVI, JUDY STEWART, Sixth Grade Teacher; *b:* Chattanooga, TN; *m:* William Stuart; *c:* Amber M. Levi Batson; *ed:* (BS) Elem Ed, Univ of TN Chattanooga 1976; (MA) Admin/Supervision, TN Technological Univ 1984; *cr:* Kndgtn Teacher 1976-77, 1st Grade Teacher 1977-89, 6th Grade Teacher 1989- Soddy Elem; *ai:* Awds, Local Scholars, Scheduling Comm; Valentine Poetry Comm Chairperson; Hamilton Cty Ed Assn, TN Ed Assn, NEA 1976-; PTO Pres 1976-78, Schlsp; Chattanooga Adult Literacy Movement; Taught Adult Rdng; Sci Curr Channel 45; *home:* 11481 Holly Cir Soddy-Daisy TN 37379

LEVIN, DAVID, 3rd Grade Teacher; *b:* Philadelphia, PA; *m:* Linda; *c:* Sarah, Rebecca, Susannah; *ed:* (BS) Elem Ed, Univ of PA 1978; *cr:* 3rd/5th Grade Teacher Cranberry Pines Elem Sch 1978-; *ai:* Sch Liaison Comm Chm; Intramural Supervisory Asst; Medford Ed Assn (Exec Bd Mem 1987-, Assn Rep 1987-, Faculty Rep 1980-, Philanthropic Fund Trustee 1989-); Nom NJ Governors Awd 1988; *office:* Cranberry Pines Elem Sch 400 Fairview Rd Medford NJ 08055

LEVIN, VICTOR S., English Teacher; *b:* Philadelphia, PA; *c:* Robert, Traci; *ed:* (BS) Elem Ed, Cheyney St 1965; Grad Courses Temple Univ 1968; *cr:* Teacher Morrison Sch 1965-; *ai:* Drama Club Coach; PATHS Mem; Creative Writing Team & Faculty; ASCD Mem 1989-, Certicates 1989-; Nom Rose Lindenbaum Awd Outstanding Teacher 1989-; *office:* Morrison Sch 3rd & Duncannon Philadelphia PA 19120

LEVINE, ARLENE GAY, Teacher of Gifted Education; *b:* New York, NY; *m:* Alan; *ed:* (BA) Ed - Magna Cum Laude, Queens Coll 1969; (MA) Early Chldhd Ed, NY Univ 1971; Grad Stud Writing; *cr:* Early Chldhd Ed Teacher PS 48 1972-76; Elem Ed Teacher PS 133 1977; Gifted Ed Teacher PS 346 1977-; *ai:* Phi Beta Kappa, Kappa Delta Pi Natl Ed Honor Society 1968; Intnl Womens Writing Guild 1990; Haiku Society of America 1990; NY Times Company Fnd Schlshp Awd 1986; Honorable Mention Writers Digest Natl Screenwriting Comp; Published Articles; *office:* PS 346 1400 Pennsylvania Ave Brooklyn NY 11239

LEVINE, RONALD STUART, Superintendent/Prin/Teacher; *b:* Cleveland, OH; *m:* Suzin; *c:* Jason, Arthur, Elizabeth, Justin, Joshua; *ed:* (BS) Anthropology, CA St NorthRidge 1974; Ed, Fresno Pacific; *cr:* Playground Dir Los Angeles Unified 1972-74; Teacher Visalia Unified 1974-78; Supt/Prin Buena Vista Elem 1978-; *ai:* 4th-6th Grade Ftbl, Bsktbl, Soccer, Bsbl Coach; ACSA Regional Dir; Area Wide Admin Comm Pres 1978-; Tulare Noon Lions VP 1985-; Little League (Coach, Pres, Bd Mem) 1982-; Amer Youth Soccer Organization Coach 1978-; Awarded 2 Mini-Grants; Presenter Several Local Curr Conf; *office:* Buena Vista Elem Sch 21660 Rd 60 Tulare CA 93274

LE VISEUR, VIRGINIA LOUISE, 4th Grade Teacher/Chairperson; *b:* Youngstown, OH; *ed:* (BA) Ed, Univ of Dallas 1965; Various Academic Trng Courses Level III TX Career Ladder; *cr:* 3rd Grade Teacher J O Schultz 1965-66; 3rd/4th/5th Grade Teacher Brandenburg 1966-; *ai:* Safety Patrol Spon, 5th Grade Math Club Spon; Dist Math Comm, Dist Productivity Comm; ATPE (Pres 1980-81 & 1986-87, Treas 1989-) Local Teacher of Yr; PTA (Secy 1988-89, Treas 1989-90, Pres 1986-88 & 1990-); PTA Terrific Teacher Awd 1983; Assn of TX Prof Educators, Teacher of Yr 1986; *office:* John J. Brandenbury 2800 Hillcrest Dr Irving TX 75062

LEVORSON, RUTH HELEN, First Grade Teacher; *b:* Lake Mills, IA; *ed:* (BSE) Ed, Dr Martin Luther Coll 1965; *cr:* 1st-8th Grade Teacher Zum Kripplein Christi 1962-67, Zion 1967-70; 1st-2nd Grade Teacher 1970-74, 1st Grade Teacher 1974- Mt Olive; *ai:* Lib Adv; Musical Dir; SAT Mem; IRA, WSRA, NCTE.

LEW, ANN R., English Teacher; *b:* Yokohama, Japan; *m:* Kenneth; *c:* Kristin, Derek; *ed:* (BA) Sociology, Univ of CA Berkeley 1967; Ed, Univ of San Francisco 1970; San Francisco St Univ; Univ of CA Berkeley; *cr:* Teacher Balboa HS 1971-79, Lincoln HS 1980-82; Teacher/Cnslr Court Schls 1982-84; Teacher Burton HS 1984-; *ai:* Literary Magazine Spon; Faculty Cncl Mem; CA Assn Teachers of Eng 1990; Hum, Ed, Research, Lang Dev Project Mem 1990; Bay Area Writing Project Teacher Consultant 1990; Japanese-Amer Lib 1990; Project STAR San Francisco Mayors Office; *home:* 35 Watt Ave San Francisco CA 94112

LEW, LINDA CHIN, Teacher of Gifted Math; *b:* New Orleans, LA; *m:* Nging Wing; *c:* Donna, Dana, Kevin, Blaine, Erin; *ed:* (BS) Math Ed, Univ of New Orleans 1967; (MST) Math, Loyola Univ New Orleans 1988; *cr:* Math Teacher Joseph Kohn Jr HS 1967-68, John Kennedy HS 1968-69; Teacher of Gifted & Honors Math Benjamin Franklin HS 1981-; *ai:* Homecoming Act, Keyettes Girls Service Club, Key Club Spon; NCTM, LA Cmptr Using Educators, New Orleans Math Collaborative; Alpha Sigma Nu Loyola Coll; Woodrow Wilson Natl Sci & Math Leadership Prgm 1988-89; Internship at Southern Regional Research Lab USDA 1989.

LEWANDOWSKI, ROBERT GERALD, Teacher/Program Coordinator; *b:* Buffalo, NY; *ed:* (BS) Bus Ed/Ec, 1974, (MS) Ed, 1976 St Univ of NY Buffalo; Bryant & Stratton Bus Inst; *cr:* Accounting Clerk Niagara Mohawk Power Corporation 1968; US Army/Supply 25th Infantry Division USARHAW 1970-71; Teacher Buffalo Bd of Ed 1974-; *ai:* Acad of Finance Prgm Coord & Advisory Bd; Lafayette Sch Bookstore Adv; Financiers Club; BEAWNY Mem 1975-; Parent Cmmty Teachers Assn Faculty Adv 1979-85; Natl Acad Fnd Buffalo Prgm Coord 1986-; *office:* Lafayette HS 370 Lafayette Ave Buffalo NY 14213

LEWE, CHRISTOPHER KELLER, Fourth Grade Teacher; *b:* Trenton, NJ; *m:* Cynthia Kantack; *c:* Lindsay, Lauren; *ed:* (BFA) Comm, 1979, (MA) Elem Ed, 1981 Jacksonville Univ; *cr:* 4th Grade Teacher J Allen Axson Elem 1981-; *ai:* Cmptr Club Spon; J Allen Axson Teacher of Yr Awd 1990; *home:* 11519 Kelvyn Grove Pl Jacksonville FL 32225

LEWELLEN, SCOTT JAY, Earth Science Teacher; *b:* Jamestown, NY; *m:* Brenda Jean Eckwahl; *c:* Carrie, Beck, Todd; *ed:* (BA) Environmental Ed, Dartmouth Coll 1974; Various Institutions Toward Permanent Cert; *cr:* Teacher/Coach Randolph Cntrl SCh 1974-79; Management Trng Bankers Trust Corp 1979-80; Teacher/Coach Bemus Point Cntrl Sch 1980-; *ai:* Jr Class, Environmental Club Adv; Jr HS Boys Bsktbl Coach; Bemus Point United Meth Church Parsonage Comm Head 1985; Chautauqua Lake Assn 1984-; Nom Natl Sci Fnd Presidential Awd 1990; *office:* Bemus Point Cntrl Sch Dutch Hollow Rd Bemus Point NY 14712

LEWERS, SHARON FAE, Fifth Grade Teacher; *b:* Greenville, SC; *ed:* (BS) Elem Ed, SC St Coll 1980; *cr:* 5th Grade Teacher 1980-81, 3rd Grade Teacher 1981-82, 5th Grade Teacher 1982- Altama Elem Sch; *ai:* GA Assn of Educators Mem 1980-; Alpha Kappa Alpha Mem 1988-; St Paul Baptist Church Youth Dir Asst 1989-; Appointed by Prin as Steering Comm Mem for the 10 Yr Self Study at my Sch 1983-84; *office:* Altama Elem Sch 5505 Altama Ave Brunswick GA 31520

LEWIEN, KAREN WOODMAN, Third Grade Teacher; *b:* Syracuse, NY; *m:* John Robert; *c:* Kathryn E.; *ed:* (BA) Elem Ed/ Music, SUNY Fredonia 1970; (MS) Elem Ed, Syracuse Univ 1974; *cr:* Kndgtn/1st/3rd Grade Teacher Baldwinsville Acad & Cntrl Sch System 1970-; *ai:* Beta Sigma Phi; Teach Gourmet Cooking BOCES Trng Center; Church Organist & Choir Dir; NEANY Local Sch Rep 1970-; Beta Sigma Phi (Pres, Secy, Treas) 1975-, Sister of Yr 1978-81; *office:* Mc Namara Elem Sch O Brien Rd Baldwinsville NY 13027

LEWINSKI, PATRICIA ANN, Mathematics Teacher; *b:* Toledo, OH; *c:* Nathan, Nicholas; *ed:* (BE) Elem Ed, 1976, (MAST) Admin/Supervision, 1982 Toledo Univ; *cr:* Teacher Libbey HS 1976-; *ai:* Stu Government & Jr Class Adv; OCTM 1990; *office:* Libbey HS 1250 Western Ave Toledo OH 43609

LEWIS, ANDREA DEORIA, Fourth Grade Teacher; *b:* New Orleans, LA; *m:* Virgil D.; *c:* Alisha, Cameron; *ed:* (BA) Elem Ed/ Spec Ed/Emr, Univ of N CO 1980; Working Towards Masters in Remedial Rdng, Univ of N CO; *cr:* 5th/6th Grade Teacher Washington Park Elem 1980-84; 6th Grade Teacher Stedmen Elem 1982-84; 4th Grade Teacher Bromwell Elem 1984-; *ai:* Denver Classroom Teachers Assn; Omar Blair Outstanding Black Educator Awd 1990; *office:* Bromwell Elem Sch 2500 E 4th Ave Denver CO 80206

LEWIS, BABE ELAINE, 8th Grade Teacher; *b:* Chicago, IL; *c:* Heather; *ed:* (BA) Ed, Chicago St Univ 1964; (MS) Guidance/ Counseling, Roosevelt Univ 1975; Working on Master in Sci; Woodrow Wilson Fnd Math & Physics Summer Prgm 1989; *cr:* Teacher Lawless Upper Grade Center 1964-80, Westcott 1990; *ai:* Museum of Sci & Industry Mem 1988-; Wesley United Meth Church (Cncl on Ministries Asst Membership Secy 1990, Women Chairperson for New Mems 1990, Act Asst); Filmmaking Gifted Grant 1977; Lawless Upper Grade Center Teacher of Yr; *office:* Westcott Elem Sch 409 W 80th St Chicago IL 60620

LEWIS, BARBARA SLOAN, Third Grade Teacher; *b:* Wellsville, NY; *m:* Douglas E.; *c:* Gabe D.; *ed:* (BA) Interdisciplinary Elem Ed, Brockport St Coll 1970; Rdng, Alfred Univ 1973-75; *cr:* 3rd Grade Teacher Bolivar Cntrl Sch 1970-72, Scio Cntrl Sch 1972-; *ai:* Dental Hlth Coord Scio Elem Sch; Delta Kappa Gamma Schlsp Chm 1988-90; Scio Teachers Assn Pres 1980; Delta Kappa Gamma Schlsp Chm 1988-; AAUW Amer Assn Univ Women Schlsp Chm 1976-78; Scio Planning & Beautification Comm 1985-; *home:* 4303 Nickerson Ave Scio NY 14880

LEWIS, BETTY RITZ, 6th Grade Science Teacher; *b:* Hurley, NM; *ed:* (BA) Elem Ed, 1961, (MA) Ed, 1965 W NM Univ; Grad Stud Sci, Math, Cmptrs; *cr:* 3rd Grade Teacher Willcox Public Schls 1961-62; 7th/8th Grade Sci Teacher 1962-63, 4th-6th Grade Teacher 1963-72 Cobre Consolidated Schls; 5th/6th Grade Teacher Silver Consolidated Schls 1972-; *ai:* Family Life Ed Plan; Mill Levy Comm; Delta Kappa Gamma Treas 1985-86; Silver City Ed Assn (Area Rep, Secy 1989-); NEA Life Mem 1965; Epsilon Sigma Alpha Pres 1958-59; Order of Rainbow Girls Grand Cross of Colors 1960; *office:* Silver Consolidated Schls 2810 N Swan St Silver City NM 88061

LEWIS, BRUCE, Guidance Counselor; *b:* Columbus, GA; *m:* Martha Ruth Graves; *c:* Sharon J., Marsha A.; *ed:* (AA) Bible, AL Chrstn Coll 1970; (BA) Speech/Bible, David Lipscomb Coll 1973; (MED) Admin, TN St Univ 1983; Grad Work Bible, Harding Grad Sch of Religion; Psych, AL A&M Univ; *cr:* Bible Teacher Nashville Chrstn Sch 1980-82; Asst Prin Chrstn Schls of Beaumont 1983-84; Prin Atlantic Chrstn Acad 1984-86; Guidance Cnslr Madison Acad 1987-; *ai:* Rifle Team Coach; 2 Articles Published; *office:* Madison Acad 301 Max Luther Dr Huntsville AL 35811

LEWIS, CARDIE BRADLEY, 6th Grade Soc Stud Teacher; *b:* Saratoga, AR; *m:* John H.; *c:* Frederick F.; *ed:* (BS) Home Ec, 1963, (BSE) Elem Ed, 1968 AM&N UAPB; Henderson St Univ, OBU; *cr:* 6th Grade Teacher 1963-64, 1st Grade Teacher 1964-66 Childress Elem; 6Th Grade Teacher Nashville Elem 1966-; *ai:* Personnel Policies Comm; Building Rep; AR Cncl for Soc Stud; AR Ed Assn Negotiations 1989-; NEA 1970-; Classroom Teachers Assn Salary Comm 1978-; Nashville Ed Assn Salary Comm 1987-; Saratoga Concern Citizen Secy 1975-; Ladies Auxiliary Vice Chairperson 1984-86; Saratoga Loins 1984-; PTA 1980-; *office:* Nashville Elem Sch 415 N 4th Nashville AR 71852

LEWIS, CARLA ROSS, Language Arts Teacher; *b:* Springfield, OH; *m:* Seth B.; *c:* Carrie, Emily, Katie; *ed:* (BS) Scndry Ed, 1973, (MS) Scndry Ed, 1978 IN Univ; Gifted & Talented, Rdng Endorsement; *cr:* Teacher Jimtown HS 1973-74, Fulton Jr HS 1975-; *ai:* Academic Coach; Natl Jr Honor Society Faculty Cncl & Gifted/Talented Excel Broad Base Team Mem; Sr Choice Honoree 1987-88; Excl in Ed Honoree 1988; *office:* Fulton Jr HS 7320 W 10th St Indianapolis IN 46234

LEWIS, CAROL S., English Teacher; *b:* Lachine, MI; *m:* Russell; *c:* Steven, Suzanne Knight; *ed:* (BA) Eng, Oakland Univ 1967; (MA) Scndry Ed, Cntrl MI Univ 1973; *cr:* Teacher Alpena Public Schls; *home:* 6310 M 65 N Lachine MI 49753

LEWIS, CAROLYN MAURINE (WOOLERY), Business Education Teacher; *b:* Clinton, MO; *m:* James Arthur; *c:* Tina M., Brian A.; *ed:* (BS) Bus Ed, 1966, (MS) Ed/Voc Office Occupations, 1970 Cntrl MO St Univ Warrensburg; Assoc Degree Secretarial Sci; Cmptr Applications Course; *cr:* Bus Teacher Adrian R-II Sch 1966-73, Hermitage R-IV Sch 1983-85; Bus Substitute Teacher Green Ridge R-VIII 1985-86; Bus Teacher Lincoln R-II Sch 1986-; *ai:* Lincoln HS Sr Class & Bus Club Spon; Bates Cty Teachers Assn (Secy, Treas) 1967-69; MO St Teachers Assn, MO Bus Ed Assn, MO Voc Bus Ed Assn Mem 1966-73, 1983-; Delta Kappa Gamma Mem 1988-; 4-H Club (Project, Club, Asst Leader) 1982-, Pens, Cards; Amer Cancer Society Public Ed Chm 1975-78, Plaque 1978; Cncl on Child Abuse & Neglect VP 1981; MO St Teachers Assn Delegate St Convention; Whos Who in Leaders of Amer Scndry Ed; Prof Dev Comm Mem 1988-; Career Ladder Comm 1989; St Fair Comm Coll Advisory Bd 1989-; *office:* Lincoln HS 101 Lamine St Lincoln MO 65338

LEWIS, CLAUDIA CHAPMAN, Science Teacher; *b:* Baltimore, MD; *m:* Charles W.; *c:* Claudia Clark, Ian K., Gaelan O.; *ed:* (BA) Sci Ed, 1965, (MS) Genetics/Scndry Ed, 1973 Univ of MD; *cr:* Laboratory Asst Virology Johns Hopkins Medical Sch 1966-67; Sci Instr Univ of MD Baltimore Cty 1967-74; Sci Teacher Westminster HS 1974-; *ai:* Chm Westminster Thinking Skills, Mem Writing Across Curr Comms; Amer Assn for Advancement Sci, ASCD; League of Women Voters, Sierra Club; Nom Carroll Cty Outstanding Teacher 1990; *office:* Westminster HS 1225 Washington Rd Westminster MD 21157

LEWIS, COLLEEN TOMLIN, Secondary Bus/English Teacher; *b:* Temple, TX; *m:* Lamar Oslin; *c:* Lindsay, Lauren; *ed:* (BS) Ed/Bus/Eng, Univ of Mary Hardin Baylor 1986; *cr:* Office Ed Teacher Temple Ind Sch Dist 1986-89; Eng/Bus Teacher Detroit Ind Sch Dist 1989-; *ai:* NCTE 1986-; AVA; Delta Kappa Gamma.

LEWIS, DEBORAH HOYLAND, Science Teacher; *b:* South Bend, IN; *m:* Michael E.; *c:* Allison, Kyle; *ed:* (BS) Bio, IN Univ 1976; (MS) Bio, De Pauw Univ 1979; Gifted/Talented Ed; Math; *cr:* Sci Teacher Ben Davis Jr HS 1976-79, Fulton Jr HS 1981-; *ai:* Natl Jr Honor Society Comm; G/T Teacher; NCA Comm Chairperson; PTA; IN Assn of Gifted; Seniors Choice Awd; Excl in Ed Awd; *office:* Fulton Jr H S 7320 W 10th St Indianapolis IN 46214

LEWIS, DEE DUNHAM, Fourth Grade Teacher; *b:* Chanute, KS; *m:* Al; *c:* Brad L., R. B.; *ed:* (BA) Elem Ed, Buena Vista Coll 1972; (MSE) Elem Ed Sch Admin, Drake Univ 1984; *cr:* Rdng Teacher 1973-74, Kndgtn Teacher 1974-77, 3rd Grade Teacher 1977-80, 4th Grade Teacher 1980- Storm Lake Cmmty Schls; *ai:* Cooperating Teacher; Presenter Plains Intl Rdng Assn Regional Conference, Mini-career Course Day, Arrowhead Ed Agency, Ed Fair; Quint Cty Rdng Cncl Pres 1989- Rdng Teacher of Yr 1988; Storm Lake Educl Assn Instructional & Prof Chairperson 1981-; Amer Field Service Pres 1980-88; NEA & IA St Educl Assn 1974-; Storm Lake Educl Assn 1973-; Intl Rdng Assn 1981-; IA St Assn (Presenter 1987) 1981-; *office:* Storm Lake Cmmty Schs 210 E 3rd St Storm Lake IA 50588

LEWIS, DIANA R., Rdng Teacher/Rdng Specialist; *b:* Chicago, IL; *m:* Brian; *c:* R. J., Erin *ed:* (BA) Elem Ed, Ball St Univ 1975; (MA) Curr/Inst Rdng, Univ of Milwaukee 1980; Course Work Admin Ed 1987-; License Admin Leadership; *cr:* Elem Teacher Blue River Valley 1975-76; 6th Grade Teacher Burlington Jr HS 1976-83; Ad Hoc Instr Univ of WI Milwaukee 1984-85; Mid Sch Rdng Teacher/K-8th Grade Rdng Specialist Stone Bank Sch 1983-; *ai:* 8th Grade Annual Play Co-Dir; Instruction Comm; Lang Art Consortium; WI St Rdng Assn 1983-; Intnl Rdng Assn 1983-; *home:* 2121 Harris Highland Waukesha WI 53188

LEWIS, DONNA BETHUNE, Director of Admissions; *b:* New Orleans, LA; *m:* Donald W.; *c:* Allison, Melissa Lewis Michals; *ed:* (BS) Elem Ed, LA St Univ 1963; (MED) Ed, Tulane Univ 1976; *cr:* 1st Grade Teacher East Side Elem 1963-64; 2nd Grade Interim Teacher St Martins 1973; 1st Grade Teacher 1973-86, Dir of Admissions 1986- St Martins Episcopal; *ai:* St Martins Key Club Co-Spon; Kappa Delta Pi; Ladies Leukemia League (Treas, Secy) 1972-; *office:* St Martins Episcopal Sch 5309 Airline Hwy Metairie LA 70003

LEWIS, DONNA POLOFF, Teacher of Gifted & Talented; *b:* Bridgeton, NJ; *m:* Frank H.; *c:* Mary M., Peter B.; *ed:* (BA) Sociology, Catowba Coll 1969; *cr:* 8th Grade Teacher New England Towne Day Sch 1973-79; Teacher of Gifted & Talented Bridgeton Public Schls 1979-; *ai:* Cognetics Adv; Bridgeton Ed Assn, NJ Ed Assn, NEA 1979-; *office:* Bridgeton Mid Sch Broad St Bridgeton NJ 08302

LEWIS, DONNA SPOOR, 5th Grade Mathematics Teacher; *b:* Weimar, TX; *m:* Carl R. Jr.;; *c:* Kadon, Trenton; *ed:* (BAT) Elem Ed, 1972, (MED) Ed /Counseling, 1977 Sam Houston St Univ; Math; *cr:* 3rd Grade Lang Art Teacher Palacios Ind Sch Dist 1972-73; 1st/3rd Grade Teacher Humble Ind Sch Dist 1973-77; 1st/2nd/5th Grade Teacher Angleton Ind Sch Dist 1977-; *ai:* Head Teacher; New Elem Sch Site & Planning Comm; Delta Kappa Gamma Secy 1984-86; Angleton Child Study Club (VP 1989-, Treas 1988-89, Pres 1990); Sunday Sch Teacher Holy Comforter Episcopal Church 1988-; Conference of Advancement of TX Math Teachers Presenter & Speaker.

LEWIS, DORA JEAN-JACOB, 8th Grade English Teacher; *b:* Columbia, MS; *m:* Cornelius Jr.; *c:* Versana M. Polidore, Sharon R. Weber, Travis L. Lewis; *ed:* (BA) Religion/Philosophy/ Sociology, Dillard Univ 1971; Type A Certificate, Southwestern Univ 1976; Certificate Early Chldhd Dev, Lafayette Regional Voc Tech Coll 1990; *cr:* Teacher Franklin Jr HS 1967-; *ai:* 4-H Leader 1967-; Coord In-Service Wkshps in Eng; Mem Pilot Spelling Implementation Prgm; Building Facilitator Creative Writing Prgm; NEA Mem 1970-89; LA Ed Assn Mem 1970-89; St Mary Parish Ed Assn Mem 1970-89; Chez-Hope VP 1985-; Natl Assn Univ Women 1st VP 1987-; US Achievement Acad Spon Merit Medal 1985, Outstanding Spon 1985; LA Outstanding Educator 1981; Teacher of Yr 1989 Franklin Jr HS; Mentor for Graduating Sr; Published 4 Articles by Chrstn Echo 1975/1985/1988/1989; *home:* 312 2nd St Franklin LA 70538

LEWIS, DOROTHY HOERTER, English Teacher; *b:* Ft Knox, KY; *m:* John Mc Cauley; *c:* Amye L.; *ed:* (BA) Eng, Univ of KY 1971; (MA) Ed, Union Coll 1980; Advanced Placement Trng; Several Gifted Ed Seminars & Wkshps; *cr:* Eng Teacher Middesboro Mid Sch 1978-86, Middlesboro HS 1986-; *ai:* Morning Prayer Group Spon; Sch Creative Writing Club Adv; St Julian Cath Church Various Parish Offices; *home:* 414 N 24th St Middlesboro KY 40965

LEWIS, ELAINE THIBODEAUX, Mathematics Teacher; *b:* Lafayette, LA; *m:* Walter L.; *c:* Walter II, Brandon, Corey; *ed:* (BS) Math Ed, 1978, (MED) Scndry Ed, 1981 Univ of SW LA; Shell Oil Company Cmptr Trng 1984-85; *cr:* Math Teacher Breaux Bridge HS 1979-81, Evan E Worthing HS 1982-89, Hartman Mid Sch 1989-; *ai:* Sr Spon & Adv; Number Sence Spon; NCTM; Houston Ind Sch Dist Outstanding Young Educator 1984-85; *home:* 7347 Kingsway Dr Houston TX 77087

LEWIS, ERIC STEPHEN, 8th Grade Teacher; *b:* Los Angeles, CA; *ed:* (AA) Music, El Camino Coll 1972; (BA) Sociology, CA St Univ Long Beach 1975; Cmptr Repair, Cascio Sch of Cmptr Technology; Sci Discovery Connection, Torrance Unified Sch Dist; Summer Cmptr Inst Pepperdine Univ; *cr:* Teacher/Cmptr Coord Nativity Sch 1981-; Lecturer/Teacher Mt St Marys Coll 1989-; *ai:* Choir Dir; Cmptr Club, Young Astronaut, Yrbk Adv; *office:* Nativity Sch 2371 W Carson St Torrance CA 90501

LEWIS, EVELYN R., Rdg/ESL Teacher; *b:* Waukegan, IL; *ed:* (BS) Eng, Univ of ME Farmington 1968; (MSED) Rdng, Univ of ME 1982; *cr:* 4th Grade Teacher Belgrade Cntrl Sch 1968-69; 7th Gr Lang Arts Teacher Williams Jr HS 1969-76; Title I Rdng Teacher Etna Dixmont Sch 1976-84; Rdng/ESL Teacher Campbell HS 1986-; *ai:* NHS Adv; Academic Coord; Intnl Rdng Assn 1986-; TESOL 1989-; Taught Eng in the Peoples Republic of China Summers of 1986/1988; *office:* Campbell H S 3295 S Atlanta Rd Smyrna GA 30080

LEWIS, JANN R., Fifth Grade Teacher; *b:* Somerset, KY; *ed:* (BS) Elem Ed, Cumberland Coll 1978; (MS) Elem Ed, TN Tech Univ 1983; *cr:* 3rd Grade Teacher 1978-79; 5th Grade Teacher 1979- Oneida Elem; *ai:* Attendance Comm; Text Book Comm; TN Ed Assn 1978-; Bus & Prof Women VP/Pres 1987-; Oneida Alumni Assn Secy 1985-89; *home:* 301 Main St Oneida TN 37841

LEWIS, JOAN CAROL, Science Department Chairman; *b:* Dayton, OH; *ed:* (BS) Chem, 1982, (MA) Chem Ed, 1983 E KY Univ 1983; Inst for Chemical Ed Univ of CA Berkeley; *cr:* Chem Teacher Bellevue HS 1983-, N KY Univ 1990; *ai:* Cheerleading & Academic Team Coach; BEST & Family Life Curr Comm; NEA, KEA, BEA (VP, Soc Chairperson 1985-); PTA Teacher Rep 1983-, Teacher of Yr 1987; NSTA 1983-; Inst for Chemical Ed Univ of CA Berkeley; KAPS Convention Presenter; *office:* Bellevue HS 215 Center St Bellevue KY 41073

LEWIS, JOHN STEPHEN, English Department Chair; *b:* Tattnall Cty, GA; *ed:* (BSED) Eng, 1966, (MST) Eng, 1968, (EDS) Eng, 1969 GA Southern Coll; Univ of GA 1973-74; *cr:* Eng Teacher Tattnall Cty Schls 1968-73, 1979-85, Pinewood Chrstn Acad 1974-79; Eng Instr Brewton-Parker Coll 1974-85; Eng Teacher Evans Cty Schls 1985-; Eng Instr GA Southern Coll 1985-; *ai:* Yrbk, Newspaper, Radio Spon; Literary Coach; Eng Dept Chm; PAGE Building Rep 1985-; Little Theater Dir 1986-87; STAR Teacher 1972, 1976, 1989; Teacher of Yr 1968, 1976, 1989; GA Southern Coll Writing Inst Fellowship; Articles Published; *home:* Rt 1 Box 275 Glennville GA 30427

LEWIS, LARRY GEORGE, Guidance Director; *b:* Escanaba, MI; *m:* Pam Collins; *c:* Adam, Travis; *ed:* (BS) Scndry Ed, 1972, (MA) Guidance/Counseling, 1976 N Mi Univ; AODA Counseling & Group Facilitation; Several Guidance Wkshps & Seminars; *cr:* Teacher Menominee Cath Cntrl 1972-75; Guidance Cnslr Heritage Mid Sch 1977-79; Owner/Mgr Coast To Coast Store 1979-87; Guidance Dir All Saints HS 1987-88, Waterford Union HS 1988-; *ai:* Gifted & Talented; At Risk; Academic Stans; Schlsp Comm; Sporting Activity Game Worker; Peer Listening Prgm Facilitator; *office:* Waterford Union HS 110 S Center St Waterford WI 53185

LEWIS, LAURA GOFFNEY, Elementary Teacher; *b:* San Jacinto, TX; *m:* John Lee Sr.; *c:* Jareld L., John L. Jr.; *ed:* (BA) Health/Phys Ed, Paul Quinn Coll 1959; Elem Ed, Tx Southern Univ; *cr:* Elem Ed Maynad Cty Sch 1958-65; Elem Ed 1965-85, Phys Ed 1985- Street Elem; *home:* Rt 2 Box 779 Willis TX 77378

LEWIS, LAWRENCE R., Science Teacher; *b:* Cincinnati, OH; *ed:* (BS) Earth Sci Comprehensive, 1970, (MED) Supervison, 1978 OH Univ; PhD Candidate Educl Leadership, OH Univ 1990; Space Acad Univ of AL; Teacher Intern Young Experimental Scientist Prgm Center of Sci & Industry; *cr:* Sci Teacher Amelia Mid Sch 1970-83; Grad Assoc OH Univ 1983-84; Sci Teacher Amelia Mid Sch 1984-; *ai:* Young Astronauts Spon; Space Club Adv; St Sci Olympid Judge; Phi Delta Kappa, Kappa Delta Pi 1983-; NSTA Life Mem; Sci Educl Cncl of OH (Bd of Dirs 1987-89) 1977-; OH Cncl of Elem Sch Sci (Bd of Dirs 1987-) 1985-; West Clermont Ed Assn (VP 1981-82) 1970-; Center of Sci & Industry 1988-; Young Mens Chrstn Assn 1985-; *home:* 455 S Broadway Williamsburg OH 45176

LEWIS, LUANN, 7th Grade Eng/Rdng Teacher; *b:* Grand Rapids, MI; *ed:* (BA) Eng, W MI Univ 1976; *cr:* Adult Ed/Rdng Teacher Caledonia Cmmty Schls 1977; HS Eng/Rdng Teacher Newaygo Public Schls 1977-84; 7th Grade Eng/Rdng Teacher Caledonia Cmmty Schls 1984-; *ai:* Mid Sch Spelling Bee Coord; MI Rdng Assn; Leighton United Meth Church (Sunday Sch Secy 1973-, Ed Chairperson 1987-89); *office:* Caledonia Mid Sch 9749 Duncan Lake Rd Caledonia MI 49316

LEWIS, MARTHA CUNNINGHAM, Remedial Reading Teacher; *b:* Murray, KY; *m:* Richard Hayes; *c:* Laura E. Lewis Maze, Cynthia J., Katherine H.; *ed:* (BS) Elem Ed, 1960, (MA) Ed, 1969 Murray St Univ; Working Toward Admin & Supervision Cert; *cr:* 5th Grade Teacher Lindbergh Sch Dist 1960-61, Fort Knox Dependent Schls 1961-62; 6th Grade Teacher Lexington City 1963-65; 8th Grade Teacher Benton City Schls 1963-66; Remedial Rdng/6th Grade Teacher Marshall Cty Schls 1978-; *ai:* Academic Team Spon; Delta Kappa Gamma; MEA, KEA, NEA; Benton Womens Club; 1st Baptist Church Choir; Murray St Univ Alumni Assn (Dir, Schlsp Comm); Task Force Ed Curr; Commonwealth Inst Teacher; Marshall Cty Teacher of Yr; Excl of KY Comm; *home:* Rt 8 Box 507 Benton KY 42025

LEWIS, MARVIN, History Teacher/Coach; *b:* Columbus, MS; *m:* Katherine Jane Brown; *ed:* (AA) Elem Ed, E MS Jr Coll 1976; (BS) ELem Ed, Jackson St Univ 1978; *cr:* Title I Math Teacher Newton Jr HS 1978-80; Eng Teacher/Coach SE Lauderdale HS 1980-86; His Teacher/Coach Richlands HS 1990; *ai:* Asst Coach Jr HS Ftbl & Bsktbl, HS Ftbl & Bsbl; Jr HS Letterman Club Spon; Kappa Kappa Psi Mem 1990; *home:* 1925 W Cty Line Rd Jackson MS 39213

LEWIS, MARY LOREAN (TURNER), 5th Grade Teacher; *b:* Columbus, MS; *m:* Ronald C.; *c:* Raneatha J.; *ed:* (BA) Elem Ed, Governors St Univ 1972; Soc Cultural Processes-Sociology; *cr:* 3rd Grade Teacher Medgar Evers Sch 1973-74; Home/Sch Rdng Coord Coolidge Sch 1974, 1976; 5th Grade Teacher Chateaux 1976; *ai:* Pod Leader; Soc Comm Chairperson/Coord; Challenge Prgm Teacher; Prof Advisory Rep; Apple Cmptrs for Stu Coord; NAACP 1989; 5 & 10 Yr Achievement Awds; *office:* Chateaux Sch 3600 Chambord Ln Hazel Crest IL 60429

LEWIS, MARY STATT, Mathematics Teacher; *b:* Buffalo, NY; *m:* Steven A.; *c:* Kristin, Betsy; *ed:* (BA) Ed, Wilmington Coll 1971; Alcohol & Drug Intervention Trng; Math; Teacher Expectation Stu Achievement Trng; *cr:* 4th Grade Teacher 1983-84, 6th Grade Math/Algebra I Teacher 1984- Washington City Schls; *ai:* Mathcounts Club; Drug Cncl; Math Comm; WA Ed Assn Rep 1983-85; OH Cncl Teacher of Math 1984-; Lioness Treas 1987-88; Beta Sigma Phi (Pres, Treas) 1978-79, 1980-81.

LEWIS, OZIE POWELL, Teacher; *b:* Blakely, GA; *m:* Irving Nelson Sr.; *c:* Phyllis, Irving Jr., Reginald, Robert, La Don; *ed:* (BS) Voc Home Ec, Fort Valley St Coll 1955; (MS) Elem Ed, GA Southwestern 1971; Cert Adult Ed, Univ of GA; Grad Stud Cmptr Literacy; *cr:* 5th Grade Teacher Kestler Elem 1956-57; Voc Home Ec Teacher Long Cty HS 1958-59; 6th/7th Grade Teacher Surrency Elem 1959-60; 1st-3rd Grade Teacher Appling Cty Elem 1960-63; Owner/Kndgtn Teacher Tiny Tots of Early Cty 1963-64; K-4th Grade Teacher Early Cty Elem 1964-; Adult Ed Center Teacher 1979-; *ai:* PTO Pres 1969-70; Literacy Task Force Rep for Adult Ed 1989-; Early Cty Assn of Educators Pres 1956-; GA Assn of Educators, Natl Assn of Educators; Washington HS Alumni Assn (Pres 1970-73, Secy 1973-76); GSA Parent; Womens Society Club of AL; Early Cty Historical Society 1979; Mt Olive Missionary Baptist Church (Various Comms, Mem Various Bds); Article Growth of Negro Ed in Early Cty; *home:* 513 Evergreen St Blakely GA 31723

LEWIS, PATRICIA A. (CROTHERS), English Teacher; *b:* Peebles, OH; *c:* Patrick A., Timothy W.; *ed:* (BS) Phy Ed/Health/Eng, Cntrl St 1970; Working Towards Masters Wright St; *cr:* Teacher Eng/Phys Ed/Health, 1970-80; Eng/Rdng Teacher Greenview Schls 1980-; *ai:* Spelling Bee Coord 1980-; Sch Paper Adv 1988-; Stu Asst Team Mem 1990; Adv Comm 1987-89; Order of Eastern Star All Offices 1954-70; Bowling Assn Pres 1960-; Delta Kappa Gamma Schlsp; *home:* 16 E High St Jeffersonville OH 43138

LEWIS, PATRICIA MONEY, Mathematics Teacher; *b:* Greenville, TX; *m:* Charles R.; *c:* Kyle R., Joni Lewis Mays; *ed:* (BS) Math/Scndry Ed, Baylor Univ 1967; (MS) Counseling/Guidance, E TX St Univ Commerce 1981; Grad Stud Univ of TX Dallas, Richardson; *cr:* 8th Grade Math Teacher Brame Jr HS 1968-69, Pearch Jr HS 1969-71, Wiesbaden Jr HS Germany 1971-74, Marlin Jr HS 1974-76; 7th Grade Math Teacher Brandenburg Mid Sch 1976-77; 7th/8th Grade Math Teacher Williams Mid 1977-; *ai:* Explorers Club Spon; Univ Interscholastic League Coach; Number Sense; Assn of TX Prof Educators 1981-; NCTM; Superior Performance Awd Dept of Army 1973-74; *home:* 4018 Bachman Blvd Garland TX 75043

LEWIS, PATSY JANE SHANKS, Fourth Grade Teacher; *b:* Johnson City, TN; *m:* Boyd Jr.; *c:* Jada M.; *ed:* (BS) Home Ec, 1971, (BS) Elem Ed, 1973 E TN St Univ; Rdng, E TN St Univ 1986; Aerospace Ed, E TN St Univ 1988; *cr:* Home Ec Teacher Dobyns Bennett 1972; 3rd Grade Teacher Sulphur Springs 1973-78; 4th Grade Teacher Jonesboro Elem 1978-; *ai:* Sci Chairperson; NEA 1986-89; Civil Air Patrol 1989-; E TN St Univ Grant; *office:* Jonesboro Elem Sch 306 Forest Dr Jonesborough TN 37659

LEWIS, ROBERT BRUCE, JR., Sixth Grade Teacher; *b:* Blackberry City, WV; *m:* Julia E. Warner; *c:* Diane Joyce L. Cintron, Rbt. B. Ryan, Debora June, Robin Annette; *ed:* (BA) Elem Ed/Lang Arts/Soc St, Marshall Univ 1972; (MS) Occupational Health/Safety, Marshall Univ 1979; Marshall Univ/WVCOGS 1989; *cr:* Substitute Teacher Cty-Wide 1978-79; 6th Grade Teacher Thorn Elem 1979; *ai:* Chairperson for St Judes Mathathon; Coord for Safety Patrols; PDK 1986-; Mercer Cty Rdng Cncl 1984-; Masonic Lodge 1978-; Mercer Cty Farm Bureau 1981-; Mercer Cty Livestock Protection Assn Pres 1987-; Southern States Coop Bd Mem Chm 1988-; Teacher of Yr 1987-88; *office:* Thorn Elem Sch 201 Thorn St Princeton WV 24740

LEWIS, ROBERT JAMES, JR., Physical Education Teacher; *b:* Oakland, CA; *m:* Jane Sulak; *c:* Lindsay, Reagan, Jason; *ed:* (BA) Philosophy/Phys Ed/Eng, St Marys Univ 1980; (MA) Educl Admin, SW TX St 1986; *cr:* Phys Ed Teacher/Coach St Thomas More Sch 1971-74, Holy Spirit Cath Sch 1974-77; Phys Ed Teacher/Athletic Dir St Lukes Cath Sch 1977-; *ai:* Boys & Girls Cross Cntry, Boys Soccer, Bsktbl, Track Coach; San Antonio Archdiocese Phys Ed & Phys Ed Curr Guide Comms; NCEA Mem 1971-; Intnl Traveling League Assoc Mem 1979-; San Antonio All Star Youth Bsbl Dir 1979-; *office:* St Lukes Cath Sch 4603 Manitou Dr San Antonio TX 78228

LEWIS, SHAREN C., Lang Art Teacher & Curr Coord; *b:* Cleveland, OH; *c:* Michael; *ed:* (BSED) Eng, Kent St Univ 1964-; Ed Courses La Verne Coll, Univ S FL Tampa, Manatee Comm Coll; Staff Dev Sarasota Cty; *cr:* 9th/10th/12th Grade Eng Teacher Shaw HS 1964-68; 7th-9th Grade Eng Teacher Sarasota Jr HS 1969-72; Eng Teacher/Dept Chairperson Venice Jr HS 1972-82; Adult HS Eng Teacher 1977-89; Eng Teacher/Team Leader Venice Mid Sch 1982-; *ai:* Team Leader; Lang Art Curr Coord; Wkshp Consultant Natl Resource Center for Mid Grades Coll of Ed Univ of S Fl Tampa; SCTA Mem 1972-; FL Rdng Assn, Sarastoa Rdng Cncl; Delta Kappa Gamma Pres 1978-; Local PTA Civic Assn; Sarasota Cty Teacher of Yr 1989-; Many Educl Materials Published; *office:* Venice Area Mid Sch 1900 Center Rd Venice FL 34293

LEWIS, WESLEY CLYDE, Art Teacher; *b:* Gary, IN; *m:* Lois Cecelia Simmons; *c:* Wesley Jr., Valorie, Jelani, Jabari, Jamil; *ed:* (BSE) Art Ed, Emporia St Univ 1969; *cr:* Teacher/Coach Bonner Springs HS 1969-75, Washington HS 1975-; *ai:* Track & Head Wrestling Coach; Art Club Spon; NEA Area Rep 1976-79; Highland Park Townhouses Incorporated (Pres, Bd of Dirs) 1978-83; New Century Best of Show Art Awd 1974; *home:* 610 N 9th Kansas City KS 66101

LEYSHON, DEBORAH DANEKER, Music Teacher; *b:* Jersey Shore, PA; *m:* Robert John II; *ed:* (BM) Cert Music Ed, Mansfield Univ 1978; Private Vocal Trng Ed; *cr:* Vocal Music Teacher Locust Street Elem, Nippenose Elem Sch, Salladasburg Elem Sch 1978-80, Shawnee Intermedia e Sch 1980-; *ai:* Shawnee Musical Costumer 1980, Choreographer 1981-, Vocal Dir 1984-; Shawnee Chorale Vocal Dir, Choreographer, Costumer 1980-; Shawnee Chorus Dir 1980-; PA Music Educators Assn 1976-80; Cntrl Moravian Church Choir (Soloist, Asst Conductor) 1980-; Jacksonville Summer Theater Vocal Dir 1987-, Leading Role Hello Dolly 1988; Shawnee PTA Service to Stu Commendation 1985; Solo Recitals Moravian Coll 1986, 1989; *office:* Shawnee Intermediate Sch 1010 Echo Trail Easton PA 18042

LEYVA, CHARLES B., Spanish Teacher; *b:* Worland, WY; *m:* Polly M.; *c:* Debra L. De Lay, Sophia A. Gomez, Charles M.; *ed:* (BA) Scndry Ed Span, Univ of WY 1972; Natl Peace Officer Trng Organization; *cr:* Family Life Instr Cnslr Mountain Plains Career Ed 1972-76; SW ID Migrant Educl Teacher SE Migrant Ed 1976-77; Liaison Jr HS Teacher Burley ID Mid Sch 1977-83; Ombudsman for Governor Salt Lake City UT 1983-84; HS Teacher Tremonton UT 1985-; *ai:* Girls Track, Asst Wrestling, Cross Cntry Coach; Sr Class & Span Class Adv; Univ of WY Past Span VP; Span Club UW VP 1971-72; PTA/Span Super Teacher Awd 1988; NEA 1976-; UT Ed Assn, Bear River Ed Assn 1984-; Natl Defense Educl Loans & Other Educl Grants; Chicano Educl Grants at Univ of WY; *home:* PO Box 117 Tremonton UT 84337

LEYVA, LUIS E., Art Teacher; *b:* Cuidad Acuna, Mexico; *m:* Belinda Ann; *c:* Luis P., Vanessa L.; *ed:* (BA) Art/Span/His, Angelo St Univ 1976; Elem Cert Sulross St Univ 1978; (MA) Art/His, TX Womans Univ 1979; *cr:* Teacher San Felipe Del Rio Consolidated Ind Sch Dist 1979-; *ai:* Art Club Spon; Prom Decoration Dir; Curr Writer; Art Dept Head; Advisory Comm Mem; Campus Improvement Plan; TSTA, NEA (Mem 1986-, Chm 1989-); Del Rio Art Cncl 1986-; Del Rio Art League 1989-; *office:* Del Rio HS 100 Memorial Dr Del Rio TX 78840

LIBBY, SOPHIA MARY, Social Studies Teacher; *b:* Greenfield, MA; *c:* Michael; *ed:* (BS) His, Worcester St Teachers 1949; (MED) Poly Sci, Univ of MA 1962; *cr:* 7th/8th Grade Teacher Montague Center Sch 1949-51; 8th Grade His Teacher Turners Falls Jr HS 1951-73; Soc Stud Teacher/Dept Chairperson Turner Falls HS 1973-85; 8th Grade World Cultures Teacher Great Falls Mid Sch 1985-; *ai:* Team Leader 8th Grade Math/Lang Art/Sci Teacher; New England League of Mid Schls Steering Comm.

LIBEN, DAVID MARK, Mathematics Teacher/Grade Head; *b:* New York, NY; *m:* Meredith Judy; *c:* Zach, Lucas; *ed:* (BA) Psych, Univ of WI Madison 1973; (MS) Ed Admin, Columbia Teachers Coll 1985; *cr:* 4th/5th Grade Teacher New Glarus Elem Sch 1973-74; 5th/6th Grade Teacher Prof Childrens Sch 1974-77; 6th Grade Teacher Fieldston Lower Sch 1977-81; 7th-9th Grade Teacher Sports Sch 1981-85, New York Prep 1985-; *ai:* Coach; *office:* New York Prep Sch 315 E 113th St New York NY 10029

LIBERSON, SHIRLEY ALTER, First Grade Teacher; *b:* Chicago, IL; *c:* Mark Jeffery, Barry Scott, Richard Glenn; *ed:* (BE) Ed, Chicago Teachers Coll 1951; (MA) Admin & Supv Ed, De Paul 1958; *cr:* Teacher Shepard Elem 1951-58, George Washington Elem 1958-; *ai:* Comm Mem Forming Stu Cncl; Hammond Hadassah Pres 1965-66 Pin 1966; Munster Hadassah Pres 1970-71 Pin 1971; North Shore Jewish Singles Soc Chm 1985-.

LIBERT, NANCY PORTA, 6th Grade Teacher; *b:* Bayshore, NY; *m:* Calvin C.; *c:* Darien Libert Logan, Leslie Libert Pompeo; *ed:* (BA) Ed, St Univ of NY Stony Brook 1973; (MA) Ed, Adelphi Univ 1977; (MA) Linguistics, St Univ of NY Stony Brook 1985; Eng, Journalism, Hofstra Univ 1954-58; *cr:* 1st Grade Teacher 1973-74, 3rd Grade Teacher 1974-77, 5th Grade Teacher 1978-79 Cordello Avenue Sch; Eng as Second Lang Teacher Mulligan Sch 1980-81; Eng Phonology Teacher St Univ of NY Stony Brook 1985; 6th Grade Teacher Francis J O Neill Sch 1982-; *ai:* Francis J O Neill Sch Textbook Comm; Islip Schls Citizen Advisory Comm 1984-85; Old South Islip Civic Assn (Founding Bd Mem 1980-, Pres 1985-87, Ed Neighborhood News); Islip Sch-Age Child Care (Founding Bd Mem 1985-89, Publicity Chairperson); Maud S Sherwood Schlsp Fund Trustee; Presbyn Church (Sunday Sch Teacher 1967-87, Sunday Sch Dir 1987-, Vacation Bible Sch Musical Dir 1987-, Chrstn Ed Comm Mem, Sr Choir Mem 1975-, Ed 1980-); Suffolk Cty Educl Comm Cncl Multi-Media Awd 1979; Teachers Center Mini Grant 1987, 1989; *home:* 88 Monell Ave Islip NY 11751

LIBORDI, FRANCIS ANDREW, American History Teacher; *b:* Hornell, NY; *ed:* (BA) Amer His, Alfred Univ 1986; (MA) Ed, Elmira Coll 1991; *cr:* Amer His Teacher Hornell HS 1986-; *ai:* Asst Ftbl Coach; Attendance Comm Pres; Knights of Columbus 1984-; BPO Elks 1988-; Presidential Schlsp Grant.

LI CALSI, LYNN, Latin Teacher; *b:* Hempstead, NY; *m:* John Carrinton Gibert; *ed:* (BA) Eng, Wellesley Coll 1981; Roman His/Italian/Ger, Harvard Extension Sch; *cr:* Latin Teacher Westover Sch 1981-83; Latin/Etymology/Semantics/Poetry Teacher Phillips Acad 1981-85, 1989; Latin Teacher Dana Hall Sch 1983-; *ai:* Latin Club Adv; Admission & Curr Comm Mem; Classical Assn of New England, Amer Classical League, Classical Assn of MA, Vergilian Society 1981-; Phi Beta Kappa; Cum Laude Society Pres; MA Jr Classical League Adv to VP; Fulbright Grant Study at Amer Acad Rome, Villa Vergiliana Cuma; Tufts Univ Continuing Ed Grant Teachers; Wellesley Coll Scholar; Virginia Wainright Sonnet Prize; *office:* Dana Hall Sch 21 Dana Rd Wellesley Hills MA 02181

LICATA, GUY THOMAS, Biology Teacher; *b:* New York, NY; *m:* Ann T. Manzo; *c:* Theresa Paff, Thomas J., Stephen P.; *ed:* (BS) Bio, St Johns Coll 1957; (MS) Bio, St Johns Grad Sch 1961; Advanced Study Certificate St Univ New Paltz 1976; Bio, NY Univ & St Univ New Paltz; *cr:* Sci Teacher 1957-68, Sci Dept Chm 1965-68 Marlboro Cntrl Sch; Bio Instr Dutchess Cty Comm Coll 1974-78; Bio Teacher John Jay HS 1968-; *ai:* Primary Author Bio Review; John Jay HS NHS Teacher of Yr; *office:* John Jay HS Rt 52 Hopewell Junction NY 12533

LICHATIN, ROSANNE STANGO, Social Studies Teacher; *ed:* (BA) His, Kean Coll of NJ 1975; Working Towards Masters East Stroudsburg Univ; *cr:* Soc Stud Teacher Westwood Regional Schls 1978-79, Columbia Sch 1979-81, West Orange Public Schls 1981-83, Summit Public Schls 1983-84, William Annin Mid Sch, Madison HS 1985-87, West Morris Cntrl HS 1987-; *ai:* Future Educators of America Club Coord; NJ Cncvl for Soc Stud.

LICHNOVSKY, BILLY JOE, 8th Grade Mathematics Teacher; *b:* West, TX; *m:* Erika; *c:* Andrew E. Rosenkranz; *ed:* (BS) Phys Ed, Baylor Univ 1961; *cr:* Teacher South Jr HS 1961-72, Lake Air Mid Sch 1972-; *ai:* TSTA 1961-; NEA 1990; Waco Class Teachers Assn; *home:* Rt 10 Box 335 F Waco TX 76708

LICHT, WILLIAM BRET, Principal/Social Stud Teacher; *b:* Lancaster, PA; *m:* Susan M. Leatherman; *c:* Ryan, Erika; *ed:* (BS) Soc Stud Ed, 1980, (MS) Educl Admin 1981 Bob Jones Univ; Pensacola Chrstn Coll, W WA Univ; *cr:* 6th Grade Teacher/Admin Asst Calvary Chrstn Sch 1981-84; Scndry Soc Stud Teacher/Prin Calvary Baptist Sch 1984-; *ai:* Yrbk & Sr Class Adv; Athletic Dir; Admin Fellowship Assn of Chrstn Schls Intnl 1987-; Cntrl Comm Republican Party Clallham Cty Exec Bd 1987-; Calvary Baptist Church (Vice-Chm, Deacon Bd) 1989-; *office:* Calvary Baptist Sch 3415 S Peabody St Port Angeles WA 98362

LICHTENBERG, GLORIA BLAZVICK, Fourth Grade Teacher; *b:* North Canton, OH; *m:* John A.; *ed:* (BA) Music Ed, Silver Lake Coll 1965; *cr:* Music Teacher Cath Sch Systems 1948-70; 4th Grade Teacher Sacred Heart Sch 1971-72; 5th Grade Teacher San Roque 1972-73; Music Teacher C W McGraw 1973-76; 4th Grade Teacher O C Johnson 1976-78, Immaculate Conception Cath 1980-; *ai:* NCEA; Pope John XXIII Minister; Immaculate Conception Church Organist; Yuma Providing Ground Organist; Book Published; *home:* 416 S 21st Ave Yuma AZ 85364

LICHTENSTEIN, BERNADINE CZERNIKOWSKI, 2nd Grade Teacher; *b:* Sayreville, NJ; *w:* John P. (dec); *c:* Barry J. (dec), Jeffrey P., Pamela Roberts; *ed:* (BA) Elem Ed, Newark St 1973; (MA) Interdisciplinary Stud, Kean Coll 1978; *cr:* 2nd Grade Teacher Selover Sch 1973-74; 2nd Grade Teacher 1974-76, 1st Grade Teacher 1976-88, 2nd Grade Teacher 1988- Wilson Sch; *ai:* Dist Building Sci Coord; Dist Math Comm Mem; Middlesex Cty Rdng Assn, NJ Rdng Assn, Cncl for Elem Sci, Alpha Delta Kappa; Sayreville Free Public Lib Bd of Trustees 1980-; Middlesex

Cty Mental Health Bd 1975-79; Governors Teacher Recognition Prgm 1987; *home:* 14 Pearl St Sayreville NJ 08872

LICHTFUSS, FRANK GEORGE, JR., Middle School Science Teacher; *b:* Appleton, WI; *m:* Gloria J. Pionke; *c:* Bryan, Heather; *ed:* (BS) Meteorology, Univ of WI-Madison 1980; Ed Cert, Univ of WI-Oshkosh 1982; *cr:* Sci Teacher St Vincent De Paul Sch 1983-84, Berlin Cath Sch 1984-; *ai:* Building Coord; Ski Club Adv; NCEA; Knights of Columbus 3rd Degree 1982-; *office:* Berlin Cath Sch 315 Sw Ceresco St Berlin WI 54923

LICKTEIG, SHARON WARREN, English Teacher; *b:* Tampa, FL; *c:* James, Cara, Crista; *ed:* (BS) Eng Ed, FL St Univ 1973; (MA) Eng, Univ Cntrl FL 1978; (EDS) Admin, Nova Univ 1987; *cr:* Teacher Evans HS 1974-75; Teacher Lake Howell HS 1975-; Teacher Seminole Comm Coll 1979-; *ai:* PTA Exec Bd; NCTE; NEA; SEA; Casselberry Elem VP 1989-; Sch PTA; Helped Implement Our Dual Enrollment Prgm Which Makes Coll Level Classes Available to Talented Students; *office:* Lake Howell H S 4200 Dike Rd Winter Park FL 32792

LICONA, KATHERINE LUPTON, English Teacher; *b:* Lubbock, TX; *m:* Guillermo; *ed:* (BA) Speech/Eng, West TX St Univ 1966; (MA) Eng/Ed, Sam Houston St Univ 1976; *cr:* Teacher Las Cruces Schls 1966-68, Loving NM 1968-70; Speech Dir Tomball HS 1970-74; Eng Teacher Cy-Fair Ind Sch Dist 1974-77, El Paso Schls 1977-; *ai:* Ready Writing Coach; 1 Act Play Coach; Team Leader & Dept Chm; Paso Del Norte Cncl of Teachers of Eng Parliamentarian; NCTE; *home:* 12 Sutton Pl El Paso TX 79912

LICONA, MIGUEL M., Science Department Chair; *b:* El Paso, TX; *c:* Laura, Evi, Mikela, Miguel; *ed:* (BA) Bio, Sam Houston St Univ 1973; (MS) Bio, NM Highlands Univ 1979; Cmptrs in Sci Laboratory Trng Univ of WY 1989; Phys Sci Laboratories Tulsa 1989; *cr:* Sci Teacher Canntillo HS 1973-76, St Michaels HS 1976-79; Bio/Phys Sci Teacher Santa Fe HS 1979-84; Sci/Math Chm Radford Sch 1984-85; Sci Teacher Gadsden Jr HS 1985-; *ai:* After Sch Study Hall & Remediation Dir; Sci Dept Chm; NSTA, TSTA, Natl Biological Society; Beta Beta Beta Mem 1972-73; Cmmty Fnd Grant Recipient 1985; Title II Trng for Teachers in Dist 3 Yr Grant; *office:* Gadsden Jr HS Rt 1 Box 196 Anthony NM 88021

LIEB, JAY EDWARD, Middle School Teacher; *b:* Miami, FL; *m:* Cheryl Christine Muehlberg; *c:* Joshua E.; *ed:* (BA) His, Luther Coll 1968; (BA) Elem Ed, KS Wesleyan 1971; IA Writers Wkshp Math, Univ of IA 1982, 1988; Human Relations, Mary Crest 1981-82; Assertive Discipline, DrakeUniv 1989; Quest Trng; *cr:* Prgm/Youth Dir YMCA Ellis Branch 1969-71; Youth Dir YMCA 1971; 5th-6th Grade Math Teacher Augusta KS 1973; Mid Sch Teacher Benton Cmmty 1973-; *ai:* 7th Grade Girls Vlybl & Bsktbl Coach; 7th-8th Boys Track Asst; Orienteering Coach; Benton Cmmty Ed Assn Pres 1972-; IA Mid Level Ed Assn Bd Mem 1986-; IA Coaches Assn 1986-; *office:* Benton Cmmty Sch 400 1st St Van Horne IA 52346

LIEBER, DAVID THOMAS, Physical & Health Ed Teacher; *b:* Philadelphia, PA; *m:* Roben Nelson; *c:* Amanda, Steven; *ed:* (BS) HPER, PA St Univ 1973; (MED) Phys/Health Ed, Trenton St Coll 1978; Working Doctorate in Sports Admin Temple Univ; *cr:* Phys Ed Specialist Lawton Elem Sch 1974-83; Supvr Natl Jr Tennis League of Philadelphia 1975-; Phys/Health Ed Demonstration Teacher Masterman 1983-; Mgr Arthur Ashe Youth Tennis Center 1983, 1989-; *ai:* Var Boys & Girls Vlybl, Boys Mid Sch Bsktbl, Girls Var Tennis Coach; 9th Grade Spon Adv; Discipline Comm; Mid Sch Reorganization; Dir Co-Founder of Philly Kids US Jr Dev Vlybl Club 1987-; Asst Coach US Maccabiah Rugby Team 1985; Amer Vlybl Coach 1989-; USTA, MSTA 1987-; PTA Coach of Yr 1988; PA HFERD 1976-; USVBA 1989-; Philadelphia Service Awd 1990; Blackthorn Rugby Club (Dir 1980-81) 1975-; Easter Seal Bsktbl Shootout 1987-89; Walk for Life Chairperson 1989; *office:* Masterman Demonstration & Lab 17th & Spring Garden St Philadelphia PA 19130

LIEBERMAN, LIBBY SHULL, First Grade Teacher; *b:* Philadelphia, PA; *m:* Neil; *c:* Josh, Larry; *ed:* (BA) Philosophy, Temple Univ 1961; (MA) Counselling, Trenton St Coll 1971; Grad Studs Ed & Sch Psych; *cr:* Kndgtn Teacher Delanco NJ 1960-61; 2nd Grade Teacher Easthampton NJ 1961-62; 3rd Grade Teacher Buckingham Elem Sch 1962-67, Univ Sch MKE 1972-74; 1st Grade Teacher Chadwick Sch 1975-; *ai:* Chadwick Sch 1978 Pascoe Teaching Awd 1978; Dir Summer AC Prgm K-8th, Mem CAIS & WASC Evaluating Teams; Author 2 Books Ed Published; *office:* Chadwick Sch 26800 S Academy Dr Palos Verdes Pnsla CA 90274

LIEBMANN, DONALD EDWARD, Elementary Guidance Counsler; *b:* Milwaukee, WI; *m:* Margaret C. Pitzner; *c:* Megan, Melissa; *ed:* (BA) Elem Ed/Phys Ed, Carroll Coll 1974; (MS) Elem Guidance, Whitewater Univ 1980; AODA Spec Trng for Stu Asst Programming HS & Elem Areas; *cr:* 5th/6th Grade Teacher 1974-79, Elem Guidance Cnslr 1979-84, Elem Guidance/Phys Ed Teacher 1984- Johnson Creek Sch Dist; *ai:* Curr Advisory Bd; Stu Asst Prgm Group Leader; HS Var Ftbl, Bsktbl, Bsbl, Track Coach; Johnson Creek Ed Assn (VP 1986-87, Pres 1988-89); WI Sch Cnslr Assn 1980-; Ducks Unlimited, WI Bowhunters 1980-; Whitetails Unlimited Banquet Comm Mem 1985-; Active Participant St Fellowship Grant; *home:* W 7974 Oakwood Ln Fort Atkinson WI 53538

LIEBOWITZ, RELLY ROSELLEN, Fourth Grade Teacher; *b:* New York City, NY; *c:* Steven, Caryn Bonosevich, Phillip; *ed:* (BA) Lit, Hunter Coll 1957; Elem Ed Cert, Newark St Coll; Writing, Spec Ed, Cmptrs, Math, Calligraphy, Lit, Brookdale Comm Coll; *cr:* Kndgtn/3rd-5th Grade Teacher Southwood Elem Sch 1963-; *ai:* Township Sci & Lang Art Comms; NJEA Assn Rep 1975-87; PTA Southwood Sch Pres 1983-85, 1986-88, Life Membership 1985; PTA Pres Cncl Coord 1988-; Governors Recognition Prgm Teacher of Yr 1988-89; *office:* Southwood Elem Sch 64 Soutwood Dr Old Bridge NJ 08857

LIEDERBACH, KATHY REEF, Mathematics Teacher; *b:* Detroit, MI; *m:* Frederick III; *c:* Mary B., Patrick; *ed:* (BAED) Math, Cntrl MI Univ 1980; *cr:* Math Teacher Littlefield Public Sch 1980-; *ai:* Mathcounts Coach; Yrbk Adv; Stu Asst Team; St Judes Childrens Research Hospital (Organizer, Chairperson) 1990; *office:* Littlefield Public Sch 7400 North St Alanson MI 49706

LIEFKE, MARY ANN MAVIS (VORPAHL), Third Grade Teacher; *b:* Shawanu, WI; *m:* Harry; *c:* Caroline, Melissa, Ephraim; *ed:* (BS) Lower Elem Ed, Univ of WI Oshkosh 1972; *cr:* Elem Librarian Shiocton Elem Sch 1968-69; 4th Grade Teacher 1969-83, 3rd Grade Teacher 1983- Oconto Unified Schls; *ai:* 8th Grade Girls Bsktbl Coach 1973-76; Alcohol/Drug Abuse Steering Comm 1989-; Public Relations Comm 1989-; Ocont Ed Assn 1969-; *office:* Oconto Unified Sch Michigan Ave Oconto WI 54153

LIEKE, RICHARD FREDERICK, Chemistry Teacher; *b:* New York, NY; *m:* Evelyn B. Hallett; *c:* E. Ayesha, Rae E.; *ed:* (DC) Chiropractic, Chiropractic Inst NY 1951; (BS) Ed, Univ of ME Orono 1962; (MTSC) Chem, Univ of NH 1972; *cr:* Chiropractor 1951-57; Sci/Math Teacher NY & ME 1957-68; Chem Teacher Brunswick ME 1969-; *ai:* Sci Subcomm of Curr Evaluation Brunswick Sch System Chm; Faculty Advisory Comm; BTA (Pres 1974) 1963-; MTA, NEA 1963-; MST 1975-; Curr Dev Grant 1987-89; Developed Numerous Sci Courses Brunswick HS; *office:* Brunswick HS Spring St Brunswick ME 04011

LIENHART, PATRICIA FLYNN, First Grade Teacher; *b:* Columbus, IN; *m:* Carl L. Jr.; *c:* Michael, Christopher; *ed:* (BS) Elem Ed, Mt St Joseph Coll 1977; Several Wkshps & Continuing Ed Seminars; *cr:* 2nd Grade Teacher 1965-68, 1977-82, 1st Grade Teacher 1982- St Therese of the Little Flower; *ai:* Summer Festival Childrens Raffle Faculty Coord; NCEA 1977-; Greater Cincinnati Cncl of Math Teachers 1985-; La Salle HS PTA (Secy 1984-86, Pres 1986-88); *office:* St Therese Little Flower Sch 5555 Little Flower Ave Cincinnati OH 45239

LIETZ, CASSANDRA LIN, Art Teacher; *b:* Kingston, PA; *m:* Paul James; *c:* Paul J. III; *ed:* (AA) Art Ed, Ocean Cty Comm Coll 1976; (BA) Art Ed, High Point 1978; *cr:* Phys Ed Teacher St Joseph Acad 1985-86; Gymnastic Coach Childrens Village Gymnastics 1982-; Art Teacher St Augustine HS 1986-; *ai:* Village Gymnastics Asst Coach; *office:* Saint Augustine HS 3205 N Varella St Saint Augustine FL 32084

LIEVENS, GRACE SINENI BUNN, 5th Grade Teacher; *b:* Chicago, IL; *m:* Ronald; *c:* John Bunn; *ed:* (BS) Elem Ed, Bradley Univ 1956; Seminars, Wkshps, Classes Bradley Univ & Univ of IL; *cr:* 3rd Grade Teacher Blaine Sumner 1956-59; 4th Grade Teacher Smith Sch 1959-60; 4th/5th Grade Teacher Ward Grundy 1962-; *ai:* NEA Political Action Coord 1986-89; IL Ed Assn Bd of Dir 1956-; Alpha Delta Kappa Pres 1965-, 25 Yr Leadership Pin 1989; Morton Educators Assn VP; Cursillo 1970-; Toastmasters Intnl 1986-88; Peace Network 1985-; *home:* 108 Sycamore Morton IL 61550

LIFKE, JAMES MICHAEL, Substance Abuse Coordinator; *b:* Mishawaka, IN; *m:* Janet Schelstraete; *c:* Jill Ellis, Janice, Steve; *ed:* (BS) Industrial Ed/Phys Ed/Health, 1965, (MS) Industrial Ed/Phys Ed/Health, 1967 IN St Univ; IN Dept of Ed Drug Abuse Trng; Level I & II Intervention Trng, Fairbanks Trng Inst; IN Univ Sch of Continuing Stud; Substance Abuse PRIDE Trng; *cr:* Industrial Ed Teacher/Coach Laville Jr/Sr HS 1965-69, Hobart City Schls 1969-73; Substance Abuse Coord/Industrial Ed/Health Teacher Heritage Hills Jr/Sr HS 1973-; *ai:* Support Group Faciliator; Peer Ed Adv; Private Victories Spon; Paren to Parent Faciliator; Caring Parents Chm 1990; St Bd of Ed IN Advisory Bd Drug Abuse 1990; N Spencer Coaliation for Drug Free Cmmty Chm 1990; Youth Drug Task Force Bd Mem 1990; IN St Bd of Ed Substance Abuse Curr Comm; Drug Free Schls Cmmty Grant; Newspaper Articles Published; *office:* Heritage Hills Jr-Sr HS R R 1 Lincoln City IN 47552

LIGGET, NOEMI CASTILLO, American History Teacher; *b:* Weslaco, TX; *m:* James Ray; *c:* Kristen, Iliana; *ed:* (BS) Ed/His, Pan Amer Univ 1978; Working Towards Masters; *cr:* Teacher Pharr-San Juan-Alamo Ind Sch Dist 1978-81, Pasadena Ind Sch Dist 1981-; *ai:* TX St Teachers Assn Mem 1985-; *office:* Jackson Intermediate Sch 100 E Jackson Pasadena TX 77506

LIGGET, ROBERT COPE, History Teacher; *b:* Bryn Mawr, PA; *m:* Joy Tressa Morris; *c:* Amy J., Sarah, Robert; *ed:* (BA) Anthropology, George Washington Univ 1975; Grad Stud Univ of PA, Univ of UT; Anthropology & Persian Stud; *cr:* His/Eng Teacher 1982, His Dept Chm 1983-84, Dir of Discipline 1984-88, His Dept Chm 1988-89, His Teacher 1990 Rowland Hall-St Marks Sch; *ai:* Stu Service Comm Mem; Bsbl Coach 1985-87; Equestrian Team Coach 1985-86; ASCD, NCSS, UT Historical Society; *office:* Rowland Hall-St Marks Sch 843 Lincoln St Salt Lake City UT 84102

LIGHT, BETTE HENDRIX, Kindergarten Teacher; *b:* Greensboro, NC; *m:* James Madison Jr.; *c:* James Madison III; *ed:* (BS) Early Chldhd, East Carolina Univ 1953; Wake Forest Univ; UNC-G Univ; Guilford Coll; *cr:* 2nd Grade Teacher Brooks Sch 1954-56; Myers Park Sch 1956-57; 4th Grade Teacher Moore Sch 1957-59; 3rd Grade Teacher Plumosa Sch 1959-60; 2nd Grade Teacher Murphey Sch 1960-64; 3rd Grade Teacher Lindley Sch 1971-73; K/ Teacher Green Price Sch Jones 1973-; *ai:* NEA; NCAE; Delta Kappa Gamma Beta Gamma Chapter Mem Chm 1988-; Muirs Chapel United Meth Church Parsonage Comm 1980-82 & 1989-; Published Article NCAE Journals; NEA; Price Traditional Sch Teacher of Yr 1979-80; 1st Runner Up Greensboro Schls Teacher of Yr 1979-80; *home:* 6402 Friendly Rd Greensboro NC 27410

LIGHT, TINA RAE, Second Grade Teacher; *b:* Sacramento, CA; *m:* Reiner; *c:* Derrick; *ed:* (BA) Liberal Stud/Elem Ed, Chico St Univ 1983; Several Courses; *cr:* 2nd Grade Teacher 1985, 7th/8th Grade Teacher 1986 St Thomas Cath Sch; 3rd/4th Grade Teacher St Thomas More Cath Sch 1986-88; 2nd Grade Teacher Wyandotte Avenue Sch 1988-; *ai:* Phi Delta Kappa; *office:* Wyandotte Avenue Sch 2795 Yard St Oroville CA 95965

LIGHTFOOT, JANET Y. (FRENCH), Sixth Grade Teacher; *b:* Batesville, AR; *m:* Richard C.; *c:* Sara; *ed:* (BS) Ed/Eng, 1978, (MS) Ed, 1983 TX Wesleyan Univ; Various Inservices; *cr:* Lead Teacher 1981-88, 6th Grade Teacher 1979- Beatrice Short Elem; *ai:* Cultural Arts Chairperson; Arlington Rdng Assn Building Rep 1988-; Assn of TX Prof Educators; Lake Arlington Baptist Church (Childrens Choir Teacher, Adult Choir Mem); PTA Bd; Comm for Writing Teachers Manual Team Leader; TX Career Ladder; *office:* Beatrice Short Elem Sch 2000 California Ln Arlington TX 76015

LIGHTSEY, MELVA JANE, History/English Teacher; *b:* Pidcoke, TX; *ed:* (BS) Ed/Soc Stud/Eng, Univ of TX 1959; (MS) Religious Ed, SW Theological Seminary; *cr:* Teacher Gatesville Sch 1959-61, New Braunfels HS 1961-62, Monterey HS 1962-63, Jonesboro Ind Sch Dist 1963-68; Missionary S Baptist Home Mission Bd 1970-76; Teacher Jonesboro Ind Sch Dist 1977-; *ai:* Beta Club, Sch Newspaper, Frosh Class Spon; Assn of TX Prof Educators, Delta Kappa Gamma 1964-68, 1978-; Jonesboro Baptist Church Sunday Sch Teacher; Conservation Teacher Yr Hamilton-Coryell Soil and Water Conservation Dist; *home:* Rt 1 Jonesboro TX 76538

LIGON, DIANE (SHAMLEY), Former Match Instructor; *b:* Wolf Point, MT; *m:* Dion F.; *c:* Taber T., Natalie J., Toby J., Chelsey L.; *ed:* (BA) Math, Carroll Coll 1973; Working Towards Masters, Various Coll MT; *cr:* Math Instr Sacred Heart HS 1973-75, Poplar Mid Sch 1975-76, Lambert HS 1976-80, Lambert HS 1985-89; *ai:* Chrldr, Pep Club Adv; Stu Cncl Spon; Girls Bsktbl, Girls Track Asst Coach; Mathcounts, MCTM Team Coach; MT Cncl of Teachers of Math 1980-89; MT Ed Assn 1976-77; PTA 1973-89; St Theresas Altar Society Pres 1982-84; 4-H Leader 1976-78; *home:* 617 Foster Ln NE Bremerton WA 98310

LIGON, MARIANNE WYNNE, Foreign Language Chairperson; *b:* Warren, AR; *m:* Robert Stark; *c:* Sarah, Star III; *ed:* (BA) Classics, Converse Coll 1976; 2nd Degree French Lang Univ of AR Monticello; *cr:* Latin I, II, III Teacher Mt St Mary Acad 1977-78; Eng, Honory, French III, & Latin I Teacher Warren HS 1984-; *ai:* Foreign Lang, Sr Play Spon; Duty Teacher Every Other Week; NC Teachers of Eng, A Clamic League 1988-; AR Foreign Lang Assn 1984-; 1st United Meth Church (Bd Mem 1989-90, Sunday Sch Teacher 1984-90; *office:* Warren HS 803 N Walnut Warren AR 71671

LIKINS, JUDITH ANN, Choral Director; *b:* Morgantown, WV; *m:* William Blaine Jr.; *c:* Micaela L., William III; *ed:* (BAED) Music/Secretarial Stud, Fairmont St Coll 1968; (MAT) Choral Conducting, WV Wesleyan 1982; *cr:* Choral/Typing Teacher Washington Irving HS 1968-70; Scndry Music Teacher Hampshire HS & Romney Jr HS 1970-; Extension Class Teacher Shepherd Coll 1987; Adult Ed Teacher Hampshire Cty Career Trng Center 1989; *ai:* Travel Extensively with Choirs; MENC (Regional Chm, All St Chm, Pres) 1968-; ACDA Pres Elect 1985-; WVEA, HCEA 1985-; Church Choir 1985-; Hampshire Cty Teacher of Yr; Whos Who Among Amer Women; Delta Kappa Gamma; *office:* Hampshire HS Rt 50 East Romney WV 26757

LIKNESS, ARLIN ELSWORTH, US History/Government Teacher; *b:* Rutland, ND; *m:* Kristine L. Nelson; *c:* Jordan P., Kara S.; *ed:* (BSED) Soc Sci/Phys Ed/Health Composite, Northern St Univ 1979; *cr:* 7th-8th Grade Soc Sci/Phys Ed Teacher Hamlin Jr HS 1979-85; 11th-12th Grade His/ Government/Phys Ed/Health Teacher Hamlin HS 1985-; *ai:* Head Ftbl; Asst Bsktbl & Track; Sr Class Adv; SD Ftbl Coaches Assn Regional Dir 1989-, Regional Coach 1988; SD Bsktbl Coaches Assn Asst Coach of Yr 1986-87; Hayti Luth Church Pres 1990; *office:* Hamlin HS Box 298 Hayti SD 57241

LILES, KANDI KAY, English & Art Teacher; *b:* South Bend, IN; *m:* Robert Land; *c:* Crystal A., Daniel R.; *ed:* (MA) Interdisciplinary Study, Univ of TX Tyler 1979; *cr:* Teacher Elkhart Ind Sch Dist 1975-77, Palestine Ind Sch Dist 1980-; *ai:* NCTE 1989-; Piney Woods Art Assn 1986-; *office:* Palestine HS Loop 256 E Palestine TX 75801

LILIE, GERALDINE J., 6th Grade Teacher; *b:* Brooklyn, NY; *m:* Martin; *c:* Julia Altman, Steven, Barbara, David; *ed:* (BS) Elem Ed, St Johns Univ 1963; (MA) Elem Ed, Adelphi Univ 1972; *cr:* 1st-3rd/5th/6th Grade Teacher Connetquot Elem Sch 1963-69; Ungraded Teacher Idle Hour Elem Sch 1969-72; 6th Grade Rdng Teacher Ronkonkoma Jr HS 1972-79; 3rd/4th Grade Teacher Sycamore Avenue Elem Sch 1980-88; 6th Grade Teacher Idle Hour Elem Sch 1989-; *ai:* 6th Grade Service Club Adv; NY St Teachers Assn, NEA 1963-; Connetquot Teachers Assn 1969-; *office:* Idle Hour Elem Sch Idle Hour Blvd Oakdale NY 11769

LILL, MICHAEL FRANCIS, Music Teacher; *b:* Evanston, IL; *m:* Manette St Leger; *ed:* (BA) Scndry Ed Instru Music Northeastern IL Univ 1985; *cr:* Assist Dir of Music Good Counsel HS 1984-; *ai:* Chicago Fed of Amer; Intnl Trumpet Guild; *office:* Good Counsel H S 3900 W Peterson Chicago IL 60659

LILL, WILLIAM H., 5th Grade Teacher; *b:* Port Huron, MI; *m:* Donna M.; *c:* Jennifer, Andrea; *ed:* (BA) Ed, 1964, (BA) Ed, 1968 MI St; Grad Stud Wayne St Univ; *cr:* 4th Grade Teacher Wadhams Elem 1963-67, 4th-5th Grade Teacher 1968-Michigamme Elem; *ai:* K-5th Grade Sci Book Selection & Cty Sci Review Comms; NEA, MEA, PHEA; Red Cross Volunteer 1962-; YMCA Bd of Dirs 1982-85; United Way Volunteer 1980-85; *office:* Michigamme Sch 2855 Michigan Rd Port Huron MI 48060

LILLARD, HERMAN EUGENE, 7th Grade Teacher; *b:* Leaksville, NC; *ed:* (BA) Ec/Bus Admin, Univ NC Greensboro 1969; (BS) Elem Ed, Univ NE Omaha 1975; (MA) Elem Ed, Appalachian St Univ 1983; *cr:* 7th Grade Teacher Fieldale Elem Sch 1975-88, Drewry Mason Mid Sch 1988-; *ai:* Math Club Spon; NEA 1975-89; *office:* Drewry Mason Mid Sch Rt 3 Box 27 Ridgeway VA 24148

LILLARD, SANDRA LYNN DOZIER, English/Spanish Teacher; *b:* Barbourville, KY; *c:* Randolph P.; *ed:* (AA) General, Univ of KY N Comm Coll 1967; (BA) Scndry Ed/Span/Eng, Univ of KY Lexington 1970; (MA) Scndry Ed, N KY Univ 1975; (Rank I) Psych, KY Univ 1979; Ed Admin Cert N KY Univ 1985; Addl Stud Numerous Wkshps 1985; *cr:* Teacher Grant Cty HS 1970-; *ai:* Span Club, The Totem Literary Magazine, Soph Class Spon; Faculty Vlybl Team Mem; Appeals Bd for Evaluation Discrepencies; KY Cncl Teachers Eng (Mem 1975-, Pres, Pres Elect 1988-); NCTE Mem 1969-; KY Ed Assn (Mem 1970-, Instr Prof Dev Comm 1988-); ASCD 1986-; Phi Delta Kappa Secy 1990, Mem of Yr 1990; Kappa Delta Pi 1987-; Amer Assn of Teachers of Span/Portuguese 1969-; Grant Cty Ed Assn (Pres, Pres Elect, Secy, Treas, Reporter) 1970-; Phi Delta Theta 1985-; Appalachia Ed Lab (Classroom Inst Comm, Bd of Dirs) 1987-; Grant Cty YMCA (Bd of Dirs, Secy) 1981-85; KY Dept of Ed & Legislature Writing Grant for Trng Teachers in Mid Sch & HS The Writing Process; Consultant, Grant Implementer 1985; Grant Cty HS Faculty Peer Awd for Professionalism 1986; *home:* 7780 Bridgegate Ct Florence KY 41042

LILLEBERG, DARRELL EUGENE, Math & Computer Sci Teacher; *b:* Willmar, MN; *c:* Lori L. Ziegler, Karla K.; *ed:* (BS) Math, St Cloud St Univ 1958; (ME) Math, SD St Univ 1965; Grad Work Math & Cmptr Sci; *cr:* Math Teacher Mills Sr HS 1958-59, Bemidji St Univ 1970; Math/Cmptr Sci Teacher Benson Sr HS 1959-; *ai:* MN Cncl Of Teachers of Math, NCTM, W Cntrl Cncl Teachers of Math (Pres 1964) 1964-; VFW Commander 1978-80; Lions Club Pres 1988-89; NSF Grant Cmptr Sci 1968-69.

LILLEY, JOAN CATANZARO, Kindergarten Teacher; *b:* Buffalo, NY; *m:* James J.; *c:* James J., Jonathan D.; *ed:* (AAS) Elem Ed, Immaculate Coll 1968; (BS) Elem Ed, D Youville Coll 1970; (MS) Elem Ed, Canisius Coll 1974; *cr:* 2nd Grade Teacher Blasdell Annex 1970-86; Kndgtn Teacher Balsdell Elem 1986-; *ai:* Developmental Kndgtn; NY St Univ Teachers, AFT, Blasdell PTA, Frontier Cntrl Teachers Assn Mem 1970-; Amer Cancer Society Volunteer 1988-; *office:* Blasdell Elem Sch 3780 S Park Ave Blasdell NY 14219

LILLEY, MELISSA DAWSON, English Teacher; *b:* Joplin, MO; *m:* Michael W.; *c:* Tristan; *ed:* (BA) Eng/Lang Art, 1982, (ME) Admin, 1987 SE OK St Univ; Wkshps Addl Trng Adolescent Lit & The Renaissance Age; *cr:* Eng Teacher Durant HS 1982-; *ai:* Comm Public Relations for Durant Ed Assn; Durant HS Academic Team Coach 1990; Durant Ed Assn, OK Ed Assn, NEA 1982-; NCTE 1989-; 1st Presbyn Church (Organist, Music Dir) 1984-; *office:* Durant HS 8th And Walnut Durant OK 74701

LILLIE, KAY, English Teacher; *b:* Flint, MI; *m:* Thomas B.; *ed:* (BA) Eng, Central MI Univ 1974; (MA) Tching Eng/Sec Sch, Univ of MI; Post Masters Studies Eastern MI Univ; *cr:* English Tchr Mt. Morris Jr. HS 1974-79; E.A.J. HS 1980-; *ai:* MI Jaycettes: Pres Burton Chapter, District Sec.

LILLY, BEVERLY LYNN, Kindergarten Teacher; *b:* Youngstown, OH; *m:* Gary J.; *ed:* (AA) Liberal Arts, Henry Ford Comm Coll 1967; (BA) Ed, 1969; (MA E 1973 Univ MI; *cr:* 3rd Grade Teacher 1969-70; 4th Grade Teacher 1970-71; 5th Grade Teacher 1971-75; Kndgtn Teacher 1975-76; 1st Grade Teacher 1976-77; 4th Grade Teacher 1977-84; Kndgtn Teacher 1984-Trenton Public Schls; *ai:* Monroe Kennel Club Obedience Chm 1987-; US Kerry Blue Terrier Club 1987-; *office:* W C Taylor Elem Sch 3700 Benson Dr Trenton MI 48183

LILLY, DONNA WOJAHN, 5th Grade Teacher; *b:* Nashville, TN; *m:* Rodman G. Jr.; *c:* Todd, Brent; *ed:* (BA) Elem Ed, Old Dominion Univ 1971; *cr:* 6th Grade Teacher Brown Elem 1973; 3rd Grade Teacher 1973, 4th-6th Grade Teacher 1978-Wessington Place Elem; *ai:* 5th/6th Grade Chm; Field Trips, Recognition Night Coord; Cheerleading Spon; Budget, Math, Sci Comm; TN Stu Cncl; NEA, TEA 1973-; SCEA (RA Rep, Public Relations Chm) 1973-; Intnl Rdng Assn; Madison Church of Christ Sunday Sch Supvr; Teacher of Yr; Pres Ronald Reagan Phone Call; *home:* 107 Ervin St Hendersonville TN 37075

LIM, DONNA, Kindergarten/Strings Teacher; *b:* San Francisco, CA; *ed:* (BA) Eng/Music, San Francisco Univ 1971; Talent Ed Inst Degree Suzuki Violin Teacher Matsumoto Japan 1985; *cr:* Part-Time Math Tutor/Jr HS Eng/Art/General Chorus Teacher St Michael Elem 1971-73; Suzuki Violin Instr San Francisco St Univ 1972-76; Kndgtn Strings Teacher Round Valley Elem Sch 1977-; *ai:* Round Valley Teachers Assn (Pres 1979) 1977-; CA Teachers Assn 1978-; Suzuki Assn of Americas 1974-; Suzuki Music Assn of CA Bd 1986-89; Covelo Volunteer Fire Dept (Firefighter, Emergency Medical Technician) 1986-, Fireman of Yr 1989; Music Round Valley Concert Series (Dir, Founder) 1977-; Covelo Womens Club (Pres 1986, 1987) 1981-; Symphony of Redwoods Violinst 1987-; Inter-Tribal Cncl Head Start Bd 1986, 1980; *home:* PO Box 32 Covelo CA 95428

LIM, LLOYD M., Math/Rdng/Phys Ed Teacher; *b:* Honolulu, HI; *ed:* (BED) Elem Ed, 1974, (MED) Elem Ed, 1975 Univ of HI; Summer Sch Courses; *cr:* Teacher Maryknoll Grade Sch 1976-; *ai:* Elem Girls & Boys Vlybl, Bsktbl, Track Coach; *office:* Maryknoll Grade Sch 1722 Dole St Honolulu HI 96822

LIMA, SALLY MURPHY, Sixth Grade Teacher; *b:* Philadelphia, PA; *m:* Robert F. Jr.; *c:* Mark X., Keith E., Michele B., Debra C.; *ed:* (AB) Chem, Rosemont Coll 1962; (MA) Ed Theory & Policy, 1984, (PHD) Ed Theory & Policy, 1990 Penn St Univ; Grad Stud Math, Penn St Univ; Various Seminars; *cr:* Research Chemist Rohm & Haas Co 1962-64; Elem Teacher Our Lady of Victory Sch 1979-; *ai:* Our Lady of Victory Cmptr Coord; NCEA 1980-; Alpha Phi Schlsp Adv 1976-80; Confraternity of Chrstn Doctrine Prin Jr HS 1974-79; Rite Chrstn Initiation of Adults Teacher of Adult Ed; Natl Sci Fnd Grant; Dessertation Moral Ed in Public Sch; *office:* Our Lady of Victory Sch 800 Westerly Pkwy State College PA 16801

LIMBAUGH, PATRICIA PEPPER, 6th Grade Teacher; *b:* Ashland, AL; *m:* Paul Daniel; *c:* Kelley, Paul D. II; *ed:* (BA) Elem Ed, Univ of AL 1974; *cr:* Spec Ed Teacher Childersburg HS 1974-76; 5th/6th Grade Combination Teacher 1976-77, 6th Grade/Phys Ed/Soc Stud Teacher 1977-80, 5th Grade Teacher 1980-89 Wheatley Mid Sch; 6th Grade Teacher Childersburg Mid Sch 1989-; *ai:* Soc Comm Chairperson; AL Ed Assn 1984-; Childersburg Little League Bd Mem 1989-; Childersburg United Meth Church Family Missions Chairperson 1987-; *home:* 121 River Run Rd Childersburg AL 35044

LIMES, WILLIAM E., JR., Science Instructor; *b:* Iola, KS; *m:* Sharon Kay Phillips; *c:* Mark W., Pamela K. Limes Jobe; *ed:* (BSED) Bio, 1966, (MS) Bio, 1973 Pittsburg St Univ; Grad Stud NEOSU, KS Univ, Emporia St Univ; *cr:* Bio Instr Meadowbrook Jr HS; Pharmaceutical Rep Lederle Laboratories 1967-69; Bio Instr Olathe HS 1969-79; Sci Instr Grove Sr HS 1979-86, Olathe South HS 1986-; *ai:* R C Model Airplane Clubs; NABT, NEA; Kiwanis Pres 1970-71; R C Barnstormers Secy 1988-89; Volunteer Fire Dept Instr 1984-86; Grove OK City Cncl 1986; Outstanding Young Educator Awd 1971; *home:* 1520 W Forest Olathe KS 66061

LINAWEAVER, JULIA HOVERMALE, Third Grade Teacher; *b:* Berkeley Springs, WV; *w:* George W. (dec); *c:* Dale William, Larry Brenton; *ed:* (AB) Elem Ed/Eng, Shepherd Coll 1954; *cr:* Teacher Hancock Elem Sch 1954-57; Berkeley Springs Grade Sch & Widmyer Elem Sch 1965-; *ai:* NEA; WVEA; Delta Kappa Gamma Area Coord 1986-88; Alpha Delta Kappa Treas; OES; First United Meth Church Officer; Outstanding Elem Teachers of Amer; Delta Kappa Gamma; *office:* Widmyer Elem Sch Rt 522 S Berkeley Springs WV 25411

LIND, JOHANNA SHERYL (SMITH), Chapter I Reading Teacher; *b:* Monahans, TX; *m:* David Walter; *ed:* (BS) Elem Ed, 1972, (MAT) Rdng, 1977 NM St Univ; *cr:* 1st Grade Teacher Holloman Primary Sch 1972-73, Buena Vista Elem 1973-76; 2nd Grade Teacher 1976-80, 1st Grade Teacher 1980-87 Buena Vista Elem; Chapter I Rdng Teacher Holloman Primary Sch 1987-; *ai:* Intnl Rdng Assn Building Rep; Golden Poet Awd 1989; *office:* Holloman Primary Sch PO Box 1209 Holloman AFB NM 88330

LIND, WILLIAM ROBERT, Mathematics Teacher; *b:* Saline, MI; *m:* Linda Katherine Carlson; *c:* Kari, Sarah, Angela, Kyle; *ed:* (BSED) Math, 1972, (MSED) Math/Ed, 1977 Univ of WI Whitewater; *cr:* Math Teacher Greenfield HS 1972-; Asst Professor of Math Lakeland Coll 1981-; *ai:* Group Facilitator; Stu Asst Prgm; Mathematical Assn of America; NCTM; NEA; *office:* Greenfield HS 4800 S 60th St Greenfield WI 53220

LINDAUER, PATRICIA CARROLL, Elementary Teacher; *b:* Henderson, KY; *m:* Darrel W.; *ed:* (BA) Elem Ed, Univ of Evansville 1971; (MA) Cnslr Ed, W KY Univ 1974; Rank I Cert Cnslr Ed; Cert Elem Principalship, Supvr, Dir of Pupil Personnel; Admin; *cr:* 1st Grade Teacher Audubon Grade Sch 1971-76; Cnslr Henderson Cty Schls 1976-77; 3rd-6th Grade Teacher Cntrl Grade Sch 1977-89; 1st Grade Teacher E Heights Elem Sch 1989-; *ai:* Cmptr Comm; Henderson Cty Assn (Pres, VP 1973-75); KY Ed Assn, NEA, Phi Delta Kappa; Henderson Cty Litercy Cncl (Pres, VP) 1984-; Rotary Club Sargeant-at-Arms 1990; United Way Speakers Bureau 1989-; *home:* 2951 Briarcliff Trail Henderson KY 42420

LINDBERG, DIANE MARIE, 7th Grade Mathematics Teacher; *b:* Bronx, NY; *m:* John David; *c:* Lisa M., John B.; *ed:* (BS) Ed, 1983, (MA) Ed, 1987 SUNY Cortland; *cr:* 7th Grade Math Teacher Chadwicks Jr HS 1983-; *ai:* Stu Cncl Adv; Union Rep; Mid Sch Transition Team; Sch Wide Jeopardy Tournament Organizer; Natl Mid Sch Assn 1989-; NY St Assn of Math Teacher 1987-89; Sauquoit Valley Youth Assn Coach 1990; PTO Rep; Empire St Regents Schlsp Math & Sci Teachers; *office:* Chadwicks Jr HS 3354 Oneida St Chadwicks NY 13319

LINDBERG, LOIS RUTH (SCHARSICH), Fifth Grade Teacher; *b:* Oak Park, IL; *m:* Robert; *c:* Steven, Susan Johnson, David, Carol, Lewis; *ed:* (BA) Ed, N IL Univ 1954; *cr:* 5th Grade Teacher River Forest 90 1971-; *home:* 925 Prospect Elmhurst IL 60126

LINDELOF, ROGER HADLEY, District Reading Coordinator; *b:* Auburn, CA; *m:* Mina Nielsen; *c:* John; *ed:* (BS) Geography, Univ of WI Superior 1969; (MS) Rdng, Univ of WI River Falls 1979; *cr:* 7th-12th Grade Geography/Eng/Rdng Teacher 1969-89; Dist Rdng Coord 1989-; *ai:* Jr HS Forensics Coach; Intnl Rdng Assn, WI St Rdng Assn; *home:* PO Box 164 Glenwood City WI 54013

LINDEMAN, CHERYL DE WYER, Biology Instructor/Advisor; *b:* Cleveland, OH; *m:* L. Dean; *c:* Sarah, Kristen, Allison; *ed:* (BA) Bio, W Henberg Univ 1971; (MS) Bio, Univ of Akron 1973; (EDD) Higher Ed/Environmental Sci, Univ of VA 1984; Advanced Training in Cell & Molecular Bio, Cath Univ of Amer 1988; BioTechnology Institute; NSF Fellowship Univ of Rochester Sch of Medicine 1989; Electron Microscopy Wkshp; VA Tech Plant Sci 1987; *cr:* Phys Sci Teacher Amherst Cty Jr HS 1973-75; Bio Teacher Amherst Cty HS 1975-77; Adjunct Assist Professor of Bio Cntrl VA Comm Coll 1975-89; Instr/Adv Cntrl VA Governors Sch Sci Technology 1985-; *ai:* Adv Stud Activities Bd; Coord Internship Prgm; Sci Fair Adv; Natl Consortium for Specialized Scndry Sch of Math Sci/Technology Bd of Dir/Mem 1988-; VA Acad of Sci 1986-; NABT 1986; Outstanding Bio Teacher Honorable Mention 1989; Natl Assn for Industry Ed Cooperative 1988; Natl Utilization Awd 1988; Electron Microscopy Society of Amer 1989-; Amer Institute Biological Sci 1988-; Phi Delta Kappa 1986-; NSF Fellowship 1989; Biotechnology Institute Univ of Rochester; Published in VA Journal of Sch; IL Journal for Gifted Children; *office:* Central VA Governors Sch 3020 Wards Ferry Rd Lynchburg VA 24501

LINDEMANN, REGINA MICHELLE (GWOZDECKA), 4-8th Grade Lang Arts Teacher; *b:* Paterson, NJ; *m:* John C.; *c:* John, Marc, Matthew (dec); *ed:* (BS) 1st-8th Elem Ed, William Paterson Coll 1954; *cr:* 2nd Grade Teacher B F Gibbs Sch 1954-56; 3rd Grade Teacher 1966-69, 6th-8th Grade Lang Arts Teacher 1970-76, 4th-8th Grade Lang Arts Teacher 1976- Zion Lutheran Sch; *office:* Zion Lutheran Sch 1st Ave & Elm St Westwood NJ 07675

LINDENMUTH, DOUGLAS D., Mathematics Teacher; *b:* Catasauqua, PA; *m:* Elsie Mae Thomas; *c:* Duane, Lisa, Denise; *ed:* (BS) Math, E Stroudsburg Univ 1958; Math Related Subjects Various Insts; *cr:* Math Teacher Northampton Sch Dist 1958-63, Parkland Sch Dist 1963-; *ai:* Golf Coach; Parkland Ed Assn Pres 1970-71; PA Math 1980-; Natl Sci Fnd 1959; *home:* 826 Liberty St North Catasauqua PA 18032

LINDER, RAYMOND ANDERSON, Mathematics Teacher; *b:* Tarentum, PA; *m:* Ann; *c:* Jeffrey, Gregory; *ed:* (BA) Ec, Hamilton Coll 1969; (MA) Math, SUNY Brockport 1975; *cr:* Math Teacher Webster HS 1969-; Adjunct Professor Monroe Comm Coll 1978-.

LINDERER, ROBERT JOSEPH, Guidance Counselor; *b:* Festus, MO; *m:* Maranetta Angela Avina; *ed:* (AA) Pre-Ed, Jefferson Coll 1984; (BA) His/Poly Sci, Maryville Coll 1986; Guidance Counseling, SE MO St Univ 1990; *cr:* Teacher 1986-88, Cnslr 1988- Hillsboro Sr HS; *ai:* Ftbl Coach; NEA 1986-; Jefferson Cty Sch Cnslrs Assn Voc Dept Chairperson 1989-; Crystal City Park Bd VP 1988-; *office:* Hillsboro Sr HS 12 Hawk Dr Hillsboro MO 63050

LINDERMAN, JUDY ANN, Principal; *b:* Detroit, MI; *m:* John; *c:* Kim, Heidi; *ed:* (BA) Math, Univ of Detroit 1964; (MA) Ed, Univ of MI 1970; Univ of North TX Mid Mgmt Cert; *cr:* Teacher Dearborn Ind Schls 1964-66, Los Angeles Unified Schls 1967-72/1971-86; Asst Prin 1986-89, PriN 1989 Arlington ISD; *ai:* Responsible for Schl (K-6) 675 Students 70 Faculty/Staff Members; TX Elem Prin Supervisors Assn 1986-; Phi Delta Kappa 1986-; PTA 1984 TX Terrific Teacher of Yr; Teacher of Yr Ditto Elem 1983; *office:* Johns Elem-Arlington 1900 Sherry Arlington TX 76010

LINDGREN, MONA G., Social Studies Teacher; *b:* Geneva, IL; *m:* Mark; *c:* Ryan, Jason, Todd; *ed:* (BS) Elem Ed, 1970, (MS) Ed, 1972 N IL Univ; Grad Work Beyond MS Gifted Ed; *cr:* Jr HS Soc Stud Teacher Thompson Jr HS 1970; *ai:* Sch Dist 303 Curr & Mid Sch Comms; Teachers Encouraging Colleges; IEA, NEA 1970-; SCEA Rep 1971-72; 20 Yr Service Awd; *office:* Thompson Jr HS 705 W Main St Saint Charles IL 60174

LINDGREN, NINA B., English Teacher/English Chair; *b:* Pryce, KY; *m:* Carl W.; *c:* Steven; *ed:* (BAED) Eng/Speech, 1969, (MAED) Ed, 1983 Akron Univ; *cr:* Eng Teacher Akron North HS 1969-70; Speech/Eng Teacher 1970-, Eng Dept Chairperson 1987-Springfield HS; *ai:* Schlsp & Inservice Comm; Haromano Adv; NEA, OH Ed Assn 1980-84; Springfield Local Assn of Classroom Teachers (Schlsp Chairperson, Teacher Ethics & Responsibilities Chairperson) 1986-, Htan Henitae 1988-89, 1990; Springfield Local Cable Comm Bd Chairperson 1982-88, Trustees Citation 1988; Process of Writing Grant; OH St Dept Grant; Early Eng Composition Accessment Prgm Natl Grant 1984; Springfield Township Citation for Service to Youth 1975-76; Summit Cty PTA Springfield HS Outstanding Teacher of Yr 1990; *home:* 2220 Ritzmanor Dr Uniontown OH 44685

LINDGREN, RUSSELL EDMUND, JR., Soc Sci Dept Chair; *b:* Berkeley, CA; *m:* Nancy Lynn Ettelson; *c:* Kristin, Rusty; *ed:* (BA) Amer His/Poly Sci, Univ of CA Santa Barbara 1969; (MA) Amer His, CA St Univ Hayward 1973; ABD Amer His; *cr:* Instr/Cnslr Tennyson HS 1975-77; Instr/Coach Ohlone Coll 1975-79, Foothill HS 1977-79, Sonora HS 1979-; *ai:* Close-Up & His Day Coord; Academic Decathlon Coach; Curr Comm; Juvenile Justice & Delinquency Prevention Commission Chm; AHA 1972-; CAWEE Pres 1987-88; OAH 1973-; Society for His Ed 1972-; Sonora Faculty Assn Pres; Lions Clubs Intnl Bd of Dir 1980-86; *office:* Sonora HS 430 N Washington St Sonora CA 95370

LINDLEY, DELORIS RAE (ORR), Business Teacher; *b:* Calvin, OK; *m:* Paul Melvin; *c:* Judy Schornick, Paula Sharp, Cheryl Tawes, Paul Jr.; *ed:* (BS) Home Ec, 1962, Bus Ed, 1970 East Cntrl Univ; Post Grad Work Elem Ed, Durant OK & Ada OK; *cr:* Elem Teacher Yeager Elem Schls 1962-66; Bus Teacher Calvin Public Schls 1966-; *ai:* Jr Class Spon; Academic Bowl Coach; Interscholastic Meet Coord; NEA; OK Ed Assn; Hughes Ed Assn; Teacher of Yr Awd 1984; *office:* Calvin Public Schls P O Box 127 Calvin OK 74531

LINDMAN, ROBERT ALLAN, Sixth Grade Teacher; *b:* Duluth, MN; *m:* Marilyn Edgar; *c:* Keri; *ed:* (BA) Elem Ed, Bethel Coll 1966; (MA) Elem Ed, Univ of MN 1976; Grad Stud Various Insts; *cr:* Intermediate Grade Teacher Edgerton Elem 1966-; *ai:* Chorus Dir; Sch Hospitality, Sch Dist Art Curr, Building Cmptr Comms; Track Coach; MEA; Trinity Baptist Church 1966-; Ed Venture Fund Grant 1989-; Dist Achievement Awds; *office:* Edgerton Elem Sch 1929 Edgerton St Saint Paul MN 55117

LINDMARK, MARIE NELSON, Elementary Teacher of Gifted; *b:* Danville, PA; *c:* Jeff, Steve, Sarah; *ed:* (BA) Elem Ed, Augustana Rock Island IL 1965; (MS) Gifted Ed, W IL Univ 1990; *cr:* 3rd Grade Teacher Denkmann Sch 1981-84; 8th Grade Teacher Edison Jr HS 1985; 2nd Grade Teacher Ridgewood Sch 1986-87; Mgr/Teacher of Gifted Ed Rock Island 1988-; *ai:* Gifted Ed Comm Chairperson; After Prom Party Co Chairperson; Drama Boosters Officer; IEA, NEA, IL Gifted Cncl; Jr Symphony Bd, St Paul Luth Church (Comms, Choir); Luth Church in America Grad Grant; *office:* Rock Island Public Schls 6th Ave & 21st St Rock Island IL 61201

LINDOW, BRADLEY T., Mathematics Teacher; *b:* Park Rapids, MN; *ed:* (BS) Math, ND St Univ 1987; *cr:* Stu Teacher Moorehead Jr HS 1986; Math Instr Dover-Eyota HS 1987-; *ai:* Head Bsbl, C-Squad Ftbl, Bsktbl, Math League Coach; NEA, MN St Coaches Assn; *home:* Box 93 Eyota MN 55934

LINDQUIST, SANDRA SKODACK, Fourth Grade Classroom Teacher; *b:* Chicago, IL; *m:* Fred R.; *c:* F. Russell, Alexander S.; *ed:* (BS) Ed/Scndry Soc Stud Univ of CO Boulder 1970; (MA) Elem Ed, Univ of CO Colorado Springs 1985; Grad Stud; *cr:* Soc Stud Teacher Pueblo South HS 1970-71, Pueblo Corwin Mid Sch 1971-72, Pueblo East HS 1972-75; 4th/5th Grade Teacher Pueblo Irving Elem Sch 1977-81, Pueblo Jefferson Elem Sch 1983-; *ai:* Team Leader Jefferson Elem; Soc Stud Curr Comm Pueblo Dist 60; NEA, CO Ed Assn, Pueblo Ed Assn 1970-; BSA (Faculty Liaison, Asst Den Leader) 1989-; US Dept of Ed Elem Sch Recognition Prgm Certificate of Merit Jefferson Elem Faculty Mem; Newspapers in Ed Rdng Act Published; *office:* Jefferson Elem Sch 401 S Prairie Ave Pueblo CO 81005

LINDQUIST, TARRY CLIFTON, 5th Grade Teacher; *b:* Aberdeen, WA; *m:* Malcolm H.; *c:* Tia, Tani Lih; *ed:* (BA) Elem Ed, 1962, (MED) Childrens Drama, 1964 Cntrl WA Univ; Grad Stud Developmental Rdng, Multicultural, Global Ed, Law-Related Ed; *cr:* 3rd Grade Teacher Mercer Crest Elem 1962-63; Elem Teacher Malem South Pacific 1964-66; Teacher Bellevue Comm Coll 1968-69, Ponope Teacher Ed Center 1969-75; HS Teacher 1976-75, 5th Grade Teacher 1980- Mercer Island Public Schls; *ai:* Stu Cncl Adv; Drama Choreographer; Dist Soc Stud Articulation Comm; WA St Cncl for Soc Stud Pres 1988-, WA St Soc Stud Teacher of Yr 1986-87; NCSS Continued Prof Dev Task Force 1988-; Center for Civic Ed Regional Consultant 1989-; Natl PTA, Honorable Mention Phoebe A Hearst Awd 1985; Fulbright Group Travel Scholar to China 1986; *office:* Lakeridge Elem Sch 8215 S E 78th Mercer Island WA 98040

LINDSAY, DONNA JEANNE, Physical Ed/Health Teacher; *b:* Davenport, IA; *m:* Robert Mathew Jr.; *c:* James M.; *ed:* (BS) Phys Ed, Univ of IL 1973; *cr:* Phys Ed/Health Teacher Churchill Jr HS 1974-; *ai:* 8th Grade Class Spon; PEO Chaplin 1988-; *office:* Churchill Jr H S 905 Maple St Galesburg IL 61401

LINDSAY, MARCIA A., English/Social Studies Teacher; *b:* Ft Meade, MD; *c:* Nathan; *ed:* (BA) His, 1976, (MA) His, 1990 Angelo St Univ; *cr:* Teacher Ballinger Ind Sch Dist 1978-80, Veribest Ind Sch Dist 1980-; *ai:* Sch Annual Spon; Effective Schls, Cmmty Drug, Cmmty Gifted/talented Selection Comms; Phi Delta Kappa 1985-; ATPE 1988-; TX Assn For Gifted & Talented 1989-; Article Published in Fort Concho Journal; *home:* 2514 Harvard Ave San Angelo TX 76904

LINDSAY, ROBERT BRUCE, Science Teacher; *b:* Ventura, CA; *m:* Dreena O'Connor; *c:* Sarah M.; *ed:* (BA) Environmental Stud, Univ of CA Santa Barbara 1978; *cr:* Sci Teacher Carpinteria HS 1985-; Hourly Instr Santa Barbara City Coll 1985-; *ai:* Sci Club & Campus Act Adv; Kappa Delt Pi 1985-; Santa Barbara Audubon Society (Pres 1982-85, Newsletter Ed 1981-85); *office:* Carpinteria HS 4810 Foothill Rd Carpinteria CA 93013

LINDSAY, VERNIECE OLIVER, Math Teacher/Math Dept Chair; *b:* Halsell, AL; *c:* Stephanie D.; *ed:* (BA) Ed, Governors St 1977; *cr:* 4th Grade Teacher Kich Sch 1977-79; Math Consultant Garfield Sch 1979-80; Math Teacher Rosa L Parks 1980-; *ai:* Comm to Revise Report Card, Promotion Criteria, Develop a Philosophy of Ed, Statement of Mission, Goals, Prgm Objectives, Curr, Instructional Objectives, Evaluation Stans; AFT, IFT Local 1698 VP 1980-; *office:* Rosa L Parks Mid Sch 147th & Robey Dixmoor IL 60426

LINDSEY, BARBARA H., Headmaster; *b:* Dothan, AL; *m:* John D.; *c:* Kim, Katie, John; *ed:* (BA) Soc Sci, Troy St Univ 1969; *cr:* Soc Stud/French Teacher Abbeville HS 1970-75; Soc Stud/French Teacher Abbeville Christian Academy 1981-89; Headmaster Abbeville Chrstn Acad 1989; *ai:* NASSP 1989; Appris Study Guild Pres; *home:* PO Box 518 Abbeville AL 36310

LINDSEY, HARRY LEE, Mathematics Teacher; *b:* Canton, MS; *c:* Adrian; *ed:* (BA) Math, Jackson St Univ 1968; (MS) Math Ed, Southern Univ 1974; Phillip Jr Coll & Univ of AR Pine Bluff; *cr:* Teacher Pilate HS 1969-71, Helena-W Helena Sch 1972-; *ai:* NEA, AEA, CTA 1974-; *home:* PO Box 2049 West Helena AR 72390

LINDSEY, JAMES ROBERT, Vocal Music Instructor; *b:* Kansas City, MO; *m:* Julie Lynn Koonce; *c:* Terryn, James III; *ed:* (BA) Music Ed, Lincoln Univ 1983; *cr:* Vocal Music Instr/Choir Dir NE Law Public Service-Military Magnet HS 1985-; *ai:* Concert Choir Dir; Jazz Ensemble; Voice Coaching; *office:* NE LPS Military Magnet HS 415 S Van Brunt Kansas City MO 64124

LINDSEY, JANET CHAUDOIN, First Grade Teacher; *b:* Pike View, KY; *m:* Jimmy Ray; *c:* Jonathan, Jeremy, Joshua; *ed:* (BS) Elem Ed, 1974, (MS) Elem Ed, 1980 W KY Univ; *cr:* 1st Grade Teacher Lincoln Trail Elem Sch 1974-; *home:* 300 White Oak Dr Elizabethtown KY 42701

LINDSEY, MARIE EVON POE, 3rd Grade Teacher; *b:* Lynchburg, VA; *m:* Leroy; *c:* Monica Y.; *ed:* (BA) Sociology, VA Seminary Coll 1960; (BS) Scndry Ed, St Pauls Coll 1965; (MA) Supervision & Admin, Bowie Univ 1974; (MED) Rdng, Towson Univ 1977; Certified Income Tax; *cr:* 1st-5th Grade/8th-12th Grade Teacher; Cashier West Point Military Acad; Income Tax Consultant H & R Block; Admin/Supvr Lindseys TV & Radio; Human Relations Chairperson; Dir A A Cty Credit Union; Kndgtn-12th Grade Rdng Teacher Towson Univ & Loyola Coll & Morgan Univ; *ai:* Cmmty Meeting for Civic Improvements; Political, Democratic Party of MD; Leader for Charitable Organizations; GSA Aide; Church & Sunday Sch Leader Teacher; NCO Organization West Point Acad Mem; A A Cty Federal Credit Union Secy; Eastern Star (Mem, Organizer of Schlsp Benefit Prgm); NEA, MSTA, TAAC, St & Local Ed Assn Mem; *home:* 909 Wanda Rd Linthicum Heights MD 21090

LINDSEY, NINA ATKINSON, 4th Grade Teacher; *b:* Danville, VA; *m:* Robert E.; *c:* Megan L., Rob; *ed:* (BS) Elem Ed, Radford Univ 1972; (MS) Curr/Instruction Gifted Ed, 1989; *cr:* 4th-6th Grade Teacher Whitmell Elem 1972-; *ai:* Gifted Coord; Cheerleading Spon; Co-Chm Self Study Comm; 4-H Adv; Delta Kappa Gamma 1980-83; VA Assn Gifted Educators 1988-; Sylvania Garden Club Pres 1987-89 June Tucker Awd 1987; Spring Garden Women of Church Pres 1986-88; Outstanding Young Woman America 1980; *home:* Rt 2 Box 323 Dry Fork VA 24549

LINDSEY, REVA STALLINGS, Second Grade Teacher; *m:* John Seldon; *c:* Nancy L., Kenneth H.; *ed:* (BA) Ed/Psych, Carson Newman Coll 1962; Grad Work Univ of TN 1977; *cr:* 7th Grade Teacher Dandridge Elem 1955; 5th-8th Grade Teacher Mt Horeb Sch 1955-58; 7th Grade Teacher Dandridge Elem 1958-59; EMR Class Teacher 1959-64, 2nd Grade Teacher 1964- Jefferson Elem; *ai:* Project Star Prgm Developed by TN St Dept Ed 1987-88; Chairperson Grade Level, Building Comm; NEA 1955-; TN Ed Assn 1955-, Over 30 Yr Certificate 1989; E TN Ed Assn 1955-; Jefferson Cty Ed Assn Chairperson 1955-; Golden Apple Awd 1988-89; *home:* 1301 Leon Dr Jefferson City TN 37760

LINDSEY, WANDA J. GOLDSMITH, Computer Teacher/Coordinator; *b:* Morris, OK; *m:* Robert G.; *c:* Jason, Erin; *ed:* (BA) Math, Southwestern Coll 1971; Wichita St Univ; KS St Univ; Emporia St Univ; *cr:* Cmptr Stud Teacher 1971-, Cmptr Coord 1984- Haysville Campus HS; *ai:* Discipline & Attendance Comm; Cmptr Curr Comm Chairperson; Dist Curricular Cncl; Jr Class Spon; Mid-America Assn Cmptrs in Ed 1984-; Haysville Ed Assn, KS Ed Assn, NEA 1971-; Order of Eastern Star, White Shrine of Jerusalem 1967-; Amer Red Cross Volunteer 1971-85; Civil Preparedness Volunteer 1972-89; Cmptr Files Published; *office:* Haysville Campus HS 2100 W 55th St S Wichita KS 67217

LINDSKOG, MARJORIE O., Fifth Grade Teacher; *b:* Rochester, MN; *ed:* (BA) Sociology, CO Coll 1959; Teaching Certificate Univ of S CO 1966; (MAT) Liberal Art, CO Coll 1972; Educl Admin, Educl Kinesiology, Format Right-Left Brain, CO Elem Math Retreat, Several Wkshps, Family Math, Whole Lang; Volunteer Achievement Certificate-Cty Credit Union League; *cr:* Field Adv/Camp Dir Columbine Girl Scout Cncl 1959-66; Dir WY St Girl Scout Camp 1966-67; Teacher Sunset Park Elem 1966-; Dir St Albans Girl Scout Camp 1968-69; Instr Univ of S CO 1990; *ai:* Elem Math Inservices; Phi Delta Kappa 1981-, (VP Membership 1986-87, Treas 1989-, Newsletter 1983-86, 1987-89) Editor 1983-; NCTM 1988-; CO Cncl Teachers Math 1988-, Outstanding Elem Math Teacher 1989; NEA, CO Ed Assn, Pueblo Ed Assn 1966-; Columbine Girl Scout Cncl (Bd of Dirs 1975-76, 1983-84) Thanks Badge 1984; Amer Camping Assn (Standards Visitor, Outdoor Leadership Trainer) 1967-; Altrusa Intnl Service Club 1989-; Pueblo Teachers Credit Union (Chairperson 1988-, Credit Comm 1986-); Bronco Mathmania Math Lessons Ftbl Statistics for Newspapers in Ed 1987-89; Creativity Grade Teacher Article; *home:* 2810 7th Ave Pueblo CO 81003

LINDSLEY, JOYCE WICKHAM, 7th/8th Grade Music Teacher; *b:* Syracuse, NY; *m:* Robert; *c:* Janice, Michael; *ed:* (AAS) Music, Onondaga Comm Coll 1969; (BA) Music, SUNY Potsdam 1971; Performance Certificate Ed; Grad Work Syracuse Univ & SUNY Oswego; *cr:* Elem Vocal/Instrumental Teacher 1971-80, Jr HS Instrumental Teacher 1981- Cntrl Square Schls; *ai:* Performances Rotary Club, Lions Club, Little League, Sr Citizens; Jazz & Marching Band Dir; HS Marching Band; Cntrl Square Sch Dist Music Newsletter; Jr HS Musical; Music Educators Natl Conference Secy 1970-71; BSA Hiawatha Cncl Music Badge Cnslr 1979-; Brewenton Meth Church Organist 1981-83; Campus Sch Stu Teacher 1973; SUNY Potsdam Hearing Impaired Experimental Prgm; All Cty & Area All St Band Adjudicator; Guest Conductor Elem All Cty Band; Performed with Syracuse Symphony; *home:* 5781 Bartell Rd Brewerton NY 13029

LINDSTROM, GORDON T., Science Teacher; *b:* Mt Carmel, IL; *m:* Harriett Gross; *c:* Ann; *ed:* (BA) Zoology, S IL Univ 1960; (MAT) Sci Ed, Univ of MT 1968; (PHD) Sci Ed, S IL Univ 1974; Tour of Selected Lang & Sci Schls Soviet Union; Narrow Canal Study Cruise England; Madeline Hunter Seminars; Rdng Wkshp at Elmhurst Coll; *cr:* Epidemiologist US Public Health Service 1960-62; Sci Teacher Armstrong HS 1962-64; Chem Teacher Alton Sr HS 1964-65; Bio Teacher Mc Clure HS 1965-66; Phys Sci/Physics Teachers Proviso E HS 1970-; *ai:* Working with HS Drop Outs; IL Sci Teachers Assn, NSTA, Museum of Sci & Industry; Art Inst of Chicago; Fellowship S IL Univ While Studying for Advanced Degree; Co-Author General Sci Curr 1971; Author Spec Report on Math & Sci IL St Bd of Ed 1980; *office:* Proviso E HS 807 S First Ave Maywood IL 60153

LINDSTROM, RHEA LETETIA, Consultant; *b:* Los Angeles, CA; *m:* Ronald E. Engel; *ed:* (BA) Poly Sci, 1953, (MA) Scandinavian Stud, Univ of CA 1963; (MA) Ed, George Mason Univ 1971; Fil Can Sociology, Univ of Stockholm Sweden 1964; PhD Prgm Comparative Ed & Poly Systems, Univ S CA 1979; *cr:* Demonstration Teacher Univ of CA 1959-64; Teacher of Gifted Falls Church 1965-71; Coord/Teacher of Gifted & Talented Fairfax Cty 1971-87; Domestic/Intnl Consultant Self Employed 1987-; *ai:* Volunteer & Coord Literacy Prgms; Pi Lambda Theta; OT Civic Assn; Fairfax Sch Bd Outstanding Contributions to Sch System Recognition; Numerous Articles Gifted & Curr Dev; Univ of CA Newhouse Grant; Natl Endowment Hum Fellowship; Teacher of Yr Nominee; Agnes Meyer Outstanding Teacher of Yr Nominee; John Hopkins Univ Certificate of Academic Distinction.

LINDSTROM, ROSELYNN MARY, Mathematics Department Chair; *b:* Escanaba, MI; *c:* Colleen; *ed:* (BA) Math/Eng, N MI Univ 1968; Eng, N MI; Math, Univ of NV Reno; *cr:* Eng/Math St Lawrence HS 1968-69, Gladstone HS 1969-70, St Xaviers Acad 1970-71; Math Teacher Bishop Manogue HS 1971-; *ai:* Academic Team, NHS, Sodality Adv; Math Dept Head; Schlsp & Academic Comm; Washoe Cty Math Assn VP 1989-; N CA Math Assn 1989-; NCTM, NCEA; Holy Cross Cath Church Secy Parish Cncl 1985-87; Our Lady of Snows Sch Secy Sch Bd 1989-; Nom Presidential Awd 1987-; *office:* Bishop Manogue Catholic HS 400 Bartlett St Reno NV 89512

LINDVAHL, CRAIG A., Director of Bands; *b:* Taylorville, IL; *m:* Beth Ann Meyer; *ed:* (BS) Music Ed, E IL Univ 1979; *cr:* Bands Dir Teutopolis Dist 50 1979-; *ai:* NBC HS Band Music Video Projects; NEA, IL Ed Assn 1979-; Teutopolis Ed Assn (VP, Treas, Pres)1979-; Intnl Fed of Musicians 1973-; Peace Child Intnl Musical Dir 1988-; Nom Applegate Dorros Awd for Peace & Intnl Understanding 1990; Excl in Ed Awd S IL Univ 1988; Those Who Excel Awd IL St Bd of Ed 1988; IL Teacher of Yr Finalist 1988; IL Distinguished Educator Awd IL St Bd of Ed & Milken Family Fnds 1989; *office:* Teutopolis Dist 50 Box 700 Teutopolis IL 62467

LINER, RODNEY WADE, History Teacher; *b:* San Mateo, CA; *m:* Patricia A. Terrill; *c:* Daniel R., Thomas S.; *ed:* (BA) His/Eng, Claremont Mens Coll 1966; (MA) Ed, Stanford Univ 1967; Oxford Tutorial Coll 1970; *cr:* His Teacher San Carlos HS 1967-82, Sequoia HS 1982-; *ai:* Faculty Spon; SADD; Faculty Forum Mem; Sch Site Cncl; NEA 1967-; CA Cncl for Soc Stud 1988-; CA Teachers Assn 1967-; European Lecturer & Tour Guide 1976-; Wrote & Directed Video 1989; *home:* 1926 Eucalyptus Ave San Carlos CA 94070

LING, LARRY K., Spanish/French Teacher; *b:* New York, NY; *ed:* (BS) Foreign Lang Teaching, NY Univ 1985; (MA) Span, Middlebury Coll 1989; *cr:* Summer Sch Span Teacher Xavier HS 1985-86; Span/French Teacher Regis HS 1985-; *ai:* Regis Open House Asst; Co-Moderated Sch Dances, Hockey Club, Regis in Spain & Mexico & Span Club; Pi Lambda Theta/Rho Chapter 1985-; Natl Honors Prof Assn in Ed 1985-; Amer Assn Teachers of Span & Portuguese 1985-; AATF 1988-; Translated for NY Landmarks Preservation Commission; *office:* Regis H S 55 E 84th St New York NY 10028

LINGENFELTER, MARY REINHARDT, 7th Grade Math Teacher; *b:* Aurora, IL; *c:* Amy; *ed:* (BS) Phys Ed, Spaulding Univ 1968; Counseling/Cmptrs & Math; *cr:* Phys Ed Teacher Cntrl HS 1968-73; Math Teacher/Sftbl Coach McKinley Jr HS 1974-81; Bus Ed Teacher/Sftbl Coach Southwestern HS 1981-88; Math/Bus Ed Teacher McKinley Mid Sch 1988-; *ai:* Asst Jr Var Sftbl Coach Herton HS; Involved Parent; Work with at Risk Stu; MI Bus Ed Assn 1984-88; MI Ed Assn 1968-; NEA 1968-; United Teachers of Flint 1968-; Burton Eagles Conductor 1989-; Whos

Who Among Amer Coll & Univ 1968; *home:* 4285 E Atherton Rd Burton MI 48519

LINGER, MARTHA JANE, 1st/2nd Grade Teacher; *b:* Fairmont, WV; *m:* Paul W.; *c:* Amy, Erin; *ed:* (BA) Elem Ed, Fairmont St Coll 1971; Speech Comm, WV Univ; *cr:* Teaching Prin Greenwood Elem Sch 1971-72; Elem Teacher Baxter Grade Sch 1972-85; 1st/2nd Grade Teacher Fairview Elem Sch 1985-; *ai:* NEA, WVEA 1972-; Intnl Rdng Assn 1990; *home:* 925 Virginia Ave Fairmont WV 26554

LINGERFELT, CHARLENE HEAD, 7th Grade Language Art Teacher; *b:* Jacksonville, FL; *m:* Terry E;; *c:* Cheri, Wendy, Thomas; *ed:* (BA) Elem Ed, Berry Coll 1967; Mid Sch Courses for Cert, Data Collecting, Mentor Trng, Cmptr Ed, Supervising Teacher; *cr:* Early Chldhd/1st-4th Grade Teacher Rome City Schls 1967-79; 5th-8th Grade Sci Teacher Berry Acad 1980-83; Mid Sch Teacher Floyd Cty Schls 1983-89; *ai:* Mid Sch Grades Stu Support Team; FCEA, GEA, NEA 1967-; Baptist Women (Pres 1986-87) 1984-89; *home:* 273 Morrison Cpgd Rd Rome GA 30161

LINGLE, MURIEL ELLEN ANDERSON, Fourth Grade Teacher; *b:* Sundown Township, MN; *m:* Dale A.; *c:* Barbara J., Tamara J.; *ed:* (BS) Elem Ed, Union Coll 1968; (MA) Elem Ed, Univ of NE Lincoln 1976; *cr:* K-8th Grade Teacher Rural Sch Dists 114 & 61 1959-62; Cntrl Dist 147 1963-67; 1st Grade Teacher Helen Hyatt Elem Sch 1968-70; 1st-6th Grade Teacher Crete Elem 1970-75; 4th Grade Teacher Crete Public Elem Sch 1975-; *ai:* NEA, NE St Ed Assn 1959-; *office:* Crete Public Elem Sch 11th & Linden Crete NE 68333

LINK, BARBARA MARIE, Social Studies Teacher; *b:* Peoria, IL; *ed:* (BA) His/Scndry Ed, Bradley Univ 1969; (MA) US His, Notre Dame Univ 1983; Ed, Soc Sci, Theology; *cr:* Jr HS Soc Stud Teacher Epiphany Grade Sch 1969-71; Soc Stud Teacher Bergan HS 1971-79, Acad Spalding HS 1979-88, Peoria Notre Dame HS 1988-; *ai:* Soc Stud Dept Head; Honors & North Cntrl Cert Comm Mem; NCSS 1975-; Peoria Area Peace Network 1984-; Sisters of St Francis 1967-; IL Migrant Cncl Governing Bd 1973-74; IL Master Teacher 1984; Published US His Curr & Enrichment Materials 1985; Curr Reviews Univ of IL Harvard Published; Newletter Articles Published; Conducted Wkshps Creative Teaching Strategies; *office:* Peoria Notre Dame HS 5105 N Sheridan Rd Peoria IL 61614

LINKE, DONNA KARLIN, Third Grade Teacher; *b:* Hays, KS; *m:* Arlyn; *c:* Steven L., Sandra Condit, William R., John T.; *ed:* (BS) Elem Ed, USAO Chickasha 1976; OK Univ, Seattle Pacific, ECU; *cr:* 3rd Grade Teacher Velma Alma Elem 1977-; *ai:* NEA, OEA; AVAE (Secy, Treas), Teacher of Yr 1984.

LINKFIELD, DIANE JANE (CRUMM), 5th Grade Teacher; *b:* Monroe, MI; *m:* Timothy G.; *c:* Andrea M. *ed:* (BS) Sci/Math, 1973, (MA) Rdng 1982 Central MI Univ; Assertive Discipline Trng; Drug/Substance Abuse Trng; Cmptr Trng; *cr:* HS/Mid Schls Math Teacher DOD Schls 1975; Headstart 1978-80, Adult Ed Math 1979-80 Pine River Area Schls; 5th/6th Grade Teacher Jefferson Schls 1980-; *ai:* Cmptr Club Adv; Crossstitch Club Adv; Cntrl Cncl-JEA Cmptr Facilitator; MEA/JEA 1980-; NEA 1980-; Jefferson Adult Booster 1980- Adult Boosters Pres Awd 1989; Curr Cncl 3 Yrs; *office:* Jefferson Hurd Rd Elem Sch 1960 E Hurd Rd Monroe MI 48161

LINKOUS, DONNA HARDY, Mathematics Teacher; *b:* Squire, WV; *m:* Howard C.; *ed:* (BA) Eng, Bluefield Coll 1980; (MS) Scndry Ed, Radford Univ 1983; Grad Stud WVCOGS; Trainers Wkshp on Applied Measurement in Math 1987; Tech Math Wkshp 1986; *cr:* Math Teacher Bradshaw Jr HS 1980-84; Adjunct Faculty Mem Bluefield St Coll 1984-86; Math Teacher War Jr HS 1984-; *ai:* Math Team Coach; Academic Adv; 8th Grade Class Spon; Detention/Discipline & Cmptr Coord; Cty Inservice Presenter; Big Creek HS Ftbl Team Statistician 1987-; Mc Dowell Cty Math Teachers Pres 1988-; Delta Kappa Gamma, NCTM 1985-; Calvary Baptist Church Choir Dir 1977-; Faith Musical Group (Pianist, Vocalist) 1977-; Writing Fellow WV Summer Writing Project 1984; Honorable Mention Merrill Publishing Company Natl Teacher Contest; Published Teaching Ideas 1987; *office:* War Jr HS Box 967 War WV 24892

LINN, SANDY BIAS, Oral Communications Teacher; *b:* Huntington, WV; *ed:* (AB) Speech/Eng, Marshall Univ 1972; (MA) Oral Comm, WV Univ 1985; Ed, Cmptr Trng; *cr:* Oral Comm Teacher Huntington East HS 1972-; *ai:* Forensic Team Coach; Stu Cncl Adv; Cty Lang Arts Comm; Lang Arts Dept Chairperson; Sec/Tres WV Comm Assn 1987-; Pres WV Interscholastic 1985-; Mem Forensic Leag Natl Forensic League 1980-; Teachers Acad Graduate; Cty Curr Cncl Mem-Former; *office:* Huntington E H S 2850 5th Ave Huntington WV 25702

LINNERUD, MARK A., Chemistry Teacher; *b:* Chicago, IL; *m:* Lorraine Bewersdorf; *c:* Christine; *ed:* (BS) Chem, N IL Univ 1972; (MS) Chem, Roosevelt Univ 1975; *cr:* Sci Teacher Morgan Park Acad 1975-; *ai:* NSTA, ISTA, Amer Chemical Society; Fermilab Summer Inst for Chem Teachers; Woodrow Wilson Fnd Inst on Phys Sci; Hope Coll Summer Inst for Advanced Placement Chem Teachers; *office:* Morgan Park Acad 2153 W 111th St Chicago IL 60643

LINSCOMBE, RUTH DAVID, 5th Grade Teacher; *b:* Gueydan, LA; *m:* Robert Gregory; *c:* Jeb, Thea, Seth; *ed:* (BA) Elem Ed, 1969, (MED) Elem Ed, 1972, 1985 Mc Neese St Univ; *cr:* Teacher Lake Arthur Elem 1969-72, Cohn Elem 1972-73, Gueydan Elem 1975-76, Lake Arthur Elem 1977-; *ai:* Associated Prof Educators of LA; Jefferson Davis Assn of Teachers of Math Pres 1988-; Jefferson Davis Task Force on Chemical Health Treas 1989-; *home:* Rt 1 Box 242-C Gueydan LA 70542

LINSE, DEE ANN (DISHMAN), Science Teacher; *b:* Scottsbluff, NE; *m:* Curtis A.; *c:* Linda L. Smrcina, Roger A., Brian S.; *ed:* (BA) Bio, NE St Univ Chadron 1961; (MS) Sci, Univ of NE Omaha 1984; Grad Stud; *cr:* Substitute Teacher/Secy to Supt Stuart Public Sch 1962-64; Substitute Teacher Neligh Public Sch 1965-67, Papillion Public Schls 1967-78; Teacher Papillion Jr HS 1978-; *ai:* 7th Grade Vlybl Coach; Extra-Duty Pay Comm; Papillion-La Vista Wellness Comm Rep & Schlsp Comm; Waste Control Study Group; Odyssey of Mind Competition Judge; Phi Delta Kappa 1985; *office:* Papillion Jr HS 423 S Washington Papillion NE 68046

LINSEMIER, GERRI A., Language Arts Teacher; *b:* Cleveland, OH; *c:* Matthew, Benjamin; *ed:* (BS) Home Ec/Eng, Siena Heights Coll 1964; (MA) Lang Art, MI St Univ 1981; APEX; Cooperative Learning; *cr:* Teacher Eaton Rapids 1964-79, Eaton Rapids Mid Sch 1980-; *ai:* Odyssey of Mind Coach; Rdng Coord; Soc Stud Olympiad Coach; Literary Publication Ed; High Potential Youth Adv; EREA, MEA, NEA 1964-; NCTE 1987-; MAMSE 1981-; Eaton Rapids Cmmty Theater 1989-; *office:* Eaton Rapids Mid Sch 301 Greyhound Dr Eaton Rapids MI 48827

LINTHICUM, TERRY BLAINE, English Teacher; *b:* High Point, NC; *m:* Paige Leigh Hollingsworth;; *c:* Mandy L.; *ed:* (BS) Phys Ed, 1981, (BA) Eng, 1984 Univ of NC Greensboro; *cr:* Teacher/Coach Randleman HS 1983-; *ai:* Asst Ftbl & Head Girls Var Bsktbl Coach; NC Coaches Assn; Sophia Baptist Church Music Dir; Cty Bsktbl Coach of Yr 1982, 1990; Conference Coach of Yr Vlybl 1983 & Bsktbl 1990; *office:* Randleman HS Box 485 Randleman NC 27317

LINTON, BEVERLAY MORGAN, Junior High School Teacher; *b:* Texmple, TX; *m:* Gerald Wayne; *c:* Krystal Curtis, Kim Richards, Gerald; *ed:* (BSED) Elem Ed, Mary Hardin Baylor 1974; Working Towards MSED Tarleton Univ; *cr:* 3rd/4th Grade Teacher Moody Ind Sch Dist 1975-78; 4th Grade/Jr HS Teacher Axtell Ind Sch Dist 1978-; *ai:* Elem & Jr HS Math, Spelling, Calculator UIL Coach; Textbook Comm; TX St Teacher Assn (Secy 1986, Pres Elect 1987, Pres 1988-, Region 12 House of Delegate 1986-89); PTA Secy 1986, Life Mem 1985; FHA Parent of Yr 1984; TX St Bd of Ed Comm on Technology 1990; *home:* Rt 1 Box 54V Axtell TX 76624

LINTON, LYNDA HECK, Business Education Teacher; *b:* LaMesa, TX; *m:* Fred L.; *c:* Christopher, Christin; *ed:* (BBA) Bus Ed, TX Tech Univ 1968; (ME) Bus Ed, TX Tech Univ 1988; *cr:* Bus Ed Teacher Denver City HS 1968-74, Monahans HS 1984-; *ai:* Univ Interscholastic League Keyboarding Contest, UIL Shorthand Contest, Jr Class Spon; TX St Teachers Assn 1968-; NBEA 1986-; TX Bus Ed Assn 1985-; Amer Assn Univ Women (Pres 1984-86) 1983-87; PTA (Edwards Forum VP 1981-83, Tatom LIFE VP 1983-84, Tatom LIFE Pres 1984-85); *office:* Monahans HS 809 S Betty Ave Monahans TX 79756

LINTON, MARY GOURLEY, Sixth Grade Teacher; *b:* Magna, UT; *m:* William Fowler; *c:* Kenneth W., Thomas C., Daniel J.; *ed:* (BS) Elem Ed, Univ of UT 1973; Elem Curr, Sci Area; *cr:* 6th Grade Teacher Hillsdale Elem Sch 1973-; *ai:* Teacher Career Ladder Comm Chm; Safety Patrol Adv; UT Sci Teachers Assn Elem Rep 1975-80; UT Sci Teachers Assn Outstanding Contributions Spec Awd 1980; Energy & Mans Environment St Level Rep 1980-84; Project Learning Tree St Level Rep 1979; *office:* Hillsdale Elem Sch 3275 W 3100 S West Valley City UT 84119

LINTZ, BARBARA LEE, 4th Grade Teacher; *b:* Shreveport, LA; *ed:* (BA) Elem Educ, Shepherd Coll 1975; (MA) Elem Educ, WV Univ 1982; WV Teachers Acad 1989; *cr:* 4th Grade Teacher Eydmyer Elem Sch 1975-; *ai:* Wydmyer Elem Staff Adv Cncl; Morgan Cty Ed Assn Secy 1983; Rdng Cncl Pres 1982; WV Minigrant; *office:* Widmyer Elem Sch 200 Myers St Berkeley Springs WV 25411

LINVILLE, MARTIN RICHARD, Learning Center Teacher; *b:* Indianapolis, IN; *m:* Dolores Colunga; *c:* Martin, Joshua; *ed:* (BS) Scndry Ed, Univ of CO 1979; Spec Ed Endorsement, SW Tx 1988; *cr:* Soc Stud Teacher Wiley Consolidated Schls 1980-82; 8th Grade Teacher Notre Dame Sch 1985-88; Ed Teacher Somerset HS 1988-89, Chisholm Trl Mid Sch 1989-; *ai:* TX Dept of Health Spinal Screener; NCEA 1985-88; PTA 1989-; Jr Beta Club Spon 1986-87; Phi Alpha Theta Mem 1978-79; *office:* Chisholm Trail Mid Sch 1311 Round Rock Ave Round Rock TX 78681

LIOZZI, BRUCE NICHOLAS, 5th Grade Teacher; *b:* Staten Island, NY; *m:* Elizabeth Michaelsen; *c:* Stephen S.; *ed:* (BS) Elem Ed, Wagner Coll 1964; (MS) Elem Ed, Richmond Coll CUNY; Elem Sch Admin, Richmond Coll CUNY; *cr:* 4th Grade Teacher Mt Pleasant Sch 1964-66; 6th-12th Grade Teacher of Emotionally Handicapped Public Sch 10 1966-72; 3rd-5th Grade Teacher Public Sch 3 1972-; *ai:* United Fed of Teachers 1967-; Delta Nu Alumni Assn Bd of Dirs 1987-; Staten Island Hospital Assn Pres 1978-80; *office:* Public Sch 3 80 S Goff Ave Staten Island NY 10309

LIPINSKI, HELEN KOLAKOWSKI, 5th Grade Teacher; *b:* Hamtramck, MI; *m:* John A.; *c:* Ann, Marie, Carol, Barbara (dec), Daniel; *ed:* (BS) Elem Ed/Soc Stud, St Mary of Springs 1953; Cmptr, AIMS, Math, Sci; *cr:* 1st-3rd Grade Teacher Mc Kinley Elem 1953-55, 4th Grade Teacher 1963-65, 5th Grade Teacher 1965- Owens Elem; *ai:* MADD Secy 1982-85; MI Society of Autistic Citizens; Jaycees Outstanding Educator of Yr 1982.

LIPP, EVELYN M., World History Teacher; *b:* Denver, CO; *m:* Stan; *c:* Stephen, Suzanne; *ed:* (BS) Soc Stud/Eng, 1981, (MS) World His/Rdng/Eng, 1983 IN Univ Ft Wayne; *cr:* Eng/Amer His/Rdng Teacher Village Woods Jr HS 1981-86; Eng/Rdng Teacher Leo HS 1986-88; World His Teacher South Side HS 1988-; *ai:* Project SET, St of IN Future Teachers Drama Club Adv; Bus Mgr; Sch Climate Comm; Phi Delta Kappa, AAUW, IN Cncl of Soc Stud, NEA; Amnesty Intnl Philharmonic Womens Comm; Jewish Temple Bd Mem 1986-88; *office:* South Side HS 3601 S Calhoun Fort Wayne IN 46807

LIPPARI, RUSSELL JOSEPH, Music Coordinator; *b:* Chicago, IL; *ed:* (BM) Music Ed, E IL Univ 1977; (MS) Educl Admin, IL St Univ 1985; *cr:* General Music Teacher Posen-Robbins Dist 143 1/2 1978-80; Band Dir Gompers/Washington Jr HS 1980-87; Music Coord Joliet Public Schls #86 1987-; *ai:* Contest Adjudicator; Festival Chm for IMEA; Conductor HS & Cmmty Musical Theater & Joliet All-City Band; Music Educators Natl Conference 1980-; IL Music Educators Assn 1980-; *office:* Joliet Public Schls #86 420 N Raynor Ave Joliet IL 60435

LIPPMANN, RICHARD D., Social Studies/Hum Teacher; *b:* Brooklyn, NY; *m:* Mary L. Roundtree; *c:* Stephanie; *ed:* (BA) His, Univ of MD 1968; (MA) Ed, George Washington Univ 1976; *cr:* Soc Stud Teacher Carter G Woodson Jr HS 1968-; *ai:* Gifted & Talented Coord; Hum Chm; 7th Grade SAT Preparation Coord; DC Cncl for Soc Stud 1986-; A FT 1968-; 1st in Class George Washington Univ 1976; Article Published 1968; *office:* Carter G Woodson Jr HS 4101 Minnesota Ave NE Washington DC 20019

LIPSETT, WYNONA WIETING, Choral Director; *b:* Waco, TX; *m:* Donald H.; *c:* Carolyn M. Lipsett Wilson, David C.; *ed:* (BMED) Music Ed, 1961, (MMED) Music Ed, 1982 S Meth Univ; *cr:* Class Piano Teacher Arcadia Park Elem 1960-61; Elem Music Teacher L K Hall & N Hawthorne Elems 1961-64, Hanby & Tisinger Elems 1974-76; Choral Music Teacher W Mesquite HS 1976-; *ai:* Spon & Dir of Choirs; Accompanist & Performer for Various Dist Events; Mu Phi Epsilon (Intnl VP 1974-80, Asumnae Pres 1970-72, Convention Delegate 1970); Memorial Fnd Bd of Dirs 1989-; TX Music Adjuticators Assn Choral Judge 1987-;TX Music Educators Assn Region Vocal Chm 1976-; TX Choral Dirs Assn 1976-; PTA (Treas, VP) 1972-, Outstanding Teacher 1981; Dallas Symphony Chorus Section Leader 1979-, Soloist European Tour 1985; Mesquite Civic Chorus (Founding Mem 1986-, Soloist 1986-); Delta Kappa Gamma (Music Chm 1988-, St Music Comm, St Pianist 1989-); Compositions Published in Society Songbook 1990; *office:* W Mesquite HS 2500 Memorial Pkwy Mesquite TX 75149

LIPSKI, JEAN JOHNSON, English Teacher; *b:* Kingston, PA; *m:* Philip Joseph; *c:* Lauren, Jaime, Michael; *ed:* (BA) Eng/Ed, Wilkes Univ 1978; Lit & Ed Courses; Accepted for Masters of Comm; *cr:* Scndry Eng Teacher Lake Lehman HS 1978-; *ai:* Drama, Sr HS Head Field Hockey, Wrestling Chldrs Coach; Class Night Adv; Lake Lehman Ed Assn 1978-; PSEA, NEA 1978-; Lehman United Meth Church Supt 1986-; *office:* Lake Lehman HS Old Rt 115 Lehman PA 18627

LIPTAK, MARY ANN ELIZABETH, Dean of Academic Affairs; *b:* Trenton, NJ; *ed:* (BA) Eng/Fr, 1966, (MA) Sch Admin, 1988 Rider Coll; Cert in Supervision/Prin; Grad Stud Trenton St Coll, Rider Coll, St Frances Coll; *cr:* Fr/Span Teacher Mc Corristin HS 1966-72; Fr/Eng Teacher 1972-77, Eng Dept Chm 1977-87, Asst Prin 1987-89; Advanced Placement Eng Teacher 1977-, Dean of Academic Stud 1989- Notre Dame HS; *ai:* Advanced Placement Stud, Notre Dame HS Stu Teacher Placement, Interdisciplinary & Learning Styles Prgms Coord;Grants Writer to Assist Building Educl Needs; NCTE, NCEA 1975-; ASCD 1985-; NJASCD 1987-; Notre Dame HS PTA Exec Bd 1988-89; Articles Submitted to Ed Journals; Grant Notification Pending; *office:* Notre Dame HS 601 Lawrence Rd Lawrenceville NJ 08648

LIPUT, PRICILLA REESE, Third Grade Teacher; *b:* Kingston, PA; *m:* John M.; *c:* Colin M., Justin J.; *ed:* (BS) Elem Ed, Bloomsburg St COll 1973; (ME) Elem Ed, St of PA 1976; Post Masters Studies, Wilkes Coll; PA St Univ; *cr:* 4th Grade Teacher 1973-75; 2nd Grade Teacher 1975-78; 3rd Grade Teacher 1978- Dallas Sch Dist; *ai:* NEA 1973-; PA St Ed Assn 1973-; DEA 1973-; Back Mt Mem Library Auction-Chm Book Booth 1980-; Amer Lgn Aux Post 672 1989-; Back Mt Rpblcn Assn 1988-; Dallas United Meth Church (Supt of Sunday Sch 1987-/Mem Cncl on Ministries 1985-/Mem Adm Bd 1985-/Chm Work Area on Ed 1987-); WVIA-TV Public Tv 1986-; WY His & Geological Socty 1986-; Westmoreland Elem PTO 1984-; Dallas Elem PTO 1988-; Musical Box Socty Intl 1989-; Meadows Nursing Ctr Aux 1984-; Whos Who Among Young Amer Prof 1988-89; Whos Who in Amer Ed 1989-; *home:* 166 Church St Dallas PA 18612

LISANDRELLI, ELAINE SLIVINSKI, 7th Grade English Teacher; *b:* Pittston, PA; *m:* Carl A.; *ed:* (BA) Eng/Scndry Ed 1973, (MS) Scndry Counseling, 1976 Marywood; 1973; Grad Studs; *cr:* 1st Grade Eng Teacher North Pocono Mid Sch 1973-; Prof Marywood Coll 1987-; In-Service Inst NEIU 19 1986-; *ai:* Literary Magazine Adv; Spelling Bee Coord; Kappa Gamma Pi 1973-; Society of Childrens Book Writers; PSEA 1973-; North Pacomo Women Teachers 1985-; Co-Authored Levels G & H of Easy Writer Series Developed & Published by ERA/CCR Inc Nyack; Co-Authored Study Skills Workout; Appointed to the PA Writing Assesment Advisory Comm 1989-; *office:* North Pocona Mid Sch Church St Moscow PA 18444

LISH, PAUL EVAN, Kindergarten Teacher; *b:* Pocatello, ID; *m:* Mary Luana Smith; *c:* Nathan, Amanda, Cy, Bradon, Emalee; *ed:* (BA) Elem Ed, ID St Univ 1976; *cr:* Kndgtn/1st Grade Teacher Lava Hot Springs Elem 1976-78; 2nd Grade Teacher 1978-86, 3rd Grade Teacher 1986-89, Kndgtn Teacher 1989- Inkom Elem; *office:* Inkom Elem Sch 300 Holstein Inkom ID 83245

LISTER, LEILANI LETWIN, Computer/Algebra Teacher; *b:* Honolulu, HI; *m:* Ronald C.; *c:* Theodore, Bryant, Patrick; *ed:* Elem Ed/Math, Univ of HI; *cr:* 1st Grade Teacher Banneker Elem 1969-70; 1st Grade Teacher 1985-86, Cmptr/Algebra Teacher 1986 St Edward; *ai:* Stu Cncl & Math Club Adv; Math & Sci Comm Chm; NCEA 1985-; Sarah D Barder Fellow-Johns Hopkins Univ 1989; Center for Academically Talented Youth; *office:* St Edward Sch 500 Merrill St Corona CA 91720

LISTER, ROGER EDWARD, Fourth Grade Teacher; *b:* Sanford, ME; *m:* Beverly Ann; *c:* Scott, Joanne; *ed:* (BS) Elem Ed, Univ of ME Farmington 1972; *cr:* 4th Grade Teacher Hanson Sch 1966-; *ai:* Sci Fair Dir; Cmptr Adv; MTA, NEA 1966-; *home:* R R 2 Box 2057 Sanford ME 04073

LISTORTI, ROBERT V., Mathematics Specialist; *b:* Bridgeport, CT; *m:* Christine Kennedy; *c:* Michael, Bradley; *ed:* (BA) Elem Ed, S CT St Univ 1972; Bus Trng Univ of New Haven; Thinking/Critical Skills Trng, St Josephs Coll; Nutritional Ed Prgm, Univ of Bridgeport; *cr:* 6th-8th Grade Teacher/Math Specialist Wilbur Cross; *ai:* Bridgeport Math League & CT Stock Market Adv; Math Textbook Comm; ATOMIC 1986-; Bridgeport Ed Assn Building Delegate 1988-; Milford United Soccer 1988-; Milford Road Runners 1984-, Grand Prix Winner 1989; Outstanding Service 1988; PAC Awd; Jr Achievement 1986-; *office:* Wilbur Cross Sch 1775 Reservoir Ave Bridgeport CT 06606

LITCHKO, JOSEPH MICHAEL, Science Teacher; *b:* Ashland, PA; *ed:* (BS) Elem Ed, Bloomsburg St Coll 1974; Grad Stud Bloomsburg Univ of PA; *cr:* Teacher Assumption BVM Sch 1976-85, Holy Spirit Sch 1985-; *ai:* Cmptr Jr HS Coord; NCEA; *office:* Holy Spirit Sch 250 West Ave Mount Carmel PA 17851

LITFIN, JERRY GLEN, Physical Education Chair; *b:* Watertown, MN; *m:* Gayle; *c:* Grant, Garrett; *ed:* (BS) Phys Ed/Health, Mankato St Univ 1973; (MS) Ed/Phys Ed, Univ of MN 1983; *cr:* Teacher/Coach Delano HS 1973-; *ai:* Head Boys Bsktbl; Asst Bsbl; MN Bsktbl Assn 1975-, Region Coach of Yr 1982, Dist Coach of Yr 1982, 1984, 1989; Delano Park Commission Secy 1983-; St Peters Church (Eucharistic Minister, Youth Cncl Mem) 1986-; *office:* Delano HS 700 E Elm Ave Delano MN 55328

LITTLE, ANNETTE MARTIN, Third Grade Teacher; *b:* Roanoke, VA; *c:* Kristi A.; *ed:* (BA) Psych, Roanoke Coll 1970; (MEED) Elem Ed, Univ of VA 1989; *cr:* Classroom Teacher 1970-, Relief Prin 1984- Lincoln Terr Elem Sch; *ai:* Kappa Delta Pi Mem 1985; Roanoke Valley Rdng Cncl, Roanoke Ed Assn, VA Ed Assn, NEA; Lincoln Terrace PTA Secy 1985-87, Distinguished Service Awd 1986; *home:* 4226 Arlington Hills Dr SW Roanoke VA 24018

LITTLE, DEL DOUCET, Mathematics Teacher; *b:* Lake Charles, LA; *m:* Bobby E.; *ed:* (BS) Math, Southern Univ 1968; Masters Equivalency 1986; *cr:* Math Teacher Marion HS 1970-71, Barb HS 1973-74, Episcopal Sch 1971, East HS 1975-; *ai:* NEA, Anchorage Ed Assn 1975-; Delta Sigma Theta (AK Alumnae Financial Secy 1981-84, Chairperson Schlsp Comm 1985-88); *office:* East HS 4025 E 24th Anchorage AK 99504

LITTLE, DOUGLAS DAVID, Chemistry/Biology Teacher; *b:* Meridian, MS; *m:* Sandra Elizabeth Camp; *c:* Douglas D. Jr.; *ed:* (BS) Bio, 1974, (MS) Bio/Ed, 1975 Livingston Univ; AA Cert Chem, Univ of S MS 1982; Specialist & AAA Cert Bio, Chem 1990; AA Cert Admin; NTE Physics 1990; *cr:* Teacher Southeast Lauderdale; *ai:* Girls Sftbl Coach; NSTA, MSTA; Mason, Shriner; STAR Teacher; *office:* Southeast Lauderdale HS Rt 7 Meridian MS 39301

LITTLE, JUDY BUTLER, Sixth Grade Teacher; *b:* Martinsville, VA; *m:* Jack V.; *c:* Susan White Dobbs, Brian S. White, Lorri J.; *ed:* (BS) Elem Ed, 1982, (MA) Elem Ed, 1985 Jacksonville St Univ; Ed Specialist Elem Ed, Univ of AL; *cr:* 5th Grade Classroom Teacher 1982-83, 1st Grade Classroom Teacher 1984, 6th Grade Classroom Teacher 1985- Fort Mc Clellan Elem Sch; Adjunct Faculty Jacksonville St Univ 1986-88; *ai:* Kappa Delta Pi (Secy 1981-82, Pres 1985-86); Kappa Delta Epsilon (Secy 1981-82, Pres 1982-83); 1st United Meth Church; *home:* 607 Riddle Ave Piedmont AL 36272

LITTLE, KATHLEEN D. (SCHMIDT), Elementary Teacher; *b:* Doylestown, PA; *m:* Dana; *c:* Jennifer, Stephanie; *ed:* (BS) Elem Ed, Kutztown 1971; Various Courses, Kutztown St, Penn St, BCIU; *cr:* Teacher Most Blessed Sacrament 1971-73, 1978-; *ai:* NCEA 1989-; NCTM 1990-; GSA Leader 1985-; *office:* Most Blessed Sacrament Sch 7th & Pine St Bally PA 19503

LITTLE, LINDA BLACKMON, Teacher; *b:* Lancaster, SC; *w:* Kenneth Richard (dec); *c:* Richard K., Lindsay K.; *ed:* (BS) Elem Ed, Benedict Coll 1972; *cr:* Teacher 1972-; *ai:* Teacher Union Asst Building Rep 1988-; Cub Scouts Asst Den Mother 1989-; St Lucille Amer Zion Church (Deaconess, Pres) 1989-; Asst Developing & Intergrating Sci Curr for Model Sci Prgm at Anne Beers Elem Sch 1985, 1986; *office:* Anne Beers Elem Sch 36 Pl & Alabama Ave SE Washington DC 20020

LITTLE, LINDA CIRCOSTA, Second Grade Teacher; *b:* Bellaire, OH; *c:* Thomas; *ed:* (BS) Elem Ed, OH Univ 1966; *cr:* 1st Grade Teacher Wayne Local 1963-65, Powhatan Elem 1966-69; Kndgtn/2nd/3rd Grade Teacher St Mary Cntrl 1975-; *ai:* OCEA; Church Organist.

LITTLE, MARY ANN, Biology Teacher; *b:* Leeds, AL; *m:* James J.; *c:* James G.; *ed:* (BS) Bio/Chem, Samford Univ 1982; (MA) Gifted Ed, UAB 1985; Adv Placement Bio Instr & Adv Lab Instr; *cr:* Bio Teacher Duran Jr HS 1982-84; Bio/Gifted Teacher Gardendale HS 1984-; *ai:* Jr Scholars Bowl Coach; Sci Textbook Comm Study Skills Comm; Faculty Adv Comm; Curr Comm; Sch Brochure Comm; Sci Dept Chairperson; AL Ed Assn 1982-; AL Sci Teachers Assn 1986-; 1st Baptist Church 1986-; Dev Printed Course Selection Guide; Appointed Dist Coord for Seeds Project; *office:* Gardendale H S 850 Mt Olive Rd Gardendale AL 35071

LITTLE, PATRICK LEE, 6th Grade Teacher; *b:* Monterey, TN; *m:* Karen; *c:* Patrick Lee Jr., Leann; *ed:* (BS) Ag, Tn Tech 1976; (BS) Ag Ed, 1977, (MS) Ed, 1980 Univ of Tn; *cr:* 4th Grade Teacher 1979-83, 6th Grade Teacher 1983- Clarkrange Elem; *ai:* Boys & Girls 6th Grade Bsktbl Coach; Boys & Girls 4th Grade Bsktbl Coach; Boys & Girls Sftbl Coach; Tn Ed Assn 1979-; Fentress Cty Ed Assn 1979-; NEA 1979-; Fentress Farmers Coop Secy/Bd of Dir 1986-; Fentress Soil Conservation Service Bd of Dir 1989-; Clarkrange Meth Church Pastor Parish Relations Comm 1989-; *home:* P O Box 38 Clarkrange TN 38553

LITTLE, RICHARD WILLIAM, Fifth Grade Teacher; *b:* Lancaster, OH; *ed:* (BS) Elem Teaching, OH Univ 1965; (MED) Teaching, Wright St Univ 1971; Cmptr Sci, Univ of Dayton, Miami Univ, Univ of VT, Boston Coll; *cr:* Teacher Beavercreek Sch System 1965-; *ai:* Beavercreek Schls Technology Comm; Beavercreek Township Trustee 1980-; Beavercreek Sch System Teacher of Yr 1986; Greene Cty & Miami Valley Regional Planning Commissions; Challenge 95 Strategic Planning; *office:* Shaw Sch 3560 Kemp Rd Beavercreek OH 45431

LITTLE, SUE MARIE (PLUGGE), 5th Grade Elementary Teacher; *b:* Fremont, NE; *m:* Robert Michael; *c:* Eric M., Kate M.; *ed:* (BA) Elem Ed, Bethany Coll 1978; (MED) Educl Admin, Univ of NE Lincoln 1985; *cr:* 6th Grade Teacher Ralston Public Schls 1978; 2nd Grade Teacher 1979-80, 5th Grade Teacher 1980- NE City Public Schls; *ai:* Delta Kappa Gamma Comm Chm 1987-89; Phi Delta Kappa; NE City Jaycees Young Educator of Yr Awd 1987; *office:* Hayward Elem Sch 306 S 14th St Nebraska City NE 68410

LITTLEFORD, STANLEY DAVID, Math Teacher/Coach; *b:* Minneapolis, MN; *m:* France G. Davidson; *c:* Carmen E.; *ed:* (BA) Phys Ed/Math, Quanchita Baptist Univ 1986; *cr:* Math Teacher 1986-; Coach 1987 Rogers Jr HS; *ai:* Coaching/Ftbl/Bsktbl/Track; Teach Honors Algebra I; *home:* 1314 W 8th El Dorado AR 71730

LITTRELL, RICHARD LEE, Fifth Grade Teacher; *b:* Henderson, KY; *ed:* (BS) Elem Ed, Univ of Southern IN 1979; (MS) Elem Ed, IN St Univ 1983; *cr:* 5th Grade Teacher Sturgis Elem Sch 1979-; *ai:* KEA 1980-; NEA 1980-; CESI 1989-; *home:* 124 N Fencerow Ln Henderson KY 42420

LITTWIN, JAMES PATRICK, English Teacher; *b:* Chicago, IL; *m:* Suzette Wanat; *c:* Kristin, Michael; *ed:* (BA) Eng, Loyola Univ of Chicago 1973; (MA) Lit, NE IL Univ 1979; *cr:* Eng Teacher St Viator HS 1973-77, Niles Township HS West 1978-79, Niles Township HS East 1979-80, Barrington HS 1980-; *ai:* Faculty Adv Nuance Literary Magazine 1985-89; Teacher Summers Northwestern Univ Center Talent Dev for Gifted Stu; IL Arts Cncl Awd; Ragdale Fnd Grants; Whetstone Prize for Poetry; Poetry & Prose Published; *office:* Barrington HS 616 W Main St Barrington IL 60010

LIVELY, GENE D., Language Art Teacher; *b:* Highland Park, MI; *m:* Kathleen; *c:* Daniel E., Andrew D.; *ed:* (BA) Eng, E MI Univ 1967; Wayne St Univ; *cr:* Teacher E Hills HS 1967-68; IMCM Teacher IMC Music Center 1968-74; Teacher Gulf Mid Sch 1974-; *ai:* 1st Assembly of God Childrens Church Dir 1975-; Gulf Mid Sch Teacher of Yr 1979-80; *office:* Gulf Mid Sch 6419 Louisana Ave New Port Richey FL 34653

LIVELY, JUDY SANDERSON, Teacher of Gifted/Talented; *b:* Hot Springs, AR; *m:* Joe Allen; *c:* Jeffrey, Jayme; *ed:* (BSE) Elem Ed, 1968, (MSE) Elem Ed, 1973 Henderson St Univ; Gifted Ed, Univ of HI Manoa; *cr:* 6th Grade Teacher 1968-73, 2nd Grade Teacher 1976-79 Jones Elem; 6th Grade Teacher 1979-86, 4th-6th Grade GiftEd Facilitator 1986- Lake Hamilton Sch; *ai:* Intermediate Sch Newspaper Spon; Natl Assn of Gifted Children, Arkansans for Gifted & Talented Ed 1986-; NEA 1968-; Delta Kappa Gamma St 2nd VP 1989- Travel/Study Grant 1988; AR Dept of Ed Teacher Recognition 1984; Antioch Baptist Church Mem; Amer Assn of Univ Women; Band Parents Pres 1989-; PTA Secy 1988-; Teacher of Yr 1984; *office:* Lake Hamilton Intermediate Sch 107 N Wolf Dr Pearcy AR 71964

LIVELY, KAREN MC NEW, 2nd Grade Teacher; *b:* El Centro, CA; *m:* James Ray; *c:* Jason R., Michael S.; *ed:* (BS) Elem Ed, TX Coll of Arts & Industries 1967; Post Grad Stud Ed, Sci, Cmptrs *cr:* 2nd Grade Teacher Alma A Pierce Elem 1967; 6th/7th Grade Math Teacher Jackson Intermediate 1967-68; 3rd Grade Teacher Kruse Elem 1968-69, Spring Valley Elem 1969; 6th Grade Sci Teacher Scott E Johnson 1973-76; 2nd Grade Teacher Mary Mc Ashan Gibbs Elem 1976-; *ai:* Math Curr & Goals Comm; Univ Methods Prgm; Delta Kappa Gamma (Recording Secy 1986-88, 2nd VP 1988-); *office:* Mary Mc Ashan Gibbs Elem Sch 441 FM 2821 E Huntsville TX 77340

LIVELY, LINDA REECE, English & French Teacher; *b:* Hope, AR; *m:* David Allen; *c:* Rainna K., David A. II; *ed:* (BA) Eng, Southern St Coll 1971; (MSE) Eng, Henderson St Univ 1988; *cr:* Teacher Hope HS 1971-72, Plain Dealing Acad 1972-73, Hope HS 1973-74, Laneburg HS 1974-87, Bodcaw HS 1987-88, Nevada HS 1988-; *ai:* Sr Class & Fr Club Spon; Teacher Quiz Bowl Team; *office:* Nevada HS Po Box 50 Rosston AR 71858

LIVESAY, DENNIS LON, 6th Grade Teacher; *b:* Jefferson City, TN; *m:* Rebecca Campbell; *c:* Robyn, Matthew; *ed:* (BA) Elem Ed, Carson Newman Coll 1975; (MS) Curr/Instruction, E TN St Univ 1977; *cr:* 5th Grade Teacher 1975-79, 4th/6th Grade Teacher 1979-80, 6th Grade Teacher 1980- Bean Station Elem; *ai:* NEA, TEA 1975-; Buffalo Trail Baptist Church 1980-; Amer Amateur Radio League, Lakeway Amateur Radio Club 1984-; *home:* 3214 Horner Dr Morristown TN 37814

LIVESAY, GLENDA KAYE, 6th Grade Math Teacher; *b:* Kingsport, TN; *ed:* (BS) Elem Ed, East TN St Univ 1973; *cr:* 6th Grade Church Hill Elem Sch 1973-79; 8th Grade Math/Pre-Algebra Teacher 1980-88; 6th Grade Math Teacher 1988- Church Hill Mid Sch; *ai:* Stu Cncl Adv; Annual Spon; Needlework Club Spon; Hawkins Cty Ed Assn- Public Relations Comm 1989-; TN Ed Assn; NEA; Calvary Baptist Church Yth Cncl 1986-; *office:* Church Hill Mid Sch PO Box 38 Church Hill TN 37642

LIVESAY, JAYNE SANDIDGE, Second Grade Teacher; *b:* Somerset, KY; *m:* John R.; *c:* Stewart, Matthew, Jill; *ed:* (BS) Elem Ed, 1970, (MA) Elem Ed, 1974 Eastern KY Univ; *cr:* Classroom Teacher Eubank Elem 1970-; *ai:* Eubank Elem Acad Coach; PTA Scholastic Comm; Eubank Baptist Ch Pianist/Sun Sch Teacher 1980-; *home:* PO Box 190 Eubank KY 42567

LIVESAY, KATHY ANN, A P Chemistry Teacher; *b:* Roanoke Rapids, NC; *ed:* (BS) Sci Ed, WAke Forest Univ 1980; (MED) Educl Admin, Coll of William & Mary 1989; *cr:* Teacher First Colonial HS 1980-; *ai:* Jr Class Adv; JETS Coach; Schlsp Comm; NSTA, VAST; *office:* First Colonial HS 1272 Mill Dam Rd Virginia Beach VA 23454

LIVINGSTON, CAROLE ANN, Fifth Grade Teacher; *b:* Lock Haven, PA; *m:* Thomas Raymond; *c:* Christina Livingston-Locey, Jennifer Livingston-Paucke; *ed:* (BS) Elem/Early Chldhd, Lock Haven Univ 1959; Grad Stud Environmental, CO Univ; *cr:* 5th Grade Teacher Flemington Elem 1959-61; Jr HS Spec Ed Teacher Bald Eagle Nittany HS 1961-67; 4th/5th Grade Teacher 1967-68, 5th/6th Grade Teacher 1968-69, 6th Grade Teacher 1969-74, 5th Grade Teacher 1974- Lamar Township Elem; *ai:* Intramural Sftbl Adv; Head Teacher Lamar Township Elem 1968-87; Delta Kappa Gamma Music Chm 1989-; Salona United Church of Christ (Consistory Pres 1974-77, Organist, Choir Dir 1961-); *home:* RD 1 Box 44 Mill Hall PA 17751

LIVINGSTON, DEAN RICHARD, Bio Teacher/Boys Bsktbl Coach; *b:* Saint Paul, MN; *m:* Donna Marie Douglas; *c:* Caleb, Tyler; *ed:* (BS) Health/Phys Ed, Freed-Hardeman Coll 1983; *cr:* Phys Ed Teacher Greater Jacksonville Chrstn Sch 1984-85; Health/Phys Ed/Bsktbl Coach Metro Chrstn Sch 1985-89; Phys Ed/Bsktbl & Vlybl Coach Crowleys Ridge Acad 1989-; *ai:* Jr & Sr Boys Bsktbl; Jr & Sr Gor;s Vlybl; Scndry Teacher of Yr Greater Jacksonville Chrstn Sch 1984-85; Coach of Yr-4B West Conference 1988-89; *office:* Crowleys Ridge Acad 626 Academy Dr Paragould AR 72450

LIVINGSTON, DONNA SUE (HOWARD), Fourth Grade Teacher; *b:* Olney, IL; *m:* James L.; *ed:* (AS) Olney Cntrl Coll 1972; (BS) Elem Ed, E IL Univ 1974; *cr:* 5th Grade Teacher Albion Elem 1974-75; 6th Grade Teacher 1975-87, 4th Grade Teacher 1987-88, Dept Lang Arts/Hist Teacher 1988-89, 4th Grade Teacher 1989-Oblong Elem; *ai:* Jr Beta Club Co Spon; Oblong Elem Sch Cty, Regional & St His Fairs in IL Former Spon; Oblong Elem Sch DAR Essay Contests Spon; Delta Kappa Gamma (Finance Comm Chm 1986-88, Schlsp Comm Chm 1988-); Kappa Delta Pi Honor Society Ed 1973; Prairie-licking Fire Dept Auxiliart; Former Jr/Sr HS Sunday Sch Teacher 1979-88; *office:* Oblong Elem Sch 600 W Main St Oblong IL 62449

LIVOTI, STEPHEN J., World Geography Teacher; *b:* Tiffin, OH; *m:* Kathryn Butdorf; *c:* Kara, Anthony; *ed:* (BS) Soc Stud, Bowling Green St Univ 1978; Course Work Univ of Toledo, Heidelberg Coll, Tiffin Univ, IN Univ; *cr:* Soc Stud Teacher Lakota Jr HS 1978-; *ai:* Head Boys & Girls Track Coach Lakota HS; NEA, OH Ed Assn, Lakota Ed Assn 1978-; Elks Organization Trustee 1986-88; Tiffin Bd of Realtors 1976-; Nom Ashland Oil Teacher of Yr; *home:* 496 Hedges St Tiffin OH 44883

LIZOTTE, CHRIS, Director of Bands; *b:* Niles, MI; *m:* Kelly; *ed:* (BSE) Music Ed, Univ of AR 1984; Music Performance, Univ of AR 1986; *cr:* Dir of Bands/Coord of Instrumental Music Mtn Grove HS 1986-; *ai:* MSTA Prgms Comm; MO Music Educators Assn, MO St Teachers Assn, MO Bandmasters Assn; Mtn Grove Chamber of Commerce Prof of Yr 1988; *home:* 1005 Hubbard Mountain Grove MO 65711

LLEWELLYN, PETER MICHAEL, English/Biology Teacher; *b:* Bay City, MI; *m:* Marilyn Sue Magner; *c:* Timothy J., Heather; *ed:* (BA) His/Eng/Bio, Univ of TX Austin 1960; Grad Stud Wayne St Univ, TX A&I, Sam Houston St Univ; *cr:* Eng Teacher Weslaco HS 1960, Mercedes HS 1961; Sci/Eng Teacher Highland Park Scndry Schls 1965-67; Sales/Mrktg Management 1967-68;

Bio/Eng Teacher Aldine HS 1968-; *ai:* Tutoring Eng & Sci; New Liaison Person Aldine HS Local Press; Metropolitan Area Teachers of Sci 1988-; Natl Audubon Soc 1980-; Natl Conservary 1982-; Natl Rifle Assn 1975-; Articles & Poem Published; *office:* Aldine HS 11101 Airline Dr Houston TX 77037

LLOYD, BARBARA SHIREY, English Teacher; *b:* Connellsville, PA; *m:* Harold Scott; *c:* Gareth; *ed:* (BS) Scndry Ed/Eng, Penn St Univ 1974; *cr:* Eng Teacher Connellsville Jr HS West 1974-; *office:* Connellsville Area Sch Dist 215 Falls Ave Connellsville PA 15425

LLOYD, EDNA MARIE/BANKS, Science Department Teacher; *b:* Jackson, MS; *m:* Ralph Martin; *c:* Natalie, Ericka, Stephanie; *ed:* (BS) Soc Stud, 1971, (MS) Guidance, 1973 Jackson St Univ; Criminal Justice, Spec Ed; *cr:* Girls Cnslr George Washington Sch 1973-74; Cnslr Prairie Hills Jr HS 1974-79; Home/Sch Coord Field Crest 1979-80; Sci Teacher Highlands 1980-; *ai:* Dance Troop Spon; Chrldr Coach; IL Ed Teacher Rep 1980-; Teacher of Yr Chairperson 1985-86 Certificate 1985; PTO Rep 1985-; Juvenile Court Rep 1974 Letter 1974; Big Sisters Coord 1975 Letter 1976; Schlsp Guidance Jackson St Univ; Fellowship Sangamon St Univ; 144 Sch Dist Awds; *office:* Highlands Sch 3420 Laurel Ln Hazel Crest IL 60429

LOBAUGH, DONNA PASCARELLA, 6th Grade Teacher; *b:* Pittsburgh, PA; *m:* Ross O. Jr.; *ed:* (BA) Elem Ed, WV Univ 1972; (MS) Elem Ed, Univ of Pittsburgh 1976; Cmptr Courses; *cr:* 4th Grade Teacher Renton Elem Sch 1973-87; 6th Grade Teacher Regency Park Elem Sch 1987-; *ai:* Soc Stud Curr Comm Chairperson; Spon Annual Washington DC Field Trip; NEA, PSEA; *home:* 328 Comstock Dr North Huntingdon PA 15642

LOBAUGH, GLENDA G., Fifth Grade Teacher; *b:* Shawnee, OK; *m:* Larry; *c:* David, Michael; *ed:* (BS) Elem Ed, OK Southwestern Univ 1964; (MS) Elem Ed, Univ of OK 1986; Post Masters Stud Curr, Univ of OK; Childrens Lit Based Writing Strategies Learn His Univ of OK; *cr:* Kndgtn Teacher Burns Flat Elem 1964-65, Hobart Elem 1968-75; 4th-6th Grade Teacher Ranchwood Elem 1975-; *ai:* Teacher-Consultant OK Writing Project; Delta Kappa Gamma (Pres) 1982-; NCTE, OK Cncl Teacher of Eng, Intnl Rdng Assn, OK Rdng Assn 1980-; NCSS, OK Cncl Soc Stud 1985-; Phi Dela Kappa 1988-; OK Anthropoligical Society, Friends of Lib, Stage Door Cmmty Theatre 1986-; Pets for People Prgm 1990; Yukon Rdng Cncl Pres 1983-84; Natl Endowment Hum Project OK St Univ Staff Mem; Yukon Teacher of Yr; Semi-Finalist OK Teacher of Yr 1987; Articles Published; *home:* 2501 Sequoia Park Dr Yukon OK 73099

LOBDELL, JAMES MARSTON, Social Studies Teacher; *b:* Youngstown, OH; *ed:* (AB) Poly Sci, 1984, (MA) Ed, 1986 Stanford Univ; *cr:* Soc Stud Teacher Milpitas HS 1986-1 Assoc Dir Teachers Curr Inst 1989-; *ai:* Boys & Girls Swimming Coach; Amnesty Intnl Staff Adv; CA Cncl Soc Stud 1986-; NCSS 1990; NCAA Volunteers for Youth Stu Dir 1983-84; Curr Inst Founder; *office:* Milpitas HS 1285 Escuela Pkwy Milpitas CA 95035

LOBSINGER, BEVERLY J. (OLSON), 2nd Grade Teacher; *b:* Balfour, ND; *m:* Richard Rollin; *c:* Amy N. Lobsinger Cody, Kay L.; *ed:* (BA) Elem Ed, Valley City St Univ 1979; Elem Ed, Univ Of ND, M St Univ; *cr:* Elem Teacher Valley City Public Sch 1968-69, Sacred Heart Parochial Sch 1969-70; Substitute Teacher Glasow & Williston Public Schls 1970-79; Elem Teacher Willison Public Schls 1979-; *ai:* NEA, ND Ed Assn 1981-; Williston Ed Assn Building Rep 1981-, Golden Apple Awd 1990; Teacher Forum Mem 1988; Whos Who Amer Ed 1989-; Contract Negotiating Team Mem 1988-; *home:* 910 16th Ave W Williston ND 58801

LOCHHEAD, LOUISE KEISER, Business Dept Chairperson; *b:* Salt Lake City, UT; *m:* Donald G.; *c:* Laura M., Donna V., Mark J.; *ed:* (BS) Bus Ed/Eng, Univ of UT 1963; Grad Stud; *cr:* Bus Teacher Skyline HS 1963-66; Eng Teacher USIA Eng Sch 1966-67; Bus/Eng Teacher 1967-69, Bus Teacher/Dept Chairperson 1979- Davis HS; *ai:* FBLA Adv; Joint Staff Study, Career Ladder Evaluation, St Stans, Objectives, St Competency Accounting, Dist Articulation Comms; UT Bus Ed Assn VP 1988-87, UBEA Action Awd 1987; UT Acad of Sci Arts, Letters; Distinguished HS Teaching Awd 1987; Salt Lake City Chamber of Commerce Distinguished Service Awd Competitive Enterprise Finalist 1985; DEA, NEA, UEA, NBEA; Amer Assn of Univ Women Rights & Responsibilities Chairperson 1987-88; Church Parish Cncl 1990-; Co-Author Book 1988-89; Forum Author 1984, 1988; *office:* Davis HS 325 S Main Kaysville UT 84037

LOCHOTZKI, MARY PAULA, SND, 8th Grade Jr HS Teacher; *b:* Sandusky, OH; *ed:* (BA) Ed/Eng, Mary Manse 1974; (MA) Psych, Marywood 1988; Practitioner Trng Cert Neuro-Linguistic Programming 1990; Advanced Religious Ed Cert; *cr:* 4th Grade Teacher Sacred Heart 1970-71; 5th Grade Teacher GESU 1971-73; 6th-8th Grade Teacher St Marys 1973; 2nd/3rd Grade Teacher Holy Rosary 1974; 7th Grade Teacher St Mary 1974-75; 8th Grade Teacher St Augustine 1975-77, Christ the King 1977-80, Our Lady of Carmel 1980-82, Immaculate Conception Sch 1983-; *ai:* Academic Quiz Bowl & Mathcounts Team Coach; HS CCD Teacher; Revised Eng Curr 1984-87; Amer Psychological Assn 1987-; Hearts Up Bellevue Bd 1986-; Articles Published; *office:* Immaculate Conception Sch Main & Broad Sts Bellevue OH 44811

LOCHRIDGE, PAMELA ELLIS, English/Speech Teacher; *b:* Temple, TX; *m:* Thomas Jeffry; *c:* Jordan R., Logan E., Caitlan PAige; *ed:* (BSED) Bus Admin/Eng, SW TX St Univ 1977; Library Sci, Theater, Drama; *cr:* Eng Teacher Fannindel Ind Sch Dist 1977-79; Asst Cashier San Antonio Bank & Trust 1979-82; Eng Teacher Windom Ind Sch Dist 1982-84, Honey Grove CISD 1984-; *ai:* Class & Stu Cncl Spon; UIL Coord; Coach & Dir for One-Act Play; TJCTE 1988-; NCTE 1982-; Outstanding Young Educator Awd Bonham Jaycees 1983; *office:* Honey Grove CISD 107 Bois D arc Honey Grove TX 75446

LOCK, FRANK DANIEL, Chemistry/Physics Teacher; *b:* Buffalo, NY; *m:* Mary Lou Kwandranc; *c:* Jennifer, Megan; *ed:* (BS) Scndry Ed/Chem, Buffalo St Coll 1974; Grad Stud Scndry Ed; *cr:* Sr HS Sci Teacher Barker Cntrl Sch 1974-79; Chem/Physics Teacher Charlotte HS 1979-80, Lemon Bay HS 1980-; *ai:* Swimming, Cross Cntry, Soccer Coach; Chess, Astronomy, Engineering Club Adv; AAPT, Amer Chem Society Div of Chem Ed; Gulf Coast Swim Assn (Pres 1985-87, Secy 1987-); Book Review Published 1986; *office:* Lemon Bay HS 2201 Placida Rd Englewood FL 34224

LOCK, JO ELLYN BIDNER, 4th Grade Teacher; *b:* Paxton, IL; *m:* Vernon Andrew; *c:* Eric, Julie; *ed:* (BA) Ed, IL St Univ Normal 1958; (MA) Ed, N AZ Univ 1970; Primary Specialist, AZ 1959; Rdng Specialist, AZ Jr Coll 1973; *cr:* 1st Grade Teacher Reedswood Sch 1958, Phoenix Elem #1 1959, Glendale Elem Sch 1960-68; Summer Rdng Clinic Dir Glendale Comm Coll 1974-; 4th Grade Teacher Litchfield Elem Sch 1974-; *ai:* Glendale Dir FUMC Mothers Decade Style Show 1972; Kappa Delta Gamma Pres 1956-58, IL NEA Natl Rep 1956; Delta Kappa Gamma 1976-; Pop Warner Parent Organization (Cheer Mother 1977-79, Dir 1974-77), Spirit Awd 1976; Meth Church Sunday Sch Teacher 1973-77; Spinal Cord Walk Back Fnd VP 1986-88, Fnd Awd 1987; Spinal Cord Walking Free Finance Chm 1984-85, Ingenuity Awd 1985; Childrens Academic Nursery Glendale Comm Coll 1971-73; Grand Canyon Coll Evening Classes Wrote Decoding Courses AZ St 1975-76; Wrote Jr Coll Courses Academic Classes 1976-80.

LOCKART, DAVID ROYCE, Vocal Music Teacher; *b:* Seattle, WA; *m:* Linda Caldwell; *c:* Jason, Heather; *ed:* (BM) Vocal Music Ed, Westminster Choir Coll 1978; (MM) Choral Music, Univ of IL 1979; Advanced Choral Conducting & Arranging Westminster; Supervisory Cert Trenton St Coll 1990; *cr:* Vocal Music Teacher North Hunterdon HS 1980-; *ai:* Theater Musical & Asst Marching Band Dir; Curr Comm; MENC, NJMEA 1980-; ACDA 1989-; Published Articles & Lectured on Group & Choral Techniques; *office:* North Hunterdon HS 14 Rt 31 Annandale NJ 08801

LOCKART, SUSAN MALONY, 2nd/3rd Grade Teacher; *b:* Detroit, MI; *m:* Robert W.; *c:* Kevin; *ed:* (BS) Elem Ed, W MI Univ 1963; (MA) Cmptr Ed, Lesley Coll 1986; Cmptr Ed; Child Welfare; *cr:* 3rd Grade Teacher L Anse Cruse Sch 1963-66; 2nd-5th Grade Chapter I Teacher 1987-89, 2nd-5th Grade Teacher 1966- Dist #60; *ai:* Building Specialists Team Leader; Discipline, Building & Chapter I Advvisory Comm; IRA 1983-; NEA, CEA, PEA 1966-; *office:* Hyde Park Elem Sch 2500 W 18th Pueblo CO 81003

LOCKE, JON DAVID, Director of Bands; *b:* Parsons, KS; *ed:* (BA) Music, TX Tech Univ 1986; *cr:* Asst Band Dir 1986-88, Dir of Bands 1988- Lubbock-Cooper Ind Sch Dist; *ai:* TX Tech Band & Orch Camp; TX Music Educators Assn, TX Bandmasters Assn Mem 1986-; Kappa Kappa Psi Pledge Trainer 1981-86; Delta Sigma Phi Pledge Master 1984-86; Teacher of Month 1989; *office:* Lubbock-Cooper HS Rt 6 Box 400 Lubbock TX 79412

LOCKE, LINDA J., First Grade Teacher; *b:* Ripley, MS; *m:* Jimmy; *c:* Jayna, Jim; *ed:* (BA) Elem, Blue Mountain 1970; (MS) Elem, Univ of MS 1979; *cr:* 1st Grade Teacher Pine Grove ELem 1970-; *ai:* 5 Yr Planning Comm; 1st Grade Bsktbl Coach; Alpha Delta 1983-89; MAE, STAE; PTO 1970-89; Heritage Society; *home:* Rt 2 Box 377 Ripley MS 38663

LOCKER, HOLLAND A., Principal; *b:* Fresno, CA; *ed:* (BS) Ed, CA ST Univ 1980; (MS) Ed/Admin, Univ San Francisco 1983; *cr:* 4th Grade Instr Weldon Elem 1980-82; 6th Grade Instr Bethune Elem 1982-86; Vice Prin Burroughs Elem 1986-89; Prin Ayer Elem 1989-; *ai:* Spon Sci Club; Vlybl Coach; Bsktbl Coach; Phi Delta Kappa Pres 1987-88; ACSA Membership Comm 1989; *office:* Ayer Elem Sch 5272 E Lowe Fresno CA 93727

LOCKER, LINDA SUE, First Grade Teacher; *b:* Danville, KY; *ed:* (BA) Elem Ed, 1973, Early Chldhd, 1983 Univ of KY; *cr:* 4th Grade Teacher 1974, 2nd Grade Teacher 1974-77, 1st Grade Teacher 1977- Blue Grass Baptist Sch; *ai:* Yrbk Adv; *office:* Blue Grass Baptist Sch 1330 Red River Dr Lexington KY 40517

LOCKETT, EMMA WALTERS, Seventh Grade Lead Teacher; *b:* Americus, GA; *m:* Eddie Lee; *c:* Roderick B. Mc Grady, Corey T.; *ed:* (BS) Elem Ed, 1974, (MED) Mid Grades Ed, 1975, (EDS) Mid Grades Ed, 1989 GA Southwestern Coll; *cr:* 5th Grade Teacher 1974-76, 4th Grade Teacher 1976-85 Vienna Elem Sch; 6th Grade Teacher Southeast Elem & Sumter Mid Sch 1985-88; 7th Grade Lead Teacher Sumter Cty Mid Sch 1988-; *ai:* Beta Club Spon; St Dev Advisory Comm; GA Assn of Ed Pres 1985-86; NEA; *home:* 302 Buttercup Ln Americus GA 31709

LOCKETT, MARJORIE ANDERSON, Third Grade Teacher; *b:* Pittsburgh, PA; *m:* Donald; *c:* Candice, Monica; *ed:* (BS) Elem, IN Univ of PA 1964; Cmptr Trng Courses; *cr:* Teacher Jennette Sch Dist 1964-66, New Kensington-Arnold Sch Dist 1966-; *ai:* Sci & Soc Stud Comm; NEA, PSEA; NKEA Building Rep 1987-; Church Treas 1985-; PTA 1966-; Tutored Children; *office:* Martin Elem Sch 7th Rd New Kensington PA 15068

LOCKHART, DORIS MATHERLY, Mathematics Dept Chair/Teacher; *b:* Dott, WV; *m:* Eugene G.; *c:* Canessa Stafford, Veneicia, Eugene Jr., Mimi; *ed:* (BS) Math, Concord Coll 1966; (MS) Ed, Marshall Univ 1979; Ed Trng; *cr:* 3rd Grade Teacher Nathan Hale Sch 1961-66; Math Teacher Athens HS 1966-; *ai:* Math Counts & Math Field Day Coach; St Judes Mathathon & Sr Class Spon; NEA, WVEA, MCEA 1966-; Order of Eastern Star Worthy Matron 1971-; *office:* Athens Jr/Sr HS State St Athens WV 24712

LOCKHART, JONE E. (TIBBETTS), Art Teacher; *b:* Brush, CO; *c:* J. S., Christine; *ed:* (Ba) Art Ed, Univ of Northern CO 1972; *cr:* K-12 Art Teacher Arickaree Sch 1973-74; K-8 Art Teacher Weld Re-1 Schls 1974-; *ai:* Suicide Prevention Team Mem; Gifted/Talented Comm; Drug/Alcohol Task Force; La Salle 4-H Club Leader 1979-89; Co-Author WCSD Re-1 Art Curr.

LOCKHART, TERESA ANN, English Teacher; *b:* Manchester, TN; *m:* Kenneth E.; *ed:* (BS) Eng, Mid TN St Univ 1985; Working Towards Masters; *cr:* Eng Teacher Cntrl HS 1986-; *ai:* Sch Newspaper Spon; TN Ed Assn, NEA, Coffee Cty Ed Assn; 1st Baptist Church of Summitville; MTSU Grad Eng Teaching Asst; Article Published; Teacher of Week; *office:* Cntrl HS 2001 Mc Arthur St Manchester TN 37355

LOCKLEY, ELIZABETH LOU RHEINLANDER, Fourth Grade Teacher; *b:* Houston, TX; *c:* Kevin, Brooke; *ed:* (BS) Elem Ed, Sam Houston St Univ 1967; Grad Stud; *cr:* 1st Grade Teacher Spring Branch Ind Sch Dist 1967-68; Kndgtn/2nd Grade Teacher Houston Ind Sch Dist 1971-72; 3rd Grade Teacher Holy Rosary Cath 1972-74; 7th-8th Grade Rdng/Math Teacher Wallis-Orchard Ind Sch Dist 1978-85; 4th-7th Grade Lang Art Teacher Stafford Municipal 1985-; *ai:* TX St Teachers Assn 1989-; Brazos Jr HS Teacher of Yr 1981, 1982, 1984, 1985.

LOCKRIDGE, DARRELL JAY, Asst Principal/Algebra Teacher; *b:* Galveston, TX; *m:* Nicki Foley; *c:* Mandy, Joe, Nick, Kara, Sean; *ed:* (BS) Ec, Univ of Houston 1972; Working Towards Masters Mid Management; Prins Certificate; *cr:* Teacher Mt Carmel HS 1972-83, Langham Creek HS 1983-85; Teacher/Admin Mt Carmel HS 1985-; *ai:* Head Ftbl & Bsktbl Coach; Asst Prin Stu Act; *office:* Mt Carmel HS 6700 Mt Carmel Dr Houston TX 77087

LOCKWOOD, NOLAN D., Mathematics Teacher; *b:* Redlands, CA; *ed:* (BS) Math, Univ of Redlands 1960; (MS) Math, N AZ Univ 1969; CA Teaching Credential, CA St Univ Long Beach; *cr:* Math Teacher Twentynine Palms HS 1961-; *ai:* Stu Act Dir; Phi Delta Kappa 1967-; NCTM 1968-; NEA Life Mem; CA Teachers Assn 1961-; Morongo Basin Former Pres; Phi Delta Kappa Treas; Morongo Teachers Assn; *office:* Twentynine Palms HS 6051 Datura Ave Twentynine Palms CA 92277

LOCKWOOD, RONNIE LEWIS, 4th-6th Grade Science Teacher; *b:* Brooken, OK; *m:* Nell Jean Collard; *c:* Steve N., Leshian J.; *ed:* (BA) Elem Ed, 1974, (MS) Elem Ed, 1985 East Cntrl Univ; Admin Certificate; *cr:* Coach/Prin/4th-6th Grade Teacher Paoli Public Sch 1974-76; Coach/Prin/K-8th Grade Teacher Whitefield Public Sch 1976-79; Coach/4th-6th Grade Sci Teacher Quinton Public Schls 1979-; *ai:* OEA Quinton Pres 1981-82; *office:* Quinton Elem Sch P O Box 67 Quinton OK 74561

LOCKWOOD, VICKIE JANE, Lang Art Teacher/Dept Chair; *b:* Ft Wayne, IN; *ed:* (BS) Elem Ed, 1974, (MS) Elem Ed, 1979 IN Univ; *cr:* 6th Grade Teacher Okeechobee Elem 1974-75, J E Ober Elem 1976-81; 6th-7th Grade Teacher Lake Travis Mid Sch 1982-84; 7th/8th Grade Teacher Eanes Ind Sch Dist 1985-; *ai:* Lang Art Dept Chairperson; West Ridge Management Team; Eanes Dist Textbook Comm; UIL Academic Coach; Odyssey of Mind Regional & St Judge; Natl Awd Winning Yrbk Adv 1986-89; Appletree Cmptrs for Stu Chm; Assn of TX Prof Educators 1989-; TX St Teachers Assn, NEA 1981-89; Nom Teacher of Yr Rotary Club 1990; Nom for Dist Teacher of Yr; NSPA Yrbk Adv Won All Amer; Gold Crown CSPA; All Southern SIPA; Top St Awd 1988, 1989; St Police Drug Ed Awd; *office:* West Ridge Mid Sch 207 Lowell St Austin TX 78733

LODES, MIKE G., 7th/8th Grade Math/Sci Teacher; *b:* Sheboygan, WI; *m:* Kathryn Ann Gottinger; *c:* Lori, Jeffrey; *ed:* (BS) Bio, Univ WI Oshkosh 1969; Grad Work Phys Sci, Univ WI OShkosh; AODA Prgm; *cr:* Elem Sci Teacher S S Peter & Paul Sch 1969-70; Sci/Math/His Teacher Holy Rosary Sch 1970-; *ai:* Cath Schls Week Chm; Hunter Safety Instr; 8th Grade Class Adv; NCEA Mem 1969-; Kiel Fish & Game (VP 1978-79, Secy 1981-89); Delta Sigma Phi 1967-; Sci World Instr Nominee DPI Prgm; *office:* Holy Rosary Sch 1814 Madison St New Holstein WI 53061

LOEB, WENDY GARTENGERG, Math Teacher; *b:* Chicago, IL; *m:* David; *c:* Bobby, Jordan, Bradley; *ed:* (BS) Elem Ed, Univ of IL 1978; Grad Cmptr; Gifted Ed & Math Ed; *cr:* Math Teacher Twin Groves Sch 1978-; *ai:* Gifted Comm; NEA/DEA 1980-; Natl Gifted Assn 1984-; *office:* Twin Groves Jr H S 1072 Ivy Hall Ln Buffalo Grove IL 60089

LOEBER, ED R., AP American History Teacher; *b:* New York City, NY; *m:* Betty Reed; *ed:* (BA) Scndry Ed, Univ of MS 1967; (MA) Supervision, Memphis St 1973; Economic Ed, Rjr Inst 1968; Law Ed Constitutional Rights Fnd 1987; *cr:* Teacher Bartlett HS 1967-72, Millington HS 1972-74; Teacher/Coach Raleigh Egypt HS 1974-; *ai:* Citizen Bee Coord; Head Coach Girls Track; Knowledge Bowl, Academic Decathlon & Knowledge Master Adv; Memphis City Schls Amer His Textbook Comm; Asst Girls Bsbl

Coach; Nom for Rotary Club Teacher of Yr; *office:* Raleigh Egypt HS 3970 Voltaire Memphis TN 38128

LOEWEN, MARY LOUISE, Religious Studies Teacher; *b:* Kenosha, WI; *ed:* (BM) Music Ed, Coll of Racine 1959; (MED) General Scndry Ed, 1968, Ed Sp General Scndry Ed, 1971 Wayne St Univ; Courses & Wkshps Religious Ed; *cr:* Teacher Assumption Sch 1964-76; Dir of Ed Sacred Heart Parish 1976-80; Facilitator Archdiocese of Detroit 1977-; Teacher Regina HS 1981-; *ai:* Pride of Regina HS Comm; Costume Coord Drama Club Production; Wayne St Univ Alumni Organization 1969-; NCEA 1981-; Founders Society Detroit Inst of Arts 1989-; Friends of Roseville Lib 1989-; Natl Sci Fnd Grant Colgate Univ & Univ of Detroit; *office:* Regina HS 20200 Kelly Rd Harper Woods MI 48225

LOFGREN, CAROL WEBB, Latin Teacher; *b:* Atlanta, GA; *m:* Mark Allan; *c:* Leigh E. Mc Chesney; *ed:* (BSED) Latin, Univ of GA 1971; (MAT) Latin, Emory Univ 1975; *cr:* Latin Teacher Cross Keys HS 1971-80, Northside HS 1980-81, Dunwoody HS 1981-; *ai:* HS Swim Team Coach; Latin Club Spon; Mentor Prgm; Stu Concerns Action Team Mem; NHS Faculty Comm; Vergilian Society Amer Classical League, Classical Assn of Midwest & South 1971-; Foreign Lang Assn of GA 1971-, Latin Teacher of Yr 1976; GA Classical Assn (Classical Journal Ed 1989-) 1979-; Teacher of Yr Cross Keys HS 1980; STAR Teacher Cross Keys HS 1980; St of GA Latin Teacher of Yr 1976; *office:* Dunwoody HS 5035 Vermack Rd Dunwoody GA 30338

LOFTIS, ANN ELLISON, Compensatory Teacher; *b:* Belton, SC; *m:* Frank Edward; *c:* Debra D.; *ed:* (BA) Elem Ed, Limestone 1970; (MAT) Elem Ed, Winthrop 1974; (MA) Admin, USCS 1986; *cr:* Bookkeeper Rice Mills 1956-58, Ellison Millings Company 1958-64, Jeffrey Manufacturing 1965-66, Bank of Gaffney 1966-68; Classroom Teacher 1970-85, Compensatory Teacher 1985- Corinth Elem; *ai:* BSAP Remedial Rep Comm; Public Relations Comm; NEA, SC Ed Assn 1971-; Cherokee Cty Ed Assn (Human Relations Chm, Sch Rep) 1971-; Beta Sign Phi 1969-, Outstanding Young Women of America 1971; Cherokee Gladiolus Society 1974-89, Personalities of South Awd 1973; Teacher of Yr Corinth Sch 1978-79; *home:* 105 Trenton Rd Gaffney SC 29340

LOFTIS, LEMAN DEAN, English Teacher; *b:* Gainesville, MO; *m:* Margaret Rose Todt; *c:* Justin K.; *ed:* (BA) Eng, the Sch of the Ozarks 1974; (MED) Eng Ed, Drury Coll 1976; Teacher Effectivenss Trng/Advanced Trng Prgm for Learning Styles; *cr:* Eng Teacher Blue Eye HS 1973-84, Hollister HS 1984-; *ai:* Coord for Learning Styles Project; Weighted Classes Comm; Dramatics Coach; Absentee Comm Mem; Curr Comm; Jr HS Transition Coord; Faculty Adv; Adjunct Faculty; Mem for Tarkio Coll Extension Degree Prgm; NCTE 1974-; MO Assn for Supervision & Curr Dev 1988-; Pres of Blue Eye Cmmty Teachers Assn; Voted Teacher of Yr By Blue Eye Faculty; Conducted Wkshp on Classroom Management for Sch of Ozarks; *office:* Hollister R-V H S BB Hwy Hollister MO 65672

LOFTON, JIMMY L., State Government Teacher; *b:* Pulaski, MS; *m:* Margarett R. Sturkin; *c:* Jimmy Jr., Devarious; *ed:* (AA) Soc Stud, Coahoma Jr Coll 1968; (BS) Soc Stud, Alcorn St Univ 1970; Masters Work Univ of S MS, William Carey & Jackson St Univ; *cr:* Teacher Raleigh Jr HS 1970-85, Raleigh HS 1985-; *ai:* Raleigh Jr Historical Society & YAC Spon; MAE; Voters League VP 1987; NAACP Smith Cty Pres 1972-; BSA Scoutmaster 1976-84, Pine Burr 1980, Scout Master of Yr 1982; Faculty Awd 1986-87; History Dept Head 1989; *home:* Star Rt Box 38A Pulaski MS 39152

LOFTON, MARY (CAMPBELL), Reading Teacher; *b:* Memphis, TN; *m:* John Norment; *c:* Janeen, Jonelle; *ed:* Comm/Fr, Lane Coll 1969; Rdng Specialist, S IL Univ 1990; *cr:* 7th-9th Grade Rdng Teacher Dr M L King Jr HS; Curr Cnslr St Louis Univ; *ai:* Cmptr Sci Spon; IL St Bd Lang Art Mem 1987-; Rdng/Lang Art Mem 1969-; Jack & Jill of America Treas 1985-87; JUGS Secy 1986-; Delta Sigma Theta Mem 1965-; Evangelical Childrens Home.

LOFTON, VERNELL THIGPEN, Phys Ed Teacher/Coach/Chair; *b:* Rose Hill, MS; *m:* Howard Lamar; *c:* Orlando H.; *ed:* (BS) Health/Phys Ed, MVSU 1967; USM, MS St Univ; *cr:* Teacher/Coach William J Berry & Heidelberg HS; *ai:* 7th-9th Grade Coach & HS Asst Coach; AFT; GSA Leader; Friend of Children Head Start Policy Cncl; *office:* William J Berry Elem Sch PO Drawer O Heidelberg MS 39439

LOFTUS, CLAUDIA BURNHAM, Guidance Counselor; *b:* Birmingham, AL; *c:* Tony, David, Gregory; *ed:* (BA) Psych, Fisk Univ 1965; (MA) Guidance/Counseling, 1975, Advanced Certificate Guidance/Counseling, 1986 Brooklyn Coll; *cr:* Classroom Teacher 1980-85, Rdng Teacher 1985-89, Guidance Cnslr 1989- Public Sch 92; *ai:* Co-Chairperson; Drug Awareness Comm Chairperson; Parent Involvement Prgm Mem; Lib Renovation Comm Recorder; Sch Improvement Prgm; Teacher of Yr Awd Parents Action Comm 1987; Teacher of Yr Awd Parent Teachers Assn of Public Sch 92 1985; *office:* Public Sch 92 601 Parkside Ave Brooklyn NY 11226

LOFTUS, JOYCE BRENKE, 5th Grade Teacher; *b:* Belle Plaine, MN; *m:* Thomas V.; *c:* Christine, Mark, Beth, Anne, Amy; *ed:* (BS) Elem Ed, Wartburgh Coll 1963; Working Towards Masters Religious Ed, Coll of St Thomas 1984-84; *cr:* 6th Grade Teacher New Hampton Elem Sch 1963-65; 4th Grade Teacher St Martins Cath Sch 1980-81; 5th Grade Teacher St Michaels Parish Sch 1982-; *ai:* Theatre Co-Dir 1989-; Negotiation Comm 1989-; NCEA 1982-; Cncl of Cath Women (Pres 1980-82, Mem) 1976-.

LOFTUS, MICHEAL K., Social Studies Teacher; *b:* Stoughton, WI; *m:* Mary Joanis; *c:* Martin, Carrie; *ed:* (BA) Anthropology, Beloit Coll1969, (MAT) Soc Stud, Beloit Coll 1970; Univ of WI Platteville; Univ of ND; Univ of WI Whitewater; *cr:* Intern Hononegah HS 1969-70; Soc Stud Teacher Evansville HS 1970-; *ai:* H a Dept Head; K-12 Curr Coord WI Cncl Soc Stud 1972-; Evansville Jaycees Pres 1979-80 Jaycee of Yr 1980; NEH Stipend to Univ of ND; Outstanding Young Educator; WI Archaeologist 1975-77 & 79; Occasional Publications in Anthropology No 3 James Madison Univ 1978; *office:* Evansville H S 420 S 4th St Evansville WI 53536

LOGAN, ARGIE PETERS, First Grade Teacher; *b:* Shubuta, MS; *m:* Eddie Will; *c:* Phelix F.; *ed:* (AA) Elem, Harris Jr Coll 1958; (BA) Elem, Rust Coll 1960; (MA) Elem, MS St Univ 1976; Jackson St Univ, Southern Univ, MS Coll, Delta St Univ; *ai:* K-1st Chairperson; Elem Bsktbl, Chrldr, Boys & Girls Track Coach; MAE, NEA; *home:* 519 Bain Durant MS 39063

LOGAN, DAVID MICHAEL, Spanish Teacher; *b:* Kansas City, MO; *m:* Judith Stahl; *c:* Mark, Sean; *ed:* (BA) Span, Univ of Tulsa 1960; (MA) Ed, Univ of MO Kansas City 1966; Span Inst MDEA Murray St Univ; *cr:* Sales Rep Intnl Bus Machines 1961-65; Span Teacher O Hara HS 1966-68, Helena Sch Dist 1 1968-; Author/Publisher Buglin Bull Press 1987-; *ai:* Span Club; MT Inst of Art, W Folklife Center, Outdoor Writers Assn of Amer; Author Poetry Books; Articles & Photographs Published; *office:* Capital HS 100 Valley Dr Helena MT 59601

LOGAN, DONALD DEAN, Guidance Counselor/Psychology; *b:* Manchester, IA; *m:* Janet Sue Dykstra; *c:* Emily, Alicia; *ed:* (BA) His/Psych, Central Coll 1970; (MA) Cnslr Ed, Univ of IA Iowa City 1973; Grad Trng Cnslr Ed & At-Risk Counseling; *cr:* Soc Stud Teacher 1970-, Guidance Cnslr 1987- Benton Cmmty Schls; *ai:* Soph Ftbl; Mid Sch Peers; Stu Government; Benton Cmmty Fnd; HS Leadership At-Risk Coord; Volunteer Services Coord; Benton Cmmty Ed Assn Pres 1978-79; IA Assn of Stu Cncls Dir 1984- Adv of Yr 1987-88; IA Bsktbl Coaches Assn 1978-; Van Horne Lions Club Pres 1982-83; United Meth Church Lay Leader 1984-; Van Horne Cmmty Club Pres 1979-80; Van Horne City Cncl Mem 1982-87; Published Report in Several Counseling Journalist Periodicals 1974/1975; *office:* Benton Community Sch 400 1st St Van Horne IA 52346

LOGAN, ELIZABETH NOLL, Art Teacher; *b:* Ft Mc Clellan, AL; *m:* Russell; *c:* Jeremy; *ed:* (BS) Art Ed, Auburn Univ 1978; (MS) Ed, Univ of Houston 1985; *cr:* Art Teacher Howell Intermediate Sch 1981-89, Martin Intermediate & Opelika Mid 1989-; *ai:* Southern Assn Accredidation Comm; Art in Ed Comm Mem 1982-89; NAEA 1981-; AL Art Ed Assn 1989-; TX Art Educators Assn, TX Classroom Teachers Assn 1981-89; Beta Sigma Phi (Pres, VP, Treas) 1984-, Woman of Yr 1988; Phi Kappa Phi 1984-; Outstanding Adult Leader Victoria TX 1986; *office:* Opelika Mid Sch 1206 Denson Dr Opelika AL 36801

LOGAN, JUDY EAVES, Vocational Business Ed Teacher; *b:* Birmingham, AL; *m:* William Douglas; *c:* Matthew; *ed:* (BS) Bus Ed, 1970, (MS) Scndry Ed, 1974 Jacksonville St Univ; *cr:* Bus Ed Teacher Emma Sansom HS 1971-; *ai:* FBLA Co-Spon; Jr & Sr Prom Chairperson; NEA, AEA, AVA; Prof Assn Of Gadsden Educators; Alpha Delta Kappa (VP 1976-78, Treas 1979-81, Schlsp Comm Chairperson 1988-); Emma Sansom HS Teacher of Yr 1989; *office:* Emma Sansom HS 2210 W Meighan Blvd Gadsden AL 35904

LOGAN, LEILA F., Kindergarten Teacher; *b:* Wister, OK; *m:* Jay V.; *c:* Allyson Logan Nelson; *ed:* (BS) Early Chldhd, OK ST Univ 1954; (MS) Elem Ed, Northeastern ST Univ 1969; *cr:* Kndgtn Teacher First Meth Church 1954-55, Tulsa Public Sch 1955-; Headstart Teacher 1985; *ai:* Tulsa Classroom Teacher Delagate; Prin Adv Comm; Discipline Comm; OK Ed Assn; Tulsa Classroom Teachers Assn; OK Kndgtn Teacher Assn; NEA; *office:* Alice Robertson Sch 2720 W 48th Tulsa OK 74107

LOGAN, LINDA NUTTER, Business Education Teacher; *b:* Middletown, MO; *m:* Vincent N.; *c:* Melissa L., Matthew R.; *ed:* (BS) Bus Ed, Univ of MO Columbia 1970; *cr:* HS Bus Ed Teacher Van-Far HS 1970-73, N Callaway R-1 HS 1973-75, 1985-; *ai:* Future Bus Leaders of America Spon Bd Dir for St of MO 1990; Salary Comm; MO Voc Assn, MO Bus Ed Assn, Cmmty Teacher Assn 1985-; Ebenezer Baptist Church Clerk 1989-; *office:* N Callaway R-1 Sch Dist P O Box 33 Kingdom City MO 65262

LOGAN, RUSSELL MAHLON, Band Director; *b:* Wetumpka, AL; *m:* Elizabeth Mary Noll; *c:* Jeremy; *ed:* (BS) Music Ed, 1976, (MM) Applied Music Performance, 1978 Auburn Univ; (DA) Music Theory, Univ of MS 1981; *cr:* Band Dir Monroe Acad 1976-77, Victoria HS 1981-89, Auburn HS 1989-; *ai:* Band Dir; AL Music Educators Assn, Music Educators Natl Conference 1989-; TX Band Masters Assn; TX Music Educators Assn Dist Band Chm 1981-89; *home:* 820 Tullahoma Dr Auburn AL 36830

LOGAN, SAM T., Social Studies Teacher; *b:* Abbeville, MS; *m:* Marilyn; *c:* Marinda, Tyra; *ed:* (BA) Poly Sci, Rust Coll 1971; (MSS) Soc Sci, Univ of MS 1976; *cr:* Quality Control Supvr Merson Electric Company 1971-73; Coord/Cmmty Relations Northwest Jr Coll 1976-78; Oxford Park Commission Supvr Park Commision 1984-; Teacher Lafayette Jr HS 1971-; *ai:* MS Ed Assn Local Pres 1976-77, Certificate 1977; NEA; Masons Secy 1981-83, Certificate 1983; Omega Psi Phi; Providence United Meth Church Sunday Sch Teacher Certificate of Achievement; *office:* Lafayette Jr HS Rt 5 Oxford MS 38655

LOGAN, SHERYL WOOD, Fourth Grade Teacher; *b:* Columbus, OH; *m:* Larry Dean; *c:* Lindsey; *ed:* (BS) Elem Ed, OH St 1968; Xavier Univ 1975; *cr:* 5th Grade Teacher Circleville City Schls 1968-73; 3rd Grade Teacher Mariemont Schls 1973-76; 3rd-5th Grade Teacher Circleville City Schls 1976-; *ai:* AAUW; Delta Kappa Gamma 1986-; *home:* 497 Willow Ln Circleville OH 43113

LOGAN, SHIRLEY ANN (HILLIARD), Guidance Counselor; *b:* Dyersburg, TN; *c:* Michelle Williams, Patti; *ed:* (BA) His/Ed/Eng, MI St 1962; (MS) Guidance & Counseling, Troy St Univ 1976; Univ of West FL; *cr:* Teacher St Adelaides Sch 1972-73; Ponderosa Elem 1973-74; Pryor Jr HS 1976-78; Bruner Jr HS 1978-81; Cnslr/Teacher Dyersburg Mid Sch 1981-; *ai:* Spon Just Say No Club; Member TN No Team; Mayors Task Force on Youth Problems; TN Assn for Conseling & Dev 1987-; TN Assn for Supervision Curr & Dev 1989-; Dyersburg Ed Assn 1981-; TN Ed Assn/NEA; Amer Cancer Society Bd of Dir FL & TN 1980-89; Dyersburg Chamber of Commerce 1987-; DEA Rep Assembly; Teacher of Yr-Building & System Wide 1986-87; Teacher of Yr 1978; *home:* Rt 1 Box 138 Dyersburg TN 38024

LOGAR, DIANNE L., English/Writing Teacher; *b:* Ely, MN; *m:* Cyril M.; *c:* Brian, John; *ed:* (BS) Eng Ed, Univ of ND 1970; (MA) Ed Admin WV Univ 1981; *cr:* Coordng/Study Skill Univ of MN 1970-71; Eng Teacher Alvarado Public Schls 1971-72; Eng/Writing Cheat Lake Jr HS 1980-; *ai:* Advisor Anchor Line; AFT; *office:* Cheat Lake Jr H S Rt 7 Box 153 Morgantown WV 26505

LOGES, LA VELLA ANN (SCHULTZ), Eng/Sci/Home Ec Teacher; *b:* Meno, OK; *m:* Nolan; *c:* Todd, Christy (dec); *ed:* (BS) Elem Ed, 1963, (MS) Elem Ed, 1969 Northwestern St Teachers Coll; Univ of OR, Univ of AK Southeast; *cr:* Elem Teacher Attica Grade Sch 1963-69, Wellington Sch Dist 1969-71; Elem Method Classes Coll Teacher Baptist Bible Coll 1971-73; Home Ec Teacher Kake City Sch Dist 1978-; *ai:* Peer Coaching Supvr; Jr HS & HS Girls Bsktbl Coach; Chrldr Adv; Hiring Comm with Supt to Hire Teachers & Prins; 8th Grade Class Spon; Kake Ed Assn Pres 1981-82, 1984-87; AK Ed Assn, AK Rural Concerns Comm Mem 1986-87; Kake Booster Club (Organizer, VP) 1986-87; Recognized as Teacher of Yr Elem Sch 1984; *office:* Kake HS Box 450 Kake AK 99830

LOGSDON, GARY WILLIAM, 4th Grade Teacher; *b:* Fremont, OH; *m:* Charlene Ann Kalo; *c:* Eric, Quinn, Brad; *ed:* (BA) Geography, Bowling Green St Univ 1968; Elem Cert, Grad Stud; *cr:* Mid Grade Teacher St Joseph Elem 1968-; *ai:* St Joseph Cntrl Cath Var Wrestling & Cross Cntry Coach; Grade Sch Yrbk Adv; NCEA; BSA Asst Scout Master 1982-; Fremont Elite Runners Club Youth Race Dir Service Awd 1988; Lions Club Pres; Inducted St Joseph Cntrl Cath HS Athletic Hall of Fame 1989; *office:* Fremont St Joseph Elem Sch 716 Croghan St Fremont OH 43420

LOGSTON, STEPHEN KENNETH, Sixth Grade Teacher; *b:* East Liverpool, OH; *m:* Claudia Lamm; *c:* Brian, Willie, Jessica; *ed:* (BA) Elem Ed, Shepherd Coll 1975; (MS) Elem Ed, Univ Dayton 1985; Inst of Childrens Literature; *cr:* 5th Grade Teacher Mathias 12 Yr Sch 1975-76; 4th Grade Teacher Mac Donald Elem Sch 1978-82; 6th Grade Teacher Fairview Elem Sch 1982-; *ai:* Head Bsbl Coach Wellsville HS; NEA/OEA/WCTA Uniserv Rep 1985-86; *office:* Fairview Elem Sch 1151 Oakdale Ave Wellsville OH 43968

LOHMANN, JUDITH LEITH, 8th Grade Reading Teacher; *b:* Bryn Mawr, PA; *m:* Watson M.; *c:* Watson Jr., David, Kimberly; *ed:* (BS) Elem Ed, Lebanon Valley Coll 1961; *cr:* 5th Grade Teacher Kindle Elem Sch 1978-80; Compensatory Ed Teacher 1980-81, 8th Grade Rdng Teacher 1981- Pitman Mid Sch; *ai:* Mid Sch Yrbk Adv; Delta Kappa Gamma Corresponding Secy 1990; South Jersey Rdng Cncl; Mc Cowan Lib (Pres, Bd of Trustees) 1983-; Borough of Pitman Councilperson 1975-78; Pitman Recreation Commission 1980-; Pitman Womans Club; Governors Teachers Recognition Prgm 1987; *office:* Pitman Mid Sch E Holly Ave Pitman NJ 08071

LOHMANN, MARY G., Teacher/Academically Talented; *b:* New York City, NY; *m:* Robert; *c:* Barbara, Loretta; *ed:* (BA) His, Ursinus Coll 1955; (MA) His/Soc Stud, Hunter Coll 1960; (CAS) Interfield Major, Wesleyan Univ 1985; *cr:* Soc Stud Teacher Washington Jr HS 1956-59; Eng/Soc Stud Teacher Bedford Park Acad 1969-71; Soc Stud Teacher Brookfield HS 1971-; *ai:* Career Ed Coord; Teacher of Academically Talented Prgm Designer; Stus of Service Adv; Systemwide Curr & Stu at Risk Comms; BEA, CEA, NEA (Rep 1973-79, Chm of Prof Rights & Responsibilities 1984-86); Phi Delta Kappa 1989-; Sierra Club (St Exec Comm 1989) 1980-; Amnesty Intnl 273 Case Coord 1988-; BHS Teacher of Yr 1989; Developed Prgm for Academically Talented; Awarded St Support Through Funding for Gifted; Received Grant to Develop Career Ed Curr Guides K-8; Conducted Wkshps in Career & Gifted Ed Through St Agencies; Appointed by St Commissioner of Ed to Comm on Teacher Preparation Prgms; *office:* Brookfield HS 45 Longmeadow Hill Rd Brookfield CT 06804

LOHR, GAIL ANN (STICKNEY), Middle School Science Teacher; *b:* Detroit, MI; *m:* David Edward; *c:* Eric C., Lindsay M.; *ed:* (BS) Elem Ed, Oakland Univ 1977; Classes in Wildlife Management & Environmental Stud; Scuba Asst Instr Oakland Univ & MI St; *cr:* 3rd Grade Teacher Webber Elem Sch 1977-78; 6th Grade Teacher Blanche Sims Elem Sch 1978-79; 3rd Grade Teacher 1979-80, 4th Grade Teacher 1980-81 Stadium Elem Sch; Sci/Math Teacher Lake Orion Jr HS 1985-87, Lake Orion Mid Sch 1987-88, Lake Orion Jr HS 1988-89, Lake Orion Mid Sch 1989-; *ai:* Prof Dev & Sci Objective Comm; MI Ed Assn, NEA, Lake Orion Ed Assn; Natl Assn of Underwater Instrs Asst Instr;

Underwater Photographer for Scuba Presentations; *home:* 879 Central Lake Orion MI 48035

LOHRENTZ, VICKY SUE, Special Education Teacher; *b:* Hutchinson, KS; *ed:* (BS) Elem/Spec Ed, Bethel Coll 1987; Grad Stud Behavior Disorders & Learning Disabilities Wichita St Univ; *cr:* Teacher of Mentally Handicapped Buhler Grade Sch 1987-; *ai:* Preassessmen, Cooperative Learning, WALK Teams Mem; Prof Dev Cncl; Teachers Advisory Comm; Knight Acad Leader; Spec Olympics Coach; Summer Sch Teacher; KS Rdng Assn, Reno Cty Retarded Citizens Assn 1987-; CEC 1985-; Buhler Memonite Church Mem 1979-; Nutrition Grant; Reno Cty Ed Cooperative Prof of Yr 1989; Numerous Athletic & Academic Schlsps; Positive Discipline Wkshp Presenter; *office:* Buhler Grade Sch 808 N Main Buhler KS 67522

LOHRMANN, PATRICIA POLING, English/Composition Teacher; *b:* Terre Haute, IN; *m:* Gregory E.; *c:* Ehren E. Shannon E.; *ed:* (BS) Eng, 1969, (MS) Eng, 1973, (CAS) Eng, 1988 IN St Univ; *cr:* Eng Teacher Benton Cntrl HS 1969, Rockville HS 1969-; Eng Teaching Asst IN St Univ 1985-; *ai:* Sch Improvement Team Mem; Sr Spon; NCTE, IN Cncl Teachers of Eng, IN St Teachers Assn; Phi Kappa Phi 1988-; Sigma Tau Delta 1969-; Kappa Kappa Kappa Pres 1978-79; *home:* RR 4 Box 226AA Rockville IN 47872

LOKEN, WILMA AUDREY (RINGEN), Mathematics Teacher; *b:* Kindred, ND; *m:* A. E.; *c:* Marc C., Kent D., Naomi R. Wilkins, Beth K. Cherryholmes, Paul L.; *ed:* (BA) Math/Ger, Concordia 1951; *cr:* 7th-8th Grade Math Teacher/Lib New Town HS 1965-67; 7th-8th Grade Math Teacher Appleton Jr HS 1969-71; Math Teacher/Lib Herreid HS 1973-75; Math Teacher Philip HS 1978-79; Math/Chapter Math Teacher Marty Indian HS 1983-; *ai:* Mem of Sch Team for Sch Improvement; Jr, Frosh, Sr Class, Stu Cncl, NHS Adv; *home:* Box 247 Marty SD 57361

LOLA, CHARLENE HELEN NEKUDA, Fourth Grade Teacher; *b:* Sargent, NE; *w:* Richard (dec); *c:* Connie Philbrick, Jeri Phillips, Kathryn Bienhoff, James; *ed:* (BA) Elem Ed, Kearney St Coll 1969; Grad Stud Univ of NE Lincoln, Wayne St Coll, Chadron St Coll, Kearney St Coll; *cr:* K-8th Grade Teacher Rural-Valley-Howard-Custer Ctys 1946-50, 1955-65; 5th Grade Teacher Arcadia Public 1965-69; 5th Grade Teacher 1969-85, 4th Grade Teacher 1985- Ord Public Sch; *ai:* Supts Advisory Comm; OEA (Secy, VP, Treas, Grieviance Chm); ADK (Pres, Secy, St Officer) 1972-76; NE Cncl for Soc Stud 1970; Ord City Cncl Ward 2 1978-86; BPW Secy 1988-, Women of Yr 1984; Amer Heart Assn Treas 1982-; City Planning Commission 1978-82; Valley Cty Planning Commission 1966-68; Taft Inst Grant; Valley Cty Rural Teacher of Yr 1956; Published Article 1970; *home:* 417 N 17th Ord NE 68862

LOLLINI, DOROTHY LOGONOVEACH, 7th-8th Grade Rdng Lit Teacher; *b:* Tiltonsville, OH; *c:* William J., Randall C., Mary L. Scherer; *ed:* (BSED) Elem Ed, OH Univ 1973; (MSED) Guidance Teacher, Univ of Dayton 1981; *cr:* 3rd Grade Teacher Martins Ferry City Schls 1973-74; Remedial Rdng Teacher St Marys 1974-75; Rdng Lit Teacher St Clairsville-Richland City Schls 1976-; *ai:* Coord Right to Read Week Act; OH Univ Alumni Bd of Trustees 1981-; *home:* 107 Park St Saint Clairsville OH 43950

LOLLO, MICHAEL ANTHONY, Jr HS & HS Spanish Teacher; *b:* Zanesville, OH; *m:* Cynthia Ann Jorgenson; *ed:* (BA) Span, Otterbein Coll 1979; Working Towards Masters Ed, Ashland Coll; *cr:* Span Teacher Watkin Memorial HS 1979-81, Crooksville HS 1982-84, New Lexington HS 1984-; *ai:* Span Club Adv; Pi Sigma Iota 1979-; *home:* 136 E Broadway St New Lexington OH 43764

LOMAS, WILLIAM THOMAS, JR., Principal; *b:* Colorado Springs, CO; *m:* Mary; *c:* Brian, Amy; *ed:* (BS) Soc Stud, S IL Univ 1978; (MA) Admin, NE IL Univ 1988; *cr:* Soc Stud Chm 1978-87, Asst Prin 1987-89, Prin 1989- Shady Lane; *ai:* Extracurricular Supvr; Soc Stud Curr Chm 1978-88; *office:* Shady Lane Sch 101 Hawthorne Ln Fox Lake IL 60020

LOMAX, ELLEN BOECKEL, Teacher of Gifted; *b:* Washington, DC; *m:* Joseph Logan; *c:* Peter L.; *ed:* (BS) Elem Ed, Cedar Crest Coll 1964; Masters Prgm Monmouth Coll; Gifted Ed, Widener Univ; *cr:* 4th Grade Teacher Lenola Sch 1964-65; 4th-6th Grade Teacher Knollwood Sch 1965-73; 6th Grade Sci/7th Grade Math/6th-8th Grade Gifted & Talented Lang Art/Math Teacher Mid Sch 1973-; *ai:* Rock Hound Club & Stu Cncl Adv; Gifted & Talented Work Study Comm; NEA, NJEA 1964-; NJ Ed of the Gifted & Talented 1989-; 4-H Fnd Secy 1983-, Service Awd 1989; Hospital Horse Show (Co-Chairperson, Chairperson) 1984-88, Service Awd 1988; Guest Lecturer NJ Assn of Prin& Supvrs 1987; Wildlife Lecturer 1968-85; Dist Teacher of Yr 1978; Unit Publication 1981; *home:* PO Box 834 Cape May Ct Hse NJ 08210

LOMBARDO, JOSEPH PAUL, Fifth Grade Teacher; *b:* Jamestown, NY; *m:* Sally M. Hamilton; *c:* Chasity, Christina, Jonathan; *ed:* (AA) Soc Sci, Jamestown Comm Coll 1973; (BS) Elem Ed, 1975, (MS) Elem Ed, 1981 SUNY Fredonia; Jr Participation 4th Grade Cassadaga Elem Sch 1974; Stu Teaching-6th Grade Southwestern Mid Sch, Kndgtn Celeron Elem Sch 1975; *cr:* Substitute Teacher 1975-77; 4th Grade Teacher Fletcher Elem Sch 1977-85; Teacher of At Risk Stus Jamestown HS 1985-88; Comp Ed Math Teacher Love Elem Sch 1988-89; 5th Grade Teacher Jefferson Sch 1989-; *ai:* Var Bsbl Coach Jamestown HS; Asst Ftbl Coach Washington Sch; Dist Scheduling, Building IMPACT, Stu Recognition Comm; NEA, NY Ed Assn 1977-; Jamestown Teachers Assn Liason/Grievance Chairperson 1977-; Amer Bsbl Coaches Assn 1986-; Coll Stadium Tenants Organization 1985-; Chaut Co 16-18 Babe Ruth Organization, Jamestown Babe Ruth Assn 1984-85; S S Peter & Paul Church 1986-; Magazine Articles Published 1984, 1988; *home:* 176 Stowe St Jamestown NY 14701

LONDON, REGINA MARTIN, Secondary Mathematics Teacher; *b:* Reidsville, NC; *m:* Charles S. II; *c:* Blake Addison; *ed:* (AB) Math/Ed, Univ of NC Chapel Hill 1986; *cr:* Math Teacher Lee Cty Sr HS 1986-; *ai:* Math Club Adv; NC Cncl of Math 1987-; *office:* Lee County Sr HS 1708 Nash St Sanford NC 27330

LONG, ALLENE STOLT, Retired Teacher; *b:* Petoskey, MI; *m:* Phillip D.; *c:* Christopher W., Barry E., Melissa Long Seabra, Camilla J. Martin; *ed:* (BA) Sociology/Ed, Alma Coll 1954; (MA) Rdng/Lang Art, Oakland Univ 1980; *cr:* 2nd Grade Teacher Johannesburg Elem Sch 1955, Hightstown Elem Sch 1955-56; K/1st Grade Teacher Pellston Elem Sch 1957-68; 1st Grade Teacher Gerrish Higgins Elem Sch 1969-72; 1st/2nd/4th Grade Teacher Reed City Elem 1969-72; 4s At Risk Teacher Reed City Public Schls 1988-; *ai:* MEA Building Rep 1955-88; MI Rdng Assn 1974-88; Project Homes 1989-; Delta Kappa Gamma 1st VP 1980-82; Recycle Mecosta Cty Chairperson 1989-; The United Church Elder; MEA & NEA Outstanding Person in Ed Region 158 1985-86; *home:* 13990 New Mill Pond Rd Big Rapids MI 49307

LONG, AMELIA GRAHAM, Mathematics Teacher/Dept Chair; *b:* Tyndall AFB, FL; *m:* Kerry Antwan; *ed:* (BA) Math, Univ of NC Charlotte 1986; *cr:* Math Teacher Cummings HS 1986-87, Hillside HS 1988, Durham HS 1988-; *ai:* Jr Class Adv; Upward Bound & Mu Alpha Theta Asst; Math Chairperson; Durham Math Cncl Steering Rep 1990; NCAE, DEA, NEA Mem 1988-; NCTM Mem 1987-.

LONG, CAROLYN GILLISPIE, Fifth Grade Teacher; *b:* Hays, KS; *m:* John A. III; *c:* Paula C. Grimm, John A. IV; *ed:* (BA) Elem Ed, OK St Univ 1972; *cr:* 5th Grade Teacher Marlin E Crowder Elem 1972-; *ai:* Fairfax Ed Assn Treas 1989-; Fairfax Hospital Auxiliary Pres 1987-89; Osage Cty Democratic Precinct (Pres 1988-89, VP 1987-88); *office:* Marlin E Crowder Sch 715 W Mulberrry Fairfax OK 74637

LONG, CHARLES HAROLD, JR., 5th Grade Teacher; *b:* Charleston, SC; *m:* Judith Lubs; *c:* Charles, Amanda; *ed:* (BS) Bus Admin, Newberry Coll 1972; (MAT) Scndry Sch Admin, The Citadel 1976; Elem, Mid Sch, HS Cert; Gifted & Talented Performing Arts; *cr:* 9th-12th Grade Teacher Country Day Sch 1972-74; K-12th Grade Prin Country Day Sch & St Pauls Acad 1974-77; 5th Grade Teacher Stono Park Elem 1977-; *ai:* Co-Dir Charleston Youth Company Cty-Wide Prof Performing Arts Prgm & Sch Chorus; Teach Piano & Voice; Adolescents & Improvement Cncl; Classy Kids Performing Arts Dir; Phi Mu Alpha Pres 1971; The Madrigalians Pres 1969-72; Blue Key 1972; Phi Delta Kappa 1986-; Ger Friendly Society Charleston; Palmetto St Teachers; St Andrews Dist Teacher 1985; Charleston Cty Teacher of Yr 1985; SC St Teacher of Yr 1986; Charleston Jaycees Outstanding Young Educator; *office:* Stono Park Elem Sch 1699 Garden St Charleston SC 29407

LONG, CHARLES L., Sixth Grade Teacher; *b:* Clayton, KS; *m:* Mary Eleanor Nolan; *c:* Charles Jr., Laura Mc Millan, Mary Pahls, William; *ed:* (BS) Elem Ed, KS St Univ 1966; (MS) Elem Admin, Fort Hays St Univ 1971; *cr:* Elem Teacher Lone Hill Rural Sch 1956-57, Junction City Public Schls 1957-63, USD 273 1966-; *ai:* Mem Beloit Imprvmt of Curr Comm; Mem Lang Arts Curr Comm; NEA; KS NEA; East Mitchell Cty Teachers Assn Treas 1972; Outstanding Young Educator Awd 1971; Port Lib Bd of Dir; Bankers Conservation Awd 1989; *home:* RFD 4 Beloit KS 67420

LONG, CHRISTOPHER JAMES, English Teacher; *b:* San Francisco, CA; *m:* Laney W.; *c:* Amanda, Ian, Abbie; *ed:* (BS) Eng, Westminster Coll 1978; *cr:* Teacher/Coach Bingham HS 1978-83, Judge Memorial 1983-; *ai:* Head Wrestling Coach; Summer Sch Dir; UT Wrestling Coaches Assn Pres 1982-83; NCTE 1983-; Writing & Wasatch Founder & Teacher; *office:* Judge Memorial Cath HS 650 S 1100 E Salt Lake City UT 84102

LONG, DEBORAH LYNN, Mathematics Dept Chairwoman; *b:* Mount Airy, NC; *ed:* (BS) Math, 1972, (MA) Math, 1978 Appalachian St Univ; *cr:* Math Teacher Fred T Foard HS 1972-; *ai:* Beta Club; Girls Athletic Club; Math Dept Chm; Mentor; NC Assn of Educators 1972-; NC Cncl Teachers of Math 1980-; Teacher of Yr 1983; *office:* Fred T Foard Sch Rt 1 Box 295 Newton NC 28658

LONG, ETOYIL F., English Teacher; *b:* Pottas Camp, MS; *ed:* (BA) Eng, MS Industrial Coll 1954; (MA) Eng, Univ of MS 1975; Memphis St Univ, Delta St Univ, Univ of MS; *cr:* Eng Teacher Walton Chapel HS 1954-67, N Panola Voc HS 1968-74, N Panola HS 1975-; *ai:* Annual Staff Adv; Eng Dept, Frosh Class Chairperson; N Panola Dist Assn of Educators Asst Secy 1989-; MS Cncl Teachers of Eng 1954-; NCTE 1954-; 4-H Club; Heroine of Jericho; Eastern Star; Teacher of Yr; 4-H Club Schlsp; *office:* N Panola HS PO Box 278 Hwy 51 N Sardis MS 38666

LONG, GARY EDWARD, HS Social Studies Teacher; *b:* Jeffersonville, IN; *m:* Shannon Beth Hensley; *c:* Matthew R., Tyler J.; *ed:* (BA) Soc Stud/Psych, Univ of Evansville 1981; (ME) Scndry Ed, IN St Univ 1986; *cr:* Soc Stud Teacher Union Cty HS 1981-; *ai:* Boys Bsktbl, Bsbl, Cross Cntry, Track Coach; His Club Spon; KY Ed Assn 1981-; NEA; Holy Name Cath Church 1981-; *office:* Union Cty HS Rt 4 Box 61 Morganfield KY 42437

LONG, HELEN LUCY MARUCA, 1st Grade Teacher; *b:* Houston, TX; *c:* Lu Becca, Lacy; *ed:* (BAT) Elem Ed, Sam Houston St Univ 1976; *cr:* 1st Grade Teacher Webb Elem 1976-; *ai:* Ready Writing - UIL 1990 - 3rd Grade; Chosen By Supt of Olton ISD to Head Rdng Comm Regarding Standardized Test Scores 1988; ATPE 1976-86; AFT 1987-89; TSTA 1976-78; Published in Caprock Area Writing Project Anthology TX Tech Univ 1987; *home:* Box 744 Olton TX 79064

LONG, JANET TAFF, Business Teacher; *b:* Fort Smith, AR; *m:* Gary; *c:* Amanda, Melissa; *ed:* (BS) Bus Ed, Univ of Ozarks 1979; *cr:* Bus Teacher Ft Smith Chrstn Sch 1981-; *ai:* Sr Class Spon; *office:* Ft Smith Christian Sch 4201 Windsor Dr Fort Smith AR 72904

LONG, JOHN WILLIAM, Mathematics Teacher/Dept Chair; *b:* Platteville, WI; *m:* Agnes Brickl; *c:* Jim, Jan Van Dallwyk, Eric; *ed:* (BS) Math/Sci, Univ of WI Platteville 1952; (MS) Math/Sci Ed, Univ of WI Madison 1957; Univ of ND 1957, Inst of Technology 1958, Univ of WI Madison 1959-61; Univ of WI Oshkosh; *cr:* Teacher Livingston WI 1952-54; Teacher Univ of WI Fox Valley 1965-85; Teacher 1954-89, Dept Chm 1958-89 Menasha HS; *ai:* WI Math Cncl 1970-; Natl Sci Fnd Schlsp 1956-57; Teacher of Yr Menasha HS 1971, 1988; *home:* 786 Pleasant Ln Menasha WI 54952

LONG, KAREN BURRELL, Remedial Reading Teacher; *b:* Kingsport, TN; *m:* Mike; *c:* Chris, Rachel; *ed:* Elem Ed, TN Wesleyan; (BS) Elem Ed, Univ of TN 1974; (MS) Elem Ed/Curr/Instruction, Mid TN St Univ 1989; *cr:* 3rd/4th Grade Teacher Knoxville City Schls 1974-76; 4th Grade Teacher Jenkins Cty Schls 1978-80; 4th Grade Remedial Rdng Teacher Rutherford Cty 1982-; *office:* Walter Hill Elem Sch Rt 3 Box 171 Murfreesboro TN 37129

LONG, KAREN SUE, 4th Grade Teacher; *b:* Hamilton, OH; *ed:* (BA) Elem Ed, 1977, (MA) Elem Ed, 1986 Marshall Univ; *cr:* 3rd Grade Teacher New Haven Elem 1977-79, Sunnyside Elem 1979-81; 5th/6th Grade Teacher Mt Flower Elem 1982-86; 4th Grade Teacher Beale Elem 1986-; *ai:* Mason Cty Prof Cncl; Beale Elem Advisory Cncl; Mason Cty Teachers Assn Building Rep 1986-; WV Ed Assn 1977-; NEA 1977-; Main Street Baptist Church 1966-; Main Street Restoration Comm 1989-; Awarded a Grant for Classroom Project/St of WV 1988; *office:* Beale Elem Sch Gallipolis Ferry WV 25515

LONG, LARRY CHRIS, Jr High Teacher/Asst Principal; *b:* Indianapolis, IN; *m:* Dorothy J. Akers; *c:* Matthew; *ed:* (BS) Ed, IN Univ 1971; (MS) Admin, Xavier Univ 1978; *cr:* Teacher/Asst Prin St Aloysius 1975-; *ai:* Speech Coach; Divisional Coord; Share the Vision Comm; Project Bus; NCEA 1975-; St Johns Ed Commission 1989-; *office:* St Aloysius Gonzaga Sch 4390 Bridgetown Rd Cincinnati OH 45211

LONG, LEON H., English Teacher; *b:* Hillsboro, OR; *m:* Aulda Elaine Brummels; *c:* Michael, Nikki; *ed:* (BS) Phys Ed, Coll of ID 1963; (MS) Ed/Phys Ed, Wayne St Coll 1973; *cr:* Teacher/Coach Wilder HS 1963-68, Nampa HS 1968-; *ai:* Athletic Dir; ID Cncl Teachers of Eng; US Bsbl Fed St Chm 1985-, Amateur Coach of Yr 1988; ID St Coaches Assn St Coach of Yr 1982; 3rd Dist Coaches Assn (A-1 Bd of Control Rep), Bsbl Coach of Yr 6 Times; St Bsbl Coaches Assn (Secy, Treas); Article Published.

LONG, LOREACE HOPKINS, World History Teacher; *b:* Meridian, MS; *m:* Carl; *c:* Keith, Marcus; *ed:* (BS) Soc Stud, Alcorn St Univ 1971; (MS) His, SE MO St Univ 1983; *cr:* Geography Teacher Carver Jr HS 1971-72; Soc Stud Teacher Charleston HS 1972-73; Geography Teacher Sikeston HS 1973-85; His Teacher Denton HS 1985-; *ai:* Phi Delta Kappa, NCSS, Assn of TX Prof Educators; Delta Kappa Gamma; *home:* 2109 Fairfax Denton TX 76205

LONG, MARGARET WALKER, Science Teacher; *b:* Springfield, MO; *m:* James C.; *c:* Clifton Ross; *ed:* (BA) Bio/Pysch/Scndry Ed, Drury Coll 1970; (MAT) Sci Ed, Webster Univ 1980; Star Drug Prevention Prgm; *cr:* 7/8/9 Grade Sci Teacher Grandview East Jr HS 1970-75; 6/8 Grade Sci Teacher West St Paul 1975-76; 9-12 Grade Sci Teacher Lindbergh HS 1976-80; 7/8/9 Grade Sci Teacher Ervin Jr HS 1980-89; *ai:* Sci Club Stu Cncl Co-Spon; NEA 1980-89; MNEA 1980-89; PTA 1980-89; Lees Summit Boosters Club 1989; Excl in Teaching Awards 1985-87 & 89; Nominee Consolidated Sch Dist #1 Teacher of Yr 1989; Nominee Sigma Chi Sci Teaching Awd 1988; *office:* Ervin Junior HS 10530 Greenwood Rd Kansas City MO 64134

LONG, MICHAEL DARWIN, Science Teacher; *b:* Inglewood, CA; *m:* Laura; *c:* Ethan; *ed:* (BS) Sci, TX Tech Univ 1983; Attended Carpentry Sch Las Vegas NV; *cr:* Sci Teacher Amarillo Ind Sch Dist 1983-86, Silverton Ind Sch Dist 1986-; *ai:* Sr Class Spon; Youth Task Comm; BSA Scout Master 1978-80; Published Several Environmental Editorials; *office:* Silverton Ind Sch Dist 700 Loreta Silverton TX 79257

LONG, MYRTICE CARR, Second Grade Teacher; *b:* Perdido, AL; *m:* Homer J.; *c:* Jeffrey, Kara; *ed:* (BSED) Elem Ed, SW MO St Univ 1962; *cr:* 2nd Grade Teacher Springfield Public Schls 1962-63; 3rd Grade Teacher 1977-83, 2nd Grade Teacher 1983- Logan-Rogersville Schls; *ai:* Textbook Selection Comm; MO St Teachers Assn; PTA (Secy 1974-75, Pres 1975-76); *office:* Logan-Rogersville Elem Sch Rt 2 Box 88 Rogersville MO 65742

LONG, NANCY TRIFFON, Language Arts Teacher; *b:* Columbus, OH; *m:* Michael J.; *c:* Terry R.; *ed:* (BA) Eng Ed, Univ of South FL 1972; *cr:* 7th Grade Lang Arts Teacher Dunedin Mid Sch 1974-; *ai:* Hospitality Comm; Pinellas CTE; Pinellas Classroom Teachers Assn; NEA; Daughters of Penelope (Secy Treas Dist Secy); *office:* Dunedin Highland Mid Sch 896 Union St Dunedin FL 34698

LONG, PATRICK HENRY, Agriculture Ed Teacher; *b:* Chico, CA; *m:* Jean Armstrong; *c:* William H., Patrick E.; *ed:* (BA) Agriculture Ed, 1976, (MS) Agriculture Ed, 1981 NM St Univ; Grad Trng Educl Management, NM St Univ; *cr:* Agriculture Instr Socorro HS 1981-82, Dora HS 1982-85, Gadsden HS 1985-; *ai:* Gadsden FFA Adv; NM Voc Agriculture Teacher Assn Pres 1989-; Honorary St FFA Degree 1989; *office:* Gadsden HS Rt 1 Box 268 Anthony NM 88021

LONG, SONDRA FOSTER, 8th/Rding Advisory Coord; *b:* Abilene, TX; *m:* George W.; *c:* Amy, Jason, Mitch; *ed:* (BS) Eng/Phys Ed, Hardin-Sim Mons Univ 1971; East TX St Univ; *cr:* PTMS 9D Teacher Valwood Elem 1971-73; Blanton Elem 1974-77; 8th Grade Teacher Ford Mid Sch; *ai:* Yrbk Adv; Advisory Coord; KeysOne Acad; Alpha Delta Kappa Corresponding Secy 1985-; Assn TX Prof Educators 1988-; *office:* Ford Mid Sch 630 Park Place Allen TX 75002

LONG, SUSAN WHITE, English/Speech Teacher; *b:* Mc Rae, GA; *m:* Allen Norris; *ed:* (AA) Ed, Mid GA Coll; (BS) Eng/Speech Ed, (MED) Eng Ed, Univ of GA; Specialist in Ed GA Southern Coll; Advanced Placement Eng Trng Prgm Univ of GA; *cr:* Teacher Ben-Hill Irwin Tech 1982-83, Mercer Univ 1988-89, Dodge Cty HS 1989-; *ai:* Co-Chairperson of Literary Club; Beta Club Adv; Honors Night Co-Coord; One Act Play Co-Spon & Coach; Oral Inteepretation & Extemporaneous Speaking Coach; NCTE, Dodge Prof Educators; STAR Teacher 1989-; *office:* Dodge Cty HS Cochran Hwy Eastman GA 31023

LONG, TIM L., Sociology/Psychology Teacher; *b:* Tompkinsville, KY; *m:* Charlene Reagan; *c:* Chris, Sarah, Leeann; *ed:* (BS) Scndry Ed/Eng, 1977, (MA) Eng, 1980 TN Tech; *cr:* Teacher Red Boiling Springs HS 1977-80, Warren Cty Sr HS 1983-; *ai:* Churches of Christ Minister; *home:* 322 Hickory Blvd Mc Minnville TN 37110

LONG, VIGINIA, 1st Grade Classroom Teacher; *b:* Baker City, OR; *m:* Keith R.; *c:* Mark A., Malinda R. Gates; *ed:* (BS) Elem Ed, E OR St CoLL 1966; Brigham Young Univ; *cr:* 2nd/4th Grade Teacher S Baker Elem 1966-68; Spec Ed Teacher Union Elem Sch 1968-69, Riveria Elem Sch 1969-70; 1st/2nd Grade Teacher Baker Summer Sch 1967-79; 1st Grade Teacher S Baker Elem 1970-; *ai:* Delta Kappa Gamma VP 1988-; E OR Teacher of Yr & Runner-Up OR Teacher of Yr 1979-80; *office:* S Baker Elem Sch 1285 3rd St Baker City OR 97814

LONGAN, KAREN CRAWFORD, Spanish/Theatre Arts Teacher; *b:* Seymour, TX; *m:* Billy Don; *c:* Kacy D., Andrea D., Kandis K., William W.; *ed:* (AA) Drama, Clarendon Coll 1972; (BSED) Drama, Midwestern St Univ 1974; Cmptr Literacy Cert Mid Sch Level; *cr:* Span/Theatre Arts Teacher Munday HS 1974-; *ai:* Jr Class, One Act Play; Jr HS UIL Individual Speech Events; Debate, Cmmty Life Involvement Cncl Spon; ATPE VP 1990-; Delta Kappa Gamma 1989-; Future Teachers of America St Adv, Adv of Yr Awd 1979-80; City Cty Lib Bd 1980-87; Whos Outstanding Young Women of America 1975; *home:* 621 N 3rd Munday TX 76371

LONGENBERGER, SALLY S., Chemistry Teacher; *b:* Kingston, PA; *m:* Drue R.; *c:* Amy; *ed:* (BA) Bio, Gettysburg 1960; Working Towards Masters Duke Univ & PA St Univ; *cr:* Jr Research Tech Hoffman-La Roche Pharmaceuticals 1961-62; Teacher Salisbury HS 1964-66, Parkland HS 1966-; *office:* Parkland HS Rt 309 Orefield PA 18069

LONGEST, ETHEL BROWN, First Grade Teacher; *b:* Evanston, IL; *c:* Carol E. Murphy, Thomas K.; *ed:* (BS) Psych, 1950, (MED) Guidance/Counseling, 1952 Univ of IL; Nutrition, Cornell Univ; Guidance, Syracuse Univ; *cr:* Music Teacher Camp Point Cmmty Cntrl Sch 1951-52; Research Asst Cornell Univ 1953-55; Music/Flute/Piano/Nursery Sch Teacher 1958-68; K-1st Grade Teacher Newfield Cntrl 1970-; *ai:* Math Comm; NY St Fed of Teachers Local Secy 1986-; Finger Lakes Rdng Cncl; *home:* 106 1/2 Homestead Cir Ithaca NY 14850

LONGO, ANN MARIE, French-Spanish Teacher; *b:* Milford, MA; *ed:* (BA) Fr, Worcester St Coll 1967; (MA) Fr, Assumption Coll 1971; Post Grad Courses, Span Alliance Francaise Paris France; Framingham St Coll; *cr:* Teacher Stacy Jr HS 1967-71, Mid Sch W 1972-87, Mid Sch E 1987-; *ai:* Chosen by Amer Assn Teachers of Fr for Study Grant in France 1976; Milford Teacher of Yr 1988; Horace Mann Grant Recipient 1989-; *home:* 13 Reade St Milford MA 01757

LONGO, MARY TASSIELLI, Fourth Grade Teacher; *b:* Newark, NJ; *m:* Donald J. Sr.; *c:* Donald J., Joanne Longo Fagan, Peter, Mary J.; *ed:* (BA) Fr, Coll of St Elizabeth 1951; Grad Stud Fr, Univ of Montreal Canada; Elem Cert at Newark St Coll; *cr:* 4th Grade Teacher Belleville Sch 2 1951-58; Kndgtn Teacher Belleville Sch 1 1956; 6th Grade Teacher Columbia Sch 1958-60; 3rd/4th Grade Teacher Gillette Sch 1960-83; 4th Grade Teacher Millington Sch 1983-; *ai:* All Schls Cncl Chairlady; Passaic Township Ed Assn VP 1965-66; NEA, NJ Ed Assn; Outstanding Elem Teachers of America 1972; Governors Teacher Recognition Prgm Outstanding Teacher 1987-88; *home:* 13 Ellers Dr Chatham NJ 07928

LONGO, MICHAEL SHARKEY, High School Teacher; *b:* Chicago, IL; *ed:* (BA) Music Ed, 1972, (MA) Music Ed/Hum, 1975 De Paul Univ; (MA) Religious Stud, Mundelein Coll 1986; Religious Stud, Hum; *cr:* Music Teacher Private Studio 1969-85; HS Teacher Resurrection HS 1978-; *ai:* Key Club Adv; Campus Coord Peace & Justice Global Act at HS; Lend Support to Music Prgm & Act; Pax Christi 1986-; Kiwanis Club Adv 1985-; Resurrection HS Golden Apple Awd 1988, Faith Witness Awd 1986; Catholic Youth Office Nomination Awd 1989; Koles Fnd Nomination Global Ed 1990; *office:* Resurrection HS 7500 W Talcott Ave Chicago IL 60631

LONGSHORE, JUNE USRY, Principal; *b:* Gadsden, AL; *m:* E. L. Jr.; *c:* John W.; *ed:* (BS) Elem Ed, 1956, (MS) Guidance/Elem Ed, 1971 Jacksonville St Univ; (AA) Admin, Univ of AL Birmingham 1975; *cr:* Elem Teacher 1956-65, Rdng Supvr 1966-72 Gadsden City Schls; Prin Mitchell Elem Sch 1973-76, General Forrest Mid Sch 1977-84, Cory Mid Sch 1985-; Part Time Coll Instr Jacksonville Univ; *ai:* Delta Kappa Gamma 1st VP 1986-88, Outstanding Educator Awd 1990; AL Cncl Sch Admin & Supvrs Bd of Dir 1985-86, Leadership Awd 1987; AL League of Mid Schls (VP 1983-85, Pres 1985-87), Leadership Awd 1986; AL PTA (Parent Ed Chm, Legislative Chm 1980-85), Life Membership 1978; AL Assn Mid Level Admin Pres 1986, Outstanding Service Awd 1986; Macedonia Baptist Church Sunday Sch Teacher 1965-89; Phi Delta Kappa 1980-; Presenter Natl Mid Sch Assn, AL Assn Mid Level Admin, AL Congress PTA, AL Eng Teachers Assn Conferences; Articles Published; *home:* Rt 6 Box 248 Macedonia Rd Gadsden AL 35901

LONGSHORE, MARY LYLE, English Teacher; *b:* Valley Head, AL; *c:* Charles Ethan Acres, Christopher Alan Satcher; *ed:* (BA) Eng, Jacksonville St Univ 1970; Univ of AL; *cr:* Librarian Gadsden-Elizabeth Shores Curr Center 1970-72; Librarian/Eng Teacher De Kalb Cty Sch 1973-84; Lynn HS 1987-; *ai:* Beta Club Spon; Yrbk Adv; Track Coach; AEA/NEA 1970-; *home:* 2824 18th Ave Haleyville AL 35565

LONGSTAFF, DANNIELLE KASPROWSKI, Language Arts Teacher; *b:* Wheeling, WV; *m:* Mark E.; *c:* Aslan, Caitlin; *ed:* (BSED) Eng, OH Univ 1972; *cr:* Eng Teacher John Hancock Jr HS 1972-73; Lang Arts Teacher Powhatan Elem 1974-; *ai:* 8th Grade Spon; OH Ed Assn, NEA 1974-; Sch Bd Mem St John Cntrl Grade Sch; *home:* 55259 Mt Victory Rd Powhatan Point OH 43942

LONGWELL, ZELLA RUTH WELCH, Retired Teacher; *c:* Kenalea R. Longwell Johnson, James W.; *ed:* (BS) Soc Stud, Drury Coll 1959; NM Highlands Univ; CO St Univ Ft Collins; NM St Univ Las Cruces; Adams St Coll; *cr:* 1st-8th Grade Teacher Mt Comfort Sch Dist 1953-59; Teacher Mt Vernon Elem Sch 1959-67, Aztec Municipal Schls 1967-84.

LONGWILL, ROBERT M., Science Teacher; *b:* Clovis, NM; *m:* Bonnie Jean Bentley; *c:* Travis, Kelsey, Nicole, Bobby, Dusty; *ed:* (AA) Sci, NM Military Inst 1967; (BS) Bio, E NM Univ 1970; (MA) Ed Admin, NM St Univ 1974; *cr:* Teacher Clayton HS 1970-73, 1974-81, Clayton Jr HS 1981-; *ai:* Ski Club Spon; NM Sci Teachers Assn 1980-; Sedan Cmmty Corp Pres 1984-87; Union Co Sheriffs Posse (Secy/Treas) 1987-; Union Co Crime Stoppers Pres 1987-; Participated in Summer Teacher Enrichment Prgm 1986; Worked at Inhilation & Toxicology Research Inst in Albuquerque; *office:* Clayton Jr HS 323 S 5th Clayton NM 88415

LOO, DIANA LYNNE, Mathematics Teacher; *b:* Philadelphia, PA; *ed:* (BS) Math, Stanford Univ 1987; (MA) Math Ed, Columbia Univ Teachers Coll 1988; *cr:* Math Teacher Phillip & Sala Burton Academic HS 1988-; *ai:* Burton HS CA Schlsp Fed Comm; San Francisco Math Teachers Assn Mem 1988-; NCTM 1988-; Stanford Alumni Assn Mem 1987-; Mellon Fnd Masters Schlsp; *office:* Phillip & Sala Burton HS 45 Conkling St San Francisco CA 94124

LOOFT, THOMAS ALLAN, Mathematics/Algebra Teacher; *b:* Estherville, IA; *c:* Joel R., Jodi S.; *ed:* (BA) Jr HS Ed, Univ of N IA 1976; *cr:* Jr HS Math Teacher Harris-Lake Park Schls 1976-79; 7th/9th Grade Math/Algebra Teacher Bondurant-Farrar Schls 1979-; *ai:* Var Girls Vlybl & Bsktbl Head Coach; Var Girls Track Asst Coach; NEA, IA St Ed Assn, IA Cncl Teachers of Math; IA Assn of Track Coaches; *office:* Bondurant-Farrar Jr/Sr HS 300 Garfield SE Bondurant IA 50035

LOOKER, ROBERT JAMES, 6th Grade Teacher; *b:* Olean, NY; *m:* Paula Ann Baldoni; *c:* Lance, Allison; *ed:* (BS) Elem Ed, Lock Haven St Coll 1968; (MS) Ed Guidance, St Bonaventure Univ 1971; Grad Stud Ed; *cr:* Elem Teacher/Prin Eldred Township Elem; Elem Teacher Boardmanville Elem; *ai:* Var Ftbl & Bsktbl Coach; Jr Var Bsbl Coach; Jr HS Ftbl Coach; Elem Intramural Dir; NEA 1968-; NYEA, OTA 1971-; PSEA 1968-71; Eldred Lions Club Dir 1982-86; Eldred Conservation Club; Developed Dist Elem Health Curr; *home:* 15 Edson St Eldred PA 16731

LOOKIS, JILL ESTELLE, Language Art & French Teacher; *b:* Alton, IL; *m:* Richard C.; *c:* Jeremy; *ed:* (BA) Fr, S IL Univ Edwardsville 1974; (MS) Ed/Rdng, W IL Univ 1984; *cr:* Teacher Washington Mid Sch 1974-; *ai:* Stu Cncl Spon; Spelling Team Coach; Springfield Ed Assn; *office:* Washington Mid Sch 2300 E Jackson Springfield IL 62703

LOOMAN, MARY LOUISE (FRUM), Retired Third Grade Teacher; *b:* Logan, OH; *m:* Ralph Eugene; *c:* Carol J. Mick, Donald L., Beverly K. Mike; *ed:* (BA) Elem Ed, Fairmont St Coll 1968; *cr:* 2nd Grade Teacher Annabelle Sch 1968-70; 4th-6th Grade Teacher/Prin Kingmont 1970-76; 3rd Grade Teacher White Hall 1976-86; *home:* RR 7 Box 332 Fairmont WV 26554

LOOMER, SHARI LYNN, Science/Phys Ed Teacher; *b:* White Settlement, TX; *ed:* (BSED) Phys Ed, Stephen F Austin Univ 1982; *cr:* Teacher/Coach Haltom Jr HS 1983-87; Phys Ed Teacher Grace E Hardeman Elem 1987-89; Teacher Haltom Mid Sch 1989-; *ai:* CARE Team; Birdville Phys Ed Assn, TX Assn of Phys Ed Recreation Dance, Assn of TX Prof Educators; *office:* Haltom Mid Sch 5000 Dana Dr Haltom City TX 76117

LOOMIS, COLLEEN S., First Grade Teacher; *b:* Ashtabula, OH; *m:* James E.; *ed:* (BSED) Elem/Spec Ed, Kent St Univ 1974; (MS) Elem Curr, Youngstown St Univ 1981; Courses/Wkshps, John Carrol Univ, Kent St & Mt St Joseph; *cr:* 2nd Grade Teacher Kingsville Elem Sch 1974-80, Ridgeview Elem Sch 1980-85; 1st Grade Teacher N Kingsville Elem Sch 1985-; *ai:* Sch & Dist Right To Read Week Comm; OEA, NEA, NEOEA, BEA; *office:* N Kingsville Elem Sch 1343 E Center North Kingsville OH 44068

LOOMIS, GAIL ASHCROFT, Spanish Teacher; *b:* Cortland, NY; *m:* Robert P.; *c:* Michele, Matthew; *ed:* (BA) His/Poly Sci, Keuka Coll 1963; Universidad De Los Andes; (MSE) SUNY Cortland 1976; In-Service Cuernavaca Mexico &Costa Rica; *cr:* Admin Asst/Secy Congressman S S Stratton US House of Rep 1963; Adv Asst Flax Newman Adv 1964-66; Resident Cnslr Good Shepherd Sch for Girls 1967-70; Teacher/Cnslr Marathon Cntrl Sch 1971-; *ai:* Art & Foreign Lang Club Adv; NY Ed Assn, FLACNY; Cortland Cty Dem U Club; Rotary Fellowship 1964; Sabbatical Leaves 1987-89; *office:* Marathon Central Sch 1 Main St Box 339 Marathon NY 13803

LOOMIS, STAN LEE, Math Teacher; *b:* Warren, OH; *m:* Marie Elena Di Battiste; *c:* Mary Beth, Cheri Lynn, William Dominic; *ed:* (BA) Math, Kent St Univ 1971; *cr:* Math Teacher W G Harding HS 1971-; *ai:* Ski Club Spon 1973-; Warren Ed Assn Faculty Rep 1971-; Elks 1986-; Eastside Girls Sftbl President/Treas/Trustee 1982-; Thunder Girl Natl Traveling Sftbl Team-Coach; *office:* Warren G Harding H S 860 Elm Rd Ne Warren OH 44483

LOOP, MARTHA A., English Teacher; *b:* Morgan Cty, IN; *m:* Ernest H.; *c:* Coral J.; *ed:* (BED) Lang Art Ed, 1963, (MAT) Eng/Journalism, 1971 IN Univ; Teaching Gifted Purdue Univ; *cr:* Eng Teacher Ben Davis HS 1963-68; Eng Teacher/Publications Adv Whiteland Cmmty HS 1968-; *ai:* Future Educators Club Spon; Newspaper & Yrbk Adv; IN HS Press Assn 1970-74, 1987-; Eastern Star Worthy Matron 1970; Kappa Kappa Sigma (VP, Pres) 1974-75; Morgantown 1st Chrstn Church (VBS Dir 1988-, Teacher of Sr Citizens Class 1983-); IN Future Educators in Action Rep; IN St Division Stu Act Comm 1984-; IFEA Sponsors Cncl 1982-; Dept of Ed Steering Comm Project Set 1988-; *office:* Whiteland Cmmty HS 300 Main St Whiteland IN 46184

LOOPER, SANDRA KAY (SAVAGE), Elementary Principal; *b:* Oklahoma City, OK; *m:* Benny Ray; *c:* Staci L., Aaron J.; *ed:* (BS) Elem Ed, SW OK Univ 1971; (MA) Counseling, E Cntrl Univ 1982; Admin Cert 1985; Project Leadership in Educl Admin Dev; Site-Based Sch Improvement Participant 1989-; Early Prevention of Sch Failure; Initial & Advanced Trng 1989; *cr:* Teacher of Migrant Butler Sch 1971-72; 3rd Grade Teacher Arapaho Sch 1973-74; 1st Grade Teacher 1974-79, 6th Grade Teahcer 1979-84 Byng Schl; Prin Homer-Byng Elem 1984-; *ai:* Staff Dev, Career Ed, Curr Comm; Pontotoc Cty Rdng Cncl (Pres, VP, Secy) 1979-, Outstanding Rdng Admin 1987; OK Assn of Elem Prin Curr Comm 1986-, Outstanding Admin of Yr Dist 12 1989-; Phi Delta Kappa Researcher Stu At Risk 1987-; Young Homemakers of OK (Pres, VP, Secy) 1975-80, Outstanding Homemaker-Pontotoc Cty 1978; GSA Leader 1978-80; Trinity Baptist Church Sunday Sch Teacher 1974-; St Wide Task Force Yr of Young Reader; OK Fnd for Excl Nominee; Presenter Ed Fair; Encyclomedia OK Rdng Cncl; OK St Dept of Ed; Whos Who Amer Ed; *office:* Homer-Byng Sch Rt 6 Box 44 Ada OK 74820

LOOSEMOORE, MARIE K., Science Teacher; *b:* Milford, MA; *m:* William J.; *c:* Mary S., W. Stuart; *ed:* (BS) Math/Sci, 1970, (MED) Guidance, 1989 Worcester St Coll; *cr:* Math Teacher Westboro Jr HS 1970-73; Sci Teacher 1984-; Teacher of Gifted/Talented 1984-87, Coord of Gifted/Talented 1986-87 Auburn HS; *ai:* Yrbk Faculty Bus Manager; Class Adv 1990; Schlsp Comm; Sch Improvement Cncl; NSTA 1986-; NEA, MA Teachers Assn, Auburn Ed Assn 1984-; Camp Fire Incorporated 1977; *office:* Auburn HS 99 Auburn St Auburn MA 01501

LOOSEMORE, WILLIAM JAMES, History Teacher; *b:* Worcester, MA; *m:* Marie K. Weatherhead; *c:* Mary S., Stuart; *ed:* (BA) His, Worchester St Coll 1969; (MA) His, Assumption Coll 1974; *ai:* Bartlett HS Faculty Comm, NHS; NEA, MA Teachers Assn 1969-; Webster Teachers Assn Pres 1974-76; Campfire Elizabeth Ann Seton Awd; Natl Endowment Hum Inst 1988; *office:* BArtlett HS Lake Pkwy Webster MA 01570

LOOZE, RICHARD C., Social Studies Teacher; *b:* Florence, AZ; *m:* Victoria L. Seidel; *c:* Amy, Marcus; *ed:* (BSE) Geography, 1970, (MST) Geography, 1974 Univ of WI Whitewater; Various Insts; *cr:* Teacher J F Luther Jr HS 1970-88, Essex England Davenant Fnd 1988-89, Ft Atkinson HS 1989-; *ai:* Ft Atkinson HS SADD Organization Adv; Ft Atkinson Ed Assn (Pres 1974-75, Grievance Chm 1975-81); WI Cncl Soc Stud 1970-, WI Soc Stud Teacher of Yr 1983; NCSS, Natl Cncl Geographic Ed 1970-; United Way Bd of Dir 1978-81; Amer Field Service (VP, Pres) 1979-80; Fulbright Fellowship for Summer in India 1988; England Fulbright Teacher 1988-89; *office:* Ft Atkinson HS 310 SE 4th St Fort Atkinson WI 53538

LOPASHANSKI, BARRY L., Inter Elem Math & Sci Teacher; *b:* Berwick, PA; *m:* Carol J. Johnson; *c:* Alex, Nicholas, Steven, Susan; *ed:* (BS) Elem Ed, 1970, (MED) Guidance, 1973 Bloomsburg SC; PENN St & Bloomsburg St Coll & Wilkes Coll & Luzerne Intermediate Unit; *cr:* Teacher Hazle Elem 1970-73, Locust St Elem 1973-; *ai:* Math & Sci Curr Comm; Coaching Elem Bsktbl Grades 4 5 & 6; NEA/PSEA/HAEA 1970-86; Slavonic-Amer Club Treas 1980-; *home:* 435 E Front St Berwick PA 18603

LOPEMAN, LINDA RAE, Dept Chair/Vocational Dir; *b:* Safford, AZ; *m:* Richard J.; *c:* Jay R., Marc B., Nicole; *ed:* (AA) Scndry Ed, Eastern AZ Coll 1971; (BS) Scndry Ed/Bus, Northern AZ Univ 1974; Admin Curr, NAU; *cr:* Bus Teacher 1974-; Dept Chm 1980-Show Low HS; 1980-; Vocational Dir Show Low Unified Dist 10 1985-; *ai:* Cheer Spon; Sr Grad Chm; FBLA Adv; AZ BEA 1980-; NBEA 1987-; Pi Omega Pi 1974-; Nom Teacher Yr St of AZ; Teacher Yr Chamber of Commerce Show Low; Named Outstanding Scndry Teacher; *office:* Show Low HS 1350 N Central Show Low AZ 85901

LOPER, ROBERT GEORGE, Mathematics Teacher; *b:* Somers Point, NJ; *ed:* (BA) Math Teacher, Glassboro St Coll 1969; *cr:* 7th Grade Math/Sci Teacher Belhaven Avenue Sch 1969-70; 6th Grade Math/Sci Teacher Poplar Avenue Sch 1970-71; 6th Grade Math Teacher 1971-75, 8th Grade Math 1975- Belhaven Avenue Sch; *ai:* Bowling, Golf, Sports Collectors Club Adv; Vlybl Coach; Comm Math Curr Chairperson; NJ Ed Assn, NEA, AMTNJ, Linwood Ed Assn Treas 1969-; NJ Governors Teacher Recognition Awd 1986; Book Published Graphing Pictures 1977; *office:* Belhaven Ave Sch Belhaven Ave Linwood NJ 08221

LOPES, RUDY J., Social Studies Teacher; *b:* Union City, NJ; *m:* Fran Richman; *c:* Noel, Brett; *ed:* (BA) Soc Sci, Jersey City St Coll 1968; Grad Stud His; *cr:* Soc Worker Hudson Cty Welfare 1968; 7th/8th Grade Teacher Old Bridge Bd of Ed 1968-; *ai:* Dudley Mens Sftbl League Pres 1975-77; Old Bridge Ed Assn (VP 1973-74) 1968-; NEA, NJ Ed Assn 1968-; *office:* Carl Sandburg Mid Sch Rt 516 Old Bridge NJ 08857

LOPEZ, ELIA, Foreign Language Dept Coord; *b:* Moroleon, Mexico; *m:* Charles A. Schabes; *ed:* (BA) Span/Fr, Mundelein Coll 1975; (MA) Span, Northwestern Univ 1977; Stage Pedagogique, Grenoble France 1978; Goethe Inst; Ger Intermediate, Goethe Inst; Immersion in Lang, Inst in Paris 1990; *cr:* Fr/Span Instr/Dept Coord Morton Comm Coll 1977-82; ESL/Fr Instr Homer Sch 1982-85; Span Instr St Patrick HS for Boys 1985-86; Span/Fr Instr/Coord IL Math & Sci Acad 1986-; *ai:* Stu Cncl Co-Spon; AATSP Corresponding Secy 1985-; ICTFL, AATF, IFLTA, ACTFL; Teaching Fellowship Northwestern Univ; Schlsp Actfl & Fr Cultural Services; *office:* Il Math & Science Acad 1500 W Sullivan Rd Aurora IL 60506

LOPEZ, FRANK D., JR., Social Studies Teacher/Coach; *b:* Santa Rita, NM; *m:* Patsy G.; *c:* Christopher; *ed:* (BA) His/Soc Stud, 1978, (MA) Sch Admin, 1986 W NM Univ; Sch Bus Trng, 1st Aid, W NM Univ; *cr:* Soc Stud Teacher Hatch Jr HS 1978-89; Civics Teacher Hatch HS 1989-; *ai:* Asst Ftbl & Head Bsbl Coach; Soph Class Stu Cncl, Bears Club Adv; S All Stars Bsbl Coach; NEA Hatch Pres 1985-86; NMHSCA Mem 1978-; Dist Coach of Yr 1982; 3 Class AA St Bsbl Championships; *home:* PO Box 34 Hatch NM 87937

LOPEZ, GRACE EVERETT, 12th Grade English Teacher; *b:* Corpus Christi, TX; *m:* Lucrano Martinez Jr.; *c:* Raul M., Geneva A., Rueben D., Aramis M.; *ed:* (BA) Eng, Univ of MD 1984; (Ms) Eng, TX a & I Univ 1990; *cr:* Registrar Boston Univ Europe 1984; Teacher Neubrucke Child Dev Ctr 1984-85; San Diego ISD 1985-; *ai:* UIL Coord; Prose Coach; Poetry Coach; Literacy Criticsm Coach; Drama Club Spon; NHS Comm; TCTA Treas 1986-88; Short Story Published in Readers BLOC; Voted Most Favorite Teacher By Students 4 Yrs; *office:* San Diego H S 609 Labbe San Diego TX 78384

LOPEZ, HERMINIA VELA, Mathematics Teacher; *b:* Nuevo Laredo Tamp, MX; *c:* Rita G., Esteban S.; *ed:* (BS) Elem Ed, TX A&I Laredo 1974; Working on MS Scndry Ed; Cert Gifted & Talented; *cr:* Pre-K Teacher TX Migrant Cncl 1974-75; Kndgtn-6th Grade Teacher H B Zachary Elem 1977-83; Math Teacher Memorial Mid Sch 1983-; *ai:* Stu Cncl Spon; Univ Interscholastic League Cmptr Coach; Faculty Club Pres; PTA Secy 1986-87, Life Membership 1987; *office:* Memorial Mid Sch 2002 Marcella Laredo TX 78040

LOPEZ, JANIE ZAMORA, World History Teacher; *b:* Alice, TX; *m:* Jose Alonzo; *c:* Josef A.; *ed:* (BS) His/Sociology, TX A&I Univ 1980; *cr:* World His Teacher 1980-, World His Teacher/ Debate Coach 1987- San Diego HS; *ai:* Cross Examination Debate Coach; Flag Corps Spon; *office:* San Diego HS 609 Labbe San Diego TX 78384

LOPEZ, LEONARD M., Sixth Grade Teacher/HS Coach; *b:* Flagstaff, AZ; *m:* Lisa F. (Rousseau); *c:* Carissa, Christopher, Jordan; *ed:* (BS) Elem Ed, N AZ Univ 1981; *cr:* Teacher/Vlybl/ Bsbl Coach Ajo Jr/Sr HS 1981-; *ai:* Vlybl & Bsbl Head Coach; NEA 1981-; Vlybl Coaches Assn 1989-; All Star Coach; 2 A W Coach of Yr 1988-; 3 A-1A S AZ Coach of Yr 1989-; *office:* Ajo Public Schls PO Box 68 Ajo AZ 85321

LOPEZ, MICHAEL PAUL, Jr High Math Teacher; *b:* Elizabethtown, NY; *m:* Karen Kanaly; *c:* Chad, Melanie, Nicole; *ed:* (BS) Scndry Math, 1972, (MS) Ed Scndry Math, 1978 PSUC at Plattsburgh; *cr:* Jr HS Math Teacher Ausable Valley Cntrl Sch 1972-73, Willsboro Cntrl Sh 1973-; *ai:* JV & V Boys Bsktbl, Varsity Tennis Coach; Elks Club Mem 1974-; Keeseville Youth Commission Mem 1973-84; *home:* Tanglewood Dr Port Kent NY 12975

LOPEZ, PHYLLIS RUTH, 6th Grade Teacher; *b:* Detroit, MI; *m:* Lawrence Anthony; *c:* Kristin, Christopher; *ed:* (BA) Elem Ed, Marygrove Coll 1963; (MA) Educl Psych, Univ of MI 1971; Educl Psych, Univ of MI; *cr:* 6th Grade Sci Teacher Sacred Heart 1964-67; 1st Grade Teacher St Marthas 1968-70; 7th/8th Grade Sci Teacher Our Lady Star of the Sea 1970-74; 6th Grade Sci Teacher St Paul Grosse Pointe Farms 1975-; *ai:* Co-Coord Sci Dept; Forensics Coach; NCEA 1985-; League of Cath Women 1987-; Natl Right to Life 1988-; *office:* St Paul Elem 170 Grosse Pointe Blvd Grosse Pointe Farm MI 48236

LOPP, STAN EDWARD, English Teacher; *b:* Maderia, CA; *ed:* (BS) Elem Ed, Mid TN St Univ 1977; (MS) Elem Ed, Univ of North AL 1983; Supv & Admin, TN St Univ 1990; *cr:* Teacher/ Asst Prin Ethridge Elem 1977-; *ai:* Spon A-Team; Bus Duty Supv; Chm Eng Dept; Kappa Delta Phi 1983-; Sigma Club 1977-; City Park Youth Supv 1978-85; *home:* 410 Beuerlein St Lawrenceburg TN 38464

LO PRESTI, PRISCILLA ANSCHUTZ, Fourth Grade Teacher; *b:* Ellsworth, KS; *m:* Ted; *ed:* (BA) Elem Ed, Bethany Coll 1971; Masters of Sci, Emporia St Univ 1987; *cr:* 4th Grade Teacher USD 469 1971-; *ai:* Curr & Negotiations Comm; Intnl Rdng Assn 1984-; KS Natl Ed Assn, NEA 1971-; *home:* 1417 Jeanne Ct Leavenworth KS 66048

LORBINENKO, NINA, French Teacher; *b:* Rockford, IL; *m:* Walter Krebs; *c:* Harrison Krebs; *ed:* (BA) Fr Ed, Univ of IL 1978; (MS) Curr/Supervision, N IL Univ 1985; *cr:* Fr Teacher Stillman Valley HS 1978-; *ai:* Fr Club; NHS; AATF; IL Assn Teachers of Fr; *office:* Stillman Valley HS Pine & Grant Streets Stillman Valley IL 61084

LORD, GEORGE E., Driver Education Instructor; *b:* La Jose, PA; *m:* Shirley J. Rummel; *c:* Louise, Lisa, Georgia, Tina, Cynde; *ed:* (BSED) Geography, Clarion St Coll 1959; Indiana Univ of PA & Clarion St Coll; *cr:* 7th Grade Eng/His Teacher 1959-61, 8th Grade His Teacher 1960-62, Classroom/Roadphase Driver Ed Teacher 1959- Purchase Line Jr/Sr HS; *ai:* Ftbl, Boys Var Bsktbl, Girls Sftbl Statistician; NEA, Purchase Line Ed Assn 1959-; PA St Ed Assn Life Membership 1959-; PA Safety Ed Assn 1986-, Certificate of Recognition 1986; Mohaffey Fire Dept Life Membership 1955-; Cambria Cty Volunteer Firemens Assn 1956-; Greensburg Tribune Review Motorcycle Trng Prgm Feature; Interview Stu for Scholastic Magazine; *home:* RD 2 Box 260 Cherry Tree PA 15724

LOREA, NELLA BUTTA, Mathematics/Science Teacher; *b:* Eskdale, WV; *m:* Frank; *c:* Steven, Bobby; *ed:* (BS) Math, Sci, WV Univ 1963; *cr:* Teacher Cedar Grove Cmmty Sch 1963-66, 1986-; *home:* 175 Hillside Ave Boomer WV 25031

LOREE, JOAN MURPHY, Pre-First Grade Teacher; *b:* Hornell, NY; *m:* William C.; *ed:* (BS) Elem Ed, ST Univ at Geneseo 1957; Graduate Courses Suny at Geneseo, Suny at Buffalo and Elmira Coll; *cr:* 2nd Grade Teacher Gillette Elem 1957-59; 3rd Grade Teacher 1959-70; 1st Grade Teacher 1970-71 North Hornell Elem Sch; 1st Thru 6th Grade Rdng Teacher Hornell Elem Sch 1971-73; 3rd Grade Teacher Columbian Intermediate 1973-89; Pre-First Grade Teacher Columbian Primary Sch 1989-; *ai:* 1988-89 Mem Bldg Leadership Team at Intermediate Sch; Hornell Educators Assn 1959-; NEA 1979-; Delta Kappa Gamma 1970-76; St Ann's Parish Cncl Pres 1989-; *office:* Columbian Primary Sch 25 Pearl St Hornell NY 14843

LOREE, SUSAN DIANE, English Teacher; *b:* Youngstown, OH; *ed:* (BSED) Eng, Kent St Univ 1972; (MSED) Scndry Admin, Youngstown St Univ 1979; *cr:* Teacher Rayen Sch 1972-; *ai:* NCTE, Youngstown Ed Assn, OH Ed Assn, NEA; YWCA; *office:* Rayen Sch 250 Benita Ave Youngstown OH 44504

LORENTZ, TERESA ALDERA, English Teacher; *b:* Storm Lake, IA; *m:* Richard David; *c:* Catherine, David, Gerrianne Musso, Tom; *ed:* (BS) Speech/Drama, Creighton Univ 1952; Dramatic Imagination; *cr:* Teacher Beatrice HS 1952-53, St Pius X 1958-72, Bishop Lynch HS 1972-; *ai:* Blackfriars Moderator; Plays Musical Dir, Producer; Faculty Cncl; SAT Supvr; Liturgical Comm; Sacred Music Assn 1973-; St Pius X (Choir Dir 1975-, Ladies Society Chm 1974); Dallas Cath Choir 1969-; Salsburg Music Festival 1974; Music Festival Mexico City 1976; St Pius X Music Ministry; Cath Ed Diocese of Dallas 30 Yr Service 1988; John F Kennedy Awd 1988; *office:* Bishop Lynch HS 9750 Ferguson Rd Dallas TX 75228

LORENZ, PAUL H., 6th Grade Teacher; *b:* Lincoln, NE; *m:* Linda E. Jorgensen; *c:* Michelle, Mark; *ed:* (BS) Elem Ed, 1975, (MED) Ed Admin, 1983 Univ of NE Lincoln; *cr:* 6th Grade Teacher Raymond Cntrl 1975-; *ai:* Academic Achievement, Sci Curr & Camp Fontenelle Comms; NEA, NE Ed Assn; Cntrl Public Ed Assn Pres 1979-80; BSA Leader 1978-79; Church Quorum Secy 1989-; NE Natl Guard (Plans, Operations) 1969-; *office:* Raymond Cntrl Sch 406 E 3rd Valparaiso NE 68065

LORENZ, VIRGIL GLENN, Social Science Teacher; *b:* O Neill, NE; *m:* Gay A. Hornback; *c:* Andra, Glenn; *ed:* (BA) Soc Sci, 1968, Ed, 1969, (MA) Poly Sci, 1975 San Jose St Univ; Poly Sci, His, Statistics; *cr:* Teacher Valley Chrstn Jr HS 1969-; *ai:* Stu Cncl & Stu Store Adv; Assn Chrstn Schls Intnl 1969- Teacher of Yr 1974; Seminar Leader Assn Chrstn Sch Intnl; Paper Published By Passports San Jose St Stu Stud IN His 1979; Selected By Yrbk Stu Valley Chrstn Yrbk Dedication Twice; *home:* 15775 Sanborn Rd Saratoga CA 95070

LORENZEN, JEANNE MARIE NIEMEIER, 3rd Grade Teacher; *b:* Beatrice, NE; *m:* Richard Melvin; *ed:* (BS) Ed, 1968, (MA) Teacher of Rdng Endorsement Ed, 1986 Concordia Coll; *cr:* K-3rd Grade Teacher 1st Luth Sch 1968-71; 3rd Grade Teacher Trinity Luth Sch 1971-; *ai:* Worship Comm; 6th Grade Confirmation Class; Luth Ed Assn; Luth Womens Missionary League (Local Pres 1984-85, Membership Developer 1986-); Amer Guild of Organists, River City Theater Organist Society, Amer Theater Organist Society; *office:* Trinity Luth Sch 1200 N 56th St Lincoln NE 68504

LORENZEN, ROBIN DEBORAH, Choral Music Educator; *b:* Avalon, CA; *ed:* (BA) Music Ed/Therapy, Wartburg Coll 1980; *cr:* Music Therapist/Educator St Marys Hill Hosp 1980-85; Music Educator Cleveland Jr HS 1985-86; Music Educator/Choral Dir Harding Sr HS 1986-; *ai:* Musical Theatre Dir Knight Sounds; Curriculum Comm; WI Chapter for Music Therapy Chairperson/ Clinical Practices Comm 1982-84; Natl Assn of Music Therapy; Amer Choral Dir Assn; Music Educators Natl Conference; Mu Phi Epsilon; St Paul Neighborhood Energy Consortium (Bd 1987-/ Vice-Chair 1989-) Greenpeace; Dist 7 Planning Cncl Recycling Coord 1987-; Dale Warland Symphonic Chorus 1987-89; Milwaukee Choristers 1982-85; Bayshore Players VP 1982-85; Integrated Arts Festival Wkshp Presenter Alverno Coll 1980; Regional Music Therapy Conference Presenter 1983; *office:* Harding Sr High 1540 E 6th St Saint Paul MN 55106

LORENZETTI, GERARD D., Director of Bands; *b:* Elizabeth, NJ; *m:* Deborah; *c:* Matthew, Sarah, Andrew, Bethany; *ed:* (BA) Music Ed, Newark St Coll 1972; (MA) Ed Admin/Supervision, Kean Coll 1980; *cr:* Instrumental Music Teacher Linden Public Elem Schls 1972-80; Dir of Bands Linden HS 1980-; *ai:* Concert & Marching Band; Jazz Ensemble; Sch Play Dir & Musical Dir; Linden Ed Assn, NJEA, NEA, Music Educators Natl Conference; *office:* Linden HS 121 W St George Ave Linden NJ 07036

LORIMIER, LYNDE, Physical Education Teacher; *b:* Tyler, TX; *m:* Dirk Edward; *c:* D. J.; *ed:* (BAT) Phys Ed, 1981, (MS) Phys Ed, 1982 Sam Houston St; *cr:* Grad Asst Sam Houston St 1981-82; Phys Ed Teacher/Coach C C Hardy Mid Sch 1984-; *ai:* Vlybl, Bsktbl, Track Coach; TX Assn of Health, Phys Ed, Recreation, Dance; TX Girls Coaches Assn; *office:* C C Hardy Jr HS 701 S Gerald St Willis TX 77378

LORRAINE, WILLIAM VINSON, HS Science Coordinator; *b:* Chicago, IL; *m:* Joan Frances Duty; *c:* Vanessa, Leah, Nathan; *ed:* (BS) Bio, 1971, (MED) Ed, 1974 SW TX St Univ; Mid Management TX A&I Univ; *cr:* Jr HS Sci Teacher San Antonio Ind Sch Dist 1973-74; Sci Teacher Natalia HS 1974-80, Jourdanton HS 1981-84; Sci Coord Devine HS 1984-; *ai:* JETS Club; Sr Class Spon; TX St Teachers Assn, NEA Medina Cty Pres 1976-77; Sci Teachers Assn of TX 1983-89; *home:* RR 2 Box 160B Devine TX 78016

LOSH, DARYL RUSSELL, 5th Grade Teacher; *b:* Pontiac, MI; *ed:* (AB) Elem Ed, 1969, (MA) Elem Sch Admin, 1972 Cntrl MI Univ; *cr:* Teacher Walled Lake Consolidated Schls 1969-; *ai:* Ski Club Spon; MAEOE 1986-; Walled Lake Teacher of Yr 1985; *office:* Oakley Park Sch 2015 Oakley Park Rd Walled Lake MI 48088

LOTAKIS, KATINA CABINOS, Assistant Principal; *b:* New York, NY; *m:* George Paul; *c:* James, Christopher; *ed:* (BS) Bio, 1968, (MS) Bio/Ed, 1973 City Coll of NY; (PHD) Admin, Iona Coll 1985; *cr:* Sci Teacher 1968-84, Chm Sci Dept 1984-89, Asst Prin 1989- Michelangelo Intermediate Sch; *ai:* Faculty Adv Sch Sci Magazine, Leaders Club; Teacher Trainer; Founder Adopt-A-Grandparent Prgm; Dist Staff Developer; Bronx Borough Asst Dir Sci Fair; NY Bio Teacher 1985-; NY St Teachers Assn 1986-; Bronx Rdng Cncl 1989-; NY-Tokoyo Teacher Exch Mem Sony Corporation; Co-Author NY City Sci Safety Manual; Correlator Harcourt Brace Jonvanovitch Sci Texts; *office:* Michelangelo Intermediate Sch 2545 Gunther Ave Bronx NY 10469

LOTANO, ERNEST JOSEPH, Social Studies Teacher; *b:* Schenectady, NY; *m:* Carol Mc Donald; *c:* Daniel, Michael; *ed:* (BA) Soc Stud, (MA) His/Ed, Coll of St Rose; *cr:* Soc Stud Teacher Linton HS 1965, Van Corlaer Jr HS 1966-77, Mont Pleasant HS 1977-; *ai:* Schenectady Fed of Teachers VP 1989-; Public Service Awds Boys Club Volunteer, Academic & Sports Commitment; *home:* 2137 William St Schenectady NY 12306

LOTT, BUFFI LEE, Mathematics Teacher; *b:* Waycross, GA; *m:* Jeffrey Steven; *ed:* (BSED) Math, Univ of GA 1984; (MED) Math, 1988, (EDS) Math, 1990 Valdosta St Coll; *cr:* Math Teacher Pierce Cty HS 1984-; Part Time Math Instr Waycross Coll 1988-; *ai:* 9th Grade Head Spon; Sr Beta Club; GCTM 1985-; *office:* Pierce Cty HS Rt 1 Box 712-A Blackshear GA 31516

LOTT, DIANETRA RUTH, Fifth Grade Teacher; *b:* Brooklyn, NY; *c:* Candis, Shenice; *ed:* (BA) Elem/Early Chldhd, Univ of N FL 1978; *cr:* 5th Grade Teacher Jacksonville Heights Elem 1979-; *office:* Jacksonville Heights Elem Sch 7750 W Tempest St S Jacksonville FL 32210

LOTT, JACKIE RUTLAND, 4th Grade Teacher; *b:* Hattiesburg, MS; *m:* Scott L.; *c:* Leslie L., Andrew S.; *ed:* (BA) Elem Ed, Univ Southern MS 1976; (MS) Elem Ed, William Carey Coll 1982; *cr:* 1st Grade Teacher 1978-79; 2nd Grade Teacher 1979-80; 4th Grade Teacher 1980- W L Smith Elem; *ai:* Grade Level Chm-4th

Grade; MS Fed Teachers 1980- Outstanding Bldg Rep 1988; Amer Fed Teachers 1980-; Petal Fed Teachers 1980-; Petal-Harvey Bapt Church 1976-; W L Smith Elem PTA 1978-; South MS Rdng Assn 1978-; *home:* 173 Wildwood Trl Petal MS 39465

LOTT, JACQUELYNE MARIE, 8th Grade Mathematics Teacher; *b:* Hattiesburg, MS; *ed:* (BS) Elem Ed, Univ of S MS 1974; (MED) Elem Ed, William Carey Coll 1982; *cr:* 1st/2nd Grade Teacher Beaumont Elem Sch 1974-80; Jr High Math Teacher Beaumont HS 1980-83; Jr High Math Teacher Perry Cntrl HS 1983-; *ai:* Jr HS Chrldr Spon; MS Prof Educators Assn 1988-; Perry Cntrls Teacher of Yr 1988; *home:* PO Box 26 Beaumont MS 39423

LOTT, LUE B., 9th Grade World His Teacher; *b:* Indianola, MS; *m:* Jarrett E. Jr.; *c:* Jarrett III, Teisha, Tashara; *ed:* (BS) Elem Ed, MS Valley St Univ 1968; (MA) Educl Leadership, Wayne St Univ 1981; Assertive Discipline, EEEI, Law Related Ed, Coalition of Labor Union Women; *cr:* Teacher Drew Elem Sch 1967-68; Eng Teacher Carver Elem Sch 1968-69; Librarian Sill Elem Sch 1970-72; Math Teacher Ellis Elem Sch 1973-74; Soc Stud Teacher Columbian Elem 1974-75; 7th-9th Grade Soc Stud Teacher Cerveny Mid 1975-; *ai:* Black His Prgm Chairperson Cerveny Mid Sch 1977-89; Wayne St Alumni Chairperson 1987-88; Secy of New Testament COGIG; Detroit Fed of Teachers, MI Fed of Teachers, NAACP; AFT 1970-; Young Women Chrstn Cncl (Pres 1988-, VP 1982-88); Dist #3 MI Women Dept Secy 1979-85, Service Awd 1983; Elected Outstanding Teacher 1987; Bus Womens Leadership Skills Certificate 1986; Service Awd 1986; Career Guidance 1988; Educl Leadership Impact Prgm 1987; MI Law Related Ed 1988; Afro-Amer Child Placed in Conf 1989; *home:* 24320 Berkley Oak Park MI 48237

LOTT, MARVIN JAMES, Band Teacher; *b:* Gainesville, GA; *m:* Okie L. Cox; *c:* Melanie J., Omar J. Lanier; *ed:* (BS) Music Ed, Knoxville Coll 1969; (MS) Admin/Supervision, Univ of TN Chattanooga; Grad Stud Admin & Supervision; *cr:* Band Dir Monroe Area HS & Carver Jr HS 1969-73; Band Dir/Coach Alton Park Mid Sch 1973-; *ai:* Asst Ftbl & Head Bsktbl Coach; Instrumental Music Competency Test Comm; Chattanooga Ed Assn, TN Ed Assn, Music Ed Natl Conference, Kappa Delta Pi; New Monumental Baptist Deacon; Chattanooga Area Urban League, Omega Psi Phi, Phi Mu Alpha; Push Excl Teacher of Yr 1985; Band Division I Rating Strawberry Festival 1987; Winner Armed Forces Day Parade Jr HS Division 1973-86; Coached Undefeated Bsktbl Team 1986-88.

LOTT, MARY LOUISE, Language Arts Teacher; *b:* Marion, KS; *m:* Dolen E.; *c:* Jaime, Alissa; *ed:* (BSE) Eng/Scndry Ed, Emporia St Univ 1970; *cr:* 8th Grade Lang Art Teacher Haysville Jr HS 1970-71; 7th/8th Grade Eng Teacher Waukee Schls 1972-75; 8th Grade Lang Art Teacher Haysville Jr HS 1981-; *ai:* Spelling Bee Spon; Scholar Bowl Judge; NEA 1970-; NCTE 1981-; *office:* Haysville Jr HS 900 W Grand Ave Haysville KS 67060

LOTT, ROBERT GRODON, Science Teacher/Athletic Dir; *b:* Flint, MI; *m:* Darlene May Curell; *c:* Joshua G., Josie A., Jared P.; *ed:* (BS) Spec Ed, TN Tech Univ 1977; Cntrl MI Univ; *cr:* Teacher North Branch Wesleyan Acad 1977-; *ai:* Athletic Dir; Var Vlybl Coach; Sunday Sch Supt 1989-; Childrens Church Dir 1980-88; *office:* North Branch Wesleyan HS 3164 N Branch Rd North Branch MI 48461

LOTT, TAMARA NEUFELD, English/Speech Teacher; *b:* Jadcherla, Southern India; *m:* Edward Morgan III; *ed:* (BA) Eng/Comm, Biola Univ 1986; *cr:* Eng/Speech Teacher Milpitas HS 1986-; *ai:* Club Adv; Speech Club; *office:* Milpitas HS 1285 Escuela Pkwy Milpitas CA 95035

LOTT-SHELBY, LEMOYNE, 1st Grade Teacher; *b:* Vicksburg, MS; *m:* Toby Shelby;; *c:* Chaille Shelby; *ed:* (BAE) Elem Ed, 1974, (MA) Elem Ed, 1978 Univ of MS; Stu Assessment Prgm Trng, Charter Lakeside; *cr:* 1st Grade Teacher Horn Lake Elem 1975-; *ai:* Public Relations, Adopt-A-Sch, Sch Improvement Comms; 4-H Club Spon; Ed of Annual; Grade Chairperson; Cooperating Teacher for 3 Stu Teachers Coord of Booth for St MAE/NEA Convention, MTAI Trained Evaluator; Star Sch Recognition, SACS Chairperson Comm; Alpha Delta Kappa 1988-; Horn Lake Elem PTA; Mid-South Daffodil Society Secy 1987-; Presented St MACA Wkshps; Teacher of Yr Horn Lake Elem 1986, De Soto Cty 1986; *home:* 4800 W De Soto Rd Walls MS 38680

LOTZ, SHARON HOGAN, Business Department Chair; *b:* Grand Junction, CO; *m:* David H.; *c:* Le Ann, Michael; *ed:* (AA) Secy Sci 1966; (BA) Bus Ed Graceland Coll 1968; Addl Studies in Svc Prgms *cr:* Bus Teacher Grand Junction Jr HS 1968-69; Bus Teacher Fort Osage HS 1 970-74; Voc Accounting 1981-87; Accounting/Dept Chair Fort Osage HS 1987-; *ai:* FBLA Spon; Cmmty Ed Assn Hospitality Comm; North Cntrl Comm-Bus Dept Chm/Curr Comm Mem; Cmmty Ed Assn 1987-; MO Voc Assn 1988-; MO St Teachers Assn 1987-; FBLA 1987-; Greater Kansas City Bus Ed Assn 1987-; Buckner Elem/PTA (Corr Secy 80-83/VP 82/Room Mother/Cultural Arts 79- 87); Middle Sch PTA Pres 1985-86; Womensdept Leader 1982-83; Music Dir 1983-84; Adult Choir 1975-; Sunday Sch Teacher 84-87; Greater Kansas City Area Teacher of Yr 1988; *office:* Fort Osage HS 2101 N Twyman Rd Independence MO 64058

LOTZ, VIVIAN EVELYN, Counselor; *b:* Paterson, NJ; *ed:* (BA) Psych, Douglass Coll 1965; (MED) Spec Ed, 1966, (MED) Counseling, 1972, (PHD) Spec Ed, 1984 Temple Univ; *cr:* Personnel Asst Ford Fnd 1965-66; Teacher Sch Dist of Philadelphia 1966-72; Cnslr Episcopal Hospital Sch of Nursing 1972-77; Dir SW Cmmty Action Group Incorporated 1972-79; Cnslr Sch Dist of Philadelphia 1972-; *ai:* Team Leader; Restructuring Effort Co-Chairperson; Career Fairs 1987-; Coll Access Center Advisory Comm; Temple Univ Exemplary Schls Liason; Counseling Assn of Greater Philadelphia 1972-; Piaget Society 1984-89; Philadelphia Fed of Teachers 1966-; Assn for Severely Handicapped 1984-88; SW Cmmty Action Group Incorporated VP 1973-78; Chapel of Four Chaplains Awd; Philadelphia Assn of Retarded Children Awd; Sch Dist of Philadelphia Commendations; *office:* William Penn HS Broad & Master Strs Philadelphia PA 19122

LOUCKS, RICHARD D., English Teacher; *b:* Tiffin, OH; *c:* Christopher A.; *ed:* (BS) Eng/Amer Stud, Bowling Green Univ 1975; (MA) Sch Cmmty Relations, Kent St Univ 1982; *cr:* Eng Teacher/Head Track/Cross Cntry Coach Thomas W Harvey HS 1975-; *ai:* Voice of Red Raiders; Class Adv; Scholastic Coach Magazine Coaching Awd 1987; N E OH Coach of Yr 1982; NAACP Coaching Awd 1987; Conference Coach of Yr 1986-89; Dist & Regional Coach of Yr 1983-89; *office:* Thomas W Harvey HS 167 W Washington St Painesville OH 44077

LOUDIN, JEAN SNYDER, 8th Grade Science Teacher; *b:* Valley Bend, WV; *m:* Larry J.; *c:* David, Susan Loudin Clark; *ed:* (BS) Home Ec/Sci, WV Univ 1957; *cr:* Teacher Kingwood HS 1957-59, Barrickville HS 1974-77, Sutton Mid Sch 1977-; *ai:* NSTA; Daughters of Amer Revolution; *office:* Sutton Mid Sch 411 N Hill Rd Sutton WV 26601

LOUDIS, ANTHONY ALAN, Broadcast Journalism; *b:* Kansas City, MO; *m:* Vanessa Jean Annis; *c:* Barry, Kyle, Nicole; *ed:* (AA) Music/Theatre, Penn Valley Coll 1973; (BSED) Speech/Theatre/Media/Ed, SW MO St Univ 1978; *cr:* Instr Kickapoo HS 1978-; *ai:* Media Club & Youth-in-Government Spon; General Mgr Arrowhead Audio Cable 19; Assemblies Comm; DSA & NASSP; Ticket Mgr Springfield R-12 Schls; Public Relations Officer for Kickapoo HS; Educl Satellite Network Coord; Alpha Psi Omega Mem 1975-; MO Interscholastic Press Assn Mem 1978-87; Journalism Ed Assn Mem 1978-; Amatuer Sftbl Assn Natl Tournament Umpire 1985-88; Springfield Ad Club Ed Comm Consultant 1984-; St Electronic Media Dir MO Youth Government; Teaching Faculty for Annual WA Journalism Conference; Published Ozark Empire Fair 1934-84; *office:* Kickapoo HS 3710 S Jefferson Springfield MO 65807

LOUGHLIN, JUDY BUCHHOLZ, Kindergarten Teacher; *b:* Wellsville, NY; *m:* Bob; *c:* Patrick, Jennifer; *ed:* (BS) Ed, SUNY Brockport 1966; *cr:* K/2nd/3rd Grade Teacher Whitesville Cntrl Sch 1966-; *ai:* Alleghany Cty Teachers Assn Treas 1980-85; Kanadea Rdng Cncl Building Rep 1980-; Amer Assn Univ Women (EPF Chm, PR Chm) 1978-; Early Literacy Inservice Course, Tutor; Staff Tutor; Ernest C Hartwell Awd 1966; *office:* Whitesville Cntrl Sch Main St Whitesville NY 14897

LOUGHNER, HELEN L., Chemistry Instructor; *b:* Greensburg, PA; *ed:* (BS) Pre Med, Penn St Univ 1976; (MED) Sci Ed, 1976, (PHD) Sci Ed, 1987 Univ of Pittsburgh; *cr:* Chem Instr Penn-Trafford HS 1978-; *ai:* Chess Club Spon; NHS Advisory Comm; Author & Co-Author 24 Publications; 3 HS Equipment Grants Spectroscopy Society of Pittsburgh; Winner Natl Chem Day Competition; Penn-Trafford Pride Awd for Excl in Teaching 1987; *office:* Penntrafford H S R R 130 Harrison City PA 15636

LOUGHRY, RICHARD BERNARD, Spanish Teacher; *b:* Canton, OH; *m:* Carol Lynn Humphrey; *c:* Eric, Alicia; *ed:* (BS) Span, 1963, (ME) Span, 1968, (EDS) Scndry Admin, Kent St; *cr:* Span Teacher Canton Mc Kinley 1963-; *ai:* Curr Comm Mem; E Cntrl OH Teachers Assn, OH Ed Assn, NEA, OH Foreign Lang Teachers Assn, Amer Assn of Teachers of Spanish & Portuguese, Kappa Delta Pi; Mc Kinley Booster Club Bd Mem; Greenpeace; Defenders of Wildlife; Friends of Animals; Animal Protection Inst of Amer; Stark Cty Humane Society; *home:* 2177 Saddle Creek St NE North Canton OH 44721

LOUIS-PRESCOTT, LEE ANN, Religion Department Chair; *b:* Jackson, MI; *m:* Jay; *c:* Steven, Yvonne; *ed:* (BA) Sociology, W MI Univ 1975; (MA) Scndry Sch Admin, E MI Univ 1979; Private Pilots License 1975-; Certified Yoga Instr 1978; *cr:* Campus Minister/Educator/Cnslr Lumen Chrstn HS 1975-79; Campus Minister/Moderator/Teacher St Mary HS 1979-83; Campus Minister/Religion Dept Chairperson Shrine HS 1985-; *ai:* Personal Counseling; Teacher of Sexuality & Chemical Dependency, Morality, Bio-Ethics; Aircraft Owners & Pilots Assn 1975-; Elected By Sr Class to Give Commencement Address; Wrote & Produced Yoga Video 1990; *office:* Shrine HS 3500 W 13 Mile Rd Royal Oak MI 48071

LOUIS-PRESCOTT, LEE ANN, Religion Department Chairwoman; *b:* Jackson, MI; *m:* Jay Louis; *c:* Steven, Yvonne; *ed:* (BA) Sociology/Span/Speech, W MI Univ 1975; (MA) Sncdry Sch Admin, E MI Univ 1979; Certified Pilot 1975-; Certified Yoga Instr 1978-; Sexuality & Ed Specialist; Chemical Dependency & Ed Specialist; *cr:* Dorm Asst Dir W MI Univ 1972-74; Childrens Camp Dir San Anselmo 1980; Educator Various Schls 1975-; Yoga Instr 1978-; *ai:* Dept Chairwoman; Class Moderator; Cheerleading Adv; Faculty Planning Comm; Bd of Discipline; Sftbl Coach; Retreat Planning Comm; Guitar Group; Aircraft Owners & Pilots Assn 1975-; Local Nursing Home Volunteer 1971-76; 1st Female to Give Commencement Address Sr Class Graduation 1988; Commencement Address CA 1980, 1981; *office:* Shrine HS 3500 W Thirteen Mile Royal Oak MI 48072

LOUK, LESLIE KAYE (GAINER), First Grade Teacher; *b:* Lancaster, OH; *m:* Phillip J.; *ed:* (BA) Elem Ed, Fairmont St Coll 1979; Addl Studies, WV Univ; *cr:* 3rd/4th Grade Teacher Pickens Sch 1979-80; 4th Grade Teacher 1980-82; 1st Grade Teacher 1982- North Elem; *ai:* Elkins Juniorette Adv; Sch Store Adv; Elkins Jr Womens; Forest Festival-Queens Dept Chm 1980-; *home:* Rt 3 Box 430-2 Elkins WV 26241

LOUKAS, ROBERTA BEYER, 4th Grade Teacher; *b:* Jersey City, NJ; *m:* Alexander William; *c:* Bradford B., David D.; *ed:* (BS) Ed, Beaver Coll 1955; *cr:* Kndgtn Teacher New Milford 1955-61; 4th/5th Grade Teacher Rochelle Park 1974-; *ai:* Textbook Selection, Attendance Policy Update, Constitution Revision Comm; Rochelle Park Ed Assn 1974-; Bergen Cty Ed Assn, NJ Ed Assn, NEA 1955-61/1974-; Beaver Coll Alumni Assn Class Agent 1988-; Luth Church of Redeemer 1974-; Midland Sch PTA Cultural Arts 1985-; Auxiliary Hackensack Med Center Exec Bd 1980-; Recipient Fellowship Awd BergeRn Cty Cncl PTA 1989; Nom Phoebe Apperson Hearst Natl Educator 1989-; *home:* 65 Somerville St Rochelle Park NJ 07662

LOUTHAN, CHUCK, Math/Science/Phys Ed Teacher; *b:* Bluefield, WV; *m:* Faye Viar; *c:* Scott, Stacy; *ed:* (BS) Elem Ed, Bluefield St 1969; (MS) Elem Admin/Supervision, Radford Univ 1981; *cr:* 6th Grade Teacher Tazewell Elem 1969-70, Graham Intermediate 1970-81; 6th/7th Grade Sci/Math/Soc Stud/Phys Ed Teacher Graham Mid 1981-; *ai:* Mid Sch Ftbl & HS Track Coach; FCA Spon; VAST 1989-; VA Mid Sch Assn 1987-; *home:* 607 Cardinal St Bluefield VA 24605

LOVATO, LORI GOEHL, Jr HS English/Science Teacher; *b:* Del Norte, CO; *m:* Timothy N.; *c:* Emily C., Nathan T., Erin E.; *ed:* (BA) Elem Ed, Adams St Coll 1983; *cr:* 6th Grade Teacher 1983-88, Jr HS Teacher 1988- Mountain Valley Sch; *ai:* Jr HS & HS Knowledge Bowls; 7th Grade Spon; Curr Comm; San Luis Valley Intnl Rdng Assn (Pres 1988-89, VP 1987-88); 4-H Leader 1989-; Mountain Valley Outstanding Teacher of Yr 1987, 1988; *office:* Mountain Valley Sch Box 127 Saguache CO 81149

LOVE, ADRIENNE DAVIS, English Teacher; *b:* Detroit, MI; *m:* Cicero; *c:* Cicero, Sojourner, Jamale, Seneca, Alston; *ed:* (BA) Soc Stud, Univ of MI 1977; *cr:* Eng Teacher Kettering HS 1978-; *ai:* Coord Kettering HS Honors Prgm; Kettering HS Schlsp Comm Mem; Midwest Academically Talented Coach Stus of Detroit Public Schls; Univ of MI (HS Liaison Comm 1987-, Coll Entrance Exam Preparation Coach 1988-); Wade Mc Cree Schlsp Comm 1988-; Guest Speaker at Natl Alliance of Black Educators Convention; Wrote Educl Prgms 1977; *office:* Kettering HS 6101 Vandyke Detroit MI 48213

LOVE, ALYCE MARIE, Social Science Teacher; *b:* Dumas, AR; *ed:* (BS) Sociology/His, Univ of AR Pine Bluff 1973; (MAED) Urban Ed, Univ MA Amherst 1974; Natl Endowment for Hum Inst 1980; Cadre Partner KS City MO Sch Dist 1987-89; Rdng Comprehension & Cognitive Dev Prgm; *cr:* Teacher Ballou HS 1974-80; Trng Rep Mead Data Cntrl 1980-86; Fashion Consulant A&A Sewing Assoc 1986-87; Teacher NE Law/Public Service Military & Magnet HS 1987-; *ai:* Stu Cncl Co-Spon; Youth In Government & Stu In Local Government Adv; NE Stu Discipline Comm; ASCD 1989-; Linwood YMCA 1989-; Natl Endowment for Hum Fellowship 1980; *home:* 5819 E 19th Terr Kansas City MO 64126

LOVE, DIANE LOUISE, 7th Grade Eng & Rdng Teacher; *b:* Dayton, OH; *ed:* (BA) Elem Ed, Cedarville Coll 1974; (MRE) Religion/Ed, Mid America Baptist Theological Seminary 1980; Working Towards Masters in Gifted Ed & Counceling, Wright St Univ; *cr:* 2nd/3rd/5th Grade Teacher Mad River Green Local Schls 1974-78; 8th Grade Eng/Rdng Teacher Dayton Chrstn Schls 1980-85; 7th Grade Eng/Rdng Teacher Northwestern Schls 1985-; *ai:* Jr HS Track, 7th & 8th Grade Girls Bsktbl, 7th Grade Girls Vlybl, Girls Var Bsktbl Coach; Jr HS Chrldr & Bible Adv; OH Ed Assn, NEA, Dist Assn 1985-; Chrstn Life Center 1982-; *home:* 515 Homewood Ave Dayton OH 45405

LOVE, KARL W., His/Eng/Geography Teacher; *b:* Middlewater, TX; *c:* Karlyn, Matt; *ed:* (BA) His/Eng/Philosophy, Abilene Chrstn Univ 1965; (MED) Ed, OR St Univ 1972; *cr:* Instr/Admin Columbia Chrstn Coll 1956-60; Minister Churches of Christ 1960-75; Teacher Brasilian Schls 1968-; *ai:* Track, Field, Bsbl, Ftbl, Bsktbl Coach 1956-89; NEA, OEA, OCEA.

LOVE, MARIAH DAVIS, English/Social Studies Teacher; *b:* Louisburg, NC; *m:* Lenwood; *ed:* (BA) Eng, NC Cntrl Univ Durham 1969; Univ of AR, Fayetteville, Univ of NC Chapel Hill, NC St Univ Raleigh; *cr:* Teacher Edward Best HS 1969-70, Holton Mid Sch 1970-; *ai:* Y-Teen Adv; 4-H Club Adv/Coach; Drop-Out Prevention Comm; Drama Coach; Choir Dir; NC Eng Teachers Assn 1985-; Durham City Assn of Educators, NEA 1970-; YWCA Youth Adv 1985-89; Church Minister of Music 1970-; Natl Endowment for Hum Fellow 1985; Nom Durham City Schls Teacher of Yr 1990; *home:* 612 Elmira Ave Durham NC 27707

LOVE, SALLY, English & Reading Teacher; *b:* Hico, TX; *ed:* (BA) Scndry Ed/Eng, 1977, (ME) Rdng, 1979 Clemson Univ; Rdng, Clemson; *cr:* Teacher Clover HS 1978, Jonesville HS 1979-80, Laurens Dist 55 HS 1980-; *ai:* Adv Natural Helpers; Mem Dist Rdng Comm; Tutor; NEA 1985-; Piedmont Cncl Teachers of Eng 1986-; Mauldin Church of Christ 1985-; Mu Beta Psi Natl Editor 1976-78; *office:* Laurens Dist 55 H S Box 309 Princeton Hwy Laurens SC 29360

LOVE, SCOTT SCOTT, English Teacher/Coach; *b:* Spring Lake, NY; *m:* Judith Kelly; *c:* Jason, Caitlin; *ed:* (BA) Creative Writing, 1977, (MA) Amer Lit, 1981 Syracuse Univ; TAC Level II Distance Cert, US Olympic Trng Center 1989; *cr:* Eng Teacher St Marys Sch 1978-79, Paul V Moore HS 1982-; *ai:* Cross Cntry Coach 1971-; Track Coach; Onondaga HS League Coaching

Achievement Awd 1988; AFS Abroad Poona India 1971; *office:* Paul V Moore HS Caughdenoy Rd Central Square NY 13036

LOVE, THOMAS EUGENE, Mathematics Dept Chairman; *b:* Mechanicsburg, OH; *m:* Mary Elaine Casar; *c:* Nicole; *ed:* (BSED) Math/Physics, Bowling Green St Univ 1968; (MED) Math Ed, Kent St Univ 1973; (MSED) Cmptr Ed, Univ of Akron 1988; Continuing Ed Certificate Cmptr Application Software, Wayne Coll & Tech Coll 1985; *cr:* Teacher Worley Jr HS 1968-71, Timken HS 1971-72, Lehman HS 1972-76, Adult Evening Sch 1972-78, Canton Summer Sch 1974-76, Migrant Summer Sch 1976-78, Mc Kinley Sr HS 1976-, Wayne General & Tech Coll 1978-, Univ of Akron 1980-, Governors Summer Inst 1986-, Univ of Ashland 1988-; *ai:* Our Lady of Peace Stu, Teacher, Parent Micro-Cmptr Instr; Cmptr Programming & Applications Curr Dev Mc Kinley Sr HS; Math & Sci Curr Textbook Comm Canton Cty Schls; Faculty Advisory Comm Mc Kinley Sr HS; OH Cncl Teachers of Math, AAPT; Canton Prof Educators Assn (Exec Comm, VP), Educator of Month 1980; E Cntrl OH Educators Assn, OH Educators Assn, NEA; Educl Cmptr Consortium of OH; Wayne Coll Learning Center Staff Certificate of Appreciation 1983; Mc Kinley Sr HS Future Teachers Club Best Lecturer Awd 1988; Jackson Local Schls Continuing Ed Certificate of Appreciation 1984; Wayne General & Tech Coll Distinguished Instr Awd 1987; Univ of Akron Summer Physics Wkshp Certificate of Appreciation 1987; Numerous Presentations & Publications; *office:* Mc Kinley Sr HS 2323 17th St N W Canton OH 44708

LOVEJOY, DAWN DEDOLF, AP Biology & Chemistry Teacher; *b:* Gettysburg, PA; *m:* William Anderson Jr.; *c:* Allison M., Geoffrey W., Matthew J.; *ed:* (AB) Bio/Chem, Immaculata Coll 1982; Coursework for Cert, Cabrini Coll; Working Towards Masters Degree, Im maculata Coll; *cr:* Lecturer Gwynedd-Mercy Coll 1984-86, Immaculata Coll 1983-; Teacher Villa Maria Acad 1983-; *ai:* SADD Adv; St Prom Comm Mem; Thornbury Township Park & Recreation Bd Mem 1988-; *office:* Villa Maria Acad HS Greentree Malvern PA 19355

LOVEL, SUSAN GAYE, Guidance Counselor; *b:* Moline, IL; *m:* Victor; *c:* Larry; *ed:* (BA) Eng/Ed, 1970, (MS) Guidance/Educl Psych, 1981 S IL Univ; *cr:* Cnslr 1985-88, Prin 1987-88 Tamaroa HS; Cnslr Pinckneyville HS 1988-; *ai:* Frosh Spon; Soc Arrangements Comm; IEA, NEA; Phi Kappa Phi 1981-; *office:* Pinckneyville HS E Water St Pinckneyville IL 62274

LOVELACE, DOROTHY L., English Teacher/Eng Dept Chair; *b:* Prosperity, SC; *w:* Joe F. (dec); *c:* Clare R. Lovelace Turner; *ed:* (BS) Ed/Bus/Eng - Magna Cum Laude, Newberry Coll 1956; *cr:* Bus Teacher Hartsville HS 1956-57, Newberry Coll 1957-58; Secy Prof Walter Summer CPA 1958-59; Eng Teacher Mid-Carolina HS 1960-; *ai:* Jr Class & Jr-Sr Prom Spon; Basic Skills Assessment Prgm Coord Eng Dept; Developed Lang Art Guides Course Outlines & Objectives; NEA, Ed Assn, Newberry Cty Ed Assn 1989-; St Adoption Eng Textbook Comm Mem 1988-89; Mid Carolina HS Yrbk Proofreader Natl Awd 1984-85; MI STAR Teacher of Yr 1968-69; Employ the Handicapped Essary Contest Spon 1968-69; Mid Carolina Teacher of Yr 1985-86; Palmetto Girls St 1950-51; Valedictorian 1950-51; *home:* Rt 3 Box 41 Prosperity SC 29127

LOVELACE, SANDRA STOWE, Guidance Counselor; *b:* Danville, VA; *m:* Bobby L.; *c:* Lee; *ed:* (BS) Elem Ed, Averett Coll 1974; (MED) Elem Ed, Univ of VA 1977; Grad Stud Radford, Univ of VA; *cr:* 5th Grade Teacher Whitmell Elem Sch 1974-89; Guidance Cnslr Whitmell/Union Hall Elem 1989-; *ai:* After-Sch Tutorial Prgm Whitmell & Union Hall; Teaching After-Sch Class for Gifted & Talented; Sch Based Assistance Team Whitmell & Union Hall Elem Schs; Pittsylvania Cty Supt Advisory Cncl; Delta Kappa Gamma (Pres 1988-, Chm Prof Affairs 1986-88, Chm Research 1984-86); Mt Hermon Baptist Church (Sunday Sch Youth Dir, Mem, Youth Sunday Sch Teacher, Church Cncl Mem, Comm for Ed); Whos Who Outstanding Young Women 1987; *office:* Whitmell Elem/Union Hall Elem Rt 1 Box 322 Dry Fork VA 24549

LOVELL, BARBARA (SKIDMORE), Remedial Reading Teacher; *b:* Ft Eustus, VA; *m:* Dennis James; *c:* Krista L., Eric J.; *ed:* (BS) Elem Ed, Frostburg St Univ 1977; (BS) Elem Ed, WV Univ 1984; Grad Stud WV Univ; *cr:* 5th Grade Teacher Washington Jefferson Elem 1977-79; 6th-8th Grade Teacher of Gifted Ellsworth Mid Sch 1979-81; 4th Grade Teacher 1981-89; 1st-6th Grade Chapter I Remedial Rdng Teacher 1989- Sistersville Elem Sch; *ai:* Sistersville Elem Sch Improvement Team, Advisory Cncl, K-4 Curr Dev Team; Soc Stud Fair 1982-89; Young Writers Contest Coord; Power of Positive Stus Instr 1988-89; Effective Schls Research Cadre 1987-88; Project Charlie Instr 1987-88; APL Participant 1989-; Nom Teacher of Yr Tyler Cty 1988-89; *home:* Rt 2 Box 64 Sistersville WV 26175

LOVELL, MARY LOU (BINGHAM), Junior HS Principal; *b:* Wynne, AR; *w:* Milton H. (dec); *c:* Milton L.; *ed:* (BSE) Eng, 1963, (MSE) Eng, 1983 AR St Univ; Grad Stud; *cr:* Eng Teacher Marked Tree HS 1963-78, Crosett Schls 1978-89; Prin Norman Jr HS 1989-; *ai:* Chrldr, Newspaper, Annual, Literary Magazine, Spon; AR Cncl Teachers of Eng VP 1986-, L C Lead Distinguished Service Awd 1989; Delta Kappa Gamma Shlsp 1980; Sunday Sch Teacher 1st Baptist Church; Chm AR Writing Project; *home:* 1307 Elm Crossett AR 71635

LOVELOCK, PATRICIA ANNE, Language Arts Teacher; *b:* New York, NY; *m:* Robert J.; *c:* Kerry J. Bazany; *ed:* (BA) Poly Sci/Pre-Law, Fordham Univ 1970; *cr:* Eng Teacher St Nicholas of Tolentine 1970-75; Lang Art Coord St Columba Sch 1979-; *ai:* Coord Christmas Pageant; NCEA 1979-; *office:* St Columba Sch Rt 82 Box 368 Hopewell Junction NY 12533

LOVERSIDGE, PATRICIA COHILL, Third Grade Teacher; *b:* Charleroi, PA; *m:* John; *c:* Trisha, Tara, Trenna; *ed:* (BS) Elem Ed, CA Univ 1971; Georgian Court Coll Grad Sch; *cr:* Elem Teacher Keansburg Sch Dist 1971-; *ai:* Textbook Selection, Stu Recognition, Curr Comm; Sch Newspaper Ed; Keansburg Teachers Assn, Monmouth Cty Ed Assn, NJ Ed Assn, NEA 1971-; Ladies Altar Rosary Society (Pres 1987-89, VP 1985-87); NJ Dept Environmental Protection Contest Winner; *home:* 4 Jumpingbrook Dr Neptune NJ 07753

LOVETT, LOIS ELAINE, Second Grade Teacher; *b:* Lufkin, TX; *ed:* (AAB) Bus, Angelina Coll 1971; (BS) Elem Ed, Baptist Bible Coll 1977; *cr:* Substitute Teacher Lufkin, Diboll, Hudson Ind Dists 1971-72; 6th Grade Teacher 1987-88, 2nd Grade Teacher 1977-87, 1988- Canyon Creek Chrstn Acad; *ai:* Chrldr Spon 1977-78, 1985-86; Journalism Teacher Yrbk & Sch Paper 1987-88; Vlybl Coach/Asst Coach 1977-78, 1985-; *office:* Canyon Creek Chrstn Acad 2800 Custer Pkwy Richardson TX 75080

LOVETT, MARVA NORTON, Science Teacher; *b:* Jamaica, West Indies; *m:* Tommy L.; *c:* Stephen; *ed:* (BA) Nursing/ Sociology/Ed, Univ of Cntrl FL 1979; Working Towards Masters Bio; *cr:* Math Teacher Jones HS 1979-80; Sci/Math Teacher Colonial HS 1980-81; Sci Teacher Tuskawilwa Mid Sch 1981-88, Oviedo HS 1988-; *office:* Oviedo HS 601 King St Oviedo FL 32765

LOVETT, V. TROY, Algebra II/Calculus Teacher; *b:* Jellico, TN; *m:* Karen Kidd; *c:* Peter A., Jeannie K.; *ed:* (BA) Math, Cumberland Coll 1969; Counseling Emphasis Prgm W KY Univ; MI St Teachers Project Participant Mid Sch & Basic HS Math; *cr:* Television/Team Math Teacher Fern Creek Jr HS 1969-76; Algebra II/Calculus Teacher Fern Creek Sr HS 1976-; *ai:* NHS Screening Comm; Sr Honors Night Master of Ceremonies; Jefferson Cty Math Bowl Judge; Thoroughbred Chorus 1989-; Cumberland Coll Alumni Bd of Dir 1985-88; Cumberland Coll One Hundred Distinguished Alumni Mem; *office:* Fern Creek HS 9115 Fern Creek Rd Louisville KY 40291

LOVING, NELDA FAY, Second Grade Teacher; *b:* Kennard, TX; *m:* Julius I.; *c:* J. Eugene, Laura J., Tanya K.; *ed:* (BS) Elem Ed, Sam Houston St Univ 1955; *cr:* 2nd Grade Teacher Cleveland Ind Sch Dist 1955-56, Dayton Ind Sch Dist 1956-59; 1st Grade Teacher Pasadena Ind Sch Dist 1959-61; 2nd Grade Teacher Crockett Ind Sch Dist 1961-62, Kennard Ind Sch Dist 1966-; *ai:* UIL; Curr Writing; Class Spon; TSTA Life Mem; 4-H Several Comms 1974-78; *home:* Rt 1 Box 152 Kennard TX 75847

LOVINGOOD, DARLENE SHELL, Chapter 1 Reading Teacher; *b:* Harriman, TN; *m:* Bob; *c:* Robbie, Jeffrey, Andy; *ed:* (BS) Elem Ed, MTSU 1975; (MS) Bus Admin, LMU 1989; *cr:* Resource Teacher MT Pleasant HS 1975-76; Elem Teacher Tellico Plains Elem 1976-85; Elem Teacher Vonore Elem 1985-88; Chapt 1 Teacher Vonore Jr HS 1988-; *ai:* Beta Club Adv; Sunday Sch Teacher; ABE Teacher; MCEA (SEC) 1976-; *home:* Rt 4 Madisonville TN 37354

LOVINS, DOROTHY HOESSLE, Second Grade Teacher; *b:* Charlestown, IN; *m:* Freddie Ray; *c:* Kerri, Shelly; *ed:* (BS) Elem Ed, IN Univ 1968; (MS) Elem Ed, SE IN Univ 1972; *cr:* 3rd Grade Teacher 1968-69, 1970-73 Henryville Elem; 2nd Grade Teacher Borden Elem 1974, Henryville Elem 1974-; *ai:* Future Problem Solving Coach 1985-86; Odessy of Mind Coach 1986-87; Drug Comm 1988-89; Book Adoption Chairperson 1983; West Clark Teachers Assn Building Rep 1987-88; PTA Teachers Rep 1986-87; Cath Chrstn Doctrice Primary Teacher 1973-80; *office:* Henryville Elem Sch Ferguson St Henryville IN 47126

LOVTANG, PRUDENCE ELAINE, Guidance/English Teacher; *b:* Arroyo Grande, CA; *m:* Roy; *c:* Kari, Jens Christian; *ed:* (BS) Soc Sci, CA St Univ 1964; Univ of CA Santa Barbara, Fullerton St Univ, Sonoma St; *cr:* San Luis Jr HS 1965-67; 9th Grade Alternative Class Teacher San Luis Obispo 1974-76; Los Osos Jr HS 1976-; *ai:* Dir Stu Act; ASB Adv; Chrldr Adv; CTA Extra-Duty Comm; Credentials Comm; Sch SIP Rep; Stu Assistance Team; Dist Advisory Comm Drug Abuse; Self-esteem; Phi Delta Kappa, CA Teachers Assn; San Luis Vocal Arts Ensemble Pres 1985-87; Vocal Arts Ensemble Handbell Choir; Babe Ruth Bsbl League Scorekeeper; European Tour Comm Chairperson 1985; Mentor Teacher 1987-89; Yrbk Dedication 1983; Mini-Grant Career Opportunity Study 1985; Project Grant Madonna Plaza Merchants 1989; *office:* Los Osos Jr H S 1555 El Moro St Los Osos CA 93402

LO VULLO, ANGELO M., Jr High Social Studies Teacher; *b:* Pittston, PA; *m:* Helen Esis; *c:* Deborah Connors, Donna Golden, Diane Spoth, John; *ed:* (BS) Soc Stud, 1952, (MS) Ed, 1979 Canisius Coll; *cr:* Substitute Teacher Buffalo Bd of Ed 1972-76; 7th/8th Grade Soc Stud Teacher Buffalo Public Sch 21 1976-80, Buffalo Public Sch 43 1980-82, Buffalo Public Sch 64 1982-85, Buffalo Public Sch BUILD Acad 1985-; *ai:* Class Adv; Buffalo Teachers Fed, NEA 1976-; *office:* BUILD Academy 340 Fougeron St Buffalo NY 14211

LOW, SHARON RUTH, 1st Grade Teacher; *b:* Altoona, PA; *m:* James R.; *c:* Nancy L. Moran, Steven R.; *ed:* (BS) Early Chldhd Ed, Kent St Univ 1965; (MA) Early Mid Chldhd Ed, OH St Univ 1983; *cr:* Kndgtn Teacher Maple Heights Elem 1963-66; 1st Grade Teacher Bedford OH 1968-69, Newark OH 1970-; *ai:* NCTE/ NTA/OEA 1988-; Order of Eastern Star 1958-; Rdng Recovery Teacher; *office:* W E Miller Elem Sch Granville Rd & Country Club Newark OH 43055

LOWDERMILK, DONNA J., History Teacher; *b:* Terre Haute, IN; *m:* Robert S.; *c:* Shelly; *ed:* (BS) Soc Stud Ed - Summa Cum Laude, 1980, (MS) Soc Stud Ed, 1985 IN St Univ; *cr:* US His Teacher North Vigo HS 1982; *ai:* IN Cncl Soc Stud 1988; Vigo Cty Teachers Assn 1982; IN St Univ Hines Memorial 1980 & Jr Scholar Awd 1979; *office:* North Vigo HS 3400 Maple Ave Terre Haute IN 47805

LOWE, BETTY BURTIS, 5th Grade Teacher; *b:* Des Moines, IA; *m:* John L.; *c:* Elizabeth Hiza, John Burtis Lowe, Martha Mills; *ed:* (BA) Speech/Arts, CO St Univ 1959; (MA) Ed, Western St Coll 1987; *cr:* 5th Grade Teacher Columbian Las Animas 1959-62; 6th Grade Teacher East La Junta 1962-67; 5th Grade Teacher 1967-84, 5th Grade Speech Teacher 1984-85 E Otero R1; *ai:* Chm Dist Lang Art Curr Comm; La Junta Ed Assn 1963-; Co Ed Assn, NEA 1959-; Delta Kappa Gamma Pres 1981-; PEO 1963-; CO Teacher of Yr Honorable Mention; Bus & Prof Club Outstanding Young Women; Metropolitan Opera Guild Natl Teacher Wkshp; *home:* 1504 Topeka La Junta CO 81050

LOWE, EDWARD PAUL, 7th-12th Grade Principal; *b:* Kearney, NE; *m:* Peggy Loyd; *c:* Bradley, Daniel; *ed:* (BA) Industrial Art, Kearney St 1980; (MS) Admin of Ed, NW MO Univ 1987; *cr:* 7th-12th Grade Industrial Art Johnson-Brock HS 1981-87; 7th-12th Grade Prin Ewing Public Schls 1987-; *ai:* Head Coach Var Ftbl, Weightlifting & Track; Jr HS Bsktbl, Ftbl & Track Coach; Athletic Dir; Stu Cncl; NASSP 1987-; NCSA 1988-; NCA, NEMCA 1981-; United Meth Church Cncl Mem 1989-; *office:* Ewing Public Schls PO Box 98 Ewing NE 68735

LOWE, JANE TYREE, His Teacher/Soc Stud Chair; *b:* Valdosta, GA; *m:* William Terry; *c:* Tara R., Tiffany J., William T.; *ed:* (BS) His Ed, Valdosta St Coll 1976; *cr:* His Teacher Echols Cty HS 1976-86; His Teacher/Soc Stud Dept Chairperson Hamilton Cty HS 1986-; *ai:* Beta Club Spon; Southern Assn of Colls & Schls Rep; 1st Yr Teachers Peer Teacher; Field Trip Spon 1989; Delta Kappa Gamma 2nd VP 1989-; New Hope Baptist Church HS Sunday Sch Teacher 1984-; Echols Cty Teacher of Yr 1980; FL Cncl for Soc Stud Teacher of Yr 1988; Speaker Echols Cty HS Graduation Exercises 1986; *home:* Rt 3 Box 198 Jasper FL 32052

LOWE, JANET SUTTON, Mathematics Teacher; *b:* Hinton, OK; *m:* C. Ruell; *c:* Darla, Katherine, Alan; *ed:* (BS) Math, SW OK St Univ 1967; OK Univ 1971-72; *cr:* Math Teacher Corn Public Sch 1967-69; Math/Eng Teacher Hydro Public Sch 1968-70; Math Teacher Purcell Public Sch 1970-71, Lexington Public Schls 1973-78, Borger Ind Sch Dist 1978-; *ai:* Chrstn Youth Fellowship Dir; Chrstn Ed & Textbook Adoption Comm; Teaching Assistantship OK Univ 1970; Critic Reader Math Book; *office:* Borger Mid Sch Tristram & Florida Borger TX 79007

LOWE, KAREN LOUISE, World Studies Teacher; *b:* Denver, CO; *ed:* (BS) His, Appalachain St Univ & Radford Univ 1968; Grad Study at Radford Univ, Wake Forest Univ, Univ of NC; Numerous Wkshps; NCAE Leadership Trng 1989; *cr:* Teacher 1968-73, Teacher 1975-76 W S Creecy HS; Teacher Gaston Jr-Sr HS 1976-88, Garysburg Elem Sch 1980-82, Gaston Jr HS 1982-; *ai:* Stu Cncl Adv; Mentor Teacher; Northampton Cty & Gaston Jr HS Improvement Teams; Yrbk Staff; Public Information Officer; Soc Stud Dept Chairperson; Span Club Spon; Ethnographer for Mastery in Learning; Northampton Cty Ed Assn (Secy, VP) 1970-; NC Ed Assn Sch Improvement Cadre 1990; NC Teachers Assn Dist Secy 1980; NCSS 1986-; NCAE Faculty Rep for Gaston HS; ASCD 1987-; Chairperson of Northampton Cty Soc Stud Teachers 1987-89; Whos Who in Amer Ed 1988; Northampton Cty HS Consolidation Comm 1982; Gaston Jr HS Teacher of Yr 1983, 1988; Northampton Cty Teacher of Yr 1983; Mini-Grant Winner 1986-89; Subsidiary of Prentice Hall Published by Croft; Taught Wkshps on Mastery in Learning; Project NEA; Teacher Effectiveness Trng; *office:* Gaston Jr HS School St Gaston NC 27832

LOWE, LINDA DIANE (HADSALL), Jr HS Science Teacher; *b:* Hillsboro, IL; *m:* Richard S.; *ed:* (BSED) Zoology, Eastern IL Univ 1974; *cr:* Sub Teacher Wilt & Nokomis IL 1974-76; Sci Teacher Edwards Cty Sch Dist 1976-; *ai:* Stu Cncl Adv; Girls Vlybl Coach 1977-80; IEA Membership Chairperson 1978-81; Edwards Cty Arts Assn; PTA Treas 1977-78; Conservation Teacher of Yr 1978; *office:* Edwards Cty K-12 361 W Main St Albion IL 62806

LOWE, LORETTA BOND ALLRED, Third Grade Teacher; *b:* Akron, OH; *m:* Anthony Paul; *c:* Megan Allred, Julia Lowe; *ed:* (BS) Elem Ed, Akron Univ 1971; *cr:* 3rd Grade Teacher Brimfield Elem Sch 1971-; *ai:* Field Local Teachers Assn; OEA; NEA; NE OH Univ Coll of Medicine Research Asst; Editor for Book Published 1984-85; Edit Proposed Research Grants Submitted by NEOUCOM Staff to Various Governmental Dept; *home:* 4635 Estes Dr Kent OH 44240

LOWE, RICHARD THOMAS, Science Teacher; *b:* Anniston, AL; *m:* Teresa Carol Spencer; *ed:* (BS) Bio, E KY Univ 1985; Working Towards Masters Ed/General Sci; *cr:* HS Sci/Bio Teacher George Ross Clark HS 1985-; *ai:* Asst HS Ftbl Coach; NSTA 1985-; *office:* George Rogers Clark HS 620 Boone Ave Winchester KY 40391

LOWE, SANDRA HOUSTON, Fourth Grade Teacher; *b:* Dalton, GA; *m:* Everette Paul; *c:* April M., Audra F.; *ed:* (BS) N GA Coll 1968; Continuing Ed, Univ of GA, Lee Coll; *cr:* 5th Grade Teacher Antioch Elem 1969-74; Chapter I Teacher Eastside Elem 1978-81; 4th Grade Teacher Cohutta Elem 1981-; *ai:* Soc Stud Sch Chm 1981-; Whitfield Ed Assn Cty Membership Chm 1972-73;

GA Assn of Educators, NEA; Cohutta Elem Teacher of Yr 1987-88.

LOWENBERG, GEORGINA ORELLANA, Third Grade Teacher; *b:* El Paso, TX; *c:* Jennifer A.; *ed:* (BS) Elem Ed, Univ of TX El Paso 1965; Univ of TX El Paso, St Thomas Univ; *cr:* 5th Grade Teacher Clardy Elem Sch 1965-70; 3rd Grade Teacher Eastwood Heights Elem Sch 1980-; *ai:* Assn of TX Prof Educators Regional Treas 1985-86; Rio Grande GSA Cncl; Scotsdale Sch PTA Pres 1978-81 TX Life Mem 1981; Eastwood Heights PTA Parliamentarian 1982; Ysleta Ind Sch Dist PTA Cncl Cultural Arts Chm 1979-80; TX St Textbook Comm Mem; Ysleta Ind Sch Dist Teacher of Yr Finalist; UIL Storytelling Coord; Eastwood HS Band Booster & Speech Booster Secy; *office:* Eastwood Hts Elem Sch 10530 Janway Dr El Paso TX 79925

LOWERY, DONNA THOMAS, 4th Grade Teacher; *b:* El Dorado, AR; *m:* John S. Sr.; *c:* John S. Jr., Johnna R.; *ed:* (BS) Elem Ed, 1964, (MED) Ed, 1965 Univ of AR Fayetteville; *cr:* 1st Grade Teacher Norphlet Elem 1964; 4th Grade Teacher Fairview Elem 1965-; *office:* Fairview Elem Sch 2708 Mt Holly Rd Camden AR 71701

LOWERY, JACQUELINE LEE, Physical Education Teacher; *b:* Johnson City, NY; *ed:* (BA) Phys Ed, AZ St Univ 1978; Counseling Northern AZ Univ; *cr:* K-8th Grade Phys Ed Teacher 1978-80, 1st-8th Grade Phys Ed Teacher 1981-82 WA Elem Sch; 1st-6th Grade Phys Ed Teacher Ocotillo Elem Sch 1982-; *ai:* Stu Cncl Adv; Faculty Soc Comm; after Sch Sports Prgm; Noon Intramurals; Yrbk Comm; *office:* Ocotillo Elem Sch 3225 W Ocotillo Rd Phoenix AZ 85017

LOWERY, KATHRYN JOHNSTON, Third Grade Teacher; *b:* Bluffton, OH; *m:* Allen R.; *c:* Heather, Megan, Steven; *ed:* (BS) Elem Ed, Univ of Findlay 1977; Grad Stud BGSU; *cr:* 1st Grade Teacher 1977-78, 2nd Grade Teacher 1978-83, 1987-88, 3rd Grade Teacher 1986- Jacobs Elem Sch; *ai:* Findlay HS Jr Var Girls Bsktbl Coach 1977-79; Karate Instr; Whos Who Among Amer Coll Stus; Univ of Findlay Scholar/Athlete Awd 1977; *home:* 1317 Shady Ln Findlay OH 45840

LOWID, JOSEPH K., 6th Grade Science Teacher; *b:* Pennsgrove, NJ; *m:* Kathleen; *c:* Millsisa, Elena; *ed:* (BA) Elem Ed, Univ of KY 1966; (MA) Advanced Elem Ed, Glassboro St 1972; Various Courses in Sci Teaching, Cmptrs, Drug Ed; *cr:* 6th Grade Teacher Elkton Mid 1966-69, Pennsville Dist 1969-; *ai:* Pennsville HS Jr Var Bsktbl Coach 1979-81; Servicemens Club, Moose Club; *home:* 28 Penn Beach Dr Pennsville NJ 08070

LOWMAN, KAREN MONTGOMERY, 7th Grade Science Teacher; *b:* Beaver Falls, PA; *m:* Lon Edward; *ed:* (BS) Bio Ed, Indiana Univ of PA 1979; Masters Equivalent Sci Ed, PA Dept of Ed 1989; *cr:* Sci & Gifted Teacher Indiana Area HS 1979-; *ai:* Astronomy-Aviation-Aerospace Club Adv; Gray Matter Team Coach; Teacher Induction Comm; IN Univ of PA Teacher Ed Coord Cncl; PA Sci Teachers Assn, NSTA, Phi Delta Kappa; PA St Ed Assn, NEA; Penelec Educl Advisory Bd Secy 1988-; *office:* Indiana Area Jr HS 245 N 5th St Indiana PA 15701

LOWRANCE, YVONNE MATHIASKO, Assistant Principal; *b:* Stockholm, Sweden; *ed:* (BA) Eng, Univ of CA Davis 1970; (MA) Ed, CA St Univ San Bernardino 1978; Grad Stud Ed; *cr:* Teacher 1971-88, Asst Prin 1988- Preston Elem; *ai:* Site Budget & Citizenship Comm; Dist Outdoor Ed Comm; CA St Univ Ed Alumni Comm Chairperson, Schlshp Comm 1981-; Alpha Delta Kappa Schlsp Comm 1980-; ACSA 1988-; REA, CTA, NEA Mem 1971-88; PTA 1988 Honorary Awd 1981, Schlsp 1976; Inland Empire Cncl for Soc Stud Mem 1974-81; CTIIP Grants 1985, 1987; Recognition Rialto Schls 1986; Rialto Chamber of Commerce Services Ed Awd 1985; PTA Honorary Awd 1981; PTA Schlsp Recipient 1976; *office:* Preston Elem Sch 1750 N Willow Rialto CA 92376

LOWREY, BOBBY WAYNE, Science Department Chairperson; *b:* Booneville, MS; *m:* Peggy Elaine Robertson; *c:* Dena Marie, Kelly Ann, Amy Carol; *ed:* (BS) Bio/General Sci, MS St Univ 1972; Graduate Hours MS St; Univ of MS; *cr:* Teacher & Coach Booneville HS 1973-77, Iuka HS 1977-; *ai:* Sci Club Spon; Jr Class Spon; Tennis Coach; Curr Comm; MS Assn of Educators 1973-; Natl Assn of Educators 1973-; Bass Anglers Sportsmen Society 1976-; Tri-St Bassmasters Pres 1981-82 & 1989-; Star Teacher Awd; Outstanding Teacher Awd Iuka Sch Dist 1987-88; *office:* Iuka H S 507 W Quitman St Iuka MS 38852

LOWREY, SANDRA SERAPHINE, 7th/8th Grade English Teacher; *b:* Denver, CO; *m:* Jack O.; *c:* Clay, Wade; *ed:* (BA) His/Elem Ed, W St Coll 1965; (MED) Rdng Specialist, TWU Denton 1980; *cr:* 3rd/4th Grade Teacher Colorado Springs CO 1965-68; 6th Grade Teacher Midlothian TX 1968-69; 4th-6th Grade Teacher Dallas TX 1969-73; 6th Grade Teacher Red Oak TX 1974-85; 7th Grade Teacher Melissa TX 1986-87; 3rd/7th/8th Grade Teacher Trenton TX 1987-; *ai:* ATPE 1973-; Teacher of Yr Red Oak TX 1980, 1982; *office:* Trenton HS Box 5 Trenton TX 75490

LOWRIE, MYRNA WALLACE, 1st Grade Teacher; *b:* Wakefield, MS; *m:* Bobby F.; *c:* Michelle A., Guyla S.; *ed:* (BA) Elem Educ, Mil 1958; (ME) Elem Educ, Univ MS 1961; *cr:* 1st Grade Teacher Denver CO 1958-60; 1st/3rd Grade Teacher Shelby Cty 1962-70; 1st Grade Teacher Hillcrest Acad 1971-73; 1st/3rd Grade Teacher Magnolia Heights 1973-; *home:* Rt 4 Box 105 Coldwater MS 38618

LOWRY, LOIS CHARLES, Kindergarten Teacher; *b:* St Martinville, LA; *m:* Eugene; *c:* Lydia, Kevon, Kelly; *ed:* (MS) Housing, OK St 1964; (BS) Housing/Interior Design, Southern Univ 1961; Post Masters Studies Housing City Planning Cornell Univ 1967-1968; *cr:* Jr Exec Trainee Macys 1961-62; Research Fellow OK St Univ 1962-64; Asst Prof-Plattsburgh St Univ 1964-67; Cornell Univ 1967-68; Classroom Teacher CNUSD 1968-; *ai:* Kndgtn Connections Facltr Univ of CA Riverside; Awds Comm Highland Sch; His Day Comm CNUSD; Omicron Nu Sec 1965-66; CA Early Chldhd Assn; Assoc of Housing Educators; Corona-Norco Teachers Assn; CA Teachers Assn; Natl Ed Assn; CA Elem Ed Assn; Assn of Housing Ed; Sch Site Cncl 1980-82; PTA Bd 1985-87; St Matthews Church Parish Cncl 1987-89; Research Fellowship Cornell Univ; Master Teacher Corona Norco Schls; Corona-Norco Unified Schls Math Grant; *office:* Highland Elem Sch 2301 Alhambra St Norco CA 91760

LOWRY, MARILYN DENHAM, Jr HS Speech/English Teacher; *b:* Tulsa, OK; *m:* David P.; *c:* Cody; *ed:* (BA) Voc Home Ec/Speech/Eng, Univ of OK 1970; *cr:* Jr HS Sci Teacher Sapulpa OK 1970-71; Eng/Speech Teacher Mounds OK 1971-74, Kellyville OK 1979-; *ai:* Drug Free Cmmty Bd; Dept Head Jr HS Eng; KCTA; Teacher of Yr 1988; *office:* Kellyville Jr HS P O Box 99 Kellyville OK 74039

LOWRY, MICHAEL LOUIS, Social Studies Teacher; *b:* Maryville, TN; *m:* Janet L Henson; *c:* Mia; *ed:* (BS) Soc Sci, TN Wesleyan Coll 1975; Univ of TN Knoxville; *cr:* Teacher Vonore HS 1975-; *ai:* Stu Taking a Right Stand Public Relations Chm; Governors Study Partner Prgm & Stu Cncl Spon; Monroe Cty Ed Assn, TN Ed Assn, NEA 1975-; Ft Loudoun Assn Bd of Dir 1989-; Monroe Cty Teacher of Yr 1988-89; *office:* Vonore HS Box 219 Hwy 411 Vonore TN 37885

LOWRY, PAMELA TUCKER, 8th Grade Teacher; *b:* Winston Salem, NC; *m:* Ken; *c:* Brad; *ed:* (BA) Eng, Limestone Coll 1968; *cr:* Eng Teacher Blacksburg HS 1968-70; 5th Grade Teacher St Annes Sch 1970-71; 8th Grade Teacher Hiddenite Sch 1971-72, New Hope Sch 1978-81; 10th-12th Grade Eng Teacher Rustburg HS 1981-83; 6th-8th Grade Teacher Aycock Mid Sch 1983-; *ai:* Stu Cncl Spon; NC Assn of Educators; Lay Teacher of Yr 1980; Ben L Smith Teacher of Yr 1986; Article Published; *office:* Aycock Mid Sch 811 Cypress St Greensboro NC 27405

LOWRY, SUSAN SCHAFFNER, English Teacher; *b:* Hudson, MI; *m:* Jeff; *c:* Katherine; *ed:* (BS) Eng Ed, 1978, (MA) Eng Ed, 1987 OH St; *cr:* Eng Teacher Pettisville HS 1978-79, Fairbanks HS 1981-; *ai:* NHS Adv; Vlybl Coach; Play Dir; Teacher of Yr; *office:* Fairbanks HS 11158 St Rt 38 Milford Center OH 43045

LOWY, RITA LANDWEBER, Mathematics Teacher; *b:* Brooklyn, NY; *m:* Robert; *c:* Dana, Allison; *ed:* (BA) Math, Queens Coll CUNY 1969; (MS) Math, Adelphi Univ 1971; *cr:* Math Teacher Roslyn HS 1969-71, Tappan Zee HS 1971-72, Newport HS 1983-; 9-12 Curr Specialist Bellevue Public Schls 1987-89; *ai:* Natural Helpers Coord; Faculty Senate; Century 21 Comm; NCTM 1969-; ASCD; Puget Sound Math Teachers Cncl; Bellevue Sch Dist Math Advisory Cncl; Natl Sci Fnd Grant for Completion of Masters Degree; *office:* Newport H S 4333 128th Ave SE Bellevue WA 98006

LOXLEY, KATHRYN HARLEMAN, 5th Grade Teacher; *b:* Darke, OH; *m:* O. B.; *c:* Connie Wharton, Ted, Cheryl, Carolyn Hanks; *ed:* (BS) Elem, OH Univ 1962; Rdng, Morehead St 1986; Ec/Environmental Ed, OH St 1986-88; *cr:* 5th Grade Teacher Milton 1958-64; 4th Grade Teacher 1964-89, 5th Grade Teacher 1989- Kinnison Sch; *ai:* Jackson HS Future Teacher Adv; NEA; OEA (Commissioned TEPS, Human Relations 1978-87) 1986; Jackson City Ed Assn Pres 1980-81; Jackson Chrstn Church (Elder, Sunday Sch Teacher); Nom St Teacher of Yr; Soc Stud Teacher of Yr; Human Relations Gov Arbor Day Awd; Regional Conservation Teacher of Yr; Ec Teacher of Yr; Life Long Environmental Teacher of Yr.

LOY, DELILA VICKERY, 2nd Grade Teacher; *b:* Seminole, OK; *m:* Gerald; *c:* Lajuana Twa, Lisa Burrows, Steve; *ed:* (BS) Home Ec/Elem Ed, E Cntrl Univ 1956; Grad Work Elem Ed, Prof Wkshps; *cr:* 5th Grade/Home Ec Teacher Excelsior 1956-58; 2nd Grade Teacher Eugene Field Elem 1965-; *ai:* Staff Dev Comm; NEA, OEA 1956-; McAct Building Rep 1965-; PTA, Victory Park Baptist Church 1965-; Valley Forge Freedom Fnd Awd; Natl Sci Fnd Environmental Study Grant; Project Wild Study Grant; *office:* Eugene Field Elem A & Walker Mc Alester OK 74501

LOY, LINDA MANN, Lang Art Demonstration Teacher; *b:* Burlington, NC; *m:* Dennis Kirk; *c:* Kevin Kirkpatrick, James Kirkpatrick; *ed:* (AB/BS) Span/Eng, E Carolina 1962; (MED) Gifted & Talented Ed 1985, (CAS) Supervision, 1989 Univ NC Greensboro; Enhancing Stu Thinking Through Collaborative Teaching Strategies, Cooperative Learning, Natl Trng Center; Cadre Teacher, Mentor/Support Team Trng NC St Dept; *cr:* Teacher Burlington City Schls 1962-68; Consultant Encyclopaedia 1966-68; Teacher Alamance Comm Coll 1974-80; Teacher/Supvr Alamance Cty Schls 1979-; *ai:* Sch Based Leadership Team; Delta Kappa Gamma 1st VP 1990-91; NC Eng Teachers Assn, Natl Cncl of Teachers of Eng 1979-; Assn for Supervision & Curr Dev 1985-; Burlington Shrinettes Pres 1970; Garden Club Pres 1966; Excl in Teaching Awd 1980-81, 1983-84; E Alamance Teacher of Yr 1988-89; *office:* Alamance Cty Schls PO Box 358 Graham NC 27253

LOY, SUSAN GUENTHER, Mathematics Teacher; *b:* Ann Arbor, MI; *m:* Darell; *c:* Justin, Katherine; *ed:* (BA) Math, Univ of MI 1970; (MA) Scndry Teaching, E MI Univ 1978; *cr:* Teacher Summerfield HS 1970-; *ai:* Class Adv; NCTM, MI Cncl Teachers of Math; Teacher of Yr 1987-88; *office:* Summerfield HS 17555 Ida West Rd Petersburg MI 49270

LOYA, EUGENE S., Latin/English Teacher; *b:* Portage, PA; *m:* Nikolette E. Medvigy; *c:* Victor, Peter, Alex, Gregory; *ed:* (BED) Foreign Lang/Eng, 1959, (MED,) Scndry, 1973 Duquesne Univ; Specialist Counseling, 1972; *cr:* Naval Aviator US Navy 1960-71; Teacher Steel Valley HS 1972-73, Hempfield Sr HS 1973-; *ai:* Latin Club Spon; Hempfield Enrichment Prgm Coord for Gifted Students; Homebound Instr; Private Industry Cncl Instr; PSEA, NEA 1973-; Knights of Columbus Chancellor 1988-89; St Nicholas Church Trustee 1985-; ARC Coord 1986-87; Hempfield Area Sch Dist Coord; Keep America Beautiful Campaign PENNDOT Coord; *office:* Hempfield Sr HS Greensburg PA 15601

LOYD, LINDA LONG, Third Grade Teacher; *b:* Dalton, GA; *m:* Frank R.; *c:* Benjamin C., Rachel M.; *ed:* (BS) Early Chldhd Ed, West GA Coll 1971; (MED) Early Chldhd Ed, Brenau Coll 1982; (ED SP) Early Chldhd Ed, West GA Coll 1987; *cr:* 1st Grade Teacher Dug Gap Elem 1971-72; 1st Grade Teacher 1972-81, 3rd Grade Teacher 1982- Chatsworth Elem; *ai:* Lead Teacher for 3rd Grade 1988-; Delta Kappa Gamma Secy 1986-88; Murray Assn of Ed; Building Rep 1988-; Gideon Auxiliary Pres 1988-; Womens Missionary Union Secy 1981-; *home:* P O Box 454 Chatsworth GA 30705

LOYD, RONDALD, Teacher/Department Head; *m:* Weslee Rose Sarment; *c:* Eric R., Amber R.; *ed:* (BA) Art/Phys Ed, CA St Univ Sacramento 1965; CA St Univ Fresno; Univ of CA San Luis Obispo; Chapman Coll; *cr:* Stu Asst Coach Sacramento St Univ 1964; Teacher/Coach/Dept Head Mt Whitney HS 1965-; *ai:* Stu Against Substance Abuse Club, Crafts Club, Sr Class Adv; Head Ftbl, Wrestling, Track Coach; Asst Fine Arts Dept Head; Visalia Unified Teachers Assn, CA Teachers Assn; NEA; Parent, Teachers, Stu Assn; CA Art Ed Assn; Tulare Cty Art League Officer; Tulare Cty Regional Arts Cncl; Developed/Taught Art Nite Class for Gifted Stu; Articulation Bd for Arts Pres; *office:* Mount Whitney HS 900 S Conyer St Visalia CA 93277

LOZANO, ROBERT CATANO, Assistant Principal; *b:* Artesia, CA; *m:* Marla; *c:* Autumn, Brittney; *ed:* (BS) Elem Chrstn Ed, Johnson Bible Coll 1980; (BS) Elem Ed, Univ of TN 1980; (MS) Educl Admin, CA St Univ Fullerton 1988; Ed, Oxford Grad Sch; *cr:* 6th Grade Teacher Inglewood Chrstn Sch 1980-81; Adult Instr Riverside Chrstn Life Sch 1981-82; 6th Grade Teacher 1982-84, Asst Prin 1984- Eastside Chrstn Schls; *ai:* Amer Assn of Bible Colls, Delta Epsilon Chi 1980; *office:* Eastside Chrstn Schls 9300 Middlebrook Pike Knoxville TN 37921

LUBARSKY, MARILYN E., Social Studies Teacher; *b:* Los Angeles, CA; *ed:* (BA) His, Scripps Coll 1974; (JD) Law, Univ of Santa Clara 1974; CA Teaching Credential Cal Poly; Taft Seminar for Teachers 1989; Acultural His of Modern Mid E, A Natl Endowment for Hum Summer Inst Fordham Univ 1990; *cr:* Soc Stud Teacher Upland HS 1987-; Soc Stud Mentor Teacher Upland Unified Sch Dist 1990; *ai:* Mock Trial Team Coach; Soph Class Adv; NHS Faculty Advisory Bd; Gifted & Talented Ed Task Force; Baldy Vista Cncl of Soc Stud Legislative Liason 1990-; NCSS, CA Cncl of Soc Stud; CA Cncl on Soc Stud Conference Presenter 1989-90; NCSS Conference Presenter 1990; *office:* Upland HS 565 W 11th St Upland CA 91786

LUBERT, ROSE ANGELA (MORAN), Fourth Grade Teacher; *b:* Orlando, WV; *m:* John R.; *ed:* (BA) Elem Ed, Fairmont St Coll 1962; Classes at Kent St Univ & Youngstown St Univ; *cr:* 4th Grade Teacher 1962-74; 5th Grade Teacher 1974-77; 4th Grade Teacher 1977- Mc Kinley Elem Sch; *ai:* Golf Leagues-Monday Church Leag-Pres & Treas; Tuesday Ladies Leag-Pres & Handicap Chm; Wednesday Hi Hopes Leag-Handicap Chm; Thursday Pro Dubbers Leag-Pres & Handicap Chm; Sunday Couples Leag-Pres & Handicap Chm; Bowling Leagues-Monday Couples Leag; Friday Couples Leag; Sunday Mixed Leag-Sgt of Arms; Show West Highland White Terriers; Delta Zeta Natl Sorority Alum Chapt Silver Awd 25 Yrs Membership; Sec; Membership Chm 1974-82 Warren Fed of Teachers; Mem 1962-74/1982- Warren Edu Assn; Mem 1962-74/1982- OH Ed Assn; NEA Mem 1962-74/1982-; North Eastern OH Teachers Assn Mem 1962-74/1982-; Nom Natl Teacher of Yr-1989; Trumbull Memorial Hosp Volunteer Svc Trophy 1989; American Cancer Society Volunteer; March of Dimes Volunteer Sunday Sch Teacher; Mem Church Choir; Church Soloist; Scripture Reader; Mem Church Parish Cncl; Renew Grp Ldr/Speaker; Bike a Thon for Needy Volunteer; Hearing Society Volunteer; Summer Playground Ldr; Bingo Worker; Eucharistic Minister;Summer Golf Teacher; Teacher Training Conducted: Assertive Discipline (Lee Canter) Wkshps; Handmade Games Wkshp;Individualized Rdng Wkshp; Devlpd Hndbk for Parents; Taught Cmptr Course to Parents; Tutored; Devlpd Sch Newspaper; Summer Sch Math Teacher; Unit C Coord; Stu Cncl; Aided in Adoption of Sch Motivation Prgm; Started Spelling Bees; Textbook Comm; New Teacher Buddy; Helped Teachers Org Run Bargining Election; Handled Corres & Membership for Ed Assn; *office:* Mc Kinley Elem Sch 1321 Elm Rd NE Warren OH 44483

LUCA, MARY KAY MINEHART, ASWAS Teacher; *b:* Clarksburg, WV; *c:* Robert J., Christopher T.; *ed:* (BA) Eng/Speech/Drama, Fairmont St Coll 1971; Pastoral Counseling, St of MD; *cr:* Headstart Teacher/Coord WV Headstart Pgrm 1970-71; 6th Grade Teacher Monongalia Cty 1971-72; Eng Teacher Pikesville Baltimore Cty 1972-76; Home/Hospital Teacher Baltimore Cty 1976-85; *ai:* Cmmty Service Comm; Wrote Curr & Made Film; *home:* 9 Bright Star Ct Baltimore MD 21206

LUCARELLI, DIANNE KAPANAK, Business Teacher; *b:* Braddock, PA; *m:* Angelo M.; *c:* David M., Joni T.; *ed:* (BS) Bus Ed, 1982, (MS) Bus Ed, 1985 Indiana Univ of PA; *cr:* Secy US Steel Corp 1966-69; Exec Secy Westmoreland Cty Comm Coll 1977-80; Bus Teacher Yough HS 1982-; *ai:* FBLA Spon; PA Bus Ed Assn; Tri-St Bus Ed Assn; Delta Pi Epsilon Secy 1986-87; *office:* Yough HS 99 Lowber Rd Herminie PA 15637

LUCAS, ALICE R., History/English Teacher; *b:* Indianapolis, IN; *c:* James B., Stacey A., Joseph A.; *ed:* (BS) Journalism, Butler Univ 1950; Teaching Credential Trng San Francisco St Univ; Lang Dev Specialist, San Francisco Unified Schls; *cr:* Teacher San Francisco Unified Sch Dist 1968-; *ai:* Cambodian Club & Multi-Cultural Fair Spon; NCSS, CCSS 1980-; SFCSS (Pres 1990-) 1980-; CATESOL; San Francisco Ed Fund Grants 1986, 1987; Zellerbach Family Fund Grant 1989, 1990; Published Bi-ling Folktales; *home:* 75 Carl St San Francisco CA 94117

LUCAS, BARBARA LOGAN, Third Grade Teacher; *b:* Washington, DC; *m:* Joseph H.; *ed:* (BS) Elem Ed, D C Teachers Coll 1958; (Masters) Child & Curr Elem Ed, Columbia Univ 1965; Post Masters Studies Amer Univ; MD Univ; Trinity Coll; *cr:* Teacher Buchanan Elem Sch 1958-78; Watkins Elem Sch 1978-86; Peabody Elem Sch 1986-87; Capital Hill Cluster Sch 1987-89; *ai:* NEA 1959-63; WA Teachers Union 1964-89; Outstanding Service Awd Research Club 1975; Watkins Sch 1980; Outstanding Teacher of the Yr Awd Peabody Sch 1987; Superintendents Perfect Attendance Awd 1987-89.

LUCAS, BERNIE A., JR., Fourth Grade Teacher; *b:* Bangor, ME; *m:* Catherine M. Goodwin; *ed:* (BS) Elem Ed, Univ of ME Presque Isle 1975; (MED) Ed, Univ of ME Orono 1980; *cr:* 4th Grade Teacher Helen Hunt 1975-80; 4th/5th Grade Teacher Lewis-Stairs 1980-83; 3rd/4th Grade Teacher Herbert Gray 1983-84; 4th Grade Teacher Helen Hunt 1984-; *ai:* Cooperating Teacher for Stu Teachers; Prof Preparation Team; Building Rep; Cmptr Instr Old Town Adult Ed Prgm; Old Town Math Curr Comm Mem; Old Town Teachers Assn, ME Teachers Assn, NEA 1975-; Phi Kappa Phi Honor Society 1981-; Contributor ME Studs Curr Project 1979, Instr & Teacher 1982, Teaching Tips from Kodak 1983; *office:* Helen Hunt Sch 47 S Brunswick St Old Town ME 04468

LUCAS, CAROLYN A., Chemistry Teacher; *b:* LaPorte, IN; *ed:* (BS) Chem, 1969, (MS) Chem, 1970 Purdue Univ; Grad Stud Sci Ed & Chem; *cr:* Chem/Math Teacher Winamac Cmmty HS 1970-77; Chem Instr Purdue Univ 1977-81; Chem Teacher Yorktown HS 1981-; *ai:* Super Bowl Academic Coach for Sci; NSTA, Hoosier Assn of Sci Teachers Inc, Amer Chemical Society, IN Alliance of Chem Teachers Inc; Delta Kappa Gamma Pres 1988-; Woodrow Wilson Dreyfus Inst at Princeton 1986; Hope Coll Inst for Teachers of AP & Honors Chem 1987; Outstanding Teachers Rose Hulman Inst of Technology 1989; *office:* Yorktown HS 700 E Smith St Yorktown IN 47396

LUCAS, CLIFFORD JOSEPH, Mathematics Dept Chairman; *b:* Alexandria, LA; *m:* Betty L. Bruce; *c:* Bradley P., Brandan J., Brittany L.; *ed:* (BS) Math, 1967, (MS) Math/Ed, 1974 Northwestern St; *cr:* Math/Algebra I & II Teacher Buckeye HS 1970-; *ai:* Beta Club Spon; *home:* 114 Hilton Ct Pineville LA 71360

LUCAS, DOROTHY, Eighth Grade Reading Teacher; *b:* Cordele, GA; *ed:* (BS) Textiles/Clothing, Savannah St Coll 1973; (MED) Elem Ed, GA St Univ 1976; Data Collector; *cr:* Lang Art/Math Teacher A S Clark Mid Sch 1977-; *ai:* ASCD 1990; Natl Mid Sch Assn 1987-89; La Carte Club; Teacher of Yr 1987-88; PTSA VP 1987-88; *office:* A S Clark Mid Sch 401 N 15th St Cordele GA 31015

LUCAS, JEANETTE LOWE, First Grade Teacher; *b:* Newton, MS; *m:* Jerry; *c:* Jerrell K., Jeffrey K., Jane Lucas Givens; *ed:* (BS) Elem Ed, Univ of S MS 1957; (MS) Elem Ed, MS Coll 1983; Grad Stud Spec Ed; Working Towards Specialist Degree; *cr:* Elem Teacher 1960-61, 1962-64, Spec Ed Teacher 1964-66, Rdng Specialist 1966-67 Franklin Cty Schls; Spec Ed Teacher G B Cooley Home for Mentally Retarded 1967-68, Quachita Parish Schls 1968-69; Elem Teacher Centreville Acad 1969-70, Franklin Cty Chrstn Acad 1970-71, Brookhaven Acad 1971-; *ai:* Kndgtn & Elem Sch Curr Supvr; MS Private Sch Educl Assn St Chm of Gifted Ed; Daughters of Amer Revolution, Parent Teacher League.

LUCAS, MARIE DAWN, Math Teacher; *b:* West Hamlin, WV; *ed:* (BA) Bus Ed/Math 1978, (MA) Scndry Ed/Mid Chldhd Ed, 1985 Marshall Univ; *cr:* Math Teacher Harts Jr/Sr HS 1979-81, Chapmanville Jr HS 1981-; *ai:* Math Field Day Team Coach; NEA, WV Ed Assn 1979-; Logan Cty Ed Assn 1981-; *office:* Chapmanville Jr HS P O Box 309 Chapmanville WV 25508

LUCAS, MARSHA GAY, Science Dept Chairperson; *b:* Savannah, GA; *m:* Thomas V.; *c:* Jonathan, Jeremy, Sarah; *ed:* (BS) Chem - Sigma Cum Laude, Armstrong St Coll 1979; Sci Ed, Woodrow Wilson; Chem, Dryfus Inst 1983; *cr:* Chem/Phys Sci Teacher St Vincents 1979-80, Lynchburg Chrstn Acad 1980-87, Pathway Chrstn 1988-89; Chem/Physics/Adv Bio Teacher Calvary Baptist Day Sch 1989-; *ai:* Tennis Coach; Class Spon; NHS; GA Sci Teachers Assn; Baptist Church (Sunday Sch, Childrens Church, Youth Group); Participant in Woodrow Wilson Chem Wkshp; Teacher of Yr Lynchburg Chrstn Acad 1985-86; *office:* Calvary Baptist Day Sch 4625 Waters Ave Savannah GA 31404

LUCAS, PAUL LEROY, JR., Social Studies Teacher; *b:* Sanford, NC; *m:* Irene Vasquez; *c:* Paul-Joseph, Christopher; *ed:* (BS) His/Soc Stud, Appalachian St Univ 1975; *cr:* Soc Stud Teacher New Hanover HS 1975-76, Emsley A Laney HS 1976-; *ai:* Stu Cncl Assn Adv; Stu Activity Dir; Mentor & Mem Religion Comm; Mem Multicultural Ed/Black Stud Comm; Asst T-Ball Coach; Mem New Hanover Cty Graduation Celebration Comm, Sensitivity Today & Respect Tomorrow Advisory Bd; NCSS, NC Cncl Soc Stud, Cape Fear Cncl for Soc Stud, NC Assn of Educators, NEA Mem; Article Published 1989; Regional Recipient Governors Bus Awd Ed for Soc Stud 1987; Nom New Hanover Cty Teacher of Yr 1987; *office:* Emsley A Laney HS 2700 N College Rd Wilmington NC 28405

LUCAS, RANDY JOE, Mathematics Department Chm; *b:* Dumas, TX; *m:* Pamela Dianne Baxter; *c:* Randee R., Cody J.; *ed:* (BS) Math/Cmptr Sci, Cntrl St Univ 1982; Weapons & Weapons Systems Trng; Electronic Trng Navy; Cmptr Trng Various Wkshps; *cr:* Missle Technician US Navy 1972-76; Welder Oil Companies 1976-81; Cmptr Operator William E Davis Companies 1981-82; Teacher/Coach Jones HS 1983-; *ai:* Ftbl & Bsbl Coach & Asst; OEA 1985-; OK Coaches Assn 1983-; *home:* Box 513 Mc Loud OK 74851

LUCE, MARILYN CAROTHERS, Language Arts Teacher; *b:* Abilene, TX; *c:* Jerry R., Susan K.; *ed:* (BS) Eng, Angelo St Univ 1981; *cr:* Teachers Aide Snyder Ind Sch Dist 1973-76, Bellville Ind Sch Dist 1977-79; Teacher Schelicher Cty Ind Sch Dist 1981-82, Christoval Ind Sch Dist 1982-; *ai:* Frosh Class Spon; Literary Coach for Ready Writing; Impromtu Speaking; Oral Rdng Prose & Poetry; One Act Play Dir; TX St Teachers Assn 1989-; Christoval Mothers Club 1979-, Teacher of Yr 1983; *office:* Christoval Jr HS Box 162 Christoval TX 76935

LUCE, REBA D., Mathematics Teacher/Dept Head; *b:* Lamesa, TX; *m:* Jack R.; *c:* Russ Lovejoy, Ella R. Bishop; *ed:* (BA) Ed, E NM Univ Portales 1974; (MED) Ed, E NM Univ 1977; Re-Learning Conference 1989-; *cr:* Math Teacher Highland Jr HS 1974-75; Elem Teacher Three Way Schls 1975-81; Elem Teacher 1982-84, Scndry Math Teacher 1985-, Math Dept Chairperson 1989- Tatum Municipal Sch; *ai:* Jr Class Spon; Phi Kappa Phi 1974; Tatum Schls Coalition of Essential Schls & Re-Learning Pilot Project.

LUCE, WILLIAM OLIVER, History Teacher; *b:* St Joseph, MO; *m:* Sharon Rose Shadduck; *c:* Tamela M.; *ed:* (BSED) Soc Sci, 1971, (MA) His, 1974 NW MO St; Applied Ec; 19th Century Europe; Improving Listening in Classroom; *cr:* His Teacher Hamilton R-II 1972-76, Savannah R-III 1976-; Cmmty Ed Dir Savannah R-III 1987-; *ai:* Soc Stud Club; Brain Bowl Coach; Tournament Dir Savannah Quiz Bowl; Class Spon; Curr Comm; Past Chm of Sch Improvement Comm; Cmmty Teachers Assn VP 1975-76; Savannah Ed Assn (VP 1980-81, Pres 1981-82, Treas 1979-80); Academic Quiz Bowl Natl Title Coach Citation St of MO; *home:* 3301 N 7th St Saint Joseph MO 64505

LUCERO, A. EUGENE, 5th Grade Teacher; *b:* Tucumcari, NM; *m:* Gloria M. Pacheco; *c:* Pete M. Serna, Eugene E., Eugena M.; *ed:* (BS) Elem Ed Univ of NM 1970; *cr:* 3rd Grade Teacher 1970-1972; 5th Grade Teacher 1972- John Baker Elem Sch; *ai:* Lulac 8020; Sons of Amer Legion; *office:* John Baker Elem Sch 12015 Tivoli Ave Ne Albuquerque NM 87111

LUCERO, CONNIE T., 2nd Grade Teacher; *b:* Las Vegas, NM; *m:* Abel; *c:* Ron; *ed:* (BA) Elem Ed, 1971, (MA) Rdng/Eng, 1972 Highlands Univ; Cmptr Sci Open Classroom Concepts, Scientific Systematic Approaches to Learning; *cr:* Teacher St Dept of Ed 1971, Highlands Univ 1972, W Las Vegas Schls 1990; *ai:* Class Spon; Homecoming Parade, Sch Act Chairperson; AFT Mem 1985-, Mem in Good Standing Awd 1988; Alpha Delta Kappa Pres 1980-85, Prof Awd 1985; Jr Rough Riders Drill Leader 1979-85, Buckles Cert 1980-83; Weight Watchers Leader Lecturer 1980-, Cert 1989; Aerobics Leader 1988-, Cert 1988; Various Research; *home:* 745 Lee Dr Las Vegas NM 87701

LUCERO, EDUARDO E., 5th Grade Teacher; *b:* Anton Chico, NM; *m:* Emily Peralta Lucero; *c:* Alexandra, Jacqueline, Joseph; *ed:* (BA) Elem Ed, NM Highlands Univ 1975; *cr:* 5th/8th Grade Teacher Santa Rosa Consolidated Sch 1975-; *ai:* Coaching-8th Grade Bsktbl; *office:* Anton Chico Elem School Gen Del Anton Chico NM 87711

LUCERO, MELVIN O., Assistant Principal; *b:* Alamosa, CO; *m:* Evelyn; *c:* Leigh A., Melanie, Steven, David; *ed:* (BA) Chem, 1966, (MA) Scndry Ed, 1967 Adams St Coll; NSF Inst Univ of CA Berkley 1969, Univ of N CO 1970; *cr:* Sci Teacher Centauri HS 1966-67, Windsor HS 1967-70, Palmer HS 1970-75; Admin/Sci Teacher Doherty HS 1975-88; Sci Teacher Coronado HS 1988-89; Asst Prin Wasson HS 1989-; *ai:* Sch Climate Cncl; Phi Delta Kappa 1966-, Pikes Peak Educator of Yr 1988; ASCD 1988-; CO Assn of Sch Execs 1984-; CO Outstanding Young Educator 1969; *office:* Wasson HS 2115 Afton St Colorado Springs CO 80909

LUCHONOK, REGINA MARIE (GATTO), Second Grade Teacher; *b:* Carbondale, PA; *m:* Nicholas; *c:* Lindsey; *ed:* (BA) Elem Ed/Chldhd Ed, Bloomsburg Univ 1982; Working Towards Masters Elem Ed; *cr:* 5th/6th Grade Sci Teacher 1983-88, 2nd Grade Teacher 1988- Fell Elem; *office:* Fell Elem Sch John St Simpson PA 18407

LUCHT, KATHLEEN A., Gymnastics Coach; *b:* Cleveland, OH; *m:* Roy A.; *c:* Heidi K., Holly K.; *ed:* (BS) Elem Ed, Kent St Univ 1968; (MS) Elem Ed Rdng, Old Dominion Univ 1970; Regional Gymnastics Trng; *cr:* Elem Teacher Gadsden Cty 1968-69, Hampton VA Schls 1969-70, Ithaca NY Schls 1971-75, Los Alamos NM Schls 1975-79; Gymnastics Coach Los Alamos Sch of Gymnastics 1984-; *ai:* Ballet & Tap Dance Instr; Ithaca Teachers Assn Sch Rep 1973-75; Natl Assn of Women Gymnastics Judges 1989-; Most Influential Teacher Rotary Club; Stu of Month 1989; *home:* 90 Loma Del Escolar Los Alamos NM 87544

LUCIA, GEOFFREY ALLEN, Mathematics Teacher; *b:* Copenhagen, NY; *m:* Sally Jarasek; *ed:* (BA) Math Ed, Niagara Univ 1977; (MAT) Math Ed, Univ of Chicago 1978; Numerous Conferences & Wkshps Advanced Placement Calculus; *cr:* Math Teacher/Coach/Dorm Head Western Reserve Acad 1978-85; Math Teacher/Coach Providence Day Sch 1985-; *ai:* Math Club; Sr Class Asst; SAT Review; PPS Summer Sch Prgm; Var Bsbl Asst Coach; Athletic Dept Comm; NCTM 1978-; NC Cncl Teachers of Math 1985-; Charlotte Choral Society Bd of Dirs 1985-; Advanced Placement Calculus Exams Reader; *office:* Providence Day Sch 5800 Sardis Rd Charlotte NC 28226

LUCKETT, LILLIAN HODGES, Kindergarten Teacher; *b:* Monesson, PA; *m:* Malvone Woodrow; *c:* Kevin; *ed:* (BA) Home Ec, VA St Coll 1947; (MED) Penn St 1957; Cert James Madison Univ; Univ VA & Univ of R; *cr:* Home Ec/Health/Phys Ed/Eng IV Teacher Rosenwald HS 1947-65; Kndgtn Teacher Wayne Hills-Wenonah, Shenandoah Heights, Kate Collins 1966-89; *ai:* WEA, VEA, NEA; *home:* 424 Smith Waynesboro VA 22980

LUCKEY, JEANIE HUGO, Social Studies Teacher; *b:* Centralia, IL; *m:* James M.; *c:* Craig R., Jay D.; *ed:* (BS) Geography/Poly Sci, 1971, (MSED) Instructional Materials/Curr, 1972 Southern IL Univ Carbondale; Chemical Intervention Awareness Trng; Cooperative Learning Trainer of Teachers; *cr:* Librarian/Dir of Stu Act Downers Grove Cmmty HS South 1972-80; Teacher/Dept Chairperson Raymond Cree Mid Sch 1985-; *ai:* CA His Day Competition Coach & Cty Winners 1986-89; Odyssey of Mind Coach & Regional Winner 1988; Coord Natl Geography Bee; Chm Palm Springs Dist Curr Cncl; Sch Site Cncl; Cooperative Learning Trainer of Teachers Staff Dev; NCSS, NCTE, ASCD, NEA, CA Teachers Ed Assn; Delta Kappa Gamma Intnl 1986-; Lyceum of Desert 1985-; Palm Springs Unified Sch Dist Mentor Teacher & Teacher of Yr 1989-; Raymond Cree Mid Sch Teacher of Yr 1985-86, 1989-; Daughters of Amer Revolution Cahvilla Valley Soc Stud Teacher of Yr 1987; *office:* Raymond Cree Mid Sch 1011 Vista Chino Palm Springs CA 92262

LUCKEY, MARY JEAN (SHANNON), 5th Grade Teacher; *b:* Cincinnati, OH; *m:* Thomas A.; *c:* Michael, David, Thomas, Nicholas, Mary J. Schablein, Jeffrey; *ed:* (BA) Liberal Arts, Marian Coll 1956; (MED) Admin/Supervision, Univ of Cincinnati 1968; *cr:* Teacher St Catharine Parish 1954-56; Teacher/Music Dir St Michael & St Bernadette 1958-60; Teacher St Aloysius 1960-63; Teacher/Music Dir St Christopher 1963-66; Teacher Fairview 1960-70, Cntrl Fairmount 1970-; *ai:* Awds & Stu Service Chairperson; Soc Stud Liaison; Clean Cincinnati Inc Sch Chairperson 1985-86, 1st Place For Elem Schls 1986; *office:* Cntrl Fairmount Elem Sch 2475 White St Cincinnati OH 45214

LUCKHARDT, ALICE KERSHAW, World Geography Teacher; *b:* Orlando, FL; *m:* Greg E.; *ed:* (AA) Ed, Miami-Dade Jr Coll 1970; (BS) Soc Sci Ed, FL St Univ 1972; Stud Williamsburg Va; Cmptr Scl at Martin Cty; *cr:* World Geography Teacher Stuart Mid Sch 1972-; *ai:* Grade Organizer for 7th Grade Incentative Trip; Local Effective Sch Comm Mem; Schls Sunshine Fund Chairperson; FL Cncl for Soc Stud Mem 1973-88, Teacher of Yr 1986; PTA Mem 1976-; Stuart Heritage Mem 1989-; Outstanding Soc Stud Teacher Mid Schls in Martin Cty 1986; Organized & Lead Mid Sch/HS Stus on European Tours 1977, 1983; Wrote Curr Guidelines FL Dept of Ed 1985; *office:* Stuart Mid Sch 575 Georgia Ave Stuart FL 34994

LUCZOWSKI, THOMAS ANDREW, 5th Grade Teacher; *b:* Buffalo, NY; *m:* Theresa Sovinski; *c:* Eric, Andrea; *ed:* (BS) Elem Ed, 1969, (MS) Elem Ed, 1973 St Univ Coll Buffalo; *cr:* 5th/6th Grade Teacher Buffalo Elem Schls 1969-; *ai:* CSIP Comm; AIDS Wkshp; Human Growth & Dev Coord; Oceanography Infusion of Lib Skills into Classroom; NYSTA, BTF, NEA; NCAAA (Boy Base Coord 1988-, Little League Coach 1981-89); Cheektowaga Hockey Mgr 1986-87, 1989-; *office:* Waterfront Sch 95 4th St Buffalo NY 14202

LUDES, ILDIKO TUNDE, Art Teacher/Fine Arts Chair; *b:* Nagyuarad, Hungary; *c:* Chryseis Blue, Margaret J.; *ed:* (BA) Art - Summa Cum Laude, Bowie St Univ 1980; *cr:* Art Instr Arthur Middleton Elem 1974-78; Restaurant Mgr Golden Bull 1981-86; Art Instr Queen Anne Sch 1986-; *ai:* Yrbk Adv; Studio Art Classes Teacher of Advanced Placement Art His & Hum; Foreign Travel Spon; Yoga Teacher; *office:* Queen Anne Sch 14111 Oak Grove Rd Upper Marlboro MD 20772

LUDLOW, DICK, Science Dept Chair; *b:* Portland, OR; *m:* Donald, Leslie;; *ed:* (AS) Bio, Snow Coll 1968; (BS) Biological Composite, UT St Univ 1970; Grad Stud Phys Sci; *cr:* Sci Teacher 1971-80, Sci Dept Head 1980- Hillcrest Jr HS; *office:* Hillcrest Jr HS 126 E 5300 S Murray UT 84107

LUDLUM, TED WARREN, American History Teacher; *b:* Chanute, KS; *m:* Vicki Lynn; *c:* Brandi, Sheri, Chase; *ed:* (BS) Journalism/Ed, KS St Univ 1977; Curr, Instruction, Counseling; *cr:* Journalism Teacher Norton HS 1977-78; Soc Stud Teacher/Coach Paxico Jr HS 1978-80; Amer His Teacher Junction City HS 1980-; *ai:* Co-Chm of N Cntrl Evaluation on Grading, Developing Criterion Reference Exams for Amer His Classes Comm Junction Cty HS; *office:* Junction City Sr HS 9th & Eisenhower Junction City KS 66441

LUDWICK, NANCY ANN, Fifth & Sixth Grade Teacher; *b:* Philippi, WV; *ed:* (ABED) Elem Ed, Fairmont St Coll 1975; Grad Stud WV Univ; Cmptr Classes; Lions Quest Trng; Prin Acad Follow-Up; *cr:* 4th Grade Teacher 1975-77, 4th/5th Grade Teacher 1977-78, 3rd/4th Grade Teacher 1978-80, 4th Grade Teacher 1980-81, 4th/5th Grade Teacher 1981-82, 5th Grade Teacher 1982-84, 4th/5th Grade Teacher 1984-85, 6th Grade Teacher 1985-87, 5th/6th Grade Teacher 1987- Haymond Elem Sch; *ai:* WV St Cert Appeals Bd; Cncl on Effective Schls; Benedum Project; Lang Art Camp Teacher WV Univ; Textbook Selection Comm; Task Force on Drug Abuse Advisory Cncl; Intnl Rdng Assn, WV St Rdng Cncl 1989-; Taylor Cty Rdng Cncl Pres 1986-; WV Ed Assn 1975-; Taylor Cty Ed Assn Past Secy 1975-; Amer Cancer Society VP 1988-; Taylor Cty League for Service 1975-78, Most Service Hrs; PTO 1975-; Grafton Blueville Church of Nazarene (Pianist, Jr Choir Dir, Church Bd Mem); Started 1st Sch Newspaper at Haymond Sch; *home:* Rt 3 Box 237 Grafton WV 26354

LUDWIG, EDMUND BRUCE, Biology/Physics Teacher; *b:* Cortland, NY; *m:* Marcia Clemens; *ed:* (BS) Bio, 1985, (MSED) Bio, 1989 SUNY Cortland; *cr:* Adjunct Instr Tompkins Cortland Comm Coll 1987, SUNY Cortland 1988; Bio/Physics Teacher De Ruyter Schls 1985-; *ai:* Girls Jr Var Vlybl & Bsktbl Coach 1986-88; SUNY Cortland Bio Club Pres 1984-85, Outstanding Contribution to Bio 1985; Natl Wild Turkey Fed 1990; SUNY Cortland NSF Grant in Physics 1989; Penn St NYSEG Grant in Nuclear Physics 1986; *office:* De Ruyter Central Sch 711 Railroad St De Ruyter NY 13052

LUDWIG, JANET E. (NIEBAUM), 2nd Grade Teacher; *b:* Fremont, NE; *m:* Raymond; *c:* John, Daniel; *ed:* (BS) Soc/Ed, Midland Coll; (MS) Elem Ed, Univ of NE Omaha; Grad Work Kearney St, Wayne St; *cr:* Rural Teacher Timpe Sch 1955-57; 1st Grade Teacher 1957-58, K-2nd Grade Teacher 1972- Arlington Elem; *ai:* Co-Founder Local NE Assn for Ed of Young Children; Arlington Ed Assn, NEA 1972; Amer Univ Assn 1976-80; Order of Eastern Star Worthy Matron 1954-; Friends of Arlington Public Lib Secy 1981-; *office:* Arlington Elem Sch Box K Arlington NE 68002

LUDWIG, SHERYL ANN, 7th/8th Grade Teacher; *b:* Mt Clemens, MI; *m:* H. Thomas; *c:* Tom, Paul, Melissa; *ed:* (BA) His/Eng, Univ of MI 1966; Numerous Wkshps & Conferences; *cr:* Teacher Mt Clemens Public Schls 1966-67, Dekalb Public Schls 1967-69, Sault Ste Marie Public Schls 1969-79, Big Rapids Public Schls 1980-; *ai:* Stu Cncl, NJHS, Memory Book Adv; Gifted & Talented Resource & Curr Comm; Eng Curr Comm; OM Coach; Sch Improvement Core Team; Big Rapids Figure Skating Club Secy 1987-; Confratute Grant; *office:* Big Rapids Mid Sch 215 North State Big Rapids MI 49307

LUDWIG, STEPHEN M., Secondary English Teacher; *b:* Oakley, KS; *m:* Deborah M. Sperry; *c:* Matthew B., Zachary M., Gregory E., Emily E.; *ed:* (BS) Lang Art, Univ of KS 1976; Adams St Coll; Univ of Northern CO; CO St Univ; Fort Hays St Univ; *cr:* Eng Teacher Marion HS 1976-77, Basehor HS 1977-81; Athletic Dir/Eng Teacher Sargent HS 1981-87; Salesman Century 21/Valley Realty 1987-88; Eng Teacher Phillipsburg HS 1988-; Composition Instr Colby Comm Coll 1989-; *ai:* Sr Class Adv; Curr Cncl & Prof Dev Cncl Mem; NCTE 1975-; KS Assn of Teachers of Eng 1990; ASCD 1988-; BSA (Instr/Badge) 1984; Cub Scouts Leader 1987-88; Parish Cncl Secy 1983-86; Dow Jones Newspaper Fund Fellowship; *office:* Phillipsburg Sch 410 S 7th Phillipsburg KS 67661

LUDWIG, WILLIAM CHARLES, III, English Teacher/Dept Chairman; *b:* Janesville, WI; *ed:* (BA) Eng/His, Northland Coll 1957; Bangor Theological Seminary; Western Univ; *cr:* Eng Instr Talas Amer Orta Okulu Talas Turkey 1957-61; Eng Teacher Erie HS 1961-; *ai:* Sr Spon; Honor Society Adv; NEA, IEA, ETA; Erie Lib Bd 1972-78, 1983-85, 1988-89; Amnesty Intnl; *office:* Erie HS 616 6th St Erie IL 61250

LUEBBERT, DIANNE KEY, English Teacher; *b:* Henderson, KY; *m:* Gary; *c:* Scott, Eric; *ed:* (BA) Eng, KY Wesleyan 1968; (MA) Scndry Ed, W KY Univ 1978; *cr:* Eng Teacher Apollo HS 1968-85, Henderson Cty Sr HS 1985-; *ai:* Teen Leadership Conference; NEA, KEA 1968-; HCEA 1985-; *office:* Henderson Cty Sr HS 2424 Zion Rd Henderson KY 42420

LUEHRING, TERRI HYNDMAN, Ath Dir/Social Studies Teacher; *b:* Jefferson, IA; *m:* Roger; *c:* Sara, Ryan; *ed:* (BA) His/Phys Ed, Westmar Coll1977; Graduate Classes Univ Northern IA; Quest Intnl; *cr:* HS Soc Stud Teacher Gladbrook Cmmty Schls 1977-87; Mid Sch Soc Stud Teacher 1987-, Ath Dir 1986- Gladbrook-Reinbeck Schls; *ai:* Athletic Dir; HS Girls Vlybl Coach; IA HS Athletic Dir Assn; ISEA Local Pres 1989-; *office:* Gladbrook-Reinbeck Comm Schls 307 Washington Gladbrook IA 50635

LUGO, JOSEPHINE REYES, Mentor-Resource Eng Teacher; *b:* Corona, CA; *m:* Gumersindo; *c:* Christopher, Charlotte, Matthew; *ed:* (BA) Eng, San Jose St 1961; Rdng & Cooperative Learning Teacher; Consultant San Jose St Writing Project; *cr:* Teacher Woodrow Wilson Jr HS 1961-65; Teacher/Soc Worker Epiphany Center 1965-72; Teacher San Jose Unified 1972-82, Part-Time Teacher West Valley Jr Coll 1974-76; Teacher Silver Creek HS 1989-; *ai:* Consultant Writing Project 1981-; Eastside Union HS Dist Eng Mentor 1988-89; Lang Art Mentor Teacher Silver Creek HS 1989-; Resource Teacher Cooperative Learning Eng & Math; Poetry & Philosophy Club Adv 1988-; Intnl Rdng Assn, NCTE, CA Rdng Assn, Santa Clara Cty Rdng Cncl; Teacher of Yr San Jose Unified 1965; Achievement Awd League of Amer & Mexican Women Recognition for Service & Devotion to Cmmty 1966; Certificate of Appreciation Faithful Service to Ed Cmmty 1981; Mentor Teacher Certificate Recognition & Commendation; *home:* 841 Willow Glen Way San Jose CA 95125

LUGO, ROBERT L., English Teacher; *b:* El Paso, TX; *m:* Rosa M. Guardado; *c:* Christopher, Nicholas, April R; *ed:* (BS) Eng/Span, Univ of TX 1975; Advanced Academic Trng; Eng; Assertive Discipline; Wrtng/Gifted & Talented; Psych of Sch Child; Classroom Man Anagement; Media; Cmptrs; Mid Sch Conf; *cr:* Eng Teacher Riverside HS 1976-83; Ysleta HS/Jr HS, Bel Air HS, Clint HS/Jr HS 1983-; *ai:* CYO San Lorenzo, Music Ministry St Pius Church; Clint Jr HS Tennis Coach 1989; UIL Spon Spelling, Dictionary Skills, Span Poetry, Choral Rdng; Santa Lucia Church Choir Dir 1972-76; *office:* Clint Jr HS Clint Ind Sch Dist PO Box 779 Clint TX 79836

LUISI, FRANK A., English Teacher/Football Coach; *b:* Astoria, NY; *m:* Francine; *c:* Oliver; *ed:* (BA) Eng/His, Univ of VT 1974; (MA) Psych/Ed, SUNY Stony Brook 1980; Certificate Sports Medicine Adelphia Univ; *cr:* Eng Teacher/Asst Ftbl Coach Bellport HS 1974-75; Eng Teacher/Asst Var Ftbl Coach Sochem HS 1975-86; Eng Teacher/Head Ftbl Coach Oceanside HS 1986-; *ai:* Dir Oceanside Weight Trng & Fitness Prgm; Selected Dean on Spec Assignment Oceanside to Combat Drug & Alcohol Problem; Nassau Cty HS Ftbl Coaches Assn Pres 1989-; Suffolk Cty HS Ftbl Coaches Assn VP 1980-86.

LUJAN, JAMES B., Athletic Director/Teacher; *b:* El Paso, TX; *c:* Frances; *ed:* (BS) Health/Phys Ed, 1978, (MED) Phys Ed, 1988 Sul Ross St Univ; TX Teacher Appraisal Trng; *cr:* Teacher/Coach Sierra Blanca Ind Sch Dist 1978-; *ai:* Athletic Dir/Coach; Sch Cnslr/Teacher; Eng as Second Land & Testing Coord; TX HS Coaches Assn 1978-88; Sierra Blanca Ind Sch Dist Dedicated Services Awd; Sch Bd of Trustees 1983-88; *home:* PO Box 112 Sierra Blanca TX 79851

LUKE, CAROLYN HAYCOCK, United States History Teacher; *b:* Benjamin, UT; *m:* James John Hirst; *c:* Phoebe Trebell, Ted Trebell; *ed:* (BA) Fine Art, Univ CA Santa Barbara 1963; Univ of CA Santa Barbara, Univ of CA Riverside, CA St San Bernardino; *cr:* Ed Instr Coll of Desert CMC 1976-80; Art Teacher Yucca Valley HS 1978-83; Eng/Math/His Teacher 1983-84, Eng/His Teacher 1984-87 Twentynine Palms Jr HS; Drawing Instr Coll of Desert CMC 1980-; US His Teacher Twentynine Palms Jr HS 1987-; *ai:* Class Adv 1984-; Asst Class Adv 1988-; Chi Omega Alumnae 1961-, Life Mem 1963; CA Schlsp Fed 1955-, Life Mem 1959; NEA 1978-89; CA Teachers Assn 1978-89; Morongo Teachers Assn 1978-89; BSA Eagle Scout Cnslr 1974-; Church of Jesus Christ of LDS, Young Womens Pres 1973-77, 1987-88; Ten Yr Pin Morongo Unified Sch Dist; *office:* Twentynine Palms Jr HS P O Box 1209 Twentynine Palms CA 92277

LUKE, DOROTHY HARRINGTON, First Grade Teacher; *b:* Hartfield, NY; *m:* Lester W.; *c:* Timothy, Tamara; *ed:* (BS) Ed, Fredonia St Teachers Coll 1955; *cr:* K-1st Grade Teacher 1955-63, 1st Grade Teacher 1965-67 Frewsburg Cntrl Sch; 1st Grade Teacher Jamestown Public Schls 1967-; *ai:* Intnl Rdng Assn 1960-; Natl PTA Life Membership 1989; Stillwater United Meth Church 1955-; *office:* S G Love Sch 624 Pine St Jamestown NY 14701

LUKE, SUE HUFF, Music & Piano Teacher; *b:* Jackson, MS; *m:* Delane; *c:* Jim, Danny; *ed:* (BA) Music Ed, MS St Univ 1971; *cr:* Piano Teacher Beulah Hubbard 1978-79; Chorus/Piano Teacher Union 1979-80; Music Teacher Neshota Cntrl Elem 1980-; *ai:* Neshoba Jr Music Club Adv; Insurance Comm; MEA Dist Rep; MENC; Piano Festival Chm 1988-; Dist IIA (Chm, VP) 1989-; Pres Elem Music Division St of MS; Dist Pres Elem Music; *home:* Rt 3 Box 410 Philadelphia MS 39350

LUKER, DEBORAH HOOKS, English Teacher; *b:* Tuscaloosa, OK; *m:* Robert T.; *ed:* (BS) Scndry Ed Eng Univ of AL 1978; *cr:* Eng Teacher Bibb Cty JHS 1979-; *ai:* Natl Jr Honor Society Spon; Steering Comm for Accreditation Southern Assn; *office:* Bibb County Jr HS 335 Walnut Centreville AL 35042

LUKMANN, LYNN FRANCES, Science Teacher; *b:* Gary, IN; *ed:* (BA) Elem Ed, St Mary Coll & Notre Dame 1978; (MS) Elem Ed, Purdue 1983; *cr:* 7th Grade Teacher Nativity of Our Savior Sch 1978-89; Sci Teacher St Mary Sch 1989-; *ai:* Sci Fair Spon; *home:* 3073 Swanson Rd Portage IN 46368

LUMAN, CAROLYN SUE, Teacher; *b:* Gallia Cty, OH; *ed:* (BS) Elem Ed, Rio Grande Coll 1967; (MS) Elem Ed/Lib Sci, Marshall Univ 1970; Post Masters Courses Univ of UT, OH Univ, Univ of Dayton, Ashland Univ; *cr:* Teacher Cadmus Elem 1962-85, Southwestern Elem 1985-; *ai:* Gallia Cty Local Ed Assn, OH Ed Media Assn, OH Teachers of Math; Gallia Cty Schls Teacher of Yr 1988.

LUMBLEY, WILLIAM D., Science Department Chairman; *b:* Superior, WI; *m:* Nancy Sue Skelton; *c:* Stephanie Wrye, Cynthia, Patrick; *ed:* (BS) Chem/Math Ed, Purdue Univ 1958; (MAT) Chem, IN Univ 1963; Sci Ed; *cr:* Chem Teacher T C Howe HS 1959-65; Radiation Lecturer IN Univ 1965-67; Chem Teacher S Bloomington HS 1967-, IN Univ 1977-; *ai:* Sr Class Spon; Tech Prep Curr, Performance Accreditation Steering, Sch Restructuring, Educl Planning Comms; Natl Assn of Sci Supvrs, Hoosier Assn of Sci Teachers, IN Assn of Chem Teachers; Monroe Cty Councilman 1976-80; Township Bd Chm 1972-76; Soil & Water Conservation Bd Chm 1973-75; IN Corporation for Sci & Technology 1980-84; IN Technology Dev Grant; Alpha Chi Sigma Awd for Contributions Chem Ed; Sigma Xi Outstanding Sci Teacher; IN Univ Pilot Teacher Coll Project Collaboration Prgm; *office:* Bloomington HS South 1965 S Walnut Bloomington IN 47401

LUMMUS, CARL RUSSELL, History Teacher/Coach; *b:* Amarillo, TX; *m:* Della Lois Satterwhite; *c:* Wesley W., Jamie L.; *ed:* (BA) His/Phys Ed, W TX St Univ 1983; *cr:* Teacher/Coach Amarillo Ind Sch Dist 1983-87, Highland Park Ind Sch Dist 1987-; *ai:* Var Ftbl, Jr HS Bsktbl, Var Boys & Girls Golf Coach; TX Coaching Assn 1984-; *office:* Highland Park Ind Sch Dist PO Box 30430 Amarillo TX 79120

LUMPKIN, BETTY STEWART, Librarian; *b:* Anniston, AL; *m:* Roy L. Jr.; *c:* John D.; *ed:* (BS) Scndry Ed, Univ of Chattanooga 1959; (MED) Aerospace Ed, Mid TN St Univ 1973; Grad Stud IN Univ, Univ of TN; *cr:* Teacher Rivermont Sch 1966-67, Tyner Jr HS 1967-74; Librarian 1974-75, Ooltewah HS 1979-; *ai:* Night Class Comm; Chattanooga Area Lib Assn Pres 1987-88; TN Lib Assn Bd Mem 1987-88; Amer Bus Womens Assn Pres 1988-89, Women of Yr 1988; Lyndhurst Grant 1988; Career Ladder Level III TN St Dept of Ed; *office:* Ooltwah HS 6112 Snow Hill Rd Ooltewah TN 37363

LUMPKIN, BEVERLY WRIGHT, 7th Grade Mathematics Teacher; *b:* Bastrop, LA; *m:* Andy E.; *c:* Stephanie Spaulding, Jeff, Tricia; *ed:* (BS) Elem/Math, E TX St Univ 1983; Working Toward Masters Counseling; *cr:* 7th-8th Grade Math Teacher Wilkinson 1984-87; 6th Grade Teacher 1987-88, 7th-8th AR/Regular Math Teacher 1988-89, 7th Grade Regular/At Risk Math Teacher 1989- A C New; *ai:* 6th Grade Stu Cncl; Worked With Psychologist Success in Schls Prgm; Alpha Delta Kappa 1988-; Kappa Delta Pi 1982-88; Amer Business Womens Assn 1984-87; *home:* 4324 Crestover Mesquite TX 75150

LUMPKIN, CYNTHIA RAWLS, 7th/8th Grade English Teacher; *b:* Paris, TN; *m:* John W.; *ed:* (BS) Scndry Ed/Eng/His/Poly Sci 1973, (MS) Ed Admin/Supervision Univ of TN Martin 1986; Working Towards Masters; *cr:* Classroom Teacher Briarwood Mid Sch 1974-; *ai:* BCEA, TEA, NEA, Delta Kappa Gamma; Outstanding Young Women in America 1981; *office:* Briarwood Mid Sch Briarwood Ave Camden TN 38320

LUMPKIN, DARLENE SCHOLL, 5th Grade Teacher; *b:* Lima, OH; *m:* Fred D.; *c:* Caron Stoltz, Ted, Rick, Sand a Brewer; *ed:* (BA) Elem Ed, Wright St Univ 1971; (MS) Elem Ed, Ball St Univ 1976; *cr:* 5th Grade Teacher Ansonia Local Schls 1968-; *ai:* Outdoor Ed Spon; Intervention Team; Ansonia Ed Assn VP 1980; Western OH Ed Assn; OH Ed Assn; NEA; *home:* 3959 St Rt 47 W Ansonia OH 45303

LUMPKIN, DOUGLAS E., 6th Grade Teacher; *b:* Waterbury, CT; *ed:* (BS) Elem Ed, 1969, (MS) Sci, 1973 Central CT St Coll; Sci Univ of RI 1978; Pimms Fellow Sci Wesleyan Univ 1989; *cr:* 4-6th Grade Teacher Bristol Sch System 1969-; Instr Univ of RI Energy Ed Dept 1980-84; *ai:* CT Energy Cncl for Teachers VP 1980- Service 1986; Pimms Fellowship 1989-; *office:* Jennings Sch 291 Burlington Ave Bristol CT 06010

LUMPKIN, JOHN WAYNE, Science Teacher; *b:* Humboldt, TN; *m:* Cindy Rawls; *ed:* (BS) Natural Sci, Univ of TN 1969; (MS) Wildlife Bio, TN Tech Univ 1972; Sci & Ed; *cr:* Teacher Jackson City Schls 1969-70, Benton Cty Bd of Ed 1972-; *ai:* BCEA, TEA, NEA; TN Conservation Educator of Yr 1980; *home:* Rt 2 Box 244 Camden TN 38320

LUMPKIN, SANDRA BARRIER, Math & Computer Teacher; *b:* Brownfield, TX; *m:* H. J. Jr.; *ed:* (BA) Elem Ed, Baylor Univ 1970; Testing, Southwestern Univ; Cmptr, Temple Jr Coll, Austin Comm Coll; *cr:* Math Teacher 1970-, Cmptr Teacher 1982- Taylor Mid Sch; *ai:* Pep Squad Chrldr; UIL Number Sense; Team Math; TSTA 1970-74; TCTA Local Pres 1970-74; ATPE Mem St Dir Bd 1975-; Natl Music Club (VP, Pres) 1988-89; United Meth Women Local (Pres 1978-80, District Pres 1976-80, Conference Publicity 1982-84); *office:* Taylor Mid Sch 410 W 7th St Taylor TX 76574

LUNA, BELLA PENA, Sixth Grade Teacher; *b:* Orani Bataan, Philippines; *ed:* Teacher Certificate Elem Ed, Philippine Normal Sch 1950; (BSED) Elem Ed, Philippine Normal Coll 1960; (MA) Elem Ed, Univ of HI 1967; Eng as 2nd Lang Cert, SE Asia Ministers of Ed Center Singapore; Mid Management, Supervisory, Univ TX Brownsville; *cr:* 4th Grade Elem Teacher 1950-55, 5th Grade Teacher 1955-58, 6th Grade Teacher 1958-65, Stu Teachers/Peace Corps Volunteer Cooperating Teacher 1958-65 Orani Elem;Intermediate Teacher Kaunakakai Sch 1967-68; Area Supvr Dept of Ed 1968-71; 5th Grade Teacher Victoria Heights Sch 1971-77, El Jardin Sch 1977-78; 6th Grade Teacher Russell Elem Sch 1978-; *ai:* Math Bee Contestants Spon; Climate Improvement Comm; East-West Fellowship Mem 1965-, Schlsp 1965-68; NEA, TX St Teachers Assn Mem, Assn of Brownsville Educators Mem 1971-; Eng as 2nd Lang Pilot Teacher; Schlsp Grant East-West Center Univ of HI Honolulu; Peace Corps Volunteer Cooperating Teacher Bataan Philippines; Fellowship SE Asia Ministers of Ed Center; *office:* Russell Elem Sch 800 Lakeside Brownsville TX 78520

LUNA, TERESA LONG, History Teacher; *b:* Jackson, TN; *m:* Anthony Lynn; *c:* Lauren, Justin; *ed:* (BA) His, Union Univ 1979; (MS) Counseling, Memphis St Univ 1982; Various Seminars & Inservice Trng Sessions; *cr:* Cnslr Union Univ 1979-84; Teacher Crockett Cty HS 1986-88, Jackson Cntrl Merry HS 1988-; *ai:* Academic Decathlon Tutor 1988-; Jr & Sr Class Spon 1987-88; Textbook Selection Comm 1989-; Alpha Delta Kappa Membership Comm 1989-; Jackson Ed Assn (Secy, Exec Bd) 1988-; TN Ed Assn Instructional Prof Dev Comm 1988-; Exec Bd Transitional Sch Educl Assn 1989-; W Jackson Baptist Church (Chm Family

Life Comm 1985-88, Youth Leader 1984-89, Schlsp Comm 1989-); *office:* Jackson Cntrl-Merry HS Allen Ave Jackson TN 38301

LUND, BRENT E., Physical Education Teacher; *b:* Ogden, UT; *m:* Midge Ranson; *c:* Travis, Matthew, Troy, Angela; *ed:* (AA) Distributive Ed, 1973, (BS) Psych, 1974 Weber St Coll; (MA) Phys Ed, Brigham Young Univ 1981; Teacher Ed, Weber St Coll 1976; Sports Medicine Certificate, UT St Univ 1978; *cr:* Phys Ed Teacher/Coach Central Jr HS 1976-77; Phys Ed/Math Teacher/ Coach N Layton Jr HS 1977-83; Phys Ed/Health Teacher/Coach Clearfield HS 1983-; *ai:* Head Ftbl, Strength & Conditioning Coach; Mt Ogden Dist Lake Bonneville Cncl Scoutmaster Troup 271 1985-; Natl Strength & Conditioning Assn St Comm 1978-, HS 1985; UT Ftbl Coaches 1983-; Natl Ftbl Assn 1985-; Davis Ed Assn 1977-; NEA, UT Ed Assn 1976-; *office:* Clearfield HS 931 S Falcon Dr Clinton UT 84015

LUND, DEBRA K., Earth Science Teacher; *b:* Plentywood, MT; *ed:* (BS) Geology, 1982, (ED) Scndry Ed, 1984 Rocky Mountain Coll; *cr:* Geography Teacher Miles Comm Coll 1983; Math Teacher O Leary Jr HS 1984-85; Math/Sci Teacher Capital HS 1985-; *ai:* HS Gymnastics & Mid Sch Track Coach; Sci Curr Comm; MT Sci Teachers Assn (Membership Chairperson 1988-, Mem) 1985-; MT Ed Assn Mem 1985-; Delta Kappa Gamma 1988-; MT Distinguished Teacher Solar Energy Research Inst Fellowshp 1988; Designed & Implemented Honors Level Earth Sci Course; *office:* Capital HS 100 Valley Dr Helena MT 59601

LUND, JACKIE DALE, Mathematics Teacher; *b:* Hamilton, MO; *m:* Barbara Ann Mc Guire; *c:* Meri D., Bryan T., Shannon R., Tracy E., Jarrod T., Justin H.; *ed:* (BSED) Math, NW MO St Univ 1967; NW MO St 1971-73; *cr:* Teacher Stanberry R-II Schls 1967-74; Laborer Allison Concrete Products 1974-77; Teacher Savannah R-III Schls 1977-; *ai:* Ftbl & Girls Track Coach; Jr Class Stand Spon; R-III Salary, R-III Budget Comm; Cty Teachers Assn 1983-; *home:* Suburban Hills Lot 38 Savannah MO 64485

LUNDAHL, CHRISTY BRECKLE, 2nd Grade Teacher; *b:* Cedar Rapids, IA; *m:* Roger; *c:* Ryan, Elizabeth; *ed:* (BSED) Elem Ed, IL St Univ 1976; *cr:* 5th Grade Teacher 1976-77, 6th Grade Teacher 1977-87, 2nd Grade Teacher 1987- Riverdale Elem; *ai:* Hospitality Comm; IL Ed Assn 1976-; *office:* Riverdale Elem Sch 9424 256th St N Port Byron IL 61275

LUNDBERG, DOUGLAS T., Science Teacher; *b:* Atlanta, GA; *c:* Claire J.; *ed:* (BS) Bio, Wayne St Univ 1970; (MA) Sci Ed, Adams St 1985; IN Univ 1982-83; Ball St 1986; *cr:* Teacher Northwestern Jr HS 1971-73, Upwey HS Melbourne Australia 1973-75, Air Acad HS 1975-; *ai:* Knowledge Bowl, Genetic Engineering Club Spon; Pikes Peak Ed Assn Pres 1981-85; Acad Ed Assn Pres 1979-82; NSTA, NABT; Published Article 1987; Human Chromosome Preparation Bio Teacher 1990; Co-Author Monograph Advances Genetic Engineering BSCS; Outstanding Dist Teacher 1989; *office:* Air Acad HS USAF Academy CO 80840

LUNDBERG, VINSON, Chemistry Teacher; *b:* Gheen, MN; *ed:* (BA) Geology, Univ of MN Duluth 1956; (BS) Phys Sci, Moorhead St Coll 1960; (MST) Physics, Univ of WI Superior 1968; *cr:* Chem/Physics/Math Teacher Granite Falls HS 1959-61; Chem/Math Teacher Duluth Cntrl HS 1961-; *ai:* Chm of Duluth City Wide Sci Curr Comm; Earth Sci Curr Project Consultant; Test Center Dir; MN Sci Teachers Exec Bd Regional Rep 1964-75; Duluth Fed Teachers Building Rep 1961-; Lake Superior Geology Club Pres 1962-68; Lake Superior Sci/Math Teachers Club Pres 1965-76; Elks 1957-; *office:* Duluth Cntrl HS 800 E Cntrl Entrance Duluth MN 55811

LUNDEEN, SAMUEL, 5th Grade Teacher; *b:* Crookston, MN; *m:* Angela Fitzhugh; *c:* Gairdt, Bjorn; *ed:* (BA) Art, Humboldt St Univ 1968; Advanced Courses in Ed; *cr:* Art Teacher Brownsville Mid Sch 1969-70; Elem Teacher Arcata Elem 1971-; *ai:* Sch Site Cncl Comm Mem; Art Task Force; CA Quality Prgm Review Team Mem; Master Teacher Credential Prgm; NHTA Pres 1972-73; NEA, CTA Mem 1971-; Certificate Commendation For Teaching Excl 1989-; *office:* Sunset Elem Sch 1125 16th St Arcata CA 95521

LUNDQUIST, KAREN BLOM, Health/Phys Ed Teacher/ Coach; *b:* Jamestown, NY; *ed:* (BS) Phys Ed/Health, Akron Univ 1969; (MS) Ed, Univ of Dayton 1984; *cr:* Health/Phys Ed Teacher Edison North HS 1969-; *ai:* Developed & Supervised 16 Sport Intramural Prgm for Boys & Girls, Girls Var Track, Bsktbl, Vlybl Edison North HS; Head Coach Vlybl, Track & Field 1976-, Bstkbl 1975-81; Head Coach Track & Field Edison North HS 1976-; Amer Alliance for Health, Phys Ed, Recreation & Dance, OH Assn for Health, Phys Ed, Recreation & Dance 1972-; NEA, OH Ed Assn 1969-; Edison Local Ed Assn 1978-;E Dist Track & Cross Cntry Coaches Assn 1980-; Dist 5 Vlybl Coaches Assn 1983-; E Buckeye Track & Field Ofcls Assn 1980-; OH HS Athletic Assn 1976-; Edison North Athletic Boosters Assn 1970-; Ashland Oil Nom; Jump Rope for Your Heart Articles; Motivation Articles; Jefferson Cty Mini-Grant; E Dist, OVAC, All Area Coach of Yr 1988; Selected to Coaching Staff Mid-West Champions Meet 1989; Citizens Awd 2nd Place 1988, 1989; Yrbk Dedication 1978; OH Valley Athletic Conference Season Champion 1989; *office:* Edison North HS Box 158 Hammondsville OH 43930

LUNDQUIST, PEGGY LYNNE ABRAHAMSON, Kindergarten Teacher; *b:* Superior, WI; *m:* Thomas G.; *c:* Allison; *ed:* (BS) Elem Ed, Univ of WI Superior 1973; *cr:* 1st/2nd Grade Teacher 1974-78, Kndgtn Teacher 1978- Maple Sch Dist; *ai:* Alpha Delta Kappa, WI Kndgtn Assn 1987-; Lake Superior Rdng Cncl 1986-; Lake Nebagamon PTO Pres 1989-; *office:* Maple Sch Dist Maple WI 54854

LUNDT, KAREN KRONWALL, Sixth Grade Teacher; *b:* Elkhorn, WI; *m:* Robert W.; *c:* Andrew, Daniel; *ed:* (BSE) Ed, Univ of WI Madison 1972; (MST) Elem Ed, Univ of WI Oshkosh 1977; Drug & Alcohol Group Trng, Various Univs; *cr:* 6th Grade Teacher Maplewood Jr HS 1972-73, Butte Des Morts Jr HS 1973-; *ai:* Stu Cncl Adv; Dist Rdng, Dist Gifted & Talented, Honor Society, Teacher of Yr, High Risk Comm; Core Team; Menasha Sch Dist Mid Sch Teacher of Yr 1987 & Distinguished Service Awd 1988; *office:* Butte Des Morts Jr HS 501 Tayco St Menasha WI 54952

LUNDVALL, DOUG E., Pres Lake Washington Ed Assn; *b:* Kirkland, WA; *ed:* (BA) His, Whitworth Coll 1974; (MA) His, E WA St Univ 1976; Teaching Certficate Ed, Univ of WA 1978; *cr:* Teacher Kirkland Jr HS 1978-88, Lake Washington HS 1988-89; Pres Lake Washington Ed Assn 1989-; *ai:* Bsbl, Bsktbl Coach; Dept Chairperson; Lake Washington Ed Assn (VP 1986-88, Pres); Parent Teacher Stu Exec Comm Assn 1989-, Special Service Awd 1990; E WA St Univ Grad Teaching Fellow; *office:* Lake Washington Ed Assn 1753 NE Union Hill Rd Ste 290 Redmond WA 98052

LUNDY, BARBARA ANN, 2nd Grade Teacher; *b:* Hancock, MI; *m:* William H.; *c:* Melissa, Mark, Erin; *ed:* (MA) Elem Ed, 1972, (BA) SocioLogy, 1969 Univ of MI; *cr:* 2nd-5th Grade Teacher Holy Rosary Elem Sch; *ai:* Sci Coord; Coord of Genesee Cty Cath Spelling Bee; *office:* Holy Rosary Elem Sch 5199 Richfield Rd Flint MI 48506

LUNSFORD, BETTY TEMPLETON, 4th/5th Grade Teacher; *b:* Statesville, NC; *m:* Tommy Gene; *c:* Cindy L. Rhyne, Eddie, Wendy L. Gray; *cr:* 4th/5th Grade Teacher Ebenezer Elem Sch 1971-; *ai:* NCEA Sch Rep 1971-; Assn of Classroom Teachers (Sch Rep, Cty Treas) 1971-; Union Grove United Meth Church (Youth Choir Dir 1963-79, Admin Secy, Choir Mem 1968-); Sch Teacher of Yr Awd; Sch & Cty Terry Sanford Awd; *home:* Rt 1 Box 180 Olin NC 28660

LUNSFORD, JOHNNA MILLER, Elementary Principal; *b:* Waterloo, OH; *m:* Alan; *c:* Nicholas, Grant, Gretta; *ed:* (BA) Elem Ed, 1974, (MA) Elem Ed, 1977 Morehead St; Admin, Univ of Dayton; *cr:* Kndgtn Teacher 1974-78, 2nd Grade Teacher 1978-89, Prin 1989- Symmes Valley; *ai:* Rehobeth Church (Pianist 1970-, Youth Choir Dir 1980-); *home:* R 1 Box 33-B Waterloo OH 45688

LUNT, JOHN S., Computer Coordinator; *b:* New Haven, CT; *m:* Jane P. Colcock; *c:* Lisa L. Phelan, Holly S; *ed:* (AB) Government, Bowdoin 1961; (MAT) His, Brown 1974; (MED) Cmptrs in Ed, Lesley 1988; *cr:* Teacher/Dept Chm Hebron Acad 1961-70; Teacher/Dir Upper Sch Providence Cntry Day Sch 1970-80; Teacher/Prin Southport Cntrl Sch 1980-85; Cmptr Coord Boothbay/Boothbay Harbor CSD 1985-; *ai:* Support System Steering & Cmptr Technology Comm Chm; Cmptr Club Faculty Adv; Adult Ed Instr; Sysop Midcoast BBS; ASCD 1988-; ME Cmptr Consortium; Intnl Society for Technology in Ed; RI Cncl for Ec Ed 1st Place Teaching Unit; Blaine House Scholar 1987; *office:* Boothbay/Boothbay Harbor CSD 156B Townsend Ave Boothbay Harbor ME 04538

LUPTON, MARY DOREEN (EVANS), Fifth Grade Teacher; *b:* Quinter, KS; *w:* Earl Dana (dec); *c:* Jana Von Richards; *ed:* (BS) Elem Ed, Ft Hays St Univ 1956; Speech Clinician Cert, KS Univ Grad Sch; *cr:* Speech Clinician Dodge City Public Schls 1956-58; 3rd Grade Teacher 1958-59, 5th Grade Teacher 1973- Unified Sch Dist #371; *ai:* Teacher in Charge Grade Sch; Selected Teacher of Yr 1989-; *home:* Box 44 RR Montezuma KS 67867

LUPTON, RON E., Art Teacher; *b:* Portsmouth, VA; *m:* Donna Jean Axtell; *c:* John, Matthew, Mindi; *ed:* (BA) Fine Arts, 1967, (MA) Fine Arts, 1968 Univ of Northern CO; *cr:* Art/Eng Teacher Olathe HS 1968-70; Art Instr CO Western Coll 1969-70; Elem Art Specialist 1971-81, Art Teacher 1981- W Irving Jr HS Colorado Springs; *ai:* After Sch Stu Mural Painting Gemstone Cutting Instr; SPA 1971-81 Recognition 1981; CEA/CSEA 1982-; Various 1-Man Shows of Artworks 1967-; Author in Residence Awd 1989; Winner Stars of Tomorrow Competition-UNC 1968; Article Published Aug 1984 Lapidary Journal;2 Cut Stones Accepted By SmithSonian Institution WA DC 1989; *office:* Washington Irving Jr H S 1702 N Murray Blvd Colorado Springs CO 80915

LURATE, LAUREN MILLETTE, Chemistry I Teacher; *b:* Pascagoula, MS; *m:* Leigh Yerger; *ed:* (MEA) Bio/General Sci, Univ of MS 1985; (MS) Sci Ed, Univ of S MS 1986; Grad Stud Chem; *cr:* Sci Teacher Gautier Jr HS 1986-87, Hillcrest Chrstn Sch 1987-89; Bio Teacher Hinds Comm Coll 1988, 1989; Chem Teacher Jackson Preparatory Sch 1989-; *ai:* Sci Club & Jr Class Spon; Publicity Photographer; *office:* Jackson Preparatory Sch PO Box 4940 Jackson MS 39216

LUSHER, PAMELA CLARKSON, Language Art Teacher; *b:* Grafton, WV; *m:* Byron Christopher; *ed:* Assoc, Parkersburg Comm Coll 1976; (BA) Eng/Journalism, 1978, (MA) Scndry Ed/ Eng, 1983 Marshall Univ; Dental Assisting Certificate Parkesburg Comm Coll 1976; *cr:* 9th-12th Grade Rdng/Eng Teacher Ripley Mid Sch 1979-80; 9th-12th Grade Journalism/Basic Lang Art/ Advanced Lang Art Teacher Hurricane HS 1980-; *ai:* Key Club Spon; PCEA (Secy 1984-85, VP 1985); Phi Delta Kappa 1983-89; WVEA 1984-85; UMW Church Publicity Coord 1988-; *office:* Hurricane HS 3350 Teays Valley Rd Hurricane WV 25526

LUSTER, DELORES CATCHINGS, Fourth Grade Teacher; *b:* Dublin, MS; *m:* Floyd Sr.; *c:* Floyd Jr., Toni D.; *ed:* (AA) Elem Ed, Coahoma Jr Coll 1969; (BS) Elem/Phys Ed, Jackson St Univ 1971; Spec Ed; Working Towards Masters; *cr:* 4th Grade Teacher Lyon Elem Sch 1972-; *ai:* GSA Troop 109 Asst Spon; Delta Sigma Theta Mem; *home:* 10880 Hwy 322 Clarksdale MS 38614

LUTES, MERLENE S., 7th/8th Grade Math Teacher; *b:* Carbondale, IL; *m:* Dallas D.; *c:* Preston, Margaret A. L. Slade; *ed:* (BA) Elem Ed, 1968, (MA) Rdng in Ed, 1971, Sci/Math, 1985 LA Tech Univ; Cmptr Literacy Courses 1986-88 & Algebra in Elem Grades, 1988 LA Tech Univ; *cr:* 2nd/3rd Grade Teacher Bethel Chrstn Sch 1968-70; 3rd Grade Teacher 1970-71, 6th Grade Teacher 1971-79 Hico Elem; 7th/8th Grade Sci Teacher Ruston Jr HS 1983-84;7th/8th Grade Math/Rdng Teacher Choudrant HS 1984-; *ai:* Natl Jr Honor Society Spon; Math Counts & Pentathlon Coach; N LA Math Improvement Project Co-Dir 1988-89; Delta Kappa Gamma Pres 1988-; A Plus Pel (Lincoln Parish Pres 1988-89, St Bd 1989-); Lincoln Parish Rdng Cncl, N LA Rdng Cncl 1985-; NCTM 1987-; Littera Club 1965-; John Knox Presbyn Church; Square Shooters Square Dance Club St Bd Rep 1987-89; Teacher of Yr Choudrant Jr HS 1986-89; Teacher of Yr Lincoln Parish Jr HS 1988; Master Math Teacher Lincoln Parish 1987; *office:* Choudrant HS P O Box 220 Choudrant LA 71227

LUTHER, BRIAN DOUGLAS, English/Media Teacher; *b:* Lexington, NE; *m:* Tammy; *c:* Chelsea; *ed:* (BA) Eng/Phys Ed, 1985, Media Endorsement 1988 Kearney St Coll; Working Towards Masters Eng; *cr:* Asst Girls Bsktbl Coach Kearney HS 1982-85; Eng/Media Teacher Oxford Cmmty Schls 1985-; *ai:* Head Boys Bsktbl, Boys & Girls Track; Co-Spon Frosh Class; NSEA, NE Coaches Assn 1985-; Oxford Ed Assn (Secy, Treas) 1987-88; Cambridge All Star Game Head Coach 1988; Oxford Teachers Negotiations Team 1988; *office:* Oxford Cmmty Schls Box 7 Oxford NE 68967

LUTHER, DONALD STEPHEN, Social Studies Teacher; *b:* Bethlehem, PA; *ed:* (BS) Scndry Ed/Soc Sci, West Chester Univ 1969; (MA) Modern European His, 1974, (PhD) Modern British His, 1979 Univ of DE; *cr:* Adjunct Instr Univ of DE 1975-80; Temporary Asst Professor Franklin & Marshall Coll 1979-80; Adjunct Asst Professor Univ of TX San Antonio 1982-85; Soc Stud Teacher Univ Sch of Jackson 1985-; His Instr Jackson St Comm Coll 1986-; *ai:* Vlybl, Sftbl & Speech Asst Coach; Faculty Comm; NHS; Amer Historical Assn 1981-; Several Articles Published 1950-62, 1986; *office:* Univ Sch of Jackson 1981 Hollywood Dr Jackson TN 38305

LUTHER, SUSAN JAYNE, Media Director; *b:* Fremont, NE; *ed:* (BS) Home Ec/Lib Sci, Wayne St Coll 1972; Grad Work Ed; *cr:* Media Dir SE Consolidated Sch 1979-; *ai:* Sci Club Adv; Class Spon; NEA, NSEA 1973-; SENCSEA Pres 1973-; Delta Kappa Gamma 1986; NE Lib Assn; Research Club; Order of Eastern Star; *office:* SE Consolidated Sch Box 73 Stella NE 68442

LUTHY, BRIAN HOWARD, Science Teacher; *b:* Parma, OH; *ed:* (BA) Comprehensive Sci/His, Muskingum Coll 1989; *cr:* Bsktbl Coach Zanesville-Rosecrans HS 1986-88; Bio Teacher John Glenn HS 1989; Track Coach Case-Western Reserve Univ 1989-; Sci Teacher Stryker Local Sch 1989-; *ai:* Boys Var Bsktbl, Boys & Girls Var Track Asst; Local Sci Fair Coord; Williams Cty Academic League Quiz Bowl Team Adv; NHS Faculty Cncl Mem 1989-; OH Acad of Sci Mem 1989-; Article Published; Girls Bsktbl St Semi Finalist Coach 1988; All Amer Decathlete Coach 1987-; *office:* Stryker Local Sch PO Box 624 S Defiance St Stryker OH 43557

LUTHY, JIM E., Chemistry Teacher; *b:* Bellaire, OH; *m:* Nancy Morris; *c:* Chris, Melissa; *ed:* (BS) Chem, Marietta Coll 1963; (MAT) Chemical Ed, IN Univ 1967; Engineering Curr Project, Univ of IL; Ed, Guidance, Sci, OH Univ; *cr:* Teacher Warren HS 1963-67, Marietta HS 1967-; *ai:* Marietta Ed Assn, OH Ed Assn, NEA, NSTA; Natl Sci Fnd Schlsp IN Univ 1963-67, Univ of IL 1969; Martha Holden Jennings Scholar 1973-74; Academic Excl Marietta City Sch Dist 1988, 1990; *office:* Marietta HS 208 Davis Ave Marietta OH 45750

LUTKUS, LYNNE (ADAMS), 4th Grade Teacher; *b:* Kendallville, IN; *m:* Allan L.; *c:* Andrea, Jannette; *ed:* (BS) Math/ Ed, Cntrl MI Univ 1969; Cntrl MI Univ; *cr:* Kndgtn Teacher 1969, 3rd Grade Teacher 1969-72 Greenville Public Schls; 1st Grade Teacher 1978-79, 4th Grade Teacher 1980- St Charles Sch; *ai:* NCEA 1978-; Alpha Gamma Delta 1965-; *office:* St. Charles Cath Sch 502 S. Franklin St. Greenville MI 48838

LUTTRELL, JEANNE M., Bus Teacher/Chm Votec Dept; *b:* Irvington, VA; *m:* William F. (dec); *c:* John W.; *ed:* (BS) Bus Ed, Longwood Coll 1953; Cmptr Studies; *cr:* Bus Teacher Middlesex HS 1953-61, Lancaster HS 1966-; *ai:* Spon Sr Class; FBLA Spon; Evaluation Self Study Steering Comm; Lancaster Ed Assn Secy; VA Bus Assn.

LUTZ, JOHN MARVIN, Fifth Grade Teacher; *b:* Milwaukee, WI; *ed:* (BS) Elem Ed, Concordia Teachers Coll 1966; (MA) Rdng/Elem Teacher, Cardinal Stritch Coll 1976; *cr:* 7th-8th Grade Teacher Peace Luth Sch 196-67; 4th Grade Teacher 1967-83, 5th Grade Teacher 1983- Willow Glen; *ai:* St Francis Ed Assn Negotiating Team; NEA, WEA, SFEA 1967-; *office:* Willow Glen Elem Sch 2600 E Bolivar Ave Saint Francis WI 53207

LUTZ, REGAN ANN (RICHARDSON), Social Studies Dept Chair; *b:* Rochester, IN; *m:* Lonnie R.; *c:* Aaron Fetrow, Megan, Devan; *ed:* (BED) Ed/His/Eng/Poly Sci, 1977; (MA) His, 1982 Univ of Toledo; *cr:* Teacher Toledo Public Schls 1977-80; Grad Asst Univ of Toledo 1980-82; Teacher St Ursula Acad 1982-; *ai:* Afro Amer Club Moderator; St Ursula Advisory Cncl Mem; Phi Alpha Theta 1981-; NCEA 1982-; NCSS 1986-; ASCD 1990; Comm Mem Formulated Toledo Diocesan Soc Stud Curr 1986-88; North Cntrl Evaluation Team Mem 1989; *office:* St Ursula Acad 4025 Indian Rd Toledo OH 43606

LUTZ, TOM V., 7th Grade Science Teacher; *b:* Bloomfield, NJ; *ed:* (BA) Biological Sci, 1970, (MS) Zoology, 1980 AZ St Univ; Ed Admin Cert N AZ Univ 1990; *cr:* Sci Teacher Colegio Jorge Washington 1972-73, Orangewood Elem 1973-82, Royal Palm Jr HS 1982-83; Sci Teacher/Management Resource Team Palo Verde Jr HS 1983-; *ai:* Homework Club Coord; WA Dist Sci Acad Staff; AZ Sci Teachers Assn 1983-, AZ Mid Sch Sci Teacher of Yr 1982; Phi Delta Kappa 1988-; WA Prof Educators Assn VP 1983-; AZ Young Life Volunteer Leader 1975-; AZ Army Natl Guard Chief Instr 1970-; *office:* Palo Verde Jr HS 7502 N 39th Ave Phoenix AZ 85051

LUX, DOUGLAS CRAIG, Math Teacher; *b:* Lockport, NY; *m:* Sandra Elaine Welbaum; *c:* Nicola S., Laura; *ed:* (BA) Math Ed, 1964, (MS) Math Ed, 1968 Buffalo St Coll; *cr:* Math Teacher 1964-84; Math Dept Head 1975-78 Clarence Jr HS; Math Teacher Bluffton Harrison Mid Sch 1984-; *ai:* Head Coach Academic Bowl Team; Coach Math Academic Bowl Team; Long Range Planning MSD; Acreditation Comm; *home:* 1120 Ridgewood Ln Bluffton IN 46714

LUX, THOMAS DAVID, Chemistry Teacher; *b:* San Diego, CA; *m:* Juliette Whiteman; *ed:* (BA) Phys Ed, San Diego St Univ 1977; (MA) Ed, Azusa Pacific 1982; *cr:* Chem Teacher Mira Mesa HS; *ai:* Mira Mesa HS Cross Cntry Coach; San Diego Teachers Assn; CA Jr Coll Coaches Assn Secy, Coach of Yr 1982; *office:* Mira Mesa HS 10510 Reagan Rd San Diego CA 92126

LUYK, DAVID MARTIN, Language Arts Teacher; *b:* Grand Rapids, MI; *m:* Janice Marie Groelsema; *c:* Kristin, Barry; *ed:* (AB) Eng/Psych/Phys Ed, Calvin Coll 1969; Grad Work Lang Art & Psych; *cr:* Mid Sch Teacher Oakdale Chrstn Sch 1969-; *ai:* 8th Grade Class Spon; Head Varsity Ftbl Coach Grand Rapids Chrstn HS; 8th Grade Womens Bsktbl Coach Oakdale Chrstn Mid Sch; MI HS Coaches Assn & MI HS Ftbl Coaches Assn 1980-; *office:* Oakdale Chrstn Sch 1050 Fisk S E Grand Rapids MI 49507

LYBARGER, LEN W., Health Teacher; *b:* Granite City, IL; *m:* Susan Elaine; *ed:* (BS) Phys Ed, Mac Murry Coll; (BS) Health/ Phys Ed, 1973, (MS) Guidance & Counseling 1975 S IL Univ; *cr:* Health Teacher Granite City Sr HS 1973-; *ai:* Sr HS Ftbl Coach; AAHPER; Masonic Lodge 177; Designed & Wrote Health Curr for Sr HS Level; *office:* Granite City Sr HS 3101 Madison Ave Granite City IL 62040

LYBARGER, SUSAN ELAINE, Sixth Grade Teacher; *b:* Granite City, IL; *m:* Lenny Jr.; *ed:* (BS) Elem Ed, 1968, (MS) Guidance Counseling, 1977 S IL Univ Evanston; Post Grad Work Gifted Ed; *cr:* Primary Teacher 1968-79, Gifted Ed Teacher 1985-89, Intermediate Teacher 1979- Edwardsville Sch Dist #1; *ai:* Sci Fair & Math Olympiad Team Spon; Edwardsville Dist #7 Staff Dev Comm Mem; Phi Delta Kappa, NEA, IEA; EEA (Policy Comm Chm, Negotiator); PTO; Co-Author Book; *home:* RR 1 Box 689 Worden IL 62097

LYCAN, SHIRLEY DALTON, English/Humanities Teacher; *b:* Charleston, WV; *m:* Mark A.; *c:* Heather, Melissa; *ed:* (BA) Philosophy, 1980, (MA) Eng, 1983 Marshall Univ; *cr:* Teacher Burch HS 1983-84, St Joseph Grade Sch 1984-86, St Joseph Cntrl Cath HS 1986-; *ai:* Var Cheering Coach; Hum Comm; NCEA 1986-; NCTE 1989-; *office:* St Joseph Cntrl Cath HS 600 13th St Huntington WV 25701

LYDE, CATHERINE ERLENE, Chemistry Teacher; *b:* Brunswick, GA; *ed:* (BA) Chem, Duke Univ 1979; (MED) Sci, GA Southern Coll 1984; Currently Enrolled in Educl Specialist Degree Prgm; *cr:* Chem Teacher Brunswick HS 1982-; *ai:* Jr Class Adv; Staff Dev & Sci Curr Comm; NSTA 1984-; GA Sci Teachers Assn 1984-; NEA 1987-; GA Assn of Educators 1987-; Natl Assn Advancement of Colored People; Kappa Delta Pi; Alpha Kappa Alpha; Glynn Cty Fed of Democratic Women; Young Woman of Yr; *office:* Brunswick H S 3920 Habersham St Brunswick GA 31520

LYDICK, DONALD HOWARD, Fifth Grade Teacher; *b:* Wheeling, WV; *c:* Michelle D., Nicole R.; *ed:* (BS) Mrktg/Ec, W Liberty St Coll 1965; WV Univ Morgantown & OH Univ Athens; *cr:* 6th Grade Teacher Colliers Elem Sch 1965-68; 5th-6th Grade Teacher Pleasant Hill Elem Sch 1968-; *ai:* NFIOA 1986-; IAABO 1988-; *home:* 36 15th St Wellsburg WV 26070

LYKINS, BEULAH DAVIS, Guidance Counselor; *b:* Pineville, KY; *m:* James O.; *c:* Jimmy, Suzanne; *ed:* (BA) Eng, E KY Univ 1964; (MED) Counseling, Xavier Univ 1970; Grad Stud; *cr:* Teacher Boone Cty HS 1964-69, Lloyd HS 1969-71; Teacher 1983-86, Cnslr 1986- Bellevue HS; *ai:* Just Say No Club; KY Assn of Sch Administrators, N KY Assn of Counseling Dev, Parents, Teachers & Stu Assn; *home:* 2833 Campus Dr Crestview Hills KY 41017

LYLE, BARRY WILLIAM, US/World History Teacher; *b:* Framingham, MA; *m:* Charlene G.; *c:* Christopher, Travis, Jared, Timothy; *ed:* (BS) Recreation Admin, Univ of MA 1975; (MA) Ed/His, Framingham St 1982; Natl Executive Inst BSA; Digital Equipment Corporation Ed Dept; *cr:* Teacher Marlboro Jr HS 1977-81, Hollis Jr HS; *ai:* Asst Scoutmaster Troop 12 Framingham; Jr HS Track & Soccer Coach; Cubmaster Pack 12 Framingham; NE Region Aquatic Sch Faculty BSA; NE Man Dance Officer; Amer Indianist Society Past Bd Mem; Amer Historical Society 1978-81; Amer Indianist Society Cncl Mem 1972-, Peter Reidy Awd 1983; BSA (Cubmaster, Scoutmaster) 1961-, Eagle Scout 1967, Silver Beaver 1989; NEA 1987-; *office:* Hollis Jr HS 11 Drury Ln Hollis NH 03049

LYLE, KAREN L., 4th Grade Teacher/Tennis Coach; *b:* Spokane, WA; *ed:* (AA) Spokane Falls Comm Coll 1975; (BA) Phy Ed, Whitworth Coll 1977, (MED) Admin, Whitworth Coll 1989; Admin, Whitworth Coll 1989; *cr:* PE/Sci Teacher Glover Jr HS 1978; K-12th Grade Phys Ed/Jr HS Sci Teacher 1978-; HS Coach 1978-; Kndgtn/Elem Rdng/Math Teacher 1978- Davenport Sch Dist 207; *ai:* HS Tennis Coach; Annual Sch Jog-A-Thon Coor; Sch Self Study Coord; WEA 1978; Sr HS Friday Morning Prayer Breakfast Leader-Music 1978-; Presenter Adult Class Preparing for Drug Free Yrs; *office:* Davenport Grade Sch PO Box 8 Davenport WA 99122

LYMAN, TREASA KATE, 7th/8th Grade Lang Art Teacher; *b:* Bloomington, IL; *m:* Robert Dennis; *c:* Kerry Lyman O Donnell, Robert, Michael, Timothy, William; *ed:* (BS) Elem Ed, Edgewood Coll 1967; (MS) Elem Ed, N IL Univ 1978; *cr:* 7th Grade Teacher Visitation 1967-68; 7th/8th Grade Teacher Eisenhower Jr HS 1976-; *ai:* Sch Newspaper Spon; IL Assn Teachers of Eng 1980-; Our Lady of Peace Cncl of Catholic Women Pres 1970-; *office:* Eisenhower Jr HS 1410 75th St Darien IL 60559

LYMAS, RALPH E., History Teacher/Coach; *b:* Hastings, FL; *m:* Neredya G.; *c:* Monica, Re Nada C., Daimille; *ed:* (BA) Health/Phys Ed, St Edwards Univ 1980; *cr:* Bsktbl/Ftbl Coach Alamo Jr HS & Midland Lee 1981-83; Head Bsktbl/Ftbl Coach Floresville HS 1983-85; Head Bsktbl Coach/Defensive Coord La Pryoro HS 1985-88; 1st Asst Defense Coord Presidio HS 1988-; *ai:* Head Coach Track, Boys & Girls Bsktbl; Ftbl Defensive Coord; Soph Spon; TX HS Coaches Assn 1979-; TX HS Bsktbl Coaches Assn 1988-; Bsktbl Coach of Yr 1988-89; Wrote Articles; Teacher of Yr Presidio HS 1988-89; Coach of Yr Floresville HS; *home:* PO Box 1197 Presidio TX 79845

LYNCH, BARBARA A., Social Studies Coordinator; *b:* Salem, OH; *ed:* (BS) Soc Stud, Kent St Univ 1959; (ME) Ed, Westminster Coll 1968; *cr:* Teacher Ursuline HS 1959-69, E Palestine HS 1969-; *ai:* Pep Club & Youth in Government Adv; Soc Stud Coord; EPEA, OEA, NEA, OCSS, NCSS; Area Women Aware, Chamber of Commerce, Booster Club; *office:* East Palestine HS 360 W Grant St East Palestine OH 44413

LYNCH, CAROLYN WILLIFORD, History Teacher; *b:* Haleyville, AL; *m:* Russell; *c:* Jonathan, Jennifer; *ed:* (BS) Phys Ed, 1974, (MS) His/Phys Ed, 1981 Univ of N AL; *cr:* Teacher Hackleburg HS 1974-; *ai:* Beta Club Co-Spon; Jr Class, Var Chrldr Spon; Jr-Sr Prom; AL Ed Assn, NEA, Marion Cty Ed Assn Mem 1974-; Mt View Church of Christ, Hackleburg Alumni Assn Mem; Hackleburg Schlsp Fund Mem 1989-; *office:* Hackleburg HS Nix Rd Hackleburg AL 35564

LYNCH, DEBBIE MIX, Fourth Grade Teacher; *b:* Baton Rouge, LA; *m:* Francis F.; *c:* Brad, Laurie; *ed:* (BS) Elem Ed, 1976, (MED) Elem Rdng/Spec Ed, 1983 LA St Univ; Various Wkshps; *cr:* Teacher East Baton Rouge Parish Schls 1976-; *ai:* Various Sch Comm; United Givers & Food Bank Drive Head; Capital Area Rdng Cncl St & Local Mem; St Alphonsus Cath Parish (Church Mem, Liturgy Comm Mem, Bible Sch Teacher, Coord); GSA Brownie Leader; Teacher of Yr 1989-; *home:* 3436 Canyonland Dr Baton Rouge LA 70814

LYNCH, DENNIS M., Mathematics Instructor; *b:* Oakland, CA; *ed:* (BA) Math, San Jose St Univ 1970, (MS) Math, Univ of Santa Clara 1982; *cr:* Math Instr Campbell HS 1971-76, Prospect HS 1976-88; Evening Math Instr West Valley Coll 1983-; Math Instr Leigh HS 1988-; *ai:* Chaperone Act; Santa Clara Valley Math Assn 1975-77, 1981-83; CTA, NEA 1971-; Los Gatos Chrstn Church 1980-; *office:* Leigh HS 5210 Leigh Ave San Jose CA 95124

LYNCH, DOROTHY G. CLARK, Primary I Teacher; *b:* Savannah, GA; *m:* Jonathan Oris; *c:* Randall G., Allen du Bignon, Vedrice J., Khiah J.; *ed:* (BSED) Early Chldhd Dev, Albany St Teachers Coll 1953; Fellowships to Atlanta Univ Grad Sch, Wayne St Univ, MI St Univ Oakland; *cr:* Primary II Teacher Dwyer Sch 1960-63; 3rd Grade Teacher Keidan Sch 1963-66; Pimary I Teacher Cooke Sch 1966-; *ai:* Elem Sch Curr Comm; Future Teacher Spon; United Torch Drive Comm; Primary Unit & UNCF Chairperson; NEA, MEA 1960-; ASCD 1989-; Detroit Rdng Cncl Building Rep 1969; Detroit Inst Arts Founders Society 1988-; Delta Sigma Theta Historian 1952-54; St John CME Church Stewardess 1976-; St Coll Schlsp; Alpha Kappa Mu Honor Society Awd; Educators Achievement Awd 1989; Banquet for Excl Teacher 1987, 1990; *office:* Cooke Elem Sch 18800 Puritan Ave Detroit MI 48223

LYNCH, EDWARD J., Social Studies Teacher; *b:* New York, NY; *m:* Donna Hughes; *c:* Edwart T., Maura J.; *ed:* (BS) Bus Ed, Spring Hill Coll 1952; (MA) 20th Century His, St Johns Univ 1967; Grad Work Several Universities; *cr:* Teacher Thibodaux Coll, St Stanislaus Coll, Aloysius HS, St Joseph Elem, St Rose Elem 1952-62; Chm Mc Clancy HS, Bishop Reilly HS, Nyeri Sr Scndry 1962-68; Headmaster Nkubu Sr Scndry, Bell Mid Sch 1969-; Adj Instr Mount St Mary Coll 1986-87; Teacher Robert E Bell Mid Sch 1969-; *ai:* Stu Advocacy, Homework, Philosophy Comm; Faculty Cncl; Bishop Reilly HS Dept Chm 1964-67; Bell Sch Chm SS 1972-76; Stu Poll Top Teacher First 1984; Natl Assn Smithsonian 1990; Newberry Lib Fellowship; Kiswahili Grant UCLA; Poverty in USA SUNY Albany; *office:* Robert E Bell Mid Sch 50 Senter St Chappaqua NY 10514

LYNCH, EILEEN SCHUMACHER, Reading Specialist; *b:* Neptone, NJ; *m:* Kevin; *c:* James, Daniel, Thomas; *ed:* (BS) Ed, St Francis Coll 1974; (MS) Ed/Rdng Specialist, C W Post Center Long Island Univ 1978; William Paterson Coll, IN Univ of PA; *cr:* Elem Teacher Altoona Area Sch 1975-76; Rdng Specialist/Gifted & Talented Math Teacher Wyandanch Public Schls 1976-78; Rdng Specialist Sylvan Ave Mid Sch 1978-79, Lakeland Regional HS 1979-; *ai:* NEA 1979-; *office:* Lakeland Regional HS 203 Conklintown Rd Wanaque NJ 07465

LYNCH, ISABEL (LAMPE), Mathematics Teacher; *b:* Geneva, NY; *c:* Jason E., Amanda L.; *ed:* (BA) Math, SUC Potsdam 1971; Grad Stud SUC New Paltz; *cr:* Math Teacher Roy C Ketcham HS 1971-72, Wappingers Falls Jr HS 1972-76, Myers Corners Sch 1976-86, Wappingers Falls Jr HS 1986-; *ai:* Service, Achievement Club, Natl Jr Honor Society Adv; DCMTA, AMTNYS, NCTM; *office:* Wappingers Falls Jr HS Remsen Ave Wappingers Falls NY 12590

LYNCH, JAMES PATRICK, Language Art Teacher; *b:* New York, NY; *m:* Jaclyn Chisholm; *ed:* (MA) Comm, 1984, (BA) Eng/Journalism/Mass Comm, 1975 Univ S FL; *cr:* Eng Teacher Horace Mann Jr HS 1976-88; Lang Art/Journalism Teacher Van Buren Jr HS 1989-; *ai:* Van Buren Crew Stu Newspaper Adv; Phi Delta Kappa Mem 1990; Article Published 1990; *office:* Van Buren Jr HS 8715 22nd St N Tampa FL 33604

LYNCH, MICHAEL P., 6th-8th Grade Math Teacher; *b:* Bayonne, NJ; *m:* Barbara Bielen; *c:* Todd M., Stephanie M.; *ed:* (BA) Elem Ed, 1970, (MA) Guidance, 1981 Jersey City St; *cr:* Teacher Mary J Donohoe 4 1970-; *ai:* Dist Elem Intramural Vlybl, Bsktbl, Cheerleading Prgm Coord; NJEA, Bayonne Teachers Assn 1970-; Natl Fed HS Umpires Assn 1984-; Amateur Sftbl Assn Umpire 1975-; Mary J Donohoe Teacher of Yr Awd Bayonne Dist 1986; *office:* Mary J Donohoe Sch 5th & Dodge Sts Bayonne NJ 07002

LYNCH, NANCY TANCABEL, High School Math Teacher; *b:* Chisholm, MN; *m:* Robert; *c:* Annie, Michael, Kevin; *ed:* (AS) Hibbing Comm Coll 1971; (BS) Math/Ed, Bemidji St 1973; *cr:* 7th Grade Math Teacher Little Falls Mid Sch 1973-84; Math Teacher Little Falls Cmmty HS 1984-; *ai:* Math Curr Comm 1973-; MN Cncl Teachers of Math 1988; *office:* Little Falls Cmmty HS 1001 Se 5 Ave Little Falls MN 56345

LYNCH, ROBERT STEPHEN, Mathematics Department Teacher; *b:* Amelia Cty, VA; *m:* Jean Dollyligh; *c:* Stephanie, Bryan; *ed:* (BS) Math, Guilford Coll 1964; (MS) Elem Ed, Radford Univ 1975; *cr:* Teacher East Surry HS 1964-65, White Plains Elem 1965-76, J Sam Gentry Mid Sch 1976-; *ai:* 7th/8th Grade Ftbl, Mathcounts Team Coach; Bsbl Asst Coach; NCAE, NEA Building Rep; NCTM; Ruritan Club All Local Club Offices, Ruritan of Yr 1985; *home:* Rt 1 Box 403 Lowgap NC 27024

LYNCH, WILLIAM JUNIOR, JR., His/Psych Teacher-Chairperson; *b:* Manchester, KY; *m:* Dian Spurlock; *c:* Koula Z., Brandon S.; *ed:* (AA) General Ed, Sue Bennett Coll 1967; (BS) His/Poly Sci, Cumberland Coll 1969; (MA) Ed/His/ Poly Sci, 1974, (Rank I) Sch Admin/Supervision/Scndry Sch Prin, 1981 Union Coll; Foxfire, 20th Century Russia, Civil War in KY, Appalachian Cultures Trng Wkshps; *cr:* Teacher Livingston HS 1971-73; Teacher/Chairperson Rockcastle Cty HS 1973-; *ai:* NEA, KY Ed Assn 1970-; E KY Teacher Network 1988-; Pittsburg Christian Church (Elder, Music Dir, Sunday Sch Supt, Adult Sunday Sch Teacher); Mellon Fnd Advisory Bd at Berea Coll; *home:* 211 Watts Ave London KY 40741

LYNN, ALBERT CHARLES, III, 6th Grade Teacher; *b:* McKeesport, PA; *m:* Dianne M. Bilesimo; *c:* Ryan, Patrick, Nicholas; *ed:* (BS) Ed, Clarion St Coll 1972; (MS) Ed, Duquesne Univ 1978; Admin Cert; Elem Prin 1979; *cr:* 5th Grade Teacher Scull Elem 1973-81; 6th Grade Teacher Hillcrest Elem 1981-; *ai:* Jr HS Track Coach; Asst Varsity Ftbl Coach; Math Club Spon; Norwin Teachers Credit Union Secy 1986-; Outstanding Young Educator Awd 1983; Hillcrest Outstanding Teacher of Yr Awd 1988-89; *home:* 1571 Guffey Rd North Huntingdon PA 15642

LYNN, ANITA FORD, Pre-School Montessori Teacher; *b:* San Antonio, TX; *m:* Fred L.; *c:* Mark, Jennifer, Kirk; *ed:* (BSED) Elem Ed, SW TX St Univ 1964; Montessori Pre-Primary Certificate St Nicholas Trng Center, London England 1974; Amer Montessori Society Pre-Primary Certificate OK City Univ 1979; *cr:* 3rd Grade Teacher 1964-66, 1st Grade Teacher 1966-68 Bellaire Elem Sch; 1st Grade Teacher 1971-72, Montessori Asst Teacher 1973-74, Montessori Teacher 1974- St Marys Hall; *ai:* Volunteer Hugger TX Spec Olympics; Amer Montessori Society, TX St Rdng Assn; 1st Baptist Church Sunday Sch Teacher; Holt-Dupont Fnd Grant 1986; *office:* St Marys Hall Sch 9401 Starcrest San Antonio TX 78217

LYNN, JOYCE MC MINN, Kindergarten Teacher; *b:* Oklahoma City, OK; *w:* Joe D. (dec); *c:* Ruby Soutiere, James, Amy, Kent; *ed:* (BS) Elem Ed, OK St Univ 1952; Grad Work OK St, Eastern NM Univ, Adams St, Coll of the Southwest; *cr:* 2nd Grade Teacher Fairfax OK 1952-53, Toano VA 1953-54; Kndgtn

Teacher Llano Elem 1971-1973; Migrant Teacher Lovington Schls 1973-76; Kndgtn Teacher Lea Elem 1976-; *ai:* Kappa Delta Pi; AAUW.

LYNN, LULA HALE, 8th Grade Mathematics Teacher; *b:* Minter, AL; *m:* Donald; *c:* Jo Nique D., Donald J.; *ed:* (BS) Chem, AL A&M Univ 1974; (T4) Chem/Math, GA St Univ 1980; *cr:* Math/Sci Teacher Henry Cty Mid Sch 1974-76, Abbeville HS 1977-79, Briarwood HS & Russell HS 1979-88; 8th Grade Math Teacher Woodland Mid Sch 1988-; *ai:* Jr Beta Club; *office:* Woodland Mid Sch 2816 Briarwood Blvd East Point GA 30034

LYNN, PEGGY ANN, Mathematics/Computer Teacher; *b:* Billings, MT; *m:* Kurt Westenbarger; *ed:* (AAS) Math/Surveying, Flathead Valley Comm Coll 1981; (BS) Math, MT St Univ 1985; *cr:* Math Teacher West Yellowstone HS 1985-; *ai:* NHS Adv; NCTM, MCTM 1983-; ICCE, MCCE 1985-; NEA, MEA, WYEA (Pres 1989-) 1985-; Natl Sci Fnd Integrated Math Prgms & Cmptr Technology Grant.

LYNN, RICHARD ARTHUR, 7th & 8th Grade Sci Teacher; *b:* St Louis, MO; *ed:* (BS) Ed, Univ of TN Martin 1981; *cr:* Jr HS Math/His Teacher Kenton Elem Sch 1981-82; HS His Teacher Dyersburg HS 1983; Jr HS Eng Teacher Kenton Elem Sch 1984-85; Jr HS Sci Teacher Black Oak Elem Sch 1985-; *ai:* Sci Club Spon 1988-; Yrbk Co-adv 1990; OCEA 1981-; Teacher Study Cncl Rep 1986-88; Black Oak Teacher of Yr 1989; Obion Cty Teacher of Yr 1989; *office:* Black Oak Elem Sch Box 38 Shawtown Rd Hornbeak TN 38232

LYNN, SARA SALLY ESTILLE, 5th Grade Teacher; *b:* Elizabeth, NJ; *c:* Jeffrey, Tracey; *ed:* (BA) Ed Soc Stud, Baldwin-Wallace Coll 1962; (ME) Ed Rdng Specialist, CA Univ of PA 1977; *cr:* 7th Grade Soc Stud Teacher Elyria Sch Dist 1962-63; Rdng Specialist Teacher 1970-80, 5th Grade Elem Teacher 1980- Connsville Sch Dist; *home:* RD 1 Box 21 A Vanderbilt PA 15486

LYNUM, BETTYE H. HEAD, Teacher/Mathematics Chair; *b:* Quitman, GA; *m:* James D.; *c:* Brandon, Nicole; *ed:* (BA) Elem Ed, Fort Valley St Coll 1968; (MS) Mid Grades, GA St Univ 1981; *cr:* Teacher Doaly Cty Bd of Ed 1968-70, Atlanta Public Sch 1970-; *ai:* Math Club; Atlanta Assn of Ed, GA Assn of Ed; Integrating Cmptrs Math; Old Natl Athletic Assn; *home:* 3755 Benchmark Dr College Park GA 30349

LYON, BARBARA BROOKS, Eighth Grade Teacher; *b:* Galax, VA; *m:* Danny D.; *c:* Noah, Danna; *ed:* (BS) Home Ec Ed, Appalachian St Univ 1972; (MA) Mid Grades/Jr HS ASU 1982; Admin Cert, ASU 1989; Mentor Cert 1989; *cr:* 5th-8th Grade Sci/Health Teacher 1972-73, 4th Grade Teacher 1973-87, 8th Grade Teacher 1987- Glade Creek Sch; Asst Prin 1988-; *ai:* Phys Ed Coord; Awards Day Coord; Sci Olympiad Spon; Annual Spon; Southern Assn Accreditation Steering Comm; NEA 1972-; NCAE 1972-; Alleghany NCAE Secy 1974; Career Homemakers Pres 1974; Glade Creek Boosters Club Secy 1988-, Outstanding Service 1988; Outstanding Young Women of America 1983; Delta Kappa Gamma Society 1984; *home:* Rt 1 Sparta NC 28675

LYON, DIANNE FRANCESCONI, Social Studies Chair; *b:* Chicago, IL; *m:* Porter A.; *ed:* (BA) His, Coll of Notre Dame 1960; (MA) His, Marquette Univ 1964; Grad Stud; *cr:* Teacher Hampstead Hill Jr HS 1960-63; House Mother Marquette Univ 1964; Teacher Eastern HS 1964-65; Instr Coll of Notre Dame 1965-67; Teacher Immaculata Coll HS 1986-; *ai:* His Club; Mid Sts Comm; Amer Historical Assn 1990; Amer Italian Historical Assn 1976-; Meal-On-Wheels Route Chairperson 1976-86; Marquette Schlsp to Complete Grad Stud; *office:* Immaculata Coll HS 12301 Academy Way Rockville MD 20852

LYON, DONALD J., Mathematics Teacher; *b:* Hopkinsville, KY; *m:* Katherine Stephenson; *c:* Joe; *ed:* (BA) Math, 1966, (MA) Ed, 1969 W KY Univ; *cr:* Math Teacher Koffman Jr HS 1966-70, Chrstn Cty Mid Sch 1970-; *office:* Chrstn Cty Mid Sch Glass Ave Hopkinsville KY 42240

LYON, JUDEE (ROWLAND), Art Teacher/Fine Arts Chairman; *b:* Clinton, OK; *m:* Philip B.; *c:* Brooke, Brennon; *ed:* (BAED) Art/Speech/Theatre, Southwestern St Coll 1968; *cr:* Speech/Drama Teacher/Debate Coach Putnam City West HS 1968-71; Art/Eng Teacher W Oaks Jr HS 1974-; *ai:* Art Club Spon; NEA, OK Ed Assn, Assn Classroom Teachers 1968-; Beta Sigma Phi (Pres 1986-87, Corresponding Secy 1989-, VP 1982-83, 1985-86); *office:* Western Oaks Jr HS 7200 NW 23rd St Bethany OK 73008

LYON, THOMAS EDWARD, Earth Science/Biology Teacher; *b:* Normal, IL; *m:* Darlene Rust; *ed:* (BS) Bio, Ball St Univ 1988; *cr:* Sales San Diego Fire Equipment Company 1982-84; Labor United Parcel Service 1984-88; Teacher Daleville Jr Sr HS 1988-; *ai:* Var Girls Vlybl & 8th Grade Boys Bsktbl Coach; Gamma Theta Upsilon 1988-; Sierra Club 1984-; *office:* Daleville Jr/Sr HS P O Box 525 Daleville IN 47334

LYONS, EARL JAMES, English Department Chair; *b:* Minneapolis, MN; *m:* Sandra Dale; *c:* Christopher, Scott, Elizabeth; *ed:* (BA) Eng Ed, 1960, (MS) Ed/Psych, Univ of MN; Grad Stud; *cr:* Teacher Lincoln HS 1962-64, Kennedy HS 1965-69; Jefferson HS 1970-; *ai:* Dept Head; Textbook Adoption, AV, Project Re-Entry Screening Comms; Faculty Seante Pres 1988-89; Excl in Ed Awd 1987; *office:* Bloomington Jefferson HS 2001 W 102nd St Bloomington MN 55437

LYONS, JAMES EVERETT, History & Spanish Teacher; *b:* Augusta, GA; *m:* Ruth Laurel Peterson; *c:* Sara J., Elizabeth A., Joshua J., Susanna R.; *ed:* (BS) Pastoral Theology, 1978, (MED) Ed, 1980 Hyles Anderson Coll; *cr:* Teacher 1st Baptist Sch 1978-82, Riverview Chrstn Sch 1982-83, Grace Chrstn Sch 1984-; *ai:* Chess Club Coach; Span Club Spon; Grace Baptist Church (Adult Trng Union Teacher 1984-, Jr Church Preacher 1985-); Articles Published Chrstn Womanhood Magazine; *office:* Grace Chrstn Sch 2915 14th Ave Columbus GA 31904

LYONS, JUDITH C., English Teacher; *b:* New Britain, CT; *m:* Thomas J.; *ed:* (BS) Ed/Eng/Rdng, Teachers Coll of CT 1961; (MS) Ed/Rdng, Cntrl CT St 1970; Cooperating Teacher & Mentor Prgm CT St Dept of Ed 1989; *cr:* 7th-9th Grade Eng Teacher Myron J Michael Jr HS 1961-63, Silas Deane Jr HS 1963-68; 1st-6th Grade Rdng Teacher Fred Wish Sch 1968-69; 7th-9th Grade Rdng Teacher Clifford Miller Jr HS 1969-70; 9th Grade Rdng Teacher Hartford Public HS 1970-74; 9Th-10th Grade Eng Teacher Bulkley HS 1974-; *ai:* Tutor-adv Financial Aid Coll Prep Stus & Stu Athletes; Bulkeley 10 Yr Accreditation Evaluation; Extracurricural Activity Chairperson; Bulkeley Parent Newsletter Editorial Bd; Japanese Educators Visit Participating More Effective Schls Comm & rapport Comm; Crisis Prevention Team Chaperone; Trinity Coll Upward Bound Prgm Cnslr & tutor; NCTE 1961-; Hartford Stage Co 1986-; Hartford Fed of Teachers 1974-; Eagle Scout Spon 1988-89; Boricuas Unidos Park St Youth Service Center Supporter 1989; Teacher of Month Bulkeley Stu Body 1983/88; Teacher of Yr Bulkeley Staff 1989-; Hartford Public Schls ExemplarY Teacher 1989-; *office:* Bulkeley H S 300 Wethersfield Ave Hartford CT 06114

LYONS, KAREN SUE (MILLER), Third Grade Teacher; *b:* Elizabethton, TN; *m:* Anthony W.; *c:* Renee; *ed:* (BS) Elem Ed, East TN St Univ 1969; *cr:* Librarian Wallace Elem 1969-70, Glen Alpine Jr HS 1970-71, Abingdon HS 1971-72, Happy Valley Elem 1972-80; 3rd Grade Teacher Happy Valley Elem 1980-; *ai:* Carter Cty Ed Assn; TN Ed Assn; Gap Creek Chrstn Church Ladies Circle Pres 1986-; Charter Mem of TN Teachers Advisory Cncl; *home:* Rt 4 Box 2625 Elizabethton TN 37643

LYONS, KIMBERLY PEVELER, Business Education Instructor; *b:* Greenville, KY; *m:* David C.; *ed:* (BS) General Bus/Distributive Educ, 1982; (MS) Scndry Ed, 1985 Western KY Univ; Endorsement for Accounting 1983; Endorsement for Basic Bus 1988; Elem Educ Univ of Louisville 1989; *cr:* Bus Teacher Breckinridge Area Vocational Educl Ctr 1982-84; St Romuald HS 1984-85; Mrktg Teacher Meade Cty Vocational Educl Ctr 1985-88; Bus Teacher/Co-Op Coord Meade Cty HS 1988-; *ai:* Adv to Future Bus Leaders Amer; Former Adv Distributive Ed Clubs Amer; KY Vocational Assn 1982-88; Mrktg Educators 1985-88; KY Educators Assn/NEA 1988-; Regional Distributive Ed Teacher 8th Yr 1988; St Distributive Ed Awd for Outstanding Work with Amer HS Students 1989; *home:* PO Box 280 Hardinsburg KY 40143

LYONS, MICHAEL LAWRENCE, 8th Grade English Teacher; *b:* Missoula, MT; *m:* Cheryl Lynn Burgmaier; *c:* Danielle, Jace; *ed:* (BA) Eng, Univ of MT 1981; Working Towards Masters Admin; *cr:* Var Ftbl Coach Sentinel HS 1981-; Eng Teacher Rattlesnake Mid Sch 1984-; *ai:* Ftbl & Bsktbl Coach; Yrbk & Cmptr Club Spon; Speech & Drama Coach Rattlesnake Mid Sch; Phi Delta Gappa 1987-; Presenter Natl Mid Sch Conference; Articles Published; Bus Week Awd; *office:* Rattlesnake Mid Sch 120 Pineview Missoula MT 59802

LYONS, PORTIA NICELY, First Grade Teacher; *b:* Latrobe, PA; *m:* William Larry; *c:* Christian L., Patrice L.; *ed:* (BS) Ed, Clarion Univ 1969; Grad Stud Slippery Rock Univ; *cr:* 3rd Grade Teacher Hempfield Schls 1969-70; 5th Grade Teacher 1970-72, 6th Grade Teacher 1972-73 Laurel; 3rd Grade Teacher 1978-80, 5th Grade Teacher 1980-82, Kndgtn/Teacher of Gifted Class 1982-84 Wilmington Sch; Kndgtn Teacher 1984-86, 1st Grade Teacher 1988- New Bedford Elem Sch; *home:* RD 3 Box 165 A Volant PA 16156

LYONS, REGINA NADINE, Lang Art Teacher/Dept Chair; *b:* Tarboro, NC; *ed:* (BS) Elem/Intermediate Ed, NC Wesleyan 1982; (MED) Mid Grades Ed/Lang Art, Campbell Univ 1985; *cr:* 7th Grade Lang Art Teacher Phillip Mid Sch 1983-; *ai:* Beta Club Spon; Sch Publicity Comm; 7th Grade Dept Chairperson; Cultural Art & Guidance Comm; Mentor Teacher 1989-; NC Assn of Educators; Prgm for Excl Mini-Grant 1986-87, 1988-89; *office:* Phillips Mid Sch PO Box 203 Battleboro NC 27809

LYONS, SARA K., 6th/7th Grade Math Teacher; *b:* Sharon, PA; *m:* Lynn D.; *c:* Michelle, Jeffery; *ed:* (BS) Elem Ed, Univ of Slippery Rock 1964; Masters Equivalent Math Ed, W MD Coll 1985; *cr:* 4th Grade Teacher Hickory Township Sch Dist 1964-65; 4th Grade Teacher Berkshire Elem 1965-70; 6th/7th Grade Teacher Charles Cty 1978-; *ai:* M M Somers Team 6-7 Team Leader; Promoting Success for All Stu Comm; Univ of MD Clinical Supvr; Charles Cty Ed Assn, MD St Teachers Assn, NEA 1978-; St Pauls Episcopal Church Teacher 1976-82; Somers PTA Best Teacher Awd 1987-88; MD St Dept of Ed Teacher Assistance Team 1986-87; *office:* Milton M Somers Mid Sch Box A La Plata MD 20646

LYONS, SHARON M. (ANDERSON), Sixth Grade Teacher; *b:* Cincinnati, OH; *m:* Robert T.; *c:* Ashleigh; *ed:* (BS) Ed, Univ of Cincinnati 1973; *cr:* 6th Grade Teacher Madisonville Elem 1973-74, Cntrl Fairmount Elem 1974-; *office:* Cntrl Fairmount Elem Sch 2475 White St Cincinnati OH 45214

LYTLE, PATRICIA (LUKOWICZ), Mathematics Teacher; *b:* Warwick, RI; *m:* John P.; *c:* John P. III, Christopher F., MArissa L.; *ed:* (BA) Math/Scndry Ed, RI Coll 1976; Grad Stud; *cr:* Teacher Lockwood Jr HS 1978-79, Aldrich Jr HS 1979-87, Winman Jr HS 1987-; *ai:* Cheerleading Adv; Steering Curr Comm Secy; Private Math Tutor; NCTM, ATMNE 1979-; *office:* Winman Jr HS 525 Centreville Rd Warwick RI 02886

LYTLE, TAMRA MC LENDON, Fourth Grade Teacher; *b:* Fort Pierce, FL; *m:* Randall; *c:* Kobey; *ed:* (BS) Early Chldhd Ed, 1980, (MED) Early Chldhd Ed, 1989 GA Southern Coll; Supervising Teacher Services; *cr:* 4th Grade Teacher Jeff Davis Mid Sch 1980-; *ai:* NEA, GAE 1980-89; Eureka Baptist Church (Childrens Church Dir 1986-, Ladies Circle Secy 1987-); *office:* Jeff Davis Mid Sch 108 Coffee St Hazlehurst GA 31539

M

MAAS, DOROTHY HAUCK, Fourth Grade Teacher; *b:* Watertown, SD; *m:* Kenneth Grant; *c:* Jay K.; *ed:* Elem Ed, Northern St Teachers Coll 1963, 1971; Elem Ed, Spec Ed, Learning Disibilities, Northern St Coll; *cr:* 2nd Grade Teacher Gettysburg Public Schls 1963-66, Howard-Hedger Sch 1966-67, O M Tiffany Sch 1967-71; 4th Grade Teacher O M Tiffany Sch 1971-; *ai:* Soc Stud Comm Mem; SDEA, NEA, Local Ed Assn 1963-; Intnl Rdng Assn 1989-; Dakota Gals Pres 1985-87; Luth Church Ladies Aide Pres 1984-86; Luth Church Circle (Pres, Secy, Treas) 1980-; *home:* 1109 North Dakota St Aberdeen SD 57401

MAAS, KENNETH, Mathematics Teacher; *b:* Elmhurst, IL; *m:* Kathleen A.; *c:* Jason; *ed:* (BS) Math, 1970, (MS) Scndry Ed, 1976 N IL Univ; Admin Certificate, N IL Univ; Prof Learning Services Courses; *cr:* Teacher Minooka HS 1970-71; US Army Fort Lewis WA 1971-73; Teacher Minooka HS 1973-; *ai:* Math Coach; ICTM, NCTM; *office:* Minooka HS P O Box 489 Minooka IL 60447

MABE, LINDA FULTON, English Teacher; *b:* Eden, NC; *m:* Doug; *c:* David; *ed:* (BSB) Eng, Appalachian St Univ, 1973 (MED) Exceptional Ed, Univ of NC Greensboro 1981; Mentor Support Certified; Ed S Admin & Supervision, Appalachian St Univ; *cr:* Eng Teacher Rockingham Cty Schls 1973-; *ai:* Stu Cncl Adv; Eng Dept Chairperson; High IQ Team Coach; Sch Improvement Comm; Advisory Cncl; Leader of Stus to Europe; NC Assn of Educators 1973-; NEA 1973-; NCTE 1973-89; NC Eng Teachers Assn 1973-89; Delta Kappa Gamma Secy 1986-; Gibsonville United Meth Church 1987-; Local Teacher of Yr 1988, 1889; Runner Up Regional Teacher of Yr 1988;NC Stu Cncl Adv of Yr 1980; Outstanding Young Woman in Amer 1987; *office:* Rockingham Cty Sr HS PO Box 41 Wentworth NC 27375

MABRY, JANIS MELTON, Chemistry Teacher; *b:* Memphis, TN; *m:* Steven L.; *c:* Misty, Drew; *ed:* (BS) Bio Ed, 1975, (MED) Sci Ed, 1979 MS St Univ; Grad Stud Chem, Delta St Univ; *cr:* Jr HS Sci Teacher Fifth St Jr HS 1978-81; Bio Teacher Greenville Chrstn 1982-83; Bio/Chem/Biochem Teacher St Joseph Cath HS 1984-86; Chem Teacher Tuscaloosa Cty HS 1987-; *ai:* TCEA Rep 1988-89; *office:* Tuscaloosa Cty HS 2200 24th St Northport AL 35476

MABRY, LINDA ARMENT, 6th Grade Teacher; *b:* Xenia, OH; *c:* Adrianne L.; *ed:* (AA) Bus, Clark Tech Coll 1974; (BS) Elem Ed, Urbana Coll 1981; Working on Masters Ed, Wright St Univ; *cr:* 6th Grade Teacher Triad Elem 1981-; *ai:* Asst Band Dir; Textbook Adoption Comm; Writing Math Competency Policy; Prin Advisory Comm; OH Jaycee Auxiliary (Local-Internal/External VP, Secy, Dist Coord/Natl Chairperson for Juvenile Diabetes 1979-80; *office:* Triad Elem Sch 7920 Brush Lake Rd North Lewisburg OH 43060

MABRY, MARY HUFFMAN, Third Grade Teacher; *b:* Commerce, TX; *m:* Marshall Whit; *c:* Michael G., Sharon K. Fontanella, Vicki L. Booth; *ed:* (AA) McLennan Comm Coll 1967, (BA) Elem Ed, 1969, (MS) Ed, 1972 Baylor *cr:* 1st Grade Teacher Midway Ind Sch Dist Woodway Elem 1969-77, 3rd Grade Teacher Midway Ind Sch Dist Woodway Elem & Spring Valley Elem 1977-; *ai:* TX St Teachers Assn, NEA Dist Exec Comm; Midway Educators Assn Pres; Alpha Delta Kappa Recording Secy 1984-86, 1988-; Midway PTA Pres 1962-63.

MABRY, TERRY THRONEBURG, Drafting Teacher; *b:* Navasota, France; *m:* Robert Andrew; *c:* Megan L.; *ed:* Assoc Engineering, Wingate Coll 1978; Engineering, UNCC; *cr:* Drafting Teacher Anson Sr HS 1980-; *ai:* VICA Club Adv; Co Chm Prom; Sftbl Coach; Civitan Teacher of Month.

MACALUSO, MARK J., History Teacher/Coach; *b:* Trinidad, CO; *m:* Lori Watson; *ed:* (AA) Ed, Trinidad St Jr Coll 1975; (BA) Phys Ed, Univ of S CO 1978; Scndry Ed, Univ of S CO, Adams St Coll; *cr:* Teacher/Coach Sierra Grande HS 1979-81, Kim HS 1981-84, Branson HS 1984-88, Hoehne HS 1988-; *ai:* Head Boys

Var Bsktbl Coach, Asst Track Coach; CHSCA League Rep 1984-; *office:* Hoehne HS PO Box 91 Hoehne CO 81046

MAC ARTHUR, THOMAS PIERCE, Mathematics Teacher; *b:* Cheboygan, MI; *m:* Martha Joyce Brazones; *c:* Timothy, Steven; *ed:* (BS) Chemical Engineering, MI Technological Univ 1969; Teacher Cert, Univ of N CO; Grad Stud, W MI Univ; *cr:* Math Teacher Willcox HS 1974-76; Sci Teacher Pecos Jr HS 1976-79; Bus Owner Fort Mackinew Candy Factory 1979-85; Math Teacher Hopkins HS 1985-; *ai:* Var Girls Bsktbl & 8th Grade Boys Bsktbl Coach; MI Cncl of Teachers of Math, MI Ed Assn, Natl Fed of Interscholastic Coaches Assn 1985-; *home:* 503 N Maple St Hopkins MI 49328

MACCABEE, SARA KATHRYN, English Teacher; *b:* Aurora, IL; *m:* David William; *ed:* (BA) Eng, 1984, (MAT) Eng/Scndry Ed, 1986 Univ of IA; Rotary Fnd Schlsp, Grad Study Abroad; Medieval Stud, Univ of Bristol England; *cr:* Eng Teacher Sterling HS 1987-88, Riverdale HS 1988-; *ai:* Yrbk Adv; Speech Team Coach; Pi Lambda Theta 1986; *office:* Riverdale Sr HS 9622 256th St N Port Byron IL 61275

MACCAGNANO, VINCENT PHILIP, Physics/Chemistry Teacher; *b:* Brooklyn, NY; *m:* Patricia Ann Jesek; *c:* Jennifer; *ed:* (BA) Biological Sci, S IL Univ Carbondale 1974; (MS) Bio, Chicago St Univ 1981; Various Studs; *cr:* Chem Teacher George Washington HS 1975-76; Chem/Phys Ed/Phys Sci Teacher South Shore HS 1976-77; Chem Teacher Calumet HS 1977-79; Chem/Phys/Phys Sci Teacher South Shore HS 1979-83; Bio/Chem/Physics Teacher Bogan HS 1983-; *ai:* Var Ftbl Asst & Line Coach; Defense Coord; Acad Olympics Sci Team; IL Sci Teacher Assn 1987-; PTA 1983-; IL HS Ftbl Coaches Assn 1988-; Avalon Trail Improvement Assn 1985-; Eucharistic Minister St Florian R C Church 1984-; Nom for Presidential Awd Excl in Sci Teaching 1991; Chicago Public Schls Monetary Incentive Awd 1984; Inspirational Sci Teacher Awd IL Inst of Technology; *office:* Bogan Cmptr Tech HS 3939 W 79th St Chicago IL 60652

MAC CONNELL, MARSHA A., Kindergarten Teacher; *b:* Rochester, NY; *m:* James R.; *c:* Terry, Christopher; *ed:* (BA) Elem Ed, St Univ of NY Brockport 1973; Grad Stud; *cr:* 6th Grade Teacher 1973-84, Kndgtn Teacher 1984- Byron-Bergen Elem Sch; *ai:* Variety Shows, Faculty Plays, Stu Play Dir; Stu Assistance Advisory & Teachers Mentor Prgm Steering Comm Mem; Fundraising Co-Chairperson; Delta Kappa Gamma 1983-; PTA Teacher Rep 1987-, Teacher of Month 1988; Order of Eastern Star (Various Offices, Matron) 1978-; Church Sunday Sch Teacher; Staff Mem of Month 1988; *home:* 2 Munger St Bergen NY 14416

MAC DONALD, CRAIG LINDSAY, Teacher; *b:* Brooklyn, NY; *c:* Amy L., Matthew T.; *ed:* (AA) Liberal Arts, Adirondack Comm Coll 1968; (BS) Eng Ed, Castleton St Coll VT 1970; (MS) Eng Plattsburg St 1975; Institute of Children Literature 1975; Institute Children Literature Graduate 1975; *cr:* 7th/8th Grade Eng Teacher Hudson Falls Jr HS 1970-; *ai:* NYSTUS; NETE; South Glens Falls Bd of Ed VP 1985-89; Mac Donalds Musings; Published in Image Magazine/The Post-Star; Instr of Yr-Chois Tae Kwon Do; Martial Arts Instr 1987.

MACDONALD, JENNIFER LEE, English Instructor/Dept Chair; *b:* Middletown, OH; *m:* Jerome; *c:* Kyle, Devin; *ed:* (BA) Eng, 1973, (BA) Ed, 1974 Univ of AZ; (MAT) Ed/Eng, Univ of AZ & W NM Univ 1987; *cr:* Eng/Math Remedial Teacher Alpine Conservation Center 1979; Eng Instr Reserve HS 1980-; *ai:* Spon Spectrum HS Newspaper 1989-; General Excl Awd NM Press Womens Assn Competition; Spon Mock Trial Team 1989-; NCTE 1987-; Teacher of Yr Reserve Sch Dist 1988-89; *office:* Reserve HS P O Box 347 Reserve NM 87830

MAC DONALD, LINDA ANN, 8th Grade Lang Arts Teacher; *b:* Upland, PA; *ed:* (BS) Elem Ed, West Chester Univ 1963; (MEQ) Penn St & Widener & Marywood 1983; *cr:* 3rd Grade Teacher Stetser Elem 1963-68; 4th-6th Grade Teacher Rose Tree Media Sch Dist 1968-; 8th Grade Teacher Springton Lake Mid Sch 1981-; *ai:* Yrbk, SLYC Spon; 8th Grade Team Leader; Rose Tree Media Ed Assn 1968-; PA St Ed Assn, NEA 1963-; NCTE 1989-; Sch Dist Grant; Dist & Sch Service Awds; *home:* 3449 Commerce Ave Brookhaven PA 19015

MAC DONALD, PAULA WORLEY, Music Teacher; *b:* El Paso, TX; *m:* Lloyd William III; *c:* Michelle, Christopher, Sean; *ed:* (BA) Music Ed, Southwest TX St Univ 1978; Elem Ed 1984; *cr:* Music Teacher Edgemere Elem Sch 1978-84, Edgemere Elem & Mesa Vista Elem & Lancaster Elem 1986-87; *ai:* 5th & 6th Grade Choir 1978-84; Teach Piano Lessons; Mac Dowell Club 1978-; AAUW 1978-80; GSA (Brownie Troop Leader, Asst) 1987-; Hillrise Elem PTO (Mem, Secy) 1988-.

MAC DONALD, RICHARD EMERSON, Science Teacher; *b:* Fairbanks, AK; *m:* Grace Diane Christie; *c:* Jennifer N., Kristen M.; *ed:* (BS) Earth Sci, VA Tech 1974; (MED) Earth Sci, Univ of VA 1986; *cr:* Sci Teacher Benjamin Syms Jr HS 1974-85, Kecoughtan HS 1985-; *ai:* Girls Fast Pitch Sftbl Coach; *home:* 125 Nottingham Trl Newport News VA 23602

MAC DOUGALL, DONALD K., 6th Grade Teacher; *b:* Rochester, NY; *m:* Joanne Sillman; *c:* Sean P., Colin K.; *ed:* (AAS) Mechanical Technology, SUNY Alfred 1962; (BS) Elem Ed, SUNY Oswego 1970; *cr:* 4th Grade Teacher 1970-73, 6th Grade Teacher 1973- Sodus Cntrl Sch; *ai:* Var Soccer, Bsktbl, Tennis; Sch Store; Effective Schls Dist & Building Teams; Intermediate Cross Cntry Ski Club; NEA 1970-; US Tennis Assn 1989-; US Prof Tennis Registry Instr 1988-; N Rose Fire Dept Ambulance Service Captain 1970-76; Presenter NY St Whole Lang Conference 1989, BOCES Conference Lit Based Rdng; *office:* Sodus Cntrl Schls Box 220 Mill St Sodus NY 14551

MAC DOWELL, KAREN CHONKA, Reading & English Teacher; *b:* New Brunswick, NJ; *ed:* (BA) Elem Ed, Trenton St Coll 1965; (MA) Curr & Instruction Rdng & Writing Process, NY Univ 1989; *cr:* 3rd Trade Teacher Hillcrest Sch 1965-66; 3rd & 4th Grade Teacher Mac Afee Rd Sch 1966-80; 7th & 8th Grade Rdng & Eng Teacher Sampson G Smith Int Sch 1981-; *ai:* Franklin Twp Teachers Assn Treas 1967-68; Somerset Cty Teachers Assn Treas 1965-; NJ Teachers Assn NEA Treas 1965-; NCTE 1987-; *office:* Sampson G Smith Int Sch Amwell Rd Somerset NJ 08873

MACE, MYRA ANNETTE, Phys Sci/Gen Math/Life Sci; *b:* Latta, SC; *m:* Tim Gomez; *c:* Greg, Timisha; *ed:* (BS) Bio, Benedict Coll 1975; (MS) Cell Bio, Univ of CT 1977; Howard Univ Sch of Dentistry; *cr:* Sci Teacher DC Public Schls 1978-83, P G Cty Public Schls 1983-; *ai:* Safe & Orderly Environ Comm Mem; Girls Bsktbl Coach; Girls Jump Rope Group Adv; PTA Howard Cty Mem; AFT 1980-; Zeta Phi Beta Mem 1975-; PTA Mem 1988-; Natl Assn For The Advancement of Colored People 1988-; Zeta Phi Beta & SC Grants; Univ of CT Fellowship; Cum Laude Benedict Coll 1975; *office:* Nicholas Orem Mid Sch 6100 Editors Press Dr Hyattsville MD 20784

MACEJKO, RUBY MARIE, Fourth Grade Teacher; *b:* Youngstown, OH; *m:* Joseph Robert; *c:* Joseph R., Andrew J., Andrea D.; *ed:* (BSED) Elem Ed/Kndgtn/Gifted/Learning Disabilities, Youngstown St 1959; Cmptr Sci; Numerous Wkshps & Inservice Lang Art Prgms; *cr:* 2nd/3rd Grade Teacher Addison Elem 1959-61; 4th/5th Grade Teacher Cleveland Elem 1962-67; 4th Grade Teacher Lincoln Elem 1968-; *ai:* Elem Cheerleading 1961-67; Advanced/Intermediate Stu Cncl 1984-; Intermediate Tutor 1959-; Curr Cncl 1966-70; New Book Stud Comm 1973-75; WIBC Teachers Bowling League 1964-74; Say No Spon Intnl Level 1985-; YEA ADHOC (Chairperson 1964-68) 1959-; OEA, NEA 1959-; Intnl Rdng Assn 1959-; Amer Eng Cncl 1959-89; PTA Treas 1979-83; *office:* Lincoln Elem Sch 1415 Charlotte Youngstown OH 44506

MAC EWAN, M. BRUCE, 7th Grade Soc Stud Teacher; *b:* New Brunswick, NJ; *m:* Diane Karlkvist; *c:* Jennifer; *ed:* (BA) His/Poly Sci, Hiram Coll 1972; (MA) Ed Admin, Glassboro St Coll 1983; *cr:* Teacher Ocean City Intermediate Sch 1976-; *ai:* Earth Day Comm; NEA, NJ Ed Assn, Ocean City Ed Assn; *office:* Ocean City Intermediate Sch 19th & Bay Ave Ocean City NJ 08226

MACHALEC, PAUL G., Biology Teacher; *b:* Houston, TX; *m:* Elizabeth; *c:* Garrett; *ed:* (BS) Animal Sci, Stephen F Austin St Univ 1983; Teacher Cert SW TX St Univ 1985; *cr:* Bio Teacher Marion HS 1985-; *ai:* Sci Club Spon; Asst Bsbl Coach 1987-89; Assn of TX Prof Educators VP 1988-89; *office:* Marion HS P O Box 127 Marion TX 78124

MACHEN, GARY LEE, American History Teacher; *b:* Pittsburgh, PA; *m:* Elizabeth Lucko; *c:* Jonathan, Joshua; *ed:* (BA) Ed, Univ of Pgh 1971; *cr:* Amer His Teacher Gateway Sr HS 1972; Gateway Jr HS 1990; *ai:* Gateway Ed Assn VP 1989-; *office:* Gateway Sr H S Mosside Blvd Monroeville PA 15146

MACHUGA, SHARON ROSE, Second Grade Teacher; *b:* Youngstown, OH; *ed:* (BS) Elem Ed, 1979, (AD) Child Care Technology, 1980, Remedial Rdng 1981 Youngstown St Univ; *cr:* Elem Teacher St Joseph Cath Sch 1979-; *ai:* Public Rel Chairperson St Joseph Sch; Stu Cncl Adv; 1st Reconciliation Facilitator; 1st Communion Facilitator; Intnl Rdng Assn 1979-; East OH CTAS Co Sci Awd 1989; *office:* St Joseph Cath Sch 4565 New Rd Austintown OH 44515

MACIAG, GEORGE, Biology Teacher; *b:* Allentown, PA; *m:* Stephanie A. Winton; *ed:* (BA) Bio Ed, 1971, (MED) Bio Ed, 1977 Kutztown St Univ; *cr:* Bio Teacher Salisbury HS 1971-; *ai:* Scholastic Scrimmage Coach; NSTA; Lehigh Valley Assn of Biologists Planning Comm; NEA, PA St Ed Assn; Salisbury Ed Assn Building Rep; *office:* Salisbury Township Sch 500 E Montgomery St Allentown PA 18103

MACIAS, HERMINIA, Counselor; *b:* Piedras Negras, Mexico; *ed:* (BA) Math, Univ of TX Austin 1976; (MED) Ed, Sul Ross St Univ 1978; Grad Stud Counseling; *cr:* Math Teacher Eagle Pass Jr HS 1976-86, Memorial Jr HS 1986-89; Cnslr Ray H Darr Elem 1989-; *ai:* Attendance, Campus Wide Project Comm Mem; Math-A-Thon Spon; Girls Vlybl & Sftbl Team Mgr; Partners in Rdng Parental Involvement Organization & Cmptr Laboratory Coord; Pi Mu Espilon Life Mem; Delta Kappa Gamma Treas 1986-; TX St Teachers Assn, NEA 1976-; PTA Mem; *home:* 252 Blanco St Eagle Pass TX 78852

MACK, BONNIE JEAN (GIBSON), 7th & 8th Grade Teacher; *b:* Jackson, MS; *m:* Austin; *c:* Pamela; *ed:* (BA) Liberal Art, Tougaloo Coll 1969; (MA) Guidance & Counseling, Bradley Univ 1975; *cr:* Teacher Trewyn Mid Sch 1970-; *ai:* Trewyn Sch Dev Prgm; Sch Dist 150 Efficiency Seminar; AFT; Natl Urban League; *office:* Trewyn Mid Sch 1419 S Folkers Ave Peoria IL 61605

MACK, JILL ELAINE, 6th Grade Teacher; *b:* Defiance, OH; *m:* John Thomas; *c:* Rachel, Zachary, Elaina; *ed:* (BS) Elem Ed, Defiance Coll 1977; *cr:* 8th Grade Teacher St Johns Sch 1977-78; 7th/8th Grade Teacher St Augustine Sch 1978-81; 4th-6th Grade Math Teacher St Marys Sch 1981-; *ai:* Fundraising Chairperson 6th Grade; 1st Eucharist Comm Chairperson; NCEA; St Marys Church Various Comms; GSA Brownie Troop Leader; St Augustine Teacher of Yr 1978-79; *office:* St Marys Sch 702 Washington Ave Defiance OH 43512

MACK, JOHN STEVEN, Agriculture Science Teacher; *b:* San Juan, TX; *m:* Gail Ann Wadsack; *c:* Sarah; *ed:* (BS) Ag Ed, Tarleton St Univ 1977; (MS) Ag Ed, SW TX St Univ 1988; Meat Sci & Technology Cert; Ag Mechanics Cert; *cr:* Teacher Moore Haven HS 1977-80; Belton HS 1981-82; James Madison 1983-; *ai:* FFA Youth Organization Officer; Madison HS Courtesy Comm; FFA Leadership & Judging Team Coach; TX FFA Honorary Lone Star 1986; Prof Rodeo Cowboy Assn Mem 1981-83; TX Cattle Woman Assn, Outstanding Service 1990; FL Dept of Ag Grant; *office:* James Madison HS 5005 Stahl Rd San Antonio TX 78247

MACK, POLLY ANNMARIE, 1st Grade Teacher; *b:* Madison, WI; *m:* James Thomas; *c:* Kelly, Kerry; *ed:* (BA) Elem Ed 1972, (MA) Elem Ed 1975 AZ St Univ; Whole Lang & Rdng; *cr:* 3rd Grade Teacher 1972-73, 4th Grade Teacher 1973-83, 1st Grade Teacher 1983- Meyer Elem Sch; *office:* Meyer Elem Sch 2615 S Dorsey Ln Tempe AZ 85282

MACK, ROBERT D., Senior Marine Instructor; *b:* Uhrichsville, OH; *m:* Ruth I. Jacobson; *c:* Robert D. Jr., Kellie Jo, Bailey; *ed:* (BGS) Kent St 1984; Instr/Stu Various Milwaukee Schls; *cr:* Master Seargent US Marine Corp 1951-71; Master Seargent Retired MCJROTC Beaver Local HS 1972-; *ai:* Cadet Club, Drill Team, Color Guard Adv; Rifle Team & Orientering Coach; DAV, Amer Legion, VFW; *office:* Beaver Local HS 13187 State Rt 7 Lisbon OH 44432

MACK, RUTH KERN, Retired; *b:* Slatington, PA; *w:* Claude E. (dec); *ed:* (BS) Elem Ed, Kutztown Univ; Music-Piano & Organ Private Lessons; *cr:* 1st-4th Grade Teacher Peters Elem 2-Room Sch 1939-55; 1st Grade Teacher Peters Elem New Schl 1955-84; Head Teacher of Building 1976-81; *ai:* Taught Phonetic Keys to Rdng; Northern Lehigh Teachers Assn Comm 1953-84; PA St Ed Assn 1939-84; NEA 1939-84; Slatington 3 Star Points 1964-67; Order of Eastern Star Organist 1967-; 25 Year Pin & Certificate 1986-87; WA Grange 1763 (Pianist & Master 1985- Lecturer 1943-51 Chaplain 1941-43); Neffs U C C Church (Choir Sub Organist/Sun Sch Organist/Church Consistory 1985-89); Leader & Teacher Bible Sch 1940-85; Serve on Comm; Played & Sang for Weddings of Former Pupils; Mem Friedens Fire Co Aux Pres; Heart Fund/United Fund; *home:* R 3 Box 224 Slatington PA 18080

MACK, WES D., Health Teacher/Coach; *b:* Lanesboro, MN; *m:* Karen Detert; *c:* Kristine, Melissa; *ed:* (BA) Bio, Phys Ed, ST Olaf Coll 1963; (MS) Health Ed, Univ WI at Lacrosse 1980; *cr:* Bio, Phys Ed Ceylon HS 1963-69; Health Ed Viroqua HS 1969-; *ai:* Ftbl Coach, Adv Letterwinners' Club, Adv SADD, Faculty Athletic Code Comm; Viroqua Ed Assn Bldg Rep Welfare Comm Outstanding Young ED Awd 1975; WI Assn Health Dist VP 1972-74; Phy Ed Dance VP Sports 1989-; Amer Assn Health, Phy Ed, Rec & Dance 1969-; Viroqua J C's 1971-73, Outstanding Young Ed Awd 1975; Good Shepherd Lutheran Church Pres 1986; Boy Scouts of Amer Comm 1967-69; Sugar Creek Bible Camp 1975-80; *office:* Viroqua Area H S Blackhawk Drive Viroqua WI 54665

MACKAY, DENNIS J., Teacher; *b:* Grand Haven, MI; *m:* Christine Wessel; *c:* Jason, Ryan; *ed:* (AS) Automotive, Muskegon Comm Coll 1967; (BS) Voc Ed, 1973, (MA) Voc Ed, 1987 W MI Univ; *cr:* Teacher Mona Shores 1973-79, Muskegon Public Schls 1979-; *ai:* Excl in Teaching Awd 1984; *office:* Muskegon Area Voc Consortium 80 W Southern Ave Muskegon MI 49441

MACKEN, ITA L., Sci/His/Rdng Teacher; *b:* Akron, OH; *ed:* (BA) His/Government, Univ of Akron 1970; *cr:* Teacher Our Lady of Angels 1968-; *ai:* Stu Cncl, Stu Court Adv; *office:* Our Lady of Angels 3644 Rocky River Dr Cleveland OH 44111

MACKEY, BARBARA ELLIS, 1st-5th Grade Computer Teacher; *b:* Hale Cty, TX; *c:* Jay, Eric, Doug, Joel, Carman L. Boss; *ed:* (BS) Ed, W TX Univ 1962; *cr:* 1st Grade Teacher Plainview-Lakeside Elem 1962-63, Mesquite-Motley Elem 1963-65, Plainview-Thunderbird Elem 1966-67; 2nd Grade Teacher Union Grove Elem 1968; 5th Grade Teacher 1976-80, 1st-5th Grade Cmptr Teacher 1984- Arp Ind Sch Dist; *ai:* UIL Spon; Picture Memory; Fund Raising for Cmptr Lab; ATPE; *home:* 11162 Cr 233 Arp TX 75750

MACKEY, CHERYL BRYAN, 6th Grade Language Art Teacher; *b:* New York, NY; *m:* Warren Cornell; *c:* Warren, Nonya; *ed:* (BA) Elem Ed, Fisk Univ 1970; Multiple Handicap Admin & Supervision, Geroge Peabody Coll for Teacher, Univ of TN Chattanooga; *cr:* Accounting Clerk Amer Express Company 1967, Capital Intnl Airlines 1975-76; Teacher Chattonooga Public Sch 1976-; Sales Assn Parisian 1989-; *ai:* CEA 1978-82; Amer Cancer Society 1989-; Jack & Jill of Amer Recording Secy 1988-; *home:* 4202 Lake Haven Ln Chattanooga TN 37416

MACKIEWICZ, BARBARA THERESA, Sophomore Guidance Counselor; *b:* Long Island, NY; *ed:* (BS) Ed, Brentwood Coll 1971; (MS) Religious Ed, Fordham Univ 1978; Sociology, St Johns Univ 1973-75; *cr:* 1st/2nd/4th Grade Teacher Holy Name of Jesus Sch 1971-75; Scndry Level Teacher/Religious Ed Chairperson Our Lady of Perpetual Help HS 1975-88; Guidance Cnslr Bishop Kearney HS 1988-; Religious Stud Teacher Stella Maris HS 1990; *ai:* Facilitator Rap Groups Drug Prevention Prgm; Faculty Cncl; NCEA, NACST; *office:* Bishop Kearney HS 60th St And Bay Pwky Brooklyn NY 11204

MACKIFIELD, BARBARA DAVIS, First Grade Teacher; *b:* Nassau, Bahamas; *m:* Ernest C. Sr.; *c:* Peggy M., Ernestine C., Ernest Jr., John A.; *ed:* (BS) Elem Ed, Itta Bena MVS 1965; (MS) Rdng/Supervison, FL Atlantic Univ 1975; *cr:* Classroom Teacher John F Kennedy 1965-67, Markham Elem 1967-87, Pompano Beach Elem 1987-; *ai:* Broward Cty Rdng Cncl Corresponding Secy 1988-; Intnl Rdng Cncl, FL Rdng Cncl 1988-; *home:* 8311 SW 20th St North Lauderdale FL 33068

MAC LEAN, BRUCE EDWARD, Social Studies Dept Chairman; *b:* Weymouth, MA; *m:* Margaret Dodd; *c:* Alexandra; *ed:* (BA) His, Univ of MS Amherst 1975 (MA) Russian & E Europe His, Univ of VT 1986; Natl Ednowment Hum Russian Stud Prgm Harvard 1985; *cr:* 7th/8th Grade His/Phys Ed Teacher Anglo-Amer Sach Moscow Soviet Union 1976-77; 9th-12th Grade His Teacher Amer Sch of Aberdeen Scotland 1977-78, Oxbow HS 1978-80; 5th-8th Grade Teacher Anglo-Amer Sch Sofia Bulgaria 1980-81; 5th-8th Grade Phys Ed Teacher Amer Sch Warsaw Poland 1981-82; 8th-12th Grade His Teacher Oxbow HS 1982-; *ai:* NEA, Oxbow Teachers Assn Pres 1982-83; Newburg Historical Society Pres 1983-84; *home:* Box 187 Newbury VT 05051

MAC LEAN, MARY ANN (DUFFY), 6th Grade Teacher; *b:* Pierre, SD; *m:* Daniel; *c:* Martin, Matthew, Margo Mac Lean Tomasi, Moira, Michael; *ed:* (BA) Elem Ed, Univ of AZ 1961; Post Grad Work; *cr:* 4th Grade Teacher Glendale Elem 1961-62; 2nd/5th Grade Teacher Frank Sch 1963-65; 2nd/6th Grade Teacher Mount Carmel 1978-; *ai:* Rainbow for Gods Children Facilitator; *office:* Mount Carmel 2121 S Rural Rd Tempe AZ 85282

MAC LEAN, RAY DONALD, Instrumental Music Director; *b:* Ottawa, KS; *c:* Lindsay; *ed:* (BME) Music Ed, Univ of Evansville 1972; Wayne St Univ, Univ of MI Flint, MI St Univ; *cr:* Elem Music Teacher Reid Elem Sch 1973-76; Jr HS Band Teacher Mc Grath Jr HS 1976-79; HS Band/Orch Teacher Flint Cntrl HS 1979-82; Band/Vocal Teacher/FL St Dir Salvation Army 1982-86; HS Band Teacher Davison HS 1986-; *ai:* Marching & Jazz Band; Small Ensembles; Vlybl & Bsktbl Coach; All City Band & Choir; The Salvation Army (Flint & Port Huron Band Dir, Flint & Port Huron Choir Dir); First Presbyn (Chancel Choir, Chamber Choir); Selected to Adjudicate Bank & Vocal; Dir Ensembles in Various Sts; *office:* Davison HS 1250 N Oak Rd Davison MI 48423

MAC LEOD, JAMES LEWIS, Teacher of Gifted; *b:* Allen Parish, LA; *ed:* (BA) Liberal Arts, WA & Lee Univ 1955-59; (MA) Teaching, Emory Univ 1967; Doctoral Scndry Ed, MS St 1972; Admin Specialist MS St 1968; *cr:* Teacher De Kalb Cty Schls 1968-72; Prin Oakwood Sch 1972-74; Dept Head Screven Cty 1975-87; Teacher of HS Gifted Prgms Glynn Acad 1988-; *ai:* Model United Nations Adv; Fulbright Alumni Assn, Phi Delta Kappa, GA Educl Assn; Assn of Scottish Clan Cncls; Published Book; Fulbright-India-Scndry 1980; Natl Endowment for Hum Scndry 1986; *office:* Glynn Acad PO Box 1678 Brunswick GA 31520

MAC LEOD, JOAN CONRAD, Social Studies Chair/Vice-Prin; *b:* Camden, NJ; *m:* David Alan; *c:* Bruce A., Jeanne M., Chip, Daniel L., Stephen C.; *ed:* (BS) Elem Ed, Glassboro St Coll 1954; Grad Stud; *cr:* 6th Grade Teacher Haddon Township Sch System 1954-59, Baumholder Sch W Germany 1959-60; 1st-8th Grade Teacher Burgoon One Room Sch 1961-62; 4th-6th Grade Teacher Smithville Consolidated Sch 1962-63, Jusmag Sch Republic of Philippines 1969-71; 6th-8th Grade Teacher Sts Peter & Paul Schls 1973-76; 7th/8th Grade Teacher St Marys Sch 1976-80; 5th-8th Grade Teacher St Francis de Sales Sch 1980-; *ai:* 8th Grade Homeroom; Government Related Class Trips; Annual Chesapeake Bay Fnd Canoe Trip; Project Bus Jr Achievement; Safety Patrol; Eastern Shore Rdng Cncl 1987-; Knights of Columbus Ladies Guild 1987-; *office:* St Francis de Sales Sch 500 Camden Ave Salisbury MD 21801

MAC MILLAN, MARTHA SMALLEY, Mathematics Teacher; *b:* Cheyenne, WY; *m:* William A. III; *c:* Laruie J.; *ed:* (BA) Math Ed, Univ of WY 1968; (ME) Ed, Azusa Pacific Univ 1989; Various Univs; *cr:* Math Teacher Palomares Jr HS 1968-75; Resource Teacher 1973-75, Math Teacher 1975- Hemet Jr HS; *ai:* Math Field Day; Mathcounts; CA Math, Natl Math, Continental Math Leagues; Golden St Examination; Sigma Math Contest; Bullpup Honors Awds Comm; San Diego Math Cncl, Riverside Cty Math Cncl 1980-; NCTM 1985-; Hemet Teachers Assn, CA Teachers Assn, NEA 1968-; 4-H Leader 1975-; Easter Seal Society; Teacher of Yr 1989-; Outstanding Math Teacher 1984-85; Presidential Awds for Excl 1990; *office:* Hemet Jr HS 831 E Devonshire Ave Hemet CA 92343

MAC NELLY, ANNIE SUE LOPE, Bus Office Services Teacher; *b:* Raymondville, TX; *m:* Rayburn; *c:* Jane Gillis, Warren; *cr:* File Clerk TX Gas & Pipeline Corporation 1956-57; Secy 1966-71, Teacher 1971- Brownsville Ind Sch Dist; *ai:* BSA Dist Awd of Merit 1986; *home:* 37 Meadow Ln Brownsville TX 78521

MACOMBER, KATHY DAVIS, Sixth Grade Teacher; *b:* Freer, TX; *m:* John C.; *c:* John Jr., Tom; *ed:* (BS) Elem Ed, TX A&I Univ 1969; Span, Berlitz; Eng & Eng as a Second Lang; *cr:* Teacher Beeville Ind Sch Dist 1969-73, Mission Consolidated Ind Sch Dist 1973-79, United Ind Sch Dist 1979-; *ai:* Univ Interscholastic League Ready Writing; Report Card Comm; TESA Wkshp; Alpha Delta Kappa Sargeant-At-Arms 1988-89; *office:* Nye Elem Sch 101 Del Mar Blvd Laredo TX 78041

MAC PHAIL, MARION JANE, First Grade Teacher/Asst Prin; *b:* Springfield, MA; *ed:* (BS) Elem Ed, Univ of S ME 1971; *cr:* 2nd Grade Teacher 1971-74, 3rd Grade Teacher 1974-78, 2nd Grade Teacher 1978-80, 1st Grade Teacher 1980-, Asst Prin 1981- Emery Sch; *ai:* Steering Comm Cert; Pre-Referal Spec Ed Services; Peer Coaching; NEA, ME Teachers Assn, Biddeford Teachers Assn 1971-; ASCD 1988-; *office:* Emery Elem Sch 83 Birch St Biddeford ME 04005

MAC PHERSON-ALLEN, DAWN, Honors English/AP Coordinator; *b:* Greenville, ME; *c:* Daina M., Thomas P.; *ed:* (BA) Eng, Bates Coll 1968; (MED) Ed, 1973, (CAS) Teaching/Gifted Ed, 1988 Univ of ME; *cr:* Eng Teacher Mt View HS 1968-71, Sedomocha Jr HS 1972-89; 6th-12th Grade Gifted & Talented Coord MSAD 68 1988-; Honors Eng Teacher Foxcroft Acad 1989-; *ai:* Hi-Q Team Adv; Gifted & Talented Comm Chm; Phi Kappa Phi Membership 1973; Delta Kappa Gamma Pres 1988-, 1st Founders Fund Schlsp; ME Educators of Gifted & Talented 1988-; Monson Acad Trustee 1975-; Monson United Church of Christ Clerk 1982-88; *office:* Foxcroft Acad & MSAD 68 PO Box 98 High St Dover-Foxcroft ME 04426

MACRINA, DENISE ROSE, 7th-8th Grade Lang Art Teacher; *b:* Herkimer, NY; *ed:* (AS) Child Dev, Maria Regina Coll 1974; (BA) Scndry Ed/Eng, Nazareth Coll 1976; Educl Admin, N AZ Univ Flagstaff; *cr:* 9th-12th Grade Eng Teacher Waterloo HS 1976-81; Teacher of Gifted/7th/8th Grade Eng Teacher Frank Borman Jr HS 1981-; *ai:* Var Sftbl Coach; Yrbk & Stu Cncl Adv; Stu at Risk Comm Chairperson; New Teacher Mentor; Interdisciplinary & Gifted Coord Peer Mediation Comm Mem; ACUMEN Leadership Prgm; AFT, AZ Eng Teachers Assn, AZ Gifted & Talented Assn, AZ Interscholastic Assn 1981-; St Francis Xavier Parish Lector 1989-; AIA Certified Ofcl 1976-; *home:* 3035 W Colter #B Phoenix AZ 85017

MACZUZAK, JANE BRICKER, Sci Teacher/Outdoor Ed Coord; *b:* Monongahela, PA; *m:* Theodore Michael; *c:* Matthew, Benjamin, Samuel; *ed:* (BSED) Bio, CA Univ 1975; (MSED) Higher Ed Instruction, Cleveland St Univ 1979; Forestry Course, Kent St Univ 1985; Primatology, Earthwatch Birute Galdikas Borneo 1988; *cr:* Sci Teacher Cleveland Public Schls 1975-78; Sci Teacher/Outdoor Ed Coord Lake Ridge Acad 1978-; *ai:* Bio Olympics Coach; Curr Review Comm, Faculty Dev, Environmental Intern Coord; Spring Trip Organizer; Sr Class Spon & Adv; Discipline Comm Mem; Challenge Organizer; NABT, North Amer Assn for Environmental Ed 1989-; NSTA 1986-; Earthwatch 1987-; Lorain Cty Metropolitan Park Dist Volunteer Naturalist 1982-; United Presbyn Church Elder 1986-89; Published Newsletter; *office:* Lake Ridge Acad 37501 Center Ridge Rd North Ridgeville OH 44039

MADARA, LINDA LOUISE, Business Teacher & Chairperson; *b:* Shamokin, PA; *c:* James (dec), Michael (dec), *ed:* (BS) Bus Ed/ Accounting, 1970, (MS) Bus Ed 1982- Bloomsburg Univ; Advanced Econ Ed, Various Cmptr, Leadership Trng Courses; *cr:* Bus Teacher Lackawanna Trail Sch Dist 1970-71; Accountant Fisher Clark Lauer CPA 1971-72; Bus Teacher Line Mountain Sch Dist 1972-; *ai:* Mid St Assn Steering Comm Chairperson; FBLA St Bd of Dir Chairperson, Cntrl Dist Adv Rep, Adv; FBLA Cntrl Dist Rep 1982- Outstanding Adv 1985; LMEA, PSEA, NEA (faculty Rep, VP, Pres) 1970-; Audubon Society; Smithsonian Inst; Outstanding Achievement Line Mountain 1986-88, Cntrl Susquehanna Intermediate Unit 1987; Outstanding Adv Recognition Natl FBLA 1989; *office:* Line Mountain H S RR 01 Box 1660 Herndon PA 17830

MADAY, THEODORE F., JR., Middle Sch Teacher/Principal; *b:* Ladysmith, WI; *ed:* (BS) Scndry Ed/Life Sci, 1975, (BS) Scndry Ed/Math, 1975, (BS) Elem Ed, 1985 Mt Senario Coll; Environmental Ed Project Wild, Project Learning Tree Facilitator; Health Ed Project Safe, QUEST, Values & Choices Sex Ed, AIDS Ed, Suicide Trng, Power of Positive Stus, Gifted & Talented Class; *cr:* Teacher 1975-78, Teacher/Prin 1978-81 Our Lady of Sorrows Sch; Teacher 1981-, Building Prin 1989- Hawkins Elem Sch; *ai:* Bsktbl Coach; Environmental Ed Task Force; Secy Steering Comm & Sci Subcommittee; Stu Cncl Adv; Gifted & Talented Comm, Task Force on Suicide Prevention; Knights of Columbus 1975-; *office:* Hawkins Elem Sch 510 Main St Hawkins WI 54530

MADDEN, JERRY EUGENE, Teacher/Mathematics Dept Chair; *b:* Sturgeon Bay, WI; *m:* Andrea Lynn Hanson; *c:* Andrew, Thomas; *ed:* (BS) Math Ed, Univ of WI Stevens Point 1961; (MA) Math Ed, N MI Univ 1965; Kent St Univ, Univ of WI Oshkosh; *cr:* Teacher Denmark HS 1961-63; Teacher/Dept Chm Green Bay W HS 1963-; *ai:* Sr Class Adv; Green Bay Ed Assn, NCTM, WI Ed Assn, WI Math Cncl, NE WI Ed Assn; *office:* Green Bay W HS 966 Shawano Ave Green Bay WI 54303

MADDEN, JOYCE JEMELKA, Fifth Grade Teacher; *b:* Yoakum, TX; *m:* Donald Reid; *c:* Kevin, Kalleen, Kendall; *ed:* (BA) Elem Ed, SW TX St 1969; (MED) Elem Ed, Univ of Houston 1986; *cr:* 3rd Grade Teacher Yorktown Primary Sch 1977-81; 6th Grade Teacher St Joseph Elem 1981-86; 5th Grade Teacher Hunt Elem 1986-; *ai:* 5th Grade UIL Number Sense Spon; TX Classroom Teachers Assn 1986-.

MADDEN, THERESA MARIE, 8th Grade Math Teacher; *b:* Philadelphia, PA; *ed:* (BA) Soc Sci, Neumann Coll 1977; Working Towards MS of Ed-Math Concentration; *cr:* 2nd Grade Teacher St Anthony Sch 1971-73, St Mary-St Patrick Sch 1973-74; 4th Grade Teacher Queen of Heaven Sch 1974-77; 1st/3rd/4th Grade Teacher St Bonaventure Sch 1977-78, 1979-84; 2nd Grade Teacher St Stanislaus Sch 1978-79; 8th Grade Teacher St Cecilia Sch 1984-; *ai:* Math Coord; Stu Cncl Moderator; Completed Certificate for Lay Prin for Archdiocese of Philadelphia.

MADDEN, TIMOTHY EDWARD, Assistant Principal; *b:* Port Angeles, WA; *m:* Melanie Brigham; *c:* Justin, Tyler, Marlisa; *ed:* (BA) Health Ed, 1977, (MS) Health Ed, 1990 Cntrl WA Univ; *cr:* Teacher Baker Jr HS 1977-78; Health/Math/Phys Ed Teacher 1979-89, Dean of Stus 1989-, Asst Prin 1990 Enumclaw Jr HS; *ai:* Activity Coord; Drug Abuse Intervention Team; WA Ed Assn 1977-; ASCD; Our Saviours Baptist Church Deacon 1985-87; *office:* Enumclaw Jr HS 550 Semanski St Enumclaw WA 98022

MADDOCK, CATHERINE, 5th Grade Teacher; *b:* Blaengwynfi, S Wales Britain; *m:* Maldwyn Jarvis; *c:* Ceri, Debbie, Christopher; *ed:* Cert of Ed Puppetry/Lit/Eng Lit, Hereford Coll for Women 1960; (BA) Elem Ed Kean Coll 1972; Span, Union Coll; *cr:* Teacher Kempsey England 1960-61; Sub Teacher Spec Ed Hebres Day Sch 1976-77, Saint Patrick Sch 1978-; *ai:* Eng Dept Coord; NJCT; Probation Volunteer Trng Certificate 1977; *home:* 152 Effingham Pl Westfield NJ 07090

MADDOCK, LESLIE GARTH, 3rd Grade Teacher; *b:* Ogden, UT; *m:* Paula Butterfield; *c:* Jeffrey G., Heather, Eric P., Amy, R. Michael, Ashley; *ed:* (BS) Botany, 1973, (BS) Elem Ed, 1980 Weber St Coll; *cr:* Teacher Latter Day Saints Church 1973-75; Paper Hanger Precision-Built Homes 1975-77; Meat Cutter Latter Day Saints Church Welfare 1977-80; Teacher Weber Sch Dist 1980-; *ai:* NEA, UT Ed Assn, Weber Ed Assn 1980-; *home:* 450 Cross St Ogden UT 84404

MADDOX, BETTY JESSIE, Language Art Teacher; *b:* Columbus, GA; *m:* Aubrey R.; *c:* Eric, Kirk, Tazanya; *ed:* (BA) Eng/Ed, Morris Brown Coll 1964; Atlanta Univ, GA St, Oglethorpe Univ; *cr:* Teacher Fairmont HS 1964-65, S H Archer HS 1966-70, George HS 1970-72; Home DayCare 1974-78; Summer Prgms Teacher Morris Brown Coll 1986-87; Teacher Charles Lincoln Harper HS 1978-; *ai:* Debate Team & Oratorical Public Speaking Group Spon; SAT After-Sch Prgm Instr; SECME Teacher; NCTE 1985-; GA Forensics 1988-89; GCTE 1987-89; YMCA Contributor; United Meth Women (Pres 1979-83, Dist Chairperson of Nom, Publications & Public Relations 1984-87) Service Awd 1987; Academic Incentive Awd Lang Art; Star Teacher 2 Yrs; Teacher of Yr; *office:* Charles Lincoln Harper HS 3399 Collier Dr NW Atlanta GA 30331

MADDOX, CYNTHIA JERNIGAN, Reading Specialist; *b:* Wichita, KS; *m:* Randolph Peyton; *c:* Ryan P.; *ed:* (BA) Elem Ed, Hendrix Coll 1981; (MED) Rdng, Univ of AR Little Rock 1986; *cr:* 1st Grade Classroom Teacher 1981-85, 2nd Grade Classroom Teacher 1985-87, K-6th Grade Rdng Specialist 1987- Little Rock Sch Dist; *ai:* Cntrl AR Rdng Cncl 1987-; Daughters of Amer Revolution, PEO 1981-; *home:* 1412 Point West Dr Little Rock AR 72211

MADDOX, MARY HARDING, Third Grade Teacher; *b:* Byers, TX; *m:* James Coe; *c:* Pamela Payne, Darwin, Kathy Mc Ghee; *ed:* (BS) Home Ec, TX Tech 1947; Grad Work Midwestern St Univ; *cr:* Home Ec Teacher Henrietta HS 1947-50, Byers HS 1957-60; Elem Classroom Teacher Wichita Falls Ind Sch Dist 1960-68, Henrietta Ind Sch Dist 1968-; *ai:* Pep Squad Spon; Vlybl Coach; FHA Adv 1947-50, 1957-60; NEA, TX St Teachers Assn 1947-70; TX Classroom Teachers Assn 1960-68; Assn TX Prof Educators 1968-; Baptist Church (Mem, Organist) 1980-; West Fnd Grant for Rdng 1990; *office:* Henrietta Ind Sch Dist 1600 E Crafton Henrietta TX 76365

MADDOX, PHYLLIS MC GUILL, Assistant Elementary Principal; *b:* Beeville, TX; *m:* Ancel D.; *c:* Holly; *ed:* (BS) Elem, SW TX St Univ 1965; (MS) Scdry Ed, Stephen F Austin Univ 1989; Gifted & Talented Trng Prgm; Effective Teaching Practices; TX Teacher Evaluator; *cr:* Elem Teacher Pearland Elem 1965-67, Humble Elem 1977-78; 6th Grade Teacher Humble Mid 1978-89; Asst Elem Prin Foster Elem 1989-; *ai:* Safety Patrol; Stu Attitude & Teacher Morale Comm; Cmmty Volunteer Prgm; TX Teachers of Eng, ATPE 1982-89; PTA Pres 1975; TEPSAI 1989-; *office:* Foster Elem Sch 1800 Trailwood Vlg Kingwood TX 77339

MADDOX, SANDRA J., 6th Grade Teacher; *b:* Takoma Pk, MD; *m:* Notley G. Jr.; *c:* Melissa, Gregory; *ed:* (BA) Eng, Atlantic Union Coll 1972; (MED) Elem/Lang Art, Miami Univ 1986; *cr:* Worcester Public Lib 1972-73; Teacher Spring Valley Acad 1973-75, Pewee Valley Jr Acad 1980-82, Spring Valley Acad 1982-; *ai:* K-12th Grade Lang Art Curr Comm Chairperson 1988-; North Cntrl Evaluation Steering Comm 1986; NCTE, ASCD, OCTELA; MADD; Master Teacher Awd 1986-87; *office:* Spring Valley Acad 1461 E Spring Valley Rd Centerville OH 45458

MADDOX, SHAREN ELLIS, Mathematics Teacher; *b:* Sanford, NC; *m:* Thomas Donnie; *c:* Meredith C., T. Seth; *ed:* (BS) Math Ed/Sci Ed, E Carolina Univ 1971; Accounting, NC St Univ; *cr:* 8th Grade Teacher Robersonville Jr HS 1971-72; 6th-8th Grade Teacher W B Wicker Sch 1972-78; 8th Grade Teacher West Lee Jr HS 1978-88; 10th Grade Teacher Lee Cty Sr HS 1988-; *ai:* SADD Spon; NEA, NCAE, Lee Cty Chapter of NCAE, NCTM; *office:* Lee Cty Sr HS 1708 Nash St Sanford NC 27330

MADDUX, CHARLES E., Social Studies Teacher; *b:* Ft Worth, TX; *m:* Deborah Ann Taylor; *c:* Kirsten, Jeb, Beau; *ed:* (BS) His/ Government, 1971, (MA) Liberal Arts, 1988 TX Chrstn Univ; Univ of Helsinki Finland, Univ of Edinburgh Scotland, US Naval Security Group, Univ of Arlington; *cr:* Teacher Carter-Riverside HS 1974, Wedgwood Mid Sch 1974-; *ai:* Whiz Quiz, Annual Staff, Newspaper, His Fair Spon; Wedgwood Sch Management Team; Campus Coordinating, Sister Cities of World, Academic Awds Comm; Soc Stud Tutor; Ft Worth Classroom Teachers Assn (Faculty Rep 1980, 1989-) 1974-; Soc Stud Advisory Cncl Sch Rep 1988-89; TX St Teachers Assn, NEA 1974-; Shulkey Sugar Daddies (Pres 1988-89, VP 1987-88); PTA 1974-, Life

Membership 1986; Shulkey Sch Management Team 1988-89; TX Career Ladder Level III 1986; Wedgwood Teacher of Yr 1983; *office:* Wedgwood Mid Sch 3909 Wilkieway Fort Worth TX 76133

MADDY, TERESA HELMS, Mathematics Teacher; *b:* Christianburg, VA; *m:* W. H. Jr.; *c:* W. Hunter; *ed:* (BS) Math Ed, 1974, (MA) Curr/Instruction, 1978 VA Tech; Advanced Placement Wkshp W KY Univ 1989; *cr:* Math Instr Blacksburg HS 1974-; *ai:* VA Math League; Key Club; Blue Ridge Cncl Teachers of Math, NEA, VEA; Church; *office:* Blacksburg HS Patrick Henry Dr Blacksburg VA 24060

MADER, JAN LANDIS, Physics Teacher; *b:* Kalispell, MT; *m:* Michael Ray; *c:* Carrie, Kristin; *ed:* (BS) Physics, MT St Univ 1976; Grad Stud in Statistics, MT St Univ; Grad Prgm in Physics, Prisms Teacher Trainer, Univ of N IA; *cr:* Sci Teacher Bigfork HS 1976-77, Physics Teacher Great Falls HS 1977-; *ai:* Bisonette Drill Team & Sci Olympiad Coach; MT Assn of Physics Teachers, AAPT 1985-; MT Acad of Sci Bd Mem; NSTA, MT Sci Teachers Assn 1985-; Great Falls Lamaze Assn (Secy, Treas) 1980-; Vision 2000 Sci Center Bd Mem 1990; Natl Diffusion Network Teacher Trainer in Physics; Sci Teaching Inst of Rockies Task Force; *office:* Great Falls HS 1900 2nd Ave S Great Falls MT 59405

MADEUX, GEORGE JAMES, Fifth Grade Teacher; *b:* Torrington, CT; *m:* Patricia T. Halloran; *c:* Michele, James, Brian; *ed:* (BS) Elem Ed, 1963, (MA) Ed, 1968 W CT St Univ; Grad Studs Beyond Masters; *cr:* 5th Grade Teacher 1964-66, 6th Grade Teacher 1967-80 Brookside Elem; 6th Grade Teacher 1981-83, 5th Grade Teacher 1984- Crompond Elem; *ai:* Field Trip Coord; Retired Bsbl Coach; NYSTA, NEA, PTA 1964-; Intnl Assn of Approved Bsktbl Ofcls Pres 1980-81, 20 Yr Awd 1989; Grant Yorktown Sch System for Extended Study 1971-73; *office:* Crompond Elem Sch Manor Rd Yorktown Heights NY 10598

MADISON, VERA JOHNSON, Independent Study Teacher; *b:* San Bernardino, CA; *c:* Toni N.; *ed:* (MA) Ed, Azusa Pacific Univ 1982; (BA) Bio, CA St San Bernardino 1969; Admin Clear Credential 1983; *cr:* Teacher Frisbie Jr HS 1971-88, REACH Alternative Center & Milor HS 1988-; Adult Ed Teacher Eisenhower HS 1989- *ai:* Sch Base Coordination Plan Comm; Site Cncl; Instruction Improvement Prgm Dist Mem; Assn of CA Sch Admin 1987-; ASCD 1986-; CA Consortium for Ind Study 1988-; Minorities Advancement Prgm Coord 1986-87; Mentor Teacher; Excellent Teacher Awd; Dist Rep Sci Can Happen; Dist Rep Sci Ambassadors Wkshp; Dist Sci Curr Comm Chm; Dist Discipline Comm; IIP Grant; Master Teacher; *office:* REACH/Milor HS 266 W Randall Ave Rialto CA 92376

MADLUNG, PAUL DAVID, Seventh Grade Teacher; *b:* Milwaukee, WI; *m:* Jane Ann Dondlinger; *c:* Timothy, Joshua, Maria; *ed:* (BS) Pre/Early Adolescent Ed, Univ of WI Milwaukee 1977; Grad Stud; *cr:* 7th/8th Grade Soc Stud/Lang Art Teacher New Holstein Elem Sch 1978-81; 7th Grade Soc Stud/Lang Art Teacher Northview Elem Sch 1981-; *ai:* Chairperson Howards Grove Soc Stud Curr Comm; Peer Helper Faculty Adv; Organize Stu Trip Washington DC; WI Cncl for Soc Stud, NEA, WI Ed Assn Cncl 1981-; Gloria Dei Luth Church Cncl Mem 1983-85; New Holstein Recreation Dept (Asst Soccer, Bsbl Coach 1987-); Taft Fellowship 1981; *home:* 2401 Hickory Ln New Holstein WI 53061

MADONIA, DIANE (LOPIPERO), Mathematics Teacher; *b:* Brooklyn, NY; *m:* Bruce; *c:* Christopher, Eric; *ed:* (BS) Early Scndry Ed, Suny Oneonta 1971; (MS) Ed, C W Post Coll 1975; *cr:* Math Teacher Great Hollow Intermediate Sch 1971-; *ai:* Li Math Fair Mentor & Judge; *office:* Great Hollow Intermediate Sch Southern Blvd Nesconset NY 11787

MADSON, SUSAN K., 6th-8th Language Art Teacher; *b:* Boise, ID; *m:* Andy; *c:* Heidi, Molly, Patrick, Mike, Christina; *cr:* 7th-8th Lang Art Teacher Meridian Jr HS 1975-78; 6th-8th Lang Art Teacher St Marks 1982-; *ai:* Gifted & Talented Class Spon.

MAEDGEN, CYNTHIA BECK, English Teacher; *b:* Yoakum, TX; *m:* James; *c:* Brody; *ed:* (BS) Ed, Mc Murry Coll 1971; (MA) Eng Supervision, Angelo St Univ 1987; *cr:* Eng Teacher Lohn Ind Sch Dist HS, Santa Anna Ind Sch Dist HS, Novice Ind Sch Dist HS, Coleman Jr HS, San Angelo Cntrl HS; *ai:* Spon UIL Ready Writing; Cntrl HS Literary Magazine Spon; Teach Sat Preparation Course; NCTE, TX Prof Educators Assn; New Womans Guild; Southland Baptist Church; BSA Troop Comm Mem; Delta Kappa Gamma Mem; *home:* 6010 Winners Cir San Angelo TX 76904

MAEHLING, SHIRLEY RAYE, Third Grade Teacher; *b:* Terre Haute, IN; *w:* Robert (dec); *c:* Jan Wrin, Robert, Stephen; *ed:* (BS) Elem Ed, IN St Univ 1949; *cr:* Primary Grade Teacher Vigo Cty Sch Corp 1949-52, 1959-; *ai:* NEA Life Mem; IN St Teachers Assn, Vigo Cty Teachers Assn, Wabash Valley Rdng Cncl; Delta Kappa Gamma; Excl in Teaching Awd; *office:* Davis Park Elem Sch 310 S 18th St Terre Haute IN 47803

MAESTAS, ELLA MARY MONTOYA, 4th Grade Teacher; *b:* Las Sauces, CO; *m:* Robert E.; *c:* Eugene, Ronald, Ellen Maestas Waller; *ed:* (BA) Elem Ed, Adams St Coll 1961; Type A1 Teaching Certificate; *cr:* 1st/2nd Grade Teacher Las Sauces Elem; 4th/6th Grade Teacher Sanford Elem; *ai:* Accountability Comm; Sanford Dist Teacher of Yr 1989; *home:* 309 14th St Alamosa CO 81101

MAESTAS, JULIA MONTANO, 6th Grade Teacher; *b:* Las Vegas, NM; *m:* Nicasio T.; *c:* Pamela Ann Lopez; *ed:* (BA) Elem Ed, 1976; (MA) Bi-Ling Elem Ed, 1978 NMHU; Bi-Ling Cert; *cr:* 1st-2nd Grade Teacher 1976-79; K-1st Grade Teacher 1980-82; 4th Grade Teacher 1983-84; 5th-8th Grade Teacher 1985- Anton Chico Sch; *ai:* Stu Cncl Spon; Spelling Bee Adv; Sch Newspaper Adv; NEA 1976-; Health Ctrs of Northern NM Secy 1982-89; PTO Secy/Treas 1976-89; *office:* Anton Chico Elem Sch PO Box 268 Anton Chico NM 87711

MAGALA, JOHN FRED, JR., Mathematics Teacher; *b:* Coatesville, PA; *m:* Patricia Sharon Staggs; *c:* Valarie A., John III, Robert, Ted; *ed:* (BS) Scndry Ed/Math, West Chester St Coll 1968; Grad Courses, Lafayette Univ, Penn St, West Chester St Coll; *cr:* Math Dept Head Clifton Heights Sch 1968-69; Math Teacher Wilson Cntrl Jr HS 1969-88; Math Teacher Wilson HS 1988-; *ai:* Academic Challenge Team & Chess Club Adv; Jr Var Bsbl Team Coach; Intramural Bsktbl Prgm Asst; Jr HS Intramural Bsktbl Prgm Head; Swim Prgm Staff; Slovak Cath Sokols, AFT; Sinking Spring Park & Recreation Bd Pres; *home:* 22 Penn Ave Sinking Spring PA 19608

MAGEE, RAYMOND CHARLES, 7th Grade Science Teacher; *b:* Freeport, NY; *m:* Rita C. Matthews; *c:* Erin L., Lucas I.; *ed:* (AS) Lib Arts, Suffolk Cty Comm Coll 1971; (BS) Early Scndry Sci Ed, SUNY Cortland 1973; (MS) General Prof Stud, SUNY Albany 1977; Post Masters Credits HS Admin; *cr:* Teacher Mohonasen Cntrl Schls 1973-74, Coxsachie Athens Cntrl Schls 1974-; *ai:* Yrbk & Ski Club Adv; Girls Var Vlybl & Girls Jr Var Sftbl Coach; Scholar Recognition Prgm Univ Albany & St Univ of NY 1990; Amer Scholastic Journalism 1st Place Yrbk Awd 1988-89; *home:* PO Box 248 Ravena NY 12143

MAGEE, RITA MATTHEWS, Physical Education Teacher; *b:* Levittown, NY; *m:* Raymond Charles; *c:* Erin, Lucas; *ed:* (AS) Ed, Suffolk Cty Comm Coll 1971; (BSE) Phys Ed, SUNYA Cortland 1973; (MS) Ed, SUNYA Albany 1977; Educl Admin; *cr:* Phys Ed Teacher Coxsackie-Athens Cntrl Sch 1973-; *ai:* Var Field Hockey & Sftbl Coach; Jr Var & Var Cheerleading, Var Assn, Gymnastics Club Adv; Yrbk Co-Adv; ASHPERD 1979-; *office:* Coxsackie-Athens Cntrl Sch Sunset Blvd Coxsackie NY 12051

MAGENNIS, DANIEL CHARLES, Science Teacher; *b:* Grand Rapids, MI; *m:* Deborah Ann Groeneveld; *ed:* (BS) Bio, Ferris St Univ 1978; (MA) Scndry Ed, Grand Valley St Univ 1985; Certified Reproductive Health Inst, Instructional Theory into Practice; *cr:* Substitute Teacher Grand Rapids Public Schls 1978-79; Sci Teacher Godwin Heights Mid Sch 1979-80, Crestwood Mid Sch 1980-; *ai:* Mid Sch Swimming Coach; Communicable Disease, Teacher Evaluation, Sci Curr Comms; Kentwood Ed Assn Building Rep 1980-; *office:* Crestwood Mid Sch 2674 44th St SE Kentwood MI 49512

MAGGART, MONTY CLIFF, Math/Science/Health Teacher; *b:* Logansport, IN; *m:* Joyce Caroleen Meadors; *c:* Heather, Daniel, Joshua, Christopher; *ed:* (BS) Elem Ed, 1973, (MS) Elem Ed/Sci Endorsement, 1976 IN Univ; Various Seminars & Wkshps in Rdng, Sci & Math; *cr:* Sci/Math Instr Eastern Elem & Eastern-Howard Sch Corporation; *ai:* Safety Patrol Spon; 7th/8th Grade Girls Vlybl; Sci Club Co-Spon; Cmptr Comm; Summer Cmptr Robotics Instr; EEE Curr Comm; E Howard Classroom Teachers Assn Pres 1979-85; IN St Teachers Assn, NEA; Hoosier Assn Sci Teachers Membership 1989-; Foursquare Church Cncl 1988-; Loyal Order of Moose 1973-; United Commercial Travelers 1969-; Outstanding Teacher for 1989; Title II Sci Grant Recipient 1989; IN Sci & Technology Grant 1990; *office:* Eastern Elem Sch 301 S Meridian Greentown IN 46936

MAGIDSON, CAROL BICKFORD, 5th Grade Teacher; *b:* Oceanside, CA; *m:* David L.; *c:* Rebecca, Benjamin; *ed:* (BED) Elem Ed, Univ of Miami 1970; *cr:* 5th Grade Teacher Dade Elem 1970-71; 5th/6th Grade Teacher Sylvania Heights Elem 1971-; *ai:* Grade Group Chm; Act Comm Chm; FL Rdng Cncl; *office:* Sylvania Hts Elem Sch 5901 S W 16th St Miami FL 33155

MAGNANI, GEOFFREY STEVEN, Dir of Elem Instrumental Music; *b:* Johnson City, NY; *m:* Cynthia Louise Hartzell; *c:* Bradford, Seth, Matthew; *ed:* (BM) Music Ed, Crane Sch of Music Potsdam St Univ 1977; (MSM) Music Ed/Performance, Ithaca Coll 1982; *cr:* Music Dir Oxford Acad HS 1977-82, Fabius-Pompey Jr-Sr HS & Fabius-Pompey Elem Sch 1985-; *ai:* Jr HS Marching Band Instr; Mid Sch Transition Team; Drum-Line Percussion Instr, Writer; NY St Sch Music Assn, Percussive Arts Society 1977-; NY St Band Dir Assn 1986-; Cncl Pres 1989-; Reference Consultant Pro-Tuner Corporation; NYSSMA All-St Adjudicator; Percussion Clinician; Concert Band Adjudicator; Guest Conductor for Band Festivals; *home:* 7 Scott St PO Box 738 Oxford NY 13830

MAGNARELLI, THOMAS J., Social Studies/History Teacher; *b:* Syracuse, NY; *m:* Kathleen Klimas; *c:* Thomas M.; *ed:* (BA) Amer Stud Concentration, 1972, (MS) Scndry Ed/Soc Sci, 1976 Syracuse Univ; *cr:* Soc Stud Teacher Cathedral Acad 1972-75, Durgee Jr HS 1975-76, Ray Jr HS 1976-79, C W Baker HS 1979-; *ai:* Amnesty Intnl Chapter Adv; NY St Cncl for Soc Stud; Cntrl NY Cncl for Soc Stud; Led Group of 31 Stu to Soviet Union April 1989; *office:* C.W. Baker H S East Oneida St Complex Baldwinsville NY 13027

MAGNER, PHILIP STEVENSON, Mathematics Teacher; *b:* Benton Harbor, MI; *m:* Alice Ann Malmstadt; *c:* Jonathan H., Paul P.; *ed:* (AS) Math, Lake Michigan Coll 1969; (BS) Math, 1974, (MA) Math Ed, 1983 W MI Univ; *cr:* Teacher Springfield HS 1976-81, 1st Assembly of God Chrstn HS 1981-83, Modesto Chrstn HS 1983-88, Downey HS 1988-; Part-Time Teacher Modesto Jr Coll 1987-; *ai:* Jr Class Adv; Renaissance Comm Acad Excl; Stanislaus Math Cncl VP 1987-; CA Math Cncl 1988-; CA Assn for Gifted 1989-; MI Cncl Teachers of Math 1980-82; Northern CA Ofcls Assn 1986-; *office:* Thomas Downey HS 1000 Coffee Rd Modesto CA 95355

MAGNUSON, FRANK EARL, Math Teacher; *b:* Birmingham, AL; *m:* Sand Elliott; *ed:* (BSED) Math, Univ of AL 1970; Teaching the Gifted Stu Univ of AL 1971-72; Math 1986, Teaching the Gifted Stu 1987-89 Univ of New Orleans; Working Towards Masters Art, Sci, Math, Loyola; *cr:* Math Teacher Shades Valley HS 1970-72, W A Berry HS 1972-73, Highlands Day Sch 1973-75, Benjamin Franklin HS 1987-; *ai:* City Wide Homework Asst TV Show Spon; NCTM 1988-; *office:* Benjamin Franklin HS 2001 Leon C Simon Blvd New Orleans LA 70122

MAGNUSON, GAYLE GLASCOCK, School Social Worker; *b:* E Chicago, IN; *m:* James; *ed:* (BA) Soc Work, W MI Univ 1970; (MSW) Soc Work, Univ of IL 1974; *ai:* IL Assn of Sch Soc Work; *office:* Victor J Andrew HS 171st & 90th Ave Tinley Park IL 60477

MAGNUSON, JOHN DAVID, Teacher/Coach; *b:* St Paul, MN; *m:* Kathy Frimanslund; *c:* Mara, Julie, Carl; *ed:* (BA) His/Poly Sci, Conordia Coll 1971; *cr:* Recreation Dir St Paul Parks & Rec 1972-74; Teacher St Paul Public Schls 1974-; *ai:* Asst Girls Vlybl, Head Boys & Girls Cross Cntry Skiing & Track Coach; Langford Booster Club VP 1987-; *office:* Saint Paul Harding Sr HS 1540 E 6th St Saint Paul MN 55106

MAGNUSSEN, MACEL J., 5th/6th Grade English Teacher; *b:* Royal, IA; *m:* W D; *c:* Paula Di Mascio, Pamela Ironside; *ed:* (BA) Elem Ed, Buena Vista Coll 1965; *cr:* 5th Grade Teacher 1957-58, 6th Grade Teacher 1960-63 Royal Cmmty Sch; 5th Grade Teacher Clay Cntrl Cmmty Sch 1965-76; 5th/6th Grade Eng Teacher Hartley Cmmty & Hartley-Melvin Cmmty 1976-; *ai:* NEA Life Mem; ISEA 1957-; ICTE, HMEA; *home:* 1237 W 11th St Spencer IA 51301

MAGRUDER, GARY L., English Teacher; *b:* Kankakee, IL; *ed:* (BA) Art Comprehensive, IL St Univ 1964; (MA) Ed, Roosevelt Univ 1972; Creative Writing; *cr:* Art Teacher Parkview Elem 1964-67; Art Dept Chm/Gifted Challenge Prgm Westview Jr HS 1968-79; Art His/Ed Methods Teacher Coll of St Francis 1975-78; Eng Teacher Romeoville HS 1980-; *ai:* Natl Eng Ed Assn, IL Eng Ed Assn; NCTE Academic Excl; Benevolent Order of Elks 1985-; ACLU 1988-; IL Writing Project Prgm Grad; Instr Stonegrange Cooking Sch; Poetry Published; IL Math Sci Acad Awd of Excl 1989; *office:* Romeoville HS 100 N Independence Blvd Romeoville IL 60441

MAGUIRE, MARTHA ELLEN, English Teacher; *b:* Newbridge, Ireland; *ed:* (BA) Speech/Eng, Incarnate Word Coll 1967; (MA) Drama/Theatre, St Louis Univ 1973; *cr:* Elem Teacher IL, MO, TX Elem Schls 1951-66; Prin Our Lady of Valley Sch 1967-69; Eng/Speech Teacher Incarnate Word Acad 1969-74, Archbishop Chapelle HS 1974-79;Jr HS Eng/Religion Teacher St Catherine of Siena Sch 1979-88; *ai:* NHS Co-Spon; Liturgy Comm Mem; NCEA; AAA Sch Safety Patrol (Coord, Supvr) 1982-88, Outstanding Achievement Supvr of Yr 1988; *office:* Archbishop Chapelle HS 8800 Veterans Blvd Metairie LA 70003

MAHAFFIE, RICK LEWMAN, Social Studies Teacher; *b:* Monterey, CA; *m:* Claudia Ray; *ed:* (BA) His, Mercer 1976; (MED) Soc Sci, Univ of GA 1978; Ed Spec Soc Sci, Augusta Coll 1987; *cr:* Soc Stud Teacher Acad of Richmond Cty 1978-; *ai:* Rotary Club Spon; Golf Coach; Asst Rowing Team Coach; PAGE.

MAHAN, BUDD POWELL, Science Teacher; *b:* Westminster, TX; *ed:* (BS) Bio/Phys Ed, 1966, (MED) Guidance/Counseling, 1971 E TX St Univ; *cr:* Sci Teacher West Jr HS 1966-; *ai:* Yrbk Spon 1980-; Assn of Children with Learning Disabilities Essay Winner 1987; Assn of Prof Educators St Finalist Christa Mc Auliffe Awd 1987; TX St Teachers Assn, NEA; Poetry Society of TX Bd of Dir 1982-; *office:* Richardson West Jr HS 1309 Holly Dr Richardson TX 75080

MAHAN, GARY DOUGLAS, English Teacher; *b:* Las Vegas, NM; *m:* Connie Jane Bowman; *c:* Doug, Ken, Glenn; *ed:* (BS) Eng/His, Univ of TN 1966; (MED) Eng, Univ of GA 1972; (EDS) Eng, W GA Coll 1979; Fr Courses; *cr:* Teacher Halifax Cty HS, Lafayette HS; *ai:* Ftbl, Tennis Coach; Yrbk Spon; Page; *office:* Lafayette HS 301 N Cherokee St La Fayette GA 30728

MAHAN, MOZELL ANITA, Teacher of Social Studies; *b:* Camden, NJ; *ed:* (BA) Ed/His, Rutgers Univ 1976; *cr:* S S Dept Chairperson Hatch MidSch 1978-87, East Camden Mid Sch 1988-89; Soc Stud Teacher Camden HS 1989-; *ai:* Hatch Mid Sch Pageant Spon 1976-86 Service 1986; *office:* Camden H S Baird & Park Blvd Camden NJ 08103

MAHER, DANIEL PATRICK, Superintendent; *b:* New York, NY; *m:* Deborah Irene Van Roo; *c:* Gerald, Scot, Marcus; *cr:* Teacher 1987-89, Supt 1990 New Covenant Chrstn Sch.

MAHER, JAMES PATRICK, Phys Ed/Health Teacher/Coach; *b:* Garland, TX; *m:* Nada Lynette Ishee; *ed:* (BSED) Phys Ed/Health, 1978, (MSED) Mid-Management Admin, 1985 Stephen F Austin St Univ; *cr:* Teacher/Coach Hardin Ind Sch Dist 1978-80, Harmony Ind Sch Dist 1980-82, Texas City Ind Sch Dist 1982-83, Beckville Ind Sch Dist 1983-; *ai:* Asst Var Ftbl & Head Var Bsbl Coach; Phys Ed Comm Chm; 6th Grade UIL Music Memory Team Spon; Classroom Teachers Assn 1982-; TX HS Coaches

Assn 1978-; TX HS Bsbl Coaches Assn 1980-; Coach of Yr Bsbl Dist 22-AA 1985; Co-Coach of Yr Bsbl Dist 21-AA 1986; *office:* Beckville HS PO Box 37 Beckville TX 75631

MAHER, TERENCE R., Director of Pupil Services; *b:* New York, PA; *m:* Margaret Lavin; *c:* Megan, Kathryn, Timothy; *ed:* (BS) Comprehensive Soc Stud, Bloomsburg Univ 1973; (MS) Cnslr/Scndry Ed, Marywood Coll 1975; Grad Stud Univ of Scranton; *cr:* Soc Stud Teacher Northeastern Educl IU 19 1974-75; Cnslr Cardinal Brennan HS 1975-76; Cnslr 1976-88, Dir of Pupil Services 1988- Lehighton Area Sch Dist; *ai:* NASSP, PASSP, ASCD, PA Assn of Pupil Personnel Admin 1988-; BPO Elks (Secy 1980-89, Exalted Ruler 1987-88); *office:* Lehighton Area Sch Dist 200 Beaver Run Rd Lehighton PA 18235

MAHLANDT, LOUISE ANN, Speech & Forensics Teacher; *b:* St Joseph, MO; *m:* Simon Barbosa; *c:* Joseph Barbosa; *ed:* (BS) Eng/Speech, 1980, (MA) Eng/Speech, 1986 NWMSU; *cr:* Teacher Valley Falls KY 1980-82, St Joseph MO 1983-; *ai:* Coast Forensic Team Lafayette; Jr Class Spon; Co-Dir Dist Speech Contest; MO St Teachers Assn 1983-; Speech/Theatre Assn MO 1987-; Robidoux Resident Theatre (Actor, Dir); Star Commty Dev Mem; PSTA, Boo Club; Natl Forensics League Double Ruby Mem; *office:* Lafayette HS 5th & Highland Saint Joseph MO 64502

MAHLSTADT, KATHY SHUPE, Retired Kindergarten Teacher; *b:* Indianola, IA; *m:* Jon P.; *c:* Chris, Jennifer Mahlstadt Davey; *ed:* Kndgtn/Primary, Univ N IA 1954; *cr:* Kndgtn Teacher Cherokee Cmmty Schls 1954-56, Indianola Cmmty Schls 1959-60, 1967-88; *ai:* NEA 1954-; IA Ed Assn 1954-88; Indianola Ed Assn 1967-88; *home:* 1103 North D Street Indianola IA 50125

MAHNKE, GLENN RONALD, Minister of Music/Teacher; *b:* Milwaukee, WI; *m:* Marie Annette Bilyea; *c:* Joy, Liesl, Gretchen, Amanda; *ed:* (BA) Ed/Music, 1969, (MMUS) Church Music, 1980 Concordia; *cr:* Minister of Music/7th Grade Teacher Grace Luth Sch 1968-76, St Pauls Evangelical Luth Sch 1976-; *ai:* Dean of Chapel; Childrens Handbell Choirs, Church Sr Choir, Adult BellChoir Dir; Church Music Dir & Head Organist; Amer Guild of Organists Mem Exec Comm Local Chapter 1978-; Amer Guild of Eng Handbell Ringers, Choristers Guild 1981-; Luth Counseling & Family Service (Bd Mem, Bd Secy) 1974-76; Prof Church Workers Conference Comm Chm 1990; S WI Dist Teachers Conference Comm Mem 1976; Organ Instr-Ago/Concordia; *office:* St Pauls Ev Luth Sch 210 E Pleasant St Oconomowoc WI 53066

MAHNKEN, CHARLOTTE BLANKE, 1st-8th Grade Art Teacher; *b:* St Louis, MO; *m:* Jack Paul (dec); *c:* Linda Ford, Kathleen Weiss; *ed:* (BS) Art Ed, Harriss Stowe St 1984; *cr:* Teacher Edwardsville Public Schls 1952-54; Substitute Teacher St Louis Cty Public Schls 1963-70; Art Teacher Harris Stowe ST Coll 1984-89; St Simon 1970-; *ai:* Art Wkshps for Teachers & Curr Comm Archdiocese of St Louis; MO Art Ed Assn 1984-; Book Color, Form, Line Shape, Texture Copywright 1987; *office:* St Simon Sch 11019 Mueller Rd Saint Louis MO 63123

MAHOLTZ, MICKEY, Sci Dept Head/Physics Teacher; *b:* Jersey City, NJ; *m:* Helen Marie Leonard; *c:* Michael, Jay, Nkole; *ed:* (BS) Electronics, Penn St Univ 1961; (BS) Ed, Clarion Univ 1964; (MST) Physics, Univ of WI 1972; Prin Cert Elem Scndry, Penn St Univ 1980; Grad Stud Several Univs; *cr:* Sci Dept Head Curwensville Area HS 1961-; *ai:* Sci Projects Stu Adv; PA Prism Physics Coord 1988-; PSTA, POE Advisory Bd Sci Ed 1989; Physics Teaching Resource Agent 1986-; Regional Sci Fair Dir 1976-; Organzied Sch-Wide Act; PA Jr Acad of Sci (Wkshp Leader, St Chm 1978-88); PA Sci Talent Search Interview Bd; NSTA Regional Wkshp Leader 1987; PSTA Wkshp Leader 1987-89; Superior Sci Teacher 1970; PA Sci Teachers Assn, PA Sci Supvrs Assn; AAPT Staff Mem Innovative Physics Teacher Awd 1972; PRTA Agent; PA Acad of Sci; Natl Sci Supvrs Assn; Penn St Alumni Assn,; Alunmi Schslp Comm Leader; Huston Township Alumni Assn Pres; Bennetts Valley Kiwanis Schlsp Comm; Bennetts Valley Road & Gum Club; Penfield PTA; Little League Bsbl Mgr; Miss Hemisphere Incorporated Pageant Judge; Penfield Firemans Assn; Outstanding Scndry Educators Awd 1974; Presidential Awd Finalist 1988, Winner 1989; Conducted Several Wkshps; Public Speaking Rotary Clubs; Developed & Taught Several Grad Metric Courses for Teachers; *home:* Horseshoe Dr Curwensville PA 16833

MAHON, ANN B., English Department Chair; *b:* Schenectady, NY; *m:* John F.; *c:* Kathryn, Sean, Elizabeth; *ed:* (BA) Eng, Le Moyne Coll 1971; Grad Stud SUNY Albany & Elmira Coll; *cr:* 9th-12th Grade Eng Teacher Fonda-Fultonville 1972-; *ai:* Newspaper Adv; AIDS Comm; Sch Improvement Comm 1988-; FFTA (HS Faculty Rep) 1988-; St Cecilia Church Religious Ed Coord 1983-89; PTA; *office:* Fonda-Fultonville HS Cemetary St Fonda NY 12068

MAHONEY, DANIEL JAMES, Physical Education Teacher; *b:* Sioux Falls, SD; *m:* Mary Lynn Coyle; *ed:* (BS) Phys Ed, Black Hills St Coll 1979-83; *cr:* K-8th Grade Phys Ed/11th Grade Amer His/6th Grade SD His Teacher Philip HS 1985-; *ai:* Jr HS Ftbl; Head Coach Var Wrestling; 7th Grade Class Adv; NASSP; SDHSCA 1985-, Nom Wrestling Coach of Yr 1990; 2nd & 4th Place Wrestling St of SD; *office:* Philip HS P O Box 730 Philip SD 57567

MAHONEY, JAMES JOSEPH, Chemistry Teacher; *b:* New York, NY; *m:* Karen D. Zanata; *c:* Stephen, James, Kevin, Brian, Daniel, Kathleen, Patrick, Kerry; *ed:* (BS) Chem, Iona Coll 1954; Grad Stud Scndry Ed, Hofstra Univ 1959-60; Chem/Physics/Math, Renssalaer Polytech 1960-61; Chem/Math/Cmptrs Stonybrook Univ 1988; *cr:* 1st Lieutenant US Marine Corps 1954-58; Teacher Copiagne HS 1958-; *ai:* Var Bsktbl Coach 1966-; NY St Sci Teachers Assn 1980-; NY St Bsktbl Coaches Assn 1984-; Suffolk Cty Bsktbl Coaches Assn 1966-; Natl Sci Fnd Inst Grants 1960-61; *office:* Copiague HS 1100 Dixon Ave Copiague NY 11726

MAHONEY, JANE MC EVILLY, Retired Teacher; *b:* Albany, NY; *m:* David L.; *c:* Daniel J., Ellen M. Floyd, William L.; *ed:* (BA) Bus Admin, Marymount Coll 1950; (MSED) Elem Ed, St Univ of NY New Paltz 1955; Numerous Courses Rdng, Math, Lang Art, Cmptrs; *cr:* 3rd Grade Teacher North Street Sch 1950-52; Substitute Teacher 1958-70, Elem Teacher 1970-88, Substitute Teacher 1989- Little Falls Cntrl Schls; *ai:* Church Society Pres; Cath Charities Bd of Dir; Cty Celebration Comm 1991; *home:* RR 2 Box 42M Little Falls NY 13365

MAHONEY, PAUL JULIAN, Physics/Chemistry Teacher; *b:* Louisville, KY; *ed:* (BA) Chem, Cath Univ of America 1954; (MS) Physics, Notre Dame 1969; *cr:* Teacher Mt St Joseph HS 1954-60, Good Counsel HS 1960-63, St Joseph Preparatory 1963-68, St Xavier HS 1968-86, Central HS 1986-; *ai:* Faculty Courtesy Comm; *office:* Central HS 1130 W Chestnut Louisville KY 40203

MAHONEY, SUSAN SULLIVAN, 2nd Grade Teacher; *b:* Pawtucket, RI; *m:* H. Edward; *ed:* (BA) Elem Ed, Mt St Joseph Coll 1970; (MED) Providence Coll 1975; *cr:* 1st Grade Teacher 1970-75, Pre-Primary Teacher 1975-78, 3rd Grade Teacher 1980-86, 2nd Grade Teacher 1986- Agnes Little Sch 1986-; *ai:* Alpha Delta Kappa; *office:* Agnes E Little Sch 60 S Bend St Pawtucket RI 02860

MAHONEY, SYLVIA GANN, English Teacher; *b:* Levelland, TX; *m:* John R.; *c:* Lesli Laughter, Raburn Benge; *ed:* (AA) Eng, NM Jr Coll 1970; (BA) Eng, 1972 E NM Univ 1975; *cr:* Eng Teacher Hobbs HS 1972-77; Eng Professor NM Jr Coll 1977-87; Dir of Museums Lea Cty Cowboy Hall of Fame 1977-87; Rodeo Coach NM Jr Coll 1977-84; Eng Teacher Quanah HS 1987-; *ai:* Debate Coach; Sr Class Spon; Delta Kappa Gamma (Research 1987-) 1977-; Amer Assn of Univ Women VP 1987-; Assn of TX Public Educators 1987-; TX Folklore Society; NM Jr Coll Professor of Yr 1984, 1986; Whos Who in Amer Jr Colls 1970; Outstanding Young Women of America 1968; Free Lance Writer & Photographer; Writing Book; Weekley Radio Prgm 1982-85; *office:* Quanah HS PO Box 4150 Quanah TX 79252

MAIBERGER, ELIZABETH ANN, Home Economics Teacher; *b:* Columbus, OH; *c:* (BA) Home Ec Ed, OH St Univ 1977; (MA) Personal Management, Cntrl MI 1984; *cr:* Home Ec Franklin Alternative Jr HS 1978-80, South HS 1980-; *ai:* Chrldng 1980- & Asst Track Coach 85-; Majorette Adv 80-; Asst Marching Band Dir 80-; FHA; Athletec Eliqibility Reform Comm; Cntrl OH Teachers Assn 78-; Columbus Home Ec Teachers Assn (Treas, VP, Pres) 1978-; Big Brothers/Big Sisters 5 Yr Service 1982-88; Elizabethian Guild; Teacher of Yr 1985; *office:* South HS 1160 Ann St Columbus OH 43206

MAIDEN, ULA K., 7th Grade English Teacher; *b:* Boston, MA; *c:* John Spittal, David Spittal, Eric Spittal; *ed:* (BA) Eng, Augustana Coll 1966; (MS) Ed, Long Island Univ 1980; Post Grad Stud Coll of New Rochelle; *cr:* 6th Grade Teacher Winston Churchill Sch 1968-69; 7th/8th Grade Teacher Peekskill Mid Sch 1974-75, Strang Mid Sch 1975-; *ai:* NMSA; Articles & Books Published; *office:* Mildred Strang Mid Sch 2701 Crompond Rd Yorktown Heights NY 10598

MAILAT, JOANNE MARIE (URDEA), French Teacher; *b:* Canton, OH; *m:* Charles Dan; *c:* Douglas M.; *ed:* (BS) Fr, OH St Univ 1961; Grad Work Univ of Akron; *cr:* Fr Teacher Glenwood HS 1961-75; Fr Instr Walsh Coll 1968-70; Fr Teacher Canton S HS 1975-; *ai:* Adv Foreign Lang Club; Chm Dist Foreign Lang Comm; OH Foreign Lang Assn; Delta Kappa Gamma 2nd VP 1988-; ACFTL, AATF; NDEA Summer Lang Inst Univ of Pittsburgh 1964; *home:* 2510 Ridgedale Ave Nw Canton OH 44708

MAINES, DONNA RODE, English/Enrichment Teacher; *b:* Suffern, NY; *m:* Robert James; *c:* Amenda, Richard; *ed:* (BS) Ed/Eng, SUNY Brockport 1974; (MA) Elem Ed, SUNY New Paltz 1977; *cr:* 6th Grade Teacher West Road Sch 1974-75; Substitute K-12th Grade Teacher Arlington Sch Dist & Hyde Park Sch Dist 1975-76, Jersey Shore Area Sch Dist 1976-77; Eng/Enrichment Teacher Jersey Shore Jr HS 1977-; *ai:* Chairperson Academic Awds Comm; Odyssey of Mind Coach; Jersey Shore Jr HS Enrichment & Peer Tutoring Club Adv; Jersey Shore Area Ed Assn Chairperson Soc Comm 1978-79; PA St Ed Assn, NEA; Amer Legion Auxiliary Pres 1978-85; Red Cross Volunteer Service To Military Families 1981-, Outstanding Volunteer 1984; *home:* RD 4 Box 310A Jersey Shore PA 17740

MAINS, PAMELA SCHLUETER, 3rd Grade Teacher; *b:* Covington, KY; *d:* Wm. David; *c:* Michael, Bridget; *ed:* (BA) Elem Ed, 1974, (MA) Elem Ed, 1978 Northern KY Univ; *cr:* 6th Grade Teacher 1974-75, 1st Grade Teacher 1975-82, 3rd Grade Teacher 1982- Northern Elem; *home:* R 1 Box 157 Butler KY 41006

MAINWARING, JOHN ROSSER, Music Teacher; *b:* Wilkes-Barre, PA; *m:* Linda Neher; *c:* Jennifer; *ed:* (BS) Music Ed, Wilkes Coll 1974; *cr:* Music Teacher Wilkes-Barre Township Jr HS 1976-80; Band Dir GAR Memorial HS 1980-84; Band/Choral Dir Wilkes-Barre Township Jr HS 1984-; *ai:* PA Music Educators Assn; Masons 1976-; Shrine Dir of Music 1977-; 1st Welsh Presbyn Church Dir of Music 1979-; *home:* 22 Elm St Mountaintop PA 18707

MAIO, NORMA GIARDINO, Retired Third Grade Teacher; *b:* Aguilar, CO; *m:* Ernest James; *c:* Samuel, Gina Corradino, Gino; *ed:* (AA) Elem Ed, Trinidad Jr Coll 1949; (BA) Elem Ed, Univ of NC Greeley 1952; Adams St Coll, Univ of S CA, Univ of CO Boulder; *cr:* 2nd/4th Grade Teacher Sopris CO 1952-54, Kndgtn Teacher Aguilar CO 1960-62; Title I Rdng Teacher 1966-70, 2nd-4th Grade Teacher 1970-88 Trinidad CO; *ai:* Attending TSJC; Taking Art Classes; Trinidad Ed Assn, NEA 1960-76; Amer Assn of Univ Women 1966-68; *home:* 260 Nona Ave Trinidad CO 81082

MAIORCA, GRACE LERCARA, Language Art Teacher; *b:* New York City, NY; *w:* Joseph (dec); *c:* Joseph, Regina Maiorca Sullivan; *ed:* (BA) Lang Art, 1977, (MS) Ed, 1980 Queens Coll; Writing Competency, Rdng Wkshps; Public Sch HS Entrance Application Preparation; *cr:* 6th Grade Lang Art Teacher 1977, 6th-8th Grade Lang Art Coord/Rdng Teacher/6th-8th Grade Lang Art Teacher 1978- St Francis Assisi; *ai:* Drama Club; Liturgy & Rdng Comm; *office:* St Francis Assisi Sch 400 Lincoln Rd Brooklyn NY 11225

MAJEK, LINDA, History Teacher; *b:* Carrizo Springs, TX; *ed:* (BS) Ed, SW TX St 1979; (MS) Ed, SUL Ross 1988; Seminar, Univ of TX; *cr:* Teacher/Coach Carris Srings Jr HS 1979-85; Teacher Carrizo Springs HS 1985-; *ai:* NHS Spon; Cadre of Leaders Mem; Delta Kappa Gamma 1989-; PTA 1989-; *office:* Carrizo Springs HS Farm Rd 1556 Carrizo Springs TX 78834

MAJOR, CLARENCE LEE, History Teacher; *b:* Sylacauga, AL; *m:* Sharon Harmon; *c:* Jason, Kevin; *ed:* (BA) His/Poly Sci, 1969, (MED) Admin, 1971 Univ of Montevallo; Cmptr Prgm & Operation; *cr:* Teacher Chelsea HS 1969-71; West Blocton HS 1971-89; Prin Woodstock Elem Sch 1989-90; Teacher West Blocton HS 1990-; *ai:* Jr Class & Chrstn Fellowship Club Spon; Advanced Placement His Teacher; BEA VP/Pres 1973-75; AEA Delegate 1973-75; NEA; Gideions Intnl Chaplain 1979-91; *office:* West Blocton HS General Delivery West Blocton AL 35184

MAJOR, JACQUELINE DAVIS, Guidance Counselor; *b:* Melbourne, FL; *m:* Louis Charles; *c:* Catherine A., Jonathan L.; *ed:* (BA) Chrstn Ed, FL Beacon Coll 1966; (BA) Ed, 1975, (MA) Cnslr Ed, 1989 Univ of S FL; *cr:* Choral Music Teacher Temple Heights Chrstn Sch 1966-69; Elem Teacher Mitchel L Black Elem 1975-86; Math Teacher Delores S Parrott Mid Sch 1986-88; Guidance Cnslr Springstead HS 1988-; *ai:* Hernando Cty Teachers Assn 1975-; Hernando Cty Assn of Counseling & Dev 1988-; *office:* Springstead HS 3300 Mariner Blvd Spring Hill FL 34609

MAJORS, TERRI B., Teacher of Gifted; *b:* New Castle, PA; *ed:* (BA) Elem/Early Chldhd Ed, Clarion St Coll 1979l (MS) Elem/Gifted Ed, Slippery Rock Univ 1985; *cr:* Teacher of Gifted Mohawk Area Schls 1979-; *ai:* Academic Games & High-Q Adv; Citizen Bee & US Academic Decathlon Coach; NEA Delegate 1982-89; CEC 1987-; PA Assn for Gifted Children 1982-; Mohawk Ed Assn Pres 1988-; PA St Ed Assn (Retirement Comm 1987-, Credentials & Elections Chairperson 1987-); Lawrence Cty Poly Action Comm for Ed Chairperson 1986-; *office:* Mohawk Area Schls Mohawk School Rd Bessemer PA 16112

MAKELKY, JEFF A., History Teacher; *b:* Miles City, MT; *m:* Vicki; *c:* Aaron, Eric; *ed:* (BA) His, Dickinson St Univ 1982; Phys Ed, Drivers Ed; *ai:* Close Up Prgm Coord; Head Ftbl Coach; MT Ftbl Coach of Yr 1984.

MAKELY, DANIEL LAVERGNE, Sixth Grade Teacher; *b:* Albany, NY; *m:* Doris Chapman; *c:* Jo-Ann Paquette, Lynne Paquette, Thomas Paquette, Andrea Paquette, William Paquette, Daniel L. III; *ed:* (AA) Liberal Art, Adirondack Comm Coll 1969; (BA) Elem Ed, New England Coll 1971; (MED) Elem Ed, Plymouth St Coll 1976; Learning Disabilities, Cmptr Sci, Math; *cr:* Title I Rdng Teacher Rowell Sch 1971-; 6th Grade Teacher Belmont Elem Sch 1971-; *ai:* Math Team Adv; Drama Club, Math Curr, Rdng Curr, Report Card Comms; NEA, NCTM; Congregational Church (Youth Services 1983-86, Membership Chm 1986-88); City of Laconia Selectman 1990; Math Summer Inst Plymouth St Coll & Diversity St of NH Dartmouth Coll Grants; *office:* Belmont Elem Sch BEST Street Belmont NH 03220

MAKENAS, VICKIE LYNN (SWAIN), Math/Computer Science Teacher; *b:* Pontiac, MI; *m:* Bruce James; *c:* Jennifer; *ed:* (BS) Math, Univ of IL 1975; Grad Stud WA St Univ; *cr:* Math Teacher Rantoul Township HS 1976-78; Math/Cmptrs Teacher Hanford Scndry 1978-; *ai:* Jr HS Math Coach; Dist Math Comm; Regional Math Contest Coord; WA St Math Cncl Government Relations Leaders Conference Chairperson 1989-; NCTM 1973-; Richland Ed Assn 1978-; Northwest Cncl of Cmptr Educators 1982-; GSA Leader 1986- St Math Stans Team; NORCUS Residence in Sci & Technology; Richland Sch Bd Certificate of Outstanding Math Achievement; *office:* Hanford Scndry Sch 450 Hanford Richland WA 99352

MAKEPEACE, TERRY JOSEPH, Mathematics Instructor; *b:* Watertown, SD; *c:* Shawna, Kesley; *ed:* (BSSE) Math, Northern St Univ 1971; Elements of Effective Learning Styles, Stress & the Family; *cr:* 7th-12th Grade Teacher Appleton HS 1971-; *ai:* Appleton Ed Assn Pres 1977-78; *office:* Appleton HS 128 S Hering Appleton MN 56208

MAKI, JUDITH, English Teacher; *b:* Eveleth, MN; *m:* Walter A.; *c:* Jon, Alissa; *ed:* (AA) Pre-Ed, Mesabi Comm Coll 1965; (BS) Scndry Ed, Univ of WI Oshkosh 1987; *cr:* Teacher Wrightstown HS 1987-; *ai:* Yrbk, Newspaper, Jr Class Adv; SEC Rdng, Lang Art, Lib Comm; Kappa Delta Pi, NCTE.

MAKI, RUSSELL WILLIAM, Computer Coordinator; *b:* Chisholm, MN; *m:* Judie K.; *c:* Otto, Bekki, Eric; *ed:* (BS) Elem Ed, 1963, (MS) Elem Admin, 1981 Bemidj St Univ; 6th Yr Elem Admin, Univ of MN 1983; Ed Tech & Aerospace Ed; *cr:* Elem Teacher 1963-86C Cmptr Coord 1986-89 Chisholm Public Schls; Elem Prin ISD #695 & IDS #692 1989-; *ai:* Chisholm Fed of Teacher Treas 1966-; Phi Kappa Phi 1983-; Elem Prin Assn 1989-; Moose Club Governor 1977; Masonic Lodge Master 1984; Grand Masters Awd 1984; Eastern Star Patron 1984; Bash Schlsp to Teach in Thailand 1988; Candidate for Teacher-In-Space Proj; Class Pictures Pub Life Mag & Smithsonian Mag; *office:* Chisholm Pub Schls 3rd Ave & 3rd St SW Chisholm MN 55719

MAKIN, STEVE, Social Science Teacher; *b:* Kansas City, MO; *m:* L. Cathy; *c:* Giselle, Genevieve, Mark; *ed:* (BA) His, CSU Fullerton 1971; (MA) Ed Admin, Univ of San Francisco 1982; *cr:* Teacher Mater Dei HS 1973-78, Paramount HS 1978-89; *ai:* CA Schlsp Fed Adv; *office:* Paramount HS 14429 S Downey Ave Paramount CA 90723

MAKRAVITZ, CAROL A., Biology/Accel Physics Teacher; *b:* Wilkes Barre, PA; *ed:* (BS) Bio, Marillac Coll 1970; (MS) Bio, 1972, (PHD) Bio, 1975 Fordham Univ; Physics, Drew Univ; Bioethics, Kings Coll; *cr:* Teacher Bishop Mc Devitt HS 1974-84, Morris Cath HS 1984-86, Bishop O'Reilly HS 1986-; Instr Assumption Coll for Sisters; *ai:* Sci Dept Chairperson; Admin Cncl Rep; NSTA, NABT, Natl Assn of Physics Teachers; Diocese of Scranton Ethics Commission 1987-; Fellowship Fordham Univ; Conducted Several Wkshps on Bioethics; Conducted Peer Counseling Prgm for HS Stus; Developed Peer Counseling Trng Manual; *office:* Bishop O'Reilly HS 316 N Maple Ave Kingston PA 18704

MAKRIS, GEORGE J., French & Spanish Teacher; *b:* Norwood, MA; *m:* Karen Valdura; *c:* Gregory, Jeffrey; *ed:* (BA) Fr, Suffolk Univ 1962; (MA) Hum, Hofstra Univ 1970; Sch Dist Admin Certificate, C W Post Coll 1981; *cr:* Fr/Span Teacher NY Avenue Jr HS 1962-82, Accompsett Intermediate Sch 1983-; *ai:* Dist Comm on Grading 1990-; Volunteer Adv/Advisee 1989-; NYSFLT; STA Local Building Rep 1965-69; NYSUT, AFT; St James Civic Assn 1988-; Comm for Litter Elimination & Neatness 1989; NDEA Grant for Advanced Stud in Fr Wells Coll 1965; Text Contributor Harcourt Brace & Jananovich of Tests for Nouveaux Copains 1989; *office:* Accompsett Intermediate Sch 660 Meadow Rd Smithtown NY 11787

MAKSIN, PATRICIA LICKERT, Sixth Grade Teacher; *b:* Mc Keesport, PA; *m:* Arthur J.; *c:* Allison, Amanda, Anna, Alexis; *ed:* (BS) Elem Ed, PA St Univ 1973; PA St Univ; *cr:* 6th Grade Teacher Lincoln Elem Sch 1973-81; Cornell Mid Sch 1981-; *ai:* Partnerships Ed Mon Valley Ed Consortium with Mc Keesport Daily News; Liaison Comm Cornell Mid Sch; Mc Keesport Area Ed Assn Recording Sec 1980-82; Mc Keesport Coll Club; Mc Keesport Alumni Assn; Psu Alumni Assn; Mini-Grant Awd Mon Valley Ed Consortium; *office:* Cornell Mid Sch 1600 Cornell St Mc Keesport PA 15132

MAKSYM, JEANNE MARY HURLEY, Kindergarten Teacher; *b:* Detroit, MI; *m:* Anthony S.; *c:* Helen M., Catherine A., Anne M., John, Roy; *ed:* (BA) Ed, Univ of Detroit 1957; (MA) Ed, Oakland Univ 1981; (PHD) Curr/Instruction, MI St 1985; Assertive Discipline Course; *cr:* Teacher Roseville Bd of Ed; *ai:* Teacher in Charge; Wrote Developmental Proposal; Curr Comm; Soc Stu Task Force; Licensed Gesell Admin; Phi Delta Kappa 1985-; Detroit News Teacher of Yr 1968; Univ Angola IN; MI St Univ; Guest Speaker Madelyn Hunter; Drive in Conference; *home:* 15321 Windmill Pointe Dr Grosse Pointe MI 48230

MAKURAT, CELINE, Junior High School Teacher; *b:* Detroit, MI; *ed:* (BS) Bus Ed, Nazareth Coll 1965; *cr:* Teacher St Robert Bellarmine 1967-; *ai:* Safety Squad Coord; Bowling League Mgr; *home:* 30134 W Warren Westland MI 48185

MALASKY, RONALD K., Chemistry Teacher; *b:* Quakertown, PA; *ed:* (BA) Bio/Chem, La Salle Univ 1986; Alternate Route Prgm; *cr:* Chem Teacher Camden HS 1988-, Univ of Medicine & Dentistry of NJ 1989-; *ai:* NJ Sci League; Schls of Excl Comm; Amer Chemical Society; Articles Published 1989, 1990; *office:* Camden HS Park & Baird Blvds Camden NJ 08104

MALAY, GAIL T., Third Grade Teacher; *b:* Rochester, NY; *c:* Laura, Lindsay, Leslie; *ed:* (MA) Admin, 1988, (MA) Elem Ed, 1980 NA Univ; Evaluators Trng; *cr:* 3rd/6th Grade Teacher Starline Elem; Substitute Prin; *ai:* PTA Teacher Adv; Substitute Prin; Level Leader; Ascd; Phi Kappa Phi; Az Sch Admin; *office:* Starline Elem Schl 215 Starline Dr Lake Havasu City AZ 86403

MALCHOW, JANICE HOPKINS, Fine Arts Chair; *b:* Rensselaer, IN; *m:* Robert; *c:* Adam T., Grant A.; *ed:* (BMUSED) Music Ed, (BMUS) Music Performance 1974 Univ of Evansville; (MA) Admin, IN Univ 1980; Working on Ed Sp Degree Ball St Univ; *cr:* Elem Music Teacher N White Sch Corporation 1975-79, Fine Art Chairperson,Choral Dir N White Jr-Sr HS 1979-; *ai:* HS Swing Choir; Mem N Cntrl Visitations & Steering Comm; NHS; Faculty Adv Comm Mem; Delta Kappa Gamma, ASCD 1989-; Sigma Alpha Iota 1971-; *home:* Box 960 Monon IN 47959

MALCOLM, HAROLD EDWARD, JR., 6th Grade Teacher; *b:* Pineville, WV; *m:* Debra R.; *c:* Hutch, Josh; *ed:* (AS) Pre-Teaching, Southwest VA Comm Coll 1970; (BS) Elem Ed, Pikeville Coll 1972; (MS) Elem Sch Admin, Radford Univ 1975; *cr:* 3rd Grade Teacher Jefferson Elem Sch 1972-74; 6th Grade Teacher Pulaski Mid Sch 1974-; *ai:* Morning Activity Coord; Intramural Supervisor for Flag Ftbl, Soccer, Boys Bsktbl/Co-Rec Sftbl; Asst Coach for Wrestling & Track; Career Day Comm; Pulask Cty Ed Assn 1972-; Va Ed Assn 1972-; NEA 1972-; Natl Coaches Assn 1985-; Pulaski Jaycees Dir 1978-83; Pulaski Recreation Dept Little League Coach 1981-; *office:* Pulaski Mid Schl 500 Pico Terr Pulaski VA 24301

MALCOM, MARIANNE VENUTI, Mathematics Teacher; *b:* Camden, NJ; *m:* Stephen D.; *ed:* (BA) Math, Rutgers Univ 1977; Math Ed, Glassboro St Coll; Probability & Statistics Wrkshp, Rutger Univ; *cr:* Math Teacher Absegami HS 1977, Cherokee HS 1977-; *ai:* Girls Swim Head Coach 1977-; Math Club & Mu Alpha Theta Adv; S Jersey Swim Coaches Assn Pres 1984-87, Coach of Yr 1986; NCTM 1977-; AMTNJ 1987-; Camden Cty Cncl of GSA Outstanding Women in S Jersey Hnrbl Mention 198; *office:* Cherokee HS Willow Bend & Tomlinson Mill Marlton NJ 08053

MALDONADO, BEATRIZ, Math Teacher; *b:* San Antonio, TX; *ed:* (BA) Elem Ed, TX Womans Univ 1962; (MA) Lang Arts; NY Univ 1973; Lincoln Center Institute; Columbia Univ; Julliard Sch; Grad Work, T Rinity Univ; *cr:* 3rd Grade Teacher Overseas Dependent Sch Hamura Elem 1967-68; 5th Grade Teacher Northside Independent Sch Valley Hi Elem 1969-72; 5th & 6th Grade Teacher Englewood Sch Dist Lincoln Elem 1973-85; 6th Grade Teacher Dismus Mid Sch 1986-; *ai:* Math Club Spon; Elected Sch Improvement Comm; Criterion Testing Develeper; Family Math Teacher; Englewood Teachers Assn; NJ Ed Assn; NEA; Amer Legion Awd; *office:* Dismus Mid Sch Tryon & Liberty Rd Englewood NJ 07631

MALDONADO, MILAGROS, Secretarial Studies Teacher; *b:* Ponce, PR; *ed:* (AAS) Secretarial Sci, Manhattan Comm Coll 1967; (BS) Bus Ed, 1970, (MA) Bus Ed, 1972, Sixth Yr Prof Degree Bus Ed, 1974 NY Univ; Word Processing & Cmptrs Teacher Trng Wkshps; *cr:* Teacher Norman Thomas HS 1971-; *ai:* Safety Evacuation, Curr/Accreditation, Time-Clock, Schlrshp, Graduation, Academic Planning Sessions Comm; Future Secretaries Assn Adv; NY St Bus Teachers Assn Clinton A. Reed Awd 1989; NY Bus Ed Assn, Delta Pi Epsilon, Kappa Delta Pi, Pi Lambda Theta, NBEA, Prof Secretaries Intnl; NY Univ Alumni Fed Bd of Dir 1980-, Leadership Awds 1984, 1985; Natl Aeronautics & Space Admin Teacher in Space Prgm Recognition & Commendation Awd 1985-86; NY Univ Bus Ed Dept (Pres, Stu Rep), Stu Cncl Service Awd 1970; Norman Thomas HS Distinguished Occupational Teacher Schlrshp 1989; Adult Trng Center Proposals; Featured in Bus Exchange 1986.

MALECHUK, EDWARD FRANK, English-Speech Teacher; *b:* Peshtigo, WI; *m:* Marcella P. Godlewski; *c:* Brian, Renee; *ed:* (BA) His/Eng, UW Madison 1959; (MA) Eng, N MI Univ 1968; MI St Univ, Spencerian Coll; *cr:* His/Eng Teacher Stephenson HS 1959-60; Eng/Speech Teacher Menominee HS 1960-; *ai:* Forensic & Debate Coach; Tri-Y Club; Jr/Sr Class Adv; NEA; MEA Secy 1967-69; BSA Scoutmaster 1975-80; Fed Grant Eng Inst 1965-66; Peshtigo Township Zoning Bd Adv; Peshtigo Bd of Ed Pres; St Marys Church Trustee 1975-78; *home:* N 1910 Hale Rd Peshtigo WI 54157

MALEDY, CINDY RUETER, Counselor; *b:* Springfield, MO; *m:* Charles R.; *c:* Grant; *ed:* (BS) Phys Ed, Southwest MO St Univ 1974; (MS) Guidance & Counseling, Lincoln Univ 1987; Specialists Degree Elem Admin, Southwest MO St Univ; *cr:* Phys Ed Teacher 1974-75, Elem Teacher 1976-86, Elem Cnslr 1987- Salem R-80 Sch Dist; *office:* Salem Mid Sch E 10th St Salem MO 65560

MALESIC, DONA GROUP, Librarian; *b:* New Castle, PA; *m:* C. Michael; *c:* Nicole, Matthew; *ed:* (BS) Lib Sci, Slippery Rock SC 1976; (MLS) Lib Sci, Univ of Pitt 1980; *cr:* Elem Librarian 1976-79, Mid Sch/HS Librarian 1979- Mc Guffey Sch Dist 1979-; *ai:* HS Lib Club Spon; Act 178 Staff Del Comm; Act & Staff Dev In-Service Prgms; Pride Task Force Chairperson; NEA, MEA 1976-; PA Sch Lib Assn 1976-; Cncl of Sch Librarians 1986-; Aspire Consortium; *office:* Mc Guffey HS/Mid Sch Box 219 RD 1 Claysville PA 15323

MALESKI, THERESA S., Mathematics Dept Chair/Teacher; *b:* Seneca Falls, NY; *ed:* Math/Sci/Lang, Romulus Cntrl Sch 1969; (BA) Math/Ed - Cum Laude, Suny New Paltz 1973; (MS) Ed, Nazareth Coll of Rochester 1978; Elements of Ed, Advanced Elements of Ed; *cr:* 7th-12th Grade Math Teacher 1973-, K-12th Grade Math Coord 1983- Romulus Cntrl Sch; *ai:* Discipline Code, Attendance Policy, Advisory to Honor Society, Prin Advisory Comms; Romulus Faculty Assn (Pres, Secy, Treas, Financial Officer) 1973-; Delta Kappa Gamma Financial Officer 1983-; Assn of Cmptr & Math Educators Secy 1987-; NY St Assn of Math Teachers 1987-; NY St Assn of Math Supvrs 1988-; Univ of Rochester Teacher of Yr 1988; Romulus Cntrl Sch Teacher of Yr 1989; *office:* Romuluc Cntrl Sch 5705 Main St Romulus NY 14541

MALEVICH, SANDRA ROSNELL (STIMAC), 4th Grade Teacher; *b:* Astoria, OR; *m:* Tony C.; *c:* Ryan, Tarrah; *ed:* (BS) Ed, Univ of MN 1971; Several Univs; *cr:* Elem Teacher Sauk Centre Public Elem 1971-82/1984-; *ai:* MEEP Mem; Per Mem for Art; NEA Mem 1971-82; MEA Mem 1984-; SCEA Mem 1984-; PTA 1989-; St Michaels Hosp Aux; Comm Concerts 1989-; *office:* Sauk Centre Elem Sch 4th And Oak Sauk Centre MN 56378

MALEY, MARY CAMPLIN, First Grade Teacher; *b:* Anderson, IN; *m:* Timothy Eugene; *c:* Thomas C., Sarah E.; *ed:* (BS) Elem Ed, 1975, (MA) Ed, 1980 Ball St Univ; *cr:* 4th Grade Teacher Charlottesville Elem 1975-76; 3rd Grade Teacher E Hancock Cmmty Sch Corporation 1976-77; 1st Grade Teacher Mount Vernon Cmmty Sch Corporation 1978-79; 3rd Grade Teacher 1979-87, 1st Grade Teacher 1987- Charles A Beard Cmmty Sch Corporation; *ai:* Delta Kappa Gamma; United Meth Church; Tri Kappa; *office:* Knightstown Elem Sch RR 2 PO Box 275 Knightstown IN 46148

MALICH, THERESA MARIE, Language Arts Teacher; *b:* Gig Harbor, WA; *m:* Rand A. Mueller; *ed:* (BA) Ed, Cntrl WA 1974; Working Towards Masters; *cr:* 3rd/4th Grade Teacher Purdy Elem Sch Peninsula Schls 1974-82; Art Teacher Purdy Treatment Center For Women 1977-78; 6th Grade Teacher Goodman Mid Sch 1982-86, 1988-; Drug/Alcohol Abuse Research Asst The Amer Coll of Ob-Gyns 1986-88; *ai:* Odyssey of Mind, Future Problem Solvers, Young Writers Conference Coach; Peninsula Sch Dist Lang Art Comm; Peninsula Ed Assn (Public Relations, Treas, VP) 1976-80; Olympic Uniserve Cncl Mem 1978-80; Sign & Mime Theatre Troupe Performing Mem 1981-86; *office:* Goodman Mid Sch 9010 Prentice Ave Gig Harbor WA 98335

MALIHA, SHERYL ELIZABETH DITTER, Business Education Teacher; *b:* Columbus, NE; *m:* Donald Lee; *c:* Angie, Brian; *ed:* Phys Ed, 1972, Bus Ed, 1980 Kearney St Coll; *cr:* Kndgtn-6th Grade Phys Ed Teacher Council Bluffs Cmmty Sch 1972-73, Westside Cmmty Schls 1973; 7th-12th Grade Bus Ed Teacher Clarkson Jr/Sr HS 1980-; *ai:* Class Spon; NE St Ed Assn 1980-; NE St Bus Assn 1975-; Leigh Civic Club 1987-; Instructional Improvement Cncl 1988-; *office:* Clarkson HS 6th & Maple Box G Clarkson NE 68629

MALIK, SHAGUFTA ADEEB, 9-12th Grade Math Teacher; *b:* Lahore, Pakistan; *m:* Mohammad K.; *c:* Parooq, Humaira, Rabia, Shazia; *ed:* (MS) Math & Physics, Funjab Univ; Physics CA St Univ Los Angeles; *cr:* Math & Physics Lahore Coll 1969-72; Math Teacher Hollywood HS 1975-85, El Camino Real HS 1985-; *ai:* Spon Kingsmen Club; Spon Stu League; Hands Across Campus; Foriegn Exchange Club; Staff Assn Treas 1988-89; TLA Treas 1989; CTA; NEA; Los Angeles Ed Partnership Grant; *office:* El Camino Real HS 5440 Valley Circle Blvd Woodland Hills CA 91367

MALIS, LUCY ELLEN, Second Grade Teacher; *b:* Butler, PA; *m:* James Joseph; *ed:* (BS) Elem Ed, Slippery Rock Univ 1974; *cr:* Kndgtn Teacher 1974-75, 2nd Grade Teacher Oakland Elem 1975-; *office:* Oakland Township Elem Sch 545 Chicora Rd Butler PA 16001

MALKASIAN, CLAIRE TASHJIAN, Reading/English Teacher; *b:* Providence, RI; *m:* Enoch; *c:* Matthew H., Mark A.; *ed:* (BA) Ed/Eng, Sacramento St Univ 1959; (ME) Rdng, Worcester St Coll 1982; Advanced Courses Eng & Rdng, San Francisco St Univ, Los Angeles St Univ, Univ of CA Berkeley; *cr:* 5th/6th Grade Teacher/Librarian Oak Ridge Elem Sch 1959-62; Eng Teacher Sam Brannan Jr HS 1962-65, Grafton Jr HS 1966-67; Rdng/Eng Teacher Grafton Mid Sch 1976-; *ai:* Sch Newspaper Sponsorship; 5th-8th Grade Lang Arts Team Leader; Book Fair Chairperson; 5 Yr Curr Planning Comm; Promotion Day Assembly Prgm Chairperson; Cntrl MA Rdng Assn, MA Rdng Assn; Natl Assn of Armenian Stud & Research; *home:* 57 Prospect St Whitinsville MA 01588

MALLARD, IDA R., Retired Elem School Teacher; *b:* Pineville, SC; *w:* Ernest L. (dec); *c:* Henry J. Stewart, Gloria S. Gadsden, Ernest R., Samuel C.; *ed:* (BA) Elem Ed, Avery Inst 1934; (BA) Elem Ed, Morris Coll 1951; (BA) Elem Ed, SC St Coll; SC St Coll; Citadel; Univ of SC; *cr:* Elem Teacher J K Gourdin Elem 1935-84; *ai:* Sunday Sch Teacher; Pres Missionary Bd, Assn Choir, United Chrstn Women & Queen for Yr; Berkeley Cty (Pres 1960-62) Teacher of Yr 1954-55; SC Retired Educator (Historian 1989-) Teacher of Yr 1974; Natl Assn Life Mem (House Delegates 1942-62) TV Honor 1983; Amer Legion Auxiliary Pres 1962-89 Outstanding Work Awd 1973; GSA Leader; Outstanding Elem Teacher Amer 1974; Spelling Contest Named in Honor; Book Published; Outstanding Citizen Berkeley Cty 1966; *home:* Rt 1 Box 29 Pineville SC 29468

MALLORY, WILLIAM K., Retired Teacher; *b:* Clark, MO; *m:* Rheba Gibbs; *c:* Doug, Greg, Jerry; *ed:* (BS) Ag, 1946; (MED) Voc Ag, MO Univ 1960; *ai:* MOVATA; Lions Club; Shrine; Scotish Rite; FFA; *home:* 310 N Main Cross Bowling Green MO 63334

MALLOY, LAUREL M., Theatre Arts Teacher; *b:* Chicago, IL; *m:* Robert; *c:* Anthony; *ed:* (BFA) Theatre Arts, Southwest TX St Univ 1984; *cr:* Theatre Arts Teacher E M Pease Mid Sch 1985-; *ai:* Pentathlon, Drama Club Spon; Literary Team Coach; Amer Assn Univ Women, Kappa Delta Pi, TX Ed Theatre Assn; Sierra Club; *office:* E. M. Pease Mid Sch 201 Hunt Ln San Antonio TX 78245

MALON, PATRICIA GLASER, Social Studies Teacher; *b:* Pittsburgh, PA; *m:* Henry C.; *c:* Paul, Carolyn Malon-Moran, Andrea, Diane, Matthew; *ed:* (BA) His - Cum Laude, 1956, (MA) Soc Stud, 1961 Hunter Coll; (PHD) Geography, Columbia Univ 1981; *cr:* Soc Stud Teacher/Dept Chairperson Newtown HS 1973-77; Adjunct Lecturer Hunter Coll 1978-86; Soc Stud Teacher BX HS Sci 1981, St Johns Preparatory Sch 1984-; *ai:* Faculty Advisory Cncl; AAG 1978-; NCSS 1990; Womens Club of Forest Hills 1975-; St Johns Lay Faculty Assn Treas; St Francis Coll Awd Outstanding Contribution to Higher Ed 1989.

MALONE, CAMILLE SHIELDS, Mathematics Dept Chairperson; *b:* Tulsa, OK; *m:* H. Dennis Wilkerson; *c:* Jay D.; *ed:* (BA) Math, Univ of N TX 1969; (MA) Inter Disciplinary Stud, Univ of TX Dallas 1981; Math, Univ of TX Dallas; *cr:* Teacher Bryan Adams HS 1968-71, S Oak Cliff HS 1975-84; Instr Eastfield Jr Coll 1982-86; Teacher/Math Dept Chair Skyline HS 1984-; *ai:* Chm Faculty Advisory Comm; Spon Univ Interscholastic

League Math Team Comm Mem; Sch Cmmty Safety Comm; Assn for Supervision Math 1989-; NCTM 1985-; Humane Society of the US 1986-; Green Peace 1980-; Jim Collins Outstanding Teacher Awd 1986; Skyline Teacher of Yr 1990; *office:* Skyline HS 7777 Forney Rd Dallas TX 75227

MALONE, GEORGIA RISNER, Bus Office Services Teacher; *b:* Georgetown, TX; *c:* John R.; *ed:* (BBA) Bus/Economics/Scndry Ed, Southwestern Univ 1967; *cr:* St Dept of Public Welfare St of TX 1951-60; Asst Dean Arts/Sci Southwestern Univ 1960-67; Math/Bus Teacher Liberty Hill Ind Sch Dist 1967-69; Voc Office Ed 1970-80, Voc CVAE-ODP 1980- Leander Ind Sch Dist; *ai:* Spon Bus Prof of America; Prior Spon of Office Ed Assn/Voc Office Careers Clubs of TX; Founding Spon of Both Groups at Leander HS; OEA 1970/VOCCI 1980/BPOA 1989; Voc Office Ed Teachers Assn of TX 1989-; Amer Assn of Univ Women Pres 1969-71; Amer AAUW Treas 1971-75; America Voc Assn; World Bible Sch Austin Tx; Stu in Nigeria West Africa; Taught in Kona HI; Securing Visa to Budapest Hungary for Teaching of Eng 1990; *office:* Leander HS 3301 S Bagdad Rd Leander TX 78641

MALONE, JAMES LELAND, JR., Science Department Chair; *b:* Philadelphia, PA; *m:* Susan E.; *c:* Molly, Jessica; *cr:* Math/Sci Teacher Mercersburg Acad 1979-; *ai:* Asst Ftbl Coach; Canoeing & Rock Climbing Supvr; NCTM 1979-; AAPT 1989-; Article Published in Math Journal on Quadratic Functions; *office:* Mercersburg Acad Mercersburg Acad Mercersburg PA 17236

MALONE, JEANIE BLACKWOOD, Social Studies Teacher; *b:* Union, SC; *m:* Charles Jackson; *c:* Anna E.; *ed:* (BA) Soc Sci/Scndry Ed, Winthrop Coll 1981; *cr:* Soc Worker/Admissions Coord Oakmont of Union 1981-85; 7th Grade Teacher Sims Jr HS 1985-; *ai:* Academic Challenge Quiz Team 7th Grade Adv; Natl Fed of Music Clubs Union Chapter Mem; Natl Guild of Piano Teachers; Union Jr Charity League Mem 1981-.

MALONE, RONALD JAMES, Math Dept Chair; *b:* Havre, MT; *ed:* (BS) Math, N MT Coll 1987; *cr:* Math/Cmptr/His Teacher Turner HS 1987-; *ai:* Jr HS Bsktbl Coach; Class & Prom Adv; MT Cncl Teachers of Math, NCTM 1988-; *home:* Box 93 Turner MT 59542

MALONE, SANDRA ELAINE, Seventh Grade Teacher; *b:* Nashville, TN; *ed:* (BS) Elem Ed, Mid TN St Univ 1975; (MS) Educl Admin, George Peabody Coll 1977; Ed, W GA Coll; *cr:* 2nd Grade Teacher Grassland Elem Sch 1978-81; 7th Grade Lang Art Teacher Westside Mid Sch 1981-; *ai:* Beta Club Spon; Lib Comm; *office:* Westside Mid Sch 580 Lafayette Rd S W Rocky Face GA 30740

MALONE, SARAH GOOCH, Teacher/Instructor; *b:* Milton, TN; *m:* Branious Andrew I; *c:* Sesilee A., Branious A. II; *ed:* (BS) Biological Sci, Stillman Coll 1967; Grad Work Soc Sci, Univ of CA Los Angeles, Univ of CA Santa Barbara, Chapman Trevecca Nazarene, TN St Univ; Keeping Healthy Instructional Model; Writing Connection; Math Prep Module, Test Taking Technique, Ed Module-Motivation Designer Presenter; Pepper/Salt Module Developer; Study Skills Module Designer; Career Ladder Team Evaluator; TN Instructional Model; *cr:* Teacher Lompoc Unified Schls 1967-73, 1975-76; Consultant Wkshp Coord Center of Ed 1974-80, 1983; Teacher Bellwood Elem 1973-; Owner/Coord Salt Ed Services 1980-; Instr/Cnslr Mid TN St Univ 1984-; *ai:* 4-H Adult Volunteer Leader, Alumni Assn; Youth Ed Schlsp Cnslr; Life Act Enrichment Prgms Coord; Spec Events, Cmmty Relations Advisory Comm; Youth Cncl Adv; Tanzania I Operations Crossroads Africa Ed Participant Scholar; Math Club Competition Spon; Math Skills Correlations, Math, Sci, Soc Stud, Textbook, Rdng Skills Checklist Comm; United Teachers (Building Rep, TERS Comm, Teacher Welfare) 1967-, WHO Awd 1971-72, We Honor Ours 1971-72; Mid TN Math Assn 1985-; TN Math Teachers Assn; TN Rdng Assn Mary Tom Berry; Amer Bus Womens Assn (VP 1988-89, Membership Chm 1989-, Registration Hostess 1989); Heart of TN; TN Extension Service 4-H 1973-, Pearl Clover Pin 1989; Concerned Educators 1985-, Certificate 1985; Thinking Corporation Pilot Prgm; *office:* Bellwood Elem Sch Mid TN St Univ PO Box 1495 Murfreesboro TN 37130

MALONEY, SUSAN ANN, 5th Grade Teacher; *b:* Norman, OK; *m:* Dennis D.; *c:* Jennifer E.; *ed:* (BS) Elem Ed, 1977, (MED) Admin, 1982 NSU; Gifted & Talented, OCU; *cr:* Kndgtn-3rd-5th-10th Grade Eng Teacher Schulter Sch 1974-77; 7th/8th Grade Teacher/Boys Coach Pretty Water Sch 1980-82; 12th Grade Eng Teacher Central HS 1982; Owner/Dir Alphabet Day Care Center 1982-83; 1st-5th Grade/Teacher of Gifted & Talented Adams Elem 1983-; *ai:* Safety Patrol Spon, Gifted & Talented, Cmptr, Spec Events Comm Mem; Bus Driver 1980-82; OK Ed Assn Mem 1974-88; Channel 5 Awd 1988; Norman Public Schls Recognition 1985-88; Coach of Yr 1981-82; Sports Act Fund Raiser 1981-82; *office:* Adams Elem Sch 817 Denison Norman OK 73169

MALPASS, MARY HOURIGAN, Mathematics Teacher; *b:* Wilkes Barre, PA; *m:* Charles James; *c:* Charles H., Augusta J.; *ed:* (BS) Math, Marywood Coll 1972; Masters Equivalency; *cr:* Teacher Holy Name of Jesus 1973-77; Permanent Substitute Teacher Dallas Area Sch Dist 1981-83; Teacher Lake-Lehman Sch Dist 1983-; *ai:* Natl Jr Honor Society Adv; Delta Kappa Gamma Treas 1986-; Parent Teacher Guild (VP, Mem Officer) 1984-; *office:* Lake-Lehman Jr HS Lake-Lehman School Dist Lehman PA 18627

MAMER, JAMES MICHAEL, History/Social Science Teacher; *b:* Los Angeles, CA; *m:* Jessica Puma; *ed:* (BA) Poly Sci/Ec, Cal Poly Pomona 1970; (MA) Intnl Affairs, Immaculate Heart Coll 1989; Span Lang Stud Columbia 1981, Mexico 1982, Ecuador 1983, Span 1986; Sabbitical Stud Fr in Paris 1985-86; *cr:* Teacher Venado Mid Sch 1977, Irvine HS 1978-; *ai:* Soc Sci & His Mentor; Sch Site Cncl Faculty Rep; NCSS 1980-; Felbright-Hayes Stud Grant India 1978; COE Fellowship Amer His Stanford 1984; USC-Danforth Fellowship Intnl SAtud 1987-; *office:* Irvine HS 4321 Walnut Ave Irvine CA 92714

MANA, DAVE PAUL, English Department Chairman; *b:* St Louis, MO; *m:* Judith Ann Sutka;; *c:* Deborah, John, Frank; *ed:* (BS) Scndry Educ, Univ of MO 1972; (M ED) Scndry Teaching, Univ of MO 1975; 52 Addl Hours at Northeast MO St Univ, Southeast MO St Univ, McPherson Coll; *cr:* Teacher/Coach DeAndreis Archdiocesan HS 1972-74; English Dept Chm Mehlville Sr HS 1974-; Asst Prin-Summer School Mehlville Sr HS 1986-; *ai:* Curr Cncl 1977-; Chm NCA School Staff & Admin Comm; MHC Crisis Management Team Mem; NCTE 1977-; Boy Scouts of America Webelos Coord 1987-88; Girl Scouts of America Leadership Awd 1987; *office:* Mehlville Sr H S 3200 Lemay Ferry Rd Saint Louis MO 63125

MANAILOVICH, ADELE C., Kindergarten Teacher; *b:* Franklin, NJ; *m:* John; *ed:* (BS) Elem Ed, Trenton St Coll 1971; *cr:* K-2nd/4th-6th Grade Teacher Hardyston Twp Sch 1971-; *ai:* Cheerleading & Gymnastics Coach; Stu Cncl Adv; Hardyston Township Ed Assn Pres 1982-85; NJ Ed Assn, NEA; Assn of Kndgtn Educators; *office:* Hardyston Township Sch 50 Rt 23 Franklin NJ 07416

MANASCO, BOBBIE MC ADAMS, Fifth Grade Teacher; *b:* Jasper, AL; *m:* Kenneth Paul; *c:* Alyson; *ed:* (BS) Elem Ed, 1972, (MA) Elem Ed, 1976 Univ of AL; *cr:* Teacher Talladega City Schls 1972-73, Jefferson Cty 1974-76, Walker Cty Schls 1976-; *ai:* 5th-8th Grades Academic Bowl Spon; *home:* Rt 10 Box 146 A Jasper AL 35501

MANCIEL, DEBORAH FAY, Sixth Grade Writing Teacher; *b:* Detroit, MI; *ed:* (BA) Early Chldhd Ed, MI St Univ 1979; (MS) Early Chldhd Ed, Wayne St Univ 1984; *cr:* Kndgtn/1st Grade Teacher Pulaski Elem 1979-80; Primary Teacher Dossin Elem & Vetal Elem 1980-; 8th Grade Eng/Soc Stud Teacher Emerson Mid Sch 1980-81; Eng/8th Grade Teacher Murphy Mid Sch 1981-82; Primary Teacher Burns 1982-83; 8th Grade Eng Teacher Jackson Mid Sch 1983; 7th/8th Grade Eng/Rdng Teacher Cerveny 1983-88; 6th/8th Grade Eng/Rdng/Writing Teacher Taft 1988-; *ai:* Tutorial Prgms Eng, Rdng & Writing; 6th-8th Grade Sch Newspaper Adv; Inservice Parents Wkshp; Writing & Compact Course; Chm Curr, Achievement, Young Writers Cooperative Learning Inservice Comms; Instructional Asst At Risk Stu; Writing Contest Adv; MI Assn Supervision & Curr Dev 1980; Area C Curr Achievement Awd; Detroit Blueprint for Rdng Inservice Ed Prgm 1988-89; Perfect Attendance Awd 1983, 1987-88; Prof Growth Awds 1989; Detroit Free Press Honor; *office:* Taft Mid Sch 19501 Berg Rd Detroit MI 48219

MANCINELLI, JOSEPH ALBERT, Mathematics Teacher; *b:* Monongahela, PA; *m:* Cynthia Jo Mc Cathren; *c:* Meghan; *ed:* (BSED) Scndry Math, 1973, (MED) Scndry Math, 1981 California Univ of PA; *cr:* 10th-12th Grade Math Teacher Monongahela HS 1973-74; 7th-9th Grade Math Teacher Finleyville Jr HS 1974-86; 9th/10th Grade Math Teacher Ringgold HS 1986-; Math Instr California Univ of PA 1989-; *ai:* First Chrstn Church of Monongahela (Elder 1986-, Stewardship Comm Chm 1988-); *office:* Ringgold HS Rt 136 Monongahela PA 15063

MANCINELLI, KATHLEEN ELIZABETH, Fifth Grade Teacher; *b:* New Eagle, PA; *ed:* (BS) Elem Ed, 1975, (MED) Elem Ed, 1980 California Univ of PA; *cr:* 2nd Grade Teacher Ginger Hill Elem Sch 1977-81; 5th Grade Teacher Roosevelt Elem Sch 1981-82; 2nd Grade Teacher Elrama Elem Sch 1982-83; 6th Grade Teacher Monongahela Elem Center 1983-85; 5th Grade Teacher Gastonville Elem Center 1985-; Adult Basic Ed Night Class Monongahela Elem Center 1985-; *ai:* Spring Musical Guitar Accompaniament 1986, Special Slide Presentation 1987, Choreographer 1988; Delta Kappa Gamma (Prof Affairs Chairperson 1986-88, Recording Secy 1988-, Prof Affairs Comm St Level 1990-92, Corresponding Secy 1990-92); Monongahela Area Historical Society, United Way Team Player; First Chrstn Church (Deaconess, Asst Treas); Pittsburgh Press Writing Contest Winner 1986; PA Dept of Ed Teacher Exch & Home Stay Prgm in Japan 1989; Nom Natl PTA Outstanding Educator Awd 1990.

MANCINI, ALPHONSE F., JR., 6th Grade Teacher; *b:* Long Branch, NJ; *m:* Mildred Merten; *c:* Marin, Mark; *ed:* (BA) Elem Ed, Glassboro St Coll 1971; WV Univ; *cr:* 4th-5th Grade Teacher Swimming River Sch 1971-74; 6th Grade Math/Sci Teacher Gihon Sch 1974-; *ai:* Math Field Day Spon 1976-81; Sci Fair Judge Elem & Jr HS 1977-86; AFT 1984-; St Francis Xavier R C Church (Lay Minister 1980-83, Sunday Sch Teacher 1981-84).

MANCINI, RICK GUY, 6th Grade Teacher; *b:* Canton, OH; *m:* Sherry Moushey; *c:* Jennifer, Damon; *ed:* (BS) Ed, Kent St 1971; (MS) Elem Admin, Akron Univ 1974; Working towards Doctoral Admin; *cr:* Teacher Roosevelt 1971-74, Washington 1974-77, Allen 1977-80, Worley 1980-; *ai:* J P Adv; Cmptr Comm; Prof Comm; Phi Delta Kappa; Jennings Scholar Awd 1971-72; Dist Teacher of Yr 1987; *office:* Worley HS 1340 23rdst N W Canton OH 44709

MANCUSI, MICHAEL MARY, CRSP Amer Government Teacher; *b:* Brooklyn, NY; *ed:* (BS) Soc Sci, Fordham Univ 1973; (MSED) Scndry Ed, Canisius Coll 1976; (STB) General Theology, 1978, (MTH) Spiritualty, 1979 Angelicum Univ; Drug & Alcohol Abuse Prevention & Intervention, Intermediate Unit 20; *cr:* Stu Teacher Julia Richmann HS 1972-73; 5th-9th Grade Teacher Stella Niagara Ed Park 1973-74; 10th-12th Grade Teacher Bethlehem Cath HS 1979-; *ai:* Key Club; SADD; Stu Peer Counseling; Amnesty Intnl; Stu Act Mid St Evaluation Comm Chairperson; Homecoming Comm; PA Assn for Soc Stud 1979-, Teacher of Yr 1989; Lehigh Valley Assn for Soc Stud 1979-, Teacher of Yr 1989; Natl Math Ed Assn 1979-; Kiwanis (Pres, VP, Secy) 1980, Kiwanian of Yr 1984; Lehigh Valley Bd on Alcoholism Bd Mem 1980, Bronze Awd 1986; Spina Bifida Assn Bd Mem 1980-, Man of Yr 1985;Ancient Order of Hibernians Chaplain 1988-; Key to City by Bethlehem Mayor Marcincin for Youth Work; Various Religious Historical Articles Published; Book to be Published 1990; Key Club Golden Key of Service 1987; *home:* 4301 Hecktown Rd Bethlehem PA 18017

MANDEL, MICHAEL WALTER, English Teacher; *b:* Suffern, NY; *c:* Jessica L.; *ed:* (BA) Eng, St Michaels 1983; *cr:* Eng Teacher Wayne Hills HS 1983-; *ai:* Poetry Club; Head Bsktbl Coach & Asst Bsbl Coach; *office:* Wayne Hills HS 272 Berdan Ave Wayne NJ 07470

MANDEVILLE, ANNE M., Italian/Spanish Teacher; *b:* Providence, RI; *m:* Richard J.; *c:* Seth, Jessica, Matthew; *ed:* (BA) Italian, Univ of RI 1969; (MED) Counseling, RI Coll 1974; Eng & Span, Comm Coll of RI; Span, Providence Coll; Critic Teacher, RI Coll; *cr:* Italian/Span Teacher Johnston Sr HS 1969-; *ai:* Homework Policy, Sch Improvement, Curr Revision, Awds Comm; Ind Span III, Span IV; Basic Educl Prgm Evaluator; RI Foreign Lang Assn 1975-; RI Teacher of Italian 1975-85; Smithfield Republican Town Comm Secy 1988-; *office:* Johnston Sr HS 345 Cherry Hill Rd Johnston RI 02919

MANDEVILLE, LEONARD, Mathematics Department Chair; *b:* Detroit, MI; *ed:* (BS) Ind Eng, Univ of MI 1969; (MA) Math Ed, Wayne St Univ 1978; *cr:* Teacher Benedictine HS 1974-; *ai:* Chess & Bowling Club; NCTM; *office:* Benedictine HS 8001 W Outer Dr Detroit MI 48235

MANDIGO, CRAIG MARTIN, 4th Grade Teacher; *b:* Syracuse, NY; *ed:* (Ba) Psych, SUC Brockport 1976; (MS) Ed, SUNY Potsdam 1982; *cr:* 1st/2nd/4th Grade Teacher Parishville Hopkmton 1977-; *ai:* Stage Mgr Sch Musical; Collect Chairperson Campbells Soup Labels; Parishville Hopkinton Tchrs Assn Pres 1984-; BPOE Elks 1988-; Awd from Parishville Hopkinton Bd of Ed Invlvmt in Extra Curr Act; Awd Music Dept for Invlvmt; *office:* Parishville-Hopkinton Cntrl School St Parishville NY 13672

MANESS, JOAN JENSEN, Second Grade Teacher; *b:* Albuquerque, NM; *m:* George A.; *c:* Richard, George III, Gregory; *ed:* (AA) Soc Sci, Coll of Sequoias 1968; (BA) Liberal Stud, CA St Univ Bakersfield 1988; Grad Stud Rdng, Specialist Credential, Ed; *cr:* K-8th Grade Substitute Teacher Tulare City Sch Dist 1968-72; Elem Teacher St Aloysius Parochial Sch 1972-; *ai:* CA Math Cncl 1987-; NSTA 1988-; Tulare Cty Rdng Cncl 1982-; NCEA 1978-; Cath Daughters of America Secy 1978-82; Natl Fed of Republican Women Secy 1985-87; *home:* 3388B E Tulare Ave Tulare CA 93274

MANFRED, GERALD A., Mathematics Instructor; *b:* Colfax, WA; *m:* Susan K. Adamson; *c:* Gerry Jr., Paul, Stephen, John; *ed:* (BA) Math Ed, 1962, (BS) Math Ed, 1966 Gonzaga Univ; Grad Courses; *cr:* Math Instr Cheney HS 1962-63, University HS 1963-; Adjunct Math Professor Gonzaga Univ 1985-; Math Instr Spokane Comm Coll 1986-; *ai:* Permanent Sr Class Adv; Events Mgr; Consultant for Coll Bd Advanced Placement Calculus; / CVEA Pres 1971, Special Service 1972; WA Math Teachers, NCTM; St John Vianney (Parish Cncl, Lay Minister) 1970-; Cntrl Valley Teacher of Yr 1981; St Runner-Up Teacher of Yr 1981; Nom Excl in Ed 1990; *office:* University HS E 10212 9th Spokane WA 99206

MANFRED, ROSEMARY PUSATERE, Math Dept Chair/Teacher; *b:* Homestead, PA; *m:* Kenneth James; *c:* Julianne, Beth A.; *ed:* (BS) Math/Scndry Ed, Indiana Univ of PA 1973; *cr:* HS Math Teacher Wilkensburg Sch Dist 1973; Mid Sch/HS Math Teacher 1973-, Math Dept Chairperson 1986- Steel Valley Sch Dist; *ai:* NCTM, PA Cncl Teachers of Math, Math Cncl of W PA, PA St Teachers Assn; Steel Valley Sch Dist Teacher of Yr 1985-86; Outstanding Teacher 1988-89; *office:* Steel Valley HS 3113 Main St Munhall PA 15120

MANFREDI, KRISTA, Theatre Teacher/Director; *b:* Sharon, PA; *m:* John M.; *c:* Zachary, John; *ed:* (AB) Theatre, Youngstown St Univ 1970; (MED) Ed Tech, Wayne St Univ 1975; Theatre Classes Ohio Univ; *cr:* (1) Teacher Troy Sch Dist 1973-; (2) Actress Performing Artists Unlimited 1983-; (3) Actress Attic Theatre 1984-; (4) Dir Actors Alliance Theatre Co 1986-87; (5) Dir Richmond Cmmnty Theatre 1987-88; *ai:* Theatre Dir; Thespian Society Spon; Chrldr Coach; ATA 1975-90; MTA 1977-90; NCET 1975-89; Attic Theatre Board Mem 1987-90; Dinosaur Hill Nature Preserve 1989-90; MCA Grants 1975-77; *office:* Troy Athens H S 4333 John R Troy MI 48098

MANGANARO, CAROL JEAN (DITTRICH), Mathematics Teacher; *b:* Tilden, NE; *m:* John; *c:* Tony, Nicholas, Marcus; *ed:* (AA) General Ed, NE Comm Coll 1975; (BA) Math, Wayne St Coll 1978; *cr:* Math Teacher Hartington Public Schls 1979-82, Laurel Concord Public Schls 1984-; *ai:* Head Vlybl Coach; Jr Class Spon; NEA 1978-82, 1984-; LCEA 1984-; *office:* Laurel Concord Public Schls 5th & Wakefield St Laurel NE 68745

MANGINI, ROSANNE CAMPANELLA, 7th & 8th Grade Teacher; *b:* New York, NY; *m:* Robert J.; *c:* Robert B., Susanne; *ed:* (BS) Elem Ed, St Johns Univ 1965; Grad Study Queens Coll 1965-67; *cr:* 5th/6th Grade Teacher PS 123 1965-67; 7th/8th Grade Teacher St Margarets Sch 1977-; *ai:* Organizer &

Moderator Stu Tutoring Prgm & Stu Service League; Moderator & Chaperone Dance Comm; 5th-8th Grade Prgm Coord 1987-88; Pearl River Environmental Assn Treas 1978-83; Study Grants from Syracuse Univ 1980 & Emmanual Coll 1982; *office:* St Margarets Sch 33 N Magnolia St Pearl River NY 10965

MANGO, ANTONIA MARIE, First Grade Teacher; *b:* Pittsburgh, PA; *ed:* (BS) Elem Ed, IN St Teachers Coll 1957; (ME) Elem Ed, Duquesne Univ 1965; Catechetical Formation Religion; *cr:* Kndgtn Teacher Kiski Area 1957-64; 2nd Grade Teacher St Gertrude 1964-68; 1st Grade Teacher St Marys 1968-69, St Anthianasius 1969-70, St Benedicts 1970-71, Immaculate Conception 1971-; *ai:* Eucharistic Minister; Parish & Sch of Immaculate Conception Liturgy Comm; NCEA 1964-, Miriam Farrell Outstanding Teaching Awd 1989, Region PA & NJ Teacher of Yr 1989; Republican Comm; Articles Published; *office:* Immaculate Conception Sch 308 2nd St Irwin PA 15642

MANGUM, EVELYN LEE, Third Grade Teacher; *b:* Marshville, NC; *m:* Fred L.; *c:* Fred L. Jr., Cynthia L.; *ed:* (BS) Home Ec/Sci, 1955, Early Chldhd Cert, 1971 UNCG; Mentor & Teacher Effectiveness Trng; *cr:* Teacher Boonville Elem Sch 1970-72, East Bend Elem Sch 1972-; *ai:* Re-Accreditation Chm Southern Assn of Colls & Schls Comms; Alpha Delta Kappa Treas; *home:* 600 Ravenscar Ct Winston-Salem NC 27104

MANGUS, DAN CARL, HS English/Mathematics Teacher; *b:* Pensacola, FL; *m:* Karen Ward; *c:* Brannon, Dani B., Brent, Bryce; *ed:* (BA) Hum, Univ of Louisville 1984; *cr:* Asst Prin/Teacher Landmark Chrstn Acad 1981-; *ai:* Athletic Dir for Sch; ASA Umpire; IBOA Referee; *office:* Landmark Chrstn Acad 6502 Johnsontown Rd Louisville KY 40272

MANGUS, THOMAS EUGENE, Band Director; *b:* Oklahoma City, OK; *m:* Jennifer Erin; *c:* Greg, Andrew; *ed:* (BME) Music Ed, 1975, (MME) Music Ed, 1979 Cntrl St Univ; *cr:* Band Dir Big Cabin Schls 1975-76, Maud Schls 1976-79, Crescent Schls 1979-82; Professor/Band Dir NE OK St A&M Coll 1982-86; Supvr/Band Dir/Instrumental Music Teacher Miami Public Schls 1986-; *ai:* Marching & Concert Band; HS Jazz Ensemble; Assist 6th-9th Grade Band; OK Music Educators Assn, OK Band Masters Assn 1976-; Amer Fed of Musicians, DEA, NEA 1974-; Miami Assn of Classroom Teachers 1986-; Rotary Club 1977-78; Outstanding Sr Male Cntrl St Univ; *home:* 2004 L Southwest Miami OK 74354

MANIGLIA, RONALD JOSEPH, AP Physics/Chemistry Teacher; *b:* Bucks Cty, PA; *ed:* (BS) Bio - Cum Laude, St Josephs Univ 1978; (MED) Educl Admin, Rider Coll 1990; *cr:* Teacher Holy Cross HS 1978-; *ai:* Cmptr Club Moderator; Cmptr Systems Admin; NACST 1987-; Knights of Columbus 1990; Tandy Distinguished Sci/Math Teacher 1990; *office:* Holy Cross HS 5035 Rt 130 S Delranco NJ 08075

MANIGO, CARRIE B., 5th Grade Teacher; *b:* Savannah, GA; *c:* Sharon A.; *ed:* (BS) Elem Ed, Savannah St Coll 1977; *cr:* 5th Grade Teacher Richmond Hill Elem Sch 1978-; *ai:* Math Comm & Grade Level Rep; GA Assn of Educators; Cleveland Schlsp Fnd VP 1989-; *office:* Richmond Hill Elem Sch Hwy 144 PO Box 820 Richmond Hill GA 31324

MANKER, ROBIN C., Mathematics Teacher; *b:* Beardstown, IL; *m:* Patricia J. Bradshaw; *c:* Bradley R., Tyson L.; *ed:* (BA) Math, IL Coll 1971; (MA) Math, Miami Univ 1973; *cr:* Teacher Jacksonville HS 1973-; *ai:* IL Cncl Teachers of Math, NCTM 1977-; Articles Published; *office:* Jacksonville HS 1211 N Diamond Jacksonville IL 62650

MANKIN, PATRICIA STIGER, 4th Grade Teacher; *b:* Lyons, KS; *m:* Samuel Ashley; *c:* Andrew B., Ashley C.; *ed:* (BSED) Elem Ed, Abilene Chrstn Univ 1965; *cr:* Teacher Houston Ind Sch 1965-67, Jefferson Parish Sch 1967-68, Muscogee Cty Schls 1968-69, DeKalb Cty Schls 1969-71, Greater Atlanta Chrstn 1970-; *ai:* Lower Sch Greater Atlanta Chrstn Sch Math Chairperson; GA Cncl Teachers of Math, NCTM; Greater Atlanta Chrstn Sch Teacher of Yr 1982; *office:* Greater Atlanta Chrstn Sch Box 4277 Norcross GA 30091

MANLEY, GAY BROTHERS, Fourth Grade Teacher; *b:* Maysville, KY; *m:* Melvin S. Jr.; *c:* Dax, Josh, Jenna; *ed:* (Ba) Elem Ed, 1972, (MA) Elem Ed, 1973 Morehead St Univ; *cr:* 7th/8th Grade Sci Teacher 1973-78; 6th Grade Teacher 1978-80 Mason Cty Mid Sch; 5th Grade Teacher 1980-85, 4th Grade Teacher 1985- Straub Elem; *ai:* Cultural Arts Chairperson Straub Elem; *office:* Straub Elem Sch 387 Chenault Dr Maysville KY 41056

MANLEY, PATRICIA E., Instructor; *b:* Rochester, MN; *m:* Burnell; *c:* Kelly, Theresa, Marcus; *ed:* (AA) Rochester Comm Coll, Rochester Jr Coll 1965; (BS) Elem Ed, 1972 (MS) Elem Ed, 1984 Winona St Univ; Great River Writing Project, Developmental & Remedial Rdng Concentration, Remedial Rdng Cert; *cr:* Teacher Winona Cath Area Schls 1976-88; Coord/Tutor Winona Adult Literacy Prgm 1985-88; Teacher Winona Cmmty Ed 1985-; Instr Winona St Univ 1988-; *ai:* Enrollment Management & Adult Literacy Comm; MN Teachers of Eng to Speakers of Other Lang; Inter Faculty Organization; MN Ed Assn, NEA, MN Teachers of Eng 1988-; SE MN Rdng Assn Bd Mem 1983-86; MN Rdng Assn Bd Mem 1979-86; Intnl Rdng Assn 1985-88; Certificate of Commendation Governor R Perpich Teaching Basic Skills to Adults 1989; *office:* Winona St Univ Student Support Services Gl 123 Winona MN 55987

MANN, ARTHUR HAROLD, JR., Eng-Soc Stud 7th Grade Teacher; *b:* Madison, WI; *m:* Sharon E. Pierce; *c:* Kathryn Bredesen, Mary Prendergast, James; *ed:* (BS) His, UW Madison 1956; (MS) Ed/His, UW Madison 1961; *cr:* Teahcer J B Young Jr HS 1957-62; West Jr HS 1962-71; Cherokee Mid 1971-; *ai:* Madison Crime Stoppers Chm 1982-84; Past Pre Madison Teachers Inc; Bd of Dir Madison Teachers Inc; *office:* Cherokee Heights Sch 4301 Cherokee Dr Madison WI 53711

MANN, CHERYL SCOTT, 3rd Grade Teacher; *b:* Muskogee, OK; *m:* Harvey; *c:* Kiristie Snow; *ed:* (BA) Elem Ed, 1966, (MA) Elem Ed, 1976 Northeastern Univ; *cr:* 3rd Grade Teacher J J Izard Elem 1967-70; 5th/6th Grade Teacher Kansas Grade Sch 1971-72; 2nd Grade Teacher 1973-; 3rd Grade Teacher 1974- Stigler Grade Sch; *ai:* Owner of Cheryls Tots-Teens & Jr Specialty Shop; OK Ed Assn, NEA 1971-; Stigler Classroom Teachers Assn 1973-; ESA of Stigler (Mem 1974-, Pres 1980, Secy 1978), Sweetheart Mem of Yr 1990; Stigler Assembly of God Church (Asst Organist & Pianists, Childrens Church Asst); *home:* Rt 2 Box 447 Stigler OK 74462

MANN, JEAN PRICE, 4th Grade Teacher; *b:* Waukegan, IL; *m:* Roger; *c:* Tricia; *ed:* (BA) Elem Ed, IA Wesleyan Coll 1967; Addl Stud IL St, N IL Univ, W IL Univ; *cr:* 3rd Grade Teacher Toulon Elem Sch 1967-69; 4th Grade Teacher Ben Funk Elem Sch 1969-70; Title I Rdng Teacher Wethersfield Elem Sch 1970-72; 4th Grade Teacher Wethersfield Elem Sch 1974-; *ai:* IL Cncl Teachers of MA; NCTM; IEA, NEA, WEA; Beta Sigma Phi Secy 1970-; Fellowship from Univ of IL-Cmptr Trng; *office:* Wethersfield Elem Sch 439 Willard St Kewanee IL 61443

MANN, JUDY J., Health & Physical Ed Teacher; *m:* Ronald; *c:* Rodney; *ed:* (BS) Health/Phys Ed, Soc Sci, Concord Coll 1966; *cr:* Teacher Giles HS 1966-; *ai:* Chm Phys Ed Dept; Spon SADD; Teacher Appreciation Awd Presented by Key Club; *office:* Giles H S Drawer G Pearisburg VA 24134

MANN, KARL, Mathematics Teacher; *b:* San Antonio, TX; *m:* Frances T.; *c:* Tony Tolito, Natalie; *ed:* (BS) Math, Univ S MS 1974; Functional Literacy Trng; MS Teachers Assessment Instrument; *cr:* Teacher/Coach D Iberville HS, Columbia Acad, N Gulfport, E Marion; *ai:* Mathcounts, Jr HS Ftbl & Bsktbl Coach; STAR Teacher 1980-81, 1989.

MANN, PERRI ROBERTS, English Teacher; *b:* Gulfport, MS; *m:* Johnny; *c:* Candice C.; *ed:* (BS) Eng, 1977, (MA) Ed, 1982 Univ S MS; MS Teacher Trng Assessment Instrument; *cr:* Eng Teacher Long Beach Jr HS 1977-84, Long Beach Mid Sch 1984-; *ai:* Beta Club & Stu Cncl Spon; Long Beach Mid Sch Intnl Optimist Club Oratorical Contest Coord; Chrldr Spon 1990; MS Assn of Educators 1977-82; AFT 1984-86; NCTE, MS Cncl Teachers of Eng 1983-89; MS Prof Educators 1987-89; St Thomas Cath Church 1972-; Coast Catamaran Club 1988-; Long Beach Yacht Club 1989-; Long Beach PTO 1988-; Long Beach Sch Dist Supt Bd of Ed & Bd Certificates of Merit; Staff Dev Planning Comm 1990; *office:* Long Beach Mid Sch Cleveland Ave Long Beach MS 39560

MANN, ROBERT WAYNE, English Dept Chm/Teacher; *b:* Sanford, NC; *ed:* (AA) Louisburg Coll 1964; (BS) Eng, E Carolina Univ 1966; Univ of NC Wilmington Writing Inst; *cr:* Eng Teacher/Dept Chm Charles B Aycock HS 1966-; *ai:* Yrbk Adv; Quiz Bowl Adv; NC Assn of Educators Pres 1980-81; NC Assn of Educators Bd of Ed 1979, Teacher of Yr 1979; NC Bus Comm for Ed 1988, Governors Awd Excl 1988; *office:* Charles B Aycock HS PO Box 159 Pikeville NC 27863

MANN, ROGER, Mathematics/Computer Teacher; *b:* Washington, IA; *m:* Jean; *c:* Tricia; *ed:* (BS) Math, IA Wesleyan Coll 1965; (MS) Math, IL St Univ 1970; Summer Inst Cmptrs, Univ of IL & Sci, Math Teachers, Fermilab; *cr:* Math Teacher Galva HS 1965-69; Grad Asst IL St Univ 1969-70; Math/Cmptr Teacher Wethersfield HS 1970-; *ai:* Class Spon; Blackhawk Cmptr Group (VP, Treas) 1987-; ICTM; NEA, IEA Regional Cncl Rep 1983-; Univ of IL Summer Inst Cmptrs Teacher Asst; IL Math & Sci Acad Awd of Excl.

MANN, VIRGIL CHARLES, Advanced Placement Eng Teacher; *ed:* (BA) Eng Ed, Bluffton Coll 1971; (MS) Educl Admin, Univ of Dayton 1982; *cr:* Eng Teacher 1971-85, Asst Prin 1985-86, Advanced Placement Eng Teacher 1986- Lima Sr HS; *ai:* Academic Quiz Team Coach; Bluffton Coll Teacher Advisory Bd (VP 1988) 1984-; Nom Teacher of Yr 1988-; *office:* Lima Sr HS 600 S Pierce Lima OH 45804

MANN, WILLIAM EDWARD, French Teacher; *b:* Washington, DC; *m:* Susan; *c:* Tuesdee Long, Lisa, Hannah, Kristen; *ed:* (MA) Fr Lang/Lit, WV Univ 1974; ABD Curr/Instruction, WV Univ; *cr:* Fr Teacher Webster Cty HS 1984-; *ai:* Fr Club Spon; Bi-Annual Study Tour Paris France Travel Coord; Summersville 7th Day Adv Church Sch Bd Chm 1988-; Fulbright Travel Grant France 1968; Teaching Assistantship Appointment by Fr Ministere De L'Ed 1968; *home:* Hwy 41 Box 1627 Summersville WV 26651

MANNEL, KAREN RUTH, Second Grade Teacher; *b:* Broken Bow, NE; *ed:* (BA) Human Dev/Elem Ed, Univ of NE Lincoln 1979; Endorsement Gifted Ed, Kearney St Coll 1986; *cr:* Remedial Rdng Teacher 1980, 2nd Grade Teacher 1979- Geneva Public Schls; *ai:* Budget, Sci, Lang Art Comm; Phi Upsilon Omicron 1979-, Honorary 1979; Geneva Ed Assn (Secy 1983-85, Treas 1983-85, Public Relations Co-Chairperson) 1979-; Delta Kappa Gamma 1988-; NE Assn for Gifted 1986-; NE St Ed Assn 1978-; NEA 1979-; York Extension Club (News Reporter 1989-, Secy 1987-88, Historian 1986-87); York Hospital Auxiliary 1988-; *office:* Geneva Public Schls 1410 L Geneva NE 68361

MANNING, DEBORAH LYNN, English Teacher; *b:* Chicago, IL; *m:* Donald R.; *c:* Chelsea M., Laura, William; *ed:* (BA) Ed Eng/Speech, TX Tech Univ 1977; Hum; *cr:* 7th Grade Lang Art Teacher Alderson Jr HS 1977-79; 8th Grade Reg/Honors Newman Smith 1979-81; Eng Teacher S Garland HS 1981-84, L V Berkner HS 1984-; *ai:* Diving Coach Swim Team; Berner HS; Academic Coach; Soph Eng Coord; Peer Helper Spon; *office:* L V Berkner 1600 E Spring Valley Richardson TX 75081

MANNING, DOROTHY JOHNSON, Mathematics Teacher/Dept Chair; *b:* Jackson, MS; *c:* Tommy, Tammy; *ed:* (BS) Elem Ed, Jackson St 1973; Guidance & Counseling; Writing Across the Curr Consultant; Using Manipulatives in Classroom & Writing Project Trainee; Jackson St & MS St Presenter; *cr:* Teacher Nichols Mid Sch 1973-77, Alternative Elem 1977-83, Bailey Magnet Sch 1983-, Jackson Public Sch 1985-; *ai:* Drill Team & NHS Spon; Grade Level & Courtesy Comm Chairperson; Honors & Parent-Cmmty Involvement Comm; MCTM 1985-; Blacks Chapel Church (Clerk 1987-, Choir Pres 1989-); Lucy C Holliday OES Secy 1988-; Jackson Public Sch Good Apple, Silver Apple, Gold Apple Awd 1987; Ed Fnd Trust Grant Winner; 7th Grade Math Curr Reviser 1987; *office:* Bailey Magnet Sch 1900 N State St Jackson MS 39202

MANNING, NANCY JOAN (RIZZI), Math Department Chair/Teacher; *b:* Troy, NY; *m:* Randy Joseph; *c:* Alexandria, Zachary; *ed:* (BS) Math Ed, SUNY Oneonta 1979; Working Towards MS Advanced Classroom Teaching Math, SUNY Albany 1990; *cr:* Math Teacher 1979-, Math Chairperson 1985- Acad of the Holy Names; *ai:* Class Adv; Math Club Moderator; Curr Comm; NCTM 1986-; NY St Math Teachers Assn 1988-; Empire St Challenger Fellowship; *home:* 115 South St Ballston Spa NY 12020

MANNING, PAULETTE CUNNINGHAM, Mathematics Teacher; *b:* Hondo, TX; *m:* Gary Lon; *c:* Troy L., Tami L.; *ed:* (BA) Ed, Univ of Mary Hardin-Baylor 1971; (MED) Ed/Cmptr, Wayland Baptist Univ 1986; *cr:* Math Teacher La Vega HS 1972-75, Travis Mid Sch 1976-77, Temple HS 1978-82, Plainview HS 1982-; *ai:* Supts Cabinet; Gifted & Talented Comm; NCTM, TX Assn for Gifted & Talented; PTA 1986-88; TX St Teacher Assn; Delta Kappa Gamma Pres 1990; 1st Baptist Church (Sunday Sch Teacher, Secy, Finance Comm Mem); Assn of Couples for Marriage Enrichment; Plainview Chamber of Commerce Teacher of Week; *office:* Plainview HS 1501 Quincy Plainview TX 79072

MANNING, THOMAS RAY, Physical Education Teacher; *b:* Santa Fe, NM; *m:* Rose Ellen Marquez; *c:* Lisa, David, Mark; *ed:* (BA) Phys Ed, NM St Univ 1973; (MA) Phys Ed, NM Highlands Univ 1982; Admin Certificate NM Highlands Univ 1986; *cr:* Phys Ed Instr Conlee Elem 1973-79; Phys Ed Instr/Head Coach De Vargas Jr HS 1979-85; Phys Ed Instr/Coach Santa Fe HS 1985-87; Phys Ed Instr/Head Coach De Vargas Jr HS 1987-; *ai:* Head Ftbl Coach De Vargas Jr Hs; Head Golf Coach Santa Fe HS; Las Cruces Classroom Teachers Assn 1973-; Las Cruces Boys Club Bd Mem 1973-79; Santa Fe City Parks Recreation Commission 1983-85; Teacher of Yr De Vargas Jr HS 1985; *home:* 2083 Placita De Vida St Santa Fe NM 87505

MANNION, ANGELA, Jr HS Religion/Family Minister; *b:* Galway, Ireland; *ed:* (BA) Eng, Mc Master Univ Hamilton Ontario Canada 1972; (MRE) Religious Ed, Univ of San Francisco 1975; Trained Teacher in Scotland 1949-52; Advanced Catechist Minister 1990; *cr:* Primary Teacher St Catherine Labouve Sch 1952-58; Prin St Josephs Sch Hamilton 1958-64; Asst Novice Dir Cluny Novitiate 1964-72; Jr HS Teacher 1972-88, Jr HS Religion Teacher/Family Minister 1988- Sts Peter & Paul Sch; *ai:* Family Minister; Bd of Dirs of Poverty Prgm Wilmington CA; Sts Peter & Paul Poverty Prgm (Founder, Dir) 1982-83; Religious Sister; *home:* 943 Lagoon Ave Wilmington CA 90744

MANNS, VIRGINIA KELLER, Third Grade Teacher; *b:* Connellsville, PA; *m:* Thomas J.; *c:* Erin L.; Brittany L.; *ed:* (BS) Elem Ed, Slippery Rock Univ 1971; *cr:* 3rd Grade Teacher Dawson Vanderbilt Elem 1971-76, Bullskin Elem 1976-; *ai:* CAEA, PSEA, NEA; Trinity United Meth Church Admin Bd Mem; Fayette Striders Running Club.

MANOLI, CHERYL ELLEN, Mathematics Teacher; *b:* Framingham, MA; *ed:* (BS) Math, 1968, (MED) Math Ed, 1972, (MA) Math, 1976, (CAES) Educl Research, 1987 Boston Coll; *cr:* Math Teacher North Quincy HS 1968-; Cmptr Teacher Quincy Jr Coll Summer Inst for Gifted & Academically Talented Stu 1982-; *ai:* Calculus Team Coach; NCTM 1984-; Pi Lambda Theta 1982-; MA Teachers Assn, NEA 1970-; Natl Sci Fnd Grant 1972-75; *office:* North Quincy HS 316 Hanlock St North Quincy MA 02171

MANS, ELLEN MARIE GRADY, Second Grade Teacher; *b:* Waukon, IA; *m:* John Carroll Mans; *c:* Caitlin; *ed:* (BA) His, Mt Mercy Coll 1971; (MA) Rdng/Lang Art, Univ of N IA 1989; Learning Disabilities, IA St; *cr:* 2nd Grade Teacher Riceville Cmmty Schls 1971-; *ai:* Elem Building Secy; Lector, Extraordinary Minister, Church Singing Group Mem; St Public Relations Comm Mem; IA Rdng Assn 1984-; NEA 1971-; NEIEU Uniserve Public Relations Chairperson 1982-85; Watanye (Secy, VP) 1985-.

MANSBACH, ARTHUR CRAIG, Teacher of Learning Disabled; *b:* Pittsburgh, PA; *ed:* (BSED) Learning Disabilities-Behavior Disorders/Elem Ed, Kent St Univ 1947; *cr:* Teacher of Learning Disabilities W Huskingum Mid Sch 1975-78, N Ridgeville Jr HS 1978-; *ai:* Girls Jr HS Vlybl Head Coach; WY

Field Studs Instr & Founder; Out of Doors Sch Prgm Instr; Cleveland Music Natl His Vol 1985-90; Midwest Biosphere Coalition/Speaker 1990; Founder WY Field Studs Prgm; Nordson Fnd Grant Develop Sci Materials Under-Achievers; Co-Founder Sch Dist Out of Door Sch Prgm; Developed Prgm Reduce Suspension Rate Jr HS Stus; *home:* 2657 Canterbury Cleveland OH 44118

MANSFIELD, AGNES LOUISE, Business Teacher; *b:* Clifton Forge, VA; *ed:* (BS) Bus Ed, Hampton Univ 1958; FL A&M Univ, VA St Univ, Univ of VA, Radford Univ; *cr:* Bus Teacher Jefferson HS 1958-62; Bus Eng Teacher Carver Heights HS 1962-68, Clifton Forge HS 1968-83, Alleghany HS 1983-; *ai:* Natl Beta Club & Frosh Class Spon; Alleghany Highlands Ed Assn, VA Ed Assn, NEA, VA Bus Ed Assn 1990; Clifton Forge Redevelopment & Housing Authority, Alleghany Regional Hospital Bd of Dirs, Main Street Baptist Church Choir Dir, Clifton Forge Architectural Review Bd; Outstanding Scndry Educators of America 1973; NAACP Youth Service Awd 1988; *home:* 920 Church St Clifton Forge VA 24422

MANSFIELD, GAIL WINGFIELD, Art & English Teacher; *b:* Denver, CO; *m:* Monte Eugene; *ed:* (BA) Comm/Speech, Univ of N CO 1969; Grad Stud Univ of N CO; *cr:* Lang Art Teacher Buchanan Jr HS 1970-73; Art/Rdng/Eng Teacher Idalia Sch 1976-; *ai:* 7th/8th Grade Class Spon; Speech Coach; Dist Inservice & Insurance Comm; Idalia Study Skills Curr Comm; Wray Art Guild (Stu Division Chm 1983-87, Mem 1979-); Accountability Comm Mem RJ-2 Dist; Appointed In-Charge When Idalias Admin is Absent; NE CO BOCES & EC BOCES Presenter; YW-KC League Art Teacher of Yr 1989; *home:* 12945 Cty Rd HH Idalia CO 80735

MANSFIELD, JOANNE HUTCHISON, Language Arts Teacher; *b:* Reading, PA; *c:* Orion; *ed:* (BA) Eng, York Coll 1973; *cr:* Area Supvr of Womens Wear Jeffersons 1974-77; Asst Buyer Lerner Shops 1977-78; Collections Account Rep Eastern Airlines 1978-86; Lang Art Teacher Brownsville Mid Sch 1986-; *ai:* Drama Club, Alpha Omega Writing Club Spon; Team Leader; Excl Fnd Grant 1986-87, 1987-88; *office:* Brownsville Mid Sch 4899 NW 24th Ave Miami FL 33142

MANSFIELD, LUTHER ALBERT, JR., Junior High Teacher; *b:* Peoria, IL; *ed:* (BA) Industrial Arts, Western IL Univ 1962; Addl Studies IL ST Univ; Bradley Univ; *cr:* 7th & 8th Grade Teacher West Jersey Sch 1962-64; Jr High Teacher Edelstein Grade Sch 1964-75; Jr High Teacher Princeville Grade Sch 1975-; *ai:* Boy's Bsktbl Coach; Girl's Bsktbl Coach; Athletic Dir; IL ED Assn 1962-; NEA 1962-; Princeville Unit ED Assn 1962-; Pres 1980-82; IL Bsktbl Coaches Assn 1976-; *office:* Princeville Grade Sch 602 N Town Ave Princeville IL 61559

MANSKE, TAD PETER, Social Studies Teacher; *b:* Anniston, AL; *m:* Ruth Ann Huffcut; *c:* James, Julie Hart; *ed:* (BS) His, Bowling Green St Univ 1964; Grad Work Bowling Green St Univ; *cr:* Teacher Alfred Almond Cntrl Sch 1971-; *ai:* 7th Grade Adv; NY St Cncl for Soc Stud; Amer Legion Post #397; F & AM Lodge #558.

MANSOR, SUSAN MARIE, Social Studies Teacher; *b:* Methuen, MA; *ed:* (BS) Soc Sci/Ed, Fitchburg St 1978; (MS) Human Services/Ed, New England Coll 1990; *cr:* Teacher Hillsboro-Deering HS 1985-; *ai:* Sr Class, Stu Cncl, Winter Carnival, NH His Day Adv; Bsktbl & Sftbl Head Coach; Staff Dev Comm; NH Coaches Assn, NH Soc Stud Assn, NH Advs Assn, NH Prins Assn; Big Sisters.

MANSOUR, THOMAS JOHN, History/Sociology Teacher; *b:* Atlanta, GA; *ed:* (BA) His, 1979, (MA) His, 1981 GA St Univ; (EDS) Soc Sci Ed, Univ of GA 1984; *cr:* Teacher/Coach SW DeKalb HS 1979-86, Redan HS 1987-; *ai:* Girls Var Bsktbl Coach; Key Club, Red Cross Blood Drive Spon; *office:* Redan HS 5247 Redan Rd Stone Mountain GA 30088

MANTHE, MATTHEW DAN, Fifth & Sixth Grade Teacher; *b:* Mankato, MN; *m:* Ruth Koeller; *ed:* (BSE) Ed, Dr Martin Luther Coll 1980; Ed, Univ of WI Whitewater 1990; *cr:* Instr Martin Luther Preparatory Sch 1980-82; Teacher St Peters Luth Sch 1982-; *ai:* 5th-8th Grade Girls & 4th-6th Grade Boys Bsktbl Coach; *office:* St Peters Luth Sch PO Box 117 Hwy 18 Helenville WI 53137

MANTHO, HENRY ALLEN, Social Studies Dept Chair; *b:* Canton, OH; *m:* Karen Lynn Dick; *c:* Melissa A., Rebecca L., Lauren E.; *ed:* (BA) Soc Stud, Univ of Akron 1974; (MED) Admin/Supervision, 1986, (EDS) Admin/Supervision, 1990 GA Southern Univ; *cr:* Teacher/Coach Calvary Baptist Day Sch 1979-83, Memorial Day Sch 1983-84; Dept Chm/Coach Calvary Baptist Day Sch 1984-; *ai:* Var Girls Sftbl Coach; Admin Asst to Headmaster; Savannah Parochial Athletic League Exec Secy 1989; Southeastern Assn Ind Schls Sftbl Coach of Yr 1980, 1982.

MANTOOTH, SANDRA RAE, Head of English and Spanish; *b:* Antlers, OK; *ed:* (BA) Span/Eng, 1966, (ME) Eng/Span, 1985 East Cntrl Univ; Univ of OK/Univ of TX at Arlington; *cr:* HS Teacher Talihina HS 1966-68, Ninnekah HS 1968-70, Tupelo HS 1970-; *ai:* St Class Spon; Span Club Spon; Academic Bowl Coach; Tupelo Arts Comm; Sch Photographer; Coal Cty St Teacher of Yr Awd 1973; Coal Cty Ed Assn Pres 1985-86, Pres Plaque 1986; OK Ed Assn Delegate 1987-88; Prof Dev Chairperson Network East Cntrl Univ 1980-85; Ada Evening News Terrific Teacher Awd 1990; Amer Quarter Horse Mem OK St QH Racing Comm; OK Heritage Assn; Stuart OK His Awd Excl in Teaching 1990; Tupelo Teacher of Yr 1983; East Cntrl Univ Appointed Bd of Dir of Teach Ed Cncl; *home:* Rt 5 Box 321 Ada OK 74820

MANUEL, HARRIETTE E., Earth Science Teacher; *b:* Chicago, IL; *c:* Perri L. Manuel Inmen; *ed:* (BS) General Sci/Ed, Roosevelt Univ 1962; (MS) Bio, Chicago St Univ 1969; Grad Stud Geology & Earth Sci; Certified Financial Planning, Roosevelt Univ; *cr:* Sci Teacher Hirsch HS 1962-66; Earth Sci Teacher Kenwood Acad 1967-75; Asst Prin 1975-80, Earth Sci Teacher 1980- Whitney M Young Magnet HS; Pres Realty Tech Assn Inc 1985-; *ai:* Sci Fair Coord; Judge & Research Teaching Methods; Fond Placement & Trng Prgm Univ Chicago; Curr Writing Comm Earth Sci Curr; IL Chapter Master Appraisers Pres; IL Chapter NAMA Sec; Natl Presidents Cncl NAMA Bd of Dir; Chicago Bd of Realtors Mem Membership Comm; NSTA, AFT, ISTA; Museum of Natl His Life Mem; Museum of Sci & Industry Art Inst of Chicago; Friends of Parks Auxiliary of Chicago Urban League 5 Yr Pin; Lake MI Fed Open Lands Project; IESTA Secy; Golden Apple Awd; Conducted Research Under Dr Qutub Northeastern Il Univ; Argonne Laboratories Talented Stus Summer Prgm Coord; *office:* Whitney M Young Magnet HS 211 S Laflin Chicago IL 60607

MANUEL, LEWIS ALFRED, Sixth Grade Math Teacher; *b:* Durban, South Africa; *m:* Sheila Moodley; *c:* Devan, Romola; *ed:* (BA) Eng/His, Univ Natal SA 1965; (MA) Elem Ed, East TX St Univ 1983; Admin ETSU; Univ of Alberta 1973-74; *cr:* Teacher Merebank HS 1964-69, St Andrews High Prairie RC Sch 1970-73, Parkdale Elem 1975-81, Adelle Turner 1981-86, Sequoyah 1986-89, Adelle Turner 1989-; *ai:* Math Coach; Phi Delta Kappa Mem 1982-84; Amer Heart Fnd Volunteer 1989-; Crime Watch Block Captain 1983-88; *office:* Adelle Turner Elem Sch 5505 S Polk St Dallas TX 75232

MANUEL, ROSE MILLER, 6th Soc Stud/7th Lib Arts; *b:* Dry Creek, LA; *m:* Daniel; *c:* Michael Gallien, Richard Gallien, Keith, Vicki G. Shirley, Linda Greene, Kent; *ed:* (BA) Elem Ed, 1973; (MA) Elem Ed, 1977 Mc Neese St Univ; *cr:* Teacher 1973-; Rdng Coord 1977-81 East Beauregard; *ai:* Chrldr Spon 1973-78; Jr HS News Spon 1975; Beauregard Assn of Educators 1973; LA Assn of Educators 1973-86; Assn of Prof Educators of LA 1986; LA Rdng Cncl 1976-88; Beauregard Rdng Cncl (Bd Mem 1976-77, Mem 1976-88); Comm Write Parish Sci Curr 1973-75; Textbook Selection Comms 1976; 1978; 1982; Parish Walk-Thru Comm for Right to Read 1977-78;Spur 1980-82; *office:* East Beauregard H S Star Rt 2 Box 61 De Ridder LA 70634

MANWARING, DOLORES KUNZ, Sixth Grade Teacher; *b:* Montpelier, ID; *m:* Fred W.; *c:* Genae M. Turpin, Whitney K., Lorene M. Clark, Ferron W., Janis; *ed:* Cert Elem Ed, Univ of ID 1946; (BS) Elem Ed, UT St Univ 1950; Adult Ed/Individual Study, Brigham Young Univ 1964-65, 1967, 1981-83; Individual Study, ID St Univ 1981-82; *cr:* 3rd Grade Teacher Soda Springs Elem 1946-48; 4th Grade Teacher Gunnison Elem 1950-51; 3rd Grade Teacher Groveland Elem 1964-71; 6th Grade Teacher Blackfoot Mid Sch 1980-; *ai:* Philosophy & Goals Comm, 6th Grade Spelling Bee Chairperson; Coordinating Cncl Comm Mem; Dist Discipline & Appeals Panel; Eng Dept Coord; Ed Honor Society, Future Teachers Mem 1944-46; IEA, NEA, BEA Mem 1948-; PTA Cncl (VP 1981-83, Building Rep 1980-82); Cmmty Cancer Drive Chairperson, Lang Art Curr Guide 1983-84; Teacher of Yr Awd 1987; Elks Teacher of Month 1990; *office:* Mountain View Mid Sch Mitchell Ln Blackfoot ID 83221

MANZER, BETH M., Business Educator; *b:* Norfolk, NE; *m:* Steven Paul; *c:* Jennifer, Leah, Tracy; *ed:* (MS) Bus Ed, 1981, (BA) Bus Ed, 1976 Wayne St Coll; *cr:* Bus Educator Osmond Cmmty Schls 1976-; *ai:* FBLA Adv; Sr Class Spon; Bus Competition Day Adv; Delta Kappa Gamma Nom 1982-; NSEA/NEA Secy 1977 1976-; Bus Ed Assn 1988-89; NETA 1988-; Legion Auxiliary 1976-; Hospital Auxiliary 1976-; Centennial Youth Organizer 1989-; UNL Comm of Bus Educators to Promote Bus Ed in NE; Handbook for All Teachers; Grieving Stu Comm in Sch; *office:* Osmond Community Schl P O Box 458 Osmond NE 68765

MANZO, NADELE STEWART, Seventh Grade Team Leader; *b:* Hollywood, CA; *m:* Rudolph O.; *c:* Marji Baumann, Martha Furtado, Michael; *ed:* (BS) Elem Ed, Lewis & Clark Coll 1962; (MA) Person Centered Ed, USIU 1990; *cr:* 4th-6th Grade Teacher Ladera Palma Sch 1962-66; 3rd-6th Grade Teacher Sierra Vista Sch 1972-83; 6th-8th Grade Washington Mid Sch 1983-; *ai:* CA Teachers Assn 1962-; Lattabra Teachers Assn Pres 1986-87; NEA; PTA Honorary Service Awd 1983; 1st Chrstn Church Woman of Yr 1982; *office:* Washington Mid Sch 716 E La Habra Blvd La Habra CA 90631

MAPLE, BEVERLY ANN, 7th Grade History Teacher; *b:* Whittenburg, TX; *ed:* (BA) Ed/His, Sacramento St Univ 1959; *cr:* K-8th Grade Teacher Penryn Elem 1955-67; Teacher Oak Avenue/Sunrise Elem 1967-77, Twin Lakes Elem 1977-83, Barrett Mid Sch 1984-; *ai:* CA Assessment Prgm Rdng Advisory Comm Mem 1979-88; CBEST Rdng Advisory Comm Mem 1980-84; CA Congress of Parents & Teachers Incorporated Lifetime Service Awds Penryn Elem Sch 1967 & Sunrise Elem 1977; *office:* Barrett Mid Sch 4243 Barrett Rd Carmichael CA 95608

MAPP, M. LYNN, Fourth Grade Teacher; *b:* San Diego, CA; *m:* Mitchell Jerome; *c:* Adam, Russell, Andrew; *ed:* (AA) Sociology, Long Beach City Coll 1973; (BA) Sociology, ID St Univ 1976; Working Towards Masters; *cr:* 1st Grade Teacher 1978-80, 1st-4th Grade Teacher 1981- Eagle Elem; *ai:* Horizons Rdng Cncl 1987-; Eagle Elem Teacher of Yr 1983-84.

MAR, NANCY, High School Science Teacher; *b:* Fort Worth, TX; *ed:* (BS) Phys Ed, Univ of TX 1979; (MS) Bio, TX Womans Univ 1989; *cr:* Sci/Phys Ed Teacher Rockdale HS 1981-82; Sci Teacher Midlothian HS 1982-; *ai:* Sr Class Spon; Chrldr Spon; TX St Teachers Assn 1980-; Pres 1986-87; VP 1984-86 Midlothian Teachers Assn; TX Tennis Coaches Assn 1981-87; Aerospace Teachers Assn 1987-; Civil Air Patrol 1987-.

MARABLE, MARY A. MC CALL-BLACK, Teacher; *b:* Fairfield, AL; *m:* Edward S Jr.; *ed:* (BS) Elem Ed, Miles Coll 1964; *cr:* Teacher Whitman Street Sch 1964-65, Fultondale Elem Sch 1965-; *ai:* AFT; AL Jazz Hall of Fame Vocalist Music Awd; *home:* 301 60th St Fairfield AL 35064

MARADEN, DAVID E., Reading Teacher; *b:* Pittsburgh, PA; *m:* Joann Cannon; *c:* Kara, Michael; *ed:* (BS) Eng, 1970, (MED) Rdng Specialist, 1975 Edinboro Univ; Grad Stud; *cr:* Eng Teacher Acad HS 1971-73, Wilson Jr HS 1974-76; Eng/Rdng Teacher New Direction Center 1977-81; Rdng Teacher Wilson Mid Sch 1981-; *ai:* Stu Cncl Adv; Academic Awds Banquet; 8th Grade Trip; PTSA Comm; NEA, PSEA, EEA, Natl Rdng Cncl, Northwest Teacher of Eng 1990; Cub Scouts Cubmaster 1988-; Teacher of Yr 1987; *office:* Wilson Mid Sch 718 E 28th St Erie PA 16504

MARAGH, MAE RAMEY, 5th Grade Teacher; *b:* Grundy, VA; *m:* Reneval; *c:* Rene; *ed:* (BA) Elem Ed, Pikeville Coll 1971; (MS) Urban Teacher Ed, Governors St Univ 1976; Ed; *cr:* Elem Ed Teacher Chicago Bd of Ed 1971-; *home:* 1841 W Belle Plaine Chicago IL 60613

MARANO, CHRISTOPHER JOHN, Biology Teacher; *b:* Hoboken, NJ; *m:* Maria Buscaglia; *c:* Cristian D.; *ed:* (BS) Pre-Med/Eastern Religion, Columbia Univ 1981; (MA) Sci Ed, Columbia Teachers Coll 1986; *cr:* Religion/Math/Cmptrs Teacher St Joseph of Palisades HS 1984-86; Bio Teacher Piscataway HS 1987-; *ai:* Stu Concerned About Our Environment & Destruction Adv; HS Environmental Club; Rutgers Meditation Club Instr; Chan Meditation Center Bd of Trustees Main Ed 1986-; Magazine & Book Ed; *office:* Piscataway HS Behmer Rd Piscataway NJ 08854

MARASCO, FLOYD C., Mathematics/Computer Sci Instr; *b:* Washington, PA; *m:* Sonya Jean Sinclair; *c:* Debra, Angela; *ed:* (BSED) Scndry Math, 1974, (MED) Scndry Math, 1977 California Univ of PA; *cr:* Math Instr Monessen HS 1975-76;Cmptr Instr Mc Guffey HS 1976-; *ai:* Chm HS Faculty Specific Curr, Facilities & Maintenance Comm; Grading, Finals, Prerequisite Comm Mem; Mc Guffeys Math Team Entry Spon; PA Sr Math League; PA St Ed Assn, NEA 1975-; Mc Guffey Ed Assn 1976-; W PA Math League 1989-; Friendship Cmmty Church (Pres, Bd of Dir) 1975-80; Windy Gap United Presbyn Church Elder 1987-; Chrstn Patriots (VP, Choral Group) 1980-; Published Masters Project; *office:* Mc Guffey HS RD 1 Box 219 Claysville PA 15323

MARBLE, ANNE, 2nd Grade Teacher; *b:* Brooklyn, NY; *ed:* (BFA) Fine Arts, Coll of William & Mary 1954; William Paterson Coll/Seattle Univ; *cr:* 2nd Grade Teacher Tisdale Sch 1958-69; Dater Sch 1969-; *ai:* Ramsey Teachers Assn Secy 1972-74; Bergen Cty Ed Assn; NJ Ed Assn; NEA; *office:* John Y Dater Sch School St Ramsey NJ 07446

MARBLE, JUDY PERSCHBACHER, Third Grade Teacher; *b:* Murphysboro, IL; *m:* Robert F.; *c:* Wiley C. Thompson, Shannon N. Thompson; *ed:* (BS) Elem Ed, NM St Univ 1977; Grad Work NM St Univ, Eastern NM Univ 1978-86; *cr:* 2nd Grade Teacher Jornada Elem Sch 1977-84, Hillrise Elem Sch 1984-86; 3rd Grade Teacher Highland Elem Sch 1986-; *ai:* Textbook Evaluation Comm Mem Las Cruces Public Schls 1988; Prin Evaluation Comm Highland Elem Sch Chairperson 1989-; Phi Delta Kappa 1979-; Phi Kappa Phi; Las Cruces Classroom Teachers; Letter of Appreciation Volunteer Services; Las Cruces Public Schls Teacher Center Auxiliary Staff 1988; *office:* Highland Elem Sch 5221 N Main Las Cruces NM 88005

MARCEAUX, RAYMOND JOSEPH, Chemistry Teacher; *b:* Abbeville, LA; *m:* Marcie Patricia Plauche; *c:* Michelle Le Doux, Stephanie Le Doux; *ed:* (BS) Health/Phys Ed/Bio, Univ of SW LA 1971; (MED) Admin/Supervision, Mc Neese St Univ 1976; Aides, Drug, Chemical Safety Ed; *cr:* Teacher New Iberia Sr HS 1987-; Operations Manager A & D Enterprise 1980-87; Teacher Abbeville HS 1971-80; Stu Asst Univ of SW LA 1969-70; *ai:* Class Spon; Parish Chemical Safety & Drug Inservice Coord; EZffective Sch & Parish Sci Fair; Chem Curr Chm; NSTA 1989-; LA Sci Teacher 1989-; Summer Youth Prgm 1987-; Drug Rehabilitation Coord 1989-.

MARCEAX, PEGGY THERESA, English Teacher; *b:* Abbeville, LA; *ed:* (BS) Health/Phys Ed, Lamar Univ 1970; (MA) Eng/British Lit, Univ of Houston CLear Lake 1987; Houston Area Writers Project Univ of Houston CLear Lake 1986; Advanced Placement Cert Hockaday 1990; *cr:* Teacher/Coach Huffman Ind Sch Dist 1970-72; Teaching Fellow Univ of Houston 1972-73; Teacher/Coach St Agnes Acad 1973-76, Alvin HS 1976-87; Teacher Smithson Valley HS 1987-; *ai:* UIL Literary Criticism & Ready Writing; NCTE, TJCTE, NEA, TSTA; TX Joint Cncl Teachers of Eng Bay Area Chapter Pres 1986-87; *office:* Smithson Valley HS 4041 Hwy 46 W Spring Branch TX 78070

MARCEK, MARIANNE GALITZ, Teacher of Gifted Students; *b:* Clinton, IA; *m:* Kent Steven; *ed:* (BA) Elem Ed, Univ N CO 1972; (MS) Supervision/Curr, W IL Univ 1980; *cr:* 4th Grade Teacher Pleasant Valley Schls 1972-78; Project TEACH Instr Performance Learning Systems 1974-78; Consultant Mobile

In-Service Trng Lab 1976-80; Teacher of Talented & Gifted Bettendorf Sch Dist 1978-; *ai:* Future Problem Solving Coach; Pleasant Valley Ed Assn In-Service Dir 1972-78; NEA 1972-; IA Talented & Gifted Assn 1978-, TAG Distinguished Service Awd 1987; Cornbelt Running Club 1978-; Articles Published 1975; 1st Place Intnl Future Problem Solving Team Coach 1986; World Conference for Gifted Children Presenter 1987; Scott Cty Outstanding Educator 1989; *office:* Bettendorf Mid Sch 2030 Middle Rd Bettendorf IA 52722

MARCELL, PHILLIP H., 6th Grade Elementary Teacher; *b:* Burlington, VT; *m:* Patricia Kasprzak; *c:* Phillip III, Bradley; *ed:* (BS) Elem Ed/His, Mc Kendree Coll 1970; Ed Admin, Castleton St Coll; *cr:* 4th Grade Teacher 1970, 5th Grade Teacher 1970-71, 6th Grade Teacher 1971-72, Adult Ed Teacher 1972-73 E St Louis IL; 6th Grade Teacher Rutland Public Schls 1973-; *ai:* Coached Castleton St Coll Sftbl 1980-82 & 5th/6th Grade Bsktbl; Lions Tail Twister 1973-75; Photography Grant; Canadian Stud Grant; *home:* PO Box 1541 Main St Castleton VT 05735

MARCELLA, TERESA ANN CARDONE, Business Ed Dept Chairperson; *b:* Nanticoke, PA; *m:* John R.; *c:* Mary F. Marcella Escudero, John A., Daniel, David; *ed:* (BA) Bus Ed, Marywood Coll 1961; (MED) Bus Ed, Trenton St Coll 1973; Grad Stud Several Colls; *cr:* Teacher Willingboro HS 1961-62, Bensalem HS 1968-; Bus Ed Dept Chairperson Bensalem HS 1976-; *ai:* Stu Volunteer Adv; FBLA Co-Adv; Bensalem Township Ed Assn, PA St Ed Assn, NEA, Bucks Cty Bus Ed Assn 1968-; Article Published 1975; *office:* Bensalem HS 4319 Hulmeville Rd Bensalem PA 19020

MARCH, RICHARD PAUL, II, English & History Teacher; *b:* York, PA; *m:* Phyllis M.; *c:* Richard III, Matthew; *ed:* (BS) Soc Stud, His, Shippensburg Univ 1971; (MLA) Eng, Western MD Coll 1975; *cr:* Eng/His Teacher Dover Area Sch Dist 1972-; *ai:* Mem Exec Bd of Dir Dover Area Aquatics Club; PA St Ed Assn 1972-; NEA 1972-; NCSS 1989-; *office:* Dover Area Sch Dist School Ln Dover PA 17315

MARCHELLETTA, JANET LYNNE (KOVACH), Third Grade Teacher; *b:* Uniontown, PA; *m:* Ronald D.; *c:* Michelle, Michael; *ed:* (BS) Elem Ed, Penn St Univ 1973; (MS) Curr/Instruction, WV Univ 1975; Real Estate Licensing Classes; *cr:* 3rd Grade Teacher German Cntrl Elem 1973-; *ai:* PSEA 1973-; Team Leader 3rd Grade Teachers; Responsible for Arts Grant; *home:* 323 Skyline Dr Belle Vernon PA 15012

MARCHESSEAULT, MARIAN SAMMATARO, Kindergarten Teacher; *b:* Westerly, RI; *w:* Peter (dec); *c:* Michael, Stephen; *ed:* (BS) Child Dev, Univ of RI 1969; Early Chldhd Ed, E CT St Coll 1976; *cr:* Kndgtn Teacher Plainfield Bd of Ed 1969-; *ai:* Contributing Ed Sch Newspaper; Plainfield Ed Assn, CT Ed Assn, NEA 1969-; PTO 1969-; *home:* 38 Stearns St Danielson CT 06239

MARCHMAN, JUDITH B., AP English Teacher; *b:* Macon, GA; *m:* Wilton A.; *c:* Drew, Megan; *ed:* (BA) Eng, Mercer Univ 1964; (MED) Eng Ed, W GA Coll 1970; (EDS) Eng Ed, GA St Univ 1976; *cr:* Eng Teacher Fulton HS 1964-67, Riverdale Jr HS 1969-73, N Clayton HS 1974-83; AP Eng Teacher Jonesboro HS 1984-; *ai:* Spon Zephyr Lit Magazine; PAGE 1978-; GA Cncl Teachers of Eng 1970-; NCTE 1980-; Alpha Delta Kappa Secy 1978-; MADD Mem 1987-; STAR Teacher; Outstanding Educator 1984; GCTE & NCTE Publications; *office:* Jonesboro HS 7728 Mount Zion Blvd Jonesboro GA 30236

MARCIL, JOY DEMARSE, English Teacher; *b:* Malone, NY; *m:* Joseph L. Jr.; *c:* Jaclyne, Jorja; *ed:* (BA) Eng/Ed, 1976, (MS) Ed, 1979 SUNY Plattsburgh; *cr:* Eng Teacher Plattsburgh HS 1977-; Adjunct Faculty SUNY Plattsburgh 1981-; *ai:* Future Educators Club Adv; Faculty Comm; NHS ; NCTE; Parish Cncl (Pres 1987, Secy 1985-87); *office:* Plattsburgh HS Rugar at Adirondack Plattsburgh NY 12901

MARCINEK, JULIE ANN, Journalism Advisor; *b:* E Chicago, IN; *ed:* (BA) Journalism, 1984, (MS) Ed, 1990 IN Univ; Numerous Wkshps Gettysburg Coll, Univ of SC, Univ of NC; *cr:* Instr IN Univ; Publications Adv/Journalism Teacher Griffith HS 1984-; *ai:* Newspaper; Yrbk; Chrldrs; IN HS Press Assn (Pres 1989-, Bd Mem 1985-89); *office:* Griffith HS 600 N Wiggs St Griffith IN 46319

MARCINKO, THOMAS JOHN, Science Teacher/Dept Chair; *b:* Philipsburg, PA; *m:* Diane Belko; *c:* Jennifer, Ryan; *ed:* (BSED) Bio/General Sci, Clarion St 1977; Grad Stud PA St Univ; *cr:* Life Sci Teacher/Dept Chm Moshannon Valley Jr/Sr HS 1977-; *ai:* Union Building Rep; Ftbl Coach; *office:* Moshannon Valley Jr/Sr HS Rd 1 Box 314 Houtzdale PA 16651

MARCOALDI, JOSEPH JOHN, Junior High School Teacher; *b:* Canton, OH; *m:* Patricia Mc Carty; *c:* Julie, Joey; *ed:* (BA) Ed, Walsh Coll 1968; Seminars, Wkshps, Courses; *cr:* 5th Grade Teacher Waynesburg Elem 1968-70; 7th-8th Grade Teacher Sandy Valley Jr-Sr HS 1970-; *ai:* St Johns Villa Christmas Project Coord; Lori Sickafoose Awd Dir; NEA, OEA; SVEA Pres 1986-87; St Anthonys Church Parish Cncl 1986-89; Canton Sftbl Assn Mem 1970-80; Martha Holden Jennings Awd; Nom Greater Canton Teacher of Yr; Sandy Valley Jr HS Teacher of Yr; *home:* 1789 Clearview SE East Sparta OH 44626

MARCOTTE, JOSEPH A., Pastor/Headmaster; *b:* Worcester, MA; *ed:* (AB) Classics, Holy Cross Coll 1965; (STB) Theology, Gregorian Univ 1970; *cr:* Assoc Pastor Our Lady Immaculate 1970-75, Christ the King 1975-80, St Bernard 1980-84; Pastor/Headmaster St Louis 1984-; *ai:* St Louis Sch Advisory Bd; Diocese of Worcester Mother Seton Awd 1990; *office:* St Louis Sch 50 Negus Webster MA 01570

MARCUS, JACQUELINE POLLAK, 4th Grade Teacher; *b:* New York, NY; *m:* Elliott; *c:* Jenny Katz, Emily Katz, Rosie, Ariel; *ed:* (MS) Child/Individualized Curr, City Coll 1975; Grad Courses Ed & Human Relations; *cr:* Coll Instr Farleigh Dickinson Univ 1978-79; Elem Teacher Hillside Sch 1973-.

MARCUSON, ROBERT WADE, Science Teacher; *b:* Spokane, WA; *m:* Susan Lynne Goedde; *c:* Jeremy, Joshua; *ed:* (BAED) Earth Sci, E WA Univ 1970; *cr:* Sci Teacher Riverside Sch Dist 1971-; *ai:* 7th Grade Ftbl 1989; 8th Grade Boys & Girls Bsktbl 1990; Intramurals Sci Fair; NEA, WEA 1971-; Sci Grant 1975; *office:* Riverside Mid Sch Rt 1 Box 278 Chattaroy WA 99003

MAREK, COLLEEN JONES, Teacher; *b:* Troup, TX; *m:* Clarence Edward; *c:* Clay E., Lynda C.; *ed:* (AA) Bus, Tyler Jr Coll 1958; (BS) Bus/Eng, Stephen F Austin 1961; (MED) Scndry, Sw TX St 1981; Gifted & Talented, Curr Dev; *cr:* Teacher Smiley Ind Sch Dist 1961-63, Hallettsville 1963-64, Gonzales Ind Sch Dist 1964-, Victoria Coll 1980-; *ai:* UIL Typing; TX St Teachers Assn 1970-; NCTE 1985-; Mountain Plains Bus Assn 1968-; ASCD 1989-; 4-H Adult Leader 1975-, Pearl Clover 1989; Delta Kappa Gamma Numerous Comms 1976-, Schlsp 1978; Poetry Published For Local Church Bulletins & Luth Digest; *office:* Gonzales Ind Sch Dist Drawer M Gonzales TX 78629

MARES, KENNETH E., Music Teacher & HS Band Dir; *b:* Las Vegas, NM; *m:* Ruth Diane Martinez; *c:* Erin M., Rachael D., Esther E.; *ed:* (BA) Music/Music Ed, NM Highlands 1979; *cr:* Music Teacher Cuba Ind Schls 1979-81, W Las Vegas Schls 1981-; *ai:* HS & Mid Sch Band; Jazz Ensemble; Private Music Lessons for Stu at Arm & Hammer United World Coll of Amer W; Music Ed Natl Conference 1979-; NM N Cntrl Music Educators Pres 1981-; E Romero Hose & Fire Co Volunteer Fireman 1981-84; Outstanding & Superior Ratings for Band Dist & St Festivals; *office:* W Las Vegas Schls 157 Moreno St Las Vegas NM 87701

MARETT, CECIL DAN, Science Teacher; *b:* Senica, SC; *m:* Cynthia Cramp; *ed:* (BS) Phys Ed/Health, Carson Newman Coll 1987; *cr:* Voc Assesment Spec Jefferson Cty HS 1987-88; Sci Teacher Hart Cty HS 1988-; *ai:* Athletic Trainer; Fellowship of Chrstn Athletes Adv; Natl Athletic Trainers Assn 1988-; FCA 1989-; Woodmen of World 1989-; Sardis Baptist Church Deacon 1988-; *office:* Hart Cty HS Campbell Dr Hartwell GA 30643

MARETT, PAULA BARNHILL, Science Department Chairperson; *b:* Gaffney, SC; *m:* Thom R.; *c:* Chad, Chan, Cort; *ed:* (BA) Bio & Span, Winthrop 1963; (MAT) Educ 1974; *cr:* Teacher Hartsville Jr. HS 1967-69; Monroe Area HS 1969-70; Loganville HS 1970-72; Teacher/Dept Chair East Jr. HS 1972-; *ai:* Sci Club Spon; Energy Bowl Coord; Sci Fair Asst; NEA 1974-; SC Educ Assn 1974-; Cherokee Co Educ Assn 1970-; SC Sci Cncl 1987-; *home:* 310 Blackwell Road Blacksburg SC 29702

MARGAN, DAVID WALLACE, Health/Phys Ed Teacher; *b:* Durham, NC; *m:* Kathryn Setser; *c:* Kyle, Kayla; *ed:* (BA) Health/Phys Ed, Mars Hill Coll 1973; Teacher Macon Cty Schls 1973-; *ai:* FCA Club Adv; Cross Cntry & Boys Bsktbl Coach; Sunday Sch Teacher Deacon; Nautilus & Raquetball Instr at Fitness Center; Coach of Yr Boys Track 1988; Coach of Yr Cross Cntry 1988-89; *home:* 30-A Foxridge Cir Franklin NC 28734

MARGHEIM, LINDA HALE, Fifth Grade Teacher; *b:* Narrows, VA; *m:* Dale E.; *c:* Chance; *ed:* (BA) Elem Ed, Sam Houston St 1965; (MA) Curr/Instruction, VA Polytechnic Inst & State Univ 1973; *cr:* 5th Grade Teacher Houston Ind Sch Dist 1965-68; 3rd/5th Grade Chapter I Rdng/Math Teacher Giles Cty Schls 1968-; *ai:* NEA, VEA, GEA 1968-; New River Valley Cncl of Rdng 1976-79; *home:* 802 Summit Dr Blacksburg VA 24060

MARGRAVE, ROBERT, Pre-Calculus/AP Eng Teacher; *b:* Birmingham, AL; *ed:* (BA) Eng, William & Mary 1975; *cr:* Teacher Falls Church HS 1978-; *ai:* Literary Magazine & ITS Academic Team Spons; NCTE 1978-; Falls Church HS Teacher of Yr 1988-89.

MARIANT, PHILIP J., Science Teacher; *b:* San Jose, CA; *m:* Barbara M.; *c:* Deborah M. Kuhs, Michael A.; *ed:* (BA) Bio, 1966, (MA) Sci Ed, 1974 San Jose St Univ; ISISS, San Jose St Univ; *cr:* Sci Teacher Burnett Sch 1967-74; Curr Coord Morgan Hill Unified Sch Dist 1974-76; Sci Teacher Britton Sch 1976-80; Mentor Teacher Morgan Hill Unified Sch Dist 1984-86; Sci Teacher Murphy Sch 1980-; *ai:* Sch Improvement Prgm; Leadership, Sch Climate, Retention Comms; Sci Task Force; Sci Budget Rep; Resident Teacher for Stu Teacher; CTA, AFT, CSTA; *office:* Martin Murphy Sch 141 Avenida Espana San Jose CA 95139

MARIN, MICHELE HARBIN, Foreign Language Dept Chair; *b:* Bryan, TX; *c:* Michael; *ed:* (BA) Fr, Trinity Univ 1969; (MA) Fr, Univ of TX Austin 1971; *cr:* Teacher Univ of TX Austin 1970-71, S San Antonio HS 1977-80; Teacher 1981-, Teacher/Chairperson 1988- Marshall HS; *ai:* Fr Club & Fr Honor Society Spon; AATF 1985-; TX Foreign Lang Assn 1981-; Nom Outstanding HS Teacher TX Ex-Stus Assn; *office:* John Marshall HS 8000 Lobo Ln San Antonio TX 78240

MARINARO, VINCENT PAUL, Fifth Grade Science Teacher; *b:* Pittsfield, MA; *ed:* (BA) Bio, St Anselm Coll 1970; Red Cross Trng First Aid, CPR, Water Safety Instruction; *cr:* Water Treatment Tech Crane & Co Paper 1970-71; Sci Teacher Cath Cntrl Mid Sch 1973-76, St Marks Mid Sch 1976-78, Sacred Heart Elem Sch 1978-; *ai:* Founder & Adult Adv Cath Youth Center Service Society; Var Soccer & Jr Var Sftbl St Josephs HS; Bantam Bsktbl Coach Cath Youth Center; Day Camp Dir Cath Youth Center; Knights of Columbus 1969-; Cath Youth Center (Asst Dir 1970-, Volunteer) Volunteer of Yr 1976, Staff Appreciation Awd 1981-82; Awd of Appreciation Amer Heart Assn; *office:* Sacred Heart Sch 1 Meadow Ln Pittsfield MA 01201

MARINE, STEVEN MURPHY, English Teacher; *b:* Kansas City, MO; *m:* Jennifer Severens; *c:* Tom, Rick; *ed:* (AB) Psych, 1983, Univ of GA; Working Towards Masters Eng Ed, Univ of GA; *cr:* Eng Teacher Winder-Barrow HS 1986-; *ai:* Debate Coach; Prof Assn of GA Educators 1986; Psi Chi; *office:* Winder-Barrow HS 5th Ave Winder GA 30680

MARINELLO, FRED R., Visual/Performing Arts Teacher; *b:* Jewett City, CT; *ed:* (BFA) Advertising Design, Rochester Inst of Tech 1962; *cr:* Volunteer Peace Corps Philippines 1962-65; Sargeant USMC 1966-69; Teacher San Dieguito Union HS Dist 1970-; *ai:* Supts Advisory; Art Club Adv; Technology Advisory, Stu-At-Risk Comm; Apple Tech, San Diego Inst of Art Coord; Advance Placement/Gifted & Talented Ed Instr; Safety & Disaster Team; San Diego Chapter Amer Truck Historical Society Pres 1981-; Antique Truck Club of America 1986-; Motor Transport Museum (Bd Mem, Secy) 1984-; Master Teacher 1975-; Fullbright Teacher Exchange 1980; Mentor Teacher 1987-88; Sabbatical Study League 1976; Coord Artist Residence Problem CA Art Cncl 1985-86; RI Sch of Design Higher Ed; Honor Schlshp 1984; Teacher ofYr Awds 1979, 1989; *office:* Torrey Pines HS 710 Encinitas Blvd Encinitas CA 92024

MARINICH, MARCIA LEE PERSON, 5th Grade Teacher; *b:* Iron Mountain, MI; *ed:* (BS) Eng/Math/Sci Ed, 1975, (MA) Rdng, 1978 N MI Univ; Prof Dev & Positive Relations; Inst of Childrens Lit Cert; *cr:* 4th-5th Grade Combined/5th Grade/6th-8th Grade Eng Teacher Hillcrest Elem in Aurora 1975-; *ai:* Hillcrest 5th-8th Grade Spelling Club Founder & Adv; Winter Games Coach; Educl Comm, Soc, Building Sunshine Chm; Gifted & Talented Curr Comm Mem; Local Ed Assn Secy; Articles & Poems Published; Wrote Childrens Book; *home:* N 3628 Moon Lake Dr Iron Mountain MI 49801

MARION, JO ANN STAMM, Associate Professor; *b:* Oakland, NE; *m:* L. M.; *ed:* (BS) Elem Ed, 1961; (MS) Elem Ed, 1969 Univ NE; *cr:* Teacher Lincoln Public Schls 1961-68; Instr/Teacher 1968-73; Asst Professor/Teacher 1973-85; Assoc Professor/Teacher 1985- Northwest MO St Univ; *ai:* Sigma Svc Society Spon; Intnl Rdng Assn (Pres 1968-) Literacy Awd 1989; Assn for Chldhd Ed Pres 1968-80; Phi Delta Kappa 1987-; Natl Gifted Assn 1975-; Assn for Early Chldhd Ed 1980-; Natl Assn Univ Lab Schls 1989-; Soroptimists (Past Mem) Youth Awd 1979; Whos Who Amer Ed 1990; Outstanting Young Educator Awd 1970; MACE Awd from Univ 1979; Focus on Gifted Article; MO Reader Article on Whole Lang; Sparrowgram Poem 1990; Southern Poetry Poem 1990.

MARISA, MARY LOU SPANG, Nursery Sch Teacher; *b:* Hershey, PA; *m:* Stephen E.; *c:* Juliann; *ed:* (BS) Elem Ed, Univ of Pittsburgh 1974; (MA) Elem Ed, Penn St 1977; *cr:* 2nd Grade Teacher 1974-76, 1st Grade Teacher 1976-86, Art Teacher 1986-88 St Joan of Arc Sch; Nursery Sch Teacher U-GRO Nursery Sch 1988-; *ai:* Childrens Book to be Published; *home:* PO Box 305 Market St Rear Campbelltown PA 17010

MARISCO, RONNIE WALLACE, Fifth Grade Teacher; *b:* Yonkers, NY; *c:* Lee Ann, Michael, Patricia, Karen; *ed:* (BS) Elem Ed, Univ of NY Cortland 1960; *cr:* 5th Grade Teacher Fabius-Pompay Elem Sch 1978-.

MARITERAGI, VICTORIA N. K., Stu Act/Leadership Teacher; *b:* Honolulu, HI; *m:* Raymond Toae; *c:* Jon R., Alvin, Clint; *ed:* (BS) Phys Ed/Health, Brigham Young Univ HI 1970; *cr:* Phys Ed/Health/HI His Teacher Kailua Intermediate 1970-74; Phys Ed/General Math Teacher 1974-75, Phys Ed Teacher 1975-85, Act Coord/Leadership Teacher 1985- Kahuku HS; *ai:* Morale Sch Climate Comm; Sch Advisory Cncl; Windward Dist Stu Cncl Adv; Intersch Sports & Fun-Tramurals Coord; Homecoming, May Day Events; Sr Class & Graduation Head Adv; Var Bsktbl Fundraisers; Leadership Wkshp; Conference Planner All Intermediate Act; Asst HS Act; *office:* Kahuku HS P O Box 308 Kahuku HI 96731

MARK, STEVE K., Band Director; *b:* Minneapolis, MN; *m:* Marty Horton; *c:* Gina, Sara, Alex; *ed:* (BMUS) Music Ed, Univ of N IA 1979; *cr:* Dir of Bands Orchard Hill Elem Sch 1979-; *ai:* Dir Elem Jazz Band; IA Bandmasters Assn 1987-; *office:* Southdale Elem Sch 627 Orchard Dr Cedar Falls IA 50613

MARKART, DANA TRAYLER, Mathematics Teacher; *b:* Borger, TX; *m:* Arthur Davis; *c:* Tara, Kelly Markart Brown, ArtHur II, William; *ed:* (AA) Math, Frank Phillips Coll 1966; (BS) Math, W TX St Univ 1969; Grad Stud Memphis St Univ; *cr:* Math/Eng Teacher Rosemark-Tipton Acad 1977-78; Math/Eng Teacher W Memphis Chrstn Sch 1978-84; Math Teacher Memphis Harding Acad 1984-; *ai:* Math Club Mu Alpha Theta Spon; Math Bowl Coach; Girls Club & Jr Class Spon; SACS Sch & Cmmty Comm Mem; AR Teachers Educl Assn 1978-84; Annual Dedication 1988; ALgebra II Pilot Prgm 1988-89; *office:* Memphis Harding Acad 1100 Cherry Rd Memphis TN 38117

MARKEGARD, BEVERLY LEE, 5th Grade Teacher; *b:* Peterson, MN; *m:* Arless R.; *c:* Michael, Raymond; *ed:* (BS) Elem Ed, Winona St Univ 1968; Elem Ed; *cr:* 5th Grade Teacher Caledonia Elem Sch 1968-; *ai:* Elem Sch Comm Parent-Teacher Conference; Report Card; Open House; Cmptr; I Love to Read; Math; Caledonia Ed Assn 1968; MN Ed Assn 1968-; NEA 1968-; Amer Legion Aux; Kappa Delta Pi Double Guard Awd Schlsp and Service; Purple Key Gold Key Awd Honor Awd Schlsp Coll and Commty Service; *office:* Caledonia Elem Sch W Main St Caledonia MN 55921

MARKER, KATHY LYNETTE, Science, Biology Teacher; *b:* Union City, IN; *ed:* (BME) Music Ed, Georgetown Coll 1973; (MA) Health/Safety, Ball St Univ 1981; Numerous Courses for Enrichment; *cr:* Elem Music Teacher Tri-Village Local Schls 1973-74; Music/Sci/Bio/Drivers Ed Teacher Bradford Exempted Village Schls 1974-; *ai:* Drivers Ed; Spon Jr Class; NEA, OEA 1973-; Amer Fed of Musicians 1968-; Union City Fire Dept Paramedic 1984-; Village of Union City Dispatcher Hillgrove Church Organist 1962-; Nom Teacher of Yr 1990; *office:* Bradford Exempted Village Schl 712 N Miami Ave Bradford OH 45308

MARKER, LARRY DUANE, Asst Principal/Athletic Dir; *b:* Richmond, IN; *m:* Jane Ellen Sponsler; *c:* David, Kathy, Karen; *ed:* (BS) Bus Ed/Phys Ed, 1964, (MS) Bus Ed/Phys Ed, 1970, Admin/Supervision, 1976, Life License Admin/Supervision, 1982 Ball St Univ; Health Certificate; Driver Ed; *cr:* Teacher Northeastern HS 1964-76; Asst Prin/Athletic Dir Randolph Southern 1976-; *ai:* 7th-12th Grade Athletic Dir; Schedule Convocations; Local Schlsp Comm Head; Natl Athletic Dirs Assn; *office:* Randolph Southern Jr/Sr HS PO Box 305 Lynn IN 47355

MARKETT, MARY CHILTON, Fourth Grade Teacher; *b:* Montgomery, AL; *m:* Edward (dec); *c:* Paula M Thomas, Sharon M. Malone, Gina M. Johnson; *ed:* (BS) Scndry ED, AL ST Univ 1950; (MA) Human Learning & Dev, Governors ST Univ 1975; *cr:* 7th Grade Teacher 1959-69; Master Teacher 1969-72; Acting Asst Prin 1972-74; 4th Grade Teacher 1974- Joseph Medill I & U; *office:* Joseph Medill I & U 1326 W 14th Pl Chicago IL 60608

MARKEY, EUGENIA WOODWARD, First Grade Teacher; *b:* Maysville, KY; *m:* Thomas III;; *ed:* (BA) Elem Ed, Morehead St Univ 1969; (MED) Early Chldhd Ed, Univ of Cincinnati 1972; *cr:* 5th Grade Teacher 1969-79, 3rd Grade Teacher 1979-82, Half Day Kndgtn/1st Grade Teacher 1982-83, 1st Grade Teacher 1982-83 Germantown Elem Sch; 1st Grade Teacher Taylor Elem Sch 1988-; *ai:* NEA, KEA, BCEA 1969-; Church Sunday Sch Teacher 1969-; Brite-Siders Homemakers 1975-; Germantown PTO Treas 1975.

MARKEY, FRANCES JANCZYK, Third Grade Teacher; *b:* Newark, NJ; *m:* John J.; *ed:* (BA) Elem Ed, 1967, (MA) Rdng, 1974 Jersey City St Coll; Open Court Rdng Wkshp 1974; *cr:* 2nd Grade Teacher 1967-74, 3rd Grade Teacher 1974- Franklin Sch; *ai:* NEA, NJ Ed Assn, Hudson Cty Ed Assn, Kearny Ed Assn 1967-; Amer Cancer Society Volunteer 1988-; *office:* Franklin Sch 100 Davis Ave Kearny NJ 07032

MARKHAM, BARBARA ABSHIRE, Second Grade Teacher; *b:* Roanoke, VA; *m:* Floyd Murray; *c:* Jennifer L., Jason D.; *ed:* (BS) Elem Ed, Radford Coll 1957; Grad Classes for Renewal of Teaching Cert 1957; *cr:* 3rd Grade Teacher Buchanan Elem 1957-60; 1st/3rd-5th Grade Teacher Belmont Sch 1960-66; 2nd/3rd & 6th Grade Teacher Buchanan Elem 1974-; *ai:* Self Study Steering Comm; After Sch Sci Club Co-Spon; Supt-Teacher Communication Comm Building Rep; NEA, VEA, BEA (Building Rep 1957-66, 1974-) 1958; Roanoke Valley Rdng Assn Mem 1988-; Lioness Comm Mem 1987-; PTA Historian 1985-86; Church (Youth Class Teacher, Vacation Bible Sch Asst Dir, Librarian, Asst Clerk); Adult Leader Botetourt Cty 4-H 5 & 10 Yr Pin Awds.

MARKHAM, E. LYNDA JAMESON, Coord/Instr/Mentor Teacher; *b:* Los Angeles, CA; *m:* Leonard; *c:* Ian J., Misty R.; *ed:* (BA) Eng, Univ of CA Santa Barbara 1974; (MA) Ed, Point Loma Nazarene Coll 1990; *cr:* Classroom Teacher Enterprise Jr HS 1975-76; Dept Chairperson/Classroom Teacher 1982-85, New Teacher/Special Project Coord/Mentor Teacher 1985-87, Admin Asst/Mentor/Curr/Instruction Teacher 1987- Sun Valley Jr HS; *ai:* Creative Writing, Journalism, Speech, Media & Academic Pentathlon; LAUSD Outstanding Recognition 1988; Eng Cncl of LA Outstanding Teacher 1989; Phi Delta Kappa 1985; Women in Educl Leadership 1986; Co-Author; Instr Dist Intern Prgm; Dir Curr/St Prgms; *office:* Sun Valley Jr Hs 7330 Bakman Ave Sun Valley CA 91352

MARKHAM, LYNN KENNEDY, Third Grade Teacher; *b:* Bethesda, MD; *m:* Blain; *c:* Joseph Tucker, David, Angela; *ed:* (BS) Elem Ed, 1974, (MED) Elem Ed, 1987 E TX St Univ Texarkana; *cr:* 2nd/3rd Grade Teacher Redwater Elem Sch 1974-; *ai:* Univ Interscholastic League Literary Dir; Fall Festival Chairperson; PTA Historian 1988-; TX St Teachers Assn 1978-86; *office:* Redwater Ind Sch Dist P O Box 347 Redwater TX 75573

MARKLEY, LOIS HOLZHAUSER, English Teacher; *b:* St Joseph, MO; *m:* Richard E.; *c:* Jill Dickerson, Brian; *ed:* (BS) Soc Stud Ed, KS Univ 1962, (MS) Eng Ed, Univ of MO Kansas City 1967; Greater Kansas City Writing Project; *cr:* Eng Teacher Benton HS 1962-64, Ruskin HS 1971-72, Hickman Mills HS 1972-76; Soc Stud Teacher Cass Midway 1978-86; English Teacher Raymore-Peculiar HS 1986-; *ai:* Scholar Bowl & Project Graduation Spon; NCTE 1985-; Lord of Love Luth Church 1979-; *office:* Raymore-Peculiar HS 211 St & School Rd Peculiar MO 64078

MARKO, ANDREW PAUL, JR., Advanced Placement Eng Teacher; *b:* Kingston, PA; *m:* Janet Thimm; *c:* Danielle; *ed:* (BA) Eng, Kings Coll 1964; (MA) Eng Ed/Admin Cert, Scranton Univ 1968; Grad Work Oxford Univ England, Scranton Univ, Penn St Intermediate Unit 17 AP Insts; *cr:* Eng Teacher/Wrestling Coach Kingston PA; Advanced Placement Lit Teacher Wyoming Valley West HS; Vice Prin 1981, 1990; *ai:* Publications Financial, Sch Newspaper, Literary Magazine Adv; Literary Club; PSEA, NEA; Councilmen Mem; *office:* Wyoming Valley West HS Wadhams St Plymouth PA 18651

MARKOSKY, RITA WHETSELL, Spanish Teacher; *b:* Mc Keesport, PA; *m:* Mark Anthony; *c:* Jessica, Jacob; *ed:* (BS) Scndry Ed/Span, Edinboro Univ 1974; (MS) Rdng Specialist, Duquesne Univ 1980; *cr:* Span Teacher Mc Keesport Jr HS 1974-76; Chapter I Prgm Rdng Specialist Mc Keesport Area 1977-85; Span Teacher Mc Keesport Sr HS 1985-; *ai:* NHS Comm; Stu Assessment Prgm; Core Team Mem; Amer Field Service AFS Exchange Prgm Adv 1985-89; PMFLA 1989-; PSEA, NEA 1974-; *office:* Mc Keesport Area HS 1960 Eden Park Blvd Mc Keesport PA 15132

MARKS, COLLEEN MC DONALD, Second Grade Teacher; *b:* Biwabik, MN; *m:* Bobby Kees; *c:* Denice, Donna Marks Hall; *ed:* (BS) Home Ec - Magna Cum Laude, Lamar St Univ 1956, (MED) Elem Ed, Univ of AR 1963; Introduction to Cmptr Ed 1984; Advanced Academic Trng; *cr:* 4th Grade Teacher South Park Ind Sch Dist 1956-57; 6th Grade Teacher Ft Smith Ind Sch Dist 1957-58; 5th Grade Teacher Carrolton Ind Sch Dist 1959-60; 4th Grade Techer Aldine Ind Sch Dist 1960-61; 6th-7th Grade Teacher Huntsville Ind Sch Dist 1961-63; 4th Grade Teacher Prairie Grove Ind Sch Dist 1963-64; 2nd Grade Teacher Huntsville Ind Sch Dist 1976-; *ai:* Stu & Methods Teachers Supvr; Assn of TX Prof Educators Membership Chairperson 1987-88; Delta Kappa Gamma 1988-; TX St Teachers Assn; Sam Houston St Univ Women Club Pres 1969-70; Hunstville Study Club (Pres, Teas, VP); GSA Brownie Leader 1971-74; Elkins Lake Baptist Church (VBS, Choir, Teacher, Comm Chairperson); Phi Kappa Phi; Whos Who Among Stus Amer Univs & Colls 1955-56.

MARKS, JANET WOOD, Teacher; *b:* Hampton, VA; *m:* Donald P.; *c:* Brent C., Kevin T.; *ed:* (BS) Bio/Gen Sci, James Madison Univ 1964; *cr:* Teacher Fairfax HS 1964-65; Jefferson Davis Jr HS 1965-67; Christiansburg Elem Sch 1967-71; Christiansburg Mid Sch 1975-; *ai:* Steering Comm Self Study; MCEA; VEA; NEA; Blacksburg United Meth Church; Admin Bd 1987-; *home:* 2814 Glade Rd Blacksburg VA 24060

MARKS, JOHNNIE MAE, Assistant Principal; *b:* Lafayette, LA; *m:* Calvin; *c:* Crystal, Jacquelyn; *ed:* (BS) Home Ec, 1976, (MED) Scndry Ed, 1985, (MED) Admin, 1988 Univ of SW LA; *cr:* Home Ec Teacher Church Point HS 1976-79, Acadiana HS 1979-82, Carencro HS 1982-; Asst Prin Acadiana HS 1990; *ai:* FHA Adv; Phi Delta Kappa (Treas, VP) 1989-; LA Voc Assn, NEA, LAE; Lafayette Parish Voc Ed Assn, AVA; Delta Sigma Theta (VP, Secy) 1973-88; GSA Leader; *office:* Acadiana HS 315 Rue Du Belier Lafayette LA 70506

MARKS, MARY BRENT BARBOUR, Senior English Teacher; *b:* Washington, DC; *m:* Alan J.; *c:* Alexander F.; *ed:* (BA) Eng, Univ of MD 1970; (MA) Human Resources Dev, Webster Univ 1990; *cr:* 7th Grade Eng Teacher Milton Somers Mid Sch 1970-72; 8th Grade Eng Teacher John Hanson Mid Sch 1972-76; Eng/Frosh Honors/Gifted & Talented/Sr Eng Teacher James Madison HS 1977-; *ai:* Sr Class Spon 1986-; Jr Class Spon 1979-86; Cooperating Teacher Univ of TX & SW TX St Univ; NCTE, TX Classroom Teachers Assn Mem; His Article Published 1976; *home:* 2611 Pebble Dawn San Antonio TX 78232

MARLA, LOIS MAC LEOD, English/Social Studies Teacher; *b:* Boston, MA; *c:* Stephen, Geoffrey, Juliette, Jennifer; *ed:* Gen Ed, Boston Univ 1959-61; (BA) Pre-Law, 1967, (MA) Eng, 1969 ID St Univ; *cr:* Part Time Instr ID St Univ 1967-71; Teacher Turlock HS 1971-83, Modesto Jr Coll 1979, Davis HS 1983-; *ai:* Bear Valley Ski Club Race Team, Masters Ski Team; Modesto Youth Soccer Spon; CTA Faculty Rep; Lit Curr Comm; Phi Delta Kappa 1979-; Turlock Teachers Assn (VP, Negotiations Team, Soc Chairperson) 1971-83; *office:* Davis HS 1200 W Rumble Rd Modesto CA 95350

MARLER, BRENDA KELLY, 7th-8th Grade English Teacher; *b:* Dayton, TN; *c:* Andrew, Catherine; *ed:* (BS) Eng/His Ed, Univ TN 1970; Adm/Supvsn TN Tech 1978; Spec Ed/Gifted Univ TN 1988; *cr:* Eng/Soc Stud 7th/8th Grade Teacher Spring City Elem 1970-71; Soc Stud/Rlgn 7th/8th Grade Teacher St Paul Sch 1971-73; Soc Stud Teacher 7th/8th Grades 1976-78; 7th/8th Grade Eng Teacher 1978 Dayton City Sch; *ai:* Jrnlsm Club Spon; Chrldn Spon; Adopt-A-Sch Comm; NCTE 1969-73/81-; Delta Kappa Gamma Schlsp Chm 1986-; PTO (VP 1985 Mem 1976-); Stride 1988-; *office:* Dayton City Sch 502 Cherry St Dayton TN 37321

MARLETON, LOIS TROAST, Fifth Grade Teacher; *b:* Passaic, NJ; *m:* Roy; *c:* Bob; *ed:* (BA) Elem Ed, Paterson St Coll 1960; (MA) Eng, Montclair St Coll 1966; *cr:* 3rd/6th Grade Teacher Euclid Sch 1960-62; 3rd Grade Teacher Sch 2 1962-69; K-5th Grade Teacher Saddle Brook Chrstn Sch 1972-73; 3rd/4th Grade Teacher Bible Baptist Chrstn Sch 1973-75; K/2nd-5th Grade Teacher Liberty Chrstn Sch 1975-76; Teacher Ocean Cty Chrstn Sch 1977-78; 2nd/3rd/5th/6th Grade Teacher Rochester Hills Chrstn Sch 1978-; *ai:* Sch Newspaper; Grandparents Day & Curr Comm; Chapel Pianist; Kappa Delta Pi 1960; NJ Ed Assn 1960-69; MI Assn of Chrstn Schls 1978-; *office:* Rochester Hills Chrstn Sch 3300 S Livernois Rd Rochester MI 48063

MARLOW, LINDA MAY (MURPHY), German/French Teacher; *b:* Highland Park, MI; *m:* Robert J.; *c:* Daniel, Peter; *ed:* (BA) Ger/Lib Arts/Scndry Ed, Oakland Univ 1973; (MA) Ger, Univ of MI 1975; (PHD) Modern Lang Art, Wayne St Univ 1985; Sommerkurs Friedrich Alexander Univ Erlangen W Germany 1976; *cr:* Teaching Fellow Univ of MI 1975-76; Grad Teaching Asst Wayne St Univ 1977-79, 1980-81; Instr Marygrove Coll 1981-82, Schoolcraft Comm Coll 1984-85; Teacher/Chairperson Plymouth Chrstn Acad 1985-; *ai:* 1990 Graduating Class Faculty Adv; Schls Delta Epsilon Phi & Schls Societe Honoraire de Francais Adv; Ed Curr Comm Mem; MLA, AATF, AATG, MI Acad; Book The Concept of Tugend An Alternative Method of 18th Century Ger Novel Classification 1988; Received Stipend from Goethe Inst Berlin to Participate in Seminar at Inst Fur Intereuropaische Studien Berlin 1990; *office:* Plymouth Chrstn Acad 43065 Joy Rd Canton MI 48187

MARLOW, LINDA SUE, Fine Arts Department Chairman; *b:* La Follette, TN; *m:* Robert C.; *c:* Robert H., Lindsie M. (dec); *ed:* (BS) TN Technological Univ 1969; Grad Work TN Tech, Belmont; *cr:* Elem Music Teacher Oneida Elem Sch 1969-81; Eng Teacher 1981-86, Fine Arts Dept Chairperson 1986- Oneida HS; *ai:* Piano Stu Teachers Supvr; 1st Baptist Church (Pianist, Youth Dir, Adult Choir Mem); MENC; Mu Phi Epsilon Officer 1969; Intnl Society of Pianist Mem; TN Ed Assn, NEA, Oneida Ed Assn; Level II Teacher on Governors Career Ladder; Robert Pace Piano Cert; Intnl Society of Pianists Prof Cert; *office:* Oneida HS P O Box 439 Oneida TN 37841

MARLOW, SANDRA SCHUMANN, Third Grade Teacher; *b:* Duluth, MN; *m:* Kent Bryan; *ed:* (BS) Elem Ed, 1975, (MS) Elem Ed, 1981 NW MO St Univ; *cr:* Spec Ed Teacher Albany Regional Diagnostic Center 1975; 2nd Grade Teacher 1975-82, 3rd Grade Teacher 1982- Gentry Cty R-II Sch; *ai:* MO St Teachers Assn Mem 1975-; Stanberry Ed Assn (Secy 1983-84, Treas 1986-87, Revisions Comm Chm); Birthright Mem 1988-89; *office:* Gentry Cty R-II Sch N Park St Stanberry MO 64489

MARONEY, JAMES THOMAS, Social Stud Instr/Head Coach; *b:* Victoria, TX; *m:* Connie Marie; *c:* Kimberly A., James K.; *ed:* (BS) His/Phys Ed, TX A&I Univ 1971; (MED) Guidance/Counseling, Prairie View A&M Univ 1977; Free Enterprise Practicum, Univ of TX Austin 1980; *cr:* Teacher Devereaux Fnd 1971-72; Coach/Teacher Bloomington Ind Sch Dist 1972-80, Howell Intermediate Sch 1982-; *ai:* Howell Intermediate Sch Athletic Coord, Head Coach; Victoria Ind Sch Dist Communications Comm; TX St Teachers Assn, TX HS Coaches Assn 1972-; YMCA 1989-; Volunteer Fire Dept 1985-; United Meth Church 1963-; Free Enterprise Practicum Grant Dupont Univ of TX Austin; *home:* Rt 2 Box 151-B Victoria TX 77901

MAROTTOLI, RALPH THOMAS, JR., 6th Grade Teacher; *b:* New Haven, CT; *m:* Donna Forlano; *ed:* (BS) Elem Ed, 1972, (MS) Elem Ed, 1977 S CT St Univ; *cr:* 6th Grade Teacher Kay Avenue Sch 1972-79, Live Oaks Sch 1979-89, Pumpkin Delight Sch 1989-; *home:* 53 Painter Ave West Haven CT 06516

MARQUARDT, KATHARINE TURLEY, Biology Teacher; *b:* Manhattan, NY; *m:* Robert James; *c:* Katharine, Jennifer, Robert Jr.; *ed:* (BA) Bio, St Josephs Coll 1968; (MA) Bio, SUNY Albany 1974; Essential Elements of Instruction Wkshps for Teachers & Admin Presentor 1986-; Critical Thinking Skills Wkshps Presentor 1989-; *cr:* Regents/General Bio Teacher Newtown HS 1968; General Bio/9th Grade Sci Teacher 1968-69, Regents/Honors Bio Teacher 1969-70 Niskayuna HS; 7th/8th Grade Sci/Bio II/Regents Bio Teacher Indian Lake Sch 1973-76; Advanced Placement Coord Warrensburg Sch System 1981-; Advanced Placement/Regents/General Bio Teacher Warrensburg Cntrl Sch 1981-; *ai:* Yrbk Financial Adv 1983-; Ski Club Adv 1982-; Athletic Events Ticket Salesperson 1987-; Class of 1984 Adv 1980-84; Class of 1979 Adv 1976-79; Amer Society for Curr Dev, NSTA, Sci Teachers of NY St; Lake George Bus & Prof Womens Assn Schlsp Chm 1988-; *office:* Warrensburg Cntrl Sch 1 James St Warrensburg NY 12885

MARQUARDT, TONI LYNN, Mathematics & English Teacher; *b:* Washington, IA; *m:* Wally A.; *c:* Jacqueline; *ed:* (BS) Scndry Ed/His/Eng, WI St Univ Platteville 1970; (MS) Scndry Ed, Purdue Univ 1974; Elem Cert, IL St Univ; *cr:* 7th Grade Teacher Highland Jr HS 1970-74; 7th Grade Rdng/Eng/Gifted/Math & 6th Grade Soc Stud Teacher 1975- Washington Jr HS; *ai:* Curr Advisory Comm VP; Discipline Comm Mem; Annual Young Writers Contest Supv for Jr HS; Starved Rock Rdng Cncl 1975-80, 1990; NEA 1970-; IEA 1975-; ASCD, IL Rdng Cncl; Oglesby Union Church (Trustee Bd Secy 1988-, Youth Group Spon 1985-89); Little League Sftbl Coach 1990; GSA Leader 1987-; PTA (Finance Comm Mem 1987-88) 1975-; *office:* Washington Jr HS 10th & Rock St Peru IL 61354

MARQUART, MITZI LYNN, Mathematics Teacher; *b:* Altus, OK; *ed:* Assoc Math/Phys Ed, Amarillo Jr Coll 1982; (BS) Math/Phys Ed, W TX St Univ 1984; Grad Work, E TX St Univ; *cr:* Math Teacher/Coach Stratford Ind Sch Dist 1984-87, Princeton Ind Sch Dist 1987-; *ai:* Head Coach Girls Vlybl & Bsktbl; Favorite Teacher 1984-85; *home:* Rt 5 116 Hope St Princeton TX 75077

MARQUES, STEVE JOSEPH, Accounting & Computer Teacher; *b:* New Bedford, MA; *m:* Marilyn Herbst; *c:* Steven Jr., Christopher; *ed:* (BS) Accounting, Univ of RI 1966; (MBA) Financial Management, Syracuse Univ; (MED) General Ed, Sul Ross St Univ; (MPS) Pastoral Stud, Loyola Univ of Chicago 1989; US Army Command & General Staff Coll; *cr:* Officer US Army 1966-86; Professor Loyola Univ 1983-86; Teacher Providence HS 1988-; *ai:* Cmptr Club Spon; Church Dir of Religious Ed; TX Bus Educators Assn 1988-; TX Computed Educators Assn 1989-;

Alamo Personal Cmptr Organization 1989-; Amer Society of Military Comptrollers 1972-; Knights of Columbus Trustee 1962-, Knight of Month 1988 & 1990; US Army Bronze Star, Legion of Merit, Defense Meritorious Service Medal, Army Meritorious Service Medal, Air Force Commendation Medal, Vietnamese Medal of Honor; *office:* Providence HS 1215 N St Marys San Antonio TX 78215

MARQUETT, KATHY DENISE, 9th Grade English Teacher; *b:* Cle Elum, WA; *m:* Gale E.; *c:* Dan, Stephanie; *ed:* (BA) Eng/Phys Ed, Cntrl WA Univ 1973; Numerous Classes; *cr:* 8th Grade Lang Art/Phys Ed Teacher Mountain View 1973-78; Eng/Phys Ed Teacher 1978-84, Dept Chairperson 1984-86, 1988-, Eng Teacher 1984- W Valley Jr HS; *ai:* 9th Grade Class Adv; Weekly After Sch Studs; NCTE, St & Local Cncl of Teachers of Eng (VP 1982) 1973-; W Valley Ed Assn Negotiations Team 1990; Youth Soccer Assn 1982-88; Natl Faculty Grant; *office:* W Valley Jr HS 7505 Zier Rd Yakima WA 98908

MARQUEZ, ELIZABETH LOCKHOVEN, Mathematics Teacher; *b:* New York, NY; *m:* Anthony P. Johnson; *c:* Alison, Elizabeth; *ed:* (BA) Math, Montclair St Coll 1967; (MA) Math, Cntrl MO St Univ 1970; *cr:* Math Teacher Knob Noster Jr HS 1967-69, Linwood Jr HS 1972-73; Adjunct Teacher Kean Coll 1983-85, Middlesex Cty Coll 1984; Math Teacher North Brunswick Township HS 1973-; *ai:* Affirmative Action Officer North Brunswick Twp HS; North Brunswick Township Ed Assn VP 1987-; NCTM 1967-; Princeton Univ Awd for Distinguished Scndry Sch Teaching 1984; NJ Bus/Industry/Sci Ed Consortium Grant for Tutorial Videos 1986; *office:* North Brunswick Township HS Rt 130 North Brunswick NJ 08850

MARQUEZ, LINDA, English Teacher; *b:* Slaton, TX; *m:* Ricardo; *c:* Diandra; *ed:* (BS) Ed, TX Tech Univ 1983; *cr:* Teacher Andrews Mid Sch 1983-; *ai:* ATPE Secy 1987-88; *office:* Andrews Mid Sch 405 NW 3rd St Andrews TX 79714

MARR, GRACE HALSEY, Fourth Grade Teacher; *b:* Pittsfield, MA; *m:* George; *c:* William L., Tracy L., G. Scott; *ed:* (BA) Elem Ed, William Paterson 1972; *cr:* 5th Grade Teacher 1972-74, 4th Grade Teacher 1974- Walnut Ridge Primary Sch; *ai:* Highland Lakes Swim Team, Aqua Gems Swim Team Marshall 1972-80; VTEA (Legislative Chairperson 1977-79, Grievance Chairperson 1982-84, Nominating Chairperson 1985-86, Faculty Rep 1975-); St Thomas Episcopal Church (Wkshp Comm 1987-, Planning Comm 1987-).

MARR, LYNETTE HAHN, Teacher of Gifted; *b:* Orrville, OH; *m:* James D.; *c:* Lindsey, Andrew; *ed:* (BS) Elem Ed, Ashland Coll 1978; (MS) Rdng Supervision, Univ of Akron 1984; Rdng & Gifted; *cr:* 4th Grade Teacher North Sch 1978-82; 6th Grade Teacher Oak St Sch 1982-86; Gifted & Talented Orrville Jr HS 1986-; *ai:* Jr HS Academic Challenger Adv; EAO 1978-; OEA 1978-; NEA 19788-; Friends of Orrville Lib 1989; People to People 1982-86; Teacher of Yr North Sch 1980; *home:* 14821 Rehm Rd Orrville OH 44667

MARRARA, CARL JOHN, High School Counselor; *b:* Clearfield, PA; *m:* Mary Ann Walters; *c:* Carl A.; *ed:* (BS) Phys Ed/Bus Ed, Dickinson St Coll 1971; (MS) Ed/Counseling/Guidance, ND St Univ 1978; Admin Ed, ND St Univ; *cr:* Teacher 1971-74, Cnslr 1974-79 Turtle Mountain Cmmty Sch; Cnslr Valley City Jr/Sr HS 1979-83, Danville Area Sr HS 1983-; *ai:* SADD Adv; Amer Personal & Guidance Assn 1974-83; ND Personal & Guidance Assn VP 1982; Susquehanna Valley Sch Cnslrs Assn Pres 1988-89; *office:* Danville Area Sr HS Northumberland Rd Danville PA 17821

MARRIOTT, CONNIE ROBERTS, 2nd Grade Teacher; *b:* Ogden, UT; *m:* Bruce P.; *c:* Jennifer, Christine, Nicholas, Brent, Annie, Joshua; *ed:* (BA) Elem Ed, Weber St Coll 1970; *cr:* 3rd Grade Teacher Lorrin Farr Elem 1970; 5th Grade Teacher 1972-74, Kndgtn Teacher 1974-76 Mt View Elem; Kndgtn Teacher Gramery 1976-78, Horace Mann 1978-86; 2nd Grade Teacher Hillcrest Elem 1986-; *ai:* Teacher Asst Team; Lang Art Rep; Code of Conduct Comm; UT Ed Assn; Latter Day Saints Church Young Womens Pres 1989-; Standard Examiner Newspaper Apple Teacher Awd.

MARRIOTT, LORI SHEA, A G Teacher K-3; *b:* Buffalo, NY; *m:* William J.; *c:* Sally, Matthew; *ed:* (BS) Elem Ed, SUNY Coll Buffalo 1972; (MED) Early Childhood Ed, Univ NC Chapel Hill 1978; *cr:* 5th Grade Teacher 1973-75, 1st Grade Teacher 1976-82 Hillandale Sch; Kndgtn St Marys Sch 1983-84; 5th Grade a G Teacher 1984-85, K-3rd Grade Explorations a G Teacher 1986- Hillandale Sch; *ai:* Hillandale Teacher of Yr 1981-82; *office:* Hillandale Elem Sch 2107 Hillandale Rd Durham NC 27705

MARRON, BETTYANNE A., 1st Grade Teacher; *b:* Camden, NJ; *ed:* (BA) Elem Ed, Glassboro St Univ 1974; (MS) Ed Theory, Rutgers 1981; Elem Sci, Glassboro St 1987; Motivation-Power to Teach/Energy to Learn St Josephs Univ 1988; *cr:* Nursery Sch Merrytyme 1976-79; 3rd Grade Teacher St Charles 1979-86; 1st Grade Teacher Delaware Avenue Sch 1986-; *ai:* Jr Unit Leader; Read Aloud, Report Card Comm; Taught Summer Sch; *office:* Delaware Ave Sch Delaware Ave Palmyra NJ 08065

MARROU, JANICE F., World History Teacher; *b:* Houston, TX; *ed:* (BA) His, 1971, (MA) His, 1976 Lamar Univ; Advanced Trng Gifted & Talented Ed; *cr:* 9th Grade Eng Teacher Franklin Jr HS 1971-72; 8th Grade Eng/His Teacher Henderson Jr HS 1972-82; His/Geography Teacher/Chairperson Hardin-Jefferson HS 1982-; *ai:* Gifted & Talented Field Trip TX Renaissance Festival; TX St Teachers Assn 1972; TX Cncl of Soc Stud, NCSS, TX Assn for Gifted & Talented 1989; NEA 1972-; Amer Mensa Deputy Local Secy 1983-; Nom TX Cncl of Hum Grant; Articles Published; *office:* Hardin-Jefferson HS PO Box 639 Hwy 326 Sour Lake TX 77659

MARSH, ARLETTA JANNINGS, Third Grade Teacher; *b:* Donnellson, IA; *m:* William V.; *c:* Deborah S. Stence, Tom W.; *ed:* (BA) Elem Ed, IA Wesleyan 1966; Grad Stud; *cr:* 1st-8th Grade Teacher Warren 1947-51; 1st-4th Grade Teacher Primrose 1951-52; K-8th Grade Teacher Jefferson 1959-60; 3rd Grade Remedial Rdng/3rd-5th Grade Teacher Harmony Cmmty Sch 1960-; *ai:* NEA Life Membership; IA St Ed Assn; Harmony Ed Assn Treas; PEO (Pres, Chaplain, Guard); *home:* 401 S Front St Farmington IA 52626

MARSH, BARBARA JANE, World Geography Teacher; *b:* Sudbury ON, Canada; *m:* Stewart O.; *c:* Kira L.; *ed:* (BA) Soc Sci/Scndry Ed, St Univ of NY Oswego 1972; (MED) Ed, Westminster Coll 1979; Admin Endorsement UT St 1990; *cr:* 8th Grade US His Teacher Roxboro Road Mid Sch 1972-74; Alternative Prgm World Geography Teacher Eisenhower Jr HS 1975-80; St Government/World Geography Gifted Prgm Teacher Bennion Jr HS 1980-; *ai:* Stu Government; Ski Club; Standards & Promotion Comm; St Accreditation Steering Comm Chairperson 1983-84; *home:* 7453 S Stone Rd Salt Lake City UT 84121

MARSH, CAROLYN LUCILLE, Third Grade Teacher; *b:* Oil City, PA; *ed:* (BSED) Elem Ed, 1967, (MSLS) Lib Sci, 1970 Clarion St; Cmptr Courses; *cr:* Teacher Cranberry Sch Dist 1967-; *office:* Pinegrove Elem Sch RD 1 Venus PA 16364

MARSH, DONALD HARRY, II, Social Studies Teacher; *b:* S Williamson, KY; *ed:* (BS) Mass Comm, 1979, (MED) Curr/Instruction, 1987 VA Commonwealth Univ; Inst of Biblical Trng 1980; *cr:* Soc Stud Teacher New Kent HS 1983-; *ai:* VA St Governors Sch Contributions as a Teacher Awd 1989; *home:* 3506-K King James Ct Richmond VA 23223

MARSH, HARRIET REDD, Social Studies Teacher; *b:* Goodman, MS; *m:* Theodore M.; *c:* La Tanya R., Shedrick D., Tyra M., Marquita S.; *ed:* (BS) Soc Stud, MS Valley St Univ 1973; Courses Towards Masters; *cr:* Teacher Harrison Cntrl 9th Grade Sch 1978-; *ai:* MS Fed of Teachers; Little Rock Missionary Baptist Church (Secy Sr Choir, Jr Matrons Auxiliary, Young Womens Auxiliary Mem).

MARSH, JEAN THOMPSON, Graduate Research Assistant; *b:* Montreal, Canada; *m:* John H.; *c:* John W., Alice; *ed:* (BA) Bio, 1963, (MAT) Sci/Eng, 1966 Harding Univ; (EDS) Curr/Instruction, Mid TN St Univ 1988; Doctoral Prgm Curr & Supervision 1988-; Various Elem Guidance Prgms; *cr:* Teacher Centerville Chrstn Sch 1981-83; Teacher/Admin Agape Chrstn Acad 1983-86; Teacher Kingston Springs Elem 1986-88; Grad Asst Vanderbilt Univ 1988-; *ai:* ASCD 1989-; Kappa Delta Pi 1987-; Full Tuition Assistantship Vanderbilt Univ 1988-; Grad Honor Cncl Vanderbilt 1989-; Presented Papers at Natl Assn for Research in Sci Teaching & Amer Educl Research Assn 1990; *home:* 111 Old Hickory Blvd 124 Nashville TN 37221

MARSH, MARYLOU SMITH, Fourth Grade Teacher; *b:* Spartanburg, SC; *m:* Harry H.; *c:* Audrey A., Jared H.; *ed:* (BA) Early Chldhd, Mars Hill Coll; *cr:* 5th Grade Teacher Carnesville Elem 1977-78; 2nd Grade Teacher 1978-79, 4th Grade Teacher 1978- Hartwell Elem; *ai:* Church-Choir; Mission Friend Leader; Former Chrldr Spon; Jr Service League 1982-86; *office:* Hartwell Elem Sch 302 College Ave Hartwell GA 30643

MARSH, PATRICIA MARSHALL, Sixth Grade Teacher; *b:* Detroit, MI; *m:* Donald L.; *c:* Jamal, Casey, Horatio; *ed:* (BS) Ed, Univ of OH Akron 1979; *cr:* Teacher Dalton Public Schls 1980-; *ai:* NEA, GA Assn of Educators; Dalton Assn of Educators Treas 1986-89; Womans Cmmty Club; *office:* Fort Hill Elem Sch Fort Hill Terr Dalton GA 30720

MARSH, ROBERT AMIL, Technical Education Teacher; *b:* Rupert, ID; *m:* Ranaye Janene Bewley; *c:* Robert J.; *ed:* (BS) Industrial Ed, Univ of ID 1969, (MA) Curr/Instruction/Voc Ed, 19772, (EDD) Curr/Instruction/Educl Media, 1978 Univ of N CO; Robotics Wkshp, Coll of S OH 1984; Principles of Technology & Instrs Trng 1986-87, Energy Resource, CO Sch of Mines 1989; *cr:* Teacher Malheur Cty 1969-70, Cole Jr HS 1970-82, East HS 1982-, Metropolitan St Coll 1985-; *ai:* Odyssey of Mind Creative Problem Solving Coach; DCTA, CEA, NEA 1970-88; CO Industrial Arts Assn 1986-88; Model T Club of America 1989-; North Cntrl Accreditation Teams; Teacher on Special Assignment; St Funded Grant Awd Denver Public Schls; *office:* East HS 1545 Detroit St Denver CO 80206

MARSH, STEPHEN DAVID, World/American History Teacher; *b:* Bell, CA; *m:* Lorraine Langbell; *ed:* (BS) His/Soc Sci, E MT Coll 1969; Grad Stud; *cr:* S/Sargent USAF 1961-67; Stu E Mt Coll 1967-69; Teacher Billings Sch Dist 2 1969-; *ai:* Stu Cncl Adv; MT Ed Assn 1969-; Phi Delta Kappa 1981-; Billings Ed Assn Building Rep 1970-71; NEA 1969-; Masons Worship Full Master 1982-88; Al Bedoo Shrine Potentate 1990; Youth Court 1976-86; Grace United Meth Church (Nominating Comm, Childrens Church Teacher); Order of Demolay Legion of Honor, Chevalier, Adv of Yr 1975-76; Scottish Rite; York Rite Bodies; Yellowstone Assn Retarded Children Outstanding Servicce 1969; Order of De Molay St Dad Adv 1979-87; Amer Legion Citation for Meritorious Service 1988; West HS Outstanding Teacher 1988; Cmmty Intervention Grant 1981; *home:* PO Box 20827 Billings MT 59104

MARSHALL, CHARLES R., Mathematics Dept Chairman; *b:* Irvine, KY; *m:* Doris M.; *c:* Robert, Kahenina M. Bianco; *ed:* (AB) His, CO Coll 1959; (MA) Ed, E KY Univ 1966; *cr:* Jr HS Math Teacher Widefield/Security 1957-60; 5th Grade Teacher Pueblo CO 1960-68; 6th Grade Teacher 1968-80, Jr HS Math Teacher 1980- Huntington Local 1980-; *ai:* Huntington Local Ed Assn 1975-76, Teacher of Yr 1975; Adult Educator of Yr Awd 1971.

MARSHALL, CLARICE HAIRSTON, Extended Learning Teacher; *b:* Uralde, Texas; *m:* A. Jay Jr.; *c:* Randall Jay; *ed:* (BA) Elem Ed, Southern Meth Univ 1970; (MA) Elem Ed, Lindenwood Coll 1987; Several Wkshps; *cr:* 1st Grade Teacher Richardson Independent Sch Dist 1970-72;2nd-6th Grade Teacher St Charles City Schls 1973-81; 3rd Grade Teacher Extended Learning G/T Humble Independent Sch Dist 1981-; *ai:* Participating/Promoting Formation Young'Authors Prgms; Intnl Rdng Assn 1984-; TX St Cncl IRA 1981- Honor Teacher 1988; Great Er Houston Area Rdng Cncl IRA VP 1990 Teaching Grant 1987; Delta Kappa Gamma Society Intnl 1987-; *office:* Timbers Elem Sch 6910 Lonesome Woods Trls Humble TX 77346

MARSHALL, DANE HAMMONS, Mathematics Teacher; *b:* Monroe, LA; *m:* William Cook; *c:* Melanie, Melissa; *ed:* (BSED) Math, 1969, (MED) Math 1974, (EDS) Math 1982 Univ of GA; *cr:* Teacher Oconee Cty HS 1974; Evening Class Teacher Univ of GA 1989; *ai:* Acad Bowl & Math Team Spon; Sr Beta Co-Spon; NCTM, GCTM, Delta Kappa Gamma; EPOCHS Secy 1986-; STAR Teacher 1979, 1983-87; GA Textile Ed Fnd Seminar; 10th Dist HS Math Teacher of Yr; Ger-Amer Teacher Exchange Prgm; *office:* Oconee Cty HS PO Box 534 Watkinsville GA 30677

MARSHALL, DELORES NICHOLS, Second Grade Teacher; *b:* Philadelphia, PA; *M:* Thomas J. Jr.; *c:* Clifton A.; *ed:* (BS) Home Ec, Drexel Univ 1954; Elem Ed, Temple Univ 1956-62; *cr:* 5th Grade Teacher Pratt Arnold Sch 1954-55; 2nd/3rd Grade Teacher William Dick Sch 1955-56/1958-64; 1st/2nd Grade Teacher John Story Jenks Sch 1964-; *ai:* Creative Dramatics John Story Jenks Sch; Home & Sch Assn 1964-; Janes United Meth Church Drama Group Spon 1988-; *office:* John Story Jenks Sch Southampton & Germantown Aves Philadelphia PA 19118

MARSHALL, DONALD KENNETH, Drama & Speech Teacher; *b:* Painesville, OH; *ed:* (BA) Poly Sci, Hiram Coll 1962; (MA) Curr/Soc Sci, Columbia Univ 1967; CA St Fullerton & UCI; *cr:* Teacher/Film Make Buckeye Schls 1962-67; MGM Teacher Garden Grove 1968; GATE/Drama Teacher Tustin Schls 1969-; *ai:* Drama; Grant & Curr Writing Comms; Mentor Teacher; Fine Arts Coordinating Cncl; TEA, OTA, NEA Building Rep 1975, 1978, 1968-; John Hopkins Univ Center for Advancement Academically Talented Youth SDB Recognition Prgm Awd 1990; *office:* Hewes Mid Sch 300 South C Street Tustin CA 92680

MARSHALL, DOROTHY MARIE, Sixth Grade Teacher; *b:* Noble, KY; *ed:* (BA) Ed/His, 1969, (MA) Ed/His, 1975, Elem Endorsement Classroom Teaching, 1975 E KY Univ; *cr:* Teacher Caney Consolidated Sch 1969-85, Marie Roberts Elem 1985-; *ai:* KY Ed Assn, Upper KY River Ed Assn; Jackson Womans Club Press Book Chm 1988-, Press Book St Champion 1989; *home:* Box 251 Jackson KY 41339

MARSHALL, GLORIA J. (BENNETT), 7th/8th Grade Eng/Rdng Teacher; *b:* Viola, WI; *m:* John W.; *c:* Annette Sebranek, John W. Jr., Maureen Swingle, Georgia Bursack, Gloria Dregne, Barbara, Rosemary Dregne, Patrick, Paul; *ed:* Elem Ed, Richland Teachers Coll 1948; (BS) Elem Ed, Univ of WI Platteville 1971; Grad Level Elem Ed, Univ of WI Platteville; *cr:* 1st-8th Grade Elem Teacher Lower Camp Creek 1948-54; Rdng Teacher Kickapoo Area Schls 1967-72; 3rd Grade Teacher Kickapoo Elem Sch; 7th/8th Grade Teacher Kickapoo Jr HS 1973-; *ai:* Jr HS Class Adv; Kickapoo Teachers Assn 1967-; Hidden Valley Rdng Cncl 1986-; Viola United Meth Church Sunday Sch Teacher 1950-; Sylvan United Meth Church Sunday Sch Supt 1980; Richland Cty 4-H Clubs Leader 1960-78; Sylvan Skyliners 4-H Club (Leader, Pres 1966); Vernon Cty Land Conservation Awd 1977, 1982; Richland Cty Land Conservation Awd 1984; Help Local Author Edit & Publish Book 1989; *home:* R 2 Box 141 Viola WI 54664

MARSHALL, IDA DEGRAFINRIED, Language Arts Teacher; *b:* Mason, TN; *m:* Frank Lewis; *c:* Frakeetta L., Faith L.; *ed:* (BA) Elem Ed, Lane Coll 1974; (MS) Educl Admin/Supervision, Memphis St Univ 1989; *cr:* Teacher Northwest Elem Sch 1974-; *ai:* 8th Grade Adv; Non-Paid Asst Prin; Chrldr Coach; NEA, TN Ed Assn, Fayette Cty Ed Assn, Kappa Delta Pi; St Bd of Regents Grad Minority Schlsp 1987-89; *office:* Northwest Elem Schl Rt 1 Box 10-C Mason TN 38049

MARSHALL, JACQUELYN WARD, Biology Teacher; *b:* Akron, OH; *m:* W. Earl III; *c:* Daun Marshall Cioban, Laurie Marsahll Jackson, Tonda Marshall Watson; *ed:* (BS) Bio, Mercer Univ 1950; Grad Work; *cr:* Bio Teacher Perry HS 1958-69, Westfield Schls 1970-; *ai:* Debate Team Coach; Literary Act Coord; Sr Class Spon; Natl Teachers Organization 1958-; NSTA 1985-; Tawasi Club Pres; City of Perry Bicentennial Comm; Perry United Meth Church (United Meth Women, Church Choir); STAR Teacher Five Different Yrs; Academic STAR Stu; Teachers Awd WPTA 1988; *home:* 815 Keith Dr Perry GA 31069

MARSHALL, KEVIN KARR, Science/Health Teacher; *b:* Hutchinson, KS; *m:* Debra Gay Gerber; *c:* Tyler C.; *ed:* (BS) Ed, 1985, (MA) Ed, Univ of CO; *cr:* Substitute Teacher Sch Dist #11 1984-85; Math/Sci/Health Teacher Washington Irving Jr HS 1985-; *ai:* Golf Coach; Sci Club Spon; Sci Olympiad Coach/Spon; Talent Show Spon; NEA, CEA, CSEA 1985-; NSTA, CSTA

1985-86; *office:* Washington Irving Jr HS 1702 N Murray Blvd Colorado Springs CO 80915

MARSHALL, OSIE ROBERSON, Fourth Grade Teacher; *b:* Longstreet, LA; *m:* Lewis James; *c:* Connie J. Smith, Bonnie J. Berry, James D.; *ed:* (BA) Elem Ed, TX Coll 1950; Elem Ed, Grambling St Univ; TX S Univ, Northwestern St Univ, Stephen F Austin St Univ; *cr:* Teacher Holly Elem 1950-53; Teacher/Coach Marion Anderson HS 1954-55; Teacher Johnson Elem 1966-68, Mansfield Elem 1968-79, Logansport Rosenwald Elem 1979-; *ai:* Sci Fair Comm Mem; De Soto Ed Assn, LA Ed Assn, NEA 1966-; LA PTA 1981-, Distinguished Membership Scroll 1989; Outstanding De Soto Parish Educator Plaque 1985-86; *home:* PO Box 86 Joaquin TX 75954

MARSHALL, RICHARD LEE, History Teacher; *b:* Seymour, IN; *m:* Paula Rebecca Rudd; *c:* Danielle, Laura; *ed:* (BA) Religion, Southern Coll of 7th Day Adv 1977; Working Towards Master of Arts Teaching; *cr:* 6th Grade Teacher Sligo Elem Sch 1978-82; Prin/Teacher Claremore 7th Day Adv Elem Sch 1982-85; Teacher/Vice Prin Sligo Elem Sch 1985-87; His Teacher Tulsa Adventist Acad 1987-; *ai:* Jr Class & Stu Assn Spon; Bsktbl Coach; *home:* 112 Riverbend Dr Claremore OK 74017

MARSHALL, RUBY J. BENNEFIELD-SMITH, Science Teacher; *b:* Birmingham, AL; *m:* Oliver Jr.; *c:* Robbin K. Marshall Williams, Carol J.; *ed:* (BS) Bio/Comprehensive Scis, Wilberforce Univ 1961; (MA) Educl Theory/Supervision, Rutgers Univ 1983; K-8th Grade Cert Courses, Glassboro St Coll 1962-65; Phys Sci, Boston Univ 1982-83; Environmental Courses, Montclair St Coll 1976; Numerouse In-Services; *cr:* Teacher Samuel Miller Sch 1961-64, Hattie Britt & Parkway Sch 1965-70; EOF Sci Instr Rutgers Univ 1982-89; Sci Teacher William W Allen III Mid Sch 1970-; *ai:* Creative Play Directing; Ecology Field Trip Supvr & Organizer; Elocution; Singing; Sewing; Quilting; Gardening; Zurbrugg Hospital Volunteer; NEA, NJ Ed Assn, Moorestown Ed Assn, NJ Sci Teachers Assn, Natl Assn of Bio Sci Teachers, Sigma Omega, Kappa Delta Pi; Rutgers Univ Alumni 1984-; Wilberforce Univ Alumni 1961-; *home:* 603 Flynn Ave Moorestown NJ 08057

MARSHALL, SHIRLEY HOWELL, Third Grade Teacher; *b:* Irondale, OH; *m:* William L.; *c:* Cindy, Mark, Kristine; *ed:* Assoc General Stud, 1974, (BS) Elem Ed, 1975 Kent St Univ; (MS) Elem Ed, Univ of Dayton 1986; *cr:* Teacher Calcutta Beaver Local Sch 1976-; *ai:* Spelling & Testing Comm; PTO VP 1979-81; BLEA 1976-; BPW 1986-89; St Clair Civic 1990; *office:* Calcutta Beaver Local Sch St Rt 170 Calcutta OH 43920

MARSHALL, TERESA FLAUGHER, Biology Teacher; *b:* Ashland, KY; *m:* Mitchell I.; *ed:* (BS) Bio, 1983, (MA) Ed, 1986 Morehead St Univ; *cr:* Bio Teacher East Carter HS 1983-; *ai:* NEA 1983-; Nominee Ashland Oil Teacher Achievement Awd 1989-; *home:* PO Box 477 Grayson KY 41143

MARSHALL, THOMAS A., Student Services Director; *b:* Beaver Dam, WI; *m:* Joanne Scott; *c:* Jennifer, Christopher, Benjamin; *ed:* (BS) Ed, 1964, (MS) Ed, 1968 Univ of WI La Crosse; (PHD) Counseling, Univ of WY 1972; *cr:* Phys Ed Teacher Stevens Point Schls 1964-65; Asst Dir Admissions Univ of WI La Crosse 1966-68, Univ of WI Milwaukee 1968-70; Stu Services Dir Lincoln HS 1972-; *ai:* WI Sch Cnslrs Assn 1980-; Rotary Pres 1977-, Paul Harris Awd 1988; United Way Pres 1979-80; YMCA Bd Mem 1982-; South Wood Cty Citizen of Yr 1982; *office:* Lincoln HS 1801 16th St S Wisconsin Rapids WI 54494

MARSHALL, THOMAS ROBERT, Mathematics Department Teacher; *b:* Grosse Pointe Farm, MI; *m:* Kathryn U.; *c:* Elizabeth A., Rebecca L.; *ed:* (BS) Ec/Bus Admin, Cntrl MI Univ 1968; Cert Elem Ed/Soc Sci, 1971, (MA) Ec, 1975 Wayne St Univ; *cr:* 6th Grade Teacher 1968-80, 7th/8th Grade Teachers 1981- Marysville Public Schls; *ai:* 8th Grad Boys Track Coach; Math Coach MCTM Competition; Ec Instr St Clair Cty Comm Coll Bus Dept; Marysville Ed Assn (Treas 1971-73, Building Rep 1975-77, Regional Rep 1980-83); St Clair Cty Ec Dev Corporation (Pres 1978-81, Treas 1981-); *office:* Marysville Intermediate Sch 400 Stadium Dr Marysville MI 48040

MARSHALL, VICTORIA (ADDISON), Mathematics Teacher; *b:* E St Louis, IL; *m:* David Hamman; *c:* Ryan, Jeff; *ed:* (BS) Math, S IL Univ Carbondale 1973; (MA) Math, E IL Univ 1987; Ed/Math N IL Univ & Univ of IL; *cr:* Math Teacher Marquette HS 1974-80, Richland Comm Coll 1982, Mt Zion HS 1982-; *ai:* Jr Var Scholastic Bowl Coach; Math Team Head Coach; JETS Team Spon; IL Cncl of Teachers of Math 1982-; NCTM 1988-89; First Baptist Church of Mt Zion; First Baptist Churches of Dupot Bethalto (Youth Choir Dir, Church Pianist, Sunday Sch Teacher, Vacation Bible Sch Dir & Bible Drill Dir) 1987-; Song Published 1983; Article Published 1988; *office:* Mt Zion HS 305 S Henderson Mount Zion IL 62549

MARSHALL, WILBUR LANE, Counselor; *b:* Chicago, IL; *m:* Lillian John; *c:* Kenneth, Susan; *ed:* (BA) Ed, Sacramento St Coll 1957; (MA) Soc Sci, Univ of Pacific 1962; Pupil Personnel Credential, St Univ Stanislaus; *cr:* Teacher 1957-66, Cnslr 1966-69, Teacher 1969-89, Cnslr 1990 Turlock Sch Dist; *ai:* Stu Cncl Adv; Phi Delta Kappa 1962-68; *home:* 2145 Hawkeye Ave Turlock CA 95380

MARSKE, KAY MERRETTE (DETLEFSEN), Third Grade Teacher; *b:* Clinton, IA; *m:* Herbert W.; *c:* Tal, Eric, Tim; *ed:* (BA) Elem Ed, Marycrest Coll 1974; *cr:* 1st Grade Teacher Durant Cmmty Sch 1957-61, Fort Campbell KY Base Sch 1961-62; 3rd Grade Teacher Bettendorf Cmmty Sch 1976-; *ai:* Bettendorf Ed Assn, NEA, IA St Ed Assn 1976-; Jr League of Quad Cities.

MARSOUN, WILLIAM J., JR., Mathematics Teacher; *b:* Moline, IL; *m:* Cathy Mc Niel; *c:* Elizabeth, Richard; *ed:* (BS) Math, IL St 1969; *cr:* Math Teacher Washington Jr HS 1969-; *ai:* Cmptrs; Quad City Music Build TEC Dir 1970-88, Quad City Music Guild Hall of Honor 1988.

MARTEL, PAUL R., Spanish/French Teacher; *b:* Fall River, MA; *ed:* (BA) Fr/Scndry Ed, SE MA Univ 1972; (MA) Fr Lit, Univ of RI 1976; *cr:* Foreign Lang/Eng Teacher Fall River MA Public Schls 1972-; *ai:* NEA, MTA 1972-; Club Richelieu (Treas, Secy) 1978-; Big Brothers/Sisters of Fall River (Bd of Dirs, Big Brothers) 1974-; MA Archaeological Assn 1988-; Earthwatch/ Mustard Seed Fnd Grant Mallorca Spain 1989; *office:* Morton Mid Sch 376 President Ave Fall River MA 02720

MARTENS-ROSENBOOM, MARCIA A., Eng/Speech/ Drama/TAG Teacher; *b:* Sheldon, IA; *m:* Joel Arthur; *ed:* (BA) Philosophy/Drama, 1975, (MA) Eng, 1984 Augustana Coll Sioux Falls; Teaching Higher Order Thinking Skills, NW IA Technical Coll; Talented & Gifted Seminar, IA City & Des Moines; Talented & Gifted Credit Hours Augustana 1989; *cr:* Eng Teacher Paullina Cmmty Sch 1975-76; Journalist Lyon Cty Reporter 1977-78; Eng/ Speech/Drama Teacher George Cmmty Sch 1979-; *ai:* Large Group & Individual Contest Speech; HS Plays; Jr Class, Stu Cncl, Drama Club Spon; NCTE, IA Cncl Teacher of Eng, NEA, ISEA, GEA; Certified IA Speech Assn Judge; Tomorrows Leaders Today 1989-;George Cmmty Dev Bd of Dir 1990; Lyon Cty Democrats (Secy, Dir) 1990; Teaching Shakespeare Inst Through the Folger Shakespeare Lib; *office:* George Little Rock Cmmty Sch 500 E Indiana Ave George IA 51237

MARTIN, ALLAN DAVID, Music Teacher; *b:* Casablanca, Morrocco; *ed:* (BMUS) Music Ed, Univ of Cincinnati 1975; (MED) Music Ed, Xavier Univ 1989; *cr:* Music Teacher Norwood Jr HS 1975-87, Xenia HS 1987-89, Norwood Mid Sch 1989-; Choirmaster/Organist 7th Presbyn Church 1976-; *ai:* Music Dir Annual Sch Stage Musical; Accompanist of HS Show Choir; HS Stage Musical; Bell Choir Dir Mid Sch; NEA, OH Ed Assn, Music Ed Natl Conference, OH Music Ed Assn 1975-; *office:* Norwood Mid Sch 2060 Sherman Ave Norwood OH 45212

MARTIN, AMMIE G., Third Grade Chapter I Teacher; *b:* Martinsville, VA; *m:* Billy D. Sr.; *c:* Billy Jr., Robin; *ed:* (BS) Elem Ed, Winston Salem St Univ 1959; Working on Cert Rdng Specialist; Grad Stud Univ of VA, Radford Univ, VA Tech; *cr:* 2nd Grade Teacher East Martinsville Sch 1961-62, Leatherwood Elem Sch 1963-64; Remedial Rdng Teacher Machias Elem Sch 1964-67; 1st Grade Teacher Lee Waid Elem Sch 1967-88; Chapter I Teacher Rocky Mt Elem 1988-; *ai:* FCEA, VEA, NEA; *home:* 619 Parkview Martinsville VA 24112

MARTIN, ANDREA MAE, 4th Grade Teacher; *b:* Taylorsville, MS; *m:* Robert; *c:* Gloria Gammage, Alesia Gammage, Carlos, Robert Jr., Veronica E.; *ed:* (BS) Elem Ed, Alcorn St Univ 1965; Working Toward Masters Univ Southern & William Carey; *ai:* Jones Cty Assn Educators (Building Rep, Membership) 1987; Alcorn St Alumni Club Secy, Alcornite of Yr 1985, 1987; AEE Mem.

MARTIN, ANITA PENDRY, Fifth Grade Teacher; *b:* Glen Morrison, WV; *m:* Robert George; *c:* Kimberly Martin Jackson; *ed:* (BS) Elem Ed, Bluefield St Coll 1974; Various Courses VA Tech, Lynchburg Coll, SW VA Comm Coll, WV Coll of Grad Stud; Extension Classes Univ of VA, Condord Coll; *cr:* Secy/Bookkeeper Pineville Furniture Company 1953-55; Secy Coppinger Machinery Service 1955-59, Mutual Insurance Agency 1965-69; 5th Grade Teacher Falls Mills Elem 1974-89; *ai:* PTA Cultural Arts Chm; 4-H Club Leader; NEA, VA Ed Assn 1974-89; Tazewell Cty Ed Assn Building Rep 1974-79; United Meth Women Circle Leader; Bluefield Trillium Garden Club Pres 1969-71; Outstanding Young Women in America; Grant from VA Commission of Arts Falls Mills Elem; Grant to Study Appalachian Folk Culture VPI; *home:* 1312 Montclair St Bluefield WV 24701

MARTIN, BLANDIE J. STEWART, Teacher; *b:* Panama City, FL; *m:* Donald L. Sr.; *c:* Donald L.; *ed:* (BA) Elem Ed, Univ of W FL 1976; Early Chldhd Dyslexic Trng; *cr:* Teacher St Paul Sch 1982-; *ai:* Mem Sch Bd 1989-; Orton Dyslexia Society Mem 1989-; PTA Pres 1989-; *office:* St Paul Cath Sch 2609 Park St Jacksonville FL 32205

MARTIN, BOBBY GENE, Math Dept Chair/Asst Prin; *b:* Sharp, LA; *m:* Gwen; *c:* Robert, Kyle, Kristi; *ed:* (BS) Math, 1953, (MED) Ed, 1960 Sam Houston Univ; Univ of TX, TX Tech, Lamar Univ; *cr:* Teacher Honey Island HS 1953-54, Aldine HS 1956-57, Silsbee HS 1957-63; Teacher/Prin/Asst Prin Warren HS 1963-; *ai:* Beta Club Spon; Sch Dist Management Team Mem; Sch Bus Driver; TSTA Life Mem 1964-; Tyler Cty Teachers Assn (Pres, VP) 1968-69; Warren Ed Assn (Treas, VP, Pres) 1964-; Warren Church of Christ Bible Class Teacher; Warren Lions Club Charter Mem; Democratic Party Precinct Chm; Natl Sci Fnd Grants Univ of TX 1957, 1963; *home:* Rt 2 Box 1390 Warren TX 77664

MARTIN, BRUCE EDWARD, Business Education Teacher; *b:* Berea, OH; *m:* Pamela Lynn Arbaugh; *c:* Brittanie, Tara, Elise; *ed:* (BA) Bus Admin, Adrian Coll 1974; *cr:* 7th/8th Grade Math Teacher 1974-78, Bus Ed/Bus Law/Accounting/General Bus Teacher 1978- W Holmes Jr HS; *ai:* Head Boys Bsktbl Coach; Bsbl & Sftbl Umpire; W Holmes Ed Assn, OH HS Coaches Assn, Wayne Cty Ofcls Assn; *home:* 9 Fairview Millersburg OH 44654

MARTIN, CANDYE PATRICIA, 8th Grade Earth Sci Teacher; *b:* Delhi, LA; *ed:* (BS) Scndry Ed Bio, 1971; (MED) Scndry Ed Bio, 1976 Lamar Univ; *cr:* Bio Teacher L W Higgins HS 1971-74; John Ehret HS 1974-75; 7th Grade Math Teacher 1975-77; 8th Grade Earth Sci Teacher 1977- Henderson Jr HS; *ai:* UIL Sci Competition Spon; Dist Career Ladder Comm; NSTA 1985-; TX Sci Teachers Assn 1983-; Phi Kappa Phi 1971-; *office:* Henderson Jr H S PO Box 278 China TX 77613

MARTIN, CAROL LOUISE, Health/Physical Ed Teacher; *b:* New Kensington, PA; *ed:* (BS) Health/Phys Ed, Slippery Rock St Coll 1974; *cr:* Health/Phys Ed Teacher Shaler Area Sch Dist 1974-; *ai:* Sr HS Vlybl, Jr HS Sftbl Coach; AAHPER; PA Vlybl Coaches Assn 1988-; Gift of Time Tribute Amer Family Inst; *office:* Shaler Area HS 381 Wible Run Rd Pittsburgh PA 15209

MARTIN, CATHERINE ROBERTS, Principal; *b:* Little Rock, AR; *m:* Tommy Lee; *c:* Hunter, Melissa, Ashley; *ed:* (BSE) Elem Ed, Henderson St Univ 1970; Admin, Univ of AR Little Rock; *cr:* Elem Teacher Little Rock Public Schls 1970-72, Stuttgart Public Schls 1972-85; Prin Holy Rosary Cath Sch 1985-87; Teacher 1987-89, Prin 1989- Immaculate Heart of Mary; *ai:* NCEA 1985-; AR Non-Public Sch Accreditation Assn 1989-; Beta Sigma Phi (Pres, VP, Secy, Treas) 1973-; GSA Asst Leader; Parish Cncl; Teacher of Yr Stuttgart AR Public Schls; *office:* Immaculate Heart of Mary Sch Rt 9 Box 2-244 North Little Rock AR 72118

MARTIN, CATHERINE VERGE, Computer Teacher; *b:* Newfoundland, Canada; *m:* Gary Ray; *ed:* (BA) Bus Admin/Ec, CA St Univ San Bernardino 1984; Drug Abuse Intervention Facilitator; *cr:* Math Teacher Golden Valley Mid Sch 1986; Math Teacher 1986-87, Cmptr Literacy Teacher 1987-, Stu Government/Publications Teacher 1988- Arrowview Mid Sch; *ai:* After Sch Act Coord & Photographer; Sch Yrbk Coord; CA St Univ San Bernardino Intern Selection Panel 1988-; San Bernardino Chamber of Commerce Outstanding Teacher Awd 1989; Kiwanis Club Teacher Achievement Awd 1989; CA St Univ San Bernardino Most Outstanding Graduating Sr in Finance Schlsp Grant 1985; *office:* Arrowview Mid Sch 2299 North G Street San Bernardino CA 92405

MARTIN, DAVID H., 5th/6th Grade Teacher; *b:* Fort Wayne, IN; *m:* Catherine Hein; *c:* Becky, Seth; *ed:* (BA) His, Hanover Coll 1965; (MS) Ed, IN Univ 1970; *cr:* 6th/7th Grade Teacher Ogilville Sch 1965-68; 5th/6th Grade Teacher Jackson Sch 1968-71, Rockcreek Sch 1971-73, Lincoln Elem Sch 1973-; *ai:* Rdng Games & Awds Prgm Chm; Columbus Educators Assn, IN St Teachers Assn, NEA; Brown Cty Public Lib Bd Secy 1987-; Brown Cty Mid Sch Building Corporation Secy 1980-; BSA Troop Comm Chm 1985-; Artists Colony Assn Pres 1988-; Brown Cty Chamber of Commerce 1989-; Brown Cty Art Guild 1982-; Allen Cty Fort Wayne Historical Society 1961-; *home:* RR 3 Box 76 Nashville IN 47448

MARTIN, DEBRA GOLEY, Guidance Counselor; *b:* Covington, KY; *m:* David Wayne; *c:* Erin, Lauren, Caitlin; *ed:* (BS) Bio/ Chem, 1976, (MAED) Ed, 1980 N KY Univ; (Rank I) Counseling, Xavier Univ 1988; *cr:* 7th-12th Grade Sci Teacher Williamstown Jr/Sr HS 1976-78; Teacher Ockerman Jr HS 1978-79; Teacher 1979-88, Guidance Cnslr 1988- R A Jones Jr HS; *ai:* 7th-9th Grade Chrldrs Spon; Vlybl Coach; Start Project Coord; Sci Dept Chairperson; NSTA, N KY Assn for Counseling Dev, NEA, NACD; Whos Who in Sci Teachers; Nom for KY Sci Teacher Awd; *office:* R A Jones Jr HS 8000 Spruce Dr Florence KY 41042

MARTIN, DENISE MARIE (BLAZEK), Principal; *b:* Uniontown, PA; *m:* Jeffrey V.; *c:* Christopher, Jesse; *ed:* (BS) Scndry Math Ed, CAlifornia Univ of PA 1973; (MA) Ed Admin, 1976, (EDD) Ed Admin, 1983 WV Univ; Alcohol & Drug Wkshp; *cr:* Jr HS Math Teacher Randolph Jr HS 1973; Math Teacher 1973-77, Math/Cmptr Sci Teacher German Jr HS 1986-77, Fa irchance Jr/Sr HS 1986-87; Math/Cmptr Sci Teacher Tri-Valley Sr HS 1987-; *ai:* Coach Head Sftbl 1975-79 & Asst Bsktbl 1974-78; Math Comm 1987-89; NHS Spon; Phi Delta Kappa 1984-; WV Alumni Assn Past VP 1985-86; NAASP 1989-; PA St Ed Assn 1973-; Published Article 1986; *office:* Tri Valley North Jr HS Box 100 Mc Clellandtown PA 15458

MARTIN, DENNIS JOHN, English/History/Gifted Teacher; *b:* Cincinnati, OH; *m:* Janet V.; *c:* Scott A., Trent A.; *ed:* (BS) His, 1969, (MED) Soc Stud, 1973 Xavier Univ; *cr:* 7th/8th Grade Teacher St Martins Elem 1968-70; 7th-12th Grade Teacher Finneytown HS 1970-; *ai:* Var Mens Bsktbl & Var Womens Sftbl Coach; NCTE, OH HS Bsktbl Coaches Assn, NEA, OEA, FEA; *office:* Finneytown HS 8916 Fountainbleu Terr Cincinnati OH 45231

MARTIN, DONNA, Social Studies Teacher; *b:* Pittsburgh, PA; *m:* Paul L.; *ed:* (BS) Scndry Ed/Soc Stud, Univ of Slippery Rock 1967-71; (MS) Cmmty Ed/Counseling Services, Duquesne Univ 1990; *cr:* Teacher St Leo 1973-; *ai:* Project Bus Jr Achievement; Catechetics-Confirmation; Deanery Enrichment Project Rep; Natl Geography Society.

MARTIN, DONNA RUSHING, English Teacher; *b:* Winnsboro, LA; *m:* Wayne; *c:* Scott; *ed:* (BA) Eng, 1976, (MED) Eng, 1983 NE LA Univ; Trained to Be Assessor in New LA St STAR Cert Prgm as Master Teacher; *cr:* Teacher Crowville HS 1976-; *ai:* Annual Staff Spon; *office:* Crowville HS P O Box 128 Crowville LA 71230

MARTIN, DONNA WOLFE, DCT Coordinator; *b:* Ramsey, IN; *m:* Gary R.; *c:* Jeffrey, Robert; *ed:* (BA) Bus Ed, Harding Univ 1971; *cr:* Diversified Cooperative Trng Teacher/Coord Newberry HS 1988-; *ai:* Club Adv Cooperative Ed Clubs of FL; Diversified Cooperative Trng Assn of FL, Alachua Cty Bus Ed Assn, Alachua Cty Voc Assn; *office:* Newberry HS P O Box 339 Newberry FL 32669

MARTIN, DOROTHY AYERS, Business Education Teacher; *b:* Billingsley, AL; *m:* Curley L.; *c:* Felicia Walker; *ed:* (BA) Bus Ed, Stillman Coll 1967; (MA) Bus Ed, Univ of AL 1974; Class AA Cert Univ of AL 1980; *cr:* Bus Ed Teacher, West Blocton HS 1967-; *ai:* Sch Newspaper and Yrbk Spon; Bibb Cty Prof Dev Comm; BCEA Retirement Comm; Admin Evaluation Dev Comm; NEA (Mem 1967-;) AL Ed Assn (Mem 1967-;) Delta Phi Epsilon (Treas 1980-82:) Zeta Phi Beta Sorority Corresp Sec 89-; Weeping Mary Bapt Church Mem 1981-; JLS Gospel Choir Treas 1981-; 1987 Nom Teacher Hall of Fame; *office:* West Blocton H S P O Box 218 West Blocton AL 35184

MARTIN, ELLEN C., English Department Chairman; *b:* Brookhaven, MS; *m:* Bobby R.; *c:* Jim, Buck, Dehna; *ed:* (BA) Eng, MS Univ for Women 1963; (MED) Sch Counseling, Univ of Southern MS 1990; Advanced Work Southern Lit Ms Coll & Southern Ms; *cr:* Eng Teacher West Jr HS 1963-68, Brookhaven Acad 1972-; *ai:* Adv for Stu Cncl, Yrbk, Sch Newspaper & Drama Club; Phi Kappa Delta; NCTE; Amer Society of Curr Dev; ASCA; NASSP; Mortar Board Society; Amer Psychological Assn; Outstanding Young Educator CO 1964; Star Teacher MS Economic Cncl 1972-85; *office:* Brookhaven Academy P O Box 946 Brookhaven MS 39601

MARTIN, ELLEN K., Biology Teacher; *b:* Lebanon, MO; *c:* Erica, Robert, Bond, Colleen; *ed:* (BS) Ed, SW MO St Univ 1982; (MED) Ed, Drury Coll 1989; *cr:* Sci Teacher Lebanon Jr HS 1983-; *ai:* Bio Club Spon; Outdoor Classman Comm; Lebanon Ed Assn Building Rep 1983-; SB 40 Bd 1986; Laclede Early Ed Bd 1988-; Boswell Grant 1986, 1988; *office:* Lebanon Jr HS 500 N Adams St Lebanon MO 65536

MARTIN, FRANKIE G., Asst Principal/Bus Teacher; *b:* Pampa, TX; *m:* Thomas E.; *c:* Stan, Dan; *ed:* (BS) Bus Ed, Univ of OK 1973; (MS) Scndry Admin, Univ of OK 190; Prin Cert; Certified Gymnastic Coach; *cr:* Administrative Secy Cleveland Co Health Dept 1964-73; Bus Teacher 1973-, Asst Prin 1987- Wayne HS; *ai:* NHS, Gifted & Talented Adv; Challenge Bowl & Cheerleader Coach; OEA 1973-; US Gymnastic Fed Coach 1980-88; St Timothys Episcopal Church Mem; Mc Clain Cty Teacher of Yr 1981; *office:* Wayne HS P O Box 40 Wayne OK 73095

MARTIN, GAE VONNE RUE, Fifth Grade Teacher; *b:* Ada, OK; *c:* Todd A., Ashley D.; *ed:* (BS) Elem Ed, 1977, (MS) Rdng Specialist Ed, 1982 E Cntrl Univ; Summer Foreign Lang Inst, OK Univ 1988; *cr:* 5th Grade Teacher Hayes Elem 1978-; *ai:* OK Ed Assn, NEA 1978-; NCTE 1985-86; *office:* Hayes Elem Sch 500 S Mississippi Ada OK 74820

MARTIN, GARY JAMES, Language Arts Instructor; *b:* East Tawas, MI; *ed:* (BA) Soc Sci, 1974; (MA) Elem Ed, 1980; (MA) Educl Systems Dev, 1983 MI St Univ; *cr:* HS Teacher 1974-79; 3rd Grade Teacher 1979-80; Mid Sch Teacher 1980- Brighton Area Schls; *ai:* Gifted Ed Advisory Comm; Brighton Ed Assn; MI Ed Assn; Teacher of Yr Nom 1986.

MARTIN, H. LE ROY, Elem Phys Ed/Music Teacher; *b:* Boulder, CO; *m:* Carolyn K.; *c:* David L.; *ed:* (BA) Music Ed, Univ of CO 1972; (MA) Creative Art, Lesley Coll 1989; Grad Stud Phys Ed; *cr:* K-12th Grade Music Teacher Ellicott Sch Dist 22 1972-86; K-6th Grade iusic Teacher Ellicott Elem 1986-; *ai:* Jr HS Bsktbl; Jr Var Bsktbl; Playground Comm; CAPERD 1988-; *office:* Ellicott Elem Sch 350 S Ellicott Hwy Calhan CO 80808

MARTIN, H. NOREEN MILLS, Social Studies Chairperson; *b:* New Brunswick, NJ; *m:* Keith A.; *ed:* (BA) Amer Stud/Poly Sci, Marist Coll 1980; (MS) Geography/Ed, SUNY New Paltz 1986; Post Grad Work Toward Prof Masters in Admin & Supervision, Fordham Univ; *cr:* Soc Stud Teacher Wappingers Cntrl Sch Dist 1980-81, 1982-84; Soc Stud Teacher/Chairperson Bulkley Sch 1981-82; Soc Stud Teacher Arlington Cntrl Sch Dist 1984-85; Soc Stud Chairperson Holy Trinity Sch 1985-; *ai:* Yrbk Adv; 7th Grade Act; Soc Stud Chairperson; Prin Assistance; Jr HS Team Leader; Phi Delta Kappa 1989-; City of Poughkeepsie Little League Volunteer 1979-, Service Awd 1989; CYO Adv 1985-, Archdiocesan Service to Youth & Cardinal Cookie Service Awd 1989; Mt Carmel Parish Eucharistic Minister; Skills for Adolescence Cert; Archdiocesan Schlsp Fordham Univ; *office:* Holy Trinity Sch 20 Springside Ave Poughkeepsie NY 12603

MARTIN, IONE, 1st Grade Teacher; *b:* Aurora, IA; *m:* Jerry L.; *c:* Cindy Doherty, Lisa Mort, Scott; *ed:* (BA) Elem Ed, Upper IA Univ 1968; Grad Stud; *cr:* 3rd Grade Teacher Morrow Cty Schls 1965-74; 1st Grade Teacher Hermiston Schls 1976-; *home:* 730 W Highland Hermiston OR 97838

MARTIN, JAMES DAVID, Science Teacher; *b:* San Jose, Costa Rica; *m:* Peggy N.; *c:* Angela, Deanna, Steve; *ed:* (BS) Bio, E Mennonite 1975; *cr:* Sci Teacher Rocky Ford 1975-80, Cheraw 1981-; *ai:* Class of 1990 Spon; *office:* Cheraw 31 HS 110 Lakeview Cheraw CO 81030

MARTIN, JEFFREY JAY, General Music, Band Teacher; *b:* Harrisburg, PA; *m:* Jane Marie Cryder; *ed:* (BM) Instrumental Music, 1977, (MM) Instrumental Music, 1985 AZ St Univ; *cr:* Music Teacher Pomeroy Sch 1979-87, Frost Sch 1987-; *ai:* Band & Chorus Instr; Mesa Ed Assn 1978-; Music Educators Natl Conference 1980-85; *office:* Frost Elem Sch 1560 W Summit Pl Chandler AZ 85224

MARTIN, JOAN THOMPSON, 6th Grade Teacher; *b:* Clifton Forge, VA; *m:* Robert Malcolm; *c:* Robert M., Dawn K.; *ed:* (BS) Ed, James Madison Univ 1954; Grad Stud Univ of VA, Lynchburg Coll; *cr:* Home Ec Teacher Stonewall Jackson Jr HS 1954-55; 6th/7th Grade Teacher Bedford Hills Elem 1958-77; 6th Grade Teacher Dunbar Mid Sch 1977-81; 6th Grade Teacher 1981-84, Staff Dev Specialist 1984- Linkhorne Mid Sch; *ai:* Lynchburg City Schls Rdng & Mid Sch Planning Comms, Planning Cncl; Linkhorne Mid Sch Staff Dev, Stu Cncl, Gifted Comms, Advisory Cncl, 6th Grade Coord; Bedford Hills Elem & Dunbar Mid Unit Leader; Lynchburg Ed Assn, VA Ed Assn, NEA Pres 1974-75; Delta Kappa Gamma Pres 1980-82; ASCD 1953-; Kappa Delta Pi; *home:* 3444 Ivylink Pl Lynchburg VA 24503

MARTIN, JOHN LEWIS, Biology/Chemistry Teacher; *b:* Covington, KY; *m:* Mary Jo Akin; *c:* Molly J., Joshua; *ed:* (BS) Bio, William Carey Coll 1967; (MA) Bio, W KY Univ 1976; *cr:* Teacher Callahan HS 1967-68, Boone Cty Schls 1968-; Teacher/Sci Chm Conner Sr HS 1989-; *ai:* BEST Comm; *office:* Conner Sr HS Box 36 Limaburg Rd Hebron KY 41048

MARTIN, JOLENE HOHENADEL, Mathematics Department Chair; *b:* Lancaster, PA; *m:* John Robert; *c:* Jordan R.; *ed:* (BS) Math Ed, 1971, (MED) Math Ed, 1975 Millersville Univ; Grad Stud Math & Cmptr Sci; *cr:* Math Teacher 1971-84, Math Dept Chairperson 1984- Columbia HS; *ai:* Adv Stu Cncl; Mem NHS Faculty Cncl; Columbia Ed Assn, PA Ed Assn, NEA, Cntrl PA Cncl Teachers of Math, PA Cncl Teachers of Math, NCTM; Pi Lambda Theta; Jaycees Outstanding Young Educator 1982; *office:* Columbia HS 901 Ironville Pike Columbia PA 17512

MARTIN, JOSEPH ANDREW, Social Studies Teacher; *b:* St Marys, PA; *m:* Darcy E. Hanes; *ed:* (BA) His, Alfred Univ 1983; *cr:* Teacher W Seneca Sch System 1983-86, Eric Boces 1 1986-87; Success Teacher Parkdale HS 1987-; *ai:* Ftbl & Track Coach; Class Adv; *home:* 11941 Beltsville Dr Beltsville MD 20705

MARTIN, JUDITH KLEIN, Fifth Grade Teacher; *b:* Newark, NJ; *m:* James; *ed:* (BS) Ed, 1966, (MA) Rdng, 1969 Seton Hall Univ; *cr:* 1st Grade Teacher 1966-69, 2nd Grade Teacher 1969-72, 4th Grade Teacher 1972-86 Woods Road Sch; Triangle Sch 1986-87; 5th Grade Teacher Triangle Sch 1987-; *ai:* Hillsborough Exec Bd 1983-; Ed Assn; Bd of Trustees Hillsborough Public Lib (VP 1990) 1989-; *office:* Triangle Elem Sch 156 Triangle Rd Somerville NJ 08876

MARTIN, JUNE SOPHIA, French/Spanish Teacher; *b:* Buffalo, NY; *ed:* (BA) Fr/Ed, Daemen Coll 1965; (MED) Foreign Lang/Ed, St Univ of NY Buffalo 1976; Summer Sessions Universite Laval Quebec, Universite De Rennes France, Middlebury Coll; *cr:* Fr/Span Teacher/Chairperson of Lang Dept Cardinal O Hara HS 1965-89; Fr/Span Teacher Clarence Jr HS 1989-; *ai:* NY St Fed of Foreign Lang Teachers 1965-; Bishop Head Outstanding Teacher Awd 1978; Elizabeth Ann Seton Outstanding Educator Awd 1988; *home:* 729 West Ave Buffalo NY 14213

MARTIN, KATHY MILANO, English Teacher; *b:* Cleveland, OH; *m:* Timmy W.; *c:* Christopher, Kelly; *ed:* (BA) Eng, W GA Coll 1986; *cr:* Eng Teacher Loganville HS 1986-; *ai:* Beta Club Spon 1987-; Asst Girls Track Coach 1989-; One Act Play Dir 1989-; Teacher of Yr 1986-89; *office:* Loganville HS 150 Clark Mc Cullers Dr Loganville GA 30249

MARTIN, LAWRENCE CLYDE, Physical Education Instructor; *b:* Urbana, IL; *m:* Patricia Rogers; *c:* Michael R.; *ed:* (BA) Phys Ed, W IL Univ 1968; (MS) Phys Ed, N IL Univ 1972; *cr:* Instr Grayslake Cmmty HS 1968-; *ai:* SADD Adv; Asst Ftbl Coach; Var Bsbl Coach; Driver Ed Supvr; IAHPER, IDEA, IHSBCA; Amer Red Cross Instr; *office:* Grayslake Cmmty HS 400 N Lake St Grayslake IL 60030

MARTIN, LINDA DOWDY, 3rd Grade Teacher; *b:* Pontotoc, MS; *m:* Bennie J.; *c:* Michael J,; *ed:* (BS) Elem Ed, Blue Mountain Coll 1970; (MA) Elem Ed, Univ of MS 1976; *cr:* 1st/3rd Grade Teacher 1970-71, 3rd Grade Teacher 1970-71 Ecru HS; 3rd Grade Teacher North Pontotoc Attn Center 1971-; *ai:* MAE, Delta Kappa Gamm, PTO; Harmony Baptist Church Sunday Sch Teacher Youth Leader; Selected Outstanding Elem Teacher of America 1974; *home:* Rt 6 Box 381 Pontotoc MS 38863

MARTIN, LINDA FLEENOR, Fourth Grade Teacher; *b:* Tuscaloosa, AL; *m:* Sidney Franklin; *c:* Katherine L.; *ed:* (BS) Elem Ed, 1974, (MA) Elem Ed, 1976 Univ of AL; *cr:* 4th Grade Teacher Holt Elem 1974-; *ai:* Mastery Math Learning; Citizenship; Soc Stud Fair; Disicpline Comm; Dropout Prevention; Honors Day Prgm; AL Ed Assn, NEA, Tuscaloosa Cty Ed Assn 1974-; *office:* Holt Elem Sch 1001 Crescent Ridge Rd Tuscaloosa AL 35404

MARTIN, LINDA LACKEY, Third Grade Teacher; *b:* Martinsville, VA; *m:* Robert Price; *c:* Kristin, Heather; *ed:* (BS) Elem Ed, VA Commonwealth Univ 1969; *cr:* 3rd Grade Teacher Figsboro Elem 1969-76, Mt Olivet 1977-; *ai:* Family Life, Comptr Comm; 3rd Grade Rep; Delta Kappa Gamma 1985-; NEA 1969-; *home:* Rt 7 Box 380 Martinsville VA 24112

MARTIN, LISA SPENCER, English Teacher; *b:* Stuart, VA; *m:* Adam Laughton; *c:* Alexander; *ed:* (BA) Eng, Longwood Coll 1983; Grad Stud Radford Univ; *cr:* Eng Teacher Covington HS 1983-84, Patrick Cty HS 1984-; *ai:* Literary Magazine & Sr Class Adv; NCTE 1983-; NEA 1985-; VA Ed Assn 1985-; VA Jaycees 1984-87, Outstanding Young Amer 1986; Woolwine United Meth Church 1984-; Outstanding Young Educator 1985; *office:* Patrick Cty HS Rt 5 Box 14-A Stuart VA 24171

MARTIN, LOREN EDWARD, Math/Computer Science Teacher; *b:* Schenectady, NY; *m:* Nancy Gradel; *ed:* (BA) Math, Univ of CA Santa Cruz 1973; (MS) Ed, USIU San Diego 1987; *cr:* Teacher Del Mar HS 1974-80, Leigh HS 1980-; *office:* Leigh HS 5210 Leigh Ave San Jose CA 95124

MARTIN, LUCILLE MUMFORD, Sixth Grade Teacher; *b:* Bennettsville, SC; *c:* Graylon; *ed:* (BS) Elem Ed, Winthrop Coll 1970; *cr:* 4th Grade Teacher Robert Smalls Elem 1971-74; 6th Grade Teacher Deep River Elem 1974-; *ai:* 6th Grade Faculty Rep; Chairperson Steering Comm, Comm Skills Comm, on Southern Assn of Coll & Sch; Mem Media Services for SAC; Spon for Stu Government Assn at Deep River Sch; NEA; NCAE; PACE; Named Designee Asst Prin 1986-89, Nominated Teacher of Yr 1981 & 88 Deep River Sch; Team Mem Taught "Teacher Effectiveness Trng"; Served Visiting Team of SAC for Cumberland Cty Sch; *office:* Deep River Elem School 7908 Deep River Rd Sanford NC 27330

MARTIN, LYDIA RUSSELL, Fifth Grade Teacher; *b:* New York, NY; *m:* Emmett C.; *c:* Brian, Nicole; *ed:* (BSED) Elem Ed, WV St Coll 1964; (MA) Curr & Instruction, Cleveland St Univ 1981; *cr:* Teacher Cleveland Sch Dist 1964-; *ai:* Staff Led Team Chairperson; Alpha Kappa Alpha 1965-.

MARTIN, MARGARET GATELY, First Grade Teacher; *b:* Teaneck, NY; *d:* Phillips H.; *c:* Paul H., Patrick W., Thomas P.; *ed:* (BA) Eng, 1950; (MA) Elem Ed, 1953 Hunter Coll; Grad Courses, SUNY; *cr:* 2nd/3rd/4th Grade Teacher P S 5 1950-53; 2nd Grade Teacher Wappingers Central 1953-55; 1st Grade Teacher Jamestown Schls 1968-90; *ai:* Report Care Comm 1st Grade Chairperson Lincoln Sch; AAUW Pres 1978-80 EFP Honoree 81; Delta Kappa Gamma Secy 1989-90; Jamestown Inter Club Cncl Pres 1987-89; Jamestown Teachers Assn Secy 1985-87; Green Thumb Garden Club Pres 1986-88; *office:* Lincoln Sch 301 Front St Jamestown NY 14701

MARTIN, MARJORIE PARR, Sixth Grade Teacher; *b:* Lockport, LA; *m:* Russell Peter Sr.; *c:* Jane M. Meaux, Lynne M. Frear, Russell P. Jr.; *ed:* (BA) Elem Ed, Nicholls St Univ 1974; *cr:* 6th Grade Teacher Lockport Upper 1970-71; 2nd Grade Teacher Lockport Lower 1971-72; 5th Grade Teacher Raceland Upper 1974-75; 6th Grade Teacher Lockport Upper 1975-; *ai:* 4-H Leader; Headed Fr Class with Sr Citizens; Chairperson Plays & Musical Performances; Liaison Person for Adopt-A-Sch Prgm; Friends of Lib Pres 1980-; Holy Savior Parish Cncl Pres 1982-Bishops Medal 1985; Represent Church Lions Club Citizen of Yr Awd.

MARTIN, MARTHA HAMILTON, Fifth Grade Teacher; *b:* Anniston, AL; *m:* Floy Harlis; *c:* Randy, Phyllis Broom, Patricia Patterson; *ed:* (BS) Elem Ed, 1971; (MS) Elem Ed, Jackson St Univ 1976; *cr:* 3rd Grade Teacher Thankful Elem 1971-73; 4th Grade Teacher Mechansville Elem 1973-81; 5th Grade Teacher Wellborn Elem 1981-; *ai:* Mem of Sch Bldg Base Comm; Mem of Effective Sch Comm; Chairperson on Accrediation Section Sch & Commty; West Park Heights Baptist Church; Nom for Teacher of the Year; AL Teacher of the Year; *home:* 423 Hutto Hill Anniston AL 36201

MARTIN, MATTHEW DALE, Biology Teacher; *b:* Alamogordo, NM; *ed:* (MAT) Bio Ed, 1987, (BS) Bio, 1984 NM St Univ; *cr:* Mgr Lamar Liquor 1979-84; Teacher Las Cruces Bujutskan 1984-87, Alamogordo Mid HS 1987-; *ai:* Sci Club Spon; Boxing Coach; NMSTA 1987-89; Alamogordo Public Schls Sci Teacher of Yr 1988-89; 5th Dan Shotokan Karate Do; *office:* Alamogordo Mid HS 1211 Hawaii Ave Alamogordo NM 88310

MARTIN, MERCIE L., Kindergarten Teacher; *b:* Brownfield, TX; *m:* John L.; *c:* Darwin K.; *ed:* (BA) Elem Ed, Prairie View A&M 1962; Kndgtn Endorsement TX Tech 1972; Working Towards Masters in Ed Univ of E NM Univ; *cr:* Lang Art Teacher Carver HS; 5th Grade Teacher Wheatley Elem; Kndgtn Teacher Oak Grove Elem, Colonial Heights Elem; *ai:* TSTA 1962-; *home:* 1108 E Ripley Box 852 Brownfield TX 79316

MARTIN, MICHELLE MARGARET (KLITZ), Fourth Grade Teacher; *b:* Chicago, IL; *m:* Keith Dale; *c:* Megan Ruth, Molly Ruth; *ed:* (BS) Ed, Valparaivo Univ 1982; *cr:* 4th Grade Teacher Hope Luth Sch 1983-; *ai:* Coach Soccer/Girs Bsktbll/Track; Vacation Bible Sch Organiziation; *office:* Hope Lutheran School 6416 S Washtenaw Chicago IL 60629

MARTIN, MURIEL LEA, Social Studies Teacher; *b:* Washington, DC; *c:* Freida J., Christina; *ed:* (BA) His, Federal City Coll 1975; (MA) Adult Ed, Univ of DC 1980; Labor His Univ of WI; Group Process, Government of DC; Teaching/Ed Support Systems, DC Public Schls; *cr:* Academic Standing Coord/Prgm Specialist 1974-84, Womens Prgm Mgr 1980-84 Univ of DC; Adult Educator DC Dept of Corrections 1984-86; Soc Stud Teacher DC Public Schls 1986-; *ai:* Faculty Adv; Stu Cncl Spon; Stu Leadership Inst; Leo Club Co Spon; Academic Advisement Comm; ASCD 1989-; PTA Pres 1988-89; Pres Youth Forum Mem 1990; Cripus Attucks Museum & Performing Art Bd Mem 1988-89; Labor His Fellowship Univ of WI; Natl Endowment for

Hum Alternate; *office:* Paul Laurence Dunbar HS 1301 New Jersey Ave NW Washington DC 20004

MARTIN, NANCY LEA (BROWN), Third Grade Teacher; *b:* Springfield, MO; *m:* Thomas J.; *c:* Thomas R., Travena M.; *ed:* (BA) Elem Ed, Sch of The Ozarks 1972; (MS) Spec Ed, Drury Coll 1979; Various Stud; *cr:* Kndgtn/HS Phys Ed Teacher Blue Eye R-5 1971-72; Day Care Curr Dir Jeans Day Care 1972-73; K-6th Grade Substitute Teacher 1973-74, Kndgtn Teacher 1974-77 N Kansas City Sch; Spec Ed Teacher 1977-82, 7th Grade Teacher 1982-86, 2nd/3rd Grade Teacher 1986- Blue Eye R-5; *ai:* Produce & Directed Musicals & Plays All Levels; Coord Sci Fair, Lang Art Contest, Young Authors; Tutor Spec Needs & High Risk Stu; Organized 1st Stone Cty Just Say No Parade; MO St Teachers Assn Pres 1984-85, 1988-89; Intnl Rdng Assn Local Chairperson; Lang Art Assn Local Chairperson 1988-; Young Authors Dir 1987-; Stone Cty Reserve Sheriffs Auxiliary 1989-; PTA (Cultural Arts Chairperson 1989-, Entertainment Chairperson 1988-89, Legislative Comm Prgm Coord); Rape Crisis Cnslr 1990; Stone Cty Rep Woman Pine B 1990; Sunday Sch Teacher 1988-; Stone Cty Child Protection Team; Republician Comm Person; St & Local Prof Wkshps; *home:* HCR 1 Box 230 Lampe MO 65681

MARTIN, NATALIE ANN, Mid Sch Mathematics Teacher; *b:* Columbus, OH; *ed:* (BA) Math/Phys Ed, 1982, Adrian Coll; *cr:* 7th/8th Grade Math Teacher Circleville City Schls 1982-; *ai:* Girls Var Bsktbl Coach 1983-; OEA Mem 1982-; Jennings Schlsp Awd Winner; *office:* Everts Mid Sch 520 S Court St Circleville OH 43113

MARTIN, NORMA S., English Teacher; *b:* Birmingham, AL; *c:* Pat, Susan, Russell; *ed:* (BS) Eng, Univ of AL 1952; Grad Stud Jacksonville St Univ; *cr:* 4th Grade Teacher Friendship Sch 1965-72; Eng Teacher Oxford HS 1972-; *ai:* Sr HS Girls Omni Spon;eng Dept Service Club Chm City of Oxford (Mayor Pro-Tem, Cncl Mem) 1984-; Fellowship House Bd Mem 1982-; Oxford Arts Cncl 1980-; Cheaha Acres Womens Club 1970-; L Amica Federated Womens Club 1972-; *office:* Oxford HS 915 Stewart St Oxford AL 36203

MARTIN, PATRICIA ANN, Fifth Grade Teacher; *b:* Oakland, MD; *ed:* (AA) Elem Ed, Garrett Comm Coll 1978; (BS) Elem Ed, 1979, (MA) Curr/Instruction, 1987 Frostburg St Univ; *cr:* 4th/5th Grade Teacher Crellin Elem 1979-83, Red House Elem 1983-; *ai:* GCTA, MSTA, NEA; *office:* Red House Elem Sch Rt 2 Box 177 Oakland MD 21550

MARTIN, PATRICIA L., Third Grade Teacher; *b:* David City, NE; *ed:* (BS) Elem Ed, Univ of NE 1971; *cr:* 3rd/4th Grade Teacher Raymond Cntrl at Raymond 1971-73; 3rd Grade Teacher Raymond Cntrl at Ceresco 1973-83, Raymond Cntrl at Valparaiso 1983-; *ai:* Prof Growth, Rdng Promotion, Young Authors, Achievement Test Comm; Cntrl Public Ed Assn Treas 1971-; NE St Ed Assn, NEA Mem 1971-; *office:* Raymond Central Public Sch 406 E 3rd Valparaiso NE 68065

MARTIN, PATRICIA MC KEON, Kindergarten Teacher; *b:* Dodgeville, WI; *c:* Mary A., Brian, Erin; *ed:* (BS) Elem Ed, Univ of WI-Platteville 1969; (MED) Elem Ed, FL Atlantic Univ 1985; *cr:* 1st Grade Teacher Sch Dist 68 1969-72; St Angela Sch 1972-74; Chapt I Comm Skills Teacher Palm Beach Cty Schls 1976-85; Kndgtn Teacher Lantana Elem 1985-; *ai:* Mem Rif; Chm Staff & Admin Section 5 Yr Review; Cty Teachers Assn 1985-; NEA; Outstanding Teacher 1988-89; Finalist Palm Beach Cty William Dwyer Awd for Excl in Teaching 1989; *office:* Lantana Elem Sch 710 W Ocean Ln Lantana FL 33462

MARTIN, PATRICIA TYLER, Mathematics Teacher; *b:* Washington, DC; *c:* Ann T.; *ed:* (BA) Fr, George Peabody Coll oF Vanderbilt Univ 1970; Math, Univ of AL Birmingham; *cr:* Fr Teacher Mt Juliet HS 1970-73; Math Teacher Hueytown HS 1984-85, Briarwood Chrstn HS 1985-; *ai:* Soph Class Spon; Women of God Club Adv; Career Club Adv; Scholar Team Coach; Citizens Bee Team Coach; NHS Spon; Beeson Fellow Samford Univ.

MARTIN, PHYLLIS JEAN, Third Grade Teacher; *b:* North Hampton, OH; *m:* Paul W.; *c:* Michelle Quick, Timothy, Greg; *ed:* (BS) Elem Ed, Wittenberg Univ 1974; Wright St Univ, Univ of Dayton; *cr:* 3rd Grade Teacher Oscar T Hawke 1973-77, Medway 1977-; *ai:* Lang Art Curr Comm; Martha Holden Jennings Scholar 1977-78; *home:* 4638 W National Rd Springfield OH 45504

MARTIN, RICHARD NEAL, Sixth Grade Teacher; *b:* Pittsburgh, PA; *m:* Linda Ritchings; *c:* Jeremy D., Ericka L.; *ed:* (BBA) Bus Admin, OH Univ 1968; (MBA) Elem Ed, Lehigh Univ 1978; *cr:* 5th Grade Teacher John C Mills Sch 1977-89; 6th Grade Teacher Pleasant Valley Mid Sch 1989-; *ai:* Pleasant Valley Sch Dist Supt Advisory Bd, Faculty Staff Dev Cncl, Technology Dev Comm; NEA, PA St Ed Assn 1977-; Faith Alive Ministries (Secy, Treas) 1985-; Pen Argyl Boro Cncl Councilman 1988-; PTO Pres 1978-80; *home:* 502 Robinson Ave Pen Argyl PA 18072

MARTIN, RONALD D., Mathematics Teacher; *b:* White Hall, IL; *m:* Carol Hayes; *c:* Julie E. Martin Wyman; *ed:* (BS) Eng, W IL Univ 1959; (MS) Admin, Sangamon St Univ 1979; *cr:* Teacher Roodhouse Dist #108 1959-63, Champaign Dist 1963-64, North Greene Dist #3 1964-69, 1974-; *ai:* Roodhouse Fire Protection Dist Secy 1974-; Lib Bd 1987-; Cemetery Bd Pres 1987-; Lions Club Charter Mem; Fellowship in Fr 1962 Coe Coll; *office:* North Greene Jr HS W North St Roodhouse IL 62082

MARTIN, RUMALDO LUNA, Spanish Teacher; *b:* Victoria, TX; *ed:* (BA) Eng/Span, Stephen F Austin St Univ 1988; *cr:* Span Teacher Schulenburg HS 1988-; *ai:* Stu Cncl; Span Club; UIL Poetry & Prose; Gifted & Talented Coord; *office:* Schulenburg HS 150 College Schulenburg TX 78956

MARTIN, SUE M., English Teacher; *b:* Fairfax, VA; *m:* Gregg G.; *c:* Kenny, Kelly; *ed:* (BS) Soc Stud/Eng, NM St Univ 1980; Cnslng; *cr:* Eng Teacher Caton Jr HS 1981-83; Highland Jr HS 1984-86; Gadsden Jr HS 1986-88; Mayfield HS 1988-.

MARTIN, SUE MARIE, Fourth Grade Teacher; *b:* Youngstown, OH; *ed:* (BS) Elem Ed, 1978, (MED) Gifted & Talented, 1987 Youngstown St Univ; *cr:* Learning Disabilities Tutor Niles City Schls 1980; 4th Grade Teacher Holy Name Cath Sch 1980-81, C H Campbell Elem 1981-; *ai:* NEA, OH Ed Assn, Canfield Ed Assn; *home:* 5612 Callaway Cir Youngstown OH 44515

MARTIN, SUE SWEARINGEN, First Grade Teacher; *b:* New Orleans, LA; *m:* David Bryan; *c:* Laura E., David B. Jr.; *ed:* (BSED) Elem Ed, Univ of AR Fayetteville 1969; (MSED) Elem Ed, Univ of AR Monticello 1982; Planned Effective Teaching; Assertive Discipline; AR Writing Project; *cr:* 1st Grade Teacher Grand Prairie Sch Dist 1969-70; Storyteller Bradley Cty Lib 1976-78; 1st Grade Teacher Eastside Elem 1977-; *ai:* Staff Dev Comm Warren Sch Dist; AR Ed Assn Chairperson Public Relations Comm 1986-89; Warren Classroom Teachers Assn Public Relations Comm 1986-88; Warren Jr Auxiliary 1975-82, Outstanding Mem 1978; Warren PTA Pres 1984-85; SE AR Arts Cncl Bd of Dirs 1990; 1st Presbyn Church Elder; Governors Commission on Teaching Excl; Potlach 1st Grade Cmptrs Grant; *home:* 1 Maple St Warren AR 71671

MARTIN, SUSAN SIMMONS, Social Studies Teacher; *b:* Derby, CT; *m:* Edward; *ed:* (BS) His/Soc Stud, 1972, (MS) Geography/Soc Stud, 1976 S CT St Univ; Admin, Sacred Heart Univ; *cr:* Teacher Shelton HS 1973-; *ai:* Stu Cncl Adv 1984-; Gaelette Sports Club Schlsp Comm 1986-; Shelton HS Graduation Comm 1982-; CT Cncl of Soc Stud 1988-; CT Mentor & Cooperating Teacher 1989-; Shelton Democratic Ladies (Mem, Town Comm 1980-) 1978-; Shelton Jaycees Outstanding Educator 1987; Nom Shelton Teacher of Yr 1988-.

MARTIN, SUZANNE SPRADLING, Science Teacher; *b:* Palo Alto, CA; *m:* Robert S.; *c:* Stacy, Saraday; *ed:* (AB) Bio, Wesleyan Coll 1967; (MED) Sci Ed, GA St Univ 1989; AP Bio Instr Course; Studied Volcanoes, ME Audubon Society Wkshp on Birding, Advanced Genetics Seminar, Clemson Univ; *cr:* Sci Teacher Milton HS 1967-68, St Johns Sch 1976-77, Gulf Breeze HS 1977-78, E Cobb Mid Sch 1978-80, Wheeler HS 1980-; *ai:* Stu Cncl, Jr Class, Prom Spon; Stu Support Team Leader; Kappa Delta Pi 1989; NSTA, GA Sci Teachers Assn, Natl Marine Ed Assn; Navy Relief Society 1970-76; Keflavik Iceland Officers Wives Assn Pres 1975-76; Yrbk Dedication 1989; Teacher of Yr Nomination 1984-85, 1988; *office:* Wheeler HS 375 Holt Rd Marietta GA 30068

MARTIN, VERNETA D. HAWKINS, 6th Grade Teacher; *b:* Steubenville, OH; *m:* John Henry; *c:* Shaun, Dana, John M.; *ed:* (BS) Elem Ed, Cntrl St Univ 1967; Advanced Trng Kent St Univ, WV Univ; *cr:* 4th-6th Grade Teacher Jefferson Elem Sch 1967-; *ai:* WV Ed Assn, NEA 1968-; *home:* 805 Commerce St Wellsville OH 43968

MARTIN, VICTORIA BOONE, English Teacher; *b:* Norfolk, VA; *m:* Thomas Michael; *ed:* (BA) Eng/Fr, Univ of NC Chapel Hill 1969; (MA) Eng, Old Dominion Univ 1972; Teaching of Writing, Research in Writing, Wake Forest Univ 1982; Cert Teaching of Gifted Stu, Norfolk Public Schls 1988; Mentorship Trng Teaching Thinking Skills to Gifted Stu, Univ of VA 1989-; *cr:* Eng/Journalism Teacher S Stokes HS 1972-75, Zebulon HS 1975-76; Eng Teacher Ben L Smith HS 1976-77, Orange HS 1978-79, N Forsyth HS 1979-80; Eng/Drama Teacher John F Kennedy HS 1980-83; Eng Teacher Thomas Nelson Comm Coll 1983-85, Campostella Mid Sch 1986-87; Eng Teacher/News Production Lake Taylor HS 1987-; *ai:* Sch Newspaper Adv; Sch Correlate Comm; Vertical Team for Sch Improvement Ranforth Fnd/Norfolk Public Schls; Mentorship for Teaching Thinking Skills to Gifted Stus; AFT 1986-; VA Assn Teachers of Eng 1987; 9th VA Volunteer Infantry (Civil War Living His & Re-Enactment); NC Writing Project Fellow Wake Forest Univ 1982; Preface & General Contribution to Poetry NC Dept of Ed 1983; Presenter NC Writing Project Summer Inst 1983 & Four Ctys NC 1982-83; Curr Comm Writing Mythology Curr Guide Norfolk Public Schls 1989; Selected to Teach Global Stud 1990; Presenter Task Analysis Old Dominion Univ Stu Teacher Prgm 1989; *home:* 1037 Westover Avenue Norfolk VA 23507

MARTIN, WANDA LEE, Phys Ed/Health Teacher; *b:* Ward, WV; *m:* David L.; *c:* Lori D., Lesley D., David L. Jr.; *ed:* (BS) Phys Ed/Soc Stud, WV Inst of Technology 1971; (MA) Rdng, WV Coll of Grad Stud 1976; Rdng, WV Coll of Grad Stud; *cr:* Teacher Craigsville Elem Sch 1971-78, Glade Elem Sch 1978-89, Webster Cty HS 1989-; *ai:* Webster Cty HS Hi-Y Club Spon & Faculty Adv; Alpha Delta Kappa (Treas 1987-89, Secy 1985-87); Sch Outstanding Teacher of Yr 1971-72.

MARTIN, WILLIAM HENRY, 9th-12th Grade Math Teacher; *b:* Lake City, FL; *m:* Carole; *ed:* (BS) Engineering, US Naval Acad 1968; (MS) Educl Leadership, Univ of W FL 1989; *cr:* Lieutenant US Navy 1968-73; Salesman Old Towne Industries 1973-76; Recruiter Management Recruiters 1976-79; Teacher Escambia HS 1979-; *ai:* Coach Var Cross Cntry 1981-, Asst Ftbl 1983-84, Asst Bsktbl 1979-86, Asst Bsbl 1986-87; Naval Reserve Captain 1973-; Escambia Cty Teachers of Math 1981-; Church Single Adult Sunday Sch Teacher 1976-; *office:* Escambia HS 1310 N 65th St Pensacola FL 32506

MARTIN, WILLIAM J., 5th Grade Teacher; *b:* Chicago, IL; *m:* Vivian Alvarez; *c:* Robert, Yvette; *ed:* (BA) His, St Procopius Coll 1969; (MA) Admin/Supervision, Roosevelt Univ 1985; *cr:* 4th-6th Grade Teacher Gower Sch Dist #62 1969-; *ai:* Soccer Coach; IEA, NEA 1969-; Gower Ed Assn Pres 1971-72/1983-84; *office:* Gower Mid Sch 7941 S Madison Burr Ridge IL 60521

MARTIN, YOLANDA ALEXANDRA, Eng, Span & Writing Teacher; *b:* Jackson, MS; *m:* Perry B. Sr.; *c:* Zina Martin Sawyer, Renee, Perry Jr.; *ed:* (BS) Eng, 1975, (MA) Eng, 1979 Jackson St Univ; Teaching Span; Inst for Thinking/Writing from Delta St; Journalism; *cr:* Teacher Brandon Attendance Center 1973-75, Jackson Public Schls 1976-; *ai:* Sch Newspaper Spon; Eng Dept Chairperson; Phi Kappa Phi Mem 1979-; Good Apple Awd 1987: Bd of Recognition Awd Local Sch Bd 1988; Outstanding Young Women of America 1982; *office:* Chastain Jr HS 4650 Manhatten Rd Jackson MS 39206

MARTIN-MAESTAS, MARY L., English Teacher & Chairperson; *b:* Roy, NM; *c:* Patricia J. Guenther; *ed:* (BA) Eng/Sociology Ed, 1960, (MA) Admin/Soc Sci, 1970 NM Highlands; Sensitivity Trng Psych; Rdng in Content Area; *cr:* Secy KFUN Radio Station 1957; Teacher Pecos Independent Sch 1960-62, West Las Vegas Sch System 1962-; *ai:* Class Spon; Chess Club Spon; Spelling Bee Comm Mem & Chairperson.

MARTINA, CAMILLE ANNE, Communications/English Teacher; *b:* Dansville, NY; *ed:* (BA) Eng, 1979, (MS) Ed, 1985 Nazareth Coll; Oxford Univ Exeter Coll Intnl Graduate Sch Prgm Reisley House 1985; *cr:* Comm/Eng Joseph C Wilson Magnet HS 1985-; *ai:* Wrap Team; Drug/Alchoal Case Worker Intervention; Earth Day 6 Week Environmental, Extra Curr Chairperson; NY St Youth Media Competitors Tech Adv at Wilson; Comm Resource Teacher; Media Arts Teacher Assn 1990; Natl & Local Sierra Club 1988-; Nalt & Local Audubon Society 1988-; Ingress Home Owners Assn Secy 1989-; Candidate Fulbright Exch United Kingdom 1990; *office:* Joseph C Wilson Magnet HS 501 Genesee St Rochester NY 14611

MARTINA, JOSEPH PHILIP, Mathematics Teacher; *b:* Chicago, IL; *m:* Judi Ellyn Dombrowski; *c:* Eric, Jason; *ed:* (BS) Math, Univ of IL 1974; (MS) Math Ed, N IL Univ 1978; *cr:* Math Teacher Elm Sch 1974-76, Daniel Wright Jr HS 1976-79, Fremd HS 1979-; *ai:* Asst Girls Bsktbl Coach; Sr Powder Puff Ftbl Spon; Timer & Scorer for Jr Var Soccer; AFT, IFT 1979-; Huntley Park Dist Coach 1989-; *office:* Fremd HS 1000 S Quentin Rd Palatine IL 60067

MARTINA, MARY LOUISE, Chair/Business Ed Teacher; *b:* Fairchance, PA; *m:* Rudy B.; *c:* Deborah J.; *ed:* (BS) Bus Ed, WV Univ; (MED) Bus Ed, Univ of Pittsburgh; Bus Ed, Columbia Univ; Bus Ed, OH St Univ; Bus Ed Temple Univ; *cr:* Teacher Uniontown Area HS; *ai:* Religious CCD Teacher; Chairperson Bus Ed Teacher; Bus Ed Advisory Cncl; NBEA; Tri St Bus Ed Assn Secy 1987-91; Bus & Prof Womens (2nd VP 1989-90, 1st VP 1990-91); Delta P Epsilon 1970-; Amer Assn Univ Women Secy 1990-91; Cath Bus & Prof Women Pres 1984-86; PSEA, UAEA (Treas 1974-80 Service Awd 1980); Uniontown Coll Club 1961-; Treas, Uniontown Area Ed Assn Service Awd 1974-80; *office:* Uniontown Area H S 146 E Fayette St Uniontown PA 15401

MARTINAT, JEANNE MARIE, Spanish Teacher; *b:* Kansas City, MO; *m:* Steve; *c:* Stephanie, Stevie; *ed:* (BA) Span, Benedictine Coll 1975; (MA) Ed/Span, UMKC 1985; *cr:* ITA Intnl Translator 1973-78; Span Teacher KCK Dist 500, Rosedale Mid Sch, J C Harmon HS 1978-; *office:* J C Harmon HS 2600 Steele Rd Kansas City KS 66106

MARTINDALE, LINDA THOMPSON, Third Grade Teacher; *b:* New Albany, MS; *m:* Don Reed; *c:* John A., Donna L.; *ed:* (BS) Elem Ed, Blue Mountain Coll 1978; *cr:* 3rd Grade Teacher Falkner Elem Sch 1978-; *ai:* Textbook Selection Comm; NEA, MS Ed Assn 1980-; *home:* Rt 4 Box 160C Ripley MS 38663

MARTINEK, DENNIS EUGENE, Seventh Grade Language Teacher; *b:* Topeka, KS; *m:* Pamela Sue Hawkins; *c:* Nicole M.; *ed:* (BED) Elem Ed, Washburn Univ 1978; *cr:* 5th-8th Grade Teacher Delia Grade Sch 1978-80; 6th Grade Teacher 1982-84, 7th Grade Teacher 1984- Silver Lake Grade Sch; *ai:* Asst Jr HS Vlybl, HS Girls Bsktbl, HS Track; Head Jr HS Girls Bsktbl; KS Bsktbl Coaches Assn 1986- Jr HS Girls Coach of Yr 1986; *office:* Silver Lake Grade Sch 200 Rice Rd Silver Lake KS 66539

MARTINEZ, ALMA LYDIA, 8th Grade Mathematics Teacher; *b:* Alice, TX; *m:* Humberto Mario Jr.; *c:* Alan D., Arianna D.; *ed:* (BA) Eng/Math, TX A&I Univ 1975; (MS) Scndry Ed/Cmptr Specialization, Corpus Christi St Univ 1990; Math Manipulatives Inst 1985; St Trainer for St Module #23 Cmptrs; *cr:* Teacher Gregory-Portland Jr HS 1975-; *ai:* Natl Jr Honor Society Spon; NCTM 1978-; TX St Teachers Assn (Local VP 1988-, Dist Pres 1990-); Portland Lioness Club (Secy, Dir) 1985-87, 1989-, Secy Awd 1985-87, 1989-; St Bd of Ed Contact for Dist II; *office:* Gregory-Portland Jr HS 4200 Wildcat Dr Portland TX 78374

MARTINEZ, ANDREW WILLIAM, 5th Grade Teacher; *b:* Albuquerque, NM; *m:* Brandie L. Elfers; *c:* Casandra I., Danielle G.; *ed:* (BA) Ed, UNM 1976; Psych & Lib Sci; *cr:* 6th Grade Teacher Mountain View Elem 1977-79; 5th Grade Teacher Whittier Elem 1979-83; 3rd/5th Grade Teacher Lavaland Elem 1983-85; 4th Grade Teacher Barcelona Elem 1986; 4th/5th Grade Teacher Lavaland Elem 1986-; *ai:* Lavaland PTA Pres; Whittier

Elem Stud Cncl Spon; Lavaland Elem Yth Leadership Spon; Lavaland PTA Faculty Rep; PTA Pres 1988-89; *home:* 1316 Cordova NW Albuquerque NM 87107

MARTINEZ, ERLINDA ROBERTSON, Middle School Principal; *b:* Santa Rita, NM; *c:* Maria A.; *ed:* (BA) Math/Scndry Ed, 1974, (MA) Sch Admin, 1986 Western NM; *cr:* Math Teacher 1974-83, Asst Prin 1983-86, Prin 1986- Los Lunas Mid Sch; *ai:* NM Cncl of Teachers in Math 1974-; NM Cncl Cmptr Users in Ed 1983-; NM Mid Sch Task Force 1988-; Center for Dispute Resolution Bd of Dir 1988-; NM St Dept of Ed Sch Health Advisory 1989-; *office:* Los Lunas Mid Sch 220 Luna St Los Lunas NM 87031

MARTINEZ, FELIPE VICHARELI, English Teacher; *b:* Laredo, TX; *m:* Leticia Azalea Vela; *c:* Felipe Jr., Fernando R., Melissa M.; *ed:* (AA) Laredo Jr Coll 1969; (BA) Certified Eng/Span, TX A&I Univ Laredo 1971; (MS) Bi-ling Ed/Span, Laredo St Univ 1977; Supervision; Military Service 1971; Trained in Stock, Control & Accounting, Fort Lee VA; *cr:* Teacher Laredo Ind Sch Dist 1971-80; Eng/ESL Instr Laredo Jr Coll 1980-84; Teacher Laredo Ind Sch Dist 1984-; *ai:* Univ Interscholastic League Competition Judge; Santo Nino Elem Faculty Club Pres 1977; TX St Teachers Assn, Laredo Ed Assn 1971-; NCTE 1982-84; TX Jr Coll Assn 1980-84; San Martin de Porres Church CCD Teacher; Military Service Rank E-5 Honorable Discharge; *home:* 2517 E Locust Laredo TX 78043

MARTINEZ, GEORGE LUIS, Mathematics Teacher; *b:* Campo Largo, Argentina; *c:* Forest; *ed:* (BA) Math, Univ of CA Santa Cruz 1978; *cr:* Math Teacher Santa Cruz HS 1978-; *ai:* Sch Site Cncl Mem; Latinos Unidos Adv; Affirmative Action & Schlsp Comm; AFT Building Rep 1986-; *office:* Santa Cruz HS 415 Walnut Ave Santa Cruz CA 95060

MARTINEZ, RAYMOND ISRAEL, Fourth Grade Teacher; *b:* Espanola, NM; *m:* Ernestine Ortiz; *c:* Angelica, Raymond III; *ed:* (BS) Elem Ed, Univ of NM 1974; Grad Courses Univ NM, La Verne Univ, Denver Univ; *cr:* 2nd Grade Teacher New Haven Schls 1974-75; 5th Grade Teacher 1975-80, 2nd Grade Teacher 1980-83, 4th Grade Teacher 1983 Lavaland Sch; *ai:* Youth Leadership Grade Level Chairperson; Talent Show Coord; Fiesta Comm Mem; AFT 1982-; *office:* Lavaland Elem Sch 501 57th St NW Albuquerque NM 87105

MARTINEZ, REBECCA PARADA, Reading Teacher; *b:* El Paso, TX; *m:* Federico; *c:* Michael, Melissa, Melinda; *ed:* (BSED) Eng/Elem Ed, Univ of TX El Paso 1980; *cr:* Drama/Eng Teacher Eastwood Knolls Sch 1980-83; Teacher/Supvr Fine Art Prgm Ysleta Ind Sch Dist 1983-85; Drama Teacher Clint HS 1985-89; Drama/Rdng Teacher Clint Jr HS 1989-; *ai:* Drama Club; Chrldr Spon; TX St Teachers Assn 1989-; Teacher of Yr Finalist Eastwood Knolls Sch 1983; *home:* PO Box 805 Clint TX 79836

MARTINEZ, SERGIO LORENZO, Mathematics Teacher; *b:* Monterrey, Mexico; *m:* Marina; *c:* Vanessa R.; *ed:* (BA) Psych/Ed, CA Univ Santa Cruz 1976; *cr:* Cnslr Neighborhood Youth Corps 1974; Teacher/Asst 1976-77, Lang Art Teacher 1977-79 San Andreas Continuation HS; Math/Phys Ed Teacher Rancho San Justo Mid 1979-; *ai:* Boys & Girls Bsktbl, Track Coach; After Sch Tutoring Prgm; Prin Advisory Cabinet; Mexican-Amer Comm on Ed (Mem 1980, Schlsp Comm Chm), 1st Schlsp 1972; Mexican-Amer Tennis Assn VP 1977-, Most Valuable Player 1987; Coll Opportunity Grants 1972-76; Math Dept Chm; *office:* Rancho San Justo Mid Sch 1201 Rancho Dr Hollister CA 95023

MARTINEZ, SUSAN WILLIAMS, 6th Grade Teacher; *b:* Pueblo, CO; *m:* Rey C.; *c:* Andrew, Thomas; *ed:* (BA) Behavioral Sci, Univ S CO 1969; (MA) Elem Ed, Univ N CO 1979; Type D Cert; *cr:* 1st/2nd Grade Teacher Sacred Heart 1969-70; 6th Grade Teacher Durango Sch Dist 9-R 1970-74, Denver Public Sch 1974-75; 5th/6th Grade Teacher 1975-80, 4th-6th Grade Teacher 1980- Jefferson Cty Sch Dist 9-R; *ai:* Durango Ed Assn (Pres 1989-, VP 1987-89); *home:* 707 Clovis Durango CO 81301

MARTINEZ, TERESA GUZMAN, 1st Grade Teacher/Chairman; *b:* Beeville, TX; *m:* Roberto L.; *c:* Morri, Mandi, Marli; *ed:* (AA) Elem Ed, Bee Cty Coll 1972; (BS) Elem Ed, TX Womans Univ 1974; Learning Styles in Classroom/TESA; *cr:* 1st Grade Teacher FMC Elem 1974-75, Tyler Elem 1975-; *ai:* Tyler-Maddera Flourney Elem PTO Bd Mem; Thomas Jefferson Jr HS PTO Mem; NEA 1974-; TX St Teachers Assn 1974-; Beeville Faculty Assn 1974-; NEA 1974-; TX St Teachers Assn Campus Rep 1978-; Beeville Faculty Assn 1978-; PTO VP 1988-; 1st Grade Level Chairperson; Building Leadership Team Mem; Apple Achvt Awds Comm Mem; *home:* 107 W Fannin Beeville TX 78102

MARTINEZ, THOMAS JACOB, 7th/8th Grade Soc Stud Teacher; *b:* Santa Fe, NM; *m:* Mary E. Turner; *c:* Brandon P., Blaine P.; *ed:* (BA) Soc Stud/Composition His, Coll of Santa Fe 1969; His, Ed, Admin, Drug Ed, Sch Law Related Wkshps; *cr:* Field Rep Coll of Santa Fe 1969-70; Soc Stud Curr Coord Santa Fe Public Schls 1978-85; Soc Stud Teacher 1971-, Soc Stud Dept Chm 1974- De Vargas Jr HS; *ai:* Santa Fe HS Var Girls Bsktbl Coach 4978-87; Jr HS Boys & Girls Bsktbl, Boys Ftbl, Girls Track Coach; NM Coaches Assn Mem 1978-87; Historical Society of NM Mem 1974-77; Boys Club (Coach, Cnslr) 1965-69; Civitans Mem 1970-76; ZIA United Meth Church (Chm 1988-89, Usher & Alter Society); *office:* De Vargas Jr HS Llano Rd Santa Fe NM 87501

MARTINEZ-BROOME, MIQUELITA, 6th Grade Lit/Lang Art Teacher; *b:* Fairview, NM; *m:* Paul E.; *ed:* (BS) Scndry Ed/Speech/Drama/Eng, NM St Univ 1978; *cr:* 10th-12th Grade Eng/Speech Teacher Cuba HS 1978-81; 6th-8th Grade Lang Art/Speech Teacher Truman Mid Sch 1981-; *ai:* Core Team & Connect Team Leader; Team Against Substance Abuse; Contact Person Truman Mid Sch; AFT, NM Fed of Teachers, Albuquerque Teachers Fed 1978-; Big Brothers/Big Sisters 1989-; St Vincent De Paul Society 1988-89; Linker Trainer AFT Educl Research & Dissemination Prgm; Facilitating Support Group Contact Person Truman Mid Sch; *home:* 1809 Britt NE Albuquerque NM 87112

MARTINEZ-MEELER, KATHLEEN, High School Counselor; *b:* Santa Fe, NM; *m:* Ernest Meeler; *c:* Marisol; *ed:* (BA) Art Ed, 1973, (MA) Guidance/Counseling, 1974 NM Highlands Univ; CA Migrant Parent Trainer, Classroom without Borders Facilitator; *cr:* Upward Bound Asst Dir NM Highlands 1973-75; Art Teacher Nueva HS 1975-79; Cnslr Shafter HS 1979-; *ai:* Math, Engineering, Sci Achievement Adv; Mecha Co-Adv; Lang Minority Task Force; Mem Migrant St Conference Comm; CA Ed Assn, Natl Teacher Assn 1974-; Kern HS Dist Cnslrs Assn 1979-; Hispanic Teacher Assn 1988-; Mexican Amer Political Assn 1982-; Kern Cty Lulac Teacher of Yr 1988; Univ of Santa Barbara Partnership Cnslr Awd Kern Cty 1983, 1984; MESA Adv of Yr 1984, 1985, 1986, 1987; *office:* Shafter HS Kern HS Dist 526 Mannel Ave Shafter CA 93263

MARTINEZ-RAMOS, ALBERTO, History Teacher; *b:* Havana, Cuba; *m:* Carmen Blanco; *ed:* (BA) His, 1973, (MA) His, 1979 Univ of Miami; *cr:* Teacher Loyola Sch 1975-79, St Brendan HS 1979-; *ai:* Amer Red Cross Blood Drive Coord; *office:* St Brendan HS 2950 Sw 87 Ave Miami FL 33165

MARTINSEN, ERIC LAURENCE, English Teacher/Drama Dir; *b:* Bay Shore, NY; *ed:* (BS) Scndry Eng Ed, SUNY Plattsburgh 1964; (MA) Liberal Stud, SUNY Stony Brook 1971; *cr:* Eng Teacher Liverpool Mid Sch 1965-67; Mount Anthony HS 1967-69; Eng Teacher/Drama Dir Connetquot HS 1969-; *ai:* Dir Drama/Musical Productions Connetquot HS; Summer Rdng Prgm Comm; Honors Curr Comm; Basic Prgm Comm; NY St Theatre Ed Assn (Bd Dir & Exec Secy 1983-87); Natl Endowment for Hum Grant Awd 1987; *office:* Connetquot HS 7th St Bohemia NY 11716

MARTINSEN, WANDA JOHNSON, Pre-1st Grade Teacher; *b:* Madison, WI; *m:* Robert L.; *c:* Kobi S. Caracci, Melissa J.; *ed:* Elem Ed, Richland Cty Teacher Coll 1960; (BS) Elem Ed, 1965; (MS) Elem Ed, 1968 Univ Wi; *cr:* 2nd/3rd/4th Grade Teacher Lakeside Sch 1960-61; 5th-6th Grade Ridgeville Sch 1961-62; Kndgtn Remedial Rdng Haz Green Elem 1965-67; 7th/8th Grade Rdng Dodgeville Elem 1967-68; 1st/2nd Grade 1968-84; Pre-1st Grade 1984 WI Heights Schls; *ai:* Inservice Comm Rep 1988; Building Rep WI Heights Fed Teachers 1986; Instr Teachers Wkshp Math Their Way 1980; Supervising Teacher WI Madison Stu Teachers; WI Math Cncl Bus Exective Bd WMC 1987-89; Kappa Delta Pi Honor Society 1968; Madison Area Rdng Assn 1980-82; Intnl Rdng Assn 1967-69; Dane Cty Ed for Employment Primary Soc Stud Curr Writing Comm 1988; WIHeights Assn Teachers (Pres 1969-70 Building Rep 1968-69); WI Heights Fed of Teachers 1971-; VT Badgers 4-H Club Adult Leader 1971-73; Our Saviours Luth Church Mem 1945-; Nom WI Teacher Yr 1987; Rdng Awd of Excl; 1966 Graduate NDEA Rdng Institute Schlsp UW-Platteville; Speaker/Presentor Math Their Way-Natl Cncl of Teachers of Math Sioux Falls SD 1983; Milwuakee WI 1985 & Madison WI 1990; WI Math Cncl Green Lake WI 1984/1986/1989 and Platteville 1984 & Madison 1986; Teaching Teachers Wkshps in Math Their Way in WI/IL/IA/MN/MT/CA; *office:* Black Earth Elem Sch 1133 Center St Black Earth WI 53515

MARTINSON, JERRY KEITH, Mathematics/Computer Teacher; *b:* Wakefield, MI; *m:* Lynn Marie Wasley; *c:* Eric, Jonathan, Luke; *ed:* (BA) Math, 1971, (MA) Scndry Ed, 1986 N MI Univ; Employee Assistance Prgm Resource Prgm Trng, Cmptr Resource Trng; *cr:* Math Teacher 1971-, Cmptr Teacher 1984- Pulaski Cmmty Schls; Adult Ed Cmptr Teacher NE WI Tech Coll 1988-; *ai:* 7th Grade Boys Ftbl & 7th Grade Girls Bsktbl Coach; 7th-8th Grade Math Tournament Adv & Coach; Metricathon & Dist St Urho Day Act Coord; Dist Cmptr & Math Comm Mem; Pulaski Ed Assn Teachers Union Rep 1971-; WI Ed Assn, NEA; WI Math Cncl Mem; Abrams & Oconto Falls Wrestling Club 1983-; Oconto Gospel (Asst Sunday Sch Supt 1985-, Boys Club Leader 1983-); PTA (Teacher Rep 1986-87, Mem 1980-); Employee Assistance Prgm Dist Resource Person 1975-; Merit Pay 1978-80, 1987; Jr HS Teacher of Yr Awd Pulaski Dist, CESA 7 Dist 1987; *office:* Sunnyside Sch 720 Cty C Sobieski WI 54171

MARTY, GEORGE ALLAN, HS Mathematics Teacher; *b:* Martins Ferry, OH; *m:* Amy Kennon; *c:* Michelle; *ed:* (BSED) Math, OH Univ 1976; MASMED Wheeling Jesuit Coll; *cr:* Math Teacher Bellaire HS 1976-78, Bridgeport HS 1978-; *ai:* Asst Bsktbl Coachl; *office:* Bridgeport HS 501 Bennett St Bridgeport OH 43912

MARTYN, HARRY ALLEN, Science Teacher; *b:* Pueblo, CO; *m:* Marilyn Adell Goughnour; *c:* Joshua H., Aurora D., Katelyn Woods; *ed:* (BS) Bio, Westmar Coll 1972; (MA) Bio, Univ of SD Vermillion 1977; *cr:* Bio Lab Instr Univ of SD Vermillion 1976-77; Sci Instr NE Indian Comm Coll 1977-89; Anatomy/Philosophy Instr St Joe Sch of Nursing for Briarcliff Coll 1979-80; 7th-12th Grade Sci Instr Morningside Chrstn Sch 1983-; *ai:* Sioux City Baptist Church (Sunday Sch Teacher 1974-, Youth Group Worker 1974-); Project Dir for Natl Sci Fnd Grant; Developed Book; *office:* Morningside Chrstn Sch 6100 Morningside Ave Sioux City IA 51106

MARTZ, BEVERLY DOBOS, English Teacher; *b:* Youngstown, OH; *c:* Michele Hodge; *ed:* (BA) Eng, 1984, (MA) Eng, 1990 Youngstown St Univ; *cr:* Eng Teacher Struthers HS 1984-; *ai:* Eng Festival & Cmptr Lab Tutor Coord; OH Cncl Teachers of Lang Art 1987-; Phi Kappa Phi 1984-; NCTE 1983-88; OH Ed Assn Exec Comm 1989-; Red Cross Volunteer 1976-; OH Dept of Ed Inservice Advisory Bd 1990-; Barbara Brothers Writing Awd for Teachers 1985-86, 1989; Lewis & Pauline Fifield Prize in Early Stud, Ball St Univ; Design Software for Teaching Eng Concept; Whos Who in Amer Colls & Univs 1984; *office:* Struthers HS 111 Euclid Ave Struthers OH 44471

MARTZ, LAURIE JANE, English Teacher; *b:* St Joseph, MO; *m:* Ronald D.; *c:* Sean, Jon; *ed:* (BSED) Eng/Soc Stud, NW MO St Univ 1977; Grad Stud; *cr:* Eng/Soc Stud Teacher Atchison Jr HS 1977-81; Eng Teacher Lathrop HS 1985-; *ai:* Soph Class Spon; Academic Bowl Coach; NEA 1977-81, 1985-; NCTE 1986-; *office:* Lathrop HS 612 Center St Lathrop MO 64465

MARUT, JANICE BEVERLEY, 5th-8th Grade Language Teacher; *b:* Richmond, VA; *m:* John Keith; *c:* Jonathan Keith, Julie Kristin; *ed:* (BS) Ed, Radford Univ 1971; *cr:* 7th-9th Grade Teacher Stafford Jr HS 1971-73; 5th-8th Grade Teacher St Paul Luth Sch 1983-; *ai:* Teacher Sch Newspaper & Literary Magazine; TCTE 1984-; LEA 1983-; TACLD 1988-89; *office:* St Paul Lutheran Sch 1800 W Freeway Fort Worth TX 76102

MARVIN, JAMES PAUL, Theatre Instructor; *b:* Lansing, MI; *ed:* (BFA) Drama/Acting, Univ of IL Champaign-Urbana 1975; (MFA) Drama/Play Writing, Trinity Univ 1979; *cr:* Resident Company Mem Dallas Theater Center 1976-82; Head-Drama Dept Appel Farm Arts & Music Center 1984-88; T heatre Instr Fillmore Arts Center 1984-; Dir Fillmore Arts Camp 1989-; *ai:* After Sch Theatre Project & Jr Shakespeare Company Dir; Actors Equity Assn, Dramatists Guild; Ruby Loyd Absey Playwriting Contest Winner; Produced at Prof Theatres Around US; *home:* 3206 18th St NW Washington DC 20010

MARVIS, BRYAN EDWARD, 7th/8th Grade Lang Art Teacher; *b:* French Camp, CA; *m:* Judith Ann Schmitt; *ed:* (BA) Elem Ed, 1977, (BA) Eng, 1985 Portland St Univ; Working Towards Masters Eng & Stan Teaching Cert; *cr:* 4th Grade Teacher Coroner Elem Sch 1977-79; Head Teacher Oak Sch 1979-80; 7th & 8th Grade Lang Art Teacher Beaver Grade Sch 1980-; *ai:* 8th Grade Trip Fundraising Spon & Adv; OR Cncl of Teachers of Eng 1987-, Poetry 1988; Pacific Northwest Writers Conference 1988-, Screenplay 1989; Clarke Awd Portland St Univ 1984; Willamette Writers Awd 1987; *office:* Beaver Grade Sch PO Box 77 Beaver OR 97108

MARYLAND, ANNA LUCILE PATTERSON, Language Arts Teacher; *b:* Autaugaville, AL; *m:* Clinton; *c:* Michael; *ed:* (BS) Elem Ed, 1962, (MAED) Elem Ed, 1985 AL St Univ; Rdng, Univ of GA; *cr:* Teacher Crawford Cty Elem Sch 1972-77, Loveless Elem Sch 1977-82, Dannelly Elem Sch 1982-; *ai:* Accreditation Comm; Montgomery Teacher Center Chairperson 1986-87; System-Wide Art Prgm Dannelly Rep 1987-88; Montgomery Public Sch Curr & Inservice Cncl Primary Academic Comm Mem 1987-88; Mc Dougald Elem Sch Cub Scout Pack Leader 1965-72, Plaque 1965; AL St Univ Adopt-A-Family for Educl Excl Proctor 1987-, Appreciation Plaque 1990; R L Mc Dougald Elem Teacher 1963-72, Teacher of Yr 1966; Developed Inservice Meeting Corrective Remedical Teaching Strategies for 1st-3rd Grade Teachers 1965; Montgomery Public Schls System Wide Wkshp Presentor 1989-; *home:* 3736 Hunting Creek Rd Montgomery AL 36116

MARZOLF, RICHARD ARTHUR, Mathematics Teacher; *b:* St Paul, MN; *m:* Mary Elizabeth; *c:* Mary B. Kissling, Thomas, Michael, Anne M.; *ed:* Philosophy, Univ of Detroit 1960; (MA) Guidance/Counseling, Coll of St Thomas 1974; Advanced Stud in Math & Physics, Univ of Detroit, Marygrove Coll, Univ of MN, Carlton Coll; *cr:* Math/Physics Teacher Cardinal Mooney Latin Sch 1961-67; Staff Announcer WAVN Radio Stillwater MN 1968-69; Math/Sci Teacher St Thomas Acad St Paul 1969-74; Math Teacher Convent of the Visitation Sch 1974-; *ai:* Convent of the Visitation Sch Faculty Admin Liason Team Mem; MN Cncl Teachers of Math, NCTM 1969-; MN Personnel & Guidance Assn 1971-76; US W Outstanding Teacher Prgm Letter of Commendation 1988; Ashland Oil Company Golden Apple Teacher Achievement Awd 1989; Math & Physics Stud Natl Sci Fnd Grant 1960-66; *home:* 1092 Fairmount Ave St Paul MN 55105

MASCOLA, CORINNE ANDERSON, Counselor; *b:* Harlingen, TX; *c:* Scott A.; *ed:* (BFA) Eng/Theatre Arts, Chrstn Univ 1965; (BA) Elem/Scndry Ed, 1979, (MS) Ed, 1981 Pan Amer; Counseling Cert; *cr:* Performer Broadway & Television NY 1966-76; Eng/Theatre Art Teacher Pace HS 1978-83, Porter HS 1988-89; Cnslr Brownsville Ind Sch Dist 1989; *ai:* Stu Teacher Coord; Presenter TSC & Pan Amer Univ; Univ Interscholastic League One Act Play Dir; Spon Intnl Thespian Society; Presenter Brownsville Ind Sch Dist In-Service Wkshps; Kappa Delta Pi, Alpha Psi Omega 1963-64; Actors Equity Assn, Amer Guild of Variety Artists 1966; Most Prominent Educators of TX Listing 1983; *home:* PO Box 4064 Brownsville TX 78520

MASHELL, LINDA COOPER, Third Grade Teacher; *b:* Shreveport, LA; *m:* James R.; *c:* Kendrick, Jason; *ed:* (BS) Elem Ed, Grambling St Univ 1973; (MED) Elem Ed, Northwestern St Univ 1981; Elem Ed, Northwestern 1986; Supvr Stu Teaching; *cr:* Teacher 1973-84, Elem Coord 1984-85, Teacher 1985- W

Shreveport Elem; *ai:* Supvr Stu Teaching; Grambling St Univ Shreveport Alumni Secy; LEA, NEA 1973-; LA Rdng Assn 1989-; Educator of Yr Awd W Shreveport 1989-; *office:* W Shreveport Elem Sch 2226 Murphy St Shreveport LA 71103

MASIDONSKI, BEVERLY BENDURE, President; *b:* Akron, OH; *m:* David J.; *c:* Brandon; *ed:* (BS) Ed, Kent St 1968; Grad Courses Kent St; *cr:* 1st Grade Teacher Hotchkiss Sch 1968-74; Remedial Rdng Teacher Gallopolis City Schls 1974-75; 1st Grade Teacher 1975-78, 1st-3rd Grade Combination Teacher of Talented & Gifted 1978-81, Federal Hocking Schls; *ai:* Effective Personal Leadership Prgm; Cascade Club Mem; Builders Exch; Akron Exec Assn (Trustee, Pres); Wita Womans Organization; Alpha Gamma Delta (Adv 1978, 1979) 1967-; Phi Delta Kappa; Jennings Scholar; Runner Up OH Teacher of Yr 1979; Manufacturers Keyperson for Midwest; *office:* Tel-Com Systems of Ohio 2745 S Arlington Akron OH 44312

MASIELLO, DON CARL, Mathematics Department Chair; *b:* Monterey Park, CA; *m:* Diane Le Pawte; *c:* Gina, Donna, Dominic; *ed:* (BA) Math, CA St Univ Los Angeles 1968; (MA) Ed, Univ of Redlands; *cr:* Math Teacher La Salle HS & Rosemead HS; *ai:* Bible Study Adv; Driver Trng Instr; PTA Service Awd; *office:* Rosemead HS 9063 E Mission Dr Rosemead CA 91770

MASKEY, DAVID LEE, Mathematics Teacher; *b:* Hannibal, MO; *ed:* (BA) Math, Univ of MO Rolla 1981; Working Towards Masters Degree in Sci, Math from Drury Coll; *cr:* Math Teacher Lebanon R-III Schls 1981-; *office:* Lebanon Jr HS 500 N Adams Lebanon MO 65536

MASLAR, NANCY JOLLEY, Kindergarten Teacher; *b:* Mt Gilead, OH; *m:* James P. (dec); *c:* James E., Joseph P., Melissa A.; *ed:* (BS) Elem Ed, Miami Univ 1961; Grad Stud Kndgtn Certificate OH St; *cr:* 1st Grade Teacher Montgomery Cty Schls 1961-64; Teacher Mt Gilead Schls 1975-; *ai:* Former Asst Childrens Librarian; OH Ed Assn, NEA, Mt Gilead Teachers 1975-; Intnl Rdng Assn 1987-; Martha Holdings Jenning Scholar; Mt Gilead Teachers Incentive Grant Rdng & Sci.

MASON, AMELIA JANE, 6th-8th Grade Teacher; *b:* Parkersburg, WV; *m:* Michael Owen; *c:* Jacqueline M.; *ed:* (AA) Applied Sci, WV Univ 1971; (BA) Art, Salem Coll 1975; (BS) Elem Ed, Glenville St 1984; Cmptr Sci; *cr:* Artist Fenton Art Glass Co 1978-82; Art Teacher 1983, Lang Art/Rdng Teacher 1984-Frontier Bd of Ed; *ai:* Dist Cmptr Coord; Cheerleading, Stu Cncl, Yrbk, Newspaper, Natl Knowledge Bowl Adv; Textbook Adoption, St Eng Composition Cty Level, Eng Study Revision, Cmptr Study Comm; Frontier Local Ed Assn, OH Ed Assn; Democratic Womens Club; *home:* 16 Kittle St Williamstown WV 26187

MASON, ANNETTE MARIE, Mathematics/Phys Sci Teacher; *b:* Greencastle, IN; *m:* Frank Sherard; *ed:* (BS) Chem, Purdue Univ 1985; (MS) Chem, IN St Univ 1989; Gifted Ed Trng Level I & II; *cr:* Math/Phys Sci Teacher Chrisman HS 1985-; *ai:* Soph Class & Peer Group Spon; Chrisman Ed Assn 1985-; Xi Kappa Xi 1989-; Spec Teacher FFA 1989-; Presenter Gifted & Talented Conference Spring 1990; *office:* Chrisman HS N State St Chrisman IL 61924

MASON, CAROL A., Media Specialist; *b:* Kalamazoo, MI; *ed:* (BM) Public Sch Music, 1965; (MSL) Librarianship, 1967 Western MI Univ; *cr:* Librarian Flint Public 1967-73; West Jr HS 1973-86; Media Specialist West Mid Sch 1986-; *ai:* Video Club-Spon; Stu Media Adv-Spon; MI Assn Media in Ed Region Bd 187-88; NEA/MEA/REA 1973-; MI Assn for Media Ed St Conf 1988; *home:* 1809 Vanhill Ct Rochester Hills MI 48309

MASON, DALE A., Fifth Grade Teacher; *b:* Princeton, IN; *m:* Susan K. Fisher; *c:* William, Kathryn; *ed:* (BS) Elem Ed, Univ of S IN 1974; (MS) Elem Ed, IN St Univ 1979; Advanced Trng TESA, Inductive Reasoning, Concept Attainment, Synectics; Trng in Cooperative Learning; Gifted & Talented Ed, Purdue Univ; *cr:* 5th Grade Teacher Lowell Elem 1974-; *ai:* 5th Grade Bsktbl Coach 1974-75, 1980-81; NGEA VP 1988-; ISTA, NEA 1974; Youth Coalition Bd Mem 1990; Princeton Cmmty Pride Awd for Cmmty Service 1985, Excl in Ed 1988; Outstanding Young Educator of Yr 1989; *office:* Lowell Elem Sch Hart & Water Sts Princeton IN 47670

MASON, ELIZABETH MARIE, OP, Vice Prin & 8th Grade Teacher; *b:* Hibernia, NJ; *ed:* (BA) Ed, Caldwell Coll 1958; *cr:* 1st/5th/8th Grade Teacher Holy Spirit 1943-57, 1960-62; 6th/8th Grade Teacher St Mary 1957-59; 6th Grade Teacher St Philip 1959-60, St Catherine 1960-66; Prin St Theresa 1966-72; 7th Grade Teacher Our Lady of the Lake 1972-73; 8th Grade Teacher Saints Peter & Paul 1973-; *ai:* Moderator Academic Bowl Team; Asst Librarian; Rdng Coord; Religious Ed Coord; Archdiocean Evaluation Team (Mem, Chairperson) 1978-80; Religious Ed Comm 1967-71; *home:* 408 Hudson St Hoboken NJ 07030

MASON, GARRY R., II, Chemistry/Physics Educator; *b:* New Martinsburg, WV; *ed:* (BS) Chem Engineering, Grove City Coll 1982; Working Toward Masters Robert Morris Coll; *cr:* Educator Shaler Area HS 1985-87, Hopewell Area HS 1987-; *ai:* Class of 1991 Spon; Stu Cncl; Coach; Odyssey of Mind; *office:* Hopewell Area Sr HS 1215 Longvue Ave Aliquippa PA 15001

MASON, JUDY MARIE (SHORT), First Grade Teacher; *b:* Baileysville, WV; *m:* Thomas Michael; *ed:* (BS) Elem Ed, Bluefield St Coll 1972; *cr:* 3rd-5th Grade Teacher Elk Lick Grade Sch 1967-69; 1st Grade Teacher 1969-70, 3rd Grade Teacher 1970-71, 2nd Grade Teacher 1971-77, 1st Grade Teacher 1977- Baileysville Elem & Jr Hs; *ai:* WV Ed Assn, NEA 1967-; WY Cty Rdng Cncl 1989-; *home:* PO Box 115 Fanrock WV 24834

MASON, PATRICIA ANN (WALTHER), Middle School Teacher; *b:* Chicago, IL; *m:* James Stanley; *c:* James S., David L., Ross A., Pamela J.; *ed:* (BS) Sci/Elem Ed, W MI Univ 1975; Grad Stud Ed; *cr:* 3rd Grade Teacher 1975-76, 4th Grade Teacher 1977-79, 4th/5th Grade Teacher 1980-81, 5th Grade Teacher 1981-85, 6th-8th Grade Teacher 1985- Marcellus Cmmty Schls; *ai:* Quest Skills Adolescence Coord; Just Say No Club Spon; Cedar Lake Recreaction Assn Treas 1985-; *home:* 28990 Cedarama Marcellus MI 49067

MASON, ROY, Social Studies Teacher; *b:* Raymond, MS; *m:* Cora; *c:* Latangela, Felisha; *ed:* (BS) Soc Sci, Jackson St 1971; Educl Admin, Supervision, Jackson St Univ; *cr:* Soc Stud Teacher Vaiden HS 19 1-76, Terry HS 1977-78, Utica HS 1978-; *ai:* Stu Cncl Adv; Hinds Cty Schls Outstanding Staff Dev Awd 1986; *office:* Utica HS P O Box Drawer H Utica MS 39175

MASON, TERRI GILMORE, US His/World Geography Teacher; *b:* Oklahoma City, OK; *m:* Raymond G.; *c:* Jennifer, Kristin; *ed:* (BAED) Soc Sci - Cum Laude, OK St Southwestern Univ 1974; (MAED) Scndry Ed/Geography - Magna Cum Laude, Cntrl St Univ 1982; Cert Eng, Akron Univ 1985; Working towards Cert Bio, Univ of OK 1982-; *cr:* Scndry Teacher Moore Cntrl HS 1974-84, Rittman HS 1984-; *ai:* 1989 Leadership & 1990 Gifted & Talented Comm Mem Rittman HS; NEA 1974-; OH Ed Assn, Rittman Ed Assn 1984-; OH Cncl for the Soc Stud 1985-; NCSS, OK Ed Assn, Moore Ed Assn, Natl Geographic Society, Smithsonian, OK Historical Society; Phi Alpha Theta Secy; Kappa Delta Pi (Pres, VP, Corresponding Secy); Outstanding Young Women of America 1986; Fulbright Fellowship Exch Teacher to the Netherlands 1986-87; Teacher at Fivel Coll Delfzijl Netherlands; Teacher Merit Pay Article Published; Whos Who Among Stu in Amer Univs & Colls; Teacher of Month; Deans & Pres Honor Roll; Panhellenic Schlsp Awds; *office:* Rittman HS 200 Saurer Rittman OH 44270

MASONBRINK, JOHN J., Science Teacher; *b:* Stella, NE; *m:* Gail Ankrom; *ed:* (BS) Math, Peru St Coll 1970; (MS) Sci Ed, Northwest MO St Univ 1974; *cr:* Sci Teacher Tarkio Jr HS 1970; Falls City HS 1970-; *ai:* Southeast NE Sci Educators 1986-; NEA 1970-; NE St Ed Assn 1970-; Falls City Ed Assn 1970-; Elks Lodge 963 1962-.

MASQUELIER, GARY L., English Teacher/Dept Head; *b:* Pittsburgh, PA; *m:* Laurie Vanderveer; *c:* Jessie; *ed:* (BA) Eng, Houghton Coll 1977; (MA) Eng Lit, N IL Univ 1983; Lit, Counseling, Scndry Ed; *cr:* Teacher Wheaton HS 1977-; *ai:* Academic Comm Head; Drama Dir; Poetry Club Adv; Weaton Chrstn HS Teacher of Yr 1979; *office:* Wheaton Chrstn HS 2 N 120 Prince Crossing Rd West Chicago IL 60185

MASS, ANTHONY JAMES, Soc Stud Teacher/Athletic Dir; *b:* Toledo, OH; *m:* Elizabeth Bergman; *c:* Anthony II, Aaron, Austin; *ed:* (BE) Comprehensive Soc Stud, Univ of Toledo 1977; *cr:* 7th Grade Teacher Walbridge Saint Jerome 1977-80; 8th Grade Teacher Huron Saint Peter 1980-85; Soc Stud Teacher Calvert HS 1985-; *ai:* Athletic Dir; Head Boys Bsktbl Coach; Soc Stud Dept Chm; OH Bsktbl Coaches Assn 1977-; Dist VI Bsktbl Coaches Assn 1985-, Coach of Yr 1989; Tiffin VFW Educator of Yr 1989-; *office:* Calvert HS 152 Madison St Tiffin OH 44883

MASSENGALE, MARY WOFFORD, Retired 3rd-5th Grade Teacher; *b:* Athens, TX; *m:* Maynard L.; *ed:* (BS) Scndry Ed/ Home Ec, TX Women Univ 1943; (MS) Elem Ed, Univ of Houston 1955; *cr:* Home Ec Teacher Cross Roads HS 1943-45; 2nd/3rd Grade Teacher San Antonio Ind Sch Dist 1950-57; 3rd-5th Grade Teacher Athens Ind Sch Dist 1957-82; *ai:* Athens Classroom Teachers Assn Local Unit Pres 1961-63; TX St Teacher Assn Local Unit Pres 1965-66; TX Retired Teachers Assn (1st VP, 2nd VP); Bus & Prof Womens Assn (Pres, VP, Secy, Treas, Comm Chm); *home:* Rt 2 Box 2072 Athens TX 75751

MASSENGILL, BELINDA BARBER, Science Teacher; *b:* Luxora, AR; *m:* Ollice A. Jr.; *c:* Steve, Kevin, Karen; *ed:* (BS) Sci Ed, Blue Mountain Coll 1981; Sci Ed, MS St Univ; Natl Sci Fnd Wkshp, Rust Coll 1985; *cr:* Sci Teacher Western Union Attendance Center 1983-88, Hickory Flat Attendance Center 1988-; *ai:* Beta Club, Chrldr Spon; MS Prof Ed 1986-; Beta Club Teacher of Yr 1989; *home:* Rt 1 Box 289 Hickory Flat MS 38633

MASSER, MARY VIRGINIA (GRAMS), German Teacher; *b:* Frederick, MD; *m:* Glenn E.; *c:* Robert E., Philip R., Mark A.,; *ed:* (BA) Eng 1974; (MA) Eng, 1977 Wright St Univ; Post Masters Studies, German, Bowling Green St Univ; OH Calvin Coll; 1979-82; *cr:* Eng Teacher Spencerville Mid/HS 1975-76; Eng/Ger Teacher Parkway Mid/HS 1978-; Adjunct Eng Instr Wright St Univ 1978-; *ai:* Coach - Parkway Scholastic Bowl Team-1978-; Co-Sopn-Foreign Lang Club-1989-; Parkway Ed Assn 1978-; OH Ed Assn 1978-; Natl Ed Assn 1978-; Merc Cty Mental Health Bd 1975-86, (President 1984-85, Personnel Comm 1975-83); Mem OH Teachers Forum - 1986; Organized and Led Tour Group to Germany Austria Switzerland Summer 1988; *office:* Parkway H S 401 S Franklin St Rockford OH 45882

MASSER, PEGGY BIRDENA (HAVEN), 5th Grade Teacher; *b:* Flint, MI; *m:* Robert Eugene; *c:* Jeremy, Brian; *ed:* (BA) Elem Ed/Sci/Math, Adrian Coll 1976; (MA) Elem Ed, Saginaw Valley St Univ 1987; *cr:* 7th Grade Math/Sci Teacher 1976-79, 5th Grade Teacher 1979- Montrose Cmmty Schls; *ai:* 5th Grade Sci Fair Dir; Montrose Baptist Church Deaconness 1990; *home:* Box 132 Montrose MI 48457

MASSEY, ALMA MOORE, Business Teacher; *b:* Corning, AR; *m:* Donald Eugene; *c:* Joy, Wade; *ed:* (BSE) Bus, 1967, (MSE) Bus, 1971 AR St Univ; *cr:* Teacher Tuckerman HS 1967-71, Newport HS 1971-; *ai:* Sr Class, FBLA Spon; Stu Bank Bd; Delta Kappa Gamma; First Baptist Church; *office:* Newport HS Remmel Park Newport AR 72112

MASSEY, DONALD R., Zoology/Earth Science Teacher; *b:* El Dorado, AR; *m:* Renee L.; *c:* Donna R., Donald Jr., Dennis, Denise, Delois; *ed:* (BA) Bio, 1965, (BA) General Sci, 1965 UAPB; Ed Leadership E MI Univ; *cr:* Math/Physics/Chem/Bio Teacher Holly Grove HS 1965-69; Chem/Bio Teacher Brinkley HS 1969-73; Bio Teacher Central HS 1973-78; General Sci Teacher Beecher HS 1980-81; Zoology/Earth Sci Teacher Northern HS 1984-; *ai:* Sci & Math Tutor; United Teachers Assn, MI Ed Assn; Harris Temple Church (Sunday Sch Teacher 1983-, Evening Sch Teacher 1984-); Golf Assn (Pres, Teacher) 1986-; Church Man of Yr 1988.

MASSEY, GAIL WHEALTON, Math Teacher; *b:* Newport News, VA; *m:* Norman; *ed:* (AA) Natural Sci, 1983, (BS) Math, 1985, (MS) Ed Admin, 1990 Eastern NM Univ; *cr:* 7th-8th Grade Math Teacher Berrendo Mid Sch 1985-; *ai:* Mem Sch Governance Comm; Chairperson Faculty Sch Improvement Team; NCTM; ASCD; Kappa Delta Pi; NEA Building Rep 1988-; *office:* Berrendo Middle School 800 Marion Richard Rd Roswell NM 88201

MASSEY, JESSE LEE, Mathematics Teacher/HS Coach; *b:* Albany, GA; *c:* Janelle; *ed:* (BS) Mid Grades Ed, Albany St Coll 1980; Working towards Masters in Ed, Albany St Coll; *cr:* Teacher/Coach Fitzgerald City Schls 1980-85, Appling Cty Bd Ed 1985-; *ai:* Scndry Ftbl, Boys/Girls Cross Cntry, Boys Track Var Coach; PAGE Crew Mgr 1985-; Boys Club Volunteer 1982-; NYSP Instr 1975-, Service Awd 1989; Omega Psi Phi 1980-; Mem GA Comm in Writing GA Basic Skills Test & GA TCT 1986-87; Natl Deans List 1979-80; *office:* Appling Jr/Sr HS 200 E Allen St Baxley GA 31513

MASSEY, JO ANN ANNE, Soc Stud Teacher/Chairperson; *b:* Goldsboro, NC; *ed:* (BA) Soc Stud, NC St Univ 1973; Mentor Trng; *cr:* Soc Stud Teacher Saratoga Cntrl HS 1974-78; Soc Stud Teacher 1979-, Soc Stud Chairperson 1986- Beddingfield HS; *ai:* His Club Co-Adv; Beddingfield HS SACS Steering, Awds Comm Mem; NHS Screening Comm; NCAE 1974-; FTA Educator of Month 1989; Nom Wilson Cty Teacher of Yr 1988-89; *office:* Beddingfield HS Rt 3 Box 100 Wilson NC 27893

MASSEY, LINDA BACON, English Teacher; *b:* Camp Springs, MD; *m:* Harry D.; *c:* Chris, Michelle; *ed:* (BS) Elem Ed, MS St Univ for Women 1966; (MS) Elem Ed, Washburn Univ 1979; *cr:* 3rd/4th Grade Teacher Netawaka Grade Sch 1966-68; 1st Grade Teacher CO Grade Sch 1970-83; 7th/8th Eng Teacher Holton Mid Sch 1984-; *ai:* Jr Kayette Spon 1984-; NEA 1970-; Holton Bus Women Pres/VP 1980-; Pilot Intnl VP/Bd Mem 1975-80; First Baptist Church Circle Pres 1980-; First Baptist Choir 1970-; *home:* 425 Cherokee Holton KS 66436

MASSEY, LORRAINE MC NEIL, Mathematics/Science Teacher; *b:* Olive Branch, MS; *m:* Alvin Wayne; *c:* Lori R., Leveda R., Alvin W. II; *ed:* (BS) Math, Le Moyne-Owen Coll 1976; Cmptr Sci, St Tech Inst; Enrichment Wkshps, Le Moyne-Owen Coll; Ed, Memphis St Univ; *cr:* Quality Control Intnl Harvester 1976-81; Teacher Memphis City Schls 1982-; *ai:* Drug Free Schls; TN No Team; Just Say No Adv; Class Mother; Clue Driver; Frayser Cmmty Leader; Childrens Corner Spon; PTO Treas; Just Say No Club of Yr 1989; Nom Rotary Parent 1990; Alpha Kappa Mu Honor Society Teacher of Day; Nom Outstanding Teacher Memphis City Schls 1990; *office:* Frayser HS 1530 Dellwood Memphis TN 38127

MASSEY, NORMAN, World History/English Teacher; *b:* Del Rio, TX; *m:* Gail; *c:* Randi; *ed:* (AA) SW TX Jr Coll Uvalde 1964; (BA) Eng/Anthropology, Univ of TX Austin 1966; (MA) His/ Sociology, TX A&M Kingsville 1973; *cr:* Teacher Memorial Jr HS 1966-67, Dove Creek HS 1967-70, Edenburg Jr HS 1970-72, Robert H Goddard HS 1972-; *office:* Robert H Goddard HS 701 E Country Club Roswell NM 88201

MASSEY, RICHARD ELLSWORTH, English Teacher; *b:* Appleton, MN; *m:* Susan Kay; *c:* Jacob, William; *ed:* (BS) Ed, Moorhead St Univ 1972; *cr:* Eng/Lang Arts Frost Public Schls 1972-77, Madison Public Schls 1978-80, Appleton Public Schls 1980-; *ai:* Spelling Bee-Announcer for Sports Events; Frost Ed Assn Pres 1974-76; Pioneer Public TV Adv Bd 1977-82; Field Ed for MN Sportsman Magazine 3 Yrs; Currently Contribute to Bowhunting World/Field & Stream/Mn Sportsman/Petersens Hunting/Outdoor Life/Sports Afield; *home:* 237 E Ronning Appleton MN 56208

MASSEY, SHARON FISHER, First Grade Teacher; *b:* Camden, NJ; *c:* Shavonne; *ed:* (BA) Elem Ed, Rider Coll 1978; *cr:* 1st Grade Teacher Northeast Sch 1978-; *ai:* Soc Comm; Grade Level Chairperson 1986-88; Mary H Thomas Day Care Bd Mem 1986-; *office:* Northeast Elem Sch 7th & Vine Sts Camden NJ 08102

MASSIE, ANNETTE ALBAN, 3rd Grade Teacher; *b:* Ironton, OH; *m:* Larry Keith; *ed:* (BS) Elem Ed, 1978, (MS) Elem Ed, 1981 OH Univ; Grad Stud; *cr:* Teacher-Aide Ironton City Sch Dist 1974-77; Teacher Campbell Sch 1978-; *ai:* Career Day Dir; Spelling Bee Pronouncer & Judge; Right to Read Comm; Ironton Ed Assn Secy 1987-88; OH Career Ed Mem 1984-; Career Ed Building Rep 1984-, 6 Yr Service Awd 1990; Just Say No Club

Act Organizer 1989-; Bd of Chrstn Life Bd Mem 1987-; Master Teacher Trng; *office:* Campbell Elem Sch 1111 S 6th St Ironton OH 45638

MASSOTH, RUTH PETTET, 4th Grade Teacher; *b:* Rensselaer, IN; *m:* Henry; *c:* Jill; *ed:* (BS) Elem Ed, 1967; (MS) Elem Ed, 1972 IN St Univ; *cr:* 5th Grade Teacher Kankakee Valley Sch Corp 1967-71; Tri County Sch Corp 1971-78; Kndgn Teacher Wanatah Sch Corp 1981-82; 4th Grade Teacher Washington Twp Sch 1983-; *ai:* Gifted/Talented Comm; Sch Accreditation Comm; Bldg Base Assessment Team Mem; Cty Teacher Evaluation Comm; PCTA Pres 1989-90; ISTA; NEA; Psi Iota XI; *office:* Washington Twp Sch 383 E St Rd #2 Valparaiso IN 46383

MASTANDREA, DIANE MARIE, Spanish Teacher; *b:* Boston, MA; *ed:* (BA) Span/Ed, Westfield St Coll 1977; Latin, Harvard Univ; Cmptr Sci, Northeastern Univ; *cr:* Substitute Teacher 1977-78, Tutor/Interpreter 1978-79, Teacher 1979-83 Norwood Public Schls; Teacher N Middlesex Reg HS 1984-; *ai:* NHS Comm; Kappa Delta Pi 1975-; MA Foreign Lang Assn 1980-; NEA 1980-; Merit Awd Westfield St Coll Foreign Lang Dept 1977; Mid Sch Foreign Lang Implementation Grant 1987; *home:* 334 Fitchburg Rd Townsend MA 01469

MASTERS, ARLEEN VERONICA, 7th-9th Grade Teacher; *b:* Cleveland, OH; *ed:* (AS) Ed, Lord Fairfax Comm Coll 1978; (BA) Eng, Mary Washington Coll 1981; *cr:* 9th/10th Grade Eng Teacher Strasburg HS 1981-85; 11th/12th Grade Eng Teacher James Wood HS 1985-86; 7th-9th Grade Eng Teacher Capon Bridge Jr HS 1986-; *ai:* Textbook Adoption Comm; WV Ed Assn 1986-; NEA; *office:* Capon Bridge Jr HS Capon Bridge WV 26711

MASTERS, ELIZABETH MC MARTIN, Secondary English Teacher; *b:* Ogdensburg, NY; *m:* William Arthur; *c:* Vickie A., David W., Daniel R., Valerie L. Masters Kelly; *ed:* (BA) Eng/Bible, Houghton Coll 1951; (MSED) Eng Ed, SUNY Potsdam 1970; Counseling Prgm, St Lawrence Univ; *cr:* Scndry Eng/Latin Teacher Frenchburg HS 1951-52; Substitute Teacher Heuvelton Cntrl 1952-55, Hogansburg 1955-59; Scndry Eng Teacher Lisbon Cntrl 1967-; *ai:* Jr Class Adv; Spelling Bee Coord; Forensics Team Coach & Coord; Yrbk Adv; Effective Schls & Negotiations Comm; Kappa Delta Gamma Intnl Recording Secy 1990; Teachers Assn (Pres 1978-80, VP 1981-89); 4-H Leader 1968-81, 10 Yr Leadership Awd 1979; Eastern Stars 1987-; United Meth Church Part-Time Minister 1982-; Amer Legion Commendation for Contribution in Stu Speeches; *home:* R 1 Box 268 Heuvelton NY 13654

MASTERS, LIBBY WOODS, Teacher of Gifted Education; *b:* Atlanta, GA; *m:* Gerald Roy; *c:* Casey, Blake; *ed:* (BS) Scndry Eng Lit, Univ of GA 1970; (MED) Math/Gifted/Mid Grades, GA St Univ 1976; Grad Courses in Scndry Math, Gifted Ed, Mid Grades, Elem Grades; *cr:* Teacher Commerce GA City Schls/Commerce Jr HS 1970-72; Lead Teacher Head Start Jackson Cty 1970-71; 6th Grade Teacher Hall Cty Schls/Sardis Elem 1972-74; 7th Grade Teacher Mimosa Elem 1974-75, Sandy Springs Mid Sch 1975-80; 8th Grade Teacher/Gifted/Algebra/Pre-Algebra/Math Holcomb Bridge Mid Sch 1983-; *ai:* Mathcounts Team Spon 1989-; League of Ind Fulton Educators 1988-; Sandy Springs Mid Sch Teacher of Yr 1977-78; 1st Runner Up Fulton Cty Teacher of Yr 1977-78; *office:* Holcomb Bridge Mid Sch 2700 Holcomb Bridge Rd Alpharetta GA 30201

MASTERS, MICHAEL LYNN, World History Teacher; *b:* Baytown, TX; *c:* Kristen, Cody; *ed:* (BAT) Phys Ed/Soc Stud, Sam Houston St Univ 1976; Masters of Ed, SFA; *cr:* Amer His Teacher Horace Mann Jr HS 1977-80; World His Teacher Humble HS 1981-; *ai:* Ftbl & Bsbl Coach; Textbook Comm; Close Up Spon; TX HS Coaches Assn 1977-; Assn of TX Prof Educators 1981-; TX Cncl for Soc Stud 1989-; *office:* Humble HS 1700 Wilson Rd Humble TX 77338

MASTERS, MORGAN L., Science Instructor; *b:* Oskaloosa, IA; *m:* Mary E. Borglum; *c:* Marc, Lori; *ed:* (BA) Gen Sci, NE MO St Univ 1969; (MS) Sci Ed, Univ of IA 1990; *cr:* Sci Instr Chariton Cmmty Schls 1969-; *ai:* Boys & Girls HS Cross Cntry; Asst HS Boys Track; 8th-12th Grade Sci Club Spon; NSTA Mem 1980-; NEA, IA St Ed Assn Mem 1969-; Natl Assn for Sci/Technology Society Mem 1987-; Kiwanis Intnl Exec Bd 1988-89; Chariton Chamber of Dev Corporation Cmmty Betterment VP 1987-; Presidential Awd Excl in Math & Sci Teaching 1988; Sci & Technology Society Consultant Silver, Burdett & Ginn; IA Cmmty Ed Assn Awd; Articles Published; *home:* 1415 Court Ave Chariton IA 50049

MASTIN, EUGENE ARTHUR, Guidance Counselor; *b:* Dansville, NY; *m:* Cheryl Tillman; *ed:* (BS) Health Ed, SUNY Brockport 1976; (MS) Ed/Coaching, 1981, (MS) Cnslr Ed, 1985 Alfred Univ; Certificate of Advanced Study Cnslr Ed, Alfred Univ 1990; *cr:* 5th Grade Teacher Cuba Cntrl Sch 1976-79, Cameron Cty Sch Dist 1979-83; 2nd Grade Teacher Hornell City Sch Dist 1983-85; Guidance Cnslr Hornell HS 1985-; *ai:* Hornell HS Head Ftbl Coach; *office:* Hornell HS Maple City Park Hornell NY 14843

MASTRINE, DIANA NEDOCK, Second Grade Teacher; *b:* Spangler, PA; *m:* Ronald A.; *c:* Matthew, Malissa; *ed:* (BS) Elem Ed, 1976, (MSED) Elem Ed, 1979 St Francis Coll; *cr:* 2nd Grade Elem Ed Teacher Cambria Elem Sch 1977-; *ai:* PA St Ed Assn, NEA, Cntrl Cambria Ed Assn 1977-; Holy Name Cath Church Mem 1979-; *office:* Cambria Elem Sch RD 4 Box 800 Rt 422W Ebensburg PA 15931

MATAMOROS, MARY ANNETTE, Theatre Director; *b:* Kansas City, MO; *c:* Matthew T., Erik T., Samantha E. Ford, Sheila K.; *ed:* (BA) Theatre/His, Incarnate Word 1979; Grad Stud Theatre; *cr:* His/Theatre Teacher S San Antonio West Campus 1979-; 6th-8th Grade Teacher Sheperd Jr HS 1988-; Upward Bound Rdng Teacher 1989-; *ai:* UIL Prose, Poetry, One Act Play, Drama Club; ATEP 1988-; TETA 1979-; Off Stage Incorporated House Mgr 1979-; NCO Pres; Ft Sam NCO VP; 97th General Hospital Behavior Management Clinic Pres; Frankfort Germany Military Wife of Yr 1972; *office:* S San Antonio West Campus Sch 5622 Ray Ellison Dr San Antonio TX 78242

MATARAZZO, MARION, English Teacher; *b:* Newark, NJ; *m:* Sam; *ed:* (BA) Eng/Bio, Montclair St Coll 1951; Elem Cert, Kean Coll 1953; (MA) Eng, Montclair St Coll 1955; Guidance/Admin/Supervision Cert, Seton Hall Univ 1971; PhD Equivalency Seton Hall Univ; *cr:* 5th-7th Grade Eng Teacher Grove Street Sch 1951-53; 5th/6th Grade Teacher Mt Vernon Elem Sch 1953-55; Eng Asst Vailsburg Jr HS 1955-59; Eng Asst/Title I Cultural Coord/Dir-Stu Tutoring Prgm/ESOP III Prgm Coord East Side HS 1959-; *ai:* Coach BRITE Team; Future Teachers of Newark Club, In-Sch Tutorial Prgm Coord; East Side HS Adv Sr Class 1959-68, Chrldrs 1962, Yrbk 1960, Sch Newspaper 1980, Stu Cncl 1981-; Chairperson Hospitality & Mid St Evaluation Comm 1962; Vailsburg Jr HS Graduating Class Adv 1958; Chairperson Handbook Comm 1958, Faculty 1955-59; Welfare Comm; Grove Street Sch Adv Sch Newspaper 1951-53, Sch Magazine 1951-53; Initiated & Coached Boys Bsktbl Team 1951-53; PTA Faculty Liason (1st VP) 1951-75; Intnl Rdng Assn Mem; NABE Mem; NJ St Opera; Amer Italian Historical Assn (Secy, Treas); Damini Fnd Co-Founder; United Nations Assn; Princeton Univ Distinguished Teaching Awd 1988; Governors Excl in Teaching Awd 1989-; Newark Teacher of Yr 1989-; Essex Cty Teacher of Yr 1989-; At for Kids Teacher Network Awd 1990; *office:* East Side HS 238 Van Buren St Newark NJ 07105

MATEJCIK, CHRISTINE CASSIDY, Fourth Grade Teacher; *b:* Gouverneur, NY; *m:* Peter Jr.; *c:* Michael P., Gregory S.; *ed:* (BA) Psych, 1974, (MS) Rdng, 1979 SUC Potsdam; *cr:* 4th Grade Teacher Gouverneur Cntrl Sch 1975-; *ai:* Excl & Accountability Prgm; Dist Planning & EAP Building Comm; Parents & Teachers of Fowler Sch; Delta Kappa Gamma 1989-; Comm to Advance & Revitalize Edwards; Cub Scouts Leader 1987-89; *home:* RD 1 Box 140 Edwards NY 13635

MATERESE, RICHARD ANGELO, 8th Grade Social Stud Teacher; *b:* Binghamton, NY; *m:* Mary J. Kroboth; *c:* Christopher K., Mary Katharine, Elizabeth; *ed:* (BA) His, Poly Sci, Philosophy, Eng, Ed Lemoyne Coll 1976; *cr:* 9th/10th Grade Soc Stud/Summer Sch/Alternate Ed Teacher Union Endicott HS: 7th/8th Grade Soc Stud Teacher Jennie F Snapp Mid Sch; Permanent Substitute Teacher/Detention Center Moderator Seton Cath Cntrl 1976-77; *ai:* Public Safety, Emergency Services Comm; Health, Ed, Recreation, Childcare Task Force, Partnership Cncl Comm Mem; Union Endicott HS Boys Var Soccer Head Coach 1980-; Jennie F Snapp Girls Modified Bsktbl Coach 1983-84; Seton Cath Cntrl Boys & Girls Head Track/Field 1982-85, Head Indoor Track/Field 1978-82, Head Boys Track/Field 1980, Modified Track/Field Boys & Girls 1977-79 Coach; Seton Mid Sch Modified Soccer Coach 1978-79; NY St Congress of Parents & Teachers, Honary Life Mem; Village of Endicott Trustee 1986-89; Town of Union Parks & Recreation Youth Prgm Dir 1976-77; Towns Boys Bsbl & Girls Sftbl Summer League Dir 1977; Broome Cty Spec Deputy Park Ranger 1977-80; Triple Cities Soccer Assn 1979-; Jr Achievement Prgm Participant; Broome Cty Legislater 14th Dist 1989-; *office:* Jennie F Snapp Mid Sch 101 Loder Ave Endicott NY 13760

MATHE, IRIS SUZANNE, 5th Grade Teacher/Dept Chair; *b:* Gainesville, FL; *m:* Liam P.; *c:* Christopher F., Kara L.; *ed:* (AA) Psych, Santa Fe Comm Coll 1975; (BAE) Ed, Univ of FL 1980; (MA) Ed, Univ of N FL 1987; *cr:* Teacher Price Mid Sch 1981, Interlachen Elem 1981-; *ai:* Inservice Comm; Math Curr Cncl; Peer Teacher; Putnam Fed of Teachers United 1983-; *home:* PO Box 1081 Interlachen FL 32148

MATHENA, RICHARD D., English/History Teacher; *b:* Linton, IN; *ed:* (AS) Soc Stud, SE Chrstn Coll 1967; (BS) US His, Oakland City Coll 1969; (MS) IN St Univ 1974; IN Univ Religious Stud Inst 1983; New England Inst of Art & Sci 1988; Work on Scndry Prin License 1989; *cr:* Teacher NE Dubois HS 1969-; Instr Vincennes Univ 1978-; *ai:* Frosh Class Spon; Coach For Academic Bowl; NCTE, NEA; Family Hospice of Dubois Cty 1987-; *home:* P O Box 155 Dubois IN 47527

MATHENY, JOSEPH CHARLES, Mathematics Teacher; *b:* Marietta, OH; *m:* Nancy Dawn Rhodes; *c:* Rebekah L., John M.; *ed:* (BS) Math, 1975, (MS) His, 1989 Marietta Coll; *cr:* Math Teacher St Marys Mid Sch 1975-76, St Joseph Prep Seminary 1976-77, Marietta HS 1977-; *ai:* Var Golf, Frosh Bsktbl Coach; Curr Advisory Comm; OH Cncl Teachers of Math 1989-; Mens Assn Pres 1989-; Washington Cty Historical Society 1986-; Honor Educator 1989-; Martha Holden Jennings Fnd; *office:* Marietta City Schls Davis Ave Marietta OH 45750

MATHERLY, MELISSA DIANE, Middle School Teacher; *b:* Newton, KS; *m:* Richard Bruce; *c:* Gabriel M.; *ed:* (BA) Art, 1974, (BA) Ed, 1975 Western St Coll; (MA) Ed, CO St Univ 1990; Prof Design, MT St Univ; *cr:* K-2nd Grade Certified Aide O Leary Elem; 2nd Grade Teacher 1977-80, 4th Grade Teacher 1980 Basalt Elem Sch; 5th Grade Teacher Glenwood Springs Elem 1981; 1st Grade Teacher Bolitho Elem 1982; Kndgtn Teacher Basalt Elem 1983-85; 5th/7th/8th Grade Teacher Basalt Mid Sch 1985-; *ai:* Stu Cncl Adv; Accountability, At-Risk Child, TESA Trainers, Soc Stud, 5th Grade Dept Comms; NEA 1976-; ASCD 1988-; Buddies Pre-Sch VP 1982-; Aspen Substance Awareness Trainer 1989-; CO Governors Excl Teaching Awd 1988; Mc Donalds Mid Sch Teacher of Yr 1990; *office:* Basalt Mid Sch Box Z Basalt CO 81621

MATHERS, DANIEL JOSEPH, 6th Grade Teacher; *b:* Espanola, NM; *m:* Ellen Marie Sheridan; *c:* Joshua, Christopher; *ed:* (BA) Soc Sci/His, 1974, (MA) Educl Admin, 1982 CA St Univ; *cr:* Scndry Teacher Baker Valley HS 1975-78, Yucaipa HS 1978-80; 6th Grade Teacher Yucaipa Mid Sch 1980-; *ai:* Baker Valley Educators Assn Pres 1977-78; Human Life Fnd Mem 1985-; Elks Mem 1980-89; San Bernardino Pregnancy Counseling Center Cnslr 1985-; San Bernardino-Riverside Ctys Industrial Cncls Teacher of Yr 1978; *office:* Yucaipa Mid Sch 12358 6th St Yucaipa CA 92399

MATHEWS, BENA ELIZABETH, 3rd Grade Teacher; *b:* Fayetteville, AR; *m:* Ted O.; *c:* Jill A., Holly B. Martin; *ed:* (BA) Elem Ed, Seattle Pacific Univ; Advanced Trng Wildlife, Music, Geography, Rdng; *cr:* 1st/2nd Grade Elem Teacher Maple Grove Sch 1941-43; 1st Grade Teacher 1952-57; 1st-7th Grade Teacher Sultan WA; 1st/3rd/4th Grade Teacher Kettle Falls WA 1973-; *ai:* NEA, WEA 1952-; Delta Kappa Gamma 1979-; *home:* 797 Applegate Rd Colville WA 99114

MATHEWS, MARILYN JO-FAUBER, 8th Grade Life Science Teacher; *b:* Wilmington, OH; *m:* Robert E.; *ed:* (BA) Elem Ed, Wilmington Coll 1974; (MA) Elem Ed, Xavier Univ 1977; TESA Trng Xavier Univ; PRIDE Trng Coll of Mount St Joseph; *cr:* 6th Grade Sci Teacher Marshall Elem Sch 1974-80; 8th Grade Sci Teacher Hillsboro Jr-Sr HS 1980-; *ai:* Frosh Chrldr Adv; Teenage Inst Adv; Sci Olympiad Team Coach; Career Educl Coord; Mem Drug Free Sch Adv Cncl; Hillsboro Ed Assn; OH Ed Assn; NEA; NSTA; Appalachian Front Audubon Soc Treas 1977-78; Hillsboro Church of Christ; Miami Univ Wkshp 1986-87; Teaching Sci with Toys; Chemical Ed Wkshp Summer 1989.

MATHIAS, MARSHA A., Vocal Music Teacher; *b:* Baltimore, MD; *ed:* (BS) Applied Piano/Scndry Music Ed, 1974, (MLA) 1980 W MD Coll; *cr:* Music Teacher Westminster E Miid Sch 1974-; *ai:* Choral Dir & Coach; Talent Show Co-Dir; Cultural Act Chairperson; *office:* Westminster East Mid Sch Longwell Ave Westminster MD 21157

MATHIAS, NEELAM ADIEL, 2nd Grade Elementary Teacher; *b:* Lahore, Pakistan; *m:* Yousaf H.; *c:* Jessica L., Joseph E.; *ed:* (BA) Elem Ed, Coll of St Rose 1979; (MS) Spec Ed, Russell Sage Coll 1983; *cr:* Elem Teacher Albany Public Sch #20 1979-; *home:* 274 Tampa Ave Albany NY 12208

MATHIEU, BERNARD CHARLES, Business Teacher; *b:* Holyoke, MA; *m:* Sandra Weinberger; *c:* Bernard Jr., Jeffrey; *ed:* (BS) Bus Ed, 1968, (MED) Ed, 1990 Amer Intnl Coll; Grad Stud Accounting, Amer Intnl Coll; *cr:* Bus Teacher Chicopee Comprehensive HS 1968-; *ai:* Chicopee Ed Assn Treas 1974-; MA Teachers Assn, NEA 1968-; Teacher of Yr Awd; *home:* 110 Shoreline Dr Ware MA 01082

MATHIS, BERNARD DUANE, Art/Indstrl Technolgoy Chair; *b:* Sterling, CO; *m:* Melverie Jo Keller; *c:* Stephanie, Jacquelyn; *ed:* (BA) Industrial Art, 1972, (MA) Industrial Art, 1979 Univ of N CO; *cr:* Industrial Art/Art & Crafts Teacher Carmel Jr HS 1973; Industrial Art/Woods Teacher Janitell Jr HS 1973-74; Industrial Art/Woods/Crafts Teacher 1974-77, Industrial Art/Drafting/Technology Teacher 1977- Sterling HS; *ai:* Co-Spon Intnl Thespian Society; Tech Dir all Schls Dramatics Productions; Head Spon of Soph Class; Supts Advisory, Dist Technology Ed Planning, Dist Health Insurance, NE CO Boces Conference Planning Comms; CO Industrial Art & Technology Ed Assn, Intnl Technology Ed Assn; Jaycees Outstanding Young Educator 1984; *office:* Sterling HS 407 W Broadway Sterling CO 80751

MATHIS, LARRY BOYNTON, Band Director/Supervisor; *b:* Griffin, GA; *m:* Elizabeth Fadell Faison; *c:* Janeen L., Stefan R.; *ed:* (BA) Music Ed, Clark Coll 1965; (MMED) Music Ed, Van Der Cook Coll of Music 1976; *cr:* Band Dir Lyons Industrial HS 1965-66, Drake HS 1966-68, Carver HS 1968-69, Westside HS 1969-71; Elem Band Dir Henry Cty Schls 1971-82; Band Dir Spalding Jr HS 1982-85; Band Dir/Supvr Griffin HS 1985-; *ai:* Dir Griffin HS Marching Band of Gold; NEA 1965-; GAE Local Pres 1976; MENC 1960-; GACT, TOTY Awd 1987; NAACP; Mt Zion Baptist Church Supt 1985-89; NEA Grassroots Lobbyist; Bd of Dir Henry Cty Fed Credit Union; *office:* Griffin HS 1617 W Poplar St Griffin GA 30223

MATHIS, PAM MARTIN, 6th Grade Science Teacher; *b:* Russellville, AR; *m:* Maxie L. Jr.; *c:* Maxie L. III; *ed:* (BS) Elem Ed 1970; (MS) Elem Ed, 1980 AR Tech Univ; Elem Ed, ATU 1980-; *cr:* 3rd Grade Teacher Scott Elem 1970; 4th-6th Grade Teacher Sequoyah Elem 1972-76; 3rd-5th Grade Teacher Dwight Elem 1976-80; 6th Grade Sci/Gt Sci Teacher 1980-; *ai:* AR Ed Assn; Russellville Ed Assn; NEA; Beta Nu Chapter Delta Kappa Gamma; Phi Delta Kappa; NEA; Russellville Sch Dist Employee of Month 1988; 1st United Methodist Church-Sunday Sch Teacher; 1988 Co-Dir Vacation Bible Sch 1989; Co-Chm Ed Comm.

MATHISON, LORNA WILLARD, GED Instructor; *b:* Alma, MI; *m:* James S.; *c:* Mark, Todd; *ed:* (BA) Eng/Sociology, Coll of Wooster 1960; (MS) Ed of Deaf, Gallaudet Univ 1963; Univ of Rochester, Univ of MI, AR Tech Univ, Webster Univ; *cr:* Instr Rochester Sch for Deaf 1962-65; ESL Instr Escola de Guerra 1977-80; Instr Immaculata HS 1982-89, KS Correctional Institution 1989-; *ai:* Immaculata HS Stu Cncl Spon; KS Rdng

Assn; KS Assn Teachers of Eng, Wkshp Presenter 1990; Scotopic Sensitivity Screener Irlen Clinic 1990; PEO Sisterhood Pres 1989-; YWCA Bd of Dirs 1986-88; Ft Leavenworth Musettes, Pres 1981-82; Leavenworth-Lansing Leadership Group; Outstanding Young Women of America 1968; Patrons of Lib Bd Mem; *home:* Rt 5 Box 508 Leavenworth KS 66048

MATLICK, PAMELA SHEPHERD, Vocal Music Teacher; *b:* Louisville, KY; *m:* Eldon Roy; *c:* Jeremy R.; *ed:* (BME) Music Ed, Eastern KY Univ 1974; (MA) Secondary Ed, Murray St Univ 1983; Post Masters Studies Indep Study Univ of OK; *cr:* Choir/Band Dir Webster Cty Public Sch 1975-77; Choir Dir Caldwell Cty Public Sch 1977-78; Irving Mid Sch 1983-; *ai:* Girls Chorus; Boys Chorus & Mixed Chorus; MENC 1975-; ACDA 1983-; OEA 1983-; COCDA Sec/Treasurer 1984-; MacDowell Society Historian 1984-86; McFarlin Chancel Choir V P 1986-87; *office:* Irving Mid Sch 1920 E Alameda Norman OK 73071

MATLOCK, DEBRA LYNN, Math Teacher; *b:* Wewoka, OK; *m:* Jimmi Lee; *c:* Deetra, Jeremy; *ed:* (BA) Math, 1973, (MS) Math Ed, 1976 Southwestern St Univ; *cr:* Math Teacher Anadarko HS 1973- *ai:* 4-H Leader Anadarko HS, East Elem; Attendance Comm Mem; Anadarko Ed Assn Building Rep 5 Yrs; OEA, AEA 1973-; OK Cncl Math Teachers 1988-; Teacher of Yr 1986; *office:* Anadarko H S 1400 Warrior Dr Anadarko OK 73005

MATNEY, CHARLES T., Band Director; *b:* Ft Worth, TX; *m:* Jean; *c:* Katherine Hill, David, Mark; *ed:* (BME) Music Ed, TX Chrstn Univ 1954; SW Baptist Theological Seminary; *cr:* Band Dir Sanderson Ind Sch Dist 1954-56, Canton Ind Sch Dist 1956-57, Fort Worth Ind Sch Dist 1957-; *ai:* TX Bd Dir Assn, TX St TeachersAssn, Ft Worth Classroom Teachers Assn 11989-; TX PTA Life Mem; *home:* 5008 Cockrell Fort Worth TX 76133

MATNEY, KAYE VARNEY, First Grade Teacher; *b:* Pikeville, KY; *m:* Jackie C.; *c:* Jack B.; *ed:* (BS) Elem Ed, Pikeville Coll 1971; (MA) Elem Ed, Morehead St 1978; *cr:* Teacher Homebound & Hospital Prgm 1974-77, Greasy Creek Elem 1977-; *office:* Greasy Creek Elem Sch Rt 1 Box 175 Shelbiana KY 41562

MATROW, PETER FRANCIS, 5th Grade Teacher; *b:* Palmer, MA; *m:* Eizabeth L. Dusza; *c:* Robert F.; *ed:* (BS) Elem Ed, Framingham St Coll 1973; (MED) Admin, Westfield St Coll 1980; Cmptr Courses Springfield Tech Comm Coll; Management Univ of MA; *cr:* 5th Grade Teacher 1973-80, 6th Grade Teacher 1980-81, 3rd Grade Teacher 1981-83, 5th Grade Teacher 1983- Monson Public Schls; *ai:* Monson Sch Building Comm Educl Consultant 1990; Math Curr Comm 1982; Main Street Candy Drive Spon & PTO 1983; Monson PTO 1978-; Main Street PTO Liason & PTO Exec Bd 1978-80; Curr & Facility Needs Comm 1989; Main Street Sch Improvement Cncl 1985-87; Health Ed Advisory Cncl 1982-86; Health Curr Writing Comm Chm 1980-82 & Needs Study Comm 1979-80; Basic Skills Test Correcting Comm 1985-86; Enrichment Rdng Prgm Comm 1983-84; Monson Teachers Assn (Treas 1984-, Bargaining Team 1981-, Exec Bd 1973-, Pres 1981-83, VP 1979-81, Building Rep 1973-79); Horace Mann Grant Selection Comm Secy 1986-87; Saint Patricks Parish (Lector, Minister of Eucharist 1981-, Cncl 1984-86); Monson Democratic Comm Assoc Mem 1981-.

MATSON, HEATHER MITCHELL, Social Studies Teacher; *b:* Waltham, MA; *m:* Timothy Andrew; *c:* Timothy; *ed:* (BS) Scndry Ed/Eng, Boston Univ 1968; *cr:* Teacher Hudson Memorial Sch 1968-; *ai:* Washington DC 8th Grade Class Spon & Chaperone 1982-; Hudson Fed of Teachers Pres 1989-; *office:* Hudson Memorial Sch 1 Memorial Dr Hudson NH 03051

MATSON, JOAN BUCKLEY, Third Grade Teacher; *b:* Hartford, CT; *m:* Robert E.; *ed:* (BA) Sociology, Trinity Coll 170; (MA) Elem Ed, St Joseph Coll 1979; *cr:* 3rd Grade Teacher Coventry Grammar Sch 1970-; *ai:* Staff Liaison Comm; Prof Dev Sch Collaborative Team Mem Univ of CT 1988-; Natl Governing Bd of CT Trinity Coll Alumnae Assn (Pres, VP, Elected Mem); Manchester CT Jr Womens Club VP 1989-.

MATSON, KAREN KRAMER, Third Grade Teacher; *b:* St Peter, MN; *m:* Ronald P.; *c:* David, Joel, Phillip; *ed:* (BS) Ed, Concordia Coll 1963; Natl Coll of Ed, Univ of IL; *cr:* 3rd Grade Teacher Trinity Luth Sch 1963-64, Hope Luth Sch 1964-65; 3rd/4th Grade Teacher Concordia Luth Sch 1965-66; 3rd Grade Teacher General George S Patton Sch 1969-; *ai:* Homework Policy Comm 1989-; IL Fed of Teachers; Hillcrest Soccer Booster Club Pres 1987-89; Hillcrest Wrestling Booster Club VP 1987-; *office:* General George S Patton Sch 137th & Stewart Ave Riverdale IL 60627

MATSUKAWA, NANCY FUJIKAWA, Math Teacher/Dept Chair; *b:* Lihue Kauai, HI; *m:* Michael; *c:* Robert, James; *ed:* (BED) Phys Sci, Univ of HI 1969; OR Coll of Ed 1976; *cr:* Chem Teacher Kauai HS 1969-71; Math Teacher Parrish Jr HS 1971-76, Kealakehe Intermediate 1978-; *ai:* Mathcounts Coach; 7th Grade Level & Math Dept Chairperson; NCTM, HI St Teachers Assn, Alpha Delta Kappa Treas 1988-; Cntrl Kona Union Church (Secy, Sunday Sch Teacher); *office:* Kealakehe Intermediate Sch 74-5062 Onipaa St Kailua Kona HI 96740

MATTA, ANN ATKINS, Third Grade Teacher; *b:* Waynesboro, PA; *m:* Lynn E.; *c:* Michael L., Kristin A.; *ed:* (BS) His/Ed, Univ of MD 1959; Addl Studies Univ of CA; *cr:* Rdng Specialist Fountain Valley Schl Dist 1976-79; Elem Teacher 1979-; Mentor Teacher 1983- Irvine Sch Dist; *ai:* Mentor Teacher; Writing Process Seminar Presenter/UCI/Irvine Dist; GATE Sch Coord Gifted & Talented Ed; ASCD 1983-; Intnl Rdng Assn 1976-; KIWI US Olympic Fund Raiser; Fellowship/UCI Writing Project; Irvine Unified Sch Dist Teacher of Yr 1983; Bank America Grant Awd Winner-Sci; Irvine Educl Fnd Awd Winner-Sci Exchange Prgm; 2 Articles-CA Sci Teacher; *office:* Meadow Park Sch 50 Blue Lake S Irvine CA 92714

MATTACHIONE, LOUIE E., Speech/Theatre Dept Chair; *b:* Canton, OH; *ed:* (BSED) Speech/Dramatic Arts, Bowling Green St Univ 1961; Speech/Comm, Akron Univ 1971; Speech/Theatre, Kent St Univ 1981; *cr:* Teacher/Theatre Dir/Speech/Forensic Coach Massillon Perry HS 1961-; *ai:* Speech Team Coach; Childrens Theatre & Broadway Musical Theatre Dir; OH Ed Assn, NEA, OH HS Speech League, OH Theatre Assn; OH Sons of Italy; OH Speech Teacher of Yr 1975; Charter Mem Speech Coaches Hall of Fame OH; Natl Forensic League 4th Diamond Key Coach; Theatre Rededicated as Mattachione Theatre; *office:* Massillon Perry HS 3737 Harsh Ave SW Massillon OH 44646

MATTEO, ALICIA, First/Second Grade Teacher; *b:* Hazleton, PA; *m:* John D.; *c:* Justin; *ed:* (BS) Elem Ed/Early Chldhd Ed, Bloomsburg Univ 1979; Minor Hearing Impaired Ed, Cert Religious Ed; *cr:* 5th/6th Grade Teacher 1980-81, 3rd/4th Grade Teacher 1982-83, 1st/2nd Grade Teacher 1983- St Stanislaus Elem Sch; *ai:* Curr Planning Comm Mem; Faculty Secy 1983-85; NACT Sr Mem 1980-; *home:* 647 Roosevelt St Hazleton PA 18201

MATTERN, DAVID BRUCE, Fifth Grade Teacher; *b:* Harrisburg, PA; *m:* Sheryl L. Young; *c:* Marcia, Melissa; *ed:* (BA) Elem Ed, Cntrl Coll 1974; (MS) Educl Admin, IA St Univ 1982; *cr:* 3rd Grade Teacher Ringrose Elem Sch 1975-77; 3rd-6th Grade Teacher 1977-83, 5th Grade Teacher 1983- Lovejoy Elem Sch; *ai:* Curr Specialist; Textbook Adoption Comm; NCTM, ICTM 1990; Des Moines Math Advisory Bd; Wrote Dist Objective Based Math Tests Grade 5; Finalist Math ICTM Awd for Excl in Elem Math Teaching; *home:* 5505 SE 7th St Des Moines IA 50315

MATTERN, MARGARETTE ALBARRAN, Science Teacher; *b:* Leesville, LA; *m:* Lloyd Alexander; *ed:* (BS) Bio, Southwest TX St Univ 1975; (MA) Ed, Tarleton St Univ 1979; Assoc Cmptr Sci, Univ of Cntrl TX 1986; *cr:* Teacher Rancier Mid Sch 1976-79, Ellison HS 1979-85, South Grand Prairie HS 1985-; *ai:* SADD; STAT Mem 1989-; Kiwanic Club Youth Service Chm 1989-; Nom Presidential Awd Excl in Math & Sci Teaching 1989; Whos Who in Amer Ed 1988-89.

MATTES, FRANCES BROCKMAN, English Teacher; *b:* Murphy, NC; *m:* Warren E.; *c:* W. Andrew, Brock A.; *ed:* (BA) Eng, IN Wesleyan Univ 1958; *cr:* Art Teacher Greentown Elem 1958-59; Eng Teacher Alexandria HS 1959-60, Trapp HS 1960-61, Johnny Appleseed Jr HS 1961-73, Lucas HS 1974-; *ai:* Mid Sch Academic Challenge; Youth Club; NEA 1958-; OEA, LTA 1960-; OCTELA 1989-; United Meth Church of Cross; *home:* 224 Bowland Rd Mansfield OH 44907

MATTESKY, VIRGINA JOHNSON, 5th/6th Grade Teacher; *b:* Paterson, NJ; *m:* Robert Cruger; *c:* Robert E., Marc R.; *ed:* (BA) Elem Ed, William Paterson Coll 1971; Instructional Theory into Practice I & II; Learning Styles; Technology for Children; *cr:* 6th Grade Teacher North End Sch 1972-75; 5th Grade Teacher Leonard R Parks Sch 1975-78, South End Sch 1978-; *ai:* Cmptr Lead Teacher; Spelling Bee Coord; Assembly Chairperson; Reorganization, Rdng Curr, Soc Stud Curr, Testing Gifted & Talented Comm; NEA, NJ Ed Assn 1972- ; Family Sch Assn 1985-; Recipient of Governors Teacher Recognition Awd 1987; *office:* South End Sch Harper Terrace Cedar Grove NJ 07009

MATTHEIS, DOLORES (REESE), Teacher/Librarian; *b:* Graceton, MN; *c:* Patricia Mattheis Haviland *ed:* (BS) Math/Eng, 1969, Ed, 1970 Mary Coll; Grad Work at Univ of MT Missoula; *cr:* 1st-8th Grade Teacher Streeter ND 1948-50; Jr HS Teacher Burnstad Sch 1952-57; Math Teacher/Librarian Linton Sch 1957-69; Math/Eng Teacher/Librarian St Regis Sch 1970-; *ai:* Concessions; Jr HS Class Adv 1978-80; Pep Club Adv 1970-74; Delta Kappa Gamma Outstanding Stu Teacher Awd 1970, Selected by Admin 1989; Five Valleys Read 1978, Rdng Literacy Awd; Church Treas 1980-88; Math Grant 1966; Concordia Valedictorian Schlsp; Jamestown Coll Schlsp; *home:* 10 Four Mile Rd Saint Regis MT 59866

MATTHEWS, ANITA SUE, Business Teacher; *b:* Pittsburg, TX; *m:* Marvin; *c:* Susan; *ed:* (BA) Bus Ed, E TX St 1983; Working Toward Masters; *cr:* Teacher Pittsburg HS; *ai:* Bus Prof of America, Nike Club, Jr Class Spon; TSTA, NEA 1983-; Bus Prof of TX 1989-; Bus Prof of America, AVA 1983-; Honor Stu E TX St; *office:* Pittsburg HS 300 Texas St Pittsburg TX 75686

MATTHEWS, BETTYE RUTH, 6th Grade Teacher/Sci Dept Chm; *b:* Ozark, AL; *ed:* (BS) Elem Ed, Tuskegee Univ 1975; (MS) Elem Ed, AL St 1981; *cr:* Teacher Washington Public 1976-; *ai:* Washington Public Sch Prgm Chm; Help with Extracurricular Act, Textbook Comm; Macon Cty Ed Assn 1976-; PTA 1987-; *home:* 2005 Colvert St Tuskegee Inst AL 36088

MATTHEWS, CHERYL BUTLER, Sci/Eng/Home Ec Teacher; *b:* Jackson, TN; *m:* Larry; *c:* Don, Jimmy; *ed:* (BS) Home Ec, Univ TN 1968; *ai:* Sci Olympiad Coach; Instr and Prof Dev Comm; Sch Rep; Delta Kappa Gamma; *home:* 11 Brenda Cove Jackson TN 38301

MATTHEWS, CYNTHIA ANN, Sales Representative; *b:* Buffalo, NY; *ed:* (BS) Interdisciplinary Arts for Children, St Univ NY Coll Brockport 1973; (MS) Human Resources, St Univ of NY Coll Buffalo 1977; Sales Trng 1979, Sr Sales Trng 1980 Burroughs Corporation; Sales Trng L M Berry & Company 1982; *cr:* 4th Grade Teacher Tonawanda City Schls 1974-76; 1st Grade Teacher 1976-77, Kndgtn Teacher 1977-79 Depew Public Schls; Sales Rep Burroughs Corporation 1979-81; Trng & Dev Instr Fisher Price Corporation 1981-82; Sales Rep L M Berry & Company 1982-; *ai:* Newman Discussion Group, Newman Center; St Univ NY Coll Buffalo; L M Berry & Company Sales Achievement Club 1983, Pres Club 1986, 1987; Jr League of Buffalo 1984-89; *home:* 1692 Ruie Rd North Tonawanda NY 14120

MATTHEWS, DANIEL JOSEPH, First Grade Teacher; *b:* West Milford, NJ; *m:* Loretta Cera; *c:* Christine, Eileen; *ed:* (BA) Elem Ed, William Paterson Coll 1960; (MA) Rdng, Seton Hall Univ 1968; *cr:* 5th Grade Teacher Wanaque Bd of Ed 1960-62, Dept of Army Okinawa 1962-63; 1st-5th Grade Teacher Milford Bd of Ed 1963-; *ai:* West Milford Jaycees Outstanding Educator Awd 1973-74; Paradise Knoll Sch Teacher of Yr Awd; St of NJ Awd 1988-89; *office:* Paradise Noll Elem Sch 103 Paradise Rd Oak Ridge NJ 07438

MATTHEWS, DEBBIE LYNNE, 2nd Grade Teacher; *b:* Dumas, TX; *m:* Jim Bob; *c:* Stephanie, *ed:* (BA) Elem Ed, Panhandle St Univ 1979; (MS) Ed, Wayland Baptist Univ 1985; ESL Cert W TX St; WSI Water Safety Instruction Red Cross; *cr:* 3rd Grade Teacher 1979-88, Alternate Classroom Teacher 1988-89, 2nd Grade Teacher 1989- Dalhart Elem; *ai:* Grade Level Chairperson 3rd Grade; Campus Improvement & Revision Curr Guide Comm; Dalhart Classroom Teachers Assn 1987-; TX Teachers Assn 1979-85; Beta Sigma Phi VP Membership 1980-, Woman of Yr 1982; Dolhart Womens Club (Pres, VP, Historian) 1980-; 1st Chrstn Church Choir Youth Group Spon 1988-; Dalhart Womens Division of Chamber 1980-85; *office:* Dalhart Elem Sch 1401 Tennessee Dalhart TX 79022

MATTHEWS, DON W., 7th Grade Soc Stud Teacher; *b:* Atlantic, IA; *m:* Mary G. Walkup; *c:* Christie, Michael; *ed:* (BS) Soc Sci, 1964, (MS) Colonial/Const His, 1972 Northwest MO St Univ; Trial Teacher HS Geography Project 1968-69; *cr:* Soc Sci Teacher Jefferson HS 1964-68; Amer His & Geo Teacher East HS 1968-69; Soc Sci Teacher Jefferson HS 1969-78; 7th Grade Soc Stud Teacher Washington Mid Sch 1978-; *ai:* Historical Research Class Spon; 8th Grade Boys/Girls Bsktbl Coach; Spon Stu Cncl; Natl Mid Sch Assn 1988-; Natl Geographers Assn 1986-89; MO St Teachers Assn 1964-; Assn of Curr & Supervision 1988-; Teacher of Yr Maryville RI Sch Dist; Chairperson Dist Instructional Improvement Cncl; Fellowship 1966 MO Teachers His Inst; 7th Grade Interdisciplinary Team Leader; *office:* Washington Mid Sch 1st And Vine Sts Maryville MO 64468

MATTHEWS, IRENE B., Principal; *b:* Lima, OH; *m:* G. Donald; *c:* Melissa Sedlis, Jeffrey; *ed:* (BS) Elem Ed, 1963, (ME) Elem Ed, 1969 Miami Univ; Grad Stud Miami Univ; *cr:* Teacher Adams Elem Sch 1962-70; Asst Prin Harrison Elem Sch 1970-72; Prin Adams Elem Sch 1972-; *ai:* Delta Kappa Gamma (Secy 1975-76) 1969-; Hamilton City Organization Sch Admin & Supervision (Pres 1981-82) 1970-; OH Assn of Elem Sch Admins 1970-; Hamilton Elem Prins Assn (Pres, Secy) 1970-; PTA (Honorary VP 1972-) 1962-; Metropolitan Womens Club (Historian, Secy) 1984-; *office:* Adams Elem Sch 450 South F Street Hamilton OH 45013

MATTHEWS, IRENE LYNCH, English/Journalism Teacher; *b:* Fullerton, CA; *m:* Edgar L.; *c:* Bryan, Todd, Craig; *ed:* (AA) Eng, Fullerton Jr Coll 1962; (BA) Eng, CA St Univ Fullerton 1969; *cr:* Teacher/Adv Yorba Jr HS 1972-77, Orange HS 1977-; *ai:* Sch Newspaper Adv; Orange Cty Journalism Ed Assn (Pres 1981-85) 1972-; S CA Journalism Ed Assn (Secy 1990, Prgm Chairperson 1989); NCTE 1972-; Orange Nazarene Church; PTA Service Awd; Articles Published; *office:* Orange HS 525 N Shaffer Orange CA 92667

MATTHEWS, KAREN HODGES, 6th Grade Teacher; *m:* Kim K.; *c:* Kirk, Kyle; *ed:* (BA) Ed, Lenoir-Rhyne Coll 1978; (MA) Mid Sch Ed, Appalachian St Univ 1982; Mentor Trng; Effective Teacher Trng; Performance Trng; TESA Instr Trng; *cr:* Teacher Forbush Elem 1978-82, East Bend Elem 1982-; *ai:* Cheerleading Coach; Effective Teacher Trng Instr Cty; NCAE; East Bend Teacher of Yr 1984; *office:* East Bend Elem Sch P O Box 129 East Bend NC 27018

MATTHEWS, KENNETH LEE, Social Studies Teacher; *b:* Altoona, PA; *m:* G. R. Wolf; *c:* Lori, Joni; *ed:* (BA) Soc Sci, Univ of PA 1973; *cr:* Teacher Theodore Roosevelt Jr HS 1973-82; Altoona Area HS 1982-; *ai:* NEA 1973-; PA St Ed Assn 1973-; Altoona Area Ed Assn 1973-; *office:* Altoona Area HS 6th Ave 13-15 Sts Altoona PA 16602

MATTHEWS, KEVIN W., Director of Bands; *b:* Marquette, MI; *m:* Karen; *c:* Nicole; *ed:* (BA) Music Ed, E MI Univ 1985; *cr:* Dir of Bands White Pigeon 1986-; *ai:* Marching, Pep, Jazz Bands; Percussion Ensemble; MI St Band & Orch Assn Co-Chairperson Solo & Ensemble 1989-; Kalamazoo Concert Band 1986-.

MATTHEWS, KIM K., Assistant Principal; *b:* Winston-Salem, NC; *m:* Karen H.; *c:* Kirk F., Kyle H.; *ed:* (MA) Admin, Appalachian St Univ 1981; (BA) Intermediate Ed, Lenoir-Rhyne Coll 1978; *cr:* 7th/8th Grade Sci Teacher W Yadkin Elem 1978-79; 7th/8th Grade Math/Sci Teacher Fall Creek Elem 1979-84, E Bend Elem 1984-87; Asst Prin W Yadkin Elem 1987-89, Forbush HS 1989-; *ai:* NC Assn of Ed Office Personnel 1989-; NC Teacher Assn of Prins & Asst Prins 1988-; E Bend Sch Teacher of Yr 1984-85.

MATTHEWS, LESLIE G., Business Education Teacher; *b:* Muskegon, MI; *m:* Lois E. Rice; *c:* Ronald L.; *ed:* (BA) Bus Ed, Ferris St Coll 1963; (MA) W MI Univ 1967; Cmptr Sci; *cr:* Bus Ed Teacher Muskegon HS; Part Time Instr Muskegon Comm Coll; *ai:* MEA, NEA, Prof Accounting Assn; MBEA; *office:* Muskegon HS 80 W Southern Ave Muskegon MI 49441

MATTHEWS, LONA BETHEL, Language Arts Teacher; *b:* Miami, FL; *m:* Jerome Matthews; *ed:* (AA) Liberal Arts, Miami Dade Comm Coll 1967; (BA) Eng, Scndry Ed, 1970, (MS) Ed, 1979 FL A&M Univ; *cr:* Lang Art Teacher North Dade Mid Sch 1970-; *ai:* Mid Sch Cadre Mem; Hospitality Club Spon; United Teachers of Dade; NCTE; Zeta Phi Beta 1968-; NAACP; St Philips Cath Church Womens Guild; North Dade Mid Teacher of Yr 1977/1987.

MATTHEWS, MARY BUSH, 5th Grade Teacher; *b:* Hollandale, MS; *m:* Roosevelt; *ed:* (AA) General, Chicago City Coll 1967; (BS) Elem Ed, Chicago Teachers Coll 1969; (MA) Elem Ed, De Paul Univ 1973; Spec Ed, Univ of Chicago Natl Coll of Ed; *cr:* Curr Teacher 1973-74, Teacher 1969- Chicago Bd of Ed; *ai:* Supt Albany Youth Center Sunday Sch; Mem Local Teacher, Parent & Cmmty Comm; Elected to Serve on Steering Comm of Lang Art Dept 1971-75; Wrote Teaching & Learning Objectives Speaking & Listening; *home:* 535 N Aztec Dr Carol Stream IL 60188

MATTHEWS, PATTI DUNCAN, First Grade Teacher; *b:* Jeffersonville, IN; *m:* Ronald Doyle; *c:* Bobby, Audrey P.; *ed:* (BS) Elem Ed, Northeastern St Univ 1975; Grad Stud Early Chldhd Ed; *cr:* 1st Grade Teacher Edison Elem Sch 1976-; *ai:* OEA, NEA 1976-; Elem Level Teacher of Yr 1986-87; Class of 1940 Teacher Awd 1987-88; *office:* Edison Elem Sch 134 W 9th St Bristow OK 74010

MATTHEWS, RONALD BURDETT, 5th Grade Teacher; *b:* Murray, UT; *m:* Pamelin S. Saur Matthews; *c:* Brent, Brian, Bryce; *ed:* (BS) Elem Ed, 1968; (MED) Educ Admin, 1971; Educ Specialist Educ Admin, 1973 Brigham Young Univ; Addl Studies Eng As 2nd Lang/Gifted Ed/Educ Admin Northern AZ Univ; *cr:* 5th Grade Teacher Whittier Elem Sch 1968-70; 6th Grade Teacher Dugway Elem Sch 1971-75; Prin Grand Canyon Unified Sch Dist 1975-76; Teacher Tuba City Public Sch Dist 1976-; *ai:* Head Building Rep; Chm Prof Growth Comm; Tuba City Ed Assn Pres 1981-82; NEA 1968-; AZ Gifted & Talented Teachers Assn 1981-84; Rotary Club Occupational Info Chm 1975-76; Cub Scouts Cub Master 1982-84; BSA Troop Comm Chm 1972-75/1984-86; *home:* 4245 St Moritz Way Flagstaff AZ 86004

MATTHEWS, SAMUEL, 9th-12th Grade History Teacher; *b:* Georgetown, Guyana; *m:* Sharon Ann Saunders;; *c:* Tara, Thaddeus; *ed:* (AB) His, Xavier Univ 1965; (MED) Soc Fnds, 1969, (EDD) 1984 Univ of Cincinnati; Trng on Adolescent Chemical Dependency; *cr:* Instr Stowe Adult Sch 1967-68, Mc Millan Adult Sch 1969-86; Teacher Withrow HS 1987-; *ai:* Core Team for Drug Prevention Mem; African-Amer Awareness Organization Co-Spon; Local Sch Advisory Comm Mem; Articles in Publications.

MATTHEWS, SANDRA J., Mathematics Teacher; *b:* Albuquerque, NM; *c:* Preston, Lisa; *ed:* (BS) Math, NM St Univ 1970; (MAT) Math Ed, Univ of NM 1972; *cr:* Math Teacher Eldorado HS 1972-; *ai:* NCTM; Gold Star Wives VP 1983-84.

MATTHEWS, SANDRA K., Gifted & Talented Facilitator; *b:* Hot Springs, AR; *m:* Mike Scroggins; *ed:* (BSE) Elem Ed, Ouachita Baptist Univ 1973; Gifted & Talented Ed, Univ of AR Little Rock, AR Tech Univ; *cr:* Classroom Teacher Hot Springs Public Schls 1973-76; Classroom Teacher 1976-84, Gifted & Talented Facilitator 1984- Lake Hamilton Public Schls; *ai:* Supt Advisory & Staff Dev Comm Mem; NEA 1973-; AR Ed Assn 1973-; Lake Hamilton Classroom Teachers Assn (pres 1979-80, Mem 1976-); Certified Womens Leadership, Talents Unlimited, Cooperative Learning Teacher; *office:* Lake Hamilton Primary Sch 106 S Wolf Dr Pearcy AR 71964

MATTHEWS, SUSAN B., Teacher of Academically Gifted; *b:* Southern Pines, NC; *m:* Timothy Brigman; *ed:* (BA) Intermediate Ed, Meredith Coll 1977; Gifted & Talented Cert; *cr:* Teacher J W Turlington 1977-88, Pauline Jones 1988-89, Edgewood 1989-; *ai:* SGA Club Adv; NCAE Pres 1982-; Teacher of Yr Sch Rep; Cty Coord for Jump Rope for Heart 1983-88; *home:* 108 B Lake Clair Pl Fayetteville NC 28304

MATTHEWS, VIRGINIA WOODARD, Kindergarten Teacher; *b:* Camden, NY; *m:* James; *c:* Peter, Jill Matthews Boadway; *ed:* (BS) Elem Ed, Oswego St Univ 1959; (MS) Ed, St Univ Potsdam 1979; Nurmerous Courses Potsdam St; *cr:* 3rd Grade Teacher 1959-60, Elem Substitute Teacher 1965-66, 4th Grade Teacher 1966-83, Kndgtn Teacher 1983- Massena Cntrl; *ai:* Mentorship Prgm; NY St United Teachers; St Lawrence Cty Farm Bureau Chm Citizenship Awd Comm 1979-; Womens Club Recording Secy; Massena Grange Mem; Church (Pres Church Ladies, Piano Player, Sunday Sch Teacher Aid); Massena Rescue Squad Awd; *office:* Massena Cntrl Sch Highland Ave & Nightengale Ave Massena NY 13662

MATTHEWS, WILLIAM BROOKS, Biology Teacher; *b:* Raleigh, NC; *m:* Rosa Marie Hurtarte; *c:* Maria S., Jennifer B., Heather L.; *ed:* (BS) Bio, 1976, (MED) Sci, 1979, (MS) Sch Admin, 1988 Campbell Univ; Sch Admin, Campbell Univ; *cr:* HS Bio/AP Bio/Chem/Physics/Phys Sci Teacher Cape Fear Chrstn Acad 1976-79; Bio/AP Bio Teacher Dunn HS 1979-85, Triton HS 1985-; *ai:* Girls Var Bsktbl Coach; Asst Athletic Dir; NEA, NC Assn of Educators 1985-; Natl Fed of Coaches 1986-87; NC Coaches Assn 1985-; NC Athletic Dirs Assn 1989-; Girls Bsktbl Coach of Yr 1988-; Boys Tennis Coach of Yr 1983-84; *home:* Highland Dr PO Box 294 Buies Creek NC 27506

MATTHYS, JOHN WILLIAM, Mathematics Teacher; *b:* Schulenburg, TX; *m:* Bess Elaine Haseman; *ed:* (BA) Phys Ed, TX Luth Coll 1972; Working Toward Masters Admin & Mid-Management Certificate; *cr:* Teacher Dulles HS 1986-; *ai:* Teams at Risk Tutoring; Jr & Sr Powder Puff Ftbl Game & Act; Ft Bend Cncl of Teachers of Math, NCTM, Classroom Teachers Assn 1986-; Targeting Success Awd, Ft Bend Ind Sch Dist Recognition of Outstanding Teachers; *office:* John Foster Dulles H S P O Box 1004 Sugar Land TX 77487

MATTICK, GLORIA PALACIOS, Chem Teacher/Sci Dept Head; *b:* Laredo, TX; *m:* Stephen D.; *c:* Anthony D.; *ed:* (BA) Sci/Math, TX A&I Univ 1963; (MAT) Chem, IN Univ Bloomington 1967; Natl Sci Fnd Summer Inst, Pratt Inst Brooklyn, Woodrow Wilson Summer Inst, Butler Univ Indianapolis; *cr:* Chem Teacher Martin HS 1963-66; Chem Teacher 1967-, Sci Teacher Dept Head 1985- Franklin Cmmty HS; *ai:* Sci Club Spon 1980; Sci Dept Head; Delta Kappa Gamma Pres 1986-88; Franklin Cmmty Best Teacher Awd 1988; Psi Iota Secy 1974-82; *office:* Franklin Cmmty HS 625 Grizzly Cub Dr Franklin IN 46131

MATTINGLY, ANNA CATHERINE, Lang Art/Soc Stud Teacher; *b:* Hardinsburg, KY; *ed:* (BA) His/Poly Sci, Univ of KY 1971; (MA) Scndry Ed, 1977, (Rank I) Scndry Ed, 1988 W KY Univ; *cr:* 5th-6th Grade Teacher 1972-83, 7th-8th Grade Lang Art Teacher 1983-86, 5th-8th Grade Soc Stud Teacher 1986-88, 6th-8th Grade Soc Stud/Lang Art Teacher 1988- Howevalley Elem; *ai:* Howevalley Instructional Comm Mem; Lang Art Rep; Girls Bsktbl Coach; KY Ed Assn; Hardin Cty Ed Assn Building Rep 1977-79; St James Church Choir (Alto Singer 1977-) 1976-.

MATTINGLY, SHARON, Third Grade Teacher; *b:* Henderson, KY; *ed:* (BA) Elem Ed, Univ of Evansville 1975; (MA) Elem Ed, 1977, (Rank I) Admin, 1988 W KY Univ; *cr:* K-6th Grade/Chapter I Rdng Teacher Corydon Elem Sch 1975-; *ai:* Girls & Boys Bsktbl Coach; Henderson Cty Ed Assn, KY Ed Assn, NEA; Resource Teacher KY Internship Prgm; Faculty Adv Comm Rep; *home:* 5371 US 41 Alt Henderson KY 42420

MATTIS, CHRISTINE MORETTINI, Mathematics/English Teacher; *b:* Springfield, IL; *m:* Richard; *c:* Jason, Victoria; *ed:* (BS) Elem Ed, E IL Univ 1973; Working Towards Masters in Ed, E IL Univ & S IL Univ; *cr:* 4th Grade Teacher 1973-76, 7th/8th Grade Teacher 1976- Holy Ghost Sch; *ai:* 8th Grade Algebra Honors Class; Fitness Instr; Dance Stu Lewis & Clark Comm Coll; Idea Organization for Fitness Prof 1983-; *office:* Holy Ghost Sch 309 N Washington St Jerseyville IL 62052

MATTNER, JANICE CAROLYN, Math/Eng/His/Art Teacher; *b:* Washington, DC; *m:* Gilbert W.; *c:* Kyle, Lorne; *ed:* (BA) Art/Eng, Beloit Coll 1957; *cr:* Art/Eng Teacher Cudahy HS 1957-58; Artist Ken Cook Co 1958-60; 6th Grade Teacher Olive View Sch 1969-72; 2nd Grade Teacher Pinecrest Sch 1972-77; Eng/His/Math/Art Teacher St Nicholas Greek Sch 1977-; *ai:* 8th Grade Adv; Friends of Children are our Future Pres 1989-; *office:* St Nicholas Greek Sch 9501 Balboa Blvd Northridge CA 91325

MATTOX, DEBRA ELAINE, Soc Stud Dept Chairperson; *b:* Memphis, TN; *c:* Kristin; *ed:* (BS) His/Sociology, 1972, (MA) Ec/Curr/Dev, 1979 Memphis St Univ; Educl Admin, Supervision, Adult Ed, Laubach Literacy Trng; *cr:* Admin Asst MARC House 1972-73; Soc Stud Teacher Craigmont HS 1973-80; Curr/Developer Memphis City Schls 1975-81; GED/Adult Ed Teacher SW Voc Tech 1975-88; Ec Teacher Southside HS 1981-; *ai:* Southside Marching Band Spon 1981; Auxiliary Units Flag Corps & Majorettes Awd; Pep Club Adv 1982-88; NCSS Mem 1973-; Natl Assn of Female Exec Mem 1988-; Girls Club of Memphis Inc Mem 1985-; Delta Sigma Theta Mem 1969-; Springdale Baptist Church (Co-Dir Vacation Bible Sch) 1985-89, Service Awds 1985-89; Outstanding Young Woman of America Awd 1979; St Technical Inst of Memphis Outstanding Teacher of Year 1986-89; Jr Achievement of Memphis Incorporated Best Teacher of Yr Awd 1987-88; City-Wide Textbook Selection Comm Chairperson 1984, 1990; *office:* Southside HS 1880 Prospect Memphis TN 38106

MATTOX, SUE MILLER, Fourth Grade Teacher; *b:* Grand Rapids, MI; *m:* Arthur D.; *c:* Robyn R., Stephanie I., Carrie A.; *ed:* (BS) Elem Ed, 1975; (MS) Elem Ed, 1982; (EDSP) Elem Ed, Jacksonville St Univ 1987-; *cr:* 1st Grade Teacher 1975-78; 4th Grade Teacher 1979- Mellow Valley HS; *ai:* Handbk Comm 1988-; Textbk Comm 1985 1988-; Courtesy Comm 1984-87; Dress Code Comm 1987-; AEA Faclty Rep 1980-85; Girl Scouts of Amer Leader 1987-89; AEA 1975-; NEA 1975-; Twentieth Century Club 1972-76; Fav Teacher 1979-80; *office:* Mellow Valley H S Rt 1 Cragford AL 36255

MATTUCCI, FRANK ANTHONY, Educator/History Teacher; *b:* Chicago, IL; *m:* Diane C. Mirochna; *c:* Joey; *ed:* (BA) European His, 1975, (MA) European His, 1977 De Paul Univ; Spec Ed, Natl Coll of Ed; *cr:* His Teacher Notre Dame HS 1976-78; Soc Stud Teacher New Trier HS 1978-87; His Teacher DePaul Univ 1987-88, N Chicago HS 1988-89; Hum Teacher Adlai E Stevenson HS 1989-; *ai:* Head Var Girls Bsktbl; Career Mrktg; Amer His Assn; Society Preservation Landmarks Society; IL Bsktbl Coaches Assn; DePaul Grad Sch Internship & Fellowship 1976-77; Fully Paid Grad Tuition & Teaching Stipend; Vassar Coll Teacher of Yr 1983; Class A Coach of Yr; *office:* Adlai E Stevenson HS 16070 W Hwy 22 Prairie View IL 60069

MATULKA, YVONNE M., 8th Grade Teacher; *b:* Lincoln, NE; *m:* Donald D.; *c:* Christopher, Sean, Michelle, Tracey; *ed:* (BS) Elem Ed, Univ of NE 1972; *cr:* K-8th Grade Teacher Butler Cty Dist 23 1972-74; 8th Grade Teacher Bellwood Public Sch 1974-; *ai:* Butler Cty Ed Assn Trea 1978-79; Bellwood Faculty Assn Pres 1986-87; Alpha Delta Kappa His 1980-82; St Marys Catholic Church Parish Cncl 1987-; St Marys Catholic Sch Cncl 1987-; David City Lib Bd & Fnd 1989-; Butler Cty Citizens for Decency/Pres 1988-; *office:* Bellwood Pub School PO Box 100 Bellwood NE 68624

MATURKO, JOAN IMPERATI, Kindergarten Teacher; *b:* New Haven, CT; *m:* Melvin Frank; *ed:* (BA) Early Childhood Ed, Univ of CT 1964; Ed, UCLA; Art Ed Training, Getty Institute; *cr:* Kndgtn Teacher Seth Haley Sch 1964-65, Jefferson Sch 1968-; *ai:* Cmptr Coord; Coord of Sch Improvement Prgm; Mem of Dist Inservice Resource Team for Discipline; Based Art Ed; NEA 1968-; CTA 1968-; RBCTA Faculty Rep 1989-; Parks & Recreation Commission Commissioner 1978-; Cultural Arts Comm 1981-85; Dominquez Brand Awd Outstanding Educator 1989; *office:* Jefferson Elem Sch 1401 Inglewood Ave Redondo Beach CA 90278

MATUSOFF, SEYMOUR BERNARD, Mathematics Department Chair; *b:* Brooklyn, NY; *m:* Cynthia Packer; *c:* Vicki G. Foreman, Nancy J. Childerston; *ed:* (BEE) Electrical Engineering, 1944, (BSME) Mechanical Engineering, 1947, (MED) Ed, 1959 Univ of DE; Command & General Staff, US Armed Forces Inst; *cr:* Instr Univ of DE 1947-48; Engineer Many Companies 1948-58; Teacher Wilmington HS 1958-; *ai:* Wrestling Coach 1960-65; Golf Team Coach 1972-77; US Army Engineers Active Duty, Reserve, Retired Colonel; Taught 10 Summmers 1st Army Intelligence Sci Ft Meade MD; *home:* 614 Loveville Rd Hockessin DE 19707

MATYAS, EILEEN HEILES, Spanish Teacher; *b:* New Kensington, PA; *m:* R. James; *c:* Megan, Patrick; *ed:* (BS) Span Ed, Indiana Univ of PA 1974; Univ of Valladolid, Penn St Univ; Ger Cert Prgm, Indiana Univ of PA; *cr:* Teacher Kiski Area Sch Dist 1973-74, Kennett Consolidated Sch Dist 1974-75, N K Arnold Sch Dist 1986-; *ai:* Interact & Span Club, Soph Class Spon; Stu Assistance Prgm Mem; PSEA, NEA; Parish Cncl 1990; Tri City Soccer 1985-86; Church Ed Comm 1983-86; *office:* Valley HS Stevenson Blvd New Kensington PA 15068

MATZ, HENRY RICHARD, Chemistry/Phys Science Teacher; *b:* Tucson, AZ; *ed:* (BS) Bio, 1976, (MBA) Accounting, 1982 Univ of AZ; *cr:* Math Teacher Doolen Jr HS 1987; Sci Teacher Rincon HS 1987-; *office:* Rincon HS 422 N Arcadia Blvd Tucson AZ 85711

MATZA, NATHAN, Health Teacher; *b:* Bronx, NY; *m:* Jeannette; *c:* Eric, Jennifer, Sara; *ed:* (AA) Bio, El Camino Coll 1966; (BS) Zoology, 1968, (MA) Ed, 1972 CA St Long Beach; Working Towards PhD Public Health, Loma Linda Univ; Supplemental Credentials in Scndry, Supervision, Health Ed *cr:* Teacher Westminster HS 1970-; Univ Asst Professor CA St Univ Long Beach 1983-; *ai:* Tobacco Ed Comm; Girls Soccer Coach; Sr Class Adv; Mentor Teacher 1984-87; CASHE Secy 1987-; APHA, CTA, NEA; Cmptr Ed & Video Role Playing Grants; *office:* Westminster HS 14325 Goldenwest St Westminster CA 92683

MATZKE, CHERYL GLASER, Scndry Eng Teacher/Dept Chair; *b:* Fargo, ND; *m:* Robert A.; *c:* Nicole, Erika, Erin, Christopher, Heidi; *ed:* (AA) Liberal Arts, 1968, (BA) Eng/Lang Art, 1970 Concordia Coll; Coaching Cert 1977, Scndry Developmental Rdng 1982, Bemidji St Univ; *cr:* Eng Teacher Lafayette HS 1970-; *ai:* Stu Cncl, Sr Class Adv; Sch Bd Cmmty Ed, Cooperative Prgms Comm; NEA, MN Ed Assn 1970-; Red Lake Falls Sftbl Assn Pres 1985-; Aid Assn to Luths (Pres 1987-, Lamplighter Team 1989-); Amer Legion Auxiliary 1987-; Twin Rivers 4-H Club Key Leader 1989-; Red Lake Falls Sftbl Umpires Assn 1988-; Amer Sftbl Assn 1986-; City Park & Recreation Bd 1988-; Teacher of Yr 1989; Mem of Blandin Cmmty Leadership Prgm 1989; *office:* Lafayette HS 404 Champagne Ave PO Box 399 Red Lake Falls MN 56750

MATZKE, NORMA JEAN, 8th Grade Teacher; *b:* Upland, CA; *c:* Kurt; *ed:* (BS) Eng Stud, OR St Univ 1973; (MED) Ed, Univ of Portland 1988; *cr:* 7th/8th Grade Lang Art Teacher Newport Mid Sch 1974-; *ai:* NCTE; Supts Awd Lincoln Cty Sch Dist 1986; Articles Published; OR Coast Cncl for Arts Teacher as Writer Awd 1986; *office:* Newport Mid Sch 311 NE Eads St Newport OR 97365

MATZNER, BARBARA J., HS English Teacher; *b:* M, New York; *m:* Gad; *c:* Jennifer, Daniel; *ed:* (BA) Eng, City Coll of CUNY 1965; (MA) Eng Ed, City Coll 1969; (PD) Supervision/Admin, Brooklyn Coll CUNY 1989; *cr:* Eng Teacher W W Niles Jr HS 1965-71, Deer Park Schls 1976-83; Sci Teacher Ind Sch 320 Bklyn 1984-86; Eng Teacher Bayside HS 1986-; *ai:* Natl Honor Society Adv; NCTE Mem 85-; Natl Ed Honor Society.

MAUCH, MARILYN TULLAR, Secondary Mathematics Teacher; *b:* Jewell, KS; *m:* Glenn V.; *ed:* (BS) Math, 1959, (MS) Ed, 1970 Ft Hays St Univ; Ed Spec/Rdng, Ft Hays St Univ 1984; *cr:* 1st Grade/Jr HS Math Teacher Chapman Elem 1959-62; 1st Grade Teacher Shawnee Mission KS 1962-66, Unified Sch Dist 208 1966-68; 3rd Grade Teacher Unified Sch Dist 489 1968-74: Lab Sch Instr 1970, Rdng Grad Asst 1983-84 Ft Hays St Univ; Chapter I Rdng Teacher Unified Sch Dist 489 1985-86; Math Teacher Jessieville Schls 1986-; *ai:* NCTM 1986-; *home:* 2 Cullera Ln Hot Springs Vlg AR 71909

MAUCK, DOLORES GERZINA, Kindergarten Teacher; *b:* James City, PA; *m:* Paul L. Sr.; *c:* Linda R. Ongley, William E. Ross, Paul L. Jr., Thomas E. Ross, Cathy Mauck Ragans, Kevin L. Ross, Robert A., Brenda R. Sunday; *ed:* (BS) Elem Ed, Edinboro St Coll 1971; *cr:* 6th Grade Teacher 1971-72, Kndgtn Teacher 1972- Chattahoochee Elem; *home:* 320 Lancaster Dr Tallahassee FL 32304

MAUCK, SANDRA MILLER, Language Arts Teacher; *b:* Wheeing, WV; *m:* James J. Jr.; *c:* Bradley R. Joseph; *ed:* (AB) Eng/Speech, West Liberty St Coll 1970; (MA) Comm, WV Univ 1983; Grad Stud Ed; *cr:* Media Specialist Madison Jr HS 1969-70; Eng Teacher Triadelphia HS 1970-71, Warwood Jr HS 1972-76; Substitute Teacher OH Cty Schls 1981-83; Lang Art/Journalism Teacher Bridge Street Jr HS 1983-; *ai:* Yrbk Spon; Speech Team Coach; Rdng Dept Chairperson; Public Relations Comm; Graduation Comm Chairperson; NEA, WV Ed Assn, WV Assn for Mid Level Ed, OH Valley Lang Art Cncl; OH Valley Jaycees Women 1976-85, US Jaycees Congresswomen 1981; Warwood United Meth Church Trustee 1989-; Showcase Awd for Outstanding Sch Yrbk; Presentor at Several WV Mid Sch Conferences & WV Prins Acad; *office:* Bridge Street Jr HS Junior Ave Wheeling WV 26003

MAUER, CHARLES M., 5th Grade Teacher; *b:* Milwaukee, WI; *m:* Karen L.; *c:* Paul, Mark; *ed:* (BA) Ed-Magna Cum Laude 1968, Ed 1972 St Martins Coll; Photography & Advanced Audio/Visual Presentations; *cr:* 5th Grade Teacher 1968-75, 3rd Grade Teacher 1975-79 Lydia Hawk Elem; Teacher of Gifted Lacey Elem 1979-87; 5th Grade Teacher Pleasant Glade Elem 1987-; Adjunct Faculty St Martins Coll, Seattle Pacific Univ, Pacific Luth Univ; *ai:* Sci Fair Coord; N Thurston Sch Dist Soc Studs & Mid Sch Lang Arts Comm; NEA Life Mem 1968-; WA Ed Assn 1968-; N Thurston Ed Assn Pres Elect 1968-; Lydia Hawk PTA (Treas 1970-71, Pres 1976-77, VP 1975-76); Recipient Dist Employee Recognition Awd 1987; WA St Cert Guidelines/Comm Chm 1986; St Martins Coll Cert Prgm Dev Comm 1985-86; *home:* 3916 18th Ave NE Olympia WA 98506

MAUERSBERGER, YUDITA G. YUNKERIS, Foreign Lang Dept Chair; *b:* Kaunas, Lithuania; *m:* Paul Dieter; *c:* Lisa A., Mark D.; *ed:* (BA) Ger, Roosevelt Univ 1959; (MA) Ed; Grad Courses Middlebury Coll; *cr:* Ger Teacher Lane Tech HS 1961-80; Teacher/Dept Chairperson Amundsen 1980-82; Teacher Morgan Park 1982-85; Teacher/Dept Chairperson Lane Tech HS 1985-; *ai:* Ger Club Spon; AATG 1961-; Daughters Pres 1980-83; Fullbright Schlsp; *home:* 907 Hirsch Ave Melrose Park IL 60160

MAUGHMER, LOIS GILES, Mathematics Teacher; *b:* Chillicothe, OH; *c:* Tab; *ed:* (BS) Soc Stud, 1978, (MA) Ed Fnds & Research, 1980 OH St Univ; *cr:* Instr Columbus Tech Inst 1978-81; Teacher OH Youth Dept Trng Inst of Columbus 1981-82, Ridgeview Mid Sch 1982-89, Champion Mid Sch 1989-; *ai:* Mathcounts Coord Coach; Worth Extra Effort Coord; NEA, Columbus Ed Assn, OH St Univ Alumni Assn, PTA; US Army Reserve Sergeant 1st Class 1974-; Mt Herman Baptist Church Choir Mem 1981-; ASCD Mem 1989-, Certificate 1990; Teacher of Yr Nom 1986; OH Cncl of Baptist Churches Grad Schlsp; Ashland Oil Teacher of Yr Nom 1988; *office:* Champion Mid Sch 1270 Hawthorne Ave Columbus OH 43203

MAULDIN, ESTHER LOWERY, 7th Grade Mathematics Teacher; *b:* Pasadena, TX; *c:* Krystal K.; *ed:* (BS) Phys Ed/Math Ed, Stephen F Austin St Univ 1975; *cr:* 9th-12th Grade Math Teacher Leveretts Chapel Ind Sch Dist 1976; 9th/10th Grade Math Teacher W Rusk Ind Sch Dist 1976-78; 6th/7th Grade Math Teacher Jefferson Ind Sch Dist 1978-; 0 *ai:* UIL Coord; Consultation Comm; TSTA; *home:* 506 E Elizabeth Jefferson TX 75657

MAULDIN, LYNDA KING, American History Teacher; *b:* Dothan, AL; *m:* Wayne; *c:* Amy, Wayne Jr.; *ed:* (BA) Soc Sci/His, Troy St 1973; Working Towards MS His, Troy St; *cr:* His Teacher Girard Mid Sch 1973-; *ai:* Dothan Ed Assn, AL Ed Assn, NEA 1973-; *home:* PO Box 9 Pinckard AL 36371

MAULDIN, MELBA RIVES, Sixth Grade Teacher; *b:* Robert Lee, TX; *m:* Donald M.; *c:* Donald G., Jana Mauldin Smith; *ed:* (AA) Applied Arts, San Angelo Coll 1965; (BS) Elem Ed, Angelo St Coll 1968; (MED) Counseling, Angelo St Univ 1980; *cr:* 4th Grade Teacher San Angelo Ind Sch Dist 1968-69; Jr HS Eng Teacher 11969-74, 5th Grade Teacher 1975-83, 6th Grade Teacher 1983- Robert Lee Ind Sch Dist; *ai:* Jr HS/HS Chrldrs; Beta Club; Many Class Organizations Spon; Coke Cty TX Assn Cmnty Schls 1975-; Coke Cty TX St Teachers Assn (Secy 1970-71, Treas 1972-73); Beta Sigma Phi (VP 1973-74, Pres 1974-75, Secy 1976-77) Woman of Yr 1975; Process of Writing Geneology Book About the Rives Family; *office:* Robert Lee I S D HC 6 Box 303 Robert Lee TX 76945

MAUNTEL, MARGARET SCHLUTER, 6th Grade Rdng/Sci Teacher; *b:* Lexington, VA; *m:* Jacob C.; *c:* Matthew C., Jennifer J., Nicole M.; *ed:* (BS) Elem Ed, 1973, (MS) Guidance/ Counseling, 1977 IN St Univ; Spec Ed; Professionalization of Counseling Degree; *cr:* 3rd/5th Grade Teacher Lafayette Cty C-1 Sch Corporation 1973-75; 6th Grade Teacher/Cnslr Dubois Mid Sch 1977-; *ai:* 6th Grade Girls Bsktbl Coach; Phi Delta Kappa 1977-; Alpha Delta Kappa (Chaplain 1985-87), 1984-; IN St Teachers Assn Pres of Local CTA 1977-; Bus & Prof Women (Pres, St Bd 1981-83) Woman of Yr 1989; Jasper Jaycettes Pres 1978-79; 4-H Leader 1988-89; MS Grad Assistantship; Initiated BSA Cub Chapter; Bible & HS Sunday Schls Teaching Awd; *home:* RR 7 Box 203 Jasper IN 47546

MAUNU, JOHN RAYMOND, Social Studies Instructor; *b:* Cloquet, MN; *m:* Johanna Meger; *c:* Michael, Kristen, Matthew; *ed:* (BS) His, Univ of MN Duluth 1970; (MA) His, Univ of WI Platteville 1975; Grad Stud E MI Univ; *cr:* Instr Riverdale Sch Dist 1970-73, Grosse Ile Township Schls 1973-; *ai:* Intramural Weight Lifting Supvr/Coach; Asst HS Wrestling Coach; Soc Stud Dept Chm; Riverdale Sch Dist Head Negotiator 1971-72; Wayne Cty Intermediate Sch Dist Plaque for Outstanding Educator, Technology & Curr Dev 1989; *office:* Grosse Ile HS 7800 Grays Dr Grosse Ile MI 48138

MAUPIN, DIANE C., Language Arts Teacher; *b:* Kansas City, MO; *m:* Rick W.; *c:* Laura, Christina, Caleb; *ed:* (BSE) Eng, Cntrl MO St Univ 1975; *cr:* Lang Arts Teacher Holden Mid Sch 1977-; *ai:* Yrbk Spon; MO St Teachers Assn 1978-; Holden Teachers Assn Building Rep 1989-; PTA 1980-; *home:* Rt 1 Box 58B Kingsville MO 64061

MAUPIN, MILDRED LEE, English Teacher; *b:* Englewood, TN; *ed:* (BS) Elem Ed, 1956, (MED) Guidance/Educl Psych, 1964 Univ of Chattanooga; *cr:* Teacher Pond Springs Elem Sch 1954-55, Rossville Jr HS 1955-56; Teacher/Cnslr Charleston Sch 1956-63; Teacher Mayfield Elem Sch 1963-66, Arnold Jr HS 1966-71, Cleveland Jr HS 1971-; *ai:* Spelling Bee Coord; Bradley Cty Ed Assn Secy; Cleveland Ed Assn Secy; TN Ed Assn; NEA Life Mem; Big Spring United Meth Church (Ed Chairperson, Admin Cncl Secy); Cleveland Jaycees Outstanding Young Teacher of Yr Awd 1958-59; *office:* Cleveland Jr HS 880 Raider Dr Cleveland TN 37311

MAUPIN, VICKI TOLLISON, Computer Literacy Teacher; *b:* Borger, TX; *w:* Larry (dec); *c:* JoAnna, Mark; *ed:* (BS) Elem Ed, 1980, (MED) Ed, 1983 W TX St Univ; Cmptr Literacy & Curr; *cr:* 3rd Grade Teacher Skellytown Elem 1980-84; Cmptr Literacy Teacher Borger Mid Sch 1984-; *ai:* Cmptr Technology Comm; TX Classroom Teachers Pres 1987-88; TX Cmptr Ed Assn 1984-; Delta Kappa Gamma; *home:* 117 Houston Borger TX 79007

MAURER, JOHN ROBERT, Music Director & Dept Chair; *b:* New York, NY; *m:* Dawn Ann De Benedetto; *c:* Michelle L.; *ed:* (BA) Music Ed, Fredonia St Univ 1984; *cr:* Music Teacher Sunnyvale Elem Sch Dist 1984-87; Music Dir James Lick HS 1987-; *ai:* Marching Band, Jazz Band, Color Guard & Winter Guard; Music Educators Natl Conference 1984-; CA Band Dir Assn 1987-; CA Teachers Assn, NEA 1984-; San Jose Childrens Musical Theater Bd Mem 1985-89; *office:* James Lick HS 57 N White Rd San Jose CA 95127

MAURER, PETER JAMES, Science Teacher; *b:* Saginaw, MI; *m:* Carol Denise Vandenberg; *c:* Rebecca M., John A. II; *ed:* (BA) Sci/Ed, Univ of MI 1978; (MAT) Rdng, Oakland Univ 1987; *cr:* Sci Baker Mid Sch 1978-; *ai:* Girls Track Team Coach; Union Building Delegate; Troy Ed Assn, MI Ed Assn, NEA 1978-; *office:* Baker Mid Sch 1291 Torpey Dr Troy MI 48083

MAURER, SELMA CHERNY, Third Grade Teacher; *b:* Brooklyn, NY; *c:* Amy Peschke, Lisa Neurohr; *ed:* (BA) Poly Sci, Brooklyn Coll 1951; (MS) Elem Ed, Hofstra Univ 1965; *cr:* Teacher Woodward Parkway Elem Sch 1966-; *ai:* Farmingdale Fed of Teachers Building Rep 1987-; The Lighthouse Assoc Spon 1990; *office:* Woodward Parkway Elem Sch Woodward Pkwy Farmingdale NY 11735

MAURINO, JOSEPH, Teacher; *b:* Waterbury, CT; *m:* Marina De Prisco; *c:* Marc, Gregory, Lara; *ed:* (BA) Fr/Italian; (MA) Fr/ Italian; Currently in Masters of Soc Work Prgm at Rutgers Univ; *cr:* Teacher N Valley Regional HS 1968-; *ai:* Italian Club; Rap Group; Paramus Unico Recording Secy 1985-89; Teacher of Yr N Valley Regional 1986.

MAUTNER, MEG W., Science Teacher; *b:* Yakima, WA; *m:* Paul F.; *ed:* (BS) Bio, Willamette Univ 1983; Lewis & Clark Coll; *cr:* Sci Teacher Sunset HS 1986, Aloha HS 1987, Cedar Park Intermediate 1987-; *ai:* Cadre; 7th Grade Adv; Dist TAG Comm; CARE Team; 9th Grade Swim Coach; *office:* Cedar Park Intermediate Sch PO Box 200 Beaverton OR 97075

MAUZY, HARRIET LYNN, 8th Grade Social Stud Teacher; *b:* Houston, TX; *ed:* (BA) His, Rice Univ 1966; Grad Stud Univ of Houston; *cr:* Teacher Fondren Jr HS 1966-78, Welch Mid Sch 1978-; *ai:* Welch Stu Cncl Spon; Houston Ed Assn Pres 1976-77; TX St Teachers Assn (Exec Comm 1978-82, Dist IV Bylaws Chm, Dist IV legislative Chm); NEA Affiliate Relations Comm 1976-78, 1980-84; Houston Educators Political Action Comm Chm 1974-76; United Way Evaluation Comm; Houston-Galveston Area Cncl Ed Comm; Outstanding Young Educator Fondren Jr High; Teacher of Yr Welch Mid Sch 1979; Bylaws Chm Dist IV TX St Teachers Assn; *home:* 3518 Cloverdale Houston TX 77025

MAXCY, WILLIAM PATRICK, American History Teacher; *b:* Houston, TX; *m:* Charlotte Mericle; *ed:* (BA) His, TX Tech Univ 1974; (MED) Ed, Prairieview A&M Univ 1990; *cr:* Teacher/ Coach Spring Forest Jr HS 1975-79, Spring Branch HS 1979-83; Teacher Cypress Creek HS 1987-; *ai:* Stu Adv Cncl; Class Spon; Dist Insurance Comm; *office:* Cypress Creek HS 9815 Grant Rd Houston TX 77070

MAXEY, ELOISE EVELYN, Director of Gifted/Talented Ed; *b:* Washington, DC; *m:* Simeon Donovan; *c:* Jerry D., Jon D.; *ed:* (BA) Bus Ed/Elem Ed, 1962, (MA) Math/Counseling, 1967 Northeastern St Coll; Post Grad Work in Gifted Ed, Tulsa Univ; Cmptr Ed, Tulsa Jr Coll; *cr:* Elem Teacher OK City Public Schls 1962-65; Jr HS Teacher Muskogee Public Schls 1965-70; Teacher 1970-84, Gifted/Talented Ed Teacher 1984- Bixby Public Schls; *ai:* Fine Arts Dir; Newsletter Ed; Public Speaker; Tour Dir Amer Stu Travel; Cmptr Challenge Coach; Video Tape Productions Producer; Comm Resource Person; Tulsa Cty Teachers Assn Secy 1970-80, Teacher of Yr 1976; OK Ed Assn, NEA 1962-; OK Assn of Gifted Creative & Talented Secy 1984-; Intnl Visual Literacy Assn, Prof Photographers Assn; Asbury United Meth Church; Republican Party; Full Coll Schlsps; OK Arts & Hum Grant; OK Bar Assn Fellowship; Published Articles & Photography; *home:* 8806 E 107th St S Tulsa OK 74133

MAXEY, SILAS OTIS, 5th/6th Math/Soc Stud Teacher; *b:* Rock, WV; *m:* Marjorie Janice Thomas; *c:* Sheri R., Crystal D.; *ed:* (BS) Ed, Concord Coll 1967; (MPA) Public Admin, WV Coll of Grad Stud 1976; (MA) Comm Stud, WV Univ 1987; Post Masters Studies Project TEACH Duquesne Univ; PRIDE Teaching Through Learning Channels; Patterns for IDEAS Salem-Teikyo Univ; Dev By Performance Learning Systems; *cr:* 6th Grade Teacher Switchback Elem 1967-69; 5th/6th Grade Teacher Pinnacle Elem 1969-70; 5th/6th Grade Geography Teacher Welch Elem 1970-71; Management & Personnel in Private Sector 1971-83; 5th/6th Grade Math/Soc Stud Teacher Bradshow Jr HS 1983-; *ai:* Spon BJHS Soc Stud Lecture Series; Chairperson BJHS 6th Grade Teachers; McDowell Cty Teachers of Math Publicity Chairperson 1989-; McDowell Cty Ed Assn; West VA Ed Assn; Mountain St RR & Logging Historical Assn; Friends of Ft New Salem; *home:* P.O. Box 143 Bud WV 24716

MAXEY, VERONICA ANN, Third Grade Teacher; *b:* La Porte, IN; *m:* Rick; *c:* Bryan; *ed:* (BA) Elem Ed, 1971, (MED) Elem Ed, 1976 Stephen F Austin St Univ; *cr:* Rdng Teacher Troup Elem Sch 1973-74; Soc Stud/Music Teacher Whitehouse Ind Sch Dist 1974-75; 1st Grade Teacher Longview Ind Sch Dist 1975-80; 3rd Grade Teacher Pine Tree Ind Sch Dist 1980-; *ai:* Delta Kappa Gamma 1978-; *home:* 2604 Northview Longview TX 75605

MAXWELL, DAWN LEEAL, School-Age Parent Teacher; *b:* Appleton, WI; *ed:* (BS) Ed, UW Whitewater 1983; *cr:* Homebound Teacher 1983-85; Schage Parents Teacher 1985- Appleton Area Sch Dist; *ai:* JV Sftbl Coach West High 1983-; JV Vllybl Coach West High 1989-; JV Coach Einstein Jr HS 1984-88; Natl Orgnztn on Adolescent Preg & Parenting 1988-; WI Vlybl Coaches Assn 1989-; Meth Church Womens Role in Church 1988-; Natl Deans List 1982-83; *office:* Appleton West HS 610 W Badger Ave Appleton WI 54914

MAXWELL, JERRY H., History Teacher; *b:* Smithville, TN; *m:* Carlene Raines; *c:* Brent C., Holly S.; *ed:* (BA) His/Eng, Adrian Coll 1964; (MA) His, E MI Univ 1968; *cr:* Teacher East Mid Sch 1964-69, North Farmington HS 1969-; *ai:* Bsbl, Bsktbl & Ftbl Coach; Boys & Girls Bsktbl Ofcl; MI Civil War Round Table Pres 1971-; 4 Times Bsbl Coach of Yr; Published Civil War Articles; Finishing Book; Speaker Historical Groups, Univs, Prisons; 3 Time St Champion Civil War Round Tables Civil War Trivia; *office:* North Farmington HS 32900 W 13 Mile Rd Farmington Hlls MI 48018

MAXWELL, LINDA ELAINE, Fourth Grade Teacher; *b:* Montgomery, AL; *m:* Marvin Joel Jr.; *c:* Meredith L., Joel A.; *ed:* (BA) Elem Ed, 1978, (MA) Elem Ed, 1981 UAB; *cr:* Teacher All Saints Episcopal Sch 1979-80, Edgewood Elem Sch 1980-; *ai:* Guest Speaker Gulf Coast Writing Conference; Delta Kappa Gamma 1986-; Homewood Patriot Youth Bsbl League Secy 1986-88, Service Awd 1989; Grad Stu of Yr UAB 1979; Outstanding Young Women of America Awd 1979; Published Workbook on AL His for 4th Graders 1986; *home:* 1742 Wellington Rd Homewood AL 35209

MAXWELL, MIKE A., Leadership/Activities Advisor; *b:* Van Nuys, CA; *ed:* (BA) Speech Comm, San Francisco St Univ 1986; *cr:* Study Hall Supvr 1984-, Act Adv 1985-, Stu Government Teacher 1985- MOnte Vista HS; *ai:* Block M V Club, Youth & Government Club, Act, & Chrldr Adv; Jr Var Ftbl; Jr Var Bsbl Head Coach; Danville Arts Cncl Mem 1989-; Jr HS Leadership Coord; Logistics Coord CA YMCA Model Legislature & Court; *office:* Monte Vista HS 3131 Stone Valley Rd Danville CA 94526

MAXWELL, NANETTE WEST, Fourth Grade Teacher; *b:* Cisco, TX; *c:* Teresa; *ed:* (BA) Journalism, TX Chrstn Univ 1975; (BS) Elem Ed, Tarleton St Univ 1975; *cr:* 5th Grade Teacher Morton Elem 1976-78; 6th Grade Teacher 1979-80, Chapter I Rdng Teacher 1980-81, 4th Grade Teacher 1981- Cisco Elem; *ai:* UIL Ready Writing Spon; ESL Textbook & Gifted & Talented Comm; *office:* Cisco Elem Sch Ave H & W 11th St Cisco TX 76437

MAXWELL, RICHARD RUSSELL, Physics Teacher; *b:* Orange, NJ; *m:* Cassandre Chalson; *c:* Christine; *ed:* (BS) Sci, Penn St Univ 1965; (MED) Ed, Temple Univ 1969; Sci Supervisory Cert, Villanova; *cr:* Sci Prgm Coord 1985-88, Physics Teacher 1967- Upper Darby HS; *ai:* Sci Club Adv; Sci Olympiad Team Coach; Schlsp Comm; PA Sci Supvrs Assn 1985-; Upper Darby Ed Assn, PSEA, NEA 1967-; NSTA 1987-; Philadelphia Sci Cncl Bd of Dirs 1970-; Received Patent on Light Meter 1970; Nom Tandy Sci Teacher of Yr 1989; Regional & St Event Supvr for Sci Olympiad 1986-; *office:* Upper Darby HS Lansdowne Ave & School Ln Upper Darby PA 19082

MAXWELL, STEVEN ROBERT, Social Studies Instructor; *b:* Coral Gables, FL; *m:* Catherine E. Templeton; *ed:* (BA) Poly Sci, Univ of FL 1975; (MPA) Public Admin, Univ of Dayton 1976; (EDS) Del/Higher Ed, FL St Univ 1982; Doctoral Candidate FL St Univ; *cr:* Lecturer Sinclair Comm Coll 1976-77; Adjunct Instr Edison Comm Coll 1978-81; Instr Sch Bd of Lee Cty 1978-80; Adjunct Professor St Thomas of Villanova Univ 1984-85; Adjunct Instr Edison Comm Coll 1988-89; Instr Sch Bd of Lee Cty 1985-;

ai: Chairperson Drug Free Schls Comm; Faculty Adv Stu Government Assn, SADD, Interact Club For Cape Coral Rotary; NEA, FL Teaching Profession; Lee Cty Human Relations Review Bd Mem; Public Admin Quartely Editorial Bd Mem; Amer Society for Public Admin Ed, Prof, Organizational Dev Bd Mem; Sanibel-Captiva Islands Charter Club Mem 1979-80; *home:* 232 Lagoon Dr Fort Myers FL 33905

MAXWELL, WILLIE PICKREN, Science Dept Chairperson; *b:* Mc Rae, GA; *m:* Gregory Daniel; *c:* Lindsey, Allison S; *cr:* Teacher Wills HS 1969-70, Monroe HS 1970-77, A S Clark Mid Sch 1977-79; Teacher 1979-88, Sci Dept Chairperson Americus HS 1988-; *ai:* Sci Dept Chairperson; GA Sci Teachers Assn; GA Assn of Educators; Natl Assn of Educators; Sumter Cty Cncl Child Abuse; Star Teacher 1988-89, 1989-; *office:* Americus HS 805 Harrold Ave Americus GA 31709

MAY, BESSIE HILL, Social Studies Dept Chair; *b:* Uniontown, AL; *m:* James Franklin; *c:* Katrice V., Keita S.; *ed:* (BSED) His/Music, AL St Univ 1960; (MED) Ed/His, Univ of Montevallo 1976; Numerous Wkshps His Inst, Tuskegee Inst 1969; *cr:* Soc Stud Teacher Robert C Hatch HS 1961-; *ai:* Sr Class Spon; NHS & Yrbk Adv; AEA, NEA, PCEA; Uniontown Recreation Bd Chairperson 1977; Uniontown Bicentennial Comm Vice Chairperson 1975-76; Perry Cty Textbook Comm 1973-74; NDEA His Inst 1969; R C Hatch HS Teacher of Yr 1980-81; *home:* PO Box 24 Uniontown AL 36786

MAY, DENNIS KEITH, Teacher/Coach; *b:* Borger, TX; *m:* Rozanna San Miguel; *c:* Robert S., Richard S.; *ed:* (BS) Phys Ed, SE OK St Univ 1973; (MED) Ed, N TX St Univ 1979; Prof Ftbl Clinics; *cr:* Head 8th Grade Ftbl/Bsktbl/Track Coach Travis Jr HS 1973-74; Ftbl/Track Coach Broken Arrow HS 1974-75, R L Turner HS 1975-77, Newman Smith HS 1977-79, SE OK St Univ 1979-82; Defensive Coord Newman Smith HS 1983-85; Defensive Coord 1985-87, Head Ftbl Coach 1987-89 Tuloso Midway HS; *ai:* Head Ftbl Coach; Defensive Coord; Amer Ftbl Coaches Assn, US Track & Field Coaches Assn, TX Coaches Assn, Fellowship of Chrstn Athletes; *office:* Tuloso-Midway HS 9760 La Branch Corpus Christi TX 78410

MAY, ERNESTINE M., Kindergarten Teacher; *b:* Biscoe, AR; *m:* Floyd; *c:* Andre Holloway, Don Holloway, Kelly, Mona; *ed:* (AA) Associated Art, Shorter Jr Coll 1962; (BA) Elem Ed, AM&N Coll 1965; (MS) Elem Ed, IN Univ NW 1975; Lib Sci, Eng; *cr:* Librarian De Valls Bluff Sch Dist 1966-69; Teacher Gary Public Sch 1969-; *ai:* Nobel Family Skating Spon; Character Ed Comm; Primary Awds Day Chairperson; AFT 1969-; Gary Rdng Cncl 1970-; Gary Educators for Christ Historian 1986-; Soc Stud Cncl Mem 1989-; Miller Citizens Corporation 1985-; NAACP Mem 1986-; Certificate Nobel Sch Journalism, Spelling Bee, Stu Cncl, Charm & Modeling Spon; *office:* Nobel Elem Sch 8837 Pottawatomi Trl Gary IN 46403

MAY, JOYCE VOLPE, English Teacher; *b:* Bristol, PA; *m:* William J.; *c:* Stephen, Andrew (dec); *ed:* (BSED) Eng/Scndry Ed, Shippensburg Univ 1980; *cr:* Eng Teacher Delran HS 1981, Fisher Jr HS 1981-82, Ewing HS 1982-; *ai:* Soph Orientation Comm; NEA, NJEA, ETEA 1981-; Glendale Civic Assn 1986-; *office:* Ewing HS 900 Parkway Ave Trenton NJ 08618

MAY, KAREN CAIN, World History Teacher; *b:* Louisville, KY; *c:* Matthew, Jeffrey; *ed:* (AB) His/Art, E Ky Univ 1971; (MED) Ed/Soc Sci, Univ of Louisville 1976; *cr:* Teacher Gottschalk Jr HS 1971, Du Pont Manual/Magnet HS 1971-; *ai:* Academic Coord; Quick Recall/Academic Teams Coach; Audubon Park Garden Club Pres 1988-; KY Academic Assn Coaches Comm; Jefferson Cty Academic Coach of Yr 1989; Facilitator for Coaches Cert Statewide Inservice; *office:* Du Pont Manual/Magnet HS 120 W Lee St Louisville KY 40208

MAY, KARRI E., 6th-8th Grade Art Teacher; *b:* Houston, TX; *ed:* (BS) Phys Ed, Stephen F Austin St Univ 1984; Working on Masters; *cr:* Teaching Asst Univ of Houston 1985; Teacher/Coach Hildebrandt Intermediate; *ai:* 7th Grade Track & 8th Grade Bsktbl Coach; Natl Strength & Conditioning Assn; Stephen F Austin Alumni Assn; N Houston Art Ed Assn; *office:* Hildebrandt Intermediate Sch 22800 Hildebrandt Rd Spring TX 77389

MAY, MARTHA, Math Dept Chm/Cmptr Coord; *b:* Rhinebeck, NY; *ed:* (BS) Math/Sci, 1961, (MS) Math/Sci, 1966 New Paltz St Univ Coll; Math, Cmptr Wkshps; *cr:* Math/Sci Teacher 1961-72, Math Teacher 1961-, Math Dept Chm 1972-, Jr HS Cmptr Coord 1984- Red Hook Cntrl Sch; *ai:* Stu Cncl & Yrbk Adv; Dist Cmptr, Mid Level Ed, Gifted, Gifted Evaluation Prgm Comms; Assn of Math Teachers NY St, St Assn of Math Supvrs, NDTM, ASCD, Dutchess Cty Math Teacher Assn, NY St United Teachers; Delta Kappa Gamma Society Intnl (1st VP 1978-80, Pres 1980-82, Music Chm 1982-); Rhinebeck Reformed Church (Choir Secy, Treas 1974-, Greater Consistory, Church Womens Guild Pres 1984-86, 1989-); Kappa Delta Pi, Agonian Alumni Assn; Math, Sci Schlsp Awd New Paltz St Univ Coll 1962; *home:* 940 NY Rt 9G Hyde Park NY 12538

MAY, NORMA LEA (HINKLE), Elementary Music Teacher; *b:* Springfield, MO; *m:* Gregory Lynn; *c:* James G., Legha L.; *ed:* (BSED) Music, 1974, (MSED) Music, 1979, SW MO St Univ; *cr:* K-12th Grade Music Instr Blue Eye Public Schls 1975-78; K-6th Music Instr Reeds Spring Public Schls 1978-; *ai:* NEA 1987-; South Cntrl MO Music Educators Assn (Elem VP 1981-83) 1975-; MO Music Educators Assn 1975-; Mu Phi Epsilon Alumni 1973-; Delta Kappa Gamma Mem 1983-; Outstanding Young Women of America 1981; *office:* Reeds Spring Elem Sch P O Box 129 Reeds Spring MO 65737

MAY, PATRICIA A., 2nd Grade Teacher; *b:* Elmira, NY; *m:* Jack T.; *c:* Angela Armbruster, Toni Herring, Michael Trippi, Teresa Trippi; *ed:* (BA) Elem Ed, SUNY Geneso 1969; Grad Stud SUNY Geneseo; *cr:* K-3rd Grade Teacher Friendship Cntrl Sch; *office:* Friendship Cntrl Sch Main St Friendship NY 14739

MAY, SANDRA WEAVER, Elementary Principal; *b:* Union, KY; *m:* Robert A.; *c:* R. Bryan, Jenna L; *ed:* (MA) Elem Ed, Eastern KY State Univ; (BS) Home Economics, Western KY Univ 1964; (Rank I) Elem Admin, Eastern KY Univ; *cr:* Classroom Teacher, Meade Cty Sch System, Carroll Cty Sch System; Principal, Kathryn Winn Elem; *ai:* KEA, Dist Bd Mem 1973-75; CCEA, Pres 1972-73; KASA 1988-; Excel in Ed of Carroll Cty, Sec 1989-90; CC Planning Commission, 1988-; Carroll Cty Democratic Comm, Treasurer 1988-; First Commonwealth Inst for Teachers Mem; Past-Pres Carroll Cty Education Assn; *office:* Kathryn Winn Elem Sch 907 Hawkins St Carrollton KY 41008

MAY, SHARLA GODFREY, English Teacher; *b:* Baltimore, MD; *m:* Jeffrey R.; *c:* Ashley La Chelle; *ed:* (BS) Eng/Soc Stud, Bluefield St Coll 1983; (MA) Comm Stud, WV Univ 1987; *cr:* Teacher of Eng/Careers Princeton Jr HS 1984; Teacher of Geography/English Spanishburg HS 1984-; *ai:* Var Cheerleading & Forensics Coach; Future Educators of America Spon; WV Eng Lang Art Cncl; *office:* Spanishburg HS PO Box 7 Spanishburg WV 25922

MAYA, MARYLN, Marketing & Distributive Coord; *b:* Cabo Rojo, PR; *m:* Jose Luis Esteves Ponce DeLeon; *c:* Jose L. III; *ed:* (BA) Bus Admin, CAAM 1978; Minor Field in Mrktg & Ed; *cr:* Teacher Luis Munoz Marin HS II 1979-; *ai:* Distributive Ed Club of America Adv; Responsibilities-Coord Act with Students; Club DECA DIP 1989-, 1st Prize on Funds Raised for Jerry Lewis Telethon 1989-; Assn of Teachers Dip 1979-; *home:* Box 504 Cabo Rojo PR 00623

MAYBAUM, KAY LYNN REICHER, Third Grade Teacher; *b:* Cedar Lake, IN; *m:* Randall C.; *ed:* (BS) Elem Ed, IN St Univ 1975; (MS) Elem Ed, Purdue Univ 1979; *cr:* 3rd Grade Teacher Jane Ball Elem Sch 1975-; *ai:* Book Adoption, Performance Based Accrediation Comm; IN St Teachers Assn, NEA 1980-; *office:* Jane Ball Elem Sch 13313 Parrish Ave Cedar Lake IN 46303

MAYBERRY, BETTY PATE, Algebra Teacher; *b:* Nashville, TN; *m:* Ronald Edward; *ed:* (BA) Math, 1975, (MST) Math, 1978 Mid TN St Univ; NCTM Regional & Natl Wkshps; *cr:* Teacher Knox Doss Jr HS 1975-78, Benton Jr HS 1978-79, Westmoreland Sr HS 1979-85, Gallatin Sr HS 1985-88, Riverdale Sr HS 1988-; *ai:* Beta Club; Quiz Bowl; Math Coach; Pride Drug Free Prgm; MT2 Pres 1978-; TMTA, NCTM, REA, MTEA, TEA, NEA; APTA, Delta Kappa Gamma, Alpha Delta Kappa; Woodrow Wilson Inst Algebra; TN Collaborative Acad; Teacher of Yr Upper Cumberland Dist; Belmont Round Table Teacher of Yr; *home:* 2602 Charter Ct Murfreesboro TN 37129

MAYBERRY, LATHA MC KUIN, Fourth Grade Teacher; *b:* Plumerville, AR; *c:* Michael, Mark; *ed:* (BS) Elem Ed, AR St Univ Jonesboro 1956; (MS) Elem Ed, St Francis Coll 1968; *cr:* 2nd Grade Teacher Deering Public Schls 1951-54; 3rd Grade Teacher Kennett Public Schls 1954-66; 2nd Grade Teacher East Allen Sch System 1966-71; 4th Grade Teacher Ashley Elem 1971-; *ai:* Spon-Little Hoosiers His Club; Teacher-Admin Liaison Comm Mem; Pokagon Rdng Cncl-Building Rep; Dekalb Educators Assn Building Rep 1975-78/1988-89; NEA; Alpha Delta Kappa St Historian 1969-70; Ashley Elem 4-Star Sch for 1989-; *home:* 80 Castle Ct Auburn IN 46706

MAYER, CELINA KARAM, Second Grade Teacher; *b:* Nogales, AZ; *w:* Richard (dec); *c:* Richard, Steve, Tom, Alice, Lorraine Soto, Jeanne; *ed:* (BA) Elem Ed, Dominican Coll 1952; (MS) Teaching, Univ of AZ 1977; ESL/Bi-ling Ed; *cr:* 3rd Grade Teacher Mill Valley CA 1952-53, Lincoln Sch 1953-54; 4th Grade Teacher Lincoln Sch 1954-56; 2nd Grade Teacher A J Mitchell Sch 1971-; *ai:* At Risk 5th Grade Tutoring; ESL/Adult Basic Ed Night Classes; Prof Educators of Nogales Rep; *home:* 331 Kolver St Nogales AZ 85621

MAYER, GEORGE J., JR., Math/Cmptr Literacy Teacher; *b:* Shiner, TX; *m:* Angeline Vincik; *c:* Amy L., Laurie B., Christie D.; *ed:* (BS) Math, SW TX St Univ 1972; (ME) Math Ed, Univ of Houston 1976; *cr:* Math/Cmptr Teacher Bloomington Ind Sch Dist 1972-; *ai:* Natl Jr Honor Society Spon; Math & Technology Comm; Number Sense, Calculator Spon; TSTA 1973-78; Athene Study Club Teacher of Yr 1989-; *office:* Bloomington Ind Sch Dist P O Box 158 Bloomington TX 77951

MAYER, HELOISE (CARR), English/Drama Teacher; *b:* Providence, RI; *m:* Tansie Joseph Jr.; *c:* Tansie J. III, Gerald S.; *ed:* (BA) Ed, Stowe Teachers Coll 1947; (MAT) Comm, Webster Univ 1976; Experimental Theatre & Directing, Univ of S CA 1949; Music, WA Univ; *cr:* Kndgtn Music Teacher Cote Brilliante Sch 1947-55; 7th/8th Grade Music Teacher Simmons Elem Sch 1956-59; 6th Grade Teacher Cupples Sch 1960-64; Teacher/Music Specialist St Louis Public Schls 1965-72; Eng/Drama Teacher Metro HS 1973-; *ai:* Dramatic Productions Dir; AFT St Louis Public Schls Teacher of Yr 1987; Pilgrim Congregational Church Chrstn Ed Bd Pres 1988-, Outstanding Educator 1988; Whos Who Among Grad Stus at Webster Univ 1976; North Adams Univ Natl Endowment for Hum 1987; Univ of MO St Louis Socratic Method Seminar 1984; *office:* Metro HS 5017 Washington Ave Saint Louis MO 63108

MAYER, JEANNIE BERCIER, 2nd Grade Teacher; *b:* Opelousas, LA; *m:* Charles R.; *c:* Karl, Maureen; *ed:* (BA) Elem Ed, Univ of Southwest LA 1957; *cr:* 3rd Grade Teacher Lawtell Elem 1957-69; 1st Grade Teacher Opelousas Cath 1977-82; 5th/6th Grade Teacher Acad of Sacred Heart 1983-86; 2nd Grade Teacher Opelousas Cath 1986-; *ai:* Long Range Planning Comm; Curr Planning Comm; Delta Kappa Gamma Intnl; NCEA; Natl Right to Life; AARP; Amer Inst for Cancer Research; Opelousas Cath Outstanding Elem Teacher of Yr 1988-89; *home:* 650 E Bellevue St Opelousas LA 70570

MAYER, MARY K., English Teacher; *b:* Alexandria, MN; *m:* David P.; *c:* Paul, Mark, Ann, Kate; *ed:* (BA) Eng, Coll of St Benedict 1963; Grad Stud Hofstra Univ, Stanford Univ, St Cloud St Univ, Carlton Coll; *cr:* Teacher Glenwood HS 1963-66, Hosterman Jr HS 1966-67, Sauk Centre HS 1982-; *ai:* MN Cncl Teachers of Eng Mem 1984-; MN Chamber Fnd Excl Ed Awd 1989; MN Ed Assn; NEA; Sauk Centre Ed Assn (Pres 1989-) 1982-; *office:* Sauk Centre HS 9th & State Rd Sauk Centre MN 56378

MAYERCIK, JOHN EDWARD, JROTC Instructor; *b:* Danbury, CT; *c:* Michael, Mark; *ed:* (BS) Ed, Columbus Coll 1973; (MED) Ed Admin, 1980, (EDS) Ed Admin, 1983 Mid TN St Univ; *cr:* Sr Army Instr JROTC Oakland HS 1978-; *ai:* Coach Drill Team, Adventure Trng Team, Mock Trial, Orienteering Team, Color Guard; Lions Club (Pres 1980-81), Superior Club Extension Awds 1981; Leo Club Adv 1980-88; *office:* Oakland HS Oakland Dr Murfreesboro TN 37130

MAYERNICK, ARTHUR MICHAEL, Assistant Principal; *b:* Milford, CT; *m:* Glenda Gay Burgess; *c:* Ruth M., Mike, Mandy; *ed:* (BS) Health/Phys Ed, Belmont Coll 1961; (MA) Admin/Supervision Austin Peay St Univ 1969; Grad Stud Admin/Scndry Ed, Univ of TN, Fisk Univ, Wayne St Univ, TN St Univ, Azusa Pacific Coll; *cr:* Teacher Cumberland HS 1961-69, Neelys Bend Mid Sch 1969-85; Teacher/Asst Prin Davidson Acad 1985-; *ai:* Var Girls Bstkbl & Asst Bsbl Coach; Stu Life Comm; NEA, TEA, MNEA 1961-; AAHPER 1965-70; TN Coaches Assn 1985-; York Rite Mason 1980-; Neelys Bend Mid Sch Teacher of Yr & Runner-Up Metro Nashville Teacher of Yr 1984; *office:* Davidson Acad 1414 Old Hickory Blvd Nashville TN 37207

MAYES, ARLENE FAYE (MATNEY), Jr HS Language Arts Teacher; *b:* Buffalo, KS; *m:* Carl W.; *c:* Jonathan C., Lacie J.; *ed:* (AA) Elem Ed, Allen Cty Cmmty Jr Coll 1968; (BA) Elem Ed, 1970, (MS) Elem Ed, 1973 Pittsburg St Univ; Admin KS St Univ; Whole Lang, Emporia St Univ; Continuing Ed, Univ of KS; *cr:* 5th Grade Teacher 1970-72, 6th Grade Teacher 1972-73, Jr HS Sci Teacher 1973-78 Carbondale Sch; 6th Grade Teacher Gardner Sch 1978-79; Jr HS Lang Arts Teacher Carbondale Sch 1979-; *ai:* Concession Stand Dir; Cheerleading; Dist Curr & Lang Art Curr Comm; Yrbk; 8th Grade Spon; Spelling Bee Coord; BSA Den Mother 1986-89; PTA Carnival Concessions; *office:* Carbondale Sch 315 N 4th Carbondale KS 66414

MAYES, DEBBIE DUNCAN, Fifth Grade Teacher; *b:* Owensboro, KY; *m:* Larry Dean; *c:* Erik T., Jason R., Brian D.; *ed:* (BS) Elem Ed, 1979, (MA) Elem Ed, 1981 W KY Univ; *cr:* 6th Grade Teacher 1979-85, 2nd Grade Teacher 1985-87 Beaver Dam Elem Sch; 3rd Grade Teacher Wayland Alexander Elem Sch 1987-88; 5th Grade Teacher Beaver Dam Elem Sch 1988-; *ai:* Cheerleading Spon; Sch Newspaper Adv; KY Ed Assn 1979-; Alpha Delta Kappa Secy 1986-88; Beaver Dam Baptist Church 2nd & 3rd Grade Choir Dir 1989-; *office:* Beaver Dam Elem Sch Rt 3 Louisville Rd Beaver Dam KY 42320

MAYES, MARY ANN KOVACHICH, English Teacher; *b:* Herrin, IL; *m:* Thomas G.; *ed:* (BA) English, Southern IL Univ 1967; (MS) English, Southern IL Univ at Edwardsville 1973; Post Masters Studies Eng; Word Processing; *cr:* Eng Teacher East St Louis Sr HS 1967-; *ai:* Faculty Comm Mem NHS; Faculty Comm Mem in Charge of Sr Week Act & Graduation Each Yr; Kappa Delt Pi 1973-; IL Assn Teachers Eng 1970-; SIU Alumni Assn 1975-; *office:* East Saint Louis Sr High 4901 State St East Saint Louis IL 62205

MAYES-ROBINSON, DEBORA, English Teacher; *b:* Detroit, MI; *m:* Charles E. Robinson; *c:* Brandi, Dorothy, Daniel; *ed:* (BA) Eng Lit, Univ of Detroit 1976; (MA) Spec Ed, Mercy Coll of Detroit 1986; EEEI, Instrumental Enrichment , Thinking Skills Prgms, Madeline Hunter; *cr:* Switch Bd Operator Brent Hospital 1973-76; Eng Teacher Osborn HS 1977-; *ai:* Sr Spon; Pep Club Adv; Contest Coord; Delta Sigma Theta 1972-; NAACP 1963-; Volunteer Service for NCTE; *office:* Osborn HS 11600 E 7 Mile Detroit MI 48205

MAYESKY, GARY JOHN, Mathematics Teacher; *b:* Youngstown, OH; *ed:* (BE) Math Ed, Univ of Toledo 1985; *cr:* Math Teacher Toledo Scott HS 1985-87, Toledo Macomber HS 1987-88, Toledo Woodward HS 1987-; *ai:* Var Ftbl, Frosh Bsktbl, Jr Var Bsbl Coach; Greater Toledo Cncl Teachers of Math, OH Cncl Teachers of Math, NCTM, Mathematical Assn of America; *home:* 2701 Kendale #101 Toledo OH 43606

MAYFIELD, D. DONALD, English Teacher; *b:* Camas, WN; *m:* Janice C. Brock; *c:* Douglas S., Dianne S. Aalseth, Jeffrey S.; *ed:* (BA) Phys Ed, Univ of Portland 1953; Grad Stud; *cr:* Teacher/Coach Condon HS 1953-57; Teacher Mc Loughlin Mid Sch 1957-; *ai:* Intramural Coord; *home:* 6213 Montana Ln Vancouver WA 98661

MAYFIELD, DONNA ELLIOTT, Spanish Teacher; *b:* Enid, OK; *m:* Phillip D.; *c:* Donita, Misty, Phillip D. II; *ed:* Span/ Elem/ Sec/Soc Stud, NW OK St Univ 1971; Advanced Stud Cntrl St Univ; *cr:* Span Teacher Jet-Nash Schls 1971-76, Wakita Schls 1981-83, Chisholm Public Schls 1986-; *ai:* Jr Spon; Span Club Adv; Chisholm Teachers Membership Comm Chm; OK Ed Assn 1971-76; NEA 1981-83; OK Foreign Lang Teachers 1986-; Beta Sigma Phi Pres 1976-82; OK Young Homemakers Reporter 1976-79; Band Boosters Parent Organization Calling Comm Chm 1982-89; Alumni (Pres, VP, Secy) 1979-82; Phi Kappa Phi 1969-70; Kappa Delta Pi 1970-71; Jet-Nash Teachers Organization Pres; Jet-Nash Schls Teacher of Yr Awd; Whos Who in Amer Colls & Univs 1971.

MAYFIELD, VALARIE JEAN RAMSEY, Pre-Kindergarten Teacher; *b:* Houston, TX; *m:* Keith; *c:* Jared, Lauren; *ed:* (BS) Ed, Abilene Chrstn Univ 1980; *cr:* 4th Grade Teacher Shreve Chrstn Sch 1980-82; Kndgtn Teacher T L Rodes Elem 1982-84; 1st Grade Teacher Turner Elem/Mid Sch 1984-87; Pre-K/Kndgtn Teacher Walter Floyd Elem 1987-; *ai:* Stu At-Risk Comm; TX Prof Educators Assn; PTA; LA Prof Improvement Prgm 1982-87; *office:* Walter Floyd Elem Sch 3025 Hickory Tree Rd Mesquite TX 75180

MAYHEW, RONALD DALE, Social Studies Teacher; *b:* Maitland, WV; *m:* Gwenn Cook; *c:* Christopher D.; *ed:* (BA) Soc Stud, Morris Harvey Coll 1967; (MA) Scndry Ed, WV Coll of Grad Stud; Grad Stud, Sch of Modern Photography; *cr:* A/IC US Air Force 1959-67; Sanitarian II Wyoming Cty Health Dept 1967-70; Teacher/Coach Wyoming Cty Bd of Ed 1970-; Sociology Teacher WV Comm Coll 1980-82; *ai:* Head Bsbl & Asst Bsktbl Coach; Athletic Trainer Ftbl; Amer Legion Post 133 Commander 1983-87; Pineville Little League Bd of Dirs 1968-; Bd Wyoming Cty Solid Waste Auhority; Pres Wyoming Cmmty Action; Oceana Jaycees Past Secy; Pineville Jaycees; Wyoming Cty Mental Health Assn; Wyoming Cty Freshman Bsktbl Assn; *home:* Box 787 Pineville WV 24874

MAYHUGH, PATSY MARIA, 3rd-5th Grade Teacher; *b:* Basalt, CO; *m:* Lonnie L.; *ed:* (BA) Elem Ed, Univ of Northern CO 1963; *cr:* 3rd Grade Teacher Eagle Cty Schls 1963-75; 1st-3rd Grade Teacher 1979-88, 3rd-5th Grade Teacher 1988- Gateway Sch; *ai:* Chrldr Spon; MVEA, CEA, NEA 1979-; PTO Historian 1983-86; *home:* 319 Taos Dr Grand Junction CO 81503

MAYLE, PATRICIA WOOLSEY, Kindergarten Teacher; *b:* Oklahoma City, OK; *m:* Fred Wm.; *ed:* (BSED) Elem Ed, Cntrl St Univ 1969; Numerous Colls; *cr:* Classroom Teacher Black Hawk Elem Sch 1969-; *ai:* Sch Climate, Rdng/Lang Art, Kndgtn Grade Level Comms; NEA, IA St Ed Assn, Burlington Ed Assn 1969-; ACEI; Alpha Delta Kappa Treas 1984, 1986; Intnl Rdng Assn 1980-84, 1988; IA Assn Chldhd Ed Intnl, Local Assn Chldhd Ed Intnl (Secy, Treas, 1st VP, 3rd VP); Burlington Hospital Auxiliary 1978-; *office:* Black Hawk Sch 2804 S 14th Burlington IA 52601

MAYLONE, LINDA SPINDEN, Second Grade Teacher; *b:* Iowa City, IA; *m:* Jack D.; *ed:* (BA) Elem Teaching, Univ of N IA 1970; Talented & Gifted Ed; *cr:* 2nd Grade Teacher W Liberty Cmmty Schls 1970-; *ai:* Nature Nuts Club Leader, Presidential Awd 1987; Merit Badge Consultant BSA/GSA; Environmental Ed Newsletter; W Liberty Ed Assn (Secy 1983-84, 1989-, Pres 1990); Kappa Delta Pi 1970-; Univ of N IA Alumni Assn 1970-; Environmental Ed Comm Pres 1978-; Muscatine Cty Fair Supt of Fine Arts1984-; Midwest Cntrl Railroad Historical Society 1967-; W Liberty Historical Society 1990; Teacher of Yr 1981; St Conservation Awd 1990; NACD St Conservation Awd 1981; Outstanding Conservation Teacher 1990; Outstanding Young Iowan 1982; Friend of Conservation 1987; Dist Conservation Teacher 1980, 1989; *office:* West Liberty Cmmty Schls 823 N Elm West Liberty IA 52776

MAYNARD, BRENDA STANLEY, English Teacher; *b:* Pikeville, KY; *m:* Roger Douglas; *c:* Allison B.; *ed:* (BS) Eng, Pikeville Coll 1973; (MED) Scndry Ed, 1977, Supervision, 1983 Morehead St; *cr:* Eng Teacher Runyon Elem 1975-77, Johns Creek Elem 1977-79, Johns Creek HS 1980-; *ai:* Yrbk Adv; E Ky Cncl Teachers of Eng; *office:* Johns Creek HS Rt 1 Box 870 Pikeville KY 41801

MAYNARD, CATHY PIKE, French/English Teacher; *b:* Dallas, TX; *m:* Russell Leslie; *ed:* (AA) Eng, Eastfield Coll 1973; (BA) Eng, N TX St Univ 1975; (MED) Rdng, E TX St Univ 1981; Teaching the Gifted Child; *cr:* Eng Teacher/Dept Leader Vanston Mid Sch 1975-86; Eng/Fr Teacher Poteet HS 1986-; Developmental Rdng Teacher Eastfield Coll 1985-; *ai:* Intnl Club Spon; Mesquite Ed Assn 1975-; NCTE 1986-88; TX Foreign Lang Assn 1989-; AATF 1990; Amer Cncl Teachers of Foreign Lang 1990; Educator of Month 1989; *office:* Dr Ralph H Poteet HS 3300 Poteet Dr Mesquite TX 75150

MAYNARD, CLEO, Retired Substitute Teacher; *b:* Logan, WV; *c:* Betty Simms, Mrs. Neil Hunter; *ed:* (AB) Marshall Univ 1969; *cr:* Prin/1st-8th Grade Teacher Milum Elem 1950-51, Honey Trace Elem 1951-52, Beechy Branch Elem 1952-53; Prin/5th-8th Grade Teacher Brush Creek Elem 1960-63; 3rd Grade Teacher East Lynn Elem 1964-89; *ai:* Volunteer Work At Wayne Continuous Care; NEA Mem 1950-53; Classroom Ed Assn Mem 1963-89; NHS Mem 1950; PTA Treas 1984-; Local Fair Bd Comm Treas 1989-; WCARSE Mem 1989-; Outstanding Elem Teacher of A er 1974; *home:* Star Rt Box 35 East Lynn WV 25512

MAYNARD, DELYLIA GAIL (RAMEY), Fourth Grade Teacher; *b:* Cleveland, OH; *m:* Dewey; *c:* Christopher R., Sean M., Brent J.; *ed:* (AB) Elem Ed, Marshall Univ 1973; Working Towards Masters; *cr:* Classroom Teacher Buffalo Elem 1974-; *ai:* Youth Ftbl, Bsbl, Bsktbl Prgm; Team Mother & Treas; Jr Var Cheerleading Spon; Plan 4th Grade Trip to Washington DC or NY Annually; Alpha Delta Gamma Hospitality Chairperson 1990; Alpha Delta Kappa; First Baptist Church of Ceredo (Sunday Sch Teacher 1975-85, Pastor Search Mem, Vacation Bible Sch Dir 1988); *home:* 54 Pine Hill Estates Kenova WV 25530

MAYNARD, DIANNA LYNN, Athletic Trainer; *b:* Williamson, WV; *ed:* (BS) Phys Ed/Recreation, Univ of KY 1981; (MS) Sports Med, Marshall Univ 1990; Amer Red Cross CPR, First Aid, Lifesaving/Water Safety Instr, Univ of WA; Athletic Health Care System; WV Scndry Schls Act Commission Project Target; *cr:* Phys Ed/Coach Burch HS 1982-85; Athletic Trainer Logan Sr HS 1985-; *ai:* Teach CPR, First Aid Logan Cty Personnel; Fellowship Chrstn Athletes Spon; Athletic Insurance Logan HS; Literacy Cncl Teaching Adults to Read; WV Athletic Trainers Assn 1985-; Natl Teachers Assn 1982-; Logan Cty Coaches Assn Secy 1988-; Delta Psi Kappa, Sigma Kappa Alumni 1982-; Devised & Implemented Athletic Trng Prgm/Facility & Stu Handbook Logan HS; Athletic Trng Handbook Logan Cty Bd of Ed; *office:* Logan Sr HS Midelburg Island Logan WV 25601

MAYNARD, JERILYN OUIMETTE, Guidance Counselor; *b:* Exeter, NH; *m:* Ronald F.; *ed:* (BS) Phys Ed/Health Ed, Boston Univ 1966; (MED) Sch Counseling, Boston St & Univ of MA 1974; *cr:* Phys Ed Teacher Model Demonstration HS 1968-69; Phys Ed Teacher 1969-75, Guidance Cnslr 1975-77, Phys Ed Teacher 1977-83, Guidance Cnslr 1983- East Boston HS; *ai:* Girls Var Bsktbl Coach; Girls Sftbl Commissioner; AIDS Ed Coord & Peer Leader Adv; US Army Reserve SSG Admin 1976-, Achievement 1982; NCOIC Medals 1986; Horace Mann Teaching Grant; Girls Bsktbl Coach of Yr 1982; *office:* East Boston HS 86 White St East Boston MA 02128

MAYNARD, JIM, 5th Grade Teacher; *b:* Missoula, MT; *m:* Joann Alice Mc Elravy; *c:* Kim, Dallas, Stephanie, Michael; *ed:* (BA) Phys Ed/Health/Prof Ed, W WA Univ 1962; *cr:* 5th/6th Grade Elem Coach/4th-12th Grade Phys Ed Coach Crescent Consolidated Schls 1962-64; 7th Grade Homeroom/7th-8th Grade Teacher/9th Grade Phys Ed Coach/Health Teacher Roosevelt Jr HS 1964-80; 9th/12th Grade Alternative Coach Evergreen Alternative Prog 1982; 5th/6th Grade Teacher Crescent Consolidated Schls 1982-.

MAYNARD, PHELECIA JANE, 5th Grade Teacher; *b:* Tahlequah, OK; *m:* Jerry Lee; *c:* Kylie D.; *ed:* (BS) Elem Ed, 1975, (MA) Rdng, 1978 Northeastern St Univ; Rdng Specialist Certificate Northeastern St Univ 1978; *cr:* 6th-8th Grade Teacher Jay Mid Sch 1976-77; 3rd Grade Teacher 1977-82, Pre-K/Kndgtn Teacher 1982-87, 5th Grade Teacher 1987- Jay Elem Sch; *ai:* OK Ed Assn 1975-; OK Kndgtn Teachers Assn 1982-87; OK Rdng Cncl 1989-.

MAYNARD, SUSAN SMITH, Coord/Lead Teacher; *b:* Dayton, OH; *m:* James M.; *c:* John R.; *ed:* (BS) Elem Ed, Mid TN St Univ 1969; (MA) Ed/Spec Ed, Austin Peay St Univ 1981; *cr:* 1st Grade Teacher Metropolitan Bd of Ed 1969-72, Poplar Bluff Bd of Ed 1972-74, Hickman Cty Bd of Ed 1974-89; Developmental Pre-Sch Dir Developmental Services of Dickson Cty 1989-; *ai:* Hickman Cty Ed Assn, TN Ed Assn 1974-; NEA 1969-; Mid TN Talent Show Organizing Comm 1987-; Foster Care Review Bd 1986-89; Poplar Bluff Outstanding Young Educator Awd 1974; East Hickman Sch Teacher of Yr 1987-89; Hickman Cty Teacher of Yr 1987-88; *home:* RR 2 Box 218 Bon Aqua TN 37025

MAYNE, JOHN ROBERT, Assistant Principal & Teacher; *b:* Williamsburg, KY; *m:* Patricia Louise Gardner; *c:* Ritchie, Robert, Renea, Jason; *ed:* (BS) Elem Ed, 1963, (MA) Sch Admin, 1970 E KY Univ; Grad Stud; *cr:* Teacher Goshen/Lebanon OH 1959-66, Woodstock Elem 1966-74; Prin/Teacher Hogue Elem 1974-87, Woodstock Elem 1987-89; Asst Prin Northern Jr HS 1989-; *ai:* 7th Grade Girls Bsktbl Coach; NEA 1959-; KY Ed Assn, Pulaski Cty Ed Assn 1966-; Waynesburg Area Rescue Squad 1974-.

MAYNER, EDITH, Teacher of Gifted & Talented; *b:* Roselle, NJ; *ed:* (BS) Elem Ed, Wilberforce Univ; Masters Stud, Kean Coll; T&C Trng Trenton St; Cmptr Ed, Univ of VT; *cr:* 2nd/4th Grade Teacher Lincoln Sch; Teacher of Gifted & Talented Lincoln & Harrison Schls 1985-; *ai:* OEA Past Treas; NJEA, NEA; Alpha Kappa Alpha Pres 1982-84; Teacher of Yr Roselle NJ 1987; *office:* Lincoln Sch Warren St Roselle NJ 07203

MAYO, SHERRY ELLIS, Social Studies Teacher; *b:* Cape Girardeau, MO; *c:* Gloria; *ed:* (BS) Soc Stud, 1972, (MAT) His, 1986 SE MO St Univ; *cr:* Soc Stud Teacher Scott City Jr HS 1978-; *ai:* Jr HS Stud Cncl Spon; Capaha Correspondence Sch Soc Stud Curr Writer.

MAYO-ALBRECHT, KAREN, 9th/10th Grade English Teacher; *b:* Chickasha, OK; *m:* Richard Carl; *c:* Ryan, Bonnie; *ed:* (BA) Eng, Univ of Sci & Arts 1974; (MA) Hum/Eng/Lit, Univ of Houston 1982; Evaluation of Writing Techniques Acting, Gifted & Talented, Debate Theory, Contest Debate; *cr:* Frosh Eng Teacher Univ of OK 1975-76; Eng/Speech Teacher Pasadena HS 1978-80, Clear Lake HS 1980-88; Eng Teacher Clear Brook HS 1988-; *ai:* Academic Decathlon Coach; Faculty Club Pres; Girls Bsktbl; Alvin Youth Livestock Arena Assn 1987-; Teacher in Space Prgm; *office:* Clear Brook HS 4607 FM 2351 Friendswood TX 77546

MAYS, KELLI KATHLEEN, Reading Teacher; *b:* Idaho Falls, ID; *m:* Martin Calvin; *c:* Mackenzie; *ed:* (BA) Eng Ed, ID St Univ 1981; *cr:* Rdng Teacher S Bonneville Jr HS 1984-; *home:* 373 Contor Ave Idaho Falls ID 83401

MAYS, O'JOY OAKS, 2nd Grade Teacher; *b:* Akron, OH; *c:* Trey Phillips, Leslie Phillips Sisiam; *ed:* (BS) Ed, Univ of GA 1954; Child Psych; Stud of Amer Indians; Cmptr Trng; *cr:* Teacher Waynesboro Elem Sch 1955-56; Diving Instr Camp Nakanawa for Girls 1955-56; Fashion Richs Incorporated 1958-61; Teacher South Jackson Elem Sch 1973-; *ai:* Peer Coaching; Inter Sch Liaison & Cmmty-Sch Relations Comms; Rebun Gap Nacoohee Jr Guild 1956-70, Service Awd 1968; Kappa Kappa Gamma Founding Advisory to Emory 1965; Boggs Chapel United Meth Church Ofcl Bd 1988-; Art in Elem Sch Grant; Math Grant; *office:* South Jackson Elem Sch Rt 2 Athens GA 30607

MAYS-BUKKO, DEBRA, English Instructor; *b:* Merced, CA; *m:* Ashour Shlimon; *ed:* (BA) Eng/World His, 1986, Credential Eng/ World His, 1988 CA St Univ Stanislaus; *cr:* Eng Instr Ceres HS 1988-; *ai:* Service Club & Soph Class Spon; NCTE 1989-; CTA, CUTA 1988-; *office:* Ceres HS 2320 Central Ave Ceres CA 95307

MAZANEC, THOMAS PAUL, Music Teacher; *b:* Bozeman, MT; *m:* Beth Pope; *c:* Michael, Nicholas; *ed:* (BAME) Vocal/ Instrumental, MT St Univ 1980; *cr:* Band/Choral Teacher Terry HS 1980-83, Helena Mid Sch 1984-88; General Elem Music Teacher Helena Schls 1988-; *ai:* Summer Band Teacher; MENC 1980-; Helena Civitan Club Pres 1987-88; St Capital Band Bd of Officers 1990; BSA Scoutmaster 1984-, Bronze Bear 1990; *home:* 2218 8th Ave Helena MT 59601

MAZNER, VIOLET M., 3rd/4th Grade Teacher; *b:* Hurley, WI; *m:* Edward J.; *c:* Thomas; *ed:* (BS) Primary Ed, Univ of WI Superior 1952; Rdng, Alverno Coll; Univ of WI Milwaukee & Viterbo Coll; *cr:* Phys Ed Teacher Hurley HS 1952-62; 3rd/4th Grade Teacher St Rita 1969-; *ai:* NCEA 1969-; League of Cath Home & Sch Assn Certificate of Outstanding Service; *home:* 2535 S 70th St Milwaukee WI 53219

MAZUR, DIANE QUINN, Physical Ed/Health Dept Chair; *b:* Chicago, IL; *m:* Jeffrey; *c:* Jamie, Kevin, Sarah; *ed:* (BA) Scndry Phys Ed, NE IL 1979; CPR Certified, Amer Heart Assn; *cr:* Teacher 1979-, Phys Ed Chairperson 1988-, Athletic Dir Resurrection HS; *ai:* Jr Var & Var Bsktbl, Head Sftbl Coach; Booster & Health Careers Clubs, GAA Moderator; Drug Free Sch & Curr Comm; IL Assn for Health, Phys Ed, Recreation Mem 1984-; Amer Alliance for Health, Phys Ed, Recreation Mem 1986-; Amer Red Cross Volunteer 1979-, 10 Yr Service 1989; *office:* Resurrection HS 7500 W Talcott Chicago IL 60631

MAZUR, RICHARD JOSEPH, Mathematics Teacher; *b:* Rochester, PA; *m:* Mary Ann Raybuck; *c:* Michelle, Tracy; *ed:* (BS) Math, Edinboro St Coll 1965; (MED) Math, Univ of Pittsburgh 1969; *cr:* Math Teacher 1965-, Math Dept Chm 1986-88 Hopewell Memorial Jr HS; *ai:* Algebra Contest Spon; HS Statistician; Hopewell Ed Assn VP 1987-; NCTM Life Mem; St Vladimir Church Bd Pres 1983-85; Whos Who in Ed 1986; *office:* Hopewell Memorial Jr HS 2121 Brodhead Rd Aliquippa PA 15001

MAZZARELLA, MARY GUOKAS, Jr HS English Teacher; *b:* Philadelphia, PA; *m:* Louis J.; *c:* Joseph Tyrrell, Patrick B. Tyrrell; *ed:* (BS) Elem Ed, St Joseph Univ 1965; Masters Equivalency St Josephs, Temple Univ; *cr:* 5th Grade Teacher Kirkbride Sch 1965-67; Jr HS Eng Teacher Ocean City Intermediate 1975-; *ai:* Mem Instructional Cncl & Affirmative Action Comm; *office:* Ocean City Intermediate Sch 19th St & Bay Ave Ocean City NJ 08226

MAZZOULA, SANDRA LEE, 7th Grade Teacher of Gifted; *b:* Stockton, CA; *ed:* (AA) Eng, San Joaquin Delta Coll 1966; (BS) Soc Sci, Univ of Pacific 1968; Grad Courses; *cr:* 7th Grade Teacher Carden Sch of Stockton 1971-72; 6th Grade Teacher King Elem Sch 1972-77, El Dorado Elem Sch 1978-79; 7th/8th Grade Teacher Hamilton Mid Sch 1980-; *ai:* Video Crew & Prolific Thinkers Club Spon; Yrbk & Journalism Adv; NCTE 1988-; Amer Assn of Univ Women 1976-; C-TIP Grant; Article Published; Produced Commercial with Stus; *office:* Hamilton Mid Sch 701 N Madison St Stockton CA 95202

MC ADA, DEE-DEE, Fifth Grade Teacher; *b:* Alton, IA; *m:* Hampton; *c:* Wayne; *ed:* (BA) Elem Ed/Phys Ed, Westmar Coll 1981; His & Elem Ed; *cr:* 3rd Grade Teacher 1982-84, 5th Grade Teacher 1984- Hutchinson Elem Sch Dist; *ai:* UIL Coach; Absentee Comm; ATPE 1988-; Red Cross Volunteer 1978-; On Level 2 of the TX Career Ladder.

MC ADAMS, GEORGE ALAN, History Teacher/Chairman; *b:* Twin Falls, ID; *m:* Carol J. Dalos; *c:* Doug, Gina Dawn; *ed:* (AS) Law Enforcement, Coll of Southern ID 1967; (BA) Phys Ed/Soc Stud, ID St Univ 1971; Intermediate Degree Law Enforcement; *cr:* Wrestling Coach Kimberly 1972-76; Teacher Kimberly Jr HS/HS 1972-96; *ai:* Asst Wrestling Coach; Weight Lifting Club Spon; 7th Grade Spon; ID Ed Assn 1989-; Kimberly Lions Club Tail Twister 1989-; Kimberly City Cncl Cnclmn 1990-94; Dist Wrestling Coach of Yr; Booster Club Awd.

MC ADAMS, JUNE ALLEN, Physical Science Teacher; *b:* Lufkin, TX; *m:* Hollis R.; *c:* Scott, April; *ed:* (BS) Chem/Bio, Stephen F Austin Univ 1970; Grad Work Bio & Ed; *cr:* Teacher Lufkin Intermediate 1971-72, Lufkin Jr HS 1972-73, Cntrl Ind HS 1979-81, Lufkin Jr HS West 1981-; *ai:* TX St Teachers Assn 1971-88; TX Classroom Teachers Assn 1989-; NSTA 1990.

MC ADAMS, TINA BURKS, Eighth Grade Earth Sci Teacher; *b:* Texas City, TX; *c:* John, Reid, Cody; *ed:* (BS) Elem Ed, 1983, (MED) Elem Ed, 1986 Lamar Univ; *cr:* 5th Grade Teacher Kirbyville Elem 1983-87; 8th Grade Teacher Buna Jr HS 1987-; *ai:* Stu Cncl Spon; UIL Sci Coach; TSTA Faculty Rep 1989-;

Baptist Young Women Pres 1975-78; *home:* PO Box 74 Buna TX 77612

MC ADOO, LISA GAIL, Mathematics Teacher; *b:* Marlow, OK; *ed:* (BS) Math, SW OK St Univ 1985; *cr:* Math Teacher Velma-Alma HS 1985-88, Bridge Creek HS 1988-89, Jones HS 1989-; *ai:* Chrldr & Jr/Sr Spon; Math Club Adv; N Cntrl Evaluation Comm; Mu Alpha Theta Co-Spon.

MC ADOW, SHERRIE FITE, Mathematics/Physics Teacher; *b:* Benton, AR; *m:* James D.; *c:* Allison, Vanessa; *ed:* (BSE) Math, Univ of AR Little Rock 1986; Dance Ed; *cr:* Math Teacher Robinson HS 1986-87, Harmony Grove HS 1987-; *ai:* Sr Class Spon; Stu Cncl; AEA, NEA; Riggs Dance Company Dir; *home:* 2711 Bristol Benton AR 72015

MC AFEE, BEATRICE FOWLER, English Teacher; *b:* Wiergate, TX; *m:* John Douglas Jr.; *ed:* (BA) Eng, TX Coll 1967; (MA) Eng Lit, Cntrl MI Univ 1975; *cr:* 11th/12th Grade Eng Teacher Cmmty HS 1967-68; 8th/9th Grade Eng Teacher Cntrl Jr HS 1968-; *ai:* Sch Newspaper Adv; Cheerleading & Girls Vlybl Coach; Saginaw Ed Assn, MI Ed Assn 1968-; NEA 1967-; *home:* 3837 Mackinaw Saginaw MI 48602

MC AFEE, CHARLES HAMILTON, JR., Fifth Grade Teacher; *b:* York, PA; *m:* Beverly E. Hollinger; *c:* Amy J. Beddia; *ed:* (BS) Elem Ed, Millersville St Univ 1963; (MS) Elem Ed Admin/Supervision, W MD Coll 1967; PA St Univ 1963-73; Marywood Coll 1971-76; Shippensburg 1986-87; *cr:* Elem Teacher 1963-66, Asst Prin 1967-72 York City Sch Dist; Prin Northeastern Sch Dist 1972-74, W York Area Sch Dist 1974-76; *ai:* Curr Comm; Help Organize Sci Fairs; W York Area Ed Assn 1976-; PA St Ed Assn 1976-; NEA 1963-; York YMCA (Building Comm 1972-73, Fund Raising 1972); *home:* 2601 Sunset Ln York PA 17404

MC AFEE, SUSAN J., Language Arts Teacher; *b:* Los Angeles, CA; *m:* Robert R.; *c:* Jack, Lani; *ed:* (BA) Eng, E MT Coll 1969; Ed Admin, N AZ Univ Flagstaff; *cr:* Lang Art Teacher Lake Havasu JR HS 1981-; *ai:* Yrbk Adv 1982-88; *office:* Lake Havasu Jr HS 98 Swanson Plz Lake Havasu City AZ 86403

MC ALEXANDER, CHARLOTTE DUER, English/Vocal Music Teacher; *b:* Fletcher, OH; *m:* Donald; *c:* Debra Marchal, Anthony, Cinda; *ed:* (BA) Elem Ed/Music Ed, Wright St 1969; Courses in Eng & Scndry Ed, Wright St; *cr:* Teacher Fairlawn HS 1966-; *ai:* Sr Class Adv; Jr & Sr Show Choirs; Drama Yearly Broadway Musical; Greenview United Church of Christ (Organist, Choir Dir) 1960-; *home:* 3717 Tawawa Maplewood Rd Sidney OH 45365

MC ALISTER, KATHRYN JOYCE FREEMAN, Chairperson/Reading Department; *b:* Sentinel, OK; *m:* Robert J.; *c:* Michael J., Steven P.; *ed:* (BA) Phys Educ/Elem Educ, Southwestern St Teachers Univ 1962; (MED) Public Sch Admin, Tarleton St Univ 1976; Rdng, North TX St Univ; Classroom Mgmt and Discipline Prgm; *cr:* Phys Ed/Jr HS Girls Bsktbll Coach/Sayre Public Sch 1962-63; Elem/Phys Ed Teacher Amarilo Public Sch 1963-66; 7/8th Lang Art Teacher Heizer Jr HS 1966-67; Elem Phys Ed Teacher Albuqurque Public Sch Dist 1967-68; Elem Ed 6th Grade Teacher Pampa ISD 1968-69; Girls Phys Ed Teacher Pampa Jr HS 1969-73; Homebound/Spec Ed White Settlemark ISD 1973-78; Life Sci Lib/TX His 1978-80; Rdng Dept 1980- Brewer Mid Sch; *ai:* Dont Do Drug Prgm; Heart Assn BMS Jump-A-Thon; Discipline Mgmt Comm; Campus Planning Comm; ATPE; PTA; Cmmty Chest Comm Mem 1989-; BMS Drug Prog Spon 1989-; City Lib Bd of White Settlement Mem 1980-; *office:* Brewer Mid Sch 1000 A Cherry Ln Fort Worth TX 76108

MC ALISTER, MARY TERRELL, English Teacher/Dept Chair; *b:* Atlanta, GA; *ed:* (AB) Eng, GA St Univ 1962; (MED) Eng, Clemson Univ 1981; Bread Loaf Sch of Eng; *cr:* Eng Teacher Southwood Jr HS 1976-85, Westside HS 1985-; *ai:* Poetry, Short Stories Published; *office:* Westside HS 806 Pearman Dairy Rd Anderson SC 29625

MC ALLISTER, LESIA JEAN, Fifth Grade Teacher; *b:* Tacoma, WA; *ed:* (BS) Ed, 1977, (MA) Spec Ed/Gifted, 1983 Wright St Univ; *cr:* K-8th Grade Substitute Teacher Piqua City Sch 1978-79; 5th Grade Teacher 1979-81, 2nd Grade Teacher 1981-84, 5Th/6th Grade Math Teacher 1984-85, 5th Grade Teacher 1985- Favorite Hill Elem; *ai:* Rdng & Math Curr Comm; Piqua Ed Assn (VP 1988-, Pres 1990); Church of Christ Curr Adv 1987-; Mini Grant Cmptr Materials Creating Classroom Newspaper; *office:* Favorite Hill Elem Sch 950 South St Piqua OH 45356

MC ANDREW, MARY JORDAN, Third Grade Teacher; *b:* Scranton, PA; *m:* Robert G.; *c:* Maureen, Margaret, Kathleen, Michael; *ed:* (BA) Elem Ed, 1979, (MS) Rdng, 1986 Marywood Coll; *cr:* Kndgtn Teacher 1979-82, 3rd Grade Teacher 1982- St Clare Sch; *ai:* Marywood Coll Alumni Bd Secy; Saint Andrea Society; *office:* St Clare Sch 2215 N Washington Ave Scranton PA 18509

MC ANELLY, ELIZABETH ANN BOWYER, Bio Teacher/Chm Science Dept; *b:* Stamford, TX; *m:* Rex H.; *c:* Laura C.; *ed:* (BS) Pre-Med, TX Womens Univ 1948; Hardin Simmons Univ; Univ of NM; Univ of Northern CO; Univ of Ok; West TX St Univ; Tarleton St Univ; Univ SW OK; Pepperdine Univ; *cr:* MS Sci Anson Ind Sch Dist 1948-50; 4th Grade Teacher Brooksmith Ind Sch Dist 1950-51; MS Lang Art Edcoud Elsa Ind Sch Dist 1955-56; HS Sci Pampa Ind Sch Dist 1960-; *ai:* Leadership Team Pampa HS; Teacher Training Coord-PISD; TX Classroom Teachers Assn; Sci Teachers Assn TX; Delta Kappa Gamma; NSTA; Teacher Yr Pampa HS 1972 & 1979; Natl Bio Assn Inst 1967 1968 & 1969; Bio Teacher Yr TX 1968; Nom Outstanding HS Teacher TX 1989.

MC ANELLY, LINDA BURLESON, English Department Chairperson; *b:* Lubbock, TX; *m:* Phillip Aaron; *c:* Lance, Matt; *ed:* (BS) Eng/Speech, TX Tech Univ 1973; (MA) Curr/Instruction, Univ of TX San Antonio 1978; SOI Trng; Jr Great Books; Gifted & Talented Wkshps; *cr:* Rdng/Eng Teacher Tahoka HS 1973-74; 2nd-8th Grade Rdng/Eng Teacher of Gifted & Talented Devine Elem 1976-77, 1982-84; Rdng Specialist Hondo HS 1977-81; Eng II & IV Teacher Devine HS 1984-; *ai:* Interscholastic League Poetry & Oral Rdng Coach; Jr Prom Spon; TX St Teachers Assn, NCTE; Devine Current Events Secy 1984-85; Devine Jr Miss Comm Mem; Eng/Lang Art Dept Head; *office:* Devine Sr HS 1225 W Hondo Ave Devine TX 78016

MC ANINCH, VIVIEN DURHAM, Biology Teacher; *b:* Greenwood, IN; *m:* Marshall F.; *c:* Sherri, Frank; *ed:* (BS) Bio, 1971, (MA) Bio Ed, 1972; Supervision, 1976; Scndry Prin, 1982 E KY Univ; Internship Prgm KY; *cr:* Bio Teacher Madison Cntrl HS 1972-86, Madison Southern HS 1986-; *ai:* Adopt-A-Sch Co-Chm Madison Cty Schls Richmond Chamber of Commerce; Dir of Mentor Shadowing Prgm Madison Southern HS; KY Sci & Tech Cncl Inst Mem 1989-; NABT, KY Sci Teacher Assn, NEA, KEA; Homemakes Club VP; E KY Univ Alumni Assn; Nom Outstanding KY Bio Teacher; KY Ed Fnd Grant to Develop Mentor Shadowing Prgm; Numerous Comm & Cncls.

MC ARDLE, MARTIN WALTER, Secondary Mathematics Teacher; *b:* Pigeon, MI; *c:* Darcy L., Greg M.; *ed:* (BS) Math, 1971, General Ed Admin, 1980 Cntrl MI Univ; *cr:* Math Teacher Laker Jr HS 1971-75, Vassar HS 1975-; *ai:* Academic Math Team Adv; *office:* Vassar HS 220 Athletic St Vassar MI 48768

MC ARTHUR, JOHN ERWIN, Director of Bands; *b:* Waynesboro, MS; *ed:* (BM) Music Ed, Univ of MS 1985; Grad Work, MS St Univ; *cr:* Jr HS Band Dir Kosciusko Public Schls 1985-89; Dir of Bands Quitman Public Schls 1989-; *ai:* East Cntrl Band Dir (Pres 1990, Officer 1987-); MS Bandmasters Assn; Gulf Coast Judges Assn; Natl Band Assn; Articles Published; Outstanding Young Men of America; *office:* Quitman HS 211 S Jackson Quitman MS 39355

MC BRADY, MARY SIEFERT, Kindergarten Teacher; *b:* Graceville, MN; *m:* Joseph; *c:* Peg Plaggerman, Barb, Dan, Betty Thomes, Jerry, Carol, Pat, Mary P. Mc Brady Stifter; *ed:* (BS) Elem Ed, St Cloud Univ 1972; Early Chldhd Ed 1991; *cr:* Teacher Rosolt Cntry Sch 1950-51, St Timothys 1967-68, Maple Lake Elem 1968-; *ai:* Bible Study & Baptism Class Teacher; Quality Schls Comm; NAEYC, MN Kndgtn Assn, MEA, MFT; *home:* R 1 Box 75 Maple Lake MN 55358

MC BRIDE, BETTY SINGLEY, 7th/8th Grade Math/Sci Teacher; *b:* Butler, AL; *m:* Vernon G.; *c:* Nicole, Kimberly; *ed:* (BS) Elem Ed, 1977, (MED) Elem Ed, Livingston Univ; Special Cert Adult Ed, Univ of AL; *cr:* Teacher East Choctaw Jr HS 1977-80, Windward Preparatory 1980-84, East Choctaw Jr HS 1984-; *ai:* Beta Club & Prom Spon; Chm at Risk Prgm at East Choctaw; Sci Textbook Comm for Cty; Adult Ed Teacher; CCEA (VP, Pres) 1988-89; AEA, NEA Delegate 1989; Appointed to Serve on East Choctaws Asset Team; Currently Writing Projects on Cooperative Learning for AL A&M; *home:* 507 Gloria Dr Butler AL 36904

MC BRIDE, JUDITH LEWIS, Instrumental Music Teacher; *b:* Whitmire, SC; *m:* Gerald J.; *c:* James A., Geralee J.; *ed:* (BMED) Music Ed, Murray St Univ 1959; (MED) Admin/Supervision, The Citadel 1977; *cr:* Music Teacher Walnut Creek Elem 1959-63, Elmwood Public Sch 1963-67; Instrumental Music Goose Creek HS 1967-; *ai:* Spirit of Gold Marching Band Dir, Goose Creek HS Symphonic Band, Concert Band, Jazz Ensemble; SC Bd Dir Assn, SC Music Educators Assn; Amer Sch Band Dir Assn St Chm 1989-; Trident Cmmty Band; *office:* Goose Creek HS 1137 Redbank Rd Goose Creek SC 29445

MC BRYDE, MARY ALICE, Mathematics Teacher/Coach; *b:* Gonzales, TX; *ed:* (BS) Phys Ed, Univ of TX 1979; *cr:* Math Teacher/Coach Austwell-Tivoli HS 1979-83, Industrial Jr HS 1983, Industrial Jr HS 1983-; *ai:* 7th Grade Girls Bsktbl, track, 8th Grade Girls Vlybl Coach; 6th Grade UIL Spon in Number Sense & Calculator Contest; Assn of TX Prof Educators 1983-; TX Girls Coaches Assn 1979-; TX Assn of Bsktbl Coaches 1983-; *office:* Industrial Jr HS Box 208 Lolita TX 77971

MC BURNETT, STEPHEN WARE, Jr HS Science Teacher; *b:* Milwaukee, WI; *m:* Jenny Crocker; *c:* Stephen W. Jr., Joshua D.; *ed:* (BA) Government, Harvard Coll 1968; (MED) Univ of MO Columbia 1970; Chem, WA Univ; *cr:* Jr HS Sci Teacher St Louis Public Schls 1970-72; Elem Ed Teacher Valley R-6 Schls 1973, 1974; Jr HS Sci Teacher Viburnum Schls 1975-; *ai:* Var Cross Cntry & Var Track Coach; Educl Fair Chm; Sch Newspaper Adv.

MC BURNEY, DONALD EVANS, Science Teacher; *b:* Ashland, OH; *m:* Denise Lovano; *ed:* (BS) Bio, OH Northern Univ 1983; Curr/Instr, Kent St Univ; OH Ed Assn Leadership Acad; Natl Sci Teachers Assn Conventions; Sci Ed of OH Conventions; *cr:* Sci Teacher/Athletic Trainer Trinity HS 1983-86; Sci Teacher/Classroom of the Future Coord Ravenna HS 1986-; *ai:* Key Club Adv; Ski Club Adv; Frosh Class Adv; Tennis Coach; Sci Olympiad Coach; Dist Coord-Classrooms of the Future; Sci Ed of OH Convention Exhibits Chm/Bd Mem 1990-; NSTA Mem 1986-; NEA/OEA/Ravenna Ed Assn Dist Treas 1986- St New Leader Awd 1989; Kiwanis Intnl Youth Services Co-Chm 1989-; Dist Teacher of Yr 1989; OH Dept of Ed Mentor Teacher Trng 1989-; OH Dept of Ed Classrooms of the Future; Comm of Participating Institutions 1990; North Cntrl Evaluation Visiting Team Mem; Teachers for The Levy Campaign; *office:* Ravenna H S 345 E Main St Ravenna OH 44266

MC BURROWS, FRANCES JACKSON, Physical Education Teacher; *b:* Chicago, IL; *m:* John Wesley Jr.; *c:* Aisha, Faith, John IV; *ed:* (BA) Scndry Phys Ed, 1974; (BA) Elem Ed, 1974 Northeastern IL Univ; *cr:* Guidance Coun Bryn Mawr Elem 1975-76; 2nd Grade Teacher Schneider Elem 1977-78; Kdngtn Teacher Wheaton Christin Ctr Acad 1982-83; Elem/Sr HS Phys Ed Mary a Yates 1983-; *ai:* Coach 5th & 6th Grade Girls Bsktbl; Dir & Coord Black His Prgms; Stu Intervention Team Against Drugs; *home:* 5702 Crestwood Rd Matteson IL 60443

MC CABE, BEVERLY KELLEY, 8th Grade Math/English Teacher; *b:* Evergreen Park, IL; *m:* William E.; *ed:* (BSED) Phys Ed, 1964, (MSED) Outdoor Ed, 1968 Northern IL Univ; Graduate Work Eng/Writing Southern IL Univ 1981-86; Agronomy Univ IL 1970-71; *cr:* 4th-12th Grade Phys Ed Teacher Lanark 1964-65; 9th-12th Grade Phys Ed Teacher/Chairperson Sycamore HS 1965-78; K-6th Grade Phys Ed Teacher Carrier Mills 1978-83; 8th Grade Eng/Math Teacher Our Lady of Mt Carmel 1985-; GED/Adult Ed Teacher John A Logan 1988-; *ai:* Girls Sports, Coached Var Bsktbl, Track & Field, Sftbl, Badminton, Field Hockey; Dance Show Spon; Girls Sports Coord; Gymnastics Show Spon; Initiated Leadership Prgm Sycamore; Earthday Prgm, Yrbk, 8th Grade Class, Creative Mag Spon; NCTE 1987-; IL Cncl Teachers of Math 1990; NCEA; St Frances De Sale Church Trustee 1989-; Amer Angus; Amer & IL Farm Bureau 1974-; Trained Several Stu Teachers; Leaders of Amer Scndry Ed 1972; Published Phys Ed Outdoor Ed Articles; Competency Testing Prgm Curr Mem; North Cntrl Assn & St Evaluator; *office:* Our Lady of Mt Carmel Sch 300 W Monroe Herrin IL 62948

MC CABE, DENNIS ROBERT, Social Studies Teacher; *b:* Milwaukee, WI; *m:* Margaret Erchul; *c:* Ann, Lily; *ed:* (BS) His, Univ of WI Milwaukee 1969; *cr:* 7th/8th Grade Soc Stud Teacher Merton Elem 1973-; *ai:* 7th/8th Grade Team Leader; NEA 1973-; *office:* Merton Elem Sch 6881 Main St Merton WI 53056

MC CABE, FRANK JAMES, Sales & Sales Trng; *b:* Boston, MA; *m:* Susan Nancy Bray; *c:* Jamie, Scott, Dana; *ed:* (BS) Earth Sci, 1972, (MSED) Earth Sci, 1976 Boston St Coll; *cr:* Teacher Mary E Curley Mid Sch 1972-82; Sales/Sales Trng Smith Kline & French Labs 1982-; *ai:* Bsktbl & Bsbl Coach; Boston Juvenile Court Probation Officer Asst; Milton Hospital Bd; New England Aquarium Teacher; Milton Town Meeting Mem; *office:* Smith Kline & French Labs 37 Belvoir Rd Milton MA 02186

MC CABE, ROBERT, 5th Grade Teacher; *b:* Scranton, PA; *ed:* (BS) Ed, 1957, (MA) Philosophy, 1971 Rutgers; *cr:* Teacher Monroe Township Sch Dist 1957-61; Mamaroneck Sch Dist 1961-; *ai:* Dir of Spring Musical; NYSTA, NEA; *office:* Chatsworth Avenue Sch Forrest Park Ave Larchmont NY 10538

MC CABE, SANDRA PETIKA, French Teacher; *b:* Canonsburg, PA; *m:* John T.; *c:* John S.; *ed:* (BA) Fr, Univ of Pittsburgh 1959; *cr:* Fr Teacher Canon-Mc Millan Sr HS 1959-62; Fr/Eng Teacher Washington Sr HS 1963-; *ai:* Fr Club Adv; Character Building Comm; *office:* Washington Sr HS Allison & Hallam Ave Washington PA 15301

MC CAFFERTY, EILEEN PATRICIA, 2nd Grade Teacher; *b:* Philadelphia, PA; *ed:* (BS) Elem Ed, St Josephs Univ 1990; Certificate Religious Studies St Charles Seminary; *cr:* 2nd Grade Teacher Our Lady of Loreto 1972-; *ai:* Math Coord; NCEA; *office:* Our Lady Of Loreto Sch 2412 S 62nd St Philadelphia PA 19142

MC CAIN, JEAN GEIPEL, Fourth Grade Teacher; *b:* St Louis, MO; *m:* Paul Burdette; *c:* Paul T., Philip J.; *ed:* (BSED) Lit/Sci, Concordia Teachers Coll 1955; Grad Stud Pre-Sch Ed & Scndry Lang Art; *cr:* 1st/2nd Grade Teacher/Admin Redeemer Luth Sch 1955-57; 4th/5th Grade Teacher Immanuel Luth Sch 1957-61; 1st/2nd/7th/8th Grade Teacher Redeemer Luth Sch 1961-65,1974-85; 6th Grade Teacher St Peter Luth Sch 1985-89; 4th Grade Teacher St John Luth Sch 1989-.

MC CAIN, MELISSA SMITH, Fourth Grade Teacher; *b:* Tallapoosa, GA; *m:* Ralph Stanley; *c:* John, Josh, Joseph; *ed:* (BA) Psych/Socialogy, Tift Coll 1972; (MED) Mid Grades, W GA Coll 1977; Gifted Add-On, W GA Coll 1982; *cr:* Teacher Cty Schls 1974-83, Bremen City Schls 1983-; *ai:* Bremen Ed Assn VP 1988-; NEA; GA Ed Assn; Delta Kappa Gamma; *office:* H A Jones Elem Sch Lakeview Dr Bremen GA 30110

MC CAINE, GLORIA MOORE, 7th Grade Soc Studies Teacher; *b:* Cleveland, MS; *m:* Craig E.; *c:* Tanya L.; *ed:* (BS) Ed, Univ of Mo 1977; Addl Studies MO St Univ; Nort Heast MO St Univ; *cr:* Stu Teacher/Teacher Riverview Gardens Jr HS 1976-77; His Teacher Riverview Gardens HS 1977-78; Soc Stud Teacher Riverview Gardens Mid Sch 1978-; *ai:* Add Hoc Comm; NEA 1989-; MNEA 1989-; Riverview Gardens NEA 1989-; Bus/Prof Women Fed 1988-; *office:* Riverview Gardens Mid Sch 9800 Patricia Barkalow Drive Saint Louis MO 63137

MC CALL, CHARLENE N., French Teacher; *b:* Camden, NJ; *c:* Christine, Billy; *ed:* (BA) Fr Ed, Rutgers Univ 1971; Various Prgms Aimed at Improvement of Foreign Lang Instruction; Summer Study Dickenson Center Toulouse France; *cr:* Fr Teacher Haddonfield Memorial HS 1971-73, Swarthmore HS 1980-84, Strath Haven HS 1980-84, Highland Reg HS 1985-; *ai:* Fr Club

Adv; Chairperson Mid Sts; Dept Comm AFS Adv; AATF, MLA NJ 1971-; Univ of DE Project on Artificial Intelligence & Foreign Lang 1987; Commonwealth Fellow, Partnership 1988; NJ Governors Outstanding Teacher Awd 1989; *office:* Highland Reg HS Erial Rd Blackwood NJ 08012

MC CALL, DAVID L., Spanish Teacher; *b:* Abingdon, VA; *ed:* (BA) Span, Concord Coll 1968; (MA) Scndry Ed, WV Univ 1974; *cr:* Span/Eng Teacher 1968-70, FL Chm 1968-70 Martinsburg Sr HS; Span Teacher 1970-, FL Chm 1973- St Clairsville HS; *ai:* Span Club, Soph Class Adv; NHS Selection Comm; Yrbk Adv 1970-73; St Clairsville Ed Assn Treas 1978; NEA, OH Foreign Lang Assn; OH Ed Assn 1970-; Study Tours Cnslr Spain, France, Portugal, Mexico; *office:* Saint Clairsville HS 108 Woodrow Ave Saint Clairsville OH 43950

MC CALL, JANICE LYNNE, Speech Teacher; *b:* Austin, TX; *m:* John Holmes Jr.; *ed:* (BS) Speech Comm, 1987, Teaching Certificate Biological Sci, 1988 Univ of TX Austin; *cr:* Classroom Teacher Parkhill Jr HS 1988-; *ai:* Speech Club Spon; Teens Offering Peer Support Co-Spon; Musical Dir; REA, PTA 1988-; *office:* Parkhill Jr HS 16500 Shadybank Dr Dallas TX 75248

MC CALL, MARGARET CARTER, Mathematics Teacher; *b:* Atlanta, GA; *m:* Jerry Wayne; *c:* Jeremy, Stephanie; *ed:* (BS) Math, 1977, (MED) Math-Ed, 1981 N GA Coll; K-12th Grade Gifted Cert; *cr:* Teacher S Hall Jr HS 1979-88, S Hall Mid Sch 1988-; *ai:* NEA, GAE, HCEA 1980-; NCTM 1983-87; Delta Kappa Gamma 1987-; Beta Sigma Phi (Extension Officer 1983-84, Corresponding Secy 1988-89, Mem 1982-); Mc Ever Road United Meth Church Chairperson of Higher Ed 1990; *office:* S Hall Mid Sch Poplar Springs Rd Gainesville GA 30501

MC CALL, MARQUERITE DYE, Fifth Grade Teacher; *b:* Elbert Co, GA; *M:* Silvey A. (dec); *c:* Mark A., Jan Bowers; *ed:* (BS) Elem Ed, GA Southern 1955; (MED) Elem Ed, Univ of GA 1975 *cr:* 4th Grade Teacher Nancy Hart Memorial 1955-63; 5th-7th Grade Teacher Beaverdam Elem 1969-71; 5th Grade Teacher Falling Creek Elem 1971-; *ai:* ECTA (Secy 1970-71 Mem 1955-63; GAE/NEA/PTA 1969-; Outstanding Elem Teachers Awds of Amer 1973; Outstanding Educator of Elbert Cty 1988-89; *office:* Falling Creek Elem Sch 1050 Washington Hwy Elberton GA 30635

MC CALL, MELBA JUNE (MATNEY), Retired Teacher; *b:* Palo Pinto Cty, TX; *m:* Charles Franklin; *c:* Charles Jr., Stephen, Jack; *ed:* Certificate ELem Ed, Weatherford Jr Coll 1946; (BS) Elem Ed, Hardin-Simmons Univ 1955; (TECAT) Elem Ed, TX Ed Agency 1986; Cmptr Applications, Western TX Coll; Advanced Ed, TX Technological Coll; *cr:* 4th Grade Teacher Rotan Elem Sch 1946-48; 6th Grade Rdng/Eng/HS Commercial Teacher 1952-53, 4th Grade Teacher /HS Secy 1953-54 Rotan Elem & Rotan HS; 3rd Grade Teacher 1956-80, 3rd Grade Homeroom/4th Grade Rdng Teacher 1981-82, 4th Grade Teacher 1983-87 Rotan Elem Sch; *ai:* UIL Story Telling, Picture Memory & Spelling; Career Ladder 1985-87; TX St Teachers Assn, Fisher Cty Teachers Assn, Rotan Classroom Teachers Assn 1946-48, 1953-87; Delta Kappa Gamma Society 1959-74; Rolling Plains Retired Teachers 1987-; 1st Baptist Church; *home:* 713 E Johnston Rotan TX 79546

MC CALL, VERA MITCHELL, Teacher; *b:* West Point, MS; *m:* Chester; *c:* Ricky, Byron; *ed:* (BS) Elem Ed/Soc Stud, Alcorn Univ 1963; (MA) Elem Ed, TN St 1970; Columbus MS; *cr:* Teacher Amory Elem 1964-; *ai:* GSA Leader; Pres Alumni Mary Holmes Jr Coll; Secy West Amory Act Funds; MAE Building Rep 1974; NAACP 1965; Prof Ed Assn 1964; BTU Pres 1960; Sunday Sch Teacher 1959-64; Baptist Choir Secy 1958-63.

MC CALL, WILLIAM P., II, Life Science Teacher; *b:* Leitchfield, KY; *m:* Dorothy L Basham; *c:* William P. III; *ed:* (BA) Ed Biological Sci, Univ of KY 1960; (MED) Ed Biological Sci, Univ of VA 1963; (PHD) Sci Ed Bio Sci, Univ of IA 1972; Various Univ; *cr:* Scndry Sci Teacher 1960-64; Elem Teacher 1957-59; Asst Professor Mid TN St Univ 1964-69; Botany/Zoology/Geology Teacher/Bsktbl Coach/Athletic Dir Ancilla Coll 1972-73; Part Time Admin/Teaching Asst Univ IA 1969-72; Assoc Professor/Asst Dir Model Lab Sch E KY Univ 1973-76; Prin Marion Cty HS 1979-82; Life Sci Teacher Grayson Cty Schls 1984-; *ai:* Honorable Order of KY Colonels; Faculty Senate E KY Univ; Ed Speaker Australia; Inservice Act for Teachers Co ord; NEA, KY Ed Assn 1984-; Phi Delta Kappa 1969-; Chrstn Church; Chamber of Commerce; NASSP; NSTA; Faculty Senate, EKU; Univ of IA Alumni Assn Life Mem; Numerous Fund Raising Drives Coord 1972-; Jaycees (Secy, Treas) 1964-69; Amer Legion 1977-, Service Awd 1989; Visiting Sr Lecturer in Ed; Gourburn Coll of Adv Ed; NSW Australia; NSF Summer Inst; Univ of NE; Yale Univ; Academic Yr Inst Univ of VA; Cert of Appreciation US Postal Service; Numerous Articles Published; *home:* 200 Mill St Leitchfield KY 42754

MC CALLUM, BRIAN NEIL, 6th Grade Math/Sci Teacher; *b:* Grand Rapids, MI; *m:* Beverly Lou Chapman; *c:* Ryan; *ed:* (BA) Eng, MI St Univ 1970; Grad Course Work MI St; *cr:* 6th Grade Teacher Grand Rapids Sch 1969-70; 5th/6th Grade Teacher Sparta Area Schls 1970-; *ai:* 8th Grade Girls & Boys Bsktbl Coach; 7th Grade Vlybl Coach; 6th Grade Camping Prgm Dir; Project Learning Tree, Outdoor Biological Instructional Strategies, Acclimatization Facilitator; MEA, NEA 1969-; SEA 1969-, Teacher of Yr 1975-76; MI Sci Teachers Assn Outstanding Teacher Awd Finalist 1981; W MI Environmental Assn Bd Mem 1978-79; *office:* Sparta Mid Sch 240 Glenn Sparta MI 49345

MC CAMBRIDGE, ELIZABETH TURBES, Soc Stud Dept Chairperson; *b:* Minneapolis, MN; *m:* Carleton S.; *ed:* (BA) Scndry Soc Stud, Univ of MN 1979; *cr:* 7th Grade Adult Eng as Second Lang Teacher St Paul Public Schls 1980-84; 7th/8th Grade Soc Stud Teacher Cleveland Jr HS 1984-; *office:* Cleveland Jr HS 1000 Walsh St Saint Paul MN 55106

MC CANCE, MARY SUSAN, Assistant Principal; *b:* Glendale, CA; *ed:* (BA) Eng/Comp Lit, 1977, (MS) Counseling, 1981 CA St Univ Fullerton; Admin, Univ of CA Irvine; Chemical Abuse Prevention Prgms Trng; *cr:* Eng/Bus/Leadership Teacher L Raney Jr HS 1977-81; Eng/Span Teacher Walnut HS 1981-82; Eng as 2nd Lang Teacher South Jr HS 1982-84; Cnslr Orangeview Jr HS 1984-89; Asst Prin Ball Jr HS 1989; *ai:* Stu Act, ASB, 9th Grade Class, Newcomers Club, Newspaper, Journalism Adv; CA Assn Dir of Act (Area F Bd Rep 1988-, Leadership Camp Steering Comm 1984-) Outstanding Area Mem 1990; Natl Assn Wkshp Dir 1987-; Leadership Assn S CA Pres 1984-88, Pres Awd 1987; Speak to Stus on Comm, Stress & Leadership Skills; Speaker at CA Assn Dir of Act Leadership Camps & St Conferences; *office:* Ball Jr HS 1500 W Ball Rd Anaheim CA 92804

MC CANDLESS, ELIZABETH M., 4th Grade Teacher; *b:* Pittsburgh, PA; *m:* William C.; *c:* William H., Mary M. Palin; *ed:* Penn St; *cr:* 2nd Grade Teacher Duxbury MA Elem Sch 1951-52; Elkton Elem Sch 1952-53; Kndgtn Teacher 1959-66 4th Grade Teacher 1968- Pine Richland; *home:* Box 397 Gibsonia PA 15044

MC CANN, ANN MARIE COX, First Grade Teacher; *b:* Pawtucket, RI; *m:* William Joseph; *c:* William J., Beth L.; *ed:* (BED) Ed, Rhode Island Coll 1964; Grad Stud; *cr:* 2nd Grade Teacher Center Sch 1964-65; Kndgtn Teacher Coggeshall Sch 1970-76; Kndgtn Teacher 1976-88, 1st Grade Teacher 1988- Elmhurst Sch; *ai:* Cmptr, Gifted & Talented, Health Ed Curr Cncl; Crisis Intervention Comm; Amer Assn of Univ Women (VP of Prgms 1985-86, Mem) 1982-; Delta Kappa Gamma Society Intnl Mem 1987-; Intnl Rdng Assn (Delegate 1989-, Mem) 1986-; RI Artist in Residence Grant 1985; Native Amers RI Princs Grant 1989-; Salt Water Aquarium St Sci Grant 1989-; *office:* Elmhurst Elem Sch Glen Rd Portsmouth RI 02871

MC CANN, JOHN LEO, JR., Social Sci Dept Chairperson; *b:* Stockton, CA; *m:* Patricia Yvonne Caylor; *c:* Michael, Sean; *ed:* (BA) His/Cultural Geography, Univ of CA Berkeley 1977; *cr:* His Teacher Red Bluff Union HS 1979-80; Soc Sci Teacher Lassen Union HS 1980-; *ai:* Sr Class Adv Lassen Cty Soc Sci; Curr Specialist; Soc Sci Dept Chm; NCSS 1986-; Assn for Curr Dev 1989-; Fulbright Assn 1989-; City of Susanville Mayor Pro Ten 1986-; Lassen Cty Transportation Commission Chm 1987-; Fulbright Fellowship South Korea 1986; CA Mentor Teacher Awds 1984-85, 1988; *office:* Lassen Union HS 1110 Main St Susanville CA 96130

MC CANN, JOSEPHINE ANNE, Principal; *b:* Butte, MT; *m:* Alfred Watterson; *c:* Maureen Randall, Martin, Patrick; *ed:* (BE) Ed, Seattle Univ 1956; (MAD) Admin, Gonzaga Univ 1985; W WA Coll, E WA Univ; *cr:* 4th/5th Grade Teacher St Johns 1955-56; 2nd-4th Grade Teacher Marblemount 1956-59; Pre-Sch Teacher Lakewood Pre-Sch 1966-70; Spec Tutor Dist 81 1975; 2nd/3rd Grade Teacher All Saints Primary 1978-82; Prin St Francis Xavier/Assisi 1982-; *ai:* Spokane Schls Drug/Alcohol, Curriculum, Teacher Evaluation, Athletic Comm; NCEA; Principals Assn Secy 1983-84; Childrens Hospital Guild Pres 1964-65; Spokane Newcomers (VP 1971-72, Pres 1972-73); *office:* St Francis Xavier/Assisi E 544 Providence Spokane WA 99207

MC CANN, LORRAINE DOROTHY-JEAN, 4th Grade Teacher; *b:* Long Island City, NY; *ed:* (BS) Ed, SUNY Potsdam 1961; (MSED) ED, Queens Coll 1968; Post Masters Studies MSED Post Coll; Univ of CO; *cr:* Teacher Schenectady NY 1961-64; Teacher South Huntington S.D. #13 1964-; *ai:* Teacher Ctr Policy Bd Mem 1988-89; Retirement Comm; Textbook Selection Comm; NYSTA; SHTA; AAUW Bd Mem 1984-85; Field Researcher for NYS Sci Civ.

MC CANN, MARGUERITE ROY, Retired Elem Ed Teacher; *b:* Hessmer, LA; *c:* Johnny; *ed:* (BS) Home Ec, Univ of SW LA 1971; *cr:* Home Ec Teacher 1957-60, Elem Ed Teacher 1964-82 Hessmer HS; *ai:* Alpha Delta Kappa Secy 1976-78; Avoyelles Teachers Assn 1957-82; Avoyelles Retired Teachers Assn 1982-; Woodmen of the World Woman of Yr 1974; Church (Altar Society Treas 1976-78, Cncl 1978-80); *home:* PO Box 116 Hessmer LA 71341

MC CANN, NANCY MILLER, Retired Elem Teacher; *b:* Mechanicsville, PA; *m:* James Patrick; *ed:* (BS) Elem Ed, Villa Maria Coll 1965; (MS) Elem Math, Clarion St Coll 1973; Soc Stud, Indiana Univ of PA; Rdng, Sci, Edinboro St Coll; *cr:* Elem Teacher Erie Diocese Parochial Schls 1953-68; Math Teacher North Clarion Elem 1968-70; Math Teacher 1970-73, Elem Teacher 1973-89 Warren Cty Sch Dist; *ai:* Math Comm Mem; Art & Lib Coord; NEA, PA St Educl Assn 1968; Warren Cty Educl Assn 1970-; St Granger 1968-; Sweet Adelines 1973-76; Amer Red Cross Mem 1973-79; *home:* RD 1 Box 98 Clarion PA 16214

MC CANNEY, TERRA BAKER, Spanish Teacher/Chair; *b:* Galion, OH; *m:* Thomas Owen; *c:* Andrea, Mark; *ed:* (BA) Span/Home Ec, Otterbein Coll 1968; OH St Univ, Carleton Coll, Otterbein Coll; *cr:* Span Teacher/Chairperson/Jr HS Home Ec Teacher Buckeye Cntrl HS 1968-74; Span Teacher/Chairperson Big Walnut HS 1984-; *ai:* Span Club & Span Dancers Adv; NHS Co-Adv; Piano Teacher 1974-84; OH Foreign Lang Assn 1968-; Amer Assn of Teachers Span, Portuguese 1968-; Sociedad Honoraria Hispanica Adv 1968-; OH Valley Consortium of Foreign Lang Teachers 1990; Humane Society Delaware Cty 1989-; Handbell Choir Dir 1980-; United Meth Church Worship Comm 1988-; Golden Apple & Leaders of Scndry Ed Awd; Developed Advanced Placement Prgm in Span Grammer & Lit; Accompany Stu to Mexico; Presenter at Area Coll on Teaching Methods; *home:* 3044 Carters Corner Rd Sunbury OH 43074

MC CANTS, DESSIE MC NEILL, Bus/Office Education Teacher; *b:* Erwin, NC; *m:* Moses A.; *c:* Cynthia E.; *ed:* (BS) Bus Ed, Barber-Scotia Coll 1959; (MA) Ed Admin/Supervision, NC Central Univ 1989; *cr:* Bus Teacher Harnett HS 1967-68; Angier HS 1968-70; Dunn HS 1970-85; Triton HS 1985-; Secy Sci Instr Rutledge Coll 1989-; *ai:* Sr Spon; Bus & Office Ed Chairperson; FBLA Spon; NC Ed Assn 1967-; NEA 1959-; ASCD 1987-; Cape Fear & Southwestern JT Union Sec 1983-; Riverside Cmmty Organization 1967-; *office:* Triton H S Rt 1 Box 210 Erwin NC 28339

MC CANTS, LILLIAN GAYLE, Gifted/Talented Teacher; *b:* Bogalusa, LA; *ed:* (BA) Elem Ed, SE LA Univ 1970; (MED) Elem Ed/Psych, Nicholls St Univ 1975; Academically Gifted Cert, Leadership Trng Inst; *cr:* 4th Grade Teacher St Mary Parish Schls 1970-74; Statistical Data Clerk Rutger Univ 1971; Grad Asst Nicholls St Univ 1974-75; 6th Grade Teacher 1975-76, 5th Grade Teacher 1976-78, Gifted/Talented Resource Teacher 1978- Bogalusa City Schls; *ai:* After Sch Peer Tutoring Prgm; Job Trng Prgm Assistantship; Kappa Delta Pi Secy 1971-72; LA Assn of Educators 1970-; Assn for Classroom Teachers Pres 1972-73; Kappa Kappa Iota Pres 1979-81; Assn for St Exec Bd 1985-87; Russian Winter Ed Festival 1971; Outstanding Young Educator 1972; Presenter at 29th Annual Convention Natl Assn for Gifted 1982; Article Published; *home:* 105 Lee Cir Bogalusa LA 70427

MC CARROLL, NORMA CAMPBELL, 6th Grade Reading Teacher; *b:* Independence, MO; *m:* Roger N.; *c:* Debra Vahldick, Virginia Miller, Leigh A. Williams, Scott; *ed:* (BS) Elem Ed, Cntrl MO St Univ 1968; (MA) Elem Ed with Math Emphasis, Univ of MO Kansas City 1974; Psych, Rdng & Teaching Skills; *cr:* Self-Contained 6th Grade Teacher Isley Elem Sch 1968-73; Block Classes Lang Art Teacher 1974-76, Accelerated Lang Art Teacher 1977-88, Span/Rdng Teacher 1988- Lewis Mid Sch; *ai:* 5-Core Subject Team Chm; MNEA Legislative 1975-; ESEA Pres 1975-; NEA, Intnl Rdng Assn 1975-; Kappa Delta Pi 1989-; Amer Assn of Univ Women VP Membership 1983-, Woman of Distinction 1990; Optimists Bd of Dir 1987-; Excelsior Springs Historical Society 1981-; Independence Cmmty Messiah Choir 1974-; Blood Bank Dir/Chm 1977-85; Park & Recreation Bd Excelsior Springs MO; Mid-Continent Lib Bd; Learning Exchange Act Published; *office:* Lewis Mid Sch Leavenworth & Concourse Excelsior Springs MO 64024

MC CARRON, JAMES P., Fifth Grade Teacher; *b:* Chicago, IL; *ed:* (BSED) Spec & Elem Ed, 1972, (MSED) Spec Ed, 1977 N Il Univ DeKalb; Real Estate License; Numerous Courses; *cr:* Spec Ed Teacher Oswego Jr HS 1972-76; 4th Grade Teacher 1976-87, 5th Grade Teacher 1987- Boulder Hill Elem Sch; *ai:* Technology & Report Card Comms 1989; Sch Improvement Team 1989; Mentor Teacher 1989; Intramural Sports Coach 1980-89; NEA, PTA 1976-.

MC CARTER, LARRY DAN, Mathematics Department Teacher; *b:* Fort Smith, AR; *m:* Connie Rhea Johnson; *c:* Bradley S., Karissa D., Landon B.; *ed:* (BS) Math, SW MO St Univ 1963; (MED Admin, Univ of MO 1967; *cr:* Jr HS Teacher Hickory Hills 1963-68, Jarrett 1968-78, Cherokee 1978-; *ai:* Math Events Club & Natl Jr HS Honor Society Spon; Springfield Ed Assn Pres 1963-; Phi Delta Kappa; *home:* 1536 E Holiday St Springfield MO 65804

MC CARTER, MARGARET ANNE (MAINS), Kindergarten Teacher; *b:* Newville, PA; *m:* Arthur Barrett III; *ed:* (BS) Elem Ed, 1964, (ME) Guidance/Counseling, 1968 Shippensburg Univ; *cr:* 1st Grade Teacher Stevens Elem 1964-72; 5th-8th Grade Lang Art Teacher 1972-73, 4th/5th Grade Teacher 1973-74 Usdesea; Kndgtn Teacher Carlisle Area Sch Dist 1974-; *ai:* Soc Comm Co-Chm; Carlisle Area Ed Assn; Newville Historical Society Nominating Comm; Presbyn Women (Officer of Least Coin, Church Choir, Handbell Chairperson); *home:* 375 Big Spring Rd Newville PA 17241

MC CARTER, TAMRA PAUL, Gifted Math/English Teacher; *b:* Jena, LA; *m:* Allen G.; *c:* John A.; *ed:* (BA) Eng/Math, LA Tech 1982; (MED) Admin Supervision, NE LA Univ 1985; Completed Cert in Gifted Ed; *cr:* Teacher Riser Jr HS 1982-83; Grad Asst N LA Univ 1983-; Instr NE LA Univ 1984-85; Teacher Wossman HS 1985-; *ai:* Frosh, Soph, Jr Class Spon; *home:* 2012 University Ave Monroe LA 71203

MC CARTHY, DAVID R., Daniel Sargent Master of Eng; *b:* New York, NY; *c:* Andrew, Elizabeth, Judith, Sara, Teresa, Daniel; *ed:* (BBA) Management, Univ of Notre Dame 1955; (MA) Eng, Columbia Univ 1960; Anglo-Irish Lit, Univ Coll Dublin; Post Grad Stud Eng Lit, Brown Univ; *cr:* Eng Instr Assumption Coll 1958-60; Eng Assoc Prof Stonehill Coll 1960-71; Daniel Sargent Master of Eng Portsmouth Abbey Sch 1972-; *ai:* Sch Newspaper & Portsmouth Bulletin Ed; Co-Dir Portsmouth Elder Hustle; Amer Conference Irish Stud 1985-; Articles & Stories Published; *office:* Portsmouth Abbey Sch Corys Ln Portsmouth RI 02871

MC CARTHY, DIANE ELIZABETH, Health Education Teacher; *b:* Grand Rapids, MI; *ed:* (MS) Phys Ed, Univ of NM 1982; (BS) Phys Ed, MI St 1979; Grad Stud Health Ed; *cr:* Teacher/Instr Univ of NM 1980-82; Teacher 1982-, Teacher/Coach 1982- Valley HS; *ai:* Track & Cross Cntry Coach; City HS Body Building Competition Organizer; Core Team Comm; Fitness Club Spon; AAHPER 1976-; NPA 1988-; Red Cross 1978-;

Norton Kalishmen Awd Health Promotion; Articles Published; Foreign Stud Schlshp; NM Body Building Champion; *office:* Valley HS 1505 Candelaria Albuquerque NM 87109

MC CARTHY, DONNA KANNER, Spanish Teacher; *b:* Holyoke, MA; *m:* Terrence Michael; *ed:* (BS) Span/Ed, S CT St Univ 1970; (MED) Bi-Ling Ed, Amer Intnl Coll 1977; Scndry Sch Admin, Westfield St Coll; *cr:* ESI Teacher Kelly Sch 1970-71; Span Teacher JFK Jr HS 1971-82, Enrico Fermi HS 1982-; *ai:* Sr Class Adv 1990; Effective Schls Comm; Prins Advisory Cncl; Amer Cncl on Teaching Foreign Langs; *home:* 154 Russell Ave Suffield CT 06078

MC CARTHY, EDNA DAVIS, Retired; *b:* Boonville, MO; *m:* Thomas E.; *c:* Thomas O., Jack D.; *ed:* (BS) Elem Ed, Bus, Central MO St Univ 1942; *cr:* 1st-8th Grade Teacher East Oakland Rural Sch 1933-35; Billingsville Rural Sch 1935-37; Concord Rural Sch 1937-39; Bell Air Rural Sch 1939-41; Clear Spgs Rural Sch 1950-55; 1st Grade Teacher New Franklin Elem Sch 1955-80; *ai:* Alpha Phi Delta Ed Hnr Society CMSU; Kappa Delta Phi Natl Ed Society; Intnl Society Bus Ed; Delta Kappa Gamma Intnl Honorary Prof Organization; Amer Assn Univ Women; NRTA; Retired Teachers Assn Life Mem; Cooper Cty Teachers Assn Pres; Howard Cty Teachers Assn Pres; Outstanding Elem Teachers of Amer 1974; *home:* Rt 1 Box 438 Boonville MO 65233

MC CARTHY, GLENN A., Math Teacher/Asst Principal; *b:* New York, NY; *ed:* (BA) Psych, Iona Coll 1973; Theology Immaculate Conception Seminary 1979; Religious Stud, Archdiocese NY; *cr:* Cnslr Lincoln Hall Sch for Boys 1973-75; Teacher Our Lady of Fatima Sch 1975-76; Teacher 1976-, Asst Prin 1987- Saint Gabriel Sch; *ai:* Boys Pee-wee & Jr Var Bsktbl Head Coach; Girls Varsity Bsktbl Asst Coach; Commissioner Sr Divison South Riverdale Bsbl League; Graduation Journal & Video Adv; Parish-Sch Planning Bd; Ed Comm; Elmwood Park Little League Coach 1977-78 All-star Coach 1977-78; South Riverdale Little League Coach 1981-83; South Riverdale Little League Commissioner 1982-; Cath Youth Organization Parish Volunteer Awd 1983 & 1986; St Gabriel Sch Journal Dedication Awd 1986; *office:* Saint Gabriel Sch 590 W 235 St Bronx NY 10463

MC CARTHY, JOANN BUSCH, Fourth Grade Teacher; *b:* Fresno, CA; *c:* Michael; *ed:* (AA) Liberal Arts, Fresno City Coll 1973; (BS) Child Dev, CA St Univ Fresno 1975; Post Baccalaureate Work CSU Fresno to Receive Standard Elem Credential 1975-76; Working on Learning Handicapped Credential; *cr:* L H Teacher Madison Sch 1979, Laboratory Sch of Natural Sci 1981-82; 5th Grade Teacher 1982-85, 4th Grade Teacher 1985- Westside Elem Sch; *ai:* CA Teachers Assn Treas 1988-; Fresno Area Rdng Cncl 1990; *office:* Westside Sch 19191 W Excelsior Ave Five Points CA 93624

MC CARTHY, JOSEPH R., Social Studies Teacher; *b:* Bronx, NY; *ed:* (BA) Philosophy/His, Manhattan Coll 1986; Working Toward Masters in Philosophy, NY Univ; *cr:* Soc Stud Teacher Msgr Scanlan HS 1984-; *ai:* Drama Club, Christmas Assembly, Stu Cncl, Graduation Exercises Dir; FCT 1965-; Phi Alpha Theta Mem 1984-; Epsilon Sigma Phi Mem 1984; *office:* Monsignor Scanlan HS 915 Hutchinson River Pkwy Bronx NY 10465

MC CARTHY, JUDITH M., Social Studies Teacher; *b:* Kingston, Jamaica; *ed:* (BS) Scndry Ed/Soc Sci, 1978, (MS) Developmental Counseling, 1984 St Thomas Univ; Diploma Shortwood Teachers Coll; *cr:* Teacher Trench Town Comprehensive HS 1977-79, St Monica Cath Sch 1980-89, Miami Springs Mid Sch 1989-; *ai:* Caribbean Women Network VP 1989-; United Teacher of Dade 1989-; Learn to Read Volunteer 1987; *home:* PO Box 2503 Carol City FL 33055

MC CARTIN, BRIAN, Social Studies/Science Teacher; *b:* Flushing, NY; *m:* Debra Sue Schneider; *c:* Kellie R.; *ed:* (BA) His, Coll of Holy Cross 1975; *cr:* Soc Stud Teacher Brian Piccolo Intermediate Sch 1977-79; Spec Ed Teacher Assn for Help of Retarded Children 1981-84; Math Teacher Monroe Jr Coll 1989-; Sci/Soc Stud Teacher St Johns Prep HS 1986-; *ai:* Strength & Conditioning, Phys Fitness Team, Intramural Ftbl Coach; Track Field Events Asst Coach; Natl Strength & Conditioning Assn 1988-; Phi Beta Kappa 1990; Poppenhauser Inst Boxing Coach Achievement Awd for Disadvantaged Youth 1985-86; *office:* St Johns Preparatory HS 21-21 Crescent Astoria NY 11105

MC CARTY, CHERYL ANN, English Teacher; *b:* Springfield, MO; *ed:* (BSED) Eng, Southwest MO St 1971; Ed, Eng, Guid Counseling; 1 Yr Univ of MO Kansas City Law Sch; *cr:* Eng/Phys Ed Teacher Study Jr Hs 1971-74; Eng Teacher Hillcrest HS 1974-80; Special Tutor St Marys Hospital Psychiatric & Drug Rehab 1981-85; Eng Teacher Hillcrest HS 1985-; *ai:* Spon/Coach of Lit; Spon of Joplin Field Day Competition in Eng; Spon Chrldrs & our Drum & Bugle Corps; NEA, SNEA, NCTE; *office:* Hillcrest HS 3319 N Grant Springfield MO 65803

MC CARTY, LINDA JEAN, First Grade Teacher; *b:* Gladwin, MI; *m:* Gordon; *ed:* (BA) Elem Ed, Univ of MI Flint 1971; (MA) Elem Rdng, Cntrl MI Univ 1974; Math Trng; *cr:* 1st Grade Teacher Meridian Public Schls 1971-; *ai:* MI Ed Assn, NEA 1971-; Meridian Ed Assn Secy 1986-87; Midland Cty Rndg Cncl 1985-87; TOPS Secy 1989-.

MC CARTY, MARY S., Mathematics Teacher; *b:* Opelika, AL; *c:* Lauren, Melanie; *ed:* (BS) Aviation Management, Auburn Univ 1982; (MA) Scndry Ed/Math, Univ of AL 1989; Cert Scndry Ed/ Math, Univ of Montevallo; *cr:* 7th-8th Grade Math Teacher Duran Jr HS 1986-; *ai:* Yrbk Assoc Adv; NCTM, ASCD 1988-89; GSA Troop Leader 1988-89; United Meth Youth Fellowship Adv 1988-89; *office:* Duran Jr HS 309 12th St S Pell City AL 35125

MC CARTY, PATRICIA LOBPRIES, High School Math Teacher; *b:* Houston, TX; *c:* Preston J., Jacquelyn A.; *ed:* (BS) Ed, Univ of TX 1970; (MED) Math, Univ of AR 1975; (MS) Admin, Corpus Christi St Univ 1989; *cr:* Math Teacher Corpus Christi St Univ 1980; Algebra Teacher Del Mar Jr Coll 1980-81; Math Teacher Cullen Jr HS 1985-87, Roy Miller HS 1987-; *ai:* Key Club Spon; Homework Comm; Number Sense Contests; Strategic Planning Team; MENSA; Amer Assn of Univ Women (VP, Membership) 1981-83; Sierra Club TX Assn for Gifted & Talented; Speaker Natl, Regional, St, Dist, Local Math Conventions; Typed Weekly Bullentin Roy Miller HS; *home:* 2410 Indian Wells Corpus Christi TX 78414

MC CARTY, SUSAN WERTZ, Biology Teacher; *b:* Dayton, OH; *m:* Philip; *ed:* (BS) Ed/Biological Sci, Miami Univ 1978; Registered Cytotechnologist, Miami Valley Hospital 1985; *cr:* Bio Teacher Heath City Schls 1978-81, Clinton Massie Schls 1981-; *ai:* Frosh Class Adv; OEA, NEA; *office:* Clinton Massie Sch 2556 Lebanon Rd Clarksville OH 45113

MC CARY, DIANE BARNES, 4th Grade Teacher; *b:* Baltimore, MD; *m:* Ralph C. Jr.; *ed:* (BA) Elem Ed, Frostburg St Univ 1968; (MAE) Elem Ed, Coll of William & Mary 1977; *cr:* 4th Grade Teacher Rockland Elem 1968-72, Aberdeen Elem 1972-78, Barron Fundamental Elem 1978-; *ai:* Stu Cncl Assn Co-Spon; MD St Techers Assn 1968-72; Hampton Ed Assn 1972-; VA Ed Assn 1972-; NEA 1968-; Howard Cty Teachers Assn 1968-72; *office:* Barron Fundamental Elem Sch 45 Fox Hill Rd Hampton VA 23669

MC CASKEY, THEODORE JOHN, Biology Teacher; *b:* New Castle, PA; *m:* Nancy R. Mc Farland; *c:* Lyndsey, Elise; *ed:* (BS) Bio, Westminster Coll 1986; *cr:* Bio Teacher Halifax Cty Sr HS 1986-; *ai:* Asst Ftbl Coach 1986-; Asst Bsktbl Coach 1986-89; *home:* Rt 1 Box 161 Clover VA 24534

MC CAULEY, DAVID A., Social Studies Teacher; *b:* Bridgeport, CT; *m:* Ingrid Otten; *ed:* (BS) Teaching/Soc Stud, New Haven St Teachers Coll 1959; Grad Asst/Teaching Asst, Amer Univ; Grad Stud New York Univ; *cr:* Teacher Fairfield CT System 1959-60; Grad Stu Amer Univ 1960-62; Teacher Masuk HS 1962-66, Danbury HS 1966-; *ai:* Danbury Ed Assn, CT Ed Assn, NEA; Newtown CT Land Trust Bd of Dir 1988-; Newtown Bridge Lanes Assn Bd of Dir; NDEA Summer Inst 1969; *office:* Danbury HS Clapboard Ridge Rd Danbury CT 06811

MC CAULEY, JACQUELINE ROBINSON, English Teacher; *b:* Cleveland, OH; *m:* Marvin N.; *c:* La Ravi M.; *ed:* (BA) Eng, Johnson C Smith 1979; *cr:* Eng/Span Teacher Harding HS 1985; Eng Teacher N Mecklenburg Sr HS 1985-; *ai:* Project Graduation Co-Spon; NCTE 1987-; Sigma Tau Delta 1979-89; Kappa Delta Pi 1985-89; *office:* North Mecklenburg Sr HS PO Box 16512 Charlotte NC 28297

MC CAULEY, KATHI CLAY, Teacher; *b:* Liberal, KS; *m:* Richard E.; *c:* Bradley, Scott, Clay; *ed:* (BA) Lang Art, SWOSU 1979; *cr:* Teacher Reydon HS 1981-; *ai:* Reydon All-Sports Assn Pres; Lang Art Chm; 10-Day Rule & Curr Comm; Class Spon; NCTE; *office:* Reydon HS Box 36 Reydon OK 73660

MC CAULEY, KEVIN JAMES, Biology Teacher; *b:* Los Angeles, CA; *m:* Renee K. Vasey; *c:* Brian, Ian, Lauren; *ed:* (BS) Bio, Univ of CA Irvine 1974; (MS) Bio, Univ of OR 1976; Grad Teaching Fellowship Univ of OR 1974-77; *cr:* Bio Teacher/Sci Chm Marist HS 1977-84; Bio Teacher N Eugene HS 1984-; *ai:* Staff Pres; Staff Comm Chm; Keynote Speaker Marist HS Commencement Exercises; Articles Published 1980 & 1988; N Eugene HS Teacher of Month 1986.

MC CAULEY, RONALD JAMES, Electronics Instructor; *b:* Braddock, PA; *m:* Renee E. Mazanek; *c:* Justin, Ryan; *ed:* (AA) Electronic Technology, Penn Tech Inst Pittsburgh 1979; Voc I Voc Ed, Univ of Pittsburgh 1988; Voc Ed, IN Univ; *cr:* Electronic Technician TX Instruments; Electronic Scale Specialist Toledo Scale; Cmptr Technician/Instr Greensborg Inst of Technology; Teacher Lenape Voc-Tech Sch, Cntrl Westmoreland Area Voc-tech; *ai:* VICA Adv; Tutor for Homebound; PSEA, NEA Assoc Mem; BSA Spon; PA Mayors Assn, PA St Boroughs Assn Assoc Mem; Mayor of E Vandergrift Borough Westmoreland Cty PA 1986-; Author of Numerous Research Papers; Guest Speaker Many Public & Private Schls; *office:* Cntrl Westmoreland Vo-Tech Sch 240 Arona Rd New Stanton PA 15672

MC CAWLEY, KATHLEEN ANN, Sci/Religion/Spanish Teacher; *b:* Kankakee, IL; *ed:* (BA) Elem Ed, Coll of St Francis 1982; *cr:* Sci Teacher St Rose Sch 1982-85, St Jude Sch 1985-; *ai:* Conflict Mgr Prgm Coord; IL Foreign Lang Teachers Assn, NSTA, IL Sci Teachers Assn; Pax Christi; IL Summer Migrant Ed Prgm Teacher 1979-83, On-Site Facilitator 1984; Oneida Summer Session Teacher 1986-88.

MC CAY, MARY L., American History Teacher; *b:* Decatur, AL; *ed:* (BS) Eng/Scndry Ed, Jacksonville St Univ 1966; (MA) Scndry Ed/His, Univ of AL 1970; (AA) Supervision/His, 1974 Univ of AL Birmingham 1974; British His, Cultural Stud, Univ of City of London 1976; *cr:* Classroom Teacher Gardendale HS 1966-; *ai:* Health Careers Club; Bank Bd Spon; Sr Class Spon; NEA 1966-; AEA 1966-; JCEA (Building Rep 1969-70) 1966-; Alpha Delta Kappa 1978-; Warrior United Meth Organist 1970-; Steering Comm 10 Yr Evaluation Study 1989; Outstanding Young Women of Amer; Comm Play Published in Jeff Cty Publication Compiled Self-Study Report 1989; *office:* Gardendale H S 850 Mount Olive Rd Gardendale AL 35071

MC CLAIN, BOBBY L., Teacher/Soc Stud Dept Chairman; *b:* Staley, NC; *m:* Sandra Robinson; *c:* Ryan L., Justin S.; *ed:* (BS) His/Poly Sci, Fayetteville St Univ 1971; (MA) Admin, E Carolina Univ 1989; *cr:* Teacher/Coach Woodbury HS 1971-72, Jacksonville HS 1972-; *ai:* His Club Adv 1986-, Co-Adv 1989-; Soc Stud Dept Chm 1981-; Cross Cntry & Boys Track Coach 1979-; NEA, NCAE, OCAE, ASCD Mem 1984-; Waity Missionary Baptist Church Deacon 1988-; Jacksonville HS Teacher of Yr 1989-; Mid East 4A Conference Cross Cntry Coach of Yr 1988-89; Boys Track Coach of Yr 1989; *office:* Jacksonville HS 1021 Henderson Dr Jacksonville NC 28540

MC CLAIN, ELIZABETH LEE, Second Grade Teacher; *b:* Portland, ME; *w:* Robert H. W. (dec); *c:* Patricia A. Bennett, Kathleen Bonaccorsi; *ed:* (BS) Elem Ed, Gorham Teachers Coll 1945; Boston Univ, Univ of NH, Lesley Coll. Plymouth & Keene St; *cr:* 2nd Grade Teacher Frisbee Sch 1945-46; 3rd Grade Teacher Burleigh Sch 1946-53; 5th Grade Teacher Marston & Centre 1953-; 2nd Grade Teacher Hampton Schls 1957-; *ai:* NEA; Seacoast Ed Assn (Pres, VP, Secy, Treas); NH Ed Assn (Exec Bd, Resolutions Comm, Constitution Comm, Judicial Comm); Con Con (Mem, Natl Resolutions Comm, Natl Conventions Delegate); Seacoast Federal Credit Union (Incorporator, First Treas) 1967-70; *home:* 18 Grandview Terr North Hampton NH 03862

MC CLAIN, THERESA NALEPA, Science Teacher; *b:* Mc Keesport, PA; *m:* Patrick J.; *c:* Brian, Jennifer; *ed:* Sci, Boyce Comm Coll 1968; Bio/General Sci, Clarion Univ 1970; Grad Stud Penn St 1971, IN Univ 1972; *cr:* Sci Teacher Norwin Jr HS East 1970-; *ai:* Soccer & Sftbl Coach; Bsbl & Sftbl League Secy; CCD 6th Grade Teacher 1986-; EAAA Bd of Dirs; EA Band Parents Assn Mem; *office:* Norwin Jr HS East 1 Main St North Huntingdon PA 15642

MC CLANAHAN, DONNA GAIL, English Teacher; *b:* Grundy, VA; *ed:* (BA) Eng, Lincoln Memorial Univ 1982; *cr:* Eng Teacher Garden HS 1985-87, Hurley HS 1987-; *ai:* Hurley HS Journalism Staff, Newspaper, Ftbl Cheerleading, Drama Spon; NEA 1985-89; Word Evangelistic Outreach Choir Secy 1988-; *home:* PO Box 43 Hurley VA 24620

MC CLARDY, ALICE R., First Grade Teacher; *b:* Whitesboro, NJ; *w:* Ernest (dec); *c:* Ursula M., Robert E.; *ed:* (BS) Kndgtn/ Primary Ed, Glassboro St Teachers Coll 1952; Rdng, Cmptr, New Math, Writing, Sci Wkshp; *cr:* 1st Grade Teacher Mannheim Amer Army Sch Germany 1960-62, Edison Township 1952-60, 1962-; *ai:* Rep on Sch Curr Comm; Head Teacher of 1st Grade; In Charge of Soda Machine; Rep of Teachers Assn; Charge of Sunshine Fund Comm; NJ Ed Assn, NEA, PTA, Cty Teachers Assn Mem 1952-; Edison Teachers Asssn Rep 1952-; Supported Olympic, Cerebral Palsy, Polio, Jerry Lewis Telethon Organizations 1985-; Contribute to Teachers Schlsp Fund; Nom for St Best Teacher Awd 1989-; *home:* 359 Durham Ave Metuchen NJ 08840

MC CLAUGHERTY, CAROL THORN, French/Spanish Teacher; *b:* Princeton, WV; *m:* A. Herbert; *c:* Alicia, Heather; *ed:* (BS) Fr/Span, Concord Coll 1969; (MA) Speech Comm, WV Univ 1983; Grad Stud WV Coll; Admin, Advanced Placement Inst; St Johnsbury Acad, WV Teachers Acad; *cr:* Teacher Fairview Jr HS 1969-70, Athens HS 1980-; *ai:* Spon Foreign Lang Club; Sch Improvement & Mercer Cty Schls Comm Team; AHS; Phi Delta Kappa 1985-; ACTFL, WVFLTA 1988-; Mercer Cty Academic Boosters Chm 1987-88; Mercer Cty Schls Mini-Grant 1988; WV Dept of Ed Grant Effective Teaching; AHS Teacher of Yr 1986-87; *office:* Athens HS PO Box 608 Athens WV 24712

MC CLAY, BRUCE EDWARD, His/Religion/Eng/Sci Teacher; *b:* Pensacola, FL; *m:* Mary Ruth Froelich; *c:* Johanna C., Douglas B.; *ed:* (BA) Religion/His, Columbia Union Coll 1968; (MA) Religion/Church His, Andrews Univ 1971; His, Ed, Eng, Microcomputers; *cr:* Prin/Teacher Morganton Elem Sch 1968-69; 9th/10th Grade Teacher Albany Elem 1969-70; His/Eng/Religion Teacher Hinsdale Jr Acad 1971-85, Anchorage Jr Acad 1985-; *ai:* 10th Grade Class Spon; Lake Union Conference Textbook Selection Comm; 7th Day Adv Church (Elder, Deacon, Sabbath Sch Teacher, Dir of Youth Cammp 1974) 1968-; Presented Wkshp on Strategies for Teaching Eng, Grammer, Mechanics at N Pacific Union Conference Teachers Convention 1988; Comm to Develop NW His Curr Guide for N Pacific Union Conference & Soc Stud Curr Guide for Lake Union Conference; Learning in Affective Domain; Chrstn Leadership Seminar; *office:* Anchorage Jr Acad 5511 O Malley Rd Anchorage AK 99516

MC CLELLAN, BEVERLY SUE, English Teacher; *b:* De Land, FL; *ed:* (BA) Speech/Eng, Southwest Baptist Univ 1971; (MRE) Speech/Religion, Southwestern Seminary 1974; GA Southern Univ, Univ of GA, SW MO St Univ; *cr:* Eng/Speech Teacher Naylor HS 1971-72, Toombs Cntrl HS 1975-78; Eng Teacher David Emanuel Acad 1982-85, Reidsville HS 1985-; *ai:* Co-Dir One Act Play; PAGE 1985-; Delta Psi Omega 1971-; Church of God of Prophecy 1976-; STAR Teacher Toombs Cntrl Sch 1978; *office:* Reidsville HS Brazell St Reidsville GA 30453

MC CLELLAN, BRENDA BOULDIN, English/Speech Teacher; *b:* Dumas, TX; *m:* Ronnie; *c:* Finnan, Briah; *ed:* (BS) Eng/Speech Ed, 1974, (MA) Eng, 1984 W TX St Univ; *cr:* Eng Teacher Amarillo HS 1974-75; Eng/Speech Teacher Dimmitt Jr HS 1975-78, Dimmitt HS 1978-81, Hereford HS 1983-84, Stratford HS 1984-; *ai:* 1 Act Play Competition; UIL Forensics, Debate, Interpretation; Speech Club & Soph Spon; TFA Speech Coach; UIL Advisory Comm; TX St Teachers Assn (Pres 1989-)

1974-; TX Speech Comm Assn (Dist Chairperson 1989-) 1978-; TX Forensic Assn Mem 1978-; Natl Forensic Assn Mem 1984-; Alpha Chi 1971-74; Sigma Tau (Pres 1974) 1971-74; Nu Beta 1984-89; Eng Grad Schlsp 1981; Faculty Favorite 1985-86, 1989-; Poetry Published; St Speech Qualifiers Coach; *home:* PO Box 588 Stratford TX 79084

MC CLELLAN, CAROL, Music Teacher; *b:* Santa Ana, TX; *ed:* (BS) Music Ed, Mc Murry Coll 1960; Various Summer Wkshps; TMEA Conference In-Service Trng; *cr:* Music Teacher Bowie Elem 1960-; *ai:* TX St Teachers Assn (Dist XIV Pres 1980-81, Local Pres 1979-80, 1988-); 1st Cntrl Presbyn Church Deacon 1986-89; *home:* 3 Lake Point Abilene TX 79606

MC CLELLAN, JESSIE MC DONALD, Fifth Grade Teacher; *b:* Sanderson, TX; *m:* Reid; *c:* Rob, Michael; *ed:* (BS) Elem Ed, Sul Ross St Univ 1962; *cr:* 3rd Grade Teacher Sanderson Elem 1962-64; 6th Grade Teacher Kermit Jr HS 1964-66; 5th Grade Teacher Sanderson Elem 1966-; *ai:* UIL Spelling Spon; TX St Teachers Assn 1962-; NEA; *home:* 306 Cargile Ave Box 639 Sanderson TX 79848

MC CLELLAN, JOHN L., Science Teacher/Chair; *b:* New Edinburg, AR; *m:* Sue Dell; *c:* Detri Brech, Doug; (BSE) Sci/Biological Soc Sci, AR A&M 1962; *ed:* Grad Stud Univ of AR Pine Bluff, Univ of Cntrl AR, AR Tech; *ai:* Stu Cncl Spon; CTA Pres 1980-81; AEA, NEA; Quorum Court, Masonic Lodge; Farm Co-Op Pres; US Army Reserve Lieutenant Colonel; *office:* Warren Sch Dist 308 W Pine St Warren AR 71671

MC CLELLAN, MICHAEL CHARLES, Eng Teacher; *b:* Ft Worth, TX; *m:* Denise C Locke; *c:* Meghan, Kaitlin; *ed:* (BA) Eng/His, Univ of AZ 1975; (MED) Scndry Ed/Rdng AZ St Univ 1979; Taft Inst of Government N AZ Univ 1976; AZ Cncl of Ec, 1976; *cr:* Eng Teacher Ft Thomas HS 1975-77, Fremont Jr HS 1977-81, Dobson HS 1981-; *ai:* Literary Arts Club Spon 1982-85; Dobson Chapter of Amnesty Intnl Spon; NEA 1977-88; Valley Citizens League 1989-; Ed Task Force Mem 1990; Teacher of Yr Fremont Jr HS 1981; Dobson HS Pres, Faculty Senate 1984; Coll Bds for Advanced Placement Consultant 1985; *office:* Dobson HS 1501 W Guadalupe Rd Mesa AZ 85202

MC CLELLAND, JOHN W., Choir Director; *b:* Erie, PA; *m:* Jane Magnetta; *c:* Rick, Ron, Laurel, John, Erin; *ed:* (BS) Music Ed, 1959, (MED) Music Ed, 1964 IN Univ of PA; *cr:* Choir Dir Kiski Area HS 1959-; *ai:* Kiski Area HS Jazz Rock Ensemble Swing Choir; Responsible for Concerts & Related Act 9th Grade Chorus, Mixed Chorus, Concert Choir; PA Music Educators Assn; Music Educators Natl Conference; Westmoreland Cty Music Educators Assn, 25 Yr Plaque 1986; Somerset Cty Chorus Guest Conductor 1979; Armstrong Cty Chorus, Rotary Choral Festival Guest Conductor 1988; Maintained 3 Large Mixed Choruses in HS; *home:* 1301 Dallas Ave Natrona Heights PA 15065

MC CLELLAND, LINDA MORGAN, 6th-8th Grade Jr HS Teacher; *b:* Atlanta, GA; *m:* Joseph P. Sr.; *c:* Clay Hoard, Joyce; *ed:* (BA) Ed, W GA Coll 1964; Ed, Tift Coll of Mercer Univ; *cr:* Librarian Fulton Cty Sch System 1964-65; 1st Grade Teacher Butts Cty Sch System 1966-71, Indian Springs Acad 1971-79; Jr HS Teacher Piedmont Acad 1979-; *ai:* Jr HS Coord; *office:* Piedmont Acad P O Box 231 Monticello GA 31064

MC CLELLAND, PHYLLIS DITTMAN, German/Spanish Teacher; *b:* Yonkers, NY; *m:* Fay; *c:* Phyllis M., D. Keith, Lane I., Rise M. Kagan; *ed:* (BA) Music, Cornell Univ 1943; (MA) Ger, Rutgers Univ 1971; Courses at Temple Univ, Marywood Coll, Villanova Univ, La Salle Univ Center for Hispanic Stud; *cr:* Ger Teacher Vestal Cntrl HS 1966-67, Neshaminy HS 1971-77, Neshaminy-Maple Point HS 1977-82; Ger/Span Teacher Philadelphia HS for Girls 1983-; *ai:* Mentor of Mentally Gifted; Spon of Ger & Ukrainian Clubs; AATG 1971-; Amer Guild of Organists 1955-; Rockefeller Fnd Fellowship 1988; *home:* 538 Lenape Cir Langhorne PA 19047

MC CLELLAND, RICKEY LEROY, Jr HS Science Teacher; *b:* Starkville, MS; *m:* Cathy Hoggle; *c:* Brian, Rickey; *ed:* (BS) Phys Ed, 1975, (MA) Phys Ed/Scndry Sch Admin, 1976 MS St Univ; *cr:* Teacher Hale Cty HS 1976-; *ai:* Hale Cty HS Ftbl & Bsktbl Coach; AL Ed Assn 1976-; Outstanding Young Educators of America 1988; *office:* Hale Cty HS Box 188 Moundville AL 35474

MC CLENAGAN, BRENDA HOWELL, 1st Grade Teacher; *b:* Guymon, OK; *m:* Michael; *c:* Jason; *ed:* (BS) Elem Ed, Panhandle St Univ 1972; *cr:* 1st Grade Teacher Salyer Elem 1972-; *ai:* Educl Cncl; Textbook Comm; Stud Teaching Trng Prgm Panhandle St Univ; NEA; OEA; IOEA; *office:* Salyer Elem Sch P O Box 1307 Guymon OK 73942

MC CLENDON, LYNN PRICE, English Teacher; *b:* Vallejo, CA; *m:* Joe; *c:* Carrie, Laura; *cr:* Teacher Marsh Jr HS 1967-73, Berkner HS 1984-; *ai:* TX Joint Cncl Teachers of Eng; Womens Cncl Dallas Cty; Dallas Lawyers Wives Club; *office:* Berkner HS 1600 E Spring Valley Rd Richardson TX 75081

MC CLENDON, MARCIA KAY (SIECKO), Computer Teacher; *b:* Ganado, TX; *m:* Ralph Odell Jr.; *c:* Mark O., Ross J.; *ed:* (BA) Sci Ed/Math/Cmptr Sci, SW TX St Univ 1985; Logo Math Project, SW TX St Univ; *cr:* Cmptr Teacher Dahlstrom Mid Sch 1985-; *ai:* Stu Cncl Adv; 7th-8th Grade UIL Oral Rdng Coach; Co-UIL Coord; ATPE, TX Cmptr Ed Assn; *office:* Dahlstrom Mid Sch 1001 FM 967 Buda TX 78610

MC CLOUD, SUSAN WILLIS, Sci/Math/Soc Stud Teacher; *b:* Columbia, KY; *m:* Michael Kent; *c:* Alexandria, Evan K.; *ed:* (BA) Elem Ed, 1980, (MA) Elem Ed, 1982 W KY Univ; KY Cert Elem Prin, Supvr, or Supt; *cr:* Head Teacher 1980-82, 6th Grade Teacher 1982- Adair Cty Bd of Ed; *ai:* Curr Comm 1984-; Ashland Oil 1989- Nom Teacher Achievement 1990; *office:* John Adair Mid Sch Greensburg Rd Columbia KY 42728

MC CLUNG, DIANE DEAN, Fourth Grade Teacher; *b:* Iuka, MS; *m:* Ben R.; *c:* Stephanie, Josh; *ed:* Elem Ed, NE MS Comm Coll; (BS) Elem Ed, 1975, (MA) Elem Ed, 1985 Univ of N AL; *cr:* 1st Grade Teacher 1975-82, 2nd Grade Teacher 1983-85, 4th Grade Teacher 1985- Iuka Elem; *ai:* Sci Chm; Soc Stud Comm; MAE Treas; MPE; Delta Kappa Gamma 1987-89; PTA VP; *office:* Iuka Elem Sch 1500 Whitehouse Rd Iuka MS 38852

MC CLUNG, KAREN THORSEN, French Teacher; *b:* Pasadena, CA; *m:* William Lacey; *ed:* (BA) Fr, CA St Univ Fullerton 1983; *cr:* Fr Teacher Troy HS 1984-; *ai:* Fr Club & Yrbk Adv; Foreign Lang Assn of Orange Cty; CA Foreign Lang Teachers Assn; AATF; *office:* Troy HS 2200 E Dorothy Ln Fullerton CA 92631

MC CLURE, D. LANCE, 6th Grade Teacher; *b:* Springfield, OH; *m:* Ellen Mary Cook; *c:* Carrie B., Marcie A., Andrew L.; *ed:* (BA) Elem Ed, 1974, (MA) Elem Ed, 1981 AZ St Univ; *cr:* 6th Grade Teacher Adams Elem Sch 1974-; *ai:* Intermediate Chairperson; Dist Test Coord; Rocketry Club Spon; Bsktbl Coach; Mesa Independent Prof Educators 1986-; AZ St Prof Educators 1986-; Mesa Public Sch Dist Educator of Month 1989; Perfect Attendance Teaching 1986-89.

MC CLURE, J. SCOTT, 5th Grade Teacher; *b:* Oklahoma City, OK; *m:* Tissie Lester; *c:* Jared, Tyler, Tissa L.; *ed:* (BS) Phys Ed, Panhandle St Univ 1974; Elem Ed, Central St Univ 1983; Post Grad Work Cntrl St Univ 1977-83; Ec 1970-74; *cr:* Elem Phys Ed Teacher 1974-79, 5th Grade Teacher 1979- Eastside Elem; *ai:* 4th-6th Grade Ftbl & Track & Field Coach; 5th-6th Grade Bsbl Coach; Sch Improvement Comm 1988-; Legislative Rep Eastside 1987-; OK Ed Assn 1974-; Assn of Classroom Teachers, NEA 1974-; *office:* Eastside Elem Sch 600 N Key Blvd Midwest City OK 73110

MC CLURE, JEAN SUMMERS, 5th Grade Teacher; *b:* Bowling Green, KY; *m:* William David; *c:* C. David, Paul D.; *ed:* (BS) Elem Ed/his, Murray St Univ 1963; (MED) UNC Charlotte 1990; *cr:* Teacher Jefferson Cty Schls 1963, Unit 5 Schls 1964-66, Charlotte Mecklenburg Schls 1977-; *ai:* Charlotte Teachers Assn, NEA; BSA Merit Badge Cnslr.

MC CLURE, JOE RIVERS, Math Instructor; *b:* Pulaski, TN; *ed:* (BS) Math, TN A&I ST Coll 1944; (MS) Math TN ST Univ 1955; Lecture Series in Aerospace Sci Engrng 1967; US Army Missile Command & Marshall Flight Ctr Redstone Arsenal; *cr:* Teacher Bridgeforth HS 1947-60; Prin Bridgeforth Elem Sch 1960-66; Teacher Elkton Sch 1966-89; Teacher Giles Cnty 1989-; *ai:* Instr in Adult Basic Ed; Coached Jr Bsktbl Serving on Sr Citizen Advisory Bd; Beta Kappa Chi Charter Mem 1944-; NEA Mem 1947-; TN Ed Assn Mem 1947-; Natl Sci & Math Assn Mem 1947-; TN Math Teacher Assn 1947-; Amer Natl Red Cross 1947-; 30 Yrs Serv Pin 1977; Amer Legion Vice-Commander 1950-55; Giles Cnty Historical Society 1980-; TN Ag & Industrial ST Univ; Golden Anniversary Alumni Assn Citation As An Educator; Co-Authored History of Black Education in Giles County 1920-70; *home:* 912 N 3rd St Pulaski TN 38478

MC CLURE, JOY ALEXANDER, Fifth Grade Teacher; *b:* Vandalia, IL; *m:* Nelvin L.; *c:* Shawn, Seth, Polly, Heidi, Gretchen; *ed:* (BA) Eng/Performing Art, Millikin Univ 1967; *cr:* Teacher Stephen Decatur HS 1967, Lakeview HS 1967-68, Moweaqua Jr HS 1974-75, Ramsey Elem 1981-; *ai:* Alpha Chi Omega 1964-; *home:* RR 1 Box 24 Bingham IL 62011

MC CLURE, MICHAEL CRAIG, Science Department Chair; *b:* Rosebud, TX; *ed:* Mid-Management Internship & Coursework; *cr:* Stu Teacher Navasota HS 1977-78; Teacher 1978-, Sci Chm 1983- Spring HS; *ai:* Jr Engineering Tech Society Club Adv; NHS Faculty & Campus Improvement Comms; STAT 1979-; MHCTA, ACT2, NSTA 1988-; Spring HS Teacher of Yr 1982-83; Admin Intern 1984; Advancement of Sci Teaching Conference Presenter 1989; Dist Level Wkshp Presenter; *office:* Spring HS 19428 IH 45 Spring TX 77373

MC CLURE, SALLY VAN LANDINGHAM, 7th-8th Grade Science Teacher; *b:* Dallas, TX; *m:* John C.; *c:* Kristi L.; *ed:* (BS) Animal Sci, 1985, (BS) Ag Ed, 1986 TX A&M Univ; *cr:* Teacher/Aide Mumford Ind Sch Dist 1986-87; Sci Teacher Venus Ind Sch Dist 1987-; *ai:* Jr HS Spon; Venus Jr HS UIL Dir & Sci Coach; Chm Homeroom/Tutorial Comm; Annual Adv 1990; Color Guard Coach 1990; Sci Teachers Assn of TX 1987-; *office:* Venus Jr/Sr HS 1 Bulldog Dr Venus TX 76084

MC CLURE, SANDIE RUTH, 6th Grade Teacher; *b:* Phoenix, AZ; *c:* Lauren; *ed:* (BA) Ed, Phoenix Coll 1966; (BSED) Elem Ed, N AZ Univ 1969; Grad Stud AZ St Univ; *cr:* 6th Grade Teacher Larkspur Elem 1969-76, Liberty Elem 1976-87; 2nd Grade Teacher 1987-88, 6th Grade Teacher 1988- Sandpiper Elem; *ai:* Paradise Valley Sch Dist Teacher Evaluation, Drug & Alcohol Abuse Advisory Comm; Sandpiper Sch Drug Resistent Prgm Chairperson & Club Spon, Sch Theme Comm; Paradise Valley Ed Assn (Mem, VP 1978-80, 1988-, Exec Bd 1973-87, 1988-, Membership Chairperson 1974-75, Prof Rights & Responsibilities Chairperson 1974-77, Public Relations Chairperson 1985-86, Bargaining Team Mem 1979-84, 1987-) 1969-; Phi Delta Kappa Mem 1987-, Distinguished Service Awd 1990; Az Ed Assn (Mem, Leadership Dev 1975-77, Prof Rights & Responsibilities 1977-78) 1969-, Internal Comm Sch Bell Awd 1990; NEA Mem 1969-; Greater Paradise Valley Chamber of Commerce Ed Comm 1988-89; Learning Leader Awd 1985-86, Pride Awd; Paradise Valley Sch Dist (Math Scope & Sequence 1979-81, Drug Ed Comm 1974-78, Human Growth & Dev 1977-78, 5 Yr Planning Comm 1984-85, Cmmty Drug Task Force St Level 1974, Natl Level 1975) AZ Teacher of Yr 1985, Best in West 1987; Teacher Venture Grant 1988-89, 4th Place Winner 1988-89; Salt River Project St Finalist 1988-89; Presenter at Various Conferences & Wkshps 1986-; Ed Standard & Dialogue Newsletters 1984-85; Math Explorer Pilot Prgm 1989-; Governors Alliance Against Drugs Trainer 1989-; *office:* Sandpiper Elem Sch 6724 E Hearn Rd Scottsdale AZ 85254

MC CLURE, SANDRA DAVIS, Spanish Teacher; *b:* Spartanburg, SC; *m:* Barry; *ed:* (BA) Scndry Ed/His, Clemson Univ 1984; Span, Univ of SC 1987; Grad Stud Span, Univ of SC; *cr:* His/Span Teacher Mabry Jr HS 1985-87; Span Teacher Chapman HS 1987-; *ai:* Span Club Spon; Vlybl Coach; Foreign Lang Dept Head; Mexico Trip Coord; Piedmont Foreign Lang Collaborative 1989-; Chapman HS Teacher of Yr 1988-89; *office:* Chapman HS 35 Oakland Ave Inman SC 29349

MC CLURE, THOMAS MATTHEW, Mathematics Teacher; *b:* Casper, WY; *ed:* (AA) General Ed, San Joaquin Delta Coll 1974; (BS) Ed/Math, S OR St Coll 1977; *cr:* Math Teacher Ashland Jr HS 1977-78, Hermiston HS 1978-79, Boise HS 1979-82, Riverside HS 1982-; *ai:* Dist Math Curr Comm; HS Curr Comm; Dist Experimental Ed Comm; NCTM 1985-; OR Cncl Teacher of Math 1987-; Mathematical Assn of America 1990; Assn For Experimental Ed 1990; Spokane Mountineers 1986-; WSU & Gonzaga Univ Summer Math Insts; *office:* Riverside HS Rt 1 Box 277 Chattaroy WA 99003

MC CLURG, JOSEPH ALLEN, Cmptr Lab Coord/Math Teacher; *b:* Lancaster, OH; *m:* Jill M. Palmer; *c:* Caitlin Marie; *ed:* (BA) Math Ed, Miami Univ 1976; *cr:* Math Teacher Liberty Union HS 1976-78; Math Teacher/Cmptr Lab Coord Stanberry Frosh Sch 1978-83; Math Applications Teacher Thomas Ewing Jr HS 1983-; *ai:* Cmptr Lab Coord; Cmptr Club Adv; Ftbl Coach; LEA 1976-; OEA & NEA 1976-90; OH Teachers of Math 1976-; Emanuel Lutheran Church Mem 1985-; St Participant New Building Resource Prgm; Faculty Organization VP 1986-87 & Pres 1987-88; *home:* 243 Lake St Lancaster OH 43130

MC COLL, CAROLYN WALKER, Latin Teacher; *b:* Winston-Salem, NC; *m:* David Kenneth; *c:* Elizabeth Mc Coll Quattlebaum, Lynn, Mary M.; *ed:* (BA) Latin/Ed, Univ of NC 1960; Eng, Appalachian St Univ; Eng, Clemson Univ; Classics, Furman Univ; Amer Acad at Rome; Vergilion Society Summer Study; *cr:* Latin/Eng Teacher Heathwood Hall 1968-72; Latin/Eng Teacher 1972-80, Latin Instr 1980- Christ Church Episcopal; *ai:* Mid Sch Stu Cncl; Latin Club; 9th Grade Class Adv; Amer Classical League Membership Chm 1985-; Jr League 1973-; Christ Church Sunday Sch Teacher 1988-; City of Greenville AD HOC Recycling Comm 1990; Amer Acad Rome & Vergilion Society Sch Cumae Fulbright Grant 1989; *office:* Christ Church Episcopal Sch 100 Cavalier Dr Greenville SC 29607

MC COLLAM, ROBERT LEE, 4th-6th Grade Math Teacher; *b:* Iowa City, IA; *m:* Donna Louise Chapman; *c:* Cynthia A. Bucknam, Robert P., Daniel L.; *ed:* (BA) Elem Ed, Parsons Coll 1962; Grad Stud Univ of N IA, MO St Teachers Coll, W IL; *cr:* Coach/7th/8th Grade Sci/Math Teacher Pleasant Plain Sch 1962-64, Blue Grass Sch 1964-67; Coach/Mid Sch Math Teacher/Class Guide Bettendorf Mid Sch 1967-74; 6th Grade Homeroom/Wrestling Coach Blue Grass Elem & Walcott Jr HS 1974-75; 4th-6th Grade Math Teacher/Jr HS Wrestling Coach Walcott Elem & Jr HS 1975-; *ai:* Upper Elem Dept Head; 4th-6th Grade Boys Wrestling Clinic; NEA, IA St Ed Assn, Davenport Ed Assn, IA Cncl of Math Teachers, Nom Outstanding Teacher of Elem Math 1984, 1987; Blue Grass Presbyn Church Elder 1966-, SE IA Outstanding Lay Leader 1988, Commissioner General Assembly Philadelphia 1977; Natl Sci Fnd Grant Univ of N IA Jr HS Math; Nom Humanity Awd 1978; Davenport Sch Dist Jr HS Coach of Yr 1984; *office:* Walcott Elem & Jr HS 545 E James St Walcott IA 52773

MC COLLUM, DOROTHY HOOTS, 2nd/3rd Grade Teacher; *b:* Winston-Salem, NC; *c:* Lou A. Dennison, David L; *ed:* (BA) Ed, High Point Coll 1956; *cr:* Teacher 1952-60; Teacher 1965- Forbush Elem Sch; *ai:* Chm Steering Comm-Southern Assn for Accreditation; NCAE-Local Assn Rep 1988-; *home:* Rt 2 Box 773 East Bend NC 27018

MC COLLUM, MARK, Band Director; *b:* Waynesburg, PA; *m:* Patricia Mary Kinneavy; *ed:* (BME) Music Ed, WV Univ 1979; *cr:* Substitute Teacher 1979-88, Music Teacher 1980-81 Cntrl Green Sch Dist; Band Dir W Greene Mid Sch & Sr HS 1988-; *ai:* Prof Freelance Musician 1979-; Marching, Concert, Pep Band; MENC, PMEA 1989-; Natl Assn of Jazz Educators VP 1978-79; *office:* W Greene Mid Sch & Sr HS RD 5 Box 36A Waynesburg PA 15370

MC COLLUM, TIMOTHY DAVID, Science Instructor; *b:* Chicago, IL; *m:* Rita Jean Schroeder; *c:* Monica L., Kyle T.; *ed:* (BS) Ed, 1973, (MS) Zoology, 1977 E IL Univ; *cr:* Sci Instr/Sci-Math Dept Chm Charleston Jr HS 1973-; *ai:* Sci Fair Act Coord, Site Coord NASA Videoconferences OSU; Consultant Educl Service Center Wkshps & Inservices on Space Sci; IL Jr Acad of Sci (Regional Chm 1984-89, St Bd Dirs 1985); NSTA, IL Sci Teachers Assn; NEA, IL Ed Assn; Charleston Kiwanis Club Pres 1988-; Immanual Luth Church Bd of Dir 1988-; Recipient IL St Bd of Ed Sci Literacy Grant; IL Math & Sci Acad Awd of Excl;

Chapter II Mini Grant; Charleston Cncl of Bus & Industry for Better Ed Awd; Jaycees Outstanding Young Educator; Teacher of Yr; Invited to NASA Hubble Launch Educators Conference 1990, Jet Propulsion Laboratory Galileo Launch Educators Conference Kennedy Space Center 1989; *office:* Charleston Jr HS 920 Smith Dr Charleston IL 61920

MC COMBS, BARBARA JUDY, Teacher; *b:* Dayton, OH; *m:* Timothy C.; *c:* Megan, Ben; *ed:* (BS) Ed, OH St Univ 1979; *cr:* 3rd Grade Teacher William E Miller Elem Sch 1980-83; 5th Grade Teacher Kettering Elem Sch 1983-84; Substitute Teacher Upper Arlington City Schls 1985-86; *ai:* Newark Teachers Assn 1980-84; Creative Living Incorporated Service Bd 1989-; Upper Arlington Luth Church Kndgtn Sunday Sch Teacher 1989-; TWIG Childrens Hospital 1989-; Neward PTO 1980-84; *home:* 1589 Berkshire Rd Columbus OH 43221

MC COMBS, JUDITH ANNE, Religious Education Director; *b:* Bluffton, OH; *ed:* (BA) Eng/Soc Stud, OH Dominican Coll 1969; (MA) Pastoral Stud, Loyola Univ Chicago 1985; Beginnings & Beyond Inst N Amer Forum on Catechumenate; *cr:* 5th/6th Grade Elem Teacher St Joseph Sch 1969-71; 5th Grade Elem Teacher St Francis Xavier Sch 1971-75; Elem Lang Art Teacher Holy Cross Sch 1975-76; 3rd Grade Teacher St Benedict the Moor Sch 1977-79; 2nd/3rd Grade Elem Teacher St Patrick Sch 1979-81; 3rd/4th Grade Elem Teacher 1981-84, Religious Stud Coord 1984-85 Corpus Christi Sch; Religious Ed Dir St Cecelia Church 1985-; *ai:* Chairperson AIDS Awareness; Youth Advisory Bd; NCEA 1980-; Diocesean Religious Ed (Rep for Deanery, Advisory Bd) 1986-89; Sacramental Guidelines, Curr Guidelines for Religious Ed Diocese of St Petersburg; Guest Lecturer on Family Catechesis Sacramental Ed.

MC COMIC, JOHN ALVIS, American History Teacher; *b:* Dallas, TX; *m:* Carolyn Dee Cleary; *c:* Sasha, Alesha; *ed:* (BA) His/Eng, Univ of TX 1968; (MED) Personal Supvr, Stephen F Austin 1971; *cr:* Teacher Kilgore Ind Sch Dist; *ai:* 4-H Adv; Kilgore Youth Stand Superior in Elminating Drugs, Drug Free Group Spon; TX St Teachers Assn, NEA, Natl Historical Assn, TX Assn of Prof Educators.

MC CONN, MABLE BALINDA NARUM, Second Grade Teacher; *b:* Douglas, ND; *m:* Charles L.; *c:* Nancy J. Mc Conn Burke; *ed:* (BS) Ed, Minot St Univ 1970; Univ of MN, Univ of ND; *cr:* 1st/2nd Grade Teacher Glenburn Public Sch 1946-48; 2nd Grade Teacher Stanley Public Sch 1948-50, Minot Public Sch 1950-56, Surrey Public Sch 1967-71, 1972-; *ai:* Comm Mem Young Authors Conference, Sch Improvement Process; Sch Contact Person Teacher Learning Center; Surrey Sch & Natl PTA, NEA, ND Ed Assn, Surrey Sch Ed Assn, IRA, N Cntrl ND Rdng Assn; *home:* 1828 9th St SW Minot ND 58701

MC CONNELL, BRIAN KEITH, 5th Grade Teacher; *b:* Canonsburg, PA; *c:* Rhonda L., Bradley K.; *ed:* (BS) Elem Ed/Phys Ed, Clarion Univ 1974; *cr:* 4th-6th Grade Teacher Live Oak Elem Sch 1976-; *ai:* Hospitality Comm; Campus Improvement Team; *office:* Live Oak Elem Sch 12301 Welcome Dr San Antonio TX 78233

MC CONNELL, JILL GENTRY, English Teacher; *b:* Owensville, IN; *m:* Richard L.; *c:* Amy S. Mc Connell Page; Jason P., Todd G., Richard J.; *ed:* (BS) Scndry Ed Eng, Oakland City Coll 1971; (MA) Hum/Eng, Univ of Evansville 1976; Curr & Instr, IN Univ; *cr:* Eng Teacher Francisco Schl, Princeton Mid Sch; *ai:* Sch Newspaper Spon; Plays, Drama Dir; Spell Bowl, Spelling Bee Dir; Teachers Teaching Teachers; Alpha Delta Kappa 1976-; Sigma Kappa Sigma 1970-; Pi Lemba Theta 1988-; NCTE, NCTW 1985-; Tri Kappa 1985-; *office:* Princeton Mid Sch 410 E State St Princeton IN 47670

MC CONNELL, LORI ANNE, Special Education Teacher; *b:* Altoona, PA; *ed:* (BS) Pre Phys Therapy Univ of NM; (BS) Scndry Ed, Univ of TX El Paso 1987; *cr:* Spec Ed Teacher Parkland HS 1988-; *ai:* Head Jr Var & Asst Var Girls Bsktbl Coach.

MC CONVILLE, EDWARD JOSEPH, Third Grade Teacher; *b:* Kittanning, PA; *c:* Julianne, Jennifer; *ed:* (BS) Elem Ed, IN Univ of PA 1968; (MA) Elem Admin, OH Univ 1973; OH Univ & Ashland Univ; *cr:* 6th Grade Teacher Franklin Twp Elem 1968-69; 2nd-3rd-4th-5th Grade Teacher Medill Elem 1969-88; 3rd Grade Teacher East Elem 1988-; *ai:* Safety Patrol Adv; Entry Yr Mentoring Relationships Comm; NEA; OH Ed Assn; Lancaster Ed Assn; Martha Holden Jennings Schlsp Awd; *office:* East Elem Sch 751 E Wheeling Lancaster OH 43130

MC COOL, BRENDA BELL, English Teacher; *b:* Greenwood, MS; *m:* Johnny; *c:* Melanie, John K.; *ed:* (BSE) Eng/Speech, 1971, (ME) Eng, 1972 Delta St Univ; Grad Stud MS St Univ; *cr:* Scndry Eng Teacher Leflore Cty HS 1972, Eupora HS 1972-73, East Side HS 1973-74, N Sunflower Acad 1974-75; *ai:* HS Annual Staff & Sr Class Spon; MS Assn of Educators 1977-87; MS Prof Educators 1987-; St Luke United Meth Church Mem; STAR Teacher 1979.

MC COOL, DEBORAH JOYCLYN, Chemistry Teacher; *b:* Johnstown, PA; *m:* William R.; *c:* Bryan, Jeffrey, Eric, Sean; *ed:* (BS) Bio, Univ of Pittsburgh Johnstown 1974; (MED) Ed, St Francis Coll 1990; *cr:* Chem Teacher Penn Cambria Sr HS 1984-; *ai:* Coach Scholastic Quiz Team & Sci Olympiad Team; Cntrl PA Assn of Chem Teachers, NSTA, NEA, PA St Ed Assn 1985-; Cntrl Western Scholastic Quiz League Secy 1985-; Spectroscopic Society of Pittsburgh HS Equipment Grant 1984-88; Title II Grant for Hands on Sci Wkshp for Dist Elem Teachers 1990; *office:* Penn Cambria Sr HS 4th St And Linden Ave Cresson PA 16630

MC CORD, EMMA MC GINNIS, Language Art Teacher; *b:* Maysville, KY; *m:* William R.; *c:* William D.; *ed:* (BA) Elem Ed/His, 1969, (MS) Elem Ed, 1972, (Rank I) Elem Ed, 1982 Morehead St; Process Writing Wkshps; *cr:* 1st Grade Teacher Washington Elem 1969-75; 1st Grade/Chapter I Teacher Ewing Elem 1975-81; 7th/8th Grade Lang Art/Teacher of Gifted Simons Mid 1981-; *ai:* Academic Coach; KEA, NEA, FCEA Secy; NCTE; WCG Secy; Homemakers; Commonwealth Inst for Teachers 1988; *office:* Simons Mid Sch 242 W Water St Flemingsburg KY 41041

MC CORD, SCOTT ANTHONY, Honors/AP Chemistry Teacher; *b:* Orlando, FL; *ed:* (BA) Limnology/Music Ed, Univ of Cntrl Fl 1980; (MME) Music EZd, IN Univ 1985; Working Towards Doctorate in Curr & Instr/Sci Ed, Univ of Cntrl Fl; *cr:* Chem Instr 1983-, Advanced Placement Chem Instr 1984- Titusville HS; *ai:* Chem Honor Society Adv; Marching & All-St Band; Solo/Ensemble Contest Adjudicator; Private Music Instr; NAST (Mem, Sch Dist Regional Convention Rep 1987, , Asst Ed 1988-); FL Assn of Sci Teachers, FL Bandmasters Assn, Amer Assn for Advancement of Sci; Cntrl FL Percussion Ensemble (Composer, Conductor); Percussive Art Society, Union of Concerned Scientists, Sierra Club; Amer Chemical Society (Mem) Outstanding Chem Teacher Awd 1986-88, 1990; Brevard Cty Laboratory Safety Comm Mem 1987; Published Article 1988; Sci Honors Symposium 1990; Chematon Chem Competition 1st Place St Teacher Awd 1985-86, 1988, 1990; Univ of Cntrl FL Outstanding Chem Teacher Awd 1988; USAF Acad Honorary Liaison Officer 1986-; *office:* Titusville HS US 1 Titusville FL 32780

MC CORKLE, CECELIA RUSSAK, Home Ec Teacher/Dept Chair; *b:* Wilkinsburg, PA; *ed:* (BS) Home Ec Ed, Indiana Univ of PA 1969; *cr:* Teacher Norwin Sr HS 1969-; *ai:* Home Ec Ed Assn, Amer Home Ec Assn; *office:* Norwin Sr HS 251 Mc Mahon Rd North Huntingdon PA 15642

MC CORMACK, M. KATHLEEN THOMAS, IHM, Junior High School Teacher; *b:* Philadelphia, PA; *ed:* (BA) Sociology/Theology, Immaculata PA 1972; (MA) Elem Ed, Glassboro St 1980; EDD Candidate, Univ San Francisco 1989; Private Sch Admin; *cr:* 8th Grade Teacher St Joseph, St Philomena, Incarnation, Our Lady of Ransom, St Martin of Tours, BVM 1967-83; Prin Holy Family Sch 1983-84; Teacher Ed Instr Immaculata Coll 1984-85; Jr HS Teacher St Simon Sch 1985-; *ai:* Jr HS Confirmation Prgm & Spiritual Dir; Youth Group Lecturer; Phi Delta Kappa, Pi Lambda Theta, ASCD; Curr Wkshp Presenter 1974-; Published Teaching Kits 1973-74; Revised Eng Texts Loyola Company 1981-83; Adult Ed Lecturer 1977-; Self-Esteem Seminar Presenter 1985-; *office:* St Simon Sch 1840 Grant Rd Los Altos CA 94024

MC CORMACK, THOMAS HUSTON, Teacher; *b:* Cincinnati, OH; *m:* Ruth; *c:* Rob; *ed:* (BS) Earth Sci/Geography, Miami Univ 1967; (MA) Guidance, Xavier 1972; Geography; *cr:* Teacher Sycamore Jr HS 1967-; *ai:* Jr NHS Adv; Awds Comm Chm; Sycamore Ed Assn, OH Ed Assn, NEA 1967-; Planning Commission Sch & Cmnty; *office:* Sycamore Jr H S Cooper Rd Cincinnati OH 45241

MC CORMACK, WILLIAM DANIEL, History Department Chair; *b:* Shirley, NY; *m:* Janet Ann Sullivan; *c:* Melissa, Heather; *ed:* (BA) His, Houghton Coll 1986; Millersville Univ; *cr:* His Teacher 1986-87, His Dept Head 1987- Lancaster Chrstn Sch; *ai:* Var Bsktbl & Bsbl Coach; Sch Philosophy & Educl Policy Comm; Jr Class Adv; Cmptr Service Coord; Phi Alpha Theta Secy 1965-86; Apple Programming & Developing Assn, Organization Amer Historians 1990; PA Natl Guard 1983-; *home:* 950A Village Rd Lancaster PA 17602

MC CORMICK, GAIL LYNN, Physical Ed/Health Teacher; *b:* Prior Lake, MN; *m:* Kevin Joseph; *ed:* (BA) Phys Ed/Health/Ed, Wiona St Univ 1986; *cr:* Phys Ed/Health Teacher Caledonia HS 1986-; *ai:* Var Gymnastic & Asst Vlybl Coach; Stu Asst Team, Staff Wellness, Sch Discipline Comm; YMCA Aerobic Instr 1987-; *office:* Caledonia HS W Main St Caledonia MN 55921

MC CORMICK, GARY ALAN, English/Amer History Teacher; *b:* Covington, KY; *ed:* Assoc Eng, 1988, (BA) His, 1988 Thomas More Coll; *cr:* Amer Lit Teacher 1988-89, Eng/Amer His Teacher 1989- Ludlow HS; *ai:* Acad Team, Head Jr Var & Asst VAr Soccer Team Coach; Supt & Prins Advisory Cncl; NCTE, NCSS 1989-.

MC CORMICK, JOYCE WORCESTER, Third Grade Teacher; *b:* Eunice, NM; *m:* Gary Grau; *c:* Kimberly M.; *ed:* (BA) Elem Ed/His, Wayland Baptist Univ 1975; Work Towards Masters Degree, Advanced Academic Trng in Bi-ling/ESL, Gifted & Talented, Lang Art; *cr:* 4th Grade Teacher R C Andrews Elem 1975-79; 3rd Grade Teacher College Hill Elem 1979-; *ai:* TX Classroom Teachers Assn 1987-; Assn TX Public Educators 1983-87; TX St Teachers Assn 1975-83; PTA (Treas 1989-, 2nd VP 1988-89, Secy 1986-88), Life Membership 1989; *office:* College Hill Elem Sch 707 Canyon Plainview TX 79072

MC CORMICK, KAREN E., Spanish I & II Teacher; *b:* Neenah, WI; *m:* James; *c:* Danny L., Scott, Allen, Marty Mendenhall; *ed:* (BS) Elem Ed/Span, Univ of WI 1964; Working Towards Masters Univ of Evansville; *cr:* 3rd Grade Teacher Green Bay WI 1964-65, Long Beach CA 1965-66; 4th Grade Teacher Johnston City IL 1966-67; 5th/6th Grade Teacher Rockport IN 1968-70; 4th Grade Teacher/EMR Gallatin TN 1973-74; 7th-12th Grade Teacher Hendersonville TN 1977-; *office:* Hendersonville Chrstn Acad 355 Old Shackle Island Rd Hendersonville TN 37075

MC CORMICK, NANCY SANDS, 4th-6th Grade Elem Teacher; *b:* Springfield, OH; *m:* Richard Barry; *c:* Andrew, Clare A.; *ed:* (BA) Elem Ed, Marietta Coll 1972; Grad Work OH Univ & Marietta Coll; *cr:* 2nd-6th Grade Teacher Beverly Elem Sch 1972-; *ai:* OH Cncl Teachers of Math 1986-; Ft Frye Teachers Assn (Pres, Negotiator); OH Ed Assn Resolutions Commission; SE OH Ed Assn Exec Comm; Alpha X Delta Alumni Pres 1978; Barlow Vincent Elem PTA Secy 1988-89; Washington Cty Credit Union Audit Comm; *office:* Beverly Elem Sch Box 98 Beverly OH 45715

MC COWAN, MICHAEL O'MELIA, Sixth Grade Teacher; *b:* Fort Knox, KY; *m:* Marla Jean Messer; *c:* Nathan R.; *ed:* (BED) Elem Ed/Speech Comm, Univ of AK 1983; Post Grad Stud Elem Ed, Univ of AK; *cr:* 6th Grade Teacher Delta Junction Sch 1983-; *ai:* Elem Sci Curr Comm Chairperson; AK Dog Mushers Assn Race Marshall 1980-; *office:* Delta Junction Sch Pouch 1 Delta Junction AK 99737

MC COWN, JOAN M., Fifth Grade Teacher; *b:* Ville Platte, LA; *m:* Larry; *c:* Michael, Gregory, Patrick; *ed:* (BS) Elem Ed, 1961, (MS) Elem Ed, 1986 Lamar Univ; *cr:* 4th Grade Teacher Houston Ind Sch Dist 1961-62, Sheldon Ind Sch Dist 1962-66; 5th Grade Teacher All Saints Episcopal 1976-81; 4th-6th Grade Teacher Lumberton Ind Sch Dist 1981-; *ai:* Grade Level Chm; Textbook Selection Chm; TX St Teachers Assn 1981-; NEA; TX Assn of Gifted & Talented 1986-89; Lumberton PTA Bd 1981-, Teacher of Yr 1988; *home:* 4755 Hardwood Beaumont TX 77706

MC COWN, MARGARET HALBERT, Retired Science Teacher; *b:* Dialville, TX; *m:* Rayburn; *c:* Patrick, Tim, Andy, Julie Cruz; *ed:* (BS) Soc Stud/Eng, 1951, (MED) Elem, 1957 Stephen F Austin Univ; Advanced Sci Trng A&M Summer Prgms Stephen F Austin Univ; *cr:* Soc Stud/Eng Teacher Gallatin Public Sch 1951-52; 6th Grade/Eng Teacher New Summerfield Sch 1953-54, 1958-64; Head Start 1966-67; 6th Grade Sci Teacher 1968-81,Teacher of 6th-8th Grade Gifted/Talented Sci 1981-89 Jacksonville Mid Sch; *ai:* Established Gifted & Talented Prgm Jacksonville Ind Sch Dist; St Exemplary Awd 1984-85; Delta Kappa Gamma; TSTA; St & E TX Assn of Gifted Sci Teachers; 1st Baptist Church All Areas Ed 1955; TX Gifted/Talented Curr Dev Regional Team Mem; Level III TX Career Ladder; Teacher of Yr Jacksonville Ind Sch Dist 1985; Nom Natl Teacher of Yr; Interdisciplinary Curr Conference Comm; *home:* Rt 7 Box 206-A Jacksonville TX 75766

MC COY, BERNADINE MARIE (HECK), 3rd Grade Teacher; *b:* Allentown, PA; *m:* Charles R.; *c:* Michael J., Marti J.; *ed:* (BS) Elem Ed, Bloomsburg Univ 1959; *cr:* 3rd Grade Teacher Linglestown Elem 1959-60; 3rd Grade Teacher 1960-63, Kndgtn Teacher 1963-64 Woodward Township; 2nd/3rd Grade Teacher Hudson Sch Dist 1970-; *ai:* Buddy Prgm Between Class & Local Nursing Home; Monthly after Sch Act.

MC COY, CAROL L., Teacher; *b:* Flora, IL; *m:* Herbert A.; *c:* Michael, Jonathan, Mary; *ed:* (BS) Ed, 1961, (MS) Ed, 1972 Cntrl MO St Univ; Adult Basic Ed, Cntrl MO St Univ; *cr:* 5th Grade Teacher Grandview Schls 1961-62; Adult Basic Ed Teacher Raytown Schls 1976-85; 6th Grade Teacher Lees Summit R-7 Dist 1985-; *ai:* Westview Stu Cncl & Spelling Bee Coord; Young Authors Conference; NEA Intnl Rdng Assn 1985-; Nom Kansas City Start Learning Exch Prgm Excl in Teaching; *office:* Westview Elem Sch 200 N Ward Rd Lees Summit MO 64063

MC COY, DELMAS BOYD, Physical Ed/Health Teacher; *b:* Webster Springs, WV; *m:* Susanna Marie Arthur; *c:* Annette M., Lisa D.; *ed:* (AB) K-8th Grade Elem Ed, Glenville St Coll 1965; Grad Stud; *cr:* 8th Grade Teacher/Asst Prin Richwood Jr HS 1965-70; 8th Grade Teacher/Coach Beaver Grade Sch 1971-74; Asst Prin/Prin 1975-78, Classroom Teacher/Phys Ed/Health Coach 1979- Webster Springs Elem; *ai:* Jr HS Boys Bsktbl & Sftbl Coach; WV Ed Assn 1965-; NEA, WVEA, CEA Building Rep; *home:* Rt 3 Box 4 Webster Springs WV 26288

MC COY, HANNAH LITTLES, Social Studies Teacher; *b:* Hazlehurst, MS; *m:* Joe L.; *c:* Lakeyra G.; *ed:* (BS) Soc Sci, Alcorn St Univ 1968; (MS) Soc Sci Ed, MS St Univ 1981; *cr:* Soc Stud Teacher T Y Fleming 1968-70, Sam Baltan 1970-81, Amando Elzy HS 1981-; *ai:* Drug Awareness Comm; Courtesy Comm; Leflore Co Assn Educators 1968-; MS Assn of Educators 1968-; Natl Assn of Educators 1968; Amer Legion Auxilary 1974-; Magnolia Chapter No 38 OES 1987; *home:* 506 State St Greenwood MS 38930

MC COY, MAE TAYLOR, High School Reading Teacher; *b:* Crystal Springs, MS; *c:* Travis; *ed:* (BA) Sociology, Jackson St Univ 1966; (MA) Rdng, Univ of MO 1970; Specialist Rdng, Univ of MO Kansas City 1970; (PHD) Sociology, Walden Univ 1978; *cr:* Teacher Miles Coll 1970-72, Pinellas Cty Schls 1972-78, US Virgin Islands St Thomas 1979-82, Hazlehurst HS 1982-; *ai:* Staff Dev Comm Chairperson; Literacy Teacher & Cmmty Youth Cnslr Volunteer; Intnl Rdng Assn 1970-; Amer Peace Corps Volunteer 1966-68; Campfire Girls (Trainer, Leader) 1967-78, Certificate 1978; Child Dev Assn Rep 1978-, Certificate 1988; Articles Published 1980, 1988; *office:* Hazlehurst HS 101 S Haley St Hazlehurst MS 39083

MC COY, MARY LOU LOU (BAUGHN), 4th Grade Teacher; *b:* Henry Cty, IN; *m:* Donald R.; *c:* David, Lou A.; *ed:* (BS) Elem Ed, Ball St Teacher Coll 1956; (MA) Ball St Univ 1965; *cr:* Teacher New Castle Herny Twp Sch 1956-57; Thurston Olympia Sch 1957-58; New Castle Herny Twp Sch 1958-68; Shenandoah Sch Corp 1968-; *ai:* Head Teacher; SEA Mem at Large Secy Negotiation Team; Delta Kappa Gamma 1985-.

MC COY, MARYBETH HALVORSON, 6th Grade Language Art Teacher; *b:* Brainard, MN; *m:* Lloyd C.; *c:* Lee C. Markwell, David M. MarkWell; *ed:* (AA) Elem Ed, Concordia 1964; (BS) Elem Ed, Mt Mercy Coll 1974; Grad Stud Various Colls; *cr:* Elem Teacher Immanuel First Luth Sch 1964-67; Elem Teacher Aide Center Point Cmmty Sch Dist 1972-74; Elem Teacher Cedar Rapids Sch Dist 1974-76, 6th Grade Lang Art Teacher S Tama Sch Dist 1977-; *ai:* IA Cncl Teachers of Eng 1985-; Tama Cty Extension Cncl Secy 1982-84; *office:* S Tama Cmmty Sch Dist 201 S Green St Toledo IA 52342

MC COY, PATRICIA GALLION, Fourth Grade Teacher; *b:* Webbville, KY; *m:* John C.; *ed:* (BA) Elem Ed, 1968, (MA) Elem Ed, 1974, (Rank I) Elem Ed, 1978 Morehead St Univ; *cr:* 4th Grade Teacher Prichard Elem Sch 1968-; *ai:* Carter Cty Ed Assn, KY Ed Assn, NEA.

MC COY, REBECCA SMITH, Chapter I/Science/Eng Teacher; *b:* Bridgeport, AL; *m:* Marcus Ted; *c:* Eula B., James D.; *ed:* (BA) Elem Ed, Auburn Univ 1977; Working on Masters in Elem Ed; *cr:* 1st Grade Teacher 1977-82, 2nd Grade Teacher 1982-86, Chapter I Teacher 1986-88 Bridgeport Elem; Chapter I/Eng/Sci Teacher Bridgeport Mid Sch 1988-; *ai:* Yrbk Spon; Sci Textbook Comm; NEA, AEA, JCEA; *home:* HCR 62 Box 72 Stevenson AL 35772

MC CRACKEN, EUGENE KEITH, Business & Drivers Ed Teacher; *b:* French Lick, IN; *m:* Jancie Kay Hawkins; *c:* Thaddeus, Jameson; *ed:* (BS) Bus Ed, Oakland City Coll 1972; (MS) Bus Ed, IN Univ 1975; Drivers Ed Endorsement IN Univ; *cr:* Bus Teacher Switzerland Cty Cmmty Schls 1972-73; Bus/Drivers Ed Teacher Mitchell Cmmty Schls 1973-; *ai:* Spon Sch Newspaper & Yrbk; Spon Quill & Scroll Club; NEA; IN St Teachers Assn; Mitchell Ed Assn; IN Bus Ed Assn; Elks Lodge #826; Mitchell Comm Schls Teacher Excl Awd 1989; Pres Mitchell Ed Assn 1987-; Lawrence Cty Chm of Hoosiers for Safety Belts; *office:* Mitchell H S 1000 Bishop Blvd Mitchell IN 47446

MC CRACKEN, JAY KENT, 5th Grade Teacher; *b:* Amboy, IL; *m:* Kimbearly Crutcher; *c:* Megan M.; *ed:* (AA) Ed, Sauk Valley Coll 1974; (BS) Ed, Northern IL Univ 1976; Ed, IL St Univ & Western IL Univ; *cr:* 1st & 2nd Grade Teacher Senachwine Grade Sch 1976-79; 5th Grade Teacher Henry-Senachwine Grade Sch 1979-; *ai:* Literary Coach; Phi Kappa Phi Nalt Honor Society 1976-; Henry Elem Teachers Assn Pres 1984-85; City of Henry (Alderman 1985-86, Mayor 1989-); Henry Cmmty Amb Service 1982-84; Marshall Putnam Youth Service Bd of Dir 1986-; Written Educls Curr for Educl Service Region; *home:* 1217 3rd St Henry IL 61537

MC CRACKEN, JUDY GARLAND, First Grade Teacher; *b:* Rabun Cty, GA; *m:* Carl Michael; *c:* Jennifer, Jonas, Micah; *ed:* (AA) Reinhardt Coll 1966; (BS) Home Ec, W Carolina Univ 1969; (MS) Ed/Early Chldhd, N GA Coll 1980; *cr:* 5th Grade Teacher Clayton Elem 1968-69; Home Ec Teacher Bureau of Indian Affairs 1970-71; 1st Grade Teacher Rabun Gap Cmmty Sch 1977-; *ai:* Landscape, Sci, Health Insurance Comms; Alpha Delta Kappa Pres 1988-, Cornacopia Awd 1990; GA Assn of Educators Building Rep 1981-83; Natl Teacher Assn 1977-; Womens Missionary Union Dir 1989-; *office:* Rabun Gap Cmmty Sch PO Box 127 Rabun Gap GA 30568

MC CRACKEN, RICHARD E., Science Teacher; *b:* Litchfield, IL; *m:* Wilma Reinwald; *c:* Mark, John, Matthew; *ed:* (BS) Bio, Elmhurst Coll 1961; (MS) Bio, Northern IL Univ 1966; Natl Sci Fnd Grants Summers 1969-70; Admin Cert 1981; *cr:* Sci Teacher 1961-, Math/Sci Dept Chm 1968- O Neill Jr HS; *ai:* Stu Cncl Adv 1970-; Curr Advisory Cncl HS Dist; Staff Dev Comm; Sci Fair Comm; NEA; IEA; Downers Grove Elem Ed Assn; NSTA; IL Sci Teachers Assn; Natl Assn of Wkshp Dirs; Downers Grove Human Service Commission Chm 1983-; Cmmty Coordinating Cncl 1989-; Dir Summer Leadership Camp for IL Assn of Jr HS Stu Cncls 1982-; *office:* O Neill Jr H S 635 59th Downers Grove IL 60516

MC CRACKEN, SHARILYN LYONS, Fourth Grade Teacher; *b:* Wheeling, WV; *c:* Roger D. II; *ed:* (BA) Elem Ed, W Liberty St Coll 1969; (MA) Elem Ed, WV Univ 1976; Piano, Organ Trng; *cr:* 1st Grade Teacher First Ward Sch 1968-69; 2nd Grade Teacher Cntrl Grade Sch 1970-71; 6th Grade Teacher 1971-84, 4th Grade Teacher 1984- Cameron Elem Sch; *ai:* PTA; CYF Leader; Yrbk Adv; Alumni Assn; Homebound Teacher; Tutoring; NEA, WVEA, MCEA 1968-; Eastern Star (Worthy Matron 1981-82, Organist 1988-); Chrstn Church Organist 1968-; *home:* RD 5 Box 14 Cameron WV 26033

MC CRACKEN, WILLIAM JAMES, Social Studies Chair; *b:* Philadelphia, PA; *m:* Janice Parsons; *c:* Megan; *ed:* (BSED) His/Government, Univ of TX Austin 1969; (MA) Admin/Supervision, Univ of S FL 1976; Grad Work His, Purdue Univ; *cr:* Teacher Wilbur Watts Mid Sch 1969-73, Sarasota Jr HS 1973-76; Pine View Sch 1976-; *ai:* Soc Stud Chm; Shared Decision Making Team Pine View Sch; Organization of Amer Historians, Amer Historical Assn 1984-; Western His Assn 1985-; Phi Alpha Theta 1986-; Sarasota Coastal Credit Union Supervisory Comm 1982-85; NSF Sociology OR Coll of Ed 1972, Anthropology Univ of S FL 1977-78; NEH Federalist Papers Harvard Univ 1984, Classics of Amer West Univ of CA Davis 1987.

MC CRARY, HERDIS W., Dept Chm-Lang Arts Teacher; *b:* Green Bay, WI; *m:* Nancy J. La Combe; *c:* Candace De Marlin, Mitchel, Karen, Linda Lawler, Christine Van Alstine, Patrick; *ed:* (BA) Bus/Economics, Univ of WI Madison 1956; (MS) Eng, Univ of WI Oshkosh 1968; Grad Stud Univ of WI Madison/Green Bay/Oshkosh, Bemidji St, Lesley Coll Grad Sch, St Olaf Coll, Winona St Univ; *cr:* Teacher Appleton West HS 1958-64; Dept Chm Ashwaukenon HS 1965-; Instr/Ad-Hoc Univ of WI Green Bay 1978/1980/1984; Instr St Norbert Coll 1968-; *ai:* Scndry Ed Consortium Exec, Gifted & Talented, Sch Improvement, Credit Review, Dist Lang Art Comms; Swim Coach; NEA, WI Educl Assn, Ashwaubenon Ed Assn; WI Cncl Teachers of Eng Distinguished Service Awd; NCTE Distinguished Service Awd; Amer Legion Service Awd; Disabled Amer Veterans Service Awd; Jr Chamber of Commerce Service Awd 1957; Green Bay Packer Organization & Hall of Fame Founders Univ of WI Green Bay Founders Club; Univ of WI Madison W Club; Shrines Club Spec Recgonition Awd; Grad Study Fellowship Creighton Univ Omaha NE; Teacher Recgonition Awds from Various Schls; *home:* 920 Mancel Ln Green Bay WI 54304

MC CRAW, SALLY, Reading Teacher; *b:* Baker, OR; *m:* Mike; *c:* Joel, Cassie; *ed:* (BS) Elem Ed, E OR St Coll 1975; Rdng Endorsement E OR St Coll 1988; *cr:* 5th Grade Teacher 1975-89, Rdng Teacher Union Elem 1989-; *ai:* Rdng Comm Chairperson; Ski Group Coord; Lang Art Comm; MURC, ORA; NEA, OEA 1980-; UEA (Pres 1982-84) 1980-; Little League Treas 1989-; Union Elem Teacher of Yr 1989; *home:* 62139 Evergreen Rd La Grande OR 97850

MC CRAW-ORLANDO, ANN, Science Coordinator/Teacher; *b:* Birmingham, AL; *m:* Joseph; *ed:* (BA) Psych/Ed, Kean Coll 1972; Grad Stud Instruction/Curr, Kean Coll; Dance Instr Trng, NY & Arthur Murray; *cr:* Owner/Operator Miss Anns Dance Studio 1966-76; Instr Arthur Murray Dance Studio 1979-82; Security Supvr Major Retail 1976-80; Teacher St Josephs The Carpenter 1980-; *ai:* St Josephs Afterschool Prgm Dir; Sci Fair & Olympiads Coord; Safety Patrol Adv; NCEA Mem 1981-; NSTA Mem 1990; Dance Educators of America Mem 1963-76; *office:* St Joseph The Carpetner Sch 140 E 3rd Ave Roselle NJ 07203

MC CRAY, LIZA BATES, Fourth Grade Teacher; *b:* Pine Top, KY; *m:* Watson; *c:* Larry, Venida G. Mc Cray-Hyde, Timothy; *ed:* (BS) Eng/Soc Sci, E MI Univ 1963; (MS) Elem Ed, N AL Univ 1979; *cr:* 1st-8th Grade Teacher 1945-46, 3rd-5th Grade Teacher 1947-59 Letcher Cty Schls; 2nd Grade Teacher Woodhaven Schls 1962-73; 4th Grade Teacher Hamilton Elem 1973-; *ai:* Woodhaven Ed Assn Pres 1969-70; Marion Cty Ed Assn Pres 1980-81; Order of Eastern Star (MI Worthy Matron 1972-73, AL Worthy Matron 1974-87); Prof Rights & Responsibilities; Legislative Rep to Delegate Assembly 19680; Prof Dev Ethics; Chairperson on Numerous Comms; *home:* Rt 4 Box 327 Hamilton AL 35570

MC CRAY, MARY ANNE, Language Art Chair; *b:* Live Oak, FL; *m:* Keith O.; *c:* Neil, David, Ashley; *ed:* (AA) General, NFJC 1977; (BA) Eng, Univ of FL 1980; HRMD; Grad Stud Univ of FL; *cr:* Teacher Patterson HS 1980-81, Suwannee HS 1981-85, Lafayette HS 1986-; *ai:* Academic Team Coach; *office:* Lafayette HS Rt 2 Box 270 Mayo FL 32066

MC CRAY, WILLIE JAMES, Math Department Chairperson; *b:* Mc Comb, MS; *m:* Youlinda Harris; *c:* Elizabeth A., Luther O., Tralanda N.; *ed:* (AA) General Admin, US Marine Corp Admin Sch 1973; (BS) Scndry Math Teaching, 1980, (MS) Ed Emphasis In Math, 1990 Alcorn St Univ; Microcomputer Operator/Analyzer; *cr:* Admin/Postal Clerk US Marine Corps 1972-75; Supvr/Coord South Pike Sch Dist 1979-80; Math Teacher/Coach Memphis City Schls 1980-84, South Pike Consolidated Sch Dist 1984-; *ai:* Jr HS/HS Ftbl Coach; 9th Grade Bsktbl Coach; MS Assn of Coaches 1984-; NCTM 1979-84; Prince Hall Masonic Order Sr Warden 1984-; Received Academic Schlsp for High Score on ACT; *home:* 850 Garland St Magnolia MS 39652

MC CREA, DEBI CATUCCI, Teacher/Comm Facilitator; *b:* Cincinnai, OH; *m:* Michael V.; *c:* Natalie, Alicia; *ed:* Assoc Early Chldhd Ed, 1977, (BA) Elem Ed, 1979 Univ of Cincinnati; (MS) Ed/Rdng Specialist Xavier Univ 1985; *cr:* Teacher Cincinnati Public Schls 1979-; *ai:* Forensics Coach; Drama Club Spon; Eng Dept Chairperson; *home:* 8639 Heritage Dr Florence KY 41042

MC CREA, PHILIP R., Sixth Grade Teacher; *b:* Bronx, NY; *ed:* (AA) Liberal Arts, Nassau Comm Coll 1969; (BS) Elem Ed, 1971, (MS) Elem Ed, 1973 SUNY Cortland; *cr:* 5th Grade Teacher 1971-78, 6th Grade Teacher 1978-80, 5th Grade Teacher 1980-86, 4th Grade Teacher 1986-89, 6th Grade Teacher 1989- Chenango Valley Sch Dist; *ai:* Odyssey of Mind Coach; NYSUT 1971-; BSA Scoutmaster 1973-76; *office:* Chenango Valley Cntrl Schls 768 Chenango St Binghamton NY 13901

MC CREARY, BETH CHRISTINE, 1st Grade Teacher; *b:* Kansas City, MO; *m:* David Charles; *c:* Amy, Dane; *ed:* (BS) Elem Ed, OK St Univ 1974; *cr:* 1st Grade Teacher Chisholm Elem 1974-; *ai:* Spring Fling Comm; Chisholm Ed Assn Parlimentarion, OK Ed Assn, NEA 1974-; Kappa Kappa Iota (VP, Reporter/Historian) 1976-; *office:* Chisholm Elem 300 Colorado Enid OK 73703

MC CREARY, PETER W., JR., Mathematics Teacher; *b:* Chicago, IL; *m:* Geraldine Tiner; *c:* Kimberly, Amira, Janelle; *ed:* (BS) Math, St Louis Univ 1972; *cr:* Area Mgr Southwestern Bell Telephone 1972-87; Math Teacher Parkway Schls 1987-; *ai:* Head Coach Girls Track & Field; NCTM 1987-89; MCTM, MEGSL 1987-; Baptist Church Pastor 1981-; *office:* Parkway South Sr HS 801 Hanna Rd Manchester MO 63021

MC CREARY, RICHARD OLIVER, Head Teacher; *b:* Kansas City, KS; *m:* Veronica U. Armstrong; *c:* Richshaunda; *ed:* (BA) Elem Ed, Park Coll 1974; *cr:* 6th Grade Head Teacher 1986-88, Assertive Discipline/Math/Rdng/Sci Head Teacher 1988-Blenheim Elem Sch; *office:* Blenheim Elem Sch 2411 E 70th Terr Kansas City MO 64132

MC CROHAN, ROSEANN STRANGE, Reading Teacher; *b:* Augusta, GA; *c:* Erin, Heather; *ed:* (BA) Span/Eng, Montclair St 1965; (MS) Rdng Spec, Monmouth Coll 1989; *cr:* Span/Eng Teacher Matawan Regional HS 1965-67; 1st Grade Teacher West Freehold Elem Sch 1967-68; Kndgtn Teacher West Freehold Sch/Erikson Sch 1969-71; 3rd Grade Teacher Erickson EleM Sch 1976-81; Gifted & Talented Rdng Teacher Dwight David Eisenhower 1981-; *ai:* Forensic, Debate, Track, Drama Coach; AAUW 1974-75; NJ Governors Teachers Grant; Grant Drama Dir Montclair St 1966; Forensic Exec Bd NJ Forensic League; *office:* Dwight D Eisenhower Sch Burlington Rd Freehold NJ 07728

MC CROSKY, CAROLIN SKYDEN, Kindergarten Teacher; *b:* Memphis, TN; *m:* Harvey A. Jr.; *c:* Alex, Bea; *ed:* (BAE) Elem Ed, Univ of MS 1967; Univ of MS; *cr:* 1st Grade Teacher Holly Springs Seperate Sch Dist 1967-68, Clear Creek Sch Dist 1968-69; 1st Grade Teacher 1973-79, Elem Remedial Rdng Teacher 1981-82, Kndgtn Teacher 1983- Marshall Acad; *ai:* MS Private Sch Assn (Dist Chm 1973-, Dist Art Chm); TX Teachers Assn 1968-69; MS Teachers Assn 1967-68; Marshall Cty Democratic Executive Parliamentarian 1988-; Holly Springs Garden Club Comm Pres 1987-88; Amer Heart Assn Marshall Cty Dist Chairperson 1990; Marshall Cty Public & Private Schls Teacher of Yr 1974; *office:* Marshall Acad 100 Academy Dr Holly Springs MS 38635

MC CUE, KERMIT CLARE, English Department Chairperson; *b:* Alexandria, NE; *c:* Lori L.; *ed:* (BA) Eng/His, 1959, (MA) Eng, 1963 Univ of NE; Doctor of Ed - Honorary, Doane Coll 1982; Univ of NE 1966-67; Rutgers Univ 1981; Univ of Chicago 1984; *cr:* Eng/Journalism Teacher/Dept Chm Barr Jr HS 1959-; *ai:* Journalism Adv; NE Cncl Teachers of Eng Pres 1976-77; Phi Delta Kappa 1965-; NE Jaycees Outstanding Educator Awd 1970; Omaha World Herald Distinguished Teacher Awd 1985; Amer Assn of Univ Women Teaching Awd 1988; First Presbyn Church Elder; Fellowship in Eng Univ of NE 1966-67, Rutgers Univ 1981, Univ of Chicago 1984; *home:* 1631 Coventry Ln Grand Island NE 68801

MC CUE, LEO FRANCIS, JR., Social Studies Dept Chair; *b:* Lowell, MA; *m:* Maureen Smyth; *c:* Kathleen, Kelly; *ed:* (BA) His, Lowell Univ 1969; (MA) US His, 1971, (PHD) US His, 1979 Boston Univ; Fellow The Well-Built Constitution Inst 1990; *cr:* Lecturer Northeastern Univ 1972, Boston Univ 1972-79; Visiting Instr Pine Manor Coll 1978-79; Teacher Cntrl Cath HS 1979-; *ai:* Cross Cntry Asst Coach; Yrbk Moderator; NCSS; F Lauriston Bullard Fellow 1970; Harry S Truman Fellow 1974; *office:* Central Catholic HS 300 Hampshire St Lawrence MA 01841

MC CULLAGH, NANCY JONES, Third Grade Teacher; *b:* Chicago, IL; *m:* Eugene P.; *c:* Cindy, Susan Populorum; *ed:* (BE) Elem Ed, Chicago Teachers Coll 1953; Gifted, Rdng, Sci, Govern St; *cr:* 1st/3rd Grade/Art Teacher Ffoulkes Elem 1953-55; 1st/3rd Grade Teacher Worth Elem 1955-60; 3rd Grade Teacher 1960-63, 3rd/4th Grade Teacher 1970- Dolton Dist 148; *ai:* IEA, NEA 1953-; S Sub Rdng Cncl 1970-; GSA Troup Leader 1974-; Methodist Church Sunday Sch Teacher 1970-75; *office:* Roosevelt Elem Sch 146th & La Salle Dolton IL 60419

MC CULLAH, L. DOLPHYNE, Librarian; *b:* Jay, OK; *m:* George E.; *c:* Vinnie R., Celya D.; *ed:* Voc Certificate OK St Univ Stillwater 1975; Lib Certificate NE OK St Univ Tahlequah 1989; *cr:* Bus Ed Teacher Fairland HS 1971-76; Voc Bus Ed Teacher Grove HS 1976-78; Bus Teacher/Lib Stratford HS 1979-85; Lang Art Teacher/Lib Sulphur Mid Sch 1985-; *ai:* Stu Cncl Chapter II Comm; 4-H; Acad Team; OK Ed Assn, NEA 1971-; Sulphur Ed Assn 1987; Delta Kappa Gamma Secy 1981; OK Lib Assn 1988-; Friend of Speech Awd; Honorary Chapter Farmer; SE Dist Outstanding Young Homemaker; SE Dist YHO VP; Delta Kappa Gamma Schlsp; FFA Mother of Yr; Fairland Teacher of Yr; Stratford Teacher of Yr; Garvin Cty Teacher of Yr; Outstanding Young Woman of Amer 1982; *home:* PO Box 552 Sulphur OK 73086

MC CULLAR, MARY M., Spanish Teacher; *b:* Memphis, TN; *m:* Edward; *ed:* (BS) Eng/Ed, Memphis St 1964; Univ of OK; Univ of Western KY; Memphis St; *cr:* Spanish Teacher Blytheville HS 1964-65; Tigrett Jr HS 1965-68; Bartlett HS 1968-; *ai:* Spon Spanish Club; Spon Sociedad Honoraria Hispanica; Faculty Rep Shelby Cty Ed Assn (SCEA); NEA/TEA/SCEA; TFLTA; Amer Assn of Teachers of Spanish & Portuguese; NDEA Inst Ap Wkshp Grant (Advanced Placement); *home:* 3086 Altruria Rd Bartlett TN 38134

MC CULLAR, ROGER MARK, History Teacher; *b:* Houston, TX; *m:* Mary Virginia Atkinson; *ed:* (BSED) His/Eng, Abilene Chrstn Univ 1985; *cr:* Grad Asst Abilene Chrstn Univ 1985; 10th Grade His Teacher Willowridge HS 1986-88; 11th Grade Amer His Clements HS 1988-89; 10th Grade His Teacher Kempner HS 1989-; *ai:* Phi Alpha Theta Pres 1984-85; Kappa Delta Pi Mem 1984-85; Grad Fellowship to Study His of 3rd Reich Abilene Chrstn Univ; *home:* 12707 Murphy Rd #42 Stafford TX 77477

MC CULLOCH, BECKY CLARY, 6th Grade Teacher; *b:* Gaffney, SC; *m:* Jere William; *c:* Mary C., Jere W. Jr.; *ed:* (BA) Music Ed, Limestone Coll 1972; (MED) Elem Ed, Univ of SC 1977; *cr:* 6th Garde Teacher Corinth Sch 1973-; *ai:* SC Basic Skills Writing Comm; Dist Coord of Young Writers Contest & Lt Governor Essay Contest; SC Ed Assn, NEA; First Baptist Church; Corinth Teacher of Yr 1988; *home:* 705 Union St Gaffney SC 29340

MC CULLOCH, CAROL STAMEY, Third Grade Teacher; *b:* Norfolk, VA; *m:* Larry W.; *c:* Larry M., Kathryn Mc Culloch Martin; *ed:* (BS) Elem Ed, Univ of TN Knoxville 1978; *cr:* Teacher Aide Tellico Plains Elem Sch 1970-74; 3rd Grade Teacher Madisonville Elem Sch 1978-; *ai:* Monroe Cty Teacher Assn (Newsletter Ed, Newsletter Comm) 1985-88, Awd of Distinction 1986-88; 1st Baptist Church Mission Friends Teacher 1988-; *office:* Madisonville Elem Sch Monroe Cir Madisonville TN 37354

MC CULLOCH-VISLISEL, SUSAN, English Dept Chair/ Teacher; *b:* San Francisco, CA; *m:* David John; *ed:* (BA) Eng, Univ of WA 1967; (MA) Ed, Stanford Univ 1968; Gifted Ed Endorsement; Louisville Writing Project; *cr:* Eng Teacher Lincoln Sch 1968-70; Adult Ed Teacher WIN Prgm 1970-71; Eng Teacher Woerner Mid Sch 1971-76, Brown Sch 1976-; *ai:* 9th Grade Adv & Spon; Chairperson Eng Dept; Chairperson Coalition of Essential Sch, Scheduling, Comp Comm; NCTE 1967-; Greater Louisville Eng Cncl; Spouse Abuse Center Volunteer; Leadership Ed 1985-86; Hambleton-Tapp Historical Society Grant; Univ of Louisville & Jefferson Cty Public Schls Cooperative Grant; Gheens Fnd Grant; KY Arts & Hum Grant; Mellon Scholar; *office:* The Brown Sch 546 S 1st St Louisville KY 40202

MC CULLOUGH, BARBARA ZINN, English Teacher; *b:* Parkersburg, WV; *c:* Megan; *ed:* Assoc Secretarial, Parkersburg Comm Coll 1974; (BS) Eng/Bus, Blenville St Coll 1980; Grad Work Oral Comm 1983-84; Dev Rdng, 1988; *cr:* Classroom Teacher Jackson Jr HS 1981-; *ai:* Dev Rdng Prgm Curr; Textbook Selection Comm; NEA Local Rep 1981-85; Jaycees 1987, Young Educator of Yr; WLELAC, Wood Cty Ed Assn 1981-; OH Valley Lit Group Exec Dir; Published Writing Strategies Wkshps; Artsbridge & OH Valley Lit Group Grants; Ed Lit Magazine Marietta Coll; Free Lance Writer; *office:* Jackson Jr HS 1601 34th St Vienna WV 26105

MC CULLOUGH, BUNDERLAI SOUTO, Spanish Teacher; *b:* Merida, Venezuela; *c:* Jessika, Kristin, Ryan; *ed:* (BA) Span, 1974, (MA) Span Lit, 1978 Univ of TN; Cert in Graphic Design 1979; Master Span Lit, Eng Lit Grad Level; *cr:* Teacher Memphis City Schls 1974-75; Interpreter/Translator Backman Laboratories Inc 1975-77; Teacher/Tutor Blount Cty Schls 1977-80; Teacher Knox Cty Schls 1985-; *ai:* Span Club & Frosh Class Spon; Advanced Placement & Guidance Comm; CORE Team Mem; Amer Assn Teachers of Span, TN Teaching Assn, NEA 1987-; Natl Teaching Assn; Published Thesis; Teacher of Month 1988, 1989, 1990; Teaching Assistantship 1973; *office:* Bearden HS 8352 Kingston Pike Knoxville TN 37919

MC CULLOUGH, CLAUDIA ELISSA, English Teacher; *b:* Altoona, PA; *ed:* (BS) Scndry Ed/Eng, PA St Univ 1976; Grad Stud PA St, Millersville & Wilkes Coll; *cr:* Eng Teacher Roosevelt Jr HS 1977-; *ai:* Sch Newspaper Adv; Faculty Rep to Parent Advisory Comm; PIAA Track & Field Official; Altoona Area Ed Assn Rep on Exec Comm; Coalition of Altoona Prof Mem; *office:* Roosevelt Jr HS 6th Ave & 15th St Altoona PA 16602

MC CULLOUGH, DEKOTA GRIER, Lang Art/Soc Stud Teacher; *b:* Charlotte, NC; *m:* John A. Jr.; *c:* Jonathan D., Jessica D.; *ed:* (BA) Intermediate Ed, NC Cntrl Univ 1981; Ed Admin, Univ of NC Charlotte; Extensive Trng in Effective Teaching, Teaching Rdng in Content area. Mid Grades Ed, Interdisciplinary Teaching, Co-Operative Learning, Teaching Writing; *cr:* Teacher/ Observer/Evaluator Various Schls 1985-86; Career Dev Asst Berryhill Elem, Derita Elem, Coulwood Mid Schls 1988-89; Teacher Spaugh Mid Sch 1981-; *ai:* Faculty Advisory Cncl, Career Dev & Staff Dev Comm Chairperson; Mem Charlotte Mecklenburg Rdng Curr Comm; Cheerleading Adv; Track N Fields Coach; Reward Activity of Month Spon; Team Leader 8th Grade Teachers; NEA, NC Assn of Educators 1981-; Natl Cncl of Negro Women 1989-; Natl Assn for the Advancement of Colored People 1989-; Friendship Baptist Church; West Side Coalition 1985-86; *office:* Spaugh Mid Sch 1901 Hubert Spaugh Ln Charlotte NC 28208

MC CULLOUGH, DIANE R., Social Studies Chair; *b:* Kansas City, MO; *m:* J Edward; *c:* James, Laura; *ed:* (BS) Elem Ed, Univ of MO Columbia 1960; (MA) Guidance/Counseling Univ of MO Kansas City 1968; *cr:* 1st-2nd Grade Teacher Wyman Elem Sch 1961-63; 2nd Grade Teacher Westview Elem Sch 1964-69; 1st-3rd/5th Grade Teacher Isley Elem Sch 1969-82; Soc Stud Teacher Lewis Mid Sch 1982-; *ai:* His Club Co-Spon; Soc Stud Dept Chm; MO Ed Assn; *home:* Rt 1 Excelsior Springs MO 64024

MC CULLOUGH, FANNIE ROGERS, Fourth Grade Teacher; *b:* Baltimore, MD; *m:* Melvin; *c:* Ronald Tatum, Michael, Matthew; *ed:* (BS) Elem Ed, 1979, (MS) Elem Ed, 1988 Coppin St Coll; *cr:* 4th Grade Teacher Patapsco Elem 1979-; *ai:* Tap Dance & Drama Teacher; Coord Black His Month; Home Teacher Tutor; NAACP 1980-; Church Choir Dir 1970-82; *office:* Patapsco Elem Sch 844 Roundview Rd Baltimore MD 21225

MC CULLOUGH, JOYCE ANN, English Teacher; *b:* Nashville, TN; *ed:* (BS) Eng, 1976, (MED) Curr, 1985 Mid TN St Univ; *cr:* Teacher Manchester Cntrl HS 1976-; *ai:* Coffee Cty Ed Assn, TN Ed Assn, NEA, NCTE; Cumberland Presbyn Women; *office:* Central HS 2001 Mc Arthur St Manchester TN 37355

MC CULLOUGH, NANCY KILLION, English Teacher; *b:* Terre Haute, IN; *m:* Jack; *c:* Jeffrey, Michael; *ed:* (BA) Eng, IN St Univ 1967; (MS) Ed/Eng, De Pauw Univ 1973; *cr:* Eng Teacher Van Buren HS 1967-84, N Clay Jr HS 1984-; *ai:* Delta Kappa Gamma, Beta Psi; *office:* N Clay Jr HS RR 13 Box 48 Brazil IN 47834

MC CULLOUGH, SOPHIA AGORIS, Kindergarten Teacher; *b:* Canonsburg, PA; *m:* Clarence Jr.; *c:* Kathy M. Mc Cullough-Testa, Shawn H.; *ed:* (BS) Elem Ed, CA St Teachers Coll 1959; Cert, Univ of Pittsburgh; *cr:* 2nd Grade Teacher Canon-Mc Millan Sch Dist 1959-60; 1st Grade Teacher 1960-85, Kndgtn Teacher 1985- Chartiers-Houston Sch Dist; *ai:* Various Educl Comms Relating tO Curr Dev; NEA, PA St Ed Assn, Chartiers-Houston Ed Assn 1959-; Beta Zeta Chapter, Delta Kappa Gamma Society Intnl 1982-; Order of Eastern Star Chartier Chapter #97 1961- Worthy Matron 1969-70; Order of the White Shrine Monongahela Valley Shrine #9 1964-.

MC CURDY, CAROLYN SMITH, Mathematics Teacher; *b:* Atlanta, GA; *m:* John Burford Jr.; *c:* Celina Mc Curdy Garrett, Rhonda Mc Curdy Vanderford, Carl B., Tanya L.; *ed:* (BA) Scndry Math, Agnes Scott Coll 1960; (MA) Scndry Math, GA St Univ 1985; *cr:* Math Teacher Aberdeen Jr/Sr HS 1957-58, Avondale HS 1961-62, Columbia HS 1979-81, Stone Mountain HS 1982-84, Stone Mountain Jr HS 1985-.

MC CURRY, CHERYL FOSTER, Health & Physical Ed Teacher; *b:* Asheville, NC; *c:* Weston C.; *ed:* (BS) Health/Phys Ed, Limestone Coll 1977; *cr:* Teacher/Inter Hill Street Mid 1979-80; Teacher Candler Elem Sch 1980-86, Enka Mid Sch 1986-; *ai:* Team Leader; Sftbl Coach; Supervision Comm; Mentor Teacher; NCAE 1979-; NCHPERD 1981-; Pole Creek Baptist Church Youth Comm 1989-; *office:* Enka Mid Sch 390 Asbury Rd Candler NC 28715

MC CURTAIN, RITA JANE, Teacher; *b:* Pauls Valley, OK; *m:* James M. Jr.; *c:* Amber; *ed:* (BS) Ed/Eng, Univ of OK 1980; Cntrl St Univ; Higher Ed, Univ of OK 1991; *cr:* Advanced Placement Eng Teacher/Coord Western Heights HS 1980-; *ai:* Mock Trial Team Coach; Leadership Educl Apprenticeship Prgm Spon & Instr; OK Cncl of Eng Teachers; NEA, OEA; PTA; Western Heights HS Teacher of Year 1985; Advanced Placement Eng Exam Reader; Carnegie/Mellon Advanced Placement Eng Grant 1989; *office:* Western Heights HS 8201 SW 44th Oklahoma City OK 73179

MC CUTCHEON, CONSTANCE THOMAS, Social Studies Teacher; *b:* Oak Hill, WV; *m:* Harold R;; *ed:* (BA) His/Speech, Marshall Univ 1964; *cr:* Teacher East Dover Sch 1964-67; Intermediate East 1967-; *ai:* St of NJ Governors Teacher Recognition Prgm; Teacher of Yr 1987-88 Toms River Intermediate East; *office:* Toms River Intermediate East Hooper Ave Toms River NJ 08753

MC CUTCHEON, EMOGENE S. SMALL, Retired Science Teacher/Chair; *b:* Wiona, WV; *m:* Harry D.; *c:* Carl E., Harry L.; *ed:* (BS) Sociology, Cumberland Coll 1971; (MS) Sch Soc Work, E KY Univ 1977; Scndry Sci, Morehead Univ 1977; *cr:* Teacher Powell Cty HS 1971-89; *ai:* NABT 1977-89; NEA, KY Ed Assn 1971-89; Powell Cty Teachers Assn (Pres 1973-74) 1978-79; Powell Cty HS Teacher of Yr 1983-84; Natl Assn of Sci Teachers Grant; *home:* 237 Maple St Stanton KY 40380

MC CUTCHEON, JOIE C., Third Grade Teacher; *b:* Pittsburgh, PA; *m:* William L.; *c:* Sarah, Russell, Mark, David, John, Michael; *ed:* (BA) Elem Ed, 1970, (MA) Rdng, 1980 Kent St Univ; *cr:* 1st Grade Teacher Westgate Elem 1960-62; 4th Grade Teacher 1965-66, 5th Grade Teacher 1969-70, 2nd Grade Teacher 1970-74, 3rd Grade Teacher 1974- Mac Donald Elem; *ai:* Delta Kappa Gamma 1975-; *home:* 705 Riverside Ave Wellsville OH 43968

MC DANIEL, BARBARA MARIE, 3rd Grade Teacher; *b:* Wagoner, OK; *m:* William E.; *c:* Jayna, Dana; *ed:* (BS) Elem Ed - Summa Cum Laude, Urbana Coll 1979; *cr:* Elem Ed Teacher Triad Schls 1979-; *ai:* Triad Elem Volunteer Work; Lady Liberty Fund Raiser Dir 1983; Tribes Prgm 1984; Taught Substance Abuse Course 1985; Triad Ed Assn; Delta Kappa Gamma Mem 1984-86; North Lewisburg Meth Church Sunday Sch Teacher; Dixie Brand Hatch Schlsp 1979; Martha Holden Jennings Scholar 1989-; Urbana Univ Academic Society Mem; Deans List 1978, 1979; Lady Liberty Fund Raiser Dir 1983;African Relief Auction 1985; Urbana Red Cross Citation 1985; *home:* Box 133 North Lewisburg OH 43060

MC DANIEL, BRENDA SEBREN, 5th/6th Grade Lang Art Teacher; *b:* Malvern, AR; *m:* Fred W.; *c:* David; *ed:* (BSE) Elem Ed/Eng, 1967, (MSE) Rdng/Elem Ed, 1980 Henderson St Univ; Teachers Expectations Stu Achievement, Cooperative Learning, Plan for Effective Teaching, Tactics for Thinking; *cr:* 2nd/5th Grade Teacher Prattsville Public Schls 1967-69; 6th Grade Teacher Ouachita Public Schls 1969-71, Malvern Public Schls 1976-79; 5th/6th Grade Teacher/Chapter I Coord Ouachita Public Schls 1979-; *ai:* Local Sch Dist Personnel Policy Comm Chairperson; Terrific, Outstanding, Polite Stus Spon; AR Ed Assn Local Pres 1980-; Spec Ed Stud Schlsp AR St PTA; Innovative Rdng Incentive Prgm AR Power & Light Company Grant; *home:* Rt 1 Box 75 Donaldson AR 71941

MC DANIEL, CAROLYN MARIE PETERSON, English Teacher; *b:* Nevada City, NV; *m:* William Charles; *c:* James, John, Michael, Robert; *ed:* (AA) Liberal Arts, Sacramento Sierra Jr Coll 1971; (BA) Eng, CSU 1973; Graduate Work CSUS-Ed; *cr:* Substitute Teacher Grass Valley Sch 1975-77; Reader for Eng Dept 1974-84; Long-Term Substitute 1984-85; Eng Teacher 1985- NV Union HS; *ai:* Goldpan Adv; CSF; Frosh Class Adv; Jeanc 1987-; NUHSTA 1985-; Gold Cntry Soccer League Sec/Registrar 1984-; Grass Valley Little League Womens Aux Pres 1986-; Rich Marin Awd Little Leag Service Club; Active Club; Active Youth Service Awd; Mem Comm Writing Journalism; *home:* 104 Cathy Dr Grass Valley CA 95949

MC DANIEL, CYNTHIA LEMLEY, 6th Grade Soc Stud Teacher; *b:* Greenville, AL; *m:* Tommy; *c:* Beth; *ed:* (BS) Elem Ed, Samford Univ 1969; Jacksonville St Univ Grad Stu; *cr:* 4th/5th Grade Teacher Gardendale Elem 1969-72; 5th Grade Math Teacher Rocky Ridge Elem 1972-75; 3rd Grade Teacher Saks Elem 1976-78; 6th Grade Soc Stud Teacher Saks Mid 1979-; *ai:* AL St Soc Stud Fair; Sch Rep; Judge Cty Dist, & St Levels; NEA, AEA 1969-; CCEA 1975-.

MC DANIEL, DENNIS MICHAEL, Assistant to Superintendent; *b:* Grand Junction, CO; *m:* Mary Lou; *c:* Charles, Sean, Ann Geiser; *ed:* (BA) His, Regis Coll 1960; (MA) Elem Ed, Univ of CO 1966; *cr:* Teacher 1960-67, Prin 1968-89 Western Hills Elem; Asst to Supt Dist #1 Adams Cty 1990; *office:* Sch Dist #1 Adams Cty 591 E 80th Denver CO 80229

MC DANIEL, EVELYN HUTTON, 7th Grade Soc Stud Teacher; *b:* Bristol, VA; *m:* Robert Roland; *c:* Elaine Mc Daniel Ryder, Ellen Mc Daniel Staton; *ed:* (BA) Ed/Soc Stud, VA Intermont Coll 1975; *cr:* Sch Attendance Office 1964-75, Classroom Teacher 1975- VA Jr HS; *ai:* Stu Cooperative Assn Spon; East End Chrstn Church (Organist 1950-, Bible Sch Teacher 1950-); Bristol Historical Assn Charter Mem; *home:* 504 Euclid Ave Bristol VA 24201

MC DANIEL, GEORGIA COCKERHAM, 5th Grade Teacher; *b:* Monroe City, IN; *m:* Stanley Keith Sr.; *c:* Stanley K. Jr., Kimberly A. Mc Daniel Maples; *ed:* (BA) Elem Ed, 1962, (BA) Home Ec, 1976 Humboldt St Univ; (MA) Cmptrs in Ed, Lesley Coll 1988; *cr:* Teacher Cutten-Jacoby Creek Elem 1963-69, Knox Cty Elem Sch 1977-; *ai:* TEA, NEA; Jr League of Knoxville Cmptr-Video Project Grant 1988-89; *office:* Gap Creek Elem Sch 1920 Kimberlin Hts Rd Knoxville TN 37920

MC DANIEL, JANET BARBER, 8th Grade Science Teacher; *b:* Fort Carson, CO; *m:* Robert Miller III; *c:* Robbie; *ed:* (BS) Bio/ Scndry Ed, Gardner Webb Coll 1982; Grad Stud Appalachian St Univ; *cr:* Teacher W Correctional Youth Inst 1982-84, Hildebran Jr HS 1984-87, E Burke Jr HS 1987-; *ai:* Yrbk Spon; Coach for Sci Olympiad Team; Steering Comm for S Assn Evaluation; Media & Cmptr Adv Comm; Faculty Handbook Comm; NCAE, NEA 1983-88; NC Sci Teachers Assn, NSTA 1983-; Foothills Deaf Lioness Club Treas 1985-89, Lioness of Yr 1987; Interpreter for the Hearing Impaired, First Baptist Church Morganton; Teacher of Yr 1985-86; Host Comm Co Chairperson Regional Sci Olympiad 1987-; PICA Awd Jostens Yrbk 1987, 1989, 1990; *office:* East Burke Jr HS Miller Bridge Rd PO Box 1150 Icard NC 28666

MC DANIEL, JOANN PETTIGREW, Principal; *b:* Nettleton, MS; *m:* Eugene; *c:* Phillip, Joanna; *ed:* (BS) Elem Ed, 1959, (MA) Admin/Elem Ed, 1972 MS St Univ; *cr:* Teacher Verona Elem & Nettleton Elem 1957-69; Prin Nettleton Primary 1969-72; Elem Supvr Lee Cty Sch 1972-74; Teacher Nettleton Elem 1974-89; Prin Nettleton Primary 1989-; *ai:* Delta Kappa Gamma Mem; *home:* PO Drawer N Nettleton MS 38858

MC DANIEL, JOYCE NOLLMANN, Spanish Teacher; *b:* Deadwood, SD; *m:* James Lee; *c:* Adam; *ed:* (BA) Span/Latin Amer Studs, SD St Univ 1973; Art; *cr:* Span Teacher Brookings HS 1973-; *ai:* Span Club Adv; Span Travellers Trip Cnslr; SDEA, NEA, BEA; Jobs Daughters 1965-69, Honored Queen 1969; PEO; Wesleyan Church Mem; Whos Who Young Career Woman; *office:* Brookings HS 530 Elm Ave Brookings SD 57006

MC DANIEL, JUDITH E., Office Technology/Bus Instr; *b:* Powers Lake, ND; *c:* Lance, Layne; *ed:* (BS) Bus Ed, Minot St Coll 1965; Masters Prgm Moorhead St Univ; *cr:* Bus Ed/Ger Teacher Max Public Sch 1965-66, Kenmare Public Sch 1966-68; Office Technology Teacher 1988, Bus Teacher 1974- ND St Coll of Sci; *ai:* ND St Coll of Sci Flextime Ed Microcomputer Course Developer, Single Parent/Homemaker & Prof Dev Inst Advisory Bd, Wrestling Chrldr Adv, Prof Staff Mem Articulation Meetings & Numerous Campus Comm; Prof Secys Intnl (VP 1988-89) 1983-; Bethel Luth Church; Developed & Presented Numerous Bus Seminars; Excl Teaching Awd for Bus Division 1988-89, 1989-; Jaycee Outstanding Young Educator Kenmare 1967-68; *office:* ND St Coll of Sci Main #210 Wahpeton ND 58075

MC DANIEL, RANDY GLENN, Biology Teacher; *b:* Joplin, MO; *m:* Kimberly Jean Bekebrock; *c:* Victoria A.; *ed:* (BS) Bio, 1983, (MS) Ed Admin, 1990 Pittsburg St Univ; Ed Admin Pittsburg St Univ; Drug & Alcohol Crisis Intervention Wkshp; *cr:* Bio Teacher East Cntrl HS 1984-85, Galena HS 1985-, Labette Comm Coll 1986-; *ai:* Var Boys Bsktbl, Var Boys & Girls Track Coach; Frosh Class Spon; Curr, Evaluation Tool, Attendance Comm; AAU Summer Track Volunteer Head Coach 1986-89; Nom USD 499 Golden Chalk Awd Teacher of Yr; Pittsburg St Univ Deans List; *home:* Box 421 Galena KS 66739

MC DANIEL, RHONDA GWEN, VIP English/Math Teacher; *b:* Coalmont, TN; *ed:* (AA) Martin Meth Coll 1984; (BS) Eng Ed, TN Wesleyan Coll 1986; *cr:* 6th-8th Grade Phys Ed/Eng Teacher North Elem 1986-89; VIP Eng/Math Teacher Grundy Cty HS 1990; *ai:* Elem Boys & Girls Bsktbl & HS Sftbl Coach; Elem Newspaper, Just Say No, 8th Grade Spon; Grundy Cty Ed Assn Faculty Rep 1986-89; TN Ed Assn, NEA 1986-; Shoot-Out for Easter Seals Coord 1986-89; Jump Rope for Heart Amer Heart Assn Coord 1986-89; *home:* PO Box 1381 Tracy City TN 37387

MC DANIEL, TIM V., Language Arts Teacher; *b:* Dodge City, KS; *m:* Julia L. Thorpe; *c:* Melora, Sean, Marisa, Melaney, Monique; *ed:* (BS) Elem Ed, St Mary of Plains 1967; (MA) Elem Ed, KS St Univ 1977; Certified Gifted Ed Elem; *cr:* 5th/6th Grade

Teacher Sacred Heart 1967-69; 7th/8th Grade Soc Stud Teacher Jetmore Jr HS 1969-72; Remedial Math/Rdng Teacher Montezuma Grade Sch 1973-75; 5th-8th Grade Lang Art Teacher Spearville Unified Sch Dist 381 1976-; *ai:* 7th/8th Grade Pep Club Spon & Track; Curr Core Supt Cncl; KS Ed Assn (Pres, VP); *home:* Box 163 Spearville KS 67876

MC DANIEL, WILLIAM MATTHEW, Physical Ed/Health Teacher; *b:* Saint Louis, MO; *m:* Susan D. Lee; *c:* Thomas, Sarah; *ed:* (BS) Phys Ed, Southeast MO St Univ 1978; (MS) Admin & Supervision Ed, Southern IL Univ 1982; *cr:* Phys Ed Teacher Crawford County R-II 1978-79, Thomas Elem Sch 1979-84, Lemasters Elem Sch 1984-89; *ai:* Intramurals; MSTA 1978-82; AAHPER 1975-83; *office:* Lemasters Elem Sch 1826 Crown Point Dr Saint Louis MO 63136

MC DERMOTT, CAROL KECK, Math Teacher/Department Chair; *b:* St Louis, MO; *m:* Joseph G.; *c:* Michele Stone, Karen Bennett, John, Beverly, Joe, Patrick; *ed:* (BBA) Merchandising/Management, SMU 1964; Completed Cert Math, Ed, N TX St Univ Grad Sch 1983-85; *cr:* Math/Sci Teacher Good Shepherd Sch 1974-77; Math/Cmptr/Sci Teacher 1980-, Dept Head/Math/Cmptr Teacher 1984- St Patrick Sch; *ai:* Math Textbook Adoption Comm; Math & Cmptr Chm; Math Tutor; Math Contests Coach; GSA (Leader 1983-83, Religious Awd Chm 1980-89), St Anne Awd 1984; Diocese of Dallas Service Awd 1990.

MC DERMOTT, TARA ZETLER, 4th Grade Teacher; *b:* Mc Keesport, PA; *m:* John Allen; *ed:* (BS) Elem Ed, CA Univ of PA 1986; *cr:* 7th Grade Teacher 1986-88, 4th Grade Teacher 1988- Mc Keesport Cntrl Cath; *ai:* Coach JV & Varsity Chrldrs; *home:* 5201 Walnut St Mc Keesport PA 15132

MC DONALD, ANNE, Resource Teacher; *b:* Scranton, PA; *m:* John; *c:* Alice, John, Michael; *ed:* (BS) Elem Ed, GA Court Coll 1959; Grad Stud George Mason Univ, VPI, Univ VA; *cr:* Classroom Teacher Orange Hunt Elem 1978-88; Resource Teacher Area IV Office 1988-; *ai:* Greater WA Rdng Cncl; Local Ed Assn, St Ed Assn, NEA Mem.

MC DONALD, BARBARA DAVIDSON, Home Economics Dept Chair; *b:* Emporia, KS; *m:* David M.; *c:* Lisa Novak, Jill; *ed:* (BS) Home Ec, Emporia St Univ 1969; (MS) Adult/Voc Ed, KS St Univ 1980; *cr:* Teacher Turner Unified Sch Dist 202 1969-72, Johnson Cty Comm Coll 1972-76; Teacher/Dept Chairperson Turner Unified Sch Dist 202 1976-; *ai:* Turner Unified Sch Dist Human Sexuality & AIDS Ed Comm Chairperson; Spon KS Assn for Youth; Amer Home Ec Assn, Greater KS City Home Ec Assn, NEA; KS St Dept of Ed Trainer for Human Sexuality & AIDS Ed; *office:* Turner Unified Sch Dist 1312 S 55th St Kansas City KS 66106

MC DONALD, BARBARA LOUISE, 4th Grade Teacher; *b:* York, PA; *m:* Terry R.; *c:* Bradley, Lisa; *ed:* (BS) Elem Ed, Indiana Univ of PA 1964; Working Towards Cert; *cr:* 3rd Grade Teacher Trimmer Elem Sch 1964-68; Remedial Math Teacher Loucks Elem Sch 1977-80; 4th Grade Teacher Trimmer Elem Sch 1980-; *ai:* NEA, PSEA, W York Ed Assn 1964-68, 1980-.

MC DONALD, CORA EDNA (POE), 8th Grade Sci Teacher/Dept Chm; *b:* Pecos, TX; *m:* Herschel C. Jr.; *c:* Scott H., H. C. III, Kelli C.; *ed:* (BS) Bio, Sul Ross Univ 1978; Composit Sci 1979; *cr:* Sci Teacher Crockett Jr HS 1979-85; Sci Teacher/7th Grade Girls Coach 1980-84; Sci Teacher/Building Chariperson for Sci Pecos 1986-; *ai:* UIL Sci Spon Adv & Coach; NSTA Mem 1981-89; Sci Teachers Assn of TX Mem 1987-89; Lady Elks Club 1984-89; Nominee for Presidential Awd for Sci Teachers 1988-89; *home:* Rt 1 Box 41 Balmorhea TX 79718

MCDONALD, DONNA J. S., Teacher of Human Ecology; *b:* Hackensack, NJ; *m:* William M.; *c:* Dane B., Dorian T.; *ed:* (BS) Home Ec, Marywood Coll 1975; *cr:* Teacher of Human Ecology Belvider HS 1975-; *ai:* Sr Class Adv; Belvidere Ed Assn Soc Comm; Belvidere Ed Assn; Warren Cty Ed Assn; NJ Ed Assn; NEA: Voc Ed Assn 1975; Forks Twsp PTA 1987-; *office:* Belvidere H S Oxford St Belvidere NJ 07823

MC DONALD, JOHN WILLIAM, Mathematics Teacher; *b:* Bath, NY; *m:* Cynthia Richards; *c:* Jessica; *ed:* (BA) Math - Magna Cum Laude, Lycoming Coll 1972; *cr:* Math Teacher 1972-86, Asst to Prin 1986-87, Math Teacher 1987- Hollidaysburg Jr HS; *ai:* Head Wrestling & Bsbl Coach Hollidaysburg Sr HS; Stu Asst Prgm Leader; NEA, PSEA, NCTM 1972-; PA Stu Asst Prgm 1990; *office:* Hollidaysburg Jr HS 501 Hewitt St Hollidaysburg PA 16648

MC DONALD, JUDITH ANN, Social Studies Teacher; *b:* Ottumwa, IA; *ed:* (BA) Soc Sci, William Penn Coll 1974; (MS) Curr Instruction, Northern IL Univ 1982; Ed Admin Cert Scndry Level; *cr:* CEDA Tutor Lincoln Mid Sch 1975-76; Soc Sci Teacher Eisenhower Jr HS 1976-; *ai:* Newspaper Spon; Soc Stud Task Force; Variety Show Co-Dir; PTA Teacher Rep; Mid Sch Comm; PTA Newsletter Chairperson; SEA Building Rep; SEA, IEA, NEA; *office:* Eisenhower Jr H S 800 Hassell Rd Hoffman Estates IL 60195

MC DONALD, JUDITH IWEN, Religion Teacher; *b:* Salem, OR; *m:* Ron; *c:* Alison; *ed:* (BA) Fr, Marylhurst Coll 1970, 1975; (MA) Theology, St Marys Coll 1981; Admin & Cmptr Courses; Post Grad Work Fr & Theology; *cr:* Foreign Lang/Religion Teacher/Dept Head St Marys Acad 1970-77; Teacher/Admin Sacred Heart Acad 1977-81; Teacher/Pastoral Minister Kennedy HS 1981-; *ai:* Stu Retreats All Sch Liturgies; ASB Pres Summer Grad Theology Prgm St Marys Coll 1979; My Class was Voted Favorite Sr Class 1988; *office:* Kennedy HS 140 S 140th Seattle WA 98168

MC DONALD, MARY JUNE HENNESSEY, Kindergarten Teacher; *b:* Iowa City, IA; *m:* James E.; *c:* Jamie, Sean, Brigid Mc Donald Gifford; *ed:* (BA) Elem Ed, Briar Cliff Coll 1961; *cr:* Kndgtn/1st Grade Teacher Monti Consolidated 1957-59; 1st Grade Teacher Howard Kennedy 1961-63; Kndgtn Teacher Johnston Elem 1972-; *ai:* NEA, IA St Ed Assn, Maquoketa Valley Ed Assn; St Patricks Church & DE Cty Porkettes; *home:* R R 2 Box 13 Delhi IA 52223

MC DONALD, NORMA SUMMERLIN, Math Teacher & Dept Chairman; *b:* Kinston, NC; *m:* Irvin Ray; *c:* I. Ray Jr., William M.; *ed:* (BS) Primary Ed, 1962, (MA) Elem Ed, 1972, Cert Admin/Supervision, 1990 E Carolina Univ; *cr:* Primary Teacher Brogden Sch 1962-65; Math Teacher Mt Olive Jr HS 1974-; *ai:* Beta Club Spon; Delta Kappa Gamma Society Chairperson of Schlsps 1989-; NEA, NC Assn of Educators, NC Cncl of Math Teachers; Chamber of Commerce Comm, Mental Health, Red Cross Bd of Dirs; Schlsp to Summer Inst in Sci & Math at Univ of NC; Schlsp from Wayne Cty Chambers Industrial Relations; Teacher of Yr; Young Educator of Yr; *office:* Mount Olive Jr HS Wooten St Mount Olive NC 28365

MC DONALD, SHIRLEY BROGAN, Third Grade Teacher; *b:* Gibbon, NE; *c:* James, Sherri Spale, Donald; *ed:* (BS) Elem Ed, Concordia Coll 1977; *cr:* 4th-8th Grade Teacher Bruno Sch 1950-51; 1st/2nd Grade Teacher Rural Sch 1954-55; 4th-8th Grade Teacher Garrison Sch 1959-69; 3rd Grade Teacher Bellwood Public Sch 1961-; *ai:* NE St Ed Assn, NEA 1951-; Butler Cty Ed Assn (Pres 1988-89) 1961-; Bellwood Faculty Assn (Secy 1982-88) 1982-; KOLN Spec Teacher Awd 1989.

MC DONNELL, SUE S., Substitute Teacher; *b:* Cody, WY; *m:* Tom G.; *ed:* (AA) Elem Ed/Spec Ed, Northwest Comm Coll 1974; (BA) Elem Ed, MT St Univ 1984; Cmptr in Ed, Math Their Way, Advanced Art Courses, Lee Cantors Discipline, Red Alert; *cr:* Mid Sch Eng/Math/Rdng/1st-8th Grade Art/5th/6th Grade Soc Stud Teacher Willow Creek Sch 1984-88; *ai:* Class Spon; Drama Dir; Childrens Crusade for Kids, Red Alert Wkshps, Establishing Lee Cantors Assertive Discipline; *home:* 532 Vista Dr Castle Rock CO 80104

MC DONOUGH, MARY T., First Grade Teacher; *b:* Holyoke, MA; *ed:* (BA) Sociology, Coll Our Lady of Elms 1960; Grad Stud Westfield St Coll 1990; *cr:* 1st Grade Teacher Morgan Sch 1960-65, Joseph Metcalf Sch 1965-; *ai:* Holyoke Teachers Assn, MA Teachers Assn, Natl Teachers Assn 1960-; Birthright 1981-; *home:* 24 Lindbergh Ave Holyoke MA 01040

MC DONOUGH, ROBERT R, Jr HS Soc Stud/Phys Ed Teacher; *b:* Turlock, CA; *m:* Beth; *ed:* (BA) His, CA St Univ Stanislows 1972; *cr:* Jr HS Teacher Chatom Sch 1973-; *ai:* Coach-Boys Ftbl/Soccer/Bsktbl/Track; Stu Cncl Adv; Union Negotiator; CA Teachers Assn 1973-; NEA 1973-; Parent Teachers Club 1973-; *office:* Chatom Union Elem Sch 7201 Clayton Ave Turlock CA 95380

MC DONOUGH, SUSAN COTTER, English Teacher; *b:* Winchester, MA; *m:* Mark B.; *ed:* (BA) Eng, 1971, (MA) Eng, 1981 Salem St Coll; Grad Stud; *cr:* Eng Teacher Nashua Public Schls 1971-73, Wakefield HS 1976-; *ai:* Co-Spon Soc Awareness & Responsibility Club; Wakefield HS Basic Stud Prgm Coord; Writing Contest Judge; Regional Cncl Teachers of Eng 1990; Wakefield Teachers Assn Prof Rights & Responsibilities 1988-89; NEA; MA Teachers Assn 1976-; Big Sister Assn of Greater Boston 1986-; Greenpeace 1989-; Por Cristo 1987-; Founding Mem Honorary Fellows of John F Kennedy Lib; *office:* Wakefield HS 60 Farm St Wakefield MA 01880

MC DOUGALD, LA VERNE LOMAX, 10th Grade Counselor; *b:* Gastonia, NC; *m:* Wallace Jr.; *c:* Wesley H., Vincent E., Lynn A. Jerrod O.; *ed:* (BS) Bus Ed, Livingston Coll 1959; (MA) Cnslr Ed, NC Cntrl Univ 1977; Certificate Career Ed, NC Dept of Public Instruction 1972; *cr:* Secy Leonard Trng Sch 1959-64; Teacher I Ellis Johnson HS 1965-69, Washington Park Elem Sch 1970-72; Cnslr/Coord Washington Park Elem Sch 1973-83; *ai:* Home Ec Dept Advisory Comm; Southern Assn Accreditation Steering Comm; Sch Based Comm Exceptional Children; NC Cnslrs Assn, NC Educators Assn; *office:* Scotland HS 1000 W Church St Laurinburg NC 28352

MC DOUGALL, NANCY BROWN, Elementary Counselor; *b:* San Antonio, TX; *m:* Michael H.; *c:* Jeff, Kenneth, Matthew; *ed:* (BA) Bio, 1971; (MED) Cnslng, 1976 Trinity Univ; *cr:* Mid Sch Teacher Kingsville ISD Memorial Jr HS 1971-72; HS Teacher Center Sch/Alternative Sch 1972-75; Mid HS Teacher Madison HS/Wood Mid 1976-80; Elem Cnslr Dellview Elem 1984-86; Windcrest Elem 1987-88; Redland Oaks Elem 1989-; *ai:* South TX Assn for Guidance Cnslng; TX Assn for Cnslng & Dev; United Methodist Women Pres 1984-86; *office:* Redland Oaks Elem Sch 16650 Redland Rd San Antonio TX 78247

MC DOUNOUGH, JOSEPH PETER, Mathematics Teacher; *b:* Brooklyn, NY; *m:* Maryellen Dickinson; *c:* Thomas, Meave; *ed:* (BS) Math, Manhattan Coll 1968; (MA) Scndry Ed, Hofstra Univ 1974; Grad Stud St Johns, CCNY, C W Post, SUNY Stony Brook, Manhattan Coll; *cr:* HS Teacher Peace Corps Volunteer 1968-71; Math Teacher Elmond Memorial HS 1971-; *ai:* Jr Math Team Coach; Talented & Gifted Mentor; Nassau Bd of Womens Ofcls Bsktbl Ofcl 1978-; Nassau Cty Math Teacher, Finalist Teacher of Yr 1988-89; Natl Sci Fnd Grant 1979; *office:* Elmont Memorial HS 555 Ridge Rd Elmont NY 11003

MC DOWELL, DAVID SAMUEL, Life Science Teacher; *b:* Piqua, OH; *m:* Kimberly; *c:* Tiffany E.; *ed:* (BS) Bio, Rio Grande Univ 1979; (MS) Speech Comm, WV Univ 1984; Mid Sch Cert; Group Counseling Trng; Educl Wkshps; *cr:* Bio/General Sci Teacher Ridgedale HS 1979-80; Life Sci Teacher Pleasants Cty Mid Sch 1980-; *ai:* 5th-8th Grade Bsktbl Coach; Photography Club, Bio Club, Prom, Plant Comm Adv; Head Yrbk Photography; Cty Sci Fair Coord; Textbook Comm Chm; Sch Faculty, Sunshine, Activity, Time-Out Comms; Counseling Group Leader; PCEA Building Rep 1981-85; NEA 1979-; NSTA 1981-; Christ Luth Church Cncl Pres 1983-84; Neighborhood Watch Captain 1981-84; March of Dimes Organizer Chm 1982; PCEA Building Rep; Chairperson for Sch Textbooks Comms; *office:* Pleasants Cty Mid Sch Box 469 Belmont WV 26134

MC DOWELL, EMILY, Choir Director; *b:* Cynthiana, KY; *ed:* (BA) Music Ed, OH St Univ 1971; Advanced Music Ed, Bus Admin; *cr:* Choir Dir Northern Tioga Sch Dist 1973-80; Elem Music Teacher Laredo Ind Sch Dist 1980-81, 1984-87; Choir Dir J W Nixon HS 1988-; *ai:* Extracurricular Choral Act Adv; Music Educators Natl Conference 1973-80; TX Music Educators Assn 1985-; *office:* J W Nixon HS 2000 Plum St Laredo TX 78043

MC DOWELL, JUDITH ANN, Choral Music Teacher; *b:* Huntington, WV; *m:* William A.; *c:* Susan H. Barker; *ed:* (BA) Music Ed, 1970, (MA) Ed Admin, 1985 Marshall Univ; Practitioner Cert Neuro-Linguistic Programming-Zermatt Switzerland; Master Cert Neuro-Linguistic Programming, Tampa FL; *cr:* Elem Music Teacher Greenup Cty Schls 1970-71; 1st Grade Teacher Pocohontas Cty Schls 1971-72; Music Teacher Mason Cty Schls 1972-80, Cabell Cty Schls 1980-; Choral Music Dir Huntington East HS 1990; *ai:* Mem Cabell Cty Music Curr Comm 1986-89; Chm Cabell Cty HS All Cty Music Festival 1986-89; Chm Music Comm Huntington East HS N Cntrl Evaluation; Spon Huntington East HS Lads & Lassies Show Choir; ASCD 1990; Music Educators Natl Conference 1986; Natl Assn of Neuro-Linguistic Programming 1990; Bethesda Meth Church Choir Dir 1983-86; Trinity Episcopal Church Mem 1970-; Recipient WV Arts & Hum Cncl Mini Grant 1989-; Guest Organist St Johns Episcopal Church Zermatt Switzerland; Co-Founder, Co-Dir Appalachian Center for Trng & Therapeutic Services, Mid-Atlantic Center of Neuro-Linguistic Programming; *office:* Huntington East HS 2850 5th Ave Huntington WV 25702

MC DOWELL, LINDA GUYETTE, Math Teacher; *b:* Ashland, KY; *m:* Ricky L.; *ed:* (BS) Math, 1978, (MA) Scndry Ed, 1982 Morehead St Univ; Scndry Ed; *cr:* Math Teacher Summit Jr HS 1978-; *ai:* Adv Summit Chapter of Natl Jr Beta Club; NEA 1978-; KEA 1978-; Phi Beta Kappa *office:* Summit Jr H S 1226 Summit Rd Ashland KY 41101

MC DOWELL, ROSIA HALL, 5th-6th Grade Reading Teacher; *m:* Roosevelt James; *ed:* (BS) Elem Ed, 1972, (MS) Elem Ed, 1980 AL St Univ; Wkshp Inservice Trng Elem Ed; *cr:* Elem Ed Teacher Lowndes Cty 1972-; *ai:* Jr Beta Club Spon; Textbook Comm, Honors Day, Courtesy Comm Chairperson; AL Ed Assn, NEA 1972-; Zeta Phi Beta (Asst Secy 1986-87, Secy 1988-); *office:* Lowndes County Mid Sch P O Box Drawer P Fort Deposit AL 36032

MC DOWELL, SALLY FITZGERALD, Social Studies Teacher; *b:* Oneida, NY; *m:* Walter Jr.; *c:* Matthew, Courtney; *ed:* (BA) His, 1967, (MA) Soc Stud, 1968 SUNY Albany; Teaching Advanced Placement Amer His, Manhattan Coll 1989; Drug & Alcohol Counseling Courses, Russell Sage 1988-89; *cr:* Soc Stud Teacher Queensbury HS 1984-; *ai:* Sr Class Adv; Cheerleading Coach; Crisis Response Comm; Straight Group Facilitator; Honors Comm; QHS Faculty Assn Building Rep 1988-; PTSA Treas 1982-83; Welcome Wagon VP 1978-79; Amer Cancer Society Fashion Show Chairperson 1979-80; Planned Parenthood, Hyde Museum Volunteer; Implemented Queensburys First Advanced Placement Amer His Prgm; *office:* Queensbury HS 99 Aviation Rd Queensbury NY 12804

MC DUFFIE, CATHERINE DE MARA, Teacher of Gifted & Talented; *b:* Tresckow, PA; *m:* Harold L.; *c:* Justine; *ed:* (BS) Eng, Mansfield St Coll 1961; (MED) Curr, Rutgers Univ 1965; Gifted Ed, Univ of AR; *cr:* Teacher Roosevelt Jr HS 1961-65, Quibbletown Jr HS 1965-68, Kamay Jr HS 1968-69, Springdale HS 1971-; *ai:* Odyssey of the Mind Coach; SEA, AEA, NEA 1971-; Gifted St Organization 1989-; Outstanding Teacher Awd Springdale System 1981; *home:* Rt 1 Box 201 Fayetteville AR 72703

MC EACHEN, AVIS R., ELP Teacher; *b:* Rolla, ND; *m:* Lawrence A.; *c:* Michael, Meghaan; *ed:* (BA) Eng, 1976, (MAE) Eng Ed, 1978 AZ St Univ; Various Wkshps in Gifted Ed; *cr:* Eng/Soc Stud Teacher Trevor Browne HS 1976-80; Eng/Soc Stud/Teacher of Gifted Mesa Jr HS 1980-; *ai:* Natl Jr Honor Society Spon; 8th Grade Academic Soc Stud Team Coach; Natl His Day Spon; Phi Kappa Phi 1976-; NCSS 1989-; AEA, NEA 1976-; *office:* Mesa Jr HS 828 E Broadway Mesa AZ 85204

MC ELHANEY, JODY PATRICK, 7th Grade Science Teacher; *b:* Norman, OK; *m:* Denice Dick; *c:* Taylor Allene; *ed:* (BS) Phy Ed, 1983, (MS) Ed Scndry, 1988 Cntrl ST Univ; *cr:* 7th Grade Sci Teacher Mustang Mid Sch 1984-; *ai:* Fellowship of Christian Athletes-Head Spon; 8th Grade Girls Bsktbl-1 Yr; 7th Grade Ftbl-5 Yrs; 8th Grade Boys Bsktbl-6 Yrs; 7th/8th Grade Boys Track-6 Yrs; OEA; NEA; OAHPERD; FCA; Chisholm Heights Baptist Church; Mustang Track Club Head Spon 1985-87; *office:* Mustang Mid Sch 906 S Heights Dr Mustang OK 73064

MC ELHANEY, THOMAS A., Band Director; *b:* Huntington, IN; *m:* Janice Mc Combs; *c:* Douglas, Michael, Barbara; *ed:* (BM) Music Ed, De Pauw Univ 1963; (MA) Ball St Univ 1964; *cr:* Band Dir De Kalb Central USD 1964-65, Huntington Cty Cmmty Sch 1965-66, Southern Wells Schls 1966-72, Huntington Cty Cmmty Schls 1972-; *ai:* Dir Stage Band; IN Band Masters Assn 1979-; IN St Teachers Assn 1964-; Outstanding Jr HS Classroom Teacher 1983-84; Huntington Rotary Club; *office:* Crestview Mid Sch 929 Guilford Huntington IN 46750

MC ELHINNY, MARY GERTRUDE, SC, Fifth Grade Teacher; *b:* Pittsburgh, PA; *ed:* (BS) Elem Ed, Seton Hill Coll 1963; DuQuesne 1965-67, Carlow 1971, Dayton, Mid-Western Intermediate Univ 1983; *cr:* Elem Teacher Sisters of Charity Parochial Schls 1953-65, Johnstown & Greensburg 1965-69, Our Lady of Mercy 1965-67, St Bruno Sch 1967-70, Pittsburgh 1970-78, St Michael Sch 1978-; *ai:* Elem Prin 6 Yrs; Educator of Yr; Prin St Brunos 1968; St Michael Sch Cath Schls Week Teacher Tribute 1987; *home:* RD 1 Box 180 Hartstown PA 16131

MC ELREATH, MARY HELEN, Health/Phys Ed Teacher/Coach; *b:* Macon, GA; *ed:* (MED) Health/Phys Ed, GA Southern Univ 1980; (BA) Health/Phys Ed, Tift Coll Mercer 1975; Educl Specialist Degree Augusta Coll; Models of Teaching Prgm Richmond Cty; *cr:* Teacher/Coach Langford Jr HS 1975-80, Glenn Hills HS 1980-; *ai:* Var Sftbl/Girls Bsktbl Coach; SAC Comm Chm Plant & Facilities; GA Sftbl All Star Comm; GA Athletic Coaches Assn 1980-; Tennis Coach of Yr 1984; Womens Bktbl Coaches Assn; GA Assn of Health, Phys Ed & Recreation; Natl Hills Baptist Church 1960-; Amer Red Cross Volunteer 1983-; Outstanding Young Women of Amer; Models of Teaching Cadre Mem; *office:* Glenn Hills HS 2840 Glenn Hills Dr Augusta GA 30906

MC ELROY, LISA CARD, Second Grade Teacher; *b:* Fayetteville, AR; *m:* Gary Duane; *c:* James W., Jennifer A.; *ed:* (BA) Elem Ed, S AR Univ 1978; (ME) Elem Ed, AR Tech Univ 1985; *cr:* 3rd Grade Teacher Ozark Public Schls 1978-80; 4th Grade Teacher Crawford Elem 1980-87; 2nd Grade Teacher Sequoyah Elem 1987-; *ai:* AR Ed Assn, NEA 1979-; Russellville Ed Assn 1980-; AR Childrens Hospital Support Group 1989; United Meth Church Mem 1980-; *office:* Sequoyah Elem Sch 1601 W 12th St Russellville AR 72801

MC ELROY, STEVE CHARLES, History Department Chair; *b:* Las Vegas, NM; *m:* Karen Kruse; *c:* Cheryl, Erika, Thomas; *ed:* (BA) Soc Sci, 1971, (MA) Soc Sci, 1973 NM Highlands Univ; Cmptr Sci & Sch Admin Courses; *cr:* Teacher Las Vegas City Schls 1971-; *ai:* Phi Gamma Mu Mem 1970-71; Nom Teacher of Yr 1985, 1987, 1988; *office:* Las Vegas City Schls 901 Douglas Las Vegas NM 87701

MC ELVEEN, DONNA NELL (MC ALLISTER), Fifth Grade Teacher; *b:* Lake City, SC; *m:* Carey S.; *c:* Shane, Carmon; *ed:* (BS) Elem Ed, 1975, (ME) Elem Ed, 1981 Francis Marion Coll; *cr:* Teacher J C Lynch Elem; *ai:* Scranton Baptist (Pianist, Asst Organist, Youth Choir Dir); Florence Cty Dist 3 Lieutenant Governors Creative Writing Awd; *home:* PO Box 130 Church St Scranton SC 29591

MC ELVEEN, GAIL MARIE, 7th Grade/Life Science Teacher; *b:* Houston, TX; *ed:* (BS) Life Sci/Bio, 1977, Cert Bio/Eng, 1982 Sam Houston St Univ; Working Toward Masters Theological Stud S TX Bible Coll 1989; Cert Bovine Artificial Insemination Technician Cntrl OH Breeding Assn 1981; *cr:* Laboratory Technician Asst Long Point Medical Square 1972-76; Houston Zoological Gardens 1978-79; Owner/Mgr Whispering Pines Dairy 1979-82; 6th Grade Sci Teacher Leal Mid Sch 1984-87; 9th Grade Eng Teacher Robert E Lee HS 1985, Churchill HS 1986; 7th Grade Sci Teacher Leal Mid Sch 1987-; *ai:* Livingway Chrstn Church 1988-; Prin Advisory Comm; Wrote 7th Grade Life Sci Curr for Harlandale Curr Guide; *home:* 4858 Castle Lance San Antonio TX 78218

MC ELVEEN, TERRI LYNN, American History Teacher; *b:* Waycross, GA; *m:* John Philip; *c:* Meredith, Andrew; *ed:* (BS) Soc Sci, Auburn Univ 1982; (MED) Soc Sci, W GA Coll 1986; *cr:* Amer His Teacher W Rome HS 1982-; *ai:* Y Club 1982-84; Tennis Coach 1982-86; Pep Club 1985-87; Jr Class Trip Adv; NCSS 1982-85; NEA 1982-87; PAGE 1987-; Delta Kappa Gamma 1987-; *office:* W Rome HS 2500 Redmond Cir Rome GA 30161

MC ELWAIN, ROBERT DOUGLAS, Social Studies Teacher; *b:* Panama City, FL; *m:* Lorraine Marie Bartell; *c:* Emily M.; *ed:* (BA) Poly Sci, 1973, (MED) Scndry Ed, 1979 Univ of IL; Jr Coll Level Cmptr Courses; *cr:* 7th/8th Grade Soc Stud Teacher Paxton Jr HS 1977-83; 7th Grade Soc Stud/Rdng Teacher J W Eater Jr HS 1983-; *ai:* Shakespeare Play Festival Spon; Asst Boys Bsktbl Coach; Scholastic Bowl Coach; Gifted Stu Field Trip Spon; NCSS 1982-87; Rantoul Bicentennial Commission Mem 1987-88; Amer Luth Church Deacon 1982-85; Up With Ed Exhibition 1984; G ifted Drama Stu St Grant 1987-88; *home:* RR 1 Box 11C Thomasboro IL 61878

MC ELYEA, WANDA HAND, Fourth Grade Teacher; *b:* Henderson, TX; *m:* Lewie B.; *c:* Pamela D. Mc Elyea Curtis, Malcolm W.; *ed:* (BS) Elem Ed, Sam Houston 1956; (MS) General Ed, TX A&I 1962; Numerous Courses in Ed; *cr:* 4th Grade Teacher Corpus Christi TX 1956-58; 5th/6th Grade Teacher Kingsville TX 1958-62; 7th-9th Grade Eng/6th Grade Soc Stud Teacher Edna Jr HS 1965-66; 3rd Grade Teacher Olalla Elem 1970-78; 4th Grade Teacher Burley Glenwood 1978-; *ai:* 4th Grade Team Leader; Ceramic Adv; Rainbow Girls Mother Adv 1987-89; Sigma Iota Chi Pres 1954; Masonic Outstanding Teacher Awd 1988; *home:* 3988 Menzie Rd SE Port Orchard WA 98366

MC ENANEY, JUDY ANDERSON, Teacher; *b:* Lansing, MI; *m:* Stephen A.; *c:* Melissa Mc Enaney Hardy, Matthew; *ed:* (BA) Art Ed, 1969, (MA) Art Ed, 1989 MI St Univ; *cr:* HS Teacher Ovid-Elsie Public Schls 1969-70, St Johns Public Schls 1970-; *ai:* Yrbk & Natl Art Honor Society Adv; NEA, MEA, SJEA; MAEA Liasion 1987-89; Interscholastic Press Assn Region Dir 1987-89; Clinton Cty Arts Cncl, Lansing Area Schlsp Alert Bd Mem 1987-89; *office:* St Johns HS 501 W Sickles Saint Johns MI 48879

MC ENANEY, NICHOLAS WILLIAM, English Teacher; *b:* Butte, MT; *m:* Sandra; *c:* Cory, Chris; *ed:* (BA) Eng, MT Tech 1975; (BA) Ed, Univ of MT 1975; Working Towards MA Eng, Univ of MT; *cr:* Eng Teacher Butte Cntrl HS 1975-78; Cnslr/Revisor MT Tech 1978; Eng Teacher MCHS Big Sky 1979-; *ai:* Frosh Boys Bsktbl, Head Girls Bsktbl & Sftbl Coach; *office:* Missoula Big Sky Sch 3100 South Ave W Missoula MT 59801

MC ENIRY, JOHN T., Cmptr Programming/Math Teacher; *b:* Sedalia, MO; *m:* Cheryl Ann Berger; *c:* Sean T., Kelly Padraic, Ashley C.; *ed:* (BA) Scndry Math Ed, 1976, (MA) Scndry Math Ed, 1979 Univ of MO Kansas City; *cr:* Math Teacher/Dept Head Oak Park HS 1976-79; Math/Cmptr Teacher Rockhurst HS 1979-; *ai:* Cmptr Club; Academic Competition Spon; NCTM Mem 1976-; *office:* Rockhurst HS 9301 State Line Rd Kansas City MO 64114

MC ENTIRE, JOYCE A. NAVA, 6th Grade Teacher; *b:* Clifford, IL; *m:* James Jr.; *c:* Tony; *ed:* (BMED) Music Ed, Southern IL Univ 1960; *cr:* 6th Grade Music Teacher Johnston City Unit 1 1961-62; 7th Grade Music Teacher Energy Sch 1962-63; 6th Grade Music Teacher 1963-65, 1st Grade Teacher 1971-73, Title I Rdng Aide 1977-80, 6th Grade Teacher 1980- Herrin Unit 4; *ai:* Delta Kappa Gamma; Mu Phi Epsilon; Union Gospel Mission Youth Leader/Piano Player/Sunday Sch Teacher; *office:* Herrin Unit Dist 4 700 S 14th Herrin IL 62948

MC ENTIRE, MERRILL JOE, Arts Chairperson; *b:* Old Fort, NC; *m:* Sally Wren; *c:* Denise Baker, Yvonne Painter, Gary, Amy J., Tamara; *ed:* (BS) Art Ed, Appalachian St 1966; Penland Sch, E TN St Univ, Univ of NC Greensboro; *cr:* Art Teacher NE Guilford HS 1966-67; Art Supvr Mc Dowell Cty Schls 1967-75; Art Teacher Mc Dowell HS 1976-89; *ai:* NC Art Ed Assn, Natl Art Ed Assn; *home:* Rt 2 Box 173-A Old Fort NC 28762

MC ENTURFF, ARIE PUTRAIE FAULK, 4th Grade Teacher; *b:* Barbour Cty, AL; *m:* Don C.; *c:* Wanda K. Parker, Donald T.; *ed:* (BS) Elem Ed, East TX St Univ 1973; *cr:* Title I Rdng Teacher 1973-74; 6th Grade Math Teacher 1974-75; 4th Grade Teacher 1974 Fruitvale ISD; *ai:* Local Textbook Comm; Alpha Chi TX Lambda; *home:* Rt 1 Box 91-B Edgewood TX 75117

MC EWEN, RALPH EDWIN, HS Literature/Drama Teacher; *b:* Salem, OR; *m:* Vernita Berlee Harvey; *c:* Sarah M., Joel A.; *ed:* (BS) Bio, Univ of Puget Sound 1969; Grad Stud Univ of OR, Univ of CA Santa Cruz, Seattle Pacific Univ, Prairie Bible Inst, Univ of Louisville; *cr:* Lit Teacher Mobile Open Classrooms 1977-79, Sweet Home Chrstn Sch 1979-84, E Linn Chrstn Acad 1985-; *ai:* Drama Dir; OR Citizens Alliance 1987-89; NEH Summer Seminar Univ of OR Russian Lit 1987; NEH Summer Seminar Univ of CA Santa Cruz British Lit 1988; Robert Taft Inst in Government Seminar Univ of OR 1989; Fnd in Ec Ed Seminar Irvington NY; *office:* E Linn Chrstn Acad 30337 Fairview Rd Lebanon OR 97355

MC FADDEN, MARY CLARE ROMANS, Physical Education Teacher; *b:* Baltimore, MD; *m:* Michael Patrick; *c:* Caitlyn C.; *ed:* (BA) Phys Ed/Health, Univ of Richmond 1982; *cr:* Sales Rep TDY Systems Inc 1982; Coach Garrison Forest 1983; Teacher/Coach Maryvale Preparatory 1983-; *ai:* Head Field Hockey, Head Lacrosse, JR Var Bsktbl Coach; Athletic Assn Faculty Adv; Assn of Ind Schls (Secy, Treas) 1986-87; US Womens Lacrosse Assn 1983-; US Womens Field Hockey Assn 1983-; Lacrosse for Leukemia Coach 1987-89; *office:* Maryvale Preparatory Sch 11000 Falls Rd Brooklandville MD 21022

MC FADDEN, PAMELA ECHOLS, 8th Grade English Teacher; *b:* Tupelo, MS; *m:* Patrick M.; *c:* Cory M., Megan M.; *ed:* (BSED) Elem Ed, Baldwin-Wallace Coll 1983; *cr:* 8th Grade Teacher St Ambrose Sch 1983-89; *ai:* Writing Contest Spon; *office:* St Ambrose Sch 929 Pearl Rd Brunswick OH 44212

MC FADIN, JUANITA JONES, 8th Grade Amer History Teacher; *b:* Ottawa, KS; *c:* Cynthia Ann; *ed:* (BS) Ed/SS, 1955, (MS) Soc Sci, 1972 Northwest MO St Univ; *cr:* 6th Grade Teacher South Park 1951-67; 7th/8th Grade Teacher Humboldt 1967-73; 8th Grade Teacher Robidoux Mid Sch 1973-; *ai:* Soc Stud Curr Planning St Joseph Schls; Newspaper Adv; Textbook Comm; MO St Teachers Assn 1951-; NEA 1951-70; PTSA 1951-.

MC FALL, DANIEL SCOTT, Advanced Curr Math Teacher; *b:* Gadsden, AL; *m:* Connie Machen; *c:* Jay; *ed:* (BS) Math/Phys Ed, 1983, (MS) Math/Phys Ed, 1986 Jacksonville St Univ; Working Towards AA Cert Math, Univ of AL; *cr:* Math/Phys Ed Teacher Geraldine HS 1983-84; Coach/Math Teacher Pisgah HS 1984-; Math Professor NE AL St Jr Coll 1988-; *ai:* Math Club, Sr Class, Stus for Christ Spons; Asst Ftbl, Head Frosh Bsktbl Coach; Church Youth Comm; Natl Educl Organization, AL Educl Organization 1983-; Jackson Cty Educl Organization 1984-; Pisgah Baptist Church (Sunday Sch Teacher 1984-, Nominating Comm Chm); *home:* Rt 2 Box 23-A Pisgah AL 35765

MC FALL, PEGGY GREEN, Sixth Grade Teacher; *b:* Williams Cmmty, AL; *m:* Sidney H.; *c:* Heather, Matthew; *ed:* (BS) Elem Ed, Jacksonville St Univ 1974; *cr:* 1st Grade Teacher Weaver Elem Sch 1974-80; 4th/5th Grade Teacher 1982-83, 6th Grade Teacher 1983- Pleasant Valley; *ai:* 6th Grade 4-H Club; Textbook & Curr Comm; AL Ed Assn; Calhoun Cty 4-H Club of Yr 1986-88; *office:* Pleansant Valley Sch 4141 Pleasant Valley Rd Jacksonville AL 36265

MC FANN, JANE CATHERINE, English Teacher; *b:* Newark, DE; *ed:* (BA) Eng, 1974, (MS) Linguistics/Lit, 1976 Univ of DE; Grad Stud; *cr:* Eng Teacher Glasgow HS 1974-; *ai:* NHS Co-Adv; Academic Recognition Comm Chairperson; Mid Sts Steering Comm; NCTE; Author of Novels; *office:* Glasgow HS 1901 S College Ave Newark DE 19702

MC FARLAND, JAMES DALE, Government/History Teacher; *b:* Rupert, ID; *m:* Linda Ashcraft; *c:* Jeffery D., Bradley J.; *ed:* (BA) Phys Ed, Magic Valley Chrstn 1963; Grad Stud Abilene Chrstn Coll; *cr:* Elem Teacher Lava Grade Sch 1963-66; His/Government Teacher Marsh Valley HS 1966-; *ai:* Asst Coach Var Ftbl; Athletic Trainer; Class Adv; Close-Up Fnd Teacher; ID Athletic Trainers Assn, NEA, ID Ed Assn; Lava Lions Club VP 1969; Lava Ambulance; Lava City Councilman; *home:* PO Box 322 Lava Hot Spgs ID 83246

MC FARLAND, JANE ANN TEAGUE, Fourth Grade Teacher; *b:* La Follette, TN; *m:* Willard Gerald; *ed:* (BS) Elem Ed, Cumberland Coll 1968; (MS) Curr/Instruction, Univ of TN 1983; ST Career Ladder; *cr:* Pre-Sch Teacher Ridgewood Elem 1966; 4th Grade Teacher Westside Elem 1968-72, E La Follette Elem 1973-80, Jacksboro Elem 1981-; *ai:* Delta Kappa Gamma; NEA, TN Ed Assn, Campbell Cty Ed Assn 1973-; *office:* Jacksboro Elem School PO Box 437 Jacksboro TN 37757

MC FARLAND, ROBERT J., Math Teacher; *b:* New York, NY; *m:* Brenda Diane Mc Carter; *c:* David, Douglas; *ed:* (BS) Bus Admin, Carson-Newman Coll 1970; East TN St Univ; Cert at Univ of TN; *cr:* Bus Teacher De La Warr HS 1970-75; Adjunct Prof Typing Walters St C C 1980-87; Bus/Math Teacher Sevierville Mid Sch 1975-; *ai:* Spon-Bsbl Card Club Sevierville Mid Sch; Mem Sevier Cty Bsktbl Referees Assn; Coach-Bsbl Sevier Cty HS 1980-86; NEA 1970-; TN Assn of Mid Schls 1985; Sevier Cty Schls Federal Credit Union (Treas 1977-80 Loan Officer 1980-); *office:* Sevierville Mid Sch 520 High St Sevierville TN 37862

MC FARLAND, WILLIAM, Eng/Bus/Journalism Teacher; *b:* Dyer, TN; *ed:* (AA) Scndry Ed, Freed-Hardeman Coll 1969; (BS) Bus Admin/Ed, Harding Univ 1971; (MS) Admin/Supervision, Univ of TN Martin 1978; Eng Cert Lambuth Coll; *cr:* Teacher Dyer HS 1972, Kenton HS 1973, Gibson HS 1974-80, Gibson Cty HS 1980-; *ai:* Sch Information Dir; Yrbk Adv; Chrldr Spon; NEA, TN Ed Assn, Gibson Cty Ed Assn; Gibson Cty Sch Dist Teacher of Yr 1982; Outstanding Teacher 1989; Attended W TN Teacher Banquet; *office:* Gibson Cty HS Box 190 Dyer TN 38330

MC FEELY, EDWARD CARY, JR., Fifth Grade Teacher; *b:* Lansdowne, PA; *m:* Jeanne Roux; *c:* Kristin, Scott; *ed:* (AA) Ed, Keystone Jr Coll 1964; (BA) Ed, Shippensburg St 1967; Graduate Work, West Chester Univ; *cr:* 4th & 5th Grade Teacher Rainbow Elem 1967-70; 7th & 8th Grade Teacher South Brandywine Mid Sch 1970-75; 3rd & 5th Grade Teacher Caln Elem 1975-; *ai:* After School Bsktbl League; Ski Club; Outstanding Service Awd 1978; Outstanding Service Awd 1984; Outstanding Teachers Awd 1987; *home:* 1513 Doyle Dr Downingtown PA 19335

MC FERREN, CLARK DAVID, English Teacher/Dept Chair; *b:* Davenport, IA; *m:* Laurence Anne Begin; *c:* David; *ed:* (BA) Eng, Univ of IA 1978; *cr:* Teacher Spalding Public Sch 1978-79; Teacher/Coach Louisa-Muscatine HS 1979-; *ai:* Vlybl & Asst Girls Bsktbl Coach; Stu Cncl & Drama Club Adv; Spring Play Dir; NCTE 1978-; *office:* Louisa-Muscatine HS Letts IA 52754

MC GAHAN, JAMES EUGENE, Science Department Chairman; *b:* Wallace, NE; *m:* Martha Ida Willhoft; *c:* Ellen, Steven; *ed:* (BS) Phys Sci, Kearney St Coll 1966; (MS) Phys Sci, Emporia St Univ 1971; (EDD) Sci Ed, Univ of N CO 1978; PSSC Physics, Univ of IA; Nuclear Physics, Univ of CO; Chem, Univ of AZ; *cr:* Jr HS Sci Teacher Cntrl City Public Schls 1966-68; Chem/Math Teacher Northwest HS 1968-76; Sci Consultant NE Dept of Ed 1976-77; Chem/Cmptrs/Physics Teacher Northwest HS 1978-; *ai:* NE Prof Practice Commission Peer Reviewer; NW Ed Assn; NE Sci Cadre Mem; Greater NE Assn Teachers of Sci (Pres, Bd of Dir) 1987-89; NE Educl Technology Assn Bd of Dir 1985-88, Teacher of Yr 1986; NE St Ed Assn PRR&R Commission Chm 1987-; Grand Island Chamber of Commerce Bd of 2M 1986-, Outstanding Educator 1976; Hall Cty Civil Defense Radiological Officer 1986-; Blessed Sacrament Cath Church 1980-; Hall Cty Democratic Party 1970-, Delegate 1980, 1984, 1990; Univ of AZ ICE Chemical Demonstrator; Wilson Fellowship in Physics Princeton Univ; Physics Teaching Resource Agent AAPT; Doing Chem for ACS; Sourcebook Project Univ CA Berkeley; Articles Published; Dreyfus Fellowship in Chem at Princeton; *office:* Northwest HS 2710 North Rd Grand Island NE 68803

MC GAHEE, BARBARA ANN, Social Studies Teacher; *b:* Augusta, GA; *ed:* (BA) Soc Stud, Mercer Univ 1960; (MED) Soc Stud, Augusta Coll 1976; *cr:* Teacher Butler HS 1960-78, Westside HS 1978-; *ai:* Delta Kappa Gamma 1976-; STAR Teacher.

MC GAHEY, ELIZABETH ANN HUNT, Fourth Grade Teacher; *b:* Ardmore, OK; *m:* Ray; *c:* Joyce, RaeAnn, Alvin; *ed:* (BS) Home Ec, 1977, Elem Ed, 1980 SE OK St; *cr:* Teacher Olney HS 1978-79; 4th Grade Teacher Rad Ware Elem 1983-; *ai:* 4-H; Little League Girls Bsktbl; Writing & Oral Rdng Coach; TX St Teacher Assn 1987-; *home:* Rt B Box 298 Kingston OK 73439

MC GARRY, CYNTHIA KNIGHT, Religious Education Director; *b:* Westbrook, ME; *m:* Owen P.; *c:* Michael, Matthew, Melinda Gregory; *ed:* Ed, Gorham St Teachers Coll; Catechical Inst 1984-; *cr:* Sub Teacher Windham Sch System 1968-69, S Berwick Sch System 1969-74; His Teacher St Patricks Sch 1976-84; Dir of Religious Ed 1984-; *ai:* ME Irish Childrens Prgm; ME Right to Life Movement; St Patricks PFTA; Cheverus HS Mothers Club Pres 1985-86, 1990-91; *office:* Saint Patricks Sch 1251 Congress St Portland ME 04102

MC GAUGH, POLLY POLING, First Grade Teacher; *b:* Halstead, KS; *m:* Cecil Bartlett; *c:* Lisa; *ed:* (BA) Elem Ed, 1969, (MS) Elem Ed, 1973 Wichita St Univ; *cr:* 1st Grade Teacher Lincoln Elem Sch 1969-; *ai:* Multi Cultural Comm Co-Chairperson; Sch Improvement & Substance Abuse Prevention Team Comm Chairperson; Positive Discipline & Rdng Portfolio Comm Mem; NEA Rep 1973-86; *home:* 1120 E 46th S Wichita KS 67216

MC GEE, BETTY ANN BENSON, Retired Third Grade Teacher; *b:* Stevens, AR; *m:* John Edward Jr.; *c:* Marcia L., Lisa A. Mc Gee Gaker, Julie Mc Gee Leighton; *ed:* (BM) Music, Henderson St Univ 1950; Ed 1953; Ed & Cert Miami Univ 1967-73; *cr:* 3rd-4th Grade Music/Piano Teacher Crossett Public Sch & Arkadelphia Public Sch 1950-53; 2nd Grade Teacher Carlisle Public Schs 1966-69; 2nd-3rd Grade Teacher Middletown Public Schls 1969-87; *ai:* Kappa Delta Pi Life Mem 1950-; Meth Church; Middletown Music Club 1965-80; *home:* 4608 Wicklow Dr Middletown OH 45042

MC GEE, BRENDA K. HUMPHREY, 4th Grade Teacher; *b:* Elizabethton, TN; *m:* Johnny Wayne; *c:* Jeremy, Kasey; *ed:* (BS) Elem Ed, E TN St Univ 1970; *cr:* Teacher Central Elem 1970-; *ai:* TEA, NEA 1970-; *home:* Rt 11 Box 1015 Elizabethton TN 37643

MCGEE, CARL OWEN, Social Studies Teacher/Coach; *b:* Kinder, LA; *m:* Lori Jane Nelson; *ed:* (BS) Health/Phys Ed, 1983, (MED) Health/Phys Ed, 1986 Mc Neese St Univ; *cr:* Teacher/Coach South Beauregard HS 1983-; *ai:* Coach Ftbl & Bsktbl; Jr Beta Co-Spon; LAE, NEA, BEA, LHSAA 1983-; Teacher of Yr South Beauregard 1987; *home:* Rt 13 Box 384 Lake Charles LA 70611

MC GEE, DIANE CHIARIELLO, Mathematics Teacher; *b:* Brooklyn, NY; *m:* Joseph Doren; *c:* Maureen, Erin; *ed:* (BA) Elem Ed, 1977, (MA) Rdng, 1980 Clemson Univ; Math, Cmptr; *cr:* Learning Disabilities Resource Teacher Walhalla Elem Sch 1977-79, East End Sch 1979-80; Lang Art Teacher Belton Mid Sch 1980-86; Math Teacher Woodmont Mid Sch 1986-; *ai:* Yrbk & Mathcounts Adv; Recycling, Honors, Awds Comm; NEA, SCEA 1986-; Teacher of Yr 1988; Article Published; *office:* Woodmont Mid Sch 325 Flat Rock Rd Piedmont SC 29673

MC GEE, DONNA ELIZABETH, Fifth Grade Math Teacher; *b:* Detroit, MI; *m:* Allen; *c:* Amanda, Mark; *ed:* (BSE) Elem Ed, AR St Univ 1978; *cr:* 3rd Grade Teacher Tuckerman Public Schls 1978-79; 5th Grade Teacher Mc Crory Public Schls 1981-; *ai:* Gifted & Talented OM Coach; Natl Tae Kwon Do Fed of America (Mgr, Instr 1987-) Black Belt 1988; *home:* Rt 3 Box 394-A Newport AR 72112

MC GEE, JAMES WILLIS, Mathematics Teacher; *b:* Hattiesburg, MS; *m:* Virgie Jones; *c:* James III, Virnessa; *ed:* (BS) Poly Sci, Univ of S MS 1975; *cr:* Math Teacher Gulfport Public Schls 1977-; *ai:* Admin Asst Cntrl Jr HS; Bsktbl Coach; W Gulfport Civic Pres 1980; Elks 1288 Entertainment Chm 1988-89; Outstanding Teaching Performance & Attendance Awd; Cntrl Jr HS Yrbk Dedication; *home:* 1502 Rich Ave Gulfport MS 39501

MC GEE, JUDY RHODES, Lang Art & Soc Stud Teacher; *b:* N Wilkesboro, NC; *m:* John Franklin; *c:* William F., Julie M. Shepherd, Keith M.; *ed:* (BS) Elem Ed, Appalachian St Univ 1963; *cr:* 4th Grade Teacher 1961-63, 7th Grade Teacher 1964-69 Union Elem; 7th/8th Grade Teacher Mulberry Elem 1969-; *ai:* Tarheel Jr Historian Club; NC Soc Stud Assn 1975-; NC Assn of Educators 1961-63, 1965-; Bible Study Group Pres 1988-; Wilkes Cty Mini-Grant; Mulberry Sch Teacher of Yr; *office:* Mulberry Elem Sch Rt 1 Box 664 North Wilkesboro NC 28659

MC GEE, PAMELA JO, English Teacher/Dept Chair; *b:* Greeley, CO; *c:* Aaron W., Bryan S., Kyle M.; *ed:* (BA) Eng/World His/Fine Art, UNC 1967; Grad Stud Mid Sch Ed; *cr:* Teacher Aurora Public Schls 1967-70, Boron Unified Sch Dist 1970-71, Douglas Cty Schls 1980-; *ai:* Curr Comm 1985-86; NCTE 1988-; Natl Mid Sch Assn (Presenter 1985-86, 1988) 1985-; CO Mid Sch Assn Presenter 1985-88; Mid Sch Article Published; Comm Grant; *office:* Parker Jr HS 6651 Pine Lane Ave Parker CO 80134

MC GEE, SARA G., First Grade Teacher; *b:* Washington, GA; *m:* Gordon H.; *c:* Heather L.; *ed:* (BS) Elem Ed, Tift Coll 1964; *cr:* Classroom Teacher Columbia Cty; *ai:* Various Curr Comms; PAGE, Alpha Delta Kappa, Women of GA Power; First Baptist Church.

MC GEE, SUSAN MONTELARO, Third Grade Teacher; *b:* Eunice, LA; *m:* Gordon James; *c:* Kimberly, Denise; *ed:* (BA) Elem Ed, Univ of SW LA 1971; (MED) Supervision of Stu Teaching, LA St Univ 1975; Master Teacher LA Teaching Internship & Teacher Evaluation Prgm; STAR Assessor; Prof Improvement 1980-85; *cr:* Teacher St Landry Parish Sch Bd 1972-; Supervising Teacher Mc Neese StUniv 1975-; Master Teacher LA Teaching Internship & Evaluation Prgm 1990; *ai:* Quiz Bowl Spon; Math Club Co-Spon; Read-A-Thon Project Chm; Drug Awareness Week Comm; Mc Neese St Univ Cooperating Supvr; Academic Excl Mem; Gift & Floral Fund Comm; Associated Prof Educators of LA Mem 1987-; Eunice Camp Fire Cncl Leader 1984-87, Camp Fire Super Achievement Awd 1987; Eunice Girls Sftbl Incorporated Coach 1975; Acadian Womens Assn VP 1984-87; Parent Teacher Club Attendance Chm 1980-, Service Awd 1986; Outstanding Young Educator by Eunice Jaycees; Teacher of Yr East Elem 1975-76, 1989-; *home:* 1320 Yukon Eunice LA 70535

MC GEE, V. WAYNE, Mathematics Teacher; *b:* Brookhaven, MS; *ed:* (BS) Math, Univ of S MS 1969; *cr:* Math Teacher Brookhaven Public Schls 1969-84, Copiah Cty Schls 1984-; *home:* Rt 1 Box 310 Hazlehurst MS 39083

MC GEEHIN, CYNTHIA MARIE SEARS, Science Department Chair; *b:* Tacoma, WA; *m:* John P.; *ed:* (BS) Geology, 1980, (MA) Enviromental Policy, 1990 George Washington Univ; Global Environmental Change, Bermuda Biological Station; *cr:* Geologist US Geological Survey 1975-83; Sci Teacher 1983-89, Sci Dept Chairperson 1989- Holton-Arms Sch; *ai:* Environmental Awareness Club & 9th Grade Class Adv; Long Range Curr Planning Comm Mem; Multi Cultural Assessment Prgm Mem; NSTA 1983-; Amer Inst Biological Sci 1986-; Geological Society of Washington 1976-; Klingenstein Fellowship Awd 1988; Exxon Fellowship Awd 1989; *office:* The, Holton-Arms Schl 7303 River Rd Bethesda MD 20817

MC GEHEE, JOHN HIRAM, Physics Teacher; *b:* Jackson, MS; *m:* Susan Glennon Harlow; *c:* John H. IV, Margaret E. Ostler; *ed:* (BS) Physics, Univ of CA Los Angeles 1965; (MA) Phys Sci, CA St Univ Long Beach 1969; *cr:* Physics/Math Teacher Lakewood HS 1966-67; Physics Teacher Rolling Hills HS 1967-; *ai:* Physics Club; AAPT 1966-; CA Teachers Assn, PV Teachers Assn, NSTA 1985-; Presidential Awd for Excl in Sci Teaching 1985; Natl Sci Fnd Inst Project Physics; Organizer of Physics Stus; *office:* Rolling Hills HS 27118 Silver Spur Rd Rolling Hills Ests CA 90274

MC GEHEE, JUDY DANNER, Mathematics Teacher; *b:* Amory, MS; *m:* Paul Glenn; *c:* Hollie, Justin; *ed:* (BA) Math, 1974, (MAT) Ed, 1979 MS St Univ; *cr:* Teacher Smithville HS 1974-76, Starkville Jr HS 1976-79, Laurel HS 1981-82, Franklin HS 1982-; *ai:* Daughters of the Amer Revolution (Chaplain, Registrar) 1984-; Homochitto Heritage Club 1982-89; Star Teacher 1987.

MC GHEE, DEBRA NOWELS, Second Grade ESEA Teacher; *b:* Chicago, IL; *m:* Derrick; *c:* Deadra, Donnell; *ed:* (BA) Spec Ed, Univ of WI Whitewater 1978; (MA) Concordia Coll 1986; Seminar Trng St Johns Coll; *cr:* EMH Teacher Raster Branch Sch 1979-80, Holmes Sch 1980-82; K-3rd Grade Teacher Nathan Goldblatt Sch 1982-; *ai:* Cal Pk Rams Chrldr Coach, Safety Comm; Cal Pk Convenant Choir 1988-; *office:* Nathan R Goldblatt Sch 4257 W Adams Chicago IL 60624

MC GHEE, LESLIE LONNIE, African-Amer History Teacher; *b:* Magnolia, MS; *m:* Linda A. Webster; *c:* Yonakish, Leslie Jr., Brandi J.; *ed:* (BS) HS Soc Stud, Chgo ST Univ 1971; (MA) Comm Sci Emphasis in Educational Technology, Governors ST Univ 1976; Post Masters Studies Photography Apprentice Cam Era Studios 1981; *cr:* 5th Class Finance Specialist US Army 1965-68; Teacher Chgo Bd of Ed 1971-; Teacher Chgo City Coll 1985-86; *ai:* Coach for TV Game Show; Pan African Pen Pal Assn Spon; African-Amer Hist Prgm Comm Chm; Prof Problems Comm; Prof Personnel Adv Comm; *office:* Morgan Park H S 1744 W Pryor Ave Chicago IL 60643

MC GHEE, MARSHALL LARRY, Fourth Grade Teacher; *b:* Caryville, TN; *m:* Shirley Ann Housley; *ed:* (BS) Elem Ed, Lincoln Memorial Univ 1962; *cr:* Teacher Campbell Schls 1960-62, Briceville Elem Sch 1962-; *ai:* 4-H Club Leader; Building Level Supvr; Anderson Cty Ed Assn, TN Ed Assn, NEA 1962-; PTO Treas 1977; Caryville Lodge #665 F&AM 1960-, 25 Yr Pen; OES Caryville Chapter #415 1960-; Salvation Army Public Relation Chm 1987-; Lake View Baptist Church Music Dir; Caryville City Cncl 1985; Golden Apple Awd 1986; Inducted Careyville Literary Hall of Fame 1988, Lincoln Memorial Univ Hall of Fame 1988; Published Books; *home:* Butter & Egg Rd Caryville TN 37714

MC GHEE, WANDA ROBERTS, Sixth Grade Teacher; *b:* Sparta, TN; *m:* John Douglas; *c:* James D.; *ed:* (BS) Elem Ed, 1972, (MA) Early Chldhd Ed, 1979 TN Tech Univ; *cr:* 4th/5th Grade Teacher 1972-74, 3rd Grade Teacher 1974-76, 5th/6th Grade Teacher 1976-80, 6th Grade Teacher 1980- Cassville Elem; *ai:* 7th/8th Grade Tutor 1986-; Girls Bsktbl Coach 1972-76; Cheerleading Spon 1977-78, 1980-82, 1985-86; Public Relations 1976-80; White Cty Ed Assn; WCEA (Rep 1982-85, Bd of Dir 1982-86) 1972-, Service Awd 1984; NEA, TN Ed Assn Mem 1972-, Service Awd; Teachers Study Cncl (Pres Elect 1983-84, Pres 1984-85) 1983-86, Service Awd 1984-85; Sparta Jaycees Bd of Dir 1980-84, Outstanding Educator Awd 1983; Minor League Asst Coach 1988, Service Awd 1988; Just Say No Rep 1980-, Recognition Awd; *home:* 306 Gillen Dr Sparta TN 38583

MC GILBRAY, SHIRLEY ANN (SMALL), Third Grade Teacher; *b:* Ottawa, KS; *m:* Delvin Craig; *c:* Darren C., Jacqueline D., De Lynn C.; *ed:* (BSE) Elem Ed, Emporia St Univ 1965; (MS) Spec Ed, Wichita St Univ 1982; Trained in WTA&A Model for USD #259; *cr:* 3rd Grade Teacher Little Elem Sch 1966-71; 2nd-4th Grade Teacher Meridian Elem Sch 1971-77; Pre-Kndgtn Teacher Fairmount Elem Sch 1968; 3rd Grade Teacher Buckner Elem Sch 1977-; *ai:* Teacher in Charge of Building; Discipline & Multicultural Affairs, Career Ladder Design Comm; Substance Abuse Team; Health, Rdng Resource, Cooperating Teacher for Stu Teachers; NEA; Nazarene Christian Life Teacher 1977-; Young Adult Group VP 1987-; Teacher of Yr 1983; *home:* 2500 N Belmont Wichita KS 67220

MC GILL, DARLENE JO (DEAN), Reading Teacher; *b:* Logan, WV; *m:* Thomas Allen; *c:* Chantelle, Stephanie, Todd; *ed:* (BS) Elem Ed, Kent St Univ 1969; (MED) Elem, Edinboro Univ 1983; Grad Stud Ashland Coll; *cr:* 2nd Grade Teacher 1969-72, 3rd Grade Teacher 1975-83, Jr HS Teacher 1983- Buckeye Local Schls; *ai:* Provide Statistical Input Yearly DPPF Grants; Responsible for Yearly Right to Read Celebration; NEA, OEA, NEOTA, BEA 1969-; IRA 1983-; Co-Author Local Chapter II Grant for Rdng Lab; *office:* Wallace Braden Jr HS 3436 Edgewood Dr Ashtabula OH 44004

MC GILL, STAN ALAN, Choir Director; *b:* Sikeston, MO; *m:* Laurie Ann Windham; *c:* Sean A., Heath G.; *ed:* (BS) Music Ed, William Jewell Coll 1975; (MME) Choral Music, AZ St Univ 1980; *cr:* Choir Dir Camdenton Jr/Sr HS 1975-79; Asst Choir Dir S Garland HS 1979-80; Choir Dir Lake Highlands HS 1980-82, S Garland HS 1982-; *ai:* Amer Choral Dirs, TX Choral Dirs; TX Music Educators (VP 1989, St VP, Voacl Chm); Region Vocal Chm 1983-84; *office:* S Garland HS 600 Colonel Dr Garland TX 75043

MC GINNESS, J B, Teacher; *b:* Huntsville, AL; *m:* Cleone J. Kiel; *c:* Jay H., Jeriel L., Jenel B.; *ed:* (BS) Elem Ed, 1958, (MA) Elem Ed, 1961 Harding Univ; Grad Work At Numerous Univs; *cr:* Teacher 1958-59, Prin 1959-61 Parma ID Sch; Teacher 1961-66, Prin 1966-70 Freeport IL Schls; Teacher Pearl City IL 1970-; *ai:* VP Parma Ed Assn 1959-61; Cntrl Planning Cncl 1962-66; Sci Fair Dir; Gifted Prgm; Church of Christ (Asst Minister 1961-70, Ed Dir 1965-70); Mc Ginness Genealogy Awd TN & AL 1986; Stephenson Cty Outstanding Young Educator Awd, Jr Chm of Comm; Outstanding Young Men of America; Outstanding Elem Teachers of America; *home:* 2365 Chelsea Ave Freeport IL 61032

MC GINNIS, GERTRUDE WILLIAMSON, 8th Grade English Teacher; *b:* Belleville, NJ; *m:* Augustus William; *c:* Raymond, Lee A. Vones; *ed:* (BA) Lang Art, Upsala Coll 1953; *cr:* 5th Grade Teacher Belleville Sch #5 1954-55; 7th/8th Grade Eng Teacher Belleville Sch #8 1956-61; 8th Grade Teacher 1966-69, 8th/9th Grade Eng Teacher 1969- Fords Mid Sch; *ai:* Team Leader; AFT, Woodbridge Township Ed Assn, NJ Ed Assn, NEA; Governor Recognition Awd 1990; *office:* Fords Mid Sch Fanning St Fords NJ 08863

MC GINNIS, JUDITH MC CLELLAND, Fifth Grade Teacher; *b:* Lake Charles, LA; *m:* Gordon Edwin; *c:* Rebekah Senith; *ed:* (BA) Elem Ed, 1966, (MED) Elem Ed, 1971, (EDS) Rdng Specialist, 1980 Mc Neese St Univ; Admin/Supervision, Rdng Laboratory, Creative Writing, Rdng in Classroom; *cr:* 7th/8th Grade Rdng/Soc Stud Teacher Iowa HS 1966-69; 5th Grade Teacher Riverside Elem 1969-74; 6th-8th Grade Rdng Laboratory Teacher De Quincy Mid Sch 1974-79; 3rd/5th Grade Teacher Westwood Elem 1980-; *ai:* 3rd/5th Grade Sch Testing Coord; LA Week Act Co-Chm; Calcasieu Educators Assn, LA Educators Assn, NEA 1966-; Houston River Baptist Church; Teacher of Yr Westwood Elem 1988-; *home:* 2924 Roy Bunch Rd Sulphur LA 70663

MC GINNIS, LINDA (FRYE), 4th Grade Teacher; *b:* Indiana, PA; *m:* Donald R.; *c:* Donald E., Scott A.; *ed:* (BS) Elem Ed, 1973, (MED) Elem, 1981 IN Univ of PA; *cr:* Elem Teacher Marion Center Area Sch Dist 1976-; *ai:* Instructional Dev Comm Mem; Aide at Track Meets; Chaperones Sch Dances Skating Parties; NEA, DSEA 1976-; Marion Center Ed Assn Pres 1976-; in Cty Coord Cncl V P 1988-; PTSA 1989-; *home:* RD 1 Box 506 Marion Center PA 15759

MC GINNIS, SHIRLEY A., 5th Grade Teacher; *b:* Detroit, MI; *c:* Stacy, Sharita; *ed:* (BA) Elem Ed, 1971, (MS) Spec Ed, 1980 Wayne St; Grad Stud Admin Trng Prgm 1988-89; Natl Consultant AIMS Fnd Trng, Fresno Pacific Coll 1989-; *cr:* Teacher Detroit Public Schls 1971-72; Owner/Admin Playmates Daycare Center 1976-80; Teacher Oak Park Sch Dist 1972-; *ai:* Safety Patrol Service Squad Spon; Alpha Delta Kappa (Pres-Elect 1986-, Pres 1990); Certificate of Commendation MI Civil Rights Commission 1989; Finalist Newsweek WDIV Outstanding Teacher Awd; *office:* Key Sch 23401 Morton Oak Park MI 48237

MC GINNITY, HELENE CAREY, 3rd Grade Teacher; *b:* Brooklyn, NY; *m:* Frank; *ed:* (BA) Eng/Ed, Siena Heights Coll 1960; Grad Summer Sci Wkshp, Plattsburg St 1961; Grad Study, Columbia Univ 1962-64; *cr:* 2nd Grade Teacher Valley Cntrl Sch 1960-64; 1st Grade Teacher Mountain Lakes Wildwood Elem 1964-67; 3rd Grade Teacher Minisink Valley Cntrl Sch 1967-; *ai:* Gifted Comm; Grade Level Chm; PTO, NYSTA, NEA; Horton Memorial Hospital Volunteer 1981-; CCD Teacher; Brownie Leader; *office:* Minisink Valley Cent Sch PO Box 217 Rt 6 Slate Hill NY 10973

MC GIRR, HARRIET GLADINE (VAUGHN), Retired Substitute Teacher; *b:* Wessington, SD; *w:* Gerald Thomas (dec); *c:* La Vaughn Mc Girr Busse, Kay Mc Girr Cady; *ed:* (BS) Elem Ed, Northern St Univ 1969; Renewed Cert by Traveling & Writing Papers; *cr:* Teacher Collins Cntry Sch 1944-45, Thompson Cntry Sch 1945-46, Sand Creek Consolidated 1947-48, Pratt 1959-61, Douglas 1961-63; 6th Grade Teacher Highmore Elem 1963-83; *ai:* Recruitment for Cotty Coll Centrl SD Health & Ed Fnd PEO Bd; Univ Week for Women; Church (Active Mem, Choir); Historical Society Robinson Certificate of Recognition 1990; NEA, SDEA, Hyde Cty Ed Assn; Highmore Civic League 1960-79; Cmmty Volunteerism 1989-, Certificate of Recognition; PEO; Order of Eastern Star; Amer Legion Auxiliary Educl Chm; Published Poetry & Spec Articles; Public Speaking Engagements; SD His Teachers Prgm for 6th Grade Stus.

MC GLAMERY, NANCY ANN (CHANEY), Teacher of Gifted Education; *b:* Eugene, OR; *m:* Lawrence Marvin; *c:* James L., John R.; *ed:* (BA) Elem Ed, Univ of OR Honors Coll 1962; Working Towards Masters Gifted & Talented Ed, Univ of OR 1986-88; *cr:* 5th/6th Grade Teacher Sch Dist 48 1962-67; 4th/5th Grade Teacher Dept of Defense Overseas Schls 1967-73; Substitute Teacher 1982-83, 3rd-6th Grade Teacher of Gifted 1983- N Thurston Sch Dist; *ai:* Lacey Elem In-Service Comm; Gifted Advisory Cncl; NEA 1962-; OR Ed Assn Membership Chm 1965-66; Overseas Ed Assn 1967-73; WA Ed Assn, N Thurston Ed Assn 1983-; Natl Assn for Gifted Children 1986-; Army Cmmty Service Trainer 1978-83, Volunteer of Quarter 1981, 500 Hr Plaque 1982; Citizens Curr Advisory Co M 1981-83; Luth Church (Cncl, Comm Mem 1980-, Cncl Pres 1985); Dept of Army Certificate of Achievement 1973; Asst Prin Chitose Amer Elem Sch Japan 1967-68; *home:* 1701 Alder St SE Lacey WA 98503

MC GLOCKLIN, MARY BURGOYNE, Science Department Chair; *b:* Harrisville, MI; *m:* Jeffrey L.; *c:* Cailyn; *ed:* (BS) Biological Scis, Cntrl MI Univ 1974; Bio, OH St Univ; Geology, Univ of Akron; Bio, Cntrl MI Univ; *cr:* Teacher Luke M Powers HS 1974-79; Dept Chairperson St Francis De Sales HS 1979-; *ai:* NHS Adv; *office:* St Francis De Sales HS 4212 Karl Rd Columbus OH 43224

MC GLONE, MARSHA MARTIN, English Teacher; *b:* Atlanta, GA; *c:* Bobby Crutchfield; *ed:* (BS) Ed, GA Southwestern; GA St Univ; *cr:* Teacher Morrow Sr HS, Stockbridge Jr/Sr HS; *ai:* Head Chrldr, Drama Coach; Voice of Democracy Awd Veterans Foreign Wars Awd 1988-89.

MC GLOTHIN, PAT O'DONNELL, Fourth Grade Teacher; *b:* Danville, KY; *c:* Suzanne Meyer; Patrick Meyer; *ed:* (BS) Elem Ed, Univ of Louisville 1966; (MA) Elem Ed, Morehead St Univ 1977; In Service/Ed Always in Progress; Cooperative Lrng Wrkshp 1989; *cr:* Substitute Montgomery Cty System 1973-74; 4th Grade Classroom Teacher Mt Sterling Elem 1974-; *ai:* NEA 1974-; KEA 1974-; MCEA (Secy) 1974-; Kiwanis Club Chm Major Emphasis Comm 1988-; Teacher of Yr 1984 M S Elem; *office:* Mt Sterling Elem 212 N Maysville St Mount Sterling KY 40353

MC GLOTHLIN, BETTY FOLEY, Teacher/Vocational Dept Chair; *b:* Bath Cty, KY; *m:* Robert Steele; *c:* Mary B. McGlothlin Rouse, Laura S.; *ed:* (BS) Home Ec, Univ of KY 1961; (MA) Scndry Ed, 1982, (Rank I) Scndry Ed, 1989 Morehead St Univ; *cr:* Teacher Boyd Cty HS 1961-63, 1970-; *ai:* FHA Club Adv; Region 10 Home Ec Teacher (VP 1977-78, Treas 1987-89); KY Assn Voc Home Ec Teacher 1970-; *office:* Boyd Cty HS 12307 Midland Trail Rd Ashland KY 41101

MC GLOTHLIN, BRIAN H., HS Social Studies Teacher; *b:* Kirksville, MO; *m:* Debra Ann Crager; *c:* Kelli, Christopher; *ed:* (BSE) Poly Sci, 1975, (MA) Scndry Soc Sci, 1988 NE MO St Univ; *cr:* Teacher Linn Cty R-1 1975-778 Knox Cty R-1 1977-78, Brookfield R-3 1979-80, Marceline R-V 1980-; *ai:* Soph Class Spon; Marceline CTA Salary Chm 1987-; MSTA 1987-; Jaycees VP 1988-; Kinderland Presch Bd Mem 1988-; *office:* Marceline R-V 314 E Santa Fe Marceline MO 64658

MC GLOTHLIN, MARY KATHRYN RUARK, Sixth Grade Teacher; *b:* Ashland, KY; *m:* Daniel V.; *c:* David L., Amy L.; *ed:* (AB) Elem Ed, 1970; (MA) Rdng Specialist, 1976; Rank I Elem Ed, 1983 Morehead St Univ; Writing Process Wkshp; Career Ladder; Teacher Expectation Stu Achvmt Wkshp; Talking with Your Stu About Alcohol; *cr:* Teacher Cannonsburg Elem 1959-60; Haney-Hatfield 1960-63; Crestwood 1964-68; Ewing Elem 1971-; *ai:* NEA 1959-; KY Ed Assn 1959-; Ewing Womens Club (Pres 1974;) 4-H Cncl Outstanding Leader 1982; Flemingsburg Evening Homemakers KY Colonel 1989; PTA (Treas 1970, Chairperson Spending Comm); *home:* Rt 2 Box 239 Ewing KY 41039

MC GLYNN, JACQUELINE MARIE, Mathematics Teacher; *b:* Naperville, IL; *ed:* (BA) Math, N Cntrl Coll 1989; *cr:* Math Teacher/Coach Waubonsie Valley HS 1989-; *ai:* Girls Var Bsktbl Asst; Soph Sftbl; Fed Chrstn Athletes Spon; NCTM 1988-; *office:* Waubonsie Valley HS 2590 Ogden Ave Aurora IL 60504

MC GOVERN, VINCENT JOHN, Chemistry Teacher; *b:* San Francisco, CA; *c:* Stefan V.; *ed:* (BA) Cellular Bio, Univ of CA Berkeley 1977; (MS) Molecular Bio, Univ of AZ 1983; Credential Life Sci/Chem, San Francisco St Univ 1984; *cr:* Student Teacher Ben Franklin Mid Sch 1983-84; Chem Teacher St Ignatius Coll Preparatory 1984-; *ai:* Sci Club Co-Moderator; Recycling Club & Jr Prom Comm Moderator; NSTA 1984-; CA Assn Chem Teachers 1985-; Inst for Chemical Ed 1985; Impact of Hazardous Materials on Humans & Environment 1988; Regional Lead Teacher Chem Video Disc Series; *office:* St Ignatius Coll Preparatory 2001 37th Ave San Francisco CA 94116

MC GOWAN, CHARLES CLINTON, History/Earth Science Teacher; *b:* Wauseon, OH; *ed:* (BS) Comprehensive Soc Stud, Bowling Green St Univ 1974; Grad Work, Kent St Univ; *cr:* Amer His Teacher 1974-, Earth Sci Teacher 1986- Wayne Cty Schls Career Center; *ai:* Wayne Cty Schls Career Center NHS Faculty Cncl Mem; Schls Environmental Awareness Club Adv; Unified Ed Assn Pres 1986-87, 1988-89; Wayne Cty Joint Voc Dist Ed Assn Pres 1985-86; Wayne Cty Schls Career Center Teacher of Yr 1987; *office:* Wayne Cty Schls Career Center 518 W Prospect Smithville OH 44677

MC GOWEN, BILLIE JO, Mathematics Teacher; *b:* Tulsa, OK; *m:* Benny D.; *c:* Josh, JilAnn; *ed:* (BA) Elem Ed, Cameron Univ 1978; *cr:* 5th/8th Grade Math Teacher 1978-80, 1st Grade Remedial Math Teacher 1980-82, 6th Grade Teacher 1982-84 Meridian Elem; 8th Grade Pre-Algebra Teacher Comanche Mid Sch 1984-; *ai:* Coach; Cheerleading; Stu Cncl; Gifted & Talented;Math-A-Thon Coord; Stu Won Regional Awd in Video Section OK Beautification Project; 8th Grade Won 2nd in Nation Natl Math League; *office:* Comanche Public Sch Box 310 Comanche OK 73529

MC GOWIN, JIM ALLEN, Fifth Grade Teacher; *b:* Poplar Bluff, MO; *m:* Marsha Ann Steinmeier; *c:* Eric, Julie; *ed:* (BS) Elem Ed, 1971, (MA) Elem Admin, 1975 SE MO St Univ; *cr:* Elem Teacher Egyptian Unit #5 1971-; *ai:* BSA Asst 1987-; Waterfowl USA Mem 1987-; First Baptist Church Mem 1978-; *office:* Egyptian Sch R R 1 Tamms IL 62988

MC GRADY, BETTY SHUMATE, Fifth Grade Teacher; *b:* North Wilkesboro, NC; *m:* Ronald B.; *c:* Susan, Rebecca; *ed:* (BA) Elem Ed, Univ of NC Greensboro 1972; *cr:* 5th Grade Teacher Mulberry Elem Sch 1972-; *ai:* NCAE, NEA; *home:* Rt 6 Box 113 North Wilkesboro NC 28659

MC GRADY, C. NADINE SEHL, Chemistry/Physics Teacher; *b:* Larned, KS; *m:* Donald James; *c:* Aaron, Olen, Jennifer; *ed:* (BSE) Phys Sci, 1973, (MS) Earth Sci, 1978 Emporia St Univ; Working Towards Advanced Study in Supervision Certificate, Univ of NC Natl Sci Fnd Project; *cr:* 9th Grade Earth Sci/ Geology/Astronomy/Meteorology Teacher Emporia HS 1974-78; Chem/Applied Chem/Gen Sci/8th Grade Earth Sci Teacher Newton HS 1978-81; Chem/Physics Teacher Hoke Cty HS 1985-; *ai:* Sci Club Spon; NHS Faculty Advisory Bd; Academicaly Gifted Sch Base Comm; Flexible Funding; AAPT 1989-; NC Sci Teachers Assn 1989-; NSTA 1989-; NEA 1974-81, 1985-; Women of Church, Greenpeace, Natl Geographic Society; Thanks to Teachers, Teacher of Yr, Teacher of Month Nom; Rep Hoke HS TV Show on Ed; Grad Asst Emporia St Univ 1973-74; *office:* Hoke Cty HS 600 Bethel Rd Raeford NC 28376

MC GRADY, RUTH SUE GARDNER, Retired Elementary Teacher; *m:* Jordan Dawes; *ed:* (BS) Elem Ed, Radford Univ 1957; *cr:* 1st-3rd Grade Elem Teacher Mt Tabor 1949-54; 3rd Grade Elem Teacher St Paul 1954-55; 3rd-5th Grade Elem Teacher Sylvatus 1955-61; 3rd/4th Grade Elem Teacher Hillsville Elem 1961-75; 3rd-5th Grade Elem Teacher Dugspur Elem 1979-85; *ai:* Bus Duty; 4-H Club; Carroll Ed Assn Treas; St Ed Assn; NEA; Daughters of Amer Revolution 1970-72; United Meth Church Pres; *home:* PO Box 452 Hillsville VA 24343

MC GRATH, PATRICK CARREL, Teaching Assistant; *b:* Washington, DC; *ed:* (BA) Eng Lit, 1976, (MA) Eng Lit, 1979, (MA) Ger Lit, 1981 Univ Of MD; *cr:* Asst Teacher Universitat Des Saarlandes 1981-83; Teacher Hudson HS 1983-89; Asst Teacher Univ Of MD 1989-; *ai:* PhD Candidate, The Gompers Papers Translating Consultant; United Sch Employees of Pasco Mem 1983-; Phi Beta Kappa Mem 1976-; Published In Samuel Gompers Papers, & FL Eng Journal; Reviews Modern Lang Journal & Die Unterrichtspraxis 1990; *office:* Univ Of MD Dept Of German Univ Of MD College Park MD 20742

MC GRAW, LINDA LARGENT, Teacher; *b:* Winchester, VA; *m:* Jerald; *c:* Wyatt; *ed:* (BA) Ed, Shepherd Coll 1969; (MA) Ed, WV Univ 1979; Guidance & Counseling, WV Univ; *cr:* Fr Teacher Mc Connellsburg HS 1969-70; Eng Teacher Chrstn Cty Mid Sch 1970-71, Lake Forest HS 1972-73; Eng Teacher Berkeley Springs HS 1973-; *ai:* Yrbk Adv; Morgan Cty Educl Assn Pres 1973-; WV Ed Assn, NEA 1973-; NCTE 1976-; Delta Kappa Gamma (Corresponding Secy, Comm Chm) 1978-; *office:* Berkeley Springs HS 836 Concord Ave Berkeley Springs WV 25411

MC GRAW, NANCY SIMONE, 7th Grade Teacher; *b:* Fort Lauderdale, FL; *m:* Gary Earl; *c:* Gary E Jr., Walter S., Christopher L.; *ed:* (BA) Soc Stud, Univ of MI 1962; (MED) E TN St Univ 1988; *cr:* Stu Teacher Univ of Sheffield England 1961; 2nd/3rd Grade Teacher Corl Street Sch 1962-62; Adult Ed Teacher Berkeley CA 1965-67; 5th Grade Teacher Miller Perry 1978; 7th Grade Teacher E TN St Univ Sch 1984-; *ai:* Jr HS Math Club & His Club SpoN; Franklin Math Bowl Region Coord; TN Ed Assn Local Pres 1990; NEA; NCTM; Upper E TN Cncl Teachers of Math; Franklin Historical Society; BSA Dist Cub 1970-79, Pioneer Awd; 1st Presbyn Church Hunger Comm; Established Franklin Math Bowl TN Career Level III Teacher.

MC GREGOR, ROBERT G., 6th Grade Science/Math Teacher; *b:* Enderlin, ND; *m:* Jacqueline Joann Pfeiffer; *c:* Kinsey, Kaali; *ed:* (BS) Math/Chem, Valley City St Coll 1968; (MS) Sci Ed, OR St Univ 1974; Cooperative Learning, Curr Alignment, Bay Area Writing Project, Assertive Discipline; Several Cmptr Classes, Aerospace Ed, Project Wild, Energy Conservation; *cr:* Chem/ Physics Teacher Ashley HS 1968-70; Math/Sci Teacher Blatchley Mid Sch 1970-; *ai:* Sitka Ed Assn Pres 1975, 1978; AK Ed Assn St Bd of Dir 1981-83; NCTM 1972-76; Sitka Luth Church Treas; HSS Swimming 1984-; Elks Club 1970-; Natl Sci Fnd Ed Grant St Cloud St 1969, OR St Univ 1970-74; Natl Geographics Hello Prgm 1987-88; *home:* 321 Wachusetts St Sitka AK 99835

MC GRIFF, GEORGIANA MENAPACE, Lang Art/ Journalism Teacher; *b:* Ludwigsburg, Germany; *m:* Mark D.; *c:* Dustin, Rachel, Maggie, Patrick; *ed:* (BA) (BSE) Eng, MSSC Joplin 1979; Comm, SMSU Springfield 1988-89; *cr:* Eng Teacher Mc Auley HS 1979-80; NIE Coord/Secy Joplin Globe 1980-81; Ad Salesperson Ad-Vantage 1981-82; Lang Art Teacher/ Publications Adv Carl Junction HS 1982-; *ai:* Knight Yrbk, Courier-Journal Newspaper Adv; North Cntrl Assn Steering, Career Ladder Comm Mem; Journalism Ed Assn 1988-; Ozarks Publications Advs 1987-; Amer Scholastic Press Assn 1985-, 1st Pl NSP 1985-88, 2nd Pl NSP 1989; NEA Publicity Chm 1987-89; MO Southern St Coll Alumni Assn (Publicity Chm 1983-88, Secy 1989-); *office:* Carl Junction HS PO Box 4 W Allen & Broadway Carl Junction MO 64834

MC GROARTY, TONY THOMAS, Biology Chair; *b:* Tamaqua, PA; *ed:* (BS) Bio/Phys Ed, 1969, (MA) Ed, 1971 Murray St Univ; Curr Dev for Gifted & Talented Prgm City of Paducah 1986-; Curr Dev & Implementation for Governors Scholars Prgm W KY Univ & Murray St Univ; *cr:* Sailor US Navy 1959-62; Coll Stu IN St Univ/Murray St 1962-69; Bio Chm Lone Oak HS 1962-; Teacher Governors Scholars Prgm 1988-; *ai:* Spon Key Club, Bio Club, Medical Explorers; Asst Ftbl, Head Boys & Girls Track Coach; Mc Cracken Cty Ed Assn VP 1978-79; NSTA Mem 1970-; Outstanding Educator City of Paducah 1988; Paducah Cystic Fibrosis Fund Raising Chm 1975-78; KY Colonel 1988; AR Traveler Awd 1989; *office:* Lone Oak HS College Ave Paducah KY 42001

MC GUINESS, SHERRY G., Business Education Teacher; *b:* New Rockford, ND; *m:* Bruce; *c:* Michael; *ed:* (BS) Bus Ed, Dickinson St Univ 1969; (MS) Voc Ed, Univ of AK 1984; *cr:* Librarian Soldotna Jr HS 1969-80; Bus Ed Teacher Soldotna HS 1980-; *ai:* Teacher Rights Rep; KPEA, NEA (Pres, Secy, Treas) 1973-83; AK Ed Assn (Pres Elect, Regional Dir) 1975-77; NBEA, Amer Voc Assn; AK Prof Teaching Practices Commission 1988; *office:* Soldotna HS 425 W Marydale Soldotna AK 99669

MC GUIRE, BETTY JONES, Social Studies Teacher; *b:* Malvern, AR; *m:* James A.; *c:* Vicky Hohrine, Mary Todd; *ed:* (BSE) Soc Sci, 1970, (MSE) Soc Sci, 1977 Henderson St Univ; *cr:* 7th/8th/9th Grade Teacher Malvern Jr HS 1970-79; 11th/12th Grade Teacher Malvern HS 1980-; *ai:* Model United Nation; Mock Trial; Citizen Bee; Class Spon; Malvern Ed Assn Pres/Secy/ Treas 1985-; AR Ed Assn Bd of Dir/Pace Exec Comm 1989-; AR Cncl of Soc Stud; NCSS; Malvern Planning Commission Bd 1975-80; Hot Spring Cty Democratic Comm.

MC GUIRE, EILEEN R., Learning Center Director; *b:* Scott Cty, IN; *ed:* (BA) Elem Ed/Soc Stud, Asbury Coll 1954; (MA) Ed Admin, 1959, (MS) Ed, 1959 IN St Univ; Intensive Phonics, N AZ Univ; *cr:* Elem Teacher Public Schls IN 1952-60; Elem Teacher 1960-85, Elem Prin 1961-71, Learning Center Dir/HS Teacher/Elem Coord SW Indian Sch 1986-; *ai:* Co-Spon Chrstn Service Club; Spon Chrstn Stu Fellowship; Helping Indian Reservation Churches with Vocation Bible Schls; Seminar Speaker for Assn of Chrstn Schls Intnl; *office:* SW Indian Sch 14202 N 73rd Ave Peoria AZ 85381

MC GUIRE, GEORGETTE MARIE, Fifth Grade Teacher; *b:* Hermann, MO; *m:* Danny W.; *c:* Danette, Michael; *ed:* (AA) St Marys Jr Coll 1973; (BA) Elem Ed, Maryville Coll 1977; *cr:* 3rd/ 4th Grade Teacher St Theodore Sch 1973-76; 4th/5th Grade Teacher All Saints Sch 1977-78; 5th Grade Teacher Assumption Sch 1978-; *ai:* Christmas Play & Sch Talent Show Dir; Soc Stud Chairperson; NCEA; Assumption Athletic Assn 1977-82; St Dominic Parents Club Treas 1980-86; Assumption Parish Cncl Secy 1984-87; *home:* 40 N Meadow Dr O'Fallon MO 63366

MC GUIRE, JULIA LYNN, Mathematics Teacher; *b:* Atlanta, GA; *ed:* (BA) Math, 1986, (MED) Math, 1988 Univ of GA; *cr:* Teacher Univ of GA 1987-88, Sylvan Learning Ctr 1987-88, Parkview HS 1988-; *ai:* Jr Var Math Team & Flag Corps Spon; *office:* Parkview HS 998 Cole Dr Lilburn GA 30247

MC GUIRE, KIMBERLEY KAYE, Secondary Teacher; *b:* Cincinnati, OH; *ed:* (BSED) Health Ed, Univ of Cincinnati 1985; (MSED) Educl Admin, Univ of Dayton 1987; *cr:* Sci Teacher 1985-89, OWA Teacher 1989- Kiser Intermediate; *ai:* Bsktbl & Track Coach; NEA, OH Educators Assn, Dayton Educators Assn 1985-; US Army Reserves 1982-88, Army Achievement Medal 1984; Athletic Dir 1988-89; Poetry & Lyrics Published 1985; *home:* 1840 Hewitt Ave Kettering OH 45440

MC GUIRE, PATRICIA RUTH, Learning Disabilities Teacher; *b:* St Louis, MO; *c:* Michael S., Patrick S.; *ed:* (BA) Elem/Spec Ed/Eng/Bus Management, S IL Univ 1978; Grad Stud; *cr:* 6th Grade Teacher Marissa Grade Sch 1978-79; Eng/Lit Teacher Marissa Jr/Sr HS 1979-85; 4th Grade Teacher 1985-87, Teacher of Spec Ed Learning Disabilities 1987- Marissa Grade Sch; *ai:* 7th Grade Spon; Eng Dept Chairperson; NEA, IEA (VP 1982-83, Schlsp Comm); Kappa Delta Phi NHS 1978-83; Yrbk Dedicated by Sr Class 1990; *home:* 6 Algonquin Forest Millstadt IL 62260

MC GUIRE, PATRICK MICHAEL, Fifth Grade Teacher; *b:* Massena, NY; *m:* Jean Livingston; *c:* Megan, Ian; *ed:* (BA) His, SUNY at Potsdam 1972; SUNY at Potsdam; St Lawrence Univ; *cr:* 6th Grade Teacher 1972-79, 5th Grade Teacher 1980- Lisbon Cntrl Sch; *ai:* Head of Gifted/Talented Prgms & Var & JV Girls Bsktbl Prgm; Lisbon Teachers Assn VP 1983-85; NYSUT 1972-; Lisbon Recreation Comm Chm 1982-; St Lawrence Golf & CC 6th

Man Team Event 1985-; Teacher of Yr 1987; Lisbon Sch Support Group; ITV 3rd Place Awd for TV Production; *home:* Rt 1 Box 284 Hall Rd Lisbon NY 13658

MC GUIRE, ROD L., Sixth Grade Teacher; *b:* Pine Bluff, AR; *m:* Phyllis Albrecht; *c:* Kevin, Tricia; *ed:* (BSBA) Management/ Mrktg, 1967, (MA) Elem Ed, 1972 Univ of AR; Ec Ed & Cmptr Ed; *cr:* 5th Grade Teacher Watson Elem Sch 1970-72; Jr HS Math/Soc Stud Teacher Eureka Springs HS 1972-75; 6th Grade Teacher Eureka Springs Elem Sch 1975-; *ai:* 6th Grade Spon; Sr Trip Coord; Track & Field Record Keeper; City Parks & Recreation Comm Chm; Elem Sch Cncl NW AR Delegate 1975-82; Cath Youth Organization Spon 1974-; St Elizabeth Parish Cncl Pres; Classroom Teacher Organization, Elem Classroom Teachers Organization Pres; *home:* 18 Judah St Eureka Springs AR 72632

MC GUIRE, ROSE MARY, Science Teacher; *b:* Chicago, IL; *c:* Joslyn, Brenda; *ed:* (BA) Sci Ed, FL St Univ 1981; Apprenticeship Hyperkinesis & Dyslexic Teaching; Developmental Courses The Mid Sch Concept, Skill Oriented Sci; *cr:* Teacher Woodlawn Acad, Griffin Mid Sch, Adult & Cmmty Ed; *ai:* Beta Club Co-Spon; Sci Fair Coord; Most Stu Awds in Regional Sci Fair Coord 1988; *office:* Griffin Mid Sch 800 Alabama St Tallahassee FL 32304

MC GUIRE, ROSEMARY GILKISON, 5th Grade Teacher; *b:* Emporia, KS; *m:* Cecil Junior; *c:* Deanna, Dustin; *ed:* (BSE) Elem Ed, 1974, (MA) Master Teacher, 1982 Emporia St Univ; *cr:* Kndgtn Teacher/HS Coach Unified Sch Dist 252 1974-75; 5th Grade Teacher Burkburnett Sch Dist 1976-82, Unified Sch Dist 389 1982-; *ai:* Negotiations Comm; Earth Day Comm Cmmty Coord; Delta Kappa Gamma; KS Assn of Teachers of Sci Bd of Dir 1987-; NSTA, NEA; Meth Church Childrens Choir Dir 1983-; *home:* 614 S 3rd Madison KS 66860

MC GUIRE, ROSEMARY GILKISON, 5th Grade Teacher; *b:* Emporia, KS; *m:* Cecil Junior; *c:* Deanna, Dustin; *ed:* (BSE) Elem Ed, 1974, (MA) Master Teacher, 1982 Emporia St Univ; *cr:* Kndgtn Teacher/HS Coach Unified Sch Dist 252 1974-75; 5th Grade Teacher Burkburnett Sch Dist 1976-82, Unified Sch Dist 389 1982-; *ai:* Negotiations Comm; Earth Day Comm Cmmty Coord; Delta Kappa Gamma; KS Assn of Teachers of Sci Bd of Dir 1987-; NSTA, NEA; Meth Church Childrens Choir Dir 1983-; *home:* 614 S 3rd Madison KS 66860

MC GUIRE, TERESA K., Health/Bio/Math Teacher; *b:* Mt Vernon, WA; *m:* Michael J.; *ed:* (BA) Sci/Ed, WA St Univ 1983; ed, W Wa Univ 1986; Drug/Alcohol Trng; Natural Helpers Trng; *cr:* Migrant Summer Sch Teacher Burlington-Edison HS 1983-84; 7th/8th Grade Teacher Ferndale-Vista Mid Sch 1983-87; 8th/9th Grade Teacher Mukilteo-Olympic View Jr HS 1987-; *ai:* Track Coach; Up with People Week Adv; Natural Helper; Health Comm Mem; Developed Health & Sci Curr; NEA, WEA, MEA Mem 1983-; Bell Awd for Outstanding Accomplishments in Teaching from ASB; Canned Food Drive Public Service Awd; *office:* Olympic View Jr HS; 2602 Mukilteo Dr Mukilteo WA 98275

MC GUIRT, CAROLYN JOYCE SCONIERS, Kindergarten Teacher; *b:* South Bend, IN; *m:* Milford W.; *c:* Andrea, Shavonne; *ed:* (BA) Elem Ed, Univ of IA 1978; (MS) Early Chldhd Ed, IN Univ 1983; GA St/Mercer Univ; *cr:* Teacher South Bend Comm Schls 1978-86, De Kalb Cty Schls 1986-; *ai:* Alpha Kapp Alpha Dean of Pledges 1977; *home:* 1635 Links Overlook Stone Mountain GA 30088

MC HALE, KATHLEEN ANNE, Sixth Grade Teacher; *b:* Philadelphia, PA; *ed:* (BA) Elem Ed, 1974, (MA) Elem Admin, 1984 Glassboro St Coll; Grad Stud; *cr:* 3rd Grade Teacher 1974-85, 5th Grade Teacher 1985-88 Evans Sch; 6th Grade Teacher Marlton Mid Sch 1988-; *ai:* Phi Delta Kappa VP 1988-; NJ Ed Assn 1974-; NEA; Marlton Ed Assn Pres; Evesham Township Ed Assn; Cath Sch Bd Secy 1988-; Confraternity of Chrstn Doctrine 8th Grade Teacher 1988-; Beginning Teacher Induction Center Advisory Bd Glassboro St Coll 1987-; Volunteer Teach Bible Sch to Appalachian Children; NJ Governors Teacher Recognition Awd 1988; *office:* Marlton Mid Sch Tomlinson Mill Rd Marlton NJ 08053

MC HALPINE, CATHY NIGHTENGALE, Health Education Teacher; *b:* Charlotte, MI; *c:* Suzanne, Matthew; *ed:* (BS) Health Ed, 1973, (MA) Ed Admin, 1989 Cntrl MI Univ; Elem Ed Endorsement; ITIP; Quest; Peer Coaching; *cr:* Grad Asst CMU 1973-74; Teacher Mt Pleasant HS 1974-81, West Intermediate 1983-; *ai:* Stu Cncl, Class Adv; Quest Instr; Sex Ed, Family Planning, Health Ed Curr, Drop-Out Comm; Policy Review Bd; LSIP Building Team; Amer Red Cross First Aid Instr 1974-81, Service Awd 1976; *office:* West Intermediate Sch 440 S Bradley Mount Pleasant MI 48858

MC HARGUE, JACKIE RUSHING, History Teacher; *b:* Dallas, TX; *m:* Marvin Wendell; *c:* Gary B., Mark L., Lynn E. Mc Hargue Nitcher; *ed:* (BA) His, 1975, (MA) His, 1984 Univ of TX Arlington; Numerous Seminars & Conferences on Gifted Ed; *cr:* Teacher Duncanville HS 1976-; *ai:* Honors & GATE Classes Spon; Local Level Natl His Day Contest; Assn of TX Prof Ed; Lake Ridge Baptist Mission Sunday Sch Teacher 1988-; Other Baptist Churches Asst Pianist 1952-; *office:* Duncanville HS 900 W Camp Wisdom Duncanville TX 75116

MCHATTIE, TONY ARTHUR, English Teacher; *b:* Grand Rapids, MI; *ed:* (BA) Eng/Span, 1967; (MA) Eng, 1968 Western MI Univ; Biblical/Counseling; *cr:* Chm/Eng Dept/Coach 1968-79; Asst Prin/Athletic Dir/Coach 1979-83; Eng Instr/Coach 1983-88; Eng Instr 1988- White Cloud HS; *ai:* Quiz Bowl Coach; Spelling Bee Coach; Jr HS Stu Cncl Adv; Young Authors Coord; 8th Grade Class Spon; MI HS Athletic Assn; Registered Official Track & X-Country; Sch DJ; 1974 Runner-Up X-Cntry Coach of Yr; Class 1987 Natl Coaching Awd in X-Cntry; 1971-72 White Cloud Teacher of Yr; 4-Time Recipient Outstanding Ed Awd Newaygo Cty; *home:* 2687 Bingham White Cloud MI 49349

MC HENRY, PAULA L., Kindergarten-1st Grade Teacher; *b:* Eureka, CA; *M:* Jack R.; *c:* Brad, Janine Averill; *ed:* (BE) Elem Ed, Humboldt St Univ 1965; Humb St Univ; Univ of CA; *cr:* K-6th Grade Teacher Hydesville Elem Sch 1959-70; K-4th Grade Teacher Cuddeback Elem Sch 1970-; *ai:* Sch Improvement Prgm Mem; PTA; Delta Kappa Gamma 1983-; Mem of MAR Team; *home:* Box 174 Hydesville CA 95547

MC HUGH, PHYLLIS MEADOWS, Mathematics Teacher; *b:* Ft Meade, MD; *c:* Paul A., Julia B.; *ed:* (BA) Math, Centre Coll 1970; (MED) Scndry Ed, Univ of Louisville 1985; *cr:* Math/Eng Teacher Junction City Sch 1970-71; Math Teacher St Rita Sch 1971-75, Mercy Acad 1984-85, Pleasure Ridge Park HS 1985-; *ai:* Greater Louisville Cncl Teachers of Math; *office:* Pleasure Ridge Park HS 5901 Greenwood Rd Louisville KY 40258

MC HUGH, STEVE, Social Studies Dept Chairman; *b:* Painesville, OH; *m:* Lauren Carr Boggs; *ed:* (BSED) Soc Stud, Duquesne Univ 1971; (MED) His, Memphis St 1979; *cr:* Amer His Teacher Fairport HS 1972-74, Overton HS 1979-84; World His/ Psych/Sociology Teacher Wooddale HS 1986-; *ai:* Key Club, TN Tomorrow Club Spon; Soph Class Adv; Boys & Girls Tennis Coach; TN Cncl for Soc Stud, Great Memphis Area Cncl for Soc Stud 1989-; *office:* Wooddale HS 5151 Scottsdale Memphis TN 38118

MC INERNEY, JUDITH STRAUSBAUGH, Math Teacher; *b:* Cleveland, OH; *m:* Kevin J.; *c:* Sean, Megan, Patrick, Daniel; *ed:* (BS) Math, St Bonaventure Univ 1968; (MSED) Scndry Math Ed, Elmira Coll 1984; *cr:* Teacher Horseheads Mid Sch 1968-72, Notre Dame HS 1981-84, Horseheads HS 1984-; Ed Consultant Steuben-Alleghany BOCES 1989-; *ai:* Inservice & Buddy Teacher; Jr Class Adv; Assn of Math Teachers 1984-; St Mary Our Mother Choir 1972-; Mini Grant Transformational Geometry; NHS Teacher of Yr 1989; Co-Author; *home:* 101 Snake Hill Rd Horseheads NY 14845

MC INISH, BETTY MC KEE, Third Grade Teacher; *b:* Hartselle, AL; *m:* James H Jr.; *c:* Paul, Pamela; *ed:* (BS) Elem Ed, 1971, (MA) Elem Ed, 1975 Univ of N AL; *cr:* 2nd/3rd Grade Teacher Sheffield Bd of Ed 1971-73; Title I Rdng Teacher 1973-78, 3rd Grade Teacher 1978- Lauderdale Cty Bd of Ed; *ai:* Soc Stud Comm for Accreditation Chm; NEA, AL Ed Assn; Lauderdale Cty Ed Assn Faculty Rep 1987-; Lauderdale Cty Textbook Comm 1982-88; Phi Kappa Phi Honor Society; Kappa Delta Pi Ed Honor Society; *office:* Wilson Elem Sch Rt 5 Box 111 Florence AL 35630

MC INROY, RICHARD OLIVER, HS Mathematics Teacher; *b:* Hornell, NY; *m:* Cynthia Amelia Brown; *c:* Jessica, James; *ed:* (BS) Math, St Univ of NY Geneseo 1983; (MS) Math Ed, Alfred Univ 1988; *cr:* Jr/Sr HS Math Teacher Arkport Cntrl Sch 1983-88; HS Math Teacher Canisteo Cntrl Sch 1988-; *ai:* Frosh Class Adv; Negotiations Comm; Canisteo Fire Company Volunteer 1988-; Recipient Empire St Teachers Schlsp; *home:* 17 Bennett St Canisteo NY 14823

MC INTIRE, CAROLYN JEAN (METCALF), Fourth Grade Teacher; *b:* Waynesburg, PA; *m:* Edmond F. Jr.; *c:* Kathleen, Traci; *ed:* (BS) Elem Ed, 1968, (MA) Elem Ed, 1976 CA Univ of PA; Grad Stud in Elem Admin; Extensive Trng in Innovative Teaching Techniques; *cr:* Teacher Trinity Area Sch Dist 1968-77, SE Greene Sch Dist 1977-; *ai:* SE Greene Ed Assn, PSEA, NEA, Delta Kappa Gamma; *home:* 308 Ringneck Rd Carmichaels PA 15320

MC INTOSH, BEVERLY A. (WORTZ), Biology Teacher; *b:* Coldwater, MI; *m:* David D.; *c:* Brent A., Brenda A. Jewell, Bonni A., Brad A.; *ed:* (BA) Biological Sci, Marion Coll 1962; (MA) Home Ec/Sci, Ball St Univ 1968; Project Wild; Water Management, Aerospace, Energy Seminar, OK St Univ; Cell Bio, Genetics Seminar, Tulsa Univ; *cr:* Teacher Fairmount Schls 1962-66, Carmel-Clay Schls 1966-70, Columbus Chrstn HS 1971-73; Adult Ed Teacher Marion IN 1977; Teacher Madison Jr HS/Bartlesville Mid Sch 1978-; *ai:* Local, St, Intnl Sci Fair & Interscholastics Spon; Courtesy & Textbook Comm; NEA, OK Ed Assn, Bartlesville Ed Assn 1978-; OK St Teachers Assn; Audubon Society, OK Acad of Sci.

MC INTOSH, HAL WINSTON, Soc Stud/Theatre Arts Teacher; *b:* Birmingham, AL; *ed:* (BS) Comprehensive Soc Stud, 1975; (BA) Theatre, 1976 Auburn Univ; Recertification - Univ of Montevallo 1986; *cr:* Teacher Hewitt-Trussville HS 1986-; *ai:* Adv-Troup Spon Local Troup; ITS; Dir Sch Plays; Actor & Dir Arts Cncl Trussville Area; AL Cncl Soc Stud 1986; AL Speech Comm Theatre Assn Pres 1987-; *office:* Hewitt-Trussville H S 5275 Trussville - Clay Rd Trussville AL 35173

MC INTRYE, JOHN THOMAS, High School Art Teacher; *b:* Syracuse, NY; *m:* Lori Lynn; *c:* Sean, Chuck, Christi; *ed:* (BFA) Ed, Univ of AZ 1970; Working Towards Masters Ceramics, N AZ Univ; *cr:* Art Teacher Ft Grant Trng Center 1971-72; Staff Dev Specialist AZ Dept of Corrections Statewide 1972-74; Diagnostic Emotionally Handicapped Evaluation Specialist AZ Dept of Corrections Adobe Mt Sch 1974-79; Art Teacher Camp Verde HS 1979-; *ai:* Stu Class Adv; Head Var Ftbl, Bsbl & Track Coach; AZ Art Ed Assn; N AZ Rep; Kiwanis Intnl; Artist in Ed Prgm Adobe Mt Sch 1978-79, Camp Verde HS 1988-89; Art Collections, Mountain Bell, Glendale Coll AZ, N AZ Univ; Private Collections AZ, CA, NY, MA, IL; *office:* Camp Verde HS PO Box 728 Camp Verde AZ 86322

MC INTYRE, AMY BEDELL, English Teacher; *b:* Jeffersonville, IN; *m:* Bradford Morris; *c:* Lana, Brett; *ed:* (BA) Eng/Scndry Ed, 1980, (MS) Scndry Ed/Eng/Speech/Drama, 1989 IN Univ Southeast; *cr:* Teacher IN Univ Southeast 1988-89, Henryville HS 1980-; *ai:* Sr Play Dir; Class Spon; Stu Cncl Spon; Newspaper Spon; NHS Faculty Comm Mem; Textbook Adoption Comm Chairperson; NCTE Mem 1988-; NEA Mem 1980-; IN St Teachers Assn Building Rep 1988-; *office:* Henryville HS 213 N Ferguson Henryville IN 47126

MC INTYRE, BRENDA KELLEY, Science Dept Head/ Teacher; *b:* Belle Glade, FL; *m:* Travis L.; *c:* Joshua Rodning; *ed:* (AA) Elem Ed, Palm Beach Jr Coll 1968; (BS) Elem Ed, Univ AL 1970; (MEd) Elem Ed, Livingston Univ 1976; Guidance & Counseling 1990; *cr:* 4th & 6th Grade Teacher Chrstn Day Sch 1970-72; 5th & 6th Grade Teacher Grove Hill Elem Sch 1972-75; 6th & 12th Grade Teacher Meadowview Chrstn 1975-76; 7th & 8th Grade Teacher Wilson Hall Mid Sch 1976-; *ai:* Sci Dept Chairperson; Sci Fair Spon; Steering Comm Mem SACS; Sci Fair Judge & Consultant; AL Ed Assn Mem 1970-75 1976-; NEA 1970-75 & 1976; Amer Assn for Counseling & Dev 1989-; Clarke Cty Ed Assn 1970-75 1976-; City of Grove Hill Zoning Bd Mem 1984-; Grove Hill Baptist Church Mem 1978-; Order of Eastern Star Mem Organist 1980-; Outstanding Young Woman of Yr 1979; Nom AL Teacher Hall of Fame; *office:* Wilson Hall Middle School P O Box 906 161 Carter Dr Grove Hill AL 36451

MC INTYRE, MIKE E., Phys Sci/Health Teacher; *b:* Memphis, TN; *m:* Linda R.; *c:* Trace, Mandy; *ed:* (BA) Health/Phys Ed, 1978, Phys Sci Endorsement, 1982, (MS) Health/Phys Ed, 1983 Memphis St Univ; Educl Admin Endorsement Memphis St Univ; *cr:* Teacher/Coach Mt Pisgah 1978-83, Kirby HS 1983-86, Germantown HS 1986-88, Bolton HS 1988-; *ai:* Golf & Var Bsktbl Head Coach; Stu Assistance Prgm Mem; TN Ed Assn, Shelby Cty Ed Assn Mem 1978-; TN Coaches Assn Mem 1983-, Coach of Yr 1988-89; TN Scndry Schls Athletic Assn Mem 1983-, St Champions 1988-89; Shelby Cty Coaches Assn VP; Best of Preps Coach of Yr; *office:* Bolton HS 7323 Brunswick Rd Arlington TN 38002

MC INTYRE, MIKE WAYNE, Scndry Sch Math/Sci Teacher; *b:* Flint, MI; *m:* Cheryl Sue; *c:* Geoffrey W., Monica L.; *ed:* (BA) Soc Sci, Spring Arbor Coll 1968; Grad Work Univ of TX Tyler; *cr:* Teacher/Coach Lancaster Ind Sch Dist 1968-72, Windom Ind Sch Dist 1978-79, Athens Ind Sch Dist 1980-84; Teacher Martins Mill Ind Sch Dist 1984-, Sun Down Ranch-Chemical Abuse Recovery Center; *ai:* Psychiatric/Specialist Univ Park Hospital; Coaching; Sr Trip & NHS Adv; Assn of TX Prof Educators 1985-; Natl Assn of Scndry Curr Dev 1988-; FHA Service Awd 1988; *office:* Sun Down Ranch Campus Rt 2 Box 280 Ben Wheeler TX 75754

MC INTYRE, SHEILA (HIMMEL), Teacher; *b:* Cleveland, OH; *c:* Robert, Stacy, Darcy Hocevar, Richard; *ed:* (BS) Elem Ed, 1967, (MS) Elem Admin, 1974, (MS) Guidance/Counseling, 1975 St John Coll of Cleveland; Psych, Multi-Image Media, Ed, Slide Photography, Kent St Univ; Chemical Dependency Facilitator Trng, Geology, Videography, Underwater Photography, Univ of Akron; Cmptr Courses, Ashland Coll; Certified SCUBA Instr Natl Assn of Underwater Instrs; *cr:* 1st Grade Teacher Towslee Sch 1971; 8th Grade Sci/Lang Art Teacher Willetts Mid Sch 1976-81; 2nd Grade Teacher 1982, 6th Grade Teacher 1983 Towslee Elem; Soc Stud Teacher Edwards Mid Sch 1986-; *ai:* 8th Grade Girls Vlybl, Bsktbl, Track Coach; AFS Host Family; Brunswick Ed Assn (Building Rep 1986-89, Grievence Chairperson 1988-, Negotiator 1982-); NE OH Teachers Assn Publicity Comm 1988-; OH Ed Assn Assembly Delegate 1986-88; St Ambrose (Womens Guild Pres 1969-70, Parish Cncl Pres 1975-77, Parish Lector 1980-); NOAA & Marine Resource Center Marine Life Grant 1989; Curr Research Brunswick Schls 1971-85; NASA Project Teacher in Space Candidate; City of Brunswick Cmmty Civic Service Awd; Medina Work-Study Prgm Commendation; *home:* 4155 Regal Pkwy Brunswick OH 44212

MC INTYRE, VELMA LUCILLE, 5th-8th Grade Math Teacher; *b:* Ravenna, NE; *m:* Kenneth Leo; *c:* Larry K., Kathleen K. Mc Intyre Baxley; *ed:* Ed, Highland Jr Coll 1950; (BSED) Soc Stud/Comp/Elem/General, Benedictine Coll 1966; Grad Stud Ed; *cr:* 1st-8th Grade Teacher Iola Rural Sch 1938-42, Willow Springs Rural 1942-45, Klipple Rural 1945-47; 7th/8th Grade Soc Stud Teacher Highland Grade Sch 1947-50; Teacher St Josephs Atchison 1959-60, Sacred Heart Atchison 1960-70, Atchison Cath Elem Sch 1970-86, St Josephs Nortonville 1986-88; 5th-8th Grade Math Teacher Atchison Cath Elem Sch 1989-; *ai:* 8th Grade Commencement Speaker; 8th Grade Service Club, Concession Stand for Home Athletic Events, Math Contestants Regional Contest Spon; Atchison Cty Spelling Contest Chm; Math Comm Mem 1958-59; Arcjdopcesam Math Evaluation Comm; ASCD 1989-, Certificate 1989; Natl Chinchilla Breeders Assn of America (Corresponding Secy, Recording Secy) 1948-53; Victory 4-H Club (Organizer, Leader) 1944; 4-H Club (Float, Booth & Window Display, Finance & Buying Chm, Advisory Comm 1970-72); Doniphan Cty Teachers Assn Secy 1944; Geography Club Emporia St Teachers Coll Secy 1940; Willow Springs Alumni (Secy 1986-89, Pres 1989-); Anti Child Abuse 1982-87, Certificate; United Way, Heart Fund, Muscular Dystrophy 1983-89; Outstanding Educator Awd 1978; Certificate & Listed in Outstanding Leaders Elem & Scndry Ed; Nom KS Master Teacher Awd 1989; Chosen to Give Response for Our 50th Anniversary of Graduation From Troy HS 1987; St Teachers Convention Delegate 1944; *home:* 1601 Commercial Atchison KS 66002

MC KAY, MARY FRANCES, English & Art Teacher; *b:* Winnsboro, LA; *c:* Stephen M., Mark P.; *ed:* (BSE) Ed, Univ Cntrl AR 1952; Memphis Acad of Fine Arts, East TX Univ, Ouachita Baptist Univ, Henderson St Univ; *cr:* Elem Teacher Brinkley Public Sch 1951-53, 1962-67, Clarendon Public Sch 1954-62; Scndry Teacher Gillette Public Sch 1968-72; Elem Teacher El Dorado Public Sch 1972-74; Scndry Teacher Ashdown Public Sch 1974-; *ai:* Mentor For Gifted Art; Remedial Summer Sch; General Adult Ed; Lang Art Chairperson; NEA, AR Ed Assn 1951-; Ashdown Classroom Teachers Assn (Pres) 1974-; AR Cncl Teachers of Eng 1974-; 1st Meth Church (Mem; Adult Sunday Sch Teacher; Prgm Dir) 1977-85; Little River Cty Spelling Bee Chairperson 1984-87; Ozark Folk Center Comm of 100 1975-77; First Arts & Hum Inst Participant 1966; *home:* 1560 Leona Dr Ashdown AR 71822

MC KEATHERN, JAMES ALVIN, Dept Chm/Science Teacher; *b:* Richmond, VA; *m:* Gertrude Bennett; *c:* Margaret, Elizabeth; *ed:* (BS) Bio, VA St Coll 1955; VA Commonwealth Univ; Longwood Coll; VA St Univ; *cr:* Sci Teacher Park View Mid Sch 1979-; *ai:* Math/Sci Conference Spon & Treas; Mecklenburg Ed Assn Rep 1986-; St Marks Episcopal Church (Treas 1989- Lay Reader 1979-); Southside VA Chapter; Retired Officers Assn Mem 198 5-; *office:* Park View Mid Sch Rt 1 Box 921 South Hill VA 23970

MC KEE, DIANE K., Fourth Grade Teacher; *b:* Connellsville, PA; *ed:* (BS) Elem Ed, Shippensburg St Coll 1972; (MED) Elem Ed, Penn St Univ 1976; *cr:* Elem Teacher Juniata Valley Sch Dist 1972-; *ai:* Juniata Valley HS Drama Club Adv; *home:* RD 1 Box 410B Alexandria PA 16611

MC KEE, HAZEL GRACE, Business Education Dept Head; *b:* Saltillo, MS; *m:* Archie; *c:* Sturdy, Jennifer, Beth; *ed:* (BS) Eng, Austin Peay St Univ 1964; (MA) Bus Ed, Univ of S FL 1975; Doctorate Stud Bus Ed; *cr:* 7th/8th Grade Math Teacher Fernwood Jr HS 1968-69, Sligh Jr HS 1970-71; Eng/Bus Teacher Middleton Jr HS 1971-73, Buchanan Jr HS 1973-76; Bus Ed Teacher Hillsborough HS 1976-77; Teacher Univ of S FL Coll of Ed 1977-80; Bus Ed Teacher Jefferson HS 1982; Eng Teacher Eisenhower Jr HS 1982-84; Bus Ed Teacher/Dept Head D H Jefferson HS 1984-85, East Bay HS 1985-; *ai:* FBLA Adv 1984-; Stu Government Adv 1987-88; Sch Newspaper Adv 1972-73, 1982-84; Many Sch & Cty Comms; NBEA, Natl Vocation Ed Assn 1977-80; FL Bus Ed Assn, FL Voc Assn; Beta Sigma Phi (VP, Scrapbook Chairperson) 1985-; Merit Teacher St of FL 1985-88; Phi Kappa Phi Honor 1975; *office:* East Bay HS 7710 Big Bend Rd Gibsonton FL 33534

MC KEE, PATRICK RUSSELL, Social Studies Teacher; *b:* Yonkers, NY; *m:* Cherie M. Fernandez; *c:* Danielle, Cherie; *ed:* (BA) His, Marist Coll 1970; (MA) His, Seton Hall 1976; Poly Sci, Taft Inst; Success Motivation Inst; *cr:* Teacher Toms River Intermediate 1970-; *ai:* Tour Dir Educl Fnd; His Club Adv; Geography Comm; Toms River Ed Assn Building Rep 1970-; NJ Ed Assn, NEA 1970-; Toms River Fire Cty Secy 1981-86; Dover Township Rent Bd Public Mem 1984-85; Ocean Cty Water Advisory Bd 1989-; Educl Fnd Volunteer Area Rep 1990; Taft Inst Grant Study Poly Systems; Honorable Mention Natl Geographics Geography Project; Amer Inst Foreign Study Intnl Travel Awareness Awd; *office:* Toms River Intermediate Sch 1519 Hooper Ave Toms River NJ 08753

MC KEE, RALPH K., II, Life Science Teacher; *b:* Danville, KY; *m:* Nancy D. Daugherty; *ed:* (BS) Bio, 1975; (MAED) Bio, 1978 Eastern KY Univ; *cr:* HS Bio Teacher Lee Cty HS 1975-76; Casey Cty HS 1977-79; Burgin Independent HS 1979-84; 8th Grade Life Sci Teacher Cntrl Intermediate 1984-85; Boyle Cty Mid 1985-; *ai:* Sci Fair; Ftbl Coach; Cave Expeditions; KY Native Plant Society 1986-; Elected Favorite Teacher 3 Consec Yrs at BCMS; *office:* Boyle Cty Mid Sch Perryville Rd Danville KY 40422

MC KEE, SHERI WEST, Math & Physics Teacher; *b:* Millington, TN; *m:* Rick; *c:* Scott, Leslie; *ed:* (BS) Math, 1973; (MED) Math, 1976 Univ of Montevallo; *cr:* Math Teacher Jemison HS 1974-85; Math/Physics Teacher Chilton Cty HS 1985-; *ai:* Physics Team Spon; Sci Club Spon; Sage Spon; SGA Spon; Scholar Bowl Teem Coach; Citizens Bee Coach; Cty Scholars Bowl Tourn Coord; Sci Fair Coord; Chilton Cty Ed Assn, Pres 1987-88; AL Schlstc Competition Assn, Treas 1988-89; *office:* Chilton County HS 1214 7th St S Clanton AL 35045

MC KEE, TERESA LEE (SMITH), Chemistry Teacher; *b:* Kittanning, PA; *m:* Jonathan David; *ed:* (BA) Chem, 1981, (BS) Chem Ed, 1984 IN Univ of PA; Supervision of Sci Cert & Masters Degree Prgm Duquesne Univ; *cr:* Physics Teacher Edgewood Sr HS 1983-84; Chem Teacher Dayton HS 1985-86, Redbank HS 1986-87, Kittanning Sr HS 1987-; *ai:* Young Chemists Assn & Sci Video Club Spon; Long-Range Planning Comm Mem; Spectroscopic Society of Pittsburgh Equipment Grant 1988; GTE Fellow & Grant Winner 1990; *home:* Box 131 Worthington PA 16262

MCKEE, THOMAS JOHN, English Teacher; *b:* Darby, PA; *m:* Kathleen; *c:* Garin, Elena, Veronica, Christopher; *ed:* (BA) Eng Lit, La Salle Univ 1973; (MA) Eng Lit, Rutgers Univ 989; *cr:* Eng Staff Teacher Highland HS 1973-; Adjunct Staff Teacher Burlington Cty Coll 1987-, Glassboro St Coll 1989-; *office:* Highland Regional HS Erial Rd Blackwood NJ 08012

MC KEEL, JIM WEBB, Physics/Chem Teacher/Dept Head; *b:* Paragould, AR; *m:* Sunnye June Banister; *c:* Jamie L., Jason L.; *ed:* (BSE) Sci, AR St Univ 1964; (MAT) Sci, Murray St Univ 1974; Various Natl Sch Fnd Insts; Electronics, Advanced Class Amateur Radio Operator; *cr:* Sci/Bio Teacher Senath-Hornersville HS 1964-68; Physics/Chem/Bio/Advanced Bio/Phys Sci/Cmptr Teacher New Madrid Cty R-1 1968-; *ai:* Cmptr Usage Adult Instr; JETS Spon; Sch Bd Teacher Rep; Cmmty Teachers Assn Rep 1969-73; CTA (Treas 1972, Pres 1988-89); MO St Teachers Assn Comms 1990; Semo Weather Watch Trng Officer 1971-74; Headstart Advisory Bd Pres 1871; Nom Teacher of Yr 1984-86, 1988-89; US Navy Spec Merit Awd 1985; US Navy Distinguished Teacher of Physics 1986; *home:* 205 Clover Ln Portageville MO 63873

MC KEIVIER, JAMES A., III, Teacher/Coach/Athletic Dir; *b:* Winnsboro, LA; *m:* Ellen M. Bergeron; *c:* Archie, Robert, Rebecca, Rocky, Donald; *ed:* (BA) Phys Ed, Tulane Univ 1973; (MED) Admin, Nicholls St Univ 1978; PIPS Prgm Nicholls St & Mc Neese St Univ; *cr:* Teacher/Coach South Terrebonne HS 1973-79, Sulphur HS 1979-83, H L Bourgeois HS 1983-87; Teacher/Coach/Athletic Dir Merryville HS 1987-; *ai:* Head Ftbl & Bsbl Coach; Athletic Dir; CORE Group Mem; LA Assn Prof Educators, NFICA, LA HS Coaches Assn; T-Club; *office:* Merryville HS Drawer B Merryville LA 70653

MC KELVAIN, TRICIA M., Counselor; *b:* Temple, TX; *m:* Joe; *c:* Amy, Meghan; *ed:* (BS) Eng/His, Univ of Mary Hardin-Baylor 1967; (MED) Counseling, East TX St Univ 1973; *cr:* Teacher Belton Jr HS 1967-68; Killeen HS 1968-75; Cnslr Nolan Mid Sch 1976-; *ai:* TX Assn for Counseling Dev 1976-; Delta Kappa Gamma 1983-; Phi Delta Kappa 1985-; Jr Svc League 1989-; Rotary Educator of Month Nov 1989; *office:* Killeen ISD 505 E Jasper Killeen TX 76541

MC KENNA, EILEEN MARIE, Sixth Grade Teacher; *b:* Chicago, IL; *ed:* (AA) Ed, Santa Rosa Jr Coll 1951; (BA) Elem Ed, San Francisco St Univ 1953; *cr:* 5th Grade Teacher Jedediah Smith Sch 1953-56, Village Elem 1956-58; Asst Prin Village Elem 1960-88; Prin Rincon Valley Union Sch Dist 1974-76; 6th Grade Teacher 1958- Village Elem; *ai:* Stu Council Adv; Rincon Valley Union Teachers Assn (Pres 1958-59, VP 1970-72, 1987-88, Secy 1974-75), Teacher of Yr 1981; Appointed Mentor Teacher 1988-; Qualified as Lead Reviewer for Cty of Sonoma CA; *office:* Village Elem Sch 900 Yulupa Ave Santa Rosa CA 95405

MC KENNA, MARY KAY, Religion/English Teacher; *b:* South Bend, IN; *c:* Samantha, Pierce; *ed:* (BA) Theatre Arts, Barry Univ 1973; Ed, Univ of S MS; Moral Theology, St Charles Seminary; *cr:* Teacher Sacred Heart Acad 1975-77; Trng Mgr Bambergers Macy Incorporated 1978-80; Teacher Bishop Kenrick 1980-81, Bishop Mc Devitt 1981-; *ai:* Peer Ministry; Pro-life; Soc Justice Issues; Homecoming; Inasense Performers 1989; *office:* Bishop Mc Devitt HS Royal Ave At Mulford Rd Wyncote PA 19095

MC KENNEY, EDWARD GARLAND, II, 6th Grade Teacher/Admin Asst; *b:* Richmond, VA; *m:* Kathy Thomas; *c:* Eddie, Jeanelle; *ed:* (BS) Elem Ed, Univ of Akron 1975; *cr:* 6th Grade Teacher Maury Elem Sch 1975-80, Walker-Grant Mid Sch 1981-; *ai:* Sci & Math Dept Chm; Crisis Planning, Assembly, Public Relations, TV Act, Awds, Parent Advisory Comm; Fredericksburg Ed Assn, VA Ed Assn, NEA; Admin Asst 1989-; Incentive Awd 1988; Jaycees Outstanding Educator 1990; *office:* Walker-Grant Mid Sch 1 Learning Ln Fredericksburg VA 22401

MC KENZIE, BRENDA WYLIE, Computer Math & Sci Teacher; *b:* Groesbeck, TX; *m:* Michael Crosby; *c:* Kimberly, Sara; *ed:* (BBA) General Bus/Information Systems, Baylor Univ 1987; *ai:* Cmptr Club; Sr Spon; Prom & Flag Comm; Waco Classroom Teachers Assn Area Rep 1988-; TX St Teachers Assn, NEA 1988-.

MC KENZIE, DENISE, Campus Minister/Instructor; *b:* Lackawanna, NY; *ed:* (AAS) Liberal Art, Trocaire Coll 1972; (BA) Religious Stud, 1973, (MA) Religious Stud, 1973 Canisius Coll; *cr:* Teacher Mt Mercy Acad 1973-89; Lecturer Trociare Coll 1983-89; Campus Minsiter/Instr D Youville Coll 1989-; *ai:* Coord Adopt-A-Grandparent Prgm Local Nursing Home; My Group Serves Dinner to Homeless Monthly; Advise Group Ice Skates with Blind & Handicapped Children; Spon 3 Children from Chrstn Childrens Fund; NACST 1973-; W NY Peace Center for Justice 1973-; *office:* D Youville Coll 320 Porter Ave Buffalo NY 14201

MC KENZIE, MARTHA FAYE, 2nd Grade Teacher; *b:* Scottsboro, AL; *ed:* (BS) Elem Ed, 1974, (MS) Elem Ed, 1978 Jacksonville St; *cr:* 1st/2nd Grade Teacher 1974-76, 3rd Grade Teacher 1976-81, 2nd Grade Teacher 1981- Pisgah HS; *ai:* NEA, AEA 1974-; United Meth Church Treas 1980-84; Upper Sand Mountain Parish Treas 1983-87; Childrens Sunday Sch Teacher.

MC KENZIE, PATRICIA ROBERTS, 5th Grade Teacher; *b:* Manchester, CT; *m:* William Edgar; *c:* Pamela A. Jackson; *ed:* (BA) Elem Ed, 1973, (MED) Elem Ed, 1977 Univ of SC; *cr:* 2nd Grade Teacher Boundary Street Sch & Speers Street Sch 974-83; 4th Grade Teacher 1983-87, 5th Grade Teacher 1987- Lucille Moore Elem; *ai:* Assn of Bay Cty Educators (Exec Bd 1984-86, 1988-); FTP, NEA, PAC Cncl Mem 1990; B-L Womans Club Pres 1968-82; *home:* 3169 Wood Valley Rd Panama City FL 32405

MC KENZIE, SHARON K., Teacher; *b:* Gastonia, NC; *ed:* (AA) Gaston Coll 1967; (BA) Soc Stud, Pfeiffer Coll 1970; *cr:* Teacher Albemarle Sr HS 1970-73, Ashbrook HS 1973-; *ai:* Producer & Dir Miss Ashbrook Pageant; Adv Jr Marshals; Spon PCA Sr Spirit Club; Co-Chm Sr Class Bar-B-Que; Announcer & Scorekeeper Boys & Girls Track Teams; Sch Wide Candy Sale Comm; Dir Miss South Point Pageant; Sr Class Adv 1985; Inter Club Cncl Adv 1973-76; Stu Cncl Adv 1979-82; Jr Heart Bd Adv 1979-80; Jr Class Adv 1970-73; NC Assn of Educators, NEA 1970-; Intnl Order of Rainbow for Girls (Chm Advisory Bd 1982-, Mem Advisory Bd 1979-82); Miss Gastonia Pageant Comm Mem 1980-; Jr Miss Comm Mem 1990; *office:* Ashbrook HS 2222 S New Hope Rd Gastonia NC 28054

MC KENZIE, SUZAN MARTIN, 4th-6th Grade Science Teacher; *b:* Meridian, MS; *m:* Larry Daniel; *c:* Suzan Tabory, Nancy E., Robert M.; *ed:* (BS) Elem Ed, Livingston St Coll 1965; (MED) Elem Ed, Livingston Univ 1969; *cr:* 5th/6th Grade Elem Sci Teacher Butler Elem 1965-68; 4th-6th Grade Elem Sci Teacher Lisman Jr HS 1969-; 5th/6th Grade Elem Sci Teacher Butler Elem 1970-; *ai:* NEA, AL Ed Assn, Choctaw Cty Ed Assn; Delta Kappa Gamma Pres 1982-83; *home:* Rt 1 Box 286 Lisman AL 36912

MC KEON, ELAINE ELIZABETH, Math Teacher; *b:* East Orange, NJ; *m:* James L.; *c:* Kristin, Dan; *ed:* (AB) Math, Rosemont Coll 1970; Adv Ed Courses UC Berkley; *cr:* Math Teacher Springstowne HS 1970-71, W Essex HS 1973-74, Mary Lawn HS 1975-78, De Paul HS 1980-; *ai:* Class, Mock Trial, Math Team Adv; NCTM; Healing the Children Secy 1979-82; Confirmation Coord 1987-; 110 Percent Awd 1988; *office:* De Paul HS 1512 Alps Rd Wayne NJ 07470

MC KIBBAN, JOSEPH L., III, English Teacher; *b:* Phila, PA; *ed:* (BA) Eng Ed, Glassboro St 1975; *cr:* Eng Teacher Gloucester City HS 1984-; *ai:* Var Girls Bsktbl, Jr Var Bsbl, Jr Var Soccer Coach; Nom Governors Teacher Recognition Prgm in NJ 1988-; *office:* Gloucester City Jr Sr H S Rt 130 & Market St Gloucester City NJ 08030

MC KIBBIN, KAREN MC CLURE, Chemistry Teacher; *b:* South Bend, IN; *m:* Scott W.; *ed:* (BS) Life Sci Ed/Math, IN St Univ 1972; (MS) Chem Ed/Bio/Math, IN Univ South Bend 1977; Woodrow Wilson Inst for Teachers of HS Chem, Butler Univ 1987-88, Teacher Expectations & Stu Achievement Teacher & Coord 1988; Project Sci Teachers Awareness Raising Seminars, Notre Dame Trng 1989-; *cr:* Chem/Bio/Math Classroom Teacher La Salle HS 1972-; Methods Professor IN Univ South Bend 1990; *ai:* Quizmaster for Home & Televised Quiz Bowl Matches; Sideline-Ten Yard Marker Mover Ftbl Games; Intramural Bowling & Class Spon; St Marys Coll Cooperative Cncl for Teacher Ed 1984-; IUSB Alumni Assn Distinguished Alumnus Awd 1988; NEA, ISTA 1978-; Hoosier Assn of Sci Teachers Inc 1983-; IN Alliance of Chem Teachers 1980-; Delta Kappa Gamma 1989-; Crop Walk Hunger Relief Prgm Honorary Lead Walker 1989; St Peters United Church of Christ Elder 1982-85; Sagamore of the Wabash by IN Governor; Key to City from South Bend Mayor; IN Teacher of Yr 1989; St Joseph Cty YWCA Woman of Yr 1989; Honorary Doctor of Laws Degree Notre Dame Univ 1989; Chem Sourceview Project IN Univ Bloomington 1990; *office:* La Salle HS 2701 W Elwood Ave South Bend IN 46628

MC KIE, GERALD, Phys Sci Ecology Teacher; *b:* Salley, SC; *m:* Deborah Elizabeth Mc Gee; *c:* Melanie, April; *ed:* (BS) Scndry Bio, Voorhees Coll 1975; *cr:* Teacher/Coach Graniteville HS 1975-79; Teacher Midland Valley HS 1979-; *ai:* Bus Driver; Book Selection Comm; Aiken Cty Ed Assn, SC Ed Assn, NEA 1975-; Youngstorm Branch Deacon 1977-, Citizenship 1979; *office:* Midland Valley HS Mustang Dr Langley SC 29834

MC KIE, ROSALYN ANITA, Second Grade Teacher; *b:* Aiken, SC; *ed:* (BS) Elem Ed, Paine Coll 1977; Elem Ed, SC St Coll; *cr:* 1st Grade Teacher Sand Bar Ferry Elem Sch 1977-82, Peter H Craig Elem Sch 1982-84; 2nd Grade Teacher Peter H Craig Elem Sch 1984-88, Jamestown Elem Sch 1988-; *ai:* Spec Olympics Advisory Bd; Sch Communicator; NEA Building Rep 1988-89; GA Assn of Educators, Richmond Cty Assn of Educators Building Rep 1989-; Tau Gamma Delta Pres 1975-77; PTA Adv; Peter H Craig Elem Teacher of Yr 1986-87, Jamestown Elem 1990-91; *home:* 3132 Truxton Rd Augusta GA 30906

MC KILLOP, DAVID J., Social Studies Teacher; *b:* Riverhead, NY; *m:* Alice Abraldes; *ed:* (BA) Scndry Soc Stud, SUNY Cortland 1982; (MA) Sch Admin/Leadership, LIU-C W Post 1986; *cr:* Soc Stud Teacher Riverhead HS 1982-; Adjunct Instr Syracuse Univ 1989-; *ai:* Head Coach Var Ftbl; JV Coach Boys Bsktbl; NCSS 1984-88; Natl Assn for Curr Dev 1986-88; Bsktbl Coach of Yr 1986-; *office:* Riverhead HS 700 Harrison Ave Riverhead NY 11901

MC KIM, LOUISE WOOTON, English Teacher; *b:* Hazard, KY; *m:* Keith E.; *c:* Kathleen, Kristina, Michal; *ed:* (BS) Elem Ed, TN Temple Univ 1970; *cr:* Teacher Chattanooga City Schls 1970-71, Berea Public Schls 1978-79, Westside Baptist Schls 1979-80, Faith Chrstn 1981-; *ai:* Yrbk Adv; ASCD 1989-; Faith Baptist Church; *home:* 4690 Crumrine Rd Greenville OH 45331

MC KINNELL, MARCIE L., 7/8th Grade Sci/Health Teacher; *b:* Kansas City, MO; *m:* Mike Mc Clure; *ed:* (BS) Bio, Emporia St Univ 1977; (MA) Sci Curr, Wichita St Univ 1989; *cr:* 7th/8th Sci/Health Teacher North Reno 1978-; *ai:* Stu Cncl Spon; Girls Bsbl Coach 1978-85; Sci Chairperson; Human Sexuality Curr Chm; Sci Textbook Comm Chm; Sci Curr Comm Chm; KS Assn of Bio Pres 1989-; Teachers Ed Assn 309 Pres 1984-86; KS Natl Ed Assn Commission Mem 1985; Girl Scouts Leader 1979-84; Amer Red Cross CPR Instr 1986-; Presnter Reg Natl Sci Teacher Conf; Presenter Natl Symposium of Adolescents & Health; Elemplary Teaching Wkshp 1984; *office:* North Reno Elem Sch 1616 N Wilshire Hutchinson KS 67501

MC KINNEY, GENEVA VAUGHN, Sixth Grade Teacher; *b:* Baxley, GA; *m:* Norman L.; *c:* Jetta Lightsey, Leon, Keith; *ed:* (BS) Elem Ed, 1978, (MED) Elem Ed, 1982 GA Southern Coll; Completed Requirements for Dual Certificate; *cr:* 3rd Grade

Teacher 1978-84, 6th Grade Teacher Altamaha Elem Sch 1985-; *ai:* 4-H Club Adv; Chm of Textbook & Curr Comm; Chm of Fluoride Rinsing Prgm; Hospital-Homebound Instr; Appling Cty Assn of Educators (Treas 1982-83, Pres 1985-86, Faculty Rep 1980-81, 1987-88), Honor Roll Membership 1985-86; NEA 1978-; GA Assn of Ed (Mem 1978-, Convention Delegate 1985-86); Woodmen of the World Baxley Lodge 518 (Pres 1986-87, Secy 1990); Appling Cty Bicentennial Comm 1976-80; *home:* Rt 3 Box 115 Baxley GA 31513

MC KINNEY, JOAN MARY ALTGILBERS, Substitute Teacher; *b:* Quincy, IL; *m:* Ivan Edward; *c:* Mary K. Mc Kinney Burnett, Jean E. Mc Kinney Hatfield, Carl I., Earl E.; *ed:* (BA) Sociology, Quincy Coll 1951; Grad Stud Quincy Coll, Univ of AZ, W St Gunnison, CO St Univ, Univ of CO Denver; *cr:* Dean of Women Quincy Coll 1952-53; File Clerk Air Research 1953-54; Techer Norwood Schls 1954-87; *ai:* Masons Awd of Excl 1989-; GSA Field Dir 1951-52; Elem Teacher of Yr Norwood Sch 1987; *home:* PO Box 155 3775 Rd Redvale CO 81431

MC KINNEY, JOHN HUSTON, Math/Social Studies Teacher; *b:* Sylacouga, AL; *m:* Gloria Jean Burress; *c:* Vincent, Ashley, Markese; *ed:* (BS) K-12th Elem, Wilberforce Univ 1978; WISE Prgm, Wright St Univ; *cr:* Teacher/coach Trotwood-Madison City Schls 1978-; *ai:* Coaching Jr HS Girls Vlybl, Jr HS Boys Bsktbl, HS Boys Track; Sci Ed Comm; Heritage Days Parade Comm; City Bsktbl Coach 1972- Plaque 1984-; City Sftb Coach 1984-88 Trophy 1985; City Awd 1985 & 1987 Recognition of Services; Inducted HS Hall of Fame 1987; Jr HS Coach of Yr 1987; Received Recognition 1st Coach to Win 100 Games & More in League Jr HS Boys Bsktbl; *office:* Trotwood-Madison Park Elem Sch 301 S Broadway Trotwood OH 45426

MC KINNEY, MARTHA ANN (MORLEY), First Grade Teacher; *b:* Niles, MI; *m:* Charles Roger; *c:* Heather; *ed:* (BA) Soc Stud/Eng, Cntrl MI Univ 1966; (MA) Teaching of Rdng, W MI Univ 1979; *cr:* 2nd Grade Teacher 1966-76, 1st Grade Teacher 1976- Oakview; *ai:* NEA, MI Ed Assn, Muskegan City Teachers Ed Assn; *office:* Oakview Elem Sch 1420 Madison St Muskegon MI 49442

MC KINNEY, TAMMY ANN CANTERBURY, English/Reading Teacher; *b:* Mullens, WV; *m:* Clifford A.; *c:* Clint Houck, Amber, Blaine A.; *ed:* (BA) Eng/Lib Sci, Concord Coll 1972; (MA) WV Coll 1978; *cr:* Kndgtn Teacher Summerlee Elem 1972-74; Teacher Collins HS 1974-76, Pineville HS 1976-77, Mullens Jr HS 1977-79, Mullens Mid Sch 1984-; *ai:* Stu Cncl, Yrbk Spon; Newspaper Adv; NHS Co-Spon; Assembly Coord; WVEA; *home:* 104 Crystal Ave Beckley WV 25801

MC KINNEY, WANDA MEWBOURN, 2nd Grade Teacher; *b:* Canton, TX; *m:* Curtis; *c:* Tanya, Roper, Greg; *ed:* (BA) Elem Ed, E TX St Univ 1963; *cr:* 6th Grade Teacher Kerens Elem Sch 1963-64; Phys Ed/Coach/Teacher Blooming Grove 1965-68; Chapter I Rdng Teacher Mildred Ind Sch Dist 1969-71; 2nd Grade Teacher Mildred Elem 1971-; *home:* Rt 1 Box 2520 Corsicana TX 75110

MCKINNEY, WILLIAM ANTHONY, Supervisor; *b:* Reidsville, NC; *m:* Vicki Stanfield; *c:* Leigh, Ben; *ed:* (BS) His, Appalachian St Univ 1979; *cr:* Technician NC Gas Service 1979-81; His/Sci Teacher Cmmty Baptist Sch 1981-86; Supvr Amer Express TRS 1986-; *ai:* Sch Bd Cmmty Baptist Sch; Former Vlybl Bsktbl Sftbl All Girls Coach 1981-86; Challenge Bsktbl Club Adv; Dir; Sch Prgm 1985; Jr HS Bsktbl/Vlybl Offica L; Great Performer Awd Amer Express 1987; Golden Headset AMEX 1987; Service Awd Cmmty Baptist Sch 1986; Annual Dedication Cmmty Baptist Sch 1985; *home:* Rt 10 Box 206 Reidsville NC 27320

MC KNIGHT, GLADYS GWENDOLYN, Choral/Keyboard Music Teacher; *b:* Mc Comb, MS; *ed:* (BMUSED) Music, Xavier Univ 1972; (MMUSED) Music, Univ S MS 1973; Univ of CO Boulder, Jackson St Univ; *cr:* Teacher Sam Houston HS 1973-76, Washington HS 1976-83, La Grange HS 1983-84, Washington-Marion Magnet HS 1987-; *ai:* Class Adv, Spon & Chairperson; LA Ed Assn, NEA, Music Educators Natl Conference, Amer Choral Dir Assn Mem 1973- Alpha Kappa Alpha Schlsp Chairperson 1983-; Natl Assn Univ Women Music Chairperson 1978-; *office:* Washington-Marion Magnet HS 2802 Pineview St Lake Charles LA 70601

MC KNIGHT, NORMA LYNCH, Retired Teacher; *b:* International Fall, MN; *w:* James M. (dec); *c:* Larry T., Nancy A., Karen Mc Knight Casey, David J.; *ed:* (BA) His, Aquinas Coll 1964; Grad Courses, Aquinas Coll, W MI Univ, MI St Univ; Seminars; *cr:* 2nd-4th Grade Teacher St Francis Xavier Sch 1965-89; *ai:* Art & Rdng Coord; Taught Cmmty Ed Classes; Red Cross Teacher Spon; Diocese of Grand Rapids Curr Comm; NCEA 1979-89; Curr & Dev Assn 1975-80; Phi Alpha Theta Pres 1967-68; Amer Red Cross Outstanding Voluntary Contributions to Youth Services Awd 1989.

MC KOWN, JEANNE YOUNG, 3rd Grade Teacher; *b:* Washington, PA; *m:* Robert M. Mc Kown Sr.; *c:* Robert Jr., Christopher, Susan Mc Kown Holihan; *ed:* (BS) Ed, PA St Univ 1951; (MA) Ed, St Univ of NY 1975; *cr:* 2nd Grade Teacher Reiffton Sch 1951-52; 4th Grade Teacher 1968-78, 3rd Grade Teacher 1978- Sandy Creek Cntrl Sch; *ai:* Co-Adv Elem Stu Cncl; Northern Oswego Cty Health Services Inc Bd Mem 1988-; *home:* PO Box 299 9050 S Main Sandy Creek NY 13145

MC KOWN, JOAN LOUISE HEFFELFINGER, History Teacher; *b:* Lakewood, OH; *m:* M. James; *c:* Kristalyn L., Gary R.; *ed:* (BA) His/Poly Sci/Sociology, Adrian Coll 1968; *cr:* Teacher Lucas Local Schls 1987-; *ai:* Stu Cncl & Class Adv; OH Cncl for Soc Stud, OH Ed Assn 1988-; *office:* Lucas Local Schls Lucas North Rd Lucas OH 44843

MC KOY, ALVIN L., 6th Grade Teacher; *b:* Leland, NC; *m:* Pecolia Mc Rae; *c:* Kelvin L., Javonne L.; *ed:* (BS) Elem Ed, Fayetteville St Univ 1964; (MA) Admin & Ed, Appalachian St Univ 1973; *cr:* Teacher Lincoln Elem Sch 1964; Dir Adult Ed Lincoln HS 1965; Resource Teacher NC Advancement Sch 1966; Asst Site Admin Cochrane Jr HS 1984; Teacher Piedmont Mid Sch 1990; *ai:* NEA; NCAE; Masons Secy; *home:* 6411 Farmlake Dr Charlotte NC 28227

MC LAIN, KATHERINE J., Band Director; *b:* Ft Riley, KS; *c:* Christopher; *ed:* (BME) Music Ed, 1973, (MME) Music Ed, 1984 Morehead St; Post Masters Stud; *cr:* Band Dir Evans Elem Sch 1980-81, Evans HS 1981-83, Northumberland HS 1984-86, Enslow Mid Sch 1986-; *ai:* Curr Comm; All Cty Band Chairperson; Percussion Exploratory Class; *office:* Enslow Mid Sch Coliss Ave Huntington WV 25702

MC LAMORE, TOM J., Science Teacher; *b:* Natchitoches, LA; *m:* Ginger Fuller; *c:* Angela, Eric; *ed:* (BS) Bio/Phys Ed, E NM Univ 1974; NM St Univ, Univ of NM; *cr:* Teacher/Coach Grants HS 1974-78, Farmington HS 1978-; *ai:* Head Bsbl Coach; *office:* Farmington HS 2200 Sunset Ave Farmington NM 87401

MC LANAHAN, BRUCE DAVID, Bible/History Teacher; *b:* Indianapolis, IN; *ed:* (BA) Bible, 1981; (MDIV) Bible, 1985 Bob Jones Univ; *cr:* Teacher/Athletic Dir Faith Chrstn Sch 1986-; *ai:* Athletic Dir; Var Soccer, Girls Bsktbl, Sftbl Coach; Faith Baptist Church Youth Pastor 1986-; *home:* Rt 1 Box 49 Ramseur NC 27316

MC LANE, MARK DENNIS, English Department Chairman; *b:* South Bend, IN; *c:* (BS) Eng, 1973, (MAE) Eng, 1980 Ball St Univ; *cr:* Eng Chm Brookville HS 1976-89, Franklin Cty HS 1989-; *ai:* NHS & Sch Newspaper Spon; Long Range Planning Comm & Gifted & Talented Prgm, Steering Comm North Cntrl Accreditation Team, Eng Dept Chm; IN Cncl Teachers of Eng 1976-, Hoosier Teacher of Eng 1989; NCTE 1976-; I-STAR Teacher 1985-87; Sch Bd Recognition & Commendations; St Supt of Public Instruction & Governor Orr Commendation; Hoosier Commended Scholar; *office:* Franklin Cty HS 10156 Oxford Pike Brookville IN 47012

MC LAREN, HAROLD WINFRED, Assistant Principal; *b:* Stanford, KY; *m:* Patsy Wall; *c:* Susan J., Allissa L., Harold B.; *ed:* (BA) Art Ed/Bus, 1967, (MA) Sch Admin, 1980, (Rank I) Sch Admin, 1980 E KY Univ; *cr:* Art/Bus Teacher Stanford Elem & HS 1967-76; Design Consultant Stanford Wood Products Incorporated 1976-78; Jr HS Sci Teacher Hustonville Elem 1978-84, Stanford Elem Sch 1984-89; Asst Prin Lincoln Cty HS 1989-; *ai:* Lincoln Cty HS Athletic Dir; Ftbl, Bsktbl, Soccer, Track, Bsbl, Sftbl, Tennis, Golf & Cheerleading Direct Supervision Dir; Stanford & Hustonville Jr HS Beta Club Spon; KY Assn of Sch Admin, Phi Delta Kappa 1979-; KY Sci Teachers Assn 1984-; *office:* Lincoln Cty HS US Hwy 27 S Stanford KY 40484

MC LARTY, KAREN SHEPHERD, Mathematics Teacher; *b:* Lubbock, TX; *m:* Danny; *c:* Kristi, Mandy; *ed:* (BS) Scndry Ed, 1969, (MA) Math, 1986 TX Tech Univ; *cr:* Math Teacher Olton Ind Sch Dist 1970, Lubbock Ind Sch Dist 1970-73, 1980-81; Teaching Asst TX Tech Univ 1981-86; Math Teacher Frenship Ind Sch Dist 1986-; *ai:* NCTM 1989-; TX S Plains Cncl Teachers of Math, Pres Elect 1989-; Jr League of Lubbock 1985-88; Outstanding Teacher Awd 1989-; Tandy Technology Scholar at Frenship HS; *office:* Frenship HS P O Box 100 Wolfforth TX 79382

MC LAUGHLIN, FREDERICK ARTHUR, Band Director; *b:* Des Moines, IA; *m:* Jean Kay Zimdars; *c:* Frederick C., Shelley D.; *ed:* (BME) Music Ed, 1968, (MSED) Scndry Sch Admin, 1988 Drake Univ; *cr:* Percussionist US Army 1968-71; Music Teacher Collins Comm Schl 1971-73; Band Dir Des Moines Public Schls 1973; *ai:* North Side Cmmty Band Dir; Elem Instrumental Task Force Mem; IA Bandmasters Assn 1971-80, 1989-; Des Moines Ed Assn, IA Ed Assn, NEA 1973-; Honor Grad US Army Element Navy Sch of Music 1969; *home:* 4414 Amick Des Moines IA 50310

MC LAUGHLIN, MARK F., AODA/SAP Coordinator; *b:* Clintonville, WI; *ed:* (BS) Ed, Univ WI Oshkosh 1973; (MS) Guidance/Counseling, Univ WI 1990; AODA Trng, Heitzinger Assocs Teen Suicide, Eating Disorders, Sexuality, Children of Alcoholics, Univ WI Platteville; *ai:* Ftbl Coach; WI Dept Public Instruction & WIAA Target Team Facilitator; Children at Risk & WI Drug Abuse Cncl; WI Ftbl Coaches Assn 1975-; WEA 1975-85; WHSFCA, WHSCA 1975-; CESA 2 & DPI AODA Grant; Outstanding Young Man in America 1989-; *office:* Mc Farland HS 5101 Farwell St Mc Farland WI 53558

MC LAUGHLIN, MARY FRANCES, Assistant Principal; *b:* Utica, NY; *ed:* (BA) His, Regis Coll 1967; *cr:* 6th Grade Teacher St Raphaelis 1967-68; 5th Grade Teacher 1968-78, 7th-8th Grade Teacher 1978-, Asst Prin 1986- St Clements Elem; *office:* St Clement Elem Sch 589 Boston Ave Somerville MA 02144

MC LAUGHLIN, PAUL FRANCIS, Mathematics Teacher; *b:* Cincinnati, OH; *m:* Rebecca; *c:* Fred, Elmo; *ed:* (BA) His, (MED) Elem Admin, Xavier Univ; NSF Sci, Drug Counseling & Racial Awareness US Military; *cr:* Dir Joy Ed Center 1974-75, Tippecanoe YMCA Ed 1976-78; Teacher St Andrew Sch 1977-83, St Ann & St Alogsius 1984-88, St William 1988-; *ai:* Homework Club; Tutor & Math Study Group; Assn of Interpative Naturalist 1975-77; OH Cath Ed Assn 1976-; NSTA 1977-83; Cincinnati Zoological Assn 1976-; Morgan Ross Atheletic Assn 1987-; St Alogsius Parish Cncl 1990.

MC LAUGHLIN, RUSSELL LOWELL, Retired Science Teacher; *b:* Audubon, IA; *c:* Holly J., Kirk E., Verna J., Pat J., Laury J., Jamie J.; *ed:* (BSE) Phys Ed, Drake Univ 1950; Grad Stud Sci Ed; *cr:* Ftbl/Bsktbl/Bsbl/Track Coach/Teacher Odebolt HS 1950-54; Ftbl/Bsbl Coach/Math Teacher Rockwell City HS 1954-55; 7th-8th Grade Sci Teacher/Coach Audubon Mid Sch 1955-88; *ai:* NSTA 1960-87; Lions Club 1988-; Presbyn Church 1938-; *home:* 602 Washington Audubon IA 50025

MC LAUGHLIN, TED I., Mathematics Teacher/Dept Chair; *b:* Saginaw, MI; *m:* Beth E. Corwin; *c:* Lea A., Tonya A. Mc Laughlin Gray; *ed:* (BS) Math, 1966, (MA) Math, Cntrl MI Univ; Courses Cmptr Ed; *cr:* Math Teacher Saginaw Public Schls 1967-, Delta Coll 1988-; Cmptr Teacher Carrollton Public 1985-88; *ai:* Wrestling Tournament Dir; Math Curr Dev; Math Textbook Selection Comm; Natl Cncl Math Teacher, MI Cncl Math Teacher; *office:* Saginaw HS 3100 Webber Saginaw MI 48601

MC LAUGHLIN, THELMA GOOCH, 6th Grade Teacher; *b:* Pinehurst, NC; *m:* V. Augustus; *c:* Charles E. Jr.; *ed:* (BS) Elem Ed, Fayetteville St Univ 1949; (MS) Team Teacher Trng, Herbert H Lehman Coll City Univ 1972; Ed/Supervision, Brooklyn Coll, Yeshiva Univ, Fordham Univ 1974; Admin/Supervision, William Paterson Coll 1988-89; *cr:* Teacher Harnett HS 1949-56; Group Teacher Colony House Day Care Center 1959-64; Teacher CS 21 1964-69, CS 134 1969-; *ai:* NYC Comprehensive Sch Improvement Plan Comm Mem; NYC Bd of Ed Mentor Inexperienced Teachers; Adv 6th Grade Cheering Squad & Peer Tutoring; ASCD 1987; United Fed of Teachers 1964; Natl Assn for Negro Corresponding Secy 1983-84; Bus & Prof Women Financial Secy 1984-87; Alpha Kappa (Chaplain 1979, Charter Mem); Bergen Cty Urban & Urban League Guild 1979-83; Pi Lambda Theta 1988; Benjamin G Brawley Awd for Excl in Lit; HS Honor Grad; *office:* City Sch 134 1330 Bristow St Bronx NY 10459

MC LEAN, CHRISTINE FIONA, Civics & Geography Teacher; *b:* Pugwash NS, Canada; *ed:* (BS) Soc Stud Ed, 1984, (MED) Scndry Ed/Soc Sci/Eng/Rdng, 1986- LA St Univ; *cr:* Grad Supvr Asst Undergraduate Soc Stud LA St Univ 1985-86; Amer His Teacher Woodlawn HS 1987; Civics/Geography Teacher Scotlandville Magnet HS 1987-; *ai:* Tri-Hi-Y Youth in Government; TARS Teenage Rupublicans; SPILES Bible Study; Kappa Delta Epsilon (Rush Chm 1983-84) 1982-84; Heartbeat 1983-; Chi Alpha Chrstn Fellowship 1980-86; Phi Kappa Delta 1987-88; *office:* Scotlandville Magnet HS 9870 Scotland Ave Baton Rouge LA 70807

MC LEAN, DONALD JESS, History Teacher; *b:* Waubay, SD; *m:* Donna M. Moir; *c:* Deborah, Christensen, Donita Serr, Darci Winthers; *ed:* (BA) His Ed, Dakota Wesleyan Univ 1956; (MED) Ed, SD St Univ 1967; Northern St Univ; Univ SD Vermillion; *cr:* His Teacher/Coach Ethan HS 1956-59; Plano HS 1959-61; His Teacher Mitchell Jr HS/Mid Schl 1961-; *ai:* Coaching Ftbl/Bsktbl/Track; Athletic Referee Ftbl/Bsktbl; Mitchell Ed Assn; SD Ed Assn; NEA; SD Cncl Soc Stud Bd Dir 1989-; SD HS Act Assn; Ducks Unlimited; Davison Cty Sportsman Club; Presbyn Church; *home:* RR 3 Box 294 Mitchell SD 57301

MC LEAN, EMILY LEIGH, English Teacher; *b:* Charlotte, NC; *m:* Robert F.; *c:* Mark, Heather, Laura, Courtney; *ed:* (BA) Eng, Univ of NC Greensboro 1961; *cr:* Teacher Mc Clenaghan HS 1961-63, Wilson HS 1982-; *ai:* Soph Class Spon; NEA, SCEA Mem 1982-; Jr League Past Pres 1973; First Presbyn Bible Teacher 1990; *home:* 823 Mohawk Dr Florence SC 29501

MC LEAN, MARY ANN, Jr HS Coord/7-8 His Teacher; *b:* Hoboken, NJ; *ed:* (BA) His, Coll St Elizabeth 1968; Soc Stud, Seton Hall Univ & Jersey City St Coll 1973; *cr:* 6th Grade Teacher St Marys 1968-69; 7th-8th Grade Teacher St James 1969-73, St Pauls 1974-; *ai:* Jr HS Grade Level Coord; Newspaper, Forensics Moderator; Schls in Crisis Faculty Rep; NCEA Nom Miriam Joseph Farrell Awd Distinguished Teaching Elem Ed 1987; Faculty Sch Bd Rep; Sch Financial Comm Adv; Grant for Developing Drug Prgm; Co-Author Document U S Dept of Ed for Sch of Excellence Recognition ; *home:* 4 Begonia Ct Sayreville NJ 08872

MC LEAN, SARA CUNNINGHAM, World History Teacher; *b:* San Pingelo, TX; *c:* Heather; *ed:* (BS) His/Ed/Phys Ed, 1964, (MA) Ancient European His, 1976 TX Chrstn Univ 1976; Offical US Government Guide for Palace of Knossos Crete/Greece; Archaelogical Trng in Greece/Israel/Italy; *cr:* His Teacher Cntrl HS 1964-65/1967-68, Crowley HS 1985-; *ai:* AFS; Stu Cncl; NHS Selection Comm; Assn of Prof Educators 1986-; Daughters of Am Rev Historian 1983-86; Daughters of Confed Historian 1983-86; Girl Scouts Leader/Adult Trainer1977-; Outstanding Adult Trainer Sadie Tucker Awd Girl Scouts 1984 & 1985; Recognized By Jewish Cmmty for Cmmty Service, Dan Dancinger Jewish Cmmty Center 1980-; HS Teacher of Yr Crowley HS 1986-87; Recognized By Tarrent Cty for Cmmty Service 1976; Book Published the End of the High Bronze Age Civilization in Crete 1976-; Poems Published 1959 & 1960; *office:* Crowley H S 1005 W Main Crowley TX 76036

MC LELLAN, JUDY COMBES, Sixth Grade Teacher; *b:* San Diego, CA; *m:* Michael Scott; *c:* John M., Sarah A.; *ed:* (BA) Ed, Humboldt St Univ 1975; (MA) Curr/Instruction, Univ of WY 1988; *cr:* Kndgtn Teacher Van Duzen Elem Sch 1975-76, Alcova Elem Sch 1979-80; Spec Rdng/Eng as a 2nd Lang Teacher Jefferson 1981-82; Kndgtn Teacher Jefferson & Sagewood Elem Schls 1982-; 6th Grade Teacher Sagewood Elem Sch 1990; *ai:* Vlybl, Spelling Bee Coach; Dist His Day Judge; Invent America Coord; Writing Assessment Comm; WY Shriners Teacher of Yr Awd; Wrote Pre-Primers for Early Readers 1990; Grant to Help Write, Produce Sch Musical; WY Teacher of Yr Finalist 1989-; *office:* Sagewood Elem Sch 2451 Shattuck Ave Casper WY 82601

MC LENDON, BARBARA GILES, Science Teacher/Science Chair; *b:* Winston-Salem, NC; *m:* Charlie; *c:* Tracy S., Derrick M.; *ed:* (BS) Chem, Benedict Coll 1963; (MED) Phys Sci Ed, Univ of GA 1979; Univ of GA, Columbia Univ, New York City Coll; *cr:* Teacher Martha Schofield HS 1963-64, Blackwell Memorial HS 1964-66, Blackwell Jr HS 1970-76, Elbert Cty Mid Sch 1976-; *ai:* Beta Club, Stu Goverment, Sci Club, Homeroom Group Guidance Adv; NEA, GA Sci Teachers Assn, GA Assn of Ed; Elbert Cty Assn of Ed 1982-83; Single or Displaced Homemaker Chairperson; Elbert Cty Teen-Age Pregnancy Awareness; EXCEL Club (Founder, Organizer, Adv); GA 250 Yr Celebration Steering Comm; Elbert Cty Athletic Booster Bd Mem; Cancer Fund Bd; Natl Assn for Advancement of Colored People; Elbert Cty Mid Sch Teacher of Yr 1988-89; Elbert Cty Sch System Liaison Cncl Pres 1989-; *home:* Rt 5 Box 466 Elberton GA 30635

MC LENDON, ELIZABETH LEE, Russian Department Chair; *b:* Ponca City, OK; *m:* David; *c:* Jason, Jonathan; *ed:* (BA) Russian, OK Univ 1965; (MED) Admin/Russian, Univ of Houston 1977; Russian, Northwestern Univ 1964, IN Univ & USSR 1965, Bryn Mawr Coll, Jherzen Inst Leningrad; *cr:* Russian Instr Bellaire HS 1963-70, Univ of Houston 1974-76, Bellaire Foreign Lang Acad 1977-; *ai:* US-USSR Academic Partnership Leader & Coord; Slavic NHS Spon; Bellaire Russian Club Spon; Amer Assn Teachers Russia (VP, Bd of Dirs) 1985-87; SLAVA NHS USA Pres 1987-; TX Foreign Lang Assn 1989, Teacher of Yr; Houston Area Teachers Foreign Lang, Russian Chair 1965, 1968, 1970, 1977, 1986, 1988; Houston BAKU Sister Cities VP 1989-; Bellaire HS Teacher of Yr 1988-89; Rice Univ Media Center Bd of Dir 1987-; Natl Defense Ed Act Schlsp; Fulbright-Hayes US-USSR Teacher Exch Schlsp; US-USSR Lung Cancer Research Team; Appollo-Soyuz Editor & Translator; Travel Magazine Writer.

MC LENDON, RICHARD CHARLES, Band Director; *b:* Troy, AL; *m:* Michelle B.; *ed:* (BS) Music, Jacksonville St Univ 1977; (MM) Music Performance, Univ of Southwestern LA 1979; *cr:* Grad Asst in Percussion Univ of Southwestern LA 1977-79; Band Dir Murray Ind Sch System 1979-80; Percussi on Instr Murray St Univ 1981-82; Colquitt Cty Jr HS 1984-; *ai:* Phi Mu Alpha 1974-; Pi Kappa Lambda Natl Music Honor Society 1979-; Percussive Arts Society 1977- 3rd Place 11th Annual Composition Contest 1984; Music Ed Natl Conference 1984-; GA Music Educators Assn 1984-; Moultrie Colquitt Co Chamber of Commerce 1985; Moultrie Optimist Club 1985; BSA 1964-, Eagle Scout 1967; Grad Assistantship Univ of Southwestern LA; *office:* Colquitt Co Jr H S 5th St S W Moultrie GA 31768

MC LENDON, STEVE, Band Director; *b:* Ozark, AL; *m:* Marolyne Dasinger; *c:* Marc, Amanda; *ed:* (BME) Music Ed, Troy St Univ 1977; (MA) Music Ed, Univ of N AL 1984; *cr:* Band Dir Fairview HS 1977-88, Dothan HS 1988-; *ai:* AL Band Master Assn, AEA, Menc.

MC LEOD, BONITA YVONNE, 7th Grade Math Teacher; *b:* Broxton, GA; *m:* James D.; *c:* Lisa R., Nathan J.; *ed:* (BS) Mid Grade Ed, Tift Coll 1983; (MS) Mid Grad Ed, Valdosta St Coll 1987; *cr:* Math Teacher Jeff Davis Jr 1984-; *ai:* Chrldr Spon; GAE Pres 1987-89; *home:* Rt 2 Box 417 Hazlehurst GA 31539

MC LEOD, JOYCE LEE, 5th Grade Teacher; *b:* Raleigh, NC; *m:* Michael Reginald; *c:* Michelle, Michael Jr.; *ed:* (BA) Elem Ed, St Augustines Coll 1969; Child Psych, Sci; *cr:* Teacher Franklinton City Schls 1969-; *ai:* Yrbk Comm Chm; Improve CA Achievement Test, Lang Art Improvement, Budget Comms; NC Sci Teachers Assn 1989-; NCAE 1969-; GSA Dean Mother 1979-84; Sci Fellowship; Teacher of Yr 1983-84; Math Teacher of Yr 1985; *office:* Franklinton Elem Sch 418 S Hillsboro St Franklinton NC 27525

MC LIN, ANNE WILLIAMS, Developmental Teacher; *b:* Tchula, MS; *m:* Robert L.; *c:* Aaron, Nkenge; *ed:* (BA) Elem Ed/ Psych, NE IL Univ 1969; *cr:* 4th Grade Teacher Dvorak Elem Sch 1969-71; 1st Grade Developmental Teacher Schneider Elem Sch 1974-; *ai:* Extended Learning Prgm & Rdng Resource Building Rep; N IL Rdng Cncl Mem at Large; IL Lang Experience, Whole Lang Spec Interest Cncl Mem at Large; Aurora Ed Assn Building Rep; *office:* Schneider Elem Sch 304 Banbury Rd North Aurora IL 60542

MC LOCKLIN, MELANIE NEAL, Home Economics Dept Teacher; *b:* Atlanta, GA; *m:* Wayne David; *c:* Rachel Elizabeth; *ed:* (BSHE) Home Ec Ed, 1981, (MS) Home Ec Ed, 1982 Univ of GA; *cr:* Home Service Adv Jackson Electric Membership Corp 1982-83; Home Ec Teacher Cntrl Gwinnett HS 1983-; *office:* Central Gwinnett H S 564 W Crogan St Lawrenceville GA 30245

MC LOUGHLIN, PATRICK JOSEPH, Mathematics Teacher; *b:* Decatur, IL; *m:* Betty Wilcott; *ed:* (BS) Philosophy, 1967, (MS) Math, 1980 Univ of IL; *cr:* Math Teacher Taft HS 1968-74; Math Tutor Univ of IL 1974-79; Math Teacher University HS 1979-; *ai:* Math Team Coach; Sr Class Spon; IL Cncl Teachers of Math 1985-; Articles Published; *office:* University HS 1212 W Springfield Ave Urbana IL 61801

MC LUCKEY, ROBERT ALLEN, Principal; *b:* Uniontown, PA; *m:* Rebecca Sisson; *c:* Kimberly, Robert; *ed:* (BA) Poly Sci, Washington & Jefferson Coll 1972; (MS) California Univ of PA 1986: Admin Prgm for Prin, California Univ of PA; *cr:* Soc Stud Teacher Uniontown Area Sr HS 1974-78; Connellsville Jr HS West 1978-87; Asst Prin Connellsville Area Sr HS 1987-88; Prin Connellsville Jr HS East 1988-; *ai:* SADD Club Spon; Helped OrganizE PTG Organization in our Sch; Ftbl, Bsktbl, Track Coach; PA Assn of Scndry Sch Prin; NASSP; Connellsville Lions Club VP 1990-; Wesley Mens Bible Class Teacher 1976-; Nom for Whos Who Among Americas Young Leaders; *home:* 110 Falcon Dr Connellsville PA 15425

MC LUCKIE, GLORIA LINDSEY, Theatre Teacher; *b:* Gladewater, TX; *m:* George Francis III; *c:* Azure; *ed:* (AA) Theatre, Kilgore Jr Coll 1980; (BA) Theatre/Speech, E TX St Univ 1985; Brigham Young Univ; Working on Masters Univ of TX Tyler; *cr:* Costumer/Actress E TX St Univ Summer Repertory 1981-82; Theatre/Eng Teacher New Diana HS 1987-88; Theatre/ Speech Teacher Jr/Sr HS 1988-; *ai:* One Act Play Dir; UIL Speech Coach for Jr/Sr HS & Elem; Jr HS Chrldr Spon; Delta Kappa Gamma 1990; Upshur Cty Arts Cncl Bd 1989-; Jr HS Teacher of Yr 1987-88; Dist/Area/Regional/St One Act Play Winner; *office:* New Diana HS PO Box 26 Hwy 154 Diana TX 75640

MC MACKIN, MARY BRENDA, Third Grade Teacher; *b:* Bennettsville, SC; *ed:* (BA) Ed, Columbia Coll 1962; (MA) Soc Fnds of Ed, Univ of VA 1981; *cr:* 2nd Grade Teacher Mecklenburg Cty 1962-64; 2nd/5th Grade Teacher Charleston Public Schls 1964-68; 2nd-4th Grade Teacher Alexandria Public Schls 1968-; *ai:* Faculty Cncl Chairperson; Sch Soc Comm; Red Cross Sch Rep; Curr, Grounds, Building Comm; Tutoring Prgm Volunteer; EEA, VEA, NEA 1968-; Delta Kappa Gamma 1984-; SC Jaycee Organization Outstanding Young Ed Nominee 1965; Head Start Prgm Teacher & Building Dir 1965-67; Adult Ed Prgm 1960; *office:* Geroge Mason Elem Sch 2601 Cameron Mills Rd Alexandria VA 22302

MC MAHON, MARY SMITH, Teacher of Mentally Gifted; *b:* Chester, PA; *m:* Kevin K.; *ed:* (BS) Ed, Mary Rogers Coll 1964; (MS) Counseling, Temple Univ 1968; Cmptr Ed; Leader of Jr Great Books; *cr:* Teacher Peace Corps 1964-66, George W Childs 1966-74; 6th-8th Grade Teacher of Mentally Gifted 1974-; *ai:* Jr Great Books Club; *office:* Andrew Hamilton Public Sch 57th & Spruce Sts Philadelphia PA 19139

MC MAINS, STUART ALLEN, Science Teacher; *b:* Ottumwa, IA; *m:* Ginny Greening; *c:* Zachary, Jacob; *ed:* (BSE) Biological Ed, 1970, (MA) Biological Ed, 1975 NE MO St; Univ of MO Columbia; Univ of IN; Univ of S IL Edwardsville; *cr:* Sci Teacher Brookfield R-III Schls 1970-; *ai:* Sci Club; Brookfield R-III Schls Career Ladder Comm; Cmmty Teachers Assn Exec Comm; Instr K-7th Grade Math & Sci Prgm; NSTA 1989-; MO Alliance for Sci 1988-; Sci Teachers of MO 1986-; MO St Teachers Assn 1988-; Brookfield Public Lib Pres 1988-; N Cntrl Energy Symposium Co-Dir; Union Electric Company Grants; *office:* Brookfield R-3 Mid Sch PO Box 230B Brookfield MO 64628

MC MANUS, LOIS TIERNEY, Spanish Teacher; *b:* Oneida, NY; *m:* Paul E.; *c:* Brian, Amy, Allison; *ed:* (BA) Span, SUNY Albany 1968; SUC Oswego & Cortland; Elmira Coll; *cr:* Span Teacher N Syracuse Cntrl Sch 1968-69, Oneida HS 1969-72, Cazenovia Cntrl Sch 1984-86, De Ruyter Cntrl Sch 1986-; *ai:* Stu Cncl Co-Adv; Sch Improvement Team; Stu Assistance & Congruency Team; NY St Assn Foreign Lang Teachers 1968-; *office:* De Ruyter Central Sch 711 Railroad St De Ruyter NY 13052

MC MATH, JOSEPHINE ROSA, Fourth Grade Teacher; *b:* Sharpsville, PA; *m:* Melvin J.; *c:* Michael P.; *ed:* (BS) Ed, Slippery Rock St Univ 1969; *cr:* 6th Grade Teacher Gamble Elem 1969-77; 5th Grade Teacher Wengler Elem 1977-82; 4th Grade Teacher Case Avenue Elem 1983-; *ai:* Kappa Delta Pi; Coll Club of Sharon; *home:* 55 Victory Dr Sharpsville PA 16150

MC MICHAEL, EDWARD JOHN, HS Bio/Chem/Marine Bio Teacher; *b:* Philadelphia, PA; *m:* Mary Walton; *c:* Edward R., Ian D.; *ed:* (BS) Bio, Lynchburg Coll 1975; (MS) Marine Sci, Univ of S FL 1979; Exercise Sci, NE LA Univ; *cr:* Teacher St Petersburg Cath HS 1980-84; Soccer Coach NE LA Univ 1984-86, Huntingdon Coll 1986-87; Teacher Roanoke Valley Governors Sch 1987-; *ai:* Boys Soccer Head Coach Patrick Henry HS; Amer Alliance of Phys Ed, Recreation & Dance; NABT, NSTA; St Olympic Dev Prgm St Soccer Coach 1990; Article Published; *home:* 9009 Poor Mountain Rd Bent Mountain VA 24059

MC MILLAN, ANN ELEANOR (BARNES), Second Grade Teacher; *b:* Riverside, CA; *c:* Steven, Laura; *ed:* (BA) Elem Ed, San Diego St Univ 1963; Completed 27th Unit Extension Courses & Plan to Begin Work on Masters; *cr:* 2nd Grade Teacher Las Palmas Elem 1964-65; 2nd-3rd Grade Teacher Bostonia Elem 1967-; *ai:* Stu Cncl Co-Adv; Phys Ed Cncl Rep; Staff Soc Comm; PTA (Talent Show Dir 1978-, Historian 1972, 1986), Honorary Service Awd 1981, Continuing Service Awd 1987, 1989; Granite Hills HS Booster Bd Prgm Dir 1981-84; Cajon Valley Ed Assn 1967-85, 1989-; Cajon Valley Sch Bd Recognition Awd 1990; *office:* Bostonia Elem Sch 1390 E Broadway El Cajon CA 92021

MCMILLAN, BONNYE BRINK, Second Grade Teacher; *b:* Buffalo, NY; *m:* Robert K.; *c:* Megan Brink; *ed:* (BS) Elem Ed, Shippensburg St 1972; *cr:* Teacher Berrysburg Elem 1972-; *office:* Berrysburg Elem Sch Box 266 Berrysburg PA 17005

MC MILLAN, ELIZABETH WORTH, 6th Grade Teacher; *b:* Chicago, IL; *c:* David; *ed:* (BSED) Elem Ed, N IL Univ 1960; *cr:* 3rd/4th Grade Teacher Burlington Cntrl Dist #301 1960-63; 5th/ 6th Grade Teacher Malta Unit Dist #433 1963-; *office:* Malta Unit Dist #433 507 N 3rd St Malta IL 60150

MC MILLAN, JEANETTE MC GLOHON, Third Grade Teacher; *b:* Pitt Cty, NC; *w:* David F. (dec); *c:* Karen Mc Millan Knight, David Jr.; *ed:* (BS) Primary Ed, East Carolina Coll 1955; *cr:* 2nd-3rd Grade Teacher Bradley Creek Sch 1955-70; Rdng Lab Teacher Sunset Elem Sch 1971-72; 2nd-3rd Grade Teacher Bradley Creek Sch 1973-; *ai:* 2nd/3rd Grade Chm; Media Adv Comm; Supervising Teacher for UNCW Stu Teacher; NHCAFT 1980-; NCCIRA 1980-; NCCTM 1980-; NCSTA 1980-.

MC MILLAN, VIOLA BROWN, Mathematics Teacher; *b:* Pitt Cty, NC; *m:* Arthur Samuel; *c:* Arthur S. Jr., Linda K. Mc MilLan Pritchard, Brice B., Eva J.; *ed:* (BS) Math, E Carolina Coll 1958; (MA) Math, E Carolina Univ 1964; Lehigh Univ 1970-71, Kent St Univ 1974-75, Univ of San Francisco, E Carolina Univ 1975; *cr:* Math Dept Chairperson E Knox Schls 1958-64, Danville HS 1965-68; Math Teacher River View HS 1970-; *ai:* Home Tutoring; Jr Class Adv; Monthly Math Dept Meeting; OH Ed Assn, E OH Teachers Assn, NEA, NCTM, River View Ed Assn, OH Cncl of Teachers of Math 1990; Warsaw United Meth Church (Missions Chairperson 1990, Jr HS Sunday Sch Teacher 1987-); NSF Grant Lehigh Univ 1971-72, Kent St Univ 1974, Baldwin-Wallace Coll 1989; Math Camp for Teachers 1989; *office:* River View HS 26496 State Rt 60 N Warsaw OH 43844

MC MILLEN, GAYLE CONNER, Band Director; *b:* Wichita, KS; *m:* Jane Lorraine Callaway; *c:* Jennifer Brooke, Katherine Conner; *ed:* (BA) Music, Southwestern Coll 1971; (MME) Instrumental Music, Wichita St Univ 1976; Grad Stud Emporia St Univ, KS St Univ, KS Univ, Washburn Univ; *cr:* Band Dir South Haven KS 1971-73; Admissions Cnslr KS Wesleyan Univ 1973-75; Band Dir Solomon KS 1976-78, Salina KS 1978-; *ai:* Curr Revision; Sch Improvement Sub-Comm; KS Bandmasters Assn (Exec Secy 1989-, Past Pres 1985); KS Music Educators Assn (Dist III Jazz Chm 1980-83, 1989-, St Jazz Chm); Music Educators Natl Conference, Intnl Assn of Jazz Educators, Natl Band Assn, Phi Beta Mu, NEA, KEA; Trinity United Meth Church Pianist 1974-; Conductor KMEA Dist V Jr HS Honor Band 1988; Teacher Excl Unified Sch Dist 305 1985; *office:* Roosevelt-Lincoln Mid Sch 7th & Mulberry Salina KS 67401

MC MILLEN, JOHN CHARLES, Fourth Grade Teacher; *b:* Moorhead, MN; *m:* Joan Ellen Marshall; *c:* Jason, Jana, Jared; *ed:* (BS) Elem Ed/Geography, Valley City St Univ 1967; (MS) Elem Admin, Moorhead St Univ 1977; Working Toward Specialist Degree Elem Admin; *cr:* 5th Grade Teacher 1967-68, 4th Grade Teacher 1968-69 Grent Falls Public Schls; 4th Grade Teacher Pelican Rapids Public Schls 1969-; *ai:* Cmptr Comm; Teachers Assisting Teachers; Continuing Ed Comm; NEA, MN Ed Assn 1969-; Pelican Rapids Ed Assn Pres 1976; United Fund Pres 1988-89; BSA Scout Coord 1980-; *home:* Rt 4 Box 32 Pelican Rapids MN 56572

MC MILLIN, JUDITH ANN (OSBORN), Fourth Grade Teacher; *b:* Altus, OK; *m:* Bobby J.; *c:* Johnelle, Lissa; *ed:* (BS) Bus Ed, 1965, (MED) Elem Ed, 1974 SWOSU Weatherford; *cr:* Remedial Teacher Altus Public Sch 1966-67; HS Bus Teacher 1967-70, Migrant Teacher 1971-75, 4th Grade Teacher 1975- Blair Public Sch; *ai:* Yrbk, 4-H Club, Jr & Sr CLass Spon; Jr & Sr Play Dir; Blair Ed Assn Pres 1985-86; OK Ed Assn, NEA; Blair Sorosis Club Pres 1980-81; Blair First Baptist Church Organist 1978-; *office:* Blair Public Sch PO Box 428 Blair OK 73526

MC MILLIN, MARY ZICK, Fourth Grade Teacher; *b:* Webster, SD; *m:* Michael Charles; *c:* Michelle, Michael, Mitchell; *ed:* (BS) Elem Ed, Univ of WI Platteville 1969; *cr:* 2nd/3rd Grade Teacher Gays Mills Elem 1962-64; 1st/3rd Grade Teacher Germantown Elem 1964-68; 3rd Grade Teacher Spring Green Elem 1969-71; 4th Grade Teacher Ithaca Elem 1975; 1st Grade Teacher Rockbridge Elem 1975-80; 4th Grade Teacher Jefferson Elem 1980-; *ai:* Host Teacher for Ed Stus Doing Observation Univ of WI Richland; Jaycettes (Secy 1973, Pres-Elect 1974, Pres 1975); Reedsburg St Johns Luth Church (Assisting Minister, Lector, Sunday Sch Teacher, Choir Mem); Scout Leader; *office:* Jeffeson Elem Sch 586 N Main St Richland Center WI 53581

MC MILLION, MADELINE CARLEY, Seventh Grade Teacher; *b:* Rome, NY; *m:* Edward Houston; *c:* Geoffrey, John; *ed:* (AB) Elem Ed, Marywood Coll 1964; (MED) Elem Ed, Univ of SC 1984; *cr:* Teacher/Health Ed Adv US Peace Corps 1964-66; Spec Ed Teacher Hurricane Elem Sch 1966-67; 4th Grade Teacher First Ward Elem Sch 1967-68; 4th/6th/7th Grade Teacher Chapin Elem Sch 1979-; *ai:* Stu Cncl Spon; NEA, SCEA 1979-; Lexington Medical Center Advisory Cncl 1973-; AAUW VP 1976-77; Chapin Cmmty Theatre Bd of Dir 1988-; Returned Peace Corps Volunteers 1987-; Outstanding Young Women of America 1970; *home:* 368 St Thomas Church Rd Chapin SC 29036

MC MILLION, PATRICIA MADAR, Fifth Grade Teacher; *b:* Princeton, WV; *m:* James M.; *c:* David A., Cynthia L.; *ed:* (BS) Elem Ed, Concord Coll 1967; (MED) Elem Ed, AL A&M Univ 1978; Admin & Supervision, AL A&M 1985; *cr:* 5th Grade Teacher Montview Elem 1973-76; 1st Grade Teacher E Clinton Elem 1982; 3rd-5th Grade Teacher Creative Learning Center 1982-84; 5th Grade Teacher Acad free Academics & Arts 1984-;

ai: Staff Dev Sch Rep; Wkshp AL Cncl on Economic Ed; Huntsville Ed Assn, AL Ed Assn, NEA 1969-; Ruth Hindman Fnd Fellow 1984; Teacher of Yr Huntsville 1986; AL Teacher Hall of Fame Nom 1987; AL Elem Economics Teacher of Yr 1987-88; *office:* Acad For Academics & Arts 2800 Poplar Ave Huntsville AL 35816

MC MULLEN, CAROL (PANCOST), Food Service Instructor; *b:* New Roads, LA; *m:* Wayne William; *c:* Jennifer; *ed:* (BSED) Home Ec, Kent St Univ 1963; Culinary Arts, Johnson & Wales Univ; Management, Baldwin Wallace Coll; Project Teach, Coll of Mount Saint Joseph; *cr:* Food Service Mgr Coll of Saint Teresa 1963-67; Home Ec Teacher Medina HS 1968-69; Dietary Mgr Medina Hospital 1970-71; Food Service Instr Lorain Cty Voc Center 1971-; *ai:* FHA/HERO Club Adv; Regional Rally Chm FHA/HERO; Amer Culinary Fed 1986-; OH Cncl Hotel/Restaurant, Institutional Ed Treas 1985-; Lorain Cty Home Ec Assn Pres 1971-; Delta Kappa Gamma Mem; *office:* Lorain Cty Voc Center 15181 Rt 58 S Oberlin OH 44074

MC MULLEN, M. SHARON, Reading/English Teacher; *b:* Leesville, LA; *c:* Shavonn D.; *ed:* (BS) Elem Ed, Sam Houston St Univ 1965; (MED) Ed, Stephen F Austin St Univ 1978; Cert Counseling K-12, OR St Univ 1985; Rdng Specilization; *cr:* 3rd-6th Grade Phys Ed Teacher Spring Branch Elem 1969-73; 7th Grade Rdng/Eng/Soc Stud Teacher Anson Jones Sch 1974-75; 6th Grade Lang Art Teacher Olle Mid Sch 1975-77; 7th Grade Lang Art Teacher Lufkin Intermediate Sch 1977-78; 4th-8th Grade Lang Arts Teacher Mat Su 1978-; *ai:* Advisory Counseling Prgm; Vlybl Boosters Pres; 7th Grade Girls Bsktbl Coach; AK Teachers of Eng; Lang Art Curr Comm; AK Assn of Rdng; Adult Children of Alcoholic Group Co-Leader; Amer Assn of Counseling; AK Writing Consortium 1985-; Mat Su Ed Assn 1980-; TX St Teachers Assn (Treas 1976-77) 1969-78; NEA 1969-; Homeowners Assn VP 1988-; Delta Kappa Gamma 1989-; *home:* PO Box 872715 Wasilla AK 99687

MC MULLIN, CRAIG, Social Studies Teacher; *ed:* (BS) Geography, 1967, (MED) Ed, 1972 TX Univ; (PHD) Multi-Disciplinary, Univ of N TX 1987; *ai:* Amer Geographical, Oral His Society; Great SW Vietnam Veterans; Colonel, US Army Reserve; *office:* Wylie HS PO Box 490 Wylie TX 75098

MC MULLIN, JOHN JOSEPH, French Teacher; *b:* Philadephia, PA; *ed:* (BA) Fr, St Josephs Univ 1980; (MA) Fr Lit, Bowling Green St Univ 1982; (EDD) 2nd Lang Acquisition/Foreign Lang Ed/Scndry Ed, Temple Univ 1988; LA Sorbonne Paris Certificat de Langue Francaise; Fr Immersion Prgm Universite de Montreal; *cr:* Teaching Asst Bowling Green St Univ 1980-81; Fr/ESL Teacher Valley Forge Military Acad 1981-83; Fr Teacher Morgan Village Mid Sch 1983-85, Upper Merion Area Sch Dist 1981-; Fr/ESL Teacher Berlitz Lang Sch 1982-; Fr Teacher Camden HS 1985-; *ai:* St Josephs Univ Ice Hockey Club Asst Coach; Camden HS Academic Excl Comm; Foreign Lang Educators of NJ Exec Bd Mem 1984-; Published Dissertation, Article; Fr Honor Society Elected Mem; *office:* Camden HS Baird & Park Blvds Camden NJ 08103

MC MULLIN, SHEILA DANIEL, Sixth Grade Teacher; *b:* Beckley, WV; *c:* Nicole; *ed:* (BS) Elem Ed, Concord Coll 1980; (MS) Voc Ed, Marshall Univ 1984; *cr:* Elem Teacher Spanishburg Elem Sch 1981-; *ai:* Chm of Sch Soc Stud Fair; Supts Comm Team; WV Ed Assn; Spanishburg Teacher of Yr 1988-89; *home:* 1004 Reynolds Ave Princeton WV 24740

MC MURRAY, SANDRA K., US History/Journalism Teacher; *b:* Mc Cook, NE; *m:* A. Lindsey; *c:* Sean; *ed:* (BAE) Eng/US & World His, Univ of NM 1976; Grad Stud; *cr:* His/Journalism/Eng/Lang Art Teacher Hoover Mid Sch; *ai:* Spon Sch Paper & Yrbk; Sch Improvement Team; Scheduling & At Risk Comms; *office:* Hoover Mid Sch 12015 Tivoli NE Albuquerque NM 87112

MC MURRY, DOYLE RAY, Science Teacher; *b:* Memphis, TX; *m:* Peggy Irene Tolle;; *c:* Sheila, David; *ed:* (BS) Chem/Bio, Southwestern St Coll 1964; (MST) Chem/Physics, Univ of MO Rolla 1973; TX Tech Univ; Southwestern OK St Univ; Princeton Univ; Univ of AZ; *cr:* Teacher Lubbock Public Schl 1964-69; OK City Public Schls 1969-70; Clinton Public Schls 1970-; *ai:* Sci-Mat Club; Sci Fair Dir; Fellowship of Chrstn Athletes; Sci Fair Judge; 9th/10th/11th/12th Grades Class Spon; Wkshp Instr; North Cntrl Assn Comm; OK Sci Teachers Dir 1970-77; Clinton Ed Assn VP & Pres 1980-81; OK Ed Assn 1970-; Amer Chem Socty of Ed 1986-; NSTA 1964-; NEA Wkshp Presentaion 88; Assn for Physics Teacher 84-; TX St Teacher Assn 1964-; Woodrow Wilson Fellowship Princeton Univ; Univ of AZ Ice Wkshp; Natl Sci Fnd Univ of MO Rolla;Sunday Schl Dir; Deacon Elem Scndry Awd; Outstanding Ldrs in Ed; *office:* Clinton HS 2130 Gary Freeway Clinton OK 73601

MC NABB, BETTYANN ABBE, Third Grade Teacher; *b:* Rust, MI; *c:* Kamela, Lynnada, Malisha, Nichelle; *ed:* (BS) Bio/Sociology/Home Ec/Music, Central MI Univ 1967; *cr:* K-8th Grade Teacher Hammond Rural Sch 1961-62, Yond Rural Sch 1962-63; 5th/6th Grade Teacher Sumner Elem Sch 1963-65; 3rd Grade Teacher Ithaca Elem Schls 1965-; *ai:* Sch Improvement Comm & Stu at Risk Team Mem Ithaca Public Schls; Ithaca Ed Assn, MI Ed Assn, NEA; Ithaca Church of God.

MC NABB, WILLIAM MICHAEL, Biology Teacher; *b:* Chattanooga, TN; *m:* Sarah Patton Mc Kinney; *ed:* (BS) Bio Ed, 1974, (MS) Curr/Instr, Univ of TN Knoxville; (Rank I) Univ of Louisville; *cr:* Teacher/Dept Head Shawnee HS 1975-84; Teacher Doss HS 1985-; *ai:* Sr Class & Sci Club Spon; NSTA; Amer Bio Teacher; KY Sci Teacher; Teachers Summer Sci Inst-Teacher Coord 1985; NSF Fellowship 1989-; Woodrow Wilson Master Teacher 1990; *office:* Doss HS 7601 St Andrews Church Rd Louisville KY 40214

MC NAIR, LINDA A., English Teacher; *b:* Lakeland, FL; *m:* Roy; *c:* Leslie, Lance; *ed:* (BA) Eng Ed, FL A&M Univ 1970; TABA Strategies Course 1974; HSPT Wkshp 1989; *cr:* Afro Amer His Teacher 1970-74, Eng Teacher 1974-84 Memorial Jr HS; Eng Teacher John F Kennedy HS 1984-; *ai:* Mem Natl Jr Honor Society Faculty Cncl; Staff Dev & 9th Grade Soc Comm; NCTE, Willingboro Ed Assn, NEA; NCTE Seminar Convention 1989; *office:* John F Kennedy Jr HS John F Kennedy Way Willingboro NJ 08046

MC NAIR, VIKKI JENKINS, Secondary Math Dept Teacher; *b:* Philadelphia, MS; *m:* John B.; *c:* Austin; *ed:* (AA) Scndry Math, East Central Jr Coll 1982; (BA) Scndry Math, MS St Univ 1984; *cr:* Math Teacher Neshoba Central HS 1984-; *ai:* Jr HS & HS Chrldr Spon 1984-; LA Sertoma; PTO Secy 1988-; *office:* Neshoba Central HS 1125 Golf Course Rd Philadelphia MS 39350

MC NAMARA, CLARE AGNES, English Teacher; *b:* New York, NY; *ed:* (BA) Eng, Coll of New Rochelle 1936; (MA) Eng, 1945, (MS) Guidance, 1949 St John Univ; Grad Stud Theology; *cr:* Eng Teacher Mary Louis Acad 1941-49, Bishop Mc Donnel Memorial HS 1949-57, 1969-71; Theology Teacher St Joseph Novitiate 1957-64; Eng Teacher Stella Maris HS 1971-.

MC NAMARA, DONALD JOSEPH, Physics Teacher; *b:* Providence, RI; *m:* Valerie E. Pepe; *c:* Holly, Emily; *ed:* (BA) Pre Med, Providence Coll 1970; (MED) Cmptrs in Ed, Lesley Coll 1990; Teacher Cert Bridgewater St Coll; Advanced Grad Study Chem, Clarkson Coll of Technology; *cr:* Sci Teacher Somerset HS 1970-; *ai:* ASCD 1989-; Little League Coach 1990; Article Published 1987; Sci Prgms Cmptrs Software Published; Horace Mann Grant 1988-; Nom Pres Awd Excl in Sci Teaching 1985; Presenter MA Assn Advancement of Individual Potential 1986; *office:* Somerset HS Grandview Ave Ext Somerset MA 02726

MC NAMARA, EDWARD EUGENE, AP American History Teacher; *b:* Duquesne, PA; *m:* Nancy Lee Tack; *c:* Michael, Shelly, Shannon, Heather; *ed:* (BS) Soc Stud, Edinboro St Univ 1961; PA St, Glassboro St, Mt Mercy Coll, Taft Sch, Fleisher Sch of Art; *cr:* 7th Grade World His Teacher Butler Jr HS 1961-63; 7th Grade Self Contained Teacher 1963-68, Amer His/Advanced Sociology Teacher 1968-72, US His Teacher of Art Lit/Music Teacher 1972-87, Advanced Placement His Teacher 1987- Overbrook Sr HS; *ai:* Audio Visual Aids Dir; Girls Sftbl Coach; NJ Ed Assn, NEA; Barrington Democratic Campaign Chairperson 1980-86; Chrstn Life Cmmty; St Francis De Sales Church Renewal Co-Chairperson; Penn St Labor Schlsp; Natl Defense Ed Act; Rdng Teacher Mt Mercy Coll; Taft Sch Advanced Placement His Teacher; *office:* Overbrook Regional HS Turnersville Rd Pine Hill NJ 08021

MC NAMARA, JOHN ROBERT, Social Studies Teacher; *b:* Chicago, IL; *m:* Souphanh Phasouk Chitdamrong; *c:* Rattanarangsy, Kittiyarath, Soumalee; *ed:* (BS) Soc Stud, Miami Univ 1973; *cr:* Soc Stud Teacher Gilbert Jr HS 1976, Gilbert HS 1976-80, Gilbert Jr HS 1980-88, Gilbert HS 1988-; *ai:* Frosh Vlybl Coach; *office:* Gilbert HS 140 S Gilbert Rd Gilbert AZ 85234

MC NAMARA, KATHLEEN MARIE, Music Educator; *b:* Cedar Rapids, IA; *m:* Phaedra;; *ed:* (BA) Music Ed, Mt Mercy Coll 1966; Working Towards Masters Univ of IA Iowa City; *cr:* K-12th Grade Music Teacher Alburnett Cmmty Sch 1966-73; K-5th Grade Music Teacher Coolidge Sch 1973-; *ai:* Coolidge Honor Choir Dir; Music Productions Choreographer; Educl Dance Theatre Dir & Founder; Childrens Musicals Composer, Writer, Dir; Cedar Rapids Dist Fine Art Comm; Zeta Phi Eta Pres 1989-; Cedar Rapids Follies Choreographer 1980-89; Jefferson HS Hononary Degree 1989; IA Arts Cncl Model Prgm Team Task Force 1990; Outstanding Young Woman of IA 1979; *office:* Coolidge Elem Sch 6225 1st Ave SW Cedar Rapids IA 52404

MC NAMARA, LOUISE, Eighth Grade Teacher; *b:* New York City, NY; *m:* Gerald F.; *c:* Teresa; *ed:* (AA) Liberal Arts, Queensborough Comm Coll 1969; (BA) Ed, 1971, (MS) Ed, 1974 Queens Coll; Facilitor Skills Trng; Dev of Human Potential Group Skills Prgm; *cr:* 3rd Grade Teacher Immaculate Conception Sch 1972-77; 6th Grade Teacher 1984-, 8th Grade Teacher 1985- Blessed Virgin Mary Help of Chrstns; *ai:* RAP Group Leader; Sch Mission Coord; NCEA 1985-; 108 Precinct Cmmty Cncl 1988-; Citizens of Elmhurst & Maspeth Together 1990; Office of Cath Ed 5 & 10 Yr Merit Awd; Advanced Cathechist Awd; *office:* BVM Help of Christians Sch 70-20 47th Ave Woodside NY 11377

MC NAMARA, PATRICIA SANDERA, Chapter I Teacher; *b:* Oak Park, IL; *c:* Kelly Daghita, Molly Cercone; *ed:* (BED) Elem Ed, Univ of Miami 1963; (AA) Kndgtn Ed, Southern Seminary 1959; *cr:* Teacher Harris Cty Schls 1979-; Substitute Teacher Palm Beach Cty Schls 1965-75; *ai:* PAGE 1987-; Harris Cty Lib Bd Treas 1981-; Sigma Kappa Alumni Pres 1967-69; Courts of Praise 1989-; *office:* Park Elem Sch P O Box 428 Hamilton GA 31811

MCNAMARA-ELISEO, NANCY TESMER, 5th Grade Teacher; *b:* Rockford, IL; *m:* Dr. Thomas S.; *c:* Michael; *ed:* (BS) Elem Ed, 1964, (MS) Elem Ed, 1970 Northern IL Univ; *cr:* 1st Grade Teacher David Fairchild Elem 1964; Teacher J A Riverdahl 1964-74; 3rd-6th Grade Teacher R K Welsh 1974-; *ai:* Rockford Ed Assn; IL Ed Assn; NEA; Educl & Philanthropic Sisterhood.

MC NAMEE, JOHN RAYMOND, Mathematics Teacher; *b:* Mahnomen, MN; *ed:* (BA) Math, St Johns Univ 1986; *cr:* Math/Cmptr/Physics Teacher Cathedral HS 1986-; *ai:* Chess Club Adv; Budget Comm; Prof Assn of Cath Teachers Treas 1989-; Mathematical Assn of America; New Ulm Chorale (Treas 1988, VP 1989); Univ of CO Doctoral Fellowship Awd 1990-91.

MC NANEY, WENDY SUE (JOCHIM), First Grade Teacher; *b:* Denver, CO; *m:* Michael; *ed:* (BA) Elem Ed, Univ of WY 1985; *cr:* 6th Grade Comm Block Rdng/Eng/Soc Stud/Spelling/7th Grade Soc Stud Teacher Mountain View Mid Sch 1985-86; 1st Grade Teacher Alma Elem Sch 1986-87; 3rd Grade Teacher Sarah Milner Elem 1987-89; 1st Grade Teacher Mary Blair Elem 1989-; *ai:* Dist Curr Cncl; I Love to Read Month Chm; Thompson Ed Assn 1987-; *home:* 2631 Wapiti Rd Fort Collins CO 80525

MC NATT, CAROL DOWDY, English Teacher; *b:* Dallas, TX; *m:* Charles William; *c:* Kristin, Blake; *ed:* (BA) Eng, Univ of TX 1961; Grad Stud; *cr:* Teacher Athens HS 1976-; *ai:* UIL Poetry Interpretation; TX Classroom Teachers Assn (Faculty Rep 1987-, 2nd VP 1986-87, Secy 1990); *office:* Athens HS 708 E College Athens TX 75751

MC NATT, DONNA JEAN, Mathematics Department Chair; *b:* Dennison, OH; *m:* James Robert; *ed:* (BS) Phys Ed, Malone Coll 1980; (MS) Phys Ed, Delta St Univ 1984; *cr:* Math Teacher North Sunflower Acad 1983-84, Heritage Chrstn Sch 1984-; *ai:* Sr Class Adv; Girls Bsktbl Coach; Grad Assistantship Phys Ed Delta St; *home:* 13357 N Main Beloit OH 44609

MC NEAL, ANN ELIZABETH, Science Department Chairperson; *b:* San Augustine, TX; *ed:* (BS) Bio, Morehead St Univ 19984; Getit Prgm, GA Southern Univ 1988; *cr:* Asst Dir Pine Camp; Sci Teacher Thomson HS; *ai:* Cheerleading Spon; Sr Class Adv; Asst Girls Var Track; Teen Adventure Prgm Volunteer; Teacher of Yr 1987-88; Nom Rookie of Yr 1985-86; *office:* Thomson HS 511 Main St Thomson GA 30824

MC NEAL, BERTHA BARBEE, Vocal Music Teacher; *b:* Shannon, MS; *c:* Martin A., Melva J.; *ed:* Assoc Music Ed, Flint Jr Coll 1960; (BA) Music Ed, 1963, (MA) Music Ed, 1975 W MI Univ; Music Ed, MI St Univ 1980, 1989; *cr:* Auditor W MI Univ 1965-67; Teacher/Tutor Para Sch Learning Center 1972-76; Vocal Music Teacher Edison Elem Sch 1976-81, Milwood Mid Sch 1981-; *ai:* Voluntary Action Center for Greater Kalamazoo; Keyboard Accompanist for Weddings, Soloists, Churches & Choirs; Prof Entertainer; Sch Choir Concert & St Convention; MI Sch Vocal Assn 1987-; Kalamazoo Ed Assn, MI Ed Assn 1976-; YMCA 1987-; NAACP 1982-; 1st United Church Childrens Choir Dir 1983-85; Kalamazoo Black Arts Festival Awd Entertainment Chairperson 1986; Certificate of Appreciation Kalamzoo NAACP 1988; Music Dept Alumni Celebrity of Month Showcase 1985; Boys/Girls Club of Kalamazoo Spec Awd 1985; Music Lady Clubhouse for Kids 1974-78; Childrens One World Festival, Entertainment Chairperson 1986; *office:* Milwood Mid Sch 2916 Konkle St Kalamazoo MI 49001

MC NEAL, EVELYN BOYK, Teacher of Gifted Speech; *b:* Davenport, WA; *m:* Edgar; *c:* Kim Meline, Kerry Morrison, Kelly; *ed:* (BA) Ed, WA St Univ 1957; (MED) Ed, Univ of Puget Sound 1971; Grad Work Numerous Univs; *cr:* Soc Stud Teacher Naches HS 1959; 2nd Grade Teacher North East Sch 1959-60; Elem Teacher Tacoma & Franklin Pierce Schls 1962-80; Honors/Gifted Teacher Franklin Pierce Schls 1980-; *ai:* Drama, Speech, Future Problem Solving Coach; Project Achieve Comm; WA St Educl Delegation Mem Peoples Republic of China 1984, 1986; Fulbright-Hays Scholar Seminar in Egypt 1988; *office:* Ford Mid Sch 1602 E 104th St Tacoma WA 98445

MC NEAL, MARY MARTINDILL, Geography Teacher; *b:* Denver, CO; *m:* Johnny Ray; *c:* Joshua, Sarah; *ed:* (BA) His, Augusta Coll 1986; *cr:* 7th Grade Soc Stud Teacher Greenwood Lakes Mid Sch 1986-; *ai:* Spirit, Building Comm; Natl Cncl Geographic Ed 1987-90; NCSS; *office:* Greenwood Lakes Mid Sch 601 Lake Park Dr Lake Mary FL 32746

MC NEELY, BECKY PAYNE, Sixth Grade Teacher; *b:* Pelahatchie, MS; *m:* Don Keith Sr.; *c:* Mrs. Grant Holland, Lee Jones, Keith, Gwen; *ed:* (BS) Elem Ed, Midwestern Univ 1972; (MED) Elem Ed, Univ of MS 1974; Drafting, Residential Drafting, Real Estate; *cr:* 1st Grade Teacher Lafayette Cty 1972-74, Burnsville 1974-76; 1st-4th/6th Grade Teacher Iuka Elem Sch 1976-; *ai:* SWEEP; Art Festival Spon; Lib Supporter; MPE 1987-; PTA VP 1974-; *home:* Rt 3 Box 370 Iuka MS 38852

MC NEER, BEVERLY KING, Social Studies Teacher; *b:* Laurel, MS; *m:* Maxie Eugene; *c:* Marc E., Scott E.; *ed:* (AA) Scndry Ed, 1968; (BS) Eng/His, USM 1970; PET Trainer & Teacher; USM & William Carey Coll; *cr:* Teacher Bay Springs HS; *ai:* PET Trainer & Staff Dev Teacher; Soc Stud Chm; St Soc Stud Input Comm; Beta Club & Chrldr Spon; MS Ec Commission 1979-80, 1988-89, STAR Teacher; Mae Del 1980; Union Seminary; Baptist Church; *office:* Bay Srpings HS Box 389 Hwy 18 Bay Springs MS 39422

MC NEIL, JAMES MICHAEL, 7th Grade Soc Stud Teacher; *b:* Burlington, VT; *ed:* (BA) Soc Stud/Lang Art/Phys Ed/Rdng, Univ of VT 1981; *cr:* Soc Stud South Burlington HS 1981-82, Camels Hump Mid Sch 1982-; *ai:* Bsktbl, Track, Bsbl & Intramurals Coach; VT Ed Assn 1983-; VT Waterski Assn Pres 1976-, VT Water Ski Champ 1976; Partners of Amer YMCA Certified Scuba Diver 1989; *office:* Camels Hump Mid Sch Brown Trace Rd Richmond VT 05477

MC NEIL, JESSE A., JR., 6th Grade Teacher; *b:* Mound City, IL; *m:* Emma Brooks; *c:* Kerry, Tabitha, Jared; *ed:* (BA) Elem Ed, Wilber Force Univ 1971; (MS) Elem Admin, Southeast MO Univ 1982; *cr:* Staff Trainer 1971-74; 5th Grade Teacher 1975-82; 4th Grade Teacher 1982-86; 6th Grade Teacher 1987- Meridian Elem; *ai:* Track; Sftbl; Meridian Elem Assn 1971-; IL Ed Assn 1971-; NEA 1971-; Masonic Lodge 1973-78; Mound City City Cncl Alderman 1975-76.

MC NEIL, MARTIN D., 4th Grade Teacher; *b:* White Plains, NY; *m:* Judith Shuebruk; *c:* Brian, Ian; *ed:* (BS) Elem Ed/His, Buffalo St Teachers Coll 1961; (MS) Elem Sch Admin, Columbia Univ 1967; *cr:* US Army 1961; 6th Grade Teacher 1961-76, 5th Grade Teacher 1976-80, 4th Grade Teacher 1980- Trinity Elem Sch; *ai:* Larchmont Jr Soccer League Coach 1980-; New Rochelle Fed of United Sch Employees Exec Bd 1970-; NY St Schlsp to Study Geometry Columbia Univ 1970; *office:* Trinity Sch 180 Pelham Rd New Rochelle NY 10805

MC NEILL, CHARLES BISHOP, Teacher/Mathematics Dept Chair; *b:* Kansas City, MO; *c:* Madeline, M. David, Brian; *ed:* (BS) Soc Stud/Econ/Anthropology, Santa Clara Univ 1971; Grad Stud Notre Dame, Gonzaga Univ; *cr:* Teacher Moreau HS 1974-75, St Francis HS 1973-74, 1975-76, St Anthonys HS 1976-77, St John Vianney 1977-; *office:* St John Vianney Sch N 501 Walnut Rd Spokane WA 99206

MC NEILL, STEPHANIE SLOAN, Spanish/English Teacher; *b:* Davenport, IA; *m:* Tim; *ed:* (BA) Eng/Span Scndry, Univ of IA 1988; *cr:* Span/Eng Teacher E Union HS 1988-; *ai:* Yrbk; Newspaper; Cheerleading; NEA 1988-; Nom St of IA Top 6 Educators 1989; *office:* E Union HS 1000 Eagle Dr Afton IA 50830

MC NELLIS, MARJORIE KATHLEEN, Asst Dir Bilingual Project; *b:* Butte, MT; *ed:* (BA) Eng, Univ of MT 1972; (MED) Admin, MT St Univ 1986; Ed/General Sch Admin, MT St Univ 1987, 1990; *cr:* Eng Teacher Whitehall Public Sch Dist 1983-87; Asst Dir Bi-Ling Project MT St Univ 1989-; Supt Roy Public Sch Dist 1990; *ai:* Kappa Delta Pi Pres 1989-; Phi Delta Kappa 1990; Article, Assoc Ed Big Sky Admin 1989; Developed, Presented Study Skills Wkshp; *office:* MT St Univ MT St Univ Bozeman MT 59719

MC NIEL, RAE COCHRANE, Gifted Consultant; *b:* Brockton, MA; *m:* Robert N.; *c:* Mark M., Michael G., Alan C., Brian A.; *ed:* (BA) Ed, Univ of CO 1956; (MA) Counseling/Guidance, Wichita St Univ 1979; Gifted Ed; Sch Psychologist Trng; *cr:* Elem Teacher Billings Sch Dist 1956-57; Private Pre-Sch Teacher YMCA 1970-78; GTC Teacher of Gifted Unified Sch Dist #260 1980-; *ai:* Soph Class Head Spon; Suicide Prevention Comm; Scholars Bowl, Future Problem Solving Team, Odyssey of the Mind Team Coach; N Cntrl Evaluation Team; Delta Kappa Gamma 1989-; Prof Advocates of Gifted Ed Pres 1984-; Eastminster Presbyn Church; Chi Omega; KS Honor Teacher Univ of KS Awd; St of KS Evaluator Future Problem Solving; Presentations for Dist Suicide Prevention; Teacher Effectiveness Trainer; *home:* 9110 Autumn Chase Wichita KS 67206

MC NINCH, STACY H., Mentor/Eng/Rdng/His Teacher; *b:* Coalinga, CA; *ed:* (BA) Sociology/Anthropology, Univ of CA Santa Barbara 1979; Working Toward Masters Ed, CA St Univ Bakersfield; CA Single Subject Teaching Credential Soc Sci, Eng; Basic & Advanced Trng Cooperative Learning, Johnson & Johnson; *cr:* Teacher Lakeside Union Sch Dist 1980-85, Visalia Unifield Sch Dist 1985-; Mentor Teacher Visalia Unified Sch Dist 1989-; Instr College of Sequoias 1989-; *ai:* Var Girls Bsktbl Coach; Visalia Unified Rdng In-Depth Study, Instructional Materials Selection, Valley Oak Advisory, At Risk Comm; Lakeside PTA 1980-85, Honorary Service Awd 1984; Cooperative Learning Presenter 1989 & St CATE Conference 1989; Curr Conference Presenter 1990; Visalia Unified Sch Dist Mentor Teacher 1989; *office:* Valley Oak Mid Sch 2000 N Lovers Ln Visalia CA 93291

MC NULTY, MOLLY BETH, 7th/8th Grade Lang Art Teacher; *b:* Eugene, OR; *m:* Richard A. Revoyr; *ed:* (BS) Psych, 1972, (MS) Rdng,1973 Univ of OR; (MA) Rhetoric/Composition, W WA Univ 1988; *cr:* K-6th Grade Title I/Rdng Teacher Jefferson Elem 1974-79; 7th/8th Grade Lang Art Teacher La Venture Mid Sch 1979-81; Frosh Composition Teacher W WA Univ 1981-82;7th/8th Grade Lang Art Teacher La Venture Mid Sch 1982-; *ai:* Asst Track Coach 1984-85; HS Drama 1982-84; Odyssey of Mind Regional Dir 1985-89; Research Paper Skagit Valley Coll 1989; *office:* La Venture Mid Sch 1200 La Venture Rd Mount Vernon WA 98273

MC NUTT, PATRICIA MC CUNE, Mathematics Teacher; *b:* Oil City, PA; *m:* Larry W.; *c:* Carla; *ed:* (BS) Elem Ed, Slipper Rock 1963; *cr:* 6th Grade Teacher Sandycreek Elem 1963-68; 4th Grade Teacher 7th Street Elem 1971; 5th Grade Teacher Utica Elem 1972-79; 6th Grade Teacher Sandycreek Elem 1979-86; 8th Grade Teacher Franklin Mid Sch 1986-; *ai:* Wrestling Chrldr Adv 1982-88; Fox St Church of God (Sunday Sch Teacher 1987-89, Youth Cnslr 1986-); *home:* RD 1 Miller Rd Franklin PA 16323

MC PEAK, PATRICIA RAPPUCCI, English Teacher; *b:* Philadelphia, PA; *m:* James Anthony III; *ed:* (BSED) Speech Comm, West Chester Univ 1987; Working Towards Masters Scndry Ed, West Chester Univ; *cr:* Eng Teacher West Philadelphia Cath HS for Girls 1987-89, West Cath HS 1989-; *ai:* Drama Club Moderator; SAP 1987-, Certificate 1988.

MC PECK, CHARLES LEE, 5th Grade Teacher; *b:* Muncie, IN; *m:* Betty Jean Skaggs; *c:* Betsy Swoape, Charles E., Lonna Williams, Steven L., Anissa R.; *ed:* (BSED) Elem Ed, 1966, (MAED) Admin, 1972 Ball St Univ; (MA) Chrstn Ed, United Theology Seminary 1981; Bible Stu in Yokefellow Bible Class; *cr:* 3rd-6th Grade Teacher Garfield Elem 1966-76; 4th-5th Grade Teacher Claypool Elem 1976-; *ai:* Girls Vlybl Team & Boys Flag Ftbl Team Coach; NEA, ISTA 1966-; MTA Bldg Rep 1966-; Muncie Area Rdng Cncl 1966-; Substance Abuse Prevention Team; (MATCH) Continuing Ed Ball St Univ 1988-; Trinity United Meth Outreach Prgm Coord of Cmmty Ed 1984-88; N IN Conference of United Meth Church Certified Lay Speaker 1987-; Paul V Lefler Cmmty Service Awd 1970; Rev JC Williams Ed Day Awd for Meritorious Service for Christ & People in Indigenous Cmmty 1986; *home:* 4208 N Redding Rd Muncie IN 47304

MC PHEE, SHARON WHITEIS, English Teacher; *b:* St Cloud, MN; *m:* Neil P.; *c:* Daniel, Heather, Jessica; *ed:* (BA) Eng, Framingham St Coll 1981; Fr, St Cloud St Coll 1964-67; Grad Courses, Northeastern Univ; *cr:* Teacher 1967-79; Part Time Stu 1972-79; Eng Teacher Natick Public HS 1980-86, St Sebastians Cntry Day Sch 1986-; Eng as Second Lang Teacher Japanese Prgm Walnut Hill Sch 1984-; *ai:* Sch Newspaper Adv; NCTE, NEATE; *office:* St Sebastians Cntry Day Sch 1191 Greendale Ave Needham MA 02192

MC PHEETERS, GEORGE MADISON, JR., Science Instructor; *b:* Mt Vernon, IL; *m:* Dianne L. Gregory; *c:* Kathryn; *ed:* (AA) Sci, Mt Vernon Comm Coll 1966; (BS) Biological Sci, 1968, (MSED) Zoology, 1973 S IL Univ; *cr:* Sci Instr Pinckneyville HS 1968-; Cmmty Coord Rend Lake Coll 1978-; *ai:* Sci Dept Chair; Faculty & Negotiating Comm; NEA, IL Ed Assn 1968-; Yrs of Service Awd Rend Lake Coll; Bio Teachers Inst S IL Univ; *office:* Pinckneyville HS E Water St Pinckneyville IL 62274

MC PHERSON, DEBORAH STANDRIDGE, English Department Chair; *b:* Lawton, OK; *m:* Daniel W.; *c:* Scott, Linda, Lane; *ed:* (BA) Eng, Cameron Univ 1976; *cr:* Eng Teacher Apache Schls 1976-80, Tuttle Schls 1980-; *ai:* Staff Dev Comm 1988-; Tuttle Ed Assn 1980-; OK Ed Assn 1976-.

MC PHERSON, DORIS JEAN MADISON, Sixth Grade Teacher; *b:* Portland, OR; *c:* Kathleen S. Walls, Donald S., Gordon S., Curtis S., Kenneth S.; *ed:* (BS) Elem Ed, W OR St Coll 1984; Cnslr Trng, OR St Univ 1975, 1978; Guidance Services, OR St Univ 1974; *cr:* Soc Worker II Bush Elem Sch 1976-77; Soc Worker II 1977-78, 3rd/4th Grade Teacher 1978-80 W Salem Elem Sch; 6th Grade Teacher Newport Mid Sch 1982-; *ai:* Stu Assistance Prgm; Co-Facilitator; NEA, OR Ed Assn 1975-; Lincoln Cty Ed Assn, Poly Involvement in Ed 1982-; Amer Assn of Univ Women 1975-; Appointed Commissioner Welfare Review Commission 1971-73; 1st Single Foster Parent in St of OR; 16 Yrs Foster Parent; *office:* Newport Mid Sch 311 NE Eads St Newport OR 97365

MC PHERSON, KATHARYN ANN (ROSS), 5th Grade Teacher; *b:* Mart, TX; *m:* Ballard D.; *c:* Nefeterius, Tamara; *ed:* (BBA) Bus, 1971; (ME) Elem Ed, 1981 TX Tech Univ *cr:* 4th Grade Teacher Beaumont Ind Sch Dist 1977-78; 5th Grade Teacher Killeen Ind Sch Dist 1978-; *ai:* PTA Pres 1982-83; Grade-Level Leader 1984-87; Curr Comm Rep; Dist Comm Rep; TEA Rep TEAMS/TAAS 1986-; Career Ladder Selection Comm Mem 1986-87; Admin Selection Comm Mem 1986-87; Excel Trainer 1988-; TSTA/NEA 1988-; Sugar Loaf PTA 1979-; Educator of Month 1986; Nom for Teacher of Yr 1986-87; *home:* 3100 June St Killeen TX 76543

MC PHERSON, LINDA AUSTIN, Fourth Grade Teacher; *b:* Jackson, TN; *c:* William III, Sue, Jay; *ed:* (BS) Elem Ed, GA Coll 1972; Staff Dev Project Read-Write; Transient Stu Wkshps, GA Southern, Valdosta St, GA Southwestern; Grad Work GA Coll; *cr:* 4th Grade Teacher Gatewood Schls 1972-74, Jeff Davis Mid Sch 1974-; *ai:* Jeff Davis GA Assn of Ed Treas 1980-81; Prof Assn GA Educators, NEA; First Baptist Church Mem; Grant by Union Camp Corp for Teachers Environment & Technology Inst GA Southern Univ 1990; *office:* Jeff Davis Mid Sch Box 625 Hazlehurst GA 31539

MC PHERSON, OSCAR MILTON, Business & Office Ed Teacher; *b:* Autryville, NC; *m:* Betty Warren; *c:* Alicia R., Heidi E.; *ed:* (BS) Bus/Office Ed, Campbell Univ 1975; Pursuing Masters Bus & Office Ed, NC Cntrl Univ; *cr:* Teacher/Coach Dunn HS 1975-85; Teacher Triton HS 1985-; *ai:* FBLA Adv, Cmptr Lead Teacher, Faculty Rep NCAE; Attendance Comm; FBLA Dist Adv 1975-; NCEA (Pres, Treas, St Delegate) 1975-; Beauty of Dunn Lodge #155 1980-; Edward Evans Consistory 1985-; Amer Legion Post 193 1975-; *office:* Triton HS Rt 1 Box 210 Erwin NC 28339

MC PHERSON, RUTH RICH, Retired Primary Teacher; *b:* Pingree, ID; *m:* Alan I.; *c:* Rita Carole Donce, Ella Marie Gingerich, Deanna Susser, Rodney A., Karen; *ed:* (BA) Ed, ID St Univ 1983; Brigham Young 1937, Univ of ID Moscow, UT St Univ Logan, Univ of NM Albuquerque; *cr:* 1st Grade Teacher Blackfoot Dist 1942-46; Music Teacher Moriority 1948; Substitute/Kndgtn Teacher Albuquerque 1949-55; 1st-3rd Grade Teacher Wapello Sch 1950-54; 1st-3rd Grade/Head Teacher Snake River Dist 52 1956-83; *ai:* Pingree Elem Head Teacher; IEA Secy 1959; NEA; Classroom Teacher Pres 1961-65; Right To Read Grant; Thom McAnn Distinctive Merit Awd; Nom Govenor Cecil Andrus Friend of Ed Natl Awd New Riverside Sch 1974; Blackfoot News Gold Medallion Awd 1968-69.

MC PHILLIPS, BERNICE BOYUM, Second Grade Teacher; *b:* Kasson, MN; *m:* Ronald D.; *c:* Sharol Mc Phillips O Brien, Patricia, Jill; *ed:* Stan Elem Ed, Minot St Teachers Coll 1956; (BA) Elem Ed, 1959, (MA) Elem Ed, 1983 Univ of MT; *cr:* 5th-8th Grade Teacher Grilley Sch 1955-56; 1st-3rd Grade Teacher Ethridge Sch 1956-57; Editorial Dept Encyclopaedia Britannica 1957; 5th Grade Teacher Hawthorn Sch 1959-60; 5th Grade Teacher 1961-62, 6th Grade Teacher 1962-63, 1st Grade Teacher 1964-66 Meadowlark Sch; Elem Music Teacher Shelby Schls 1969-76; 2nd Grade Teacher Bitterroot Sch 1976-; *ai:* Sci Curr Comm; Delta Kappa Gamma; Shelby Outstanding Teacher of Yr 1983; Univ of MT Alumni Bd of Delegates Mem.

MC PIKE, KARLYN KORSGAARD, German/French Teacher; *b:* Cleveland, OH; *m:* James I.; *c:* Michael, Matthew, Sean; *ed:* (BS) Ger/Fr, Bowling Green St Univ 1972; NEH Summer Ger Inst Westminster Coll 1989; *cr:* Substitute Teacher 1972-84, Ger/Fr Teacher 1984- Hicksville HS; *ai:* Foreign Lang Club; OEA, NEA, OFLA, AATG; United Meth Women Dist Officer 1985-88; United Meth Church Dist Lay Leader 1988-; BSA Comm Mem 1988-; Jennings Fnd Wkshps Fr 1986 & Ger 1987; *office:* Hicksville HS Corner Of Smith And Main Hicksville OH 43526

MC QUEEN, DORTHY TURNER, 8th Grade Math/Soc St Teacher; *b:* Millry, AL; *m:* Robert Lee Jr.; *c:* Robert L. III, Rashad L.; *ed:* (BA) Elem Ed, Daniel Payne Coll 1967; (MS) Elem Ed, Livingston Univ 1987; *cr:* Teacher Shady Grove Jr HS 1967-68, Cmmty Team Work Head Start 1968-76; Instructors Aide Greater Lowell Regional Vocational Tech HS 1976-83; Teacher Shady Grove Jr HS 1984-; *ai:* 8th Grade Adv; AL Ed Assn 1988-; NEA 1988-; *office:* Shady Grove Jr H S Rt 1 Box 229-F Silas AL 36919

MC QUEEN, GWEN, Business Teacher; *b:* Laurel, MS; *m:* Pete; *c:* Greg, Mitch; *ed:* (BS) Bus Ed, Univ S MS 1965; (MA) Bus Ed, GA ST Univ; *cr:* Teacher Sumrall HS 1965-67, Forest Park Sr 1967-69, Morrow HS 1969-.

MC QUIAG, MERIAM RANDALL, Fifth Grade Teacher; *b:* Ocala, FL; *ed:* (BA) Religion, John B Stetson Univ 1950; (MS) Teaching Eng to Speakers of Other Langs, Nova Univ 1988; *cr:* 2nd Grade Teacher Waresboro Sch 1951-52; 4th/5th Grade Teacher 1952-54, 5th/6th Grade Teacher 1954-56 Belleview Elem; 6th Grade Teacher Cntrl Elem & Eighth St Sch 1959-68; 4th-6th Grade Teacher Laura Dearing Elem 1968-72; 6th Grade Math Teacher Jo Mackey 6th Grade Center 1972-77; 5th Grade Teacher Hoggard Elem 1977-81, Rose Warren Sch 1981-; *ai:* Clark Cty Classroom Teachers Assn Senator 1985-87; *home:* 5280 Ganado Dr Las Vegas NV 89103

MC RAE, CAROL REEVES, 8th Grade Teacher; *b:* Memphis, TN; *m:* Thomas C.; *c:* Angela, Clay; *ed:* (BA) Eng/Public Speaking, Univ of MS 1979; Phi Delta Kappa Write More Learn More; Writing Across Curr; Basic Skills & FLE Writing Components Evaluation Trng, Measurement Incorporated; *cr:* Teacher Grenada HS 1987-88, Grenada Jr HS 1980-; *ai:* Var Ftbl, Jr HS Ftbl, Jr HS Bsktbl Cheerleading Spon; NCTE; Grenada HS Band Publicity Chm 1989-; Emmanuel Baptist Church Drama Dir 1989-; Modern Woodmen of America Creative Writing Essay Contest Chm; DAR Amer His Essay Contest Final Judge; MS Teacher Assessment Instruments Evaluator; *office:* Grenada Jr HS Jones Rd Grenada MS 38901

MC REAVY, SHARON TREADWELL, First Grade Teacher; *b:* Texas City, TX; *m:* Richard T.; *c:* Chris, Laura, Holly; *ed:* (BS) Elem Ed, SW TX St Univ 1970; *cr:* 1st Grade Teacher Lackland City Elem 1970-72, Reagan Cty Elem 1974-; *ai:* Lead Teacher; Mem Campus Plan Comm; Delta Kappa Gamma Local Chairperson 1978-; Laubach Literacy; 1st United Meth Church (Pianist, Mem); *home:* 803 Pennsylvania Big Lake TX 76932

MC REYNOLDS, MARY FRANCES, Spanish/French Teacher; *b:* Tulsa, OK; *m:* Samuel Alan; *c:* Taryn, Frances; *ed:* (BS) Span/Fr Ed, NE OK St Univ 1971; Ed, OK St Univ & San Diego Univ; *cr:* Span Teacher Bixby Jr HS 1971-72; 8th-9th Grade Span/Fr Teacher Sapulpa OK 1972-; *ai:* Foreign Lang Dept Head 1980-; United Sapulpa Educators Pres 1977-78; Kappa Kappa Iota 1973-78; OK Foreign Lang Stu of Yr 1971; Stu Cncl Teacher of Yr 1985; Supts Distinguished Service Awd 1986; *home:* PO Box 621 Sapulpa OK 74067

MC ROBERTS, DENNYSE, Guidance Counselor; *b:* Chicago, IL; *m:* Edward; *c:* Eric; *ed:* (BA) His/Poly Sci, Roosevelt 1958; (MA) Guidance/Counseling, Governors St 1976; (MA) Admin/Supervision, Natl Coll of Ed 1976; *cr:* Soc Stud Teacher Fenger HS 1958; Primary Grade Teacher Lawson Elem Sch 1959-68, Hinton Elem 1968-81; Rdng Resource Admin Team 1981-86; *ai:* Teen Service; Mc Knight Achievers; Young Adult Chorus; Medical Center Volunteer; Job Occup & College Bound Adv; Chicago Area Rdng Assn; Broward Teachers Union; NEA, IL Ed Assn; NAACP, Zeta Phi Beta, Urban League, People United to Save Humanity; Incentive Teacher Awd; Teacher of Month.

MC ROY, REBECCA PEOPLES, Fourth Grade Teacher; *b:* Fayetteville, NC; *m:* Phillip Mayhew; *c:* Jessica; *ed:* (BS) Intermediate Ed, 1975, (MA) Elem Ed, 1983 E Carolina Univ; *cr:* 4th-6th Grade Teacher Pungo Chrstn Acad 1975-76; 4th Grade Teacher Chocowinity Primary Sch 1976-; *ai:* Jr Var Chrldr Adv; Beaufort Cty Assn of Educators VP 1983-84; NC Assn of Educators Pres 1984-85; Hobie Fleet 257 Commodore 1988-89; Nom Chocowinity Primary Sch Teacher of Yr Awd 1983; *home:* PO Box 88 Bath NC 27808

MC SHANN, DORIS YARBROUGH, Social Studies Teacher; *b:* Athens, AL; *m:* Charles E.; *ed:* (BS) Home Ec Ed, 1962, (MS) Scndry Ed, 1975 AL A&M Univ; *cr:* Teacher Dogwood Jr HS 1962-68; Prof Case Worker Limestone Cty Bd of Ed 1972-75; Teacher East Limestone Sch 1968-72, 1975-; *ai:* Spon E Limestone HS Jr Beta Club; Limestone Cty Teachers Assn, AL Ed Assn, NEA; Alpha Kappa Alpha Pres 1981-85, Pres of Yr SE Region 1985; Teacher of Yr 1990; *home:* 6506 Eric St Huntsville AL 35810

MC SPARIN, PHILLIP A., English Teacher; *b:* New Orleans, LA; *ed:* (BSED) Eng/Speech, MS Coll 1980; Working Towards Masters Ed, 1990; *cr:* Eng Teacher All Saints Episcopal Sch 1981-82, Chamberlain Hunt Acad 1982-85; Eng/Speech Teacher Woodland Hills Baptist Acad 1985-; *ai:* Sch Play Dir; Sr Class Spon; STAR Teacher 1988; *office:* Woodland Hills Baptist Acad 5055 Manhattan Rd Jackson MS 39206

MC SWAIN, MARTHA WAIT, 5th Grade Teacher; *b:* Birmingham, AL; *c:* Preston Daniel; *ed:* (BME) Music Ed/Piano, Birmingham-Southern Coll 1960; (MA) Elem Ed UAB 1978; Orff Cert- Level I; *cr:* Choral Teacher Shades-Cahaba/Rocky Ridge/ Roebuck Plaza 1960-66, Crumley Chapel/Hillview 1968-78; Classroom Teacher Hillview Elem 1978-; *ai:* Multi-Media Adv; Chairperson of 5th Grade Jef Co Ed Calendar Skills Comm; NEA/AEA/JCEA 1960-; ACT 1978-; Altrusa Intnl 1988-; VP 1990-91; *home:* 605 Manchester Ln Birmingham AL 35209

MC SWEENEY, CONNIE JUNE (WARD), Mathematics Teacher; *b:* Ashland, KY; *m:* Robert Allen; *c:* Sarah B., Luke A., Laura R., Mitchell A.; *ed:* (AB) Math, Marshall Univ 1974; Working Towards Masters; *cr:* Math Teacher Wayne Jr HS 1974-77; Math/Cmptr Literacy Teacher Wayne HS 1977-; *ai:* Sch Math Field Day & WV Math League Sch Group Adv; *office:* Wayne HS P O Box940 Wayne WV 25570

MC VAUGH, CHARLES P., JR., US History Teacher; *b:* Wilmington, DE; *m:* Anne Simmons; *c:* Charles S., Peter M.; *ed:* (BA) His/Eng, 1968, (MA) British His, 1970 Univ of DE; Economics, His, Eng Lit, Ed Admin; *cr:* Teaching Asst Univ of DE 1969-70; His/Eng Teacher Conrad HS 1971-78; His Teacher Mc Kean HS 1978-80, Glasgow Hs 1980-; *ai:* Glasgow Weightlifting Club 1980-; Center for Economics Ed Teacher Participant 1984-; Avon Grove Little League (T-Ball Dir 1989-, Coach 1987-); European Cmmty Seminar Univ ofDE 1989, 1990 & Washington DC 1989-; Teacher Exchange in UK & Ireland June 1990; Distinguished Military Grad Univ of DE 1970; *office:* Glasgow HS 1901 S College Ave Newark DE 19702

MC VEY, MARJORIE M., Business Teacher; *b:* Nelsonville, OH; *m:* Jack L.; *c:* Kristy, Mary Beth; *ed:* (BS) Ed, OH Univ 1958; *cr:* Bus Teacher Starr-Washington HS 1958-73, Logan HS 1973-74, Tri-Cty Voc Sch 1974-; *ai:* Bus Prof of Amer; Youth Club Adv; OH Bus Teachers; Eastern Stars; Shorthand Transcription 1st Place Regional/St 3rd in Natl 1977; Promotional Display 1st Place Regional 2nd St 6th Natl 1987; 1st Place Regional/St 10th Natl Competition 1989; *home:* Rt 1 Box 77 New Plymouth OH 45654

MC VEY, PHYLLIS JANE, Chapter I Teacher; *b:* Martins Ferry, OH; *m:* John Michael; *c:* Rebekah, Brooke; *ed:* (BS) Elem Ed, OH Univ 1970; (MA) Elem Ed, WV Univ 1974; Grad Stud Univ of Dayton; Sci Wkshps OH Univ; *cr:* 4th Grade Teacher 1970-75, 5th-7th Grade Teacher 1976-80, 4th Grade Teacher 1980-85, 5th Grade Teacher 1986-88, Chapter I Rdng Specialist 1988- Rose Hill Elem; *ai:* Bellaire City Schls Rdng Comm; PTO 1970-; Amity Meth Church Choir 1984-; *office:* Rose Hill Elem Sch 3400 Franklin St Bellaire OH 43906

MC VICKER, LINDA JANSSENS, English Teacher; *b:* Pittsburgh, PA; *m:* Richard J.; *ed:* (BSED) Eng/Rdng, Slippery Rock St Coll 1970; (MSED) Ed, Penn St 1985; Grad Stud; *cr:* 7th Grade Eng Teacher 1970-72, 8th Grade Eng Teacher 1973- Montour Jr HS; *ai:* Spelling Bee Club Spon; NCTE; Mc Donald Womans Club Secy 1988-.

MC WHIRTER, PATRICIA WEBB, Third Grade Teacher; *b:* Corpus Christi, TX; *ed:* (BS) Elem Ed, Univ of Houston 1973; Teacher Effectiveness Trng, Gifted & Talented, Project AIMS, Univ of St Thomas; Inst of Chemical Ed Univ of N CO 1989; *cr:* 5th Grade Teacher 1973-75, 3rd Grade Teacher 1976- Betsy Ross; *ai:* Ross Elem Teacher of Yr 1985; *office:* Betsy Ross Elem Sch 2819 Bay Houston TX 77026

MC WHORTER, CAROL ANDESS, 6th Grade English Teacher; *b:* Port Arthur, TX; *ed:* (BA) Ed, Lamar Univ 1964; *cr:* 6th Grade Eng Teacher Silsbee Ind Sch Dist 1964-; *ai:* 6th Grade Math Team Coach; Gifted/Talented Comm; NEA, TSTA, SEA; PTA Outstanding Teacher Awd 1985; *office:* Laura Reeves Elem Sch 695 Woodrow Silsbee TX 77656

MC WILLIAMS, EDNA PLANT, Lang Art/Mathematics Teacher; *b:* Andalusia, AL; *m:* David H.; *c:* David Jr., Steven, Jake, Angela I. Vaughan; *ed:* (BA) Elem Ed, 1969; (MED) Ed Leadership, 1985 Univ of W FL; *cr:* K-5th Grade Music Teacher 1969-72, 5th Grade Teacher 1973 Rhodes Elem Sch; 7th Grade Soc Stud Teacher Hobbs Mid 1974-79; 6th Grade Teacher Hobbs Mid Sch 1979-; *ai:* Sch Inservice Rep; *office:* Hobbs Mid Sch 309 Glover Ln Milton FL 32570

MC WILLIAMS, JEAN PHILLIPS, Real Estate Associate; *b:* Granite Falls, NC; *m:* Clayton T. Jr.; *c:* Clayton III, Linda; *ed:* (BA) Eng, Univ of Montevallo 1962; *cr:* Eng Teacher Lee Jr HS 1962-65, Madison HS 1965-67; 5th Grade Teacher 1970-73, Phys Ed Teacher 1977-80, Eng Teacher 1981-87 Madison Acad; *office:* Madison Realty PO Box 643 Madison FL 32340

MC WILLIAMS, KELLY LYNN, English Teacher; *b:* Canton, OH; *ed:* (BS) Eng Ed, 1987, Rdng Cert 1987 OH St Univ; *cr:* Eng Teacher Felicity-Franklin HS 1987-; *ai:* Academic Team Coach 1987-; 7th Grade Class Adv; Pi Lambda Theta 1986-, Awd of Membership 1986; *office:* Felicity-Franklin HS 415 Washington St Felicity OH 45120

MC WREATH, CYNTHIA L., English Teacher; *b:* Doylestown, PA; *ed:* (BS) Eng, CA Univ 1971; *cr:* Eng Teacher Burgettstown Area Jr/Sr HS 1971-; *ai:* 8th Grade Class Spon; PA St Ed Assn, NEA 1971- ; Presidential Scholar CA Univ of PA; *office:* Burgettstown Jr-Sr H S Old Bavington Rd Burgettstown PA 15021

MEACHAM, GRACE AUSTIN, English Teacher; *b:* Helena, AR; *c:* Monique J., Emil C.; *ed:* (BA) Eng, Le Moyne Coll 1961; (MS) Rdng, Syracuse Univ 1968; Memphis St Univ; Real Estate St Tech Inst Memphis; *cr:* Fr/Eng Teacher George W Carver HS 1961-62; Spelling/Eng Teacher J S Phelix HS 1962-63; Eng/Rdng Teacher Shelby Cty Bd of Ed 1963-69; Eng/Rdng/Black Lit/ Drama Teacher Memphis Bd of Ed 1969-; *ai:* Yrbk Adv; Guidance, Mr & Miss Carver HS Pageant, Africa-In-Africa Comm; African Amer His Month Assembly Spon; W TN Ed Assn, Shelby Cty Teachers of Eng; Memphis Calligraphy Guild 1989-; Memphis Amateur Radio Assn 1981-89; Memphis Black Writers & Artists 1989-; Natl Defense Ed Act Grant De Pauw Univ 1966; Experienced Teacher Fellowship Syracuse 1967-68; Guest Columnist 1987-89; Manuscript TN Journal of Health, Phys Ed, Recreation, Dance 1988; Teaching Assistantship Temple Univ 1990; *home:* 1615 Crider St Memphis TN 38111

MEACHAM, KAREN VICKREY, Vocational Office Educ Teacher; *b:* Huntsville, AL; *m:* John Russell Jr.; *c:* Jenny E.; *ed:* (BS) Bus Ed, Austin Peay St Univ 1969; Voc Cert APSU 1978; Office Admin/Cmptr Course APSU 1987; *cr:* Bus Teacher Clarksville HS 1969-70; Bus/Voc Office Ed Teacher Northwest HS 1970-; *ai:* Adv Bus Profs of America; Sr Class Spon; Prins Advisory Comm; Mem St Evaluation Team Sumner Cty; Steering Comm Voc Evaluation; Graduation Coord; Clarksville-Montgomery Cty Ed Assn, TN Ed Assn, NEA 1969-; 1st Baptist Church (5th Grade Sunday Sch Teacher 1989-, 2nd Grade Vacation Bible Sch Teacher 1985-); Chamber of Commerce Mem 1984-85; Austin Peay Alumni Assn; Amer Voc Assn 1987-88; *office:* Northwest HS 800 Lafayette Rd Clarksville TN 37042

MEACHUM, TONY FRANKLIN, History Teacher; *b:* Wadesboro, NC; *m:* Ellen Morris; *ed:* (BS) His/sci, Wingate/ UNCC 1983; (MS) Admin, NC A&T St 1989; CPR, Effective Teacher Trng, Cmptr Competency & Critical Thinking Skills Mentor; *cr:* Teacher Allen Jay Mid 1983-86, Jamestown Mid 1986-87; Lead Teacher/Team Leader Allen Jay Mid 1987-; Summer Sch Site Supvr Guilford Cty 1986-89; *ai:* Bsbl Coach; TV Network Chairperson; Jr Historian Club; Bsktbl Scorekeeper; Video Club; Lead Teacher; Team Leader; Drug Awareness Coord; NC Assn of Educators Rep 1986-88; Allen Jay Teacher of Yr 1984; Archdale Chamber of Commerce Bd Mem 1988-; Archdale Planning Bd Commission; Natl Honors Society; Mentor Teacher; *office:* Allen Jay Mid Sch 1201 E Fairfield Rd High Point NC 27263

MEAD, BARBARA GALE (WINNETT), 5th Grade Teacher; *b:* Louisville, KY; *m:* James L.; *c:* Jennifer L.; *ed:* (BA) Elem Ed, Univ of Evansville 1969; (MS) Elem Ed, IN Univ Southeast 1980; *cr:* 5th Grade Teacher Mid Road Elem Sch 1977-81; Wilson Elem Sch 1981-; *ai:* Intermediate Unit Leader; Bookstore Spon; Spelling Bee Chairperson; GCEA 1979-; ISTA 1979-; NEA 1979-; Kappa Kappa Kappa Rec Secy 1965; *office:* Wilson Elem Sch 2915 Charlestown Jeff Rd Jeffersonville IN 47130

MEAD, GRETCHEN ZALOGA, 3rd Grade Teacher; *c:* Jeffrey R., Alyson; *ed:* (BS) Ed, St Univ of NY 1961; Graduate Courses, Southampton Coll 1972-; *cr:* 5th Grade Teacher Main Sch 1961-62; 2nd/3rd/5th Grade Teacher Phillips Ave Sch 1966-69; 5th Grade Teacher Lincoln Ave Sch 1971-72; 3rd/4th/5th/6th Grade Teacher Westhampton Beach Elem Sch 1972-; *ai:* Cutural Arts Comm; Black Stud Comm; Lit Magzn Adv; Gifted and Talented Comm; Evaluation Comm; Positive Reinforcement Comm; Bldg Adv Team; Frnch/Amer Exch Comm; Open House Comm; Wiehauken Curriculum Wrtg Comm; Conf Comm; Rotary Teacher of Month 1985; Bide-A-Wee Animal Shelter Adopt a Teacher 1989; Natl Minigrant Nutrtn; Westhampton Bch Bd of Educ Teacher of Month March 1990; *office:* Westhampton Beach Elem Sch Mill Rd Westhampton Beach NY 11978

MEAD, ISABEL DELORES, 7th & 8th Soc Stud Teacher; *b:* Sidnaw, MI; *ed:* (BED) Soc Stud, 1963, (MS) Soc Stud, 1972 UW Whitewater; *cr:* 7th/8th Grade Soc Stud Teacher Johnson Creek Sch 1963-; *ai:* Adv to Jr HS Stu Cncl; Chairperson Soc Stud Curr Comm; Johnson Creek Ed Assn (Pres, Treas); WI Ed Assn, NEA 1968-; NCSS; St Mary Magdalene Church Cncl 1966-69/1989-92; Johnson Creek Village Bd Past Mem 1975-81; Attended Taft Institute 1974 ; *home:* 116 South St Johnson Creek WI 53038

MEAD, TONI DIERSTEIN, Second Grade Teacher; *b:* Princeton, IL; *m:* David K.; *c:* Susan; *ed:* (BA) Sociology/Elem Ed, Monmouth Coll 1967; *cr:* 5th Grade Teacher Colchester IL 1967-68; 5th Grade Teacher 1968-69, 1st Grade Teacher 1969-70 Prairie City IL; 2nd Grade Teacher Ohio IL 1973-; *ai:* Educl Dev Comm; *home:* 616 Hidden Lake Dr Princeton IL 61356

MEADE, FRANCIS J., Business Education Teacher; *b:* Ashland, PA; *m:* Joan Sasso; *c:* Timothy, Maria, Teresa; *ed:* (BS) Bus Ed/ Accounting, Bloomsburn Univ 1967; (MED) Scndry Sch Admin, Villanova Univ 1973; Prin Cert Scndry Sch; *cr:* Bus Ed Teacher Downingtown Sr HS 1967-76, Lionville Jr HS 1976-; *ai:* Team Leader 9th Grade; Supervisor of Admin Detention Area; Downingtown ATA; PA St Ed Assn; NEA; Holy Name Society; Our Lady of Rosary Church; Knights of Columbus Financial Secy 1980-90; Parents Music Club; *office:* Lionville Jr H S 50 Devon Dr Downingtown PA 19335

MEADE, GLENN LOUIS, English Teacher; *b:* Waukegan, IL; *m:* Diane Hermanson; *c:* Eric, Kevin, Kelli; *ed:* (BSED) Journalism/Eng, N IL Univ 1974; (MSED) Scndry Ed/Curr, Concordia Coll 1989; *cr:* Journalism/Eng Teacher Dundee HS 1974-78; Eng Teacher Canton Mid Sch 1981-; *ai:* Mid Sch Ftbl & HS Bsbl Coach; Canton Mid Sch Eng Dept Rep; Journalism Ed Assn 1974-78; Streamwood Little League Commissioner 1989-; *office:* Canton Mid Sch 1100 Sunset Circle Streamwood IL 60107

MEADE, HAZEL HELEN (HEASTIE), K-8th Grade Teacher/ Director; *b:* Belle Glade, FL; *m:* Richard Peter; *c:* Mary Meade Montaque, Karen Meade Wilson; *ed:* (BA) Early Chldhd Ed/ Speech, 1971, (MS) Elem Ed/Rdng, 1978 Brooklyn Coll; Grad Stud Curr Ed, Atlantic Union Coll, Andrews Univ; *cr:* K-8th Grade Teacher Brooklyn 7 Adv Sch 1971-89; Summer Instr Atlantic Union Coll 1979; 9th/10th Grade Summer Rdng Teacher Greater NY Acad 1982; Teacher/Founder/Dir Innovate Schls for Gifted & Talented Young People 1989-; *ai:* Greater NY Acad & Greater NY Conference of 7 Day Adv Trustee; Atlantic Union Conference Chairperson; Kappa Delta Pi Mem 1971-, Scholastic Honors 1971; Greater NY Teachers Assn (Pres 1979-83) 1976-88; United Parent Assn Delegate 1963-64; Amer Bible Society Scripture Volunteer 1982-; Atlantic Union Coll Trustee 1982-86; Whos Who in Religion 1984; Hospital Audiences Incorporated Reader for Mentally Ill Service Awd; Articles Published; *home:* 1680 Bedford Ave 5B Brooklyn NY 11225

MEADE, PRISCILLA GAIL COMBS, Social Studies Teacher; *b:* Lackey, KY; *c:* Cecilia A.; *ed:* (CA) Soc Stud, Alice Lloyd Coll 1968; (BA) Soc/Emp Soc Work/Psych, Morehead St Univ 1970; (MS) Ed/Soc Stud, MSU 1976; *cr:* Teacher Knott Cty HS 1971-75, Knott Cty Mid Sch 1975-76, Knott Cty Cntrl HS 1976-; *home:* HC 80 Box 5050 Langley KY 41645

MEADE, ROBERT, Math/Science Chair; *b:* Los Angeles, CA; *c:* Patti, Margaret A., Paul, Thomas, Mark; *ed:* (AB) Biological Sci, Univ of S CA 1947; Grad Sch Univ of S CA; Claremont Grad Sch; *cr:* Teacher Arrowview Jr HS 1949-53, Franklin Jr HS 1953-57, Pacific HS 1957-81; Math/Sci Chm & Teacher Notre Dame HS 1984-; *ai:* Notre Dame HS Sr Class Adv; USC Inland Empire Pres 1979-84; Kiwanis Intnl Club Secy 1985-88; *office:* Notre Dame HS 7085 Brockton Ave Riverside CA 92506

MEADE, VELMA SUE (PAINTER), 6th Grade Teacher; *b:* Snead, AL; *m:* Troy E.; *ed:* (AA) Elem Ed, Lee Coll 1956; (BS) Elem Ed, Jacksonville Univ 1959; Grad Stud; *cr:* HS/4th-6th Grade Teacher Susan Moore; *ai:* 6th Grade 4-H Club; NEA, AEA, BCEA 1957-; Mt Zion Church of God Chrstn Ed Dir, YPE Pres of Yr 1961; *home:* PO Box 563 Blountsville AL 35031

MEADOR, BETSY LOWE, French/Journalism Teacher; *b:* Lebanon, TN; *m:* John Benton; *c:* Jay, Bill, Robert, Doug; *ed:* Foreign Lang Inst Univ of AR 1986, 1988; *cr:* Eng/Journalism Teacher 1970-72, Fr/Journalism Teacher 1972-76, 1978- Fordyce HS; *ai:* Jr/Sr Plays Dir; Quiz Bowl & Fr Club Spon; Newspaper Adv; Teacher/Cnslr European Tours; AR Assn Teachers of Foreign Lang, AR Assn Fr Teachers, AATF; Delta Kappa Gamma VP 1987-89; Sesame Club Reporter 1987-89; 1st Baptist Church Choir; Dallas Cty Teacher of Yr; St Foreign Lang Handbook & St Curr Guideline Comm Mem; Educl Media Contest Winner; *office:* Fordyce HS 1800 College St Fordyce AR 71742

MEADOR, CONNIE JEAN, Fifth Grade Teacher; *b:* Glendale, CA; *m:* William John; *c:* Courtney A., Jarrod J.; *ed:* (BA) Eng, Univ of La Vern 1971; Post Grad Stud Continuing Ed Classes, Univ of La Vern; *cr:* Teacher Walnut Avenue Elem 1972-; *ai:* 4th-6th Grade Level Co-Chairperson; ACT Site Rep 1988-; CTA, NEA 1972-; *office:* Walnut Avenue Elem Sch 5550 Walnut Ave Chino CA 91710

MEADOUGH, BARBARA GEORGE, Health/Phys Ed Teacher; *b:* Houston, TX; *m:* Joshua Bill; *c:* Erica M., Joshua B. Jr.; *ed:* (BS) Health/Phys Ed, TX Southern Univ 1964; (MED) Ed, Univ of Houston 1972; *cr:* Health/Phys Ed Teacher Wharton Trng HS 1964-68, Booker T Washington Sr HS 1969-70, S P Waltrip Sr HS 1970-72, Mc Reynolds Jr HS 1973-79; Family Life Health Ed/Phys Ed Teacher Louie Welch Mid Sch 1979-; *ai:* Coach Girls Cross Cntry, 8th Grade Girls Bkstbl Team, Houston Bsktbl Congress Intnl; Spon Bows & Arrows Spirit Club; Houston Fed of Teachers, TX HS Coaches Assn, Jackis Aerobic Prgm Certified Dancing Instr; Mt Hebron Baptist Church (Beginner Class Teacher, Dir Childrens Church, Youth Bible Study Inst); *office:* Louie Welch Mid Sch 11544 S Gessner Houston TX 77051

MEADOWS, ANNETTE, Social Studies Teacher; *b:* Moultrie, GA; *ed:* (BS) Scndry Ed/His, 1982, (MED) Scndry Ed/His, 1986, (EDS) Scndry Ed/Soc Stud, 1989 Valdosta St Coll; *cr:* Spec Ed Teacher Doerun Elem 1982-83; Soc Stud Teacher Pineland Sch 1983-84, Colquitt Cty Jr HS 1984-; *ai:* Beta Club Spon; GA Assn of Educators, NCSS, Phi Alpha Theta; *office:* Colquitt Cty Jr HS 5th St SW Moultrie GA 31768

MEADOWS, BETTY FOSTER, Spanish Teacher; *b:* Atlanta, GA; *m:* Rodney Glenn; *c:* Mandy J., Monica E.; *ed:* (BS) Span, GA Southern 1972, (MA) Span, Univ of CA Long Beach 1975; *cr:* Span Teacher Winder Barrow HS, Heritage HS, Eagles Landing HS 1990; *ai:* Natl Span Honor Society, Sr Class Spon; FLAG, GA AATSP; *home:* 838 Conyers Rd Box 734 Mc Donough GA 30253

MEADOWS, GAIL T., Assistant Principal; *b:* Langdale, AL; *ed:* (BS) Phys Ed, 1971, (MA) Elem Ed/Ed Admin, 1987 Troy St Univ; *cr:* Title I Teacher Fairfax Elem 1971-73; 2nd Grade Teacher Huguley Elem 1973-74, Fairfax Elem 1974-80; 6th Grade/Rdng/Soc Stud Teacher Fairfax Elem 1980-86; Asst Prin Valley Jr HS 1986-; *ai:* Chambers Cty Ed Assn, AL Ed Assn, NEA 1971-; *office:* Valley Jr HS 292 Johnson St Valley AL 36854

MEADOWS, JEFFREY T., Assistant Band Director; *b:* Maysville, KY; *m:* Jennifer Mangin; *ed:* (BME) Music, Morehead St Univ 1986; Ed Prgm Univ of Louisville; *cr:* Asst Band Dir Meade Cty Schls 1986-; *ai:* Marching Band; Music Educators Natl Conference; KY Music Educators Assn; Percussive Arts Society; *home:* 804 Allen Ct #3 Brandenburg KY 40108

MEADOWS, JUDITH SANDRA, Girls Athletic/Phys Ed Coord; *b:* Dallas, TX; *ed:* (BS) Phys Ed, TX Chrstn Univ 1957; (MED) Phys Ed, Univ of N TX 1961; Guidance & Counseling, W TX St Univ 1967; Educl Admin, Univ of N TX 1980; *cr:* Teacher/Coach Castleberry HS 1957-61, Olton HS 1961-68; Teacher/Coach/Coord Duncanville HS 1968-; *ai:* Head Girls Bsktbl Coach; Coord All 7th-12th Grade Girls Sports; TX Girls Coaches Assn Pres 1967-68, 1978-79, All-Star Coach 1975, 1981, 1990; TX Assn Bsktbl Coaches Coach of Yr 1989-90; TX Assn Prof Educators; Chamber of Commerce Woman of Yr 1989-90; Served on Staff for Abausa with Two Natl Bsktbl Teams which Played Intnl Tournaments Poland, Yugoslavia, Taiwan, South Korea; *office:* Duncanville HS 900 W Camp Wisdom Rd Duncanville TX 75116

MEADOWS, VICTOR LYLE, US History Teacher; *b:* Lynchburg, VA; *ed:* (BA) His, James Madison Univ 1971; (BMED) Guidance/Counseling, Longwood Coll 1976; *cr:* US His Teacher 1971-75, Guidance Cnslr 1975-78, US His Teacher 1978- Appomattox Mid Sch; *ai:* SCA Spon; Soc Stud Dept Chm; Curr Coord Soc Stud; Chm Curr Coord; NEA Local Pres 1982-84; Chamber of Commerce 1980 Teacher of Yr 1980; *office:* Appomattox Mid Sch 300 N Church St Rt 2 Appomattox VA 24522

MEADS, SARAH AGNES (OWNLEY), Fifth Grade Teacher; *b:* Elizabeth City, NC; *m:* Joseph Moody; *c:* Daphnne Meads Stevenson, Janice Meads Gray, J. S., Terry B., Howard M.; *ed:* (BS) Intermediate Ed, East Carolina Univ 1971; Diploma Practical Nurse Ed, Coll of Albemarle 1966; Licensed Practical Nurse St of NC; *cr:* Nurse LPN Pasquotank Cty Schls 1966-69; Teacher Perquimans Cty Schls 1971-72; Part Time LPN Britthaven of Edenton NC 1982-87; Teacher Perquimans Cty Mid Sch 1989-; *ai:* Sch Assistance Team, Improvement Plan Chapter 1, Sch Beautification Comm; PTSA Mem; NCAE/NEA (Sch Rep 1971-75, Mem 1971-); NC Licensed Practical Nurse 1966-; Alzheimer Disease Chapter 1985-; Parkville Holiness Church (Pianist 1945-, Sunday Sch Teacher 1949-); Prospective Teacher Schlsp St of NC 1969-71; Florence Nightingale Awd; Graduation Coll of Albemarle 1966; Teacher of Yr Hertford Grammar Sch 1979-80; *home:* 182 Winslow Rd Elizabeth City NC 27909

MEAGHER, THOMAS WALTER, Music Dept Chair/Orch Dir; *b:* Salina, KS; *m:* Patricia Ann Brungardt; *c:* Angela, William, Jennifer, Matthew, Melissa; *ed:* (BME) Music Ed, 1979, (MS) Ed Admin, 1989 Ft Hays St Univ; Working Towards Eds Ed Admin; *cr:* Orch Dir Hays HS 1979-81; Music Instr St Marys Grade Sch 1981-85; Orch Dir/Music Chm Hays HS 1985-; *ai:* K-12th Grade Math Study Comm Chm; Curr Cncl; KS St Orch Chairperson; Music Educators Natl Conference, KS Muisc Educators Assn, ASCD, NEA; *office:* Hays HS 2300 E 13th Hays KS 67601

MEANEY, PETER JOSEPH, Guidance Cnslr & Math Teacher; *b:* Kingston, NY; *ed:* (BA) Philosophy/Ed, Seton Hall Univ 1944; (MA) Religious Ed/Psych, Catholic Univ 1957; Various Wkshps-Inst & Summer Pgrms; Theology, Immaculate Concepcion Seminary St Marys Abbey 1951; *cr:* Math/Religion/Latin Teacher 1947-, Track Coach 1947-70, Campus Minister 1953-62, Chm Religious Ed Dept 1953-68, Guidance Cnslr 1980- Del Burton Sch; *ai:* St Marys Abbey Sr Bd of Trustees; Morris Cty Guidance Cnslrs Assn Mem 1979-89; NJ Cath Track Conf Former Pres 1970-75, Recognition 1975; NJ Civil War Roundtable 1980-; Civil War Society Mem 1981-; SCV/MOSB Mem 1980-; Our Lady of Mt Parish Asst Priest 1965-; Published Civil War Book & Civil War Articles 1983; *office:* Delbarton Sch 270 Mendham Rd Morristown NJ 07960

MEANS, ELEANOR WEBB, First Grade Teacher; *b:* Effingham, IL; *ed:* (BS) Elem Ed, 1958, (MSE) Elem Ed, 1964 Eastern IL Univ; *cr:* 1st Grade Teacher Hickory Hill Sch 1958-60; 2nd Grade Teacher South Shores Sch 1960-61; 1st Grade Teacher East Side Sch 1961-69, Judith Giacoma Sch 1969-70, Chrisman Grade Sch 1970-; *ai:* Chrismen Ed Assn Secy 1984-85 Mem 1970-; IL Rdng Assn 1988-; IEA-NEA 1970-; Chrisman United Meth Church Secy Nominating Comm 1970 Mem 1977-; *office:* Chrisman Elem Schl 111 N Pennsylvania Chrisman IL 61924

MEANS, SHIRLEY LACY, First Grade Teacher; *b:* Fall River, KS; *m:* Le Roy Dale; *c:* Michael Walters, Kenneth Walters, Dave, Rick; *ed:* (BS) Elem, Harris Teachers Coll 1967; *cr:* 2nd Grade Teacher Brown Elem 1967-68; 4th Grade Teacher 1968-86, 1st Grade Teacher 1986- Kyle Trueblood Elem; *home:* 210 S 6th Conway Springs KS 67031

MEARES, CHERYL HOOTMAN, Fifth Grade Teacher; *b:* Lebanon, IN; *m:* Joseph; *ed:* (BS) Elem Ed, IN St Univ 1981; *cr:* 5th Grade Teacher Valley Mills Elem 1984-; *ai:* Math Club, Stu Cncl Spon; *office:* Valley Mills Elem Sch 5101 S High School Rd Indianapolis IN 46241

MEARIEWEATHER, PATRICIA, 8th Grade Teacher; *b:* Gainesville, GA; *c:* Paula E.; *ed:* (BS) Ed, S IL Univ 1972; (MA) Counseling, Governors St Univ 1981; *cr:* 6th-8th Grade Teacher Dunne Sch 1972-73; 7th/8th Grade Teacher West Pullman Sch 1973-80; 5th/7th/8th Grade Teacher Dumas Sch 1980-84; 7th/8th Grade Teacher West Pullman Sch 1984-; *ai:* West Pullman Sch Cncl Mem; LSC (Teacher, Mem) 1989-; *office:* West Pullman Sch 11941 S Parnell Chicago IL 60628

MEBANE, JANICE HARRISON, Teacher; *b:* Suffolk, VA; *m:* Simon L.; *c:* Ronald M., Ryan K.; *ed:* (BA) Elem Ed, Shaw Univ 1962; VA St Univ, OLD Dominion Univ, Hampton Univ; *cr:* 1st Grade Teacher Andrew J Brown 1962-63; 4th Grade Teacher Georgia Tyler 1963-69; 7th Grade Math Teacher Windsor Elem 1969-; *ai:* All 7th Grade Act; Debate Team; VA Ed Assn, NEA, Isle of Wight Ed 1962-; AKA; Prof Women Club; Grant 1963, 1964; *home:* 1420 Kate Dr Chesapeake VA 23320

MEBANE, NANCY L., English Teacher; *b:* Kingston, PA; *m:* Richard Franklin; *ed:* (BA) Eng/Scndry Ed, Wilkes Coll 1974; Cert Penn St Univ; *cr:* Teacher Wyoming Valley West; *ai:* NHS Adv; Vertical Curr & Faculty Advisory Comm; Luzerne Cty Rdng Cncl; *office:* Wyoming Valley West Mid Sch Chester St Kingston PA 18704

MECKEY, MARYLYNNE LEARISH, 9th Grade English Teacher; *b:* Clearfield, PA; *m:* Timothy A.; *c:* Matthew, Kurt; *ed:* (BS) Scndry Ed/Eng, Clarion Univ 1979; Work Begun on Masters in Rdng; *cr:* 9th Grade Eng Teacher Clearfield HS 1979-; *ai:* Coached Girls Sftbl, Vlybl, Bsktbl; PSEA 1979-; Womens Group at Church, Non Local Womens Club; *office:* Clearfield Area H S P O Box 910 Clearfield PA 16830

MEDER, DELORES BALLEW, Gifted/Talented Prgm Teacher; *m:* Daniel L.; *c:* Samantha A., Erin L.; *ed:* (BSE) Elem Ed, 1967, (MSED) Elem Ed, 1978 Cntrl MO St Univ; Working Toward Specialist Degree in Process; *cr:* 4th Grade Teacher Belton Schls 1967-69; 5th Grade Teacher Macon Schls 1969-70; 5th Grade Teacher 1970-, Gifted/Talented Teacher 1990 Kearney Schls; *ai:* Curr & Teacher Benefit Comms; MNEA 1984-; NEA Life Mem 1984-; KNEA Local, Past Pres 1984-; NCSS 1989-; Excl in Teaching Awd Nominee 1986, 1990; Outstanding Elem Teachers of America 1972; Local, Dist Reaching for Excl Awd 1984; *office:* Kearney RI Schls Kearney MO 64060

MEDFORD, MAISIE COON, 4th Grade Teacher; *b:* Stafford, OK; *m:* Bruce L.; *c:* Susan Smith, Mary A. Beers, Christine Appling; *ed:* (BA) Geology, TX Tech Univ 1946; Learning Disabilities Ed, Ed, Bi-ling; *cr:* Teacher Sterling City TX, Alice TX, Corpus Christi TX, San Antonio TX; *ai:* Grade Level Academic Coord; Amer Assn Prof Geologists 1944-47, Outstanding Stu 1944; W TX Geologists Society Outstanding Geology Stu; *office:* David Crockett Elem Sch 2215 Morales San Antonio TX 78216

MEDIAVILLA, ROSARIO, Fourth Grade Teacher; *b:* Villosilla De La V, Spain; *ed:* (BA) Philosophy/Letters, Nunez De Arce 1974; (BA) Liberal Stud, 1986, (MS) Ed, 1980 Fresno St; *cr:* 1st/2nd Grade Teacher St Anne 1977-83; 3rd Grade Teacher 1983-89, 4th Grade Teacher 1989- Sacred Heart; *ai:* Religion Coord; Outstanding Achievement Awds Project Wild & Energy & Environment Seminars 1984.

MEDICUS, JULIA ANN (KALLENBAUGH), 8th Grade Eng/Rdng Teacher; *b:* Youngstown, OH; *c:* Amy J., David C.; *ed:* (BME) Music Ed, Dana Sch of Music 1975; (MSE) Master Teacher Curr, Youngstown St Univ 1990; Teacher Trng in Drug Intervention & Prevention Prgms; *cr:* Vocal Music Teacher Warren City Schls 1975-78; Elem Teacher Girard City Schls 1978-; *ai:* Sch Newspaper Faculty Adv; Asst Coach Sci Olympiad Team; Youngstown St Univ Eng Festival Asst; NEA 1975-; Music Educators Natl Conference 1975-78; Girard Ed Assn (Building Rep, Labor Relations Bd) 1988-89; Wickliffe Chrstn Church Choir Dir; Career Ed Grant 1985-86; Outstanding Young Women of America 1984; Schlsp Recipient Masters Prgm 1989-; *office:* Prospect Jr HS 700 E Prospect St Girard OH 44420

MEDLIN, WANDA HINSON, 5th Grade Teacher; *b:* Monroe, NC; *m:* Richard W.; *c:* Matthew D., Raina L.; *ed:* (AS) Elem Ed, Wingate Coll 1972; (BS) His, Univ NC Charlotte 1974; (MA) Intermediate Ed, Wingate Coll 1987; *cr:* 5th Grade Teacher Unionville Elem Sch 1974-; *ai:* Yrbk; Lit Team Coach; *home:* 3905 Sincerity Rd Monroe NC 28110

MEDLOCK, ANGELA HIGHT, Business Teacher; *b:* Rockford, IL; *m:* Michael Joe; *c:* Jered, Jillian, Jessica; *ed:* Bus, Cmptr; *cr:* Telephone Operator Continental 1972-76; City Clerk Fayetteville AR 1976-80; Bus Teacher Alma HS 1983-87, Mulberry HS 1988-; *ai:* Soph Class & FBLA Spon; USTA; Womens League 1985-87; United Meth Church Act; Foothills Little Theater; *home:* Rt 2 Box 45 Mulberry AR 72947

MEDLOCK, LINDA SUE, Physical Education Teacher; *b:* Salem, IN; *m:* Larry W.; *ed:* (BS) Phys Ed, 1983, (MS) Ed/Spec Ed, 1986 IN Univ; *cr:* Phys Ed Teacher Bradie Shrum Elem; *ai:* Track & Field Coach; Sch Improvement for St Acceleration; Spokesperson Red Ribbon Week; AIDS Seminar; Be Kind to Animals Week; Earth Week 1990; Amer Heart Pepi Jump Rope; IN St Teachers Assn, Salem Classroom Teachers Assn; Washington Cty Humane Society Pres 1988-; Amer Heart Assn Region 12 IN; *office:* Bradie Shrum Elem Sch R 3 Box 500 Salem IN 47167

MEDVE, ELEANORA EVANS, First Grade Teacher; *b:* Suffern, NY; *ed:* (BA) Elem Ed, 1970, (MS) Spec Ed, 1978 Butler Univ; Grad Stud Continuing Ed; *cr:* 2nd Grade Teacher Sch 32 1970-73; 1st-3rd Grade Teacher Elder W Diggs 42 1973-; *ai:* Human Relations Comm-Coord; Grade Level Chairperson; Teachers Advisory & Textbook Adoption Comm; NEA, IN St Teacher Assn, Indianapolis Ed Assn 1970-; PTA (VP 1984-86, Secy 1986-88); GSA 1972-73; Alpha Chi Omega 1968-; *office:* Elder W Diggs Sch 42 1002 W 25th St Indianapolis IN 46208

MEDVIG, KAY JOHNSON, 3rd Grade Teacher; *b:* Humboldt, TN; *m:* A. Stephen; *c:* Stephanie K. N.; *ed:* (BS) Elem Ed, Univ of TN 1977; Human Dev Trng, Perceptional Trng; *cr:* 1st-4th Grade Teacher Oakland Elem 1967-68; 2nd Grade Teacher Mt Juliet Elem 1968-77; 3rd Grade Teacher St Pius Tenth Elem Sch 1977-; *ai:* Jumprope Team & Asst Speech Coach; Math Textbook Comm 1977; 1st-4th Grade AV Equipment Room Co-Chm 1974-77; ADA Budget Comm 1971, 1976; Local Teachers Assn (Faculty Rep 1971, 1976, Public Relations Chm 1976, Chm Election Comm 1972, 1973, 1975); St Ed Assn Voting Delegate 1974; PTA VP 1975; Cty Cancer Assn Treas 1974-76; Outstanding Young Woman of America 1977; St Legislature Honorary Staff 1977; Preliminary to Miss America Pageant Co-Dir 1967-77; *home:* 91 S Eagle Cir Aurora CO 80012

MEECH JR., PAUL COLLINS, Science Teacher; *b:* Adrian, MI; *m:* Carol Sue Meyer; *c:* Britt Bulla, Brad Bulla; *ed:* (BS) Geology, Guilford Coll 1973; (MED) Sci Ed, Univ of GA 1975; *cr:* Teacher Clarke Mid Sch 1975-; *ai:* Clarke Assn of Cty Educators (Governing Bd 1976-78, VP 1986-87, Pres 1987-88); 1st Baptist Church Assoc Deacon 1989-; Clarke Cty Teacher Advisory Bd; *office:* Clarke Mid Sch 1235 Baxter St Athens GA 30606

MEEK, CONNIE MARIE, Business Education Teacher; *b:* Raton, NM; *m:* Charles R.; *c:* Jason Wallace, Beau, Ron II, Cheryll; *ed:* (BA) Bus Ed, Southern CO St Coll 1970; (MA) Bus Teacher Ed, Univ of Northern CO 1982; Post Masters Studies 60 Hrs; *cr:* Bus Teacher, Seton HS 1970-71; Pueblo Cmmty Coll 1971-77; Central HS 1973-82; Centennial HS 1982-; *ai:* FBLA Adv 1970-; NBEA 1970-; Co Educators Sec 1975-77 Schlsp 1981-; PEA/CEA/NEA 1973-; Delta Kappa Gamma 1987-; CEFAB Schlsp 1981-; Co Teacher Awd 1988-; *office:* Centennial H S 2525 Mountainview Dr Pueblo CO 81008

MEEK, JANIS GAYLE (PAYNTER), Home Economics Teacher; *b:* Warrenton, NC; *m:* Oscar L.; *c:* Ginger, Sam; *ed:* (BS) Home Ec Ed, Univ of NC Greensboro 1971; (MS) Home Ec Ed, NC Central Univ 1990; *cr:* Teacher John Graham HS 1971-81; Warren Cty HS 1981-; *ai:* Sr Class Adv; Mentor Teacher; FHA & HERO Adv; Leadership Team Mem; NC Voc Assn Home Ec Div Pres 1987-88; Amer Home Ec Assn Certified Home Economist 1988; NC Assn of Educators; Delta Kappa Gamma Chapter Pres 1988-; FHA Regional Adv 1985-86; Chapter Adv of Yr & Master Adv 1988; Teacher of Yr 1983; Wkshp Presenter; Outstanding Young Educator 1982; Published Teacher Resource Materials.

MEEKS, DAN, Instrumental Music Teacher; *b:* Cleveland, OH; *m:* Barbara Suzan Franz; *c:* Bonnie, Patrick; *ed:* (BM) Music Ed, Miami Univ 1977; *cr:* Band Dir Wm Henry Harrison Jr Sch & HS 1977-; *ai:* HS Percussion Instr; Jazz Band Dir; Dept Head Jr HS; 8th Grade Bsktbl Coach; OH Music Ed Assn Contest Chair 1988-; Jr HS Bands Perform at Opryland 1987-88/Disney World & Sea World 1990; Superior Ratings at OMEA Contests 1986/1988/1989; 1st Place Natl Music Festival Orlando 1980; *office:* Wm Henry Harrison Jr H S 9830 West Rd Harrison OH 45030

MEEKS, DARRELL JAMES, Mathematics Teacher; *b:* Richmond, IN; *m:* Pamela Sue Cobb; *c:* James, Julie; *ed:* (BS) Math/Scndry Ed, Univ of Dayton 1968; (MED) Sch Admin, Miami Univ 1971; *cr:* Teacher C R Coblentz Schls 1968-69, Trotwood-Madison City Schls 1969-; *ai:* Bsktbl Coach; Girls Sftbl Coach; TMEA 1969-; OEA 1968-; NEA 1970-; Preble Cty Mental Health Bd 1989-; *office:* Trotwood-Madison City Schls 229 E Trotwood Blvd Trotwood OH 45429

MEEKS, FRANCINE CELESTE (GARRETT), 4th-6th Grade Science Teacher; *b:* Baltimore, MD; *m:* Lloyd David; *c:* Lloyd J.; *ed:* (BA) Eng Lit/Ed, 1974, (MA) Instructional Systems in Ed, 1986 Univ of MD Baltimore; Several Wkshps; *cr:* 4th/5th Grade Sci/Soc Stud Teach 1974-88, 4th-6th Grade Sci Dept Teacher 1988- St Philip Neri Elem Sch; *ai:* St Philip Neri Stu Cncl Moderator; Bantams 10 Pin Bowling Coach; St Philip Neri Sci Curr Coord; Univ of MD Baltimore Teaching Grant 1970-74; *office:* St Philip Neri Elem Sch 6401 Orchard Rd Linthicum Heights MD 21090

MEENACH, DEBORAH LEWIS, Home Economics/Science Teacher; *b:* West Liberty, KY; *m:* Danny; *c:* Steven, Matthew; *ed:* (BS) Area Home Ec, 1977, (MS) Voc Home Ec, 1980 Morehead St Univ; *cr:* Teacher Carter Cty Bd of Ed 1978-; *ai:* 7th Grade Beta Club Adv; NEA, KY Ed Assn 1978-; KY Area Voc Home Ec Teachers 1988-; Grayson Jaycees 1987-, Outstanding Mem 1988; Bagby Memorial Meth Ladies Circle Telephone Meeting Reminder 1988-; Riverview Homemakers 1988-; Nom for Ashland Oil Teacher Achievement Awd 1989; *office:* Prichard Elem Sch 401 E Main Grayson KY 41143

MEGGS, KATHERINE NOLAN, English/Dramatics Teacher; *b:* Tupelo, MS; *m:* C. Lawrence; *c:* Scott L., Chad L.; *ed:* (BA) Speech, Mc Kendree Coll 1969; Grad Stud S IL Univ; *cr:* Teacher Freeburg HS 1969-; *ai:* Thespians, SADD, Lifesavers Spon; NCTE, IL Speech & Theatre Assn; Freeburg Ed Assn (Pres 1976-78, Secy 1974-75); IL Ed Assn; Outstanding Educator 1984; Worked in Prof Theatre; *home:* 212 N Vine St Freeburg IL 62243

MEGLIO, NORMA-JEAN J., High School Teacher; *b:* Providence, RI; *ed:* (BA) Eng, Providence Coll 1982; Working towards MAT Eng, RI Coll; *cr:* Teacher St Patrick HS 1982-84, Bishop Keough HS 1985-; *ai:* Stu Cncl Moderator; Model Legislature; Drama; RI Cncl Teachers of Eng Mem 1982-; RI Soc Stud Assn Mem 1985-; Providence Coll Alumni Assn Mem 1982-; Prof Proofreader-Observer Publications Inc; Free-Lance Writer; *office:* Bishop Keough HS 145 Power Rd Pawtucket RI 02861

MEGNIN, JULIA KING, Elementary Teacher of Gifted; *b:* Goshen, IN; *m:* Donald F.; *c:* Martin King, Daniel F.; *ed:* (BS) Elem Ed, Manchester Coll 1953; (MA) Comparative Ed, Syracuse Univ 1965; Boston Univ Sch of Theology; *cr:* 5th Grade Teacher Mt Morris IL 1953-55; 6th Grade Teacher Pinckney Sch 1955-57; 8th Grade Unified Stud Teacher Shawnee Mission Jr HS 1957-58; Teacher of Elem Gifted Center Township Sch & Emily Brittain Sch & Broad Street Sch 1978-; *ai:* Butler Area Sch Dist Instructional & Prof Dev Cncl 1988- & Cmptr Comm 1981-84; NEA 1953-58; PSEA 1978-; PAGE Butler Chapter Organizer 1980-; Experiment in Intnl Living Co-Leader 1962, Group to Germany; Rotary Grande (176 Stu to Germany 1976, 20 Stu to Germany 1984 Co-Leader); Organized Nursery Sch Slippery Rock PA 1966-68 & Musoorie India 1966; *office:* Butler Area Sch Dist 167 New Castle Rd Butler PA 16001

MEHAFFEY, MARK E., Secondary Art Teacher; *b:* Ann Arbor, MI; *m:* Rose Marie; *ed:* (BFA) Art/Art Ed, MI St Univ 1973; Numerous Painting Seminars & Wkshps; *cr:* Art Teacher Lansing Sch Dist; *ai:* Discipline & Sch Improvement Comm Chm; Natl Watercolor, MI Watercolor, Mid-West Watercolor Society Bd of Dir 1990-91, Inter-North Fnd Awd 1987; Numerous Awds for Excl Watercolor Painting.

MEHARG, CARRIE NOLAND, Chemistry Teacher; *b:* Durango, CO; *m:* Neil; *ed:* (BS) Chem, N AZ Univ 1985; *cr:* Chemist Westinghouse ID Nuclear Company 1985-86; Chem Teacher Cibola HS 1988-; *ai:* Chem Challenge Contest & Academic Decathalon Coach; ACS 1985-86; AEA, NSTA 1988-; Research Corporation Grant; *office:* Cibola HS 4100 20th St Yuma AZ 85364

MEHEW, DEBORAH ESKRIDGE, Debate/Drama Coach; *b:* Muskogee, OK; *c:* Katherine Lees; *ed:* (BA) Speech, Northeastern St Coll 1873; (MSED) Scndry Speech Ed, NE OK St Univ 1977; *cr:* New Stud Cnslr NE OK St Univ 1976-77; Homebound Teacher 1977-78, Speech/Eng Teacher 1978-81, Debate/Drama Coach 1981- Muskogee Public Schls; *ai:* Children Theatre; Competitive Drama Prgm; Debate Coach; Bus Driver; All Sch Play Dir; Speech Tournament Host; Muskogee Ed Assn, OK Ed Assn, NEA 1977-; Kappa Kappa Iota 1981-; Muskogee Cmmty Theatre Bd of Dir 1987-89; Schlsp Adults Art Inst; Children Theatre & Child Abuse Grants; *office:* Muskogee HS 3200 E Shawnee Muskogee OK 74403

MEHLBERG, JOHN ELDON, Head Fifth Grade Teacher; *b:* Effingham, IL; *m:* Julie Rapp; *c:* Kristen, Elizabeth; *ed:* (BA) Ed, IL Wesleyan Univ 1978; (MS) Educl Admin, IL St Univ 1986; *cr:* 4th Grade Teacher 1978-79, 5th Grade Teacher 1979-, Head Teacher 1981- Washington Elem Sch; *ai:* Building Gifted Coord; Staff Dev Trainer; Inservice, Parent Advisory, Cmptr, Report Card Comm; St Paul Luth Church (Deacon 1982-85, Sunday Sch Supt 1988-); Present Creative Writing Wkshps for Teacher Insts; *home:* 1205 E Blackhawk Pl Pontiac IL 61764

MEHLBRECH, TERRANCE L., Chemistry Instructor; *b:* Bridgewater, SD; *m:* Jerilynn Schrupp; *c:* Michelle, Michael, Kristin; *ed:* (BS) Chem, Northern St Univ 1970; Grad Stud Physics & Chem; *cr:* Instr Langford HS 1970-71, W Cntrl HS 1971-74, Granite Falls HS 1974-77, Brandon Valley HS 1978-; *ai:* Detention Supvr; Head Coach Youth Bsbl 1985 & Sftbl 1984-88; NEA, SDEA; BUEA Pres Head Negotiator 1984-87; YMCA Bsktbl Coach 1986-, 5 Yr Awd 1990; *office:* Brandon Valley HS 304 Splitrock Brandon SD 57005

MEHLON, MICHAEL A., Jr HS Mathematics Teacher; *b:* Batesville, IN; *m:* Mary J. Hoyer; *c:* Jake, Joe; *ed:* (BA) Math, IN Univ 1977; (MS) Jr HS Mid Ed, Ball St Univ 1982; *cr:* Math Teacher Laurel Jr HS 1977-; *home:* 2143 St Rd 229 Batesville IN 47006

MEIDELL, STEPHEN JACOB, English Department Chairperson; *b:* Malden, MA; *m:* Frances M. De Rubeis; *c:* Julie, Erica, Amy, Christopher; *ed:* (BA) Eng, 1969; (MA) Educl Media, 1976 Boston Univ; (MA) Scndry Admin, Rivier Coll 1980; Writing Process Wrkshp Inst Univ of MA; Project Style MIT; Amer Stud Inst Tufts Univ; *cr:* Eng Teacher Chelmsford HS 1969-83; Eng Lecturer Middlesex Cmmty Coll 1977-81; Eng/Ed Instr Rivier Coll 1983-; Eng Dept Chair Chelmsford HS 1983-; *ai:* Adv Chs Jrnlsm Page Newsweekly; Prin Adv Cncl; NCTE 1988-; New England Assn of Teacher of Eng 1975-; MA Cncl Teachers of Eng 1973-; Chelmsford Fed of Teachers Pres 1977-80; US Army Off of Protocal West Point 1970-72 Supt Awd 1972; Horace Mann Grants 1987-88; Horace Mann Gmnt Admin 1988; Presenter NEATE Full Conf; Presenter Belmont Public Sch; Prof Dev Day; Presenter Merrimac Educl Ctr; *office:* Chelmsford HS 200 Richardson Rd North Chelmsford MA 01863

MEIER, BEVERLY LOEFFLER, Science Curriculum Dir/ Teacher; *b:* Baltimore, MD; *m:* Thomas J. Sr.; *c:* Thomas Jr., John H.; *ed:* (BS) Distributed Math/Physics/Chem, 1963, (MA) Ed/ Geology, 1969 Univ of CO; CO Sch of Mines, Univ of N CO, Metropolitan St Coll; *cr:* Sci/Chem/Phys Sci Teacher Cherry Creek HS 1963-65; Math Teacher Bonneville Jr HS 1965-66; Teacher/Dept Chairperson Boulder Valley Sch Dist 1977-; Teacher/Research Assoc US Dept of Energy & Solar Energy Research Inst 1989-; *ai:* CO St Sci Fair Advisory Comm; Boulder Valley Sch Dist Sci Fair Dir; Talented & Gifted Spon; Curr & Environmental Comm; NSTA, Phi Delta Kappa; NSTA Publications 1988; Newspaper Article Published 1984; Governor CO Environmental Awd; VFW Awd for Distinguished & Meritorious Service; Boulder Daily Camera Awd; Volunteer Committment to Sci Fair; Teacher Research Assn US Dept Energy; *office:* Broomfield Heights Mid Sch 1555 Daphne St Broomfield CO 80020

MEIER, DAVID G., Math/Computer Science Dept Chm; *b:* Neillsville, WI; *m:* Miriam Von Bergen; *c:* Lynn, William; *ed:* (BS) Math, Univ of WI Stevens Point 1967; (MS) Math Ed, Univ of WI Oshkosh 1985; *cr:* Math Teacher Coleman HS 1967-70; Math/ Cmptr Sci Teacher Reedsville HS 1970-; *ai:* Inservice Comm; Class Adv; WI Math Cncl 1970-; WI Ed Assn, NEA 1967-; *office:* Reedsville HS 340 Manitowoc St Reedsville WI 54230

MEIER-FISHER, PAMELA SUE (BEISER), Mid Sch/High Sch Teacher; *b:* Mishawaka, IN; *m:* Wayne J.; *c:* Christian, Ashley; *ed:* (BS) Eng, 1972, (MAE) Eng, 1976 Ball St Univ; Advanced Trng in Teacher Effectiveness; *cr:* Composition/Fine Art Appreciation Teacher Wes-Del HS 1972-; *ai:* Focus Corporation Newsletter Staff; Mid Sch Newspaper & Yrbk; HS Fine Art Super Bowl Coach; Gifted & Talented Planning Comm; Phi Delta Kappa, NCTE 1988-; Natl Endowment for Hum Ind Study Grant 1990; Lilly Teacher Creativity Fellowship 1989; Newspapers in Ed Grant Recipient 1989; *office:* Wes-Del HS R R 1 Gaston IN 47342

MEINERDING, ALLEN AUGUST, 7th-8th Grade Soc Stud Teacher; *b:* Celina, OH; *m:* Janet Carmean; *c:* Marcie, Isaak, John, Jakob, Samantha, Katie; *ed:* (BS) Amer Stud, Bowling Green 1969; (MS) Guidance/Counseling, St Francis 1972; *cr:* 7th-8th Grade Geography/His Teacher Mc Broom Jr HS 1969-; *ai:* Schlastic Bowl Coach; Saturday Sch Teacher; SMEA, OEA, NEA; Knights of Columbus Treas; FOE; Nom for Outstanding Young Educator 1974; *office:* Mc Broom Jr HS 5 Front St Saint Marys OH 45885

MEISCH, KATHERENE TUTTLE, Chemistry Teacher; *b:* Penn Yan, NY; *m:* John Harper; *ed:* (BA) Chem, Keuka Coll 1958; Numerous Univs; *cr:* Chem Teacher Webster HS 1958-; *ai:* JETS Team & Sci Olympiad Team; ACS Natl Sci Teachers Assn HS Test Comm 1978-79; Regents Examination Comm Chem Exam 1964-67; Debate Club Asst 1962-64; Adv Stu Cncl 1962-65, NHS 1965-67, Jr Engineers Tech Society, Sci Olympiad Team; Nom Stus for Natl Youth Sci Camp; Gave Natl Sci olympiad Chem Exam; Delta Kappa Gamma Mem 1971; NYS Advisory Comm Mem 1986-88; Webster Teachers Assn (Membership VP 1979-89, Exec Cncl Mem 1979-89, Educl Opportunity Comm 1980-89; HS, Jr HS Reorganization Sci Subcommittee 1980-82); Webster Teachers ASsn (Past Chm, Elections Comm 1977-79); Finger Lakes Sci Teacher Secy; New England Assn of Chem Teachers 1964-89; Church (Youth Sunday Sch Teacher, Admin Bd 1983-, Finance Comm 1985-87, Finance Comm Chm 1987-); Sci Educators Assn, Natl Sci Teachers of America; Lions Club Awd 1962; Webster Sch dist Career Teachers Awd 1974; NSF Prgm for Continuing Ed of Scndry Sch Teachers; HS Chem Teacher Awd 1976; NE Regional ACS Teacher Awd 1982; Keuka Coll Prof Achievement Awd 1958; Ind Colls & Univs Commission; Wayne Cty Conference 1968; Educl Opportunities Comm Scholastic Rep; EAstman Kodak Intnl Sci & Engineering Fair Awd 1982; Chosen for Honors Polymer & Cmptr Wkshp by NSTA 1985; *home:* 2792 St Paul Blvd Rochester NY 14617

MEISSNER, BARBARA GRAHAM, English Teacher; *b:* Farmington, MI; *c:* Kirk, Erik; *ed:* (BS) Ed/Bio/Eng, Cntrl MI Univ 1960; (MED) Admin, Sam Houston St Univ 1984; *cr:* Teacher KS Sch Dist 1961-62, Consolidated Sch Dist #2 1964-73, Klein Ind Sch Dist 1973-; *ai:* Assn of TX Prof Educators Building Rep 1985-; *office:* Klein Oak HS 22603 Northcrest Dr Spring TX 77389

MEISSNER, DONALD WAYNE, Life Science Teacher; *b:* Fort Lauderdale, FL; *m:* Nancy Lee; *c:* Natalie A., Nicole M.; *ed:* (BA) Bio/Ed, Greenville Coll 1968; (MS) Bio, Univ of IL Champagn-Urbana 1976; (PHD) Sci Ed, Univ Southern Ms 1988; Manty Courses and Wkshps; *cr:* Coll Instr Coll of Lake Cty; Sci Teacher Kenneth Murphy Jr HS 1968-; *ai:* 8th Grade Chm, Spon; NSTA, IL Sci Teachers Assn, NABT; Zion Benton Lib Trustee 1988-89; Article on Sci and Children; Conducted Wrkshp Sci Teaching for Lare Cty Teachers; *office:* Kenneth Murphy Jr HS 11315 W Wadsworth Rd Beach Park IL 60099

MEISTER, LINDA S., English & Reading Teacher; *b:* Tango, WV; *m:* Thomas A.; *ed:* (BA) Eng/Soc Stud, Charleston Univ 1961; Cert Rndg, OH St Univ; *cr:* 9th Grade Eng Teacher Midway & Du Pont Jr HS 1961-63; 11th Grade Eng Teacher Du Pont HS 1963-65; 6th/7th Grade Soc Stud Teacher Mt Vernon Elem & Fairfield Jr HS 1965-67; 11th Grade Rdng Teacher IN St Laboratory Sch 1967-69; Rdng Specialist Columbus Public Schls 1969-71, Kilbourne 1972; 7th-12th Grade Rdng/Eng Dept Teacher Grandview Heights Sch Dist 1972-; *ai:* Jr HS Yrbk & Drama Club Adv; Dist Dev Cncl; Top Cat Club, Essential Elements of Instruction, Lang Art CBE Comm; Ferguson-Florissant Project; Grandview Heights Ed Assn Building Rep 1988-, Teacher of Yr 1988-89; OH Ed Assn, NEA; OH Teacher of Yr Finalist 1988-89; OH St Univ Outstanding Service Cooperating Teacher 1989; Articles Published.

MEJLAENDER, JOHN ROBERT, English Teacher/Coach; *b:* Seattle, WA; *ed:* (BA) Eng/Scndry Ed, Western WA Univ 1983; (MA) Educl Admin, Seattle Univ 1988; *cr:* Teacher/Coach Tolt Mid Sr HS 1983-; *ai:* Head Track Coach; Natural Helper Coord; Honor Society Adv; Mid Sch ASB Adv; Substitute Prin; Assn of WA Sch Prin Mem 1989-; Project Lead Schlsp; *office:* Tolt Mid Sr HS 3740 Tolt Ave Carnation WA 98014

MELANSON, LYNDA GARRETT, Speech/Debate Coach; *b:* Miami, FL; *c:* Melissa; *ed:* (BS) Ed/Speech/Eng, Univ TX El Paso 1983; *cr:* 9th-12th Grade Speech Teacher Eastwood HS 1983-84; 9th-12th Grade Speech Teacher/Coach Hanks HS 1984-; *ai:* Speech & Debate Coach; Natl Forensic League Spon; W TX Writing Project Consultant 1984-; TSCA Public Relations 1988-; TX Forensic Assn 1984-; Coach of Natl Dramatic & TX 5 A UIL St Poetry Champion; W TX Writing Project Charter Fellow; *office:* Hanks HS 2001 Lee Trevino El Paso TX 79935

MELASKY, JEANETTE BETH, Math Teacher; *b:* Houston, TX; *ed:* (BS) Elem Ed, U of Houston 1971; Grad Classes at Univ of Houston; *cr:* 5th Grade Teacher Livingston Ind Sch Dist 1917-73; 3rd Grade Teacher North Ind Sch Dist 1974-78; 8th Grade Teacher Lamar CISD 1979-; *ai:* Chrldr Spon; NJ HS Faculty Cncl; NCTM 1980-; TCTA 1979-; *office:* George Jr HS 4601 Airport Rd Rosenberg TX 77471

MELBOURNE, CAVEL ANDREA (BECKFORD), Social Studies Teacher; *b:* Westmoreland, Jamaica; *m:* Bertram; *c:* Yolande, Maurice, Launice; *ed:* (BA) His, West Indies Coll 1982; (MA) His, Andrews Univ 1984; *cr:* Soc Stud/Phys Ed Teacher Frome Jr Scndry 1970-71; 6th Grade Teacher Cokes View Elem 1971-72; Soc Stud/Phys Ed Teacher Maggotty Jr Scndry 1972-74; Soc Stud/Eng Teacher Harrison HS 1974-78, W Indies Coll H S 1978-81; Soc Stud Teacher John Nevins Andrews Jr HS 1986-; *ai:* Stu Cncl Spon 1987-89; Columbia Union Evaluation Supervison Comm Mem; NCSS 1989-; Phi Kappa Phi 1989-; Article Published; *home:* 8121 Lockney Ave Takoma Park MD 20912

MELDRUM, JOSEPH REUEL, Biology/Physiology Teacher; *b:* Spanish Fork, UT; *m:* Stacey Smith; *c:* Adam, Ameri; *ed:* (BS) Zoology/Comp Teaching, Brigham Young Univ 1987; *cr:* Bio Teacher Nebo Sch Dist Payson HS 1987-; *ai:* Wrestling Coach; Taking Group on Sci Field Trip to FL; Voted Favorite Teacher Payson HS 1988-89; *office:* Payson HS 1050 S Main Payson UT 84651

MELEASON, GERALYN UHL, 7th Grade Soc Stud Teacher; *b:* St Marys, PA; *m:* Paul M.; *c:* Paul J., Marie G.; *ed:* (BA) Scndry Ed/Soc Stud, Gannon Univ 1979; *cr:* 8th Grade Teacher St Paul Sch 1979-84; 7th Grade Soc Stud Teacher Sacred Heart Sch 1984-87; *ai:* St Paul Sch Patrols, Cheerleading, Newspaper; Sacred Heart Sch Newspaper; Jr PSEA NW Regional Pres 1977-78; Gannon Ed Club Pres 1977-78; Archbishop John Mark Gannon Awd for General Scholastic Excl 1979; Highest Grade Point Average Grad 1979.

MELEDANDRI, CAESAR FRANCIS, High School English Teacher; *b:* Brooklyn, NY; *m:* Judith A. O Brien; *c:* Marc; *ed:* (BS) Theatre, 1967, (MA) Educl Theatre, 1972, NY Univ; *cr:* 9th-12th Grade Speech Teacher Arlington Heights HS 1967-68; 10th-12th Grade Eng Teacher Summit Sr HS 1968-69; 9th-12th Grade Eng Teacher Pascack Hills HS 1969-77, Inter-Lakes HS 1982-; *ai:* Var Soccer Coach; Drama Club Dir; Curr Dev Comm; NEA, NCTE, NEATE 1977-; ASCD 1988-; NH Army Natl Guard SFC 1982 Army Commendation Medal 1990; Diocesene Parish Cncl 1989-; *office:* Inter-Lakes H S Rt 25 Meredith NH 03253

MELENDEZ, MARY ALICE, Honors English I Teacher; *b:* El Paso, TX; *ed:* (BS) Ed/Rdng/Eng, Univ of TX El Paso 1985; Writing & Study Skills Projects; *cr:* Teacher Socorro Ind Sch Dist 1985-; *ai:* Frosh Chrldr Spon; LIFT Project Presenter; Co-Developer Practical Writing Study Skills Course; Literacy Day Comm Mem; NCTE 1984-; Intnl Rdng Assn 1988-; Paso Del Norte Teachers of Eng 1988-; Impact II Awd Socorro Ind Sch Dist 1988; Stephen F Austin St Univ Title VII Grant 1990; *office:* Socorro HS 10150 Alameda Ave El Paso TX 79927

MELLEMA, THOMAS E., Math/Science Teacher; *ed:* (BS) Bio, 1969, (MS) Fisheries Bio, 1972 MI St Univ; *cr:* 8th Grade Math/Sci Teacher Fruitport Mid Sch 1969-; *office:* Fruitport Mid Sch Pontaluna Rd Fruitport MI 49415

MELLER, PAULA DETRIXHE, Eng/Theatre Arts/Span Teacher; *b:* Higgins, TX; *m:* Robert Kay; *c:* Ryan, Roger, Amy; *ed:* (BA) Eng Ed, W TX St Univ 1972; Several Grad & Advanced Academic Courses; *cr:* Eng/Speech Teacher Horace Mann Jr HS 1972-73; Dir/Teacher Pre-Sch Place 1984-87; Eng/Theatre/Span Teacher Higgins Ind Sch Dist 1987-; *ai:* Local Dir of Annual UIL One-Act Contest Play; Local & Dist UIL Dir HS Ready Writing & Spelling; Class Spon; Gifted & Talented, Sch Improvement Comm Mems; NE Panhandle Teachers Federal Credit Union 1987-; TX Educl Theatre Assn 1990; Gem Baptist Church Youth Teacher 1977-; Higgins Chamber of Commerce Dir of Summer Cmmty Play 1987, 1990; *office:* Higgins Ind Sch Dist 406 N Main Box 238 Higgins TX 79046

MELLOY, SAMUEL H., English Department Chair; *b:* Sturgis, KY; *m:* Linda Dale Berry; *c:* Kyle D.; *ed:* (BA) Eng, Murray St Univ 1975; (MA) Eng, 1980, (Rank I) Sch Admin, 1984 W KY Univ; *cr:* Eng Teacher 1975-, Eng Chm 1983- Meade Cty HS;

Adjunct Eng Instr W KY Univ 1983-; *ai:* NHS Adv; Academic Team Coach; KY Cncl Teachers of Eng, NCTE 1980-; KY Ed Assn, NEA 1975-; Democratic Party Precinct Chm 1981-89; Stu Teacher of Yr Carlisle Cty HS 1975; *home:* 325 Monroe St Brandenburg KY 40108

MELONE, JOHN IRVIN, JR., Retired Physics Teacher; *b:* Ruckersville, VA; *m:* Wanda Fay Graves; *c:* Donna Lynn Bilko, Kathleen; *ed:* (BSED) Gen Sci, 1955, (MED) Bio, 1963 Univ of VA; US Army Air Defense Sch; *cr:* Gen Sci/Bio Teacher Wm Fleming HS 1956-58, 1960-62, Lane HS 1963-65, Buford Mid Sch 1965-66; Physics Teacher Thomas Jefferson HS for Sci & Technology 1967-89; *ai:* NSTA Life Mem; Phi Delta Kappa, Kappa Delta Pi; *home:* 7404 Floyd Ave Springfield VA 22150

MELTON, ANITA, 7th-8th Grade Teacher/Prin; *b:* Woodbury, TN; *ed:* (BS) Elem Ed, 1976, (MED) Curr/Instruction, Mid TN St Univ 1981; *cr:* Teacher 1977-88, Teacher/Prin 1988- Short Mountain Elem; *ai:* Bsktbl Spon; 4-H Club, Just Say No Leader; Cannon Cty Ed Assn Faculty Rep 1980-81, Cannon Cty Teacher of Yr 1987; TN Ed Assn, NEA; New Short Mountain United Meth Church Ed 1979-; New Short Mountain United Meth Women (Pres 1986-89, Secy 1982-85); Short Mountain Cmmty Correspondent for Cannon Collier; *office:* Short Mountain Sch Rt 2 Box 66 Woodbury TN 37190

MELTON, BEVERLY DUNN, 5th Grade Teacher; *b:* Milan, TN; *m:* Danny Joe; *c:* Justin, Jantzen; *ed:* (BA) Scndry Ed/Elem Ed, Univ of TN Martin 1973; *cr:* 4th-8th Grade Teacher Gleason Sch 1973-; Adult Basic Ed Dresden Voc Sch 1987-; *ai:* Just Say No Club; NEA, TEA; *office:* Gleason Sch Front St Gleason TN 38229

MELTON, CYNTHIA BLACKWELL, Mathematics Teacher; *b:* Mobile, AL; *m:* Charles Joel; *c:* Jordan, Patrick, Lee; *ed:* (BS) Phys Ed, Troy St Univ 1973; (MS) Phys Ed, Univ of W FL 1978; *cr:* Phys Ed/Sci Teacher Chumuckla HS 1973-75; Phys Ed Teacher Gulf Breeze Mid Sch 1975-80; CAD Analyst Teacher Litton Guidance & Control Systems 1981-83; Phys Ed Teacher Pace Mid Sch 1984-85; Math/Phys Ed Teacher Central HS 1985-; *ai:* Fellowship of Chrstn Athletes Adv; Var Vlybl, Bsktbl Coach; NEA 1987-; Pensacola News Journal Vlybl Coach of Yr 1986, 1989; Dist 1 Vlybl Coach of Yr 1989; *office:* Central HS Rt 6 Box 230 Milton FL 32570

MELTON, LOUISE MC CLAIN, Home Economics Teacher; *b:* Pelham, GA; *m:* Luther A.; *c:* Melanie Melton Collins; *ed:* (BS) Home Ec, GA Coll 1959; Grad Sch Auburn Univ, GA Coll; *cr:* Home Ec Teacher Dublin HS 1959-62; Elem Teacher Central Elem 1962-63, West End Elem 1964-65; Home Ec/Elem Teacher Rockdale Cty Schls 1965-; *ai:* Chairperson Home Ec Dept; FHA Adv; GEA, NEA 1959-76; Pilot Club Secy 1988-89; GA Teacher Hall of Fame Nom 1978; *office:* Heritage HS 2400 Granade Rd Conyers GA 30207

MELTON, MARTHA LAWRENCE, Fifth Grade Teacher; *b:* Altus, OK; *m:* Billy Don; *c:* Scott Mitchell, Melanie Mitchell, Melissa Mitchell, Leonard, Angela; *ed:* (BS) Ed, TX Technological Coll 1966; *cr:* 6th Grade Teacher Posey Elem 1966; 4th Grade Teacher Alameda Elem 1967; 5th Grade Teacher Frostwood Elem 1967-68; 4th Grade Teacher Armstrong Elem 1976-77; 5th Grade Teacher Eastview Elem 1977-; *ai:* TX St Teachers Assn Local Pres 1982-83; TX Classroom Teachers Assn; *home:* 18448 FM 15 Troup TX 75789

MELTON, RAMONA JUNE BAYLEY, Business Teacher/ Librarian; *b:* Siloam Springs, AR; *m:* Roy Don; *c:* Deanna M.; *ed:* (BS) Secretarial Sci, Union Coll 1961; (MED) Voc Ed, Univ of AR 1986; Grad Stud Lib Media Specialist Cert; *cr:* Secy SW Adventist Coll 1960-64, Union Coll 1964-69; Bus Teacher/Secy Ozark Adventist Acad 1971-; *ai:* Alumni Coord; NBEA, Amer Lib Assn, AR Lib Assn 1989-; Zapara Excl in Teaching Awd 1989; *home:* Rt 1 Box 107 A Siloam Springs AR 72761

MELTZER, MICHAEL R., Physics Teacher; *b:* Syracuse, NY; *m:* Sandra L.; *c:* Dawn, David, Steven; *ed:* (BS) Ed, 1963, (MS) Sci, 1964, (MS) Sci Teaching, 1974 Syracuse Univ; Environmental Sci, Syracuse Univ; *cr:* Sci Teacher E Syracuse-Minoa Cntrl HS 1964-; *ai:* Jr Engineers & Ham Radio Club Adv; NY St Regents Exam Evaluation & Exam Item Writing Comms; NY St Physics Syllabus Revision Comm; Radio Amateurs of Greater Syracuse Pres 1984-88; Published Articles; Honor Societys Excl in Teaching Awd 1989; NY St Best Sci Teachers 1988; *office:* E Syracuse-Minoa Cntrl HS Kirkville & Fremont Rds East Syracuse NY 13057

MELVILLE, BEVERLY LURVEY, English Teacher; *b:* Locke Mills, ME; *m:* Richard F.; *c:* Dana, Nancy Melville Snyder; *ed:* (BS) Lang Arts, Univ of ME Farmington 1975; Masters Prgm, Univ of ME; Summer Session in Eng Writing & Lit, Bread Loaf Middlebury Coll; *cr:* Eng Teacher Rumford HS 1975-77; Eng/Eng Composition Teacher Berlin HS 1977-78; Eng/Soc Stud Teacher Telstar Mid Sch 1978-86; Eng Teacher Telstar HS 1986-; *ai:* ME Aspirations Fnd Mentor in Prgm at Telstar; Eng Curr Review Co-Chairperson; Academics Standard Steering Comm Mem; Sr Class & Career Week Adv; SADD Adv; Chairperson 3 Self Groups; NCTE, New England Assn of Teachers of Eng 1975-; ME Cncl of Eng & Lang Arts; Locke Mills Union Church (Organist, Choir Dir) 1955-; Delta Kappa Gamma World Fellowship & Other Comm 1978-; Amer Legion Auxiliary (Past Pres, Past Secy, Girls St Chairperson) 1953-, Outstanding & Dedicated Service 1989; Order of Eastern Star 1978-; *office:* Telstar HS R R 26 Bethel ME 04217

MELVIN, DOROTHY EILEENE, Physical Education Teacher; *b:* Burlington, IA; *ed:* (BA) Phys Ed, 1969, (MS) Phys Ed, 1976 IL St Univ; *cr:* Teacher Trewyn Jr HS 1969-70; Teacher 1970-, Athletic Dir 1985-, Phys Ed Dept Head 1985- East Peoria Cntrl; *ai:* Sftbl, Vlybl, Track Head Coach; Sftbl, Bsktbl Asst Coach; Stu Cncl Adv; EPEEA Pres 1984-86; AAHPERD 1988-; Tazewell Cty Sch Credit Union Vice Chm of Bd 1989-; Inducted to IL St Univ Athletic Hall of Fame; *office:* East Peoria Cntrl 601 E Washington East Peoria IL 61611

MELVIN, LINDA JEAN, Science Teacher; *b:* Boone, IA; *c:* Jennifer, Heather, Leah, Jeffrey, Scott; *ed:* (BA) General Sci, Univ of N IA 1976; Working Towards MA, Univ of IA; *cr:* 8th/9th Grade Sci Teacher Freeport Schls 1978-80; 7th-9th Grade Sci Teacher Preston Cmmty Schls 1980-; *ai:* Jr HS Cheerleading & Class Spon; *office:* Preston Comm Schls Box 12 Preston IA 52069

MENA, MANUEL R., Mathematics Dept Chairperson; *b:* Havana, Cuba; *m:* Elena F. R.; *c:* Raul R., Vivien M.; *ed:* (BS) Curr Instruction - Cum Laude, Univ of Albuquerque 1973; (MS) Math/Curr, 1975, Ed Specialist Bi-ling Ed, 1978 Univ of NM; Cmptr Sci Teacher; Ford Motor Technician; Span Teacher; Bi-ling Ed Teacher; *cr:* Show Room Inspector Ford Motor Company 1966; Mgr INCO Service Gas Station 1970, Standard Oil Company 1972; Teacher Albuquerque Public Sch 1990; *ai:* Cmptr Club Spon, Math Dept Chairperson Ernie Pyle Mid Sch; Cuban Club Pres 1986; Rio Grande Cluster Sch Prgm Mem 1988; Parent Teacher Stu VP; Wrote Book for Cmptr Sci Class; Published Books for Bi-ling Classes; *home:* 1615 Robert Dale NE Albuquerque NM 87112

MENA, ROSA NATALIA, Third Grade Teacher; *b:* Salamanca, Mexico; *ed:* (AA) Office Occupations, Austin Comm Coll 1976; (BS) Elem Ed, Pan Amer Univ 1980; *cr:* Teacher/Trainee TX Migrant Cncl 1970-72; Teacher Child Incorporated 1974-75, Donna Ind Sch Dist 1980-; *ai:* UIL & Spelling Bee Coach; TSTA Mem 1986-; *office:* Runn Elem Rt 1 Box 48 Donna TX 78537

MENARD, ALBERT ERNEST, Fourth Grade Teacher; *b:* Woonsocket, RI; *ed:* (BS) Elem Ed, 1972, (MED) Elem Ed, 1976 RI Coll; GEO VISTA Summer Prgm to Thailand 1989; *cr:* 3rd Grade Teacher Social Street Sch 1973-74; 4th Grade Teacher E Woonsocket Elem Sch 1974-; *ai:* Sci Textbook Evaluation Comm 1990; Adopt-A-Sch Comm 1987-; Court Appointed Special Advocate 1984-; 1st Prize Creative Teaching Ec Awd; RI Cncl Ec Ed 1989; *office:* E Woonsocket Elem Sch 990 Mendon Rd Woonsocket RI 02895

MENARD, CLAY ANTHONY, Physics Teacher; *b:* Eunice, LA; *m:* Cora Chachere; *c:* Jeffery, Andre, Jeanne; *ed:* (BS) Bio/ Wildlife Management, USL 1970; (MS) Zoology, Univ of SW LA 1975; *cr:* Grad Asst Univ of SW LA 1970-73; Teacher/Dept Head Opelousas Cath HS 1973-78, Eunice Jr HS 1978-85; Teacher Eunice HS 1985-; *ai:* Physics Club, Scuba Club, Chess Club Spon; LAE, NEA; Eunice Biddy Bsktbl Asst Dir 1987-89; Eunice Girls Sftbl Bd of Dirs 1990; Eunice Jaycees Teacher of Yr 1978; *office:* Eunice HS Bobcat Ln Eunice LA 70535

MENDELSOHN, WILLIAM L., Social Studies Dept Chair; *b:* Cincinnati, OH; *m:* Margaret E.; *c:* Matthew; *ed:* (BA) His, Yale Univ 1974; (MA) Ed, 1979, (EDS) Ed Evaluation, 1981 Stanford Univ; *cr:* Teacher The Foote Sch 1973-74, Bund Brook HS 1974-77; Teacher Kirkwood HS 1981-, Soc Stud Chair 1987- Kirkwood HS; *ai:* Lit Ed Team Coord; NCSS; Conference of Ed Bd of Dir Mem 1988-; Intnl Ed Consortium Bd of Dirs Mem 1989-; Kirkwood Sch Dist Teacher of Yr 1988-89; Emerson Electrics Excl Teaching Awd 1989; *office:* Kirkwood HS 801 W Essex Kirkwood MO 63122

MENDENBALL, JACK LEONARDO, Biology Instructor; *b:* Rochester, PA; *m:* Veronica Huchko; *c:* Todd; *ed:* (BS) Bio Pre Medical, Geneva Coll 1967; MEDS Sci, Univ of Pittsburgh 1972; *cr:* Instr Aliquippa Sch Dist 1966-68; Hopewell Area Sch Dist 1968-; Park Dir Hopewell Township 1980-; Agent Greek Cath Union 1982-; Instr Anatomy/Physiology/Bio I-II Beaver Cty Cmmty Coll 1972-88; *ai:* Act 178 Educl Comm; Adv to Counservation/Fishing/Hunting Club; Cmmty Service Prgm Comm; Asst Health Careers Club; Hopewell Township Park Dir 1982-; Citizens Awd 1983; Womens Civic Club Cmmty Service 1980; Aliquippa Chamber of Commerce Outstanding Man of Yr Service 1986; Buhl Planetarium Outstanding Sch Teacher 1968; Hopewell PTA Outstanding Educator 1982; Greek Cath Union Outstanding Service; Beaver Cty Conservation Dist Conservation Educator of Yr 1979; *home:* 4312 Beverly Dr Aliquippa PA 15001

MENDENHALL, DEANNA DUDLEY, Third Grade Teacher; *b:* Tulsa, OK; *m:* Mike; *c:* Robin A., Todd D.; *ed:* (BS) Elem Ed, OK St Univ 1970; Grad Stud OK St Univ; *cr:* 1st Grade Teacher Pratt Elem 1970-73; 1st Grade Teacher 1973-81, 3rd Grade Teacher 1981- Cntrl Elem; *ai:* Sci Textbook Selection Comms; SSEA, OEA, NEA Sch Rep 1986-89; NEFL Grant OK St Univ 1987; *office:* Cntrl Elem Sch P O Box 970 Sand Springs OK 74063

MENDENHALL, SHARON LYNCH, 7th Grade Teacher; *b:* Norfolk, VA; *m:* Ted A.; *c:* Traver, Amy; *ed:* (BA) His, NC Wesleyan Coll 1969; *cr:* 4th Grade Teacher King Elem Sch 1969-77; ESL Teacher Project Lift 1977-78; 7th/8th/9th Soc Stud Teacher Ruffner Jr HS 1978-83; 7th Grade Soc Stud Teacher Northside Mid Sch 1983-; *ai:* Sch Climate Comm 1986-; Behavior & Attitude Reform Comm Cnslr 1988-; NCEA/NEA 1969-71; VA Cncl for Soc Stud 1978-82; VA Mid Sch Assn 1988-; *office:* Northside Mid Sch 8720 Granby St Norfolk VA 23503

MENDEZ, DEBORAH SUE, Drill/Dance Team Director; *b:* Victoria, TX; *ed:* (BS) Dance, SW TX St Univ 1986; *cr:* Asst Dance Teacher Jan Moore Sch of Dance 1981-83; Youth Organizations Unlimited SW TX St Univ 1985-86; Dance/Drill Dir Stroman HS 1986-; *ai:* Stroman HS Raider Belle Dance Team Dir; TX Drill & Dance Team Dir Assn 1989-.

MENDEZ, LORELENA, Eng as Second Lang Teacher; *ed:* (BA) Span, 1985, (BA) Fr, 1985 Univ of TX El Paso; Eng as Second Lang Teaching Endorsement Certificate 1986; *cr:* Eng As Second Lang Teacher Burges HS 1987-; *ai:* Foreign Lang Tournament Coach; Close-Up Prgm Spon; *office:* Burges HS 7800 Edgemere Blvd El Paso TX 79981

MENDOZA, CHARLES PHILLIP, Biology/Phys Science Teacher; *b:* Redlands, CA; *m:* Julie Powell Schofield; *ed:* (BS) Psych/Bio, Univ of CA Riverside 1985; Masters Ed/Phys Ed; Basic Teaching Credits, CA St San Bernardino 1985-86; E End Sci Consort 1986-87; Curr Dev, CA St San Bernardino 1987-88; NSF Sci Leadership Instr, UCR 1988-89; Physics Teachers Instr, NSF/ UCR; Project Wild Teacher Instr; *cr:* Sci Teacher Cope Jr HS 1985-; *ai:* Phys Sci Club Spon; Asst Ftbl, Bsbl, Track Coach; Ski Club Adv; CTA, AAPT, NEA 1985-; San Bernardino Cty Supt Drug Force Comm Mem; *office:* Cope Jr HS 1000 W Cyprus Ave Redlands CA 92373

MENENDEZ, OSCAR, Second Grade Teacher; *b:* Havana, Cuba; *m:* Rosa Hilda Gamboa Orozco; *ed:* (BA) Soc Sci, LaVerne Coll 1980; (MA) Ed, CA Poly Pomona 1989; *cr:* 5th Grade Teacher Dean L Shively 1982; 4th Grade Teacher New Temple 1982-85, Dean L Shively 1985-89; 2nd Grade Teacher New Temple 1989-; *ai:* Migrant Ed Teacher; Cmmty Recreation Tennis Instr; *home:* 541 N Pasadena Azusa CA 91702

MENICUCCI, JILL MARIE, Sixth Grade Teacher; *b:* Reno, NV; *m:* Donald C.; *c:* Matthew; *ed:* (BS) Elem Ed, UNR 1978; *cr:* Recreation Cnslr Natl Judicial Coll 1975-79; 6th Grade Teacher OBrien Mid Sch 1979-81, Grace Warner Elem 1982-; *ai:* IBM USA Today Current Events Contest; Young Writers Contest; Sch Patrol; Masters Equivalency Comm; 6th Grade Writing Field Test Comm; Child Study Team; SPURS Secy 1975-78; Kappa Alpha Theta Pledge Adv 1975-78; NEA, NSA, WCTA Rep 1979-81; *office:* Grace Warner Elem 3075 Heights Dr Reno NV 89503

MENIZE, ELENA ORVANI, Math Teacher; *b:* Milford, MA; *m:* James Ronald; *ed:* (AB) Math, Bridgewater St Coll 1971; *cr:* Math Teacher Franklin HS 1971-; *ai:* Class Adv; Schlsp & Early Dismassal Comm; Organizer of Schl Fundraiser; MA Teachers Assn, NEA, Franklin Ed Assn, Norfolk Cty Teachers Assn 1971-; Franklin Historical Society 1980-; Horace Mann Grant; *office:* Franklin H S Oak St Franklin MA 02038

MENKE, GEORGIANN, Fourth Grade Teacher; *b:* Amarillo, TX; *ed:* (BS) Elem Ed, W TX St Univ 1971; (BA) Bible Theology, Moody Bible Inst 1974; CA Teaching Cert, CA St Univ Hayward; *cr:* 4th Grade Teacher Redwood Chrstn Schls Inc 1974-; *ai:* Academic Meet Supvr; Redwood Chapel 1980-; *office:* Redwood Chrstn Schls Inc 19300 Redwood Rd Castro Valley CA 94546

MENSH, BARRY ALAN, Biology Teacher; *b:* Washington, DC; *ed:* (BS) Scndry Ed/Bio, Old Dominion Univ 1979; Numerous Courses; *cr:* Consumer Chem Teacher 1984-85, Bio Teacher 1979- George C Marshall HS; *ai:* Head Boys & Girls Cross Cntry & Track Coach; Jr Class Spon; Gifted & Talented & Mentoring Comms; AFT 1980-; PTA Faculty Rep, Teacher of Yr 1988; Freemasons Worshipful Master 1987-88; Fairfax Hospital Blood Bank Blood Coord 1986-; Kena Temple Shrine Mem 1987-; NHS Teacher of Yr 1988; VA Masonic Blood Prgm Seymore Jonas Levy Awd 1987-; *home:* 1793 Ivy Ct Woodbridge VA 22191

MENTUS, L. TAMMY, Sci/Youth Challenge Teacher; *b:* Stoneham, MA; *m:* Michael John; *c:* Tambrey Pomeroy; Tennyson Pomeroy; *ed:* (BS) Earth Sci, Univ of MA Amherst 1969; (MED) Counseling/Guidance, Salem St Coll 1990; Project Adventure Inc; Madeline Hunter Trng; *cr:* Sci Teacher North Reading HS 1969-78, Manchester HS 1983-; *ai:* Class Adv; Coaching Cross Country, Bsktbl, Tennis; Manchester Teachers Assn, MA Teachers Assn; GSA Troop Leader 1988-; 1st Parish Church Sunday Sch Supt 1987-; *office:* Manchester Jr Sr H S Lincoln St Manchester MA 01944

MEOLI, PATRICIA ANN, 10th & 11th English Teacher; *b:* Brooklyn, NY; *m:* Peter John; *c:* Anthony, Michael; *ed:* (AAS) Liberal Arts, Ulster Cty Comm Coll 1968; (BA) Eng, 1970, (MS) Admin, 1990 SUNY New Paltz; *cr:* 7th-12th Grade Eng Teacher Ellenville Cntrl Sch 1970-72; Rdng Teacher Migrant Prgm Rondout Valley Cntrl Sch 1972; 9th-12th Grade Eng Teacher Fallsburg Cntrl Sch 1983; 10th-11th Grade Eng Teacher Rondout Valley Cntrl Sch 1983-; *ai:* Yrbk Adv Literary; Rondout Valley Fed Teachers Schlsp Comm; Natl Honor Society Comm Mem 1985-87; Building Rep Rondout Valley Fed of Teachers & Sch Related Personnel; Ulster Cty Rdng Cncl Secy 1978-80; *office:* Rondout Valley Central Kyserike Rd Accord NY 12446

MERCADO, LUCY, Social Studies Chair/Teacher; *b:* New Orleans, LA; *ed:* (BA) Eng His, Loyola Univ of South 1967; Ed, Univ of Houston, TX A&M Univ; Curr, Instruction, TX A&I Univ; *cr:* 7th Grade Teacher St Louis King of France 1963-65; 4th Grade Teacher St Mary of the Angels 1965-67; 4th-8th Grade Soc Stud/Lang Art/Math/Span/Cmptr Teacher St Ambrose 1967-; *ai:* Stu Cncl, Chrldr, Yrbk Spon; Speech Meet, Prep Bowl, Soc Stud Contest, Academic Rally Coach & Spon; NCEA 1980-; TX Cmptr Ed Assn 1987-; *office:* St Ambrose Sch 4213 Mangum Rd Houston TX 77092

MERCER, CHERIE, English Teacher; *b:* Topeka, KS; *m:* Stephen A.; *c:* Scott E., Stephen M.; *ed:* (BA) His, Washburn Univ 1978; (MS) Ed, Emporia St Univ 1987; Phd 3rd Yr Stu; Educl Psych & Research KS Univ; *cr:* Eng Teacher Paxico Jr HS 1978-81; Harveyville Jr HS 1981-87; *ai:* Phd Stu; KNEA Local Secy 85-87; Phi Alpha Theta 84-; AERA 1990; *home:* Box 104 Harveyville KS 66431

MERCER, DONALD J., English Teacher; *b:* Alpena, MI; *m:* Rebecca Marie Stoller; *ed:* (BA) Eng, Spring Arbor Coll 1981; *cr:* Eng/Soc Stud Teacher Midland Chrstn Sch 1981-85; Eng Teacher Santiago Chrstn Sch 1985-; *ai:* Var Bsktbl Coach; Adv HS Quiz Team; Spring Arbor Coll Young Leader of Yr 1987; Teacher of Yr; *home:* Apartado 62 Santiago Dominican Republic

MERCER, JAMES LOUIS, Life Skills Coord; *b:* Lubbock, TX; *m:* Wanda Turvey; *c:* B. J., Adam, Jamie; *ed:* (BAT) Phy Ed, 1975; (MED) Phy Ed, 1977 Sam Houston St Univ; *cr:* Teacher/Coach Clear Creek ISD 1978-79; Employment Supv Monsanto Chemical 1979-80; Teacher Longfellow Elem/Manuel Jr HS/Alvin HS 1980-89; Life Skills Coord Alvin ISD 1989-; *ai:* Dist-Wide Prof Dev Comm; Sch Climate Comm; Curr Comm; High Expectations Comm; Search Comm Head Coach; TX St Teachers Assn 1980-; NEA 1980-; Assn of TX Prof Educators 1988-; Longfellow Elem Teacher of Yr 1987; TSTA St Human Rel Awd 1985; YMCA Awd Vol Svc 1980; *office:* Alvin ISD 903 House St Alvin TX 77511

MERCER, KAREN MOORE, Speech/Lang Pathologist/Coord; *b:* Wilson, NC; *m:* Millard Daniel; *c:* Caroline R.; *ed:* (BS) Speech/Lang/Auditory/Pathology, 1974, (MS) Audiology 1977 E Carolina Univ; Mentor Trng; Prgm Admin Spec Ed Prgms; *cr:* Coord Title VI-B Prgm Coord Sampson Cty Clinton Schls 1976-78; Speech/Lang/Pathologist/Coord E NC Sch for Deaffor Deaf 1978-; Adjunct Professor Hearing Impaired Ed Prgm Atlantic Chrstn Coll 1979-80; *ai:* Jr Class Spon; Governors Page, Creative Arts Festival Coord; Signing Choir Adv Supvr; Speech/Lang Audiology Comm Chm; Comprehensive Clinic Rep; Deaf Awareness Wk Co-Chairperson; ASCD; NC Assn of Educators; Speech/Hearing Area Resource Exchange Secy 1990-; St Employees Assn of NC; Wilson Cancer Society Bd Mem 1987-; Wilson Arts Cncl 1989-; Outstanding Young Educator Sampson Cty 1977 Clinton Jaycees; E NC Sch for Deaf Employee of Yr 1988; Governors Excl Awd 1987; Whos Who in Amer Ed; *office:* Eastern NC Sch for the Deaf Mc Adams Hall Hwy 301 N Wilson NC 27894

MERCER, MARYILYN SYLVESTER, Fifth Grade Teacher; *b:* Yuma, AZ; *c:* Matt; *ed:* (BA) Elem Ed, AZ St Univ 1956; Grad Stud Various Wkshps, Champs Trng Peer Leadership; *cr:* 5th Grade Teacher Andalucia 1956-58, Cordova Sch 1958-; *ai:* Sch Cmmty Cncl; Team Leader; Promotion-Retention Comm; Honor Court; Champs Scheduling & Benevolent Comm; Alpha Delta Kappa (Pres, Secy, Treas) 1970; Classroom Teachers Treas 1975-77; Valley Youth Soccer League Treas; AZ Youth Soccer Assn (Secy 1978-79, Vice Commissioner 1979-80); Dist Employee of Month 1987; *office:* Cordova Sch 3455 W Montebello Phoenix AZ 85017

MERCHANT, BEATRICE BYRD, English Teacher; *b:* Washington, DC; *c:* Marcia; *ed:* (BA) Eng, VA Union Univ 1970; Span & African Amer Course, VA Commonwealth Univ, George Washington Univ; Re-Cert Teaching Courses; *cr:* Teacher Martha Winston Jr HS 1978-79, Friendship Ed Center 1980-83, Coolidge Sr HS 1984-; *ai:* Drama Club Dir, Coach, Writer; Public Speaking Competition Coach; DC Commission for Hums & the Art Comm Mem 1984-85, Drama Awd 1984; African-Amer African Outreach Club Spon 1989-; Amer Bus Women Assoc Mem.

MERCHANT, DIANE BOWERS, 7th Grade Reading Teacher; *b:* West Grove, PA; *m:* Roy Douglas Sr.; *c:* Tamisha Armstrong; *ed:* (BS) Elem Ed, 1978, (MS) Ed, 1983 Univ of Houston; Various Wkshps & Seminars; *cr:* Rdng Teacher Scndry Guidance Center 1978-79, Weis Mid Sch 1979-87, Cntrl Mid Sch 1987-; *ai:* Dist Advisory Cncl Rep; Discipline Management & Strategic Planning Comm; Set-Net Team Mem; Leadership Dev Seminar; Galveston Ed Assn Secy 1982-84; Bay Area Rdng Cncl Secy 1987-88; TX Southern Rdng Cncl 1989; Krewe of Togetherness Outstanding Teacher Awd 1988-89; Holy Rosary Church Secy 1979-, Distinguished Service Awd 1988; NAACP; AKA Historian 1988-; Teacher of Yr 1988-89; Most Effective Teacher 1982-83; Teacher Acad I 1987-88, Acad II 1988-89; *office:* Cntrl Mid Sch 3014 Sealy Galveston TX 77550

MERCHANT, LESLIE CAROL, English Teacher; *b:* New York, NY; *ed:* (BA) Eng - Magna Cum Laude Univ of Rochester 1968; (MAT) Eng, Yale Univ 1969; Writers Inst Teachers Coll Columbia Univ 1988; *cr:* Eng Teacher Woodmere Jr HS North 1969-79, Woodmere Mid Sch 1979-; *ai:* Essay Published 1969; Editied Poems & Prose Booklet 1989; *office:* Woodmere Mid Sch 1170 Peninsula Blvd Hewlett NY 11557

MERCHANT, ROLAINE MANN, Sixth Grade Teacher; *b:* Birmingham, AL; *m:* John C.; *c:* Martha M. Griffin, Barbara Merchant Hendershott, Conley, Clay; *ed:* (AB) Music, Birmingham S 1953; (MA) Elem Ed, Univ of AL 1981; *cr:* 6th Grade Teacher Woodrow Wilson Sch 1954-55; Music/Art Teacher Oneonta Elem 1955-56; 5th Grade/Music Teacher Curry Elem 1956; Music Teacher Jones Valley 1957-59; 6th Grade/Art Teacher Jackson Elem 1962-63; 5th Grade Teacher Rockdale Cty 1964-65; 7th Grade/Music Teacher Dekalb Cty 1965-66; His/Choir Teacher 1972-77, 6th Grade Teacher 1977- Susan Moore; *ai:* 4-H Spon; NEA, AEA, AL Cncl for Soc Stud, NCSS; Phi Beta Kappa; Kappa Delta Epsilon; Mu Alpha; *office:* Susan Moore Sch Rt 3 Blountsville AL 35130

MERDIAN, PATRICIA V., Language Arts Department Chair; *b:* Mc Keesport, PA; *c:* Brian; *ed:* (BS) Ed/Eng, 1967, (MA) Eng, 1984 CA Univ of PA; Post Grad Courses Advanced Placement Eng, 1988-, Advanced Placement Trng, Carnegie Mellon Univ; *cr:* Eng Teacher 1967-83, Eng Teacher/Lang Arts Chairperson 1984-, Advanced Placement Instr 1987-, Adult Ed Prgm Teacher 1989- Yough Sr HS; *ai:* Stu Newspaper Spon; NCTE 1980-82; Yough Ed Assn (Secy 1985-, Exec Bd 1980-); PA St Ed Assn; NEA 1967-; St Edwards Church Commentator 1984-; Excl Eng Awd Seton Hill Coll; Excl Prgm for Effective Teaching Belle Vernon Area Sch Dist; Presenter In-Service Wkshp Writing Across the Curr; *office:* Yough Sr HS 99 Lowber Rd Herminie PA 15637

MEREDITH, DAVID EARL, Mathematics/Geometry Teacher; *b:* Tallulah, LA; *m:* Marjorie Dunlap; *c:* Ariel S.; *ed:* (BA) Math, Southern Univ 1969; (MS) Math, NW St Univ 1976; Supvr of Stu Teaching, Parish City Sch Supvr of Instruction; Admin, LSUS 19 8; *cr:* Teacher Walnut Hill Jr HS 1969-78; Math/Sci Coord Oak Terrace Mid Sch 1978-84; Math/Sci Dept Head Turner Mid Sch 1984-87; Math Teacher Huntington HS 1987-; *ai:* Soph & Oakterrace Jr HS Builders Club Spon; NEA, LEA, CEA 1969-; Twilight Meadows Civic Club Secy 1979-; Parent Teacher Stu Assn Faculty Adv; Huntington HS PTA Certificate of Appreciation; Turner Tigers Appreciation Awd; *office:* Huntington HS 6801 Rasberry Ln Shreveport LA 71129

MEREDITH, JOYCE ADAMS, Fourth Grade Teacher; *b:* Fullerton, NE; *m:* James E.; *c:* Todd, Joseph, Jerry, Jason; *ed:* (BA) Elem Ed, Midland Coll 1985; *cr:* 4th-6th Grade Teacher Holy Family Sch 1968-; *ai:* Stu Assistance Team for Spec Ed; NEA; Amer Legion Auxiliary 1985-; 4-H Vision Ed Comm 1985-86; Legion of Mary; *home:* 802 Beaver Saint Edward NE 68660

MEREDITH, KAY GILLUM, English Teacher; *b:* Buckhannon, WV; *m:* William Wingfield III; *c:* Laura A., William E.; *ed:* (BS) Eng Ed, Radford Univ 1965; Grad Work at VCU & Wake Forest Univ; *cr:* Eng/Soc Stud Teacher Fred Lynn Jr HS 1965-67; Eng Teacher Arbutus Jr HS 1967-68, Lindsay Jr HS 1968-69, ShugarT Jr HS 1971-72, Suitland HS 1975-76, Powhatan HS 1978-; *ai:* Jr Class Head Spon; VATE, NCTEA 1988-; *office:* Powhatan HS 4135 Old Buckingham Rd Powhatan VA 23139

MERENDA, ROBERT F., Principal; *b:* Wyoming, PA; *m:* Marie E.; *c:* Kimberly A., Scott R.; *ed:* (BA) Eng, Kings Coll 1963; (MA) Hum, 1971, (MA) Admin, 1973 Newark St Coll; *cr:* Eng Teacher Madison Cntrl HS 1963-86; Dir of Cmmty Schls/Federal Funds 1986-89, Adult HS Prin/Federal Funds 1989- Old Bridge Sch Dist; *ai:* Eng Curr Dev Chm 1965-71; Madison Cntrl HS Lib Evaluation Comm Chm 1973-74; Developed Rdng & Math Curr For Adult Basic Skills Prgm 1975-76; Developed 1st In-Sch Suspension Prgm Madison Cntrl HS 1974-75; Drug Free Sch Prgm Curr Approval 1986-87; Supervise Revision of Curr Packets for Adult HS 1986-; NEA, NJ Ed Assn 1963-; Old Bridge Admin Assn, Adult HS Network of NJ, NJ Assn of Lifelong Learning, Amer Assn for Adult & Continuing Ed 1986-89; Old Bridge Lib Literacy Volunteer, Theatre Guild, Advisory Bd to Cmmty Sch 1986-; 1st Aid & Rescue Squad; Letters of Accomodation Cty Supts Office; *office:* Old Bridge Adult HS Rt 516 Old Bridge NJ 08857

MERGEN, CHERYL KAY (AKER), Third Grade Teacher; *b:* Madison, SD; *m:* Mark; *c:* Mitchell, Jesse, Kyle; *ed:* (BA) Elem Ed, Dakota St Coll 1974; *cr:* Spec Ed Teacher, Third Grade Teacher Dell Rapids Public Sch; *office:* Dell Rapids Public Elem Sch 613 State Dell Rapids SD 57022

MERIDETH, DUANE ALLEN, Biology Teacher; *b:* Oklahoma City, OK; *m:* Melanie Hughes; *ed:* (BS) Phys Ed, 1984, (MS) Admin, 1986 S E OK St Univ; *cr:* Teacher/Coach 1984-87, Teacher 1988- Sherman HS; *ai:* TX St Teacher Assn 1984-; *office:* Sherman HS 2201 E Lamar Sherman TX 75090

MERKEL, DAVID PAUL, Business Education Teacher; *b:* Cincinnati, OH; *m:* Sylvia A. Dalton; *c:* Ashley L., Kaitlynn A.; *ed:* (BSED) Bus Ed, 1967, (MA) Bus Ed, Univ of Cincinnati; *cr:* Bus Teacher Mt Healthy HS 1967-; *ai:* Wrestling, Boys & Girls Tennis Coach; *office:* Mt Healthy HS 2046 Adams Rd Cincinnati OH 45231

MERKEL, ELIZABETH, First Grade Teacher; *b:* St Louis, MO; *ed:* (BA) Ed, Fontbonne Coll St Louis 1959; (MA) Ed, Loyola Univ New Orleans 1971; *cr:* 1st Grade Teacher St Thomas Long Beach 1949-54; 6th Grade Teacher St Josephs New Orleans 1954-55; 2nd Grade Teacher St Patricks San Francisco 1955-56; 1st Grade Teacher St Thomas Long Beach 1956-64, St Boniface Perryville 1964-66; Primary Departmental Rdng St Joseph New Orleans 1967-75; 1st Grade Teacher/Prin St Boniface Perryville 1975-83; Prin Our Lady of Victory Beeville 1983-89; 1st Grade Teacher St Marys Odessa 1989-; *ai:* Intnl Rdng Assn Pres 1973-75, Pres Plaque 1975; New Orleans Intnl Rdng Past Pres; NCEA 1949-; Teacher of Week Awd Odessa TX; *office:* St Marys Cntrl Cath Sch 1703 N Adams Odessa TX 79761

MERKEL, GRACEANN (CAESAR), Second Grade Teacher; *b:* Lafayette, IN; *m:* Willard Franklin; *c:* Lara Lee, Ryan Willard; *ed:* (BS) Elem Ed, Ball St Univ 1970; (MS) Elem Ed, Purdue Univ 1976 Advanced Work Toward Spec Ed Degree Purdue Univ; *cr:* 2nd Grade Teacher Klondike Elem 1970-; *ai:* Organizer of the Core Group for Purdue Problem-Centered Math Curr 1988-; Tippecanoe Ed Assn; NEA in St Teachers Assn Mem & Assn Rep; Alpha Delta Kappa-Chaplain 1980-82; Honor Society of Phi Kappa Phi; Mentor Prgm St of IN; IN Council of Teachers of Math Lions Club 1989; Youth MinistRy at Our Church Chairperson 1989-; Articles in Arithmetic Teacher 1988; NCTM Yrbk 1989-; Semi-Finalist in Teacher Yr 1990; Runner-Up in Tippecanoe Golden Apple Awd in CTM *office:* Klondike Elem Sch 3310 N Co Rd 300 W West Lafayette IN 47906

MERKEL, TERRY M., Sixth Grade Teacher; *b:* Birdseye, IN; *m:* Karen E. Roberts; *c:* Clint, Julie, Kara; *ed:* (BA) Elem Ed, 1972, (MS) Elem Ed, 1978 IN St Univ; *cr:* 6th Grade Teacher Benton Cmmty Sch 1972-75; Elem Phys Ed Teacher 1975-76, 5th Grade Teacher 1976-79 N Lawrence Sch Corporation; 5th Grade Teacher 1980-83; 6th Grade Teacher 1983- Brown Cty Sch Corporation; *ai:* Boys & Girls Elem Bsktbl Coach; Ed Assn 1972-; *home:* PO Box 731 Nashville IN 47448

MERKERSEN, CARLETHA LOPER, 3rd Grade Teacher; *b:* Live Oak, FL; *c:* Willie J. II, Craig L.; *ed:* (BS) Phys Ed/Health, Bethune Cookman Coll 1960; Cert Elem Ed/Eng/Soc Stud/Sci; *cr:* 2nd Grade Teacher Jre Lee 1962-65; 5th Grade Teacher Rosenwald Sch 1965-66; 6th Grade Teacher 1966-70; Health Teacher 1970-73; 5th Grade Teacher 1973-86; 3rd Grade Teacher 1986 English Estates; *ai:* Grade Rep Rdng & Soc Stud; Seminole Ed Assn 1966-; FL Teachers Prof 1966-; Alpha Kappa Alpha 1975; Evergreen Temple 321 Improved Benevolent Protective Order of Elks Daughter Ruler 1988-; Bethune Cookman Coll Medallion; *office:* English Estates Elem Sch Oxford Rd Fern Park FL 32730

MERKORD, LANNY DEAN, Science, Phys Ed, Math Teacher; *b:* Taylor, TX; *m:* Deborah Anne Kretzmann; *c:* Jordan L.; *ed:* (BS) Elem Ed, Concordia Coll 1977; Teaching Certicate Renewal Classes, St Cloud St, Univ of MN Morris; *cr:* 5th-8th Grade Math/Sci/Phys Ed Teacher Grace Luth Sch 1977-81; 5th-8th Grade Sci/Phys Ed/7th-8th Grade Math Teacher Zion Luth Sch 1981-89; *ai:* Athletic Dir; Soccer, Bsktbl, Track, Sftbl Coach; *home:* 1022 Bridgeport Ln Alexandria MN 56308

MERKX, KATHRYN C, 11th Grade English Teacher; *b:* Chickasha, OK; *ed:* (BA) Eng, Univ of OK 1975; OK Writing Project, Univ of OK 1989; *cr:* 7th/8th Grade Eng Teacher Monroney Jr HS 1975-76; 11th Grade Eng Teacher Midwest City HS 1976-77; 9th Grade Eng/Art Teacher Carl Albert Jr HS 1977-78; 11th Grade Eng Teacher Midwest City HS 1978-; *ai:* Pom Pon Squad Head, Chrldr & Spirit Cncl Asst, Soph Class Spon; Dist Eng Curr, Dist Criterion Referenced Test, Dist Textbook, Midwest City HS Improvement Comms; Act Midwest City HS Rep 1988-; OEA, NEA 1988-; *office:* Midwest City HS 213 Elm Dr Midwest City OK 73110

MERONEY, RICHARD FRANCIS, History Teacher; *b:* Philadelphia, PA; *m:* Mary O'Hagan; *c:* Michael, Sandra; *ed:* (BA) Soc Stud, La Salle Coll 1964; Working Towards Masters Equivalency His, Temple Univ, Villanova Univ; *cr:* His Teacher Father Judge HS 1964-65, Furness Jr HS 1965-76, Girls HS 1976-; *ai:* Var & Jr Var Bowling Coach; Girls Lacrosse Coach;PIAA & IAABO Bsktbl Ofcl; *office:* Philadelphia HS for Girls Broad St at Olney Ave Philadelphia PA 19141

MEROW, CRAIG BANKS, District Mathematics Coord; *b:* Philadelphia, PA; *m:* Donna June Snider; *c:* Rebecca, Katharine; *ed:* (BA) Geology, 1973; (MED) Ed, 1975 Temple Univ; PhD Candidate, Universidad Nacional Federico Villarreal, Lima, Peru, Univ of PA; Villanova; *cr:* Sci Teacher Sun Valley HS 1973-77; Math Dept Chm Germantown Acad 1978-86; Dist Math Coord Delaware Valley Sch Dist 1986-; *ai:* Mu Alpha Theta Adv; NCTM Referee/Reviewer for Math Teacher 1983-; MAA/COMAP 1983-; Cornell Univ Fellow 1977-78; Germantown Acad Bd Trustees Outstanding Teacher Awd 1979-80/1983-84; Search for Excl Fellowship 1988-89; Semifinalist PA Teacher of Yr 1990; Published Articles in Sci & Math Ed; *office:* Delaware Valley Sch Dist Rt 6 Box 209 Milford PA 18337

MERRIFIELD, ROBERT PAUL, Biology Teacher; *b:* Springfield, MA; *m:* Sharon Maguire; *ed:* (BS) Bio, St Lawrence Univ 1977; Grad Work Ecology, Univ of NC Chapel Hill; *cr:* Naturalist Wilderness SE Inc 1979-81; Bio Teacher Blair Acad 1981-; *ai:* Outdoor Skills Prgm Dir; Alpine Skiing Coach; Geraldine R Dodge Fellow for Tropical Forest Stud; *office:* Blair Acad Blairstown NJ 07825

MERRIL, G. DENISE, Kindergarten Teacher; *b:* Commerce, GA; *m:* Jeff; *c:* Jonathan, Ashley; *ed:* (AA) Bellevue Comm Coll 1972; (BA) Sociology/Elem Ed, Univ of WA 1974; Early Chldhd, W WA Univ 1979; Early Prevention of Sch Failure, Math Their Way, Whole Lang, Gesell Dev Testing; *cr:* Kndgtn Teacher Lockwood Elem 1974-82, Shelton View Elem 1982-83, Hollywood Hill Elem 1983-; *ai:* Discipline Comm; WA Organization of Rdng Dev 1985-; Northshore Ed Assn 1974-; Alan Buchanan Kiwanis Prof Schlsp 1988; Florence Sperling Rdng Schlsp 1989; *office:* Hollywood Hill Elem Sch 17110 148th Ave Ne Woodinville WA 98072

MERRILL, JUDY KEVER, Chapter I Supervisor; *b:* Ft Polk, LA; *m:* Joseph A.; *ed:* (BSE) Soc Stud/Bus Ed, Univ of Cntrl AR 1979; (MSE) Rdng Specialist, AR St Univ 1987; Elem Cert AR St Univ 1986; *cr:* Bus Ed Teacher Tyronza Public Sch 1984-86; Soc Stud Teacher Weiner Public Sch 1986-88; Rdng Teacher/Lecturer Univ of AR 1988-89; Chapter I Supvr West Fork Public Sch 1989-; *ai:* NW AR Rdng Cncl (Treas, Membership Chm, Officer 1990, Mem) 1989-; Weiner HS Teacher of Yr 1987-88; *home:* 1206 N Oakland Fayetteville AR 72703

MERRILL, SUZANNE E., Spanish & English Teacher; *b:* Mc Alester, OK; *m:* Michael Alan; *c:* Lauren, James; *ed:* (BS) Span, Univ of OK 1970; (MA) Guidance/Counseling, NE OK St Univ 1980; Inst of Span Stud Valancia Spain; *cr:* Span/Eng Teacher

Cleveland Jr HS 1971-83, Mc Lain HS 1983-84, Edison HS 1984-; *ai:* Impact Comm; Span Club Spon; La Mesa Redonda Schlsp; *home:* 4803 E 46th St Tulsa OK 74135

MERRYMAN, JANE MERIGIAN, Kindergarten Teacher; *b:* Sanger, CA; *m:* Roger L.; *c:* Elizabeth, Rachel; *ed:* (BA) Eng, Univ of CA Santa Barbara 1972; Project AIMS; Music Ed; *cr:* Kndgtn Teacher Vandalia Elem Sch 1973-; *ai:* Vandalia Sch Key Planner; Porterville Schls Early Chldhd Comm Mem; Porterville Educators Assn, CTA, NEA 1976-; Amer Assn of Univ Women Newsletter Ed 1989-; *office:* Vandalia Elem Sch 271 E College Ave Porterville CA 93257

MERTA, DAVID JOSEPH, Social Studies Teacher; *b:* Palo Alto, CA; *ed:* (BA) Poly Sci, Univ of San Francisco 1966; *cr:* Soc Stud Teacher Carlmont HS 1967-89; *ai:* Soph Class Adv; Advanced Placement European Independent Study Prgm; NEA, Carlmont Teachers Assn; Mentor Teacher 1987-88; *office:* Carlmont HS 1400 Alameda Belmont CA 94062

MERTENS, IRENE MEDVECZ, Seventh Grade Teacher; *b:* Wausau, WI; *m:* James P.; *c:* Mary Marren, Darlene Balgord, Joseph, Steven, Anthony; *ed:* (BS) Ed, Silver Lake Coll 1970; (Ms) Curr/Instruction Univ of WI Milwaukee 1977; Teachers License Stevens Point Teachers Coll; *cr:* 1st-8th Grade Teacher Fond du Lac Cty Rural Sch 1947-51; 4th Grade Teacher S S Peter & Paul Cath 1957-59; 4th/5th/7th Grade Teacher Kiel Public Schls 1964-; *ai:* Work With Children of Alcoholic Families; Phi Delta Kappa 1979-; ASOC 1977-; Rdng Cncl Pres; WI Ed Assn Cncl (Comm Mem, Comm Chairperson, Uniserve Bd); Chrstn Mothers Secy 1957; Cty Extension 1951-; Toast Masters 1980-; *home:* W 687 Hwy 149 Kiel WI 53042

MERTZ, INEZ M., Retired; *b:* Sleepy Eye, MN; *ed:* (BS) Elem Ed, Mankato Univ 196 Grad Stud; *cr:* Teacher Rural Sch Dist 44 1934-36, Rural Sch Dist 29 1936-39, Rural Sch Dist 44 1939-40, Rural Sch Dist 36 1940-53; 1st Grade Teacher St Marys Cath Sch 1953-83; *ai:* MN Ed Assn Mem; SW Rdng Cncl; Brown Cty Retired Teachers Pres 1985-86; AARP & MN Retired Assn Mem; Delta Kappa Gamma Pres 1984-86; Qui Vive Womans Club Pres; Dist Federated Clubs Treas; Taught Summer Sch Sleepy Eye Public Sch; *home:* 635 Prairie Center Dr Eden Prairie MN 55344

MERZ, FRANK J., Middle School Reading Teacher; *b:* Williams, IA; *m:* Joan M. Wheeler; *c:* Holly, Hope, Heather, Heath; *ed:* (BA) Elem Ed/Phys Ed, William Penn Coll 1970; Real Estate License; *cr:* 8th Grade Teacher Ellsworth Comm Schls 1955-56; Acting Elem Prin Owasa Comm Schls 1960-64; 6th Grade Teacher 1965-67, Mid Sch Rdng Teacher 1969- Iowa Falls Comm Schls; *ai:* Boys & Girls Bsktbl Coach; Little League Bsbl, Jr HS Track Coach; IFTA Pres 1971-72, CTF 25 Yrs Plus Active Teaching; NEA 1990; Hardin Cty Sch-Masters 1961-67; IA St Ed Assn 1990; Kiwanis 1972-73; Elks 1972-78; Athletic Club 1960-61; City Clerk Owasa IA 1961-64; *office:* Iowa Falls Comm Schls 1124 Union St Iowa Falls IA 50126

MESCHKE, DOROTHY DOMAGALA, 5th/6th Grade Lang Art Teacher; *b:* Bowman, ND; *m:* Carl; *c:* Sara, Cal, Faye; *ed:* (BA) Elem Ed, Dickinson St Univ 1973; 5th Grade Teacher Brockton MT 1973-74; 5th/6th Grade Lang Art Teacher Bowman Mid Sch 1980-; *ai:* NEA, ND Ed Assn 1980-; 4-H Leader 1984-; Bowman Cty 4-H Cncl (Secy, Treas) 1988-; *home:* RR 1 Box 86 Bowman ND 58623

MESEKE, F. GALE, Principal; *b:* Vandalia, IL; *m:* Helen Boyd Stephens; *c:* Sarah D., Rachel L.; *ed:* (Bs) Poly Sci, IL St Univ 1969; (MS) Educl Admin, E IL Univ 1988; Coursework at S IL Univ Edwardsville, Univ of IL, E IL Univ, Natl Coll of Ed; *cr:* Teacher Vandalia Cmmty HS 1969-89; His Teacher Kaskaskia Coll 1988-; Prin Shobonier Elem 1989-; *ai:* IL Prins Assn 1989-; IL Educl Assn Regional Cncl 1986-89; Vandalia Unit Teachers Assn (Pres 1972-74) 1986-88; IL Extension Exec Comm Pres 1981-85; Fayette Cty Youth Extension VP 1981-85; Immanuel of Augsburg Church Cncl Secy 1977-; Fellowship-Inst in Cmptrs for Elem Sch Teachers Univ of IL 1990; *office:* Shobonier Elem Sch Box 10 Shobonier IL 62885

MESEKE, HELEN STEPHENS, Mathematics Teacher; *b:* Centralia, IL; *m:* F. Gale; *c:* Sarah, Rachel; *ed:* (BA) Math, Lawrence Univ 1968; Data Processing, Kaskaskia Coll 1983-85; *cr:* Math Teacher Forsythe Jr HS 1968-69, Vandalia HS 1969-70, Vandalia Jr HS 1970-74; Adjunct Data Proc Instr Kaskaskia Coll 1984-85; Math Teacher Vandalia HS 1985-; Adjunct Data Proc Instr Kaskaskia Coll 1990; *ai:* Class Spon; Faculty Cncl Advisory Comm 1989-; Stu Cncl Adv 1987-89; Vandalia Unit Teachers Assn 1970-74, 1985-; Delta Kappa Gamma 1987-; IL Cncl Teachers of Math 1970-74, 1987-; Participant Integrating Problem Solving into Math Teaching S IL Univ Carbondale Published Teaching Module 1987; Participant Natl Sci Fnd Advance Placement Prgm Carleton Coll 1989; Monetary Awd S IL Univ Edwardsville for Excl in Teaching Math 1989; Vandalia Cmmty Schls Awd for Excl in Teaching Math 1989; *office:* Vandalia Cmmty HS 1109 N 8th St Vandalia IL 62471

MESEROL, HANNAH KATHLEEN, Science/Health Teacher; *b:* Medina, OH; *ed:* (BSED) Health Ed, OH St Univ 1974; Working Towards Masters OH St Univ; *cr:* Sci Teacher Columbus Public Schls 1974-; *ai:* Dominion Mid Sch Game Mgr, Sci Fair Coord, Sch Energy Facilitator, Scientific Leader; Columbus Ed Assn, Cntrl OH Teachers Assn 1974-; Cntrl OH Sci Cncl HS Registration Chm 1987-; PTA Linmoor Mid Sch Educator of Yr 1984-85; PTA Dominion Mid Sch Educator of Yr 1990; Young Scholars Prgm OH St Univ 1988; *office:* Dominion Mid Sch 330 E Dominion Blvd Columbus OH 43214

MESHEY, EDWARD FRANKLIN, Bible Teacher; *b:* Philadelphia, PA; *m:* Judith Ann Johnson; *c:* Christian, Karis, Kyle, Colin; *ed:* (AA) Bible, 1971, (BRE) Bible Ed, 1973 Baptist Bible Coll of PA; *cr:* Elem Teacher 1973-87, Jr HS Teacher 1987-89, HS Teacher 1989- West Chester Chrstn Sch; *ai:* Stu Cncl Adv; Fall Fundraising Chm; Bible Quiz Team Coach; Keystone Chrstn Ed Assn Teacher Recognition Certificate; *office:* West Chester Chrstn Sch 1237 Paoli Pike West Chester PA 19380

MESKER, GLEN E., Biology Teacher; *b:* Henderson, MN; *c:* Greg, Jay, Scott; *ed:* (BS) Bio, Mankato St Univ 1961; Grad Stud; *cr:* Sci Teacher Chandler Public Sch 1961-64, Fergus Falls Jr HS 1964-80, Fergus Fall Sr HS 1984-; *ai:* Local Assn Pres; MEA, NEA 1964-; United Fund Bd 1980-83.

MESLER, JUDITH COUGHLIN, Teacher; *b:* Pittsfield, MA; *m:* James; *c:* Katherine; *ed:* (BS) Spec Ed/Elem Ed, Westfield St Coll 1978; (MS) Specific Learning Disabilities, Nova Univ 1988; *cr:* Resource Room Teacher of Learning Disabilities Pittsfield Public Schls 1978-82; 6th Grade Teacher 1982-83, 3rd Grade Teacher 1983-84 Blessed Trinity Sch; Kndgtn Teacher St Gregory Sch 1984-85; *ai:* Cheerleading Advisory St Gregory Sch 1984-85; Spina Bifida Assn (VP 1989-, Newsletter Ed 1986-, Parent Advocate 1986-); *home:* 2816 SW 81st Terr Davie FL 33328

MESSERLY, LARRY L., Business & Computer Ed Teacher; *b:* Ft Dodge, IA; *m:* Susan E.; *c:* Ben, Mandy, Marcy; *ed:* (BA) Bus Ed/Phys Ed, 1968; Grad Stud; *cr:* Teacher Reinbeck HS 1968-88, Gladbrook/Reinbeck HS 1988-; *ai:* ISEA; *office:* Gladbrook Reinbeck HS Blackhawk St Reinbeck IA 50669

MESSIAH, HENRY ROBERT, Graphic Arts Teacher; *b:* New Orleans, LA; *m:* Elouise Jones; *c:* Kenneth, Brian; *ed:* (BFA) Art, Art Inst Chicago 1953; Photography, Graphic Arts, Total Drafting, Lettering; *cr:* Graphic Arts Teacher Doot-Russell 1953-67; Graphic Layout Artist Chicago Defender 1968-69; Art/Graphic Arts Teacher Chicago Voc Sch 1969-87; *ai:* Lensmen Spon & Photography Class; Yrbk Adv; Cavaliers for Christ Advertising Club; Stu Cncl; Human Relations; *home:* 8215 S La Salle St Chicago IL 60620

MESSICK, TIMOTHY B., English Department Chair; *b:* Long Island, NY; *m:* Susan Cleary; *c:* Elizabeth, Rebekah, Sarah, Anne, Joan; *ed:* (BA) Span, St John Fisher Coll 1971; (MA) Eng, St Univ of NY Cortland 1980; *cr:* Eng Teacher Rome Cath HS 1971-; Adjunct Professor Mohawk Valley Comm Coll 1987-; *ai:* NY St Fed of Cath Sch Teacher of Yr John the Baptist de La Salle Awd; Poetry Published; *office:* Rome Cath HS 800 Cypress St Rome NY 13440

MESSIER, DAVID CHARLES, Principal; *b:* Manchester, NH; *m:* Ruthanne Linehan; *ed:* (BA) Eng, St Anselm Coll 1969; (MED) Admin, 1980; (CAGS) Ed Admin/Career Ed, 1982; *cr:* Teacher Manchester HS West 1969-82; Acting Dir Greater Manchester Chamber of Commerce 1982-83; VP Operations J J Moreau & Son True Value Hardware 1983-84; Teacher/Prin Southside Jr HS 1984-; *ai:* MEA Treas 1972-75; Teamsters 1988-; Riverfest General Chm 1982-87, City Key 1983; Lions Club 1st VP 1984-; SVDP Pres 1984-; City of Manchester Educl Rep to Taichung Taiwan ROC 1989; *office:* Southside Jr HS 140 S Jewett St Manchester NH 03103

MESSINA, PATRICIA HART, First Grade Teacher; *b:* Rochester, NY; *c:* Alyce, Emily; *ed:* (BA) Elem Ed/His/Soc Stud, NY St Univ Coll Potsdam 1967; (MS) Elem Ed, NY St Univ Coll Brockport 1971; *cr:* Kndgtn Teacher 1967-69, 1st Grade Teacher 1969- Herman Avenue Elem; *ai:* Herman Avenue Parents Rdng Mem; Partners Comm; Auburn Teachers Assn, NY St United Teachers; Sacred Heart Rosary Society; Outstanding Elem Teachers of Amer Awd 1973; *office:* Herman Avenue Elem Sch Herman Ave Auburn NY 13021

MESSINGER, KATHLEEN FUGATE, Fifth Grade Teacher; *b:* Du Bois, PA; *m:* Gary Richard; *c:* Gary R. Jr., Brandyn L., Amy K., Todd A.; *ed:* (BS) Ed, Elizbethtown Coll 1968; Working Towards Masters in Ed, Penn St Univ; *cr:* 1st Grade Teacher 1968-69, 5th Grade Teacher 1970-71 N Lebanon; Pre-Sch Teacher Ono United Meth Church 1981-82; 5th Grade Teacher N Lebanon 1982-; *ai:* Cooperating Teacher; Amer Ed Comm Chm; N Lebanon Ed Assn 1988-; Lebanon Cty Educl Honor Society 1990; N Lebanon Booster Club (Secy 1987-, Pres 1990); Ono United Meth Church (Secy Pastor Parish Relations Comm, Sunday Sch Teacher); *office:* Fredericksburg Elem Sch N Pine Grove St Fredericksburg PA 17026

MESSNER, LARRY KENT, Principal; *b:* Berkeley Springs, WV; *m:* Katherine Lou Potter; *c:* Kent, Kristopher, Katie; *ed:* (BA) Elem Ed, Shepherd Coll 1975; (MA) Ed Admin, WV Univ 1983; *cr:* Teacher N Jefferson Elem 1975-81, Hedgesville Mid Sch 1981-85; Dropout Prevention Coord RESA VIII 1985-89; Prin N Berkeley Elem 1989-; *ai:* TESA Coord & Trainer Morgan Cty Schls; Phi Delta Kappa VP 1986-; *office:* N Berkely Elem Sch 213 Harrison Ave Berkeley Springs WV 25411

MESTEMAKER, KAREN WISNIESKI, Lang Arts Chairperson/Teacher; *b:* Flint, MI; *m:* Duane; *c:* Kay, Sara; *ed:* (BA) Soc Sci, Olivet Coll 1976; (MA) Teaching in Elem, Western MI Univ 1983; Instructional Supervision ITIP I/II/III 3 Yrs 1985-87; Cognative Coaching 1988; Quest Skills for Adolescnece 1986; Elks Drug/Alcohol Prevention 1987; Cooperative Learning; *cr:* 4th-8th Grade Teacher Olivet Mid Sch 1977-; *ai:* Young Authors Magazine Adv; Future Problem Solving Adv/Coach; NEA 1977-; MI Ed Assn 1977-; Calhous Cty Rdng Cncl 1988-; *office:* Olivet Mid Sch 255 1st St Olivet MI 49076

MESYK, JOHN, Mathematics Teacher/Dept Head; *b:* Chicago, IL; *m:* Roxanne Ruth Iwaskiw; *ed:* (BA) Math/Ed, Trinity Coll 1976; Working Towards Masters Cmptrs & Psych; *cr:* Math Teacher Twin Groves Jr HS 1976-83, Tri-County HS 1983-; *ai:* Quiz Bowl Coach; Cntrl WI Math League Spon; HS Math Curr Comm Chm; *office:* Tri-County Area Schls P O Box 67 Plainfield WI 54966

METALLO, JOAN ANN P. LARATTA, 8th Grade Math/Eng Teacher; *b:* Newark, NJ; *m:* Nicholas Carmen; *c:* Victor, Claudine; *ed:* (MA) Ed, 1981, (BS) Elem Ed, 1968 Seton Hall Univ; Music, Art, Religious Teachers Filippini; *cr:* 2nd Grade Self-Contained Teacher St Joachims 1955-56; 4th Grade Self-Contained Teacher St James 1956-57, St Peters 1957-64; 6th Grade Self-Contained Teacher Sacred Heart 1964-65, 7th-8th Grade Eng Dept/3rd Grade Self-Contained Teacher Alexander Street Public Sch 1966-69; K-8th Grade Teacher Bloomfield Nutley & Elmwood Park Sch Systems 1969-77; 7th-8th Grade Eng Dept Chairperson/7th Grade Religion Teacher Holy Family 1977-81; Adjunct Professor Math Dept Seton Hall Univ 1987-; *ai:* Reorganized Math Dept; Designed & Implemented Accelerated Prgm for Advanced Stus; Math & Religion Text Selection; *home:* 79 Claremont Ave Montclair NJ 07042

METCALF, JOHN, Volunteer History Teacher; *b:* Sureka, MT; *ed:* (BA) His, Univ of MT 1947; (MA) Poly Sci, Mc Gill Univ 1949; *cr:* Teacher Federal Way HS 1962-88.

METCALF, PHILIP LESLIE, HS Mathematics Teacher; *b:* North Webster, IN; *m:* Karilyn Sue Fetterhoff; *ed:* (BS) Math, Ball St Univ 1970; (MS) Math, St Francis Coll 1975; *cr:* Math Teacher Milford Jr HS 1971-84, Wawasee HS 1984-; *ai:* Prom Chairperson; Concessions Mgr; Sr Class Spon; Wawasee Cmmty Educators Pres 1981; Natl Ed/IN St Teachers Dist Cncl Chm 1984/1986 & 1988-89; IN Natl Cncl Teacher of Math; Lions Bd of Dir 1985-; Sigma Alpha Epsilon; Governor to St Study Comm on STandards Bd; Elected in St Delegate to NEA Prof; Rep Assembly; *office:* Wawasee H S 1 Warrior Path Syracuse IN 46567

METELITS, MELVIN, 6th Grade Retired Teacher; *b:* Philadelphia, PA; *m:* Roberta Coleman; *c:* Letetia Coleman, Sabre Coleman, Michael, Wendy Coleman, Chandler Coleman, Cassandra Coleman Thomas; *ed:* (BS) Elem Ed, Temple Univ 1954; *cr:* Teacher Philadelphia Sch Dist 1954-68, St Thomas-St John Sch Dist 1968-70, Philadelphia Sch Dist 1970-89; *ai:* Eng as 2nd Lang Teacher to Immigrants; Ed Columnist; Current Events Lecturer; Philadelphia Fed of Teachers (Exec Bd, Chm Cmmty Relations Comm 1980-84) 1954-89, Excl Drive for Collective Bargaining 1964; Teachers for Peace Co-Chm 1966-68; Frederick Douglass Home & Sch Assn 1970-89, Cmmty Service 1984; Sch Employees Action Caucus (Mem, Co-Chm 1970-78), Service Awd 1984; Emma Johnson Schlsp Temple Univ 1953; Volunteer Integration Transferee 1965; Certify Long Term Substitutes Comm 1966-68; Basic Ed Summer Study Fellowship Cncl 1987; Dr Ruth Hayre Schlsp Fund Cmmty Service Awd 1989; *home:* 7101 Boyer St Philadelphia PA 19119

METHVIN, KOLETA GILES, 2nd Grade Teacher; *b:* Winters, TX; *c:* Melissa, Lindsey, Kelly; *ed:* (BS) Elem Ed, TX Tech Univ 1974; *cr:* 1st/2nd/3rd Grade Team Teaching Erasmo Seguin 1975-78; 2nd Grade Teacher St Marys Sch 1978-; *ai:* Chm Stu Assistance Team; *office:* St Marys Sch 1101 E 5th St Natchitoches LA 71457

METKE, DONNA RAWLINGS, English Teacher; *b:* Chicago, IL; *m:* L. Michael; *c:* Jennifer, John; *ed:* (BS) Eng/Scndry Ed, 1970, (MSE) Rdng, 1979 Univ of WI; *cr:* Lang Art Teacher St Marys Elem 1971-75, Maplewood Jr HS 1975-79; Eng/Honors Eng/Advanced Rdng Teacher Harlingen HS 1980-; *ai:* Honors Chairperson; Intnl Baccalaureate Coord; Quill & Scroll, NHS Spon; Stu Literary Publication Adv; Parent Teacher Stu Assn Faculty Liaison; Schlsp Comm Mem 1988-89; Steering Comm & SACS Mem 1988; Supts Faculty Advisory Comm Pres 1980-81; 7th-12th Grade Lang Art Moderator; NCTE, TX Joint Cncl Teachers of Eng 1982-; TX Assn of Gifted & Talented 1988-; Kappa Delta Pi, Delta Kappa Gamma; Cub Scout Den Leader 1989-; Friends of Lib Bd of Dirs; TX League of Intnl Baccalaureate Schls Presenter 1989; TECAT Presenter & Trainer; Region I Conference Presenter 1989; St Gifted & Talented Conference Presenter 1989; Coll Resource Room Volunteer; Academic Decathlon Guest Lecturer, Riofest Cmmty Volunteer & Exhibit Tent Chm 1988; *office:* Harlinge HS 1201 E Marshall Harlingen TX 78550

METOYER, KATHY BRADLEY, Special Education Teacher; *b:* New Orleans, LA; *m:* Nicholas Anthony; *c:* Neil A., Melissa F.; *ed:* (BA) Elem Ed, Univ of New Orleans 1974; *cr:* Spec Ed Teacher New Orleans Public Sch System 1974-; *ai:* Stu Building Level Comm 1987-; Spec Ed Chairperson 1983, 1985; UTNO Rep 1979-81, 1984-87; AFT 1980-; BSA Den Leader 1984-86; GSA 1989-; Soc Services Food Baskets 1984-; Garden Club 1989-; *office:* Mc Donogh No 24 Sch 421 Burdette St New Orleans LA 70118

METROKA, ELIZABETH R., Mathematics Dept Chair; *b:* Honolulu, HI; *m:* Gary M.; *c:* Jaclyn, Laura, Michael, Katherine; *ed:* (BA) Math, Rosemont Coll 1977; (MA) Math, Ball St Univ 1987; *cr:* Math Teacher Archbishop Carroll HS 1977-78, Charles Boehm 1978-79, Tri Jr/Sr HS 1981-; *ai:* NHS Spon; Math Academic Competion Team, Coach; Faculty Cncl; Math Dept Chairperson; NCTM, ICTM; E Cntrl IN Sch Dist, Individual Stu/Teacher Awd Recognition 1986; *office:* Tri Jr/Sr HS Rt 1 Box 98 Straughn IN 47387

METTE, PATSY ANN, Mathematics Teacher; *b:* Macon, MO; *m:* Keith A.; *c:* Serena A.; *ed:* (BSED) Math, NE MO St Univ 1970; *cr:* Math Teacher Hoech Jr HS 1970-72, Palmyra HS 1972-; *ai:* Soph Class Spon; NCTM, MO St Teachers Assn, Palmyra Cmmty Teachers Assn; *office:* Palmyra HS S Main St Palmyra MO 63461

METTLER, JOHN H., Fifth Grade Teacher; *b:* Bethlehem, PA; *m:* Janet E. Scapura; *c:* John J.; *ed:* (BS) Elem Ed, 1971, (MED) Elem Ed, 1975 The PA St Univ; *cr:* 5th Grade Teacher Tamaqua Area Schls 1971-; *ai:* Tamaqua Ed Assn Pres 1987-88; PSEA, NEA; *office:* Tamaqua Area Sch Dist Box 112 Tamaqua PA 18252

METZ, BARBARA DOTSON, 4th Grade Teacher; *b:* Charleston, WV; *c:* James, Vicki, Nora, John; *ed:* (BA) Elem Ed, Univ of FL 1970; (MS) Elem Ed, Univ of Cntrl FL 1984; *cr:* 2nd/3rd Grade Classroom Teacher Bronson HS 1970-71; 3rd/4th Grade Teacher Eustis Heights 1971-; *ai:* Discipline Comm Chm; Quality Circle Instr Teacher Ed Center; Chairperson Teaching Team Mini Sch; Lake Cty Rdng Cncl Pres; Lake Cty Ed Assn Bd of Dir; Natl Organization for Women, Democratic Party, Cancer Society; Eustis Heights Teacher of Yr 1989-; Assoc Master Teacher Awd 1986; *office:* Eustis Heights Elem Sch 310 W Quayle Ave Eustis FL 32726

METZ, CAROLYNN E. (WOJCIK), First Grade Teacher; *b:* Detroit, MI; *c:* Frederick G., Carolynn M.; *ed:* (BA) Soc Sci, MI St Univ 1964; Perceptual Trng & Thematic Integrated Instruction; *cr:* Kndgtn Teacher 1963-69, 4th Grade Teacher 1970-71, 1st Grade Teacher 1972-85, 1st-2nd Grade Teacher 1987- Greenwood Elem; *ai:* Cmptr Technology & Sch Improvement Comm; PTO Rep; Teacher of Yr Awd 1980; *office:* Greenwood Elem Sch 27900 Joan Saint Clair Shores MI 48081

METZ, GLORIA L. BELTZNER, Social Studies Teacher; *b:* Newton, NJ; *m:* Richard D.; *ed:* (BA) Soc Stud, 1974, (MA) Stu Personnel Services, 1976 Montclair St Coll; Univ of Cntrl FL, Jersey City St Coll; *cr:* Teacher Hackettstown Mid Sch 1974-85, Titusville HS 1985-; Adjunct Faculty Brevard Comm Coll 1990; *ai:* Frosh Class Spon; *office:* Titusville HS 150 Terrier Trail Titusville FL 32780

METZ, INGRID C., Latin Teacher; *b:* Washington, DC; *c:* Danielle, Brian; *ed:* (BA) Latin, Mary Washington Coll 1969; (MAT) Latin, Vanderbilt Univ; *cr:* Eng/Latin Teacher Ritenour Sr HS 1970-71, Falls Church HS 1972-76; Eng Teacher 1977-78, Latin Teacher 1981- Brunswick HS; *ai:* Latin Club; Latin NHS; Elem & Mid Sch Foreign Lang Comm; Foreign Lang Assn of GA 1986-; Amer Classical League 1982-; GA Classical League Teacher of Yr 1982-; Amer Cncl Teaching of Foreign Lang 1985-; Elem Teachers of Classics 1988-89; STAR Teacher 1988-89; Teacher of Yr Brunswick HS & Glynn Cty 1989-; GA Teacher of Yr Finalist 1990; *office:* Brunswick HS 3920 Habersham St Brunswick GA 31523

METZ, SUSAN LYNN, Second Grade Teacher; *b:* Kansas City, KS; *ed:* (BS) Elem Ed 1967; (MS) Elem Ed Curr Instr, Univ KS 1979; *cr:* 2nd/3rd Grade Teacher Wm Allen White Sch 1968-69; 2nd Grade Teacher Abbott Sch 1969-71; 2nd Grade Teacher Douglass Sch 1972-; *ai:* Core Curr Comm Drug/Alcohol Abuse Trng; Critical Thinking Comm; NEA 1968-; Intnl Rdng Assn Recording Secy 1980; Ira VP 1981-82; *office:* Douglass Sch 9th Washington Blvd Kansas City KS 66101

METZELFELD, KATHLEEN MCCARTAN, 5th Grade Teacher; *b:* Milwaukee, WI; *m:* Alan W.; *c:* Pam Mifflin, Polly, Paul, Paula, Peter; *ed:* Elem Ed, Racine Kenosha Normal 1950; (BA) Elem Ed, Univ of WI Whitewater 1969; Rdng/Writing Connection; Spec Ed; Teaching Literature Rdng; *cr:* 1/2/5/8 Grade Teacher Marcy Elem 1950-60; 3rd/4th Grade Teacher St John Vianney 1960-61; 4th & 5th Grade Teacher 1962-69, 3/4/5th Grade Teacher 1971-87 Marcy Elem; 5th Grade Teacher Templeton Mid Sch 1987-; *ai:* Soc Stud Comm; Drug/Alcohol Comm Curr; Writing Curr Comm; Lang Arts Curr Comm; Waukesha Cty Rdng Assn; WI Rdng Assn; NEA; WEA; Brookfield Lioness Club (Pres Secy 1970-75/1980 & 1982); Lioness Dist 27A2 Cabinet Secy Area Chr 1983-88; Teacher of Yr 1982; Nom Hamilton Sussex Sch Dist Teacher World 1989; *office:* Templeton Mid Sch 759 W 22490 Silver Spring Sussex WI 53089

METZGAR, VICKI HOPKINS, Biology Teacher; *b:* Madison, TN; *c:* Kelly A., Amanda K.; *ed:* (BA) Scndry Sci Ed, Univ of TN 1974; (MST) Bio, Mid TN St Univ 1980; Advanced Placement Bio Trng Wkshp; *cr:* Classroom Sci Teacher Isaac Litton Jr HS 1975-79; Bio Teacher Whites Creek HS 1979-81; Sci Teacher Ewing Park Mid Sch 1981-85; Bio Teacher Whites Creek HS 1985-; *ai:* Sci Olympiad Spon; Sci Assn TN Bd of Dir 1985-; NSTA 1985-; NEA Mem 1975-; St Anns Episcopal Church Sr Warden 1988-89; Mary Reynolds Babcock Fnd Earthwater Grant 1984; Career Ladder III Teacher; Brotherhood-Sisterhood Awd; Mid Sch Sci Curr Comm; Teacher of Yr 1985, 1988; Distinguished Classroom Teacher 1989; *office:* Whites Creek Comprehensive HS 7277 Old Hickory Blvd Whites Creek TN 37189

METZGER, JOHN MATHIAS, Mathematics Teacher; *b:* Lima, OH; *m:* Elizabeth Sierra; *c:* Rob La Count; *ed:* (BSED) Elem Ed, Bowling Green Univ 1969; NASA Newmast 1985; Project Excels 1987; Math Specialization, AZ St Univ 1984; Chisanbop Instr & Trainer 1979; Support Teacher & Facilitator 1986; *cr:* 5th Grade Teacher Dublin Elem 1969-71; 6th Grade Teacher Meyerholz Elem 1971-77; 7th/8th Grade Teacher Pine Elem Sch 1977-82, Palo Verde Mid Sch 1982-; *ai:* At-Risk Cmptr Tutoring Prgm; Curr Leader; Support Teacher Facilitator Mentor Prgm; Cooperative Learning Inservice Instr; Beginning Teacher Trainer; Math Curr Cmptr Use Inservice Instr; NCTM 1988-; AATM, ASPE 1989-; Nom AZ Teacher of Yr 1990; *office:* Palo Verde Mid Sch 7502 N 39th Ave Phoenix AZ 85051

METZGER, MARY FOUTS, Fourth Grade Teacher; *b:* Rockwell City, IA; *m:* Glenn; *c:* Jennifer; *ed:* (BA) Fr, Briar Cliff Coll 1975; Various Courses To Renew Certificate; *cr:* 5th Grade Teacher 1975-80, 7th/8th Grade Teacher 1982 St Peter & Paul Sch; 4th Grade Teacher West Bend Cmmty Sch 1982-; *ai:* Sch Building Comm Mem; West Bend Ed Assn, IA St Ed Assn, NEA 1982-; West Bend Women of Today 1989-; *office:* West Bend Cmmty Sch 3rd Ave W West Bend IA 50597

METZLER, C. LEHMAN, Ag Teacher/Dept Chairperson; *b:* Holtwood, PA; *m:* Alta M. Boll; *c:* Jonathan A., Joel A.; *ed:* (BS) Ag Ed, PA St Univ 1968; (MS) Dairy Sci, MI St Univ 1972; Trng Intnl Economics & Rural Sociology Grad Level PSU; Trng Bible & Sociology Dev Eastern Mennonite Seminary; Span Lang Stu Costa Rica 1969; Ger Lang Stud Paraguay 1973; *cr:* Teacher Damascus HS 1968; Ag Dev Lancaster Mennonite Conf 1969-71; Grad Asst MI St Univ 1971-72; Ag Dev Mennonite Cntrl Comm 1973-79; Teacher Lancaster Mennonite HS 1980-; *ai:* Future Agriculturalists of Amer Faculty Adv; Resourse Dev Comm Secy & Mem; Chairperson Cmptr Study Comm; Lancaster Cty Vo Ag Teachers 1981-; PA Vo Ag Teachers Assn 1981-; Natl Vo Ag Teachers; Laurel Street Mennonite Church Leadership Team 1984-; Founding Organization Inter-Sch Competition Known as Ag Tech Week Specifically Designed for Stus Enrolled Ag & Technology Courses Mennonite Scndry Ed Cncl; *home:* Rt 2 Box 91 A Airville PA 17302

MEUNIER, CAROL ANN, Teacher & Math Team Leader; *b:* Canton, OH; *m:* Edward P.; *ed:* (BA) Ed, Univ of Akron 1972; *cr:* 7th Grade Teacher 1972-78, Math Team Leader/8th Grade Teacher 1978- Taft Mid Sch; *ai:* 8th Grade Field Trip Adv & Awds Prgm Organizer; Taft Teacher Recognition Awd 1982; Local Nom Myrtle Miller Outstanding Teacher Awd; *office:* Taft Mid Sch 3829 Guilford NW Canton OH 44718

MEUNIER, FRANCES VITALI, 2nd Grade Teacher; *b:* New Britain, CT; *m:* Norman J.; *c:* Laurie, Susan; *ed:* (BA) Romance Lang/Eng, Smith Coll 1946; Addl Studies Smith Coll; Westfield St Coll; Univ of MA; North Adams St Coll; *cr:* Eng Teacher Hawley Jr HS 1957-60;Kndgtn Teacher Vernon St Sch/Jackson St 1975-80; 4th Grade Teacher 1980-84; 2nd Grade Teacher 1984-89 Jackson St Sch; *ai:* Mem Bd Dir VINS; MTA; NTA; Hampshire Cty Smith Club; Cooley Dickinson Hosp Aux; Northampton Zoning Bd; *home:* 17 Prospect Heights Northampton MA 01060

MEUTH, SALLY WILLIAMS, English Teacher; *b:* Zanesville, OH; *m:* David; *c:* Mason; *ed:* (BS) Eng, Murray St Univ 1979; (MS) Scndry Ed, Western KY Univ 1987; *cr:* 7th/8th Grade His Teacher Sikeston Jr HS 1979-80; Gifted Ed Teacher 1980-84; Eng Teacher 1987- Henderson Cty HS; *ai:* Comm Admin Assessment; Comm Restructuring Scndry Schls; *office:* Henderson Co H S 2424 Zion Rd Henderson KY 42420

MEVES, SHARON BROMLEY, Eng Lang Art Teacher; *b:* Streator, IL; *m:* Richard E.; *c:* Ericka, Sarah; *ed:* (BS) Music Ed/Eng, 1968, (MA) Musicology, 1969 Ball St Univ; *cr:* Music Teacher Boylan Cath HS 1969, Music Meridian Dist 223 1970-84; Eng/Lang Art Teacher Meridian Jr HS 1984-; *ai:* NEA, IEA, SVEA 1974-; Contact Crisis Hotline 1971-72; Spring Creek Church Choir Dir 1984-; Meves Music Studio; *office:* Meridian Jr HS 305 W Main St Stillman Valley IL 61084

MEYER, BETTY EASTON, Kindergarten/Elem Music Tchr; *b:* Hebron, NE; *m:* Steven A.; *c:* Spencer, Cassandra; *ed:* (BA) Elem Ed/Vocal Music, Univ of NE Lincoln 1975; (MA) Vocal Music Ed, Univ of NE 1979; Educl Media Specialist, Kearney St Coll 1990; Endorsement in Early Chldhd Ed 1987; *cr:* Elem Music Teacher Lincoln Public Sch 1975-77; Elem Music/Kndgtn Teacher Bruning Public Sch 1977-; *ai:* Music Prgrms Grandparents Day; Amer Ed Week; Holiday Prgms; Taught Guitar Class; Mu Phi Epsilon 1973-; NE Music Educators Assn 1975-; Natl Music Educators 1975-; NE St Ed Assn 1975-; Natl Ed Assn 1975-; NAEYC 1981-; NE Assn for Ed of Young Children 1981-; South Cntrl Assn for Ed of Young Children (Treas 1988-) 1981-; Bruning Ed (Pres, VP, Secy, Treas) 1977-; NE Rdng Cncl 1985-; Intl Rdng Assn 1985-; Wkshps Midwest Convention for Ed Young Children 1988; NE Rdng Cncl 1987; NE Assn for Ed Young Children 1986; Outstanding Stu Teacher Awd 1975; Published Art Act Mailbox Magazine; *office:* Bruning Public Sch 340 Carroll St Bruning NE 68322

MEYER, BILL RICHARD, Social Studies HS Teacher; *b:* Harrisburg, PA; *m:* Tina Leigh Sheets; *ed:* (BA) Soc Stud Ed, VPI & SU 1983; *cr:* US Govt Teacher Pulaski Cty HS 1984-; *ai:* Sr Class Spon; Sr Steering Comm Adv; Stu Schlsp Comm; NEA 1989-; *office:* Pulaski County HS P O Box 518 Dublin VA 24084

MEYER, CHARITA, Sixth Grade Teacher; *b:* Huntington, IN; *ed:* (BA) Ed, 1973, (MS) Ed, 1982 St Francis Coll; *cr:* 3rd/4th Grade Teacher St Agnes Sch 1970-71, St Francis Xavier Sch 1971-72, St Agnes Sch 1972-74; 5th/6th Grade Teacher St Lawrence Sch 1974-75; 6th Grade Teacher St John Evangelist Sch 1975-76; 5th/6th Grade Teacher St George Sch 1976-79, St Lawrence Sch 1979-82; 6th Grade Teacher St John Evangelist Sch 1982-; *ai:* Guitar Teacher; Liturgical Music Instr; Sci Fair Coord; *office:* St John The Evangelist Sch 9400 Wicker Ave Saint John IN 46373

MEYER, DEBORAH LYNN (BAIN), Fourth Grade Teacher; *b:* Indianapolis, IN; *m:* Roy G.; *c:* Tamara, Tricia; *ed:* (BS) Elem Ed, Univ of Indianapolis 1971; (MS) Spec Ed, IN Univ 1983; Rdng, Elmhurst Coll 1989; *cr:* 7th/8th & 4th Grade Teacher St Anthonys Sch 1972-74; 5th/6th Grade Teacher 1979-83, 5th Grade Teacher 1983-84, 4th Grade Teacher 1984-Kingsford Heights Elem Sch; *ai:* Systemwide Prgm Planning Comm; Spelling Bee Comm; Report Card Comm; La Porte Fed of Teachers Negotiating Team & Executive Bd; Delta Kappa Gamma Treas 1984-; Amer Assn of Univ Women 1982-86; Intnl Rdng Assn 1987-; La Porte Area Rdng Cncl 1986-; Welcome Wagon Treas 1979-84; Kingsbury PTA Treas 1979-87; Bahais of Scipio Twp Treas 1978-; *office:* Kingsford Hts Elem Sch 460 Evanston Rd Kingsford Heights IN 46346

MEYER, DOUGLAS B., Science Teacher; *b:* Spokane, WA; *m:* Susan E.; *c:* Adam D.; *ed:* (BAED) Chem/Bio-Chem/Health Ed, E WA Univ 1980; Chem, Sci Teaching Degree; *cr:* Phys Sci Teacher North Cntrl HS 1982-83; Biological Sci Teacher Summer Sch Dist 81 1982-85; Sci Teacher Worley HS Dist 1984-; *ai:* Sr Class Adv; Drama Coach; Drug & Alcohol, HIV/AIDS Dir; Curr Dev; ASCD 1989-; Fraternal Order of the Eagles Aire #2 1975-; BSA Leader; Nom for Teacher of Yr; DevelopEd HIV/AIDS Activity Curr for Grades 7-12 State Wide; Advisory Panel; Drug Free Schls Prgm Kootenai Cty; *home:* 6027 N Washington Spokane WA 99205

MEYER, EDWIN C., Technology Department Chair; *b:* Cold Spring, MN; *m:* Mary Lou Zierden; *c:* Mary B. A., Mike, Mark; *ed:* (BS) Industrial Art, St Cloud St Univ 1961; (MS) Industrial Art, Mankato St Univ 1969; Grad Stud Various Univs; *cr:* Industrial Art Teacher Midwest HS 1963-66; Industrial Art Chm Kenyon HS 1966-69; Technology Dept Chm Litchfield HS 1969-; *ai:* MEEP Team Mem; Hutchinson Tech Coll Advisory Comm; MTEA 1969-, Problem Solving 1990; ITEA 1987-; CMTEA 1969-; Prairie Chippers Pres 1985-, Best Fish 1987-88; St Philips Choir 1983-; VFW Voice of Democracy Chm 1969-, Achievement Awd 1984; Feature Articles Natl Publications; Feature Speaker Sci & Technology Teachers Huntington Beach 1990; Presenter St Conventions; *office:* Litchfield HS 901 N Gilman Litchfield MN 55355

MEYER, ELIZABETH HATCH, Spanish Teacher; *b:* Pasadena, CA; *m:* David E.; *c:* Angela L., Jeffrey D.; *ed:* (BS) Ed, N AZ Univ 1966; (MA) Rdng Specialist, CA St Univ San Bernardino 1985; *ai:* Span Club Spon; Delta Kappa Gamma 1985-; Peace Corps Volunteer Venezuela 1966-68; *office:* Twentynine Palms HS 6051 Datura Ave Twentynine Palms CA 92277

MEYER, GINNY MERRELL, Third Grade Teacher; *b:* Columbus, OH; *c:* Jennifer, Jaclyn; *ed:* (BA) Elem Ed, 1972, (MS) Elem Ed, 1974 Univ of Evansville; Grad Stud Soc Stud; *cr:* 1st Grade Teacher Clarke Elem 1972-75; 2nd Grade Teacher 1976-77, 3rd Grade Teacher 1977-81 Loge Elem; 4th Grade Teacher 1981-87, 3rd Grade Teacher 1987- Sharon Elem; *ai:* Cheerleading Coach; Curr Coord; Reg Ed Rep Spec Ed Dept; Univ of Evansville Chrldr Alumni Assn; Newburgh United Meth Church (Youth Coord, Family Ministries Chm, Sunday Sch Teacher); *home:* 2166 Union Dr Newburgh IN 47630

MEYER, HERBERT THEODORE, 2nd-3rd Grade Teacher; *b:* Mt Clemens, MI; *m:* Michele Annette Boccia; *c:* Anne Meyer Hoef, Michael, Elizabeth; *ed:* (BM) Music, 1961, (MMUS) Music, 1962 Univ of MI; Elem Cert Elem Ed, E MI Univ 1971; *cr:* Music Teacher Brookside Sch 1962-64; Music Teacher 1964-71, Classroom Teacher 1971- Birmingham Schls; Classroom Teacher Meadow Lake Sch 1975-; *ai:* Stu Services; Mem of Lang Art Curr Dev & Textbook Selection Bghm Schls; Mi, NAE 1964-; MI Sch Band & Orch Assn 1962-; Natl ASCD; Holy Name Church Music Ministry; *office:* Meadow Lake Elem Sch 7100 Lindenmere Birmingham MI 48010

MEYER, JAMES GEORGE, Fourth Grade Teacher; *b:* Sauk Centre, MN; *m:* Patty Ann; *c:* Adam; *ed:* (BS) Phys Ed, 1988, (BS) Elem Ed, 1989 St Cloud St Univ; *cr:* Coaching Sartell HS 1987-88; Phys Ed Teacher/Coach Rocori Sch Dist 1988-89; 4th Grade Teacher/Coach Cold Spring Elem 1989-; *ai:* Head Cross Cntry, Asst Track Coach; PTA 1990; MEA 1988-89; MN Coaches Assn 1987-; VP of The Rocori Coaches Assn; *office:* Cold Spring Elem Sch 533 Main St Cold Spring MN 56320

MEYER, JOETTE ANN KRALL, Kindergarten Teacher; *b:* Iowa City, IA; *m:* James Paul; *c:* Matthew; *ed:* (BA) Elem Ed, Univ of N IA 1973; *cr:* 1st Grade Teacher Holy Family Sch 1973-74; 3rd Grade Teacher 1974-85, Kndgtn Teacher 1985- Solon Cmmty Sch; *ai:* Recognition & Advisory Comm; Solon Ed Assn (Pres, VP, Secy, Treas) 1979-80, 1985-; St Marys Altar Society (Treas) 1978-79, 1984-89; *office:* Solon Cmmty Schls PO Box 279 Solon IA 52333

MEYER, JOSEPHA, Third Grade Teacher; *b:* St Marys, PA; *ed:* (BA) Ed, Villanova Univ 1960; Various Courses & Univs; *cr:* 3rd Grade Teacher Sacred Heart Sch 1951-54; 3rd/4th Grade Teacher St Callistus Sch 1954-56, St Joseph Sch 1956-58; 1st/2nd Grade Teacher St Boniface Sch 1958-59; 1st Grade Teacher Sacred Heart Sch 1959-60; 1st/2nd Grade Teacher St Joseph Sch 1960-67; 1st Grade Teacher Sacred Heart Sch 1967-68, St Marys Parochial 1968-71, Queen of the World 1971-87; 3rd Grade Teacher St Ann Sch 1987-; *ai:* NCEA; Benedictine Cmmty (Renewal Team 1967-70, Cncl to Prioress 1968-87, Treas 1969-71, Procurater 1971-79, Sub-Prioress 1979-87); *home:* 526 Fairview St Emmaus PA 18049

MEYER, JUNIA MARIE (SCHLINKERT), Home Ec Teacher; *b:* Minneapolis, MN; *m:* Douglas Henry; *ed:* (BS) Home Ec Ed, SD St Univ 1971; *cr:* Home Ec Teacher 1972-, Elem Phys Ed Instr 1982-85, 1987- Willow Lake Sch; *ai:* FHA Adv; AVA, AHEA, SDHEA; *home:* Cemetery Rd Box 186 Willow Lake SD 57278

MEYER, KAREN SCHROEDER, Sixth Grade Teacher; *b:* Ledyard, IA; *m:* Larry C.; *c:* Todd, Julie, Timothy; *ed:* (BA) Elem Ed, UNI 1979; Grad Stud; *cr:* 3rd Grade Teacher 1958-63, 6th Grade Teacher 1979- Wellsburg Cmnty Sch; *ai:* Phase III, PBP Comm; Hardy Rdng Cncl, IA Rdng Assn 1980-; *office:* Wellsburg-Steamboat Rock Comm 609 S Monroe Wellsburg IA 50680

MEYER, KONNIE EICKHOFF, Third Grade Teacher; *b:* Mansfield, OH; *m:* Bruce Ervin; *c:* Ryan B., Anita L.; *ed:* (BA) Elem Ed, Wittenberg Univ 1973; *cr:* 3rd Grade Teacher Patrick Henry-Hamler Elem 1973-88, Patrick Henry Malinta Elem 1988-; *ai:* Jr Great Books Leader; PHEA, OEA, NEA 1973-; Immanuel Luth Church 1965-; PH Athletic Boosters Lifetime Mem 1965-; Martha Holden Jennings Scholar 1982-83; Patrick Henry Teacher of Yr 1985-86; *office:* Patrick Henry Malinta Elem 204 N Henry Malinta OH 43535

MEYER, LLOYD EUGENE, 7th/12th Grade Bible Teacher; *b:* La Salle, CO; *m:* Joanne M. Ackerman; *c:* Marilyn Broyles, Beverly Weaver, Steve; *ed:* (THM) Theology, 1951, (DD) 1968 Arlington Baptist Coll; New Testament Moody Bible Inst; Supvrs Pensacola Chrstn Coll; *cr:* Pres Baptist Temple Sch 1958-69, Orlando Chrstn Sch 1968-; Calvary Baptist Sch 1979-81; *ai:* Assn of Supervision 1988; Metropolitan Baptist Church (Minister, Pastor, South & Cntrl Amer, Europe Radio Minister) World Baptist Fellowship Pres; Missions World Baptist Fellowship Bd Mem.

MEYER, MARGARET, Third Grade Teacher; *b:* Carrollton, IL; *ed:* (BS) Elem Ed, Quincy Coll 1975; (BA) Eng, Quincy Coll 1975; (MS) Elem Ed, Southern IL Univ 1986; *cr:* Teacher, St John Sch 1975-81; Teacher, Carrollton HS 1982; Teacher, St John School 1982-; *ai:* Articles Published in Good Apple, Teacher, Instructor, and The Miraculous Medal; *office:* St John Sch 3rd & Locust St Carrollton IL 62016

MEYER, MARY DICKINSON, Kindergarten Teacher; *b:* Keokuk, IA; *m:* Ronald E.; *c:* Elizabeth, Charles; *ed:* (BA) Ed, NE MO St 1973; Sci Ed, Stu At Risk, Lang, Rdng Courses; *cr:* Kndgtn Teacher Keokuk Cmmty Sch Dist 1974-77, 1986-; *ai:* Early Chldhd Study & Safety Town Comm; ISEA, NEA, KY Ed Assn 1986-; United Meth Women Pres 1984-86, Mission Awd 1987; BSA Asst Leader 1986-87; GSA Asst Leader 1985-; Safety Town Teacher 1984-; PTA Rep; *office:* Torrence & Lincoln Sch 17th Fulton Keokuk IA 52632

MEYER, NORMA WEINTRAUB, Orchestra Director; *b:* Philadelphia, PA; *m:* Joshua Lee; *c:* Adam, Ranaan; *ed:* (BM) Applied Music-Performance, Philadelphia Music Acad 1968; (MM) Applied Music-Performance, Temple Univ 1970; Cert Teaching Courses,Temple Univ, Philadelphia Coll of Performing Arts, Glassboro St Coll; *cr:* K-8th Grade General Music/Chorus Teacher Vare Elem 1974-78; Private Piano Teacher 1964-; Mid/HS Orch Dir Washington Township 1985-; *ai:* Orch Dir Washington Township HS & Chestnut Ridge Mid Sch; ASTA NJ St Bd Dir 1989-91; Cong Bnai Tikvah Bd Dir 1989-91; GPBL Swim Club Bd Dir 1989-92; WTHS Orch Patrons Adv 1988-; Public Performances in Chamber Music Groups & as Accompanist; Built Current String Prgm in Washington Township Schls; *office:* Washington Township HS RD 3 Sewell NJ 08080

MEYER, SUE ANN, Music Teacher; *b:* Rensselaer, IN; *m:* Donald; *c:* Kurt, Mark; *ed:* (BME) Music, 1961, (MME) Music, 1964 IN Univ; *cr:* Music Teacher M S D Perry Township 1961-70, Univ of Indianapolis 1974-78, M S D Perry Township 1977-; *ai:* Music Ensembles; Sigma Alpha Iota, DKT; *office:* Mary Bryan Sch 4355 E Stop 11 Indianapolis IN 46237

MEYER, WIL J., AP US His/Ger/Soc Stud Chair; *b:* Luebeck, Germany; *m:* Phyllis Peterson; *c:* Jon, Greg, Jacki, Ryan, Chad; *ed:* (BA) Ger, 1969, (MS) His, 1978, (MED) Ed, 1979 Univ of UT; *cr:* Teacher/His Dept Chm Murray HS1969-; *ai:* Ger Club Adv; Exec Bd Mem Dist Level; Leader Close Up Prgm; Academic Decathlon Adv; *office:* Murray HS 5440 S State St Murray UT 84107

MEYER, WILLIAM JOSEPH, 7th/8th Grade Math Teacher; *b:* Piqua, OH; *m:* Peggy L.; *c:* Bryan, Erik; *ed:* (BS) Soc Stud, 1971, (MS) Rdng, 1980 Wright St Univ; Working Towards Masters; *cr:* Soc Stud Teacher Lehman HS 1972-74; 4th Grade Teacher Marion Local HS 1974-83; 7th/8th Grade Teacher Minster Local Schls 1983-; *ai:* Head Var Bsbl & Golf Coach; OEA, NEA, OHSAA Coach; Eagles; *home:* 155 N Frankfort Minster OH 45865

MEYERS, BERNARD L., Assistant Principal; *b:* Tidioute, Indonesia; *ed:* (BA) Sociology, St Univ of NY Binghamton 1963; (MS) Elem Ed, Cortland 1970; *cr:* Textile Salesman M Lowenstein 1963-65; Teacher 1966-87, Coord of Basic Skills 1987-89, Asst Prin 1989- Johnson City NY; *ai:* NY Educators Assn (Bd of Dir, Building Rep) 1974-82.

MEYERS, CINDY LU, 2nd Grade Teacher; *b:* Reno, NV; *m:* John W.; *c:* Thomas E., John J., Jeffrey P., Kaye L.; *ed:* (BS) Elem Ed, 1978, (MED) Educl Admin, 1981 Univ of NV Reno; *cr:* 1st/2nd/3rd Grade Teacher Imlay Elem 1978-84, Lovelock Elem 1984-; *ai:* Young Astronauts Club; Emergency 911 Fund Raiser; Pershing Co Classroom (VP/Pres 1983-; Teachers Assn NV St Ed Assn 1983-; NEA 1983-; Beta Sigma Phi VP 1985-; Pershing Co Teacher of Yr 1983; Univ of NV Alumni Day 1983; *office:* Lovelock Grammar Sch Box 621 Elmhurst Lovelock NV 89419

MEYERS, DEBBIE BOETZ, 8th Grade English/Rdng Teacher; *b:* Montpelier, OH; *m:* Richard Alan; *c:* Craig, Dustin; *ed:* (BA) Elem Ed/Early Chldhd, Univ of Toledo 1985; Working Towards Masters; *cr:* 8th Grade Eng Teacher Montpelier Superior Mid Sch 1986-; *ai:* Pi Lambda Theta, Phi Kappa Phi, NAEYC 1985; OH Child Conservation League (Secy 1987-88, VP 1989-); *office:* Montpelier Superior Mid Sch Rt 3 Montpelier OH 43543

MEYERS, DOROTHY PAZDERNIK, Sixth Grade Teacher; *b:* St Louis, MO; *m:* John Christian; *c:* William, David; *ed:* (BA) Ed, Fontbonne Coll 1965; (MAT) Soc Stud, Webster Univ 1969; Working on Gifted/Talented Cert; *cr:* 5th Grade Teacher 1965-68, 6th Grade Teacher 1969- Bayless Mid; *ai:* Mentor; Judge at St Louis Sci Fair; Teacher Advisory Bd to Post Dispatch; I CARE Comm; MNEA; Seven Holy Founders Teacher 1985-; *office:* Bayless Mid Sch 4530 Webster Rd Saint Louis MO 63123

MEYERS, JACQUELINE GUNNS, Seventh Grade Math Teacher; *b:* Tacoma, WA; *m:* William; *c:* Jennifer, Barbara; *ed:* (BA) Ft Wright Coll 1954; Math, Sci, Gonzaga Univ; Grad Work Several Univs; *cr:* 6th Grade Teacher St Francis Sch 1960-68; 7th Grade Teacher 1968-69, Prin 1967-70 St Annes Sch; Vice Prin/7th Grade Teacher All Saints Mid Sch 1970-85; 7th-8th Grade Teacher Cataldo Sch 1985; *ai:* Coach Mathcounts; Adv Stu Cncl & Sch Patrol; Coord John Hopkins Talent Search; Stu Sci Wkshps; Energy & Mans Environment Vice Chairperson 1975-; Helped Write Dist Curr; Several Math Grants; Taught Numerous Wkshps for Teachers Credit Local Univs & Colls.

MEYERS, LINDA SUE, Science Teacher; *b:* Monroe, MI; *c:* Bryan Diroff; *ed:* (BA) Art/Bio, 1968, (MA) Curr, 1985 E MI Univ; Numerous Wkshps; *cr:* Art/Bio Teacher St John HS 1968-70; Sci Teacher Stevenson Jr HS 1971-; *ai:* Coaching & Judging Sci Olympiad; *office:* Stevenson Jr HS 38501 Palmer Rd Westland MI 48185

MEYTHALER, ERIC LANZ, 2nd Grade Teacher; *b:* Appleton, WI; *m:* Gwendolyn June Hofman; *ed:* (BA) Poly Sci/Philosophy, 1975, (MAT) Elem Ed, 1977 CO Coll; *cr:* Dir/Title I Math Teacher 1977-80, 2nd Grade Teacher 1980- Longfellow Elem; *ai:* Accountability & PN Comm; Bsktbl Coach; NCTM 1977-80; NEA 1977-; Salida Youth Soccer Assn Sr Referee 1981-; High Cntry Fine Arts Assn (Treas 1984-86) 1980-; First Luth Church Chm of Trustees 1985-; BSA Service Awd; Sequel Published Through Project Wild; *office:* Longfellow Elem Sch 8th & I Streets Salida CO 81201

MEZA, RAYMOND P., Principal; *b:* Del Rio, TX; *m:* Bertha A. Ybarra; *c:* Raymond, Paul, Adam; *ed:* (BS) Elem Ed, 1971, (MA) Scnd Y Ed, Sul Ross State Univ; TX Teacher Appraisal Sys Cert; Sign Lang Cert; *cr:* Kndgtn Teacher Sam Houston Sch 1971-79; 6th Grade Teacher Santa Rita Elem 1979-80, Memorial Sch 1980-85; Prin Austin Pre-Sch 1985-; *ai:* Pres-San Felipe Lions Club; VP South TX Head Start Dir; Mem of Val Verde Child Welfare Bd; TX Elem Prin Assn 1985-; Natl Head Start Dir Assn 1986-; Southwest TX Head Start Dir Assn 1986-; San Felipe Lions Club Pres 1980- Outstanding Service 1988-89; BSA Awds Chairperson 1987-88; Instr Teacher of Yr Nom; Head Start Dir San Felipe Del Rio Head Start Prgm; Prin-San Felipe Del Rio Prekndgtn Prgm; *home:* 305 W 9th Del Rio TX 78840

MEZGER, GAIL EILEEN (MC MANUS), 7th/8th Grade Math Teacher; *b:* Bremerton, WA; *m:* Walter Louis III; *c:* Sarah C., Darren K.; *ed:* (BA) Math/Eng, Seattle Pacific Univ 1972; Ed, W WA Univ 1975; (MED) Supervision/Leadership, Univ of Portland 1989; Working on Ad Credentials at Portland St Univ; *cr:* Teacher Cascade Mid Sch 1972-; *ai:* Math Contest Coach; Self Study, K-12 Math, Retention, Eval of Mid Sch, Steering Comms; NCTM, NEA, ASCD; *office:* Cascade Mid Sch 2821 Parkview Dr Longview WA 98632

MIAMIDIAN, MADELYN BORRELLI, Business Teacher; *b:* Salem, NJ; *m:* Raymond; *ed:* (BS) Bus Ed, Rider Coll 1970; (MED) Bus Ed, Temple Univ 1980; *cr:* Teacher Riverside HS 1970-75, Washington Township HS 1975-; *office:* Washington Township HS P O Box 513 R R 12 Sewell NJ 08080

MICETICH, JOEL PHILLIP, Jr HS Teacher; *b:* Morris, IL; *ed:* (BS) Health/Phys Ed, Eureka Coll 1980; Math, Joliet Jr Coll; *cr:* Teacher South Wilmington Grade Sch 1981-; *ai:* Boys Jr HS Bsktbl, Bsbl, Track Coach; IL Bsktbl Coaches Assn 1981-; *home:* 593 N 2nd Ave Coal City IL 60416

MICHAEL, CYNTHIA KENNEDY, 11th Grade Soc Stud Teacher; *b:* Ft Worth, TX; *m:* Charles William Jr.; *c:* Matthew; *ed:* (BS) Religion, 1974, (BS) Intre Soc Sci, 1976 TX Weslevan Univ; *cr:* Sales-Acct Leorards Dept Stores & Auto Centers 1967-71; Buyer-Sales Career Fashions 1971-74; Buyer J C Penney 1974-76; Teacher Birdville Ind Sch Dist 1976-; *ai:* Sr Class Spon; Birdville Prof Educators, TX Prof Educators, Mid-Cities Cncl for Soc Stud 1979-; Phi Mu Alumnae of Ft Worth 1974-; *office:* Richland Sr HS 5201 Holiday Ln Fort Worth TX 76180

MICHAEL, KEVIN LEE, Math/Computer Science Teacher; *b:* Clearfield, PA; *m:* Cindy Joy Hatten; *ed:* (BS) Math Ed/Music Ed, Clarion Univ of PA 1981; Grad Stud Clarion Univ of PA, Univ of MD; Admin, Supervision, George Washington Univ 1990; *cr:* Math Teacher Northern HS 1982-; *ai:* NHS & Cmptr Team Spon; Calvert Cty Curr, Math Textbook Selection, Cmptr Study Comms; MD Cncl Teachers of Math, NCTM, ASCD 1988-; Northern HS Teacher of Yr 1990; *office:* Northern HS 2950 Chaneyville Rd Owings MD 20736

MICHAEL, MELINDA VOGEL, AP Math Teacher; *b:* Terre Haute, IN; *m:* Timothy A.; *ed:* (BS) Math Ed, 1970, (MA) Math Ed, 1975 OH St; (MS) Math, Univ of Cincinnati 1979; *cr:* Math Teacher East HS 1970-71, Mc Guffey Jr HS 1971-75, Upper Arlington HS 1975-77; Math Instr/Stu Univ of Cincinnati 1978-80, 1981-84; Advanced Placement Math Teacher St Xavier HS; *ai:* MAA 1988-; NCTM 1989-; GCTM 1987-; Cincinnati Zoo Volunteer 1989-; *office:* St Xavier HS 600 N Bend Rd Cincinnati OH 45224

MICHALIK, PEGGY ANN, 6th Grade Teacher; *b:* Sandusky, OH; *m:* Louis; *c:* Viki Rogers, Lori; *ed:* (BA) Elem Ed, Bowling Green St Univ 1973; *cr:* 6th Grade Teacher Townsend Elem 1973-; *home:* 2811 E Bayview Ln Sandusky OH 44870

MICHALSKI, CAMILLE BUCK, Jr High Social Studies Teacher; *b:* Chicago, IL; *m:* Thaddeus S.; *ed:* (BA) Political Science, Loyola Univ 1972; *cr:* Jr High Soc Stud Teacher St Isidore Sch 1966-68; Jr High Soc Stud Teacher St John of God Sch 1968-80; Jr High Soc Stud Teacher St Bede Sch 1980-; *ai:* NCEA; Natl Assn of Soc Stud Teachers; Polish Women's Alliance of Amer; Outstanding Elem Teachers of Amer 1974; *home:* 24952 West Forest Dr Lake Villa IL 60046

MICHALSKI, DONNA L., Art Teacher 8-9/Dept Chair; *b:* Natrona Heights, PA; *ed:* (BS) Art, IN Univ of PA 1969; (MED) Art, Univ of Kutztown; Post Masters Studies Univ of VT; West Chester Univ; *cr:* Art Teacher (6th-8th Grade) Windham Village Exempted Sch Dist 1969-70; Art Teacher (7th-8th Grade) 1970-74; Dept Chair 1974- Phoenixville Area Sch Dist; *ai:* NEA; PA St Ed Assn; Phoenixville Area Ed Assn Grievance Chair 1980-89; Negotiator 1981-82; PA Art Ed Assn; Delta Kappa Gamma Ways & Means 1980-81; Philadelphia Art Alliance; Dev 2 Small Art Related Bus HMS Critters & Nuclear Novelties; *office:* Phoenixville Area Sch Dist 1330 S Main St Phoenixville PA 19460

MICHALYK, CATHERINE J., Spanish/English Teacher; *b:* Farrell, PA; *ed:* (BA) Span, Thiel Coll 1984; Bi-ling Teaching Certificate, El Inst De Filologia Hispanica Saltillo Coahuila Mexico; *cr:* Span Teacher Osbourn Park HS 1984-88; Span/Eng Teacher Jamestown HS 1988-; *ai:* Span Club Adv; Spon LA Sociedad Honoraria Hispanica Capitulo Saltillense; AATSP 1986-; Thiel Womens Club 1984-; VA St Teachers of Foreign Lang Travel & Study Grant 1987; *office:* Jamestown HS 204 Shenango St Jamestown PA 16134

MICHAUD, DAVID R., Business Teacher; *b:* E Millinocket, ME; *m:* Joan L.; *c:* Kelley, Kerry, Jennifer; *ed:* (BSED) Bus Ed, WA St Teachers Coll 1968; *cr:* Bus Teacher Lee Acad 1968-74, Schenck HS 1974-; *ai:* Natl Rifle Assn Hunter Safety, ME Snowmobile Safety, Canoe Safety Instr; EMTA Building Rep 1987-; BEAM, MTA Mem 1968-; NBEA 1985-; *office:* Schenck HS 31-40 North St East Millionocket ME 04430

MICHEL, ANTONIA LA ROSA, 5th Grade Teacher; *b:* Mc Keesport, PA; *m:* Donald E.; *c:* Donna M., Donald J., John P., Joanne E.; *ed:* (BA) Psych, Seton Hill Coll 1983; Diocesan Catechist Formation Prgm; Prof Level Cert Religion; *cr:* 5th Grade Teacher Immaculate Conception Sch 1983-; *ai:* Liturgical Planning Comm; Sci Dept Self Study Comm Chm; NCEA 1983-; Chrstn Mothers Past VP 1973-; Parent Teacher Guild Past VP 1977-; *office:* Immaculate Conception Sch 308 2nd St Irwin PA 15642

MICHEL, SHARON LANTZ, Sixth Grade Teacher; *b:* Baltimore, MD; *m:* Robert Paul; *c:* Lori A., Lance P. (dec); *ed:* (BS) Elem Ed, Cntrl St Univ 1978; *cr:* 2nd Grade Teacher Harvest Hills Elem 1978-79, J L Dennis Elem 1979-81; 3rd Grade Teacher 1981-83 6th Grade Teacher 1983- J L Dennis Elem; *ai:* Vertical Team Chm; Math Spon; Math Olympiad Team; BEO Treas 1989-; Invited Excl in Ed Awds Banquet 1989; *office:* James L Dennis Elem Sch 11800 James L Dennis Dr Oklahoma City OK 73162

MICHEL, STEVEN HAROLD, Science/Phys Ed Teacher; *b:* Princeton, IN; *m:* Sherry Marginet; *c:* Stuart, Stacey; *ed:* (BS) Life Sci, IN St Univ Evansville 1979; (MS) Ed, IN St Univ 1982; *cr:* Sci Teacher Haubstadt Public Sch 1979-.

MICHELSEN, WILLIAM C., HS Mathematics Teacher; *b:* Bismarck, ND; *m:* June Nelson; *c:* Debra Doctor, Candace Glanville, Pamela Wolff, Timothy; *ed:* (BA) Math, Valley City St 1954; Grad Work Univ of ND Grand Forks & ND St Univ Fargo; *cr:* HS Teacher Hesper ND 1950-51; 6th-8th Grade Teacher Denhoff ND 1951-54; HS Teacher Regan ND 1954-60; Supt Deering ND 1960-62; HS Teacher Wing ND 1962-; *ai:* NDEA 1950-; Wing Lions Past Pres 1962-; City Cncl Mayor 1980-; Wing Ec Dev VP 1987-; *home:* Box 144 Wing ND 58494

MICHIE, HELEN S., 6th Grade Teacher; *b:* Salt Lake City, UT; *ed:* (AS) Elem Ed, Richs Coll 1968; (BS) Elem Ed/Psych, Brigham Young Univ 1970; *cr:* 5th Grade Teacher Linden Park Sch 1970-73; 5th Grade Teacher 1973-81, 6th Grade Teacher 1981-88 J A Taylor Sch; 6th Grade Teacher Jennie P Stewart 1988-; *ai:* Stu Body Faculty Rep 1981-87; Safety Patrol Leader 1985-88; Davis Ed Assn, UT Ed Assn, Natl Ed Assn 1973-; Intermountain Sexual Abuse Treatment Center Co Therapist 1984-87; Chorus Conductor for 4th-6th Grades Bicentennial St Win; Wrote Article Local Medical Group; *home:* 66 W Brookside Ln Centerville UT 84014

MICHIE, JEAN STROHMETZ, First Grade Teacher; *b:* Philadelphia, PA; *m:* James Campbell; *c:* David, Keith; *ed:* (BS) Elem, W Chester PA St Teachers Coll 1953; In Service Wkshps; *cr:* 1st Grade Teacher Bristol PA 1953-54, Coatesville PA 1954-55; Kndgtn-2nd Grade Teacher S Brunswick NJ 1966-; *ai:* Early Chldhd Comm; S Brunswick Teachers Assn (Sch Rep 1985-87, Head Sch Rep 1987-); Governor Teacher Recognition Comm Elem Rep 1987-; PTO (Teacher 1970-73, Rep 1988-); Summer Grant to Make Learning Stations; ; *office:* Constable Elem Sch; Constable Rd Kendall Park NJ 08824

MICIR, SYLVESTER MARK, 8th Grade Math Teacher; *b:* Pittsburgh, PA; *m:* Ann Marie Willard; *c:* Emily A., Addie E.; *ed:* (BS) Mechanical Engr, Univ of PA 1971; (MA) Math Ed, Temple Univ 1979; *cr:* 8th Grade Math Teacher William Penn Mid Sch 1977-; *ai:* Ftbl, Bsktbl, Sftbl Coach; NCTM; *home:* Box 7018 Wrightstown PA 18940

MICKELSEN, KAY LYNN BROADHEAD, Colorguard Advisor; *b:* Pocatello, ID; *m:* Chris; *c:* Jody, Christian, Zachary, Marci; *ed:* (AD) Poly Sci, Ricks Coll 1972; (BS) Phys Ed, Brigham Young Univ 1975; (MA) Comm, ID St 1990; *cr:* Colorguard Adv Blackfoot HS 1982-; *ai:* Flag & Rifleteam Adv; NW Speech Communicators 1990; Church Youth Leader 1976-89; Cub Scouts Den Mother; Gymnastic Booster Pres 1988-89; AYSO Soccer Coach 1985-89; Natl Outstanding Young Women 1988.

MICKELSEN, MARVA ANN, First Grade Teacher; *b:* Bancroft, ID; *ed:* Assoc Elem Ed, Ricks Coll 1945, (BS) Elem Ed, UT St Univ 1962; *cr:* 1st Grade Teacher Marsh Valley Sch Dist 1945-51, N Gem Sch Dist 1952-; *ai:* Delta Kappa Gamma (Pres 1954-56, 1978-80, Secy 1989-); IEA, NEA; Bancroft Literary Society (Pres, VP, Secy) 1960-61; Amer Legion Auxiliary Pres; *home:* 22 S 1st West Bancroft ID 83217

MICKELSON, EDWARD JAY, Latin/German Teacher; *b:* Mobridge, SD; *m:* Beverly Kaye Allison; *c:* Allison J., Andrew R. T.; *ed:* (BA) Latin/Ger, 1971, (MA) Classics, 1976 Univ of SD; Deutsche Sommerschule Pazifik Portland St Univ; Capitol Univ Center, SD St Univ, Macalaster Coll; Life of the Mind; *cr:* Teacher Asst/Derivatives Univ of SD 1970-71; Instr Capitol Univ Center 1983-88; Teacher Wolfgang Borchert Gymnasium West Germany 1986-87, Pierre Public Schls 1971-; *ai:* Latin Club; Ger Club; AFS Foreign Stu Club; Foreign Stu Adv; Pierre Ed Assn Pres 1974-75; SD Foreign Lang Assn (Treas, Secy) 1985-; Classical Assn of Mid West & South 1970-; AATG 1988-; SD Art Cncl Bd Mem 1980-86; Pierre Players 1971-; Pierre Cmmty Chorus 1980-; Teacher of Yr 1977, 1978; SD Bd of Regents Coll Entrance Requirements Comm; SD Ed Assn Cmmty Excl Awd; SD Teacher in Space Semi-Finalist 1985; 1st Natl Teachers Forum SD Rep 1986; *home:* 236 W Prospect St Pierre SD 57501

MICKLEY, ARLENE WILLIAMS, Kindergarten Teacher; *b:* Thief River Falls, MN; *m:* Jerry E.; *c:* Dale Mickley Griffin, Tracy J., Jill Mickley Dobis; *ed:* (BS) Eng/Phys Ed/Coaching, 1952, (BS) Elem/Kndgtn Endorsement, 1976 Moorhead St Univ; Grad Classes Moorhead St Univ, ND St Univ, St Thomas Univ; *cr:* Phys Ed, West Fargo HS; Rdng Teacher 1960-61, Kndgtn Teacher 1961-64, St Francis De Sales, 1st Congregation 1964-67, Edison Sch 1967-; *ai:* Mem PER Ind Sch Dist 152, Early Chldhd Study, Music Curr Comm; 10-59 Regional Coop Task Force Mem; MN Kndgtn Assn St Bd; Red River Rdng Cncl; NEA, MN Ed Assn, 1967-, Moorhead Teacher of Yr 1983, MN Teacher of Yr of Excl 1983; Cmmty Ed Appreciation Awd 1989; Phi Delta Kappa Recognition Awd 1983; Moorhead Lib Bd, Lake Aggasiz Regional Lib Bd, Moorehead Housing Bd Mem; *office:* Edison Sch 1110 S 14th Moorhead MN 56560

MICKSON, SANDRA WISWELL, Biology Teacher; *b:* Fitchburg, MA; *m:* Warren A.; *c:* Heather, Rebecca; *ed:* (BSED) Sci Ed, 1969, (MED) Ed, 1974 Fitchburg St Coll; DNA Sci Wkshp SUNY Stony Brook; *cr:* Bio Teacher N Middlesex Regional HS 1969-; *ai:* NABT, ABT; NSF Grant Bucknell Univ 1975; *office:* N Middlesex Regional HS Main St Townsend MA 01469

MICOL, RAYMOND THOMAS, 7th Grade Sci/Health Teacher; *b:* Valdese, NC; *m:* Judy Campbell; *c:* Angela E., Bradley R.; *ed:* (BS) Bio, Appalachian St Univ 1968; *cr:* 7th Grade Sci Teacher Eastway Jr HS 1968-70; 7th Grade Sch/Health Teacher S Ray Lowder Sch 1970-75, Lincolnton Jr HS 1975-; *ai:* Sci Dept & Sci Comm for Review Chm; Sci Fair Coord; Media Advisory Comm; Outstanding Young Educator 1971, 1976; Lincoln Jr HS Teacher of Yr 1979; Lincoln Cty Sci Teacher of Yr 1985; *office:* Lincolnton Jr HS 511 S Aspen St Lincolnton NC 28092

MICULKA, JAMES RAY, Instrumental Music Dept Chm; *b:* Floresville, TX; *m:* Cheryl Kathleen; *c:* Jay E., Jennifer E.; *ed:* (BA) Music Ed, St Marys Univ 1975; (ME) Mid-Management Admin, Univ of TX San Antonio 1978; Mid-Management Admin Cert 1990; TX Teaching Ladder Career Level III; *cr:* Private Trumpet Instr San Antonio TX 1971-79; Asst Band Dir 1975-77, Band Dir 1977-79 E M Pease Mid Sch; Asst Band Dir 1979-81, Band Dir 1981- John Marshall HS; *ai:* TX St Teachers Assn, TX Music Educators Assn, TX Bandmasters Assn, Phi Delt Kappa, Phi Beta Mu; Battle of Flowers Assn of San Antonio Band Festival Chm 1987-89; Mayors Citation of Excl; Statue of Liberty Celebration Awd for Excl; ERIC Document Publication Univ of TX San Antonio; *home:* 731 Heavenly Sky San Antonio TX 78258

MIDCALF, RANDALL W., English Department Chair; *b:* Saginaw, MI; *m:* Cynthia A Lohn; *c:* Steven, Kendall; *ed:* (BS) Eng Ed, Bob Jones Univ 1981; (MA) Eng, Oakland Univ 1989; Journalism, Oakland Univ; *cr:* Eng Dept Chm/Yrbk Adv Bethany Chrstn Sch 1981-; *ai:* Graduation Coord; Yrbk Adv; Speaker MI Assn of Chrstn Schls 1987; Speaker Young Writers Conference Oakland Univ 1988; Reporter 1986-87; *office:* Bethany Chrstn Sch 2601 John R Rd Troy MI 48083

MIDDLEBROOKS, DIANE SOLOMON, Principal; *b:* Abilene, TX; *m:* Robert Lee Jr.; *c:* Jennifer, Travis; *ed:* (BA) Eng, 1972, (MED) Admin, 1984 Univ of N TX; *cr:* Teacher Brownsville Ind Sch Dist 1971-72; Teacher 1978-84, Prin 1984- St Marys Sch; *ai:* Math Curr Comm; Ft Worth Diocese Sch Annual Spon; Citizens Advisory Comm Secy 1986-; NCEA, TX Assn Nonpublic Schls; 1st United Meth Church Stewardship Chairperson/Mem of Administrative Cncl 1986-; *office:* St Marys Sch 931 N Weaver Gainesville TX 76240

MIDDLETON, BETTY FLOWERS, Fifth Grade Teacher; *b:* Meridian, MS; *m:* James Willard; *c:* Julaine N. Knight, Robin M. Holland; *ed:* (BA) Soc Stud/Music, William Carey Coll 1955; Grad Stud Several Univs; *cr:* 5th Grade Teacher W C Griggs Sch 1979-; *ai:* Mobile Opera Guild; Bayou Allied Art Cncl; Choir Dir; Performing Soloist; Spelling Bee Spon; St Textbook Comm; NEA, AEA 1979-; MCEA Building Rep 1989-; La Luna Sevante 1987-; Irvington Baptist Church Soloist; PTA Lifetime Membership Outstanding Service; Outstanding Teacher of Yr CA & AL; Outstanding Cmmty CA Service Awd; Celebration Singers Prof Singing Group Television Mini Mem; *office:* W C Griggs Sch 3 Notch Rd Mobile AL 36619

MIDDLETON, CAROL DE VONE, Physical Education Teacher; *b:* Houston, TX; *ed:* (BA) Phys Ed, 1976, (MS) Phys Ed, 1983 TX S Univ; *cr:* Phys Ed Teacher Deady Jr HS 1977-85, Milby Sr HS 1985-; *ai:* Head Girls Bsktbl & Cross Cntry & Track; Women Bsktbl Assn, Houston Fed Teachers; Teacher of Yr 1978; *home:* 6210 Flamingo Houston TX 77087

MIDDLETON, CINDY SANDERS, Mathematics Dept Chairperson; *b:* Pocatello, ID; *m:* Albert Paul; *c:* Becky; *ed:* (BA) Ed, ID St Univ 1980; *cr:* Teacher Owyhee HS 1980-82, Blackfoot Alternate Sch 1982-84; Math Dept Head Alameda Jr HS 1984-; *ai:* Drill Team Adv Asst; *office:* Alameda Jr HS 845 Mckinley Ave Pocatello ID 83201

MIDDLETON, DONNA RAHM, Language Art Teacher; *b:* Evansville, IN; *m:* William Dale; *c:* Justin; *ed:* (BA) Elem Ed, 1969, (MS) Elem Ed, 1974 Univ of Evansville; TESA; *cr:* Teacher St Phillips 1969-70, Evansville/Vanderburgh Sch Corporation 1970-; *ai:* Lang Book Adoption, Curr Guide Writing, Performance Based Accreditation Comm; Phi Delta Kappa, Delta Kappa Gamma; IN Mid Sch Assn; Amer Red Cross Canoe Assn Treas; BSA; PTO; Governor Conference Talks with Teacher; Scholastics Scope Advisory Bd; *office:* Thompkins Mid Sch 1300 W Mill Rd Evansville IN 47710

MIDDLETON, JIMMY, Teacher; *b:* Laurel, MS; *ed:* (BA) Eng/His, Belhaven Coll 1966; (MED) Ed/Eng, Univ of S MS 1985; NTE for Speech Comm Cert; *cr:* Teacher Jackson Ind Sch Dist 1966-68, French Camp Acad 1983-89, Channelview Ind Sch Dist 1969-70, Deer Park Ind Sch Dist 1989-; *ai:* French Camp Acad Beta Club & Class Spon; Drama Dir of Plays; Staff Dev & Lib Comm; MS STAR Teacher 1988; *home:* 3819 Washington Pasadena TX 77503

MIDDLETON, LUTHER CLAY, Asst Principal for Instruction; *b:* Brady, TX; *m:* Mary Lou Dodds; *c:* Courtney, Natalie; *ed:* (BS) Eng/Speech, Hardin-Simmons Univ 1967; (MS) Admin, Univ Houston-Victoria 1985; TX Provisional Teaching & Mid Management Certificates; *cr:* Rdng/Eng Teacher Coliad Mid Sch 1967-72; Eng/Speech Teacher Crain Intermediate Sch 1972-85; Asst Prin Howell Intermediate Sch 1985-; *ai:* TX Teacher Appraisal System Advisory Cncl; Goliad Local St Teachers Assn Pres 1971-72; Mid Coast Assn of Supervision & Curr Dev Pres 1988-89; Article Published; *office:* Howell Intermediate Sch 2502 Fannin Dr Victoria TX 77902

MIDDLETON, MARGARET ANN, English Teacher; *b:* Pine Bluff, AR; *m:* Edward C.; *c:* Beth, Jerry, Susan, Wendy; *ed:* (BA) Eng, MS Coll 1963; (MED) Scndry Ed/Eng Concentration, Francis Marion Coll 1989; *cr:* 7th Grade Teacher Oxford Elem Sch 1963-64; 8th Grade Eng Teacher Millbrook Elem Sch 1964-65; Eng Teacher St Johns HS 1986-; *ai:* Team Coord; Project REACH; Jr Classical League Adv; NCTE, SC Cncl Teachers of Eng 1987-; Palmetto St Teachers Assn 1989-; Jack & Jill Pre-K Sch of Camp Pendleton Bd Chm 1975-76; Camp Pendleton Day Care Center Bd Vice Chm 1975-77; Naval Construction Battalion Center Chapel Religious Ed Dir 1977-79; Naval Officers Wifes Club Pres 1984-85; Project REACH Grants; Darlington Writing Project; *office:* St Johns HS 545 Spring St Ext Darlington SC 29532

MIDDLETON, ROSALIE ROW, 6th Grade Teacher; *b:* Tulsa, OK; *m:* Whitwell Newton; *c:* William W., John R., James F.; *ed:* (BA) Elem Ed, W GA Coll 1961; *cr:* 1st Grade Teacher Mt Olive Elem 1961-65; 6th Grade Teacher Donelson Chrstn Acad 1981-; *office:* Donelson Chrstn Acad 3151 Stafford Dr Nashville TN 37214

MIDDLETON, SANDRA SUE, Third Grade Teacher; *b:* Plymouth, IN; *m:* John A.; *c:* Susan Terpstra, Kelly Lynch; *ed:* (BS) Elem Ed, Otterbein Coll 1965; (MS) Elem Ed, Purdue Univ 1977; *cr:* Elem Teacher Culver Cmmty Schls 1967-; *ai:* 3rd Grade Teacher of Gifted & Talented; Church Choir; *home:* 17441 16th Rd Culver IN 46511

MIDDLETON, WANDA BREWSTER, Language Arts/Speech Teacher; *b:* Moran, TX; *m:* Don A.; *c:* Michael; *ed:* (BS) Scndry Ed, Univ of North TX 1959; (MS) Adm & Supervision, TX Womans Univ 1980; *cr:* Teacher Odessa TX ISD 1959-67, Jefferson CTU ISD 1967-68, Carrollton ISD 1968-78, Mesquite ISD 1978-; *ai:* Spon Natl Jr Honor Society; Mesquite Educl Assn 1978-; *home:* 3012 Manchester Mesquite TX 75150

MIDEY, MICHAEL JOHN, 7th-8th Grade Science Teacher; *b:* Seneca Falls, NY; *m:* Mary A. St Thomas; *c:* Sean A. Roulan; *ed:* (BA) Environmental Stud, Alfred Univ 1982; (MS) Cmptr Literacy Ed, Nazareth Coll 1990; *cr:* 7th/8th Grade Sci/Cmptr Teacher Romulus Cntrl Sch 1984-; *ai:* Ski, Cmptr Club Adv; Technology Advisory, Effective Schls Comms; Natl Youth Sports Coaches Assn 1989-.

MIDKIFF, RICHARD NORMAN, Mathematics Department Teacher; *b:* Midland, TX; *m:* Rebecca Mattingly; *c:* Greg, Robert, Laura; *ed:* (BS) Elem Ed, Stephen F Austin Univ 1972; *cr:* 5th/6th Grade Teacher Harker Heights Elem 1972-83; 6th Grade Math Teacher Nolan Mid Sch 1983-; *ai:* Nolan Effective Sch Team Trainer; TX St Teachers Assn; Killeen Daily Hearld Outstanding Teacher Awd 1989.

MIDURA, PATRICIA MULHALL, Mass Media Chair/Lit Teacher; *b:* Utica, NY; *m:* Edmund Michael; *c:* Christopher, Jennifer, Jonathan, Abigail; *ed:* (BA) Utica Coll of Syracuse 1960; (MA) Speech Comm, Penn St Univ 1965; (MA) Mass Comm, Amer Univ Cairo 1979; Working Towards Doctorate in Policy Stud, Univ of MD Baltimore Cty; *cr:* Sr Lecturer Towson St Univ; Coll Writing Teacher Amer Univ Cairo 1977-78; Eng His Teacher Cairo Amer Coll 1978-80; Eng/His Teacher/Moderator of Gifted Gulliver Preparatory Sch 1980-85; Media Moderator/Eng Teacher Maryvale Preparatory Sch 1985-; *ai:* Yrbk & Newspaper Moderator; Long Range Planning Comm Faculty Mem; Assn of Ind Schls 1980-; Assn Teachers of Eng; *office:* Maryvale Preparatory Sch 11300 Falls Rd Brooklandville MD 21022

MIEDEMA, ANDREW HENRY, Counselor; *b:* Hospers, IA; *m:* Joan Van Leeuwen; *c:* Brenda, Barry, Robert, Bonnie, Bradley; *ed:* (AA) Ed, Northwestern Jr Coll 1951; (AB) Scndry Ed, Calvin Coll 1957; (MA) Ed Psych & Guidance, Univ of SD 1970; KS St Univ; Univ of MN; *cr:* Teacher Western Chrstn HS 1957-66; Prin Southwest Chrstn HS 1966-68; Cnslr Unity Chrstn HS 1968-76; Maurice-Orange Cty Jr HS 1976-; *ai:* NWIPGA 1963-79; Teachers Alliance Pres 1963-66; Church Cncl Elder 1971-73; 1985-87; Sch Bd Pres 1963-66; 3 Grants Study/Research Te Aching Disadvantaged Youth; *home:* RR 1 Alton IA 51003

MIEFERT, DIANNE WEBER, Third Grade Teacher; *b:* Meadville, PA; *m:* John F. Jr.; *ed:* (BS) Ed, Ashland Univ 1972; Grad Stud; *cr:* 4th Grade Teacher Stadium Elem 1972-75; 3rd Grade Teacher Brinkerhoff 1975-; *ai:* Faculty Advisory Cncl; Grade Card Comm Chairperson; Mansfield Support Ed Assn (Building Rep, Past Elections Chairperson) 1972-; Amer Assn of Univ Women; Mansfield Art Center; *office:* Brinkerhoff Elem Sch 240 Euclid Ave Mansfield OH 44903

MIELNIK, GEORGEANN PASSIALIS, 7th Grade Teacher; *b:* Chicago, IL; *m:* Matthew; *ed:* (BA) Sociology, Rosary Coll 1975; (MA) Rdng, NE IL Univ 1980; *cr:* Kndgtn Teacher Holy Rosary Coll 1975-77; 1st/2nd/5th/6th Grade Teacher St Genevieve 1977-86; 5th-8th Grade Teacher St Bede 1986-87; 7th Grade Teacher Northwood Jr HS 1987-; *ai:* Dist 200 Rdng Coord; Mid Sch Action Team; ASCD 1988-; Assn of IL Mid Schls 1987-; Grad Merit Schlsps NE IL Univ; Dist 200 Recognition Awd 1988; *office:* Northwood Jr HS 2121 N Seminary Woodstock IL 60098

MIER, JOE A., Chemistry Teacher; *b:* Santa Fe, NM; *m:* Carmela C. De Baca; *c:* Jeremy A., Kimberly M.; *ed:* (BS) Bio, Coll of Santa Fe 1972; (MS) Chem/Bio, Highlands Univ 1980; Cmptr Ed, Univ of NM; *cr:* Chem Teacher Santa Fe HS 1972-; Curr Coord Santa Fe Public Schls 1978-; Sci Dept Chm Santa Fe HS 1986-; *ai:* Scndry Sci Curr, Sci/Math Center, Los Alamos Stu Prgm Coord; Health & N Cntrl Evaluation Steering Comm Mem; Key Club Spon; ASCD 1989-; NSTA 1984-85; NEA Building Rep 1972-; Elks (Exalted Ruler 1988-89, Trustee 1989-); Cath Church Usher 1988-; Exceptional Chem Teacher Amer Chemical Society; Nom Twice Outstanding Teacher NM; *home:* 2209 Brilliante Santa Fe NM 87505

MIESNER, STAN, Social Studies Teacher; *b:* Cole Camp, MO; *m:* Elizabeth Winters; *c:* Stan, Scott, Chris King; *ed:* (BS) His, Drury Coll 1971; (MA) His, SW MO St Univ 1976; Grad Seminar, Freedoms Fnd 1985; *cr:* Part Time His Instr SW MO St Univ 1978-79, 1988; Gifted Prgm Coord 1979-82, Soc Stud Teacher 1971- Reed Jr HS; *ai:* Reed Jr HS Intramural Prgm Spon 1972-88; NEA, NCSS; Fellowship Ind Stud Hum Cncl for Basic Ed 1989; *office:* Reed Jr HS 2000 N Lyon Springfield MO 65803

MIESNIK, ALICE J., English Instructor; *b:* Wilmington, DE; *ed:* (BA) Eng Teaching, Univ of DE 1981; (MA) Eng, Villanova Univ 1988; Certificate Prgm Cmptr Programming; *cr:* Eng Dept Chairperson Immaculate Conception HS 1981-86; Eng Instr Marish HS 1987-; Eng Adjunct Professor Montclair St Coll 1987-; *ai:* Academic Quiz Bowl Moderator; Music Club; Writing for Coll Bound Lab; Ski Club; Natl Cncl Teachers of Eng 1981-; Published Pamphlet; Taught in Egypt 1989; Archdiocese Newark Scndry Eng Teacher Lecturer 1986.

MIETUS, MARYANN, 4th Grade Teacher; *b:* New Bedford, MA; *ed:* (BS) Early Chldhd Ed, Boston St Coll 1977; *cr:* 4th Grade Teacher 1977-; VP 1987- St Stanislaus Sch; *ai:* Suffolk Cty Jr Miss Prgm; Scholastic Achievement Judge; NCEA; Nom 1989 Miriam

Joseph Farrell Awd Distinguished Teachers Spon By NCEA; *office:* St Stanislaus Sch 181 Chestnut St Chelsea MA 02150

MIHOCKO, JANICE N., French Teacher; *b:* Chicago, IL; *m:* David J.; *c:* Beth, Cory, Emily; *ed:* (BA) Fr, Wheaton Coll 1969; Eng Minor, W MI Univ 1987; *cr:* Fr Teacher Ipswich HS 1970-73; Substitute Teacher Quincy Cmmty Schls 1983-86; Eng Teacher Franklin Adult Ed 1983-86; Fr/Eng Teacher Hamilton Cmmty SchLs 1986-; *ai:* Fr Club Spon; HS Academic Super Bowl Spon & Eng Coach; *office:* Hamilton Cmmty Schls R 1 Box 208 Hamilton IN 46742

MIKEL, JEFFREY TODD, Elem Phys Ed Teacher; *b:* Kirksville, MO; *m:* Chris Ann Reese; *c:* Brett, Ashley; *ed:* (BSE) Phys Ed, NE MO 1984; *cr:* Driver Ed/Phys Ed/Health Teacher Kirksville R-III Sr HS 1985-87; Phys Ed Teacher Kirksville Ray Miller Elem 1987-; *ai:* Head Coach Var Girls Bsktbl, Girls Sftbl, Boys Bsbl; Kirksville R-III Welfare Comm 1989-; NEA 1989-; MSTA 1985-89; City of Kirksville Traffic Comm 1988-89; *office:* Kirksville R-III Sch 1300 S Cottage Grove Kirksville MO 63501

MIKES, JANICE (COATS), English Teacher; *b:* Alamo, GA; *m:* Willie G.; *c:* Marshall R. Troup, Martisse R. Troup, Mickey, Micheal; *ed:* (BA) Fr, Albany St Coll 1971; (MS) Eng, GA St Univ 1976; Leadership Seminars Marquette & Atlanta Univ; Advanced Placement Teachers Seminar Univ of Cntrl FL; *cr:* Eng Teacher Terrell Cty Schls 1972; Eng Specialist Upward Bound Prgm 1974-79; Curr Coord Upward Bound Spec Services Prgm 1979-83; Eng Teacher Terrell Cty Schls 1983-84, Albany St Coll 1984-, Monroe HS 1984-; *ai:* Academic Bowl Spon; Debate Coach; Annual Writing Festival Coord; Writing Consultant; Alpha Kappa Alpha SAT Coord; Upward Bounds Teacher of Yr 1984, 1986, 1989; Monroe HS Teacher of Yr 1985; Terrell Cty HS Teacher of Yr 1983; *home:* 1215 Augusta Dr Albany GA 31707

MIKESELL, CHRISTINE LOUISE, Mathematics Teacher; *b:* Hamburg, NY; *m:* Carl Richard; *c:* John D.; *ed:* (BS) Math, (BA) Eng, Western St Coll 1973; (MS) Scndry Rdng Ed, Univ of CO Denver 1985; Human Resource Dev; *cr:* Math/Eng Teacher Centennial Jr HS 1973-78, Ken Caryl Jr HS 1980-; Math Teacher E Arvada Jr HS 1980-82, Ken Caryl Jr HS 1983-84, Columbine Sr HS 1985-; *ai:* Cty Process Consultation Cadre Facilitator; Cmptr Use, Stu Needs & Advisement Comm; N Cntrl Sub Comm Chm; Sr Class Spon; Co-Chair Annual All Sch Retreat; NCTM Mem 1989-; Volunteer for Arapahoe Cty Advocates for Children 1988-; Teacher of Yr Columbine Sr Staff 1989-; *office:* Columbine Sr HS 6201 S Pierce St Littleton CO 80123

MIKETA, CONSTANCE GENOVA, Mathematics Teacher; *b:* Pueblo, CO; *m:* Robert L.; *c:* Terrianne Drake, Tina, Rob; *ed:* (BA) Math, Univ of N CO 1961; (MA) Cmptr Ed, Lesley Coll 1987; Grad Stud Adams St Coll, Western St Coll, Univ of S CO; *cr:* Math Teacher Central HS 1961-62, Alamosa HS & Jr HS 1962-63, 1972-73, Pueblo Cty HS 1965-, Univ of S CO 1989-; *ai:* Chrldr Spon, Math Club Spon; CO Teachers of Math 1975-; CO Ed Assn 1961-; Pueblo Cty Ed Assn 1961-; NEA 1961-; Okolitza Tamburitzans Costumes 1975-; Shrine of St Thearse Catechism Teacher 1976-89; *home:* 28 Loyola Ln Pueblo CO 81005

MIKLES, CHRISTINE METHORN, Math Teacher/Coach; *b:* Annapolis, MD; *m:* Scott Allen; *c:* Allen, Andrew; *ed:* (BS) Math, Cal Poly San Luis Obispo 1972; Teaching Credential K-12, CA Luth Coll 1976; Tri Ctys Math Project; Assertive Disc Cmptr Classes; Equals; Involvement in Math A&B; Madelein Hunter Courses; *cr:* 5th-8th Grade Teacher St Thomas Aquinas Sch 1972-76; 5th-6th Grade Teacher El Rio Sch 1976-79; 9th-12th Grade Teacher Ventura HS 1984-; *ai:* Soccer, Swimming, Vlybl, Tennis Coach; Non Traditional Career Day for Girls; NCTM, CMC 1988-; VCMC 1989-, Teacher of Yr; AYSO (Regional Commissioner 1986-89, Bd of Dir/Division Dir 1984-86); NAWIC Mem 1982-85; Tri Ctys Math Fellow UCSB; Mentor Teacher VUSD; *office:* Ventura HS 2155 E Main St Ventura CA 93002

MIKLESH, ROBERT LOUIS, Biology Teacher; *b:* Ironwood, MI; *m:* Sandra Jean Aho; *c:* Robert M., James W.; *ed:* (AA) Teaching, B Gogebic Comm Coll 1967; (BS) Bio/His, 1969, (MA) Elem Ed, 1973 N MI Univ; *cr:* Jr HS Teacher 1969-78, Bio Teacher 1978- Ironwood Area Schls; *ai:* HS Var Bsbl Coach.

MIKODA, ROSLYN ANNE, Second Grade Teacher; *b:* Sarasota, FL; *ed:* (BS) Elem Ed, FL St Univ 1975; (MS) Admin/ Supervision, 1979, (MS) Early Chldhd, Troy St Univ 1981; *cr:* Classroom Teacher West Bainbridge Elem 1976-79, Thompkins Kndgtn 1979-82; Jr Coll Instr Wallace Coll 1983; Classroom Teacher Lisenby Elem 1982-; *ai:* Chairperson for Schl Renewal Project 1989-; NEA, AEA, OEA 1979-; Alpha Delta Kappa 1988-; Kappa Delta Pi 1975-; GSA Brownie Leader 1989; Friends of Lib 1980-; Teacher of Yr 1988; Finalist in AL Teacher of Yr 1988; Book Published; *office:* Lisenby Elem Sch 800 Faust St Ozark AL 36360

MIKOVICH, THEODORE J., Fifth Grade Teacher; *b:* Nesquehoning, PA; *m:* Joanne Marouchoc; *c:* Gregory D., Christopher A.; *ed:* (BS) Elem Ed, 1967, (MED) Elem Ed, 1970 E Stroudsburg Univ; Ed, Christ The Savior Orthodox Seminary; *cr:* 5th Grade Teacher Salisbury Township Sch Dist 1967-; *ai:* Salisbury Ed Assn (Pres, Chief Negotiator) 1970-83; Suicide Hot Line Volunteer 1985; Firefighter Volunteer 1974-85; *home:* 5261 Bow Ln Emmaus PA 18104

MIKSIC, ROBERT MICHAEL, English Teacher; *b:* Milwaukee, WI; *ed:* (BA) Eng, Dominican Coll 1972; *cr:* 7th/8th Grade Teacher St Jerome Sch 1972-75; 6th-8th Grade Eng Teacher Stone Bank Sch 1975-; *ai:* Sch Newspaper; Dramatics; Outdoor Environmental Ed Coord; *home:* 6470 Bayview Rd Oconomowoc WI 53066

MIKULASCH, MICHAEL PETER, Social Studies Teacher; *b:* Elkhorn, WI; *ed:* (BSE) His, UW Whitewater 1983; *cr:* Substitute Teacher Lake Geneva Sch Dist 1983-84; Ger/Soc Stud Teacher Badger HS 1984-85; Substitute Teacher Lake Geneva Sch Dist 1985-86; Soc Stud/Ger Teacher Catholic Cntrl HS 1986-; *ai:* Coach Girls Var Bsktbl; *office:* Catholic Cntrl HS 148 Mc Henry St Burlington WI 53105

MIKULEC, JO ANN MARIE (GRAZIANO), English Teacher; *b:* Albany, NY; *m:* Robert A.; *c:* Robert, Gregory, Lisa; *ed:* (BS) Elem Ed, Coll of St Rose 1964; Hard of Hearing Courses; *cr:* Teacher of Hard of Hearing 1964-65, Spec Ed Teacher 1965-66 Albany PubLic Schls; Eng Teacher Christ the King 1983-; *ai:* 8th Grade Adv; Ronald Mc Donald House Bd Mem 1983-89; *office:* Christ The King Schl 2 Lamarck Dr Snyder NY 14226

MIKULENCAK, MARSHA OVERTON, 8th Grade English Teacher; *b:* Temple, TX; *m:* Lanny W.; *c:* Marissa, Brance; *ed:* (BA) Eng, Mary Harding Baylor 1969; Gifted and Talented; *cr:* 12th Grade Eng Teacher Georgetown HS 1969-70; 8th Grade Eng Teacher Bonham Jr HS 1970-74; Beverly Hills Int 1974-; *ai:* Spon of Sch Newspaper; Spon of Schl Yrbk; Co Chm of Awds Assem; Schls Publ Person; NCTE; Delta Kappa Gamma Sec 1978-; TX Assn of Gifted and Talented; Teacher of Month - 1st of Dist Sep 1984; Places Career Level Initial Yr; *home:* 10606 Sagevale Ln Houston TX 77089

MILAM, DALE ERIC, Math/Sci/Religion/Phys Ed; *b:* Takoma Park, MD; *m:* Darla Jean; *ed:* (BA) Bio/Chem/Scndry Ed, Columbia Union Coll 1984; *cr:* 7th-10th Grade Math/Sci/Phys Ed/Religion Teacher Eastern Shore Acad 1984-; *ai:* Work with Local Pathfinder Club, Intermural Sports, Backpacking & Birdwatching Trips, Running Club; Bsktbl CoaCh; Cmmty Service Projects; Eastern Shore Acad Athletic Field Was Named for Me; *office:* Eastern Shore Acad RD 1 Box 54-B Sudlersville MD 21668

MILANA, VIOLA P., Language Art Department Chair; *b:* Vineland, NJ; *c:* Linda Errickson, John A., Laurie A., Robert; *ed:* (AA) Cumberland Cty Coll 1974; (BA) Elem Ed, 1977, (MA) Elem Ed, 1983 Glassboro St Coll; Post Baccalaureate Certificate in Math; *cr:* 6th Grade Teacher Reber Sch 1976-77; 3rd-5th Grades Teacher Rossi Sch 1977-81; 6th/8th Grades Teacher Memorial Intermediate Sch 1981-; *ai:* Governors Awd Recipient Comm Mem; Ticket Person Sch Play; Ticket Chairperson 8th Grade Dinner Dance; Lang Art Core Curr Comm; Rdng Cncl of S NJ 1985-; NJ Cncl Teachers of Eng 1987-89; Alpha Delta Kappa Sargeant at Arms 1986-; Singing Ambassadors 1984-; Recipient of Governors Teacher Recognition Awd 1986; *office:* Memorial Intermediate Sch 424 S Main Rd Vineland NJ 08360

MILANT, JACQUELINE, Third Grade Teacher; *b:* Milwaukee, WI; *ed:* (BSED) Elem Ed, WI St Univ Whitewater 1970; (MBA) Bus Admin, Ca St Univ Fullerton 1985; *cr:* 2nd-4th Grade Teacher Armstrong Elem 1970-78; 3rd Grade Teacher Mendoza Elem 1978-79, Decker Elem 1979-; *ai:* Pomona Dist Mentor Teacher 1989-; NEA, Associated Pomona Teachers 1970-; Literacy Volunteers of America 1990; CTIIP Grant; Whos Who of American Women 1983-84; Pomona Candidate Teacher of Yr.

MILBURN, DEBRA GIANNINY, Biology/Earth Science Teacher; *b:* Charlottesville, VA; *m:* Donald S.; *c:* Ashley P.; *ed:* (BS) Bio/Botany, VA Polytechnic Inst & St Univ 1978; Various Bio, Cmptr, Horticulture Courses, 1979-85; Educl Courses for MD Cert 1984-85; *cr:* Continuing Ed/Horticulture Teacher Garrett Comm Coll 1984-85; Earth Sci Teacher 1986, Bio/Earth Sci Teacher 1986- South Garrett HS; *ai:* Floral Designs Activity Classes; Faculty Soc Comm 1987-88; 10th Grade Adv 1986-87; Garrett Cty Teachers Assn, NEA 1986-87; Garrett Cty Teachers Fed, AFT, MD Bio Teachers Assn 1987-; St Pauls United Meth Church Admin Bd Mem 1990-; Nature Conservancy 1983-; Defenders of Animal Rights 1982-; *office:* Southern Garrett HS 1100 E Oak St Oakland MD 21550

MILBY, PATRICIA BELL, Senior Counselor; *b:* Greensburg, KY; *m:* Gordon E.; *c:* Tonya M. Wilson, Kathryn H.; *ed:* (BS) Voc Home Ec, Morehead St Univ 1968; (MA) Guidance, 1976, (Rank I) Counseling/Guidance, 1980 W KY Univ; *cr:* Home Ec Teacher Butler HS 1968-79; Cnslr Iroquois Mid Sch 1979-85, Pleasure Ridge 1986-; *office:* Pleasure Ridge Park HS 5901 Greenwood Rd Louisville KY 40258

MILES, ANNETTE (BIGBEE), English Teacher; *b:* Springfield, MO; *:* Steven C.; *ed:* (BSED) Eng, Southwest MO St Univ 1986; *cr:* Eng Teacher Coll Heights Chrstn Sch 1986-88/1989-; Eastvue Baptist Acad 1988-; *ai:* Sr Class Spon; *home:* 1819 Bird Joplin MO 64804

MILES, GERALDINE SYKES, Sixth Grade Teacher; *b:* Elams, NC; *m:* Albert; *ed:* (BS) Elem Ed, Elizabeth City St Univ 1965; (MSED) Educl Admin/Supervision VA St Univ 1980; *cr:* 6th/7th Grade Teacher Garysburg Elem Sch 1966-72; Dean Stu Affair St Pauls Coll 1972-76; 6th Grade Teacher Meherrin-Powellton Elem 1976-; *ai:* Meherrin-Powellton Sch Advisory Comm; Delta Sigma Theta (Pres, VP); Univ Women General Alumni Assn Elizabeth City St Univ Recording Secy 1979; NEA 1976-; Intnl Toastmistress Secy 1976; Brunswick Educl Assn 1976-; United Bd for Coll Dev 1980-81; Patillo Chapel Baptist Church (Youth Group Adv, Secy); *home:* Star Rt Box 20 Henrico NC 27842

MILES, JANET FINCH, Third Grade Teacher; *b:* Russellville, KY; *m:* Nathaniel; *c:* Natalie Nicole, Miles, Paula Denise, Miles; *ed:* (BS) Ed 1977, (MA) Ed, 1980, Rank I Ed, 1982 Austin Peay St Univ; *cr:* Teacher Olmstead Elem Sch 1977-; *ai:* Phys Ed/ Health/Safety Textbook Comm; Stu Evaluation/Grading Comm; NAACP 1982-; Human Rights Commission Secy 1982-; *home:* 3055 S Beauchamp Rd Russellville KY 42276

MILES, JOHN RAYMOND, Math Dept; *b:* Utica, NY; *m:* Pamela Genest; *c:* Jason, Christopher, Jennifer; *ed:* Psych, SUNY Potsdam 1970; Grad Work SUNY Geneseo 1972; *cr:* K-5th Grade Teacher 1970, Head Teacher 1978, Curr Coord/Math Teacher Penn Yan Cntrl Schls; *ai:* Asst Boys Var Bsktbl & Girls Modified Bsktbl Coach; Penn Yan Dept Secy 1978-; Rochester Bd of Officials 1978-.

MILES, OMA VELMA, Team Leader; *b:* Valdosta, GA; *m:* John; *c:* John Le Vell; *ed:* (BS) Elem Ed, 1977, (MA) Mid Sch, 1980 Valdosta St Coll; Working on Six Yr Degree Mid Sch; *cr:* Team Leader Lowndes Mid Sch 1980-; *ai:* Stu Cncl Adv; Washington DC Trip, Family Day & His Club Spon; Libr Comm; Lowndes Assn of Educators Pres 1980-81; GA Assn of Educators, NEA Mem 1977-; GSA Adv 1985-88; United Way Group Leader 1988-; Camp Relitso VP 1977-, Cmmty Service 1981; European Countries Study Tour; Presidents Awd for Adv to Youth; GA Sch Bell Awd; *home:* Rt 6 Box 428 Valdosta GA 31601

MILES, REBECCA HARRISON, First Grade Teacher; *b:* Paintsville, KY; *m:* James R.; *c:* James B.; *ed:* (BA) Elem Ed, Belmont Coll 1968; (MA) Elem Ed, Univ of Northern CO 1976; *cr:* 2nd Grade Teacher Lakeside Elem 1968-69; Primary Grade Teacher Goodlettsville Elem 1969-; *ai:* Excl Teacher Grade 1; Chairperson Multiculture; Chairperson Rdng Comm; Amer Ed Comm; UTP Teacher of Yr 1988; Cum Laude 1968; Delta Kappa Gamma Teachers Sorority 1989-; Awd Life-Time Mbrshp Parent-Teacher Assn 1990; *office:* Goodlettsville Elem School 514 Donald Ave Goodlettsville TN 37072

MILES-HUTCHESON, BEATRICE, Physical Education Teacher; *b:* Crane, TX; *m:* George E.; *c:* Ronald, Crystol; *ed:* (BA) Phys Ed, Sul Ross St Univ 1971; Working Towards Masters Counseling, TX Women Univ; License Pract Cnslr; *cr:* Phys Ed Teacher Hutcheson Jr HS 1971-; *ai:* Head Coach 9th Grade Bsktbl, 8th Grade Vlybl, 7th-9th Grade Track; TSTA, NEA; Mt Olive Baptist Church; *home:* 1811 Guenivere Arlington TX 76014

MILHON-CRESS, CANDACE LYNN, Assistant Principal; *b:* Bloomington, IN; *m:* Connie E.; *ed:* (BS) Elem Ed, IN Univ 1975; (MAT) Elem Ed, De Pauw 1978; (PHD) Ed Admin, IN St 1990; *cr:* Teacher Mill Creek Sch Corp 1975-87; Grad Fellow IN St Univ 1987-88; Consultant IN Dept of Ed 1988-89; Asst Prin MSD of Wayne Township 1990-; *ai:* Phi Delta Kappa 1987-; IN Assn of Elem Mid Sch Prin Dist, NAESP 1989-; Friends of Lib 1990; Fred Swalls Awd; *office:* MSD Wayne Township 3820 W Bradbury Indianapolis IN 46241

MILLARD, GARY A., Chemistry/Math Teacher; *b:* Yakima, WA; *ed:* (BS) Chem, WA St Univ 1987; *cr:* Teacher Juanita HS 1987-; *ai:* Track & Field Cross Cntry Head Coach; Soph Cabinet Adv; Lake Washington Ed Assn, WA Ed Assn, NEA 1987-; *office:* Juanita HS 10601 NE 132nd Kirkland WA 98034

MILLEA, BETTY TINDALL, 3rd Grade Teacher; *b:* Graettinger, IA; *m:* Thomas; *c:* Tim, John, Mary, Mike, Dan, Katie; *ed:* (BA) Elem Ed, Buena Vista Coll 1977; Rdng Endorsement; *cr:* 2nd Grade Teacher Lincoln Cntrl Sch 1953-55; 1st-4th Grade Teacher Wallingford Sch 1955-56; 3rd Grade Teacher 1969-70/1969; Chapter I Rdng Teacher 197 Graettinger Cmmty; *ai:* Rdng Cncl Secy 1976-78; IA Rdng Cncl & Mem 1974-; Womans Club; Catholic Daughters Grand Regent 1980-82; Rosary Society Pres 1969; *home:* 306 Cedar St Graettinger IA 51342

MILLER, A. NELL, English Teacher; *b:* Louisburg, NC; *m:* Gilbert; *c:* Jeri Vaughn, David Vaughn; *ed:* (BA) Eng, Barry Coll 1971; (MA) Eng, Barry Univ 1989; *cr:* Teacher Yale Sch 1977-79, Madison Jr HS 1979-85, Hialeah Miami Lakes Sr HS 1985-; *ai:* North Dade Lioness Club Pres 1974-75, 1982-83, Pres Golden Chain Governors Appreciation Awd; *home:* 6901 SW 38th St Miramar FL 33023

MILLER, AGATHA LOUISE, 6th Grade Teacher; *b:* Norfolk, VA; *ed:* (BS) Elem Ed, Univ WI Platteville 1969; Grad Stud; *cr:* 5th Grade Teacher Hickory Grove Sch 1969-79; 6th Grade Teacher Orchard Lane Sch 1979-; *ai:* Staff Dev Comm Mem; WEA, NEA 1969-; Delta Kappa Gamma 1986-89; *office:* Orchard Lane Sch 2015 S Sunnyslope Rd New Berlin WI 53151

MILLER, ALAN EUGENE, Social Science Teacher; *b:* North Platte, NE; *m:* Kristy; *c:* Talia; *ed:* (BA) Soc Sci, Kearney St Coll 1982; *ai:* Girls Vlybl, Boys Bsktbl, Track Head Coach; Lettermans Club Spon; NSEA Pres 1986; *home:* Box 2 Tryon NE 69167

MILLER, ALICE BLACKMON, 5th Grade Teacher; *b:* Haw River, NC; *m:* Lenis J.; *c:* James, Neal, Barry, Jeffrey; *ed:* (BA) Elem Ed - Cum Laude, Elon Coll 1968; (MED) K-12th Grade Rdng, Univ of NC Greenboro 1977; *cr:* 5th Grade Teacher N Graham Elem 1969-; *ai:* Elem Task Force Alamance Cty 1989-; Sch Based Leadership & N Graham Budget Comm 1989-; Alamance Cty Assn of Educators, NC Assn Educators, NEA 1969-; Alpha Delta Kappa Sergeant at Arms 1987-88; N Graham Teacher of Yr 1973-74; Outstanding Elem Teacher America 1974; *home:* 1005 E Hanover Rd Graham NC 27253

MILLER, AMY (KIPP), Second Grade Teacher; *b:* Lincoln, NE; *m:* Don E.; *c:* Donnie St Pierce, Gregg, Judith L. Cynthia; *ed:* (BA) Elem Ed, Univ KS 1956; Certified-Remedial Rdng Stu; *cr:* 1st Grade Teacher Lincoln Sch 1956-57; 2nd Grade Teacher Doloris 1967-68, Rolla Public Sch 1980-; 6th Grade Teacher Newburg Elem 1969-70; Rolla Public Sch 1980-; *ai:* Delegate Treas Rolla Cmmty Teacher Assn; MO St Teachers Assn Delegate 1979-80; Kappa Kappa Iota Pres 1984-85; Episcopel Church Women; Cntrl Dist Square Dance Assn VP 1989-; Girls Town Federated Club Pres 1985-81; Recipient-Kappa Kappa Iota Schlsp; *home:* 1807 Belmont Ct Rolla MO 65401

MILLER, ANNIE BLACKWELL, Business Dept Chm/Teacher; *b:* Memphis, TN; *c:* Patricia Gay, Andrea, Carolyn; *ed:* (BA) Bus Ed, TN St Univ 1963; (MS) Counseling/Guidance, Chicago St Univ 1977; Information Word Processing, Speedwriting/ Superwrite Shorthand, Electronic Office Procedures; *cr:* Secy Chicago Amer Newspaper 1960-63; Substitute Teacher Chicago Public Schls 1964-67; Teacher Altgeld Elem Sch 1967-71; Bus Dept Chm Jones Metropolitan HS 1971- *ai:* 40-50-60 Typing Club; Faculty Fund Comm; Bulletin Bd Club; Prof Problems Advisory Comm; Bus Advisory Cncl; Chicago Bus Ed Assn 1976-; Chicago Area Alliance of Black Sch Educators 1990; United Negro Coll Fund 1981-; Chicago Teachers 1971-; AFT 1976-; Public Service; Adult Ed Univ of IL; *office:* Jones Metropolitan HS 606 S State St 606 S State St Chicago IL 60605

MILLER, BARBARA ANN FEAST, Fifth Grade Teacher; *b:* Paducah, KY; *m:* Jerry Lee; *c:* Teresa Bishop, Peggy Wright, Jennifer Garrison; *ed:* (AA) Ed, Univ of KY 1971;(BS) Elem Ed/ Soc Work, 1973; (MA) Ed-Cum Laude, 1980 Murray St Univ; *cr:* 2nd Grade Teacher Hendron Elem Sch 1973, Farley Elem Sch; 6th Grade Teacher Farley Elem Sch; 5th Grade Teacher Reidland Elem Sch 1973-1990; *ai:* Spon 4-H Speech Contest Annually; Womens Health Issues Comm; Kappa Delta Pi Chapter Delta Omega 1972-; NEA 1973-; KY Ed Assn 1973-; MC Cracken Cty Ed Assn 1973-; United Meth Church Martha Group Life Mem 1986; Reidbud Elem PTA Pres/Life Mem 1966; *home:* 301 Riverside Dr Paducah KY 42003

MILLER, BARBARA JEAN, Teacher of Handicapped; *b:* Denver, CO; *ed:* (BA) Elem Ed/Spec Ed EMR, 1978, (MA) Learning Disabilities, 1988 Univ of Northern CO; *cr:* 5th-6th Grade Teacher Ralston Elem 1978-79; 1st/2nd/4th/5th Grade Teacher 1979-88, E H Resource Teacher 1988- Warder Elem; *ai:* Stud Teacher Supervising Teacher; Building Level Consultant; Intervention & Prevention Team 1988-; Writing Wkshp Publishing Center; Jefferson Cty Sci Inservice Leader 1983-88; Curr Revision & Inservice Sci Trng 1987-89; Intnl Rdng Assn, CO Cncl of Intnl Rdng Assn 1980-; CO Cncl for Exceptional Children (Regional Odyssey Rep 1989-) 1988-; Jr League of Denver 1989-; Arvada Cmmty Zoning Study 1987-88; N Seffco Cmmty Band 1984-; Cherry Hills Cmmty Church 1990; Denver Museum of Natural His (Mem, Volunteer) 1987-; AIDS Ed for Elem Stus Jefferson Cty Schls; Developed & Taught Course Through CO Sch of Mines; Jefferson Cty Prevention Task Force Awd; Warder Team Mem; *office:* Warder Elem Sch 7840 Carr Dr Arvada CO 80005

MILLER, BARBARA VINCIQUERRA, HS Special Education Teacher; *b:* Cleveland, OH; *m:* Lawrence R.; *c:* Thomas R., Raelyn; *ed:* (BS) Health/Phys Ed/Recreation, 1971, (MA) Spec Ed, 1975 OH Univ; *cr:* Phys Dev Spec Teacher Athens Cty 1971-74; Teaching Asst OH Univ 1974-75; Spec Ed Teacher Athens Cty 1975-78, Bonner Cty 1978-85, Riverside Sch Dist 1976-; *ai:* Sr Class Adv; Stu Assistance Team; Curr Comm; Riverside Ed Assn Building Rep 1988-; Riverside Outstanding Teacher 1989; Bonner Cty Outstanding Teacher 1985; *office:* Riverside Sch Dist 416 Rt 1 Box 277 Chattaroy WA 99003

MILLER, BETTY JANE, English Teacher; *b:* Kline, SC; *c:* Burton R.; *ed:* (BS) Scndry Ed/Eng/His, Newberry Coll 1959; FL St Univ, Rollins Coll, Winter Park, SC St Coll Orangeburg, Univ of SC Columbia; *cr:* Lexington Elem 1959-60; Springfield Elem 1960-61; Park Avenue Elem Sch 1961-62; Allendale-Fairfax HS 1963-67; Bamberg-Ehrhardt HS 1969-71; Andrew Jackson Acad 1971-81; Smoaks Mid Sch 1981-83; Wade Hampton HS 1983-; *ai:* NEA, SC Ed Assn, NCTE; SC Historical Society; Natl Society US Daughters of 1812 (Historian 1973-76, 1981-82, Corresponding Secy 1976-79); Natl Society Daughters of Amer Revolution (SC St Historian 1979-82, SC St Chm Public Relations 1982-85); FL Merit Teacher 1963; STAR Teacher Bamberg Ehrhardt 1971; *office:* Wade Hampton HS Airport Rd Hampton SC 29824

MILLER, BETTY JEAN, English Department Chairperson; *b:* Union Springs, AL; *m:* Kenneth; *ed:* (BA) Eng, IL St Univ 1966; (MA) Eng, Chicago St Univ 1972; Chicago Bd of Ed Human Relations Courses, Improving Critical Thinking Skills, Proposal Writing; Modern Approaches to Literary Analysis Univ of Chicago; *cr:* ECIA Summer Coord Chicago Bd of Ed 1984; Curr Specialist IL Bd of Ed 1985-86; Eng Teacher Lindblom HS 1966-; Curr Writer Chicago Bd of Ed 1985-; *ai:* Sch Newspaper Co-Adv; NHS Consultant; Writing Across Curr Comm; Chicago Area Rdng Assn & Intnl Rdng Assn 1980-; Trinity Luth Church (Mem, Cncl mem 1984-) 1975-; Univ of Chicago Summer Seminar Fellowship; Chicago Bd of Ed Orals Bd for Cert Interviewer; St of IL Bd for Eng Cert Comm Mem; Chicago Public Schls Writing Conference Speaker; *office:* Lindblom Tech HS 6130 S Wolcott Ave Chicago IL 60636

MILLER, BEVERLY JOHNSON, 1st Grade Teacher; *b:* Rawlins, WY; *m:* Joseph Paul; *c:* Matthew, Max; *ed:* (BA) Elem Ed, 1974, (MED) Ed Admin, 1985 Univ of WY; Post Grad Stud Technology, Media, Elem Ed; *cr:* K-2nd Grade Teacher Mountain View Elem Sch 1974-; *ai:* Technology, Criterion Reference Testing, Plans & Priorities Curr Comm; Teacher Comm Bd; Sch Screening, Technology, Wellness Building Comm; Carbon Cty Dist I Teachers Assn Treas 1974-; Intnl Rdng Assn NIE Chm 1982-; Delta Kappa Gamma (Secy, Treas) 1979-; 1st United Meth Church 1964-; BSA Den Leader 1989-; PTA 1976-; Sch Bd Recognition for Initiating Cmptr Logo & Walk to Learn Prgms; Spec Arts Festival & WY St Sci/Math Conference Presenter; *office:* Mountain View Elem Sch 11th & Birch St Rawlins WY 82301

MILLER, BILL, Junior High Science Teacher; *b:* San Antonio, TX; *m:* Dinah Patton; *c:* Ann, Lyle; *ed:* (BS) Ag/Animal Sci, 1970, (MS) Ag Industries, 1977 S IL Univ; Grad Stud Educl Admin; *cr:* Sci Teacher/Coach Sparta Comm Dist 1971-74, Anna Jr HS 1977-; *ai:* Jr HS Track & Bsbl Coach; NSTA 1977-; Phi Deta Kappa 1980-; SIL Alumni Assn 1977-; Elem K-8th Grade Dist Bd Mem; *home:* RR 2 Box 209 Makanda IL 62958

MILLER, BILL WAYNE, Biology Teacher; *b:* Columbus, TX; *m:* Dayna S. Newberry Miller; *c:* William C., Mary K.; *ed:* (BA) Scndry Ed, TX Luth Coll 1977; (MS) Admin Ed, Sam Houston St Univ 1982; *cr:* Bio Teacher/Coach Spring Woods HS 1977-85, Judson HS 1985-; *ai:* Asst Ftbl Coach; Head Bsbl Coach; Fellowship of Chrstn Athletes Spon; TX St Teachers Assn; TX HS Coachs Assn (Adv Bd Mem 1988) 1977-; TX HS Bsbl Coaches Assn Region VIII Dir 1990-; HS Bsbl San Antonio HS Bsbl Coach of Yr 1989; *home:* 960 West Coll New Braunfels TX 78130

MILLER, BOBBIE TOLLIVER, Language Arts Teacher; *b:* Bandy, VA; *c:* Letitia; *ed:* (BS) Eng Ed, VA Commonwealth Univ 1969; Grad Classes Radford Univ; Univ of VA; *cr:* 6th Grade Teacher Rivermont Elem Sch 1970-80; 6th Grade Lang Arts Teacher 1980-89, 7th Grade Lang Art Teacher 1989- Richlands Mid Sch; *ai:* Coach RMS Academic Competition Team; Co-Spon RMS Drama Club; Tazewell Ed Assn, VA Ed Assn &NEA 1970-; VA Mid Sch Assn 1987 *office:* Richlands Mid Sch Rt 460 Richlands VA 24641

MILLER, BONNIE RUTH (MAX), Fourth Grade Teacher; *b:* Sherman, TX; *m:* Bruce A.; *c:* Kevin, Danny, Rainee De La Garza; *ed:* (BA) Elem Ed, Austin Coll 1961; Lee Canters Assertive Discipline; Learning Inst Science on a Shoestring; Bill Hallorans Rdng 1989; *cr:* 1st/2nd Grade Teacher Howe ISD 1964-65; Kndgt Teacher Kern Valley Consolidated 1965-68; 4th Grade Teacher Bells ISD 1968-69; 3rd Grade Teacher TX 1970-79; 4th Grade Teacher 1979-90 Scherte Cibolo Universal City ISD; *ai:* Grade Level Chm; Textbook Comm; Soc Sci Contact Person; Sci Fair Chm; Cibolo Valley Educators Assn Campus Rep 1987-90; TX St Teachers Assn; NEA; 1987-88; Pres 1989-90 South Central TX Rdng Cncl; Vice Pres 1988-89; Beta Sigma Phi Inter Sorority (VP 1978-79/Pres 1979-80/Sec 1985-86/Treas 1989-) Woman of Yr 1980; *office:* Wiederstein Elem Schl 200 Schlather Rd Cibolo TX 78108

MILLER, BRENDA MANUEL, Third Grade Teacher; *b:* Eunice, LA; *m:* Russell J.; *c:* Renee, Kayla, Stephanie; *ed:* (BA) Elem Ed, Mc Neese St Univ 1969; Prof Improvement Prgm; *cr:* 4th Grade Teacher Central Elem Lake Charles 1969-70; 1st Grade Teacher Central Elem Jennings 1970-71; 5th/6th Grade Math Teacher Basile HS 1971-72; 1st-3rd Grade Teacher W W Stewart Elem 1972-; *ai:* LA Ed Assn, NEA 1969-; *home:* 931 N 6th Eunice LA 70535

MILLER, BRICE HYMAN, Fourth Grade Teacher; *b:* Logansport, IN; *m:* Alexandra Stewart; *c:* Erica, Erin, Jill; *ed:* (BA) Elem Ed, 1974, (MS) Elem Ed, 1976 Ball St Univ; *cr:* 4-5th Grade Teacher 1974-78; 4th Grade Teacher 1978- Grissom Memorial Elem; *ai:* Lang & Spelling Book Adoption Comm; Soccer & Flag/Ftbl Coach Elem; Drug Ed & Young Authors Comm Chairperson; Muncie Teachers Assn 1978-; NAtl Teachers Assn 1978-; IN St Teachers Assn 1978-; Riverside Avenue Baptist Church Deacon & Trustee 1976-; Baptist Houses Bd Mem 1988-; YMCA 1979-; *office:* Grissom Memorial Elem Sch 3201 S Macedonia Ave Muncie IN 47302

MILLER, BRUCE GERARD, Science Teacher; *b:* Colorado Springs, CO; *m:* Pamela Jean Hulin; *c:* Jefferey Justin; *ed:* (MED) Creative Arts Ed, Lesley Coll 1989; (BA) Scndry Sci Ed, Univ of Northern CO 1979; *cr:* Sci/Rdng Teacher Grand Cty Mid Sch 1979-81; Sci Teacher Scott Carpenter Jr HS 1981-83; Sci/Gifted Talented Carmidy Jr High 1983-; *ai:* Gifted/Talented Prgm Adv; Coach Bsktbl & Track; NEA 1979-; Nom for PTA Teacher of Yr 1987; Sci Ed Mem of Writing Team; *office:* Carmody Jr H S 2050 S Kipling St Littleton CO 80227

MILLER, CAROL BRAUN, 5th Grade Teacher; *b:* Toledo, OH; *m:* David D.; *c:* Jennifer; *ed:* (BED) Elem Ed, 1973, (MED) Elem Ed, 1977 Univ Toledo; *cr:* 6th Grade Teacher Dorr Street Elem Sch 1973-74; 4th & 5th Grade Teacher Crissey Elem Sch 1974-; *ai:* Writing Across Curr Comm; Competency Based Ed Comm; Departmental Chm; Rdng Curr; Springfield Ed Assn 1973-; OH Ed Assn 1973-; NEA 1973-; Natl Sci Fnd Schlsp to Study Marine Bio; *office:* Crissey Elem Sch 9220 Geiser Rd Holland OH 43528

MILLER, CAROL SACKS, First Grade Teacher; *b:* Chicago, IL; *m:* Charles E.; *c:* John T. Sacks Jr., Jill M. Sacks, Cathy L. Sacks; *ed:* (BS) Elem Ed, N IL Univ 1963; Grad Stud Rdng Disabilities, Survey of Exceptional Child, Cmptr Ed, Educl Research & Dissemination; *cr:* 1st Grade Teacher Fry Sch 1970-75; 4th Grade Teacher Tobin Sch 1975-77; 1st Grade Teacher Fry Sch 1977-; *ai:* 7th & 8th Grade Bsktbl Cheerleading Coach; Curr Cncl; Rita Quaid Schlsp, Sci/Health Textbook, 1st Grade Testing, SRA Field Research, Sci/Health Textbook Selection Comm; AFT; Womens Club Chancel Guild Treas 1983-89; Chippewa Soc Club 1975-; *office:* Harry E Fry Elem Sch 78th & Mobile Burbank IL 60459

MILLER, CAROLYN JONES, 6th Grade Teacher; *b:* Dallas, TX; *c:* Billy, Tina Miller Easley, Christy; *ed:* (BS) Elem Ed, N TX St Univ 1976; (MS) Guidance & Counseling, E TX St Univ 1980; Working on Mid-Management Certificate in Educl Admin; *cr:* 3rd Grade Teacher 1976-84, 3rd/4th Grade Combination Teacher 1983-84, 2nd Grade Teacher 1984-85, 6th Grade Teacher 1985-, 5th/6th Grade Gifted Combination Teacher 1989, 6th Grade Teacher 1985- Shands Elem; *ai:* PTA Exec Bd; Comm for Reorganization of Curr; Guides in Lang Art/Writing for MISD; Avid Bridge Player; Loves Rdng & Church Act; MEA, ATPE 1976-; PTA (Treas 1986-88, 2nd VP 1988-90, Pres Elect 1990-91), Life Membership Awd 1988; *office:* Shands Elem Sch 4836 Shands Dr Mesquite TX 75150

MILLER, CHARLIS, Business Teacher; *b:* Drew, MS; *ed:* (BS) Bus Ed, Jackson St Univ 1973; (MS) Bus Ed, Delta St Univ 1977; Grad Stud Cmptr Sci, Delta St Univ; Cmptr Sci Wkshps; *cr:* Teacher Goahoma Comm Coll 1989-, Ruleville Cntrl HS 1973-; *ai:* Sr Class & NHS Spon; Honors Club; Sunflower Cty Educators Secy 1979-83, Certificate 1981; Zeta Pi Beta 1977-, Certificate 1981, 1988; Natl Cncl of Negro Women 1977-, Certificate 1987, 1988; Drew Sch Alumni Assn Bus Mgr 1982-, Plaque 1982, 1984; Holly Grove United Baptist Church Youth Dir; Numerous Awds & Certificates; STAR Teacher 1980, 1982, 1989; Services Rendered Placques; *office:* Ruleville Cntrl HS 360 N Division Ruleville MS 38771

MILLER, COLETTE MARY, 6th Grade Teacher; *b:* Fort Worth, TX; *m:* Dennis R.; *ed:* (BA) Elem Ed, 1971, (MED) Elem Ed, 1974 Univ of North Tx; Gifted & Talented Trng; *cr:* 5th Grade Teacher 1971-88, 6th Grade Teacher 1988- Carrollton Elem; *ai:* TX Fed of TX 1989-; TX Math 1989-; PTA Treas 1971-; Selected VIP Sch Dist 1989; *office:* Carrollton Elem Schl 1805 Pearl St Carrollton TX 75006

MILLER, CURTIS H., Physics Teacher; *b:* Des Moines, IA; *m:* Dorothy Griggs; *c:* Roxanne, Kimberly, Kristina; *ed:* (BA) Math/ Physics, 1965, (MA) Math, 1966 Univ of N CO; Electrical Engineering, Univ of CO; *cr:* Teacher Jefferson HS 1966-88, Wheatridge HS 1988-; *ai:* Bicycle Ride Organizer; AAPT 1980-; NEA 1966-; Jefferson Cty Tech Ed Assn 1980-; VMI Honors Physics Wkshp; Woodrow Wilson Physics Inst at Princeton; Physics Teaching Resource Agent Prgm at Univ of MD; Microcmptr Based Laboratory Tufts Univ; Lab-Net Telecommunications Tufts Univ; PRISMS Prgm Univ of N IA; *office:* Wheatridge HS 9505 W 32nd Ave Wheat Ridge CO 80033

MILLER, DAVID KELL, Social Studies Teacher; *b:* Lansing, MI; *m:* Patricia Margaret George; *c:* Ashleigh; *ed:* (BAED) Eng/ Soc Stud, 1970, (MA) Educl Admin, 1975, (MA) Guidance/ Counseling, 1981 MI St Univ; *cr:* Soc Stud/Creative Writing/ Math/Phys Ed/Drama/Lang Art Teacher Kinawa Mid Sch 1971-; *ai:* Phi Delta Kappa 1975-80; *home:* 5915 E Sleepy Hollow Ln East Lansing MI 48823

MILLER, DEBORAH RUTH (MOCK), 7th-8th Grade Spanish Teacher; *b:* Latrobe, PA; *m:* Lawrence Edward; *c:* Scott, David; *ed:* (BA) Span/Scndry Ed, WV Wesleyan Coll 1968; (BA) Eng/ Scndry Ed, IN Univ of PA 1972; Span, IN Univ of PA; *cr:* Eng Teacher Ligonier Valley Sr HS 1968; Span Teacher Greater Latrobe Sr HS 1968-78, Greater Latrobe Jr HS 1984-; *office:* Greater Latrobe Jr HS Country Club Rd Latrobe PA 15650

MILLER, DENNIS EUGENE, 6th Grade Teacher; *b:* Lock Haven, PA; *m:* Linda Carol Munro; *c:* Joelle Lingenfelter, Duane, Brad; *ed:* (BS) Elem Ed, Lock Haven Univ 1965; Grad Stud Rider Coll, Glassboro St Coll, Monmouth Coll; *cr:* 6th Grade Teacher 1965-79, Dept Chm 1972- Johnstone Sch; 6th Grade Teacher Memorial Mid Sch 1980-; *ai:* Head Wrestling Coach Vineland HS; NEA, NJ Ed Assn, Cumberland Cty Ed Assn, Vineland Ed Assn Mem; S Jersey Wrestling Ofcls & Coaches Assn, S Jersey Coaches of Boys Athletics; Memorial Sch Teacher of Yr 1987; Region 8 Coach of Yr 1985; *office:* Memorial Mid Sch 424 S Main Rd Vineland NJ 08360

MILLER, DIANE, 6th Grade Teacher; *b:* Independence, KS; *m:* John M.; *c:* Kristin; *ed:* (BA) Ed, 1964, Psych/Rdng, 1971 Cntrl WA Univ; Various Courses; *cr:* 1st Grade Teacher Anacortes WA Public Sch 1964-66, DODS Nurnberg Germany 1966-71; 2nd Grade Teacher Chelalis WA Public Schls 1972-73; Grad Asst Cntrl WA Univ 1971-72; 1st/5th/6th Grade Teacher Oregon City OR Public Schls 1973-; *ai:* Outdoor Sch Teacher; Coaching Vlybl & Bsktbl 1975-85; Bldg Recycling Adv; Dist Sci Comm; Bldg CORE Team; Prin Advisory Comm; NEA, OCEA 1973- OEA Awd 1988; *office:* Holcolmb Elem Sch 14625 S Holcolmb Blvd Oregon City OR 97045

MILLER, DIANNE EWING, Second Grade Teacher; *b:* Mounds, IL; *m:* Vance Allen; *c:* Stephanie Caldwell; *ed:* (BS) Ed, S IL Univ 1966; Grad Work Memphis St Univ; *cr:* Bruce Elem 1966-71; Stafford Elem 1971-; *ai:* Grade Chairperson; Curr Coord; Building Leadership Team; NEA, TEA, MEA 1966-; *home:* 9220 Fletcher Trace Pkwy Memphis TN 38133

MILLER, DONALD BRUCE, Mathematics Department Chair; *b:* Fort Worth, TX; *m:* Patricia A. Wittrock; *c:* Darcy, Drew, Deirdre; *ed:* (BS) Math, 1972, (MS) Educl Admin, 1983 OK St Univ; *cr:* Math Instr Pawnee HS 1974-; *ai:* OEA, NEA, OCTM, NCTM; MENSA; Teacher of Yr 1987-88; Yrbk Dedication 1987-88; *home:* 408 Cleveland Pawnee OK 74058

MILLER, DOROTHY FREEMAN, Fifth Grade Teacher; *b:* Crossmore, NC; *m:* Grady Lynn; *ed:* (AS) Elem Ed, Wingate Coll 1968; (BS) Elem Ed, Appalachian St Univ 1970; *cr:* 6th Grade Teacher 1970-77, 3rd-4th Grade Teacher 1977-78, 5th Grade Teacher 1978 Lower Creek Elem Sch; *ai:* NC Assn of Educators Faculty Rep; *home:* Rt 1 Box 400-A Granite Falls NC 28630

MILLER, EDNA A., 9th Grade English Teacher; *b:* Danville, IL; *c:* Alfred, Russell Panepinto; *ed:* (BS) Eng, 1972, Permanant Cert, 1976 St Univ of NY Geneseo; Grad Stud Trng, Elements of Instruction; *cr:* Remedial Eng Teacher 1981-83, ABE Instr 1981-86 Genesee Cmmty Coll; 7th-12th Grade Eng Teacher Oakfield-Alabama HS 1972-; *ai:* Effective Schls, Career Day, Home Sch & Peer-Tutor Partner Comms; Delta Kappa Gamma 1985-; Teacher Excl & Peer Partnering Participant; *office:* Oakfield-Alabama HS Lewiston Rd Oakfield NY 14125

MILLER, EDNA GARCIA, Math Teacher; *b:* Bakersfield, CA; *m:* Gary Joseph; *c:* Melissa; *ed:* (BS) Math/Soc Sci, Santa Clara Univ 1974; *cr:* Teacher Our Lady of Perpetual Help 1974-75; Math Teacher Peter Burnett Jr HS 1975-80, Yerba Buena HS 1980-; *ai:* Math Club Adv; Math Contest Coach; Natl Sci Fnd Honors Wkshp; SCVMA 1980-82; *office:* Yerba Buena H S 1855 Lucretia Ave San Jose CA 95122

MILLER, EDWARD HOHMAN, Russian Lang & History Teacher; *b:* Baltimore, MD; *m:* Billie Frances Mitzelfelt; *c:* Gretchen M., Amy E., Henry J., Heidi A.; *ed:* (BA) His, Loyola Coll 1951; (MA) Russian Area Stud, Georgetown Univ 1968; Middlebury Coll Summer Russian Lang Sch; Univ of MD-Salzburg, Austria Branch-Russian Lang; *cr:* Russian Lang Instr Baltimore City Adult Ed 1956-66; Russian Lang Instr/Evening Adult Ed Loyola Coll 1966-69; 9th-12th Grade Teacher/Russian Lang/His Instr John Carroll Sch 1970-; *ai:* Slavic Honor Society Moderator; John Carroll Foreign Exchange Prgm Coord; Baltimore City Odessa, Sister City Comm 1988-; Balto City Intnl Visitors Organization 1975-; John Carrolls Teacher of Yr Awd 1989.

MILLER, ELIZABETH HOGAN, Retired; *b:* Rush, KY; *w:* Joe F. (dec); *c:* Joe H., Ruth A. Miller Dunn; *ed:* (BA) Elem Ed, Morehead St Univ 1962; Math, Morehead St Univ; *cr:* Teacher Hazeldale Elem 1933-34, Davis 1934-35, Hazeldale 1944-45, Longbranch 1956-57, Garner Elem 1957-82; *ai:* KY Retired Teachers, KY Ed Assn, E KY Ed Assn; KY Parent Teacher Life Mem 1980-; E Fork United Secy Admin Bd 1988-; Meth Church Adult Sunday Sch Teacher 1989-; *home:* 22429 State Rt 3 Rush KY 41168

MILLER, ELLEN TINSON, Special Education Teacher; *b:* Blakely, GA; *m:* Teddy; *c:* Tiffany; *ed:* (BS) Mental Retardation, Albany St Coll 1981; *cr:* Teacher Early Cty Bd of Ed; *ai:* Spec Ed Curr Comm; *office:* Early County Mid Sch Columbia Hwy Blakely GA 31723

MILLER, FANNY KNIGHT GAILLARD, History Teacher; *b:* Atmore, AL; *m:* William Neil; *c:* William W. *ed:* (BA) His 1970, (MA) His, 1974 Univ of AL; *cr:* Jr HS Teacher Alston Summerville Mid Sch 1971-73, Rosman Mid Sch 1974-78; HS Teacher W Columbus HS 1978-80; His Teacher J P Knapp Jr HS 1980-85; Advanced Placement Teacher E Wake HS 1985-; *ai:* Senate Bill 2 Stu Achievement Comm; NCAE 1974-; Mirian Rebecca Frazer Univ of AL Awd; *office:* East Wake HS Rt 4 Box 254 Wendell NC 27591

MILLER, FAY BROWNLEE, Third Grade Teacher; *b:* Indianapolis, IN; *m:* Carl Edward; *c:* Carl Jr., Cameron, Christopher; *ed:* (BS) Elem Ed, Ball St Univ 1963; (MS) Curr/Instruction/Ed, Cleveland St Univ 1985; *cr:* 1st Grade Teacher Cleveland Public Sch; 3rd Grade Teacher Shaker Heights; *ai:* Ludlow Sch Stu Cncl & Safety Patrol Adv, United Way Chairperson, Career Dev Rep; Cleveland Black Alliance Sch Educators Mem; UCC Plymouth Church Teacher; Leukemia, Heart Assn Volunteer; *office:* Boulevard Shaker Heights Sch 14900 Drexmore Shaker Heights OH 44120

MILLER, FREDA DILLON, Sixth Grade Teacher; *b:* Rich Creek, VA; *m:* William J.; *c:* Suellen M. Johnston, Bethany D.; *ed:* (BSED) Elem Ed, Concord Coll 1969; Grad Work Radford Univ; *cr:* 5th Grade Teacher Plumsted Township Elem 1962-64; 6th Grade Teacher Petertown Elem 1971-; *ai:* Choir Dir; NEA, MCEA; *office:* Peterstown Elem Sch College Dr Peterstown WV 24963

MILLER, GARY ALLEN, Acting Principal; *b:* Alttona, PA; *m:* Kay Ann Kylor; *ed:* Gary A. Jr., Cheri L., Adam S., Anne M.; (BS) Elem Ed, 1976, (MED) Curr/Instruction, 1978, (PHD) Educl Admin, 1990 PA St; *cr:* Teacher Altoona Area Sch Dist 1976-88; Grad Research Asst PA St 1988-89; Prin Bellefonte Area Sch Dist 1989-; *ai:* PA Assn Elem Sch Prins; Blair Cty Solid Waste Authority Mem 1976-78; BSA (Chm, Scoutmaster), Woodbadge 1984; Grad Assistantship PA St; *home:* RD 2 Box 225 Williamsburg PA 16693

MILLER, GINA MONTELEONE, 4th Grade Teacher; *b:* Hampton, SC; *m:* Christopher C.; *c:* Cameron C.; *ed:* (BS) Early Chldhd Ed, Winthrop Coll 1983; (MED) Elem Ed, Converse Col L 1988; *cr:* 5th Grade Teacher 1983-84, 6th Grade Teacher 1984-89, 4th Grade Teacher 1989- Duncan Elem Sch.

MILLER, GLADYS (WILSON), Reading Teacher; *b:* Boise City, OK; *m:* Larry; *c:* Chad, Chase; *ed:* (BS) Elem Ed, Panhandle St Univ 1980; Post Masters Studies Rdng, West TX St Univ 1990; *cr:* Migrant Teacher 1980-81; 3rd/4th Grade Teacher 1981-88 Felt Public Sch; Rdng/Lang Arts Boise City Public Schls 1988-; *ai:* Delta Kappa Gamma 1986-; Cimarron Cty Teachers Assn Pres 1985-87; Whos Who of Amer Young Women; Delta Kappa Gamma Socty Intnl Schlsp 1990; Omega Chapter Schlsp 1990; *home:* Box 742 Boise City OK 73933

MILLER, GLORIA CASH, French Teacher; *b:* Cliffside, NC; *m:* Thomas Carl; *c:* Kim Burnett, Michelle Clem, Bethany; *ed:* (BS) Fr/His, 1966, (MA) Fr/Jr Coll Ed, 1972 Appalachian St Univ; Radford Coll, Univ of VA; *cr:* Fr Teacher St Margarets Sch for Girls 1966; Fr Teacher/Dept Chm Woodbridge Sr HS 1966-71; Fr/His Teacher/Dept Chm Graham Park Mid Sch 1971-79; Fr Teacher/Dept Chm Potomac Sr HS 1979-; *ai:* Foreign Lang Dept Chairperson; Textbook Adoption, Effective Schls & Curr Comm; Foreign Exch Stu Coord; Prince William Ed Assn, VA Ed Assn, NEA 1966-; Delta Kappa Gamma Parliamentarian 1977-; Modern Lang Assn of VA, Amer Cncl Teaching of Foreign Lang, AATF; Cornerstone Baptist Church (Pianist, Adult Sunday Sch Teacher); NDEA Schlsp to Study Fr 1968; Distinguished Foreign Lang Teacher of VA 1977; Washington Post Agner Meyer Teacher of Yr 1983; Prince William Cty Teacher of Yr 1978; *home:* 11213 Beauclaire Blvd Fredericksburg VA 22401

MILLER, HARVEY JAMES, Teacher; *b:* Tillamook, OR; *m:* Elizabeth Stewart; *c:* Catherine E., Samanth L., *ed:* (BS) Elementary Ed, Eastern OR State College 1977; *cr:* Teacher Fir Grove Elem Sch 1977-82, Calapooia Mid Sch 1982-89, Memorial Mid Sch 1989-; *ai:* Asst Bsbl Coach, Linn Benton Comm Coll; Amer Bsbl Coaches Assn 1989-; National Geographic Society; Takena Kiwanis, Sec 1984-, Bd of Dir 1984-85, 1989-; Selected Asst Bsbl Coach of the Year 1987-88.

MILLER, HAZEL HENRY, 4th Grade Teacher; *b:* Cardington, OH; *m:* Robert Paul Jr.; *ed:* (BA) Elem Ed, Malone Coll 1966; Grad Stud OH St Univ, Bowling Green Univ; *cr:* Perry Local Schls 1965-72; Fulton Elem 1972-82; 4th Grade Teacher Cardington Lincoln 1982-; *ai:* Young Authors & Right to Read; CLFA (Treas 1980) 1972-; OEA, NEA 1972-; Intnl Rdng Assn; Jennings Scholar; *home:* 2436 SR 61 Marengo OH 43334

MILLER, HENRY A., English Teacher; *b:* New York, NY; *m:* Sandra Yeakel; *c:* Tammy Miller Strempel, Drew; *ed:* (BS) Ed/Eng, Temple Univ 1963; (MED) Ed/Eng, Beaver Coll 1974; Grad Stud; *cr:* Eng Teacher Colonial Sch Dist 1963-; *ai:* Guidance Advisory Comm; Team Leader; Walkathon Montgomery Cty Assn for Retarded Citizens; Young Authors Conference; Colonial Ed Assn, NEA, PA St Ed Assn, NCTE 1963-; Brigade of Amer Revolution Corporal 1975-; Excl Ed Awd 1980-81; *office:* Colonial Mid Sch 716 Belvoir Rd Norristown PA 19401

MILLER, HOLLAND LEE, Mathematics Teacher; *b:* Cleveland, OH; *c:* Justin, Katherine; *ed:* (BA) Ec/Bus Admin, Heidelberg Coll 1972; Supervision/Teacher Trng, Emory Univ; Math, W GA Coll; Ec, Univ of Nottingham England; *cr:* Math Teacher Shamrock HS; *ai:* Key Club Spon; Study Table Tutor; PAGE; *office:* Shamrock HS 3100 Mount Oliver Dr Decatur GA 30033

MILLER, IRMA JEAN (IMLER), 8th Grade Math & Sci Teacher; *b:* Altoona, PA; *m:* Robert Edward; *c:* Michael, Jason, Crystal, Matthew; *ed:* (BA) Elem Ed, Penn St Univ 1973; Diagnostic & Prescriptive Math, Physics for Elem Classroom, Lead Teacher Prgm; *cr:* 7th/8th Grade Sci/6th-8th Grade Math Teacher St Marys 1979-; *ai:* Mathcounts Coach 1988-; Jr Acad of Sci Spon & Coach 1989-; Set Up Sci Fair & Quiz Bowl; Responsible for Christmas Parade Float & 8th Grade Grad Ceremonies; Natl Cath Teacher Assn, PA Sci Teachers Assn, PA Math League, NCTM; St Marys PA Dept of Ed Curr Conference Rep; *office:* St Marys Sch 1400 4th Ave Altoona PA 16602

MILLER, JACK RICHARD, Chapter I/Cmptr Teacher; *b:* Fort Bragg, NC; *m:* Gweneth Joy Osborne; *c:* Richard O., Monique C.; *ed:* (BA) His/Ec, Univ of CO 1963; (MA) Educl Media, Univ of N CO; *cr:* Sci/His Teacher Buchanan Jr HS 1967-68; Teacher Sherman Elem Sch 1968-87; Librarian Fort Morgan HS 1987-88; Cmptr/Chapter I Teacher Fort Morgan Mid Sch 1988-; *office:* Ft Morgan Mid Sch 300 Duel St Fort Morgan CO 80701

MILLER, JACKIE MERCER, English Teacher; *b:* Clinton, NC; *m:* Kenneth Neil; *ed:* (BA) Scndry Ed in Eng 1985, (MED) Admin Supervision 1990 Clemson Univ; *cr:* Teacher Newberry Jr HS 1985-; *ai:* Natl Jr Beta Club Spon; SC Ed Assn Rep 1988-; *office:* Newberry Jr HS 1829 Nance St Newberry SC 29108

MILLER, JAMES EDWARD, Social Studies Teacher; *b:* Upper Darby, PA; *m:* Janis Talhelm; *c:* Jo Lynn, Adam; *ed:* (BS) Comprehensive Soc Stud, Mansfield St 1966; *cr:* Teacher Williams Valley Sch Dist 1966-; *ai:* Golf & Girls Var Bsktbl Coach; PSEA, NEA 1966-; Liberty Hose Company #1 Williamstown Volunteer Firefighter 1969; *office:* Williams Valley Jr/Sr HS Rt 209 Tower City PA 17980

MILLER, JANE HOFFMAN, Fifth Grade Teacher; *b:* Upland, PA; *m:* Glenn Stevens; *c:* Andrew Torgrimson, Stephanie; *ed:* (BA) Eng, James Madison Univ 1966; (MED) Rdng, Northwestern St Univ 1977; Advanced Studies Admin & Supervision, Univ of VA 1980-84; *cr:* 1st Grade Teacher Stafford Cty Schls 1966-68; 5th Grade Lang Art Teacher Stafford Cty Schls 1969-70; Eng Teacher 1972-74, ESA Teacher 1974-75 King George Cty Schls; Admin Asst 1984-88, Educl Television Coord 1976-85, 5th Grade Teacher 1975- King George Elem; *ai:* Grade Level Chairperson; 4-H Teacher, Spon; Intnl Rdng Assn, Rappahannock Area Rdng Cncl 1988-; BSA (Den Leader Coach 1981, Troop Comm) Scouting Awd 1981; Dahlgren Swim Team Refreshment Chairperson 1979-83; Peace Luth Church Sunday Sch Teacher 1988-; King George HS Band Boosters VP 1986-88; Staff Dev Wkshp Rdng; *office:* King George Elem Sch Rt 3 Box 79 King George VA 22485

MILLER, JERRY D., Mathematics/Phys Ed Teacher; *b:* Welch, WV; *m:* Jennifer Surber; *c:* Alan, Quinn; *ed:* (BA) Phys Ed, Concord Coll 1973; Athletic Trng, Marshall Univ; *cr:* Teacher/Coach Gilbert HS 1974-; *ai:* Head Ftbl Coach 1974-88; Girls Sftbl Coach 1985-86; Head Bsktbl Coach 1989-; AAHPERD 1974-; WV Coaches Assn 1974-; Williamson Daily News Ftbl Coach of Yr 1976; *home:* PO Box 358 Gilbert WV 25621

MILLER, JETANNA HUSKEY, Sci Dept Chairperson; *b:* Gaffney, SC; *m:* Clarence Everette; *c:* Travis, Taryn; *ed:* (BS) Bio, Limestone Coll 1969; (MAT) Ed, Winthrop Coll 1975; *cr:* Teacher East Jr HS 1969-74; Teacher 1974-, Sci Dept Chairperson 1986- Blacksburg HS; *ai:* Spon Future Teachers Club & Varsity Chrldrs; NSA, SCSA, CCEA; *office:* Blacksburg HS 201 Ramseur Dr Blacksburg SC 29702

MILLER, JILL D. TORMEY, 6th Grade Teacher; *b:* Summit, NJ; *m:* Arthur; *ed:* (BA) Elem Ed, 1976, (MA) Rdng Specialist, 1981 Kean Coll; Grad Stud Admin, Supervision, Continuing Ed; *cr:* Rdng Teacher 1977-80, 6th Grade Teacher 1980- Silver Bay; *ai:* Cheerleading Coach; Yrbk, Sch Fair, Spelling Bee Comms; NEA, NJ Educl Assn, Intnl Rdng Assn; Grad Thesis Published in ERIC Files; *office:* Silver Bay Elem Sch Silver Bay Rd Toms River NJ 08753

MILLER, JODY ROBERT, English Teacher; *b:* Bethlehem, PA; *c:* Elizabeth; *ed:* (BA) Eng, Moravian Coll 1970; (MA) Eng Ed, Beaver Coll 1979; Lehigh Univ; *cr:* Eng Teacher Freedom HS 1972-; Eng Teacher Supvr Freedom HS 1976-79; Teaching Asst Lehigh Univ 1979; Speech Resource Moravian Theological Seminary 1980; *ai:* NCTE 1972-89; Historic Bethlehem 1980-; Sun Inn Preservation 1980-; Early Amer Society 1975-; IDEA 1989-; Outstanding Young Men of America 1977/1980; Certificate of Excl White House Commission on Presidental Scholars 1985; *home:* 3537 Sutton Pl Bethlehem PA 18017

MILLER, JOHN P., Social Studies Teacher; *b:* Lebanon, PA; *m:* Linda L. Loose; *c:* Suzanne L., Ryan P., Kelly E., John B.; *ed:* (BS) Soc Stud, 1969, (MA) His, 1974 Millersville Univ; Additional Courses Elizabethtown Coll; *cr:* Teacher 1969- Soc Stud Dept Chm 1972- Palmyra Area Sch Dist; *ai:* Stu Cncl Adv; Var Bsbl Coach; Sch Dist Announcer for Ftbl Games; Palmyra Area Ed Assn Pres, PA St Ed Assn, NEA 1969-; NCSS 1985-; Annville-Cleona Recreation Assn Bd Mem 1978-; Palmyra Rotary Club Teacher of Yr 1990; *office:* Palmyra Area Sch Dist Cherry St Palmyra PA 17078

MILLER, JOHN WILLIAM, Science Teacher; *b:* Pittsburgh, PA; *m:* Debra Kay Lechner; *c:* Sara; *ed:* (BA) Bio, Univ of Richmond 1975; (AAS) Forest Technology, Flathead Valley Comm Coll 1977; Teacher Cert Univ of Denver; *cr:* Sci Teacher Parker Jr HS 1982-84, Will James Jr HS 1984-86, Billings West HS 1986-; *ai:* Track Coach; Club Adv West HS Outings Club; Focus Team Mem Helping Stus Under Stress; NSTA, MT Sci Teachers Assn 1986-; NEA 1984-; Natl Wildlife Fed, Defenders of Wildlife, Great Bear Fnd, World Wildlife Fund; *home:* 703 Highland Park Dr Billings MT 59102

MILLER, JOSEPH ALVIN, History & Anthropology Teacher; *b:* Waukegan, IL; *m:* Jennifer Gail Yos; *ed:* (BSED) Poly Sci, 1974, (MS) His, 1982 IL St Univ; Grad Work His; *cr:* Soc Sci Dept Teacher Lincoln Way Cmmty HS 1974-; *ai:* Schls Tutorial Prgm & Effective Schls Comm; NCSS 1975-77, 1989-; *office:* Lincoln-Way Cmmty HS Rt 30 New Lenox IL 60451

MILLER, JOYCE DEBOLT MILLER, Lang Art/Soc Stud Teacher; *b:* Lake Lynn, PA; *m:* Richard Ralston; *c:* Roderick K., Cheryl K. Miller Scarvey; *ed:* (BA) Bio/Psych, Bridgewater Coll 1954; Various Courses His & Ed, James Madison Univ; *cr:* 5th Grade Classroom Teacher Bridgewater Elem Sch 1954-58, Grohoes Elem Sch 1958-59; 4th/5th Grade Classroom Teacher Bridgewater Elem Sch 1965-67; 6th Grade Classroom Teacher Pleasant Valley Elem Sch 1970-76; 7th Grade Classroom Teacher John W Wayland Intermediate Sch 1977-89, Wilbur S Pence Mid Sch 1989-; *ai:* Speech & Drama Coach; RCEA, VEA, NEA; Jr Womans Club Pres 1958-62.

MILLER, JOYCE THOMAS, Mathematics Teacher; *b:* Elizabethtown, KY; *m:* Larry S.; *c:* Bartley, Amanda; *ed:* (BS) Math, Univ of KY 1972; (MA) Sci Ed, W KY Univ 1976; Rank I Univ of Louisville 1987; *cr:* Math Teacher North Hardin HS 1972-73; Sci Teacher Cntrl City HS 1973-75; Math Teacher Cloverpool HS 1975-76, Woodford Cty HS 1976-77; Sci Teacher Walton Verona HS 1978-79; Math Teacher Simon Kenton HS 1979-82, Meade Cty HS 1982-; *ai:* Delta Kappa Gamma 1983-; Alpha Gamma Chapter Secy 1988-, Gertrude Collins Golden Anniversary Schlsp 1987; KY Assn for Gifted Ed 1987-; *office:* Meade Cty HS Old State Rd Brandenburg KY 40108

MILLER, JUDITH ANN (STOCKLIN), Gifted Coordinator/Librarian; *b:* Chillicothe, OH; *m:* John R.; *c:* Carol A. Cottrill, John C., Don E., Mark A., Beth S. Crone; *ed:* (BSED) Elem Ed, OH Univ 1963; (MS) Lib Sci, OK St Univ 1981; Gifted Ed 24 Hrs; Sch Admin 26 Hrs; *cr:* 1st Yr Primary Allen Elem 1960-71; 3rd Grade Teacher Central Elem 1971-81; Lib/Teacher of Gifted 1st-6th Angus Valley Elem 1981-83; Gifted Coord/Librarian Central Elem 1983-; *ai:* Political Action Comm Mem & Interviewer; Dept Head Elem Librarians/Gifted Prgm; Staff Dev Comm Mem & Presentor; SSEA/OEA/NEA (Lobbyist Bldg Rep 1971- Pacesetter Awd 1987); OK Assn for Gifted (1st VP 1981-

Bldg Teacher of Yr 1982/88/89); OK Lib Assn Presentor/State Conf 1991; United Way Ed Prgm Lib Coord 1990; Sand Springs Heard Assn Sch Prgm Coord 1990; Sand Springs Constitution Comm 1987-; State Grants for Libraries 6 Yrs; NEH Constitution Grant; NSF Master Teacher Sci Grant; Fed Grant for Computerizing Libraries; *office:* Central Elem Sch P O Box 970 Sand Springs OK 74063

MILLER, JUDITH BISHOP, Fourth Grade Teacher; *b:* McMinnville, TN; *m:* Steven Michael; *c:* Mary M.; *ed:* (BS) Elem Ed, David Lipscomb Coll 1978; *cr:* 3rd Grade Teacher William Biles Elem 1978-79; 1st-6th Grade Teacher TN Preparatory Sch 1979-82; 4th Grade Teacher William D Robbins Elem 1982-; *ai:* Safety Patrol Spon; Bible Sch Teacher at Alpine Hills Church of Christ; Mobile Cty Schls 1983-84, AL Teacher of Yr; *home:* 9872 Sky Vista Dr Semmes AL 36575

MILLER, JULIE MORIN, Third Grade Teacher; *b:* Seymour, IN; *m:* Richard Franklin; *ed:* (BS) Elem Ed, 1981, (MS) Elem Ed, 1984 IN Univ; In-Service Trng; *cr:* 4th Grade Teacher 1981-87, 3rd Grade Teacher 1987- Graham Creek Jennings Cty; *ai:* Grants, Fund Raising for Parent-Teachers, Positive Reinforcement Comm; NEA, IN St Teachers Assn, Jennings Cty Classroom Teachers Assn 1981-; CEC; Tea Creek Baptist Church; PTA 1981-; IN Univ Honor Society; Certificate of Appreciation Indianapolis Public Schls; Graduated IN Univ with Distinction; *home:* 101 Davis St Apt 6 North Vernon IN 47265

MILLER, KAREN AUSTIN, 8th Grade Lang Arts Teacher; *b:* Decatur, IL; *m:* Thomas V.; *c:* Jennifer, Kathleen; *ed:* (BA) Eng 1965, (MED) Rdng Specialist 1983 Univ of Louisville; *cr:* 10th Eng Teacher Philip Barbour HS 1976-79; 7th Eng Teacher Oldham Cty Mid Sch 1983-86; 9th Eng Teacher Oldham Cty HS 1986-88; 8th Eng Teacher South Oldham Mid Sch 1988-; *ai:* Academic Coach; Governors Cup Competition; Lang Arts and Eng Composition; Team Leader 8B; NCTE 1982-; KY Mid Sch Assn 1983-86/1990; Published Article in Notes Plus Sept 1986; *office:* So Oldham Mid Sch 6403 W Hwy 146 Crestwood KY 40014

MILLER, KATHLEEN HAYES, English/Speech/Drama Teacher; *b:* Mason City, IA; *m:* Robert F.; *c:* Elizabeth, Joseph, Robert; *ed:* (BA) Eng, Marycrest Coll 1966; MA Candidate Univ of IA; *cr:* Eng Teacher Marycrest Coll 1966-70; Rdng Teacher Caterpillar 1973-75; Eng/Math Teacher Sudlow Jr HS 1981-85; Eng/Speech/Drama Teacher J B Young Jr HS 1985-; *ai:* Annual Musical Drama, 9th Grade Play Dir; Drama Club Adv; St Paul The Apostle Church (Jr HS Religious Ed Supvr 1987-, Music Ministry 1983-); *office:* J B Young Jr HS 1709 Harrison St Davenport IA 52803

MILLER, KATHRYN MARIE (BROWN), Latin Teacher; *b:* Logan, UT; *c:* Kellie L., Lori A., Michelle M.; *ed:* (BA) Latin/ Eng, Hope Coll 1965; Eng, MI St Univ 1966, Cntrl MI Univ 1982; *cr:* Eng/Latin Teacher Dwight Jr HS 1965-68, Bangor Public Schls 1977-84, Klein HS 1984-; *ai:* Newspaper Adv; Vlybl, Sftbl, Cheerleading Coach; Class, Latin Club, Latin NHS Spon; NEA, MEA, BEAM 1965-68, 1977-84; TSTA, NEA, KEA 1986-, Nominee Teacher of Yr 1989-; Delta Kappa Gamma Iota Epsilon 1987-; JC Auxiliary Pres 1971-75; Bay City Hospital Bd of Mental Health; *office:* Klein HS 16715 Stuebner Airline Spring TX 77379

MILLER, KATHY B., Music Teacher; *b:* Boone, NC; *m:* Edward Dee; *c:* Mariea B., Matthew B.; *ed:* (BS) Music Ed/Fr, W Carolina Univ 1965; *cr:* Music Teacher Reidsville City Schls 1965-71, Mitchell Cty Schls 1975-; *ai:* NEA; Delta Kappa Gamma Treas 1980-; *office:* Mitchell HS 217 School Rd Bakersville NC 28705

MILLER, KAY SMITH, Second Grade Teacher; *b:* Foreman, AR; *m:* Elton Eugene; *c:* Michael; *ed:* (BS) Elem Ed, Univ of AR 1968; *cr:* 2nd Grade Teacher Jones Elem 1968-69, Crestview Elem 1969-71; 2nd/3rd Grade Teacher Foreman Elem 1974-77; Remedial Rdng C D Franks Elem 1977-79; 3rd Grade Teacher Burke Street Elem 1979-89; 2nd Grade Teacher C D Franks Elem 1989-; *ai:* Grade Level Chm 1979-85; Burke Street Elem Test Coord 1980-86.

MILLER, KAYE GRAHAM, Science Department Chair; *b:* Arkadelphia, AR; *m:* Cloyce H.; *c:* Stacey, Scott; *ed:* (BS) Bio, Univ of AR 1967; Grad Courses Lamar Univ, Univ of Indianapolis, Univ of St Thomas; *cr:* 6th Grade Sci Teacher Guess Elem 1967-68; Bio Teacher Forest Park HS 1968-73; Life Sci Teacher Campbell Jr HS 1981-84; Sci Dept Chairperson Langham Creek HS 1984-; *ai:* UIL & Jets Spon; NSTA, NABT, Assn for Supervision & Sci Teachers of TX; TX Excl Awd Outstanding HS Teaching 1987; Teaching Excl Awd Cty Fair Ind Sch Dist 1987; *office:* Langham Creek HS 17610 F M 529 Houston TX 77095

MILLER, KENNETH R., Instrumental Music Director; *b:* Joliet, IL; *m:* Joy L. Sebastian; *c:* Kyle, Allison; *ed:* (BMED) Instrumental Music Ed, 1963, (MMED) Instrumental Music Ed, 1973 Vandercook; Several Wkshps; *cr:* Band Dir Dakota HS 1963-73, Dundee Crown HS 1973-, Imperial Scots 1982-; *ai:* Bsktbl & Ftbl Pep Band; Girls & Boys Sports; Various Marching Bands; IL Ed Assn, NEA, Music Ed Natl Conf, IL Music Educators Mem 1963-; Mid-America Competing Band Dir VP 1972-73; *office:* Dundee-Crown HS 1500 Kings Rd Carpentersville IL 60110

MILLER, LAURIE CROUCH, Principal; *b:* Poteet, TX; *m:* Adrian; *c:* Leslie, Lyle; *ed:* (BS) Elem Ed, SW TX St Univ 1971; (MS) Admin, Univ of TX San Antonio; Leadership Trng; *cr:* Teacher Harlandale Ind Sch Dist 1972-80; 4th/5th Grade Teacher Pecan Valley Elem 1980-81, Sinclair Elem 1980-87; Vice Prin Harmony Elem 1987-; *ai:* Alamo City Heat Fan Club Creator & Spon; ASCD, NAESP, TX Assn for Supervision & Curr Dev; TX Elem Prin & Supvrs Assn (Secy 1989-, Treas 1990); Assn of TX Prof Educators (Secy 1982-83, Pres 1983-84); E Cntrl Dist Cncl PTA 2ND VP; Teacher of Yr Sinclair Elem; *office:* Harmony Elem Sch 10625 Green Lake San Antonio TX 78223

MILLER, LAVONNA FAYE (ROSE), Business Education Teacher; *b:* Patriot, OH; *m:* Larry F.; *c:* David W., Aaron L.; *ed:* (BS) Scndry Bus Ed, Univ of Rio Grande 1987; (MS) Educl Admin, Univ of Dayton 1990; Voc Cert; *cr:* Part-Time Adult Ed Teacher Pike Cty Public Schls 1987; Bus Ed Teacher Vern Riffe Joint Voc Sch 1987-; *ai:* Bus Prof of America Adv; OH Assn Coach; Parliamentary Procedure Team; Seminar Speaker for Bus Prof of America OH Assn; OH Bus Teacher (Asst Membership, Parliamentarian) 1986-; OH Voc Assn Public Relations Bus Ed Division, Life Mem 1989; Prof Secys Intnl (Corresponding Secy 1988-89, Schlsp Chm 1989); Jr Federated Womens Ed Chm 1983; Co-Authored Video Script for Bus Ed; Authored Article for Ova Reporter; Bus Ed New Prof Awd Winner; *office:* Vern Riffe Joint Voc Sch 23365 SR 124 Piketon OH 45661

MILLER, LEONARD M., Mathematics/Computer Chair; *b:* Scranton, PA; *m:* Carolyn; *c:* Mark; *ed:* (BS) Scndry Ed, 1961, (MED) Math, PA St Univ 1968; (MBA) Accounting, Univ of Az 1982; *cr:* Math Teacher Hanover Park HS 1961-62; Math/Sci Teacher 1962-67, Prin 1968-70 Chilex Sch; Math/Cmptr Teacher Sahuarita Jr HS 1971-; *ai:* Chess & Cmptr Club; SEA, AEA, NEA Pres 1983-88; NCTM 1981-; Masonic Secy 1966-; Tucson Stamp Club Treas 1982-; *office:* Sahuarita Jr HS P O Box 26 Sahuarita AZ 85629

MILLER, LEONARD M., English Teacher; *b:* Cambridge, MA; *ed:* (BA) Eng, N Adams St Coll 1972; Grad Work Salem St Coll, Simmons Coll, Rivier Coll, TX A&M Univ; *cr:* Eng Teacher Alvirne HS 1972-79; Dir Boston Bartender Sch of America 1980-86; Eng Teacher Alvirne HS 1986-; Owner Boston Bartenders Sch of America; *ai:* Drama Adv 1986-; Alvirne HS Drama Society; Sr Play Dir; Hudson Fed of Teachers VP Candidate 1990-91; Awd Grant to Study Mark Twains Huckleberry Finn from Natl Endowment for Hum TX A&M Univ Coll Station 1988; *office:* Alvirne HS Derry Rd Hudson NH 03051

MILLER, LEWIS WILLIAM, 7-9th Grade German Teacher; *b:* Beatrice, NE; *m:* Marlene Donnette Stewart; *c:* Kelly Jean; *ed:* (BA) Ger/Eng, Kearney St Coll 1968; Univ of NE Omaha; *cr:* Ger Teacher Grand Island Sr HS 1968, West HS 1968-79, Norris Jr HS 1981-; *home:* RR 1 PO Box 305 Fort Calhoun NE 68023

MILLER, LILLIAN CRAWFORD, Science Teacher; *b:* Bainbridge, GA; *m:* Peter J. Jr.; *c:* Joseph C.; *ed:* (BS) Bio, Bluefield St Coll 1973; Physics Scndry Teachers, Albany St Coll, Biological Institute, Albany St Coll, Physics Institute, Albany St Coll; *cr:* Sci Teacher Bainbridge HS 1973-75, Plains HS 1977-78, Southside Mid Sch 1979-84; Dougherty Comprehensive HS 1984-; *ai:* Natl Ed of Educators 1973-; GA Assn of Educators 1973-; PTA 1983-; Dougherty Cty Assn of Educators 1973; Order of Eastern Star Recording Sec 1985-; Delta Sigma Theta 1970-72.

MILLER, LINDA RUETER, Eighth Grade Science Teacher; *b:* Michigan City, IN; *m:* Jerry Lee; *c:* Kelly L., Kristen L.; *ed:* (BS) Bio, 1970, (MA) Bio, 1974 Ball St Univ; *cr:* 7th Grade Sci Teacher Barker Jr HS 1970-72; 8th Grade Sci Teacher New Prairie Jr HS 1972-; *ai:* New Prairie Jr HS Yrbk, Girls Track; New Prairie Sr HS Girls Golf; IN HS Girls Golf Assn; La Porte Lady Elks BPOE #396; Rolling Prairie Conservation Club; *office:* New Prairie Jr HS 5331 N Cougar Rd New Carlisle IN 46552

MILLER, LOIS MORK, Kindergarten Teacher; *b:* Rice Lake, WI; *m:* Richard; *c:* Brian, Brent, Bradley; *ed:* Elem Ed, Barron Cty Teachers Coll 1959; (BS) Elem Ed, Univ of WI Eau Claire 1978; Courses at Univ of WI Stout, River Falls, Stevens Point, Eau Claire; *cr:* 3rd Grade Teacher Bloomington Elem 1959-60; 3rd/4th Grade Teacher Rice Lake Elem 1960-63; 1st Grade Teacher 1964-65, 2nd Grade Teacher 1965-66, Girls Phys Ed Teacher 1968-69, 4th Grade Teacher 1978-69; Kndgtn Teacher 1985- Cameron Elem; *ai:* Math Guidance & Lib Comm; Vlybl Act Assistant; Kndgtn Teachers Assn 1985-; Chrstn Bus & Prof Women Chm 1988-; *home:* 1248 19 9th St Cameron WI 54822

MILLER, LORETTA DOWLING, 6th Grade/Head Teacher/ Prin; *b:* Panhandle, TX; *w:* Bill R. (dec); *c:* Glen R.; *ed:* (BA) Ed, Highlands Univ 1958; Working on Admin Degree; *cr:* 3rd Grade Teacher White Pine Cty Schls 1963-64; Natrona Cty Schls 1964-76; 5th Grade Teacher 1977-87; 6th Grade/Head Teacher/ Prin 1987- Grants-Cibola Cty Schls; *ai:* Stu Cncl Adv; Admin Cncl; Prin of Elem Sch K-6; Treas 1987-88; Mem 1963- NEA; Nm Sch Admin 1987-; NM Assn Elem Sch Prin 1987-; *office:* Grant-Cibola Cty Schls P O Box 8 Grants NM 87020

MILLER, LORRAINE CRAIG, 8th Grade English Teacher; *b:* Memphis, TN; *m:* Samuel A.; *c:* Scott; *ed:* (BA) Elem/Spec Ed, 1978, (MS) Spec Ed, Memphis St 1980; *cr:* 6th Grade Teacher 1978-79, 4th Grade Teacher 1979-80, 6th Grade Teacher 1980-86, 8th Grade Teacher 1987- Woodstock; *ai:* Natl Jr Beta Club; Rdng Club; Yrbk, Newspaper, Lang Art Dept Chm; Book Adoption Lang Art Chm; Shelby Cty Ed Assn (Rep 1983-84, Research Comm 1984-85); West TN Ed Assn Rdng Chm 1985-86; BSA Act Comm 1980-; NCTE; IntnlRdng Assn; Natl Teachers Study Cncl; Memphis St Dept of Instruction Nom for Distinguished Teacher 1988; Nom Commercial Appeal Thanks to Teachers 1990; *office:* Woodstock Sch 5909 Woodstock-Cuba Millington TN 38053

MILLER, LOUISE QUILLIAM, French Teacher; *b:* Verdun PQ, Quebec Canada; *m:* Tony R.; *c:* Tonya; *ed:* (BA) Sociology, Furman Univ 1963; *cr:* Patients Rep/Information Supvr Greenville General Hospital 1963-68; Medical Secy E H Williams MD 1969-70; Eng/Fr/Typing Teacher 1982-88, Fr/Typing Teacher 1988- Heritage Chrstn Sch; *home:* 109 Salem Rd Gaffney SC 29340

MILLER, MARC HOWARD, 4th Grade Teacher; *b:* Mount Clemens, MI; : Jo Woolrich; *c:* Todd J,. Joshua C.; *ed:* (BS) Ed, Central MI Univ 72;(MA) Ed, Saginaw Valley St Coll 1976; *cr:* 5th Grade Teacher 1972-77; 4th Grade Teacher 1977-; *ai:* Sci Olympiad Coach; Sci Fair Leader; 1st United Meth Church Admin Bd Mem 1987-89; *office:* Ojibwa Elem Sch 46950 Heydenreich Mount Clemens MI 48044

MILLER, MARGARET GALLAGHER, Second Grade Teacher; *b:* St Marys, PA; *m:* John A. Jr.; *c:* Jamie L. *ed:* (BS) Elem Ed, Clarion St Coll 1973; *cr:* 4th Grade Teacher St Boniface Sch 1973-76; 2nd Grade Teacher Fox Twp Elem Ed 1976-83; 6th Grade Teacher St Marys Area Mid Sch 1983-89; 2nd Grade Teacher Fox Twp Elem Sch 1989-; *ai:* Organized & Sponsored St Marys Area Mid Sch Chapter Young Astronausts; St Marys Area Educational Assn; PA St Educational Assn; NEA; St Boniface Rosary Society; *home:* Box 142 Kersey PA 15846

MILLER, MARIA JOY MC CORKLE, Business Teacher; *b:* Pittsburg, KS; *m:* Billy W. Jr.; *c:* Meagan N., Jonathan A.; *ed:* (BS) Bus Ed, Cntrl St Univ 1981; *cr:* Teacher Kiefer HS 1981-83, Olive HS 1984-; *ai:* Sr Spon; Staff Dev, Guidance, Schlsp Comm; *home:* Rt 1 Box 100 Beggs OK 74421

MILLER, MARK LEROY, Soc Stud Teacher/Team Leader; *b:* Frederick, MD; *m:* Constance Marie Stehman; *c:* Marybeth, Mark Jr.; *ed:* (BA) Soc Sci, Elizabethtown Coll 1964; (MED) Elem Ed, West Chester St Univ 1969; Post Grad Stud Sch Admin, Univ of DE 1970; Grad Stud Cmptr Sci; *cr:* Teacher Stanton Elem Sch 1964-66; 6th Grade Teacher Heritage Elem Sch 1966-69; Asst Prin 1979-81, 7th-9th Grade Teacher 1969- Skyline Mid Sch; *ai:* Skyline Mid Sch Amateur Radio Club Spon & Faculty Adv; Skyline Soccer Coach 1969; St of DE Soc Stud Advisory Comm; NEA Life Mem; DE St Ed Assn, Red Clay Ed Assn 1964; Living His Organization Revolutionary Period (Amer 2nd PA Regiment, British 43rd Regiment of Foot); Ebenezer United Meth Church (Admin Bd Chm, Bd of Trustees Chm); Licensed FCC Amateur Radio Operator; Military Affiliate Radio Service Affiliation; *office:* Skyline Mid Sch 2900 Skyline Dr Wilmington DE 19808

MILLER, MARY ALICE, First Grade Teacher; *b:* Newark, NY; *c:* Susan Meyer, Jennifer, Pamela, Christopher; *ed:* (BS) Elem Ed, SUNY 1964; Early Literacy Inservice Course; Project Intervention for Elem Children; *cr:* 1st Grade Teacher 1964-67; Kndgtn Teacher 1967-84; 1st Grade Teacher 1984- Marion Elem; *ai:* Play Dir 1985-88; Chrldng Coach 1973-88; Mentor for Support Group of Elem Children; Marion Teachers Assn 1964-; NY St Teachers Assn 1964-; 2nd VP 1984-86; Pres 1986-88 Delta Kappa Gamma; Girl Scouts of America Leader 1964-70; United Church Marion (Sunday Sch Teacher/Mem of Bd Chrtn Ed/Mem of Ofclbd); Marion-Save Our Cmmty Group; Teacher of Yr 1981; *home:* 4540 Dormedy Hill Rd Marion NY 14505

MILLER, MARY C. LIPKE, Secondary Physical Ed Teacher; *b:* Mendota, IL; *m:* Donald; *c:* Griff, Lindsay; *ed:* (BS) Phys Ed, IL St Univ 1965; Grad Stud in Ed, Psych & Phys Ed at UW LaCrosse, Northern IL Univ, Drake Univ & IL Valley Comm Coll; *cr:* Phys Ed Teacher Kenosha Elem Schls 1965-66, Tremper HS 1966-68, Mendota HS 1972-; Health & Phys Ed Teacher Dixon HS 1968-72; *ai:* Vlybl Coach; Jr Class Chm; Prom Adv; Schlsp Selection Comm; IL Ed Assn, NEA 1968-; Mendota Ed Assn 1972-; Amer Vlybl Coaches Assn; United Way Campaign Contributer; Mendota Elks Club Honorary Mem; Holy Cross Cath Church Mem; Recognition Dinner; Vlybl Coach Soph 1987-, Asst Var 1987 & 1990; *office:* Mendota Twnshp H S 302 16th St Mendota IL 61342

MILLER, MARY JANE, Chemistry/Physical Sci Teacher; *b:* Jenning, LA; *ed:* (BS) Bio/Gen Sci Ed, 1971, (MED) Scndry Ed/ Bio, 1974 Univ of SW LA; Grad Stud; Cert Chem; *cr:* Sci Teacher Comeaux HS 1972-; *ai:* Sci Club; Jr Class Spon; Substance Abuse Prevention Ed Team; NEA, LAE, LPAE 1986-; LPACT Rep 1975-86; *office:* Comeaux HS 100 W Bluebird Lafayette LA 70508

MILLER, MARY JANE (ELLIS), Third Grade Teacher; *b:* Shawnee, OK; *m:* Ronald Ray; *c:* Scott Ray, Stacie Marie; *ed:* (BS) Elem Ed, OK St Univ 1970; *cr:* First Grade Teacher El Dorado Springs Elem 1970-71; Third Grade Teacher Stockton Elem 1971-; *ai:* MSTA; STA; Stockton Chrstn Church; *home:* 805 Petty Ln Stockton MO 65785

MILLER, MARY LYNN, Third Grade Teacher; *b:* Casper, WY; *c:* Christian; *ed:* (AA) Elem Ed, Casper Coll 1966; (BA) Elem Ed, Univ of WY 1968; Grad Stud; *cr:* 1st Grade Teacher 1968-84, 4th Grade Teacher 1985-86, 3rd Grade Teacher 1968-85 Univ Park Sch; *ai:* Drama Univ Park Sch; NEA, WEA 1968-.

MILLER, MATTIE ELINORA BRITTAIN, Third Grade Teacher; *b:* Morganton, NC; *m:* Raymond K.; *c:* Richard K., Michael K., Sharon M. Schwartz; *ed:* (BS) Elem Ed, E KY Univ 1967; (MA) Early Chldhd, Appalachian St Univ 1987; *cr:* Classroom Teacher Burke Cty Public Schls 1967-; *ai:* Mentor Teacher; Co-Coord Volunteer Prgm; Alpha Delta Kappa (Chaplain 1985, Secy 1988-); NEA, NCAE 1967-; NC Cncl Teachers of Math 1988-; Wrote & Received Sci & Cultural Arts

Grants; *office:* Hillcrest Elem Sch Tennessee St Morganton NC 28655

MILLER, MAXINE KLINK, Fifth Grade Teacher; *b:* Meyersdale, PA; *m:* Jeffery T.; *ed:* (BS) Elem Ed, 1984, (MED) Admin & Supervision, 1986 Frostburg St Coll; (MED) Curr & Instruction, Frostburg St Univ 1990; *cr:* Grad Asst Frostburg St Coll 1985; Math/Eng Teacher S Garrett HS 1985-88; 4th Grade Teacher 1988-89, 5th Grade Teacher 1989- Accident Elem Sch; *ai:* Accident Elem Rural Schls Enhancement Comm Mem; Supervised Coll Stu Asst; Cty Rep Quantitative Literacy Conference; Attendance Math Symposium FSU; Mem Comm to Revise Cty Math Scope & Sequence; Phi Delta Kappa (Treas 1987-88, Secy 1988-89) 1986-; NCTM 1986-; ASCD 1987-; Amer Assn of Univ Women Life Mem 1985-; Young Prof Hall of Fame 1987; Met With Iris Educators Travel-Study Tour 1990; Teacher Tips Published Classroom Magazine 1990; Who Whos Amer Ed 1988-89; *home:* 204 Grant St Ext P O Box 573 Grantsville MD 21536

MILLER, MICHELLE MURRAY, English II & III Teacher; *b:* Oswego, NY; *m:* Frank E.; *c:* Robert K.; *ed:* (BA) Ger/Psych, Jacksonville Univ 1980; Working Toward Masters Guidance & Counseling, Univ of N FL; *cr:* Ger/Eng Teacher Middleburg HS 1986-88, Episcopal HS 1988-89; Eng/Ger Tutor Middleburg HS 1989-; *ai:* Games Club Spon; Intnl Club 1986-88; Clay Cty Rdng Cncl 1986-87, 1989-; Willing Hands 1984-86; MS North FL Chapter 1986-89; Avondale Meth Youth Choir Dir 1988-; *office:* Middleburg HS 3750 County Rd 220 Middleburg FL 32068

MILLER, MILTON MAXWELL, Fifth Grade Teacher; *b:* Altoona, PA; *m:* Cynthia Kay Leipold; *c:* Russ, Melanie; *ed:* (BA) Elem, 1972, (MED) Curr/Instruction, 1976 Penn St; Cmptr Ed, Univ of Pittsburgh Johnstown; *cr:* 5th Grade Teacher Hollidaysburg Area Sch Dist 1972-; *ai:* Tennis Coach; Cmptr Comm; Hollidaysburg Area Ed Assn, PA St Ed Assn, NEA 1972-; Altoona Bible Church (Deacon 1986-89, Sunday Sch Supt 1983-89); *home:* 114 25th Ave Altoona PA 16601

MILLER, MILVERN JORDAN, Second Grade Teacher; *b:* St Louis, MO; *m:* Maurice; *c:* Maurita, Michael, Marleen; *ed:* (BS) Elem Ed, IN Univ Indianapolis 1974; (MS) Elem Ed, IN Univ South Bend 1980; *cr:* 5th Grade Elem Teacher Indianapolis Public Sch 57 1974-75; 4th Grade Elem Teacher Ardmore 1975-76l; 3rd/4th Grade Teacher Coquillard 1976-81; 2nd/3rd Grade Teacher James Madison 1981-; *ai:* Madison Sch Contactperson Ec Ed, SBCSC Black His; Madison Building Based Team Mem; Effective Instruction Seminar; NEA; Circle of Mercy Nursery Sch (Regional Bd, Parent Bd Mem, CDA Parent Adv) 1973-74.

MILLER, NANCY A., Mathematics Teacher; *b:* Jackson, OH; *m:* Stephen F.; *c:* Jennifer, Erik; *ed:* (BS) Math, Rio Grande Coll 1968; (MS) Math, OH Univ 1982; *cr:* Math Teacher Warren Local Sch Dist 1968-69; Math Dept Chairperson 1982-88, Math Teacher 1969- Ft Frye HS; Math Instr Washington Tech Coll 1988-; *ai:* OH Cncl Teachers of Math (VP 1982-83, Mem 1968-), Outstanding Math Teacher OH 1984; Ft Frye Teachers Assn 1968-; OH Ed Assn, NEA 1968-; Beverly United Meth Church; Zeta CCL; Natl Sci Fnd Grant; OCTM Convention Chm 1982-83; Outstanding Young Educator; *home:* 509 Fairview Ave Box 9 Beverly OH 45715

MILLER, NANCY LYNN (SCHAEFER), Fourth Grade Teacher; *b:* Jackson, MS; *c:* William T. II, Mary A.; *ed:* (BS) Elem Ed, Univ of S MS 1975; (MS) Elem Ed, William Carey Coll 1986; Remedial Rdng Cert Univ of S MS 1989; *cr:* Remedial Rdng Teacher 1975-76, 4th/5th Grade Teacher 1976- Sumrall Attendance Center; *ai:* Sumrall Elem Public Relations Comm; Video Documentary Producer; Teachers Strike Panelist; Sumrall Elem Fundraising Projects Chairperson; Sunrall Attendance Center Ten-Yr Self-Study Evaluation Math Comm Chairperson; Lamar Cty Amer Fed of Teachers (VP 1982-83, Exec VP 1983-84, Pres 1984-86, 1987-88); Delta Kappa Gamma Research Comm Chairperson 1985-86; Phi Kappa Phi 1975-76; PTA Legislative Conference MS Congress Speaker 1985; Dist Wide Lamar Cty Inservice Speaker; *home:* 502 Hacienda Ave Hattiesburg MS 39402

MILLER, NANCY MC CORD, Kindergarten Teacher; *b:* Marion, IN; *m:* Donald C.; *ed:* (BA) Elem Ed - Summa Cum Laude, IN Wesleyan 1977; (MA) Elem Ed - Summa Cum Laude, Ball St Univ 1982; Sign Lang; *cr:* 3rd Grade Teacher 1978-80, 4th Grade Teacher 1980-87, Kndgtn Teacher 1987- Marion-John W Kendall Elem; *ai:* Comm to Revise Entire Kndgtn Curr Marion Cmmty Schls; Math Adoption Comm; ISTA, NEA 1978-; Kings Four Ministries (Bd Mem, Pianist) 1973-; Teacher Expectations & Stu Achievement Course Certificate of Recognition 1987; Excl Teaching Awd 1987; Working with Deaf Cmmty in Marion; *office:* Kendall Elem Sch 2009 W Kem Rd Marion IN 46952

MILLER, NEUCEDIA ISON, Fourth Grade Teacher; *b:* Isom, KY; *m:* Winfred R.; *c:* Gregory; *ed:* (BS) Elem Ed, Univ of KY 1953; (MA) Elem Ed, 1979, (Rank I) Elem Ed, 1980 Morehead St Univ; *cr:* Teacher Ashland Ind 1970-; *ai:* ASA Bd; Sick Bank; Governors Cup Coach Poage; Math Olympiad; Cheerleading; Sch Protal; AEA Bd; KEA, NEA; Beta Sigma Phi Girl of Yr 1987; First Baptist Church; Alpha Delta Kappa Treas; PTA Nom Teacher of Yr, Life Membership 1989; Nom Ashland Ind Teacher of Yr 1988-89; *home:* 2344 Ranch Rd Ashland KY 41101

MILLER, ODUS JAMES, Mathematics Teacher; *b:* Spartanburg, SC; *m:* Shirley Ann Hileman; *ed:* (BA) His, Carson-Newman Coll 1957; (MM) Math, Univ of TN Knoxville 1966; Post Grad Courses E TN St Univ & Univ of TN Knoxville; *cr:* Math Teacher Whitesburg HS 1958-59, Morristown HS 1959-65; Sr Process Eng Amer Enka Corporation 1966-83; Math Teacher Cocke Cty HS 1984-; *ai:* Algebra I Math Team Coach; Sr Class Spon; NEA, TN Ed Assn, E TN Ed Assn, Cocke Cty Ed Assn; Lions Club (Secy-Treas 1968-69, VP 1969-72, Secy 1969); Alpha Delta Kappa Mens Assn (TN Pres 1982-86, Intnl Pres 1989-); Buffalo Trail Baptist Church (Deacon Chm 1988-, Ushers Chm 1985-); Natl Sci Fnd Schlsp TN Tech 1959, Univ of TN Knoxville 1965-66; *home:* 2007 Morningside Dr Morristown TN 37814

MILLER, PAMELA HART, School Psychologist; *b:* Booneville, MO; *m:* John B.; *ed:* (BS) Elem Ed, Univ of MO Columbia 1974; (MA) Counseling Psych/Cnslr Ed, 1987, ED SPEC Counseling Psych/Cnslr Ed, 1989 Univ of MO Kansas City; *cr:* Elem Teacher 1974-86, Sch Cnslr 1986-88 West Platte R-II Sch Dist; Sch Psychologist Platte Valley Ed Cooperative 1988-; *ai:* Delta Kappa Gamma Charter Mem 1986-89; Pi Lambda Theta Secy 1986-89; Amer Assn of Counseling & Dev, MO Sch Cnslr Assn 1986-; Platte Cty Eleeomosynary Society 1985-; W Platte PTA Pres Awd 1987; *office:* Platte Valley Ed Cooperative Box 339 Smithville MO 64089

MILLER, PATRICIA WILSON, English Teacher; *b:* Fort Bragg, NC; *m:* Jon Charles; *c:* Amy; *ed:* (BA) Fr, Salem Coll 1965; (MAT) Eng, Univ of NC at Chapel Hill 1973; *cr:* Eng Teacher Durham HS 1969-78, Northern HS 1978-; *ai:* Yrbk; Published Articles in HS Press Journals; Judge Columbia Scholastic Press Assn; Yrbk Division; *office:* Northern Durham H S 117 Massey Rd Durham NC 27712

MILLER, PRISCILLA SOUMIS, 1st Grade Teacher; *b:* Highland Park, MI; *m:* Douglas S.; *c:* Brandon, Clinton; *ed:* (BA) Sci/Soc Stud, Univ of Detroit 1974; (MA) Rdng, Oakland Univ 1979; Certified MI Model Educator; *cr:* 3rd Grade Teacher 1974-75, 1st Grade Teacher 1975- Beacon; *office:* Beacon Elem Sch 19475 Beaconsfield Harper Woods MI 48225

MILLER, ROBERT CASSIUS, English Teacher; *b:* Albany, NY; *m:* Elizabeth Ann; *c:* Sarah, Robert, Stephanie; *ed:* (AA) Liberal Arts, Adirondack Comm Coll 1967; (BA) Eng Ed, 1969, (MS) Eng Ed, 1974 Plattsburgh St Univ; *cr:* Eng Teacher Berlin Jr-Sr HS 1969-; *ai:* Team Management System 7th Grade Team Leader; NYSUT 1969-; Cub Scouts Den Leader 1987-, Service Awd 1990; 4-H 1984-; *office:* Berlin Jr-Sr HS Rt 22 Cherry Plain NY 12040

MILLER, ROBERT FULTON, JR., 6th Grade Social Stud Teacher; *b:* Reading, PA; *c:* Jason, Ethan; *ed:* (BS) Elem Ed, 1968, (MS) Elem Counseling, 1974 Kutztown Univ; *cr:* 6th Grade Soc Stud Teacher Schuylkill Valley 1968-; *ai:* Jr HS Asst Bsktbl Coach; In Charge of Intramural Act; PA St Ed Assn, NEA, Schuylkill Valley Ed Assn 1968-; Schuylkill Valley PTO 1968-; Antietam Sch Athletic Boosters 1980-; Dist Teacher of Yr 1980; *office:* Schuylkill Valley Sch RD 1 Leesport PA 19533

MILLER, RONALD DALE, SR., Fourth Grade Teacher; *b:* Chicago, IL; *m:* Carolyn Chandler; *c:* Ronald Jr., Gerald, Francesca; *ed:* (BA) Early Chldhd Ed, Chicago St Univ 1974; Working on MS in Admin; *cr:* Teacher Englewood Center for Handicapped 1974-76, S Cntrl Sch for Handicapped 1976-78, Kellar Jr HS 1978-; *ai:* Teachers Union Local 1173 Pres; *office:* Thomas J Kellar Jr HS Lydia And Mc Breen Sts Robbins IL 60472

MILLER, ROSALIE KAY, Third Grade Teacher; *b:* Richmond, IN; *ed:* (BA) Elem Ed, Purdue Univ 1972; (MA) Elem Ed, Marshall Univ 1978; Grad Work Marshall Univ; *cr:* Kndgtn Teacher Mt Olive Sch 1972-73; 3rd Grade Teacher Ordnance Sch 1973-; *ai:* Yrbk Adv; Effective Schls Comm; Academic Cncl; Mason Cty Rdng Cncl (Recording Secy 1978-79, Pres 1980-81, 1982-84, Pres Elect 1981-82) 1977-; WV Assn for Supervision & Curr Dev 1989-; Christ Church Vestry Registrar 1981-87, 1989-; Tu-Endie-Wei Garden Club 1981-; Alpha Xi Delta 1969-; Jaycees Outstanding Young Teacher of Yr; Mason Cty Rdng Cncl Teacher of Yr; Outstanding Young Women of America; *home:* Rt 1 Box 63 Point Pleasant WV 25550

MILLER, SALLY SHANNON, English Teacher; *b:* Weeksbury, KY; *m:* Hugo E.; *c:* Kimberly Hall, Jeffry; *ed:* (BA) Eng/Art, Pikeville Coll 1965; (MA) Ed, 1983, (Rank I) Supervision, 1985 Morehead St Univ; *cr:* Classroom Teacher Floyd Cty Bd of Ed 1965-; *ai:* Drama Club, Chrldr, Yrbk, Speech League, Jr/Sr Prom, Honor Banquet Spon; NEA, KY Ed Assn 1965-; Delta Kappa Gamma 1978-; *office:* Mc Dowell HS Mc Dowell KY 41647

MILLER, SANDRA ANN (STERNBERG), Second Grade Teacher; *b:* Huntingburg, IN; *c:* Ross, Trent; *ed:* (BS) Elem Ed, 1970, (MS) Elem Ed, 1973 IN St Univ; *cr:* Teacher Ireland Elem 1970-; *ai:* Jasper Classroom Teachers Assn Discussion Team Mem, NEA, Dubois Cty Cncl of IN Rdng Assn, IN St Teachers Assn; Alph Delta Kappa (Corresponding Secy 1984-86, Pres Elect 1988-, Pres 1990); Luncheon Optimist Club Mem; St Marys Church (Mem, Vaction Bible Sch Teacher 1986-); Jasper HS Positive Educator Awd; *office:* Ireland Elem Sch Green St Ireland IN 47545

MILLER, SANDRA G., Mathematics Teacher; *b:* Erie, PA; *ed:* (BS) Scndry Ed/Math, PA St Univ 1963; Hofstra Univ; *cr:* Math Teacher Dodd Jr HS 1963-68, Mc Dowell HS 1968-; *ai:* MEA (Treas 1973-80, Building Rep 1972-73); PSEA, NEA 1968-; MENSA 1990; Erie Theatre Arts Inst (Pres 1985-, Costume Design 1976, Property Design 1975); Sweet Adelines Music Staff 1984-; Erie Playhouse Asst Dir 1977-; Erie Opera Company Staff 1987-; *office:* Mc Dowell Intermediate HS 3320 Caughey Rd Erie PA 16506

MILLER, SHIRLEY PHILLIPS, Mathematics Teacher; *b:* Dornsife, PA; *m:* Carl O.; *ed:* (MED) Natural Sci, Univ of DE 1969; (BA) Math, Bridgewater Coll 1964; *cr:* Teacher Lord Baltimore Sch 1964-66, Milton Jr HS 1966-; *ai:* Coach Mathcounts Team, DE interscholastic Math Team, Cmptr Faire Calculator Team; DE Cncl Teachers of Math Pres 1987-88; NCTM, NEA, DE ST ED Assn; Presidential Awd Excl in Math Teaching 1985; Milton Jr HS Teacher of Yr 1985; *home:* RD 4 Box 144 Georgetown DE 19947

MILLER, STEVE, Mathematics Teacher; *b:* Mason City, WV; *m:* Roberta Jean Ord; *c:* Kamille, Kay; *ed:* (BS) Math, OH Univ 1973; (MA) Scndry Ed, AZ St Univ 1986; Grad Work in Cmptrs, Math, Ed; *cr:* Math Teacher Shadow Mountain HS 1974-; *ai:* Academic Decathlon Coach; AATM, NCTM, AEA, NEA; PVEA Building Rep; Mu Alpha Theta Spon; GTE Grant 1987-88; *office:* Shadow Mountain HS 2902 E Shea Blvd Phoenix AZ 85028

MILLER, STEVEN DENNIS, Science Department Chairman; *b:* Los Alamos, NM; *m:* Nadine A. Trujillo; *c:* Steven N.; *ed:* (BA) Bio, 1980, (MA) Bio, 1983 WNMU; Various Wkshps in Bio & Environmental Ed; *cr:* Bio Teacher 1980-, Sci Dept Head 1987-, Sci Fair Dir 1981- Silver HS; *ai:* Dir/Spon Silver Schls Sci Fair; NEA 1980-; Gila Wildlife Rescue Dir 1984-; Sci Fair Spon of Yr SW NM 1982-85 & 1987-89; St Sci Fair Spon of Yr NM 1989; Humanitarian of Yr NM Veterinarians Assn 1989; Outstandng Young Men America 1988; *office:* Silver HS 3200 North Silver Silver City NM 88061

MILLER, STEVEN J., United States History Teacher; *b:* Joplin, MO; *m:* Connie D.; *ed:* (BS) Scndry Ed, 1975, (MS) Ed Admin, 1981 OK St Univ; Grad Stud Ed Admin; *cr:* Teacher Union Mid Sch 1975-78, Union HS 1978-; *ai:* Teacher of the Month 1985; Awarded Regional Teacher of Yr Daughters of the Amer Revolution.

MILLER, STUART EARL, 7th/8th Grade Science Teacher; *b:* Martins Ferry, OH; *m:* Shawn Kathleen; *c:* Jordan; *ed:* (BS) Elem Ed, OK Univ 1983; (MS) Sch Counseling, Univ of Dayton 1990; *cr:* 7th/8th Grade Teacher Union Local Sch Dist 1984-; *office:* Belmont Elem Sch P O Box 27 Belmont OH 43718

MILLER, SUSAN TERESA, 7th & 8th Grade Math Teacher; *b:* Philadelphia, PA; *m:* Joseph T.; *c:* Joseph Jr., Stephanie, Melissa, Jeffrey; *ed:* (BA) Ed, Neumann Coll 1985; Numerous Courses; *cr:* Teacher St George Sch 1970-73, 1979-81, St Robert Sch 1977-78, St Francis of Assisi 1983-; *ai:* Yrbk Adv & Ed; Math Dept Chm; Mathcounts Coach; Math Competition Dir; Math Club Moderator; NCEA; Parish Cncl 1988-89; Nom Distinguished Cath Educator Awd 1987; *home:* 722 15th Ave Prospect Park PA 19076

MILLER, TONY, Social Studies Teacher; *b:* Ft Campbell, KY; *m:* Kathleen Suzanne; *c:* Elisabeth, Daniel; *ed:* (BA) Soc Stud, Shepherd Coll 1978; (MA) Psych/Sociology, Hood Coll 1986; *cr:* Soc Stud Teacher Linganore HS 1979-; *ai:* Frederick Cty Teacher-Historian 1987; *office:* Linganore HS 12013 Old Annapolis Rd Frederick MD 21701

MILLER, VIVIAN ARLENE, Kindergarten Teacher; *b:* Dequincy, LA; *m:* George Eugene;; *ed:* (BA) Early Chldhd, 1976, (MED) Ed, 1984 Mc Neese Univ; *cr:* Headstart Teacher Starks Government 1970-72; 2nd Grade Teacher 1976-84, Kndgtn Teacher 1984- Starks HS; *ai:* Active Mem PTO; CAE/NEA 1976-87; Fed of Teachers 1987-; Teacher of Yr Starks HS 1989-.

MILLER, WALTER ROBERT, JR., Ath Director/Math Teacher; *b:* Dallas, TX; *m:* Toni Klidas; *c:* Kristi, Walter III, John; *ed:* (BS) Phys Ed/Math, Univ North TX 1975; Phys Ed/Math, KS St; Phys Ed/Math, Henderson Cty Jr Coll; *cr:* Teacher/Coach Kemp TX, Polytechhnie Ft Worth, Western Hills; *ai:* Head Track; Def Coord Ftbl; Ath Dir Head Ftbl; Assn of TX Prof Educators; Ft Worth Coaches Pres 1985-89; TX HS Coaches; US Army E-4 1971-73 DAV 1973; Teacher of Yr Western Hills 1989; *office:* Western Hills H S 3600 Boston Fort Worth TX 76116

MILLER, WANDA HAIRE, Third/Fourth Grade Teacher; *b:* Winston Salem, NC; *m:* Tommy Sr.; *c:* Renee; Tommy L. Jr., Danita, Chris, Jerry Miller; *ed:* (BS) Elem Ed, 1968, (MA) Mid Sch, 1983 Appalachian St Univ; Effective Teaching Trng Prgm Instr, Teacher Performance Appraisal & Mentor Support Team Trng Prgm; *cr:* Teacher Yadkin Cty Bd of Ed 1968-78; Educl Consultant NW Regional Ed Center for ARC Model Classroom Teacher Improvement Project 1978-; Teacher Yadkin Cty Bd of Ed 1980-; *ai:* Yadkinville Elem Sch Hospitality Comm; NEA 1968-; NC Assn of Educators Faculty Rep 1968-; Yadkin Cty Assn of Educators (VP 1972-73, Pres 1973-74) 1968-; Center United Meth Church; Yadkin Cty PTA 1968-; Natl PTA 1988-; Forbush HS Music Boosters Club (Secy 1987), 1984-87; Cub Scouts of Amer Asst Den Mother; Susanna Wesley Circle United Meth Church (Pres, Vacation Bible Sch Dir, Teacher); Center United Meth Church Co-Chairperson; PTA Citizenship Comm; Yadkin Cty Ed Dev Cncl 1975; Yadkin Cty Teacher of Yr 1976; Southern Assn of Colls & Schls Visiting; Alexandr Cty Comm 1982; Natl Teachers Esam Job Analysis Study Participant 1989; *office:* Yadkinville Elem Sch PO Box 518 Yadkinville NC 27055

MILLER, WANDA SUE, 8th Grade Soc Stud Teacher; *b:* De Ridder, LA; *c:* Bruce B. II; *ed:* (BA) Upper Elem, (MA) Admin/Supervision, 1975 Mc Neese St Univ; *cr:* Teacher Houston Ind Schls 1965-70, Vidor Jr HS 1970-; *ai:* GED Teacher Jefferson Cty

Jail; TSTA; Vidor Jr HS Teacher of Yr 1988; *office:* Vidor Jr HS Tram Rd Vidor TX 77662

MILLER, WAYNE C., Counselor; *b:* Clinton, MO; *m:* Mary Barbee; *c:* Leslie, Lauren, Nathan; *ed:* (BS) Phys Ed, Univ of MO Columbia 1966; (MS) Scndry Admin, 1975, Ed Spec Scndry Admin, 1982 Cntrl MO St Univ; Cert in Guidance & Counseling, Cntrl MO St Univ 1987; *cr:* Teacher/Coach Leeton HS 1970-72, Knob Noster Mid Sch 1973-75; Prin Knob Noster Mid Sch 1976-87; Cnslr/Coach Knob Noster HS 1988-; *ai:* Jr Class Spon; Asst Vlybl Coach; Girls Bsktbl Head Coach; MO St Teachers Assn; Phi Delta Kappa; Knob Noster Chrstn Church Elder 1982-; Educator of Yr Knob Noster Optimist Club 1984; Article Published 1972; *office:* Knob Noster HS 504 S Washington Knob Noster MO 65336

MILLETT, KATE SANDEROFF, Social Studies Teacher; *b:* Hemel Hempstead, England; *m:* Anthony Derek; *c:* Richard A.; *ed:* (BA) Soc Stud/Eng - Summa Cum Laude, Oakland Univ 1975; Permanent Certificate Qualification Oakland Univ 1981; Archaeology, Leeds Univ England; Prof Dev Oakland Univ; *cr:* Personnel Asst United Nations 1945-48; Publishing Asst Economist Newspaper 1948-51; Sales Dir Personal Asst Firestone Tyre & Rubber Company 1951-56; Soc Stud Teacher Roeper City & Cntry Sch 1976-; *ai:* 6th Grade Cnslr; Soc Act Spon; Sch Trip Coord; *office:* Roeper City & Cntry Sch PO Box 329 Bloomfield Hills MI 48013

MILLEVILLE, BRENDA STURM, 7th Grade Teacher; *b:* Springfield, IL; *m:* Dan E.; *c:* Derek, Darin; *ed:* (BS) Sociology/Anthropology, Sangamon St Univ 1973; Educl Admin; *cr:* 4th/6th/Jr HS Teacher Little Flower Sch 1973-89; Jr HS Teacher St Patrick Sch 1989-; *ai:* Rainbows for all Gods Children Facilitator; NCEA 1973-; Big Brother Big Sister 1983-86; Partners in Ed Grant; Teacher of Yr 1988; *office:* St Patrick Sch 412 N Jackson Decatur IL 62523

MILLIGAN, CONSTANCE FRY, Mathematics Teacher; *b:* Kansas City, MO; *m:* Jerry L.; *c:* Lisa, Christopher, Patrick; *ed:* (BA) Math, Loretto Heights Coll 1959; Grad Stud Math & Ed; *cr:* Math Teacher Shawnee Mission Sch Dist 1959-64, Moscow Jr HS 1976-; *ai:* Mathcounts Coach; NCTM 1980-; ID Cncl Teachers of Math 1985-; Article Published 1983.

MILLIGAN, JOHN DAVID, Biology Teacher; *b:* Levelland, TX; *m:* Lu Ann Johnson; *c:* Mallory A.; *ed:* (BS) Bio/Phys Ed, Angelo St Univ 1984; Working Toward Masters TX Tech Univ; *cr:* Teacher Denver City Jr HS 1984-85; Teacher Denver City HS 1985-; *ai:* Jr Var Ftbl & Bsktbl Coach; *office:* Denver City HS 601 Mustang Ave Denver City TX 79323

MILLIGAN, JUNE MOORE, English Teacher; *b:* Norfolk, VA; *m:* William E. Jr.; *c:* Sharon Reeves, Donna Newland, Laurie; *ed:* (BA) Eng/Math, 1974, (MA) Eng, 1983 Univ of Houston; *cr:* Eng/Math Teacher Seabrook Intermediate Sch 1974-82; Eng Teacher Clear Lake HS 1982-; *ai:* Clear Lake HS UIL Spelling Team Coach; Clear Lake HS Chapter Young Conservatives of TX Spon; Phi Kappa Phi 1974-; TX St Teachers Assn 1975-; Bessie Ebaugh Eng Schlsp Univ of Houston; Outstanding Young Woman of Yr 1967; *office:* Clear Lake HS 2929 Bay Area Blvd Houston TX 77062

MILLIGAN, MICHAEL, III, Third Grade Teacher; *b:* Paterson, NJ; *m:* Margaret Mary Slisz; *c:* Michael IV; *ed:* (BA) Elem Ed/Spec Ed, Mercyhurst Coll 1980; *cr:* Teacher Rev Geo A Brown Mem Sch 1980-84, Cherry Hill Sch 1984-; *ai:* Affirmative Action, Rdng Networking, Writing Process, Thinking Skills, Cmptr, Gifted & Taltented, Standardized Testing Dist Comm Mem; NEA, NJEA 1984-; NJ Governor Teacher Recognition Awd 1988; *home:* PO Box 127 Layton NJ 07851

MILLIGAN, VALERIE GAYLE JONES, Biology Teacher; *b:* Clinton, LA; *m:* Columbus; *c:* Meagan K.; *ed:* (BS) Scndry Ed/Bio, 1985, (Med) Scndry Ed, 1989 Southern Univ; *cr:* Math Teacher Scotlandville Mid Sch 1986; Bio Teacher Woodlawn HS 1986-; *ai:* Advisory Cncl Chairperson; Tri-Hi-Y Co-Spon; Incentive Club Dropout Intervention Spon; Cmmty Assn for Welfare of Sch Children 1986-; E Baton Rouge Parish Dropout Collaborative; Tri-Beta Biological Honor Society 1987-; Minority Women in Sci 1987-; Advisory Cncl Appointment & Chairperson; *home:* 17007 Culps Bluff Ave Baton Rouge LA 70817

MILLNER, GWENDOLYN DALTON, Mathematics Teacher; *b:* Roanoke, VA; *m:* Clarence F. Jr.; *c:* Elizabeth M.; *ed:* (MS) Math/Bio, Longwood Coll 1965; (MED) Admin, Lynchburg Coll 1980; *cr:* Teacher Roanoke City Sch 1965-67, George Washington HS 1967-; *office:* George Washington HS 701 Broad St Danville VA 24540

MILLNER, RUTH RAIBON, Middle School Choral Director; *b:* Tyler, TX; *m:* Authur D.; *c:* Rachelle, Williams A. III, Michael D.; *ed:* (BS) Music, Butler Coll 1955; SMU Dallas/Grambling Coll LA/UT Austin; *cr:* Teacher Central HS 1955-57, Pleasant HS 1958-59, Hill HS 1960-64, Dallas Ind Sch 1964-; *ai:* Minister of Music Local Church; Pres/VP Dallas Music Educators Assn; Chairperson Region XX Mid Sch Vocal Division; Soc Comm Chairperson Present Employment; Choral Dir; Girls Bsktbl Coach; Chrldr Spon; Prgm Comm Church Comm in Local Building; Music Select Comm; Dalls Music Educators Assn (Pres 1980-, VP 1972-79); Soc Comm Chairperson 1980-; Region XX Vocal (Division Chairperson 1981-82, Vice Chairperson); Choral Dir Assn; Music Educators Assn; Classroom Teachers Of Dallas; NEA; Porter Temple CME Church Minister of Music 1974-, Service 1980; Feature Teacher of Yr 1972; PTA Life Membership 1978; Dedicated Book; Teacher Of Yr 1981; Nominee For Perot Awd 1984/1986/1987; Most Outstanding in Dept 1987; Most Outstanding in Choir Competition 1986-; Earned Sweepstakes in Choral Competitions and City 1980-; Best of Kind Ensemble in City 1975-; Fun Fest/Best Choirs of The Season 1984-; *home:* 336 W Brownlee Dallas TX 75224

MILLS, ANITA TROXELL, Fourth Grade Teacher; *b:* Buckhannon, WV; *m:* Lewis Ferrell; *c:* Kent, Heather; *ed:* (BA) Ed, WV Wesleyan 1968; (MA) Elem Ed, Marshall Univ 1980; *cr:* Eng Teacher Lewis Cty HS 1968-69; 7th Grade Teacher Ravenswood HS 1969-71; 4th Grade Teacher East Lynn Elem 1974-78, Wayne Elem 1978-; *ai:* Sch Math Field Day Dir; Sch Advisory Comm Mem; Wayne United Meth Church (Sunday Sch Teacher, Choir, Chm of Ed Comm, Bible Sch Dir) 1974-; *home:* PO Box 176 Wayne WV 25570

MILLS, BENNY RAY, Language Art Dept Chair; *b:* Mullens, WV; *ed:* (BA) Scndry Ed - Magna Cum Laude, Univ of Charleston 1980; (MA) Spec Ed, WV Coll of Grad Stud 1986; Advanced Placement Trng Eng; *cr:* 12th Grade Eng Teacher Wirt Cty HS 1980-82; Spec Ed Teacher Guyan Valley Sch 1982-85, Stephenson Grade Sch 1985-86; 11th-12th Grade Eng Teacher Herndon HS 1986-; *ai:* Drama, Jr HS Girls & Boys Bsktbl Coach; Quiz Bowl, Honor Society Spon; Mark of Excl WVCOGS; WV Mini Grant Awd Winner; *home:* PO Box 6 Itmann WV 24847

MILLS, BRENDA (LEWIS), Elementary School Counselor; *b:* San Pedro, CA; *m:* Michael A.; *ed:* (BAED) Ed Soc Stud/Earth Sci/Coaching/Psych, E WA Univ 1980; (MAED) Sch Counseling, Cntrl WA Univ 1990; Counseling Related Curr; *cr:* 7th/8th Grade Teacher Selah Jr HS 1980-81; HS Var Track & Cross Cntry Coach 1982-85, 5th Grade Teacher 1981-86 Selah Intermediate Sch; Cnlsr Lince Intermediate Sch 1987-; *ai:* Stu Cncl; WA Ed Assn, Selah Ed Assn; PTA; Outstanding Young Amer Woman Awd 1983; Outstanding Educl Service Awd 1989; *office:* Lince Intermediate Sch 316 W Naches Ave Selah WA 98942

MILLS, C. EDWARD, Biology Teacher; *b:* Hagerstown, MD; *m:* Patricia Ann Paone; *c:* Nicole, Bradley, Christopher; *ed:* (BS) Bio/General Sci I, Shepherd Coll 1970; Post Grad Stud VA Polytechnic Institute & St Univ, Univ of VA, WV Univ, Salem Coll, Shenandoah Coll & Conservatory; *cr:* Life Sci/ Earth Sci/Phys Sci Teacher Fred M Lynn Mid Sch 1970-79; Life Sci Teacher Parkside Mid Sch 1980-82; Phys Sci Teacher Frederick Cty Mid Sch 1982-86; Bio Teacher James Wood HS Amherst Campus 1986-; *ai:* Frederick Cty Night Alternative Prgm Teacher; NEA, VEA, FCEA Rep 1985-86; Published in Potomiac Newspaper for Greenhouse Club; Published in Baltimore Sun & Washington Post for Nature Walk Guidance; *office:* James Wood HS Amherst 1313 Amherst St Winchester VA 22601

MILLS, CHARLES E., Chemistry Instructor; *b:* Oakland City, IN; *m:* Karen Sue Wira; *c:* Bill, Kevin; *ed:* (BS) Scndry Ed, Oakland City Coll 1965; (MS) Scndry Ed, IN St Univ 1970; Chem, Univ of the Pacific 1971; Technology, CO St Univ 1972; *cr:* Sci Teacher Jackson Township HS 1965-66, Barr-Reave HS 1966-69, Haubstadt HS 1969-74; Chem Teacher Gibson Southern HS 1974-; *ai:* Sci Club; NEA, IN Assn of Chem Teachers; Haubstadt Chamber of Commerce; Gibson Cty Councilman-Elected Office 1973-; *office:* Gibson Southern HS RR 1 Box 496 Fort Branch IN 47648

MILLS, CYNTHIA ALPERS, Math Department Teacher; *b:* Mc Allen, TX; *m:* Danny R.; *c:* Tiffany, Kylie; *ed:* (BA) Scndry Ed/Math, TX Luth Coll 1972; (MA) Scndry Ed/Supervision, Pan Amer Univ 1981; *cr:* Substitute Teacher Asmara Dependent Sch 1972; Math Teacher Lincoln Jr HS 1972-74; Mc Allen Memorial HS 1983-; *ai:* Frosh Class Spon; Campus Improvement Plan Comm; Soph Class Spon; Learning Styles Club; Rio Grande Valley Math Teachers Assn; Mc Allen Jr League Teen Court Chairman 1989- Lizzie Service Awd 1981-88; *office:* Mc Allen Memorial HS 101 E Hackberry Mc Allen TX 78501

MILLS, D. JEAN, Classroom Teacher; *b:* Detroit, MI; *m:* Garnett Arley Sr.; *c:* Jeanene M. Allen, Garnett A. Jr., Sally M. Tyree, Thomas E., Dinah M. Babb; *ed:* (BS) Scndry Soc Stud, Cntrl CT St Coll 1967; (MED) Soc Stud, William & Mary 1973; Grad Courses Bowie St Coll, Longwood Coll, Univ of VA, Lynchburg Coll; *cr:* 5th Grade Teacher Windsor Elem 1967-72; 7th-10th Grade Teacher Northern HS 1972-73; 6th Grade Teacher Appomattox Elem Sch 1973-; *ai:* Grade Chm; Building & Grounds Comm; Piedmont Rdng Cncl 1973-; Cntrl VA Fed of Teachers Pres 1981-; Phi Delta Kappa 1990-; PTA 1960-; *office:* Appomattox Elem Sch 600 W Confederate Blvd Appomattox VA 24522

MILLS, DONNA MAEDA, 1st/2nd Grade Teacher; *b:* Ontario, OR; *m:* Lon R.; *c:* Lindy D., Jennifer L.; *ed:* (BA) Elem Ed, EOS Coll 1971; Grad Stud; *cr:* 1st Grade Teacher Halfway Elem Sch 1971-73; Opportunity Teacher 1973-75, 1st/2nd Grade Teacher 1975- Harrisburg Elem; *ai:* Lang Art & Textbook Selection Comm; NEA, OR Ed Assn 1971-; Harrisburg Ed Assn (Secy, Treas) 1971-; *office:* Harrisburg Elem Sch PO Box 217 Harrisburg OR 97446

MILLS, DORIS ANN, K-8 Dist Guidance Counselor; *b:* Jersey City, NJ; *ed:* (BS) Ed, 1960; (MED) Soc/Philo Fdn of Ed, 1963 Rutgers Univ; Stu Personnel Svcs Kean Coll; Rutgers Univ; Douglass Coll 1954-56; *cr:* 7th Grade Teacher Township of Raritan Public Schls 1956-58; 8th Grade Teacher Highlands Public Sch 1958-60; 6th-8th Grades Soc Stu Teacher 1960-87; K-8th Grade Dist Guidnc Cnslr 1987- Mendham Borough Schls; *ai:* Coord of Act; Stu Cncl; Bd/Adv Comm; MCCEA 1956-; Natl Local Cncls for Soc Stu 1970-87; NEA 1956-; NJEA 1956-; Counseling Organizations 1990; MBEA 1960-; Republican Club; 1st Recipient of Delbarton Medal 1975; DAR Awd for Excellence in Teaching Morris Cnty 1984; Governors Teacher Recognition Prgm 1986-87; Commissioners Sympsm 1987; *office:* Mendham Borough Schs Mountain View School 100 Dean Rd Mendham NJ 07945

MILLS, GEORGE W., Teacher; *b:* Bremerton, WA; *m:* Lila Hedlund; *ed:* (BS) Physics, 1969, (MED) Math, 1978 Seattle Pacific; *cr:* Teacher Toledo HS 1970-78, Napavine HS 1981-; *ai:* NHS Adv; Sci Team Coach; WA Ed Assn 1981-; Prof Photographers of America 1986-; Cowlitz Prairie Baptist Church Elder 1981-; Several Article & Photographs Published Natl Magazines; *office:* Napavine HS P O Box 357 Napavine WA 98565

MILLS, JAMES OWEN, History Teacher; *b:* Brewton, AL; *M:* Judy Beth; *c:* Julie; *ed:* (BS) Phys Ed, Univ of Montevallo 1978; Educl Leadership, FL Institute of Technology; *cr:* Teacher/Coach Sebastian River Jr HS 1980-; *ai:* Head Ftbl Coach 1983-; Head Bsktbl Coach 1980-86; *office:* Sebastian River Jr HS 9400 State Rd 512 Sebastian FL 32958

MILLS, JEANNE M., 1st/3rd Grade Teacher; *b:* Saint Petersburg, FL; *m:* Stanley R.; *c:* Colby A.; *ed:* (AA) St Pete Jr Coll 1966; (BS) Elem Ed/Early Chldhd, FL St Univ 1968; (MS) Admin/Supervision, Univ of South FL 1981; (EDD) Early & Mid Chldhd; Suncoast Area Teacher Training Supervisor of Interns from USF; Beginning Teacher Prgm; FL Performance Measurement System; Classroom Collegial Coach; *cr:* 1st Grade Teacher Shore Acres Elem 1968-73; Sanders Memorial Elem 1977-78; 1st/3rd Grade Teacher Hudson Elem 1978-89; *ai:* Beginning Teacher Prgm Peer Teacher; Classroom Collegial Coach Coaching Veteran Teachers Prof Dev Plans; SCATT Supervisor; Jr Service League (Corres Secy, Treas, Mem); Childrens Service Cncl Secy 1990; Co-Authored Rdng Prgm 1st Graders; Wrote Practicun Doctoral Accepted Into ERIC; Developing & Implementing Kndgtn Sci Curr Pasco Cty; Inservicing & Teaching Kndgtn Classes Sci Center; Wrote Childrens Book Marine Sci.

MILLS, JOHN G., German/AP European His Teacher; *b:* Ogden, UT; *m:* Krystal Larsen; *c:* John, Megan, Bin, Adam, Jaren; *ed:* (BA) His/Ger, Weber St Coll 1974; (MA) European/Amer His, Univ of NE 1976; Admin Endorsement UT St Univ 1990; *cr:* Adj Instr UT St Univ 1987-89; Teacher Clearfield HS 1976-; *ai:* Head Soccer Coach; Ger Club & Model United Nations Club Adv; UT St Concurrent Enrollment Oversight Comm; Sch Dist Civil Rights Comm Mem; Davis Ed Assn Sch Rep 1976-; UT Ed Assn 1976-; NCSS Mem 1989-; *office:* Clearfield HS 931 S Falcon Dr Clearfield UT 84015

MILLS, JOY BOATRIGHT, Fifth Grade Teacher; *b:* Swainsboro, GA; *m:* David G.; *c:* Vicki, Kaci, Ashlei; *ed:* (BA) Elem Ed, E GA Coll 1980; (BS) Elem Ed, 1982, (MED) Elem Ed, 1985 GA Southern Univ; EDS Elem Ed, GA Southern Univ 1989; *cr:* 6th Grade Teacher 1982-85, 5th Grade Teacher 1985- Emanuel Cty Inst; *ai:* GA Assn of Educators, NEA, Emanuel Assn of Educators 1982-; Twin City 1st Baptist Church Sunday Sch Teacher; *home:* Rt 1 Box 229 Garfield GA 30425

MILLS, JUDITH ZILLA, Chair-Language Arts Teacher; *b:* Springdale, PA; *m:* Kenneth W.; *c:* Jeffrey, Steven; *ed:* (BSED) Ed/Eng, Indiana Univ Of PA 1964; (MED) Scndry Ed/Rdng, OH Univ 1971; *cr:* Sr Eng Teacher Freeport HS 1964-66; 7th Grade Rdng Teacher Evans City Jr HS 1966-67; HS Eng Teacher Athens HS 1967-69; 7th-8th Grade Rdng/Eng Teacher Grove City Jr HS 1978-85; 9th/11th Grade Eng Teacher Dept Chairperson Grove City HS 1985-; *ai:* NCTE; Delta Kappa Gamma Women Educators; Grove City Comm Lib Bd (Pres 1984-86) 1982-86; Gen Electric Fellow Career Ed 1983; *office:* Grove City H S 511 Highland Ave Grove City PA 16127

MILLS, KAREN (BREWER), First Grade Teacher; *b:* Winchester, IN; *m:* Robert L.; *c:* Tammy, Trent; *ed:* (BS) Elem Ed, 1974, (MA) Elem Ed, 1978 Ball St Univ; *cr:* 1st Grade Teacher Monroe Cntrl Schls 1976-; *ai:* Sch Advisory Cncl; Guidance Comm; *home:* RR Box 464 Selma IN 47383

MILLS, LOIS ANNE, Retired; *b:* Corry, PA; *m:* David R.; *c:* Tammi Lyn Wagner, Denise, Scott; *ed:* (BA) Music, Cedarville Coll 1960; (BS) Elem Ed, Wilberforce Cntrl St Univ 1961; *cr:* Substitute Teacher Newaygo/Saginaw/Grand Rapids/Xenia Schls 1962-73; Pre-K Teacher Blackhawk Chrstn Sch 1973-75; K-1st Grade Rdng Teacher Berean Baptist Schl 1975-81; 5th-6th Grade Speech/Rdng Teacher Ridgewood Baptist 1981-89; *ai:* Musical Prgm & Act; Drama Coach; Librarian; OEA 1962-64; *home:* 712 Pierce St Maumee OH 43537

MILLS, MARY ANN, Principal; *b:* Houston, TX; *m:* Milton A.; *ed:* (BA) Psych, TX S Univ 1970; (MA) Admin Ed; *cr:* Prin Kiddie Wondland 1977-81, Woodland Acres Chrstn Sch 1982-; *ai:* Writer Sch Song; Founding Bd Mem Woodland Acres; Cnslr; Delta Sigma Theta Pres 1981-82; Chrstn Womens Bus League 1979-; *office:* Woodland Acres Chrstn Sch 12919 Sarahs Ln Houston TX 77015

MILLS, MARY LYNN, Third Grade Teacher; *b:* St Louis, MO; *ed:* (BS) Elem Ed/Spec Ed, Univ of MO Columbia 1971; Working Towards Masters at Numerous Univs; *cr:* Spec Ed Teacher EH Spec Sch Dist 1970-72; 3rd/4th Grade Teacher Seminary Hill Sch 1973-89; 3rd Grade Teacher Mt Lebanon Sch 1989-; *ai:* Earth Day Comm; NEA, Lebanon Ed Assn; Sierra Club; NH Environmental Teacher of Yr 1990; *office:* Mt Lebanon Elem Sch 5 White Ave West Lebanon NH 03784

MILLS, MELINDA BOZETT, 7th Grade Life Science Teacher; *b:* Centralia, IL; *m:* W. Ron; *c:* Jeremy; *ed:* (BS) Bio, 1969, (MS) Bio, 1971 Austin Peay St Univ; *cr:* 9th Grade Phys Sci Teacher Greenwood Jr HS 1971-73; 9th Grade Bio Teacher White Oak Int Sch 1974-77; Dept Head/Bio Teacher Santa Fe HS 1979-83; 7th Grade Life Sci Teacher Clear Lake Int Sch 1983-; *ai:* Spon Sci Fair Participants; NSTA Obaus Awd 1990/Innovations in Sci Teaching 1990; Contributor Articles Sci Scope 1986/1990; Most Prominent Ed TX 1983; Nom Outstanding Sci Teacher Awd 1984; Nom Pres Awd for Excl Sci/Math Teaching 1985; Nom TX Outstanding Bio Teachers Awd 1990.

MILLS, MICHAEL L., Sixth Grade Teacher; *b:* Joseph, UT; *m:* Lynette Acheson; *c:* Shannon, Amanda; *ed:* (BA) Ed, Brigham Young Univ 1968; Post Grad Stud; *cr:* 4th-6th Grade Teacher Valley View Elem 1968-77; 6th Grade Teacher Centerville Elem 1977-; *home:* PO Box 583 Centerville UT 84014

MILLS, MILTON ALEXANDER, Math & Phys Ed Supervisor; *b:* Detroit, MI; *m:* Mary Ann; *ed:* (BA) Phys Ed, KY St Univ 1970; Grad Stud; *cr:* Supvr Woodland Acres Chrstn Sch 1983-; *ai:* Woodland Acres Founding Bd Mem; Bsktbl, Vlybl, Bsbl Head Coach; Debate Team Spon; Houston Coaches Assn VP 1984-85; NAACP, Chrstn Mens Bus League 1983-.

MILLS, PAMELA BOLTON, 6th Grade Teacher; *b:* Montgomery, AL; *m:* James Richard; *c:* Jonathon, Christopher; *ed:* (BS) Elem Ed, Judson Coll 1973; (MED) Elem Ed, Auburn Univ 1976; Teacher Trng Wkshp E AL Regional Inservice Center; *cr:* Kndgtn Teacher Stillman Coll 1973-74; 5th Grade Teacher Tallassee City Schls 1974-80; 1st Grade Teacher 1980-81, 6th Grade Teacher 1981- Elmore Cty Schls; *ai:* Sci Curr, Textbook Accreditation Comm; Sci Fair Spon; Drug Coord WES II; AL Ed Assn, Elmore Cty Teachers Assn, NEA; *home:* 700 Company St Wetumpka AL 36092

MILLS, PAMELA D'EON, Senior English Teacher; *b:* Dodge City, KS; *ed:* (BS) Eng, 1972, (MA) Eng, 1979 W TX St Univ; *cr:* Eng Teacher Seminole HS 1972-78, Ulysses HS 1978-; *ai:* Yrbk Newspaper; Stu Cncl; KS Ed Assn; Delta Kappa Gamma 1980-86; Teaching Assistanship TX Tech Univ; Teacher of Yr Grant Cty 1988; *office:* Ulysses HS 501 N Mc Call Ulysses KS 67880

MILLS, RONALD MICHAEL, Math Teacher; *b:* Norton, VA; *ed:* (BS) Ed, 1973, (MS) Curr/Instruction, 1984 Univ of TN; *cr:* Teacher Morristown-Hamblen HS East 1980-; *ai:* Beta Club Spon; Fellowship of Chrstn Atheletes Spon; Golf Coach; Hamblen Cty Assn 1980-; East TN Ed Assn 1980-; TN Ed Assn 1980-; NEA 1980-; *office:* Morristown Hamblen H S E 405 S James Morristown TN 37813

MILLS, SHARON ELLIS, 5th Grade Teacher; *b:* Jacksonville, FL; *m:* David Rayburn Sr.; *c:* David R. Jr., Gregory E.; *ed:* (BS) Elem Ed, Jacksonville Univ 1967; *cr:* 4th-5th Grade Teacher San Mateo Elem 1967-69; 4th Grade Teacher Carter G Woodson Elem 1969-70; 4th-5th Grade Teacher 1970-, Advanced Projects Teacher 1985- Dinsmore Elem; *ai:* Grade Level Chm; Sci & Cmptr Lead Teacher; Steering Comm for Southern Assn for Coll & Schls; Kadet Spon; Duval Rdng Cncl, PTA Mem; Duval Teachers Union (Mem, Building Rep); Faculty Forum Rep; Teacher of Yr Dinsmore Elem 1984-85; *office:* Dinsmore Elem Sch 7126 Civic Club Rd Jacksonville FL 32219

MILLS, SONIA ROSE VIDAL, Foreign Language Chair; *b:* Dagupan Pangasinan, Philippines; *m:* C. Ralph; *c:* Margaret R., Rachel A., Sarah E.; *ed:* (BS) Elem Ed, Philippine Normal Coll 1962; (MA) Elem Ed, Geo Peabody Coll 1965; (MA) Chrstn Ed, Scarritt Coll 1967; (BS) Span, Marshall Univ 1973; Voice Trng, Oscar Mc Cullough Hollins Coll 1971; *cr:* Supervising Teacher Elem Dept Philippine Chrstn Coll 1962-64; Span Instr TN Tech Univ 1967-68; Span Teacher Putnam Cty Sr HS 1967-68; Teacher Mt Pleasant Sch 1968-71; Span Instr Marshall Univ 1972-76; Span Teacher Cntrl Jr HS 1978-80; Teacher Rocky Gap Schls 1977-78, Whitethorn Elem 1980-85; Foreign Lang Chairperson/Span Teacher Pine Forest Jr HS 1985-; *ai:* Adv & Spon Span Club; Textbook Comm Foreign Lang; Cumberland Cty Foreign Lang Cncl Span Rep; NCAE 1985-; NEA 1971-; Amer Assn of Teachers of Span & Portuguese 1972-77; Amer Guild of Organist Charter Mem 1973-; Amer Guild of Eng Handbell Ringers 1971-77; Girl Scouts of The Philippines (Adult Leader, Officer) 1962-64; Delta Kappa Gamma Intnl Honorary Society for Women Educators 1973-; Outstanding Teacher 1977; Outstanding Young Women of America 1978; Altrusa Intnl Grants; PEO Sisterhood, Bd of Missions United Meth 1964-67.

MILLS, SUSAN WEBER, English/Psychology Teacher; *b:* Kansas City, MO; *m:* Barry La Mont Sr.; *c:* Heather L., Barry L. Jr.; *ed:* (BA) Eng/Scndry Ed/Psych, Univ of NM 1983; Numerous Courses; *cr:* Ad Copy Writer Kansas City Star 1963-65; Secy/Receptionist John J Ramm Engineering 1965-66, Helio Aircraft Corporation 1966-67; Secy to Chm Child Psych KS St Coll 1968; Secy/Crisis Cnslr Desert Samaritan Mental Health Center 1972; Secy to Pres AZ League of Women Voters 1973; Teacher Amiguitos Sch 1977-80; Head Teacher Corrales Alternative Sch 1980-82; Crisis Cnslr Shelter for Victims of Domestic Violence 1982-83; Coord Univ of NM Mental Health Center 1982-83; Teacher Valley HS 1983-; *ai:* El Valle Chapter, NHS Spon 1987-; Touchstones, St Johns Great Ideas Seminar Adv 1989-; Cnslr/Facilitator Life Support Dept Stu Support Group 1985-; N Cntrl Evaluation Team; Philosophy/Objectives, Attendance, Room Assignment, Instructional Interruptions, Discipline, Steering, Issues Comms 1989-; Peer Tutors 1988-, Handicapped Awareness Day 1987- Adv; Celebrate Youth Spon/Mentor 1988-; General Equivalency Exam Tutor 1985-; AFT 1983-, Distinguished Service Awd 1989; NM Fed Teachers (St Delegate 1989) 1983-; Albuquerque Teachers Fed (Fed Rep 1987-, Grievance Rep 1989-) 1983-; NASSP 1987-; Natl Assn Stu Act Adv; NCTE (St Delegate 1985) 1983-; Adobe Cmmty Theater of Corrales Bd of Dir 1987-; Comm for Passage of Mill Levy for Albuquerque Public Schls 1989-; People to People (Teacher, Leader 1988), Certificate of Appreciation 1988; Amer Intnl Stu Exch (Cnslr 1982-88), Distinguished Service Awd 1988; Shelter for Victims of Domestic Violence (Volunteer, Coord) 1982; YWCA of Albuquerque (Bd of Dir 1977-80, VP 1980); Service to Academic Achievement Valley HS 1988-; Albuquerque Public Schls Employee of Week 1990; In-Service Wkshp SW Indian Polytechnic Inst 1987-88; Masterwork Study Grant Natl Endowment for Hum 1989-; SW Lit for HS Teachers Contributing Writer 1990; Albuquerque Public Schls Radio Announcements Writer 1989; Albuquerque Public Schls Chm; Comm Curr Dev for Communication Skills; Writer & Ed Resource Book 1987; Instr Teaching Comm Skills 1987; Grammar Wkshps Facilitator HS & Mid Sch 1985-; *office:* Valley HS 1505 Candelaria NW Albuquerque NM 87107

MILLS, SYLVIA ANNE, 5th Grade Teacher; *b:* Carlsbad, NM; *m:* Sidney Lane; *c:* Marquesa, Kim, Kris; *ed:* (BA) Elem Ed, Mc Murry Coll 1964; Grad Classes, Univ of NM; *cr:* Teacher 1964-68, 1975- Albuquerque Public Schls; *ai:* Knowledge Master Open Cmptr Contest Spon; Past Pres HS Soccer Booster Club & Band; Zuni Cmptr Club Spon; NEA, NM Cmptr Users in Ed; Christa Mc Auliffe Fellow for NM 1990; IBM NM Teacher of Yr 1990; *office:* Zuni Elem Magnet Sch 6300 Claremont Ave NE Albuquerque NM 87110

MILLWARD, JACK MIKEL, Anatomy & Physiology Teacher; *b:* Oakland, CA; *m:* Ann Alice; *c:* Keith, Scott; *ed:* (BA) Phys Ed, 1967; (MA) Phys Ed, 1970; Anatomy & Physiology; *cr:* Teacher Fairfield HS 1968-; *ai:* Voted Outstanding Teacher by Local Newspaper 1989; *home:* 107 Vista View Dr Vacaville CA 95688

MILNE, GLORIA J., 4th Grade Teacher; *b:* Flushing, NY; *ed:* (BA) Elem Ed, 1972, (MS) Spec Ed, 1974 Queens Coll; Grad Courses Marine Bio, Univ S FL, Fast Approach to Sci, Univ of HI; *cr:* Teacher Freeport Sch Dist 1972-75, Pasco Cty Sch Dist 1976-; *home:* 7874 Raintree Dr New Port Richey FL 34653

MILNE, JANE MARIE, Physical Ed/Health Teacher; *b:* San Jose, CA; *ed:* (BS) Phys Ed, Judson Baptist Coll 1984; *cr:* Coach Cascade Chrstn HS 1984-85; Teacher Rogue Comm Coll 1984-85; Teacher/Coach Eagle Point HS 1985-; *ai:* Head Vlybl Coach; Athletes in Action; First Baptist Church Mem 1970-; *office:* Eagle Point HS PO Box 198 Eagle Point OR 97524

MILNER, LYNDA MINOR, Science Teacher; *b:* Albany, GA; *c:* Ronetta, Tonia Minor, Avais Kyles, Tiera Minor; *ed:* (BS) Bio, Savannah St Coll 1970; NE LA Univ, Armstrong St Coll, GA S Univ; *cr:* Sci Teacher Edward J Bartlett Mid Sch 1972-; *ai:* Quiz Bowl Adv; 8th Grade Appreciation Comm; NSTA, GA Sci Teacher Assn, NEA, GA Assn of Educators; *home:* 120 Quail Forest Ct Savannah GA 31419

MILOT, JOHN L., History Department Chair; *b:* Fern Glen, PA; *m:* Rosemary C. Corradini; *c:* Christine, John F.; *ed:* (BA) His, Kings Coll 1959; (MA) His, Lehigh Univ 1961; Supvrs Certificate; *cr:* Teacher 1960-75, His Teacher/Dept Chm 1975- West Hazleton HS; *ai:* Sch Spirit Club & Presidential Classroom for Young Amer Adv; *home:* 11 Cindy St West Hazelton PA 18201

MILOTTE, JANE L., 4th Grade Teacher; *b:* Laconia, NH; *ed:* (BS) Phys Ed, 1959, Elem Ed, Univ of NH; *cr:* Phys Ed Teacher Hampton Acad 1959-67, Ousley River HS 1967-69; Elem Teacher Frank Jones Sch 1969-82, Dondero Sch 1982-; *ai:* Portsmouth Writing Comm; NEA, NHEA; Assn of Portsmouth Teacher Rep 1986-; *office:* Dondero Sch Van Buren Ave Portsmouth NH 03801

MILOVICH, CHARLENE M., Teacher/English Dept Chairman; *b:* Price, UT; *m:* Ted; *c:* Kelle, Todd, Scott; *ed:* (BS) Eng, UT St Univ 1972; Gifted & Talented Endorsement; *cr:* Teacher Mont Harmon Jr HS 1971-; *ai:* Speech & Drama Coach; Phi Kappa Phi; Delta Kappa Gamma; Outstanding Teacher Mont Harmon Jr HS 1986-87; *office:* Mont Harmon Jr H S 60 W 4th N Price UT 84501

MILSTEAD, VIRGINIA LUCAS, Counselor; *b:* State Line, MS; *m:* Jimmy J.; *c:* Virginia M. Conn, J. Martin, L. Kellee; *ed:* (BS) Home Ec, 1959, (ME) Sch Counseling, 1973 Univ Southern MS; Home Ec Masters Cert; *cr:* Home Ec Teacher Bassfield HS 1959-60, Colmer Jr HS 1967-88; Cnslr Pascagoula HS 1988-; *ai:* Alpha Delta Kappa (Pres, Treas, Chap) 1973-; Phi Delta Kappa 1980-; MS Assn Ed, Amer Home Ec Assn, NEA; *office:* Pascagoula HS 2903 Pascagoula St Pascagoula MS 39567

MILTON, MARK GLENN, Math Teacher; *b:* Glendale, CA; *m:* Joan Knoll; *ed:* (BA) Phys Ed, Whittier Coll 1978; (MS) Phys Ed, Eastern NM Univ 1984; Math Credentail, Eastern Nm Univ; *cr:* Teacher Nogales HS 1982-83; Grad Asst Eastern NM Univ 1983-84; Teacher Clovis HS 1984-86, Apple Valley HS 1986-; *ai:* Ftbl, Bsktbl, Bsbl Coach; Natl Fed Interscholastic Coaches Assn & CA Coaches Assn 1986-; *office:* Apple Valley Sr H S 11837 Navajo Rd Apple Valley CA 92308

MILZA, JO ANN BRADLEY, Fifth Grade Teacher; *b:* Kearny, NJ; *m:* Paul L.; *c:* Paul, Kathleen Furman, Michael, Peter; *ed:* (BA) His, St Josephs Coll 1959; His, Duquesne Univ; *cr:* Teacher 1959-62, Substitute Teacher 1962-80 New Dorp HS; Teacher St Charles 1980-; *ai:* Cath Conference Coll Alumnae Pres 1965-75; St Teresas Mothers Guild Pres 1976-78.

MIMS, JUDY MELTON, Fourth Grade Teacher; *b:* Clanton, AL; *m:* Troy O Neal; *c:* Leslie O Neal, Brett A.; *ed:* (BA) Elem Ed, 1970, (MED) Elem Ed, 1976, Elem Ed, 1986 Univ of Montevallo; *cr:* 7th Grade Math Teacher 1970-71, 5th Grade Teacher 1972-78 Henry M Adair; 1st Grade Teacher 1979-80, 4th Grade Teacher 1980- Clanton Elem; *ai:* Chilton Cty Ed Assn, AL Ed Assn, NEA; Alpha Delta Kappa (Pledge Chm, Altruistic, Treas); Liberty Hill Baptist Church (Mem, Bible Sch Teacher, Choir); *office:* Clanton Elem Sch 1000 Cloverleaf Dr Clanton AL 35045

MIMS, SANDRA DIANNE, Spanish Teacher; *b:* Evanston, IL; *ed:* (BA) Span, Southern IL Univ 1975; Addl Studies Intensive Lang Institute; *cr:* Span Teacher James Roy Skiles Mid Sch 1975-77; Chute Mid Sch 1981-; *ai:* Span Club; Teaches 6th Graders Culture, Vocab, Act after Sch; Amer Assn of Teachers of Span & Portuguese; IL Foreign Lang Teachers Assn; *office:* Chute Mid Sch 1400 Oakton St Evanston IL 60202

MIMS, VERNON EUGENE, JR., English Teacher; *b:* Chicago, IL; *ed:* (BA) Eng, 1964, (MA) Eng, 1979 Roosevelt Univ; Various Seminars; Fry Summer Inst, Univ of Chicago 1985; Summer Inst Curr Dev Gifted Ed 1981; Fellow in Mellon Literacy Prgm Univ of Chicago 1990; *cr:* 9th Grade Eng Teacher Wendell Phillips HS 1964-65; 7th-8th Grade Lang Art/Soc Stud Teacher Spry Upper Grade Sch 1965-70; Lit Teacher N Park Coll 1986; 11th/12th Grade Eng Teacher 1970-, 12th Grade Advanced Eng Teacher 1980- Lane Tech HS; *ai:* Spon Lane Tech Chess Club 1981-; Alpha Phi Alpha 1961-; Univ of Chicago Outstanding Teacher Awds; *office:* Lane Tech HS 2501 W Addison Chicago IL 60618

MINCEY, PATRICIA JENKINS, English as Second Lang Teacher; *b:* Eatonton, GA; *m:* Willie; *c:* Mikell; *ed:* (BS) Fr/Eng Ed, Morris Brown Coll 1960; (MA) Rdng, Atlanta Univ 1975; Advanced Stud, Univ of MD 1969-70; Overseas Prgm of Stud, Kadena AFB Okinawa Japan; ESOL Cert, GA St Univ; *cr:* Fr/Eng Teacher Tompkins HS 1960-68; Fr Teacher DOD-Overseas Ed System 1972; Graduate Asst Atlanta Univ 1974-75; ESOL Teacher Shuman Mid Sch 1975-; *ai:* Rep for Supt Teacher Talks 1989-; Yrbk Adv; ESOL Club Adv 1989-; Steering Comm 1989-; Intnl Rdng Assn 1986-; Chatham Assn of Ed Bd of Dir 1980-82; GAE GA 1975- Certificate of Service 1987; NEA; MBC Alumni VP 1976- Civic Achievement 1980; MBC Natl Alumni 1976- Purple & Black Service 1979; Pickens Circle Pres 1975- Outstanding Service 1989; Lamarville Cmmty Assn VP; Grant Fr Inst Saint Lawrence Univ; Graduate Asst Rdng Spelman Coll; Atlanta Univ; *office:* Shuman Mid Sch 415 Goebel Ave Savannah GA 31404

MINCH, DAVID L., Social Studies/English Teacher; *b:* Elwood, IN; *m:* Susan K. Galbraith; *c:* Kevin M., Marcia K.; *ed:* (BA) His, Albion Coll 1966; (MA) Guidance/Counseling, E MI Univ 1971; Gifted & Talented & Spec Fundamental Stus Teaching Trng; *cr:* Teacher Mary Lyon Jr HS 1966-81, Churchill Jr HS 1981-; *ai:* Churchill Girls Sftbl & Bsktbl Coach; Churchill Stu & Teacher Recognition Comm Chm; Athletics Scoreboard Operator; Gifted & Talented & Dist Soc Stud Comm; NEA, MI Ed Assn, Royal Oak Ed Assn 1966-; YMCA Indian Guides Feather Merchant 1977-83, Fed Honor Awd 1982; St Johns United Meth Church 1967-; Co-Author 8th Grade Prgm; *office:* Churchill Jr HS 707 Girard Ave Royal Oak MI 48073

MINCK, STUART JAMES, Health & Anatomy Teacher; *b:* Yonkers, NY; *m:* Noelle Yvonne Moffitt; *c:* Meghan L.; *ed:* (BS) Phys Ed, Pittsburg St Univ 1981; (MS) Sports Medicine/Athletic Trng, Univ of AZ 1982; Certified First Aid & CPR Amer Red Cross; *cr:* Teacher/Athletic Trainer Del Valle HS 1982-83, Widefield HS 1983-85, Lyman HS 1985-89, Rio Grande HS 1989-; *ai:* Certified Athletic Trainer; Natl Athletic Trainers Assn 1980-; US Swimming Team Trainer 1983-85; *office:* Rio Grande HS 2300 Arenal Rd SW Albuquerque NM 87105

MINDER, JUDITH MOWRY, Jr HS Social Studies Teacher; *b:* Greensburg, PA; *m:* Walter J.; *c:* Michael J., Lisa A.; *ed:* (BA) Liberal Arts/His/Art, 1963, (BA) Scndry Ed, 1973 West Liberty St Coll; Graduate Work/His, WV Univ 1973-74; Rdng at WV Univ; *cr:* Substitute Teacher OH Cty Schls 1968-73; Teacher St Mary Cntrl Sch 1973-; *ai:* Spon His Day Competition; Instr for Rainbow; Arts Day & 100 Yr Celebration Chairperson; OH Cath Ed Assn, NCEA; Winner St OH His 1979 & 1983; Comm Mem St Cath Teachers Convention 1984; Chairperson of Art Curr Comm; Judge OH His Day; Diocese of Steubenville 1989-; *home:* 2216 Marshall Ave Wheeling WV 26003

MINDERLEIN, PHILIP JOSEPH, Social Studies Dept Chairman; *b:* Bel Air, MD; *m:* Patricia Ann Leland; *c:* Michael, Jennifer; *ed:* (BA) His, WV Wesleyan 1969; (MED) Ed, Towson St 1974; Staff Dev Seminar - MD St Dept Ed; *cr:* Teacher Bel Air HS 1970, Edgewood Mid Sch 1972-78, Fallston HS 1978-79; Teacher/Dept Chm Southampton Mid Sch 1979-; *ai:* Lacrosse and Soccer Coach; Lacrosse Referee; Mem-Harford Cty Public Schls Mid Sch Soc Stud Curr; Mem Southampton Curr Comm; Mem-Southampton Instructional Leadership Team; MCSS 1987-; NCSS 1984-87; Natl Geographic Society 1981-; American Legion 1987-; BSA Asst Scout Master 1972-79; Chm-Southampton United Way; *office:* Southampton Mid Sch 1200 Moores Mill Rd Bel Air MD 21014

MINER, JOHN RALPH, Science Teacher; *b:* Grand Rapids, MN; *c:* Gregory, Michele Puglisa; *ed:* (BS) Bio, St Johns Univ 1962; (MS) Bio, Bemidji St Univ 1966; *cr:* Chem Tech Asst Bemidji St Univ 1965-66; Bio/Chem Teacher Rush City 1965-66; Phys Sci Teacher Columbia Heights 1966-67, Grand Rapids Mid Sch 1967-89; *ai:* Mid Sch Bsbl & Ftbl 1970-80; Helping Able Kids Sci Coord 1981-89; MN Mid Sch Sci Teacher of Yr 1989; MN

Acad of Sci Teacher of Yr 1985; *home:* 816 4th Ave SW Grand Rapids MN 55744

MINER, SHERL MAX, 5th Grade Teacher; *b:* Payson, UT; *m:* Cheryl A. Ransom; *c:* Olivia, Angela, Alexis, Amanda, Steven; *ed:* (BA) Elem Ed, Brigham Young Univ 1975; *cr:* Educ Internship Grant Sch, Nebo School District 1974-75; 3rd Grad Teacher Shelley Schl, 1975-77; 3rd/5th Grade Teacher Barratt Sch 1977-; Soc Stu Instr Brigham Young Univ 1989-; *ai:* Rep Sch Instructional Improvement Comm; Dist Exploring Commissioner; UT Natl Parks CNC Boy Scouts of America; UEA 1975-; Phi Kappa Phi 1974-; Boy Scouts America Scouting Coor 1985-89.

MINESSALE, JOANNE STEFFEN, Second Grade Teacher; *b:* Sheboygan, WI; *m:* James A.; *c:* James M., Steve; *ed:* (BA) Elem Ed, Oshkosh St Univ 1967; (MS) Ed Prof Dev, Whitewater St Univ 1983; Coll of St Thomas, Timber Lake Stevens, Whitewater Univ 1984-; *cr:* Teacher St Cloud Cath Sch 1964-66, New Holstein Public Sch 1967-69, Wauwatosa Public Sch 1969-; *ai:* Phi Kappa Phi 1982; *home:* W288 N8443 N Bay Rd Hartland WI 53029

MINGHETTI, RITA ANN, Theology Teacher/Dept Chair; *b:* Youngstown, OH; *ed:* (BSED) Elem Ed, Youngstown St Univ 1969; (MAED) Religious Ed, Boston Coll 1976; Grad Stud Counseling; *cr:* Elem Teacher St Charles Sch 1967-69; Jr HS Teacher St Joan of Arc Sch 1969-73; Theology Teacher Ursuline HS 1973-74; Dir Religious Ed Holy Family Parish 1974-80, St Michael Parish 1980-87; Theology Teacher Ursuline HS 1987-; *ai:* Minorities & Environmental Stu Organization Club Adv; NCEA; Amnesty Intnl, Bread for World; Youngstown Diocesan Catechetical Awd 1985; *office:* Ursuline HS 750 Wick Ave Youngstown OH 44505

MINICHELLI, JOHN A., Social Studies Teacher; *b:* Brooklyn, NY; *m:* Anna Martinez; *c:* Elena, Joymarie, Justin; *ed:* (BA) Poly Sci, 1969, (MA) Amer His, 1973 Brooklyn Coll; *cr:* Teacher Jr HS 275 1969-77, Jr HS 324 1977-81, Tildon HS 1981-87, Wagner HS 1987-; *ai:* Mock Trial Coord; Grace Dodge Fnd US Constitution; *office:* Susan Wagner HS 1200 Manor Rd Staten Island NY 10314

MINICK, LISA MARSH, Language Arts Teacher; *b:* Statesboro, GA; *m:* Jay; *c:* Jon; *ed:* (BS) Eng, 1983, (MED) Rdng, 1987 GA Southern Coll; *cr:* Lang Art Teacher Hinesville Mid Sch 1983-84, William James Mid Sch 1984-; *ai:* Jr Beta Club Spon; Lang Art Dept Chairperson; PAGE 1983-; Statesboro Service League; *office:* William James Mid Sch 150 Williams Rd Statesboro GA 30458

MINICK, MITZI KNIGHT, 5th Grade Teacher; *b:* Statesboro, GA; *ed:* (BS) Ed, 1977, (MS) Ed, 1984 Univ of GA; Local Staff Dev Courses; *cr:* 7th Grade Math Teacher 1977-78, 4th Grade Teacher 1978-80 Rockdale Cty Bd of Ed; 5th/6th Grade Teacher Gwinnett Cty Bd of Ed 1980-; *ai:* Grade Level & Soc Stud Chm; Local Sch Plan for Improvement & Media Comm; Cub Safety Patrol Spon; Field Trip Organizer; Media Research Processing; NEA, GEA 1977-86; PAGE 1986-89; Smoke Rise Baptist Church Mem 1977-; Gwinnett Republican Women Mem 1989-; Phi Kappa Phi; Nom Alpha Delta Kappa & Teacher of Yr; *home:* 700 Pepperwood Trl Stone Mountain GA 30087

MINKLER, SANDRA LYNN, Phys Ed & Home Arts Teacher; *b:* St Louis, MO; *m:* David Lee; *c:* Reid, Bradlee; *ed:* (BS) Phys Ed, Univ of IL 1965; Grad Stud Phys Ed & Home Arts; *cr:* Phys Ed Teacher Champaign HS 1965-68; Phys Ed/Home Arts Teacher El Segundo Jr HS 1969-71; Aerobics/Fitness Instr Adult Ed Inglewood HS 1970-72; Phys Ed/Home Arts Teacher Kingman Jr HS 1981-; *ai:* Girls Sftbl Coach 1981-89; Dress Code & Assertive Discipline Comm; Chrldr & Pon Pom Spon; Alpha Sigma Nu 1965; Ski Hawks West 1985-; *home:* 3473 Hodges Rd Kingman AZ 86401

MINKOFF, SANDRA RITA (COHEN), Counselor; *b:* Chicago, IL; *m:* Robert; *c:* Michael, Eileen; *ed:* Assoc General, Wright Comm Coll 1956; (BED) Ed, Chicago Teachers Coll 1957; Teacher Ed, Inst of Psychoanalysis 1972; (MA) Counseling & Guidance, NE IL Univ 1984; Building Fairness, Sex Equity, Child Sexual Abuse Prevention, Drug Wrkshp; Psychological Issues of Chldhd, Sci Prgm for Teachers Learning Disabilities, Implementing Mastery Learning, Intensive Rdng Improvement Prgm; *cr:* Kndgtn Teacher Bright & Bradwell Schls 1955-56; 6th-8th Grade Teacher Beal Sch 1957-58; Nursery Teacher Kitty Coll 1966-67; Kndgtn/3rd Grade Teacher Stone Sch 1967-82; Rdng Resource Teacher 1982-88, Cnslr 1988- Stone Scholastic Acad; *ai:* Prof Problems Advisory Comm; Sch Soc Club; PTA 1967-; Cnslr Assn 1988-, Excl in Teaching & Counseling 1989; *office:* Leander Stone Scholastic Acad 6239 N Leavitt St Chicago IL 60659

MINKS, STANLEY JAY, English Teacher; *b:* Logansport, IN; *m:* Barbara Ann Koetz; *c:* Cara, Alicia; *ed:* (BS) Speech/Drama, Taylor Univ 1969; (MS) Guidance Counseling, Butler Univ 1976; *cr:* Eng Teacher Blackford Cty HS 1969-70, Arsenal Tech HS 1970-; *ai:* Drama Club, Thespian Society Spon; Fall All Sch Play & Musical Drama Dir; NEA, Indianapolis Ed Assn, IN St Teachers Assn 1975-; Natl Forensics League 1970-; Intnl Thespian Society 1978-; Above & Beyond the Call of Duty Awd.

MINNER, FREDERICK, Soc Stud Teacher, Chairman; *b:* St Louis, MO; *c:* Kevin J., Tracy L. T.; *ed:* (BA) Soc Work, 1979, (MS) Ed Scndry/Adult 1986 Univ of MO St Louis; (MS) Scndry/Ed, NE MO St 1990; Assoc Degree in Human Services, Cmptr Trng Inst; *cr:* Cmptr Operator/Rep Monsanto Chemical Co 1975; Soc Worker De Paul Hospital 1980; Teacher Brittany Woods Mid Sch 1983; *ai:* District Wide Social Studies Comm Chairperson/Soc Stud Dept; Comm Mem Enhancing Sch Climate; Prof Dev & Sch Improvement Cncl; Sch Recognition Comm Nation; Mentor for Teacher, Tutor Saturday Sch; Stu Cncl Chm; AFT Union VP 1987-, Teacher of Yr Finalist 1987-88; Parent to Parent Network 1988; Alpha Phi Alpha 1980; Brittany Woods Barber Shop Spon 1989; Affiliation With Big Brothers/Sisters Assn 1986; Trinity Mt Carmell Church (Appointed Deacon, Sunday Sch Teacher); Deans List Univ of MO Status; *home:* 7636 Horatio Dr Bel-nor MO 63121

MINNER, SIDNEY RODD, Mathematics Teacher; *b:* Marion, IL; *m:* Donald E.; *c:* William C., Kathryn M.; *ed:* (AFA) Music, William Woods Coll 1955; (BS) Ed, S IL Univ 1967; (MED) Intermediate Ed, Univ of NC Greensboro; *cr:* Elem Teacher Poplar Bluff MO 1967-74; GED/ABE Teacher John A Logn Comm Coll 1975-76; 7th/8th Grade Teacher E L Brown Mid Sch 1978-; *ai:* Delta Kappa Gamma Pres 1982-84; NCTM, NEA, NCAE; Lexington Music Study Club Secy 1990; *office:* E L Brown Mid Sch 1145 Kendall Mill Rd Thomasville NC 27360

MINOLFO, ANDREA SUSAN, 6th Grade Math Team Leader; *b:* Portsmouth, VA; *m:* Dominick; *c:* Salvatore, Trina, Daniel; *ed:* (BA) Elem Ed, 1981, (MSED) Elem Ed, 1984 Univ of SC Aiken; *cr:* 6th Grade Teacher Leavelle Mc Campbell Mid Sch 1981, Jackson Mid Sch 1982-; *ai:* Stu Cncl Adv; 8th Grade Prom Chairperson; Talent Show Coord; Sch Improvement Comm; ASCD Mem 1989-; Phi Beta Kappa Mem 1990; Teacher Incentive Awd Winner 1987, 1989-90; *home:* Rt 5 Box 144A Aiken SC 29801

MINOR, DONNA SAMUELS, Second Grade Teacher; *b:* Tulsa, OK; *m:* J. Vernon; *c:* Matthew, Seth; *ed:* (AA) Art, Labette Cty Cmmty Jr Coll 1972; (BS) Elem Ed, KS St Univ 1974; Grad Stud Elem Ed; *cr:* Spec Ed Teacher Parsons St Hospital & Training Center 1974; 2nd Grade Teacher Thayer Elem 1975-; *ai:* KNEA Building Rep 1987-; *office:* Thayer Elem Sch Box 278 Thayer KS 66776

MINOR, ELEANOR TRUE, Vocal/General Music Teacher; *b:* Cheverly, MD; *m:* Richard Paul; *c:* Jason, Kristen, Embrey; *ed:* (BS) Music Ed, 1975, (MED) Ed/Child Dev, 1989 Univ of MD; *cr:* Vocal/General Music Teacher Nicholas Orem Mid Sch 1975-89, Martin Luther King Jr Mid Sch 1989-; *ai:* Music Dept Chairperson; Show Choir Dir/Choreographer; MENC, MMEA; *office:* Martin Luther King Jr Mid Sch 4545 Ammendale Rd Beltsville MD 20705

MINOR, JAMES BEAUREGARD, JR., Social Studies Teacher; *b:* Ridgeland, SC; *m:* Carrie Williams; *c:* James III, Jeffrey; *ed:* (BA) His, 1978, (MS) Ed, 1986 Univ of SC; *cr:* Soc Stud Teacher/Admin Asst CR-Irmo Mid Sch 1978-; *ai:* Model United Nations Club Spon; Textbook & 9th Grade Soc Stud Curr Writing Comms; SC Jaycees Pres 1976-77; Teacher of Yr 1980-81; Lyons Club Second Mile Awd 1981-82; *office:* Irmo Mid Sch 6051 Wescott Rd Columbia SC 29212

MINOR, TOM W., Chemistry/Physic Teacher; *b:* Dayton, OH; *m:* Mary Ellen Brady; *c:* Faith E. Minor Powell, Matthew, Elizabeth, J. P.; *ed:* (BA) Chrstn Ed, Asbury Coll 1970; (MED) Scndry Classroom/Cmptr Sci, Wright St Univ 1975; Numerous Wkshp; *cr:* Summer Chemist Instr Howard Laboratories 1978-89; Summer Sci Teacher Wright St Univ 1986-89; Teacher Dayton Chrstn Schls 1970-; Teacher/Sci Dept Chm Dayton Chrstn HS 1980-; *ai:* Sci Fair Coord; Soccer Coach; Sci Curr Comm; Montgomery Cty Sci Day (Mem 1978-88, Chm 1988-); West Dist Sci Day Mem 1980-; S OH Section Amer Assn of Physics Teachers Mem 1983-; Huber Heights Church of God Sunday Sch Teacher 1972-89; S OH Assn of Chrstn Schls Intnl Sci Fair Chm 1983-; Governors Awd for Excl Youth Sci 1985, 1989-; Outstanding Sci Teacher Battelle Acker Awd; Commendation from Intnl Sci & Engineering Fair 1987-89; *office:* Dayton Chrstn HS 325 Homewood Ave Dayton OH 45405

MINSHALL, MELINDA S., French Teacher; *b:* Stillwater, OK; *ed:* Certificat d Assiduite Fr, Univ de Grenoble France 1976; (BA) Fr, 1978, (MED) Scndry Admin, 1989 Univ of OK; Certified Trainer of Trainers; Developing Capable People Seminar; Effective Skill Dev for Adolescents; *cr:* Fr Teacher Del City HS 1978-79, Edmond Mid Sch & HS 1979-80; Foreign Lang Teacher Irving Mid Sch 1980-86; Fr Teacher Cntrl Mid Sch & HS 1986-; *ai:* Spon Fr Club, Societe Honoraire de Francais, Stu Cncl; Foreign Lang Advisory Bd; Organizer & Spon Annual Stu Trip to France; AATF, OK Foreign Lang Teachers Assn 1978-; NASSP, ASCD 1989-; Friends of Intnl Stus 1990; *office:* Central Mid HS 215 N Ponca Norman OK 73071

MINTER, BARBARA TIMS, Advanced Placement Eng Teacher; *b:* Meridian, MS; *m:* George E. Jr.; *c:* Elizabeth A., Laura M.; *ed:* (AA) Eng, Jones Cty Jr Coll 1969; (BS) Eng/British Lit, 1971, (MS) Eng/British-Amer Lit, 1973 Univ of S MS; Gifted & Talented, William Carey Coll 1988; Gifted & Talented Licensing Trng 1988; *cr:* 6th-8th Grade Eng Teacher Collins Jr HS 1972; 8th Grade Eng Teacher Jefferson Mid Sch 1973-76; 7th-12th Grade Eng/Speech Teacher Oak Grove Sch 1976-78; 9th/10th Grade Eng Teacher 1980-88, 9th-12th Grade Advanced Placement Eng Teacher 1988- Forrest Cty Ag HS; *ai:* Lang Art Dept Chairperson; Prom, Artisan Club, Soph Class Spon; Exec Planning Comm for Alumni Homecoming Assn; MS Cncl Teachers of Eng, NCTE; Phi Theta Kappa Pres; Lambda Iota Secy; Pineview Baptist Church (Sunday Sch Teacher, Bible Sch Teacher); Band Booster Club Mem; Univ of S MS Teaching Fellowship; Forest Cty Ag HS STAR Teacher 1988-, Teacher of Yr 1989-; Univ of S MS Honor Grad; *home:* Rt 6 Box 1150 Hattiesburg MS 39401

MINTON, JACQUELYN BEELER, Eighth Grade Teacher; *b:* Knoxville, TN; *m:* Robert L.; *c:* Jessica; *ed:* (BS) Scndry Sci Ed, Univ of TN 1979; *cr:* Chapter I Teacher 1980-81, 8th Grade Teacher 1981- Midway Elem; *ai:* Jr Beta Club Spon; Claiborne Cty Ed Assn Secy 1987-88; Intnl Order of Demolay Hats Off for Meritorious Services Awd 1989; *office:* Midway Elem Sch Rt 2 Box 286 New Tazewell TN 37825

MINTON, SARNIA MURPHY, Jr/Sr Social Studies Teacher; *b:* Springfield, MO; *m:* Fred L.; *c:* Tim, Tommy; *ed:* (BSE) Soc Stud, Univ of Cntrl AR 1968; Elem Teacher Cert 1977; *cr:* 1st Grade Teacher Murfreesboro Elem 1975-85; Scndry Teacher Murfreesboro HS 1985-; *ai:* Yrbk Spon; Soph Adv; Murfreesboro Ed Assn (Pres 1984-85, Secy, Treas 1989-); Murfreesboro Jaycettes VP 1977-78, Jaycette of Yr 1978; Murfreesboro Band Boosters VP 1986-87; Murfreesboro Cmmty Fnd (VP 1982-83), 1989-; Murfreesboro PTA Secy 1980-81; Murfreesboro Teacher of Yr 1989; *office:* Murfreesboro HS P O Box 339 Murfreesboro AR 71958

MINTON, TONY RAY, Sixth Grade Teacher; *b:* Hammond, IN; *ed:* (BS) Elem Ed, 1981, (MA) Elem Ed, 1987 Western KY Univ; *cr:* 4th/5th Grade Teacher Western Elem 1982-85; 6th Grade Teacher Beaver Dam Elem 1985-; *ai:* 6th Grade Quick Recall Team Coach Governors Cup Team; 4th/5th Grade Sci Team Coach Govenrors Cup Team; Math, Lang Arts & Composition Coach; In-Sch Cmptr Coord; Court House Players Cmptr Coord 1990; Outstanding Young Educator OH Cty Jaycees 1985; *home:* 452 Kentucky St Beaver Dam KY 42320

MIOTKE, CHERI L., Kindergarten Teacher; *b:* Viroqua, WI; *m:* Michael John; *c:* Anthony; *ed:* (BS) Elem Ed, UW-La Crosse 1975; *cr:* Kndgtn Teacher 1975-1978, 1st Grade Teacher 1978-1981, Kndgtn Teacher 1981-Howards Grove Schls; *ai:* Howards Grove Ed Assn; WI Ed Assn; NEA; Elem Teacher of Yr Howards Grove Schls 1982; *office:* Howards Grove Elem Sch 437 N Wisconsin Dr Sheboygan WI 53083

MIRACLE, KAY HUFFMAN, 6th Grade Teacher; *b:* Grayson, KY; *m:* David Russell; *ed:* (BA) Elem Ed, 1967, (MS) Elem Ed, 1972 Morehead Univ; *cr:* 4th Grade Teacher Prichard Elem 1967-70; 6th Grade Teacher Campbell Elem 1970-71, Worthington Elem 1972-; *ai:* 4-H Spon; RWEA Local Pres 1986-87; NEA, KEA; Order of Eastern Star Officer 1967-; *office:* Worthington Elem Sch Worthington Ave Worthington KY 41183

MIRANDO, LUCILLE GAROFALO, Computer Teacher; *b:* Trenton, NJ; *ed:* (BA) Psych/Elem Ed, Immaculate Coll 1969; (MED) Rdng, Rutgers Univ 1983; Cmptrs & Their Applications in Ed; Classroom Cmptr Assisted Instruction in Management; *cr:* 3rd Grade Teacher Wilson Elem 1969-70; 5th Grade Teacher Mott Sch 1970-75; 6th Grade Teacher Kilmer Sch 1975-78; 1st Grade Teacher 1978-88, Cmptr Teacher 1988- Mott Sch; *ai:* Cmptr Club Adv; Sci Fair, Apples for Stu Coord; Talent Show Comm Mem; Faculty Soc Fund Pres; Mott Sch Census Coord 1990; NJ Ed Assn 1969-; Intnl Rdng Assn 1985-; Phi Delta Kappa 1986-; Colonial Lakelands Civic Assn; Building Teacher of Yr 1988-89; Pacesetters Symposium Apple Cmptr Incorporated Awd 1986.

MIRELES, SYLVIA, Biology Teacher; *b:* Rio Grande City, TX; *ed:* (BS) Bio, 1972, (MED) Counseling/Guidance, 1974 Pan Amer Univ; *cr:* Bio Teacher Weslaco HS 1972-; *ai:* Stu Cncl, Jr Class, Sr Class, Keywanettes Spon; VICA Cosmetology Co-Spon; STAT, ATPE, RGVSA Mem; *home:* 1602 S Oregon #B Weslaco TX 78596

MIRIZIO, FRANK P., History Teacher; *b:* East Orange, NJ; *ed:* (BA) Ed/Poly Sci, AZ St Univ 1987; *cr:* Teacher Marcos De Niza 1987, Corona Del Sol HS 1987-; *ai:* Frosh Bsbl & Jr Var Ftbl Coach; Sr Class Spon; Spirit Club Dir; Study Skills Comm; Stress & Depression Group Facilitator; Voice of Aztecs for Bsktbl & Wrestlng; Tempe Little League Mem 1983-85; Pop Warner Ftbl 1980-84; *office:* Corona Del Sol HS 1001 E Knox Tempe AZ 85284

MIRRA, FRANK A., English Teacher/Curr Coord; *b:* Flushing, NY; *ed:* (BA) Educl Psych, Queens Coll 1969; (MA) Educl Psych, SUNY New Paltz 1976; Curr Coord Lang Art K-12; *cr:* Eng/Span Teacher Marlboro Cntrl Schls 1970-76; Eng Teacher/Curr Coord Ellenville HS 1978-; *ai:* Curr Coord; Mid States Comm; Kappa Delta Phi 1970-80; NY St Teachers Assn 1970-; NEA 1970-; Teacher of Yr Awd 1980; *home:* 276 Fosler Rd #16 Highland NY 12528

MISCHEL, KAREN WILDERMAN, Librarian; *b:* Evansville, IN; *m:* Michael; *c:* Chris, Brian, Dana; *ed:* (BA) Elem Ed, Brescia Coll 1973; (MA) Elem Ed, 1977, (Rank I) 1981 Western Ky Univ; *cr:* 4th Grade Teacher Blessed Mother 1973-78, Whitesville Elem 1978-84, Tamarack Elem 1984-89; Librarian Masonville/Whitesville Elem 1989-; *ai:* KEA, NEA, IRA; Youth Bsbl Auxiliary Pres 1988-89; *home:* 2511 Middleground Dr N Owensboro KY 42301

MISCHKE, SANDRA ANNE MC CARTY, Language Arts Teacher; *b:* Wichita, KS; *m:* Charles Russell; *c:* Michelle, Matthew; *ed:* (BA) Elem Ed/Bus, Westmar Coll 1967; Post Grad Stud; *cr:* 1st-5th Grade Elem Teacher Dubois Elem Sch 1964-70; 6th-7th Grade Teacher Worland Mid Sch 1970-; *ai:* Lang Art Dept Head; Soc Comm; Sch Paper Curr Coord Comm; WEA, NEA 1964-; Worland Ed Assn Secy 1970-, Master Teacher 1989; Delta Kappa Gamma Secy 1972-; PEO (VP, Pres, Corresponding Secy, Treas, Chaplain) 1981-; Outstanding Elem Ed Awd; *office:* Worland Mid Sch 1200 Culbertson Worland WY 82401

MISENHIMER, LINDA SPIELER, Student Project Coordinator; *b:* San Angelo, TX; *m:* Gregory R.; *c:* Joshua G.; *ed:* (BS) Bio, Angelo St Univ 1976; (MS) Bio/Ed, TX Tech Univ 1981; Natl Sci Teachers Assn Honors Cmptr Wkshp; NASA Educl Wkshp for Math & Sci Teachers; *cr:* Teacher O'Donnell Ind Sch Dist1977-79; Teaching Asst TX Tech Univ 1979-81; Teacher Ysleta Ind Sch Dist 1981-87; High Potential Stu Project Coord Univ of TX El Paso & Comprehensive Regional Center 1989-; *ai:* Sun Cntry Sci Fair Scientific Review Comm; Ysleta Ind Sch Dist Mid & HS Sci Contest Coord, Univ Interscholastic League, Academic Decathlon Interview Competition Coord; NSTA 1984-; Amer Assn of Univ Women 1983-; El Paso Cty Medical Society Auxiliary 1989-.

MISHLER, DANIEL J., Chem Teacher/Sci Dept Chair; *b:* Lansing, MI; *m:* Martha Pixley; *ed:* (BA) Bio, Olivet Coll 1976; Aquatic Bio; Cmptrs; Teacher Effectiveness; *cr:* Sci Teacher Roseville Baptist Acad 1977-78; Mid Sch Sci Teacher Hartland Farms Mid Sch 1978-82; Sci Teacher Northport Public Sch 1982-84; Chem Teacher/Sci Dept Chm Hartland HS 1984-; *ai:* Sci Olympiad Coord; MI Sci Teachers Assn; MI HS Bsbl Coaches Assn; *office:* Hartland HS 9525 Highland Rd Hartland MI 48029

MISITIS, JAN H., History/Geography Teacher; *b:* Pittsburgh, PA; *m:* Mary Ella Mangan; *ed:* (BA) His, Univ of Miami 1974; (MS) Soc Stud Ed, FL Intnl Univ 1986; *cr:* Soc Stud Teacher Miami Jackson Sr HS 1987-; *ai:* NCSS 1987-; FL Cncl for Soc Stud 1988-; Fellowship St of FS for Advanced Degree 1986-87; *office:* Miami Jackson Sr HS 1751 NW 36th St Miami FL 33142

MISTRETTA, PHILIP J., 5th Grade Teacher; *b:* Newark, NJ; *m:* Jo Ann Kozlowski; *c:* Nicholas J., Michael A.; *ed:* (BS) Ed, Seton Hall Univ 1974; *cr:* 5th Grade Teacher Deerfield Sch; *ai:* Lunchtime Supvr; Little League Coach; *office:* Deerfield Sch 26 Troy Ln Short Hills NJ 07078

MISTRO, NANCY NESTA, Sixth Grade Teacher; *b:* Pittsburgh, PA; *m:* Angel M.; *c:* Gina, Angelica; *ed:* (BA) Span Mercyhurst Coll 1964; (MED) Elem Ed, Duquesne Univ 1970; *cr:* 6th Grade Teacher Carlynton Sch Dist 1968-; *ai:* Amer Fed of Teachers 1970-; Carlynton Fed of Teachers 1970-; Span Cultural Club of Pittsburgh 1980; *office:* Carnegie Elem School Franklin Ave Carnegie PA 15106

MITCHAM, BETTY TAYLOR, Sixth Grade Teacher; *b:* Dawson, TX; *m:* Donald E.; *c:* Donna Mitcham Blankenship, Kristy; *ed:* (BBA) Bus Ed, N TX Univ 1958; (ME) Supervision, Stephen F Austin Univ 1982; *cr:* Teacher Dawson Elem Sch 1968-; *office:* Dawson Ind Sch Dist PO Box 278 Dawson TX 76639

MITCHAM, MARGRET, Health Teacher; *b:* Roswell, NM; *ed:* (BS) Phys Ed, SW TX St Univ 1985; Working Towards Masters Counseling, SW TX St Univ; Bio, Univ of TX San Antonio; *cr:* Grad Asst SW TX St Univ 1985-86; Eng Teacher 1986-87, Bio Teacher 1987-88, Health Teacher 1988- Clark HS; *ai:* Jr Var Vlybl & Bsktbl, Track Asst Coach; Delta Psi Kappa VP 1984-85; TX Girls Coaches Assn 1990; *office:* Tom C Clark HS 5150 De Zavala Rd San Antonio TX 78249

MITCHELL, A. DIANE DORN, Advanced English Teacher; *b:* Augusta, GA; *m:* James Daniel Jr.; *c:* Athena D., Dana M., James D. III; *ed:* (BA) Eng, 1970, (MED) Rdng Specialist, 1981 Augusta Coll; *cr:* Spec Ed Dept Glenn Hills HS & Josey HS & Butler HS & Hephzibah HS; 7th Grade Teacher/Instr of Hospital & Homebound Richmond Cty Schls 1970-82; 7th Grade Eng Teacher Whittier Mid Sch 1982-83; 11th/12th Advanced Eng Teacher Harlem HS Natl Sch of Excl 1983-89; *ai:* Literary Competitions Spon, Coach, Asst; Drama Club & One-Act; Sch Newspapers; Yrbk Jr & Sr Proms; Jr Advisory Cncl; Y-Club; Faculty Morale Booster; Newsletter;Pep Rally Skits; Teacher of Yr & Natl Sch Of Excl Comms; Acad Booster Club Charter Mem; Delta Kappa Gamma Society Intnl Music Chairperson 1982-; Prof Assn of GA Educators Page 1985-; NEA, GA Assn of Ed 1974-82; Word of Life Church Music Dir 1986-; Augusta Track Club 1979-82; PTO Poetry Contest Judge 1989-, Appreciation Awd 1989-; Teacher of Yr 1988-89; Natl Sch of Excl Winner 1988-89; Various Appreciation Awds; Poems Published Literary Section of Yrbk; Mentor/Teacher Supvr Augusta Coll: *office:* Harlem HS Box 699 Hwy 221 Harlem GA 30814

MITCHELL, A. MARIA, English Teacher; *b:* Savannah, GA; *c:* Rebecca, Robert A., David A.; *ed:* (BA) Eng, 1969, (MA) Eng/Hum, 1977 Univ of TX Arlington; (EDD) Adult/Continuing Ed, TX Womens Univ 1983; Prof Stud Peabody Conservatory of Music 1950; Prof Trng Lepperts Bus Coll 1954; Test Preparation Trng Project Early Options 1986-; *cr:* Orch Leader/Musician 1953-72; Secy 1953-57; Teacher 1967-, Admin Trainee 1976- Dallas Ind Sch Dist; *ai:* NHS Faculty Cncl Chairperson; D W Carter HS Faculty Comm Mem; Leader of 11th Grade Eng Teachers; Project Early Options Seminar Leader 1986-, Seminar Leader Awd 1987-88; TX Assn of Scndry Prin 1982-86; Musicians Union 1953-73; PTA 1963-; Phi Delta Kappa 1982-86; Various Coll Schlsps 1948-50, 1968-70, 1983; Doctorate Dissertation Published 1983; Poetry Published; Notable Women of TX 1984-85; *office:* David W Carter HS 1819 Wheatland Dallas TX 75232

MITCHELL, BARBARA, Fourth Grade Teacher; *b:* Bethany, MO; *m:* David; *c:* Lance, Amy; *ed:* (BS) Elem Ed, 1971, (MS) Elem Ed, 1990 NWMSU; *cr:* Elem Teacher St Joseph MO Sch System 1972-73, Maysville Sch System 1974-75, Lawson MO Sch System 1975-76, Unionville MO Sch System 1976-; *ai:* Chrldr Spon; Sunday Sch Teacher; Vacation Bible Sch Teacher; *home:* Rt 3 Unionville MO 63565

MITCHELL, BETTY GOODMAN, 5th Grade Teacher; *b:* Sumter Cty, SC; *c:* Millicent, Michelle; *ed:* (BS) Elem Ed, Morris Coll 1965; Working Towards Masters Elem Ed, Univ of SC; *cr:* Teacher Royalgate 1968-69, Narimasu 1971-73, St Alphonsus 1974-75, R E Davis 1976-; *ai:* SCEA Rep; IRA Mem; SC Ed Assn, Intnl Rndg Assn; United Meth (Youth Adv, Sunday Sch Teacher); Teacher of Yr 1983; *office:* R E Davis Sch Rt 5 Sumter SC 29150

MITCHELL, BRENDA DEARING, Fourth Grade Teacher; *b:* Morristown, TN; *m:* Edgar V. II; *ed:* (BS) Elem Ed, Carson-Newman Coll 1970; Univ of VA; East TN St Univ; Univ of TN; *cr:* 5th Grade Teacher McIntire Elem 1970-74; 4th/5th Grade Teacher Manley Elem 1974-; *ai:* Teachers Study Cncl Hamblen Cty; Building Planning Comm; Awds Night; Lakeway Rdng Cncl 1974-; Cert Recognition 1984; Morristown-Hamblen Cty Gifted Ed Assn; Cert Recognition 1981; Hamblen Cty Educ Assn Sch Rep 1974-83; TN Educ Assn 1974-83; Outstanding Elem Teacher Amer Book & Cert 1973; Alpha Bapt Church (Trng Dir 1980-88; Adult Discipleship Trng Dir 1988-); Scholastic Bowl Coach 1983-88; Cty Champions 1983; Txtbk Adoption Comm; Lead Math & Rdng Insvc for Teachers; TN Instructional Model for Staff Dev; St Paperwork Cutting Forum; St Model for Local Evaluation; Insvc Comm; *office:* Manley Elem 3685 W Andrew Johnson Hwy Morristown TN 37814

MITCHELL, BRENDA J. R., English Department Head; *b:* Vacherie, LA; *m:* Leroy Sr.; *c:* Rachelle, Kyle, Leroy Jr., Terrence; *ed:* (BS) Eng, 1966, (MED) Eng, 1975 Southern Univ; Rdng, Nicholls Univ 1980; Advanced Placement Coord; Writing Success for HS Stus; Classroom Management; *cr:* Teacher W St John HS 1966-; Real Estate Developer 1990; *ai:* Lay Religion Teacher; Drama Spon; Activity Dev Comm; Wantu Wazuri; St John the Baptist Church Lecter; Crystal Apple Awd 1988-89; *office:* W St John HS P O Box 66 Edgard LA 70049

MITCHELL, CAROL LACINAK, Mathematics Department Chair; *b:* New Orleans, LA; *m:* Royal Judson; *ed:* (BA) Ed, 1971, (MED) Curr/Instruction, 1976 Univ of New Orleans; Grad Stud; *cr:* Math Teacher Edna Karr Jr HS 1971-72, John Mc Donogh Sr HS 1972-81, Seton Acad 1984-; *ai:* NHS Spon; Sr Class Act; Scheduling Stus for Next Sch Yr; NCTM 1983-; LA Cncl Teachers of Math, Greater New Orleans Teacher of Math 1988-; Phi Delta Kappa 1976-81, 1983-; Kappa Delta Pi 1985-; *office:* Seton Acad 3222 Canal St New Orleans LA 70119

MITCHELL, DIANE MILLER, English/Journalism Teacher; *b:* Corbin, KY; *m:* Wendal; *c:* Christina; *ed:* (BA) Eng/Fr, 1962, (MA) Ed/Eng, 1969 Union Coll; Advanced Trng Journalism, Process Writing, Foxfire Teaching Method; *cr:* Teacher Ft Knox Dependent Schls 1962-65, Corbin HS 1965-; *ai:* Sch Newspaper, Yrbk, Literary Magazine, Writers Guild Adv; Younger Bus & Prof Womens Club Pres 1967-69, Club Woman of Yr 1968; Ossoli Club of Corbin 1985-; KY 5th Dist Outstanding Service to Ed Awd 1987; NDEA Grant Univ of KY 1967; Newspaper Fund Grant Univ of KY 1971; Mellon Fellowship Berea Coll 1989; Teacher of Yr 1987; *office:* Corbin HS 19th & Snyder Sts Corbin KY 40701

MITCHELL, DOUGLAS S., French Teacher; *b:* Greenup, KY; *ed:* (BA) Fr, 1962, (MS) Ed, 1967 Northern IL Univ; Fr Studies, Universite De Reims France; *cr:* Fr/His Teacher Kaneland HS 1962-67, Prospect HS 1968-; *ai:* Foreign Exch & Foreign Stu Adv; Teacher of Yr Prospect HS 1984-85; Little Brothers Friends of Elderly Volunteer Awd 1990; *office:* Prospect HS 801 W Kensington Mount Prospect IL 60056

MITCHELL, GAIL BRITT, Eng Dept Chair/AP Coordinator; *b:* Grafton, IL; *m:* Robert W.; *c:* Sharon L. Barnes, Lori T. Sailiata; *ed:* (BS) Eng/Speech, IL St Univ 1957; (MA) Comparative Hum, 1975, (PhD) Asian Stud, 1981 NY Univ; Japanese Lang/Philisophy & World Religion, Univ HI 1972/1986-; *cr:* Eng Instr Vienna HS 1961-; AP Eng Instr/Eng Dept Chm Oswego Cmmty HS 1966-; Eng Instr 1982-87, Japanese Instr 1987 Waubonsee Comm Coll; *ai:* JETS Adv; AP Coord; WCC Site Coord; Interactive Television Teacher of Japanese; Head Sr Class Spon; Track Aide; NEA 1957-; IEA 1957-; OEA 1966-; Fulbright Scholar to India; Runner Up for IL Teacher of Yr; Kendall Ctt Teacher of Yr; White Schoolhouse Awd for Excl in Teaching; *office:* Oswego Community H S Rt 71 Oswego IL 60543

MITCHELL, JANELLE SISTRUNK, 6th/8th Grade Math Teacher; *b:* Orangeburg, SC; *m:* Maurice V.; *c:* De Vona J., Maurice II; *ed:* (BS) Math, Claflin Coll 1977; (MED) Math Ed, SC St Coll 1987; *cr:* Math Teacher Tubman Jr HS 1977-81, Davidson Fine Arts Sch 1981-83, Bennett Mid Sch 1984-; *ai:* 6th Grade Cluster Leader; Natl Jr Honor Society Advisory Cncl; Dist 5 Math Comm Mem; Sch Improvement Cncl; Orangeburg #5 Ed Assn, SC Ed Assn, NEA 1984-; Alpha Kappa Alpha Secy 1988-; Silhouettes 1985-; *home:* 4743 Edgewood Dr Orangeburg SC 29115

MITCHELL, JIMMIE EUGENE, Science Teacher; *b:* Lumberton, MS; *ed:* (BS) Bio, Univ of S MS 1965; (MED) Guidance Cnslr, Nicholls St Univ 1972; Sci/Ed, LSU, Univ of New Orleans, Univ of VA, Loyola Xavier Univ; *cr:* Bio Teacher Terrebonne Parish Schls 1965-74; Guidance Cnslr Spotsylvania Sch Bd 1974-77; Cardmember Service Rep Amer Express Company 1977-82; Sci Teacher New Orleans Public Schls 1982-; *ai:* NSTA, La Earth Sci Teachers Assn; *home:* 10501 Curran Apt 13G New Orleans LA 70127

MITCHELL, JOAN BETAR, First Grade Teacher; *b:* Bridgeport, CT; *c:* Leslie, Heather, Lorne; *ed:* (BS) Elem Ed, Cntrl CT St Coll 1960; (MA) Elem Ed, Fairfield Univ 1973; Certificate of Advanced Stud, Fairfield Univ 1989; *cr:* Kndgtn Teacher Timothy Dwight Sch 1960-63, 1967-69; 1st Grade Teacher N Stratfield Sch 1974-77, Roger Sherman Sch 1977-; *ai:* Delta Kappa Gamma (Mem, Chm) 1986-87; Intnl Society for Women Educators, FFA, CFA, NEA; Fairfield Ed Assn Schlsp Comm Chm 1986-; United Way Rep; *home:* 556 Old Post Rd Fairfield CT 06430

MITCHELL, JOHN GILBERT, JR., Science Teacher; *b:* Clarksburg, WV; *ed:* (BA) Bio Sci, Fairmont St 1979; (BA) Curr/Instruction, WV Univ; Grad Stud Curr, Instruction, WV Univ; Aerospace Curr Dev, NEWMAST, Sky Sch; IBM Cmptr Trng; *cr:* Bio/Astronomy/Geology/Zoology Teacher Liberty HS 1979-82; Life/Earth Sci Shinnston Mid Sch 1982-85; General/Phys Sci/Chem Teacher Lincoln HS 1985-; *ai:* Sci Club Spon; Bsktbl Statistician JR Var & Var; WVEA HCEA Building Rep; PAC Steering Comm; Jr/Sr Prom Comm; Faculty Advisory Comm; WVSTA 1982-; NRAO Adv 1987, Graduate 1987; BSA Eagle Scout 1967-79; Amer Chem Society Mem 1975-79; Tri-Beta Biological Society Mem 1976-79; NASA Teacher in Space Prgm; Natl Radio Astonomy Assoc Sky Sch Cadet & Spon; NEWMAST NASA Graduate 1988; Lincoln HS Teacher of Yr 1986, 1987; *office:* Lincoln HS Rt 1 Box 300 Shinnston WV 26431

MITCHELL, JOLETTE, Band Director; *b:* Marianna, FL; *ed:* (BME) Music Ed, UTA 1980; (MM) Flute, NTSU 1984; *cr:* Band Dir Hedrick Mid Sch 1980-84, Euless Jr HS 1984-; *ai:* Band; TMEA 1978-; TBA 1980-; Arlington Wind Symphony 1989-; *office:* Euless Jr HS 306 W Airport Frwy Euless TX 76039

MITCHELL, JOSEPH CHARLES, Fourth Grade Teacher; *b:* Auburn, NY; *m:* Joanne Leonard; *c:* Joseph Jr., William, John, Laura; *ed:* (BS) Elem Ed, 1961, (MS) Elem Ed, SUNY Oswego; Grad Stud; *cr:* Elem Teacher Genesee Street Sch 1961-63, Mark Loveless Elem 1963-78, Morgan Rd Elem 1978-; *ai:* Natl Parent Teachers Local Pres 1974-75, Honorary Life Membership 1974; United Liverpool Faculty Assn VP 1974-75; NY St United Teachers 1970-; Liverpool Center Schls Prof Planning Staff; BSA Advisory Bd; *office:* Morgan Rd Elem Sch Morgan Rd Liverpool NY 13090

MITCHELL, KAREN TATMAN, French Teacher/Dept Chair; *b:* Santa Monica, CA; *m:* Robert R.; *ed:* (BSED) Ed/Fr/Music, Univ of MO 1964; (MS) Admin Sci, Univ of AL Huntsville 1979; *cr:* Fr Teacher Binghamton Cntrl HS 1964-68; Fr/Music Teacher White Oak Jr HS 1968; Fr/Eng Teacher Lee HS 1969; Fr / Russian Teacher Huntsville HS 1969-72; Fr Teacher Johnson HS 1972-73; Fr/Russian Teacher Huntsville HS 1973-; *ai:* Jr Class, Fr Club, Fr NHS Spon; AATF 1975-; Phi Delta Kappa 1985-; AAFLT 1980-; NE AL Foreign Lang Collaborative Secy 1985-; Outstanding Admin Sci Grad Awd 1978; AL St Dept of Ed Hum Task Force 1978, Course of Stud Comm 1982-85; Huntsville City Sch System Exec Dev Prgm 1987-88, Christa McAuliffe Fellowship Nom 1989; Co-Author Elem Sch Stu Fr Video Series 1988; Optimists Club Outstanding Scndry Sch Teacher Awd 1989; *office:* Huntsville HS 2304 Billie Watkins Dr Huntsville AL 35801

MITCHELL, KENNETH O., Science Teacher; *b:* Terre Haute, IN; *m:* Claudia Marie Cain; *c:* John, Darren; *ed:* (BA) Bio, 1970 (MS) Ed, 1975 IN St Univ; *cr:* Teacher Clinton HS 1970-71; Edgewood HS 1971-; *ai:* Homecoming Spon; Edgewood SADD; Hoosier Assn of Sci Teachers Incorporated 1986-; NEA; IN St Teachers Assn; Ellettsville Chrstn Church Elder; Monroe Cty Soil/Water Dist Conservation Teacher of Yr 1990; *home:* 9540 W State Rd 48 Bloomington IN 47401

MITCHELL, LARRY ALAN, Fourth Grade Teacher; *b:* Muncie, IN; *m:* Vickie Lynn Garringer; *c:* Jacob, Jennifer, Sarah; *ed:* (BS) Elem Ed, Huntington Coll 1974; (MA) Elem Ed, Ball St Univ 1977; *cr:* 4th Grade Teacher Monroe Cntrl Sch Corp 1974-; *ai:* 5th Grade Girls Bsktbl Coach; Monroe Cntrl Classroom Teachers Assn Building Rep 1986-; Randolph Cty Classroom Teachers Assn; in St Teach Ers Assn; NEA; Bethel United Church of Christ Deacon 1974-89; Bethel United Church of Christ Supt; Bethel United Church of Christ Sunday Sch Teacher 1987-; BSA Asst Scoutmaster 1990; Jr Pro Bsktbl Coach Boys & Girls 1987-; Minor League Bsbl Asst 1988; Bethel United Church of Christ Mens Fellowship VP 1989; DE Church Bowling League Secy 1974-75; *office:* Monroe Central Elem Sch State Rd 32 East Parker City IN 47368

MITCHELL, MADIE WASHINGTON, Third Grade Teacher; *b:* Concord, NC; *m:* Ernest Jr.; *c:* Lafayette, Valerie M. Davis, Kris; *ed:* (BS) Elem Ed, Barber Scotia Coll 1959; (MA) Early Childhood Ed, VA St Univ 1977; Attend Numerous Wkshp & Conferences in Ed; *cr:* 1st Grade Teacher Bessie Mason Sch 1960-62; 3rd Grade Teacher Harry E James Sch 1962-70, Patrick Copeland Sch 1970-; *ai:* Cooperating Teacher Stu Teachers; Chm for Odyssey of Mind Team; 3rd Grade Mentor Teacher & Chairperson; Co-Chm & Presented Wkshps for Colleague and Beginning Teachers City-Wide; Served on City-Wide Textbook Comm; Attended Wkshp to become Mentor Teacher; Hopewell Ed Assn; VA Teachers Assn; Natl Teachers Assn; Zeta Phi Beta ; First Baptist Church; Appointed Steering Comm for Accrediation of Sch; Assisted with Dev of Colleague Teacher Handbook & PCS Stu Teacher Handbook.

MITCHELL, MARGARET SHOCKLEY, English/Literature Teacher; *b:* Georgetown, DE; *m:* Earl P.; *c:* Kelly Jones, Stephen; *ed:* (BS) Elem Ed, 1977;(MS) Curr & Dsgn, 1989 DE St Coll; Post Masters Studies; *cr:* Eng/Lit Teacher Sussex Jr HS; *ai:* Artist in Residence Chm; NEA 1977-; NCTE 1985-; Sussex Cty Arts Cncl; Sussex Heart Assn 1987-89; Sussex Sftbl Girls Leag Pres 1969-72; Georgetown Majorettes Club Organizer 1972-74; Millsboro Historical Society Pres 1989-; *office:* Sussex Central Jr H S State St Millsboro DE 19966

MITCHELL, MARIE SHAMBURGER, Mathematics Dept Chairperson; *b:* Meridian, MS; *m:* Zola Monty; *c:* Elizabeth, Leigh A., Melissa; *ed:* (BS) Math, MS Univ for Women 1972; (MED) Math, MS St Univ 1980; *cr:* Math Teacher Hamilton Jr HS 1972-75, Hall Cty Jr HS 1976-78; Math Dept Lecturer MS St Univ 1978-84; Math Teacher Caldwell HS 1984-; *office:* Caldwell HS 820 N Browder Columbus MS 39702

MITCHELL, MARY ELIZABETH, 8th Grade US History Teacher; *b:* Bogalusa, LA; *ed:* (AA) His, Pearl River Jr Coll 1968; (BA) Soc Stud, Univ of S MS 1970; (MS) His/Ed, William Carey on Coast 1978; *cr:* Soc Stud Teacher Moss Point Schls 1970-; *ai:* Stu Cncl Spon 1985-; Jackson Teachers Lobby Rep 1983; His Dept Head 1971-80; Discipline Comm 1980-; Project Bus Co-Teacher 1983-; MS Youth Legislature Spon 1973-; Moss Point PTA 1970-80; MS Assn of Educators 1983-; MS Assn of Educators 1983-; Church of God (Mem & Pianist) 1970-, Woman of Yr 1985; Natl Affais Conference MS Cnslr 1989-; Outstanding Young Women of America 1985; Annual Yrbk Dedication 1973; STAR Teacher 1989-; Outstanding Teacher of Yr 1972; MS Dept of Ed Soc Stud Teachers Curr Guide 1973; *office:* Magnolia Jr HS Magnolia St Moss Point MS 39563

MITCHELL, MARY MARGARET, English Teacher; *b:* Denver, CO; *ed:* (BA), (MA) Univ of Co; *cr:* Eng Teacher Niwot HS 1983-; *ai:* NHS Spon; NEA, NCTE; NEH Fellowship 1986; Published Literary Criticism & Poetry in Journals; *office:* Niwot HS 8989 E Niwot Rd Longmont CO 80501

MITCHELL, PATRICIA HAMILTON, 7-12th Grade English Teacher; *b:* Pekin, IL; *ed:* (BA) English, IL Coll 1964; (MA) Human Dev Cnclng, Sangamon ST Univ 1990; *cr:* English Teacher Jacksonville HS 1964-66; Robert E Lee HS 1966-68; Routt HS 1968-69; Balyki HS 1978-; *ai:* NHS Adv; Oratorical Contest Dir; Asst Play Dir; Sponsored Class of 1979, 87 and Currently 8th Grade Class; IEA, NEA 1964-; NCTE 1964-; Chi Sigma Iota NHS of Cnslrs 1989-; ASCA 1989-; Chi Beta 1960-64; Beta Sigma Phi 1963-; *home:* 1607 Chilton Jacksonville IL 62650

MITCHELL, ROBERT EDWARD, Computer Science Teacher; *b:* Camden, NJ; *c:* Robert Jr., Renee; *ed:* (BA) Elem Ed, 1972, (MA) Elem Ed, 1977 Glassboro St Coll; *cr:* Math Teacher St Lawrence Sch 1969-72; 5th Grade Teacher Robert B Jaggard Sch 1972-82; Cmptr Sci Teacher Marlton Mid Sch 1984-; *ai:* Evesham Township Ed Assn Pres 1982-87; Ind Umpires Assn (Assignor 1987-, Pres 1981, Rules Interpretor 1980); St of NJ Mini-Grant 1973; *office:* Marlton Mid Sch Tomlinson Mill Rd Marlton NJ 08053

MITCHELL, SARAH L., Biology/Science Teacher; *b:* Watertown, WI; *ed:* (BS) Sci, Univ of WI Oshkosh 1987; *cr:* Bio Teacher E E Worthing HS 1988-; *ai:* Var Tennis Coach; Explorers Sci Club & Jr Class Spon.

MITCHELL, SHIRLEY W., 9th Grade English Teacher; *b:* Wayne, WV; *m:* Donald E.; *c:* William D., Nancy, Jason; *ed:* (BA) Eng/Soc Stud, 1981, (MA) Scndry Ed, 1986 Marshall Univ; Eng, WV Wesleyan Coll; *cr:* Rdng Teacher E Lynn Mid Sch 1981-85; Eng Teacher Ft Gay HS 1985-86, Wayne HS 1986-; *ai:* Frosh Spon; Homeroom Teacher; WV Ed Assn; Advanced Placement Wkshp Concord Coll 1986; Seminar Participant WV Wesleyan Coll 1989; *office:* Wayne HS Rt 3 Craig Rd Wayne WV 25570

MITCHELL, THOMAS STEVEN, Band Director; *b:* Sheffield, AL; *m:* Rhonda Ann; *c:* Brad, Emily, Sara; *ed:* (BS) Music Ed, Univ of AL 1976; (MMED) Music Ed, LA St Univ 1984; Natl Trombone Wkshp; *cr:* Band Dir Westlawn Mid Sch 1976-88; Dir of Jazz 1985-88, Instr of Trombone 1985- Univ of AL Huntsville; Band Dir Challenger Mid Sch 1989-; *ai:* Prin Trombonist Huntsville Symphony Orch; Phi Beta Mu 1987-; Phi Mu Alpha 1984-; MENC 1976-; AL Bandmasters Assn Dist (Chm 1986-88, St Bd Mem); NEA, AEA, HEA; Huntsville Symphony Orch (Bd of Trustees, Orch Rep) 1986-87; Conductor LA Ind Sch Assn St Honor Band; *office:* Challenger Mid Sch 13555 Chaney Thompson Rd Huntsville AL 35803

MITCHELL, VERNA JEAN (COLE), English Teacher; *b:* Cincinnati, OH; *m:* H. Leon; *c:* Dennis L., Debra L. Cheap; *ed:* (BA) Eng, IN Wesleyan Univ 1958; Trng for Cert Gifted Ed; Numerous Grad Courses in Teaching Writing; *cr:* Eng/Span Teacher Van Buren HS 1958-61; Eng Teacher Wallace HS 1961-65, Indian Trail Elem 1965-67, Cochrane Jr HS 1967-68, Quail Hollow Jr HS 1968-; *ai:* Eng Dept Chairperson; Curr Comm; Quail Hollow Jr HS Teacher of Yr 1986; Charlotte Teachers Assn, NCTE; Textbook Consultant Ginn Eng Prgm 1983; *office:* Quail Hollow Jr HS 2901 Smithfield Church Rd Charlotte NC 28210

MITCHELL, VIRGINIA DALE, Fourth Grade Teacher; *b:* Louisville, MS; *ed:* (AA) Elem Ed, E Cntrl Jr Coll 1970; (BS) Elem Ed, 1972, (MED) Elem Ed, 1980 MS St Univ; *cr:* 2nd Grade Teacher Eastside Elem 1972-78; 4th Grade Teacher Louisville Elem 1978-; *ai:* MS Prof Educators 1989-; *office:* Louisville Elem Sch 300 N Columbus Louisville MS 39339

MITCHELL, WILLIAM DONALD, Eng/Literature Dept Teacher; *b:* Chicago, IL; *m:* Gail Annette Wardlow; *c:* Scott R., Jeffrey J.; *ed:* (BA) Eng/Lit, Sioux Falls Coll 1978; Working Towards Masters; *cr:* Teacher Beresford Mid Sch; *ai:* Drama, Declam, Ftbl, Track Coach; Building Rep; Inservice Comm; Church Sunday Sch Supt 1986-88; Teacher of Yr Awd Sch Dist; Teacher of Month Awd Local TV Station KSIT; *office:* Beresford Mid Sch 201 S 4th Beresford SD 57004

MITCHELL, WILMA DUFFIELD, Teacher of Gifted/Talented; *b:* Gassaway, WV; *m:* Raymond L.; *c:* Lorelei Gunnoe, Christina, John, James; *ed:* (BS) Elem Ed, 1972, (MED) Elem Ed, 1981 Kent St Univ; Course Work Teaching Gifted & Talented; *cr:* Elem Teacher 1966-79, Teacher of Gifted & Talented 1979- Katherine Thomas Elem Sch; *ai:* Compentency Based Ed Dev & Give a Boost Comm; NEA, NE OH Teachers Assn, OH Teachers Assn 1970-; Windham Teachers Assn 1966-; OH Assn Gifted Children 1980-; Originated & Continued Help Develop Gifted Prgm Share Windham Schls; *office:* Windham Exempted Village Sch Community Rd Windham OH 44288

MITCHUM, FULTON J., Soc Stud Teacher/Dept Head; *b:* Washington, DC; *m:* Nancy L. Ahlgrim; *c:* Travis D., Joshua A.; *ed:* (BA) Psych/His, Milligan Coll 1973; (MAT) Ed, Citadel 1979; PET Instr; Title IX Sports Medicine; *cr:* 7th/8th Grade Teacher Blackville Mid Sch 1973-74; 9th-12th Grade Teacher Macedonia HS 1974-; *ai:* Jr Class Spon; Womens Sftbl Coach; SADD; Coord Inservice & Psych Wkshps; Textbook Adoption Comm; Sch Improvement Cncl; Natl Coaches Assn, NEA 1973-; Bonneau Beach Civic Club; Amer Red Cross Blood Drive Publicity Chm; Moncks Corner Recreation Dept Head T-Ball Coach; Berkeley Cty Dept of Soc Service Foster Parents; Local Cub Scout Pack Volunteer; First Chrstn Church (Mem, Vice-Chm, Eldership, Chrstn Mens Fellowship, Chrstn Singles Ministry Coord, Sftbl & Vlybl Teams Mem, Gospel Chords Mem, Most Outstanding Young Men in America 1983; Teacher of Yr 1985; Coach of Yr 1984; Television Appearances on Midday; Teacher Incentive Awd 1988-89; Nom Incentive Awd 1989-; Article Published; *home:* HCR 69 Box 438 B Moncks Corner SC 29461

MITSTIFER, ARWOOD E., 4/5/6 Grade Soc Stud Teacher; *b:* Williamsport, PA; *m:* Walburga R. Scholz; *c:* Romy D. Young; *ed:* (BS) Sociology, Lycoming Coll; (MED) Elem Ed, PA St; *cr:* Teacher 1963-, Head Teacher 1966-75 Liberty Elem Sch; *ai:* PSEA 1963-; NEA 1963-; *office:* Liberty Elem Sch RD 1 Box 2C Liberty PA 16930

MITTAN, KENNETH D, Jr HS Math GATE Teacher; *b:* Chadron, NE; *m:* Cathy Mc Dermott; *c:* Meghan, Janie, Mark; *ed:* (BA) Ed, Univ CA Santa Barbara 1955; (MS) Ed Admin, Univ Southern CA 1965; Minority His/Gifted & Talented Ed/Math/Admin/Eng; *cr:* 8th Grade Teacher 1959-64; 3rd Grade Teacher 1965 Ocean View Sch Dist; 5th/6th Grade Teacher Sespe Sch 1966-79; 7th/8th Grade Teacher Math Lit GATE Fillmore Unified Sch Dist Jr HS 1979-; *ai:* Honor Soc; Chess Club; Coord Parent GATE Jr HS; CA Assn Gifted 1981-; NEA 1967-; CA Teachers Assn 1961-; Fillmore Unified Teachers Assn Pres Beginning Team 1966-; Fillmore Boosters 1987-; Amer Legion Treas 1980-; Grant Minority His Study 1969; Book Teacher Pleaser of Potentially Gifted; Study Units Discovery & Going where Presenter CA Assn of Gifted Ventura Cty Wkshps; *office:* Fillmore Jr HS 2nd & Palm Fillmore CA 93015

MITTNACHT, KATHERINE L'HOMMEDIEU, High School English Teacher; *b:* San Francisco, CA; *m:* Peter; *c:* Anne, Henry; *ed:* (BA) Amer Lit, Middlebury Coll 1982; Grad Stud Drew Univ; *cr:* Eng Teacher Suffield Acad 1982-83, Pingry Sch 1983-86, Lawrenceville Sch 1986-; *ai:* Suffield & Pingry Field Hockey & Lacrosse Coach; Housemaster; Small Acapella Womens Group Dir; Lawrenceville Lacrosse 3rd Team Coach; *office:* Lawrenceville Sch P O Box 66060 Lawrenceville NJ 08648

MIXON, LISA EDENS, Spanish Teacher; *b:* Johnson City, TN; *ed:* (BA) Span/Eng, Carson-Newman 1971; (MS) Foreign Lang Ed, Univ of TN 1976; Univ Guadalajara Mexico; *cr:* Teacher Cocke Cty HS 1971-75, Jefferson Cty HS 1976-85, Halls HS 1985-; *ai:* Sr Spon; Span Honor Club; Y Teens; Knox Cty Ed Assn Building Rep 1989-; TN Foreign Lang Teachers Assn 1971-; League of Women Voters (VP 1981-82, Pres 1982-84); PTA 1982; Master Teacher; *office:* Halls HS 4321 Emory Rd Knoxville TN 37938

MIXSON, PATRICIA SMITH, Spanish Teacher; *b:* Jersey City, NJ; *m:* Michael I.; *c:* Ariane, Anais, Michael; *ed:* (BA) Span, 1967, (MA) Span Lit, 1974, (MA) Comparative Lit, 1977 Montclair St; *cr:* Span Teacher Neptune HS 1967-; *ai:* Span Club Adv; Russian Class Facilitator; Advanced Placement Coord; Reader for Span Advanced Placement Examinations 1988, 1989, 1990; *office:* Neptune HS 55 Neptune Blvd Neptune NJ 07753

MIYANO, STEVEN CLIFFORD, Biology/Marine Biology Teacher; *b:* Petaluma, CA; *m:* Janice G. Shafer; *c:* Phillip, Sam; *ed:* (BA) Life Sci, San Jose St Univ 1975; Sea Marine Bio Trng; *cr:* Sci Teacher Awalt HS 1977-81, Mountain View HS 1981-; *ai:* Coach Var Golf & Jr Var Girls Tennis; Asian Club, Class, Ski Club Adv; Encina Fnd Fellowship 1988; Los Altos Rotary Club Service Above Self Awd 1986; *office:* Mountain View HS 3535 Truman Ave Mountain View CA 94040

MIZELLE, TERESA K., English Teacher; *b:* Washington, NC; *ed:* (BA) Eng, VA Wesleyan Coll 1978; (MA) Eng, 1981, (CAS) Educl Admin, 1987 Old Dominion Univ; *cr:* Teacher Deep Creek HS 1978-; *ai:* Asst Eng Dept Chairperson; Coach Its Academic; Chesapeake Challenge & Knowledge Master Open Teams; Administrative Cncl Mem; Inst for Teacher Dev Task Force; NCTE, TATE-T, VATE, ASCD; Delta Kappa Gamma Treas 1986-; Teacher of Yr 1986; *office:* Deep Creek HS 2900 Margaret Booker Dr Chesapeake VA 23323

MLINARICH, JOHN JOSEPH, Social Studies Teacher; *b:* E Pittsburgh, PA; *m:* Susan; *c:* Matthew, David; *ed:* (BS) Soc Stud Ed, Clarion St Coll 1965; (MED) His Ed, IN Univ of PA 1971; Kent St Univ 1967; Univ of Pittsburgh, Carnegie Mellon Univ 1971-72; *cr:* Soc Stud Teacher N Braddock Sch Dist 1965-71, Smithtown HS East 1972-; *ai:* Regents Action Planning Comm; NCSS; Sachem Youth Advisory Group Sponsorship Dir 1988-; Police Athletic League Dir 1990; NDEA Schlsp Kent St Univ 1967; Doctoral Fellowship Univ of Pittsburgh 1971-72; *office:* Smithtown HS East Northern Blvd Saint James NY 11780

MOADE, MARY JAMES (HOLSEN), Retired Substitute Teacher; *b:* Mount Carmel, IL; *m:* Donald Ray; *c:* Donald P., Lynn A. Moade Burton; *ed:* (BA) Elem Ed, Univ of Evansville 1966; Natl Sci Fnd 1970, Grad Stud Towards Masters Degree 1975-80 Univ of Evansville; *cr:* 5th Grade Teacher 1960-65, 7th Grade Eng Teacher 1966-70, Spec Ed Teacher 1970-72, 8th Grade Sci Teacher 1972-89 North Mid Sch; *ai:* Sci Fair Spon 1972-89; Pom Pom Girl Spon 1971-89; Chrldr Spon 1965-89; 8th Grade Play Production 1979-89; Fundraiser Chm 1975-89; IL Jr Acad of Sci (Pres 1970-71, Treas 1971), Prof Contributions 1979; Wabash Cty Ed Assn (Treas 1988-89, Secy 1972-73); Beta Sigma Phi (Pres 1970-71, Secy 1971-72); Sigma Sigma Sigma Treas 1974-75; Amer Legion Auxiliary Pres 1974-75; Jr 4-H Fair Awds Comm 1975-; *home:* 1026 Market St Mount Carmel IL 62863

MOAK, LYNN DAVIES, English Teacher; *b:* New Orleans, LA; *m:* Stacey; *c:* Paul D., Ashley L.; *ed:* (BS) Bus/Eng Ed, LA St Univ 1967; Wkshps & Seminars; *cr:* Prgm Specialist LA St Bd of Ed 1967-74; Teacher St Theresa of Avila 1980-; *ai:* FBLA Exec Secy; Chrldr, Stu Cncl, Stock Market Game Moderator; NCTE, LCTE, NCEA; St Theresa of Avila Teacher of Yr 1989-; *office:* St Theresa of Avila Sch 212 E New River Gonzales LA 70737

MOBERG, MARTHA JANE TULLY, 6th Grade Science Teacher; *b:* Camp Grove, IL; *m:* Eldon Sam Jr.; *ed:* (BS) Ed, Mary Rogers Coll 1964; Standard Prof Cert 1975-82; (AAC) Advanced Prof Cert 1982-83; Grad Maryknoll Lang for Swahili, Musoma, E Africa 1964; Curr Dev in Elem Sch, George Washington Univ; Biographical Stud in His, Towson Univ 1975; *cr:* 3rd/7th Grade Rdng Teacher Sci Corpus Christi Sch 1964; Upper Level/Form IV Geography/New Testament/Lower Level Domestic Sci Teacher/Music/Drama Dir Rosary Girls Scndry Sch 1965-69; 8th Grade Soc Stud Teacher St James Sch 1970; Remedial Rdng/5th Grade Teacher High Point Elem Sch 1971; *ai:* Sci Club 1978-; Stu Against Name Calling Comm Mem; CAC Mem; Finance Comm; Sci Dept Chairperson; John Hopkins Ed Psych Recent Dev 1972; 6th Grade Family Life & Human Dev Prgm 1974; Triple A Alcoholism Control Admin 1980; Rosary Yrbk Production 1966-68; PTA (Secy, Treas 1971-73, Bd Mem 1978-), Sch Achievement 1971-75, Life Membership Awd 1986, 1st Place MD Outstanding Educator of Yr, Golden Apple Awd 1985, Awd of Recognition in Ed 1973-89; MD Rdng Assn Mem 1971-74; TAAAC, MSTA, NEA Mem 1971-89; MD Mid Sch Assn Mem 1975-89; Cty Supt Oil Can Awd 1986; Cmmty Talent Assn (Founding Bd Mem, Active Artist 1978-89) 1989-; Church (Cantor 1975-84, Choir 1976-85); Nom for Natl Phoebe Hearst Awd, Masonic Awd for Outstanding Contributions to Ed & Cmmty; Human Relations Comm George Fox Ethnic Fair 1982-85; Recognized Tanzanian Government Dept of Ed Best Organized Geography Lab in Nation 1968 & Cambridge Top Level IV Highest Percentage of Geography; Poetry Published in Magazine 1964; Maryknoll Magazine Double Page Photo Published 1966; Univ of Akron Elem Sci Wkshp 1971; Several In-Services & Wkshps; *office:* George Fox Mid Sch 7922 Outing Ave Pasadena MD 21122

MOBILIA, MARIA DE PALMA, Fifth Grade Teacher; *b:* Milford, MA; *m:* Michael; *ed:* (BA) Elem Ed, Notre Dame Coll 1975; *cr:* 3rd Grade Teacher Memorial Sch 1975-77; 5th Grade Teacher 1977-81, 1st Grade Teacher 1981-82, 3rd Grade Teacher 1982-88, 5th Grade Teacher 1988- Woodland Sch; *ai:* PTO Teacher Rep; MA Teachers Assn, NEA 1975-; Amer Legion 1989-; Nom Teacher of Yr 1988; Woodland Sch Teacher of Yr 1988; *office:* Woodland Elem Sch N Vine St Milford MA 01757

MOBLEY, MIKE COLIN, Choral Act/HS Choir Dir; *b:* Breckenridge, TX; *ed:* (BME) Choral Music/Scndry, 1985, (MM) Choral Conducting, 1987 W TX St Univ; Teacher Expectation & Stu Achievement; *cr:* Choir Dir Spearman Ind Sch Dist 1987-88, Seminole Ind Sch Dist 1988-; *ai:* TX Music Educators Assn 1983-; *office:* Seminole HS Po Box 900 Seminole TX 79360

MOBLEY, PEGGY HAM, Mathematics Teacher; *b:* Andalusia, Covington; *c:* Carrie; *ed:* (BS) Math, Univ of Montevallo 1967; (MS) Scndry Ed, Troy St 1975; *cr:* Teacher Florala HS 1967-68, Andalusia HS 1968-69, Terrebonne Parish 1969-70, Pleasant Home Sch 1970-; *ai:* Jr Class & Chrldr Spon; NEA Alternate Dir 1986-; AL Ed Assn St Bd of Dir 1987-; Alpha Eplison (VP 1988-, Treas 1986-); AL Democratic Party Mem St Exec Comm 1986-; Andalusia Pee Wee Ftbl League Chrldr Coord 1984-85; Andalusia Star News Readers Advisory Comm 1987-88; Coord Kumon Math Supplemental Prgm Pleasant Home 1989; Birmingham Post Herald AL All St Academic Judge 1989-; *office:* Pleasant Home Sch Rt 7 Andalusia AL 36420

MOBLEY, SONYA COLLINS, 2nd Grade Teacher/Chair; *b:* Daytona Beach, FL; *m:* Wallace Sr.; *c:* Wallace Jr.; *ed:* (BA) Sociology, Bethune-Cookman Coll 1969; Additional Stud Steson Univ & FL A&M Univ; *cr:* Teacher R J Longstreet 1969-; *ai:* Grade Level Chairperson; Lang Art Contact; Sch Chairperson United Negro Coll Fund; Volusia Cty Educators; Natl Cncl of Negro Women, Jack & Jill Interest Group, Alphabets, Longstreet PTA; *home:* 220 Garden St Daytona Beach FL 32114

MOBLEY, VIVIAN ANDERSON, Geography Teacher; *b:* Bulloch Cty, GA; *m:* Harris W.; *c:* Stephen M., L. Jane Mobley Carrie, J. Mark; *ed:* (BSED) Soc Stud, 1971, (MST) Soc Stud, 1975, (EDSP) Soc Stud, 1977 GA Southern; *cr:* Teacher Julia P Bryant Sch 1971-72, William James Sch 1972-82, Statesboro HS

1982-; *ai:* Debate Team Coach 1984-86; Academic Quiz Bowl Spon/Coach 1986-; *office:* Statesboro H S 10 Lester Rd Statesboro GA 30458

MOCCIA, REGIS, SC, English Department Chm/Teacher; *b:* Brooklyn, NY; *ed:* (BA) His/Eng, Spring Hill 1948; (MS) Eng, St Johns Univ 1963; NY St Advanced Placement Eng Prgm, Colgate Univ; Natl Prgm for Eng Teachers, Univ of VA; Enrichment, Fordham Univ & Loyola Univ; *cr:* Eng Dept Chm Mc Clancy HS 1961-65, Bishop Reilly HS 1966-72, St Josephs HS 1973-; *ai:* Literary Magazine Adv; Moderator Volunteer Work Nursing Home; NCTE 1963-88; NJ Cncl Teachers of Eng 1980-85; BQ Teachers of Eng VP 1970-75; Natl Grant Study Univ of VA; Outstanding Teacher Metuchen Diocese 1989-; Nom Outstanding Teacher Princeton Univ Awd 1989-; Published Books & Eng Handbook; Organized & Operate Rdng & Writing Clinic; Conduct Wkshps Eng Teachers to Improve Motivational Approach & Understand Youth Better; Conduct Prgms Parents ConcersConduct Wkshps Eng Teachers to Improve Motivational Approach & Understand Youth Better; Conduct Prgms Parents Concerning Youth; *home:* 145 Plainfield Ave Metuchen NJ 08840

MOCK, MARTHA THORNTON, Latin/English Teacher; *b:* Macon, GA; *m:* Isaac Henry; *c:* Jennifer L. Wyatt, Christin K. Wyatt, Shelley R. Wyatt; *ed:* (BS) Home Ec, Univ of Ga 1972; (MED) Eng, GA Coll 1984; Licensed Real Estate Agent- GA Real Estate Commission; *cr:* Teacher Beechwood Sch 1973-76; Home Ec Teacher Univ of GA Extension Service 1972-73; Public Relations Dir Citizens Bank Fort Valley GA 1978-81; Eng Teacher Gordon Jr Coll 1984-88; Teacher Piedmont Acad 1982-; Owner Martha T Mock Interiors 1988-; *ai:* Var Chrldr Coach 1981-89; Sr Class Adv 1983-; Yrbk Adv 1986-; Phi Upsilon Omicron 1971-72; Star Teacher 1984-88.

MOCKRY, JEAN WADE, 12th Grade English Teacher; *b:* Glens Falls, NY; *m:* John Anthony Jr.; *c:* Brian W., Katelyn Wade; *ed:* (AA) Liberal Stud, Adirondack Comm Coll 1972; (BA) Eng/Ed, 1975, (MS) Ed, 1977, (CAS) Guidance Counseling, 1987 SUNY Plattsburgh; *cr:* K/4th-6th Grade Elem Teacher Abraham Wing Sch 1976-79; 9th-12th Grade Eng Teacher 1979-, Guidance Cnslr 1988- Mount Assumption Inst; *ai:* Sr Class & Newspaper Moderator; NY St Assn for Counseling & Dev 1988-; League of Women Voters (Mem 1986-, VP 1987-89); Cornell Cooperative Extension Home Ec Prgm Comm Mem 1990; Clinton Cty Recycling Comm Chairperson; North Cntry Cath Weekly Freelance Journalist; *home:* 59 Oak St Plattsburgh NY 12901

MODARELLI, MARIANNE ORLANDO, Kindergarten Teacher; *b:* Youngstown, OH; *m:* Nicholas E.; *c:* Nicholas A.; *ed:* (BS) Elem Ed, 1973, (MS) Early Chldhd Ed, 1978 Youngstown St Univ; *cr:* Teacher Roosevelt Elem Sch 1974-; *ai:* NEA, OH Ed Assn, Hubbard Ed Assn (Exec Bd Mem, Soc Comm); Delta Kappa Gamma Honorary Corresponding Secy 1988-; Mahoning Cty Bar Assn Auxiliary (Historian, Corresponding Secy) 1983-84; St Patrick Church Choir; Roosevelt Sch Parents Assn Mini Grant Awd; *office:* Roosevelt Elem Sch 110 Orchard Ave Hubbard OH 44425

MODEC, THOMAS JACK, Math Dept Chair/Math Teacher; *b:* Eveleth, MN; *m:* Elizabeth Vonder Haar; *c:* Tom, Dave; *ed:* (BS) Math Ed, Univ of MN Duluth 1960; (MS) Math Ed, St Cloud Univ 1972; *cr:* Math Teacher Kimball Jr HS 1961-66, Larkin HS 1967, Anoka Jr HS 1968, Jackson Jr HS 1969-; *ai:* Ftbl, Bsktbl, Bsbl Coach; Gifted & Talented Comm Mem; Math Dept Chairperson; Anoka-Hennedin Educl Assn, MN Ed Assn, NEA 1967-; MN Cncl Teachers of Math 1989-; Natl Math Fnd Grant Carleton Coll 1967; *home:* 321 Mc Cann Ave NW Anoka MN 55303

MODENBACH, PATRICIA FULKERSON, English Dept Chair/Dev Dir; *b:* Denver, CO; *m:* Le Roy John Jr.; *c:* Neil, Christine, Mark, Scot; *ed:* (BA) Eng, Incarnate Word Coll 1968; *cr:* Teacher St Catherine of Sienna Elem 1968-70, Incarnate Word HS 1971-72, St John Elem 1983-84; Teacher/Dev Dir/Head of Eng Dept St John Interparochial HS 1984-; *ai:* Adv Literary Magazine; Something Literary Dev Dir; Coord Alumni Act, Fundraising, Capital Campaigns, Public Relations, Publicity; MS Teacher Assessment Instrument Evaluator; Gulf Coast Chamber 1989-; MS Theater Assn 1988-; Gulfport Little Theaters Dir Bd 1988-; STAR Teacher 1988; *office:* St John Interparochial HS 620 Pass Rd Gulfport MS 39501

MODESTO, ROBERT, English Department Chair; *b:* Gary, IN; *m:* Julie Mc Cracken; *c:* Maureen A.; *ed:* (BA) Ed/Comm, Purdue Univ 1984; *cr:* Wrestling & Track Coach W Lafayette Jr HS 1982-84; Eng Teacher Mid West Military Acad 1985-86; Eng Dept Chair St Francis De Sales HS 1983-; *ai:* Stu Cncl; NCTE 1987-; *home:* 4232 E 7th Ave Miller IN 46403

MODLIN, JAMES KENNETH, Retired Mathematics Teacher; *b:* Picher, OK; *m:* Pauline Sue Hunt; *c:* James M., John K.; *ed:* (BS) Math, 1950, (MS) Math, 1953 KS St Pittsburg; Grad Stud Several Univ; *cr:* Math Teacher Crawford Cmmty HS 1950-53, Bellflower HS 1953-89, Cerritos Coll 1976-77; *ai:* Stu Act Chm; Faculty Club VP; Math Dept Chm; Bellflower Ed Assn 1953-89; Kappa Mu Epsilon, Alpha Gamma Taw 1948-50; PTA Life Membership, Continued Ed Awd; NEA, CA Teachers Assn, CA Math Cncl, NCTM; Stu Act for CASSA Accreditation Chm; Los Angeles Cty Drivers Ed Assn; Natl Sci Fnd Grants Univ CA Los Angeles 1959-61 & USC 1962-66; Nom Presidential Awd of Excl; CA Math Teacher of Yr; Faculty Recognition Awd; Whos Who for Outstanding Scndry Educators; Dept of Water & Power Eng Awd; Annual Dedication; *home:* PO Box 1003 Twin Peaks CA 92391

MOEGLING, LAWRENCE ANTHONY, Spanish Teacher; *b:* Canton, OH; *m:* Mary Lou Bennett; *c:* Lori, Lee Ann; *ed:* (BSED) Span/Eng, 1975, (BA) Span/Eng, 1975 Bowling Green St Univ; (MA) Span/Eng, Marietta Coll 1981; (MED) Span/Eng, OH Univ 1989; Grad Stud Purdue Univ 1984; *cr:* Span Teacher Fort Frye HS 1975-; *ai:* Span Honor Society; OH Foreign Lang Assn, OH Ed Assn 1975-; Knights of Columbus; Martha Holden Jennings Scholar; NEH Grant to Purdue Univ 1984; *home:* 516 3rd St Marietta OH 45750

MOEHLE, ELLEN MILLER, Third Grade Teacher; *b:* Burlington, IA; *m:* Robert; *c:* Michael, Bryan, Jeffrey; *ed:* (BA) Elem Ed, IA Wesleyan Coll 1976; Various Classes; *cr:* Elem Ed Teacher Mediapolis Cmmty Sch 1976-; *ai:* Rdng, Math, Sci, Cmptr Comm; Comm for Prgm & Facilities; New to Dist Teacher Asst; Performance Base Pay Observation Trng; IA Rdng Assn Past Mem; Mediapolis Cmmty Ed Assn; Meth Church (Past Sunday Sch Teacher, Choir Mem, Educl Comm, Sunday Sch Accompanist) 1990; *office:* Mediapolis Cmmty Sch 725 N Northfield Mediapolis IA 52637

MOEN, DIANA, French Teacher; *b:* Tacoma, WA; *ed:* (BA) Fr, Univ of WI Oshkosh 1976; (MED) Fr, Univ of MN Minneapolis 1988; Fr Bus Rockefeller Fellowship 1987; Fr Lang & Culture, AAFT Sch 1984; *cr:* Fr/Eng Teacher Northdale Jr HS 1979-80; Eng/Soc Stud Teacher Caloosa Mid Sch 1980-81; 9th-12th Grade Fr Teacher North Branch HS 1982-85, Rosemount HS 1985-; *ai:* Declamation Speech Coach; AATF 1980-, Schlsp 1984; Speaker Northeast Convention NY City 1988, Cntrl States Conference Minneapolis 1990; *office:* Rosemount HS 3335 142nd St W Rosemount MN 55068

MOEN, MONA L., Physical Education Teacher; *b:* St Paul, MN; *ed:* (BS) Phys Ed, La Crosse St Univ 1966; *cr:* Phys Ed Teacher Woodrow Wilson Jr HS 1967-; *ai:* Bsktbl/Track Coach; Manitowoc Ed Assn 1966-; WI Ed Assn 1966-; NEA 1966-; Manitou Girl Scouts Sr Leader 1967-78; Windstar Fnd 1984-; *office:* Woodrow Wilson Jr H S 1201 N 11th St Manitowoc WI 54220

MOEN, PAMELA NEUHARTH, Kindergarten Teacher; *b:* Pierre, SD; *m:* Daniel; *c:* Eric, Adam, Seth; *ed:* (BA) Spec/Elem Ed, Augustana Coll 1973; Grad Work in Elem Ed; *cr:* Spec Ed Teacher Bedford Cmmty 1973-75; Elem Teacher W Lyon Cmmty Sch; *ai:* Sch Climate, Rdng Month, Phase III Advisory Comms; NWIRC Legislative Chairperson 1988-; IRA 1989-; ISEA, NEA 1973-; Inwood Summer Recreation Pres 1987-; Bethlehem Luth Church Womens Club 1976-80; *office:* West Lyon Cmmty Sch Hwy 182 Inwood IA 51240

MOESKER, MARTHA GARLAND, English Teacher; *b:* Baltimore, MD; *m:* Joseph Albert; *c:* Susan, Matthew, Sarah; *ed:* (BA) Eng, E KY Univ 1969; Eng, Georgetown Univ; Eng/Ed/Hum, Xavier Univ; Ferguson-Florissant Writers Project; Jennings Scholar Lecture Series, Univ of Dayton; *cr:* Educl Therapist Overbrook Childrens Center 1970-71; Eng Teacher US Army Prep Prgm 1971-72, Blanchester HS 1982-86, Goshen HS 1986-; *ai:* Goshen Ed Assn Building Rep 1988-89; OH Ed Assn, NEA; Governors Awd for Spec Ed 1986; *office:* Goshen HS 6692 Goshen Rd Goshen OH 45122

MOFFATT, G. CARROL, Band Director; *b:* Caddo, OK; *m:* Klaasje de Vries; *c:* Rene Day, Carolynne Wells, G. Carrol Jr.; *ed:* (BS) Music Ed, 1960, (MM) Music Ed, 1970 Hardin-Simmons Univ; *cr:* Band Dir Throckmorton Ind Sch Dist 1962-64, Anson Ind Sch Dist 1964-71, Killeen Ind Sch Dist 1971-81, Moody Ind Sch Dist 1988-; *ai:* Choir Dir Moody Ind Sch Dist; TMEA, TBA 1963-81, 1988-; Salado Church Choir Minister of Music 1979-89; Harker Heights Church Choir Minister of Music 1989-; *home:* 2003 Valley Oaks Dr Harker Heights TX 76542

MOFFETT, DAVID WARD, Social Studies Chair; *b:* Cincinnati, OH; *m:* Sandra Steffen; *c:* Mary-Margaret, Elizabeth A.; *ed:* (BS) His/Journalism, 1978, (MA) Public Relations/Philosophy, 1979, Teaching Certificate Soc Sci, 1988 Ball St Univ; *cr:* Realtor Moffett Company Incorporated 1980-86; Soc Stud Chm Bellmont HS 1988-; *ai:* Adams Cty Recycling Center Organizer; Stu Cncl Adv; Jr Class Spon; Phi Delta Kappa; IN Cncl Soc Stud St Citizens Awd 1990; Geography Educators Network IN, NCSS; ICSS Grant Database Cmptr Applications 1989; Ball St E European NEH Grant 1990; IN St Ecology Awareness Prgm 1st Place 1990; Governors Awd Excl in Recycling 1990; Outstanding Young Man of America 1985; *office:* Bellmont HS 1000 E N Adams Dr Decatur IN 46733

MOFFITT, JUDI LYNN CRAVEN, 7th/8th Grade Lang Arts/Soc St; *b:* Asheboro, NC; *m:* James Randall; *ed:* (BS) Intermediate Ed Grades 4-9 Lang Arts/Soc Stud, 1985, (MA) Mid Sch Ed/Rdng, 1989 Univ of NC; Jr Great Books Wrkshp 1989; Certified Seminar Leader; *cr:* 7th/8th Grade Lang Arts & Soc Stud Teacher Coleridge Elem Sch 1985-; *ai:* Stu Cncl Spon; Beta Club Spon; Senate Bill 2 Comm; Natl Ed Week Comm; SACS Comm; NC Assn of Educators Mem 1985 ; Nom Teacher of Yr 1987-88 Representing Coleridge Elem Sch; *home:* 2003 Lambert Dr Asheboro NC 27203

MOFFITT, TERRY ERVIN, Government/Ec/Academic Dean; *b:* Hendersonville, NC; *m:* Cynthia Hackler; *c:* Holly; *ed:* (AB) Scndry Soc Stud, Univ of NC Chapel Hill 1981; Admin, Supervision, Univ of NC Greensboro; *cr:* 7th-12th Grade Soc Stud Teacher Westchester Acad 1981-84; Training Mgr Kay Chemical Company 1984-87; Academic Dean/Government/Ec Teacher Wesleyan Acad 1987-; *ai:* ASCD 1988-; NASSP 1990; NOLPE 1988-; High Point City Cncl Councilman 1989-; Conservatives for Freedom St Advisory Bd 1988-; Guilford Cty GOP Exec Bd 1988-; Key Chemical Company Sales Engr of Yr 1985; Conference Soccer Coach of Yr 1983; NCSSA Region 6 Soccer Coach of Yr 1983; Full Grant to Study Ec Fnd for Ec Ed 1989; *home:* 3102 Woodview St High Point NC 27265

MOGAN, GREGORY LEE, Science Teacher/Dept Chair; *b:* Terre Haute, IN; *m:* Debra Sue Wright; *c:* Jeri J., Nikki L.; *ed:* (BA) Elem Ed, IN St Univ 1975; (MAT) Ed, DePauw Univ 1979; Red Cross Certified CPR Trng; *cr:* 5th Grade Teacher Van Duyn Elem Sch 1976-84; Sci Teacher N Clay Jr HS 1985-; *ai:* Sci Curr Comm; Sci Dept Chm; Jr HS Track Coach; Union United Meth Church Gospel Quartet Living Water 1981-; *office:* N Clay Jr HS Rt 13 Admin Office Brazil IN 47834

MOGLE, NANCY FRANCIS, Math Teacher; *b:* Wilmington, DE; *m:* Robert Alan; *c:* Shelly L. Ashley A.; *ed:* (BSED) Scndry Math Ed, 1975, (MED) Educl Psych, 1983 IN Univ of PA; *cr:* Math Substitute Teacher North Allegheny & North Hills Sch Dist; Accrual Unit/Non-Performing Loans Melon Bank; Cost Accounting Dept/Engr Technician Robert Shaw Controls; Private Math Tutor; Math Teacher Marion Center HS; *ai:* 8th Grade Spon; Marion Center Area Ed Assn, PSEA, NEA 1980-; Naughty Pines Western Square Dance (VP 1980-81, Pres 1981-82); Alpha Phi (Alumni Pres, Financial Adv); *home:* RD 1 Box 14 Marion Center PA 15759

MOHLENHOFF, BRUCE R., Eighth Grade Teacher; *b:* Staten Island, NY; *ed:* (BA) His, 1971, (MSED) Scndry Ed, 1974 Wagner Coll; *cr:* Teacher St Adalbert Sch 1971-; *ai:* Summer Co-op Sch, Soc Stud Fair, Graduation Coord; St & Local NCSS; Fed of Cath Teachers Union Delegate; Staten Island Historical Society 1971-; St Johns Luth Church Finance Comm Chm 1986-; *office:* St Adalbert Sch 355 Morningstar Rd Staten Island NY 10303

MOHLMAN, DEAN GERALD, Life Science Teacher; *b:* Yankton, SC; *ed:* (BS) Health Ed, TX A&M Univ 1985; Masters Ed, E TX St Univ; *cr:* Teacher/Coach T H Mc Donald Mid Sch 1985-; *ai:* 7th Grade Ftbl Coach; 7th/8th Grade Track Coord; Fellowship of Chrstn Athletes Spon; *office:* T H Mc Donald Mid Sch 2930 Town East Mesquite TX 75150

MOHORIC, FRANKLIN JOSEPH, Third Grade Teacher; *b:* Cleveland, OH; *ed:* (BS) Elem Ed, 1969, (MED) Admin/Elem Ed, 1978 Kent St Univ; Grad Stud; *cr:* 4th/6th Grade Teacher Erwine Sch 1969-71; 5th Grade Teacher T Jefferson Sch 1971-80; 4th Grade Teacher Noble Sch 1980-83; 3rd Grade Teacher Glenbrook Sch 1983-; *ai:* Safety Patrol Supvr; Talent Show Organizer; Traditional Sch Comm Mem; ETA Rep; Euclid Teachers Assn; *home:* 22671 Arms Ave Euclid OH 44123

MOHPRASIT, DIANNE CARTER, History/Computer Teacher; *b:* New Orleans, LA; *c:* Jason; *ed:* (BA) His, Univ of Montevallo 1967; (MA) His, MS St Univ 1972; *cr:* Teacher Adair Mid Sch 1966-68, Sparkman HS 1968-70, Isabella HS 1970-71; Grad Asst MS St Univ 1971-72; Teacher Uttaradit Teachers Coll 1974-75, Dallas Cty HS 1976-; *ai:* Yrbk Spon; NEA, AL Ed Assn, Dallas Cty Ed Assn; 1st United Meth Church; Univ of Montevallo Alumni Assn Chilton Cty Excl Awd in Teaching 1989; Dallas Cty Sch System Teacher of Yr 1987.

MOHR, CAROLYN HUPP, Work Adjustment Coordinator; *b:* Springfield, OH; *m:* Charles; *c:* Donald Cavanaugh, Cathy Cavanaugh; *ed:* (BA) Elem Ed, 1959, (MS) Early Mid Chldhd, 1984 OH St; *cr:* Teacher Huy Elem 1962-79, Medina Mid Sch 1980-88; Occupational Work Adjustment Coord Medina Mid Sch 1988-; *ai:* Athletic Dir; Advisory Comm; Columbus Ed Assn Building Rep 1965-69, Outstanding Building Rep Awd 1964; *office:* Medina Mid Sch 1425 Hwy Rd Columbus OH 43224

MOHR, DAVID, Science Department Chair; *b:* Ellwood City, PA; *m:* Kathleen R. Wenkhous; *c:* Melissa, Christina; *ed:* (BS) Bio, Geneva Coll 1976; *cr:* Sci/Math Teacher Beaver Valley Chrstn Acad 1985-; *ai:* Chess Club Spon; Floor Hockey & Geneva Coll Womens Soccer Coach; Beaver Cty Soccer League (Pres, VP) 1982-; Fellowship of Chrstn Athletes 1989-; *office:* Beaver Valley Christian Acad 350 Adams St Rochester PA 15074

MOHR, MARJORIE JEAN (JACKSON), 3rd Grade Teacher; *b:* Lansing, MI; *w:* Dennis W. (dec); *ed:* (BA) Bio, Albion Coll 1968; Various Classes & Wkshps; *cr:* 2nd Grade Teacher 1968-77, 2nd/3rd Grade Teacher 1978-79, 3rd Grade Teacher 1979- Springport Public Sch; *ai:* Various Textbook Comms; Labels for Ed Coord; 6th Grade Classroom Aides Supvr; Elem Storytelling Group Spon; MI Rdng Assn; Albion Cmmty Band Librarian 1980-; Jackson Cmmty Concert Band; Springport Academic Booster of Yr 1984; *office:* Springport Public Sch W Main St Springport MI 49284

MOHR, NORMA JEAN (BATESON), Sixth Grade Teacher; *b:* Tontogany, OH; *m:* Royce E.; *c:* Sondra Roberts, Ronda Braatz; *ed:* (BS) Elem Ed, Bowling Green St Univ 1960; *cr:* 7th-8th Grade Teacher Milton Center 1960; 4th Grade Teacher 1960-76, 6th Grade Teacher 1976- Grand Rapids Elem; *ai:* OH Ed Assn; Otsego Educators Secy 1984-87; NEA; NW OH Ed Assn Outstanding Service Awd 1986-87; Meth Church Chm of Bd 1986-; Eastern Stars Starpoint 1987-; Otsego Educators Negotiations; Otsego Sch Dist Teacher of the Yr 1986; Grant from Wood Cty Ed to Study Water Pollution Through OH Wildlife Division; *home:* 24249 W 2nd St Grand Rapids OH 43522

MOKRY, PATRICIA RAESENER, Science Teacher/ Chairperson; *b:* Llano, TX; *m:* Fred Marion; *c:* Carole M., Michael A., Phyllis M. Mokry Fink; *ed:* (BSMT) Medical Technology, Univ of TX 1965; (MA) Biological Sci/Ed, Univ of TX Austin 1989; Bio Laboratory Wkshp 1987, 1989; *cr:* Medical Technician Holy Cross Hospital 1965-66; Medical Technician/Instr Brackenridge Hospital 1966-70; Medical Technician Medical Parkway Clinical Laboratory 1970-76, Austin Neurodiagnostics 1977-81; Sci Teacher Westlake HS 1982-; *ai:* Sci UIL Coach; Spon Stu Action Volunteers for Environment; Technology Comm Mem; Prof Growth Comm; Kappa Delta Pi 1987-; Natl Society of Sci Teacher 1982-; NABT, TX Assn of Bio Teachers; TX Assn for Supervision & Curr Dev Presenter 1986; Eanes Area Recycling Group; St Austins Cath Church (Ed Comm, Parish Cncl Secy 1988); Conference for Advancement of Sci Teaching Presenter 1988; Golden Apple Awd 1989; *office:* Westlake HS 4100 Westbank Dr Austin TX 78746

MOLANDER, JUDY SCHONDELMAYER, 5th Grade Teacher; *b:* St Joe, IN; *m:* Frank G.; *c:* Terre L., S. L.; *ed:* (AA) Soc Sci, Ohlone Coll 1970; (BA) His - Magna Cum Laude, CA St Univ 1972; *cr:* 6th Grade Teacher 1973-84, Cmptr Specialist 1984-87; 5th Grade Teacher 1987- Warm Spring Sch; *ai:* Elem Cmptr Teachers Pres 1988-; CA St Univ San Jose Master Teacher 1984; CA St Univ Hayward Master Teacher 1987; ASCD 1990; Mentor Teacher 1984-86; Environmental Ed Asst Dir; *office:* Warm Springs Sch 47370 Warm Springs Blvd Fremont CA 94539

MOLDENHAUER, MARLENE LATHAM, Science Department Chairperson; *b:* Detroit, MI; *m:* Ralph R.; *c:* Alex S., Victoria M.; *ed:* (BA) His, Albion Coll 1957; (MS) Bio, Sam Houston St Univ 1987; Ed-Cmptr-Sci-Gifted & Talented-Occupational Ed; *cr:* Kndgtn Teacher Milford MI 1957-59; 1st Grade Teacher Lansing MI 1959-60; Pullman WA 1961-62; Kndgrtn Teacher Corvallis OR 1962-68; 6th Grade Sci Teacher Huntsville TX 1980; 7th Grade Sci Teacher Coldspring TX 1980-; *ai:* Sci Fair Organizer; UIL Sci Team Coach; NSTA; Sci Teacher Assn of TX; Bio Teacher Assn of TX; Natl Audubon Assn Editor/Secy/Treas/Ed Chm; *office:* Lincoln Jr HS P O Box 39 Coldspring TX 77331

MOLE, LAURA A., English Teacher; *b:* Charleston, SC; *ed:* (BA) Drama, Furman Univ 1986; (MAT) Eng, The Citadel 1988; *cr:* Teacher Goose Creek HS 1988-; *ai:* Yrbk Adv; Drama Club Spon.

MOLEDOR, ELIZABETH WINNEFELD, Third Grade Teacher; *b:* Rootstown, OH; *m:* Lamar C.; *c:* Barbara, Carl, Ann M.; *ed:* (BED) Elem/Spec Ed, 1954, (MAED) Spec Ed Developmentally Handicapped, 1969 Kent St Univ; Religion Cert Diocese Youngstown 1979/1986; Grad Stud Ed & Religion; *cr:* Teacher Developmentally Handicapped Happy Day Sch 1954-55; 2nd-4th Grade Teacher St Patrick Sch 1955-; *ai:* Soc Stud Chairperson; Sci Fair Comm; Public Relations Diocesan Bi Weekly Exponent Newspaper; Kappa Delta Pi 1953-60; Natl Cath Ed Assn 1955-; Intnl Rdng Assn 1960-81; Northeastern OH Teachers Assn 1954-65; Cath Daughters of Amer 1954-75; Infant of Prague Guild 1954-75; PTO Kent Public Schls 1960-89; Home & Sch Assn St Patrick Sch 1955-90; Kent St Univ Alumni Assn 1954-88; Chapter I Rdng Parent Rep 1975-81; Recognized Youngstown Diocese Teaching Awd; *office:* St Patricks Sch 127 Portage St Kent OH 44240

MOLINARO, RUTH ANN SWARNER, 6th Grade Teacher; *b:* Erie, PA; *m:* John Joseph; *ed:* (BA) Elem Ed. Muskingum Coll 1959; Univ of CO/Edinboro St Coll; *cr:* 5th & 6th Grade Teacher Russell Erwine Sch 1959-75; 6th Grade Teacher Glenbrook Elem Sch 1975-87; 6th Grade Teacher Forest Park Elem Sch 1987-; *ai:* Sch-6th Grade Choir Dir; System Sch Rep to Public Relations Comm; Euclid Teachers Assn 1959-Teacher of Yr 1973-74; Jennings Scholar Greater Cleveland Fnd Awd 1978-79; Leaders of Amer Elem Ed 1971; Delta Kappa Gamma-Women Educators Honorary Assn 1973-; OH Ed Assn; NEA Delegate to Natl Conv; Euclid Teachers Assn; North East Greater Cleveland Math Assn; OH Teachers Assn; *home:* 833 E 250th St Euclid OH 44132

MOLIX, WILLIE MAE, Math Teacher & Dept Chair; *b:* St Gabriel, LA; *m:* David Jr.; *c:* Darold J., Rhonda J. Molix-Smith, Karen E. Molix-Charleston, David W.; *ed:* (BS) Math, Southern Univ 1958; (ME) Curr/Instruction, Univ of TX El Paso 1979; Prof Supvr, Utep; Grad Stud Southern Univ; Various Wkshps; *cr:* HS Math Teacher Thomas A Levy 1959-60, Loretta Acad 1968-69; Math Teacher Bel Air Jr HS & Ranchland Hills Mid Sch 1969-; *ai:* Adv UIL Number Sense Team; Chm Hospitality Comm; Transition & Fund Raiser Comm Mem; Tutor Honor Stus for SAT; Local Cncl of Teachers of Math, NEA 1969-; Mem Writing Team for Mid Level Ed; St Textbook Comm; 20 Yrs Service Ysleta Ind Sch Dist; Trainer TX Examination of Current Admin & Teachers; *office:* Ranchland Hills Mid Sch 7615 Yuma Dr El Paso TX 79915

MOLK, BONNIE JEAN, Spanish Teacher; *b:* Waynesburg, PA; *ed:* (BS) Scndry Ed/Lang, CA St Coll 1973; Univ of Valencia Spain 1971; *cr:* Span Teacher Laurel Highlands Sr HS 1973-; *ai:* Foreign Lang Dept Head 1984-87; PA St Modern Lang Assn 1972-; Laurel Highlands Ed Assn, PA St Ed Assn, NEA 1973-; St Michaels Altar Society 1984-.

MOLLING, THOMAS CLARENCE, 8th Grade Math Teacher; *b:* Port Washington, WI; *m:* Joan Elizabeth Collard; *c:* Laura, Scott; *ed:* (BS) Math, Marian Coll 1974; *cr:* Teacher West De Pere Jr HS 1974-; *ai:* Bsktbl Referee, WI St Tournament Referee 1985-86/1988-89; Sftbl Umpire; *office:* W De Pere Jr H S 665 Grant St De Pere WI 54115

MOLSTAD, KERRY LYNN, Health Education Teacher; *b:* Ladysmith, WI; *ed:* (BS) Health/Phys Ed, Univ of WI La Crosse 1979; Working Toward MS in Health Ed; *cr:* Elem Phys Ed Teacher Faribault Public Schls 1980-81, St Marys Sch 1982-85; Health Ed Teacher Portage Jr HS 1985-; *ai:* Asst Var Vlybl & Jr HS Girls Track Coach; Kids on the Block Puppet Troupe Coord; WI Assn of Health Phys Ed Recreation & Dance; Fellowship of Chrstn Athletes; *office:* Portage Jr HS C/O Rusch Jr HS 117 W Franklin Portage WI 53901

MOLTER, KAREN S., English Teacher; *b:* Rensselaer, IN; *m:* Michael D.; *c:* Megan, Joshua; *ed:* (BS) Phys Ed, IN St Univ 1973; (MS) Ed, Purdue Univ 1980; Eng Cert Purdue 1979; Acceleration Course for Teachers of Advanced Placement, Earlham Coll 1987; *cr:* Phys Ed Teacher N Newton Sch Corp 1975-78; Spec Ed Teacher Goodland Elem 1979-81; Eng Teacher S Newton HS 1981-; *ai:* Stu Cncl Spon; IN Teachers of Writing 1984-; NCTE 1988-; Tri Kappa (Pres 1988-89, St Schlsp Comm 1989-); ITW Conference Presenter 1986, 1987; *office:* S Newton HS R R 1 Kentland IN 47951

MONACO, DON, English Teacher; *b:* Cleveland, OH; *c:* David, Dina; *ed:* (BA) Psych, John Carroll Univ 1966; (MS) Ed, Youngstown St Univ 1982; Various Wkshps; *cr:* Eng Teacher John Adams HS; *ai:* Co-Adv Poetry Writing Club; Mem Curr Comm John Adams HS; Cleveland Teachers Union 1967-; Cleveland Ed Fund Writing Collaborative Co-Chm Teachers Advisory Group 1989-; SW General Hosp Volunteer 1988-, 300 Hr Pin 1989; Small Grant Awd Cleveland Ed Fund; Selected to Attend Andover Breadloaf Writing Wkshp 1989; *office:* John Adams HS 3817 Martin Luther King Jr Dr Cleveland OH 44105

MONAHAN, DENNIS P., Spanish Teacher/Coordinator; *b:* Chicago, IL; *ed:* (BA) Span, Benedictine Coll 1964; (MED) Second Lang, Natl Coll of Ed 1982; Cas Sch Admin, Natl Coll of Ed 1983; *cr:* 7th/8th Grade Teacher St Paul of The Cross Sch 1964-69; Span Teacher CCSD 15 Palatine 1969-; *ai:* Sandburg Chorus Co-Dir; Hip Comm; Staff Dev Comm; AATSP 1987-; IFLTA 1987-; *office:* Carl Sandburg Jr H S 2600 Martin Ln Rolling Meadows IL 60008

MONCERET, MILLIE JO J. LILES, Retired English Teacher; *b:* Lauderdale Cty, AL; *m:* Arthur; *c:* Patricia A. Albright, Arthur T., Kathy J. Monceret Koonce, Timothy A.; *ed:* (BS) Elem Ed, Florence St Coll 1967; (MA) Elem Ed, Florence St Univ 1969; Ed Specialist Elem Ed, Univ of N AL 1977; Cmptr Trng; *cr:* 6th Grade Teacher Rogers Sch 1967-72; 4th/6th/8th Grade Rdng Teacher TN Valley Authority 1972-73; 6th Grade Eng Teacher Rogers Sch 1973-89; *ai:* Textbook Comm; Womens Society of Chrstn Service (Pres 1955-60, 1990), Pin 1962; 4-H Leader of Yr Awd, Outstanding Dedicated Service 1986; *home:* Rt 5 Box 126 Killen AL 35645

MONCREIF, CATHY PETERKA, Spanish Teacher; *b:* Somerdale, NJ; *c:* Kelly, Shannon; *ed:* (BA) Span, Montclair & Rutgers 1971; (MA) Span Curr, Glassboro 1981; *cr:* Span Teacher Washington Township HS 1971-; *ai:* Sftbl Coach 1972-74; Stu Cncl 1973-75; Span Club 1980-; Lindenwold Bsbl Athletic Assn (Commissioner, Coach) 1983-; *office:* Washington Township HS RR 12 Box 513 Sewell NJ 08080

MONCRIEF, EARL DOUGLAS, Fifth Grade Teacher; *b:* Anniston, AL; *ed:* (BS) Scndry Ed/Psych, 1973, (MAED) Admin, 1976 Jacksonville St Univ; *cr:* Asst Prin Saks Elem Sch 1976-77, Soaks HS 1977-78; Private Bus 1978-83; Classroom Teacher Ft Mc Clellan Elem Sch 1983-; *ai:* NEA, AEA, OEA; FMEA Pres 1984-85; Civitan 1980-82; *home:* 604 Wendover Terr Anniston AL 36206

MONDOUX, MARVIN JOSEPH, Sixth Grade Teacher; *b:* Glens Falls, NY; *m:* Joyce Marie Fisher; *c:* Vicki, Michael, Mark; *ed:* (BA) Economics, Siena Coll 1959; Intensive Teacher Training PrgM, Oneonta St Coll; *cr:* Elem Teacher Stillwater Cntrl Sch 1963-; *ai:* Stillwater Teachers Assn VP 1971-72; NYSUT; NEA; Amer Legion VP 1970-72; Veterans Pres 1972-75; Memorial Home Assn; Stillwater Booster Club VP 1971-72; *home:* 352 N Hudson Ave Stillwater NY 12170

MONDRONE, LOUIS ANTHONY, Seventh Grade English Teacher; *b:* Somerville, NJ; *ed:* (BS) His/Eng, 1957, (EDM) His, 1964 Rutgers Univ; *cr:* 9th Grade Eng Teacher South River HS 1957-61; 9th Grade Eng/World His Teacher South River Jr HS 1961-77; 7th/8th Grade Eng/7th Grade Rdng Teacher South River Mid Sch 1977-; *ai:* Walking Club; Yrbk Adv 1966-77; NEA, NJ Ed Assn, Middlesex Cty Ed Assn 1957-; South River Ed Assn 1957-, 33 Yrs Dist Service 1989-; *office:* South River Mid Sch Thomas St South River NJ 08882

MONETTE, LYLE GAYLYN, Business Teacher; *b:* Muskegon, MI; *m:* Judith Chapman; *c:* Craig, Lynelle, Keri, Laurel; *ed:* (BS) Distributive Ed, 1965, (BBA) Personnel, 1968 W MI Univ; Grad Work Vocal Sch Admin; *cr:* Teacher/Coord Holland Public Schls 1965-66, Muskegon Public Schls 1966-; *ai:* Excl in Teaching Awd Comm; United Way HS Chairperson; MI Voc Coords Assn (Pres, Treas) 1965-, Life Mem 1978; Excalibur Club (Pres, Secy, Treas) 1966-85, Life Mem 1975; *office:* Muskegon HS 80 W Southern Muskegon MI 49442

MONEY, JACK ALAN, History Teacher; *b:* Middlesboro, KY; *m:* Geralyn Sue; *c:* Jason, Michael; *ed:* (AS) His - Cum Laude, Monroe Comm Coll 1972; (BS) His - Cum Laude, 1974, (MA) Ed - Cum Laude 1978 E MI Univ; Sex Ed; Tai Kwon Do; Interactive Television; Assertive Discipline; Alternative Ed; ITIP; *cr:* Soc Stud Teacher Brake Jr HS 1974-76; Alternate Ed Teacher TITAN Prgm 1977-80; Alternate Ed Dir FORCE Prgm 1980-82; Bio Teacher Surline Mid Sch 1982-86; His Teacher Ogemaw Heights HS 1986-; *ai:* Soph Class Adv; Var Ftbl Coach; MI Assn for Ed Options NE MI Rep 1980-82; Phi Theta Kappa 1972-; Deans List 7 Times; *office:* Ogemaw Heights HS 960 S M-33 West Branch MI 48661

MONEY, NORMAN ALLEN, Technology Teacher; *b:* Ft Bragg, NC; *m:* Karen J. Childers; *c:* Amanda L., Megan L.; *ed:* (BSED) Industrial Art Ed, 1975, (MED) Ed, 1981 Univ of GA; *cr:* Instr Lanier Area Tech Sch 1981-83; Teacher Forsyth Cntrl HS 1975-; *ai:* Technology Stu Assn Spon; Forsyth Cty BOE Ed Comm; Intnl Technology Ed Assn, AVA 1980-; GA Industrial Technology Ed Assn 1975-, Educator of Yr 1983, Prgm of Excl 1989; NEA, GA Assn of Educators 1986-; GA Voc Assn (Industrial Art Division VP 1986-89) 1980-, Educator of Yr 1983; Kappa Delta Pi; Forsyth Cty Lions Club Secy 1984-86; Jim Coffey Inspirational Teacher Awd 1987; *office:* Forsyth Cntrl HS 518 Tribble Gap Rd Cumming GA 30130

MONFERDINI, SUSAN SCHULTZ, Third Grade Teacher; *b:* Joliet, IL; *m:* Michael B.; *c:* Michael B. II; *ed:* (AA) Liberal Arts & Sci, Joliet Jr Coll 1975; (BS) Elem Ed, IL ST Univ 1977; *cr:* Third Grade Teacher Bonfield Grade Sch 1977-; *ai:* Sftbl Coach 1978-87; Amer Federation of Teachers 1985-; PTA Bd/Prgm 1983-85; Bldg Rep 1985-89, Schlsp Comm 1986-89 Unit 2 Classroom Teachers; PTA Bd/Publicity 1987-89; *office:* Bonfield Grade Sch P O Box 96 Smith St Bonfield IL 60913

MONITTO, MARYANN, English Teacher; *b:* Copiague, NY; *m:* John Peter; *c:* Katey; *ed:* (BA) Scndry Eng Ed, SUNY Cortland 1981; (MS) Liberal Stud, SUNY Stonybrook 1989; *cr:* Eng Teacher Amityville Memorial HS 1983-; *ai:* HS Newspaper & Echo Adv; *office:* Amityville Memorial HS Merrick Rd Amityville NY 11701

MONK, GEORGE EDWARD, Science Teacher; *b:* Sidney, NE; *m:* Lisa Rose Stoecklein; *ed:* (BA) Sci Ed, Cntrl Meth Coll 1988; *cr:* Teacher Cooper Cty R-IV 1988-; *ai:* Jr Class Spon; Sci Fair Coord; Boys & Girls Sftbl & Bsbl Coach; Sci Teachers of MO 1990; Knights of Columbus 1978-; Outstanding Bio Sr 1988; Cntrl Meth Coll Hall of Spons Schlsp; *office:* Cooper Cty R-IV Box 110 Bunceton MO 65237

MONKEN, SUSAN MARY, 5th Grade Teacher; *b:* St Louis, MO; *m:* Glenn A.; *ed:* (BS) Elem Ed, 1973; (MS) Cnslr Ed, 1978 Southern IL Univ; Admin Cert, Southern IL Univ 1988; *cr:* Teacher Highland Comm Unit Sch Dist 5 1974-; *ai:* Sci Fair Spon; Enriched Summer Sci Teacher; Highland Ed Assn/IEA/NEA Pres; IL Sci Teachers Assn; NSTA; ASCD; Kappa Delta Pi; Delta Gamma Society; Wrote Mini-Grant Sci Fair Prgm Grades 5 and 6; Wrote Enriched Summer Sci Prgm Gifted 4th-5th and 6th Graders.

MONROE, BEATRICE HILL, English/Language Arts Teacher; *b:* Tallahassee, FL; *c:* Katrina, Glynis; *ed:* (BA) Eng, FL A&M Univ 1967; Working Towards MS Degree Aduld Ed 1990; *cr:* Teacher Camilla Consolidated Sch 1968-69; Typist WCTV Television Station 1969-71; Teacher Griffin Mid Sch 1971-; *ai:* Black His Month Act Coord; Black His Brain Bowl Team Coach; FL Teaching Profession, NEA; Tallahassee Urban League; Griffin Mid Sch Teacher of Yr 1975-76, 1984-85; *office:* Griffin Mid Sch 800 Alabama St Tallahassee FL 32304

MONROE, BEVERLY JEANNE, 9th Grade English Teacher; *b:* Oahu, HI; *c:* Lynsey, Shannon, Steve, Diana; *ed:* (BA) Elem Ed, Humboldt 1963; Grad Work Sonoma & San Francisco St Univ; *cr:* Teacher Pacifica Sch Dist 1963-69, Santa Rosa City Schls 1983-; *ai:* Yrbk Honors Eng Adv; Phi Delta Kappa 1987-; Bennett Valley Sch Site Cncl Pres 1980-81; SSU Bay Area Writing Project Fellowship; Nom Teacher of Yr; *office:* Herbert Slater Jr HS 3500 Sonoma Ave Santa Rosa CA 95405

MONROE, DUNCAN ALLEN, Social Studies Lead Teacher; *b:* Raleigh, NC; *m:* Claudia Lee Anker; *c:* Aaron, Rhonda; *ed:* (BSED) His/Poly Sci, Univ of NV Reno 1971; Washoe Cty Sch Dist Masters Equivalency 1990; *cr:* Teacher Swope Mid Sch 1971-; *ai:* Stu Government Adv; Photo Club; Washoe Cty Teachers Assn Building Rep 1971-; NV Army Natl Guard Colonel 1966-; 6th Army Liaison Officer to Headquarters NV Natl Guard Colonel 1990; Distinguished Service Awd Washoe Cty Teachers Assn; *home:* 5590 St Andrews Ct Reno NV 89502

MONROE, HEIDI KURBJEWEIT, 7th Grade Phys Science Teacher; *b:* Langendiebach, West Germany; *m:* David Dubois; *c:* Adam D., Scott W.; *ed:* (BA) Bio/Phys Sci, 1967, (MA) Bio, 1976 Montclair St; *cr:* 7th Grade Sci Teacher W Essex Regional Jr & Sr HS 1967-; *ai:* Cheerleading Adv; W Essex Ed Assn Exec Bd 1988-; NJ Sci Teachers Assn; Hope Parent Teacher Club VP 1985-87; St Lukes Episcopal Church (Sunday Sch Teacher, Alternate) 1986-; *office:* W Essex Regional Jr HS West Greenbrook Rd North Caldwell NJ 07006

MONROE, JANET M., Principal; *b:* Wadsworth, OH; *m:* Robert S.; *c:* Tera; *ed:* (BS) Elem Ed, Kent St Univ 1970; (MS) Elem Admin, Univ of Akron 1978; Doctoral Stu Ed Admin, Univ of Akron 1989-; *cr:* 3rd/4th Grade Elem Teacher 1970-83; 6th/8th Grade Amer His Teacher Copley-Fairlawn City Schls 1983-86; Elem Prin Ft Island Sch 1986-; *ai:* Kiwanis Builders Club Adv; Copley Fairlawn Schls Fnd Educl Adv; Drug Free Cmmty Comm Mem; OH Assn of Elem Sch Admin 1986, Hall of Fame 1989; Summit Cty Elem Admin Pres 1988-; OH Mid Schls Assn 1989-; Fairlawn Kiwanis Bd Mem 1989-; Ft Island Park Commission 1988-.

MONROE, JOY ANN SAUERBRUN, Retired Teacher; *b:* Warren, OH; *m:* Carl Collister; *c:* David L. Perry, Laura L. Perry; *ed:* (BA) Art Ed/Eng, 1956, (MA) Curr, 1975 MI St Univ; Numerous Conferences, Seminars, Wkshps; *cr:* 6th-12th Grade Art Teacher Holt HS 1956-57; 7th-8th Grade Art Teacher Derby Jr HS 1957-60; Art/Eng/Soc Stud/Sci/Ind Study/Creative Writing Teacher C H Smart Jr HS 1970-88; *ai:* NEA, MEA, Walled Lake Ed Assn; Daughters of Amer Revolution Schlsp 1986-; *home:* 11275 Katrine Fenton MI 48430

MONROE, KAREN KINSLOW, Fourth Grade Teacher; *b:* Cookeville, TN; *m:* Brian Wade; *c:* Rachel, Cole; *ed:* (BS) Elem Ed, Mid TN St Univ 1980; *cr:* 4th Grade Teacher Mid TN Chrstn Sch 1980-; *ai:* TN Rdng Assn 1987-; Mid TN Chrstn Sch Elem Teacher of Yr 1986-87, 1988-89; *office:* Mid TN Chrstn Sch 100 Mtcs Rd Murfreesboro TN 37130

MONROE, PAMELA TURNER, Social Studies Teacher; *b:* Laredo, TX; *m:* Dana E.; *c:* Laura, Clayton, Taylor; *ed:* (BAED) His, Sam Houston St Univ 1974; *cr:* Soc Stud Teacher Trinity Mid Sch 1978-; *ai:* Natl Jr Beta Club Spon; UIL Oral Rdng Coach; TX Heritage Project of TX Historical Fnd 1982; *office:* Trinity Mid Sch P O Box 752 Trinity TX 75862

MONTAG, MARY JEAN, 1st/2nd Grade Teacher; *b:* Windom, MN; *m:* Donald Norman; *c:* Judith Fesko, Debra, Stefanie, Jon; *ed:* (AA) Elem Ed, Concordia Coll St Paul 1956; (BA) Elem Ed, Concordia Coll River Forest 1972; Rdng, Slippery Rock St Univ; *cr:* 1st-4th Grade Teacher 1956-61, Kndgtn Teacher 1961-74, 1st/2nd Grade Teacher 1974- St Lukes Luth; *ai:* K-6th Grade Music Theory; 6th-8th Handbell Dir; 5th-8th Grade Sci & Nature Club; Operetta & Orch Dir; Church (Organist, Sr Choir Dir); *office:* St Lukes Luth Sch 314 Hannahstown Rd Cabot PA 16023

MONTAGUE, ARNETT GLENN, Teacher; *b:* Memphis, TN; *m:* Valeria Shields; *c:* Arnett G. II, Karla P. Montague-Brown, Kevin D.; *ed:* (BS) Bio, KY St Univ 1958; (MS) Chem, AZ St Univ 1964; (EDD) Ed Admin/Supervision, Univ of TN Knoxville 1976; Licensed Pest Control Operator; *cr:* Sci Instr/Dept Chm Owen Coll 1958-60, Memphis City Sch System 1960-77; Educl Researcher Univ of TN Knoxville 1972-74; General/Early Chldhd Ed Dept Chm Shelby St Comm Coll 1976-77; Exec Dir TN Commission Human Dev 1977-79; Stu Finance Dir/Ed Assoc Professor Oakwood Coll 1979-81;Life/Phys Sci Instr Baltimore MD 1981-84; Bio/Sci Technology/Cmptr Sci Instr Fayette-Ware Comprehensive HS 1986-; Adult Basic Ed Teacher John S Wilder Youth Dev Center 1989-; *ai:* Sci Club Spon; NSTA, NEA, WTEA, TEA 1960-; FCEA 1986-; NAACP 1960-; Inst African Affairs Chm 1988-; Omega Psi Phi 1955-; Outstanding Educator of Yr; Natl Sci Fnd Awd 1963-67, 1987; Oak Ridge Assn Univ STRIVE 1989; TN St Job Trng Partnership Act Cncl; Attended Several Natl Sci Fnd Insts; *home:* 501 Shofner Memphis TN 38109

MONTAGUE, JACQUELINE MINOR, Special Education Teacher; *b:* Bridgeport, CT; *c:* Michelle; *ed:* (BS) Ed, Bluefield St Coll 1963; (MA) Spec Ed, Univ of CT 1967; (MS) Clinical Psych Natl Univ 1985; *cr:* Spec Ed Teacher Eastford Grammar Sch 1967-68; 4th Grade Teacher John Adams 1974-75; Supplemental Spec Ed Teacher S Plainfield Mid Sch 1977-78; Resource Teacher Collier Jr HS 1978-83; Small Group Instr Pershing Jr HS 1985-; *ai:* Club Adv Stu on Saturday Jr Amer Music Show; Schlsp Comm Delta Kappa Gammas; NEA Mem 1986-; Delta Kappa Gamma Mem 1987-; Alpha Kappa Alpha Mem 1963-; YWCA Bd Mem 1989-; Black Psychologist of San Diego Mem 1990; Fellowship Work on Master Degree Spec Ed from Univ of CT; Recognition Awd Outstanding Adv for Stus on Saturday Jr Amer Show; *home:* 8557 Hudson Dr San Diego CA 92119

MONTAGUE, NANCY JEANNE, Theatre Director; *b:* Wilmington, DE; *ed:* (BA) Theatre, N TX St Univ 1980; *cr:* Theatre Dir Diamond Hill HS 1983-86, Nimitz HS 1986-; *ai:* ITS Spon; Fall, Spring, UIL One Act Play; Childrens Theatre Production Dir; Theatre Ed Assn, TX Educl Theatre Assn; Teacher of Yr 1985; *office:* Nimitz HS 100 W Oakdale St Irving TX 75060

MONTANO, JOSEPH EDWARD, Mathematics Teacher; *b:* San Antonio, TX; *ed:* (BA) Math, Trinity Univ 1986; *cr:* Math Teacher Mayde Creek Jr HS 1986-87, Harlandale HS 1987-; *ai:* Lighthouse Club & Sr Class Asst Spon; Math Tutorial Adv; Sch on Saturday Math Tutor; Dist Textbook Math Rep; *home:* 440 W Mayfield San Antonio TX 78211

MONTANO, ROBERT A., 4th Grade Teacher; *b:* Los Angeles, CA; *m:* Ruth Escamilla; *ed:* (AA) Liberal Arts, East Los Angeles Coll 1970; (BA) Sociology, CA St Univ Long Beach 1974; Teaching Credential Elem, CA St Univ Long Beach 1976; *cr:* Teachers Aide Long Beach Unified Sch Dist 1972-76; Bi-Ling Teacher Lucia Mar Unified Sch Dist 1976-; *ai:* Stu Cncl Adv Oceans Schl; Dist Limited Eng Proficient Rep; CA Teachers Assn 1980-; Assn of MX-Amer Ed Chap Pres/VP/St Regional VP 1976-; CA Poly-San Luis Obispo Adjunct Professor 1987-88; *office:* Oceano Elem Sch 17th & Wilmar Ave Oceano CA 93445

MONTEFORTE, STEPHANIE LUPO, 1st Grade Teacher; *b:* Erie, PA; *m:* David Paul; *c:* Philip, Anthony; *ed:* (BS) Elem Ed/Early Chldhd, St Marys of Notre Dame 1976; Masters Equivalent Elem, Edinboro & Gannon Coll 1989; Ethnic Cooking Courses; *cr:* 7th Grade Teacher Our Lady of Mt Carmel 1976-77; 4th-8th Grade Teacher St Boniface 1977-79; 7th-8th Grade Teacher Saegertown Mid Sch 1980-85; 1st Grade Teacher Euclid Elem Sch 1985-; *ai:* Cheerleading & Stu Cncl Adv; Health & Sci Curr Comm; NEA, PSEA 1980-; St Mary Church Rosary (Financial Secy 1987-89, Publicity Chm 1985-87); Public Service Awd; Penelec Safety Awd; *office:* Euclid Elem Sch 420 North St Saegertown PA 16433

MONTEMAYOR, ELIA IRENE (PALOS), Computer Literacy Teacher; *b:* Laredo, TX; *m:* Juan Jesus; *c:* Jessica J., Elias J.; *ed:* (BS) Elem with Bi-ling Cert, Laredo St 1980; Cmptr Sci; *cr:* Eng/Rdng Teacher Clark Mid Sch 1980-84; 5th Grade Teacher Clark Elem 1984; Rdng/Soc Stud Teacher Trautmann Annex 1985-86; 8th Grade Cmptr Literacy Teacher United Intermediate 1987-; *ai:* Girl Scout Leader Sr, Cadettes; Cmptr Literacy Competition Spon; Literacy Group; Laredo Jr Coll Upward Bound Lit Teacher; Laredo Womens Center Choices Prgm for Young Women; TX Cmptr Ed Assn Mem 1987-; Kappa Delta Phi Mem 1980-; Girl Scouts (Prgm Chair 1987-88, Leader) 1980-, Super Leader 1990; *home:* 3218 Rosario Laredo TX 78043

MONTEMAYOR, JUAN JESUS, English Teacher; *b:* Laredo, TX; *m:* Elia Irene Palos; *c:* Jessica J., Elias J.; *ed:* (BS) Eng/Span, TX A&I Laredo 1974; (MS) Elem Bi-ling Ed/Span, Laredo St Univ 1976; Trng in Teacher Corps; *cr:* Kndgtn Bi-ling Teacher Fennville Elem 1974-75; 2nd Grade Teacher Zapata Elem 1975-77; Scndry Spec Ed Teacher Martin & Wixon HS 1977-79; Scndry Migrant Eng Teacher/Tutor Martin HS 1979-83; 5th Grade Sci Teacher Trautmann Annex & Clark Mid Sch 1983-85; Eng Teacher United HS 1985-; *ai:* Laredo Jr Coll Upward Bound Lit, Eng Teacher/Cnslr; AFT Mem 1977-85; Kappa Delta Phi Mem 1974-; Stu Rdng Group Organizer/Mem 1988-; Saturday Tutorial Sessions Teacher 1989-; *home:* 3218 Rosario Laredo TX 78043

MONTEMAYOR, MARTINA LONGORIA, Teacher; *b:* San Benito, TX; *m:* Gustavo C.; *c:* Cynthia Jude, Debra A. Willadsen, Gus Jr.; *ed:* (BA) Ed, SW TX St 1958; (MA) Ed, Stephen F Austin 1978; Supervision, Admin; Bi-ling Cert; *cr:* Teacher Ebony Heights 1956-59, Olmito Elem 1959-78, Villa Nueva Sch 1978-; *ai:* Girls Sftbl & Vlybl Coach; Outstanding Elem Teacher 1974; *home:* Rt 8 Box 870 Brownsville TX 78520

MONTGOMERY, BETTY J., 3rd Grade Teacher; *b:* Gloster, MS; *m:* Betty C.; *c:* Keisha D., Frederick, Kristie; *ed:* (BS) Elem Ed, MS Valley St Univ 1970; (MA) Elem Ed, 1974; Specialist Elem Ed, 1979 Jackson St Univ 1979; *ai:* MAE 1990; 69er Club Chaplin 1990; Herion 1990; *home:* 101 Stansberry Dr Durant MS 39063

MONTGOMERY, BOBBYE KEY, Second Grade Teacher; *b:* Little Rock, AR; *ed:* (BSE) Home Ec, Univ Cntrl AR 1949; Creative Writing; *cr:* Teacher Wilmot Public Sch 1949-52; Home Service Adv AR Power & Light 1952-54; Teacher Warren Elem 1955-; *ai:* Insurance Comm Chm; Parent Volunteers Comm; AR Ed Assn 1955-; NEA 1961-; Classroom Teachers Assn Secy; Jr Auxillary 1956-60; United Meth Women Circle Secy 1987-; Church Admin Bd 1989-; *home:* 604 Bond Warren AR 71671

MONTGOMERY, DEBORAH (SKINNER), Counselor; *b:* Benton Harbor, MI; *m:* Thomas Leonard; *c:* Melanie Droghetti, Beth; *ed:* (BS) Elem Ed/Eng, 1971, (MA) Guidance/Counseling, 1974 Western MI Univ; Suicide Prevention, Crisis Team Trng; Stephen Ministry Leadership Trng Conference; *cr:* Kndgtn/4th Grade Teacher Eau Claire Public Schls 1971-74; Cnslr Marysville Public Schls 1974-; *ai:* Adv Natl Jr Honor Society; Sch Improvement, Sch Safety, Child Abuse Comm; Sch Crisis Team; MI Assn Cnslr & Dev Mem, MI Assn Sch Cnslrs Mem 1974-; MI Elem Sch Cnslrs Bd of Dir 1978-80; Stephen Ministry Leadership Team 1986-; Child & Family Services of MI Bd of Dirs 1977-81; *office:* Marysville Intermediate Sch 400 Stadium Dr Marysville MI 48040

MONTGOMERY, DIANE E., Teacher of Gifted & Talented; *b:* Jonesboro, AR; *m:* Larry; *c:* Kerry; *ed:* (BSE) Elem Ed, 1980, (MS) Gifted/Talented/Creative, 1989 AR St Univ; *cr:* 4th Grade Teacher 1980-84, Teacher of Gifted & Talented 1985- Brookland Sch; *ai:* Quiz Bowl Spon; Sr HS Cheerleading Coach; AR for Gifted & Talented Ed; Civil Air Patrol; *home:* Rt 2 Box 83 Lake City AR 72437

MONTGOMERY, ERNEST DAVID, English Teacher; *b:* Philadelphia, PA; *ed:* (BA) Ed, 1979, (MED) Ed, 1981 Allegheny Coll; *cr:* Eng Teacher Audubon/Patrick Henry HS 1979-81; Rdng Instr Clevleland Job Corps Center 1981-83; Eng Teacher Shaw HS 1983-85, Valley Forge/Parms HS 1985-; *ai:* Table Tennis Team Adv; Frosh Wrestling Coach; Parma Ed Assn 1985-; OH Ed Assn 1983-; Teaching Assistanship Univ of AL 1981; Poems Published 1978; Outstanding Teacher Dist-Wide Newsletter 1981; *office:* Parma SR HS 6285 W 54th St Parma OH 44129

MONTGOMERY, JOHN DAVID, Sixth Grade Teacher; *b:* Philadelphia, PA; *m:* Mary Ellen Heitz; *c:* Chad; *ed:* (BS) His/Poly Sci, Bloomsburg St Coll 1967; Grad Stud CA St Los Angeles; *cr:* Teacher Ewing HS 1967-68, Trapp Elem Sch 1968-73, Eisenhower HS 1973-78, Preston Elem Sch 1978-; *ai:* Alta Loma HS Var Bsktbl Parent Rep; Alta Loma HS Advisory Club; Alta Loma HS Sports Booster Club; Rialto Ed Assn (Sch Rep, Mem) 1973; CA Teachers Assn, NEA Mem; Amer Youth Soccer Organization Referee 1977-80; Rialto Sch Dist 20 Yr Service Awd; *home:* 6368 Opal St Alta Loma CA 91701

MONTGOMERY, JOHN RAY, Mathematics Teacher; *b:* Philpot, KY; *m:* Peggy Jorene Smith; *c:* Christina, Timothy, Thomas; *ed:* (BS) Math/His, Brescia Coll 1971; Ed, W KY Univ; *cr:* Prin St Alphonsus Elem 1974-75; Amer His Teacher Owensboro Cath HS 1975-76; 5th-8th Grade Soc Stud Teacher 1976-80, 5th-8th Grade Math Teacher 1986- Mary Carrico Memorial; *ai:* Coach & Organizer Mathcounts; Diocese of Owensboro Cath Educators Mem 1989-; Renew Prgm Publicity Chm 1986; *office:* Mary Carrico Memorial Sch 9546 KY 144 Philpot KY 42366

MONTGOMERY, JOYCE BELLE, Sixth Grade Teacher; *b:* Washington, DC; *m:* John Rorthwell; *c:* Steve, Brad, Doug; *ed:* Liberal Arts, Marion Coll 1959; (BS) Phys Ed, Univ of Richmond 1961; *cr:* Phys Ed/Bio Teacher Powhatan HS 1961-62; Phys Ed Teacher Albert Hill Jr HS 1962-66; 5th Grade Teacher Frankford Elem Sch 1973-77; 6th Grade Teacher Ronceverte Elem Sch 1977-; *ai:* Hoop Shoot Contest; Scoliosis Testing; Attending Meeting on Phys Ed; Greenbrier Cty Ed Assn; WVEA; Alpha Delta Kappa (Sargent at Arms 1982-84, Chaplain 1986-88, Recording Secy 1990-); *home:* 606 Pocahontas Ave Ronceverte WV 24970

MONTGOMERY, KAREN JEANETTE, 4th & 5th Grade Alternative Ed; *b:* Quonset Point, RI; *m:* Mark Allen; *ed:* (AA) Elem Ed, Pensacola Jr Coll 1978; (BA) Early Chldhd/Elem Ed, 1980, (MA) Elem Ed, 1984 Univ of West Fl; *cr:* 4th Grade Teacher 1980-89, 4th-5th Grade/Alternative Ed Teacher 1989- West Pensacola Elem; *ai:* Phi Beta Kappa Mem 1985-88; Escambia Ed Assn (Faculty Rep 1980-) Most Positive Person 1987-89; Pensacola Bay Baptist Assn Fact Team Mem 1985-; Pensacola Acts Bd Mem 1984-; Warrington Baptist Church Sunday Sch Teacher, Trng Leader, Vacation Bible Sch Dir 1983-; ECCPTA Local Unit Person of Yr Awd 1985; Wildlife Rescue Awd 1985; Jr League Grant 1986; Escambia Ed Assn Most Positive Person 1987-89; Teacher of Yr 1988; *office:* West Pensacola Elem 801 N 49th Ave Pensacola FL 32506

MONTGOMERY, LAWANNA HARGROVES, 8th Grade Language Art Teacher; *b:* Waycross, GA; *m:* Chester Revere; *c:* Sharmane T.; *ed:* (BA) Eng, Paine Coll 1975; *cr:* Teacher Waycross Day Care Center 1975-76, Bacon Cty Jr HS 1976-85, Center Jr HS 1985-; *ai:* Newsletter Coord Center Jr HS; Schls Bicentennial Celebration, Writing Club, Stu Recognition Comm Men Center Jr HS; GAE, Phi Delta Kappa Parliamentarian 1987-; Mission in Action (Bd of Dir, VP 1988-); Laubach Literacy Action Volunteer Teacher 1989-; Bryants Theological Sch Communicative Art Teacher 1989-; *home:* 829 Homer St Waycross GA 31501

MONTGOMERY, MARGARET MEI MEI ROGERS, 4th Grade Teacher; *b:* Saint Louis, MO; *c:* Phil, Meg Kilday, Cindy; *ed:* (BA) Elem Ed, Washington Univ St Louis 1959; (MS) Ed Psych/Research; Univ of KS 1981; *cr:* 4th Grade Teacher Flynn Park Sch 1959-62; 2nd/4th Grade Teacher Riverside Sch 1974-77; 3rd/5th Grade Teacher Pickney Sch 1977-; *ai:* Dist Curr Comms; PTO VP.

MONTGOMERY, MARIE TRESCOTT, First Grade Teacher; *b:* Warsaw, NY; *m:* Terry; *c:* Sean P., Patrick R.; *ed:* (BS) Elem Ed, Suny Geneseo 1972; Early Childhood Suny Geneseo; *cr:* 5th Grade Teacher St Monicas Sch 1964-65; 3rd Grade Teacher St Patricks Sch 1970-72; 1st Grade Teacher Keshequa Elem Sch 1975-; *ai:* Summer Sch Teacher; Soc Stud Comm; Home-Sch Comm; NEA/Neany 1975-; Genesee Valley Teachers Assn Teacher of Year 1986; KTA SecY 1975-; Teacher of Yr 1986; Published Article Instructor Magazine 1981; *home:* 2826 Rte 258 Mt Morris NY 14510

MONTGOMERY, MICHAEL JOE, Physical Education Teacher; *b:* Hale Center, TX; *m:* Dorena Joy; *c:* Joy, Bethlyn, Jane; *ed:* (BED) Phys Ed, Univ of AK Anchorage 1980; (MA) Phys Ed, Univ of N CO 1981; *cr:* Phys Ed Teacher Hanshew Jr HS 1983-; *ai:* Jr HS Girls Gymnastics & Soccer, HS Var Girls Soccer Coach; Natl Soccer Coaches Assn of America AK St Soccer Coach 1987-88; Natl HS Athletic Coaches Assn Nom AK St Soccer Natl HS Coach of Yr 1989; AK St Youth Soccer Assn Rep 1989-, Coach of Yr 1987-89; *home:* 7001 O Malley Rd Anchorage AK 99516

MONTGOMERY, RONALD CLELL, Teacher/Family Leader; *b:* Louisville, KY; *m:* Marilyn Flener; *c:* Teresa; *ed:* (BA) Soc Sci, W KY Univ 1966; (MAED) Ed, Spalding Univ 1975; Rank I Admin, 1976, Rank I Supervision 1979 Spalding Univ; *cr:* Teacher 1971-75, Instructional Coord 1976-81 Thomas Jefferson HS; Teacher Thomas Jefferson Mid Sch 1981-; Media Production Instr Spalding Univ 1989-; *ai:* Patriots Production; Learning Choice Prgm; Family Leader; Bookstore Mgr; Horizons Unlimited Gifted Prgm; Natl Mid Sch Assn, KY Mid Sch Assn Presenter 1981-; KY Ed Assn, NEA 1971-; NMRA, NTRACK, KSONS; KY Video & Script Competition Awd of Excl 1988, 1989; KY Educl Television Utilization Awd; Natl Deans List; *office:* Thomas Jefferson Mid Sch 4401 Rangeland Rd Louisville KY 40219

MONTGOMERY, ROSALIE MERTZ, Resource Teacher; *b:* Rogers City, MI; *m:* Monte; *c:* Mary C. Montgomery Smith, Erin S. Montgomery Bothwell; *ed:* (BA) Elem Ed, Univ of AZ 1954; Grad Stud Univ of AZ; *cr:* 2nd Grade Teacher Pueblo Gardens 1954-55; Demonstration/Classroom Teacher Lineweaver 1956-71, Special Projects Center Lineweaver 1967-69; Demonstration/Resource Teacher Tucson Unified Sch Dist Curr Dept 1971-74; 3rd/4th Grade/K-4th Grade Resource Teacher Collier 1974-89; *ai:* 1st-3rd Grade Monday Marathon Prgm; Primary Field Day Co-Chairperson; Soc Comm; Educl Support Personnel Appreciation Day; NEA Life Mem; AZ Ed Assn, Tucson Ed Assn 1954-; PTA Favorite Teacher Awd 1985-86; Tucson Public Schls Up Date; Tucson Unified Sch Dist Supplementary Materials Pads Lang Art; *office:* Collier Elem Sch 3900 N Bear Canyon Rd Tucson AZ 85749

MONTGOMERY, ROSE WINNER, Second Grade Teacher; *b:* Lonaconing, MD; *m:* Robert L.; *c:* Susan, Robert, William, John; *ed:* (BA) Elem Ed, Frostburg St Uni 1958; *cr:* 2nd Grade Teacher Western Port Elem 1958-60; Piedmont Elem 1964-71; Midland Elem/Georges Creek 1972-; *office:* Georges Creek Schl Rt 36 North Lonaconing MD 21539

MONTIERTH, CONSTANCE OVERALL, First Grade Teacher; *b:* Morenci, AZ; *m:* J. Rex; *c:* Benjamin; *ed:* (AA) Elem Ed, Eastern AZ Coll 1969; (BA) Elem Ed, AZ St Univ 1971; (MA) Elem Ed, Northern AZ Univ 1989; Rdng Specialist; *cr:* 4th Grade Teacher Solomonville Elem 1971-72, Douglas Unified Sch 1972-73; 1st Grade Teacher Thatcher Unified 1973-; *ai:* Grade Level Chm Curr Dev; AZ Ed Assn Local Rep 1971-; NEA 1971-; Thatcher Ed Assn 1973-; Phi Kappa Phi; Womens Relief Society Mem 1961-; Primary Childrens Organization 2nd Cnslr 1988-; Young Womens Organization Adv 1984-88; *office:* Thatcher Unified Sch 1154 N High School Ave Thatcher AZ 85552

MONTO, MARILYN ANN, Fifth Grade Teacher; *b:* Toledo, OH; *ed:* (BSED) Elem Ed, Miami Univ 1961; (MED) Curr, Univ of Toledo 1972; *cr:* 4th-6th Grade Horizons/Gifted Teacher 1976-81; 4th/5th Grade Teacher Oakdale Sch 1961-; *ai:* Toledo Fed of Teachers 1962-; Alpha Delta Kappa (Chapter Pres 1970-72, 1980-82, NW OH Dist Chm 1974-78); Jennings Scholar 1979-80; *office:* Oakdale Elem Sch 1620 E Broadway Toledo OH 43605

MONTOYA, SALLY TRIVIZ, Consultant & Adv for Teachers; *b:* Fort Bayard, NM; *m:* Mauro A.; *c:* Ana Montoya Green, Mauro Jr., Robert; *ed:* (BA) Span/Sociology, Univ of NM 1949; Leadership Trng Phys Ed, Cooperating Teacher, Univ of NM; *cr:* 3rd-8th Grade Teacher A Montoya Sch 1950-55; 2nd Grade Teacher Holy Ghost Sch 1966-68; 6th Grade Teacher East San Jose 1969-72; K-5th Span Teacher Whittier Sch 1971-87; Consultant & Adv for Teachers 1987-; *ai:* Albuquerque Teacher Advisory & Dev Plan Comm; Consultant & Adv in Team Learning; NEA Wkshp Leader 1976-84, Certificate 1984; Instructional Improvement & Professional Dev Commission 1976-84; Alpha Delta Kappa Pres 1955-56, Plaque 1956; Delta Kappa Gamma Mem 1980-82, Cert 1979; Bi-ling Assn Chm 1976, Certificate 1976; Federal Judicial Commission; Book & Articles Published; Best Teacher Dedication in Book 1980; *home:* 1013 Dakota SE Albuquerque NM 87108

MOODY, BETTY GOODALE, Retired Kindergarten Teacher; *b:* Indianapolis, IN; *m:* J. Preston; *c:* Orville (dec), Janyce Wilson, Bruce; *ed:* (BS) Ed, Albion Coll 1941; (MA) Ed, Ball St Univ 1957; Northwestern Univ & Huntington Coll; *cr:* Kndgtn Teacher Albion Public Sch 1941-46, Battle Creek Public Sch 1946-47, Downey Public Sch 1947-48, Huntington Public Sch 1948-84; *ai:* Delta Kappa Gamma (Local Pres 1978-80, St VP 1981-83, Corresponding Secy 1983-85) 1981-88; NEA Comm 1955, 1980-84; Sigma Eta St Pres; IN St Teachers Assn Local Pres 1960-; Psi Iota Xi Pres 1970-; Zeta Tau Alpha Comm 1940-, Alumnae Merit 1974; Amer Assn of Univ Women 1971-; Daughters of Amer Revolution (Local Pres, St Librarian 1987) 1943-; Eastern Star 1969-; Chrstn Church Bd Trustee 1965-; Outstanding Educator 1972; *home:* R 1 Box 194 Angola IN 46703

MOODY, CAMILLE ROSE, Span/Life Management Teacher; *b:* Frankfurt, Germany; *m:* Michael Allen; *c:* Kyle B., Leah M.; *ed:* (BSED) Phys Ed, Univ of TX El Paso 1974; Ed, TX Womens Univ; Phys Ed, Midwestern St Univ; *cr:* Phys Ed Teacher/Vlybl/Track/Bsktbl Coach Eastwood Jr HS 1974-76; Phys Ed Teacher/Tennis Coach Burkburnett Jr HS 1976-; *ai:* 7th & 8th Grade Tennis Coach; TSTA Building Rep 1977-78, 1989-; Outstanding Young Women of America 1978; *office:* Burkburnett Jr HS 104 S Avenue D Burkburnett TX 76354

MOODY, FRANK COZBY, Biology Teacher; *b:* Sweetwater, TX; *ed:* (AS) General Stud, Arlington St Coll 1950; (BA) Anthropology, Univ of TX Austin 1955; (BS) Geology, TX Chrstn Univ 1971; (MLA) His, S Meth Univ 1973; (AA) Ag, 1989, (AAS) Ag Bus, 1989 Weatherford Coll; Certificate Ranch Management Prgm, TX Chrstn Univ 1980; Certificate Publishing Prgm, Rice Univ 1987; *cr:* Geology Teaching Asst Columbia Univ 1957-58; Paleontology Research Asst Amer Museum of Natural His 1957-58; Medical Genetics Research Asst NY St Psychiatric Inst 1958-59; Reference Librarian NY Acad of Medicine 1959-60; General Sci Teacher Ft Worth Ind Sch Dist 1968-69; Bio Teacher Birdville Ind Sch Dist 1969-; *ai:* Richland HS Sci Instruction Comm; NEA, Natl Wildlife Fed, The Sierra Club, Natl Trust for Historic Preservation; USMC Reserve Private 1948-50, Honorable Discharge 1950; US Army (1st Lieutenant, 2nd Lieutenant) 1952-57, Honorable Discharge 1957; Research at TX A&M Univ 1966-67, N TX St Univ 1973-74, S Meth Univ 1971-73, Rice Univ 1984-87, Harvard Univ 1988; *home:* 2300 Park Pl Apt 14 Fort Worth TX 76110

MOODY, PAUL H., Fourth Grade Teacher; *b:* Chicago, IL; *m:* Jane W. Jackson; *ed:* (MA) Elem Ed, SW Baptist Univ; *cr:* 6th Grade Teacher Golden Elem 1970-73; 6th Grade Teacher 1974-77, 5th Grade Teacher 1978-86, 4th Grade Teacher 1987- Camp Point Elem; *ai:* CU3EA Teachers Organization VP 1989-; IL Heart Assn Spec Events Comm Mem; *office:* Cntrl Elem Sch 107 School St Camp Point IL 62320

MOOG, HELENE OPDYCKE, Fourth Grade Teacher; *b:* Bryan, OH; *m:* Lyle D.; *c:* Tony, Jennifer; *ed:* (BS) Elem Ed, Bowling Green St Univ 1970; *cr:* 2nd Grade Teacher West Unity Schls 1968-71; 4th Grade Teacher Bryan City Schls 1971-; *ai:* NEA, OH Ed Assn, Bryan Ed Assn; Bryan Tree Commission Secy 1989-; Wesley Meth Church; *office:* Bryan City Schls 510 Ave A Bryan OH 43506

MOON, BARBARA JEAN, Mathematics Teacher; *b:* Auburn, NY; *ed:* (BA) Math, Russell Sage Coll 1970; (MS) Math, Syracuse Univ 1972; *cr:* Math Teacher Blodgett Jr HS 1972-78, Lemoyne Coll Upward Bound Prgm 1975-85, Fowler Sr HS 1978-; *ai:* Math Dept Chairperson; Instructional Leadership Team; Sch Improvement & Dist Math Steering Comm; NEA, STA, OCMTA, AMNYSTA; Rainbow Coalition, Syracuse Golf Assn, Neighborhood Organization; Natl Sci Fnd Pres Excl Teaching Awd Nom 1990; *office:* Fowler Sr HS 227 Magnolia St Syracuse NY 13204

MOON, ELIZABETH JEAN (GUDDLE MOORE), Retired Mathematics Teacher; *b:* Neodesha, KS; *m:* Vernon L.; *c:* Carolyn Preston, Cynthia Jesseph, Bernard Moore; *ed:* (BA) Ed, Newnan Coll 1962; Math Specialist WSU, Emporia, KS Univ Lawrence, Washburn; *cr:* Teacher St Margaret Mary 1956-64; Colwich Grade Sch 1964-89; Substitute Teacher 1989-; *ai:* Started Block Mother for Civil Defense 1955; NEA Civil Defense 1955-57; KS Univ Lawrence 25 Yr Teacher; Natl Camper & Hikers Treas 1968-70; Phi Kappa Phi 1981; Math & Sci Grant Washburn; *home:* 3243 S Fern Wichita KS 67217

MOON, NORMA NILDA (MARTINEZ), English Teacher; *b:* Kingsville, TX; *m:* John Daniel; *c:* Kristy N., Meghan R. Martinez; *ed:* (BS) Scndry Ed/Eng/Journalism, 1971, (MS) Ed Admin/Mid Management, 1982, TX A&I Univ; Grad Work in Teaching Eng as 2nd Lang; *cr:* 8th Grade Eng/Journalism Teacher Austin-Pearce Jr HS 1971-74; 9th Grade Eng Teacher Corpus Christi-Wynn-Seale Jr HS 1974-76; 10th-12th Grade Eng/Newspaper Teacher Robstown HS 1979-81; Prgm Coord/Master Teacher Migrant Dropout Prevention Prgm TX A&I Univ 1987-89; Eng I Honors Teacher Bishop HS 1981-; *ai:* Sr Class Spon; UIL Spelling Coach; Building Leadership Team Mem; NHS Selection Comm; Teacher Advisory Cncl to Supt; NEA; Bishop Educators Assn (Pres 1986-88, Secy 1985-86), Newsletter Pride in Comm 1989; TSTA Dist II (Elections Chairperson 1989-, Organizational Affair Chairperson 1990); Amer Assn of Univ Women Kingsville Branch VP Membership 1990); Appointed Mem S TX Teacher Center Advisory Bd TX A&I Univ; *office:* Bishop HS Box 39 Bishop TX 78343

MOON, PATRICIA ANITA (HAMMOND), 3rd Grade Teacher; *b:* Lakeland, FL; *m:* Joseph A.; *c:* Marybeth Hammond, Shannon, Matthew, Brian; *ed:* (BA) Elem Ed, FL Atlantic Univ 1971; *cr:* 4th Grade Teacher Wahneta Elem 1971-74; 3rd Grade Teacher Padgett Elem 1974-; *ai:* Polk Ed Assn 1971-; FL Teaching Prof 1971-; NEA 1971-; *office:* Edgar L Padgett Elem 110 Leelon Dr Lakeland FL 33809

MOONINGHAM, LAURA J., Sr English/Journalism Teacher; *b:* Langley Field, VA; *m:* James Daniel; *c:* James B., Kamara L.; *ed:* (BA) Eng/Ed, 1967, (MA) Eng/Ed, 1968 AZ St Univ; *cr:* Teacher East HS 1968-70, Carl Hayden HS 1970-72, Trevor Browne HS 1972-74; *ai:* Yrbk & Newspaper Adv; Newsletter Ed; Sch Improvement Team; Literary Magazine Adv; NEA, AEA, CTA, JEA 1968-; *office:* Trevor Browne HS 7402 W Catalina Phoenix AZ 85033

MOORE, AMANDA LOUISE OWENS, 5th Grade Teacher; *b:* Birmingham, AL; *m:* John A.; *ed:* (BA) Elem Ed, AL A&M 1960; Rdng/Childrens Lit; *cr:* Teacher Cecil Ave Elem 1963-78; Resource Teacher Fremont Elem 1979-80; Mentor Teacher 1987-; Teacher 1981-; Albany Park; *ai:* Oral Lang Coach Grades 5 & 6; Mem Sch Site Child Study Team; Delta Kappa Gamma Pres 1974-76; Delano Union Teachers Assn Pres 1967-68; Kern Rdng Assn Treas 1990-91; Beta Sigma Phi Pres 1979-81; Girl of Yr 1983; Albany Park PTA/PTA Svc Awd 1988-89; 1988 Ed Awd Outstanding Svc to Cmmty By Delano HS Black Stu Union; Co-Writer CA Teachers Instr Improvement Grant 1984; *office:* Albany Park North Sch 235 W 20th St Delano CA 93215

MOORE, ANNE RUSSELL, Mathematics Teacher/Dept Chair; *b:* Pampa, TX; *c:* Darren; *ed:* (BS) Elem Ed, 1968, (MED) Elem Ed, 1972 W TX St Univ; Scndry Ed Cert Math/Speech, 1972; *cr:* Teacher Amarillo Ind Sch Dist 1968-71, 1976-; *ai:* Stu Cncl Spon 1986-; Math Dept Chairperson 1988-; Teach Tap & Ballet; Kappa Kappa Iota 1968-73; Kappa Delta Pi 1985-; San Jacinto Baptist Church 1975-.

MOORE, B. JEANNETTE, Phys Ed & Health Teacher; *b:* Farmville, NC; *ed:* (BA) Phys Ed/Health, Univ NC Wilmington 1984; *cr:* Phys Ed/Health Teacher Trexler Mid Sch 1984-; *ai:* Health Dept Head Chairperson; Coach Girls Sftbl, Bsktbl, Vllybl, Track 1984-; NEA, NC Assn of Educators 1984-; Natl Fed Interscholastic Coaches Assn 1984-; *office:* Trexler Mid Sch PO Box 188 Foy St Richlands NC 28574

MOORE, BARBARA CAMP, Principal/Teacher; *b:* Los Angeles, CA; *c:* Donald, Warren, Christopher; *ed:* (BA) Bio, Loma Linda Univ 1953; Ed Courses; *cr:* Teacher/Prin Oakhurst Adventist Sch 1967-; *ai:* Area Ski Prgm.

MOORE, BARBARA HOLTON, 5th Grade Teacher; *b:* Oneida, NY; *m:* Kenneth Dale; *c:* Chris, Leslie; *ed:* (BA) Elem Ed, 1960, (MA) Elem Ed, 1980, (RI) Elem Ed, 1984 Eastern KY Univ; *cr:* 1st Grade Teacher 1963-72, 5th Grade Teacher 1972-89 Lancaster Elem; *ai:* Teacher of Yr 1973; *home:* 115 Hagan Ct Lancaster KY 40444

MOORE, BENNIE DORIS TEAGUE, 6th Grade Lang Art Teacher; *b:* Brady, TX; *m:* Jaroy; *c:* Greg, Meredith; *ed:* (ABS) Elem Ed, Tarleton St Univ 1961; (BS) Elem Ed, Sam Houston St Univ 1963; *cr:* 5th Grade Teacher Pecos Barstow Toyah 1972; 6th Grade Lang Arts Teacher Pecos Barstow Toyah 1973-; *ai:* UIL Spelling Coach; Lamar Elem & Austin Elem Public Relations Comms; Delta Kappa Gamma Parlimentarian 1988-; Pecos Barstow Toyah PTA Historian 1988-89; TSTA Building Rep 1989-; 20th Century Club Pres 1985-86; Chamber of Commerce Ladies Division; Lamar Elem 6th Grade Teacher of Yr 1989-; *home:* 1836 Jackson Blvd Pecos TX 79772

MOORE, BETTYE GRIFFIS, Teacher Elem Gifted/Talented; *b:* Italy, TX; *m:* Earl Gene; *c:* Marla Moore Ferguson, Steven E., Robert E., John G.; *ed:* (BS) Elem Ed, TX Tech 1956; (MS) Ed, Baylor Univ 1967; Gifted Ed, TWU, E TX Univ, Univ of Dallas, Southwestern St; *cr:* 5th Grade Teacher 1962-64, Elem Librarian 1964-66 Marlin Ind Sch Dist; 1st Grade Teacher 1967, 1972-78, Elem Teacher of Gifted & Talented 1980- Ennis Ind Sch Dist; *ai:* Assn of TX Prof Educators 1980-; TX St Teachers Assn 1962-79; TX Assn of Gifted & Talented 1980-; Tabernacle Baptist Church Adult Teacher 1970-88; Presented Gifted & Talented Wkshps for TX Region X Educl Service & St Convention; *office:* Austin Elem Sch Austin Dr Ennis TX 75119

MOORE, BEVERLY JONES, Sixth Grade Teacher; *b:* Kirksville, MO; *m:* Pearl Edward; *c:* Debra Groeper, Cheryl Cramp, Carol Baker, Shane; *ed:* (BSE) Elem Ed, 1971, (MA) Elem Admin, 1972 NMSU; Univ of Columbia; *cr:* 6th Grade Teacher Adair Cty R-1 Sch 1971-; *ai:* Acad Bowl Grades 4th-6th; Local & Dist Spelling Bee Word Pronouncer; Cmmty Teachers Assn (Pres 1973-74, Treas 1981-84, Secy 1985-); MSTA Legislative Comm; NCTE; Alumni Assn NMSU Life; Teacher of Month 1977; Alpha Phi Sigma Schlsp; *office:* Adair County R-1 PO Box Hwy 149 Novinger MO 63559

MOORE, BRENDA HUFFSTATLER, HS Social Studies Teacher; *b:* New Albany, MS; *m:* Thomas; *ed:* (BA) Soc Stud, Blue Mountain Coll 1970; (MS) Ed, Univ of MS 1977; *cr:* Eng Instr Algoma HS 1970-72, S Pontotoc Attendance Center 1972-74; Soc Stud Instr N Pontotoc Attendence 1974-; *ai:* N Pontotoc Attendance Center Jr & Sr Class, Chrlder, Beta & Peb Club Spon; MS Prof Educators Pres 1987-88; Phi Delta Kappa 1987-, Pontotoc Cty Educator of Yr; Delta Kappa Gamma 1988-; STAR Teacher; *home:* PO Box 301 Ecru MS 38841

MOORE, CAROL SMITH, Third Grade Teacher; *b:* Eugene, OR; *m:* Richard D.; *c:* Amy; *ed:* (BS) Elem Ed, OR Coll of Ed 1970; Grad Stud; *cr:* 5th/6th Grade Teacher Whitworth Elem 1970-72; 1st/4th/6th Grade Teacher Bailey Hill Elem 1972-76; 1st-3rd Grade Teacher Douglas Gardens & Centennial Elem 1976-; *ai:* Young Authors Comm; OEA, SEA; ADK Corresponding Secy 1988-; *office:* Centennial Elem Sch 1315 Aspen Way Springfield OR 97477

MOORE, CHARLES MICHAEL, Biology Teacher; *b:* Bristol, TN; *m:* Jane Canter; *c:* Stephen, Jennifer, Jeremy; *ed:* (BS) Bio, E TN St Univ 1975; Grad Stud; *cr:* Bio Teacher John S Battle HS 1983-; *ai:* Ftbl & Bsbl Coach; Sch Philosophy & Objectives Comm Mem; WA Cty Ed Assn Building Rep 1983-89; NSTA 1984-; Amer Welding Society 1976-81; BSA Scoutmaster 1974-82; Emory & Henry Coll Adjunct Faculty Mem 1989; *office:* John S Battle HS Rt 5 Lee Hwy Bristol VA 24201

MOORE, CHARLINE V., Science Teacher; *b:* Sandersville, GA; *w:* Charles H. (dec); *c:* Cathy M. Etheridge, Charles S., Michael Grayson; *ed:* (BS) Elem Ed, 1972, (MED) Mid Grades, 1980 GA Coll; *cr:* Sci Teacher Sandersville Elem Sch 1972-85, T J Elder Mid Sch 1985-; *ai:* Spelling, Drama, Soc Club Adv; NSTA; *office:* T J Elder Mid Sch 608 Hines St Sandersville GA 31082

MOORE, CONNIE DE LONG, Teacher; *b:* Atlanta, GA; *m:* Terry A.; *c:* Guy I., Joshua I.; *ed:* (BS) Physics/Scndry Ed, 1971, (MS) Physics, 1990 Univ S MS; Math, Univ of S MS 1980-81; Several Wkshps; *cr:* Teacher Pearl HS 1971-73, Reed Jr HS 1973-74; Adjunct Instr Univ S MS 1987-89; Teacher Oak Grove HS 1976-; *ai:* Stu Cncl Adv; Exec Comm Mem Advisory Bd MS St; Assn of Stu Cncls; Oak Grove Quality Circle; Sigma Pi Sigma Mem 1975-; Amer Assn of Physicists Mem 1980-; NSTA Mem 1982-; MS Sci Teachers Assn Mem 1982-; MS Cncl of Teachers of Math Mem 1982-; Natl Assn Stu Activity Advs Mem; MS Assn of Physicists HS Rep to Exec Comm 1989, Outstanding Physics Teacher of MS 1984; Delta Kappa Gamma Mem 1989-; Teacher in Space Educl Fnd Charter Mem 1986-; Outstanding Stu Cncl Adv St of MS 1980, 1987, Honorable Mention 1986, 1989; Star Teacher 1980, 1982, 1984, 1988; Outstanding Young Woman of America 1984; Sci Teacher Recognition Awd for Outstanding Teaching Sigmi Xi USM 1986; NASA Teacher in Space Prgm MS Finalist 1985; Lamar Cty Teacher of Yr 1990; Teacher of Yr MS 5th Congressional Dist 1990; Educl Consultant for Space Ed Stennis Space Center 1987-88; Regional Ed Journal; *office:* Oak Grove HS Rt 4 Box 1121 Hattiesburg MS 39402

MOORE, CYNDIA DUNEVANT, 2nd Grade Teacher; *b:* Memphis, TN; *m:* Larry Dean; *c:* Jennifer L., Julie C.; *ed:* (BS) Home Ec, Stephen F Austin 1973; (MED) Elem Ed, E TX St 1976; Post Grad Stud in Admin; *cr:* Sci Teacher Greiner Mid Sch 1974-77; 4th Grade Teacher 1977-82, 6th Grade Teacher 1982-85, 2nd Grade Teacher 1985- Edna Rowe Elem; *ai:* Ed Sch Yrbk 1987-88; Girls Soccer Coach; Newspaper Staff Spon 1982-85; Safety Patrol Spon 1982-85; Young Astronauts 1985-86; Early Chldhd Educators; Natl Rdng Assn; Intnl Rdng Assn News Asst Ed 1985-87; Advancement Soc Stud Bi-ling Educators 1985-89; PTA Bd Mem 1975-87, Life Membership 1985; GSA Troop Leader 1988-; PTA Life Membership; *home:* 2913 Churchill Way Garland TX 75042

MOORE, CYNTHIA LYNN, Chapter I Mathematics Teacher; *b:* Goldsboro, NC; *ed:* (BS) Math, IL St Univ 1988; *cr:* Math Teacher Manual HS 1988, Douglas Mac Arthur HS 1988-89; Chapter I Math Teacher Mound Mid Sch 1989-; *ai:* Mid Sch & HS Pom-Pon Spon; DEA, NEA, ICTM, NCTM 1987-; *home:* 3954 Camelot Dr #2D Decatur IL 62526

MOORE, DAVID WAYNE, Technology Education Teacher; *b:* Pikeville, KY; *m:* Mary Ellen Lazenby; *c:* Daniel I.; *ed:* (BS) Industrial Ed, Morehead St Univ 1982; (MS) Industrial Ed, Univ of WI Stout 1986; *cr:* Teacher Nelson Cty HS 1982-; *ai:* Academic Problem Solving Team Coach; Technology Stu Assn Club Adv; KY Industrial Arts Assn, KY Ed Assn, NEA 1982-; *office:* Nelson Cty HS 1070 Bloomfield Rd Bardstown KY 40004

MOORE, DEBORAH JOAN, Third Grade Teacher; *b:* Muskogee, OK; *ed:* (BA) Elem Ed, Mary Hardin-Baylor Coll 1971; *cr:* 5th Grade Teacher Donna Ind Sch Dist 1971-75; Rdng Teacher 1975-78, 3rd Grade Teacher 1978-88 Fowler Elem; 3rd Grade Teacher Mountain View Elem 1988-; *ai:* Effective Schls Comm; Grade Level Chm; TX St Teachers Assn, PTA 1975-; TX Classroom Teacher Assn 1976-; Rotary Club Teacher of Month Fowler Elem & Mountain View Elem; Terrific Teacher Awd Fowler Elem; *office:* Mountain View Elem Sch 500 Stagecoach Rd Harker Heights TX 76543

MOORE, DONALD R., Principal; *b:* Fresno, CA; *m:* Peggy Hambleton; *c:* Sarah, Jeff; *ed:* (BA) Eng/Phys Ed, Univ of CA Davis 1966; CA St Univ Stanislaus; *cr:* Teacher Travis Unified Sch Dist 1971-74, Soulsbyville Sch Dist 1974-76; Eng Teacher 1976-88, Prin 1989- Twain Harte Sch Dist; *ai:* Mentor Teacher 1988-89; Masonic Teacher of Yr 1981; Teachers Honor Roll 1985; *office:* Twain Harte Sch PO Box 339 Twain Harte CA 95383

MOORE, EDWARD C., Computer Literacy Teacher; *b:* Houston, TX; *m:* Gertrude Loretta O'Reilly; *c:* Brian, Linda; *ed:* (AA) Geology, S TX Jr Coll 1970; (BS) Elem Ed, 1973, (MED) Sci Ed, 1976 Univ of Houston; Admin & Evaluation; *cr:* Teacher Clear View Elem Canada 1974-75; Sci Teacher Singapore Amer Sch 1976-80; Elem Teacher Sheldon Schls 1980-88; Cmptr Literacy Teacher C E King Jr HS 1988-; *ai:* Cmptr Club Spon; ATPE 1980-; Cmmty Assn (Chm, Treas) 1986-; Published Software Author; *home:* 4909 Dairy Oaks Dr Crosby TX 77532

MOORE, EDWARD F., Science Department Chair; *b:* Warners, NY; *m:* Anne C. Farley; *c:* Robert, Kathleen Moore Guertin; *ed:* (BS) Ed/Sci, ECSU 1974; (MA) Instructional Media, Univ of CT 1981; Phd Candidate Educl Leadership Univ of CT; *cr:* Electronics Instr US Coast Guard 1963-71; Earth Sci Teacher Bennet Jr HS 1974-.

MOORE, ELSA LUTZ, Teacher; *b:* Brooklyn, NY; *m:* Jimmy Dave; *c:* David B., Joanna M. Moore Price, Christopher S., Melissa A., Joseph A.; *ed:* (BA) Math, MS St Univ 1964; (MA) Math/Cmptr Sci/Gifted, Univ of TX 1982; Admin, TX A&I 1978; Advanced Teaching Math, A P Calculus, Univ of TX 1985; Advanced Academic Trng, St of TX; *cr:* Teacher Starkville Municipal Sch Dist 1965-66, Rutherford HS 1967-70, Pinson Jr/Sr HS 1971-73, Gardendale HS 1975; Teacher/Math Dept Chm Round Rock HS 1976-81, Westwood HS 1981-87; Teacher Waco HS 1987-; *ai:* Sr & Mu Alpha Theta Spon; TX Math League & HS Math Exam Coord; Academic Decathlon Coach; Dist Textbook Adoption, Athens Acad, Dist Testing Comm; Phi Kappa Phi 1982-; Assn of TX Prof Educators 1978-, Phi Kappa Phi Awd 1982; Classroom Teacher Assn; NEA 1965-76; NCTM; Zeta Tau Alpha (Chapter Pres 1962, Mem Chairperson 1961, Chapter Adv 1964-66); Grant Women in Sci Univ of TX 1981-82; *office:* Waco HS 2020 N 42nd St Waco TX 76710

MOORE, EURYDICE ANN, Vocational Education Teacher; *b:* Chicago, IL; *c:* Rita, Nashell, Mc Clendon; *ed:* (BS) Health Arts, Coll of St Francis 1984; (MS) Human Services Admin, Spertus Coll of Judaicia 1986; *cr:* Medical Laboratory Techician Cook Cty Hospital 1975-78, Rush-Presbyn St Luke 1979-85; Teacher/Coord/Voc Ed Teacher Lucy Flower HS 1985-; *ai:* Prof Problems & Prof Personnel Advisory Comm; Big Sister, Little Sister Spon; Amer Society of Clinical Pathologists 1977-; Ambassadors for Christ Church Assoc Minister 1990; Family Cares Mission Soc Worker 1985-; *office:* Lucy Flower HS 3545 W Fulton Chicago IL 60624

MOORE, GARY ANN (SISTRUNK), Mathematics Teacher; *b:* Union, MS; *m:* Truman G.; *c:* Amanda, Donna; *ed:* (AA) Math Ed, E Cntrl Comm Coll 1968; (BSE) Math Ed, 1970, (MSE) Math Ed, 1974 Delta St Univ; *cr:* Math Teacher S Leake HS 1970-73, Sebastopol HS 1973-74, S Leake HS 1974-84; Carthage HS 1984-; *ai:* MS Prof Educators 1980-; MS Cncl Teachers of Math, NCTM; STAR Teacher 1974, 1981, 1987, 1989, 1990; *office:* Carthage HS School St Carthage MS 39051

MOORE, GARY LEE, Assistant Principal; *b:* Sullivan, IN; *m:* Mary Wallace; *c:* Matthew, Thomas; *ed:* (BS) Phys Ed, 1972, (MS) Ed/Admin Services, 1985 Cal Poly SLD; *cr:* Phys Ed Teacher Orchard Sch 1975-76; Phys Ed/Sci Teacher Paulding Intermediate 1976-86; *ai:* Act & Athletic Coord Dir; Yrbk; Newspaper Leadership; CA Act Dir Assn 1982-86; Mentor Teacher; *office:* Paulding Intermediate Sch 600 Crown Hill Arroyo Grande CA 93420

MOORE, GENIENE CARTER, Second Grade Teacher; *b:* Macon, GA; *m:* Larry; *c:* Shannon, Jeff; *ed:* Assoc Elem Ed, Abraham Baldwin Ag Coll 1970; (BA) Early Chldhd/Elem Ed, GA Coll Milledgeville 1972; Augusta Coll; Gifted Ed, UGA; *cr:* 4th Grade Teacher 1972-73, Teacher of Gifted 1973 Madison Elem; 5th-8th Grade Teacher Oak Park Elem 1973-74; 4th Grade Teacher Monroe Elem 1974-75; 2nd-4th Grade/Chapter I Teacher Columbia Cty Sch System 1975-; *ai:* Yrbk Staff; Grade Chm; Sunshine & Climate Comm; PAGE 1986-; ADK; Teacher of Yr; Published Articles 1981; *office:* N Columbia Elem Sch Rt 1 Box 10 Appling GA 30802

MOORE, HARRIETT POWELL, Kindergarten Teacher; *b:* Little Rock, AR; *m:* Samuel Hale; *c:* Courtney E., Katherine H.; *ed:* (BS) Ed, Univ of N Tx 1968; *cr:* 1st-3rd Grade Teacher Ft Worth Ind Sch Dist 1968-74; Montessori Childrens House 1981-83; Pre-Sch Level Teacher Kinderplatz of Fine Arts 1984-86; 1st Grade Teacher Crowley Ind Sch Dist 1986-87; Kndgtn Teacher Trinity Sch 1976-78, 1987-; *ai:* TVS Auction Comm; TVS Kndgtn Admissions Evaluator; Delta Kappa Gamma 1973-, Achievement Awd 1990; Ft Worth Assn for Ed of Young Children; Ft Worth Jr League 1990; Delta Gamma Alumnae Pres 1990, Outstanding Alumnae 1982; Outstanding Young Women of America 1980; *office:* Trinity Valley Sch 6101 Mc Cart Fort Worth TX 76133

MOORE, JACQUELINE GRAY, 4th Grade Teacher/Chairman; *b:* Jacksonville, NC; *m:* Barry Carl; *ed:* (BS) Elem Ed, Fayetteville St Univ 1973; Sponsored Wkshps; *cr:* Teacher Bell Fork Elem 1976-78; Teacher/Grade Chm John J Wright Sch 1981-83; Teacher/Chm Bell Fork Elem 1983-; *ai:* Lang Art Rep; Chm Sci Accreditation Comm; Mentor for Beginning/Nontenured Teachers; Trainer Teacher Effectiveness Trng Prgm; Onslow Co Assoc of Educators Sch Rep 1987-88, Distinguished Service; Fayetteville St Alumni Corresponding Secy 1985-; Democratic Precinct Treas 1989-; *home:* 721 Dennis Rd Jacksonville NC 28540

MOORE, JACQUELINE RUSSELL, Library/Media Specialist; *b:* Morgantown, WV; *m:* Lloyd G.; *c:* Justin Ross, Jared Cole; *ed:* (BA) Elem Ed, Fairmont St Coll 1976; (MA) Elem Ed, WV Univ 1981; *cr:* 4th Grade Teacher Blacksville Elem Sch 1976-84; 2nd/3rd Grade Teacher Jakes Run Elem 1987-88; Lib/Media Spec Blacksville/Daybrook/Jakes Run/Pentress & Wadestown 1988-; *ai:* Blacksville Area Sch Bond Steering Comm; Eng & Handwriting Textbook Adoption Comm; Alpha Delta Kappa Honorary Women Educators 1989-; Monongalia Cty Rdg Cncl 1989-; NEA/WVEA/MCEA 1976-; WVCTM 1987-89; WV Educl Media Assn 1988-; Golden Glow Rebekah Lodge #299 1973-; West Warre Baptist Church 1962-; Wadestown Sch PTA 1987-89;Wadestown Sch PTO 1989-; *home:* Rt 1 Box 50 Burton WV 26562

MOORE, JAMES GLENN, Science Teacher; *b:* Rock Hill, SC; *m:* Kathie Horlacher; *c:* Susan, Caroline; *ed:* (BA) His/Sci, Univ of SC 1971; (MED) Ed, Winthrop Coll 1974; *cr:* Teacher York Rd Elem Sch 1971-73; Coach Lewisville Mid Sch 1973-80; Asst Prin Great Falls Mid Sch 1980-84; Teacher York Jr HS 1984-; *ai:* Palmetto St Teachers Assn 1979-; Phi Delta Kappa 1984-; Mc Connells Town Cncl Councilman 1972-; *office:* York Junior H S 1280 Johnson Rd York SC 29745

MOORE, JANICE A., 5th Grade Teacher; *b:* Louisville, KY; *m:* Dennis L.; *c:* Andrew, Laura; *ed:* (BA) Elem Ed, 1964, (Rank II) Rdng, 1989 Univ of KY; *cr:* 1st Grade Teacher 1965, Headstart Teacher 1965 Eastern Elem; 2nd Grade Teacher Stonewall Elem 1965-69; 5th Grade Teacher Eastern Elem 1973-; *ai:* Dir 5th Grade Wax Museum; Consultant to Various Writing Projects; Young Authors Conference Chairperson; Scott Cty Academic Showcase Writing Co Chairperson; Steering Comm Mem for New Writing Across the Curr; Scott Cty Ed Assn Secy 1978-79; KY Ed Assn, NEA; Tates Creek Chrstn Church; Accepted in 1st Bluegrass Writing Project 1987; Grants for Project WRITE Wkshp NJ 1986, Sci Equipment; *office:* Eastern Elem Sch 3407 Newtown Pike Georgetown KY 40324

MOORE, JERRY JOE, Physical Education Teacher; *b:* Daleville, IN; *m:* Mary Ann Beck; *ed:* (BS) Elem Ed, Ball St 1965; (MS) Elem Ed, IN St 1971; Phys Ed, Ball St 1986; *cr:* 6th Grade Teacher Garfield Elem 1965; 5th/6th Grade Teacher Chesterfield Elem 1966-86; Phys Ed Teacher Meadowbrook Elem 1986-, Southview Elem; *ai:* Elem Bsktbl, Track Coach; Anderson Fed of Teachers; Kiwanis Club Secy 1969-70; Jaycees DSA Awd 1969; *home:* Box 273C RR 1 Daleville IN 47334

MOORE, JOHN BRENDAN, Latin/Religion Teacher; *b:* New York, NY; *ed:* (BS) Ed, Fordham Univ 1950; (MA) Religious Ed, Catholic Univ 1956; St Xaviers Coll Latin, Span, Art 1958-70; *cr:* Elem Teacher Sacred Heart Sch 1944-50; Sr HS Teacher Iona Preparatory Sch 1950-57, Brother Rice HS 1957-89; *ai:* Head Tennis Coach 1963-86; Asst Tennis Coach 1958-63; Head of Latin Dept Brother Rice; NCEA; Chicago Cath League Coaches Assn 1963-86; Chicago Cath League 1976, Coach of Yr 1976; Brother Rice HS Hall of Fame 1984, HS Alumni Assn Man of Yr 1987; Seleect Circle Coaching Awds, Gold Awd Tennis 1987; Chicago Cath League Hall of Fame 1987; *office:* Brother Rice HS 10001 S Pulaski Rd Chicago IL 60642

MOORE, JOHN MORTON, Biology Teacher/Computer Prof; *b:* Elizabeth, NJ; *m:* Cathy Lynne Hinkley; *c:* Michael E., Bethanie L., Daniel R.; *ed:* (BS) Bio, Taylor Univ 1972; (MA) Bio, 1978, (EDD) Sci/Bio, 1989 Ball St Univ; *cr:* Teacher Justice Jr HS 1973-83, Marion HS 1983-; Professor Adjunct Taylor Univ 1985-; *ai:* Novus Sci Club; Sci Curr Comm; NABT; Phi Delta Kappa; NSTA, Hoosier Sci Teachers Assn; Amer Red Cross Aquatics Dir 1980-; Upland Youth Bsbl League 1988-; Fellowship Ball St Univ; Curr Dev Grant; N Cntrl Assn Evaluation Team; Outstanding Educator Awd 1989; *home:* 413 W Payne Ave Upland IN 46989

MOORE, JOSEPH, Chemistry Teacher; *b:* Mahanoy City, PA; *ed:* (BS) Scndry Ed, PA St Univ 1974; (MED) Chem Ed, Bloomsburg Univ 1981; AP Chem Trng, Duke Univ; Microcomputer Trng, Wilkes Univ; *cr:* Chem Teacher N Pocono HS 1975-; *ai:* Amer Chem Society 1976-; PSEA 1975-; *office:* N Pocono HS Chruch St Moscow PA 18444

MOORE, JUDY DAVIS, Sixth Grade Teacher; *b:* Milford, DE; *m:* Lynn Wilson; *c:* Lisa A., Christy L.; *ed:* Assoc Legal Secy, DE Tech & Comm Coll 1970; (BA) Elem Ed, Salisbury Univ 1979; Counseling, Liberty Univ 1990; *cr:* Secy/Cmptr Operator Townsends Incorporated 1970-72; Secy John F Farquhar DDS 1972-14;l 4th Grade Teacher Frankford Elem Sch 1979; 5th Grade Teacher Phillip Showell Elem Sch 1980-83; 6th Grade Teacher Georgetown Elem Sch 1983-; *ai:* Textbook Selection & Cheer Comm; Sch Spirit Comm Chairperson; Epworth Chrstn Var Bsktbl Chrldrs & Georgetown Sr League Sftbl Team Coach; Intnl Rdng Assn 1989-; Big Brothers & Big Sisters of America Big Sister 1989-; Epworth Fellowship Church (Comm, Sunday Sch Teacher) 1975-; Georgetown Elem Teacher of Yr 1984-85; *office:* Georgetown Elem Sch West Market St Georgetown DE 19947

MOORE, KATHRYN WARREN, Resource Teacher; *b:* Lakewood, OH; *m:* Albert; *c:* Lissa M. Beckley, Seth M. Beckley; *ed:* (BS) Early Chldhd Ed, Kent St Univ 1963; (MA) Spec Ed, Univ of NM 1981; Excl in Math Instruction Teacher Trng Prgm 1985; Elem Sci Teaching Wkshp Amer Indian Sci/Engineering Society Natl Sci Fnd 1985; Math/Sci Summer Inst Haskell Jr Coll 1986; *cr:* Kndgtn Teacher Moreland Hills Elem Sch 1963-64, The Plains Elem Sch 1964-65; 3rd Grade Teacher Heights Cath Sch 1965-66; Instr in Ed Univ of KS 1968-69; Tutor Union Cty Head Start 1970-71; Co-Founder/Head Teacher Kinderfolk Pre-Sch 1971-73; Creative Arts Teacher Geisinger Medical Center 1974-75; Elem Teacher S Pueblos Agency 1975-77; Kndgtn Teacher Santa Clara Day Sch 1977-82; Exceptional Ed Prgm Santa Clara Day Sch 1982-; *ai:* Prgm Coord Kinderfolk Pre-Sch 1973-75; Related Arts Comm Mem Lewisburg Elem Schls 1974-75; Creative Dramatics Consultant Cntrl Susquehanna Intermediate Unit 1974-75; Mem Lewisburg Prison Project 1972-75; Volunteer Suicide Prevention Center 1976; Chairperson Rdng is Fundamental Santa Clara Day Sch 1981-84; Prgm Chairperson San Gabriel Historical Society 1984-86; NSTA, NCTM Mem 1984-; Intnl Rdng Assn Mem 1987; CEC (Intnl Convention 1984, 1987, 1988; NM Convention 1987,, Presenter 1988, 1989, Mem 1984-); AFT, Natl Cncl BIA Educators 1988-; Los Alamos Choral Society, Espanola Valley Chorale Mem 1983-86; San Gabriel Historical Society Prgm Chm 1984-86; Several Sci Teaching Wkshps 1985-87; Project Wild 1985; N Pueblo Agency Merit Awd 1985, Teacher of Month 1989; Instr Math/Sci Summer Wkshp 1986, Native Amer Sci Ed Assn Teacher Trng Prgm 1986; *office:* Santa Clara Day Sch PO Box HHH Espanola NM 87532

MOORE, KENNETH DALE, Social Studies Teacher; *b:* Warfield, KY; *m:* Barbara Holton; *c:* Christopher, Leslie; *ed:* (BA) His, E KY Univ 1959; Certified Elem Ed; *cr:* Coach/Teacher Garrard Cty HS 1963-70; Teacher Garrard Elem System 1971-; *ai:* Sch Related Act; KEA, NEA; Jaycees 1963-72; Optimist Pres 1968-; *home:* 315 Hagan Ct Lancaster KY 40444

MOORE, KIM CHARLENE, Third Grade Teacher; *b:* Great Falls, MT; *m:* Daniel K. Webster; *c:* Lyndsay, Kimball G., Cody F.; *ed:* (BS) Elem/Spec Ed, E Mt St Coll 1976; 5th Yr Cert Cntrl WA St Univ; *cr:* Intermed-EMR Teacher Napi Elem 1976-78; K-12th Grade Resource Rm Teacher 1978-80, 3rd Grade Teacher 1980- Brewster Elem; *ai:* Jr Women 1976-88; Garden Club 1980-; *office:* Brewster Elem Sch PO Box 97 Brewster WA 98812

MOORE, LARRY EUGENE, Math Teacher/Asst Principal; *b:* Heber Springs, AR; *m:* La Donna K. Betts; *c:* Heath, Nicole; *ed:* (BSE) Math/Phys Ed, 1971, (MSE) Educl Admin, 1988 Univ of Cntrl AR; Grad Stud Scndry Sch Admin; *cr:* Math Teacher/Coach Wilburn HS 1971-76; Math Teacher 1976-88, Asst Prin 1988- Pangburn HS; *ai:* AASSP 1988-; *home:* 2660 16th Hwy Searcy AR 72143

MOORE, LILLIE M., 9th Grade English Teacher; *b:* Marion, AL; *c:* Anthony, Cheryl, Charlotte; *ed:* (BA) Eng, AL A&M Univ 1953; (MA) Ed, Natl Coll of Ed 1984; Certificates in HS Rdng, TESL, Soc Stud; *cr:* Eng Teacher Parker-Paul Robeson HS 1962-; *ai:* Sch Newspaper & Yrbk Spon; Team Leader Eng I Teachers; Speech & Drama; NCTE 1980-; NEA 1966-; IL Ed Assn 1966-; AFT 1966-; Lilydale 1st Baptist Church Sunday Sch Teacher 1963-, Teacher of Yr 1985; Ed Grant from Univ of Chicago 1963; *office:* Paul Robeson HS 6835 S Normal Blvd Chicago IL 60621

MOORE, LINDA ANN WEILITZ, Sci Dept Head/Biology Teacher; *b:* St Louis, MO; *m:* William Reginald Jr.; *ed:* (BS) Scndry Ed/Bio, SE MO St Univ 1977; Working Towards Masters in Scndry Ed, Univ of MO St Louis; Sci Ed Wkshp & Seminars; *cr:* Sci Teacher Richland HS 1977-78; Bio Teacher Windsor HS 1978-; *ai:* Sci Club Spon; Dist Sci Fair Coord; N Cntrl Sci Comm & Sci Dept Head; NEA 1984-; NABT 1979-; Rock Presbyn Church (Ordained Elder 1987-, Bd of Session 1987-, Outreach/Fellowship Chairperson 1987-); *office:* Windsor HS 6208 Hwy 61-67 Imperial MO 63052

MOORE, LINDA MAE (JENNER), First Grade Teacher; *b:* Dickinson, ND; *m:* Le Roy R.; *c:* Robby, David; *ed:* (BA) Elem Ed, VCSU 1975; Grad Stud Numerous Univs; *cr:* Math Teacher Jamestown Jr HS 1975; 1st Grade Teacher Bismarck Public Schls 1975-84, Williston Public Schls 1985-; *ai:* Rdng Conventions Speaker; Delta Kappa Gamma 1985-; Beta Sigma Phi 1984-87; Williston Ed Assn Public Relations 1989-; Entertainment Incorporated 1987-, Outstanding Actress 1988; Teachers

Convention Presenter Rdng Awd; Intnl Sch of Alcohol & Drug Abuse Schlsp; *home:* 201 E 14th St Williston ND 58801

MOORE, LYNDA STROUD, Third Grade Teacher; *b:* El Paso, TX; *m:* Charles E.; *c:* Cheryl, Christopher, Cathleen; *ed:* (BS) Elem Ed, Univ of TX El Paso 1969; Bill Martin Literacy Conference; Beyond Assertive Discipline; Exemplary Center for Rdng Instruction; Alphabetic Phonics 1990; *cr:* 3rd Grade Teacher Pecos-Barstow CISD 1969-72; 2nd Grade Teacher Ysleta Ind Sch Dist 1972-77; 5th Grade Teacher 1978-80, 3rd Grade Teacher 1977- Allen Ind Sch Dist; *ai:* 3rd Grade Team Leader; UIL Coach; Assn of TX Prof Educators (Building Rep 1989-, Mem 1979-); Orton Dyslexia Society 1989-; ASCD 1988-; Persons Reaching Individuals for Dyslexic Ed 1987-; Allen Cmmty Ed Advisory Cncl 1990; Nom Allen Ind Sch Dist Teacher Excl Awd 1986, 1988, 1990; *office:* Alvis C Story Elem Sch 1550 Edelweiss Dr Allen TX 75002

MOORE, MARCELLA COE, Fourth Grade Teacher; *b:* Poplar, KY; *m:* Harley W.; *c:* Barbara Barnett, Daniel, Mary Mirre; *ed:* (BA) Elem Ed, Univ of KY 1972; (MA) Elem Ed, 1978, (Rank I) Elem Ed, 1986 E KY Univ; *cr:* 3rd-6th Grade Teacher Harlow Elem 1973-84; 4th/5th Grade Teacher Harrodsburg Elem 1984-; *ai:* HEA, KY Ed Assn, NEA 1972-; *office:* Harrodsburg Elem Sch 371 E Lexington Harrodsburg KY 40330

MOORE, MARGARET HENDERSON, 2nd Grade Teacher; *b:* Somerset, KY; *:* William D.; *c:* Matthew, Michael; *ed:* (BME) Music, Memphis St Univ 1977; Elem Ed Univ of KY 1979; Elem Ed Eastern KY Univ; ORFF Schulwerk Memphis St Univ 1977: *cr:* Music Teacher Fairley Elem Sch 1977-78; Elem Teacher Perryville Elem Sch 1980-; *ai:* Sch Based Magegement PTO Task; KEA-NEA 1980-; *office:* Perryville Elem Sch West 4th St Perryville KY 40468

MOORE, MARILYN BRACEY, Employability Skills Teacher; *b:* Alexandria, VA; *c:* Constance Moore Jones, Lewis S.; *ed:* (BS) Bio, VA St Univ 1966; (MED) Stu Personnel Admin, Howard Univ 1975; Grad Studs Howard Univ, Univ of DC, Southeastern Univ, Johns Hopkins Univ; *cr:* Bio Teacher Jefferson Jr HS 1968-72; Teacher/Coord Roosevelt Sr HS 1972-76, Teacher/Coord 1977-86, Employability Skills Teacher 1986- Woodson Sr HS; *ai:* FBLA Co-Adv; Annual Career Fair Co-Spon; ASCD, Earthwatch, Natl Career Dev Assn; Alpha Kappa Alpha; Laverne Noyes Fellowship Awd; *office:* Woodson Sr HS 55th & Eads St NE Washington DC 20019

MOORE, MARILYN JOYCE WALLUK, Third Grade Teacher; *b:* Bridgeport, CT; *m:* Thomas William; *c:* Thomas J.; *ed:* (BS) Ed, Cntrl CT St Coll 1971; (MS) Ed, Southern CT St Coll 1974; Ed, St Josephs, Baptist Univ 1989-; Best Prgm for St of CT; *cr:* 3rd Grade Teacher Garden Sch 1972-80, Center Sch 1980-83; Kndgtn Teacher Franklin Sch 1984-89; 3rd Grade Tea cher Eli Whitney Sch 1989-; *ai:* Mentor for BEST Prgm; Nom for Teacher of Yr Town of Stratford 1989; *home:* 15 Brinsmayd Ave Stratford CT 06497

MOORE, MARTINE, Fifth Grade Teacher; *b:* Timpson, TX; *c:* Tracy; *ed:* (BA) Elem Ed, TX Southern Univ 1972; Chem Sci, Univ of Houston 1990; Math/Lang HISD 1979, 1980; Advanced Media Production 1980; HISD Crime Prevention Drug Ed Wkshp 1979; *cr:* K-6th Grade Teacher Blackshear Elem 1972-; *ai:* Parent-Teacher, Safety Patrol, Character Ed Comm 1989-; Houston Teachers Assn 1972-; Church of God in Christ Treas 1983-, Certificate of Appreciation 1989; Houston Bus Comm for Educl Services 1987; Teacher Mini Grant; *office:* Blackshear Elem Sch 2900 Holman Ave Houston TX 77004

MOORE, MARVA ANN (RUCKER), Guidance Counselor; *b:* Crystal, WV; *m:* Gerald; *c:* Jacqueline A., Juliette A.; *ed:* (BS) Bio/Chem, Bluefield St Coll 1958; (MS) Guidance Counseling, Wright St Univ 1976; Grad Work Univ of Dayton, Wright St Univ; *cr:* Teacher Dunbar HS 1967-70; Teacher/Unit Leader Longfellow Mid Sch 1973-81; Teacher/Cnslr E J Brown Jr HS 1981-85; Cnslr Patterson Career Center 1985-; *ai:* Class & Leadership Conference Stu adv; Faculty Cncl Mem; NEA, OEA, DEA, OH Cnslrs; Delta Sigma Theta 1955-, 35 Yr Awd 1990; NAACP 1987-; Mt Enon Baptist Church 1985-; *office:* Patterson Career Center 118 E 1st St Dayton OH 45402

MOORE, MARY B., 7th/8th Grade Religion Teacher; *b:* Omaha, NE; *ed:* (BA) His/Phys Ed, Creighton Univ 1974; In Grad Prgm Pastoral Ministry, Creighton Univ; *cr:* Phys Ed Teacher Council Bluffs Public Schls 1974-75; Substitute Teacher Omaha Public Schls 1975-76; Teacher St Marys of Bellevue 1976-; *ai:* Cross Cntry Coach; Planning Comm for Human Relations; Attitude & Skills Course for Teachers; Talent Show Coord; Liturgy Planner on Self Study Comm for Sch; NE Against the Death Penalty 1987-89; NE for Peace 1986-; *office:* St Marys Sch 903 W Mission Bellevue NE 68005

MOORE, MELISSA KOWALSKI, English Teacher; *b:* Huntingdon, PA; *m:* Glenn T.; *ed:* (BA) Eng, Juniata Coll 1974; *cr:* 7th Grade Teacher Lewistown-Granville HS 1974-75; Tyrone Area HS 1976-79; 9th Grade Teacher Jefferson Davis Jr HS 1979-80; 10th Grade Teacher Tyrone Area HS 1984-; *office:* Tyrone Area H S Clay Avenue Ext Tyrone PA 16686

MOORE, MORNA RUTH WRIGHT, 3rd Grade Teacher; *b:* Corsica, PA; *m:* Robert I.; *c:* John Hamel, Morna K., James K., Sheila, Adam, Melody G. Troup, Robert E.; *ed:* (BS) Elem, Maryville Coll 1952; Grad Stud OH St Univ; *cr:* Stevens Sch 1952-56; Fair Avenue Sch 1956-96; Substitute Teacher New Waterford 1963-66; Washington Sch 1971-74; Hawthorn Sch 1976-; *ai:* PSEA, NEA; Redbank Valley Ed Assn; Bus Prof Women 1976-77; GSA, Camp Fire Girls; Church (Sunday Sch Teacher, Choir Mem); *home:* RD 3 Box 59H New Bethlehem PA 16242

MOORE, NANCY JANE, English Department Chairperson; *b:* South Boston, VA; *ed:* (BS) Ed, Radford Coll 1969; (MS) Ed, Old Dominion Univ 1979; *cr:* Eng Teacher D H Truitt Jr HS 1969-; *ai:* Forensics Coach; Odyssey of Mind Coach; Child Study Team Chm; Tidewater Assn Teachers of Eng Treas 1975-76, 1989-; VA Assn Teachers of Eng Svc Awd 1984; Chesapeake Rdng Cncl Mbrshp Dir 1988-89; VA St Rdng Assn; Chesapeake Ed Assn; VA Ed Assn; NEA; NCTE; Teacher of Yr 1977 & 1987; *office:* Dorothy H Truitt Jr High 1100 Holly Ave Chesapeake VA 23324

MOORE, NANCY LEE (MADSEN), 7-8th English Teacher; *b:* Spencer, IA; *m:* Dennis D.; *ed:* (BA) Eng, William Penn Coll 1.71; *cr:* Eng/Span/Journalism Teacher DUrant Community HS 1971-78; Teacher Durant Comm Sch 1979-; *ai:* Spelling Bee Coord; Young Writers Confernce Spon; Publisher/Editor Stu Publication Reflections of the Mind; Durant Ed Assn Mem 1985-; IA Cncl Teachers Eng Chairperson 1988-; Berean Bapt Church Sunday Sch Teacher 1978-; Cornbelt Running Club 1988-; Article Published Journal NATL Assn Coll & Teachers Agriculture Written By Dr Conrad Whiten in Collaboration with Nancy Madsen Moore & Debbie Williams; *office:* Durant Cmmty Sch 408 7th St Durant IA 52747

MOORE, NEAL F., Chemistry & German Teacher; *b:* Bay City, MI; *m:* Elsie Ann Felice; *c:* Geoffrey A., Anne E., Meghan M.; *ed:* (BA) Chem/Ger/Bio, Albion Coll 1964; Scndry Ed, 1968, (MA) Sociology, 1974 E MI Univ; Grad Stud at Numerous Univs; *cr:* German Teacher C S Mott HS 1968-70, Univ of WI Milwaukee 1970-71; Chem/German Teacher Warren HS 1971-; *ai:* Sci Olympiad Coach; WEA, MEA, NEA 1968-; Aikidy Uoshinkai Assn of North Amer Instr 1980, 2nd Degree Black Belt 1988; Ger Consulate Stipend for Goethe Inst; Warren Garden Club Stipend; AEC Stipend; 2 Articles Published from Conservation Sch Seminar; Past Contributor to TPR Lang Periodical; *office:* Warren HS 5460 Arden Warren MI 48092

MOORE, NELL BRACKETT, Sixth Grade Teacher; *b:* Mobile, AL; *m:* Joseph Perry; *c:* Joseph, Stephanie, John; *ed:* (BS) Elem Ed, MS Coll 1954; (MRE) Religious Ed, New Orleans Baptist Theo Seminary 1958; *cr:* 2nd Grade Teacher Sidon Elem 1954-55; 5th Grade Teacher Semmes Elem 1958-59; 7th Grade Teacher Houma Elem 1960; 6th Grade Teacher Arlinton Elem 1961-72, W C Griggs; *ai:* 4-H & Traffic Patrol Stu Leader; Youth Club Adv; Volunteer Asst Prin; Volunteer Traffic Officer; Mobile Cty Young Women Assn Dir; Mobile Cty Ed Assn Sch Rep 1965-68; Mobile Cty Public Sch Teacher of Yr 1980, 1983, Heart of Gold 1989; *home:* 7801 Fordham Dr Mobile AL 36619

MOORE, NORMA GADDIE, Guidance Counselor; *b:* Deatsville, AL; *m:* James A.; *c:* Traci E.; *ed:* (BA) Home Ec, AL Coll 1969; (MA) Home Ec, Univ of AL 1976; (MS) Counseling/Human Dev, Troy St Univ 1979; Numerous Educl Wkshps, Meetings; *cr:* 3rd Grade Teacher Robinson Springs Elem Sch 1969-70, S Highlands Elem 1970-71; Home Ec Teacher 1972-88, Cnslr 1988- Opp HS; *ai:* Anchor Club & FHA Spon; Delta Kappa Gamma (VP 1988-, Pres 1990-92); OEA, AEA, NEA; *office:* Opp HS 502 N Maloy St Opp AL 36467

MOORE, ODIE, Director; *b:* Marshall, TX; *m:* Elbert; *c:* Brenda, Linda; *ed:* Child Dev, East Field 1988; Cosmotology; *ai:* NAEYC; PTA Pres, Advisory Comm Pres; *home:* 2807 52nd St Dallas TX 75216

MOORE, PAMELA EDWARDS, 7th/8th Grade Teacher; *b:* Ft Eustis, VA; *m:* Carter Grayson; *c:* Brian, William; *ed:* (BS) Elem Ed, Trevecca Nazarene Coll 1978; (MED) Elem Ed, TN St Univ 1989; *cr:* Teacher/Coach Pioneer Chrstn Acad 1978-79; Teacher Richland Elem Sch 1982-; *ai:* Chm Sci Fair Comm; Spon Rhythmettes Drill Team; Communicator Giles Cty Negotiations Comm; GCEA (Secy 1988-89) 1982-; TEA, NEA 1982-; TRA 1988-; Historical Society 1990; Giles Cty Teacher of Yr 1988; *office:* Richland Sch Rt 1 Box 215 Pulaski Hwy Lynnville TN 38472

MOORE, PAMELA WETZEL, Vocal Music Teacher; *b:* Eugene, OR; *m:* Glen Eugene; *c:* Sean, Connemara; *ed:* (BA) Music Theory/Lit, Seattle Pacific 1968; (MA) Ed, Univ of WA 1971; Post Grad Stud Music & Ed; *cr:* Intern/Corps Teacher Seattle Public Schls 1970, 1971; Asst Teacher Sharples Jr HS 1972; Elem Music Teacher Port Angeles Public Schls 1977-84; Vocal Music Teacher Stevens & Roosevelt Mid Schls 1985-; *ai:* Music Co-Curricular Performance; Building & Performing Art Steering Comm; Prof Musician; MENC 1985; Delta Kappa Gamma 1988; *home:* 809 Ridge View Dr Port Angeles WA 98362

MOORE, PATSY MARTIN, Fourth Grade Teacher; *b:* Tupelo, MS; *m:* Jerry H.; *c:* Whitney, Kevin; *ed:* (BS) Scndry Ed, MS St Univ 19 9; *cr:* 7th Grade Rdng Teacher Nettleton Elem 1969-70; 4th Grade Teacher Dorsey Elem 1970-; *ai:* NEA 1969-; *office:* Dorsey Elem Sch Rt 5 Box 500 Fulton MS 38843

MOORE, PRENTISS, II, Health/Science Teacher; *b:* Bennettsville, SC; *m:* Bonnie Faye Dozier; *c:* La Toya, Quianna; *ed:* (BS) Bio, Morris Coll 1970; Towson St Univ, Morgan St Univ, Teachers Coll NY Univ; *cr:* Sci Teacher Fleming Sch 1970-73, Woodbourne Mid Sch 1973-74; Sci/Health Teacher Roland Park Mid Sch 1974-; *ai:* Stu Government & Natl Jr Honor Society Adv; Supvr of Cafeteria; Coord Health Related Projects; Site Facilitator SCE Summer Prgm; Facilitator AIDS Awareness Session for Cntrl Office; Just Say No Club Coord; AFT, Baltimore Teachers Union 1974; Most Worshipful Prince Hall Grand Lodge Lecturer 1988-; United Supreme Cncl Grand Inspector General 1984-; Prince Hall Grand Lodge Bd of Trustees Dev Comm Chm 1988-; Certificate of Appreciation Baltimore City Public Schls Office of Sci & Health; Roland Park Mid Sch Teacher of Yr 1988; Certificate of Honor Baltimore Polytechnic Inst Recommended as Outstanding & Inspirational Teacher of Former Stus; Nom Thanks To Teachers Excl 1990; *home:* 6200 Northwood Dr Baltimore MD 21212

MOORE, REBECCA LENEGAR, Sixth Grade Teacher; *b:* Oakland, CA; *m:* Jeff C.; *c:* Joshua; *ed:* (MSED) Guidance/Counseling, Loyola-Chicago 1985; *cr:* 5th Grade Teacher Francis Campanelli Elem Sch 1978-83; 6th Grade Teacher Edwin Aldrin Elem Sch 1983-; *ai:* Stu Cncl; Rdng Tutor; *office:* Aldrin Elem Sch 617 Boxwood Dr Schaumburg IL 60193

MOORE, REBECCA SUE (HARVEY), 4th Grade Teacher; *b:* Marion, IN; *m:* John Victor; *c:* Paul S., Jeffrey S., Brent A., Mark A.; *ed:* (BS) Elem Ed, Taylor Univ 1967; (MA) Elem Ed, Ball St Univ 1973; *cr:* 1st Grade Teacher Mississinewa Cmmty Sch Corporation 1967-71; 3 & 4 Yr Old Teacher Lakeview Chrstn Pre Sch 1982-83; 4th Grade Teacher Lakeview Chrstn Sch 1983-; *home:* 2560 W 1100 S Fairmount IN 46928

MOORE, RHONDA AIKENS, English Teacher; *b:* Quitman, GA; *m:* Ronnie L.; *ed:* (AA) N FL Jr Coll 1973; (BA) Lib Sci, FL St Univ 1975; (MS) Eng, Nova Univ 1986; Delta Sigma Theta Prof Enhancement Prgm 1988; *cr:* 5th Grade Teacher Madison Mid Sch 1976; Eng Teacher Madison Cty HS 1977-; *ai:* NHS Co-Adv; Yrbk Adv; Madison Cty HS Media Specialist Comm; FL Cncl Teachers of Eng; Eng Dept Madison Cty HS 1986; SSAT Team Winner 1986; Delta Sigma Theta Secy 1982-86, Achievement 1986; Mt Zion AME Church Active Involvement; Natl Cncl of Negro Women 1986-; Madison Cty HS Teacher of Yr 1987; Outstanding Young Woman of Yr 1986, 1988.

MOORE, RHONDA GRAFTON, Science Dept Chair/Teacher; *b:* Honolulu, HI; *m:* Jerry Pat; *c:* Mandolyn, Meredith; *ed:* (BS) Bio, William Carey Coll 1977; Sci Ed; NSF Chem Wkshp; *cr:* Teacher Stringer HS 1977-80, Northeast Jones HS 1980-81, Taylorsville HS 1987-; *ai:* Math & Sci Team; *office:* Taylorsville HS Box 8 Taylorsville MS 39168

MOORE, RITA FAYE, Science Teacher; *b:* Memphis, TN; *ed:* (BSE) Scndry Ed, 1971, (MSE) Curr/Instruction, 1987 Memphis St Univ; *cr:* Sci Teacher Richland Jr HS 1973-80, White Station HS 1980-; *ai:* Jr Engineering Tech Society; After Sch Tutorial Prgm; ACT & SAT Wkshps; Sci Assn of TN, NSTA 1989-; NAACP 1989-; Prof Women Treas 1990; Rotary Teacher Initiative Grant; Rotary Awd for Teacher Excl; Sigma XI Research Societies Outstanding Sci Teacher; *home:* 3245 Crete Memphis TN 38111

MOORE, ROBERT, Health Teacher; *b:* Des Moines, IA; *m:* Frances Paulaine Cleaver; *c:* Margaret Carabine, Catherine Parker, Christine; *ed:* (BA) Industrial Ed, 1956, (MA) Ed, 1960 CA St Univ Long Beach; *cr:* Teacher 1957-60, Cnslr 1960-64 Narbonne HS; Teacher Huntington Beach HS 1964-; *ai:* Drug Intervention & Stu Support Groups; Amateur Radio Club; CTA, CASHE; *office:* Huntington Beach HS 1905 Main St Huntington Beach CA 92648

MOORE, ROBERTA DOSSIE, Prep Specialist; *b:* Abbeville, AL; *m:* John W.; *c:* Marsha T.; *ed:* (AA) Gen Ed, Edward Waters Jr Coll 1957; (BA) Elem Ed/Early Chldhd Ed, Univ of West FL 1975; *cr:* Sub Teacher a D Harris Elem Sch 1959-60; Kndgtn Teacher Redemption Luth Church Sch 1960-64; Owner/Oper 1964-66; Owner/Supv 1966-69 Moores Kndgtn; Teachers Aide/Classroom Teacher Lucille Moore/Hiland Park Elem Sch 1966-84; Primary Spec Hiland Park Elem Sch 1985-; *ai:* Guidance Comm; Staffing Comm; ABCE/NEA 1975-; Natl Phi Delta Kappa Tamias 1987-88; La Reno De Clubo Bridge Club Pres 1986-87; Panastics Gymnastics Bd Mem 1984-85; D.O.E. St Cncl Mem Special Materials; Initial Cert Test Pre-K Writing Team Mem; Inservice Sharing Best Practices Level Kndgtn Consultant; *office:* Hiland Park Elem Sch 2507 Baldwin Rd Panama City FL 32405

MOORE, RONALD LEE, Lang Arts/Jr High Teacher; *b:* Zanesville, OH; *m:* Marjorie L.; *c:* Brian, Jennifer; *ed:* (BA) Eng, OH Univ 1974; Lang Arts; Ed Leadership; Prin Cert; *cr:* 4th/6th Grade Teacher York Elem 1968-71; 6th/8th Grade Teacher Mc Connlsville Elem Sch 1971-; *ai:* Building Coord; Textbook Comm; Newspaper & Safety Patrol Adv; Morgan Local Ed Assn; Morgan Local Ed Assn Building Rep 1984-85; Jennings Scholar; Good Apple Awd; *home:* 9760 N Pisqah Ridge Rd NW Mc Connelsville OH 43756

MOORE, RONALD LEWIS, Social Studies Teacher; *b:* Chattaroy, WV; *m:* Linda Allen; *c:* Melissa, Shannon, Kristen; *ed:* (BA) Soc Stud, Morehead St Univ 1986; *cr:* Soc Stud Teacher Paul G Blazer HS 1986-; *ai:* Head Coach Frosh Ftbl & Weightlifting; Young Historians Spon; Jr Class Co-Spon; KY Ed Assn; *home:* 1901 High St Ashland KY 41101

MOORE, RONNIE MITCHELL, Assistant Principal; *b:* Falkville, AL; *m:* Sharon Rose Tapscott; *c:* Melanie, Laura, Joshua; *ed:* (BA) Sociology/His/Ed, Univ of AL Huntsville 1973; (MA) Educl Leadership, Univ of AL Birmingham 1979; Army Natl Guards & Army Reserves Mem; *cr:* Media Aide Morgan Cty Bd of Ed 1973-74; 4th/5th Grade Teacher Eva Jr HS 1975-79; 6th Grade Teacher Sparkman Elem Sch 1979-87; Asst Prin Cotaco Jr HS 1987-; *ai:* Sch Building Staff Support Team Admin; Morgan Cty Ed Assn Bd of Dir 1977-86; First Meth Church (Admin Bd

1987-88, Health Chm 1990, Welfare Chm 1990); *home:* 1902 Bluff St Hartselle AL 35640

MOORE, SHEILA GAIL, English Teacher; *b:* Tullahoma, TN; *ed:* (BS) Elem Ed, 1976, (MED) Elem Ed, 1985 Mid TN St Univ; *cr:* 2nd/4th/6th Grade Teacher 1976-88, 7th/8th Grade Eng Teacher 1988- Stevenson Mid Sch; *ai:* Yrbk Spon & Ed 1984-; Drug Awareness Coord Stevenson Mid Sch 1989; Kappa Delta Pi; Amer Assn of Univ Women; Stevenson Elem PTO Exec Bd 1985-88; *home:* 1300 Cedar Ln Apt I-7 Tullahoma TN 37388

MOORE, SHERIDA BURGMEIER, English Teacher; *b:* Seymour, IN; *m:* Tom; *c:* Terri, Tricia, Tommy, Trent, Trevor; *cr:* Eng Teacher Morehead Univ 1960-61, Jennings Cty HS 1964-; Composition Instr Purdue Univ 1982-; *ai:* Jr, Sr, Soph Spon; NHS; Delta Kappa Gamma, IN Cncl Teachers of Eng, IN St Teachers Assn; St Vincent De Paul 1985-; Morehead Univ Grad Asst; De Pauw Amer Stud Fellowship.

MOORE, STACEY LEE, Spanish/German Teacher; *b:* Vero Beach, FL; *ed:* (BA) Span/Ger, GA Southern Coll 1986; Working Toward MEd in Span, GA Southern Coll; *cr:* Span/Ger Teacher Statesboro HS 1986-; *ai:* Intnl Club Adv; Foreign Lang Assn of GA, Prof Assn of GA Educators 1986-; GA Assn of Educators 1989-; Crisis Pregnancy Center Bd of Dirs 1989-; Adoptive Parents Assn; Foreign Lang Oratorical Competition; *office:* Statesboro HS 10 Lester Rd Statesboro GA 30458

MOORE, STEPHEN WAYNE, Science Teacher; *b:* Crawfordsville, IN; *m:* Diane Marshall; *c:* Scott, Jill; *ed:* (BS) Life Sci, 1966, (MS) Life Sci, 1969 IN St Univ; *cr:* 7th/8th Grade Sci Teacher Otter Creek Jr HS 1966-68; Chem/Phys Sci Teacher Garfield HS 1968-71; Chem/Zoology Teacher Terre Haute North HS 1971-; *ai:* Var Bsbl Coach; SADD, Fellowship of Chrstn Athletes, Blood Drive, Academic Decathlon Team Spon; Prof Based Accreditation Comm; IN Acad of Sci; Terre Haute Authority VP 1987-; Vigo Cty Sheriff Reserve 1983-; Natl Sci Fair Finalists & NSF 1st Place Winner Spon; *home:* 500 Cannon Ct B Terre Haute IN 47803

MOORE, THOMAS EDWARD, Sixth Grade Teacher; *b:* Wilkes Barre, PA; *m:* Mary T. Mc Donagh; *c:* Michael T., Mary E.; *ed:* (BA) Ec, Kings Coll 1964; Working Towards Masters Equivalency St Univ of NY & Various PA Colls; *cr:* 5th Grade Teacher St Patricks Elem Sch 1964-65; 4th Grade Teacher Chenango Forks Sch Dist 1965-68; 6th Grade Teacher Wilkes-Barre Area Sch Dist 1968-; *ai:* Wilkes Barre Area Ed Assn Building Rep 1968-; PA St Ed Assn, NEA 1968-; Donegal Society, Friendly Sons of St Patrick, Ancient Order of Hiberians; *home:* 158 Willow St Wilkes-Barre PA 18702

MOORE, THOMAS EDWARD, III, Chemistry Teacher; *b:* Auburn, NY; *m:* Carrollee Valentine; *c:* Alexander T., Heather L., Matthew S.; *ed:* (BA) Bio/Chem, San Jose St Univ 1965; *cr:* Sci Teacher Foothill Intermediate Sch 1969-84; Chem Teacher San Ramon Valley HS 1984-; *ai:* Jr Var Girls Bsktbl, Asst Girls Var Bsktbl, Frosh Bsbl Coach; Mt Diablo Ed Assn Treas 1974-75; Mustang Soccer League Fields Supvr 1983; Danville Little League Big League VP 1990; *office:* San Ramon Valley HS 140 Love Ln Danville CA 94526

MOORE, THOMAS FREEMAN, On-Campus Supervisor; *b:* Ft Lauderdale, FL; *c:* Teri L. Moore Holmstrom, David F.; *ed:* (BSED) Health/Phys Ed, Cntrl St Coll 1966; (MED) Scndry Sch Admin, Cntrl St Univ 1987; *cr:* Teacher/Coach Kerr Jr HS 1966-83, Del City HS 1984; Teacher Kerr Jr HS 1985-; *ai:* Former Wrestling & Track Coach; OK Jr HS Wrestling Coach of Yr 1975; OK Wrestling Ofcl of Yr 1985; Natl Sci Fnd Earth Sci Grant OK St Univ 1969-70; *office:* Kerr Jr HS SE 22nd & Linda Ln Del City OK 73115

MOORE, TRACEY LA FEVERS, Mathematics Teacher; *b:* Goldsboro, NC; *m:* Harry Ballard III; *ed:* (BA) Scndry Math Ed, Univ NC Chapel Hill 1986; *cr:* Math Teacher Sanderson HS 1986-; *ai:* Southern Assn Math Chairperson; Faculty Cncl; Fellowship of Chrstn Athletes Spon 1986; Fellowship of Chrstn Athletes Coach of Yr 1989; *home:* 2724 Anderson Dr Raleigh NC 27608

MOORE, VICKIE LORENE (OWEN), English/French Teacher; *b:* Marshall, TX; *m:* Mike; *c:* Amanda M.; *ed:* (BSED) Eng/Fr, TX Chrstn Univ 1982; Grad Work Univ of TX Arlington; *cr:* Eng/Fr/Newspaper Teacher Hutcheson Jr HS 1982-85; Eng/Fr Teacher Sam Houston HS 1985-; *ai:* Fr Club; AATF 1985-; TX St Teachers Assn; Tarrant Cty Jr Coll Fr Teachers Oral Proficiency Wkshps Grants 1987-88; *office:* Sam Houston H S 2000 Sam Houston Dr Arlington TX 76014

MOORE, YVONNE, Third Grade Teacher; *b:* Smithdale, MS; *c:* Edwin D.; *ed:* Elem Ed, Prentiss Jr Coll 1961; (BS) Elem Ed, Alcorn St Univ 1963; Early Chldhd Ed, Bank Street Coll; Early Chldhd & Elem Ed, Univ of S MS; *cr:* Elem Teacher Amite Cty Sch Dist 1963-66; Dir of Ed SW MS Child Dev Cncl/Project Head Start 1967-73; Elem Teacher Amite Cty Sch Dist 1974-; *ai:* MS Ed Assn, NEA; PTA Secy 1976-85; Ford Fnd Leadership Dev Prgm 1971-72; *home:* Rt 1 Box 203 Smithdale MS 39664

MOORE, YVONNE MATHEWS, Kindergarten Teacher; *b:* Bartow, FL; *c:* Pamela; *ed:* (AA) Elem Ed, Polk Comm Coll 1970; (BA) Elem Ed, 1972, (MA) Elem Ed, 1976 Univ of S FL; Early Chldhd; Culyer Rdng Prgm; Process Writing; *cr:* Kndgtn Teacher Eagle Lake Elem 1972-; *ai:* Polk Cty 4-H Advisory Cncl, Yth Adv, Leader; PEA, NEA; Grand Union Pallbearers; Good Hope Missionary Baptist Church Secy; Polk Cty Kndgtn Grant 1978; *office:* Eagle Lake Elem Sch 400 Crystal Beach Rd Eagle Lake FL 33839

MOOREHEAD, LAWRENCE EDWARD, JR., 7th Grade Math/English Teacher; *b:* Fayetteville, TN; *m:* Tauna Warren; *c:* Hugh Douglas, Wendy R.; *ed:* (BA) Elem Ed, Athens St 1978; *cr:* Teacher Evangle Sch 1972-77, Monrovia Mid Sch 1978-; *ai:* Coach Girls Vlybl/Bsktbl/Sftbl Monrovia Sch; Spon Madison Cty 4H Club; NEA 1978-; NCTM 1989-; AL Cncl of Teachers of Math 1989-; Madison Cty Cncl of Teachers of Math 1989-; PTA VP 1978-; Natl Young Speakers Assn 1972-; Huntsville JCs 1970-71; *home:* 2518 Birchfield St Huntsville AL 35810

MOOREHEAD, STANLEY LEON, Fifth Grade Teacher; *b:* Benton, MS; *ed:* (BSEd) Amer His, 1973, (MSEd) Elem Ed, 1975, (EdS) Elem Ed, 1988 Jackson St Univ; MS/Jackson St Univ; *cr:* Intern Isable Elem Sch 1973-75; Teacher Lester Elem Sch 1975-; Summer Sch Teacher John Hopkins Elem Sch 1984-89; Asst Instr Jackson St Univ 1988; *ai:* Grade Chm; Team Leader; Local Advisory Comm; Sch Improvement Comm; PTA Exec Secy; Safety Comm; Test Coord; Comm on Soc Disease in Public Schls; JAE/NEA Mem 1975-; Exec Trng Trainee 1987, Cert 1987; Good Apple Awd Peer 1987-89, Cert 1988; Nate 19758 Membership 1975-; Cmmty Inst Chm 1978-79, Plaque & Cert 1979; Ole Miss Nutrition Public Schls 1980-81, Cert 1980; NAACP Schlsp/Fellowship Jackson St Univ; Fellowships Through Jackson Public Schls; *office:* Lester Elem Sch 2350 Oakhurst Dr Jackson MS 39204

MOORER, LISA WILLIS, Senior English Teacher; *b:* Baton Rouge, LA; *m:* William B. Jr.; *c:* William L.; *ed:* (BS) Eng/Scndry Ed, Univ of S MS 1986; Working on Masters Univ of S MS 1990; *cr:* Jr Eng Teacher 1988-89, Sr Eng Teacher 1989- Moss Point HS; *ai:* Sr Class Spon; Teacher Intervention Prgm, Teacher Stu Relations Awds Comm; Phi Kappa Phi; Pascagoula Civic League (Pres, VP, Fund Raising Chm); Pascagoula-Moss Point Jr Auxiliary (VP, Public Relations Chairperson, Projects Chm); Lagniape Schlsp Recepient; Grad with Highest Honors from Univ S MS; *office:* Moss Point HS Weems St Moss Point MS 39563

MORALES, NANCY LEE, Home Ec Teacher; *b:* San Francisco, CA; *m:* Frank Jr.; *ed:* (BS) Home Ec, Univ of AZ 1972; *cr:* Home Ec Sunnyside Jr HS 1972-73; Home Ec Wade Carpenter Mid Sch 1973-; *ai:* Stud Cncl Spon; Natl Honor Society Spon; North Central Outcomes Accreditatiion-Pilot Project Chairperson; Phi Kappa Phi 1972-; Omicron NU 1972-; Pi Lamba Theta 1972-; Nogales Dist 1 Teacher of Yr 1987-88; Democratic Precinct Comm Chm 1986-; Pima Coll Adv Comm 1986-; *home:* 1556 N Royal Rd Nogales AZ 85621

MORAN, BARBARA CAROL, First Grade Teacher; *b:* Huntington, WV; *m:* Daniel; *c:* Jim; *ed:* (BA) Kndgtn/Primary, Marshall Univ 1956; *cr:* 1st/3rd Grade Teacher Pea Ridge Elem 1959-62; 1st Grade Teacher Louis J Morris Elem 1966-; *ai:* NEA 1959-; AL Ed Assn, Huntsville Ed Assn 1966-; Sherwood Park Civic Assn, Madison Cty Bar Auxiliary 1966-; Alzheimers Support Group Assn 1988-; *home:* 502 Delaney Rd Huntsville AL 35806

MORAN, FRANCES RUSSELL, 4th Grade Teacher; *b:* Edgemont, SD; *m:* Robert J.; *c:* Thomas J., Mary A. Allison; *ed:* (BS) Elem Ed, Clarion Univ 1970; Univ of Denver 1944-46; *cr:* Ballet Mistress St Stephen Sch 1964-70; 4th Grade Teacher Lincoln Elem 1970-; *ai:* NEA 1970-; PSEA 1970-; OCEA 70-; Outstanding Elem Teachers of Amer 1975; *home:* 316 Innis St Oil City PA 16301

MORAN, JAMES PATRICK, Bio & Marine Ecology Teacher; *b:* Yonkers, NY; *m:* Judith Anne Gostic; *c:* Alison; *ed:* (BA) Bio/General Sci, Iona Coll 1960; (MA) Sci Ed, NY Univ 1964; Fundamentals Admin I & II, NY Univ; Fnds of Astronomy in Physics, Hunter Coll; Tutorial Rdngs SUNY Stony Brook; Introduction to Cmptrs Bd of Cooperative Ed; Marine Ecology Suffolk Environmental Bio & Suffolk Cty Organization Promotion of Ed; *cr:* Sci Teacher Rice HS 1960-61, Isaac E Young Jr HS 1961-66, Elwood Jr HS 1966-86; Scuba Instr SUNY Stony Brook 1974; Sci Teacher Elwood Mid Sch & John Glenn HS 1986-; *ai:* NYS United Teachers 1966-; Elwood Teachers Alliance 1968-; NABT 1990; Amer Red Cross; Prof Assn of Diving Instrs Certified Instr 1975; Natl Assn of Underwater Instrs Certified Instr 1969; Natl Assn of Skin Diving Schls Open Water Instr 1971; Scuba Schls Intnl Advance Open Water Instr 1982; NY St Dept Environmental Conservation (Hunter Trng Prgm Certified Bow Hunting Instr 1982, Asst License Issuing Officer 1979); Natl Sci Fnd Grant; Published Article Intnl Divers Guide; Owner & Pres North Shore Sch of Skin Diving 1969-81; Discovered Living Seven-Armed Starfish While Scuba Diving; Article Published Intnl Divers Guide; 3rd Place Underwater Photography Winner; Produced & Directed Underwater Symposium & Film Festival 1974, 1975; Published Photographs Newsday; Author Marine Ecology, Human Psych, Bio/Earth Sci/Bio Curr; *office:* John H Glenn HS 478 Elwood Rd East Northport NY 11731

MORAN, MARY, Mathematics Department Chair; *b:* Ryton, England; *m:* Mark Francis; *c:* Mark F.; *ed:* (BS) Math/Music, Univ Of Southampton 1962; (FIL) Italian, London 1965; (MS) Math, Lehigh Univ 1969; Grad Work W IL Univ, Univ of Scranton, IUP, ESU, Marywood, Lafayette; Supvrs Cert, Lehigh Univ; *cr:* Teacher Gilmoss Liverpool England 1962-64, St Josephs Upminster England 1964-65, Pocono Cntrl Cath 1965-67, Pleasant Valley HS 1967-; *ai:* PA Math League AHSME Coord; NCTM 1967-; PCTM, PCSM Membership Chairperson 1970-; PSEA Retirement Comm Chairperson 1967-; NEA, PVEA 1967-; PDK 1975-; Stans for K-12 Sch Math Prgms in PA & NCTM Stans Dissemination Team Mem; *office:* Pleasant Valley HS Rt 209 Brodheadsville PA 18322

MORAN, MELODY JOY, English/Speech Teacher; *b:* Mcconnellsburg, PA; *m:* Kevin B.; *ed:* (BS) Speech Ed, 1986, (MS) Scndry Ed, 1987 Pensacola Chrstn Coll; *cr:* Speech Instr Pensacola Chrstn Coll 1986-88; Speech/Eng Instr New Castle Baptist Acad 1988-; *ai:* Drama & Girls Sftbl Coach; *office:* New Castle Baptist Acad 901 E Basin Rd New Castle DE 19720

MORAN, SHERYL LEE, Drafting Instructor; *b:* Richmond, NY; *m:* Cary M.; *ed:* (AA) Drafting/Design, Jefferson Davis 1983; (BA) Industrial/Voc Ed, Univ S MS 1988; *cr:* Drafting Technician Civil Engineering Assoc 1983-85; Drafting Instr Harrison Cty Voc Tech 1985-; *ai:* Voc Industrial Clubs of America 1985-; Var Chrldng Spon 1986-; *office:* Harrison Cty Voc Tech 15600 School Rd Gulfport MS 39503

MORAVEK, GEORGE MICHAEL, Music/Strings/Vocal Teacher; *b:* Red Cloud, NE; *ed:* (BME) Vocal Music, NE Wesleyan 1968; Westminister Choir Coll, Hofstra Univ, Post Univ; *cr:* Music/Vocal Instr Ruskin Public Schls 1968-69; Vocal/Music Teacher Imperial Public Schls 1969-70, Patchogue Public Schls 1970-72, Riverhead Public Schls 1972-; *ai:* HS Drama Dir; Amer Guild Organist, SCMEA, MENC Mem 1980-; St Marks Episcopal Church Organist & Dir; Teacher of Yr Riverhead Schls; Riverhead Faculty Theatre Founder & Dir; *office:* Riverhead Sch Dist 600 Harrison Ave Riverhead NY 11901

MORDEN, JOETTE MARIE, Life Management Teacher/Chair; *b:* Wyandotte, MI; *m:* William E. Jr.; *c:* Joseph, Phillip; *ed:* (BS) Home Ec/Bus, W MI Univ 1974; (MS) Consumer Affairs, E MI Univ 1988; *cr:* Fashion Mgr Montgomery Wards 1974-77; Office Mgr Island Assocs Incorporated 1977-82; Teacher Harrison HS 1983-; *ai:* Aids Ed Facilitator; Stu Assistance Team Mem; AHEA, MEA, FEA, NEA, MOEA, MHEE 1983-; *office:* Harrison HS 29995 W 12 Mile Rd Farmington Hills MI 48018

MORE, JAMES E., Counselor; *b:* Cut Bank, MT; *m:* Diane F.; *c:* Mandy, Jason; *ed:* (BA) Eng, MT St 1974; (ME) Guidance & Counseling, N MT Coll 1985; *cr:* Eng Instr Browning Jr HS 1975-78, Browning HS 1978-79; K-12th Grade Guidance Cnslr Troy Public Schls 1979-; *ai:* Girls Bsktbl & Head Golf Coach; Stu Cncl Adv; Curr Comm; MACD Cnslr 1987-; NEA, MEA 1979-; TEA Pres 1984; Troy Youth Recreation Assn (Secy, Treas) 1988-; Troy Stu Loan Fund 1983-; Bd of Dirs Flathead Valley CC Lincoln Cty Campus 1988-; St Cert Review Bd 1977; Nominee Coach of Yr 1987; *office:* Troy HS Drawer O Troy MT 59935

MOREAU, BARBARA OBRIG, Third Grade Teacher; *b:* Ridgewood, NJ; *m:* William; *c:* Jim Hennig, Cheryl Hennig; *cr:* Teacher Travell Elem 1956-57, Pine Beach 1957-60, Selzer Sch 1960-65, Walnut Street Elem Sch 1965-; *ai:* St, Curr, Dist Coord; Delta Kappa Gamma Recording Secy 1984-; Ocean Cty Teachers Assn Delegate 1989-; Young Astronauts St Coord 1984, Leader of Yr 1989, US Delegate Japan 1989; Air Force Assn 1987-, Natl Medal of Merit 1989; Aerospace Ed Assn 1987-, Aerospace Ed Awd 1989; Ocean Cty Historical Society Dir Jr Historial Society 1980-, James Murray Awd 1986; BPO Elks 2 Ladies Auxiliary Pres; Toms River Teacher of Yr 1989; *office:* Walnut Street Elem Sch Walnut St Toms River NJ 08753

MOREFIELD, BARBARA RUTH (HARMON), 6th Grade Teacher; *b:* Columbia, MO; *m:* Paul D.; *c:* Eric, Brian, Sarah; *ed:* (AA) Psych, 1966, (BA) Psych/Sociology, 1968 Southwest Baptist Coll; (ME) Elem Curr, Univ of MO Columbia 1988; George Warren Brown Sch of Soc Work WA Univ; *cr:* Caseworker Dallas Cty Welfare Office 1968-69; Substitute Teacher Meramec Valley Schls R-III 1969-72; Secy Clow Corporation 1974-75; Insurance Sales Secy Fidelity Union Life Ins Co 1972-77; 6th Grade Teacher Southern Boone Cty Schls RI 1980-; *ai:* VP Cmmty Teachers Assn; Sci Comm; NSTA 1987-; Ashland Baptist Church (Sunday Sch Dir 1989- Church Recorder 1980-85); Grants from Union Elec for Classroom Sci Projects; *office:* Southern Boone County R-1 Sch P O Box 168 Ashland MO 65010

MOREHEAD, JEANNETTE EILEEN, 6th Grade Teacher; *b:* Akron, OH; *ed:* (BS) Elem Ed, Univ of Akron 1972; Cmmty Intervention-Drug Prevention & Abuse; *cr:* 2nd Grade Teacher 1973-77, 4th Grade Teacher 1977-79, 5th Grade Teacher 1979-89, 6th Grade Teacher 1989- Nordonia Hills Bd of Ed; *ai:* PTA Teacher Rep 1985-88 Lee Eaton Teacher of Yr 1987; OH Mid Sch Assn 1989-; *office:* Nordonia Hills Mid Sch 73 Leonard Ave Northfield OH 44067

MOREL, DIANE (CAPONE), Social Studies Teacher; *b:* Medford, MA; *m:* Raymond V.; *c:* Raymond, Michael; *ed:* (BA) His/Scndry Ed, St Francis Coll 1972; (MA) His, Providence Coll 1989; *cr:* Jr HS Soc Stud Teacher St Rocco Sch 1983-85; HS Soc Stud Teacher St Mary Acad Bayview 1985-; *ai:* Model Legislature & In-Site RI Adv; RI Soc Stud Assn Exec Bd Mem 1988-; RI St Geography Bee Steering Comm 1989-; *office:* Saint Mary Acad Bayview 3070 Pawtucket Ave East Providence RI 02915

MOREL, DONNA WAHL, Jr High School Teacher; *b:* Sterling, IL; *m:* Richard; *c:* Jennifer Buyens, Marsha Gapinski, Rhonda Morel; *ed:* (BS) Lang Art, N IL Univ 1975; *cr:* Teacher Peru Cath Sch 1967-; *office:* Peru Cath Sch 1305 6th St Peru IL 61354

MOREL, PHILIP E., Fourth Grade Teacher; *b:* Hays, KS; *m:* Judi Ann Jensen; *c:* Derek, Mica; *ed:* (BS) Elem Ed, Ft Hays St Univ 1978; *cr:* 5th Grade Teacher 1978-86, 4th Grade Teacher 1987- Eisenhower Elem Sch; *ai:* 5th/6th Girls Bsktbl & Track Coach; Sch Dist Math & Sci Curr Comm; *office:* Eisenhower Elem Sch Eisenhower Dr Norton KS 67654

MORELAND, WILLIAM THOMAS, JR., Mathematics Teacher; *b:* Abington, PA; *m:* Debra Muhl; *c:* Colsey, Allie, William III; *ed:* (BS) Math, Elizabethtown Coll 1968; (MS) Math, Univ of DE 1970; *cr:* Math Teacher Abington HS 1970-72, Lower Cape May Regional 1972-73, Mainland Regional 1973-79, Ocean City HS 1 79-; *ai:* Math Club Adv; Math Curr Comm; Boys Cross Cntry, Winter Track, Asst Boys Track Coach; NJ Assn of Math Teachers 1979-; NJEA, NEA 1973-; Ocean City Cmmty Center (Bd of Dir, VP, Pres) 1980-86; Runaway Athletic Club (Pres 1980-86, VP 1989-); Teaching Assistanship Univ DE; *home:* 9 Braden Dr Marmora NJ 08223

MORELLI, ALBERT, Social Studies Teacher; *b:* Chicago, IL; *ed:* (AA) Soc Stud, Wright Jr Coll 1958; (BPH) Soc Stud, Northwestern Univ 1964; (MA) Admin, Concordia Coll 1978; *cr:* Teacher Washington Sch 1966-72, Lincoln Sch 1972-; *ai:* IEA 1966-67; IFT (Elected Pres 1968-69) 1967-.

MORENO, LESLIE ANN (HARVEY), 7th/8th Grade Health Teacher; *b:* Eureka, CA; *m:* Martin; *c:* Jeffrey, Jeanette, Tracy; *ed:* (BA) Phys Ed, Humboldt St Univ 1971; *cr:* 6th-8th Grade Sci/Phys Ed Teacher French Camp Elem 1974-76; 7th/8th Grade Math Lab Teacher 1980-82, 7th/8th Grade Health Teacher 1984-El Portal Mid Sch; *ai:* Drug & Alcohol, Health Comm; CTA 1984-, Young Educator 1985; Amer Red Cross CPR Instr; *office:* El Portal Mid Sch 805 1st St Escalon CA 95320

MORENO, LYDIA MARTINEZ, Fifth Grade Teacher; *b:* Santa Fe, NM; *m:* James; *c:* James C., Phillip R.; *ed:* (BA) Elem Ed, Univ of NM 1980; Effective Teacher Trng, Collaborative Consultation Trng; *cr:* 2nd Grade Teacher 1980-82, 5th Grade Teacher 1982-83, 3rd/4th Grade Combination Teacher 1983-84; 4th/5th Grade Combination Teacher 1984-85, 5th Grade Teacher Albuquerque Public Schls 1985-; *ai:* Spelling Bee Spon; Support Staff Mem; 5th Chairperson; Delta Kappa Gamma Mem 1986-88; *office:* Bel-Air Elem Sch 4725 Candalaria NE Albuquerque NM 87110

MORETZ, VIRGINIA BRIDGES, 8th Grade Science Teacher; *b:* Forest City, NC; *m:* Elmo Earl; *c:* Anne, Patricia Mc Carty, Sabena; *ed:* (BA) Bio, Univ of NC Greensboro 1952; (MS) Elem Ed, E KY Univ 1974; *cr:* 8th Grade Sci Teacher NC 1952-58; Bio Teacher Dade Cty 1958-61; Adult Ed Teacher Comprehensive Employ & Trng 1974-81; 3rd/4th Grade Teacher St Marks Sch 1981-83; 8th Grade Sci Teacher Clark Moores Sch 1983-; *ai:* NSTA 1983-; KY Sci Teachers Assn 1983-; GSA (Troop Leader, Trainer) 1963-84, Thanks Badge 1980; Madison Cty Conservation Awd for Teachers 1988; *office:* Clark Moores Mid Sch 1143 Berea Rd Richmond KY 40475

MOREY, NORITA A. (MORFORD), 2nd Grade Teacher; *b:* Big Rapids, MI; *m:* Richard G.; *c:* Jeffery R., Vicky L. Dewe; *ed:* (BS) Elem Ed, 1972, (MA) Chldhd Ed, 1976 Central MI Univ; *cr:* Teacher Reed Sch 1956-57; 2nd Grade Teacher Stanwood Elem 1972-; *ai:* Chm-Patriotic Week; Coord Sci Van; MEA (Negotiator 1977/1983 Building Rep 1980 Cncl Multi Sch 1978-80 & 1988); *home:* 13694 Seneca Big Rapids MI 49307

MORGAN, BARBARA KORNER, 5th Grade Science Teacher; *b:* Cincinnati, OH; *M:* James R.; *c:* Jessie L., Jason T.; *ed:* (BS) Elem Ed, Univ of Cinti 1974; (MA) Elem Ed, Morehead St Univ 1980; *cr:* K/4th/5th Grade Teacher Remedial Rdng 1974-82, Gifted Teacher/Coord 1982-86 Germantown Elem Sch; 5th Grade Sci Teacher Bracken Cty Mid Sch 1990; *ai:* Spon Annual Bracken Cty Sci Fair; *home:* Rt 3 Box 338 Brooksville KY 41004

MORGAN, BETTY DELAMARTER, 4th Grade Teacher; *b:* Pontiac, MI; *m:* Thomas David; *c:* Richard, Victoria Morgan Mc Ferran, Valarie M. Scott, Douglas; *ed:* (BS) Sociology/Ed/Psych, Greenville Coll 1960; (MS) Elem Ed, S IL Univ Edwardsville 1977; Working Towards Specialist Degree Counseling, S IL Univ Edwardsville 1968; *cr:* 6th Grade Teacher Kansas Public Schls 1960-61; 7th/8th Grade Music/Eng Teacher Harter Sch 1961; Part-Time Teacher of Handicapped & Emotionally Disturbed Stu Canton Public Schls; K-8th Grade Music Teacher 1968-74, 4th Grade Teacher 1974-79, 3rd Grade Teacher 1979-84 Hillsboro Cmmty Dist; *ai:* NEA; AFT Life Mem; F M Church Pastors Cabinet Mem; Greenville Coll (Alumni Bd, Ed Advisory Cncl Elem Teacher); Spring Arbor Coll Bd of Trustees; *home:* 322 E Main St Greenville IL 62246

MORGAN, BETTY JEAN WILIAMS, Mathematics Teacher; *b:* Aiken, SC; *m:* Charles B.; *c:* Blaine L., Deadra C.; *ed:* (BS) Math, Allen Univ 1966; (MED) Ed/Math, Univ of SC 1980; NSF Cmptr Sci 1986, Math 1985, Earth Sci 1971; *cr:* Teacher A L Corbett 1966-71, Paul Knox 1971-86; Researcher Natl Sci Center 1989; Teacher Aiken HS 1986-; *ai:* Jack & Jill of America Treas; SC Cncl Teacher of Math VP 1985-87; NCTM 1966-; Alpha Kappa, Alpha Chaplain 1986-88; Teacher Incentive Awd 1985-89; Teacher of Yr Paul Knox Mid Sch 1985-86; Reviewer Charles E Merrill Algebra I 1989; Speaker SCCTM Fall Conference; *office:* Aiken HS 211 Rutland Dr Aiken SC 29801

MORGAN, BILLIE SUE MOORE, Kindergarten Teacher; *b:* Ridgely, TN; *c:* Paula Sue, Jordan; *ed:* (BA) Eng & Psych, Union Univ 1960; Psych & Ed; *cr:* K-1st Grade Teacher Lara Kendall Sch 1960-; *ai:* Private Music Teacher; Pianist 1st Baptist Church Abundant Life Fellowship; Abundant Life Advisory Bd; LCEA; Delta Kappa Gamma 1982-84; TEA; NEA; Ridely Womans Club Pres 1968-72; *home:* 404 Poplar St Ridgely TN 38080

MORGAN, BONNIE LEE, Counselor; *b:* Manchester, NH; *m:* James F.; *c:* Christopher, Brendan; *ed:* (BE) Teaching Scndry Eng, Plymouth St 1964; (ME) Sch Counseling, Rioien 1978; *cr:* Eng Teacher Punkerton Acad 1968-69, Cntrl HS 1971-72; Admin/Adult Ed Cnslr/Dir Ed Cntrl HS 1981-; *ai:* NH Cnslr Assn; Amer Legion Post 79 Booster Club; PAC Organization; Cntrl HS Booster Club; *office:* Cntrl HS 207 Lowell St Manchester NH 03104

MORGAN, CLEVE, Social Science Dept Chair; *b:* Malad, ID; *m:* Kay Tovey; *c:* Jo-Ellen, Kirk; *ed:* (BS) Phys Ed/Health/Rec, Ricks Coll 1955; (MPE) Phys Ed, ID St 1967; Univ of ID, BYU, UT St; *cr:* Teacher/Coach Marsh Valley HS 1955-67, Snow Coll 1967-72, Soda Springs HS 1972-; *ai:* Athletic Dir; Head Ftbl & Wrestling Coach; ID Educators Assn, Soda Springs Educators Assn Local Pres 1965-80; Rotary 1971-72; Caribou Historical Society 1980-; His Summer Grants; *office:* Soda Springs HS 3rd E 1st N Soda Springs ID 83276

MORGAN, DEBRA BURROUGHS, Second Grade Teacher; *b:* Bessemer, AL; *m:* Stephen Bennett; *c:* Stephanie, Ben; *ed:* (BA) Elem Ed, 1974, (MA) Elem Ed, 1982 Univ of AL Birmingham; *cr:* 1st Grade Teacher Katherwood Chrstn Sch 1974-75, Greenwood Elem 1975-79; 2nd/3rd/8th Grades Teacher Greenwood Elem 1983-; *ai:* Amer Red Cross Bd of Dir; Natl Kidney Fnd Mem; Bessemer City Schls Teacher of Yr 1987-88; Spine Rehabilitation; Fed Grant to Write Curr to Prevent Spinal Cord Injury; *home:* 1319 7th St Pleasant Grove AL 35127

MORGAN, DOROTHY MARIE (BROZ), Government & Economics Teacher; *b:* Bellville, TX; *m:* Emmett Colvin Jr.; *c:* Kevin, Christy, Lori, Jason; *ed:* (BS) Poly Sci/Government/His/Ec/Eng, SW TX St Univ 1968; *cr:* Poly Sci Teacher Brenham Ind Sch Dist 1968-; *ai:* Chrldr & NHS Spon; TSTA VP 1974; BCTA VP 1978; City of Brenham (Mayor 1982-, Dir Local Bds, St & Local Organizations); Outstanding Young Women Awds; Outstanding Southern Women Awd; *home:* 808 Geney Brenham TX 77833

MORGAN, ELAINE KING, Title I Reading & Math Teacher; *b:* Blakely, GA; *m:* Harvey Clay; *c:* Terry, Tanya; *ed:* (BS) Elem Ed, Ft Valley St 1959; Lib Sci, Albany St 1963; Elem, Columbus Coll 1973; Rdng Courses & Educl Psych; *cr:* 1st Grade Teacher 1959, Teacher/Librarian 1964 Bluffton Elem Sch; Kndgtn Teacher 1972, Title I Teacher 1989- Clay Elem Sch; *ai:* GAE; Eastern Star Worthy Matron 1964-66; Church Youth Dept Dir 1990; *home:* Rt 1 Box 406 Fort Gaines GA 31751

MORGAN, GAY DAVIS, English Teacher; *b:* Laurel, MS; *m:* Ben C.; *c:* David, Kathy Daniels, Angela; *ed:* (BS) Scndry Eng, 1977, (MED) Scndry Eng/Admin 1981 Univ of S MS; *cr:* Eng Teacher Jones Jr HS 1977-; *ai:* Sch Newspaper Spon; MTAI Evaluator; 5 Yr Evaluation Comm; MS Cncl Teachers of Eng; Delta Kappa Gamma Secy 1986-88; Gideons Auxiliary (Pres 1973-76, Chaplain 1980-83, 1987-89, St Coord 1980-83); Phil Hardin Fnd Grant 1985; MS Dower Fnd Grant 1989; Jones Jr HS Teacher of Yr 1988-89; *office:* Jones Jr HS 1125 N 5th Ave Laurel MS 39440

MORGAN, JUDY A., English Teacher; *b:* Snyder, TX; *m:* Sterling; *ed:* (BA) Eng - Summa Cum Laude, Sul Ross St Univ 1973; Advanced In-Service Trng/Gifted Talented Conference; *cr:* Eng Teacher John Glenn Jr HS; Rdng Teacher Quail Valley Jr HS; Eng Teacher Alamo Jr HS & Greenwood Jr HS; *ai:* 7th Grade Speech Coach; TX St Teachers Assn Secy 1976-77; Alpha Chi, Sigma Tau Delta 1971-73; Church Lay Leader; *office:* John Glenn Jr HS 2201 University San Angelo TX 76904

MORGAN, KATHERINE WILLIAMS, 4th Grade Teacher/Chair; *b:* Whitesboro, TX; *m:* Weldon Clement; *c:* John W.; *ed:* Assoc Bus, E OK Coll 1959; (BS) Bus Ed, 1963, (MS) Elem Ed, 1967 NE OK Univ; *cr:* Teacher Ft Wingate Elem 1960-62, Huslia AK 1962-63, Gallup Jr HS 1963-70, Richardson Ind Sch 1970-; *ai:* Soc & Site Based Management Comm; Grade Level Chairperson; Assn of TX Prof Educators 1975-; Richardson Ed Assn 1970-; Intnl Rdng Assn 1980-; N TX IRA 1980-; Delta Kappa Gamma 1981-; Alpha Delta Kappa 1963-; Intnl Rdng Assn 1985-; Nom Ross Perot Teacher Awd 1987; TX Career Ladder I, II, III 1985-; *office:* Richardson Heights Elem Sch 101 N Floyd Rd Richardson TX 75080

MORGAN, KIMBERLY BROWN, Art & Photography Teacher; *b:* Lynwood, CA; *m:* Robert Arthur; *ed:* (BA) Art Studio/Art His, Univ of CA 1971; Various Continued Arts Ed; Brooks Inst of Photography; *cr:* Art/Photography Teacher Placer HS 1972-82; Stu Brooks Inst 1982-84; Art/Photography Teacher Placer HS 1984-; *ai:* Coord Leader for Stu Summer Travel; Placer Teachers Soc Comm 1989-; Articulation Comm Photo Dept Sierra Coll; NAEA, CAEA Mem; ARTCETERA Mem 1980-, Classroom Grant 1989-; ATP, NEA, CTA Teachers Union Mem 1972-; Auburn City Grant 1984; Artcetera, City of Auburn, Placer Cty, CA Arts Cncl Grant & Re-Grant; Nom for Thank to Teacher 1990; Art, Photo Recognition & Shows 1974-; *office:* Placer HS 275 Orange St Auburn CA 95603

MORGAN, M. SUE, School Psychologist; *b:* Elwood, IN; *w:* Wm. L. Morgan (dec); *c:* Jennifer Draper, Melissa, Charles, Anne, Mark; *ed:* (BS) Elem Ed, 1959, (MA) Ed, 1969, (PHD) Sch Psych, 1988 Ball St Univ; Rdng Specialist Prgm; *cr:* Teacher Elwood Cmmty Sch 1959, Frankton Schls 1960-63, Tipton Cmmty Sch 1965-70, Sch Psychologist Madison-GranT USC 1984-86, Cumberland Cty Schls 1986-; *ai:* Parent Ed on Developmental Placement; NC Test Review Comm; Intern Supvr; Natl Assn of Sch Psychologists 1983-; IN St Teachers Assn 1960-83; Amer Ed Research Assn 1983-86; Teaching Fellow Ball St Univ 1985-86; IN Academic Allstar Prgm Teacher Awd 1989; *office:* Cumberland County Schls 2121 Skibo Dr Fayetteville NC 28303

MORGAN, MARY ANN, Second Grade Teacher; *b:* Scranton, PA; *c:* James B., Rhonda L.; *ed:* (BA) Elem Ed, 1979, (MS) Elem Ed, 1983 Wilkes Univ; Rdng Cert, Temple Univ 1982; Gesell Readiness Screening Wkshp, Elmira Coll 1985; ITEC Course Information Technology Ed for Commonwealth, Wilkes Univ 1987; *cr:* Teacher Wyoming Seminary Lower Sch 1979-; *ai:* Primary Coord; Way & Means Chairperson; Women in Ind Schl Liaison; Luzerne Cty Rdng Cncl (Pres 1985, Ways & Means Comm, Charter Mem), Mem of Yr 1989; Delta Kappa Gamma 1986-; Papas Evaluating Team Comm Mem 1988; Published Articles 1982; KSRA Conference Presenter; *office:* Wyoming Seminary Lower Sch 1560 Wyoming Ave Kingston PA 18704

MORGAN, MARY HELEN, Fourth Grade Teacher; *b:* Delavan, IL; *w:* Ken (dec); *c:* Kelly A. Stanek, Allison Worman, Mary K.; *ed:* (BS) Home Ec, Bradley Univ 1952; Univ of IL, NE MO, Quincy Coll; *cr:* 4th Grade Teacher Seymour Grade Sch 1967-; *ai:* NEA; Outstanding Elem Teachers of America 1973; *home:* 307 E State St Payson IL 62360

MORGAN, MELBA CALDWELL, 8th Grade English Teacher; *b:* Piedmont, AL; *m:* T. C. (dec); *c:* Joan Matthews, Melba Blevins, Linda E.; *ed:* (A) Elem Ed, Stillman Inst 1948; (BA) Elem Ed, Stillman Coll 1956; Post Masters Studies - Ed Univ of Cincinnati; *cr:* Teacher Tuscaloosa Public Schls 1956-69; Cincinnati Public Schls 1969-; *ai:* Eng Dept Cochair; Black His Month Comm; Teacher Bldg Comm; Modeling Club Adv; Cincinnati Federation of Teachers; Delta Sigma Theta Sorority Inc (Pres & VP & Parliamentarian 1988-) Outstanding Leadership & Cmmty Svc Awd 1987; *home:* 7948 Greenland Pl Cincinnati OH 45237

MORGAN, NANCY EPTING, 5th Grade Teacher; *b:* Columbia, SC; *m:* James Michael; *c:* Jeremy O Neal, Michael Clary; *ed:* (BA) Elem Ed, Univ of SC 1975; *cr:* 2nd Grade Teacher Greenville Street Elem 1976-77; 1st Grade Teacher John C Calhoun Elem 1982-83; 5th Grade Teacher Greenville Street Elem 1983-; *ai:* Sci Academic Team Coach 1988; Basic Skills Team Leader; NEA 1976-77/1982-; SC Ed Assn 1976-77/1982-; Incentive Awd Academic Excl; Campus Model for Teacher Excl 1989; *office:* Greenville Street Elem Sch Greenville St Abbeville SC 29620

MORGAN, NINA PERRY, Second Grade Teacher; *b:* Jasper, AL; *m:* William A.; *c:* Anna N.; *ed:* (BS) Eng, 1970, (MA) Elem Ed, 1988 Univ of AL; *cr:* Title I Eng Teacher 1970-71, Title I Math Teacher 1971-73, 2nd Grade Teacher 1973- Sand Rock Elem Sch; *ai:* NEA 1972-; AEA, CCEA 1970-; Jacksonville St Univ Inservice Ed Cncl Bd Mem 1985-87; Cherokee Cty Teacher of Yr Nom Sand Rock Elem Sch 1985-86; *office:* Sand Rock Elem Sch Rt 1 Leesburg AL 35983

MORGAN, PATRICIA DEESE, Math/Science Teacher; *b:* Monroe, NC; *m:* J. N.; *c:* Brittany L.; *ed:* (BS) Bio, Lenoir-Rhyne Coll 1986; *cr:* Teacher Calvary Chrstn 1986-87; Sci/Math Teacher United Faith 1987-; *ai:* Yrbk Spon/Adv; Stu Government/Spon Adv; Zeta Tau Alpha Secy 1984-85; *home:* 517 S Jackson St Waxhaw NC 28173

MORGAN, PATRICIA M., Eng, Drama, Bus Law Teacher; *b:* Palo Alto, CA; *c:* Desnie M.; *ed:* (BA) Lang Art, Chico St Coll 1954; Mc George Coll of Law; Advanced Instruction, Chico St Coll; *cr:* Eng/Drama Teacher Yuba City HS 1956-58, Grant Sch Dist 1961; Eng/Bus Law Teacher Marysville HS 1962-64; Eng/Drama/Bus Law Teacher Marysville Joint Dist 1974-; *ai:* Drama Coach; GATE Rep; CA Curr Comm Visual & Performing Arts Chairperson; CA Assn Teachers of Eng 1977-; Peach Bowl Lioness Dir 1985-88; *office:* Lindhurst HS 4446 Olive Dr Olivehurst CA 95961

MORGAN, PATTY MYERS, Language Art Teacher; *b:* Jefferson City, TN; *m:* Jan; *c:* Nicholas, Dustin, Mitchell; *ed:* Assoc Bus, Draughons Jr Coll 1974; (BS) Elem Ed, Carson-Newman 1986; *cr:* Lang Art Teacher Joppa 1986-87, Bean Station 1987-88, Joppa 1988-; *ai:* Beta Club, Cheerleading Spon; Scholars Bowl Rep; His Textbook Comm; GCEA, TEA, NEA 1986-; *home:* Rt 1 Box 80 Rutledge TN 37861

MORGAN, REBECCA L. (STEPHENS), 5th/6th Grade Teacher; *b:* Canton, IL; *m:* Paul; *c:* Rachel, Emmy; *ed:* (BS) Elem Ed, W IL Univ 1972; Levels I & II Certificates in Gifted Ed; *cr:* 3rd-6th Grade Teacher Bolipi Schls 1972-; *ai:* 1st-6th Grade Head Teacher; IEA; First Baptist Church & Choir Mem; *home:* 315 N Broadway Havana IL 62644

MORGAN, ROBERT KEITH, High School Guidance Counselor; *b:* Kalamazoo, MI; *m:* Marilyn Jean Caines; *c:* Jodie L. Kellam, Todd J.; *ed:* (BA) Sociology, Kalamazoo Coll 1963; (MA) Guidance/Counseling, W MI Univ 1968; Grad MO Auction Sch; *cr:* Teacher/Coach Galesburg-Augusta Schls 1964-; *ai:* Asst Ftbl Coach; Ski Club Spon; 4-H Dodge-Minor 1988; *home:* 10350 V W Ave Vicksburg MI 49097

MORGAN, ROBERTA LEONARD, Fourth Grade Teacher; *b:* Logan, OH; *m:* Dorsey Gene; *c:* Marcus, Jeffrey; *ed:* (BS) Elem Ed - Cum Laude, OH Univ 1972; (MA) Ed, Coll of Mt St Joseph on the OH 1986; *cr:* 1st Grade Teacher 1972-77, 4th Grade Teacher 1977- Central Elem; *ai:* Delta Kappa Gamma 1986-; Trinity United Meth Church Trustee 1985-; *home:* 45 N High St Logan OH 43138

MORGAN, ROGER JAMES, Lang Art/World His Teacher; *b:* Banner Elk, NC; *ed:* (BS) Eng, E TN St Univ 1969; *cr:* Self Contained Classroom Teacher Old Fort HS 1969-71; 7th/8th Grade Lang Art Teacher Cloudland HS 1971-76, 1983-; *ai:* 9th Grade Spon; 7th/8th Grade Boys Bsktbl Coach; TEA; *home:* PO Box 147 Roan Mountain TN 37687

MORGAN, ROSA GAINES, English Teacher; *b:* Birmingham, AL; *m:* Isom James Sr.; *c:* Isom Jr., Rosalyn; *ed:* (BA) Eng, Miles Coll 1950; (MS) Eng Ed, AL A&M Coll 1973; *cr:* Teacher Dunbar HS & 2nd Avenue Mid Sch & James A Davis Mid Sch 1959-; *ai:* Spelling Bee Coord; Class Day Adv; Sch Closing Act; NEA, AL Ed Assn 1959-; NCTE 1965-89; Alpha Pi Chi Secy 1979-, Soror of Yr 1987; Cmmty Aid Club Financial Secy 1984-; Club El Barrett Financial Secy 1989-; Miles Coll Alumni Citation for Service; Trinity Baptist Church & Vacation Bible Sch Recognition for Service; Outstanding Scndry Educators of America; *home:* 1600 Avenue H Ensley Birmingham AL 35218

MORGAN, SALLY (BURROWS), Biology/Science Teacher; *b:* Bridger, MT; *m:* James A.; *c:* James F., Shannon M.; *ed:* (BS) Bio, 1970, (MS) Sci Ed, 1973 IN Univ; *cr:* Sci Teacher Pierce Jr HS 1970-; *ai:* Performance Based Accreditation Evaluation Comm; NEA, IN St Teachers Assn, Hoosier Assn of Sci Teachers 1970-; Merriville Cmmty Teachers Assn Building Rep; St Michaels Womens Guild VP 1988-89; Schererville Town Bsbl League Team Mother 1988-; Lake Cntrl Youth Bsktbl League Team Mother 1986-; *office:* Pierce Jr HS 199 E 70th Pl Merrillville IN 46410

MORGAN, SANDRA KAY RADER, 4th Grade Teacher; *b:* Morristown, TN; *m:* Richard Lee; *c:* Casey, Kara; *ed:* (BS) Elem Ed/Early Chlhd Dev, Univ of TN 1972; *cr:* 5th Grade Teacher Hillcrest Elem; 6th Grade Teacher Davidson Academy; 4th Grade Teacher Morningside Elem; *ai:* TEA, NEA 1974-79; Jr Rdng Circle Parliamentarian 1980-84; Baptist Young Women Pres 1978-82; Nashville Teacher of Week; Featured on Channel 2 News; *home:* 3870 Vauxhall Roanoke VA 24018

MORGAN, SHELLY J., 7th Grade English Teacher; *b:* Valley City, ND; *c:* Lindsay M.; *ed:* (BSE) Eng/Soc Sci, Valley City St Univ 1981; Univ of ND; *cr:* 7th-9th Grade Eng Teacher Williston Public Sch Dist 1982-; *ai:* Paper & Annual Staff Adv; Williston Ed Assn Pres 1986-87, Appreciation Awd 1987; ND Ed Assn Commission Mem 1986-; NEA; Leadership Conferences 1987, 1988; Bus & Prof Womens Young Careerist Finalist; *office:* Williston Jr HS 612 1st Ave W Williston ND 58801

MORGAN, TAMELA HOUSTON, Kindergarten Teacher; *b:* Fort Payne, AL; *m:* Ben; *ed:* (BA) Early Chldhd Ed, 1985, (MS) Early Chldhd Ed, 1987 Jacksonville St Univ; *cr:* Kndgtn Teacher Geraldine Elem Sch 1986-; *ai:* Chrldr Spon Jr HS 1987-; Homecoming Comm Chairperson 1987-; AL De Kalb Assn Young Children Pres 1988-89; De Kalb Ed Assn Sch Rep 1987-89; Lusk Chapel Meth Church (Mem, Youth Dir) 1986-; Brownie Troop 302 Silent Spon 1988-; Appointed to Field Testing for AL Kndgtn Checklist; *office:* Geraldine Elem Sch PO Box 145 Hwy 11 Geraldine AL 35974

MORGAN, TERRY LEE, Language Arts Teacher; *b:* Wilkes-barre, PA; *M:* Edward M. Grala; *c:* Morgan Grala; *ed:* (BS) Elem Ed, 1974, (MED) Eng , 1978 Mansfield Univ; Rdng Specialist Cert K-12 1977; *cr:* Intermediate Lang Arts Teacher Liberty Elem Sch 1977-; *ai:* Head Teacher 1984-; Admin Cncl; Mentor Teacher 1989-; Lang Arts Comm 1980-; Summer Writing Wkshp; Elem Stu Cn L Adv; PA St Ed Assn 1977-; NEA 1977-; Teaching Asst Eng 1975-76; Ed 1976-77 Mansfield Univ; *office:* Libert Elem Sch RD 1 Box 2C Liberty PA 16930

MORGAN, VANESSA GOODWIN, Kindergarten Teacher; *b:* Selma, AL; *m:* Gary; *ed:* (BS) Early Chldhd, AL St Univ 1979; *cr:* Upward Bound Dorm Cnslr Selma Univ 1976-78/1980-86; Kndrgtn Teacher Cedar Park Elem Sch 1979-80; Edgewood Elem Sch 1980-; *ai:* Sunday Sch Teacher and Asst Secy; Youth Choir Dir; Odyssey of Mind Coach; Grade Level Chairperson; Selma City Schls Assessment Team Mem; AL Ed Assn; Selma Ed Assn; NEA; Negro Bus and Prof Womens Club Youth Dir 1985-87; Venussettes Club; Odyssey of Mind Team; Whos Who Among Amer Coll & Univ; Whos Who Among Amer Women; *home:* 217 Hickory Ave Selma AL 36701

MORGAN-HILL, CHARLENE M., English/Journalism Teacher; *b:* Asheville, NC; *ed:* (BA) Lit, Univ of NC Asheville 1967; Eng, W Carolina Univ 1970; Mentor Teacher Trng 1988-; *cr:* Eng/Journalism Teacher N Buncombe HS 1969-; Summer Sch Instr Asheville Buncombe Tech Coll 1973; *ai:* Sch Newspaper N Buncombe HS Spon/Adv 1970; NEA, NC Assn of Educators, Buncombe Cty Assn of Educators 1969-; NC Teachers of Eng 1986-; Delta Kappa Gamma 1990; Nom Teacher of Yr N Buncombe HS 1990-; *office:* N Buncombe HS 890 Clarks Chapel Rd Weaverville NC 28787

MORGENROTH, GERRY ROHAN, Electives Department Chair; *b:* San Marcos, TX; *m:* Malcolm; *c:* Kyle, Dustin; *ed:* (BS) Bus, 1969, (MED) Admin/Bus/Sociology, 1974 SW TX St; *cr:* Teacher Floresville Intermediate 1968-69, East Cntrl HS 1969-73; Teacher/Dept Chairperson East Cntrl HS 1978-; *ai:* NHS Spon; UIL Accounting Coach; Assn TX Prof Educators Mem 1981-; East Cntrl Ind Sch Dist Teacher of Yr 1984; *office:* East Cntrl HS 7173 FM 1628 San Antonio TX 78263

MORIARTY, BRIGID, Teacher; *b:* Kill, Ireland; *ed:* (BA) Ed, Point Park Carlow Coll 1971; Child Care Seminar Certificate, St Louis MO; Rdng, Math, Sci Wkshps; *cr:* Ed Child Care St Paul Orphanage; Ed Primary Level John F Kennedy, St Colman, St Paul Cathedral.

MORIARTY, LUCY CATHERINE, English Teacher; *b:* Winclendon, MA; *ed:* (BA) Eng/Ed, 1962, (MS) Guidance, 1967 Fitchburg St; *cr:* Eng Teacher Murdock Jr Sr HS 1962-67, Gardner Jr HS 1967-; *ai:* Gardner Ed Assn, MA Teachers Assn, NEA 1967-; Democratic Town Comm Delegate to St Convention 1980; Delta Kappa Gamma (1st, 2nd VP 1979-82) 1979-; *office:* Gardner Jr HS Waterford St Gardner MA 01440

MORKIN, SHARON BRYSON, Second Grade Teacher; *b:* Salem, IL; *m:* Don; *c:* Mike, Matt; *ed:* (BA) Elem Ed, (MS) Curr/Instruction, IL St Univ; Grad Work; *cr:* 2nd Grade Teacher Oakland 1966-; *ai:* Bloomington Ed Assn, IL Ed Assn, NEA, IL Sci Teachers Assn, Cncl for Elem Sci Intnl; Comm for Dev & Preservation of Anglers Lake City Project Educl Rep; Article Published; Nom Pres Awd for Outstanding Elem Teacher in Sci 1990; Selected for Honors Project for Outstanding Elem Teachers of Sci in IL; Mid Sch Presented at IL Sci Teachers Convention 1989; *office:* Oakland Grade Sch 1605 E Oakland Ave Bloomington IL 61701

MORLAN, PAMELA P., English Teacher; *b:* Brownwood, TX; *m:* Milton Jay; *c:* Jay D.; *ed:* (BS) Bus, Howard Payne Univ 1983; Counseling, Tarleton St Univ; *cr:* Eng Teacher Brownwood HS 1983-; *ai:* Conduct Teams Remediation Wkshps Math/Lang Art; Wrote Teams Remediation Course West Cntrl TX Cncl of Governments; *home:* Rt 6 Box 25 Wellington TX 79095

MORLEY, DIANE BEAN, 4th Grade Teacher; *b:* Price, UT; *m:* Richard H.; *c:* Dickson, Natalie Mantz, Jedd, Roseanne, Marcia; *ed:* (AS) Carbon Coll 1958; (BS) Elem Ed/Music/Drama, Brigham Young Univ 1960; Ed with Emphasis in Music; *cr:* 1st Grade Teacher Reeves Elem 1959-60, Carlton Elem 1960-61, Roosevelt Elem 1961-62, Altamont Elem 1962-64; Instr Pullman Pre-Sch 1968-70; 4th Grade Teacher Durrant Elem 1980-; *ai:* Taught Private Piano 20 Yrs; Direct Boys Choir-Sing for Civic & Church Orgnizations 1987-; Sing & Accompany Groups in Comnty; Write Direct & Produce Musicals for Church & Schl Functions; UEA 1980-; NEA; UT Music Teachers Assn Pres Local Chapt 1978; Castle Valley Chorale 1987; LDS Church Cnslr Music Dir 1988.

MORNINGSTAR, LARRY MICHAEL, Mathematics Teacher; *b:* South Bend, IN; *ed:* (BS) Math, 1966, (MAT) Ed, 1967, (MS) Math, 1974 Univ of Notre Dame; *cr:* Math Teacher Clay Jr HS 1967, Jackson HS 1967-75, Riley HS 1975-; *ai:* Boys Cross Cntry Coach; AFT, NEA; *office:* James Whitcomb Riley HS 405 E Ewing South Bend IN 46613

MORONE, LEON A., English Teacher/Drama Director; *b:* Jersey City, NJ; *m:* Valerie Barbetta; *ed:* (BS) Eng/His/Ed, Monmouth Coll 1969; *cr:* Asst Drama Dir 1980-84, Eng/His Teacher 1974-, Drama Dir 1984- Brick HS; *ai:* Voice of Democracy Speech Coord; *office:* Brick Township HS 346 Chambers Bridge Rd Brick NJ 08723

MOROSS, MARK S., Senior High Literature Teacher; *b:* Philadelphia, PA; *ed:* (BA) Philosophy, La Salle Coll 1977; (MA) Ed, Univ of VI 1989; Grad Stud Various Colls; *cr:* Teacher St Croix Cntrl HS 1979-; Lecturer Univ of VI 1983-86; Visiting Scholar Harvard Univ 1985, 1988; Fellow Univ of Haifa Israel 1986; *ai:* VI Quiz Bowl; Territorial Task Force Lang Art Curr; Textbook Selection Comm; Jr Class Adv; NCTE, NASSP; St Croix Tai Chi Assn VP 1985-; Natl Assn of Underwater Instrs; AFT; Teacher of Yr; Eng Teacher of Yr; Most Inspirational Teacher of Yr; Fellow Natl Endowment for Hum; Highest Honors Univ of VI 1989; Numerous Publications; *home:* Estate Castle Nugent Box 3492 Christiansted VI 00822

MORPER, SHERI RAE (MATHIS), 4th/5th/6th Grade Teacher; *b:* Tucumcari, NM; *m:* Grant J.; *c:* Robert G. *ed:* (BA) Elem Ed, E NM Univ 1965; *cr:* 5th-6th Grade Teacher Mountain View Elem 1962-70; 6th Grade/Head Teacher Granger Elem 1970-74; 6th Grade Teacher 1974-80, 4th Grade Teacher 1980-87 Mountain View Elem; *ai:* Tucumcari Ed Assn, NEA Secy 1962-87; Delta Kappa Gama; PEO (Pres 1972, Treas 1983-).

MORRAH, ANNETTE HERRING, 5th Grade Teacher; *b:* Greenwood, SC; *m:* John W. III; *c:* Elizabeth Lee, Miranda Britt, Cassandra Jones; *ed:* (MS) Elem Ed, Clemson Univ 1970; *ai:* BSAP Corr; *office:* S Pine St Elem Sch Walhalla SC 29691

MORRIL, LORRAINE ANN, Science Department Teacher; *b:* Norway, MI; *c:* Christopher W., William T.; *ed:* (AA) Elem Ed, Outagamie Teachers 1971; (BS) Elem Ed, Univ of WI Coll Stevens Point 1977; UW Superior Physics 1973; Summer Sch UW Stevens Point 1981; *cr:* 6th Grade Practice Teacher Outagamie Cty Teacher Coll 1971; 3rd Grade Sub Teacher Schiocton Grade Sch 1971; 1st/2nd Grade Teacher Florence Grade Sch 1977-78; 4th/5th Grade Teacher St Pauls Sch 1972-; *ai:* Built a Sci Lab; Cert of Scholastic Acheivement UWSP Highest Honors; Awd from Awds Banquet for Very Important Parent; La Crosse Diocese Cert of Awd for Reinstatement; Eisenhower Grant-CESA; *office:* St Pauls Catholic Sch 404 High St Mosinee WI 54455

MORRILL, CONNIE NELL, Cnslr/Home Economics Teacher; *b:* Springfield, MO; *m:* Charles A.; *c:* Tammy, Kayla, Joshua; *ed:* (BA) Voc Home Ec, Southwest MO St Univ 1982; (BS) Bio, Drury Coll 1985; (MS) Guidance & Counseling, SW MO St U 1990; *cr:* Cnslr/Home Ec Teacher Chadwick R-1 1987-89; *ai:* Jr HS Chrldr Adv; FHA, FBLA, 7th Grade Spon; MSTA 1987-89; *office:* Chadwick R-1 Hwy 125 Chadwick MO 65629

MORRILL, EMMET FRANCIS, 6th Grade Teacher; *b:* Worcester, MA; *m:* Jeanne M. Gagne; *c:* Thomas, Daniel; *ed:* (BS) Ed, Bridgewaer St Coll 1968; (MS) Ed, Westfield St Coll 1975; *cr:* 6th Grade Teacher C M Granger Sch 1968-73; Agawam Mid Sch 1974-; *ai:* Dir Mid Sch Intramurals; Agawam Ed Assn 1968-; Hampden Cnty Teachers Assn 1968-; MA Teachers Assn 1968-; NEA 1968-; Amer Legion Post 124 Sons of Erin Bd of Dir 1985; Westfield Yth Soccer Assn (Bd of Dir 1985- Pres 1990-92); Westfield Little League Bd of Dir 1985-88.

MORRILLY, ELIZABETH JEFFERS, Elementary Guidance Counselor; *b:* Wakefield, RI; *m:* John Thomas; *c:* Phillip, MaryKate; *ed:* (BA) Elem Ed, 1965-; (MS) Guidance, Fitchburg St 1979; Grad Stud; *cr:* 4th Grade Classroom Teacher Crocker Elem 1965-67; 3rd Grade Teacher Sheridan Elem 1972-75; 2nd Grade Teacher Hosmer Elem 1975-87; Elem Guidance Cnslr South St Elem 1987-; *ai:* Gold Book Club 1988-; Weekly Recognition of Good Citizens South St Elem; FTA Negotiating Comm 1989; Performing Arts Comm 1987; Fitchburg Teachers Assn (Exec Bd 1984-86, Membership 1970-); MA Teachers Assn, NEA 1970-; Sch Improvement Cncl 1986-87; Lang & Math Skills Achievement Monitoring Comm 1977-78; *office:* South St Elem Complex 366 South St Fitchburg MA 01420

MORRING, DOROTHY WILSON, Kindergarten Teacher; *b:* Colerain, NC; *m:* Don Michael; *c:* Deanna, Don Jr., Dalan; *ed:* (BS) Elem Ed, Elizabeth City St Univ 1975; (MS) Elem Ed, E Carolina Univ 1988; *cr:* 2nd Grade Teacher 1975, 3rd Grade Teacher 1978, Kndgtn Teacher 1987- Perquimans Cntrl Sch; *ai:* Mentor; NC Assn of Educators Building Rep 1975-; NEA 1975-; ASCD 1989-; NC Center for Advancement of Teaching Alumna; PTA Nominating Comm 1985-; Parent Teacher Stu Assn 1989-; NC Natl Guard Auxiliary Life Mem; Jack & Jill Inc 1988-; MADD 1988-; Outstanding Young Educator Sch & Cty 1984; Outstanding Elem Math Teacher Cty 1985; NC Center for Advancement of Teaching 1987; NC Career Ladder Forum Mem 1988; *home:* 1508 Herrington Rd Elizabeth City NC 27909

MORRIS, ALICE M., High School Math Teacher; *b:* Sardis, MS; *m:* Larry D.; *c:* Kathy; *ed:* (BS) Math, MS Valley St 1969; (MA) Math, DePaul Univ 1990; Andover-Darmouth Inst for Math Teachers 1987; *cr:* Teacher Grenada Public Sch 1969-71, Amundsen HS 1971-72, Von Stueben HS 1972-73, Prosser Voc HS 1973-; *ai:* NHS Adv; IL Cncl of Math Teacher 1986-; Gold Apple Awd 1985; *office:* Prosser Voc HS 2148 N Long Ave Chicago IL 60639

MORRIS, ANGELA MC DANIEL, 5th Grade Teacher; *b:* Baxley, GA; *M:* Joffre L.; *c:* Breanna R.; *ed:* (BS) Mid Chldhd, 1983, (MS) Mid Chldhd, 1986, (EDS) Elem Ed, 1987 GA Southern Univ; *cr:* 3rd/4th Grade Teacher Lanier Elem 1983-84; 5th Grade Teacher Appling Cty Elem 1984-; *office:* Appling Co Elem Sch Rt 7 Box 250 Baxley GA 31513

MORRIS, BARRY SHERMAN, Mathematics Department Chair; *b:* Richmond, VA; *m:* Frances Emily; *c:* Geoffrey S., Tracy L.; *ed:* (BS) Math, Randolph-Macon Coll 1971; (MED) Curr/Instruction, VA Commonwealth Univ 1983; US Naval Officer 1974-79; *cr:* Teacher Gumberry HS 1971-72, Floyd Cty HS 1972-73, Fluvanna Cty HS 1979-; *ai:* Asst Ftbl Coach; *home:* PO Box 804 Columbia VA 23038

MORRIS, BEVERLY WILSON, 7th & 8th Grade Eng Teacher; *b:* Laurel, MS; *m:* Johnny Denson; *c:* Melanie, Mandy; *ed:* (BS) Elem Ed, Univ of S MS 1972; *cr:* 6th Grade Eng Teacher Raleigh Elem Sch 1973-74; 7th/8th Grade Eng Teacher South Jones HS 1974-; *ai:* Fidelia Club Pres 1985-86; Federated Womens Clubs of MS VP 1989; *home:* Rt 3 Box 479 Jordon Loop Ellisville MS 39437

MORRIS, BRENDA PACE, Third Grade Teacher; *b:* Russellville, AL; *m:* Charles Larry; *c:* Tyler S., Carla F.; *ed:* (BA) NW AL St Jr Coll 1973; (BS) Elem Ed, 1975, (MA) Elem Ed, 1980 Univ of N AL; *cr:* 1st/2nd Grade Teacher Mt Hope Elem 1975-77, Rockwood Elem 1977-78; 4th-6th Grade Rdng/Soc Stud Teacher 1978-86, 3rd Grade Teacher 1988- Hackleburg Elem; *ai:* Marion Cty Vlybl Coach of Yr 1979; *home:* Rt 3 Box 472 Russellville AL 35653

MORRIS, CARON CAMP, Gifted/Talented Coordinator; *b:* Oklahoma City, OK; *m:* William T.; *c:* Lucas, Jacob; *ed:* (BS) Elem Ed, Univ of AR Monticello 1976; (MS) Elem Ed, S AR Univ 1980; *cr:* 6th Grade Teacher 1976-86, 1st Grade Teacher 1986-87, Gifted/Talented Coord 1987- Stamps Schls; *ai:* Odyssey of Mind & Quiz Bowl Coach; AR Ed Assn Resolution Comm 1976-; Stamps Ed Assn Pres 1976-; Delta Kappa Gamma VP 1980-; Order of Eastern Star 1978-; PTO 1976-; Teacher of Yr 1987; *office:* Stamps Public Schls P O Box 309 Stamps AR 71860

MORRIS, CLAIRE ANN, Third Grade Teacher; *b:* Washington, DC; *ed:* (BA) His/Elem Ed, W MD Coll 1982; (MA) Curr, Loyola Coll 1987; *cr:* 5th Grade Teacher 1982-86, 3rd Grade Teacher 1986- Our Lady of Mercy Sch; *ai:* 3rd Grade Girls Soccer Coach; NCEA 1982-; W MD Coll (Young Alumni Assn Pres 1989-, WA Area Young Alumni 1985-89), Distinguished Young Alumni of Yr 1989; Our Lady of Mercy Faculty Delegate Prin Search Comm & Cmptr Assn of Ind Schls; *office:* Our Lady of Mercy 9222 Kentsdale Dr Potomac MD 20854

MORRIS, CLIFFORD WILLIAM, Business & Physical Ed Teacher; *b:* Butte, MT; *m:* Diana Jeannette Mahugh; *c:* Josh, Mindy; *ed:* (BS) Bus Ed/Phys Ed, W MT Coll 1970; Drivers Ed, Athletic Trng; *cr:* Teacher/Coach Sch Dist #1 1971-73, Waldport HS 1973-76, W Yellowstone Schls 1976-; *ai:* Head Ftbl Coach;

Close Up Coord; Sr Class Spon; W Yellowstone Ed Assn Negotiator 1976-, Teacher of Yr 1981-83, 1985, 1988; Mt Coaches Assn, Mt Voc Assn 1976-; Natl Strength & Conditioning Coaches Assn; W Yellowstone Booster Club 1980-; W Yellowstone Snowmobile Club 1976-; *office:* W Yellowstone HS PO Box 460 West Yellowstone MT 59758

MORRIS, CONSTANCE ELIZABETH BARTH, 5th Grade Teacher; *b:* Girard, OH; *c:* Michael J., Matthew A.; *ed:* (BS) Elem Ed, 1975; (MS) Elem Curr, 1978 Youngstown St Univ; *cr:* 5th Grade Teacher 1975-; *ai:* Initiated Sch Newspaper; Dir Sch Plays; Dir/Chrngrphr HS Majorette & Flag Line; Attended Croft Wkshp; Coached Jr HS Girls Bsktbl; Attended Tampeel Outdoor Environmental Learning Experience; MEA Sec 1976-77; OEA; NEOEA; Vlg of McDonald Progrss/Partcptn Comm 1989-; Trumbull Cty Panhellenic Assn; Our Lady of Perpetual Help Chldrns Choir Dir 1989; Map & Globe Skills Grant; Lang Arts Grant; Writing Skills Grant; *office:* Roosevelt Elem 400 Illinois Ave Mc Donald OH 44437

MORRIS, CRYSTAL JAMES, 10th Grade English Teacher; *b:* Baltimore, MD; *m:* Warren Hamilton; *c:* Alex, Warren J.; *ed:* (BA) Eng, Morgan St Univ 1963; (MA) Rdng, Bowie St Univ 1972; Howard Univ, Trinity Coll; *cr:* Teacher Banneker & Chopticon HS 1963-67; Eng/Rdng Teacher Spaulding Jr HS 1967-76; Eng Teacher Francis Scott Key Mid Sch 1977-87; Eng Teacher Northwestern HS 1988-; *ai:* FTA, Chrldrs, PA Announcers; Dance Group, Newspaper, Yrbk, Jr Class Spon; PG Cty Educators Assn, NEA, MD St Teachers Assn; Washington DC Alumnae (Recording Secy 1977-, Historian 1980-82); Somerset HS Alumni Assn 1959-83, Plaque 1983; Nom Twice Outstanding Educators Assn; Received Plaque from Amer Inst for Stu of Foreign Study; *home:* 5817 Chillumgate Rd Chillum MD 20782

MORRIS, DEBORA LYNN KOUNOVSKY, Math Teacher; *b:* Wichita, KS; *m:* Robert W.; *c:* Amy, Robert, Emily; *ed:* (BA) Elem Ed, WSU 1976; *cr:* 8th Grade Teacher St Patrick Sch 1977-78; 7th/8th Grade Teacher Magdalen Sch 1978-81; Math Teacher Derby HS 1981-; *ai:* Frosh Class Spon; Chrldr Spon 1987-88; *office:* Derby Sr HS 801 E Madison Derby KS 67037

MORRIS, DENNIS ELDEN, Third Grade Teacher; *b:* Cumberland, MD; *m:* Monica Sulava; *c:* Lydia A., Aubrey L.; *ed:* (BS) Journalism, WV Univ 1973; Cert Elem Ed, Frostburg St Univ 1979; (MA) Elem Ed, WV Univ 1985; Elem Ed, WV Univ; *cr:* Teller Farmers & Merchants Bank 1973-77; 3rd/4th Grade Classroom Teacher Fountain Primary Sch 1979-; *ai:* PTA (Devotional Leader 1983-, Treas 1989-), Lifetime Mem 1988-89; *office:* Fountain Primary Sch Rt 2 Box 9 Keyser WV 26726

MORRIS, ELIZABETH ANN (BARTLETT), History Teacher; *b:* Charleston, SC; *c:* Jason B.; *ed:* (BA) Scndry Ed, Clemson Univ 1977; *cr:* Teacher Easley Chrstn Sch 1977-78, Bonds-Wilson HS 1978-85, Alice Birney Mid Sch 1985; *ai:* Stu Cncl Adv; Sch Improvement Cncl; Sch Based Management; Charleston Cty Sch Dist Comm; Charleston Fed of Teachers Mid Sch VP 1983-; *home:* 7023 S Kenwood Dr Charleston SC 29418

MORRIS, ELIZABETH ANN ROBERTS, First Grade Teacher; *b:* Washington, DC; *m:* Roderick Harvey; *c:* Rick, Robert D.; *ed:* (BS) Voc Home Ec, E Carolina Coll 1959; K-3rd Grade Early Chldhd, Pembroke St Univ 1974; Mentor Trng; *cr:* Teacher Pemberton Township Sch 1959-60, Tar Heel Sch 1960-62; Voc Home Ec Teacher Elizabethtown HS 1963-68; Kndgtn Teacher Elizabethtown Primary Sch 1974-76; 1st Grade Teacher Bladenboro Primary Sch 1976-; *ai:* Supervising Teacher for Stu Teacher Pembroke St Univ 1989; NCAE; Teacher of Yr Bladenboro Primary 1989 & Bladenboro Sch 1980; *office:* Bladenboro Primary Sch PO Box 820 Bladenboro NC 28320

MORRIS, ELIZABETH GOETZ, Teacher/Coordinator of Gifted; *b:* Flint, MI; *m:* Mike E.; *ed:* (BS) Spec Ed, 1981, (MA) Elem Ed, 1984 TN Tech Univ; Talents Unlimited Certified Trainer K-12; *cr:* Resource Teacher Houston Cty Sch System 1982-84; Teacher of Gifted 1984-85, Teacher/Coord of Gifted 1985- Robertson Cty Sch System; *ai:* Future Problem Solving Prgm St Evaluator Coach; Prof Relations Comm Robertson Cty Ed Assn; Spec Ed Monitoring Team; TN Assn for the Gifted 1984-, Outstanding Teacher of Gifted/Talented 1989; Robertson Cty Ed Assn (2nd VP 1984-, Prof Advisory Cncl Spec Ed Rep 1987-89); Optimist Club 1990; Our Lady of Lourdes Cath Church (Parish Cncl Mem 1989-, Coord 3 Yr Renew Prgm 1987-), 1984-; Presented Paper World Cncl for Gifted Intnl Conference Salzburg Austria 1988; Presentor Scndry Level Gifted Prgm TN Assn for Gifted Conference Memphis 1988.

MORRIS, ELLEN L., Social Studies Teacher; *b:* Painesville, OH; *m:* James W.; *ed:* (BA) Soc Stud Comp, 1968, (BS) Scndry Ed, OH St Univ 1969; (MS) Cnslr of Ed, Univ of Dayton 1989; Working on Masters; Alcohol & Drug Counseling, Meth Theological Sch of OH 1989; *cr:* Teacher Groveport Madison HS 1970-; *ai:* Stu Cncl Adv 1979-89; OH Honor Cncl Adv Level; Groveport Madison Ed Assn Soc Chm 1989-; GMLEA Grievance Chm 1971; OH Ed Assn, NEA; 1st Presbyn Church Elder 1986-; Bloom Township (Emergency Medical Technician, Volunteer Firefighter) 1986-; *office:* Groveport-Madison HS 4475 S Hamilton Rd Groveport OH 43125

MORRIS, GWEN A., Business Teacher/Coordinator; *b:* St Louis, MO; *m:* Jan G.; *c:* Alison, Brady; *ed:* (BA) Bus Ed, SW Baptist Univ 1968; Voc Bus & Office Cert 1977; *cr:* Teacher 1967-, Teacher/Coord 1977-, Bus Dept Chairperson 1986- Fox Sr HS; *ai:* FBLA Faculty Adv; Jr Class Spon; Cmmty Teacher Assn (Corresponding Secy 1986-88) 1967-; Jefferson Cty Bus Ed Assn (Pres 1985-87) 1980-; MO Voc Assn 1977-; *office:* Fox Sr HS 745 Jeffco Blvd Arnold MO 63010

MORRIS, JEFF BLAKE, Mathematics Teacher/Dept Head; *b:* Cambridge, OH; *c:* Kristopher C.; *ed:* (BA) His/Math, Muskingum Coll 1978; (MS) Ed Admin, OH Univ 1988; *cr:* Math Teacher Roosevelt Jr HS 1978-79, Caldwell HS 1979-81; Prin/Teacher Caldwell Elem 1987-88; Math Teacher Caldwell Jr HS 1981-; *ai:* 8th Grade Girls Bsktbl Coach; Textbook Adoption Comm; OH Ed Assn, NEA 1978-; *office:* Caldwell Elem Sch 44350 Fairgrounds Rd Caldwell OH 43724

MORRIS, JOHNATHAN E., Agriculture Instructor; *b:* Bloomington, IL; *ed:* (BS) Ag Ed, W IL Univ 1983; *cr:* Ag Instr Franklin HS 1983-; Dist Mgr Golden Harvest Seeds Incorporated 1983-; *ai:* FFA Adv; Soph Class Spon; NHS Selection & Teachers Union Public Relations Comms; IAVAT Section 15 Chm 1989-, Top Mrktg Prgm Awd 1987, 1988; NVATA, AVA 1983-; *home:* RR 2 Box 22 Franklin IL 62638

MORRIS, JON PHILLIP, Assistant Principal; *b:* Indianapolis, IN; *m:* Rebecca Koenig; *c:* Jeffrey, Melissa; *ed:* (BS) Elem Ed, 1963, (MA) Elem Admin/Elem Supervision & Cnslng 1966 Ball St Univ; *cr:* 5th Grade Teacher Crooked Creek Elem 1963-65; 5th/6th Grade Teacher Abraham Lincoln Elem 1965-69; 7th/8th Grade Teacher Meridian Mid Sch 1969-75; 4th Grade Teacher Winchester Village Elem 1975-85; Asst Prin Clinton Young Elem 1985-88; Douglas Mac Arthur Elem 1988-; *ai:* Stu Cncl Spon; Citizens Advisory Cncl; Performance-Based Accreditation Comm; IN Assn of Elem & Mid Sch Prin 1985-; Phi Delta Kappa; ACSD; School Corporation Liaison with Indianapolis Zoo-Ed Bd; *office:* Douglas Mac Arthur Elem Sch 454 E Stop 11 Rd Indianapolis IN 46227

MORRIS, JUDY CARVER, Spanish Teacher; *b:* Red Boiling Spring, TX; *m:* D. Keith; *ed:* (BA) Eng, High Point Coll 1977; Eng, Span Univ of NC Greensboro, TN Tech Univ Cookeville, Mid TN St Univ, Univ of TN Knoxville; *cr:* Eng/Span Teacher Lucy Ragsdale HS 1977-81; Span Teacher Red Boiling Springs HS/Macon Cty HS 1987-88, Macon Cty HS 1988-; *ai:* Span Club & Jr Class Spon; AATSP St Bd Mem 1989-; TFLTA, NEA, TEA, MCEA; Local Collaboraters at TTU, MTSU (Bd Mem, Chairperson); Partners of Americas Bd Mem 1990; *office:* Macon Cty HS 401 Meador Dr Lafayette TN 37083

MORRIS, JUDY WEAVER, Fifth Grade Teacher; *b:* Greensboro, NC; *m:* John G. Jr.; *c:* John G. III; *ed:* (BS) Elem Ed, Campbell Univ 1968; *cr:* 5th Grade Teacher Paul Braxton Elem 1968-70, 1975-77, Siler City Elem 1977-; *ai:* Mentor Teacher; Quiz Bowl Spon; Teacher Assistance Team Mem; Southern Assn Accreditation Schls & Colls Co-Chairperson; Delta Kappa Gamma VP 1987-; NC Teachers of Math 1988-; Siler City Elem Teacher of Yr 1987; *home:* 807 Cliftwood Dr Siler City NC 27344

MORRIS, MARCIA HUMPHREY, First Grade Teacher; *b:* Vallejo, CA; *m:* Dean W.; *ed:* (BA) Soc Sci, San Diego St 1970; Post Grad Stud Sch of Ed; *cr:* 1st-3rd Grade Teacher Warner Union Sch 1972-; *ai:* Prgm/Assembly Dir; Parent Teacher Club Treas 1972-; Warner Faculty Assn Negotiator 1977-; Cuyamaca Volunteer Fire Company Firefighter 1975-77; Julian Planning Group Exec Comm 1975-77; Greater San Diego Rdng Assn Commendation 1982; Mentor Teacher 1987-; Nom Outstanding Teacher of Yr 1975; *office:* Warner Union Sch PO Box 8 Warner Springs CA 92086

MORRIS, MARGARETT SUE, 6th Grade Teacher; *b:* Loveland, OK; *m:* David; *c:* Pat Tidwell, Dee; *ed:* (BS) Ed, Southeastern OK St Univ 1967; *cr:* 1st/4th Grade Teacher Little Beaver 1943-44; 1st/8th Grade Teacher Sage 1944-46; Kndgtn-8th Wilburton Public Sch 1967-68; Kndgtn-11th Red Oak Public Schls 1968- *ai:* 7th Grade Spon; Kndgtn Spon; 6th Grade Spon; Honorary Spon of 1990 Srs; Building Decoration Comm; Latimer Cty Teachers 1967-; OK Ed Assn 1967-; NEA 1967-; Order of Eastern Star (Ester Assn Conductress) 1970-; Conductress Assn Matron 1976; Amer Legion Aux Secy/Treas 1967-; *home:* PO Box 10 Red Oak OK 74563

MORRIS, MARGO LANE, Phys Ed/Health Teacher/Coach; *b:* Salisbusy, MD; *m:* Kenneth E. Long Sr.; *c:* Kenneth Long II, Marcus Long; *ed:* (BS) Phys Ed, Univ of MD 1968; *cr:* Phys Ed Teacher Beaver Run Elem/Willards Elem/Pittsville Elem & Powellville Elem 1968-70; Laurel Jr & Sr HS 1970-73; Laurel Mid Sch 1973-; *ai:* Mentor; Field Coach; Varsity Sftbl Coach; Chair Person Olympiad Comm; Mem Discipline Comm; Mem Athletic Advisory; NEA 1968-; DE St Ed Assn 1970-; DE Interscholastic Players Selection Coaches Assn Comm 1987-; Womens Intnl Bowling Congress League Sec 1970- Most Improved 1973; Modified Sftbl Player 1984-85 St Champs 1985; Womens Fast Pitch Captain 1964-85 League Champs 1965-85; Henlopen Conference Coach Yr 1986; Mentor Honors 1987 & 88; *office:* Laurel Mid Sch 801 Central Ave Laurel DE 19956

MORRIS, MARY DANIELS, Second Grade Teacher; *b:* Jamesville, NC; *m:* Fentress T.; *c:* Fenita, Markitta; *ed:* (BS) Early Chldhd, Elizabeth City St Univ 1969; (MAED) Elem Ed, E Carolina Univ 1985; *cr:* 2nd Grade Teacher Cntrl Elem Sch 1970-; *ai:* Jack & Jill of America Tutoring Prgm; River City Marching Unit; Phi Delta Kappa 1986-; Alpha Kappa Alpha 1976-; Natl Assn of Univ Women; Chums Incorporated Treas; *home:* 201 Harvey St PO Box 1032 Elizabeth City NC 27906

MORRIS, NANCY DRINKWATER, 4th Grade Teacher; *b:* Shawnee, OK; *c:* Jesse D.; *ed:* (BA) Art Ed , 1973, (MED) Elem Ed, 1978 SW OK St Univ; OK Aerospace Ed 1989; Energy Awareness Wkshp 1988; *cr:* Sped Teacher Tulsa Public Schls 1973-74; 2nd/3rd Grade Teacher Pleasant Grove Sch 1976-78; 4th Grade Teacher Grove Elem Sch 1978-; *ai:* Yrbk; Elem Sci Fair; Grove Ed Assn Pres 1986, 1988, Teacher of Yr 1987-88; Natl Endowment for Hum Constitution Project III OK St Univ 1989; *office:* Grove Elem Sch 2800 N Bryan Shawnee OK 74801

MORRIS, PEGGY L., 5th & 6th Grade Teacher; *b:* David City, NE; *ed:* (BS) Elem Ed, Manchester Coll 1972; (MS) Elem Ed, IN Univ 1975; Post Grad Work Cmptr, Gifted & Talented; *cr:* 5th/6th Grade Teacher Metro North Elem Sch 1972-; *ai:* Former Elem Girls Vlybl, Bsktbl Coach; PTO Officer; North Cntrl Assn Self-Study Comm Chm; Various Schl Comm; Pi Lambda Theta 1976-87; Church of the Brethren Mem; *home:* RR 1 Box 58 Macy IN 46951

MORRIS, RONALD GROVER, Elementary Teacher; *b:* Anniston, AL; *m:* Alice K.; *c:* Nathan T.; *ed:* (BS) Elem Ed, Geneva Coll 1970; (MS) Admin/Supervision, Morgan St Univ 1978; *cr:* Teacher Baltimore Cty Bd of Ed 1970-78, Calhoun Cty Bd of Ed 1978; *ai:* Adopt-A-Highway Prgm Spon; MD St Teachers Assn Faculty Rep 1970-78; Calhoun Ed Assn Faculty Rep 1978-; NEA 1970-; Cty Teacher of Yr; *home:* Rt 2 Box 216 Nicut WV 26633

MORRIS, RONALD SCOTT, Social Science Teacher; *b:* Centralia, WA; *m:* Alice Mc Intosh; *c:* Cherise, Kristine; *ed:* (BA) Soc Sci, 1968, (MA) Ed Admin/Curr, 1982 CA St Univ Los Angeles; Taft Inst for 2 Party Politics S Sacramento St Univ 1988; Natl Endowment for Hum Inst Univ CA Los Angeles 1990; *cr:* Soc Sci Teacher Arcadia HS 1969-80; Advanced Placement Government Teacher 1987-; *ai:* Advanced Placement Government Class Bicentennial 1989; Taft, NEH Inst; Advanced Placement Government Class 1989-.

MORRIS, RUTH F., Teacher; *b:* Marshall, TX; *m:* Ray F.; *c:* Ray II, Rhonda, Ryan, Ricky, Rolanda; *ed:* (AA) Span, Los Angeles City Coll 1960; (BA) Span, TX Southern Univ 1966; (MA) Span, Stephen F Austin Univ 1974; *cr:* Teacher Lockhart HS & Marshall Public Sch; *ai:* Faculty Affairs; TSTA, NEA Building Rep; AATSP; Kappa Delta Pi; OES 2 Secy 1974-; Bethesda Baptist Church; PTA Life Membership 1977; *office:* Marshall HS 1900 Maverick Dr Marshall TX 75670

MORRIS, SANDRA NELSON, First Grade Teacher; *b:* Holton, KS; *M:* Timothy B.; *c:* Stephanie, Katherine, Erin L.; *ed:* (BE) Elem Ed, Washburn Univ 1973; (MS) Curr/Instr, Emporia St Univ 1978; Rdng Spec Cert Emporia St Univ *cr:* 2nd Grade Teacher 1973-75, Kndgtn Teacher 1975-86, 1st Grade Teacher 1986 Mayetta Grade; *ai:* Inservice Cncl 1987-; Sch Impvmt Team 1989-; Intnl Rdng Assn 1987-; Topeka Area Cncl Intnl Rdng Assn 1987-89; Educl Homemakers Unit Pres 1983-85; Greater KS City Dairy Cncl Ed Citation 1987-1989; 1st Pl in Alliance for Bus of Ed & Innovator in Ed Awd; *office:* Mayetta Elem Sch 155 Mayetta KS 66509

MORRIS, SONYA K., 5th Grade Teacher; *b:* Brookyn, NY; *m:* Eugene; *c:* Beth S., Stephen J.; *ed:* (BS) Elem Ed, Lesley Coll 1956; *cr:* 6th Grade Teacher Newton Public Sch 1956-57; Math Curr Head Dentsville Sch Dist 1957-58; 6th Grade Teacher Richland Cty Sch 1958-59; 5th Grade Teacher Hopewell Area Sch 1966-; *ai:* NEA 1966-; PSEA 1966-; Hopewell Ed Assn Building Rep 1987-; Hopewell Elem Fndrs Day Awd-Schlrsp.

MORRIS, SUE JUANITA PERTEET, English Dept Chairman; *b:* Griffin, GA; *m:* Otis; *c:* Yolanda Morris Thomas, Lisa Morris Holland, Otis Jr., Juanitress; *ed:* (AB) Eng, Spelman Coll 1949; (MA) Eng Ed, Atlanta Univ 1968; Several Wkshps Univ of GA Athens, Univ of IL Illini, Mercer Univ; *cr:* Eng/Music Teacher Dickerson HS 1949-50; Eng/Music/Span Teacher Bailey-Johnson HS 1951-60; Eng Dept Chairperson/Teacher Griffin HS 1960-; *ai:* Sr Class Adv 1973-; GAE, NEA; St Eng Organization 1988-; GA Eng Cncl of Teachers 1980-; NCTE 1988-; Phi Beta Kappa 1986-; PTA Emancipation Proclamation Comm (Past Secy, Treas, Chm); Excl in Achievement Organization Pres 1985-; Rising Star Baptist Church Youth Dept Directress, Mother of Yr, Appreciation Plaque 1983, Achievement Plaque 1990; Bailey-Johnson Teacher of Yr 1958; Griffin-Spalding System Teacher of Yr 1970; *home:* 520 Futral Rd Griffin GA 30223

MORRIS, TIMOTHY L., Math/Cmptr Sci/Physics Teacher; *b:* Kenmare, ND; *m:* Kim Eltz; *ed:* (AS) Math, ND St Univ Bottineau 1973; (BS) Bio, Minot St Univ 1977; Drivers Ed Courses; Working Towards MAT Math, Minot St Univ; *cr:* Sci Teacher Lansford HS 1978-79; Math Teacher Sherwood HS 1980-; *ai:* Jr Class Adv; ND Ed Assn 1978-; NCTM 1987-; NEA Book Review Comm Mem; City of Sherwood (Mayor 1985-, Cmmty Pride Leadership 1984); ND Farm Bureau 1981-; Sherwood Fire & Ambulance Squad 1980-; *office:* Sherwood HS PO Box 9 Sherwood ND 58782

MORRIS, VICTOR LEWIE, American History Teacher; *b:* Keokee, VA; *m:* Lunelle; *c:* Richie, Lewis, Amy, Daniel; *ed:* (BS) Phys Ed, Cumberland Coll 1964; *cr:* Teacher Cumberland Elem 1964-; *ai:* Cumberland HS Bsbl Coach; NEA, KEA; *home:* Box 106 B Totz KY 40873

MORRISEY, REBECCA WALKER, Mathematics/History Instructor; *b:* Atwood, KS; *m:* Shawn; *c:* Adam, Christopher, Erin; *ed:* (BA) Math, St Mary of Plains Coll 1983; *cr:* Jr HS Math/His Teacher Spearville Grade Sch 1984-86; Math/His Teacher

Spearville Jr/Sr HS 1986-; *ai:* Head Womens Bsktbl & Vlybl Coach; KBCA 1988-, 2A Coach of Yr 1989; KVA 1989-; KNEA, STA Local Pres 1984-; Spearville Hospital Auxiliary; Minerva Club Prgm Comm 1984-; *office:* Spearville Jr/Sr HS P O Box 158 Spearville KS 67876

MORRISON, ANNE MARIE, 5th Grade Teacher Gifted Prgm; *b:* Los Angeles, CA; *ed:* (BA) Phys Ed, CA St Univ Northridge 1973; *cr:* Teacher Our Lady of Grace 1976-78, Belvedere Elem 1978-80, Gates St Elem 1980-; *ai:* Garden Club Coord; Sci Club Spon; Teach for America LAUSD Stu Greater Los Angeles Teachers of Sci Assn 1986-88; United Teachers of Los Angeles 1986-; ASCD; Classroom Teacher Instructional Improvement Prgm Grant 1985-86; Los Angeles Beautiful Contest 1st Place Sch Beautification 1988-89; Office of Speaker of House Civic Achievement Awd Prgm 1988-; *office:* Gates St Elem Sch 3333 Manitou Ave Los Angeles CA 90031

MORRISON, BEVERLY JANE, English Teacher; *b:* Bamberg, SC; *ed:* (BA) Eng, Furman Univ 1982; (MAT) Eng, Univ of SC 1983; *cr:* Eng Teacher Greenwood HS 1984-; *ai:* SADD & Acknowledge Christ Today Spon; Prom Comm Mem; S Main Street Baptist Church 1984-; *office:* Greenwood HS Hwy 254 Greenwood SC 29646

MORRISON, BRIAN LEE, Assistant Band Director; *b:* Philpot, KY; *m:* Leeann Riley; *ed:* (BME) Music Ed, Univ of KY 1984; *cr:* Asst Band Dir Hamilton HS 1984-86, N Hardin HS 1986-; Band Dir Radcliff Mid Sch 1986-; *ai:* HS Marching, Concert, Pep, Mid Sch Concert Bands; HS & Mid Sch Solos & Ensembles; Lessons for All St & All Dist Band, Lessons for Schlsp Auditions; KY Bandmasters Assn Dist Rep 1989-; Phi Mu Alpha Sinfonia Treas 1981-83; *office:* N Hardin HS 801 S Logsdon Pkwy Radcliff KY 40160

MORRISON, CARLA NELSON, History Teacher; *b:* Hannibal, MO; *m:* Jon; *c:* Patrick; *ed:* (BA) His, Quincy Coll 1979; (MA) Lib Sci, Univ of MO Columbia 1989; *cr:* Lib Dir John Wood Comm Coll 1981-86; Teacher Payson HS 1986-; *ai:* His Curr Advisory Comm; NCTE, NEA; Jr Womens Club.

MORRISON, CATHERINE BRYANT, Third Grade Teacher; *b:* Birmingham, AL; *m:* Cecil Ray; *c:* Morgan Elizabeth Amick; *ed:* (BS) Home Ec Ed, Samford UNIV 1970; (MA) Early Childhood Ed, UnIV AL Birmingham 1981; *cr:* 3rd Grade Teacher 1st Bapt Church Sch 1979-81, George W Scott Elem 1981-; *ai:* Delta Kappa Gamma-Alpha Lambda Chapter 1989-; *office:* George W Scott Elem Sch 1517 Hibernian St Birmingham AL 35214

MORRISON, EDWARD JAMES, Teacher; *b:* Bridgeport, CT; *c:* Laura Downs, Edward J. Jr., Briggs W.; *ed:* (BS) Elem Ed, 1955, (MS) Sci Ed, Univ of Bridgeport; (MA) Ed Admin, 1960, (MA) Cnslr, 1978 Fairfield Univ; *cr:* Teacher Roger Ludlow Elem 1955-56, Roger Sherman 1956-61, Burr Farms Elem 1961-81, Coleytown Mid Sch 1981-; *ai:* Sci Club, Teaching, Swimming, Sailing; NEA, CT Ed Assn, Westport Teachers Assn; *office:* Coleytown Mid Sch North Ave Westport CT 06881

MORRISON, JACK HARLEY, Electronics Teacher; *b:* Buckhannon, WV; *m:* Lois V. Yates; *c:* Medina, Erin, Kristen; *ed:* (BT) Theology, Apostolic Bible Inst 1980; Ed, OH Univ; Electronics, USMC; *cr:* Minister United Pentecostal Church 1980-82; Teacher Asheville HS 1982-; *ai:* Vica & Electronics Club Adv; Bsktbl Time Ofcl; Sch Soc Comm; Faculty Cncl; Trade & Industrial Ed Dept Chairperson; NC Curr Dev Comm for Electronics; Regional Leadership Cncl Chairperson 1989-; NC Voc Teachers Assn, NC Electronics Teachers 1982-89; Published Poem in Amer Anthology of Poets 1989; Teacher of Month 1989; Selected for NC Extern Leadership Trng; *office:* Ashville HS 419 Mc Dowell St Asheville NC 28803

MORRISON, MARY NAPOLEON, Choral/Piano Teacher; *b:* Monroe, LA; *c:* Frederick I. Jones; *ed:* (BS) Voice/Piano/Instr, Grambling St Univ 1959; (MMED) Music Choral/Voice, NE LA Univ 1970; Grad Stud Univ CA Berkley, San Francisco Univ, Holy Name Coll, CA St Univ Hayward; *cr:* 9th-12th Grade Teacher Ouachita Parish Sch Bd 1959-68, Caddo Parish Sch Bd 1968-70; 7th-9th Grade Teacher Oakland Unified Sch Dist 1971-; *ai:* Choral Act Spon Oakland Unified Sch Dist; Music Educators Natl Conference; CA Music Ed, NEA, CA Teachers Assn, Oakland Ed Assn; Natl Assn of Negro Musicians Inc Music Youth Schlsps; Beta Pi Sigma; Oakland Music Ed Assn Pres 1978-80; B & P Society ATBC Mem; Outstanding Musical Achievements; Chancel Choir Choral Dir 1973-88; Whos Who in the West 1984-86; *office:* Oakland Unified Sch Dist 1025 2nd Ave Oakland CA 94606

MORRISON, MICHAEL G., Athletic Director/Teacher; *b:* Tyler, TX; *m:* Jan Eubanks; *c:* Michael, Amanda, Matthew; *ed:* (BS) Scndry Ed/His/Health/Phys Ed, East Tx Baptist Coll 1977; MID Management Cert TX; *cr:* Teacher/Coach Marshall HS 1977-81, West Rusk HS 1981-85; Athletic Dir/Teacher West Rusk HS 1985-; *ai:* Head Ftbl Coach; Golf Coach; TSTA 1981-; THSCA 1977-89; *home:* 203 N Paradise Overton TX 75684

MORRISON, NANCY STUPP, Second Grade Teacher; *b:* Bellefontaine, OH; *m:* Terry W.; *c:* Brian, Jennifer; *ed:* (BA) Ed, Capital Univ 1972; Rdng/Lang Arts, OH St Univ; *cr:* 1st/2nd Grade Teacher Lakewood Local Schls 1971-75; 1st Grade Teacher Gahanna Schls 1975-77; 1st/2nd Grade Teacher Plain Local Schls 1978-; *ai:* Curr Design Team; Literacy Connection 1987-; Childrens Hospital Twig Bazaar Chairperson 1976-83; Forrest Park Civic Assn Block Chairperson 1976-80; Cmmty Volunteer for Aged 1978-80; Franklin Cty Mini-Grant for Lang Arts Prgm; Presented Whole Lang Inservices to Franklin Cty Schls; Fredericktown Schls & Sch Study Cncl of OH; *office:* New Albany Elem Sch 6425 New Albany-condit Rd New Albany OH 43054

MORRISON, SARAH ELIZABETH, K-12th Grade Counselor; *b:* Wabash, IN; *m:* Roy; *c:* Shelby A., Sharla K., Sherri L.; *ed:* (BAED) Speech/Eng, Univ of AZ 1969; (MAED) Psych, W TX St Univ 1973; Mid Management Cert TX Tech Univ; Counseling Cert W TX St Univ; *cr:* Teacher Dumas Ind Sch Dist 1969-076, Hays Ind Sch Dist 1982-83; Jr HS Prin 1986-89, Cnslr 1981-Smyer Ind Sch Dist; *ai:* Univ Interscholastic League Cross Debate Coach, Lincoln Douglas Debate; Informative & Persuasive Speaking; Natl Jr Honor Society, SADD Spon; Delta Kappa Gamma 1974-; TX St Teachers Assn, NEA 1981-; TX Assn of Scndry Sch Prins 1986-; TX Assn of Speech Educators 1986-; Amer Legion Auxiliary 1968-; Order of E Star 1964-; Delta Kappa Gamma Schlsp TX Tech Univ Study Mid-Management; *office:* Smyer Ind Sch Dist 4th & Lincoln Box 206 Smyer TX 79367

MORRISON, SCOTT R., 4th Grade Teacher; *b:* Hanover, NH; *m:* Sue V.; *c:* Matthew; *ed:* (BA) His, Pittsburg St Univ 1970; (MS) Elem/Learning Dis, Northeastern St Univ 1975; *cr:* 6th Grade Teacher Alexander Elem Commerce 1970-73; LD Teacher Commerce Jr HS 1973-83; 4th Grade Teacher Alexander Elem 1983-; *ai:* Soc Stud Curr Comm; Grade Level Chm; OK Ed Assn 1970-; Classroom Teachers Bldg Rep/Head Negotiator; 1st Baptist Church; *home:* Rt 5 Box 128 Miami OK 74354

MORRISON, SUE, Fifth Grade Teacher; *b:* Miami, OK; *m:* Scott; *c:* Matthew; *ed:* (BA) Elem Ed, 1970, (MS) Elem Ed, 1975 Pittsburg St; *cr:* Teacher Commerce Public Schls 1970-; *ai:* NEA Congressional Contact Team 1975-88; OK Ed Assn 1970-; OEA Bd of Dir 1976-79; Outstanding Young Women of America 1980; *office:* Commerce Public Schls 601 6th St Commerce OK 74339

MORRISSEY, MARGARET ANN, Choral Director; *b:* Sibley, IA; *m:* Robert L. Jr.; *c:* Robin, Molly Sterner; *ed:* (BA) Music Ed, Northwestern Coll 1967; (MA) Elem Admin, NE MO St Univ 1982; *cr:* Teacher Eddyville Cmmty Schls 1967-68, Blakesburg Cmmty Schls 1972-76, Eddyville Cmmty Schls 1976-, William Penn Coll 1988-; *ai:* Choreographer & Swing Choir Dir; Fall & Winter Color Guard Coach; Faith Cmmty Church Bd Clerk 1986-; Support Our Comm Kids Founding Mem 1986-89; SE IA Orff-Schulwerk Assn & NW IA Orff-Schulwerk Assn Clinician.

MORRISSEY, STEPHEN A., Retired 6th Grade Teacher; *b:* Albany, NY; *m:* Claire L. Barry; *c:* Christine Janetti, Clare M., Jeanne Noble, Kathy Green, Therese Snowden, Stephen, Peter, Martha Petrisky; *ed:* (BA) His, Russell Sage Coll 1969; (MS) Elem Ed, Plattsburgh St Univ Coll 1973; Grad Stud Outdoor Ed & Environmental Sci; *cr:* Plant Mgr NY Telephone 1947-66; Dist Mgr General Telephone Company 1966-69; 6th Grade Teacher Queensbury Mid Sch 1969-89; *ai:* Outdoor Ed Comm Chm 1977-89; Metric Comm Mem 1975-80; Sci Comm Mem 1986-89; NY St Outdoor Ed Assn Mem 1970-80; Queensbury Faculty Assn Treas 1983-85; Sch Bd Mem 1968-73; Rotary Intnl Mem 1966-69; BSA Scout Master 1976-81; Zoning Bd Mem 1978-82; Zoning Commission Chm 1982; Adirondack Mountain Club 1988-; Adirondack Trusteeship (Mem, Schlsp Bd) 1985-; *home:* RR 01 Box 01 Landon Hill Rd Chestertown NY 12817

MORRISSON, LINDA URAM, Social Studies Teacher; *b:* Pittsburgh, PA; *m:* Robert H.; *c:* Laura, Elizabeth; *ed:* (BA) His, PA St Univ 1962; (MA) His/Poly Sci, Univ of MS 1966; Univ of FL, Emory Univ, W GA Univ; *cr:* Soc Stud Teacher Therrell HS 1962-68; Teacher/Dept Chairperson N Cobb HS 1979-; *ai:* Stu Cncl, Interact Club Adv; Model United Nations Spon; GA Cncl Soc Stud 1980-; NCSS 1981-; League of Women Voters 1967-87; STAR Teacher 1983, 1985, 1987; Cobb Cty Teacher of Yr 1984; *office:* North Cobb HS 3400 Old 41 Hwy Kennesaw GA 30144

MORROW, ADRIENNE VIDA, Third Grade Teacher; *b:* New Haven, CT; *m:* Adrienne A. Vida; *ed:* (BS) Elem Ed, S CT St Univ 1957; (MAT) Elem Ed, 1989, Elem Ed, 1991 Sacred Heart Univ; *cr:* 2nd/3rd Grade Teacher Region 15 1957-76; 2nd-4th Grade Teacher Oxford 1984-; *ai:* Curr Advisory & Planning Cncl; Staff Dev Chairperson; CT Ed Assn, NEA 1957-; Oxford Ed Assn 1984-; Foreign Stu Exch Chairperson 1961; *office:* Oxford Center Sch 462 Oxford Rd Oxford CT 06483

MORROW, CHERYL BINDSEIL, 8th Grade Math Teacher; *b:* Des Moines, IA; *m:* Jeff; *c:* Travis, Todd; *ed:* (BSE) Health/Phys Ed, 1974; (MA) Sports Admin, Northeast MO St; *cr:* Phys Ed Teacher 1974-80; Math Teacher Clark Cty R-I 1980-84; Math Teacher Kirksville R-III 1984-; *ai:* Varsity Girls Track Volunteer; Local Pres/VP/Treas MO St Teachers Assn 1974-; NCTM 1983-; MO Cncl Teachers of Math 1983-; Beta Sigma Phi (Pres 1978- VP 1978- Treas 1978-); *office:* Kirksville Jr H S 1515 S Cottage Grove Kirksville MO 63501

MORROW, ELAINE STOLP, Principal; *b:* Geneva, NY; *m:* Douglas R.; *c:* Jessica, Jeffery, R. Cody, Leah; *ed:* (BA) Eng, Ithaca Coll 1972; (MA) Educl Admin, SUNY Brockport 1988; Permanent Teaching Cert SUNY Oswego, SUNY Geneseo, Elmira Coll, Coll of St Rose 1978; *cr:* Teacher St Stephens Sch 1972-80; Teacher 1980-89, Admin Asst 1984-85, Admin Intern 1988-89, Principal 1989- St Francis deSales-St Stephens Sch; *ai:* Various Comms; Parish Staff, Cncl Mem, Sch Bd; Yrbk Adv 1985-87; 8th Grade Class Adv 1972-89; Cheerleading Moderator 1973-75; Admin Asst 1984-85; Scheduling Coord 1972-82; Jr HS Coord 1975-89; NCEA 1972-; CSAANYS 1989-; St Stephens Church Parish Cncl Mem 1984-86; St Francis deSales-St Stephens Sch Bd Planning Bd for Consolidation 1983-84; *home:* 31 Elmwood Pl Geneva NY 14456

MORROW, JEFFERY DALE, Math Teacher; *b:* Paris, TX; *m:* Karen Ann Wilkinson; *c:* Julie, Bryan; *ed:* (BA) Music, Denison Univ 1969; (MM) Music Ed, East TX St Univ 1974; Musicology, Univ of CA Berkeley 1969-70; Teacher Cert Prgm, SMU & ETSU 1970-72; Doctoral Prgm Supervision, Curr, Instruction, E TX St Coll 1982; *cr:* Choral Dir John B Hood Jr HS 1970-76; Asst Choral Dir 1976-79, Theater Arts Dir 1979-84 W W Samuell HS; Math Teacher Skyline HS 1984-; *ai:* Pre-Calculus Course Coord; NEA, Greater Dallas Cncl Teachers of Math, TX Cncl Teachers of Math 1984-; NCTM 1988-; Classroom Teachers of Dallas, TX St Teachers Assn 1970-; Eastminster Presbyn Church Session Mem 1988-; *office:* Skyline HS 7777 Forney Rd Dallas TX 75227

MORROW, JULIA S., Fourth Grade Teacher; *b:* Boligee, AL; *c:* Kim; *ed:* (BS) Elem Ed, Grambling St Univ 1973; *cr:* Teacher Carver Elem Sch 1973-; *office:* Carver Elem Sch P O Box 659 Eutaw AL 35462

MORROW, KATHLEEN SMITH, Second Grade Teacher; *b:* Rockville Center, NY; *m:* James Kevin Sr.; *c:* James Jr., Richard P.; *ed:* (BS) Elem Ed/Hist, Cabrini Coll 1970; (MS) Rdng/Elem Ed, Long Island Univ 1974; Grad Studies; *cr:* 5th Grade Teacher St Marys Sch 1970-71, Jericho Public Sch 1971-72; 2nd/3rd/5th Grade Teacher Babylon Grade Sch 1972-; *ai:* NY St United Teachers 1972-; Bayblon Teachers Assn 1972-; St Matthews Couples Club Religious Comm 1979-89; *office:* Babylon Elem Sch 169 Park Ave Babylon NY 11702

MORROW, MARJORIE, Second Grade Teacher; *b:* Enon, MO; *ed:* (BS) Ed, Cntrl MO St Univ 1956; Grad Stud Lincoln Univ; *cr:* Teacher Enon Sch 1948-50; 2nd Grade Teacher Cole R-1 1950-; *ai:* CTA Teacher Welfare Comm; Cmmty Teachers Assn Treas 1987-88; MO St Teachers Assn; Enon Baptist Church Organist 1950-; *home:* Rt 1 Box 271 A Russellville MO 65074

MORROW, SCOTT A., Third Grade Teacher; *b:* Newcastle, WY; *m:* Lori D. Herrud; *c:* Abbie M., Jared S.; *ed:* (BS) Elem Ed, Univ of WY 1982; *cr:* 4th Grade Teacher 1983-87, 3rd Grade Teacher 1987- Gertrude Burns Elem; *ai:* 4th-6th Grade Boys Bsktbl Coach; Lions Club 1984-; *home:* 214 Frontier Newcastle WY 82701

MORROW, TOMMY, Mathematics Dept Chair; *b:* Houston, TX; *m:* Barbara Anne Ornelar; *c:* Willow, Dove; *ed:* (BS) Math, 1973, (MA) Ed, 1985 NM St Univ; *cr:* Teacher/Jr Var Coach Deming HS 1984-85; Teacher/Boys Bsktbl/Girls Track/Head Coach Hot Springs 1985-; *ai:* Boys Bsktbl & Girls Track Head Coach; NEA; *office:* Hot Springs HS Box 952 Truth or Consequen NM 87901

MORS, CHRISTINE K., Third Grade Teacher; *b:* Waukegan, IL; *c:* Julie, Peter; *ed:* (AA) Elem Ed, Coll of Lake Cty 1976; (BS) Elem Ed, IL St Univ 1978; *cr:* 2nd Grade Teacher Carman Sch 1978-79; 3rd Grade Teacher Our Lady of Humility 1979-; *ai:* Cheerleading Moderator; *home:* 539 Meadow Ln Zion IL 60099

MORSE, JENNIFER JUNE, Science Teacher/Chairperson; *b:* Santa Barbara, CA; *m:* Brian Scott; *ed:* (BS) Bio, Seattle Pacific Univ 1988; *cr:* Sci/Cmptr Teacher Cascade Chrstn HS 1988-; *ai:* Chrstn Service Club Adv; Sr Class Adv; Girls Varsity Vlybl Coach; Girls Varsity Bsktbl Coach; NSTA 1988-90; *office:* Cascade Christn HS 608 N Bartlett Medford OR 97501

MORSE, OPAL MARIE (ROSE), Biology Teacher/Sci Dept Chair; *b:* Gallipolis, OH; *m:* Stephen Leslie; *c:* Wendy Vaughan, Jessica; *ed:* (BA) Biological/General Sci, 1968, (MA) Ed/Psych, 1974 Marshall Univ; Working Towards Masters Ed, Marshall Univ; Advanced Placement Trng Bio, WV Univ; *cr:* Bio/Speech Teacher 1968-, Chairperson/Sci Dept 1974-79, 1988- Point Pleasant HS; *ai:* Forensic & Drama Coach; Jr Class Prom & Sr Class Graduation Comm; Thespian & Billiards Club Adv; NEA, WV Ed Assn, Mason Cty Teacher Assn 1968-; WV Speech Comm Assn 1984-; Natl Forensic League 1984-, Degree of Spec Distinction 1989; Title I Federal Grant Psych 1983, Broadcast Journalism 1987; Spec Distinction US Postal Service Public Relations 1988; *office:* Pt Pleasant HS 2312 Jackson Ave Point Pleasant WV 25550

MORSS, WAYNE, History Instructor; *b:* Avon, IL; *m:* Sharon Kay Woods; *c:* Teresa K. Morss Webb, David W., Randolph E., Wesley A.; *ed:* (BS) Phys Ed, Bradley Univ 1958; (MA) Scndry Ed, St Univ of IA 1970; Several Courses & Wkshps; *cr:* Phys Ed/Soc Stud Teacher Gardner S Wilmington HS 1960-62; Phys Ed Teacher 1962-63, Phys Ed/His Teacher 1963-65, His Teacher 1965- Dixon HS; *ai:* Teach Advance Placement Courses; DEA 1962-; IEA, NEA 1960-; 1st Meth Church (Church Bd, Sunday Sch Teacher); AL Morrison Bsbl Schedule Chm; Dixon Teachers Credit Union Pres; *office:* Dixon HS Lincoln Statue Dr Dixon IL 61021

MORTON, CHARLES BRADLEY, III, Mathematics Department Chair; *b:* Orange, NJ; *m:* Sandra Diane Kaufhold; *ed:* (BBA) Bus Management, TX A&M Univ 1983; Masters Courses in Ed & Math, E TX St Univ; *cr:* Lancaster HS 1986; Red Oak Jr HS 1986-; *ai:* Natl Jr Honor Society Founder & Adv; UIL Calculator Application Team Coach; Ftbl & Bsktbl Game Announcer; Santa at Christmas for Stus; S W Dallas Cty A&M Club Pres 1985-86; TX Cncl Teachers of Math; Assn of TX Prof Educators; PTA Mem; Red Oak Jr HS Teacher of Yr 1987-88; PTA Natl Educator of Yr Nom 1988-89; Outstanding Teacher Awd 1987-88; Recognized for Superior Achievement in Conducting Math-A-Thon Fundraiser; *home:* 1819 Carrington Dr Desoto TX 75115

MORTON, DAVID L., Counselor/Coach; *b:* New Orleans, LA; *m:* Nancy; *c:* Zachary, Melissa; *ed:* (BS) Ed/Soc Sci, OK St Univ 1974; (MED) Ed/Counseling, Cntrl St Univ 1980; Licensed Prof Cnslr 1986; OK St Dept of Mental Health Certificate #821; *cr:* 4th-8th Grade Teacher Christ the King Sch 1974-79; 5th-8th Grade Teacher New World Sch 1979-80; Teacher/Cnslr/Coach Bishop Mc Guinness HS 1981-; *ai:* Fellowship of Chrstn Athletes; OK Inst for Child Advocacy; Mc Guiness Prgm REACH for Learning Disabilities Coll Bound Stu; Mc Guiness 9th Grade Say it Straight Drug Ed Prgm Grant; Region 8 Cross Cntry Coach of Yr 1984, 1985, 1987, 1989 & Track Coach of Yr 1989, 1990; OK Track Coach of Yr 1988; Boys & Girls Cross Cntry St Champions 1984, 1987, 1988; Boys & Girls Track & Field St Champions 1989, 1990; *office:* Bishop Mc Guinness HS 801 NW 50th St Oklahoma City OK 73118

MORTON, DEBORAH CRIDDLE, Reading Dept Chair/ Teacher; *b:* Charleston, SC; *m:* Samuel Thomas Jr.; *c:* Marcus A.; *ed:* (BS) Elem Ed, Coll of Charleston 1982; Cmptrs, Classroom Management, Effectiveness Trng for Teachers; *cr:* Teacher Sedgefield Mid Sch 1984-; *ai:* Drama Club Spon; Curr Advisory; Rdng Dept Chairperson; 8th Grade Recognition Ceremony Coord; Cntry Curr Comm Mem 1989-; Berkeley Rdng Cncl Mem 1985-; St Instructional Television Advisory Comm 1989-; SC Forum on Cognition Cty Rep 1989; Friendship Baptist Church (Mem 1967-, Childrens Church Dir 1978-89, Sunday Sch Teacher 1982-, Vacation Bible Sch Dir 1986-87); *office:* Sedgefield Mid Sch Charels B Gibson Blvd Goose Creek SC 29445

MORTON, PATRICIA HOWLEY, Jr HS Language Arts Teacher; *b:* Wheeling, WV; *m:* R. Clark; *c:* Neal E., Scott G., Teresa E., Deidre E.; *ed:* (BA) Amer His/Eng, Seton Hill Coll 1951; (MA) Curr/Instr, Univ of Detroit 1980; Creative Writing, WV Univ & Marshall Univ; *cr:* Asst Supt of Recreation City of Wheeling 1951-57; 3rd Grade Teacher St Catherines 1957-58; 8th Grade Teacher Corpus Christi 1976-77, Blessed Trinity 1977-80; 7th/8th Grade Lang Art Teacher St Michael 1980-; *ai:* Newspaper Adv; Co-Dir Spring Musical; Sch Librarian; Quality Ed Comm Mem; Assn of Curr & Instruction; City of Wheeling Recreation Commission (Mem 1976-, Pres 1985-87); WV Writing Assessment Test Scoring Team Mem; OH Cath Educators Convention 1989; *office:* St Michael Sch 1221 National Rd Wheeling WV 26003

MORTON, RUTH YVONNE (MUNGO), English Teacher; *b:* Greenville, SC; *m:* George Cleveland; *c:* Marlon T.; *ed:* (Ba) Eng, Livingstone Coll 1965; (MA) Eng 1977; (MS) Displinary Measures 1984 St Univ of NY; Cert Elem Ed, Benedict Coll 1967; *cr:* Teacher Lancaster Cty Sch System 1965-72; Soc Worker Cath Charities of Buffalo 1972-73; Teacher Niagara Falls NY Sch System 1973-79; Buffalo NY Sch System 1979-; *ai:* Coach the Richmond Speaking Contest; Coach the Harriet Tubman Speaking Contest Curr Dev Comm; NEA; NY Ed Assn; Buffalo Teachers Fed; NCTE; Delta Sigma Pheta; the Buffalo Innovators Founder & Pres a Resolution for Leadership 1987; Natl Cncl of Negro Women Inc; Written & Copyrighted Prose & Poetry; *office:* Buffalo Trad Sch 450 Masten Ave Buffalo NY 14209

MORTON, SHEILA ANNETTE, Mathematics/Computer Teacher; *b:* Lorain, OH; *m:* Phillip; *ed:* (BS) Ed/Math, OH St Univ 1983; Cmptr Sci, Bowling Green St Univ; Beyond Assertive Discipline, Baldwin Wallace; *cr:* Auxiliary Services for Lorain Cath HS 1983-86; HS Math Teacher Lorain City Schls 1983-; Admiral King HS 1986-; *ai:* Adv & Spon Stu Bible Study & SAT Study Helps; Phi Delta Kappa 1988-; Lake Erie Math Assn 1986-; OH Cncl Teachers of Math 1983-; *office:* Admiral King HS 1020 W 7th St Lorain OH 44052

MORTON, SONDRA W., Teacher; *b:* Harrisburg, PA; *m:* Frank M. III; *c:* Hunter; *ed:* (BA) His - Cum Laude, Christopher Newport Coll 1979; Grad Stud Univ of VA, Old Dominion Univ, VA Commonwealth Univ; *cr:* Doubleday Publishers 1961-63; Colonial Williamsburg Fnd 1965; Dow Badische Company 1968-71; Menchville HS 1979-; *ai:* Group Leader Stu Tour; Stratford Hall Seminar Fellowship; *office:* Menchville HS 275 Menchville Rd Newport News VA 23602

MORTON, THOMAS RICHARD, 5th Grade Teacher/Head Teacher; *b:* Corry, PA; *m:* Paula L. (Sankey); *c:* Karen J. Edwards, David P. Hauser, T. Ryan; *ed:* (BS) Elem/Scndry Ed, Slippery Rock Univ 1970; Grad Stud Westminster Coll & Slippery Rock Univ; *cr:* 3rd Grade Teacher 1970-84, 5th Grade/Head Teacher 1984- Dassa Mc Kinney Elem Sch; *ai:* Academic Games Coach Adv; Lang Art & Rdng Comm Chm; Moniteau HS Asst Coach Track 1970-74 & Ftbl 1971-73; NEA, PSEA; Moniteau Ed Assn Pres 1972-74; W Sunbury Little League (Organizer, Pres) 1970-72; *home:* Box 74 West Sunbury PA 16061

MORTON, WILLIAM DUNBAR, Second Grade Teacher; *b:* Hollywood, CA; *m:* Jetty Lou; *c:* Kathlene Saunders, Todd, Donald, Glen, John; *ed:* (AA) Bus Management, Los Angeles Valley Coll 1955; (BA) Elem Ed, Chico St 1962; *cr:* 7th/8th Grade Teacher Thermalito Elem Sch Dist 1962-66; 4th Grade Teacher Paradise Unified Dist 1966-68; 2nd/4th/5th Grade Teacher N Kitsap Sch Dist 1968-; *ai:* Veterans of Foreign Wars 1952-89.

MORTSOLF, GAYLE J., 2nd Grade Teacher; *b:* Lafayette, IN; *ed:* (BA) Elem Ed, Purdue Univ 1970; (MA) Elem Ed, Miami Univ 1975; *cr:* 2nd Grade Teacher Arlington Primary 1970-80; Lockland Elem 1980-; *ai:* Soc Stud Curr Revision Comm; Sci Textbook Selection Comm; Teacher Eva Luation Comm; St Excl in Ed Application Comm; NEA; OH Ed Assn; Lockland Ed Assn Bldg Rep 1982-83; *office:* Lockland Elem Sch 210 N Cooper Ave Cincinnati OH 45215

MORZUCH, ROBERT EUGENE, Sci Teacher/Dept Chairperson; *b:* Chicago, IL; *m:* Jane Joelson; *c:* Beth, Michael, Joseph; *ed:* (BA) Sociology, 1969, (MSED) Educl Admin, 1977 N IL Univ; Bio/Chem/Geology, Coll of Lake Cty; *cr:* Jr HS Teacher St Joseph Sch 1969-73; Jr HS Sci Teacher Westfield Sch 1973-; Asst Prin Spring Bluff Sch 1986-; *ai:* Sci Fair Spon & Coord; IL Prin Assn 1986-; *office:* Westfield 2309 W 9th St Winthrop Harbor IL 60096

MOSCHELL, BONITA JONES, Mathematics Dept Chairperson; *b:* Salt Lake City, UT; *m:* Richard L.; *c:* Amy, William; *ed:* (BS) Chem, Univ of MN 1964; (MED) Natural Sci/ Cmptr, Carthage Coll 1987; *cr:* Math Teacher Woodbridge Jr HS 1964-65, Math/Sci Teacher St Anthony Village 1965-66; Math Teacher Red Lake Indian Reservation 1966-67, Kenosha Unified Sch Dist #1 1967-; *ai.* Scndry Evaluation Consortium Math Chairperson; Math Teams Adv; Teachers Cmptr Use, Math Curr, Textbook Selection Comms; Milwaukee Ed Cmptr Assn, NCTM, WMC; Black Watch Band Treas 1986-; *office:* Bullen Jr HS 2804 39th Ave Kenosha WI 53142

MOSELEY, CASSANDRA LANE, Fourth Grade Teacher; *b:* Snow Hill, NC; *m:* Michael; *c:* Jeremy M.; *ed:* (BS) Intermediate Ed, Fayetteville St Univ 1972; Grad Stud; *cr:* 3rd/4th/6th Grade Teacher C H Bynum Elem Sch 1972-79; 2nd/3rd Grade Teacher Northwest Elem Sch 1979-82; 4th Grade Teacher J H Sampson Elem Sch 1982-; *ai:* NCAE Faculty Rep; Kinston City Schls Initial Cert Team; Facilitator NC Effective Teacher Trng Prgm; Super Kid Proposal Comm; Art & Sch Coord; NEA; NC Assn of Educators Unit Treas 1990; St Augustus Church; Alpha Kappa Alpha; Teachers Memorial PTO VP 1988-89; Kinston HS Choral Guild; Kinston City Schls Teacher of Yr 1989-, Finalist 1985-86; NC Mentor Suport Team; Consortium Advancement Public Ed Scholar; Southern Assn Accrediation Team; Lenoir Cty Friends of Public Schls & Kinston Grass Roots Grant Recipient; Accelerated PACE Prgm Teacher; Outstanding Young Women of America; *home:* 2412 Linden Ave Kinston NC 28501

MOSER, C. STEVE, Science Teacher; *b:* Loundon, TN; *m:* Joy Rhea Duggan; *ed:* (BA) Scndry Ed, Lee Coll 1977; (MS) Elem Ed, Univ of TN Knoxville 1983; Career Ladder III Status; Grad Stud; *cr:* Interim/Multiple Handicap Stu Everett Spec Ed Center 1978; 7th/8th Grade Teacher Eagleton Mid Sch 1978-84; 9th-12th Grade Sci Teacher William Blount HS 1984-; *ai:* Coach Frosh Ftbl & Asst Var Girls Bsktbl; NEA, TN Ed Assn, Blount Cty Ed Assn 1978-; Lovell Heights Church of God Sunday Sch Teacher 1982-; *office:* William Blount HS Rt 11 Cty Farm Rd Maryville TN 37801

MOSER, CHARLES PAUL, Science Teacher; *b:* Denver, CO; *m:* Roxanna L. Vader; *c:* Timothy I., Thomas P.; *ed:* (BS) Ag, CO St Univ 1979; (BS) Sci/Ed, Univ of WY 1984; Trng in Cmptr & Laser Disc Technology; Desktop Publishing; *cr:* Sci Teacher Lyman Jr/Sr HS, N Park Jr/Sr HS, Oak Harbor Jr HS; *ai:* Girls HS Soccer Coach; Jr HS Discipline Comm Mem; NEA; *office:* Oak Harbor Jr HS 8115 800th Ave W Oak Harbor WA 98277

MOSER, MELODY (PHILLIPS), 5th Grade Teacher; *b:* Anacortes, WA; *c:* Brenden, Tysen, Robin; *ed:* (BA) Spec Ed, Cntrl WA Univ 1973; Cntrl WA Univ 1978; *cr:* HS Home Ec Teacher 1973-74, 2nd Grade Teacher 1973-78 Pateros Sch Dist; Kndgtn Teacher 1978-84, 1st Grade Teacher 1984-88, 5th Grade Teacher 1988- Manson Sch Dist; *ai:* NEA 1973-; WA Ed Assn 1973-; Manson Ed Assn (secy 1989-) 1978-; Co-author Health Curr Grant for Dist; Bi-Ling Teacher Trainer in Bi-Ling Teaching Strategies; *office:* Manson Elem Sch Box A Manson WA 98831

MOSES, JEANNE KERR, First Grade Teacher; *b:* Newton, NC; *m:* James Hardin; *c:* Mindy, Andy; *ed:* (BA) Sociology, Catawba Coll 1968; Teachers Cert Early Chldhd, Lenoir Rhyne Coll 1970; Masters Trng Lenoir Rhyne Coll; *cr:* Spec Ed Teacher Maiden Elem 1968-69; Early Chldhd Ed Teacher Celeste Henkel Elem 1970-89; *ai:* Educl Testing Comm Chairperson; Southern Assn of Schls & Colls Steering Comm; NEA, NC Assn of Educators 1975-89.

MOSES, LILIAN, Mathematics Teacher; *b:* Eagle Pass, TX; *ed:* (BA) Math, TX Womens Univ 1976; *cr:* Math Teacher Eagle Pass HS 1976-; *ai:* Spelling Team Coach; Campus Improvement & Textbook Comm; Delta Kappa Gamma 1989-; AEGUS 1988-; NCTM 1987-; Math Assn of America 1988-; TX Classroom Teachers Assn; TX Excl Awd for Outstanding HS Teachers; *office:* Eagle Pass HS 2020 2nd St Eagle Pass TX 78852

MOSES, NELL JOHNSON, First Grade Teacher; *b:* York, SC; *m:* James Kenneth; *c:* Brad, Jan; *ed:* (BS) Elem Ed, 1972, (MED) Elem Ed, Winthrop Coll 1980; *cr:* 5th/6th Grade Teacher Ebenezer Avenue Sch 1973; 1st Grade Teacher 1973-75, 2nd Grade Teacher 1975-82, 1st Grade Teacher 1982- Kinard Elem; *ai:* Teacher Cadet Spon; Classroom Management System Dist Comm Rep; Saint Paul United Meth Church (Chairperson Ed & Evangelism Lit 1989-, Secy 1990); *office:* Kinard Elem Sch 201 Pressley St Clover SC 29710

MOSHER, DAVID BYRON, Spanish/Eng 2nd Lang Teacher; *b:* Chattanooga, TN; *m:* Jama Lynn Moorhead; *c:* Laurel F., James D.; *ed:* (BA) Span, Carson Newman Coll 1977; (MS) Foreign Lang Ed, Univ of TN 1990; *cr:* Spec Ed Teacher Crystal River Mid Sch 1977-78; Youth Dir 1st Baptist Church 1978-79; Eng/ Speech Teacher Valley Baptist Acad 1979-85; Span/Eng as 2nd Lang Teacher Harrison-Chilhowee Baptist Acad 1985-; 000 *ai:* Stu Work Prgm Dir; 1st Baptist Church Seymour Chm of Deacons 1989-; *office:* Harrison Chilhowee Baptist 202 Smothers Rd Seymour TN 37865

MOSIER, EARLENE A., Mathematics Teacher; *b:* Sentinel, OK; *c:* William C., Mary E., Rebecca A., Roberta L.; *ed:* (BSED) Math, Southwestern Univ 1963; Grad Stud Various Univs; *cr:* Scndry Math Teacher Dill City Schls 1963-65; HS Math Teacher Bloomfield Schls 1965-71, Moriarty Schls 1978-; *ai:* Math Dept Head; Teach Summer Sch; Core Team; GED Night Sch; Run Clock for Vlybl Games; NEA (Treas 1968) 1963-71, 1978-88, 1990; United Meth Church Trustee 1983-88; NFL Fellowship Grant Tulane 1967; *office:* Moriarty HS PO Drawer 20 Moriarty NM 87035

MOSIER, ROSEMARY JOHNSON, 5th Grade Teacher; *b:* Nashville, TN; *m:* Thomas Addison; *c:* Sondra K., Andrew K.; *ed:* (BA) Ed, Belmont Coll 1967; (MAED) Rdng, TN St Univ 1985; *cr:* 3rd-5th Grade Teacher Stratton Elem 1967-72; 3rd-6th Grade Teacher Old Center Elem 1975-83; 5th Grade Teacher Brick Church Mid Sch 1983-; *ai:* Red Cross Spon; Mid Sch Rep; Math Dept Chm; NCTM, NCTM, Mid Sch Assn; *home:* 3075 Patton Branch Rd Goodlettsville TN 37072

MOSLEY, BARBARA GALLOWAY, Mathematics Teacher; *b:* Raleigh, NC; *m:* Howard C. Jr.; *c:* Chanell, Shauna, Tarren; *ed:* (BS) Math/Ed, Cheyney St Univ 1969; (MS) Math/Ed, Penn St Univ 1981; Grad Stud, Drexel Univ, Temple Univ, IIT, Univ S CA; *cr:* Teacher Fels Jr HS 1969-70, Gillespie Jr HS 1970-75, W Philadelphia HS 1975-78, Philadelphia HS for Girls 1978-; *ai:* PFT Building Comm 1989-; NCTM, ATMOPAV 1989-; Alpha Kappa Alpha Grad Adv 1973-76, Grad Adv of Yr 1976; Natl Sci Fnd Grant 1971-72; *office:* Philadelphia HS for Girls Broad & Olney Aves Philadelphia PA 19141

MOSLEY, CHARLES WILLIAM, Chem/Math/Physics Teacher; *b:* Kansas City, MO; *m:* Sondra Jane Schutte; *c:* Jennifer, Kenneth; *ed:* (BS) Chemical Engineering KS Univ 1965; (MA) Ed, N AZ Univ 1980; Grad Stud Ball St Univ, Univ of AR, W FL Univ, Univ of S CA, Univ of KS; *cr:* Officer/Pilot USAF 1965-86; Faculty KS Univ 1982-85; Stu Teacher F L Schlagle HS 1987-88; Teacher Sumner Acad 1988-; *ai:* Asst Ftbl Coach; St Quiz Bowl Competition Moderator; NSTA, KS Assn Sci Teachers 1987-; Kiwanis Club Youth Organization Chm 1982-85; Eisenhower Math/Sci Grant KS Math Wkshp 1990; *office:* Sumner Acad of Arts & Sci 8th & Oakland Kansas City KS 66102

MOSLEY, CLARENCE MARLON, Principal; *b:* Vidalia, GA; *m:* Teresa Sue Worley; *c:* Lance; *ed:* (BA) His, Univ of N TX 1976; Supvr/Prin Trng, Accelerated Chrstn Ed Headquarters Lewisville TX; *cr:* Head Supvr/Prin 1st Baptist Chrstn Sch 1976-; *ai:* Girls Vlybl & Bsktbl Coach; TX Baptist Athletic Conference (Vice-Commissioner 1987-89, Commissioner 1989-); *office:* First Baptist Chrstn Sch 5800 Denton Hwy Fort Worth TX 76148

MOSLEY, GLORIA ALINE, Language Art Teacher/Librarian; *b:* Mangum, Oklahoma; *m:* Randy Wayne; *c:* Brandon; *ed:* (BA) Eng Ed, 1971, (MS) Eng, 1986 Southwestern OK St Univ; *cr:* Eng Teacher 1971-76, Eng/Fr Teacher 1982-89; Lang Art Teacher/ Lib Media Specialist 1989 Snyder HS; *ai:* NCTE 1971-; Amer Lib Assn 1989-; OK Lib Assn 1989-; OK Assn of Teachers of Fr 1984-; AATF 1984-; OK Ed Assn 1971-76/1981-; NEA 1971-76/ 1981-89; *office:* Snyder HS 515 9th St Snyder OK 73566

MOSLEY, PATRICIA ROBERTS, Sixth Grade Teacher; *b:* Meridian, MS; *m:* Billy A. Sr.; *c:* Winoka Stokley, Billy A. Jr.; *ed:* (BS) 1969, (MED) 1971 Livingston Univ; *cr:* Teacher Butler Elem 1969-70, South Choctaw Acad 1970-; *ai:* Town of Toxey Councilman 1976-87; BPW Choctaw Cty, Natl Bus & Prof Womens Club 1978-; *home:* PO Box 303 Toxey AL 36921

MOSLEY-JENKINS, SHIRLAN WOODBURY, Mathematics Teacher; *b:* Marion, SC; *m:* Rodger; *c:* Donyale, Christopher; *ed:* (BA) Phys Ed, AZ St 1973; (MED) Scndry Ed, Univ of SW LA 1975; Pet Sysmatic Effective Teaching; *cr:* Teacher/Coach Univ of ND 1975-81, Steven HS 1981-84, Edisto HS 1984-; *ai:* Var Girls Bstkbl, Track & Field; SC Cncl Of Supvr of Math; SC Womens Sports 1989-; Edisto Booster Club 1989-; PTA; Teacher Incentive Awd 1989-; *office:* Edisto HS PO Box 101 Cordova SC 29039

MOSNER, ANN LA RUSSO, Vocal Music Teacher; *b:* Cheektowaga, NY; *m:* James L.; *ed:* (BS) Music Ed, Rosary Hill Coll 1978; (MED) Elem Ed, SUNY Buffalo 1984; Turnkey Trained, NY St Ed Dept; Grad Work in Curr, Vocal Techniques; *cr:* Vocal Music Teacher Buffalo Public Sch 1978-80, W Hertel Acad 1980-83, City Honors Sch 1983-; *ai:* Music & Artistic Dir of Spirit of Youth; Erie Cty Music Educators Assn (Bd of Dir 1983-85, VP 1985-); Music Educators Natl Conference NY St Sch Music Assn; Cheektowaga Comm Coll (Asst Dir, Accompanist) 1979-; Infant of Prague Church Choir.

MOSS, CYNTHIA BOGGS, Mathematics Dept Chairperson; *b:* Ducktown, TN; *m:* Ronny; *ed:* (BS) Ed, Univ TN Knoxville 1978; *cr:* Teacher Polk Cty HS 1978-; *ai:* Academic & Math Team Coach; Awds Prgm Comm Chairperson; Math Assn of America 1986-88; NCTM, TN Math Teachers Assn 1987-; Teacher of Yr 1983; *office:* Polk Cty HS School House Hill Benton TN 37307

MOSS, GLORIA SALINAS, 7th/8th Grade Science Teacher; *b:* Harlingen, TX; *m:* Ray B.; *c:* Wesley R., Ashley D.; *ed:* (BA) Elem Ed/Bio/Phys Ed, 1975, (MS) Diagnostician, 1976 Univ of TX PAU; TMR Endorsement, LLD, EMR; Phys Ed with Aerobic, TESA Certificate; Reality Therapy; *cr:* Teen Bd Coord Sears & Company 1974-76; 6th Grade Teacher Lincoln Jr HS 1976-78; 5th Grade Teacher Zavala Elem 1978-82; ESL Teacher Mc Allen Sch Adult Ed 1982-86; Aerobic Instr Glorias Energetics Stud 1981-; 7th/8th Grade Teacher Brown Jr HS 1982-; *ai:* Teens Against Drugs 1985-; S TX Engineering, Math, Sci Prgm Spon 1987-88;

Cmptr Club 1989-; Spon Quiz Bowl Zavala Elem & Brown Jr HS; Springfest & Health Fairs; TSTA Mem 1975-85; NEA Mem 1985-87; TCTA Mem 1987-; Mc Allen Chamber of Commerce Mem 1988-; Arthritis Fnd Mem; Muscular Dystrophy, Spec Olyumpics Cmmty Service Mem; Mc Allen Ind Sch Dist Teacher of Yr 1988-89, St of TX Ed Nom Teacher of Yr 1989-; *home:* Rt 1 Box 156A Mission TX 78572

MOSS, LINDA FAYE, English Teacher; *b:* Clarksville, TN; *ed:* (BS) Eng, Austin Peay St Univ 1973; Guidance/Cnslng Austin Peay St Univ; Murray St Univ; *cr:* Eng Teacher Greenwood Jr HS 1973-83; Northwest HS 1980-; *ai:* NEA 1973-89; TN Ed Assn 1973-89; Clarksville-Montgomery Cty Ed Assn 1973-89; Delta Sigma Theta Sorority Inc 1970-; Order of Eastern Star 1989-; *home:* 908 Austin Dr Clarksville TN 37040

MOSS, MARCIA STEWART, Third Grade Teacher; *b:* Canal Zone, Panama Republic; *ed:* (BS) Early Chldhd Ed, Radford Coll 1977; Ed Law & Psych Ed Assessment, Univ of VA; *cr:* Teacher Hurt Park Elem 1978-; *ai:* Staff Dev Advisory Cncl; United Fund Chairperson; Clean Valley Cncl & Oratorical Contest Coord; Roanoke Ed Assn (Faculty Rep) 1984-88; VA Minority Caucus, Blue Ridge Cncl Teachers of Math 1990; VA Ed Assn, NEA 1978-; Blue Ridge Cncl Cub Scouts Den Leader 1980-82; Roanoke Certificate of Appreciation 1989; *office:* Hurt Park Elem Sch 1525 Salem Ave Sw Roanoke VA 24016

MOSS, PAULA ALLEN, Band Director; *b:* Spartanburg, SC; *m:* Gilbert F.; *ed:* (BA) Music Ed, Newberry Coll 1978; (MED) Ed, Univ of SC 1989; Gifted Ed, Furman Univ; *cr:* Band Dir Laurens Dist 55 Schls 1978-; *ai:* Youth Arts Center; Beta Siga Phi, Music Educators Natl Conference, SC Band Dir Assn, SC Ed Assn, Laurens Cty Ed Assn, Delta Omicron Intnl Music, Cardinal Key NHS; Teacher Incentive Awd 1988-89; *office:* Hickory Tavern Sch W Main Laurens SC 29360

MOSS, RELDA ANN, 2nd Grade Teacher; *b:* Dayton, OH; *ed:* (BS) Elem Ed, Central St Univ 1972; (MS) Educ Admin, Univ of Dayton 1975; *cr:* Teacher Central Elem 1972-82; East Elem 1982-; *ai:* Fairborn Ed Assn; NEA; OH Ed Assn; Future Teachers of Amer Past Mem; Tri-Hi-Y Past Mem & Treas; Leadership Recognition Awd 1968, Natl Honor Society 1969, Awd of Distinction 1969 Jefferson Twnshp Sr High; Cum Laude, Central St Univ 1972; Jennings Teacher/Scholar 1977-78; *home:* 3609 S Union Rd Dayton OH 45418

MOSS, STEPHEN S., Art Teacher; *b:* Shelby, NC; *m:* Philomena Sealey; *ed:* (BFA) Art, MA Coll of Art & Atlanta Coll of Art 1977; (MFA) Art, 1984, (MAED) Art Ed, 1985 Univ of GA; Doctoral Candidate Univ of GA; Skidmore Coll Fellowship 1990; *cr:* Art Teacher Lincolnton HS 1984-85, Walton HS 1986-; *ai:* Walton Stus for Promotion of Environmental Awareness Spon; Natl Art Honor Society Spon; Cobb Cty Intercultural Comm; GA Art Ed Assn, NAEA 1985-; Ford Fnd Fellowship 1980-81, Materials Grant 1980; Skidmore Coll Fellowship 1990; *office:* George Walton HS 1590 Bill Murdock Rd Marietta GA 30062

MOSS, WANDA (USSERY), English Teacher; *b:* Mc Rae, GA; *m:* Michael D.; *c:* Christopher, Adam; *ed:* (BA) Eng, GA S Coll 1976; (MED) Ed, Converse Coll 1983; Assessments of Performance in Teaching Trng, Prgm for Effective Teaching Trng, GRI Lab Using Cmptrs for Remedial Rdng Stu Trng; *cr:* Eng Teacher Effingham Cty HS 1976-77, Byrnes HS 1978-; *ai:* Spon of Serteen Club; Prom Adv; Teacher in Survive Five Alternative Sch; Stu Advisory Comm Mem; *office:* James F Byrnes HS PO Box 178 Duncan SC 29334

MOSTAD, C J. CHRISTIANSEN, 2nd Grade Teacher; *b:* Alexandria, MN; *m:* Dennis A.; *c:* Daniel, Jolinda Mostad-Kreider; *ed:* (BS) Elem Ed, Mary Hardin 1965; (MS) Ed, Baylor Univ 1966; U of HI/HI Pacific/U C Berkley/HI Loa Coll/Church Coll HI; *cr:* Pre-Sch Teacher Verdun 1959-63; K-1st Grade Teacher Munich Elem 1966-68; 7th-9th Grade Spec Ed Teacher Chula Vista Jr HS 1968-69; Kndgtn Teacher Helemann Elem 1969-70; 3rd Grade Teacher Wheeler AFB 1970-76; 2nd Grade Teacher Molulele Elem 1988-; *office:* Dept of Ed 1304 14th St Hickam AFB HI 96818

MOSTYN, MARGIE IRWIN, Algebra/Geometry Teacher; *b:* Joliet, IL; *m:* John P.; *c:* Mollie, Jay; *ed:* (BA) Ed, Lewis Univ 1977; Grad Work Counseling, IL St Univ; *cr:* 4th-8th Grade Teacher St Joseph Sch 1977-80; Math Teacher Providence Cath HS 1983-; Algebra Teacher Joliet Jr Coll 1988; Geometry Teacher IL Math & Sci Acad 1989-; *ai:* Alumni Correspondent & Communicate with Coll Alumni; IL Cncl Math Teachers 1989-; Jr Cath Womens Club Chair Fund Raisers 1970-78, Lifetime Mem Awd; Article Published 1988; *office:* Providence Cath HS 1800 W Lincoln Hwy New Lenox IL 60441

MOTA, EDMUNDO, 7th Grade History Teacher; *b:* Ajo, AZ; *ed:* (BSED) Phys Ed, Univ of AZ 1958; (MAED) Ed, N AZ Univ 1965; *cr:* His/Phys Ed Teacher Gila Vista Jr HS 1960-; *ai:* Bsktbl Team Jr HS; Amer Legion, Elks 1969-; Knights of Columbus 1965-.

MOTA, LYDIA, Special Education Teacher; *b:* Texas, TX; *m:* Jack;; *c:* Michael, Lee, Alma, Jacques; *ed:* (BA) Elem Ed/Lang Arts, Bi-Ling Eastern NM St Univ 1972; (MED) Sch Admn, Sul Ross St Univ 1974; Spec Ed; Mid-Mgmt; Gifted & Taalented; *ai:* Val Verde TSTA (PAC Chm 1977-78 Awds Comm 1977-78 Treas 1972-73); Gov Blue Ribbon Comm Mem 1978-79; Mayors Comm Mem 1979-80; Sch Yrbk Spon Elem Sch; Sch Newspaper Spon Elem & Middle Sch.

MOTE, OLGA JEAN, Retired Jr High School Teacher; *b:* Newcastle, TX; *m:* Billy Donald; *c:* Linda, Brent, Kevin; *ed:* (BA) Ed, San Diego St Univ 1965; *cr:* Teacher of Gifted Brier Patch Elem 1965-69; Eng Teacher Palm Jr HS 1969-85; Retired; *ai:* CA Ombudsman 1988; *home:* 4529 Lyons Dr La Mesa CA 92041

MOTE, PATRICIA TAYLOR, Senior High School Teacher; *b:* Ft Knox, KY; *m:* Doyle Kirby; *c:* John A., David T.; *ed:* (MED) Sci Ed, Univ of GA 1975; *cr:* Research Microbiologist Centers for Disease Control; Teacher Stone Mountain HS; *ai:* Sci Olympiad Team; Sr Beta Club; NHS; Sci Teachers of De Kalb (Secy 1982-83, VP 1987-88), Sci Teacher of Yr 1983; NSTA 1973-; GA Sci Teachers Assn 1973-, 4th Dist Sci Teacher of Yr 1978; Friends of Fernbank 1985-; Friends of Atlanta Zoo 1975-; Stone Mountain HS Teacher of Yr; De Kalb Cty Teacher of Yr; STAR Teacher; Microbiology Articles Published; *office:* Stone Mountain HS 4555 Central Dr Stone Mountain GA 30083

MOTLEY, ANNA ASHLOCK, Substitute Teacher; *b:* Burkesville, KY; *m:* William; *c:* Judith M. Bobbitt, Joan E. Nevins, J. Katherine Dickert; *ed:* (BA) Elem Ed, 1955, (MA) Counseling/Guidance, 1963 W KY St Univ; Gifted & Talented, AZ St Univ 1970-86; Elem Ed; *cr:* 1st-8th Grade Teacher KY 1935-42; 1st-3rd Grade Teacher Potter Orphans Home 1949-54, Bowling Green City Schls 1955-66; 2nd Grade Teacher 1966-75, 1st-5th Grade Teacher/Coord of Gifted 1975-86 Flowing Wells Dist #8; *ai:* Univ of AZ Teacher Prep Prgm 1970-74, AZ St Testing Comm; AZ St Dept of Ed Task Force on Pupil Achievement Testing Mem; Bowling Green Ed Assn Pres; PTA (Pres, Treas); Flowing Wells Ed Assn (Pres) 1966-, Plaque of Appreciation; AZ Ed Assn 1966-; NEA 1956-; Phi Delta Kappa Mem 1977-; Church of Christ Sunday Sch Dir; Univ of AZ Certificate of Appreciation 1974, Outstanding Teacher of Gifted 1985; AZ St Dept of Ed Certificate of Appreciation 1986; Area Rdng Cncl Letter of Appreciation; Outstanding Elem Teachers of America 1972; *home:* 2292 W Paseo Cielo Tucson AZ 85741

MOTLEY, KATE RICHARDS, English Teacher; *b:* Alton, IL; *m:* John R.; *c:* Krista, Mark; *ed:* (BA) Theatre, William Woods Coll 1976; Musical Comedy CA Inst of Arts 1974; *cr:* Eng/Soc Stud Teacher Edwardsville Jr HS 1985-87; Eng Teacher Edwardsville Sr HS 1987-; *ai:* Drama Dir; Thespian Troupe Spon; NCTE 1986-; IL Theatre Assn 1988-; YMCA (Bd of Dir, Secy 1980-84), Achievement Awd 1978-84, Service Awd 1988-91; St Johns United Meth Church; Wildey Arts Center Project 1985-86; Jaycee Service Awd 1986; *office:* Edwardsville Sr HS 145 West St Edwardsville IL 62025

MOTT, ELIZABETH LAVURN, First Grade Teacher; *b:* East Mc Keesport, PA; *m:* Charles Howard; *c:* Charles L., Marshall L., Melanie D. Cooper, Lisa L. Schreiber, Kevin D., Stephen H.; *ed:* (AB) Chem/Bio, Asbury Coll 1952; (MA) Elem Ed, GA Southwestern 1977; *cr:* Teacher Dougherty Cty 1959-60, Lee Cty 1960-61, Dougherty Cty 1973-; *ai:* Girl Scout, Cub Scout, Church Choir Leader; Church Youth Worker; DCAE, GEA, NEA 1975-89; *home:* 1913 Forest Glen Rd Albany GA 31707

MOTTO, MARY LOU (MULLER), 5th-6th Grade Science Teacher; *b:* Teaneck, NJ; *c:* Richard, David, Michael (dec); *ed:* (BS) Elem Ed, Seton Hall Univ 1965; (MA) Rdng, Jersey City St 1971; Certificate Learning Disabilities Teacher-Consultant, Montclair St 1989; Various Courses Admin, Academically Talented, Media; *cr:* 3rd Grade Teacher Cresskill Bd of Ed 1965-68; Title I Rdng Teacher Fair Lawn Bd of Ed 1971-77; 3rd Grade Teacher 1977-79; Rdng Specialist Elmwood Park Bd of Ed 1979-80; Rdng Specialist/Academically Talented/Supplemental Teacher Carlstadt Public Schls 1980-85; *ai:* NJ Teachers Academically Talented; *office:* Carlstadt Public Schls 3rd St Carlstadt NJ 07072

MOTZ, KAREN ZABELL, French Teacher; *b:* Detroit, MI; *m:* John P.; *c:* Laura, John; *ed:* (AB) Fr/Ger, Univ of MI 1977; (MED) Foreign Lang Curr/Instruction, Cleveland St Univ 1983; Courses in Foreign Lang Translation, Marygrove Coll 1977; *cr:* Substitute Teacher Clarke Cty Public Schls 1977; Nursery Sch/Kdgtn Teacher Dunoon Armed Services Center Scotland 1978-80; Fr Teacher Magnificat HS 1980-89; *ai:* Cleveland Diocesan Foreign Lang Assn (VP, Mem, Officer 1982-86) 1980-.

MOTZ, STEFFANIE, Social Studies Teacher; *b:* Oakland City, IN; *m:* Raymond Lee; *c:* Benjamin; *ed:* (BS) Soc Stud/Ed, IN Univ 1970; (MA) Ed, Univ of Evansville 1975; *cr:* 5th/6th Grade Teacher Culver Elem Sch 1971-72; 2nd-7th Grade Teacher Thompkins Elem Sch 1972-84; 6th/8th Grade Soc Stud Teacher Thompkins Mid Sch 1984; *ai:* Faculty Cabinet Mem; Phi Delta Kappa; Delta Kappa Gamma Treas 1988-; NCSS, IN Cncl of Soc Stud, IN Mid Sch Assn, Evansville Mid Sch Assn; Evansville Teachers Assn Building Rep; Evansville Philharmonic Guild 1986-; Evansville Courier Mid Sch Teacher of Yr 1990; *office:* Thompkins Mid Sch 1300 W Mill Rd Evansville IN 47710

MOULDER, JOSEPH A., Chem/Physics/Earth Sci Teacher; *b:* Newberry, MI; *m:* Harriet Goddard; *c:* Thadius, Gretchen; *ed:* (BS) Bio/Chem, 1971, (MS) Sci Ed, 1975 W MI Univ; Grad Stud Geology, Physics, Chem, Ed MI St, Oakland Univ, W MI Univ, Hope Coll; *cr:* Sci Teacher Lee HS 1972-; *ai:* Ski Club; Sci Olympiad; MI Ed Assn 1972-; Godfrey Lee Ed Assn (Negotiatior, Pres); MI Sci Teachers; MEA, PAC Rep 1981-; Wrote Event for Sci Olympiad.

MOULTON, GLADYS MAYO, Retired; *b:* Springfield, TN; *m:* John L.; *c:* Janyth Moulton Henry, John C.; *ed:* (BS) Elem Ed, 1971; (MA) Curr/Instr Ed, 1974 Austin Peay St Univ; *cr:* Teacher Lamont Sch 1940-43; Orlinda Sch 1944-45; Coopertown Sch 1951-86; *ai:* Sub Teacher at Coopertown Sch; Pres-Robertson Cty NRTA; Church Organist for 38 Yrs; NEA Mem; TEA; RCEA; Robertson Cty Retired Teachers Assn Pres 1988-; Jesse Holman Jones Hosp Aux 1986-; 1978 Merit Teacher in Robertson Cty TN; 1978/1983 Teacher of Yr Runner-Up Robertson Cty-TN; *home:* 5057 Hwy 49 W Springfield TN 37172

MOUNTAIN, LILLIAN TIERNEY, Third Grade Teacher; *b:* Worcester, MA; *m:* Robert H.; *c:* Tammy A.; *ed:* (BS) Elem Ed, Gorham St Teachers Coll 1953; Grad Work Univ of S ME & Boston Univ; *cr:* 3rd Grade Teacher 1953-58, 4th Grade Teacher 1958-63, 5th Grade Teacher 1963-64, 4th-6th Grade Rdng Teacher 1964-65 Soccarappa Sch; Nursery Sch Teacher Gorham Co-op 1970-74; 3rd Grade Teacher Millett & Narragansett Schls 1974-; *ai:* GTA, MTA, NEA; *office:* Narragansett Elem Sch 284 Main St Gorham ME 04038

MOUNTAIN, PATRICIA L. (KURTH), Social Studies Teacher; *b:* Eau Claire, WI; *m:* John; *c:* Patrick, J. Michael, David, James, Thomas, Richard, William; *ed:* (BS) Eng/Psych, Marquette Univ 1955; (MA) Ed, 1980, (Rank I) Guidance, 1986 W KY; Catechical Cert 1981, Update 1988; Continuing Ed Counseling 1990; *cr:* Soc Stud Teacher Immaculate 1972-89; Guidance/Teacher Owensboro Cath Mid Sch 1989-; *ai:* Soc Stud Dept Head; Soc Stud Curr Comm; Religion Master Schedule; Diocese of Owensboro Cath Educators (Pres 1987-) 1985-; NCEA 1972-; Amer Assn for Counseling & Dev 1989-; Public Defenders Office 1988-; Task Force Sch Consolidation 1987-89; Immaculate Parish (Cncl 1988-89, Personnel Comm 1987-, Eucharistic Minister 1983-, Lector 1978-).

MOUNTS, DANIEL CHARLES, Sixth Grade Teacher; *b:* Houston, TX; *m:* Beth Ann Palmer; *c:* Jessica N., Dylan B.; *ed:* (BA) Accounting, Mid America Nazarene Coll 1976; (MS) Rdng, SW MO St Univ 1984; *cr:* 3rd Grade Teacher 1980-84, 6th Grade Teacher 1984- Republic Sch Dist; *office:* Republic Mid Sch 518 N Hampton Republic MO 65738

MOUSE, MELANI MARQUE, Bio/Anatomy Physiology Teacher; *b:* Weatherford, OK; *ed:* (BS) Bio Ed, 1985, (MS) Scndry Sch Admin, 1987 SW OK St Univ; Doctoral Prgm Curr/Admin, Univ of OK; Working on Superintendancy Cert; *cr:* Teacher/Coach Mustang HS 1985-; *ai:* HS Girls Bsktbl Asst Coach; Jr Var Soph Head Coach Girls B-Ball; Asst Girls Track; NEA 1986-; Amer Educl Research Assn 1989-; Received a Fellowship for Grad Study in Doctoral Prgm at Univ of MI; Mustang HS Recognizing Excl Awd 1988-89; *office:* Mustang HS 906 S Heights Mustang OK 73064

MOUSEL, RONALD E., Principal; *b:* Eau Claire, WI; *m:* Elizabeth Misch; *c:* John, William, Michelle, Patrick; *ed:* (BA) Phys Ed, Univ of WI La Crosse 1964; (MS) Ed, N IL Univ 1967; (MA) Park/Recreation Admin, Cntrl MI Univ 1971; *cr:* Teacher Rice Lake Schls 1967-69; Professor West Shore Comm Coll 1969-81; Teacher 1982-86, Prin 1986- Pentwater Schls; *ai:* NASSP, MASSP, MEMSPA 1986-; Red Cross (Bd of Appeals Chm 1972-) 1969-, Volunteer of Yr 1989; *office:* Pentwater Public Schls 600 E Park St Pentwater MI 49449

MOUSSEAU, ANDY W., HS Mathematics Teacher; *b:* Pontiac, MI; *m:* Laura Barringer; *c:* A. J.; *ed:* (BS) Math, Aquinas Coll 1987; *cr:* Math Teacher Grand Haven Sr HS 1987-; *ai:* Asst Track Coach; Allendale Weslyan Church (Youth Group, Choir); *office:* Grand Haven Sr HS 900 Cutler Grand Haven MI 49417

MOUTON, PATRICIA PENLAND, English Teacher; *b:* Biltmore, NC; *m:* Stephen; *c:* David, Joanna; *ed:* (BA) Eng, Maryville Coll 1961; (MS) Rdng Ed, Syracuse Univ 1979; Trng as Adjunct Professor at Syracuse Univ; *cr:* Rdng Teacher Gillette Road Mid Sch 1961-70; Eng Teacher Cicero HS 1979-81, Liverpool HS 1981-; *ai:* Yrbk Adv 1985-89; Cultural Diversity Cncl; Restructuring II; Delta Kappa Gamma Secy; NYSEC Newsletter Ed 1984-87; Cty N Human Services Cncl 1975-76; US Distinguished Teacher 1986; NY Eng Teacher of Excl 1989; NEH Seminar on Fairy Tales; NEH Inst on Greek Mythology; *home:* 8316 Redwing Dr Liverpool NY 13090

MOWERY, BRENDA LEE, Sixth Grade Teacher; *b:* Rolla, MO; *ed:* (BS) Elem Ed, Univ of MO Columbia 1985; *cr:* 6th Grade Teacher West Boulevard Elem Sch 1986-87; 6th Grade Teacher 1987- Madison C-3 Public Sch; *ai:* Drug Awareness Advisory Comm; Jr Concession Stand; Madison Booster Club 1988-; CTA 1987-; Intl Rdng Assn 1989-; *home:* 100 Comb Madison MO 65263

MOWREY, ROMILDA NEAL, Health/Phys Ed Teacher; *b:* Nicholas City, WV; *w:* John Wesley III (dec); *c:* John W. IV, Kristina F.; *ed:* (BA) Health/Phys Ed/Art, Glenville St Coll 1968; Grad Stud Medical Aspect Sports, Marshall Univ & WV COGS Prgm 1981; *cr:* Phys Ed Teacher N Burlington Jr/Sr HS 1968-69; Art Teacher Gauley Bridge HS & Grade Sch 1970-74; Dental Asst Doctor Tom Vodak 1977-78; Health/Phys Ed Teacher Summersville Jr HS 1980-; *ai:* WV St AIDS Curr; Writing Comm; Asst Spon Natl Jr Honor Society; Pep Club Spon; Summerville Jr HS Sch Improvement Team & Health/Phys Ed Dept Head; WV Ed Assn 1988-; Kappa Delta Pi; Summerville Baptist Church (Missions Chairperson 1985-85, Memorial Comm Treas 1988-); *home:* 502 Scarlet O Hara Dr Summersville WV 26651

MOWRY, JOHN CHARLES, Speech/Language Pathologist; *b:* Eustus, FL; *m:* Lou Gillean; *c:* Kevin; *ed:* (BA) Speech/Lang Therapy, 1969, (MAT) Speech/Lang Therapy, 1972 Harding Univ; Grad Stud SE MO St Univ 1978-79; *cr:* Speech/Lang Pathologist Potosi R-3 Schls 1969-, Private Practice 1980-; *ai:* City Park Tennis Dir; Potosi R-3 Sch Cmptr & Gifted Comms; MO St

Teachers Assn, Cmmty Teachers Assn, MO Speech/Hearing Assn 1969-; Potosi Church of Christ Song Leader 1969-; Church Youth Rally Chm 1987; Clothing & Food Drive for Needy 1972-; Outstanding Young Men of America 1982-83; *home:* PO Box 412 Potosi MO 63664

MOWRY, LOU (GILLEAN), Learning Disabilities Teacher; *b:* Paragould, AR; *m:* John Charles; *c:* Kevin; *ed:* (BA) Bio, Harding Univ 1969; (MAED) Spec Ed, SE MO St Univ 1979; Grad Work Univ of MO Columbia; *cr:* Life Sci Teacher Potosi Jr HS 1969-72; Adult Sewing Class Teacher Potosi HS 1972-74; Learning Disabilities Teacher John Evans Mid Sch 1976-; *ai:* Nutrition Comm 1988- & Prof Improvement Comm 1988-89 Potosi Mid Sch; MO St Teachers Assn 1969-; Cmmty Teachers Assn Schlsp Comm 1969-; Potosi Church of Christ Clothing & Food Drive for Needy 1969-; Outstanding Young Women of America 1983; *home:* PO Box 412 Potosi MO 63664

MOXLEY, GLENDA VAUGHN, Fourth Grade Teacher; *b:* Etowah Cty, AL; *m:* Robert B.; *c:* Tammey Kilpatrick, Tracy Crawford, J. Farrell Hammett; *ed:* (BS) Elem Ed, Jacksonville St Univ 1974; (MA) Elem Ed, 1976, (EDS) Sch Admin, 1988 Univ of AL; Addl Grad Stud, Peabody Coll & Auburn Univ; *cr:* 1st Grade Teacher 1974-80, 4th Grade Teacher 1980-86, 4th Grade Teacher/Vice Prin 1986- West End Elem; *ai:* Vice-Prin; Alpha Delta Kappa Recording Secy 1988-; PTO Recording Secy 1986-; Walnut Grove UMC (Pianist 1986-, Trustee 1986-88); West End Elem Teacher of Yr 1986-87; *office:* West End Elem Rt 1 Box 211-B Altoona AL 35952

MOXLEY, MARIE T., English Teacher; *b:* Troy, AL; *m:* Marvin R.; *c:* Susan M., Molly M.; *ed:* (BA) Eng, Troy St Univ 1969; *cr:* Teacher Fitzgerald HS 1969-83, Vidalia HS 1983-84, David Emanuel Acad 1985-; *ai:* Yrbk & 9th Grade Adv; Delta Kappa Gamma 1980-83; PAGE 1989-; GAE, NEA 1969-83; Jr Womans Club VP 1970-80, Outstanding Family 1972; STAR Teacher 1989-; City of Cobbtown Cncl Woman 1987-; *office:* David Emanuel Acad PO Box 77 Stillmore GA 30464

MOXLEY, WARREN DONALD, Science Teacher/Coach; *b:* Bowling Green, KY; *m:* Ellen Whitner; *c:* Donald, Kimberly; *ed:* (BS) Pre-Med, St Augustines Coll 1654; Bank St Coll, Kean Coll, NY Univ, OH Wesleyan Univ; *cr:* Teacher/Coach Kentucky-Owensboro & Franklin 1654-59; Teacher Chicago Public Schls 1960-67; Juvenile Probation Officer Cook Cty IL 1968; Teacher/Coach New York Public Schls 1971-83; Teacher Eastside HS 1983-84; Teacher/Coach Irvington HS 1984-; *ai:* 8th Grade Ftbl, Jr Var & Asst Var Bsktbl Coach; NEA, Irvington Ed Assn, NJ Ed Assn 1984-; Kappa Alpha Psi 1954-; Natl Sci Fnd Grants 1966, 1967.

MOYER, EDWARD LLEWELLYN, JR., 7th Grade World His Teacher; *b:* York, PA; *m:* Carolyn Elizabeth Miller; *ed:* (BSED) Soc Stud/Ancient His, Millersville Univ 1968; Grad Stud York Coll of PA, Penn St Univ; *cr:* Teacher York Suburban Sch Dist 1968-; *ai:* Jogging Club Mid Sch; Tells Awd Comm; NEA, PA St Ed Assn, York Suburban Ed Assn 1968-; York Twirling Assn 1984-; Grace Luth Church Act 1970-.

MOYER, LINDA D., Spanish Teacher; *b:* Kermit, TX; *m:* Dennis K.; *c:* Kathryn; *ed:* (BA) His, Ursinus Coll 1966; Hispanic Stud, Univ of Madrid 1966; *cr:* Span Teacher Upper Perkiomen HS 1966-; *ai:* Learning Styles, Paideia, Peer Coaching, Induction Comms; Montgomery Cty Teachers of Foreign Lang; NEA, PSEA, Local Ed Assn Secy 1978-81; PA Ger Society, Goschenhoppen Historians, Peter Wentz Farmstead Society; Mentor Teacher; Oustanding Young Educator Awd; *office:* Upper Perkiomen HS 2 Walt Rd Pennsburg PA 18073

MOYERS, ANNE A., Fifth Grade Teacher; *b:* Independence, MO; *m:* William G.; *c:* Glennon, Carol A. Morgan; *ed:* (BS) Ed, Cntrl WA St Univ 1963; (MA) Ed, Lewis & Clark 1976; Grad Stud; *cr:* Teacher Edmonds Sch Dist 1963-65, Head Start 1968-69; Substitute Teacher Auburn Sch Dist 1969-70; Teacher St Johns Episcopal Sch 1970-72, Columbus Public Schls 1972-73, Vancouver Public Schls 1973-; *office:* Felida Elem Sch 2700 NW 119th St Vancouver WA 98685

MOYERS, DEBBY ANN (WARNER), English Teacher; *b:* Moline, IL; *m:* Jewel I.; *c:* Zachary; *ed:* (BS ED) Eng, IL St Univ 1969; TESA Critical Thinking; Writing Wkshp; Rdng Ed; *cr:* Eng Teacher Tremont 702 1969-; *ai:* Yrbk Echo Co-Spon; NCTE; Western IL Univ Distinguished Teaching Awd 1989; Natl Endowment for the Hum; Bradley Univ Study Amer Lit; Cooperative Learning Wkshp; *office:* Tremont H S 400 W Pearl Tremont IL 61568

MOYERS, JOHN RUSSEL, Social Studies Teacher; *b:* Petersburg, WV; *m:* Erma Shirley Berg; *c:* Meredith Jeanene, John Frederick; *ed:* (AB) Phys Ed, Fairmount St 1970; (MS) Phys Ed, WVU; *cr:* Traveling Phys Ed Teacher Monongalia Cty 1970-72; Grant Cty 1973; 6th Grade Teacher Petersburg Elem 1974-82; Phys Ed Teacher Maysville Elem 1983-85; Soc Stud Teacher/Coach Petersburg HS 1986-; *ai:* Wrestling Coach; *office:* Petersburg HS Jefferson Ave Petersburg WV 26847

MOYERS, PATTI HIXSON, 4th Grade Teacher; *b:* Lexington, KY; *ed:* (BA) Soc Sci, Bethel Coll 1969; (MS) Curr & Instruction, Univ of TN Martin 1977; *cr:* Title I Teacher Cayce Elem 1970-72; EMR/Resource Teacher Eastside Elem/Cntrl Elem 1972-74; Resource/5th Grade Teacher Dixie Elem 1974-84; 4th Grade Teacher Lake Road Elem 1985-; *office:* Lake Road Elem Sch 1130 E Hwy 22 Union City TN 38261

MOYNIHAN, MICHAEL FRANCIS, English Teacher; *b:* Glens Falls, NY; *m:* Kaye E.; *c:* David, Barbara Gillis; *ed:* (BS) Eng Ed, Siena Coll 1963; (MS) Eng Ed, SUNY New Paltz 1968; Cmptr, Tech/Bus Writing Adirondack Comm Coll; *cr:* Eng Wappingers Cntrl Sch 1963-65, Granville Cntrl Sch 1965-67, Hudson Falls 1972-89, Corinth Cnrtrl Sch 1967-; *ai:* Jr HS Boys & Girls Track Team Coach; Ski Club Asst Dir; Ft Edward Little League Pres 1975-76; Ft Edward Rescue Squad Mem 1975-76; Ft Edward Lions Club Mem 1972-77; Active Tech Promotional Writer; *home:* 84 Northwinds Queensbury NY 12804

MOZINGO, ANNE LYNCH, 7th/8th Grade Teacher; *b:* Goldsboro, NC; *m:* Carl; *c:* Amanda M. Hill, Jonathan; *ed:* (BS) Elem Ed, E Carolina Univ 1964; *cr:* 6th-8th Grade Teacher Greenwood Jr HS 1965-81, Spring Creek Sch 1981-; *ai:* Spring Creek Sch PTA Exec Bd & Inservice Comm; NEA, NCAE 1965-; Delta Kappa Gamma Society 1965-; Order Eastern Star 1978-; *home:* Rt 5 Box 200 Lagrange NC 28551

MROCZEK, DAVID J., Social Science Teacher; *b:* Loup City, NE; *m:* Mary Jo Knapp; *c:* Sydney, Adam, Molly; *ed:* (BA) His/Phys Ed/Soc Sci/Coaching, Kearney St Coll 1988; *cr:* Teacher Deshler HS 1988-; *ai:* 8th Grade Class Spon; Head Ftbl Coach; Asst Var Bsktbl & Var Track Coach; Jr Bsktbl Coach; Deshler Ed Organization 1988-; Lion Club 1989-; Knights of Columbus 1978-; *office:* Deshler HS 3rd & Plum Deshler NE 68340

MROZ, JAMES F., Technology Education Teacher; *b:* Norway, MI; *m:* Mary Mackie; *c:* Stephanie L., Sara K.; *ed:* (BS) Phys Ed, MI St Univ 1970; Grad Stud MI St Univ, Cntrl MI Univ; *cr:* Teacher St Charles HS 1971-; *ai:* Stu Cncl & Technology Club Adv; Jr Var Ftbl Coach; N Cntrl Accreditation Steering Comm Co-Chairperson; Saginaw Cty Teachers Ed Curr Dev; MI Industrial & Tech Ed Society; *office:* St Charles HS 881 W Walnut St Saint Charles MI 48655

MROZ, ROGER W., Director of Music; *b:* Buffalo, NY; *m:* Judith Ann Dulkiewicz; *c:* Janel L., Tiffany A.; *ed:* (BFA) Music Ed, 1969, (MED) Music Ed, 1973, SUNY Buffalo; (CAS) Sch Admin, St Coll at Buffalo 1978; (EDD) Curr Planning, SUNY Buffalo 1982; *cr:* Music Dir Tonawanda Public Schls 1969-; *ai:* Spring Musicals Orchestral Dir, La Salle Flute Club & Saxaphone Club Adv; Tonawanda Jazz Renaissance Dir; Erie Cty Music Educators Assn, Music Educators Natl Conference, Ny St United Teacher, Tonawanda Educators Assn, Natl Assn of Jazz Educators; NY Congress of Parents & Teachers Honorary Life Mem; Jenkins Memorial Service Awd; Book Published; *office:* Tonawanda HS Fletcher & Hinds Sts Tonawanda NY 14150

MRUZ, LINDA ROLFSMEYER, Physiology & Chemistry Teacher; *b:* Lincoln, NE; *m:* Daniel Joseph; *c:* Danielle, Erin; *ed:* (BS) Bio, NE Wesleyan Univ 1978; Bio; *cr:* Bio & Chem Teacher 1978-79, Bio Teacher 1979-82, Bio & Physiology Teacher 1982-87, Physiology & Chem Teacher 187- Fremont Sr HS; *ai:* Asst Girls Track Coach 1978-87; Asst Girls Vlybl Coach 1979-88; Spon Girls Letter Club; Spon Fellowship Chrstn Athletes 1980-; NE St Ed Assn 1978-; Fremont Ed Assn 1978-; St Patricks Cath Church 1984-; Fellowship of Chrstn Athletes 1980-; Nom Fremonts Young Educator of Yr 1981; Produced Instructional Videotapes Dissection of Various Organisms Major Sci Supply Co.

MUCKELVANY, SYLVIA A., 5th Grade Teacher; *b:* Yonkers, NY; *m:* Theodore R.; *c:* Paul, Alycia; *ed:* (BSED) Elem Ed, Mills Coll of Ed 1971; (MSED) Rdng, Coll of New Rochelle 1976; Trng Human Relations Facilitator Yonkers Bd of Ed Human Relations Dept; *cr:* Pre K Teacher P S #25 1972-73; 5th Grade Teacher Museum Sch of the Arts & Sci 1973-; Cooperating/Master Teacher Sarah Lawrence Coll 1987 & 1990; *ai:* PTA VP; Sch Improvement Plan; Mem Former Teacher in Charge; ASCD Mem 1989-; PTA (VP 1988-89) 1972- Life Membership Jenkins Awd 1987; Yonkers Fed of Teachers Mem; NAACP Mem Lifelong; Yonkers Alliance of Minority Sch Educators Mem 1983-; Mem Summer Inst Sarah Lawrence Coll, Guest Presenter 1989; *office:* Museum Sch #25 579 Warburton Ave Yonkers NY 10701

MUCKERHEIDE, PAUL ROBERT, Mathematics Teacher; *b:* Winona, MN; *ed:* (BA) Ec/Math, St Johns Univ 1970; Teachers Cert Univ of WA 1975; (MS) Sports Sci, US Sports Acad 1985; *cr:* Math Teacher Kennedy HS 1972-; *ai:* Coach Head Boys Cross Cntry, Head Girls Cross Cntry, Bsktbl, Track & Asst Boys Track; WA Coaches Assn; North Puget Sound League Cross Cntry Coach of Yr 1978-79, Track Coach of Yr 1981-83; *office:* John F Kennedy HS 140 S 140th Seattle WA 98168

MUDD, MAGGIE WEBER, Retired; *b:* Yarrow, MO; *m:* Otho D.; *c:* Larry D.; *ed:* (BS) Home Ecs, Northeast St Univ 1942; (MS) Elem, Teachers Coll; *cr:* Teacher Yarrow Rural Sch 1942-43; Hazel Creek Rural Sch 1949-51; Oak Dale Rural Sch 1952-53; Willard Elem Sch 1954-86; *ai:* MO St Teachers Assn; Delta Kappa Gamma.

MUELLER, CONNIE FREDERICK, Curr Coord/Rdng Teacher; *b:* New Richmond, WI; *m:* Gerald; *c:* Steve, Lori; *ed:* (MS) Rdng Specialist, Univ of WI River Falls 1978; Curr Coord Cert; *cr:* 1st Grade Teacher Baldwin-Woodville Sch Dist 1973-76; Elem Teacher 1976-89, SEC Curr Chairperson/Rdng Teacher 1989-, Curr/Gifted & Talented Coord 1990 St Croix Cntrl Sch Dist; *ai:* Sch Evaluation Consortium Chairperson; Rdng Comm; St Croix Valley Rdng Cncl, ASCD, WI Ed Assn; Roberts-Warren Rescue Squad; United Church of Christ Sunday Sch Supt; *home:* Rt 1 Box 168 New Richmond WI 54017

MUELLER, JANIE SCHIEFFELIN, Chemistry Teacher; *b:* Denver, CO; *m:* Dean; *ed:* (BS) Bio, CO St Univ 1982; (MS) Exercise Sci, Chapman Coll 1988; *cr:* Sci Instr Fountain-Ft Carson HS 1982-; *ai:* Fellowship of Chrstn Athletes Spon; Head Girls Bsktbl Coach; Weighting Comm; CO Chem Teachers 1988-; Church Praise Band 1987-; *office:* Fountain-Ft Carson HS 515 Santa Fe Fountain CO 80817

MUELLER, MARLENE MEYER, 2nd Grade Teacher; *b:* Fillmore Cty, MN; *m:* Donald Wayne; *c:* David W., Kimberly J. Black, Michelle M.; *ed:* (BS) Elem Ed, Univ of NE Omaha 1972; Bi-ling Ed Trng Inst 1979; Math Solution Leadership Trng 1984; Relations in Classroom; *cr:* 1st-4th Grade Teacher St Johns Luth 1955-56; 3rd-4th Grade Teacher 1960-61, 1st Grade Teacher 1963-64 Zion Luth; 1st-2nd Grade Teacher St Johns Luth 1966-67; 3rd-4th Grade Teacher 1st Good Shephard 1967-68; 1st Grade Teacher Omaha Public Schls 1972-73; 3rd Grade Teacher San Felipe Del Rio Ind Sch Dist 1978-79; 2nd-4th Grade Teacher/Departmentalized Northeast Ind Sch Dist 1979-; *ai:* Math, Cmptr Coord; Bi-ling Teacher; Grade Level Leader; ARD Rep for Prin; Stu Teachers 1978-79; PTA (Bd, Family Life Chm) 1987-89, TX Honorary Life Membership 1988; Kappa Delta Pi 1972-; Gamma Theta Upsilon Charter Mem 1968-69; Lutherans for Life Presentation Chm 1984; AFT Building Rep 1989-; Luth Womens Missionary League; Right To Life Bd; Broadway Group; Concerned Women for America; Windcrest Teacher of Yr 1982; Instrumental in Rdng Methods Course for Teachers Sal Ross Univ; *office:* Windcrest Elem Sch 465 Faircrest San Antonio TX 78239

MUELLER, MICHAEL, Physical Education Teacher; *b:* St Louis, MO; *m:* Janet Collins; *c:* Brett, Stacey; *ed:* (BS) Phys Ed, Univ of MO Columbia 1968; Grad Work NE MO St Univ Kirkville; *cr:* Phys Ed Teacher Mc Cluer HS 1968-; *ai:* Head Ftbl & Bsbl Coach; NEA, MSTA, FFTA; *office:* Mc Cluer HS 1896 S Florissant Rd Florissant MO 63031

MUELLER, MICHAEL JOHN, Math/English Teacher; *b:* Milwaukee, WI; *m:* Dorothy Bernard; *c:* Fred, Chaucer, Koenig, Caesar; *ed:* (BA) Eng Ed, Mercy Coll 1972; *cr:* Soc Stud Harding Jr HS 1974-76; 6th Grade Eng Sci Teacher St Scholastica Sch 1977-79; Eng Teacher Webber Mid Sch 1979-82; Eng/Math Teacher Murphy Jr HS 1982-; *ai:* Adv Photo Club; Sch Security Comm; Kappa Delta Pi (Pres 1976-70 1972-73) Honors; A.H.S.A. 1987; U.S.D.F. 1985-; M.D.A. 1985-; Book Photography Hote Ecole of HS Horse By C D Grant Article for Les Chevaus Mag; *office:* Murphy Jr HS 23901 Fenkel Detroit MI 48223

MUELLER, OLLIE WATTS, 6th Grade Teacher; *b:* Cincinnati, OH; *m:* Frank J. III; *c:* Cynthia, Mark; *ed:* (BSED) Elem Ed, Univ Cincinnati 1971; (MED) Elem Ed, Xavier Univ 1976; Rdng Supvr; *cr:* Elem Teacher St Dominic Sch 1968-; *ai:* Rdng Coord; Chairperson Soc Comm; IRA OH Cncl; Eunice Combs Local Chapter; *home:* 218 Solarama Ct Cincinnati OH 45238

MUELLER, RICHARD W., 4th Grade Teacher; *b:* Fort Atkinson, WI; *m:* Nancy C.; *c:* Monica, Melissa Beckman; *ed:* (BS) Elem Ed, Lakeland Coll 1961; Grad Work N IL Univ; *cr:* 5th Grade Teacher Lake Geneva WI 1961-62; 7th Grade Teacher Harvard IL 1962-67; 3rd-5th Grade Teacher Sussex WI 1967-; *ai:* Staff Dev Advisory, Strategic Planning, Building Improvement Comm; Salem Meth Church Mens Club Pres 1986-88; Jaycees VP 1964-65, Nom Outstanding Young Man Runner Up 1965; *home:* 265 Fisk Ave Waukesha WI 53186

MUELLER, SUSAN JANE, Science Teacher/Science Coord; *b:* Evansville, IN; *ed:* (BA) Sci Ed, 1971, (MA) Sci Ed, 1976, (MA) Sch Admin, 1978 Univ of Evansville; *cr:* Teacher St Matthews Elem Sch 1968-70; Lab Technician General Foods 1969-71; Sci Teacher Barret Mid Sch 1972-77; Sci Teacher/Coord South Jr HS 1977-; *ai:* Spon Stu Research; Sci Acad Coach; Sci Club Spon; KJAS Sci Bowl; South Sci Fair Dir; Developed & Conducted Numerous Wkshps & Trng Sessions 1989-; Developed & Conducted Inservice Prgm 1988; Served Dist Comm Developing & Implementing Gifted Ed 1985; Developed & Conducted Wkshp on Implementing Family Life Skills Curr Scndry Schls 1989; Implemented Project Equals Sci Curr 1987-; KY Sci Teachers Assn Bd of Dir 1973- Outstanding Sci Teacher 1986; KY Acad of Sci 1986- Outstanding Sci Teacher 1988; Phi Delta Kappa 1979-; Assn Progress Bd of Dir; NSTA/NEA/KEA/HEA/KAGE Mem; Univ of EvansvillE Advisory Bd; Sch of Ed; 2nd Dist Math/Sci Alliance Bd of Dir; KJAS Bd of Dir; Leag of Women Voters Bd of Dir 1986-; Univ of Evansville Sch of Ed Adv Bd 1987-; Natl Sci Fnd Grant FL St Univ 1973; Awd of Excl U of E Alumni Assn 1987; Presidential Awd Excl-Sci Teaching/Certificate of Honor 1987; Curr Coord Project REAP; Outstanding Sci Teacher of KY KAPS 1986; Outstanding Teacher South Jr HS 1987; Univ of Evansville Alumni Assn Awd Excl 1987; Presidential Awd Excl Sci Teaching St Awd 1987; *office:* Henderson Cty South Jr HS 800 S Alves St Henderson KY 42420

MUELLER, VIVIAN SANTROCK, 8th Grade English Teacher; *b:* Wadsworth, OH; *m:* Don Sheridan; *c:* Carl F., Cathy Mueller Galligan; *ed:* (BA) Eng, MI St Univ 1959; Grad Stud Counseling & Guidance; *cr:* Teacher Berrien Cty Schls 1948-52, Lansing Public Schls 1954-59, Dansville Ag Sch 1964-68, De Witt Mid Sch 1968-73, Croswell Lexington Mid Sch 1972-; *ai:* N Cntrl Evaluation Team De Witt Mid Sch; Eng Dept Chm 1974-80 Croswell Lexington Schls; Lib Mgr Croswell Lexington Schls 1985-; MEA, NEA, NCTE; *office:* Croswell-Lexington Schls 5485 E Peck Rd Croswell MI 48422

MUENSTRAMAN, KATHY JOYCE (HILL), 6/7th Grade Reading Teacher; *b:* Evansville, IN; *m:* Albert J.; *c:* Mike, Terri, Kristy; *ed:* (BS) Elem Ed, IN St Univ 1969; *cr:* 2nd Grade Teacher Remington Grade Sch 1969-70; 4th Grade Teacher Willie Harris

1971-72; 6th & 7th Grade Rdng Teacher Orchard Farm Mid Sch 1984-85; *ai:* Co-Dir Orchard Farm Mid Sch Play & Spon Orchard Mid Sch Newspaper Staff; ITFS Video Comm; Writing Across Curr Comm; OFCTA Mem 1984-; IRA Local Mem 1986-; Celebrotian Fellowship Childrens Church Yth Group Leader 1984-87 Sunday Sch Teacher 1989-; Booster Club Mem 1984-; *home:* 702 Apricot Dr St Charles MO 63301

MUERY, JUDY ORR, 4th Grade Teacher; *b:* Shamrock, TX; *m:* A. Talley; *c:* Rebecca G. Muery Newman, Talley F., Adam T.; *ed:* (BS) Elem Ed, Univ of TX 1982; Advanced Academic Trng; *cr:* Cmptr Operator Southwestern Bell Telephone Company 1967-69, Austin Police Dept 1972-76; 4th/5th Grade Teacher Pflugerville Ind Sch Dist 1982-; *ai:* Headed Up Lang Textbook Comm for Campus; Classroom Teachers Assn; Grade Level Leader; Teacher of Yr 1985-86; Level II of Career Ladder 1985-86; Graduated With Honors Univ of TX; *office:* Timmerman Elem Sch 700 W Pecan St Pflugerville TX 78660

MUFFET, JANET BROWN, English/Drama Teacher; *b:* Lancaster, OH; *m:* Michael George Jr.; *c:* Mallory, Molly, Donald, Trey; *ed:* (BA) Eng, Mt Union Coll 1967; *cr:* 7th Grade Eng Teacher Chippewa Mid Sch 1967-68; 8th Grade Eng/Girls Phys Ed Teacher Wapakoneta Jr HS 1968-69; 9th Grade Teacher Green HS 1969-71; 7th Grade Eng Teacher Green Jr HS 1971-72; HS Eng Teacher Buckeye Trail HS 1988-; *ai:* Theatre Production, Drama; OEA; NEA; United Meth Women Pres 1984-88; Teacher of Yr Buckeye Trail HS 1989; *office:* Buckeye Trail HS 65555 Wintergreen Rd Lore City OH 43755

MUHLENBRUCK, RICHARD OWEN, 7th/8th Grade Sci/His Teacher; *b:* New York, NY; *m:* Eileen Brennan; *c:* James, Lucy, Jill; *ed:* (AAS) Phys Ed, Queens Comm Coll 1972; (BA) Sci Ed/Phys Ed, CUNY York Coll 1975; Phys Sci Trng Monmouth Coll 1982; Audubon Ecology Trng Greenwich Nature Center 1980; *cr:* Substitute Teacher Brielle Elem Sch 1978-84; Sci/His Teacher Spring Lake Heights Sch 1984-; *ai:* Bsktbl Coach 1984-; Sch Rocket Club Adv; NJ Teacher of Yr Spring Lake Heights Sch 1987; *office:* Spring Lake Heights Sch Rt 71 Spring Lake Hts NJ 07762

MUILENBURG, MARGO A. (MOET), Elem Facilitator of Gifted; *b:* Sibley, IA; *m:* Lloyd; *c:* Greg, Jeff, Sheri; *ed:* (BA) Elem Ed, Westmar Coll 1963; (MS) Gifted, KS St Univ 1988; *cr:* 2nd Grade Teacher Sheldon Public Sch 1955-56; 3rd-5th Grade Teacher Epworth Public Sch 1956-59; 2nd-3rd Grade Teacher Amer Elem Sch Germany 1971-74; Kndgtn-12th Grade Eng Teacher Salina Public Sch 1978-82; 5th-6th Grade Teacher 1982-86, Facilitator of Gifted 1986- Topeka Pub Sch, Highland Park Cntrl; *ai:* Delta Kappa Gamma (Pres 1990-92, VP 1986-88), Schlsp Awd 1988; Phi Kappa Phi 1988-; Church Choir; *office:* Highland Park Cntrl Sch 2717 Illinois Topeka KS 66605

MULCHAY, NORANNE, Biology/Chemistry Teacher; *b:* Glens Falls, NY; *ed:* (BA) Bio, Coll of New Rochelle 1966; (MS) Bio, Long Island Univ Brooklyn 1970; *cr:* Sci Teacher Ft Edward HS 1969-; *ai:* Class,Former Stu Cncl, Bio Club, Activity Club Adv; Vlybl & Jr Var Bsktbl Coach; Sci Teachers Assn of NY St 1972-74, 1980-; NABT, NSTA 1985-86; Ft Edward Teachers Assn Former Pres; Natl Sci Fnd Union Coll Prgm.

MULDER, JON, English Dept Chair/Teacher; *b:* Holland, MI; *m:* Vicki Lynn Kempkers; *c:* Pamela M., Jonathan M., David V.; *ed:* (BA) Eng, Calvin Coll 1968; Several Courses Hope Coll, Grand Valley St Coll, W MI Univ, MI St Univ; *cr:* Eng Teacher S Chrstn HS 1969-71, Holland Chrstn Schls 1972-; *home:* 472 64th St Holland MI 49423

MULE, CAROL JEAN SCHMIDT, Fifth Grade Teacher; *b:* Orange, NJ; *m:* Daniel A.; *ed:* (BS) Elem Ed, Trenton St Coll 1973; (MS) Ed, Univ of UT 1982; Cmptr Programming for Educl Applications Logo 1984, Programming Applications-Basic 1983, Cmptr Programming for Educl Applications-Basic 1983; Educl Applications of The Microcmptr 1982, Univ of UT Salt Lake City; Murray Cmmty Ed Introduction to The Macintosh, Desktop Publishing, Word Processing Word Perfect 1989; Logo, Cmptr Sci, 1983, Basic Concepts in Cmptrs Management Systems Corporation; *cr:* 1st Grade Teacher 1974-75, 4th Grade Teacher 1975-76 Webster Elem Salt Lake City Sch Dist; Gifted Prgm 5-6th Grade Teacher 1977-78, 3rd/4th Grade Teacher 1978-79, 4th Grade Teacher 1979-86 Meadowlark Elem Salt Lake City Sch Dist; 3rd Grade Teacher The Waterford Sch 1986-87; 6th Grade Teacher 1987-89, 5th Grade Teacher 1989- Meadowlark Elem Salt Lake City Sch Dist; *ai:* Deseret News Spelling Bee Coord & Cmptr Club Spon Meadowlark Elem; Logo & Logo Writer Instr 1987-; NEA; UT Ed Assn Mem 1974-; PTA 1974-; UT Cncl for Cmptrs in Ed Mem 1982-87; UT Sci Teachers Assn Mem 1983-86; Cmptr Programming for Educl Applications Logo Univ of UT Instr 1985; Cmptr Lab Mgr Trainee/Teacher The Waterford Sch 1986-87; Teacher Leader Meadowlark Elem Sch 1985-86; Cmptr Lab Coord Salt Lake City Sch Dist 1985-86; Instr Logo Programming Wkshp Meadowlark Elem Sch 1985; Instr Educl Applications of Microcmptr Salt Lake City Sch Dist 1984; Cmptr Leader Meadowlark Elem Sch 1983-86; Sandy City Chamber of Commerce The Waterford Sch Teacher of Month 1987; Salt Lake City Teacher of Yr Finalist Salt Lake City Sch Dist 1984; Technology Using Educator of Yr Honorable Mention Awd Recipient Electronic Learning Magazine 1983; Natl Apple Cmptr Club Spon Meadowlark Elem Sch 1983-86; Instr Microcmptr Seminar for Educators Management Systems Corporation 1983; Teacher Specialist Assn Contact Teams Peer Adv Salt Lake City Sch Dist 1981-82; *office:* Meadowlark Elem 497 Morton Dr Salt Lake City UT 84116

MULKEY, JUDITH MULLIS, 8th Grade Language Arts; *b:* Charlotte, NC; *m:* James Franklyn; *c:* Angie Marshall, Ginger Marshall; *ed:* (BS) Elem Ed, Winthrop Coll 1967; (MS) Ed, Univ of SC 1976; Carolina Journalism Inst; *cr:* Elem Teacher Sunter Sch Dist 17 1967-81; 8th Grade Teacher Irmo Mid Sch Campus I 1982-; *ai:* Newspaper Adv; Sch News Coord; Teacher Forum Mem; Model Mid Sch Mem, Lang Art, Faculty Advisory, Textbook Adoption Comm; Bus Duty Captain; Visiting Comm for SACS Mem; SC Scholastic Press Assn V Chm of Exec Bd 1988-; S Interscholastic Press Assn Bd of Judges 1989-; Carolina Power & Light Ed Adv 1980-81; Teacher of Yr Irmo Mid Sch Campus I 1989-; Teacher of Month Greater Columbia Chamber of Commerce; Teacher Incentive Campus Awd 1988-89; *office:* Irmo Mid Sch Campus I 6949 St Andrews Rd Columbia SC 29212

MULL, SHIRLEY SUTTON, 7th Soc Stud Teacher/Dept Chm; *b:* Salisbury, NC; *M:* Eugene; *ed:* (BS) Soc Stud, Appalachian St Univ 1968; NC St Univ Raleigh; *cr:* 8th Grade Teacher Cannon Jr HS 1968-71; 7th Grade Teacher Knox Jr HS 1971-73, Lowes Grove Elem 1973-76; 11th & 12th Grade Teacher Chapin HS 1976-79; Ninety Six HS 1979-80; 7th Grade Teacher Chewning Jr HS 1981-; *ai:* Spon/Adv Chewning Jr HS Natl Jr Honor Society; Mem Stud Asst Comm; NC League Mid Schools Mem 1988-; Delta Kappa Gamma Mem 1986-; NEA Mem 1968-76; NCAE Mem 1981-; NCCSS 1989-; NCAE Awd; Terry Sanford Awd Creativity & Innovation in Teaching 1971; Chewning Jr HS Teacher of Yr 1985-86 & 1989-; Presenter NC Mid Sch Conference 1989-; Certified NC Mentor/Trainer 1986-; *home:* 4 Wedgewood Rd Chapel Hill NC 27514

MULLEN, EVELYN (KUETER), HS English Teacher/Dept Chair; *b:* Bellevue, IA; *m:* Michael G.; *c:* Mike, Sue, Sara; *ed:* (BA) Eng, Viterbo Coll 1965; Grad Stud Curr Dev, Effective Teacher Trng, Positive Attitude Toward Learning Trng; *cr:* Eng Teacher K D Waldo 1965-67, Reeseville HS 1967-68, Cntrl Jr HS 1968-69, St John the Baptist 1972-74; Eng Teacher/Dept Chairperson Seymour HS 1977-; *ai:* Academic Decathlon Coach; Class Adv; 7th-12th Grade Lang Art Curr Coord; SEA, WEA, NEA, NCTE, WCTE; Curr & Teaching Articles Published; *home:* 627 Lee St Seymour WI 54165

MULLEN, JAMES ELWIN, Head Band Director; *b:* Jackson, MS; *m:* Phylis Geiger; *c:* Lynn, Don, David, Jimmy; *ed:* (BMED) Music, MS Coll 1965; (MM) Music, Univ of MS 1970; Univ of Southern MS; *cr:* Head Dir Forest Hill HS 1978-83, Grand Prairie HS 1983-87; Head Dir/Chm of Fine Arts Granbury HS 1987-; *ai:* Stage Band HS Musicals; TX Music Educators Assn 1983-; TX Band Masters Assn 1983-; Phi Beta Mu 1979-; MS St Textbook Selection Comm Music; Awarded Outstanding Teacher Jackson Public Sch Bd; Nom Outstanding Band Dir By Phi Beta Mu; *office:* Granbury H S 2000 W Pearl Granbury TX 76048

MULLEN, JAMES L., Secondary English Teacher; *b:* Woodstock NB, Canada; *m:* Darice Dawn Beardsley; *c:* Jessica R.; *ed:* (BA) Eng, Houghton Coll 1986; Grad Trng Geneseo Univ; *cr:* 11th/12th Grade Teacher Elba Cntrl Sch 1987-88; 7th-12th Grade Scndry Eng Teacher Fillmore Cntrl Sch 1988-; *ai:* Bsktbl & Soccer Coach; Class Adv; NEA Mem 1988-; Houghton Wesleyan Church Mem 1983-; *home:* 117 W Main St Fillmore NY 14735

MULLEN, JANELLE ALDERSON, Jr HS Administrator; *b:* Alliance, NE; *ed:* (BA) Span, Univ of Mankato MN 1976; (MS) Admin, Univ of NE Omaha 1987; *cr:* Span Teacher Morton Jr HS 1977-84, Bryan Jr HS 1984-89; Admin Nathan Hale Jr HS 1989-; *ai:* Discipline & Athletic Dir; Federal Lunch Prgm; Transportation, Intramurals, Spec Projects; *office:* Nathan Hale Jr HS 6143 Whitmore St Omaha NE 68152

MULLEN, SUE MOORE, Health Teacher; *b:* West Palm Beach, FL; *c:* Jody S., Joell P., Jonie M.; *ed:* (BA) Bio/Sci/Phys Ed, KS St Univ 1962; Working Towards Masters Bio, Univ of MO 1967; *cr:* Health/Phys Ed Teacher Cntrl Jr HS 1962-64; Bio/Health Teacher Tonganoxie HS 1965-67; Health/Phys Ed Teacher Cntrl Jr HS 1967-69; Health Teacher Leesburg HS 1970-; *ai:* Cheerleading, Gymnastics, Tennis, Track, Sftbl, Vlybl, Swimming, Diving Coach; St Textbook Adoption Cncl; FAAPHER 1983-89; Coach of Yr; Quality Circle & CPR Trainer; *office:* Leesburg HS 1401 Meadow Dr Leesburg FL 34748

MULLER, MARCEE MAREE, Mathematics Teacher/Dept Chm; *b:* Wakefield, NE; *ed:* (BA) Math Ed, Gustavus Adolphus Coll 1961; Grad Stud Phys Ed & Math; *cr:* Teacher Ceylon Public Sch 1961-64, Tecumseh Public Sch 1964-; *ai:* 8th Grade Class Spon; NEA, NE Ed Assn 1961-; Tecumseh Ed Assn (Pres 1976-77, Pres-Elect 1975-76, Secy 1983-84, Treas 1969-73, 1985-); NCTM, St Math Assn; Phi Delta Kappa; NE Sftbl Assn Service Awd 1981; United Meth Church; NE Womens Bowling Assn Dist Dir 1982-; Natl Womens Bowling Assn; Tecumseh Bowling Assn (Pres 1976-80, Treas 1971-73, Secy 1981-); NE Math Scholars Prgm Fellowship 1986-88; Peter Kiewit Fnd Awd 1990; Tandy Technology Scholars Prgm Awd 1990; Honorable Mention Presidential Awd Excl in Math Teaching 1987; *office:* Tecumseh Public Sch 358 N 6th Box 338 Tecumseh NE 68450

MULLER, RICARD CHARLES, Math & Cmptr Sci Teacher; *b:* Chicago, IL; *ed:* (BA) Math, 1963, (MA) Math, 1966 Loyola Univ; *cr:* Math/Cmptr Sci Teacher St Patrick HS 1964-; *ai:* Math Club; NCTM; IL Cncl Teachers of Math St Contest Comm; Math Teachers Assn Chicago Secy Master Teacher Awd 1986; Metropolitan Math Club Chicago Ed 1979-89; Distinguished Lafallian Educator Awd 1988; Article Published 1977; *office:* St Patrick HS 5900 W Belmont Ave Chicago IL 60634

MULLICAN, DOROTHY FINLEY, Mathematics Teacher; *b:* Brookhaven, MS; *m:* Danny L.; *c:* Jake, Patrick; *ed:* (BA) Math, SW TX St Univ 1972; *cr:* Teacher Poteet HS 1972-80, Waxahachie HS 1980-; *ai:* NHS Co-Spon; TX Cncl Teachers of Math; *office:* Waxahachie HS Hwy 77 N Waxahachie TX 75165

MULLICAN, GAIL BROWN, Teacher of Gifted & Talented; *b:* Tyler, TX; *m:* Jimmy Randall; *c:* Kristi; *ed:* (AA) Ed, Tyler Jr Coll 1978; (BS) Ed, Univ of TX Tyler 1980; Working Towards Masters in Gifted & Talented Ed, Art; Jr Great Books Cert; *cr:* 5th Grade Teacher Jacksonville Ind Sch Dist 1980-; *ai:* UIL Oral Rdng & Knowledge Master Open Coach; Spon Jr Historians; Assn of TX Prof Educators Pres 1982, 1986, 1989; TX Assn for Gifted & Talented 1982-; TX Rdng Assn 1987-; Alpha Delta Kappa 1984-; Bullard Eastern Star 1967-; Rotary Club 1967- , Rotary Awd 1967; Outstanding Teacher Regional His Fair E TX Baptist Coll 1983; *home:* 12236 FM 344 E Whitehouse TX 75791

MULLIGAN, MAXINE ROGERS, 9th/10th Grade Coll English; *b:* Vineland, NJ; *m:* Rodney William; *c:* Kelly J.; *ed:* (BA) Scndry Sch Eng, 1980, (MA) Scndry Sch Eng, 1987 Glassboro St; *cr:* Educl Secy Vineland Sch System 1954-80; Eng Teacher Vineland HS N 1980-; *ai:* Eng Club Co-Adv; Spirit Club & All-Sports Booster Club; Shakespeare Birthday Celebration Coord; Serving as Chairperson & Comm Mem on Selection Comm for Teachers Recognition Awd for Governor 1987-; Vineland Ed Assn Rep 1983-; Cumberland Cty Ed Assn 1980-; NJEA, NEA 1980-; Liasion VHS N & Bd of Ed 1987-; All-Sports Booster Club 1987-; Teacher of Yr-Governors Teachers Recognition Prgm 1986; Whos Who in Amer Ed 1989-; Present Seminar on Charles Dickens in Cape May 1990; *office:* Vineland HS N 3010 E Chestnut Ave Vineland NJ 08360

MULLIGAN, REGINA, Earth Science Teacher; *b:* Detroit, MI; *ed:* (BS) Sci Ed, 1969, (MA) Soc Fnds of Ed, E MI Univ; *cr:* 7th Grade Math/Sci Teacher 1969-70, 8th-9th Grade Sci Teacher 1970-71, 9th Grade Sci Teacher 1971-83, Home Track Meets Ofcl 1972-80, 8th Grade Sci Teacher/Dept Chm 1983-89 South Mid Sch; Supervising Teachers EMU Stu Teachers 1979-89; *ai:* Tech Writer for MI Educl Assesment Prgm 1989; Playground Leader Wyandotte Recreation Dept 1966-67; Supvr Summer Recreation Prgm Wyandotte Recreation Dept 1968-70; Jr HS Girls Summer Camp Cnslr Cedar Lake Camp in Chelsea 1984-87; MI Sci Teachers Assn Mem 1985-89; MI Earth Sci Teachers Assn (Mem 1986-89, Bd Mem, Regional Focus Person 1988-89); Natl Earth Sci Teachers Assn 1986-89; Earth Sci Seminar Spon by Natl Sci Fnd at Univ of MI 1988; 1989 Newsweek & WDIV Outstanding Mid Sch Teacher in Wayne Cty; 1990 Finalist for MI Sci Teacher of Yr; 1990 Nominee for Presidential Awd for Excl in Math & Sci Teaching; *office:* South Mid Sch 45201 Owen St Belleville MI 48111

MULLIKIN, MICHAEL CRAIG, 5th Grade Teacher; *b:* Oakland, CA; *m:* Jackie; *c:* Shilo, Shandy, Lacie; *ed:* (BA) Liberal Stud, CA St Univ Sacramento 1979; *cr:* 1st Grade Teacher 1979-83, 5th Grade Teacher 1983- Mills Elem Sch; *ai:* 5th Grade Ftbl, Bsktbl, Sftbl Coach; Field Day Coord; Phys Ed & Lang Art Comms; CTA 1979-; BTA (Site Rep 1981-83, 1989-) 1979-; PAL Sftbl Coach 1988-; *office:* Mills Elem Sch 401 East K Street Benicia CA 94510

MULLIN, ELIZABETH BROWNLOW, Retired Kindergarten Teacher; *b:* Philadelphia, PA; *w:* John James (dec); *c:* Ruthanne, Margaret L. M. King (dec), Robert B.; *cr:* Kndgtn Teacher Booth Sch 1938-42, Barrington RI 1947-48, US Navy Base 1950-52, Smith Sch 1954-57, Navy Base RI 1957-59; 2nd Grade Teacher St Piux X 1961-66; Librarian Navy Base Puerto Rico 1966-69; Kndgtn Teacher St Pius X 1969-88; *ai:* Sr Scout Troop Adopted Grandmother; After Sch Prgm Volunteer 1960-86; Dancing Master of America, Dance Educators of America 1936-43; US Navy Waves 1st Class Petty Officer 1943-46, Good Conduct, World War II Medals; GSA (Brownie, Scout Leader), 35 Yr Pin, Golden Eaglet Awd 1937.

MULLIN, PATSY DONOHUE, Spanish Teacher; *b:* Winfield, KS; *m:* Daniel John; *c:* Mary K., Margaret A., John P.; *ed:* (BA) His/Span, St Mary of Plains Coll 1968; Latin Amer Stud, N IL Univ; Span, Universidad Iberoamericana Mexico; *cr:* 6th-7th Grade Teacher St Patricks Sch 1958-59; 7th Grade Teacher St Rose Sch 1961-68, Dighton Sch 1968-70; 5th Grade Teacher Dept of Defense 1971-73; IL Migrant Educl Coord/Eng 2nd Lang IL Migrant Cncl 1975-79; Span Teacher Sterling HS, Chadwick HS 1984-85, Mount Morris HS 1985-; *ai:* Span Club & Stu Cncl Adv; Mount Morris Ed Assn Exec Bd; Summer Sch 4th/6th Grade Gifted Span; Alpha Chi 1968; Grad Magna Cum Laude 1968; St Patricks Church Choir 1974-; Grad Teaching Assistantship N IL Univ; *office:* Mount Morris HS 105 W Brayton Rd Mount Morris IL 61054

MULLIN, RITA MC ALISTER, Fifth Grade Teacher; *b:* Hagerman, NM; *m:* Ottis Lee; *c:* William B., Norman H., Jena L. Mulling Mc Claine; *ed:* (BS) Elem Ed, 1968, (MS) Elem Ed, 1972 W TX St Univ; *cr:* 4th Grade Teacher 1968-72, 3rd Grade Teacher 1972-84 Silverton Elem; 5th Grade Teacher Crestview Elem 1984-89, 5th Grade Teacher Woodland Elem 1989-; *ai:* Dir Class Prgm; Cmmty & Sch Coord Comm 1986; Hospitality Comm 1986-87; Supt Comm Cncl 1988-89; Career Ladder I, II, III; Career Ladder Selection Comm 1985-86; ATPE Pres 1988-89, Outstanding Achievement 1989; Delta Kappa Gamma Piano Player 1983-84; Study Club Pres; TSTA 1982-84; Order of Eastern Star Past Worthy Matron 1963-64; Rainbow for Girls Worthy Adv 1952; Outstanding Young Woman of Amer 1967; Teacher of Yr 1982; Graham Educator of Month 1989; *home:* Rocky Mound Rd Graham TX 76046

MULLINAX, CAROLYN VANDERGRIFF, Third Grade Teacher; *b:* Lebanon, TN; *m:* Kenneth Ray; *c:* Kevin, Wesley; *ed:* (BA) Elem Ed, Mid TN St 1963; (MS) Elem Ed, TN Tech Univ 1976; *cr:* Teacher Coll Street Elem, Dowelltown Elem, De Kalb West Elem; *home:* Box 36 Liberty TN 37095

MULLINEAUX, JEANNE H., Fourth Grade Teacher; *b:* Sidney, NY; *ed:* (BA) Elem Ed, Baptist Bible Coll 1974; *cr:* 3rd Grade Teacher High Point Baptist Acad 1974-84; 1st Grade Teacher Horseheads Chrstn Sch 1987-89; 4th Grade Teacher Cntrl Baptist Chrstn Acad 1989-; *ai:* Articles Published; *office:* Cntrl Baptist Chrstn Acad 1606 Upper Front St Binghamton NY 13901

MULLING, ARTHUR L., Teacher; *b:* New York, NY; *m:* Marilyn Flatter; *c:* Carol, Craig; *ed:* (BA) His, Baldwin-Wallace Coll 1957; (MED) His/Ed, Kent St Univ 1964; *cr:* Teacher Harding Mid Sch 1957-89; *ai:* OH Ed Assn Lifetime Mem 1957-; Greater Cleveland Cncl for Soc Stud; Lakewood Teacher Assn Exec Bd Mem; Kiwanis; NDEA Inst for Scndry Teachers Soc Stud Union Coll 1968; *home:* 375 Fern Dr Berea OH 44017

MULLINS, BRENDA MCKEEHAN, 2nd Grade Teacher; *b:* Athens, TN; *m:* David R.; *ed:* (BS) Elem Ed, East TN St Univ 1973; *cr:* Teacher Riceville Elem Sch 1973-; *ai:* TBN Ed Assn; NEA; McMinn Cty Ed Assn; Beta Sigma Phi; Womans Missionary Union; *home:* 129 Woodacre Dr Athens TN 37303

MULLINS, CATHERINE THAXTON, First Grade Teacher; *b:* Atlanta, GA; *m:* Charles M.; *ed:* (BS) Elem Ed, Mercer Univ 1978; *cr:* 6th Grade Teacher 1978, 2nd Grade Teacher 1978-80, 1st Grade Teacher 1980-87 Peachtree City Elem; 1st Grade Teacher Oak Grove Elem 1987-; *office:* Oak Grove Elem Sch 101 Crosstown Rd Peachtree City GA 30269

MULLINS, DELORES WILLIAMS, 8th Grade Algebra/Math Teacher; *b:* Pensacola, FL; *c:* Lance, Marquez; *ed:* (AB) Chem, 1977, (MA) Comm, 1985 Univ of N CO; Facilitating Youth Support Groups; Drug Intervention/Prevention; Cooperative Learning/Trng; Dist Crisis Team Trng; *cr:* Track Coach 1978-80, Vlybl Coach 1978-81 Gorman Jr HS; Mesa Adv CO Minority Engineering Assn 1981-88; Gifted Facilitator Mid Sch TAG Prgm 1986-88; 2nd Chance Tutor & Cnslr Harrison HS Drop Out Prgm 1987-; Math Club Spon Gorman Mid Sch 1988-; Supvr Scndry Summer Sch Dist HS 1988-; *ai:* Youth Support Group, Drug Intervention Team Facilitator 1988-; Dist High Risk Task Force Comm 1988; Dist Rdng Curr Comm 1979-80; Dist Sci Curr Comm 1980-81; Drug Preventation Advisory Comm 1984-85; Advisee Adv Planning Comm 1979-80; A Better Chance Selection Comm 1983-84; First Aid Instr 1984-85; Staff Trng for Ed Progress Rep 1984-88; Skateboard Club Founder 1986-87; Accountability Comm (Parent/Patron Rep 1989-) 1988-; Inservice Instr Walsenberg Sch Dist 1985; Gorman Mid Sch Teacher of Yr 1984-85; Outstanding St Math Engineering Sci Achievement Adv 1984-85; Math Conference Dist Rep.

MULLINS, JACQUALIN GRUBBS, English/Spanish Teacher; *b:* Memphis, TN; *m:* James Paul; *ed:* (BA) Span, Memphis St Univ 1970; Grad Courses Memphis St Univ, Lambuth Coll; Span Courses, Inst Technilogico Mexico; *cr:* Span Teacher Memphis Technical HS 1971-72, Riverview Jr HS 1972-82; Span/Eng Teacher Raleigh Egypt Jr HS 1972-; *ai:* TEA, NEA, MEA 1971; *home:* 5389 Ravendale Memphis TN 38134

MULLINS, JAMES ALLISON, Social Studies Dept Chairman; *b:* Clintwood, VA; *m:* Thelma M.; *c:* James, Douglas; *ed:* (BA) His/Poly Sci, 1962, (MA) Educl Admin, 1965 E Tn St Univ; *cr:* Dept Head 1st Natl Bank of Arlington 1959-60; Soc Stud Teacher Cedar Bluff Elem 1962-65, Richlands HS 1965-75; Spec Asst to Congressman US House of Reps 1975-83; Civics Teacher Richlands Mid Sch 1984-; *ai:* Just Say No To Drugs Spon; Debate & United Nations Debate Coach; VA Ed Assn Human Relations & Civil Rights Cmmty Awd 1978, Peace & Intnl Relations Awd, Natl Ed Awd; US House of Reps Congressional Staff Dir 1980-82, Outstanding Staff Mem Awd; Tazewell Ed Assn VP 1989-; Richlands Rotary Chm Intnl Comm 1990; *office:* Richlands Mid Sch Rt 460 Richlands VA 24641

MULLINS, JIMMY J., SR., Air Force Junior ROTC Instr; *b:* Bonnie Blue, VA; *c:* Jimmy J. Jr., Michael T.; *ed:* (BS) Management/Human Resources, Park Coll 1989; Working Towards Masters Degree in Counseling, Liberty Univ; *cr:* Chief Master Sergeant USAF 1958-88; USAF Jr ROTC Instr Tecumseh HS 1988-89, Wayne HS 1989-; *ai:* Air Force Jr ROTC Drill Team & Color Guard; Sr Enlisted Adv, Postal Mgr, Theater Clark Air Base; Top Secret Armed Forces, Base Career Adv; Personnel Supt; Chiefs Assn Secy 1986-87; Air Force Assn 1986-; Amer Legion 1989-; Air Force Jr ROTC Outstanding Instr Awd 1990; Earned Many Significant Military Decorations; Oak Leaf Clusters, Joint Service Commendation Medal USAF Commendation Medal; *office:* Wayne HS 5400 Chambersburg Rd Huber Heights OH 45424

MULLINS, KIMBERLY WRIGHT, English/Speech Teacher; *b:* Laramie, WY; *m:* James Robert; *ed:* (BS) Ed, TN Temple Univ 1986; Working Towards Masters Ed, Univ of TN Chattanooga; *cr:* Eng/Speech Teacher East Ridge HS 1986-; *ai:* Class, Cheerleading, SSS Spon; Pioneer Highlight & Homecoming Comm; NEA; *office:* East Ridge HS 4320 Benntt Rd East Ridge TN 37412

MULLINS, MARY JANE (NEAL), First Grade Teacher; *b:* Nashville, TN; *m:* Charles T.; *c:* Charles T. Jr., Susan K. Mullins Smiley; *ed:* (BS) Elem Ed, David Lipscomb Univ 1957; Mid TN St Univ, Belmont Coll; *cr:* 7th-9th Grade Teacher Pulaski TN 1957-58; 3rd/4th Grade Teacher Tom Joy 1959-60; 2nd Grade Teacher UNA 1960-62; Substitute/Math Lab Teacher Charlotte-Mecklenburg 1969-76; 1st Grade Teacher MTCS 1977-; *ai:* Curr Guides for Rdng, Handwriting, Spelling, Listening, Math; Comm to Formulate Philosophy & Objectives K-12th Grade; MTCS for Southern Assn & Served on Sch Plant Comm; Chm of Selection for New Rdng Prgm at MTCS; TN Rdng Assn, Intnl Rdng Assn 1987-; Murfreesboro Civitian 1986-89; *home:* 502 E Clark Blvd Murfreesboro TN 37130

MULLINS, ROBERT S., Dir of TV Services/His Teacher; *b:* Morris, IL; *m:* Ellen Mackiewicz; *c:* Carl, Nathaniel; *ed:* (BS) Ed/Comprehensive Soc Stud, 1974, (MED) Instructional Media, 1976 West Chester Univ; Doctoral Stud Temple Univ; *cr:* Media Specialist Girard Coll 1974-79; TV Production 1979-, AP US His Teacher 1988- Salesianum Sch; *ai:* WSAL TV Studio Dir; Homeroom Show & Vlybl Moderator; Phi Alpha Theta, Pi Gamma Mu, Kappa Delta Pi 1974; Sharpley Civic Assn Rep 1990; *office:* Salesianum Sch 18th & Broom St Wilmington DE 19802

MULLIS, MELANIE HOVIS, Sixth Grade Teacher; *b:* Charlotte, NC; *m:* Wayne; *c:* Anna, Danny; *ed:* (BA) Eng, Univ NC Charlotte 1971; (MA) Intermediate Ed, Gardner Webb Coll 1989; *cr:* 4th Grade Teacher 1971, 6th Grade Teacher 1973-76 O L Kiser Elem; 2nd Grade Teacher Springfield Elem 1978-84; 6th Grade Teacher O L Kiser Elem 1984-; *ai:* Just Say No Club Spon; NEA, NCAE; *office:* O L Kiser Elem Sch 311 E College St Stanley NC 28164

MULVANEY, PATRICK ROBERT, Teacher of Gifted & Talented; *b:* Jersey City, NJ; *m:* Eileen Reilly; *c:* Tiffany; *ed:* (BA) Spec Ed, Jersey City St Coll 1973; (EDM) Creative Art Ed, Rutgere Univ 1984; *cr:* Spec Ed Teacher Central Sch 1974-80; Teacher of Gifted/Talented Peter Muschal Sch 1980-84, Spec Services Coop of Wamego 1984-86, Ocean City HS 1986-; *ai:* Mock Trial & Adacemic Team Coach; Dramatics Asst Coach; Ocean City Ed Assn Mem 1986; NEA Mem 1973-; NJ Ed Assn Mem 1973; *office:* Ocean City HS 6th & Atlantic Ave Ocean City NJ 08226

MULVANY, BYETA M., English Teacher; *b:* Peoria, IL; *c:* Ian M., Aaron P.; *ed:* (BS) Speech, IL St Univ 1969; (MA) Lit, Sangamon St Univ 1982; *cr:* Eng/Speech Teacher Mt Zion HS 1969-71; GED Instr Richland Comm Coll 1979; Eng Teacher Illiopolis Jr HS 1977-89; Composition/Lit Instr Springfield Coll 1984-; Eng Teacher Riverton HS 1989-; *ai:* Frosh Class Spon; Sch Morale & Discipline Comm; IL Assn of Teachers of Eng, NCTE; 1st Presbyn Church Deacon 1988-; *home:* 541 S Douglas Ave Springfield IL 62704

MULVIHILL, SERAPHINE, Retired Principal; *b:* New York, NY; *ed:* (BA) Eng, St Norbert Coll 1948; Grad Work, Guidance Admin; *cr:* Elem Teacher St Joseph Sch Fond Du Lac 1930-40, St Joseph Sch Fort Wayne 1941-51; Elem Prin St Joseph Fond Du Lac 1952-58; Prin Sacred Heart HS 1959-67; *home:* 475 Gillett St Fond Du Lac WI 54935

MUMMERT, MICHAEL ALVIN, Business/Computer Dept Chair; *b:* Hanover, PA; *m:* Lizabeth Ann Marchio; *ed:* (BS) Bus Ed, Shippensburg St Coll 1983; (MBA) Management/Personnel, Mt St Marys Coll 1989; *cr:* Teacher Walkersville HS 1983-; Supvr Universal Investment Company 1986-; Entrepreneur Miller & Mummert Home Improvement Incorporated 1988-; *ai:* Asst Bsktbl Coach; Staff Dev Coord; Combined Charities Campaign Rep; FBLA Adv; MSTA, NEA 1983-; *office:* Walkersville HS 81 Frederick St Walkersville MD 21793

MUNA, MITRI JOHN, Industrial Arts/Tech Dept Head; *b:* Jerusalem, Palestine; *m:* Jane Donkhorst; *c:* Katie, Amber, John, Jami, Jessika; *ed:* (BA) Industrial Art, 1975, Te ch Credit Industrial Art, 1976 CA Poly San Luis Obispo; *cr:* Sargeant US Army 1969-72; Stu CA Poly San Luis Obispo 1972-76; Teacher Millcreek Jr HS 1976-; *ai:* Wrestling & Track Coach; Sch Friendship Comm; Internation Technology Ed Assn 1989-; *office:* Millcreek Jr HS 245 E 1000 S Bountiful UT 84010

MUNAO, JAN FRANK, Jr High English Teacher; *b:* Chicago, IL; *m:* Nancy E. Cahill; *c:* Christopher, Hallie; *ed:* (BS) Ed, Northern IL Univ 1973; *cr:* Teacher St Anne Sch 1975-; *ai:* Yrbk Adv; NCTE; S Barrington Park Dist Dir 1975-77; *office:* St Anne Sch 312 E Chestnut St Barrington IL 60010

MUNCK, MIRIAM HOFFMAN, Science Teacher; *b:* Walla-Walla, WA; *m:* Gordon Walter; *c:* Thomas, Heather; *ed:* (BS) Chem, 1974, (MS) Ed, 1982 E OR ST; *cr:* Lab Technician City of Pendleton 1974-75; 7th-8th Grade Teacher Morrow Cty Schls 1980-83; Sci Teacher Albuquerque Public Schls 1983-88, Moriarty Sch Dist 1988-; *ai:* Yrbk, Photography; Amer Assn of Univ Women, NM Sci Teachers Assn; *office:* Moriarty HS P O Drawer 20 Moriarty NM 87035

MUNDAY, NANCY WYCKOFF, Third Grade Teacher; *b:* Washington, DC; *c:* J. B. Wilson, Tamara L. Wilson; *ed:* (BA) Elem Ed, Coll of William & Mary 1962; (MED) Elem Ed, Univ of VA 1967; Grad Stud; *cr:* 2nd Grade Teacher Westmore Elem 1962-68; 5th Grade Teacher Central Elem 1974-77; 3rd-4th Grade Teacher Greenbriar West Elem 1978-; *ai:* Team Leader; Co-Sci Lead Teacher; Fairfax Ed Assn, VA Ed Assn, NEA, Natl Assn of Teachers of Math; *office:* Greenbriar West Elem 13300 Poplar Tree Rd Fairfax VA 22033

MUNDEN, LYNN K., 8th Grade Lang Art/G T Teacher; *b:* Commerce, TX; *m:* David Van; *c:* Michele, Cody; *ed:* (BS) Journalism/Eng, Southwest TX St Univ 1972; Guidance & Counseling Angelo ST Univ; *cr:* Eng Teacher South San Antonio HS 1973-75; Spec Ed Teacher Mineola Jr HS 1976-77; Eng/Journalism Teacher Bridgeport HS 1977-83; Lang Arts/Gifted & Talented Teacher Brady Jr HS 1983-; *ai:* 8th Grade UIL Literary Ready Writing, Spelling; Twirling Spon; Gifted & Talented Comm; Phi Delta Kappa 1989; TX Classroom Teachers Assn (Pres 1987, VP 1986, Secy 1988-89); *home:* Rt 1 Box 13 Rochelle TX 76872

MUNDY, JAMES PATRICK, Social Studies Teacher; *b:* Baltimore, MD; *m:* Catherine; *c:* Alexandria; *ed:* (BA) His, Wake Forest Univ 1973; (MMS) Modern Stud, Loyola Coll & Pepperdine Univ 1978; *cr:* Teacher Howard HS 1974-80, Glenelg HS 1982-; *ai:* Tennis Coach; Faculty Advisory Steering Comm; Howard Cty Ec Coord 1978-80; NEA, MSTA; Howard Cty Ed Assn Pres 1980-82; Glenelg HS Parent Teacher Stu Assn Faculty Rep 1990, Howard Cty Teacher of Yr; Howard Cty Assn of Stu Cncls, Howard Cty Chamber of Commerce Howard Cty Teacher of Yr 1990; Taft Inst of Government Fellowships 1975, 1977; Co-Chm of Howard Countian for Cncl Districting.

MUNDY, TWYLA G., Math Teacher; *b:* Latrobe, PA; *m:* Wayne A.; *c:* Matthew, Andrew, Nathan; *ed:* (BS) Math, IN Univ PA 1970; Univ AK; *cr:* Math Teacher Anchorage Sch Dist 1970-89; *ai:* Jr Class Adv; Prom Coord; Swimming Referee; Natl Ed Assn AK; AK Cncl Teachers of Math; NCTM; KNIK Swim Club Pres; *office:* Chugiak HS P O Box 770218 Eagle River AK 99577

MUNIZ, FRANCES GARCIA, Kindergarten Teacher; *b:* Brownsville, TX; *c:* Belinda S. Hernandez, Irma Clough, Melba Solis; *ed:* (BA) Elem Ed, Pan Amer Univ 1971; Bi-ling & Kndgtn Certificate; *cr:* 1st Grade Teacher El Jardin Elem 1960-62; Kndgtn Teacher Sch for Migrants 1967-70, R L Martin Elem 1971-; *ai:* Lead Kngdtn Teacher; Kndgtn Curr Writer 1982; PTA Secy; Local Best Teachers Awd 1977; Golden Poet Awd 1989; Whos Who in Poetry 1990; Poems Published; *home:* 1754 Loma Linda Brownsville TX 78520

MUNLEY, ELIZABETH ANN, Latin/Spanish Teacher; *b:* Scranton, PA; *m:* Paul Joseph; *c:* Paul, John, Kevin, Brian; *ed:* (BA) Latin/Fr, Marywood Coll 1965; (MS) Scndry Ed, Elmira Coll 1981; Fr Laval Univ Quebec Canada; *cr:* Latin/Fr Teacher Windsor Cntrl Schls 1965-68; Span Instr Broome Comm Coll 1981-84; Latin/Span Teacher Johnson City HS 1984-; *ai:* Career Awareness Comm; Pep Band Adv; *office:* Johnson City HS 666 Reynolds Rd Johnson City NY 13790

MUNOZ, LORETTA LEE, K-6th Grade Math Teacher; *b:* Napa, CA; *ed:* (BA) Elem Ed, San Francisco St Univ 1965; *cr:* 5th Grade Teacher Green Valley Elem 1961-63; 4th/5th Grade Teacher David A Weir 1963-82; 4th Grade Chapter I Teacher Fairview 1982-; *ai:* PTA Teacher of Yr 1980; *home:* 4499 Green Valley Suisun City CA 94585

MUNOZ, MINERVA AGUILAR, Kindergarten Teacher; *b:* Wharton, TX; *m:* Joe Frank; *c:* Jeffrey J.; *ed:* (BS) Elem Ed, Univ of Houston 1972; Kndgtn Endorsement Certificate; Math Curr; *cr:* Kndgtn Teacher Abell Street Sch 1973-89; *ai:* TX St Teachers Organization 1973-89; Delta Kappa Gamma 1984-89; *home:* 1713 Linwood Dr Wharton TX 77488

MUNRO, JOHN JOSEPH, History Teacher; *b:* New York, NY; *c:* Meredith; *ed:* (BA) His, Iona Coll 1966; (MA) Asian Stud, Seton Hall Univ 1971; Spec Ed Cert; *cr:* His Teacher Bergen Cath HS 1966-69, River Dell HS 1969-; *ai:* Stu Government Organization Adv; NEA, NJEA, BCEA, ROEA; Chinese Lang Proficiency Awd; Track Coach of Yr 1979; NJ Governors Awd for Excl Teaching 1989; *office:* River Dell Sr HS Pyle St Oradell NJ 07649

MUNSEE, SANDRA NUPP, Math Teacher; *b:* Erie, PA; *m:* Lloyd L.; *c:* Andrea, David; *ed:* (BS) Sec Ed-Math, 1971; (MED) Sec Ed-Math, 1974 PA St Univ; *cr:* Scndry Math Teacher Philipsburg-Osceola Sch Dist 1971-82; Southwestern Central Sch Dist 1982-; *ai:* Natl Jr Honor Socty Adv; Pi Lambda Theta 1970-; NCTM 1971-; AMTNYS 1982-; Sugar Grove Presbyn Church Elder 1987- S S Teacher/Sun Sch Supt 1990; *office:* Southwestern Cntrl Sch Dist 600 Hunt Rd W E Jamestown NY 14701

MUNSEY, NETA KIMBROUGH, Science Teacher; *b:* Ocoee, TN; *w:* Ronnie L. (dec); *c:* Russell L., Timothy W.; *ed:* (BS) Health/Phys Ed/Bio, Lincoln Memorial Univ 1962; Elem Cert 1980; *cr:* Teacher/Prin Riverside Elem 1961-62, Buffalo Elem 1962-63; Teacher Bearden HS 1963-67; Owner/Operator Munsey IGA Supermarket 1967-80; Teacher Soldiers Memorial Mid Sch 1980-85, Claiborne Cty HS 1985-; *ai:* Claiborne HS Girls Bsktbl & Sftbl Coach; NEA 1980-; TEA (Delegate 1986) 1980-; CCEA (Pres 1985-86) 1980-; *home:* PO Box 443 New Tazewell TN 37825

MUNSON, ALAN W., Math/Computer Science Teacher; *b:* Carrington, ND; *m:* Karol Micheals; *c:* Ryan, Tonya, Eric; *ed:* (BS) Math, Mayville St Coll 1970; (MA) Math, Minot St Univ 1990; *cr:* Math Teacher Tintah HS 1970-72, Campbell-Tintah HS 1972-79, Kenmare HS 1979-; *ai:* Class Adv; Ftbl & Wrestling Coach.

MUNSON, HOWARD ADELBERT, III, 7th/8th Grade Teacher; *b:* Niles, MI; *m:* Marjorie June Davis; *c:* Vashti, Howard IV; *ed:* (BA) His, 1974, (MED) Scndry Admin, 1986 Walla Walla Coll; *cr:* 7th-8th Grade Teacher Milwaukee Jr Acad 1974-77, Yakima Jr Acad 1977-; *ai:* Yrbk & Class Spon; North Pacific Assn of Teachers 1977-; North Pacific Assn of Teachers; Teaching Innovation Awd 1987; Magazine Article; *home:* 4406 N Rozalee Way Yakima WA 98901

MUNY, ROBERT GAYLORD, 5th Grade Teacher; *b:* Beaver Falls, PA; *m:* Anna M. Antonini; *ed:* (BA) His, Geneva Coll 1968; Permanent Cert, Elem Cert, Penn St Univ; Beaver Campus Geneva Coll; *cr:* 5th Grade Teacher Ridge Road Elem 1968-71; 6th Grade Teacher 1971-86; 5th Grade Teacher 1986- State Street Elem; *ai:* Head Teacher 1971-; Baden Economy Ed Assn Secy 1969-71; Ambridge Area Ed Assn 1971-; PA St Ed Assn 1968-; NEA 1968-; Amer Legion Post 19 1966-; Baden PTO Faculty Liason 1987- Schlsp 1976-77; VFW 165-Ambridge 1988-; Golf/Bowling Leags Secy; Co-Spon 11 Yrs Jump Rope for Heart Project Amer Heart Assn; Statue of Liberty Restoration Chm 1985; Annual Organizer Campaign for Give-A-Christmas; New Brighton Ftbl Boosters Club Awd for Distinguished Service 1975; Sports Coorespondent for Post-Gazette Pittsburgh PA; *office:* State Street Elem Sch Harmony Rd Baden PA 15005

MUNZA, DIANA JOHNSON, Mathematics Teacher; *b:* Fairmont, WV; *m:* Ronald Lee; *ed:* (AB) Ed/Math, Fairmont St Coll 1974; (MS) Ed/Math, WV Univ 1979; Cmptrs; *cr:* Math Teacher Fairmont Sr HS 1974-; Adjunct Staff Fairmont St Coll 1982-; *ai:* Cmptr Club Spon; WV Univ Benedum Project Teaching Disciplines Team; Curr Cncl; In-Service Speaker; WV Cncl of Teachers of Math, Delta Kappa Gamma VP 1988-; NCTM, NEA, WV Ed Assn, Marion Cty Ed; MT Improvement Assn; MT United Meth Church (Secy, Asst Teacher); St Presidential Awd of Excl for Math Teachers; Cty Nom for Leaders of Learning Awd; Regional Math Field Day Dir; WV Teachers Forum; *office:* Fairmont Sr HS Loop Park Fairmont WV 26554

MURAKAMI, VICKI ANNE, Fourth Grade Teacher; *b:* Boise, ID; *ed:* (BA) Elem Ed, 1974, (MA) Curr/Instruction, 1983 Boise St Univ; *cr:* 4th Grade Teacher Ustick Elem 1975-; *ai:* NEA, ID Ed Assn, Meridian Ed Assn 1975-; *office:* Ustick Elem Sch 4535 E Ustick Rd Meridian ID 83642

MURCHISON, SUSAN HARPER, English Teacher; *b:* Mobile, AL; *m:* Thomas Randall; *c:* Kevin, Kristy; *ed:* (BA) Eng, Mercer Univ 1973; (MED) Ed, GA Coll; *cr:* Eng Teacher Northside HS 1973-; *ai:* Jr Class Spon; FTA Co-Spon; PAGE 1985-; *office:* Northside HS 926 Green St Warner Robins GA 31093

MURDOCCA, LORRAINE YANNO, Mathematics Teacher; *b:* Hazleton, PA; *m:* Anthony C.; *c:* David A., Robert V.; *ed:* (BA) Chem/Phys Sci/Math, Holy Family Coll 1958; (MA) Ed/Psych, Temple Univ 1963; Elem Ed, Phys Sci, Math, Eng Teaching Cert 1975; *cr:* Eng Teacher Nativity BVM Sr HS 1958-60; Math Teacher Milton Hershey Sr HS 1960-62; Louis E Dieruff Sr HS 1962-63; Lower Dauphin Sr HS 1963-67; Rdng/Math Teacher Capital Area Intermediate Unit 1973-79; Math Teacher Mechanicsburg Area Intermediate Sch 1979-; *ai:* Cmmty & Careers; Kiwanis Builders Club; Scrabble Club; Alpha Room Tutorial Services; Math Clubs; Past Photography, Journalism & Yrbk Club; NCTM 1960-67; Phi Delta Kappa (Prgm Chairperson, VP, Pres) 1978-89, Presidential Awd 1981; NEA, PA St Ed Assn 1962-; PA Dept of Ed Evaluation Team Mem; W Shore Soccer Club Prgm Chairperson 1975-83; Sun & Splash Swim Club Membership Awds Chairperson 1973-83; Harrisburg Swim Club (Exec Comm, Newsletter Ed) 1976-82; Univ of Pittsburgh, Kings Coll, Dickinson Coll Evaluating Team Mem; *office:* Mechanicsburg Intermediate Sch 100 E Elmwood Ave Mechanicsburg PA 17055

MURDOCK, LARRY G., Accounting Instructor; *b:* Coffeyville, KS; *m:* Helen Marie Beason; *c:* Nathan, Susan, Justin, Brendan; *ed:* (BSBA) Accounting 1969, (BS) Ed/Bus Ed, 1971, (MS) Ed/ Bus Ed, 1975 Pittsburg St Univ; Grad Stud Bus Admin Trng As Operations Manager 1980-82; *cr:* Bus Teacher 1970-76, Dir Cmmty Volunteer Ed 1976-80 Independence HS; Operations Manager Georges Cafeteria 1980-82; Dir Youth & Bus Trng Prgm 1982-85, Accounting Instr 1985- Field Kindley HS; *ai:* Active Citizens Through Service Club Spon; Past Chm of Bus Ed Dept; Local Teacher Assn Treas 1975-78; NEA Life Mem; KS Bus Ed Assn; Kiwanis Intnl Secy 1982-; Advisory Comm for Cmptr 1989-; Sci Dept of Coffeyville Cmmty Coll; Outstanding Thesis/Research Paper Awd Grad Sch on Accounting at Pittsburgh St Univ; Natl Awd for Excl Youth & Bus Prgm at Field Kindley; *home:* RR 4 Box 46 Coffeyville KS 67337

MURDOCK, THOMAS MELVIN, Business Department Chairman; *b:* Huntington, WV; *m:* Barbara Ruth Hensley; *c:* Michael; *ed:* (BA) Bus Ed/Journalism, 1971, (MA) Educl Admin, 1977 Marshall Univ; CPR Trng, Apple Cmptr Trng on Mac Intosh, IIGS, IIE; *cr:* Salesman JC Penny Co 1966-70; Soldier US Marine Corps Reserve 1971-77; Teacher 1972-78, Bus Dept Chm 1978- Chesapeake HS; *ai:* Adv & Ed Stu Literary Magazine; Camera Club, Bus Lab Assts Adv; OBTA, NEA, OEA; CLTA Pres 1989-; Little League Bsbl Coach 1988-89; Church of Christ Mem 1964-; TESSA Group; *office:* Chesapeake HS P O Box 458 Chesapeake OH 45619

MURIE, CRAIG ROBERT, Mathematics Teacher; *b:* Grafton, ND; *m:* Karen Corrine Hansen; *c:* Kyle R.; *ed:* (BA) Math/HPER, Valley City St Coll 1973; *cr:* Math/Phys Ed/Health Teacher Raymond MN 1975-77; Math Teacher Harvey ND 1978, Shanley HS 1979-; *ai:* Head Girls & Boys Bsktbl Coach; ND Coaches Assn 1978-, Coach of Yr 1980-81; Eagles 1972-; *office:* Shanley HS 705 13th Ave N Fargo ND 58102

MURKOVICH, SALLY ANNE, Fourth Grade Teacher; *b:* Portland, OR; *m:* Edward P.; *c:* James, Diane; *ed:* (BA) Elem Ed, Univ of NV Reno 1963; *cr:* 3rd Grade Teacher Brown Sch 1963-68; 2nd Grade Teacher Lena Juniper Sch 1968-70; 3rd/4th Grade Teacher Virginia City Elem 1970-71; 5th Grade Teacher 1979-89, 4th Grade Teacher 1989- Hugh Gallagher Elem; *ai:* Storey Cty Ed Assn (Pres 1988-89, Secy 1989-); Comstock PTA Pres 1978-79.

MURPHREE, MARIETTA JONES, First Grade Teacher; *b:* Duck River, TN; *c:* Barbara Murphree Bates, Betty Murphree Allen, W. M. III; *ed:* (BS) Elem Ed, Austin Peay St Univ 1971; *cr:* Secy Hickman Soil Conservation Dist; 1st Grade Teacher East Elem 1971-77, Centerville Elem 1977-; *ai:* Delta Kappa Gamma Intnl Secy 1987-89; Hickman Cty Ed Assn (Secy 1972-73, Treas 1982-83); TN Ed Assn, NEA 1971-; PTO; *home:* 790 Murphree Rd Centerville TN 37033

MURPHY, BARBARA BRESLIN, Latin Teacher; *b:* Somerville, MA; *m:* Thomas William; *ed:* (BA) Latin, Regis Coll; (MA) Latin, Boston Coll; Choral Conducting, Voice, Ithaca Coll; Choral, Boston Univ; Oberlin Conservatory of Music; Teachers Performance Inst; Tufts Univ; Suffolk Univ; *cr:* 5th/7th Grade Teacher St Mary 1949-54; 7th/8th Grade Teacher St Joseph Sch 1954-59; HS Latin/Fr/Choral Teacher Cardinal Spellman 1959-62; Latin/Fr/Choral Music Teacher Matignon 1962-67, Pope John XXIII HS 1967-71; Latin/Span Teacher Woburn Sr HS 1971-; *ai:* Glee Club & Madrigal Choirs Conducter & Dir 1959-71; Latin Classics Club Adv 1971-; Vocation Dir 1969-71; Classical Assn of MA, Natl Jr Classical League, Classical Assn of New England; Classical Assn of MA Excl in Teaching Latin Awd 1985; Choral Music Article; Music Educators Rockefeller Grant Oberlin Conservatory of Music; Villa Vergiliana Rome Italy Schlsp; *office:* Woburn Sr HS 88 Montvale Ave Woburn MA 01801

MURPHY, BARBARA WHITE, Fourth Grade Teacher; *b:* Rock Hill, SC; *m:* Solomon Jesse; *c:* Merchelle, Demetria, Monica; *ed:* (BA) Elem Ed, Clark Coll 1967; (MS) Elem Ed, Winthrop Coll 1987; Working Towards Masters; *cr:* Teacher Carolina Cmmty Action Head Start 1968-70, Ft Mill Sch Dist 4 1970-; *ai:* Ft Mill Primary Sch Advisory Comm; NEA, York Cty Ed Assn, SC Ed Assn 1971-; Phi Delta Kappa Certificate of Recognition, Teacher of Yr; Ft Mill Elem Sch Teacher of Yr.

MURPHY, CAROL JENISON, Mathematics Teacher/Dept Chair; *b:* Tulsa, OK; *m:* Joseph T.; *c:* Paula R.; *ed:* (BS) Math, 1965, (MED) Guidance Counseling, 1983 SD St Univ; Math, Sch of Mines & Tech, Univ of Phoenix; *cr:* Math Teacher Colman HS 1965-67, Sioux Valley HS 1967-69; Math Instr Natl Coll 1974-77; Guidance Cnslr 1988, Math Teacher/Math Dept Chairperson 1977- Cntrl HS; *ai:* R C Dist Math Curr Comm; Sr Class Adv; NEA, SDEA, RCEA (VP, Chief Negotiator 1987-88); Delta Kappa Gamma; SD Cncl of Teachers of Math Regional Conference Publicity Chairperson 1989; NCTM; Colman Ed Assn (VP & Pres); Amer Assn of Univ Women Pres 1988-, Women of Worth 1983; Pennington Cty Drainage Commission Vice Chairperson 1989-; Affirmative Action Comm 1985-88; Teacher Rep on Title IV Parent Comm 1986-87; Natl Guard Wives Local Assn (VP, Pres); Rapid City Womens Center (Treas, Pres); Sigma Xi Scientific Research Society Awd; Article Published; Appointed to North Cntrl Accreditation Teams 1983, 1988-89; *home:* 3727 Reder St Rapid City SD 57702

MURPHY, CAROLYN MARIE, 6th Grade Teacher; *b:* Cleveland, OH; *m:* Michael D.; *c:* Bridget; *ed:* (BS) Chem, St Francis Coll 1970; Registered Medical Technologist, Intnl Society for Clinical Laboratory Technology; *cr:* 8th Grade Math/Sci Teacher St Joseph Sch 1971-76; Medical Technologist Dukes Memorial Hospital 1976-84; 5th Grade Teacher 1984-88, 6th Grade Teacher 1988- St Charles Sch; *ai:* Elem Vlybl Clinic Faculty Spon; Diocese of Lafayette Task Force For Dev of Liturgy & Sacramental Guidelines Mem; Visions & Values Leadership Team; Sch Public Relations Chairperson; Intnl Society for Clinical Laboratory Technology 1978-; NCEA 1971-76, 1984-; St Charles Worship Comm (Chairperson 1989-91) 1982-; *office:* St Charles Sch 80 W 5th St Peru IN 46970

MURPHY, CHARLOTTE V., Business/Mathematics Teacher; *b:* Valdosta, GA; *m:* Jimmy M.; *c:* Angela, Jamie; *ed:* (BS) Bus Ed, GA Southwestern Coll 1985; *cr:* Instr Darton Coll 1986-88; Teacher Sherwood Baptist Chrstn Sch 1988-; *ai:* Annual Staff Adv; *office:* Sherwood Chrstn Sch 2200 Stuart Ave Albany GA 31707

MURPHY, CLARIE LISENBE, 4th Grade Teacher; *b:* Sacramento, CA; *m:* Marlan T.; *c:* Glenn, Jeffery, Amy; *ed:* (BS) Sociology, MS St Univ for Women 1971; MS St Univ Med 1980; *cr:* Elem Teacher West Lauderdale HS 1974-; *ai:* MPE 1987-; Alpha Delta Kappa 1980-84; Bethel S M Church Secy 1980-; *office:* West Lauderdale Sch Collinsville MS 39325

MURPHY, CYNTHIA, Home Economics Teacher; *b:* Cambridge, MA; *m:* Raymond Jr.; *c:* Raymond III; *ed:* (ABS) Massasoit Comm Coll 1978; (BS) Home Ec, Univ of MA 1981; Hairdresser, Brockton Beauty Acad; *cr:* Sewing/Ind Living Teacher Littleton HS 1981-83; Cooking Teacher Normandin Jr HS 1983-84; Child Care Teacher New Bedford HS 1984-; *ai:* FHA & Class Adv; Cheering Coach; NH Home Ec Assn Pres 1982-83; *office:* New Bedford HS 230 Hathaway Blvd New Bedford MA 02740

MURPHY, ELDON E., Industrial Art/Phys Ed Teacher; *b:* Wyandotte, MI; *m:* Kathleen Clement; *c:* Lance, Nathan; *ed:* (BA) Art Ed, 1967, (MA) Art Ed, 1971 MI St Univ; *cr:* Voc Teacher Peace Corps Ethiopia 1964-66; 7th-12th Grade Teacher Camden-Frontier Sch 1967-; *ai:* Ftbl & Girls Track Var Head Coach; Camden-Frontier Sch Retention Comm; CFEA, MEA, NEA (Pres, Chief Negotiator, Assn Rep); S Cntrl Athletic Assn Pres; *office:* Camden-Frontier Sch 4971 Montgomery Rd Camden MI 49232

MURPHY, EMMA JEAN, Fifth Grade Teacher; *b:* Lovely, KY; *m:* Arnold; *c:* Medra D., Harmon; *ed:* (BA) Elem/Soc Stud - Cum Laude, Marshall Univ 1971; (Rank II) Morehead Univ 1978; Resource Teacher & Leadership Trng; *cr:* Teacher Warfield Elem 1970-; *ai:* Spelling Team Coach; Prof Stu Cncl, Soc Services, Academic Banquet Comm; Delta Kappa Gamma Prof Affairs Comm; *home:* Box 29 Lovely KY 41231

MURPHY, GLEN, Athletic Dir/His Teacher; *b:* St Louis, MO; *m:* Mary Claire Lagman; *c:* Daniel, Francis, Eileen Panter, Timothy, Tommy; *ed:* (BS) His, Spring Hill Coll 1953; Grad Stud St Louis Univ, Univ of S MS; *cr:* His Teacher De Andries HS, Duchesne HS; Ath Dir/His Teacher Resurrection Cath HS; *ai:* Ftbl, Bsbl, Bsktbl Coach; Letter Club; Natl Fed of Coaches, NCTA; Conference Coach of Yr; *office:* Resurrection Cath HS Corner Of Watts & Magnolia Pascagoula MS 39567

MURPHY, GWENDOLYN GIBBS, Sixth Grade Teacher; *b:* Cherry Pt, NC; *c:* Dentriss, Shamar; *ed:* (BA) Elem Ed, NC Cntrl Univ 1975; *cr:* Teacher Pamlico JR HS 1978-; *ai:* Spring Carnival & Amer Ed Week Coord; Calligraphy; Academic Awds Banquet Comm 1989-; *home:* PO Box 439 Hwy 55 Oriental NC 28571

MURPHY, HOPE STEWART, Mathematics Teacher; *b:* Baltimore, MD; *m:* John S. III; *c:* Tammy Murphy Gowe, Julia Murphy Milligan; *ed:* (BS) Math, 1973, (MED) Math/Ed, 1980 Salisbury St Univ; *cr:* Teacher Bennett Jr HS 1973-75, Parkside Sr HS 1975-85, Easton HS 1985-; *ai:* Coach Chrldrs; Chairperson Stu Assistance Prgm; Talbot Cty Ed Assn 1985-; MD St Teacher Assn, NEA 1976-; *office:* Easton HS Mecklenburg Ave Easton MD 21601

MURPHY, JAMES EDWARD, English/History Teacher; *b:* Titusville, PA; *ed:* (BA) Soc Stud, 1960; (MS) Ed, 1966 Edinboro Univ; Gannon Univ; *cr:* Teacher Randolph-East Mead HS 1960-75; Maplewood Mid Sch 1975-; *ai:* Drama Coach; Activity Leader; Hiking Club; PSEA Pres 1965-66 Life Mem; NEA; Northwestern Cncl of Teachers of Eng; Knights of Columbus; CCD Teacher; Parish Mem; *office:* Maplewood Mid Sch R D 1 Townville PA 16360

MURPHY, JANET COMPTON, Fifth Grade Teacher; *b:* Latrobe, PA; *m:* Paul M.; *c:* Brian, Stephen; *ed:* (BS) Elem Ed, 1972, (MS) Elem Ed. 1981 Indiana Univ of PA; *cr:* Elem Substitute Teacher Blairsville-Saltsburg Sch Dist 1974-77; 5th Grade Teacher Third Ward 1977-78; 6th Grade Teacher 1978-79, 5th Grade Teacher 1979-81 Willard; 4th Grade Teacher Willard-Saltsburg Elem 1981-86; 5th Grade Teacher Saltsburg Elem 1986-; *ai:* Leader Great Books; NEA, PA Ed Assn, Blairsville-Saltsburg Ed Assn 1977-; Trinity Presbyn Church (Sunday Sch Teacher 1974-79, Secy 1985-87, Chrstn Ed Comm 1975-); PTA ; *home:* RD 1 Box 573 Saltsburg PA 15681

MURPHY, JEANINE SCHWINN, Kindergarten Teacher; *b:* Leavenworth, KS; *w:* Samuel (dec); *c:* Samuel Jr.; *ed:* (BS) Elem Ed, St Marys Coll 1978; (MS) Elem Ed, Emporia St Univ 1989; *cr:* 5th Grade Teacher 1978-81; Kndgtn Teacher 1981 Easton Grade Sch; *ai:* NAEYC 1988-; Intnl Rdng Assn 1988-89; Bell 4-H Club (Cmmty Leader) 1989-; *office:* Easton Grade Sch PO Box 219 Easton KS 66020

MURPHY, JEFFRY WRIGHT, European History Teacher; *b:* Bennettesville, SC; *m:* Joseph Charles; *c:* Michael A. Thrasher, Jeffry C. *ed:* (BA) European His, Univ of AL Huntsville 1970; *cr:* Teacher Evangel Sch 1970-72, Huntsville HS 1972-; *ai:* NEA, AL Ed Assn, Huntsville Cncl of Soc Stud Teachers; Huntsville Ed Assn Building Rep 1972-75; *office:* Huntsville HS 2304 Billie Watkins Ave Huntsville AL 35801

MURPHY, JOHN E., Fourth Grade Teacher; *b:* Watertown, SD; *m:* Lori Andrea Woldt; *c:* Kelly, Angy; *ed:* (BS) Elem, Dakota St Coll 1973; *cr:* 6th Grade Teacher Canova Elem 1974-76; 7th/8th Grade Teacher Canova Jr HS 1976-78; 4th Grade Teacher Baltic Elem 1978-; *ai:* Baltic Teacher Assn (VP 1980-81, 1984-85, Pres 1981-82); Dorney Art Schlsp Dakota St Coll 1972; *office:* Baltic Elem Sch Box 309 Baltic SD 57003

MURPHY, JOHN PATRICK, Chemistry Teacher; *b:* Wilkes Barre, PA; *ed:* (BS) Pharmacy, Temple Univ 1958; Teacher Cert, Kings Coll 1960; Grad Work Chem, Wilkes Univ; *cr:* Chem Teacher 1960-66, Vice Prin 1965-66 Hazle Township HS; A-V Coord ESEA Hazleton Area Sch Dist 1963-73; Chem Teacher Hazleton HS 1973-; *ai:* Luzerne Cty Sci Teachers Assn 1973-; NEA, PSEA, HAEA 1960-; Hazleton Art League 1980-89; *home:* 905 Elmira St White Haven PA 18661

MURPHY, JOSEPHINE STRUKEL, 6th-8th Grade Science Teacher; *b:* Brooklyn, NY; *w:* Vincent E. (dec); *c:* Maureen, Edward, Mark; *ed:* (BA) Sci, Montclair St 1952; (MA) Liberal Stud, Stonybrook Univ 1980; *cr:* 5th Grade Teacher Lincoln Sch 1952-53; Engineering Aide Sperry Gyroscope Company 1953-57; Substitute Teacher Neighboring Sch Dists 1969-78; 6th-8th Grade Sci Teacher Sacred Heart Seminary 1978-81; 7th/8th Grade Sci Teacher St Rose of Lima 1981-85; 6th-8th Grade Sci Teacher Our

Lady of Perpetual Help 1985-; *ai:* Sci & Technology Coord; Yearly Sci Fairs; *office:* Our Lady of Perpetual Help Sch 240 S Wellwood Ave Lindenhurst NY 11757

MURPHY, JOSEPHINE TAGLE, Bilingual Second Grade Teacher; *b:* Manila, Philippines; *c:* Christine, Michael A.; *ed:* (BS) Soc Sci, San Diego St Univ 1968; (MA) Music/Dance Ed, CA St Univ Fullerton 1986; Grad Stud Ed, Univ of S CA; *cr:* Teacher San Diego Diocese Schls 1963-71, Placentia Unified Sch Dist 1972-; Part Time Eng as 2nd Lang Teacher N Orange Cty Comm Coll Dist 1988-; *ai:* Grade Level Chairperson; Fine Art & Visual/Performing Art Comm; NEA 1972-; CA Teachers Assn 1972-, Schlsp 1989; Amer Orff-Schulwenk 1979-86; Orange Cty Performing Art Center Volunteer 1988-; St Juliana Cath Parish Lector 1977-; Academic Schlsp Philippine Coll 1958, San Bernardino Coll 1960; Stanford Univ Inst of Microcomputers 1984; Master Teacher Schlsp CA St Univ Fullerton 1986-88; Fulbright-Hays Grant Univ of S CA 1987; CA Teachers Assn Human Rights Schlshp 1989; Selected by Univ of S CA to Develop Units of Study in China 1985; *office:* Ruby Drive Sch 601 W Ruby Dr Placentia CA 92670

MURPHY, JULIA MARY, OP, Social Studies/Science Teacher; *b:* New York, NY; *ed:* (BA) His, Molloy Coll 1972; (MS) His/Ed, C W Post 1976; *cr:* 8th Grade Teacher Cure of Ars Sch 1957-61, St Agnes Cathedral Sch 1961-67; Soc Stud Teacher St Catherine of Sienna Sch 1967-73; Soc Stud/Sci Teacher St John the Baptist Diocesan HS 1973-; *ai:* Long Island Cncl for Soc Stud 1965-; *office:* St John the Baptist HS 1170 Montauk Hwy West Islip NY 11795

MURPHY, KATHLEEN A., Eighth Grade Teacher; *b:* High Ridge, MO; *m:* John T.; *c:* John M., Michael D., Thomas J.; *ed:* (BS) Ed, SE MO St 1980; Religious Ed Certificate Archdiocese of St Louis; *cr:* 7th Grade Homeroom Teacher St Pauls Sch 1980-84; 8th Grade Homeroom Teacher St Anthonys Sch 1984-; *ai:* Jr HS Sci, 5th-8th Grade Teacher Coord; Beallarmine Speech Team Coach & Judge; NCTA 1980-; Bellarmine Speech League Bd of Dirs 1986-; Presented Wkshps Interface Conference, Archidocesean Sch Teachers; *office:* St Anthonys Sch 3005 High Ridge Blvd High Ridge MO 63049

MURPHY, KATHLEEN A., Gifted & Talented Teacher; *b:* Addison, MI; *m:* Eldon E.; *c:* Lance E., Nathan L.; *ed:* (BA) Elem Ed/Sci, 1961, (MA) Elem Ed, 1967 MI St Univ; *cr:* 4th-6th Grade Teacher Lansing Public Schls 1961-67; Peace Corps Teacher Sci HS Ethiopia 1964-66; 6th Grade Teacher Rdng Cmmty Schls 1967-69; Teacher/Dir Head Start 1969; 5th-6th Grade Teacher Hillsdale Cmmty Schls 1976-; *ai:* Coach Quiz Bowl; Mem Dist Wide Sch Improvement, Building Sch Improvement, Dist Sci Comm; Delta Kappa Gamma Secy; NEA, MEA, HEA Negotiator; *office:* Davis Mid Sch 30 N West St Hillsdale MI 49242

MURPHY, KATHLEEN RITA SULLIVAN, HS Mathematics Teacher; *b:* Chicago, IL; *m:* Patrick J.; *ed:* (BS) Math, Univ of IL Champaign Urbana 1987; Math, Chicago St Univ; *cr:* HS Math Teacher Queen of Peace HS; *ai:* Jr Class Moderator; The Math Assn of America 1990; Published 10 Manual Supplements for Coll Math Textbooks; *office:* Queen of Peace HS 7659 S Linder Burbank IL 60459

MURPHY, KENNETH MICHAEL, Science Teacher; *b:* Thomasville, GA; *m:* Tanya Sparks; *c:* Kris, Scott, Kyle; *ed:* (BS) Bio Ed, Valdosta St Coll 1973; Working Toward Masters Sci Ed, Valdosta St Coll; *cr:* Sci Teacher Tift Cty HS 1973-; *ai:* Sci Olympiad Team; Sci Bowl Team Coach; Sci Symposium Participants; Sci Club Adv; Co-Adv Friends Against Alcohol & Drugs; GA Sci Teachers Assn (Dist Dir 1988-89) 1985-, Dist Sci Teacher of Yr 1989; NABT 1988-; HS Teacher of Yr 1981, 1988; Tift Cty Sch System Teacher of Yr 1988; Sigma Xi Outstanding Sci Teacher 1982, 1987; SW GA Regional Sci Fair Teacher Awd 1983, 1986-89; GA Jr Sci & Hum Symposium Teacher Awd 1986; GA Sci Olympiad Outstanding Teacher Awd 1987-; Tift Cty STAR Teacher 1987, 1990; Nom GA Dept of Energy Teacher Research Assoc Prgm 1990; GA Sci & Hum Symposium Jr Winner 1988- Spon; Natl Jr Winner 1988, Natl Participants 1984, 1986-; *office:* Tift Cty HS W 8th St Tifton GA 31793

MURPHY, LONNIE JOE, Math Teacher/Assistant Prin; *b:* Booneville, MS; *m:* Amanda Kay Strange; *c:* Joseph K.; *ed:* (BA) Math Ed, 1975, (MED) Math Ed, 1977 MS St Univ; *cr:* Math Teacher/Coach Thrasher HS 1975-81, Wheeler HS 1981-85; Math Teacher/Asst Prin Wheeler HS 1985-; *ai:* Jr Civitan Club & Stu Cncl Spon; Hunter Safety Ed Instr; Shooting Sports Team Coach; Math Limp & Insurance Comm; Sch Rep; Bus Driver; MAE, NEA 1981-; Civitan 1989-; *office:* Wheeler HS PO Box 98 Wheeler MS 38880

MURPHY, MARGUERITE J., 7th & 8th Grade Teacher; *b:* Stearns, KY; *m:* Jack W.; *c:* Terrance, Shane; *ed:* Assoc Elem Ed, Cumberland Coll 1953; (BS) Elem Ed, Xavier Univ 1974; (ME) Supervision/Curr, Miami Univ 1981; Grad Stud; *cr:* Teacher Vinton Cty Schls 1958-61, Fayetteville Perry Sch 1969-71, Mt Orab Mid Sch 1971-; *ai:* Natl Jr Honor Society Adv; Academic Team Spon & Coach; Curr Comm; NEA, OH Ed Assn; W Brown Ed Assn VP 1975-77; *home:* 3233 Pleasant Hill Rd Mount Orab OH 45154

MURPHY, MARIE KLEIN, Seventh Grade Teacher; *b:* Atlantic City, NJ; *m:* Robert P.; *ed:* (BA) Elem Ed, Georgian Court Coll 1967; Masters Level Math, Cntrl Ct St Coll; Elem Ed, Madeline Hunter Trng; *cr:* Prin Our Lady of Lourdes 1967-69, St Francis 1972-75; Teacher St Mary Cathedral 1983-86, Gregory Sch 1987-; *ai:* Stu Cncl Moderator; NJEA, TEA; Governors Awd Teacher of Yr 1989-; *office:* Gregory Sch Rutherford & Exton Ave Trenton NJ 08618

MURPHY, MARY CATHERINE, Third Grade Teacher; *b:* Phillipsburg, NJ; *ed:* (BA) Elem Ed, Alvernia Coll 1969; (MED) Elem Ed, West Chester Univ 1976; Grad Courses Penn St Univ, Millersville Univ, East Stroudsburg Univ, Wilkes Coll; *cr:* 3rd Grade Teacher Phillipsburg Elem Schls 1969-70, Daniel Boone Elem Schls 1970-; *ai:* NEA, PA St Ed Assn; *office:* Roosevelt Elem Sch 3rd & Jefferson Sts Birdsboro PA 19508

MURPHY, MARY DEAN, English Teacher; *b:* Metter, GA; *c:* Deana, Jodi; *ed:* (BA) Eng/Philosophy, La Grange Coll 1961; (MAT) Eng, GA St Univ 1966; (EdS) Eng/Ed, Univ Of GA 1973; Grad Work; *cr:* Eng Teacher Clarke Cntrl HS 1973-75, 1984-85; Eng Dept Head/Eng Teacher Jackson Cty HS 1981-84; Eng Dept Head/Advanced Placement Eng Teacher Glynn Acad 1985-; Part Time Eng Teacher FL St & N IL; *ai:* Writing Coach For Competitions; Eng Related Act; NCTE, Phi Delta Kappa, Delta Kappa Gamma; Carnegie Mellon Fellowship for Advanced Placement Teachers; *home:* 106 Armstrong St Saint Simons Isld GA 31522

MURPHY, MICHAEL H., 10th-12th Grade Eng Teacher; *b:* Burlington, IA; *m:* Julie Ellis; *c:* Matthew T., Lauren V.; *ed:* (BA) Eng, W GA Univ 1972; (MAT) Museum Ed/Amer Stud, George Washington Univ 1977; Grad Stud Kent St, Akron Univs; Personnel Management Specialist Ed Branch; Agent Trng Headquarters, WorldWide Command, Criminal Investigation Div Fort Mc Nair Washington DC US Army; *cr:* Exec Dir Family Practice Center Medical Clinic 1980-81; Eng/His Teacher Massillon Bd of Ed 1977-; *ai:* NW Jackson Soccer League & Wales Road Soccer Club Affiliate 1987-; Back Cntry Ranger; Algoma Cntrl Railroad Canada; Host Family Argentine Stu for Rotary Intnl; Natl Park Service Cuyahoga Valley Recreation Area; Volunteers in the Parks Prgm; NEA, OH Ed Assn, Massillon Ed Assn 1977-; BSA Cub Master 1988-, Service Recognition 1990; OH Archaeological Soc VP 1988-89; Natl Park Serv; Yosemite Natl Park Archaeological Site Survey/Publication; Nobles Pond Site Archaeological Project Research Dev; Staric Preservation Alliance Awd 1988; Research & Personal Writing Publisher; Heifer Project Intnl; *home:* 906 17th St NE Massillon OH 44646

MURPHY, MIRIAM, Biology Teacher; *b:* Cork, Ireland; *m:* Dermot Mc Gahern; *ed:* (BS) Pharmacology/Biochemistry, Univ Coll Dublin 1984; Higher Diploma in Ed Univ Coll Dublin Ireland; *cr:* Sci Teacher Clonkeen Coll Dublin Ireland 1984-85; Bio Teacher Aquinas HS 1986-; *ai:* NCEA; Assn of Irish Teachers 1989; *office:* Aquinas HS Belmont Ave & E 182nd St Bronx NY 10457

MURPHY, PATRICIA ELIZABETH, Social Studies Dept Chair; *b:* Detroit, MI; *ed:* (BA) Ed, Univ of S FL 1969; *cr:* Elem Teacher Lapahoehoe Sch 1969-71; Substitute Teacher Pinellas Cty 1971-73; Elem/HS Teacher Canterbury Sch 1973-86; HS Teacher St Stephens Episcopal 1986-; *ai:* Jr Class Spon; Var Boys & Girls, Jr Var Boys Tennis Coach; Soc Stud Dept Chairperson; *office:* St Stephens Episcopal Sch 315 41st St W Bradenton FL 34209

MURPHY, REBECCA HARRISON, American History Teacher; *b:* Knobster, MO; *m:* Kevin J.; *c:* Meghan; *ed:* (BS) Elem Ed/Scndry Soc Stud, 1982, (MS) Curr/Instruction, 1985 KS Univ; *cr:* Soc Stud Teacher Hillcrest Jr HS 1982-87, Westridge Mid Sch 1987-; *ai:* Stu Cncl; Homebase Coord; NCSS 1982-; Phi Delta Kappa 1988-; Alpha Delta Kappa 1988-89; Danforth Grant Project Published; KS Bankers Assn Awd Winner for Curr Dev 1982; *office:* Westridge Mid Sch 9300 Nieman Rd Overland Park KS 66214

MURPHY, SHARON MARR, Office Education Teacher; *b:* Haskell, TX; *m:* Basil T. Jr.; *c:* Renee, Basil T. III; *ed:* (BA) Bus Ed, 1974, (MAED) Voc Ed, 1980 Univ N TX; Desktop Publishing Xerox Ventura; Word Perfect; *cr:* Office Ed Teacher J Earl Selz HS 1975-82, Decatur HS 1983-84, J Earl Selz HS 1985-; Word Processing Cooke Cty Coll 1989-; *ai:* Bus Prof of America; SADD; AVA 1982-; NBEA 1975-; TCEA 1988-; *office:* J Earl Selz HS 829 S Harrison Pilot Point TX 76258

MURPHY, TERI M., Art Teacher; *b:* Beaver Dam, WI; *ed:* (BA) Studio Art, 1971, (BAE) Art Ed, 1974 Univ of WI Oshkosh; Grad Work Univ of MN, Univ of WY, Hameline Univ, Univ of WI River Falls; *cr:* K-12th Grade Art Instr Portage Public Schls 1974-80; K-6th Grade Art Instr Inver Grove Public Schls 1980-82; Jr HS Art Instr Cody Public Schls 1982-83; Elem/Jr HS Art Instr River Falls Public Schls 1986-; *ai:* Exhibit Professionally Fiber Artist.

MURPHY, THOMAS MICHAEL, Social Studies Dept Chair; *b:* Jersey City, NJ; *m:* Catherine Moran; *c:* Thomas, Karen; *ed:* (BA) His, Jersey City St Coll 1984; (MA) Ed/Admin/Supervision, St Peters Coll 1988; *cr:* US Army 1962-65; Accountant G A Fuller Company 1965-72; Controller J I Hass Company Incorporated 1972-87; Soc Stud Chm Marist HS 1987-; *ai:* Sch Newspaper, Forensics Team Moderator; *office:* Marist HS 1241 Kennedy Blvd Bayonne NJ 07002

MURPHY, VERA BRANSCUM, First Grade Teacher; *b:* New Castle, IN; *m:* Greg; *ed:* (BA) Soc Stud, Milligan Coll 1967; (MS) Elem Ed, Butler Univ 1971;; *cr:* 1st Grade Teacher Charles A Beard Sch Corporation 1967-75, Greenfield-Cntrl Cmmty Schls 1975-; *ai:* Alpha Delta Kappa; Tri Kappa; *office:* Greenfield-Cntrl Cmmty Schls 8185 N State Rd Greenfield IN 46140

MURPHY, VICKI (GEORGE), Kindergarten Teacher; *b:* Montezuma, IN; *m:* Robert T.; *c:* Katie E.; *ed:* (BS) Elem Ed, 1974; (MED) Supv, 1977 Lamar Univ; *cr:* Kndgtn Teacher 1975-76; 2nd Grade Teacher 1976-77; Kndgtn Teacher 1977-Vidor Elem; *ai:* Grade Level Chm; G/T Curr Comm; Alpha Delta Kappa Pres/Treas 1978-; PTO Treas 1980-84; Teacher of Yr 1986-87; *home:* 115 Camellia Ln Lumberton TX 77656

MURPHY, VIVIAN INGRAM, 7th Grade Geography Teacher; *b:* Jasper, GA; *m:* Michael; *c:* Christie, Joey; *ed:* (BS) Soc Stud/Sociology, Univ of GA 1970; *cr:* 7th/8th Grade Teacher Canton Elem Sch 1970-72; 11th/12th Grade Teacher 1 Pickens Cty HS 1972-73; 7th/8th Grade Teacher Canton Elem Sch 1973-86; 7th Grade Teacher Teasley Mid Sch 1986-; *ai:* Teasley Mid Sch Stu Cncl Co-Spon; Fund Raising Comm; Booster Club; NEA, GA Assn of Educators 1970-; Cherokee Ed Assn 1971-; Ball Ground Cmmty Assn 1986-; Outstanding Elem Teachers of America 1974; *office:* Marie Archer Teasley Mid Sch Rt 6 Hwy 20 W Canton GA 30114

MURPHY, WILLIAM JOSEPH, Fourth Grade Teacher; *b:* Youngstown, OH; *m:* Diane T. Di Carlo; *c:* Michael W.; *ed:* (BSED) Elem Ed, 1969, (MS) Guidance, 1974, (MS) Elem Admin, 1978 Youngstown St Univ; Grad Stud; *cr:* 5th/6th Grade Teacher Youngstown City Schls 1969-70; 4th Grade Teacher Canfield Local Schls 1970-; *ai:* Past Ftbl & Wrestling Coach; Bsktbl & Ftbl Ofcl; OH Ed Assn, NEA; Canfield Ed Assn Building Rep; Boardman, Canfield OH; Booster, Ursuline Chancery; Youngstown State Univ Alumni; *office:* Hilltop Elem Sch 400 Hilltop Blvd Canfield OH 44406

MURPHY, ZELMA DAVES, 4th Grade Teacher/Admin Asst; *b:* Atlanta, GA; *m:* Charles Havord; *c:* James; *ed:* (BA) Eng, GA St Univ 1962; Working Toward Masters, W GA Coll; *cr:* 3rd Grade Teacher 1965-78, 4th Grade Teacher 1978-87, Admin Asst/Teacher 1987- Skyview Elem; *ai:* Instr/Dir Skyview Rhythm Band; Display Comm; Staff Dev & Field Trip Coord; Sci Fair Judge; Skyview Elem Lead Teacher 1965-, Teacher of Yr 1990; PTA (Nominating Publicity Chairperson 1986, Prgm Entertainment Chairperson 1990), Ann Weeks Music Schlrsp; Pebblebrook HS Band Boosters (Uniform Chairperson, Special Projects 1977-81), Active Participation Awd 1980; Fortified Hills Baptist Church Var Offices 1950-, Participation Awd 1979; Pebblebrook HS Academic Bowl Booster (Parent 1977, Spon 1981) 1978-; S Cobb Arts Alliance 1989-; Thanks to Teacher Awd; Coord-Remedial Ed, Testing, St Standards Comm; Chairperson-Curr, Budget, St Standards; Participant-1st Yr Teachers Research Project, Univ of GA; Cty Textbook Adoption & Elem Concert Comm; Instr/Dir Bell Soloist Cty Elem Concerts, Southern Assn of Colls & Schls Steering Comms; *home:* 1550 Greenbrook Dr Austell GA 30001

MURR, CAROL VAN KUIKEN, 7th/8th Grade Teacher; *b:* Grand Rapids, MI; *m:* Robert W.; *c:* Tim Du Bois, Mark Du Bois, Melody Du Bois; *ed:* (BS) Elem Ed, Taylor Univ 1963; (MA) Curr/Instruction, MI St Univ 1987; Bible Inst Trng, Water Safety Instruction, Natl Wildlife Fed Instr Trng; *cr:* 2nd/3rd Grade Teacher Grand Rapids Bd of Ed 1963-68; 7th/8th Grade Teacher Riverside Chrstn Sch 1971-; *ai:* Sch Touring Choir K-12th Grade Dir; Sch Yrbk, Stu Cncl, Sch Art Adv; Sch Bd Rep; Victorious Women Ministries Incorporated Chm 1983-; Article Published; *office:* Riverside Chrstn Sch H #15 Lost Creek KY 41348

MURRAY, ANDERSON ONEAL, Retired; *b:* Huntsville, TX; *m:* Wanda Christenberry; *c:* Leslie, Michael; *ed:* (BA) Ind Arts, Sam Houston 1959; *cr:* 7th 9th Grade Shop Teacher Crain Intermediate 1959-64; Coach Crain and Howell 1961-73; 6th Grade Math Teacher Crain 1964-70; 6th & 7th Grade Math Teacher Howell Intermediate 1970-89; *ai:* TSTA Lifetime Mem 1959-; Crain PTA Lifetime Mem 1959-70 Lifetime Mem Awd 1968; Howell PTA Lifetime Mem 1970-89 Lifetime Awd 1972; 1st Baptist Church 1975-; Riverside Golf Assn VP 1962-68.

MURRAY, BROOKIE ANN, Fourth Grade Teacher; *b:* Cyclone, WV; *m:* Bill L.; *c:* Sharon, Michelle; *ed:* (BA) Elementary Ed Eng & Soc Stud, Morris Harvey Coll 1963; (MA) Elem Admin, WV Univ 1971; Adv Stud Admin Marshall Univ WV Univ; Cmptr Trng 1988; Trng in Identifying the Gifted Stu 1988; *cr:* Teacher/Lorado Elem 1959-61; Lundale Elem 1961-62; Christian Elem 1962-74; Acting Prin Mallory Elem 1980; Supv Teacher Mallory Elem 1988; *ai:* Spon Math Field Day Team Mallory Elem; Logan County Spelling Bee Ofcl Judge; Logan County Soc Stud Fair Comm-Judge; NEA Mem 1959-; WV Ed Assn Mem 1959-; Claypool United Meth Church (Coord of Childrens Ministeries 1975-/Sunday Sch Instr 1970-; PTA Mallory Elem VP 1980-81; Teacher of Yr VP Mallory Elem Awd-Trophy 1979; *office:* Mallory Elem Sch Mallory WV 25634

MURRAY, CAROLYN JOHNSON, Kindergarten Teacher; *b:* Memphis, TN; *m:* William L.; *c:* Anna K., Lauren A.; *ed:* (BS) Ed, 1973, (MS) Early Chldhd Ed, 1977 Memphis St Univ; *cr:* K-1st Grade Teacher Covington Elem Sch 1973-; *ai:* NEA, TN Ed Assn; Covington City Ed Assn Pres; Delta Kappa Gamma (2nd VP 1988-89, 1st VP 1989-, Pres 1990); Kappa Delta Pi, Phi Kappa Phi; *office:* Covington Elem Sch 760 Bert Johnston Ave Covington TN 38019

MURRAY, CATHERINE LOUISE, 4th Grade Teacher; *b:* Kelly Township, PA; *m:* John S. Jr.; *c:* Vaughn, Jeffrey; *ed:* (BS) Elem Ed, Bloomsburg St Coll 1960; *cr:* 3rd Grade Teacher Grant Sch 1960-65; 2nd Grade Teacher Millward Sch 1972-73; 4th Grade Teacher Montandon Elem 1973-77/1980; Milton Elem 1977-80; *ai:* Long Range Plan Adv Comm-Milton Area Sch Dist Teacher Rep to Parent Sch Assn; NEA; PA St Ed Assn; Milton Area Ed Assn Rep to Sch Bd 1989-; *home:* PO Box 242 Montandon PA 17850

MURRAY, DEBRA MONTGOMERY, Physical Education Teacher; *b:* Birmingham, AL; *m:* Kenneth M.; *c:* Jennifer, Lisa; *ed:* (BS) Phys Ed, Samford Univ 1978; (MA) Phys Ed, Univ of AL 1983; *cr:* Phys Ed/Sci Teacher 1978-79, Phys Ed Teacher 1979-81, Phys Ed/Sci Teacher 1981-87, Phys Ed Teacher 1987- Bragg Jr HS; *ai:* Vlybl Team Coach 1978-; Girls Track Team Coach 1978-; Mem Systemwide Certified Inservice Comm 1989-; AL HS Athletic Dir & Coaches Assn 1978-; NEA 1985-; JCEA/AEA 1985-; *office:* Bragg Jr H S 840 Ash Ave Gardendale AL 35071

MURRAY, DONNA BOYETTE, Second Grade Teacher; *m:* Orvil Lee; *c:* Ashley D., Avis Murray Harris, Sarah E.; *ed:* (BS) ECE, 1980, (MS) ECE, 1986 VSC; Ed Specialist Degree; *cr:* 2nd Grade Teacher Patterson Elem 1980-; *ai:* Prof Assn of GA Educators 1983-84, 1989-; Delta Kappa Gamma 1988-; *office:* Patterson Elem Sch PO Drawer 6 Hwy 6 Patterson GA 31557

MURRAY, HENRIETTA UNDERWOOD, 7th Grade Teacher/Soc Stud Dep; *b:* Fayetteville, NC; *m:* George L.; *c:* Brodrique, Genee, Jumoka, Ayesha; *ed:* (BS) Soc Stud, Fayetteville St Univ 1974; Discipline, Mentoring, Ed, Teacher Effectiveness; *cr:* Teacher (GED Prog) Fayetteville Tech Inst 1974-76; Soc Stud Teacher Williston Jr HS 1978-88f SS/Rdng Teacher Williston Mid Sch 1988-; *ai:* Teacher Mentor; 7th Grade Coord; Chairperson of Soc Stud Dept; Career Dev Cncl Rep; Rocame Adv; Self-Study Rep; NCAE 1978-; Candidate for Teacher of Yr 1984; *office:* Williston Mid Sch 401 S 10th St Wilmington NC 28401

MURRAY, JANE ROUDEBUSH, English Teacher; *b:* East Chicago, IN; *c:* Susan J.; *ed:* (BA) Eng, Univ of TN 1965; (MED) Curr/Eng, Memphis St Univ 1980; *cr:* Teacher Westside HS 1965-66, Colonial Jr HS 1966-72, Havenview Jr HS 1977-83, Corry Jr HS 1983-88, Hillcrest HS 1988-; *ai:* Chairperson Eng Dept; Amer Jr Red Cross; Service Club for Teachers; Discipline Comm Teacher & Admin; Spelling Bee Shelby Cty; NCTE, TN Cncl Teacher of Eng; Kingsway Chrstn Church Deacon 1987-; Friends of Pink Palace Museum 19 73-77; Textbook Selectiom Comm 1986; *home:* 3129 Domar St Memphis TN 38118

MURRAY, LONDALEA, First Grade Teacher; *b:* Milan, IN; *m:* Robert; *c:* Barbara Power, Brian, Brent, Bruce; *ed:* (BA) Elem Ed, 1955, (MS) Elem Ed, 1979 Ball St Univ; *cr:* 3rd Grade Teacher Greendale Sch 1955-62; 1st Grade Teacher Aurora Elem 1978-; *home:* Box 375 Dillsboro IN 47018

MURRAY, MICHAEL LEE, Assistant Principal; *b:* Washington, DC; *m:* Pamela Anderson; *c:* Sabrina, Britini; *ed:* (BS) Sci, Mars Hill Coll 1984; (MAED) Ed Admin, W Carolina Univ 1988; St Evaluators & Leadership Trng; *cr:* Physics/Chem/Bio Teacher A C Reynolds HS 1984-88; Asst Prin Sand Hill Elem Sch 1988-; *ai:* Interim Prin 1990; Sch Improvement Team, Collaberation Team, Advisory Cncl Mem; Sch Sci Curr Coord; Summer Sch Prgm Dir 1988-89; NCAE Mem 1984-88; PTO Rep; United Way Sch Rep 1988-89; Articles Published; *office:* Sand Hill Elem Sch 128 Sand Hill School Rd Asheville NC 28806

MURRAY, MILLIE COOLEY, Teacher; *b:* Gainesville, TX; *m:* Rodger E. Jr.; *c:* Steve, Belinda Zampino; *ed:* (BS) Ed, TX Womans Univ 1965; (MED) Ed, TX Tech Univ 1969; *ai:* Campus & Curr Comm; Team Leader; TX St Teachers Assn; Channelview Teachers Assn Pres 1983-84; Citizen of Yr in Youth Dev & Ed Awd Lions Club 1984; Free Interprise Awd San Jacinto Coll 1985; *office:* Channelview Ind Sch Dist 915 Dell Dale Channelview TX 77530

MURRAY, R. EILEEN WILLIAMS, Intermediate Lang Arts Teacher; *b:* Meadville, PA; *M:* Robert K.; *c:* Robert L., Vicki Prutzman; *ed:* (BS) Elem Ed, in Univ of PA 1958; Penn St Univ; *cr:* 6th Grade Teacher Seventh St Sch 1958; Spec Ed Teacher South Side JR HS 1960-63; 5th Grade Teacher Hasson Heights Elem 196-; *ai:* NEA 1958-; PA ST Ed Assn 1958-; Oil City Ed Assn 1958-; United Meth Women Pres 1987-; *home:* 1144 Grandview Rd Oil City PA 16301

MURRAY, RENEE LOGSDON, Language Arts Teacher; *b:* Hart Cty, KY; *c:* Mike, Jared; *ed:* (BS) Speech/Journalism, 1973, (MS) Comm, 1974 Murray St Univ; Working Towards Masters W KY Univ; Natl Writing Project; *cr:* Instr Cntrl MO St Univ 1974-77; VP Beverly Norman Public Relations 1976-81; Ed Hart Cty Herald 1982-86; Teacher Caverna HS 1986-; *ai:* Yrbk, Newspaper, Speech & Drama Club Adv; Public Relations; KY Cncl Teachers Eng 1989-; Hart Cty 4-H Cncl (Treas, Pres 1989-88) Feltner Leadership 1989; Mammoth Cave 4-H Fnd Secy 1989-; *office:* Caverna HS 2276 S Dixie St Horse Cave KY 42749

MURRAY, SHARON SCOTT, 7th-8th Grade Lang Art Teacher; *b:* Kewanee, IL; *m:* Lauren; *c:* Miranda, Brittany; *ed:* (BS) Elem Ed, IL St Univ 1974; Cmptr Class; *cr:* 7th-8th Grade Lang Art Teacher Galva Mid Sch 1974-; *ai:* Jr HS Pom Pon Coach; Mid Sch Stu Cncl Adv; Delta Kappa Gamma Communication Comm Chairperson 1980-; 1st United Meth Church Pre-Sch Comm Pres 1988-; *home:* 529 SE 8th Ave Galva IL 61434

MURRAY, SHIRLEY JONES, Reading Teacher; *b:* Elizabethton, TN; *c:* Mark, Shannon, Matthew; *ed:* (BA) Eng, ETSU 1955; (MAED) Ed, Tusculum 1987; Grad Stud; *cr:* 4th Grade Teacher Keenburg Elem 1955-56; 6th Grade Teacher St Simons Island Elem 1956-57; Substitute Teacher TN & GA 1975-85; Teacher Maury Mid Sch 1986-; *ai:* Co-Spon Yrbk; Jefferson Cty Ed Assn, TN Ed Assn, NEA 1986-; Meth Church (Youth Dir 1984-86, Steward 1987-); Schlsp Basic Aerospace Ed; Ec & Ed Wkshp; Profiled TN Storytelling Journal; *home:* Rt 1 Box 273 Little Bonanza Dandridge TN 37725

MURRAY, TED WILLIAM, Marketing Education Coord; *b:* Wabash, IN; *m:* Vicky Polhamus; *c:* Heath, Heather; *ed:* (AS) Bus Admin, Vincennes Univ 1970; (BA) Distributive Ed, Bowling Green St Univ 1972; (MS) Scndry Ed, Univ of Dayton 1978; *cr:* Sales Miami Industries 1972-73; Teacher Wayne HS 1973-; *ai:* DECA I Adv; OMEA, MEA, HHEA, OEA, NEA, OVA, AVA; Troy Elks 1979-; Troy Bsktbl Parents Treas 1987-; Troy Bsbl Parents All Sports Rep; Troy Teener League Pres 1987-88; *office:* Wayne HS 5400 Chambersburg Rd Huber Heights OH 45424

MURRAY, THOMAS GEORGE, High School Teacher; *b:* Oak Park, IL; *m:* Patricia Ann Lazzara; *c:* Matthew, Colleen, Timothy; *ed:* (BA) Amer His, W IL Univ 1972; (MS) Curr & Instruction, Chicago St Univ 1978; (MS) Criminal Justice, Univ of IL Chicago 1990; *cr:* Instr Polo HS 1972-75, Glenbard S HS 1975-; Adjunct Faculty Natl Louis Univ 1984-; Hunter Teacher Plainfield HS 1990; *ai:* Asst Ftbl 1975-; Mock Trial Adv 1983-; IEA, NEA Bldg Pres 1979-80; Phi Kappa Phi 1988-; IL Coaches Assn 1975-; Du Page Law Ed Wkshp for Teachers Ed Coord 1983-, Liberty Bell 1983; Outstanding Teacher Awd Univ of Chicago 1989; Outstanding Alumnus WIU His Dept 1990; *office:* Glenbard S HS Park Blvd at Butterfield Rd Glen Ellyn IL 60137

MURRAY, VICKIE HARRIS, Elementary Mathematics Teacher; *b:* Sulphur Springs, TX; *m:* Ricky John; *c:* Shawn D., Shane L.; *ed:* (BS) Elem Ed, 1976, (MS) Elem Ed, 1987 E TX St Univ; *cr:* 4th/5th Grade Teacher Sulphur Bluff Sch 1976-77; Mid Sch Math/Sci Teacher Jefferson Mid Sch 1978-80; 4th-7th Grade Math Teacher Sulphur Bluff Sch 1981-; *ai:* UIL 5th-7th Grade Number Sense & 6th/7th Grade Calculator Coach.

MURRAY, WILLIAM LEROY, Jr HS Social Studies Teacher; *b:* Newbern, TN; *m:* Mary Carolyn Johnson; *c:* Anna, Kathryn, Lauren; *ed:* (BS) Scndry Ed, 1969; (MS) Elem Ed, 1973 Memphis St Univ; Cert for Supvr of Instruction; *cr:* 5th Grade Teacher Frazier Elem 1969-70, Covington Grammar 1970-71; 4th Grade Teacher Frazier Elem 1971-74; Federal Projects Coord Covington City Schls 1974-77; 7th/8th Grade Teacher Covington Elem 1977-; *ai:* Beta Club Spon; Teachers Study Cncl (St Secy 1987-88, St Chm Elect 1983); TN Ed Assn, NEA 1969-; *office:* Covington Elem Sch 760 Bert Johnston Ave Covington TN 38019

MURRAY, WILLIAM P., Mathematics Department Chair; *b:* Charlevoix, MI; *m:* Patricia M. Russell; *c:* Angela M., Matthew J.; *ed:* (BA) Math, Cntrl MI Univ 1969; Spec Ed, Mid Sch Phil, Curr Study; *cr:* Math/Physics Teacher Roscommon HS 1969-; *ai:* Ftbl & Bsktbl Time Keeper; Head Track Timer; Bsktbl Scorer; Math/Physics Intermediate Sch Dist Rep; N Cntrl Area Credit Union Bd of Dir, Friedrich W Raiffeisen 1990; REA Pres; Contract Negotiator; *home:* 9883 N Wheeler Roscommon MI 48653

MURRELL, REBA R., 5th Grade Teacher; *b:* Church Hill, TN; *m:* Jerry; *c:* Donna Culbreth, Gary Fox; *ed:* (BS) Elem Ed, East TN St Univ 1979; *cr:* Secy 1961-79; 5th Grade Teacher 1980- Kingsley Elem; *ai:* PTA 1st VP; Grade Level Chm; PTA 1st VP 1990, Life Mem 1975; SCEA Faculty Rep 1985-86; TEA/NEA 1980-; Optimist Club Pres 1964-66 Most Val Mem 1965; Teacher of Yr 1987; Ruritan Club Teacher of Yr 1988, Kingsley Sch; Graduated Magna Cum Laude; *office:* Kingsley Elem Sch 100 Emory Ln Kingsport TN 37660

MURRELL, SUSAN SMITH, Sixth Grade Soc Stud Teacher; *b:* Parkersburg, WV; *w:* Jonathan S. (dec); *c:* Susan J. Kayden, Linda C. Gross; *ed:* (BA) Elem Ed, 1957, (MA) Elem Ed, 1958 Marshall Univ; *cr:* 5th Grade Teacher 1957-60, Remedial Rdng Teacher 1966, 6th Grade Teacher 1966-88 West Elem; 6th Grade Soc Stud Teacher Waverly North Jr HS 1988-; *ai:* Alpha Chi Omega 1953-; Alpha Delta Kappa 1967-; *office:* Waverly North Jr HS 610 E 3rd St Waverly OH 45690

MURREY, MARY (ARMSTRONG), Jr HS Language Arts Teacher; *b:* Waco, TX; *m:* Willard R.; *c:* Douglas W., Tambra M.; *ed:* (BA) Elem Ed, Baylor Univ 1965; TX Womans Univ 1978; *cr:* 3rd Grade Teacher Killeen Ind Sch 1965, Corsicana Ind Sch 1965-66; 4th Grade Teacher Hobbs Municipal Schls 1966-68; Adult Ed/1st Grade/Title I Rdng Teacher Crowley Ind Sch 1970-80; Jr HS Lang Art Teacher Bruceville Eddy Ind 1980-; *ai:* Gifted & Talented Prgm; Univ Interscholastic League Literary Coach; Intnl Rdng Assn 1989-; Mc Lennan Cty 4-H Adult Leader 1980-, TX Salute to Excl 1988; First Baptist Church of Eddy Organist 1980-; *home:* PO Box 417 Eddy TX 76524

MURTA, PHILIP H., Asst Prin/Science Teacher; *b:* Fort Smith, AR; *m:* Melody Ashworth; *c:* Evan P.; *ed:* (BS) Phys Ed, Tulsa Univ 1987; *cr:* Sci Teacher 1984-, Asst Prin 1987- Tulsa Chrstn Sch; *ai:* Varsity Boys Soccer Coach; Commissioner Tri-St Chrstn Athletic Conference; *office:* Tulsa Christian School 3434 S Garnett Rd Tulsa OK 74146

MURTAUGH, MARIANNE SANTARELLI, Social Studies Teacher; *b:* Hershey, PA; *m:* Kevin Michael; *c:* Marissa; *ed:* (BS) Ed, Shippensburg Univ 1975; (MS) His, West Chester Univ 1981; *cr:* Soc Stud Instr Susquenita Sch Dist 1975-76; Downingtown Area Sch Dist 1977-; *ai:* Band Front Adv 1977-81; NEA; PA St Ed Assn; Downingtown Area Ed Assn; *office:* Downingtown Area Sch Dist 122 Wallace Ave Downingtown PA 19335

MUSCARELLA, LOUIS MONISTERE, Science Teacher; *b:* Hammond, LA; *m:* Peter; *c:* Stephen, Melissa; *ed:* (BS) Home Ec/Sci, SE LA Univ 1969; *cr:* Sci Teacher Southwood Acad 1970-71, St Joseph Sch 1979-; *ai:* Sch Building Level & Sci Club Vision & Values Comm; Mission Moderator; Sci Fair Coord; NSTA, NCEA, ASCD; *home:* 711 Crapanzano Rd Hammond LA 70401

MUSE, MICHAEL G., Physical Education Teacher; *b:* Winston-Salem, NC; *m:* Deborah Lynne Murdock; *c:* Katie L.; *ed:* (BS) Phys Ed, Appalachian St Univ 1985; *cr:* Asst Bsktbl Coach Appalachian St Univ 1984-86; Teacher/Coach R J Reynolds HS 1986-; *ai:* Head Ftbl & Asst Bsktbl Coach; Reynolds Service Club Spon; NC Coaches Assn 1983-; NABC 1984-88; Head Coach Wigan England Bsktbl Clinic 1985; *office:* R J Reynolds Sch 301 N Hawthorne Rd Winston-Salem NC 27104

MUSLOFF, KEITH STEVEN, Reading Teacher; *b:* Milwaukee, WI; *m:* Constance Mary Forecki; *c:* Amy, Beth, Katie; *ed:* (BA) Elem Ed, Univ of WI Milwaukee 1971; (MA) Rdng Specialist, Cardinal Stritch Coll 1987; *cr:* Elem Teacher St Veronicas 1971-72; 3rd/5th Grade Teacher Mac Arthur 1972-85; 7th/8th Grade Rdng Teacher Kennedy Mid Sch 1985-; *ai:* Drama Club, Annual Play Dir; Forensics Asst, Odyssey of Mind Coach; Stu Assistance Prgm Group Leader; St Andrews Summer Day Camp Dir 1985-; GEA VP; Germantown Distinguished Service Awd Nom 1988-89; *office:* Kennedy Mid Sch W160 N11836 Crusader Ct Germantown WI 53022

MUSSACK, MARK D., English/US History Instructor; *b:* Onawa, IA; *m:* Lynette Vawser; *c:* Patrick, Emily; *ed:* (AA) Eng, Northeast Tech Comm Coll 1980; (BS) Eng/His, Univ of NE Omaha 1983; Creative Writing, Univ of IA & Northeast Tech; Civil Rights Movement His, Univ of IA; *cr:* Scndry Instr West Monona Jr/Sr HS 1984-; *ai:* Jr HS Stu Cncl Spon; Jr HS Literary Magazine Publisher; Stu Assistance Team; Drug & Alcohol Awareness Comm; NCTE Mem 1982-84; IA Cncl Teachers of Eng Mem 1986-; IA Cncl of Soc Stud Mem 1986-.

MUSSELMAN, SUSAN EDENS, English Teacher; *b:* Frankfurt, Germany; *m:* Larry L.; *c:* Cheri, Lucy Pratt, Gavin, Jason, Lauren; *ed:* (BA) Speech/Comm, Denison Univ 1968; Post Graduate Work; Akron Univ; Malone Coll; Dusquesne Univ; IN Univ of PA; Penn St; Seton Hill; *cr:* Eng Teacher Lake Local HS 1969-71; Eng Sub Teacher/Teacher Kiski Area HS 1981-; *ai:* Jr League of Pittsburgh Bd 1981-; Opportunities & Resources Bd 1987-89; Teacher of Yr 1988-89; *office:* Kiski Area H S 200 Poplar St Vandergrift PA 15690

MUSSER, ANTOINETTE LOUISE ANGLE, Third Grade Teacher; *b:* Quincy, OH; *m:* Carl E. Musser; *c:* Dale Lee, Alan Lee; *ed:* (BA) Elem, OH Univ 1966; *cr:* 3rd/4th Grade Teacher Lewistown OH 1951-52; 5th Grade Teacher De Graff OH 1952-54; 3rd Grade Teacher Grove City OH 1954-55, Amanda OH 1967-; *ai:* NEA 1983-; OEA, PTO, PTA 1951-; OCCL (Pres, Secy, VP, Treas) 1962-; Order of Eastern Star Star Point 1948-; Jennings Scholar OH Univ 1988-89.

MUSSER, SAUNDRA J., Vocal Music Teacher; *b:* Bluffton, OH; *c:* Trisha Musser Hicks, David, Steven; *ed:* (BMUSED) Music, Bluffton Coll 1959; (MSED) Ed, Univ of Dayton 1979; *cr:* Vocal Music Teacher Glenwood Jr HS 1959-64; K-6th Grade Vocal Music Teacher Whittier & Adams Elem 1974-75; Vocal Music Teacher Glenwood Jr HS 1976-; Adjunct Supvr of Stu Teachers Bowling Green St Univ 1989-; *ai:* Curr Cncl Findlay City Schls; In-Service, Staff Dev, Advisory Comms; Findlay City Schls; Performance Ensemble Glenwood; ASCAP, FEA, NEA, OMEA, OEA, AlPha Gamma, Pi Delta Society; Composer of Published Vocal Compositions; Bruce Hill Awd for Exemplary Classroom Teaching 1988; Findlay Educator of Month 1985; Martha Jennings Scholar Findlay City Schls 1982-83; ASCAP Composer Awd 1987, 1989; Composer Natl Theme Song for Music in Our Schls 1986; *office:* Glenwood Jr HS N Main St Findlay OH 45840

MUSTON, BETTY RUTH ATKINS, Third Grade Teacher; *b:* Paint Rock, TX; *c:* William E.; *ed:* (BS) Elem Ed, Hardin-Simmons Univ 1978; Span Intermediate; Cmptr Sci Introductory; *cr:* Bus Experience 1941-48, 1961-76; 3rd Grade Teacher Paducah Ind Sch Dist 1978-; *ai:* Ready Writing & Story-Telling Coach; Assn of TX Prof Educators 1978-; Delta Kappa Gamma 1983-86; Bi-Centennial Lib Bd of Dir 1986-89; Paducah Chamber of Commerce 1989-; Hendrick Mem Hosp Candy Striper; Salutatorian Christoval HS; Newspaper Ed; *home:* PO Box 601 Paducah TX 79248

MUTERT, DINAH RUTH, Sixth Grade Teacher; *b:* Augsburg, Germany; *ed:* (BSED) Elem Ed, Univ of MO Columbia 1974; Grad Work Curr/Instruction/Elem Admin, Univ of MO Columbia; *cr:* 6th Grade Teacher 1974-75, 3rd Grade Teacher 1975-76, 6th Grade Teacher 1976-81 Augusta Elem; 6th Grade/Head Teacher/Admin 1981- Labadie Elem; *ai:* Stu Cncl; Sch Beautification; Charity Fund Drives Spon; Cmptr Prgm; Pi Lambda Theta; *office:* Labadie Elem Sch 220 Locust St Washington MO 63090

MUZICHUCK, JACK F., Welding Teacher; *b:* Fairmont, WV; *m:* Charlotte A.; *c:* Zach, Seth; *ed:* Welding, Fayette Cty Voc Tech; Voc Ed, Univ of Pittsburgh 1990; *cr:* Teacher Greene Cty AVTS 1978-; *ai:* Welding VICA Club Spon; PA St Ed Assn Local Pres 1989-; Amer Welding Society 1990; *office:* Greene Cty Voc Tech RD 2 Box 40 Waynesburg PA 15370

MYCHALISZYN, KIM M., Business Education Teacher; *b:* Allentown, PA; *ed:* (AA) Bus Admin, Lehigh Cty Comm Coll 1985; (BS) Bus Ed, Bloomsburg UniM 1987; *cr:* Bus Ed Instr Lehigh Cty Comm Coll 1989; Bus Ed Teacher Lehightown Area Sr HS 1987-; Bus Ed Instr Allentown Bus Sch 1988-; *ai:* Asst Cheerleading, Wrestling, Jr Var Ftbl Coach; FBLA Asst; PBEA, NBEA 1986-; LAEA 1987-; Pi Omega Pi Secy 1986-87; Phi Beta

Lambda 1983-87; Lycoming Hall Academic Awd Bloomsburg Univ 1986; *office:* Lehighton Area Sr HS 301 Beaver Run Rd Lehighton PA 18235

MYER, DEE ANN, Language Quest Teacher; *b:* Shelbyville, IN; *ed:* (BS) Phys Ed/Health & Safety, 1980, (MS) Eng, 1985 IN St Univ; Quest Intnl Quest Cert; I-Star Wkshp I Star Cert; *cr:* Teacher/Coach Shelby East Schls 1980-; *ai:* 7th-8th Grade Vlybl, Var Gymnastics, Jr HS Gymnastics, Girls & Boys Track Coach; Book Adoption Comm; Phi Kappa Phi; Sigma Tau Delta (Secy, Pres) 1978-80; Kappa Delta Pi; Shelbyville Baptist Temple (Choir, Hand Bells, Brass); IN St Univ I Awd; Girls Clubs of America Awd; Outstanding Track Coach 1988; *office:* Morristown Jr/Sr HS PO Box 247 US Hwy 52 Morristown IN 46161

MYERS, BERTHA, Teaching/Asst Principal; *b:* Tulsa, OK; *ed:* (BA) Elem Ed, Langston Univ 1946; (MA) Ed, Wichita St Univ 1953; Further Study Columbia Univ; *cr:* 3rd Grade Teacher Dunbar Sch 1950-75; Prgm Implementor Phoenix Elem Sch Dist 1 1975-77; 4th Grade Teacher 1977-86, Teaching/Asst Prin 1986- Kenilworth Sch; *ai:* AZ Ed Assn Mem Bd of Dir 1985-; Phoenix Elem Classroom Teachers Assn Pres 1982-84; NEA Mem of Resolution Comm 1985-; Assn Honoree 1989; Citation of Appreciation Amer Legion 1981; Mem Phoenix Excl in Ed Commission 1989-; *office:* Kenilworth Sch 1210 N 5th Ave Phoenix AZ 85003

MYERS, BEVERLEY SIMMONS, Mathematics Teacher; *b:* Harrisonburg, VA; *m:* Darlene Staples; *c:* Brian S., Lorena Staples; *ed:* (BA) Math, Bridgewater Coll 1967; *cr:* Teacher/Coach Ft Defiance HS 1967-; *ai:* Jr Class Spon; Math Dept Chm; Teacher Assistance Team Mem; Valley of VA Math Teachers Assn; *office:* Fort Defiance HS PO Box 38 Fort Defiance VA 24467

MYERS, CHARLES F., Latin Teacher; *b:* Brooklyn, NY; *m:* Rosemary T. Glimm; *c:* Rosemary Myers Sherman, Carol Myers Saunders, Charles F. Jr.; *ed:* (BA) Eng/Lang/Philosophy, St Johns Univ Coll 1948; (MA) Poly Philosophy, Fordham Univ 1954; (EDD) Ed/Lang, St Johns Univ 1979; Russian, Fordham & Dartmouth; Admin & Supervision Certificate, Brooklyn Coll; Cathedral Coll; *cr:* Latin/Eng Teacher Brooklyn Prep 1949-55; Latin Teacher St Johns Coll 1951-52; Latin/Eng Teacher Levittown Division Area HS 1955-57; Latin/His/Eng Teacher/ Eng Dept Chm Plainedge HS & Jr HS 1957-86; Latin Teacher St Pauls HS 1986-88, Hewlett HS 1986-; *ai:* Latin Club Hewlett HS; Natl, St, Cty Classical Assn Past Pres 1956-; Natl, St, Cty Eng Assn 1960-; Phi Delta Kappa 1985-; St & Cty Teacher Ed Prof Stans Comm Chm; Nassau Eng Chm Assn 1965-89; Natl Defense Act Grant Russian Ed; St Grant Classics Teachers 1988; Doctoral Dissertation; *office:* G W Hewlett HS 60 Everit Ave Hewlett NY 11557

MYERS, COLLEEN BRENDEMUEHL, Third Grade Teacher; *b:* Lancaster, WI; *m:* Michael A.; *c:* Patrick, Jim, Bridgid; *ed:* (BA) Ed 1970, (MST) Ed 1973 Univ of WI-Platteville; Rdng Specialist; *cr:* 3rd Grade Teacher Bloomington Cmnty Schls 1969-; *ai:* Bloomington Teachers Assn (Pres 1987-88, Secy 1989-); Alpha Gamma Rho Rho-Mates Adv 1989-; Jamison Museum Volunteer 1989-; *home:* 987 Golf View Dr Platteville WI 53818

MYERS, DARRELL RICHARD, History Teacher; *b:* Toledo, OR; *m:* Patricia Donohue; *c:* Melina Johnson, Merry, Chrysse Lorenzen, Matt; *ed:* (BA) Ec Humboldt St Univ 1966; Ec, His, Ed, Humboldt St Univ; *cr:* Teacher Eureka Sr HS 1967-82, Winship Jr HS 1983-; Part Time Lecturer Humboldt St Univ 1967-69, 1982, 1988-; *ai:* Mem Advisory Comm CA Assessment Prgm; 8th Grade Sub-Committee Chm; Phi Delta Kappa, CA Teachers Assn; Winner CA Educator Awd 1989; *office:* Winship Jr HS 2500 Cypress Avenue Eureka CA 95501

MYERS, DEBRA SCOGGIN, Art Teacher; *b:* Tacoma, WA; *m:* Craig; *c:* Margo K.; *ed:* (AA) Fine Art, 1974, (BFA) Fine Art, 1976 Columbia Coll; (MFA) Fine Art, Univ of MO 1984; *cr:* Teaching Asst Univ of MO Columbia 1980-84; Elem Art Teacher Canton R-V 1984-86; Adjunct Instr Culver Stockton Coll 1985-; Art Teacher Highland HS 1986-; *ai:* Art Club Adv; Adv Comm; Sr Class Spon; Odyssey of Mind Coach; MO St Teachers Assn, NAEA, Coll Art Assn, Natl Womens Caucus for Arts; Canton Area Arts Cncl Prgm Bd 1988-; Bethel Colony Sch of Arts Teacher 1989-; MS River Watercolor Society 1988-; Locally & Nationally Exhibit Art Work; Juried Electronic Gallery Art Work Tour; *office:* Highland HS Hwy 6 Ewing MO 63440

MYERS, GLORIA HAY, Second Grade Teacher; *b:* Florence, AL; *m:* Melvin Woodrow; *c:* M. W. Jr., Mark A.; *ed:* (BA) Elem Ed/Lit Eng, Spring Hill 1969; (MED) Elem Ed, Univ of New Orleans 1947; Grad Southeastern 1982; *cr:* 5th Grade Elem Teacher Chickasaw Elem 1947-50; Gov Contracting Brookley AFB 1950-52; 3rd Grade Elem Teacher Kenner Mid Sch 1968-71; 2nd Grade Elem Teacher FL Ave Elem 1971-; *ai:* NEA; LA Assn of Educators; *office:* Florida Avenue Elem Sch 342 Florida Ave Slidell LA 70458

MYERS, ILEAN, First Grade Teacher; *b:* Brilliant, AL; *ed:* (AS) Brewer St Jr Coll 1971; (BS) Elem Ed, 1973, (MA) Elem Ed, 1976 Univ of AL 1976; (AA) Elem Ed, Univ of North AL 1989; *cr:* Music Teacher Private Instrucion Piano/Organ/Voice 1951-73; 1st/6th Grade Music Teacher Guin Elem Sch 1973-74; Classroom Teacher Brilliant Elem Sch 1974-89; *ai:* Various Music Activities; Private Music Instructor; Church Musician; Ladies Auxiliary; AL Ed Assn 1973-; NEA 1973-; Marion Cty Ed Assn 1973-; Delta Kappa Gamma (2nd VP 1989-91; (Schlsp 1984; Mem 1982-; Comm 1983-; Brilliant Hs Alumnus of the Y R 1988; Brilliant Elem Teacher of Yr 1989-; *office:* Brilliant Elem Sch Rt 1 Box 10ABC Brilliant AL 35548

MYERS, JAMES HOWELL, Social Studies Teacher; *b:* Martinsburg, WV; *ed:* (BA) Comprehensive Soc Stud, Shepherd Coll 1969; (MA) Scsndry Ed, WV Univ 1974; *cr:* Soc Stud Teacher North Mid Sch 1970-; *ai:* Acompanied Stus to Europe 1976-; Golden Horseshoe Academic Competition 1972-; Berkeley Cty Ed Assn, WV Ed Assn, NEA 1970-; Berkeley Cty Educator of Yr Awd 1986; A Caring Educator Awd 1988; DAR St His Teacher of Yr 1984-85; *office:* North Mid Sch 105 East Rd Martinsburg WV 25401

MYERS, JO AN BUCH, Jr & Sr High School Counselor; *b:* Glenwood, IA; *m:* Roger Owen; *c:* Bradley O.; *ed:* (BS) Scndry Ed/ Eng/Soc Stud, 1969, (MED) Scndry Counseling, 1972 LA St Univ; Graduate Stud Univ of Northern IA, Concordia Coll, Univ of NV Reno, IA St Univ, Marycrest Coll; *cr:* Cnslr & Financial Aid Dir MN Sch of Bus 1973-74, St Ansgar Cmmty Schls 1974-77, Clarksville & Plainfield Schls 1977-80, Instr Buena Vista Coll 1987, Drake Univ 1989-; Cnslr Charles City Cmmty Schls 1980-; *ai:* Employee Wellness Coord 1985-; Area Ed Agency At Risk Cncl Mem 1988-; WI, NE & IA Cadre Trainer; Local Ed Assn, IA Ed Assn, NEA 1980-; IA Assn Counseling & Dev Membership Retention 1978-; Natl Certified Cnslr 1985-; AMer Assn for Counseling & Dev 1985-; Floyd Cty Substance Abuse Cncl 1978-81; Floyd Cty Heart Assn 1989-; Co-Author Substance Abuse Prevention Prgms Article; *office:* Charles City Jr & Sr HS 318 Salsbury Ave Charles City IA 50616

MYERS, KATHY ABMYER, English Teacher; *b:* Alliance, OH; *m:* Dennis Lee; *c:* Shane, Kerri, Benjamin, Ali; *ed:* (BS) Ed, Kent St Univ 1975; *cr:* Jr HS Teacher 1977-84, HS Teacher 1985- Sebring Mc Kinley HS; *ai:* OH Ed Assn; OH Cncl of Teachers of Eng & Lang Art 1987-; NCTE 1985-; *office:* Sebring Mc Kinley HS 225 E Indiana Ave Sebring OH 44672

MYERS, KENNETH J., 5th Grade Teacher; *b:* Cassandra, PA; *M:* Mary A. Donohoe; *c:* Benjamin, Molly, Andrew, Hannah; *ed:* (BS) Elem Ed, St Francis Coll 1971; *cr:* 5th/6th Grade Teacher Penn Cambria Sch Dist 1971-78; 6th Grade Math Teacher Lilly Mid Sch 1978-79; 5th Grade Teacher Lilly Elem Sch 1979-; *ai:* PCTM; NCTM; Amer Horticulture Socty; *home:* Rd 4 Box 337 Ebensburg PA 15931

MYERS, MARY KATHRYN TOOLE, Second Grade Teacher; *b:* Pittston, PA; *m:* Sylvester T.; *c:* Michael; *ed:* (BS) Elem Ed, Misericordia Coll 1968; Masters Equivalency Elem Ed; *cr:* 8th Grade Sci Teacher 1968-69, 4th-6th Grade Rdng Teacher 1969-71, 2nd Grade Teacher 1971- Pittston Area; *ai:* Discipline Comm; Play Adv; AFT 1970-; Little League Team Mother 1987-88; *office:* Pittston City Elem Schl 1 New St Pittston PA 18640

MYERS, MICHAEL LYNN, SR., Social Studies Teacher; *b:* Little Rock, AR; *c:* Michael Jr.; *ed:* (BS) His, DE St Coll 1974; Addl Studies Curr/Instr DE St Coll 1986; *cr:* St Driver Welfare Dept 1970; Cell-Repairman Diamond Shamrock Chemical Plant 1971; Spec Promotion Intnl Playtex 1972-74; Teacher/Coach Smyrna Sch Dist HS 1974-; *ai:* Jaycee Club of America Outstanding Young Man Awd 1977; Phi Beta Sigma Pres 1977-84 Sigma Man 1976/79; NAACP Life Mem 1977-; Mount Zion AME Church Steward 1978-; *office:* Smyrna H S Duck Creek Pkwy Smyrna DE 19977

MYERS, REBECCA COPPLEY, Lang Art/Soc Stud Teacher; *b:* Lexington, NC; *m:* Malcolm Lewis Jr.; *c:* Wendy M., Malcolm L. III; *ed:* (BS) Elem Ed, Appalachian St Teachers Coll 1964; (MA) Elem Ed, Appalachian St Univ 1967; *cr:* 6th Grade Teacher Colonial Drive Elem Sch 1964-70, Pilot Elem Sch 1970-73; 5th/ 6th Grade Teacher Linwood Elem Sch 1973-78; 6th-8th Grade Teacher Cntrl Davidson Mid Sch 1978-; *ai:* Curr Coord; Senate Bill 2 Comm; Collaborative Project High Point Coll; NCEA, NEA (Treas 1965-67, Building Rep 1972-73); Delta Kappa Gamma; Jersey Baptist Church (Sunday Sch Teacher, Youth Choir Dir); Linwood Cmmty Center Bd of Dirs 1985-; Davidson Cty Teacher of Yr 1980-81; *home:* Rt 16 Box 3057 Lexington NC 27292

MYERS, ROGER WILLIAM, Mathematics Department Teacher; *b:* Wheeling, WV; *m:* Holly Jane Bennington; *c:* Derek, Katlyn, Cody; *ed:* (BA) Elem Ed/Rdng, Capital Univ 1980; (MS) Admin, Univ of Dayton 1982; *cr:* 7th/8th Grade Math/ Pre-Algebra/Rdng Teacher Kirkwood Mid Sch 1980-; *ai:* Asst Var Ftbl Coach; Phys Fitness Dir; OEA.

MYERS, SHANNON KIRBY, 5th Grade Teacher; *b:* Hickory, NC; *m:* John Alan; *c:* Kimberly; *ed:* (AB) Intermediate Ed, Lenoir Rhyne Coll 1972; (MA) Ed, Univ NC Charlotte 1985; *cr:* 7th Grade Teacher Balls Creek Elem 1972-74; 7th/8th Grade Teacher Mountain View Elem 1974-76; Math Dept Head Washington Wilkes Comprehensive HS 1976-77; 7th/8th Grade Teacher South Jr HS 1977-78; 6th Grade Teacher Brooklyn Springs Elem 1978-80; 5th Grade Teacher Waxhaw Elem 1980-; *ai:* Volunteer, Quiz Bowl, Spelling Bee Coord; Planning Team; 5th Grade Lit Team Coach; NCAE 1972-; NEA 1974-; IRA 1987-; Teacher of Yr Waxham Elem 1983; Union Cty Outstanding Math Teacher of Yr 1987; *home:* 1813 Winfield Dr Monroe NC 28110

MYERS, SUSANNE DUPUIS, Bio Teacher/Sci Dept Coord; *b:* Morgan City, LA; *m:* Jerry J.; *c:* Jeffrey, Erin; *ed:* (BS) Sci Ed, 1971, (MED) Ed, 1974 Nicholls St Univ; Grad Stud; *cr:* Sci Teacher Morgan City Jr HS 1972; Bio Teacher Morgan City HS 1972-; *ai:* Yrbk Adv; St Mary Fed of Teachers Sch Employees 1988-; LA, Amer Fed of Teachers 1988-; LA Sci Teachers Assn 1989-; LA Sci Supvrs Assn 1990; Delta Kappa Recording Secy 1986-88; Gamma Society Intnl Corresponding Secy 1988-; Outstanding Bio Teacher LA 1976; *home:* 811 Ditch Ave Morgan City LA 70380

MYERS, ZAC DAVID, Speech, Physical Ed Teacher; *b:* Lima, OH; *m:* Linda Jean Milby; *c:* Veronica E.; *ed:* (BA) Health/Phys Ed, Bluffton Coll 1981; Chicago St Univ, St Xavier Coll, Bradley Univ; *cr:* Phys Ed/Health Teacher St Paul Sch 1984-86; Adaptive Phys Ed Teacher B L Braun Center 1987-88; Phys Ed/Health Teacher Easton CUSD 1988-89; Speech/Phys Ed Teacher Illini Cntrl HS 1989-; *ai:* Frosh Soph Bsktbl & Jr HS Bsbl; Illini Cntrl Ed Assn 1989-; IL Ed Assn, NEA 1988-; IL Bsktbl Coaches Assn 1988-; IL Bsbl Coaches Assn 1988-89.

MYERS-PACHLA, DIANA M., Social Studies Teacher; *b:* Elmira, NY; *m:* Edward J. Jr.; *ed:* (BA) His, Niagara Univ 1981; (MED) Soc Stud Ed, St Univ of NY Buffalo; Coll Prgm for Teaching about Japan, Japan Study Tour Fellowship; Late Bronze Age Yrs in Crisis, Brown Univ 1989-; Global Stud, Blakesley Fellowship Clark Univ 1988; *cr:* Soc Stud Teacher Clarence HS 1983; Mid Sch Soc Stud Teacher St Ambrose Sch 1983-84; Soc Stud Teacher Foxborough HS 1984-; *ai:* Italian Exchange Coord; Newspaper & Class Adv; Hokkaido Intnl Art Youth Camp Teacher Escort MA Stus 1988; Educl Redirection & Recycling Project Policy Advisory Bd Mem 1987-; MA Teachers Assn, NEA, Norfolk Cty Teachers Assn, Foxborough Ed Assn 1985-; New England His Teachers Assn, Assn for Teaching Asian Stud 1985-; Holocaust & Jewish Resistance Summer Fellowship Prgm in Poland & Israel 1990; Horace Mann Grant India Video Presentation 1988-89, US His Curr Revision 1987; Fulbright Summer Study in India Bridgewater St Coll Regional Grant 1987; Prof Dev Grants Curr Writing 1986-88; Univ of MA Writing Project 1985; Several Wkshps on Curr Dev in Soc Stud 1985-89; Stu Travel to Italy & Greece 1988, Austria & Germany 1989; Italian Stu Exch Prgm 1989-; *office:* Foxboro HS South St Foxboro MA 02035

MYFELT, CAROL JEAN, 5th Grade Lang Arts Teacher; *b:* Elmira, NY; *ed:* (BS) Elem Ed/Comm, Mansfield Univ 1971; Addl Studies Elmira Coll & Mansfield; *cr:* 5th Grade Teacher 1971-86; 5th Grade Lang Arts Teacher 1986- W R Croman Elem Sch; *ai:* HS Play-Dir; Asst Statistician for Boys Varsity Bsktbl; 5th Grade Drama Club-Adv; NEA/PSEA 1971-; TAEA 1971-; Gamma Theta Nu Treas 1975-; *home:* R D 2 Box 115 D Ulster PA 18850

MYLES, GLENDA JEAN (MITCHELL), English Teacher; *b:* St Louis, MO; *m:* Greg Sr.; *c:* Greg Jr., Gerard; *ed:* (BS) Lang Art, Phillips Univ; Financial Management, OSU; Grad Stud, SIUE; *cr:* Stu Teacher Emerson Jr HS 1976; Sterile Technician Enid Memorial Hospital 1977; Lang Art Teacher Emerson Jr HS 1978; Lang Art/His Teacher Enid Sr HS 1978-79; Lib Technician Belton MO 1979-80; Teacher 6th St Sch 1981-82; Small Bus & Real Estate Tutor Belleville IL 1982-; Lang Art/Publications Teacher Lajes HS 1985-86; Lang Art Teacher Riverview Gardens Sr HS 1986-; *ai:* Yrbk & Newspaper Spon Azores 1985-86; Bd of Trustee Mem St Louis Comm Coll 1990; Meadows Elem Sch Room Mother 1986-87; Chrldr Phillips Univ 1976-77; Natl Honor Society Service & Dedication Awd 1987-; Black Peoples Union Phillips Univ (VP 1975, Pres 1976-77); Castle Point Park Comm Mem 1989-; Castle Point Lighting Dist Mem 1987-; Neighborhood Watch Prgm Co-Developer 1989-; Red Cross Blood Donor 1988-; Red Cross Volunteer Tutor 1985-86; Our Lady of Guadalupe Ladies Club 1988-; Founder & Admin St John Baptist Church Tutorial Prgm & Summer Sch 1988-; Co-Founder of Beth Yod Feh 2nd Baptist Church 1980; Pres Young Chrstn Women Group Progressive Baptist Church 1978-79; Various Churches Lay Leader; Stu Senate Jr & Sr Class Phillips Univ 1975-77; ACU-I Conference KS St Univ 1976-77; Phillips Univ All Univ Productions 1976-77, Univ Poetry Conference 1975-77;Cmmty Service Awd Ethnic Awareness; Pres Honor Roll & Deans List Phillips Univ 1973-77; Whos Who Among Stu in Amer Univ & Coll 1976-77; Homecoming Queen Finalist Phillips Univ 1976; Schlsps Lincoln Univ, Univ of MO Columbia, Phillips Univ 1973; Internship/Assoc Prof OK St Univ, Univ TX 1977.

MYLES, ROSA THOMPSON, Second Grade Teacher; *b:* Orlando, FL; *m:* Michael Antonio; *c:* Michanda, Michael Jr., Marcus; *ed:* (BS) Spec Ed, Morris Brown 1977; *cr:* Spec Ed Teacher Tubman Mid 1977-79, Wheeless Road Elem 1979-82; 2nd Grade Teacher Gracewood Elem 1983-89, Willis Foreman Elem 1989-; *ai:* NEA, Richmond Cty Assn of Educators, GA Assn of Educators; Alpha Kappa Alpha; Gracewood Elem Teacher of Yr 1985-86; *office:* Willis Foreman Elem Sch 2413 Willis Foreman Rd Hephzibah GA 30815

MYRES, SHELLEY BOONE, Fourth Grade Teacher; *b:* Bakersville, NC; *m:* Dean; *c:* Heather, Sarah; *ed:* (BS) Early Chlhd, Western Carolina Univ 1972; (MA) Grades 4th-6th, Appalachian St Univ 1982; *cr:* 3rd Grade Teacher Elkin Primary 1972-75; 1st-4th Grade Remedial Rdng Teacher Harris Elem 1975-76; 3rd Grade Teacher Deyton Primary 1976-79; 4th-8th Remedial Rdng Teacher 1979-81; 4th Grade Teacher Harris Mid Sch 1981-; *ai:* Sch Imprvmnt Comm; NCAE 1972-; NEA 1972-; Lily Branch Baptist Church Teacher 1978-; *home:* 117 Galax Trl Spruce Pine NC 28777

MYRICK, LINDA KIRK, First Grade Teacher; *b:* Ottawa, IL; *m:* Edward J.; *c:* James; *ed:* (BA) Elem Ed/Eng, 1973, (MA) Elem Ed, 1979 Murray St Univ; *cr:* 1st Grade Teacher Frances Elem 1973-79; 4th Grade Teacher Marion Elem 1980-82; 1st Grade Teacher 1983-, K-2nd Grade Coord 1988- Crittenden Cty Elem; *ai:* Chess Club Co-Spon; Resource Teacher 1988-; Supervising Teacher 1988-89; Kndgtn-2nd Grade Coord 1988-; KY Educators Assn (2nd VP 1988-89, 1st VP 1989-); *home:* R 4 Box 196-C Marion KY 42064

N

NAATZ, THOMAS JOHN, Jr High History Teacher; *b:* Brownsdale, MN; *ed:* (AA) Liberal Art, Austin St Jr Coll 1972; (BS) Soc Sci/Ed, Concordia Teachers Coll 1974; Grad Work, AL A&M Univ; *cr:* 5th Grade Teacher 1974-78, 6th-8th Grade Teacher 1978- Grace Luth Sch; *ai:* Sch Yrbk Ed; Educl Ministries Coord; Accreditation Comm; NCSS, ASCD 1986-; Luth Ed Assn 1974-; Southern Dist Teachers Conference Pres; Southern Dist Accreditation Comm Secy; Huntsville Ind Sch League Pres 1985-; Madison Cty Emergency Management Private Schls Coord 1985-; *office:* Grace Lutheran Sch 3321 S Memorial Pkwy Huntsville AL 35801

NABERS, VICKI L., Sixth Grade Teacher; *b:* Memphis, TN; *ed:* (BS) Elem Ed, Lambuth Coll 1977; Curr & Instruction, Memphis St Univ; *cr:* Spec Ed Teacher Maury City Sch 1977-80; 5th/6th Grade Teacher Idlewild Elem 1980-; *ai:* 6th Grade Chairperson; Discipline Comm; Spelling Bee Comm; Memphis Ed Assn 1977-; West TN Rdng Assn 1987-89; *office:* Idlewild Elem Sch 1950 Linden Ave Memphis TN 38104

NABINGER, CAROL ANN BROWN, English/Chinese Teacher; *b:* Cincinnati, OH; *c:* David E. Jr., Bethe A., Johnathan F.; *ed:* (AB) Eng, Catawba Coll 1961; Chinese, Middlebury Coll, Johannean Lang Center; Working on Masters in Ed, Akron Univ; *cr:* 2nd Grade Teacher Salisbury City Schls 1961-62; 1st Grade Teacher Valley Vista Elem 1963-64; 8th Grade Eng Teacher Willetts Mid Sch 1977-; Chinese Teacher Brunswick HS 1988-; *ai:* Delta Kappa Gamma 1987-; Brunswick Ed Assn 1977-; OH Ed Assn, NEA 1977-; Brunswick City Schls Federal Grant 1986-87; Rockefeller Fnd Grant 1988; Outstanding Classroom Teacher Providing Asst to Handicapped Youngsters 1986; Wrote Spelling & Eng Curr for 8th Graders 1987; *home:* PO Box 553 1190 N Carpenter Rd Brunswick OH 44212

NADDY, CANDACE FREYER, 7th Grade Science Teacher; *b:* Chicago, IL; *m:* Edward; *c:* Laura, Allison; *ed:* (BA) Elem Ed, UICC 1973; *cr:* Teacher Henderson Elem Sch 1974-82, Van Vlissingen Elem Sch 1982-; *ai:* Sci Fair Coord; Family Life Ed Resource; *office:* Van Vlissingen Sch 137 W 108th Pl Chicago IL 60628

NADEAU, BEVERLY M., Mathematics Teacher; *b:* Springfield, MA; *m:* Thomas R.; *c:* Lindsay; *ed:* (BA) Math, Westfield St Coll 1974; (MED) Curr/Instruction-Math, Univ of S FL 1989; *cr:* Math Teacher Gateway Regional HS 1974-79; Math Tutor Chicapee HS 1984-85; Math Teacher Gateway Refional HS 1985-86, Ft Myers HS 1986-; *ai:* FL Future Educators of Amer & Omega Club Spon; Lee Cty Math Cncl, NCTM 1986-; *office:* Ft Myers HS 2635 Cortez Blvd Fort Myers FL 33901

NADEAU, SUSAN NORRIS, 4th Grade Teacher; *b:* Baraboo, WI; *m:* Richard Harry; *c:* Angela; *ed:* (BS) Elem Ed, Westfield St Coll 1975; (MS) Elem Ed, Univ of SC 1984; *cr:* Lang Arts/Math Teacher 1978; 4th Grade Teacher 1979-88 Lakewood Elem; 4th Grade Teacher Forestbrook Elem 1988-; *ai:* Cmptr Club Adv 1980-; Ed Club Adv Coastal Carolina Coll 1988-; NEA 1979-; HCEA (Pres 1988-89, Secy 1984-88), Pres Awd 1986; Alpha Delta Kappa Treas 1986-89; Phi Delta Kappa Spec Projects VP 1989; SCEA 1979-, Cmptrs & Instructional Mini Grant, Prof Dev Mini Grant; *office:* Forestbrook Elem Sch Rt 11 Box 2000 Myrtle Beach SC 29577

NADLER, ESTELLE EPSTEIN, Sixth Grade Teacher; *b:* Kingston, NY; *m:* Errol; *c:* Scott, Jeremy; *ed:* (BA) Elem Ed, Syracuse Univ 1968; (MS) Elem Ed/Psych, St Univ of NY New Platz 1970; Assertive Discipline; Madeline Hunter Model-Effective Teaching; Cmptr Ed; Prin Acad for Effective Schls; *cr:* 5th Grade Teacher Walpole Elem Sch 1968-69; Teacher of Deaf Child Duzine Elem Sch 1970; 5th Grade Teacher Pine Bush Mid Sch 1973; Psych I Teacher Orange Cty Comm Coll 1975; Title I Math Teacher 1977, 4th-6th Grade Teacher 1977- Phoenicia Elem Sch; *ai:* Leadership Responsibilities in Effective Sch Team; Plan, Dev, Administer 1 Week Environmental Trip to ME; Woodstock Recreation Bd 1977-78; Cystic Fibrosis Assn 1975-; *home:* 15 Elwyn Dr Woodstock NY 12498

NAFZGER, GEORGANA, 2nd Grade Teacher; *b:* Shamrock, TX; *m:* Don; *c:* Wade, Jana; *ed:* (BS) Bus Ed, West TX St Univ 1963; *cr:* 2nd Grade Teacher Olton ISD; *ai:* Excl Ed Comm; Assn TX Prof Ed; Faith Circle Luth Church VP 1990-.

NAGEL, DORIS (SAUL), 4th Grade Teacher; *b:* Greenville, PA; *m:* Robert W.; *c:* Dianne Nagel Lavin, Robert Jr., Kirk; *ed:* (BS) Elem Ed, Thiel Coll 1956; *cr:* 4th Grade Teacher Sharpsville Sch System 1956-62, Reynolds Sch System 1962-; *ai:* Lang Art & Math Comms; Reynolds K-8th Grade Selecting Curr; Reynolds Ed Assn Mem; PA Sch Ed Assn; NEA; Womens Chrstn Temperance Union Educl Dir 1986-87; United Church of Christ (Organist, Elder 1986-89); Mercer Cty Historical Society Mem; *home:* 652 River Rd Greenville PA 16125

NAGEL, LISA WILKENING, K-8th Vocal Music Teacher; *b:* St James, MN; *m:* John T.; *ed:* (BA) Music Ed, St Olaf Coll 1982; Various Classes & Wkshps at Numerous Universities; *cr:* 6th-8th Grade Teacher Little Falls Mid Sch 1982-; K-5th Grad Teacher Dr S G Knight Elem 1982-84; 9th-11th Grade Teacher Little Falls HS 1984-86; K-5th Grade Teacher Dr S G Knight Elem 1986-; *ai:* Vocal Music Concerts; MEA/NEA 1982-; MMEA 1982-; ACDA 1983-; *office:* Little Falls Cmmty Schls 1000 1st Ave NE Little Falls MN 56345

NAGEM, EVELYN TRICHELL, First Grade Teacher; *b:* Oak Grove, LA; *w:* Joseph Winston (dec); *c:* David; *ed:* (BA) Elem Ed, Northeast LA Univ 1965; (MED) Elem Ed, 1969, Elem Ed, 1974 NLU Monroe; Prof Improvement for Teachers 1984; *cr:* Teacher Forest HS 1966-68, Goodwill Elem 1968-; *ai:* Sch Carnival Spon 1978-; Sch Building Level Comm 1980-; Textbook Adoption Comm 1973-83; LA Assn of Educators 1966-; NEA 1966-; Catholic Parish Cncl VP 1986-; Catholic Altar Society Secy 1982-; Teacher of Yr 1986-89; Elem Teacher of Parish 1988-89; Supervising Teacher 1988-; *office:* Goodwill Elem Rt 3 Oak Grove LA 71263

NAGLE, DOUGLAS RAYMOND, Social Studies Instructor; *b:* Bethlehem, PA; *m:* Nancy Paula Schneider; *c:* Rose, Nick, Aimee; *ed:* (BS) Scndry Ed/Comp Soc Stud, Kutztown Univ 1972; (BA) Criminal Justice, 1983, (MED) Guidance/Counseling, 1987 OH St Univ; Driver Ed, OH St Univ; Freedoms Fnd Amer Judiciary Seminary; *cr:* Teacher Ind Local Sch Dist 1975-78, Jonathan Alder Public Schls 1978-79; Instr Coshocton Joint Voc Sch 1979-; *ai:* OH Mock Trial Pgrm & OH Citizenship Bee Adv; OEA, NEA, CCJUSEA Pres 1983-86; Chi Sigma Iota, OH Sch Cnslrs Assn 1987-; Elks 1984-; Coshocton Cty Rotarys Outstanding HS Teacher of Yr 1988; Freedoms Fnd Valley Forge Seminar Schlsp Awd 1989; *office:* Coshocton Cty Voc Sch 23640 C R 202 Coshocton OH 43812

NAGLE, SHARLENE MC INTYRE, Soc Studies/Lang Art Teacher; *b:* Jesup, GA; *c:* Bekki, Kanda; *ed:* (MED) Soc Stud/Mid Grades GA Southern 1977; *cr:* Spec Ed, Claxton Elem 1972-73; 5th-6th Grade Lang Art Teacher 1974-78, 7th-8th Grade Soc Sci Teacher 1979- Collins Elem; *ai:* GA Quiz Bowl Competition; Collins GA His Fair; Collins Halloween Carnival Organizer 1975-; Collins Media & SST Mem; Collins Ben Franklin Stamp Club; GAE 1972-76; PAGE 1985-; GA Cncl for Soc Stud 1987-.

NAHIRNY, DOLORES M., Teacher; *b:* Olean, NY; *m:* Joseph; *ed:* (BS) Elem Ed, Newark St 1952; Kean Coll, Jersey City St Coll; *ai:* Grade Chairperson Curr Comm; Nutley Ed Assn, Essex Cty Ed Assn, NJEA, NEA Mem 1952-; Dist Leader Springfield 1986-; Ethics Bd Springfield Bd Mem 1984-88; Republican Nominating Comm 1980-; Springfield Ladies of Unico Pres 1984-88; Columbiettes #5560 1965-; Natl Republican Comm.

NAIL, CHARLES E., Supervisor of Music; *b:* Novice, TX; *m:* Brenda C.; *c:* Valerie, Thomas; *ed:* (BME) Music, 1963, (MA) Music, 1974 West TX St Univ; Univ of North TX/Univ of TX AUSTIN; *cr:* Officer/Pilot U S Army 1963-68; Band Dir Pecos ISD 1968-71, Bonham Jr HS 1971-72; Band/Orch Dir Permian HS 1972-89; Supervisor of Music Ector Cty ISD 1989-; *ai:* Mem-Odessa Cultural Cncl; Mem-Midland-Odessa Symphony Bd; TX Music Educators Assn VP 1985-87; Pres 1987-89; TX Orchestra Dir Assn VP/Pres/Sec/Treas 1981-85; Phi Beta Mu; Outstanding Young Band Dir 1975; Honor Band of TX 1975; Honor Orchestra of TX 1980 & 1985; *office:* Ector Cty ISD PO Box 3912 Odessa TX 79760

NAILS, RAYMOND FULTON, English Department Chairman; *b:* Coushatta, LA; *m:* Celine Gaudin; *c:* Nicole; *ed:* (BA) Ed, Northwestern St & Univ of LA 1957; San Antonio Coll, Nicholls St Univ, LA St Univ; *cr:* Teacher Thibodaux HS 1957-79, Cntrl Cath HS 1979-; *ai:* Natl Jr Honor Society & NHS; NCEA, NCTE 1979-87; Cntrl Cath HS Boosters Club, La Fourche Parish Teachers, Tuesday Club Secy; Outstanding Teacher of S Thibodaux Jr HS 1975; *office:* Cntrl Cath HS 2100 Cedar St Morgan City LA 70380

NAKAMA, PATRICIA PIILANI ONO, English/Journalism Teacher; *b:* Waiamea, HI; *m:* Clayton S.; *c:* Michelle, Carole Ann, Matthew; *ed:* (BA) Eng Elem Ed, Southern CA Coll 1966; (PD) Scndry Ed, Chaminade Univ 1984; Stapleton Sch of Real Estate Certified 1974; *cr:* Eng/Jornalism Teacher Kekaha Sch 1966-69; Eng Teacher Waimea Intermediate & HS 1969-72; Eng/Journalism Teacher HI Bapt Acad 1984-; *ai:* Eagle Eye Newspaper Adv; Quill & Scroll Adv; HI Teachers of Eng Assn 1984-; Y-Teens Adv 1967-68; Campus Life Club Adv 1966-72; Kekaha Church Supt Sunday Sch 1968-72; Dow Jones Newspaper Fund 1984; *office:* Hawaii Baptist Acad 2429 Pali Hwy Honolulu HI 96817

NAKAMICHI, JANE CHIEKO, Second Grade Teacher; *b:* Honolulu, HI; *ed:* (BA) His, Chaminade Univ 1966; (MA) Elem Ed, Univ of N CO Greeley 1967; *cr:* Elem Teacher HI Dept of Ed 1969-; *ai:* NEA, HI St Teachers Assn; Amer Cancer Society Breast Cancer Detection Project 1980; *office:* Maemae Elem Sch 319 Wyllie St Honolulu HI 96817

NAKAUE, MICHAEL, Science Department Chairperson; *b:* Chicago, IL; *ed:* (BS) Bio 1975, (MA) Ed 1978 Ca St Univ Long Beach; *cr:* Bio Teacher Westminster HS 1975-76; Life Sci Teacher Huntington Beach HS 1976-77; Sci Teacher Fleming Jr HS 1978-80; Bio Teacher Bolsa Grande HS 1980-82; Woodbridge HS 1982-; *ai:* Sci Olympiad Coach; Sci Fair Coord; Cycling Club Adv; Academic Banquet Coord; Mentor Teacher; Sci Dept Chm; NSTA; CA Sci Teachers Assn; NABT; Orange Cty Sci Ed Assn; Outstanding Sci Teacher Awd Orange Cty Sci Fair 1984/1986; Thomas Edison Awd 1987; Orange Cty Bio Teacher of Yr 1989; Textbook Consultant Addison-Wesley Publishers; *office:* Woodbridge H S 2 Meadowbrook Irvine CA 92714

NALASKI, CAROL J., English Department Chairman; *b:* Chicago, IL; *ed:* (BA) Eng/Speech, Rosary Coll 1966; (MED) Rdng Specialist, Natl Coll of Ed 1976; *cr:* Rdng Specialist Notre Dame HS for Boys 1973-76; Expository Writing Teacher 1973-83, Chairperson Eng Dept/8th Grade Eng/Lit Teacher 1983- The Willows Acad; *ai:* The Willows Acad Yrbk Co-Moderator; Intnl Rdng Assn Former Mem 1973-83; NCTE Former Mem; *office:* The Willow Acad for Girls 8200 W Greendale Niles IL 60648

NALL, DONALD E., US History Teacher; *b:* Brooklyn, NY; *m:* Ora Margaret Thompson; *c:* Kelly, Whitney; *ed:* (BA) His/Eng, Georgetown Coll 1958; (MA) Counseling/Psych, 1966, (EDS) Counseling, 1974 W KY Univ; Berea Coll Mellon Fellow 1987, 1989; NIH Soc Stud Center Univ of CO 1989; Stratford Hall Seminar 1990; *cr:* 8th Grade Lang Art/Soc Stud Teacher Daviess Cty Jr HS 1963-66; 10th/11th Grade Eng Teacher Daviess Cty HS 1966-68; Cnslr Daviess Cty Jr HS 1968-73; 8th Grade Teacher Daviess Cty Mid Sch 1973-86; US His Teacher Daviess Cty HS 1986-; *ai:* Academic Coach; NEA Bd of Dir 1975-82; KY Ed Assn VP 1984-86; KY Cncl of Soc Stud Outstanding Teacher 1989; Delivered Paper to White House Conference on Ed 1978; *office:* Daviess Cty HS 4255 New Hartford Rd Owensboro KY 42303

NANCE, MARGARET PEGGIE OELAND, Language Arts & Literature; *b:* Greenville, SC; *m:* John Drayton Jr.; *c:* Estelle Oeland; *ed:* (AA) Child Dev, 1974, (BA) Elem, 1976 Univ of SC; Post Grade Work, Furman Univ, Clemson Univ; Assessment Performance In Teaching Certified; *cr:* 7th Grade Health/Rdng/Soc Stud Teacher Northwest Mid Sch 1977-80; 7th Grade Teacher Fork Shoals Elem 1980-82; 7th/8th Grade Lang Arts/Lit Teacher Woodmont Mid Sch 1982-; *ai:* Spon Sch Newspaper; Dir Civic Oration, Creative Writing Contest; PTA VP 1986-88; NCTE 1989-; NEA, SC Ed Assn, Greenville Ed Assn 1977-; Delta Kappa Gamma VP 1981-; PTA VP 1986-88; Teacher of Yr 1982; *office:* Woodmont Mid Sch 325 Flat Rock Rd Piedmont SC 29673

NANCE, WILMA LARETTA, Fifth Grade Teacher; *b:* Trumann, AR; *m:* David F.; *ed:* (BSE) Elem Ed, AR St Univ 1978; *cr:* 5th Grade Teacher 1978-88, 7th Grade Teacher 1988-89, 5th Grade Teacher 1989- Trumann Public Schls; *ai:* Odyessy of Mind Judge; AR Ed Assn 1979-; Alpha Delta Kappa Pres 1988-; Cntrl Fire Protection Volunteer Fireman 1985-; *home:* Rt 3 Box 241 Trumann AR 72472

NANNENGA, DONNA MAE COOMBS, Orchestra Teacher; *b:* Pickardville, ND; *m:* Miles Dirk; *c:* Nathan D., Amy J.; *ed:* (BME) Music Ed, Seattle Pacific Univ 1955; String Wkshps Numerous Univ; *cr:* Elem Music Teacher Sequim WA 1954-57, Fargo Public Schls 1958-62; Elem Music Teacher, 1963-69, Orchestra Dir/Teacher 1970- Jamestown Public Schls; *ai:* 5th-12th Grade Orchestra Prgm; Cmmty String Teacher; Amer String Teachers Assn St Pres 1988-; NDEA, JEA, NEA, NDMEA, MENC; Civic Music Bd, Church Bds, Special Music for Church.

NANNEY, JOAN BATES, First Grade Teacher; *b:* Tupelo, MS; *m:* Stephen; *c:* Brian, Jole, Drew; *ed:* (BS) Elem Ed, Delta St Univ 1973; Elem Ed, Univ of MS Oxford; *cr:* Teacher Lakeview Chrstn Sch 1975-80, New Albany City Schls 1982-; *office:* Mattie Thompson Sch Cleveland St New Albany MS 38652

NANTON, ULMONT CLAUDIUS, Senior ROTC Instructor; *b:* St Croix, VI; *m:* Joyce Margery Wilson; *c:* Doris L. Edwards, Ulmont C. Jr., Gordon K.; *ed:* (BS) Chem, Hampton Univ 1958; Span, Defense Lang Inst 1971; US Army Command & General Staff Coll 1976; Post BACC Stud Bus Admin, Univ of Houston Cntrl 1980; Advanced Police Trng US Army MP Sch AL 1960-75; *cr:* Officer US Army 1958-78; Sr ROTC Instr Furr Sr HS 1978-80, Law Enforcement/Criminal Justice HS 1981-; *ai:* ROTC Drill Teams, Color Guard, Rifle Team Coach; Retired Officers Assn Mem 1978-; US Army Legion of Merit; Order of Ruben Dario Republic of Nicaraguas Awd for Humanitarian Service 1972; *office:* HS Law Enforcement & Crml Jus 4701 Dickson Houston TX 77007

NAPIER, DONALD GREEN, English Department Chairperson; *b:* Watts, KY; *m:* Barbara Williams; *c:* Kelby B.; *ed:* (MA) Eng, 1970, (Rank II) Ed/Eng, 1982 E KY Univ; *cr:* Eng Teacher Warner Jr HS 1970-72; Soc Stud/Eng Teacher Breathitt Cty Bd of Ed 1974-77; Eng Instr Lees Jr Coll 1986; Eng Teacher Breathitt Cty HS 1986-; *ai:* Breathitt Cty HS Academic Team; Red River Bsktl Team; Breathitt Cty Curr Comm; KY Educators Assn, NEA 1986-; Cub Scouts of America Den Leader 1985-88; Red River Elem PTA 1985-; Hazel Green Volunteer Fire Dept Fireman 1986-; *home:* 5210 Lee City Rd Campton KY 41301

NAPIER, ELLEN RUTH, 3rd Grade Teacher; *b:* Benham, KY; *m:* Canton; *c:* Lisa Lyn Paine; *ed:* (BA) Bus Ed, Union Coll 1961; Elem Cert, Univ of TN; *cr:* 5th Grade Teacher Hardin Valley Elem 1970-80; Fairview Elem 1980-82; 5th Grade Teacher 1983, 3rd Grade Teacher 1985- Karns Intermediate; *ai:* Teacher Ctr Rep; Environmental Comm; Textbook Comm; AAA School Safety Patrol Chaperone-Washington DC Trip; Phi Delta Kappa 1983-; Intnl 1987-; Assn 1970-; NEA 1970-; TN Ed Assn 1970-; 1st United Meth Church (Ed Commsn 1988- Admin Bd 1990); Educator of Yr Karns Intermediate 1987; TN Cncl of Arts Fellowship 1989; Career Ladder I; *home:* 116 Newridge Rd Oak Ridge TN 37830

NAPIER, RONNIE, Industrial Art Teacher; *b:* Hazard, KY; *m:* Karen Dawn Hurlbert; *c:* Katie, Monica, Roxanne; *ed:* (BS) Industrial Arts, Univ of W FL 1974; Numerous Courses at Ford & GM Trng Centers Jacksonville FL; *cr:* Teacher Mosley HS 1975-; *ai:* Bay Cty FL Voc Assn; Covenant Presbyn Church (Sunday Sch Teacher 1989-, Mem 1975-); FTP, NEA Mem 1984-; Bay Cty

Right to Life Mem 1989-; *office:* A C Mosley HS 501 Mosley Dr Lynn Haven FL 32444

NAPIERALSKI, VALERIE A., Business Teacher; *b:* Toledo, OH; *m:* John; *ed:* (BA) Bus Ed, 1974, (MA) Bus/Cmptr Tech, 1989 Univ of Toledo; *cr:* Bus Teacher Macomber-Whitney Voc Tech HS 1974-79; Comm/Trng Admin Westinghouse Electric Corporation 1979-82; Financial Analyst Prestollite Battery Corporation 1983-85; Bus Teacher Macomber-Whitney Voc Tech HS 1985-; *ai:* Local Bus Prof of America Chapter & Region 6 NW OH Adv; Bus Prof of America Adv to Macomber-Whitney Bus Club & Quiz Bowl; NW OH Bus Teachers Assn Pres 1986, 1987-88; OH Bus Teachers Assn Prof Dev Comm 1987-88, Nom Teacher of Yr 1989; Pi Lambda Theta 1987-; Assn for Retarded Citizens Exec Bd Secy 1980-82; Articles Published; *home:* 3455 Christie Blvd Toledo OH 43606

NAPIERSKI, WILLIAM, Science Teacher; *b:* Natrona, PA; *m:* Rebecca L. Green; *c:* Brian, Pam; *ed:* (AA) Liberal Arts, Comm Coll of Allegheny Cty 1969; (BS) Scndry Ed/Bio, Clarion Univ 1971; (MED) Scndry Ed/Sci, Univ of Pittsburgh 1976; Grad Stud PA St Univ; *cr:* Sci Teacher 1972-74, Bio Teacher 1974-89 Moon Area Jr HS; Sci Teacher Moon Area Mid Sch 1989-; *ai:* Mid Sch Sci Fair Co-Spon; Grading Procedures, Homework Policy Comms; Prof Rights & Responsibilities Comm Chm; Moon Jr HS Intramural Dir 1978-89; Moon Ed Assn (Pres 1983-85, VP 1981-83); NEA, PA St Ed Assn 1972-; Cub Scouts of America (Comm Man, Webelos Leader) 19880; Little League Bsbl (Coach, Mgr) 1987-; Hopewell Soccer Club Asst Coach 1989-; *office:* Moon Area Mid Sch 1407 Beers School Rd Coraopolis PA 15108

NARDONE, MARIANNE WLODKOWSKI, Assistant Superintendent; *b:* Norwich, CT; *m:* Peter S.; *ed:* (BS) Elem Ed, Cntrl CT St Univ 1968; (MA) Elem Ed, Seton Hall Univ 1969; (CAGS) Educl Admin, RI Coll 1981; (EDD) Educl Leadership, Boston Univ 1985; Supts Acad Columbia Univ 1990; *cr:* 1st-6th Grade Teacher Norwich Public Schls 1969-84; Adjunct Instr FairField Univ 1984-85; Admin Asst Supt 1984-85, Asst Prin 1985-86, Grants Coord 1986-88, Asst Supt 1988- Norwich Public Schls; *ai:* Grants Coord; Coord St & Federal Prgms; Project Mgr; Dir Summer Enrichment Prgm; Educl Policy Fellowship Prgm; CT Rep 1984-85; Bd of Trustees St Bernard HS 1988-; *office:* Norwich Public Schls Mahan Dr Norwich CT 06360

NARDONE, NANCY E., Sixth Grade Teacher; *b:* Aurora, IL; *ed:* (AA) Speech, Waubonsee Comm Coll 1973; (BA) Theatre, N IL Univ 1975; Quest Skills for Adolescents Certified Instr; *cr:* Substitute Teacher Sch Dist 131 1976; Lang Art Teacher Our Lady of Good Counsel Jr HS 1976-82; 6th Grade Teacher Holy Angels Sch 1982-; *ai:* Speech Contest Coach; City-Wide Parochial Lang Art Curr Rep 1981; NCEA; Outstanding Parochial Teacher 1984; *office:* Holy Angels Sch 720 Kensington Pl Aurora IL 60506

NARDOZZI, KATHLEEN S., English Teacher; *b:* Pittsburgh, PA; *m:* Ronald J.; *c:* Deron; *ed:* (BA) Ger/Eng, Kent St Univ 1971; Rheinische Paedagogische Hochschule, Rhine Sch of Ed Neuss West Germany 1969; *cr:* Ger/Eng Teacher Penn Hills Sch Dist 1976-; Ger Teacher Comm Coll of Allegheny Cty 1988-; *ai:* NEA, PSEA.

NARDOZZI, RONALD J., Social Studies Teacher; *b:* Pittsburgh, PA; *m:* Kathleen S.; *c:* Deron N. Nanchuk; *ed:* (BA) Poly Sci, Grove City Coll 1968; (MED) Scndry Ed, Univ Pittsburgh 1974; His/ World Affairs, Carnegie Mellon Univ Seminars; *cr:* US His Teacher Penn Sr HS, Penn Jr HS, Linton Jr HS 1972-; Soc Stud Teacher Seneca & Linton Jr HS 1972-; *ai:* NEA 1976-; Pittsburgh His Landmarks Fnd 1989-; *office:* Linton Jr HS 250 Aster St Pittsburgh PA 15235

NARETTO, JEAN TROTTER, First Grade Teacher; *b:* Mazon, IL; *m:* Louis M.; *c:* Mark, Becky N. Jones, Betsy N. Lutz, Barbara N. Petungaro; *ed:* (BS) Home Ec, 1955; Spec Cert Elem, 1971 IL St Univ; (MS) Elem Ed, Olivet Nazarene Univ 1988; Grad Stud; *cr:* Home Ec Teacher 1955-57, Chapter I Rdng 1967-71 Dwight HS; Kndgtn Teacher Goodfarm Sch 1971-78; Kndgtn-2nd Grade Teacher South Wilmington Elem 1976-; *ai:* Literary Coach South Wilmington Elem; Delta Kappa Gamma 1st VP 1986-88, IL Lambda St Schlsp 1987; Delta Kappa Gamma Pres 1990-92; Cncl Cath Women Treas 1980-86, Woman of Yr 1981; Lambda St Schlsp 1981; *office:* South Wilmington Elem Sch 5th St South Wilmington IL 60474

NASCA, DAVID MICHAEL, Mathematics Teacher; *b:* Washington, DC; *m:* Audrey J.; *c:* Ashley M.; *ed:* (BA) Math/Ed, St Leo Coll 1976; (AA) Curr/Instrtuction, VA Poly Tech Inst & VA St Univ 1982; *cr:* Math/Sci Teacher St Thomas More Sch 1976-80; Math Teacher O Connell HS 1980-; *ai:* Var Swimming Coach; Ftbl Asst Coach; Soph Class Moderator; NCEA 1980-; Knights of Columbus 1976-; *office:* Bishop Denis J O Connell HS 6600 Little Falls Rd Arlington VA 22213

NASCA, DIANA LYNN (HOSPODAR), Mathematics Teacher; *b:* Berwyn, IL; *m:* Joseph; *c:* Lauren E.; *ed:* (BS) Scndry Math Ed, IL St Univ 1984; *cr:* Math Teacher Downers Grove South HS 1984-; *ai:* Asst Math Team Coach; NCTM 1984-; *office:* Downers Grove South HS 1436 Norfolk Downers Grove IL 60516

NASH, DONNA SCHILLING, Business Education Teacher; *b:* The Dalles, OR; *m:* Richard Lee; *c:* Shannon, Mark; *ed:* (BA) Bus Ed, 1976, (EDM) Bus Ed, 1979 OR St Univ; *cr:* Bus Ed Teacher Tillamook HS 1976-; *ai:* Sr Class Adv; Onward to Excl & Advisory Comm Mem; Natural Helpers Prgm; *office:* Tillamook HS 2605 12th St Tillamook OR 97141

NASH, JOYCE SWEENEY, Mid Sch Language Arts Teacher; *b:* Borger, TX; *m:* Rex; *c:* Donna L. Houston, Glen D.; *ed:* Cmptr Literacy; Profile Writing; *cr:* 3rd/6th Grade Teacher Elkhart Schls 1969-77; 1st/2nd Grade Teacher Texhoma Elem 1978-79; 6th-8th Grade Lang Art Teacher Texhoma Mid 1980-; *ai:* 8th Grade Graduation Spon; Spelling Bee Coord; Delta Kappa Gamma 1974-81; KNEA (Local Secy 1976, Local Pres Elect 1977) 1969-77; OTEA 1978-79; ATPE 1980-; *office:* Texhoma Mid Sch Box 709 Texhoma TX 73949

NASH, MILDRED LEONARD, Teacher of Gifted & Talented; *b:* Sharon, PA; *m:* James A.; *c:* Noreen, Rebecca; *ed:* (MED) Ed/ Poetry, Harvard 1977; *cr:* Eng/Fr Teacher Rockport HS 1961-62; Eng Teacher Burlington HS 1978-83; Eng/Beam Teacher Marshall Simonds Mid Sch 1984-; *ai:* Adv HS Literary Magazine 1978-87; Coach Odyssey Mind Teams 1986-; Burlington Ed Assn; Burlington Town Meeting Elected Rep 1978-; Published Poetry Book 1989; Horace Mann Grants; Emily Dickinson Americ Poetry Society Awd; Power Dalton & Leighton Memorial New England Poetry Club Awds.

NASH, PATRICIA KAY (BLEW), Mathematics Teacher/Dept Chair; *b:* Wichita, KS; *m:* Paul Douglas; *c:* Jamie; *ed:* (BAT) Math, Sam Houston St Univ 1974; *cr:* Teacher Mance Park Jr HS 1974-; *ai:* 7th Grade Number Sense & Calculator Math Team; 8th Grade Number Sense, Calculator, Algebra Math Team; Mathcounts Coach; Math Dept Chm; SHSU Building Teacher Training; TURBCTM, NCTM; GTE Gift Grant 1987; HISD Teacher of Month 1987; *office:* Mance Park Jr HS 441 FM 2821 E Huntsville TX 77340

NASH, PATRICIA ROEBUCK, Junior High English Teacher; *b:* Buford, GA; *m:* Lamar; *c:* Larren, Casey, Keesee; *ed:* (BA) Eng, North GA Coll 1966; (MA) Counseling/Psych, Appalachian St Univ 1968; Graduate Work Univ of GA; West GA Coll; Brenau Coll; *cr:* Classroom Teacher Miami Beach Sr HS 1968-69, Gainesville Coll 1969-70, Buford HS 1970-; *ai:* Thespian Society Spon; Debate Coach; NCTE; GA Assn of Educators; NEA; Amer Bus Womens Assn Schlsp Chairperson 1985; ITS Area Rep 1981; Cancer Society; Grad Assistantship MA Prgm; *office:* Buford H S 2200 Hwy 13 Buford GA 30518

NASSEN, CHRISTINE ELIZABETH, Math/Computer Literacy Teacher; *ed:* (BS) Early Scndry Ed/Math, Oneonta St 1974; (MS) Early Scndry Ed/Math, Syracuse Univ 1979; *cr:* 5th/ 6th Grade Teacher 1974-84, PSEN-Title I Math 3rd-8th Grade Teacher 1984-85 Fort Plain Elem Sch; 6th Grade Math/Cmptr Literacy Teacher Harry Hoag Sch 1985-; *ai:* Sch Improvement Building & Dist Level Teams; Curr Dev Comm; Fort Plain Teachers Secy 1985-; CIMS Rep 1987-88; Fort Plain Bd of Ed Recognition Awd 1987; Stu Cncl Teacher of Quarter 1990; *office:* Harry Hoag Sch High St Fort Plain NY 13339

NASUTOWICZ, FRANK MARTIN, English Teacher; *b:* Munich, Germany; *m:* Wendy Marie Carr; *ed:* (AA) Hum, Jerkimer Cty Comm Coll 1972; (BA) Eng/Ed, Utica Coll of Syracuse Univ 1975; Eng/Ed, Plattsburgh St Univ Coll 1979; *cr:* 11th Grade Regents Eng Teacher New Hartford HS 1974-75; 7th Grade Eng Teacher Ticonderoga Mid Sch 1975-83; Adjunct Eng Instr North Cntry Comm Coll 1979-83; 7th Grade Eng Teacher Vernon-Verona-Sherrill Mid Sch 1983-; *ai:* Dev Implement, Monitor, Evaluate Eng Curr Comm; Prins Advisory Comm; Mid Sts Up-Date Comm; Vernon-Verona-Sherrill Exec Comm; Vernon-Verona-Sherrill Teachers Assn VP 1987-; *home:* 4935 Hill Rd Oneida NY 13421

NATALE, JAMES A., Elementary Science Teacher; *b:* Uniontown, PA; *m:* Carol A. Babich; *c:* James V., Andrew M.; *ed:* (BS) Elem Ed, California Univ of PA 1970; *cr:* Teacher Uniontown Area Sch Dist 1970-71, St Agnes Sch 1972-73, Frazier Sch Dist 1973-; *ai:* Perryopolis Lions Club Secy 1984-86; *home:* RD 1 Box 259A Fayette City PA 15438

NATALE, JOSEPH ANTHONY, English Teacher; *b:* New York City, NY; *m:* Launa Kliever; *ed:* (BA) Eng, S Meth Univ 1984; Gifted & Talented Curr Conferences; Expository Writing Conferences & Seminars; *cr:* 9th-12th Grade Teacher 1985-86, Amer Lit Teacher 1986- Wylie HS; *ai:* Gifted & Talent Coord; Mock Trial Team Spon 1986-89; NCTE; Sigma Chi; *office:* Wylie HS 516 Hilltop Ln Wylie TX 75098

NATALE, MARIAN BOWERS, Social Studies Teacher; *b:* Pittsburgh, PA; *m:* Karl J.; *c:* Katherine, Marie; *ed:* (BA) His, Marietta Coll 1965; Wkshp & Courses; *cr:* Teacher Highland HS 1967-87; Secy NBC News 1966; Teacher Triton HS 1987-; *ai:* Stu Cncl Adv 1974-76; NCSS 1989-; NJEA Unified 1967-; Black Horse Pike Ed Assn Secy 1970-74, 1977-79; Natl Trust for Historic Preservation, Colonial Williamsburg, Smithsonian; Woodbury NJ Democratic Comm Woman 1986-87; *office:* Triton HS Schubert Ave Runnemede NJ 08078

NATH, GARIE ANN MARIE, English Teacher; *b:* Trenton, NJ; *m:* E. Jeffrey; *c:* Brett, Curt; *ed:* (BA) Eng, Trenton St Coll 1972; *cr:* Teacher Jr HS #4 1972-76, Hamilton HS W 1985-; *ai:* Curr Dev, Writing, 12th Grade Curr Comm; Basic Skills Prgm Planning; 5th/6th/9th Grade Writing Comm; *office:* Hamilton HS W 2720 S Clinton Ave Trenton NJ 08610

NATH, NANCY LEE, Fourth Grade Teacher; *b:* Riverside, NJ; *m:* Donald J.; *c:* Donald Jr., Kristen; *ed:* (BS) Elem Ed, Kutztown Univ 1973; Grad Stud at Temple Univ, Villanova Univ & West Chester Univ; *cr:* 5th Grade Teacher Highland Park Elem 1974-75; 4th Grade Teacher Cardington Stonehurst Elem 1975-81, Highland Park Elem 1981-; *ai:* Math Curr Comm Upper Darby

Sch Dist; UDEA 1973-; PACE 1973-; *office:* Highland Park Elem Sch W Chester Pike & Lynn Blvd Upper Darby PA 19802

NATIONS, CATHY MILLS, Science/Ag Science Teacher; *b:* Ft Worth, TX; *m:* Loyd; *c:* Bryce; *ed:* (BS) Ag Ed, TX A&M Univ 1984; *cr:* Ag Sci Teacher Edgewood HS 1984-86; Sci/Ag Teacher Fruitvale HS 1986-; *ai:* Jr Class Spon; FFA Adv; Voc Ag Teachers Assn 1984-86; *office:* Fruitvale HS P O Box 77 Fruitvale TX 75127

NAUMAN, MARY ANN (FINKBINER), 7th Grade Soc Stud Teacher; *b:* Lancaster, PA; *m:* Ray M.; *c:* Elizabeth, Jennifer; *ed:* (BS) Comprehensive Soc Stud/Georgraphy, Kutztown Univ 1973; Grad Work; *cr:* 7th Grade Soc Stud Teacher Red Lion Jr HS 1975-; *ai:* Bowling Club Adv; *office:* Red Lion Jr HS Charles & Henrietta Sts Red Lion PA 17356

NAVAGE, RAYMOND G., Business Education Teacher; *b:* Waterbury, CT; *m:* Nedra Stevens; *c:* Lamar, Corey; *ed:* (BS) Bus, Univ of CT 1964; (MS) Ed, S CT St Univ 1974; Univ of CT Law Sch; Post Grad Stud St Joseph Coll; *cr:* Elem Teacher Wolcott Public Schls 1969-72; HS Teacher Crosby HS 1974-; *ai:* CT Bus Educator Assn, CT Ed Assn, NEA; *office:* Crosby HS 300 Pierpont Rd Waterbury CT 06705

NAVARRA, MARY JO, Second Grade Teacher; *b:* Charleroi, PA; *ed:* (BSED) Elem Ed/Early Chldhd, 1978, (MA) Rdng, 1981 WV Univ; *cr:* 2nd Grade Teacher Easton Elem Sch 1978-; *ai:* Friends of Univ Hospital Volunteer 1987-; WV Ed Fund Mini-Grant; *office:* Easton Elem Sch 2901 Pt Marion Rd Morgantown WV 26505

NAVARRE, RICK LYNN, Resource Teacher of Gifted; *b:* Sherman, TX; *m:* Brenda Mc Clain; *c:* Michael; *ed:* (BA) Psych, 1972, (MA) Elem Ed, 1973 Austin Coll; Grad Work Math, Ed of Exceptional Children, Gifted Ed; *cr:* Kndgtn Teacher 1972-81, 5th Grade Regular Teacher 1981-82, 6th Grade Teacher of Gifted/ Regular 1982-88, Teacher of Gifted Resource 1988- Plano Ind Sch Dist; *ai:* Phi Delta Kappa; NEA 1972-; Plano Ed Assn Pres 1980-81; TX Assn for Gifted & Talented 1988-; Teacher of Yr Weatherford Elem 1980-81; Teacher of Yr Aldridge Elem 1985-86; Perot Excl in Elem Teaching 1986; Forman Elem Teacher of Yr for Gifted & Talented 1988-89; *home:* 3001 Laurel Ln Plano TX 75074

NAVERT, MARY PERPETUA, First Grade Teacher; *b:* Louisville, KY; *ed:* (BA) Elem Ed, Bellarmine Coll 1970; (MA) Elem Ed, Spalding Univ 1980; *cr:* 1st Grade Teacher St Elizabeth 1965-67; 1st/2nd Grade Teacher St Helen 1967-72, St Leo 1972-74; 1st Grade Teacher St Aloysius Sch 1974-; *ai:* Trng, Cert as Resource Teacher for Intern Teachers; Assisted Interns; NCEA Mem 1972-; *home:* 1017 Plum St Shepherdsville KY 40165

NAVIN, JOHN PATRICK, Social Studies Dept Chairman; *b:* Erin, WI; *m:* Mary Braden; *c:* John J., Catherine, Matthew, Emily; *ed:* (BS) Sociology, Marquette Univ 1960; (MSED) Guidance Counseling, Northern IL Univ 1967; Numerous Stud, IL St Univ, Natl Coll of Ed, Governors St Univ, Northern IL Univ, Concordia Coll, Loyola Univ; *cr:* Teacher Sch Dist #54 1960-62; Teacher/ Team Leader/Dept Chm Sch Dist #25 1962-; *ai:* Natl Assn of Soc Stud; *office:* Thomas Jr H S 303 E Thomas St Arlington Heights IL 60004

NAVRATH, JOE, Voc-Ag Instructor; *b:* Ada, OK; *m:* Rosalie Pratka; *c:* Sheila Morgan, Sherry Hayes, Laramie; *ed:* (BA) Ag, OK St Univ Stillwater 1967; (MS) Ag, Univ of WY Laramie 1974; *cr:* Voc Ag Teacher Burns WY 1967-75, Prague OK 1975-84, Stroud OK 1984-; *ai:* FFA; Jr Class Spon; Stroud Chamber of Commerce Bd of Dir 1989-; Lions Club 2nd VP 1989-; OK Voc Ag Teachers Assn, Natl Voc Ag Teachers Assn; Outstanding Young Voc-Ag Teacher Western Region USA; Western Region Ag Careers Awd Winner USA; *office:* Stroud HS Box 410 Stroud OK 74079

NAWROTZKY, NICHOLAS, Mathematics Teacher; *b:* New York City, NY; *m:* Diane Largent; *c:* Shayna, Kirk; *ed:* (BA) Math/Ec, City Coll of NY; (MS) Math/Ed, Radford Univ; Cmptr Programming; Grad Level Math Courses; *cr:* Math Teacher Barnard/Horace Mann Sch 1968-72; Math Teacher 1974-79, Admin 1979-83, Math Teacher 1983- Fairfax Cty Public Sch; *ai:* VA Cncl of Teachers of Math, Fairfax Cty Teachers of Math 1989-; *office:* Thomas Jefferson HS Sci/Tech 6560 Braddock Rd 6560 Braddock Rd Annandale VA 22312

NAYLOR, ANN MC KINNEY, Eighth Grade Math Teacher; *b:* Winchester, KY; *m:* George L.; *ed:* (BS) Elem Ed, Cumberland Coll 1978; (MA) Spec Ed, 1982, Ed, 1985 Univ Louisville; Northern KY Univ; *cr:* 5th Grade Teacher Gethsemane Chrstn Sch 1978-79, LaGrange Elem Sch 1979-83; Spec Ed 1st-4th Grade Teacher Southern Elem Sch 1983-85; 8th Grade Math Teacher Pendleton Mid Sch 1985-; *ai:* Math Club Spon; Sch Contact Rep KY Mid Sch Assn; Academic Team Coach; Guidance Comm; Stu Achievement & Curr Comm; NCTM Mem 1985-; KY Assn for Gifted Ed Mem 1985-; Northern KY CTM Mem 1989-; Falmouth Bapt Church Youth Sunday Sch Teacher 1983-; Teacher of Year Awd 1987-88; *home:* 403 Maple Ave Falmouth KY 41040

NAYLOR, GAIL E. DOHERTY, 5th Grade Teacher; *b:* Everett, MA; *m:* David R.; *c:* Cheryl, Brooke; *ed:* (BSE) Elem Ed, Westfield St 1976; (MS) Rdng, Salem St 1980; Eng Cert; *cr:* Chapter I Teacher/ESL Tutor 1979-83, Rdng Teacher 1983-84, Rdng/Lang/Soc Stud Teacher 1984-85, Rdng/Lang Teacher 1985-86, Rdng/Lang Teacher 1987-89, 5th Grade Teacher 1989- Lynnfield Mid Sch; *ai:* MA Teachers Assn, Lynnfield Teachers

Assn 1984-; N Shore Rdng Cncl 1985-; Lynnfield Educl Trust Bd of Dirs 1990; *office:* Lynnfield Mid Sch 505 Main St Lynnfield MA 01940

NAYLOR, SANDRA PAYTON, Second Grade Teacher; *b:* Columbia, MS; *m:* Walter Jerome; *c:* Rashad; *ed:* (BS) Elem Ed, MS Valley St Univ 1972; Addl Stud Elem Ed, Univ of S MS; *cr:* Teacher E Marion Elem 1972-82, Earl Travillion Elem 1982-; *ai:* NEA; Sweet Pilrgim Baptist Church; NAACP; *home:* 311 Fairway Dr Hattiesburg MS 39401

NEAL, DAVID MICHAEL, Area Supvr Math, Math Teacher; *b:* Kendallville, IN; *m:* Susan Jane; *c:* Brian, Brad; *ed:* (BS) Math Ed, Manchester Coll 1971; (MS) Ed, Purdue Univ 1974; *cr:* Teacher Garrett HS 1971-; *ai:* N Cntrl Evaluation Comm; NEA, IN St Teachers Assn, Garrett Classroom Teachers Assn 1971-; IN Academic All Stars Certificate of Merit; *office:* Garrett HS 801 E Houston St Garrett IN 46735

NEAL, ELNORA MAY, Elementary Teacher; *b:* North Platte, NE; *m:* Terrence Jay; *c:* Trevor, Craig, Tyler; *ed:* (BA) Elem Ed, Kearney St 1971; *cr:* K-4th Grade Elem Teacher Buffalo Cty 1964-66; Elem Teacher Hall Sch 1974-78; K-2nd Grade Teacher Tryon Grade Sch 1981-84; Elem Teacher Ringgold Sch 1984-; *ai:* Sandhills Rdng Cncl; United Meth Church Organist 1974-; *home:* HC 35 Box 5-A Tryon NE 69167

NEAL, JAMES EDWARD, 8th Grade Lit/Drama Teacher; *b:* Lake Forest, IL; *m:* Janet Louise Beitzel; *c:* Jennifer, Rebecca, Kathryn; *ed:* (BSE) Speech/Theatre, 1971, (MA) Tech Theatre, 1984 N IL Univ; *ai:* 7th/8th Grade Drama Club; Stage Crew; Dir of Fall, Christmas, Spring Shows, Design & Tech Supervision of Dramatic Productions; ITS Spon 1983-; Accuca Presenter 1978-83; *home:* 118 N Chapel St Waukegan IL 60085

NEAL, JAMES KENNY, Mathematics Teacher; *b:* Greeneville, TN; *m:* Patricia Eidson; *c:* Anna; *ed:* (BS) Bus Admin, 1976, (MAT) Ed, 1978 E TN St Univ; Math Cert; *cr:* 2nd/3rd/5th/6th/8th Grade Teacher Mosheim Elem 1977-86; Math Teacher Chuckey-Doak HS 1986-; *ai:* Frosh Spon; Math Club & Stock Market Club Adv; NEA 1977-; Greene Cty Ed Assn Pres 1985-86; NCTM 1989-; Mountain Valley Church of Bretheren; *home:* Rt 6 Box 271 Greeneville TN 37743

NEAL, JANNIE M., Teacher of Gifted & Talented; *b:* Paulsboro, NJ; *ed:* (BS) Elem Ed, Cheyney Univ; *cr:* 2nd Grade Teacher 1967-89, Teacher of Gifted & Talented 1989- Loudenslager Elem; *ai:* Enrichment Comm; Glee Club Accompanist; Sigma Gamma Rho Basilus; Gloucester Cty Ed Assn Minorities Involvement Comm Chairperson; 2nd Baptist Church Organist 1980-89; Cheyney Alumni Assn; Chairperson for City Schls of Excl Grant; Outstanding Educator America for Advancement of Ed 1970; 1st Governors Teacher of Yr Awd, Teacher Symposium Mem; Cheyney Alumni Certificate of Appreciation for Outstanding & Dedicated Service 1983.

NEAL, MARIE H., Literature Teacher; *b:* Escatawpa, MS; *m:* Ronald S.; *c:* Candice L.; *ed:* (BS) Eng, Univ of S MS 1962; *cr:* Teacher Pascagoula Jr HS 1963-64, Mobile Cty Sch System 1966, 1968-; *ai:* Natl Jr Honor Society; Speech Coach; Eng Dept Chairperson; Mobile Ed Assn, ADK; Honor Society Teacher of Yr 1977, 1989; Mobile Cty Teacher of Yr.

NEAL, SARAH WRIGHT, Latin Teacher; *b:* Salem, MA; *m:* David Ditchburn; *ed:* (BA) Classics, Trinity Coll 1979; (MA) Classics, Tufts Univ 1985; Amer Sch of Classical Stud 1981; Advanced Latin Inst Univ of NY 1982; New England Classical Inst & Wkshp 1980; Tufts Univ 1983-84; *cr:* Latin/Greek Teacher The Sunset Hill Sch 1979-84; Elem Latin Instr Tufts Univ 1984-85; Latin Teacher St Sebastians Cntry Day Sch 1986-; *ai:* Latin Club; Amer Classical League 1979-; Classical Assn of New England 1985-; Alumnae, Faculty Grant Sunset Hill Sch; Arthur Patch Mc Kinlay Schlsp Amer Classical League 1981; Natl Endowment for Hum Fellow for New England 1983; Classical Inst at Tufts Univ; *office:* St Sebastians Cntry Day Sch 1191 Greendale Ave Needham MA 02192

NEALE, WILLIAM CHRISTOPHER, Computer/Music Teacher; *b:* Heidleberg, West Germany; *m:* Laura Lea Sebastian; *c:* Meredith A., Nathaniel I.; *ed:* (BME) Music Ed, Cntrl Meth CoIL 1982; (MSE) Ed/Music SW MO St Univ 1985; Kodaly & Orff Trng; *cr:* Band Dir Houston R-I Schls 1982-84; Grad Asst S MO St Univ 1984-85; 5th-12th Grade Music/Cmptr Teacher Gasconade Cty R-I Schls 1985-; *ai:* Phi Mu Alpha, MO Music Educators Assn, Music Educators Natl Conference; United Meth Church Youth Coord 1987-; River Bluff Sheltered Wkshp Bd Mem 1990; *office:* Gasconade Cty R-I Schls Hwy 100 W Hermann MO 65041

NEALON, LINDA RYAN, Russian & French Teacher; *b:* Albany, NY; *m:* Timothy Joseph; *c:* Tara, Timothy; *ed:* (BA) Russian, Syracuse Univ 1969; (MED) Counseling, Trinity Univ 1972; *cr:* Teacher Lanier HS 1970-; *ai:* Russian & Fr Club Spon; Amer Assn Teachers of Russian, AATF, NEA, TX St Teachers Assn; *office:* Sidney Lanier HS 1514 W Durango St San Antonio TX 78207

NEAR, JACQUELINE ANNE (LANKFER), 2nd Grade Teacher; *b:* Muskegon, MI; *m:* Jack W.; *c:* Jack W. II, Jacquelynne Schropp, Jillene Foran, Judith A.; *ed:* (BS) Elem Ed/Soc Sci, Western MI Univ 1967; *cr:* K-8th Grade Teacher Flower Creek & Blooming Valley 1957-60, Garver Sch 1962-64; 3-5th Grade Teacher Carpenter Sch 1964-65; Elem Teacher Thomas Read Elem 1965-; *ai:* NEA; MEA; SEA; Performing Arts Cncl; Dir of Summer Creative Arts Camp 1977-81; *home:* 65 Rankin St Shelby MI 49455

NEARY, JO ANN JOHNSON, 5th Grade Lang Arts Teacher; *b:* Mc Lean, NE; *m:* Del William; *c:* Nancy Cyr, Shari Freeman, Sally J.; *ed:* (BA) Elem Ed, Buena Vista Coll 1978; Effective Teaching, Drake Univ 1991; *cr:* Teacher Knox Cty Rural Dist 1949-50; 7th Grade Teacher Tekamah Public Schls 1951-53; 6th/7th Grade Teacher Irwin Public Sch 1953-54; 6th Grade Elem Teacher 1959-65, 5th Grade Elem Teacher 1967- Atlantic Cmmty Schls; *ai:* Atlantic Ed Assn (Treas, VP, Building Rep); ISEA, NEA; Delta Kappa Gamma (Secy 1984-86, Membership & Nominations Chm 1986-88, VP 1988); *home:* 705 E 17th St Atlantic IA 50022

NEARY, JOANN RHOLL, Physical Science Teacher; *b:* Webster City, IA; *m:* Patrick J.; *c:* Anne, Andrew; *ed:* (BA) Ed/Bio/General Sci, Univ of N IA 1970; (MS) Ed/Sci, Univ of WI Whitewater 1984; Grad Stud; *cr:* Sci/Math Teacher Oconomowoc Jr HS 1970-87; Sci Teacher Oconomowoc HS 1987-; *ai:* Pep Club & Academic Awds Adv; Summer Sch Teacher Outdoor Ed; Sci Olympiad Coach; Oconomowoc Ed Assn 1970-, Jr HS Teacher of Yr 1983; WI Society of Sci Teachers 1980-; NEA, WI Ed Assn; Our Saviors Luth Church (Cncl Mem, Sunday Sch Teacher) 1974-; Sci World Participant Awd; ICE Chem Prgm Awd; Nom for Presidential Excl Awds in Sci; *home:* N 8110 LaSalle Cir Oconomowoc WI 53066

NEATHERY, MADELYN FAYE (WILSON), Fifth Grade Teacher; *b:* Granger, TX; *m:* James W. Sr.; *c:* James Jr.; *ed:* (BS) Elem Ed, Univ of TX 1962; (MED) Sci Specialization, Sam Houston St Univ 1968; Natl Sci Fnd Earth Sci, TX A&M 1985; Natl Sci Fnd Honors Inst, TX A&M 1984; *cr:* 4th Grade Teacher Ft Worth Ind Sch Dist 1962-65; 1st Grade Teacher Galveston Ind Sch Dist 1965-66; 3rd Grade Teacher Conroe Ind Sch Dist 1966-67; 5th Grade Teacher Humble Ind Sch Dist 1968-69, Deer Park Ind Sch Dist 1969-; *ai:* TX Young Astronaut Curr Coord & Young Astronauts Chapter Leader; TX Cncl of Elem Sci Treas 1988-; St Sci Teachers Assn Area Dir 1988-; Young Astronaut Cncl (Space Lesson 1989, Delegate to Japan 1989); TX Outstanding Sci Teaching; San Jacinto Elem Teacher of Yr 1986; *office:* San Jacinto Elem Sch 601 E 8th Deer Park TX 77536

NEAVES, TRACEY BLACK, 6th Grade Science Teacher; *b:* Detroit, MI; *m:* Jeffrey Dale; *c:* Kyle R.; *ed:* (BS) Elem Ed, Univ of AL 1982; Working Towards Masters Elem Ed; *cr:* Teacher of 3/4 Yr Olds St Lukes Episcopal Sch 1982-83; 5th/6th Grade Sci/Heath Teacher St Martin Mid Sch 1984-; *ai:* Sci Dept Chm; Staff Dev Presenter; Insurance & Book Selection Comm; *office:* St Martin Mid Sch 16300 Le Moyne Blvd Biloxi MS 39532

NEBEL, ARMIN C., Intermediate Teacher; *b:* Neenah, WI; *m:* Cindy L. Michel; *c:* Lindsey, Stephen; *ed:* (BA) Elem Ed/Gen Sci, 1974, (MST) Elem Ed, 1980 UW Stevens Point; *cr:* Intermediate Teacher Plover-Whiting Sch 1974-; *ai:* Vlybl & Bsktbl Coach; Service Cadet Prgm; PTO Asvisory Comm; Neighborhood Watch Organizer 1987-; Dist Teachers 110 Percent Club Awd; *home:* 1100 Phillips St Stevens Point WI 54481

NEBLESICK, GARY DANIEL, Mathematics Teacher; *b:* Mitchell, SD; *m:* Barbara Mary Grassel; *c:* Lindsey, Leslie, Michael, Mary E.; *ed:* (BA) Phys Ed, Dakota Wesleyan Univ 1981; *cr:* Teacher/Coach Tripp HS 1982-86, Elk Point Public Sch 1986-; *ai:* Boys Bsktbl & Track Head Coach; Ftbl & Track Asst Coach; *home:* Box 696 Elk Point SD 57025

NECKER, PAULINE KNOWLES, 5th Grade Mathematics Teacher; *b:* Bristol, PA; *m:* David; *c:* Debbi, Devon, Douglas (dec); *ed:* (BS) Elem Ed, Penn St Univ 1962; (MS) Elem Ed, Converse Coll 1985; *cr:* 2nd Grade Teacher La Grande Sch 1962-63, Campobello Gramling Sch 1976-78; 5th Grade Teacher Inman Elem Sch 1979-; *office:* Inman Elem Sch Oakland Ave Inman SC 29349

NEDROS, CHARLOTTE HOBBS, 5th Grade Teacher; *b:* Taylorsville, KY; *m:* David Allen; *c:* Andrea; *ed:* (BS) Elem Ed, 1967, (MA) Elem Ed/Soc Stud, 1970, (Rank I) Admin/Supervision, 1973 W KY Univ; *cr:* 4th Grade Teacher Fairdale Elem 1967-71; 4th/5th Grade Teacher Wheeler 1971-; *ai:* 5th Grade Act & Grade Group Chm; Safety Patrol Adv; Phi Delta Kappa 1989-; JCTA Rep 1967-; *office:* Wheeler Elem Sch 5410 Cynthia Dr Louisville KY 40299

NEE, SHARON CODICK, Home Economics Teacher; *b:* Scranton, PA; *m:* Joseph; *c:* Jonathan, Brendan, Patrick, Michael; *ed:* (BS) Home Ec Ed, Marywood Coll 1971; Spec Ed & Home Ec; *cr:* Home Ec Teacher W Scranton HS 1971-74, E Scranton Intermediate Sch 1974-76, W Scranton HS 1976-; *ai:* Home Ec Club; PA Home Ec Assn, Scranton Ed Assn, PA Ed Assn, NEA; Mid States Assn of Colls & Schls 1987, 1989; *office:* W Scranton HS 1201 Luzerne St Scranton PA 18504

NEECE, ANNA M., 6th Grade Teacher; *b:* Quick City, MO; *m:* Harold O. Jr.; *c:* Christie Grant, Dennis, David, Kenneth; *ed:* (BS) Elem Ed, Grand Canyon Coll 1959; Grad Stud; *cr:* 5th Grade Teacher Post Sch 1959-61; Math Teacher Yuma HS 1961-62; Kndgtn Teacher Ajo AZ 1962-64; 6th Grade Teacher Gwyneth Ham Sch 1965-; *ai:* Spelling Bee Chm; NEA Pres 1957-59; NEA, AEA Various Offices 1959-; Spec Olympics 1970-, Outstanding Parent 1979; *home:* 2100 W 3rd St Sp 14 Yuma AZ 85364

NEEDHAM, MARJORIE LOUISE, 3rd Grade Teacher; *b:* Lynn, MA; *ed:* (BA) Eng, 1945, (MED) Elem Ed, 1957 Boston Univ; Wrkshps Curr Comm Lynnfield; *cr:* Librarian/Research Asst MA Taxpayers Fnd 1945-49; Elem Teacher Lynn Public Schls 1949-57, Springfield Public Schls 1957-66, Marshfield Public Schls 1966-68, Lynnfield Public Schls 1968-; *ai:* NEA, MA Ed Assn, Local Ed Assn 1949-; ACEI (VP, Pres) 1960-65; MA Rdng Assn 1979-; Sigma Kappa (Pres, VP) 1941-45; Phi Beta Kappa 1945-; Honor Society Valedictorian; Co-Spon of Grant to Honor 200th Anniversary of US Constitution; Cited for Outstanding Contribution to Lynnfield & St by Supt of Schls 1990; Co-Authored Pamphlet 1948; Articles on File MA St Dept of Ed 1956, 1971; Outstanding Elem Teachers of America Mem 1974.

NEELEY, CYNTHIA TILLMAN, 8th Grade Teacher/Coordinator; *b:* Chicago, IL; *m:* Argell; *c:* Cassandra Harts, Cypriana, Ines Frazell; *ed:* (BS) Speech/Home Econ, Olivet Nazarene Univ 1969; (MSED) Bilingual Bicultural Ed, Conferred at Chgo ST Univ 1980; Post Masters Studies ACT Natl Ctr for Advancement of Ed Practices; IL Insurance License, Acctng & Financial Mgt Certificate, SBA Institute of Proposal Writing & Grantship; *cr:* Teacher Curtis Sch/Goudy Sch 1969-; Coordng Spec Project NY Statue of Liberty Centennial Commissioner a Calobro 1985; Prgm Coordin CSU Parent-HS Stu Transitional Coll Prep Prgm 1985-; *ai:* 4-H Club, Sci Fair Coord, Resource Teacher Drug Ed, Curtis Black Innovators Awd Prgm, Sch Monitors & Spon of Girls Chorus; St Xavier Coll Adv Bd Mem 1984-; Natl Alliance of Black Sch Educators 1989-; Leadership Edge Dir 1988-; Far South Task Force on Excl in Ed Educational/Consultant 1984-; Curtis Local Sch Cncl Mem Cncl Sec 1989-; Beth Eden Baptist Church Mother's Bd VP 1984-; Push Excl in Ed Awd "Those Who Excel" in Ed ST of IL Unselfish Cooperation & Support Awd-DuSable Museum; Sen Emil Jones Jr Comm Serv Awd Recognition of Serv-Intnatl Rdng Assn; *home:* 849 West 111th St Chicago IL 60643

NEELEY, PATRICIA CROSS, Retired English Teacher; *b:* Alicia, AR; *m:* L. Paden; *c:* Tracy Lamberth Johnston, Christopher; *ed:* (BSE) Eng, AR St Univ 1958; Eng, Lit, Composition, Spec Ed; *cr:* Eng Teacher W Memphis HS 1958-59, Kennett HS 1959-61, Newport HS 1961-62, Egypt HS 1962-63, Alternative Sch 1979-84, Annie Camp Jr HS 1984-87; *ai:* NATE 1984-87; Natl Assn of Jr Auxiliary (Secy, Projects Chm, VP, Pres) 1965-71; United Way of Jonesboro Bd Mem 1970-72; 1st Presbyn Church (Chm, Bd of Deacons) 1970.

NEELY, FRED EUGENE, Biology Teacher; *b:* Loysville, PA; *m:* Nancy Bryant; *c:* Amanda, Burke, Clark; *ed:* (BA) Bio, Warren Wilson Coll 1974; *cr:* A I/Lab Technician Sire Power Incorporated 1976-78; Dairy Farmer 1978-86; Teacher West Perry Sr HS 1986-; *ai:* Centre Presbyn Church (Chm Chrstn Ed, Elder, Trustee, Sunday Sch Teacher); Perry Cty Soil Conservation Dist Dir; Agway & Sire Power Incorporated Dir; Warren Wilson Coll Dir Ind Research Project 1975-76; Kellogg Fnd Grant 1975-76; *home:* RD 2 Box 73 Loysville PA 17047

NEELY, TERESA YACKUBOSKEY, First Grade Teacher; *b:* Indiana, PA; *S:* James D.; *c:* Amanda, Nathan; *ed:* (BS) Elem Ed, IN Univ of PA 1977; *cr:* 1st/2nd Grade Teacher St Anthony Sch 1977-78; K-3 Remedial Math Teacher 1978-80, 6th Grade Teacher 1981-82, 5th Grade Teacher 1982-83, 1st Grade Teacher 1983- Marion Center Sch Dist; *ai:* St Anthony PTA 1989-; Citizens for Decency of IN Cty Mem 1989-; *home:* Rd 6 Box 157A Indiana PA 15701

NEFF, ANN ROUGEUX, Fourth Grade Teacher; *b:* Clearfield, PA; *m:* Jack L.; *ed:* (BS) Elem Ed, Clarion Univ of PA 1970; *cr:* 1st Grade Teacher 1970-77, 4th Grade Teacher 1977- Curwensville Area Sch Dist; *ai:* Curwensville Area Ed Assn Treas 1988-; PSEA, NEA 1970-; BPW 1978-83; *office:* Curwensville Area Sch Dist 650 Beech St Curwensville PA 16833

NEFF, DON E., Science Teacher; *b:* Chillicothe, OH; *m:* Carole; *c:* Scott, Holli, Donna, Regina, Angie; *ed:* (BS) Sci/Phys Ed, OH Univ 1959; (MS) Xavier Univ 1975; Grad Stud Various Univs; *cr:* Teacher Circleville HS 1960-65, Unioto HS 1966-; *ai:* OH HS Bsbl Coaches Assn Bd of Dir 1970-78, 100 Win 1967, 200 Win 1972, 300 Win 1977, 400 Win 1982, Hall of Fame 1977; Book Published; Teacher of Yr 1983-84.

NEFF, NANCY L., Social Studies Teacher; *b:* Mountain Home, AR; *ed:* (BA) His/Eng, Univ of TN Chattanooga 1982; Shakespeare Summer Sch Univ of Birmingham 1983; Grad Courses Eng, UTC 1982-87; *cr:* 5th-8th Grade Soc Stud Teacher Senter Sch 1982-; *ai:* Disciplinary Comm Head; Drama Club, Newspaper, Cheerleading Spon; Fine Arts Mini Course Instr; Hamilton Cty Young Democrats 1986-; League of Women Voters 1984-89; John F Kennedy Luncheon Club 1986-; Christ United Meth Church Mem; Runner-Up Clan Mc Donald Schlsp 1983; Tutor North Chattanooga Girls Home 1983-84; Jeopardy Winner 1987; *office:* Senter Sch 1512 S Holtzclaw Ave Chattanooga TN 37404

NEFF, PATRICIA ANN, Spanish Teacher; *b:* Beaumont, TX; *m:* Larry O.; *c:* Theresa S. Nelson, Gregory S.; *ed:* (BA) Span, Miami Univ 1967; Lib Sci, UW Eau Claire; Photography, UW Stout; Supervisory of Stu Teachers, UW Superior; *cr:* Span Teacher Hibbard Jr HS 1967-68; Eng Teacher Lac Du Flambeau Sch 1969; Span/Eng Teacher/Librarian Park Falls HS 1969-74; Span Instr Hayward HS 1979-; *ai:* Span Club, Yrbk, Sr Class Adv; Head Coach Forensics; SEC Comm Chm; AATSP Secy 1987-89; WI Dist Teacher of Yr 1987-88; Excl in Ed 1987-89; *office:* Hayward HS PO Box 860 Hayward WI 54843

NEGUS, IRENE BERTHA, Fifth Grade Teacher; *b:* Cleveland, OH; *m:* Melvin E.; *c:* Barbara L. Thompson; *ed:* (BA) ED, CA Western Univ 1970; (MS) ED, Pt Loma Coll 1977; *cr:* Fourth Grade Teacher 1970-74; Fifth Grade GATE 1974-89 Lindbergh Elem; *ai:* Math Repr; Conducted Staff In-Services Related to Math; Pilot Participant in Whole Lang Approach to Rdng; ASDEG League of Women Voters; Semester's Trng at UCLA in a Prgm "Law in a Free Society", Emphasis on Political Process of US; *office:* Lindberg Elem Sch 4133 Mt Albertine Ave San Diego CA 92111

NEHR, L. MARGARET, Retired Elementary Teacher; *b:* San Antonio, TX; *ed:* (BS) Ed/His/Eng, Our Lady of Lake 1963; *cr:* Elem Teacher St Joseph Sch 1949-87; *home:* 222 Dacus Ave San Antonio TX 78211

NEIGHBORS, JANET CARUSO, Second Grade Teacher; *b:* Jacksonville, FL; *m:* Donald Eugene; *c:* Bart, Brad; *ed:* (BS) Elem Ed, FL St Univ 1967; *cr:* 1st Grade Teacher Hyde Grove Elem 1967-70, Charles E Bennett Elem 1971-74; 2nd Grade Teacher Southside Elem 1976-; *ai:* Cty Curr Advisory Comm, Rdng Comm; Alpha Delta Kappa 1970-89; *office:* Southside Elem Sch 823 E Stansburg Starke FL 32091

NEILSON, CHARLES DOUGLAS, English Department Teacher; *b:* Asheville, NC; *ed:* (BS) Eng, E Carolina Univ 1965; (MA) Eng, Trinity Coll 1966; *cr:* Eng/Dept Chm/Academic Dean Stounton Military Acad 1966-76; Eng/Dept Chm Trinity Episcopal HS 1976-81; Teacher Thomas Dale HS 1981-; *ai:* Newspaper, Dorm R A, Honor Society Spon; Chesterfield Ed Assn, NEA, VEA, VA Assn of Ind Schls Evaluation Comm; *office:* Thomas Dale HS 3626 W Hundred Rd Christchurch VA 23031

NEIMAN, MARJORIE A., Counselor; *b:* Boston, MA; *ed:* (BA) Sociology, 1965; (MED) Cnslr Ed, 1966 Boston Univ; Cnslr Ed; *cr:* Cnslr Amesbury HS 1967-69; Guthne Job Corps for Women 1969-70; Salem HS 1970-77; Alcoholism Therapist Comp Alen Rehab Prgm 1977; Cnslr Silver Lake Reg HS 1978-81; Shephard Hill Reg Sch 1987; *ai:* Co-Lead Group after Sch Children of Alcoholics; Mass Sch Cnslrs Exec Bd 1980-; MA Teachers Assn Faculty Rep 1979; NEA; MSCA Task Force on Groups 1973-75; *office:* Shephard Hill Regional HS Dudley-Exford Ext Webster MA 01570

NEISEN, THOMAS P., Science/History Teacher; *b:* Marshall, MN; *m:* Marie Junker; *ed:* (BA) Soc Stud, General Beadle St 1964; (MA) Soc Stud, Western St Coll 1970; *cr:* Elem Prin 1965-86, Jr HS His/Sci Teacher 1964-, Mid Sch Sci/His Teacher 1989- Norwood Public Schls; *ai:* Knowledge Bowl & Master Open; Gifted & Talented Comm; Stu Government; CEA, NEA (Local VP 1968-69) 1988-; Planning & Zoning Mem 1976-77; Finalist St Teacher of Yr 1969; *office:* Norwood Public Schls Box 448 Norwood CO 81423

NEISES, BARBARA HORKHEIMER, 4th-6th Grade Teacher; *b:* Prairie Du Chien, WI; *m:* Christy Robert; *c:* Chris, Michael, Patrick; *ed:* (BS) Elem Ed, WI St Univ La Crosse 1971; (MA) Elem Ed, Univ of WI Platteville 1987; Ed Courses Univ of WI Plateville, Univ of WI Stevens Point, Univ of WI Eau Claire; Variuos Wrkshps, Inservices & Conferences; *cr:* 5th Grade Sci Teacher Mt Horeb Elem Sch 1971-72; Substitute Teacher 1977-85, Chapter 1 4th-6th Grade Teacher 1985-, K-12th Grade Gifted/Talented Coord 1988- West Grant Schls; *ai:* Jr HS Forensics Coach; Cmptr Resource Room Teacher; Chm of Gifted/Talented Comm; Rdng, Math Curr Comm Mem; ACDA Facilitator; Spon Coll for Kids; Hidden Valley Rdng Cncl, WEA, WSRA 1985-; Phi Kappa Phi, WAEGT, WCGT, WI Math Cncl 1988-; Homemakers Club (Pres, Secy, VP) 1977-89; *office:* West Grant Schls PO Box 78 Patch Grove WI 53817

NEISLER, FRANCES WEAVER, English Department Chairman; *b:* Sardis, TN; *m:* Romie W.; *c:* Jane Neisler Stockwell, Joe W.; *ed:* (BA) Eng, Lambuth Coll 1946; (MA) Eng, Univ of TN Knoxville 1949; *cr:* Prin Center Hill Elem Sch 1944-45; Eng Professor Univ of TN Martin 1946-47; Eng Teacher Carter HS 1947-48, Southside HS 1957-; *ai:* Future Teachers of America Club Adv; Sr Class Spon; Chm Eng Dept; Omicron Phi Tau Pres 1971-72, Sch Honor 1971-73; Delta Kappa Gamma Pres 1978-80, Teacher Society 1978-80; Church Women United Pres 1959-62, Pres Awds 1962; United Meth Women Pres 1970-82, Life Membership 1982; Southside HS PTA, Life Membership 1988; Poem Published Murray St Univ 1975; TN Arts Commission 1986-; TN Conservation League Bd Mem 1987-; Teacher of Yr 1989; *home:* 33 Elmwood Dr Jackson TN 38305

NEISS, CAROLE L., 8th Grade English Teacher; *b:* Canton, OH; *m:* Paul L.; *c:* Jennifer B., Daniel P.; *ed:* (BA) Eng/Speech, Malone Coll 1968; Akron Univ, Kent St Univ, Ashland Univ, Inst of Childrens Lit; *cr:* Teacher Dover City Schls 1968-69; Teacher/Tutor 1969-85, Substitute Teacher 1985-87 Canton Local Schls; Teacher N Canton City Schls 1987-; *ai:* 8th Grade Washington DC Trip Organizer & Chm; N Canton Ed Assn, NEA, OH Ed Assn, OCTELA 1987-; Canton Local Schls Citizens Advisory Comm Secy 1986-88; S Canton Parent Advisory Comm Pres 1988-; Published Several Short Stories; *office:* N Canton Mid Sch 200 Charlotte Ave NW North Canton OH 44720

NEITZ, HELEN BURR, 8th Grade Home Ec Teacher; *b:* Elko, NV; *m:* Robert C.; *c:* Aaron, Andrea; *ed:* (BS) Home Ec Ed, Univ of NV 1965; *cr:* Home Ec Teacher Elko Jr HS 1969-; *ai:* Elko Cty Classroom Teachers, NV St Ed Assn 1988-; *office:* Elko Jr HS 777 Country Club Dr Elko NV 89801

NEJMAN, GERARD JOHN, English Teacher; *b:* Philadelphia, PA; *m:* Deborah Mary Thomas; *c:* Kathleen, Sean; *ed:* (BA) Eng/Ed, Allentown Coll 1975; Oblate Novitiate, Childs MD, Extension Prgm Cath Univ of Amer 1971-72; Grad Sch, Villanova Univ; *cr:* Eng Teacher Archbishop Ryan HS 1975-; *ai:* Cross Cntry & Track Team Boys & Girls Asst Coach 1975-; Extraordinary Eucharistic Minister; Archbishop Ryan HS Eng Teacher 1975-, Teacher of Yr 1982-83; Del Valley Track & Field Coaches Assn Coach 1975-; Coach City of Philadelphia & Cath League Cross Cntry Champions Boys 1975-78; Coach Boys Indoor Track Cath League Champs 1976-77, 1982, 1988-89; Coach Boys PA St Champs Indoor Track 1976-79; Coach Boys Outdoor Track Cath League Champs 1976-77, 1984 & Girls 1985-89; *office:* Archbisop Ryan H S 11201 Academy Rd Philadelphia PA 19154

NEKUZA, KATHLEEN MARIE BREINDEL, 4th Grade Teacher; *b:* St Marys, PA; *m:* Lawrence Alan; *c:* Timothy A.; *ed:* (BS) Elem Ed, Villa Maria Coll 1969; Grad Stud Penn St, Clarion Univ, Gannon Univ; *cr:* 2nd-4th Grade Teacher Holy Rosary Sch 1967-68; 2nd Grade Teacher Spruce Street Sch/St Marys 1969-70; 3rd-5th Grade Teacher St Marys Parochial Sch 1971-; *ai:* Sports Events Coord; Penn Dot Clean Up Prgm; Annual Pickle Race Chm; Stu Faculty Vlybl Chairperson; St Marys Public Lib Bd Mem 1987-; Amer Red Cross Bloodmobile Volunteer 1988-; St Marys Church Eucharistic Minister; Altar Society; Erie Diocese 15 Yr Service Awd; *office:* St Marys Parochial Sch 325 Church St Saint Marys PA 15857

NELLIS, MARY ANN, English/French Teacher; *b:* Amsterdam, NY; *c:* Stacia P. Williams, Amanda J. Klump; *ed:* (BA) French Ed, St Univ Coll NY New Paltz 1970; Lit & Rdng, Russel Sage, Elmira Coll, St Univ Coll NY Oneonta; *cr:* Fr/Eng Teacher Owen D Young Cntrl Sch 1980-83, Ft Plain Cntrl Sch 1983-; *ai:* Adv Natl Jr Honor Society; 6th-12th Grade Eng Dept Coord 1983-; Stu Cncl & Class Adv 1980-83; Pres AFS 1980-83; NCTE 1980-; Silver Spur Riding Club 1956-; *office:* Ft Plain Cntrl Sch High St Fort Plain NY 13339

NELMS, SHERRY STRINGER, Sixth Grade Teacher; *b:* Valdosta, GA; *m:* Terry; *c:* Terry II; *ed:* (BS) Elem Ed, 1975, (MS) Elem Ed, 1977 W GA Coll; *cr:* Teacher Centralhatchee Elem 1975-; *ai:* GAE Stu Spelling & Essay Contest; HAE Treas 1976-77; PTA Treas 1980-81; Local Church Civic Work with Young People & VBS; *office:* Centralhatchee Elem Sch 14785 US Hwy 27 Franklin GA 30217

NELSON, ALINE COLLINS, 5th Grade Teacher; *b:* Millington, TN; *c:* Sherrye L. Nelson-Wheeler; *ed:* (BS) Elem Ed, Lemoyne-Owen Coll 1966; (MED) Admin/Supervision, Memphis St Univ 1971; Grad Stud, Memphis St Univ 1982; *cr:* Teacher Frazier Elem Sch 1966-67, Capleville Elem Sch 1967-70, Havenview Elem Sch 1970-73, Oakshire Elem Sch 1973-.

NELSON, ALLAN DALE, Science Department Teacher; *b:* Brownwood, TX; *m:* Rebecca June Roberts; *c:* Michael Allan, Markedlee Allan; *ed:* (BS) Ag Ed, 1983, (MST) Bio, 1988 Tarleton St Univ; *cr:* Sci Teacher Sidney Ind Sch Dist 1984-; *ai:* Class Spon; UIL Sci; TX St Teachers 1986-87; TX Classroom Teacher Assn 1987-; Parent Teacher Club Pres 1984-; Tarleton Astronomy Club VP 1988-84; *office:* Sidney Ind Sch P O Box 290 Sidney TX 76474

NELSON, ANGIE JUAREZ, Mathematics Teacher; *b:* Laredo, TX; *m:* Robert J. Jr.; *c:* Lisa A., James B.; *ed:* (BA) Chem, Our Lady of Lake Univ 1962; *cr:* Math/Sci Teacher Abilene HS 1982-; *ai:* Soph Class Spon; NEA, TSTA, Abilene Educators; Big Cntry Cncl Teachers of Math; *office:* Abilene HS 2800 N 6th St Abilene TX 79603

NELSON, BERTHA BRUMFIELD, Sixth Grade Teacher; *b:* Logan, WV; *m:* James Elton; *ed:* (AB) General Stud, S WV Comm Coll 1979; (BA) Elem Ed - Magna Cum Laude, Marshall Univ 1981; Soc Service Technology Counseling; Working Towards Masters; *cr:* Elem Teacher Midkiff Elem 1982-; *ai:* Field Trip Coord; Panther Pride Co-Spon; Sch Fund Raiser Spon; Prom & Graduation Coord; Kappa Delta Phi 1980-85; AFT 1988-; WVEA 1981-88; *home:* 4680 Tyler Creek Rd Salt Rock WV 25559

NELSON, BETTY LIEBENOW, 5th Grade Teacher; *b:* Barnesville, MN; *m:* Marvin LeRoy; *c:* Jeanne Peterson, Carol Nolte, Peggy Bingham, Liz Lindberg; *ed:* (BS) Elem Ed, Moorhead St 1969; Grad Stud; *cr:* Teacher/Elem Prin 1967-69, 5th Grade Teacher 1960- Gary Public Sch; *ai:* Gary Ed Assn (Pres 1972-73, 1983-84, VP 1971-72, Secy 1963-64, Treas 1966-67, 1970-71, 1980-81) 1960-; MN Ed Assn, NEA 1960-; *home:* 611 Blaine SE Fertile MN 56540

NELSON, BEVERLY JEAN, English Teacher; *b:* Wauseon, OH; *m:* Richard A.; *c:* Megan D., Jefferson W.; *ed:* Eng, Taylor Univ, (BS) Eng/His, Houston Baptist Univ 1972; Grad Stud in Rdng & Eng, Bowling Green St Univ; Univ of Toledo; *cr:* Office Mgr Stuckey and Spear Diamond Importers 1972-74; Teacher Wauseon HS 1984, Napoleon HS 1984-; *ai:* Advanced Placement Lit; NFA, OEA, NEA Local Treas 1987-; NCTE 1984-; Presidential Scholars most Influential Teacher 1989; Recipient of Hum Grant Shakespearean Stud 1988-89; *office:* Napoleon HS 701 Briarheath Dr Napoleon OH 43545

NELSON, CAROLYN VICK, 5th Grade Teacher; *b:* Providence, AL; *m:* James B.; *c:* Rob; *ed:* (BS) Elem Ed, Livingston Univ 1961; *cr:* 1st-4th Grade Teacher Demopolis City Schls 1961-69; 1st/3rd/5th-9th Grade Teacher Demopolis Acad 1970-; *ai:* Sch Calligrapher; 1st Baptist Sunday Sch Pres 1987-; *home:* 1205 Janet St Demopolis AL 36732

NELSON, CHRIS ALLEN, Mathematics Teacher; *b:* Hoopeston, IL; *m:* Nancy Lou Geiss; *c:* Tami, Staci; *ed:* (BS) Math, IL St Univ 1962; (MS) Math/Admin, N IL Univ 1968; Natl Sci Cmptr Inst NE LA 1969; Gifted Ed Trng, Advanced Math & Ed, N IL Univ; *cr:* Math Teacher Altamont HS 1962-64, Sandwich HS 1964-79, Oswego HS 1979-85; Part-Time Math Instr Waubonsee Coll 1976-; Math Teacher Yorkville HS 1985-; *ai:* Head Boys Bsktbl & Soph Girls Sftbl Coach; Yorkville Ed Assn 1962-; IL BsKtbl Coaches Assn 1985-, Coach of Yr 1987-88; Lions Club (Pres 1972-73) 1967-76; Yorkville Zoning Bd of Appeals 1974-78; Bsktbl Coach of Yr Interstate 8 Conference 1985-86, 1988-; *office:* Yorkville HS 702 Game Farm Rd Yorkville IL 60560

NELSON, COLLEEN COTHRAN, Retired Science Teacher; *b:* Greenwood, SC; *m:* Justice Peace; *c:* Cheryl Nelson Landon, Deidre Nelson Black; *ed:* (BA) Elem Ed, Erskine Coll 1950; Womans Coll, Clemson Univ, Univ SC Columbia; *cr:* Teacher Abbeville Cty Schls 1950-67; Mid Sch Sci Teacher Greenwood Cty Schls 1967-87; *ai:* Textbook Comm; Beta Club Adv; Sch Newspaper; Sci Club; NEA; SC Ed Assn; Star Teacher of Yr Dist 51 1986; Certificate SC House of Reps 1987; *home:* Rt 6 Dead Fall Rd 260 W Greenwood SC 29646

NELSON, DEBRA LYNN (MC NEA), 7th/8th Grade Science Teacher; *b:* Bottineau, ND; *m:* Marc; *c:* Travis; *ed:* (BS) Bio/Chem, Valley City St Univ 1980; Courses in Ed, Health, Life Sci, Earth Sci; *cr:* Jr HS Sci Teacher Bottineau HS 1980-; *ai:* Var Cheerleading Coach; Pep Club Adv; Co-Chm North Cntrl Evaluation 1990 & Health Comm; Teacher Adv to Teachers Advisory Comm; North Cntrl Evaluation Steering Comm 1983-84; NASSP, NEA, Bottineau Ed Assn 1980-; Bottineau Young Astronauts 1986-; Bottineau Trail Riders Pres 1990; North Cntrl Horse Show Assn Dir 1990; Bus & Prof Womens Assn Young Careerist 1985; Jaycees Outstanding Young Educator 1989; Project Wild & Project Wet Facilitator; Natl Sci Fnd Meteorology & Climatology Project Pilot Sch; *office:* Bottineau HS 301 Brander St Bottineau ND 58318

NELSON, DENNIS E., Mathematics Teacher; *b:* Graettinger, IA; *m:* Joan; *ed:* (BA) Math Ed, Univ of IA 1974; (MA) Ed, Marycrest 1985; *cr:* Math Teacher Moline Sch Dist 40 1974-82, Davenport Cmmty Sch Dist 1982-84, United Township HS 1984-; *ai:* Sr Staff Spon; Frosh Ftbl, Math Team Coach; Curr Comm; Union Treas; Univ of IL Cmptr Teaching of Calculus Wkshp Fellowship 1990.

NELSON, DOUGLAS RODNEY, Physical Education Teacher; *b:* Sweetwater, TN; *m:* Carolyn Marie Leamon; *c:* Christopher R., Bryan M.; *ed:* (AA) Ed, Hiwassee Jr Coll 1966; (BSED) Ed/Phys Ed/Health, Univ of TN 1968; (MS) Phys Ed, W Carolina Univ 1988; Grad Stud Various Wkshps; *cr:* Phys Ed/Health/Spec Ed Teacher Clay HS 1969-77; Phys Ed/Sci Teacher Keystone Heights 1977-82; Phys Ed/Health Teacher Stecoah Sch 1982-87, Robbinsville Elem 1987-; *ai:* Head Bsbl Coach; Kappa Delta Pi 1988-; NC Army Natl Guard Military Police 1967-; Bsbl Coach of Yr 1981; FL Crown Conference 1980; *office:* Robbinsville Elem Sch P O Box 625 Robbinsville NC 28771

NELSON, ESTHER LOUISE (MANGUS), 7th/8th Grade Science Teacher; *b:* Elkview, WV; *m:* Harold Eugene; *c:* Valerie, Angela; *ed:* (BA) 7th-12th Grade General Sci/7th-12th Grade Bio, WV Univ 1977; (MS) Scndry Admin, Marshall Univ 1982; *cr:* Teacher Hamlin HS 1977-; *ai:* Jr & Sr Beta Spon; *office:* Hamlin HS General Delivery Hamlin Hamlin WV 25523

NELSON, GLENDA GUEST, K-6th Grade Enrichment Teacher; *b:* Shreveport, LA; *m:* Donald Ray; *c:* Elizabeth A.; *ed:* (BA) Primary Ed, 1970, (MS) Rdng, 1978 Northwestern St Univ; Grad Stud Bus Ed; *cr:* 1st Grade Teacher Ringgold HS 1970-75; 1st Grade Teacher 1975-84, 3rd Grade Teacher 1988-89, Enrichment Teacher 1989- Castor HS; *ai:* Elem Homecoming & Annual Beauty Pageant; NEA 1979-84, 1989-; LA Rdng Assn 1988-; LAE 1970-84, 1988-; Honorary FHA 1980; Teacher Incentive Awd 1978; *office:* Castor HS P O Box 69 Castor LA 71016

NELSON, GRETCHEN GILDEMEISTER, Social Studies Teacher; *b:* Brooten, MN; *m:* Don E.; *c:* Mark, Tahra Doan, Marit Middlestead, Bekah Conover, Amanda; *ed:* (BA) Hum/Soc Stud/Music, Concordia Coll 1959; Long Beach St Univ, Chapman Coll, San Bernardino St Univ, Univ CA Irvine; *cr:* Soc Stud Teacher Rancho Mid Sch 1987-; *ai:* Church Choir; Some Directing; Wedding Consultant & Hostess; PTO Staff Rep; UCI Writing Fellow; *office:* Rancho Mid Sch 4861 Michelson Dr Irvine CA 92617

NELSON, HAROLD, Biology Teacher; *b:* Chicago, IL; *m:* Jean Stein; *c:* Gail B., Holly D., *ed:* (BS) Bio/Math, Northern IL Univ 1958; (MAT) Sci/Math, MI St Univ 1962; Radiation Bio, Wayne St Univ 1966; Summer Studs Univ of OK 1960, Bemidji St Coll 1950, 61, 63, 64; Comm Wkshp 1980; ITIP Trng 1986-89; *cr:* General Sci Teacher Old Mission Peninsula Sch 1958-63; Bio/Math Teacher Locust Valley HS 1963-66, Pontiac Northern HS 1966-67; Bio Teacher Traverse City Jr HS 1967-; *ai:* Ftbl Coach; Sci Club Adv; Coord Sci Fairs; Task Force Mem Mid Sch; Instr MI Health Model Inservice; Ed Assn Pres 1959-61; Sci Critical Review Mem 1987-88; NSTA 1959-; MI Sci Teachers Assn 1960-; Teachers Assn 1959-60; Chamber of Commerce Outstanding Educator 1989; Quality Control Chemist for Cherry Industry; Corp Walk Comm Mem; *home:* 10112 W Bay Shore Dr Traverse City MI 49684

NELSON, HOWARD E., Mathematics Teacher/Dept Chair; *b:* Lorain, OH; *ed:* (BA) Math/Soc Psych, Malone Coll 1975; (ME) Curr, Ashland Univ 1989; *cr:* Teacher Timken HS 1975-76; Teacher 1976-, Dept Chm 1976- Lehman Jr HS; *ai:* Cmptr Club Adv; Faculty Advisory Comm Chm; Math Curr Comm Mem; Canton City Schls Grant; *office:* Lehman Jr HS 1120 15th St NW Canton OH 44703

NELSON, JEAN BAILEY, English Teacher; *b:* Warren, OH; *ed:* (BA) Eng/Ed, NE Wesleyan Univ 1967; (MA) Eng Lit, TX Tech Univ 1970; Grad Work Technical Writing, Univ of NM; *cr:* Eng Teacher Hobbs HS 1967-69; Eng Instr Univ of NM Albuquerque 1970-72; Eng Teacher Albuquerque Public Schls 1972-; *ai:* Coach Academic Decathlon; Class & Teen Action Prgm Spon; Albuquerque Public Schls & Univ of NM Alliance; NEA 1972-; NCTE 1985-; Assn for Teachers of Tech Writing 1988-; Society for Tech Comm 1989-; Albuquerque Blue Ribbon Teacher; Teacher of Today; *office:* La Cueva HS 7801 Wilshire NE Albuquerque NM 87122

NELSON, JEANNE SAMUELSON, 5-6 Lang Arts/Soc Stud Teacher; *b:* Long Beach, CA; *m:* Guy Wayne; *c:* Guy W. Jr., Andrew D.; *ed:* (BS) Elem Ed, 1983, (MS) Educl Mid-Management, 1989 Univ of Houston/Clear Lake; Advanced Dyslexic Trng; *cr:* Teacher Bayou Road Elem 1984-; *ai:* PTA Treas; La Marque Classroom Teachers Assn (Pres Pro-Tem 1989, Pres 1990); ASCD 1990; Pilot Club of La Marque (Treas 1990) 1989-; *home:* 1405 Austin La Marque TX 77568

NELSON, JEFFREY OWEN, Biology Teacher; *b:* Hartford, CT; *m:* Irmgard Blum; *c:* Thomas, Michele Lowe; *ed:* (BA) Bio, 1971, (MA) Ed, 1988 Univ of CA Riverside; Rdng Specialist Trng 1982; Cooperative Learning 1983; Essentials of Mgmt & Supervision 1981; *cr:* Bio Teacher J W North HS 1982-83; Advanced Placement Bio/Bio Sunny Hills HS 1983-; *ai:* Ftbl, Wrestling, Track Coach; NHS Adv; Site & Leadership Cncl Comms; CA Teachers Assn Mem 1982-; Intnl Baccalaureate Higher Level Instr 1986-; PTA Mem 1982-, Teacher of Yr 1989; Amer Assn for Advancement of Sci Mem 1984-85; Sch Dist Mentor Teacher 1985; Master Teacher 1986, 1989; Advanced Placement & Intnl Baccalaureate Wkshps Presenter; NASA Teacher in Space Dist Curr Author 1986; *office:* Sunny Hills HS 1801 Warburton Way Fullerton CA 92633

NELSON, JO ANN HARLIN, K-8th Grade Gifted Ed Teacher; *b:* Independence, KS; *c:* Shelly; *ed:* (BSE) Elem Ed, Emporia St Univ 1970; (MA) Counseling, Univ of NE 1979; Ed Admin, Univ of MO; Gifted Cert, Emporia St Univ; *cr:* 2nd Grade Teacher Independence Public Schls 1970-73; 5th Grade Teacher Ralston Public Schls 1973-78; Grad Research Asst Univ of NE 1980-82; Teacher of Gifted Ed Tri Cty Spec Ed Cooperative 1984-; *ai:* NEA, KS Ed Assn 1970-; KS Gifted Teachers Assn 1984-; Amer Assn Univ Women 1977-87.

NELSON, JOHN F., Math & Economics Teacher; *b:* Newport, TN; *ed:* (BS) Bus Admin, Carson Newman Coll 1970; *cr:* Teacher Parrottsville HS 1970-71; Northport Sch 1971-75; Edgemont Sch 1975-76; Hartford Sch 1976-85; Cosby HS 1985-; *home:* P O Box 54 Newport TN 37821

NELSON, JOHN L., Middle School Science Teacher; *b:* Rolla, MO; *m:* Bonnie Ivy; *c:* Chris, Alicia; *ed:* (BS) Phys Ed/Sci, Union Univ 1974; *cr:* Teacher/Coach Stigall Elem 1976-81, Humboldt Jr HS 1981-82, Medine Sch 1984-; *ai:* Boys & Girls Vlybl & Ftbl Coach; Fellowship of Chrstn Athletes Spon; Gibson Cty Ed Assn 1984-; TN Ed Assn, NEA 1976-; NFICA, NSTA; Lions Club Intnl 1977-85; Amer Cancer Society Public Ed Chm 1988-89, Cmmty Service 1989; Amer Red Cross Cmmty Chm 1984-; Stigall Elem Teacher of Yr 1978; *office:* Medina Sch 221 2nd St Medina TN 38355

NELSON, JOYCE ANN, Sixth Grade Teacher; *b:* Magee, MS; *m:* R. D.; *c:* Reggie, Roderick; *ed:* (BS) Elem Ed, Jackson St Univ 1973; (MS) Elem Ed, William Carey Coll 1978; *cr:* Librarian Mc Cullough Jr HS 1973-74; 5th Grade Teacher Magee Elem Sch 1974-81, Magee Mid Sch 1981-88; 6th Grade Teacher Magee Mid Sch 1988-; *ai:* AFT Secy 1982-; *office:* Magee Mid Sch 501 E Choctaw St Magee MS 39111

NELSON, KENNETH E., Social Studies Teacher; *b:* Bertha, MN; *m:* Mary Ellen Loen; *c:* Jo Lynn K. Nelson Welle, Troy; *ed:* (BA) Soc Stud, St Cloud St UniV 1962; Masters Equivalent Plus Credits; *cr:* Cnslr St Cloud St Reformatory 1962-64; Teacher Sauk Centre Public Schls 1964-; *ai:* Head Golf Coach; MN Assn Ed Bd of Dir 1982-85; MN Coaches Assn Delegate 1979-83, St Golf Coach of Yr 1983; Charter Comm Mem 1988-89; St Golf Coaches Chm 1981-83; 1st Luth Church Chairperson 1980; *office:* Sauk Centre HS 9th & State Rd Sauk Centre MN 56378

NELSON, KENNETH JOHN, Director of Bands; *b:* Iowa City, IA; *ed:* (BME) Music Ed, 1982, (MME) Music Ed, 1984 Univ of Tulsa; *cr:* Music Dir Amer Theatre Company 1983-; Dir of Bands Kellyville Public Schls 1984-; *ai:* Phi Beta Mu 1990; IAJE Exec Secy 1989-; OBA, OMEA, NEA, AFM; *office:* Kellyville Schls P O Box 99 Kellyville OK 74039

NELSON, LAURA J., Chemistry Teacher/Track Coach; *b:* New Haven, CT; *m:* Stephen B.; *c:* Erik S.; *ed:* (BA) Bio, Wheaton Coll 1976; Educl Leadership Services, Old Dominion Univ 1992; *cr:* Teacher Azalea Gardens Jr HS 1976-77, Booker T Washington HS 1977-; *ai:* Cross Cntry & Outdoor Track Coach; NFT; Amer Shark Assn, MAMEA; Girls Track Team Dist & St Champions 1983-89; Girls Cross Cntry Team Dist Champions 1983-84, 1986-87; *office:* Booker T Washington HS 1111 Park Ave Norfolk VA 23504

NELSON, LE MAR ARDEN, English/Journalism Teacher; *b:* Watertown, SD; *m:* Anne Irene Hazzard; *c:* Anne Benson, Teri Mc Namara, Renee; *ed:* (BS) Eng/Journalism, General Beadle St Teachers Coll 1954; (MED) Ed/Eng, SD St Coll 1959; Admin Specialist Certificate Univ of MN 1966; NDEA Eng Inst Carleton Coll 1965; *cr:* Teacher Chester HS 1954-57, Blooming Prairie HS 1957-66; Prin 1966-71, Teacher 1971- Blooming Prairie HS; *ai:* Yrbk, Sch Paper, Jr Class Adv; Speech Dir; BPTA Secy 1987-89; Speech Assn 25 Yr Pin 1987; Journalism Advs 1971- Adv of Yr 1987; First Luth Church (Choir 1957-, Congregation Pres 1963-64); Honor Roll Teacher of Yr Runner Up 1966; MN all Publications Awds 1982, 1984, 1986, 1989; Natl Security Seminar US War Coll 1989; *office:* Blooming Prairie HS 202 4th Ave NW Blooming Prairie MN 55917

NELSON, LYNN A., Science Teacher; *b:* Waupaca, WI; *m:* Karen Kay Wilburn Nelson; *c:* Richard, Kathleen, Brittany; *ed:* (BA) Broad Field Sci, 1971, (MA) Jr HS Sci, 1976 UW-Whitewater; *cr:* 8th Grade Sci Teacher Mukwon Mid Sch 1972-; *office:* Park View Mid Sch 930 N Rochester Ave Mukwonago WI 53149

NELSON, MARJORIE CARLSON, 5th Grade Teacher; *b:* Denver, CO; *m:* Brad; *c:* Dan, Andy, Jocelyn; *ed:* (BA) Ger/Eng, CO St Univ 1971 Elem Ed Cert & Lib Endorsement MT St Univ Bozeman; Working Towards MA NMC Havre; *cr:* Ger/Eng Teacher Mitchell HS 1972; Title I Havre HS 1973; Title I/1st Grade Teacher Valier Elem 1974-78; 3rd/4th Grade Teacher/Lib/Music F E Miley Elem 1979-86; Speech Aide/5th Grade Teacher Anna Jeffries Elem 1988-; *ai:* MT Rdng Teacher, MT Lib Assn, MT Ed Assn; St Paul Luth Cncl (Chm, Music Comm) 1988-; Cut Bank Golf Assn; Carl Schurz Awd to Study in Germany 1970; *home:* 114 4th St SW Cut Bank MT 59427

NELSON, MARK WILLIAM, Fine Arts Department Chair; *b:* Belleville, IL; *m:* Jean Melton; *c:* Laura, Ryan; *ed:* (BSED) Speech Comm, E IL Univ 1971; (MA) Speech Comm, S IL Univ 1974; Admin Cert, S IL Univ 1978; *cr:* Speech/Drama/Soc Sci Teacher 1971, Eng Dept Chairperson 1979-86, Fine Art Dept Chairperson 1986- Collinsville HS; *ai:* Speech & Drama Dir; Thespian Spon; IL Ed Assn, NEA 1976-; Miners Inst Fnd Bd of Dir 1988-; Excl in Teaching Awd S IL Univ 1985; *office:* Collinsville HS 2201 S Morrison Ave Collinsville IL 62234

NELSON, MARTHA R. MC CAW, 8th Gr Earth Science Teacher; *b:* Durango, CO; *ed:* (BA) Earth Sci/Eng/Ed, Adams St Coll 1971; (MS) Sci Teaching, NM Tech 1982; *cr:* Stu Teaching Sir Isaac Newton Jr HS 1971; Earch Sci/Basic Bus/Journalism/Ecology/Remedial Math Teacher Yucaipa HS 1971-74; Earth/Life/Phys Sci Teacher Tse Bit Ai Sch 1975-; *ai:* Natl Jr Honor Society Spon; Sci Club & Pep Club; San Juan Regional Sci Fair Comm Mem & Dist Rep; NEA 1971-; NSTA, NM Sci Teachers Assn 1987-; MAER Indian Sci & Engineering Society 1987-; Amer Assn of Univ Women San Juan Branch 1971-, Pres 1989-; NASA Educators Wkshp for Math & Sci Teachers; Jet Propulsion Lab 1986; AISES Sci Teachers Wkshp 1987-89; Mt St Helens Project 1989; *office:* Tse Bit Ai Mid Sch P O Box 1873 Shiprock NM 87420

NELSON, MIRIAM, Biology I Teacher; *b:* Dallas, TX; *ed:* (BS) Bio/Math, ETSU 1985; Math *cr:* HS Resource Teacher 1986; HS Bio/Alg I 1986-87 Rains HS; HS Bio Skyline HS 1987-; *ai:* Soph Class Spon; *office:* Skyline Ctr HS 7777 Forney Rd Dallas TX 75227

NELSON, NANCY POORE, Second Grade Teacher; *b:* Jamestown, NY; *m:* Frank C.; *c:* Brenda L. Brown, Everett E., Nancy A. Clavin; *ed:* (BA) Ed, NY St Univ Brockport 1959; Various Courses, Wkshps & Schls; *cr:* 4th Grade Teacher Frewsburg Cntrl Sch 1959-60; 1st/4th Grade Teacher #8 Sch Conkey Ave 1961-63; 1st/2nd Grade Teacher Fletcher Sch 1967-; *ai:* Conducting Whole Lang Approach Wrkshp; NEA Life Mem; NY St Teachers Assn, Chautaugua Cty Rdng Assn; Tender Loving Care & Share Group; Published in Educators Monthly News; *office:* M J Fletcher Sch 301 Cole Ave Jamestown NY 14701

NELSON, NORMA ADDINGTON, 2nd Grade Teacher; *b:* Cromona, KY; *m:* Don; *ed:* (BS) Elem Ed, Pikeville Coll 1962; (MA) Elem Ed, Morehead St Univ 1981; Post Masters Studies Rank I Morehead St Univ 1981; *cr:* 2nd Grade Teacher 1955-56/1958-; Summer Head Start Teacher 1970-75; Resource Teacher 1985-; 2nd Grade Teacher 1990 Fleming-Neon Elem; *ai:* ICTO; UKREA; KEA; NEA; Rep Fleming-Neon Elem Sch Teacher Appreciation Day; *home:* Tolliver Town Rd Neon KY 41840

NELSON, PATRICIA WAY, English Teacher; *b:* Shreveport, LA; *m:* Stevan H.; *ed:* (BS) Eng, 1972, (MS) Eng, 1976 Chadron St Coll; Journalism, Univ of NE Lincoln; Cmptr Trng, Chadron St Coll; *cr:* Grad Asst Chadron St Coll 1972-73; Eng Teacher Stapleton Public Schls 1973-75, Alliance City Schls 1975-; *ai:* Annual, Dark Room Adv; Delta Kappa Gamma 1977-; NCTE 1975-88; PEO (All Offices 1976-83) 1969-; NE St Cncl for Y-Teens 1977-80; Outstanding Young Woman of America 1980; *office:* Alliance City Schls 1450 Box Butte Ave Alliance NE 69301

NELSON, REX OTTO, K-8th Grade Art Teacher; *b:* South Charleston, WV; *m:* Audrey Jeanette Hinds; *c:* Jessie N., Rana B.; *ed:* (AB) Art Ed, WV Univ 1981; (MS) Athletic Trng, Marshall Univ 1987; *cr:* Art Teacher Glade Elem 1981-; Athletic Trainer Webster Cty HS 1987-; *ai:* Webster Cty HS Asst Track Coach 1988-89, Asst Wrestling Coach 1989-; *office:* Glade Elem Sch Cowen WV 26206

NELSON, RICHARD ALAN, Health Teacher/Athletic Trng; *b:* Mount Clemens, MI; *ed:* (BS) Phys Ed, 1984, (MED) Admin/Supervision, 1987 Nicholls St Univ; *cr:* Health Teacher Thomas Jefferson HS 1987-; *ai:* Head Athletic Trainer; Natl Athletic Trainers Assn 1982-; SW Athletic Trainers Assn 1987-; Nationally Certified Athletic Trainer; Licensed Athletic Trainer St of TX; *office:* Thomas Jefferson HS 2200 Jefferson Dr Port Arthur TX 77642

NELSON, RONALD, Music Department Chair; *b:* Pontiac, MI; *m:* Glenda Irene Burke; *c:* Jacqueline, Douglas, Katie, Kelly; *ed:* (BS) Music Performance, Grace Coll 1981; (MMUS) Studio Teaching, IN Univ 1990; Grad Work in Brass, Univ of MI; *cr:* Euphonuim Specialist 298th US Army Band 1976-80; Dir of Music Calvary Chrstn Acad 1980-84, Emmanual Baptist Church Sch 1984-85; Dir Youth/Music Temple Baptist Church 1985-87; Dir of Music Elkhart Baptist Church Sch 1987-; *ai:* Marching Band, Pep Band, European Brass Choir; Dir of Parent Sch Suport Organization; Chrstn Instrumental Dir Assn 1989-; Elkhart Municipal Band 1989-; *office:* Elkhart Baptist Chrstn Sch 2626 Prairie St Elkhart IN 46517

NELSON, SANDRA LUCAS, Mathematics Teacher; *b:* Washington, DC; *m:* Harold F.; *c:* Brian K., Brandy R.; *ed:* (BS) Math, DC Teachers Coll 1970; (MED) Admin/Supervision, Bowie St Univ 1989; Grad Stud Guidance & Counseling; *cr:* Math Teacher Douglas Jr HS 1970-74, Browne Jr HS 1974-78, Richardson Jr HS 1978-81, Backus Jr HS 1981-84, Forestville HS 1984-; *ai:* Math Club; Phi Delta Kappa Asst Ed Newsletter 1989-; NCTM, MD Cncl Teachers of Math, ASCD; Delta Sigma Theta; *home:* 1709 Rhodesia Ave Ft Washington MD 20744

NELSON, ZELDA CARROLL, Fifth Grade Teacher; *b:* Peggs, OK; *m:* Tom C.; *c:* Steve, Curtis, Eric, Jim; *ed:* (BS) Elem Ed, 1960, (MS) Elem Ed, 1965 Northeastern St Coll; Elem Admin, Tulsa Univ; *cr:* 3rd Grade Teacher Fairfax OK 1960-61; 5th Grade Teacher Berryhill OK 1961-65; Typing Teacher Sinaloa Jr HS 1965-67; 6th Grade Teacher Union 1967-74; Asst Prin Union Mid Sch 1974-77; 5th/6th Grade Teacher Briargen Elem 1977-; *ai:* Dist Soc Stud Textbook Selection Comm; Valedictorian; Outstanding HS Girl Athlete; Mid Sch Teacher of Yr 1972; Nom Outstanding Scndry Educator of America 1974; Dist Teacher of Yr Union 1984; Tsa La Gi Annual Queen Candidate; Whos Who in Amer Colls & Univs; *home:* 4749 S Irvington Pl Tulsa OK 74135

NEMEC, BEVERLY LOUISE, Elementary Principal; *b:* Cleveland, OH; *m:* Thomas Raymond; *ed:* (BSE) Elem, St John Coll of Cleveland 1968; Working Toward Masters Degree in Private Sch Admin; *cr:* 5th-6th Grade Teacher St Wenceslas Sch 1968-72; 6th Grade Teacher 1972-77, 7th-8th Grade Teacher 1979-80 St Bridget Sch; 7th-8th Grade Teacher 1980-88, Prin 1988- St Raphael Sch; *ai:* Pastoral Staff; Sch Bd; Planning, Operation & Finance Comm; Parish Cncl; Home & Sch Assn; NCEA 1968-; Elem Prin Assn Diocese of Cleveland, ASCD 1988-; Bay Village Network Prgm Advisory Bd Mem 1988-; *office:* St Raphael Sch 525 Dover Center Rd Bay Village OH 44140

NEMETH, ROSEMARY LEONE, 4th Grade Teacher; *b:* Cleveland, OH; *m:* James; *ed:* (BA) Elem Ed, 1982, (MSED) Rdng, 1990 John Carroll Univ; Numerous Courses; *cr:* Aquatics Supvr Beechwood Recreation Dept 1975-; 4th-6th Grade Sci/Math Elem Sch Teacher Cleveland Cath Diocese 1982-; *ai:* Sci Club Adv; Clevelands Sts Sci Olympiad Coach; Mission Moderator; Earth Comm Chairperson; Diocesan Soc Stud Teachers Organization Membership Chairperson 1985-89; NEA; Swim for Diabetes Volunteer Pool Coord, Dir 1989-; Eastern Region Cleveland Diocese Teacher of Yr Awd 1989; *home:* 2515 Richmond Rd Beachwood OH 44122

NEMETH-BARATH, ANNE (COLLINS), English Teacher; *b:* Washington, DC; *m:* D. Jr.; *c:* Barbara A., Carolyn A.; *ed:* (BA) Eng/Sociology, Univ of MD College Park 1959; *cr:* Teacher James Wood HS Amherst Campus 1985-; *ai:* Class of 1990 Spon; Forensics Judge; Child Study, Sch Team, Supt Advisory Comm; NEA, VEA, FCEA, VATE 1985-; James Wood HS Amherst Campus Teacher of Yr 1989; *office:* James Wood HS Amherst Campus 1313 Amherst St Winchester VA 22601

NENNI, IRENE YASTREMSKI, First Grade Teacher; *b:* Kingston, PA; *m:* Roger; *c:* R. Dean, Nadine M.; *ed:* (BS) Elem Ed, Wilkes Coll 1957; *cr:* 3rd Grade Teacher Baltimore Cty Schls 1957-59; Kndgtn Teacher 1964-66, 2nd Grade Teacher 1966-68, 1st Grade Teacher 1968- Wyoming Valley West; *ai:* PSEA, NEA 1966-; *home:* 18 Valley View Dr Pringle PA 18704

NEPTUNE, LARRY EDWARD, Science Teacher; *b:* Fairmont, WV; *m:* Diane Marie Mignella; *c:* Allison; *ed:* (BA) Bio, West Liberty 1974; General Sci Cert West Liberty Summer of 1974; Math Cert West Liberty & Univ of Steubenville Summer of 1976; *cr:* Math & Sci Teacher Jefferson Union HS 1974-88; Sci Teacher Edison South HS 1988-; *ai:* Ftbl/Bsktbl/Track Coach 1974-86; Frosh Class Adv 1988-89; Edison Local Ed Assn Building Rep 1976-86; Lions Club 1972-; Served on Jefferson Cty Schls Committees Involving Courses of Study Textbook Selection and CBE Test Formation; *office:* Edison South H S R R 1 Box 308 Richmond OH 43944

NERI, ANTHONY JOSEPH, Biology Teacher; *b:* Jersey City, NJ; *m:* Sandra S (Gerak); *c:* Christopher, Theresa; *ed:* (BA) Sci Ed, 1966, (MA) Sci/Spec Ed, 1980 Jersey City St; Environmental Sci, Marine Ecology; Certified Operating Room Tech; US Navy; *cr:* Instr US Naval Natl Medical Center 1967-68; Teacher Raritan HS 1968-, Woodbridge Adult Sch 1969-74; *ai:* Adv Class of 1972 & 1991; Drill Team Coach; Front Group Adv, Sci League Adv; Co-chairperson Comm Mid State; NJ Dept of Ed; EEIS Bio Comm; 4-H Leader; Comm Pilot Test for Division of Consumer Health Ed NJ Medical Sch; NJ Ed Assn 1968-; NABT 1980-; NEA 1968-; NJ Sci Teachers Assn 1980-; St Marys Church VP 1981-87; Woodbridge Jaycees 1974-76; Iota Mu Pi Elected Officer 1964; Internship NJ Bus Industry Sci Consortium; Recipient of Governors Teacher of Yr Awd 1988; Recipient 2 Mini-Grants Public Service Awd; Veterans Foreign Wars; Article Published Natl Naval Medical Center MD; *office:* Raritan H S 419 Middle Rd Hazlet NJ 07730

NERI, MARIA ANN, 6th Grade Teacher; *b:* Peckville, PA; *ed:* (BA) Elem Ed/Early Chldhd Ed, Marywood Coll 1980; Comm Disorders & Deaf Ed; *cr:* 2nd/3rd Grade Teacher St Josephs Sch 1980-82; 6th Grade Teacher Lake Ariel Mid Sch 1982-; *ai:* Creative Writing Activity; Sch Coord Scrantonian-Tribune Spelling Bee; Hamlin-Lake Ariel PTA Membership Comm, Honorary Life Membership; Rdng Is Fundamental & Hamlin-Lake Ariel PTA Awd 1988; *office:* Lake Ariel Mid Sch RD 3 Box 1 Lake Ariel PA 18436

NESSELROAD, MICHAEL ALAN, Chemistry Teacher; *b:* Pomeroy, OH; *m:* Tania Rae Bichsel; *c:* Coree R.; *ed:* (BA) Bio/ Chem, Rio Grande Coll 1979; *cr:* Chem Teacher Greenfield McClain HS 1979-84, Delaware Hayes HS 1984-; *ai:* Asst Var Bsbl Coach; Delaware City Teachers Assn Building Rep 1987-89; OH Ed Assn 1979-89; NEA 1979-87.

NESTER, DORTHA HOLLAND, Third Grade Teacher; *b:* Geneva, NY; *:* Alan W.; *c:* Debra Baker, David, Darlene Latten; *ed:* (BS) Elem Ed, St Univ of NY Geneseo 1956; *cr:* 3rd Grade Teacher W Street Sch 1956-58; 1st/5th Grade Teacher Angelica Cntrl Sch 1958-60; 6th Grade Teacher 1971-86, 3rd Grade Teacher 1986- Penn Yan Elem; *ai:* Dist Long Range Planning, Math Curr, Dist Gifted Comm; NEA, NYEA 1971-; United Meth Church Ed Dir 1968-85; United Way Dist Rep 1980-88, Service Awd 1985; Parent/Teacher Group 1971-; *home:* 309 Keuka St Penn Yan NY 14527

NESTICO, JANE MATTHEWS, Principal; *b:* Florence, SC; *m:* Alan R.; *ed:* (BS) Elem Ed, 1974, (MED) Elem Ed, 1977 Francis Marion Coll; Educl Admin, Univ of SC; *cr:* 1st Grade Teacher J C Lynch Elem Sch 1974-84, Ashley River Creative Arts Elem Sch 1984-85; Prin J C Lynch Elem Sch 1985-; *ai:* Florence Sch Dist 3 Art Comm Chm; Art in Basic Curr St Steering Comm Mem 1987; Phi Delta Kappa 1990; SCAEMSP (Fall Conference Comm Mem 1986-88, Winter Conference Comm Mem 1988-) 1985-; Ariel Baptist Church 1965; *office:* J C Lynch Elem Sch PO Box 140 Coward SC 29530

NESTLERODE, CAROL LOUISE (DEMMY), Fourth Grade Teacher; *b:* Ephrata, PA; *m:* Bert; *ed:* (BS) Ed, 1974, (ME) Ed, 1977 Millersville Univ; Grad Courses Ed; *cr:* 6th Grade Teacher 1974-75, 4th Grade Teacher 1975- Highland Elem Sch; *ai:* PTA; *office:* Highland Elem Sch 99 Highland Ave Ephrata PA 17522

NESTOR, DANIEL E., Mathematics Teacher; *b:* Columbus, OH; *m:* Roberta Dale Haiges; *c:* Kristin, Marc; *ed:* (BS) Math, Univ of WI River Falls 1966; (MS) Math, Univ of Notre Dame 1971; *cr:* Math Teacher Kettel Moraine HS 1966-70, Lakeland HS 1971-72, Forrest View HS & Rolling Meadows HS 1972-; *ai:* Staff Dev Comm; NCTM 1972-; *office:* Rolling Meadows HS 2901 Central Rd Rolling Meadows IL 60008

NESTOR, KATHY GUTCH, English Teacher; *b:* Jersey City, NJ; *m:* Joseph; *ed:* (BA) Media Arts, 1983, Scndry Cert Ed, Jersey City St Coll 1986; *cr:* Eng Teacher St Aloysius HS 1984-; *ai:* Frosh Advisory Bd Coord; Putting on the Hits Adv; NCTE; *office:* St Aloysius HS 721 W Side Ave Jersey City NJ 07306

NESVACIL, SHEILA DAHMEN, Marketing Teacher; *b:* Madison, WI; *m:* Richard Lee Jr.; *c:* Keegan; *ed:* (BSE) Mrktg, Univ of WI Whitewater 1982; Mrktg Curr Work, Univ of WI Madison & Univ of WI Stout 1984-; Development of Competency Based Events DECA; *cr:* Mrktg Teacher Monona Grove HS 1984-; *ai:* Class & Head DECA Adv; Stu Act Audit Comm; WI Mrktg Ed Assn, Natl DECA 1984-; WI DECA (Series Dir 1985-) 1984-; MEA Dane Cty Chairpeson 1985-; Ed for Employment Mrktg Chairperson 1987-88; St of WI Voc Ed Prgm of Yr 1988-89; *home:* 6721 Franklin Ave Middleton WI 53562

NETHERCOTT, MARK A., Physical Science Teacher; *b:* Jackson, WY; *m:* Christie Bagley; *c:* Angela R., Lance A., Aaron R., Michelle C.; *ed:* Assoc Geology, Ricks Coll 1979; (BS) Geology, 1981, (MS) Geology, 1984 Brigham Young Univ; *cr:* Sci Teacher Dugway HS 1984-87, Morgan HS 1987-; *ai:* Frosh Class, Pep Club, Sci Club Spon; Sci Bowl Coach; NEA, UT Ed Assn, UT Sci Teachers Assn; Explorer Scout Leader 1985-88; Cub Scout Leader 1989-; Brigham Young Univ Distinguished Alumni Awd; Geologic Map of Deadman Canyon Quadrangle UT Geological Survey 1985, 1987; *office:* Morgan HS 55 Trojan Blvd Morgan UT 84050

NETHERCUT, JANE SWANN, Latin and English Teacher; *b:* Atlanta, GA; *m:* William Robert; *c:* Amanda J., Robert C., Jason S.; *ed:* (AB) Latin/Eng, GA St Univ 1972; Latin & Counseling, GA St Univ; *cr:* Latin/Eng Teacher Campbell HS 1972-77, Gonzales HS 1977-78; Latin/Eng/Journalism Teacher O Henry Jr HS 1978-87; Latin/Eng Teacher Lanier Sr HS 1987-; *ai:* Soc Comm Chm, Human Relations, Effectiveness Comm Mem; Jr Classical League & Jr Class Spon; Clock Keeper Girls Var Bsktbl Team; Sr Classical League Natl Pres 1971-72; Natl Comm Jr Classical League (Secy 1974-76, Chm, Membership 1974-80, Coord of States 1980-82); Classical Assn SW US Pres 1987-88; Respite Care Center For Children Pebble Project 1990; GSA Troop Leader 625; 1st Baptist Church (Educl/Soc Ministries Comm); W Hills Youth Soccer Assn (AssT Coach, Team Mother); Delta Kappa Gamma VP 1982-84, 1988-; GA Latin Teacher of Yr 1975; Eloise Roach Awd Outstanding Contributions Foreign Lang Ed 1983; Outstanding Young Women in America 1986; Teacher of Yr Lanier Sr HS 1990; *office:* Lanier Sr HS 1201 Peyton Gin Rd Austin TX 78758

NETTLETON, GWEN K., High School Biology Teacher; *b:* Filer, ID; *c:* Allen G., John M.; *ed:* (BA) Biological Sci/Secretarial Sci, NW Nazarene Coll 1961; Grad Stud; *cr:* Teacher Harper HS 1961-63; Bio Teacher 1979-, Bio Teacher/Dept Chairperson 1989- Vallivue HS; *ai:* Soph Class Adv 1990; Sci Club Adv 1982-89; Vallivue Ed Assn (Building Rep 1980-85) 1979-; ID Educl Assn 1979-; NSTA 1989-; *office:* Vallivue HS 16412 S 10th Ave Caldwell ID 83605

NETTLETON, LUCETTA CORLEY, Fifth Grade Teacher; *b:* Baton Rouge, LA; *ed:* (BS) Elem Ed, Loyola Univ 1975; Grad Sch Curr & Instruction, Cmptr Sci; *cr:* 6th-8th Grade Rdng Teacher Henry Ford Jr HS 1975-80; 5th Grade Teacher Westgate Elem 1980-; *ai:* Henry Ford Jr HS Chldr Coach, Drill Team & Art & Radio Club Spon, Yrbk Adv; Westgate Elem Stu Cncl Adv, PFC Parent Advisory Cncl, Newspaper Ed; Alpha Delta Kappa 1989-; Jefferson Fed Teachers 1978-; Outstanding Young Elem Educator 1987; Westgate Rep at Teacher Highlights 1988; *office:* Westgate Elem Sch 2504 Maine Ave Metairie LA 70003

NETTLETON, SUE NANCY, History/Language/Art Teacher; *b:* Santa Monica, CA; *m:* Richard; *c:* Shannon, Erin; *ed:* (MS) Adolescent/Childrens Literature, CA St Univ 1980; CSULB/ South Basin Writing Proj; *cr:* Elem Teacher Eastwood Sch 1977-78; Kndgtn Teacher Westminster Luth Sch 1978-80; Elem Teacher Eastwood Sch 1980-88; Jr HS Teacher Stacey Intermediate 1988-; *ai:* Chrldg Adv; Lang Art/His Mentor; Site Cncl Rep; Ad Hoc Comm; PTSA Auditor; Westminster Teachers Assn 1981-; PTSA (VP 1984-86, Secy 1986-88) Honorary Service Awd 1986; Dist PTA CNcl Honarary Service Awd 89; Westminster Teacher of Yr 1988-89; Orange Cty Semi Finalist Teacher of Yr 1988-89; *office:* Stacey Intermediate Sch 6311 Larchwood Dr Huntington Beach CA 92647

NETTNIN, THERESA STUBBS, Kindergarten Teacher; *b:* Henderson, NC; *m:* Lynn Hunt; *c:* Christina K., Elizabeth M.; *ed:* (BS) Elem Ed, NC Wesleyan 1979; *cr:* 4th Grade Teacher 1979-83, 3rd Grade Teacher 1983-87, Kndgtn Teacher 1989- Benvenue Elem Sch; *ai:* NC Assn of Educators (Nash Cty Unit Secy 1980, Pres Elect 1981-82) 1978-86, Stu Teacher Awd 1979; Jr Womans Club 1982-85, Outstanding Provisional 1982; Jr Miss Schlsp Publicity Chm 1986-88; Marvin Meth Church Mem; NC Wesleyans Outstanding Academic Achievement Awd 1979; Teacher of Yr Nom Benvenue Elem 1981; Benvenue Elem PTO Teacher of Yr 1982; *office:* Benvenue Elem Sch 2700 Nicodemus Mile Rd Rocky Mount NC 27804

NETZER, FRANK L., Sixth Grade Teacher; *b:* Selma, CA; *m:* Norma Jean Carrara; *c:* Kara, Eileen; *ed:* (BA) Phys Ed, Fresno St 1958; Grad Stud Fresno St; *cr:* Teacher Fresno Colony Sch 1958-63; Prin Ivy Sch 1963-76, Grant Sch 1976-81; Teacher Alta Sch 1981-; *ai:* Phi Delta Kappa 1963-76; CA Elem Sch Admin Assn Pres 1963; CA Teachers Assn Pres 1959; Elem Assn Research Project; Several Educl Articles Published.

NEUFELD-PRICE, NANCY ANN, Second Grade Teacher; *b:* Des Moines, IA; *m:* Francis E.; *ed:* (BSE) Elem Ed, 1968, (MSE) Educl Curr, 1988 Drake Univ; Effective Schls Trng, Project Impact, Assertive Discipline, Positive Approach to Learning, Techniques of Effective Instruction, GESA; *cr:* 3rd Grade Teacher Washington Elem Sch 1968-71, Bird Elem Sch 1971-72; 2nd Grade Teacher Findley Elem Sch 1972-; *ai:* Curr Specialist 1988-; Unit Leader IGE 1973-79; Budget Review Comm Citizen Rep 1976; Dist Desegregation Comm 1976; NEA, IA St Ed Assn; Des Moines Ed Assn (Faculty Rep 1975-80, Negotiations Comm 1977-78); *office:* Findley Elem Schl 3000 Cambridge St Des Moines IA 50313

NEUHAUS, DARLENE CHAMBERS, Fourth Grade Teacher; *b:* Durham, NC; *m:* Leslie Eugene Jr.; *c:* Les III; *ed:* (BS) Eng, Univ of TN Knoxville 1974; Grad Stud Ed; *cr:* 2nd/4th Grade Teacher Northwest Elem 1977-80; 11th-12th Grade Eng/Amer His Teacher Goshen HS 1980-81; 6th Grade Rdng/Lang Art/Soc Stud Teacher South Mid Sch 1982-85; 3rd-5th Grade Rdng/ Spelling Teacher Bearden Elem Sch 1985-; *ai:* Baton Teacher; Cheerleading Spon; Spelling Bee, Talent Show Coord; Knoxville Ed Assn Asst Sch Rep 1988-89; NEA Mem; Golden Apple Awd; Public Service Announcements WATE; *office:* Bearden Elem Sch 5717 Kingston Pike Knoxville TN 37919

NEUKAM, CARLA KAY, Fifth Grade Teacher; *b:* St Meinrad, IN; *m:* Farrell C.; *c:* Amanda; *ed:* (BS) Elem Ed, St Benedict Coll 1970; (MS) Elem Ed, IN St Univ 1973; *cr:* 5th Grade Teacher David Turnham Ed Center 1970-; *ai:* Delta Kappa Gamma 1987-; N Spencer Rdng Cncl 1970-; *office:* David Turnham Ed Center Dunn-Locust St Dale IN 47523

NEUMANN, CLARICE TURCO, Fifth Grade Teacher; *b:* Omaha, NE; *m:* John; *c:* Nicole, Chad; *ed:* (BS) Elem Ed, Coll of St Mary 1971; *cr:* Teacher St Joseph Grade Sch 1971-77; 5th Grade Teacher St Thomas More Sch 1977-; *ai:* Intermediate Coord; Adv for Girl Scout Religious Awds; CCD Teacher; NCEA 1980-; NE Assn of Teachers of Math 1980-; St Anne Medal-Outstanding Service to Spiritual Dev of Catholic Youth 1988; *office:* St. Thomas More Sch 3515 S. 48Th St. Omaha NE 68106

NEUMANN, WILMA IONE (KLAUS), Third Grade Teacher; *b:* Grinnell, IA; *m:* Herbert W.; *c:* Timothy, Sara Meyer, Jane; *ed:* (BS) Elem Ed, Dana Coll 1980; Cert Courses; *cr:* Teacher Cntry Schls 1948-53, Charter Oak-Ute Schls 1973-; *ai:* Advisory Comm 1985-86, 1988-89; IA Rdng Assn Mem; Amer Legion Auxiliary (Unit Pres, Unit Secy, Cty Pres); Ute Lib Bd (Pres, VP, Secy) 1984-; *home:* 133 E 6th Box 47 Ute IA 51060

NEUMEIER, THOMAS C., Phys Ed/Religion Teacher; *b:* Burbank, CA; *m:* Aleen Boele; *c:* Jennifer, Leslie, Amber; *ed:* (BA) Soc Sci, CA St Univ Fresno 1974; *cr:* Teacher 1976-77, Vice Prin 1977-79, Prin 1979-86, Vice Prin 1986- St Anthony; *ai:* Stu Government; Finance Comm; Youth Group Act; Coaching; Elem Athletic League 1976-; NCEA 1976-; US Dept of Ed Exemplary Schls Awd 1985-86; *office:* St Anthony Sch 5680 N Maroa Ave Fresno CA 93704

NEUSCHAFER, JULIE SULLIVAN, Mathematics Teacher; *b:* Philadelphia, PA; *m:* Daniel F.; *ed:* (BS) Math/Scndry Ed, West Chester Univ 1959; (MA) Math/Scndry Ed, Glassboro St 1970; *cr:* Math Teacher Triton Regional HS 1959-; *ai:* CCEA, NJEA, NEA; Received Outstanding Teacher of Yr Awd through Governors Teacher Recognition Prgm 1988-89; *office:* Triton Regional HS Schubert Ave Runnemede NJ 08078

NEVELES, PAULA WALKER, 5th/6th Grade Teacher; *b:* Centralia, IL; *m:* Julius E.; *c:* Nichole, Jasmine, Danielle; *ed:* Assoc Centralia Jr Coll 1966; (BA) Elem Ed, S IL Univ 1968; (MS) Instruction/Curr, Concordia Univ 1983; Paideia Coord Trng; Madeline Hunter Instruction; *cr:* Teacher S C Johnson Sch 1968-70, Rdng Thru Drama Teacher 1978-80, Paideia Coord 1983-84, Teacher of Int Gifted 1970- Goldblatt Sch; *ai:* Safety & Grading Comms Chm; Phi Delta Kappa; Teacher of Yr Goldblatt Sch 1990; *office:* Nathan Goldblatt Elem Sch 4957 W Adams St Chicago IL 60624

NEVID, BARBARA GAIL (ROTHMAN), Spanish Teacher; *b:* Burlington, VT; *m:* Maynard; *c:* Eric, Steven; *ed:* (BS) Span/Eng, Univ of VT 1959; (MA) Span, Syracuse Univ 1968; Educl Admin; *cr:* Span Teacher W Irondequoit Cntrl Schls 1961-63, Jamesville-De Witt Cntrl Schls 1963-64; Dept Chm of Foreign Lang 1967-71, Span Teacher 1965- Baldwinsville Cntrl Schls; *ai:* NY St Assn of Foreign Lang 1968-, Service Awd 1972; Foreign Lang Assn of Cntrl NY (Treas, Secy 1971, 1987-88, Exec Mem at Large 1989); Natl Assn of Teachers of Span & Portuguese 1965-71, 1989-; *office:* Baldwinsville Cntrl Schls E Oneida St Baldwinsville NY 13027

NEVILLE, CAROLYN L., 6th Grade Language Art Teacher; *b:* Springfield, OH; *m:* Frederick; *ed:* (BA) Soc Sci, Adrian Coll 1972; *cr:* Kndgtn Teacher Simon Kenton Elem 1973-77, St Catherines 1981-82; 6th Grade Lang Art/6th-8th Grade Creative Writing Teacher Homestead Mid Sch 1984-89; *ai:* Washington DC Educl Trip Spon; Mid Sch Team Leader; *office:* Homestead Mid Sch 650 NW 2nd Ave Homestead FL 33030

NEVILLE, PATSY H., Third Grade Teacher; *b:* Ritchie, KY; *m:* William E.; *c:* Suzanne; *ed:* (BS) Elem Ed, N GA Coll 1977; (MED) Early Chldhd Ed, Brenau Coll 1980; Data Collector Evaluator of New Teachers; *cr:* 3rd Grade Teacher Jasper Elem 1977-; *ai:* GAE, NAE 1977-; *home:* 173 S Brook Dr Jasper GA 30143

NEW, JOHN EMMETT, Instrumental Music Director; *b:* Milwaukee, WI; *ed:* (BM) Music Ed, St Norbert Coll 1976; (BS) Music Ed, 1983, Adv Cert Music Ed, 1984 Univ of IL; *cr:* Band Dir Girard Cmmty Unit #3 1976-82; Band/Orch Dir Dennis-Yarmouth Regional HS 1984-; *ai:* Track Coach; Phi Delta Kappa, NMEA, NEA; *office:* Dennis-Yarmouth Regional HS 210 Station Ave South Yarmouth MA 02664

NEW, PENNY LOUISE, Fourth Grade Teacher; *b:* Joplin, MO; *m:* Larry Jay; *c:* Bradley, Brittany; *ed:* (BSED) Elem Ed, Pittsburg St Univ 1983; *cr:* Math Teacher Galena Jr HS 1984-86; 4th Grade Teacher Liberty Elem Sch 1986-; *ai:* Star Lab Coord; Playground Safety Comm; PTA; Galena Ed Assn Treas 1985-86; KS Natl Ed Assn; *home:* 719 Wood St Galena KS 66739

NEW, ROBERT CHARLES, English Teacher; *b:* Marion, OH; *ed:* (BS) Eng Ed, OH St Univ 1972; *cr:* Teacher/Coach St Mary Sch 1972-88, Marion Cath HS 1988-; *ai:* Boys Head Track & Field Coach; OH Assn of Track & Cross Cntry Coaches 1982-, Dist 11 Coach of Yr 1989; Cntrl Dist Track Coaches Assn 1982-, Dist Coach of Yr 1989; Track Registry Assn of Cntrl OH 1981-; Smithsonian Assocs, Natl Fed of Interscholastic Ofcls of America; *office:* Marion Cath HS 1001 Mt Vernon Ave Marion OH 43302

NEW, WALTER, Honors & AP English Teacher; *b:* Ralls, TX; *m:* Frances White; *c:* Pamela, Michael; *ed:* (BS) Ed, TX Tech Univ 1985; *cr:* Teacher Del Rio HS 1985-; *ai:* UIL Writing Spon; Dist Advisory Comm; ATPE (Pres 1987-88, VP 1988-); Republican Party Precinct Chm 1986-; *office:* Del Rio HS 100 Memorial Dr Del Rio TX 78840

NEWBERN, ARMA JEAN, Second Grade Teacher; *b:* Guttenberg, IA; *m:* Donald T.; *c:* Dan Bilsten, Bruce, Jill Mohr; *ed:* Teachers Certificate Elem Ed, Wartburg Coll 1954; (BS) Elem Ed, Upper IA Coll 1970; Grad Stud Margcrest Coll, Univ of N IA, Laverne Coll, Drake Univ; *cr:* 2nd Grade Teacher 1954-56, 5th Grade Teacher 1959- Guttenberg Cmmty Sch; 1st Grade Teacher 1964, 2nd Grade Teacher 1965- Cntrl Cmmty Schls 1965-; *ai:* Cntrl Ed Assn Faculty Rep 1989-; N IA Rdng Assn, NEA; Bethany Luth; Bethany WELCA Various Offices; Amer Legion Auxiliary Pres 1964; Proteus Womens Club; *office:* Central Cmmty Sch 400 1st St NW Elkader IA 52043

NEWBERRY, JANE LESLIE, Eighth Grade Teacher; *b:* Bay City, TX; *m:* James W.; *c:* Emily Caldwell, Susan May; *ed:* (BA) Elem Ed, Northeast St 1963; (MED) Admin, LA St Univ Shreveport 1982; Gifted/Talented Cert; Counseling, LA St Univ Shreveport 1982; *cr:* Classroom Teacher Oak Terrace Jr HS 1963-65, Ridgewood Mid 1965-; *ai:* Spon Yrbk; Curr Comm; Soc Stud Chairperson; Phi Delta Kappa, NEA, Caddo Assn Ed, LA Ed Assn; Daughters of Amer Revolution Mag Chm 1989-; PTA Life Membership; Friends of Genealogy Trustee 1988-; First Presbyn Church Deacon 1988-; Journal Articles Published; *office:* Ridgewood Mid Sch 2001 Ridgewood Dr Shreveport LA 71118

NEWBERRY, KAY KINNE, Theatre/English Teacher; *b:* Fort Worth, TX; *c:* Michael Craig; *ed:* (BFA) Theatre Art, 1971 (MFA) Theatre Art, 1980 TX Chrstn Univ Ft Worth; *cr:* Teacher Burleson HS 1971-78; Instr N IL Univ 1980-81; Teacher Crowley HS 1981-; *ai:* One Act Play Competition Dir; ITS Spon; TX Educl Theatre Assn, TX St Teachers Assn; *office:* Crowley H S 1005 W Main St Crowley TX 76036

NEWBROUGH, WILDA R. F., Speech & English Teacher; *b:* Houston, TX; *m:* Dan E.; *c:* Danna, Marykae; *ed:* (AA) General Liberal Art, Wharton Jr Coll 1957; (BA) Speech/Eng/Ed, Univ of TX 1960; (MED) Drama/Rdng/Ed, Sam Houston St Univ 1972; Various Univs; *cr:* Speech Therapist Richland Ind Schls 1959-61; Speech Teacher of Homebound La Porte Ind Sch Dist 1965-66; Eng/Lang Art Teacher Clear Creek Ind Sch Dist 1966-74; Rdng/Eng/Lang Art Teacher Friendswood Ind Sch Dist 1974-82; Eng Teacher Private Sch O Connell; *ai:* Teach Regular & Basic 12th Grade Eng Teams; Ext Speech Club; UIL Academic Sch Coord; Stu Cncl Co-Spon; Intnl Rdng Assn Local Chapter VP 1976-77; TX St Teachers Assn (Local Chapter VP 1975-76, Pres 1976-77); NCTE 1985-; GSA Leader 1968-76; Univ of TX Ex-Stus Assn (Local Schlsp Comm 1972-) 1959-; Nom Teacher of Yr 1988; Curr Writing Friendswood Ind Sch Dist 1981 & Santa Fe Ind Sch Dist 1989; *office:* Santa Fe HS Box 370 War Path Dr Santa Fe TX 77510

NEWBURG, EDWIN E., JR., Science Teacher; *b:* Chico, CA; *m:* Sharon E. Mc Brian; *c:* Ken; *ed:* (BA) Liberal Stud, CA St Coll Stanislaus 1976; *cr:* 8th Grade Teacher Lincoln Elem Sch 1978; 7th/8th Grade Teacher Nile Garden Elem Sch 1978-80, New Haven Elem Sch 1980-85, Golden West Elem Sch 1985-; *ai:* Math Superbowl & Sci Olympiad Coach; Manteca Educators Assn; Ripon Lions Club (Pres 1987-88, Zone Chm 1989-) 1979-; Cntrl Valley Math Project Fellowship 1987, 1989; PGE Energy Grant 1988; *home:* 1061 Spring Creek Dr Ripon CA 95366

NEWBURN, MARY LOU, English/Amer History Teacher; *b:* Indianapolis, IN; *ed:* (BA) Hum, Purdue Univ 1964; (MA) Classical Antiquities, Univ of CO 1977; Womens Stud, Poly Theory; *cr:* Span/Soc Stud Teacher South Jr HS 1968-70; Soc Stud Teacher Coronado HS 1970-80; Eng/Soc Stud Teacher Air Acad HS 1985-; *ai:* Yrbk Adv; Sr Awds Selection & Building Goals Comm; NEA, CEA, Pikes Peak Ed Assn 1985-; Womens Stud Seminar San Diego NEH Awd 1989; Various Articles Published; *office:* Air Academy HS USAF Academy CO 80840

NEWBURY, RUSSELL DEAN, Band Director; *b:* Whitefish, MT; *m:* Loralee T.; *c:* Christopher, Anna; *ed:* (BA) Music Ed, Rocky Mountain Coll 1981; (MM) Euphonium Performance, E NM Univ 1983; *cr:* Band Dir Libby Sr HS 1983-86, MT St Univ 1987-88, Bozeman Sr HS 1986-; *ai:* Dir of Band Act; Bozeman Ed Assn VP 1989-; Music Educators Natl Conference, MT Band Masters 1983-; Composer of Works Concert Band; Jass Ensemble; Compositions Performed Major Music Conventions.

NEWCOMB, KATHY PALMER, First Grade Teacher; *b:* Warren, OH; *m:* Thomas L. D. Litt; *c:* Matthew; *ed:* (BS) Elem Ed, Kent St Univ 1975; (MED) Elem Ed, Westminster Coll 1982; Prof Seminars & Conferences; *cr:* 1st Grade Teacher 1975-79, 3rd Grade Teacher 1979-82, 1st Grade Teacher 1982- Bloomfield-MESPO Local Schls; *ai:* OEA/NEA 1975-; Natl Wildlife Fed 1989-; N Amer Wildlife Park Fnd 1989-; Parkman Congragational Church Mem 1984-; Several Grants Funded to Bloomfield-MESPO Local Schls; *office:* Bloomfield-Mespo Local Schol 4466 Kinsman Rd Mesopotamia OH 44439

NEWCOMB, PHYLLIS JEAN LYALL, Anatomy/Biology Teacher; *b:* Pasadena, CA; *m:* Harold Edward; *c:* Tara M., Tiffany D., Ashley L.; *ed:* (BS) Bio, Marshall Univ 1973; (MA) Comm, WV Univ 1979; *cr:* Teacher Clear Fork HS 1974-77, Woodrow Wilson HS 1977-; *ai:* Citizens Schlsp Fnd; *home:* Box 318 Bradley WV 25818

NEWCOMER, SAUNDRA KAYE, Journalism & English Chair; *b:* Van Nuys, CA; *m:* Buck; *c:* Tracy, Amanda Newcomer Arens; *ed:* (BS) Eng/Journalism, SW MO St Univ 1979; *cr:* Eng/Journalism Mt Vernon HS 1979-; *ai:* Yrbk, Newspaper Adv; Spon Academic Bowl Team; Prof Dev Comm; Career Ladder Comm; MO Journalism Ed Assn (Secy, Treas 1987-) Teacher of Yr; SW MO EducatoR of Yr; Dir Media Camp SW MO 1987-; PEO Pres 1978-82, 1990; Pres, Co-Organizer & Founder Ozarks Publications Adv; MO Interscholastic Press Assn Advisory Comm; Teacher Summer Media Camp Univ of MO; *office:* Mt Vernon HS Mount Vernon MO 65712

NEWELL, CLINTON HARRISON, French Teacher; *b:* Belleville ON, Canada; *m:* Sharon Schoming; *c:* Sharna, Sharmin; *ed:* (MS) Intnl Relations, Brockport St Univ 1967; Fr, Cmptr Sci, Public Relations, Math, Techniques of Teaching, Counseling Techniques; *cr:* Teacher Letchworth Sch Dist 1963-67, Carthage Sch Dist 1967-68, Bremerton Sch Dist 1968-; *ai:* SADD, Fr Club Adv; Drug Intervention Team; NHS Selection Comm; Bremerton Ed Assn, WA Ed Assn 1968-; NEA 1963-; Bremerton Chrstn Sch Bd Mem 1975-88; Sylvanway Baptist Church Elder 1972-82; Crossroads Neighborhood Church Elder 1984-; US Rep France 100 Percent Schlsp 1979; *home:* 3255 Almira Dr Bremerton WA 98310

NEWELL, DONNA BLAYLOCK, 6th Grade Teacher; *b:* Roxboro, NC; *m:* David Bruce Alexander; *c:* Nina, David Jr.; *ed:* (BS) Elem Ed, Appalachian St Univ 1975; *cr:* Teacher North Elem Sch 1975-; *ai:* PTA Rep 1988-; Spelling Bee Chm 1988-; Alpha Delta Kappa 1989-; Roxboro Jr Service League (Treas 1984-85) 1976-85; North Elem Teacher of Yr 1990; *home:* 402 Newell Dr PO Drawer 1098 Roxboro NC 27573

NEWELL, EUGENE L., Teacher of Gifted/Talented; *b:* Hartford, CT; *m:* Suzanne Lee Bennetch; *c:* Aimee L., Ian L.; *ed:* (BA) Eng - Cum Laude, Trinity Coll 1970; (MA) Eng, Univ of Wales 1972; Certificate of Advanced Study Interdisciplinary, Wesleyan Univ 1985; Elements of Effective Instruction, Clinical Supervision II, Hunter Model, The Writing Inst Fairfield Univ; *cr:* 10th-12th Grade Teacher 1976-86, 9th-12th Grade Teacher of Academically Gifted & Talented 1986- Brookfield HS; *ai:* Peer Counseling & Literary Magazine Adv; Hunter Coach; Curr Comm; Natl Assn of Gifted Children 1987-89; New Milford Zoning Commission 1987-89; New Milford Youth Bsbl Coach 1989-; Nom for Teacher of Yr Brookfield HS 1987-89; *office:* Brookfield HS 45 Longmeadow Hill Rd Brookfield CT 06804

NEWGARD, ROBERT DAVID, Gifted-Enrichment Prgm Teacher; *b:* Minneapolis, MN; *m:* Karen Sue Wilson; *c:* John, Brant, Vance; *ed:* (BA) Poly Sci, Univ of MN 1969; Gifted Ed Certificate Prgm Natl Coll of Ed; Ec Ed Certificate Coll of Bus & Public Admin Governors St Univ; *cr:* Jr HS Teacher 1969-75, K-8th Grade Teacher Gifted-Enrichment Prgm Teacher/Coord 1975-; DEEP Coord 1988- Sch Dist 170; *ai:* Track Team Coach; IFT Local 1260 Pres 1974; Dr Gavin Fnd Schlsp Comm Chm 1982-83; Homewood Bsbl League Coach 1990; Homewood-Flossmoor Soccer Club Coach 1985-89, H-F Cup Champion 1987; Co-Author of Two Books;1st PL Awd Ec Ed IL Cncl Ec Ed 1987, Natl Joint Cncl 1987; *office:* Sch Dist 170 25 W 16th Pl Chicago Heights IL 60411

NEWLANDS, DONNA HULL, Kindergarten Teacher; *b:* St Clair Cty, IL; *m:* Brian Frank; *c:* Brad, Carly; *ed:* (BS) Elem Ed, Univ of MO Columbia 1972; (MA) Ed, CO St Univ Ft Collins 1981; *cr:* 3rd Grade/1st-3rd Grade Summer Sch Teacher 1973, 1st Grade Teacher 1973-76 Whiteside Sch; 3rd Grade Teacher 1977, 2nd Grade Teacher 1977-83, 2nd/3rd Grade Combination Teacher 1981-82, Kndgtn Teacher 1983-88 Cache La Poudre Elem; Kndgtn Teacher Johnson Elem 1988-; *ai:* PEA 1978-; IRA; Presbyn Church; Daughters of American Revolution 1973-; Chi Omega Rush Adv 1979-81; PTA Rep; *office:* Johnson Elem Sch 4101 Seneca St Fort Collins CO 80526

NEWLIN, TERRY RYAN, Jr & Sr HS Phys Ed Teacher; *b:* Montrose, CO; *m:* Debra L.; *c:* Kevin, Denise; *ed:* (BA) Recreation Admin, 1976, Teacher Cert Phys Ed, 1985 W St Coll; *cr:* Scndry Phys Ed Teacher Mancos HS 1986-; *ai:* Head Girls Bsktbl, Asst HS Ftbl, Jr HS Track Coach; BPOE #1053; *office:* Mancos HS 355 W Grand Ave Mancos CO 81328

NEWLON, CAROL ROWE, Remedial Language Art Teacher; *b:* Baltimore, MD; *m:* Joseph Richard; *c:* Luke, Ben, Nick; *ed:* (BS) Lang Art, WV Univ 1973; (MA) Counseling, Marshall Univ 1981; WV Writing Project 1988; *cr:* Eng Teacher Grafton HS 1973-74, Milton HS 1987-89; Remedial Lang Art Teacher Cabell Cty Voc-Tech Center 1989-; *ai:* Monthly Sch Newsletter; Voc Fest 1990 Coord; NEA, WVEA; *home:* 2001 Olvie Ct Milton WV 25541

NEWMAKER, DOROTHY MARIE, Fifth-Sixth Grade Teacher; *b:* Sacramento, CA; *m:* Robert G.; *c:* Paul K., Gerald W.; *ed:* (BA) Ed/Eng, Humbolt St Univ 1966; *cr:* 1st-8th Teacher/Prin Zenia Elem Sch 1952-54; 3rd/4th Grade Teacher S Humbolt Sch Dist 1954-55; 1st/2nd Grade Teacher Casterlin Sch Dist 1958-59; 5th-7th Grade Teacher/Vice Prin Cuddeback Union Elem 1966-; *ai:* Olympics of Mind Coach; Various Comms; CA Teachers Assn, NEA; PTA (Secy, Parliamentarian, Inspirational Chm); Mentor in Lit 1984-86; Masonic Lodge Meritorious Service Awd 1981; 8th Grad Graduation Speaker.

NEWMAN, DOROTHY P., Sixth Grade Teacher; *b:* Como, MS; *m:* Floyd S. III; *c:* Mark, Eric; *ed:* (BA) Elem Ed, LeMoyne-Owen Coll 1965; Writing Across Curr; Newspaper in Classroom; *cr:* Teacher Memphis City Schls 1965-; *ai:* Fundraising Chairperson; Memphis Ed Assn, TN Ed Assn, NEA; Silhouettes of Kappa Alpha Psi Pres 1971-; Level II Career Ladder Teacher; *home:* 173 Honduras Memphis TN 38109

NEWMAN, DOROTHY PHILLIPS, Business Education Teacher; *b:* Quitman, MS; *m:* Amos Jr.; *c:* Amos, Antonio, Anthony; *ed:* (BS) Bus Ed, Alcorn St Univ 1961; (MS) Bus Ed, IN Univ 1967; Southern Univ; *cr:* Bus Ed Teacher Tylertown HS 1961-; *ai:* AKA; Progressive Lit Arts & Crafts & Crafts Club; Tylertown 1st Bapt Church; MS Assn of Educators Secy 1989-; NEA 1961-; MS Bus Assn 1971; *office:* Tylertown HS Gullege Dr Tylertown MS 39667

NEWMAN, NELL SLEMP, Business Teacher; *b:* Jonesville, VA; *m:* Barlow Jr.; *c:* Hannah, Hansel; *ed:* (BS) Accounting/Bus Ed, Union Coll 1978; *cr:* Accountant Jonesville Oil Company 1979-80; Teacher Lee Cty Sch Bd 1980-; Adjunct Teacher Mountain Empire Coll 1989-; *ai:* FBLA Spon; LCEA, VEA, NEA 1980-.

NEWMAN, ROBERT HAUSMAN, Guidance Counselor; *b:* Mt Holly, NJ; *ed:* (BA) Soc Stud, 1976, (MA) Counseling/Personnel Services, 1987 Trenton St Coll; *cr:* 5th Grade Teacher Burlington Cty Chrstn Sch 1976-78; Soc Stud Teacher 1978-87, Guidance Cnslr 1987- Life Center Acad; *ai:* Life Action Puppets Co; Super Sunday Outreach to Cmmty; Fountain of Life Burlington; Fountain of Life Center Usher; Phi Alpha Theta NHS 1975; Kappa Delta Pi 1987-; Amer Jaycees Outstanding Young Men of America 1981; *office:* Life Center Acad P O Box 457 Columbus & Old York Rd Burlington NJ 08016

NEWMAN, STEPHEN D., Science Teacher; *b:* Richmond, VA; *m:* Marilyn Schannen; *ed:* (BS) Bio, Manchester Coll 1974; (MS) Scndry Ed, St Francis Coll 1982; *cr:* Teacher Prairie Heights Mid Sch 1976-; *ai:* Mid Sch Yrbk Spon; NEA 1976-; IN St Teachers Assn 1976; *office:* Prairie Heights Mid Sch R 2 Box 604 Lagrange IN 46761

NEWMAN, VICKI ELAINE, Social Studies Teacher; *b:* Zanesville, OH; *ed:* (BSED) His/Poly Sci, OH Univ 1978; Working on Masters in Educl Admin, OH Univ 1990; *cr:* Learning Disabilities Teacher 1978-79, Amer Civics Teacher 1979-84, OH His Teacher 1982-84 Grover Cleveland Jr HS; Civics Teacher Zanesville HS 1984-; *ai:* Stu Cncl Dir; SADD Adv; Prin Advisory Cncl; Instructional Improvement Comm; Drug Task Force; OH Ed Assn 1979-; OH Cncl of Soc Stud 1987-; NEA 1979-; Amer Assn of Univ Women; GSA Evaluation Team 1989-; Martha Holden Jennings Scholar Awd 1988; OH Univ Tele Comm Advisory Cncl on Public Broadcasting; Presented Paper on Effective Study Skills Methods 1988; *home:* PO Box 2452 Zanesville OH 43702

NEWNAM, CINDY LYNN, Director of Public Relations; *b:* Reidsville, NC; *ed:* (BA) Journalism, Univ of NC Chapel Hill 1981; (MA) Ed, FL Atlantic Univ 1983; *cr:* Sports Information Dir 1981-83, Sftbl Coach 1983-84 FL Atlantic Univ; Residence Hall Dir Coll of Boca Raton 1983-85; Dir of Public Relations St Andrews Sch 1983-; *ai:* Var Sftbl, Bsktbl, Mid Sch Vlybl Coach; Yrbk Adv; Residence Hall Dir Sch Photographer; Society of Prof Journalists 1979-81; CASE 1983-; *office:* St Andrews Sch 2707 NW 37th St Boca Raton FL 33434

NEWSOM, ANGELA KAE, Special Education Teacher; *b:* Paxton, IL; *m:* John Andrew; *ed:* (BS) Spec Ed, Eastern IL Univ 1984; (MA) Elem Ed, Olivet Nazarene Univ 1988; *cr:* 5th Grade Teacher Maplewood Sch 1985; 4th Grade Teacher 1985-; L D Resource 1987-88 Limestone Sch; Spec Ed/Eng Teacher Herscher HS 1988-; *ai:* Head Vlybl Coach-Herscher HS; 8th Grade Vlybl Coach-Limestone Grade Sch; AFT 1985-; *office:* Herscher H S 501 N Main St Herscher IL 60941

NEWSOME, ANN L., 7th Grade TX History Teacher; *b:* Overton, TX; *m:* Rudolph; *ed:* (BA) Soc Sci, TX Coll 1956; (MA) Stephen F. Austin 1975; E TX St Univ, Prairie View A&M Univ, N TX St Univ, Univ of TX; *cr:* 12th Grade Civics Teacher C B Dansby HS 1957-59; TX His/Rdng Teacher Kilgore Jr HS 1970-77; TX His Teacher Maude Laird Mid Sch 1977-; *ai:* Former Chm Soc Stud Dept Kilgore Jr HS; TSTA Rep Kilgore Jr HS; CTA Rep Maude Laird Mid Sch; NEA, TX St Teacher Assn 1977-; TX Classroom Teacher 1977-89; Maude Laird Mid Sch PTA 1978-; Harmony Baptist Church (Secy, Financial & Schlsp Comm Mem, Church Financial Collector, Gospel Choir, Choir VP 1989-; Circle No 5 & Calanthe Washington Court No 124 Mem, Sunday Sch Hugh Alexander Achievement Awd Prgm Speaker, Church Annual Women Day Queen 1989-); Natl Cncl of Negro Women Mem 1989-; Miss Jabberwock Pageant (Spon 1988, Chm 1977); *office:* Maude Laird Mid Sch 2500 Shasta Way Kilgore TX 75662

NEWSON, FRANCIS DAVIS, 8th-12th Grade Headmaster; *b:* Richmond, VA; *m:* Harriette Warren; *c:* Warren, Frank; *ed:* (BA) His, Hampden Sydney Coll 1974; (MS) Ed, Longwood Coll 1985; Post Grad Prof VA; *cr:* Teacher 1974-, 8th-12th Grade Headmaster 1985- Brunswick Acad; *ai:* Asst Var Ftbl & Var Bsbl Coach; Stu Cooperative Cncl, Honor Cncl Spon; Lions Club (Pres 1984-85, VP 1983-84).

NEWTON, ANNELLE NOEL, 7th/8th Grade Math Teacher; *b:* Harrodsburg, KY; *m:* Bill Martin; *c:* Noelle P. Smith, Neely A., John B.; *ed:* (BS) Sociology/Eng, Campbellsville Coll 1970; (MA) Elem Ed, Univ of KY 1978; *cr:* 6th-8th Grade Teacher Springfield Elem #2 1970-74; 6th Grade Teacher Washington Cty Elem 1975-85; 7th/8th Grade Teacher Washington Cty Jr HS 1985-; *ai:* 7th & 8th Grade Spon; St Judes Childrens Research Hospital Math-A-Thon; *home:* Rt 1 Box 914 Springfield KY 40069

NEWTON, CHARLES WILLARD, Journalism/Eng/Photo Teacher; *b:* Longmont, CO; *m:* June Ann Debarbieris; *c:* C. Christopher, Catherine, Cynthia, Craig; *ed:* (BA) Journalism, Univ of CA Bebkeley 1950; (MA) Audio-Visual Ed, AZ St Univ 1973; Basic & Advanced Officers Courses; *cr:* Asst Professor Military Sci AZ St Univ 1967-71; Eng/Journalism/Photography Teacher Tempe HS 1971-; *ai:* Sch Newspaper, Yrbk, Photography Club

Spon; Asst Spon Sch Literary Magazine; Sigma Delta Chi 1950-; Disabled Amer Veterans, The Retired Officers Assn 1972-; Selected AZ HS Journalism Teacher of Yr by AZ Newspaper Assn 1979; Tempe HS Outstanding Eng Teacher 1990; *office:* Tempe HS 1730 S Mill Ave Tempe AZ 85281

NEWTON, DEBORAH WARD, 4th-6th Grade Music Teacher; *b:* Glendale, CA; *m:* Allen E.; *c:* Taylor, Morgan, Evin; *ed:* (BA) Fine Art, San Diego St Univ 1972; Elem Ed, CA St San Luis Obispo; Music, Sacramento St Univ; *cr:* Elem Classroom Teacher 1974-82, Jr HS Phys Ed Teacher 1982-87 Roseville City Schls; Jr HS Drama/Performing Art Teacher Eich Jr HS 1987-89; Elem Classroom Music Teacher Roseville City Schls 1990; *ai:* Elem Choirs; CA Teachers Assn; United Meth Church Childrens Choir Asst Dir; Trained in Adolescence Quest Skills; City of Loomis Soccer Coach; *office:* Eich Intermediate Sch 1509 Sierra Gardens Roseville CA 95661

NEWTON, HELEN A., Sixth Grade Teacher; *b:* Kirksville, MO; *m:* Merle E.; *c:* Jonathan; *ed:* (BCE) Chrstn Ed, Ozark Chrstn Coll 1974; (BS) Elem Ed, Southwest Baptist Univ 1984; *cr:* 4th Grade Teacher 1984-85, 6th Grade Teacher 1985- Stockton Elem; *ai:* Local Coord Young Authors Prgm; Spon 6th Grade Newspaper Staff; Coord of Annual Intnl Supper; MO St Teachers Assn 1984-; Church (Youth Choir Dir, Camp Head Cook); Outstanding Young Women of America 1987.

NEWTON, HELEN JONES, Mathematics Teacher; *b:* Omaha, NE; *c:* Mark, Lynn Baum, Tenley, Scott; *ed:* (BA) Ed, CA St Univ Northridge 1964; *cr:* 2nd Grade Teacher Vanalden Elem Sch 1964-76; 4th Grade Teacher Canoga Park Elem Sch 1976-84; Eng/Sci/Math/Hist Teacher Columbus Jr HS 1984-; *ai:* Drama & Chorus Dir; Yrbk Spon; PTA Life Membership Awd 1974; *home:* 6825 E Poppyview Dr Agoura Hills CA 91301

NEWTON, JOANNE BARRON, Mathematics Teacher; *b:* Rapid City, SD; *m:* Rickey Lee; *ed:* (BS) Scndry Ed, TX Tech Univ 1978; (MS) Ed, N TX St Univ 1985; Working on Prin Cert; *cr:* Math Teacher Lubbock Estacado HS 1978-80; Math Teacher/Asst Team Leader R C Clark HS 1980-83; Math Teacher Plano E Sr HS 1983-85; Math/Cmptr Teacher Robinson HS 1985-87; Math Teacher John Tyler HS 1987-; *ai:* Natl Jr Honor Society 1981-83; PSAT Summer Seminar 1989; SAT Seminar 1989-; ATPE 1987-89; TCTA 1989-; Written Dist Curr for Geometry 1984, FOM 1985, Pre-Algebra 1985-86, Comp Sci 1986.

NEWTON, NANCY WALKER, Third Grade Teacher; *b:* Nashville, TN; *m:* Joseph Allen; *c:* Joseph A. III, Elbert W., Andrew L. John M.; *ed:* (BS) Elem Ed, George Peabody Coll 1959; (MS) Audiology, Vanderbilt Univ 1961; Univ of Pittsburgh, Valdosta St Coll, GA Southern Coll; *cr:* Audiologist Dr A J Brizalara 1961-62; Teacher Westside Side Public Schls 1962-63; Missionary Foreign Mission Bd of SBC 1965-78; Audiologist Cloverbottom Developmental Center 1978-80; *ai:* Prof Assn of GA Educators; NCTM, NSTA; *office:* Patterson Elem Sch PO Drawer 6 Patterson GA 31557

NEWTON, RUSSELL E., Mathematics Department Chair; *b:* Harvey, IL; *m:* Robin Rene Matern; *c:* Rene C.; *ed:* (BS) Scndry Ed, Hyles-Anderson Coll 1984; Counseling, Liberty Univ; *cr:* Math Chm Shiloh Hills Chrstn Sch 1984-; *ai:* Amer Chrstn Honor Society Spon; *office:* Shiloh Hills Chrstn Sch 75 Hawkins Store Rd Kennesaw GA 30144

NEYER, SARA ROSE FELIX, English Teacher; *b:* Sheridan, WY; *m:* Tommy C.; *ed:* (BA) Span/Eng/Ed, Univ of Denver 1972; Advanced Hrs Univ of WY, Univ of NM, CO St Univ, ND St Univ; *cr:* Eng Teacher 1976-80, Gifted Teacher 1980-82 Twin Spruce Jr HS; Eng/Span Teacher Sage Valley & Twin Spruce Jr HS 1982-87, Campbell Cty HS 1987-; *ai:* Academic Competitions Coach; Sr Class Spon; Kappa Delta Pi 1971-72; NEA, Local Ed Assn, St Ed Assn Pres 1976-, Teacher of Yr 1985; PEO Pres 1981-83; Chairperson Human & Civil Rights Commission WY Ed Assn 1987-; Various Articles in WY Ed News; Campbell Cty Ed Assn Newsletter; *office:* Campbell Cty HS 1000 Camel Dr Gillette WY 82716

NIALS, LUCINDA CHAVEZ, HS Home Economics Teacher; *b:* Clovis, NM; *m:* Alfred Marvin; *c:* Alfred M. Jr., John L., Winfred A., Lauterio D.; *ed:* (BS) Home Ec Ed, NM St Univ 1965; Quest Trng 1990; Successful Leadership 1990; Flatter Your Figure 1989; Foods Optional Credit for Sci 1989; Consumer Ed for Ec Credit 1989; *cr:* Home Ec/Sci Teacher San Jon Jr/Sr HS 1965-67; Attendance Officer/Sci/Soc Stud Teacher Tucumcari Jr Hs 1968-70; Home Ec Teacher Tucumcari HS 1978-; *ai:* FHA Hero, Dist FHA Hero Adv; Jr Class Spon; Faculty Advisory Cncl; AIDS Curr Dev Comm; North Cntrl Accrediation Steering Comm; NMVHETA Public Relations Officer;Supt Advisory Comm; NM Voc Home Ec Teachers Assn (Secy, VP, Pres) 1983-88, St Exemplary Prgm 1987-88; Natl Assn of Voc Home Ec Teachers Membership Comm 1987; AVA, NM Voc Assn 1978-; NEA, NM TEA (VP, Pres) 1986-88; St Annes Church Lector 1990; Quay Cty Fair Home Arts Judge 1970-; NM Home Ec Exemplary Prgm 1988; *office:* Tucumcari HS 1100 S 7th Tucumcari NM 88401

NIBLOCK, PATRICIA, OP, 8th Grade Teacher; *b:* Bronx, NY; *ed:* (BS) Ed, St Thomas Aquinas Coll 1973; (MS) Ed, Wm Paterson Coll 1978; *cr:* 5th/6th Grade Teacher 1973-79, 7th/8th Grade Teacher Sacred Heart Sch 1979-80; 7th/8th Grade Teacher St Anthony Sch 1980-; *ai:* Yrbk Moderator.

NICHOLAS, ELEANOR ANN, Kindergarten Teacher; *b:* Evanston, IL; *m:* Richard A.; *c:* Barbara, Matthew, David, Jane; *ed:* (BS) Elem Ed, Univ of Dayton 1962; Univ of Arkon; *cr:* 1st Grade Teacher Pitts City 1962; Kndgtn Teacher St Agnes 1976-77; 3rd Grade Teacher 1977-78, Kndgtn Teacher 1980- Orrville City Schls; *ai:* Policy, Grading, Curr Comms; AAUW VP; EAO Secy; *office:* Orrville City Schls 605 Mineral Springs St Orrville OH 44667

NICHOLAS, IDA MARIE, Second Grade Teacher; *b:* Brooklyn, NY; *m:* Thomas R.; *ed:* (BA) Ed, Brentwood Coll 1965; (MS) Elem Ed, Brooklyn Coll 1971; Educl Wkshps; *cr:* 1st Grade Teacher St Philip Neri 1960-62, Our Lady of Victory 1962-67, St Finbars 1967-76; 2nd/6th Grade Teacher Our Lady of Perpetual Help 1976-; *office:* Our Lady of Perpetual Help Sch 240 S Wellwood Ave Lindenhurst NY 11757

NICHOLAS, SHARON ANDERSON, Teacher of Gifted & Talented; *b:* Louisville, KY; *m:* Norman Leslie; *ed:* (BA) Elem Ed, KY S Coll 1968; (MA) Elem Ed, E KY Univ 1974; (Rank I) Admin/Supervision, Univ of Louisville 1985; Louisville Writing Project; KY Teacher Internship Prgm; *cr:* Adult Ed Teacher 1967-68, 2nd Grade Teacher 1968-71, Advance Prgm Teacher 1971- Jefferson Cty Public Schls; *ai:* Coord/Coach Odyssey of Mind; Participatory Management Facilitator; Sci Fair & Young Authors Comm; Grade Group, Budget Comm Chairperson; Resource Teacher KY Teacher Internship Prgm; Sch Action, Guidance, Law Related Ed Comm; Natl Assn for Gifted Children, KY Assn for Gifted Children; Delta Kappa Gamma Society (Corresponding Secy 1981-84, Membership Chairperson 1982-83), Rebecca Browning Schlsp 1982; Odyssey of Mind KY St Bd of Dirs 1985-; PTA Cultural Arts Chairperson 1979-, Life Membership 1987; *office:* Kerrick Elem Sch 2210 Upper Hunters Trace Louisville KY 40216

NICHOLS, ALICE JO DAVES, 5-kindergarten Teacher; *b:* Vilonia, AR; *m:* Harrell Gene; *c:* Mike, Mark; *cr:* Kndgtn Teacher Harding Acad 1970-; *office:* Harding Acad 1100 Cherry Rd Memphis TN 38117

NICHOLS, BARBARA DARLENE, English Teacher; *b:* Woodbury, TN; *ed:* (BS) Eng, 1977, (MA) Eng, 1980 Mid TN St Univ; Grad Stud Mid TN St Univ; *cr:* Eng Teacher Cannon Cty HS 1980-; *ai:* Asst Girls Bsktbl Coach; Beta Club & Lioness Club Spon; Delta Kappa Gamma 1985-; Lions Club 1989-; Jaycees VP 1988-89; *home:* Rt 1 Box 49 Doolittle Rd Woodbury TN 37190

NICHOLS, CAROLYN KRUEGER, English/Journalism Teacher; *b:* Louisiana, MO; *w:* Robert L. (dec); *c:* Jeffrey L., Tracy W.; *ed:* (BSED) Lang Art, 1968, (MSED) Ed/Lang Art 1987 Pittsburgh St Univ; *cr:* 9th-12th Grade Eng Teacher 1969-80, Journalism/Debate/Speech Concomitantly/9th-12th Grade Eng Teacher 1982- Baxter Springs HS; *ai:* Sr & Fellowship of Chrstn Athletes Spon; Musical Bus Mgr; Lang Art Curr Cncl; Phi Delta Phi 1987-, Honor Grad 1987; Kappa Delta Pi 1968-; NEA; Delta Gamma, PEO Sisterhood 1950-; Beta Sigma Phi 1951-; Disciples of Christ Chrstn Church (Elder, Trustee); Weekly Newspaper Column; Published Book; *home:* 21 Oakcrest Cir Box 416 Baxter Springs KS 66713

NICHOLS, CHARLES LLOYD, Fifth Grade Teacher; *b:* Stillwater, OK; *c:* Charles, David; *ed:* (BA) Elem/Scndry Soc Stud, NW St Univ ALva 1969; *cr:* 5th Grade Teacher Owensville Elem 1969-81, Glencoe Public Sch 1981-; *ai:* Elem Bsktbl Coach; *office:* Glencoe Public Sch Box 218 Glencoe OK 74032

NICHOLS, DANNY MADDOX, Band Dir/Music Coordinator; *b:* Cincinnati, OH; *m:* Terry Rae Peters-Nichols; *c:* Rae C., Andrew V.; *ed:* (BS) Music Ed, Miami Univ 1979; Grad Work Univ Cincinnati, Xavier Univ, Coll of Mount St Joseph; Seeking Masters Degree in Leadership, Miami Univ; *cr:* Music Teacher 1979-, Music Dept Chm 1989- Fairfield City Schls; *ai:* Music Coord; Pep Band Dir; Chess Club Spon; Various Curr Comms; Music Ed Assn, Amer Fed Musicians 1979-; Phi Mu Alpha, Pi Kappa Lamba; Presser Fnd Scholar; A D Lekvold Schlsp; Pat Heisey Service Awd; 4 Yr Tuition Schlsp; Univ Orch Awd; *office:* Fairfield Mid Sch 255 Donald Dr Fairfield OH 45014

NICHOLS, DARLENE ANDERSON, 5th-8th Grade Soc Stud Teacher; *b:* Gilman, WI; *m:* Clarence H.; *c:* Scott A., Shannon R. Mravik; *ed:* (BS) Elem Ed, Univ Eau Claire 1969; Working Toward Masters; *cr:* 1st Grade Teacher Ladysmith Sch 1962-65; 6th Grade Teacher/5th-8th Grade Soc Stud Teacher Sheldon Elem Sch 1966-; *ai:* Chrldr & Memory Book Adv; Sch Photographer; Asst Person-in-Charge; Sch Newspaper; NEA; Presbyn Church Clerk of Session 1989-; *home:* W13754 Trucker Ln Gilman WI 54433

NICHOLS, DONALD EUGENE, Third Grade Teacher; *b:* Terre Haute, IN; *m:* Mary Beard; *c:* Leah R., Sara R.; *ed:* (BS) Elem Ed, 1969, (MS) Elem Ed, 1972 IN St Univ; *cr:* 5th Grade Teacher Logansport Schls of IN 1969; 4th Grade Teacher 1969-74, 3rd Grade Teacher 1974- Clay Cmmty Schls; *ai:* 5th/6th Grade Intermural Sftbl; IN St Teachers Assn, NEA 1969-; Wesleyan Church Treas 1970-; YWCA Girls Bsktbl Coach 1989, Championship; *home:* RR 32 Box 861 Terre Haute IN 47803

NICHOLS, DONNA KENNEDY, History Teacher & Chair; *b:* New Castle, IN; *m:* Gordon Wayne; *c:* Dale Mahurin, Kelli Mahurin Chrisman, Barry, Joe, Don Mahurin, Kevin; *ed:* (BS) Soc Stud/Eng, Purdue Univ 1961; Soc Stud/Latin/Eng, Hanover Coll; Grad Trng, Western MI Univ; Sam Houston St; *cr:* Kndgtn-8th Grade Teacher Womer Sch 1961-62; 3rd-4th Grade Spec Ed Teacher South Bend IN 1962-63; 6th-8th Grade Soc Stud/Eng Teacher Constantine MI 1964-67; Eng Teacher S San Antonio-East 1981-82; Migrant Teacher Medina Valley 1982-83; Soc Stud Teacher Alvin HS 1983-; *ai:* Curr, Textbook Adoption Comm; Alvin Teachers Assn, TSTA, NEA Faculty Rep 1987-; NCSS 1989-; 4-H Leader 1974-77; Natl Defense Ed Act Grant Univ of Eau Claire 1965; *home:* 1114 Laurel Valley Houston TX 77062

NICHOLS, E. SUSAN COWAN, Fifth Grade Teacher; *b:* Oklahoma City, OK; *c:* Charles, David; *ed:* (BA) Ed, Northwestern St Univ 1969; *cr:* 1st Grade Teacher 1970-75, 5th Grade Teacher 1975- Gasconade R-II Sch Dist; *ai:* Cty Teachers Assn Reporter 1990; MO St Teachers Assn 1970-; GSA Cadet Leader 1983-84; Cub Scouts Cub Master 1981-84; Historical Society 1987-.

NICHOLS, HENRIETTA SCALF, Sixth Grade Teacher; *b:* Pikeville, KY; *m:* R. Thomas; *c:* Donna L., Glenda R., David T.; *ed:* (BS) Elem Ed, E KY Univ 1964; Grad Work E KY Univ 1980; *cr:* 3rd Grade Teacher Cold Springs Elem 1964-71; 4th Grade Teacher Pulaski Elem 1974-81; 6th Grade Teacher Southern Elem 1982-; *ai:* Jr Beta Club Spon; Teacher Observer KY Beginning Teacher Internship Prgm; 6th Grade Beta Club Washington DC Trip Spon; KY Ed Assn, NEA 1964-; Alpha Delta Kappa 1980-; Natl Assn Women Educators Secy 1980-; Amer Cancer Society 1989-; 1st United Meth Church (Sunday Sch Teacher, Choir Mem) 1960-; Excl Teaching Awd 1990; Chosen Attend Natl Geographic Society Instructional Leadership Washington DC 1990; Wrote Curr Project Success Joint Pre-Sch GED Prgm Pulaski Cty; *home:* 126 S Central Ave Somerset KY 42501

NICHOLS, JAMES NEIL, Social Studies Teacher; *b:* Abilene, TX; *m:* Deanna E.; *c:* Noah; *ed:* (BA) His/Philosophy, Davidson Coll 1963; (MAT) His/Ed, Duke Univ 1968; Ed Specialist His/Ed, GA St Univ 1972; *cr:* Teacher Natl Univ of Iran 1963-64, Armstrong HS 1966-68, Capital Avenue Elem 1968-72, Gwinnett Cty 1973-; *ai:* Interact Club Spon; Head Teachers Ideas Wkshps; Future Teachers Clubs Liaison; NCSS 1974-; PTA Legislative Rep 1966-; Sugar Hill Betterment Comm Chm 1983-84; Sugar Hill Recreation Bd 1989-; Fulbright Grant Iran; Local Sch Teacher of Yr; HS Teacher of Yr; STAR Teacher; 3rd Pl St Instructional Fair Competition; *office:* Norcross HS 600 Beaver Ruin Rd Norcross GA 30071

NICHOLS, JOHN MICHAEL, Eighth Grade Teacher; *b:* Athens, TN; *m:* Linda Humphreys; *ed:* (BA) Eng/Ger, TN Wesleyan Coll 1974; (MS) Eng Ed, Univ of TN 1980; Educl Leadership, UTK; Governors Sch of Writing; *cr:* Teacher Mountain View Elem Sch 1974-; *ai:* Chm of Prof Advisory Cncl; Spon Project Bus; 8th Grade Spon; Mc Minn Cty Ed Assn Pres 1971-72; Mc Minn Cty Bd of Ed Teacher of Yr 1985-86, Athens Area Chamber of Commerce Teacher of Yr 1986-87; Governors Writing Acad; TN Wesleyan Coll Alumni Bd Mem; *home:* Rt 3 Box 192 Athens TN 37303

NICHOLS, KEN E., History Teacher; *b:* Valley City, ND; *m:* Deanna Merchant; *c:* Ken Jr., Chad; *ed:* (BS) Soc Sci, 1968; (MS) Ed, 1970 Bemidji St Univ; (EDD) Curr Dev UT St Univ 1981; *cr:* Project Dir Mid Sch Curr Project 1974-77; Teacher 1968- Bemidji Public Schs; *ai:* Faculty Leadership Cncl; MEA Schlsp Comm 1985-87; BSA Scoutmaster 1980-; NESA Outstanding Scoutmaster Awd 1987; Research Grant MN Dept of Ed; Publication 1975-77; *office:* Bemidji Mid Sch 1910 Mill St NE Bemidji MN 56601

NICHOLS, LOUISE, Fifth Grade Teacher; *b:* Frankfort, KY; *m:* Lenwood N.; *c:* Linda K. Morgan, Stephen L.; *ed:* (BA) Ed, Univ of KY 1957; (MS) Ed, Mount St Joe 1988; Grad Stud Wright St & Univ of Dayton; *cr:* 6th Grade Teacher Elkhorn Elem 1953-63; 4th/6th Grade Teacher Wise Cty VA 1963-69; 6th Grade Teacher Scott Cty KY 1969-74; 1st-6th Grade Substitute Teacher 1974-80, 5th/6th Grade Teacher 1981- Xenia City Schls; *ai:* PTO Treas; Xenia Ed Assn, OH Ed Assn 1981-; NEA 1974-; Churches Bible Teacher Adults 1963-; Outstanding Teacher in KY 1971-72; Spokesman Prof Negotiation Team; *home:* 178 Hardacre Dr Xenia OH 45385

NICHOLS, MARY BUTLER, Third Grade Teacher; *b:* Pittsburgh, PA; *m:* Clifford Jr.; *c:* John J. Edson, Hilary B. Edson, M. Trinity; *ed:* (BS) Ed, Univ of Pittsburgh 1954; (MS) Counseling, Duquesne Univ; *cr:* 2nd Grade Teacher N Allegheny; 2nd/3rd Grade Teacher Sewickley Acad; *ai:* Rdng Comm; Cmmty Services; PA Assn Ind Schls Sch Rep 1986-88.

NICHOLS, NANCY JO, Science Teacher; *b:* Ann Arbor, MI; *m:* Gerald E. Smith; *ed:* (BS) Eng, Univ of MI 1976; Cert Bio, Eastern MI Univ 1983; *cr:* 4th Grade Teacher Word Processor Environmental Protection Agency 1976-80; Exec Secy Grades 5/6 Veterans Memorial Medical Ctr 1980-81; Temp Ofc Aide Kelley Services Inc 1981-83; Sci Teacher B Jordan HS 1983-; *ai:* Natl Sci Teachers of Amer 1988-; Natl Disabled Amer Veterans Outstanding Svc 1981; Sci Teacher Sch Within-A-Sch Dropout Prevention Prgm 1987; Teacher of Month 1984-86; *office:* Barbara Jordan HS for Careers 5800 Eastex Freeway Houston TX 77026

NICHOLS, PATRICIA K., 2nd Grade Teacher; *b:* Northampton, MA; *m:* Erwin D.; *c:* Todd, Kyle; *ed:* (BS) Ed, Castleton Coll 1963; *cr:* 1st-3rd Grade Teacher Peru VT 1962-64; 1st Grade Teacher Lansing Ctr 1964-65; 1st-3rd Grade Teacher Schuylerville Ctr 1965-; *ai:* Schuylerville Teachers Assn 1965-; NY St United Teachers 1965-; NEA 1 62-66; Amer Fed of Teachers 1965-; NY Teachers Retirement System 1965-; NY Rdng Assn Iroquois Rdng Cncl; Amer Assn of Univ Women 1983-88; Home Bureau Saratoga Cty 1980-84; Schuylerville Cmmty Theater 1981-; Schuylerville Booster Club 1985-; Home Sch Assn 1988-; *home:* Saratoga Road Schuylerville NY 12871

NICHOLS, PHYLLIS NEWSOM, Counselor; *b:* Sherman, TX; *m:* Delbert E.; *c:* Kathy A. Weatherman, Joe D.; *ed:* (BA) Music Ed, Cntrl St Univ 1965; (MMED) Music Ed, OK Univ 1967; Counseling Cert; *cr:* Music Teacher Hoover Jr HS 1966-67, Southeast HS 1967-76; Cnslr Moore HS 1978-; *ai:* OK Ed Assn; Classroom Teacher Assn; *office:* Moore Hs 300 N Eastern Moore OK 73160

NICHOLS, SAM E., Assistant Principal; *b:* Lima, OH; *ed:* (BA) Zoology, TX Tech Univ 1974; (MA) Health Ed, TX Tech Sch of Medicine 1976; (MA) Scndry Sch Admin, E NM Univ 1986; *cr:* Dir Patient Services Norte Vista Medical Center 1976-78; Dir Staff Dev Lea Regional Hospital 1978-83; Sci Instr/Dept Chm 1983-87, Asst Prin 1987- Hobbs HS; *ai:* Cirr Revision, Cmptr Literacy, Sci, Sci Fair, Drug Intervention Team, NHS Dist Comms; *office:* Hobbs HS 800 N Jefferson Hobbs NM 88240

NICHOLS, SANDRA BAILEY CLARK, English Teacher; *b:* Robinson, IL; *m:* Roger Earl; *c:* Pamela Miller, Michael T. Clark, Rebecca Miller; *ed:* (BSED) Music/Eng, E IL Univ 1969; Music, E IL Univ 1990; *cr:* Music Teacher Jasper Unit Rural Schls 1961-69; Eng Teacher Newton HS 1969-70; Band Teacher Dieterich 1970-73; Band/Eng Teacher 1974-88, Eng Teacher 1988- Newton HS; *ai:* Sftbl Coach; *office:* Newton HS West End Ave Newton IL 62448

NICHOLS, SHARON EMILY, 4th Grade Teacher; *b:* Detroit, MI; *c:* Monique, Erica; *ed:* (BS) Sci/Eng/Elem Ed, 1965, (MA) Elem Ed, 1970 MI St Univ; *cr:* 5th Grade Teacher Beechwood Elem 1965-70; 3rd/5th/6th Grade Teacher Lake Center Elem 1970-84; 4th Grade Teacher Angling Road Elem 1984-; *ai:* Counseling Comm; *office:* Angling Road Elem Sch 5340 Angling Rd Portage MI 49002

NICHOLS, VENUS LONDREAU, 5th Grade Teacher; *b:* Dothan, AL; *c:* Diana L. Desiree Nichols Clements; *ed:* (BA) Group Sci, 1969, (MA) Rdng, 1978 W MI Univ; *cr:* 5th Grade Teacher Angell Muskegon Public; *ai:* Helped Write Curr for Rdng Seatwork & Human Reproduction; Founded & Produced Tribute Positive Role Models Honoring Dr Martin Luther King Jr with Assembly Prgm; Over 20 Yrs & Yearly Observance of African-Amer His; Served on Multi-Cultural, Dist Comm, Human Reproduction; MI Rdng Assn; Alpha Kappa Alpha Connections Chairperson; Urban League; NAACP; W MI Univ Alumni Ambassador 1988, Certificate.

NICHOLS, VIRGINIA SHIELDS, English/Social Science Teacher; *b:* Omaha, NE; *w:* Walter E. (dec); *c:* Carole Nichols Hanley, Thomas E.; *ed:* (AA) Ed, Univ of Omaha 1948; (BA) Ed, CA St Univ Los Angeles 1965; Lit, Eng, UCI Writing Project, Univ Of CA Irvine; Various Classes CA St Univ Northridge, Fullerton; *cr:* Long Beach Sch Dist 1951-52, Bassett Sch Dist 1960-63, Irvine Sch Dist 1965-; *ai:* Speech & Debate; Eng Dept Chairperson; Irvine Teachers Assn, NEA, CA Assn of Teachers of Eng; Angels.

NICHOLS, WYNELLE WHISNANT, Social Studies Chairperson; *b:* Icard, NC; *c:* Nicky, Wiley Tate; *ed:* (BS) Elem Ed, 1958, (BS) Exceptional Children, 1968 Appalachian St Univ; *cr:* Teacher Fullerwood Elem 1958-60, Caldwell Cty 1960-62, Burke Cty 1962-; *ai:* SBC & Discipline Comms; Beta Club, NC Heritage Week, Model United Nations Spon; Mentor Teacher; Sch Store; Chaperone 8th Grade Field Trip; Soc Stud Dept Chm; Security Cncl; Talent Show; NEA 1977-; NCAE 1962-; NCSS 1986-; NASAM 1989-; Lovelady Rescue Auxiliary (Pres, Secy, Charter Mem) 1967-73; *office:* East Jr HS PO Box 1150 Icard NC 28666

NICHOLSON, A. DEAN, 8th Physical Science Teacher; *b:* Des Moines, IA; *m:* Donadee Strombeck; *c:* Barbara Muench, Todd; *ed:* (BA) Phys Ed, Buena Vista Coll 1957; (MA) Phys Ed, Univ of SD 1971; *cr:* Sci Teacher Storm Lake Cmmty Sch 1957-; *ai:* 8th Grade Ftbl; 8th Grade Boys Bsktbl; Var Boys Track; IA Assn of Track Coaches 1984-, St Coach of Yr 1987 & 1988, Regional Coach 1989; *home:* 822 W 5th Storm Lake IA 50588

NICHOLSON, DAVID ANDREW, 4th Grade Elem Sch Teacher; *b:* Boston, MS; *ed:* (BS) Elem Ed, Boston Coll 1960; (MA) Elem Ed, Suffolk Univ Boston 1961; (MED) Educl Admin, Boston St Coll 1973; Math, Lang Arts, Sci, Educl Leadership, Boston Sch System; Cmptr Course Leslie Coll MA; *cr:* 4th Grade Teacher John Chrurvus Sch 1962-68; 4th-5th Grade Teacher, 1968-78, 4th-5th Grade Advanced Classes Teacher Curtis Guild Sch 1978-86; His/sci Teacher Barnes Mid Sch 1986-88; 4th Grade Teacher Longfellow Sch 1988-89, Russell Sch 1989-; *ai:* Sargeant First Class MA Army Natl Guard; Volunteer Worker Boston Childrens Hospital; World Travel Slides Soc Stud & Sci Classes; Boston Homes Sch Assn (Pres 1974-75, VP, Secy, Treas 1965-); Cath Alumni Club of Boston 1965-; Mystic Valley Railway Society 1973-; Railroad Enthusiasts 1969-; Yankee Division Club 1988; *office:* William E Russell Sch 750 Columbia Rd Dorchester MA 02125

NICHOLSON, KATHRINE TILTON, Fr/Soc Stud/Eng Teacher; *b:* Queens Village, NY; *m:* James Howard; *c:* Katherine A.; *ed:* (BA) Fr/Span, Columbia Coll 1968; (MAT) His, Citadel 1977; Intern Teaching Gifted & Talented Stu SC Governors Sch for Art 1989-; *cr:* Dir Carriage Hills Daycare Center 1972-73; Teacher St Catherines 1973, Sacred Heart 1974-75, Hanahan HS 1975-; *ai:* Dir & Spon Hanahan Players; Coach & Judge Natl Forensic League; Co-Dir Musicals & Plays Performing Art Prgm; Mrktg & Pre-Voc Comm Secy; NEA; BCEA Bd Mem 1981-82; Amer Assn of Teachers of Fr 1988-; SC Conference Foreign Lang Teaching 1988-; Natl Historic Trust 1988-; Friends of Old Exch Exec Bd 1984-; SC Legislature Awd Excl Teaching 1989; Letter of Commendation Excl Teaching 1989; Hanahan HS Teacher of Yr 1979-80; City of Hanahan Awd for Excl Teaching 1989; *office:* Hanahan HS 6015 Murray Ave Hanahan SC 29406

NICHOLSON, LARRY DEAN, Social Studies Teacher; *b:* Raymond, WA; *m:* Lisa Dee Wirth; *ed:* (BS) His/Ed, Univ of OR 1982; *cr:* Teacher Bend-La Pine Sch Dist 1983-87, La Grande Sch Dist 1988-; *ai:* Asst Ftbl Coach; Onward to Excl Comm Person; Lions Club 1988-; *office:* La Grande HS 708 K Ave La Grande OR 97850

NICHOLSON, MARGRET LEE, English/Journalism Teacher; *b:* Hattiesburg, MS; *m:* Stacy Carnes; *c:* Caleb, Courtney, Chad; *ed:* (BS) Eng/Scndry Ed, Univ of S MS 1976; Grad Stud Univ St MS, MS St, Livingston Univ; Numerous Journalism Wkshps, Univ St MS, Univ of MS, Univ of AL; Herff Jones Wkshp, Gulf Shores AL; *cr:* Eng Teacher Northeast HS 1978-83, Jefferson Davis Acad 1984-89; Eng/Journalism Teacher Patrician Acad 1989-; *ai:* Yrbk & Paper Adv.

NICHOLSON, NANCY BAGWELL, Third Grade Teacher; *b:* Cookeville, TN; *m:* Joe H.; *c:* Joseph, Clara; *ed:* (BS) Home Ec, Mid TN Univ 1960; (MA) Supervision/Admin, TN St Univ 1990; *cr:* Asst Home Agent U T Ag Extension Service 1960-67; 3rd Grade Teacher Bransford Elem 1975-; *ai:* Robt Cty Ed Assn Several Comms, Merit Teacher 1977, 1980; TEA, NEA; Bus & Prof Women VP 1967; Music Study Club (Pres, Secy, VP) 1972-80; Fed of Womens Clubs Secy 1988-; Short Story Club Secy 1987-88; *office:* Bransford Elem Sch 700 Bransford Dr Springfield TN 37172

NICHOLSON, PATRICIA ONODERA, Mathematics Teacher; *b:* Los Angeles, CA; *m:* Charles R.; *ed:* (BA) Span/Math, Univ of CA Santa Barbara 1968; *cr:* Span/Math Teacher Glen A Wilson HS 1969-; Mentor Teacher Dist Level Hacienda La Puente Unified Sch Dist 1987-; *ai:* Amerasian Club Adv; NCTM 1970-74, 1987-; Amer Assn of Teachers of Span & Portuguese 1975-85; CA Math Cncl 1987-; Teacher Consultant for Houghton Mifflins Geometry 1990; *office:* Glen A. Wilson HS 16455 E Wedgeworth Dr Hacienda Heights CA 91745

NICHOLSON, ROSANN CICCHETTI, Jr High/Language Arts Teacher; *b:* Chicago, IL; *m:* James W.; *ed:* (BS) Elem Education, IL ST Univ 1977; *cr:* Fifth Grade Teacher 1977-78; Jr High Lang Arts 1978- St Frances of Rome; *ai:* Stu Newspaper/Yrbk Adv, Special Comm Chm, Service Act Moderator, Co-Dir of Summer Tutoring Prgm; NCEA 1977-; *home:* 1441 High Ridge Parkway Westchester IL 60154

NICHOLSON, TOM C., Director of Career Education; *b:* Kewanee, IL; *m:* Carol Colvin; *c:* Ben, Lindsey, Tom; *ed:* (BS) Ag Ed, IL St Univ 1967; (MED) Ed, Univ of IL 1968; Post Masters Stud Ed; *cr:* Ag Instr 1968-69, Ag/Coop Ed/Voc Dir 1969-72, Coop Ed/Career Dir 1972- Orion Sch Dist; *ai:* Orion Sch Dist Curr Cncl Mem; Health Occupations Task List Verification Comm Chm; Academic Excl Comm Mem; Natl Cncl Voc Admin, IL Cncl Voc Admin, IL Citizens Ed Cncl, NEA, Orion Ed Assn; IL Voc Assn Bd of Dir Admin of Yr Awd 1984; IL Cncl Local Admin (Pres 1979-80, Region II Dir); North Cntrl Steering Comm Chm 1970, 1975, 1981, 1989; IL Ed Assn Outstanding Educator Awd 1974; Lynn Township Trustee 1981-; Township Ofcls of IL, Henry Cty Ofcls Assn, Bi-State Metropolitan Planning Commission Finance Comm, Daisy Dispatch/Argus Self-Help Schlsp Comm Mem; Chm 17th US Congressional Acad Appointment Bd, OEA Legislation & Poly Action Comm, Cty Bd of Henry Cty; Orion Fall Fest Bd of Dir 1987-; Henry Cty Outstanding Teacher Awd 1975; IL Teacher of Yr Awd 1975; Natl Teacher of Yr Awd 1975; ICLA Retiring Pres Awd 1980; *office:* Orion Cmmty Unit 223 1100 13th St Orion IL 61273

NICI, JOHN BARTHOLOMEW, High School English Teacher; *b:* Astoria, NY; *m:* Judith Elizabeth Bauguss; *c:* Laura, Andrew; *ed:* (BA) Eng, 1974, (MS) Eng/Scndry Ed, 1976, (MA) Art His, 1981 Queens Coll; *cr:* Eng/Art His Teacher St Agnes HS 1975-78; Eng Teacher JHS 73 1978-80; Eng/Art His Teacher Forest Hills HS 1980-; *ai:* Yrbk Adv 1982-; Produced 6 Awd Winning Yrbks; *office:* Forest Hills HS 67-01 110th St Forest Hills NY 11375

NICKELL, D., Theatre Art Teacher; *b:* Lincoln, NE; *m:* Judith A. Line; *c:* Veronica Berberich, Rochelle; *ed:* (BA) Eng/Scndry Ed, E CT St Coll 1975; (MFA) Theatre Art, Wesleyan Univ 1978; *cr:* Theatre Art Teacher Hillcrest HS 1981-; *ai:* Thespian Spon.

NICKELL, LARRY ARTHUR, Social Studies Teacher; *b:* Brush, CO; *m:* Donna Lynn White; *c:* Jeremy S., Carissa L., Rachelle R.; *ed:* (BA) Anthropology, Univ of Denver 1966; (MA) Archeology, Univ of N CO 1974; *cr:* Soc Stud Teacher Karval Public Schls; *ai:* Knowledge Bowl, Stu Cncl, Yrbk Matchwits, Spelling Bee, Soph Class, Jr HS Knowledge Bowl Spon; Photography, Yrbk Coord; E Cntrl BOCES Knowledge Bowl Host; Lions Club Secy 1989-; Pastor RLDS Genoa Branch Church 1970-; Climax Molybdenum Company Awd & Grant 1973; CO St Bd of Ed Commitment to Excl & Dedication to Teaching Awd 1987; Karval Water Users Incorporated VP; CO Plant Operators Certificate Type D; *home:* 201 Hodgson Karval CO 80823

NICKERSON, RICHARD GEORGE, Director of Choral Music; *b:* Newcastle NB, Canada; *ed:* (BME) Vocal Music Ed, Univ of ME 1986; Several Wkshps Univ of ME, Westminster Choir Coll, Pacific Luth Univ; *cr:* Substitute Music Teacher 5th Street Mid Sch 1986-87; Choral Dir Windham Jr/Sr HS 1987-; *ai:* Sch Musical; Chamber Singers; 7th Grade Boys Soccer & Bsktbl; ME Music Educators Choral VP 1990; Amer Choral Dir Assn 1984-; Music Educators Natl Conference; *office:* Windham HS 406 Gray Rd Windham ME 04062

NICKLSON, SHERRY ALLEN, 1st Grade Teacher; *b:* Cincinnati, OH; *m:* John R.; *c:* Scotty Allen, Risha Allen, Heidi Allen; *ed:* (BA) Elem Ed, Mt Vernon Nazarene Coll 1977; (MS) Elem Ed, Cumberland Coll 1984; *cr:* 6th Grade Teacher Fredericktown Elem 1976-77; 1st Grade Teacher Campground Elem 1977-78; Headstart Teacher 1977-78, 1st Grade Teacher 1978- Felts Elem; *ai:* KY Ed Assn 1977-; Felts Elem Sch Teacher of Yr 1988-89; *home:* PO Box 1851 Corbin KY 40702

NICKODEMUS, ROSE MARIE, Mathematics Teacher; *b:* Detroit, MI; *m:* John H.; *c:* Bridge Mc Kewan, Lucy Galus, Mary, John, Rose, Paul; *ed:* (BA) Math, St Marys Coll 1959; (MA) Scndry Ed, Cntrl MI Univ 1974; *cr:* Math Teacher Saginaw City Schls 1959-63, Diocese of Saginaw 1968-73; Academic Adv Saginaw Valley St Univ 1979-85; Math Teacher Center for Arts & Sciences 1985-; *ai:* Math Competition Coach; Eucharistic Minister; NEA, MEA, SEA, NCTM, MCTM; Univ of IL Statistics Inst; *office:* Center for the Arts & Sciences 115 E Genesee Saginaw MI 48602

NICKOLS, JOHN M., History Teacher/Bskbl Coach; *b:* Harrison, AR; *m:* Barbara; *c:* Eric, Molly, Mark; *ed:* (BA) His/Poly Sci, 1960, (MA) Poly Sci, 1965 Baylor Univ; *cr:* Teacher/Bsktbl Coach Shasta HS 1964-65; FBI Agent 1965-69; Teacher/Coach Mac Arthur HS 1969-71, Everman HS 1971-82, Waxahachie HS 1983-; *ai:* Head Boys Bsktbl Coach; Society of Former FBI Agents, Assn of TX Prof Educators, TX HS Coaches Assn; Masonic Lodge; Teacher of Yr Everman Ind Sch Dist 1982; Teacher of Yr Waxahachie HS 1989; Written Several Bsktbl Articles in Natl Coaching Magazines; *office:* Waxahachie HS Hwy 77 N Waxahachie TX 75165

NICKOLS, MITCHEL ANTOINE, Pastor/TV Teacher; *b:* Rochester, PA; *m:* Quandra Combs; *c:* Rachelle, Amber; *ed:* (BS) Elem Ed, Slippery Rock Univ 1974; (MED) Lang Comm, 1977, (PHD) Curr/Supervision, 1983 Univ of Pittsburgh; Coursework Pittsburgh Theological Seminary & Penn St Univ New Kensington; *cr:* K-8th Grade Rdng Specialist 1975-82, 2nd Grade Teacher 1982-83, 6th Grade Teacher 1983-84, 1975- New Kensington-Arnold Schls; Pastor/Bible Sch/TV Teacher Bibleway Chrstn Fellowship & Dayspring Bible Trng Center & Cornerstone Television 1978-; *ai:* Cty Jails, St Prison, Youth Detention Centers Speaker; Highlands Sch Dist Citizens Advisory Bd 1987-; NEA, PA St Ed Assn, New Kensington-Arnold Ed Assn 1975-84; NAACP 1985-; Cornerstone TV, Valley Cmmty Services Bd Mem 1989-; Whos Who in the East; Whos Who in Religion; *office:* Bibleway Church/Cornerstone TV PO Box 390 Tarentum PA 15084

NICLAUS, GAIL GARDINER, 3rd Grade Teacher; *b:* Passaic, NJ; *m:* John Jr.; *c:* Lisa A. Martinez; *ed:* (BA) Elem Ed, William Paterson Coll 1981; *cr:* Nursery Sch Teacher Nursery Rhymes Sch; 3rd Grade Teacher St Leos Sch; *ai:* NCEA; *home:* 9 Dapp Ct Elmwood Park NJ 07407

NICOTRE, SHERRI SHEFFIELD, Third Grade Teacher; *b:* Woodville, TX; *m:* Terry James; *c:* Kristen; *ed:* (BS) Elem Ed, 1978, (MED) Elem Ed, 1986 Lamar Univ; Rdng Specialist; *cr:* Teacher E E Sims Elem 1980-87; Remedial Rdng Teacher Hatton Elem 1987-88; Teacher E E Sims Elem 1988-; *ai:* Sims Elem Campus Improvement Comm; TX Classroom Teachers Assn 1985-; TX St Teachers Assn 1980-85; Schlsps Amer Bus Women Assn & Alpha Delta Kappa; *office:* E E Sims Elem Sch 425 Roberts Bridge City TX 77611

NIEBUHR, KITTY EVANS, Counselor; *b:* Dayton, OH; *m:* Robert E.; *c:* Jennifer, Jeff; *ed:* (BS) Elem Ed, 1980, (MED) Cnlsr Ed, 1985 Auburn Univ; *cr:* Elem Teacher Lee-Scott Acad 1980-82; Cnslr Auburn Jr HS 1985-88, Auburn HS 1988-; *ai:* Drug Ed & Stu Act Leadership Comm; Alpha Delta Kappa Chaplain 1987-; 1st Baptist Church Sunday Sch Teacher 1980-.

NIEBUR, BARBARA E., 6th Grade Teacher; *b:* Farmington, MN; *ed:* (BS) Elem Ed, Coll of St Teresa Winona 1971; *cr:* 6th Grade Teacher St Josephs Sch 1971-82; 4th-8th Grade Teacher 1982-85, 6th Grade Teacher 1985- St Anthonys Sch; *ai:* NCEA 1971-; Teacher Ed Advisory Comm; *office:* St Anthonys Sch 2410 1st St N Saint Cloud MN 56303

NIEDZWIECKI, BARBARA (DESJARDINS), Jr HS Soc Stud/Eng Teacher; *b:* Ware, MA; *w:* Charles B. (dec); *c:* Charles Jr., Cindy Niedzwiecki Krasnecky; *ed:* (BA) His, Anna Maria Coll 1960; (EDM) Ed, Worcester St Coll 1963; *cr:* Jr HS Teacher Ware Jr HS 1960-65, St Marys Sch 1971-; *ai:* Yrbk Adv; May Fair Chm; Natl Geographic Contest Coord; Bicentennial Comm; Map Contest; Concession Chm; NCEA 1971-; St Marys PTO Treas of 1-20 1985-87; *home:* 8 Crescent Terr Ware MA 01082

NIELAND, JONI LANGE, Chemistry Teacher; *b:* Sioux Falls, SD; *m:* James K.; *c:* Joshua, Amanda; *ed:* (BS) Chemical Engrg, SD Sch of Mines/Tech 1982; Teacher Cert Scndry Math/Sci, Univ of CO Boulder 1985; *cr:* Chem Teacher Martin HS 1985-; *ai:* Jr Class Adv; Attendance Comm; Chemical Use/Abuse Comm; *office:* Redwood Falls-Morton H S 4th & Lincoln Redwood Falls MN 56283

NIELSEN, GINGER MAE, Kindergarten Teacher; *b:* Hamburg, IA; *ed:* (BS) Elem Ed, 1974; (MS) Elem Ed, 1981 Cntrl MO St Univ; *cr:* Kndgtn Teacher Greenwood Elem Sch 1974-; *ai:* Sch Improvement Team Comm; MO St Teachers Assn; Lees Summit Ed Assn; Lees Summit Intnl Rdng Assn; Delta Kappa Gamma;

Pamphlet Copyrighted 1987; *office:* Greenwood Elem Sch 805 W Main Greenwood MO 64034

NIELSEN, JUDY ANN, Mathematics Teacher; *b:* Lamar, CO; *m:* Reese R.,; *c:* Derek, Dane; *ed:* (BA) Math, CO Coll 1966; Grad Stud USU & WSC; *cr:* Teacher Lahoma, Jet-Nash, Box Elder Adult Ed, Box Elder HS; *ai:* PTA & Dist Outstanding Teacher.

NIELSEN, KAREN E., English/Vocabulary Teacher; *b:* Massillon, OH; *m:* Charles A.; *c:* Edward, Melora; *ed:* (BA) Eng/Ed, Capital Univ 1966; Cmptr Sci, Ed, Advanced Placement British Lit; *cr:* Eng Teacher Roosevelt Jr HS 1966-70; LD Tutor Massillon Public Schs 1973-74; Eng & Vocabulary Teacher Tuslaw Local Schs 1975-; *ai:* NHS & Sch Newspaper Adv; NCTE 1989-; Dedicated Yrbk 1978; Nom Ashland Teacher Achievement Awd 1989-; Organized Computerized Writing Lab 1989; *office:* Tuslaw HS 1723 Manchester Ave SW Massillon OH 44647

NIELSEN, LAURI A. (FRIZZELL), Third Grade Teacher; *b:* Lansing, MI; *m:* Gary L.; *c:* Marcus, Cory, Joe, Dan, Greg; *ed:* (AA) Arts Soc Service Technician, Ferris St Univ 1974; (BS) Elem Ed, 1976, (MA) Cnslr Ed Personal Dev 1983 Cntrl MI Univ; *cr:* Teacher Chapter I Summer Sch 1980, Big Rapids Public Schls 1985; Rdng Improvement Skills Teacher RED 065 1985; Teacher Ferris St Univ 1986, Big Rapids Public Schls 1977-; *ai:* Sci, Math, Writing/Lang Art Comm Mem; MI Ed Assn, Big Rapids Ed Assn 1977-; MI Sci Teachers Assn 1984-; MI Elem Sch Cnslr Assn 1983-85; Riverview PTO 1984-; Eastwood PTO 1978-84; *office:* Riverview Elem Sch 509 Willow St Big Rapids MI 49307

NIELSEN, LENUS A., Chemistry Teacher; *b:* Beach, ND; *m:* Janice Adams; *c:* Ron, Gary, Brad; *ed:* (BA) Bio, Univ of ND Dickinson 1957; (MA) Natural Sci, Univ of WY 1961; Chem, Univ of SD 1965; *cr:* Teacher Liberty Sch 1949-50, Killdear HS 1957-58, Sheridan HS 1958-; *ai:* Academic Decathlon; Class Spon; Sheridan Cntrl Ed Assn Pres 1958-; NEA 1958-; Bighorn Execs Club Pres 1970-; Natl Sci Inst 1959, Fellowship 1960-61; *home:* 905 Beckton Ave Sheridan WY 82801

NIELSEN, LORRAINE JEANNETTE, Spanish Teacher; *b:* Berkeley, CA; *ed:* (BA) Span, 1974, (MS) Span Lit, 1976 Univ of Ar; Univ of Valencia Spain, Univ oF AR; Instituto Centroamericano de Asuntos Internacionales, San Jose, Costa Rica; *cr:* Fr/Span Teacher 1978-87, Span Teacher 1978- Searcy HS; *ai:* Jr Class, Span Honorary Spon; Span Club; Personnel Policy Comm; AR Assn of Teachers Of Span/Portuguese, Pres 1990-; Delta Kappa Gamma VP 1988; AR Ed Assn; Beta Sigma Phi Pres 1987-88; Phi Delta Kappa; AR Foreign Lang Teacher s Assn; Fullbright-Hayes Grant Study In Costa Rica 1988; Univ of AR Foreign Lang Inst Grant 1986; *office:* Searcy HS 301 N Ella St Searcy AR 72143

NIELSEN, PATRICIA TERRY, 2nd Grade Teacher; *b:* Spanish Fork, UT; *m:* James Alan; *c:* Nathan, Austin; *ed:* (BA) Elem Ed, Brigham Young Univ 1971; *cr:* 4th Grade Teacher 1975-76, 2nd Grade Teacher 1976- Wasatch Elem; *ai:* Sch Soc Stud Specialist; Delta Kappa Gamma 1979-; *office:* Wasatch Elem Sch 1080 N 1000 E Provo UT 84604

NIELSEN, SALLY SUE, Sixth Grade Teacher; *b:* Elmer Township, MI; *ed:* (BA) Eng/Soc Stud, MI St Univ 1956; Counseling, Gifted, Learning Disabled Courses; *cr:* 4th Grade Teacher Warren MI Schls 1956-58; 4th-6th Grade Teacher Arlington Cty Public Schls 1958-70; Child Dev Consultant 1971-76, 5th/6th Grade Teacher 1976- Arlington Cty Schls; *ai:* Teachers Cncl on Instruction; Arlington Ed Assn 1958-; *home:* 3442 S Wakefield St Arlington VA 22206

NIELSEN, SHIRLEY FOLKER, Seventh/Eighth Grade Teacher; *b:* Julesburg, CO; *m:* Robert J.; *c:* Wendy, Philip, Jeffrey; *ed:* (BA) Elem Ed, Kearney St Coll 1966; Working Towards Mid Sch Endorsement; *cr:* 4th Grade Teacher Clarmar Sch 1966-67; 5th Grade Teacher Karen-Western 1967-68; Soc Stud Teacher Mid Sch 1968-69; 4th Grade Teacher 1980-82, 7th/8th Grade Teacher 1983- Our Redeemer Luth; *ai:* 8th Grade Adv in Charge of Graduation; Stu Elected Teacher of Yr 1989; *home:* Box 181 Brady NE 69123

NIELSEN, VAUGHN S., Eng/Lang Art/Reading Teacher; *b:* Hyrum, UT; *m:* Jean Johansen; *c:* Jon (dec), Jeff, Cathy, David, Crystal; *ed:* (BS) Eng, 1958, (MED) Scndry Ed, 1976 UT St Univ Logan; Eng, NDEA Inst; *cr:* Teacher Box Elder Jr HS 1958-62; Teacher/Dept Head Liahona HS 1963-65; Teacher Box Elder Jr HS 1965-; *ai:* Dist Eng Lang Art Textbook Adoption Comm; Box Elder Ed Assn Secy; UT Historical Society; UT Teachers of Eng, NCTE Mem; Brigham City Museum Gallery Bd Mem, Historical Preservation Comm; Author Natl Historic Site Tour Guide & Local His; *office:* Box Elder Jr HS 18 S 500 E Brigham City UT 84302

NIELSON, JULIE, First Grade Teacher; *b:* Payson, UT; *ed:* (BS) Ed, 1976, Early Chldhd, 1977 Brigham Young Univ; *cr:* 1st Grade Teacher Wilson Elem Sch 1976-; *ai:* NEA, UEA.

NIELSON, LARRY D., Physical Education Teacher; *b:* Olympia, WA; *c:* Lisa, Anthony, Tyson; *ed:* (BA) Phys Ed, W WA Univ 1970; (MS) Psych, WA St Univ 1975; *cr:* Eng/Lit Teacher Washington Mid Sch 1975-; *ai:* Olympia HS Track & Cross Cntry 1975-81; Washington Mid Sch Ftbl Bsktbl, Wrestling; Top Citizen Awd 1983; First Amer Climb Mt Everest Without Oxygen; *office:* Washington Mid Sch 3100 Cain Rd Olympia WA 98501

NIELSON, MARILYN SHULDBERG, Third Grade Teacher; *b:* Idaho Falls, ID; *m:* Robert D.; *c:* Glen, Renee Carter, Maxine Hardy, Sharon Peterson; *ed:* (BS) Voc Home Ec, UT St 1950; Grad Stud Elem Ed; *cr:* Teacher Lynndyl Elem, Leamington Elem, Delta Elem, Delta South Elem; *ai:* Dist ODDM Comm for Sch Improvement; MEA Pres 1980-81; UEA Rep 1980-81; NEA Delegate 1981; Church of Jesus Christ of Latter Day Saints Teacher 1950-80; 4-H Club Teacher 1964-74; Millard Cty Teacher of Yr 1983-84; Runner Up for St of UT 1983-84; Cty & St Delegate for Republican Convention; *home:* Box 214 Lynndyl UT 84640

NIEMANN, ANNETTE PUPPE, Teacher; *b:* Grafton, ND; *m:* Lynn; *c:* Allison, Angie; *ed:* (BS) Elem Ed, Mayville St Coll 1980; *cr:* 1st Grade Teacher Karlstad Public Sch 1980-81; 1st-4th Grade Teacher Nash Public Sch 1981-82; 4th Grade Teacher Valley Public Sch 1982-87; *ai:* Sunday Sch (Supt, Teacher) 1982-; *home:* RR 1 Box 19 Crystal ND 58222

NIEMI, LOIS LILLIBRIDGE, Fifth Grade Teacher; *b:* Muskegon, MI; *m:* Sanfrid; *c:* Edward, Ellen Dela Rosa, Elmer; *ed:* (BS) Elem Ed, W MI Univ 1959; (MA) Counseling, MI St Univ 1967; *cr:* 1st-8th Grade Teacher Rowe Sch 1950-52; 4th-8th Grade Teacher WY #10 1952-58; Teacher Grandville Public Sch 1959-; *ai:* 4-H Club Leader; Sunday Sch Teacher; Sch Comm; *home:* 2172 Wilson NW Grand Rapids MI 49504

NIEMI, WARREN RICHARD, Social Science Teacher; *b:* Wakefield, MI; *m:* Judith Ann Pricco; *c:* Susan, Richard; *ed:* (AA) Soc Sci, Gogebic Comm Coll 1962; (BA) His, 1964, (MA) Ed, 1971 MI St Univ; *cr:* 7th/8th Grade Teacher Blissfield Mid Sch 1964-72; Asst Prin Blissfield Elem Sch 1972-76; 7th/8th Grade Teacher Blissfield Mid Sch 1976-; *ai:* 8th Grade Girls & Boys Bsktbl Coach; Blissfield Ed Assn, MI Ed Assn, NEA 1964-; Blissfield Jaycees Chm of Bd 1973-77, Bill Brownfield Awd 1975; *home:* 509 W Adrian St Blissfield MI 49228

NIEMIE, PHILIP E., JR., Fifth Grade Teacher; *b:* Honolulu, HI; *m:* Judy; *c:* Melissa, Matthew, Kirsta; *ed:* (BS) Elem Ed, CA Polytechnic St Univ 1977; (MS) Ed, OH St Univ 1986; *cr:* Elem Teacher East Elem 1977-82; Teaching Asst OH St Univ Columbus 1981-83; Mid Sch Teacher Dublin Mid Sch 1983-89; Elem Teacher Deer Run Elem 1989-; *ai:* Mid Sch Bsktbl Coach; Educl Improvement Comm; Converse Cty Outstanding Young Educator; WY Outstanding Young Educator; *office:* Deer Run Elem Sch 8815 Manley Rd Dublin OH 43017

NIEMIEC, VIRGINIA A., Fifth Grade Teacher; *b:* Jersey Shore, PA; *ed:* (BA) Elem Ed, Hobe Sound Bible Coll 1970; *cr:* 5th Grade Teacher Hobe Sound Bible Acad 1970-; *ai:* Financial Adv Elem Yrbk Sandpiper; Chapel Prgms; Hobe Sound Bible Coll Alumni Assn 1970-, Alumnus of Yr Placque 1988; FL Assn of Chrstn Schls 1970-, Teacher of Yr Trophy 1989; Touching Lives for Christ Mem 1989-; Travels Abroad to Relieve Missionaries Work Load, Daily Vacation Bible Schls, Evangelistic Services; *home:* 9284 SE Sunrise Way PO Box 1065 Hobe Sound FL 33475

NIEMOND, STEPHEN W., Social Studies Teacher; *b:* Lewistown, PA; *c:* Tricia, Heather; *ed:* (BS) Soc Stud, Shippensburg Univ 1968; Grad Credits Elem Ed, Geography, Cmptrs; *cr:* Elem Teacher Susquehanna Elem 1968-89, Monroe Elem 1989-; *ai:* Juanita Cty Ed Assn, PA St Ed Assn, NEA; *home:* PO Box 342 Mifflintown PA 17059

NIEMUTH, ROGER LAWRENCE, Fifth Grade Teacher; *b:* Plymouth, WI; *m:* Dorothy Veldboom; *c:* Todd, Troy, Tanya; *ed:* (BA) Ed, 1961, (MS) Ed, 1969 Oshkosh; AODA Coord & Simulator; *cr:* 6th Grade Teacher Mc Kinley Elem 1961-64; 4th Grade Teacher 1964-80, 5th Grade Teacher 1980- Wilson Elem; *ai:* Coaching Boys & Girls Ftbl, Bsktbl, Soccer, Hockey, Sftbl, Hardball, Vlybl, Bowling, Riflery, Rocketry, Coin & Stamp Collecting; AODA Coord; Stu Asst; Sheboygan Recreation Dept Special Service Recognition; Teacher of Yr 1987-88; Teacher of Yr 1988 City of Sheboygan Sch Evaluation Consortium; *office:* Wilson Elem Sch 1625 Wilson Ave Sheboygan WI 53081

NIETO, SHIRLEY BRIDGMAN, Anatomy/Biology Teacher; *b:* Loris, SC; *m:* Ralph Anthony; *c:* Chris; *ed:* (BA) Scndry Ed/Sci, Univ of Cntrl FL 1974; (MS) Sci Ed, Nova Univ 1990; Numerous Wkshps; *cr:* Adult Ed Credit Teacher Orange Cty Ad Ed 1973-79; Teacher Evans HS 1974-75; Teacher 1975-, Sci Dept Chairperson 1982- Lake Brantley HS; *ai:* Dept Chairperson; Previously Sponsored Stu Cncl, Sci Club, Tri-Hi-Y, Chrldrs, Interclub Cncl; Various Publications; *office:* Lake Brantley H S 991 Sand Lake Rd Altamonte Springs FL 32707

NIEVES, NORIS COLBERG, Mathematics Teacher; *b:* San Juan, PR; *m:* Rafael A.; *c:* Noris M., Raquel M.; *ed:* (BA) Eng, Univ of PR 1976; *cr:* Jr/HS Math Teacher Episcopal Cathedral Sch 1973-; *ai:* Newspaper Club; Best Teacher of Yr 1976; *office:* Episcopal Cathedral Sch PO Box 13305 Santurce Sta San Juan PR 00908

NIEVES CARABALLO, ANGEL L., Social Studies Teacher; *b:* Adjuntas, PR; *m:* Aili L. Plaza Orta; *ed:* (BA) His, 1983, Cert Ed His/Soc Stud, 1983 Cath Univ Ponce; Working Toward Masters Puerto Rican His; Working Toward Doctorates Univ of Valladolid Spain; *cr:* Soc Stud Teacher Academia San Joaquin 1983-84; Center Coord Centro De Investigaciones 1984-85; Hum Lecturer Pr Jr Coll 1985-; Soc Stud Dept Dir Colegio Ponceno 1987-; *ai:* Colegio Ponceno NHS & Sr Adv; Article Published; Wrote Historical Articles for Newspapers; *home:* Box 1130 Progreso #8 Adjuntas PR 00601

NIGGEMEYER, JANICE REA, Fourth Grade Teacher; *b:* Fort Madison, IA; *m:* Steven Wayne; *c:* Alan, Bradley, Caitlin; *ed:* (BA) Psych, Elem Ed, Simpson Coll 1977; *cr:* Chapter 1 Rdng 1977-78, 4th Grade Teacher 1978- West Central Schls; *ai:* Executive Cncl WCEA; Delta Kappa Gamma 1986-88; West Cntrl Ed Assn 1977-; IA ST Ed Assn 1977-.

NIGGEMEYER, STEVEN WAYNE, 6th Grade Mid Sch Teacher; *b:* Ft Madison, IA; *m:* Janice Marie Rea; *c:* Alan, Brad, Caitlin; *ed:* (BA) Elem Ed/Phys Ed, Simpson Coll 1977; *ai:* Coach Head Vlybl, Asst Girls Bsktbl 1978-88; NEA, ISEA 1977-.

NIGOHOSIAN, ELSIE TATOIAN, Kindergarten Teacher; *b:* Thompsonville, CT; *m:* Leon Sr.; *c:* Leon Jr., Stephan; *ed:* (BA) Elem Ed, William Paterson Coll 1977; Candidate MA Rdng, William Paterson Coll; Gesell Inst Certified Examiner; Marthas Vineyard Writing Project Writing as Process; Columbia Univ Teachers Coll Inst; *cr:* 2nd Grade Teacher Mt Carmel Sch 1977-79, Norwood Public Sch 1979-82; K-2nd Grade Teacher Alpine Public Sch 1985-; *ai:* Pres Alpine Ed Assn; Outstanding Teacher Awd 1990; St of NJ Governors Teacher Recognition Prgm; Intnl Rdng Assn; NJ Rdng Assn; NCTE; Pi Lambda Theta 1989; Daughters of Vartan VP/Secy 1972-; Cub Scouts Den Mother 1972-74; St Thomas Armenian Church Womens Guild 1972-; 16th Annual Symposium on Young Child William Paterson Coll; Wkshp for Teachers/Administrators Entitled Problem Solving Thinking; Process Skills in K & 1st Grade Based on NAEYC DAP Guidelines; Forthcoming Book by Feeley Wepner & Strickland; Teachers Share Their Literacy Prgm; *office:* Alpine Public Sch Hillside Ave Alpine NJ 07620

NIGRO, ARDATH HAGAN, Fourth Grade Teacher; *b:* Cambridge, OH; *m:* Anthony F.; *c:* Tony, Ryan, Nicole; *ed:* (BS) Elem Ed, Kent St 1977; Grad Stud; *cr:* Teacher Indian Valley Sch Dist 1967-70, Newcomerstown Sch Dist 1970-71, New Philadelphia Sch Dist 1977; 4th Grade Elem Teacher Newcomerstown Sch Dist 1977-; *ai:* Newcomerstown Teachers Assn, OH Ed Assn, NEA 1977-; Kappa Delta Pi; First Baptist Church Mem; *home:* 420 N College St Newcomerstown OH 43832

NIKNAHAD, CORAL GARMON, Sr HS Social Studies Teacher; *b:* Chattanooga, TN; *c:* Nickolas; *ed:* (BA) His/Russian, (BSE) Scndry Ed, 1982 Memphis St Univ; *cr:* Sr HS Soc Stud Instr Marshall Acad; *ai:* Jr/Sr HS His Club; Anchor Club & Jr Class Spon; MPSEA STAR Teacher 1988, 1989; MS Private Sch Ed Assn Dist Chm; *office:* Marshall Acad 100 Academy Dr Holly Springs MS 38635

NILES, RHONDA RUCKER, Reading/English Teacher; *b:* Hartford, CT; *m:* John C.; *c:* Tony A.; *ed:* (BS) Elem Ed, Cntrl CT St Coll 1981; Sch Counseling Cert; Educator Support & Trng Prgm 1989; Hartford Effective Sch Initiative; *cr:* 7th/8th Grade Rdng/Eng Teacher Batchelder Sch 1981-; *ai:* 7th/8th Grade Intramural Sports Supv; 4th-8th Grade Double Dutch Coach; Union Sch Comm Mem 1988-; CT Black Caucus 1988; Intnl Rdng Assn; Lewis W Batchelder Schlsp Awd Outstanding Service 1982-83; Teacher of Yr 1985-86; 1st Place Winner City-St-World Double Dutch Competition; 1st Place Winner Southland Recitation Contest; 1st & 2nd Place Winner City Wide Recitation Contest; Book Batchelders Multi-Ethnic Recipe Book 1986; *office:* Batchelder Sch 757 New Britain Ave Hartford CT 06106

NILIUS, TIM PAUL, Music Teacher; *b:* Omaha, NE; *m:* Twila J. Wolfe; *c:* Kristen, Erik; *cr:* (BS) Bible/Music, Faith Baptist Bible Coll 1982; Teacher Grandview Park Baptist Sch 1985-; *ai:* Var Girls Bsktbl Coach; Class of 1991 Adv; Traveling Music Group Dir; *office:* Grandview Park Baptist Sch 1701 E 33rd St Des Moines IA 50317

NILSSON, GARY DUANE, Jr/Sr HS Principal; *b:* Grafton, ND; *ed:* (BS) Bus/Phys Ed/Drivers Ed, Mayville St Univ 1967; Bemidji St Univ; *cr:* Bus Teacher/Coach Osnabrock HS 1967-69; Bus Teacher/Coach 1969-78, Prin 1978- Walhalla HS; *ai:* Bsktbl, Ftbl, Track Coach; Yrbk & Annual, Stu Cncl, Jr Class Adv; Jaycees Regional VP 1977-78, Outstanding Young Educator 1977, Outstanding Young Men of America 1977, Keyman Awd 1977; *home:* Box 1 Walhalla ND 58282

NIMS, ROSALIND MYLES, English Teacher; *b:* Tallahassee, FL; *c:* Albert Jr.; *ed:* (BS) Speech/Theatre, FL A&M 1972; *cr:* English Teacher New Smyrna Beach HS 1973-74, Jefferson HS 1975-84, Leon HS 1984-; *ai:* Future Teachers of America Club Spon; Charm-Retes Co-Spon; LCTA; Beg Bend Uni-Serve; SACS Comm to Evaluate Schls; *office:* Leon HS 550 E Tennessee St Tallahassee FL 32308

NINMAN, LARRY RAY, High School Principal; *b:* El Reno, OK; *m:* Rebecca Teresa Sterba; *c:* Elizabeth; *ed:* (BA) Soc Stud, Cntrl OK Univ 1979; (MS) Ed Admin, Southwestern St Univ 1984; *cr:* Soc Stud Teacher/BB Coach Copeland HS 1979-81, Mountain View HS 1981-84; Prin/Soc Stud Teacher/Coach Freedom HS 1984-88; Prin/Soc Stud Teacher Ryan HS 1988-; *ai:* COASA; *office:* Ryan Public Schls Box C Ryan OK 73565

NIRO, ANTONIO M., JR., Teacher; *b:* Milford, MA; *m:* Nancy L. Bodio; *c:* Francesca, Anthony; *ed:* (BA) Sociology, St Anselms Coll 1972; Ed Philosophy, Mid Sch Curr, Cmptr Ed, Phys Sci, Audio-Visual Techniques; *cr:* Research Asst Hopedale Public Schls 1972-73; Sci Teacher Milford Public Schls 1973-; *ai:* Sci Club Adv; Local/Regional Teacher In-Service Prgm Presentations/Wkshps; Developed Annual Mini-Sci Museum Exhibition; NSTA, NEA, MA Teachers Assn; Milford Teachers Assn Bd of Dir 1987-88; BSA Cub Master 1988-; Little League Asst Coach 1988-89; PTO 1988-; Worcester Area Teachers Mini-Grant 1986-87; Horace

Mann Grant 1987-89; Milford Mid Sch W Teacher of Yr 1989; *office:* Milford Mid Sch 66 School St Milford MA 01757

NISSEN, BEVERLY ANN, Reading Teacher; *b:* North Bend, NE; *m:* Walter; *c:* Stephen; *ed:* (BS) Elem Ed, 1963, (MS) Elem Ed, 1970 Univ of NE; Grad Stud Ed; *cr:* Kndgtn-8th Grade Teacher Dist 30 Dodge 1982-58; 5th Grade Teacher Fremont Public 1958-71; Kndgtn/Music Teacher Dist 93 Dodge 1972-77; Remedial Rdng Teacher Fremont Public 1977-; Part-Time Music Teacher Dist 93 Dodge 1979-; *ai:* NEA, NSEA, Fremont Ed Assn; St Charles Church Organist 1968-; CCD Teacher; *home:* RR 1 North Bend NE 68649

NISTENDIRK, VIRGINIA DI MAGGIO, 5th Grade Teacher; *b:* Kansas City, MO; *m:* David W.; *c:* Thomas; *ed:* (BA) Ed, 1972, (MS) Rdng, 1977 Univ of MO Kansas City; *cr:* 4th Grade Teacher 1972-76, 5th Grade Teacher 1976- Chapel Hill; *ai:* MO N KS City Ed Assn Mem 1972-; *office:* Chapel Hill Sch 3220 NE 67th Terr Gladstone MO 64119

NISWONGER, L. CAROL, English/Drama Teacher; *b:* Madisonville, KY; *ed:* (AA) Liberal Art, Hopkinsville Comm Coll 1968; (BA) Ed, Univ of KY 1970; (MA) Ed, 1976, (MA) Ed, 1985 Murray St Univ; *cr:* 7th/8th Grade Teacher Hanson Sch 1971-76, 1979-86; 7th-9th Grade Teacher Lakenheath Amer Jr HS 1976-79; Cnslr Educl Talent Search 1986-87; Part-Time Instr Madisonville Comm Coll 1986-; 9th/11th/12th Grade Teacher Madisonville-North Hopkins 1987-; *ai:* Drama Coach; Educl Talent Search Spon; Channel 2 News Crew; NEA, KY Ed Assn; HCEA Building Rep; Alpha Delta Kappa (Charter Mem, Recording Secy 1986-87) 1986-; Footlight Players (Exec Bd 1986-, Secy 1990, Mem) 1971-; Purchase Area Writing Project 1989; South Cntrl Bell Grant; Outstanding Elem Teachers of Amer 1972; *office:* Madisonville-North Hopkins HS 4515 Hanson Rd Madisonville KY 42431

NITTO, JOSEPH ANTHONY, Computer/Health Teacher; *b:* Jersey City, NJ; *m:* Patricia Fitzgerald; *c:* John, Maryanne, Lori, Patti; *ed:* (BS) Elem Ed, St Peters Coll 1970; (MA) Human Dev, Fairleigh Dickinson 1974; Cmptr Trng, E Stroudsburg Univ 1985; *cr:* 5th/8th Grade Teacher Mt Carmel Sch 1968-70; 6th Grade Teacher 1970-85, Kndgtn-8th Grade Teacher/Cmptr Coord 1985- Hackettstown Mid Sch; *ai:* Girls Track & Field Team, Cross Cntry Coach 1975-79; Hackettstown Ed Assn VP 1978-80; US Coast Guard Radarman 2nd Class 1963-67; Liberty Township Bd of Ed Elected Mem 1976-82; NJ Governors Teacher Recognition Awd 1989-; NJ St Minigrant Awd for Innovative Teaching Ideas 1976; *office:* Hackettstown Mid Sch 500 Washington St Hackettstown NJ 07840

NIX, ELIZABETH K., Science Teacher; *b:* Adrian, MI; *m:* Gary T.; *c:* Alisha A.; *ed:* (BA) Scndry Ed/Bio, 1973; (MS) Scndry Ed/Bio, 1976 Univ of North AL; *cr:* 7th/8th Grade Sci Teacher Haleyville City Schls 1973-90; *ai:* Natl JR Honor Society Spon; Sci Olympiad Rgnl/St Coach; Haleyville Ed Assn 1973-90; AL Ed Assn 1973-90; NEA 1973-90; Natural His Organization 1989-90; Baptist Women Mission Organization Study Chm 1987-90; Yrbk Dedication 1987-88; *office:* Haleyville H S 20st Haleyville AL 35565

NIX, EUPLE LEE BAUGHN, Third Grade Teacher; *b:* Carbon Hill, AL; *w:* James Edward (dec); *c:* Jearldine Nix Kane, Sheila Nix Franklin, Karen Nix Darty (dec), Kathryn Nix Ripley; *ed:* (BA) Elem Ed, Walker Coll 1965; (BS) Elem Ed, 1967, (MA) Elem Ed, 1974 Univ of AL; Wkshps In Service Ed; Univ of AL; *cr:* Self Contained 3rd Grade Classroom Teacher Caron Hill Elem Sch 1967-87; *ai:* NEA, AL Ed Assn 1967-88; Carbon Hill Local Ed 1967-87; *home:* PO Box 933 Carbon Hill AL 35549

NIX, SUE JACOBY, 6th Grade Elementary Teacher; *b:* Peekskill, NY; *m:* Ronald J.; *c:* Jeffrey Krakowka, Carrie Krakowka, Andrew Krakowka; *ed:* (AA) Liberal Art, Jefferson Comm Coll 1969; (BA) Elem Ed, Oswego St Univ 1972; Grad Stud SUC Oswego *cr:* 4th Grade Teacher Kingsford Park Sch 1972-73; 6th Grade Teacher Fitzhugh Park Sch 1973-; *ai:* Oswego City Sch Dist Wellness Prgm Chairperson; Dist Liaison Comm Rep; Fitzhugh Park Sch Sci Coord; Trout Unlimited Secy 1984-87; Oswego YMCA Aerobic Instr; OCTA Summer Grants in Curr Writing & Spelling 1988, Sci 1986, Health & AIDS Curr 1987; *office:* Fitzhugh Park Sch E Tenth And Bridge Sts Oswego NY 13126

NIXON, CAROLYN SUE, Doctoral Student; *b:* Rover, MO; *m:* Gregory; *c:* Donna Walker, Laura Walker, Darren, Scott; *ed:* (BS) Comm Disorders, 1980, (MS) Elem Ed, 1985 SW MO St Univ; Working Towards PhD Spec Ed, Univ of MO Columbia; *cr:* Teacher Dallas Cty R-I Sch Dist 1980-81, Half Way R-III Sch Dist 1981-89; Doctoral Stu Univ of MO Columbia 1989-; *ai:* Coll of Ed Grad Stu & External Relations Comm; Stu Cncl for Exceptional Children MO Fed Bd Rep 1989-; MO Fed Cncl for Exceptional Children (Legislative Comm, Newsletter Ed); CEC (Teacher Ed Division, Early Chldhd Division, Assn for Gifted Division) 1989-; MO St Teachers Assn 1980-89, SW Dist Educator of Yr Nom 1987-88; Halfway R-III Cmmty Teachers Assn (Pres 1987-88, VP 1986-87, Treas 1985-86) 1981-89; Dallas Cty R-III Cmmty Teachers Assn 1980-81; Buffalo PTA (Pres 1982-84, Treas 1981-82, 1984-85, Membership Comm Chairperson, Public Relation Comm Chairperson, Communication Comm Chairperson, Newsletter Ed) 1980-86; Dallas Cty Child Welfare Advisory Bd; Dallas Cty Park Bd 1988-; Church of Christ Mem; Grad Asst SW MO St Univ 1984-85; Nom MO Teacher of Yr 1987-88; Nom Natl PTA Educator of Yr 1987-88; Excl in Ed Incentive Grant Awd 1987-88; Teaching/Research Fellowship Univ of MO 1989-; Whos Who Among Stus in Amer Univs & Colls 1989-; Outstanding Young Women of America 1983; Numerous Presentations & Wkshps 1988-; *home:* Rt 2 Box 200 Elkland MO 65644

NIXON, GEORGE E., Mathematics Teacher; *b:* Morristown, NJ; *m:* Linda Euchardt; *ed:* (AB) Russian Area, Rutgers Univ 1962; (MA) Russian, 1971, (MA) Math, 1978 NY Univ; *cr:* Math Teacher Morris Knolls HS 1964-66; Capt US Army Intelligence 1966-68; Math Teacher Morris Knolls HS 1968-; *ai:* Asst Sr Class Adv; Assn Math Teachers of NJ 1964-; NCTM 1964-: Woodrow Wilson Fellowship; Dodge Grant Recipient; *office:* Morris Knolls HS 50 Knoll Dr Rockaway NJ 07866

NIXON, JAMES RUSSELL, Elementary Principal; *b:* Berkeley, CA; *m:* Julia Wendt; *c:* Laura, Rebecca; *ed:* (BA) Theology/Eng, Hanover Coll 1973; (MAT) Elem Ed, Northwestern Univ 1976; (EDS) Sch Admin, Ball St Univ 1988; Gifted & Talented, Univ of Purdue; *cr:* Teacher Bluffton-Harrison 1977-84; Prin Sch City 1984-86, Garrett-Keyser-Butler Schls 1986-89, E Noble Sch Corp 1989-; *ai:* NAESP, IAEMSP, ASCD 1984-; Presbyn Church (Elder, Choir Mem, Soc Stud Teacher) 1981-84; Garrett Chamber of Commerce; Gifted Ed Dev Grants; *office:* Kendallville Cntrl Elem Sch Diamond at Riley St Kendallville IN 46755

NIXON, KIMBERLEE ANNE (PARDON), Third Grade Teacher; *b:* Roseburg, OR; *m:* David A.; *ed:* (BA) Elem Ed, NW Nazarene Coll 1980; Grad Courses Boise St Univ & Univ of ID; *cr:* 3rd Grade Teacher Linder Sch 1980-81, Indian Creek 1981-; *ai:* Alpha Delta Kappa 1986-.

NIXON, MARY LOUISE RICH, 5th Grade Teacher; *b:* Asheboro, NC; *m:* Sammy K.; *ed:* (BS) Elem Ed, Appalachian St Univ 1969; Teacher Old Providence Sch 1970, Franklinville Sch 1970-; *ai:* Steering Comm Chairperson; Southern Assn of Colls & Schls; Comm Mem Math/Plans/Priorities; NEA 1981-; NC Ed Assn 1981-; Franklinville Sch/Randolph Cty Schls Distinguished Educator Awd 1984-85 & 1986-87; Mem 4-H Youth Advisory Bd 1989-; *office:* Franklinville Sch PO Box 258 Pine St Franklinville NC 27248

NIXON, WILLIAM, Industrial Arts Dept Chair; *b:* Easton, PA; *m:* Carol Hamlen; *c:* Tracy, Brian; *ed:* (BS) Ed, Temple Univ 1983; (MED) Ed/Supervision, E Stroudsburg Univ 1986; Journeyman Electrician, Stu Cncl Adv, Voc Ed, Blue Seal Stationary Engr; *cr:* Electricians Mate 2nd Class US Navy 1967-71; Stationary Engr Jersey Cntrl Power & Light Company 1972-74; Teacher Le High Cty Voc Tech Sch 1974-83; Teacher/Dept Chm/Adv Phillipsburg HS 1983-; *ai:* Stu Cncl Adv; Almost Anything Goes Adv; NJ Prins Assn Mem; Pilgrim Presbyn Church Elder 1987-; Sch Act Almost Anything Goes Grant; *home:* 626 Youngs Rd Phillipsburg NJ 08865

NOACK, HERBERT A., Science Teacher; *b:* Scranton, PA; *m:* Judith Hays; *c:* Alison, Faith; *ed:* (BA) Ed Psych, Barrington Coll 1962; Grad Sch Newark St 1970-72; Cert Sci Teaching Trenton St 1973-74; *cr:* Grad Asst Barrington Summer 1962; Teacher Lakewood Public Schls 1962-; *ai:* Hobley Sci Club; Rocket Club Adv; Sci Fair Coord; Gifted & Talented Ad Hoc Comm; Math Team Coach; Sci Resource Lab Room Organizer; NJEA, NEA, LEA 1962-; Ocean Grove Fire Dept (First Aid Sq Sgt 1972-73, Chief 1979), Citizen of Yr 1976; Neptune Twp Bd of Adjustment; Fire Dept Election Bd; Dist 4 Republican Committeeman; Recreation Coach; Umpire Sftbl; Cmmty Centennial Parade Chm 1976, 1986; *office:* Princeton Avenue Sch Princeton Ave Lakewood NJ 08701

NOAH, THELMA ANN (CAGE), 5th Grade Teacher; *b:* Detroit, MI; *m:* Pat; *c:* Deborah Noah Lucero, Terri Noah Fisher, Kelli; *ed:* (BS) Elem Ed/Sci, Univ of CO Denver 1973; Grad Studs; *cr:* 5th Grade Teacher 1974-76, 6th Grade Teacher 1976-89, 5th Grade Teacher 1989- Mc Elwain Elem; *ai:* 1st-6th Grade Stu Leadership Spon; Responsible Learner, Faculty Advisory, Five Star Sch Dist Math Comms; Kappa Delta Pi, CO Cncl of Intnl Rdng Assn, CO Lang Arts Society, NEA; *office:* Mc Elwain Elem Sch 1020 Dawson Dr Thornton CO 80229

NOAKES, BETTY LA VONNE-HAWKINS, Teacher; *b:* Oklahoma, OK; *w:* Richard E.; *c:* Michele M.; *ed:* (BS) Health/Phys Ed/Recreational Therapy, Cntrl St Coll 1962; (MED) Elem Ed, OK City Univ 1972; *cr:* Dir Recreational Therapy Lahoma Rehabilitation Hospital 1969-70; 4th Grade Elem Teacher Margaret Sheehy Elem 1970-71; Elem Teacher John Tyler Elem 1971-74; Pleasant Hill Elem 1974-; *ai:* Soc Stud Textbook Adoption Comm; Finder Womanhood Comm-Sorority; ASCD 1989; NEA 1970-; OEA 1970-; AAUW 1970-; NCTRC 1962-; Zeta Phi Beta Sorority 1969-; Urban League 1970-; YWCA 1960-; NACP; ASCD; Extensive Awareness Trng in Effective Sch Research *office:* Pleasant Hill Elem Sch 4346 NE 36th Oklahoma City OK 73121

NOBLE, BARBARA SEVERIN, Classroom Teacher; *b:* Akron, CO; *m:* Lanny M.; *c:* Richard M., Ryan W.; *ed:* (BA) Phys Ed, 1969, (MA) Rdng, Univ of N CO; *cr:* Classroom Teacher Yuma Mid Sch 1970-; *ai:* Girls HS Track 1974-81; 7th Grade Girls Vlybl 1984-; Civic Oration Contest Chairperson; Yuma Areans Theater Troup 1976-; United Meth Church; *office:* Yuma Mid Sch 500 Elm St Yuma CO 80759

NOBLE, FRAN ZUCKERMAN, Marketing Teacher; *b:* New York, NY; *m:* William C.; *ed:* (AA) General Stud, 1983, (AS) Fashion Mrktg, 1984 Daytona Beach Comm Coll; (BS) Aviation Bus Admin, 1986, (MBA) Bus Admin, 1988 Embry Riddle Univ; Voc Ed, Univ of Cntrl FL; *cr:* Academic Evaluator Embry-Riddle Univ 1984-87; Teacher Flagler Palm Coast HS 1988-; *ai:* Adv Distributive Ed Clubs America; Dance Line Dir; Stu of Week Selection Comm; Mrktg Ed Assn 1989-; *office:* Flagler Palm Coast HS P O Box 488 Bunnell FL 32110

NOBLE, FRANK JAMES, Fifth Grade Teacher; *b:* Holyoke, MA; *m:* Tommi L.; *c:* Cherise, Sherri, Heather, Thomas, Kaleb, Daniel, Saul; *ed:* (BS) Elem Ed, BHSU 1981; *cr:* 5th Grade Teacher Spearfish Schls 1982-; *ai:* Jr HS Wrestling, Track; Sci Comm; N Hills Rdng Cncl 1990; AAU Spearfish Pres Athletics 1986-; Spearfish Ed Assn, SD Ed Assn, NEA; Sid Grant SD His 1982, Rdng 1988, Sci 1989, 1990; *office:* East Elem Sch 400 E Hudson St Spearfish SD 57783

NOBLE, LINDA A., Physics Teacher/Sci Dept Chair; *b:* Cincinnati, OH; *ed:* (BS) Bio/Chem, Edgecliff Coll 1979; (MA) Physics/Scndry Ed, Xavier Univ 1988; *cr:* Sci Teacher Bishop Brossart HS 1979-81; Physics Teacher Lakota HS 1981-; *ai:* Jr Class & Wrestling St Spon; AAPT.

NOBLE, RALPH B., Fifth Grade Teacher; *b:* Rome, GA; *m:* Teresa R.; *c:* Sam, Caleb; *ed:* (BS) Elem Ed, Shorter Coll 1976; (MED) Mid Grades Ed, W GA Coll 1981; *cr:* Teacher Darlington Sch 1976-79, Parks Mid Sch 1979-82, Cherokee Elem 1982-; *ai:* Polk Assn Ed Pres 1984-85, 1986-87; GA Assn of Ed (Dist Dir 1987-, Exec Comm 1989-); Natl Ed Assn Rep Assembly Delegate 1984-89; *home:* 35 Gwen Dr Ringgold GA 30736

NOBLES, WAYNE, 6th Grade Teacher; *b:* Conway, SC; *m:* Karen Elizabeth Floyd; *c:* Adrianne S.; *ed:* (AA) Ed, 1974, (BA) Scndry Ed, 1975 USC-Coastal; (MED) Ed Admin, Univ of SC 1979; Prgm for Effective Teaching Cycle I & II; APT; *cr:* Teacher Conway Mid Sch 1976-; *ai:* 6th Grade Team Leader; Sch Advisory Comm Chm; SCASC Wkshp Cnslr; Stu Cncl Adv; Yrbk & Sci Club Spon; Trinity United Meth Church (Choir Mem, Youth Dir) 1989-; Teacher of Yr 1986; *home:* 4830 Youpon Dr Conway SC 29526

NOCCHI, MARTIN C., English Teacher; *b:* Hazleton, PA; *m:* Barbara Mc Carro; *c:* Teresa, Lisa, David, Martin, Daniel, Kathleen; *ed:* (BA) Eng, Kings Coll 1971; *cr:* Teacher W Hazleton Jr/Sr HS 1971-; *ai:* Hazleton Area Ed Assn 1971-; NEA Life Mem; Elks Club 1976-; W Hazleton JR HS Teacher of Yr 1981-; Yrbk Dedication 1981, 1990; *home:* 1102 Burton St Freeland PA 18224

NODEEN, ERMA FARQUER, 4th Grade/Gifted Care Teacher; *b:* Williamsfield, IL; *m:* Philip G.; *c:* John, Jerry, Linda; *ed:* (BS) Elem Ed, Bradley Univ 1971; Cert Gifted/Talented; *cr:* Teacher Galva Sch System 1971-; *ai:* Challenge Boosters Exec Comm; Phi Kappa Phi 1971-; Delta Kappa Gamma 1978-80; Writer Weekly Column Local Newspapers; Author of Book; Named Galva Author 1984; Edition of IL Authors 1985; *office:* Galva Mid Sch Morgan Rd Galva IL 61434

NOE, MARY ANN HENTSCHEL, English Teacher; *b:* Wisconsin Rapids, WI; *m:* Dennis H.; *c:* Joshua, Jessica; *ed:* (BS) Eng, Univ of WI Oshkosh 1970; (MST) Eng, Univ of WI Whitewater 1974; Grad Courses Ed & Eng; *cr:* 8th Grade Eng Teacher Woodside Sch 1969-70; Lang Art/Soc Stud Teacher Horning Mid Sch 1970-76; Eng Teacher Cath Memorial HS 1984-; Eng Methods Ed Lecturer Carroll Coll 1988-; *ai:* Yrbk Adv; NCTE, WI Cath Educators Assn; NEH Grant 1987-88; Presidential Scholar Outstanding Teacher Awd 1989; Univ of Chicago Outstanding Teacher Awd 1990; *office:* Cath Memorial HS 601 E College Ave Waukesha WI 53186

NOE, WANDA DEAN, Retired Elementary Teacher; *b:* Bellflower, MO; *m:* Wanda Dean Kamp; *c:* Judith, Tom, Judith L. Dillman; *cr:* Elem Teacher Jonesburg, Bellflower, New Florence; *ai:* MSTA Pres; CTA Pres; Order of Eastern Star Worthy Matron 1985-87; *home:* 216 E Spinsby Montgomery City MO 63361

NOEL, AMELIA GAIL M., Fourth Grade Teacher; *b:* New Orleans, LA; *m:* Willie Thomas Sr.; *c:* Chandra D., Willie T. Jr.; *ed:* (BA) Elem, Southern Univ New Orleans 1977; (MA) Admin/Supervision, Nicholls St 1981; Loyola & Delgado 1985; Prof Improvement Prgm; Wkshps Xavier Univ; *cr:* Helper St Anna Asylym 1974; 1st/2nd Grade Teacher Lafitte Elem 1978-84; 2nd Grade Teacher Woodmere Elem 1984-86; 6th Grade Teacher Woodland West Summer Sch 1986; 4th Grade Teacher Jean Lafitte 1986-; *ai:* 4th Grade Chairperson 1989-; Eng Chairperson 1987-89; Sch Chairperson; Young Authors & Young Writers; Progressive Baptist Church Choir Mem; Delta Sigma Theta; Honor Roll Schlsp; Magna Cum Grad; Poem Published; Black His Pageant Judge; Created Sci Scrapbook Units; *office:* Jean Lafitte Elem Sch 235 City Park Dr Lafitte LA 70067

NOEL, KARYL LYNNE, Health/Physical Ed Teacher; *b:* Sharon, PA; *ed:* (BS) Health/Phys Ed, Slippery Rock St Coll 1967; (MED) Health/Phys Ed, Univ of Pittsburgh 1977; PHD Prgm Admin of Phys Ed & Athletics, Univ of Pittsburgh; Several Courses & Univs; *cr:* Health/Phys Ed Teacher Bethel Park HS 1967, Wilkinsburg Elem Schls 1967-68, Peters Township HS 1968-; *ai:* Stu Against Drugs Spon; PIAA Vlybl Ofcl; Cardio Pulmonary Resuscitation Instr Amer Heart Assn; Stu Assistance Team; Girls Cross Cntry & Track Head Coach; Allegheny Cty Assn for Health, Phys Ed, Recreation & Dance (Pres Elect 1971-73, Pres 1972-73) 1970-; PA St Assn for Health, Phys Ed, Recreation & Dance 1963-; Amer Assn Health, Phys Ed, Recreation & Dance 1965-; ASCD 1989-; Peters Township Drug & Alcohol (Task Force 1987-, Comm 1988-); Amer Heart Assn Certificate Appreciation for Outstanding Service 1981; Amer Family Inst Valley Forge Gift of Time Tribute 1990; Mid Sts Assn Coll & Schls Certificate Recognition of Outstanding Service to Scndry Ed 1990; Guest Speaker PA Assn of Health, Phys Ed,

Recreation & Dance; Slippery Rock Coll Convention & IN St Univ 1977, Brentwood-Whitehall Kiwanis 1985, Baldwin Kiwanis 1990; *office:* Peters Township HS 264 E Mc Murray Rd Mc Murray PA 15317

NOEL, SHELLY CONWAY, 4th Grade Teacher; *b:* New Castle, PA; *m:* Jon David; *ed:* (BS) Ed, Youngstown St Univ 1972; (MA) Ed, Westminster Coll 1975; Wkshps Whole Lang & Trng, Cmptr Course; *cr:* Teacher Park Sch & Hillview 1973-; *ai:* Spelling & Lang Textbook Comm; Building Rep; NEA, PSEA; GCAEA Secy; Unity Church Deacon 1990.

NOEL, TREVIA GRIFFIN, Mathematics Teacher; *b:* Martinsville, VA; *m:* Wilbert E.; *c:* Tonya V. Griffin, Elijah H. Griffin; *ed:* (BS) Math, NC A&T St Univ 1971; Math/Sci Ed, George Washington Univ; Admin/Supervision, NC Agriculture & Tech Univ; *cr:* Teacher DC Public Schls 1973-89, P G Cty Public Schls 1989-; *ai:* Spon Sr Class Phelps Voc HS; Girls Bsktbl Coach Kramer Jr HS; Class Adv & Math Dept Chairperson Ft Lincoln Mid Sch; Ft Lincoln PTA Historian 1983-84; DC Public Schls Teacher 1984-89, Certificate of Achievement 1986; NCTM Participant 1986-87, Certificate 1987; Fletcher-Johnson Educl Center Summer Teacher 1984, Outstanding Service 1984; Washington Teachers Union Elections Comm Mem 1984-85, Service 1985; George Washington Univ Schlsp for Sci & Math Teachers 1987; Whos Who in America 1989-; *home:* 11916 Autumnwood Ln Ft Washington MD 20744

NOELKER, CECILY NIEBANK, Third Grade Teacher; *b:* Evanston, IL; *m:* James Eric; *c:* Alison M.; *ed:* (BS) Elem Ed, 1977, (MS) Elem Ed, 1980 IN Univ; Gifted & Talented Ed Cert Purdue Univ; *cr:* 1st Grade Teacher Crothersville Elem Sch 1977-80; 2nd Grade Teacher 1980-87, 3rd Grade Teacher 1987- Seymour Jackson Elem Sch; *ai:* Hoosier Awd Nominating, REACH Broad Based Planning Comms; Pi Lamda Theta Mem 1977-; IN Assn For the Gifted Mem 1983-; Environmental Ed Assn of IN 1980-; Friends of the Lib Pres 1980-81; Kappa Kappa Kappa VP 1982-83; Seymour Cmmty Concerts Mem 1985-87; Jackson Cty Unit of Indianapolis Symphony Society Mem 1982-; Purdue Univ Inst Summer Leadership Gifted Ed Schlsp 1982-; IN Univ Summer Rdng Conference Grant 1983; *office:* Seymour Jackson Elem Sch 1000 S Poplar St Seymour IN 47274

NOELKER, RUTH CONNOR, First Grade Teacher; *b:* Washington, MO; *m:* Dale; *c:* Amy, Bill, Bob, Sara, Elizabeth; *ed:* (BA) Soc Stud/Ed, Notre Dame 1973; Grad Stud Early Ed & Religious Ed; *cr:* 3rd-4th Grade Teacher Our Lady of Lourdes 1969-71; 2nd-3rd Grade Teacher St Gertrudes 1974; 3rd-5th Grade Teacher St Francis Borgia Grade Sch 1974-76; 1st/6th-8th Grade Teacher Our Lady of Lourdes 1976-; *ai:* Primary Coord; Sesquicentennial Comm 1989-; NCEA; *office:* Our Lady of Lourdes Sch Madison Ave Washington MO 63090

NOESSER, VINCENT PAUL, Girls Basketball Head Coach; *b:* Phoenix, AZ; *m:* Joan Cross; *c:* Vincent L., Donna S.; *ed:* (BSE) Phys Ed, S AR Univ 1962; Driver Ed; *cr:* Head Bsktbl Coach Wickes HS 1962-66, Blevins HS 1966-82; Head Girls Bsktbl Coach Prescott HS 1982-; *ai:* Girls All Star Comm Chm; St-Wide Athletic Comm; AR HS Coaches Assn (Mem, Girls Div Chm) 1987-89; Natl Fed of HS Coache Assn Charter Mem; United Meth Church Sunday Sch Supt 1978-; Prescott Sch System Finalist Teacher of Yr 1987; Wrote Lead Article St-Wide Act Bulletin 1987; St Outstanding Girls Athletic Coach 1978, 1987; St Outstanding Girls Bsktbl Coach 1978; All Star Girls Head Coach 1978; *office:* Prescott HS 736 Martin St Prescott AR 71857

NOFSINGER, JOAN M., Mathematics Teacher; *b:* Westernport, MD; *m:* Robert W.; *c:* Deborah Vickery, John A., Mary K. Kerns; *ed:* Cert Gifted Ed, WV Univ 1988; *cr:* Math Teacher Piedmont HS 1970-75, Keyser Primary Mid Sch 1975-; *ai:* Cty Math Curr Chairperson; Math Field Day Coach; Math Club Spon; WV Cncl Teacher of Math (Treas, VP), Outstanding Jr HS Math Teacher 1985; WV Math Field Day VP; St Peters Church (Lector, Eucharistic Minister) 1983-89; Co-Author; Mineral Cty Teacher of Yr 1985; Presidential Awd Excl in Math Teaching 1985; Outstanding Grad Frostburg St Univ 1986; *office:* Keyser Primary Mid Sch 700 S Water St Keyser WV 26726

NOGAY, JOSEPH F., JR., 7th-8th Grade Science Teacher; *b:* Sharon, PA; *m:* Nancy Clapper; *ed:* (BS) Comp Soc Stud, Edinboro St Univ 1976; Sci Cert, Youngstown St Univ & Kent St Univ; *cr:* Teacher Our Lady of Fatima 1976-77, La Brae Mid Sch 1977-; *ai:* Golf Coach; La Brae Teachers Assn, OH Ed Assn, NEA; Trumbull Cty Course of Study Comm 1988.

NOGLE, GEORGIA YVONNE (FULKS), Science Teacher; *b:* Chesapeake, OH; *m:* Richard H.; *c:* Richard T.; *ed:* (BS) Elem Ed, Rio Grande Univ 1967; C E Mendez Drug Trng Prgm; Clear Choices Me-ology Trng; Working Toward Masters Marshall Univ & Univ of KY; *cr:* 1st Grade Teacher Hannan Trace Elem 1962-63; 2nd Grade Teacher Middletown Elem 1963-66; 5th Grade Teacher Novi Elem 1968-70; 5th-8th Grade Sci/Health Teacher Hannan Trace Elem 1975-; *ai:* Sci Fair; Quiz Bowl; OH Ed Assn, NEA, Gallia Cty Local Ed Assn, NSTA; Delta Kappa Gamma Society Intnl, Beta Alpha 1988-; Martha Holden Jennings Scholar OH Univ; Teacher of Yr Gallia Cty Schls 1989; *home:* 1 Gallia St Crown City OH 45623

NOHAVA, PAULETTE MARIE (SERBUS), 1st Grade Teacher; *b:* Redwood Falls, MN; *m:* Stephen; *c:* Stephen, Sara; *ed:* (BS) Elem Ed, Mankato St 1973; Grad Courses St Cloud St; Hamline Univ; *cr:* 2nd Grade Paraprof St Peters Sch 1973-74; 1st Grade Teacher Holy Family Sch 1974-; *ai:* Accreditation Comm Team; Sci Curr Comm; Rdng Curr Comm; NCEA; Home & Sch Assn Hosp Chm 1983; Mrs Jaycees 1975-76; Team Leader 1985-86; Asst Princ 1987-88, 1989-; Stu Cncl Adv 1989-; *office:* Holy Family Schl P O Box 674 Albany MN 56307

NOHNER, SHIRLEY E., Campus Minister; *b:* Watkins, MN; *ed:* (BA) Theology/Scndry Ed, Coll of St Benedict 1983; *cr:* Religion Teacher 1983-86, Campus Minister 1986-88 Cathedral HS; *ai:* Chrstn Service Requirement for Jr & Sr, Peer Helper Prgm Cathedral HS; Distinguished Service Awd St Cloud Childrens Home 1987; Golden Service Awd Senator James Phelor 1989.

NOLAN, CAROL MURPHY, 5th Grade Teacher; *b:* Chicago, IL; *ed:* (BA) Ed/Speech, De Paul Univ 1958; *cr:* Announcer WTTW-Channel 11 1957-59; 2nd Grade Teacher Christ The King Cath Sch 1959-60; Substitute Teacher Chicago Bd of Ed 1960-61; 4th Grade Teacher Walter Scott Sch 1961-65, Horace Mann Sch 1965-68; 3rd/4th/5th Grade Teacher W K Sullivan Sch 1968-; *ai:* Chicago Teachers Union Delegate Rep 1964-78; Ind Cath Society Pres 1980-83; Mexican Cmmty Teacher of Yr 1976; *office:* William K Sullivan Elem Sch 8225 S Houston Ave Chicago IL 60617

NOLAN, ELIZABETH MAX, Fifth Grade Teacher; *b:* Petersbury, VA; *m:* Robert William; *c:* Robert W., Daniel O., Richard A., David A.; *ed:* (BS) His/Ed, Columbus Coll; *cr:* 3rd Grade Teacher 1959-64, 4th Grade Teacher 1964-81, Coach/Athletic Dir 1960-, 5th Grade Teacher 1981- St Anne; *ai:* St Anne Sch Sports Coord & Dir; Cath Athletic Assn Treas; Holy Childhood Chm; NCEA 1978-; Deanery Cath Parish Cncl (Pres 1978-80, Secy 1967-71); Cncl of Catholic Women Pres 1960-; Third Order of St Dominic 1960-; Eucharist Minister; CCD Dir; Greeter; Visitation Minister; Team Leader; Knights of Columbus Auxiliry.

NOLAN, JOSEPH A., Language Department Chair; *b:* Philadelphia, PA; *m:* Ann Marie Yerbury; *c:* Joseph A. Jr., Michael, Philip, Melissa White; *ed:* (BA) Philosophy/Eng/His, St Bonaventure Univ 1955; Bus, La Salle Univ; Ed CUNY & Montclair St; Theology, St Francis Coll & Holy Name Coll; *cr:* Manufacturers Rep John J Nolan & Assn 1958-59; Social Worker Cath Charities 1959-61; Teacher Cliffside Park HS & Wardlaw Sch & William Annin Jr HS & Bishop Ahr HS 1961-; *ai:* Ftbl, Bsktbl, Golf Coach; Bank Mortgage Dept; Lang Dept Chm 1979-; Foreign Lang Educators of NJ; Lions Club, Kiwanis Club; Mellutone Incorporated Manufacturers Rep of Yr 1970; *office:* Bishop George Ahr HS 1 Tingley Ln Edison NJ 08820

NOLAN, PATRICIA LAVELLE, 4th Grade Math/Science Teacher; *b:* Shreveport, LA; *m:* Earl Davis Jr.; *c:* Earl D. III, Randolph B.; *ed:* (BA) Elem Ed, SE LA Univ 1967; Natl Sci Fnd Math, Sci, Elem Specialist Prgm in E Baton Rouge Parish, Through LA St Univ; *cr:* 4th/6th Grade Teacher Walnut Hills Elem Sch 1967-69; 4th Grade Teacher 1969-88, 4th Grade Math/Sci Teacher 1988- Wildwood Elem Sch; *ai:* Natl Sci Fnd Grant; *office:* Wildwood Elem Sch 444 Halfway Tree Rd Baton Rouge LA 70810

NOLAN, SUSAN LONG, 4th Grade Teacher; *b:* Steubenville, OH; *m:* Jerry Lee; *c:* James W., Kathleen A., John P.; *ed:* (BA) Elem Ed, W Liberty St Coll 1977; Univ of Dayton, Steubenville Univ Campus, Mt of St Joseph Coll, New Philadelphia OH Campus; *cr:* 4th Grade Teacher St Anthony Grade Sch 1978-; *ai:* St Anthony Conservation Club Spon; WV Cath Ed Assn; St Anthony TAPA Secy 1988-91; St Anthony Church Lector 1988-; St Anthony Honor Society Selection Comm Chairperson 1983-89; St Anthony Golden Jubilee Comm 1988; Organized Project Hurricane Hugo Cmmty Drive; *office:* St Anthony Sch 1017 Jefferson St Follansbee WV 26037

NOLAND, PATTI M., Bio/Psych Teacher Dept Chair; *b:* Jonesville, VA; *m:* John R. (dec); *c:* Holly Nicole, Melody Noel; *ed:* (BS) Natural Sci, Univ of TN 1963; Wright St Univ; Univ of Dayton; Miami Univ; *cr:* 7th Grade Teacher Gen Sci Hampton Bennett Jr HS 1963-65; Frosh Bio/Gen Sci 1966-70, Bio Teacher 1977-82 Franklin Jr HS; Bio/Gen Sci Teacher 1983-85, Bio/Psych Teacher 1985- Franklin HS; *ai:* Sci Dept Chairperson; Sci Curr Comm; Steering Comm Mem North Central HS Accrediting Assn; United Ed Profession 1978-; Faith United Meth Church Admin Cncl Youth Cncl 1978-; *home:* 8076 E Lawn Dr Franklin OH 45005

NOLDEN, PATRICK DANIEL, PC & Basic Biology Teacher; *b:* Detroit Lakes, MN; *ed:* (BA) Life Sci, Univ of MN 1984; Earth Sci Coaching Certificate; *cr:* Bio Teacher Soldotna HS 1984-; *ai:* Head Hockey & Asst Ftbl Coach; *office:* Soldotna HS 425 W Marydale Ave Soldotna AK 99669

NOLDER, DAALA AMES, 5th Grade Teacher; *b:* Toledo, OH; *m:* Keith E. Sr.; *c:* Kimberly, Keith Jr., Kelleigh; *ed:* (BS) Elem Ed, Lindenwood Coll 1963; (MA) Elem Ed, 1983, Specialist Elem Curr, 1985 Univ of Toledo; *cr:* 3rd/5th/6th Grade Teacher Brentwood Sch Dist 1963-67; 3rd/5th Grade Teacher 1967-69, 5th Grade Teacher 1971- Anthony Wayne Sch Dist; *ai:* Chm of 5th Grade; Yrbk Adv; Phi Delta Kappa, Pi Lambdu Theta 1983-; Delta Kappa Gamma Pres 1978-, Schlsp 1983; Anthony Wayne Bus & Prof Womens (Pres 1975-77, Mem) 1970-83; *home:* 7539 Maumee Western Maumee OH 43571

NOLE, LOIS RAE, 3rd Grade Teacher; *b:* Auburn, KY; *ed:* (BS) Elem Ed, 1968; (MA) Elem Ed, Western KY Univ 1973; *cr:* Teacher Chandlers Elem Sch 1966; *ai:* TESA; Soc Stud Curr & Textbookadoption Comm; Inservice Comm; Sch Philosophy Comm; Sch Safety Comm; NEA; KEA; *home:* 113 Park St Auburn KY 42206

NOLES, JAMES CARL, Teacher-Counselor; *b:* Tonkawa, OK; *m:* Audrey Nadine Edwards; *c:* James II, Christi; *ed:* (BS) Bus Admin, Panhandle St Univ 1960; (MS) Ed/Guidance/Counseling, SW St Univ Weatherford 1973; Advance Guidance & Counseling, Drug Ed & Law Enforcement, Sch Finance, Test Admin; *cr:* Teacher/Cnslr Channing Ind Sch Dist 1959-; *ai:* Dist Test Coord; Guidance & Counseling Services; Dist UIL Coord; Literary Speech Coach; Discipline-Management Comm; TSTA Lifetime Mem; NEA, W TX Speech Assn; Numerous Teaching Awds; *office:* Channing Ind Sch Dist 10th & Greenwood Channing TX 79018

NOLFF, DALE CHARLES, Financial Planner; *b:* Monroe, MI; *m:* Glenda M.; *c:* Kelly Peters, Kristy Peters, Karry Peters, Danielle; *ed:* (BS) Math/Earth Sci, Western MI Univ 1979; Rdng, Univ S FL; *cr:* 3rd Grade Teacher Harper Creek Cmmty Schls 1978-79, Lee Cty Sch Bd 1979-81; Merchandiser J C Penney Company 1981-83; Financial Planner Amer Financial Design 1983-; *ai:* Referee HS & Coll Bsktbl; NASD Mem 1985-; Invest America Dist Mgr 1984-89, Planner of Yr 1988; Vision Ministries Church, Ind Order of Foresters, Natl Assn of Private Enterprise Mem; *home:* 1502 NE 13th Terr Cape Coral FL 33909

NOLL, LINDA LARKIN, Former Grade School Teacher; *b:* Covington, KY; *m:* Kenneth R.; *c:* Adam K., Ashlie L., Amie L.; *ed:* (BA) Elem Ed, 1975, (MA) Elem Ed, 1979 N KY Univ; *cr:* 4th Grade Teacher 1976-78, 5th Grade Teacher 1978-80, 6th Grade Teacher 1980-86 Grandview Elem Sch.

NOLLMANN, JEAN LOUISE, Fourth Grade Teacher; *b:* Bryn Mawr, PA; *ed:* (BS) Elem Ed, Sioux Falls Coll 1967; Grad Stud Math, Spec Ed, Elem Ed, Lib Materials, Cmptrs, Chem, Ec; *cr:* Elem Teacher Cypress Sch Dist 1967-69; Educl Consultant Discovery Toys 1987-88; Elem Teacher Winner Sch Dist 1969-; *ai:* Piano Accompanist; Grade Sch Chorus; Instrumental Contest; Winner Ed Assn (Negotiations, Membership Comm, Pres, Secy, Rep, Assembly Delegate 1969-); SD Ed Assn Plains Exec Bd Mem 1987-89; SD Cncl of Teachers of Math 1986-; Winner Cmmty Playhouse 1986-; Boys Club of Amer Certificate of Appreciation; *home:* 533 W 6th Winner SD 57580

NOLT, JAMES L., 6th Grade Teacher; *b:* Reinholds, PA; *m:* Gail Gehman; *c:* Lisa Nolt Copenhauer; *ed:* (BS) Elem Ed, Millersville Univ 1968; Masters Equivalency Millersville Univ, Temple Univ; *cr:* 6th Grade Teacher 1968-, Head Teacher 1988- Lincoln Elem Sch; *ai:* Sch Safety Patrol & Dramatics Adv; Ephrata Area Ed Assn (Treas 1973-76, Mem 1968-); PA Ed Assn, NEA Life Mem; *home:* 222 Marion Terr Ephrata PA 17522

NOLTING, PAUL DAVID, Principal/Social Studies Chair; *b:* Sleepy Eye, MN; *m:* Sara Fiegel; *c:* Kristen, Erin, Laura, Paul; *ed:* (BA) Ger, Univ of WI Eau Claire 1977; (CRM) Theology, Immanuel Luth Seminary 1980; Grad Stud His; *cr:* Pastor St Pauls Evangelical Luth Church 1980-86; Instr/Prin Immanuel Luth HS 1986-; *ai:* Jr Var Girls Bsktbl Coach; Mission Society Adv; Chm of Publicity Comm; Bus Mgr of Journal of Theology; Excl in Ed 1988, 1990 Cmmty Awd; Writing Staff Journal of Theology.

NOMIKOS, SYLVIA ANNA, High School Math Teacher; *b:* Brooklyn, NY; *ed:* (BA) Speech/Theater, Brooklyn Coll 1971; *cr:* Teacher Argyrios Fantos Creek Amer Sch 1970-83; 5th Grade Teacher 1983-85, 4th-6th Grade Math Teacher 1985-87 St Demetrious Mid Sch; 8th Grade Eng/11th Grade Theater Teacher 1987-88, 7th-9th Grade Math Teacher 1988-89, 7th-9th Grade Math/11th Grade Theater Teacher 1989- St Demetrios HS; *ai:* Cnslr HS Applications; Chaperone; Spelling Bee & Eng Curr Coord; Sch Book Fair; Yrbk Photographer; Yrbk, Cheerleading, Newspaper, 11th Grade Adv; Dir Sch Musical Productions; Asst to Prin; Transportation Test Coord Adv to Safety Patrol; St Constantine & Helen Cathedral Ed of Church Magazine 1977-79; Teachers Assn of NY Educator of Yr 1982; Dir Plaques 1983, 1985, 1987; PTA Awd of Service 1983; Sch Appreciation Awd 1981; *home:* 1447 E 49th St Brooklyn NY 11234

NONNEMACHER, CLARENCE MARTIN, Social Studies Teacher; *b:* Brooklyn, NY; *m:* Betty J. Brandenburg; *c:* Stephanie Meyer; *ed:* (BA) His/Phys Ed, E KY Univ 1949; Grad Stud; *cr:* Teacher/Coach Irvine HS 1950-53, Montpelier HS 1953-56, Bexley HS 1956-58; Coach 1960-67, Teacher 1960- Hilliard Jr HS; *ai:* Letter Club Spon, Salary & Building Comm; Ftbl, Bsbl, Bsktbl Coach; NEA 1950-; OH Ed Assn 1953-; F&A Masonic Lodge; Right Angle Club 1937-; Amigo Club 1990; *office:* Hilliard City Schls 5380 Scioto Darby Rd Hilliard OH 43026

NOOK, EULA ANDERSON, Language Arts Teacher; *b:* Hamburg, IA; *m:* Dale A.; *c:* Roger, Mark A., Brian C.; *ed:* (BS) Elem Ed, NE St Teachers 1955; (MA) Elem Ed, Morningside 1973; Numerous Courses; *cr:* 3rd Grade Teacher Dunlap Public 1962; 6th Grade Teacher Fountain Valley 1965-68; 4th Grade Classroom Instr Battle Creek Cmmty 1968-70; 7th-8th Lang Art Teacher Galva Holstein 1970-; *ai:* Building Head Prin; Jr HS Spelling Bee Coord; Citizens Advisory & Curr Comm; NEA Lifetime; IA Ed Assn 1968-; Galva-Hosltein Ed Assn (Pres 1974, Secy, Treas 1975-82); Cmmty Club 1987-; BSA Den Mother 1960-70; Luth Bible Camp Ambassador 1987-; Sunday Sch Supt Church Cncl; *home:* 111 E 2nd Box 545 Holstein IA 51025

NOONAN, JAMES EDWARD, Jr HS Mathematics Teacher; *b:* Dubuque, IA; *m:* Kristine E. Koob; *c:* Sean, Molly, Erin; *ed:* (BA) Ec, Loras Coll 1969; Peer Helper 1980; Teacher Leadership 1982; Stu At Risk 1989; *cr:* Soc Stud Teacher St Anthonys Grade Sch 1969-76; Rdng Teacher West Dubuque Dyersville 1976-80; Math Teacher West Dubuque Schls Farley 1980-; *ai:* Math Curr Comm Mem; Boys Head Golf Coach; Peer Helping Adv; West Dubuque Teacher Assn Pres 1984-85, Teacher of Yr 1988; IA Ed Assn,

NEA; Tri-St Ofcls Assn (Secy 1980-85, Pres 1985-); St Tournament Ofcl Ftbl, Boys & Girls Bsktbl; Officiated Finals Natl Cath Bsktbl Tournament 1986; *office:* Western Dubuque Jr HS 3rd Ave NE Farley IA 52046

NORD, PETER D., English Teacher; *b:* Cohasset, MA; *c:* Kevin, Valarie Mc Intyre, Nicole; *ed:* (BS) Eng, Bridgewater St Coll 1963; (MALS) Wesleyan Univ 1967; Master of Liberal Arts, Boston Univ Summer Prgm 1971-76; Teacher Writing Wkshp Univ of MA Summer Prgm 1986; Ind Study Master of Arts Prgm Lesley Coll 1989-; *cr:* Eng Teacher Dighton-Rehoboth Regional HS 1963-65, Hingham HS 1965-66, Scituate HS 1966-; *ai:* Yrbk Adv; Cmmty Service Supervisory Teacher; Sch Improvement Cncl; Chm Steering, Curr Dev Comm; Faculty Advisory Cncl & Senate; NEA, MA Teachers Assn 1963-; NCTE 1975-; Scituate Teachers Assn Exec Bd; Disabled Amer Veterans Commanders Club; US Marine Corps Veteran; NEASSC Self-Evalution; Teacher of Month; Univ of MA Writing Project; Project Interact; *home:* 15 Riverview Pl PO Box 9 North Scituate MA 02060

NORDELL, GERALDINE THOMPSON, Third Grade Teacher; *b:* Omaha, NE; *m:* Robert H. Jr.; *c:* Robert III, Amy Purdy; *ed:* (BS) Elem Ed, Univ of NE Omaha 1957; Grad Stud; *cr:* 3rd Grade Classroom Teacher Omaha Public Sch 1957-62; Pre-Sch Teacher YWCA 1966-69; K-3rd Grade Classroom Teacher Dist 15 Sch 1973-77; 3rd Grade Classroom Teacher Valley Public 1978-; *ai:* Teacher Evaluation Comm Mem; NEA, NSEA; VEA Secy 1986-87; Certificate of Excl 1985.

NORDGREN, LYNN LIZBETH, Fourth Grade Teacher; *b:* Mankato, MN; *c:* Nathan; *ed:* (BS) Elem Ed/Spec Ed, Mankato St Univ 1975; Experiential Ed, Mankato St Univ; *cr:* 4th Grade Regular Ed/4th-6th Grade EMR Intermediate Teacher 1976-79, 4th-6th Grade Rdng/Math Teacher 1980-81 Lincoln Elem; K-2nd Grade Teacher/EMR Primary Standish Elem 1981-82; 4th Grade Teacher/Omega Math Lab Holland Sch 1982-83; K-6th Grade Teacher of Gifted & Talented/Chapter I Olson Elem 1982-88; 3rd/4th Grade Teacher Minneapolis Public Sch Acad 1988-; *ai:* Chairperson Staff Dev, Five With Five Dist, Fine Art 1985-89, Assemblies 1986-89, Staff & Prgm Dev 1983-, Chairperson Soc Comm 1982-; Lang Art Resource Person 1984-88; Reward Day Prgm, Sch Patrol 1986-87, Sch Store Coord 1986-88; Parent Liaison Chapter I Olson Sch 1987-88; Resource Person Gifted/Talented 1983-; Dist Task Force; World Festival Days 1988-89 Creator & Coord; Minneapolis Fed of Teachers, Minneapolis Cncl Teachers of Math, Minneapolis Cncl Teachers of Sci, ASCD; PTA Bd Mem 1986, 1988-89; The Holiday Project (Chairperson 1987-89, Volunteer Coord 1985-87, Visits Coord 1985-87); Teacher Venture Fund Awd & Grant 1985-87; MN Energy Awd & Minigrant 1990; Presentor MFT St & Natl Quest Convention 1989, MN Gifted/Talented St Convention 1989; NAACP Cable TV Prgm Guest 1989; Minneapolis Urban League Conference on Sci/Math Ed 1988-89; Trainer Nominal Group Processing MFT 1989; Minigrant MN Environmental Sci Fnd Math/Sci Laboratory 1989-; Restructuring Conference 1990; Gender Fair Focus 1989; *office:* Minneapolis Public Sch Acad 919 Emerson Ave N Minneapolis MN 55411

NORDSTEN, MICHAEL JOHN, German Teacher; *b:* Springfield, OR; *ed:* (BA) Ger, OR Coll of Ed 1982; 5th Yr, Eastern WA Univ 1988; *cr:* Math/Ger Teacher James Monroe Jr HS 1982-84; Ger Teacher Hanford Scndry Sch/Richland HS 1984-; *ai:* Ger Club; Study Skills Comm; Schls of the 21st Century; Instructional Materials Comm; WA Assn of Foreign Lang Teachers; ASCD; Currently Leader Organzation Ger Teachers Tri-Cities Supported by Goethe Inst Seattle; *office:* Hanford Sec Sch & Richland H S 450 Hanford St Richland WA 99352

NORDSTROM, JEANNE BOLYARD, Sixth Grade Teacher; *b:* Springfield, IL; *m:* Jeff; *ed:* (BA) Ed, Earlham Coll 1971; (MS) Ed, IN Univ & Purdue Univ 1982; Post Masters Work; *cr:* Teacher Arthur Morgan Sch 1971-72; Elem Teacher Centerville-Abington Schls 1972-73, N Scott Schls 1973-77; Adjunct Professor IN Univ East 1982-87; Elem Teacher Tri Village Schls 1977-; *ai:* Phi Lambda Theta 1982; *office:* Tri Village Intermediate Sch S Main St Hollansburg OH 45332

NORKUS, PATRICIA LYNN, High School Art Teacher; *b:* Pittsburgh, PA; *ed:* (BS) Art Ed, Indiana Univ of PA 1972; Art, Tyler Univ & Alfred Univ; Cmptr Literacy Point Park Coll; Ed Penn St; Art Ed Univ of Pittsburgh; *cr:* Elem Art Teacher 1972-78, HS Ceramics Teacher 1979-83, HS Art/K-6th Grade HS Art/Cmptr Teacher 1984-85, HS Drawing/Painting Teacher 1986- Fox Chapel; *ai:* Spon of F C Crew Club; Set Designer & Painter for Musical; Responsibility Trng & Mini Grant Selection Comm; Fox Chapel Ed Assn Pres Elect 1988-; Festival 87 Planning Comm; Mini Grant Recipient for Art Billboards & Calendar; Art Dept Head 1984-89; *office:* Fox Chapel Area Sch Dist 611 Field Club Rd Pittsburgh PA 15238

NORMAN, CHARLOTTE PARRIS, English Teacher; *b:* Shelby, NC; *m:* John C.; *c:* Garrett C.; *ed:* (BA) Eng, Univ NC Asheville 1977; Grad Work Guidance & Counseling; *cr:* Eng Teacher/Suspension Coord E Rutherford HS 1977-; *ai:* Peer Helpers & Beta Club Spon; Hi-Q Team Coach; Faculty Coord for NCTE Writing Awds; Mc Nair Schlsp Comm Mem; NC Teachers of Eng 1988-; Sunday Sch VP 1989-; Your Gym (Aerobics Coord, Supvr) 1986-; Cty Curr Comm; Nom E Rutherford Teacher of Yr 1989-; *home:* 123 Aaron Dr Shelby NC 28150

NORMAN, DONNA VICKERY, Asst Principal for Instruction; *b:* Atlanta, GA; *m:* Michael Franklin; *c:* Kayla E., Joshua F.; *ed:* (BS) Phys Ed/Health, 1976, (MS) Mid Grades Math/Sci, 1978, (ES) Mid Grades Math/Sci 1985 GA SW Coll; Leadership in Supervision, Univ of GA 1986; *cr:* 4th-5th Grade Lang Art/Math Teacher South Elem 1976-78; 6th Grade Math/Sci Teacher Radium Springs Elem 1978-79, Morningside 6th Grade Center 1979-81; 6th Grade Lang Art/Math/Sci Teacher Sarah Cobb Elem 1981-86; Asst Prin for Instruction Staley Mid Sch 1986-; *ai:* Permanent Record Comm Chm; Oral Interpretation Comm; Asst Prin for Instruction; Academic Bowl Teams; Beta Club; One Act Play; GA Cncl of Teachers of Math, Prof Assn of GA Educators, GA Mid Sch Assn, Assn of Supervision & Curr Dirs; Kappa Delta Alumni Assn VP 1982-85, Alumni of Yr 1985; Organized & Compiled Application Which Helped Staley Mid Sch Achieve GA Sch of Excl & Nom for Natl Sch of Excl; Whos Who in American Education; *home:* Rt 2 Box 122A Pelham GA 31779

NORMAN, JUDY CAROL, 7th-9th P E/9th Grade Coach; *b:* Post, TX; *ed:* (BS) Phys Ed/Health, TX Tech Univ 1976; *cr:* Teacher/Coach Carroll Thompson Jr HS 1976-78, W B Atkins Jr HS 1978-; *ai:* Girls Vlybl/Bsktbl/Track Coach; TAHPER; NEA/TSTA; TX Girls Coaches Assn; PTA; United Meth Women; United Meth Church Admin Bd; United Meth Church Commission on Missions; Teams Won Eight Bkstbl City Championships; Three Track City Championships; Two Vlybl City Championships; *office:* Atkins Jr H S 5401 Ave U Lubbock TX 79412

NORMAN, MICHAEL DAVID, Fourth Grade Teacher; *b:* Hartford, CT; *m:* Mary Marshall; *c:* Samuel, Lawrence; *ed:* (BA) Hist, Univ of CT 1960; (MS) Soc Sci, Cntrl Ct St Coll 1972; Educl Admin, Univ of CT 1976; *cr:* Teacher Morgan Sch 1965-67, Duckley 1968-74, Keeney St Sch; *ai:* Cmptr Curr Comm; Sci Curr/Soc Stud; Manchester Ed Assn (Political Action Chairperson 1982-86 & 1990/VP 1970-71); CEA; NEA; Temple Beth Sholom VP 1980-86; Lutz Jr Museum Treas 1972-74; ManchesteR Comm for Latchkey Children 1988-; Celebration of Excl Runner-Up for Stu Run Sch Store; *home:* 275 Timrod Rd Manchester CT 06040

NORMAN, RICK W., Earth Science Teacher; *b:* San Angelo, TX; *ed:* (BS) Earth Sci, Sul Ross St Univ 1980; Earth Sci Inst Prgms; Gifted & Talented Trng; *cr:* Sci Teacher Lamesa Mid Sch; *ai:* Dir Earth Sci Club; Tx Utilities Ed & Campus Improvement Comm; Drug Free Sch Prgm Lamesa Ind Sch Dist; TX Earth Sci Teacher Assn Contributor 1987-90; Magazines & Newsletters Contributor; Nom Natl Presidential Outstanding Sci Teacher Awd 1989; Candidate Natl Sci Fdn Awds; *home:* PO Box 835 Lamesa TX 79331

NORMAND, MARCEL HENRY, Soc Sci/Religion Teacher; *b:* Arma, KS; *m:* Helen Virginia Rutledge; *c:* Timothy, Tyler, Teresa; *ed:* (BS) Soc Sci, 1957, (MS) Poly Sci, 1959 Pittsburg St Univ; Grad Work Soc Sci, Univ of WY Laramie, Newman Coll, Pittsburg St Univ; *cr:* Soc Sci/Eng Teacher Liberal HS 1957-58; Soc Sci/Fr Teacher Ft Scott HS 1960-65; Soc Sci Teacher Ft Scott Comm Coll 1965-80; Soc Sci/Religion Teacher St Marys-Colgan HS 1980-; *ai:* Sr Class Spon; Coord Project Graduation; KS Assn of Realtors Mem 1971-81; NEA, KS Ed Assn Mem 1960-75; Ft Scott Teachers Assn Pres 1964; St Marys Sch Bd Pres 1978-79; St Marys Sch & Home Assn Pres 1976-77; Fellowship Pittsburg St Univ 1958-59; Fellowship Univ of WY 1961; Precinct Committeeman of Arma 1965-79; Outstanding Young Teacher 1963; Whos Who Among Amer Educators 1970; Outstanding Educator in America 1972; *office:* St Marys-Colgan HS 212 E 9th Pittsburg KS 66762

NORRED, NORA HAWKINS, Social Studies Teacher; *b:* Roanoke, AL; *m:* Jimmy Jerry; *c:* Joseph G., Jennifer L.; *ed:* (BA) Soc Stud, La Grange Coll 1962; Grad Work, Univ of NC Greensboro; *cr:* Teacher Troup Cty HS 1962-63, Fayetteville St Sch 1963-66, Lake Placid Elem 1973-74; Teacher/Soc Stud Chairperson Lexington Sr HS 1977-; *ai:* Coach High IQ Team, Mock United Nations Team; Mentor Teacher; Quality Assurance Team; Senate Bill 2 Comm; NEA, NCAE 1977-89; NC Cncl of Soc Stud 1989; Delta Kappa Gamma Pres 1988-; Pauls Chapel UCC (Church Sch Teacher, Pastors Wife, Church Women, Pres, Youth Adv) 1974-; W Lexington Lions Club Citizen of Yr 1978; *home:* Rt 18 Box 3458 W Center Ext Lexington NC 27292

NORRIS, ANDREA HARRIS, Social Studies Teacher/Chair; *b:* Pitt Cty, NC; *m:* Bill T.; *c:* Beth, Allyson; *ed:* (BS) Soc Stud, E Carolina Univ 1965; Sch Base Management Trng Facilitator Natl Clearing House SBM; *cr:* Teacher Fike HS 1965-66, Camden HS 1966-70, Greene Cntrl HS 1970-73, 1974-; *ai:* Club Adv NHS; Quiz Bowl Club; Facilitator Greene Cntrl Teacher Leadership Cncl 1989-; Dist Leadership Cncl; Dept Head, Stu Teacher Supvr; NC Assn of Educators, NEA 1970-; NC Cncl of Soc Stud 1975-; Bonne Heuse Book Club Pres 1974-; Alpha Phi Pres of Corp Bd 1962-: Recreation Commission 1980-; Teacher of Yr Greene Cty 1976; St Nominee Governor Bus Awd for Excl in Teaching Soc Stud & Ec; E Carolina Univ His Symposium Speaker 1988; NC Center for Advancement of Teaching Participant; Delta Kappa Gamma World Fellowship Participant 1982-.

NORRIS, BARBARA ANN, Second Grade Teacher; *b:* Collins, MS; *m:* Dennis Frederick; *c:* Candace L.; *ed:* (BS) Elem Ed, Univ of S MS 1967; (MS) Elem Ed, William Carey Coll 1987; Counseling Classes, Rdng; *cr:* 1st Grade Teacher Mt Olive Sch 1967-68; 6th Grade Teacher Collins Mid Sch 1968-79; Kndgtn Teacher MS Barbaras Sch 1979-85; 5th Grade Teacher Seminary Attendance Sch 1985-86; 2nd Grade Teacher Collins Elem 1986-; *ai:* Club of 92 Spon; Okatoma Festival Float Comm Sch Chm; Cty Rdng Comm; Covington Cty Teachers Eng Writing Chm; Covington Cty Teachers Assn 1990; Covington Cty Teachers of Eng Chm 1990; MS MTAI Panel Expert 1985-; MS Cncl Teachers Eng 1990; MS Writing Across the Curr Wkshp Presentation; St Dept of Ed MTAI Panel Expert; MS Teacher Assessment Instruments Evaluator; *office:* Collins Elem Sch P O Box 160 Collins MS 39428

NORRIS, CAROL ELIZABETH, First Grade Teacher; *b:* Leavenworth, KS; *ed:* (BA) Bible, Cntrl Bible Coll 1963; (BS) Elem, Emporia St Univ 1965; Grad Stud Earaly Chldhd; *cr:* 1st Grade Teacher Easton Unified Sch Dist 1965-67; 2nd/3rd Grade Teacher Sisseton Public Schls 1967-71; 1st/2nd Grade Teacher Atchison Cty Cmmty Schls 1971-73; 1st Grade Teache East Charles Mix #102 1973-75; Easton Unified Sch Dist #449 1975-; *ai:* Negotiation/Book Adoption/Calender Adoption Comm; NEA 1965-; Easton Ed Assn 1965-67, 1975-; Sci Article Published; *office:* Easton Grade Sch Rt 1 Easton KS 66020

NORRIS, DENISE KELBAUGH, 8th Grade Earth Sci Teacher; *b:* Baltimore, MD; *m:* Michael Gene; *c:* John M., Christopher B., AmandA A.; *ed:* (BS) Bio, 1976, (BA) Span, 1976 St Edwards Univ; Composite Sci Degree; *cr:* Teacher Cutter-Morningstar 1979, Johnston HS 1980-85, Covington Mid Sch 1985-; *ai:* Just Say No Club & Sci Fair Spon; Austin Fed of Teachers 1980-83; TX St Teachers Assn 1983-86; TX Prof Educators Assn 1986-; Tracor Incorporated Covington Scholar 1986; *office:* Covington Mid Sch 3700 Convict Hill Rd Austin TX 78749

NORRIS, JEFFREY A., Social Studies Teacher; *b:* Mt Vernon, OH; *ed:* (AB) Eng/Soc Stud, Kenyon Coll 1976; OH St Univ 1975-76; OH Univ 1977; Univ NV Reno 1985; Truckee Meadows Comm Coll 1988; *cr:* Substitute Teacher Mt Vernon City Schls 1976-78; Teacher W Jefferson HS 1979-81; Part-time Instr Truckee Meadows Comm Coll 1986-87; Teacher Sparks HS 1983-; *ai:* Advanced Placement & Regional Citizen Bee Coord; Sr Class Adv; Faculty Senate; Dist Graduation, Washoe Cty Teachers Assn Awds, WCTA Dept Chm, Sparks HS Schlsp Comms; Washoe Cty Teachers Assn (Building Rep 1984-, NSEA Del 1983, 1985, 1988, Deputy Registor of Voters 1990), Washoe Cty Teacher of Yr 1989-; N NV Cncl for Soc Stud 1988-; Teachers in Politics; Journal of Divergent Amer Opinion Ed 1975-78; NV Mini Grant Excl in Ed 1987; W Jefferson Ed Assn Certificate Achievement for Distinguished Service ; Mt Vernon Educators Assn Distinguished Service Awd; *office:* Sparks HS 820 15th St Sparks NV 89431

NORRIS, LINDA FLEMING, First Grade Teacher; *b:* Columbus, MS; *c:* Elizabeth L., Mary K., Camden R.; *ed:* (BS) Elem Ed, 1966, (ME) Elem Ed, 1973 MS St Coll for Women; *cr:* Remedial Rdng Teacher Hunt Jr HS 1970, Union Elem 1971-73; 1st Grade Teacher Sale Elem 1974-; *ai:* MS Prof Educators 1985-; Columbus Classroom Teacher Assn 1983-; Fairview Baptist Church Teacher; *home:* 249 Lakeover Dr W Columbus MS 39702

NORRIS, MARY KATHRYN (BAKER), Chapter 1 Coord/Teacher; *b:* Newport, AR; *m:* Walter; *c:* Lucinda Norris Mc Clour, Kathryn, Drew; *ed:* (BSE) Elem, 1981, (MSE) Rdng, 1987 AR ST Univ; *cr:* 4th-6th Grade Math Teacher 1981-83, 5th Grade Teacher 1983-86 Weiner Elem Sch; Adult Ed Delta Vo-Tech 1984-85; Chapter 1 Rdng Teacher Weiner Elem Sch 1986-88; 3rd-10th Grade Chapter 1 Rdng/Math Teacher/Coord Weiner Sch 1988-; *ai:* Spelling Bee Coord; RIF Prgm; Parent Volunteer Prgm Coord; ASCD 1989-; Natl Rdng Cncl 1986-88; Adams Rib Pres 1983; Womens Chrstn Cncl Pres 1982; Serving on St Pre-Comm for Test Adoption 1991; *home:* P O Box 26 2nd St Weiner AR 72479

NORRIS, MAYNARD R., Teacher & Elementary Principal; *b:* Rochester, IN; *ed:* (BA) Bible, Cedarville Coll 1968; (MS) Elem Ed, St Francis Coll 1972; *cr:* Teacher N Miami Consolidated Schls 1968-71, Rochester Cmmty Schls 1971-74, W Boone Cty Schls 1975-76, Lafayette Baptist Sch 1976-77, Jackson Baptist Schls 1979-; *ai:* Prin Elem Grades K-6th; Big Brothers/Big Sisters 1982-80; Jackson Baptist Sch Teacher of Yr Awd 1982; *home:* 206 S West Ave Jackson MI 49201

NORSWORTHY, REMILLIE ANN (GOOD), French/English/Art Teacher; *b:* Presque Isle, ME; *m:* Willard Reid; *ed:* (BS) Scndry Ed/Eng, Univ of ME Presque Isle 1975; Univ of ME Orono; Univ of ME Farmington; Univ of New Brunswick Canada; St Thomas Univ; Univ of ME Portland/Gorham; *cr:* Teacher Cntrl Aroostook Jr Sr HS 1977-; *ai:* Hunter Safety Instr; Sr Class & Drama Club Co-Adv; Fr Club Adv; NHS Exec Cncl; Dist Inservice Comm Chairperson; Prgm of Studs & Academic Banquet Comm; Jr Ex-Coach; Local Foreign Lang Assn Poetry Competition & Foreign Lang Day Coord; Cntrl Aroostook Teachers Assn VP 1978-79; ME Teachers Assn 1977-; Foreign Lang Assn of ME 1988-; Regional Foreign Lang Enthusiasts Coming Together Chairperson 1986-89; Presque Isle Fish & Game Club (Exec Cncl 1988-89, Secy 1990); Natl Rifle Assn; Amateur Sftbl Umpires Assn (Secy, Assignor) 1983-88; Prof Artist Pet/House/Wildlife Portraits; Works Accepted St of ME Sportsman Show 1989, 1990; Shows at the Aroostook Medical Center 1986-88, 1990; The Eastman Gallery, Mars Hill 1989; Published Art 1988-89; *home:* RFD 2 Box 207 E Chapman Rd Presque Isle ME 04769

NORTH, CAROL ANN, English Teacher; *b:* San Antonio, TX; *ed:* (BA) Drama/Speech, Fisk Univ 1969; (MED) Curr Design Scndry Instr, Howard Univ 1985; Various Univs; *cr:* Eng Instr Univ of DC 1983-84, DC Dept of Corrections 1985-86, Frank W Ballow Sr HS 1987-89, Paul Lawrence Dunbar Sr HS 1989-; *ai:* Hospitality, Testing Comm; Ballou Stu Against Teen Pregnancy Drama Troupe; Helping our Parents Educate Team; Hum Festival Coord; Black His Month Coord; NCTE (Comm on Urban Ed 1988-, Presenter 1989) 1989; Intnl Trng in Comm 1988-, Judge Presenter 1989-; Educl Testing Service Reader for the Natl Teachers Exam 1989-; Natl Endowment for Hum Fellowship 1987; DC Cmmty Hum Cncl 1989; Cafritz Fnd Teacher Fellowship Oxford England 1989; Natl Endowment for Hum Fellowship 1990; *home:* 800 Taylor St NE Washington DC 20017

NORTH, CAROL KAY (URBAN), Teacher/Elementary Supervisor; *b:* Grand Junction, CO; *m:* Shayne Eugene; *c:* Stephanie; *ed:* (BA) Elem Ed, Cedarville Coll 1972; Open Court Rdng, Hyperactivity; Visual Auditory Kinesthetic Learning Seminar; *cr:* Teacher Dayton Chrstn Sch 1972-74, Southside Chrstn Sch 1974-78; Teacher/Elem Supvr Beth Eden Baptist Sch 1978-; *ai:* Elem Supvr; AACS Teacher of Yr 1989; *office:* Beth Eden Baptist Sch 2600 Wadsworth Blvd Denver CO 80215

NORTH, GAYLE FOZARD, Mathematics Teacher; *b:* Carbondale, IL; *m:* Mark H.; *c:* Mitchell Hayton, Eric Harris; *ed:* (BS) Math Ed, 1976, (MS) Scndry Ed/Math, 1984 S IL Univ; Advanced Math Courses; *cr:* Math Teacher Harrisburg HS 1976-77, Lewis Cty Schls 1977-78, Coulterville HS 1978-; *ai:* Coulterville HS Beta Club & Sr Class Spon; Spart HS Girls Track Asst Coach; Betsey Gimber Schlsp Selection Comm; PI Lambda Theta, Phi Kappa Phi, NCTM, IL Cncl Teachers of Math; *office:* Coulterville HS PO Box 386 Coulterville IL 62237

NORTHCUTT, STEVEN WAYNE, High School History Teacher; *b:* Mc Minnville, TN; *c:* Steffen, Jenee-Maree; *ed:* (BS) His, 1974, (MA) His, 1976, (MED) Ed Admin/Supervision, 1979 Mid TN St Univ; *cr:* 7th/8th Grade Lang Art Teacher Centertown Elem 1974-80; 6th-8th Grade His Teacher Dibrell Elem 1981-83; His/Contemporary Issues Teacher Warren Cty Sr HS 1984-; *ai:* Career Ladder Merit 1986-; *office:* Warren Cty Sr HS 200 Caldwell Mc Minnville TN 37110

NORTHRIP, ARVELLA (PITMON), English Teacher; *b:* Mill Creek, OK; *m:* Richel Ray; *ed:* (BA) Eng, E Cntrl St Univ 1963; Working Towards Masters; *cr:* Eng Teacher Mc Clave Public Schls 1963-65, Gate Public Schls 1965-67, Ringling Public Schls 1967-68, Ryan Public Schls 1968-; *ai:* Jr Class Spon; Ryan Ed Assn Pres 1988-89, Teacher of Yr; OEA, NEA; Assembly of God Church (Secy, Treas, Sunday Sch Teacher) 1987-; *office:* Ryan Public Sch E Hwy 32 Ryan OK 73565

NORTHROP, ARLENE LITTLE, Fifth Grade Teacher; *b:* Winchester, IL; *m:* Harry L.; *c:* Cynthia Schiber, Steven; *ed:* (BS) Ed, S IL Univ Edwardsville 1965; *cr:* 4th Grade Teacher 1966-67, 6th Grade Teacher 1967-89, 5th Grade Teacher 1989- Blair Elem Sch; *ai:* Delta Kappa Gamma 1989-; Amer Legion Auxiliary Pres 1966; *office:* Blair Elem Sch 300 Washington Ave East Alton IL 62024

NORTHROP, DIANE LENNICX, First Grade Teacher; *b:* Foley, AL; *m:* Medrick; *c:* Ty, Scott; *ed:* (BS) Elem Ed, Univ of S AL 1969; *cr:* 2nd Grade Teacher 1969-72, 1st Grade Teacher 1973- Fairhope Elem; *ai:* Supvr Extended Day Prgm; Baldwin Cty Ed Assn 1986-; Baldwin Cty Assn of Prof Educators 1973-86; South River Park Church of God (Sunday Sch Supt 1987-88, 1989-); *home:* 10751 Gayfer Rd Ext Fairhope AL 36532

NORTHSEA, STEVEN GEORGE, English/Journalism Teacher; *b:* Rockford, IL; *m:* Michael Rhea Rhodes; *c:* Jean, Layne, Daniel, Erin, Cole; *ed:* (BA) Elem Ed, 1968, (MA) Potentially Handicap Ed, 1970 Univ of S FL; (PHD) Educl Admin, Southwestern Univ 1980; *cr:* Teacher St Pauls Sch 1968-69; Admin Gables Acad of FL 1970-84; Teacher Marion Cty Sch Dist 1984-; *ai:* Athletic Bus Mgr; Asst Prins Detention Supvr; Quill & Scroll & Newspaper Spon; Adult Ed GED Instr; Homebound Teacher; LA ACLD Secy 1976-78; FL Rdng Cncl Secy, Treas 1985-87; IRA, NCTE, NCTM, NASSP; Riverland News Ed 1984-87; Masters Fellowship Potentially Handicapped Ed Dir of Yr 1976-78; *home:* 3517 W Cypress Dr Dunnellon FL 32630

NORTHWOOD, WILLIAM CAMPBELL, 5th Grade Teacher; *b:* Wilkinsburg, PA; *m:* Barbara Hempstead; *c:* William H., Rebecca S., *ed:* (BRE) Chrstn Ed, Baptist Bible Coll 1961; (MS) Ed, St Univ of NY 1965; Broome Cmmty Coll; *cr:* 4th Grade Teacher Floyd Bell 1961-81; Rdng Specialist Susquehanna Valley Central Sch Dist 1970; 5th Grade Teacher C R Weeks Elem 1981-90; *ai:* Chm Intermediate Multi-District Supt Conf; Windsor Teachers Assn 1961-90; Town of Conklin Zoning Brd of Appeals Chm 1970-90; Mem Cmmty Advisory Brd WSKG TV 1981-90; *home:* Tiffany Ave Rd 1 Box 286 Conklin NY 13748

NORTON, ELAINE CONNOLLY, 7th/8th Grade Lang Art Teacher; *b:* Charlotte, NC; *m:* Bobby G.; *c:* David G., Alyssa J.; *ed:* (BS) Ed, Gardner Webb Coll 1983; *cr:* Lang Art/Math Teacher East Jr HS 1983-; *ai:* Stu Cncl Adv; *home:* 325 S Center St Taylorsville NC 28681

NORTON, GEORGE R., Social Studies Teacher; *b:* Blackstone, VA; *m:* Mary Ellen Harris; *c:* Deena P., Kelli J.; *ed:* (BS) Health/Phys Ed, Troy St Univ 1963; (MS) Health/Phys Ed, Old Dominion Univ 1974; Grad Work Guidance, Counseling, Drivers Ed; *cr:* Teacher/Coach Milton HS 1963-72; Washington HS 1972-75, Pace HS 1975-84, Cntrl HS 1984-87, Pensacola Jr Coll 1985-87, Pace HS 1987-; *ai:* 11th Grade Class Spon; Bsktbl & Ftbl Coach; Fellowship of Chrstn Athletes; FL Coaches Assn 1963-85; Phy Ed Assn 1975-85; Teacher of Yr Pace HS 1980; Teacher of Yr Cntrl HS 1985; Kiwanis Club Awd 1968-69; *office:* Pace HS 407 Norris Rd Pace FL 32571

NORTON, MARGARET CRAIG HEDGEPETH, Biology Teacher; *b:* Raleigh, NC; *m:* Wilburn L. Jr.; *c:* Alvin C., Akuna L.; *ed:* (BA) Bio/Psych, NC Wesleyan Coll 1970; Grad Work Sci Ed, Univ of NC Chapel Hill; Mentor Teacher Trng; Supvr of Stu Teacher Trng; Bio Technology Trng; *cr:* Bio Teacher South Johnston HS 1970-71, Zebulon HS 1971-75; Life Sci Teacher East Millbrook Mid Sch 1975-78, West Millbrook Mid Sch 1982-86; Bio Teacher Apex Sr HS 1986-; *ai:* Field Trip Comm Mem; Prof Educators of NC 1989-; NCAE 197-78, 1982-88; Alpha Delta Kappa (Recording Secy 1990) 1987-; Mini Grant Awds 1984, 1987, 1988; Elem Sch Sci Fair Judge 1986-88; *office:* Apex Sr HS 1501 Laura Duncan Rd Apex NC 27502

NORTON, OAKLEY L., Honors Mathematics Teacher; *b:* Tucson, AZ; *m:* Sally O.; *c:* Escott, Cari, Trevor; *ed:* Intnl Affairs, Univ of Vienna 1954-55; (BA) Philosophy, 1956, Ed Credential Ed, 1957 Occidental Coll 1957; Math, Natl Sci Fnd, Univ of S CA; Cmptr Sci Prgm, Los Angeles City Coll; *cr:* Coord/Teacher of Gifted Burbank Jr HS Learning Center 1968-71, Area H Alternative Sch 1971-11, King Jr HS 1977-81; Math Chm/Teacher of Gifted Eagle Rock HS 1981-; *ai:* Magnet Math Chm; Spon Stu Cncl; Sch Leadership Cncl Faculty Rep; UTLA Sch Bd of Dir Mem; NCTM, CA Math Cncl, Los Angeles City Teachers of Math Assn 1969-, Outstanding Teacher Awd 1985; CA Gifted Educators Assn 1980-; CA Industry Ed Cncl Outstanding Teacher Awd 1980; Nom Eagle Rock HS CA Teacher of Yr 1988; John Hopkins Univ Cty Gifted Teacher Awd 1990; *office:* Eagle Rock HS 1750 Yosemite Dr Los Angeles CA 90041

NORTON, PATRICK KEVIN, Mathematics Teacher; *b:* Atlanta, GA; *m:* Becky Anne Boyd; *c:* Andrew K.; *ed:* (BS) Math Ed, Bob Jones Univ 1986; Working Towards Masters in Math Ed, Univ of GA 1990; *cr:* Math Teacher Monroe Area Comprehensive HS 1987-; *ai:* Harvest Baptist Church Youth Dir 1986-; Mu Alpha Theta Spon; *office:* Monroe Area Comprehensive HS Bryant Rd Monroe GA 30655

NORTON, SAMMYE RUTH, Mathematics Department Chair; *b:* Louisville, AL; *ed:* (BS) Bus Ed, Univ of Montevallo 1951; (MED) Ed/Math, Auburn Univ 1961; (AA) Ed/Math, Auburn Univ Montgomery 1976; *cr:* Teacher Robert E Lee HS 1957-; *ai:* NHS & Math Team Spon; Task Force Comm Math Mem; MCEA, AEA, NEA 1957-; ADK 1960-; Attended Grad Sch in Natl Sci Fnd Stripend; *office:* Robert E Lee HS 225 Ann St Montgomery AL 36107

NORVILLE, FLO P., 4th Grade Teacher; *b:* Sevierville, TN; *m:* Russell M.; *c:* Sandra K. De Bush; *ed:* (BS) Elem Ed, Univ TN Knoxville 1972; Grad Stud Ed; *cr:* Teacher Pi Beta Phi 1953-; *ai:* Sevier Cty Sci Textbook Comm Mem; NEA, TEA Rep, SCEA Rep 1953-; Natl Geographic Society; Womens Adv Comm of Sevier Cty Hosp; PTA 1953-; Teacher of Yr Sevier Cty 1980, Individual Sch 1989-; *home:* Rt 4 Box 598 Hilltop Gatlinburg TN 37738

NORWOOD, CECELIA LOUISE, 7th Grade Teacher; *b:* La Grange, GA; *ed:* (BS) Elem Ed, Radford Univ; Grad Stud Educl Admin, GA St Univ; *cr:* 7th Grade Teacher East-Point Elem Sch 1982-83; 5th/6th Grade Teacher 1983-84, 7th Grade Teacher 1984- Union City Elem Sch; *ai:* Sch Newspaper & Safety Patrol Spon; Discipline Comm Chm; PTA (Prgm Chm 1986-87, Inspiration Chm 1987-88) 1982-; Teacher of Yr 1986-87; Recipient of Fulton Cty Public Schls Fnd Mini-Grant for Sch Newspaper 1988-89; Fulton Cty Peer Asst 1987-89; GA Congress of Parents & Teachers Contributed to Ann Weeks Schlsp Fund for Music 1986-87; *home:* 3077 Vista Brook Dr Decatur GA 30033

NORWOOD, DOREEN JEANNE PENNIMAN, Home Economics Teacher; *b:* Oakland, CA; *c:* Suzanne Gionnoris, Leonard C., Patricia Walter; *ed:* (BA) Home Ec Ed, 1967, (MA) Child Dev/Family Life Ed, 1974 E MI Univ; Instruction Trng; Nutrition Ed Wkshp; Sewing Skills Seminars, Schoolcraft Coll; *cr:* Nursery Sch Teacher Oakland Unified Sch Dist 1956-58; Home Ec Teacher Flat Rock Cmmty Schls 1967-; *ai:* Soph Class Adv; Co-Dir Drama Club; Suicide Crisis Team; MI Voc Consumer Home Ec Standards Project Team; Competency Testing; N Cntrl Evaluation Comms; NEA, MEA, FREA (VP, Secy); Amer Home Ec Assn, Amer Sewing Guild, MI Voc Ed Assn; MADD; *office:* Flat Rock HS 28639 Division St Flat Rock MI 48134

NORWOOD, MACK M., Teacher/Coach; *b:* Macon, MS; *ed:* (BS) Phys Ed, MS St Univ 1984; Working Towards Masters Admin; *cr:* Teacher/Coach Pillow Acad 1985-; *ai:* Jr HS Ftbl, Bsktbl, Track Coach; Jr Hunting & Fishing Club, Sr Class Spon; MS Private Sch Assn, MS Coaches Assn Mem 1985-; *office:* Pillow Acad PO Box 1880 Greenwood MS 38930

NOSKOWIAK, PEGGY KILLOREN, English/Speech/Drama Teacher; *b:* Superior, WI; *m:* Robert P.; *c:* Julie F., Paul R.; *ed:* (BS) Eng/Speech, Univ of WI Superior 1970; Cooperative Learning, Creative Writing, Advocacy Mentally Handicapped, Acting, Theatre; *cr:* Jr HS Eng Teacher Albany Area Schls 1975-81; Eng Teacher Rocori HS 1981-82, Kimball HS 1982-83; Eng/Speech Teacher Holdingford Jr/Sr HS 1983-; *ai:* One Act Play Dir; Stu Assistance Comm; Class Adv; MN Educl Assn 1983-; Childrens Prgm of Northern Ireland Outstate Rep 1982-; Dist 19 Speech & Drama Coaches Pres 1989-; *office:* Holdingford Jr/Sr HS Holdingford MN 56340

NOUR, MARGARET ADAMS, 7th Grade Life Science Teacher; *b:* Atlanta, GA; *m:* George M.; *c:* George E., Kathleen E.; *ed:* (BA) Bio/Scndry Ed, West GA Coll 1970; Phys Sci 1985; Earth/Space Sci 1986; Life Sci/Health 1988; Sci & Cmptr Trng 1989; Supervising Teacher Course Interns FSU 1988; *cr:* 10th Grade Bio Teacher Newnan HS 1970-71; 7th Grade Life Sci Teacher Bowdon Elem Sch 1974-83; 8th GRADE PHYS SCI TEACHER 1984-86; 7th Grade Life Sci Teacher 1987 Raa Mid Sch; *ai:* Dept Chairman Sci Dept/Raa Mid Sch; Spon of Raa Mid Sch Sci Fair; Life Sci Textbook Adoption Comm-Leon Cty Schls; Leon Cty Teachers Assn 1984-; FL Teaching Profession 1984-; NEA 984-; FL Assn of Sci Teachers 1984-; 1977 Teacher the Yr-Bowdon Elem Sch; 1977 Runner-Up Teacher of Yr Carroll Cty; 1988 Teacher of Yr-Raa Mid Sch; 1989 Recipient of Mini-Grant from BEST Fund Leon Cty Schls; *office:* Agusta Raa Mid Sch 401 W Tharpe St Tallahassee FL 32303

NOVAK, BETH VAN ORMER, Former Teacher; *b:* Lancaster, PA; *m:* Michael David; *c:* Anne M., Michael V.; *ed:* (BS) Bible, Houghton Coll 1974; (MA) Ed, Millersville Univ 1979; *cr:* Jr HS Eng/Art/Elem Phys Ed Teacher 1975-78, 3rd Grade Teacher 1978-81 Lancaster Chrstn Sch; 6th Grade Teacher Faith Acad 1981-85; 6th Grade Art Teacher Lancaster Chrstn Sch 1985-89; *ai:* Manila HS Girls Cross Cntry Coach 1982-85; *home:* 101 Parkwood Dr Lancaster PA 17603

NOVAK, CARL MAXWELL, Mathematics Teacher; *b:* Charlevoix, MI; *m:* Kathy Mae Greer; *c:* Rachel M., Kayla M.; *ed:* (BS) Math, MI St Univ 1974; (MA) Ed Leadership, E MI Univ 1980; Mid Sch Cert; *cr:* Math Teacher St Louis Public Schls 1974-76, Tecumseh Public Schls 1976-; *ai:* MI Math Prize Competition Coord Tecumseh HS; NEA, Mi Ed Assn 1974-; Tecumseh Ed Assn 1976-; United Church of Christ (Diaconate Bd 1983-89, Pres 1985, VP 1984, Secy 1988-89); Tecumseh HS Teacher of Yr 1980, 1987, 1990; *office:* Tecumseh HS 307 N Maumee Tecumseh MI 49286

NOVAK, EDWARD F., Technology Education Dept Head; *b:* Cleveland, OH; *m:* Beth Patterson; *ed:* (BS) Ed, Berea Coll 1984; *cr:* Technology Education Dept Head Clarke Cty HS 1985-; *ai:* Odyssey of Mind; Epsilon Pi Tau 1985-; Technology Stu Assn; *office:* Clarke Cty HS Rt 3 Box 5578 Berryville VA 22611

NOVAK, RONALD F., Science Teacher; *b:* Chetek, WI; *m:* Janet K. Hullinger; *c:* Greg, Brad; *ed:* (BED) Broad Field Sci, Univ of WI Whitewater 1965; (MED) Admin, De Paul Univ 1968; (MS) Bio, Syracuse Univ 1970; N IL Univ & Miami of OH Univ; *cr:* Sci Teacher Downers Grove North/South HS 1965-; *ai:* IL Ed Assn (Pres 1971, VP 1970); Natl Sci Fnd Grants; Awd of Excl IL Math & Sci Acad; *office:* Downers Grove South HS 1436 Norfolk Downers Grove IL 60516

NOVAK, SUSAN MUNRO, 1st Grade Teacher; *b:* Antwerp, NY; *c:* Jessica, Clayton; *ed:* (AA) Liberal Arts, Cazenovia Coll 1968; (BA) Bio, SUNY Oswego 1970; (MA) Elem Ed SUNY Cortland 1990; Sci Ed, Syracuse Univ 1977-82; *cr:* Bio Teacher Port Byron Cntrl HS 1970-72; Sci/Planetarium Teacher 1977-84, 1st Grade Teacher 1984- E Syracuse Minoa Cntrl HS; *ai:* Lang Art Leader; NYSUT Building Chairperson 1977-; Lakecrest Womens Club 1979-; Natl Sci Fnd Grant Bio 1971, Geology 1979; *office:* E Syracuse Minoa Sch Fremont Rd East Syracuse NY 13057

NOVAK, TOMMY JAMES, Fourth Grade Teacher; *b:* Omaha, NE; *m:* Marilyn Kratzer; *c:* Cathleen C.; *ed:* (BS) Elem Ed, UNO 1969; *cr:* Classroom Teacher Pawnee Sch 1969-; *ai:* Track Coach; Stamp Club Adv; Head Teacher; NEA, NSEA; OEA Building Rep; PTA VP 1989-, St Life Recipient; TAC Natl Championship High Jump Coach; *office:* Pawnee Sch 7310 S 48th St Omaha NE 68157

NOVAK, WILLIAM, Elementary Teacher; *b:* Streator, IL; *m:* Janet; *c:* Amber, Megan; *ed:* (BS) Elem Ed., Oakland City Coll 1970; (MS) Ed, IN St Univ 1975; Reformed Theological Seminary; *cr:* 4th Grade Teacher Marlette Elem Sch 1970-71; 5th-7th Grade Math/Sci Teacher Cayuga Elem Sch 1971-72; 2nd/3rd Grade Teacher Crestview & Maple Park Schls 1972-; *ai:* Gideons Intnl; Pike Cty Right to Life; Magazines Articles Written; *home:* R 2 Petersburg IN 47567

NOVAK, WILLIAM ANDREW, English/Language Arts Teacher; *b:* Bobtown, PA; *c:* Wm., Leah, Deborah, Brian; *ed:* (BA) Eng, Waynesburg Coll 1960; Grad Stud WV Univ; *cr:* Eng Teacher Annapolis Jr HS 1960-62, Ben Franklin Jr HS 1962-64, Maple Town Jr/Sr HS 1964-; *ai:* Jr & Sr HS Var Girls Bsktbl Coach; PA St Ed Assn, NEA 1962-; SE Greene Ed Assn 1964-; *office:* Mapletown Jr/Sr HS RD 1 Greensboro PA 15338

NOVELLO, DORIS JEAN, Honors English Teacher & Chm; *b:* Youngstown, OH; *ed:* (BSE) Eng, Youngstown St Univ 1971; *cr:* Substitute Teacher Mahoning & Trumbull Counties 1971-78; 9th/11th Grade Eng Teacher Wilson HS 1979-81; 7th/8th Grade Eng Teacher Hayes Jr HS 1978-79, Princeton Jr HS 1981-; *ai:* Textbook Comm; Younstown Ed Assn 1973-; OEA 1973-; NEA 1973-; Eng Dept Chairperson (Wilson 1977-78, Hayes 1978-79, Princeton 1981-; *office:* Princeton Jr H S 2546 Hillman St Youngstown OH 44507

NOVELLO, RITA MAE (ROMEO), Spanish Teacher; *b:* Youngstown, OH; *m:* Daniel Michael; *c:* Derek M., Danielle M., Dale M.; *ed:* (BSED) Span, Youngstown St 1961; Grad Stud Universidad de San Carlos Guatemala 1962; Youngstown St Univ 1982-83, 1989; *cr:* Span Teacher Jackson-Milton HS 1961-66; Substitute Home Instr Girard HS 1966-80; Span Teacher Bristol HS 1983-88, Liberty HS 1988-; *ai:* Span Club Adv; Academic Alliance Steering Comm Youngstown St Univ; NEA, OH Ed Assn, Liberty Ed Assn, Delta Kappa Gamma; Liberty Band Boosters Pres 1983-84; Sigma Sigma Sigma; Doris Burdman Service Club VP; Youth for Understanding Public Relations 1986-; Youngstown Playhouse Membership Drive Top Salesperson; *home:* 1422 Sunny Dr Girard OH 44420

NOVITSKE, LINDA SUE (KOSOSKI), Learning Disabilities Teacher; *b:* Iron Mountain, MI; *ed:* (BS) Elem Ed, 1973, (MSE) Spec Ed, 1978 Univ WI Oshkosh; Grad Stud MSE Degree from Viterbo Coll; *cr:* 3rd Grade Teacher 1973-75, Learning Disabilities Teacher 1975- Victor Haen Elem; *ai:* Learning Disabilities Parent-Teacher Support Group; NEA, WEAC, KEA 1973-;

ACLD 1975-79; Games & Act Published in Early Yrs Magazine; *home:* 702 N Morrison St Appleton WI 54911

NOVOTA, MARLENE R., English/Language Arts Teacher; *b:* Rockford, IL; *m:* John B.; *ed:* (AA) Liberal Arts, Rock Valley Coll 1974; (BS) Eng, S IL Univ 1976; (MS) Educl Admin, N IL Univ 1989; *cr:* Eng/Lang Art Teacher Kinnikinnick Sch 1977-; *ai:* Drama Dir; Eng Curr Comm Chairperson; Gifted Curr Comm; Cheerleading Adv; ASCD, IL Assn Teachers of Eng, IL Ed Assn, NEA, Outstanding Young Women of America; *office:* Kinnikinnick Sch 5410 Pine Ln Roscoe IL 61073

NOVOTNI, CAROL A., ESEA Reading Teacher; *b:* Cincinnati, OH; *c:* Stephen; *ed:* (BA) Elem Ed, Coll of MT St Joseph 1963; (MED) Elem Admin, Univ of Cincinnati 1972; *cr:* 5th Grade S C Teacher Holy Family Elem 1963-64; 5th/6th/8th Grade Teacher St Dominic Elem 1964-71; Prin St Elizabeth Elem 1971-72; 6th Grade Teacher Kennedy Heights Elem 1974-77; 6th Grade Teacher 1977-89, 1st-3rd Grade ESEA Rdng Teacher 1989- Hays Elem; *ai:* Cincinnati Fed of Teachers 1988-; Archdiocesan Lay Teachers Assn Recording Secy 1968; *home:* 1114 Coronado Ave Cincinnati OH 45238

NOWAKOWSKI, PAMELA A., Business Education Teacher; *b:* Erie, PA; *m:* James Mark; *c:* Nicholas J., Joseph B.; *ed:* (BS) Bus Ed, Shippensburg Univ 1976; (MS) Bus Ed, Robert Morris 1983-85; *cr:* Secy PA Dept of Justice 1976-78; Bus Teacher Erie Bus Center 1977-, General Mc Lane HS 1978-79, Seneca HS 1979-; *ai:* FBLA; CORE Team Chairperson; PSEA, NEA, Tri St Bus Assn; *office:* Seneca HS 9770 Wattsburg Rd Erie PA 16509

NOWICKI, JOHN S., Business Education Instructor; *b:* Chicago, IL; *m:* Mary Therese Gedeon; *c:* Kathleen J., Emily J.; *ed:* (BSED) Bus Ed, N IL Univ 1972; Grad Stud Masters Prgm Educl Admin & Supervision Roosevelt Univ; *cr:* 6th Grade Teacher Amboy Jr *ai:* FBLA Class Spon & Adv; Home Athletic Contests Asst Adv & Public Address Announcer; Textbook/Curr Evaluation Comm; N Cntrl Evaluation Self-Evaluation Dept Chm; NBEA, IL Bus Ed Assn 1975-; DeLta Pi Epsilon 1975-80; Alpha Phi Omega (VP 1972-72) 1969-73; US Jaycees (VP 1978-80) 1977-80; N Northfield UMC Northbrook (Trustees 1986-88) 1981-; *office:* Adlai E Stevenson HS 16070 W Hwy 22 Prairie View IL 60069

NOWICKI, MARY MC DERMOTT, 5th Grade Teacher; *b:* Lorain, OH; *m:* Robert Edward; *c:* Jennifer, Michael; *ed:* (BS) Elem Ed, Kent St 1970; Grad Stud Kent, Ashland & Mt St Joseph; *cr:* 4th Grade Teacher Fairhome 1970-71; 5th Grade Teacher Kaiserslautern 1 Amer Dependent Sch Germany 1971-73; 6th Grade Teacher Amherst St Joseph 1973-74; 5th Grade Teacher Elyria St Mary 1974-76, Lorain St Peter 1976-84; 4th/5th Grade Teacher Hawthorne Acad 1984-; *ai:* Elem Stu Cncl Adv; Acad Newspaper; Intnl Rdng Assn; Natl Consortium of Gifted Ed; *home:* 2141 W 38th St Lorain OH 44053

NOWLAN, HELEN CHATBURN, Mathematics Teacher; *b:* Oklahoma City, OK; *m:* William Taylor; *c:* Patrick T., Kathy L. Nowlan Powell; *ed:* (BS) Math Ed, Phillips Univ 1959; (MAT) Math, Webster Coll 1970; (PHD) Higher Ed/Math, Univ MS 1978; *cr:* Math Teacher Florrisant Valley Comm Coll 1967-70, Shelby St Comm Coll 1972-76, Shelby Cty Sch System 1976-79, Leavenworth HS 1979-; *ai:* MAA, NCTM, NEA, KNEA, LNEA; PEO, Womens Division Chamber of Commerce; Lioness; *home:* RR 2 Box 136 Y Leavenworth KS 66048

NOWLIN, DAN, Retired; *b:* Portland, OR; *m:* Ardonnah Elligsen; *c:* Nancy, Dan Jr.; *ed:* (BS) Elem Ed, OR Coll of Ed 1954; (MA) General Stud, OR St Univ 1973; *cr:* 6th Grade Teacher Foster Elem 1954-88; *ai:* Chess Coach; *home:* 316 8th Ave Sweet Home OR 97386

NOXON, DEBORRAH CHAPIN, Reading/Writing Teacher; *b:* Charlotte Amalie, Virgin Islands; *ed:* (BA) Foreign Lang - Cum Laude, Stetson Univ 1974; Grad Stud Eng, Theatre, Ed, Univ of FL, Los Angeles Valley Coll, Univ of CA Los Angeles, CA St Univ Northridge; *cr:* 9th-12th Grade Foreign Lang Teacher Golden Hills Acad 1975-76; 6th-8th Grade Span/Drama Teacher Osceola Mid ScH 1976-79; 7th-12th Grade Span Teacher Oakwood Sch 1980-81; 8th Grade Eng Teacher Osceola Mid Sch 1981-82; 7th Grade Rdng/Writing Teacher Lake Weir Mid Sch 1983-; *ai:* Team Leader; Ocala Civic Theater (Bd Mem 1977-79, Bd of Dir 1975-); Lake Weir Mid Sch Teacher of Yr 1986-87; FL St Conference Eng Teachers Presentation; FL Beginning Teacher Prgm Peer Teacher, Panel, Comm; Offered Full Teaching Assistantship Univ of CA Los Angeles & Dean Position Mid Sch Oakwood Sch; Offered Natl Inst for Hum Fellowship 1988; Lake Weir Mid Sch Past Subject Area Leader; *office:* Lake Weir Mid Sch 10220 SE Sunset Harbor Rd Summerfield FL 32691

NOYES, GINGER WILLIAMSON, 7th Grade Life Science Teacher; *b:* Aurora, CO; *m:* Frederick William; *c:* Aaryn S.; *ed:* (BS) Health/Phys Ed, 1977, (MED) Scndry/Life-Earth Sci, 1981 Lamar Univ; *cr:* Life-Earth Sci Teacher Buna Jr HS 1978-82; Earth Sci Teacher Bedichek Jr HS 1982-83; Life Sci Teacher Buna Jr HS 1984-; *ai:* Co-Spon Stu Cncl; Tour Dir for Washington DC Stu Tours; Mem Faculty Advisory Comm 1989-; TX Classroom Teachers Assn 1984-; Buna Classroom Teachers Assn (Treas 1989-) 1984-; Sierra Club 1981-; Nom Buna Teacher of Yr 1989-; Career Ladder Level III 1985-89; Career Ladder Level IV 1989-.

NUCCIO, EDWARD ANTHONY, Instrumental Music Teacher; *b:* Chicago, IL; *m:* Mary Ellen Risdal; *c:* Mark, Bradley; *ed:* (BA) Instrumental Music, Coe Coll 1958; (MA) Scndry Sch Admin, Univ of CO Boulder 1971; Grad Stud Child Abuse, Guidance, Counseling; *cr:* Bandsman 1958-61, Band Dir 1961-62 USAF Acad; Band Dir Cheyenne Mountain Public Schls 1962-; *ai:* Instrumental Music Dept Chm; St of CO Band Contest Adjudicator & Instrumental Affairs Cncl Mem; Amer Sch Band Dir Assn Chm 1985-86; Phi Beta Mu Secy 1981, St of CO Most Outstanding Band Dir 1990; Music Ed Natl Conference, CO Music Educators Assn, NEA 1961-; Cheyenne Mountain Elem Sch Most Outstanding Teacher 1988; *home:* 612 Orion Dr Colorado Springs CO 80906

NULL, CHERIE STAPFER, Fourth Grade Teacher; *b:* Saint Louis, MO; *m:* William; *c:* Cody; *ed:* (AA) Childcare/Guidance, 1976, (BS) Elem Ed, 1978 SE MO St; (MS) Spec Ed/Learning Disabilities, Univ of MO St Louis 1988; Grad Studs; *cr:* 2nd Grade Teacher 1978-79, 3rd/4th Grade Combination Teacher 1979-81 Buder Sch; 4th Grade Teacher Marvin Sch 1981-; *ai:* Marvin Elem Dev Coord 1986-88; Alpha Gamma Nu 1986-89; Ritenour Wrting Wkshp Leader 1984-89; Ritenour Writing Improvement Team 1989-; *office:* Marvin Elem Sch 3510 Woodson Rd Saint Louis MO 63114

NULL, GAIL KNOX, Mathematics Teacher; *b:* Crowell, TX; *m:* Albert; *c:* Thomas Pitillo, Knoxie Dilger, Melissa; *ed:* (BS) Ed, 1970, (ME) Elem Ed, 1973 W TX St Univ; *cr:* 2nd Grade Teacher 1970-82, 4th-7th Grade Teacher 1983- Happy Elem Sch; *ai:* UIL Math Coach; ATPE 1987-; Kappa Delta Pi, Phi Theta Kappa, Alpha Chi Mem; *home:* Box 155 Happy TX 79042

NULL, MARJORIE MURRAY, English Dept Chairperson; *b:* Punxsutawney, PA; *m:* William H.; *ed:* (BS) Ed/Eng, 1968, (MS) Ed/Eng, 1976 Indiana Univ of PA 1976; Journalism, OH Univ Athens; *cr:* 11th/12th Grade Eng Teacher Brockway Area HS 1968-69; 12th Grade Eng Teacher 1969-89, Eng Dept Chairperson 1989- Marion Center Area HS; *ai:* Sr Class Adv; Chairperson Eng Dept; NCTE; PA Cncl Teachers of Eng; Amer Assn of Univ Women Pres 1989-; Bus & Prof Women Pres 1955, 1957; Friends of Lib VP 1989-; Grace Meth Church Pres Admin Cncl 1988-; Yrbk Adv Awds for Excl 12 Yrs; *office:* Marion Center Area HS Marion Center PA 15759

NULL, MARSHA CLARY, Phys Ed Teacher/Track Coach; *b:* Cleburne, TX; *m:* Hugh David Jr.; *c:* Stephanie, Allyson, Meredith; *ed:* (BS) Health/Phys Ed, TX A&M 1977; Grad Courses in Mid-Management, Stephen F Austin Univ; *cr:* Phys Ed Teacher/Coach Spring HS South 1977-78, North Shore Mid Sch 1979-; *ai:* 7th-8th Grade Track Coach; Jr Var Track Coach; TCTA 1981-; THSCA 1979-; Article Published 1987; *home:* 13202 Joliet Houston TX 77015

NUNEMACHER, JULIA MARTIN, Mathematics Teacher; *b:* Detroit, MI; *m:* Robert B.; *c:* Robert M., Suzanne L.; *ed:* (BS) Biochemistry, CO St Univ 1967; Post Grad Work Penn St Univ, Millersville St Univ, E Stroudsburg Univ; *cr:* Bio/Math Teacher Barnum Jr HS; Math Teacher Cedar Crest HS; *ai:* Stu Cncl Adv; *office:* Cedar Crest HS 115 E Evergreen Rd Lebanon PA 17042

NUNN, CURTIS EUGENE, Mathematics Teacher; *b:* Freeport, IL; *m:* Lu Ann Marie Martin; *c:* Zachary, Ian; *ed:* (BS) Aerospace Engineering, IA St Univ 1974; (BS) Math/Physics, Buena Vista Coll 1985; *cr:* Space Systems Officer USAF 1974-76; Manufacturing Engr Bourns Inc 1976-80; Product Line Engr Centralab Inc 1980-84; Math Teacher Indianola HS 1985-; *ai:* Yrbk Adv; Astronomy Club Spon; Intramural Bsktbl Spon; NCTM Mem 1985-89; Natl Sci Fnd Grant Recipient for Summer Wkshp a Unified Approach to Transformations Analytical Vectors & Cmptr Graphics Univ of IA 1989; *office:* Indianola H S 1304 E 1st St Indianola IA 50125

NUNN, JOYCE MARIE LAWRENCE, 5th/6th Grade ESL Teacher; *b:* Providence, RI; *m:* Edward Christopher; *c:* Adam; *ed:* (BA) Span/Ed, Salve Regina Coll 1970; (MA) Elem Ed, Univ of RI 1973; Eng as Second Lang & Bi-ling Span Endorsement RI Coll; Prin Cert Providence Coll; *cr:* Eng as Second Lang/Bi-ling Teacher Pawtucket Sch Dept 1970-72; Ed Tester URI Curr Research & Dev 1972-73; Eng as Second Lang/Portugese/Span Teacher Cntrl Falls Sch Dept 1973-; Management Consultant Hasbro Industries Incorporated 1978-; *ai:* Alpha Delta Kappa (Corresponding Secy 1985-86, Treas 1987-); N Smithfield Town Democratic Party 1983-; N Smithfield Town Cncl Mem 1982-83; *office:* Dr E F Calcutt Mid Sch 112 Washington St Central Falls RI 02863

NURIK, MARGY PAULA, Social Studies/Spanish Teacher; *b:* New York, NY; *m:* Irving; *c:* Jeffrey C., Jody, Tracey Gallagher; *ed:* (BA) Sociology, Douglass Coll 1949; (MAT) Teaching, Montclair St 1968; Inservice Courses; *cr:* Teacher Lakeside Sch 1969-; *ai:* Crisis Intervention, Report Card, Dept, Soc, Historical Comm; NJ Mid Level Ed Assn, NJ Ed Assn, NEA; Pompton Lakes Ed Assn Past VP; BSA Badge Adv; Hadassah Pres 1960-61; Congregation Beth Shalom Pres Womens Div 1963-65; Textbook Adv; *office:* Lakeside Sch Lakeside Ave Pompton Lakes NJ 07442

NUSS, BOBBYE BYRD, Second Grade Teacher; *b:* Greenbrier, AR; *m:* Mike A.; *ed:* (BS) Home Ec, 1957, (MED) Guidance/Counseling, 1962 E TX St Univ; *cr:* Teacher Texarkana Ind Sch Dist 1953-55; Home Dem Ag Teacher Titus Cty 1957-62; Cnslr Texarkana Ind Sch Dist 1962-68; Teacher Brownwood Ind Sch Dist 1968-; *ai:* Beautification Chm Northwest Elem; Phi Delta Kappa 1989-; TX Classroom Teachers 1968-; TX St Teachers Assn Teacher of Yr Awd 1988-89; *home:* 3001 Austin Ave Brownwood TX 76801

NUSS, DEBORAH HAHN, Music Specialist; *b:* St Louis, MO; *m:* Harlan A.; *c:* Jeremy R., Aaron C.; *ed:* (BME) Music Ed/Voice, Drake Univ 1972; 2nd Level Orff Cert, Memphis St Univ; 1st Level Orff Cert, N AZ Univ; *cr:* K-6th/9th-12th Grade Vocal Music Instr Dallas Cmmty Schs 1972-74; K-12th Grade Vocal Music Instr Bayard Cmmty Schls 1975-76; 1st-5th Grade Music Specialist Marshalltown Cmmty Schls 1976-; *ai:* Building Improvement & IMPACT Selection Gifted & Talented Comm; Building Developmental Comm Chm; NEA 1972-; Amer Guild of Eng Handbell Ringers, Choristers Guild, Amer Orff-Schulwerk Assn; Marshalltown Youth Orchestra Guild, 1st Presbyn Church (Dir Chancel Bell Choir, Dir J P Singers); Friendship Force of Cntrl IA Bd Mem 1983-86; Marshalltown Area Cncl for Arts (Pres, Past Pres) 1984-86; Outstanding Young Women of America 1982; Nom YWCA Women of Achievement 1984; Published Composer; *office:* Marshalltown Cmmty Sch Dist 317 Columbus Marshalltown IA 50158

NUSZKIEWICZ, DOROTHY WESTFALL, Kindergarten Teacher; *b:* Iowa City, IA; *c:* Michelle, Timothy, Jon; *ed:* (BA) Elem Ed, Marycrest Coll 1964; Graduate Work at Humboldt St Univ; *cr:* 1st Grade Teacher 1964-66, 4th Grade Teacher 1967-69 & 1973-78, Kndgtn Teacher 1978- Pine Grove Elem; *ai:* NEA 1964-; CTA 1969-; Del Norte Assn for Ed of Young Children Executive Bd 1989-; *office:* Pine Grove Elem Sch 900 Pine Grove Rd Crescent City CA 95531

NUTE, BARBARA BROWN, 5th Grade Teacher; *b:* Lawrence, MA; *m:* Eugene W.; *c:* Nancy Rolla, Frank, Dianne Young; *ed:* (BS) Elem Ed, DE St 1973; (MA) Curr/Dev, Washington Univ St Louis 1982; S IL Univ; *cr:* Teacher Estelle Kampmeyer 1976-; *ai:* 5th Grade Environmental Ed Camping Trip; SIU-E Cooperating Teacher; Sci Fair; O Fallon Classroom Teachers Assn (Pres 1987-88, Mem 1976-); *office:* Estelle Kampmeyer Elem Sch 707 N Smiley O'Fallon IL 62269

NUTTALL, JANE E., Third Grade Teacher; *b:* Wichita, KS; *m:* John P.; *c:* Lisa, Amy; *ed:* (BS) Elem Ed, Univ of CO 1970; Grad Stud Univ of AK; *cr:* 3rd-5th Grade Teacher Peterson Sch 1970-76; 3rd Grade Teacher East Sch 1978-; *ai:* Delta Kappa Gamma 1976-; Kodiak Borough Ed Assn 1970-; NEA, AEA, Natl Rdng Assn, Kodiak Rdng Assn; Assn for Retarded Citizens of Kodiak (Pres, Secy); St Paul Luth Church (Asst Sunday Sch Supv, Chm Ed Comm, Secy) 1970-; 1st Runner Up AK Teacher of Yr 1990; Kodiak Teacher of Yr 1989; *home:* 1121 Mission Rd Kodiak AK 99615

NUTTER, DONNA BOHRER, Reading Teacher; *b:* Erie, PA; *m:* James Walter; *c:* J. Christopher, Patrick, Melanie Greenman; *ed:* (BA) Eng, Villa Maria Coll 1970; (MED) Rdng Specialist, Edinboro Univ 1978; *cr:* Rdng/Lang Arts Gridley Mid Sch 1971-; *ai:* Support Teacher for New Teachers; Resource Teacher for Sch Faculty; Northwest PA Cncl of Teachers of Eng Bd Mem 1989-; Erie Rdng Assn Mem 1984-; Teacher of Yr 1984-85, 1989-; Mem Lead Teacher Consoritum NW PA; *home:* 255 Locust St Erie PA 16508

NUTTER, GLEE LELIA, Reading Teacher; *b:* White Sulphur Spgs, WV; *ed:* (BS) Elem Ed, 1973, (MA) Rdng, 1975 WV Univ; *cr:* 2nd Grade Teacher 1974-88, Chapter 1 Rdng Specialist 1988- Rupert Elem; *ai:* Yrbk Co-Spon; Intnl Rdng Assn Mem; WV Rdng Cncl Mem; Greenbrier Cty Rdng Cncl (Corresponding Secy, Mem) 1988-; PTA (VP, Stage Comm); Writer & Co-Dir Greenbrier Cty Rdng Cncl Musical Drama Produced 1989; WV Ed Fund Mini Grant Awd 1990; *home:* 516 E Main St White Slphr Spg WV 24986

NUTTER, LLOYD, JR., History Teacher; *b:* Quantico, VA; *m:* Dayle Earnest; *ed:* (BS) His, Univ of Monte Vallo 1981; *cr:* Teacher Henry Cty HS 1981-; *ai:* Soc Stud Club Spon; *office:* Henry Cty Sr HS 401 E Tomlinson St Mc Donough GA 30253

NUTTMAN, JOHN MARK, Physical Science Teacher; *b:* Lewiston, ID; *m:* Leslie Ann Haigh; *c:* Kathryn A.; *ed:* (BSED) Soc Sci, Univ of ID 1978; *cr:* Jr & Sr HS Teacher Columbia Sch Dist 206 1978-79; Jr HS Teacher 1979-81, Indian Ed Tutor/Cnslr 1982-83 Bremerton Sch Dist 100-C; MS Teacher N Mason Sch Dist 403 1983-; *ai:* Bsktbl, Wrestling, Track Head Coach Hawkins Mid Sch; Swimming Lessons Teacher Catrons Pool; Competitive Swimming Coaches & Aquatic Facilities Management & Admin Teacher; WA St Emergency Medical Technician; Amer Alliance for Health, Phys Ed, Recreation & Dance; Amer Red Cross Water Safety Chm 1981-83, 20 Yrs Service Awd 1987; Elks 1975-; Mason Cty Fire Protection (Lieutenant, EMT-O) 1984-; BSA Merit Badge Cnslr; *office:* Hawkins Mid Sch P O Box 167 Belfair WA 98528

NYAHAY, JANICE GLEITSMANN, ESOL Chairperson; *b:* Mount Vernon, NY; *m:* Edward Michael; *c:* Rebecca E., Colin E.; *ed:* (BA) Eng Ed, St Univ NY New Paltz 1972; (MS) Ed, Iona Coll 1979; ESOL, Coll of New Rochelle; *cr:* Eng Teacher Gorton HS 1972-77; Jr HS Eng Teacher Mark Twain & Hawthorne 1982-85; ESOL Teacher Emerson Jr HS 1985-; *ai:* NYS TESOL 1990; Womens Club of Valhalla 1st VP 1986; Kensico Little League Secy 1985-89; Columbus Avenue PTA Bd Mem 1984-; Valhalla HS PTO Bd Mem 1989-; *office:* Emerson Jr HS 160 Bolmer Ave Yonkers NY 10703

NYBELL, CAROLYN A., 8th Grade English/Rdng Teacher; *b:* Youngstown, OH; *m:* Douglas H.; *ed:* (BS) Elem Ed, 1972, (MS) Ed/Rdng, 1976, (MS) Ed/Cmmty Counseling, 1984 Youngstown St Univ; Lions Quest Skills of Adolescence Wkshp, NEORCA Trng Consortium High Risk Children, Inst for Childrens Lit, Wkshp in Educl Computing; *cr:* 2nd/3rd Grade Teacher 1972-79, K-4th Grade Sci Teacher 1979-80 Market St Elem; 5th-8th Grade

Teacher Glenwood Mid Sch 1980-; *ai:* Boardman Ed Assn 1972-; Chi Sigma Iota 1987-; Kappa Delta Pi 1976-; Jennings Scholar; *office:* Glenwood Mid Sch 7635 Glenwood Ave Boardman OH 44512

NYKIEL, JANET, English/Reading Teacher; *b:* Brackenridge, PA; *ed:* (BA) Sci Ed, 1972, (MA) Sci Ed, 1978 Duquesne Univ; *cr:* Teacher Burrell Jr HS & Charles A Huston Mid Sch 1972-.

O

OAKES, NORMAN C., Remedial Mathematics Teacher; *b:* New York, NY; *m:* Sandra Rae Schwartz; *c:* Christopher, Kimberly; *ed:* (BS) His, 1970, (MS) Ed, 1972 SUC Oneonta; (SAS/SDA) Admin Ed, C W Post 1990; *cr:* 5th/6th Grade Teacher 1972-89; 3rd-6th Grade Remedial Math Teacher 1988- Sachem Cntrl Sch Dist; *ai:* Employee Assistance Prgm Building Rep; Cmptr Task Force Sachem Cntrl Sch Dist; Sachem Cntrl Teachers Assn 1972-; NYSUT 1972-; ASCD 1989-; Phi Delta Kappa.

OAKLEY, BARRY LEWIS, Mathematics Department Chair; *b:* Durham, NC; *m:* Lila Dorman; *c:* Steven; *ed:* (BS) Math Ed, NC St Univ 1977; (MS) Math Ed, NC Cntrl Univ 1990; Grad Courses NC St; *cr:* Math Teacher Stanford Jr HS 1977-82, Southern Durham HS 1982-; *ai:* Mu Alpha Theta Spon; Math Dept Head; NEA 1977-83, 1989; NCTM 1990; Church of God Supt 1987-; Southern Durham Teacher of Yr 1983; *home:* 2501 E Club Blvd Durham NC 27704

OAKLEY, OTHNIEL, Jr HS Math Teacher/Chairperson; *b:* Port Antonio, Jamaica; *m:* Joslette Gorden; *c:* Alex M.; *ed:* General Subjects, Univ of Cambridge 1960; (BA) Comm, Chapman Coll 1976; (MA) Ed, Intnl Univ 1986; Grad Stud Windsor Sch, Univ of London; PhD Curr/Admin, CA Coast Univ; *cr:* Jr HS Teacher St Barbari Sch; Teacher Alpha Boys Sch 1961-66, 1973-74; Craft-Oil Painting Instr H&H Floral & Craft 1969-84; Teacher St Joseph Sch 1979-; *ai:* Math & Soc Stud Chairperson; Pentathlon Team Coach; Performing Arts & Jamaica Festival; Speech Adjudicator; Pentathlon Orange Cty Jr HS; BSA Leader 1962-64; 4-H Club Local Leader 1956-60; Inland Forensic Assn Team Mem 1970, 1st Place Awd 1970; ASCD, Educl Leadership, NCEA; Plays for Jamaican Stage; Diocese of Orange Author of Educl Festival; Presidential Awd for Excl Math Awd 1990; Rotary Club Idyllwild Schlsp; *office:* St Joseph Sch 801 Bradford Ave Placentia CA 92670

OAKLEY, VIRGINIA ALLBRITTON, Fourth Grade Teacher; *b:* Dilley, TX; *c:* Renee Anderson; *ed:* Phys Ed, Baylor Univ 1951-53; (BS) Phys Ed, N TX St Univ 1963; *cr:* Teacher Nathaniel Hawthorne Elem 1963-; *home:* 1743 Lucille Mesquite TX 75149

OAKS, GARRY GENE, Soc Stud & English Teacher; *b:* Elizabethton, TN; *m:* Regina Sneed; *c:* Brandy; *ed:* (BS) Eng/His, 1969, (MA) Scndry Ed, 1972 E TN St Univ; *cr:* Teacher/Coach Old Fort HS 1969-71, Cloudland HS 1971-; *ai:* Asst Ftbl Coach; Soph Class Spon; AFT 1972-; Ruritan Bd of Dir 1983-85; Favorite Teacher Cloudland HS 1988; *office:* Cloudland HS Rt 3 Roan Mountain TN 37687

OATES, JANICE SMITH, Business Education Teacher; *b:* Florala, AL; *m:* Frederick D.; *ed:* Recommendations Bus Ed, Collegiate Bus Inst 1964; (BA) Bus Ed, Selma Univ Jr Coll 1969; (PHD) Bus Ed, AL St Univ 1972; Bus Ed Wkshps; *cr:* Teacher Max Bruner Jr Jr HS 1974-89, Max Bruner Jr Mid Sch 1989-; *ai:* FL Voc Assn 1983-; FL Teaching Profession, NEA 1984-; Beulah Missionary Baptist Church Librarian 1985-.

OATESS, JANET SUE, English Department Head; *b:* Peru, IN; *m:* Stephen P.; *c:* Diana Oatess-Shockey, Stephanie Oatess-Imbler, Kristen L. Slusher; *ed:* (BS) Eng/Ed, 1972, (MS) Eng/Ed, 1977 IN Univ; *cr:* Adjunct Lecturer in Eng IN Univ Kokomo 1977-86; Eng Dept Head Maconaquah HS 1972-; *ai:* Sr Class, Literary Magazine Spon; Maconaquah NHS Comm Adv; Part-Time Stu of Yr 1972, Part-Time Teacher of Yr 1977 IN Univ Kokomo; *home:* 202 S Madison Converse IN 46919

OATLEY, LINDA GERHARDSTEIN, English Teacher; *b:* Bellevue, OH; *c:* Cheryl Mc Nally, Carol Franklin; *ed:* (BA) Eng/Speech, 1972, (MED) Admin, 1977 Bowling Green St Univ; *cr:* 6th Grade Teacher Townsend Elem 1969-72; Eng Teacher Margaretta HS 1972-; *ai:* Problem Solving & Schlsp Comm; Eng Dept Chairperson; Margaretta Teachers Assn Pres 1972-73, 1977-78; OH Ed Assn, NEA, Phi DeLta Kappa, NCTE, OH Cncl of Teachers of Eng; Erie Cty Super Teacher 1988; Margaretta Teacher of Yr 1986; Martha Holden Jennings Scholar 1982; *office:* Margaretta HS 209 Lowell St Castalia OH 44824

OATS, MAE ELLEN, Fifth Grade Teacher; *b:* Paris, TX; *m:* Lane W.; *c:* Malone, Terri, Trey; *ed:* (BS) Home Economics, 1970, (MED) Elem Ed, 1975 East TX St Univ; *cr:* 5th Grade Teacher Huntington ISD 1970-71; Home Economics Teacher Roxton ISD 1971-73; Teacher Prairiland ISD 1977-80; 5th Grade Teacher Delmar & Chisum1980-; *ai:* UIL Number Sense Elem Level; *home:* Rt 1 Cooper TX 75432

O'BANNON, BRENDA CARAWAY, Mathematics Teacher/ Dept Chair; *b:* Louisville, MS; *m:* John T.; *c:* Tyler; *ed:* (BS) Math Ed, MS St Univ 1979; Grad Work MS St Univ; *cr:* Math Teacher Starkville HS 1979-; *ai:* Math Dept Chairperson 1988-; MS Assn of Educators, Natl Assn of Educators 1980-; *office:* Starkville HS Yellow Jacket Dr Starkville MS 39759

O'BARA, CARRIE L. SULLIVAN, First Grade Teacher; *b:* Columbus, OH; *m:* Ronald Edward; *c:* Ashley J.; *ed:* (BA) Liberal Stud, CA St Univ Fresno 1983; Clinical Supervision of Teachers, CA St Univ Stanislaus; *cr:* Eng 2nd Lang/ESL Teacher Merced Adult Sch 1983-84; 5th Grade Teacher Mitchell Elem Sch 1984-87; K-1st Grade Teacher 1985, 3rd-8th Grade Lang Art Teacher 1986, 1st Grade Teacher 1987 Atwater Sch Dist; 1st Grade Teacher Mitchell Elem Sch 1987-; *ai:* Mitchell K-6th Grade Stu Study Team Mem, Spirit Chairperson; Stu Cncl Adv; CA Teachers Assn Mem 1984-; PTO (Rep, Prgm Planner); Delta Gamma Alumni 1983-; Sheperd of the Valley Luth Church Mem 1979-; *office:* Mitchell Elem Sch 1601 Grove Ave Atwater CA 95301

OBERBECK, RICHARD DEAN, Science Teacher; *b:* Marshfield, MO; *ed:* (Ba) Chem/Bio, 1985, (MED) Ed/Sci, 1988 Drury Coll; KSAM Instr Course; *cr:* Grad Asst Drury Coll 1985; SciTeacher Purdy R-II Schls 1987-; KSAM Instr Drury Coll 1989-; *ai:* Soph Spon; Math/Sci Club Adv; CTA Pres; Bsktbl Score Clock Worker; MSTA/CTA Pres 1989-; CTA Secy 1988-89; TIE Wkshp Participant in 1990; *office:* Purdy R-II Schls Box 248 Purdy MO 65734

OBERG, THOMAS CARL, 7th Grade Math Teacher; *b:* Minneapolis, MN; *ed:* (BS) Math, Bemidji St Univ 1979; *cr:* Teacher/Coach Sauk Centre Jr HS 1980-; *ai:* Ftbl, Hockey, Bsbl Coach; Stu Cncl Adv; SCEA Negotiations Cncl 1980-82; MEA, NEA.

OBERHOLZER, CECILIA GARVIN, Chemistry Teacher; *b:* Philadelphia, PA; *m:* John C.; *c:* John, Mark, Matthew, Christopher; *ed:* (BA) Chem - Magna Cum Laude, Holy Family Coll 1962; Sci Ed/Cmptr Sci/Chem, St Josephs Univ; *cr:* Research Chemist Exide Corporation 1962-65; Math Teacher Bishop Kenrick HS 1979-80; Cmptr Teacher NE Cath HS 1981-; Chem Teacher Little Flower HS 1982-; *ai:* Wardrobe Club, Bloodmobile; Philadelphia Area Cmptr Society; Kappa Gamma Pi Aid for Friends; Outstanding Young Women of America 1963; Distinguished Teacher Awd 1987; Co-Author Article in Journal of Appl ed Polymer Sci 1963; *office:* Little Flower Catholic HS 10th & Lycoming Philadelphia PA 19140

OBERMIER, DUANE A., Communicative Arts Dept Chair; *b:* York, NE; *m:* Bonnie; *c:* Christian Dennhardt, Adriene, Aaron; *ed:* (BS) Eng, Kearney St Coll 1965; (MS) Journalism, KS St Univ 1972; (MS) Counseling, Kearney St Coll 1986; Writing Wkshp Marquette Univ; *cr:* Classroom Teacher Hastings HS 1965-67, Grand Island Sr HS 1967-; *ai:* Stu Newspaper, Yrbk & Literary Magazine Faculty Adv; NE HS Press Assn Pres 1972, Distinguished Adv 1985; Grand Island Ed Assn Pres 1984-85; NE St Ed Assn Dir 1987-; Cooper Fnd Awd Winner; NE Teacher of Yr 1990; *office:* Grand Island Sr HS 2124 N Lafayette Ave Grand Island NE 68803

OBERSKI, ANN MILLER, English/Reading Teacher; *b:* Wauseon, OH; *m:* Robin Mark; *ed:* (BS) Elem Ed, Bowling Green St Univ 1981; Newspapers in Ed, the Writing Process; *cr:* Elem Sub Wauseon Exempted Village Schls 1981-82; 6th Grade Teacher 1982-84; 8th Grade Eng/Rdng Reacher 1984- Burr Road Mid Sch; *ai:* 7th/8th Grade Cheerleading Adv; Originator/Adv the Arrowhead the Sch Newspaper; Wauseon Ed Assn, OH Ed Assn, NEA; Amer Heart Assn, Amer Cancer Society, Lucas/Fulton Cty Humane Societies; *office:* Burr Rd Mid Sch Burr Rd Wauseon OH 43567

OBERTO, ALAN JAMES, Teacher of Gifted/Talented; *b:* Des Moines, IA; *ed:* (BA) Ed, 1970, (MA) Church His, 1972 Olivet Nazarene Univ; Teaching of Gifted Level II Trng, St of IL; *cr:* 4th Grade Teacher Bradley Sch Dist 61 1973-88; *ai:* Young Astronauts; Sch Newspaper; Prof Staff Dev Comm; NEA; IL Educl Assn Dist Rep 1978-83; BB Federal Credit Union Bd of Dir 1980-87; *office:* Bradley West Elem Sch 200 W State Bradley IL 60915

O'BOYLE, MICHAEL KEVIN, Chemistry Instructor; *b:* Kalispell, MT; *m:* Sherry L.; *c:* Sandi, James, Tara; *ed:* (BS) Forest Products, OR St Univ 1973; (MS) Chem Ed, S OR St Univ 1983; *cr:* Process Chemist Crown Zellerbach Corporation 1973-76; Chem Teacher Tillamook HS 1977-78, Mazama HS 1979-; *ai:* Key Club Adv; NSTA, OR Sci Teachers Assn; Local Elem Sch Bd Mem; Coll Instr OR Inst of Technology; *office:* Mazama HS 3009 Summers Ln Klamath Falls OR 97603

O'BOYLE, TIMOTHY F., English Teacher; *b:* Gary, IN; *ed:* (BS) Eng, 1972, (MS) Eng, 1977 IN St Univ; *cr:* Teacher Diocese of Gary Schls 1972-76, Randolph Cty Sch Corporation 1976-78, Boone Grove HS 1978-; *office:* Boone Grove HS Main St Boone Grove IN 46302

OBRECHT, ROGER ALAN, Principal; *b:* Urbaba, IL; *m:* Lindy Mary Glombicki; *c:* Sara, Jodi; *ed:* (BS) Biological Sci, S IL Univ-Carbondale 1974; (MS) Ed Admin, Univ of IL 1983; *cr:* Sci Teacher Thomasboro Grade Sch 1974-75; Sci Teacher/Coach/ Athletic Dir Gifford Grade Sch 1975-87; Prin Fisher Jr/Sr HS 1987-; *ai:* Gifted, Voc Ed, Chapter I, Drug Free Schls Coord; IPA, NASSP 1987-; Sangamon Valley Conference Treas 1989-; *home:* Box 223 Gifford IL 61847

OBRECHT, STEVEN E., English Teacher; *b:* Brooklyn, NY; *ed:* (AA) Kingsborough Cmmty 1970; (BS) Eng, Univ of S FL 1972; (MS) Eng Ed, 1975, (EDS) Educl Admin, 1979 FL St Univ; Public Admin Certificate 1981; Grad Stud FL St Univ 1985; *cr:* 4th-8th Grade Lang Art Teacher Trinity Cath Sch 1972-74; 6th-8th Grade Eng Teacher Griffin Mid Sch 1974-75; Adult Ed/ Dept Chm Lively Voc-Tech Sch 1975-85; 9th-12th Grade Eng Teacher Leon HS 1985-; *ai:* Brain Brawl Team Spon; Peer Cnslr Project Success; Phi Delta Kappa 1975-; NCTE 1972-; PTO Faculty Rep; Tallahassee Jaycees 1975-80; *office:* Leon HS 550 E Tennessee St Tallahassee FL 32303

O'BRIEN, D. SUE NICHOLS, Sixth Grade Teacher; *b:* Charleston, IL; *m:* Maynard; *c:* Carol S. Hankins, Laurel S. Hankins; *ed:* (BSED) Art/Phys Ed, 1952, (MSED) Phys Ed, 1972 Eastern IL Univ; Supervision/Admin, Univ of IL 1974-76; *cr:* Phys Ed Teacher Mattoon HS 1952-55, O Fallon Township HS 1955-57; Phys Ed Teacher/Coach Charleston Cmmty HS 1957-74; 6th Grade Teacher Jefferson Elem Sch 1977-; *ai:* Gifted Prgm Math/Cmptrs; Dist Cmptr & St Bsktbl, Vlybl Rules Comm; Pom-Pon Group; N Cntrl Evaluation Team; Kappa Pi Honorary Art (Pres 1951-52) 1950-52; IL Ed Assn; NEA 1952-; Phi Delta Kappa 1975-; Wesley United Meth Church 1941-; Charleston Cntry Club Golf Chairperson 1987; IL League HS Girls Bsktbl Assn (Pres 1970) 1967-70; PTA Dist Pres; Co-Authored Manuals Math & Soc Stud; Conducted 2 St Girls Ath Assn Wkshps; *home:* 2408 Terrace Ln Charleston IL 61920

O'BRIEN, FELCIA SHELOSKI, Second Grade Teacher; *b:* West Rutland, VT; *m:* John Thomas; *c:* Judy A. Grastorf, Beth Montrello, Margaret M. Bartkoski, Michael C.; *ed:* (BA) Early Chldhd Ed, St Univ of NY Potsdam 1958; (MS) Elem Ed, St Joseph the Provider 1979; *cr:* 2nd Grade Teacher Broad St Elem 1958-59; Art Teacher 1963-64, Kndgtn Teacher 1968-83, 2nd Grade Teacher 1983- Granville Cntrl Sch; *ai:* Delta Kappa Gamma Intl 1984-; Ed Advisory Bd Green Mt Coll 1979-84; *office:* Granville Cntrl Sch Quaker St Granville NY 12832

O'BRIEN, GERALD LEO, English Teacher; *b:* Lynn, MA; *m:* Trudy L. Cronin; *c:* Kevin, Daniel; *ed:* (BA) Hum, Merrimack Coll 1964; (MA) Ed, Suffolk Univ 1977; *cr:* Soc Stud Teacher Eastern Jr HS 1967-78; Soc Stud/Eng Teacher Lynn English HS 1978-; *ai:* Coach Jr Var Bsbl 1972-73, Var Golf 1982-; Class Adv 1983-; Babe Ruth Bsbl Mgr 1975-79; AMVETS 1967-; *office:* Lynn English HS 50 Goodridge St Lynn MA 01902

O'BRIEN, JANIE C., First Grade Teacher; *b:* Dover, DE; *c:* Wendy C.; *ed:* (BS) Elem Ed, Univ of DE 1976; (MSED) Ed, Salisbury St Coll 1980; Dist & St Inservice Courses; *cr:* 1st Grade Teacher Allen Frear Elem 1976-78; 1st Grade Teacher 1978-81, 2nd Grade Teacher 1981-86, 1st Grade Teacher 1986- General Henry H Arnold Elem; *ai:* Teach Career Wkshp Elem Teachers; Staff Dev & Arnold Texbook Comm Mem; General Henry H Arnold Faculty Pres; Kappa Delta Pi 1976, Honors 1976; NEA 1976-; PTA Exec Bd; Diamond St Ed Assn 1976-86; Caesar Rodney Ed Assn (Secy, Sch Rep, Exec Bd); Kent Cncl for Rdng 1976-; Diamond St Rdng Assn 1976-86; CREA 1976-; Caesar Rodney Sch Dist Teacher of Yr 1982, 1989; *office:* Gen Henry H Arnold Elem Sch Center Rd Dover DE 19901

O'BRIEN, JUDY E. SCHOLL, Third Grade Teacher; *b:* Holyoke, CO; *m:* John E.; *c:* Timothy, Janis, Suzette; *ed:* (BS) Elem Ed, NE Teachers Coll 1964; Grad Stud at E MT; *cr:* All Grades Teacher Dist 42 Frontier Cty 1954-56; 3rd Grade Teacher Grant Elem 1957-60, Columbus Elem 1960-71, Circle Elem 1974-.

O'BRIEN, KATHERINE JEAN (DOTY), Eng Teacher/ Speech/Drama Coach; *b:* Maquoketa, IA; *m:* Thomas E. Jr.; *c:* Timothy, Patrick, Matthew; *ed:* (BA) Speech/Drama, Clarke Coll 1962; *cr:* Eng/Span/Drama Teacher Wahlert HS 1962-63; Speech Teacher Bettendorf Mid Sch 1963-64; Jr HS Teacher St Marys 1984-88; Eng/Speech/Drama Teacher Alleman HS 1982-84, 1988-; *ai:* Fall Musical, Winter Play, All Sch Variety Show Dir; Pride, NHS, Soc Comms; Prepare Stu for Speech Contests & Chaperone; NCEA; *office:* Alleman HS 1103 40th St Rock Island IL 61201

O'BRIEN, PATRICK ANTONY, III, Social Studies Dept Teacher; *b:* Elkhart, KS; *m:* Susan Joyce Bush; *c:* Cody, Tine; *ed:* (BA) Scndry Ed His Mid Amer Bible Coll 1986; (MS) Scndry Ed Admin, Cntrl St Univ 1990; *cr:* His Teacher Grace Chrstn Acad 1986-; *ai:* Vlybl Coach; Boys Bsktbl Coach; Athletic Dir; OK Chrstn Conf VP 1988 Coach of Yr 1989-; Tri-State Conference Rep 1987- Coach of Yr 1989-; OCSAA Coach of Yr 1989-; *office:* Grace Christian Acad 4712 S Sante Fe Oklahoma City OK 73109

O'BRYAN, VIRGINIA LOIS, English Department Chair; *b:* Elgin, TX; *m:* Robert C.; *c:* Jeremy, Travis, Hilary, Caitlin; *ed:* (BSED) Eng, SW TX St Univ 1966; Univ of AK Fairbanks, Vanderbilt Univ, Univ of CA Hayward; *cr:* Teacher 1968-79, Eng Dept Head 1979- Ben Eielson HS; *ai:* NHS; NCTE, NEA, Fairbanks Ed Assn 1968-; Chairperson Dist Scndry Lang Art Comm 1988-; *home:* 3293 Lineman Ave North Pole AK 99705

O'BRYANT, ANNETTE BARNES, Mathematics Teacher; *b:* Richfield, UT; *m:* Wendell T.; *c:* Sean K., Kerri, Cory J.; *ed:* (BS) Math, Brigham Young Univ 1970; *cr:* Teacher Springville Jr HS 1971; Tax Consultant H&R Block 1979-88; Teacher Provo HS 1988-; *office:* Provo HS 1125 N University Provo UT 84604

OCH, SANDRA, 6th Grade Reading Teacher; *b:* Pittsburgh, PA; *ed:* (BS) Elem Ed, Duquesne 1978; (MED) Ed Admin, Univ of Pittsburgh 1981; Doctoral Stu in Instruction & Learning, Univ of Pittsburgh; *cr:* Teacher Diocese of Pittsburgh 1978-79, Pittsburgh Public Sch 1979-; *ai:* Drill, Dance Team Coord; Drama Club; Mentoring Comm; Pittsburgh Fed of Teachers 1979-; Pi Lambda Theta 1990; Published Article for Urban Ed Bloomsburg Univ; Allegheny Conference on Cmmty Dev, Parent Involvement Grants; *office:* Greenway Mid Sch 1400 Crucible Pittsburgh PA 15204

OCHOA, ALBERT RICHARD, JR., Art Instr/Var Tennis Coach; *b:* Laredo, TX; *m:* Diana Lynne Decenzo; *ed:* (BA) Art Ed, St Edwards Univ 1977; US Prof Tennis Assn Certified Mem; *cr:* Photo/Lab Instr St Edwards Univ 1977-80; Art Instr/Tennis Coach Burnett Mid Sch 1980-; Var Tennis Coach Anderson HS 1983-; *ai:* Anderson HS Var Tennis Coach; Burnet Mid Sch Art Club; US Prof Tennis Assn Certified Prof 1988-; Coach of Yr, Capital Area Tennis Assn 1986; Burnet Mid Sch Teacher of Yr 1987; *home:* 1902 Petunia Cedar Park TX 78613

OCHSENBEIN, DOROTHY ZIRKLE, Geometry/Algebra II Teacher; *b:* Columbus, OH; *m:* Alan Robert; *c:* Jeremy; *ed:* (BS) Math Ed, Indiana Univ of PA 1968; Math, Cmptrs, Effective Teaching; *cr:* 7th-8th Grade Math Teacher Newark Valley Cntrl Sch 1968-70; Jr HS Teacher Thomas Eaton Jr HS 1970-73; Jr/Sr HS Teacher Bartlett Begich Scndry Sch 1973-75; Secy Douglas Cty Schls 1978-82; Admin Stanley H Kaplan Educl Center 1982-84; Math Teacher Castle Rock Jr HS 1986-87, Ponderosa HS 1987-; *ai:* NCTM 1968-72, 1989-; CO Cncl of Teachers of Math 1988-; *office:* Ponderosa HS 7007 E Bayou Gulch Rd Parker CO 80134

OCHSENBEIN, JOHN THOMAS, Guidance Counselor/Dept Chm; *b:* Dayton, OH; *m:* Rebecca S. Clement; *c:* Gabriel, Gretchen, Sarah; *ed:* (BS) Soc Stud Ed, Miami Univ 1971; (MS) Stu Personnel/Counseling, Miami Univ 1972; Univ of Dayton; Wright St Univ; ON-TASC; *cr:* Grad Asst Cnslr Miami Univ 1971-72; Soc Stud Cnslr Brookville HS 1972-73; Cnslr Spinning Hills Mid Sch 1973-; *ai:* Dist Grading Sys Comm; Dist Atten Improvement Comm; Bldg Stu & Staff Support Comm; Instr/Improvement Cncl; On-Tasc Core Team; Intervention/Prevention Core Team; NEA; OEA; MREA; AACD; OACD; OSCA; Christ Cmmty Church (Adv Bd, Yth Minister 1984-89); Norma Zeppin Doer Awd Ed Handicapped; Mem Omicron Delta Kappa; Past Pres NU Chapter of Kappa Delta Pi; *home:* 3112 Braddock St Kettering OH 45420

O'CONNELL, BARBARA JUNE, Social Studies & Lit Teacher; *b:* Taunton, MA; *m:* Michael J.; *c:* Patrick, Kevin; *ed:* (BA) Ed/Lang Art, Univ of Louisville 1977; *cr:* 5th Grade Teacher Kingsolver Elem 1977-79; Jr HS Lang Art Teacher St Joseph 1980-81; Jr HS Soc Stud/Lit Teacher St Vincent de Paul 1985-; *ai:* Curr Dev Comm; Participating Teacher Two Cmmty Prgm for Jr HS Stus; Project Bus Sponsored by Jr Achievement; WEEK-TV News Game; NCEA 1985-; St Awd Economic Ed Prgm 1979; *home:* 6704 N Parkwood Dr Peoria IL 61614

O'CONNELL, EUGENIE WAUGH, Choral Dir & Music Teacher; *b:* Boothbay Harbor, ME; *m:* John William; *c:* James, Maeve; *ed:* (BM) Music, Natl Univ of Ireland 1977; Additional Trng Univ of S ME, Westminster Choir Coll; *cr:* Music Teacher Knightsbridge HS 1978-79, Southport Cntrl Sch 1979-80, Woolwich Cntrl Sch 1983-86; Choral Dir Morse HS 1984-86; Music Teacher/Choral Dir Boothbay Region Schls 1986-; *ai:* Choral Coach; Dir Chamber Singers; Staff Dev, Cmmty Public Relations, Boothbay CSD Sch Comm 1982-85; Amer Choral Dir Assn Pres Elect 1989-; Music Educators Natl Conference, ME Music Educators Assn; Boothbay Region Performing Arts Cncl, Boothbay Harbor Congregational Church; Lincoln Art Festival Founding Mem; Dir Windjammer Pageant 1982-87; Festival of Lessons & Carols Founding Dir; *office:* Boothbay Region Elem & HS 156 Townsend Ave Boothbay Harbor ME 04538

O'CONNELL, JUDITH HELEN, Modern Language Dept Chair; *b:* St Louis, MO; *ed:* (BA) Span, Univ of MO St Louis 1973; (MA) Span Applied Linguistics, St Louis Univ 1977; *cr:* Span/Fr Teacher Southwest HS 1973-74; Teacher/Dept Chairperson Vianney HS 1974-; *ai:* Sociedad Honoraria Hispanica Spon; AATSP; *home:* 8620 Gen Grant Ln Saint Louis MO 63123

O'CONNELL, THOMAS JOHN, III, 7th/8th Grade Soc Stud Teacher; *b:* Belvidere, IL; *m:* Victoria Constance Smykay; *c:* Debra L. Arabia, Sheryl A. Simms, Liz A. Nelson; *ed:* (BSED) His, N IL Univ 1965; (MA) Ed, Rockford Coll 1972; CAS Admin, N IL Univ; *cr:* Teacher Kinnikinnick Sch 1965-; *ai:* NCSS Mem; NEA Life Mem; IL Ed Assn Regional Cncl Rep Mem; Kinnikinnick Ed Assn (Mem, Co-Founder Local Assn, Pres, Secy, Building Rep, VP, Chief Negotiator); Phi Delta Kappa (Mem, Fnd & Legislative Chm); Boone Cty Cntrl Comm (Mem, Precinct Committeeman); Belvidere Fire & Police Commission (Chm, Secy); Natl Wildlife Fed Life Mem; Defenders of Wildlife Involvement Mem; Holy Trinity Episcopal Church (Mem, Vestryman); Co-Author Soc Stud & Gifted Ed Curr Kinnikinnick Curr Comm; Winnebago Cty Amer His Teacher of Yr Daughters of Amer Revolution 1988; Writer & Performer; *home:* 119 E Boone St Belvidere IL 61008

O'CONNOR, BARBARA BLOUGH, Third Grade Teacher; *b:* Avon, OH; *w:* Stan E. (dec); *c:* Amy M. Domanico, Christian E., Kevin C., Todd R.; *ed:* (BS) Elem Ed, Kent St Univ 1954; Various Univs; *cr:* 3rd Grade Teacher Justin E Rowland 1954-55; 4th Grade Teacher Greensburg Elem 1966-67; 3rd-6th Grade Teacher Non Graded Sch 1967-71; 3rd/4th Grade Teacher E Liberty Sch 1971-82; 3rd Grade Teacher Kleckner Elem 1982-; *ai:* Touch of Green Editorial Bd; Eng & Sci Graded Course of Study Comms; Intnl Rdng Assn 1979-; Kappa Kappa Iota Chronacleer 1988-89; Jefferson Grange 1945-; Weathervane Theater Boutique Treas 1981-; Outstanding Elem Teachers of America 1973; Nominee GEA Service Ed Awd 1978; Jennings Scholar 1972; *office:* Kleckner Elem Sch 1900 Greensburg Rd Greensburg OH 44232

O'CONNOR, CAROL KURNIG, Science/Social Studies Teacher; *b:* Allentown, PA; *m:* Lawrence T.; *c:* Sarah, Maureen, Daniel; *ed:* (BA) Hum, Gwynedd Mercy Coll 1967; Bethany Coll/Eastern IL Univ/Univ of Scranton; *cr:* Teacher Holy Cross Sch 1962-63, Gwynedd-Mercy Acad 1963-66, Archbishop Wood HS 1967-97, Merion Mercy Acad 1971-72, St Theresa Sch 1973-76; St Elizabeth Sch 1983-; *ai:* PA Jr Acad of Sci Spon; Religion Coord; Dir of Religious Ed St Elizabeth Parish; PA Jr Acad of Sci 1963-; Assn of Coord of Religious Ed 1984-; Natl Sci Teacher Grants 1986-70; *office:* St Elizabeth Sch 433 Pershing Blvd Whitehall PA 18052

O'CONNOR, DALE LEGGETT, Computer Ed Teacher/Dept Head; *b:* Miami, FL; *m:* William Dean; *c:* Erin K.; *ed:* (AA) Phys Ed, Miami-Dade Jr Coll 1969; (BS) Phys Ed, FL Atlantic Univ 1971; (MS) Phys Ed/Adult Ed, FL Intnl Univ 1975; Advanced Trng Cmptr Programming; *cr:* Teacher Margate Mid Sch 1971-72; Teacher/Coach South Broward HS 1972-74; Teacher/Swim/Water Polo Coach South Miami HS 1978-79; Teacher/Coach Suwannee HS 1979-; *ai:* Head Swim Coach Boys & Girls Squads; United Teachers of Suwannee Cty, NEA 1982-; FL HS Act Assn 1987-; Amer Red Cross Water Safety Instr Trainer 1966-, 25 Yr Service 1989; Cousteau Society 1971-; Audubon Society 1980-89; *office:* Suwannee HS 1314 Pine Ave Live Oak FL 32060

O'CONNOR, JOHN S., 7th-11th Grade English Teacher; *b:* New York City, NY; *m:* Claiborne Mc Clement; *c:* Sean, Brian; *ed:* (BA) Eng/His, Johns Hopkins Univ 1954; Trinity Coll, Long Island Univ, Adelphi Coll, Hofstra Coll; *cr:* Teacher/Coach Kingswood Sch 1954-60, St Louis Cntry Day Sch 1960-64, ALbuquerque Acad 1964-; *ai:* Var Wrestling & Tennis Coach; Stu Adv; NM Wrestling Coaches Assn Pres 1978-82; Village of Los Ranchos (Trustee 1984-, Fire Chief 1982-84); N Valley Neighborhood Assn Pres 1980-86; Articles Published Local Papers & Magazines; *office:* Albuquerque Acad 6400 Wyoming Blvd NE Albuquerque NM 87109

O'CONNOR, MARY KAY CONLEY, Home Economics Teacher; *b:* Lewistown, PA; *m:* John R.; *ed:* (BED) Home Ec, Indiana Univ of PA 1976; Elem Cert Elem Ed, St Francis Coll; *cr:* Teacher/Asst Prin St Mark Sch 1977-82; Home Ec Teacher 1982-, Practical Art Chairperson 1988- Bellwood Antis HS; Instr Mt Aloysius Jr Coll 1988-; *ai:* Bellwood Antis FHA Adv; PA St Ed Assn, NEA, Bellwood-Antis Ed Assn 1982-; Clothing Construction Judge for 4-H Club Competition; *office:* Bellwood-Antis HS Martin St Bellwood PA 16617

O'CONNOR, TERRY JAMES, English Teacher; *b:* Seattle, WA; *m:* Janice Watson; *ed:* (BA) Eng, Univ of WA 1968; Grad Work Univ of WA, UPS, WA St Univ, Cntrl WA St Coll, W WA St Coll; *cr:* Teacher Nathan Hale HS 1968-75; Teacher/Dept Head Garfield HS 1975-85; Teacher Auburn HS 1985-; *ai:* Asst Golf Coach; SAT Prep Instr; NEA, WA Ed Assn; Advanced Placement Eng Consultant for Coll Bd.

ODAMA, KUNIYE, Mathematics Teacher; *b:* San Jose, CA; *m:* Donald K.; *c:* Eileen, Robert; *ed:* (BS) Home Ec, Univ of CA Los Angeles 1960; *cr:* Home Ec Teacher/Cnslr Belvedere Jr HS 1961-68; 3rd Grade Teacher Mesa Robles Elem 1985; Math Teacher Mesa Robles Jr HS 1986-; *ai:* Math Count Team Coach 1989-; *office:* Mesa Robles Jr HS 16060 Mesa Robles Dr Hacienda Heights CA 91745

O'DEA, TIMOTHY JOHN, Guidance Counselor; *b:* Jersey City, NJ; *ed:* (BA) His, Jersey City St Coll 1974; (MA) Human Dev, Fairleigh Dickinson Univ 1984; NJ St Cert in Stu Personel Services, Admin & Supervision; Amer Coaching Effectiveness Prgm Certified; *cr:* His Teacher 1974-87, Athletic Coord 1983-, Guidance Cnslr 1987- Toms River Intermediate Sch West; *ai:* Boys Soccer & Bsktbl Coach; Intnl Assn of Bsktbl Ofcls 1976-; *office:* Toms River Intermediate Sch W Intermidiate West Way Toms River NJ 08753

O'DELL, FAYE LOFTIN, 7th Grade Teacher; *b:* Newnan, GA; *m:* Thomas D.; *c:* Esther M. Shellnutt, David R., Matt; *ed:* (BS) Spec Ed, Tift Coll 1984; (BS) Mid Sch, GA Coll 1985; *cr:* 5th Grade Teacher Henderson Elem Sch 1984-85; 6th Grade Teacher 1985-86, 6th/8th Grade Teacher 1986-87, 7th Grade Teacher/Team Leader 1987- Henderson Jr HS; *ai:* Newspaper Adv; Media Comm; 7th Grade Team Leader; Steering Comm Mem with Prin & Supt; PTO Secy 1987-88; First Baptist Church (Pres, Nominating Comm 1989-), Woman of the Yr 1990; *office:* Henderson Mid Sch 820 N Mulberry St Jackson GA 30233

O'DELL, JULIE MYERS, HS Business Instructor; *b:* Billings, MT; *m:* Kenneth Lee; *ed:* (BS) Bus Ed, E MT Coll 1974; (MS) Bus Ed, MT St Univ 1978; Cmptrs & Reprographics, Univ of Missoula; *cr:* Secy/Dir of Stu Act E MT Coll 1970-74, Dir of Stu Act 1974 E MT Coll; Telephone Operator Mountain Bell Telephone Company 1970-74; Travel Agent Action Travel 1988; Teacher Coord Hardin Sr HS 1974-; *ai:* Classroom Educators Advisory Cncl Mem; Western Bus Ed Assn (Awds Dir 1987-, Chairperson of Regional Conference 1986) 1974-; MT Ed Assn (VP, Secy, Treas) 1974-; PEO 1987-; NBEA 1974-; Alpha Delta Kappa Pres 1978-, Violet Awd 1986; Bus Prof of America Local Adv; MT Outstanding Bus Ed & Hardin Outstanding Citizen 1987; *office:* Hardin Sr HS 702 N Terry Hardin MT 59034

O'DELL, RALPH, Librarian/Teacher; *b:* Shrub Oak, NY; *m:* Ann Gross; *c:* Eben; *ed:* (BS) Ed, Edinboro Univ 1968; (MS) Lib Sci, Long Island Univ 1971; *cr:* Librarian 1971-, Soc Stud 1979-89 Garrison Union Free Sch; *ai:* Sch Forest Comm; Amer Ornithologists Union; Bedford Audubon Society Pres; Hudson Highlands Land Trst Dir 1989-; *home:* 360 Peekskill Hollow Rd Putnam Valley NY 10579

O'DELL, WANDA MALONE, Mathematics & Algebra Teacher; *b:* Greenwood, SC; *m:* Simuel Dennis; *c:* Travis L.; *ed:* (BA) Elem Ed/Scndry Math Ed, 1977, (MA) Elem Ed, 1979 Clemson Univ; PET Trng; CBE Trng; Mastery Learning Trng Session; *cr:* 7th Grade Lang Art Teacher Ware Shoals Jr HS 1977-79; General Math Teacher Ware Shoals HS 1979-80; 7th/8th Grade Math/Algebra Teacher Ware Shoals Jr HS 1980-; *ai:* Incentive Comm 1988-; Consensus Based Evaluation Comm; Palmetto St Teachers Assn; *office:* Ware Shoals Jr HS West Main Ware Shoals SC 29692

ODELL, WESLEY W., Ag Science Teacher/Voc Dir; *b:* Houston, TX; *m:* Minnie Ewald; *c:* Tracy, Marcy; *ed:* (BS) Ag Ed, 1968, (MED/AG) Agriculture, 1974 SWTSU; Voc Supvr; *cr:* Ag Sci Teacher Canyon HS 1968-; Voc Coord Comal Ind Sch Dist 1989-; *ai:* Adv Comal Cty Young Farmers; VATAT (Dir 1976-79) 1968-; TSTA 1968-, Life Mem; NVATA 1974-; Lions Club Pres 1977-78; Freiheit Bowling Bd 1984-86; Area Agriculture Teachers Pres 1985-86; Honorary St Farmer 1972; Honorary Amer Farmer 1985; Outstanding Conservation Teacher 1986; *office:* Canyon HS 1421 Hwy 81 E New Braunfels TX 78130

ODEN, HARTLEY CALVIN, Math Dept Chairman; *b:* Mc Keesport, PA; *m:* Catherine Pauline Hess; *c:* Sandra Lee, Virginia Gail Baker, Hartley Richard, Charles Ronald; *ed:* (BS) Math, Thiel Coll 1951; (MA) Ed, Westminster Coll 1963; Univ of Rochester; Youngstown St Univ; Slippery Rock Univ; *cr:* Math/Sci Teacher Union Township HS 1951-52; Math/Chem/Physics Teacher Bessemer HS 1952-58; Math Teacher Mohawk Jr-Sr HS 1958-; *ai:* Natl Honor Society Comm; Photo Club Adv; Math & Sci Fair Co-Chm; Mohawk Ed Assn Pres 1964-67; Midwestern PSEA Math Teachers Pres 1959-60; PSEA; NEA; PCTM; NCTM; Kappa Delta Pi; MEA; Mohawk Educator of Yr 1974; Local Barbershop Harmony Society Pres 1974-75 & 1983; Barbershopper of Yr 1973 & 1983; Bessemer Presbyn Ch Clerk of Session; *office:* Mohawk Jr Sr HS Mohawk School Rd Bessemer PA 16112

ODOM, CAROL WOOD, Third Grade Teacher; *b:* Rapid City, SD; *m:* Robert Carl; *c:* Bobby, Rebekah; *ed:* (BA) Elem, 1977, (MS) Rdng, 1986 OK Univ; Quest, Gesell Trng; TESA Instr; *cr:* Aide Monroe Elem 1973-76; Teacher Jackson Elem 1977-; *ai:* Prof Educators of Norman Rep; 1st/2nd Grade Girls T-Ball Coach; PTA Rep; Prof Educators of Norman Rep 1989-; OK Educators Assn, NEA 1980-; Mc Farlin Meth Church 3rd Grade Sunday Sch 1987-88; Jackson Elem Teacher of Yr; Jackson Elem PEN Rep; *office:* Jackson Elem Sch 520 S Wylie Rd Norman OK 73069

ODOM, MARTHA MC KENZIE, 4th/5th/6th Grade Lang Teacher; *b:* Little Rock, MS; *w:* Robert L. (dec); *c:* Yolanda, Michelle; *ed:* (BA) Bus Ed, MS Valley St Univ 1968; (BS) Elem Ed, MS St Univ 1980; *cr:* Teacher 1968-69; Secy 1969-70 Harris HS; Teacher Beulah Hubbard HS 1970-; *ai:* Newton Cty Teachers Assn; MS Assn of Ed; *home:* Rt 2 Box 50 Collinsville MS 39325

ODOM, SANDRA DARLENE, Jr HS Science Teacher; *b:* Cleveland, OH; *ed:* (BA) Ed, 1984, (MA) Ed, 1989 Univ of MS; *cr:* Sci Teacher Fairview Jr HS 1986-; *ai:* Sci Club & Fair Spon; *office:* Fairview Jr HS Rt 1 Box 268 Golden MS 38847

O'DONNELL, HUGH JOHN, JR., Social Studies/Cmptrs Teacher; *b:* Brooklyn, NY; *m:* Linda; *c:* Christopher; *ed:* (BS) Sociology, Portland St Univ 1971; Teacher Trng, Portland St Univ 1975; *cr:* Pre-Voc Coord Levi Anderson Sch 1975-76; Soc Stud Teacher Meadow Park Jr HS 1976-77; Substitute Teacher Beaverton Sch Dist #48 1979-81; Soc Stud/Cmptr Teacher/Cmptr Network Admin J W Poynter Jr HS 1981-; *ai:* Equivalency Credit & 8th Grade Soc Stud Curr Comm; ASCD 1989-; Hillsboro Ski Club Dir 1985-; NW Regional Ed Lab Sch Leadership Team 1985-89; Book Published; *office:* J W Poynter Jr HS 1535 NE Grant St Hillsboro OR 97124

O'DONNELL, JAMES PETER, 5th Grade Teacher; *b:* Newburgh, NY; *m:* Susan Dimatteo; *c:* Kathleen, Kevin; *ed:* (BA) Elem Ed, Barrington Coll 1973; (MED) Elem Admin, Providence Coll 1979; *cr:* 5th Grade Teacher Seekonk Sch Dept 1973-; *ai:* Bsktbl Coach; Teacher Evaluation; Summer Sch Cmptr Camp; Bsktbl Summer Sch Instr; NEA, MA Educators Assn 1973-; Bristol Wrestling Club VP 1988-89; Bristol Little League Mgr 1990-; Wrote Article for Providence Journal on Ed.

O'DONNELL, PATRICIA A., Kindergarten Teacher; *b:* Cortland, NY; *ed:* (BA) Elem Ed, 1972, (MS) Elem Ed, 1976 St Univ Coll-Cortland; *cr:* Kndgtn Teacher 1972-75, 1st Grade Teacher 1975-88, Kndgtn Teacher 1989- South New Berlin Cntrl; *ai:* Mem Morning Prgm Team; Mem Fac Drug/Alcohol Awareness Team; Mem Building Improvement Team; South New Berlin Fac Assn (Pres 1980-82/Treas 1985-89); Delta Kappa Gamma Corresponding Secy 1986-; Developer of South New Berlin Morning PRGM; *office:* S New Berlin Central Sch Main St South New Berlin NY 13843

O'DONNELL-SMITH, PATRICIA, Science Teacher; *b:* Havertown, PA; *m:* Patrick J. Smith; *ed:* (BS) Bio, Villanova Univ 1986; Sci/Bio Ed, Kutztown Univ 1986; (MED) Sci/Ed, Lehigh Univ 1989; Cert in General Sci; Staff Dev; Instructional

Technology Ed & Microcomputers in Ed, Lehigh Univ; *cr:* 9th Grade Substitute Bio Teacher 1986-87, 9th Grade Substitute Phys Sci Teacher 1987-88, 9th Grade Phys Sci Teacher 1988- Northampton Jr HS; *ai:* Sci Club Adv; Head Womens Cross Cntry Coach; Lehigh Univ Asst Track Coach; PA St Ed Assn, East Coast Conference Coaches Assn, Eastern Coaches Athletic COnference 1987-; Lehigh Univ Grad Assistantship to Study Sci Ed; Summer Microbiology Researcher at Lehigh Univ Biotechnology; *home:* 68 Dorothy Ave Bethlehem PA 18015

ODROBINA, PETER MARTIN, Physical Education Instructor; *b:* Buffalo, NY; *c:* Peter Jr.; *ed:* (AS) Recreation, Erie Comm Coll 1970; (BS) HPER, Univ of Buffalo 1972; Working towards Masters Health Related; *cr:* Phys Ed Instr John F Kennedy HS 1972-; *ai:* Girls Jr Var Bsktbl & Boys Var Bsbl; NYSVT, PTA 1972-; *home:* PO Box 1353 Cheektowaga NY 14225

ODUM, LANETTE BARRON, First Grade Teacher; *b:* Eastman, GA; *m:* Frank Wade II; *c:* Kreslyn, Barron; *ed:* (AS) S GA Coll 1969; (BSHEC) Child Dev, 1971, (MED) Early Chldhd Ed, 1975 Univ of GA Athens; Cates Courses, GA Southern Coll; Write to Read; *cr:* 1st Grade Teacher Odum Elem Sch 1987-; *ai:* GA Textbook Adoption Comm 1989-; Odum Elem Sunshine Comm; Univ of GA Alumni Society; Delta Kappa Gamma Society; Arch Mem; Odum First Baptist Church; Teacher of Yr Wayne Cty; *office:* Odum Elem Sch PO Box 8 Odum GA 31555

ODUM, VIOLA ROPER, 6-8 Computer Science Teacher; *b:* Hopkinsville, KY; *m:* John M. Jr.; *ed:* (BS) Music, 1970; (MS) Admin/Supervision, 1982 Austin Peay Univ; (MS) Music, Western KY Univ 1975; Cmptr Sci Endorsement; *cr:* Music Teacher Clifty Elem 1970-73; Barren Cty Schls 1973-74; Bowling Green ISD 1974-76; Clifty Elem 1976-88; Cnptr Sci Teacher Todd Cty Mid Sch 1988-; *ai:* Pres Todd Cty Ed Todd Cnty Ed Pres 1983-87/89-; Allegre Homemakers Photographer 1988-89; Teacher Observer for KY Intersnhip Prgm 1985-; *home:* 680 Blue Hole Rd Elkton KY 42220

O'DWYER, MARY CATHERINE, Science/Computer Instructor; *b:* San Francisco, CA; *ed:* (BA) General Sci, 1950, (MSE) Bio, 1957 Immaculate Heart; MAT Equivalent Math, Stanford; Environmental Engineering/Air Pollution Control, CA Poly San Luis Obispo; *cr:* Teacher Elem Schls 1935-52; Sci/Math Teacher Bellarmine-Jefferson HS 1952-60, Bishop Garcia Diego HS 1960-62, Xavier HS 1962-66, Bellarmine-Jefferson HS 1966-85; Sci/Math/Cmptr Teacher St Robert Bellarmine 1985-; *ai:* CA Jr Schlshp Fed Adv; Prins Advisory Cncl; NSTA, Natl Math Teachers; Natl Sci Fnd Grant Chem, Bio, Math; Laboratory Dedication 1987; *home:* 520 E Orange Grove Burbank CA 91501

OEFFINGER, CHERYL K., Fourth Grade Teacher; *b:* Altoona, PA; *ed:* (BS) Elem Ed, PA St Univ 1972; Grad Stud Permanent Cert; Numerous Conferences & Wksps; *cr:* 4th Grade Teacher Roosevelt Elem Sch 1972-; *ai:* Claysburg-Kimmel Ed Assn Pres 1978-79; Beta Sigma Phi Pres 1989-, Girl of Yr 1978, 1983; Cty Railroading Comm; Sch Bd Dist Contributions Recognition; *office:* Roosevelt Elem Sch Bedford St Claysburg PA 16625

OELKE, DEBBI A., Third Grade Teacher; *b:* Petoskey, MI; *m:* John; *ed:* (BA) Elem Ed/Soc Stud/Geography, W MI Univ 1977; Working Towards Masters Rdng; *cr:* 6th Grade Teacher 1979-83, 5th Grade Teacher 1983-84, 3rd Grade Teacher 1984-89 St Francis Xavier; *ai:* Yrbk Staff; Soc Comm; *home:* 1020 Jefferson Ave Petoskey MI 49770

OESCH, RUTH ASHER, 8th Grade Language Art Teacher; *b:* Blackey, KY; *m:* Daniel D.; *c:* Sarah M.; *ed:* (BA) Eng/His/Poly Sci, Union Coll 1963; Grad Work W KY Univ & Univ of Louisville; *cr:* Teacher Perry Cty Schls 1963-64, Jefferson Cty Schls 1964-70; Asst Prin 1986-88, Teacher 1984- St Barnabas Sch; *ai:* Lang Art Dept Chm; NCEA Mem 1984-; Louisville Cmmty Fnd Grant; *home:* 11104 Berwick Pl Louisville KY 40243

OFFENBORN, KATHERINE CHRISTA, Second Grade Teacher; *b:* Teaneck, NJ; *ed:* (BS) Elem Ed, St Univ of NY Oswego 1962; Katherine Gibbs Bus Course for Coll Women; Grad Stud St Univ of NY Oswego & Oneonta; *cr:* 2nd Grade Teacher Ft Plain Cntrl Sch 1964-; *ai:* NYSTA, NEA, Fort Plain Teachers Assn 1964-; Ft Klock Historic Restoration (Trustee 1978-, Treas 1987-88, 1990); Leatherstocking Spinners & Weavers VP 1988-; *office:* Harry Hoag Elem Sch High St Fort Plain NY 13339

OFFERMAN, RICHARD ALLEN, Math/Cmptr Programming Teacher; *b:* Detroit, MI; *ed:* (BS) Math, 1974, (MA) Counseling, 1982 W MI Univ; *cr:* Math/Cmptr Prgm Teacher Albion Sr HS 1976-; *ai:* Cmptr Club Co-Adv; Math Curr Review Comm; Albion Ed Assn VP 1984-86; Albion Ed Assn Pres 1986-88; MI Assn for Cmptr in Learning; *office:* Albion Sr HS 225 Watson Albion MI 49224

OFFUTT, MICHAEL LEE, Chemistry Teacher; *b:* Aurora, IL; *m:* Gay; *c:* Scott; *ed:* (BS) Chem, IL St Univ 1970; (MSED) Scndry Ed, N IL Univ 1976; Cooperative Learning; *cr:* Chem Teacher Barrington HS 1970-; *ai:* IL Sci Teachers Assn, NSTA, IL Chem Teachers Assn; Physics & Chem Song Bag; *office:* Barrington HS 616 W Main St Barrington IL 60010

O'GAVAGHAN, JOHN ALBERT, Sixth Grade Teacher; *b:* Syracuse, NY; *m:* Jennifer Neild; *c:* Heather, Colleen; *ed:* (AB) Philosophy/Scholastic, St Bernards Seminary 1967; (MS) Elem Ed, Syracuse Univ 1970; Grad Courses Theology, St Bernards Seminary 1967-68; Public Sch Admin, Syracuse Univ 1980-82; *cr:* 3rd Grade Teacher 1971-75, 2nd-4th Grade Teacher 1975-76, 4th Grade Teacher 1976-87 Fayetteville Elem Sch; 6th Grade Teacher Wellwood Mid Sch 1987-; *ai:* Building Comm; Faculty Play; NY St Teachers, NY St United Teachers; Vietnam Veterans of Amer (Secy 1986-87, Bd of Dirs 1989-), Vietnam Veteran of Yr 1987; Cntrl NY Veterans Outreach Center Bd of Dir 1990; Military Service Vietnam 1970-71; NY St Conspicuous Service Cross, Gallantry Cross Republic of Vietnam Army Commendation Medal; Published His Articles; *home:* 242 Marsh Dr De Witt NY 13214

OGDEN, SALLY NORTHWAY, French/Psychology Teacher; *b:* Denver, CO; *ed:* (BA) Fr, CO St Univ 1968-72; (MA) Curr/ Instruction, Univ of N CO 1978; Foreign Lang Leadership Inst Univ of N CO; Cooperation Natl Network Natl Hum Ed Center; *cr:* Teacher Dunstan Jr HS 1972-85, Chatfield Sr HS 1985-; *ai:* Soph Class & Sr Lock-In Spon; Chaperone 15 Stu to France; CO Congress of Foreign Lang Teachers Bd of Dir 1978-79, Natl St Teachers of Yr 1977-; CO Congress of Foreign Lang Teachers & Bd of Dir 1978-79; Delta Kappa Gamma Womens Educl Honorary; Phi Sigma Lota Romance Lang Honorary; Jeffco Cooperative Learning Team 1980-; Guidance Advisory Cncl St of CO 1977; Postitive Attudies Teacher/Stu Dunstan 1982-83; Stu Staff Responsibilities Comm; Advisory Prgm Dunstan Jr; Jeffco 2nd Lang Teachers Exec Cncl; Jeffco Schls Books Illustrator; CO Teacher of Yr 1977; CO St Univ Honor Alumni Awd 1977; Featured Denver Post Contemporary; Adjunct Instr; CO St Univ Grade Course; Consultant on Discipline; Metivation, Stress, Learning Styles & Cooperation; Featured Channel 9 News Spec on Discipline 1984; CO Teacher of Yr Selection Comm 1978-79; Promotional Video Tape for Jim Fay Discipline With Love & Logic; Honored Guest Grad Exercises Green Mountain HS 1981; *office:* Chatfield Sr HS 7227 S Simms St Littleton CO 80227

OGHIGIAN, JEANETTE LINDA, Teacher; *b:* Chicago, IL; *ed:* (BA) Soc Sci/Eng, Univ of CA Los Angeles 1967; *cr:* 2nd/3rd Grade Teacher Riviera Elem Sch 1968-.

OGILVIE, CORA LUCERO, 5th Grade Teacher; *b:* San Jose, NM; *m:* J. Richard; *ed:* (AA) Elem Ed, Trinidade St Jr Coll 1956; (BS) Elem Ed, 1959, (MA) Elem Ed, 1966- Univ of NM; Post Masters Stud Univ of NM, Univ of Denver, Univ of CO; *cr:* 4th Grade Teacher Collet Park Sch 1959-68; 5th Grade Teacher Governor Bent Sch 1968-69; Fulbright Exch Sir Alexander Mac Kenzie Sch 1969-70; 5th Grade Teacher Governor Bent Sch 1970-; *ai:* NM Acad of Sci & Sci Center Comm; Sci Fair Dir; Young Astronauts Cncl Chapter Leader; Soc Stud Rep; Grade Level Chairperson; NEA 1959-; NCSS 1987-89; Local & Natl ASCD 1987-89, Focus on Excl 1987 Alpha-Delta Kappa Honorary Society Mem 1968-84; NM Cystic Fibrosis Assn, Volunteer Service Awd 1968; Epilepsy cncl of Albuquerque 1983-; Deputy Registration Officer 1988-; US Agency for Intnl Dev Teach Corps Costa Rica 1967; Nom Natl Teacher of Yr 1984, 1987; Nom US West Comm Outstanding Teacher; Advisory Bd Soc Stud & Young Learner Prof Magazine; *home:* 1341 Vassar NE Albuquerque NM 87106

OGLE, CHARLES A., Fifth Grade Teacher; *b:* Knoxville, TN; *ed:* (BA) His, Carson Newman 1979; (MED) Admin/Supervision, E TN St Univ 1985; *cr:* 5th-8th Grade Teacher Turtletown Elem Sch 1979-82; 5th Grade Teacher Seymour Primary 1982-84; 8th Grade Teacher Catons Chapel 1984-85; 7th/8th Grade Teacher Seymour Mid 1985-89; 5th Grade Teacher Seymour Primary 1989-; *ai:* TN Assn Mid Schls 1985-; Sevier Cty Ed Assn Faculty Rep 1982-88; NEA, TEA 1979-; Sons of Confederate Veterans Recording Secy 1989-; Sevier Cty Library Bd Chm 1990; Rdng Consultant Clairmont Press 1989-; *office:* Seymour Mid Sch Pitner Rd Seymour TN 37865

OGLE, CLIFTON ROBERT, Science Teacher/Sci Dept Chair; *b:* Chickasha, OK; *m:* La Fonda Davis; *c:* Teresa K., Anna V.; *ed:* (BS) Natural Sci/Bio, 1968, (MED) Sci Ed, 1972 Central St Univ; Engineering Technology 1972; OK St Univ; *cr:* Teacher US Grant HS 1968-70, Putnam West HS 1970-72; Pres Alpha Mud & Beta Chemical 1981-85; Teacher/Dept Chm US Grant HS 1985-; *ai:* Chm Faculty Advisory 1986-; Spon SADD 1986-89; Bd Dir OKC Sci Fair 1985-; Textbook Comm 1989; Curr Comm 1989-; Asst Girls Bsktbl; Head Soccer; AFT Building Rep 1985-; Natl Sci Fnd Grants 1969/1970; *office:* U S Grant H S 5000 S Pennsylvania Oklahoma City OK 73119

OGLE, PATRICIA J., Fifth Grade Teacher; *b:* Wildwood, NJ; *m:* Samuel R.; *ed:* (BS) Ed, 1955, (MA) Advanced Elem Ed, 1966 Glassboro St Coll; Career Ed, Cmptr Ed; *cr:* 3rd Grade Teacher Northfield Public Schls 1955-57; 4th Grade Teacher 1957-62, 5th Grade Teacher 1962- Ocean City Public Schls; *ai:* Natl Jr Honor Society Faculty, Guest Reader Prgm Faculty, Rdng Curr, Affirmative Action Comms; NEA, NJ Ed Assn 1955-; Cape May Cty Ed Assn; Ocean City Ed Assn 1957-; Delta Kappa Gamma Recording Secy 1972-74; Amer Assn of Univ Women Treas 1965-70; *home:* 6 Red Oak Dr Ocean View NJ 08230

OGLESBY, JACQUELINE JACKSON, Teacher; *b:* Tuskegee, AL; *m:* Richard Donald; *c:* Dianne Holston, Keven L. Smith, Karyn L. Smith; *ed:* (BS) Elem Ed, AL St Univ 1974; *cr:* Teacher Lewis Adams Elem 1973-74, Girard Elem 1976-82, Honeysuckle Mid Sch 1982-; *ai:* Northview HS Band Booster Bd; NEA, AEA, DEA; Order of Eastern Star.

OGLIARUSO, BASILA ELIZABETH (GALLO), Second Grade Teacher; *b:* New York, NY; *m:* Michael Anthony; *c:* Michael D.; *ed:* (BA) Ed/Sci, 1959, (MS) Ed, 1963 Brooklyn Coll; *cr:* 2nd-4th Grade Teacher P S 123 Brooklyn 1959-63; 2nd/3rd Grade Teacher P S 277 Brooklyn 1963-65; 2nd Grade Teacher Gilbert Linkous Elem Sch 1971-; *ai:* Chm Design for Learning; Mem Sci Curr Comm; Sch Coord for Bus Partnership; Phi Delta Kappa 1989-; Phi Delta Kappa Outstanding Educator Awd 1989; *office:* Gilbert Linkous Elem Sch 813 Toms Creek Rd Blacksburg VA 24060

O'HAIR, STEVEN LEE, Soc Sci Teacher/Dept Chair; *b:* Beliot, KS; *m:* Trudy Ann Worley; *c:* Todd, Jennifer; *ed:* (AA) Cowley Cty Comm Coll 1968; (BS) Psych, 1971, (BSED) Scndry Ed, 1975 Pittsburg St Univ; Counseling Psych, Wichita St Univ; *cr:* Rec Therapist Sedg Cty Mental Health Center 1971-73; Head Therapist Wesley Medical Center 1973-75; Soc Sci Teacher Bishop Carroll HS 1975-79, Arkansas City Sr HS 1979-; *ai:* Head Sr Spon; Chm Soc Sci Dept; Prins Adv Comm; Curr Cncl; KNEA, NEA, ASCA; *home:* RR 1 507 Arkansas City KS 67005

O'HARA, GENE PAUL, 8th Grade Science Teacher; *b:* Louisville, KY; *m:* Pat Bonds; *c:* Katherine, Theresa, Angela Dukes; *ed:* (BS) Ed, 1978; (MA) Elem Ed, 1982 Univ of SC; Sci & Health Ed; *cr:* US Air Force 1955-77; Teacher Alice Drive Mid Sch 1978-; *ai:* Spon Rocket Club; Jr Optimist Club; Lit Club; Chm Prin Adv Comm; SC2 1985-; Amer Legion 1986-; Disabled Amer Veterans 1989-; Alice Drive Teacher of Yr 1986-87; *office:* Alice Drive Mid Sch 40 Miller Rd Sumter SC 29150

O'HEARN, JAMES BRENDAN, English Department Chair; *b:* Arlington, MA; *m:* Lynne Hedin; *ed:* (BA) Eng, Univ of MA 1964; (MED) Ed, Amer Intnl Coll 1971; IN Univ, Dept of Defense Information Sch; *cr:* Eng Teacher Birchland Park Sch 1965-67; Broadcasting Dept of Defense Information Sch 1968-69; Eng Chm Birchland Park Sch 1969-; *ai:* HS Var Soccer Coach; NEA, MA Teachers Assn, E Longmeadow Teachers Assn, NCTE; Volunteer Service Awd; NCAA II Bsktbl Natl Championship Ofcl Announcer; *office:* Birchland Park Sch 50 Hanward Hill East Longmeadow MA 01028

OHL, KAY BISH, Third Grade Teacher; *b:* Summerville, PA; *m:* Ray; *c:* Rae L. Dobson, Cindy L., Tracy A. Loftin; *ed:* (BS) Elem Ed, 1970; (MED) Elem Ed, 1972 Clarion Univ 1972; *cr:* Elem Teacher Brookville Area Schs 1970-90; *ai:* Delta Kappa Gamma Society Sec 1979; *office:* Brookville Area Sch Jenks St Ext Brookville PA 15825

OHLENBURG, DIANE CATO, English Teacher; *b:* Fort Worth, TX; *m:* Jonny K.; *c:* Jan M. Mc Bride, Kristi D. Sebera; *ed:* (BA) Eng, Univ TX San Antonio 1980; *cr:* Eng Teacher Fredericksburg HS 1980-; *ai:* Future Teachers of Amer Spon; UIL Coach Informative Speaking; Assn TX Prof Educators Mem 1987-; *office:* Fredericksburg H S 202 West Travis St Fredericksburg TX 78624

OHLFEST, SHERRY VERMILION, English Teacher; *b:* Atchison, KS; *m:* John Allen; *ed:* (MA) Eng/Lang Art, Valparaiso Univ 1972; Hum Inst Summer Course Cambridge Univ England 1983; Cmptr Summer Courses; *cr:* 10th/11th Grade Eng Teacher Griffith HS 1958-59; 9th/10th Grade Eng Teacher Morgan Township Sch 1963; 6th-8th Grade Eng/Music Teacher Madison Sch 1966-68; 9th/11th Grade Eng Teacher Portage HS 1968-; *ai:* 11th Grade Curr & Textbook Comm; NEA; IN St Teachers Assn 1959-; NCTE Writing Contest 1959-; IN Cncl Teachers of Eng 1959-, Outstanding Hoosier Teacher 1983; IN Teacher of Writing 1987-; Delta Kappa Gamma; Porter Cty Family Service Assn Pres of Bd 1975-76, Leadership Awd 1976; *office:* Portage HS East 6450 Hwy 6 Portage IN 46368

OHLGREN, SANDRA SHUEY, Learning Disabilities Teacher; *b:* Chicago, IL; *m:* Richard F.; *c:* Kevin, Brace; *ed:* (MAED) Educl Admin, 1976, Specialist Educl Admin, 1978 St Cloud St Univ; Sr Arbitrator Trng Better Bus Bureau; Arbitration Trng Amer Arbitration Assn; Mediation Trng Twin Cities Mediation Center; *cr:* Teacher St Louis Park Sch Dist 1958-64, Anoka Hennipin Ind Sch Dist #II 1965-; *ai:* Mediation Trainer & Coord; Talented & Gifted Comm; Faculty Cncl; Building Leadership Team Effective Schls Project; NEA, MN Ed Assn 1965-; AFT 1988-; Advisory Bd Mem N Hennepin Comm Coll, W Suburban Mediation Center; *home:* 1512 Boone Ave N Golden Valley MN 55427

OHM, BETTY T., 3rd Grade Elementary Teacher; *b:* Valley City, ND; *m:* Carl L.; *c:* Terri Mastel, Kathy Ward, Gary Martin, Paul Martin; *ed:* (BS) Elem Ed, Mary Coll 1968; *cr:* 3rd Grade Teacher Grimsrud Elem 1966-88, Centennial Elem 1989-; *ai:* Lecture for Church; Bismarck Ed Assn Building Rep 1986-; Parents Without Partners (Pres 1977, VP 1976, Adv); *office:* Centennial Elem Sch 2800 Ithica Bismarck ND 58501

OHMAN, JAMES KEITH, Fourth Grade Teacher; *b:* Minneapolis, MN; *m:* Geraldine J.; *ed:* (BA) Elem Ed, Bemidji St 1968; Working Towards Masters Elem Ed, Univ of WI Superior; *cr:* 4th Grade Teacher Lexington Elem Sch 1968-70; 6th Grade Teacher Montgomery Lonsdale Elem Sch 1970-76; 4th Grade Teacher Ind Sch Dist #710 1976-; *ai:* Union Negotiations Comm; MFT; *home:* 308 Van Buren Ave Eveleth MN 55734

OHMAN, JEROME C., Mathematics Department Chair; *b:* Jamestown, ND; *m:* Sandra L. Hougelman; *c:* Jerome M., Debbirah Ohman-Franscona, Johanna L., Johnette C.; *ed:* (BA) Bio, Univ of MT 1963; (MA) Teaching of Math, Wayne St Univ 1976; (ME) Public Sch Admin, Univ of LA Verne 1990; Prgm Quality Review; Cntrl Valley Math Project; *cr:* Educator Turlock Jr HS 1966-; *ai:* Math Superbowl Coach; Yr Round Ed & Stu Advisement Comm; Turlock Teachers Assn (Pres 1967-68, Treas 1969-71); CTA, NEA; PDK; Assn of CA Sch Administrators; Natl Sci Fnd Fellowship Wayne St Univ; *home:* 4718 Colorado Ave Turlock CA 95380

OHME, GREGORY ALAN, Music Teacher; *b:* Wenatchee, WA; *ed:* (BS) Ed/Music, WA St Univ 1985; *cr:* Music/Band Teacher Quincy Sch Dist 1986-; *ai:* Band; *office:* Quincy HS 16 6th Ave SE Quincy WA 98848

OHMS, DIANE MARIE, Sixth Grade Teacher; *b:* Harlan, IA; *ed:* (BS) Elem Ed, IA St Univ 1982; Grad Work Gifted Ed; *cr:* 6th Grade Teacher Lincoln Elem 1982-; *ai:* Talented & Gifted, Thinking Skills, Soc Stud Sch Dist Comms; Sch Geography Bee Organizer; His Day Coach; Spencer Ed Assn 1982-; Kappa Delta Pi 1980-; Bethany Luth Church 1982-; *office:* Spencer Cmmty Sch Dist 615 4th Ave SW Spencer IA 51301

OHMSTEDT, DIANA M. BUSTILLO, Spanish Teacher; *b:* Barranquilla, Colombia; *m:* Harry O.; *c:* Diana E. Ohmstedt-Wildermuth, Marguerite R.; *ed:* (BA) Ed/Lang, Escuela Superior de Idiomas Universidad del 1959; Liceniatura Ed/Lang, Atlantico Barranquilla 1960; (MA) Span, SUNY Albany 1966; *cr:* Eng Teacher Escuela Superior de Idiomas 1959-60; Span/Fr Teacher Mechanicville HS 1961-63; Lang Laboratory Conversational Span Teacher Skidmore Coll 1971-72; Span Teacher Saratoga Springs Jr-Sr HS 1981-; *ai:* More Effective Sch Comm Mem; NYSAFLT, SSTA, NYSUT, AFT; Natl & Local AAUW Intnl Relations Chairperson 1978-; Academic Fellowship Skidmore Coll 1958-59; *office:* Saratoga Springs Sr HS W Circular St Saratoga Springs NY 12866

OKARMA-TKACZ, JOYCE M., Mathematics Dept Teacher; *b:* Wallington, NJ; *m:* Raymond Tkacz; *ed:* (BA) Math, Paterson St Coll 1965; *cr:* Math Teacher Christopher Columbus Mid Sch 1965-; *ai:* Math Dept Helping Teacher; Dist Standard Testing, Math Articulation, Cmptr-Math, Curr Revision Comm; Affirmative Action, T & E Goal, Team Approach Comm Mem; Gifted & Talented Comm Chairperson; NEA, NJEA, CTA 1965-; CCMSH&S (Treas 1976-89) 1965-; CCMSFO VP 1965-; CCJHSFO (Nominating Comm, Treas) 1965-; Conducted Career Infusion Pgrm; *office:* Christopher Columbus Mid Sch 350 Piaget Ave Clifton NJ 07011

O'KEEFE, DONNA DARRAH, Level Coord/Lang Arts & Lit; *b:* Manchester, NH; *m:* Michael D.; *c:* Amanda; *ed:* (BA) Eng, Notre Dame Coll 1970; Creative Writing; Myths in Lit; Adolescent Coping Skills; *cr:* 5th-8th Grade Eng Teacher Sacred Heart 1970-72; 9th Grade Eng/Lit Teacher Manchester HS Cntrl 1973-77; 6th-8th Grade Lang Teacher 1987-, Arts Level Coord 1988- West Side Cath Regional; *ai:* 8th Grade Class Adv Grad HS PLacement Fund Raisers; Discipline Grades 6th-8th; NCTE; Amer Horse Show 1987-; Lions Quest 1989-; Teacher of Yr Favorite Teacher 1972; *office:* West Side Catholic Regional 281 Cartier St Manchester NH 03102

OKESON, RICHARD GARY, 6th Grade Teacher; *b:* Butler, PA; *m:* Helen Kay; *c:* Amy B., Mark R.; *ed:* (BS) Elem Ed, Slippery Rock Coll 1968; Grad Work Geology, Slippery Rock Coll; Math, Cmptr Sci; *cr:* 6th Grade Teacher Summit Township 1968-; *ai:* Soccer Coach; Butler Ed Assn Sch Rep 1968-; NEA 1968-; PA Ed Assn Delegate 1968-; *office:* Summit Township Sch 351 Brinker Rd Butler PA 16001

OKINS, JOAN PFLEGER, 4th Grade Teacher; *b:* Chicago, IL; *m:* George William; *c:* Catheleen, George Jr., Caren, Colleen, Fredrick; *ed:* Psych, Elmhurst Coll; Psych/Clerical, La Grange Jr Coll 1957; *cr:* Perm Sub Teacher Garden City Pub Sch 1978-83; Spec Ed Sub Teacher Redford Union Pub Sch 1980-83; Sub Teacher 1978-83; Teacher 1983- United Chrstn Sch; *ai:* Boys & Girls Club Leader Awd; Sunday Sch Teacher; HS Sr Adv/Spon 1986-87 & 1988-89; Yrbk Adv 1985-87; Sch Newspaper Adv; MACS; PTA Pres/VP Garden City Jr HS; PTSA Pres Garden City HS; Garden City Lay Ed Comm; *office:* United Christian Sch 29205 Florence Garden City MI 48135

OKOREN, FRANCES M., Mathematics Teacher; *b:* Boon, MI; *ed:* (BS) Math, 1966, (MA) Scndry Ed, 1971 MI St Univ; Specialist Instructional Technology, Wayne St Univ 1985; AP Calculus 1989; NSF Calculus 1988-89; NSF Honors Algebra 1987-88; NSF Pascal Programming 1986; Cobol Programming 1983-84; NSF Basic Programming 1982; ITIP Trng 1988; Cooperative Learning 1988-89; *cr:* Math Teacher St Clair HS 1966-; *ai:* Cmptr Team Spon; Teachers Advisory Cncl; Math League Team Spon; Cmptr Comm; St of MI NCTM Standards Discussion Group; Blue Water Math/Sci Cncl Secy 1987-; NCTM, MCTM, DACTM, MEA, NEA, ECEA, SSM, MAA, & MACUL 1966-; Port Huron Bus Prof Womens Club VP 1988-; Natl Sci Fnd Insts Mini Grant Calculus Materials; *office:* Saint Clair H S 2200 Clinton Saint Clair MI 48079

OKOS, MARY ANN, Third Grade Teacher; *b:* Joliet, IL; *ed:* (BA) His, Coll of St Francis 1973; *cr:* 3rd Grade Teacher St Bernards 1977-80, St Jude 1980-87, St Paul the Apostle 1987-; *ai:* NCEA; *office:* St Paul the Apostle 130 N Woodlawn Joliet IL 60436

OKRUCH, THOMAS MICHAEL, Language Art Instructor; *b:* Tonawanda, NY; *m:* Susan Marie Larrabee; *c:* Kelsey M.; *ed:* (BSE) Eng, NE MO St Univ 1981; *cr:* Lang Art Teacher/Coach Western Mid Sch 1981-; *ai:* Asst HS Ftbl & Head HS Bsktbl Coach; NCTE; MO Bsktbl Coaches Assn.

OLANDER, MARK G., Seventh Grade Math Teacher; *b:* Bristol, CT; *m:* Janice Anderson; *c:* Amy, Tim; *ed:* (BA) Eng, 1967, (MA) Comm, 1971 Fairfield Univ; Ed Univ of Bridgeport; Math Inst Wesleyan Univ 1986; Integration Inst, Mc Gill Univ 1989; *cr:* 4th Grade Teacher 1968-81, 6th Grade Teacher 1982-83 Meeting House Hill Sch; 7th Grade Teacher Mid Sch 1984-; *ai:* 7th Grade Team Leader; New Fairfield Ed Assn Pres 1974-75; Assn Teachers of Math in CT; Western CT Assn for Handicapped & Retarded (Mem, Bd Pres); Distinguished Parent Awd 1989; Assn of Persons with Severe Handicaps Mem; Distinguished Parent Awd 1989;Naugatuch Valley Society of Persons with Autism Mem; CT Society of Persons with Autism Mem; Autism Society of America (Mem, Nom Dir 1990); Knights of Columbus (Mem, Officer 1989-); St Francis Xavier Church (Mem, Active Mem, Music Ministry); Recognized for Excellence in Ed Western CT Superintendents Assn & Union Carbide Corp 1990; Nom Teacher of Yr 1990; *home:* 3 Cobbler Ln New Milford CT 06776

OLASHUK, LEANORA D. GREGORIO, Instructor-Health Assistant; *b:* Weirton, WV; *m:* John E.; *c:* Donna Olashuk Gialluco, John, Mary Olashuk Davis, Robert; *ed:* Monogalia General Hospital 1955; (BSN) Nursing, W Liberty Coll 1982; Voc Ed, Marshall Univ 1985; Grad Stud WV Univ; *cr:* Registered Nurse Weirton General Hospital 1955-59; Sch Nurse Weir Jr HS 1969-81; Instr John D Rockefeller IV Voc Tech Center 1982-; *ai:* WV Ed Assn 1970-; AVA 1984-; Delta Kappa Gamma 1985-; Amer Red Cross Past Secy; *office:* John D Rockefeller IV Voc Tech Rt 2 New Cumberland WV 26047

OLDENBURG, MIRIAM KVIGNE, Third/Fourth Grade Teacher; *b:* Viroqua, WI; *m:* Darrel; *c:* Dustin, Jordan, Kyle; *ed:* (BS) Elem Ed, Univ of WI La Crosse 1979; Working Towards Masters Prof Dev, Univ of WI La Crosse 1990; *cr:* 3rd/4th Grade Classroom Teacher Seneca Dist Schls 1980-; *ai:* Natl Sci Fnd Grant Sci Enhancement Project; *office:* Lynxville Elem Sch Seneca WI 54654

OLDHAM, DONALD G., Science/Health Teacher; *b:* Martin, TN; *w:* Lura Ann Weatherford (dec); *c:* John, Julie; *ed:* (BS) Bus Ed/D E, 1971, (MA) Bus Ed, 1976, Admin, 1979 Murray St Univ; Elem & Scndry Prin Cert; Mid Sch Sci Cert; *cr:* Jr HS Math Teacher Lowes Elem 1971-73; Jr HS Sci Teacher Wingo Elem 1973-; *ai:* Sci Fair Coord; Stu Cncl Spon; Mid Sch Ftbl Coach; Asst Prin Wingo Elem; Started & Organized Jr HS Prom; Wingo Elem Philosophy Comm; Graves Cty Ed Assn (Various Comm, Negotiations Team) 1971-; KY Ed Assn St Convention Delegate 1984; NEA Mem; Landrum Lodge 448 All Chairs 1971-, Past Master Awd 1975; 1st Assembly of God; Natl Sci Teachers Convention 1988; Regional Caucus Democrats Delegate 1985; Graves Cty Democratic Exec Comm; Lowes Elem Teacher of Yr 1972; Town & Cntry Real Estate Assoc with Coldwell Banker; *office:* Wingo Mid Sch Lebanon St Wingo KY 42088

OLDHAM, JULIA JONES, Office Education Coordinator; *b:* Poteau, OK; *m:* Stanley Raymond; *c:* Marshall, Ashley; *ed:* (BA) Ed/Bus/Eng, Baylor Univ 1974; (MSOE) Occupational Ed, Univ of Houston 1989; *cr:* Eng Teacher Caprock HS 1983-85; Eng VOE Teacher/Coord Mayde Creek HS 1986-; *ai:* Drug Awareness Team Leader; Bus Prof of America Spon 1986-; Spec Olympics Volunteer 1989-; Prof Secretaries Intnl Mem 1990; Masters Thesis Published; Helped Author Bus Prof of America Regional/St/Natl Competition 1991; *office:* Mayde Creek HS 19202 Groschke Rd Houston TX 77084

OLDHAM, MIGNON HAYES, English Teacher; *b:* Jersey City, NJ; *c:* Maiya; *ed:* (BA) Eng, Univ of MI 1971; (MED) Early Chldhd Ed, Marygrove 1974; Montessori Trng; PhD Prgm Instructional Technology, Univ of MI; *cr:* Eng Teacher Osborn HS & Pershing HS & Finney HS 1972-73, Lessenger Jr HS 1973-74, Cody HS 1974-86, Renaissance HS 1986-; *ai:* NCTE 1988-; Wayne St Univ Upward Bound (Teacher, Tutor) 1989-, Outstanding Teacher 1989; Mercy Coll Outstanding Educator 1987, 1989; Detroit Public Schls Teacher of Influence 1986-89; *office:* Renaissance HS 6565 W Outer Dr Detroit MI 48235

OLDHAM, PAMELA S., Legal Secretary Instructor; *b:* Dayton, OH; *m:* Norm; *c:* Brad; *ed:* (BS) Bus Ed, E KY Univ 1968; *cr:* Bus Ed Teacher Miamisburg HS 1968-69, Sawyer Bus Coll 1970-71; Bus Ed Teacher 1971-75, Adult Ed Teacher 1975-85, Bus Ed Teacher 1985- Montgomery Cty Joint Voc Sch; *ai:* TESA Coord Montgomery Cty Joiny Voc Sch; MCJVS Employees Assn Secy 1985-; OFT, AFT 1988-; *office:* Montgomery Cty Joint Voc Sch 6800 Hoke Rd Clayton OH 45315

OLDROYD, CAROLYN A., Mathematics/Spanish Teacher; *b:* Elmira, NY; *ed:* (BS) Math, Mansfield Univ 1972; (MS) Math, Elmira Coll 1979; *cr:* Substitute Teacher N Tioga Sch Dist & Troy Sch Dist 1972-74; Math Teacher Horseheads Chrstn Sch 1974-76; Math/Span Teacher Twin Tiers Baptist HS 1976-; *ai:* Jr Class Adv; Dir of Drama; Jackson Summit Baptist Church (Choir Dir 1979-, Sunday Sch Teacher 1980-, Sunday Sch Treas 1974-); *office:* Twin Tiers Baptist HS PO Drawer K Breesport NY 14816

OLDROYD, JERALD TODD, Fifth Grade Teacher; *b:* Glenwood, UT; *m:* May Dene Torgersen; *c:* Kathleen, Wayne, Brent, Jerry; *ed:* (BA) Elem Ed, SUSC Cedar City UT 1960; Working Towards Masters; *cr:* 7th/8th Grade Teacher Richfield Jr HS 1960-61; 5th Grade Teacher 1961-74, 4th Grade Teacher 1974-84, 5th Grade Teacher 1984- Ashman Elem; *ai:* NEA 1960-, Valley Forge Teachers Medal 1974; UT Ed Assn, Sevier Ed Assn; Army Soldier 1953-55; Town Councilman, Pres; Bishops Cnslr, HS Cncl; *home:* 255 S 1st W Glenwood UT 84730

OLDVADER, LARRY L., English Teacher; *b:* Brunswick, MO; *ed:* (BA) Eng, 1971, (MA) Eng, 1972 NE MO St Univ; Working Towards PHD in Eng, Univ of MO Columbia; *cr:* Eng Teacher/Bsktbl Coach N Shelby HS 1971-75; Eng Teacher Mexico HS 1975-; *ai:* Jr Class Spon; Sr Graduation Comm Mem; Jr-Sr Prom Spon, Organizer, Supvr; NEA, MO Natl Teachers Assn, NCTE; Baptist Church; Big Brothers; MO Writing Project Schlsp; *office:* Mexico HS 639 N Wade Mexico MO 65265

OLEKSAK, WILLIAM L., 5th Grade Science/Rdng Teacher; *b:* Kittanning, PA; *m:* Kathryn Varholla; *c:* William A., Julie; *ed:* (BS) Elem Ed, Clarion Univ of PA 1974; (MED) Elem Ed, Clarion Univ of PA 1977; Post Masters Studies Sci Ed Clarion Univ of PA; *cr:* Teacher Templeton Elem 1974-79; Lenape Elem 1979-; *ai:* Rdng Tutor Spon By PTO; Resource Facilitator for Human Sexuality Seminar Spon By Catholic Parishes Ford City; PA Sci Teachers Assn 1981-; Cncl Elem Sci Inter 1981-; Armstrong Basketball Officials Pres 1983-87; Parish Cncl VP 1981-84; Eagles 1985-; Elks 1986-; Sch Dist Grants for Anti Drug Assembly; Armstrong Conservation Dist Outstanding Educator-1986; Nom PA Teacher of Yr-1988; *office:* Lenape Elem Sch 2300 Center Ave Ford City PA 16226

OLEKSY, DEBRA ANN, Mathematics Teacher; *b:* Detroit, MI; *ed:* (BA) Philosophy, Wayne St Univ 1979; (MA) Math, Univ of Detroit 1986; Assertive Discipline, Graphing Calculator, Gifted & Talented Trng; *cr:* Self-Contained 5th Grade Teacher Moore Elem 1979-82; Homeroom/4th/5th Grade Teacher Loving Elem 1982-86; Math Teacher Martin Luther King HS 1986-; *ai:* Eligibility Chairperson; Stu of Month, Pep Club, Academic Games Team Spon; Asst Sftbl Coach; Bsktbl Statistician; Jr Class Co-Spon; Soc, Curr, Sch Improvement, Textbook Selection Comms; Detroit Fed of Teachers 1979-, Teacher of Yr 1985, 1986, 1990; Perfect Attendance Awd; *office:* Martin Luther King HS 3200 E Lafayette Detroit MI 48207

OLESZKIEWICZ, KAREN GEMBARA, Elementary Education; *b:* Chicago, IL; *m:* Anthony; *c:* Sarah, Katie, Marci, Anthony; *ed:* Elem Ed, Univ of IL Chicago 1973; *cr:* Elem Ed Teacher Chrstn Liberty Acad 1979-84, Clonlara Home-Based Educl Prgm 1984-86, Seven Pillars Home Sch 1986-.

OLFF, SHARON FAITH GETTEL, Third Grade Teacher; *b:* Lebanon, PA; *m:* Richard Edward; *c:* Richard Jr.; *ed:* (BS) Elem Ed, Bloomsburg Univ 1978; (MS) Elem Ed, Millersville Univ 1981; Elem Prin Certificate, Temple Univ 1987; Peer Coaching, Cooperative Learning; *cr:* Elem Teacher Northern Lebanon Sch Dist 1978-89; Elem Prin Pine Grove Area Sch Dist 1990; *ai:* Intramural & Jr HS Field Hockey Coach; Prof Dev Comm; Amer Ed Week Chairperson; Liason Comm; NLEA, PSEA, NEA 1978-89; NAESP, PAESP 1990; Trinity UCC Church (Deacon, Elder) 1985-; Bloomsburg Univ Alumni 1978-, Outstanding Young Alumni 1990; Millersville Univ Alumni 1981-; PA Jaycees; Outstanding Young Educator of PA 1987 & Hamburg 1986; Outstanding Young Alumna Bloomsburg Univ 1990; Outstanding Young Women of America 1986, 1987; *home:* 935 Parish Pl Hummelstown PA 17036

OLICK, STEVEN ANDREW, Social Studies Dept Chairman; *b:* Nemacolin, PA; *m:* Marianne Elizabeth Farrell; *c:* Scott M., Josech C., Steven A. III, Rosemary Bouie; *ed:* (BA) His/Government, Univ of Buffalo 1952; (MS) Educl Admin, Niagara Univ 1979; Various Univs; *cr:* 7th-12th Grade Soc Stud Teacher West Valley Cntrl 1952-53, Fillmore Cntrl 1953-56; Vice Prin Starpoint 1974-76; Instr Niagara Cty Comm Coll; 10th-12th Grade Soc Stud Teacher Starpoint 1956-; *ai:* Bsktbl Coach; NHS; Sr Class Adv; Its Academic; Scholastic Bowl; At-Risk, Staff Dev, Instructional Cncl Comm; NY St United Teachers 1952-; Syracuse, Kent St, St Lawrence, Russell Sage, Vassar NDEA Grants; Presidential Scholar Distinguished Teacher Awd 1987; *home:* 5011 Saunders Settlement Rd Lockport NY 14094

OLIPHANT, ANNIE JACKSON, 7th/8th Grade Eng/His Teacher; *b:* Natchitoches, LA; *m:* James L.; *ed:* (BA) Elem Ed, 1978, (MS) Elem Teaching, 1980 Northwestern St Univ; *cr:* Teacher Clarence Elem Sch 1978-81, Campti Jr HS 1981-; *ai:* Newspaper Spon; SBLC; Prom Adv; LAE, NEA, NAE secy 1986-88 Outstanding Service; Outstanding Chrstn Female Image 1989; *home:* Rt 4 Box 744 Natchitoches LA 71457

OLITSKY, ELEANOR ROSINSKY, Retired 6th Grade Teacher; *b:* Brooklyn, NY; *m:* Paul; *c:* Steven, Randy Thau; *ed:* (BA) Sociology, Brooklyn Coll 1945; Ed/Sociology, Brooklyn Coll & Dist 18 Office; *cr:* Substitute C B Teacher NY City Schls; 4th Grade Teacher Ramaz Sch; 6th Grade Substitute Teacher, 6th Grade Teacher/Acting Admin Asst PS 135 Brooklyn.

OLIVAS, EDUARDO R., 6th Grade Teacher; *b:* Tucson, AZ; *m:* Maria Lilia; *c:* Mercedes, Margarita; *ed:* (AA) Pre-Ed, Pima Coll 1977; (BA) Elem Ed, Univ of AZ 1981; *cr:* Educator Davis Bi-ling Learning Center 1981-87; Career Cnslr Tucson Manpower Dev Corporation 1982-89; Child Care Specialist La Frontera Center 1987-88; Educator Roskruge Mid Magnet Sch 1987-; *ai:* Yrbk Patrols; TUSD Site Based Decision Making Comm; AZ Ed Assn Human Relations 1988-; Tucson Ed Assn (Human Relations 1985-86, Minority Affairs Chm 1986-88), Tlamatinime Awd 1989; *office:* Roskruge Bilingual Magnet Sch 501 E 6th St Tucson AZ 85745

OLIVE, ANN MC FARLIN, 5th Grade Teacher; *b:* Atlanta, GA; *m:* Robert E.; *c:* Robert M., Alan K.; *ed:* (BS) Home Economic Ed, GA Coll for Women 1957; Math, Gordon Coll; Elem Educ, Tift Coll; GA St Coll; GA St Univ; *cr:* Home Ec Teacher 1957-60; Math Teacher 1960-63 Yatesville HS; 4th/5th/6th Grade Teacher Yatesville Elem Sch 1965-88; 5th Grade Teacher Upson Elem Sch 1988-; *ai:* GA Assn of Educators; Yatesville Meth Church Pianist 1980-; Yatesville Lib Club 1957-60; Upson Cty Heath Comm 1957-58; *office:* Upson Elem Sch Box 151 172 Upson Elem Dr Thomaston GA 30286

OLIVER, ERNEST L., Fourth & Fifth Grade Teacher; *b:* Arlington, GA; *m:* Dorcas L.; *c:* Deborah, Ernest Jr., Jennifer; *ed:* (BA) Ed, Univ Puget Sound 1972; 5th Yr Ed; *cr:* Lt Col US Army 1943-46, 1952-70; Teacher Tacoma Public Schls 1972-; *ai:*

Intramural Sports; Asst To Prin; Photography; Knights of Columbus Dist Deputy Family of Yr 1982; US Army Lt Colonel 1952-70, Bronz Star 1967, CIB 1967; *office:* Mc Carer Elem Sch 2111 South J St Tacoma WA 98405

OLIVER, JAYNE MULLENDORE, English Teacher; *b:* Columbia City, IN; *m:* Danny R.; *c:* Aaron, Joseph; *ed:* (BA) Eng, Purdue Univ 1977; (MS) Ed, IN Univ 1988; *cr:* 6th-8th Grade Teacher Coesse Jr HS 1986-; *ai:* Sch Newspaper, Class Spon; NEA, IN St Teachers Assn 1986-; Local Parliamentary Law & Literary Society (Parliamentarian, Historian 1986-88) 1986-; BSA Tiger Cub Organizer 1987-; *office:* Coesse Jr HS 2250 S 500 E Columbia City IN 46725

OLIVER, MICHAEL CLINTON, History Teacher; *b:* Manchester, TN; *m:* Susan Norris; *ed:* (BS) His, Trevecca Coll 1975; (MS) His, Mid TN St; *cr:* Math/His Teacher Palmer 1975-76; His Teacher North 1977-78, Pelham 1979-; *ai:* Bsktbl Coach; TEA, S Historical Society; Green Peace; *office:* Pelham Elem Sch PO Box 37 Pelham TN 37366

OLIVER, ROBIN L., Science Teacher; *b:* Lynwood, CA; *m:* Sheldon Newberger; *c:* Katie; *ed:* (BA) Bio, Whittier Coll 1977; (MA) Bio, CA St Univ Fullerton 1983; Teacher Effectiveness Trng; Critical Thinking Wkshp; Classroom Management Teacher Trainer; *cr:* Tech Biologist CSOF & Army Corps of Engineer 1978, 1980; Environmental Awareness Coord YEC US Forest Service 1978-80; Lecturer CA St Univ Fullerton 1978-82, Rancho Santiago Comm Coll 1981-86; Sci Instr 1982-, Intnl Baccalaureate Coord 1986- Sonora HS; *ai:* Sch Site Cncl; NSTA 1982-; CTA; Tri Beta 1977-; Nature Conservancy 1983-; PTA Faculty Rep 1983-; CTIPP Fully Funded Grant 1984, 1985; CA Mentor Teacher 1985, 1986; *office:* Sonora HS 401 S Palm St La Habra CA 90631

OLIVER, VIRGINIA DAKAN, Pre-Kindergarten Teacher; *b:* El Paso, TX; *m:* Charles Wayne; *c:* Paul T., Mark A., Kellie L.; *ed:* (BS) Elem Ed/Kndgtn, Univ of Houston 1974; *cr:* Kndgtn Teacher Dowell Elem 1962-63, Park Elem 1965-67, Memorial Dr Elem 1969-70, Nottingham Elem 1970-73, 1987-88, Shadow Oaks Elem 1974-84; 1st Grade Teacher Houseman Elem 1986-87; Pre Kndgtn Teacher Spring Shadows Elem 1988-; *ai:* Team Leader; Teaching Adults Eng Second Lang Night Class; Assn of TX Prof Educators 1980-84; SBEA, NEA 1975-80; United Meth Women 1983-85; PTA 1962- TX Life Mem 1980; *home:* 826 Greenpark Houston TX 77079

OLIVER, WILLIAM HERVERUS, Mathematics Teacher; *b:* Miami, AZ; *m:* Virginia Carol; *c:* William Jr., Stephen P., Karen L. E., David, Andrew T., Mary K.; *ed:* (BS) Naval Sci, US Naval Acad 1958; (BS) Aeronautical Engineering, US Naval Post Grad Sch 1966; Teaching Certificate Math Ed, CA St Univ Hayward 1979; Naval Aviator 1960-78; Grad Stud Univ of Phoenix; Cmptr Sci, Northland Pioneer Coll; *cr:* Commissioned Officer US Navy 1958-78; Math Teacher Fremont HS 1979-81, Blue Ridge Jr HS 1981-; *ai:* Math Counts Coach; Math Team Adv; Athletic Events Scorekeeper & Time Keeper; NCTM 1978-; AZ Assn Teachers of Math 1983-; BSA (Scoutmaster 1970-78, 1985-, Eagle Scout 1954, Dist Commendation Awd 1988); Luth Church (Confirmation Teacher 1988-, Congregation Pres 1983-87); *office:* Blue Ridge Jr HS PO Box 885 Lakeside AZ 85929

OLIVERIO, PAULA JONES, Special Education Teacher; *b:* Philippi, WV; *m:* Joseph R.; *ed:* (BA) Elem Ed/Spec Ed, Glenville St Coll 1986; (MS) Spec Ed, WV Univ 1990; Skin Care/Cosmetics Trng Certificate, Jafra Cosmetics Inc; *cr:* Pre-Sch Teacher of Handicapped 1987, Teacher of Gifted Ed 1987-88 Barbour Cty Schls; 1st Grade Teacher Fairmont Cath Grade Sch 1988; Spec Ed Teacher Belpre City Schls 1989, St Marys HS 1989-; *ai:* Var Cheerleading, Spec Olympic Coach; Key Club Adv; Drama Dir; WV Ed Assn; Pleasant Cty Ed Assn; CEC; Bus/Prof Womens Club 1987-89, Young Careerist 1987; Kiwanis 1990; Altar Rosary Society; Intnl Retts Syndrome Assn Outstanding Amer Women; Retts Syndrome Assn Spokes Teacher; Chairperson St Judes Childrens Research Hospital; *home:* 117 Bryan Dr Saint Marys WV 26170

OLIVERIO, ROSANNE MALFREGEOT, Third Grade/Music Teacher; *b:* Clarksburg, WV; *m:* Louis A.; *c:* Jacquline, Claudine; *ed:* (BMED) Music Ed, Coll of Mt Joseph On the OH 1962; Grad Work WV Univ; *cr:* 3rd Grade/1st-6th Grade Music Teacher St Marys Grade Sch 1962-65, 1974-; *ai:* NCEA 1962-; Heart Fund Volunteer; Jr Cath Daughters Co-Club Adv; Holy Chldhd Assn Moderator; OH Cath Ed Convention Planning Comm; *office:* St Marys Grade Sch 107 E Pike St Clarksburg WV 26301

OLIVIA, SUSAN (REHRIG), Sixth Grade Teacher; *b:* Palmerton, PA; *m:* Christopher D.; *c:* Kristin; *ed:* (AA) Elem Ed, Lehigh Cty Comm Coll 1970; (BS) Elem Ed, Kutztown Univ 1972; (MED) Rdng Specialist, Lehigh Univ 1976; Grad Courses Beyond Masters, Marywood Coll, Wilkes Coll, Intermediate Unit 21; *cr:* Teacher S S Palmer Mid Sch 1972-87, Franklin Elem Sch 1987-88, S S Palmer Elem Sch 1988-; *ai:* Sixth Sense Scholastic Scrimmage Team Adv; Palmerton Ed Assn Secy 1978-79; Palmerton Concourse Club 1976-; Bus & Prof Womens Club 1979-; Palmerton Band Parents Secy 1988-; *office:* S S Palmer Elem Sch 3rd And Lafayette Aves Palmerton PA 18071

OLKEN, DIANA, Teacher; *b:* Philadelphia, PA; *ed:* (BBA) Bus Ed, Woodbury Univ 1965; (MBA) Intnl Mrktg, W Coast Univ 1981; (MS) Sch Admin/Supervision, PepperdineUniv 1989; Advanced Trng Cmptr Ed & Industrial Technology; *cr:* Teacher La Canada Unified Sch Dist 1965-66, Watterson Coll 1985-86, Burbank Schls 1966-; *office:* Burbank Unified Schls 1111 N Kenneth Rd Burbank CA 91504

OLLIGES, GEORGE R., Marketing/Bus Law Teacher; *b:* Louisville, KY; *m:* Shirley Blunt; *c:* Ray Jr., Frederick, Julie, Joe Dotson; *ed:* (BSBA) Bus Admin, Xavier Univ 1957; (BSBA) Distributive Ed, Univ of KY 1970; Distributive Ed; *cr:* Teacher Doss HS, Bishop David HS; *ai:* DECA Club Spon; KADET; NADET; *office:* Doss HS 7601 St Andrews Ch Rd Louisville KY 40214

OLMSTEAD, LINDA TROBOUGH, Kindergarten Teacher; *b:* Kansas City, KS; *ed:* (BS) Ed, Emporia St Teachers Coll 1969; (MS) Ed, KS St Univ 1976; *cr:* 1st Grade Teacher 1969-75, Kndgtn Teacher 1975- Highland Park Cntrl Elem Sch; *ai:* NEA Mem 1969-; PTO Treas 1973-76, 1982-; Instructional Improvement Career Awd Topeka Public Schls 1989; *office:* Highland Park Cntrl Elem Sch 2717 Illinois Topeka KS 66605

OLSAVICK, KIM WILT, Third Grade Teacher; *b:* Altoona, PA; *m:* Gregory S.; *c:* Katelynn; *ed:* (BS) Elem Ed, 1977, (MED) Rdng/Lang/Comm, 1981 PA St Univ; Rdng Specialist Certificate, PA St Univ 1981; *cr:* 1st-3rd Grade Teacher Allegheny #2 Sch 1977-86; 3rd Grade Teacher Charles Longer Sch 1986-; *ai:* Blair Concert Chorale Mem; Voice Instr; Cntrl PA Heritage Festival Comm; Penelecs Educl Advisory Bd (Chairperson 1986-88, Bd Mem 1984-); PA Coll Engery Debates Judge 1988; Amer Cancer Society Blair Unit (Chairperson, Youth Ed Comm 1990-); Amer Cancer Society Bd Mem 1985-; Hollidaysburg Womens Club Mem 1986-; Pi Lambda Theta; Phi Kappa Phi; Consultant for Use of Storytelling Techniques with Folktales; Evan Pugh Scholar Awds; Presenter at Seminars Sponsored by Penelec & Amer Cancer Soc; *office:* Charles Longer Elem Sch 1320 Union St Hollidaysburg PA 16648

OLSEN, REBECCA JANE, A P European History Teacher; *b:* Salt Lake City, UT; *ed:* (BS) His/Geography, 1977, (MA) Anthropology, 1990 Univ of UT; Dissertation for PhD in Anthropology; *cr:* Teacher Brighton HS 1980-87; Anthropology Dept Teaching Asst Univ of UT 1987-88; Teacher Alta HS 1988-; *ai:* Earth Club Adv; Amer Anthropological Assn 1987-; Andean Childrens Fnd Bd Mem 1980-; UT-Bolivia Partners Pres of Women in Dev Comm 1987-; Choice Center for Humanitarian & Intercultural Exch; Fulbright Schlsps & Seminar to India 1983, Korea 1986; *home:* 575 De Soto St Salt Lake City UT 84103

OLSEN, ROBERT ALLEN, English/Music Teacher; *b:* Chicago, IL; *ed:* (BS) Scndry Ed/Eng/Music, Hyles Anderson Coll 1978; Sacred Music, Moody Bible Inst; Amer Conservatory of Music Chicago; *cr:* Teacher Hammond Baptist HS 1977-; *ai:* Sr Class Spon 1990; Dir HS Ensemble; *office:* Hammond Baptist HS 134 Joliet Schererville IN 46375

OLSEN, ROBERT STEPHEN, Orchestra/Choir Director; *b:* Marquette, MI; *m:* Dori Kay Irish; *ed:* (BME) Music Ed, Univ of WI Superior 1976; Univ of AK Fairbanks, Univ of WI, Peabody Conservatory of Music Johns Hopkins Univ; *cr:* Music Orchestra Dir 1976-, Music Choir Dir 1987- Tanana Jr HS 1987-; Music Orchestra Dir Ryan Mid Sch 1987, Lathrop HS 1988, Joy-Nordale Elem Schls 1976-; *ai:* Guitar Club Tanana Jr HS 1979-84; Fairbanks Youth Symphony Bd Mem 1981-89; Fairbanks Symphony Orchestra Mem 1976-; Arctic Chamber Orchestra Mem 1976-84, 1989; *office:* Tanana Jr HS 600 Trainor Gate Rd Fairbanks AK 99701

OLSHANSKY, PATRICIA JOAN (OLDFIELD), Science/Computer Teacher; *b:* Leechburg, PA; *m:* Donald; *c:* Marcia Carroll, Michael, Karen, Daniel; *ed:* (BS) Health/Phys Ed/Sci, Slippery Rock Univ 1961; Grad Work in Sci, Univ of PA; Cmptr, Penn St Univ; *cr:* Sci/Cmptr Teacher Leechburg Area HS 1980-; *ai:* NEA, PA Ed Assn 1980-; Leechburg Ed Assn Secy 1980-; Monday Evening Club 1962-72; *office:* Leechburg Area HS 215 1st St Leechburg PA 15656

OLSON, BETTY ELMER, Chapter I Teacher/Asst Prin; *b:* Cottonwood, MN; *m:* Palmer; *c:* Tony, Steven, Rick, Robin Olson Trader; *ed:* (BS) Elem Ed, 1967, (MS) Rdng, 1989 Moorhead St Univ; *cr:* Classroom Teacher 1967-81, Chapter I Teacher 1981-, Asst Prin 1971 South Elem; *ai:* Teacher Asst Team; Valley Rdng Cncl 1978-; Assn of Teacher Educators 1967-; *home:* 113 3rd Ave W West Fargo ND 58078

OLSON, BRIAN, Third Grade Teacher; *b:* Minneapolis, MN; *m:* Melinda Radoumis; *c:* Yancey, Ian; *ed:* (BA) Liberal Stud, CA St Univ San Bernardino 1976; *cr:* 2nd Grade Teacher Colton Elem Sch 1976; 2nd/3rd Grade Teacher Bishops Peak Elem Sch 1977-; *ai:* Intramural Sports Prgm Coord; Management Team Mem; SIP Comm Mem; *office:* Bishops Peak Elem Sch 451 Jaycee Dr San Luis Obispo CA 93401

OLSON, CLARA JEAN (WHITE), First Grade Teacher; *b:* Gooding, ID; *m:* Jack W.; *c:* Kathie D. Hull, Rick E.; *ed:* (BS) Elem Ed, Univ of NV 1969; Southern ID Coll Ed 1950-51; Eastern WA Coll of Ed 1951-52; ID St Coll Summer Schl Extension Classes; Continuous Trng UNR; Inservice Classes; *cr:* 2nd Grade Teacher Glenns Ferry ID 1952-53; 2nd & 3rd Grade Teacher Jerome Cty Sch 1953-55; 3rd Grade Teacher Jerome ID 1957-61; 1st Grade Teacher Fallon NV Northside Elem 1961-; *ai:* Textbook Comm 1989-; St Teacher of Yr Pres 1979-80; Natl/St Teachers of the Yr Charter Mem 1979-; Churchill Cty Ed Assn 1962-; Comm Service Awd 1983; Amer Assn of Univ Women (Vp 1979-81/Pres 1981-82) Woman of Yr 1983; Beta Sigma Phi Pres 1959 & 1966/ Girl of Yr 1954/65/72; PTA 1961-85; Teacher of the Yr 1978; Teacher of the Yr for St of NV 1979; St Senate Comm Upgrading Ed in NV 1982-83; Teaching Inservice Classes Rdng/Writing; *office:* Northside Elem Sch 340 Venturacci Ln Fallon NV 89406

OLSON, DAVID BRIAN, Chemistry Teacher; *b:* Omaha, NE; *m:* Bernadette A.; *c:* Ryan, Shane, Kelly, Tari; *ed:* (BS) Bio/Ed, 1973, (MS) Bio/Ed, 1978 Univ of NE Omaha; *cr:* Teacher Nathan Hale Jr HS 1973-80, Omaha Bryan HS 1980-; *ai:* Boys & Girls Cross Cntry Head Coach; Omaha Ed Assn, NE St Ed Assn, NEA; *office:* Omaha Bryan HS 4700 Giles Rd Omaha NE 68157

OLSON, DOUG JAMES, Soc Stud/Physical Ed Teacher; *b:* La Moore, ND; *m:* Carolyn C. Cox; *c:* Danielle J.; *ed:* (BS) Phys Ed, Valley City St Univ 1987; *cr:* Phys Ed/Soc Stud Teacher Goodrich Public Sch 1987-; *ai:* Asst Ftbl Coach; Soph Class Adv; Kappa Delta Pi 1986; ND Natl Guard Sergeant 1981-; *home:* 311 Sarles St Goodrich ND 58444

OLSON, LINDA MUSSER, 5th Grade Teacher; *b:* Ladysmith, WI; *m:* Richard; *c:* Erik, Kirk; *ed:* (BS) Spec Ed/Elem Ed, Univ of WI-Eau Claire 1976; Ed; *cr:* Adult Ed Teacher WITI Rice Lake 1976-77; 4th/3rd/7th Grade Chapter I Math Teacher Lac Courte Oreilles Ojibwa Sch 1977-84; Mid Sch Soc Stud Teacher 1984-88, 5th Grade Teacher 1988- Winter Public Schls; *office:* Winter H S Main St Winter WI 54896

OLSON, MARGARET ANN, High School Math Teacher; *b:* Chicago, IL; *ed:* (BA) Math, St Xavier Coll 1961; (MED) Guidance/Counseling, Loyola Univ 1967; Math & Cmptr, Ed; *cr:* Math Teacher Kelly HS 1961-84, Morgan Park HS 1984-; *ai:* NHS Spon; Math Club; NCTM, IL Math Teachers Assn, Retired Teachers Assn, Natl Cncl Retired Teachers, Chicago Teachers Union, IL Fed Teachers, AFT 1961-; Aguin Guild Treas 1980-87, Service Awd 1989; Elected Trustee Chicago Teachers Pension Fund 1973-; *office:* Morgan Park HS 1744 W Pryor Ave Chicago IL 60643

OLSON, MARY LOUISE, Language Art Teacher; *b:* Spring Valley, WI; *m:* Craig W.; *c:* Trygve, Kjersti; *ed:* (BS) Scndry Ed/Eng, 1957, Grad Study Eng, Univ of WI River Falls 1967-69; Inst for Teachers of Talented HS Stus, Carleton Coll 1983, 1989; *cr:* 11th/12th Grade Lang Art Teacher/Asst Librarian Prince George HS 1957-59; 9th-11th Grade Lang Art Teacher/Librarian Elmwood HS 1959-60; Dist 196 Librarian Rosemont Public Schls 1960-62; Asst HS Librarian Decatur HS 1962-67; 11th-12th Grade Lang Art Teacher River Falls HS 1979-; *ai:* WI Cncl Teachers of Eng; WI Republican Educators Advisory Cncl 3rd Dist Chairperson 1989-; *office:* River Falls HS 230 N 9th St River Falls WI 54022

OLSON, POLLY (LEONA) ELLIS, Science Dept Chairman; *b:* Saxis, VA; *m:* Larry Wayne; *c:* Kimberly A. Jenkins, Angela D.; *ed:* (BS) Bio, Mary Washington Coll Univ of VA 1962; (MED) Scndry Ed, George Washington Univ 1975; Teaching Gifted & Talented; *cr:* Sci Teacher Glenridge Jr HS 1962-64, Roger B Taney Jr HS 1966-67, La Plata HS 1969-; *ai:* Mid St Evaluation Co-Chm; Honors Convocation Coord; Bio Textbook Comm Chm; Delta Kappa Gamma Pres, Woman of Yr; Ed Assn Charles Cty 1969-; MD St Teachers Assn, NEA 1962-; Joint Bd of Sci & Engineering Ed Awd 1979; Charles Cty Teacher of Yr 1987; Agnes Meyer Outstanding Teacher Awd 1987; Deans Awd for Spec Achievement in Teaching 1987; Outstanding Scndry Educator 1974; *office:* La Plata HS Box 790 Radio Station Rd La Plata MD 20646

OLSON, RANDALL HOWARD, Mathematics Teacher; *b:* San Pedro, CA; *m:* Janet Mc Clean; *c:* Jessie S., Jacqueline K., Adam M.; *ed:* (BS) Soc Sci/Phys Ed, Fullerton Univ 1971; *cr:* Teacher Blessed Sacrament Sch 1972-73; Teacher of Incorrigibles 1973-76, Math Teacher 1976- Bolsa Grande HS; *ai:* Jr Var Bsktbl, Boys & Girls Var Tennis Coach; Ski Club Adv; Garden Grove Ed Assn 1989-; *office:* Bolsa Grande HS 9401 Westminster Ave Garden Grove CA 92644

OLSON, SANDRA BRENNAN, Physics Teacher/Sci Dept Chair; *b:* Louisville, KY; *m:* William A. Jr.; *c:* Carie, David, Brian; *ed:* (BS) Math/Physics, SW TX St Univ 1970; (MED) Sci Ed, Univ of Houston 1989; *cr:* Physics Teacher Richfield HS 1970-74, Taylor HS 1980-; *ai:* JETS Spon; NSTA; Sci Teachers Assn of TX; Assn of TX Prof Educators; AAPT; TX Outstanding Physics Teacher 1972; *office:* James E Taylor HS 20700 Kingland Blvd Katy TX 77450

OLSON, TERRY ROBERT, Math & Computer Teacher; *b:* St Paul, MN; *c:* Eric; *ed:* (BS) Math, Univ of MN; *cr:* Tennis Prof/Mgr Phalen Indoor Tennis Club 1974-79; Math/Cmptr Teacher Highland Park 1983-; *ai:* Head Coach HS Girls & Boys Tennis; US Prof Tennis Assn Mem 1973-79; *office:* Highland Park Complex Sch 975 S Snelling Saint Paul MN 55116

OLSZOWKA, KATHY NIEMEL, Mathematics Teacher; *b:* Buffalo, NY; *m:* Donald E.; *c:* Michael, John; *ed:* (BA) Math, Hartwick Coll 1969; Cmptr Applications, Lesley Coll 1991; *cr:* Teacher Holden Sch Dist 1969-72, Union RXI Sch Dist 1976-; *ai:* Frosh Class & Future Educators of America Spon; Union Cmmty Teachers Assn (Secy, Treas) 1976-84; NCTM 1976-; NEA; Union Ed Assn Secy 1989-; Wildcat Booster Club 1972-; Daughters of Isabella 1989-; Grant Union RXI Fnd; *office:* Union HS 1217 W Main Union MO 63084

OLWELL, LAURENCE EDWARD, Mathematics Teacher; *b:* Mitchell, SD; *m:* Marjean; *c:* Laura, Linda; *ed:* (BS) Math/Bus, GBSTC 1960; *cr:* Math Teacher Pickstown SD, W Lyon Comm Sch, Pocahontas Area Comm Sch; *ai:* NHS Adv; PEA, ISEA, NEA; *home:* 1009 3rd Ave NW Pocahontas IA 50574

O'MALLEY, MARY KAY, Fourth Grade Teacher; *b:* East Cleveland, OH; *ed:* (BA) Elem Ed, Notre Dame Coll 1980; (MED) Profession Teaching Rdng, John Carroll Univ 1988; *cr:* 4th Grade Teacher St Francis of Assisi Sch 1980-; *ai:* Stu Cncl Moderator; ASCD 1988-; IRA 1990; Cleve Cath Diocese Eastern Region #1 Teacher Awd 1988; Faculty Collaborator John Carroll Univ 1990; *office:* St Francis Of Assisi Sch 6850 Mayfield Road Gates Mills OH 44040

O'MASTA, SHIRLEY CONWAY, Chapter I Teacher/Director; *b:* Youngstown, OH; *m:* Thomas; *ed:* (BS) Elem Ed, Youngstown St Univ 1971; (MS) Rdng, MI St Univ 1975; Success Team Leadership Trng, Instructional Trng Prgm; *cr:* Teacher Pymatuning Valley Schls 1971-72; Teacher 1972-77, Chapter I Dir/Teacher 1977- Concord Cmmty Schls; *ai:* Lang Art Curr Comm; Organizer March is Rdng Month Promotion; Jackson Cty Rdng Assn Pres 1981-82; MI Rdng Assn Contract Team 1989-; Seven Cty Dirs Organization Chm 1986-87, Outstanding Compensatory Ed Teacher 1984; MI Dept of Ed; Outstanding Elem Ed Teacher Concord Cmmty Schls 1983-84; Ed & Publisher Dist Wide Creative Writing Booklet; *office:* Concord Cmmty Schls 405 S Main St Concord MI 49237

OMECENE, MARY M., 7th Grade Math/Science Teacher; *b:* St Joseph, MO; *m:* Edward John; *c:* Beth, Kristen; *ed:* (BA) Elem Ed, Cntrl MO St Univ 1973; Impact Trng; Religious Certified; Interface 90 Sci/Math Integratoin; Project STAR Trng; Baseline-Drug Ed & Awareness; Math Wkshps; *cr:* 4th Grade Teacher 1973-78, Kndgtn Teacher 1979-81, 4th Grade Teacher 1981-84, 6th-8th Grade Math Teacher/6th-7th Grade Sci Teacher/7th Grade Religion/Spelling Teacher, Lib Supvr, Asst Prin 1984- St Gabriel Sch; *ai:* Book Fairs, Math-A-Thon, Read-A-Thon Chairperson; NCEA 1973-; Ewing Kaufman Fnd Trainer for Project STAR 1989; Univ of MO Kansas City Bio Project; *office:* St Gabriel Sch 4737 N Cleveland Kansas City MO 64117

OMILIAN, MICHAEL, Dean of Students; *b:* Jersey City, NJ; *ed:* (BSME) Mechanical Engineering, NJ Inst of Technology 1982; *cr:* Contract Engineer Self Employed 1982-86; Math Instr Huntington Learning Center 1984-86; Math Teacher/Dean of Stu Vail-Deane Sch 1986-; *ai:* Stu Faculty Senate, Math Club, Peer Counseling Adv; Mathematical Assn of Amer 1989-; *office:* Vail-Deane Sch Woodacres Dr Mountainside NJ 07092

ONDASH, MADONNA L., Span Teacher/Lang Dept Chair; *b:* Wilkes-Barre, PA; *ed:* (BA) Span, 1975, (BA) Eng, 1979 Kings Coll; *cr:* Span Instr Crestwood HS 1975-76, Bishop O Reilly HS 1976-; *ai:* Span & Pen Pal Club; Society Honoraria Hispanica; Frosh Class Moderator; Amer Assn Teachers of Span & Portuguese, PA Modern Lang Assn 1976-; *office:* Bishop O Reilly HS 316 N Maple Ave Kingston PA 18704

ONDRLA, THOMAS JOSEPH, History Teacher/Principal; *b:* Chicago, IL; *m:* Christine Scott; *c:* Jennifer, Joseph, Mark; *ed:* (BA) His, Loyola 1968; (MA) His, De Paul 1972; *cr:* Teacher St Eulalia Grammar Sch 1968-74; Teacher/Admin St Laurence HS 1974-; *ai:* Summer Sch Prin 1986-; NCEA Mem 1974-89; Chicago Metro His Fair Judge 1990; *office:* St Laurence HS 5556 W 77th St Burbank IL 60459

O'NEAL, MICHAEL LEE, Life Skills Teacher; *b:* Paso Robles, CA; *m:* Marla Dawn Womack; *c:* Kelsey L., Jacob R.; *ed:* (AA) His, Fresno City Coll 1981; (BA) US His, CA St Univ Fresno 1983; Grad Stud Psych; Several Wkshps; *cr:* Long Term Substitute Teacher Escondido Sch Dist 1984-86; 7th Grade Soc Stud Teacher Hidden Valley Jr HS 1986; 11th/12th Grade Soc Stud Teacher 1986-87, 9th Grade Life Skills Teacher 1987- Hanford Union HS; *ai:* Noon Study Hall Stu with Low GPA; FHA Adv; Night Continuation Teacher; Asst Peer Facilitators; R House VP 1987-88; Teen Pregnancy Prevention Cncl 1988-89; Certificated Employee of Month 1989; Bd Recognition Coaching FHA Competitive Events; St Recognition Home Ec Dept Exemplinary Prgm; *home:* 932 Moffat Dr Hanford CA 93230

O'NEIL, J. PETER, 7th & 8th Grade Sci Teacher; *b:* Rockville Center, NY; *m:* Carol Ann Sypniewski; *c:* Kelly A., Thomas J.; *ed:* (MA) Sci Ed, Webster Coll 1972; (BA) Psych, Loyola Univ 1968; *cr:* Teacher Sacred Heart Sch 1968-73, Waunakee Mid Sch 1973-; *ai:* K-8th Grade Sci & Summer Sci Coord; Curr Consultant; NSTA Journal Reviewer 1973-; WI Society Sci Teachers 1975-; NEA, WI Ed Assn 1973-; Dane Cty Ed for Employment (Author, Presenter) 1987-89; Textbook & Writing Consultant; Author; Presenter St & Natl Conventions; Dir Cmptr Ed Project; Nom Search for Excl in Sci Ed; *home:* 119 Simon Crestway Waunakee WI 53597

O'NEILL, CAROLE J., Sixth Grade Math/Sci Teacher; *b:* Pawtucket, RI; *m:* Edward J.; *c:* Erin, Jeremiah; *ed:* (BA) Scndry Ed/Eng, RI Coll 1969; *cr:* 6th Grade Teacher 1969-77, 7th Grade Eng/Soc Stud/Rdng Teacher 1977-83, 8th Grade Eng/Soc Stud/Rdng Teacher 1983-87, 6th Grade Math/Sci/Rdng Teacher 1987- Coelho Mid Sch; *ai:* NEA 1969-; Jr Great Books Co-Leader 1974-; Amer Diabetes Assn (Youth Group Leader 1986-87, Mem 1975-); *office:* Robert J Coelho Mid Sch Brown St Attleboro MA 02703

O'NEILL, DANIEL H., Jr HS Science Teacher; *b:* Brookville, PA; *c:* Dana K.; *ed:* (BS) Earth & Space Sci, 1971, Masters Equivalent Ed, Clarion St Univ 1983; Cmptr Trng; *cr:* Jr HS Sci Teacher Seneca Valley Jr HS 1971-; *ai:* Coal Bus 1977-85; *office:* Seneca Valley Jr HS RD 1 Harmony PA 16037

O'NEILL, KATHLEEN QUINLAN, English Teacher; *b:* Mineola, NY; *m:* Sean; *ed:* (BS) Eng Ed, 1982, (MS) Counseling, 1985 Long Island Univ; *cr:* Substitute Teacher Bellmore-Merrick Sch Dist 1982; Eng Teacher Sacred Heart Acad 1982-, Woodmere Acad Summer Sch 1986-; *ai:* Speech & Debate; Spiritual Life; Rainbows; Sch Assemblies; NCTE Mem 1982-; ASCD Mem 1990; Cath Youth Organization Oratorical Judge 1986-.

O'NEILL, MARYLEE RITTER, History Department Chairman; *b:* Baltimore, MD; *m:* Anthony Ross; *c:* Julie O neill Tracy, Stephen, Elizabeth, Kathleen; *ed:* (BA) His, Goucher Coll 1963; (MA) His, 1979, (PHD) His, 1984 Boston Univ; *cr:* Teacher Ellington CT Mid Sch 1963-64; Tour Guide Historic Annapolis 1969-71; His Teacher Notre Dame Acad 1984-; *ai:* Jr Class Adv; Close-Up Fnd Transatlantic Prgm; MA Faculty Participant; NCSS Mem 1984-; NCEA 1984-; Hingham Historical Society 1975-; *office:* Notre Dame Acad 1073 Main St Hingham MA 02043

O'NEILL, PATRICIA CUFF, 3rd Grade Teacher; *b:* Montague, MA; *m:* John J.; *c:* Michael D.; *ed:* (BA) Ed, Bridgewater St Coll 1956; Various Courses; *cr:* 3rd Grade Teacher N River Sch 1956-58, Indian Orchard Elem 1958-69; 1st-3rd Grade Teacher/Enrichment Prgm West Street Sch 1969-; *ai:* Delta Kappa Gamma (Corresponding Secy 1984-85, Mem 1982-86); *home:* 85 Pearl St South Hadley MA 01075

O'NEILL, THOMAS EUGENE, Art Teacher; *b:* Teaneck, NJ; *m:* Rosalie Rizzo; *c:* Scott, Todd; *ed:* (BFA) Commercial Art, Syracuse Univ 1961; (MFA) Art Ed, NY Univ 1968; *cr:* Art Teacher Leonia HS 1968, Fair Lawn HS 1968-; *ai:* Yrbk Adv 1969-; BCAENJ, NAEA 1975-; NJEA 1975-; NJ Stu Craftmens Fair Secy 1975-; Midland Park Booster Club 1989-; Midland Park Ftbl & Bsbl Assns.

O'NEILL, WILLA JOYCE, Teacher; *b:* Sharon, PA; *m:* Donn B. Jensen; *c:* Peggy Barnes, Candy Blake, Julie; *ed:* (BS) Eng, Youngstown St 1965; (MA) Theatre, Univ of CO 1983; *cr:* Teacher Brookfield Schls 1966-69, Flint Schls 1970-; *ai:* Theatre Production Coach; MI Ed Assn, NEA 1970-; Shakespeare Festival; *office:* Whittier Mid Sch 701 Crapo St Flint MI 48503

ONEY, KAY PRATER, Sixth Grade Teacher; *b:* Salyersville, KY; *m:* S. V.; *ed:* (BA) Soc Stud, Morehead St 1964; *cr:* 6th Grade Teacher Briarfield Elem 1964-65, Jenkins Elem 1965-70, Jefferson Elem 1970-80, Washington Mid Sch 1980-; *ai:* Natl Jr Honor Society Faculty Cncl; Sch Beautification & Rdng Comm; NNEA, VEA, NEA 1965-89; Newport News Rdng Cncl 1990; Candidate for Teacher of Yr.

ONO, SAMUEL KIYOSHI, Social Studies Teacher; *b:* Honolulu, HI; *m:* Colette Hayashi; *c:* Carol Kaito; *ed:* (BA) Accounting, 1957, Soc Stud, 1961, (MED) US His, 1966, (MED) Educl Admin, 1974 Univ of HI; *cr:* Soc Stud Teacher Pearl City Highlands Intermediate Sch 1961-62, R L Stevenson Intermediate Sch 1962-; *ai:* Model-Making Club Adv; HI Cncl for Soc Stud Pres 1972-73; Palolo Toastmasters Pres 1971; *office:* R L Stevenson Intermediate Sch 1202 Prospect St Honolulu HI 96822

ONTIVEROS, RANELLE DOWNEY, Spanish Teacher; *b:* Davenport, IA; *c:* Evelena, Wilmon; *ed:* (BA) Socioloy, Mac Murray Coll 1971; Eng as 2nd Lang, Univ of AZ; *cr:* Eng as 2nd Lang Teacher Lourdes Acad 1972-84; Span Teacheer Rockridge HS 1986-; *ai:* Class of 1992 & Span Club Spon; NEA Mem; IL Migrant Cncl Teacher 1984-86; E Moline Correctional Center Teacher 1984-88; *office:* Rockridge HS 14110 134th Ave W Taylor Ridge IL 61284

OPIHORY, KATHLEEN ANN, Fourth Grade Teacher; *b:* Passaic, NJ; *ed:* (BS) Elem Ed, Ball St Univ 1966; (MS) Elem Ed/Rdng/Rdng Endorsement, St Francis Coll 1971; *cr:* Elem Teacher Passaic Public Schls 1966-69, Ft Wayne Comm Schls 1969-; *ai:* Spon Stu Cncl; Ind Educators of Ft Wayne; *office:* Pleasant Center Elem 2323 Pleasant Ctr Rd Fort Wayne IN 46819

OPPER, NANCY OKOLISH, Fifth Grade Teacher; *b:* Barberton, OH; *m:* David N.; *c:* Jessica L., Joshua D., Matthew P.; *ed:* (BA) Elem Ed, Capital Univ 1973; (MS) Curr/Instruction, Ashland Univ 1989; *cr:* 5th Grade Teacher Pleasant 1975-76; 3rd Grade Teacher Benedict 1977-81; 5th Grade Teacher Pleasant 1981-82, Maplehurst Elem 1982-; *ai:* OH Ed Assn, NEA 1975-77, 1990; OH Conservation & Outdoor Ed Assn 1989-; *home:* RR 4 1280 S Norwalk Rd Norwalk OH 44857

OPPERMANN, MARCIA EVELYN (NUTT), Foreign Language Teacher; *b:* Hot Springs, AR; *m:* Milton A.; *c:* Lori Oppermann Imhof, Kimberly Oppermann Green, William A.; *ed:* (BA) Foreign Lang Fr, Univ of NC 1957; CO Coll; Univ of N CO; CO St Univ; Univ of S CO; Univ of CO Colorado Springs; Instituto De Filologia; Instituto Fenix; Univ of Vienna; Univ of N IA Summer Prgm in France; *cr:* Substitute Teacher Ft Knox Schls 1957-59; Eng as 2nd Lang Teacher Amer Univ Assn 1967-69; Substitute Teacher Colorado Springs Area Schls 1970-71; Foreign Lang Teacher Falcon HS 1972-; *ai:* NHS Selection Comm; Falcon HS Improvement Team; Falcon HS Sunshine Comm; Jr/Sr Class Spon; Foreign Lang Club Spon; Foreign Exchange Stu Adv; Foreign Lang Dept Acting Chairperson; World Affairs Cncl Comm for Educators; CO Congress of Foreign Lang Teachers 1978-; Amer Assn of Univ Women 1987-88; Amer Cncl on Teaching of Foreign Lang 1990; World Affairs Cncl 1990; Prince of Peace Luth Church 1969-; Spon Stu Trips to Mexico 1976-; Encouraged Intnl Understanding by Promoting Interaction Between Foreign Exchange Stu & Amer Stu Through Club Act; *office:* Falcon H S 11110 Stapleton Rd Falcon CO 80831

O'QUINN, PATRICIA SUTHERLAND, Fifth Grade Teacher; *b:* Kingsport, TN; *m:* Johnny Ted; *c:* Cynthia L., Candace J.; *ed:* (BA) Elem Ed, Clinch Valley Coll 1976; (MA) Elem Ed, VPI & SU Blacksburg VA 1980; *cr:* 5th Grade Teacher Sandlick Elem 1976-; *ai:* NEA, VA Ed Assn, Dickenson Cty Ed Assn.

ORCHARD, VICKI G., English Teacher; *b:* Idaho Falls, ID; *c:* Brady J.; *ed:* (BA) Eng/His, Brigham Young Univ 1971; *cr:* Eng Teacher Bonneville HS 1972-; *ai:* Chrldr, Yrbk, Soph Class, Girls Fed Adv; Faculty Soc Comm Chairperson; Mentor St of ID; Past Eng Dept Chairperson; Bonneville HS Teacher of Month; Bonneville Teacher of Yr; Cultural Arts Fair Poetry Winner; Veterans of Foreign Wars; Citation Awd; Voice of Democracy; Herff-Jones Yrbks Gold Awd; Outstanding Leader in Scndry Ed.

ORDWAY, JANIE READ, 2nd Grade Teacher; *b:* Paulding, MS; *c:* Sara L.; *ed:* (BA) Elem Ed, Belhaven Coll 1968; (MS) Elem Ed, William Carey; Working Towards Masters in Rdng; *cr:* Teacher Howard II Elem 1969-70, NE Taconi, Sylva Bay Acad; *ai:* Sch Bd; Sftbl & Honor Society Spon; Chrldr Co Spon; *home:* Box 504 Paulding MS 39348

O'REAR, SUSAN ADAMS, Music Teacher; *b:* Abilene, TX; *m:* Dan Freeman; *c:* Caleb; *ed:* (BM) Applied Voice, Hardin Simmons Univ 1972; (MMED) Voice, Univ of N TX 1989; Level III Completed Orff Schulwerk Music Trng; *cr:* Music Teacher Colleyville Elem 1976-83, Newton Rayzor Elem 1983-87, Eva S Hodge Elem 1987-; *ai:* Choral Dir; Piano Accompanist, Voice Stus; Amer Orff Schulwerk Assn 1984-; ATPE 1976-83; *office:* Eva Swann Hodge Elem Sch 2900 Grant Pkwy Denton TX 76201

OREN, FREDERIC LYNN, Math Dept Chair & Teacher; *b:* Gas City, IN; *m:* A. Jane Clark; *c:* William C., Frederic W.; *ed:* (BS) Educ Indiana St Univ 1956; Univ of IL; Univ of CA at Davis, Sonoma, Sacramento, San Francisco; Ottawa Univ; CA Lutheran Coll; *cr:* 7th-8th Grade Teacher, Principal-Superintendent Suisun Valley Joint Union Elem Sch Dist 1958-64; 7th Grade Teacher Bransford of Fairfield Elem Sch Dist 1964-68;8th Grade Math Teacher, Dept Chm, Mentor C.L. Sullivan Mid Sch 1968-; *ai:* Spon of Coin Club, Stamp Club, B.B. Card Club, School Master Teacher, Vision and Curr Comm, Dist Math Comm, Mid Sch Network Dir, Dist Mentor; Fairfield-Suisun Teachers Assn 1964-; CA Teachers Assn 1958-; NEA 1958-; CA Math League 1968-; Regional Best 1984-; Solano Cty Math Assn; F & AM #645 1956-; Alphi Phi Omega 1954-; Cal Farley Boy's Ranch 1960-, Honorary Ranch Hand 1960; CMT-FC Union Pres,Dir 1969-; Youth Service Awd 1966, 1972; Natl Sci Fnd Grant Recipient 1969-72; $10,000 Natl Educ Recipient 1972; Newspaper Awd Outstanding Teacher 1976, Teacher of the Yr 1977, 1987, 1988; Presidential Citation Awd Candidate 1989; *office:* C.L. Sullivan Mid Sch 2195 Union Ave Fairfield CA 94533

OREN, ROSEMARY BROOME, 6th-8th Grade Grammar Teacher; *b:* Gainesville, GA; *m:* Donald Gene; *c:* Marie, Sunday, Daniel, Jared; *ed:* (BA) Poly Sci/His, Mars Hill Coll 1977; *cr:* 7th-12th Grade Grammar Teacher Gloucester Cty Chrstn Sch 1985-86; Mid Sch Grammar Teacher New Castle Baptist Acad 1986-; *ai:* Orchestra Mem 2nd Part Clarinet Player; Whos Who Among Young Amer Prof 1988-89; *office:* New Castle Baptist Acad 901 E Basin Rd New Castle DE 19720

ORFALE, LINDA SHELTON, High School English Teacher; *b:* Pontiac, MI; *m:* Alfredo; *ed:* (BA) Eng Lit - Magna Cum Laude, 1973, (MA) Eng Lit - Magna Cum Laude, 1978 Oakland Univ; Cert in Rdng; Endorsement for Rdng Specialist 1988; Grad Work Doctoral Study 1986-; *cr:* Eng Teacher Pontiac N HS 1973-80; Adult Ed Teacher Pontiac Motors Learning Center 1980-81; Soc Stud/Eng Teacher Kennedy Jr HS 1981-86; Eng Teacher Pontiac Cntrl HS 1986-; *ai:* Key Club Intnl Spon 1986-; MI Rdng Assn 1984-; Pontiac Beta Sigma Phi Pres 1987-89, Woman of Yr 1987, 1988; PTA, Clarkston Meth Church; *office:* Pontiac Cntrl Sr HS 300 W Huron St Pontiac MI 48053

ORGAIN, GLORIA JEAN GRACE, 4th Grade ESL Teacher; *b:* Oakdale, LA; *ed:* (BS) Elem Ed, Southern Univ 1965; (MA) Elem Ed, CA St Hayward; *cr:* CA St 1972-74; Univ of CA Berkeley 1975-76; Holy Names Oakland 1977-78; NSU Natchitoches 1980-84; *ai:* Youth Dir; Comm Cook Organization; Sandy Hill Bus Assn; Delta; Natl Teacher Organization Cert 1977; Church Organizations Sunday Sch Teacher 1981-; Public Service Awd; *home:* 587 Vinson Trl Pk Leesville LA 71446

ORGAN, RENEE HARRIS, Second Grade Teacher; *b:* La Porte, IN; *m:* Donald; *c:* Ashley; *ed:* (BS) Elem Ed, Ball St Univ 1973; (MS) Elem Ed, Purdue Univ 1977; *cr:* 3rd Grade Teacher Stillwell Sch 1973-79; 1st/3rd Grade Teacher F W Crichfield Sch 1979-83; Rdng Teacher Mill Creek Sch 1987-88; 2nd Grade Teacher F W Crichfield Sch 1988-; *ai:* Natl Problem Solvers Team Coach; PTA Bd Mem; Amer Assn of Univ Women 1973-77; La Porte Area Rdng Cncl, AFT 1973-; La Porte Service League Secy 1980-86; *office:* F W Crichfield Sch 336 W Johnson Rd La Porte IN 46350

ORGERON, RICHARD KEITH, Science Dept Chair/Bio Teacher; *b:* Lafayette, LA; *m:* Arleen Anne Billeaud; *c:* Kerrie R., Simone C.; *ed:* (BA) Bio, USL 1974; AIDS Ed Curr Comm; *cr:* Teacher 1974-, Sci Chairperson 1982- Carencio HS; *ai:* Sr Spon; Jr Prom; Sci Fairs; *office:* Carencro HS 721 Butcher Switch W Lafayette LA 70507

ORILLION, CHERYL SAUNEE, 8th Grade Teacher/Asst Prin; *b:* New Orleans, LA; *m:* Steve A.; *c:* Matthew, Nathan, Jonathon; *ed:* (BS) Elem Ed, 1987, (MED) Educl Admin/Supervision, 1990 Our Lady of Holy Cross; *cr:* Teacher St Christopher 1971-75, St Robert Bellarmine 1975-77; 8th Grade

Teacher 1977-, Vice Prin 1990 St Louise de Marillac; *ai:* Admin Team 1988-; Stu Cncl Adv; Soc Stud Fair Coord; Nom Miriam Joseph Farrel Distinguished Teaching Awd 1989.

ORLANDO, JEAN M., Fourth Grade Teacher; *b:* Reading, PA; *m:* Pellegrino J.; *c:* Lisa M., Amy M.; *ed:* (BS) Elem Ed, 1970, (MS) Elem Ed, 1973 Kutztown St; Post Grad Work Millersville Univ PA St Univ; *cr:* 5th Grade Teacher 1972-86, 4th Grade Teacher 1986- Brandywine Heights Area Sch Dist; *ai:* NEA, PA St Ed Assn, Brandywine Heights Area Ed Assn 1972-; *office:* Brandywine Hts Area Sch Dist Barkley St Topton PA 19562

ORLANDO, SAL, English Teacher; *b:* Watsonville, CA; *m:* Mary Ann Forni; *c:* Steven; *ed:* (BA) Journalism, San Jose St 1958; Chico St, Univ of San Francisco; *cr:* Teacher Willow Glen HS 1962-63, Overfelt HS 1963-65, Mt Pleasant HS 1965-82, Santa Teresa HS 1982-; *ai:* Coaching; Class Adv; Club Sponsorship; Phi Delta Kappa Ed 1987-; NCTE 1973-; Almaden Valley Youth Counseling Service Bd 1988-; Whos Who in Amer Ed 1989; Certificate of Excl CA Newspaper Publishers 1962; Certificate of Excl by CA Newspaper Publishers 1962; *office:* Santa Teresa HS 6150 Snell Rd San Jose CA 95123

ORLANDO, TODD MARTIN, History Teacher; *b:* Brooklyn, NY; *ed:* (AA) Management, 1984, (BA) Mrktg, 1984 Bentley Coll; *cr:* Prof Athlete European Bsktbl Assn 1984-85; Asst Bus Office Mgr Riverside Hospital 1985-88; His Teacher Bishop Kenny HS 1988-; *ai:* Coach Var Girls Bsktbl 1988- & Var Mens & Womens Tennis 1988-; Saturn Bsktbl Club Bsktbl Player 1984-85; Boston Celtics 5th Round Draft Choice 1984; Coach of Yr 1989-; *office:* Bishop Kenny HS 1055 Kingman Ave Jacksonville FL 32207

ORLEN, GERALD L., Social Studies Teacher; *b:* Holyoke, MA; *m:* Iris Paquette; *c:* Lauren, Joshua, Jonathan; *ed:* (BA) Amer His, Amer Intnl Coll 1965; (MED) Ed, Westfield St Coll 1970; *cr:* Teacher William E Norris Sch 1965-67; Educl Dir Temple Emanuel Religious Sch 1974-89; Teacher Marblehead Mid Sch 1967-; *ai:* NCSS 1967-; NEA 1965-; Natl Assn of Temple Educators 1974-; Horace Mann Grant; Exceptional Children Conference, New England League of Mid Schls, NE Regional Conference for Soc Stud Presenter; *office:* Marblehead Mid Sch Village St Marblehead MA 01945

ORLUCK, DEBBIE, 1st Grade Teacher; *b:* Oakland, CA; *ed:* (BA) Psych, Univ CA Berkeley 1977; Multiple Subject Cred Ed, CA St Hayward 1978; *cr:* 1st Grade Teacher Redwood Chrstn Schls 1978-; *ai:* Chairperson Curr Comm; Teach Class for New Teachers in Philosophy of Chrstn Ed; *office:* Redwood Chrstn Sch 19300 Redwood Rd Castro Valley CA 94546

ORMAN, JUDITH D. (JAFFE), 8th Grade Teacher; *b:* Chicago, IL; *m:* Milton; *c:* Michael; *ed:* (BS) Ed, Northwestern Univ 1947; (MA) Gifted Ed, Northeastern Univ 1985; Admin/Rdng/Math/Spec Ed; *cr:* Elem Teacher Dist 83 1947-54, Mc Kinley 1954-55; Upper Elem Teacher Funston 1955-; *ai:* Stu Cncl Adv; LSC Teacher-Cncl Mem 1949-51; Volunteer Work in Hospitals; *office:* Funston Sch 2010 N Central Park Chicago IL 60647

O'ROURKE, NANCY FOREE, 12th Grade English Teacher; *b:* Oklahoma City, OK; *m:* Edward J.; *c:* Lynda Bradshaw Hamlet, Michael R. Bradshaw; *ed:* (BA) Eng/Drama/Speech Oklahoma City Univ 1959; (MED) Scndry Admin, Cntrl St Univ 1984; *cr:* Eng/His Teacher Kerr Jr HS 1961-62; Eng Teacher Grant & NW Classen HS 1964-72, Heritage Hall Private Sch HS 1972-76, Deer Creek Public Sch HS 1976-77, Putnam City HS & Putnam City North HS 1977-; *ai:* Legislative Comm of ACT; Disciplinary Comm of PCN; Heritage Hall K-12th Grade Eng Dept Chm; Deer Creek HS 9th-12th Grade Eng Dept Chm; OK Ed Assn, NEA, Assn of Classroom Teachers; *office:* Putnam City North HS 11800 N Rockwell Oklahoma City OK 73034

ORPHEY, EARY GOINS, Science Teacher; *b:* Lake Charles, LA; *m:* Michael Wayne; *c:* Michael L., Natalie A., Willie L.; *ed:* (BS) Bus Ed, Mc Neese St Univ 1973; Post Grad Stud Mc Neese St Univ 1982-84; *cr:* Secy Calcasieu Parish Sheriffs Office 1974-76; Teachers Aide 1977-78, Prof Tutor 1978-85, Teacher 1985- Calcasieu Parish Sch Bd; *ai:* Sci Club Spon; Calcasieu Assn of Educators, LA Educl Assn, NEA; Teacher of Yr 1988-89; *office:* Reynaud Mid Sch 745 S Shattuck Lake Charles LA 70601

ORR, ADRIANNE BURR, Third Grade Teacher; *b:* New York, NY; *m:* Richard; *c:* Richard T., Greg S., Trisha J.; *ed:* (BS) Elem Ed, 1959, (MLS) Lib Sci, 1978 Butler Univ; *cr:* 2nd Grade Teacher Pike 1959-63; 3rd Grade Teacher Eagle Union 1979-; *ai:* Head Grade Level of Lang Curr; Rdng & Soc Comm; Psi Iota Xi 1965-72; Village Art & Study; St Alphonus Ladies Comm (Pres, Secy, Soc Treas) 1966-; *home:* 656 Spring Hills Dr Zionsville IN 46077

ORR, CHARLES WARREN, 8th Grade History Teacher; *b:* Cedartown, GA; *m:* Linda S. Pierce; *c:* Marie, Victoria, Margaret, Stewart; *ed:* (BA) Ed, Soc Stud Shorter Coll 1966; (MED) Soc Stud, GA Southwestern 1975; *cr:* Dept Head/Teacher Worth Cty HS 1966-68/1970-74; Teacher Cedartown HS 1974-82; Dept Head/Teacher Cedar Hill Mid Sch 1982-; *ai:* Soc Stud Dept Chm; Page; Grace Presbyn Church Deacon; Yrbk Dedication Worth Cty HS 1974; Yrbk Dedication Cedartown HS 1982; Teacher of Yr Cedar Hill Mid 89; Beta Club Teacher of Yr 1985-86; *home:* 142 Jule Peek Ave Cedartown GA 30125

ORR, CHARLES WESLEY, Teacher; *b:* Columbus, OH; *m:* Roberta Craig; *c:* Craig, Christi, Cathy; *ed:* (BA) Instrumental Music, Capital Univ 1965; (MS) Instrumental Music, OH St Univ 1970; *cr:* Teacher Beery Jr HS 1965-69, Otterbein Coll 1970-73, South HS 1970-75, Independence HS 1976-; *ai:* Fed of Musicians Local 103 Exec Bd Mem; OMEA 1965-; Phi Beta Mu 1989-; Church of the Redeemer Choir Dir 1989-; Jazz Arts Group of Columbus Lead Trumpet & Personnel Mgr; *office:* Independence HS 5175 Refugee Rd Columbus OH 43232

ORR, DEBORAH WESTER, 8th Grade Teacher; *b:* Kingman, AZ; *m:* David Edwin; *c:* Brian, Rebecca; *ed:* (BA) Phys Ed, Biola Univ 1974; Art, Sonoma St Univ 1978; *cr:* Substitute Teacher Sonoma Cty Schls 1976-77; Teacher Rincon Valley Chrstn Sch 1977-79, Santa Rosa Chrstn Sch 1980-; *ai:* Yrbk Adv; Sci Fair Coord; *office:* Santa Rosa Chrstn Sch 950 S Wright Rd Santa Rosa CA 95407

ORR, GORDON DALE, 7th/8th Grade English Teacher; *b:* Elwood, IN; *m:* Cheryl Ann Off; *c:* Kelly K., Jason J.; *ed:* (BS) Eng, IN St Univ 1971; (MA) Eng, Ball St Univ 1978; *cr:* 7th/8th Grade Eng Teacher Tipton Jr HS 1971-72, Tipton Mid Sch 1972-; GED Teacher NCIPIC Tipton Career Resources 1984-; *ai:* Yrbk; Knowledge Master Open Cmptr Challenge; IN St Teachers Assn Governance 1980-; Tipton Ed Assn Pres; *home:* PO Box 43 Tipton IN 46072

ORR, PAULINE BENGS, Third Grade Teacher; *b:* Geary, OK; *m:* Donald H.; *c:* Jeff, Beth Orr Dees, Lisa L.; *ed:* (BS) Elem Ed/Eng, OK Baptist Univ 1954; *cr:* 3rd Grade Teacher Washington Grade Sch 1952-53; 2nd Grade Teacher Ft Bragg Dependents Sch & Bowley Sch 1953-60; 4th/5th Grade Teacher Pope Sch 1961-; 3rd Grade Teacher Glendale & Ashley Elem 1977-; *ai:* Ashley Elem Sch Newspaper Spon; Delta Kappa Gamma; NC Assn of Educators; Fayetteville City Schls, Glendale Acres Sch Teacher of Yr 1982; NC Center for Advancement Teaching Participant; Talks With Teachers Facilitator; Teaching Fellows Seminar Public Sch Forum NCAAT Adv; *office:* Ashley Elem Sch 1301 Robeson St Fayetteville NC 28305

ORRELL, SARAH EVANS, Third Grade Teacher; *b:* Vardaman, MS; *m:* Charles Noel; *c:* Beth, Amy; *ed:* (BS) Elem Ed, Ms St Univ 1967; (MA) Elem Ed, Univ of MS 1977; *cr:* 3rd Grade Teacher 1967-73, 6th Grade Teacher 1976-77 Lizzie Horn Elem; 3rd Grade Teacher Carrie Dotson Elem 1977-; *ai:* Certified in MS to Train New Teachers; Chosen to Help Set up Instructional Management Prgm for Local Sch System; Have Conducted Staff Dev Prgms; Grenada Municipal Sch Dist Teacher of Yr 1986-87; *home:* 657 Old Hickory Rd Grenada MS 38901

ORRIN, KATHY GARNER, Principal; *b:* Taft, CA; *m:* Ronald E.; *c:* Mary A., Zackery; *ed:* (AA) Sociology, Taft Coll 1968; (BA) Sociology, Univ of CA Santa Barbara 1970; (MS) Learning Handicap, Univ of CA La Verne 1982; Doctorate in Progress Educl Management; *cr:* Teacher 1972-87, Admin Intern 1987-89, Prin 1989- Rowland Unified Sch Dist; *ai:* PTA Teacher Rep 1973-75; ADA Mae Warner Schlsp 1979; ACSA, ASCD; Published in Thrust Magazine 1989; *office:* Shelyn Elem Sch 19500 E Nacora Rowland Heights CA 91748

ORSBURN, DEBORAH CROW, Second Grade Teacher; *b:* Oklahoma City, OK; *m:* Howard M. III; *c:* Katie, Madison; *ed:* (BSE) Elem Ed, Univ of Cntrl AR 1980; Math Their Way, Center For Innovation in Ed Inc 1988; *cr:* 1st Grade Teacher 1980-87, 2nd Grade Teacher 1987- Dardanelle Elem; *ai:* AR River Valley Rdng Assn; *office:* Dardanelle Elem Sch 900 N 5th St Dardanelle AR 72834

ORSLAND, KATHY ROGERS, First Grade Teacher; *b:* Osage, IA; *m:* James L.; *c:* Jacob, Kaylene; *ed:* (BA) Ed, Univ of N IA 1976; BA Staff Dev & Grad Work; *cr:* 1st Grade Teacher Webster City IA 1976-77; 2nd Grade Teacher 1977-89, 1st Grade Teacher 1989- Bondurant IA; *ai:* Human Growth & Dev Comm Rep for Grades K-6; Anderson Elem 3rd Grade Stu at Risk Rep; Bondurant-Farrar Ed Assn Building Rep 1989-; IA St Ed Assn 1976-; *office:* Bondurant-Farrar Schls 4th & Garfield Bondurant IA 50035

ORTEGO, JANE MATTIS, Fourth Grade Teacher; *b:* Alexandria, LA; *M:* Cylde S.; *c:* Jennifer DePriest Shamblin, Clifford J. DePriest Jr.; *ed:* (BA) Elem Ed, Louisaiana Coll 1964; Northwestern St Univ; *cr:* Teacher North Bayou Rapids Elem 1964-; *ai:* Delta Kappa Gamma (Corres Secy/2nd VP) 1990-92; *home:* 1170 Lake Dr Woodworth LA 71485

ORTEGO, KAYREN FONTENOT, English Teacher; *b:* Ville Platte, LA; *m:* Robert Lee; *c:* Taylor E., Ryan L.; *ed:* (BA) Liberal Art, Univ of SW LA 1982; (BA) Equivalent Eng, Univ of S LA 1985; Writing Inservices; Eng Teacher Ville Platte HS 1982-88, Basile HS 1988-; *ai:* Dist & St Literary Rally Faculty Adv; NEA 1982-; LA Educators Assn Sch Rep 1988-89; *office:* Basile HS PO Box 666 Basile LA 70515

ORTIZ, BEATRICE C., 4th Grade Bilingual Teacher; *b:* Santa Fe, NM; *c:* Daniel M., Donna B. Delgado, Darla J.; *ed:* (BA) Elem/Bi-ling Ed, Coll of Santa Fe 1979; *cr:* 4th Grade Teacher 1979-, 4th Grade Teacher Asst 1978-79, 2nd Grade Teacher Asst 1976-78; 1st & 2nd Grade Teacher Asst Wood Gormley Elem 1974-76, Agua Fria Elem 1969-71; *ai:* 4th & 6th Grade Testing Chairperson; Stu Special Prgm Organizer; Teacher Soc Prgm Organizer; NM Natl Ed Assn Bldg Rep 1985-; Intl Rdng Assn Mem 1984-; *office:* Kearny Elem Sch 901 Avenida Las Campanas Santa Fe NM 87505

ORTIZ, CAROL MAUCH, 4th/5th Grade Teacher; *b:* Covina, CA; *m:* Fernando; *c:* Kristina, Anthony, Michael; *ed:* (AA) Liberal Art, Mt San Antonio Jr Coll 1972; (BA) His, San Diego St Univ 1975; Working Toward Masters in Rdng Credential; *cr:* Elem Teacher Vista La Mesa Elem; *ai:* Stu Cncl Adv.

ORTIZ, DIANE JABLONSKI, Resource Teacher; *b:* San Diego, CA; *m:* Salvador S.; *c:* Elizabeth; *ed:* (BA) Liberal Stud, San Diego St Univ 1977; (MA) Elem Curr, Northern AZ Univ 1985; Rdng Specialist Emphasis; Clinical Teaching & Supervision; *cr:* 4th Grade Teacher Miguel Hidalgo Sch/Witter Sch 1977-83; 6th Grade Teacher 1983-88, Resource Teacher 1988- Phil D Swing; *ai:* Stu Cncl Adv; Futures Comm Mem; Academic Activities Adv/Oakley Swing PTA; Honor Society of Phi Kappa Phi 1985- 4.0 MA 1985; Brawley Boys & Girls Club Bd Mem 1987-89; Mentor Teacher 1983-87; *office:* Phil Swing Elem 261 D Street Brawley CA 92227

ORTIZ, ENEIDA, Elementary School Teacher; *b:* Cidra, PR; *c:* Arnaldo, Hipolito, Orville; *ed:* (BA) Elem Ed, Interamerican Univ 1968; *cr:* Teacher Pedro MA Dominicci Sch; *ai:* PTO; Teachers Assn, Assn of Public Employees; Catechesis Teacher of Religion; *office:* S U Pedro Ma Dominicci Sch Carr 171 Km 4 Cidra PR 00639

ORTIZ, LILLY ORTEGA, Teacher; *b:* Des Moines, IA; *c:* Monica; *ed:* (BA) Phys Ed, 1972, (MS) Phys Ed, 1975 AZ St Univ; Grad Stud Bio; *cr:* Teacher Scottsdale Public SchlS; *ai:* Vlybl, Sftbl, Bsktbl, Track & Field Coach; NSTA, AZ Sci Teachers Assn 1984-; Nature Conservancy 1989-; *office:* Mohave Mid Sch 1110 Bryan Rd Scottsdale AZ 85253

ORTIZ, MARY HELEN CASTILLO, 5th/6th Grade Phys Ed Teacher; *b:* Lockhart, TX; *m:* Robert Vincent; *c:* Robert V. III, Rachel J.; *ed:* (BS) Elem Ed/Phys Ed, SWTSU 1978; *cr:* 5th Grade Teacher 1978-88, 5th/6th Grade Phys Ed Teacher 1988- Lockhart Intermediate Sch; *ai:* TSTA 1978-80; TCTA 1980-84; St Marys Ladies Altar Society Mem; *office:* Lockhart Intermediate Sch 715 Medina Lockhart TX 78644

ORTIZ, NORA IRIZARRY, English Teacher; *b:* Yauco, PR; *m:* Oscar Ortiz-Ramos; *c:* Yolanda, Martha, Maria T., Oscar L.; *ed:* (BA) Ed, St Univ of NY 1974; Bi-ling Ed, Religion; *cr:* 5th Grade Teacher Holy Rosary Sch 1960-61; Bi-ling Teacher Grand Street Sch 1972-74; Eng Teacher Academia Cristo Rey 1974-80, Colegio Ponceno 1980-; *ai:* Eng Dept Head; Eucharist Minister; Steering, Evaluating Comm Mid Sts Assn Mem; Book Ed; Teacher of Yr 1979-80; *home:* Urb Perla Del Sur 0-419 Ponce PR 00731

ORTIZ, SALLYE (HARTT), Business Dept Chairman; *b:* Farmersville, TX; *m:* F. Gilbert; *c:* Dan Japhet, Adriane Japhet; *ed:* (BBA) Accounting, Abilene Chrstn Univ 1964; (MBA) Bus Ed/Accounting, North TX St Univ 1965; PhD Work, Univ of Houston; Cmptr Sci, Mc Murry Coll; *cr:* Bus Instr Univ of Houston 1966-67; Bus Teacher Withrow HS 1967-68, North Springs HS 1968-69; Instr Galveston Coll 1975-76; Instr Asst Prof Mc Murry Coll 1976-80; Bus Teacher/Dept Chm Cooper HS 1980-; *ai:* Adopt-A-Sch Coord; TX Bus Ed Assn (Reporter & Historian 1990-, Prof Dev Comm Chairperson 1986-) Teacher of Yr 1986; Delta Kappa Gamma (VP 1990-91 & 1986-87); DAR 1975-; Republic of TX 1975-; Teaching Fellowship North TX St Univ 1966; Big Cntry Bus Teachers Pres 1986; TX Delegate to Mountain-Plains Bus Ed Assn Leadership Conference 1989; *office:* Cooper H S 3639 Sayles Abilene TX 79605

ORTLI, PATRICIA GRAYATT, General Science Teacher; *b:* Lakewood, OH; : Richard H.; *c:* Diane E., John R.; *ed:* (BS) Medical Technology, Mt Union Coll 1960; Teacher Cert Baldwin-Wallace Coll 1965; Grad Stud Numerous Univs; *cr:* Medical Technologist Louis Weiss Hospital 1961-64; Teacher Larimer Cty 1966-68; Medical Technologist Mary Rutan Hospital 1973-81; Teacher Benjamin Logan HS 1981-; *ai:* Frosh Class Adv 1982-86; Academic Team Adv 1985-; Jr Class Co-Adv 1986-87; BLEA (VP, Secy, Building Rep) 1981-; OEA Delegate Assembly Rep 1986-88; NEA, NSTA, OAS, ASCP-MT; GSA Leader 1975-80, Golden Apple Awd 1979; NSDAR Vice Regent 1976-77; Athenian Club Prgm Pres 1979-80; OH Acad of Sci Jerry Acker Outstanding Sci Teacher Awd 1989; *home:* 102 N Heather Hill Dr Bellefontaine OH 43311

ORTLIEB, CHERYL B., Mathematics Teacher; *b:* Ithaca, NY; *m:* William W.; *c:* Loreen, Amy; *ed:* (BA) Scndry Math, SUC Cortland 1970; Grad Courses SUC Cortland, SUC Utica & Rome Coll of Tech; *cr:* 8th Grade Math Teacher Southern Cayuga Cntrl Sch 1970-71; 6th-8th Grade Teacher Annunciation Sch 1973-81; Math Teacher Holland Patent Cntrl Sch 1981-82, Little Falls Cntrl Sch 1982-83, Oppenheim-Ephratah Cntrl Sch 1984-; *ai:* OETA Co-Pres Union; Scndry Building Team for Effective Schls Mem; Teach GED Classes; Herkimer Reformed Church (Elder 1990-, Deacon 1987-89).

ORTMAN, DOROTHY KLUPPING, 4th Grade Teacher; *b:* Maywood, IL; *w:* Frederick J. (dec); *c:* Frederick J. Jr.; *ed:* (AB) Phys Ed/Bio, Mac Murray 1939; (ME) Ed, Univ of La Vernge CA 1973; Grad Stud; *cr:* Phys Ed Franklin Sch 1939-40, Forest Park Jr HS 1940-41, Western Springs Jr HS 1941-42, Forest Park Jr HS 1943-48; Elem Teacher Palatine Public Sch 1957-; Supervisor Forest Pk Comm Con Sch Dist; *ai:* Stu Cncl Spon; Teacher Rep Classroom Teacher Assn; Curr Cncl Comm Dist; Classroom Teacher Assn (VP 1963-64, Pres 1964-66); IL Ed Assn; PTA Lifetime Mem; NEA; IL Sftbl Hall of Fame 1973; Treetowns Boxer Club (Secy 1957, Pres) 1957-; Palatine North Little League Secy 1964-66; Regional Dir Amer Boxer Club; Working Group Judge Amer Kennel Club; *home:* 748 N Stephan Dr Palatine IL 60067

OSBORN, MARGARET WARREN, Jr HS Language Arts Teacher; *b:* Faucett, MO; *w:* Kenneth (dec); *c:* Harlan; *ed:* (AE) Elem Ed, St Joseph Jr Coll 1940; (BS) Ed, NW MO St Univ 1963; Topics & Projects in Learning; *cr:* 1st-8th Grade Teacher Dist #11 1940-41; 5th Grade Teacher 1957-58, 6th Grade Teacher 1958-59, 7th/8th Grade Lang Art Teacher De Kalb R-IV 1959-86; *ai:* Jr HS Spon; MO St Teachers Assn; Classroom Teachers Assn Secy 1963-64; Retired Teachers of MO; *home:* Box 17 De Kalb MO 64440

OSBORN, MARJORIE LYNN, Second Grade Teacher; *b:* Ottumwa, IA; *m:* Michael; *c:* Jennifer L.; *ed:* Working Towards Masters W IL Univ; *cr:* 2nd Grade Teacher Lincoln Sch 1978-; *ai:* IA St Ed Assn, NEA, Ft Madison Ed Assn 1978-.

OSBORNE, DEBRA C., 8th Grade Teacher; *b:* Chatsworth, GA; *ed:* (BS) Broad-Field Soc Sci, Berry Coll 1987; Working Towards Masters Mid Grades Ed, Berry Coll 1991; *cr:* 8th Grade Teacher Summerville Mid Sch 1987-; *ai:* Beta Club Co-Spon; Sci Fair Coord; NCSS, Sierra Club 1987-; GA Soc Sci Journal 1988; *office:* Summerville Mid Sch Rt 1 Box 203-A Summerville GA 30747

OSBORNE, DORIS BIRD, Bio/Anatomy/His Teacher; *b:* Princeton, WV; *m:* Denver; *c:* Deborah Sumpter, Donna Chafin, Denise Stephens; *ed:* (BS) Bio/His/Poly Sci, Pikeville Coll 1967; (MA) Ed, 1974, (Rank I) Ed, 1976 Morehead Univ; *cr:* Teacher Wheelwright HS 1967-; *ai:* Wheelwright Investment Club Spon; Academic Boosters Club VP, Past Secy & Treas; Floyd Cty Educl Assn Building Rep 1974-; KY Ed Assn, NEA; Floyd Cty Forum (Mem 1985-, Bd of Dir); Sch Cmmty Partnership Mem 1985-; Amer Heritage Awd; KY Ed Fnd Amer His Grant; Nom Readers Digest Heros in Ed Awd; *office:* Wheelwright HS Box 1700 Wheelwright KY 41669

OSBORNE, GAYLE RATLIFF, 6th Grade Lang Arts Teacher; *b:* Drill, VA; *m:* John W.; *c:* John Garcel, Ann Britton; *ed:* (BS) Eng/Speech, 1972; (MS) Ed, 1975 Radford Univ; Europe 1974; *cr:* Eng Teacher Honaker HS 1972-74; Christiansburg HS 1980-83; Lang Arts Teacher Auburn Mid Sch 1984-; *ai:* Spon Mid Sch Forensics; Wellness Coord; VEA/MECA 1980-; Phi Kappa Phi 1975-; Kappa Delta Pi 1975-; Key Club Spon 1987-88; *home:* 601 Ingles St Radford VA 24141

OSBORNE, LINDA L., 6th Grade Teacher; *b:* El Paso, TX; *m:* Terry L.; *c:* Travis R., Christopher, Kari L.; *ed:* (BS) Elem Ed, Univ of TX El Paso 1969; Grad Work Univ TX San Antonio; *cr:* 3rd Grade Teacher Marion Manor Elem 1969-71; 1st Grade Teacher Booker T Washington Elem 1971-73; 6th Grade/Chapter I Teacher Live Oak Elem 1981-; *ai:* Campus Cmptr Coord; Judson Ind Sch Dist Cmptr Consultant/Trainer; ATPE 1981-; TCEA 1985-, Honorable Mention 1987, St Teacher of Yr 1988-89; Live Oak Swim Team Pres 1986-; Books & Articles Author; *office:* Live Oak Elem Sch 12301 Welcome Dr San Antonio TX 78233

OSBORNE, MARILYN, Second Grade Teacher; *b:* White Castle, LA; *c:* Sheba; *ed:* (BA) Elem Grades, 1973, (MED) Elem Grades, 1977, (MS) Elem Grades/Rdng Specialist, 1984 Southern Univ; *cr:* 4th-6th Grade Phys Ed Teacher Dorseyville Mid 1977-78; 1st Grade Teacher 1979-85, 3rd Grade Teacher 1985-68, 2nd Grade Teacher 1986- Samstown Elem; *ai:* Summer Youth Camp Spon & Leader; Track Coach; Summer Tutoring Prgm Spon; LA Assn of Educators 1989-; *home:* PO Box 66 Hebert Rd Bayou Goula LA 70716

OSBORNE, RHONDA LYNN, English Teacher; *b:* Chicago, IL; *ed:* (BSE) Eng, Drake Univ 1983; *cr:* Eng Teacher Lincoln HS 1983-86, Proviso East HS 1986-; *ai:* Sr Class Spon; *office:* Proviso East HS 807 W 1st Ave Maywood IL 60153

OSBURN, LARY, 6th Grade Teacher; *b:* Yakima, WA; *m:* Bonnie L. Coe; *c:* Chris; *ed:* (BA) Natural His, Cntrl WA Univ 1975; Accel Trng; *cr:* 5th Grade Teacher Parker Elem 1975-79; 3rd Grade Teacher 1979-82, 6th Grade Teacher Wide Hollow Elem 1982-; *ai:* Instructional Materials Comm; Educl Technology; W Valley Ed Rep 1987-; *office:* Wide Hollow Elem Sch 1000 S 72nd Yakima WA 98908

OSER, BARBARA S., Foreign Language Dept Chair; *b:* Mobile, AL; *m:* Kenneth; *ed:* (BA) Fr, 1975, (MFS) Fr, 1981 Auburn Univ; *cr:* Fr/Span Teacher Greenville HS 1975-79; Foreign Lang Chairperson/Fr/Span Teacher Milton HS 1985-; *ai:* Societe Honoraire De Francais Sr Class Spon, Stu Act Comm; Amer Assn of Teachers of Span, Portuguese, Fr.

OSETEK, FRED LEON, Science Teacher; *b:* Holyoke, MA; *m:* Patricia Voss; *c:* Laura, Scott; *ed:* (BS) Ed, Westfield St Coll 1965; (MS) Sci, Amer Intnl Coll 1976; *cr:* 5th Grade Teacher Fairview Elem Sch 1965-67; 7th/8th Grade Sci Teacher Fairview Memorial Sch 1967-70; 8th Grade Sci Teacher Bellamy Mid Sch 1970-; *ai:* AJAC Dir 1985-88; *home:* 63 Voss Ave Chicopee MA 01020

OSGER, DELORIS JEAN, Lang Arts & Geography Teacher; *b:* Iola, KS; *ed:* (BA) Ed, 1959, (MS) Ed, 1966 Emporia St Univ; *cr:* Teacher Rural Schls 1943-48; 3rd-5th Grade Teacher Reece Grade Sch 1948-49; 5th/6th Grade Teacher Virgil Grade Sch 1949-52; Jr HS Teacher/Prin Toronto Schls 1952-73; Teacher Eureka Jr HS 1973-; *ai:* Jr HS Pep Club; KS Ed Assn, Unified Sch Dist 389 ETA, NEA; Unified Sch Dist 389 Candidate Teacher of Yr 1978; KS Master Teacher 1981; *home:* 920 E 1st Eureka KS 67045

OSGOOD, MAUREEN REDDY, English Teacher; *b:* Kalamazoo, MI; *m:* Daniel J.; *c:* Ashley, Daniel; *ed:* (BA) Eng/Psych, W MI Univ 1972; Counseling, Boston St Coll; Psych, Harvard Univ; *cr:* Eng/Psych Teacher Scituate HS 1972-79, Amer Sch of Valencia 1979-84, Wuerzburg Amer HS 1984-; *ai:* Natl Jr Honor Society 1989-; Eng Dept Chairperson 1984-85, 1988-89; Sr Class Spon 1982-83; NCTE.

O'SHAUGHNESSY, WILLIAM JAMES, 7th Grade Social Stud Teacher; *b:* Lowell, MA; *m:* Patricia A. Murningham; *c:* Michael F.; *ed:* (BA) Scndry Ed, Merrimack Coll 1969; (MA) Admin/Supervision, Univ of Lowell 1976; Grad Stud Univ of Lowell 1976-; *cr:* US Military Police US Army 1971-73; Teacher Hudson Memorial Sch 1969-; *ai:* Intramurals Dir; AFT, HFT; *office:* Hudson Memorial Sch 1 Memorial Dr Hudson NH 03051

OSHIRO, EDWARD Y., Science Department Chair; *b:* Honolulu, HI; *m:* Constance Giovanni Kawaoka; *c:* Beau, Marlo, Jamie, Ryan, Wendy; *ed:* (BED) Ed/Sci, 1969, (MS) Sci, 1974 Univ of HI; Grad Stud Admin; *cr:* Scndry Sci Teacher 1969-89, Sci Dept Chairperson 1989- Radford HS; *ai:* Bsbl Coach; Club Adv; Inservice Trng Advisory Cncl Chairperson; Sch Improvement Cadre; HI St Teachers Assn 1969-; Honolulu Neighborhood Bd 1972-74; Aloha Babe Ruth League Secy 1990; Honolulu Quarterback Club Coach of Yr 1988; American Cancer Society 1969-70; *office:* Radford HS 4361 Salt Lake Blvd Honolulu HI 96818

OSINA, MARTHA A., English Teacher; *b:* Bay City, TX; *m:* George T.; *c:* Kevin; *ed:* (BS) Phys Ed/Health, TX Chrstn Univ 1963; Gifted & Talented Ed Univ of Houston; *cr:* Eng Teacher 1963-65, Eng/Phys Ed Teacher 1965-71 Travis Jr HS; Eng/Lang Arts Teacher Van Vleck Jr HS 1982-; *ai:* Assn TX Prof Educators 1982-; Alpha Delta Kappa 1984-; *home:* Rt 3 Box 137 Bay City TX 77414

OSMUNDSON, MARCELLINE MARIE OAKLAND, Sixth Grade Teacher; *b:* Fertile, IA; *w:* Robert D. (dec); *ed:* Pre Prof Elem Ed, Waldorf Coll 1956; Prof Elem Ed, Drake Univ 1965; (MA) Bus, Business Inst 1973; Working Towards Masters Ed, Drake Univ; Norwegian Music, Lang, Art, Oslo Univ 1959; Tax, Accounting; *cr:* 5th Grade Teacher Radcliffe Cmmty Sch 1956-60; 6th Grade Techer Parkersburg Cmmty Sch 1961; 4th-6th Grade Music/6th Grade Teacher Cncl Bluffs Sch 1961-62; 6th Grade Teacher/Asst Prin Rockford Cmmty Sch 1962-63; 6th Grade Teacher NV Cmmty Sch Dist 1964-; *ai:* NCEA, NTA, ISEA Mem; ATE (Mem, Presenter 1987), NV Outstanding Young Educator 1961-62; Radcliffe Commission Betterment Pres 1983-, Governors Leadership 1984; Radcliffe Dev Secy 1975-; Sunrise Apts Incorporated (Secy, Treas) 1986-; Radcliffe Historical Society (Pres, VP) 1984-; IA St Univ Speak to Future Teachers, Teacher on TV, Research & Stu Teaching Projects, NV Ed Excl Team, Taught Math Class to Elem Teaching Majors 1990; Scndry Math Class Speaker Drake Univ; Ed Panels; Developed Individual Needs Prgm; *home:* 405 Park St PO Box 220 Radcliffe IA 50230

OSSEWAARDE, DEBBIE RADOLL, English Teacher; *b:* Berwyn, IL; *m:* Mark A.; *c:* Christopher; *ed:* (BA) Religious Stud, 1976, (BA) Eng/His, 1978 Whitworth Coll; Various Courses; *cr:* His/Eng Teacher W Valley HS 1977-78; Eng Teacher Spokane Public Schls 1985-89, Juanita HS 1987-; *ai:* 1992 Class Adv; Natural Helpers; NCTE 1987-; *office:* Juanita HS 10601 NE 132nd St Kirkland WA 98034

OSTAPIEJ, MICHELLE THERESA, Compensatory Education Teacher; *b:* Queens, NY; *ed:* (BA) Elem Ed, Kings Coll Wilkes-Barre 1977; *cr:* Asst Cashier MCA Finance Co 1977-78; Teacher St Benedict Elem 1978-83; Personnel Mgr Sterns 1983-88; Teacher ECESC 1988-; *ai:* Home Bound Tutorial; Visit House Bound Elderly; Red Cross Volunteer; Rdng Coord; Recreational Asst; Sch Evaluation Team Mem; Kndgtn Curr; NEA, NJEA, ESTA 1988-; *office:* Essex Cty Educl Services 123 Cleveland St Orange NJ 07050

OSTBY, NELL MAUNEY, Staff Administrator; *b:* Kings Mountain, NC; *m:* Lon Peter; *c:* Paul, Joseph, Daniel; *ed:* (BA) Ed, Univ of NC Wilmington 1977; Writing Fellowship, Univ of NC Wilmington 1984; *cr:* Teacher Jr HS Irmagawa Japan 1960-61; Teller Southern Natl Bank 1966-70; Teacher New Hanover Cty Bd of Ed 1977-88, Cape Fear Comm Coll 1978-80, 1989-; Staff Admin Cape Fear Comm Coll 1990; *ai:* Wilmingtons 250 Anniversary Comm; Natl Assn Educators; NC Assn of Ed (Pres, Pres-Elect 1986-87), Distinguished Service 1987-88; Alpha Psi Omega 1957; Delta Kappa Gama 1988; Luth Church Women 1967; VIP Blood Donor 1980; Mem of NC Writing Fellows; Aluma of NC Center for Advancement of Teaching; Educl Articles & Interviews; *home:* 4632 Long Leaf Hills Dr Wilmington NC 28409

O'STEEN, SANDRA MAINS, Third Grade Teacher; *b:* Elmira, NY; *m:* Jerry W.; *c:* Jerry W. Jr.; *ed:* (AS) Ed, S GA Coll 1966; (BS) Ed, Valdosta St Coll 1968; (MED) Ed, GA Coll 1974; Data Collector St of GA; *cr:* 3rd/4th Grade Teacher Satilla Elem 1968-71; 3rd Grade Teacher Cntrl Elem 1971-72; 2nd-5th Grade Teacher Eatonton Grammar & Butler-Baker Sch 1972-; *office:* Butler-Baker Sch Alice Walker Dr Eatonton GA 31024

OSTERMEYER, MARYANN, GATE English & History Teacher; *b:* Indianapolis, IN; *ed:* (AB) Eng/His Classical Langs - Honors & Distinction, 1972; (MA) Ancient & Medieval, 1981 San Diego St; Project Stop Substance Abuse; *cr:* Classics/His Asst Teacher 1970-72, Latin Teacher 1972 San Diego St Univ; Eng/His/Latin Teacher Emerald Jr HS 1973-85; Teacher of Gifted & Talented Eng/His Cajon Valley Jr HS 1985-; *ai:* Kiwanis Builders Club Adv; Spearhead Campaign to Save Historical Julia Liffrieigg House; Affirmative Action Comm Cajon Valley Dist; New Mid Sch Advisoy Comm; Project Code Stop Team Mem; His Fair Adv; NEA, CTA 1973-; Friends of Classics; El Cajon Historical Society; Unified Sch Dist of 1812 VP 1985; Vision 2000 Task Force Mem Blue Ribbon Comm to Mayor of El Cajon 1989-; Summer Inst for Hum Stipend 1983; Published Article 1984; Presenter San Diego Cty Dept of Ed St Lang Art Meeting; Bea Evenson Comm of 100 Awd; Cajon Valley Union Sch Dist Educl Leadership Awd; Emerald Jr HS PTA Outstanding Teacher Recognition 1985; Cajon Valley Union Sch Dist SIP Grant 1981; *office:* Cajon Valley Jr HS 395 Ballantyne El Cajon CA 92021

OSTERWEIL, ELAINE KUHN, Teacher; *b:* New York, NY; *m:* David; *c:* Karen Walker; *ed:* (BA) Math, Hunter Coll 1944; Addl Studies Accounting; Ed; Guidance; *cr:* Math Teacher New York City HS 1944-48; Manual Training HS 1948-54; Brooklyn Tech HS 1954- ; *ai:* Adv to Long Fellows; Teacher Cnslr; NY Teachers of Math Assn 1954-; Chm of Prgm Comm; *office:* Brooklyn Technical H S 29 Fort Greene Pl Brooklyn NY 11217

OSTOYICH, MATTHEW JOHN, Social Studies Dept Chair; *b:* Hoboken, NJ; *m:* Sandra Bonesio; *c:* Joseph, Thomas; *ed:* (BA) Soc Stud/His, 1957, (MA) Soc Stud/His, 1961, SUNY Albany; Hum, Univ of Chicago 1962-63; Amer Stud, SUNY Stony Brook 1962; African Stud, Univ of Rochester 1963; Advanced Placement, Columbia Univ 1964; NDEA Fellow, Union Coll 1966; NEH Fellow, Bard Coll 1983; His, Princeton Univ 1989; PHD Cand His, SUNY Albany 1970; *cr:* Teacher 1957-, Dept Chm 1959- Onteora HS; *ai:* Honor Society, Academic Quiz Bowl, Debate, Model Congress Adv; Mid-Hudson Soc Stud Cncl (VP 1984-87, Pres 1987-), Outstanding Teacher 1986; NY St Cncl for Soc Stud, Amer Poly Sci Assn, Organization of Amer Historians; Philadelphia Coll Bd Consultant 1984-; Princeton Educl Testing Service (Reader, Amer His Table Leader) 1976-87; NCSS; Saugerties Cntrl Schls Bd of Ed Mem 1981-84; Changing Roles of Women US His Chairperson; *office:* Onteora HS Boiceville NY 12412

OSTWALD, FAITH ANN, Mathematics Teacher; *b:* North Tonwanda, NY; *ed:* (BS) Math Ed, SUC Buffalo 1969; (EDM) Math Ed, SUNY Buffalo 1972; *cr:* Math Teacher Kenmore Jr HS & Mid Sch 1969-; *ai:* NEA, NYSUT 1969-; Alpha Delta Kappa Chaplain 1987-; Immanuel Luth Church (Womens Guild Secy 1979-, Choir Secy 1963-); *office:* Kenmore Mid Sch 155 Delaware Rd Kenmore NY 14217

O'SULLIVAN, WILLIAM PETER, English Teacher; *b:* Bronx, NY; *ed:* (BA) Eng, Fordham Coll 1953; (MS) Ed, Fordham Univ 1957; Grad Stud Eng Ed; *cr:* 5th Grade Teacher Incarnation Sch 1955-57; Jr HS Teacher N Tresper Clarke Jr-Sr HS 1957-; *ai:* Jr HS Newspaper Adv; *home:* 610 Willis Ave Williston Park NY 11596

OSWALD, ANN K., Fifth Grade Teacher; *b:* Whitmire, SC; *m:* Ron; *c:* Britt, Zachary; *ed:* (BA) Elem Ed, Newberry Coll 1973; Working Towards Masters Clemson Univ 1990; *cr:* 1st Grade Teacher Carlsan Elem 1973-78; Title I Math Teacher 1978-79, 6th Grade Teacher 1979-84, 5th Grade Teacher 1984- Carver Elem; *ai:* Sch Improvement Cncl; Supt ELA Comm; *home:* Rt 1 Box 280-C Whitmire SC 29178

OSWALD, JO ANN BAUER, Physical Education Teacher; *b:* Cincinnati, OH; *c:* Kimberly A., Jennifer L.; *ed:* (BS) Health/Phys Ed, Miami Univ 1957; Grad Stud Ed Courses; *cr:* Phys Ed Teacher Mt Healthy City Schls 1957-60, North Jr HS 1967-; *ai:* Girls Vlybl & Bsktbl Coach; NEA, OEA, Mt Healthy Teachers Assn, OH Assn Health, Phys Ed, Recreation, Dance; *office:* Mt Healthy & North Jr HS 2170 Struble Rd Cincinnati OH 45231

OSWALD, JOSEPH STEVEN, Science Teacher; *b:* Brownsville, PA; *m:* Karen B.; *c:* Joel C., Paul J.; *ed:* (BS) Elem Ed, CA St Univ 1972; Towson St Univ; PA St Univ; CA St Univ; *cr:* 6th Grade Teacher Bel Air Elem 1972-80; Sci Teacher Southampton Mid Sch 1981-; *ai:* Coaching JV Bsbl; Coaching Little Leag Bsbl; HCEA; MSTA; NEA; *office:* Southampton Mid Sch 1112 Moores Mill Rd Bel Air MD 21014

OSWALT, CHERYL ROBERTS, Study Skills Teacher; *b:* Longview, TX; *m:* Michael Anthony; *ed:* (BA) Finance Management, TX A&M 1983; (MS) Voc Ed, Univ of Houston 1986; Bus Cmptrs, Programming; *cr:* Bank Officer Trainee United Bank Coll Station 1983-84; Substitute Teacher Spring Branch Ind Sch Dist 1984-86; Eng Teacher 1986-88, Study Skills Teacher 1988- Cy Creek HS; *ai:* Soph Class Spon; ATPE 1989-; *office:* Cypress Creek HS 9815 Grant Rd Houston TX 77070

OSWALT, DALE ALLEN, Fifth Grade Teacher; *b:* Hammond, IN; *m:* Laurie Brodien; *c:* Brian; *ed:* (BA) Elem Ed, 1975, (MS) Eng Ed, 1987 Olivet Nazarene Univ; *cr:* 5th Grade Teacher Hickory Elem 1976-77, Alan Shepard 1977-; *ai:* 6th Grade Track & Bsktbl Coach; Local Government Bourbonnais VIllage Clerk 1989-; *office:* Alan Shepard Elem Sch 325 N Convent Bourbonnais IL 60914

OTERSEN, JENNIE BECK, Substitute Teacher; *b:* Wadesboro, NC; *m:* Adolf Jr.; *c:* Jenelle, Mark; *ed:* (BA) Bible/Chrstn Ed/Math, Flora Mac Donald Coll 1959; *cr:* Math Teacher Piedmont Acad 1979-82, Danville Chrstn Schls 1982-83, William T Sutherlin Acad 1983-89; Substitute Teacher Danville Public Schls 1989-; *ai:* Presbyn Women VP 1985, Life Membership 1982; *home:* 714 Northmont Blvd Danville VA 24540

OTHUS, MARCELLA MC LEAN, Honors Eng/Soc Stud Teacher; *b:* Seattle, WA; *c:* John McLean, Marcia Othus Floberg; *ed:* (BS) Soc Sci/Lang Art, 1966, (Mat) Jr HS Ed, 1968 Lewis & Clark Coll; Writing Process; Cooperartive Learning; Writing Cmptr Lab; Outcome Based Ed; Freedom Fnd of Vally Forge; Civil War; *cr:* 8th Grade Eng/Soc Stud Teacher 1966-70, 9th Grade Career

Ed Teacher 1970-78 Fremont Jr HS; Soc Stud/Eng Teacher Parkrose Mid Sch 1978-; *ai:* Team Leader; Dept Coord; Steering Comm & Sch Renewal Comm; Adv Prgm Co Dir; Phi Delta Kappa 1989; IRA Assn; Freedom Fnd of Valley Forge Study Amer Government & the Civil War; *home:* 4220 NE 125th Pl Portland OR 97230

OTT, CHARLES CEARLEY, Social Studies Teacher; *b:* Santa Barbara, CA; *ed:* (BA) Poly Sci, Univ of CA Los Angeles 1970; (MA) Educl Admin, CA St Northridge 1976; *cr:* Soc Stud Teacher Culver City HS 1971-73, Culver City Mid Sch 1973-; *ai:* Soph Bsktbl & Boys Var Vlybl Coach Culver City HS; Culver City Dist Curr Comm Mem; Stu Cncl Adv; CIF Exec Comm; Boys Vlybl S CA; Parents Teachers Stu Assn Honorary Service Awd 1983; Dist Curr Comm 1984-86; *office:* Culver City Mid Sch 4601 Elenda St Culver City CA 90230

OTT, LINDA FLEMING, English Teacher; *b:* Greenville, SC; *m:* Harry L. Jr.; *c:* Russell, Kevin; *ed:* (BA) Scndry Ed/Eng, 1973, (MED) Ed/Rdng, 1976 Clemson Univ; Ed, Univ of SC; *cr:* Teacher Crescent HS 1973-75, Greenville Tech Coll 1975-76, Belleville Mid Sch 1976-78, John Ford Mid Sch 1979-84, Bennent Mid & Orangeburg-Wilkinson HS 1984-; *ai:* Faculty Staff Newsletter; Eng Dept Secy; SC Cncl Teachers of Eng 1989-; Andrew Chapel United Meth Church Sunday Sch Teacher 1980-84, 1988-89; Whos Who in Amer Ed; *office:* Orangeburg-Wilkinson HS 601 Bruins Pkwy Orangeburg SC 29115

OTT, MARK OTT STEVEN, English/Reading/Quest Teacher; *b:* Detroit, MI; *m:* Barbara Ann Willard; *c:* Jennifer, Michael, Kathleen, Christopher; *ed:* (BA) Eng/Soc Stud, 1970, (MA) Rdng, 1976 Oakland Univ; Admin Prgm MI St; *cr:* Teacher Shrine Elem Sch 1973-76, Oxford Mid Sch 1976-; *ai:* Yrbk Adv; Ftbl, Vlybl, Track Coach; Building Instructional Team; Instructional Improvement Comm; Drama Coord; MI Rdng Teachers Assn 1976-; Dads Club 1988-; *home:* 3300 W South Blvd Rochester Hills MI 48309

OTT, MARY LOU, 8th Grade English Teacher; *b:* Malvern, OH; *m:* William A.; *c:* Char; *ed:* (BA) Eng/Speech, 1971, (MA) Family Stud, 1982 Univ of Akron; Adulthood Aging Certificate; Teaching Writing to the Adolescent; *cr:* Chrstn Ed Dir 1st Chrstn Church 1983-86; Part-time Instr Wayne General & Tech Coll 1983-86; 8th Grade Eng Teacher Wadsworth City Schs 1986-; *ai:* Writing Coach; Wadsworth City Sch Staff Dev Comm; Young Authors Spon; NCTE, OCTELA; Chrstn Church of OH Bd of Dir 1989-; *office:* Wadsworth Cntrl Mid Sch 151 Main St Wadsworth OH 44281

OTT, WILLIAM L., Mathematics Department Chair; *b:* Fayetteville, NC; *m:* Joan E.; *ed:* (BA) Math, Univ of N CO 1959; (MA) Cmptrs in Ed, Lesley Coll; *cr:* Teacher South Jr HS 1959-73; Gateway HS 1973-; *ai:* Dept Chm, Accountability Comm; Asst Track Coach; NCTM, ASCD; *office:* Gateway HS 1300 S Sable St Aurora CO 80014

OTTE, LINDSAY OWEN, 5th Grade Teacher; *b:* Covington, KY; *m:* David M.; *c:* Meredith, Megan, Matthew, Michael; *ed:* (BS) Elem Ed, Georgetown Coll 1974; (MA) Ed, Xavier Univ 1979; *cr:* 5th Grade Teacher 1974-77; Title I Rdng Teacher 1978-79 Gallatin Cty Elem Schl; 3rd Grade Teacher 1979-80; 5th Grade Teacher 1980-89 Burlington Elem Sch; *ai:* Salary Comm Boone Cty Ed Assn; Formerly-Mem Comm to Start Elem Cmptrs Boone Cty Schls; BCEA/KEA/NEA; *home:* 425 Stevenson Rd Erlanger KY 41018

OTTO, DOROTHY HUNTER, Retired Choir Director; *b:* Madison, WI; *m:* Gary Lee; *c:* Derik, Ryan; *ed:* (BA) Music Ed, Cascade Coll 1969; Music Ed, W OR Coll; *cr:* Music Teacher Sheridan Public Schls 1969-71; Choir Dir N Clackamas Chrstn Sch 1973-89; *ai:* Dean of Girls; Jr Class, Sr Class & Stu Cncl Adv; Home Ec Teacher; ACSI 1982-89.

OTTO, NANCY KUSHMIDER, Biology/Scndry Sci Teacher; *b:* Hazleton, PA; *m:* Randall E.; *ed:* (BS) Scndry Ed/Bio, PA St Univ 1980; Grad Work Temple Univ, West Chester Univ, PA St Univ, Beaver Coll; *cr:* Sci Teacher Lenape Jr HS 1980-81, Holicong Jr HS 1981; Scndry Sci Teacher Plumstead Chrstn Sch 1981-; *ai:* Stu Cncl & Soph Class Adv; NSTA; *office:* Plumstead Chrstn Sch 5765 Old Easton Rd P O Box 216 Plumsteadville PA 18949

OTTO, STANLEY ALAN, Social Science Teacher; *b:* Bloomington, IL; *ed:* (BSE) His, IL St Univ 1973; (ME) Scndry Ed, Univ of IL 1978; *cr:* Soc Sci Teacher Blue Mound HS 1973-85, Bloomington HS 1985-; *ai:* Adv for Stu Who Are Accepted to Participate in Natl Civic Ed Prgm Based in Washington Dc; Presidential Classroom for Young Amer; Presidential Classroom Instr 1981-; Masonic Blue Lodge 742 1972-; Scottish Rite Consistory 1972-; Masonic Shrine 1972-; Phi Alpha Theta His Honorary Society; Grad IL St Univ with Honors; Presidential Classroom Alumnus; Amer Field Service Adv & Cmmty Coord; Nom IL Teacher of Yr; Nom IL Master Teacher; *office:* Bloomington H S 1202 E Locust St Bloomington IL 61701

OTULAKOWSKI, RONALD JAMES, Drama Teacher; *b:* Detroit, MI; *ed:* (BS) Speech/Drama, Wayne St Univ 1971; (MA) Dramatic Art, E MI Univ 1981; *cr:* Teacher Cass Tech HS 1971-; Drama Dir Thurston HS 1976-, Macomb Cty Comm Coll 1980-82; Dir/Producer Backstage Dinner Theatre 1982-; *ai:* Cass Tech HS Drama Dir; Thurston HS Theatre Dir; Grosse Pointe, Huron Civic, Wyandotte Cmmty Theatre; *office:* Cass Tech HS 2421 Second Detroit MI 48201

OTWELL, BRENDA KAYE, Fifth Grade Teacher; *b:* Jasper, AL; *ed:* (AS) Walker Coll 1970; (BS) Scndry Ed/Eng, 1972, (MA) Elem Ed, 1975, (MA) Admin, 1990 Univ of AL; Rdng Endorsement 1978; *cr:* 3rd Grade Teacher 1972-81, 5th Grade Teacher 1981-86 Lupton Jr HS; 6th-8th Grade Teacher Kitzengen West Germany 1986-88; Math/Rdng/Eng Remedial Teacher Walter Area Voc Sch 1988-89; 5th Grade Teacher Lupton Jr HS 1989-; *ai:* Rdng, St Teachers Accreditation & Cert, St Teachers Prof Evaluation Comms; St Lang Art Curr Mem; Alpha Delta Kappa (Treas 1980-82, Pres 1984-86), Young Careerist 1979; Walker Coll Concert Bd Secy 1990; 1st United Meth Church; Teacher of Yr Dist Winner; Outstanding Young Women of America; *office:* Lupton HS Rt 1 Nauvoo AL 35578

OUDERKIRK, KIM AUDREY, Science Department Chair; *b:* Albany, NY; *ed:* (BA) Geology, Bryn Mawr Coll 1982; Geology, Princeton Univ 1982-83; Ed, Univ of AL 1987-88; Inst for Chemical Ed 1988, 1989; *cr:* Laboratory Teaching Asst Princeton Univ 1982-83; Teacher Lawrence Day Sch 1983-85; Sci/Cmptr Sci Teacher Hun Sch of Princeton 1984-86; Sci/Math Teacher Tuscaloosa Acad 1986-; *ai:* Sci Club Spon; Cheerleading Coach 1984-85, 1986-87; Tennis Coach 1984-86; Environmental Protection Club Spon 1985-86, 1987-88; AL Sci Teachers Assn 1987-; Tuscaloosa Sci Teachers Assn (VP 1989-, Mem) 1987-; Nom Teacher of Yr; Presented Hands on Approach to Sci Seminars; Southern Assn of Ind Schls Speaker; *office:* Tuscaloosa Acad 420 Rice Valley Rd N Tuscaloosa AL 35406

OUIMET, JANICE M., Biology Teacher; *b:* Acushnet, MA; *m:* Charles C.; *c:* Adam, Sally; *ed:* (BA) Bio, N Adams St 1969; Numerous Courses & Wrkshps; *cr:* Sci Teacher C T Plunkett Jr HS 1969-70; Bio Teacher New Bedford HS 1971-81, Amity Sch Dist 5 1981-88, Leon HS 1988-; *ai:* Exchangettes Service Club Adv; NEA 1975-; *office:* Leon HS 550 E Tennessee St Tallahassee FL 32308

OUIMETTE, CLARE M., Second Grade Teacher; *b:* Providence, RI; *d:* Leo; *c:* Stephen, Michael, James, Thomas, Carol; *ed:* (BA) Elem Ed, RI Coll 1950; Grad Stud; *cr:* Substitute Teacher Woonsocket 1960-61; Elem Teacher E Woonsocket Sch 1962-; *office:* E Woonsocket Sch 900 Mendon Rd Woonsocket RI 02895

OULTON, GRACE DIETER, English Teacher/Vice Principal; *b:* Camden, NJ; *m:* Martin John; *c:* Heather, Bryn; *ed:* (BS) Eng, E Stroudsburg St 1967; Courses Taken at LA St Univ; *cr:* Eng Teacher Cntrl Jr HS 1967-68, 1st Assembly Chrstn Acad 1980-82; Eng Teacher/Vice Prin Cornerstone Acad 1982-; *ai:* Stu Cncl Adv; NCTE; United Meth Women; Teacher of Yr 19828 1988.

OURSO, CHARLENE GOMEZ, 7th Grade Social Studies; *b:* Donaldsonville, LA; *c:* David; *ed:* (BA) Elem Ed, Nicholls St Univ 1972; (MED) Admin/Supervision, LA St Univ 1980; Certified Instr Lions Quest Skills for Adolescence; *cr:* Teacher Donaldsonville Elem 1972-75; Jr HS Teacher Prairieville Elem 1975-; *ai:* Just Say No Club Adv; Budget Comm Prairieville Elem; 4-H Club Spon; NEA, LA Ed Assn, Ascension Ed Assn 1972-; Ascension Parish Teacher of Yr 1980-81; Ascension Parish Master Teacher 1989-; Prairieville Elem Teacher of Yr 1980-81; Certified LA Starr Assessor; *office:* Ascension Parish Schls 16200 Hwy 930 Prairieville LA 70769

OUSLEY, ANN MC KETCHEN (WRIGHT), Vocational Business Teacher; *b:* Shelbina, MO; *c:* Stephenie N., Michael R.; *ed:* (BSE) Bus Ed, 1971, (MA) Bus Ed, 1972 NE MO St Univ; *cr:* Bus Teacher Bryamer HS 1972-75, Marceline HS 1978-80; Voc Bus Teacher Brunswick R-III HS 1980-; *ai:* Class Spon; Career Ladder Review Comm Secy; Insurance & Software Comm Chairperson; MO Bus Ed Assn, NBEA, MO Voc Assn; MO Bus Ed Contest Assn (St VP 1989-, Pres 1990); GSA Troop Leader 1985-; Meth Youth Group Asst Dir 1988-; *home:* 726 W Broadway Brunswick MO 65236

OUTLAW, MARTHA BULLOCK, Eng as Second Language Teacher; *b:* Sanford, NC; *m:* Marion Moise; *ed:* (BS) Home Ec, E Carolina Univ 1968; Univ of NC Charlotte, Univ of NC Greensboro; *cr:* 1st Grade Teacher Merry Oaks Elem 1970-72; Teacher of Trainable Mentally Retarded Mc Iver Sch 1972-73; 1st/2nd Grade Teacher Wiley Elem Sch 1973-78; Eng as Second Lang Teacher Cone Sch 1978-; *ai:* Leadership Team; After Sch Rdng Club; Courtesy Comm Chairperson; Teachers To Speakers Other Langs; Neighborhood Assn (Pres 1986-88, Ed 1988-); Ben L Smith Schlsp Awd; Teacher of Yr Finalist City Schls; Teaching Mini-Grant Rdng Club; NC Center For Advancement Teaching Scholar; *office:* Ceasar Cone Sch 2501 N Church St Greensboro NC 27405

OUTLAW, NANCY MARION, 8th Grade Teacher; *b:* Raleigh, NC; *m:* Gene Quinn; *c:* Joshua, Anna; *ed:* (BS) Elem Ed, Campbell Univ 1978; (MAED) Mid Grades Ed, East Carolina Univ 1989; *cr:* 8th Grade Teacher Anderson Creek Sch 1978-79; 4th Grade Teacher Chinquapin Sch 1979-80; 7th/8th Grade Teacher B F Grady Sch 1980-86; 8th Grade Teacher E E Smith Mid Sch 1986-; *ai:* Sci Textbook Adoption Comm; Superintendents Faculty Advisory Comm; Effective Schs Cntrl Comm; Sci Fair Chairperson; Sch Leadership Team; NC Assn of Educators 1978-; NEA 1978-; NSTA 1983-; NC Sci Teachers Assn 1983-; Alumni Springs Baptist Church Youth Leader; Duplin Cty Ed Fnd Grants; NC Sci/Math Ed Network Fellowships; Telephone Pioneers Conservation Awd for NC Educator 1988; Attended East Carolina Univ Institutes; *home:* Rt 1 Box 136 Mount Olive NC 28365

OUTLAW, NINA STEPHENSON, Science Teacher/Dept Chair; *b:* Ft Worth, TX; *m:* B. Morris; *ed:* (BS) Bio, 1964, (MED) Bio, 1979 NTSU; (MT) Medical Technology, Tarleton St Univ 1985; King Fnd Prgm at M D Anderson Hospital 1986; *cr:* Teacher W A Meacham Jr HS 1963-68, Diamond Hill HS 1968-83, Keller HS 1985-; *ai:* Sci Dept Head; Sci Fair Instr; Conference for Advancement of Sci Teaching Wkshp Speaker; Sci Teachers Assn of TX 1975-; Bio Teachers Assn of TX 1986-; Amer Heart Assn Bd of Dir 1979, Cmmty Service 1979; Sci Teachers Assn of Ft Worth (Treas 1968, Secy 1969); Outstanding New Educator General Dynamics 1965; Outstanding Bio Teacher of TX 1978; Three Instructional Improvement Grants 1987-89; *office:* Keller HS 101 Indian Trail Dr Keller TX 76248

OUTT, DENNIS BRENT, Earth & Life Science Teacher; *b:* New Orleans, LA; *m:* Susan Davette Ross; *c:* Damon, Daren, Bryann; *ed:* (BS) Phys Ed, MSSC 1975; (BS) Sci, PSU 1986; Working Toward Masters in Admin; *cr:* Teacher/Coach Carl Junction Schls 1977-78, Galena HS 1979-81, Galena Jr HS 1981-; *ai:* Ftbl, Bsktbl & Track Coach; 8th Grade, Noon Hour Act & Sch Patrol Spon; Galena Ed Assn, KS Ed Assn 1984-; KS Coaches Assn 1980-; *home:* 702 N Wilson Webb City MO 64870

OVER, EDWARD N., 6th Grade Teacher; *b:* Roaring Spring, PA; *m:* Glenda Burket; *c:* Jill; *ed:* (BS) Elem Ed, Mansfield Univ 1971; (MS) Elem Counseling, Shippinsburg Univ 1977; *cr:* Elem Teacher Northern Bedford 1972-; *ai:* Jr HS Wrestling Coach; *office:* Northern Bedford Cty Elem Sch Loysburg PA 16659

OVERHEIDT-SMITH, SHERYL, English Teacher; *b:* Evergreen Park, IL; *m:* Jerry Allan; *ed:* (BSED) Ed, 1969, (MA) Eng, 1971 Chicago St Univ; Gifted Ed, Career Ed, Counseling; *cr:* Teacher Bloom HS 1972-; *ai:* Dist 206 Thinking Skills, Faculty Assn Schlsp Selection, NHS Selection Comm; Curr Advisory Cncl; Jr Class Spon; Kappa Delta Pi 1967-69, Outstanding Sr 1969; NCTE 1988-; Kappa Delta Pi Alumni 1970-; IL PTA Honorary Life Mem 1987; IL Ed Assn Convention Delegate; Faculty Assn (VP 1984-86, Governing Bd Mem 1978-); Christa Mc Auliffe Schlsp Awd 1987; NCE Curr & Instrustion Chairperson 1985; Chicago St Univ Outstanding Sr & Outstanding Eng Major Awds; *office:* Bloom HS Dist #206 101 W 10th St Chicago Heights IL 60411

OVERMAN, CHARLES SAGE, Gifted/Talented Coord/Teacher; *b:* Oklahoma City, OK; *m:* Kolleen Ra Von; *c:* Simone Starkman, Linda Nelson, Sandra Lee; *ed:* (BED) Speech Correction/Audiology, Univ of Wichita St 1957; Grad Stud at Various Univs; *cr:* Speech Therapist Childrens Hospital 1957; Grad Asst KS Univ 1957-58; Speech Corr/Audio Logan Cty 1958-59, Wichita Cty 1959-60; Speech Corr Pueblo Dist 60 1960-65; Deaf Ed Admin State of HI 1965-66; Teacher Dofferville KS 1966-69, Hawaii 1969-; *ai:* Unified Profession HI Bd/Dir 1982-84; Windward Y Mens Club 1979-83; NDEA Schlshp 1963.

OVERMAN, DEE ANN SCHRYVER, Third Grade Teacher; *b:* Sibley, IA; *m:* David Allen; *c:* Lindsay M., Brian R.; *ed:* (BA) Elem Ed, Sioux Falls Coll 1976; TESA Coord Trng; *cr:* 3rd Grade Teacher Kinsey Elem Sch 1978-; *ai:* Sci Dept Head Co-Chairperson; Sci & Health Adoption Comm; NEA, NW IA Rdng Assn, IA St Ed Assn; PEO Sisterhood; *office:* Kinsey Elem Sch 4th Ave & 10th St SE Sioux Center IA 51250

OVERMAN, MISTY M., Mathematics Teacher; *b:* Dallas, TX; *m:* Jerry; *c:* John G., Jordan A.; *ed:* (BS) Math Ed, Univ of GA 1986; *cr:* Math Teacher Greater Atlanta Chrstn Sch 1986-; *ai:* Math Team Coach; *office:* Greater Atlanta Chrstn Sch PO Box 4277 Norcross GA 30091

OVERMAN, SUSAN JOHNSON, Second Grade Teacher; *b:* Smithfield, NC; *m:* Jim; *c:* Beth, Janet; *ed:* (BA) Early Chldhd Ed, Univ of NC Greensboro 1971; *cr:* 3rd Grade ESEA/Spec Rdng Teacher Smithfield Jr HS 1971-73; 2nd Grade Teacher Albemarle Acad 1973-74, Grandy Primary 1974-; *ai:* Screening Comm Chm; Critical Analysis Performance in Ed Mem; Sci Comm Mem; Phi Delta Kappa 1987-; Alpha Delta Kappa Ways-Means Co-Chm 1989-; NEA, NC Assn of Educators 1973-; Corinth Baptist Church (Pre-Sch Teacher, Personnel Comm Mem); PTO 1974-; Camden Cty Math Teacher of Yr 1989-; *office:* Grandy Primary Sch Box 99 Camden NC 27921

OVERSTREET, CATHERINE MARSHALL, Mathematics & Biology Teacher; *b:* Charlottesville, VA; *c:* Karen O. Price, Kristi O. Forgione; *ed:* (BS) Bio, Westhampton Coll Univ of Richmond 1960; Grad Work Univ of Richmond, Univ of VA, Longwood Coll; Biotechnology Wkshp E Carolina Univ; *cr:* Math/Sci Teacher Westhampton Jr HS 1960-63; Sci Teacher 1963-64, Bio Teacher 1970-87 Halifax Cty Sr HS; Math/Bio Teacher Manteo HS 1987-; *ai:* Cheerleading, SGA, Sci Club Spon; Sci Team ACE Coach; Delta Kappa Gamma 1975-78; Outstanding Scndry Educators of America, Outstanding Ed Awd 1974.

OVERSTREET, F. TRAXLER, Third Grade Teacher; *b:* Goshen, IN; *m:* Thomas Reed; *c:* Reed, Ross; *ed:* (BA) Elem Ed, 1973, (MS) Elem Ed, 1977 Ball St Univ; *cr:* 4th Grade Teacher Ober Elem Sch 1973-74; 3rd Grade Teacher Mt Comfort Elem Sch 1975-; *ai:* NCA & PBA Chairperson of Staff & Admin Comm; Phi Delta Kappa 1974-75; *office:* Mt Comfort Elem Sch 5694 W 300 N Greenfield IN 46140

OVERSTREET, JOHANNA, Assistant Principal; *b:* Calvert, TX; *m:* Early; *c:* Gladys Overstreet Richard, Brian E.; *ed:* (BS) Dietetics/Elem Ed, Prairie View A&M Univ 1957; (MED) Ed/Supervision, 1964; Admin & Supervision 1987; *cr:* Teacher Prairie View A&M Univ 1958-60; 5th Grade Teacher Double Bayou Elem Sch 1960-65; 6th Grade Teacher Gregory Elem 1965-69; Coord 1970-84, 3rd Grade Teacher 1984-88, Asst Prin 1988- Grissom Elem; *ai:* Phi Delta Kappa 1986-; Houston Assn of Admin 1988-; Natl Women of Achievement 1986-; PTO, Mission, Civic Club;

Outstanding Service Awd; Nom Outstanding Teacher 1976 & Outstanding Elem Teacher of Yr 1975; *office:* Grissom Elem Sch 4901 Simsbrook Houston TX 77045

OVERSTREET, SARAH COLVIN, Mathematics Department Chair; *b:* Dubach, LA; *m:* Arley C.; *c:* Robin J.; Mike; *ed:* (BA) Math/Ed, 1964, (MSE) Math/Ed, 1969 LA Tech Univ; Math/Ed, NE LA Univ 1974; Prof Improvement Prgm; Advanced Placement Calculus Seminar; *cr:* Classroom Teacher El Dorado HS 1964-81; Adjunct Teacher Univ of AR El Dorado 1972, NE LA Univ El Dorado 1974, S AR Univ El Dorado 1976-77; Teacher Minden HS 1981-; Adjunct Teacher Southern Univ Shreveport 1987-; *ai:* Sr Spon; Sr Fund Making Act Co-Chairperson; Math Quiz & Bowl; NEA 1985-; Webster Assn of Ed Treas 1986-; LA Cncl Teachers of Math 1989-; NCTM 1987-; *office:* Minden HS PO Box 838 Minden LA 71055

OVIATT, DONA DAUGHERTY, Fifth Grade Teacher; *b:* Falls Creek, PA; *m:* Morris W.; *c:* Pamela Mc Cune, Marsha Knoster, Paula Long; *ed:* (BS) Elem Ed, Clarion Univ of PA 1952; Various Wkshps & In-Service Classes; *cr:* Kndgtn Teacher Warren City Schls 1952-55; 2nd Grade Teacher New Castle City Schls 1955-58; Substitute Elem Teacher Indiana, Coudersport, Austin 1958-70; 5th Grade Teacher Coudersport Area Schls 1970-; *ai:* NSEA 1952-58; CAEA, NEA Secy 1970-; Delta Kappa Gamma Secy 1973-85; Red Cross Secy 1975-; FUC New Century Club Secy 1980-; Church Organizations 1960-; Cmmty Chorus 1973-; *home:* 203 Isabella St Coudersport PA 16915

OVIATT, TED, English Teacher; *b:* Winsted, CT; *c:* Wendy A., Edward P. Jr., Jill Oviatt Tremblay, Peter G.; *ed:* (BA) Fr, Williams Coll 1955; (MAT) Ed, Wesleyan Univ 1957; Summer Prgms Univ of Grenoble France; Russian & Fr, Univ of PA; CA St Univ Northridge; Span, Moorpark Coll; *cr:* Eng Lang Teacher Lycee Jacques-Amyot 1957-58; Teacher/Coach/Asst Headmaster St Marks Sch of TX 1958-64; Headmaster The Key Sch 1964-71, Buckley Cntry Day Sch 1971-73; Asst Headmaster Staples HS 1973-76; Dir Oakwood Sch 1976-78; Headmaster W Valley Neighborhood Sch 1978-80; Eng Teacher Robert Frost Jr HS 1982-83, Belmont HS 1983-; *ai:* Filipino Club & Mock Court Spon; *home:* 5800 Kanan Rd #270 Agoura Hills CA 91301

OWEN, BILL CARL, Physical Education Teacher; *b:* Butler, KY; *m:* Dixie Louise Wyatt; *c:* Craig, Carl; *ed:* (BS) Elem Ed, E KY Univ 1963; *cr:* 4th Grade Teacher 1963-64, 5th Grade Teacher 1964-65 Butler Elem; 3rd Grade Teacher Mt Sterling Elem 1965-66; 5th/6th Grade Teacher Butler Elem 1966-72; Phys Ed Teacher Northern Elem 1972-; *ai:* Elem Soccer Dir; 5th/6th Grade Girls Bsktbl Coach & Dir; KEA, NKEA, NEA; Teacher of Yr 1989-; *home:* 402 Pendleton St Falmouth KY 41040

OWEN, CHARLES B., Mathematics Department Teacher; *b:* New Albany, MS; *m:* Anna Jane Foster; *ed:* (AA) Soc Sci, NE MS Jr Coll 1949; (BS) Soc Stud/Math, Delta St 1951; Math, MS St Univ; Cmptr, MS CC; *cr:* HS Coach/Teacher/Prin Jericho HS 1951-52; Jr HS Coach/Teacher Tippal-Union HS 1954-61; Jr HS Coach/Teacher 1961-80, Math Teacher Myrtle Attendance Center 1980-; *ai:* Class & Class Musical Spon; Time Keeper Ofcl HS Bsktbl Games; Jr HS Bsktbl Coach; MEA 1954-78; MS Prof Educators 1979-; Union Cty Teachers Assn VP 1969-70; Gideons Intnl Bible Secy 1985-87, 1989-; 4 H Club Adv 1954-70, Outstanding Adv 1959; Baptist Church (Deacon 1968-, Sunday Sch Teacher 1960-); Math & Cmptr Course Grant; *home:* Rt 3 Box 316 New Albany MS 38652

OWEN, DONNA PUGH, English Teacher; *b:* Mathews, VA; *c:* Mark, Andrea; *ed:* (BA) His, 1961, (MAT) Elem Ed, 1969 Lynchburg Coll; (EDS) Educl Admin, Coll of William & Mary 1988; Educl Admin, Coll of William & Mary; *cr:* 2nd Grade Teacher Lynchburg Public Schls; 2nd/6th Grade Gifted Teacher Falls Church City Public Schls; Management G&P Telephone Company; 6th/8th Grade Writing/Math/RdnG/Eng Teacher Mathews Cty Public Schls; *ai:* Upstream Literary Magazine Spon; Kappa Delta Pi Mem 1987; ASCD; *home:* PO Box 72 Gwynn VA 23066

OWEN, EVELYN BERNADETTE, English Teacher; *b:* Baltimore, MD; *m:* Clarence A.; *c:* Chiante L., Kahshadd J., Kjordahn R.; *ed:* (BSED) Eng, St Pauls Coll 1974; Grad Stud Univ of VA, Longwood Coll, VA St Univ; Religious Ed, Goldsboro Chrstn Inst; *cr:* Teachers Aide Brunswick Cty Public Schls 1972-74; Rdng Teacher Halifax Jr HS 1974-78; Rdng Teacher 1979-81, Eng Teacher 1981- J S Russell Jr HS; *ai:* Drama & Forensics Spon; Brunswick Ed Assn, VA Ed Assn, NEA Mem 1979-; Starlight Gospel Singers 1954-; Celebrity Storyteller 1990; Stu & Teachers Writing Wkshps Conductor; Poet; *home:* Rt 1 Box 184 Lawrenceville VA 23868

OWEN, GAYLE GRISSOM, 8th Grade Lead Teacher; *b:* Russellville, AL; *m:* Richard Barry; *c:* Richard N., Joshua R., Matthew D.; *ed:* (BS) Phys Ed/Bio/Scndry, 1974, (MS) Elem Ed, 1979 Auburn Univ; TN Elem Endorsement, Mid TN St Univ; AL Elem Endorsement, Auburn Univ; Calhoun Coll; *cr:* 5th/6th Grade Teacher Spring Hill Sch 1974-76; 5th Grade Teacher South Elem Sch 1976-79; 2nd-4th/6th-8th GradeTeacher Monrovia Sch 1979-; *ai:* Math Team Coach; Stus Against Alcohol & Drug Spon; Exec PTA Mid Sch Rep; Prof Growth Comm; Washington DC 8th Grade Trip Coord; Alpha Delta Kappa (VP, Pledge Chair) 1988-; Madison Cty Ed Assn, NEA, AL Ed Assn 1974-; AL Rdng Assn, Intnl Rdng Assn, N AL Rdng Assn 1988-; N AL Cncl Teachers Math, AL Cncl Teacher Math, NCTM 1989-; PTA 1974-; YMCA 1987-; Booster Club 1976-; Sch Yrbk Dedication Recipient 1989; Nom Teacher of Yr 1989- from Local Sch; Co-Authored Math Curr Guide & Coauthored Math Act Book used Cty Wide; *office:* Monrovia Sch 1030 Jeff Rd Huntsville AL 35806

OWEN, HARRY DAVID, Science Teacher; *b:* Salem, OH; *m:* Patricia Stubbs; *c:* Christine, David, Scott; *ed:* (BA) Phys Ed, Mt Union Coll 1972; Teaching Certificate Health Sci, Youngstown St 1975; *cr:* Phys Ed Teacher Western Reserve Schls 1973-74; Sci Teacher Western Reserve Mid Sch 1974-; *ai:* Asst Var Ftbl Coach; 7th Grade Bsktbl Coach; Jr HS Track Coach; Ruritan 1987-; *home:* 7040 Duck Creek Rd Berlin Center OH 44401

OWEN, JOAN WHISNANT, 4th Grade Teacher; *b:* Salisbury, NC; *m:* James H. Jr.; *c:* James S., Dawn C.; *ed:* (BS) Elem Ed, Appalachian St Teachers Coll 1962; *cr:* 4th Grade Teacher Cotswold Elem Sch 1961-68; 1st Grade Teacher Matthews Elem Sch 1977-78; 4th Grade Teacher Clear Creek Elem Sch 1978-; *ai:* Teacher Rep PTA Bd; Steering Comm Southern Assn of Colls & Schs; Media Advisory Comm; Soc Comm; Sci Fair Comm; Cultural Arts Comm; Order of Eastern Star 1975-; *home:* 3412 Matthews-Mint Hill Rd Matthews NC 28105

OWEN, KELLY PETERS, 5th Grade Teacher; *b:* Barre, VT; *m:* Janet Thornton; *c:* Elizabeth, Rebecca; *ed:* (ASA) Lib Art, S VT Coll 1972; (BA) Sociology, Univ of VT 1974; Grad Stud Coll of ID; *cr:* 6th Grade Teacher Cntrl Elem 1977-79; 5th/6th Grade Teacher Carnation Elem 1979-89; 5th Grade Teacher Stillwater Elem 1989-; *ai:* Stu Cncl Adv; NEA 1977-; Pacific NW Writers 1989-; *office:* Stillwater Elem Sch 11530 320th Ave NE Carnation WA 98014

OWEN, LINDA LEE, Kindergarten Teacher; *b:* Sparta, MI; *m:* Kenneth; *c:* Douglas, Thomas, Lisa M.; *ed:* (BA) Elem Ed, W MI Univ; Grad Work W MI Univ, MI St Univ, Oakland Univ; Instructional Theory in Practice Gesell Inst of Human Dev Courses; *cr:* Pre-Sch Dir Bostwick Lake Nursery Sch 1965-71; 1st Grade Teacher Cedar Springs Schls 1972-73; K-3rd Grade Teacher Rockford Public Schls 1974-; *ai:* Sci, Early Chldhd Curr, Effective Schls, Policy Bd Dist Comm; Teacher Assistance Team Mem; NAEYC, MI Assn for Young Children 1987-; Kent Cty Ed Assn Prof Dev Comm 1972-, Distinguished Service Awd 1981; Wrote & Taught Correspondence Course; Published Spelling Dictionary; *office:* Crestwood Elem Sch 6350 Courtland Rockford MI 49341

OWEN, OWENEY ELIAS, Health Education Teacher; *b:* Lebanon, KY; *m:* Sharon H.; *c:* Michael; *ed:* (BA) Health/Phys Ed Recreation, Univ of KY 1969; (MS) Scndry Ed, Morehead St 1985; Univ of KY Grad Sch Cert 1971-72; *cr:* Teacher/Coach Paris HS 1970, Harrison Cty HS 1973, Mt Sterling HS 1974-75, Montgomery Cty HS 1976-; *ai:* Head Phys Ed Dept Chairperson; Ftbl Coach Montgomery Cty HS; Modern Health Textbook Consultant 1985; *home:* 1921 Heatherway Mount Sterling KY 40353

OWEN, THOMAS S., Religion Department Chair; *b:* Hamilton, OH; *ed:* (BA) Theology, Athenaeum of OH; *cr:* Youth Ministry Dir St Vincent Ferrer Church 1981-84; Youth Services Dir Maria Stein Center 1984-85; Religion/Publications Teacher St Ursula Acad HS 1985-87; Religion Teacher/Dept Chm/Dir of Theatre Arts Stephen T Badin HS 1987-; *ai:* Asst Dir Public Relations, Dev, Alumni Affairs; Dir Theatre Badin; Soph Class Moderator; NHS Selection Comm; Literary Magazine & Liturgy Comm Co-Moderator; NCEA 1981-; Theatre Ed Assn 1989-; *office:* Stephen T Badin HS 571 New London Rd Hamilton OH 45013

OWEN-GOODLING, SUSAN GAIL, Third Grade Teacher; *b:* York, PA; *c:* Nathan, Michael W.; *ed:* (BS) Elem Ed, Lebanon Valley Coll 1974; Working Towards Masters Equivalency; *cr:* Teacher Orendorff Elem Sch 1979-; *ai:* Stu Cncl Adv; *office:* Northeastern Sch Dist Hartman St Manchester PA 17345

OWENS, CHRISTINE C., 5th Grade Teacher; *b:* West Monroe, LA; *m:* Wamul R.; *c:* Greg, Chris; *ed:* (BA) Elem Ed, NE LA St 1954; (MA) Elem Ed, MS Coll 1957; (MS) Elem Ed, NE LA St 1972; Grad Stud NE LA St; *cr:* 5th Grade Teacher Millsaps Elem 1954; 4th Grade Teacher Ransom Elem 1954-63; Kndgtn Teacher Bethel Baptist 1969-72; 5th Grade Teacher Lenwil Elem 1972-89; *ai:* 5th & 6th Grade Choir; Cub Scouts; Crisp Comm; Ouachita Teachers Assn, NEA, LA Educators Assn, PTA; Reserve Officers Assn for Ladies, BSA; Order Eastern Star Worthy Matron 1983; Bethel Baptist (Organist, Sunday Sch Teacher); Wkshps Presenter; Outstanding Elem Teachers of America 1975; *home:* 102 Ellen Dr West Monroe LA 71292

OWENS, CONSTANCE RENFRO, HS Special Education Teacher; *b:* London, KY; *m:* Michael B.; *c:* Jennifer A., Whitney L.; *ed:* (BS) Health/Allied, Cumberland Coll 1973; (MA) Ed, Union Coll 1980; *cr:* Mental Health Assoc Comprehensive Care Center 1973-74; Spec Ed Teacher Whitley Cty HS 1975-; *ai:* KY Ed Assn, NEA Mem 1976-; Wrote & Received Educl Innoviation Fund Grant St of KY; *home:* Rt 3 Box 28 Williamsburg KY 40769

OWENS, CRYSTAL J., Spanish Teacher; *b:* Zanesville, OH; *ed:* (BA) Span Ed, Mt Vernon Nazarene Coll 1980; (MA) Foreign Lang Ed, OH St Univ 1988; CA St Univ, Sacramento; Guadalajara Prgm Univ of San Diego; *cr:* Span Teacher Maysville HS 1980-81, East Knox HS 1981-; *ai:* Span Club, Sr Class Adv; OH Foreign Lang Teachers Assn 1981-; NEA (Local Secy, Local Negotiator 1981-; Heart of OH Lang Assn; Church of the Nazarene; *office:* East Knox Local Schls PO Box 127 Howard OH 43028

OWENS, GARY WAYNE, English Teacher; *b:* Monticello, KY; *m:* Joyce Faye Byrd; *c:* Ryan W., Trent A.; *ed:* (AA) Scndry Ed, Lindsey Wilson Coll 1965; (BS) Eng, Campbellsville Coll 1967; (MA) Eng, Union Coll 1975; *cr:* Eng Teacher Wayne Cty HS 1967-; *ai:* Sch Paper Adv; KEA; *home:* Rt 5 Box 513 Monticello KY 42633

OWENS, GRACE WITTIG, Spanish Teacher; *b:* Buffalo, NY; *m:* John B.; *c:* Christopher J., Mark E., Amy E.; *ed:* Span, Univ of Madrid 1964; (BA) Span, 1965, (MAT) Foreign Lang, 1966 Oberlin Coll; *cr:* Eng Teacher Academia Bilingue Normington 1983-84; Span Instr ID St Univ 1984-85; Amer Teacher Amer Lang Acad 1984-85; Span Teacher Highland HS 1985-; *ai:* Intnl Relations, Soccer, Span Club Adv; AATSP; NEA Martin Luther King Jr Awd 1987; Pocatello Human Relations Advisory Comm Chairperson 1986; Northwest Coalition Against Malicious Harassment Bd Mem 1988; Univ of Granada Spain Fulbright Professor 1970-71; *office:* Highland HS 1800 Bench Rd Pocatello ID 83201

OWENS, HELEN M., Teacher; *b:* Arkansas City, KS; *c:* Maura Zale; *ed:* (BA) Poly Sci/Psych, Coll of Emporia 1949-51; (MS) Sci Ed/Curr, Univ of KS 1964; Grad Stud Wichita St Univ; *cr:* Teacher Enterprise 1951-52, Derby Public Schls #260 1952-; *ai:* Stu Cncl; Derby Ed Assn Pres 1954-55; South Cntrl Uniserv Pres 1989-; Daughters of Amer Revolution 1986, Outstanding St His Teacher 1986; Amer Assn of Univ Women Pres 1981-83; Delta Kappa Gamma; Master Teacher; *office:* Derby Mid Sch 715 E Madison Derby KS 67037

OWENS, HENRY CLEAMON, Sixth Grade Teacher; *b:* Bermuda, AL; *ed:* (BS) Elem Ed, Mobile Coll 1972; (MED) Elem Ed, Univ of S AL 1979; *cr:* Prin Chickasaw Acad 1972-74; Teacher Nichberg Jr HS 1974-75, Whitley Elem-Nan Gray Davis 1975-; *ai:* Sch Safety Coord; Sch Philosophy, Objective & Commitments Chm; Math, Geography, Sci Clubs & Stu Cncl Spon; Cty & St Textbook Comms; Mobile Cty Ed Assn, AL Ed Assn, NEA 1975-; Prichard-Chickasaw Toastmasters, Prichard-Chickasaw Civic Forum Pres; Prichard Lib Bd Chm; Mobile Cty Republican Exec Comm Mem; *home:* 6650 David Dr S Theodore AL 36582

OWENS, JACQUELINE HOEKSTRA, Fifth Grade Teacher; *b:* Kankakee, IL; *m:* Doyle; *c:* Megan, Brandon; *ed:* (BS) Elem Ed, 1976, (MS) Elem Ed, 1985 Olivet Univ; *cr:* Summer Sch Teacher Wichert Grade Sch 1976-78; 1st Grade Teacher 1976-82, 3rd Grade Teacher 1982-86, 5th Grade Teacher 1986- St Anne Grade Sch; *ai:* Kappa Delta Pi 1975-84; IEA, NEA 1976-; *office:* St Anne Grade Sch 333 S St Louis Saint Anne IL 60964

OWENS, KAREN NEAL, English Teacher; *b:* Greenville, SC; *m:* Thomas L. Jr.; *c:* Thomas N., Amanda E.; *ed:* (BA) Ger, Columbia Coll 1971; (MA) Ed, Furman Univ 1975; APT Evaluator Trng 1988; *cr:* Eng Teacher Wade Hampton HS 1971-73, Lakeview Mid Sch 1973-77, Wade Hampton HS 1977-81, Southside HS 1981-; *ai:* Prom Spon; Past Chm Eng Dept; Greenville Cncl Teachers of Eng Mem.

OWENS, KITTYE EASTERLY, Third Grade Teacher; *b:* Lebanon, VA; *m:* Charles Allen; *c:* Angela D., Pamela E.; *ed:* (BS) Elem Ed, Radford 1968; *cr:* 2nd Grade Teacher Gilbert Linkous Elem 1968-70; 3rd Grade Teacher Wallace Elem 1971-72, 1974-; *ai:* NEA, VA Ed Assn 1968-; Washington Cty Ed Assn 1971-; Pleasant View United Meth Church; *office:* Wallace Elem Sch 1376 Wallace Pike Bristol VA 24201

OWENS, PATRICIA MC AFEE, Mathematics Teacher; *b:* Texarkana, AR; *m:* Wayne Quincey Sr.; *c:* Cana A., Wayne Q. II; *ed:* (BS) Math, Prairie View A&M Univ 1973; (MA) Math, Univ of MI 1975; Ed Admin, Univ of MI; *cr:* Math Teacher Northeastern HS 1977-82, Murray-Wright HS 1982-; *ai:* Class Spon; Dress Code, Sch Improvement Comms; NCTM, MCTM, DACTM; New Calvary Baptist Church; Zeta Phi Beta Treas 1987-; Outstanding Young Woman of America 1982; Recognized Teacher Most Influential in Stus Life 1986-87, 1989; *office:* Murray-Wright HS 2001 W Warren Ave Detroit MI 48208

OWENS, PATTY DEEL, Second Grade Teacher; *b:* Grundy, VA; *c:* Beth A.; *ed:* (AA) Liberal Arts, Warren Wilson Jr Coll 1966; (AB) Elem Ed, Morehead St Univ 1973; (MA) Elem Ed, Union Coll 1979; Grad Stud Univ of TN; *cr:* 1st/2nd Grade Teacher Prater Elem 1967-68; Kndgtn Teacher Bean Station Elem 1973-74; Resource Teacher Southern Heights 1974-78; 2nd Grade Teacher Witt Elem 1978-; *ai:* Sch Rep Lakeway Rdng, Teacher Study Cncl; Past Textbook Repl NEA, TN Ed Assn 1974-; Witt PTO Past Pres; Hamblen Cty Ed Assn Mem; Lakeway Rdng, Hamblen Cty Assn for Retarded Citizens Mem 1980-; Career Ladder Level III 1988-; Cty Teacher of Yr 1986; *home:* 1150 Mc Farland St H-T 11 Morristown TN 37814

OWENS, REBECCA FOOTE SMITH, Chemistry-Physics Teacher; *b:* Raleigh, NC; *m:* Osborne Hyde; *c:* Carrie E. Owens Jones; *ed:* (BS) 1963-65, (MED) 1978 Campbell Coll; Mentor Trng, 1985-87; Several Wkshps & Seminars; *cr:* Sci Teacher Lee Cty-Deep River 1965; Chem Teacher Sanford Cntrl HS 1965-66, Fayetteville Sr HS 1966-67; Chem/Physics Teacher Concord HS 1967-70; Bio/Chem Teacher Cabarrus Acad 1970-72; Bio/Bio II/Chem II/Physics Salisbury HS 1972-79; Chem/Chem II Goldsboro HS 1979-80; Bio/Chem/Physics Creswell HS 1980-81, Beauford Cty Schls 1981-; *ai:* Chm Sci Dept 1989-; Participated with All Classes Local Environmental Clean Up 1989; Spon Jr-Sr Prom; Chaperone Stu Trips; Sci Club & Sci Fairs; Beta Club; Graduation; Dept Chm; Mem Southern Assn Evaluation Team for Sci 1978-79; Teacher Metric Wkshps for Staff Dev 1975-76; NCAE; NCSTA; IOOF-Rebekah Nobel Grand 1983-85; Mattamuskette Medical Center Bd Chm 1984-86; Amer Legion Auxiliary Pres Local Unit 1972; Nom Presidential Awd Excl in Sci & Math Teaching 1989- ; 1989 Schlsp for Study in Sci NC Dept Public Instruction; 1989 Woodrow Wilson Fnd Chem Inst, Physics

Inst; IOOF-Rebecca Chapter Ed Schlsp Fnd Chm; *home:* 333 Front St Belhaven NC 27810

OWENS, RUTH WILMA TOWNSEL, English Teacher; *b:* Birmingham, AL; *m:* Blanton; *c:* Blanton Jr., Phil, Marc; *ed:* (BS) Ed, 1960, (MED) Ed, 1965 AL St Univ; Grad Stud IN Univ, Univ of WI Milwaukee, Cardinal Stritch Coll; *cr:* Teacher 33rd Ave Elem Sch 1960-63, 28th St Elem Sch 1963-67, Fulton Mid Sch 1967-72, Bell Mid Sch 1972-; *ai:* Chess & Youth Helping One Another Club Dir; Chrstn Bus & Prof Alliance Treas 1980-; United Negro Coll Fund; G E Grant; *home:* N12449 W15 Emily Ln Mequon WI 53092

OWENS, SUE THOMPSON, 6th Grade Teacher; *b:* Indianapolis, IN; *m:* James S.; *c:* Tony, Laura; *ed:* (BA) Elem Ed, 1967, (MED) Elem Ed, 1968 Univ of OR; *cr:* 4th Grade Teacher John Enders Elem 1968-; 4th-6th Grade Teacher Dept of Defense Schls 1970-77; 4th/6th Grade Teacher Lake Youngs Elem 1977-; *ai:* Stu Cncl Adv; KEA 1977-; OEA 1967-68; CEA 1968-70; NEA 1970-77; Accompanied Prin & Supt to Washington DC to Receive Natl Excl Awd; *office:* Lake Youngs Elem Sch 19660 142nd Ave SE Kent WA 98042

OWENS, WILLIAM JUDE, 9th Grade Soc Stud Teacher; *b:* Brooklyn, NY; *m:* Patricia Ann Arelt; *c:* Timothy, Terence, Ryan; *ed:* (BA) Liberal Arts, 1966, (MA) Liberal Arts, 1972 Adelphi Univ; *cr:* SS Teacher Hicksville Jr HS 1967-87; Eng Teacher Hicksville HS 1987-88, Hicksville Mid Sch 1988-89; SS Teacher Hicksville HS 1989-; *ai:* Coaching Soccer; BSA Scoutmaster 1988-; *office:* Hicksville HS Division Ave Hicksville NY 11801

OXANDALE, DORIS MAE (SOURK), 8th Grade Mathematics Teacher; *b:* Goff, KS; *m:* Glenn E.; *c:* Rodney, Sheri Dibbern; *ed:* (BSED) Elem Ed/Math/Soc Sci, Washburn Univ 1972; Cmptr; *cr:* 5th Grade Teacher/7th/8th Grade Phys Ed/Vlybl Teacher Stony Point 1954-55; 1st-8th Grade Teacher Lower Banner 1956-62; 5th/6th Grade Girls Bsktbl/Sftbl/Track Coach Netawaka 1962-69; 7th Grade Girls Bsktbl/Sftbl/Track Coach Whiting 1969-75; Kndgtn Teacher/Acting Prin/8th Grade Math Teacher Jackson Heights Elem 1975-; *ai:* Knowledge Bowl & Math Contestants Coach & Spon; Math Comm Chairperson; KSTA, KNEA Delegate; North Jackson Ed Assn; *home:* RR 1 Box 99 Wetmore KS 66550

OXARART, JULIANNE SCANDURA, Mathematics Teacher; *b:* Ontario, CA; *m:* John Alan; *c:* Jeffrey; *ed:* (BS) Bus Admin, CA Poly Pomona 1982; Continuing Ed, CA St San Bernardino; *cr:* Buyer Millers Outpost 1979-85; Math Teacher Montclair HS 1985, Alta Loma HS 1986-; *ai:* SADD & Pep Squad Adv; Accredidation Comm Chairperson; CTIIP Comm, Stu Intervention Team, Parent Advisory Cncl Mem; Assn of Chaffey Teachers Mem 1986-; CA Math Cncl Mem 1985-88; *office:* Alta Loma HS 8880 Baseline Rd Alta Loma CA 91730

OXHOLM, WILDA FAY GRACE, 4th Grade Teacher; *b:* Kentwood, LA; *m:* Einor; *c:* Susan; *ed:* (BA) Elem Ed, SE LA Univ 1967; Working Towards Masters Elem Ed; *cr:* 7th Grade Teacher Natalbany Elem Sch 1967; 4th Grade Teacher Kentwood Elem Sch 1967-68; 4th-6th Grade Teacher Spring Creek Elem 1968-70; 1st Grade Teacher Valley Forge Acad 1970-78; 4th Grade Teacher Chesbrough Elem 1978-; *ai:* Testing Co-Chm Coord; Stu Handbook Comm; LEA, NEA 1987-89; PTO Rep; *home:* Rt 2 Box 156 Kentwood LA 70444

OXLEY, KEVIN RAY, English Teacher; *b:* Huntingburg, IN; *m:* Leslie Geiselman; *c:* Jesse M.; *ed:* (BS) Phys Ed/Eng, Oakland City Coll 1983; (MA) Ed, Univ of Evansville 1987; *cr:* Teacher Tecumseh Jr-Sr HS 1983-; *ai:* Jr Var Boys Bsktbl; Boys Var Track Asst; *office:* Tecumseh Jr-Sr HS Hwy 68 Lynnville IN 47619

OYER, DONALD RAY, Sixth Grade Teacher; *b:* Deer Creek, IL; *m:* Martha M. Rainey; *c:* Dawn S. Robinson, Cathy J., Bradley R.; *ed:* (BS) Music Ed, 1960; (MS) Information Services & Technology, 1987 Eastern IL Univ; *cr:* 9th-12th Grade Band & Chorus Teacher 1960-78; 5th-8th Grade Band Teacher 1960-78; Sixth Grade Teacher 1978- Stew-Stras Elem Sch; *ai:* Stew-Stas Ed Assn Pres 1970; NEA 1960-; IL Ed Assn 1960-; Strasburg Lion's Club Pres 1978; *office:* Stewardson-Strasburg Elem Sch P O Box 67 Strasburg IL 62465

P

PABST, WILLIAM F., Eighth Grade English Teacher; *b:* New Rochelle, NY; *m:* Mary E. Kelly; *c:* Jennifer; *ed:* (BA) Eng/Ed, Montclair St Coll 1971; *cr:* Teacher Long Branch Mid Sch 1971-; *ai:* Audio-Visual Coord 1980-; NCTE, NEA, NJEA, Monmouth Cty Ed Assn; LBSEA Pres 1973-74; *office:* Long Branch Mid Sch Indiana Ave Long Branch NJ 07740

PACE, BARBARA AKIN, English Teacher; *b:* Sheffield, AL; *m:* Dewey B. Jr.; *c:* William G.Carey; *ed:* (BA) Eng, 1974, (MA) Ed, Univ of North AL 1976; Various Wkshps & Post Grad Classes; *cr:* Spec Ed Teacher 1974-77, Eng/Lang Arts Teacher 1977- Colbert Cty HS; *ai:* Stu Cncl Adv; Jr Class Spon; Red Cross Blood Drive Spon; St Jues Bike-A-Thon Spon; NEA, AEA, NCTE; Faculty Secy; *home:* 303 Richton Ave Muscle Shoals AL 35661

PACE, CHERYE SCOTT, 4th Grade Teacher; *b:* Camden, AR; *m:* Tom; *c:* David; *ed:* (BSE) Elem, 1967, (MSE) Rdng, 1971 Univ of Cntrl AR; *cr:* Private Rdng Tutor Little Rock AR 1970-72; Title I Teacher Conway AR 1972-74, Tuscaloosa AL 1974-76; 2nd Grade Teacher Arkadelphia AR 1976-81; 3rd-5th Grade Teacher Blowing Rock NC 1981-; *ai:* Teaching Course Appalachain St Univ; 4th-5th Grade Teacher Alliance Co-Coord; NCAE 1981-; Phi Delta Kappa 1988-; ASCD 1988-; Watauga Hunger Coalition VP 1989-; Region 7 NC Teacher of Yr 1988-; NC Teacher of Yr Finalist 1988-; Grant Alliance for 4th/5th Grade Teachers of Watauga Cty; *office:* Blowing Rock Elem Sch 228 Sunset Dr Blowing Rock NC 28607

PACE, PAULA B., English/Resource Teacher; *b:* Ogden, UT; *m:* Rudolph S.; *c:* Bradley R., David W., Brian W., Matthew D.; *ed:* (BA) Sociology/Eng, USU 1965; Spec Ed Cert, BYU 1968; Resource Cert, SUU 1989; *cr:* Eng Teacher Washington Jr HS 1966-67; Spec Ed Teacher Tarrer Jr HS 1968-69; Soc Stud Teacher Wayne HS 1976, 1978-79, Richield HS 1986-; *ai:* Natl Eng Teachers Assn, UT Cncl of Eng Teacher; *home:* Box 40 Torrey UT 84775

PACES, MILOSLAV JOSEF, Social Studies Teacher; *b:* Prague, Czechoslovakia; *m:* Dorothy Ann Farrell; *c:* Cynthia, Diane; *ed:* (BA) His, St Johns Univ 1965; (MA) His, Fordham Univ 1967; Addl Stud in Various Soc Sci Areas; *cr:* Teacher Senator Robert F Wagner Jr HS 1965-69, John Jay HS 1969-78, Erasmus Hall HS 1971-75, Walton HS 1978-85, George Washington HS 1985-; *ai:* After Sch Coord; Asst Dept Chairperson; United Fed of Teachers Chapter Exec Bd Mem 1980-84; St Patricks Church Youth Group Adult Adv 1986-87; St Patricks Church Confraternity of Chrstn Doctrine HS Parent Assn Pres 1984.

PACHECO, CATHERINE DE ROSA, 6th Grade Teacher; *b:* Joliet, IL; *c:* Cathy L. Pacheco-Munstedt, Cristy A.; *ed:* (BA) Span/Elem Ed, Coll of St Francis 1971; (MA) SW Stud, CO Coll 1986; Cert Type D Admin Elem, Scndry Univ of Denver 1988; *cr:* 6th Grade Teacher Indian Trail Jr HS 1971-75; Bi-ling/Remedial Teacher Rockdale Elem 1975-77; 5th Grade Teacher Keith Elem 1977-79; 6th Grade Teacher CO Springs Sch Dist #11 1979-; *ai:* CO Springs Ed Assn Building Rep 1981-82, 1984-87, Outstanding Rep of Yr 1986-87; *home:* 10895 Thunderhead Colorado Springs CO 80925

PACHECO, ELIZABETH LEGITS, Counselor; *b:* Santa Fe, NM; *c:* Yvette T.; *ed:* (BA) Home Ec/Ed, 1975, (MA) Counseling, 1979 NM Highlands Univ; Numerous Courses; *cr:* Home Ec Teacher 1976-89, Cnslr 1989- Santa Fe HS; *ai:* FHA/HERO & SADD Spon; North Cntrl Evaluation, Employees Assistance Comms; Home Ec Dept Chairperson; Home Ec Dist Curr Coord.

PACK, BOBBIE SUE, Guidance Counselor; *b:* Winchester, TN; *m:* James F. Jr.; *c:* Bond H. Little III, Timothy S. Little; *ed:* (BS) Bus Ed, 1962, (MED) Guidance/Counseling, 1977 Mid TN St Univ; Property & Casualty Insurance License; *cr:* Teacher Franklin Cty Bd of Ed 1962-70, Madison Cty Bd of Ed 1970-74, Mc Nairy Cty Bd of Ed 1974-75; Voc Rehabilitation Cnslr Memphis St Dept of Ed 1975-76; Cnslr Franklin Cty Bd of Ed 1976-; *ai:* Yrbk Spon; S TN Assn for Counseling & Dev.

PACKARD, ELAINE SUSAN, Program Manager; *b:* Olney, MD; *m:* Alan J. King; *c:* Dana C., Lucius E.; *ed:* (BS) Math/Scndry Ed, Simmons Coll 1963; (MED) Educl Admin, Seattle Univ 1982; Sociology of Ed, Teachers Coll & Columbia Univ; Educl Policy, Hofstra Univ; *cr:* Classroom Teacher 1973-74, Prgm Mgr 1974- Nova; *ai:* Seattle Alternative Sch Coalition; WA Alternative Learning Assn Pres 1980-81; Puget Sound Educl Consortium 1988-; Phi Delta Kappa 1982-; Katrilli Finnish Folkdancers Dir 1987-89.

PACKARD, LEE EDWARD, Sixth Grade Teacher; *b:* Framingham, MA; *m:* Annette De Luzio; *c:* Matthew, Mark, Michael; *ed:* (AA) Liberal Art, St Charles Coll 1964; (BA) Philosophy, St Bonaventure Univ 1967; (MA) Elem Ed, Worcester St Coll 1979; Grad Stud Multi Cultural Ed; *cr:* 6th Grade Teacher Dutcher Street Sch 1968-79, Hopedale Memorial Sch 1979-; *ai:* Head Teacher; Stu Cncl Adv; Artistic Dir; Soc Stud Curr Comm Chairperson; Jr Var Soccer Coach; Hopedale Teachers Assn (Secy 1970, VP 1974, Pres 1975, Exec Bd 1976); Educators for Soc Responsibility 1989; Milford Theatre Guild 1986-; Town Meeting Mem 1987-; Daughters of Amer Revolution Promoting Study of Amer Heritage; Talented & Gifted Commonwealth Inservice Inst Grant; Horace Mann Grant Supplementary Curr for Soc Stud on Prejudice; Cncl for Basic Ed Fellowship Study of Ethnicity & Relation to Global Ed; *home:* 67 East St Ext Milford MA 01747

PACKARD, LOIS M., Fifth Grade Teacher; *b:* Brighton, MI; *ed:* (BS) Lang Art/Soc Stud/Art, E MI Univ 1969; *cr:* 5th Grade Teacher Howell Public Schls 1969-; *office:* Highlander Way Mid Sch 511 N Highlander Way Howell MI 48843

PACKER, JON O., Fifth Grade Teacher; *b:* Flint, MI; *m:* Vicki Lynn Brooks; *c:* Brianna B., Allyssa L.; *ed:* (BA) Ed, W MI Univ 1973; Rdng Specialist Prgm, MI St Univ; *cr:* Teacher Vandercook Lake Public Schls 1975-; *ai:* Bsktbl & Sftbl Coach; VCLEA VP; United Meth Mens Club Pres 1988-; Young Men of America; *office:* Vandercook Lake Public Schls 800 E Mc Devitt Jackson MI 49203

PACKETT, CYNTHIA BRONNER, 8th Grade Mathematics Teacher; *b:* Richmond, VA; *m:* Randall W. Jr.; *c:* Douglas, Murphy; *ed:* (MED) Ed Curr/Instruction, 1986, (BS) Math Ed, VA Commonwealth Univ 1975; *cr:* 7th Grade Math Teacher 1975-79, 8th Grade Math Teacher 1979- Richmond Cty Intermediate; *ai:* Mathcounts Prgm Coach; Yrbk Spon; Magazine Adv; Gifted Prgm Photography Instr; NCTM 1983-; VA Cncl of Teachers of Math 1985-; Delta Kappa Gamma Society Intnl Schlsp Chairperson 1982-; *office:* Richmond Cty Intermediate Sch P O Box 705 Warsaw VA 22572

PACKEY, BETTY BARAN, Second Grade Teacher; *b:* Jackson Heights, NY; *c:* Leah, Amanda; *ed:* (BS) Elem Ed, St Johns Univ 1970; (MS) Ed, C W Post 1972; *cr:* Elem Teacher Three Village SchLs 1970-; *ai:* Math Curr Comm Mem 1978-; NY St United Teachers, 3 Village Teachers Assn 1970-; *office:* Setauket Elem Sch Main St Setauket NY 11733

PADDOCK, SANDRA STALEY, First Grade Teacher; *b:* Terre Haute, IN; *m:* M. David; *ed:* (BS) Elem Ed, E IL Univ 1963; (MS) Lib Sci, Univ of IL 1969; *cr:* 2nd Grade Teacher Kings Road Sch 1963-66; Mid Primary Teacher Flossie Wiley Sch 1966-67; 1st Grade Teacher ABL Sch System 1967-68; Librarian Buzzard Laboratory Sch 1968-71; 1st Grade Teacher Seed Sch 1971-; *ai:* Red Hill Unit 10 Gifted Ed Comm; Delta Kappa Gamma Pres 1980-82; NEA, IEA; PEO Chaplain 1987-; *office:* Seed Sch 749 Church St Bridgeport IL 62417

PADEN, CYNTHIA LEE, 8th Grade Eng/Core His Teacher; *b:* Selma, CA; *ed:* (BA) Art His/His, Fresno St 1976; Grant Natl Endowment for Hum Univ of VA 1985; SJV Writing Project 1986; Writing Project London England 1988; Constitutional Seminar Univ of CA Los Angeles 1987;Dept of Defense 1990; *cr:* His Teacher Hanford HS 1979-83; Core His Teacher Edison Computech 1983-; Soc Stud Teacher Dept of Defense Germany 1990; *office:* Computech Mid Sch 555 E Belgravia Fresno CA 93706

PADGETT, BRENDA REED, Fourth Grade Teacher; *b:* Dewitt, AR; *m:* Steven Dale; *c:* Casey L.; *ed:* (BA) Early Chldhd/Elem Ed, Univ of AR Monticello 1978; Grad Work Univ of Cntrl AR & Univ of AR Little Rock; *cr:* Kndgtn Teacher Dewitt Elem Sch 1978-79, Jacksonville Elem Sch 1979-82; 5th Grade Teacher Guy-Perkins Schls 1982-84; Migrant Ed/Gifted & Talented Ed Teacher Pangburn Schls 1984-86; 4th Grade Teacher Guy-Perkins Schls 1986-; *ai:* Parent to Parent of Faulkner Cty Secy 1989-.

PADGETT, CHRISTINE MONTGOMERY, 6th Grade Reading Teacher; *b:* Port Arthur, TX; *m:* James A.; *c:* Rebecca Smith, James Jr., Charles E., Mary Moore; *ed:* (BS) Elem Ed, Univ Houston 1969-70; Rdng Spec; *cr:* 2nd Grade Teacher 1969-70; 4th Grade Teacher 1970-76 Red Bluff Elem; 8th Grade Teacher 1976-83; 6th Grade Teacher 1983- San Jacinto Intermediate; *ai:* PTA 1st VP 1988-; San Jacinto Intermediate Club Sponsrshp; Tigers Spots Game Club Comm Mem; PISD Content Mastery Comm Former Mem; Curr Revision Comm 1985; Teacher Dress PISD Code Comm 1978; Kappa Delta Pi 1969-; Phi Theta Kappa 1968-; TSTA Building Rep 1971-76; Red Bluff Elem PTA 1st VP 1972-74; Golden Acres Bapt Church Organist 1963-; 1st Runner-Up Intermediate Sch Teacher of Yr 1979; *office:* San Jacinto Intermediate Sch 3102 San Augustine Pasadena TX 77503

PADGETT, SHARON A., Mathematics Teacher; *b:* Demopolis, AL; *ed:* (BS) Bio/Math, MS Univ for Women 1978; (MS) Math Ed, Jacksonville St Univ 1988; Ed Specialist; Attended Natl & Regional Meetings of Math Teachers 1989, 1990; *cr:* Sci Teacher Enterprise HS 1979-82; Math Teacher Pleasant Valley HS 1984-; In-Service Instr Jacksonville St Univ 1989-; *ai:* Math, Pre Algebra Math & Consumer Math Tournament Team Coach; NEA, AL Ed Assn, Calhoun Cty Ed Assn 1984-; NCTM, AL Cncl of Teachers of Math Exec Bd 1988-; Phi Delta Kappa 1987-; AL Classroon Teachers Assn 1989-; Redemption Ensemble Dir 1988-; Sanctuary Choir First Baptist Church 1983-; Serve on Advisory Panel for Coll of Ed Jacksonville St Univ; Serve as Secy for Local Ed Assn; Serve as Delegate to AL Ed Assn Rep Assembly; *home:* 2492 Hwy 204 Wellington AL 36279

PADILLA, CARLOS, Reading Teacher; *b:* Brownsville, TX; *ed:* (BA) Psych/Soc, 1985, (TCAP) Rdng, 1986 Pan Amer Univ 1986; Scndry Counseling/Guidance Currently Completing Graduate Prgm; *cr:* Soc Worker Big Brothers/Big Sisters 1985; Teacher Cummings Intermediate 1985-; *ai:* Spon UIL Modern Oratory Events 1987-88; Pan Amer Univ Highest GPA in Psych 1985; Kappa Delta Pi 1985; *office:* Cummings Intermediate Schl 1800 Cummings Pl Brownsville TX 78520

PADILLA, JOHN EDWARD, Sixth Grade Teacher; *b:* Belen, NM; *m:* Patricia F. Edweil; *c:* Jennifer, Tomas, Erin; *ed:* (BA) Elem Ed, 1974, (MA) Ed Admin, W NM Univ 1981; *cr:* 8th Grade Teacher Cochiti Elem Sch 1974-79; 6th Grade Teacher Gil Sanchez Elem 1980-85, Dennis Chavez Elem 1986-; *ai:* 6th Grade Bsktbl Coach; *home:* 1315 Gabaldon Belen NM 87002

PADILLA, ORLANDO, 6th Grade Teacher; *b:* Dexter, NM; *m:* Merlinda; *c:* Londie, Orlando, Camille; *ed:* (BA) Elem Bi-ling Ed, E NM Univ 1979; Sci, Math, Mexican Folk Dance Wkshps; *cr:* 3rd Grade Teacher 1979-83, 5th Grade Teacher 1983-85, 6th Grade Teacher 1985- Flora Vista Elem; *ai:* Youth Sports Coach 1980-; NEA 1979-; Youth Soccer Assn Pres; St Johns Cath Church.

PADILLA, ROCHELLE LE KUS, Social Studies Teacher; *b:* Brooklyn, NY; *c:* Sharon Israel, Lisa Polevoy, David Polevoy; *ed:* (BA) His, Adelphi Univ 1957; (MA) Speech Comm, Denver Univ 1974; Grad Stud CA St Univ Long Beach, CA St Univ Dominguez

Hills, CO Univ; *cr:* 3rd Grade Teacher Public Sch 81 1958-59; 4th Grade Teacher Public Sch 289 1959-60; 9th Grade Soc Stud/Eng Teacher Place Jr HS 1978-79; 9th Grade Soc Stud Teacher Lindberg Jr HS 198-85; Soc Stud Teacher Jordan HS 1985-; *ai:* Jordan HS Dropout Prevention Coord 1988-; NEA 1983-; Teacher Assn of Long Beach Faculty Rep 1983-88; Natl Organization for Women VP 1977-78; Organization for Rehabilitation Through Trng VP 1974-76; Anti Def League Speakers Bureau 1989-; Invited to Apply Business Week Magazine Natl Honorarium; *office:* Jordan HS 6500 Atlantic Ave Long Beach CA 90805

PADMORE, VIVIAN YOUNGER, Fourth Grade Teacher; *b:* Bronx, NY; *m:* Philip; *ed:* (BS) Ed, Oswego 1960; *cr:* 3rd Grade Teacher 1960-77, 4th Grade Teacher 1977- W Nyack Elem Sch; *ai:* West Nyack PTA Treas 1976-78; *office:* W Nyack Elem Sch 661 W Nyack Rd West Nyack NY 10994

PAFFORD, RONALD EVERETT, 7th/8th Grade Soc Sci Teacher; *b:* Camden, TN; *m:* Brenda Melton; *ed:* (BS) Soc Sci Endorsement, Univ of TN Martin 1976; *cr:* Teacher Benton Cty 1976-; *ai:* Benton Cty Ed Assn (Past Pres) 1976-; TN Ed Assn, NEA 1976-; *home:* PO Box 399 Camden TN 38320

PAGAN, ELBA I, Sci Teacher/Sci Dept Chair; *b:* Ponce, PR; *m:* Luis R. Vieva; *c:* Luis R., Lenys, Ernesto; *ed:* (BS) Sci/Psych, Cath Univ 1974; (MS) Ed Curr/Teaching Admin & Supervision, 1987; Master Clinical Psych; *cr:* Sci Teacher/Sci Dept Chairperson Colegio Ponceno 1978-; Prof Univ PR 1988-; *ai:* Academic Cncl; Ponce Sci Teachers Assn, Curr & Supervision Assn 1980-; Colegio Ponceno Teacher of Yr 1988; *office:* Colegio Ponceno Ponce PR 00644

PAGANO, LYNN M., Jr HS Social Studies Teacher; *b:* East Orange, NJ; *ed:* (BA) Anthropology/His, Ft Lewis Coll 1981; *cr:* Soc Stud Teacher Tse Bit Ai Mid Sch 1988-; *ai:* Responsible for Selection of Jr Honor Society Mems Tse Bit Ai Mid Sch 1988-; NM Cncl of Soc Stud Mem 1988-; Natl Jr Honor Society Comm Mem; Church World Service Mem 1989-; Grant to Attend 41st Annual Mid East Conference Washington DC to Study Conflicts & Issues in Mid East Policies 1987; *office:* Tse Bit Ai Mid Sch PO Box 1873 Shiprock NM 87420

PAGANO, MARIANNE B., Spanish Teacher; *b:* Brooklyn, NY; *ed:* (BA) Span, 1978, (MS) Ed/Foreign Lang, 1990 Queens Coll CUNY; Certificate Paralegal Stud, Queens Coll; *cr:* Dept of Romance Lang/Adjunct Lecturer/Span Teacher Queens Coll CUNY 1978-81; Span Teacher Stella Maris HS 1981-; *ai:* Moderator Stella Maris Stu Cncl; Sigma Delta Pi; *office:* Stella Maris HS Beach 112th St Rockaway Park NY 11694

PAGE, ANNIE GRACE (TATUM), Third Grade Teacher; *b:* Bay Springs, MS; *m:* Audrey Jack; *c:* Lee, Anita; *ed:* (BS) Elem Ed, MS Valley St Univ 1970; (MA) Elem Ed, MS St Univ 1974; Spec Ed Elem Ed, Univ of S MS 1987; William Carey Coll 1988; Elem Supervision, Elem Prin Admin; *cr:* 1st Grade Teacher Southside Elem Sch 1968-70; 3rd Grade Teacher William Berry Elem Sch 1970-; *ai:* Staff Dev Comm; MS Assn of Educators 1969-, Poly Act Campaign 1988; MS Assn of Women in Ed Leadership 1989-; ASCD 1990; Jasper Cty MVSU Alumni Chapter Pres 1980-, Merit Awd; Cong Contact Team CD 3 Mem 1989-; MS St Democratic Exec Comm Election Comm 1988-; Jasper Cty Democratic Exec Comm Secy; 5 Yr Educl Plan Coord; MS Teachers Assessment Instrument Evaluator; *home:* PO Box 1215 Bay Springs MS 39422

PAGE, EDWARD LEWIS, Head Teacher; *b:* Litchfield, IL; *cr:* Head Teacher Browning Grade Sch 1977-; *ai:* Ftbl, Bsktbl, Track Coach; *home:* 230 W Lafayette Rushville IL 62681

PAGE, GENEVA FORD, Fourth Grade Teacher; *b:* Fairmont, NC; *m:* Robert Franklin; *c:* Rodney, Gwendolyn, Sheila Page Hutchinson, Charmaine, Boneita, Carmaine Loleita; *ed:* (BS) Elem Ed, 1953, (MS) Elem Ed, 1987 Fayetteville St Univ; *cr:* 6th Grade Teacher Fairmont City Schls 1959-60; Spec Ed Teacher US Military Sch 1960-61; 1st/3rd/4th Grade Teacher 1963-89, 4th Grade Teacher 1989- Fairmont City Schls; *ai:* Hospitality Chairperson; Grade Leader; Cultural Growth Comm; NEA; NCEDA Recording Secy 1968-69; Natl Assn Univ Women (Treas 1987-, Finance Secy 1985-86, VP 1985-87) Woman of Yr 1986; Adult Basic Ed Instr; Teacher of Yr Marietta Elem Sch 1975; *home:* Rt 1 Box 375 Fairmont NC 28340

PAGE, GWEN, Fourth Grade Teacher; *b:* American Fork, UT; *ed:* (BS) Elem, Brigham Young Univ 1968; Creative & Talented, Math, Sci & Cmptr; *cr:* 2nd Grade Teacher Draper Park Elem; 1st/3rd Grade Teacher Midvale Elem; 4th Grade Teacher Welby Elem; *ai:* Drama Club; Jordan Dist Math Adoption Comm; Alpha Delta Kappa; Daughters of UT Pioneers; Assn of Certified Teachers VP; KSL Radio Teacher of Day 1978; *office:* Welby Elem Sch 4200 W 100 S Aprox South Jordan UT 84065

PAGE, JANE ALTMAN, Professor Foundations & Curr; *b:* Statesboro, GA; *m:* Fred Mc Dougald Jr.; *c:* Fred III, John; *ed:* (BS) Elem Ed, 1971, (MED) Elem Ed, 1974, (EDS) Instructional Supvr, 1977 GA Southern; (EDD) Curr/Instr, MS St 1979; *cr:* 2nd Grade Teacher Sallie Zetterower Sch 1971-73; 1st Grade Teacher Mattoe Lively Sch 1978-79; Coll Professor GA Southern Coll 1979-; *ai:* Faculty Adv Southern Educators; Phi Delta Kappa Active Service Citation 1990; Amer Educl Research Assn, ASCD; Univ Optimist Club; GA Southerns Awd Excl in Contributions to Instructions 1985-86; Project Innovations Spec Merit Awd 1988; Whos Who in Amer Ed 1989-; Numerous Prof Publications; *office:* GA Southern Univ L B 8144 Statesboro GA 30460

PAGE, JEAN KENDALL, 7th/8th Grade Teacher; *b:* East Chicago, IN; *m:* William J.; *c:* Mark; *ed:* (MA) Eng, N IL Univ 1981; (BA) Eng, IN Univ 1961; Working Beyond Masters Degree Ed; *cr:* Teacher Washington HS 1961-64; Substitute Teacher Oswego Comm 1973-75, Oswego & Thompson Jr HS 1975-; *ai:* Chair Faculty Sch Improvement Team; Lit & Lang Art Dist Curr Comm; Mock Trials for Gifted Stu Organizer; Sigma Tau Delta, NCTE 1981-; Phi Delta Kappa 1989-; Article Published 1989; *office:* Thompson Jr HS Boulder Hill Pass Oswego IL 60543

PAGE, JOYCIE COLEMAN, 1st Grade Teacher; *b:* Carthage, MS; *m:* Ralph William; *c:* Sederick, Steven; *ed:* (BS) Elem Ed, 1972, (MSE) Elem Ed, 1979 Jackson St Univ; *cr:* 6th Grade Teacher Poindexter Elem Sch 1975-77, Oak Forest Elem Sch 1977-82; Kndgtn Teacher 1982-85, 1st Grade Teacher 1985- Oak Forest Elem Sch; *office:* Oak Forest Elem 1831 Smallwood St Jackson MS 39212

PAGE, LINDA A., Social Studies Teacher; *b:* Mt Holly, NJ; *ed:* (BA) Ed, Rider Coll 1978; (MED) Trenton St Coll 1983; Rutgers Prgm Counseling, Psych, Guidance; *cr:* 7th/8th Grade Gifted & Talented Teacher Hopewell Valley; Soc Stud Teacer Burlington Cty Voc Tech; *ai:* Voc Industrial Clubs of America Adv; Chrldr Coach; Schlsp Comm; Phi Delta Kappa 1980-; Lumberton Emergency Squad Treas 1982-; Lumberton Historical Society; Participated Taft Inst 1986; NJ Comm for Hum 1987; *office:* Burlington Cty Voc Tech HS Hawkins Rd Medford NJ 08055

PAGE, MICHAEL FREDERICK, Fifth Grade Teacher; *b:* Jacksonville, IL; *m:* Elizabeth Ann Bettina; *c:* Emily, Benjamin, Ellen; *ed:* (BS) Soc Sci, 1976, (MED) Elem Ed, 1979 E NM Univ; *cr:* Substitute Teacher Clovis Public Schls 1977-78; 5th Grade Teacher Lovington Public Schls 1979-; *ai:* Phi Kappa Phi 1976-; Lovington Ed Assn (VP, Pres) 1983-86; NM Ed Assn Bd of Dir 1986-; Lovington Schls Teacher of Yr 1984; Honor Graduates Most Influential Teacher Awd 1989; NM St Bd of Ed Prof Status Task Force 1985; *office:* Lea Elem Sch 1202 W Birch Ave Lovington NM 88260

PAGEL, LYLE WAYNE, Biology Teacher; *b:* Wessington Springs, SD; *m:* Jessie Jo; *c:* Ramsee, Samee; *ed:* (BS) Health Phys Ed & Recreation, 1974, (MED) Teacher Ed, 1989 SD St; *cr:* Sci Teacher Colman Schls 1974-79; Bio Teacher Flandreau Schls 1979-80, Rapid City Stevens HS 1980-; *ai:* Head Boys Bsktbl Coach; Letter Club Adv; Drug & Alcohol Alternative Group Spon; SD Ed Assn, SD Coaches Assn, SD Sci Teachers Assn, SD Bsktbl Coaches Assn Region Dir 1988-; *office:* Rapid City Stevens HS 1200 44th Street Rapid City SD 57702

PAGEL, MARILYN GENTRY, 5th Grade Teacher; *b:* Quanah, TX; *m:* Frank J.; *c:* Christopher; *ed:* (BA) Eng/His, Sam Houston St Univ 1962; (MSED) Rdng/Curr/Instruction, Corpus Christi St Univ 1979; Elem, TX A&I Univ 1965, 1972, 1973; Numerous Wkshps; *cr:* 7th/8th Grade Teacher Travis Jr HS 1962-63; 5th/6th Grade Lang Art Teacher Seadrift Elem Sch 1964-66; 3rd-12th Grade Substitute Teacher Austwell-Tivoli Sch Dist 1969-71; 5th/6th Grade Teacher Tivoli Elem Sch 1971-; Adult Ed Austwell-Tivoli Sch Dist 1989-; *ai:* Elem Ready Writing Spon; TX St Teachers Assn (Pres 1973-74, Pres Elect 1972-73, Cty Secy 1988-); GFWC-TFWC Pioneer Club (Secy/Treas 1965-67, VP 1973-75, Pres 1975-77); Tivoli Presbyn Church; TX Career Ladder Level 2; *office:* Tivoli Elem Sch Rt 1 Box 995 Tivoli TX 77990

PAGEL BEWLEY, MARY JANE, Theology Teacher; *b:* Philadelphia, PA; *ed:* (BS) Elem Ed, Chestnut Hill Coll 1971; (MA) Theology, 1990, Family Treatment of Addictions, 1992 La Salle Univ; Learning Disabilities PA St; *cr:* Theology/His Teacher St Ignatius Yardley 1976-80, Villa Joseph Marie HS for Girls 1980-84; Theology Teacher Archbishop Wood HS 1984-; *ai:* Sch Newspaper; Jaycees 1976-77.

PAGLIARA, MICHAEL D., Computer Coordinator; *b:* Morristown, NJ; *m:* Marianne Rastelli; *c:* Michael, Joseph; *ed:* (BA) Soc Stud Ed, La Salle Univ 1973; Grad Stud W Chester St Univ, Villanova Univ, Rosemont Coll; Attended US Naval Acad 1969-71; *cr:* Teacher Delaware Cty IMU 1973, Neshaminy Jr HS 1973-74, Beverly Hills Mid Sch 1974-; *ai:* Dir of Intramurals Beverly Hills Mid Sch; Var Girls Vlybl Coach Upper Darby HS; Natl Apple Works Users Group 1988-; Upper Darby Ed Assn Faculty Rep 1988-89; Upper Darby Sch Dist Cmmty Service Awd 1988; Franklin Select Circle Coaching Awd Gold Medal; *office:* Beverly Hills Mid Sch Garrett Rd & Sherbrook Blvd Upper Darby PA 19082

PAGLIO, CONSTANCE OROSZ, Jr High Mathematics Teacher; *b:* Cleveland, OH; *c:* Mary, Peter, Joseph; *ed:* (BS) Elem Ed/Visual Arts, Cleveland St 1973; *cr:* 5th/6th Grade Teacher St Pauls Croatian Sch 1973-75; 5th Grade Teacher St Gregory the Great Sch 1975-79; 1st Grade Teacher St Andrews Sch 1981-82; 7th/8th Grade Teacher St Louis Sch 1984-89; 7th Grade Teacher Patrick Henry Sch 1989-.

PAGOS, PAULA ANN, English Teacher; *b:* Springfield, MA; *ed:* (BA) Eng, Springfield Coll 1978; (MED) Amer Intnl Coll 1980; *cr:* 8th Grade Elem Teacher Thorndike Grammar Sch 1981-83; HS Eng Teacher Belchertown Public Schls 1984-; *ai:* Jr Class Adv; NCTE, NEA, Belchertown Teachers Assn, US Gymnastic Fed; *office:* Belchertown Sr H S 62 N Washington St Belchertown MA 01007

PAHL, KAREN BERNATH, Fifth Grade Teacher; *b:* Wauseon, OH; *m:* Lee J.; *c:* Randall; *ed:* (BA) Elem Ed, Cedarville Coll 1972; (MS) Elem Ed, IN Univ 1982; *cr:* 5th Grade Teacher Edgerton Local Schls 1972-; *ai:* Ed Cncl Rep; NEA, OH Ed Assn, Edgerton Ed Assn Building Rep 1972-; *home:* 353 S Michigan Ave Edgerton OH 43517

PAHL, RANDALL LEE, Mathematics Department Chair; *b:* Green Bay, WI; *m:* Judith Ann Wangerin; *c:* Jason, Eric, Karen; *ed:* (AA) General Ed, WI Luth Coll 1978; (BS) Elem Ed, Dr Martin Luther Coll 1981; *cr:* Math Dept Chm E Fork Luth HS 1981-; *ai:* Boys Jr Var & Var Bsktbl Head Cnslr; Traveling Choir Dir; *office:* East Fork Luth HS Box 489 Whiteriver AZ 85941

PAHLAVAN, GHOLAM H., Science Department Chair; *b:* M I S, Iran; *m:* Marilyn; *c:* Shane; *ed:* (BS) Chem, Tehran Univ 1972; (MS) Chem, Univ of Houston & TX Southern Univ 1976, 1977; (PHD) Chem, Univ of Houston 1980; Impact Trng, Energy Consumption Trng, Access Trng; *cr:* Teaching Asst TX Southern Univ & Houston 1975-79; Asst Prof Houston Comm Coll 1978-; Sci Teacher Houston Ind Sch Dist 1988-; *ai:* Sci Fair Coord & Dept Chairperson; UIL Sci & Calculator Contest Spon; Boys Soccer Coach; Faculty Adv Comm Chairperson 1989-; *home:* 1660 W T C Jester #1201 Houston TX 77008

PAIGE, RHEA HANSEN, Retired Elem Music Teacher; *b:* Nampa, ID; *m:* Earl Eugene; *c:* Gregory E., Alison M. Paige Bear; *ed:* (BA) Music Performance, 1953, (MA) Elem Ed, 1972 ID St Univ; Grad Stud Several Univs; *cr:* Piano Teacher Northwest Chrstn Coll 1953-55; Music Educator Blaine Cty Sch Dist 61 1974-79, Joint Sch Dist 2 1979-89; *ai:* NEA 1974-89; Univ Chrstn Church Sanctuary Choir Accompanist 1979-, Sanctuary Choir Music Awd 1986-87; Meridian Sch Dist Teacher of Yr 1986-87; *home:* 11249 Barden Tower Dr Boise ID 83709

PAIGE, VIRGINIA ZIELINSKI, Third Grade Teacher; *b:* Brattleboro, VT; *m:* Edmund E.; *c:* Eric, Darcy; *ed:* (BS) Ed, Castleton St 1963; (MALS) Hum, Dartmouth 1979; *cr:* 3rd Grade Teacher Woodstock Elem 1963-65; Kndgtn Teacher Private 1966-68; 3rd Grade Teacher Woodstock Elem 1969-; *ai:* Public Sch Approval & Math Comm; NEA, VT Ed Assn 1963-; Woodstock Elem Ed Assn VP 1989-; *office:* Woodstock Elem Sch 15 South St Woodstock VT 05091

PAINTER, ROBIN LEE (EPPES), Physical Education Teacher; *b:* Leesburg, VA; *m:* Robert Louis; *ed:* (BA) Health/Phys Ed, William Jewell Coll 1976; (MS) Scndry Ed, Univ of MO Kansas City 1987; Grad Stud Conservation, Ec, Cmptrs; *cr:* Art/Phys Ed Teacher Morgan Cty R-2 Schls 1976-77; Dental Asst Endodontic Corporation 1977-79; Elem Phys Ed Teacher N Kansas City Sch Dist 1979-; *ai:* Comm for Intergrating New Rdng Series; Phys Ed Dept & Equipment Selection Inservice Comm; MO PTA 1979-, Life Membership 1989; MAAPERD; All-Dist Elem Phys Ed Demonstration Dir; Organized & Installed 1st Outdoor Ed Day Meadowbrook 1988; Various Positions on Dist Comms; *office:* Meadowbrook Elem Sch 6301 N Michigan Dr Gladstone MO 64118

PAINTER, RUTH ELIZABETH MINCEY, First Grade Teacher; *b:* Moore County, NC; *w:* Carl Jr. (dec); *c:* Terance K.; *ed:* (BS) Primary Ed, W Carolina Univ 1956; *cr:* 1st Grade Teacher Haywood Cty Schls 1956-; *ai:* Alpha Delta Kappa (Treas, Historian, VP) 1969-; NC Assn of Educators 1956-; NEA 1956-; Intnl Rdng Assn; Maggie Valley Chamber of Commerce Bd of Dir 1962-63; Haywood Cty Hospital Auxiliary Mem 1979-; 1st Baptist Church (Choir Mem 1963-, Sunday Sch Teacher); *home:* 114 Whispering Pines Dr Waynesville NC 28786

PAKRADOUNI, ROUBINE M., Kindergarten Teacher; *b:* Beirut, Lebanon; *ed:* Armenology Lang, Palandjian Armenian Cl 1954-56; ECE Pedagogy Fr Cultural Mission 1959-60; Cmptr Aided Design, Drafting, Rio-Hondo 1984; *cr:* Teacher Nichan Palandjian Armenian Coll 1954-65; Kdgtn Teacher/Head of Dept Mesrobian Armenian Sch 1965-; *ai:* Armenian Cultural Assn Hamazkayin 1970-; Armenian Revolutionary Fed 1966-; Armenian Relief Society Incorporated 1968; Armenian Textbooks for 2nd-5th Grades.

PALACIOS, LYDIA CUELLAR, 4th Grade Span/Bi-ling Teacher; *b:* Brownsville, TX; *m:* Simon Gonzales; *c:* Yvonne, Mark, Michael, Simon Jr., Daniel; *ed:* (BA) Liberal Stud, CA St Univ Fresno 1982; Grad Work Bi-ling Ed, Fresno Pacific Coll; *cr:* Sales Clerk J C Penney Company 1960-75; Substitute Teacher Brownsvil le Ind Sch Dist 1979-80; Migrant Tutor Fresno Ind Sch Dist 1980-81; Bi-ling Teacher Parlier Unified Sch Dist 1983-; *ai:* Bi-ling, Dist Advisory, Sch Site Advisory Comm; Tutoring; Fresno Cty Teacher of Year Participation Certificate 1988-89.

PALADINO, PEGGY S., Physical Sci Teacher; *b:* Albert Lea, MN; *c:* Wendy A. Turner, Sam P. Turner; *ed:* (BS) Ed/Sci, Univ of ChattanooGA 1969; (MED) Natural Sci, Univ of TN 1984; Various Wkshps; *cr:* 5th-8th Grade Sci Teacher St Jude Cath Sch 1978-80; Bio Teacher Lakeview Fort Oglethorpe HS 1980-82; Life & Earth Sci Teacher J C Booth Jr HS 1982-85; 9th Grade Teacher of Advanced & Gifted Physical Sci Fayette Cty HS 1985-; *ai:* Cheerleading & Sci Club Spon; Sci Olympiad Coach; Sci Fair Sch & Cty Level Dir; NSTA Mem 1980-, Cert of Excl 1984; Kappa Delta Pi Mem 1984-; GSTA Mem 1980-; AAPT Mem 1988-89; Fayette Cty Sci Teachers Assn Pres 1987, 1988; CCD Teacher 1978-80, 1983-84; Fayette Cty Teacher Incentive Grant 1987; NSTA Summer Wkshp; Dryefus/Woodrow Wilson Wkshp; Fayette Cty HS Teacher of Technology 1989; *home:* 804 Bedford Park Peachtree GA 30269

PALAIA, JOANN, English/Theatre Arts Teacher; *b:* Long Branch, NJ; *ed:* (BA) Theatre/Speech Comm/Eng/Ed, Monmouth Coll 1982; Amer Acad Dramatic Arts; Juilliard Sch of Music; Mannes Coll of Music; *cr:* Faculty Shore Regional HS

1982; *ai:* Govr Awd Excl in Teaching; Comm Chm; AEA Mem 1978-; NJEA Mem 1982-; Zeta Phieta Mem 1980-; Speech & Theatre; Red Oak Music Threatre Secy 1986-; Bd Dir Red Oak Music Theatre; Private Vocal Coach; *office:* Shore Regional HS Rt 36 Monmouth Park Hwy West Long Branch NJ 07764

PALEA, SUSAN YAMANAKA, Art Teacher; *b:* Hilo, HI; *m:* Robert; *c:* Tyler, Cole; *ed:* (BA) Scndry Art Ed, Univ of Puget Sound 1972; WA St, Univ of HI Hilo; *cr:* Art Instr Creative Eye Art Studio 1973-80; Art Dir Kaumana Elderly Adult Care Center 1980-81; Art Teacher Dept of Ed Art Resource 1981-85, Hilo Intermediate Sch 1985-86, Pahoa HS 1986-; *ai:* Jr Class Adv; Faculty Comm Mem for Sch Accreditation; HI St Teachers Assn, NEA 1981-; Dept of Ed Art Teachers Assn 1986-; PTSA 1981-; Beta Sigma Phi 1973-83.

PALERMO, JOSEPH ANDREW, English Teacher; *b:* Swindon, England/UK; *m:* Karen Marie; *ed:* (BS) Eng/His, SW TX St Univ 1985; Eng as a 2nd Lang Cert; *cr:* Classroom Teacher San Marcos Consolidated Ind Sch Dist 1985-; *ai:* Spon Stu Assistance Prgm; Crisis-Hotline; Sports Card Club; NCTE Mem 1990; *office:* San Marcos HS 1301 State Hwy #123 San Marcos TX 78666

PALISANO, JAMES THOMAS, History Teacher; *b:* Buffalo, NY; *m:* Mary Ann Wingerter; *c:* Karen M., Kathryn A., James F.; *ed:* (AB) His/Philosophy, 1955, (MSED) Ed/His, 1959 Canisius Coll; Law Sch Univ of Buffalo 1955-56; *cr:* His Teacher Bishop Colton HS 1957; His/Math Teacher Canisius HS 1958-; *ai:* St Textbook Council 1976-; Soc Stud Cncl of Niagara Frontier 1958-; *office:* Canisius HS 1180 Delaware Ave Buffalo NY 14209

PALISCH, BARBARA ELAINE, Second Grade Teacher; *b:* Delray Beach, FL; *m:* Theodore H.; *c:* Terry, Brenda, Beth; *ed:* (BS) Ed, Valparaiso Univ 1960; *cr:* 3rd Grade Teacher 1960-64, 2nd Grade Teacher 1976- Green Park Luth Sch; *ai:* Childrens Choir Dir; Luth Schls Week Comm; Luth Ed Assn; *office:* Green Park Luth Sch 4248 Green Park Rd Saint Louis MO 63125

PALLADINO, ANTHONY, Third Grade Teacher; *b:* Brooklyn, NY; *ed:* (BS) Elem Ed, St Johns Univ 1968; (MS) Elem Ed, C W Post 1971; Adelphi Univ; *cr:* 6th Grade Teacher New York City; 3rd/4th/6th Grade Teacher Floral Park-Bellerose; *ai:* Floral Park-Bellerose Union Pres.

PALLADINO, NICHOLAS S., 8th Grade Math Teacher; *b:* Salerno, Italy; *m:* Anna Muzzo; *c:* Mary A., Frank; *ed:* (BA) Elem Ed, Jersey City St 1969; Various Guidance & Cmptr Courses, Jersey City St Coll, St Peters Coll; *cr:* 6th Grade Teacher PS 22 1969-70; 7th Grade Teacher 1970-73, 8th Grade Teacher 1973- PS 17; *ai:* Remedial Math Tutoring; Jersey City Ed Assn, NJ Ed Assn, NEA 1969-; Hudson Cty Bd of Realtors 1989-; Marion Neighborhood Assn VP 1980-; Mayors PJP Dump Task Force 1983-85, NJ Senate Citation 1985; Governors Teacher Recognition Certificate 1988; St Grant Teaching Aids for Stus; *office:* J H Breusinger PS 17 128 Duncan Ave Jersey City NJ 07306

PALLADINO, STEPHEN D., Advanced Mathematics Teacher; *b:* Riverside, CA; *m:* Heidi Bradfield; *ed:* (BA) Geography/ Environmental Stud Univ of CA Santa Barbara 1985; *cr:* Math Teacher Mayfair HS 1986-; *ai:* Academic Decathalon Asst, Jr Var Girls Vlybl Coach; Boys Vlybl Club Adv; Kappa Delta Pi 1986-87; *office:* Mayfair HS 6000 N Woodruff Ave Lakewood CA 90713

PALLENBERG, JANE STAMLER, Social Studies Teacher; *b:* Elizabeth, NJ; *c:* Gregory, Amy, David; *ed:* (BS) Soc Stud, Temple Univ 1964; (MALS) Soc Stud, Wesleyan Univ 1981; Working Toward Masters, Wesleyan Univ; *cr:* Teacher Arthur L Johnson Regional HS 1964-67, Guilford HS 1968-69, 1977-; *ai:* Guilford Educl Assn Secy 1986-88; Democratic Town Comm Mem 1986-88; Natl Organization of Women Mem 1980-; *office:* Guilford HS New England Rd Guilford CT 06437

PALLEY, BEVERLY HALL, Mathematics Teacher; *b:* Berkeley, CA; *m:* Dan M.; *c:* Marco Marello, Lauren Strickland, Tari Strickland, Umala; *ed:* (BA) Math, CA St Univ Sacramento 1975; (MA) Sch Admin in Ed, CA St Univ Hayward 1989; *cr:* Math Teacher James Rutter Jr HS 1975-77, Valley HS 1977-80; Math Consultant Lawrence Hall of Sci UC Berkeley 1980-82; Math Teacher Oakland Unified Sch Dist 1982-; *ai:* Chrldrs Club Adv; Comm Leader Sch Improvement Prgm; NCTM, NEA, Oakland Ed Assn; *home:* 1062 View Dr Richmond CA 94803

PALLO, JANET LEE, 5th Grade Teacher; *b:* Ashtabula, OH; *m:* John David; *c:* Matthew; *ed:* (BA) Elem Ed, Kent St 1968; (MA) Elem Ed, Garfield Sr Coll 1979; Grad Stud; *cr:* 3rd-5th Grade Teacher North Kingsville; *ai:* Ashtabula Cty Adv of Gifted; Sci Fair Chairperson; Right to Read Comm; Buckeye Ed Assn Public Relations Chairperson 1986-89; Ashtabula Coin Club 1983-; Ashtabula Historical Society 1989-; Jefferson Chamber of Commerce 1989-; Owner & Curator Museum Victorian Perambulator Museum of Jefferson; Book Author; Ashtabula Cty Teacher of Yr 1987-88.

PALLOTTA, JOSEPH J., Director of Music; *b:* Queens, NY; *ed:* (BA) Music Performance, SUNY Brockport 1978; (MS) Music Ed, Aaron Copland Sch of Music 1987; Cert Music Ed, Nazareth Coll of Rochester 1978; *cr:* Music Dir Holy Cross HS 1982-, Summer Repetary Theatre Queens Coll 1986-, Grey Wig Alumni Theatre Hofstra Univ 1989-, Boradhollow Repetory Theatre Company 1990; *ai:* Holy Cross Jazz Ensemble Dir; United Fed of Musicians Local 802, NY St Sch Music Assn, Music Educators Natl Conference, Natl Assn of Jazz Educators; St Univ of NY Music Assn Pres 1977-78; St Univ Music Scholar Awds; *office:* Holy Cross HS 26-20 Francis Lewis Blvd Flushing NY 11358

PALM, VIOLET ELAINE, Science Teacher; *b:* Hannaford, ND; *ed:* (BS) Chem/Elem Ed, Valley City St Univ 1969; *cr:* 4th-6th Grade Teacher Turtle Mountain Cmmty Elem Sch 1970-83; 7th Grade Sci Teacher 1983-84, 8th Grade Sci Teacher 1984-86, 1988- Turtle Mountain Cmmty Mid Sch; *ai:* Sch Effectiveness Team Facilitator; Honor Club Adv; Mid Sch Drug & Alcohol Team Mem; Sci Fair Chairperson; Natl Fed of Federal Employees 1970-83; NEA, ND Ed Assn, Belcourt Assn for Improvement of Teaching 1983-; GSA Leader 1981-83; *home:* Box 1197 Belcourt ND 58316

PALMA, RAYMOND JOSEPH, Teacher; *b:* West Paterson, NJ; *m:* Marianne Barbara; *c:* Raymond, Lewis; *ed:* (BA) Elem Ed, 1964, (MA) Ed/Sci Concentrate, 1968 William Paterson Coll; Grad Stud Montclair St Coll 1968; *cr:* 8th Grade Sci Teacher West Paterson Schls 1964-69; Adjunct Instr Passaic Cty Comm Coll 1980-81; 4th Grade Teacher West Paterson Schls 1969-; *ai:* Passaic Evening HS Teacher 1983; West Paterson Ed Assn Pres 1969-72; West Paterson Lib Bd Trustee 1971-75; Teacher in Charge; *office:* Charles Olbon Sch Lincoln Ln West Paterson NJ 07424

PALMACCIO, RICHARD JOHN, Math Department Chairman; *b:* Newton, MA; *ed:* (BS) Math, 1966, (MAT) Math Ed, 1967 Boston Coll; *cr:* Teacher Wellesley Sr HS 1966-80; Teacher/Dept Chm Pine Crest Sch 1980-; *ai:* Faculty Adv to Stu Honor Court; - NCTM 1966-; Numerous Articles; Software Works Published; Gravity Simlation; PC Graphics; Portfolio Data Mgr; 2 Books Published; Held & Linnell Awds; *office:* Pine Crest Sch 1501 NE 62nd St Fort Lauderdale FL 33334

PALMER, ANNE CALDWELL, French Teacher; *b:* Birmingham, AL; *ed:* (BA) Eng/Theatre/Fr, Sanford Univ 1977; (MA) Eng, Univ of Birmingham 1983; (MA) Fr, Middlebury Coll 1986; Diplome Universite de Nice France 1985; *cr:* Eng Dept Chairperson/Theatre Dir Bessemer Acad 1977-81; Asst Eng Professor Southern Inst 1982-83, Sanford Univ 1982-; Eng/Fr Teacher Homewood HS 1982-; *ai:* Newspaper Ed Adv; Fr Club Spon; System Textbook, Eng Curr Comm; Delta Kappa Gamma Research Chm 1985-; NCTE 1983-; AL Cncl Teachers of Eng 1985-; AATF 1985-; Rotary Club Summer Study Grants 1988-89; Published Books of Poetry; *office:* Homewood HS 1901 S Lakeshore Dr Homewood AL 35209

PALMER, BERNICE HELEN (KAPPE), Kindergarten Teacher; *b:* Montcalm Cty, MI; *m:* Gerald G.; *c:* Dan C., Susan R. (dec), Peggy J.; *ed:* (BA) Ed, 1967, (MA) Ed, 1970 MI St Univ; *cr:* 1st Grade Teacher Lowell Public Schls 1966-69; 1st Grade Teacher 1969-74, Kndgtn Teacher 1974- Iona Public Schls; *ai:* Iona Ed Assn (Kndgtn Center Assn Rep, Soc Stud Comm Kndgtn Rep, Evaluation Comm, Early Elem Rep); Boyce Elem Teacher of Yr 1986-87.

PALMER, BETTY BONHAM, Fourth Grade Teacher; *b:* Lexington, MO; *m:* George O.; *c:* Rebecca Wendell Mc Coy, Griffin J., George T.; *ed:* (BS) Ec/Sociology, 1949, (MS) Ed/ Rdng Specialist, 1976 Northeastern St Coll; *cr:* News Ed Johnson Cty Graphic Clarksville 1949-51; Writer OK St Planning & Resources Bd 1951-53; Elem Teacher Muskogee Public Schls 1972-; *ai:* Muskogee Ed Assn, OK Ed Assn, NEA; *home:* 208 Palmer Dr Muskogee OK 74403

PALMER, CURTIS M., Mathematics Teacher; *b:* Big Rapids, MI; *m:* Susan D.; *c:* Sandra L., Suzanne E.; *ed:* (BS) Bio, Ferris St Univ 1963; Grad Work Central MI & MI St Univ; *cr:* Math/Sci Teacher Reed City HS 1963-; *ai:* Co-Chm Morley Stanwood Building Comm; Formed & Chm of Academic Comm; 7th/8th Grade Bsktbl Coach; Class Spon; Curr & Schl Improvement Comms; Reed City Ed Assn; MI & Natl Ed Assn; NSTA; MI Cncl Teachers of Math; Red City Hospital Amer Cancer Society & Heart Assn; Worked with Local Scout Troop; Reed City Teacher of Yr 1989-; MI Teacher of Yr Finalist 1989-; Trained Stu Teachers; *home:* 19516 11 Mile Rd Big Rapids MI 49307

PALMER, DEBORAH TAYLOR, French Teacher; *b:* Huntsville, AL; *m:* James Gordon; *c:* Alan S., Ryan C.; *ed:* (BA) Fr, Univ of AL Huntsville 1973; Elem Teacher Cert 1978; Span Cert 1987; *cr:* Fr Teacher Franklin Cty HS 1973-74, Randolph Sch 1980-85, S R Butler HS 1985-; *ai:* Fr Club & Fr NHS Spon; Huntsville Ed Assn, AL Assn of Foreign Lang Teachers, AATF; Schlsp from Fr Cultural Service 1986; *office:* S R Butler HS 3401 Holmes Ave Huntsville AL 35816

PALMER, ELIZABETH IMPERATORE, Fourth Grade Teacher; *b:* Mineola, NY; *m:* Charles D.; *c:* Bradley J., Andrew P.; *ed:* (BS) Elem Ed, Keuka Coll 1973; Graduate Work SUNY Oswego 1978; CAS Degree SUNY Brockport Admin Cert; *cr:* Elem Teacher North Rose Wolcott Schls 1973-; *ai:* Mem of Effective Schls; Elem Sci Curr Comm; *home:* 78 Lake Ave Wolcott NY 14590

PALMER, ERNEST ELVIN, Eighth Grade Teacher; *b:* Macon, NC; *m:* Edna Mc Pherson; *ed:* (BA) His, Lincoln Univ 1973; (MA) His, Case Western Reserve 1975; *cr:* Teacher Our Lady of Perpetual Help Sch 1982-; *home:* 91-132 Hailipo St Ewa Beach HI 96706

PALMER, JAMES GORDON, English Department Chair; *b:* Birmingham, AL; *m:* Deborah Taylor; *c:* Alan S., Ryan C.; *ed:* (BA) Eng, Univ of the South 1974; (MA) Eng, Univ of AL Huntsville 1982; *cr:* Teacher Univ of AL Huntsville 1982-87, Randolph Sch 1974-; *ai:* Boys & Girls Cross Cntry & Track Head Coach; Red Cross 1973-, 3 Gallon Donor 1989; Cmmty Watch 1987-; Church Lay Reader 1986; Track & Cross Cntry St Champions.

PALMER, JANE ELLEN, 7th Core Rdng/Soc Stud Teacher; *b:* Los Angeles, CA; *c:* Joseph Garguile, Angela Garguile; *ed:* (BA) Soc Stud, W WA Univ 1961; Working Towards Masters; *cr:* 3rd/ 6th Grade Teacher Lone Hill Elem 1961-64; 3rd/5th Grade Teacher 1964-65, 2nd Grade Teacher Oil Companies Sch 1977-78; 7th Grade Core Teacher Shuksan Mid Sch 1979-; *ai:* 7th Grade Level Chairperson; Faculty Cncl & Self Stud Steering Comm Mem; Discipline Comm; Vlybl Club Adv; Bellingham Ed Assn; Bellingham Sch Dist Grant 1983; Rdng Connection Presenter Regional Conference NCTE; W WA Univ Annual Rdng Conference Presenter; *office:* Shuksan Mid Sch 2713 Alderwood Bellingham WA 98225

PALMER, JOANN LINDA (IATAURO), Fifth Grade Teacher; *b:* Albany, NY; *m:* Richard N. II; *c:* Seth R., Bradford A.; *ed:* (AA) Liberal Arts, Hudson Valley Comm Coll 1969; (BA) Sociology, SUNY Potsdam 1971; (MS) Elem Ed/Rdng, Russell Sage Coll 1973; Grad Work Capitol Region Center for Arts Ed; *cr:* 3rd Grade Teacher 1971-81, 5th Grade Teacher 1982- Pieter B Coeymans Elem Sch; *ai:* 4th/5th Grade Benjamin Franklin Stamp Club Adv; Rdng Task Force 5th Grade Teacher Rep; Stus at Risk Task Force; Report Card Revision Comm; NY St Rdng Assn 1989-; Greater Capital Region Teacher Center 1988-; Colonie Chrstn Life Center Sunday Sch Supt 1971-80; PTO Teacher Rep Spec Prgms 1985-88; Whole Lang Integrating Soc Stud & Rdng Grant; Presenter Whole Lang Conference Rochester & Albany NY; Presenter Lang Art Conference Mid-St Teacher Center; *home:* RD 2 Box 31 Martins Hill Ravena NY 12143

PALMER, JOE DELANO, English Teacher; *b:* Trezevant, TN; *ed:* (BS) Bus Admin, Bethel Coll 1962; (MA) Eng, Memphis St Univ 1987; Eng; *cr:* Eng Teacher West Memphis Jr HS 1962-64; Bus Teacher Bruceton Cntrl HS 1964-65; Eng Teacher De La Salle HS 1965-67, St Pauls Sch 1967-72, Gibson Cty HS 1976-; *ai:* Schlsp Comm; Show Classic Movies; Phi Delta Kappa, NCTE, TN Cncl Teachers of Eng; *office:* Gibson Cty HS PO Box 190 Dyer TN 38330

PALMER, JUDY BOWLIN, 4th Grade Teacher; *b:* South Bend, IN; *m:* Warren; *c:* Andrew, Michael; *ed:* (BA) Elem Ed, Univ of NE 1971; Grad Stud Various Universities; *cr:* 4th Grade Teacher Carriage Hill Elem 1971-71; 5th Grade Teacher Basalt Elem Sch 1975-76; 5th-8th Grade Teacher Basalt Mid Sch 1976-88; 4th Grade Teacher Basalt Elem Sch 1988-; *ai:* 4th Grade Dept Chairperson Roaring Fork Sch Dist; Mem Dist Math & Steering Comm; NEA Mem 1975-; Roaring Fork Cmmty Ed Assn (VP 1976-79, Building Rep 1981-82); Nominee Governors Awd Excl Gifted & Talented Ed 1986; *office:* Basalt Elem Sch Box Z Basalt CO 81621

PALMER, LINDA MARIE, Elem Special Education Teacher; *b:* Washington, DC; *ed:* (BS) Spec Ed/Elem Ed, Univ of MD 1972; *cr:* Spec Ed Teacher Scaggsville Sch 1972-74, Templeton Elem 1974-; *ai:* Grade Level Chairperson; NEA, MD St Teachers Assn, Prince Georges Cty Educators Assn 1974-; *office:* Templeton Elem Sch 6001 Carters Ln Riverdale MD 20737

PALMER, PAMELA ELYN, US History Teacher; *b:* St Elizabeth, West Indies; *m:* Kenneth Henry; *c:* Pete, Cheryl; *ed:* 2 Yr Certificate Elem Ed, West Indies Coll 1960; (BS) Elem Ed, Columbia Union Coll 1970; (MA) Admin/Supervision, Bowie St Coll 1977; *cr:* Teacher Harrison Memorial HS 1960-62, Larchwood Sch 1970-74, Dupont Park Sch 1974-81, Buck Lodge Mid 1981-; *ai:* Vlybl Coach; MD Consortium Leader of Effective Schls Comm 1985-87, Being Instructional Leader 1986-87; Metropolitan SDA Church Sabbath Sch Supt 1989-; *office:* Buck Lodge Mid Sch 2611 Buck Lodge Rd Adelphi MD 20783

PALMER, PATRICIA (FAIX), Jr-Sr High School Librarian; *b:* Pittsburgh, PA; *c:* Timothy, Sandra, Erin, Sean; *ed:* (BED) Bio/ Scndry Ed, Duquesne Univ 1962; (MLS) Sch Libs, Univ of PIttsburgh 1976; *cr:* Teacher Glassport Jr HS 1972-78; Federal Prgm Writer S Allegheny Sch Dist 1978-85; Teacher 1978-85, Librarian 1985- S Allegheny Jr-Sr HS; *ai:* Cncl of Sch Librarians 1988-; S Allegheny Ed Assn 1972-; *office:* S Allegheny Jr-Sr HS 2743 Washington Blvd Mc Keesport PA 15133

PALMER, REBECCA ANNE, Biology Teacher; *b:* Jackson, MS; *ed:* (BS) Forest Sci, MS St Univ 1984; (MS) Forest Sci, TX A&M Univ 1989; *cr:* Image Analyst MS Remote Sensing Center 1984-85; Biological Technician Bering Land Bridge Natl Preserve 1985; Bio Teacher Southwest HS 1987-.

PALMER, REBECCA E., Junior High Science Teacher; *b:* Minneapolis, MN; *ed:* (BS) Elem Ed, Univ of WI La Crosse 1982; *cr:* 7th/8th Grade Sci Teacher Campbellsport Public Sch 1983-; *ai:* Girls Track Coach; Participant Sci World; Stu Assistance Prgm Facilitator; Finalist Dist Teacher of Yr 1989-; *office:* Campbellsport Public Sch 114 W Sheboygan St Campbellsport WI 53010

PALMER, RUTH BANTA, English Teacher/Eng Dept Chair; *b:* Los Alamos, NM; *m:* J. Dean; *c:* Amber M., Ashlyn D.; *ed:* (BA) Eng Ed, Ft Lewis Coll 1976; (MA) Eng, N AZ Univ 1980; Cmptr, Talented & Gifted Ed, Effective Elements of Teaching; *cr:* Eng Dept Chairperson/Eng Teacher Aztec HS 1976-82; Eng Teacher Air Acad Jr HS 1982-85, Air Acad HS 1985-87; Eng Teacher/ Eng Dept Chairperson/TAG Coord Liberty HS 1987-; *ai:* Lang Art Curr Task Force; Future Problem Solving Coach; Alpha Delta Kappa (Pres, St Bd), 1984-, Elected St Bds 1988-; Phi Delta

Kappa 1986-; *office:* Liberty HS 8720 Scarbrorough Dr Colorado Springs CO 80920

PALMER, WILLIAM LEE, Social Studies Teacher; *b:* Mt Eden, KY; *m:* Donna Runner; *c:* Justin C., Winona F.; *ed:* (BS) Elem Ed, 1977, (MA) Elem Ed, 1985 Univ of KY; *cr:* 8th Grade Math/Sci Teacher Spencer Cty HS 1978-79; 5th Grade Teacher Spencer Cty Elem Sch 1979-; *ai:* Math Derby; Soc Stud Comm; KY Ed Assn, NEA 1978-; Green River Archeological Society; Barbering, Auctioneering, Real Estate Cert.

PALOMO, JOE R., Sixth Grade Bilingual Teacher; *b:* Edinburg, TX; *m:* Mary E. Zapata; *c:* Jose A., Cris; *ed:* (BA) Elem Ed, 1972, (MA) Elem Ed, 1978 E NM Univ; Bi-ling Endorsement 1974; Educl Admin & Supervision 1985; *cr:* 1st Grade Teacher Llano Elem Sch 1972-73; 2nd Grade Teacher 1973-74, 3rd Grade Teacher 1974-87 Jefferson Elem Sch; 6th Grade Teacher Taylor Mid Sch 1987-; *ai:* Bi-ling Ed Advisory Comm; Lovington Ed Assn VP 1988-; NEA, NM Ed Assn Mem 1972-; St Thomas Cath Choir Dir 1976-; Youth Center Advisory Bd 1984-88; Knights of Columbus Mem 1975-76, Family/Mon 1975; Federal Bi-ling Grant to Study Span; NM Textbook Adoption Comm 1974, 1990; *home:* 1000 West Avenue P Lovington NM 88260

PALSMA, MARY (JACOBSON), Math Dept Chair & Teacher; *b:* Webster, SD; *m:* Wayne H.; *c:* Robert W.; *ed:* (BS) Scndry Ed/ Math/Eng, 1962; (MS) Classroom Teaching Math, 1967 Nor Thern St Coll; *cr:* Eng Teacher/Librarian Northville Northwestern 1962; Math Teach 1962-64; Math/Eng Teacher/Dept Chm Riggs HS 1964-68; Private Tutoring/Homebound Substitute Teaching Mitchell SD 1969-70; Math Teacher Mitchell Jr HS 1970-71; Math Teacher 1975-78; Math/Eng Teacher Dept Chair 1980 Bourgade Cath HS; Taxpaper Service Rep Internal Revenue Service 1979-80; *ai:* Hiking Club Moderator; Bookstore Mgr; SD Ed Assn Life Mem; NCEA 1980-; ASCD 1988-; Amer Assn of Univ Women (Pres 1977-79 Life Mem); Inter-Club Cncl of AZ (Pres 1987-88 Life Mem); Steering Comm for Intnl Yr of the Child Treas 1978-80; Masters Degree Thesis Published August 1967; *office:* Bourgade Catholic H S 4602 N 31st Ave Phoenix AZ 85017

PALUCH, DEBORAH LANE, First Grade Teacher; *b:* Anoka, MN; *m:* Jack Ray; *c:* Nicholas L.; *ed:* (BS) Elem Ed, UW Superior 1972; *cr:* 1st Grade Teacher Washington Elem 1972-73; K/ 2nd-3rd Grades Teacher Saints Peter And Paul Sch 1973-77; Day Care Dir Oneida Child Care Center 1977-78; K/1st/3rd Grades Teacher St Boniface Sch 1978-89; 1st Grade Teacher Marquette Elem 1989-; *ai:* Cmptr Comm; Cheerleading Coach; NCEA Mem; NE WI Talented & Gifted Univ WI Green Bay Summer Sch Teacher 1980-82; Nom for NCEA 1986 Miriam Joseph Farrell Awd for Distinguished Teaching; Awd for Outstanding Cooperating Teacher St Norberts Coll 1988; *home:* 2519 Valley Heights Dr Green Bay WI 54311

PAN, NANCY S., 3rd Grade Teacher; *b:* Oakland, CA; *ed:* (BS) Elem Ed, TN Temple Univ 81; *cr:* Teacher San Francisco Chrstn Schl 1981-; *office:* San Francisco Chrstn Sch 25 Whittier St San Francisco CA 94121

PANCHERI, AMY C., 6th Grade Teacher; *b:* Idaho Falls, ID; *m:* A. Michel; *c:* Michelle Tanner, Mathew, Suzanne, Oliver, Dan, Rachel; *ed:* (ABA) Sociology, Ricks Coll 1967; (BS) Elem Ed, ID St Univ 1981; Elem Admin; Art, Math & Law Related Ed; Economics & Leadership Trng; *cr:* Jr HS Eng & Phys Ed Teacher Shelly Jr HS 1964-65; 4th-6th Grade Teacher Longfellow Elem 1982-; *ai:* Pres Church Young Womens Group; VP Idaho Falls Ed Assn; Coach City League Sftbl 12-13 Girls; Chair Art Comm; IFEA (Building Rep VP) 1988-89; BSA Cub Master/Scout Leader Extra Miler 1984; 4-H Leader; ID Comm for Arts Grant for Working with Clay K-6 Grades; Dist Cmptr Comm; Poster Awd/ID Centennial; *office:* Longfellow Elem Sch 2500 S Higbee Idaho Falls ID 83404

PANCRAZI, MICHAEL J., Health Teacher; *b:* Yuma, AZ; *m:* Margaret Lynne Blair; *c:* Angela, Marie; *ed:* (BS) Phys Ed, NW St Univ 1971; (MS) Admin, N AZ Univ 1982; *cr:* Teacher/Coach 4th Avenue Jr HS 1973-79, Yuma HS 1980-; *ai:* Golf & Track Coach; Sch, St, Cmnty Comms; AZ Health, Phys Ed & Recreation 1980-; Natl Coaches Assn 1988-; AZ Coaches Assn 1986-; Junior Golf Instr of Golf 1980-; BSA Fundraiser Comm 1989-; AZ Girls Golf Coach of Yr 1986, 1987, 1989; Yuma HS Teacher of Yr 1988-89; *office:* Yuma HS 400 S 6th Ave Yuma AZ 85364

PANETTA, MARY CHAFFEE, Fourth Grade Teacher; *b:* Towanda, PA; *m:* Julio J.; *c:* Matthew T., David M.; *ed:* (BS) Elem Ed, West Chester St Coll 1971; *cr:* 4th Grade Teacher Perkiomen Valley Elem Sch South 1971-; *ai:* Church Organizations; *office:* Perkiomen Valley Elem Sch 200 E 3rd Ave Collegeville PA 19426

PANKE, JACQUELINE L., Sixth Grade Teacher; *b:* Utica, NY; *m:* John W.; *c:* Kari L.; *ed:* (BA) Speech/Drama, 1968, (MA) Ed, 1984 Univ of TX El Paso; *cr:* Pilot Teacher Gifted/Talented 1980-82, Curr Specialist Gifted/Talented 1982-84, 6th Grade Teacher 1984 Ysleta Ind Sch Dist; *ai:* Odyssey of the Mind Teams Coach; Trainer of Teachers in Cooperative Learning & Higher Order Thinking Skills; Ysleta Teachers Assn Pres 1988-89; TX St Teachers Assn, NEA 1970-; Phi Delta Kappa 1987-; Alpha Delta Kappa Treas 1987-88; Teacher of Yr 1980; Whos Who in Amer Ed; *office:* Glen Cove Elem Sch 10955 Sam Snead Dr El Paso TX 79936

PANKIW, MARY, Foreign Language Dept Chair; *b:* Rosenheim, Germany; *ed:* (BSED) Span/Russian, OH St Univ 1968; (MA) Span, Kent St Univ 1974; Subject Matter & Methodology; *cr:* Span/Russian Teacher Pleasant Valley Jr HS 1969-73; Span/ Russian Teacher 1973-, Foreign Lang Dept Chairperson 1980- Valley Forge HS; *ai:* Span Club Adv; NEA, OEA, NEOTA, PEA, OFLA; Presenter OFLA Conference 1990; *office:* Valley Forge HS 9999 Independence Blvd Parma Heights OH 44130

PANKOW, SHARON JOHNSON, 1st Grade Teacher & Principal; *b:* Manitowac, WI; *M:* Ronald W.; *ed:* (BA) Ed, Univ of WI 1970; *cr:* 1st-8th Grade Teacher Salt Box Sch 1962-64; 1st Grade Teacher Sharon Cmnty Sch 1964-66; 2nd Grade Teacher East Troy Cmnty Sch 1966-69; 1st Grade Teacher 1969-78; Admin 1978-88; Prin/1st Grade Teacher 1988- Reek Elem Sch; *ai:* Sci Curr Comm; Primary Sci Club Adv; NEA 1962-75; WI Ed Assn 1962-75; WI Assn of Sch Dist Admin 1978-87; Burlington Prof Womens Club 1977-82; Nom State Teacher of Yr Awd 1977; *home:* 291 Robins Run Burlington WI 53105

PANNONE, ALFRED, Spanish/Italian/French Teacher; *b:* Providence, RI; *ed:* (BA) Ed/Span/Italian, Providence Coll 1979; (MA) Comparative Literature Span/Italian/Fr, Univ of RI 1986; *cr:* Teacher Bishop Hendricken HS 1979-87; Pilgrim HS 1987-; *ai:* Amer Assn Teachers of Span & Portuguese 1979-; RI Teachers of Italian 1979-; Amer Assn Teachers of Italian 1979-; RI Foreign Lang Assn Bd Dir MeM; Dir RI Natl Span Honor Society 1986-89; *office:* Pilgrim H S 111 Pilgrim Pkwy Warwick RI 02888

PANTASON, DOROTHY I., Enrichment Resource Teacher; *b:* Plainfield, NJ; *m:* Paul; *c:* Laura Pantason Brown, Andrew, Paula; *ed:* (BSED) Elem Ed, Hofstra Univ 1959; (MS) Elem Ed, Long Island Univ 1976; Gifted & Talented Confratute Univ of CT 1985, 1988, 1989; Creative Learning & Problem Solving 1986; *cr:* 2nd Grade Teacher Plainview 1959-61; Title I Remedial Math/Rdng/ Substitute Teacher 1968-73; 4th Grade Teacher 1973-79, 5th Grade Teacher 1980-81, Gifted/Talented Project Challenge Teacher 1981-, Enrichment Resource Teacher 1989- Valley Stream #24; *ai:* 4th-6th Division I & II Coach for #24 Odyssey of Mind Competitions 1985-89; 1st Place Regional Winners 1985-89; Dist 2 Staff Dev Comm 1988-; Regional Competition Odyssey of the Mind Judge 1990; ASCD 1989-; Assn of Ed of Gifted Underachieving Stus 1988-; Advocacy for Gifted & Talented 1985-; SEPTA 1988-; Curr Dev for Gifted & Talented; Mentor & Consultant for Classroom Teachers; Dist Wide Enrichment Resource Teacher; PTA & Teacher Groups Speaker; Wkshp Presentor for Dist Acad; *office:* William L Buck Elem Sch #24 Horton Ave Valley Stream NY 11581

PANTLIK, JEAN, Cosmetology Teacher; *b:* Prague, OK; *m:* Walter; *c:* Cathy Tenne, Janice Russell, Linda, Mike; *ed:* (BS) Ed, Cntrl St Univ 1987; Cert Cosmetology, Bartlesville Beauty Coll 1969; Certificate Cmptr Literacy, Francis Tuttle Voc Tech 1987; Advanced Styling, OK Univ; Advanced Color, Clariol & Loreal; Advanced Pivot Point Trng Classes; *cr:* Salon Owner Bartlesville Beauty Salon 1966-72; Instr Tri Cty Area Voc Tech Sch 1972-85, Francis Tuttle Voc Tech Center 1985-; *ai:* Voc Industrial Club of America Adv; Natl Voc Industrial Club of America Olympics Comm Mem; OVA, AVA, T&I VP 1988-, T&I Region IV Outstanding Teacher 1987; OVA 1987-88, Outstanding Teacher 1986-87; Hair America; Iota Lamda Sigma Mem 1985-; OK Women Ed Assn Mem 1985-88; OK Policy Leadership Awd; Developed Self-Paced Competency Based Curr for Cosmetology Course; Channel V Outstanding Teacher Awd 1988-89; Five Alive Teacher of Yr 1988-89; Organized Industrial Advisory Cncl 1985-; *office:* Francis Tuttle Voc Tech Center 12777 N Rockwell Oklahoma City OK 73142

PAOLOTTO, PATRICIA MARIE, Private Tutor; *b:* Rochester, NY; *m:* David Bottar; *c:* Anna, Taylor; *ed:* (BA) Poly Sci/Math, Eisenhower Coll 1977; (MAT) Soc Stud, Colgate Univ 1980; *cr:* Soc Stud Teacher Fayetteville Manlius HS 1978-79; Math Teacher Canastora HS 1979-81; 6th-8th Grade Jr HS Teacher Blessed Sacrament Sch 1981-86; Private Tutor 1986-; *ai:* Pre-Sch Activity & Music Prgm Coord.

PAPAS, CAROLYN RUSSELL, 4th Grade Teacher; *b:* Modesto, CA; *m:* Dennis; *c:* David; *ed:* (BA) Ed, Northland Coll 1964; (MA) Comm, Webster Univ 1989; CA St Coll Fullerton 1965-66, Univ of HI 1966, Sacramento St Coll 1967; *cr:* 4th Grade Teacher Damron Sch 1964-66, Goose Bay Labrador 1966-67; Nursery Teacher St Louis Clerical 1967-68; 4th Grade Teacher Mesnier Sch 1968-69; 3rd Grade Teacher Heege Sch 1969-75, Reavis Sch 1975-81; 4th Grade Teacher Mesnier Sch 1981-84, Gotsch Intermediate Sch 1984-; *ai:* NEA, AEA.

PAPP, GREGORY JOHN, Educator/Soc Stud Teacher; *b:* Akron, OH; *m:* Glenabah Martinez; *c:* Christine; *ed:* (BA) Span/ Latin Amer Stud, 1971, (MA) Latin Amer/US His, 1973 Univ of Akron; Latin Amer/US His Univ of NM; PhD Prgm Latin Amer, Iberian, US His; *cr:* Park Dir City of Akron 1968-73; Grad Asst Univ of Akron 1971-73, Univ of NM 1973-76; Educator Albuquerque Public Schls 1976-; *ai:* Bsktbl Coach; Albuquerque Coach of Yr 1984; NM Coach of Yr 1986; Summer Inst Fellow 1988; *home:* 406 Dartmouth NE Albuquerque NM 87106

PAPPAS, HARRY JAMES, Mathematics Dept Lecturer; *b:* Erie, PA; *m:* Jean M. Kissick; *c:* Alexandra; *ed:* (BS) Math/ Physics, Edinboro St Univ 1960; (MED) Math, PA St Univ 1964; (MA) Math, CA St Univ Northridge 1972; *cr:* Math/Sci/ Geography Teacher Wesleyville Jr/Sr HS 1960-62; 7th-9th Grade Math Teacher Lincoln Jr HS 1962-63; Math Teacher Santa Monica HS 1964-89; Part Time Math Teacher Santa Monica Coll 1966-85; Math Teacher Univ of CA Los Angeles 1982; Math Teacher/SAT Review Beverly Hills HS 1986; Math Teacher CA St Univ Fullerton 1989-; *ai:* Univ Supvrs Comm; Scndry Ed Teacher Rep Comm; Math Dept Chm 1973-89; Phi Delta Kappa, NEA 1960-; CA Teachers Assn 1962-; Santa Monica Malibu Teachers Assn Treas 1988-89; New Start Bd of Dir 1988-89; Baush & Lomb Sci Awd; Outstanding Teacher Awds; Natl Sci Fnd Grants; Mentor Teacher; *home:* 90272 17193 Avenue de Santa Yuez Pacific Palisds CA 90272

PAPPAS, MARIA COUGRAS, Coord Gifted & Talented Prgms; *b:* Youngstown, OH; *m:* Paul G.; *ed:* (BSED) Elem Ed/ Rdng - Magna Cum Laude, 1979, (MSED) Gifted/Talented Ed, 1983 Youngstown St Univ; Post Grad Work in Admin & Scndry Ed, Youngstown St Univ 1985-89; *cr:* Peer Tutor Youngstown St Univ 1978-79; Elem Teacher 1979-85, Teacher/Coord of Gifted 1985-89 Girard City Schls; Coord of Gifted & Talented Prgms Youngstown City Schls 1989-; *ai:* Teacher Leader & Parent Keynote Speaker Youngstown St Univ Saturday Treasures on Campus; Inservice Act Parents, Teachers, Admin; Sunday Sch Teacher; Kappa Delta Pi (Secy, VP) 1978-79; Phi Kappa Phi; Delta Kappa Gamma 1989-; Consortium of OH Coord of Gifted 1989-; OH Assn for Gifted Children, Merit Awd 1988-; Youngstown Assn for Gifted Children Founder 1990; Daughters of Penelope (Local Chapter Offices 1980-, Dist Lieutenant Governor), Outstanding Pres 1986, Penelope of Yr 1987; PTA Phoebe Hearst Outstanding Educator Awd 1989; Articles Published 1988-; Yountstown Educl Fnd Schlsp; Outstanding Young Woman of America; Girard Liberty Rotary Club Teacher of Month; Good Apple Publishers Natl Cover Contest Winner; *office:* Youngstown City Schls 20 W Wood St Youngstown OH 44503

PAPPIN, CHARLENE PATRICIA, Professor & Math Dept Chair; *b:* Chicago, IL; *ed:* (AA) Math, Wright Coll 1958; (AB) Math, Mundelein Coll 1960; (MA) Math, 1966, (EDD) Math Ed, 1973 Columbia Univ; *cr:* Math Teacher Madonna HS 1960-66; Math Dept Chairperson 1964-66; Math Instr Wright Coll 1966-69; Asst Math Professor 1969-78; Math Professor 1978-; Math Dept Chairperson 1979-; *ai:* Coll Strategic Planning, North Cntrl Assn Visitation Steering Comm Mem; Chairperson Institutional Requirements; Chm Wright Coll Math Contest; NCTM; IL Cncl Teacher of Math (Coll Rep 1990) 1960-; Math Assn of America (Jr Coll Math Rep 1976-) 1962-; Sch Sci & Math Assn Inc 1962-; AFT 1966-; Womans Math Club of Chicago & Vicinity (Pres 1971-72) 1960-84; Phi Theta Kappa Initiation Speaker; Kappa Delta Pi Mem 1967-; Pi Lambda Theta Mem 1968-; Phi Delta Kappa Mem 1971-; Wright Coll Theta Omega Teacher of Yr 1987, 1989; Arthur Crandall Awd for Teaching Excl 1989; Stu Government Leadership Awd 1984, 1989; Various Published Works; *office:* Wilbur Wright Coll 3400 N Austin Ave Chicago IL 60634

PAQUETTE, ANNE, IHM, 7-8 Grade Religion/Eng Teacher; *b:* Marine City, MI; *ed:* (BA) Eng, Marygrove Coll 1937; (MA) Eng, Villanova Univ 1959; Admin, Wayne Univ; Speech, Univ of Detroit; Theology, Marygrove Coll; *cr:* Teacher/Admin St Mary Acad 1966-67; Admin Lumen Christi HS 1967-81; Teacher St Mary; *ai:* Mission Adv; Vocation Coord; Journalism Grant Univ of Detroit; *office:* St Mary Sch 11208 N Saginaw Mount Morris MI 48458

PAQUETTE, MARY GRACE, French/Spanish Teacher; *b:* San Mateo, CA; *ed:* (BA) Fr, 1963, (ma) Fr, 1966, (PHD) Fr Lit, 1970 Univ of CA Santa Barbara; *cr:* Lecturer in Ed Univ of CA Santa Barbara 1969-70; Professor of Fr CA St Coll 1970-81; Foreign Lang Teacher Summerville HS 1982-; *ai:* Club Adv Amer Field Service; Fr Club; Pursuing Excl Steering Comm; Tuolumne Cty His Society Pres 1985 Wheelhorse 1986; Tuolumne Cty Museum Bd of Governors Dir 1983-; Kern Cty His Society; Numerous Scholarly Articles; 3 Books 1978, 1982 & 1985; Bicentennial ,edal Fr Government 1979; Awd of Merit Scholastic Acheivement 1984; *office:* Summerville H S 17555 Tuolumne Rd Tuolumne CA 95379

PARANTO, STEVE A., Physical Education Specialist; *b:* Seattle, WA; *m:* Karen Sutton; *c:* Kourtney; *ed:* (BA) Phys Ed/Health, 1979, (MS) Phys Ed, 1985 Pacific Univ; *cr:* Phys Ed Specialist Indian Hills Elem 1979-88, Butternut Creek Elem 1989, Sexton Mountain Elem 1990; *ai:* Organizing & Teaching Sport Clubs; OR Alliance for Phys Ed Recreation & Dance; *home:* 2375 SW Augusta Pl Aloha OR 97006

PARCELL, EMMA PERDUE, Spanish Teacher; *b:* Roanoake, VA; *M:* William M. Jr.; *c:* Elizabeth S., William R.; *ed:* (BA) Span, Hollins Coll 1967; (MAT) Span, Univ of VA 1970; *cr:* Span Teacher Maggie Walker HS 1970-72; 7th Grade Teacher Snow Creek Elem Sch 1972-77; Span/Cmptr Teacher Franklin Cty Mid Sch 1977-89; Span Teacher Benjamin Franklin Mid Sch 1989-; *ai:* NEA; VEA; *home:* Rt 2 Box 52 Ferrum VA 24088

PARDI, ROBERT PAUL, Social Science Teacher; *b:* Antioch, CA; *m:* Claire J.; *c:* Maria, John; *ed:* (BS) Phys Ed, CA St Hayward 1963; Soc Sci, His CORE; *cr:* Teacher College Park HS 1964-; *ai:* Var, Frosh, Jr Var Ftbl Coach, Jr Var Bsktbl Coach; Mt Diablo Ed Assn, CA Ed Assn Mem 1964-; Italian Amer Club Bd Mem 1981-; *office:* College Park HS 201 Viking Dr Pleasant Hill CA 94523

PARDINE, JOSEPH, JR., Mathematics Teacher; *b:* Orange, NJ; *m:* Sandra Mac Gowan; *c:* Eric, Timothy, Jonathan, Andrew, Jeffrey; *ed:* (BA) Math, Montclair St Coll 1971; Working Toward Masters; *cr:* Math Teacher Elmwood Park HS 1971-72, John F Kennedy HS 1972-; *ai:* Athletic Treas; Paterson Ed Assn 1978-; NJ Ed Assn, NEA 1971-; NJ Governor Teachers Recognition Awd 1988-89; *office:* John F Kennedy HS 61 Preakness Ave Paterson NJ 07522

PARDUE, JANE ELLEN, 2nd Grade Teacher; *b:* Bloomsburg, PA; *ed:* (BA) Psych/Elem Ed, Cedar Crest Coll 1973; *cr:* Kndgtn Teacher Benton Elem 1974-75; 5th Grade Teacher Factoryville Elem 1976-77; 3rd Grade Teacher Nicholson lem 1977-78; 2nd Grade Teacher Benton Elem 1978-; *ai:* Religious Ed Dir Our Lady of Abingtons Church; Parish Cncl; Lackawanna Trail Building Rep 1980-84; Ed Assn Pres Elect 1988-89; Down Yonder Minstrel Group Pres 1979-80; *office:* Lackawanna Trail Sch Dist Benton Elem Sch Fleetville PA 18420

PARDUE, UNA HOWELL, Fifth Grade Teacher; *b:* Jacksonville, FL; *m:* Daniel Gibson Jr.; *c:* Sigrid L., Daniel G.; *ed:* (BA) Eng, Marymount Coll 1966; *cr:* 6th Grade Teachere John N C Stockton Elem 1966-69; 5th Grade Teacher San Jose Episcopal Day Sch 1983-; *ai:* Tennis Captain; Jr League of Jax Treas Thrift Shop 1981-82; Ortega Garden Circle (Transfer Chairperson 1983, Pres 1980).

PARDUE, WANDA MATHIS, 4th Grade Teacher; *b:* N Wilkesboro, NC; *m:* Joseph Daniel; *c:* Joseph C.; *ed:* (BA) Coll Transfer Prgm, Wilkes Comm Coll 1973; (BS) Elem Ed, 1975, (MA) Rdng Ed, 1979 Appalachian St Univ; *cr:* Kndgtn Aide 1975, 7th-8th Grade Soc Stud Teacher 1976, 4th Grade Teacher 1977- Mullberry Elem; *ai:* Mulberry Sch Staff Dev Coord.

PARENCIA, SHIRLEY MARIE, English Teacher/Coach; *b:* Port Lavace, TX; *ed:* (BS) Phys Ed, TX A&M Univ 1986; *cr:* Eng Teacher/Coach Kenedy HS 1986-88, El Campo HS 1988-; *ai:* Jr Var Vlybl & Bsktbl Coach; TX Bsktbl Coaches Assn 1989-; NCTE 1986-; *office:* El Campo HS 600 W Norris El Campo TX 77437

PARENT, ROBERT CHARLES, 6th Grade Teacher; *b:* Holyoke, MA; *m:* Noreen Marie Briere; *c:* Christopher, Jamie; *ed:* (BS) Ed, Westfield St Coll 1972; Grad Stud; *cr:* 6th Grade Teacher Park Sch 1972-76; 5th/7th/8th Grade Teacher 1977-84, 6th Grade Teacher 1985- White Brook Mid Sch; *ai:* Easthampton Boys & Girls Var Swim Coach; Prins Faculty Adv Comm, HS Swim League Ethics Comm Mem; NEA, MA Teachers Assn, Easthampton Teachers Assn 1972-; Town of Easthampton Town Meeting Mem 1982-88; Pioneer Valley Swim League Pres 1980-86; Jr Achievement Bus Basics 1987-; Age Group Swim Club Coach 1976-88; *office:* White Brook Mid Sch 200 Park St Easthampton MA 01027

PARHAM, ALICE MARIE, Teacher Third Grade; *b:* Bolivar, TN; *ed:* (BS) Soc Sci, KY St Univ 1953; (MA) Elem Ed, Washington Univ St Louis 1960; *cr:* Teacher Farragut Sch; Sunday Sch Teacher 3rd Presbyn Church; *ai:* Drama Club Farragut Sch; Alpha Kappa Alpha; NEA, Intnl Rdng Assn; Public Service Awd 1975; *home:* 1002 Goodfellow Saint Louis MO 63112

PARILLO, TERRI MARY TERESA, Third Grade Teacher/ Vice Prin; *b:* Macon, GA; *m:* Jack; *c:* John W., Jena Abshire, Mari P. Cely; *ed:* (BA) Elem Ed, Furman Univ 1978; Grad Stud Pre-Med; *cr:* 3rd Grade Teacher 1964-, Asst Prin 1985- Our Lady of the Rosary; *ai:* Roper Mountain Sci Center, Greenville Little Theater Mem; Sister Cities Ed Comm; Alpha Phi Chi 1947-50; PTO, Friends of Lib Mem; Outstanding Women in SC; *home:* 115 Brittany Dr Greenville SC 29615

PARIS, RODNEY MELVIN, Mathematics Teacher; *b:* Aurora, CO; *ed:* (BS) Educl Curr/Instruction, TX A&M Univ 1983; *cr:* Math Teacher Bryan HS 1983-; *ai:* Soph Class Spon; Parent Teachers Stu Organization Treas 1985-87; *home:* PO Box 13164 College Station TX 77841

PARISH, CARLA WILLIAMS, 7th/8th Grade Science Teacher; *b:* Paducah, KY; *m:* Douglas Clinton; *c:* Kyle D.; *ed:* (BS) Bio, 1985, (MA) Ed, 1990 Murray St Univ; *cr:* Sci Teacher North Marshall Mid Sch 1986-; *ai:* KY Ed Assn; Sci Careers Grant Proposal; *office:* North Marshall Mid Sch Rt 2 Calvert City KY 42029

PARISI, ELLEN W., History Teacher; *b:* Buffalo, NY; *m:* Peter; *c:* Kate; *ed:* (BS) Soc Stud Ed, St Univ 1969; (MA) Soc Stud Ed, Coll of NY Buffalo 1973; Grad Stud at SUCB, SUNY Buffalo, Canisius Coll; *cr:* His Teacher Williamsville Cntrl Schls 1969-; *ai:* Model United Nations Adv; Williamsville Schls Supt Cncl & Soc Stud Cncl; NHS Selection Comm; Niagara Frontier Soc Stud Cncl (Membership, Secy 1988-, Bd of Dir 1984-); NY St Cncl for Soc Stud, NCSS; Organization of Amer Historians; Williamsville Teachers Assn Cncl of Delegates 1984-86, NY St United Teachers, AFT; Alpa Delta Kappa 1976-81; Phi Delta Kappa 1985-; Church of Good Shepherd Ed Dir 1986-; Published Author History of Church of Good Shepherd 1988; Sci Research Assocs Consultant 1988-89; NY St Bd of Regents Soc Stud Ed Dept Consultant 1986-; Advanced Placement Amer His Reader 1985, 1987; Presenter at Various Organizations; *office:* Williamsville East HS 151 Paradise Rd East Amherst NY 14051

PARK, FAYE WHITLEY, Mathematics Teacher; *b:* Tifton, GA; *m:* Sammy; *c:* Deidre, Sam Jr.; *ed:* (BS) Elem Ed, Univ of GA 1965; (MED) Math, GA Southwestern 1978, 1982; *cr:* 3rd Grade Teacher Sylvester Elem Sch 1965-68; 4th Grade Teacher 1974-77, 6th Grade/Algebra I Teacher 1980-82, Algebra I & II/Geometry/ Trigonometry/Cmptr Sci/Math Teacher 1984-87 Worth Acad; 8th Grade Math Teacher Worth Cty Mid Sch 1987-88; *ai:* Beta Club, Stu Cncl, Chrldrs Spon; NCTM 1984-89; Star Teacher 1987-89.

PARK, HOWARD WALTER, Retired Teacher; *b:* W Dummerston, VT; *m:* Zana Czaplinski; *ed:* (BMUS) Public Sch Music, New England Conservatory of Music 1942; (MA) Elem Ed/Supervision, CO St Coll of Greeley 1950; NM St Univ Silver Cushman & Sons Contractors 1943-44; Supvr of Elem/Vocal/ Instrumental/Music/Amer His/Journalism Teacher Hot Spring Municipal Schls 1944-46; Dir Music/Amer His/Journalism Teacher Mt Berry Schls for Boys & Berry Schls & Mt Berry Coll 1946-47; Supvr of Music NH Public Schls 1947-48; Dir Elem Ed/ Dean of Men Univ of ME Aroostook St Normal 1948-49; Elem Curr/Dur Public Schls Arkansas City KS 1951-54; Assoc Prof Ed Franklin Coll of IN 1957-60; Dept Head/Eng/Soc Stud/6th Grade Teacher Julian D Coleman Sch 1968-; *ai:* HS Journalism & Stu Cncl Adv; Curr Comm; BSA (Scoutmaster, Dir) 1943-45, Eagle & Palms 1944; Phi Delta Kappa Mem, Service Key 1955; Kappa Delta Pi Honor Mem 1957-60, Key 1957; Kappa Delta Rho Adv 1958-60, Key 1958; NM Music Educators Assn Rep 1945; Lions Intnl Boy & Girl Comm 1943-45, Silver Key 1944; Precinct Committeeman Republican 1986-; Dial-A-Teacher 1980-; NH St Music Festival Accompanist 1948; Johnson Cty Civic Music Assn Pres 1958-60; City-Wide Comm of Teachers for Eng Textbook Selection Chm 1978-79; New England Conservatory of Music Dormitories (Chm, Judiciary Bd, Stu Cncl); Teacher of Yr 1968-; Lilly Educl Fnd Fellowship Grant 1989; Citation Bd of Sch Commissioners; Natl Comm on Records Music Ed by St Commission NH 1948; Univ of NH Summer Youth Music Sch Boys Glee Club Dir 1948; Keene Light Opera Company Musical Dir & Conductor; *office:* Julian D Coleman Sch 110 1740 E 30th St Indianapolis IN 46218

PARK, JACK EDWARDS, Health-Physical Ed Teacher; *b:* Elkin, NC; *m:* Juanita Beroth; *c:* Bruce, Brian; *ed:* (BS) Health/ Phys Ed/Soc Stud, Appalachian St Univ 1955; Several Courses Towards Masters; *cr:* Teacher/Coach/Athletic Dir Wilson Jr HS 1955-84, Wilson Mid Sch 1984-; *ai:* Ftbl, Girls Sftbl, Boys Bsktbl, Girls Bsktbl, Bsbl Coach; Monogram Club & Athletic Dir; Athletic Dir Assn (Pres, Coach) 1960-65, Coach of Yr; Pine Island Cntry Club (Pres, Chm of Bd) 1961-66; Nom Citizenship Awd Meek Cty 1986; *office:* Wilson Mid Sch 7020 Tuckaseegee Rd Charlotte NC 28214

PARK, LOIS ROBERTA-ALLEN, 1st Grade Teacher; *b:* Paola, KS; *m:* Gilbert N.; *c:* Gilbert N. Jr., Millie F. Mellgren, Stan E., Allen L.; *ed:* (TC) Elem Ed, KS St Coll 1953; (BE) Elem Ed, Washburn Univ 1973; (ME) Ed, Northwestern OK St 1981; Specialist Deg, Fort Hays St Univ; *cr:* 3rd/4th Grade Teacher Edgerton Elem 1953-54; 2nd/5th Grade Teacher St George Elem 1954-55; 3rd Grade Teacher Camp Spring Elem 1957-58; 1st/5th/ Rdng Teacher 1965-69; Kndgtn/5th Grade Teacher 1971-75; Kndgtn/Phy Ed/1st Grade Teacher 1976-; *ai:* Curr Comm; Building Rep; Delta Kappa Gamma Society Intnl VP 1976-; KNEA Pres 1953-55; VP 1971-; Comanche Cty Teachers Building Rep; Meth Church Sunday Sch Teacher; 4-H Project Leader 1970-82; Alumni Awd 1980; American Cancer Society 1966-; 10 Yr Awd 1988; BSA Treas 1963-80; Girl Scouts Comm Leader 1964-74; Outstanding Leader 1967; Outlook Club; Outstanding Young Woman 1968; Taught Outreach Classes Dodge City Jr Coll; Taught Summer Class Fort Hays Univ; Taught Extension Classes Fort Hays St Univ.

PARK, LORI RHAE, High School Choral Director; *b:* Waurika, OK; *ed:* (BME) Vocal Music, SW OK St Univ 1984; Process of Completing Masters Degree in Music; *cr:* Choral Dir Sayre Schls 1985-88, Moore HS 1988-; *ai:* Cheerleading Spon During Teaching Duties in Sayre; Served on Facilities & Act Comm at Moore during N Cntrl Accredidation; OK Music Educators Assn, Natl Music Educators Assn, OK Choral Dir Assn, Amer Choral Dir Assn, OK Educators Assn; *office:* Moore HS 300 N Eastern Moore OK 73160

PARKE, H. LYNN, First Grade Teacher; *b:* Missoula, MT; *m:* Charles W.; *c:* Piper A.; *ed:* (AA) Interior Design, Inter Amer Univ 1969; (BS) Elem Ed, MT St Univ Bozeman 1971; (MS) Guidance & Counseling, Northern MT Coll 1990; Numerous Courses Taken; *cr:* 3rd Grade Teacher 1971-73, 2nd Grade Teacher 1973-75 Lowell Sch; 1st Grade Teacher Lewis & Clark Elem Sch 1976-; *ai:* Odyssey of Mind Coach; Stu Teacher Supvr; Lang Arts & Ethos Comm; Great Falls Ed Assn Faculty Rep 1971-, Faculty Rep of Yr 1987; MT Ed Assn Delegate 1971-, 1986-88; NEA 1971-; Delta Kappa Gamma Prof Affairs Comm Chairperson 1985-; Naval Reserve Admin Officer 1978-, Sailor of Yr 1988; Bus & Prof Women 1972-76, Women of Yr 1974; Beta Sigma Phi (Pres, VP, Secy) 1969-76, Sweetheart 1976; Seminars & Articles Published on Behavior Management; Theme Teaching & Art Ideas for Children; *office:* Lewis & Clark Elem Sch 3800 1st Ave S Great Falls MT 59405

PARKER, AMY HOBBS, Third Grade Teacher; *b:* Thomasville, GA; *m:* James Howard; *c:* Jessica R. Christian; *ed:* (BS) Elem Ed, Womans Coll of GA 1962; (MED) Elem Ed, 1966, (SPED) Elem Ed/Lang Art, 1967 GA Southern Coll; Numerous Wkshps & Staff Dev Units; Span Stud, Saltillo Coahuila Mexico; *cr:* 2nd Grade Teacher Balfour Elem Sch 1962-64; 7th Grade Teacher Baldwin Cty 1964-65, Screven Cty 1966-67; 5th Grade Teacher 1967-69, Resource/5th Grade Classroom Teacher 1970-73 Thomasville City; 3rd Grade Teacher Thomas Cty Schls 1974-; *ai:* GA Ed Assn 1962-88; Prof Assn of GA Educators 1988-; Alpha Delta Kappa Gamma 1975-; First United Meth Church; GA Teacher Schlsp 1965-66; *office:* Garrison Pilcher Elem Sch Rt 2 Box 2 Hall Rd Thomasville GA 31792

PARKER, ANTOINETTE BOYKIN, Science Teacher; *b:* Brundidge, AL; *m:* Louis Henry I; *c:* Jacqueline L., Louis H. II (dec), John J.; *ed:* (BS) Elem Ed, AL St Univ 1970; Elem Ed, Word Processing I; *cr:* Teacher Mango Elem 1970-72, Limona Elem 1972-73, Harmon Elem Jr HS 1973-82, Ashford HS 1982-; *ai:* Houston Cty Ed; AL Ed Assn Rep 1988-; Phi Delta Kappa 1988-; Alpha Kappa Alpha 1981-; *office:* Ashford HS P O Drawer S Church St Ashford AL 36302

PARKER, BERNICE M., Fourth Grade Teacher; *b:* Illinois Bend, TX; *m:* Adrian H.; *c:* Sheila Arledge, Rex, Lisa Bellows; *ed:* (AS) CCC Gainesville 1970; (BS) Elem Ed, 1972, (MLS) Lib Sci, 1975 TX St Univ Denton; *cr:* Librarian Montague Cty Schls 1972-71; 4th Grade Teacher St Jo Ind Sch Dist 1977-; *home:* Rt 1 Box 156 Saint Jo TX 76265

PARKER, BLAINE RAY, Metals Instructor; *b:* St Anthony, ID; *m:* Mary Ann Peterson; *c:* Marilyn, Karen, Susan, Christine, Brandon, Justin; *ed:* (MIE) Industrial Ed, Brigham Young Univ 1973; (BS) Industrial Ed, UT St Univ 1970; *cr:* Metals Instr Taylorsville HS 1980-; Machine Shop Instr Salt Lake Cmmty Coll 1980-; Metals Instr Cyprus HS 1970-80; *ai:* VICA Club Adv; UIEA Life Mem; UVA; AVA; VICA; UEA; NEA; *office:* Taylorsville H S 5225 S Redwood Rd Salt Lake City UT 84123

PARKER, CHRIS, Second Grade Teacher; *b:* Martins Ferry, OH; *c:* Arik A.; *ed:* (BSED) Elem Ed, OH Univ 1966; Barry Univ, Dayton Univ, OH Univ St Clairsville, OH Univ Zanesville; *cr:* Spec Ed Teacher St Clairsville-Richland 1966-69; 1st Grade Teacher Flushing Elem 1969-72; 2nd/3rd Grade Teacher Morristown Elem 1972-; *ai:* OH Ed Assn, NEA, Assn of Classroom Teachers Union; Morristown PTA; *office:* Morristown Elem Sch PO Box 1 Bethesda-Morristown Rd Morristown OH 43759

PARKER, DELORISE, Elementary Teacher; *b:* Suffolk, VA; *ed:* (BA) Sociology/Psych, Brooklyn Coll 1975; (MS) Elem Ed, Long Island Univ 1979; *cr:* Asst Teacher 1973-74, Pre-Sch Teacher 1974-82 Together We Stand Day Care; 4th-6th Grade Elem Teacher PS 256 1982-; *ai:* Plan to Lead Comm Mem; Voluntary Tutorial After-Sch Rdng Math Prgm; Public Sch 256 Teaching Staff Common Branch Teacher Honoring Service & Excl Plaque 1986-90.

PARKER, DONNA NEAL, Senior English Teacher; *b:* Bruce, MS; *m:* Benny Joe; *c:* Benjy, Joshua; *ed:* (BA) Eng, 1975, (MS) Eng, 1978 Univ of MS; *cr:* Eng Teacher Northwest MS Cmmty Coll 1984-89, Bruce HS 1975-; *ai:* Spon Weekly Stu Newspaper; Sr Class Spon; MS Prof Educators; Bruce PTO; Booster Club Secy 1988-; Star Teacher 1984; Bruce HS Outstanding Teacher 1987; Outstanding Young Woman Amer 1982; *office:* Bruce H S PO Box 248 Bruce MS 38915

PARKER, DONNA PASCHALL, World Geography/Econ Teacher; *b:* Memphis, TN; *m:* Bobby; *c:* Ben, Dan; *ed:* (BS) Secondary Educ, Univ of TN at Martin 1984; *cr:* Teacher Obrion Co Central HS 1985-; *ai:* Pep Club Spon; SADD Spon; Faculty Adv Cncl; Chrldg Spon; Project Graduation Adv; Obion Co Educ Assn; Special Services Comm; Christian Youth Adv; NEA 1985-; TEA 1985-; First Church of God Youth Leader 1988-, Sunday Schl Teacher 1986-; *office:* Obion County Central H S Hwy 51 Troy TN 38260

PARKER, ELONEY WILLIAMS, 6th Grade Teacher; *b:* Monticello, FL; *c:* Regina, Lashawnda; *ed:* (AA) Elem Ed, N FL Jr Coll 1967; (BS) Elem Ed, FL A&M Univ 1969; Organization, Comm & Team Planning; Elem Sci Inst & Admin Leadership Trng; *cr:* Teacher Madison Mid Sch 1969-; *ai:* 6th Grade Team Leader; NEA 1969-; NAACP 1980-; *office:* Madison Mid Sch Rt 1 Box 225 Madison FL 32340

PARKER, JOSEPH VINCENT, Mathematics Teacher; *b:* Alexandria, VA; *m:* Emma Jean Brown; *c:* Joseph V. Jr.; *ed:* (BS) Health/Phys Ed, Lamboth Coll 1973; *cr:* Phys Ed/Sci Teacher Burgundy Day Sch 1972-73; Sci Teacher Haywood Jr HS 1973-74; Health/Spelling Teacher Anderson Grammar 1974-75; Math Teacher Munford HS 1977-86, Covington HS 1986-; *ai:* Frosh Boys Bsktbl Coach; Soph Class Spon; Admin of Staff, Math, Athletics, Health Comms; Tipton Cty Math Olympics Chm; NEA, TN Ed Assn, Tipton Cty Ed Assn; *office:* Covington HS Covington TN 38049

PARKER, JUANITA KAY (PEMBER), Business Education Instructor; *b:* Jetmore, KS; *m:* Arlan D.; *c:* Harlan D., Patricia A. Mc Adoo; *ed:* (BS) Bus Ed, 1958, (MS) Bus Ed, 1966 KSTC Emporia; Additional Stud Completed FT Hays St Univ, Emporia St Univ, Dodge City Comm Coll; *cr:* Bus Ed Instr Utica Rural HS 1958-60, Ness City HS 1960-; *ai:* KAY & NHS Adv; KS Bus Ed Assn (Secy, VP, Pres) 1958-; Mountain Plains Bus Ed Assn, NEA 1968-; Delta Pi Epsilon 1965-; NEA Life Mem; KS Natl Ed Assn 1958-; Ness City NEA 1970-; KNEA Resolutions Commission Mem; KNEA Rep Assembly Delegate; ASCD; Emporia St Alumni Assn 1970-; 1st Baptist Church (Sunday Sch Supt, Adult Sunday Sch Teacher, Asst Treas, Asst Clerk, Pianist, Trustee, Chairperson of Building Comm, Trustess, Auditing Comm & Nominating Comm) 1945-; Amer Baptist Women Mem; Delta Kappa Gamma (Mem, Secy, 1st VP, Pres); KS Master Teacher Local Nominee; KS Teacher of Yr, KS Teachers Hall of Fame; Leaders of Amer Elem & Scndry Ed 1971; Mountain Plains Bus Ed Leadership Trng Inst Delegate 1971; Received R B Russell Outstanding Bus Teacher of KS Awd 1983; 25 Yr Certificate of Appreciation Univ of KS; Advisory Bd KS Internship Prgm 1989, On Site N Cntrl Evaluation Team for Tribune HS 1988; *home:* 412 S Franklin Ness City KS 67560

PARKER, KATHLEEN HOWARD, Teacher of Gifted & Talented; *b:* Worcester, MA; *m:* William G.; *c:* Abigail, Nathan; *ed:* (BA) Geography/Ed, Clark Univ 1977; (MA) Gifted & Talented Ed, Univ of N CO 1986; *cr:* Teacher Brush Ranch Sch 1977-78; 4th Grade Teacher Elizabeth Elem Sch 1979-83; 6th Grade Teacher of Gifted & Talented Schls 1984-88; Teacher of Gifted & Talented Weare Schls 1988-; *ai:* Odyssey of Mind Coord; Enrichment Comm; NHAGC, NAGC; Aububon Society; GSA Leader; AAUW Scholarship 1985; *office:* Weare Schls East St Weare NH 03281

PARKER, LEROY NEAL, School Counselor; *b:* Chicago, IL; *c:* Clifford, Keorian, Clatressa; *ed:* (BS) Art, MS Valley St Univ 1965; (MS) Counseling & Educl Psych, Univ NV 1984; Post Masters Studies Substance Abuse; Marriage & Family; Voc & Career Counseling; *cr:* Teacher Greenville 1965-70; Garside Jr High 1971-72; Valley H S 1973-84; Sunset H S 1985-; *ai:* Drill Team Trnr & Dir; Asst Band Dir & Marching Instr; Human Relationship Spon; Asst Yrbk Spon & Layout Artist; Career Day Cnslr; Re-Entry Drug Cnslr; Northwest Assn of Sch & Coll Evaluation Comm; Southern NV Sch Cnslr Assn 1986-87; Clark Cty Classroom Teachers Assn 1989-; Full 4 Year Music Schlsp; Boosters Club Awd Sch Beautification Art Teacher; Pass Pres Teachers Adv Cncl; *home:* 1004 N 17th St Las Vegas NV 89101

PARKER, LINDA NADINE, Business Teacher; *b:* Buffalo, NY; *ed:* (BS) Bus/Distributive Ed, 1981, (MS) Bus/Distributive Ed, 1985 St Univ Coll Buffalo; *cr:* Bus Instr Kensington Bus Inst 1981-84, Grand Island Adult Ed 1982-84, Lake Weir HS 1984-, Webster Bus Coll 1985-; *ai:* FBLA Adv 1985-88; Marion Cty Voc Ed Assn 1984-89; Amer Bus Womens Assn 1985-87; Mem Amaranth NY ST 1976-; Mem & Beloved Queen Triangle NY ST 1971-; DeMolay Sectional Sweetheart 1976-78; Teacher of Term Awd Webster Coll; *office:* Lake Weir HS 10351 SE Maricamp Rd Ocala FL 32672

PARKER, LOIS HAWKINS, Coordinator of Gifted Programs; *b:* Decatur, IL; *m:* Christopher Robert; *c:* Rachel K.; *ed:* (BS) Elem Ed, 1975, (MED) Elem Ed, 1976 MS Univ for Women; Cmptr Programming, Cmptr Software, Gifted Ed; *cr:* 1st Grade Teacher 1975-79, Gifted Teacher 1979-85, Elem Gifted Prgm Coord 1985- Briarcrest Chrstn Schls; *ai:* Yrbk Spon; Teacher Cncl 1989; TN Assn for Gifted; W TN Assn for Gifted (Prgm Chm 1986, Bd Mem 1987); Ind Teachers of Gifted; MS Univ for Women Alumnae Assn Bd Mem 1990; Christ United Meth Church Oratorio Choir; Outstanding Young Women of America 1985, 1986; *home:* 2072 Shetland Cove Cordova TN 38019

PARKER, MARGARET ELAINE (THORBURN), Science Teacher; *b:* Oakland, CA; *m:* Edward Lawrence; *c:* William L., Katherine R.; *ed:* (BS) Animal Husbandry, 1950, Bio Sci, 1970 Univ of CA Davis; Univ of CA Davis Conservation, Environmental Stud, Area III Environmental Wkshp; Univ of CA Lawrence Hall of Sci, SCIS, Trng to Train Teachers & Stus; Natl Sci Fnd Summer Inst; Mid Sch Math/Sci Technology Inst; *cr:* K-12th Grade Sci Coord Woodland Dist 1972-75; 7th Grade Life/8th Grade Phys Sci Teacher Harriet Lee Jr HS 1975-88; Volunteer Consultant Honor Society Cmmty Project 1988-; *ai:* Chaperone Cultural, Educl & 9th Grade Playday Field Trips; March of Dimes Walk America for Total Sch Population Chairperson; 9th Grade Field Trip Ashland OR; Theatre Acts; Natl Jr Honor Society (Adv 1978-88, Act Consultant & Participant 1988-; NEA, CA Teachers Assn; Woodland Ed Assn, Elem Sci Stud Assn Former Mem; March of Dimes N CA Bd of Dir 1970-89, Distinguished Volunteer Leadership 1989; Yolo Cty Sci Cncl 1985-; Amer Assn of Univ Women 1980-; St of CA Dept of Ed Prgm Review Mem; External Assessment Team Mem to Evaluate Univ of CA Davis Teaching Prgm; St of CA Environmental License Plate Grant; CTIIPS Grant; Organized & Presented With Univ of CA Davis Natl Sci Fnd Grants; Mentor Teacher 1986-88; Outstanding Educator Woodland Sch Dist 1985; *home:* 102 Rancho Way Woodland CA 95695

PARKER, MARTHA HARRELSON, Fourth Grade Teacher; *b:* Calhoun City, MS; *m:* John R.; *c:* Timothy, Jessi; *ed:* (BSE) Elem Ed, Delta St Univ 1973; *cr:* 4th Grade Teacher Calhoun Acad 1973-; *ai:* Spelling Bee Chm 1989; MS Private Sch Assn 1973-; Brownies Leader 1988-89; Jr GSA Jr Leader 1989-; *office:* Calhoun Acad Drawer C Calhoun City MS 38916

PARKER, MARY LOUISE, Chemistry/Physics Teacher; *b:* Washington, DC; *c:* Kimberly A. Kern, Edward J. Kern Jr.; *ed:* (BS) Ed, Univ of MD 1961; Advanced Placement Chem, Taft Summer Prgm; PSSC Physics, Putney Sch; *cr:* Sci Coord Parkdale HS 1979-84; Sci Teacher Garrison Forest Sch 1984- ; *ai:* 11th Grade Adv; NSTA; *office:* Garrison Forest Sch 9819 Reisterstown Rd Garrison MD 21055

PARKER, NADINE TOMPKINS, 6th/8th Grade English Teacher; *b:* Evansville, IN; *m:* Gary J.; *c:* Laura R., Kathryn A.; *ed:* (BA) Elem Ed, Eng Endorsement, Univ of Evansville 1968; (MS) Elem Ed, Univ of Evansville 1972; *cr:* Remedial Rdng/Rdng & Eng Teacher Oak Hill Elem Sch 1968-83; Eng Teacher Oak Hill Mid Sch 1984-; *ai:* Eng Textbook Adoption;Prof Meetings Comm; Spelling Bee; Sch Renovation Comm; 8th Grade Spon; Faculty Cabinet Chm; NEA 1968-; IN St Teachers Assn 1968-; Evansville Teachers Assn 1968-; PTA 1988-; Evansville Mid Sch Assn Exec Bd 1987-; Evansville Rdng Assn 1968-; Delta Kappa Gamma Society Intnl 1982-; TESA Teacher Expectations & Stu Achievement Eli Lilly Grant; *office:* Oak Mill Mid Sch 7700 Oak Hill Rd Evansville IN 47711

PARKER, NANCY PUCKETT, Mathematics Teacher; *b:* Lebanon, VA; *m:* Jonathan Fredrick; *ed:* (BS) Math, Radford Univ 1965; (MS) Math, Univ of IL 1971; Post Grad Stud Various Colls & Univs; *cr:* Math Teacher Holston HS 1965-70, John S Battle 1970-; *ai:* Jr Class Spon; Welfare/Hospitality; SWAC Coach; Academic Chm; Mu Alpha Theta Spon; Math Month Coord; NEA, WCEA, VEA 1965-; NCTM, VCTM, SWVCTM, UETCTM 1989-; Eastern Star 1988; Church Dist Bd Ministry Commission 1988-; Rowland Crull Church of Brethren MOderator 1988; *office:* John S Battle HS Rt 5 Lee Hwy Bristol VA 24201

PARKER, NANCY S., Math Teacher; *b:* Roanoke Rapids, NC; *ed:* (BS) Scndry Math, NC Wesleyan 1970; *cr:* Math Teacher Roanoke Rapids HS 1970-79; Items Specialist Cntrl Office 1979-82; Math Teacher Chaloner Mid Sch 1982-; *ai:* Sch Base Assistance Team; Buddy Teacher; NC Cncl of Math Teachers 1975- Teacher of Yr 1981-82; Jaycees Teacher Outstanding Young Educator 1981-82; *home:* 500 Park Ave Roanoke Rapids NC 27870

PARKER, PAULETTE BYARS, Speech/Drama/English Teacher; *b:* Detroit, MI; *m:* Gene; *c:* Kelly F.; *ed:* (AA) Gen Ed, Phillips Coll 1974; (BSE) Speech/Eng, 1976, (MFA) Theatre Arts, 1990 AR St Univ; *cr:* Teacher Elaine HS 1977-; *ai:* Sr Class Spon; Drama Dir; Speech Coach; AR Speech Comm Assn 1978-; Helena Little Theatre Pres 1978-; Helena, West Helena Jaycee Women Pres 1980-85, Speak-Up 1982-84; Phillips Cty Cancer Society VP 1981-84; *office:* Elaine Sch Dist PO Box 419 Elaine AR 72333

PARKER, PHILIP A., Teacher; *b:* Rochester, NY; *m:* Kathryn O'Rourke; *c:* Kaitlin; *ed:* (BS) Math, 1968, (MA) Scndry Ed, 1972 MI St Univ; *cr:* Teacher Bendle HS 1968-81, Allen HS 1982-86, Kearsley HS 1986-87, Allen HS 1987-; *ai:* Spon Interscholastic Math Team; Mem Dist Textbook Comm; Assn of TX Prof Educators 1982-; TX Cmptr Ed Assn 1987-; Teacher of Yr Allen Ind Sch Dist 1985; Software Product Published 1988; *office:* Allen HS 601 E Main St Allen TX 75002

PARKER, ROSE DAWN, Teacher; *b:* Teague, TX; *ed:* (BS) Scndry Ed, 1974, (MED) Scndry Ed, 1977, Scndry Ed, 1978-83 Univ oF N TX; *cr:* Teacher Spruce HS 1975-, BrookHaven Jr Coll 1982-84, Booker T Washington HS for Performing & Visual Art 1984-; *ai:* Sch Newspaper, Mock Trial Team, NHS Spon; Assn of TX Prof Educators 1988-; Teacher of Yr Arts Magnet HS 1987-88; Adjunct Professor Social Sci Brookhaven Jr Coll 1987-88; Bd of Arts Jazz 1990; Dir Peace Conference Educators 1987; *office:* Arts Magnet HS 2501 Flora St Dallas TX 75201

PARKER, STELLA BAGWELL, English-Business Teacher; *b:* Pontotoc, MS; *ed:* (BS) Bus Ed/Eng, MS St Univ 1964; (MRE) Religious Ed, Southwestern Baptist Theological Seminary 1967; Cmptr Cert, MS St Univ 1989; *cr:* Teacher Univ Chrstn Sch 1971-72, Massey Bus Coll 1972-73, Southeast HS 1973-75, Pontotoc HS 1980-87, S Pontotoc Attendance Ctr 1987-; *ai:* Jr Class & Chrldr Spon; Southern Region Ed Bd & Staff Dev Comms; MEA, NEA 1980-; Algoma Baptist (Youth Leader, Puppet Team) 1988-; *home:* Rt 5 Box 211 Pontotoc MS 38863

PARKER, STEPHEN GREGG, Social Studies Dept Chair; *b:* Kendallville, IN; *m:* Pamela Jean Johnson; *c:* Bradley, Lanelle, Andrea; *ed:* (BA) Ed, Univ of Indianapolis 1972; (MA) Soc Stud/Guidance/Counseling, St Francis Coll 1982; *cr:* Soc Stud Teacher Moores Hill Sch 1972-75, Wolcottville Sch 1975-79, Lakeland Jr HS 1979-; *ai:* 8th Grade Bsktbl & Ftbl Coach; IN St Teachers Assn 1972-; *office:* Lakeland Jr HS RR 5 Box 432A Lagrange IN 46761

PARKER, TERESA O'NEAL, English Teacher; *b:* Mc Kinney, TX; *m:* William John; *c:* Jason B., Matthew S., Eric C.; *ed:* (BA) Eng, Stephen F Austin 1974; *cr:* Eng Teacher Corsicana HS 1974-; *ai:* Soph Class Spon; *office:* Corsicana HS West Hwy 22 Corsicana TX 75110

PARKER, THELMA ROBINSON, Social Studies Dept Chairman; *b:* Norfolk, VA; *m:* Addison L. Sr.; *c:* Robert Robinson, Yolanda R. Coles, Dwayne T.; *ed:* (BA) His Ed, Norfolk Div VA St Univ 1961; (MA) Urban Affairs/Ec, Norfolk St Univ 1980; Law Inst VA Commonwealth Univ; Mid East Seminar & Consumer Economics Old Dominion Univ; Writing Across the Curr Seminar of Atlantic Region Mid Sch; *cr:* Classroom Teacher Mary N Smith HS 1961-63, Madison Jr HS 1963-64, Jacox & Willard Jr HS 1965-78; Appointed Dept Chairperson of Soc Stud 1974; Summer Sch Teacher Norfolk City Schls 1972-; Dept Chairperson/Teacher Lake Taylor Mid 1978-; *ai:* Stu Cncl Assn & Natl Jr Honor Society 1979-; Norfolk Educl Assn, VA Ed Assn, NEA Lifetime Membership; VA Cncl of Soc Stud; VA Geography Conference; BTW Boosters Secy 1980-83; St Mark RZUA (Choir Pres 1977-81, Sunday Sch Pianist, Pastors Aid Secy); United Order of Tents Financial Secy; VA St Univ Fullbright Scholar 1974, 1976; Geography Teacher of Yr; VA Natl Geographic Awd 1978; Lake Taylor Mid Sch Teacher of Yr 1982, 1990; Teacher of Yr Honoree 1987; Golden Apple Awd 1987; *office:* Lake Taylor Mid Sch 1380 Kempsville Rd Norfolk VA 23502

PARKER, VIRGINIA BELL, English Teacher; *b:* Sandersville, GA; *m:* John Newton; *c:* Linda Parker Hudson, John N. Jr.; *ed:* (BA) Eng - Cum Laude, Wesleyan Coll 1947; *cr:* 3rd Grade Teacher Lafayette Elem/HS 1947-49; 3rd/4th/5th Grade Combination Teacher Warthen Elem 1956-58; 1st/4th Grade Teacher Lee Elem 1958-60; 4th Grade Teacher Beverly Shores Elem 1960-65; Eng Dept Chm Leesburg Jr HS 1965-84; Eng Teacher Leesburg HS 1985-; *ai:* NCTE; Leesburg Jr Womans Club Teacher of Yr 1970; Lake Cty Teacher of Yr 1969-70; Leesburg Jr HS Teacher of Yr 1982-83; Leesburg HS Teacher of Yr 1987-88; *office:* Leesburg HS 1401 W Meadows Dr Leesburg FL 34748

PARKERSON, ROBERT D., JR., Teacher; *b:* Lebanon, TN; *m:* Patricia Lee Blythe; *c:* Kelly; *ed:* (BS) Bio, Mid TN St Univ 1972; (MA) Elem Ed, 1981, Ed Spec Admin & Supervision, 1986 TN Tech Univ; *ai:* Boys & Girls Bsktbl Coach; DCEA Pres 1985; Lions Club Secy 1987-88; Mayor of Alexandria 1985-89; Alderman of Alexandria 1990; Cty Commissioner 1990; *home:* Box 142 Alexandria TN 37012

PARKES, SALLY ANN, Spanish Teacher; *b:* Ellensburg, WA; *m:* Ivor Roy; *c:* Curtis; *ed:* (BA) Span Ed, Cntrl WA Univ 1986; Eng Endorsement/Supt of Public Instruction 1988; *cr:* Span Teacher Ridgetop Jr HS 1987-; *ai:* Span Club Advisors; WA Ed Assn, WA Assn Foreign Lang Teachers 1987-; Tutoring Coord Ridgetop Jr HS 1988-89; *office:* Ridgetop Jr HS PO Box 8 Silverdale WA 98383

PARKINSON, BRENDA JOYCE, 9th-11th Grade English Teacher; *b:* Greenwood, MS; *ed:* (BA) His/Eng, Mobile Coll 1972; (MED) Scndry Ed/Eng, Univ of S AL 1976; Eng, Univ of S MS; Eng, Drama & Broadcasting, Univ of London; Eng, William Carey Coll; *cr:* Teacher Mobile Cty Public Schls 1972-80, George Cty Public Schls 1980-; *ai:* NEA, NASSP, NCTE, ASCD, ITS, Intnl Rdng Assn; MAE Faculty Rep; George Cty Sch for Performing Arts (Owner, Instr) 1988-; *home:* PO Box 144 Lucedale MS 39452

PARKINSON, NANCY OWENS, 7th Grade Science Teacher; *b:* Crossville, TN; *m:* R. Jeffrey; *c:* H. Cory; *ed:* (BA) Scndry Ed, David Lipscomb Univ 1980; (MED) Educl Admin, TN St Univ 1989; *cr:* 7th Grade Sci Teacher Ezell-Harding Chrstn Sch 1982-; *office:* Ezell-Harding Chrstn Sch 574 Bell Rd Antioch TN 37013

PARKINSON, WILLIAM HENRY, Religious Studies Teacher; *b:* Philadelphia, PA; *m:* Mary Ellen; *c:* William J., Gregory F., Allyson L.; *ed:* (BA) Philosophy, Villanova Univ 1974; Philosophy/Classical Lang, St Charles Coll 1972-74; Coaching Cert Level I Grad, NYU 1988; Coaching Cert Level II, NYU 1990; Working Towards Masters Scripture Stud, Villanova 1987-; *cr:* Math/His Teacher St Joseph The Worker Jr HS 1974-79; Debate/Forencis Teacher 1979-89, Religouis Stud Teacher 1979-, Cross Cntry/Track & Field Coach 1979- Notre Dame HS; *ai:* Mens Cross Cntry Indoor/Outdoor Track Head Coach; E Ct Track Coaches Assn Mem; BSA Den Leader 1988-; St Elizabeth Seton Grant for Advanced Degree Work in Scripture & Classical Lang; *office:* Notre Dame HS 24 Ricardo St West Haven CT 06516

PARKS, DAWN C. BEEBE, 6th Grade Teacher; *b:* Ithaca, NY; *m:* George H.; *c:* Cindy R. Parks Parlett, Lee J.; *ed:* (BS) Phys Ed, SUNY Cortland 1963; Grad Stud Ed & Psych; *cr:* Phys Ed Teacher East Syracuse Minoa Elem Sch 1963; 4th Grade Teacher 1972-83, 6th Grade Teacher 1983- Candor Elem Sch; *ai:* Liberty Partnership Stu-At-Risk Prgm; STEP-UP S Tier Educators Prgm; PTA Local, St, Natl; NY St United Teachers Assn, Candor Faculty Assn, NY St Teachers Retirement System; Amer Assn of Retired Persons, Square-A-Naders; GSA Leader; Sci Prgm Being Intergrated with Lang Art Article; *office:* Candor Cntrl Elem Sch Box 145 Candor NY 13743

PARKS, DEANN MIELKE, Chapter 1 Teacher; *b:* Cameron, ID; *m:* Charles Jr.; *c:* Steven, Douglas, Charlene Thomason, Brian; *ed:* (BSED) Elem Ed, Lewis-Clark St Coll 1974; *cr:* 1st Grade Teacher 1974-81, 5th Grade Teacher 1981-84, Chapter 1 Teacher 1984- Juliaetta Elem; *ai:* Negotiations; ID Cncl of Intnl Rdng Assn, Tamarack Rdng Cncl.

PARKS, DOROTHY COFFEY, Mathematics Teacher; *b:* Edmonton, KY; *m:* Charles E.; *c:* Charles Jr., David; *ed:* (AB) Math/Eng, W KY Univ 1949; (BS) Ed, IN Univ 1956; Post Grad Study W KY Univ, Moorehead St Univ; Wkshps Gifted Ed W KY Univ, St & Local Conferences; Local, St, Natl Conferences on Math; *cr:* Math Teacher Daviess Cty HS 1949-51, Central Jr HS 1951-54, Southern Jr HS 1954-57; Substitute Teacher Owensboro Public Schls 1962-66; 6th Grade Teacher Western Elem Sch 1966-67; Math Teacher Southern Jr HS 1967-72; Math Teacher/Dept Chairperson Owensboro HS 1972-81, Owensboro Jr HS 1981-88; Math Teacher Owensboro HS 1988-; *ai:* Coach of Math Team; Academic Coaching Staff; Gifted & Talented Advisory Comm; Teaches Who Care; KY NEA, KY Assn for Gifted Ed, NCTM; Pilot Intnl Pres 1990-; Friendship Force of W KY; Baptist Church Sunday Sch Dir; TX Gas Grant for Ec Ed; Invitation to Foreign Policy Conference on Ed; Chairperson Textbook Selection Comm; Math Curr Dev Comm Local St Evaluation; *home:* 1337 Hickory Ln Owensboro KY 42301

PARKS, FRANK, Fifth Grade Teacher; *b:* Orange, NJ; *m:* Ora Bragg; *ed:* (AA) General Ed, Ocean Cty Coll 1968; (BS) Elem Ed, Monmouth Coll 1972; (MA) Admin/Supervision Curr Planning, Georgian Court Coll 1989; Acad Advancement of Teaching & Mgmt; Instructional Theory Into Practice Cert; Classroom Mgmt Cert; *cr:* 5th Grade Teacher East Dover Elem Sch 1972-; *ai:* East Dover Elem Sch Cmptr Adv; Toms River Schls Summer Cmptr Instr; Toms River Ed Assn 1972-; NJ Ed Assn 1972-; NEA 1972-; American Heart Assn Neighborhood Vol 1989-; Toms River Ed Assn Schlsp Fund Vol 1978-86; *office:* East Dover Elem Sch 725 Vaughn Ave Toms River NJ 08753

PARKS, GEORGE THOMAS, Mathematics Teacher; *b:* Los Angeles, CA; *m:* Iolani Goodwin; *ed:* (BA) Chem, Univ CA Riverside 1961; (MA) Educl Psych, CA St Univ Long Beach 1970; Chem Bonding, Earlham Coll; Various Courses, UCLA; *cr:* Chem Teacher 1963-71, Guidance Cnslr 1971-79, Advanced Math Teacher 1979- Mayfair HS; *ai:* CA Schlsp Fed Spon; Sch Resource Comm for Accreditation; Bellflower Ed Assn, CA Teachers Assn, CA Math Cncl, NEA; Natl Sci Fnd Grant; CA Engineering Assn Awd; *office:* Mayfair HS 6000 N Woodruff Lakewood CA 90712

PARKS, JULIE DURBIN, Math Teacher; *b:* Wichita Falls, TX; *m:* Mike R. Jr.; *ed:* (BS) Elem Ed, Lubbock Chrstn Univ 1983; *cr:* Math Teacher Alderson Jr HS 1984-; *ai:* Stud Cncl Spon; TCTA/LCTA; Stu Teacher of Yr Awd 1983; Mem Sunset Church of Christ; *office:* Alderson Jr H S 219 Walnut Lubbock TX 79403

PARKS, K., English Teacher; *b:* Hagerstown, MD; *ed:* (BS) Bus Admin, Towson St Univ 1983; Ed, Hood Coll; Pursuing MLA Johns Hopkins Univ; *cr:* Teacher Linganore HS 1987, Boonsboro HS 1987-; *ai:* Yrbk Adv; WA Cty Teachers Assn 1987-; United Democrats of WA Cty Secy 1987-; *office:* Boonsboro HS 10 Campus Ave Boonsboro MD 21713

PARKS, KATHLEEN MONGTOMERY, English Teacher; *b:* Long Beach, CA; *m:* William A. Jr.; *c:* Meredith G.; *ed:* (BA) Eng, Univ of CA Berkeley 1971; (MA) Eng, CA St Univ Northridge 1984; *cr:* Teacher Antelope Valley HS 1972-74, Quartz Hill HS 1974-; *ai:* NCTE, CATE 1976-; Mentor Teacher 1986-; Antelope Valley HS Mentor Teacher Coord 1989-; Advanced Placement Exam Reader 1989-; CAP Essay Assessment Reader 1989-; Article Published; *office:* Quartz Hill HS 6040 W Avenue L Lancaster CA 93536

PARKS, LINDA INGLE, English Teacher; *b:* Athens, TN; *m:* Roger D.; *c:* Kristie, Tyler; *ed:* (BS) Scndry Ed/Eng/His, 1972, (MA) Psych/Cnslr Ed, 1974 TN Tech Univ; *cr:* Eng Teacher Mc Minn Cty HS 1980-; *ai:* Stu Cncl Adv; NEA 1981-86; TN Ed Assn, Mc Minn Cty Ed Assn, E TN Assn of Teachers of Eng 1988-; *office:* Mc Minn Cty HS 2215 Congress Pkwy Athens TN 37303

PARKS, MARGARET CECIL (HERSHBERGER), 4th Grade Teacher; *b:* Lima, OH; *c:* David Jr., Darrell; *ed:* (BS) Elem Ed, OH Northern Univ 1964; (MA) Counseling Elem, Univ of Dayton 1985; *cr:* 1st Grade Teacher Harrod Elem Sch 1962-65; 1st/3rd/4th Grade Teacher Allen East Sch 1965-; *ai:* Allen East Ed Assn 1968-; AlleN East Competency Based Ed Comm 1986-87; *office:* Allen East Elem Sch 9520 Harrod Rd Harrod OH 45850

PARKS, MARGARET LA VERNE, Teacher; *b:* Covington, KY; *c:* Christopher P.; *ed:* (AA) Sociology, Univ of Cincinnati 1971; (BA) Sociology, 1973, (MS) Criminal Justice, 1975, (MED) Ed/Admin, 1988 Xavier Univ; Cert Comprehensive Scndry Soc Stud 1987; *cr:* Supvr/Cnslr Citizens Comm on Youth 1976-78; Youth Job Cnslr Cincinnati Public Sch 1978-81; Supvr/Asst Admin Hamilton Cty Dept of Human Services 1982-86; Lecturer Univ of Cincinnati 1975-86; Teacher Cincinnati Public Sch 1987-; *ai:* Minority Recruitment Task Force Comm; Honor Society Adv & Spon; Frosh Chrldg Coach; Soc Stud Curr Substitute; PTA 1987-; Scndry Curr 1987-88; *office:* Taft HS 420 Ezzard Charles Dr Cincinnati OH 45214

PARKS, MARY PATRICK, Fourth Grade Teacher; *b:* Kinston, NC; *m:* Odis Lee; *c:* Reginald, Terrell; *ed:* (BS) Early Chldhd, Winston-Salem St Univ 1972; *ai:* Pupil Assistance Team; Grade Level Coord; Advisory & Curr Comms; NEA; Teacher of Yr 1989-.

PARKS, MARY TOLBERT, Health/Physical Ed Teacher; *b:* Floyd, VA; *m:* William C.; *c:* Bill; *ed:* (BS) Health/Phys Ed, Radford Coll 1965; Univ of NC Greensboro 1974; *cr:* 9th/10th Grade Health/Phys Ed Teacher Drewry Mason HS 1965-88; 8th Grade Health/Phys Ed Teacher Laurel Park HS 1988-; *ai:* Head Var Girls Bsktbl, Sftbl, 8th Grade Bsktbl; *office:* Laurel Park HS Rt 8 Box 67 Martinsville VA 24112

PARKS, RENA ELIZABETH LACEY, 7th & 8th Grade Teacher; *b:* Columbus, OH; *m:* James C.; *ed:* (BS) Eng, Cntrl St Univ Wilberforce 1964; (MED) Scndry Sch Admin/Supervision, Xavier Univ 1973; Admin, Eng, Ed Hum, Curr, OH St Univ 1981; *cr:* Eng Teacher/Newspaper Organizer Beckman Jr HS 1964-65; Spec Ed Teacher East HS 1965-67; Spec Ed/Eng/Fr Teacher Champion Jr HS 1967-74, Woodward Park Jr HS 1976-79; Eng/Soc Stud/Fr/Drama Teacher Keiller Mid Sch 1981; *ai:* Stu Body Organization Past Adv; CA Teachers Assn, San Diego Teachers Assn 1983-; NEA 1964-; Columbus Ed Assn 1964-81; Episcopal Comm Servs 1981-; Most Dedicated Teacher Eastmoor Jr HS; Fellowship Teachers Assistantship OH St 1980-81; Articles Published 1989; Poetry Book with Stus Black Experience 1971.

PARKS, ROBIN DEE (PLATTE), 6th Grade Teacher; *b:* Mondovi, WI; *m:* James De Vere; *ed:* (BS) Elem Ed, St Cloud St Univ 1972; (MA) Human Dev/Technology, St Thomas Coll 1988; Certificate Curr Design & Dev; Support Group Facilitator Tnrg, Johnson Inst; *cr:* 6th Grade Teacher Hoover Elem 1972-73; 4th Grade Teacher Washington Elem 1973-80; 5th Grade Teacher 1980-86, 6th Grade Teacher 1986- Jefferson Elem; *ai:* Anoka-Hennepin Dist 11 Rdng Comm; Support Group K-6th Grade Facilitator Self Esteem, Friendship Groups; NEA, MN Ed Assn, Anoka Hennepin Ed Assn 1972-.

PARKS, ROGER DALE, Physical Education Instructor; *b:* Athens, TN; *m:* Linda Gail Ingle; *c:* Kristie N., Jonathan T.; *ed:* (BS) HPED/Bio, 1973, (MA) HPED/Admin, 1974 TN Technological Univ; Working Towards Doctoral, Univ of TN Knoxville, Chattanooga; *cr:* Grad Asst TN Technological Univ 1973-74; Instr TN Technological Univ Housing Admin 1974-75; Teacher/Coach Putnam Cty Sch Bd 1975-77; Supvr Ralston Purina 1977-78; Teacher/Coach Putnam Cty Sch Bd 1978-80, Mc Minn Cty Sch Bd 1980-85; Head Coach/Teacher Meigs Cty HS 1985-86; Teacher/Coach Mc Minn Cty Bd of Ed 1986-; *ai:* Strength & Conditioning Coach; Ftbl Asst Coach; FCA Co-Spon; Amer Ftbl Coaches Assn 1983-87; TN Athletic Coaches Assn 1985-; AAPHER 1988-; Optimist Club 1985-.

PARKS, TRENA LA SHEA, Earth Science Teacher; *b:* Newport, TN; *m:* James Jr.; *ed:* (BS) Sci Ed, Univ of TN Knoxville 1987; *cr:* Earth Sci Teacher Cocke Cty HS 1987-; *ai:* Cheerleading Spon; Stu Cncl & Fellowship of Chrstn Athletes Adv; Phi Kappa Phi Honor Society, Golden Key NHS Mem 1986; William B Stokely Schlsp; Graduated Top of Class Coll of Ed Univ of TN; Excl in Teaching Awd Cocke Cty HS; *office:* Cocke Cty HS Hedrick Dr Newport TN 37821

PARKS, YVETTE LORRAINE, Foreign Language Dept Head; *b:* Rochester, NH; *m:* Thomas L.; *c:* Michael, Bobby; *ed:* (BA) Fr, Univ of NH 1968; (MAT) Fr/Ed, Boston Coll 1970; *cr:* Fr Teacher Norwood HS 1968; Dept Head Norwood Jr HS 1969-; *ai:* Organize Annual Stu Trips Canada & France; MA Foreign Lang Teachers Assn Speaker 1980, 1983; AATF Presenter 1982; Norwood Cncl for Art 1988-; Horance Mann Grants; Commonwealth In-Service Inst Grant; *office:* Norwood Jr HS Endean Park Norwood MA 02062

PARMA, LISA MARIE, Math/Computer Teacher; *b:* Montgomery, AL; *ed:* (BS) Scndry Math Ed, Auburn Univ 1983; *cr:* Math/Cmptr Teacher Lafayette HS 1983-84; Floyd JR HS 1984-89; Lamp Lanier HS 1989-; *ai:* Math Team Co-Spon; Future Teachers of Amer Co-Spon; Alpha Delta Kappa 1988-; Kappa Delta Phi 1983-; Paws Pet Therapy Prgm 1989-; Frazer Mem United Meth Church Lay Minister 1988-; Most Outstanding Stu Sch of Ed 1983; Most Outstanding Math St Sch of Sci 1983; Floyd JR HS Teacher of Yr 1987.

PARMALEE, EILEEN M., Resource Teacher/Math Dept; *b:* Bedford, OH; *ed:* (BSED) Elem Ed, OH Univ 1972; Kent St Univ, Ashland Coll, John Carroll Univ; *cr:* 3rd Grade Teacher 1972-79, 4th Grade Teacher 1979-80, 5th Grade Teacher 1980-82, 7th-8th Grade Math Teacher 1982-83, 8th Grade Math/6th Grade Sci/Soc Stud/Math Teacher 1983-84, 5th Grade Teacher 1984-86, 5th-6th Grade Math Teacher 1986-87, 6th-8th Grade Math/Resource Teacher/Guidance 1987- Chagrin Falls Schls; *ai:* Math Dept Chairperson; Mem Dist Curr Advisory Cncl; Tutoring Evening Resource Prgm; 7th Grade Girls Bsktbl & Var Girls Sftbl Coach; OH Cncl of Teachers of Math; Natl Mid Sch Assn; NEA, OH Ed Assn, NE OH Ed Assn; Chagrin Falls Ed Assn; OH Cnclon Supervision & Curr Dev; PTO Building Rep; Booster Club; Chagrin Falls Schls Teacher of Yr 1988; Martha Jennings Fnd Awd; Developed Individualized Accelerated Math Prgm; Presented Prgm Natl & OH Mid Sch Annual Conferences; *office:* Chagrin Falls Mid Sch 77 E Washington St Chagrin Falls OH 44022

PARMENTER, HARLEY JAMES, Science Teacher; *b:* Mojave, CA; *m:* Maidie L.; *c:* Julie D.; *ed:* (AA) General Ed, Coalinga Jr Coll 1967; (BA) Biological Sci, Chico St Coll 1971; Scndry Teacher Credential Chico Coll 1971; *cr:* Electrician US Navy 1956-60; Oil Worker Standard Oil Company of CA 1963-65; Teacher Brook Haven Sch 1971-; *office:* Brook Haven Sch 7905 Valentine Ave Sebastopol CA 95472

PARMER, BARBARA J., Teacher of Gifted; *b:* Weston, WV; *m:* David L.; *c:* Jason D.; *ed:* (BA) Eng, Glenville St Coll 1963; (MA) Rdng Ed, Coll of Grad Stud 1979; (MA) Eng, VA Tech 1988; Advanced Placement Trng, Gifted Ed Cert; *cr:* Eng Teacher Jefferson Sch 1963-65, Hedgesville HS 1965-66; Teacher of Learning Disabilities Williamsport HS 1966-68; 5th/6th Grade Teacher Bruceton Elem 1968-71; 7th-9th Grade Eng Teacher Sandstone Sch 1974-79; Teacher of Gifted/Eng Countryside 1979-; *ai:* WV Challange Academic Games Coord; RESA I Academic Bowl Cty Coord; Sch Literay Magazine & Eng Bowl Team Adv; WVEA, NEA, SCEA Secy 1978-80; Delta Kappa Gamma (VP, Pres) 1989-; WV Gifted Assn; Service Club Pres 1989-; Friends of the Lib (Pres, VP); Main Street Bd Mem 1989-; Gifted Ed Rep on Regional Task Force; *home:* 119 Ballengee St Hinton WV 25951

PARONI, GENEVIEVE SWICK, Chem/Physics/Computers Teacher; *b:* Eureka, NV; *m:* Walter A.; *c:* Andrea; *ed:* (BA) PreMed/Chem, Univ of NV Reno 1948; (MED) Sci Ed/Scndry, Univ ID Moscow 1978; Numerous Univs; *cr:* Vice Prin/Sci Teacher Eureka Cty HS 1948-60; Vice Prin/1st Grade Teacher Eureka Elem Sch 1964-66; Sci/Cmptr Teacher Wallace Sr HS 1968-; *ai:* Univ of ID Math/Sci Curr Comm; Physics Alliance for Inland Empire; Prof Dev Comm; Inland Empire Distance Learning Comm; NSTA St Mem Chairperson NV 1950, ID St Finalist Excl in Sci Teaching 1983, 1985-86; Phi Delta Kappa 1986-; Delta Kappa Gamma Wallace Pres 1973-; Wallace Dev Corp Mem 1978-84; Wallace City Cncl Mem 1970; Wallace Public Lib Bd VP 1980-; AAUW Wallace Pres 1970; Holy Trinity Episcopal Church St Warden 1990; ID Power Grant 1986; Outstanding Teacher Dist #393 1975; Numerous Westinghouse, NSF, BPA, Fellowships & Grants; *office:* Wallace Sr HS 401 River St Wallace ID 83873

PARR, MARGERET WELCH, Second Grade Teacher; *b:* Dyersburg, TN; *m:* Michael W.; *c:* Yolanda V., Michael A.; *ed:* (BS) Home Ec, TN St Univ 1970; Elem Ed, 1975, (MS) Spec Rdng 1982 Univ of TN Martin; *cr:* Rdng Aide Dyer Cty Cntrl Sch 1969-71; 2nd Grade Teacher Holice Powell Sch 1972-; *ai:* Dyer Cty Ed Assn (Membership Chm, Assn Rep); Delta Kappa Gamma Secy 1989-; NEA, PTO, TN Sci Assn, TN Rdng Assn, TN Math Assn; Delta Sigma Theta Pres 1989-; Delta Tau Nu (Spon, Adv); TEA Nom Distinguished Classroom Awd 1986; Teacher of Yr 1975, 1976, 1984, 1990; *home:* Rt 5 Box 497 Dyersburg TN 38024

PARRA, DOROTHY LEE HOLMBERG, Language Art/Soc Stud Teacher; *b:* Gloucester, MS; *m:* Armando Joseph; *c:* Linda, James, David, Jennifer; *ed:* (BA) Ed, Univ of AZ 1958; *cr:* Teacher Tucson Unified Sch Dist 1958, Oracle Sch Dist 1959, Sierra Vista Sch Dist 1960, Chinle Public Schls 1961-68, Tucson Unified Sch Dist 1968-; *ai:* Co-Chm Breakthrough Team; Audio-Visual & Chess Club; Tucson Ed Assn, NEA 1958-; Toastmasters Intnl (Club Pres 1988) 1988-; Archaeological Dig & African Violets Grant; *office:* Booth/Fickett Math-Sci Magnet 7240 E Calle Arturo Tucson AZ 85710

PARRIS, ANNA E., English Teacher; *b:* Belhaven, NC; *m:* Samuel A.; *c:* Robert, Katherine; *ed:* (BA) Practical Chrstn Trng, Bob Jones Univ 1974; *cr:* 1st Grade Teacher 1974-88, HS Eng Teacher 1989-, Music Teacher 1981- Heritage Chrstn Sch; *ai:* Music/Play Dir for Sch Productions; *office:* Heritage Chrstn Sch Rt 8 US Hwy 29 North Gaffney SC 29340

PARRISH, CARMELITA BEAL, English Teacher; *b:* Varina, NC; *w:* John Jacob (dec); *c:* Deborah J. White, Toni L. Altenburg; *ed:* (AA) Eng, Mid GA Coll 1979; (BSED) Eng, GA S Univ 1981; (MED) Eng, Valdosta St Coll 1988; *cr:* Teacher Ware Cty Sr HS; Collection Correspondent Sears Roebuck & Co; *ai:* Yrbk Adv; Sch Climate Comm; GA Cncl Teachers Eng Bd of Dir 1982-86; NCTE Stu Pres 1980-; ASCD 1988-; Pilot Club Intnl Anchor Area Leader 1976-82, Outstanding New Mem 1976; Phi Kappa Phi 1981-; GSA (Neighborhood Chairperson 1966-72, Service Citation 1969, Trainer 1967-72); STAR Teacher; Whos Who Among Amer Educators; *home:* 1003 Dean Dr Waycross GA 31501

PARRISH, PAMELA KNIGHT, English Teacher; *b:* Shreveport, LA; *c:* Stacie, Ryan; *ed:* (BA) Speech/Eng, LA St Univ Shreveport 1982; *cr:* Speech/Eng Teacher Woodlawn HS 1982-; *ai:* Drama Club & Knights for Christ Spon; Caddo Cncl Teachers of Eng VP 1989-; Caddo Heights Baptist Church (Choir Mem, Church Trng Teacher, Sunday Sch Teacher); Southern Regional Educl Bd (Woodland HS Academic, Eng Rep); *office:* Woodlawn HS 7340 Wyngate Shreveport LA 71106

PARRISH, SANDRA GRIGG, 2nd Grade Teacher; *b:* Shelby, NC; *m:* A. Leonard III; *ed:* (AA) Liberal Arts, Gardner-Webb Jr Coll 1961; (BS) Elem Ed, Appalachian St Teachers Coll 1963; *cr:* 2nd Grade Teacher Phillips Elem Sch 1963-; *ai:* Grade Chairperson 1975-; Spec Ed Case Mgr 1987-89; NEA, VA Ed Assn 1963-; Olde Colonies Uniserv (Sch Rep 1977-81) 1963-; *office:* Phillips Elem Sch 703 Le Master Ave Hampton VA 23669

PARRISH, SANDRA Y., English Teacher; *b:* Easton, PA; *m:* John D.; *c:* Mark, Lori; *ed:* (BS) Elem Ed, TN Wesleyan Coll 1973; (MS) Curr/Instruction/Media, Univ of TN Knoxville 1979; *cr:* 6th Grade Rem Teacher Allentown City Sch 1973-74; K-1 Teacher Mentor Elem/Louisville Elem 1974-79; 3rd/4th Grade Teacher Chilhowee View Elem Sch 1980-83; K-1 Teacher Union Elem Sch 1983-84; 7th/8th Grade Eng Teacher 1984-88; 2nd/3rd Grade Teacher Lanier 1988- Lanier Elem Sch; *ai:* Alpha Delta Kappa; Career Level II on TN Career Ladder; *office:* Lanier Elem School Rt 4 Box 369 Maryville TN 37801

PARRISH, WILLIAM KENNETH, II, Science & Math Teacher/Coach; *b:* Wilson, NC; *m:* Kathy Scott; *ed:* (BS) Elem Ed, Campbell Univ 1985; *cr:* 6th-8th Grade Teacher/Coach Kenly Elem 1985-87; 8th Grade Teacher/Coach Cooper Mid Sch 1987-; *ai:* Asst Ftbl, Sftbl Coach; Coopers Faculty Advisory Comm Mem; Chm Phys Ed Planning Comm for Construction of New Sch; Natl Rifle Assn 1989-; NC St Univ Math & Sci Summer Inst 1987-88; *office:* Cooper Mid Sch 849 N Mial St Clayton NC 27520

PARROTT, MARK ALFRED, Technology Education Teacher; *b:* Portage, WI; *m:* Cynthia Marie Cornell; *c:* Brianna, Kaitlynn; *ed:* (BS) Technology Ed, Univ of WI Stout 1982; Working Towards Masters; *cr:* Technology Ed Teacher Reedsburg Mid Sch 1982-; *ai:* Athletic Dir; 7th-8th Grade Boys Track Coach; Madison Area Tech Coll Athletic Hall of Fame Mem 1990, Athletic Achievment 1979; NJCAA All Amer in Wrestling; Ducks Unlimited Cmmty Mem 1987-; DNR Hunter Safety Instr 1985-; *office:* Reedsburg Mid Sch 1121 8th St Reedsburg WI 53959

PARRY, JAMES KEITH, 8th Grade Math Teacher; *b:* Canton, IL; *m:* Linda Joy; *ed:* (BA) Math/Phys Ed, 1967, (MA) Scndry Ed, 1972 Bradley Univ; Admin Endorsement, Western IL Univ; *cr:* Math Teacher/Coach Dunlap HS 1967-70, Orion Mid Sch 1970-; *ai:* 8th Grade Ftbl, Track, Athletic Dir; 7th Grade Boys Bsktbl; Fellowship of Chrstn Athletes Spon; IEA, NEA, OEA 1967-; *office:* Orion Mid Sch 802 12th Ave Orion IL 61273

PARRY, RITCHARD GEORGE, Chemistry Teacher; *b:* Kingston, PA; *m:* Charlotte Dymond; *c:* Brenda, Ritchard, Brian; *ed:* (BS) Sci, Muhlenberg Coll 1957; (MAT) Chem, Brown Univ 1962; *cr:* Teacher Council Rock HS 1957-67, Lower Moreland HS 1967-; *ai:* Bsbl Coach; LMTEA, PSEA, NEA, MESTA; Natl Sci Fnd Grants to Syracuse Univ & Brown Univ; *office:* Lower Moreland HS 555 Red Lion Rd Huntingdon Valley PA 19006

PARSLEY, JAYLENE WEHMEIER, College Mathematics Teacher; *b:* Topeka, KS; *m:* Charles H. Jr.; *ed:* (BS) Elem Ed, Concordia Coll 1980; *cr:* 5th/6th Grade Teacher Trinity Luth Sch 1980-85; Basic Math Instr Tarkio Coll 1986-; *ai:* Honey Tree Nursery Sch Bd (Asst Secy 1987-88, Pres 1988-89); Hosanna Luth Church Sunday Sch Supt; *office:* Tarkio Coll 13th & Mc Nary Tarkio MO 64491

PARSON, JOAN SCOTT, English Teacher; *b:* Mississippi Cty, MO; *m:* James W. Sr.; *c:* James Jr., Elizabeth, Scott; *ed:* (AA) Pre-Law, Jefferson Jr Coll 1979; (BS) Ed/Soc Stud, SE MO St Univ 1981; (MED) Curr/Instruction Eng, Univ of MO St Louis 1986; Photography & Writing, Jefferson Jr Coll; *cr:* Eng Teacher Cruise Sch 1981-85, Crystal City HS 1985-86; Soc Stud Teacher Hazelwood Cntrl Sr HS 1987; News Reporter Marten Publications 1987-88; Eng Teacher Cruise Sch 1988-; *ai:* Crystal City HS Yrbk & Newspaper Adv; Public Relations Dir; MO St Teachers Assn, NCTE, ASCD; Kingston CTA (Treas 1982-83, VP 1983-84, Pres 1984-85); De Soto Church of Christ Mem; Photographs & News Feature Articles Published; Writing Short Stories; Own Photography Business; *home:* 1528 Berry Dairy Rd De Soto MO 63020

PARSON, PAULA T. (MUKAI), Reading Instructor/Eng Dept; *b:* Waimea, HI; *m:* Mickey H.; *c:* Barbara, Michael, Christopher; *ed:* (BA) Ed, Cntrl WA Univ 1966; (MED) Rdng Specialist, Univ TX Pan Amer Univ 1982; Working Toward PhD Univ TX Austin; *cr:* 3rd-4th Grade Elem Teacher WA St 1966-71; Spec Ed/ Trainables Teacher East Elem 1971-72; Kndgn Teacher GraingerElem 1977-78; 4th-5th Grade Elem Teacher Brownsville Tx 1979-82; Jr HS Rdng Teacher Olveira Intermediate 1982-85; Rdng Instr TX Southmost Coll 1985-; *ai:* Ben L Brite Stu Ed Assn & Phi Beta Kappa Co-Spon; Dena J Gallic Rdng Assn Secy 1987-89; Alpha Delta Kappa Secy 1979-81; Delta Kappa Gamma Annie Blanton Schlsp 1989; TX Jr Coll Teachers Assn; Natl Assn of Developmental Educators; Prof Women Speak Prgm Chairperson 1988-; PTA Secy 1981-82; Most Valuable Alumni in Ed UT Pan Amer Univ 1989; Delta Kappa Pi Honorary Society for Grad Stus Prominent Educators of TX 1982; *office:* Texas Southmost Coll 80 Ft Brown Brownsville TX 78520

PARSONS, BARBARA ANN (KARCSAK), Secondary Math Teacher; *b:* Toledo, OH; *m:* Thomas E.; *c:* Jeffrey, Jonathan; *ed:* (BS) Math, Bowling Green St Univ 1968; (MA) Math, Siena Heights Coll 1973; *cr:* Jr HS Math Teacher & Adult Ed Monroe 1968-69; Basic Math/Coll Algebra/Alge Teacher Sierra Heights Coll 1989-; *ai:* Prin Adv Comm; Nat Honor Society Comm; Annual Honors Night Comm Chairperson; MI Teachers of Math; St Marys Church; Beta Sigma Phi; Mem the Apple Core; *office:* Deerfield HS 452 Deerfield Hwy Deerfield MI 49238

PARSONS, JAN MARIE, English Teacher; *b:* Polson, MT; *ed:* (BA) Ed/Home Ec, E WA Univ 1971; Puget Sound Writing Wkshp 1980; *cr:* Teacher Mason Jr HS 1971-80, Truman Jr HS 1980-89; Eng Teacher Stadium HS 1989-; *ai:* Stadium HS NHS Adv; Asst Drama Dir; Scorekeeper Var Girls Bsktbl Team; Ftbl Games Supervision; Sons of Norway 1984-; *office:* Stadium HS 111 North E Street Tacoma WA 98403

PARSONS, JANIS ANNETTE (MICKELSON), Fifth Grade Teacher; *b:* La Porte, IN; *m:* Kevin Kent; *c:* Sarah, Elizabeth; *ed:* (BS) Elem Ed, 1973, (MAE) Elem Ed, 1980 Ball St Univ; Multicultural Ed, IUPUI; Cmptr Ed, Warren Township; *cr:* Teacher Indianapolis Public Schls 1974-78, Warren Township Schls 1981-; *ai:* Cmptr Coord; GSA Leader; Sigma Delta Pi (Secy 1987-88) 1985-; IN Cmptr Educators 1987-; NEA, ISTA, WEA 1974-; IN St Readers Assn 1989-; *office:* Eastridge Elem Sch 10930 E 10th St Indianapolis IN 46229

PARSONS, PATRICIA MARIE, Science Teacher; *b:* Rahway, NJ; *m:* John H.; *c:* Sean A., Kathleen M.; *ed:* (BA) Soc Stud, 1972, (BS) Bus Admin, 1980 Caldwell Coll; (MA) Liberal Stud, Kean Coll 1990; Alatot Trng; *cr:* Teacher St John the Apostle 1968-73; Substitute Teacher Our Lady of Mt Carmel 1975-76; Teacher St John Vianney 1982-; *ai:* Drug Liaison Sch Diocese; NCEA 1982-; *office:* St John Vianney Sch 420 Inman Ave Colonia NJ 07067

PARTAIN, CYNTHIA, Assistant Professor; *b:* Elberton, GA; *ed:* (BA) Eng, Lander Coll 1986; (MED) Eng Ed, Univ of GA 1988; *cr:* Teacher Elbert Co Comp HS 1988-89; Asst Prof Lander Coll 1989-; *ai:* Annual Adv Eidolon 1988-; NCTE 1987-; Named Rotary Fnd Scholar; Attend Grad Sch Univ Sydney Australia; *office:* Lander Coll Humanities Dept Greenwood SC 29649

PARTIER, JOAN HANSEN, Fourth Grade Teacher; *b:* Oakland, CA; *m:* William Albert; *c:* Lauren, Leah; *ed:* (BS) Early Chldhd Ed, CA St Univ 1972; (MS) Curr & Instr, Unlv 1983; Further Training Lib Sci & Admin Sch Lib; *cr:* 5th and 6th Grade Teacher St Bedes Cath Sch 1973-75; 3rd Grade Teacher St Clements Cath Sch 1975-77; 4th Grade Teacher Laura Dearing Sch 1977-80; 4th Grade Teacher R Guild Gray Sch 1980-; *ai:* PEO Corresponding Sec 1990; Outstanding Elem Eng Teacher Southern NV Awarded By Southern MV Teachers Eng 1988; Nom Attend Excl in Ed Seminar Unlv Summer 1985.

PARTIN, JANE CARPENTER, Second Grade Teacher; *b:* Culpeper, VA; *m:* H. Le Roy; *c:* Pamela D., Donna L.; *ed:* (BS) Elem Ed, Madison Coll 1958; *cr:* 3rd/4th Grade Teacher Dumfries Elem Sch 1958-61; 3rd Grade Teacher Sycamore Park Elem Sch 1961-62, Greenbrier Elem Sch 1962-65; 2nd/3rd Grade Teacher Broadus Wood Elem Sch 1976-89; *ai:* Monticello Rdng Cncl Young Authors Contest Judge; NEA 1958-65; VA Educl Assn 1976-82; Local Educl Assns 1987-89; Spring Hill Baptist Church (Choir Dir 1971-83, Sunday Sch Teacher 1974-75, 1979-81); *home:* Rt 4 Box 281 Charlottesville VA 22901

PARTLOW, KATHLEEN LAWLER, His Dept Chair/Teacher; *b:* Lansing, MI; *m:* Fred; *c:* Daniel, Elizabeth, John; *ed:* (BA) His/ Sociology, Marquette Univ 1961-65; Grad Study in His; Trng for Certified Dyslexic Tutor; *cr:* Teacher Wells Jr HS 1965-67, Divine Savior HS 1967-69, St Gerard 1969-71, 1973-75, 1976-80, 1983-85, Jackson Cath Mid Sch 1971-73; His Teacher/Dept Chairperson Lansing Cath Cntrl 1982-83, 1985-; *ai:* Jr Class Moderator; Golf Asst; Girls His Dept & Academic Cncl Chairperson; NCEA 1967-; NEA 1965-67; Grand Ledge Cntry Club 1989-; Teacher of Yr Lansing Cath Cntrl 1987; Outstanding Educator Chamber of Commerce 1988, 1989; *office:* Lansing Cath HS 501 N Marshal Lansing MI 48912

PARTON, DANIEL RICHARD, Assistant Pastor/Bible Teacher; *b:* Harriman, TN; *m:* Robin Elizabeth Dukes; *c:* Jonathan D., Cynthia J., David P., Jack A.; *ed:* (BS) Pastoral Theology, Hyles-Anderson Coll 1979; *cr:* Asst Pastor Emmanuel Baptist Church 1979-80, 1st Baptist Church 1980-84, Lighthouse Baptist Church 1984-86, 2nd Baptist Church 1986-88, Berean Baptist Church & Acad 1988-; *ai:* Youth Choir Dir Sch & Church; Asst Pastor; Whos Who 1979; *office:* Berean Baptist Acad 751 W Maumee St Adrian MI 49221

PASARILLA, MICHAEL DAVID, Mathematics Department Teacher; *b:* New Brighton, PA; *m:* Linda A. Mc Auliffe; *c:* Paul M., Sarah R., Hannah C., Elizabeth G.; *ed:* (BS) Mechanical Engineering, Univ of OK 1981; Working on Masters of Divinity at Westminster Theological Seminary CA; *cr:* Naval Officer US Navy 1977-87; Math Teacher Covenant Chrstn Sch 1987-89, Santa Fe Chrstn Sch 1989-; *ai:* Bayview Orthodox Presbyn Church Ruling Elder 1985; Orthodox Presbyn Church Licentiate 1989.

PASCAL, FREDDIE JEAN (STEWART), 2nd Grade Teacher; *b:* Olive Branch, MS; *m:* Joe W.; *c:* Sharda, Simone; *ed:* (BA) Elem Ed, Lane Coll 1972; (MS) Elem Ed, Univ of IL Champaign Urbana 1976; *cr:* 1st Grade Teacher Collett Sch 1972-75, Northeast Sch 1975-86; 2nd Grade Teacher East Park Sch 1986; *ai:* 2nd Grade Unit Leader; Phi Delta Kappa 1985; Leadership Danville Class III 1988-89; East Park Sch Outstanding Teacher 1990; *office:* East Park Elem Sch 930 Colfax Danville IL 61832

PASCHAL, ADELE MAE, 6th Grade Science Teacher; *b:* Hannibal, MO; *m:* John W.; *c:* Jeanine, Regina, Zane; *ed:* (BS) Phys Ed, Quincy Coll 1966; Elem Cert NMSU; Hannibal La Grange Coll; Quincy Coll; Teaching Gifted , MO Univ; *cr:* Phys Ed Elem Teacher Payson Grade Sch 1966-67; Phys Ed 7th-12th Grade Teacher Palmyra HS 1967-68; Payson HS 1968-69; Phys Ed Elem Teacher Payson Grade Sch 1969;K-6th Grade Elem Teacher Hannibal Cath Schls 1975-80; 6th Grade Elem Teacher Cntrl Grade 1980-89; Hannibal Mid 1989-; *ai:* 6th Grade Young Astronaut Spon; Mid Sch Steering Comm; NEA VP 1981-83; MSTA 1985-; Sci Teachers 1988-; 4-H Club Horsemanship Club 1982-; Outstanding Project Leader 1984; Extension Club Secy/ Treas 1978-; Church Choir 1975-; Grant from MO Univ at Columbia for 6 Hr Course Teaching Gifted; *office:* Hannibal Mid Sch 4700 Mc Masters Hannibal MO 63401

PASCHAL, PATRICIA KORNEGAY, English/Literature Teacher; *b:* Warsaw, NC; *m:* Jerry Drew; *c:* Arthur G., Joan Paschal Mabry; *ed:* (BA) Elem Ed, High Point Coll 1960; (MA) Ed/Rdng, Appalachian St Univ 1976; *cr:* 4th Grade Teacher Chadbourn Sch 1960-61, Walnut Street Sch 1961-62; 6th Grade Teacher Pikeville Elem Sch 1962-67; 4th-6th Grade Teacher Goldsboro Mid Sch 1967-73; 8th Grade Eng Teacher Central Mid Sch 1973-; *ai:* Lang Art Chm; Tutor; Senate Bill II Comm; Oratorical Coach; NC Assn of Educators, NEA; Whiteville Womens Civic League (Secy, Treas, Intnl Chm); Alpha Delta Kappa (VP, Secy, Treas, Sargent at Arms); PTA; Southern Assn of Schls & Colls Evaluator; *office:* Central Mid Sch Memory St Whiteville NC 28472

PASQUINI, DAVID P., History Teacher; *b:* Hinsdale, IL; *m:* Susan Struven; *c:* Sarah; *ed:* (BA) His, 1971, (MA) His, 1977 Western IL Univ; Grad Stud Bradley Univ & De Paul Univ; *cr:* Teacher Peoria Height HS 1972-79, Glenbrook S HS 1979-; *ai:* Head Cross Cntry, Asst Track & Field Coach; Stud Cncl Adv; Sr Class Spon; IL Track & Cross Cntry Coaches Assn (Secy, All St Comm) 1982-; NCSS 1971-; Organization of Amer Historians 1987-; 20th IL Volunteer Infantry C W Re-Enactors, Northern IL Civil War Round Table 1987-; Civil War Society 1989-; Consultant Textbook With Scott Foresman Publisher; Teacher of Yr 1978; *office:* Glenbrook S HS 4000 W Lake Glenview IL 60025

PASS, LYNN THOMPSON, Special Education Resource; *b:* Birmingham, AL; *ed:* (BS) Eng/Spec Ed, Univ North AL 1978; (MA) Ed Learning Disabilities/Spec Ed/Eng Concentration, Univ AL 1989; Should Complete AA in Mild Learning Handicaps in Ed Field By Summer 1990 with Endorsement in Eng; *cr:* Teacher Cathedral Chrstn 1978-79; Eng Teacher Pinson Valley HS 1979; LD/EC Resource Teacher Emma Sansom HS/General Forrest Mid Sch 1979-; *ai:* Exceptional Child Spokesperson of Emma Sansom; Dept Head; Contact Person for Emma Sansom; Sigma Tau Delta 1977-; Kappa Delta Pi 1977-; Prof Assn of Gadsden Educators (Treas 1989-, Secy 1986-88); *office:* Emma Sansom H S 2210 W Meighan Blvd Gadsden AL 35904

PASS, SUSAN JEANETTE, PIB US History; *b:* Alameda, CA; *m:* Edward; *c:* Janette, Suzanne, Michael; *ed:* (MS) Ed, Western IL Univ 1986; (BS) Econ/His/Government/Ger, Georgetown Univ 1966; His WWII Univ of Haifa Israel 1987; *cr:* Teacher Washington Mid Sch 1982-86; I B Teacher Bellaire HS 1986-; *ai:* Swimming & Diving Team Coach; Charter Founder & Adv Jr Historians; Adv Natl His Fair; Houston Cncl of Soc Stud Educators 1987-; Houston Cncl of Educators 1987-; Chrstn Doctrine 1988-; Right to Life Comm 1987-; Fellowship HCJHS to Study WWII Univ of Haifa 1987; Outstanding Educ ator Houston Bus Cmmty 1980; Woodrow Wilson Fellowship 1st Alternate 1989; HBCEE Mini Grant Competition Winner 1990; *office:* Bellaire Sr H S 5100 Maple St Bellaire TX 77025

PASSANETE, CARL JESS, Jr High Counselor; *b:* Pueblo, CO; *m:* Denise L. Atkinson; *c:* Chace, Merrick; *ed:* (BA) Phys Ed, CO St Coll 1965; (MA) Psych/Counseling/Guidance, 1970, (EDS) Sch Psych, Univ of N CO 1971; *cr:* 5th Grade Teacher St Francis Sch Dist 1965-66, Englewood Public Sch Dist 1966-69; Sch Psychologist 1971-87, Sch Counselor 1990 Colorado Springs Sch Dist 11; *ai:* PRIDE Team Dir; Leadership Conference Co-Dir; CO Society of Sch Psychologists 1973-86; Colorado Springs Ed Assn 1989-; Colorado Springs Racquet Club (Pres 1985) 1973-87; Natl Assn St Bds of Ed Federal Grant; *office:* Sabin Jr HS 3605 N Carefree Cir Colorado Springs CO 80917

PASSARELLI, AGNES MARY, First Grade Teacher; *b:* Detroit, MI; *ed:* (BA) Math, Marygrove Coll 1970; (MA) Elem Ed, Wayne St Univ 1976; *cr:* Teacher St David Sch 1970-80; 1st-3rd Grade Teacher/Sch Librarian St Veronica Sch 1980-; *ai:* Primary Division & Mission Prgm Coord; Private Tutor Math & Rdng; NCEA Mem; Poem Published 1988; *office:* St Veronica Sch 21450 Universal Dr East Detroit MI 48021

PASSINO, JUNE M. (SPRAY), 5th Grade Teacher; *b:* Cheboygan, MI; *m:* Robert R.; *c:* Larry R.; *ed:* (BS) Eng/Math, 1966; Rdng, 1970 Cntrl MI Univ; Rdng Specialist-Chapter I Coord; *cr:* Elem Teacher Cheboygan Pub Schls 1950-66; Jr HS Teacher Pellston Jr HS 1966-72; Rdng Consultant 1972-75, Elem Mid Sch Teacher 1976- Pellston Public Schls; *ai:* Soph Class Adv; Rdng Comm; PTO Adv-Teacher; Pellston Teachers Assn Secy; Delta Kappa Gamma Treas; Cheboygan Lib Building Chm; Meth Church Teacher; Schlsps for Former Stu Nursing Field/Teaching Coll; *office:* Pellston Mid Sch Zipf St Pellston MI 49769

PASTERNACK, BONNIE GREENWALD, Fourth Grade Teacher; *b:* Passaic, NJ; *m:* Joel; *c:* Amy D.; *ed:* (BS) Elem Ed, Univ of CT 1973; *cr:* 4th Grade Teacher Abington Avenue Sch 1973-; *ai:* YM-YWHA Bd of Dir; *office:* Abington Avenue Sch 209 Abington Ave Newark NJ 07107

PASTOR, JUNE L., Spanish Teacher; *b:* Pittsburgh, PA; *m:* J. Ricardo; *ed:* Diplome Fr Lit, Universite D'aix-En-Provenee France 1970; (BA) Fr/Span, Bethany Coll 1972; (MA) Fr, WV Univ 1974; Bi-ling/Bicultural Endorsement; *cr:* Fr Teacher Springfield City Schls 1976-77; Fr/Span/Bi-ling Teacher Carrollton HS 1978-; *ai:* Travel Abroad Leader; Lang Club Spon; Lang Day Competition Coach; Teachers for Academic Excl Mem; Honors Banquet & Schlshp Selection Comms; Saginaw Valley Foreign Lang Teachers Assn 1979-83; AATF 1980; Amer Assn of Teachers of Span & Portugese; Articles Published; *office:* Carrollton HS 1235 Mapleridge Rd Saginaw MI 48603

PASZTOR, WILLIAM MICHAEL, JR., Adapted Phys Ed Specialist; *b:* Toledo, OH; *m:* Jane E.; *c:* Melissa, Melinda; *ed:* (BS) Ed, 1970, (MS) Ed, 1990 Univ of Toledo; *cr:* Phys Ed Instr Wynn Elem 1970-89; Adapted Phys Ed Specialist Oregon City Schls 1989-; *ai:* St Stephens Girls Vlbl & Bsktbl 1988-89, 1989-; St Stephen Sch VP Sch Bd 1989-; E Center for Cmmty Mental Health Bd (VP 1988, Pres 1989-); Oregonian Club 1990; Birmingham Hall of Fame Bd Mem 1988-; Birmingham Hall of Fame Athletic & Civic Achievement 1988; *office:* Oregon City Schls 5721 Seaman Rd Oregon OH 43616

PATACH, RICHARD CHARLES, Physics Teacher; *b:* Boston, MA; *ed:* (BSME) Mechanical Engineering, Northeastern Univ 1965; (MST) Physics, Univ of WI 1970; (MNS) Physics, Univ of SD 1975; ID St Univ Pocatello, Univ of WA Seattle; NSF Academic Yr Univ of WI 1969-70; NSF Summer Inst Univ of WA 1968; Sabatical Leave Univ of SD 1974-75; *cr:* Physics Teacher Holliston HS 1965-67; Physics/Math Teacher Salem HS 1967-83; Physics Teacher Marblehead HS 1983-; *ai:* Sigma Pi Sigma Treas 1970-; Northshore Physics Teachers 1965-; *office:* Marblehead HS Duncan Sleigh Sq Marblehead MA 01945

PATANE, SAMUEL VINCENT, Social Studies Teacher; *b:* Futon, NY; *m:* Valerie J.; *c:* David S., Michael M.; *ed:* (BS) Scndry Ed, 1968; Scndry Ed 1970 SUNY Oswego; Grad Courses SUNY Oswego; NYS Cert Hunter Safety Instr; *cr:* Soc Stud Teacher Hannibal Cntrl Sch 1969-; *ai:* Adv Class 1991-93; Mem Dist Adv Organization; Mem Adv Organization; Mem Negotiations Team Grievance Chm; NYS United Teachers 1969-; Oswego Cty Teachers Assn Treas 1985-; Hannibal Faculty Assn 1969-; Elks 1981-; Natl Rifle Assn 1969-; Past Pres Hannibal Central Sch Credit Union; 2nd VP Hannibal Faculty Assn 1976-77; Pres Hannibal Faculty Assn 1977-; Hannibal HS Teacher Yr 1979-83; *home:* Rd 2 Box 378 Hannibal NY 13074

PATCH, LORRAINE SHOEMAKER, Fourth Grade Teacher; *b:* Johnson City, NY; *m:* Philby O.; *c:* Valerie Huggins, Bransen, Kevin; *ed:* (BS) Ed, Eastern Nazarene Coll 1964; Grad Work SUNY Binghamton; *cr:* Teacher Johnson City Sch Dist Harry L Johnson Sch 1964-; *ai:* Odyssey of the Mind Team Coach 1986-88; Accompany on Piano Chorus & Orchestra Harry L Johnson Sch; NEA, NY St Teachers Assn 1964-; Johnson City Teachers Assn Mem Bd of Dirs; Johnson City PTA Lifetime Membership 1972; Valleyview Alliance Church (Mem, Chairperson, Music Comm) 1975-; Johnson City PTA Treas 1977-79; Pictured in Family Circle Feature Article; *home:* 184 Deyo Hill Rd RD 5 Binghamton NY 13905

PATE, JAMES EDWARD, Mathematics Dept Chair; *b:* Orange, CA; *m:* Karen Susan Mc Auley; *c:* Eric J., Matthew W.; *ed:* (BA) Chem, Pomona Coll 1961; (MED) Ed, Whittier Coll 1963; (MS) Chem, Cornell Univ 1966; Numerous Univ; *cr:* Teacher Los Altos HS 1961-65; Teacher/Math Chairperson Glen A Wilson HS 1966-; *ai:* Faculty Chm Sch Accreditation Comm; Mentor Teacher; NHS Spon; CA Math Cncl, NCTM; Faculty Assn Treas; Outstanding Math Teacher Sigma XI Club; Outstanding Teacher Inst for Advancement of Eng; NSF Grants 1965-66, 1969, 1970, 1978, 1985; Presenter Mariana Islands Math Inst; *office:* Glen A Wilson HS 16455 Wedgeworth Dr Hacienda Heights CA 91745

PATE, NAN R., History Department Chair; *b:* Anniston, AL; *m:* Benjamin Sanford Jr.; *ed:* (BS) Ed, 1967, (MED) Ed, 1968 Auburn Univ; *cr:* Teacher Jordan HS 1968-70; Teacher/Dept Chairperson Brookstone Sch 1970-; *ai:* Stu Government, Harvard Model Congress, Brookstore Leadership Forum Adv; Frosh Class Spon; GA Assn of Ind Schls Outstanding Teacher 1974; Natl Assn Soc Stud Teachers, GA Soc Stud Cncl; AP Amer Government Grader 1990; GA St STAR Teacher 1989-; Runner-up Page One Teacher of Yr 1988-89; Natl Mock Trial Team Competitions 1989, 1990; GA Championship Mock Trial Team 1989, 1990; *office:* Brookstone Sch 440 Bradley Park Dr Columbus GA 31995

PATE, PAMELA, French/English Teacher; *b:* Camp Pendleton, CA; *ed:* (BA) Art His, Rice Univ 1985; *cr:* Eng/Fr Teacher Bellaire HS 1985-87; Teaching Asst Coll Marcel Aymard Millau France 1987-88; Eng/Fr Teacher San Marcos HS 1988-; *ai:* Fr Club Spon; Gifted & Talented Comm; TX Teachers of Foreign Lang 1988-; Awarded Teaching Assistantship by Fr Government; Participated in Study of Fr Lang & Culture in Fr Antilles; *office:* San Marcos HS 1301 State Highway 123 San Marcos TX 78666

PATE, STEVE C., Teacher of Gifted; *b:* Columbus, GA; *m:* Brenda Mixon; *ed:* (BA) Elem Ed, 1977, (MS) Mid Grades, 1983 Columbus Coll; Gifted Ed, Univ of CT, Columbus Coll; *cr:* 4th Grade Teacher 1977-82; 5th Grade Teacher 1982-87; Triad/Gifted Teacher Muscogee Cty Sch Dist 1987-; *office:* Muscogee Cty Sch Dist Edgewood 3835 Forest Rd Columbus GA 31907

PATEL, MANU V., Physics Teacher; *b:* Jhalod, India; *m:* Shashi; *c:* Sonna, Rupa; *ed:* (BS) Physics, 1955, (BED) Sci/Math Ed, 1958 Gujarat Univ India; (MED) Sci Ed, M S Univ India 1960; (MS) Physics, 1970, (PHD) Physics, 1975 Univ of CT; *cr:* Grad Asst Univ of CT 1969-75; Physics Teacher T C Williams HS 1976-; *ai:* Coll Bd/ETS; Advanced Placement Phyics Exam Dev Comm; AAPT Comm on Minorities in Physics Ed; ETS, SAT, ACH Test Center Chief Supv; Advanced Placement Physics Coll Bd Exam Reader & Teachers Wkshp Consultant; AAPT 1970-; PTRA Mem 1985; Fulbright Exch Scholar 1965-66: Nom Presidential Awd Excl In Sci Teaching 1988-; Nom Washington Post Agnes Meyers Awd for Excl in Teaching 1990; *office:* T C Williams HS 3330 King St Alexandria VA 22302

PATELLA, MARIE R., English & Foreign Lang Teacher; *b:* Bronx, NY; *ed:* (BA) Eng, Caldwell Coll 1962; (MA) Philosophy, St Johns Univ 1964; Grad Stud; *cr:* Eng Teacher 1965-, Supvr of Eng & Foreign Lang 1983- Hawthorne HS; *ai:* Sch Play Dir; NCTE, ASCD, Prins & Supvrs Assn; Articles Published; *home:* 92 Lowell Rd Glen Rock NJ 07452

PATEREK, PAMELA SIGLOCH, US History/English Teacher; *b:* Elizabeth, NJ; *m:* Raymond R.; *c:* Elizabeth M.; *ed:* (BA) Soc Stud/Scndry Ed, Kean Coll 1972; Sci, Astronomy, Chem, Physics I 1978-80; *cr:* 7th/8th Grade Teacher 1974-, Soc Stud/Sci Teacher 1974-80, Soc Stud/Eng Teacher 1980 St Mary of the Assumption Elem; *ai:* Patrols, Stu Cncl, Class Plays, 8th Grade Class Yrbk Fund Raisers & Party Adv; Roselle Ambulance Corps 1973-80, 5 Pt EMT; St Marys Elem Evaluation Self Study Chairperson 1979; *office:* St Mary of Assumption Elem Sch 237 S Broad St Elizabeth NJ 07202

PATERRA, JANE FERGUSON, Language Art Teacher/Dept Head; *b:* Ft Dodge, IA; *m:* Dominic V.; *c:* Dominic V. G., Angeli H. V.; *ed:* (BS) Eng, Ball St Univ 1967; Bi-ling/ESL/SSL, Oakland Univ 1968; (MA) Ed MACT, MI St Univ 1977; *cr:* Advanced Lang Art/Journalism Teacher/Dept Chairperson Pontiac City Schls 1967-; *ai:* Newspaper & Yrbk Spon; Sch & Dist Speech Coord; NCTE, Phi Kappa Phi, Delta Kappa Gamma; MI Ed Assn, Pontiac Ed Assn 1967-; Lioness of Pontiac; Newsweek WDIV Jr HS Teacher of Yr Oakland Cty 1989; Scndry Educator of Month 1979, 1986; Outstanding Leaders in Elem & Scndry Ed 1974-76; *office:* Abraham Lincoln Jr HS 131 Hillside Dr Pontiac MI 48058

PATIL, ERNEST LOUIS, Retired Elementary Teacher; *b:* Sutersville, PA; *m:* Lavaun Smith; *c:* Louis, Kim; *ed:* (BS) Span Sci, IN St Teacher Coll 1951; (MED) Elem Ed, Univ of Pittsburgh 1956; *cr:* Elem Teacher Elizabeth Forward Sch System 1954-57, Fl Sch System Dade Cty 1957-73; *home:* 420 Industry Rd Buena Vista PA 15018

PATIN, KEITH JAMES, 8th Grade Soc Stud Teacher; *b:* Lafayette, LA; *m:* Cynthia Ann; *c:* Leah; *ed:* (BA) Scndry Soc Stud 1974, (MED) Scndry Soc Stud, 1976 Univ S LA; Grad of Ed for Living Seminars; *cr:* Teacher Lafayette Mid Sch 1974-; *ai:* Stu Cncl Spon; SACS Liason; Soc Stud Dept Chm; Phi Delta Kappa Treas 1978-80; St Edmonds Finance Comm 1988-; St Edmonds New Building Chm 1988-; *office:* Lafayette Mid Sch 1301 W University Ave Lafayette LA 70506

PATITZ, IVA M. (WRIGHT), Kindergarten/Chapter I Reading; *b:* Central City, NE; *m:* K D; *c:* Carolyn Newton, Kathy Smith, Jan Bolin; *ed:* (AA) Elem Ed, CO Womans Coll 1951, (BA) Kearney St Coll 1970; Elem Ed, Kearney St Coll; *cr:* 3rd/4th Grade Teacher Bloomfield Public Sch 1951-52; Kndgtn Teacher Bassett Public Sch 1955-58; Kndgtn/Reading Teacher 1966 Mc Cool Jct Public Sch; *ai:* NSEA 1951-; MEA Pres Sec Negotiator 1966-; Alpha Delta Kappa Sec Historian 1981-; Amer Legion Aux 1966-; Meth Women 1966-; Jobs Daughters Cncl Sociability Hospitality 1974-79; Outstanding Educator of Yr 1987-88; *office:* Mc Cool Jct Public Sch 209 S 2nd Mc Cool Junction NE 68401

PATNAUD, MARY CHISHOLM, Language Arts Teacher; *b:* Asheboro, NC; *m:* William J.; *c:* William Jr.; *ed:* (BA) Elem Ed, Univ of NC Greensboro 1960; (MED) Ed, Univ of NC Chapel Hill 1966; *cr:* Elem Teacher Fairfax Cty Schls 1960-65, 1966-71; Lang Art Teacher Greensboro City Schls 1971-; *ai:* Lang Art Dept Chm; NEA 1960-; NCAE 1971-; *office:* Aycock Mid Sch 811 Cypress St Greensboro NC 27405

PATOSKY, EDWARD JOSEPH, 6th Grade Sci & Math Teacher; *b:* Latrobe, PA; *m:* Linda Lee Smith; *c:* Michael, John; *ed:* (BA) Elem Ed, Clarion Univ 1979; (MS) Curr Instruction, DE St 1989; *cr:* 5th/6th Grade Teacher Welch Elem 1979-89; 6th Grade Teacher Dover AFB Jr HS 1989-; *ai:* Math League & At Risk Prgm Coach; Safety Patrol Supvr; Caesar Rodney Ed Assn Building Rep Lifetime Membership 1988; *office:* Dover Air Force Base Jr HS Hawthorne Dr Dover DE 19901

PATREI, GREGORY L., Mathematics Teacher; *b:* Ilion, NY; *m:* Karen Mac Gregor; *c:* Laurie; *ed:* (BS) Math Ed, SUNY Cortland 1969; (MS) Math Ed, SUNY Albany 1973; *cr:* Math Teacher Saratoga Springs HS 1969-; *ai:* Saratoga Springs Teachers Assn 1969-; Blooming Grove Nursery Sch Registrar 1988-; Golub Fnd Scholar Recognition Outstanding Teacher Recipient 1988-89; *office:* Saratoga Springs HS W Circular St Saratoga Springs NY 12866

PATRICK, CAROL CROSBY, First Grade Teacher; *b:* Tampa, FL; *ed:* (BA) His, Agnes Scott Coll 1970; (MED) Early Chldhd Ed, Univ of GA 1973; *cr:* Teacher Ila Kndgtn 1970-73; 1st Grade Teacher 30th Avenue Elem 1973-74, Clubview Elem 1974-; *ai:* Kappa Delta Pi 1973; Delta Kappa Gamma 1985-; Prof Assn of GA Educators; St Luke United Meth Church Various Offices; Clubview PTA Exec Bd; Chapter II St Advisory Comm 1983-; St Bd Drug Abuse Resistance Ed; *office:* Clubview Elem Sch 2836 Edgewood Rd Columbus GA 31906

PATRICK, CECELIA CELESTE, Science Teacher; *b:* Jackson, TN; *ed:* (BS) Bio/Scndry Ed, Univ TN at Martin 1982; (MS) Admin, Trevecca 1988; *cr:* 7th Grade Sci Teacher Riverdale 1982-; *ai:* Natl Jr Beta Club Spon; NEA; Shelby Cty Ed Assn 1982-; TN Ed Assn 1982-; Delta Sigma Theta; *office:* River Dale Elem Sch 7391 Nashoba Rd Germantown TN 38138

PATRICK, HENRY ALLEN, Marketing Education Teacher; *b:* Paintsville, KY; *m:* Elwanda Stambaugh; *c:* Brent; *ed:* (BS) Bus, 1969, Ed, Morehead St Univ; Marketing Block Univ of KY; *cr:* Bus/Marketing Ed Teacher Johnson Cntrl 1975-; *ai:* DECA Adv; *home:* PO Box 23 Wittensville KY 41274

PATRICK, JOYCE ELAINE (KARGER), Business Teacher; *b:* Parkers Prairie, MN; *m:* Cecil; *ed:* (BS) Bus Ed, Moorhead St Coll 1966; (MA) Bus Ed, W MI Univ 1972; Cmptr Instruction, E MI Univ, Albion Coll, W MI Univ; *cr:* Bus Teacher Albion Adult Ed, Albion Sr HS 1966-; *ai:* Bus Dept Chm 1973-76, 1982-; Attendance, Home Sch Relations Comms 1988-; Albion Bus Club Adv 1984-86; NBEA 1989-; NEA 1966-; MI Ed Assn 1966-; Albion Ed Assn Secy 1966-; ASCD 1990; Natl Appleworks Users Group 1989-; *office:* Albion Sr HS 225 Watson St Albion MI 49224

PATRICK, SANDRA F., 5th Grade Teacher; *b:* Corpus Christi, TX; *m:* Steve; *c:* Stephen C., Matthew B.; *ed:* (BA) Elem Ed, Univ of AL 1981; (MS) Elem Ed, AL A&M Univ 1988; *cr:* 5th Grade Teacher Page Elem 1981-; *ai:* Spon Young Astronaut Club 5th Graders; *home:* 3215 Scenic Dr Scottsboro AL 35768

PATRICK, SUZANNE T. (ROBINSON), Mathematics Teacher; *b:* Glen Cove, NY; *m:* Roderick D.; *c:* Michael, Steven, Cathy Freer; *ed:* (BA) Math, Ladycliff Coll 1957; (MA) Math, Manhattan Coll 1967; Hunter Coll, NY Univ, Univ of N CO; *cr:* Teacher St Josephs 1959-63, St Josephs 1963-67; Instr Ladycliff Coll 1967-70; Teacher St Josephs 1970-71; Teacher/Dept Chairperson Onteora Cntrl 1971-83; Dist Coord Greeley Cty 1983-85; Teacher Greeley Cntrl 1985-; *ai:* Math Assn of America 1959-; NCTM 1963-; ASCD; Alpha Delta Kappa Treas; BPOE Does Jr Cnslr 1983-; *office:* Greeley Cntrl HS 1515 14th Ave Greeley CO 80631

PATRIDGE, CAROLYN H., Remedial Math/Lab Teacher; *b:* Newberry, SC; *m:* Robert P.; *c:* Leslie, Christie; *ed:* (AB) Elem Ed, Newberry Coll 1970; *cr:* Spec Ed Teacher Whitten Center 1970-77; Cnslr Newberry Cty Family Court 1979-84; Teacher Whitmire HS 1984-; *ai:* Sr Class Spon; Stu Cncl Adv; NEA 1988-; *office:* Whitmire HS 1400 Coleman Ave Whitmire SC 29178

PATTERSON, ANN HESTER, Office Technology Teacher; *b:* Shelbyville, TN; *m:* Fred L.; *c:* Coby, Tami, Brittany; *ed:* (BS) Bus Ed, 1971, (MED) Curr/Instruction, 1973, (MED) Admin/ Supervision, 1984 Mid TN St Univ; Grad Stud Eng, Ed; *cr:* Office Technology Teacher Spotg Lowe Voc Center & Marshall Cty HS 1971-; *ai:* Bus Profs of America & Stu Cncl Adv; Soph Class Spon; Delta Pi Epsilon Charter Mem 1979-; Phi Delta Kappa 1978-; Daughters of Amer Revolution 1981-; Outstanding Young Women of America 1984; TN Career Ladder Level III; *office:* Spot Lowe Voc Center 1771 Old Columbia Rd Lewisburg TN 37091

PATTERSON, BEVERLY MAY, Fifth Grade Teacher; *b:* Beaver Falls, PA; *ed:* (BSED) Elem Ed, Geneva Coll 1970; (MSED) Spec Ed, Duquesne Univ 1974; Elem Prin Cert, Univ of PA; *cr:* Kndgtn Teacher La Croft Kndgtn 1970-78; 5th Grade Teacher Westgate Elem 1978-; *ai:* Camp Fitch Coord; St Judes Math-A-Thon, Spelling Bee, Right to Read C hm; Alpha Delta Kappa (Historian, Budget Chm) 1987-; *office:* Westgate Elem Sch 810 W 8th St East Liverpool OH 43920

PATTERSON, BONNIE HOOVER, 6th/7th Language Arts Teacher; *b:* Woodbury, TN; *m:* Eddie; *c:* Megan, Clint; *ed:* (BS) Elem Ed, Mid TN St Univ 1981; Working Towards Masters in Guidance & Counseling; *cr:* 4th Grade Teacher 1981-84, 6th Grade Lang Art Teacher 1984-87, 6th Grade Teacher 1987-89, 6th-7th Grade Lang Art Teacher 1989- Woodbury Grammar; *ai:* Girls Bsktbl Coach; 4-H Spon; Inservice Comm; Post Cannon Cty Teaching Assn Pres; Just Say No, Fellowship Chrstn Athletics Spon; Cannon Cty Ed Assn (Pres 1987-88, Faculty Rep 1984-86, Pres Elect 1986-87), Teacher of Yr 1989-; Cannon Cty Elem Coach of Yr 1984-87; *office:* Woodbury Grammar Sch 500 E Colonial St Woodbury TN 37190

PATTERSON, BRENDA VANCE, Jr HS Mathematics Teacher; *b:* Forrest, MS; *m:* Glenn; *c:* Shannon, Dawn, Matthew; *ed:* (BS) Elem Ed, 1982, (MED) Elem Ed, 1986 Univ of S MS; *cr:* Math Teacher Sumrall Jr HS 1982-; *ai:* Stu Cncl Adv; Mathcounts & MCTM Spon; Delta Kappa Gamma 1985-; MS Assn of Educators Secy 1987-; Teacher of Yr Sumrall Jr HS 1987-88; *office:* Sumrall HS Center Ave Sumrall MS 39482

PATTERSON, CINDY LOU, Foreign Language Teacher; *b:* Ashtabula, OH; *ed:* (BS) Early Chldhd Ed, 1984, (BS) Elem Ed, 1985 Kent St Univ; (BS) Spec Ed, UT St Univ 1985; Grad Courses Rdng; *cr:* Substitute Teacher Jefferson Local Schls 1984-85; Learning Disabilities Tutor 1985-87, Math/Rdng Teacher 1986-87, Foreign Lang/Rdng Teacher 1987- Wallace Braden Jr HS; *ai:* Amer Field Service; Braden Jr HS, 9th Grade Cheerleading Adv; HS Girls Track Asst Coach; Buckeye Ed Assn Building Rep 1988-; OH Ed Assn 1986-; Prin Advisory Comm Mem 1988-; Curr Dev Comm Ashtabula Cty Schls in Foreign Lang 1990; *office:* Wallace Braden Jr HS 3436 Edgewood Dr Ashtabula OH 44004

PATTERSON, CONSTANCE LEE, Scndry English/Drama Teacher; *b:* Lodi, CA; *ed:* (BA) Theatre Art, Univ of CO Boulder 1986; *cr:* Talented & Gifted Prgm Coord Casey Jr HS 1985-86; Drama/Eng Teacher Excelsior Youth Center 1987; Eng/Novels/ Drama Teacher Crane Jr HS 1987-; *ai:* Drama Spon; Yrbk Spon 1987-89; Crane Ed Assn, AZ Ed Assn, NEA Mem 1987-; NCTE 1987-89; PTA (Teacher Liason, Prgm Dir); Writer & Dir of Play; Outstanding Young Women of Yr 1987; *office:* Crane Jr HS 4480 W 32nd St Yuma AZ 85364

PATTERSON, CYNTHIA S., Teacher of the Gifted K-5; *b:* Onatrio, CA; *c:* Justin; *ed:* (BA) Elem Ed, Univ of AZ 1969; (MA) Ed, GA St Univ 1982; Advncd Trng Gftd Ed; *cr:* 1st Yr Teacher Los Ninos 1969-71; 5th Yr Teacher Fair Oaks 1972-80; Teacher Gifted K-5th Kings Springs Elem 1980-; *ai:* Asst Dir Aftersch Pgrm; Dir Kids Kapers; Art Rep; Citizens Advisory Comm; Discipline Comm; Crisis Intervention Team; Dir KS-TV Stu Video Production; NEA/AAE/SSAE 1969-71; 1972-78; 1983-89 NEA/ GAE/CCAE; Madd; Wrld Wldlf Fed 1979; Just Say No Cncl 1988; PTA Schlsp Awarded in My Name 1987; *office:* King Springs Elem-Cobb Co 1041 Reed Rd Smyrna GA 30082

PATTERSON, ELLEN CLAY, Math Department Chairperson; *b:* Boaz, AL; *m:* Frank Edwin; *c:* Ginger Anne Cooper; *ed:* (BS) Math, Scndry Ed, 1969, (MS) Math, Scndry Ed, 1976 Jacksonville St Univ; *cr:* Math/Eng Teacher Douglas HS 1969-72; Math Teacher Sardis HS 1972-; *ai:* Sr Class Spon; Mu Alpha Theta Co-Spon; Math Team Co-Spon; NEA 1969- Outstanding AL Kappa 1988; AEA 1969-; EEA 1969-; Kappa Kappa Iota (St Pres 1986-88 Pres-Elect 1984-86 Treas 1980-84); Band Parents (Treas) 1982-86; Parent-Teacher Stu Assn 1969-; Sardis HS Teacher of Yr 1988; *office:* Sardis H S Route 5 Box 269 Boaz AL 35957

PATTERSON, GENEVA NERO, Middle School Librarian; *b:* Greenwood, MS; *m:* Eugene; *c:* Susan, Traci Patterson Cook, Darryl (dec), Kevin; *ed:* (BS) Elem Ed, Dist of Columbia Teachers Coll 1956; (MS) Ed, IN Univ Bloomington 1961; (AAA) Lib Sci, Univ of S MS 1971; *cr:* Teacher Mc Laurin Street Elem Sch 1958-60; Librarian S Pike Mid Sch 1960-; *ai:* S Pike MId Sch Lib Club Spon; Public Speaking & Creative Writing Skills Supervisor & Coach; NEA, S Pike Assn Educators; MS Lib Assn, Intnl Rdng Assn, McComb-Pike Rdng Assn Corresponding Secy, Lillie Mae Bryant Federated Club Project Comm; Magnolia Lib Bd (Volunteer for Mental Health, Chm, Burn Center Chm, Heart); Pike County Democrative Exec Comm Secy; 4-H & Cmmty Dev Leader; Den Mother; MS Federated Girls Outstanding Work Awd, Dist 5 Club Women 1987; Public Speaking Awd; *home:* PO Box 374 Magnolia MS 39652

PATTERSON, JANICE WHITLAW, Chemistry Teacher; *b:* Augusta, GA; *m:* Truett Clifton; *c:* Sharon A. Patterson Meade, Carole L. Patterson Churchman; *ed:* (BS) Bio, Furman Univ 1959; Teacher Cert Scndry Sci, Carson Newman Coll 1980; (MS) Curr/ Instruction, Univ of TN Knoxville 1986; *cr:* Teachers Aide 1972-79, Teacher 1980- Jefferson Cty Bd of Ed; *ai:* Jefferson Cty HS Faculty Adv; Jefferson Cty HS Key Club Spon; NEA, TN Ed Assn 1980-; Jefferson Cty Ed Assn Negotiating Team 1980-, Outstanding Educator Awd 1985-86; NSTA 1986-; 1st Baptist Church Mem 1964-; Adult Ensemble Mem 1987-; Outstanding Faculty Adv 1989: *office:* Jefferson Cty HS R R 5 Box 385 Dandridge TN 37725

PATTERSON, JERALD WRAY, Health/Soc Stud/PE Teacher; *b:* Hemingway, SC; *ed:* (BS) Ed/Phys Ed Health, USC Columbia 1978; Cert in Psych, Soc Stud, Driver Ed; Working Masters Counseling; *cr:* Teacher-Coach R H Fulmer Mid Sch 1978-; *ai:* Bsktbl, Track Coach; Palmetto St Teachers Assn.

PATTERSON, JO TROXELL, Mathematics Department Chm; *b:* Forrest City, AR; *m:* William Glenn; *c:* Cara, Erin; *ed:* (BS) Math, MS St Univ 1974; Working on Masters AR St Univ Jonesboro; *cr:* Math Teacher Starkville MS 1975, Nathan Bedford Forrest Acad 1975-78; Math Dept Chm Palestine HS 1978-81, Lee Acad 1989-; *ai:* Soph Class Spon; Phi Kappa Phi 1974-82; Forrest City Jr Auxiliary Pres 1986-87, Service Awd, Best JA 1987; *home:* 151 Richmond Terr Forrest City AR 72335

PATTERSON, JOYCE ANN, Tenth Grade English Teacher; *b:* Ashland, AL; *ed:* (BS) His/Eng, 1959, (MS) Scndry Ed, 1970, (AA) Scndry Ed, 1978 Jacksonville St Univ; *cr:* Teacher Salter Elem Sch 1959-73, Ellis Jr HS 1973-89, Talladega HS 1989-; Part-time Instr Southern Union Jr Coll; *ai:* Talladega Schls Scndry Teacher of Yr 1989; Pilot Club Teacher of Yr 1985; Chm Curr Review Comm; Talladega Ed Assn, AL Ed Assn, NEA 1959-;

Delta Kappa Gamma, Secy; Friends of Lib; Historical Society Bd Mem; *office:* Talladega HS 1177 Mc Millan St Talladega AL 35160

PATTERSON, JOYCE BEATRICE, 2nd Grade Teacher; *b:* Boston, MA; *ed:* (BS) Ed, Boston St Coll 1968; (MED) Ed, Cambridge Coll 1989; Whole Lang Literacy Inst Lesley Coll; *cr:* 1st Grade Teacher 1968-73, 2nd Grade Teacher 1973, Co-Head Primary Dept/Teacher 1989- Longfellow Sch; *ai:* Sch Maintenance, Writing Project Steering Comms; Whole Lang Teachers Assn Mem 1989-; NCTE 1990; Horace Mann Grant 1987; M Bingham Charitable Trust Grant 1988-; *office:* Longfellow Sch 359 Broadway Cambridge MA 02139

PATTERSON, JOYCE T., Third Grade Teacher; *b:* W Warwick, RI; *c:* Tracy R., Kerry M.; *ed:* (BS) Elem Ed, St Johns Univ 1964; *cr:* Kndgtn Teacher Anna S Kuhl Sch 1964-65; Substitute Teacher Nanuet Public Sch 1977-79; 3rd Grade Teacher Anna S Kuhl Sch 1979-; *ai:* Math Comm; NY St Teachers Assn 1979-; Preservation of Erie Depot Calligrapher 1988; *office:* Anna S Kuhl Elem Sch Rt 209 Port Jervis NY 12771

PATTERSON, KATHERINE BEAM, Fourth Grade Teacher; *b:* Shelby, NC; *m:* William Thomas; *c:* William T., Katherine Beam, James A.; *ed:* (BA) Elem Ed, Univ of NC Greensboro 1962; (MA) Rdng/Lang Art Ed, ASU 1976; *cr:* 6th Grade Teacher Victory Sch 1962; Marion Sch & Oak Sch 1962-69; 8th Grade Teacher Kings Mountain Jr HS 1970; 4th Grade Teacher James Love Sch 1970-71; Teacher Country Club Circle Kndgtn 1971-72; 2nd/3rd Grade Combination Teacher 1972-73, 4th Grade Teacher 1973- Fallston Elem; *ai:* St Textbook Adoption, Sci, Eng, Calendar Comm; NEA 1962-; NCEA (Shelby City Rep 1963-64, 1966-67, Clev Cty Rep 1973-74) 1962-; IRA Secy 1965-; AAUW (Corresponding Secy, Secy 1966) 1964-68; Lionette Club 1968-71; Amer Bus Women Assn 1969-71; Taught 1st Class at Cleveland Comm Coll of Adults to Read & Write; *home:* 217 Gold St Shelby NC 28150

PATTERSON, KIMBERLY KAY, Jr High Physical Ed Teacher; *b:* Canton, IL; *ed:* (BS) Phys Ed, Western IL Univ 1984; *cr:* Jr HS Phys Ed Teacher Ingersoll Sch 1984-; *ai:* Jv & Varsity Vlybl Coach; Varsity Girls Bstkbl Coach; IAHPERD 1988-; Womens Bsktbl Coaching Assn 1984-; *office:* Ingersoll Sch 1605 E Ash Canton IL 61520

PATTERSON, L. RUTH, Mathematics Department Teacher; *b:* Provo, UT; *m:* Greg Sulik; *ed:* (AS) General, UT Tech Coll 1982; (BA) Phys Ed, UT St Univ 1984; Math Endorsement; *cr:* Phys Ed/Health/Sci Teacher Roosevelt HS 1985-86; Math Teacher Hillcrest Jr HS 1986-; *ai:* Math Counts Team; Math Week; Spec Tutoring; *office:* Hillcrest Jr HS 126 E 5300 S Murray UT 84107

PATTERSON, MARILYN AMY, English Teacher; *b:* Barrington, NJ; *m:* James G.; *c:* Daniel, Sara L.; *ed:* (BA) Eng, Glassboro St 1968; *cr:* Teacher Eastern Regional HS 1968-78, Edgewood Sr HS 1981-; *ai:* Aquila Sch Newspaper 1987-88, 1988-89, 1989-; Lower Camden Cty Teachers Assn (Assn Rep 1981-) 1989-; Journalism Ed Assn 1988-; Winslow Township Environmental Assn 1988-; Outstanding Teacher of Yr Edgewood HS 1988; *office:* Edgewood Sr HS 250 Coopers Folly Rd Atco NJ 08004

PATTERSON, MARY JANE-RUTHERS, Fifth Grade Teacher; *b:* Wheeling, WV; *m:* Victor; *c:* Vickie C. Loughery, Daniel R., Robert C.; *ed:* (BA) Elem Ed, West Liberty St Teachers Coll 1971; Grad Pgrm, OH Univ Belmont; *cr:* Teacher Elm Sch 1971-; *ai:* Martins Ferry Teachers Assn Rep; Chaperoned 7th Graders to Washington DC; Martins Ferry Ed Assn Building Rep 1988-; Short Creek Meth Church (Day Camp Dir, Vacation Bible Sch Dir) 1974-81; *office:* Elm Elem Sch Euclid Ave Martins Ferry OH 43935

PATTERSON, MARY LOUISE, First Grade Teacher; *b:* Holyoke, MA; *ed:* (BA) His, Elms Coll 1967; (MED) Ed Rdng, Westfield ST Coll 1976; *cr:* Teacher Sacred Heart Sch 1968-, Park ST Sch 1970-; *ai:* Stu Improvement Cncl; Teacher Renewal Comm for Western MA; Palmer Teachers Assn; MTA, NEA; *office:* Park St Elem Sch 85 Park St Palmer MA 01069

PATTERSON, MICHAEL DONALD, Mathematics/Science Teacher; *b:* Safford, AZ; *m:* Sheryl Dunlap; *c:* Kellen, Koby; *ed:* (BS) Earth Sci, Univ of AZ 1986; *cr:* Math/Sci Teacher Marana HS 1987-89, Willcox HS 1990; *ai:* Asst Var Ftbl & Bsbl Coach; Frosh Class Spon; Willcox Quarterback Club 1990; *office:* Willcox HS 240 N Bisbee Willcox AZ 85643

PATTERSON, PAUL SEBRON, English Teacher; *b:* Floyd, TX; *ed:* (BS) His/Eng, 1971, (MS) Elem Ed, 1978 E TX St Univ; Ed Admin; *cr:* Teacher Bland Ind Sch Dist 1971-78, Richardson Ind Sch Dist 1978-79, Princeton Ind Sch Dist 1979-82; Prin/Teacher 1982-85, Teacher 1985- Bland Ind Sch Dist; *ai:* Beta Club Honorary Organization Spon; ATPE.

PATTERSON, RICHARD JOHN, Instrumental Music Department; *b:* Aberdeen, SD; *m:* Beverly Carpenter; *c:* Shelly Hart, Wade Stratton, Derek; *ed:* (BM) Music, Univ of IA 1975; (MM) Music, Northwestern Univ 1979; (PHD) Admin, Univ of Denver; Univ of Northern IA; St Cloud St; Univ of Miami; IA St; Univ CO Denver; Univ CO Boulder; CO St Univ; Vandercook Coll; Univ of Denver Grad Studies; *cr:* Music Instr Cosmos Consolidated Schls 1975-78, Waterloo Cmnty Schls 1979-86; Music Percussion Luther Coll 1976-86; Music Instr Colorado Springs Schls 1986-; *ai:* Marching, Pep Band; Instrumental, Musical, Solo & Ensemble, Jazz Contests; Large Groups; Civic Performances; Am Sch Band Dir Assn Natl Memberhip 1978-; CO Band Assn Bd Dir 1988-; CO Assn Sch Execs 1989-; Music Ed Natl Conf 1975; Natl Band Assn; Intnl Jazz Ed Assn; MENC Exemplary Music Awd 1976; Mallet Making Care & Repair 1988; *office:* Thomas B Doherty HS 4515 Barnes Rd Colorado Springs CO 80917

PATTERSON, RICHARD JOHNSTON, Science Teacher/Dept Head; *b:* Atlanta, GA; *m:* Georgia Hightower; *ed:* (BS) Botany, 1974, (MED) Sci Ed, 1979 Univ of GA; *cr:* Sci Teacher Lakeview Acad 1974-77; Summer Inst Instr of AP Bio Teachers Univ of GA 1984, 1986-, Univ of VA 1987-89; Sci Teacher Athens Acad 1977-; *ai:* Frosh Class Faculty Spon; Honor Cncl Adv; Vlybl & Track Coach; NSTA 1977-; NABT 1977-, Outstanding Bio Teacher Awd GA 1988; Phi Delta Kappa, GA Athletic Coaches Assn; Athens Astronomical Assn 1980-; GA Herpetological Society 1985-; GA Historical Society 1989-; Advanced Placement Bio Exam Reader 1986-89; Table Leader 1990; Course Syllabus Published 1990; Question Item Writer for AP Bio Exam 1985, 1987, 1989; Natl Teachers Exam in Bio 1987, 1990; Assessment of Educl Progress Exam; STAR Teacher Awd 1981-82, 1986-89; *office:* Athens Acad P O Box 6548 Athens GA 30604

PATTERSON, ROGER L., Mathematics Teacher; *b:* Marion, OH; *m:* Karen L. Davis; *c:* Jeanette, Teresa, Stephanie; *ed:* (AB) Chem, Dartmouth Coll 1968; (MS) Math, OH St Univ 1972; Youngstown St Univ; Kent St Univ; *cr:* Math/Sci Teacher Teays Valley HS 1968-76; Math/Cmptr Sci Teacher Boardman HS 1976-; *ai:* Ftbl Coach; Intramural Supvr; OEA, NEA 1968-; NEOTA, BEA, OH Ftbl Coaches Assn 1976-; OH Cncl Teachers of Math 1987-; Boardman Meth Church Ofcl Bd Trustees 1976-; Boardman Sch Employees Credit Union (Bd Mem 1980-, Pres 1989-); Outstanding Young Teacher Pickaway Cty Jaycess; Boardman Yrbk Dedication 1981; Boardman Teacher of Yr 1989; *office:* Boardman HS 7777 Glenwood Ave Boardman OH 44512

PATTERSON, SAMUEL LATHAM, JR., Lang Art/Soc Stud Teacher; *b:* High Point, NC; *m:* Lynn Hall; *c:* Gordon K., Wesley C.; *ed:* Elem Ed/His, High Point Coll 1975; (MED) Intermediate Ed, NC A&T St Univ 1986; Prin Cert A&T St Univ 1987; *cr:* 6th Grade Teacher Millis Road Elem Sch 1976-79, Jamestown Mid Sch 1979-; *ai:* Lead Teacher; Team Leader; Mentor Teacher; Summer Sch Prin; Sch Soc Stud Olympiad Team Adv; NCAE; Sch Teacher of Yr 1989-; *office:* Jamestown Mid Sch 4401 Vickrey Chapel Rd Jamestown NC 27282

PATTERSON, STEVEN LYNN, Mathematics Teacher/Coach; *b:* Greenville, MS; *m:* Joy Lynne Crouse; *c:* Charity L.; *ed:* (AS) Math, Dyersburg St 1981; (BS) Math/Phys Ed, Union Univ 1983; (MS) Athletic Admin, Memphis St 1987; Youth & Recreation; *cr:* Teacher/Coach South Side Jr HS 1985-86, Gibson Cty HS 1986-; *ai:* Fellowship of Chrstn Athletes; Boys & Girls Var Bsktbl & Golf Coach; Friends Against Drugs; Summer League Sftbl; GCEA; TN Educl Assn, NEA 1985-l Natl Coaches Assn 1987; Outstanding Young Men of America 1987; Pinecrest Cntry Club; Sunday Sch Teacher; Bsktbl Coach of Yr 1988-89; *home:* 109 Scattered Acres Dyer TN 38330

PATTISON, JOSEPH NELSON, Industrial Art Teacher; *b:* Landstuhl, Germany; *m:* Marsha; *c:* Joseph P.; *ed:* (BS) Tech Ed, 1980, (MA) Admin, 1985 NM St Univ; Staff Trng, Orientation Center for Blind & OR Commission for Blind; Leadership Trng; Cmptr Maintenance; *cr:* Teacher Holloman Mid Sch 1980-88, NM Commission for the Blind 1988-; *ai:* Coord Transition Summer Work Prgm NM; Natl Fed of the Blind 1988-; NM Voc Spec Needs Exec Bd Mem 1989-; NM Tech Ed 1980-; Grace United Meth Men Assn; *office:* NM Commission for the Blind 408 White Sands Ave Alamogordo NM 88310

PATTISON, MARSHA TERI, Teacher; *b:* El Paso, TX; *m:* Joseph N.; *c:* Joseph P.; *ed:* (BS) Home Ec Ed, 1980, (MA) Curr/Instruction, 1985 NM St Univ; Spec Ed, AIDS Ed, Drug Prevention; *cr:* Dept Chm Alamogordo Sr HS 1980-; Teacher NM Commission for the Blind 1990; *ai:* Chm Home Ec & Alamogordo AIDS Curr Advisory Comm; NM Voc Home Ec Teachers Assn (Pres, Past Pres, Mem Advisory Comm) 1987-, Educator of Yr 1989; Delta Kappa Gamma Secy 1987-; Natl Fed of Blind, Amer Home Ec Assn 1988-; FHA, HERO (Mentor Adv 1990, Master Adv 1988, Honorary Mem 1990), Adv of Yr 1986; NASSP 1987; Phi Kappa Phi 1987-; PTA, AACT; Article Published 1986; Natl USOE Grant; Marsha Pattison Day Alamogordo Sr HS 1990; Exemplary Home Ec Prgm 1987; *office:* NM Commission for the Blind 408 White Sands Ave Alamogordo NM 88310

PATTON, BRENDA G., Fourth Grade Teacher; *b:* Rives, MO; *ed:* (BSE) Elem Ed/Sci, SE MO St Univ 1974; *cr:* Kndgtn Teacher Delta C-7 Sch Dist 1974-77, Lake City Schls 1977-78; Teacher Southland C-9 Sch Dist 1978-; *ai:* Southland Excl Comm; 4th-6th Grade Curr Comm 1989-; Southland Cmmty Teachers Schlsp Comm 1990; SADD 1987-88; Gifted Prgm 1988; Advisory Comm 1987-89; Southland Cmmty Teachers Assn (Pres 1990, VP 1989); MO St Teachers Assn 1974-77, 1978-; Veterans of Foreign Wars (Guard 1981, Trustee 1982), Voice of Democracy Awd 1981, 1982; Jonesboro Helpline Volunteer 1981; AR Volunteer Certificate 1981; Danforth Schlsp 1970; Campbell Soup Prgm Coord Gold Seal of Recognition 1983-88; March of Dimes Certificate of Recognition 1982; CTA Rep to Convention 1980; *home:* 2201 Parkside Jonesboro AR 72401

PATTON, FERN (DURHAM), Kindergarten Teacher; *b:* Loyall, KY; *w:* Lewis A. (dec); *c:* Roger C., Lewis C.; *ed:* (BS) Ed, Capital Univ 1955; *cr:* Kndgtn/1st Grade Teacher White Hall City Schls 1955-57, 1959-61; 1st Grade Teacher Dade Co FL 1957-58; Learning Disability Tutor Columbus Public Sch 1965-67; Kndgtn Teacher Brevard Co Schls FL 1971-; *ai:* Restructuring Comm Saturn Elem Sch; Prof Issues Comm, Brevard Fed of Teachers; Faculty Rep PTO Bd Saturn Elem Sch; Delta Kappa Gamma Secy 1980-82, Membership 1976-; Childrens Cmmty Theatre (Bd of Dir 1984-88, Secy 1986-88); *office:* Saturn Elem Brevard Cty Schls 880 Range Rd Cocoa FL 32926

PATTON, JOAN CUCCIAS, Mathematics Teacher; *b:* Lake City, FL; *m:* C. Edward; *c:* Patrick, Mary P., Stephanie, John, Karen; *ed:* (BS) Math, Mary Washington Coll 1966; Grad Stud Ed; *cr:* Math Teacher Robert E Lee HS 1973-; *ai:* Algebra I Review Course Organizer; Heritage Civic Assn Secy 1971-72; Annandale HS Booster Club 1989-.

PATTON, SUSAN STOWELL, Preschool Teacher; *b:* Toledo, OH; *m:* Kenneth; *c:* Jennifer Tokarski, Scott Roswell, Beth Miller; *ed:* (BA) Elem Ed, 1959, (MA) Family/Child Ecology, 1989, (ZA) Early Chldhd Endorsement, 1989 MI St Univ; *cr:* Teacher Jackson Public Schls 1959-60, 1969-; *ai:* Curr Comm 1987-88; Parent Adv 1988-89; NAEYC Jackson Steering Comm 1988-; MI Assn Ed Young Children 1989; Delta Gamma 1957-.

PATTY, SANDRA MARLIN, Third Grade Teacher; *b:* Evansville, IN; *m:* William Robert; *c:* Mary M.; *ed:* (BS) Elem Ed, TX W Coll 1966; (MED) Guidance/Counseling, Univ of TX El Paso 1968; Cmptr Sci, El Paso Comm Coll; *cr:* 3rd Grade Teacher Mackinaw Elem Sch 1961-62; 1st Grade Teacher Toulon Consolidate Sch 1962-65, Pinellas Cty Schls 1966-67; 1st/2nd Grade Teacher Ysleta Ind Sch Dist 1968-80; 3rd Grade Teacher NE Chrstn Acad 1980-; *ai:* Lib Supvr; Day Camp Organizer; NEA, TX St Teacher Assn, Ysleta Teachers Assn 1968-80; El Paso Chamber of Commerce 1978-81; Beta Sigma Phi (Secy, Treas) 1970-79; Alpha Delta Gamma 1975-80; Teacher of Yr Dolphin Terrace Sch 1969; Whos Who Among American Women 1973; *home:* 10029 Kirwood El Paso TX 79924

PATY, ORVILLE BRITT, Mathematics Teacher; *b:* Little Rock, AR; *m:* Margie; *c:* Orville W., Joe, Pam Paty Knicht; *ed:* (BE) Phys Ed, 1939, (ME) Admin, 1949 TCU; *cr:* Coach/Prin Kaufman Ind Sch Dist 1939-46; Prin Iraan Ind Sch Dist 1946-50; Supt Hermleigh Ind Sch Dist 1950-60; Prin/Teacher Roscoe Ind Sch Dist 1960-; *ai:* TSTA Pres 1948-52; Masonic Shrine Pres 1956-57; *home:* 602 Hickory Roscoe TX 79545

PATZER, RONALD LESTER, Chairman Social Studies Dept; *b:* Benton Harbor, MI; *m:* Mary E. Ressie; *ed:* (AB) Soc Stud, Univ of MI 1975; (MA) Ed, MI State Univ 1980; *cr:* Teacher/Coach River Valley HS 1975-78; Lakeshore HS 1978-82; Teacher-Coach/Dept Chm Evanston HS 1982-; *ai:* Asst Var Ftbl Coach; Grad Requirement Comm; Dept Chm Soc Stud; Prin Adv Comm; Natural Helpers Adv; Supt Adv Comm; NCSS 1985-; Evanston Ed Assoc 1982-; NEA 1975-; *office:* Evanston HS 701 W Cheyenne Dr Evanston WY 82931

PAUL, ALEXIS WHITE, First Grade Teacher; *b:* Washington, DC; *m:* Donnis W.; *c:* Christopher W.; *ed:* (BA) Elem Ed, La Grange Coll 1966; (MED) Early Chldhd Ed, GA St Univ 1972; (EDS) Early Chldhd Ed, W GA Coll 1985; *cr:* 4th-5th Grade Teacher La Grange Sch System 1967-69; 1st/4th Grade Teacher Muscogee Sch System 1969-76; 1st Grade Teacher La Grange Sch System 1976-; *ai:* System Staff Developer; Stu Support Team Mem; PAGE; GAE; NEA; Wisteria Garden; Union Womens Club Pres; Troup Band Boosters; La Grange Teacher of Yr 1989; Finalist GA Teacher of Yr 1989; Volunteer of Yr Dick Goldschmidt Awd-GA Cystic Fibrosis Fnd 1985; *office:* West Side Elem Sch Forrest Ave La Grange GA 30240

PAUL, ALICE LEE CRAIG, Kindergarten Teacher; *b:* Vandergrift, PA; *m:* Wm. F.; *c:* Wm. C., David L.; *ed:* (BS) Elem Ed, Westminster Coll 1950; Grad Courses Univ Pittsburgh; Kndgtn Wkshps, Shippensburg Univ; *cr:* Kndgtn Teacher Ellwood City Elem Sch 1950-55; 2nd Grade Teacher 1962-63, 1st Grade Teacher 1963-64 SW Butler Cty Sch; Kndgtn Teacher Connoquenessing Valley Elem Sch 1964-; *home:* 196 Northview Dr Zelienople PA 16063

PAUL, ANNE HATTEN, Mathematics/Computer Teacher; *b:* Buffalo Center, IA; *m:* John R.; *c:* Melissa Bougher, Adam; *ed:* (BS) Phys Ed/Math, W Liberty St Coll 1983; Grad Stud; *cr:* Math Teacher Bridge St Jr HS 1983-; *ai:* Math Club Adv 1984-; Math Field Day Coord 1984-; Math Counts Adv 1985-; Girls Asst Bsktbl Coach 1984-86; NCTM, WVEA, NEA 1984-; Red Cross Volunteer Night Worker 1984-, 5 Yr Service Pin 1989; Natl Math Counts Team 1985-86; *office:* Bridge Street Jr HS 1 Junior Ave Wheeling WV 26003

PAUL, DEBORAH ANNE, Teacher of the Gifted; *b:* Rochester, NY; *ed:* (BA) His, VA Intermont Coll 1974; (MED) Soc Sci Ed, Univ of GA 1977; (EDS) Scndry Soc Stud, West GA Coll 1988; Certificate Gifted Ed, GA St Univ 1979; *cr:* Economics Teacher Woodward Acad 1977-78; Soc Stud/Gifted Teacher North Cobb HS 1978-79; Soc Stud Teacher Wheeler HS 1979-83; Teacher of the Gifted Tapp Mid Sch 1984-; *ai:* Media Comm; Quiz Bowl Spon; Earth Day & SACS Comm; Cobb Cncl Exceptional Children; Taft Inst for Two Party Government; GA Mid Sch Assn; GA Conversancy High Museum of Art; Alliance Theatre Guild Zoo Atlanta; Natl Sci Fnd Economics Seminar1981; Taft Institute for Two Party Government Seminar 1987; *office:* Tapp Mid Sch 3900 Macedonia Rd Powder Springs GA 30073

PAULK, CARLA FAYE, English Teacher; *b:* Heavener, OK; *m:* Jerry Wayne; *c:* Anthony Reid, John; *ed:* (BS) Ed/Eng, Univ of Ok 1981; *cr:* Rdng Teacher Moore Public Sch 1981-87; Eng Teacher Panola Public Sch 1988-; *ai:* Sr Class, Chrldr, Yrbk, Newspaper, Pep Club, Jr Class Spon; Prof Assn Educators of Panola Pres

1989-; Staff Dev Comm Mem 1985-87; NEA Mem 1981-; Intnl Rdng Convention; Teachers Manuals; *office:* Panola HS 6 Panola Rd Panola OK 74559

PAULLIN, ROBERT L., 6th Grade Teacher; *b:* Winter Haven, FL; *m:* Catherine Hudson; *c:* Robert Jr., Laurie, Vicky Wolfe; *ed:* (AA) Ed, Polk Cmmty 1970; (BS) Elem Ed, FL S Coll 1973; *cr:* 6th Grade Math Teacher Bartow Mid 1973-79; 5th-6th Grade Teacher Lake Shipp Elem 1979-; *ai:* 6th Grade & Sci Chm; *office:* Lake Shipp Elem Sch 350 Camellia Dr SW Winter Haven FL 33880

PAULMANN, ELEANOR MARIAN, Retired 3rd Grade Teacher; *b:* Oshkosh, WI; *m:* James A. Sr.; *c:* James Jr., Anne E. Koenig; *ed:* (BS) Elem Ed, Oshkosh Teachers Coll 1948; Master Equivalency; *cr:* 5th Grade Teacher Washington Sch 1945-51; 5th/6th Grade Teacher Grant Sch 1969-70; 4th Grade Teacher 1970-83, 3rd/4th Grade Teacher 1983-85, 3rd Grade Teacher 1985-87 Washington Sch; *ai:* 1st Congregation United Church of Christ Bd of Chrstn Ed 1955-58; Sheboygan Cty Area Retired Teachers Assn, NEA, WEAC, Sheboygan Ed Assn Mem; People to People Charter Mem.

PAULONS, JANET LEIGH (JONES), World History Teacher; *b:* Peoria, IL; *m:* Brian S. Jr.; *c:* Alisha; *ed:* (BA) Sociology, Bradley Univ 1972; Scndry Ed, Soc Sci 1975; *cr:* 4th Grade Teacher St Josephs Grade Sch 1976-77; Dir Richland Baptist Day Care Center 1977-78; Kndgtn Teacher Childrens Center 1978-79; Teacher Pekin Cmmty HS 1980-; *ai:* Key Club Adv; Peoria-Pekin Cncl for Soc Stud (Secy, Treas, VP, Pres); YWCA Women of Yr; *office:* Pekin Cmmty HS West Campus Pekin IL 61554

PAULSON, ELEANOR F. LAMBERG, 1st Grade Teacher; *b:* Minong, WI; *w:* Carl V. (dec); *c:* Carl V. III, Kenneth L., Pamela Radig, Steven E.; *ed:* Ed, 1948; (BS) Elem Ed, 1961; (MS) Elem Ed, 1969 Univ of WI; *cr:* 1st/8th Grade Teacher 1948-50; 5th/8th Grade Teacher 1958-61 Rural Sch; *ai:* Helped with Sci City - 5th Graders and Sci Fairs; Stewart on Teachers Union; Alpha Delta Kappa 1976-; President-1988-; Phi Delta Kappa Tres 1986-; Right-To-Read Prgm-Teacher 1973-; Lake Superior Rdng Cncl Pres 1974-; Garden Club 1980- Sweepstake Ribbon; Fair Organization Supt of Floral Dept 1983-84 Sweepstakes Ribbon; Superior Elem Teacher of Yr 1983; Mini-Grants for Breakfast Units; Nursing Home Visits; *office:* William Cullen Bryant Elem Sch 6010 John Ave Superior WI 54880

PAULSON, JEAN O'NEAL, Chem Teacher/Sci Dept Chair; *b:* Hattiesburg, MS; *m:* Paul R.; *c:* Jenny; *ed:* (AS) Chem/Scndry Ed, Perkinston Jr Coll 1971; (BS) Math/Chem/Scndry Ed, 1973, (MS) Chem/Bio/Scndry Ed, 1975 Univ of S MS; Marine Sci; Legal Rights & Responsibilities Wkshp; *cr:* Math Teacher Pascagoula Jr HS 1972-73; Physics/Chem/Bio Teacher Stone HS 1973-74; Chem/Math/Bio/Marine Bio/Physics Teacher d'Iberville HS 1975-; *ai:* Sci Dept Chairperson; Southern Assn Accreditation Steering Comm; Sci & Math Team Spon; MSTA 1989-; Sigma Xi Outstanding Sci Teacher 1986; STAR Teacher 1980, 1983-85; Teacher of Yr North Bay 1980 & Harrison Cty 1990; *home:* Box 58 Mc Henry MS 39561

PAULSON, NANCY (NOVAK), Fourth Grade Teacher; *b:* Waupun, WI; *m:* Daniel D.; *c:* Kayla M.; *ed:* (BS) Elem Ed, Univ of WI La Crosse 1980; Univ of WI Eau Claire; *cr:* 6th Grade Teacher 1981-87, 4th Grade Teacher 1987- St Pauls Sch; *ai:* NCEA; *home:* Rt 1 Box 107 Bloomer WI 54724

PAULTER, EDWARD STEPHEN, Social Studies Teacher/Coach; *b:* Paterson, NJ; *m:* Rita Bailey; *ed:* (BA) His/Ec, Boston Coll 1972; Curr & Instruction, Seattle Univ; *cr:* Teacher/Coach Seattle Prep 1984-; *ai:* Head Var Bsbl & Jr Var Bsktbl Coach; WA St Coaches Assn 1984-; *office:* Seattle Prepatory Sch 2400 11th Ave E Seattle WA 98102

PAULUCCI, PHILLIP SAMUEL, Master English Teacher; *b:* Gowanda, NY; *m:* Sharon I.; *c:* Jason, Jeremy, Kiara; *ed:* (BA) Eng Lit, St Univ of NY Buffalo 1969; (MS) Ed, Canisius Coll 1977; Grad Work Eng Lit, Comm; *cr:* Teacher/Dept Chm Maryvale Jr HS 1973-78; Teacher/Master Teacher Clark Cty Sch Dist 1978-; Hum Instr Natl Univ 1989-; *ai:* Natl Jr Honor Society Spon; Instr & Coach Martial Arts NY St & NV; Eng Dept Chm; Consortium Mem; NCTE 1979-; Cmmty Luth Church Youth Adv 1980-; Co-Published Text; *office:* Clark Cty Sch Dist 2832 E Flamingo Ave Las Vegas NV 89121

PAULUS, JAYSON JOHN, Science Teacher; *b:* Des Plaines, IL; *ed:* (BS) Botany, Eastern IL Univ 1986; (MSEd) Outdoor Ed, Northern IL Univ 1990; Grad Natl Outdoor Leadership Sch; *cr:* Stu Teacher Barrington HS 1986; Sci Teacher IL St Gifted Prgm 1987, Warren Township HS 1987-; *ai:* Volunteer Coach Bsktbl, Strength, Weightlifting; Specific Heat Diagram; *home:* 109 Hillside Prospect Hgts IL 60070

PAULUS, MICK, Social Studies Dept Head; *b:* Cape Girardeau, MO; *m:* Becky Oehl; *c:* Andrew, Alexander; *ed:* (BSED) Soc Stud, SE MO Univ 1969; *cr:* Teacher Seton Sch 1970-71, Menfro Public Sch 1971-72, St Marys Sch 1972-79, St Vincent Sch 1979-; *ai:* Youth Club Adv; Knights of Columbus Deputy Grand Knight; MO Cmmty Betterment Volunteer of Yr; Article Published Tech of Teaching; *home:* 1130 Zita Perryville MO 63775

PAULY, VIRGINIA A. CROZIER, 2nd Grade Teacher; *b:* Hornell, NY; *c:* Cynthia S. Pauly Donovan, Douglas L.; *ed:* (BA) Art, Buffalo St Teachers 1958; Elem Ed, Elmira Coll 1975; Elem Ed, Geneseo Coll 1975; *cr:* 1st-3rd Grade Art Teacher Bath NY 1958-60; 7th-8th Grade Art Teacher Hornell Jr HS 1960-62; 1st Grade Teacher Hornell 1974-76; 2nd Grade Teacher Columbian Sch 1976-; *ai:* HEA Building Rep 1986-88; Hospital Group Pres 1968-69; Campfire Girls Leader-Training Leaders 1970-73 Bd of Dir 1973; Public Lib Rdng Prgm TV Show 1972-74; Evening Tribune Woman of Wk 1973; Articles in Chalk Talk 1980-81; BOCES Prof Dev Magazine Teaching Tips 1985; Honorable Mention ITV Utilization of TV in Ed 1987; Designed Post Card for NEA 1987;Curr Guide on Aids 1988; Comm for Rdng Prgm 1988; Designed Cover for Columbian Sch 1989; *home:* 19 Alley Ave Hornell NY 14843

PAUTLER, VERA MAE (LAUFER), First Grade Teacher; *b:* Sparta, IL; *m:* James; *c:* Jeffrey, Joseph, Jonathan; *ed:* (BA) Thelogy, Concordia Teachers Coll 1968; Grad Stud Concordia Teachers Coll, S IL Univ Edwardsville, S IL Univ Carbondale; *cr:* 1st-4th Grade Teacher 1968-69, 1st-3rd Grade Teacher 1969-70 Zion Luth Sch; 1st Grade Teacher St Johns Luth Sch 1970-; *ai:* Amer Heart Assn Jump Rope for Heart Coord; Evening Guild Treas 1984; *office:* St Johns Luth Sch 104 E South 6th St Red Bud IL 62278

PAVELLA, CHARLOTTE KATHERINE, 6th Grade Science Teacher; *b:* Beeville, TX; *m:* Jack; *c:* Jonathan; *ed:* (BS) Elem/Soc Stud, California Univ of PA 1966; Univ of MD, Penn St, Univ of IA, E Strasburg; *cr:* 1st/2nd Grade Teacher Prince George Co MD 1966-68; 2nd Grade Teacher 5th Ward Washington Park Mid Sch 1968-69, Green Mt Ind Sch 1969-72; 5th/6th Grade Teacher Gulf Stream Sch 1973; 6th Grade Teacher Clark Sch 1974-76, Washington Park Mid Sch 1976-; *ai:* AIM Corporation Study Skill & Bd Mem; Delta Kappa Gamma; Alpha Psi 1982-84; Teacher Society Chairperson; Genesis (Bd Chm, Co-Chairperson Fashion Show) 1986-; Chemical People 1984-86; *office:* Washington Park Mid Sch 801 E Wheeling St Washington PA 15301

PAVLACKA, JAMES ANTHONY, Science/Mathematics Teacher; *b:* Allentown, PA; *m:* Joanne Marie Fahringer; *c:* Jenna A.; *ed:* (BS) Biomechanics/Kinesiology, E Stroudsburg Univ 1982; (MSED) Biomechancis/Kinesiology, N IL Univ 1984; Biomechancis/Kinesiology, Univ of MD College Park; *cr:* Instr N IL Univ 1982-84, Univ of MD College Park 1984-85; Teacher St Vincent Pallotti HS 1985-; Womens Vlybl Coach Cath Univ 1988-*ai:* NHS Adv; Coach St Vincent Pallotti HS, USVBA Jr Olympic Vlybl; Deerfield Vlybl Club; USVBA (Bd of Dirs, Jr Olympic Coord) 1987-, Honorable Mention Awd 1989; NCEA Teacher Assoc 1985-; Teacher of Yr 1989-, Coach of Yr 1985-86 St Vincent Pallotti HS; *office:* St Vincent Pallotti HS 113 8th St Laurel MD 20707

PAVLAK, PATRICIA MC GINTY, English Teacher; *b:* Sedalia, MO; *m:* Stephen A.; *c:* Stephen E. II, Nancy E., Sarah E.; *ed:* (BA) Eng, Wilson Coll 1966; (MLS) Lib Sci, Univ of Pittsburgh 1971; *cr:* Lang Art Teacher 1966-70, Librarian 1970-72 Pleasant Hills Mid Sch; Substitute Teacher/Librarian Baldwin-WhiteHall Sch Dist 1984-86; Eng Teacher Thomas Jefferson HS 1986-; *ai:* Statesman Sch Newspaper Spon; Beta Phi Mu, NCTE, Wilson Coll Club of Pittsburgh; PTA (Various Offices, Cncl, Sch Bd Rep) 1978-84; *office:* Thomas Jefferson HS PO Box 18019 Pleasant Hills PA 15236

PAVLIK, JEFFREY C., Sixth Grade Teacher; *b:* Wilkinsburg, PA; *m:* Judith A. Lynch; *c:* Amy, Jill, Megan; *ed:* (MED) Elem Ed, Penn St Univ 1976; (BSED) Elem Ed, CA St Coll 1969; *cr:* 6th Grade Teacher Maple Ridge Elem Sch 1969-70, New Stanton Elem Sch 1970-74, Fort Allen Elem Sch 1975-89, W Hempfield Elem Sch 1989-, W Hempfield Mid Sch 1990; *ai:* Jr HS Girls Vlybl Coach; Sci Textbook Selection Comm; 6th Grade Co-Organizer Outdoor Ed Experience; Hempfield Area Ed Assn, PSEA, NEA; PTA Comm Mem; *office:* W Hempfield Mid Sch RD 1 Wendel Rd Irwin PA 15642

PAVONE, VICKI LYNN, Fifth Grade Teacher; *b:* Tooele, UT; *m:* George J.; *c:* Alison E.; *ed:* (BS) Elem Ed, PA St Univ Harrisburg 1971; Grad Courses Local Univs; *cr:* 5th Grade Teacher Hershey Intermediate Sch 1971-; *ai:* Writing Curr Soc Stud, Lang Art, Gifted Prgms Comms; PA St Ed Assn, Hershey Ed Assn Unions; *office:* Hershey Intermediate Sch Homestead Rd Hershey PA 17033

PAX, ROBERT, Physical Education Teacher; *b:* Freeport, IL; *m:* Mary Beth Johnson; *c:* Amy; *ed:* (BS) Phys Ed, 1979, (MS) Phys Ed, 1982 N IL Univ; *cr:* Phys Ed Teacher Dummer Jr HS 1979-; *ai:* HS Cross Cnty & Track Coach; SCTA Secy 1985-; IL Coaches Assn 1989-; *office:* Dummer Jr HS 422 S Wells Sandwich IL 60548

PAXSON, ILA JEANNE, Third Grade Teacher; *b:* Salem, OH; *m:* Neil J.; *c:* Amy, Judy, Steve Rowedda, Barbara Slaght; *ed:* (BS) Elem Ed, Mt Union Coll 1965; Grad Stud; *ai:* Health Curr Comm; SEA, OEA NEA; Salem Music Study Club Corresponding Secy 1989-; Church (Organist, Childrens Choir Dir); *home:* 333 W 10th Salem OH 44460

PAYACK, CHRISTINE ANNE, 4th/5th Grade Head Teacher; *b:* Denville, NJ; *ed:* (BS) Animal Ecology/Conservation, Univ of MA Amherst 1979; *cr:* 5th/6th Grade Head Teacher 1983-87, 6th Grade Head Teacher 1987-89, 4th-5th Grade Teacher 1989-Cambridge Public Schls; *ai:* Network of Progressive Educators 1990; Boston Writing Project (Mem, Participant) 1986-88; Prospect Archive & Center for Ed & Research; Summer Inst II 1990; Living is for Elderly Life Appreciation Awd; *office:* Tobin Elem Sch 197 Vassal Ln Cambridge MA 02138

PAYANO, PEDRO, Eighth Grade Teacher; *b:* El Seybo, Dominican Repub; *m:* Maria Then; *c:* Pedro, Hassan, Pavel, Maria; *ed:* (BA) Poly Sci, UCDEP 1986; Electronical Technician; *cr:* Technician/ESL Teacher Telecommunication 1978-82; ESL Teacher 1982-85, Governor 1984-86 Dominicano; Teacher H K Oliver 1987-; *ai:* Sch Newspaper; Lawrence Teachers Assn, MS Teachers Assn, Natl Teacher Assn 1988-; Los Trinitario Secy of Culture 1988-89; Latino Americano Secy of Culture 1987-88; Articles Published Span Newspaper; *home:* 214 Broadway Lawrence MA 01840

PAYNE, ALFRED DERREL, Special Education Teacher; *b:* Mill Creek, OK; *m:* Mitzi June Roberson; *ed:* (BS) Phys Ed, 1972, (ME) Spec Ed, 1975 E Cntrl St Univ; *cr:* Classroom Teacher Mill Creek HS 1972-73, Sulphur Public Schls 1972-; *ai:* Jr Class Spon 1972-73; 5th/6th Grade Gymnastics Coach 1973-80; Spec Ed Dir 1978-85; Foster Grandparent Bd of Dir 1985-87; OK Natl Guard Officer 1963-82; *office:* Sulphur Public Schls 700 W Broadway Sulphur OK 73086

PAYNE, BEVERLY NYMAND, Retired Teacher; *b:* Brayton, IA; *m:* Thomas J.; *c:* Thomas Jr., Paul, Robert; *ed:* (BS) Elem Ed, 1960, (MS) Elem Ed, 1971 Drake Univ; *cr:* K-8th Grade Teacher Rural Sch 1938-43; Teacher Exira Cmmty Elem Sch 1944-83; *ai:* NEA Lifetime Mem; Delta Kappa Gamma Pres 1986-88; IA Fed Womens Club (All Offices, Dist Schlsp Chm 1988-) 1942-; *home:* 202 S Jefferson St Exira IA 50076

PAYNE, EDDIE A., Social Studies Chair; *b:* Copperhill, TN; *m:* Jeannine K.; *c:* Ryan, Aaron; *ed:* (BS) His/Ed, Univ of TN Chattanooga 1975; (MAT) His, Mid TN St Univ 1981; *cr:* Teacher Fannin Cty HS 1976-; *ai:* Cross Cntry & Tennis Coach; Stu Cncl Spon; Sch Newspaper Faculty Adv; PAGE Building Rep.

PAYNE, JUDITH KAY (FELTON), 4th Grade Teacher; *b:* Somerset, PA; *m:* Douglas Harold; *c:* Benjamin D., Tiffany L.; *ed:* (BS) Bus Ed/Elem Ed, Lee Coll 1972; Grad Work NWG ATES Univ of GA, W GA Univ, UTC, Trevecca Coll; *cr:* 4th-5th Grade Eng Teacher Eton Elem 1972; 6th Grade Teacher Elm Street Elem 1972-76; 4th/5th Grade Rdng Teacher Eton Elem 1976-77; 7th-9th Grade Sci/Soc Stud/Math Teacher Edgecombe Cty Schls 1977-78; 5th Grade Teacher Roosevelt Elem 1978-79, 4th Grade Teacher Tunnel Hill Elem 1979-; *ai:* NEA, GAE, WEA Local Rep 1987-; Gamma Eta Beta Sigma Phi Secy 1985; Enetha Circle Church; *office:* Tunnel Hill Elem Sch 203 E School St Tunnel Hill GA 30755

PAYNE, LINDA MC KINNEY, Vocational Office Ed Teacher; *b:* Elizabethton, TN; *m:* Stephen B.; *c:* Stephen A.; *ed:* (BS) Bus Ed/Home Ec, 1961, (MA) Counseling/Guidance, 1970 E TN St Univ; Grad Stud Voc Ed, Univ of TN; *cr:* Home Ec Teacher Happy Valley HS 1961-65; Office Ed Teacher Herman Robinson Voc Tech Sch 1965-69; Guidance Cnslr Happy Valley Mid & HS 1973-80; Cmptr Applications/Accounting/Voc Office Ed Teacher Happy Valley HS 1981-; *ai:* Bus Prof of America; Sch Newspaper; Sr Class; TN Ed Assn; TN Office Ed Teachers Assn East VP 1988-; *office:* Happy Valley HS Rt 11 Box 3500 Elizabethton TN 37643

PAYNE, MAGGIE ANN, Applied Human Sciences Teacher; *b:* Ft Collins, CO; *ed:* (BS) Voc Home Ec Ed, CO St Univ 1979; Aerobics Instr 1985; *cr:* Teacher Natrona Cty HS 1980-81, Ft Collins HS 1981-; *ai:* Cheerleading Coach; Teacher Rep PTO; Soph Class Spon; CVA (Treas, Mem), Rookie 1983-84; AVA Mem 1978-88, CHEA, AHEA 1978-85; *office:* Fort Collins HS 1400 Remington Fort Collins CO 80524

PAYNE, MARTHA ANDERSON, Mathematics Teacher; *b:* Elk City, OK; *m:* Larry Don; *c:* Timothy, Steven; *ed:* (BS) Ed, Univ of Tulsa 1979; (MS) Math, NE OK St 1988; *cr:* Math Instr Owasso Mid Sch 1979-84, Owasso HS 1984-; *ai:* Math Curr, Math Textbook, Educl Schlsp Selection Comm; Mid Sch Math Dept Chairperson; United Meth Women Pres; Univ of Tulsa Tuition Schlsps; Whos Who in America Jr Colls 1976; *office:* Owasso HS 12901 E 86th St N Owasso OK 74055

PAYNE, PHYLLIS SMITH, Third Grade Teacher; *b:* Bloomington, IN; *m:* Robert A. Jr.; *c:* Katrina, Robert III; *ed:* (BS) Bus, IN Univ 1955; (MS) Ed, IN Univ 1958; *cr:* Teacher Mooresville 1956-58; East Elem 1958-60; Perry Twnshp 1961-64; Poston Road 1964-; *ai:* Delta Kappa Gamma Recording Sec; NEA; IN ST Teachers Assn; Phi Mu Alumnae VP 1989-; Phi Mu Corp Treas 1988-; *home:* 4030 Mahalasville Rd Martinsville IN 46151

PAYNE, ROBERT LEE, III, English Teacher; *b:* Hagerstown, MD; *ed:* (BA) Fr, Washington & Lee Univ 1968; Eng & Creative Writing; *cr:* Eng Teacher Glebe Acres Sch 1969-70, Norfolk Collegiate Sch 1976-; *ai:* Honor Court, Sch Newspaper, SADD, Kids Insisting That Smoking Stop, Jr Class Spon; *home:* 3837 Beach Ave #3 Norfolk VA 23504

PAYNE, RONALD DEAN, Director of Bands; *b:* Kings Mountain, NC; *c:* Alex, Adam; *ed:* (BM) Music, 1975, (MM) Music, 1983 East Carolina Univ; Mentor Trng & Evaluation W/Teacher Performance Appraisal Instrument; *cr:* Dir of Bands Ayden-Grifton HS 1976-84, Independence HS 1984-; Conductor/Dean of Men Winthrop Coll Summer Band Camp 1978-; *ai:* Dir Independence Band of Patriots Marching Band; Co-Adv Flagline, Letter Girls Dance & Drill Team; Phi Kappa Phi; Phi Kappa Lambda; Whos Who Among Amer Coll & Universities; Whos Who Among Americas Teachers; Clinician Pitt All Cty 7th Grade Band 1980; Guest Conductor East Carolina Univ Symphonic Wind Ensemble Spring Concert 1983; Clinician Stanly All Cty Band 1988; Clinician Gaston All Cty Band 1990; Amer Sch Band

Directors Assn; Music Educators Natl Conference; NC BandMasters Assn Bd of Directors 1988-; South Cntrl Dist Bandmasters Assn Pres 1988-; Phi Mu Alpha Sinfonia/Zeta Psi Chapter (Pres, VP, Treas) 1973-75; Students Selected All Dist Band Eastern Dist 1978-82/1984, South Cntrl Dist 1985 , St Honors Band 1982/1984/1987-; Students Participated St Solo & Ensemble Contest 1987-; *office:* Independence HS 1967 Patriot Dr Charlotte NC 28227

PAYNE, SUSAN PRICE, Health Teacher; *b:* Liberty, KY; *m:* Robert; *c:* Chad, Jason; *ed:* (BA) Health/Phys Ed, Univ of KY 1974; (MS) Elem Ed, Eastern KY Univ 1981; TWKAA Trng; Skills For Adolescence Trng; Parenting & Family Life Skills Trng; *cr:* 4th Grade Teacher Liberty Elem 1974-85; 6th-8th Health/Phys Ed Teacher Liberty Mid 1985-88; 7th-8th Grade Health/Family Life Casey Mid 1989-; *ai:* Co-Spon of Just Say No Musical Production; Chairperson of 8th Grade Graduation; Champions Against Drugs Regional Action Group Mem 1989-; *office:* Casey County Mid Sch Rt 4 Liberty KY 42539

PAYNE, WENDY HOWELL, Physical Education Teacher; *b:* San Diego, CA; *m:* Togie; *c:* Chip Wilson; *ed:* (BA) Phys Ed, 1981, (MS) Phys Ed Exercise Sci, 1989 George Mason Univ; *cr:* Bus Owner Spa Health Club 1976-81; Teacher/Coach N Stafford HS 1981-; *ai:* Var Gymnastic & VA HS Coach; AAHPERD, VHSCA, NASACA, NASPE Active Mem 1981-; VA HS League Spec Sports Comm, St Marys Church CCD Teacher 1981-; Post Coach of Yr; Potomac NewsPaper Coach of Yr; *office:* North Stafford HS 839 Garrisonville Rd Stafford VA 22554

PAYNE, WILLIAM C., History Teacher; *b:* Frankfort, Germany; *m:* Veda Eileene Connor; *c:* Carly; *ed:* (BA) Philosophy/Soc Sci, San Diego St Univ 1979; (MA) Ed/His, Univ of CA Riverside 1983; *cr:* Teacher Moreno Valley HS 1980-; *ai:* Cncl for Soc Stud 1989; Bd Mem Inland Cncl for Soc Stud; *office:* Moreno Valley HS 23300 Cottonwood Ave Moreno Valley CA 92388

PAYSON, MARTIN SAUL, 7th Grade Math Teacher; *b:* New York City, NY; *ed:* (BA) Philosophy, Monmouth Coll 1969; (MS) Elem Ed, City Univ of NY 1975; *cr:* Math Teacher Frederick Douglass Intermediate Sch of Math & Cmptr Sci 1970-84, John Philip Sousa Jr HS 1984-; *ai:* 7th Grade Math Tutor NY St After Sch Tutorial Prgm; NCTM 1987-; Assn of Math Teacher of NY St 1987-; United Fed of Teachers NY 1970-; AFT, Afl, CIO 1970-; Monmouth Coll Asst Head in Philosophy Dept 1968; Deans List Monmouth Coll 1969; Prgm Speaker 25th Annual AMTNYS Math Wkshp; Canton Univ 1987; NY St Regents Scholar Incentive Awd 1963; *office:* John Philip Sousa Jr H S 3750 Baychester Ave Bronx NY 10466

PAYSOUR, MICHAEL GLENN, 7th-8th Grade Soc Stud Teacher; *b:* Newton, NC; *ed:* (BS) Geography/His, W Carolina Univ 1974; Teacher Cert Lenoir Rhyne Coll 1976; *cr:* 7th/8th Grade Soc Stud Blackburn Mid Sch 1977-; *ai:* Jr Beta Spon; Geography Bee Coord; NC Assn of Educators 1977-; NCSS, Natl Cncl for Geographic Ed; Teacher of Yr Blackburn Mid Sch 1988; *home:* 206 6th St SW Conover NC 28613

PAZZAGLIA, SUSAN BUTCHER, First Grade Teacher; *b:* Troy, PA; *m:* David Ronald; *c:* Alexandra, Kierston, Dominic; *ed:* (BS) Elem, Mansfield St Coll 1971; *cr:* 1st/2nd Grade Teacher 1971-72, 2nd/3rd Grade Teacher 1972-73 Gillett Elem Sch; Kndgtn-6th Grade Substitute Teacher Troy Area Schls 1973-75; 1st Grade Teacher Mosherville Elem Sch 1975-; *ai:* Peer Coaching Comm; PA Game Commission Certificate of Appreciation 1987; *home:* RD 3 Box 55 Columba Crs Rds PA 16914

PEABODY, DEBRA YOUNG, Drafting/Technology Teacher; *b:* Mason, MI; *m:* Charles L.; *c:* Eileen, Marie, Amanda, Jean; *ed:* (BA) Studio Art/Industrial Design, MI St Univ 1981; (MED) Trade/Industrial Ed, GA St Univ 1987; *cr:* Drafting Teacher Stockbridge HS 1983-; *ai:* Asst Track Coach; Sr Class Spon; Amer Voc Assn, GA Voc Assn 1983-88; Principles of Technology Cncl of GA Newsletter Officer 1988-; Stockbridge HS Voc Teacher of Yr 1989; *office:* Stockbridge HS 109 Lee St Stockbridge GA 30281

PEACOCK, CAROLYN L. ELLIOTT, 2nd Grade Teacher; *b:* Oakdale, CA; *m:* Dale Edward; *c:* Ali L.; *ed:* (BE) Elem Ed, Univ of AK 1975; (ME) Learning Disabilities/Educable Mentally Handicapped, Central St Univ 1982; *cr:* 1st Grade Teacher North Kenai Elem Sch 1976-77; Kndgtn Teacher 1978-80, 2nd Grade Teacher 1981- Covington Douglas Elem; *ai:* Staff Dev Comm 1987-89; NEA; Covington Douglas Ed Assn (Secy 1985-86, Pres 1987-88); *office:* Covington Douglas Sch Drawer C Covington OK 73730

PEACOCK, DOLORES IMOGENE HOOTMAN, Lang Art/Soc Stud Teacher; *b:* Birmingham, IA; *m:* Wendell Warner; *c:* Karoline M.; *ed:* (BA) Elem Ed, Parsons Coll 1967; Grad Work Various Univs; *cr:* Elem Teacher Van Buren Cmmty Schls 1957-; *ai:* Van Buren Ed Assn, IA St Ed Assn, IA Rdng Assn; NEA Life Mem; Delta Kappa Gamma Secy 1980-82; United Meth Women.

PEACOCK, FRANCYSE SPITLER, Art/English Teacher; *b:* Lufkin, TX; *c:* Bethany Cheryl Smith, David Victor; *ed:* (BS) Speech Eng, 1958, (MED) Elem Ed, 1959, Art, 1980 East TX ST Univ; Gifted/Talented; Bi-Lingual Ed; *cr:* Elem Teacher Mc Camey TX Schls 1961-62, New Home Schls 1965-66; Carlsbad City Schls 1956-60/1966-70; Elem/HS Art/Eng Teacher Athens Ind Sch Dist 1970-; *ai:* Chairperson Fine Arts Dept; Art Club Spon; Teacher Incentives Comm; NAEA; TX Art Ed Assn/Piney Woods Art Ed Assn; Dallas Artist & Craftsman Assn; TX Classroom Teachers Assn; Athens Classroom Teachers Assn; Henderson Cty Photographers Assn; First Chrstn Church Elder 1986-; Labor of Love Secy 1988-; Henderson Cty Art League Past Pres 1985-87; Helped Build House for Habitat for Humanity; *office:* Athens H S 708 E College Athens TX 75751

PEACOCK, MARYLINE ANN, 5th Grade Teacher; *b:* Mitchell, SD; *ed:* (BA) Elem Ed, Mount Marty Coll 1968; *cr:* 3rd Grade Teacher Dell Rapids St Marys Elem Sch 1968-69; 4th-5th Grade Teacher Wilmot Public Schls 1969-; *ai:* Delta Kappa Gamma 1988-; Wilmot Ed Assn (Pres, Negotiator) 1969-; Whetstone Valley Rdng Cncl 1986-; SD Ed Assn, NEA 1969-; *home:* Box 166 Wilmot SD 57279

PEACOCK, MELVIN LEON, Sixth Grade Teacher; *b:* Mt Vernon, IL; *m:* Judy I. Winder Peacock; *c:* Carrie G., Jennifer A.; *ed:* Gen Stud, Rend Lake Jr Coll; (BA) Soc Stud, 1972; (MS) Scndry Ed, 1977 Southern IL Univ; *cr:* Teacher/Coach Bluford Comm Consol Dist 114 1972-; *ai:* Just Say No Supv; Chrldg Spon; Sftbl-Bsktbl & Track Coach; Teachers Negotiating Comm; Bluford Ed Assn Pres 1979; Bluford Puritan Club Secy 1981-83; Pres Bluford Ed Assn; Comm for Sr Olympics; *office:* Bluford Comm Consol Dist 114 Rt 2 Bluford IL 62814

PEAK, ANN G., 3rd Grade Teacher; *b:* Williamstown, PA; *m:* Jack; *c:* Dusty, Kellie Gorski, Kristin; *ed:* (BA) Elem Ed, Shippensburg Univ 1955; (MA) Elem Sch Teaching, Glassboro St 1986; Acad for Advancement; *cr:* 1st Grade Teacher Steele Sch 1959-63; 3rd Grade Teacher Penn Beach Sch 1964-67; 3rd-5th Grade Teacher Penns Grove Carneys Point Schls 1967-; *ai:* Septemberfest Comm; NEA; NJEA; SCEA; AR; Delta Kappa Gamma 1986-; Church of Our Merciful Saviour (Sunday Sch Teacher, Choir Mem, Vestry Mem) 1964-; NJ Mini Grant 1979; Article Published; *office:* Field Street Sch Field St Carneys Point NJ 08069

PEAKE, JACQUELINE STILES, Chemistry/Biology Teacher; *b:* Louisville, KY; *m:* Raymond Howard I; *c:* Raymond II, Helen Peake Triplett; *ed:* (MTASCP) Medical Technology, Nazareth Coll 1958; (BA) Bio/Chem, Spalding Coll 1971; (MA) Sci/Ed, W KY Univ 1977; Certified Medical Technologist, Amer Society of Clinical Pathologists; *cr:* Medical Technologist Lexington Clinic 1958-61; Elem Teacher St Joseph Sch 1966-74; Chem/Bio Teacher Bethlehem HS 1974-; *ai:* Yrbk & Academic Banquet Spon; Teach & Direct the Bethlehem HS Chorus; *office:* Bethlehem HS 309 W Stephen Foster Ave Bardstown KY 40004

PEAL, SHIRLEY ANN, Advanced Reading Teacher; *b:* Tyler, TX; *c:* India, Jamal, Cherette; *ed:* (BA) Ed, Bishop Coll 1970; (MSED) Eng, E TX St Univ 1981; Grad Stud Rdng; *cr:* Kndgtn Teacher 1970-71, 2nd Grade Teacher 1971-72 Mamie White Elem Sch; 8th Grade Lang Art Teacher, 1972-87, 8th Grade Advanced Rdng Teacher 1987- O W Holmes Mid Sch; *ai:* Charm Club Spon; AFRO Amer His Month Chairperson; TX St Teachers Assn 1972-; United Teachers of Dallas 1976-.

PEARCE, HELEN GELLING, First Grade Teacher; *b:* Aberdeen, MS; *m:* Abner Tyrus; *c:* Tyrus, Moree, Sue Pearce Motes-Conners, Elizabeth Pearce Sims, Carl Gelling; *ed:* (BS) Elem Ed, 1970, (MS) Elem Ed, 1976 Univ of S MS; Grad Stud Adult Ed; *cr:* 4th Grade Teacher Broom Memorial HS 1950-51; 2nd Grade Teacher 1952-53, 3rd Grade Teacher 1954-55 Van Cleve Consolidated Sch; 6th Grade Soc Stud Teacher Our Lady of Prompt Succor 1968-69; 4th Grade Teacher 1973-75, 1st Grade Teacher 1975-77 Dixie Elem; 1st Grade Teacher S Forrest Attendance Center 1977-; *home:* PO Box 42 Brooklyn MS 39425

PEARCE, HOLLIS (EDNEY), Fourth Grade Teacher; *b:* Asheville, NC; *m:* James L.; *ed:* (BS) Elem Ed, Winston-Salem St 1966; Masters Prgm, Bowie St Coll; Writing Process in Content Area, Trinity Coll; Methods of Teaching Geometry, Georgetown Univ; *cr:* Teacher Little River Elem Sch 1966-68; Supvr Recreational Act MD Capital Park & Planning Commission 1978; Teacher Harris Elem Sch 1966-; *ai:* 4th Grade Chairperson; Field Trip Comm; Soc Fund, Chapter Advisory Comm Mem; Washington Teachers Union Mem 1969-; NAACP Mem 1988-; NEA Mem; Forest Spring Condomunium Assn Mem 1985-; Neighborhood Watch Mem 1987; Mt Sinai Baptist Church Mem 1978-; Outstanding Service, Inservice Seminars & Staff Dev Participation Certificates; Teacher Appreciation Awd; *office:* Harris Elem Sch 53rd & C Streets SE Washington DC 20019

PEARCE, JAMES ALAN, English Teacher; *b:* Smithfield, NC; *m:* Susan Matthews; *ed:* (BS) Scndry Eng, E Carolina Univ 1977; *cr:* Eng/Drama/US His Teacher Columbia HS 1979-83; Eng/NC His Teacher E B Aycock Jr HS 1983-; *ai:* Pitt Cty Teachers & Academically Gifted Sch-Based Comm; Ftbl Athletic Trainer; Sch Leadership Team; Sch Fund Raiser Chairperson; NCTE 1983-; Outstanding Young Educator of Yr 1983; NC Teaching Fellows Comm 1990; Alumnus of NC Center for Advancement of Teaching 1989; Tyrrell Cty Teacher of Yr Comm Chm; *office:* E B Aycock Jr HS 1325 Red Banks Rd Greenville NC 27858

PEARCE, KATHY HILL, Mathematics Dept Chair/Teacher; *b:* Bay Springs, MS; *m:* Charles C.; *c:* Christina P., Daniel ; *ed:* (ME) Math Ed, MS St Univ 1989; (BS) Math, Univ of S MS 1972; *cr:* Teacher Pascagoula Jr HS 1972-73, Stinger HS 1973-76; Carver Jr HS 1976-78, Newton Cty Schls 1978-; *ai:* Mu Alpha Theta & Jr HS Math Club Spon; Mathcounts & Math Teams Coach; Jr & Sr Class Spon; NCTM, MS Cncl Teachers of Math 1978-; MEA, NEA 1st VP 1989; Delta Kappa Gamma; Church GA Leader; Assn GA Dir; Children Church Dir 1986-; Honors & STAR Teacher; Stans Comm Mem; *home:* 106 Staton St Union MS 39365

PEARCE, LOUISE EVANS, 1st-6th Grade Teacher; *b:* Gove, KS; *w:* Frank (dec); *c:* Cecil, Rita Kirkham, Bryan; Evan (dec); *ed:* (BS) Elem Ed, Fort Hays St Univ 1975; *cr:* Teacher Gove Cty Rural Schls; USD 241; Wallace Grade Sch; *ai:* Piano Private Lesson Teacher; United Meth Church Comm of Ed Chairperson; Busy Bee Club; Nom Ks Teacher of Yr 1989; Southwestern Bell Telephone Co Grant Local His Unit; *home:* County Rd Box 68 Wallace KS 67761

PEARCE, NANCY BECKWITH, Orchestra Director; *b:* Raleigh, NC; *m:* William M. Jr.; *ed:* (BM) Instrumental Music Ed, East Carolina Univ 1980; *cr:* Band Dir North Cntrl HS 1980-84; Orch Dir Spring Lake Jr HS 1985-; *ai:* Cumberland Cty Youth Orchestra Section Coach; Spring Lake String Ensemble Dir; Spring Lake Jr HS Band Woodwind Coach; Cumberland Cty Jr HS All Cty Orch Dir; NC Music Educators Assn Orch Contest Chairperson 1987-; Music Educators Natl Conference 1980-; *office:* Spring Lake Jr HS 612 Spring Ave Spring Lake NC 28390

PEARL, LAUREN F, Foreign Lang Dept Chair; *b:* Springfield, MA; *m:* Jeffrey T.; *c:* Edward, Lisa; *ed:* (BA) Fr/Scndry Ed, Simmons 1971; (MA) Romance Langs, Boston Coll 1972; Teaching Stu With Special Needs, Talented & Gifted Coord, Scndry Sch Rdng Teacher Wkshps; *cr:* Fr/Span Teacher John F Kennedy Jr HS 1972-74; Foreign Lang Teacher Oxon Hill Sr & Mt Rainier Jr & Thomas Johnson Mid & Cntrl Sr & B Tasker Mid 1974-; *ai:* Foreign Lang Dept Chairperson; Coord of Talented & Gifted Tasker Mid; Greater WA Assn Teachers of Foreign Lang 1978-; Temple Solel 4th-5th Grade Hebrew Teacher 1986-; Workbook Author; *office:* Benjamin Tasker Mid Sch 4901 Collington Rd Bowie MD 20715

PEARSON, ALLAN N., German Teacher; *b:* Boston, MA; *c:* Rebecca; *ed:* (BA) Modern Lang, Boston Coll 1961; (MA) Ger, Boston Univ 1962; PhD Prgm Univ of CA Berkeley 1962-64, 1965-65; Ger Government Grant Univ of Munich West Germany 1964-65; *cr:* Teaching Asst/Assoc Univ of CA Berkley 1962-64; Lecturer Univ of CA Riverside 1965-66; Tutor St Johns Coll 1971-74; Asst Professor Coll of Santa Fe 1979-81; Ger Teacher Santa Fe HS 1981-; *ai:* Ger Club Adv; Ger Amer Partnership Prgm Coord; Natl Ger Honor Society Chapter Spon; AATG (VP, Pres); Santa Fe Concert Assn Pres 1979-81; Ger Academic Exch Service Fellowship Grants Boston Univ, Univ of CA Berkeley; Opera Critic; *office:* Sante Fe HS 2100 Yucca Rd Santa Fe NM 87501

PEARSON, BARB SCHAEFER, History/Government Teacher; *b:* Bloomington, IL; *m:* John; *ed:* (BS) His, N IL Univ 1979; *cr:* Teacher Tri-Valley HS 1980-; *ai:* HS Cheerleading, Stu Cncl, Soph Class Spon; Discipline Comm; IEA, NEA; Tri-Valley Ed Assn Secy 1983-89.

PEARSON, CHARLES STEVEN, Elementary Teacher; *b:* Kalamazoo, MI; *m:* Eileen D. Armstrong; *c:* John, Samuel; *ed:* (BS) Elem Ed, 1977, (MA) Sci Ed, 1981 W MI Univ; Presenter & Model Teacher Trng; *cr:* 1st-3rd Grade Teacher Kalamazoo Public Sch 1977-; *ai:* MI Dept of Ed Hands on Sci Wkshps Presenter; Kalamazoo Area Math & Sci Center Consultant; Little League & YMCA Youth Bsktbl Coach; NSTA Mem 1986-; MI Sci Teachers Assn Dir-At-Large 1984-89; ASCD Mem 1990; Articles Published; Kalamazoo Ed Fnd Grant & Mini-Grant 1990; *office:* Kalamazoo Public Schls 1914 Cobb Ave Kalamazoo MI 49007

PEARSON, DEBORAH RICHARDSON, Third Grade Teacher; *b:* Fort Hood, TX; *m:* John Garrett; *ed:* (BA) Early Chldhd Ed, 1975, (MS) Early Chldhd Ed, 1976 GA Southwestern; Masters Degree Early Chldhd; *cr:* Kdngtn Teacher Pearl Stephens 1976-79; 3rd Grade Teacher Tucker Elem Sch 1979-; *ai:* PAGE 1981-.

PEARSON, HELEN MARIE, 2nd Grade Teacher; *b:* Minneapolis, MN; *m:* Darrel N.; *c:* Heidi M. Wyatt, Darren N.; *cr:* 1st Grade Teacher N Branch Public Schls 1955-57; Primary Teacher 1957-64, Chapter I SLD Teacher 1965-74 Ind Dist 16 Sp Lake Park; Chapter I SLD Teacher 1974-76,2nd Grade Teacher 1976- St Francis Dist 15; *ai:* Stu-at-Risk Comm; Cmptr Comm; Elem Eng 1974-; Pi Lambda Theta 1972-; MN Ed Assn, NEA 1955-; Church Endowment Fund Secy 1985-; Church Long Range Planning 1987-; Local Teacher of Yr Nominee; *home:* 1655 Viking Blvd NE Cedar MN 55011

PEARSON, JAMES GREG, History Teacher; *b:* St Joseph, MO; *ed:* (BA) His, William Jewell 1970; Grad Stud *cr:* Jr-Sr HS His Teacher West Platte R-II 1972-; *ai:* Concession Stand Dir; Asst Jr HS Girls Bsktbl; MSTA 1972-; United Methodist Church Youth Dir 1989-; PTA Honorary MO Life Membership; Stu Cncl #1 Club Faculty Awd; *office:* West Platte R-II 935 Washington St Weston MO 64098

PEARSON, NANCY MOLLINS, Communications Teacher; *b:* Fargo, ND; *m:* Paul G.; *c:* Paul C., Eric L.; *ed:* (BS) Elem Ed, Minot St Univ 1982; *ai:* Speech Team Coach; Yrbk Adv.

PEARSON, PATSY JOHNSON, 6th/7th/8th Grade Math Teacher; *b:* Selmer, TN; *m:* Terry L.; *c:* Mary B., Julie A.; *ed:* (AS) Elem Ed, Jackson St Coll 1971; (BS) Elem Ed, Univ of TN Martin 1973; (MS) Elem Admin/Supervision, Memphis St Univ 1977; *cr:* 5th Grade Teacher Bethel Springs Elem 1973-78; 4th Grade Teacher 1978-81, 6th-8th Grade Math Teacher 1981- Ramer Elem; *ai:* Beta Club Spon; Mc Nairy Cty Teachers Assn Pres 1976-77; TN Teachers Assn 1973-; *home:* Rt 2 Box 97 B1 Ramer TN 38367

PEARSON, PERRY ALAN, Sixth Grade Science Teacher; *b:* Morristown, TN; *m:* Patricia Suzanne Livesay; *ed:* (AS) Elem Ed, Walters St Comm Coll 1976; (BS) Elem Ed, 1978, (MED) Admin/Supervision, 1985 E TN St Univ; *cr:* Teacher West View Mid Sch 1978-; *ai:* 6th Grade Boys Bsktbl, Boys B-Team Bsktbl, Boys Var Bsktbl, Asst Girls Track Coach; NEA, TN Ed Assn, E TN Ed Assn, Hamblen Cty Ed Assn; *home:* 1980 Red Bird St Morristown TN 37814

PEARSON, SELENA POLLARD, Third Grade Teacher; *b:* Sheffield, AL; *m:* William A.; *c:* Christopher, Reginald; *ed:* (BS) Elem Ed, 1974, (MS) Learning Disabilities, 1978 AL A&M Univ; *cr:* 3rd Grade Teacher New Hope Sch 1974-; *ai:* AEA, NEA 1974-; *office:* New Hope Elem Sch 5300 Main Dr New Hope AL 35760

PEART, JOSLYN KRISTINA, Seventh Grade Math Teacher; *b:* Detroit, MI; *m:* Ronald Norman; *c:* Niccolle, Tanina, Kristina; *ed:* (AS) Elem Ed, Highland Park Comm Coll 1975; (BS) Soc Sci, Wayne St Univ 1977; (MA) Mid Sch Math, Univ of Detroit 1987; Master of Teaching Prgm, Univ of MI; SEED Prgm, Assertive Discipline, Cooperative Learning Trng; Cmptr Literacy; *cr:* Play Leader Highland Park Recreation Dept 1972-75; Homeroom Teacher 1977-79, Math Teacher 1979- Detroit Public Schls; *home:* 16740 Vaughan Detroit MI 48219

PEART, RONALD NORMAN, Math Instructional Specialist; *b:* Detroit, MI; *m:* Joslyn Kristina Jones; *c:* Niccolle, Tanina, Kristina; *ed:* (BA) Soc Sci, Wayne St Univ 1975; (MA) Teaching of Math, Univ of Detroit 1987; *cr:* Teacher 1975-89, Instructional Specialist 1990 Detroit Public Schls; *ai:* Distinguished Service Awd Wayne Cty; Detroit Bd of Ed Certificate of Appreciation; *office:* Detroit Public Schls 8401 Woodward Detroit MI 48202

PEASE, SOPHIA ANDRYCHUK, Sixth Grade Teacher; *b:* East Rochester, NY; *m:* Douglas S.; *c:* Shelly Woodward, David, Stephanie; *ed:* (BA) Soc Stud, Houghton Coll 1950; (MED) Elem Ed, Univ of NM 1976; Working Toward BA in Fine Arts, AZ St Univ; Univ CA Long Beach; *cr:* 4th/5th Grade Teacher Belen NM Public Schls 1967-77; 2nd/3rd Grade Teacher Wood Sch 1978-80; 5th Grade Teacher 1980-83, 6th Grade Teacher 1983- Rover Elem Sch; *ai:* Mem Supts Advisory, Art, Soc Stud Comm; Renaissance Festival Organizer; Rover Rams Newspaper Spon; NEA; AZ Teachers Assn Building Rep 1984-88; Delta Kappa Gamma; AZ Auxiliary of Gideons Intnl VP 1987-; Tempe Sister Cities 1985-88; Tempe Elem Schl Dist 3 Impact Awd 1987; AZ Republic Appreciation Certificate 1986; Ribbons for Oil Paintings.

PEAVY, BECCA HAZEL MC GRAW, 5th Grade Teacher; *b:* Moultrie, GA; *m:* Edward A.; *c:* Robert E.; *ed:* (BS) Elem Ed, Valdosta St Coll 1960; *cr:* 1st Grade Teacher Leila Ellis Elm Sch 1960-62; Winter Garden Elem 1962-63; Dover Shores Elem 1964-66; 6th Grade Teacher Sallas Mabone Elem 1967-68; 4th Grade Teacher Holiday Hills Elem 1968-70; 3rd/5th Grade Teacher Armstrong Elem 1971-; *ai:* Idea Comm Armstrong; Cultural Arts Comm; Berea Youth Assn; Summer Seminar Greenville Cty; Delta Kappa Gamma Pres 1986-88; State Comm Mem 1988-91; Palmetto Teachers Assn; Intnl Reading Assn; Alpha Delta Pi 1961-; Daughters of Amer Rev Secy 1988-; United Daughters of Confederacy 1988-; Alliance for Ed Grant 1989-; 1960-62 Mem GA St Bd New Math Prgm; Teacher of Yr; *office:* Armstrong Elem Sch 20 Martin Dr Greenville SC 29611

PEAY, SARAH ANN, 7th-8th Grade Teacher; *b:* Burgaw, NC; *ed:* (BS) Intermediate Ed 4th-9th Grades, East Carolina Univ 1980; *cr:* 5th/9th Grade Teacher 1981-, 7th-8th Grade Sci/Math Teacher 1988- Atkinson Mid Sch; *ai:* Athletic Dir 1984-86; Sch Base Comm 1987-89; Girls Vlybl/Bsktbl Coach 1985-87; Sch Calendar Comm 1986-89; Reaccreditation Co-Chm 1989-; Southern Assn of Schls & Colleges Sci Chm 1987-; Testing Coord 1987-; Intnl Rdng Assn 1982-83; NCAE 1987-89; Mem Rileys Creek Baptist Church; Atkinson Mid Sch Teacher of Yr 1986-87; Recognized for Excl Teaching Sci By Governor Jim Martin 1986-87; *home:* Rt 1 Box 359 Willard NC 28478

PECCINI, ROBERT, English Teacher; *b:* Acushnet, MA; *ed:* (BA) Eng, Boston Coll 1967; (MED) Eng, Boston St Coll 1968; *cr:* Eng Teacher New Bedford HS 1971-; *ai:* Alpha Literary Magazine Club Adv 1979-85; NCTE; *office:* New Bedford HS 230 Hathaway Blvd New Bedford MA 02740

PECK, CAROLYN CHILDERS, Choral Director; *b:* Scottsboro, AL; *m:* Benjamin Donnell Jr.; *c:* Benjamin III; *ed:* (BME) Music Ed, 1965, (MME) Music Ed, 1967 Murray St Univ; *cr:* General Music Teacher Marshall Cty KY 1965-66; Choral Music Teacher N Marshall HS 1966-67; Band/Choral Dir Madison Jr HS 1967-69; Choral Dir S R Butler HS 1969- *ai:* TRI-M Intnl Music Honor Society Spon; Music Educators Natl Conference 1965-; AL Music Educators Assn 1967-; NEA 1965-; AL Vocal Assn (Treas 1972-74, Dist Chm 1967-74); Huntsville Choral Dirs Assn (Pres, Secy, Treas); Amer Choral Dirs Assn St HS Chm 1988-89; Huntsville Cmmty Chorus 1988-; Twickenham Singers 1981-83; Outstanding Young Women of America 1981; *office:* S R Butler HS 3401 Holmes Ave Huntsville AL 35816

PECK, MARTHA KIRK, Third Grade Teacher; *b:* Fort Payne, AL; *d:* Charles Bruce; *c:* Suzanne, Misti L., Alec K.; *ed:* (BA) Ed, Northeast St Jr Coll 1968; (BS) Home Ec/Scndry Ed, Jacksonville St Univ 1970; (MED) Early Chldhd Ed, AL A&M Univ 1977; *cr:* Home Ec Teacher Sandrock HS 1970-71; Elem Teacher Henegar Jr HS 1971-77, Plainview HS 1977-; *ai:* NEA, AL Ed Assn, De Kalb Ed Assn; Alpha Delta Kappa Corresponding Secy 1988-; *office:* Plainview Sch PO Box 469 Rainsville AL 35986

PECK, STEVEN RANDAL, Fifth Grade Teacher; *b:* Enid, OK; *m:* Diane Luckett; *c:* Sean, Ian, Devin, Tristan; *ed:* (BS) Elem Ed, Univ of WI Milwaukee 1976; *cr:* 2nd/3rd Grade Teacher Lahoma Elem Sch 1976-82; 2nd Grade Teacher Cleveland Elem Sch 1982-85; 2nd/5th Grade Teacher Monroe Elem Sch 1985-; *ai:* Sch Newspaper Adv; Lahoma Teachers Assn Pres 1979-80; Enid Ed Assn; NEA; Attended Natl Endowment for Hum & OK St Univ Summer Inst 1987; *office:* Monroe Elem Sch 400 W Cottonwood Enid OK 73701

PECKALLY, JOHN A., Fifth Grade Teacher; *b:* Sayre, PA; *m:* Linda L.; *c:* Michele, Lisa, Michael; *ed:* (BS) Elem Ed, Mansfield Univ 1965; (MS) Ed, Elmira Coll 1973; Grad Stud Corning Coll of Finger Lakes; *cr:* Teacher Corning Sch Dist 1965-67, Horseheads Sch Dist 1967-; *ai:* 5th Grade & Fall Festival Ticket Chm; Dist Report Card & Dist Eng Evaluation Comms; Horseheads Teachers Assn, NY St United Teachers; Elmira Police Benevolent Assn; *office:* Gardner Road Elem Sch Gardner Rd Horseheads NY 14845

PECKHAM, DIANA MAURER, English/Publications Teacher; *b:* Springfield, IL; *m:* Richard; *ed:* (BS) Eng/Journalism, IL St Univ 1972; (MA) Journalism, Univ of MO Columbia 1979; *cr:* Eng Teacher Morton HS 1972-83; Eng/Publication Teacher Pekin Comm HS 1983-; *ai:* Pekinois Sch Newspaper, Yrbk, Quill & Scroll Journalism Honor Society Spon; IL Journalism Ed Assn Bd Of Dir 1988-; E IL Univ Press, Journalism Ed Assn 1978-; IL Ed Assn, NEA 1974-; IL Journalism Teachers (Secy, Treas 1979-81, VP 1981-83, Pres 1983-85) 1978-; Natl Scholastic Press Assn 1978-; Morton Ed Assn 1974-83; Pekin Teachers Alliance 1983-; IL St Univ Alumni Group 1973-; Univ of MO Alumni Group 1979-; Delta Kappa Gamma 1986-88; Morton Womens Club 1974-79; Blessed Sacrament Church, Cursillo in Christianity 1977-; Prison Ministry Faith, Hope, & Love Inc 1982-; Teens Encounter Christ 1978-85; Nom Yrbk Staff Best Yrbk Adv in IL, Received Awd from E IL Univ 1982; Speak Yrbk Wkshps Around Midwest; Dir of Yrbk Wkshp E IL Univ 1988-; *office:* Pekin Community HS C103 E Campus Pekin IL 61554

PECOR, MARCY JOHNSON, Fifth Grade Teacher; *b:* Rutland, VT; *m:* Richard; *c:* Michelle Pecor Herman; *ed:* (BS) Elem Ed, Univ of VT 1959; *cr:* 3rd/4th Grade Teacher Proctor VT 1959-60; 4th Grade Teacher Northwest Sch 1960-69; 5th Grade Teacher Allen Sch 1969-79, Chamberlain Sch 1979-; *ai:* Math Advisory Bd; Chorus Club Musical Theatre Productions; Stu Math Team Coach; Delta Kappa Gamma 1982-; *office:* Chamberlain Street Sch Chamberlain St Rochester NH 03867

PEDDICORD, JANE STEPHAN, 6th Grade Math/Science Teacher; *b:* Piqua, OH; *m:* Victor A.; *c:* Andrew; *ed:* (BA) Elem Ed, Capital Univ 1975; (MA) Early/Mid Chldhd Ed, OH St Univ 1979; Early Mid Chldhd & Environmental Ed Courses; *cr:* Phys Ed/Art Teacher Plain Local Schls 1975-76; Dir/Cnslr Camp Fire In corporated Summer Camp 1975-76, 1980-82, 1984-88; 5th Grade Teacher 1976-84, 6th Grade Teacher 1984- Plain Local Schls; *ai:* 6th Grade Environmental Ed Field Trip Organizer; NEA, OEA 1975-; Amer Camping Assn 1984-; Camp Fire Incorporated Camping (Comm Mem 1983-88, 1990, Leader 1981-84), Camping Awd 1988; Gethsemane Luth Church Educl Bd Mem 1989-; *office:* Plain Local Schls 6425 New Albany-Condit New Albany OH 43054

PEDERSEN, JAMES KEITH, 8th Grade Math/Science Teacher; *b:* Caldwell, ID; *m:* Joyce Ellen Williams; *c:* Wendy K., Keith E.; *ed:* (BA) Psych, 1966, (MA) Clinical Psych, 1968 Pepperdine Univ; Math, UCLA; Advanced Scndry Math Cert, Portland St Univ; *cr:* Math Teacher Lindbergh Jr HS 1968-70; Math/Sci Teacher Laurin Intermediate Sch 1973-82, Lewisville Intermediate Sch 1982-; *ai:* Stu Store Adv; Math Curr Comm Mem; HIV/AIDS Curr Comm; Battle Ground Ed Assn 1982-; Battle Ground Youth Soccer Club VP 1977-88; Fellowship Bible Church Elder 1978-; *office:* Lewisville Intermediate Sch 1001 W Main St Battle Ground WA 98604

PEDERSEN, NANCY ANN, Kindergarten Teacher; *b:* Minneapolis, MN; *ed:* (BSED) Early Childhood, 1973; (MED) Early Childhood, 1978 Columbus Coll; Staff Dev Courses & Seminars 1978-; *cr:* Remedial Rdng Teacher 1973-74, Kndgtn Teacher 1974-77 Reese Road Elem Sch; Kndgtn Teacher Dawson Elem Sch 1977-; *ai:* Mentor to New or Beginning Teachers; Dawson PTA 2nd VP; St Standards Comm Chm; NEA, GA Assn of Educators, Muscogee Assn of Educators (Asst Secy 1977-78, Ed Mercury 1976-79) Sch Bell Awd 1977-78; Alpha Delta Kappa Pres Elect 1989-; St Luke United Meth Church Single Adult Coord 1988-; Admin Bd Mem 1988-; Amer Assn of Univ Women Prgm VP 1988-; Dawson Teacher of Yr 1978-79; *office:* Dawson Elem Sch 180 Northstar Dr Columbus GA 31907

PEDERSON, THOMAS ANTHONY, Fifth Grade Teacher; *b:* Olivia, MN; *m:* Beverly Barnett; *c:* Claire, Isaac; *ed:* (BS) Elem Ed, St Cloud St Univ 1977; Grad Stud Toward Masters Degree; *cr:* Chapter I Tutor Mc Kinley Elem 1977-78; 6th Grade Teacher Five Hawks Elem 1978-80; 5th Grade Teacher Bluff View Elem; *ai:* Stu Cncl Adv; Read-In Chm; MN Ed Effectiveness Prgm Mem; Discipline Comm; NEA, MN Ed Assn 1977-; Lake City Ed Assn 1980-; Local Ed Assn Meet & Conference; Bluff View PTO Bd Mem; Lake City Jaycees 1980-85; Trout Unlimited 1987-; *home:* 110 N 6th St Lake City MN 55041

PEDIGO, PAMELA JO, Fourth Grade Teacher; *b:* Bryan, TX; *m:* Billy Ray; *c:* Jake C., Jessica A.; *ed:* (BS) Elem Ed/Art, TX Womens Univ 1977; Midwestern Univ; *cr:* 1st Grade Teacher 1977-81, 4th Grade Teacher 1988- Pilot Point Elem; *ai:* Elem Rep Textbook Adoption Comm; Classroom Teachers Assn Secy 1989-; Calvary Baptist Dir 1988-; Vacation Bible Sch; *office:* Pilot Point Elem Sch 829 S Jefferson Pilot Point TX 76258

PEDRYC, ROSE MARIE HOLBROOK, 7th Grade Teacher/Asst Prin; *b:* Chicago, IL; *m:* Wayne R.; *ed:* (BA) Elem Ed/Rdng/Psych Univ of IL Chicago Circle Campus 1975; *cr:* 5th Grade Teacher 1975-87, 7th Grade Teacher/Asst Prin 1987- St Mary of Angels Sch; *ai:* Asst Prin; Rainbows Facilitator; Purchasing Agent; CAT, Soc Stud, Annual Fundraiser Coord; Heart of Sch Awd, Chicago Archdiocese 1989; Sch Division of Mc Graw Hill Pub Cty Certificate of Excl; Outstanding Leadership Qualities in Teaching 1989; *office:* St Mary of Angels Sch 1810 N Hermitage Chicago IL 60622

PEEBLES, EDWARD M., Physics Teacher; *b:* Denver, CO; *m:* Ellen Moloney; *c:* John, Mary E., Ted, Leslie Gilman, Catherine; *ed:* (BS) Engineering, US Naval Acad 1955; (MS) Naval Architecture/Marine Engineering, MIT 1961; PMD Harvard Univ Bus Sch 1970; *cr:* Design/Construction Nuclear Submarines US Navy 1961-83; Physics Teacher Bishop Denis J O Connell HS 1983-89; *ai:* Amer Society Naval Engineers 1955-; NSTA 1983-; Amer Assn of Physics Teachers Treas 1984-; Legion of Merit Awd Given by Pres of the US 1974-83; *home:* 2343 Citation Ct Reston VA 22091

PEEBLES, PATTI JONES, French/Russian/Spanish Teacher; *b:* Dallas, TX; *m:* Jerry; *ed:* (BA) Fr, 1976, (MA) Fr, 1978 Univ of TX Arlington; Univ of Paris Sorbonne; *cr:* Fr/Russian/Span Teacher Dallas Ind Sch Dist 1977-81; Fr/Eng Teacher St Andrews Sch on the Marsh 1984-85; Span Instr Armstrong St Coll 1986-88; Fr/Russian/Span Teacher Jenkins HS 1985-; *ai:* Fr Club, Fr Honor Society, Russian Club; AATF 1977-; Amer Cncl of Teachers of Russian 1989-; Grant to Study Fr in Caen & Antibes, France 1986 & Span in Madrid, 1987; Rockefeller Fellowship to Study Russian & Produce Lang Video Soviet Union 1989; *home:* 108 Rose Dhu Way Savannah GA 31419

PEEK, OLLIE LOUIS, Mathematics Teacher; *b:* Concho County, TX; *m:* Jo Ann Lumpkin; *c:* Suzanne, Tommy; *ed:* (BA) Math, Mc Murry Coll 1949; (MED) Ed, Hardin Simmons Univ 1955; Natl Sci Inst E TX St Univ, TX Tech Univ, Sul Ross Univ Houston; *cr:* Math Teacher Crosbyton HS 1949-51, Snyder Ind Sch Dist 1951-; *ai:* NEA Life Mem 1949-; TSTA (Pres Treas, Life Mem) 1949-; TCTA VP, Pres 1953-; Local Comm for Educl Excl Chamber of Commerce Banquet Teacher of Yr 1987; Univ of TX Ed Dept St Teacher of Yr 1986; *home:* 3007 Austin Snyder TX 79549

PEEPLES, ELIZABETH SOTELO, First Grade Teacher; *b:* Bisbee, AZ; *m:* Tim Sr.; *c:* Tim, Michael; *cr:* (AA) Liberal Arts, Cochise Jr Coll 1970; (BS) Elem Ed, GA St Univ 1975; 5th Grade Eng Teacher Atkinson Elem 1975-77; 3rd Grade Teacher 1977-86, 1st Grade Teacher 1986- Orrs Elem; *ai:* Future Stock Sch Contact Person; Prof Assn of GA Educators; *office:* Orrs Elem Sch Spalding Dr Griffin GA 30223

PEEPS, RICHARD DONALD JAMES, Computer Language/Math Teacher; *b:* Toledo, OH; *m:* Rose Mueller; *c:* Antonia H., Deirdre E. Okamoto, John R.; *ed:* (BED) Math, Univ of Toledo OH 1958; Grad Stud Advanced Math, W WA Univ; Scndry Sch Guidance, Univ of WA & Seattle Pacific Univ; Scndry Sch Admin, W WA Univ; *cr:* Math Teacher Perrysburg HS 1962-65; Math Teacher 1965-67, Guidance Cnslr 1967-69, Eng Teacher 1969-72, Math/General Sci/Acre Space Sci Teacher 1969-78 Olympic View Jr HS; Math/Cmptr Lang Teacher Mariner HS 1978-; *ai:* OH & WA Var Ftbl Coach; Springboard Diving, Sailing & Chess Mariner HS; Mukilteo Ed Assn (Exec Bd, Treas, Lead Negotiator) 1965-; WA Ed Assn 1965-; NEA Lifetime Mem 1965-; Everett Sailing Assn (Bd of Dir, Treas) 1978-88; US Army Aviator 1958-62; Chm of Sch Math Curr Comm; *office:* Mariner HS 200 120th SW Everett WA 98204

PEET, JANE ELIZABETH (GUY), 4th Grade Teacher; *b:* Scranton, PA; *m:* D. Carl; *c:* Julie, Kevin; *ed:* (AA) Ed, Keystone Jr Coll 1964; (BS) Elem Ed, Kutztown St Coll 1966; Permanent Cert Univ of Scranton 1969; *cr:* 1st Grade Teacher Salem Twp Cons Sch 1966-71; Substitute Teacher Western Wayne Sch Dist 1972-79; 4th Grade Teacher 1979-85, Ungraded Teacher 1985-87, 4th Grade Teacher 1987- Hamlin Elem; *ai:* Mentor Teacher; Math & Rdng Comms; GSA Treas 1981-84; Cub Scouts Publicity & Refreshment Chairperson 1983-86; PTA Life Membership 1982; *office:* Hamlin Elem Center PO Box 55 Hamlin PA 18427

PEFLEY, STEPHEN ARLIN, 6th Grade Teacher; *b:* Coffeyville, KS; *m:* Cindy Denise Wolfe;; *c:* Richard, Chris, Lisa; *ed:* (BA) Elem Ed, Calvary Bible Coll 1977; (MA) Elem Admin, Pittsburg St Univ 1984; *cr:* 6th Grade Teacher USD 447 1977-; *ai:* Principals Advisory Cncl.

PEHANICH, PATRICIA M., 6th Grade Teacher; *b:* Oak Park, IL; *ed:* (BSED) Spec Ed/Phys Ed, N IL Univ 1974; Grad Stud Various Univs; *cr:* 4th-6th Grade Teacher of Physically Handicapped SW Cook Cty Coop 1974-77; 6th Grade Teacher Palos Cmmty Consolidated Sch 1977-; *ai:* Declamation & Speech Coach; Lang Art, Math, Sci, Rdng, Curr, Building Advisory, Soc, Discipline Comms; White Pines Ranch Outdoor Ed Coord; After Sch Phys Ed Spon; Palos Ed Assn Union Building Rep 1979-80, 1981-82, 1985-86; Teaching Futuristics Published by Dist 118; 1st Place SWIC Contest; *office:* Palos S Jr HS 131st & 82nd Ave Palos Park IL 60464

PEIFFER, GEORGE EDWARD, Fifth Grade Teacher; *b:* Toledo, OH; *m:* Dawn Denise Betz; *c:* Dayna Betz; *ed:* (BS) Elem Ed, 1975, (MED) Admin/Supervision, 1987 Univ of Toledo; *cr:* 7th/8th Grade Teacher 1986, 1988, 5th/6th Grade Teacher 1989 Woodmore Local Schls; 5th Grade Teacher Lake Local Schls 1976-; *ai:* Lake Elem Code of Conduct Comm Mem; Coach 9th Grade Ftbl 1976, 8th Grade Ftbl 1977, 8th Grade Boys Bsktbl 1977, 7th Grade Girls Bsktbl 1983-84, 8th Grade Girls Bsktbl 1985, Elem Bsktbl 1978-85; NEA, OEA, LEA 1976-; *home:* 1131 Cedar Creek Dr Northwood OH 43619

PEINE, MARIE ELAINE, Teacher of Gifted; *b:* Bowerston, OH; *m:* John D.; *c:* Mary A., Emelie; *ed:* (BSED) Soc Stud, Capital Univ 1967; (MA) His, Univ of AZ 1972; Spec Ed Cert Univ of TN Knoxville; *cr:* HS Soc Stud/Music Teacher Ridgewood Schls 1967-69, Goose Bay Labrador Canada Dept of Defense Schls 1970-71; Teacher of Gifted Sevier Cty Schls 1984-; *ai:* Future Problem Solving Team Coach; Select Girls Vocal Ensemble Instr; ASCD 1989-; TN Assn for Gifted 1985-; Sevier Cty League of Women Voters (Voter Service Chairperson 1983-, Pres 1986-87); PTA, PBP VP 1989-; St Dept of Ed Gifted Curr Comm; MI Cncl for Hum Local His Curr Grant; *office:* Pi Beta Phi Sch 180 Cherokee Orchard Rd Gatlinburg TN 37738

PEKURNEY, TUELL ANN, Language Art/Soc Stud Teacher; *b:* Corpus Christi, TX; *c:* Thomas R., Kyle M.; *ed:* (BA) Elem Ed, N TX St 1968; *cr:* 1st Grade Teacher 1977-80, 6th Grade Teacher 1980-89 Browning Heights Elem; 6th Grade/Lang Art/Soc Stud Teacher N Ridge Mid Sch 1989-; *ai:* Lang Art Coord; TX St Teacher Assn Secy; TSTA St Convention Speaker 1982; *office:* N Ridge Mid Sch 7332 Douglas Ln Fort Worth TX 76180

PELAGIO, REGINALD MATTHEW, Business Department Chair; *b:* Long Beach, CA; *m:* Virginia Dale Vorce; *c:* Jennifer L., Elizabeth M., Stephanie L., Rebecca M.; *ed:* (BBA) Bus Admin, SE MA Univ 1964; MBA Prgm, SE MA Univ 1975; Ed, Bridgewater St Coll 1965-67; Bus, Bryant Coll 1967-68; Cmptr, Providence Coll 1967; *cr:* Adult Ed Evening Instr 1965-66, Instr/Supr Potential Dropout Prgm 1968-71, Bus Ed Instr 1967-78, Career Coord Career Resource Center 1978-80 BMC Durfee HS; Typing Instr Joseph Case HS 1966-68; Teacher/Anti Poverty Prgm Intnl Ladies Garment Workers Union 1966; Teacher Morton Jr HS 1966-67; Owner/Mgr Wood Expressions Arts/Crafts 1978; Owner/Partner The Inn Store 1978-81; Instr MA Migrant Ed Prgm 1979-80; Instr/Supvr Adult Clerical Trng Prgm 1981-82, Evening Instr/Word Processing 1982- Bristol Comm Coll; Bus Dept Chairperson Pres/Partner Somerset HS 1982-; Cmptr Bus Micro Users Unlimited Incorporated 1985-; *ai:* NEA, MA Teachers Assn, New England Bus Ed Assn; Carla Whipp Shlshp Fnd Pres 1979; Marion Awd Medal Cath Diocese 1975; Recognition Awd City of Fall River; MA Migrant Ed Awd 1980; MA Dept Occupational Ed Automated Typing Instruction 1973, Career Resource Center 1978-80, Word/Data Processing Prgm Grant 1983-86; *office:* Somerset HS Grandview Ave Somerset MA 02726

PELHAM, ROMIE MC DANIEL, Social Studies Teacher; *b:* Mountain Creek, AL; *c:* Sonya P. Mc Ray, Ametria M., Katrina P. Johnson; *ed:* (BS) Soc Stud, AL a & M Coll 1956; (MED) Scndry Ed, AL St Univ 1969; Post Masters Studies Univ of AL 1985-; *cr:* Jr HS Teacher Maplesville Jr HS 1957-62; Sr HS Teacher Chilton Cty Trng Sch 1963-64; Rdng Teacher West End Jr HS 1966-69; Soc Stud Teacher Verbena HS 1969-; *ai:* Stu Cncl Spon; Fclty Courtesy Comm; Political Action Comm; NEA; AL Ed Assn; Chilton Cty Ed Assn; Amer Legion Aux; Union Baptist Church Youth Dept 1982-; Zeta Phi Beta; AEA Delg Assem; AEA Uniserv Building Rep; Leukemia Volunteer Worker; *home:* 906 Samaria Rd Clanton AL 35045

PELISCHEK, PATTI LYNN (DEGLOW), 5th Grade Teacher; *b:* Fond Du Lac, WI; *m:* Jeffrey J.; *c:* Meaghan, Joshua; *ed:* (BA) Elem Ed, Univ of WI Oshkosh 1983; Grad Stud Rdng; *cr:* 5th Grade Teacher Campbellsport Elem 1984-; *ai:* Asst Track Coach; Rolling Meadows Ladies Golf League Treas 1983-84; Published Dyslexia Articles; *office:* Campbellsport Elem Sch 114 W Sheboygan St Campbellsport WI 53010

PELKOFER, SHIRLEY JENNIGES, Third Grade Teacher; *b:* Hot Springs, SD; *m:* Dennis; *c:* Tim, Julie Waage, Pat, Linda; *ed:* (BS) Elem Ed, Chadron St Univ 1967; Northern St Univ; *cr:* 2nd Grade Teacher Valleyview 1957-60; 4th Grade Teacher Riverside 1960-61; 5th Grade Teacher Hot Springs Elem 1962-67; 3rd Grade Teacher C C Lee Elem 1978-; *ai:* Delta Kappa Gamma 1982-; St Marys Altar Society 1975-; Roncalli Auxillary 1975-; Outstanding Educator C C Lee Elem 1986; Teacher of Week Aberdeem Am News 1990; *home:* 615 N Lincoln Aberdeen SD 57401

PELL, STAFANIE A., English Teacher; *b:* Fukuoka, Japan; *m:* Richard A.; *ed:* (BA) Eng, CO St Univ 1974; (MA) Guildance/Counseling, Univ of CO Colorado Spring 1982; (MAT Learning Styles Cluster Trng, Cooperative Learning, Sch Team Approach Trainer, Project Excl; *cr:* Eng Teacher East Jr HS 1974-75, Sabin Jr HS 1975-82, Russell Jr HS 1982-83; Cnslr Doherty HS 1983-87; Eng Teacher Sabin Jr HS 1987-; *ai:* Dist Staff Dev; Phi Delta Kappa 1983-; ASTD, ASCD, NCTE 1988-; Jung Society 1987-; *office:* Sabin Jr HS 3605 N Carefree Colorado Springs CO 80917

PELLEGRINI, CAROLYN ANN, 4th Grade Teacher; *b:* New York, NY; *ed:* (BA) Liberal Stud/Ethnick Stud, CSU 1978; *cr:* 2nd Grade Teacher Osborn Elem 1979-80; 2nd-4th Grade Teacher Wakefield Elem 1980-85; 4th/5th Grade Teacher Crowell Elem 1985-; *ai:* Chm Multiculture Comm; Mem Dist Rdng Comm; Global Ed Comm; Supervising Teacher to Student Teacher; Photography Instr; GATE/Enrichment Prgm; Stanislaus Rdng Cncl 1989-; Turlock Teachers Assn Site Rep 1985-; Grant Recipient Choose Well Be Well CA St Dept Nutrition Ed 1988-89; *office:* Crowell Sch 118 North Ave Turlock CA 95380

PELLETIER, NANCY (DICKEY), Fifth Grade Teacher; *b:* New Brunswick, NJ; *m:* Richard M.; *c:* James R., Michael D.; *ed:* (BS) Elem Ed, 1971, (MED) Math/Sci Elem Ed, 1973 GA St Univ; *cr:* 5th/7th Grade Teacher Laurel Ridge Elem; *ai:* Strategic Planning for Sch Improvement Chm; Patrol Spon; Media Comm; Career Ed Comm Chm; Delta Kappa Gamma (Pres 1986-88, Secy, Treas 1988-); Teacher of Yr 1989-; *home:* 2713 Diamond Head Ct Decatur GA 30033

PELLETIER, ROGER JOSEPH, Fifth Grade Teacher; *b:* Ft Kent, ME; *m:* Caryn Brand; *ed:* (BS) Elem Ed, 1975, (MS) Ed, W MT 1983; (MS) Elem Admin, Univ of MT 1988; *cr:* 5th/6th Grade Teacher Hingham Public Schls 1975-76; 5th Grade Teacher Rudyard Public Schls 1976-79, Dillon Public Schls 1979-; *ai:* Jr HS Wrestling & Ftbl Coach; Block Grant Dispersement & Prof Dev Comm; MT Math Teachers 1984-; MT Ed Assn Local Pres 1980-; Dillon Jaycees 1979-, Outstanding Young Man 1983; Dillon Lions 1988-; *home:* 3350 Hwy 91 N Dillon MT 59725

PELLEY, ORETA M., 3rd Grade Teacher; *b:* Bakersfield, CA; *m:* Robert L. Jr.; *c:* Robert W., Michael Scott *ed:* (BS) Elem Ed, Univ Sci & Arts 1979; (MS) Rdng Ed, Univ of OK 1983; *cr:* 3rd Grade Teacher Ninnekah Elem 1979-81; 3rd Grade Teacher Rush Springs Elem 1981-; *ai:* NEA/OEA 1979-; Grady Co OEA Sec/Treas 1986-87; Grady Co Cncl Treas 1988-89; Glover Spencer Lib Lib Bd Mem 1989-.

PELLMAN, JEANETTE (THORNTON), English Teacher; *b:* Rogersville, AL; *c:* Terry; *ed:* (BA) Eng, TN Temple Coll 1962; *cr:* Eng Lang Art Teacher Miller Road Chrstn Sch 1962-67; Eng Teacher Beraehah Acad 1972-85, Thrifthaven Baptist Sch 1985-; *ai:* Sr Class Spon; AL Assn of Chrstn Schls 1981-85, Outstanding Teacher Awd 1982; TN Assn of Chrstn Schls 1985-, Thrifthaven Baptist Sch Teacher of Yr 1988; Article Published in Pen & Brush, Society of Tech Writers & Publishers; *office:* Thrifthaven Baptist Sch 3925 Chelsea Ave Memphis TN 38108

PELZEL, MICHAEL J., Third Grade Teacher; *b:* Cincinnati, OH; *m:* Nancy Thatcher; *ed:* (BA) Elem Ed, Thomas More Coll 1973; Grad Work Xavier Univ, Univ of Cincinnati, Tri-State Ger Amer Sch; *cr:* Elem Teacher St James Sch 1969-70; St Margaret Mary Sch 1970-; *ai:* Olympic Day Chairperson; Textbook Selection Comm; NCEA 1969-; Hamilton Cty Chapter OH Genealogical Society 1989-; N Coll Drug Ed Comm 1971; League for Animal Welfare 1985-; St Margaret Mary PTA (Pres 1982-83, VP 1977-82, Auditor), Life Membership Awd 1983; Archdiocese of Cincinnati Certificate of Recognition 1989; Book Published 1989; *office:* St Margaret Mary Sch 1820 W Galbraith Rd Cincinnati OH 45239

PELZL, THEODORE A., Mathematics Department Chair; *b:* New Ulm, MN; *m:* Jean; *c:* Lorry, Terry, Rick; *ed:* (BA) Math/Phys Ed, Mankato St Univ 1960; (MA) Math, Univ of SD 1972; *cr:* Math Teacher/Coach NW Luth Acad 1959-72; Ellendale-Geneva HS 1973; *ai:* Boys Var Bsktbl, Track Coach; Continuing Ed Comm; Summer Recreation Dir; Sr Class Adv; MSHCA, NHSCA; Ellendale Lions Club (Pres, Mem) 1983; 4 Summer NSF Grants.

PENA, BEVERLY STALLONS, Elementary Teacher; *b:* Hopkinsville, KY; *m:* Dean; *c:* Misty D., Lyndee L., Karrah R.; *ed:* (BS) Elem Ed, Univ of KY Lexington 1974; Murray St Univ, Clear Lake Univ; *cr:* 1st Grade Teacher Maxwell Elem 1974-75, Breckinridge Elem 1975-76, Trigg Cty Elem 1976-79; 3rd Grade Teacher Trigg Cty Elem 1979-81; 1st Grade Teacher Green Valley Elem 1981-84; Homemaker 1984-; *ai:* Assn of TX Prof Educators 1981-84; GSA (Troop Cookie Mgr 1988, Asst Brownie Leader 1989); PTO Headroom Mother 1985-89; Rdng Approach that Combines Phonetic & Basal Prgms; *home:* 158 Lancewood Cir Lufkin TX 75901

PENA, CRISTINA GUTIERREZ, US/World History Teacher; *b:* Laredo, TX; *m:* Jose Eduardo; *c:* Auriana, Mikkel; *ed:* (BA) US His, Univ of TX 1978; Eng as 2nd Lang Wkshp; *cr:* Soc Stud Teacher Cigarroa Mid Sch 1984-87, Cigarroa HS 1987-; *office:* Cigarroa HS 2600 Zacatecas St Laredo TX 78043

PENA, DIANE MACALUSO, Fifth Grade Teacher; *b:* Galveston, TX; *m:* Carlos E.; *c:* Steven, Stephanie; *ed:* (BS) Elem Ed, Univ of Houston 1978; *cr:* 3rd Grade Teacher 1978-81, 5th Grade Teacher 1981- Trinity Episcopal Sch; *ai:* Drama & Conductor Glee Club; SW Assn of Episcopal Schls Wkshp; Delta Kappa Gamma 1985-89; Jr League of Galveston Cty 1985-87; First Luth Church (Choir 1978-, Vestry 1979-82, Asst Sunday Sch Supt 1986-89); Galveston Rotary Club Teacher of Month 1983; Frenkel Awd 1988; Top 50 Teacher Galveston Academic Excl Booster Club 1984-85, 1987-88; *home:* 2719 Palm Circle W Galveston TX 77551

PENA, ESTEFANA S., 7th-8th Grade Lang Art Teacher; *b:* Hurley, NM; *ed:* (BS) General Elem Ed/Eng/His/Fr, W NM Univ 1954; Various Ed Courses; *cr:* 4th Grade/Mentally Gifted Teacher Horace Mann Sch 1954-70; His/Rdng/Eng Opportunity Class/GATE/Lit/Span Teacher Washington Jr HS 1970-; *ai:* NEA, CA Teachers Assn 1954; Bakersfield Elem Teachers Assn Building Rep; CA PTA 1954, Honorary Life Membership 1968, Honorary Service Awd 1977; Delta Kappa Gamma (Secy, Membership) 1969-89; *home:* 2326 Alta Vista Dr Bakersfield CA 93305

PENA, LEOCADITA, Fourth Grade Teacher; *b:* Rio Grande City, TX; *m:* Cipriano; *c:* Lora L., Martha E., Nina J.; *ed:* (BA) Elem Ed Pan Amer Univ 1973; Addl Studies Advanced Bilingual Classes Univ of KS; Career Ladder Level III; *cr:* Elem Teacher Edinburg 1973-; *ai:* TCTA 1973-; Teacher of the Month Awd 1984; St Theresa Parish, Pres 1985-87; 15 Year Service Awd from ECISD.

PENA, LINA VILLARREAL, Teacher; *b:* Laredo, TX; *m:* Heriberto; *c:* Heriberto, Erika; *ed:* (BS) Ed, 1979-80, (MS) Ed, 1982-83 Laredo St Univ; *cr:* Teacher Laredo Ind Sch Dist; *ai:* Expectation Comm; *office:* Memorial Mid Sch 2002 Marcella Laredo TX 78040

PENAS, MAXINE SLUKA, Bio/Chem/Physics Teacher; *b:* Roseau, MN; *m:* Albert Lee; *c:* Mary, Daniel, Samuel; *ed:* (BA) Bio/Chem, Coll of St Benedict 1968; Various Stud at Various Univs; *cr:* Sci Teacher Mid River Cmmty Sch 1969-88, Greenbush HS 1988-; *ai:* Mem Legislative Task Force on Ed, St Bd MN Rural Ed Assn; MN Ed Assn 1967-; MN Rural Ed assn Bd Mem 1989-; MN Sci Teachers Assn 1978-; St Marys Church Finance Cncl 1987-; Diocesan Pastoral Cncl 1987-; Wrote & Executed Ornithology Title II Part C Project; Technology Specialist in Sci for Project Smart, High Tech Site in MN; *office:* Greenbush HS Greenbush MN 56726

PENCE, JACKIE S., US History Teacher; *b:* Martin, KY; *m:* Charles W.; *ed:* (BA) Soc Stud, Morehead St Univ 1970; Ec Ed Law Awareness; Inservice Trng Teaching Gifted Stu; *cr:* Teacher Campbell Cty HS 1969-72; Tuskawilla Mid Sch 1976-; *ai:* Beta Sigma Phi (Pres 1976- Womn of Yr Cncl Sweetheart 1982/1985/1988); *office:* Tuskawilla Mid Sch 1801 Tuskawilla Rd Oviedo FL 32765

PENCE, MARJORIE (RAISCH), English/Spanish Teacher; *b:* Milwaukee, WI; *m:* Neal A.; *ed:* (BS) Eng, WI St Coll Superior 1967; Grad Stud at Numerous Colls; *cr:* Eng Teacher Flathead Cty HS 1962-64; Eng Teacher/Librarian Cody HS 1964-66; Eng/Speech Drama Teacher White Lake HS 1968-; *ai:* Drama; Forensics; White Lake Ed Assn Pres 1976-77, 1984-86; Tri-Cty Horse Assn (Bd of Dir 1988-89, VP 1989-); 4-H Horse Project Co-Leader 1988-; Leaders of Amer Scndry Ed 1972; Poem Published; *office:* White Lake HS White Lake WI 54491

PENDER, KAREN I. (FRANZ), 7th-8th Grade Lang Art Teacher; *b:* New York, NY; *m:* Michael J.; *ed:* (BA) Eng/Scndry Ed, 1980, (MS) Eng/Scndry Ed, 1983 Queens Coll; Prgm for Dev of Human Potential Group Facilitators Skills Trng; *cr:* 7th/8th Grade Teacher St Josephs Sch 1980-; *ai:* HS Adv; Rap Group Facilitator; 8th Grade, Lang Art, Spelling Bee, Graduation, Jr HS Dance Coord; NCTE Mem; Nature Conservancy; Kappa Delta Pi Mem; NYS Eng Cncl Excl in Teaching Awd Nom 1990; *office:* St Josephs Sch 28-46 44th St Long Island City NY 11103

PENDERGAST, SALLIE BROWN, Fourth Grade Teacher; *b:* Jacksonville, FL; *m:* Patrick J.; *c:* Meaghan, Meredith; *ed:* (BA) Elem Ed, 1978, (MS) Elem Ed, 1981 Auburn Univ; *cr:* Title 1 Teacher Wetumpka Elem & Holtville Elem 1979; 4th Grade Teacher Wetumpka Elem 1979-; *ai:* Alpha Delta Kappa Historian 1988-; Elmore Cty Ed Assn, AL Ed Assn, NEA; *office:* Wetumpka Elem Sch 1000 Micanopy St Wetumpka AL 36092

PENDERGRASS, LINDA JO (WILLIAMS), Teacher of Gifted & Talented; *b:* Ft Smith, AR; *m:* Ewell Dean; *c:* William D., Douglas A., Nagaya J.; *ed:* (BAED) Eng, Northeastern St Coll Tahlequah 1974; Scndry Ed, Univ of AR Fayetteville; Gifted/Talented Ed, AR Tech Univ Russellville; *cr:* Instr Pocola HS 1974-75; Instr/Dir Ft Smith Hope Center 1983-84; Instr Amer Coll 1984-85, Cedarville Public Schls 1985-; *ai:* Photography Club & Yrbk Adv; Personnel Policy Comm Secy; Odyssey of Mind Judge; 7th Grade Class Spon; HS & Elem Photography Coord; NEA, AEA 1974-75, 1985-; CEA Secy 1985-; AR Waterworks Pollution Control Assn 1987-; Cedarville Ed Assn Secy; Wesley United Meth Church (Youth Dir 1984-86, Ed Comm 1988, Worship Comm 1990); Ft Smith Church League Bsbl Auxiliary 1980-87; BSA Den Mother 1980-87; Spec Olympics Coaching Cert; *home:* 119 Martin Cir Fort Smtih AR 72903

PENDERGRASS, M. EILEEN, Sixth Grade Teacher; *b:* Schenectady, NY; *m:* John Robert; *c:* John Jr.; *ed:* (BS) Ed, SUNY Plattsburg 1971; Grad Work SUNY Oneonta, Coll of St Rose; *cr:* 4th/5th Grade Teacher Sharon Springs Cntrl 1971-86; 6th Grade Lang Art/Math Teacher Cobleskill Mid Sch 1986-; *ai:* Mid Level Ed Comm; Comm Adv; Teacher of Excl NY St Eng Cncl 1982; *office:* Cobleskill Mid Sch Washington Heights Cobleskill NY 12043

PENDLETON, KENT LUND, Mathematics Department Chair; *b:* Midland, TX; *m:* Lynn B. Britt; *c:* Nathan, Laura, David; *ed:* (BA) Physics, 1980, (ME) Civil Engineering, 1984 TX A&M Univ; DOE Explosives Safety Trng; Robotics Engineering Courses; *cr:* Research Engr Sandia Natl Laboratory 1984-87; Math Dept Chm Trinity Chrstn Acad 1987-; *ai:* Greater Dallas Cncl of Math Teachers 1988-; *home:* 1217 Berkeley Dr Richardson TX 75081

PENDLETON, PAULA PLASTER, Third Grade Teacher; *b:* Patrick Cty, VA; *m:* Bobby Nelson; *c:* Rene P. Coleman, Ryan N.; *ed:* (BS) Elem Ed, E Carolina Univ 1963; *cr:* Teacher Hardin Reynolds Memorial Sch 1963-72; 3rd-7th Grade Teacher Stuart Elem Sch 1973-; *ai:* Delta Kappa Gamma, NEA, VEA, PCEA; Patrick Springs Pentecostal Holiness Church (Treas 1989-, Sunday Sch Teacher); Ruritanette Ruritan Mother of Yr 1982; Patrick Springs Volunteer Fire Dept Ladies Auxiliary Secy 1982; *home:* Rt 1 Box 46 Patrick Springs VA 24133

PENDT, DIANA BURRIS, 3rd Grade Teacher; *b:* Alton, IL; *m:* Ronald V.; *c:* Terry, Kurt; *ed:* (BS) Spec Ed, 1974, (MS) Spec Ed, 1978 Southern IL Univ; Ed Admin; *cr:* Primary Teacher 1974-76, Primary LD Teacher 1976-77, Primary Teacher 1977- Blair Sch East Alton Sch Dist 13; *ai:* Just Say No Club-Blair Sch; Delta Kappa Gamma 1980-89; PTA/PTO Pres/VP 1973-77; Cmmty United for Alcohol/Drug Awareness Ed Act; Mini Grant Regional Supt for Drug Awareness Project; *office:* Blair Elem Sch 300 Washington Ave East Alton IL 62024

PENKE, DARWIN D., Soc Stud/Driver Ed Teacher; *b:* Ripon, WI; *m:* Constance L. Smack; *ed:* (BS) Soc Sci, Univ of WI Oshkosh 1965; Driver Ed Cert Univ of WI Stevens Point 1968; *cr:* Teacher Hilbert HS 1965-66, Port Edwards Schls 1966-; *ai:* Behind-The-Wheel Driver Ed; SADD, Model United Nations, Soph Class Adv; SEC Steering Comm; WDTSEA 1970-; Lions 1974-; St WEAC Comm 1986-; Uniserv Bd of Dir 1980-84; *home:* 721 Williams Ave Port Edwards WI 54469

PENN, MARSHA BARRS, World Geography Teacher; *b:* Walterboro, SC; *m:* Earl William; *c:* Christopher B.; *ed:* (BA) Eng, 1970, (MA) Soc Sci, 1976 Univ of SC; Grad Stud; *cr:* Eng/Soc Stud Teacher St Stephens Mid Sch 1970-72; Kndgtn Teacher Branchville Elem Sch 1972-73; Eng Teacher Bethune HS 1973-79; Soc Sci Teacher Woodruff Jr HS 1980-; *ai:* Beta Club & Jr Scholars Co-Spon; Spartanburg Cty Assn of Educators, SC Ed Assn, NEA 1984-; Fairforest Baptist Church 1989-; Teacher of Yr Bethune HS 1975 & Woodruff Jr HS 1985; Yrbk Dedication Bethune HS 1977 & Woodruff Jr HS 1987; *office:* Woodruff Jr HS S J Workman Rd PO Box 309 Woodruff SC 29388

PENN, MARY JANE, English/Language Art Teacher; *b:* New Berlin, PA; *c:* David, Michael, Lisa, Joel; *ed:* (BS) Music, Susquehanna Univ 1956; Wheaton Coll; Teacher Cert Univ of Albuquerque; Teacher Cert/Recertification, Univ of NM & Univ of Denver; Prof Growth Educators, Univ of Denver 1988; Jim Fays Love & Logic Wkshp 1988; Effective Teacher Trng 1987; *cr:* Study Hall Supvr Evanston Township HS 1963-64; Substitute Teacher Evanston Schls 1964-66; Classroom Teacher Parochial Sch 1966; Substitute Teacher Albuquerque Public Schls 1973-79; Eng/Lang Art Teacher Cibola HS 1979-; *ai:* Cibola HS Staff Melodrama & Comedy Actor & Singer; Choral Teacher Asst 1980; Albuquerque Teachers Fed 1989-; Sigma Alpha Iota Life Mem; NM Mt Club Librarian 1980-; Opera SW Productions Chorus; *home:* 5800 Osuna NE #206 Albuquerque NM 87109

PENNA, CECILIA A. P., Biology Teacher; *b:* Toronto, Ontario, Canada; *ed:* (BS) Bio, Montclair St Coll 1978; *cr:* Bio Teacher Toms River HS South 1978-79; Toms River HS East 1979-; *ai:* Peer Leadership; Teen Listening Ctr; Sci League; NABT 1986-; NJ Sci Teachers Assn 1986-; Amer Red Cross Volunteer Safety Services Instr 1975-; Girl Scouts Camp Dir 1979-; Canoe Team Coach 1979-; Catholic Awds Cnslr 1989-; 1989 Governor's Teacher Recognition Awd; *home:* 308 B Hastings Way Mount Laurel NJ 08054

PENNER, DIANA CHRISTINE, Scndry Level English Teacher; *b:* Newton, KS; *ed:* (BS) Ed/Eng/Ger, KS St Univ 1986; Working Toward Masters Degree in Video Production, Radio/Television; *cr:* Lang Art Teacher Manhattan HS 1987-; Stu at Risk Teacher Continuation Sch 1987-; *ai:* Advisroy Bd, Peer Asst, Building Comms; Teacher Expectations & Stu Achievement Participant; Night Course Instr of Coll Prepartory Exams; KNEA 1987-; Implemented Broadcast Journalsim; Video Commerical Won 1st Place for St of KS in NY Seltzer Contest; Educl Tape on Aids Production 1st Pl St of KS 1988; *home:* 2128 Slaon Manhattan KS 66502

PENNINGTON, B. JOLENE STOLFUS, 4th Grade Teacher; *b:* Marysville, KS; *m:* Larry William; *c:* Christopher W., Lisa M.; *ed:* (BSED) Elem/Scndry Art, Emporia St Univ 1976; (BSED) Elem Classroom, Pittsburg St Univ 1978; Fort Hays St Univ, KS St Univ, Univ of KS, Wichita St Univ; *cr:* 1st/2nd Grade Teacher Fairfield Elem 1978-86; 4th Grade Teacher Hutton Elem 1986-; *ai:* Healthy Living Curr Comm; Sci Fair Coord; Positive Action Inservicer; Synchronized Swimming Instr & Coach; Summer Sch Math Teacher; Chanute Young Career Women 1985; Chanute Bus & Prof Womens VP 1986-87; KS Ed Assn, Chanute Ed Assn Building Rep 1978-; GSA Asst; BSA; 4-H Leader; Sunday Sch Teacher; Inservice Presentations; Nom Excl in Sci Teaching 1990; *office:* James B Hutton Elem Sch 600 S Ashby Chanute KS 66720

PENNINGTON, CARMEN GONZALES, Teacher/Fine Arts Dept Chair; *b:* Albuquerque, NM; *m:* Carlton Robert Sr.; *c:* Carlton R. Jr., Jacqueline A. Matson, Patrick, Marlo M. Maxson; *ed:* (BA) Home Ec Ed, 1975, (MA) Famility Relationships/Child Dev Ed, 1980 Univ of NM; *cr:* Secy Construction Reporter 1960, 1968-70; Housewife/Homemaker 1962-68; Teacher Bernalillo Mid Sch 1975-; *ai:* Bernalillo Mid Sch FHA & Alcohol Substance Abuse Prevention Peer Counseling Spon; NMVHETA 1980-; Delta Kappa Gamma VP 1986-87; Kappa Omicron Phi Alumnus 1985-88; Univ of NM LOBO Womens Vlybl Booster, Univ of CA Santa Barbara Mens Vlybl Booster; *office:* Bernalillo Mid Sch P O Box 640 Bernalillo NM 87004

PENNINGTON, DIXIE GOZA, History Teacher; *b:* Lexington, MD; *m:* Clyde; *c:* Lisa, Michael; *ed:* (BS) His/Eng, 1985, (MSE) Scndry Ed, 1990 E TX St Univ; *cr:* Teacher Ashdown HS 1985-; *ai:* Jr-Sr Prom Chairperson; NCSS; *office:* Ashdown HS 751 Rankin Ashdown AR 71822

PENNINGTON, JUDITH DIANNE, 9th Grade Civics Teacher; *b:* Malvern, AR; *c:* Hunter, Lee; *ed:* (BSE) Bus Ed/Soc Stud/Phys Ed, Henderson St Univ 1968; *cr:* Bus/Soc Stud/Phys Ed Teacher Mills HS 1974-79; Civics Teacher Bryant Jr HS 1986-; *ai:* Bryant Jr HS Stu Cncl Co-Spon; Alpha Delta Kappa 1990; US Senator David Pryor Teacher Internship Prgm 1989; Nom Bryant Sch Dist Teacher of Yr 1989-; *office:* Bryant Jr HS 200 N W 4th Bryant AR 72022

PENNINGTON, KIMBERLEY WATSON, 7th Grade English Teacher; *b:* Madisonville, TN; *m:* R. E.; *c:* Emily J.; *ed:* (BS) Eng Ed TN Wesleyan Coll 1978; (MS) Elem Ed Univ of TN 1985; *cr:* 9th/10th/11th Grades Teacher Independence HS 1978-80; 7th Grade Teacher Madisonville Mid Sch 1980-; *ai:* Chrldr Spon 4 Yrs; JR Beta Club Spon Previously; Teacher in An Aftersch Pilot Pgrm Spon By JTPA at Risk Stu Strive for Success; Mc Minn Cty Democrat Womens Club Pres 1987-88, VP 1986-87 Parliament 1989-; *home:* P O Box 148 Niota TN 37826

PENNINGTON, LILLIAN DORIS, German/Spanish Teacher; *b:* Durbin, WV; *ed:* (BA) Ger, Hiram Coll 1973; (MA) Ger, 1979, (PHD) Ger, 1983 OH St Univ; *cr:* Teacher Olney Friends Sch 1975-78; Assoc Ed Modern Lang Journal 1981-83; Teacher Patrick Henry HS 1984-; *ai:* Ger & Span Club Adv; AATG, Amer Assn Teachers of Span & Portuguese, NEA; *office:* Patrick Henry HS St Rt 18 Hamler OH 43524

PENNYPACKER, HARRY BYRON, History Teacher; *b:* Lebanon, PA; *m:* Sally; *c:* Emily, Abigail, Molly, Helen; *ed:* (BS) Scndry Ed, 1968, (MS) European His, 1976 Millersville Univ; *cr:* 9th Grade Teacher Cedar Crest HS 1968-71; 7th/8th Grade Teacher Cedar Crest Mid Sch 1971-; *office:* Cedar Crest Mid Sch 101 E Evergreen Rd Lebanon PA 17042

PENOLI, CAROL HARWELL, Band Director; *b:* Corsicana, TX; *m:* Donald; *c:* Jason; *ed:* (BMUSED) Music, Tarleton St Univ 1975; *cr:* Band Dir Temple Ind Sch Dist 1975-77, Azle Ind Sch Dist 1977-80; Elem Music Teacher Arlington Ind Sch Dist 1980-81; Band Dir China Spring Ind Sch Dist 1982-83, Mc Gregor Ind Sch Dist 1983-86, Lorena Ind Sch Dist 1986-; *ai:* Flag Corps Spon; Sch Newspaper; Yrbk; *office:* Lorena Ind Sch Dist PO Box 97 Lorena TX 76655

PENROSE, PATRICIA WOLTERS, English Department Chair; *b:* San Francisco, CA; *c:* Christopher, Shannon, Dylan; *ed:* (BS) Eng/Soc Sci, Cal Poly 1966; (MED) Admin Services, Azusa Pacific Univ 1989; CA Writing Project, UCLA; CA Lit Project, UCI; *cr:* Eng Teacher 1981-86, Mentor Teacher 1986-, Dept Chairperson 1989- Nogales HS; *ai:* Dist Eng Lang Curr, Staff Dev Comm; Yrbk Adv; NCTE, ASCD; *office:* Nogales HS 401 S Nogales La Puente CA 91744

PENSE, DORENE SANDS, First Grade Teacher; *b:* Dodge City, KS; *m:* Harold; *c:* Chad, Marc; *ed:* (BS) Elem Ed, S Nazarene Univ 1966; (MA) Elem Ed, Central St Univ 1970; *cr:* 1st-3rd Grade Teacher Sumner Elem Sch 1966-71; 1st Grade Teacher Perry Elem Sch 1973-; *ai:* NEA, OK Ed Assn 1973-; Intnl Rdng Assn 1988-; Perry Public Schls Teacher of Yr 1988.

PENTILA, CELESTE CORINNE, English Teacher; *b:* Salt Lake City, UT; *ed:* (BA) Eng, Gonzaga Univ 1972; (MS) Creative Arts in Ed, Lesley Coll 1989; *cr:* Eng Teacher East Jr HS 1972-; Eng/Photography Teacher Cody Jr HS 1975-; *ai:* Yrbk Adv; Delta Kappa Gamma Secy 1985-87; Cody Ed Assn, WY Ed Assn, NEA; *office:* Cody Jr HS 920 Beck Ave Cody WY 82414

PENTON, MARTHA WHITE, 2nd Grade Teacher; *b:* Sulphur Springs, TX; *m:* Lon A.; *ed:* (BS) Bus, East TX St Coll 1962; (MS) Ed, Lang Arts East TX St Univ 1969; Post Masters Degree Curr; *cr:* 1st Grade Teacher Galloway Elem Sch 1967-84; 2nd Grade Teacher 1984 Hazelwood Elem Sch; *ai:* Staff Comm Comm; United Way Campaign Chm Hazelwood Sch; Experimental Class Federal Grant Through Univ WA; Hypertext Cmptr Assisted Instruction Maintaining Handicapped Students in Regular Classroom Rdng Prgm; NCTM 1976-77; Natl Sci Teachers of America 1977-78; Multiple Schlerosis Society 1985-89; Parent-Stu-Teacher Assn 1967-; TX St Teachers Assn 1967-68; Renton Ed Assn 1968-; WA Ed Assn 1968; NEA 1967-; *office:* Hazelwood Elem Sch 6928 116th Ave S E Renton WA 98056

PEOPLES, DARLENE AREY, Elementary Teacher; *b:* Polo, MO; *m:* David W.; *c:* David L., Dennis L., Kenneth H.; *ed:* (BS) Elem Ed, 1971, (MS) Rdng 1979, Cntrl MO St 1979; *cr:* Teacher MO City Elem 1970-71, E Lynne Elem 1971-; *ai:* MO St Teacher Assn 1970-; Gifted Assn of MO, Intnl Rdng Assn 1986-; MO Rdng Assn; E Lynne Teachers Assn (Pres 1975-79, VP 1986-88), Outstanding Teacher of Yr 1988-89; MO Alliance Summer Geography Inst; *home:* 205 W Walnut Blue Springs MO 64014

PEOPLES, DOROTHY SNEED, Third Grade Teacher; *b:* Mc Kenzie, TN; *m:* James Y.; *c:* Cedric G.; *ed:* (BSN) Nursing, Meharry Med Coll Sch of Nursing 1959; (MED) Elem Ed, De Paul Univ 1966; TN St Univ, Northeastern Univ, Chicago St Univ, Roosevelt Univ; *cr:* Staff Nurse/Pvt Duty, Univ of Chicago/Michael Reese 1959-64; Sch Nurse Chicago Public Sch 1964; Spec Ed Teacher Matthew Hensen Sch 1964-66; Teacher Mc Kinley & King Elem Schls 1966-; Chm Primary & intermediate Dept/Team Leader/Math Lab Martin L King Sch; *ai:* Co-Moderator Womens Assn Chatham Church; Chrstn Ed Comm; Sing In Choir; Adult Sunday Sch; Hales Franciscan Parent Assn & Awds Comm; Tau Gamma Delta Ed in Chief; Teachers Union Local 1698 Building Rep; BSA Den Leader 1981-84; Rosa L Gregg Ed & Civic Club Corr Secy; NAACP 1990; Nom Outstanding Young Women of America 1979; Outstanding Achievement iN Teaching; Spec Service Awd 1986; Staff Dev Wkshp; *home:* 7348 S Constance Ave Chicago IL 60649

PEOPLES, JAMES WENDELL, Math Teacher; *b:* Durant, OK; *m:* Janice I.; *c:* James L., Angela J.; *ed:* (BS) Math, 1966, (MS) Math, 1970 S OK St Univ; Post Grad Admin; *cr:* Math Teacher Taft Jr HS 1966-67, Kingston HS 1967-69, Silo HS 1969-; *ai:* Mu Alpha Theta Math Club, HS Scholastic Contest & OK Math League Contest Spon; OEA Bryan Cty Teacher of Yr 1978; Local OEA Silo Sch Teacher of Yr 1980; Silo Baptist Church (SS Dir 1980-, SS Teacher 1978-); Comm Mem OK Curr Improvement Commission; Prism Prin Resources in Scndry Math 1984-85; *home:* HC 30 Box 116B Durant OK 74701

PEOPLES, JOYCE LEE (DENNIS), Fifth Grade Teacher; *b:* Cambridge, OH; *m:* Timothy Eugene; *c:* Brian David, Bradley Allen; *ed:* (BA) Elem Ed, Music Ed, Muskingum Coll 1979; Cnslr Ed Univ of Dayton; *cr:* 7th/8th Grade Teacher Dexter City Jr HS 1979, 5th/6th Grade Teacher 1979-82, 5th Grade Teacher 1982-88 Caldwell Mid Sch; 5th Grade Teacher Caldwell Elem Sch 1988-; *ai:* Soc Stud Textbook Adoption Comm; Curr Comm; Math Competency Testing; NEA 1979-; OEA 1979-; Caldwell Teachers Assn 1979-; PTO 1980-81; Church of Christ Mem; *office:* Caldwell Elem Sch 44350 Fairground Rd Caldwell OH 43724

PEOPLES, LEILA OSBORN, Third Grade Teacher; *b:* Camargo, OK; *m:* Adonis; *c:* Arnold, Alan, Eric; *ed:* (BA) Elem Ed, Panhandle St 1960; Grad Stud Rdng Specialist; Working Towards Masters, NW OK St Univ; *cr:* 4th Grade Teacher Guymon Sch 1969-77; 3rd Grade Teacher Vici Sch 1977-; *ai:* Vici Adopt a Highway Chairperson; Organization of Monthly Elem Assembly; Staff Dev Chairperson Vici Sch 1984-86; OEA, NEA 1969-89; Dewey Cty Ed Assn Secy 1980-81, Teacher of Yr 1980; Vici Sch Teacher of Yr 1986-87.

PEOPLES, PATRICIA LAIRD, French/English Teacher; *b:* Florala, AL; *m:* Terry Hugh; *c:* Anais; *ed:* (BA) Eng, Auburn Univ 1979; PACER Prgm Fr, Univ of Al; *cr:* Teacher Florala HS 1987-; *ai:* Annual Staff & 10th Grade Class Adv; NEA, AEA, CEA; Florala Civic Club Corresponding Secy 1985-86; AL Commission Higher Ed Travel Grant to France; *office:* Florala HS P O Box 218 Florala AL 36442

PEPELNJAK, JOYCE CARDONI, Third Grade Teacher; *b:* Virginia, MN; *w:* Frank (dec); *c:* Jim, Joy Pepelnjak Wollenzien, Wendy Pepelnjak Senarighi, Mary Pepelnjak Rozier; *ed:* (BS) Elem, Duluth St Teachers 1946; Working Towards Masters Univ of MN Duluth 1970; *cr:* Elem Phys Ed Teacher Virginia & Jefferson & James Madison & Lincoln Elem 1946-48; 2nd Grade Teacher Franklin Sch 1948-49; Spec Ed Teacher Johnson Sch 1967-68; 1st Grade Teacher Lincoln Sch 1968-70; 3rd Grade Teacher Horace Mann Sch 1970-83, Roosevelt Sch 1983-; *ai:* VA Ed Assn, MN Ed Assn, NEA 1967-; Alpha Delta Gamma 1968-; Univ Women 1984-; VA Hospital Commission Mem 1982-85; Holy Spirit Cath Church Parish Cncl 1988-; VA Hospital Auxiliary; Jaycee Women Pres 1952-53, Todays Woman 1985; Soroptimist Intnl Bellringer Awd; Legion Auxiliary 1953-; *home:* 315 S 10th Virginia MN 55792

PEPERA, MICHAEL GERARD, Geography Teacher; *b:* Baudette, MN; *m:* Shelley M. Johnson; *ed:* (BS) Soc Stud, Univ of ND 1981; Grad Prgm Mankato Univ; *cr:* Geography Teacher Scott Highlands Mid Sch 1982-; *ai:* Mid Sch Ftbl & Bsbl Coach; Bantam A Hockey Coach 1986-89; Comparative Ed Seminar USSR; *office:* Scott Highlands Mid Sch 14011 Pilot Knob Rd Apple Valley MN 55124

PEPPER, THOMAS ANDREW, Science Department Chair; *b:* Pontiac, MI; *m:* Anita Caryl Backus; *ed:* (BS) Biological Sci, 1973, (MA) Ed, 1979 MI St Univ; *cr:* Sci Teacher Bullock Creek HS 1973-74, Vandercook Lake Cmmty Schls 1974-; *ai:* Sci Dept & Sci Curr Chm; NSTA, MI Sci Teachers Assn, MEA, NEA; Employee of Month 1989; *office:* Vandercook Lake Cmmty Schls 1000 Golf Ave Jackson MI 49203

PERALES, ARTURO, Mathematics Teacher; *b:* El Paso, TX; *m:* Rebecca Ayala; *c:* Arthur J.; *ed:* (BA) Ed, 1974, (MS) Guidance/Counseling, 1977 W NM Univ; *cr:* Math Teacher Henderson Jr HS 1974-; *ai:* Tutor Project STAR; 5 Yr Planning & Homework Planning Comm; PTA VP 1986-88, Lifetime Mem 1986; *office:* Henderson Jr HS 5505 Comanche El Paso TX 79905

PERALES-RUBIN, ALBERT, Spanish Teacher; *b:* Matanzas, Cuba; *m:* Maria A. Diaz; *c:* Laura I.; *ed:* (BA) Span, CA St Long Beach 1972; *cr:* Span Teacher Dinuba U HS 1973-; *ai:* Mecha Club Adv; Cntrl Valley Foreign Lang Assn 1980-; Dinuba Friends of Lib Treas 1985-; *office:* Dinuba U HS 1327 E El Monte Dinuba CA 93618

PERALTA, PATRICIA LA VERN, First Grade Teacher; *b:* Alcalde, NM; *m:* Orlando; *c:* Daniella; *ed:* (BA) Elem Ed, Coll of Emporia 1966; Addl Studies Highlands Univ; NMSU; Univ of NM; *cr:* Teacher Kearney Elem 1966; Chimayo Elem 1967-68; Alcalde Elem 1968-; *ai:* Chrldr Spon; Sci Spon; Spelling Spon; Art Spon; NEA; *home:* P O Box 130 Alcade NM 87511

PERCIVAL, CINDY MILLER, Mathematics Teacher; *b:* Alva, OK; *m:* Neal Jr.; *c:* Tina, Travis, Trenton; *ed:* (BA) Eng, 1970, (BS) Math, 1970, (MED) Eng Lit, 1974 NW OK St Univ; Post Masters Work HS Counseling & Clinical Psych; *cr:* Eng Teacher Cherokee HS 1972-74, Waynoka HS 1974-79; Cnslr 1979-86, Math Teacher 1986- Waynoka HS; *ai:* Academic Team Coach; Academic Bowl Coord; Curricular Advisory Comm; OEA 1971-80; Governors Cncl Teen Pregnancy 1983; Bd of Northwest Family Services 1984-88; *office:* Waynoka HS RR 1 Waynoka OK 73860

PERCIVAL, DENNIS LEE, Social Studies Teacher; *b:* Alva, OK; *m:* Kate Engel; *c:* Scott, Dianne; *ed:* (BA) Phys Ed, Phillips Univ 1967; (MED) Phys Ed/Ed, OK Univ 1968; *cr:* Phys Ed Chm/Head Ftbl/Bsktbl Coach Kennedy Jr HS 1968-69; Phys Ed Dept Chm/Head Ftbl/Bsktbl/Bsbl AZ Intermediate La Sierra HS 1971-78; Dir of Intervention Sumner HS 1980-81; Phys Ed Dept Chm/Coach Ftbl/Bsktbl/Wrestling/Bsbl Lakeridge Jr HS 1981-88; Soc Stud Teacher Lakeridge Jr HS 1989-; *ai:* Undefeated Bsbl Team 1986-87; Undefeated Girls Bsktbl Teams 1986-89; Coaching Respite 1989-; *office:* Lakeridge Jr H S 5909 Meyers Rd Sumner WA 98390

PERDUE, DANIEL STEPHEN, Music & Athletic Director; *b:* Sharon, PA; *m:* Tina Marie Roberts; *c:* Chad, Jennifer, Stephanie; *ed:* Music/Youth Phys Ed, Baptist Bible Coll 1973; *cr:* Coach/Music/Youth Athletic Dir Altamonte Chrstn Sch 1980-84; Bible Teacher/Athletic Dir/Coach 1985-89, Music Dir/Bible Teacher/Athletic Dir/Coach 1989- Bethel Chrstn Acad; *ai:* Boys & Girls Var Tackle Ftbl & Bsktbl Coach; Sr Spon; Stu Counseling; Scholastic Coach Ftbl 1987 Bronze Awd & Bsktbl Silver Awd 1987, Gold Awd 1989; Seminol Cty Chamber of Commerce Educator of Yr 1982; *office:* Bethel Chrstn Acad 1950 Michigan Ave Cocoa FL 32922

PERDUE, DEBORAH WILLIAMS, History Teacher; *b:* Pensacola, FL; *m:* Stephen J.; *ed:* (BA) Scndry Ed, TN Temple Coll 1977; (MED) Scndry Ed, Univ of TN Chattanooga 1985; *cr:* Part Time Instr East Ridge HS & Cntrl HS 1977-80; His Teacher Cntrl HS 1980-; *ai:* Beta Club Spon; Public Ed Fnd Steering Comm; Delta Kappa Gamma 1989-; TN Cncl for Soc Stud Exec Comm 1988, Outstanding Soc Stud Teacher 1988; Greater Chattanooga Area Cncl for Soc Stud (Pres 1987-88) 1985-; NCSS 1985-89; Chamber of Commerce Outstanding Teacher of Yr 1990; Japan Fnd Fellowship 1987; Laura Handley Brock Excl in Teaching Awd 1987-89; *office:* Central HS 5728 Hwy 58 Harrison TN 37341

PERDUE, KAREN JUNE, Language Arts Teacher; *b:* Welch, WV; *ed:* (Bs) Eng/Spch, Concord Coll 77; (MA) Comm Arts, WV Univ 87; 7th Grade/8th Grade Rdng; *cr:* L Arts Teacher Iaeger Intermediate 1977-; *ai:* Chrldr Spon; Spelling Bee Spon; Young Writers Contest Spon; Homecomingspon; Sch Adv Comm; WV NEA 1977-; Methodist Womens Pres 1988-; Jr Womans Club VP 1987-89; Best Overall Small Club; 20 Chrldr Trophies; Teacher Ofthe Yr 2 Yrs Iaeger Intermediate; *office:* Iaeger Intermediate Sch Box 300 Iaeger WV 24844

PERDUE, MARY KATHRYN (CLARK), 5th Grade Teacher; *b:* Welch, WV; *m:* Franklin Jay; *c:* Carrie A., Jason C.; *ed:* (AB) Psych, Guilford Coll 1973; (MA) Educl Psych/Rehabilitation Counseling, Univ of KY 1975; *cr:* 3rd Grade Teacher Fall River Elem 1975-89; 5th Grade Teacher Welch Elem 1989-; *ai:* Delta Kappa Gamma Mem 1981-; Welch Jr Womans Club (Secy 1978-80) 1976-; *office:* Welch Elem Sch Box A1 Welch WV 24801

PERDUE, NANCY CROCKETT, English Teacher; *b:* Boomer, WV; *m:* Harold; *ed:* (BA) Eng, WV Inst of Technology 1962; (MSS) His, OH Univ 1989; Grad Stud; *cr:* Teacher Liberty Union HS 1962-67, 1973-; *ai:* OH Ed Assn, NEA, LUTCTA, FCEA; Twig 6; *office:* Liberty Union HS 500 Washington St Baltimore OH 43105

PERDUE, SHARON M., Fifth Grade Teacher; *b:* Dunkirk, NY; *m:* Larry D.; *c:* Brian L.; *ed:* (BA) Scndry Soc Stud, 1966, (MS) Elem Ed, 1969 St Univ of NY Fredonia; Sci Ed Wkshps; Impact Drug/Alcohol Trng; Curr Writing BOCES; NYSUT Wkshps Negotiations Conferences; Grad Stud Syracuse Univ, St Univ of NY Fredonia; *cr:* 5th Grade Teacher Rome Public Schls Bellamy Air Force Base Sch 1966-67; K-6th Grade Summer Sch Rdng Teacher Gowanda Elem Sch 1968; 5th Grade Teacher Gowanda Elem Sch 1967-; *ai:* Stu Support Team; Values Comm; Impact, Union Negotiatiator, Curr Writing Wkshps; 5th Grade Field Trip Organizer; Sunshine Comm; Dunkirk PTA Sch 5 Pres Parents Club 1979-80; NYSUT (Negotiator 1985-, Grievance Chairperson 1967); United Meth Church (Finance Comm, Parsonage Comm, Chairperson of Ecumenical Chrstn Unity); Band Booster; Sports Booster; Little League Team Mother; March of Dimes; Amer Heart Assn Collector; Nom Teacher Recognition Prgm; Most Popular Stu 1967.

PERENNE, LINA G., Fifth Grade Teacher; *b:* Manila, Philippines; *ed:* Elem Ed, Philippine Normal Coll 1948; (BSE) Math, Philippine Womens Univ 1952; (MS) Spec Ed, Arellano Univ 1967; Univ of Whitewater 1970-74; *cr:* Primary Teacher Rafael Palma Elem Sch 1948-55; Teacher of Spec Ed Rafael Palma Elem Sch 1955-69; 5th/6th Grade Teacher Sharon Cmmty Sch 1969-; *ai:* Girls Vlybl Coach 1981-86; NEA; Big Foot Ed Assn, WI Ed Assn; Southern Lake United Educators.

PEREPECHKO, ANN VIRRUSO, First Grade Teacher; *b:* Berwyn, IL; *m:* Wayne D.; *ed:* (BA) English Elem Ed, Elmhurst Coll 1977; Addl Studies Graduate Work in Reading; *cr:* 2nd Grade Teacher St Odilo Sch 1977-84; 1st Grade Teacher Custer Sch 1984-; *ai:* Textbook Comm; Sigma Tau Delta 1977-; Dean's List 4 Yrs; Graduated High Honors.

PERESICH, MARK LEE, History Teacher; *b:* Biloxi, MS; *m:* Madelyn Elizabeth Cosh; *c:* Meg, Molly; *ed:* (AA) Soc Stud, MS Gulf Coast Jr Coll 1973; (BSE) Soc Stud, 1975, (MED) His, 1977 Delta St Univ; Bus Management, Educl Admin, Univ of S MS; *cr:* Teacher Moss Point HS 1977-; *ai:* Stu Cncl, YMCA Youth Legislature, Jr Civitan Adv; Detention Hall Supvr; Phi Delta Kappa Mem 1982-; STAR Teacher 1987, 1989; Co-Author Article 1990; *home:* 4309 Idywood Dr Pascagoula MS 39567

PEREZ, ALBERTO ZUVIA, 8th Grade English Teacher; *b:* Carrizo Springs, TX; *ed:* (BS) Elem Ed, Howard Payne Univ 1981; (MED) Counseling/Guidance, SW TX ST Univ 1988; *cr:* Eng/Journalism Teacher Carrizo Springs Ind Sch Dist 1981-83, Austin Ind Sch Dist 1983-; *ai:* Faculty Hospitality Comm; Amer Stu Travel Adv; Austin Teacher Prof Educator 1983-; Austin Resource Cncl for Independent Living 1988-; *office:* Burnet Mid Sch 8401 Hathaway Dr Austin TX 78758

PEREZ, ANNA M., Kindergarten Teacher; *b:* San Antonio, TX; *m:* Juan P. Jr.; *c:* Juan J.; *ed:* (BA) Elem Ed/Early Chldhd, Trinity Univ 1978; *cr:* Kndgtn Teacher Travis Elem & Bowden Elem & Huppertz Elem; Pre-K Teacher Huppertz Elem; Kndgtn Teacher Graebner Elem; *ai:* TX St Teachers Assn; PTA; *office:* Charles Graebner Elem Sch 530 Hoover San Antonio TX 78225

PEREZ, BLANCA DINA, Journalism Advisor; *b:* Roma, TX; *m:* Ivar; *c:* Jennifer L., Savannah I.; *ed:* (BA) Phys Ed/Journalism, PAU & Univ of TX Edinboro 1977; Grad Stud Eng; *cr:* Phys Ed Coach Houston-Rusk Elem Sch 1978-81; Journalism Adv Pharr-San Juan-Alamo HS 1981-83; Eng Teacher Porter HS 1983-85, Journalism Adv Hanna HS 1985-; *ai:* UIL Journalism; Yrbk & Newspaper Adv; *office:* Homer Hanna HS 2615 Price Rd Brownsville TX 78520

PEREZ, CONNIE LYNN (KUPER), Science/Physical Ed Teacher; *b:* Dalhart, TX; *m:* Michael Ernest; *c:* Kyle, Drew; *ed:* (BS) Phys Ed/Health, 1979, Elem Ed, 1984 NM St Univ; *cr:* Teacher/Coach Corona Public Schls 1979-82, Amistad Elem Sch 1984-89, Logan Municipal Sch 1989-; *ai:* Stu Cncl; Coach; NEA 1979-; Chi Omega 1975-77; *office:* Logan Municipal Sch Box Logan NM 88426

PEREZ, ERNESTO AMADEO, Mathematics Teacher; *b:* Alice, TX; *ed:* (BS) Civil Engineering, TX A&I 1983; *cr:* Math Teacher San Diego HS 1988-; *ai:* Sr Class of 1992 Spon; UIL Calculator Coach; *home:* PO Box 66 San Diego TX 78384

PEREZ, GRACIELA D., Junior High Counselor; *b:* Donna, TX; *m:* Noe Oscar Sr.; *c:* Noe O. Jr., Rolando J.; *ed:* (BA) Elem Ed, 1974, (MS) Counseling/Guidance, 1977 Pan Amer Univ; *cr:* K-6th Grade Elem Teacher Edinburg CISD 1974-81; Rdng Resource Teacher L B Johnson Elem 1981-84; Jr HS Cnslr South Jr HS 1984-; *ai:* TX Classroom Teachers Assn (Bd of Dir 1989-, Local Pres 1980-, Dist 1 Pres); *office:* South Jr HS 601 W Freddy Gonzalez Edinburg TX 78539

PEREZ, JOSIE MENDOZA, 4th Grade Teacher; *b:* Santa Monica, CA; *m:* Basilio Perez; *c:* Victoria J.; *ed:* (BA) Elem Ed, Pan Amer Univ Edinburg 1983; *cr:* 4th Grade Teacher Stephen F Austin 1983-; *ai:* United Interscholastic League Coach; Curr Writing for Gifted & Talented; TSTA, NEA 1987-; *office:* Donna Ind Sch Dist 503 S Hutto Donna TX 78537

PEREZ, LINDY WILLETT, Choir Director/Department Head; *b:* Dallas, TX; *m:* Ruben Antonio; *ed:* (BM) Music Ed, S Meth Univ 1984; Grad Stud E TX St Univ, Univ of TX Arlington, Univ of Dallas; *cr:* Voice Teacher N Mesquite HS 1985; Choir Dir Westwood Jr HS 1985-; *ai:* Direct Pop Ensembles; Region Choir, Solo & Ensemble Contest Vocal Coach; Musical Dir; Area Elem Choir Festival & Jr HS Choir Clinic & Festival Coord; HS Choir Accompanist; TX Choral Dir Assn, TX Music Educators Assn Mem 1985-; Pi Beta Phi Natl Music Chm 1987-89; Master Peace Religious Performing Group 1985-89; *office:* Westwood Jr HS 7630 Arapaho Dallas TX 75248

PEREZ, LORETTA BRONCHETTI, 7th/8th Grade Eng/Math Teacher; *b:* Massena, NY; *m:* Joel J.; *ed:* (BA) Eng, 1973, (MS) Rdng, 1977 St Univ Coll Potsdam; Effective Teacher Trng; Educl Research & Dissemination; *cr:* PSEN Math Teacher Massena Cntrl HS 1974-80; Eng/Math Teacher J W Leary Jr HS 1980-; *ai:* Activity Spon; Stu Cncl; Yrbk Adv; Dist Curr Comm; Dance Comm Adv; Building Leadership Team Mem; Italian-Amer Pres 1984-88; Massena Womens Bowling Pres 1979-84; Teacher Resource Linker; *home:* 21 Coventry Dr Massena NY 13662

PEREZ, MA EUGENIA SANTOS, Math Teacher; *b:* Laredo, TX; *m:* Victor.; *c:* Rene A., Sylvia D., Elizabeth M.; *ed:* (BA) Math/Eng, Laredo St Univ 1983; Addl Studies 9 Hrs; *cr:* Math Teacher, Cigarroa Midd Sch Sept 1983-; Cigarroa HS Jan 1984-; *ai:* Co-Spon Cigorra HS Courtesy Club; *office:* Cigarroa H S 2600 Zacatecas Laredo TX 78043

PEREZ, MARTA BOFILL, Spanish Teacher; *b:* Havana, Cuba; *c:* Martha E. Perez Spuhler, Ignacio J.; *ed:* (DR) Philosophy Lit, Villanova Univ 1953; (MS) Span Lit, Hunter Coll 1972; *cr:* Span Teacher Apistolate of Sacred Heart Cuba 1957-60, Our Lady of Bethleham Puerto Rico 1963-65, St Joseph by the Sea 1965-67, Farmingdale Public Schls 1967-; *ai:* Span Club Adv 1967-89; NY St Assn Foreign Lang, Teachers of Span & Portuguese 1967-; Regents Examination Items Writer NY Ed Dept; Consultant AMSCO Publica tions; *home:* 28 Lincoln St Farmingdale NY 11735

PERINE, JOHN VINCENT, Fourth Grade Teacher; *b:* Zanesville, OH; *m:* Sue Ellen Hothem; *c:* Jennifer R., Charles A.; *ed:* (BS) Elem Ed/Psych, OH Univ 1976; Title I Grant Writing Sch 1978; Dist Right to Read Supvr 1977; JEVS System Voc Testing Trng, Stout St Univ; *cr:* 5th Grade Teacher Springfield Elem 1968-72; Track Coach/Gym Teacher Hopedale Elem 1976-77; Track Coach/Title I Coord Chester Elem Sch 1976-79; 4th Grade Soc Stud Teacher Tupper Plains Elem 1979-; *ai:* Bsktbl, Elem & HS Track Coach; Textbook, Inservice & Soc Stud Curr Dev Comm; OH Ed Assn 1968-; Maysville Ed Assn Treas 1969; F&AM Belpre Lodge 609 1981-; *home:* 2529 Valleyview Dr Belpre OH 45714

PERKINS, BARBARA ANN, 12th Grade English Teacher; *b:* Houston, TX; *ed:* (BA) Eng, 1975, (MED) Curr/Instruction, 1978 Univ of Houston; Advanced Trng Understanding Blooms Taxonomy, Strategies for Effective Sch, Sch Law, Linguistics, Multi-CulturaL Ed, Effective Discipline, Management Techniques; *cr:* Curr Writer N Forest Ind Sch Dist 1981-87; Eng Teacher M B Smiley HS 1979-; Rdng Instr Harris Cty Job Trng Partnership Cncl 1988-; *ai:* NHS Spon; Secy Eng Dept; N Harris Cty Teachers of Eng, TX Joint Cncl Teachers of Eng, NCTE 1985-; TX St Teachers Assn 1983-87; Wrote Book; Fellowship Greater Houston Area Writing Project; *office:* M B Smiley HS 10725 Mesa Dr Houston TX 77078

PERKINS, CANDACE M., Journalism Teacher; *b:* Des Moines, IA; *ed:* (BS) Journalism, 1972, (MA) Journalism, 1980 N IL Univ; *cr:* Teacher/Newspaper Adv St Charles HS 1972-; *ai:* Journalism Ed Assn VP 1975-, Medal of Merit 1987; IL Journalism Ed Assn Bd 1988-; NCTE; Dow Jones Newspaper Fund Journalism Teacher of Yr 1989; Gold Key IATJL Teacher of Yr; Image Awd St Charles Chamber of Commerce; Journalism of NIU Alumni of Yr 1990; NSPA Pioneer Awd; *office:* St Charles HS 1020 Dunham Rd Saint Charles IL 60174

PERKINS, CATHERINE KOLTERMAN, Sixth Grade Teacher; *b:* Onaga, KS; *m:* Eugene R.; *c:* Alan, Adam; *ed:* (BA) Assoc of Arts, Cloud Cty Comm Jr Coll 1973; (BSED) Elem, Emporia St 1974; (MSAO) Adult/Continuing Ed, KS St 1983; *cr:* 5th Grade Teacher KCK Quindaro 1975-76; Kndgtn Teacher Mark Twain & Quindaro 1976-77;2nd-4th Grade Teacher Silver Lake 1977-82; 6th Grade Teacher Severy Elem Sch 1982-; *ai:* Delta Kappa Gamma 1983-; W Elk Ed Assn (Treas 1983-85, Secy 1989-) 1982-; United Meth Women VP 1990; Extension Homemakers Unit 1990; Elk Cty Cattlewomen 1983-; *home:* RR 1 Box 31 Howard KS 67349

PERKINS, DORIS WILSON, 4th Grade Mathematics Teacher; *b:* Braxton, MS; *m:* Billy Ray; *c:* Darcel, Felecia, Clint; *ed:* (BS) Elem Ed, 1960, (MS) Elem Ed, 1976 Jackson St Univ; Phonics the Rdng Teacher, Univ of S MS; Math Remediation, ISU; Adult Ed, Duling Sch; *cr:* 7th Grade Eng Teacher Yazoo City Tr Sch 1959-62; 5th Grade Teacher Harper Voc Sch 1962-70; 4th Grade Teacher Mendenhall Elem 1970-; *ai:* Sch Policy Comm Mem; NEA 1970-; MS Assn of Ed (Exec Comm 1974-75, Bd of Dirs 1981-83); PTA Fundraising Project Chm; Cub Scout Den Mother; Sci Grant to Study Teaching Sci in Elem Grades; *home:* Rt 1 Box 173A St John Rd Braxton MS 39044

PERKINS, JACK H., US History/Soc Stud Teacher; *b:* Memphis, TN; *m:* Paula Gates; *c:* Greg; *ed:* (BS) Scndry Ed/Soc Stud, OK St Univ 1979; *cr:* Teacher/Coach Ralston HS 1979-80, Southeast HS 1980-84, Caney Valley HS 1984-86, Ferris HS 1986-; *ai:* Soc Stud Dept Head; Instr of Gifted & Talented; FCA Spon; Asst Ftbl & Bsktbl Coach; US His Honors Teacher; Fellowship of Chrstn Athletes; *office:* Ferris HS P O Box 461 Ferris TX 75125

PERKINS, KATHY METTS, Counselor; *b:* Lufkin, TX; *m:* Jerry M.; *ed:* (BA) Eng/Psych, Stephen F Austin St Univ 1981; (MA) Counseling, Western St Coll 1989; *cr:* Teacher Olathe HS 1981-89; Cnslr Olathe Mid Sch 1989-; *ai:* Stu Government & Drug Free Youth Spon; Delta Kappa Gamma, CO Cnslrs Assn Mem 1989-; FFA 1986-, Honorary Chapter Farmer 1986; STAND 1988-; Natl Cncl on Alcoholism & Drug Abuse 1989-; Published Works Journalism & Performing Arts.

PERKINS, MURIEL YVETTE, English Teacher; *b:* Norfolk, VA; *ed:* (BA) Eng, 1977, (MA) Scndry Admin/Urban Ed, 1989 Norfolk St Univ; Eng Teacher Truitt Jr HS; Western Branch HS 1980-82, Indian River Jr HS 1982-; *ai:* Mid Sch Study & Review Steering Comm; City Wide Mid Sch Steering Comm & Sch Improvement Rep; VA Assn Teachers of Eng; Tide Water Assn Teachers of Eng 1977-; Alpha Delta Kappa 1989-; *office:* Indian River Jr HS 230 Greenbriger Rd Chesapeake VA 23325

PERKINS, ROY GARY, English Instructor; *b:* Jacksonville, FL; *c:* Pepper, Dabney P. Norman, Salty, Lynn, Mandy, Charis, Jared; *ed:* (AA) Fine Arts, Santa Fe Comm Coll 1968; (BS) Journalism/Eng, Univ of FL 1970; Grad Stud Valdosta St Coll; *cr:* Eng Instr Marion Acad 1970-72; Eng Teacher Northside Mid Sch 1972-74, Ware Cty Jr HS 1974-; *ai:* Defense Ftbl & Head Tennis Coach; Prof Assn of GA Educators; *home:* 400 Community Dr Waycross GA 31501

PERKINS, WHEATIE BALDRIDGE, First Grade Teacher; *b:* Braggs, OK; *m:* Bobby Roy; *ed:* (BS) Ed, Langston Univ 1964; Instructional Effectiveness Trng 1986; Critical Thinking Skills, Cntrl St Univ Edmond 1984; *cr:* 3rd Grade Teacher George Wright Elem 1966-68; 1st Grade Teacher Quail Creek Elem 1968-; *ai:* N Cntrl Accrediting Assn Inst for Dev Educl Act Comm Mem; Assn Classroom Teachers Outstanding Service Awd; Natl Sch Traffic Safety Awd; *office:* Quail Creek Elem Sch 11700 Thornridge Rd Oklahoma City OK 73120

PERLIS, ROBERTA MARCIA, 6th Grade Teacher; *b:* New York, NY; *ed:* (BS) Speech/Drama, NY Univ 1960; *cr:* 3rd Grade Teacher PS 3 NYC 1962-63; 2nd/3rd Grade Teacher LA Sch Dist 1964-66; 2nd Grade Teacher Dr C C Violette Sch 1966-67; 2nd/6th Grade Teacher Dodds-Chicksands England & Hof Germany 1967-80; 5th/6th Grade Teacher Newbridge Priv Sch 1980-84; 6th Grade Teacher J Miller 1984-; *ai:* Stu Cncl Adv; Sustained

Superior Awd-USDESEA (Dodds); *home:* 438 1/2 N Sierra Bonita Los Angeles CA 90036

PERLMAN, BELLA BEACH, 4th-6th Grade Lang Art Teacher; *b:* Chicago, IL; *m:* Noel B.; *c:* Samuel B.; *ed:* (BA) Elem Ed, KY St Coll 1954; (MED) Educl Generalist, Natl Coll Ed 1982; *cr:* 2nd/3rd Grade Teacher Lincoln Memorial Sch Dist 1957-67; 3rd-5th Grade Teacher 1976-87, 4th-6th Grade Lang Art/Soc Stud Teacher 1987- Faulkner Sch; *ai:* Organize Lyric Opera Trips; Chaperone Environmental Camp; *office:* Faulkner Sch 7110 S Coles Ave Chicago IL 60649

PERO, DAN LEONARD, Principal Scndry Athletic Dir; *b:* Laramie, WY; *m:* Patricia L. Hayes; *c:* Diana Maurer, Richard, Danielle Gould, Denise; *ed:* (BA) Phys Ed, Coll of ID 1961, (MS) Zoology/Botany, Univ of ID 1966; Scndry Admin, Coll of ID 1975; Emergency Medical Technician; *cr:* Teacher/Coach Homedale Jr HS 1956-57, Pinehurst HS 1957-60, Payette HS 1960-63; Vice Prin/Teacher/Coach Prospect HS 1963-73; Prin/Athletic Dir/Teacher/Coach Middleton Sr HS 1973-81; Prin/Athletic Dir/Coach New Plymouth Jr-Sr HS 1981-; *ai:* Dir Intramurals; Ftbl, Bsktbl, Bsbl, Track Coach; Bus Driver; Stu Coach; All 7th-12th Grade Classes Adv; Chrldr; Lettermens Club; Athletic Dir; Counseling; BSA Leader; Taught Boxing, Tumbling, Weight Lifting, Sport Camps; Dance Instr; Ftbl St Champion 1967; Coach of Yr 1968; Snake River Valley Conference Pres 1977-78; Western ID Conference Pres 1987-88; Cmmty Leader of Amer 1968/1973-74; Scndry Teacher of Yr 1973 & 1975; Monthly Journals Prentice Hall 1974; Prospect HS Coach of Yr Awd 1968; *office:* New Plymouth Jr/Sr H S 207 S Plymouth Ave New Plymouth ID 83655

PERO, JUDITH G. GOSS, English Teacher; *b:* Johnstown, PA; *m:* John F. Jr.; *c:* John F., Jaime L.; *ed:* (BA) Eng, 1969, (MAED) Ed, 1970 Niagara Univ; *cr:* Eng Teacher Gaskill Jr HS 1969-85, Niagara Falls HS 1985-; *office:* Niagara Falls HS 1201 Pine Ave Niagara Falls NY 14301

PERO, PAULA KEMMEEL, 7th & 8th Grade Teacher; *b:* St Louis, MO; *m:* Leonard Walter; *c:* Lance, Jason, Wynter, Cassio; *ed:* (BA) Elem Ed, Harris Teachers Coll 1967; (MS) Rdng, Natl Coll of Evanston 1981; *cr:* 2nd Grade Teacher Cole Sch 1967-68; 6th Grade Teacher Blewett Sch 1968-72; 5th-8th Grade Teacher Resurrection Luth Sch 1972-74; 7th Grade Teacher Joan Arai Mid Sch 1974-79; 5th Grade Teacher Esmond 1979-82; 7th-8th Grade Teacher Park Manor Sch 1982-; *ai:* Stu Won 4th Place De Paul Univ Stockmarket Experiment 1986; Dist Young Author 1st Place Winners 1985-86/1989; *office:* Park Manor Elem Sch 7037 S Rhodes Chicago IL 60637

PERON, EVELYN L., Spanish Teacher; *b:* Meadville, PA; *c:* Donald W.; *ed:* (BS) Span/Eng, Shippensburg Univ 1958; *cr:* Teacher Chambersburg Area Sch Dist 1958-62, James Buchanan Sch Dist 1962-64, Chambersburg Area Sch Dist 1966-; Part Time Teacher Wilson Coll 1989-; *ai:* Adv Span Club; CAEA Secy 1959-60; PSEA, NEA 1990; Chambersburg Hospital Auxilary 1978-; NDEA Schlsp to Study Span Rutgers Univ; Four Missions to Latin America; *home:* 131 N 7th St Chambersburg PA 17201

PERREAULT, STEPHEN MARK, Science/Social Studies Teacher; *b:* St Johns, Newfoundland CN; *m:* Kimberly Ann Cousins; *c:* Matthew, Branden; *ed:* (BS) Soc Stud, Univ of ME Presque Isle 1980; *cr:* Teacher Caribou Mid Sch 1980-; *ai:* Coach 8th Grade Boys Bsktbl Team; 7th/8th Grade Boys Soccer Team; Little League Bsbl (Coach 1988- Sec 1989-); Mem Caribou Recreation Commission 1988-; *office:* Caribou Mid Sch 21 Glenn St Caribou ME 04736

PERRETT, LEONARD ANTHONY, English Teacher; *b:* Bethlehem, PA; *ed:* (BA) Eng, Kings Coll 1971; (MA) Eng, Lehigh Univ 1975; (MA) Philosophy, St Johns Coll 1982; *cr:* Teacher Broughal Jr HS 1971-75, Liberty HS 1976-; *ai:* Emphasize Writing Comm Co-Chm; NEA, PEAA, BEA, NCTE; NEA Fellowship St Johns Coll 1981-82; Poems Published.

PERRICONE, JOHN MICHAEL, Health Educator; *b:* Johnson City, NY; *m:* Vicki Marolf; *c:* Loren; *ed:* (BS) Health Ed, 1981, (MS) Health Ed, 1983 SUNY Cortland; *cr:* Grad Teaching Asst SUNY Cortland 1983; 7th Grade Health Teacher West Mid Sch 1984; 11th/12th Grade Health Teacher Maine Endwell HS 1985-; *ai:* SADD, Alcohol & Drug Stu Information Prgm, Youth Cncl on Smoking Spon; Met Life Fnd Cty Health Ed Prgms Recognition; Gustav Timmel Awd; *office:* Maine Endwell HS 712 Farm-to-Market Rd Endwell NY 13760

PERRIELLO, JOSEPH E., 4th Grade Teacher; *b:* Braddock, PA; *m:* Sandra Greene; *ed:* (BA) Elem Ed, Slippery Rock 1968; Guidance; *cr:* 4th Grade Teacher Penn Hills Sch Dist 1968-; *ai:* PSEA/PHEA; *office:* Dible Elem Sch 1079 Jefferson Rd Pittsburgh PA 15235

PERRIGIN, BARBARA WALLACE, English Teacher; *b:* Roanoke, AL; *c:* Auburn Lynn; *ed:* (BSED) Eng/Soc Sci, 1970, (MSED) Eng, 1976 Auburn Univ; Grad Stud Jacksonville St Univ; *cr:* Soc Stud Instr Chambers Cty Bd of Ed 1970-72; Eng Instr Dallas Cty Bd of Ed 1972-73, Pickens Cty Bd of Ed 1973; Eng/Rdng Instr Southern Union St Jr Coll 1974-75, 1978; Eng Instr Randolph Cty Bd of Ed 1974-; *ai:* Scholars Bowl, HS Lang Art Tournament, Advanced Placement Sr Eng Spon; NEA, AL Ed Assn, Randolph Ed Assn, NCTE, AL Cncl Teachers of Eng; Sigma Tau Delta, Kappa Delta Pi; Randolph Cty Classroom Teachers Assn Past Pres; Auburn Alumni Club Secy; Randolph Cty Auburn Comm Chm; Teen-To-Teen (Instr AL Pilot Prgm, Advisory Cncl) 1989-; Pr&R Comm; Whos Who in Amer Ed; *office:* Woodland HS PO Box 157 Woodland AL 36280

PERRIGO, JANIS HOUCK, Fourth Grade Teacher; *b:* Cleveland, OH; *m:* Michael Eugene; *c:* Michelle C., Melissa S.; *ed:* (BAED) Elem Ed, OH Univ 1968; (MAED) Emerging Adolescent Ed, Cleveland St Univ 1981; Grad Work Cleveland St Univ & Baldwin Wallace Coll; *cr:* Spec Ed Teacher Ridge-Brook Elem 1968-69; 4th-5th Grade Teacher Dag Hammarskjold 1970-75; 6th Grade Teacher 1975-79, 4th Grade Teacher 1979- Ridge-Brook Elem; *ai:* Luth HS West Mothers Club Schlsp Comm 1988-; Phi Lambda Theta 1981-; Alpha Delta Kappa Secy Elect 1990-92; Parma Ed Assn (Mem 1986-89, Chairperson 1989-, Co-Chairperson 1989-); Good Bears of World Treas 1988-; Luth HS W Mothers Club Schlsp Comm 1988-; St James Friendship Circle Schlsp Comm Treas 1986-88, 1990, *office:* Ridge Brook Elem Sch 7915 Manhattan Ave Parma OH 44129

PERRIN, JAMES ADISON, Teacher/Coach; *b:* Daisy, TN; *m:* Lisa Hughes; *c:* Jimmy, Robyn, Jessica; *ed:* (BS) His, Austin Peay St 1970; (MA) Ed, Murray St 1980; *cr:* Teacher/Coach Chrstn Cty HS 1970-; *ai:* Key Club Spon; Asst Ftbl & Head Sftbl Coach; Athletic Events Mgr; KY Wrestling Coaches Assn VP 1987, Coach of Yr 1988; KY Coach of Yr 1989; Hopkinsville Human Relations & Kiwanis Phys Ed Awd.

PERRINO, JOHN ANTHONY, Mathematics Teacher; *b:* Staten Island, NY; *ed:* (AA) Liberal Art, Staten Island Comm Coll 1970; (BA) Ed/Math, Oneonta St Univ of NY 1972; (MS) Ed, Kean Coll of NJ 1977; *cr:* Math Teacher George Egbert Intermediate Sch; *ai:* Sch Bsktbl Team Coach 1976-82; After Sch Center Bsktbl Coach 1985-89; Summer Playground Coach 1978, 1982-83; Phys Ed Teacher; United Fed of Teachers 1973-89; NY St United Teachers; *office:* Egbert Intermediate Sch #2 333 Midland Ave Staten Island NY 10306

PERRY, DAVID MAX, Gifted & Talented Sci Teacher; *b:* Lansing, MI; *m:* Margaret Mary Martinez; *c:* Julian M. Reyes, Margaret E. Reyes, Kimberly A., Jennifer J.; *ed:* (BA) Bio/Ed, Spring Arbor Coll 1971; USAF Pilot Trng & Combat Crew Trng Schl; *cr:* Sci Teacher Hayes Mid Sch 1971-73; Pilot Captain USAF 1973-79; Sci Teacher H F Stevens Mid Sch 1983-; *ai:* Young Astronauts Club Spon; Crowley Educators Assn Pres 1988-; TX Assn for Gifted & Talented; TX Mid Sch Assn; *office:* H F Stevens Mid Sch 1016 FM 1187 Crowley TX 76036

PERRY, DEBBY L., Home Economics Teacher & Cnslr; *b:* Conrad, MT; *m:* Joe L.; *ed:* (BS) Home Ec, (BS) Health/Phys Ed, Univ of MT; Working Towards Masters Counseling; *cr:* Home Ed Teacher Fairfield Public Schls 1979-82; Home Ec/Phys Ed Teacher 1982-, Cnslr 1989- Brady Public Schls; *ai:* Class & Stus Active in Ed Adv; Sch Improvement Team Mem; MT Assn for Counseling & Dev 1989-; MT Assn for Health, Phys Ed, Rec, Dance; Nom MT Home Ec Teacher of Yr 1988 & West Outstanding Teacher Prgm 1988.

PERRY, DEBORAH WATTS, Elementary Teacher; *b:* Lincolnton, NC; *m:* David E.; *c:* Alicia D.; *ed:* (BA) Elem Ed, Limestone Coll 1974; (MEd) Early Chldhd Ed, Univ of SC 1979; *cr:* 1st Grade Teacher Marion Elem 1974-75; 6th Grade Spec Ed Teacher Blacksburg Annex 1975-76; 1st Grade Teacher Blacksburg Elem 1 1976-80; *office:* 401 N Granard St Gaffney SC 29340

PERRY, DONALD PAUL, Science Teacher; *b:* Altoona, PA; *m:* Marcia Ruth Davis; *c:* Paul, Charles; *ed:* (BS) Bio, 1970, (MS) Bio, 1971 N IL Univ; *cr:* Sci Teacher Huntley Sch Dist 1971-77, Dekalb Sch Dist 1977-81, Marengo Sch Dist 1983-85, Malta Sch Dist 1985-86, Genoa Sch Dist 1986-; *ai:* Sci Fair Spon; Outdoor Ed Comm; Phi Delta Kappa 1970-; Genoa Lions Club Citizens Comm 1988-; Genoa City Cncl; *home:* 316 S Hadsall Genoa IL 60135

PERRY, EDNA BURRELL, Principal; *b:* Washington, DC; *m:* Sidney L. Jr.; *c:* Angela, Andrea R.; *ed:* (BME) Music Ed/Magna Cum Laude, Howard Univ 1956; (MA) Early Chldhd Ed, Roosevelt Univ 1972; Admin/Supervision/Lib Sci; *cr:* Elem Teacher Robert Healy Sch 1957-62, Charles Wacker Sch 1962-73; Asst Prin/Cnslr/Librarian 1973-89, Prin 1990 C H Wacker Sch; Minister of Music Church of the Good Shepherd UCC 1959-; *ai:* Wacker Chorus Spon; Floating Music Teacher; Stu Cncl Spon 1972-76; Chicago Pharmacy Assn Auxliary Pres 1970-75; Natl Pharmacy Assn Auxiliary Pres 1976-79; Church of the Good Shepherd Lay Person of Yr 1980.

PERRY, JANICE O'CONNELL, Kindergarten & 1st Grade Tchr; *b:* Minneapolis, MN; *m:* James; *c:* Janis Adams, Jeffrey; *ed:* (BA) Elem Ed, Univ of MN 1960; Univ of CA; Pepperdine Univ; Univ of Southern CA; *cr:* Kndgtn-4th Grade Teacher Moffitt Sch 1960-; *ai:* Norwalk La Mirada Teachers Assn; CA Teachers Assn; Alpha Delta Pi Alumni; PTA Honorary Life Mem Awd 198 6; *office:* Thomas B Moffit Sch 13323 S Goller Ave Norwalk CA 90650

PERRY, JOAN GREGORY, Second Grade Teacher; *b:* Windsor, NC; *ed:* (BS) Primary Ed, East Carolina Univ 1967; *cr:* 2nd Grade Teacher Mary P Douglas Elem 1967-80/1981-82; Demonstration Teacher Underwood Elem Sch 1980-81; 2nd Grade Teacher Conn G/T Magnet Sch 1982-; *ai:* Grade Level Chairperson; Stu Teacher Supvr; Safety Patrol Adv; Lang Arts Curr Writer; Leadership Team SB2 Plan; PTA Bd Conn Sch; Wake Cty PTA Cncl; Arts Booster Club; NCAE/NEA 1985-; IRA 1989-; ACT 1985-; Wake Co PTA Cncl K-12 Rdng Prgms 1989-, Outstanding Teacher of Yr 1988-89; Conn PTA Faculty Rep 1982-88/1989-; Thanks to Teachers Excl Awd; Video Taped By NC Dept of Public Instruction for Integrated Curr/Effective Teaching Styles; Awd for Completing Prof Dev Plan; *office:* Conn G/T Magnet Sch 1221 Brookside Dr Raleigh NC 27604

PERRY, JOSEPH ALBERT, 6th Grade Teacher; *b:* Los Angeles, CA; *m:* Ellen Louise Farman; *c:* Michael, John; *ed:* (BA) Speech Comm, 1973, Elem Credential Elem Ed, 1975, CA St Univ Los Angeles; (MA) Educl Admin, 1986, Admin Credential Educl Admin, 1986 CA Luth Univ; *cr:* Teacher La Canada Unified Sch Dist 1975-81; Head Teacher Bellflower Unified Sch Dist 1982-89; ESL Teacher Downey Unified Sch Dist 1987-, Glendale Comm Coll 1988-; Teacher Los Angeles Unified Sch Dist 1989-, Bellflower Unified Sch Dist 1990; *ai:* Sch Site Cncl Adv; Gifted & Talented Ed Coord; Conducted Sch Plays & Awd Assemblies; Instructional Facilitator & Upper Grade Coord; PTA (Treas, Mem) 1986-87, Service Awd 1989; Compiled & Published Parent Teacher Handbooks Thomas Jefferson Elem Sch 1987-89; Head Teacher, Asst Prin Thomas Jefferson Elem 1984-; *office:* Thomas Jefferson Elem Sch 10027 E Rose St Bellflower CA 90706

PERRY, MAGGIE OLA, Social Science Department Chm; *b:* Tifton, GA; *c:* Mark D. Pollard; *ed:* (BA) Soc Sci, Paine Coll 1955; Univ of North FL; AM Univ; *cr:* Teacher Stanton Sr HS 1960, Teacher Landon Jr HS 1968-; Dir Headstart Prgm 1964-68; *ai:* Spon Future Educators Club; Dept Chm Soc Stud; Mem Cmmty Club; Duval Cty Soc Stud; NAACP; Central CME Church Sunday Sch Teacher/Youth Dir; Dir of Church Bd Evangelism Choir Mem; *office:* Landon Jr H S 1819 Thacker Ave Jacksonville FL 32209

PERRY, MARY ANNIE VERNELL, Fourth/Fifth Grade Teacher; *b:* Meridian, MS; *m:* William Henry Sr.; *c:* Theresa Gathright, William H. Jr., Bradford L.; *ed:* (BS) Ed, Jackson St Coll 1962; (MA) Elem Ed, MS St Univ 1981; Valparaiso Univ, MS St Univ, Univ Southern MS, Jackson St Univ; *cr:* Teacher West End Elem 1962-68, Oakland Heights Elem 1968; Curr Asst Meridian Public Schls; Teacher Oakland Heights Elem 1990; *ai:* Faculty Cncl; Sci Comm; Assn of Meridian Educators (Pres, Secy, Treas 1976-), Teacher of Yr 1983; MS Assn of Educators Bd of Dir 1982-83; NEA 1962-; Democratic Party Exec Comm (State 1984-88, Local 1984-), Delegate Natl 1988; NAACP 1980-88; Bowling League (Secy 1975-82, Pres 1987-); League of Women Voters 1988-; East MS St Baptist St Layman Dir 1976-; St John Baptist (Youth Dir 1975-81, Sr Choir Pres 1986-); Corona Social Club Pres 1973-78;Jackson St Univ Alumni Assn (Secy 1980-82, VP 1988-); Grant NDEA Valparaiso Univ; *office:* Oakland Heights Elem Sch 601 59th Ave Meridian MS 39301

PERRY, NANCEE VAICELUNAS, Art Teacher; *b:* Kenosha, WI; *m:* Paul L.; *c:* Kathryn, Dante; *ed:* (BA) Art Ed, Univ of WI Whitewater 1978; *cr:* Sci Teacher 1979-80, AV Coord 1980-81 Tremper HS; 5th Grade Teacher Holy Rosary Sch 1981-85; Art Teacher Kenosha Unified Schls 1985-; *ai:* Art Dept Grant; Art Contests Natl Winners; *home:* 3604 19th Ave Kenosha WI 53140

PERRY, OPHELIA JACKSON, Fourth Grade Teacher; *b:* Ailey, GA; *m:* Leroy; *c:* Bertha A. Adeniji, Janice P. Hodge, Lynita D.; *ed:* (BS) Elem Ed, Bethune-Cookman Coll 1964; Early Chldhd Ed, Univ of Cntrl FL 1987; *cr:* Teacher Seville Elem 1967-68, Starke Elem 1968-69, Longstreet & Volusia Elem 1969-70, Turie T. Small Elem 197 *ai:* Volunteer in Area Nursing Homes; Task Force Mem Creative Writing Dist Level; Sch Rep Writing Across The Discipline; Volusia Educators Assn 1967-87; AFT 1987-; Bethune-Cookman Coll Alumni Assn 1964-; Teacher of Yr 1988-89; *home:* 866 North St Daytona Beach FL 32114

PERRY, PATSY EMORY, 7th Grade Lang Arts Teacher; *b:* Durham, NC; *m:* Emmett M.; *c:* Buddy, Letitia P. Griffin; *ed:* (BA) His, Meredith Coll 1951; Certfd Rdng Teacher - Speclst ECU 1980; *cr:* 7th Lang Arts Teacher 1985; 7th ESEA Rdng Teacher 1979-85 Hawley Mid; 7th/8th Soc Stud/Lang Arts Teacher Creedmoor Elem/Hawley Mid 1966-79; *ai:* Natl Jr Honor Socty Adv;Team Ldr-7th Grade Team; Chairperson Lang Arts Dept; NEA/NCEA Bldg Rep 1988-89; Butner Exch Club 1988-; Prof Relations Bd 1975-76; *home:* 304 W Dogwood Dr P O Box 65 Creedmoor NC 27522

PERRY, PATSY PIPKIN, Business Education Teacher; *b:* Mc Coll, SC; *m:* Parrish Mitchell; *c:* Dorian T., Danika S.; *ed:* (BS) Bus Ed, Benedict Coll 1973; (MA) Bus Ed/Office Admin, Cath Univ of America 1982; Continuing Ed at Univ of DE & Dept of Public Instruction; *cr:* Application Examiner/Teacher US Securities & Exch Commission 1973-74; Exec Secy Natl Cash Register Company 1974-76, TX Rehabilitation Commission 1977; Teacher New Castle Cty Sch Dist 1978-80; Asst Professor Goldey Beacom Coll 1980-85; Teacher Newark HS 1985-; Adult Ed Teacher James Grove HS 1987-; *ai:* Newark HS Chapter Chairperson 1985-; Mid Sts Evaluation Team for Stu Act Comm 1989-; Jump Rope for Heart & america Heart Assn 1989, Black His Month 1990, Referendum Volunteer Comm as Teacher & Parent Newark HS 1990; Bus Prof of America (Adv, St Bd 1985-, Past Pres 1988-89) Adv of Yr 1988, Natl Recognition Awds 1990; DE Bus Ed Assn Mem 1980-; Jack & Jill of America Past Financial Secy 1987-89, Service Awd 1989; Chesapeake Bay GSA Brownie Leader 1989-; St John AUMP Church (Trustee Bd Secy, Sunday Sch Secy 1987-; Federal Proposal for Update of Classroom Equipment & New Accounting Computerized Prgm 1990; Spec Olymics; Drug Awareness, Membership Explosion; Gold, Mortgage Pay Off Campaihn, CARE, Club Promotions Week; *office:* Newark HS E Delaware Ave Newark DE 19711

PERRY, RAYMOND Y., Junior High School Teacher; *b:* Honolulu, HI; *ed:* St Louis Coll Prep; Cathedral Sch for Teachers; CO St; St Stephens Jr Coll; Mt St Marys Grad Division Prgm; St Josephs Coll; Numerous Courses; *cr:* Religion/His/Eng/Span

Teacher St Margaret Sch 1970-72; Religion/His/Eng/Music Teacher Nativity Sch 1972-73; Interim Prin St Matthew Sch 1973; Soc Stud/Music/Religion Teacher/Soc Stud Chm Our Lady of Peace Sch 1974-77; Religion/Soc Stud/Eng/Music Teacher Our Lady of Perpetual Help Sch 1977-78; Religion/Eng/Soc Stud/Eng Lit Music Teacher 1978-79, Span/Eng/Rdng Comprehension Teacher/Prin 1979-80, Prin/Span/Rdng Comprehension Teacher 1981-82 Our Lady of Guadalupe Sch; Jr HS Teacher/Religion Coord Our Lady of the Holy Rosary 1982-; *ai:* Dir of Altar Servers; Chm Soc Stud Dept; Consultant Cath Television; Wkshps for Teachers; Religious Ed; Chaminade Club; Chm Sodality Christmas Project, Project & Testing Comm; Carnival Comm; Mariology Contest; Clerk Bookstore; Dir Commtys Annual Christmas Prgm; Sacristan; Youth Adv; Sch Accreditation Teams; ASCD, CA Assn of Soc Stud, Assn of Pastoral Musicians, Archdiocesan Religious Educators; Veterans of Foreign Wars; Amer Legion; Confraternity of Chrstn Doctrine, Cntrl Assn of the Miraculous Medal; Blue Army of Our Lady; St Louis Alumni Assn; Sacred Heart League, Missionary Assn Mary Immaculate, Affiliate of Saint Meinrads Abbey, Drum Corps News World Magazine News Staff; Parish Extra Ordinary Minister; March of Dimes Comm; Chamber of Commerce Outstanding Man of Yr Awd; Top Honor Grad; *home:* PO Box 7982 Van Nuys CA 91409

PERRY, ROBERTA DEVAURS, Science Department Chair; *b:* Merced, CA; *m:* Michael T.; *ed:* (BS) Biochemistry/Botany, Univ of CA Davis 1980; Grad Work Pomology & Viticulture; *cr:* Lecturer CA St Univ 1984-85; Sci Teacher Corning Union HS 1987-; *ai:* Faculty Senate Mem; Pep Squad Adv; Credential Review Comm Comm; NSTA 1985-; CA Sci Teachers Assn 1986-; CA Assn of Chem Teachers 1987-; Audubon Society 1975-; Natl Wildlife Society 1971-; Amer Assn of Univ Women 1981-; Project Phys Sci Mem Univ of CA Berkeley; Lieutenant Rawlins Awd CA St Univ Chico.

PERRY, ROXIE ELLA (TAYLOR), Fourth Grade Teacher; *b:* Como, MS; *m:* James Edward; *c:* Jaime E., Joi E., Jennifer E.; *ed:* (BA) Elem Ed, IL St Univ 1969; Learning Disabled Cert, S IL Univ Edwardsville 1970; (MS) Elem Remedial Rdng, MI St Univ 1975; Administrative Intern Trng; Essential Elements of Effective Instruction; MI Model Health & Sci Wkshp; Math/Sci Wkshps; *cr:* Teacher of Learning Disabilities Venice Public Schls 1971-72; 3rd/4th Grade Teacher 1972-74, Rdng Lab Teacher 1974-79 Albion Public Schls; Teacher Battle Creek Public Schls 1979-; *ai:* Dist Sch Improvement Team; Curr Sub Comm Chairperson; Dist Curr Coordinating Cncl; Battle Creek Ed Assn (Secy 1981-82, Minority Involvement Concerns Cmmty Chairperson 1988-89); MI Ed Assn, NEA; Kiwanis Club of Battle Creek Master Teacher Awd 1988; Battle Creek Public Schls Outstanding Educator Awd 1988; Natl Assn of Negro Prof Womans Awd 1989; Bus & Prof Womens Clubs Incorporated; *office:* La Mora Park Elem Sch 65 N Woodlawn Ave Battle Creek MI 49017

PERRY, RUTH QUEEN, Third Grade Teacher; *b:* Struthers, OH; *m:* H. Kyran; *c:* Linda S. Jackson, Michelle A. Mazzarella, Susan K. Brown, David K., Dan A., Stephen W.; *ed:* (BS) Elem Ed, Malone Coll 1972; (MS) Elem Admin, Youngstown St Univ 1979; Akron Univ; *cr:* 2nd Grade Teacher Malvern Sch 1964-66; Kndgtn/Remedial Rdng Teacher 1966-67, 3rd Grade Teacher 1967- Augusta Sch; *ai:* Young Author Building Rep; Half Day Discipline Admin Duties; CEA Building Rep; OEA; Right to Life Educl Fnd, PTO; Church Mem; OH Teacher Forum Rep Dist Rep 1986; Citizens for Excl in Ed Awd 1987; *office:* Augusta Sch Box 129 Augusta OH 44607

PERRY, SULANE STONE, Kindergarten Teacher; *b:* Palatka, FL; *M:* Myles A.; *c:* Parham A., Roland K., Mylane; *ed:* (BS) Elem Ed, North GA Coll 1961; (MS) Early Chldhd, Jacksonville St Univ 1981; *cr:* 5th Grade Teacher Monroe Elem 1966-67; Preschool Teacher Oakland Army Base 1971-73; Ft Lewis Preschool 1973-76; 3rd Grade Teacher 1977-82, Kndgtn Teacher 1982 Saks Elem; *ai:* Brownie Troop Ldr; Bd Mem Cottagvilla Cncl of Girl Scouts; Sunday Sch Teacher Indian Oaks Chrstn Church; NEA 1977-90; AL Ed Assn 1977-; Calhoun Cty Ed Assn 1977-; Pilot Club of Anniston Pres 1 79-80/1987-88; Indian Oaks Ladies Cncl; Nom from Saks Elem Teacher Hall of Fame 1989; *home:* 825 Rockridge Rd Weaver AL 30655

PERRY, SUSAN DE MASTERS, Eighth Grade Teacher/ Mentor; *b:* San Francisco, CA; *m:* John Mark; *c:* Beth Covey, Ryan Covey; *ed:* (BA) Liberal Stud, Fresno Pacific Coll 1979; Grad Stud Math, Sci, Soc Stud, Lang & Rdng; *cr:* 3rd-7th Grade Teacher 1979-85, 8th Grade Teacher 1985-, Eng/Mentor Teacher 1990 Westside Elem; Adult Ed Teacher Riverdale HS 1985-; *ai:* CA Teachers Assn (Treas 1987-88, VP 1989-, Pres 1990); Riverdale Spring Festival Pres 1982-83; Natl Sci Fnd Grant to Fresno Pacific Coll; *office:* Westside Elem Sch 19191 W Excelcior Ave Five Points CA 93624

PERRY, WAYNE A., 7th Grade Mathematics Teacher; *b:* Youngstown, OH; *m:* Gloria; *c:* Marc; *ed:* (BSED) Elem Ed, 1973, (MSED) Curr, 1976 Youngstown St; *cr:* 7th Grade Soc Stud Teacher 1973-82, 7th Grade Math Teacher 1973- W S Guy; *office:* W S Guy Schl 4115 Shady Rd Youngstown OH 44505

PERRY, WILLIE FRANK, JR., Foreign Lang Dept Chair; *b:* Chicago, IL; *m:* Susan Elaine Thrall; *c:* Jennifer, Allison; *ed:* (BA) Fr/Span, Mac Murray Coll 1981; Grad Stud Ger; *cr:* Fr/Span Teacher Brown Mid Sch 1980-81, Navarre Mid Sch 1981-89; Fr/ Span Teacher/Foreign Lang Dept Chm Washington HS 1989-; *ai:* Modern Lang Assn 1984; *office:* Washington HS 4747 W Washington St South Bend IN 46619

PERRYMAN, JUDY KAY (FOWLER), First Grade Teacher; *b:* Stigler, OK; *m:* James L. Jr.; *c:* Carissa, Jaymie; *ed:* (BS) Elem Ed, SW St Univ 1970; *cr:* 2nd Grade Teacher Paden Public Schls 1970-73; Kndgtn Teacher Quinton Public Schls 1973-78; 1st Grade Teacher Stigler Public Schls 1978-; *ai:* OK Ed Assn, NEA 1970-; Stigler Ed Assn 1978-; *home:* Rt 2 Box 2810 Stigler OK 74462

PERSENSKY, MARY ANN STILL, 6th Grade Teacher; *b:* Dennison, OH; *m:* Philip Alan; *ed:* (BS) Curr/Supervision, OH Univ & Wright St 1969; (MS) Curr/Supervision Ed, Wright St 1974; Grad Stud Admin; TESA Coord; *cr:* Teacher Tuscarawas-Warwick Sch 1962-65, South Elem 1965-69, Five Points Elem 1969-; *ai:* Eng Competency Comm; Spelling Bee Coord; NEA, OEA, Phi Delta Kappa, Fairborn Ed Assn; Daughters of Isabella 1966-; Teacher of Yr 1989-; *office:* Five Points Elem Sch 4 W Dayton-Yellow Springs Rd Fairborn OH 45324

PERSHA, SUSAN R., Fifth Grade Teacher; *b:* Fond Du Lac, WI; *m:* Nickolas F.; *ed:* (BA) Elem Ed, Marian Coll 1975; *cr:* 4th Grade Teacher Holy Angels Sch 1961-68; 4th/5th Grade Teacher Mayville Public Schls 1968-; *ai:* Prof Growth Inservice Comm Cooperative Learning; Gifted & Talented Prgm; Talents Unlimited; Mayville Ed Assn, South WI Ed Inservice Organization, WI Ed Assn, WI Math Cncl, NEA, Rock River Rdng Cncl; Amer Quarter Horse Assn; Badger Quarter Horse Assn; Amateur Quarter Horse Assn; Dodge Cty Horsemens Assn; WI Quarter Horse Assn; *home:* W2441 Hwy 33 Mayville WI 53050

PERSICO, ANGELA, English Teacher; *b:* Passaic, NJ; *ed:* (BA) Elem Ed, Felician Coll 1973; *cr:* Eng Teacher/Eng Chairperson Most Sacred Heart of Jesus 1980-; *ai:* Eng Chairperson; 8th Grade Moderator; NCEA Mem 1980-; *office:* Most Sacred Heart of Jesus Sch 6 Bond St Wallington NJ 07057

PERSING, EDITH ELAINE KLENK, Senior Teacher of Psychology; *b:* Chicago, IL; *w:* Maurice H. (dec); *c:* Linda Mieras, Julie, Bonny Precord, Martha, Ted; *ed:* (BS) Med Tech/Bio, 1947, (MA) Counseling/Psych, 1968 W MI Univ; Grad Work Above Masters in Counseling & Psych; *cr:* Bio Teacher 1966-73, Psych Teacher 1973- Grand Haven HS; *ai:* Tri-Hi-Y & SADD Adv; Track Coach; Comm for Drug Ed in Schls, Lecturing to Children; Teacher of Excl 1989; *home:* 14764 172nd St Grand Haven MI 49417

PERTEET, SANDRA PLENTY, English Teacher; *b:* Sawyerville, AL; *m:* Robert Lee; *ed:* (BA) Eng/Bus Admin, Stillman Coll 1978; Cmptr Ed, Accounting, Stillman Coll; Ed, Univ of Al; Numerous Educl Wkshps; *cr:* Cashier Hardees 1978; Sales Rep Bills Dollar Store 1978; Underwriter 1979-80, Auditor Trainee 1980-82 Atlanta Life Insurance Company; Clerk/Cashier Stillman Coll 1983-85; Eng/Lit Teacher Cntrl HS West Campus 1986-; *ai:* Spon Chm of Youth Enactment for Survival; Contact Person PRIDE; Legislative Contact Team Mem; Prof Ed of Tuscaloosa Secy 1988-89, Certificate for Attending Every Meeting 1989; NEA, AL Ed Assn; Prof Ed of Tuscaloosa Exec Bd Mem 1988-89, Certificate 1989; AL Realtor License 1983; Accepted for Samford Summer Inst for Teaching Excl 1990; Nom Candidate for Summer Fellowship 1990; Summer Inst of Samford Univ Writing Project; *office:* Cntrl HS West Campus 1715 Martin L King Jr Blvd Tuscaloosa AL 35401

PERY, SHERRI WRIGHT, 5th-8th Math Teacher; *b:* Poplar Bluff, MO; *m:* James H.; *ed:* (BSE) Elem Ed, 1983; (MSE) Elem Ed, 1984 AR St Univ; *cr:* 5th-8th Grade Math Teacher Holcomb RIII Sch 1984-; *ai:* Elem Chrldng Spon; Sr Class Spon; MO St Teachers Assoc 1984-88; Cmmty Teachers Assn 1984-; *home:* Rt 1 Box 230 Caruthersville MO 63830

PERZ, ERVA K., Fifth Grade Teacher; *b:* Canton, OH; *m:* Thomas E.; *c:* Mike, David Huffman, Doug Huffman, Kathy Morse, Thomas Jr., Dann Hobson; *ed:* (BA) Elem Ed, 1964; (MA) Teacher, 1980 Kent St Univ; Workshops; *cr:* Teacher 1956-58; 1964-65; 1968-71 Canton Cty Schls; Brunswick City Schls 1972-; *ai:* Mohican Outdoor Sch Prgm; Young Auth Coord; Delta Kappa Gamma Mem 1986-; Brunswick Edctl Assn Mem/Hd Rep 1972-; Tchr of Yr Candidate; *office:* Hickory Ridge Elem 4628 Hickory Ridge Dr Brunswick OH 44212

PESCA, JOSEPH G., Math/Soc Stud Teacher; *b:* Brooklyn, NY; *m:* Neila Katzer; *c:* Michael, Lauren; *ed:* (BS) Ed, 1960, (MS) Guidance, 1962 St Johns Univ; Various Courses at Adelphi Univ, Hofstra Univ, Nassau Comm Coll; *cr:* Teacher Hewlett Elem 1960-64, Ogden Elem 1964-80, Woodmere Mid Sch 1980-; *ai:* Long Island Cncl for Soc Stud Mem 1987-; Long Island Math Teacher Mem 1989-; Hewlett Woodmere Faculty Assn (VP, Rep) 1962-83; United Soccer Coach 1978-85; *office:* Woodmere Mid Sch 1170 Peninsula Blvd Hewlett NY 11557

PESCE, LINDA D., Spanish/FLEX Teacher; *b:* Hackensack, NJ; *ed:* (BS) Span, Georgian Court Coll 1977; (MA) Span, Univ of AZ 1983; Trained & Certified Amer Cncl on Teaching of Foreign Lang to Conduct Oral Proficiency Interviews; *cr:* Span Teacher Cntrl Regional HS 1977-81; Span Lecturer/Methods of Foreign Lang Teacher Univ of San Diego 1989; Span Lecturer Georgian Court Coll 1980- ; Span Teacher Cedar Drive Sch 1981-; Span Lecturer/Methods of Foreign Lang Teacher Guadalajara Summer Sch 1990; *ai:* Yrbk & Graduation Dance Adv; NJFLE, ACTFL, AATSP 1977-; Alpha Delta Kappa Recording Secy 1988-; Governors Awd for Excl in Teaching 1990; Univ of N AZ & ACTFL Grant; *office:* Cedar Drive Sch 73 Cedar Dr Colts Neck NJ 07722

PESCHKE, PATRICIA ANNA, Business Education Teacher; *b:* Hammond, IN; *ed:* (BS) Bus Ed, Ball St Univ 1971; (MS) Bus Ed, IN St Univ 1975; Endorsement Voc Bus Ed; Participant Local, Dist, St, Natl Levels of Ed, Bus Wkshps, Seminars; Certificates Received Various Univs; *cr:* Receptionist/Switchboard Operator Smith Motors Inc 1965-86; Filing Clerk Dow Theory Forecasts Inc 1967; Secy Allied Structural Steel Co 1967-70, Ball St Univ 1967-71; Bus Ed Teacher Hammond Tech & Voc HS 1971-74, Hammond Adult Ed 1971-86; Owner/Office Mgr S&S Title Co 1973-74; Bus Ed Teacher Hammond HS 1974; Bus Ed/ Cooperative Office Ed Teacher/Coord Munster HS 1974-76; Bus Ed Teacher St Francis of De Sales Adult Ed 1976-77; Secy Blaw-Knox Foundry & Mill Machinery 1983; Asst Site Coord Pyramids Inc 1985-86; Bus Ed Teacher Purdue/Calumet 1985-87; Bus Ed/Cooperative Office Ed Teacher/Coord Hammond George Rogers Clark HS 1976-; *ai:* Class of 1990, Bus Profs of Amer, Olympia Natl Scholastic Typing Contest Spon; Bus Prof of Amer Dist 1 Coord; Clark Faculty Soc & Hammond Bus Ed Curr Comm; AFT, IN Fed of Teachers, Hammond Fed of Teachers 1971-; Delta Pi Epsilon 1972-; NBEA, N Cntrl Bus Ed Assn, IN Bus Ed Assn 1976-; IN Voc Assn 1976-; Ball St Alumni Assn 1972-; Clark PTA, Adult Booster Club 1976-; Bus Profs of Amer Dist Coords Advisory Cncl 1988-; Guest Paid Lecturer on Topics Enthusiasm, Shorthand, Voc-Bus Ed Prgms, Innovations; Office Ed Assn IN Exec Bd Mem; Co-Authored Guide Book; Consultant for Prof Secy Intnl; PSI Model Curr for Sndry Ed; *office:* Hammond George Rogers Clark HS 1921 Davis Ave Whiting IN 46394

PESHALL, DEBORAH DUNCAN, 1st Grade Teacher; *b:* Aurora, IL; *m:* Robert R.; *ed:* (BA) Hm Econ;(BS) Hm Econ, 1958 Univ of Wi; (MA) Ed, AZ St Univ 1973; Advncd Rdng/ Math, Alverno Coll 1963; *cr:* Kndgtn Teacher Fairview Elem Sch 1958-69; Top Class Teacher Newington Green Infant Sch 1965-66; Kndgtn Teacher 1969-89; 1st Grade Teacher 1989- Tempe Elem; *ai:* Tempe Sister City (Yth Adv 1980-82/Bd Mem 1980-82/ Hackett Hse Bd Mem 1988-); Fulbright Grant 1965-66; *home:* 1249 E Del Sol Dr Tempe AZ 85284

PETEANU, GERTRUDE DOLORES, Coordinator of Cosmetology; *b:* Gilberton, PA; *m:* John; *c:* Linda A.; *ed:* (BA) Voc Ed, NY St Industrial Teacher Trng 1962; *cr:* Cosmetology Teacher 1957-72, Teacher/Coord of Cosmetology 1972- Mabel Dean Bacon Voc HS *ai:* VICA Club Adv; NY Dept of St Supvr for Cosmetology; Practical Examinations 1972-; Natl Haridressers Cosmetologists Assn; *office:* Mabel Dean Bacon Voc HS 127 E 22nd St New York NY 10010

PETERIE, STANLEY TAYLOR, Seventh Grade History Teacher; *b:* Keokuk, IA; *m:* Connie Jean Minor; *c:* Tyler, Natalie; *ed:* (BS) Elem Ed, 1980, (MA) Elem Ed, 1984, Sch Admin, 1987 Western KY Univ; *cr:* 6th Grade Teacher Elkton Elem Sch 1980-81; 5th/6th Grade Teacher 1981-85, 7th/8th Grade Sci Teacher 1985-88 Rockfield Elem Sch; 7th Grade His Teacher Henry F Moss Mid Sch 1988-; *ai:* Yrbk Adv; Team Leader; PTA Rep for 7th Grade Faculty; Comm for Dist-Wide In-Service Plan for 1990-91; Supervisor for Stu Teacher; KY Ed Assn 1980-88; Intnl Rdng Assn 1989-; Nom Outstanding Young Educator for Bowling Green Warren Cty Jaycees 1982 & 1990; Nom at Sch Level for Teacher of Yr 1985; *home:* 412 Browning Rd Rockfield KY 42274

PETERMAN, DEBORAH M., Sixth Grade Teacher; *b:* Livingston, TN; *m:* David Carl; *c:* Blake; *ed:* (BS) Elem Ed, TN Tech 1981; *cr:* 4th Grade/Chapter I Teacher Rickman Elem 1981-84; 7th/8th Teacher Alpine Elem 1984-87; 6th Grade Teacher Livingston Mid Sch 1987-; *ai:* Honor Club & Lang Art Academic Bowl Spon; Summer Enrichment Prgm Instr; Intnl Rdng Assn, NEA, TEA, OCEA; Creativity Wkshps for Gifted & Talented; *home:* Rt 3 Livingston TN 38570

PETERMAN, LUCINDA (SHEIL), Jr HS Teacher; *b:* Canton, OH; *m:* David;; *ed:* (BA) Elem Ed, Walsh Coll 1979; *cr:* 4th Grade Teacher 1979-84, Jr HS Teacher 1984- St Michael Sch; *ai:* Chrldr Adv; *home:* 5022 Schuller Dr NE Canton OH 44705

PETERMANN, ALICE SCHWOERER, Seventh Grade Teacher; *b:* Manitowoc, WI; *m:* Gary L.; *c:* Laura; *ed:* (BS) Elem Ed/Spec Ed, Silver Lake Coll 1977; *cr:* 5th/7th Grade Teacher 1977-78, 4th Grade Teacher 1978-85, 7th Grade Teacher 1985- St Paul Cath Sch; *ai:* Dir Sch Play; NCEA 1977-; *office:* St Paul Cath Sch 425 Main St Wrightstown WI 54180

PETERS, CAROL KAISER, 5th Grade Teacher; *b:* Port Clinton, OH; *m:* Roger; *c:* Andrea Martin, Shaun Martin, Amy Martin; *ed:* (BS) Ed, OH Univ 1965; Bowling Green Univ; *cr:* Teacher Sylvania City Schls 1965-66, Genoa Area Schls 1966-73, Benton Carroll-Salem Schls 1975-; *ai:* Sponsored & Adv Sch Newspaper; Oak Harbor Area Ed Assn Building Rep; St John Luth Church Secy 1987-; *home:* 2240 N Leutz Oak Harbor OH 43449

PETERS, CHERYL JANET HALL, Third Grade Teacher; *b:* Ashtabula, OH; *m:* Joseph; *ed:* (BS) Elem Ed 1970, (MS) Rdng Specialization, 1989 Kent St Univ; Grad Courses Edinboro St Univ, OH St Univ, Coll of Mt St Joseph, Univ of Houston; *cr:* 5th Grade Teacher Ridgeview Elem 1966-70; Learning Disabilities/ Behavior Disorders Teacher Kingsville Elem 1970-73; 4th Grade Teacher 1973-88, 3rd Grade Teacher 1988- N Kingsville Elem; *ai:* Buckeye Ed Assn, OH Ed Assn, NEA 1966-; Helped Establish Stu Publishing Center, Wrote & Received Grants for Funding; *office:* N Kingsville Elem Sch 1343 E Center St North Kingsville OH 44068

PETERS, DARNELL, 6th Grade Teacher; *b:* Iaeger, WV; *ed:* (BS) Elem Ed, Concord Coll 1981; Soc Work, Dept of Human Services; Child Protective Services; Amer Humane Society; *cr:* Soc Worker Headstart Prgm 1972-74; Soc Worker WV Dept of Human Services 1974-80; Teacher Mc Dowell Bd of Ed 1981-; *ai:* Faculty Advisory Team Mem; WV Ed Assn, NEA 1981; Certified Child Protective Service Worker; *office:* Iaeger Intermediate Sch Box 300 Iaeger WV 24844

PETERS, DAVID JOHN, Building Principal; *b:* Dubuque, IA; *m:* Nancy Furey; *ed:* (BS) Bio, Creighton Univ 1983; Teaching Cert Univ of N IA 1984; (MS) Elem Admin, Creighton Univ 1990; *cr:* Jr HS Sci Instr St Cecilias Elem 1984-89; Building Prin All Saints Cath Sch 1989-; *ai:* Rainbows for Gods Children Coord; All Saints Cath Schls Finance & Dev Comm; NCEA 1984-; *office:* All Saints Cath Sch 2716 S 24th St Omaha NE 68108

PETERS, FRITZ S., Social Studies Chairman; *b:* Santa Fe, NM; *ed:* (BA) His/Sociology, Univ of NM 1985; *cr:* Teacher Santa Fe Tech HS 1987-; *ai:* Santa Fe Capital HS Vlybl & Sftbl Coach 1988-; Spec Olympics Coach; Financial Teaching Grant 1988; *office:* Santa Fe Tech HS 2201 W Zia Rd Santa Fe NM 87501

PETERS, GARY R., 5th Grade Teacher; *b:* Jamestown, NY; *c:* Gary Jr., Alison L.; *ed:* (BS) Elem Ed, 1974, (MS) Elem Ed/ Learning & Behavior Disorders, 1980 SUNY Coll Fredonia; *cr:* 2nd Grade Teacher Rogers Elem Sch 1982-83; 3rd Grade Teacher Bush Elem Sch 1983-86; 4th & 6th Grade Teacher Rogers Elem Sch 1986-88; 5th Grade Teacher Fefferson Mid Sch 1988-; *ai:* Asst Varsity Ftbl Coach Jamestown HS 1987-; Jamestown Teachers Assn (VP 1984-86 Pres 1986-89 VP 1989-); Chautauqua Cty United Way Executive Bd 1988; Jamestown Area Labor Management Comm Mem Bd of Dir 1987-; Governors Sch & Bus Alliance Mem Executive Bd of Dir 1988-; *office:* Jefferson Mid Sch 195 Martin Rd Jamestown NY 14701

PETERS, JAMIE (SUE) WARD, 2nd Grade Teacher; *b:* Chillicothe, OH; *m:* Steven L.; *c:* Stacie, Steffie, Steven S.; *ed:* (BA) Elem Ed, OH Univ 1978; (MA) Elem Ed, Coll of Mt St Joseph 1988; *cr:* 1st-4th Grade Rdng Teacher 1979-80, 3rd Grade Teacher 1981-82 West Elem; 2nd Grade Teacher East Primary 1982-; *ai:* Waverly Classroom Teachers Building Rep; Alpha Delta Kappa; Church of the Nazarene Mem; Waverly Adult Sunday Sch Teacher; Martha Holden Jennings Schlsp Awd; *office:* East Primary Sch 5th St Waverly OH 45690

PETERS, LYNN EDWARDS, Third Grade Teacher; *b:* Asheville, NC; *m:* Jim; *ed:* (BA) Elem Ed, Mars Hill Coll 1981; *cr:* 3rd Grade Teacher Keokee Combined Sch 1981-84, Weaverville Primary Sch 1984-85; 1st Grade Teacher Leicester Elem Sch 1985-87; 3rd Grade Teacher Keokee Elem Sch 1987-.

PETERS, MARCEE SHRIVER, Secondary Vocal Music Teacher; *b:* Long Beach, CA; *m:* Christian Kerry; *ed:* (BA) Music Ed, Univ of OR 1985; (MS) Music Ed, W OR 1990; *cr:* 5th-12th Vocal Music Teacher Cntrl Linn Sch Dist 1985-; *ai:* Drama Dir; MENC 1985-; ACDA 1987-; A2E2 Teacher of Yr 1989; *office:* Cntrl Linn Mid Sch & HS Dist 552-C Halsey OR 97348

PETERS, PATRICIA ALSUP, English Department Chair; *b:* Depew, OK; *c:* Tristan D.; *ed:* (BA) Lit, Scripps Coll 1965; (MA) Ed, Claremont Grad Sch 1968; (MA) Lit, Occidental Coll 1976; *cr:* Teacher Bassett HS 1965-66, San Luis Obispo HS 1966-67, Bassett HS 1967-; *ai:* Mentor Teacher; Proficiencies & Gifted & Talented Ed Coord; NCTE 1965-; CA Assn of Teachers of Eng; Bassett Teachers Assn 1967-; Bassett Unified Sch Dist Teacher of Yr; Prin Service & PTA Golden Apple Awds; *office:* Bassett HS 755 N Ardilla La Puente CA 91746

PETERS, PATRICIA HENNING, Home Economics Department Rep; *b:* Sioux Falls, SD; *m:* Jeffrey James; *c:* Gregory, Meggan; *ed:* (BS) Home Ec, 1974, (MED) Guidance/Counseling, 1988 SD St Univ; Grad Stud Ed, Counseling; *cr:* Teacher/Dept Rep Edison Jr HS 1974-; Curr Chairperson/Home Ec Teacher Sioux Falls Schls 1988-; *ai:* Improvisational Theatre Troupe Adv; Home Ec Major Curr Revision Chairperson; Developed Prgm for Pregnant & Parenting Teens Sioux Falls Schls; Sioux Falls Ed Assn (Comm Co-Chairperson 1989, Mem 1974-); SD Ed Assn (HCR Comm 1988-89, Mem 1974-); NEA 1974-; Cath Family Services Cnslr 1990; Sioux Falls Diocese Marriage Preparation Cnslr 1978-; SD Advocacy Network for Women Rep 1989-; Local SFEA Delegate St & NEA Rep Assembly; *office:* Edison Jr HS 2101 S West Sioux Falls SD 57105

PETERS, RENIA FULCE, HS Eng/Algebra Teacher/Prin; *b:* Dallas, TX; *m:* David Payne; *c:* Rebekah G.; *ed:* (BCH) Ed, Patriot Bible Inst 1984; Chrstn Ed; *cr:* Elem Teacher 1979-82, HS Teacher 1987- Balch Springs Chrstn Acad; Elem Prin 1983-; *ai:* Sr & Coll Testing Adv; Sr Homeroom Teacher; Elem Activity Coord; Seagoville Road Baptist Church (Sunday Sch Teacher 1979-, VP Ladies Auxiliary 1985-); Amer Heart Assn CPB Instr 1977-79; *office:* Balch Springs Chrstn Acad 11524 Seagoville Rd Balch Springs TX 75180

PETERS, SANDRA EETEN, K-8th Grade Resource Teacher; *b:* Lurvene, MN; *m:* Kennis L.; *c:* Nathan, Ross, Mitchell, Wes; *ed:* (BA) Elem Ed, St Cloud St 1979; LD/MD Cert Spec Ed, Augustana 1981; (MA) Elem Admin, SD St Univ 1986; *cr:* Spec Ed/Elem Ed Teacher Little Rock Cmmty Sch 1979-; *ai:* Little Rock Ed Assn Secy; Delta Kappa Gamma; NW IA Rdng Cncl Secy 198 9-; Little Rock Public Lib Treas 1987-; Reformed Church Women Pres 1984; *office:* Little Rock Cmmty Sch Little Rock IA 51243

PETERS, SANDRA FIECHTER, Fifth Grade Teacher; *b:* London, KY; *m:* John Marshall; *ed:* (BS) Elem Ed, Univ of TN Knoxville 1971; *cr:* Secy NC St Univ 1965-70; 5th Grade Teacher Highland Park Elem Sch 1972; *ai:* Loudon Cty Spelling Bee Comm; Chairperson Southern Assn of Colleges & Schls Accredition; Lang, Spelling Comm; NEA, TN Ed Assn, East TN Ed Assn, Loudon Cty Ed Assn 1972-; *home:* 13110 Boyd Station Rd Knoxville TN 37922

PETERS, SANDY MARCUM, English Teacher; *b:* Rotan, TX; *m:* Leonard R.; *c:* Ami, Jennifer, Mickey; *ed:* (BS) Eng/Health/ Phys Ed, Mc Murray Coll 1971; Seminars; Symposiums; Wkshps; Conventions; *cr:* Eng Teacher Lamesa Mid Sch 1971-72; Phy Ed/ Ed Teacher Richardson J J Pearce 1972-74; Eng Teacher Windthorst HS 1974-77; Shamrock HS 1978-80; Seymour Jr/Sr HS 1985-; *ai:* Natl Honor Society Spon; Debate Coach; ATPE Bldg Rep 1988-; TJCTE 1 985-; Altar Society (Pres 1988-, VP 1986-88); Several Articles Publ; Grant Summer Session Midwestern St Univ; Lit for Young Adults; *home:* Rt 3 Box 17 Seymour TX 76380

PETERS, SUSAN STEPHENS, Elementary Music Teacher; *b:* Fort Worth, TX; *m:* Joseph W.; *c:* Sara S., Andrew J.; *ed:* (BM) Scndry Vocal Music, Southwest Bapt Univ 1977; (MA) Ed/Fine Arts, Drury Coll 1985; *cr:* Elem Music Teacher Seymour Elem 1978-84; Jr High/HS Music Teacher Seymour HS 1984-88; Elem Music Teacher Ozark East/South Elem 1988-; *ai:* Prin Adv Comm; Oto Salary Comm; Music Ed Natl 1978-; NEA Pres 1982-; Amer Choral Dir Assn 1984-; *home:* 1603 Melanie Ln Ozark MO 65721

PETERS-WYNN, ZARA, NI/PI Special Ed Teacher; *b:* New Orleans, LA; *c:* Jamelle E., James E. Jr., Jonathan E.; *ed:* (BA) Elem Ed, Dillard Univ 1957; (MA) Spec Ed, 1977, (MA) Supervision/Curr 1986 Georgian Court Coll; Keane Coll; Glassboro St Coll; Fairleigh Dickinson Univ; *cr:* 3rd Grade Teacher Johnson Lockett Sch 1957-58; 3rd/5th Grade Teacher Bangs Ave Sch 1958-65; 4th/5th Grade Teacher Bond St Sch 1965-72; Supplemental Instr Asbury Park Mid Sch 1972-73; Supplemental/Resource Teacher 1973-86, NI/PI Specialist/ Resource Room 1986- Asbury Park HS; *ai:* Soph, Jr, Sr Class Adv; Graduation Comm Chairperson; Faculty Cncl Chairperson Protempore; Scndry Pursuits, Attendance, Discipline Review Comms; NEA, NJ Ed Assn; Asbury Park Ed Assn (Secy 1969-71, Bldg Rep 1986-88); Delta Sigma Theta Monmouth Cty Chapter Charter Pres 1967-69 Outstanding Service 1974; Natl Cncl Negro Women; Asbury Park HS Class of 89 Adv 1986-89 Outstanding Teacher 1989; NJ Superior Court Monmouth Cty Juvenile Conference Comm; Grant NJ Dept of Ed Career Ed Curr Writing; *office:* Asbury Park H S 1000 Sunset Ave Asbury Park NJ 07712

PETERSEN, JAMES DENNIS, SR., Principal/Business Teacher; *b:* Waterloo, IA; *m:* Lana Carol; *c:* Carla C., James Jr.; *ed:* (BS) Bus Management, Bob Jones Univ 1965; *cr:* Management JC Penney Company 1965-80; Bus Dept Head Maranatha Baptist Bible Coll 1980-86; Prin Landmark Chrstn Acad 1986-; *ai:* Athletic Dir; Yrbk Adv.

PETERSEN, JANET EVELYN (KORN), Social Studies Teacher; *b:* Jamaica, NY; *m:* Carl A.; *c:* Amy, Christina; *ed:* (BA) Evrasian His, 1971, (MA) Scndry Ed, 1976, (CAS) Admin, 1983 Hofstra Univ; *cr:* Jerusalem Avenue Jr HS 1971-73; Interdisicplinary Team Teacher 1974-80, Gifted Prgm Coord 19810-84, Dean of Stus 1984-86 Jerusalem Avenue Jr HS; Dean of Stu Grand Avenue Jr HS 1986-; *ai:* Coord Academic Competitions for Gifted Stus; Adv Yorker His Club; Joint Prof Practices Dist Comm Mem; NY St Mid Sch Assn Recording Secy 1987-; Delta Kappa Gamma 1989-; Hofstra Alumni Senate Assn Secy 1978-80; Waldorf Sch Parents Assn (Parent Chairperson 1989-, Fall Fair Chairperson 1987, 1989); Outstanding Young Woman in America 1976, 1977; Co-Presenter at ASCD Conference 1982; Co-Presenter NYSMS Conferrence 1989; Helped Organize Regional Conference on Mid Sch Issues 1989; *office:* Grand Avenue Jr HS Grand Ave Bellmore NY 11710

PETERSEN, MARLENE WOOD, Fifth Grade Teacher; *b:* Anthon, IA; *m:* Ervin; *c:* Steven, Susan Mickelson, Beverly; *ed:* (BA) Elem Ed, Wayne St Coll 1970; Learning Disabled; *cr:* 1st/ 2nd/5th-8th Grad Teacher Meadow Grove Public Schls 1962-68; 5th/6th Grade Teacher Elgin Public Schls 1969-70; K-6th Grade Teacher Dist 47 Oakdale 1971-73; 5th/6th Grade Teacher Neligh-Oakdale Public Schls 1974-; *ai:* Cmptr Curr Comm; IRA 1986-; NEA, NSEA Treas 1962-; Neligh-Oakdale Ed Assn Pres 1974-; Kappa Delta Pi 1966-; Amer Legion Auxiliary 1982-; Delta Kappa Gamma Schlsp; AK-SAR-BEN Good Neighbor Awd; Delegate Rep Assembly; *office:* Neligh-Oakdale Public Schls Box 128 Oakdale NE 68761

PETERSEN, NANCY SUTTON, Science/Biology Teacher; *b:* St Louis, MO; *m:* John Dennis; *ed:* (BSED) Bio, SE MO St Univ 1983; Natural Sci, SE MO St Univ; *cr:* Teacher Arcadia Valley R-2 Schls 1983-; *ai:* HS Vlybl & Dance Squad Coach; Class Spon; Sci Fair Organizer; MO St Teachers Assn 1983-; Cmmty Teachers Assn Pres 1985; NSTA 1988-; Alpha Delta Kappa; AR Power & Light Outstanding Teacher of Yr 1988; Natl Sci Fnd Grants; Co-Authored MO St Curr Guide for Atmospheric Scis & Field Act in Geology; *office:* Arcadia Valley Mid & HS 520 Park Dr Ironton MO 63650

PETERSON, BONNIE RAE, Chemistry/Physics Teacher; *b:* Mountain Grove, MO; *m:* Edward Dean; *c:* Marcia L. Peterson Stumpff, Deborah L.; *ed:* (BSED) Chem, SW MO St Univ 1986; Working Towards Masters Natural Sci; *cr:* Sci Teacher Ash Grove HS 1987-88; Chem/Physics Teacher Mountain Grove HS 1988-; *ai:* Prom Act Jr Class & Sci Olympiad Spon; NSTA 1987-; MSTA 1986-; SWDSTA 1988-; *home:* Rt 3 Box 226 Mountain Grove MO 65711

PETERSON, CAROL CURTIS, Health Dept Chair & Teacher; *b:* Fort Worth, TX; *m:* Fred L.; *c:* Brian; *ed:* (BS) Phys Ed, Baylor Univ 1972; (ME) Health Ed, Univ of TX Austin 1983; *cr:* Teacher/coach Rosebud-Lott HS 1973-75, Lorena HS 1975-81; Teaching Asst Univ of Tx 1981-83; Health Teacher/Dept Chairperson Pflugerville HS 1985-; *ai:* Dept Chairperson Health, Phys Ed & Drivers Ed; Power of Positive Stus Coord; Stu Assistance Prgm Mem; TX Assn for Health, Phys Ed, Recreation & Dance 1987- Health Educator of Yr 1987; TX St Teachers Assn 1973- Life Mem; ASCO 1989-; Teacher of Yr Pflugerville HS 1990; Natl Meritorious Awd Correspondence Course; Human Sexuality Univ of TX; Honorable Mention Awd HS Health Correspondence Course Univ of TX; *office:* Pflugerville H S 1301 W Pecan Pflugerville TX 78660

PETERSON, CHERRY BOYER, Teacher/Coach; *b:* Kendallville, IN; *m:* David Keith; *ed:* (BS) Phys Ed/Health, 1970, (MA) Phys Ed/Health, 1974 Ball St Univ; *cr:* Phys Ed/health Teacher/Coach Dunkirk HS 1970-73; Phys Ed/Health/Speech Teacher/Coach Carroll Jr HS 1973-; *ai:* Jr HS Vlybl & Track Coach; Cty Schls Aids Curr Comm; NEA, IN St Teachers Assn, N W Allen Cty Ed Assn; *office:* Carroll Jr HS 3905 Carroll Rd Fort Wayne IN 46818

PETERSON, DANNY A., Band Director/Fine Arts Chair; *b:* Wausau, WI; *m:* Kathryn A. Klassen; *c:* Rodrick, Wendy, Lynn; *ed:* (BME) Vocal Music/Instrumental Music, Univ of WI Oshkosh 1971; *cr:* Vocal Music Teacher New London Jr HS 1971-73, 1989; Instrumental Music Teacher New London Elem 1971-72, New London Jr HS 1973-86, New London Sr HS 1987-; *ai:* Jazz Ensemble Dir; Gifted & Talented Comm; Comm to Write Rules & Guideline for Co-Curricular Act; Bay Conference Music Educators Assn Pres 1989-; Outstanding Young Educator of Yr Awd 1978; *office:* New London Sr HS 1000 W Washington St New London WI 54961

PETERSON, DAVE ERIC, 6th Grade Teacher; *b:* Fort Dodge, IA; *m:* Audrey Lou DeJong; *c:* Kristin L., Jacalyn J.; *ed:* Summer Sch, Schiller College Kleiningersheim W Ger; (BA) Scndry Ed, 1972, Elem Ed, 1975 Buena Vista Coll 1975; (MA) Elem Admin Univ of SD 1978; *cr:* Amin Asst Ayrshire Consolidated Schls 1972-74; 7th-8th Grade Teacher Fonda OLGC 1974-75; 4th Grade Teacher 1975-77, 6th Grade Teacher 1977- Storm Lake Cmmty Schls; *ai:* Supts Advisory, Supts Staff Dev Report Card, & Soc Stud Comm; NEA, IA Ed Assn, Storm Lake Ed Assn Mem 1975-; Strom Lake Public Lib Bd of Dir 1984-; Town & Country Credit Union Bd of Dir 1985-89; Elem Ed Presenter Sch Career Day Buena Vista Coll; Sch Christmas Food Drive for Upper Des Moines Agency; *office:* West Elem Sch 1001 W 6th Storm Lake IA 50588

PETERSON, DEAN E., Vocal Music Teacher; *b:* Hendricks, MN; *ed:* (BS) Vocal Music, Northern St Coll 1974; *cr:* Vocal Music Winner HS 1974-76; Lead HS 1976-; *ai:* Stu Cncl Adv 1980-88; Co-Dir All Sch Musicals; SD Amer Choral Dir West River Chm 1989-90; Kiwanis Pres 1989-; Cmmty Concert Pres 1988-; Cmmty Choir Dir 1988-; Vocal Soloist; Outstanding Young Educator Awd; *office:* Lead HS 320 S Main Lead SD 57754

PETERSON, DIANNE DIETRICH, Fifth Grade Teacher; *b:* Buffalo, NY; *m:* Larry Gene; *c:* Nicole L., Scott M.; *ed:* (BA) Elem Ed, Peru St Coll 1972; Grad Stud Univ of NE, Peru St Coll, Kearney St Coll; *cr:* K-8th Grade Elem Teacher Sch Dist 18 1973-79; 5th Grade Teacher Nemaha Valley Sch 1979-; *ai:* Teacher Quest Skills for Adolescents; Asst T-Ball Coach; NEA, NE Ed Assn 1973-; Nemaha Valley Ed Assn Treas 1979-; Amer Fed of Teacher Educators 1989-; *office:* Nemaha Valley HS PO Box 38 Talmage NE 68448

PETERSON, DONALD ROBERT, History & Philosophy Teacher; *b:* York, NE; *m:* Erwina Hutchinson; *c:* Tania Hoar, Vanessa, Erica; *ed:* (BA) Soc Stud/Ed, NE Wesleyan Univ 1960; (MED) Eng/Ed, Univ of NE 1964; Cntrl WA Univ 1968-77; Univ of Pacific 1967; Harvard 1987; *cr:* Eng Teacher/Library Utica HS 1960-63; Eng/Hum/Soc Stud Teacher A C Davis HS 1963-; *ai:* Dept Chm Soc Stud; Dist Stu Learning Objectives Comm; WA Ed Assn Building Rep 1972-73; Phi Delta Kappa Pres 1975-79; Natl Funeral Dir Assn Arbitor; Commemcement Speaker Sr Class; Nom WA & Yakima Awd for Excl in Ed 1977, 1990; *home:* 2310 W Yakima Ave Yakima WA 98902

PETERSON, ELAINE RONE, 8th Grade Amer His Teacher; *b:* Fort Worth, TX; *m:* Gary George; *c:* David, Heather; *ed:* (AA) Government, Weatherford Jr Coll 1969; (BS) His, 1972, (BA) Scndry Ed, 1972 Tennessee Temple Univ; Grad Work Univ of TN, TX Womans Univ; Numerous AATS Law-Related Ed; *cr:* 8th Grade His Teacher Springtown Mid Sch 1986-; *ai:* Natl Jr Honor Society Spon; Stu Cncl Co-Spon; TX St Teachers Assn (Pres-Elect 1988-89, Pres 1989-); Summer Inst St Bar of TX Schlsp.

PETERSON, ELDON OREN, 8th Grade History Teacher; *b:* Saint James, MN; *m:* Barbara Kubicek; *c:* Steven, Michael, Patrick; *ed:* (BS) Soc Stud, 1958, (MS) Phy Ed, 1964 Mankato St Univ; *cr:* Teacher/Coach Welcome HS 1959-60, Fairmont Jr HS 1960-63, Lincoln Jr HS 1964-81; Teacher Mankato West Jr HS 1982-; *ai:* Coached Varsity Ftbl & Bsbl; Bsktbl; Jr HS Gymnastics; Jr HS Stu Cncl Adv; Mankato Teachers League 1959-; MN Ed Assn 1959-; Natl Ed Assn 1959-; Whos Who Amer Coll & Univ 1958; *office:* Mankato West Sch 1351 S Riverfront Dr Mankato MN 56001

PETERSON, EVERNE HORACE, Speech Teacher; *b:* Gary, IN; *c:* Valerie K.; *ed:* (BS) Eng/Speech/Drama, IN St Univ Terre Haute 1948; (MS) Management & Human Resources, Natl Coll of Ed 1982; Several Wkshps; Tour Dir Abroad & in US; *cr:* 3rd Grade Teacher Grant Sch 1948-52; Kndgtn-3rd Grade Teacher J N Thorp 1952-55; HS/Mid Sch Teacher Froebel HS/Tolleston Mid Sch 1956-; *ai:* Dept, Cultural Fair, Cmnty Sch Relations Chairperson; Oritorical Contest Coach & Judge; Travel Club Spon; Designer of Costumes; Choral Choreographer; Natl Phi Delta Kapa 1976-; Gary Natl Rdng/Eng Cncl 1957-; Natl Assn of Negro Musicians 1978-; NAACP 1960-; Lake Interfaith Families Together 1989; Outstanding Service 1972, Prof Guidance 1982, Recognition & Achievment in Speech 1984-86 Awds; Published Poems; *home:* 1736 Arthur St Gary IN 46404

PETERSON, GAIL WINTHER, English Teacher; *b:* Milwaukee, WI; *m:* Evan T.; *c:* Cristi Shaffer, Loren Bell, Valerie Van Meeteren; *ed:* (BA) Eng, 1968, (MA) Eng, 1970 Brigham Young Univ; Grad Work Theatre & Ed; CourseWork in Publishing; *cr:* Managing Ed Brigham Young Univ 1970-77; Educator Sevier Dist 1977-78, Alpine Dist 1978-; *ai:* Creative Writing; Brigham Young Univ Alumni Outstanding Teacher 1984, 1989; Writing for Adolescents & Teenagers; *home:* 415 E Continental Dr Payson AZ 85541

PETERSON, GENE MARK, 7th Grade Reading Teacher; *b:* Louisville, KY; *m:* Glenna Denton; *c:* Jody, Sarah; *ed:* (BS) Industrial Ed, 1981, (MS) Vocational Ed, 1983, (Rank I) Elem Ed, 1987 Morehead St Univ; Elem Endorsement Morehead St Univ 1985; Teacher Internship Prgm; *cr:* Teacher Brea Thitt Cty HS 1981-84, Simons Mid Sch 1984-; *ai:* Head Coach Mid Sch Ftbl Prgm; Offensive Coord HS Ftbl Prgm; Track Coach, Asst Golf Coach; KY Ed Assn 1981-; Volunteer Fire Dept 1983-; *home:* Rt 2 Box 5 A Hillsboro KY 41049

PETERSON, GEORGE E., English Teacher; *b:* Jamestown, NY; *m:* Cynthia C. Carlson; *c:* Holly R.; *ed:* (BS) Ed, 1961, (MS) Ed, 1964 SUNY Fredonia; Grad Work St Bonaventure Univ, SUNY Buffalo & SUNY Fredonia; *cr:* Elem Teacher Falconer Cntrl Schl 1961-65, Jamestown Public Schls 1965-88; Eng Teacher Jamestown Public Schls 1988-; *ai:* Safety Patrol & Sci Club Adv; Falconer Teachers Assn (Trea 1963-64, Pres 1964-65); Audubon Society, Greenpeace & Humane Society Mem; Process of Writing a Book About Teaching of Writing Skills; *office:* Persell Mid Sch 373 Baker St Jamestown NY 14701

PETERSON, GLADYS HANSON, 7-8th Grade Lang Arts Teacher; *b:* Prairie Du Chien, WI; *m:* William J.; *c:* Evalyn Nerbonne, Evonne Jordan, Ruth, Shirley Dallmann, Leroy, John, Carol; *ed:* (BS) Elem His/Soc Stud/Eng, UW-Platteville 1948; *cr:* Teacher Irish Ridge Rural Sch 1944-45, Seven Mile Rural Sch 1945-47, Lynxville St Graded 1947-48; 7th-8th Grade Lang Art Teacher Seneca Schls 1968-; *ai:* Class Adv; Ofcl Scorekeeper Girls Bsktbl; Sea Secy; 4-H General Leader 1958-; Ruby Clover 1988; Meth Church Chm Admin Bd Pastor Parish Relations Comm; Farm BUREAU 4-H Cty Chm/Dist Comm Rep 1990; Conservation Teacher of Yr; Conservation Farmers of Yr; Conservation Goodyear Awd; NFO Recognition for Teaching & Youth Work; *home:* RFD 1 Eastman WI 54626

PETERSON, GROVER A., Band Teacher; *b:* Valley City, ND; *m:* Joan B Zimmerman; *c:* Paige Ellison, Travis, Joshua, Noah; *ed:* (BS) Music, Valley City St 1965; (MS) Music Ed, Univ of IL 1969; *cr:* Band/Choir Teacher Tower City Sch 1965-67; Band Teacher St Catherine Sch 1967-70, Moorhead Public Schls 1970-74, Billing Public Schls 1974-; *ai:* MT Bandmasters Assn, MT Music Educators; *office:* Lewis & Clark Jr HS 1315 Lewis Ave Billings MT 59102

PETERSON, JAMES PARLEY, Biology/Bible Teacher; *b:* Bradenton, FL; *m:* Phillis Kay Taylor; *c:* William E., Sarah E.; *ed:* (AS) Bus Management, Jones Coll 1971; (BA) Pastoral Theology, Spurgeon Baptist Bible Coll 1979; Inst in Basic Youth Conflicts; NCR Cmptr Systems Operations, Programming Problem Solving Techniques; FL Assn ohrstn Schls; Chrstn Educators Assn; *cr:* Bio/Bible Teacher Temple Chrstn Sch 1987-; *ai:* Band Dir; Jr Class Spon; Cnslr; Give Learning Disabilities Seminar FL Assn of Chrstn Schls 1989; *home:* 208 Bobbie Cir Lakeland FL 33813

PETERSON, JEANNETTE STANTON, 2nd Grade Teacher; *b:* Denver, CO; *c:* Jill L., Randy; *ed:* (BS) Elem Ed Univ of NM 1952; *cr:* 1st Grade Teacher Canyon Sch 1952-53, King St Sch 1953-55, L Wallace &Eubank 1955-56; 1st/2nd Grade Teacher Hawthorne & D Chavez 1963-; *ai:* Nom Distinguished Teacher Wwd Albuquerque Cmmty Fnd April 1989; *office:* Dennis Chavez/Albuquerque P S 7500 Barstow N E Albuquerque NM 87109

PETERSON, JUANITA L. (COLE), Math/Computer/Art Teacher; *b:* Winner, SD; *m:* Richard Allan; *ed:* (BS) Math, Univ SD Springfield 1971; Minor in Art; Two Yr Prgm Drafting; Cmptr; *cr:* Art/Title I/Math Teacher Hebron Sch 1971-75; Math/Art Teacher Giltner Sch 1975-76; Math/Sci Teacher Yutan Sch 1976-77; Math Teacher Wall Sch System 1977-84; Math/Cmptr Teacher Hay Springs Sch 1985-86; Math/Cmptr/Art Teacher Oelrichs HS 1988-; *ai:* Jr Class Spon; Curr Comm Mem; Local Teacher Organizations, SD Ed Assn, NEA; SD Omithologist Union; *office:* Oelrichs Public Sch PO Box 65 Oelrichs SD 57763

PETERSON, JUDY RENEE, English Teacher/Dept Chair; *b:* Ft Lauderdale, FL; *m:* Everett Dale; *ed:* (BA) Eng/Scndry Ed, Univ of AZ 1971; (MA) Eng Lit, N AZ Univ 1978; Deutsch Intensive Univ of Salzburg Austria; Architecture, His of Engl 1066-1603, Fitzwilliam Coll Cambridge England; Hearldry, Univ St Andrews Scot; *cr:* Teacher Blue Ridge Sch Dist 1971-; Dept Chairperson Eng Teacher Blueridge HS 1979-; *ai:* Drama Production; Sr Class Graduation, Baccalaureate, Banquet Spon; Dist Poetry Coord; Schlsp Selection; Renaissance Club; AZ Eng Teachers Assn 1980-, Outstanding HS Eng Teacher 1988; NCTE 1971-; Delta Kappa Gamma 1st VP 1977-; Church (Cncl 1974-75, 88-, Lay Reader 1990); Foreign Exch Groups-Volunteer with Stus; PTO Steering Comm 1979; Pinetop-Lakeside Teacher of Yr 1982; Dist Co-Chairperson Lang Art Curr Study 1980; Co-Organizer Area-Wide Lang Art Dev Wkshp 1985; Dist Curr Study Rep 1988.

PETERSON, KAREN WINJE, 1st Grade Teacher; *b:* Breckenridge, MN; *m:* Wayne Allen; *c:* Derek, Tory, Waylon; *ed:* (BS) Kndgtn/Elem Ed, Valley City St 1960; *cr:* 2nd Grade Teacher Page ND 1960-61, Cannon Ball ND 1961-63; Kndgtn Teacher Kettle River MN 1964-69, Moose Lake MN 1970-73, Willow River MN 1975-78, Kndgtn/1st Grade Teacher Barnum MN 1978-; *ai:* PTA 1978-; Young Civic Women Treas 1970-71; *home:* 200 4th St Moose Lake MN 55767

PETERSON, LEE ELLA MAE SCHMIDT, English Teacher; *b:* Wadena, MN; *m:* Christian Neil; *c:* Erin; *ed:* (BA) Eng, Coll of St Catherines 1976; *cr:* Eng Teacher Simley Sr HS 1976-79, Ashby HS 1979-; *ai:* Sr Class Adv; NEA, MN Ed Assn 1976-; Ashby Ed Assn (Negotiations Chairperson, Rights & Responsibilities Chairperson, Pres) 1979; Ashby GSA Leader 1988-; Dollars for Scholars 1987-; *office:* Ashby HS Box C Ashby MN 56309

PETERSON, MARGARET GERALDINE, English Teacher; *b:* Charleston, SC; *m:* Levi Jr.; *c:* Levi III, Herschel V.; *ed:* (BA) Elem Ed, Allen Univ 1960; Elem Ed, 1974, (Rank I) Elem Ed, 1978 Univ of KY; *cr:* Teacher Murray Hill Elem Sch 1960-63, Murray La Saine Elem 1964-67, Gainesville & Lacy Elem 1968-76, Chrstn Cty Mid Sch 1976-; *ai:* Links Organization; CCEA Secy 1969-70; KEA, NEA Mem 1960-; Alpha Kappa Alpha Mem; Kappa Alpha Psi Silhouette; Pennyrile Area Dev Bd of Dir 1973-77; Hopkinsville Recreation Dept Bd of Dir 1980-82, Service Awd 1982; St Peter & Paul Church Choir Mem 1986-86; *office:* Christian Cty Mid Sch Glass Ave Hopkinsville KY 42240

PETERSON, MARJORIE BROWN, Second Grade Teacher; *b:* Bridgeport, CT; *m:* Robert A.; *c:* Kevin, Kristin; *ed:* (BS) Fine Art/Textile/Design, Russell Sage Coll 1962; (MSED) Elem Ed, Nazareth Coll 1979; *cr:* Teacher US Army Ed Center 1963-64, St Joseph Sch 1978-85, Univ of Rochester 1985-89, St Joseph Sch 1989-; *ai:* Volunteer Strong Memorial Hospital; Friends of Strong Chairperson L duco Comm 1987-89.

PETERSON, MICHAEL JOHN, Vocal Music Dir/Lang Teacher; *b:* Anchorage, AK; *m:* Susan Jane Curtis; *c:* Aaron Weaver, Christopher, Nicholas; *ed:* (BA) Music Ed, 1981, (MS) Scndry General Ed, 1988 IN Univ; Japanese Stud, Brigham Young Univ 1975; Various Additional Courses; *cr:* Vocal Coach/Teacher Batchelor Mid Sch 1978-80; Tech Adv IN Univ Theatre Dept 1980; Stu Teacher Edgewood Jr/Sr HS 1981; Resident Asst IN Univ Bloomington 1980-81; Resident Dir Shawnee Summer Stock Theatre 1980-85; Dept Head/K-12th Grade Choral Teacher Bloomfield Schls 1981-85; Custodial Service Dr Stephen Schechter 1983-88; Manager Hardees & Ponderosa 1985-88; Interim Teacher Danville HS 1987-88; Choral/Theatre Dir 1988-, Japanese Instr 1989- Frankfort Sr HS; *ai:* Choral Cncl; Sch Musical; Sr Play; Thespian Club; All St Choir Spon 1988-; Pi Kappa Lambda 1980-; Phi Kappa Phi 1975, Schlsp; ISTA 1988-; Clinton Cty Civic Theatre Voting Mem 1989-; N Cntrl Evaluation Team Kokomo 1985; Red Barn Summer Stock (Music Dir 1989, Actor 1989); Shawnee Summer Stock (Music Dir 1981-85, Actor 1981-84); Clinton Countian Honor Recipient 1989; Letter of Appreciation Governor Robert Orr 1987; Clinton Countian Frankfort Times Newspaper 1989; Natl Qualifier Regency Intnl Talent Competition Advanced Vocal Category 1984; US Army Commendation Medal US Army Spec Services 1974; Frankfort HS Stus Dir Awd 1988; True Value Cntry Showdown Nashville Letter of Appreciation 1986; Jaycees Awd of Appreciation 1985; *office:* Frankfort Sr HS 1 Maish Rd Frankfort IN 46041

PETERSON, PATRICIA SIMMONS, Business Teacher/Asst Prin; *b:* Chesbrough, LA; *m:* Johnny M.; *c:* Dwain T. (dec), Sherry Peterson Denig, John Hulon; *ed:* (BA) Bus Ed, 1960, (MED) Admin/Supervision 1974, (MED) General Ed, 1984 SE LA Univ; Drug Ed Wkshps & SAPE Wkshps 1980-; Curr Dev Seminars 1980-84; *cr:* Bus/Soc Stud Teacher Ponchatoula HS 1960-63, St Francisville HS 1966-70, Valley Force Acad 1970-74; Bus Instr SE LA Univ 1974-75, CETA Sch 1975-78, SE LA Univ 1979-80; Bus/Soc Stud Teacher Ponchatoula HS 1980-84; Teacher/Admin Sumner HS 1984-; *ai:* 7th-12th Grade Just Say No Club Spon; Southern Assn Accreditation & Evaluation Sumner HS Mem; Steering Comm Chm 1985-86; Drug Ed SAPE Mem 1982-84; Curr Guide Comm; Ponchatoula HS Sch Soc Stud Dept Chm 1980-84; Valley Forge Acad Sr Class Spon; Coll of Bus Alumni Club Bd of Dir 1978; Amite Meth Church Choir 1970-87; Daughters of Amer Revolution Prgm Dir; UDC Prgm Dir; Amite Booster Club Mem; Springview Tennis Assn Pres 1979-80; Kentwood Rotary Club Outstanding Service Awd 1989; Article Published 1975; SE LA Univ Bus Dept Mem 1975; SE LA Univ Fall Conference Co-Moderator 1974; LISA LA St Literary Rally Orgainzer & Dir; Sumner HS Outstanding Service 1985; Ponchatoula HS Outstanding Service 1984; Just Say No Natl Recognition Awd 1986-89; Sheriffs Candidate Prgm Presenter 1975; Kentwood Dairy Day Pageant (Dir 1977, 1978, Steering Comm 1977, 1978); *office:* Sumner HS Rt 4 Box 611 Kentwood LA 70444

PETERSON, RICHARD A., Mathematics/Computer Teacher; *b:* Aurora, IL; *m:* Mary Coupland; *ed:* (BS) Cmptr Sci, Northwestern Univ 1981; *cr:* Software Engineer Bally Mfg Corp 1981-86; Math/Cmptr Teacher Univ Lake Sch 1987-; *ai:* Girls Var Bsktbl Coach; Cmptr Consultant Sch Publications; Go Club Adv; Sch Scheduler; NCTM; Tandy Technology Teacher for Univ Lake Sch; *home:* 117 S Main St Oconomowoc WI 53066

PETERSON, RICHARD KURT, Band Director; *b:* Fergus Falls, MN; *m:* Pam Witikko; *ed:* (BS) Instrumental Music, Bemidji St Univ 1981; *cr:* Teacher Glenville Public Sch 1981-84, Albert Lea Jr HS 1984-89, Albert Lea Sr HS 1989-; *ai:* Dir Albert Lea HS Jazz Band, Marching Band, Pep Band, Concert Bands; MN Music Educators Assn, MN Ed Assn, NEA, Music Educator Natl Conference 1981-; Natl Rifle Assn, Fraternal Order of Eagles, Benevolent & Protective Order of Elks; *office:* Cntrl HS 504 W Clark St Albert Lea MN 56007

PETERSON, S. WAYNE, Science & Phys Ed Teacher; *b:* Duluth, MN; *m:* Martha Parrish; *c:* Paula, Sheli, Heather, Tony, Beth, Holly, Kathy, Jeffrey; *ed:* (BS) Phys Ed/Health, Gustavus Adolphus Coll 1958; (MS) Phys Ed, Mankato St Coll 1964; *cr:* Amboy HS 1958, Marshall HS 1958-59, Lake Crystal HS 1959-63, Mankato St Univ 1963-64, Bemidji St Univ 1964-65, Augustana Coll 1965-69, Rochester Jr Coll 1969-71, Univ of WI Superior 1971-73, Montevideo HS 1978-82, Sioux Falls Public Schls 1982-83, Danube Renville Sacred Heart 1984-; *ai:* Ftbl, Bsktbl, Bsbl, Ice Hockey, Track, Wrestling Coach; NEA, MEA, MSHSCA 1989; Gustavus Adolphus Coll Athletic Hall of Fame 1987.

PETERSON, STEPHANIE JOSEPHINE, Mathematics Teacher; *b:* Chicago, IL; *m:* Dean; *c:* Stacey Knudsten, Eric; *ed:* (BA) Home Ec Ed - Summa Cum Laude, AZ St Univ 1980; THA Master Prgm Math, AZ St 1986; Working Towards Masters Sch Admin, N AZ Univ; *cr:* Math Teacher 1980-89, Math Dept Chairperson 1983-89 Willis Jr HS; Math Teacher Chandler HS 1989-; *ai:* Chander HS Stu Senate, Sr Class, BSU Adv; Chander HS Management Team & Act Comm; NCTM 1983-; Phi Theta Kappa 1977; Kappa Delta Pi (Mem, Act Co-Chairperson 1980-, Office 1980); Phi Upsilon Omicron Act Co-Chairperson 1979-80; AZ Cncl of Math Teachers (Regional Convention Comm 1989) 1980-; Phoenix Cath Diocese Certified Religious Ed Instr 1968-78; J-H Maricopa Cty Leader 1980, Leadership 1980; Phoenix Coll Academic Achievement Faculty Schlsp 1978; Natl Sci Fnd Grant Microcomputer Ed 1981; Presidential Awds Excl in Math Nom 1985; Willis Jr HS Excl in Ed Awd 1986-87; *office:* Chandler HS 350 N Arizona Ave Chandler AZ 85224

PETERSON, THADA TINKER, 4th-6th Grade Science Teacher; *b:* Quantico, VA; *m:* Sidney Wm.; *c:* Sidney W. Jr., Matthew W.; *ed:* (BSE) Elem Ed, Midwestern St Univ 1969; *cr:* 3rd Grade Teacher Fowler Elem 1969-70, 1973-79; Art Teacher Ben Milam Elem 1971-72; Sci Teacher Sheppard AFB Elem 1979-; *ai:* Spon Young Astronauts Prgm; Numerous Comm & Task Forces for Sch Dist; TX Classroom Teachers Assn (Treas, Pres 1988-); TX Cncl of Elem Sci Teachers, Sci Teachers Assn of TX; W Fnd Awd for Excl in Teaching 1986-87; Teacher of Yr Sheppard Elem 1989; *office:* Sheppard Elem Sch 301 Anderson Sheppard AFB TX 76311

PETERSON, VERILYN ROXANE (POTTHOFF), Vocal Music Teacher; *b:* St Paul, MN; *m:* Kenneth F.; *c:* Vanessa, Marcia; *ed:* (BME) Music, N Cntrl Coll 1970; (MED) Music Ed, Univ of MN 1988; Grad Stud Comparative Ed, Univ of WI; Music Therapy, Univ of MN; *cr:* Teacher Johanna Jr HS 1970-82, Rhyl HS Rhyl Wales United Kingdom 1976, Chippewa Jr HS 1982-; *ai:* Vocal Dir; MENC, MMEA; SAI VP 1969-70; St Paul Mothers of Twins Pres 1985-86; Sabbatical 1987-88; *office:* Chippewa Jr HS 5000 Hodgson Rd Shoreview MN 55126

PETERSON, VIRGIL RICHARD, 4th-6th Grade Math Teacher; *b:* Cherokee, IA; *m:* Gretchen Ann Lichtenberg; *c:* Jodi A., Jay D.; *ed:* (BA) Elem Ed, Buena Vista Coll 1974; *cr:* 6th Grade Teacher 1975-84, 4th-6th Grade Math Teacher 1984-Dunlap Cmmty Sch; *ai:* Asst HS Girls Sftbl Coach; Winter Adult Recreation Night Dir; Dunlap Teachers Organization (VP 1979-80, 1984-85, Pres 1980-81, 1985-86); St John Luth Church (Cncl 1977-83, 1986-89, Pres 1981-83, 1986-89, Sunday Sch Teacher 1980-); Faculty Follies Variety Show Co-Chm 1980-88; *office:* Dunlap Cmmty Sch 1102 Iowa Ave Dunlap IA 51529

PETETT, RONALD DELANO, 4th Grade Teacher; *b:* Pasco, WA; *m:* Lola May V.; *c:* Cindy L. Aillaud, Darcy, Ronald D. Jr., Dr. J. Scott; *ed:* (BA) Eng, Univ of WA 1969; Univ of WA, Antioch Univ, Cntrl WA Coll; *cr:* 4th Grade Teacher Sunny Hills Elem 1969-71; 4th-6th Grade Teacher Apollo Elem 1971-78; Rdng Lab Teacher Maywood Jr HS 1978-84; 8th Grade Lang Arts Teacher Maywood Sch 1984-88; 4th Grade Teacher Maple Hills Elem Sch 1988-; *ai:* Coach Kndgtn & 1st Grade T Ball Team, Youth Soccer 1971-80; Natl Eng Teachers 1978-85; NEA 1969-; WEA 1969-; IEA 1969-; PTA 1961-; Public Service Commendation Coaching Youth Teams Sierra Heights PTA 1976; *home:* 2015 Union Ave NE Renton WA 98056

PETILLO, BOBBY DEAN, Developmental Reading Teacher; *b:* Sitllwater, OK; *m:* Brenda Beach; *ed:* (AS) Bio, Chrstn Coll SouthWesT 1970; (BA) Poly Sci, 1977; (Med) Elem Ed, East TX St Univ 1979; Educl Admin; Adv Academic Trng; *cr:* Remedial Math 1979-80; 3rd Grade Teacher 1980-82; 5th Grade Teacher 1982-85; 4th Grade Teacher 1985-87 Wills Pointe Elem; Developmental Rdng/Math Wills Point Intermediate 1987-; *ai:* Dist Insurance Comm; TX St Teachers Assn Treas 1980; Assn of TX Prof Educators 1982-; Parent Teacher Club Treas 1982; Superintendents Advisory Comm; Classroom Mgmt and Discipline;

office: Wills Point Intermediate Sch PO Drawer 30 Wills Point TX 75169

PETITT, WANDA (GREESON), Special Ed/Gifted & LD; *b:* Trion, GA; *m:* David Harmon; *c:* James D.; *ed:* (BA) Elem Ed, Shorter Coll 1964; (MED) Spec Ed, W GA 1976; Staff Dev Cmpt Trng & Various Other Ed Fields; *cr:* 5th-8th Grade Teacher Pennville Elem Sch 1957-70; 7th-8th Grade Teacher Summerville Jr HS 1970-74; 1st-8th Grade Teacher of Gifted Chattooga Cty Itinerant 1974-80; 5th-8th Teacher of Gifted Summerville Jr HS & N Summerville Elem 1980 -87; 6th-8th Teacher of Gifted & Learning Disabilities Summerville Mid Sch 1987-; *ai:* Jr Beta Club; NEA, GA Ed Assn, Chattooga Cty Ed Assn 1957-; *office:* Summerville Mid Sch Hwy 100 Summerville GA 30747

PETRANTO, LISA ANN, 4th Grade Teacher; *b:* Los Alamos, NM; *ed:* (BA) Elem Ed, AZ St Univ 1980; (MA) Instructional Specialist, Univ of TX El Paso 1989; *cr:* 4th Grade Teacher Clardy Elem 1980-; *ai:* El Paso Ind Public Sch Dist Sci Fair, Sci Book Adoption Comms; Intnl Rdng Assn 1982-85; PTA Various Bd Positions 1981-86, Lifetime Mem 1986.

PETRARCA, FRANCES FERRERO, Retired 7th Grade Teacher; *b:* Bessmer, MI; *m:* Paul P.; *c:* Paul A., David J., Karen, Laura Peppler; *ed:* (BA) Elem Eng, Seton Hill Coll 1974; *cr:* 7th Grade Teacher Holy Trinity 1969-73, St James 1974-88; *home:* RD 1 Box 536 Vandergrift PA 15690

PETREY, SCENA ANN (GOETZ), English Teacher; *b:* Danville, KY; *m:* Willie M.; *c:* Bradley H., Kathryn A.; *ed:* (BA) Eng, Campbellsville Coll 1972; Ed/Eng, E KY Univ 1977; *cr:* Teacher Crab Orchard HS 1972-74, Lincoln Cty HS 1975-; *ai:* Sr Spon; Yrbk, Newspaper Adv; Sftbl Coach; LCEA (Treas, Secy) 1973-74; KEA, NEA; *home:* 130 Edgewood Dr Stanford KY 40484

PETRIK, REBECCA CALVERT, Music Teacher; *b:* Pullman, WA; *m:* John Jerome; *c:* Molly, Will, Emily; *ed:* (BA) Music Ed, MI St Univ 1977; Certified Orff Instr Hamline Univ; Math, Soc Stud, Rdng, Minot St; Several Wkshps; *cr:* General Music/Choral Teacher Holdingford HS 1978-79, Capitol View Jr HS 1979-80; 1st-8th Grade General Music/Choral Teacher Holy Trinity Sch 1980-82; General Music/Choral Teacher Burlington/Des Lacs Elem 1982-; *ai:* 5th & 6th Grade Choir; Prairie Winds Orff Secy 1988-; ND Music Ed Assn Bd Mem 1990; Augustana Luth Church; Center for Adolescent Dev Volunteer Camp Cnslr; Articles Published; *office:* Burlington/Des Lacs Elem Sch 301 Wallace Burlington ND 58722

PETRISKY, ROBERT FRANKLIN, Band Director; *b:* Port Lavaca, TX; *m:* Irene Tello; *ed:* (BME) Music Ed, 1978, (ME) Music Ed, 1980 Southwest TX St Univ; Various Seminars & Wkshps Sponsored by TX Music Educators Assn; TX Bandmasters Assn; TX Luth Coll; *cr:* Asst Band Dir Edna Independent Sch Dist 1980-81, Pearsall Independent Sch Dist 1981-83, Schertz-Cibolo-Universal City Ind Sch Dist 1983-85; Band Dir Seguin Ind Sch Dist 1985-; *ai:* All Instrumental Music Act; TX Music Educators Assn 1975-; TX Bandmasters Assn 1981-; Assn of TX Prof Educators 1980-; Mid TX Symphony Orchestra Mem 1986-; San Antonio Municipal Band Mem 1989-; TX Luth Coll Band Camp Faculty Mem 1987-; Selected Clinician for TMEA Region XIII Junior HS Symphonic Band 1989; Directed Bands Which Received 8 Univ Interscholastic League First Division Superior Rating Awds for Concert Performances Including 5 Sweepstakes Awds; Dir of Bands Which Represented TMEA Region XII St Honor Band Competition 1986 & 1988; *home:* 1117 Twin Ln Schertz TX 78154

PETRO, GORDON LAWRENCE, Military Science Teacher; *b:* Greenfield, NY; *m:* Lorraine Crowley; *c:* Michael L., Michelle Petro Fitzpatrick; *ed:* (BA) Psych, Columbia Coll 1976; Advanced Systems of Sales Techniques & Sales Engineering; *cr:* Teacher Morse HS 1977-80; Dept Chm 1981-84, Teacher 1985- Hoover HS; *ai:* Jr Var Rifle Team, Male/Female Fancy Drill Team, Coed Exhibition, Individual & Flag Coach; Cadet Club Adv; *office:* Herbert Hoover HS 44474 Elcajon Blvd San Diego CA 92115

PETROSINO, VINCENT JOSEPH, Foreign Languages Dept Head; *b:* Brooklyn, NY; *m:* Patricia B.; *c:* Courteney, Francesca; *ed:* (BA) Foreign Lang, Manhattan Coll 1968; (MAT) Fr/Ger, Johns Hopkins Univ 1970; (MED) Ed, Loyola Coll 1982; Doctoral Candidate Urban Ed, Morgan St Univ; *cr:* Teacher Hamilton Jr HS 1969-74; Dept Head Northern HS 1974-79, City Coll HS 1979-80, Baltimore Sch for the Arts 1980-82; Ed Specialist Office of Bi-ling Ed 1984-86; Dept Head Northern HS 1986-; *ai:* NHS & Academic Bowl Team Adv; Graduation Comm & Curr Dev for Environmental Ed; Awds Prgm & Schlsp Comm; MD Foreign Lang Assn Pres 1986-87; MD Assn Bi-ling Ed (Pres 1987-88, Bd Mem 1988); Phi Delta Kappa 1986-; Baltimore City Public Schls ESEA Chapter VII Grant for Bi-ling Ed; Fund for Educl Excl for Foreign Lang Teaching Spec Ed Children.

PETROSKI, CAROLYN TAYLOR, Special Education Teacher; *b:* Union Cty, NC; *m:* Jeffery James; *c:* Patrick Campbell, Reggie Campbell, Shannon; *ed:* (BS) Spec Ed, Winthrop Coll 1973; Working Towards Masters in Elem Ed; Grad Stud in Supporting Fields; *cr:* Elem/Spec Ed Teacher 1973-81, Mid Sch Math Teacher 1981-87, Resource LD/EMH Teacher 1990 Lancaster Cty Schls; *ai:* Cmptr Club; Spec Olympics; Palmetto St Teachers Assn 1982-87; Republican Party Precinct Pres 1990; *home:* Rt 10 Box 1475 Lancaster SC 29720

PETRUSKA, SHARON ANN, Fourth Grade Teacher; *b:* Rochester, PA; *ed:* (BS) Elem Ed, Edinboro Univ 1971; Masters Equivalency; *cr:* 4th & 5th Grade Teacher 1971-72, 5th Grade Teacher 1972-73, 4th Grade Teacher 1973- New Brighton Elem; *ai:* Chrldng Spon 1974-75; American Assn of Univ Women 1979-80/1984-86; American Cancer Society Bd of Dir Public Ed Chairperson 1984 Awds for Public Ed 1986; Comm Concert Assn of Beaver Cty 1986-; *office:* New Brighton Elem Sch 3200 43rd St New Brighton PA 15066

PETRUSO, RONALD THOMAS, Chemistry Instructor; *b:* Meadville, PA; *m:* Bertha Louise Papp; *c:* Kimberly A., Michael T.; *ed:* (BS) Bio/Chem, Alliance Coll 1965; Cytology, Univ of PA 1977; *cr:* Chem Instr Norristown Sr HS 1966-89; Cytologist Smith Kline Laboratory 1988-; *ai:* Mid Sts Steering & Sch Dist Chemical Safety Comm; Amer Chemical Society, Amer Society of Cytology, ASCP, Natl Teachers Assn, PA Ed Assn; Laboratory Medicine Publication; Walter Reed Inst of Medical Research, Univ of DE, Woodrow Wilson Grant; Amer Family Inst Teacher Awd; Mrktg & Sci DECA Awd; *office:* Norristown Area Sr HS 1900 Eagle Dr Norristown PA 19403

PETRUZZI, JOSEPHINE A., Retired Teacher; *b:* Kittanning, PA; *c:* Fred V., Sally V.; *ed:* (MED) Elem Ed, Indiana Univ of PA 1969; Prin Cert Sch Admin, PA St Univ 1970; *cr:* Stu Teachers Supv Edinboro Univ of PA; Remedial Rdng/Team Teacher Altoona Sch Dist; 2nd Grade Teacher Armstrong Sch Dist; *ai:* Cmmty Rdng Volunteer; Pi Lambda Theta; Armstrong Sch Dist Research Study Identification & Analysis of Pupil Ancillary Services; Television PBS Prgm Remedial Rdng & Children Closed Circuit PV Prgm; *home:* 8450 Willow Pl N #1905 Houston TX 77070

PETSCHEL, SALLY JANE NEFF, Fourth Grade Teacher; *b:* Columbus, OH; *m:* Vernon J.; *ed:* (BSED) Elem Ed, Kent St Univ 1963; *cr:* 4th Grade Teacher Champion Local Schls 1963-; *ai:* Delta Kappa Gamma 1968-; NEA, OH Ed Assn, NE OH Assn 1963-; Bus & Prof Women 1966-72; Amer Assn of Univ Women 1963-72; 2nd Chrstn Church (Trustee 1989-, Diaconate 1987-); *office:* Champion Local Schls 5759 Mahoning Ave Warren OH 44483

PETTAPIECE, BOB, Teacher; *m:* Sandy Alber Howe; *c:* Lori, Erin Howe, Michelle Howe; *ed:* (BA) Hum, 1963, (BA) Religion, 1967 MI St Univ; (MED) General Scndry Ed, 1971, Educl Specialist Certificate General Scndry Ed, 1973, (EDD) Soc Stud Teacher Ed, 1980 Wayne St Univ; Inst for Advancement of Human Behavior Conferences 1979, 1980, 1982, 1989; Unicolor Teacher Trng Seminar 1979; Natl Stu Volunteer Prgm Trng Urbana Coll 1977; Trng Inst for Desegrated Ed Wkshp Northern HS 1976; *cr:* Math Teacher Greusel Jr HS 1967-68, Hutchins Jr HS 1968-71; Photography/Interpersonal Relations/1st-4th/9th-12th Grade Computing/Psych/Sociology/Soc Research Teacher Community HS 1977-89; Photography/Computing/Soc Sci Teacher Booth CEC 1989; Soc Stud Teacher Northern HS 1971-; *ai:* Booth CEC Coll Adv 1989-; Northern HS Sr Class Spon 1979; Phi Delta Kappa 1981-; MI Assn for Core Curr Treas 1973-; MI Assn for Cmptr Users in Learning; Intnl Cncl for Cmptrs in Ed 1980-; ASCD; Wayne St Univ Coll of Ed Alumni Assn Bd of Governors 1988-89; MI Cncl for Soc Stud; Metropolitan Detoit Youth Fnd, Center for Urban Ed Advisory Bd Mem; MI Atari Cmptr Ethusiasts; Wayne St Univ Grad Prof Schlsp 1975-76; Whos Who in Midwest 1982-; Articles Published; *home:* 555 Brush #2206 Detroit MI 48226

PETTENGILL, TIMOTHY OWEN, Spanish Teacher; *b:* Syracuse, NY; *m:* Lucy Velazquez; *c:* Natasha, Timothy Jr.; *ed:* (BA) Span, CA St Fresno 1983; Scndry Credential, CA St Fresno; *cr:* Span Teacher Clovis West HS 1984-; *ai:* Chess Club Coach/Adv; Intnl Club Co-Adv; Phi Kappa Phi Mem 1983; *office:* Clovis West HS 1070 E Teague Fresno CA 93710

PETTERSON, EVELYN ELIZABETH, Fifth Grade Teacher; *b:* Lowell, MA; *ed:* (BS) Elem Ed, Fitchburg St Teachers Coll 1953; (MED) Ed/Guidance, Univ of Hartford 1963; 6th Yr Spec Ed Central CT St Univ; 7th Yr Bi-Ling Ed, Univ of CT; *cr:* Elem Teacher Westlands Sch 1953-1959; Elem Teacher Consolidated Sch Dist 1959; *ai:* Soc Stud Curr Comm; Staff Dev Comm; AFT 1988; New Britain Ed Assn; CT Ed Assn; NEA; Bethany Covenant Chur Ch 1959-88; *home:* 3 Bayberry Court Cromwell CT 06416

PETTIES, JOAN ESMERALDA WOODS, Spanish Teacher/Dept Chair; *b:* Roatan, Honduras; *c:* Carla, Jennifer; *ed:* (BA) Phys Ed/Span, San Diego St Univ 1972; (MA) Ed, US Intnl Univ 1975; Bi-ling Instructional Technology, San Diego St 1986; *cr:* Teacher Gompers Scndry Sch 1972; Resource Teacher Ed Center 1989; *ai:* Advance Placement Comm; St of CA Foreign Lang Competency Project; Supervised Mexico Study Trips; Teacher Recruitment Pilot Prgm; Mentor Teacher for Span 1987-89.

PETTINGER, ANN RICHARDS, Honors English Teacher; *b:* Adel, GA; *m:* Nate; *c:* Jill, Matt, Miranda Richards, Meg Richards; *ed:* (BA) Eng, Weber St Coll 1973; *cr:* 7th/8th Grade Eng Teacher Del Rio & San Felipe Schls 1979-81, Victor Valley Jr HS 1981-; *ai:* Ski & Honors Club; Newspaper Adv; Mentor Teacher Selection Comm Chairperson; Mentor Teacher 1986-87; *office:* Victor Valley Jr HS 16925 Forrest Victorville CA 93997

PETTIT, GERMAINE, Biology Teacher; *b:* Hilldale, PA; *w:* Donald (dec); *c:* Susan; *ed:* (BS) Scndry Ed/Bio/Sci, Wilkes Coll 1959; (MS) Curr/Scndry Stud, E Stroudsburg Univ 1981; *cr:* Bio Teacher Phillipsburg HS 1959-65; Sci/Bio Teacher Wilson Area HS 1968-; *ai:* Women of Faculty Club Pres; NEA, PSEA, WAEA 1968-; *office:* Wilson Area HS 22nd & Washington Blvd Easton PA 18042

PETTIT, JONATHAN MICHAEL, Sixth Grade Teacher; *b:* Hutchinson, MN; *m:* Dorothy Fitch; *c:* Josie, Jason, Jonathan Jr., Jane; *ed:* (BS) Elem Ed, Valley City St Univ 1984; *cr:* 6th Grade Teacher Rushford Public Schls 1984-; *ai:* Head Girls Bsktbl, Head Boys Bsbl, Asst Ftbl Coach; Amer Legion Post #94 Club Bd Chm 1988-89; Natl Sci Fnd Grant 1989; *home:* Rt 2 Box 63A Rushford MN 55971

PETTIT, NANCY KEMP, English II Teacher; *b:* Martin, TN; *m:* Jim A.; *c:* James A., Scott; *ed:* (BS) Bus Admin, Univ of TN Martin 1973; (MED) Ed Curr/Instruction, Memphis St 1983; *cr:* Bus/Eng Teacher Jackson Jr HS 1975-86; Eng II Teacher Jackson Cntrl-Merry HS 1986-; *ai:* NHS & Future Teachers of Amer Spon; TEA, NEA, Phi Chi Theta, Phi Kappa Phi; JEA Secy 1984-85; Alpha Delta Kappa (Secy 1986-88 Pres 1988-); Jackson City Schls Teacher Cncl & Task Force; W TN Cncl Teachers of Eng Secy 1989-; *office:* Jackson Cntrl-Merry HS Allen Ave Jackson TN 38301

PETTIT, ROLAND LAMAR, Mathematics Teacher; *b:* Canton, GA; *m:* Sandra; *c:* Ronnie, Marty, Regena; *ed:* (BS) Physics, N GA Coll 1963; Scndry Ed Curr, Math, Jacksonville St Univ 1986; *cr:* Officer US Army 1963-84; *ai:* Natl Jr Honor Society Club Adv; Received Golden Apple Awd Outstanding Performance Sponsored Arbys & WJSU-TV 1990; *home:* 263 Silver Cir Jacksonville AL 36265

PETTUS, PAULA C., Sixth Grade Lang Art Teacher; *b:* Florence, AL; *ed:* (BS) Elem Ed, Univ of N AL 1987; Working Towards Masters in Elem Ed 1990; *cr:* 6th Grade Teacher Waterloo HS 1988-89, Rogers HS 1989-; *ai:* 6th Grade 4-H Spon; Jr HS Girls Bsktbl Team; Waterloo Var Girls Bsktbl & Sftbl Team Coach 1988-89; *office:* Rogers HS Rt 1 Box 300 Florence AL 35630

PETTY, CAROLE FELTS, Sixth Grade Reading Teacher; *b:* Lueders, TX; *m:* Harell A.; *c:* Amy Barrington, Ellen Combest, Wade, Nan Wiley; *ed:* (BS) Ed, Midwestern St Univ 1969; (MS) Ed, Sul Ross St Univ 1985; *cr:* 7th Grade Teacher Eastward Jr HS 1969-70; 1st Grade Teacher Crestview Elem 1970-71; 2nd Grade Teacher 1971-73, 1st Grade Teacher 1973-75, 5th Grade Teacher 1975-84 Stamford ISD; 6th Grade Teacher Abilene ISD 1984-85, Wylie ISD 1985-; *ai:* TSTA/NEA 1969-; Delta Kappa Gamma Society Intnl 1983; Beltway Park Baptist Church Mem; *office:* Wylie Ind Sch Dist 7650 Hardwick Abilene TX 79606

PETTY, FLORA RENSHAW, Third Grade Teacher; *b:* St George, GA; *m:* James Walter Sr.; *c:* James W. Jr., Phyllis Cowart, Angela Glisson, Greogry D., Kerry; *ed:* Math, Martha Berry Coll 1956-59; FCCJ 1980; *cr:* K-4th Grade Teacher 1971-77, 3rd Grade Teacher 1978-79, K-5th Grade Teacher 1979-81, 3rd Grade Teacher 1981- Victory Chrstn Acad; *ai:* Cheerleading Spon; Bsktbl Coach 1978, 1989; Athletic Booster Club Officer & Mem; *office:* Victory Chrstn Acad 10613 Lem Turner Rd Jacksonville FL 32218

PETTY, TAMARA SUE, Music Teacher; *b:* Columbus, OH; *ed:* (BME) Music Ed, OH St 1984; *cr:* Choir Dir Circleville City Schls 1984-; *ai:* 7th-12th Grade Vocal Music Acts; Swing Choir Dir; OH Music Ed Assn, Amer Choral Dirs Assn, Pickaway Cty Art Society; *office:* Circleville City Schls 520 S Court St Circleville OH 43113

PETTY, VENETA LA FLUER, Kindergarten Teacher; *b:* Kansas City, MO; *m:* Charles Alton; *c:* Jason, Jeffery; *ed:* (BSE) Eng, Univ of Cntrl AR 1979; Rdng Specialist Mid Sch; *cr:* Librarian 1974-79, 5th/6th Grade Rdng Teacher 1979-83 Brinkley Mid Sch; 6th Grade Teacher 1983-88, Kndgtn Teacher 1988-Calvary Chrstn Sch; *ai:* Sunday Sch Teacher 4-5 Yr Olds; *home:* 309 Laughrun Forrest City AR 72335

PETTY, WILLIAM ARTHUR, Industrial Technology Teacher; *b:* Media, PA; *m:* Barbara J. Howard; *c:* Douglas, Scott, Joel; *ed:* (BS) Industrial Arts Ed, Cheyney St Coll 1962; (MA) Industrial Arts Ed, Trenton St Coll 1967; Theory Into Practice, Acad for Advancement of Teaching 1987; *cr:* Teacher Bensalem HS 1962-64; Teacher/Coord Hunterdon Cty Adult Ed 1967-75; Teacher Night Course Kildonen Sch 1968-69; Teacher Delaware Valley Regional HS 1964-; *ai:* Boys Cross Cntry Head Coach 1970-; Boys Track 1986-; Cooperative Relationship Project; HS Honor Banquet Chairperson; Intnl Technology Ed Assn, PA Technology Ed Assn 1962-; NEA, NJ Ed Assn 1964-; St Andrews Church (Jr Warden 1979-84, Sr Warden 1984-, Vestry Person 1990); Nom NJ St Competition; NJ SIAA Coaches Assn Hall of Fame; Natl HS Silver Coaching Awd Scholastic Coach Magazine; Delaware Valley Regional Teacher of Yr; *office:* Delaware Valley Regional HS RD 1 Box 188 Frenchtown NJ 08825

PEVETO, CYNTHIA HOLECEK, English Teacher; *b:* Baytown, TX; *m:* Jerry W.; *c:* Jason Menard, Todd; *ed:* (BS) Sociology, 1969, (MS) Ed, 1989 Lamar Univ; Gifted & Talented Ed; *cr:* Eng/His Teacher Hardin-Jefferson HS 1983-; *ai:* NHS Spon; UIL Spelling Spon; Communication Comm; TX Assn Gifted & Talented, TX Joint Cncl Teachers of Eng 1988-; TX St Teachers Assn 1983-; *office:* Hardin-Jefferson HS PO Box 639 Sour Lake TX 77659

PEZLEY, PRISCILLA DIEHL, Guidance Counselor; *b:* Marion, OH; *m:* Paul D.; *c:* Daniel, Michael, David; *ed:* (BS) Ed, OH Univ 1975; (MED) Guidance/Counseling, Univ of San Diego 1976; *cr:* 11th Grade Eng Teacher Tri-Rivers Career Center 1976-78; Guidance Cnslr River Valley Jr HS 1978-; *ai:* Stu Cncl Adv; Mid Sch Transition Co-Chairperson; Phi Delta Kappa 1988-; OH Sch Cnslr Assn 1976-; 1st Presby Church Mem 1966-; *office:* River Valley Jr HS 1199 Columbus Sapdusky Rd N Marion OH 43302

PEZZINO, ESTHER MAE FALCONE, Early Childhood Educator; *b:* Frankfort, NY; *m:* Pat; *c:* Stefanie; *ed:* (BS) Home Ec Ed, 1976, (MS) Voc Home Ed, 1983 St Univ Coll Buffalo; Exec Bus Admin; *cr:* Substitute Teacher Buffalo Bd of Ed 1976-77; Consumer Homemaking Inst Buffalo Bd of Ed 1977-82; Early Chldhd Inst Erie I Bd of Cooperative Educl Services 1982-; *ai:* Dist & Chapter FHA HERO Adv; Voc Industrial Clubs of America Faculty Adv; NY St Home Ec Teacher Assn Dist Coord 1982-86, W NY Teacher of Yr 1982; Natl Assn Voc Home Ec Teachers, NY St Occupational Ed Assn, Amer Voc Assn 1976-; NAEYC 1983-; W NY Teacher of Yr 1982; NY St Curr Writing Team; Curr Piloting Team; *office:* Harkness Center/Erie I BOCES 99 Aero Dr Cheektowaga NY 14225

PFAFF, ALICE FIREBAUGH, Fourth Grade Teacher; *b:* Natural Bridge Sta, VA; *m:* Charles Thompson; *ed:* (BS) Ed, Radford Univ 1961; *cr:* 4th Grade Teacher Roanoke Cty Schls 1961-64, Pulaski Cty Schls 1964-; *ai:* VA Educl Assn, PCEA, NEA; Inglewood Garden Club; *home:* 2101 10th St Radford VA 24141

PFAFF, ANN BRIMM, Fifth Grade Teacher; *b:* Cedar Falls, IA; *m:* James L; *c:* Nicholas; *cr:* Teacher IA Annie Wittenmyer Home 1973-74; Title I Rdng Teacher Virgil grissom Sch 1974-76; 5th Grade Classroom Teacher Armstrong Sch 1976-; *ai:* Soc Stud Curr, Teacher In Service, Career Ed Comm; N Scott Ed Assn, NEA 1974-; IA ASCD 1983-; Amer Assn Counseling & Dev 1986-88; *office:* North Scott Cmmty Schls 215 E Iowa St Eldridge IA 52748

PFEFFER, INEZ GATTE, Jr HS Social Studies Teacher; *b:* Youngstown, OH; *m:* Paul; *c:* Eileen, Beth, John, Greg; *ed:* (BA) Elem, Kent St Univ 1960; Working on Masters Counseling, Duquesne Univ; Core Team Trng Drug & Alcohol St Francis Rehabilitation Center; Self-Esteem & Stress Management Trng; *cr:* Soc Stud Dept Chairperson St John the Baptist Jr HS 1978-; *ai:* Liason Between Cheerleading & Academics; Drug & Alcohol Comm Cath Diocese of Pittsburgh; Sch Philosophy Chm & Sch Soc Stud Comm St John the Baptist; NCSS 1987-; ASCD 1989-; Historical Society of Western PA 1988-89; NCEA 1978-; Plum Chemical People (Chm 1987-88, Treas 1989-), Plum Patch Proud 1987-88; Chemical People Task Force Inst of Pittsburgh Treas 1989-; Coord Teen Action Day Plum Chemical People; *office:* St John the Baptist Jr HS 444 Unity Center Rd Pittsburgh PA 15239

PFEFFINGER, CHARLA (DUMVILLE), Kindergarten/ Chapter 1 Teacher; *b:* San Francisco, CA; *m:* Lyle Edward; *c:* Christine Mingle Manley, Joseph W. Mingle, Kristie A., Brett A.; *ed:* (BA) Elem Ed, 1974, (MS) Rdng, 1978 IL St Univ; *cr:* 1st Grade Teacher Peoria PubliC Schls 1970-74; 1st Grade Teacher 1974-76, 8th Grade Teacher 1976-78, Chapter I Rdng Teacher 1978-, 1/2 D Kndgtn Teacher 1984- Rankin Elem; *ai:* Cheerleading 1978-; 8th Grade Spon 1978-; Scholastic Bowl Coach 1988-; PFK Pres 1986-; Asst Prin 1977-; 1st Chrstn Church Youth Choir Dir 1987-; Learning Magazine 1989; *home:* 229 Indian Creek Dr Pekin IL 61554

PFEIFER, DAVID ALAN, Social Studies Teacher; *b:* Passaic, NJ; *m:* Laurie Domenic; *c:* Richard, Michael; *ed:* (BA) Psych/Soc Stud, La Salle Univ 1970; Grad Stud Clinical Psych, Univ of PA; *cr:* Teacher Holy Spirit HS 1970-; *ai:* Cross Cntry & Track Head Coach Stockton St Coll; Mock Trial Adv Holy Spirit HS; NJ St Social Stud, Amer Psych Assn 1971-; NCAA Track Coaches Assn 1981-; *office:* Holy Spirit HS California & New Rd Absecon NJ 08201

PFEIFFENBERGER, ELEANOR C. ACKALUSKY, 5th-8th Grade Eng Teacher; *b:* Pottsville, PA; *m:* George Philip; *c:* Kara, Brent, Adria, Justin; *ed:* (BS) Elem Ed/Eng, Kutztown Univ 1974; Grad Stud; *cr:* Pre-Sch Teacher 1974-75, Camp Instr 1975 Wee Explorers; 6th Grade Homeroom/5th/6th Grade Eng Teacher St Marys 1975-76; 5th-8th Grade Eng Teacher St Joan of Arc 1984-; *ai:* St Joan of Arc Eng Prof, Harrisburg Diocesan Eng, Honor Roll, Sch Bd Acad Excl Comm; Eng Coord & Yrbk Co-Moderator; Hershey Hummelstown Optimist Intnl Clubs; Mc Devitt HS Forensic Tournaments Moderator, Coach, Bishop; Inductee Prgm Mentor 1986-87; NCTE Mem 1987-88; St Joan of Arc Parish Church (Cantor, Wedding Soloist); Selected to Evaluate Teacher Competency Tests at Bucknell Univ; Honored by Amer Family Inst; Golden Heart Trophy Excl in Postive Teaching 1985; Anthology Book Dedication; *home:* 22 Oakglade Dr Hummelstown PA 17036

PFEIFFER, MELVYN L., 6th Grade Elementary Teacher; *b:* Robinson, IL; *m:* Christine Jo Williams; *c:* Michael, Jon; *ed:* (BS) Elem Ed, IN Univ 1975; (MS) Ed, IUPUI 1978; *cr:* 6th Grade Intermediate Teacher Lewis W Gilfoy #113 1975-; *ai:* Sch Sci Fair & Environmental Sci Chm; Project Leadership Service Butler Univ; IEA, ISTA, NEA Exec Bd 1979-85; Bel East Little League VP 1985-89, 10 Yr Service Awd 1988; Indpls Ed Fnd Grant for Outdoor Animal Habitat; Articles Published; *office:* Lewis W Gilfoy #113 4352 N Mitthoeffer Rd Indianapolis IN 46236

PFETZING, DEBORAH SCHNEUER, English Teacher; *b:* Cincinnati, OH; *m:* Edwin Albert; *ed:* (BS) Scndry Ed, 1977 (BA) Eng Lit, 1977 Univ of Cincinnati; *cr:* Eng Teacher St Ursula Acad 1977-; *ai:* Sch Literary Magazine Adv; Natl Endowment for Hum Summer Fellowship Stratford-On-Avon 1989, Younger Scholars Adv Grant 1990; *office:* St Ursula Acad 1339 E Mc Millan St Cincinnati OH 45206

PFEUFER, BERNICE MARIE (SALTER), Mathematics/ Reading Teacher; *b:* St Marys, PA; *m:* Thomas J. Sr.; *c:* Thomas Jr., Terry P., Kelly K., Jill M.; *ed:* (MS) Elem Ed, Villa Maria Coll 1965; Penn St Univ, Gannon Univ, E Stroudsburg Coll, Carlow Coll; *cr:* 5th Grade Teacher Queen of the World Sch 1965-66; Rdng Teacher 1976-84, Elem Teacher 1984- St Marys Mid Sch; *ai:* Mid Sch Yrbk Adv; PSEA, NEA; Queen of the World Parish Cncl Mem; PTO Exec Bd of Mid Sch Rep; *home:* 1028 Lemans Rd Saint Marys PA 15857

PFISTERER, DIANE SMITH, Reading Teacher; *b:* Erie, PA; *m:* James R.; *c:* Emily, Stephen, Michael; *ed:* (BS) Elem Ed, 1968, (MED) Elem Ed, 1970 Edinboro St Coll; Rdng Specialist, Univ of PA 1980; *cr:* 3rd Grade Teacher 1968-69, 4th Grade Teacher 1969-70 Tracy Sch; 1st Grade Teacher 1978-79, 4th/5th Grade Teacher 1979-81, 3rd Grade Teacher 1982-83 Vernondale Sch; 6th Grade Rdng Specialist Westlake Mid Sch 1983-; *ai:* Millcreek Township Teacher Enhancement Comm Co-Chairperson; Millcreek Lead Teacher Consortium Mem; Disciplinary Action Task Force; Homework Hotline; PA St Ed Assn, Millcreek Ed Assn 1968-70, 1978-; Presque Isle Rotary Grant; Millcreek Township Sch Dist Teacher of Month 1988; Univ of PA Edinboro Resource Professor 1989; *office:* Westlake Mid Sch 4330 W Lake Rd Erie PA 16505

PFLASTERER, STEPHANIE BARNES, Second Grade Teacher; *b:* Winchester, IN; *m:* Duane E.; *c:* Carrie R.; *ed:* (MS) Elem Ed/Kndgtn, Ball St Univ 1971; *cr:* 3rd Grade Teacher White River Elem 1966-71; 5th Grade Teacher Willard Elem 1971-72; 1st Grade Teacher 1973-80; 2nd Grade Teacher Baker Elem 1980-; *ai:* Secy Randolph Cntrl Classroom Teachers Assn; Support Comm Working with Negotiating Team; Amer Ed Week Comm; ISTA; NEA; *home:* R 1 Box 152 Winchester IN 47394

PFORTE, DOROTHY E., 5th Grade Teacher; *b:* Castleberry, AL; *c:* Linda, Brenda P. Edwards, John; *ed:* (BS) Elem Ed, Jacksonville St 1957; Inservice Classes Cmptr/Health/Sci & Math Wkshps FSU; *cr:* Teacher Warrington Elem 1957-63; Callaway Elem 1963-66; Sneads Elem 1966-67; Cottondale Elem 1967-68; Golson Elem 1968-79; Riverside Elem 1979-; *ai:* Sch Patrol; BSA; Jackson Cty Ed Assn 1966-; NEA; Meth Womans Club Pres 1975-81; Teacher of Yr; PTO Each Yr Ofcr Several Times; Sch Comm; *home:* PO Box 104 Old Cottondale Rd Marianna FL 32446

PHAIR, SANDRA CHAET, Univ Supervisor & Lecturer; *b:* Hartford, CT; *m:* John Richard; *c:* Jonathan, Brian; *ed:* (BS) Elem Ed, 1971, (MA) Elem Ed, 1974 Univ of CT; Admin/Supervision, Cntrl CT St Univ; *cr:* 3rd Grade Teacher 1971-81, 1st Grade Teacher 1983-84, 2nd Grade Teacher 1984 Coventry Grammar Sch; Stu Teachers Univ Supvr/Lecturer/Adjunct Professor Cntrl CT St Univ 1987-; *ai:* CT Ed Assn 1973-81; Coventry Ed Assn Treas 1983-84; Amer Assn Univ Professors Assn 1973-81; Manchester Jr Womens Club Chairperson Ed Comm 1985-89; PTA 1987-; *home:* 42 Arnott Rd Manchester CT 06040

PHALEN, MARY LUCY SEGURA, Mathematics Teacher; *b:* San Antonio, TX; *m:* William J.; *c:* Joseph, Cecilia P. Abbott, Norbert, Letitia; *ed:* (BA) Span/Math, Our Lady of Lake Univ 1972; *cr:* HS Span Teacher St Francis Acad 1965-66; Elem Teacher San Antonio Cath Schls 1966-70; Bi-ling Teacher Alamo Heights Ind Sch Dist 1972-73; Math/Span/Lang/Rdng Teacher San Antonio Ind Sch Dist 1975-; *ai:* Math Coach; Tutoring; Alpha Mu Gamma, Delta Kappa Gamma, San Antonio Teachers Cncl, TX Ed Assn, NEA.

PHARIS, MICHAEL M., 8th Grade Teacher; *b:* Porterville, CA; *ed:* (AA) Liberal Art, Coll of Sequoias 1978; (BA) Liberal Stud, 1980, (MA) Ed/Counseling & Guidance, 1982 Cal Poly St Univ; *cr:* 8th Grade Teacher Alta Vista Elem Sch 1982-83, Tipton Elem Sch 1983-; *ai:* Girls Vlybl, Boys Bsktbl, Soccer, Track, Bsbl Coach; Stu Cncl, Friday Night Live Adv; Mentor Teacher; Cmptr Lab Coord; His/Soc Stud Framework Comm; Tipton Teachers Assn 1983-; Strathmore Union Elem Sch Bd of Trustee Mem 1987-; Strathmore Fire Dist Commissioner 1983-; *office:* Tipton Elem Sch 370 N Evans Rd Tipton CA 93272

PHARRIS, WILLIAM J., Band Director; *b:* Columbus, GA; *m:* Helen Miller; *c:* Stephen M., David C.; *ed:* (BME) Music Ed, FL St Univ 1956; (MME) Music Ed, Columbus Coll 1982; Admin & Supervision, Columbus Coll 1988; *cr:* Band Dir Columbus & Arnold Jr HS 1956-64, Band/Choral Dir Glenwood Sch 1973-78; Band Dir E Rome HS 1978-79, Riverdale Sr HS 1979-80, Hardaway HS 1980-86; Adjunct Grad Mu Faculty Columbus Coll 1986-87; Band Dir Albany HS 1988-, Norcross HS 1990; *ai:* Symphonic & Marching Band; Phi Beta Mu Past Secy 1980-; Natl Band Assn 1980-, Cert of Recognition 1982, 1984; Phi Mu Alpha, GA Music Educators, MENC, Sch Band Dir Assn; John Philip Souss Fnd Flag of Honor Comm 1984-; SE Clinician/ Adjudication; Distingushed Bandmaster 1981; Mid-West Band Clinic Medal of Honor 1980; Top Teacher Awd 1986; Conducted Mid-East & Mid-West Conference 1982; MENC Natl Conference 1984; 50th Presidential Inaugural Ceremonies 1985; Conducted Concert Tour Moscow & Leningrad 1986; *office:* Norcross HS 600 Beaver Ruin Rd Norcross GA 30071

PHELAN, ANDREW C., JR., Mathematics & History Teacher; *b:* Nashville, TN; *m:* Anne Scott; *c:* Jennifer L. Johanns, Christopher D.; *ed:* (BA) His, Lambuth Coll 1964; Duke Univ Divinity Sch, NC A&T, Univ of NC; *cr:* Teacher Castle Heights Military Acad 1968-69, Clio Jr HS 1969-70, Hamlet HS 1970-72, Hamlet Jr HS 1972-; *ai:* Athletic Dir; Head Var Ftbl Coach; *office:* Hamlet Jr HS 1406 Mc Donald Ave Ext Hamlet NC 28345

PHELPS, ANN, English/Journalism Dept Chair; *b:* Des Moines, IA; *c:* Angela, Renae, Jeffrey; *ed:* (BA) Eng/Journalism, Midland Luth Coll 1977; (MS) Scndry Ed, Univ of NE 1989; *cr:* Eng/ Journalism Teacher North Bend Cntrl Jr HS 1977-; *ai:* Stu Newspaper; Cls Spon; Quill & Scroll Adv; NE HS Press (Pres, Exec Bd 1987-, Format Editor 1987); Women in Cmmty Service VP 1989-; 4th-8th Grade Rdng Series Asst Writer; Paul Belz Memorial Schlsp; *office:* North Bend Cntrl HS 13th & Walnut North Bend NE 68649

PHELPS, ANN JONES, Math Dept Chair/Teacher; *b:* Marlin, TX; *m:* James Wayne; *c:* James M., David Winston; *ed:* (AA) Ed, Tarleton St 1957; (BA) Ed/Math, Baylor Univ 1959; Grad Stud AAT; *cr:* Math Teacher Rosebud Ind Sch Dist 1959-60, Temple Ind Sch Dist 1960-66; Math Teacher/Dept Chairperson Chilton Ind Sch Dist 1971-; *ai:* Stu Cncl Spon; UIL Coord; TSTA 1959-89; ATPE 1989-; United Meth Church; Outstanding Teacher 1989-.

PHELPS, CAROLYN SUE, English/Reading/Speech Teacher; *b:* Harrison, AR; *ed:* (AS) Eng, NACC 1983; (BSE) Eng, UCA 1985; Rdng/Speech; *cr:* Eng/Speech Teacher Marshall HS 1985-86; Eng/Rdng/Speech Teacher Bruno-Pyatt Sch 1986-; *ai:* Speech & Drama Club Adv; 10th Grade Class & Mock Trials Spon; Personnel Policy Comm NCTE, AR Ed Assn, NEA 1985-; VIP Teacher 1990; *home:* Rt 4 Box 55 Harrison AR 72601

PHELPS, EYELEAN D., Retired Teacher; *b:* Roundhill, KY; *m:* Kenneth T.; *c:* Kenneth Jr., William R., John R.; *ed:* (BA) Elem Ed, 1960, (MA) Elem Ed/Lib Sci, 1971 W KY Univ; *cr:* 1st-8th Grade Teacher Butler Cty KY 1947-58; 3rd Grade Teacher/ Librarian Morgantown Elem Sch 1958-75; 3rd Grade Teacher 4th Dist KY 1975-83; *ai:* KY Ed Assn Delegate; NEA, Butler Cty Assn.

PHELPS, RANDAL ROBERT, English Teacher; *b:* Long Beach, CA; *ed:* (BA) Eng, CA Luth Univ 1981; (MA) Eng, William & Mary 1987; *cr:* Teacher Brea HS 1981-82, Lafayette HS 1985-86, Lee Cty HS 1986-87, Western Hills HS 1988-; *ai:* Bsbl & Ftbl Coach; Yrbk; Journalism; FFA & Tabs Adv; Bionic Club; Academic Team; Earth Day Spon; NCTE 1985-; Teachers as Writers Grant Winner; Fellowship & Schlsp William & Mary; Natl Writing Project Grant; *office:* Western Hills HS 100 Doctors Dr Frankfort KY 40601

PHILBIN, PAULA JEAN, Social Studies Teacher; *b:* Worcester, MA; *ed:* (BS) His, 1976, (MED) His, 1988 Worcester St Coll; Research Fellowship, Univ of HI 1977-78; Harvard Univ, Intnl Relations, Gov 1987-; Amer Univ in Cairo Egypt Fulbright Seminar 1989; *cr:* Teacher Wachusett Regional HS 1976-80; Teaching Asst Univ of HI 1977-78; Private Industry & the Governments 1981-87; Lecturer Mt Wachusett Comm Coll 1987-; Teacher N Middlesex Regional HS 1988-; *ai:* Amnesty Intnl Adv; Phi Alpha Theta 1984-; Phi Delta Kappa 1988-; Fulbright Assn 1989-; Amer Assn of Univ Women 1984-; Fulbright Fellowship Egypt 1989; NEH Fellow Harvard Univ 1988; Horace Mann Grant 1989-; Governors Awd Curr Dev 1990; *office:* N Middlesex Regional HS Rt 119 Townsend MA 01469

PHILIPS, JAMES GRAY, German/History/English Teacher; *b:* Berkeley, CA; *m:* Barbara Lynne Preckwinkle; *ed:* (AA) Hum, Univ of CA Berkeley 1950; (BS) Admin, Univ of CA 1952; (MA) Ger, Middlebury Coll 1960; Univ of OR Eugene, Portland St Univ, Univ of Mainz Germany, Humboldt Univ Berlin Germany; *cr:* Assoc Univ of CA Berkeley 1957-58, Univ of CA Riverside 1962-64; Asst Professor Willamette Univ 1965-72; Teacher N Salem HS 1972-; *ai:* N Salem HS Cross Cntry, Track, Swimming, Ftbl Sports Prgm Ofcl; AATG; Fulbright Grant 1959-61; Germanistic Society of America 1959; *office:* N Salem HS 765 14th St NE Salem OR 97301

PHILLIPS, AARON W., Mathematics Teacher; *b:* Sailor Springs, IL; : Sondra K. Gaskin; *c:* Mark A.; *ed:* (BS) Math, 1963, (MS) Math/Admin, 1965, (EDS) Math/Admin, 1968 E IL Univ; *cr:* Math Teacher Charleston HS 1963-67, Belleville East HS 1967-; *ai:* NHS; AFT; *office:* Belleville East HS 2555 West Blvd Belleville IL 62221

PHILLIPS, ADRIENNE HATCHER, 7th Grade Soc Stud Teacher; *b:* Waynesboro, TN; *m:* David W.; *c:* D. Bruce Davis, Nyla R. Davis; *ed:* (BA) Elem Ed/Early Chldhd Ed, Union Univ 1971; (MA) Ed/Psych, Austin Peay St Univ 1980; Grad Stud Ed, Supervision & Admin, Univ of TN Martin; *cr:* 7th Grade Soc Stud Teacher Waverly Jr HS 1968-; *ai:* His & Drama Club Spon; Summer Sch After Hrs Tutor; Cmmty Speaker; Homecoming Local Steering Comm 1983-86; United Teaching Profession (Various Comms, Treas); TN Teacher Study Cncl (Chairperson, Secy); Delta Kappa Gamma; TN Assn of Mid Schls Mem; Intnl Rdng Assn; Warioto Rdng Assn Charter Mem; Daughters of Amer Revolution Outstanding Amer His Teacher 1985; Univ of TN Martin Outstanding His Contest Participant; *office:* Waverly Jr HS 520 E Main St Waverly TN 37185

PHILLIPS, BARBARA GIBNEY, Teacher; *b:* New York, NY; *m:* Harold B.; *c:* Oren; *ed:* (BA) Eng, Coll of New Rochelle 1961; (MS) Ed, Hunter Coll 1966; *cr:* Teacher Barnard Sch for Boys 1962-66, PS 59 1966-76, PS 8 1976-.

PHILLIPS, BARBARA HARDIE, American History Teacher; *b:* Vincent, AL; *c:* Cassandra Y., Ellen A.; *ed:* (BA) Home Ec, AL A&M Univ 1966; (MS) Soc Sci, Univ Montevallo; Inhancement Study Univ of AL Birmingham; Prof Improvement Wkshp Miles Coll Birmingham AL; Several Wkshps, Seminars, Curr Improvement Conference Jefferson Cty Area; *cr:* Home Ec/His Teacher Hale Cty Sch 1966-68; Soc Sci Teacher Jefferson Cty 1968-; *ai:* AL Ed Assn Area Rep 1984-; Sr Citzen Chairperson 1981-85; *office:* Pleasant Grove H S P O Box 69 Pleasant Grove AL 35127

PHILLIPS, BETTY JEAN JACKSON, Guidance Counselor; *b:* El Paso, TX; *m:* William Edward; *ed:* (BS) Elem Ed, Tx Western Coll 1966; (MED) Counseling, Univ of TX El Paso 1971; Grad Stud Counseling to Maintain LPC & NCC Cert; *cr:* 7th Grade Teacher 1966-75, Cnslr 1975-80 Gadsden Jr HS; Cnslr Santa Teresa Jr HS 1980-; *ai:* Facilitator & Trainer Peer Helper Prgm; Dept Head Counseling & Guidance; Delta Kappa Gamma Pres 1986-; Amer Assn for Counseling 1971; NM Assn for Counseling & Dev 1975-; *office:* Santa Teresa Jr HS PO Box 778 Strauss & Mc Nutt Rds Santa Teresa NM 88008

PHILLIPS, CAROL R., Physical Education Teacher; *b:* Whittier, CA; *ed:* (AA) Phys Ed, Rio Hondo Comm Coll 1971; (BA) Phys Ed, San Diego St Univ 1974; (MS) Educl Computing, Pepperdine Univ 1986; *cr:* 5th Grade Basic Ed/Phys Ed Teacher 1974-75, 6th & 7th Grade Basic Ed Teacher 1975-76, Phys Ed Teacher 1976-77 La Merced Intermediate 1976-77, Suva Intermediate 1977-; *ai:* Girls Athletic Assn Spon; Recreation Dir; Running Club; Vlybl, Sftbl, Track, Bsktbl, Gymnastics Coach; Phys Ed Health, Family Life Stud & Tech Curr Dev Comm; CA Assn for Health, Phys Ed, Recreation, Dance (Stu Chapter Pres) 1970-; Amer Assn for Health, Phys Ed, Recreation & Dance 1971-; PTA 1974-, Honorary Service Awd 1990; Eastern Star 1976-; Mentor Teacher 1986; Master Teacher 1976; *home:* 9256 Bonavista Ln Whittier CA 90603

PHILLIPS, CHARLES LEWIS, Geography & Reading Teacher; *b:* Bellarie, OH; *m:* Emma Joann Lambros; *c:* John C. Lewis; *ed:* (BSELED) Elem Ed, OH Univ Athens 1963; (MAELED) Elem Sch Admin, WV Univ 1973; Masters & Doctorate Courses Guidance/Educl Mentally Retarded/Sch Admin; *cr:* US Navy 1954-58; 6th Grade Teacher St Clairsville Schls 1960-61; Prin-Teacher Glencoe Elem 1962-66; HS Teacher St Clairsville HS 1967-69; 6th Grade Teacher St Clairsville Mid Sch 1969-; *ai:* Mid Sch Athletic Dir; 7-8th Boys Bsktbl Tournament Scheduling & Coord; St Clairsville Ed Assn Pres 1970-71; OH Ed Assn 1959-; NEA 1959-; Phi Delta Kappa Honorary; *home:* 101 Allen St Saint Clairsville OH 43950

PHILLIPS, EMMA JO LAMBROS, Teacher; *b:* Bellaire, OH; *m:* Charles Lewis; *c:* John C. L.; *ed:* (BS) Elem Ed, Muskingum Coll 1956; Rdng, Lang Art, WV Univ, OH Univ; Gifted Ed Wkshp Canton 1983; *cr:* K/3rd Grade Elem Teacher Shadyside Local City Sch Dist 1956-67; 2nd/5th/6th Grade Teacher of Gifted St Clairsville 1967-; *ai:* Chairperson 5th Grade Rdng Curr, Mid Sch Right to Read Prgm, Young Author Prgm, Book Fair; Mid Sch Bsktbl Tournament; Various Sch Levy & Curr Philosphy Comms 1970-; St Clairsville City Sch Dist 1987, Citations for Educl Excl; St Clairsville Ed Assn (Hospitality Chairperson, Negotiations Team Secy); Thoburn Meth Church; St Clairsville Young Womens Club 1968-72; Belmont Hills Cntry Club 1987-; Shadyside Ed Assn Pres 1966; NEA, OEA, EOTA, Sea Delegate Conference on Instruction Mem; Instructional Grant; *home:* 101 Allen St Saint Clairsville OH 43950

PHILLIPS, EVELYN MOSLEY, Head Teacher; *b:* Lumberton, MS; *c:* Adele Tyson, Carole Tyson; *ed:* (BED) Ed, Chicago Teachers Coll 1959; Early Chldhd Ed; Inner-city Stud; Small Bus Admin; Human Relations; *cr:* Teacher Medill Primary Sch 1959-71, Scott Child-Parent Center 1971-79; Parent/Resource Teacher Scott Sch 1979-81; Head Teacher Wadsworth Child-Parent Center 1981-; *ai:* Medill Sch Curr Planning Comm Mem 1963-69; Natl, Local AEYCC 1972-; Chicago Teachers Union Sch Delegate 1967-69; Sch Cncl Faculty Rep 1968-70; 69th-71st Street Block Club Secy 1986-88; Prin Selection Comm 1976, 1988.

PHILLIPS, EVERETT, 7th Grade Science Teacher; *b:* Canton, IL; *m:* Vicki Lou Dowell; *c:* Cara L.; *ed:* (AS) Bio, Spoon River Coll 1967, (BSED) Bio/General Sci, W IL Univ 1970; Grad Stud; *cr:* 7th/8th Sci Teacher VIT Unit Sch Dist 1970-73; 9th Grade Sci Teacher 1973-79, 7th Grade Sci Teacher 1979- Canton Sch Dist 66; *ai:* Sci Dept Chm; Chess Club Adv; Cmptr Hardware Repairman; Masonic Lodge 1975-; Consistory 1980-; IL Math & Sci Acad Outstanding Teacher Awd of Excl 1989; *office:* Ingersoll Mid Sch 1605 E Ash St Canton IL 61520

PHILLIPS, GENE F., Mathematics Teacher; *b:* Havre, MT; *m:* Judith A. Brunner; *c:* Jennifer, Michelle, Kelsie, Samantha; *ed:* (BS) Math, N MT 1966; (MATM) Math, Univ of MT 1971; Drivers Ed Endorsement; *cr:* Math Teacher Havre Cntrl 1966-68, Great Falls Cntrl 1968-73, Thompson Falls HS 1973-77, Havre HS 1977-82, Billings West HS 1982-; *ai:* Ftbl, Bsktbl Asst Coach; NCTM, MT Coaches Assn; Natl Sci Grant Academic Yr Inst Univ of MT 1970-71; *office:* Billings West HS 2201 St Johns Ave Billings MT 59102

PHILLIPS, JERRY H., Business Education Instructor; *b:* Woodford, OK; *c:* Marsha Phillips Dolinsky, David; *ed:* (BS) Bus Ed, SE St OK Univ 1949; Advanced Trng Various Colls; Grad Work General Ed, OK Univ & Southwestern St Univ; *cr:* Bus Ed Teacher Ryan HS 1947-48, Waurika HS 1948-49, Dundee HS 1949-52; Bus Ed/Elem Teacher Sudgen Public Sch 1952-53; Bus Ed/Home Ec Teacher Claypool Public Sch 1953-56; Bus Ed Teacher Duncan Public Sch 1956-57, 1960-74; Bus Ed/Math Teacher Empire Public Sch 1957-60; Bus Ed Teacher Comanche Public Sch 1974-; *ai:* Sr & Jr Class, Stu Cncl, 4-H Club, Yrbk Spon; Stu Teacher Supvr; Comanche Soris Club; Comanche News-Writer; OK Ed Assn, NEA, Acad Natl Advisory, Voc Home Ec Advisory, Stephens Cty Assn; Comanche Ed Assn Building Rep; Supt Advisory Cncl; NBEA, OK Bus Ed Assn; Home Demonstration Club Chm of Needy Sr Stu; Southern OK Blood Drive; St Teacher of Yr 1983-84; Governor George Nigh Leadership Conference 1982-83; Supvr of Entry Level Teachers; *home:* 1101 Jones St Duncan OK 73533

PHILLIPS, JUANITA, Third Grade Teacher; *b:* Mc Leansboro, IL; *m:* Donald D.; *c:* Sheryl Hall, Donita, Valera Peterson; *ed:* (BS) Elem Ed, S IL Univ 1970; *cr:* Teacher Richardson Elem 1950-51, Mt Pleasant 1951-55, Bixler 1956-57, Hamilton Cty Unit 10 1957-; *ai:* St Objectives Comm; IFT, AFT; *home:* PO Box 67 Broughton IL 62817

PHILLIPS, KEN A., Physics Teacher; *b:* Sewickley, PA; *m:* Kim A.; *c:* Katie A.; *ed:* (BS) Chem/Physics, OR St Univ 1986; *cr:* Physics Teacher Newberg HS 1987-; *ai:* Ftbl & Track Coach; Var Club; OR Sci Teachers 1989-; *office:* Newberg HS Elliot Rd Newberg OR 97132

PHILLIPS, LESLEY A. (ROMANICK), HS Mathematics Instructor; *b:* Boulder, CO; *m:* John W.; *c:* Heather, Bradley; *ed:* (BS) Math Ed, ND St Univ 1971; Grad Ed Courses; *cr:* Math Teacher Circle Public Schls 1971-73, Maddock Public Schls 1974-77, Washburn Public Schls 1979-; *ai:* Jr Class Adv; Washburn Ed Assn (Secy 1986-88, Treas 1989-); ND Cncl Teachers of Math; NCTM, ND Ed Assn, NEA; Natl Sci Fnd Fellowship Granted 1971; *home:* Box 853 Beulah ND 58523

PHILLIPS, LLOYD KEITH, 9th Grade Science Teacher; *b:* Marshalltown, IA; *m:* Judy Rae Winchell; *c:* Terri Lynn, Marsh, Scott David; *ed:* (BS) Bio, Univ of MS South 1961; (MA) Physics, Chem, Univ of GA 1971; Chem, Physics; *cr:* 7th Grade Sci Teacher Primghar Cmmty Schls 1961-63; 7th/8th/9th Grade Sci Teacher Twin Cedars Sch 1963-65; 9th Grade Sci Teacher Knoxville Cmmty Schls 1965-; *ai:* NSTA 1986-; ISEA 1961-; NEA 1961-; Teacher Yr for Knoxville Sch 1970; Teacher Yr for St of Ia Sci 1985; Published Book on Phys Sci Act for Teachers; Video Tapes for Sci Act; *office:* Knoxville Community Schls 308 W Marion Knoxville IA 50138

PHILLIPS, MARI ANN, 6th Grade Mathematics Teacher; *b:* Birmingham, AL; *m:* Wendele L.; *c:* Gregory Henderson, Wendell Jr.; *ed:* (BS) Elem Ed, Miles Coll 1964; (MA) Elem Ed/Math, GA St Univ 1983; Advance Stud Math, Atlanta Univ; *cr:* Teacher Mt Pleasant Elem Sch 1964-66, S R Young Elem 1966-73, North Avenue Elem Sch 1973-88, Paul West Mid Sch 1988-; *ai:* Grade Team Leader; NEA, GA Ed Assn, Fulton Cty Ed Assn; Mt Moriah Baptist Church (Choir I Pres, Trustee); Teacher of Yr; Recognition for Teaching Night Sch for Adults; *office:* Paul D West Mid Sch 2376 Headland Dr East Point GA 30344

PHILLIPS, MARY ADAIR, Eng Teacher/Spch/Debate Coach; *b:* Newton, NC; *m:* John T.; *c:* Jessie, Erin; *ed:* (BA) Eng, Wake Forest Univ 1973; *cr:* Eng Teacher/Debate Coach Bunker Hill HS 1985-; *ai:* Forensics Club Spon; Debate Team Coach; *office:* Bunker Hill H S Rt 1 Box 130 Claremont NC 28610

PHILLIPS, MARY MARTHA, Business Education Teacher; *b:* Olney, IL; *ed:* (BS) Ed/Bus Ed, 1973, (MS) Ed/Bus Ed, 1977 Eastern IL Univ; Ed, Bus Ed, Cmptr Technology, Shorthand Cmptr Transcription, Management & Job Interview Techniques; *cr:* Bus Ed Teacher Yorkville HS 1973-; *ai:* FBLA Adv; St & Natl Leadership Conferences Exam Admin; Eastern IL Univ Sch of Bus Bd Mem; Phi Beta Lambda Pres 1969-73; Future Bus Teacher of IL 1971; Placed 8th Natl Future Bus Teacher Contest 1971; Pi Omega Pi Pres 1971-73; Outstanding Sr 1973; Kappa Delta Pi Mem 1973; Delta Pi Epsilon EIU-charter Mem 1977; Delta Kappa Gamma Schlsp Chairperson 1977-; Amer Businesswomens Assn Schlsp Chairperson 1980-; IL Bus Ed Assn Mem 1973-80; NEA Mem 1973-; Voc Instr Practicum Participants Selection Comm; North Cntrl & DAVTE Team Evaluator; *office:* Yorkville H S 702 Game Farm Rd Yorkville IL 60560

PHILLIPS, MARY MILLER, Retired First Grade Teacher; *b:* Staunton, VA; *w:* Australia C. (dec); *c:* Wendell R.; *ed:* (BS) Home Ec, Hampton Univ 1943; (MED) Elem Ed, Prairie View Univ 1959; *cr:* Teacher Corsicana Ind Sch Dist 1955-75, Mexia Ind Sch Dist 1975-88; *ai:* TX St Teachers Assn, NEA, Local Ed Assn (Secy, 1958-1966, Treas 1973-75); Corsicana Ed Assn, Mexia Ed Assn 1983-85; Cntrl TX Teachers Credit Union (Secy, Bd of Dirs) 1971-80; *home:* Rt 1 Box 136 Coolidge TX 76635

PHILLIPS, PAULINE ALLEN, English Teacher; *b:* Miami, TX; *m:* Bob G.; *c:* Robert, Charlotte O'Brien; *ed:* (BS) Eng, W TX St Univ 1954; *cr:* Teacher Amarillo Ind Sch Dist 1956-62, Tulia Ind Sch Dist 1962-72, Schertz-Cibalo Universal City Ind Sch Dist 1972-75, Lefors Ind Sch Dist 1975-; *ai:* Jr HS Chrldrs & Pep Club Spon; ATPE 1980-89; Delta Kappa Gamma 1966-; Kappa Kappa Iota Pres 1985-86; TSTA, NEA 1956-72; WCS Meth Church Pres 1973-75; *home:* 2517 Duncan Pampa TX 79065

PHILLIPS, RANDY S., Health/Phys Ed Teacher; *b:* Greenville, NC; *m:* Susan Dickerson; *c:* Justin, Blair; *ed:* (BS) Health/Phys Ed, E Carolina Univ 1976; *cr:* Teacher/Coach Ayden Mid Sch 1976-83, E B Aycock Jr HS 1983-; *ai:* Asst Ftbl Coach; NC Coaches Assn; Greenville Hot Stove League; *office:* E B Aycock Jr HS 1325 Red Banks Rd Greenville NC 27858

PHILLIPS, RAY DEAN, French & English Teacher; *b:* Weaubleau, MO; *ed:* (BSED) Music /Fr, SW MO St Univ 1979; (MA) Eng, S MS Univ 1988; *cr:* HS Fr/Eng Teacher Buffalo HS 1979-; *ai:* Jr Class & Fr Club Spon; Sick Leave Pool Rep; Ozarks Foreign Lang Assn VP 1989-; PTA (Historian 1981-83, 3rd VP 1983-86); *office:* Buffalo HS P O Box 800 Buffalo MO 65622

PHILLIPS, REVONDA LEE, 6th Grade Teacher; *b:* Blairsville, GA; *m:* Roy Kenneth; *c:* Shannon; *ed:* (BA) Elem Ed, 1970, (MS) Elem Ed, 1974 N GA Coll; *cr:* 4th Grade Teacher 1970-74, 2nd Grade Teacher 1974-77, Chapter I Teacher 1978-82, 5th Grade Teacher 1982-84 Union Cty Elem Sch; 6th-7th Grade Teacher Union Cty Mid Sch 1984-; *ai:* 6th Grade Lead Teacher; Natl Assn of Educators, GA Assn of Educators; Union Cty Assn of Educators Treas 1972-74; Revival Baptist Church (Jr Teacher 1970-, Bible Sch Dir 1982-88); PTA Treas 1984-85; Union Cty Teacher of Yr 1987-88; Nom GA Teacher of Yr 1985-86; *home:* Rt 3 Box 3846 Blairsville GA 30512

PHILLIPS, RICK, Mathematics Teacher; *b:* Beardstown, IL; *c:* Julie K., Lynde M.; *ed:* (BA) Math, IL Coll 1969; *cr:* Math Teacher Jacksonville HS 1969-73, Pinckneyville HS 1973-75, Clinton HS 1975-76, Spoon River Valley HS 1976-80, Rushville HS 1980-; *ai:* Jr Class Spon; *office:* Rushville HS N Congress St Rushville IL 62681

PHILLIPS, ROGER BRUCE, Journalism Teacher; *b:* Flint, MI; *c:* Jason T.; *ed:* (AA) Liberal Arts, Alpena Comm Coll 1964; (BA) Eng/Poly Sci, 1967, (MA) Poly Sci, 1970 Cntrl MI Univ, Media Wkshp Univ CA Los Angeles; *cr:* Teacher Thunder Bay Jr HS 1967-83, Alpena HS 1984-; Part Time Instr Alpena Comm Coll 1973-; *ai:* Coaching Jr/Sr HS, Coll Bsktb l, Ftbl, Track; Stu Cncl; Thunder Bay Times, Wildcat Adv; MI Cncl Teachers of Eng 1981-; Optimist Club Pres 1981-82, Optimist of Yr 1980; Alpena Cty Bd of Commissioners (Chm 1975-84, Supvr 1988-); Alpena Township Bd of Trustees 1985-88; Golden Pen Nominee 1990; *office:* Alpena HS 3303 S 3rd Ave Alpena MI 49707

PHILLIPS, ROSE DUSCHEK, 5th Grade Teacher; *b:* Pittsburgh, PA; *m:* Jim L.; *c:* Amy B.; *ed:* Ger, Heidelberg Univ Germany 1962-63; (BA) Elem Ed, 1964, (MA) Ed, 1967 Westminster Coll; Rdng Specialist Cert Slippery Rock Univ; *cr:* Elem Classroom Teacher Grove City Area Schls 1964-; *ai:* PSEA, NEA Building Rep; Delta Kappa Gamma Secy 1976-78; ASCD; E Main Presbyn Church; Order of Eastern Star Worthy Matron 1979-80; Natl Defense Act Fellowship Rdng Univ of IL Normal; *office:* Hillview Elem Sch 482 E Main St Grove City PA 16127

PHILLIPS, ROXIE RAMSEY, 2nd Grade Teacher; *b:* Davidson, TN; *m:* Grady; *c:* Russell, Le Anne; *ed:* (BS) Elem Ed, Ball St Univ 1978; Grad Stud Office Ed & Cmptr Trng; *cr:* 5th/6th Grade Teacher Banner-Roslin Elem 1978-79; 3rd Grade Teacher Rickman Elem 1979-80; 2nd-4th Grade Teacher Wilson Elem 1980-; *ai:* Honor Club Spon; Sci Fair; OCEA Retirement Comm; TEA, NEA Mem; OCEA Mem Distinguished Teacher of Yr 1990; Hanging Limb F B Church Teacher 1987-88; Career Level II 1989; *office:* Wilson Elem Sch R R 1 Crawford TN 38554

PHILLIPS, RUTH ANN, Language Arts Chair; *b:* Lewes, DE; *m:* Keith J.; *c:* Kelly S., Pamela L., Jennifer L.; *ed:* (BA) Fr, Univ of DE 1963; Grad Work Salisbury St Coll; *cr:* Teacher Laurel HS 1970-; *ai:* Soph Class Adv; DE Teachers of Eng, DE Teachers of Foreign Lang; *office:* Laurel HS 1133 S Central Ave Laurel DE 19956

PHILLIPS, SHERRY BRANDT, 7th/8th Grade Lang Art Teacher; *b:* Freeport, IL; *m:* Joe Steven; *c:* Nathaniel, Sheyanna; *ed:* (BSED) Eng, W IL Univ 1974; *cr:* 9-12th Grade Eng Teacher Forman Manito 1974; 7th-8th Grade Eng/Rdng Teacher La Harpe Schls 1975-77; 7th-8th Grade Lang Art/Eng I Teacher Colchester Cmmty 1977-; *ai:* Honor Society, Yrbk, Newspaper Class Spon; Jr HS Vlybl Coach; Gifted Coord; Blandinsville Hore Lib Bd Trustee 1989-; United Meth Church Sunday Sch Teacher 1985; *office:* Colchester Cmmty Unit 180 Hun St Box 357 Colchester IL 62326

PHILLIPS, SUSAN M., English Teacher; *b:* Honolulu, HI; *ed:* (BA) Eng/Elem Ed, Chaminade Univ 1972; Prof Certificate, Chaminade Univ 1980; *cr:* 5th-6th Grade Teacher 1972-, 5th Grade Rdng/Religion Teacher 1972-, 5th-8th Grade Speech Coach 1972- St Patrick Sch; *ai:* 5th-6th Grade Speech Prgm; Festivals & Tournaments Competition Coach & Coord; HI Cncl Teachers of Eng; NCEA; HI Speech League; Speech Prgm Recognized by Roman Cath Diocese of Honolulu Cath Sch Dept for Excl & Significant Effect on Stus in 5th-8th Grade 1989; *home:* 94-405 Keaoopua St #189 Mililani HI 96789

PHILLIPS, TIMOTHY EDWARD, Teacher of Gifted & Talented; *b:* Pittsfield, MA; *c:* Christine E.; *ed:* (BA) His, Rutgers Coll 1979; Cmptr Sci; Adv Trng Non-Violent Crisis Intervention; *cr:* Soc Stud Teacher The Barnstable Sch 1979-80; Teacher of Gifted & Talented/Soc Stud Teacher Overbrook Jr HS 1980-84; Teacher of Gifted & Talented Edgewood Jr HS 1984-; *ai:* Coord Stu Tutorial Prgm; Audio Visual Aids Dir; Crisis Intervention Core Team Mem; NJ Educators of Gifted & Talented; NJEA, NEA Mem 1980-; Rutgers Coll Class of 1979 Pres 1979-; Amnesty Intnl Partners of Conscience (Mem, Freedom Writer); Greenpeace, Wilderness Society Mem; Phi Alpha Theta NHS 1979.

PHILLIPS, WILLIAM LEE, Social Studies Teacher; *b:* Wagoner, OK; *m:* Teddy Deanna Lorenz; *c:* Donette K., Lynette K. Phillips Jelinek; *ed:* (BS) Elem Ed, AZ St Coll 1964; (MA) Elem Ed, N AZ Univ 1970; *cr:* Elem Teacher Marshall Sch 1964-66, Thomas Sch 1966-70; Soc Stud Teacher 1970-79, Building Coord 1979-80, Soc Stud Teacher/Dept Chm 1980-85, Soc Stud Teacher 1985- East Flagstaff Jr HS; *ai:* Elem Sch Ftbl, Bsktbl, Sftbl, Vlybl, Track Coach; East Flagstaff Stu Cncl, Pep Club, Sch Act, Dances, Activity Day, Out of Town Trips Spon; Flagstaff Ed Assn Building Rep 1966-72; AZ Classroom Teacher, AZ Ed Assn Delegate 1968-75; Flagstaff Jaycees (1st VP, Pres) 1964-65, Jaycee Spoke of Yr 1965; Flag Evening Lion Club Secy 1968-71, 100 % Secy 1970; Flag Sheriffs Posse 1966-71; Flagstaff Elks 1973-79, 1989-; ASC Elem Stu Teacher of Yr 1964; Flagstaff Public Schls Scndry Mainstream Teacher of Yr 1987; *home:* 4378 N Randall St Flagstaff AZ 86004

PHILLIPS GOOD, SUSAN GERTH, Sixth Grade Teacher; *b:* Buffalo, NY; *m:* Larry W.; *c:* Sarah Beth Phillips, Adam Douglas Phillips; *ed:* (BA) Elem Ed, State U of NY Buffalo 1972; Perm Cert Nursery/K-6 Grades Univ St NY 1976; *cr:* 4th Grade Teacher 1972-1981, 6th Grade Teacher 1981-Alexander Cntrl Sch; *ai:* PTA Campbells Labels Chairperson; Faculty Sunshine Comm-Chairperson Treas; Alex United Meth Church 1985; PPR Youth Cncl 1989-; Choir 1981-; Cub Scouts; Den Asst 1989-; Tiger Cub Adult 1987-1988; *office:* Alexander Cnrtl Sch 3314 School St Alexander NY 14005

PHILPOT, DAVID L., 6th Grade Teacher; *b:* Albany, CA; *ed:* (BA) Soc Sci, CA St Univ/Stanislaus 1971; *cr:* 4th/5th Grade Teacher Keyes Union Sch Dist 1972-82; 6th Grade GATE Teacher Lakewood Sch 1983-88; 4th-6th Grade Teacher John Muir Sch 1988-; *ai:* Sch Improvement Comm; Stanislaus Math Cncl Bd of Dir 1984- CA Math Cncl Awd 1987; Keyes Teachers Assn Pres 1974-76 WHO Awd 1977; *office:* John Muir Elem Sch 1215 Lucerne Ave Modesto CA 95350

PHINNEY, PATSY E., English/History Teacher; *b:* San Angelo, TX; *m:* Gary; *c:* Lisa, Jedi J., Matthew; *ed:* (BA) His, Austin St Univ 1970; (MA) His/Eng, Sul Ross Univ 1988; Advanced Government; *cr:* Soc Stud Teacher Eola Ind Sch Dist 1970-83; His/Eng Teacher Paint Rock Ind Sch Dist 1985-; *ai:* 8th Grade Spon; UIL Dir; *home:* Rt 2 Box 53 Miles TX 76861

PHIPPS, DIANNE M., Spanish Teacher; *b:* Syracuse, NY; *m:* Howard R.; *c:* Kristen, Lauren, Karen; *ed:* (BA) Span Lang, 1964, (MS) Span Ed, 1969 Syracuse Univ; *cr:* Span Teacher Norfolk Cath HS 1964-66, E Syracuse-Minoa HS 1967-73; Adjunct Span Teacher Onondaga Comm Coll 1973-78; Span Teacher Syracuse City Schls/Levy Mid Sch 1980-; *ai:* Natl Span Honor Society, Sr Class Adv; NYSFLT; AATSP 1990; Nottingham Support Group Outstanding Teacher Awd 1989.

PHIPPS, HAROLD W., English Teacher; *b:* Jefferson, NC; *m:* Susan Kirby Shepard; *ed:* (BA) Eng, Univ of NC Greensboro 1968; (MA) Academically Gifted Ed, Appalachian St Univ 1983; *cr:* Teacher ASHE Cntrl HS 1968-; *ai:* Soph Class Spon; Homecoming & Differentiated Pay Comm; NC Assn of Educators (Bd of Dirs 1988-, Dist Pres 1984-85); NEA Convention Delegate 1986; Phi Delta Kappa Mem; Published Articles NC Ed & VA Journal of Ed; *office:* Ashe Cntrl HS P O Box 108 Jefferson NC 28640

PHIPPS, LOIS EWELL, English Teacher; *b:* New Orleans, LA; *m:* Albert H.; *c:* Courtney; *ed:* (BS) Eng Ed, Southern Univ 1969; Prof Improvement Prgm, Loyola Univ, Dillard Univ & Univ New Orleans; Working Masters Degree Counseling Xavier Univ; *cr:* Eng Teacher Reserve Jr HS 1969-70, St Gabriel the Archangel 1971-78, Eleanor Mc Main Magnet Secndry Sch 1978-; *ai:* LA Fed of Teachers 1978-; AFT 1978-; United Teacher of New Orleans 1978-; NCTE 1990-; *office:* Eleanor Mc Main Magnet Sch 5712 S Claiborne Ave New Orleans LA 70125

PHIPPS, PATSY EUBANKS, English Teacher; *b:* Dallas, TX; *c:* David; *ed:* (BFA) Radio Broadcasting, Univ of TX Austin 1948; Grad Stud E TX St Univ Commerce; *cr:* Eng Teacher Kilgore Jr HS & Maude Laird Mid Sch 1968-; Coord of Gifted & Talented Kilgore Ind Sch Dist 1978-; *ai:* Kilgore Classroom Teachers Assn Pres 1970-71; Alpha Delta Kappa Pres 1978-80; TX St Teachers Assn, NEA; Kilgore PTA (Elem Pres 1963-64, Jr HS Pres 1966-67); Kilgore City Cncl of PTAs Pres 1967-68; Kilgore Teacher of Yr of Gifted & Talented 1989; Lifetime Mem TX PTA; *home:* PO Box 793 Kilgore TX 75662

PHISTER, CARLA RUST, Reading Teacher; *b:* Topeka, KS; *c:* Wyatt; *ed:* (BED) Phys Ed, Washburn Univ 1966; (BS) Elem Ed, KS Univ 1970; (MA) Rdng, Univ of MO Kansas City 1977; Post Grad Stud; *cr:* Elem Teacher Eugene Ware Elem 1966-74; Scndry Teacher Bancroft Jr HS 1977-83, Norris Jr HS 1984-; *ai:* Positive Peer Culture Group Leader; Courtesy, Mid Sch Level Comm; Metropolitan Rdng Cncl 1983-; Phi Kappa Phi, Phi Lambda Theta 1977-; Intnl Rdng Assn 1988-; PTA 1966-, Lifetime 1970; Booster Club, Friends Assn 1989-.

PHOENIX, ELEANOR CRISP, English Teacher; *b:* Muncie, IN; *ed:* (BA) Eng, Univ of CO 1964; (MA) Eng, N AZ Univ 1970; Grad Stud Eng; *cr:* Eng Teacher Bridger Jr HS 1964-66, Rancho HS 1966-67, Hyde Park Jr HS 1968-70, Valley HS 1970-71, Boulder City HS 1971-; *ai:* Sr Class Adv; S NV Teachers of Eng 1980-, Outstanding Eng Educator 1987; Reader & Table Leader for NV Proficiency Examination in Writing; *office:* Boulder City HS 1101 5th St Boulder City NV 89005

PICARD, MARY H., Fourth Grade Teacher; *b:* Washington, DC; *m:* Ted; *c:* Evan, Bryce, Emilie; *ed:* (BA) Elem Ed, Coll of William & Mary 1976; Grad Stud, George Mason Univ; *cr:* 3rd Grade Teacher Sugarland Elem 1976-79, Hunt Valley Elem 1980-83, 1986-89; 4th Grade Teacher Hunt Valley Elem 1989-; *ai:* 4th Grade Team Leader; Talent Show Comm; Fairfax Ed Assn, PTA; Grant Awarded Media Presentation 1989; *office:* Hunt Valley Elem Sch 7107 Sydenstricker Rd Springfield VA 22152

PICCHINI, MARGARET A. MAGDON, First Grade Teacher; *b:* Olyphant, PA; *m:* Primo Thomas; *c:* Renard, Renee, Ted; *ed:* Elem Ed/Child Phys/Classroom Tech, Brookdale Comm Coll 1980; Felician Sisters Lodi NJ; *cr:* Substitute Teacher 1970, 6th Grade Homeroom/5th-8th Grade Math Teacher 1980, 1st Grade Teacher 1988 St Stephens; *ai:* Pop Warner Cheerleading Coach 1965-74; Moms & Dads Club, Cath Youth Organization 1973-; Morgan Little League; Morgan Babe Ruth League; Mt St Mary Acad Mercy Guild Secy; Monmouth Cty Election Bd Ofcl.

PICCICOLO, LEA ZAIDINS, English Department Chair; *b:* Milwaukee, WI; *m:* William P.; *ed:* (BA) Eng, 1964, (MA) Eng, 1968 Marquette Univ; Wesleyan Univ, Middletown CT; *cr:* Eng Teacher 1964, Eng Chairperson 1980- Milwaukee Tech HS; *ai:* Sr Class Act Adv; Phi Delta Kappa Natl Ed Honorary; Delta Kappa Gamma Honorary Womens; Sigma Tau Delta Honor Eng Ed; NCTE; Amer Assn of Univ Women Pres 1990; Natl Endowment for Hum Recipient Awd 1986; *office:* Milwaukee Tech HS 319 W Virginia St Milwaukee WI 53204

PICHLER, LAURA O'DELL, Advanced Placement His Instr; *b:* Dubuque, IA; *m:* Daniel Joseph; *c:* Caroline M.; *ed:* (BA) His/Government, St Marys Coll 1978; (MA) US His, Univ of Notre Dame 1979; *cr:* Teacher Mater Dei HS 1981-; *ai:* Prins Advisory Bd 1988-; *office:* Mater Dei HS 1202 W Edinger Ave Santa Ana CA 92707

PICKART, JANE ANN, English Teacher; *b:* Logansport, IN; *ed:* (BA) Eng, 1974, (MA) Eng Ed, 1976 Purdue Univ; Advanced Placement Wkshps; *cr:* Eng Teacher Haworth HS 1974-80, Morrow HS 1980-82, Stockbridge HS 1984-; *ai:* Literary & Stu Support Team; Sunshine Club; Stockbridge HS Teacher of Yr 1986; STAR Teacher 1989-; *home:* 3070 Holly Mill Run Marietta GA 30062

PICKELL-RIDLEY, DONNA MARIE, PCEN Math Lab Facilitator; *b:* New York City, NY; *m:* Andrew; *c:* Andrew C., Kevin M., Lateef C., Malik A.; *ed:* (BA) Black Stud, Herbert H Lehman Coll 1977; (MS) Rdng Ed/Spec Ed Adelphi Univ 1983; In Service Courses Teachg Gifted Child/Teachg Writing Process/Total Reading Prgm/Teachg Remediating Math Team Acclrtd Instr; *cr:* Paraprof Ps91x 1976-78; 3rd-4th Grade Teacher Ps91x 1978-80; 6th Grade Teacher 1980-87; PCEN Remed Project Teacher 1987-89; PCEN Math Lab Facltr Ann Cross Mersereau Sch 1989-; *ai:* African Dance Troupe/Chldrs/Grls Vllybl Coachg/Peer Tutoring Grp Math & Rdng; Kappa Delta Pi 1974-77; Rdng Assn 1977-; Crac Spokeswoman 1989-; Grad Magna Cum Laude Lehman 1977; Troph Grls Vllybl Tm; *office:* Ann Cross Mersereau Sch/IS206B 2280 Aqueduct Ave New York NY 10468

PICKELMAN, MAUREEN R., Fifth Grade Teacher; *b:* Bay City, MI; *ed:* (AA) Elem Ed, Concordia Coll Ann Arbor 1965; (BS) Elem Ed, Concordia Coll River Forest 1967; Cert Cntrl MI Univ 1968-70; *cr:* 5th Grade Teacher St Luke Luth Sch 1967-; *ai:* Girls Bsktbl & Vlybl Coach; Talented & Gifted Prgm Coord; Outdoor Ed Prgm & Sch Sci Fair Dir; Luth Ed Assn 1980-; NSTA 1985-; MI Assn Educators Gifted, Talented & Creative 1987-88; *office:* St Luke Luth Sch 21400 Nunneley Rd Mount Clemens MI 48043

PICKENS, CATHY JOAN, Science/Social Studies Teacher; *b:* Independence, MO; *m:* Tom; *c:* Jennifer; *ed:* (BA) Sociology, Univ of MO 1978; Grad Stud Elem Ed Teaching Cert & Mid Sch Sci/Soc Stud Extended Cert Univ of MO Kansas City; *cr:* Teacher Eastgate Mid Sch 1982-; *ai:* Sci Curr, Sci Resource, Sci Textbook Comm; 8th Grade Sci Resource Teacher; Nom Excl in Teaching Awd 1988; *office:* Eastgate Mid Sch 4700 N E Parvin Kansas City MO 64116

PICKENS, JIMMY BURTON, Earth Science Teacher; *b:* Silver City, NM; *m:* Joana Jolterman; *c:* Kathleen J. Grace, Danelle L. Frye; *ed:* (BS) Scndry Ed, NM St Univ 1957; (MED) Ed Admin, Univ of AZ 1971; Air Command & Staff Coll 1964; Industrial Coll of Armed Forces 1973; Defense Mgmt 1976; *cr:* Acad Flight Instr USAF 1957-78; Acad Instr USAF ACad 1967-70: Earth Sci Teacher Wylie Mid Sch 1981-; *ai:* UIL Sci Team Coach; Regional Sci Fair Team Spon; Stu Recongnition Comm; Asst Prin; Sch Dist Attendance Adv Comm; Dist Health Planning Comm; Phi Delta Kappa 1970-; Assn of TX Prof Educators Local Pres 1975-76; Sci Teachers Assn of TX 1981-; TX Earth Sci Teachers Assn 1985-; Abilene United Way Wylie ISD Coord 1983-87; TX St Ed Agency Top 10 Environmental Teacher Awd 1985; Participant NASA; *office:* Wylie Mid Sch 3158 Beltway S Abilene TX 79605

PICKENS, LEE FENTRESS, 5th Grade Teacher; *b:* Odessa, TX; *c:* Shera L.; *ed:* (BA) Span Eng Ed, 1957; (MA) History, 1962 TX Tech Univ; Post Masters Studies in Admin & Supervision Baylor; Econ Courses TX a & M; Advanced Academic Trng Baylor & Other Institutions; *cr:* Teacher Lubbock & Other West TX Sch 1957-64; Grad Stu/Teacher TX Tech & Lubbock 1960-62; Consultant/Ed/Flight Instr Self-Own Company 1965-78; Teacher Midway ISD 1978-; Consultant for AAT Credit Baylor, Region Service Ctrs 1985-; *ai:* 5th Grade GT Instr Reg Assignment; Part-Time History Inst McLennon Cty Coll; Ed Inst Baylor Univ; Assn of TX Prof Ed Pres/Dist Dir/Regional VP 1984-88; Delta Kappa Gamma; Assn for Supervision & Curr Dev; Alpha Lambda Delta; TX Cncl on Econ Ed Guest Speaker 1985; Alpha Delta Kappa; PTA; 2nd Place St Awd for Excl in Teaching Private Enterprise; Cert of Merit for Teaching Econ; Cert of Rec for Outstanding Contribution to Ed System of TX; *home:* 9917 Sandalwood Waco TX 76712

PICKERELL, WALT DEVON, Arts/Technology Teacher; *b:* Lebanon, IN; *m:* Debra S. Wolferman Pickerell; *c:* Heather, Shannon; *ed:* (BA) Phys Ed/Health, 1972, (MS) Phys Ed/Health, 1976 Ball St Univ; *cr:* Ind Arts Teacher Whitko HS 1972-74, Lavill Jr-Sr HS 1974-; *ai:* Head Ftbl Coach; Jr Olympic Vlybl Coach; IN Ftbl Coaches Assn 1978-; IN Industrial Technology Ed Assn 1987-89; Cty Line First Brethren Church 1976-; *office:* Laville Jr Sr HS 69969 Us 31 S Lakeville IN 46536

PICKERING, DENNIS RICHARD, 7th Grade Science Teacher; *b:* Haverhill, MA; *m:* Elizabeth Anne Herakovich; *ed:* (BS) Earth Sci, 1972, (MS) Scndry Ed, 1978 Ball St Univ; *cr:* 7th Grade Sci Teacher Madison-Grant United Schls 1974-; *ai:* Jr HS Athletic Dir; 7th/8th Grade Track Coach; *office:* Madison-Grant Jr HS 11640 S Edow Fairmount IN 46928

PICKERING, JAMES LESLIE, 8th Grade Amer History Teacher; *b:* Circleville, OH; *m:* Deborah Parsley; *c:* Christopher, David; *ed:* (BA) Soc Stud, Capital Univ 1968; *cr:* 8th Grade Amer His Teacher Teays Valley Mid Sch 1968-; *ai:* 8th Grade Ftbl & 7th/8th Grade Boys/Girls Track; DAR Amer His Teacher of Yr OH 1987; *office:* Teays Valley Mid Sch 383 Circleville Ave Ashville OH 43103

PICKETT, J. MICHAEL, Teacher/Soc Stud Chair; *b:* Corpus Christi, TX; *m:* Penny Cheryl Doss; *c:* Mark J.; *ed:* (BS) His/Government, TX A&I Univ 1971; (MA) His/Government, Corpus Christ St Univ 1975; *cr:* Soc Stud Teacher Richard King HS 1972-; *ai:* Poly Sci Club Adv; AFT, Corpus Christi Cncl for Soc Stud; *office:* Richard King HS 5225 Gollihar Corpus Christi TX 78412

PICKETT, JO BROCK, 7th Grade Math Teacher; *b:* Tyler, TX; *m:* Elmer; *c:* Teri, Ben; *ed:* (BS) Elem Ed, E TX Univ 1955; (MED) Elem Ed, Stephen F Austin 1962; *cr:* 6th Grade Teacher Kilgore Ind Sch Dist 1955-61; 7th Grade Math Teacher Adams Cty Ind Sch Dist 1962-70, Kilgore Ind Sch Dist 1977-; *ai:* TX St Teachers Assn, TX Classroom Teachers Assn, Delta Kappa Gamma, NCTM; Beta Sigma Phi; *home:* 3108 Rockbrook Kilgore TX 75662

PICKETT, STEVEN HAROLD, 8th Grade Lang Art Teacher; *b:* Danville, IL; *m:* Marlene Brumleve; *c:* Vincent, Ryan, Alexander (dec); *ed:* Assoc His, Danville Jr Coll 1966; (BS) Soc Stud/His/Eng, 1968, (MS) Soc Stud/His/Eng, 1970 Univ IL Champaign-Urbana; *cr:* 8th Grade Self Contained Classroom Teacher Gifford Grade Sch 1968-70; 7th/8th Grade Lang Art Teacher/Track & Field/6th Grade Bsktbl Coach Effingham Cntrl Sch 1970-; *ai:* Natl Assn Eng Teachers Life Mem; IL Ed Assn, NEA, Effingham Classroom Teachers Assn; Effingham Elks Club; Effingham Jaycees; Effingham Park Dist Bd (Pres, VP) 1973-; *home:* 703 N Cardinal St Effingham IL 62401

PICKLO, DAVID MICHEAL, Science Department Chair; *b:* Detroit, MI; *m:* Donna Roach; *ed:* (BS) Bio, 1966, (MS) Ed, 1980 E MI Univ; Grad Stud Bio, Geology, E MI Univ; *cr:* Sci Teacher South Jr HS 1966-80; Bio Teacher Allen Park HS 1980-; *ai:* MI Bio Teachers Assn 1987-; BPOE Trustee 1966-; *office:* Allen Park HS 18401 Champaign Allen Park MI 48101

PICKUS, JAMES PAUL, Industrial Technology Teacher; *b:* Minneapolis, MN; *m:* Suzanne Margret Martins; *c:* Stephan, Erin; *ed:* (BS) Industrial Technology, Madkato St Coll 1975; (BS) Industrial Ed, Mankato St Univ 1978; Working on Masters Mankato St Univ; *cr:* Industrial Technology Teacher New Ulm Public Schls 1978-; *ai:* Boys Var Track 1st Asst; 7th-8th Grade Ftbl; Sr HS Faculty Cncl; Sr HS Dept Chm; MN Tech Ed Assn, MN Ed Assn, NEA, Society of Automotive Engrs; MN Technology Ed Assn Anual Supermileage Competition Chm Coord; Automotive Technology/Transportation Prgm St & Nationally Recognized; *office:* New Ulm Sr HS 414 S Payne St New Ulm MN 56073

PIEDILATO, BARBARA SEYMOUR, 7th Grade Mathematics Teacher; *b:* Commerce, GA; *m:* John; *c:* Andy, Amy, Anna; *ed:* (BA) Math/Behavioral Sci, Tif Coll 1975; Univ of GA & Regional Educl Service Prgms Recertification Courses; *cr:* Math Teacher Elbert Cty Mid 1975-79, N Madison Mid 1979-80, Bleckley Cty HS 1980-82, N Madison Mid 1982-; *ai:* US Dept of Human Resources GA Division of Adolescent Services Foster Parent 1986-89; Danielsville Hard Tops Sftbl Team Coach 1989-; Teacher Assessment Prgm Data Collector; Teacher Evaluation Prgm Observer; Staff Dev Comm Mem; *office:* Madison Cty Mid Sch PO Box 690 Danielsville GA 30633

PIEGARO, KATHLEEN BRANNIGAN, Mathematics Teacher; *b:* Newark, NJ; *m:* Nicholas John; *c:* Jared, Joel; *ed:* (BA) Math, Jersey City St Coll 1963; NJ Inst of Technology; *cr:* Math Teacher Roosevelt Jr HS 1963-73, 1976-81, Edison Jr HS 1982-86, West Orange HS 1986-; *ai:* Math Team Coach; Frosh Class Adv; NCTM 1976-; NJ Ed Assn, NEA, NJ Math Teachers Assn 1963-; Natl Sci Fnd Grant 1965-66; *office:* West Orange HS 51 Conforti Ave West Orange NJ 07052

PIEMME, BETTY, Fourth Grade Teacher; *b:* Weed, CA; *m:* Albert Charles; *c:* Alice Southcott, Karen; *ed:* (BA) Soc Stud, Chico St 1969; (MA) Humanistic Ed, USIU 1975; Cmptrs, USC 1984; Cmptrs Technology & Application in Ed; *cr:* 1st-6th Grade Teacher Avocado Elem 1970-; *ai:* Cmptr Club Adv; Cmptr Chairperson; Master Teacher; Teachers Assistance Prgm; Whole Lang Cncl San Diego Hats off to Teachers Membership Chairperson 1988-, Certificate 1990; Greater San Diego Rdng Assn 1970-; Coronada Yacht Club Cruise Chairperson 1988; Cajon Valley Teacher Assn VP 1975; AB803 Grant 1985; CTIP Grant 1986; *office:* Avocado Elem Sch 3845 Avocado School Rd La Mesa CA 92041

PIEPLOW, SHARON VISE, Third Grade Teacher; *b:* Wheeler, TX; *m:* Warren Paul; *c:* Paula K; *ed:* (BSED) Elem Ed, N TX St Univ 1964; Sam Houston St Univ, W TX St Univ, TX Tech St Univ; *cr:* 1st Grade Teacher Hurst-Euless 1964-66, Spring Branch Ind Sch Dist 1966-70; 1st/2nd Grade Teacher Lubbock Ind Sch Dist 1973-76; 1st Grade Teacher Canadian Ind Sch Dist 1976-79; 4th-6th Grade Teacher El Paso Ind Sch Dist 1979-; *ai:* Primary Enrichment Prgm 3rd Grade Talented; Soc Stud Task Force Comm; PTA 1964-; Classroom Teacher Assn; Ascension Luth Church Sch Bd of Ed 1987-; Spring Branch Day Care Center Bd of Dirs 1967; Career Ladder Step 3; El Paso Ind Sch Dist Top 10 Teacher of Yr 1981; *office:* Hibbard Polk Elem Sch 940 Belvidere El Paso TX 79912

PIERA, SUSAN G., Seventh Grade Teacher; *b:* White Plains, NY; *c:* Andrew; *ed:* (BED) Elem Ed, Univ of Miami Coral Gables 1960; (MA) Admin/Supervision, Seton Hall Univ 1975; *cr:* 2nd-5th/7th Grade Teacher Sussex Avenue Sch 1971-; *ai:* NEA, NJ Ed Assn, Essex Cty Ed Assn; Newark Teachers Assn Mem 1990; Newark Teachers Union; Sussex Avenue Sch Certificate of Appreciation 1987; NJ St Dept of Ed Task Force Teacher Rep; Task Force to Develop Quality Sch Lib Media Prgms 1987; *office:* Sussex Avenue Sch 307 Sussex Ave Newark NJ 07107

PIERANGELI, STEPHEN JOSEPH, Social Studies Teacher; *b:* Philadelphia, PA; *m:* Christina Cottman; *ed:* (BS) Scndry Ed, Kutztown St Coll 1978; *cr:* Teacher/Housefather St Gabriels Hall 1978-80; Teacher/Coach/Dept Head Arthur P Schalick HS 1980-; *ai:* Jr HS Dept Chm; Head Cross Cntry, Asst Bsbl Coach; Pittsgrove Ed Assn (Pres 1984-88, VP 1988-); *office:* Arthur P Schalick HS Box 312 Elmer NJ 08318

PIERCE, CARMEN MARIA, Spanish Teacher; *b:* Vega Alta, PR; *m:* Wilson H.; *c:* Wilson H., Rachel L.; *ed:* (BS) Span Ed, Cntrl MO St 1970; (MS) Ed, IN Univ 1975; Bi-ling Endorsement; Mentor Prgm Trng; Curr Dev Gifted & Talented Essential Skills Guide; Project Successfully Teaching All Youth; *cr:* Bi-ling Teacher Edison Mid Sch 1970-72, Span Teacher West Side HS 1972-82; Adv Coll Bound JR & Sr 1982-84; Span Teacher West Side HS 1984-85; Home Ec Teacher Kennedy-King 1985-87; Span Teacher West Side HS 1987-; *ai:* Span Club Spon; West Side Hi-Y Spon; Textbook Adoption Comm Mem; Gary Rdng Cncl Mem 1987-89; AFT Mem 1970-; St Timothy Cmmty Church 1972-; Delta Sigma Theta 1968; Bi-ling Endorsement Univ Grant; *office:* West Side HS 9th & Gerry St Gary IN 46406

PIERCE, DONNA BREAUX, Librarian; *b:* Leesville, LA; *c:* David A., Jennifer A.; *ed:* (BA) Eng Ed, Univ of SW LA 1969; *cr:* Eng Teacher Crowley HS 1969-70; Eng Teacher/Librarian Vermilion Cath HS 1970-75; Librarian Mt Carmel Elem Sch 1976-79; Eng Teacher Kaplan HS 1979-80; Teacher of Scndry Gifted Acadia Parish Schls 1982-83; Librarian Crowley HS 1983-84; Lang Art Teacher/Librarian Welsh-Roanoke Jr HS 1984-; *ai:* Chrldr, Lib Club, Stu Cncl Spon; LAE, NEA, LASL, LLA; *office:* Welsh-Roanoke Jr HS PO Box 9 Hwy 90 Roanoke LA 70581

PIERCE, GLEN DE WAYNE, Computer Science Teacher; *b:* Jacksonville, TX; *ed:* (AA) Tyler Jr Coll 1979; (BS) Cmptr Sci/Math, 1981, (MSIS) Math, 1984 Univ of TX Tyler; *cr:* Teacher Longview Ind Sch Dist 1981-; *ai:* UIL Math & Sci Coach; Cmptr Sci Team Coach; NHS Spon 1984-89; TCTA, TCEA 1983-; TSTA 1981-83; *home:* Rt 2 Box 163 Cushing TX 75760

PIERCE, IRIS LANGLEY, Chem/Advanced Biology Teacher; *b:* Fordyce, AR; *m:* Herbert V.; *c:* Shawn; *ed:* (BSE) Chem/Bio, 1963, (MSE) Bio, 1968 Henderson St Univ; Ed, Chem, Gifted Ed; *cr:* Sci Teacher 1963-, Sci Dept Chairperson 1978-, Teacher of Gifted & Talented 1981-86 Dolarway HS; *ai:* NHS Advisory & Annual Awds Assembly Comm; Medical Careers Club Spon; Impact Crisis Intervention Team Mem; NSTA 1968-; AR Sci Teachers Assn, Amer Chemical Soc 1968-; Scottish Rites Fnd Schlsp; Intnl Paper Company Grants Gifted Ed; Nom Excl in Teaching Awd 1989; *office:* Dollarway HS 4900 Dollarway Rd Pine Bluff AR 71602

PIERCE, JOYCE SHRADER, Elem/EMH Special Ed Teacher; *b:* Healdton, OK; *m:* Ervin D.; *c:* Greg, Brenda Sisney, Larry; *ed:* (BS) Elem Ed, Cntrl St Univ Edmond 1960; (MA) Spec Ed, E Cntrl St Univ Ada 1970; Foreign Study Spec Ed, San Francisco St Coll 1971; Grad Stud E Cntrl St Univ 1973-74; *cr:* 1st Grade Elem Ed Teacher 1960-69, Elem Teacher of Gifted & Talented 1982-86, EMH Elem/HS Teacher 1969- Velma-Alma; *ai:* 7th Grade Class Spon; OEA, NEA Local Pres 1960-, Teacher of Yr 1968, 1983, 1990; CEC Pres 1975-78; Delta Kappa Gamma Comm Work 1975-; First Baptist Church Sunday Sch Teacher 1961-80; Democratic Women Pres 1980-83; Spec Ed Stipend 1969; Sr Play Spon 1988-89; Organized Velma OK Birthday Celebration 1986; Teacher of Yr 1968, 1983, 1990; Published 2 Books 1986; *office:* Velma-Alma Public Sch Box 8 Velma OK 73437

PIERCE, KATHLEEN MILLS, Gifted Prgm Resource Teacher; *b:* La Plata, MD; *m:* Jarvis W. Jr.; *ed:* (BFA) Art Ed, VA Commonwealth Univ 1978; Curr Design, Ed of Gifted & Talented; *cr:* Itinerant Art Teacher Beaverdam Doswell & Montpelier Elem 1978-81; Gifted Prgm Resource Teacher Hanover Cty Elem Schls 1981-82, Louisa Cty Intermediate Sch 1982-86, Louisa Mid Sch & Cty HS 1986-; *ai:* Coach LMS & LCHS Odyssey of Mind Teams; Asst Spon LCHS Art/Literary Magazine; Chairperson Higher Academic Achievement Comm; VA Assn for Ed of Gifted 1987-; Mem Steering Comm; VA Consortium of Coords of Prgms for Gifted Regional Rep of Dev.

PIERCE, LINDA ALLENE, English Teacher; *b:* Newton, IA; *ed:* (BS) Phys Ed/Eng, Marycrest Coll 1971; Ed, Drake Univ of IA, IA St Univ, Bemidji St Univ, Marycrest, NW MO St; *cr:* Teacher Algona Garrigan 1971-73; Public Relations Dir Conifer GSC 1973-74; Substitute Teacher Newton 1974-75; Teacher Union-Whitten 1975-77, Madrid 1977-; *ai:* Jr HS Girls Vlybl Coach; 8th Grade Class Spon; Young Writers Conference IA St Univ Comm Mem; NEA, Madrid Ed Assn, NCTE; UWEA Secy; *office:* Madrid Cmmty Schls Hwy 17 N Madrid IA 50156

PIERCE, LINDA DAVIS, 7th Grade Lang Arts Teacher; *b:* Ahoskie, NC; *m:* Larry Dean; *c:* Christopher, Corey; *ed:* (BS) Eng, Elizabeth City St Univ 1968; Addl Studies for Teachers of the Gifted East Carolina Univ; *cr:* Teacher, Gates Co HS 1969-1970; Hertford County Mid Sch 1970-; *ai:* Spon Sch Newspaper; NCAE Local Newspaper Ed 1987-88; NEA, PACE; Alpha Kappa Alpha Pres 1988-, Ldrship/Service 1989; Panhellenic Cncl Sec 1990; C. S. Brown Auditorium Restoration Assn, Inc. Board 1989-; Attnd NCCAT Fall 1989; Western Carolina Univ; Publ in We Learn What We Do; *home:* Route 3, Box 187C Ahoskie NC 27910

PIERCE, LINDA TALLEY, 7th Grade Life Science Teacher; *b:* Luverne, AL; *m:* Timothy William; *c:* Barrington D., Calvin Talley; *ed:* (BA) Bio/Scndry Ed, Troy St Univ 1969; (MS) Bio/Scndry Ed, 1977, (EDS) Bio/Scndry Ed, 1987 Auburn Univ; *cr:* Bio/Physiology Teacher Greenville HS 1969-73; Bio/Chem Teacher Highland Home HS 1973-74; Adjunct Bio Teacher Lurleen B Wallace Jr Coll 1972-; 7th Grade Life Sci Teacher Greenville HS 1974-; *ai:* Stu Cncl & Beta Club Co-Spon; Greenville Jr HS Sci Dept & Butler Cty Textbook Comm Chm; Alpha Delta Kappa Pres 1982-84; Univ of FL & Auburn Univ NSF Grants; NEWMAST Recipiant 1988; *office:* Greenville Jr HS Overlook Rd Greenville AL 36037

PIERCE, MARTHA PATTON, 1st Grade Teacher; *b:* Atlanta, GA; *m:* James L.; *c:* Kathy Carlson, Valorie Hooten, Loren B.; *ed:* Elem Educ, West GA Coll 1950; *cr:* Kndgtn/5th Grade Teacher Mount Vernon Bapt Church 1972-73; 1st Grade Teacher Mount Vernon Chrstn Sch 1973-86; 1st Grade Teacher/Elem Supv 1986-; *home:* 467 Panola Rd Ellenwood GA 30049

PIERCE, RICHARD JAMES, English/Gifted English Teacher; *b:* Rochester, PA; *ed:* (BS) Elem Ed, Geneva Coll 1971; (MS) Ed Admin, Penn St Univ 1976; *cr:* Elem 1972-80; Elem Gifted 1980-82; Scndry Eng 1984- Hopewell Area Sch; *ai:* Viking Voice Jr High Newspaper Spon; Forensics Team Spon; Odyssey of the Mind Club Spon; Visions-Literary Mag Spon; Beaver Cty Chapter PA Assn for Gifted Ed Pres 1983-84; Page Awd for Excl in Teaching 1988; Hopewell Mem Jr High PTSA; Nom Natl PTA Phoebe Apperson Hearst Awd 1989; PA Odyssey of the Mind Bd of Dir 1984-; Southwest PA Odyssey of the Mind Dir 1984-; Property Owners' Assn Bd of Dir 1982-; Letter of Commendation PA Governor Casey 1988; Gift of Time Tribnte Awd Amer Family Institute 1989; *office:* Hopewell Memorial Jr H S 2121 Brodhead Rd Aliquippa PA 15001

PIERCE, RUTHANNE CAUGHEY, English Dept Chair/Teacher; *b:* Dayton, OH; *m:* Daniel James; *c:* Matt, Lyndsay; *ed:* (BSE) Eng/Speech, Miami Univ 1969; Rdng Specialist Cert, John Caroll Univ 1988; *cr:* Teacher Memorial Jr HS 1969-72; Tutor Shaker Heights HS 1981-84; Teacher/Dept Head Luth HS East 1984-; *ai:* Newspaper, Pep Club, Academic Challenge Team Adv; NCTE 1987-; PTA 1977-; Parents Teachers League 1984-; *office:* Lutheran HS East 3565 Mayfield Rd Cleveland OH 44118

PIERCE, SARAH FAITH, 6th Grade Soc Stud/Chairperson; *b:* Oak Ridge, TN; *ed:* (BS) Elem Ed, 1978; (MA) Scndry Bio Sci, 1986; (EDS) Admin & Supervision, 1988 TN Tech Univ; *cr:* 3rd/6th Grade Teacher Putnam Cty Sch System 1978-; *ai:* Putnam Cty Project Dare; Comm to Pilot Project Dare for Gov McWherter; Drug Free TN Prgm; TN Dept of Ed Soc Stud Curr Revision Comm 1989-; Phi Kappa Pi 1978-; TN Ed Assn 1978-; NEA 1978-; Intnl Rdng Assn 1980; TN Task Force Comm Project Dare; Implementling Prevention Prgm in Putnam Cty Schls & Pilot for TM Sch Systems; *home:* 110 E 12th St Cookeville TN 38501

PIERCEY, JAMES NELSON, Assistant Principal; *b:* Jackson, TN; *c:* Kim, Amy, Timothy; *ed:* (BA) His/Ec, Union Univ 1968; (MA) Educl Admin, Memphis St Univ 1975; *cr:* His Teacher Tigrett Jr HS 1968-70, Merry Jr HS 1970-71; Teacher/Coach 1971-86, Asst Prin 1986- Parkway Jr HS; *ai:* Past Stu Cncl & His Club Spon; Sch Improvement Comm Co-Chm; Athletic Comm; Head Bsktbl & Asst Ftbl Coach; Jackson Ed Assn, TN Ed Assn, NEA 1968-; W TN Ed Assn Soc Stud Section Pres 1979; YMCA YBA Bsktbl Dir 1973-80; Jackson Church League Youth Bsktbl Bd of Dirs 1987-88; Jackson Little League Dir 1982-; *office:* Parkway Jr HS 1341 N Parkway Jackson TN 38305

PIERCY, MARY PETERS, Teacher; *b:* Erwin, TN; *c:* Leslie Ann, Mary Leigh; *ed:* (BA) Early Chldhd Ed, Mars Hill Coll 1977; (MA) Early Chldhd/Rdng, Western Carolina Univ 1982; Career Ladder Evaluator Trng; Mentor Teacher Trng; *cr:* Asst Teacher 1974-77, Teacher 1977- Candler Elem; *ai:* Grade Level Chairperson-Kndgtn; Mem-Hospitality Comm; Yrbk Staff; NAEYC 1980-; NC Assn of Educators 1977-; NEA 1977-; Teacher of Yr-Candler Elem 1986-87; Selected to Attend NC Center/Advancement Teaching-Western Carolina Univ 1987 & 1990; *office:* Candler Elem Sch Rt 3 Box 234 Candler NC 28715

PIERRE, MICHAEL JOSEPH, 6th-8th Grade Math Teacher; *b:* Madison, WI; *m:* Barb; *ed:* (BA) Elem Ed, 1983, (MA) Math/Ed, 1990 MT St Univ; Excl for MT Math Ed, Gender Expectations Stu Achievement; *cr:* 5th/6th Grade Teacher Melstone Public Sch 1983-84; 6th-8th Grade Math/7th Grade Lang Art Teacher Monforton Public Sch 1984-; *ai:* Monforton 5th-8th Grade Boys & Girls Bsktbl Coach 1980-83; Melstone Jr HS Jr Var & Var Asst Coach 1983-84; Monforton 5th-8th Grade Boys Bsktbl Coach 1984-85; MCTM 1986-; Big Brothers Sisters (Big Brother 1980-87, Bd Mem 1988-, Bd Pres 1990); Presidential Excl in Sci & Math Teaching Awds Finalist 1988; *home:* 1202 N Pinecrest Bozeman MT 59715

PIERRET, MADONNA MARY, Mathematics & Computer Teacher; *b:* Sherman, SD; *ed:* 2 Yr Teaching Cert, Presentation Jr Coll 1954; (BS) Ed, Northern St 1969; (MA) Ed, Univ of CA 1973; Cmptr Programming, SD St Univ 1983; Cmptr Application, Augustana 1986; Advanced Cmptr Application, Augustana 1987; *cr:* Grade Teacher St Stephens 1954-56, St Anns 1956-57, St Mary 1957-58; HS Math Teacher Sacred Heart 1969-76; Math/Cmptr Teacher St Mary 1976-; *ai:* Prom & Jr Class Adv 1980-; Cmptr Adult Ed 1984-; Sister Senate Treas 1990; NSF Grant Univ of CA 1971-73; *office:* St Mary HS 812 N State Dell Rapids SD 57022

PIERSON, GUY ROBERT, Fifth Grade Teacher; *b:* Chicago, IL; *ed:* (BSED) Education, 1968; (MED) Administration, 1970 Loyola Univ; Post Masters Studies Curr Specialist Marquette Univ 1969-71; *cr:* Adjunct Inst Natl Coll of Ed 1971-78; 4th, 5th, 6th Grade Teacher Skokie Sch Dist 69 1968-; *ai:* Phi Delta Kappa 1970-; SEA Pres 1988-89; NEA Life Mem 1968-; IL Ed Assn 1968-; Ordained Permanent Diaconate Archdiocese of Chgo 1977; Elected Treas 1983-86, Pres 1988-89 Skokie 69 Ed Assn; *home:* 909 Greenwood Street Evanston IL 60201

PIERSON, OSSEAN EUGENE, Mathematics Teacher; *b:* Watertown, MN; *m:* M. Jolene (Evans); *c:* Cheri, Paul, David; *ed:* (BSED) Math, Southwest MO St Univ 1957; (MST) Math, Univ of MO-Rolla 1970; 1 Yr of Theology Ed, Southern Meth Univ; *cr:* Math Teacher Rolla HS 1966-; *ai:* Awards Comm; Jr Class Spon; Rolla Cmmty Teachers Assn 1966-; MO St Teachers Assn 1966-; MCTM 1980-; NCTM 1970-; Optimists Dir 1980-; *home:* 30 Johnson St Rolla MO 65401

PIERSON, PATRICIA WATLINGTON, First Grade Teacher; *b:* Lynchburg, VA; *m:* Robert Lee; *c:* Susan K., Lee M.; *ed:* (BS) Elem Ed, Radford Univ 1961; (MED) Elem Ed, Univ of VA 1979; *cr:* 2nd Grade Teacher Altavista Elem 1961-67; 1st Grade Teacher Gretna Primary 1975-88, Gretna Elem 1988-; *ai:* Delta Kappa Gamma Pres 1986-88; NEA, VEA, PEA; *home:* Rt 4 Box 197 Gretna VA 24557

PIERSON, WALTER GEROLD, Vocational Agriculture Teacher; *b:* Spokane, WA; *m:* Janet Louise Bryant; *c:* Patrick, Jodi, Brandi, Jami; *ed:* (BS) Animal Sci, CA Poly San Luis Obispo 1965; (BAED) Voc Agriculture, 1967, (MS) Adult Ed, 1969 WA St Univ Pullman; Plant Genetics 1978; Cmptr Ed 1981; Chemical Applicators, 1983; First Aid Cert 1978; *cr:* Ag Educator Pateros Sch Dist 1967-69, Ephrota Sch Dist 1969-72, Lake Chelan Sch Dist 1977-; *ai:* Chelan FFA & Sr Class Adv; Wrestling Coach; WVATA Dist Pres 1981-82, Teacher of Yr 1978; WEA Mem 1967-, Educator of Yr 1988; NEA, WVA Mem 1967-; JC St Dir 1969-72, Outstanding Teacher; LCEA Mem 1977-, Teacher of Yr 1983; Dist FFA Pres 1980-81, 1983-84; Coach St Ag Mech Team 1981; St Ag Advisory Comm 1981-85; *home:* HCR Box 24 Chelan WA 98816

PIETRO, JOHN D., Math/Computer Science Teacher; *b:* Fresno, CA; *ed:* (BS) Math, CA Poly St Univ 1980; (MS) Math, CA St Univ Fresno 1990; *cr:* Math Teacher/Cmptr Sci Instr Clovis HS 1980-, Kings River Comm Coll 1984-; Math Dept Chm 1985, Cmptr/Sci Teacher/Dept Chm 1985 Clovis HS; *ai:* CO Math Club Adv; Intnl Baccalaureate Instr; Wrestling Coach; CA Math Cncl Presidential Semi Finalist 1985; Mem Assembly Bill 551 Grant Writing Comm; Developed Advanced Placement Cmptr Sci Curr Clovis Unified Sch Dist; *office:* Clovis HS/Kings River Jr Coll 1055 Fowler Ave Clovis CA 93612

PIETZ, ROSE MARIE CARLSON, 4th Grade Teacher; *b:* Estherville, IA; *m:* Albert H.; *c:* Ronald, Cindy Piest Hedquist; *ed:* Ungraded Elem Certificate Staples Teacher Trng 1951; (BS) Elem Ed, Bemidji St 1965; *cr:* 1st-6th Grade Teacher Ungraded Cntry Sch Dist #23, #9, #116 1951-58; K/1st/3rd Grade Teacher 1958-83, 4th Grade Teacher 1987- Pillager Public Dist #116; *ai:* MEA (Pres, Treas); *office:* Pillager Public Dist #116 Box 38 Pillager MN 56473

PIFER, ELOISE JANE, Music Teacher; *b:* Du Bois, PA; *ed:* (BS) Music Ed, Clarion Univ of PA 1977; (MA) Music Ed, IN Univ of PA 1980; *cr:* Music Teacher Union Sch Dist 1977, Du Bois Area Sch Dist 1977-; *ai:* Jr HS Choral Dir; Church Organist & Choir Dir; Music Ed Natl Conference 1977-; Kappa Delta Pi 1976-; PA St Ed Assn 1977-; United Church of Christ Minister of Music 1989; YMCA Youth Girls Sftbl Asst Coach 1986-; Du Bois Youth Girls Sftbl League (Secy, Treas) 1986-; Du Bois Womens Sftbl League Mgr 1986-; *home:* 23 Hand St Du Bois PA 15801

PIGG, CYNTHIA STROUD, Science Teacher; *b:* Weatherford, TX; *m:* Robert D.; *c:* Casey; *ed:* (AA) Elem Ed, Weatherford Jr Coll 1975; (BS) Elem Ed, Tartleton St Univ 1977; Model for Effective Teacher & Supervision; Beyond Assertive Discipline; *cr:* 6th Grade Teacher Granbury Mid & Elem Schls 1977-85; 7th Grade Sci Teacher 1985-88, Teacher of Gifted & Talented/7th Grade Sci Teacher 1988- Granbury Mid Sch; *ai:* UIL Literary Dir; Sci Coach; Effective Schls Project Team Mem; Granbury Mid Sch Sci Dept Head; TSTA Pres 1984-85; NEA Pres 1987-88; Delta Kappa Gamma Secy 1986-88; 4-H Spon 1985-87; Talented & Gifted Assn 1983-; *office:* Granbury Mid Sch 217 N Jones St Granbury TX 76048

PIGLIA, JACQUELINE M., Eighth Grade Teacher; *b:* Morgan City, LA; *ed:* (BA) Elem Ed, Univ of New Orleans 1984; *cr:* 5th Grade Teacher 1985, 8th Grade Teacher 1985- St Francis of Assisi; *ai:* Coord After Sch Care Prgm & Advent-Christmas Pageant; NCEA 1985-; *office:* St Francis of Assisi Sch 5951 Patton St New Orleans LA 70115

PIKE, CATHERINE BROWN, Special Education Dept Chair; *b:* La Grange, GA; *m:* R. Jeff; *c:* Christen, Joshua; *ed:* (BA) Pol Sci, GA St Univ 1981; *cr:* Soc Stud Teacher Oakwood Sch 1982-84, Cobb Cty Schls 1987-, Dade Cty Schls 1984-85; Spec Ed Division Chm Pebblebrook HS 1988-; *ai:* Accelerated Learning Prgm Sch Coord; Academic Bowl Team Coach; Guidance & NHS Selection Comm; STAR Teacher 1989; *office:* Pebblebrook HS 990 Old Alabama Rd Mableton GA 30059

PIKE, CORA SUE, 1st Grade Teacher; *b:* Elizabethton, TN; *m:* William Alfred Jr.; *c:* Brandon W., Amanda L.; *ed:* (BS) Elem Ed, E TN St Univ 1970; *cr:* 1st Grade Cntrl Elem 1970-; *office:* Cntrl Elem Sch Rt 5 Box 440 Johnson City TN 37601

PIKE, MARY E., Elementary Music Teacher; *b:* Grand Rapids, MI; *ed:* (BA) Ed Soc Sci, Mercy Coll of Detroit 1955; (BME) Music Ed Piano, Manhattanville Coll 1966; Religious Ed Cert St Norberts; Rdng Wkshps Ferris Coll; Kndgtn Wrshps Steubenville Coll; *cr:* Piano/Glee Club Teacher Mount Mercy Acad 1965-69; Music/Prin/7th/8th Grade Teacher St Patrick Schl 1969-81; Music/5th/6th Grade Teacher St Michael Schl 1981-84;music/K-8th Grades Teacher St Mary Sch 1984-; *ai:* Organist St Patrick, Parnell, ADA, MI; Dir Religious Ed St Joseph Parish; Lbrn St Francis Xavier Sch Grand Rapids; NCEA Mem 1958-; Boys/Adult Choir 1974-84; Civic Choral Group Mem 1985-87; Co-Chairperson Mansec; Liturgy Presentation at Parish Level; *home:* 245 Griggs St S E Grand Rapids MI 49507

PIKE, RUBY CRUMP, Fourth Grade Teacher; *b:* Jasper, AL; *m:* John William; *c:* Terri D. Pike Miles, John W. JR., Christopher S.; *ed:* (AS) Elem Ed, Walker Coll 1975; (BS) Elem Ed, 1976, (MA) Elem Ed, 1978, (EDS) Elem Ed, 1985 Univ of AL Birmingham; *cr:* 1st-12th Grade Teacher T W Martin HS 1977-78; K-8th Grade Teacher Townley Jr HS 1978-; *ai:* Elem 4-H Club Spon; NEA, AL Ed Assn, Walker Cty Ed Assn, AL Classroom Teachers Assn 1977-; Townley Free Will Baptist Church (Clerk, Teacher) 1965-82; Pocahontas Freewill Baptist Church (Clerk, Teacher) 1982-; *office:* Townsley Jr HS P O Box B Townley AL 35587

PILAND, BARBARA RAYMOND, 2nd Grade Classroom Teacher; *b:* Chicago, IL; *m:* Kenneth F.; *c:* Valerie Oakley, Mike, Richard; *ed:* (BS) Elem Ed, OK St Univ 1953; Gesell Inst of Human Dev; Test Pre-Sch, Sch Readiness; ITPA, Stanford-Binet; Gifted & Talented Identification; Cmptrs for Teachers, Rdng Disorders, SMSG Math; *cr:* 1st Grade Classroom Teacher Fillmore Elem 1953-56, Coronado Heights 1963-64, 1st Grade Classroom Teacher 1971-87, 2nd Grade Classroom Teacher 1987- D D Kirkland; *ai:* Grade Level Chairperson; Grade Level Vertical Chairperson; System Curr Comm; Building Math Rep; OEA, NEA, PC ACT, Building Rep; PTA Teacher of Yr 1973-74; Kappa Kappa Iota; Rndg Cncl; *home:* 4037 NW 60th Oklahoma City OK 73112

PILARCEK, BARBARA A., Spanish Teacher; *b:* Newark, NJ; *ed:* (BS) Span, Montclair St Coll 1972; *cr:* Span Teacher 1982-, Span/Fr TeAcher 1980-82 Northern Valley; *ai:* Mem Volunteens/Volunteachers of Old Tappan; Textbook Selection Comm; Foreign Lang Educators of NJ 1980-; *office:* Northern Valley Regional HS Central Ave Old Tappan NJ 07675

PILEWSKI, MARGARET ANN, OSB, 7th/8th Grade Teacher; *b:* Erie, PA; *ed:* (BS) Elem Ed, Clarion Univ 1972; (MA) Comm Art, Univ of Notre Dame 1980; *cr:* 7th/8th Grade Elem Teacher St Gregory Immaculate Conception 1969-76; Scndry Comm Teacher St Benedict Acad 1976-88; Learning Resource Teacher Villa Maria Acad 1988-89; 7th/8th Grade Elem Teacher Our Lady of Peace 1989-; *ai:* Mid St Steering & Cath Schls Week Comms; Cmmty & Leadership Self-Study for Evaluation; Sch Newspaper; Yrbk Adv 1979-88; NCEA 1988-; PA Stu Press Assn 1979-88; Public Relations Bd Mem 1988-; Eries Art Panorama Show 1986 & 1987; Photography Accepted in CA Show 1980; Outstanding Elem Teachers of Amer Awd 1975; *home:* 6101 E Lake Rd Erie PA 16511

PILLEY, CHARLES FRANKLIN, JR., Mathematics Teacher; *b:* Norfolk, VA; *m:* Judy Edland; *c:* Charles F. III, Michael B.; *ed:* (BS) Electrical Engineering, VA Military Inst 1955; (MS) Electrical Engineering, Univ of OK 1964; (MBA) Bus Admin, George Washington Univ 1967; (MS) Management, 1969, Master of Operations Research & Statistics, 1970 Rensselaer Polytechnic Inst; (MED) Educl Admin/Supervision, George Mason Univ 1990; Air Force Research Assoc, OH ST Univ 1975-76; Battelle Memorial Academic Fellow, Fort Belvoir VA 1974; *cr:* Deputy Dir of Strategic Planning HQ-USAF Pentagon USAF 1979-81; Math Teacher Madeira Sch 1981-83, W Springfield HS 1983-; *ai:* W Springfield HS Math Team Coach & Spon; Fairfax Cty Math Team, Boys & Girls Tennis, Jr Engineering Tech Society Coach; Phi Delta Kappa 1989-; Fairfax Cty Assn Teachers of Math 1983-; NCTM 1984-; Military Operations Research Society VP Prof Affairs 1972-81; Teacher of Yr Springfield VA Rotary Club 1988; W Springfield HS Golden Apple Awd 1989; Selected as Career LeveL II Teacher Fairfax Cty 1989; Recognized by Fairfax Cty Sch Bd Prof Excl & Exceptional Contributions to Teaching Profession 1990; *home:* 9261 El James Dr Fairfax VA 22032

PILLION, RICHARD JOSEPH, Mathematics Teacher; *b:* Lancaster, PA; *m:* Susan Hecker; *c:* Steven; *ed:* (BS) Math, Shippensburg Univ 1972; (MED) Math, Penn St 1977; *cr:* Math Teacher Sun Area Vo Tech 1972-77; Warwick HS 1978-; *office:* Warwick HS 301 W Orange St Lititz PA 17543

PINA, NENA HARRISON, English/Spanish Teacher; *b:* San Tome, Venezuela; *m:* Juan F.; *c:* Frank, Christine; *ed:* (BA) Eng/Span, Southwestern Univ 1968; (MA) Eng, Univ of TX El Paso 1971; *cr:* Teacher El Paso Public Schls 1968-72, Lydia Patterson Inst 1972-73, Trinity Chrstn Sch 1986-; *ai:* NCTE; *office:* Trinity Chrstn Sch 950 E St Louis Las Vegas NV 89104

PINA, ROSAMOND PERRY, Math Dept Chairperson; *b:* Alamo, TN; *m:* James; *c:* Elissa, Jaime, Adam; *ed:* (BA) Phys Ed, Harding Univ 1972; (MED) Phys Ed, TX Tech Univ 1979; Elem Ed, Bio, General Sci Cert; Currently Pursuing Counseling Masters; *cr:* 1st Grade Teacher El Jardin Elem 1972; Phys Ed Teacher Smithville HS 1972-73, Memphis Harding Acad 1973-76, Lubbock Ind Sch Dist 1976-78; Title I/Sci Teacher Thoreau Mid Sch 1978-86; 1st/3rd Grade Teacher Deming Public Schls 1986-88; 8th Grade Math Teacher Thoreau Mid Sch 1988-.

PINARD, CYNTHIA BEST, Third Grade Teacher; *b:* Gardner, MA; *m:* Roger; *ed:* (BS) Ed, Keene St 1972; *cr:* 3rd Grade Teacher 1972-87, 1st Grade Teacher 1987-88, 3rd Grade Teacher 1988- Auburn Village Sch; *ai:* Lang Art/Rdng Curr; Auburn Ed Assn (Pres 1980-81, 1989-, Treas 1987-89); *office:* Auburn Village Sch Eaton Rd Auburn NH 03032

PINGREE, ALLISON, Teaching Fellow Dept of Eng; *b:* Boulder, CO; *m:* Mark D. Cannon; *ed:* (BA) Eng, Brigham Young Univ 1985; (MA) Eng, Harvard Univ 1988; PHD Eng, Harvard Univ 1992; *cr:* Instr/Adv Brigham Young Univ 1984-86; Instr MA Advanced Stud Prgm 1989; Teaching Fellow Harvard Univ 1988-; *ai:* Non-Resident Tutor Winthrop House Harvard Univ; Phi Kappa Phi 1985; Modern Lang Assn 1988-; Harvard Dept of Eng Grad Liaison Comm 1986-88; Church of Jesus Christ of Latter Day Saints Teacher 1986-; Academic Grant for Tuition Harvard Univ 1987-89; Spencer W Kimball Schlsp Brigham Young Univ 1980-85; Mae Covey Gardner Grant 1985; Outstanding Honors Sr Brigham Young Univ 1985-86; Natl Deans List 1985; *office:* Harvard Univ Warren House Cambridge MA 02138

PINKEL, KATHRYN MARIE, 8th Grade English Teacher; *b:* Milwaukee, WI; *m:* Lawrence William; *c:* Matt, Todd; *ed:* (BS) Spec Ed, Cntrl St Univ of OK 1976; (MS) Elem Ed, Univ of NM 1984; K-12 Rdng Specialist, Cmptr Sci; *cr:* Substitute Teacher Dept of Defense RAF Woodbridge England 1976-77; Elem Teacher Heights Elem Sch 1977-80; Substitute Teacher Escambia Sch Dist 1981; Lang Art Dept Head Polk Mid Sch 1984-; *ai:* Newspaper, Yrbk, Drill Team, Toastmaster Spon; Prgm Planning Comm; Albuquerque Track Club Secy 1989-; Sch Rep for Outstanding Mid Sch Awd; *home:* 12100 Hickory Ct NE Albuquerque NM 87111

PINKNEY, LOIS BRADLEY, Fifth Grade Teacher; *b:* Birmingham, AL; *ed:* (BS) Elem Ed, 1956, (MED) Elem Ed, 1973 AL St Univ; *cr:* Teacher Rutledge Mid Sch 1987-; *ai:* AL Ed Assn, NEA; Alumni Assn; *home:* 905 Dana Dr Fairfield AL 35064

PINKSTON, CLARA BOOTH, English Teacher; *b:* Drew, MS; *m:* John Murray; *c:* John M. III, Catherine Pinkston Wilson, Corey; *ed:* (BA) Ed/Eng, Millsaps Coll 1956; (MED) Ed, MS St Univ 1978; Cmptr Literacy, Alcorn St Univ; *cr:* 3rd Grade Teacher Vicksburg Public Schls; 3rd Grade/Upper Elem Lang Art/Rdng Teacher St Francis Xavier Elem; Jr HS Eng/Math Teacher St Aloysius HS; Jr HS Eng/Heritage Teacher Vicksburg Jr HS; *ai:* NCTE, MS Cncl Teachers of Eng, Natl Fed of Teachers; Vicksburg Jr Auxiliary Past Pres; *office:* Vicksburg Jr HS 1533 Baldwin Ferry Rd Vicksburg MS 39180

PINNELL, THOMAS H., Biology Teacher; *ed:* (BA) Zoology, S IL Univ Edwardsville 1966; (MAT) Botany, Miami Univ 1972; *cr:* Sci Teacher Coolidge Jr HS 1966-73; Bio Teacher Granite City Sr HS 1973-; *ai:* Sci Club Co-Spon; NSTA, NABT 1973-; Alton-Godfrey Jaycees Ext VP 1971-79, Keyman Awd 1979; Natl Sci Fnd Grant Miami Univ 1970-72; *office:* Granite City Sr HS 3101 Madison Ave Granite City IL 62040

PINO, LEE JACK, Biology Teacher; *b:* Selma, AL; *ed:* (BS) Bio, 1986; (MS) Health Ed, 1990 Auburn Univ; *cr:* Sci Teacher Troup Cty Comprehensive HS 1987-; *ai:* Sci Club Sponsor; Assist with Sci Olympiad Team; NABT; Kappa Delta Pi Ed Honorary; *office:* Troup Cty Comprehensive H S 1920 Hamilton Rd La Grange GA 30240

PINTO, WALT HERMAN, Photography Teacher; *b:* Tucson, AZ; *m:* Judy A. Ward; *c:* Shawna, Cinamon, Amber; *ed:* (BA) Univ Stud, 1981, (MA) Educl Fnds, 1983 Univ of NM; Electronics I-TVI; *cr:* Teaching Asst Univ of NM Ed Fnds 1979-81; Art/Sci Teacher Sandia HS 1986-87; Photography Teacher Highland HS 1987-; Part Time Instr Univ of NM Art Ed 1986-; *ai:* Photography Club Spon; Join-A-Sch Comm; Grain Dealers 1986-87, Best Slide 1986; *office:* Highland HS 4700 Coal SE Albuquerque NM 87108

PIONTEK, ANNE KAZIMER, Third Grade Teacher; *b:* Pittsburgh, PA; *m:* Frank L. III; *c:* Frank L. IV, Nicole; *ed:* (BSE) Sci Ed, 1965, (MS) Ed, 1969 Duquesne Univ; *cr:* Classroom Teacher W Mifflin Area Sch Dist 1965-; *ai:* Amer Taekwondo Assn; 1st Degree Black Belt Currently Active; Mothers Club; Slippery Rock Ftbl; W Mifflin Fed of Teachers Mem; Gift of Time Tribute 1989; *office:* Homeville Elem Sch 4315 Eliza St West Mifflin PA 15122

PIPER, KARLENE S. (BAILEY), Third Grade Teacher; *b:* Emporia, KS; *m:* Theodore R. Jr.; *c:* Kirby, Laurie Piper Anderson, Sharon Piper Smith; *ed:* (BSED) Elem Ed/Eng, Washburn Univ 1958; Grad Stud Ed; *cr:* 2nd/3rd Grade Teacher Escondido Sch Dist 1960-62; 1st Grade Teacher Rich-Mar Sch Dist 1963-65; 1st-3rd Grade Teacher Jordan Sch Dist 1968-; *ai:* Jordan Ed Assn Rep; Sch Advisory Cncl Mem; JEA, UEA, NEA Rep 1968-, Teacher of Month 1989; PTA Mem 1968-; Assn for Chldhd Ed Intnl (Mem, Jordan Dist Pres 1985-) 1968-; *home:* 9777 Silica Dr Sandy UT 84094

PIPER, LINDA GAIL, Music/Spelling Teacher; *b:* Wichita Falls, TX; *ed:* (BA) Music, Midwestern St Univ 1975; (MRE) Religious Ed, SW Baptist Theological Seminary 1978; Teaching Inst Pilot Prgm; *cr:* Legal Secy Various Law Firms 1974-78; Educl/Childrens Dir FBC & Southcliff Baptist Church 1978-80; Legal Secy Various Law Firms 1980-83; Teacher Mc Gaha Elem 1983-; *ai:* Delta Kappa Gamma Recording Secy 1989-; Faith Baptist Church (2nd Grade Sunday Sch Dir, Sanctuary Choir Mem); *office:* Mc Gaha Elem Sch 1615 Midwestern Pkwy Wichita Falls TX 76302

PIPER, W. STEPHEN, Health Teacher; *b:* Uniontown, PA; *m:* Patricia Lewis; *ed:* (BS) Health/Phys Ed, Lock Haven Univ 1970; (MS) Health Sci, St Univ of NY Brockport 1977; *cr:* Health Teacher Hornell City Sch Dist 1970-; *ai:* NYS Fed of Prof Health Educators 1973-, Nom Outstanding Teacher 1977; Genesee Valley Sports Medicine Cncl 1980-; *office:* Hornell HS Maple City Pk Hornell NY 14843

PIPER, WILLIAM CARL, II, English Teacher; *b:* Altoona, PA; *ed:* (BS) Eng/Scndry Ed, Lock Haven Univ 1986; *cr:* Migrant Laborer 1982-84; Teaching Asst/Tutor Lock Haven Univ 1985-86; Eng Teacher Bishop Guilfoyle HS 1987-; *ai:* Ski Club; *office:* Bishop Guilfoyle HS 2400 Pleasant Valley Blvd Altoona PA 16602

PIPKIN, GLORIA TREADWELL, English Teacher; *b:* Gainesville, FL; *m:* Kenneth; *c:* Philip; *ed:* (BA) Eng, Univ of FL 1968; (MS) Eng Ed, FL St Univ 1985; Natl Endowment for Hum Auburn Univ 1985; *cr:* Teacher Brownsville Mid Sch 1969-75, Mosley HS 1976-77, Mowat Mid Sch 1977-; *ai:* Knowledge Master Open Team Coach; Bay Lang Art Cncl Pres 1982-84; FL Cncl Regional Dir 1982-84; Teachers of Eng Ed FL Eng Journal 1985-89; NCTE; Article Published; Natl Courage Fnd 1st Awd; *office:* Mowat Mid Sch 1903 E Hwy 390 Lynn Haven FL 32444

PIPPENGER, JANICE RAPP, 5th Grade Teacher; *b:* Syracuse, IN; *m:* Jay A.; *ed:* (BS) Elem Ed, 1966, (MS) Elem Ed, 1974 IN St Univ; *cr:* 5th Grade Teacher 1966-70, 5th-6th Grade Teacher/Prin 1970-73 Gilead Elem; 5th Grade Teacher N Miami Elem Sch 1973-; *ai:* 5th Grade Spelling Bee Chm; NMEA Building Rep; Delta Kappa Gamma Pres 1990; NMEA, ISTA, NEA 1966-; Chosen to Attend Phi Delta Kappas Maintaining Teacher Excl Inst; Miami Cty Conservation Teacher of Yr 1990; *office:* N Miami Elem Sch RR 1 Denver IN 46926

PIPPENGER, WILMA JEAN (COCHRAN), Teacher, Department Chair; *b:* Benton, TN; *m:* Johnny H.; *c:* John H. III; *ed:* (BS) Scndry Ed, TN Technological Univ 1962; Work on Masters Degree, Univ of TN Knoxville & Chattanooga; *cr:* Teacher Polk Cty HS 1962-63; Prin Linsdale Elem Sch 1963-65; Teacher Polk Cty HS 1965-; *ai:* Stu Cncl Adv; Beta Club, Jr & Sr Prom, Jr Class Spon; NEA, TN Ed Assn 1962-; Polk Cty Ed Assn Treas 1962-; TAPCAE Adult Ed Exec Comm; Beta Sigma Phi (Secy, Vice-Chm) 1964-, Girl of Yr 1970, Woman of Yr 1990; March of Dimes Exec Comm 1966-80, Service Awd 1977-78; Benton United Meth Church Secy to Admin Bd 1974-; Polk Cty HS Teacher of Yr 1989-; Exec Comm PCEA; Wildcat Marching Band Reporter; *home:* PO Box 307 Mount Herman Rd Benton TN 37307

PIPPING, CHARLOTTE HELEN, SSMI Director; *b:* Akron, OH; *ed:* (BA) Elem Ed, Youngstown St Univ 1974; *cr:* Teacher Cath Schls 1960-75, St John the Baptist 1975-81; Teacher/Prin SS Peter & Paul 1981-84; Teacher St Annes 1984-85; Dir Stamford Diocesan Office of Religious Ed 1985-; *ai:* Youth Ministry Asst to Dir; *home:* St Marys Villa-Tablerock Sloatsburg NY 10974

PIRKLE, LYNDON ELMO, 7th-12th Grade History Teacher; *b:* Oakland City, IN; *m:* Clarence Ann; *c:* Stephen L., Trudy A. Bledsoe, Lisa H. Parker, Scott Wallis, Ken Wallis; *ed:* (BA) Soc Stud/Eng, Evansville Coll 1950; IN Univ, Evansville Coll, Vincennis Univ, Murry St, IN St; *cr:* Teacher 1982-85, Prin 1985-86, Teacher 1986- Temple Chrstn Acad; *ai:* 7th-8th Grade Home Room; Counseling; Phi Gamma Mu 1950-; Union Township Trustee 1957-65; Town Bd Pres 1983-85; World War II Service 1945-47; *office:* Temple Chrstn Acad Sch 1104 S Stout St Princeton IN 47670

PIROGA, JAMES FRANCIS, Math & Computer Teacher; *b:* Sharon, PA; *m:* Mary Lynne Vaccaro; *c:* Amy L., James B.; *ed:* (BS) Ed/Math, 1972, (MED) Math, 1976 Edinboro Univ of PA; Cmptr Programming, Youngstown St Univ; Cmptr Repair & Maintenance Wkshps; *cr:* Math Teacher Lakeview HS 1973-86; Math/Cmptr Teacher Jamestown HS 1986-; *ai:* Math/Cmptr Club Spon; Bsbl Coach; Climate & Curr Comm; NEA 1973-; PA St Ed Assn 1986-; Jamestown Ed Assn VP 1986-; *office:* Jamestown Area Schls PO Box 217 Jamestown PA 16134

PIRRONE, FRANK JOHN, Science Teacher; *b:* Havre De Grace, MD; *m:* Rebecca E. Pickering; *c:* Rigel, Deneb; *ed:* (BS) Early Scndry Sci Ed - Summa Cum Laude, 1979, (MA) Early Scndry Sci Ed, 1984 St Univ of NY Coll Buffalo; Post Grad Stud Physics; Government License AA2B Amateur Radio Stud; *cr:* Laboratory Research Occidental Petroleum 1971-76; 7th-10th Grade Earth Sci/Life Sci/Phys Sci Teacher Tonawanda Jr/Sr HS 1979-; *ai:* Jr HS Cmptr & Rocketry Club Faculty Adv; Sch Dances Chaperone; NY St United Teachers 1980-; Tonawanda Ed Assn 1980-, Nom Teacher of Yr; Radio Assn of W NY (Mem, Lecturer) 1977-; Buffalo Astronomical Assn Mem 1960-; Atari Buffalo Area Users (Hardware Chm, Pres) 1981-83; NSF Physics Grant

Canisius Coll; Dist Cmptr Comm Mem; *office:* Tonawanda Jr/Sr HS Fletcher & Hinds Sts Tonawanda NY 14150

PIRTLE, DEBORAH DE CUIR, 8th Grade Earth Sci Teacher; *b:* Texas City, TX; *m:* David R.; *c:* Brett, Becky; *ed:* (BS) Bio, TX A&M Univ 1977; Cert Univ of Houston; *cr:* 6th Grade Sci Teacher Levi Fry Mid Sch 1978-84; 8th Grade Sci Teacher Blocker Mid Sch 1984-; *ai:* Sci Fair; Yrbk; TX Earth Sci Teachers Assn; Alpha Delta Kappa Corresponding Secy 1990-; TX Lib Assn; *home:* 408 27th Ave N Texas City TX 77590

PIRTLE, HAROLD N., Social Studies Teacher/Coach; *b:* Decatur, AL; *m:* Deborah Z.; *c:* Angie, Becki, Casey; *ed:* (BS) Phys Ed, Athens St Coll 1970; (MA) Ed Leadership, Univ of AL Birmingham 1988; *cr:* Teacher/Coach Hazelwood HS 1970-72, Brewer HS 1972-74, Speake HS 1974-; *ai:* Head Ftbl & Bsktbl Coach; NEA, AEA; Law Cty Coaches (Pres 1977-85, VP 1975-86) Coach of Yr 1985-87; AL Coach of Yr 1977; *office:* Speake HS 6559 Cty Rd 81 Danville AL 35619

PIRTLE, RETHA RAYMER, 3rd Grade Gifted Stu Teacher; *b:* Louisville, KY; *m:* George Thomas; *c:* Terri A.; *ed:* (BA) Elem Ed, Spalding Coll 1973; (MS) Counseling, Western Univ 1974; Grad Courses Gifted Teaching; *cr:* 5th Grade Teacher of Gifted Stu St Matthews Elem 1973-75; 3rd/5th Grade Teacher of Gifted Stu Young Elem 1975-; *ai:* KY Academic Assn; Assertive Discipline, Participatory Management, Teacher Learning Process Trng; Phi Delta Kappa Mem 1989-; Jefferson Cty Teachers Assn, KY Educl Assn 1973-; Southeast Chrstn Church Mem; Amer Cancer Society & Amer Heart Society Block Coord; Chrstn Womens Group (Dir, Adult Sunday Sch Class Teacher); Project Against Improper Television Programming (Dir, Coord); Jury Duty Forman; *office:* Young Elem Sch 3526 Muhammad Ali Blvd Louisville KY 40212

PISANO, MARY ANNE CASSIDY, K-8th Grade Reading Specialist; *b:* Lancaster, PA; *m:* Samuel F. Jr.; *c:* Christopher, Colleen; *ed:* (BA) Early Chldhd/Elem Ed, 1977, Masters Equivalent Early Chldhd/Elem Ed, 1987 Millersville Univ; *cr:* 3rd/4th Grade Teacher St Peters 1977-80; 4th Grade Teacher 1980-84, Kndgtn Teacher 1984-86 St Anne; Rdng Specialist Lancaster-Lebanon Intermediate Unit 13 1986-; *ai:* Soccer Coach; St Anne Sch-Home Assn Exec Cncl; Lancaster-Lebanon Rdng Cncl, Keystone St Rdng Cncl; Amer Family Inst Gift of Time Awd 1990.

PISCITELLI, STEVEN ANTHONY, Assistant Principal; *b:* Camden, NJ; *m:* Rosemary Espinosa; *ed:* (BA) Poly Sci, St Thomas Univ 1976; (MA) Admin, FL Intnl Univ 1986; *cr:* His Teacher 1976-77, Soc Stud Dept Chm 1977- St Brendan HS; Sociology Instr St Thomas Univ 1985-; Asst Prin St Brendan HS 1987-; *ai:* Athletic & Act Dir; Stu Cncl Moderator; Sr Class & Asst Yrbk Adv; Administrative & Academic Cncls; Religious Ed Comm 1988-; Pastors Cncl Chm 1990; Close-Up Fnd Area Coord 1979-; Good Shepherd Parish Teacher 1988-; Outstanding Contribution Awd Close Up Fnd 1979-89; St Thomas Univ Distinguished Service Awd 1975, Loyalty Awd 1976; FL Intnl Univ Outstanding Stu Awd 1984-86; *home:* 5411 SW 152nd Pl Cir Miami FL 33185

PITCHER, DANNY FRANCIS, 7th Grade Reading Teacher; *b:* New Orleans, LA; *m:* Mary Elizabeth Burns; *c:* Todd; *ed:* (BA) Mrktg, SE LA Coll 1969; (BS) Elem Ed, Univ of CO Colorado Springs 1978; *cr:* 5th Grade Teacher Pikes Peak Elem Sch 1978-80; 6th Grade Teacher Giberson Elem Sch 1980-83, Wildflower Elem Sch 1983-84; Rdng/Cmptr Teacher Panorama Mid Sch 1984-; *ai:* Conflict Management & Stu Newspaper Coord; Soccer & Bsktbl Coach; Walk for Mankind Dist Coord 1985-, Outstanding Merit 1990; Published Outdoor Ed Video for Sch Dist; *office:* Panorama Mid Sch 2145 S Chelton Colorado Springs CO 80916

PITKIN, DAVID J., African/Asian Cultures Teacher; *b:* Corinth, NY; *m:* Gail Burlett; *c:* Lisa, Daniel, John; *ed:* (AB) His, 1959, (MA) Soc Stud/Ed, 1964 SUNY Albany; Counseling, Psych, Goddard Coll 1990; *cr:* Teacher Eldred Cntrl Sch 1961-63, Oriskany Cntrl Sch 1963-68, Holland Patent Cntrl Sch 1968-71, Saratoga Jr HS 1971-; *ai:* NY St United Teachers 1961-; Saratoga Teachers Assn 2nd VP 1981; Amer Psychological Assn; *office:* Saratoga Jr HS W Circular St Saratoga Springs NY 12866

PITT, DINA COFIELD, Mathematics Teacher; *b:* Whitakers, NC; *m:* Marvin Jerome; *ed:* (BA) Scndry Math, Univ of NC Chapel Hill 1986; Working Toward Masters; *cr:* Math Teacher Rocky Mount Sr HS 1986-; *ai:* Stu Government Assembly Co-Adv; NC Assn of Educators, NC Cncl Teachers of Math; *office:* Rocky Mount Sr HS 308 S Tillery St Rocky Mount NC 27804

PITT, JUDY KAY RUSHTON, Second Grade Teacher; *b:* Alton, IL; *c:* Julia Jones, Jacqueline; *ed:* (BA) Sci Ed, Southern IL Univ 1965; Educl Wkshp; *cr:* 2nd Grade Teacher 1965- , 1st Grade Teacher 1980 Roxana Sch Dist; *ai:* Co-Chairperson of Young Authors Comm; Assisted the Phys Ed Teacher in Coaching 3rd/4th Graders; Roxana Ed Assn 1965-; Roxana Park Secy/Bd Mem 1970-85; Serve As A Park Bd Mem; *home:* 111 E Fifth Roxana IL 62084

PITTARD, MICHAEL LARRY, Choral Director; *b:* Charlotte, NC; *c:* James M., Marian E.; *ed:* (BM) Music Ed, E Carolina Univ 1968; (MA) Music Ed, Appalachian St Univ 1975; NC Summer Inst in Choral Arts UNC Chapel Hill; *cr:* Choral Dir J Mc Knitt Alexander Jr HS 1968-70, N Mecklenburg HS 1970-88, Franklin HS 1988-89, Coulwood Mid Sch 1989-; *ai:* Dir of Music First Presbyn Church; Faculty Rep Classrrom Teachers Assn; Mem Charlotte Oratorio Singers & Chamber Choir; Music Educators Natl Conference, NC Music Educators Assn 1968-; Classroom Teachers Assn 1989-; Amer Choral Dir Assn 1981-; Nature Conservancy, Sierra Club 1989-; Choral Section NC Music Educators Assn Chm 1978-80; Articles Published; Consistent Superior Ratings in St Contest & Festivals with N Mecklenburg HS Choral Groups 1970-88; *office:* Coulwood Mid Sch 1901 Kentberry Dr Charlotte NC 28214

PITTENGER, ANN CUNNINGHAM, English Teacher; *b:* Alexandria, VA; *m:* Michael H.; *c:* Bailey; *ed:* (BA) Eng, Erskine Coll 1983; (MAT) Eng, Univ of SC Columbia 1986; *cr:* Teacher Lower Richland HS 1987-; *ai:* Journalism & Newspaper Adv; *office:* Lower Richland HS 2615 Lower Richland Blvd Hopkins SC 29061

PITTMAN, CAROLYN LASSITER, Retired Teacher; *b:* Goldboro, NC; *m:* Hardy Wellon; *c:* Donna Pittman Quinn, Brian; *ed:* (BS) Elem Ed, 1977, (MAED) Elem Ed, 1984 E Carolina Univ; Certificate Advanced Study Ed; Cert Learning Disabilities; *cr:* 6th Grade Teacher Goldsboro City Schls 1977-79; 6th Grade Teacher 1979-86, 5th Grade Teacher 1986-89, Teacher of Academically Gifted 1989- Wayne Cty Schls; *ai:* Tutor Volunteer; Phi Theta Kappa 1975-; Kappa Delta Pi 1976-; Phi Kappa Phi 1977-; Alpha Delta Kappa (Corresponding Secy 1986-88, Courtesy Chairperson 1988-); NCEA Sch Rep 1984-85; NC Retired Government Employees Assn 1989-; Saulston United Meth Church (Choir Dir, Church Organist, United Meth Women Pres); Poetry Published 1989; *home:* Rt 2 Box 349 Goldsboro NC 27534

PITTMAN, KAY FERN (ELDER), English Teacher; *b:* Seagraves, TX; *m:* Dale; *c:* Jessica; *ed:* (BA) Bus, W TX St Univ 1974; Eng, Coll of The Southwest; Bus, San Angle St Univ; *cr:* Bus Teacher Woodsboro HS 1975-80, Loop HS 1980-85; Eng Teacher Wellman HS 1987-.

PITTMAN, KETURAH DRAYTON, Guidance Coordinator; *b:* St Petersburg, FL; *m:* Jerome Robert Sr.; *c:* Jerome Jr., Keisha Tajuan; *ed:* (BS) Phys Ed, 1966, (MS) Guidance & Counseling, 1979 FL A&M Univ; Substance Abuse Counseling, St Petersburg Jr Coll; *cr:* Teacher FL Memorial Coll 1966-68, Campbell Park Elem 1969-80; Cnslr St Petersburg HS 1980-; *ai:* Spectrum Club Black Culture Spon; Sch Advisory Bd; Suncoast Personel & Guidance 1980-; Alpha Kappa Alpha (Pres 1979-82) 1964-: United Way Allocation Cmmty Alliance 1984-86; Appointed to Governors Cncl on Phys Fitness; *office:* Saint Petersburg HS 2501 5th Ave N Saint Petersburg FL 33713

PITTMAN, MARTI ROBINS, Social Studies Teacher; *b:* Kansas City, MO; *m:* Charles H. Jr.; *c:* Chuck, Chris; *ed:* (BS) His, MO Southern St 1973; (MS) His, Pittsburgh St Univ Coll 1985; *cr:* Teacher Webb City Jr HS 1976-; *ai:* Spon Stu Cncl; Spon His Day; MO Cncl for Soc Stud; Jr HS Teacher of Yr 1988; MO St Teachers Org; Webb City Cmmty Teachers Org 1976-; Beta Sigma Phi 1989-; Park Bd 1989-; Lib Bd Pres/Sec 1980-89; Webb City Soccer Assn Commissioner 1983-85; Webb City Youth Bsbl/Sftbl Exec Bd 1982-84; *office:* Webb City Jr H S Washington & 1st Webb City MO 64870

PITTMAN, MARY LOU, Personal Fitness Teacher; *b:* Charleston, WV; *m:* Vernon; *c:* Scott, Brian; *ed:* (BS) Phys Ed/Sci, 1964, (MS) Health/Safety Ed, 1967 WV Univ; Grad Stud; *cr:* Teacher Lenape Regional HS 1964-66; Teacher/Dept Chairperson Cntrl Jr HS 1966-; *ai:* Cheerleading Spon; Track Coach; Various Intramural Act; Pep Club Adv; NEA, CTA, BFT, AFL, AAHPER; AAUW; Panhellenic; Alpha Beta Pi Pres 1976-78, Outstanding Alumnae 1977; WV Univ Fellowship; *office:* Central Jr HS 250 W Brevard Dr Melbourne FL 32935

PITTMAN, WANDA LUCK, Third Grade Teacher; *b:* Richmond, VA; *c:* Edward G.; *ed:* (AA) Liberal Art, VA Intermont Coll 1966; (BS) Elem Ed, Radford Coll 1968; Grad Courses Univ of VA, James Madison Univ; *cr:* 2nd Grade Teacher Seaford Elem 1968-69; 4th Grade Teacher 1969-70, 5th/6th Grade Teacher 1971-84, 3rd Grade Teacher 1984- Wenonah; *ai:* Self Study & Soc Comm; Waynesboro Ed Assn (Poly Action Comm Chairperson, VP, Substitute Rep) 1985-89; Alpha Delta Kappa (Secy, 1986-88, Pres 1988-); Main Street Meth Church (Nursery Bd, Treas 1975-77, Cncl on Ministries 1984-88, Admin Bd 1988-); Friend of Lib 1985-89; Outstanding Elem Teacher of America 1973; *home:* 116 Crompton Rd Waynesboro VA 22980

PITTS, DAN L., Math Teacher; *b:* Humansville, MA; *m:* Laura C.; *c:* Karen, Scott, Susan; *ed:* (BS) Chem, Southwest MO St Univ 1969; (MA) Curr/Inst Ed, Univ of MO 1974; *cr:* Math Teacher Mexico Jr HS 1971-79; Van Far Jr HS 1980-; *ai:* Stu Cncl Adv; 6th Grade Boys Bsktbl Coach; Teacher of Yr 1987-88; *office:* Van-Far Jr HS Hwy 54 W Vandalia MO 65301

PITTS, LARRY GUINN, Assistant Band Director; *b:* Houston, TX; *ed:* (BM) Music Ed, 1978, (MED) Curr & Instruction, 1979, (MM) Music Theory, 1983 Univ of Houston; Music Conservatory Trng & Prof Free-Lance Performing Experience Trumpet; *cr:* Asst Band Dir Sam Rayburn HS 1979-; *ai:* Marching & Symphonic Band; Campus Improvement Advisory Comm; TX Bandmasters Assn, TX Music Educators Assn Mem 1979-; Houston Prof Musicians Assn Mem 1973-; Bands Consistent Winners UIL Sponsored Events; Listed on Highest Level of Career Ladder St of TX Merit Pay System; *office:* Sam Rayburn HS 2121 Cherrybrook Pasadena TX 77502

PITTS, MISS J., Business Education Teacher; *b:* Carson, MI; *ed:* (MSED) Bus Ed, 1979, (BSED) Bus Ed, 1972 Cntrl MI Univ; Numerous Wkshps Cmptr Field; *cr:* Bus Ed Teacher Onawy HS 1975-; Cheboygan Area Schls 1980-; *ai:* NHS, Yrbk, Past Class Adv; Class Play Dir; Onoway Ed Assn (Treas 1985-, Secy 1980-85); Delta Phi Epsilon CMU; NBEA, MI Bus Ed Assn, Cntrl Bus Ed Assn; Voc Ed Assn; Onaway United Meth Choir 1980-; *office:* Onaway HS M33 South Onaway MI 49765

PITTS, SHIRLEY ANN, English Teacher; *b:* Columbus, OH; *m:* Hudson Andre; *c:* Tonnie, Tammy, Tatanisha, Hudson A. II; *ed:* (BS) Scndry Ed/Eng/Latin, OH St 1968; Grad Stud Wayne St; *cr:* Teacher Jay Jr HS 1968-77, Jackson Public Schls 1977-; *office:* Jackson HS 544 Wildwood Ave Jackson MI 49201

PITTSENBARGER, DOUGLAS EDWARD, 8th Grade Earth Sci Teacher; *b:* Greenville, OH; *m:* Valarie Coyle; *c:* Matthew, Zachary; *ed:* (BS) Elem, BGSU 1976; (MED) Admin/Supervision, UD 1981; *cr:* 5th Grade Teacher Celina City 1976-77; 4th Grade Teacher Versailles Exempted 1977-78; 6th Grade Teacher 1978-85, 8th Grade Teacher 1985- Celina City; *ai:* Asst Band Dir; Washington Trip Co-Dir; Teacher Advisory Comm; NESTA 1989-; CEA, OEA, NEA 1976-; *home:* 902 Hemlock Celina OH 45822

PITZ, PAUL NICHOLAS, English/German Teacher; *b:* Indianapolis, IN; *m:* Barbara Ann Waters; *c:* Megan, Andrew; *ed:* (BA) Ger/Eng, Wabash Coll 1968; (MA) Ger, Northwestern Univ 1971; (BED) Ger/Eng, Univ of Toronto 1976; PhD Candidate Ger, Northwestern Univ 1973; US Army Translator Worms Germany 1969-70; *cr:* Eng Teacher Etobicoke Bd of Ed 1976-83; Eng/Ger Teacher Peel Cty Bd of Ed 1983-87; Eng/Speech Teacher Amer Inst of Commerce 1987-88; Eng/Ger Teacher Durant Bd of Ed 1988-; *ai:* Stu Newspaper Adv; Jr Class Spon; AATG 1988-; Canadian Ski Instrs Alliance 1980-; NEA, IA St Ed Assn 1988-; Ontario Scndry Sch Teachers Fed 1976-87; Amer Legion 1989-; Univ & Departmental Fellowships at Northwestern Univ; Robert A King Prize for Ger; Comprehensives Wabash Coll; Grant to Study Advanced Ger 1978; Bsktbl Coaches Awd 1985; *home:* 3845 Norwich Ct Bettendorf IA 52722

PITZER, DOLORES BARBER, English Teacher; *b:* Clifton Forge, VA; *c:* Stephanie D.; *ed:* (BA) Eng, VA St Univ 1971; *cr:* Eng Teacher Albert Harris Elem 1971-76, Alleghany HS 1976-; *ai:* Black Heritage Club Spon; Martinsville Ed Assn Secy 1972-73; VA Ed Assn, NEA 1971-; 1st Baptist Church Sr Usher Bd; Delta Sigma Theta; *office:* Alleghany HS Rt 2 Valley Ridge Covington VA 24426

PIZON, JEFF A., High School Biology Teacher; *b:* Cleveland, OH; *ed:* (BS) Biological Sci/General Sci, Miami Univ of OH 1974; Grad Stud; *cr:* 9th Grade Phys Sci Teacher 1976-81, HS Bio Teacher 1982- Geneva HS; *ai:* Girls Var Cross Cntry, Bsktbl, Track Coach; Geneva Area Teachers Assn, NE OH Ed Assn 1976-; Geneva Athletic Boosters 1976-; Tri Cty Newspapers All Ashtabula Cty Coach of Yr Girls Bsktbl 1985-86; *office:* Geneva Scndry Complex Sch 839 Sherman St Geneva OH 44041

PIZON, LAWRENCE JOHN, Social Studies Teacher; *b:* Cleveland, OH; *m:* Christine Marie Sedlak; *c:* John, Anthony, Michael, Thomas; *ed:* (BS) His/Ed, 1966, (MA) His, 1970 John Carroll Univ; Guidance Cnslr; Chemical Dependency Counseling; *cr:* Soc Worker Mt St Johns 1966; Teacher/Cnslr Padua Franciscan HS 1966-; *ai:* Hockey & Golf Coach; Admin Advisory Comm; Model United Nations Adv; Adult Ed Classes Parma Sr HS; ASCD, OH Cath Educators Assn; Coast Guard Auxiliary Staff Officer 1985-, Honorary Acad Admissions Officer 1987; Knights of Columbus Deputy Grand Knight 1970-, Knight of Month 1974; St Colette Parish Pres 1984-88; Parish Religious Ed Dir 1984-; Golf Coach of Yr 1985-87; Hockey Coach of Yr 1984-85; Teacher of Yr 1986; *office:* Padua Franciscan HS 6740 State Rd Parma OH 44134

PIZZOLATO, AGNES NEWCHURCH, 8th Grade Teacher; *b:* Donaldsonville, LA; *m:* Jimmie C.; *c:* Michelle R., Bradley J.; *ed:* (BA) Elem Ed, Nicholls St Univ 1969; Grad Stud Nicholls St Univ; *cr:* Teacher Donaldsonville Elem Sch 1968-70, West Ascension Elem Sch 1970-71, Ascension Cath Mid Sch 1979-88, Ascension Cath HS 1988-; *ai:* Eng Dept Chairperson; 4-H Club Moderator; Faculty Advisory, Textbook Review, Religious Ed Comm; Jr Beta Club Co-Spon; Church & School Choir; Capital Area Rdng Cncl 1981-; Ascension Cath Mothers Club Secy 1983-86, Mother of Yr 1990; Ascension Cath Band Boosters VP 1989-; Nom Miriam Farrell Awd Teacher of Yr 1987; *office:* Ascension Catholic HS 311 St Vincent St Donaldsonville LA 70346

PJURA, MARY MADONNA, 1st Grade Teacher; *b:* Bridgeport, CT; *ed:* Certificate Ed/Teacher Trng, Notre Dame Trng Sch 1953; (BS) Ed, Notre Dame of MD 1960; Ed, Manhatten Coll 1965; Ed, Villanova Univ 1966; (MA) Ed, Fairfield Univ 1971; *cr:* Kndgtn Teacher St Michael Sch 1951-54; Kndgtn/2nd Grade Teacher St Ambrose Sch 1954-61; 3rd/4th Grade Teacher St Vincent Orphanage 1961-65; 6th Grade Teacher St Joseph Sch Manhatten NY 1965-67; 1st/2nd Grade Teacher St Joseph Sch Bridgeport CT 1967-70; 1st Grade Teacher St Mary Sch 1970-; *ai:* Took Children to Nursing Homes to Visit, Help, Entertain; Helped with Phys Therapy; SSND Proffessed Sister 1951; NCEA 1960-; Bethel Historical Singers; St Mary Ladies Guild 1970-; St Mary (Liturgical Comm, Pastoral Care); *office:* St Mary Sch 24 Dodgingtown Rd Bethel CT 06801

PLACE, ROSE ELLA (MC COY), 6-8th Grade Lang Arts Teacher; *b:* Gatesville, TX; *m:* Dwain; *c:* Allen; *ed:* (BBA) Bus Ed, Baylor Univ 1951; Lang Arts Univ of TX; Baylor; Univ of NM; Philosophy TX Tech Univ; 120 Hrs Advanced Acad Trng; *cr:* Bus Teacher Gatesville HS 1953-56; Grad Asst Baylor Univ 1956; Bus Teacher Andrews HS 1957-59; 7th Grade La Teacher Hobbs 1959-60; Nichols Jr HS 1960-65; 6th Grade Rdng Teacher

Gatesville Jr HS 1965-78; 6th/7th/8th Grade La Teacher Rice Mid Sch 1978-; *ai:* Chrldr Spon; Annual Staff Spon; Schl Newspaper Spon; Stu Cncl Spon; Spelling Bee Coach; TSTA Bldg Rep 1985-; NEA; TSTA Navarro Cty Local Unit; Lioness Club Treas 1984-86; Navarro Rgnl Hosp Aux; Womens Club Corsicana; 1st Bapt Church Dir Choir Retarded Citizens; *home:* Box 2324 Corsicana TX 75151

PLACHETKA, BETH BENJAMIN, 6th-8th Grade Lang Art Teacher; *b:* Aurora, IL; *m:* Richard J.; *c:* Pamela, Kristin, Michael; *ed:* (BS) Elem Ed, Aurora Coll 1976; *cr:* 4th/5th Grade Soc Stud Teacher 1976-77, 4th/5th Grade Math Teacher 1977-79, 6th-8th Grade Soc Stud Teacher 1980-81, 4th Grade Math Teacher 1982-85, 6th/8th Grade Lang Art Teacher 1985- Our Lady of Good Counsel; *home:* 612 Marie Ave Yorkville IL 60560

PLALE, NEAL ANTHONY, Religion Teacher; *b:* Milwaukee, WI; *ed:* (BA) Theology, St Josephs Coll 1974; *cr:* Chairperson Religion Dept 1983-89, Religion Teacher 1977- St Lawrence Seminary; *ai:* Bus Mgr St Lawrence Friary; Bookstore Mgr St Lawrence Seminary Sch Store; Study Hall Prefect; Spiritual Dir; *office:* St Lawrence Seminary 301 Church St Mount Calvary WI 53057

PLANER, MARILYN STAUFFER, English Department Chair; *b:* Humboldt, NE; *m:* Clarence F. Jr.; *c:* Todd C., Angela L.; *ed:* (BA) Eng, Doane Coll 1963; (MED) Eng Ed, Univ of NE 1970; Grad Stud Drake Univ; *cr:* Eng Teacher Pierce Sr HS 1963-65, Beatrice Sr HS 1965-70; Eng/Dept Chairperson Newton IA 1974-; Des Moines Area Comm Coll 1985-; *ai:* Scarlet Letter Adv; Mentor Teacher; NEA 1963-; NCTE, IA St Teachers of Eng; Published Pamphlet for Univ of NE Stud Series; *office:* Newton Sr HS E 4th St S Newton IA 50208

PLANK, MARY CATHERINE, 3rd Grade Teacher; *ed:* (BS) Elem/Early Chldhd, Edinboro St Coll PA 1975; Addl Stud Ed, PA St Univ, Carlow Coll; *cr:* K-6th Grade Substitute Teacher Hempfield Sch Dist 1975-77, Norwin Sch Dist 1975-77; 3rd/4th Grade Teacher Holy Family Sch 1977-79; 3rd Grade Teacher Immaculate Conception Sch 1979-; *ai:* Focus Staff Parish Newsletter Mem; Sch Survey Chairperson; Public Relations Comm Mem; Eucharistic Minister 1985-87; Parent Teachers Guild Teacher Rep 1988-; NCEA; Norwin Art League 1985-86; Westmoreland Cty Literacy Cncl Sr Tutor 1983-84; Outstanding Young Women of America 1987.

PLANT, SANDRA DALE, Fourth Grade Teacher; *b:* Floresville, TX; *c:* Christina Mikeska, James, Leslie; *ed:* (BS) Elem Ed, Mary Hardin-Baylor Univ 1976; Grad Study Ed Admin, Univ of TX San Antonio; Operation Excl Instructional Leadership Trng Prgm, Killeen Ind Sch Dist; *cr:* Teacher Killeen Ind Sch Dist 1976-78, Brenham Ind Sch Dist 1978-81, Killeen Ind Sch Dist 1981-83, San Antonio Ind Sch Dist 1983-; *ai:* Sci Fair, Black Heritage Celebration Comm; Fine Art Festival Coord; Castle Hills 1st Baptist Church Sunday Sch Teacher 1987-; *office:* San Antonio Ind Sch Dist 141 Lavaca San Antonio TX 78210

PLANTE, MARYELLEN CHILDS, 2nd Grade Teacher; *m:* Richard; *c:* Christopher, Stephanie Tuttle, Cathie; *ed:* (BS) Elem Ed, Plymouth St Coll 1971; Water Safety Instr Course, Amer Red Cross; Dynamics of Activity Centered Learning Course, NH Tech Inst; *cr:* 2nd-4th Grade Teacher Strafford Sch 1971-; *ai:* SAU 44 Comm Staff Dev Rep, Cmptr Coord, Secy; Pittsfield Recreation Dir of Pools 1989-; *office:* Strafford Sch HC 71 Box 113 Center Strafford NH 03815

PLANTZ, JAN BERG, 6th Grade Teacher; *b:* Dell Rapids, SD; *m:* Dean; *c:* Tad; *ed:* (BS) Elem Ed, Augustana Coll 1961; *cr:* 6th Grade Teacher Marshall Public Schls 1961-65; 5th Grade Teacher Fairmont Ind Schls 1965-68; 6th Grade Teacher Ankeny Comm Schls 1968-; *ai:* Co-Spon of All Nations Festival & Sci Fair; Mem Outreach Comm; NEA 1961-; Ankeny Ed Assn 1968-; IA Ed Assn 1968-; Holy Trinity Lutheran Church Evangelism Bd 1989; Ankeny Booster Club 1989-; Candidate for Teacher of Yr 1990; *home:* 325 Se 10th Ankeny IA 50021

PLAPPERT, WILLIAM F., Mathematics Teacher; *b:* Pottsville, PA; *m:* Karen Ann Solt; *c:* William Jr., Michael; *ed:* (BS) Math, Mt St Marys Coll 1968; Grad Stud Penn St; *cr:* Math Teacher Northeastern Mid Sch 1968-; *ai:* Teacher-Stu Advisory Prgm Comm; Cmptr Club; NE Ed Assn, PSEA, NEA; BSA Dover Troop 67 Comm Treas 1988-; Parish Relations Comm (Paster, Vice-Chm); *office:* Northeastern Mid Sch Hartman St Manchester PA 17345

PLASKEY, THERESA MRUGALA, Retired Teacher; *b:* Barnesboro, PA; *w:* Charles W. (dec); *c:* Charles, Christopher; *ed:* (BS) Dietetics, Villamaria Coll 1949; (BS) Ed, OH Northern Univ 1964; (MS) Counseling, Univ of Dayton 1973; *cr:* Teacher Lima City Public Schls 1964-86; *ai:* Volunteer Tutor to Disturbed Adolescents; Cmmty Latchkey Prgm; Lima Breakfast Optimist Intnl Ed Awd; Univ of Dayton Service Awd.

PLATIS, MARGARET F., English Department Chair; *b:* Los Angeles, CA; *ed:* (BA) Eng, 1981, (MA) Eng/Amer Lit, 1984 Loyola Marymount Univ; *cr:* Instr Loyola Marymount Univ 1983-84; Teaching Asst Univ of CA Davis 1984-85; Teacher St Francis HS 1985-86, St Monica Cath HS 1986-; *ai:* Jr Homeroom Teacher, Rdng Club Moderator; NCTE, CA Assn Teachers of Eng; *office:* St Monica Catholic HS 1030 Lincoln Blvd Santa Monica CA 90403

PLATT, WILLIAM G., Science Teacher; *b:* Pomona, CA; *m:* Lori; *c:* Jeremiah, Cy, Ben, Boone, Gilly; *ed:* (BA) Bio, Humboldt St 1972; *cr:* Teacher Ukiah Unified Schls 1975-; *ai:* Dept Chm; Mentor Teacher; *office:* Redwood Valley Mid Sch 700 School Way Redwood Valley CA 95470

PLATTI, RITA JANE STRANGLO, 7th Grade Math Teacher; *b:* Stockton, CA; *m:* Elvin C.; *c:* Kimberly Horner; *ed:* Math/Humanities, Dominican Coll 1943-45; (BA) Math 1947, (Gen Sec Credential) Math, 1949 Univ of Pacific; Math/Lit San Jose St 1947-52; Math San Jose St 1968; *cr:* Farmer Escalon CA 1943-; Math Teacher St Marys HS 1947-54; Chemical Analyst Escalon Winery 1949; Draftsman 1950-52; Private Practice Draftsman Stockton 1952-66;7th Grade Teacher Montezuma 1956-57; 3rd-4th Grade Teacher Davis Elem 1957-58; Rental Bus 1958-81; Math Teacher Amos Alonzo Stage HS 1961-80, Humphreys Coll 1981-83, Hamilton Jr HS 1984-; CA Real Estate Agent 1979-; *ai:* Avocations; Inventions, Math Theory/Poetry/Piano, Roman Cath, Democrat; Latest Interest Environmental Clean-up; Stockton Teachers Assn Mem 1956-; CA Teacher Assn Mem 1956-; NEA Mem 1956-; Author Math Proficiency Plateaus Published 1979; *office:* Hamilton Mid Sch 2245 E 11th St Stockton CA 95206

PLEASANT, ELIZABETH HOFFMAN, 5th Grade Teacher; *b:* Burlington, NC; *m:* Thomas Burns; *c:* Clyde A. Denny, Margaret E. Denny Boyer; *ed:* (BA) Ed/Music, Elon Coll 1952; (MED) Ed/Mid Sch, Duke Univ 1962; Grad Stud Univ of NC Greensboro., Univ of NC Chapeil Hill, Guilford Coll; *cr:* Teacher Alexander Wilson Elem Sch 1952-55, Elon Public Sch 1956-59, Alexander Wilson 1960-62, 1968; *ai:* NEA; NCAE; Delta Kappa Gamma; Phi Delta Kappa 1976-; Burlington Music Club VP; *home:* Rt 11 Box 578 Burlington NC 27215

PLEGER, CAROLYN J., Third Grade Teacher; *b:* Port Huron, MI; *ed:* (BS) Elem Ed, E MI Univ 1968; *cr:* 1st-5th Grade Teacher Seminole Elem 1968-; *ai:* Math Curr Comm; MEA, NEA 1968-; Seminole Sch PTA (Teacher, VP) 1975-77; *office:* Seminole Elem Sch 1500 Mulberry Mount Clemens MI 48043

PLESHA, JOHN F., Industrial Arts Teacher; *b:* Cle Elum, WA; *m:* Judith A.; *c:* Jared R.; *ed:* (BA) Geog, Central WA St Coll 1967; *cr:* 5th Grade Teacher Washington Elem 1967-68; 6th Grade Teacher Parker Heights Elem 1968-69; 7th-9th Grade Teacher Wapato Jr HS 1969-81; 6th-8th Grade Teacher Wapato Mid Sch 1981-; *ai:* Traffic Safety Ed Instr; Safety Comm Adv; Sch Store Mgr; WEA Local 1967-; WEA St 1967-; NEA Life Mem 1967-; Eagle Foe Mem 1971-; *office:* Wapato Mid Sch P O Box 38 Wapato WA 98951

PLESS, NANCY ELIZABETH (ARTMANN), Business Teacher; *b:* Milwaukee, WI; *m:* Tony; *ed:* (BSE) Bus Ed, Univ of WI Whitewater 1984; *cr:* Bus Teacher Wilmot Union HS 1984-85, Cath Memorial HS 1985-; *ai:* Pom Pon Adv; WI Bus Ed Assn 1984-; *office:* Cath Memorial HS 601 E College Ave Waukesha WI 53186

PLETIKAPICH, PENNY CALLAS, 6th Grade Teacher; *b:* Akron, OH; *m:* Joseph P.; *ed:* (BS) Elem Ed/Sci, Univ of Akron; Elem Ed, Univ of Akron; *cr:* 1st Grade Teacher 1978-79; 2nd/3rd Split Grade Teacher 1979-81; 3rd Grade Teacher 1981-84; 5th Grade Teacher 1984-85; 6th Grade Teacher 1985- King Elem Sch; *ai:* Safety Patrol Supv; Intnl Rdng Assn 1989-; Akron ED Assn 1978-; PTA Teacher of Yr Nom 1988-89 School Year; Recipient Awd By Supt 1988; *office:* King Elem Sch 805 Memorial Pkwy Akron OH 44303

PLETZ, MEREDITH ANNE GILMOUR, 6th Grade Teacher; *b:* Queens, NY; *m:* George Henry; *c:* Jocelyn; *ed:* (BA) Elem Ed, St Univ Oneonta 1967; (MA) Liberal Stud, St Univ Stony Brook 1972; Ed, St Univ Stony Brook; *cr:* 5th Grade Teacher Fort Salonga Elem Sch 1968-70; 6th Grade Teacher Fort Salonga Elem & W T Rogers Mid Sch 1970-; *ai:* Soc Stud Curr Comm; LI Assn Soc Stud Teachers Mem 1989-; Amer Assn of Univ Women Co-Pres 1989-; *home:* 194 Northern Blvd Saint James NY 11780

PLEXICO, HELEN MOORE, Mathematics Teacher; *b:* Summerville, SC; *m:* John O.; *c:* Brian, Jennifer, Amy, Susan; *ed:* (BS) Math, Presbyn Coll 1969; *cr:* Teacher Cross Keys HS 1969-71; Professor Midlands Tech Coll 1971-79; Teacher Allendale Mid Sch 1980-81, Du Bose Mid SC 1985-; *ai:* Just Say No Club Spon; *home:* 107 Pheasant Ln Summerville SC 29485

PLEXICO, PAMELA ARDEN, 6th Grade Language Art Teacher; *b:* Ft Campbell, KY; *m:* Kevin Le Roy; *c:* Ashley L., Bradley K.; *ed:* (BA) Elem Ed, Univ of SC 1979; *cr:* 6th Grade Lang Arts Teacher Beck Mid Sch 1983-; *ai:* Chairperson SACS; Intnl Rdng Assn 1988-; Teacher of Yr 1988-89; *office:* Beck Mid Sch 2018 Church St Georgetown SC 29440

PLIHALL, MICHELE REARDON, Sixth Grade Teacher; *b:* Fremont, OH; *m:* David; *ed:* (BA) Elem Ed, Bowling Green St Univ 1981; *cr:* Jr HS Soc Stud Teacher 1982-86, 6th Grade Math Teacher 1986- St Joseph Elem Sch; *ai:* 5th/6th Grade Quiz Bowl & 6th Grade Safety Patrol Adv; NCEA; *home:* 1645 Arrowhead Dr Fremont OH 43420

PLOURDE, MARTIN JOSEPH, Counselor; *b:* Inglewood, CA; *m:* Tracy Le Sassier; *c:* Ryan J., Matthew J.; *ed:* (BA) Comm Art, 1983, (MA) Counseling/Guidance, 1986 Loyola Marymount Univ; Univ of CA Riverside; *cr:* Teacher/Bsktbl Coach Junipero Serra HS 1982-86; Eng Teacher 1986-88, Cslr 1988- Paramount HS; *ai:* Coll Club Adv; ASCD, Assn of CA Sch Admin 1990; Families Sharing Happiness 1989-; Pre-Marriage Counseling 1989-; *office:* Paramount HS 14429 S Downey Ave Paramount CA 90723

PLUFF, DARREL A., Information Processing Instr; *b:* Baileys Harbor, WI; *m:* Patricia Gail Wood; *ed:* (AA) Accounting, Bakersfield Coll 1965; (BSC) Office Management, San Diego St Univ 1968; *cr:* Bus Ed Teacher Hiallam HS 1973-83; Instr Ashtabula Cty Joint Voc Sch 1983-; *ai:* Club & Regional Adv; Ashtabula Cty Joint Voc Sch Schlsp Comm; NBEA, OH Bus Teachers Assn 1984-; Victoria Commercial Teachers Assn 1974-83; Bus Prof of America; Heritage Hills Condo Assn Secy 1985-87; *office:* Ashtabula Cty Joint Voc Sch 1565 Rt 167 Jefferson OH 44047

PLUMMER, HELEN HOLBROOK, American History Teacher; *b:* Nacogdoches, TX; *m:* Edwin E.; *c:* Edwin E. Jr., Peggy Billingsley, Judy Chalk, Amy Covington; *ed:* (BS) His/Government, 1952, (MED) His/Government/Elem Ed, 1957 Stephen F Austin Univ; Advanced Academic Trng, Baylor Univ; Reg 12 Service Center, Stephen F Austin Univ; *cr:* Elem Teacher Dickinson Ind Sch Dist 1953-60; HS His Teacher Groesbeck Ind Sch Dist 1961-64; Elem Teacher Limestone Cty Schls 1964-65; Elem Teacher 1965-88, HS His Teacher 1988- Mexia Ind Sch Dist; *ai:* Jr Class Spon; ATPE Secy 1979, Nom St Teacher of Yr 1979; Womans Friday Club Secy 1988-; Gen Fed of Womens Club Pres Elect 1990; Sunday Sch Teacher 1989-; Delta Kappa Gamma Pres 1965-66; *home:* PO Box 501 Mexia TX 76667

PLUMMER, KATHI CAREINS, Health Occupations Teacher; *b:* Hartford City, IN; *m:* Robert Jay; *c:* R. Jay, Kara; *ed:* Diploma Nursing, Parkview Meth Sch of Nursing 1972; (BS) Health Occupations, IN Univ 1984; *cr:* Staff Nurse Ball Memorial Hospital 1972-74, Marion General Hospital 1974; Educl Services Instr Marion General Hospital 1974-80; Ed Instr Wells Cmmty Hospital 1982-85; Teacher Bluffton HS 1985-; *ai:* Health Occupations Assn; Kappa Kappa Kappa Pres 1989; *office:* Bluffton HS 428 S Oak St Bluffton IN 46714

PLUMMER, LISA GRAVES, HS Home Economics Teacher; *b:* Ashland, KY; *m:* Samuel Allen; *c:* Sara Graves; *ed:* (BS) Home Ec, Berea Coll 1982; (MS) Voc Home Ec, Morehead St Univ 1983; *cr:* Home Ec Teaching Assistantship E KY Univ 1982; Home Ec Research Assistantship Morehead St Univ 1983; Home Ec Teacher E Carter Cty HS 1983-; *ai:* Project Graduation Comm Chm; KY Assn Voc Home Ec Teachers; Incentive Grant 1987-88; *office:* East Carter Cty HS Hitchins Rd Grayson KY 41143

PLUMMER, MARSHA ANDERSON, Fifth Grade Teacher; *b:* Las Vegas, NV; *m:* Danny Eugene; *c:* Christopher M.; *ed:* (BS) Elem Ed, Winthrop Coll 1972; Univ of SC; *cr:* 5th Grade Teacher Denny Terrace Sch 1973-88, William S Sandel Sch 1988-; *ai:* Stu Cncl Spon; Chm of Soc Stud & Fire Prevention Comm; NEA 1973-80; SC Ed Assn 1973-80; Richland Ed Assn Sch Rep 1974-76; Columbia Area Rdng Cncl 1988-; Alpha Delta Kappa Pi Chapter (Pres Elect 1986-88, Pres 1988-) 1985-; Denny Terrace Teacher of Yr; Teacher Evaluation Comm for Richland Dist I; Soc Stud Curr Comm for Richland Dist I; Project Hands on for St Dept; *office:* William S Sandel Sch 2700 Seminole Rd Columbia SC 29210

PLUMMER, MARTHA W., 6th Grade Teacher; *b:* Ironton, OH; *m:* James A.; *c:* James, John, Tom; *ed:* (BS) Ed, OH Univ 1966; *cr:* Kdngtn Teacher Wellston OH 1963-69; 2nd Grade Teacher 1969-71, 6th Grade Teacher 1971- Jackson City Sch; *ai:* OEA Delegate; NEA; *home:* 209 Redondo Dr Jackson OH 45640

PLUTA, MARIA E., Physics Teacher; *b:* Frankfurt, West Germany; *ed:* (BS) Physics, 1970, (MS) 1972 De Paul Univ; Fermilab Summer Inst for Sci Teachers; PSSC Physics Wkshp-Boston Univ; Woodrow Wilson Natl Fellowship Fnd Master Teacher Inst in HS Physics; *cr:* 5th/8th Grade Teacher Math St Andrews Sch 1972-74; Sci Teacher Bolingbrook HS 1974-78; Physics Instr Coll of Du Page 1974-85; Physics Teacher Rich Cntrl HS 1978-; *ai:* Physics Club; Sica Sci Rep; Olympian Scholars Prgm Comm Mem; AAPT/NSTA HS Physics Achievement Test Writing Comm; Sica Sci Secy/Treas 1981-83; Chicago-Amer Assn of Physics Teachers (VP 1983-84/Pres 1984-85); AAPT; Distinguished Olympian Awd 1989; Certificate Of Recognition For Encouraging & Motivating Minority Stus to Pursue Careers in Engineering/Healthg Professions; IIT-CAHMCP 1986; *office:* Rich Central H S 3600 W 203rd St Olympia Fields IL 60461

PLYLER, DARLENE J., Mathematics Teacher; *b:* Meadville, PA; *ed:* (BSED) Math, IN Univ of PA 1985; Working Towards Masters Math, IN Univ of PA; *cr:* Scndry Math Teacher United Jr Sr HS 1985-; *ai:* Jr Class, Var & Jr Var CHeerleading Adv; Gymnastics Coach; Ski Club Chaperone; NCTM 1985-87; PA Cncl Teachers of Math 1985-87; Alpha Delta Pi VP of Pledge Ed 1981-; Selected to Participate in Natl Sci Fnd Project Excels Trng to Use Cmptrs to Teach Math; *office:* United HS P O Box 168 Armagh PA 15920

PLYLER, MILLIE MC ELWEE, Business Teacher; *b:* Rock Hill, SC; *m:* Tony Elwyn; *ed:* (BS) Bus Admin, 1974, (MAT) Bus Ed, 1977 Winthrop Coll; *cr:* Bus Teacher Lancaster Cty Voc Sch 1976-77, Andrew Jackson HS 1977-; *ai:* FBLA Adv; Sr Class Spon; NBEA, SC Office Ed Assn 1977-; Palmetto St Teachers Assn 1988-; *home:* PO Box 98 Liberty Hill SC 29074

PLYLER, NANNIE WILLIAMS, Retired 4th Grade Teacher; *b:* Kershaw, SC; *m:* William E. Sr.; *c:* William E. Jr., John W., Gary C.; *ed:* (BA) His, Columbia Coll 1945; Univ SC; *cr:* 5th Grade Teacher Heath Springs Sch 1945-49, St Andrews Sch 1949-50, Baron DeKalb Sch 1950-52; 4th Grade Teacher Flat Creek Elem 1955-86; *ai:* SC Ed Assn; Lancaster Cty Ed Assn; NEA; PTO 1975-86 Teacher of Yr 1985-86; *home:* RFD 3 Box 10-A Kershaw SC 29067

PLYLER, PEGGY BREWSTER, 4th Grade Teacher; *b:* Pittsburgh, PA; *m:* Henry E.; *c:* Scott, Michael; *ed:* (BS) Elem Ed, 1965, (MS) Elem Ed, 1968 Clarion Univ; *cr:* Teacher Brookville Area Sch System 1966-; *ai:* Chairperson Annual Sch Fair; Dir 4th Grade Prgm; Alpha Delta Kappa (VP 1984-86, Pres 1986-88); *home:* 101 5th Brookville PA 15825

PLYLER, ROBERT W., Social Studies/English Teacher; *b:* Butler, PA; *m:* E. Anne Davis; *c:* Christian R., Garth O., Laura A.; *ed:* (BA) His, 1970, (MA) Lit/Ed, 1971 Allegheny Coll; Univ of Durham England, St Univ of NY Fredonia; *cr:* 7th/9th Grade Soc Stud Teacher Cleveland Public Schls 1970-71; 10th/12th Grade Soc Stud/Eng Teacher Bemus Point Cntrl Sch 1971-; Government/His/Lit Teacher Mercyhurst Coll 1985-; His Instr Jamestown Comm Coll 1990; *ai:* Honors Comm; Bemus Point Faculty Assn Pres 1971-, 1977; NY Cncl for Soc Stud 1981-; Jamestown Concert Assn Pres 1985-, Outstanding Service to Arts 1987; Cty Arts Fund Funding Panel 1984-87; St Lukes Episcopal Church Lay Reader 1987-; Outstanding Young Men of America 1983; Outstanding Teacher by Rochester Inst of Technology; Delegate to Chautauga Town Meeting Riga Latvia 1986; Art Critic 1981-; Magazine Reviewer 1984-; Fellowship to Macedonian Conference Columbia Univ 1989; *office:* Maple Grove HS Dutch Hollow Rd Bemus Point NY 14712

POAG, LOIS M., Kindergarten Teacher; *b:* Cadillac, MI; *m:* Lyle; *c:* Holly M., Christopher C.; *ed:* (BA) Elem Ed, Cntrl MI Univ 1956; (MA) Spec Ed, MI St Univ 1967; *cr:* Kndgtn Teacher Royal Oak MI 1956-59, Valderes WI 1959-62, E Jordan MO 1962-63, Warren MI 1963-64; Spec Ed Mentally Impaired Ferndale 1964-68; Kndgtn Teacher/Spec Ed Cadillac MI 1968-; *ai:* Wexford Cty Planning & Zoning Bd & Bd of Appeals Mem; Lake Mitchell Improvement Bd Chairperson; Alpha Delta Kappa 1980-.

POCH, LISA MARIE, School Social Worker; *b:* Fond Du Lac, WI; *m:* Larry Stephens; *ed:* (MSSW) Soc Work, Univ of WI Madison 1986; (BSSW) Soc Work, Univ of WI Oshkosh 1983; Grad Trng in Family Therapy; Alcohol & Drug Abuse Trng Prgm; *cr:* Cnslr Luth Soc Services 1983-85, Univ of Madison Counseling Service 1985-86; Therapist Luth Soc Services 1986-87; Sch Soc Worker WI Heights Sch Dist 1987-; *ai:* Peer Helpers, SADD Adv; Natl Assn of Soc Workers 1982-; Sch Soc Workers Assn 1987-; WI Peer Helpers Assn Steering Comm 1987-; Big Brothers/Sisters Volunteer 1984-89; Homeless Shelter Volunteer 1985-89.

PODCZASKI, CATHERINE ANN, Director of Religious Ed; *b:* Wilkes-Barre, PA; *ed:* (BS) Elem Ed, 1983, (MS) Religious Ed, 1989 Marywood; Sacramental Preparation, Liturgy, Spirituality of Children & Adults Development, Marywood Coll & Religious Ed Inst Diocese of Scranton; *cr:* Elem/Jr HS Religion/Math/Eng Teacher Boston, Hartford, Allentown 1974-88; 8th Grade Religion/Math Teacher Holy Child Sch 1986-88; Pastoral Assoc/Dir of Religions Ed Holy Rosary Church 1988-; *ai:* Head of Parish Group; Scripture Class, Adult Religious Ed Teacher; Parish Music Ministry Choir & Folk Group Mem; Train Parish Lectors; Coord Childrens Liturgies; *office:* Holy Rosary Church 240 S Poplar St Hazleton PA 18201

PODHAISKY, PATRICIA JEAN, Spanish/Theology Teacher; *b:* Alliance, NE; *ed:* (BA) Span/Religious Stud, Regis Coll 1986; *cr:* Span Teacher 1987-, Theology Teacher/Dept Head 1987- Red Cloud HS; *ai:* Var Vlybl Coach; SD Vlybl Coaches Assn 1988-; *office:* Red Cloud HS Holy Rosary Mission Pine Ridge SD 57770

POE, CINDY MULLEN, Principal; *b:* Lincolnton, NC; *m:* Ronald Henry; *ed:* (BS) Elem Ed, 1976, (MA) Early Chldhd Ed, 1978, (EDS) Admin, 1982 Appalachian St Univ; Prin Executive Prgm 1986; Univ of NC Institute of Government; *cr:* Kndgtn/3rd Grade Teacher 1976-83; Prin Iron Station Sch 1983-87, Love Memorial Sch 1987-; *ai:* Lincoln Cty Prin Assn (Secy) 1983-; NC Prin/Asst Prin Assn 1989-; NC Assn of Educators 1976-; 1st Presbyn Church 1954-; Appalachian St Univ Alumni Cncl (Secy/VP) 1986-; *office:* Love Memorial Sch Rt 6 Box 367 Lincolnton NC 28092

POECK, GARY OVID, Mathematics Teacher; *b:* San Antonio, TX; *m:* Katherine Reininger; *c:* Laura, Lisa, Eric, Leslie; *ed:* (BSED) Math, SW TX St Univ 1978; *cr:* Math Teacher New Braunfels HS 1979-; *ai:* Stu Cncl & Unicorn Handlers Spon; Team Management Comm; ATPE 1979-; Adult Sftbl League Bd 1976-; Boys Little League 1989-; Eisenhower Grant Math & Sci; *office:* New Braunfels HS 2551 Loop 337 N New Braunfels TX 78130

POERTNER, LARRY PAUL, Math Dept Chair & Teacher; *b:* Traverse City, MI; *ed:* (BS) Math, 1971, (MS) Jr HS Curr, 1977 Eastern MI Univ; *cr:* Teacher Grass Lake Cmmty Schls 1971-; *ai:* MI Cncl of Teachers of Math; NCTM; Started Academic Letter Awd for HS; Started Ski Club for Jr/Sr HS; *home:* 215 Simpson Box 492 Grass Lake MI 49240

POFFENBARGER, JUDITH WATKINS, English Teacher; *b:* Lubbock, TX; *m:* Gary C.; *c:* David, Christina, Paul; *ed:* (BA) Eng, TX Tech Univ 1969; (MA) Eng, Univ of TX Austin 1971; *cr:* Eng Teacher Edna HS 1977-78, Monterey HS 1983-; *ai:* UIL Spelling Spon; Assn of TX Prof Educators 1983-; First United Meth Church (Chancel Choir, Soloist) 1983-; Various Curr Writing Assignments; LISD Inservice Trng Presenter, Soprano Soloist 1989; *home:* 4519 21st St Lubbock TX 79407

POGUE, MARY A., English Teacher; *b:* Fond-du-lac, WI; *m:* B. Lee; *c:* Matthew, Emily; *ed:* (BS) Eng/Psych, Univ of WI 1971; (MS) Guidance/Counseling, Univ of WI 1976; Cmptr Trng; Drug & Alcohol Stu Assistance Prgm Trng; Cooperative Learning; *cr:* 11th Grade Teacher Eng/Intern Oshkosh West HS 1970-71; 7th & 9th Grade Teacher Neenah Jr Sch Dist 1972-; 7th & 8th Grade Teacher Eng Horace Mann Jr HS 1972-81; 7th & 9th Grade Teacher Eng Shattuck Jr HS 1981-; *ai:* K-12 Lang Arts Comm Dist Dept Rep Neenah Ed Assn; NCTE; NEA; St Peters Congregation CCD Teacher 1989-; Adm Premarriage Inventory & Interpret to Engaged Couples 1990; *office:* Shattuck Jr H S 600 Elm St Neenah WI 54956

POHLMAN, LARRY LYNN, Band Director; *b:* Worthington, MN; *m:* Caroline Smith; *c:* Gretchen L., Gregory P.; *ed:* (BME) Music Ed, Morningside Coll 1969; (MA) Music Ed, NE MO St Univ 1972; *cr:* Band Dir Lebanon R-3 Sch Dist 1972-76, Warrensburg R-6 Sch Dist 1976-78; Band/Orch Dir Springfield R-12 Sch Dist 1978-80; Band Dir Lincoln Cty R-3 Sch Dist 1980-; *ai:* MO Bandmasters Assn Pres 1977-78; Music Educators Natl Conference, IAJE; Kiwanis Club of Troy Pres 1986-87, Distinguished Club Pres 1987; *office:* Buchanan HS 711 W College Troy MO 63379

POINDEXTER, JAMES E., Science Teacher; *b:* Ecorse, MI; *m:* Marjorie Bremer; *c:* Steven, David; *ed:* (BS) Sci/Bio, Alma Coll 1963; (MA) Sci Ed, E MI Univ 1969; *cr:* 7th Grade Sci Teacher Slocum-Truax Mid Sch 1963-80, Monguagon Mid Sch 1980-; *ai:* Stu Activity Chaperone; Swim Team Scorer; Curr Steering & Sci Curr Improvement Comm; Loyal Order of Moose 1986-; *home:* 22412 Hillcrest Dr Woodhaven MI 48183

POKORNY, SUSAN MEDHURST, 4th Grade Teacher; *b:* Galesburg, IL; *m:* Joseph J.; *c:* Maggie, Heidi, Patrick; *ed:* (BS) Ed, IL St Univ 1975. 1986; Gifted Ed Certificate; *cr:* Lang Art Teacher Havana Jr HS 1975-79; 4th Grade Teacher Havana New Cntrl 1980-; *ai:* Teaching Gifted Prgm; Red Tassel Mortar Bd 1975-; AFT, IFT Treas 1981; Town & Cntry Womens Club 1986-; Beta Sigma Phi Treas 1987-; *office:* Havana New Cntrl Elem Sch 215 N Pearl Havana IL 62644

POKORSKI, CLAIRE NEMEC, Sci Dept Teacher/Chairperson; *b:* Cleveland, OH; *m:* Conrad; *c:* Sharon, Kathleen Dombrowski, Constance Madej, Carolyn Mallinger; *ed:* (BS) Chem, Ursuline Coll 1956; Grad Courses John Carroll Univ, San Diego St Univ, FL Inst of Technology, Akron Univ; *cr:* Math Teacher Charles Eliot Jr HS 1956-58; Math/Sci Teacher 1966-72, Asst Prin 1972-75, Sci Chairperson/Chem/Physics Teacher 1976- Trinity HS; *ai:* SADD Moderator; Ecology Club; Pro-Life Group; NHS Faculty Cncl; NSTA, NEA, OH Ed Assn; Natl Sci Fnd Grant 1972; *office:* Trinity H S 12425 Granger Rd Garfield Heights OH 44125

POLAND, MARY NELL, Language Arts Teacher; *b:* Maplesville, AL; *m:* Harold; *c:* Douglas, James, Nelda P. Huddleston, Clarice; *ed:* (BS) Eng, Jacksonville Univ 1961; Various Courses, Univs; *cr:* Eng Teacher Childersburg HS 1961-63, Cook HS 1976-77; Teacher of Gifted/Eng/Art Long Cty HS 1977-; *ai:* Debate, Oral Intrepretation, Music, Essay, Beta Spon; NEA Membership Chairperson 1986-88; GAE, LAE; Garden Club Secy 1989-; Jones Creek Church Asst Pianist 1977-; STAR Teacher 1981, 1984; Made GED Video Adult Ed Univ of GA 1984; *home:* Rt 2 Box 47 Ludowici GA 31316

POLASKEY, JOAN CULLITAN, Principal; *b:* Chicago, IL; *m:* Frank C. Jr.; *c:* Frank J., Kevin M., Keith P.; *ed:* (BS) His/Eng, W MI Univ 1974; Elem Ed; Currently Working on Masters in Educl Leadership; *cr:* 3rd Grade Teacher St Joseph Cath 1975-79; 6th Grade Teacher Watervliet Public Sch 1979-81, St Joseph Cath 1981-89; Teacher of HS Completion N Berrien Comm Ed 1983-88; Prin St Joseph Cath 1989-; *ai:* Athletic & Curr Dir; Sch Newspaper, Parent Newsletter, Weekly Parish Letter News Media Contact Person; Sch Event Photographer; MI Rdng Assn 1979-; MI Assn of Non-Public Sch 1981-; Cncl for Exceptional Children Golden Nugget Awd 1984; Kalamazoo Diocesan Teacher of Yr 1987; Rdng-Recycling Classics Wkshp Presenter 1985-89; *home:* 3114 Friday Rd Coloma MI 49038

POLICASTRO, ELLEN (STANIK), German Teacher; *b:* Rochester, PA; *m:* Michael; *c:* Jacquelyn, John, Gina; *ed:* (BS) Ger Ed, Indiana Univ of PA 1977; (BS) Eng, Geneva Coll 1978; *cr:* Ger Teacher Center HS 1978-; *ai:* Ger Club & HS Steering Comm Spon; *office:* Center HS Baker Rd Ext Monaca PA 15061

POLIN, PATRICIA YOUNG, Spanish Teacher; *b:* Melville, NY; *m:* Robert D.; *c:* Kirsten Houghton, Alexander; *ed:* (BA) Span, 1970, (MS) Eng Second Lang, 1976 SUNY Albany; *cr:* Jr/Sr HS Span Teacher Kings Park Cntrl Schls 1971-; Adult Basic Ed Prgm ESL Teacher Mid Cty Sch Dist #11 1975-80; ESL Teacher Oxford Univ Intensive Sch of Eng 1985-89.

POLISENO, CAROL SEEL, Third Grade Teacher; *b:* Buffalo, NY; *m:* Raymond; *c:* Jonathan, Renee; *ed:* (BS) Elem Ed, 1972, (MS) Elem Ed, 1976 St Univ Coll Buffalo; *cr:* 1st Grade Teacher 1972-79, 2nd Grade Teacher 1981, 1st Grade Teacher 1981-89, 3rd Grade Teacher 1989- H O Brumsted Elem; *ai:* Holland Teachers Assn (Building Rep 1975-76) 1985-; GSA Troop Leader 1987-.

POLIVKA, JOHN B., History Teacher; *b:* Duquesne, PA; *m:* Arlene Jean Takacs; *ed:* (BA) His, 1959, (MED) Scndry Ed, 1969 Univ of Pittsburgh; Admin Certificate Duquesne Univ 1979; *cr:* General Sci Teacher Braddock Jr HS 1959-63; Bio Teacher 1963-65, US His Teacher 1965-67 Braddock Sr HS; US His Teacher Norwin Sr HS 1967-; *ai:* Soc Stud Dept Head; Norwin Teachers Federal Credit Union Treas 1986-; Nom PA Teacher of Yr; COE Fellowship St Univ of NY Stony Brook 1984; *home:* 14035 Easy St North Huntingdon PA 15642

POLK, SANDRA LEA, Third Grade Teacher; *b:* Indianapolis, IN; *m:* Irvin J.; *ed:* (BA) Elem Ed, 1961, (MS) Elem Ed, 1965 IN Univ; Management Systems for Teachers, Teacher Expectation Stu Achievement, Madeline Hunter Cooperative Learning; *cr:* 3rd Grade Teacher Beardsley Elem Sch 1961-62; 1st Grade Teacher Monger Elem 1962-66; 2nd Grade Teacher Middlebury Elem 1966-68; 5th/6th Grade Teacher Monger Elem 1970-74; 3rd/4th Grade Teacher Hawthorne Elem 1976-; *ai:* Discipline, Sch Improvement, PBA, Human Dev Action Cncl, Prime Time Fairs, Lang Art Curr, Selection, Soc Stud Selection Comms; Homework Hotline; Elkhart Teachers Assn Building Rep 1961-; IN Rdng Assn 1978-; Delta Kappa Gamma Secy 1978-; Grace United Meth Church (Ed Chairperson 1976-80, 1989-, Pastor Parish Relations 1982-87, Youth Dir, Puppet Team Dir); Youth for Christ Lifeline Volunteer 1963-; Research & Application of Lit mini-Grant; Exch Club Book of Golden Deeds Awd; Assisted in Revising Elkhart His Book; Based Rdng & Whole Lang; *home:* 800 Middlebury St Elkhart IN 46516

POLLACK, CHARLES, Mathematics Dept Head; *b:* Newark, NJ; *m:* Ester Neibrief; *c:* Michelle, Michael; *ed:* (BA) Math, Buena Vista Coll 1967; (MED) Math Ed, Rutgers Univ 1978; Univ of N IA; Montclair St; *cr:* Math Teacher West Side HS 1968-70; Math Teacher/Dept Head Parsippany Hills HS 1970-; *ai:* Tennis Coach; NCTM 1984-; Assn of Math Teachers of NJ 1984-; Tennis Coach of Yr 1986-87; *office:* Parsippany Hill HS 20 Rita Dr Parsippany NJ 07054

POLLAN, CECIL BARRETT, English Teacher; *b:* Natchez, MS; *ed:* (AA) Eng/Scndry Ed, Copiah-Lincoln Jr Coll 1980; (BS) Eng/Scndry Ed, 1982, (BA) Elem Ed, 1983 Univ of Southern MS; *cr:* Teacher Franklin Elem 1982-83, South Pike Jr HS 1984-89, South Pike HS 1989-; *ai:* Beta Club Co-Spon; Drama Club & 9th Grade Class Talent Spon; His/Literary Awd Copiah Lincoln Jr Coll; *office:* South Pike H S 205 W Myrtle St Magnolia MS 39652

POLLARD, DARLENE, Reading Teacher; *b:* Chicago, IL; *ed:* (BA) Ed, Chicago St Univ 1973; (MS) Ed, Governors St Univ 1976; *cr:* 3rd Grade Teacher Henry Horner Elem Sch 1974; 4th Grade Teacher 1976-78, 5th Grade Teacher 1979-83, 6th Grade Teacher 1984-86, Rdng Teacher Philip Sheridan Elem Sch 1987-; *ai:* Delta Sigma Theta VP 1990.

POLLARD, LESLIE ANN, First Grade Teacher; *b:* Clinton, IA; *ed:* (BA) Elem Ed, Univ of IA 1973; *cr:* 1st Grade Teacher St Malachys 1973-; *ai:* Religious Ed Teacher; Choir; Parish Liturgy Comm; NCEA 1973-; Richmond Hill Players; Natl Sci Fnd Grant; Outstanding Young Educator; Mirian Joseph Farrel DIstinguished Service Nom; *home:* 127 N Williams Geneseo IL 61254

POLLARD, REBECCA RAE (KREISHER), Cmptr Teacher/Coord of Gifted; *b:* Hillsboro, OH; *m:* Gerald K.; *c:* Matthew S.; *ed:* (AS) Chem, E OK St 1971; (BS) Phys Sci Ed, Univ of OK 1973; (ME) Counseling, Northeastern St Univ 1977; *cr:* Sci Teacher Nob Le Jr HS 1973-75; Sci/Math Teacher Union Mid Sch 1975-78; Phys Sci/Chem Teacher IA HS 1978-79; Sci/Cmptr Teacher/Coord of Gifted Union Jr HS 1979-; *ai:* Young Astronauts Club; Soc Comm & Awds Assembly Chm; Duty Schedule Coord; NSTA 1987-; OK Assn Gifted, Creative, Talented 1986-; NE Network 1985-; Phi Delta Kappa 1987-; Sweet Adelines Music Librarian 1989-; Mens Barbershop Auxiliary Pres 1986-; Patrian Church 1981-; PTA Teacher of Yr 1978; Educator of Month; *office:* Union Jr HS 7616 S Garnett Tulsa OK 74133

POLLEMA, DOROTHY ANNE, First Grade Teacher; *b:* Winona, MN; *ed:* (BA) Journalism, Mc Alester Coll 1961; (BS) Elem Ed, Winona St Univ 1968; *cr:* Reporter/Ed Rochester Post-Bulletin Co 1961-67; Teacher Dover-Eyota Public Schls 1968-; *ai:* Local, St, Natl Ed Assn; *office:* Dover-Eyota Elem Sch 5th St S Eyota MN 55934

POLLEY, CHRISTINE M., English Department Chair; *b:* Decatur, AL; *m:* Kevin A.; *ed:* (BS) Eng Ed, Bob Jones Univ 1987; *cr:* Eng Dept Chairperson Northside Chrstn Sch 1987-; *ai:* Sch Newspaper Spon; Homecoming Comm; *office:* Northside Chrstn Sch 7800 Northside Dr North Charleston SC 29420

POLLEY, KAREN THORNTON, 5th Grade Teacher; *b:* Petaluma, CA; *m:* Harold Lee; *c:* Harold A., Jason E.; *ed:* (BA) Soc Sci/General Elem, Ca St Univ Fullerton 1964; (MA) Ed, US Intnl Univ 1990; Cmptr Sci, Chapman Coll; *cr:* 4th Grade Teacher Mc Fadden Elem 1964-75; 3rd Grade Teacher Rio Vista Elem 1974-79; 4th/5th Grade Teacher Woodsboro Elem 1979-; *ai:* Pen & Quill Contest Coach & Judge; Soc Sci Curr; NEA 1970-; CTA, PUEA 1964-; Little League Secy 1974-75; *home:* 2997 Norco Dr Norco CA 91760

POLLEY, PHILLIP JAMES, English Teacher; *b:* Marvin, IN; *m:* Rita A Sendelbach; *c:* Kathryn, Clifford, Kirstin; *ed:* (BA) Eng, Univ of Chicago 1958; (MA) Eng Lit, N IL Univ 1966; *cr:* Eng Teacher Chicago Voc HS 1958-59, Lemont HS 1959-61; Eng Teacher/Chm Lockport HS 1961-69, Tinley Park HS 1970-; *ai:* NCTE; *office:* Tinley Park HS 6111 175th St Tinley Park IL 60477

POLLINO, JAMES ANTHONY, English-Drama Teacher; *b:* Johnstown, PA; *m:* Deborah Lonergan; *c:* David, Rebecca; *ed:* (BA) Eng, St Francis Coll 1969; *cr:* Eng/Drama/Speech Teacher/Eng Dept Chm Penn Cambria HS 1969-; *ai:* Drama Dir; Speech Coach; IU8 Speech League Treas 1987-; PA Speech & Debate Assn 1987-; *office:* Penn Cambria Sr HS 4th St & Linden Ave Cresson PA 16630

POLLINS, JOHN ANTHONY, Social Studies Teacher; *b:* Geneva, OH; *ed:* (AB) Poly Sci, Duke Univ 1984; Working Towards Masters His, S CT St Univ; *cr:* Teacher Amity Jr HS 1984-; *ai:* Jr HS Boys Bsktbl & Soccer Coach; Peer Counseling Prgm Coord; Curr Assessment Comm Mem; Amity Steering Comm Chm 1986-87; Phi Beta Kappa 1984-, Membership Awd 1984; NESTVAL Nom Distinguished Teaching of Geography 1987; Teacher Appreciation Awd Amity Jr HS 1988-89; Nom Golden Pen Awd Amity Sch Dist 1988; *office:* Amity Jr HS Ohman Avenue Orange CT 06477

POLLITT, AMY L. JOHNSON, K-6th Vocal Music Teacher; *b:* Cedar Rapids, IA; *m:* James F.; *ed:* (BA) Music, Luther Coll 1980; *cr:* K-6 Vocal Music Teacher Belmond Comm Sch 1980; *ai:* Facilitator Support Group Leader; Leadership Task Force Comm; NEA/ISEA 1980-; MENC; Belmond Concert Assn 1984-; PEO 1977-; Outstanding Young Educator 1983; *home:* 1112 Windsor Pl Belmond IA 50421

POLLOCK, GARY JOHN, Mathematics Teacher; *b:* Rochester, NY; *ed:* (BS) Scndry Ed/Math, SUNY Oswego 1984; (MS) Scndry Ed/Math, SUNY Brockport 1989; *cr:* Math Teacher Kendall Jr/Sr HS 1984-; *ai:* Sr Class Adv; Var Boys Soccer & Jr Var Boys Bsktbl Coach; USA CORE I Mem; Univ of Rochester Teacher of Yr Winner from Kendall 1988-89; *office:* Kendall Jr/Sr HS Roosevelt Hwy Kendall NY 14476

POLLOCK, JOAN CRAWLEY, Elementary Reading Teacher; *b:* New York, NY; *m:* Joseph H.; *c:* Doug, Lori Pollock Manmus, Patti Pollock Marx, Robert, Gregory; *ed:* (BA) His/Eng/Art, Colby 1948; (MS) Ed, Univ of S CA 1974; Grad Level Cmptr Trng; *cr:* 1st Grade Classroom Teacher, K-2nd Grade Classroom Teacher/Early Chldhd/Rdng Specialist Brad Oaks 1967-; *ai:* Host Foreign Exchange Stus; AKG Corr Secy; Santa Anita Rdng Cncl Dist Rep; MTA Sch Rep; Y Pres Womens Corp; PTA VP; DKG Aid Grant 1967; Sch Bd Awd 1986; U of S CA Alumni Honors Outstanding Achievement Awd 1968; Intnl Rdng Assn Speaker 1987; DKG Chi St Leadership Certificate 1988; *office:* Brad Oaks Elem Sch 930 E Lemon Ave Monrovia CA 91016

POLLOCK, KAYE TEARE, English Teacher; *b:* Grove City, PA; *m:* Burton; *ed:* (BA) Eng, Slippery Rock St Coll 1971; *cr:* Teacher Grove City; *office:* Grove City HS 511 Highland Ave Grove City PA 16127

POLLOCK, MARY KATHERINE, School Counselor; *b:* Sandy Hook, KY; *m:* Samuel Milton; *c:* Elizabeth A. Pollock Cheves, Samuel K.; *ed:* (BA) Bio, 1952, (MA) Counseling, 1969 Georgetown Coll; (Rank I) Curr Ed, Univ of KY 1981; Counseling, Univ of KY & Eastern KY Univ 1988; *cr:* 7th Grade Sci Teacher Woodford Cty Schls 1952-53; 6th-8th Grade Sci/Eng Teacher Great Crossing Elem 1954-58; 6th-8th Grade Sci Teacher Bourbon Cty Schls 1964-68; 6th Grade Teacher Garth Elem Sch 1968-72; 7th-9th Grade Teacher Scott Cty Schls 1972-81; 6th-8th Grade Cnslr Georgetown Mid Sch 1981-; *ai:* Guidance Comm; Stu Cncl; Amer Assn of Counseling & Dev, KY Assn of Counseling & Dev; CKACD; Scott Countians Against Drugs; Outstanding Woman of 1989; 4-H Cncl; *office:* Georgetown Mid Sch Clay Ave Georgetown KY 40324

POLLOCK, SUE HOBGOOD, Second Grade Teacher; *b:* Nebo, KY; *m:* Richard H.; *c:* Steven R., Anne P. Vincenti; *ed:* (BS) Voc Home Ec, Univ of KY 1955; (MAED) Elem Ed, Spalding Univ 1970; *cr:* 4th Grade Teacher Lincoln Elem 1955-56; 1st Grade Teacher 1970-73, 2nd Grade Teacher 1973- Crestwood Elem; *ai:* 2nd Grade Team Leader, United Way Rep Crestwood Elem Sch; Oldham Cty Teachers Assn, KY Ed Assn; Womans Club of Louisville KY; Presbyn Church Choir; *office:* Crestwood Elem Sch Hwy 146 La Grange Rd Crestwood KY 40014

POLS, DONNA INNIS, English Teacher; *b:* Chicago, IL; *m:* Michael D.; *c:* Beth A.; *ed:* (BS) Ed, Univ of IL 1966; (MA) Lit, NE IL Univ 1973; *cr:* Lang Art Teacher Yates Upper Grade Center 1966-67; Eng Teacher Austin HS 1967-70, Senn Metropolitan Acad 1970-; *ai:* Sr Class Spon; *office:* Senn Metropolitan Acad 5900 N Glenwood Chicago IL 60660

POLSTON, DONALD LEE, Social Studies Chairman; *b:* Chateauroux, France; *m:* Debbie S. Rayburn; *c:* Jordan, Garrett; *ed:* (BA) Ed, 1975, (MS) Soc Stud Ed, 1979 Purdue Univ; Instructional Media Design; *cr:* Teaching Asst Purdue Univ 1976; Teacher Lebanon Mid Sch 1976-; *ai:* Dept Chm; Newspaper Adv; 8th Grade Ftbl & Var Sftbl Coach; Sch Improvement Prgm; Phi Alpha Theta, NCSS; *home:* PO Box 195 Stockwell IN 47983

POLTRACK, LESLIE D., 5th Grade Teacher; *b:* Stamford, CT; *m:* David F.; *ed:* (BA) Elem Ed - Cum Laude, Georgian Court Coll 1968; (MS) Elem Ed, Univ of Bridgeport 1973; (CAS) Ed/Teaching/Fnds, Fairfield Univ 1988; *cr:* Elem Teacher New Canaan Sch System 1968-; *ai:* Math Facilitator East Sch; Integrated Lang Art Comm; New Canaan Ed Assn, CT Ed Assn, NEA Mem 1968-; Delta Kappa Gamma 1986-; New Canaan Teacher Appreciation Comm 1986-89; *office:* East Sch Little Brook Rd New Canaan CT 06840

POLZELLA, LOUIS VINCENT, SR., English Teacher; *b:* Waterbury, CT; *m:* Elizabeth O'Connor; *c:* Louis Jr., Michael, Mark, Jeanne; *ed:* (BS) Eng, Mt St Marys Coll 1965; (MS) Rdng, Cntrl CT St Univ 1974; *cr:* Eng Teacher Crosby HS 1965-; *ai:* Head Girls Swim Team Coach; Walcott Bd of Ed Mem 1989-; *office:* Crosby HS 300 Pierpont Rd Waterbury CT 06705

POLZIN, DONNA LYNN, Business Education Teacher; *b:* Salt Lake City, UT; *m:* Brian Scott; *c:* Robert D.; *ed:* (BS) Comprehensive Bus Ed, Univ of Wi Eau Claire 1984; Supervision of Stu Teachers Cert 1988; Voc License 1985; *cr:* Bus Ed Intern Tomahawk HS 1984; Bus Ed Instr N Cntrl Tech Coll 1985-87; Accounting Instr Mount Senario Coll 1988; Bus Ed Instr Colby HS 1985-; *ai:* Articulation Steering Comm; Annual Bus Skills Contest Adv; FBLA Asst Adv; WI Bus Educators Assn 1983-85; Natl Bus Educators Assn 1983-84; Colby HS Head Girls Vlybl Coach 1986-88; Colby Recreation Dept Swimming Pool Supvr 1983-84; Colby Boxboard Employees Credit Union 1987-; Audit Comm Internal Auditor 1987- & Chairperson 1989-; *office:* Colby HS N 2nd Colby WI 54421

POLZIN, ROXANN WELBORN, 2nd Grade Teacher; *b:* Kansas City, KS; *c:* Scott, Jeff; *ed:* (BS) Elem Ed, Akron Univ 1974; Artistry in Teaching Wkshps, Focuson Learning, Teaching Exceptional Children, Intro Mildly Handicapped; *cr:* 2nd Grade Elem Teacher/Transition Teacher/Coord Plain Local Sch; 5th Grade Teacher Schumacher Elem; 3rd Grade Teacher Lawndale Elem; Remedial Rdng Springfield Township; *ai:* USA Pony Club DA; 4-H Club Adv; Olympics of the Mind Omnitronic Humor & US Olympic Trials Jump Judge; *home:* 7876 Peter Hoover Rd New Albany OH 43054

POND, ANITA KAY, Third & Fourth Grade Teacher; *b:* Fairfield, IL; *m:* Richard; *c:* Kensey; *ed:* (BSED) Phys Ed, 1974, Elem Cert, 1978, (MSED) Admin, 1982 E IL Univ; *cr:* Phys Ed Teacher/Coach Washburn Jr HS 1974-76; Teachers Aide N Wayne Unit 1977-79; 3rd Grade Teacher 1979-, 3rd/4th Grade Teacher 1988- Geff Grade Sch; *ai:* Teach Renaissance Gifted Ed Classes Olney Cntrl Coll; Project Cosmic Comm; Alpha Delta Kappa (Corresponding Secy, Treas) 1980-; Phi Delta Kappa 1988-; *office:* Geff Grade Sch PO Box 68 Geff IL 62842

POND, MAXINE LISTER, 7th Grade Teacher Plus; *b:* Edmonton AB, Canada; *m:* Vernon Russell; *c:* Mark W., Elise G., Josephine A.; *ed:* (BA) Scndry Ed/Eng, NW Nazarene Coll 1970; *cr:* 11th Grade Eng Teacher Ontario HS 1970-73; 8th Grade Eng Teacher Kalispell Jr HS 1985; 7th/12th Grade Teacher Flathead Chrstn Sch 1986-; *ai:* Church of Nazarene Caravan Dir 1989-.

POND, NICHOLAS J., Debate/Speech/Theatre Teacher; *b:* Salt Lake City, UT; *m:* Janeen Gundry; *c:* D. Travis, Nicholeen, Beauen A., Preston B., Janelle; *ed:* (BA) Speech/Theatre, Brigham Young Univ 1972; (MED) Scndry, Univ of UT 1973; Minor Degrees in Japanese & Phys Ed; *cr:* Speech/Theatre Teacher Carbon HS 1973-75; Speech/Theatre Teacher 1975-, Japanese/Debate Teacher 1982-, Fine Arrts Dept Chm 1988- Murray HS; *ai:* Debate Coach; Sch Musical Dir; Dept Chm; Intnl Ed Comm; Japanese Club Adv; Natl Speech & Debate Fed Mem 1988-; Intermountain Assn of Japanese Lang Teachers (Pres, Founder) 1990; UT Speech Arts Assn Mem 1982-; St Trophies in Debate; 1st Place Championships; *office:* Murray HS 5440 S State Murray UT 84107

PONDER, TED LAMAR, English Teacher; *b:* Camden, AR; *m:* Auburn Cooley; *c:* Kelly, Ashley; *ed:* (BA) Eng 1970, (ME) Scndry Ed, 1978 Univ of AR; Prin Cert Univ of Cntrl AR; Quachita Baptist Univ; S AR Univ Technological Branch; Univ of AR Monticello; *cr:* Teacher Cassville R&IV Schls 1971-72, Adult Ed Center 1974-75, Fordyce HS 1972-; *ai:* Octagon Club; Fordyce Teachers Assn Pres 1979-80; NEA, AR Ed Assn 1972-; AR Assn of Ed Admins 1986-; AR Assn of Scndry Sch Prin 1986-; Fordyce Optimist Club Pres 1979-80, Honor Pres 1980; AR Optimist Dist Lieutenant Governor 1980-81; First Meth Church Admin Bd Chm 1989-; Grant AR Writing Project 1983; Fordyce Optimist Club 1978-; FCC Radio Operators License; *office:* Fordyce HS 1800 W College Fordyce AR 71742

PONICHTER, NADIA ANNETTE (ROBIDOUX), Drama/Eng/Spec Ed Teacher; *b:* Detroit, MI; *w:* Dennis Michael (dec); *c:* Brandon, Bethany, Nathan; *ed:* (BA) Speech/Eng, Univ of MI 1971, (ME) Spec Ed, Wayne St Univ 1974; Cert in Substance Abuse, Univ of Detroit; Summer Seminars, E MI Univ; *cr:* Eng/Speech/Spec Ed Teacher Detroit Public Schls 1971-73; Educl Coord/Teacher Barat House 1973-75; Teacher Mt Clemens Treatment Facility 1976-78; Eng/Drama/Spec Ed Teacher Mt Clemens HS 1978-; *ai:* Sch Play & Operetta Dir; Macomb Comm Coll Youth Theatre Wkshps & Shows; Drama Teacher Enrichment Classes Messmore-Utica Schls; Mt Clemens HS Summer Drama Wkshp 1989; *office:* Mt Clemens HS 155 Cass Ave Mount Clemens MI 48043

PONISCIAK, LENORA T., 6th Grade Teacher; *b:* Philadelphia, PA; *ed:* (BSED) Early Chldhd/Elem Ed, Temple Univ 1974; *cr:* 1st/3rd/4th Grade Teacher 1974-81, 6th-8th Grade Math Teacher 1981-84 St Anns; 6th Grade Teacher Phoenixville Area Cath Sch 1984-; *ai:* NCEA; *office:* Phoenixville Area Cath Elem 3rd And Buttonwood St S Campus Phoenixville PA 19460

PONTI, KAREN TRIVETT, Spanish Teacher; *b:* Banner Elk, NC; *m:* David Allan; *ed:* (BA) Span, Lenoir-Rhyne Coll 1988; Univ of Valencia Spain 1986-87; *cr:* Span Teacher Fred T Foard HS 1988-; *ai:* Jr Var Chrldr Adv; Pep Club, Span Club Spon; *home:* 1744 29th St NE Hickory NC 28601

PONWITH, MARK C., English Teacher; *b:* Mankato, MN; *m:* Laurie Bingenheimer; *c:* Josh, Jesse, Deirdra; *ed:* (BS) Eng, Northern St 1970; (MAT) Eng, Augustana Coll 1975; Grad Stud N AZ Univ, AZ St Univ, Augustana Coll; *cr:* Eng Teacher Various Schls 1970-72, 1975-77, Tuba City Public Schls 1978-83, Ray Schls 1984-, Cntrl AZ Comm Coll 1988-; *ai:* Accelerated 8th Grade Lang Art & Gifted Teacher; AEA 1978-80, 1989-; *home:* PO Box 322 Kearny AZ 85237

POOLE, BRENDA FULTON, Spanish Teacher; *b:* Hope, AR; *m:* Jerry W.; *c:* David, Kelly; *ed:* (AA) Comm, Kilgore Coll 1984; (BS) Eng/Span/Voc Ed, Univ of TX 1985; (MA) Eng/Span, Stephen F Austin St Univ 1990; ESL Endorsement 1989; *cr:* Span/Eng Teacher, Ore City HS 1986-87; Span Teacher, Gilmer HS 1987-88, Karnack HS 1988-; *ai:* Span Club Spon; State Textbook Comm; Foreign Lang Educators of East TX Secy 1989-; Phi Delta Kappa 1989-; Alpha Chi Natl Honor Society VP 1985-86; East TX Area Trail Riders Unlimited 1983-; Downtown Tyler Rotary Nom for Study Abroad Schlsp 1985; Coord Bd Schlsp for Teachers 1986; Deans List East TX Baptist Univ 1986; Natl Deans List 1986-87; *home:* Rt 2 Box 444 Diana TX 75640

POOLE, CAROLYN MEREDITH, Third Grade Teacher; *b:* Wooldridge, TN; *w:* Joe (dec); *c:* Gregory J., Meredith Poole Barth; *ed:* (BS) Elem Ed, Carson-Newman Coll 1957; *cr:* 5th Grade Teacher 1958-60; 4th Grade Teacher 1969-73, 1976-84; 5th Grade Teacher 1984-85; 3rd Grade Teacher 1986-; *ai:* Core, Lang Art, Stu Support Comms; Alpha Delta Kappa Chaplain 1989-; Epsilon Sigma Alpha Pres 1973; *home:* 4498 Kinvarra Cir Mableton GA 30059

POOLE, DONALD KENNETH, Health/Physical Ed Teacher; *b:* Camilla, GA; *ed:* (BS) Health/Phys Ed, Albany St Coll 1976; (MS) Health/Phys Ed, GA St 1978; Sch Bus Driver Trainer Prgm Pupil Transportation Safety; Motorcycle Safety Ed; Amer Heart Assn CPR Instr; *cr:* Teacher/Coach Randolph Cty HS 1976-77, Upson Cty HS 1978-87, Monroe Comprehensive HS 1987-89; *ai:* Girls Bsktbl Coach; NEA 1978-; Prof Assn GA Educators, Natl Fed Coaching Assn 1989-; GA Coaching Assn 1980-, Region Coach of Yr 1976, 1985-86; Phi Beta Sigma 1975-; *home:* 113 West Rd Albany GA 31705

POOLE, ELAINE ZETTA, Third Grade Teacher; *b:* Montgomery, AL; *m:* George Austin Jr.; *c:* Erica, Anitra; *ed:* (BS) Elem Ed, 1972, (MA) Elem Ed, AL St Univ 1987; *cr:* Chapter I Teacher Nichols Jr HS 1972-74; 1st Grade Teacher Five Points Elem Sch 1974-76; 4th Grade Teacher Valley Grande Elem Sch 1976-; *ai:* Blazer Club; Macon Cty Ed Assn 1972-74; Dallas Cty Ed Assn, AL Ed Assn, NEA 1972-; *home:* 4821 US Hwy 80 W Selma AL 36701

POOLE, ELIZABETH H., Business Education Teacher; *b:* New York, NY; *ed:* (AA) Secretarial, 1968, (BA) Sociology, 1970 Fairleigh Dickinson Univ; (MA) Speech Comm, PA St Univ 1984; *cr:* Speech Comm Instr PA St Univ 1981-83; Bus Ed Teacher Presentation of Mary Acad 1986-; *ai:* Stu Cncl Adv; Ski Club Moderator; Soph Homeroom Adv; NH Bus Ed Assn 1986-; St Thomas Aquinas Church Youth Retreat Secy 1989-; *home:* 25 E Derry Rd Derry NH 03038

POOLE, H. JOHN, Mathematics Dept Chairman; *b:* Claysburg, PA; *m:* Ann Elizabeth Inzana; *c:* Luke, Agatha, Teresa, Elizabeth, Margaret, John; *ed:* (BS) Math/Scndry Ed, St Francis Coll 1967; Cmptr Ed in Math, Scis, Univ of Pittsburgh Johnstown 1985; Numerous Wkshps & Seminars Cmptr Math; *cr:* Math Teacher 1967-, Math Dept Chm 1974- Bishop Carroll HS; *ai:* Cmptr Club 1986-88; Moderator Cmptr Team for Natl Superquest Contest 1988; St Vincent Coll Outstanding Area Educator 1989, Letter of Recognition 1989; Ind Research in Number Theory; Probability Theory-Have Just Resolved the Petersburg Paradox; *office:* Bishop Carroll HS Rt 422 & Carroll Dr Ebensburg PA 15931

POOLE, NANCY ROBERTS, Second Grade Lead Teacher; *b:* Montezuma, GA; *m:* James Roger; *c:* Charles, Carmen; *ed:* Elem Ed, GA Southwestern 1963; (BS) Elem Ed/Chldhd, Womans Coll of GA 1965; Supervising Teacher Services Univ of GA; *cr:* 2nd Grade Teacher New Era Elem 1965-66, Cherokee Elem 1966-70, Southland Acad 1970-; *ai:* Grading Comm; NEA 1965-70; *home:* 506 Dellwood Dr Americus GA 31709

POOLE, REBECCA INGRAM, Sixth Grade Teacher; *b:* Asheville, NC; *ed:* (BA) Elem Ed, Univ of NC Chapel Hill 1965; *cr:* 5th Grade Teacher Ardmore Elem 1965-67; 6th Grade Teacher Vance Elem 1967-70; Jr HS Teacher Yarnfield Jr & Infant Sch 1971-72; Soc Stud Teacher Windlesham Sch 1972-74; 6th Grade Teacher Mills River Sch 1982-; *ai:* Jr Beta Club Spon; Care Team Mem; NEA, NCAE 1982-; Meals on Wheels Coord 1977-81; Friends of Minehead Hospital Bd Mem 1980-81; Four Seasons Art Cncl (Bd of Dirs 1987-89, Secy 1988); Fulbright Exch Teacher 1971; Mills River Schls Candidate Teacher of Yr 1988.

POOLE, SUSAN TAYLOR, Kindergarten Teacher; *b:* Greenville, SC; *m:* Paul Edward; *c:* Leah, Melissa; *ed:* (BA) Math, Meredith Coll 1975; Working Towards Masters; *cr:* 4th/5th Grade Teacher Belmont Cntrl Sch 1975-77; 4th Grade Teacher Troy Elem Sch 1977-86; Media Coord Biscoe Mid Sch 1986-88; Kndgtn Teacher Troy Elem Sch 1988-; *ai:* Grade Level Chairperson 1981-86; Cty Steering Comm 1986-88; Media Advisory Comm 1989-; NEA, NC Assn of Educators 1975-; NC Cncl Teachers of Math 1982-; *office:* Troy Elem Sch 310 N Russell Troy NC 27371

POOLER, BERNARD E., Business Teacher; *b:* Watertown, NY; *m:* Lori Van Alstyne; *ed:* (BA) Bus Ed, SUNY Albany 1972; Working Toward Masters, SUC Potsdam; *cr:* Teacher Henderson Cntrl Schls 1976-81, Watertown HS 1981-; *ai:* Sftbl, Vlybl, Jr Var Ftbl, Bsbl Coach; Bsbl Ofcl Rules Interpreter 1980-; Ftbl Ofcl Pres 1988-; *office:* Watertown HS 1335 Washington St Watertown NY 13601

POOLEY, BONNIE I., English Teacher; *b:* Wilmington, DE; *c:* Kenneth T. *ed:* (BA) Eng, Univ of DE 1970; (MED) Counseling, Univ of S ME 1985; Outward Bound Instr; Wilderness First Responder; *cr:* Eng Teacher Mt Pleasant HS 1970-73, Gould Acad

1973-; Cnslr Gould Acad 1980-; *ai:* Cross Cntry Running & Ski Asst Coach; NACAC; NEACAC Governing Bd 1983-86; Bethel Conservation Commission Chairperson 1988-; *office:* Gould Acad P O Box 860 Bethel ME 04217

POORE, MITZI DRAUGHN, Business Teacher; *b:* Mt Airy, NC; *m:* James E. Jr.; *ed:* (AS) Coll Prep, Surry Comm Coll 1984; (BS) Bus, Appalachian St Univ 1986; *cr:* Bus Teacher Mt Airy HS 1988-; *ai:* FBLA Adv; Jr Class Spon; NC Assn of Educators Membership Rep 1989-; NEA; *office:* Mount Airy HS 1011 N South St Mount Airy NC 27030

POORE, TOBY ANN, Biology Teacher/Dept Chair; *b:* Middlesboro, KY; *m:* Lloyd Lee; *ed:* (BS) Bio, Cumberland Coll 1968; (MA) Ed, Union Coll 1976; Environmental Engineering; Advanced Placement Insts; *cr:* Medical Technician Louisville General Hospital 1967-69; Immunochemist Henry Ford Hospital 1969-70; Sci Teacher Right Fork Elem 1970; Bio Teacher Bell Cty HS 1970-; *ai:* Departmental Chairperson; Sci Fair Coord; NEA, KY Ed Assn 1970-; KY Assn for Progress Sci 1989-; Church (Sunday Sch Teacher 1986-, Acteens Leader 1989-); Bell Cty Teacher of Yr 1984; *office:* Bell County HS Rt 1 Box 88 Pineville KY 40977

POORMAN, RONALD J., Concert & Jazz Band Director; *b:* Hershey, PA; *m:* Karen Mellinger; *c:* Melinda, Jennifer; *ed:* (BS) Music Ed, Lebanon Valley Coll 1963; (MS) Music Ed, Ithaca Coll 1966; *cr:* Woodwind Teacher Middletown Area Schls 1963-66; Dir of Bands Pleasantville Schls 1966-73, S Regional HS 1973-; Dir of Jazz Band 553rd USAF Band 1963-69; *ai:* HS Jazz Band Dir; Band Dir on 7 European & 1 Hawaii Honor Band Tours; Jazz Band Dir Glassboro St Coll Summer Band Camp; NEA, NJ Ed Assn 1966-; Music Ed Natl Conf, NJ MEA Jazz Proced Chm 1987-89; Intnl Assn of Jazz Educators (NJ St Pres 1987-89, NJ VP 1989-); Articles Published & Author; *home:* 121m Blackman Rd RD 1 Linwood NJ 08221

POPE, CONNIE ROACH, Third Grade Teacher; *b:* Bernice, LA; *m:* Norman Lamar II; *c:* Bryn M;, Timothy W.; *ed:* (BA) Elem Ed, 1969, (MA) Elem Ed, 1976 LA Tech Univ; Grad Stud; *cr:* 3rd Grade Teacher Westwood Elem 1969-72; 4th-6th Grade Teacher Queensboro Elem 1972-73; 4th-6th Grade Math Teacher Eighty-First Elem 1973-80; 3rd Grade Teacher Summer Grove Elem 1980-; *ai:* Teacher Consultation Team 1989-; Caddo Assn of Educators (Faculty Rep 1971-72, 1983-, Co-Chm Insurance Company 1987-) 1969-; LA Assn of Educators (St Voting Delegate 1989) 1969-; NEA 1969-; NW LA Math Assn Elem VP 1980-81; Summer Grove PTA VP 1982-83; St Lukes United Meth Church (Ed Cncl 1980-, Bd of Trustees 1984-88, Sunday Sch Pres 1985-87); Linwood Mid Sch PTA Mem; Caddo Magnet HS PTA Mem; *office:* Summer Grove Elem Sch 2955 Bertkouns Ind Loop Shreveport LA 71118

POPE, DEBRA SAUGSTAD, Physical Education Teacher; *b:* Montebello, CA; *m:* Billy J.; *c:* Matthew J.; *ed:* (BS) Phys Ed, CA St Fullerton 1976; (MS) Phys Ed, CA Poly Pomona 1987; *cr:* Phys Ed Teacher Victor Valley HS 1981, Hesperia Jr HS 1981-; *ai:* Vlybl, Bsktbl, Sftbl Coach; Adv 8th Grade Grad Night; Dept Chairperson; Hesperia Educl Assn Site Rep 1989-; CA Teacher Assn, NEA; Church of the Valley; Mojave Mesa Booster Club; BSA.

POPE, DIANE DAVIS, 7th & 8th Pre-Algebra Teacher; *b:* Ft Smith, AR; *m:* John L.; *c:* Joseph L., Julie M.; *ed:* (BS) Elem Ed, Memphis ST Univ 1978; Addl Studies Comptr Engr Comptr Sci State Tech Institute; *cr:* Teacher Southaven Jr HS 1978-; *ai:* Jr HS Cncl Spon; Co-Spon Jr High Math Club; MS Assn of Ed; Alpha Delta Kappa; *office:* Southaven Jr High School 899 Rasco Rd Southaven MS 38671

POPE, GEORGE KIRK, Principal; *b:* Oberlin, KS; *m:* Janice Carolyn Bainter; *c:* Penny, Darby; *ed:* (BS) Phys Ed, 1964, (MS) Elem Admin, 1968 Ft Hays St Univ; *cr:* Teacher Leavenworth Elem 1964-65; Teacher/Prin Norton Unified Sch Dist 211 1965-76; Asst Prin Salina HS South 1978-84; Prin Haysville Jr HS 1986-; *ai:* Fellowship Chrstn Athletes; Gideons, Ftbl, Bsktbl, Track, Athletic Dir; KAMLE 1987-; NASA 1988-89; NA SP 1986-87; Optomist 1986-; Lions 1978-85; *home:* 232 Timberlane Dr Haysville KS 67060

POPE, GEORGIA NEIHARDT, Second Grade Teacher; *b:* Superior, WI; *m:* Truman Gerald; *c:* Stuart L., Stacy A., Suzy; *ed:* (BS) Ed, 1953, (MA) Ed, 1955 Ball St Univ; Ec, Purdue Univ; Sci Wkshps, Ball St Univ; *cr:* Elem Teacher Garfield Sch 1953-61, Lincoln Sch 1962-63, Roosevelt Sch 1966; Title I Rdng Prgm Sutton Elem 1968-; *ai:* Muncie Area Rdng Assn; IN Rdng Assn Building Rep 1980-; Sigma Kappa (PR 1952-53, Alumni 1953-), Homecoming Court 1952; Kappa Delta Pi 1951-; Alpha Delta Kappa Chaplin 1987-; Econ-O-Mrs Home Ec Club; Ball St Univ Wives; Intnl Rdng Assn Regional Young Authors Conference Chairperson; High St United Meth Church; Muncie Childrens Museum Advisory Comm; Muncie Civic Theater; Outstanding & Meaningful Teacher Muncie Cmmty Schls; Sutton Sch Set Up Mini YAC; Published Articles.

POPE, JAMES O., Band Instructor; *b:* Goldsboro, NC; *c:* Eric, Valencia, James Jr., Jamie, Geneva, Gina; *ed:* (BS) Music Ed, NC A&T Univ 1964; (MA) Music Ed, Morgan St Univ 1976; Phd Univ of MD Coll Park; *cr:* Band Instr Douglass HS 1965-67, Hamilton Holmes HS 1967-68; Music Ed/Choir/Band Teacher St Stevens Church Elem Sch 1968-69, King & Queen Elem 1968-69; Fr Hornist US Army Band 1969-72; Band Instr Greenspring Mid Sch 1972-85, Calverton Mid Sch 1985-; *ai:* Music Educators Natl Conference; Arch Soc Club Legal Adv 1989-; St Johns Lodge #24 F&AAYR Masons; Cntrl Rosemont Recreation Center Exec Bd Adv; *office:* Calverton Mid Sch 1100 Whitmore Ave Baltimore MD 21216

POPE, MARGIE G., Home Economics Teacher; *b:* Calhoun, GA; *m:* Guy Adam; *c:* Anita, Juanita; *ed:* (BS) Home Ec, Berry Coll 1957; *cr:* Home Ec Teacher La Fayette HS 1928; *ai:* FHA Adv; Dist Prgm Comm Person; Delta Kappa Gamma Spon; WAE Hostess Chm 1988-; Delta Kappa Gamma Pres 1986-88; Distinguished Citizen Awd; Beta Sigma Phi Citizen of Yr; Teacher of Yr for Sch/Runner-Up for Cty; *home:* Rt 3 Box 1205 La Fayette GA 30728

POPE, RICHARD BRAMLEY, 5th & 6th Grade Teacher; *b:* Little Rock, IA; *m:* Mary C. Keitges; *c:* Jeff, Mike, David; *ed:* (BS) Bus Admin, Econ, 1964; (MS) Elem Ed, 1966 Westmar Coll; *cr:* Classroom Teacher Anthon-Oto Cmmty Sch 1966-; *ai:* Phase III Performance Base Pay Comm; Coord Drug Ed for Elem Grades; Anthon-Oto Sch Bd Advisory Comm; Anthon Public Lib Bd (Pres 1978- Secy Treas); Article Published IA Sci Teachers Journal; Conservation Educator Awd 1989- By Woodbury Cty Conservation Brd; *home:* RR 2 Box 77 Anthon IA 51004

POPE, RITA JEAN (CONRAD), Business Education Teacher; *b:* Spiro, OK; *m:* Micheal Wayne; *c:* Barbara E., Duane S.; *ed:* (BS) Bus Ed, NE St Univ 1985; *cr:* Bookkeeper K-Mart 1967-69, 1973-76; Secy Spiro HS 1976-81; Teacher Arkoma HS 1985-; *ai:* 9th Grade Spon; Staff Dev Comm; NE St Univ Outstanding Bus Ed Stu 1985; OK Outstanding Bus Ed Stu 1985; Grant T White Schlsp Recipient.

POPE, SHIRLEY VIRGINIA, Retired Middle School Teacher; *b:* Lexington, VA; *ed:* (BA) His, Univ of CO 1967; (MA) Ed/Intnl Relations, Univ of Denver 1978; Certificate in Bus, OK St Univ; Cmptr Ed, CO St Univ; Archaeology Field Work, DU Center for Teaching Intnl Relations; *cr:* GED Teacher Fitzsimmons Army Hospital 1967; Soc Stud Teacher 1968-86, Cmptr Teacher 1987-89, Substitute Teacher 1990 Denver Public Schls; *ai:* Chess Club, Cmptr Club, Stamp Club Spon; City of David Jerusalem Israel Excavations Participant 1983.

POPE, STEPHANIE MARIE, Latin Teacher; *b:* Abilene, TX; *ed:* (BA) Classics, Randolph-Macon Womans Coll 1975; (MA) Classics, Univ of Cincinnati 1976; Summer Session, Amer Acad Rome 1976; *cr:* Latin Teacher Norfolk Acad 1977-; Latin Course Consultant Cambridge Univ Press 1988-; *ai:* Odyssey of Mind Coach 1990; Amer Classical League 1977-; Classical Assn of Mid West & South 1977-; Classical Assn of VA 1977-; Joint Assn of Classical Teachers 1987-; North Amer Cambridge Classics Project Secy 1987-; PEO (Recording Secy 1982-84, VP 1984-86, Pres 1986-88); Phi Beta Kappa Awd 1975; Magna Cum Laude Honors Classics Randolph-Macon Womens Coll; Semple Fellowship Univ Cincinnati; Natl Sigma Phi Summer Schlsp Study; Rome Amer Acad; Mc Kinley Schlsps Summer Stud Roman, Britain, Greece, Egypt & Israel; Charter Mem North Amer Cambridge Classics Project; NACCP Cambridge Latin Exam; Teaching Materials & 2 Articles Published; *office:* Norfolk Acad 1585 Wesleyan Dr Norfolk VA 23502

POPE, SUSAN JOE, English Teacher; *b:* Pineville, KY; *ed:* (BS) Elem Ed, 1966, (MA) Ed, 1974 Union Coll; (Rank I) Ed, 1982; *cr:* Eng Teacher Barbourville City Sch 1966-; *ai:* Jr Beta Club Spon; Curr Comm; Lib Advisory Cncl; Phi Delta Kappa, Upper Cumberland Ed Assn Bd of Dirs 1986-88; Barbourville Ed Assn Secy 1989-; Barbourville PTA 1966-; Barbourville Cmmty Chorus 1984-; Outstanding Teacher Awd 1987; Resource Teacher for KY Teacher Internship Prgm.

POPE, TAMELA LEE, English Teacher; *b:* Baltimore, MD; *m:* Ronald L.; *c:* Jeremiah, David; *ed:* (BSED) Eng Ed, Univ of Ga 1980; *cr:* Eng Teacher Jefferson HS 1980-81, Monroe Area Comprehensive HS 1981-; *ai:* Sr Class Chairperson; Graduation & Baccalaureate Chairperson; Schlsp Comm; GA Assn of Ed 1983-89; Walton Cty Assn of Ed (Treas 1987-88) 1983-89; NCTE 1983-89; Prof Assn of GA Educators 1989-; Jr Toastmasters Spon 1983-88; Academic Excl Comm Teacher of Yr; Sch & Cty STAR Teacher; *office:* Monroe Area Comprehensive HS Bryant Rd Monroe GA 30655

POPEK, JOHN JOSEPH, Choral Director; *b:* Newark, NJ; *m:* Linda Voigt; *ed:* (BS) Music Ed, William Paterson Coll 1978; Performance, Montclair St Coll; *cr:* Music Teacher Parsippany Elem Schls 1978-83; Choral Dir Parsippany Hills HS 1983-; *ai:* Classical Guitar Ensemble; Fall Variety Show; Spring Musical; Music Educators Natl Conference 1974-; Amer Choral Dir Assn 1985-; Masterwork Chorus 1980-; Natl Trust for Historic Preservation 1988-; *office:* Parsippany Hills HS 20 Rita Dr Parsippany NJ 07054

POPELKA, JULIA STINSON, Language Arts Teacher; *b:* Temple, TX; *m:* Allen; *ed:* (BA) Art His, Univ of TX 1979; NJ Writing Proj; *cr:* Teacher Bonham Mid Sch 1985-; *ai:* Coord of 7th Grade Acclrtd Fld Trip; Acad Team Comm Mem; Lang Arts Txtbk Comm; TCTA Fclty Rep 1988-; Temple JR Leag 1989-; Career Ladder Level II; *office:* Bonham Mid Sch 4600 Midway Dr Temple TX 76502

POPELKA, JULIA STINSON, Language Art Teacher; *b:* Temple, TX; *m:* Allen; *ed:* (BFA) Art His, Univ of TX 1979; *cr:* Lang Art/Rdng Teacher Bonham Mid Sch 1985-; *ai:* Academic Team Comm Mem; Curr Dev & Writing Textbook Comm; 7th Grade Accelerated Field Trip Coord; TCTA 1985-; NCTE 1986-; Jr League of Temple 1989-; *office:* Bonham Mid Sch 4600 Midway Dr Temple TX 76502

POPELKA, LA VERNE D., English Teacher; *b:* Temple, TX; *m:* Martin L.; *c:* Andrea; *ed:* (AA) Eng, Temple Jr Coll 1970; (BA) Bio, St Marys Univ 1973; (MED) Ed, Sul Ross Univ 1981; (MA) Eng, Abilene Chrstn Univ 1989; *cr:* Eng Teacher Highlands HS 1973-74, Uvalde HS 1976-80, Teague HS 1980-81, Navarro Coll 1981-86, Corsicana HS 1987-88; Bio/Eng Teacher Cooper HS 1988-; *ai:* Uvalde Annual Staff Spon; Assn of TX Prof Ed; Amer Assn of Univ Women Secy 1976-77; *office:* Cooper HS 3639 Sayles Blvd Abilene TX 79605

POPIO, JOAN KISH, Language Arts Teacher; *b:* Youngstown, OH; *m:* Ronald Frederick Sr.; *c:* Ronald Jr., Dean; *ed:* (BS) Elem Ed, Youngstown St Univ 1970; Grad Stud Youngstown St Univ 1980; *cr:* Teacher St Christine Sch 1960-82, Youngstown Chrstn Sch 1982-; *ai:* Sr & Graduation Adv; Coming Out Co-Adv; Benevolence Co-Chairperson; St Christine 8th Grade Stus 1st His Day Competition Champions Youngstown St Univ, Columbus OH & Washington DC; *office:* Youngstown Chrstn Sch 125 Wychwood Ln Youngstown OH 44512

POPOWICZ, SANDRA MAE, Sixth Grade Teacher; *b:* Jamaica, NY; *m:* Richard; *c:* Clyde Still, Alexsandra Salmon, Kerry; *ed:* (BA) Ed/Bio, 1967, (MS) Ed, 1971 Suny New Paltz; Admin Cert Whole Lang, Architecture & Curr Dev; *cr:* 2nd Grade Teacher Cahill Sch 1967-68; 5th Grade Teacher 1968-71, 2nd Grade Teacher 1971-72 Grant D Mouse; 6th Grade Teacher Mt Marion 1972-; *ai:* Sci Comm Dist; Inservice Dev Dist; Sta Sr Rep 1978-84; NYSUT; Cornell Extension Mem; 4 H Leader 1984-88; NY St Quarter Horse Judging Assn; Amer Morgan Horse, Quarter Horse , Draft Horse Assn; Curr Dev Grantsperson Chairperson; Math Comm Chm Sci Comm; Governors White Papers St Comm Cooperating Teachers St Univ NY; Cty Sci Mentor JV Bsktbl Coach; *home:* 33795 Glenerie Ln Saugerties NY 12477

POPP, BRENDA LA LONDE, Fifth Grade Teacher; *b:* Litchfield, MN; *m:* Gregg W.; *c:* Sarah, Rachael; *ed:* (BA) Elem Ed, Univ of MN Morris 1975; *cr:* Title I Kndgtn Teacher Melrose Public Sch 1975-76; Kndgtn Teacher 1976-82, 5th Grade Teacher 1982- Brownton Public Sch.

POPPLEWELL, KATHY KOGER, Mathematics Teacher; *b:* Corbin, KY; *c:* Jessica, Jared; *ed:* (BS) Elem Ed, 1972, (MA) Elem Ed, 1978 E KY Univ; Grad Hours Toward Rank I; *cr:* Elem Teacher Ferguson Elem & Hogue Elem 1972-85; Rdng/Math Teacher Shopville Jr HS 1985-87; Math Teacher Northern Jr HS 1987-; *office:* Northern Jr HS 350 Oak Leaf Ln Somerset KY 42501

PORCELLI, STEPHANIE (ADAMOWICZ), English Teacher; *b:* Ticonderoga, NY; *m:* Robert; *c:* Danielle R.; *ed:* (BA) Eng, Coll of St Rose 1967; (MS) Curr/Instruction, Rutgers Univ 1968; *cr:* Eng Teacher Westlake HS 1968-75, Kings Park HS 1976-; *ai:* Westlake HS Adv Literary Art Magazine Adv; Kings Park HS Literary Art Magazine Founder & Adv; NYSUT; Frequent Speaker & Requested Writer Columbia Scholastic Press Assn; Individual Poems Published; *office:* Kings Park HS Rte 25 A Kings Park NY 11754

PORCH, BRENDA KAY SAVAGE, Fifth Grade Teacher; *b:* Monroe, LA; *m:* Clifton Eben; *c:* Brad, Benjamin, Amy; *ed:* (BA) Elem Ed, NE LA Univ 1976; Working Towards Masters NE LA Univ; *cr:* 2nd Grade Teacher Heflin Elem 1976-77; 4th Grade Teacher Riverfield Acad 1977-80, Aldine Ind Sch 1980-81; 3rd-5th Grade Teacher Minnie Ruffin 1981-89; 5th Grade Teacher Canton Elem 1989-; *ai:* LA Assn of Educators 1981-82; AFT 1987-89; Kappa Kappa Iota 1987-89; Phi Mu Alumnae 1977-84; *office:* Canton Elem Sch 551 Marietta Hwy Canton GA 30114

PORCHER, CONNIE MITCHELL, Spanish Teacher; *b:* Dayton, OH; *m:* Melvin L.; *ed:* (BA) Span, OH Northern Univ 1973; (MA) His, Wright St Univ 1980; Grad Work His, Wright St Univ; *cr:* Span Teacher Wapakoneta HS & Blume Jr HS 1973-; *ai:* Adv Wapakoneta Sr HS Times Newspaper; OH Foreign Lang Teachers Assn 1974-; NEA, OEA, WEA 1973-; Piqua Historical Society Pres 1986-; Amer Assn of Univ Women (Prgm VP 1987-89, Schlsp Chairperson 1986-89); Ashland Oil Teacher Achievement Awd 1989; Ashland Oil Golden Apple Achiever Awd 1988; OH Assn Historical Societies & Museums Achievement Awd 1988; *office:* Wapakoneta HS 1 Redskin Trl Wapakoneta OH 45895

POROPAT, JOSEFINA LAZARO, Spanish Teacher; *b:* Cartagena, Spain; *m:* Martin P.; *c:* Edward, Joseph M.; *ed:* (BA) Soc Stud, Univ of Murgia Spain; (BA) Span Teaching, Purdue Univ; Span, Purdue Univ; *cr:* Soc Stud Teacher Escuela La Milagrosa HS 1972-79; Span Teacher Highland HS 1983-; *ai:* Span Club Spon Highland HS; Adult Ed Span; Impact Comm Mem; Assisted In Stu Exchange Prgm; Amer Assn Teacher of Span & portuguese 1986-; Croatian Fraternal Union of America Mem 1977-; Article Published Journal of Amer Assn Teachers of Span & Portuguese; *office:* Highland H S 9135 Erie St Highland IN 46322

PORT, KATHLEEN MC LEOD, 8th Grade Chair/Sci Teacher; *b:* St Petersburg, FL; *m:* Thomas Clyde; *c:* Christopher W.; *ed:* (BA) Elem Ed, Auburn Univ 1969; Grad Stud GA St Univ, W GA Coll; *cr:* Sci/Math Teacher Huntley Hills Elem 1969-70; Math/Algebra Teacher Snellville Mid Sch 1970-71; Sci Teacher Lilburn Mid Sch 1972-73; Math/Sci Teacher Snellville Mid Sch 1973-; *ai:* Stu Cncl Adv; NEA, GEA 1969-; *home:* 1341 Rock Chapel Rd Lithonia GA 30058

PORTER, ANNA BELL CARTER, 6th Grade Teacher; *b:* Morgan, UT; *m:* Keith; *c:* Anna Bennett, Dixie Porter; *ed:* (BS) Elem Ed, Weber St Coll 1966; Grad Stud UT St Univ, Brigham Young Univ, Univ of UT; Studied SA His Rio De Janerio; *cr:* 2nd Grade Teacher 1966-69, 6th Grade Teacher 1969- Morgan Elem/Mid Sch; *ai:* Morgan Ed Assn (Pres Elect 1969-70, Pres 1970-71).

PORTER, ANNE WAIT, Computer Literacy Teacher; *b:* Oxford, MS; *m:* Joel J.; *c:* Jeffrey, Emily; *ed:* (BAE) Math, Delta St Univ 1979; *cr:* Programmer Univ of MS 1979-81; Hydra Tool 1981-82; Teacher Leflore Cty HS 1987-; *ai:* MS Assn of Ed 1987-; NEA 1987-; Leflore Cty Assn of Ed 1987-; 1st Baptist Church Teacher/Mission Group & Childrens Choir 1988-; *office:* Leflore Co HS Lakeside Dr Itta Bena MS 38941

PORTER, CAROL KIERNAN, English/Eng 2nd Lang Teacher; *b:* Taunton, MA; *m:* James D.; *c:* Jeff Kiernan; *ed:* (BA) Eng, Long Beach St 1975; (MS) Ed, Coll of St Thomas 1985; Eng as 2nd Lang, Multi Dist Teacher Trng Inst 1990; Lang Dev Specialist Eng as 2nd Lang 1989; *cr:* Teacher Torrance HS 1976-80, South HS 1981-86, Calle Mayor Mid Sch 1987, Torrance HS 1988-; *ai:* Prin Advisory Comm; *office:* Torrance HS 2200 W Carson St Torrance CA 90501

PORTER, CHARLES FRANKLIN, Science Teacher; *b:* Hawkinsville, GA; *m:* Robin A.; *c:* Kristin; *ed:* (BS) Zoology, 1974, (MED) Sci Ed 1978, (EDD) Sci Ed, 1982 Univ of GA; *cr:* Teacher Cochran/Bleckly Cty HS 1976-79, Jefferson HS 1982-83, Cedar Shoals HS 1983-84, Bleckley Cty Mid Sch 1984-; *ai:* Ftbl Coach Bleckly Mid Sch; GA Sci Teachers Assn; Prof Assn of GA Educators; Kappa Delta Pi; STAR Teacher 1990; Bleckley Mid Sch Teacher of Yr 1986; Outstanding Paper Awd Natl Assn for Research Sci Teaching 1984; *office:* Bleckley Mid Sch Dublin Hwy Cochran GA 31014

PORTER, CHRISTINE ANNE, Special Education Teacher; *b:* San Francisco, CA; *m:* Jerry B.; *c:* Danielle Scott, Michelle, Adam; *ed:* (BA) Sociology, Mills Coll 1975; Teacher Cert Elem Ed Mills Coll 1976; Special Ed Cert Spec Ed Univ of ID 1986; *cr:* Kndgtn Teacher Rose Lake Elem Sch 1976-77; 3rd Grade Teacher Harrison Elem Sch 1977-78; 1st/2nd Grade Teacher Rose Lake Elem Sch 1978-83; 1st/2nd Grade Teacher Harrison Elem Sch 1983-86; Resource Room Teacher Ponderosa Elem Sch 1986-88; Post Falls Jr HS 1988-; *ai:* Faculty Adv Stu Cncl Post Falls Jr HS; Coach Odyssey of Mind Team Post Falls Jr HS; Kootenai Ed Assn Pres 1985-86; Cncl for Exceptional Children 1987-; Port of Hope Teacher 1989; Teacher of Yr Kootenai Sch Dist 274 May 1986; *office:* Post Falls Jr HS PO Box 40 Post Falls ID 83854

PORTER, CLAUDIA SIEHR, Religion & Art Teacher; *b:* Milwaukee, WI; *m:* George J.; *c:* Edward, Stephen; *ed:* (BSED) Elem Ed, Alverno Coll 1966; Candidate Master of TheologicaL Stud St Francis Seminary; *cr:* Classroom Teacher Linfield Elem 1966-69, St Alphonsus Sch 1979-85, St Johns Sch 1987-89, St Alphonsus Sch 1989-; *ai:* Religion Curr Comm Chairperson; NCEA; Meritorious Service Awd Alverno Coll 1983; *home:* 5844 Riverside Dr Greendale WI 53129

PORTER, CORNELL BURR, Religion Instructor; *b:* Provo, UT; *m:* Ruth Brady; *c:* Jason C., Stephen B., Jennifer; *ed:* (BS) Sociology 1977, (MA) Near Eastern-Ancient Stud, 1988 Brigham Young Univ; *cr:* Instr Skyline HS Seminary 1977-79; Prin Wasatch 9th Seminary 1979-84, West Lake 9th Seminary 1984-; *ai:* West Salt Lake Dist Trng Cncl; BSA Scouting Coord 1987- on M Y Honor 1989; Presentation CES Symposium at Brigham Young Univ 1981/1989; *home:* 3630 S Chatterleigh Rd West Valley City UT 84120

PORTER, EDITH M., 3rd Grade Teacher; *b:* Ft Ann, NY; *m:* John S.; *c:* Todd W.; *ed:* (BA) Elem Ed, SUNY Plattsburgh 1961; SUNY Plattsburgh, SUNY Potsdam, Marquette Univ; *cr:* 3rd Grade Teacher 1961-65, 1st Grade Teacher 1965-66, Remedial Rdng Teacher 1966-75, 3rd Grade Teacher 1975- Queensbury Elem; *ai:* Sunshine Comm; Iroquois Rdng Cncl (Pres 1966-, Past Pres 1987); NW St United Teachers 1961-, Service Awd; AFT; NY St Rdng Assn 1966-; Republican Comm Person Town of Queensbury 1986-; Sacred Heart Altar Society 1985-; Home Bureau Warren Cty; Queensbury Women of Yr Finalist 1984; Rotary Club House Exch Stu.

PORTER, GAIL GODFREY, Science Department Chair; *b:* Dothan, AL; *m:* Stanley Marion; *c:* Tricia, Tyler; *ed:* (BS) Speech Comm, FL St 1977; (MS) Educl Leadership, Univ of W FL 1989; Grad Stud Bio & Sci; *cr:* Teacher Chipley HS 1983-89; *ai:* Chrldr & Soph Spon; Womans Club 1989-; Chipley HS Teacher of Yr 1988; *office:* Chipley HS 200 N 2nd St Chipley FL 32428

PORTER, IVRIA J., Third Grade Teacher; *b:* Pocahontas, MS; *m:* Archie L.; *c:* Carol, Carol J., Melinda J., Archie L.; *ed:* (BS) Bus Ed, 1966, Recertification Elem Ed, 1970 MS Valley St Coll; (MA) Elem Ed, MS St Univ 1981; *cr:* 6th/7th Grade Teacher Gibbs Elem 1966-67; Bus Ed Teacher Kinterbish HS 1967-70; Elem Teacher Parkview Elem Sch 1973-; *ai:* MAE, NEA Mem 1971-; Church Musician; Cmmty Involvement; Teacher of Week Certificate of Merit Meridian Municipal Sch Dist 1990; AME Faculty Rep Certificate of Appreciation 1985; *office:* Parkview Elem Sch 1225 26th St Meridian MS 39301

PORTER, J. CRAIG, English Department Chair; *b:* Austin, TX; *ed:* (BA) Eng, Univ of The South 1972; (MA) Eng, TX Tech Univ 1973; PHD Prgm, Univ of TN; *cr:* Eng Instr Univ of TN 1972-77, Battle Ground Acad 1977-81; Eng Chm Randolph Macon Acad 1983-; *ai:* Spon of Honor Cncl; Dir of SAT Prgm; Cross Cntry, Track & Field, Swimmng, Tennis, Soccer Coach; Chm of In-House Self-Study Group; Asst Dir of Admissions; BSA Dist Exec 1982; *office:* Randolph-Macon Acad 201 W 3rd St Front Royal VA 22630

PORTER, LINDA RAVLIN, English Teacher; *b:* Burlington, VT; *m:* Richard; *c:* Chloe; *ed:* (BA) Eng, 1969, (MAT) Teaching, 1970 Univ of VT; *cr:* Eng Teacher Mt Mansfield Union HS 1970-; *ai:* NEA, VT Cncl of Teachers of Eng; Mt Mansfield Teacher of Yr 1986; *office:* Mt Mansfield Union HS Browns Trace Rd Jericho VT 05465

PORTER, MARY ANN, Third Grade Teacher; *b:* Conneaut, OH; *ed:* (BS) Elem Ed, 1975, (MED) Elem Ed, 1981 Edinboro St Coll; *cr:* 3rd Grade Teacher Springfield Elem 1978-; *ai:* NEA, PSEA Local Exec Cncl Mem 1987-; Springfield Township Recreation Comm Secy 1989-.

PORTER, MARY GRAFF, First Grade Teacher; *b:* Big Rapids, MI; *m:* George; *c:* Kelli Hettmansperger, Elizabeth Gibbie; *ed:* (AA) Sci, Muskegon Cmmnty 1972; (BS) Ed, Soc Std, Grand Valley St 1974; 30 Addl Hrs Prof Dev with Concentrations on Rdng; *cr:* 3rd/4th Grade Teacher St Michael 1974-76; 1st Grade Teacher Patricia St Clair Elem 1976-; *ai:* Lakeshore Rdng Cncl; MI Rdng Cncl; Teacher of Yr 1988.

PORTER, MRYTLE SLONE, 5th Grade Teacher; *b:* Knott Co, KY; *m:* Roy E.; *c:* Monica Lynne; *ed:* (BA) Elem Ed, Morehead St Univ 1974; Morehead St Univ 1978; *cr:* 1st Grade Teacher 1974-79, 5th Grade Teacher 1979-90 Hitchins Elem; *ai:* 4-H Adv; Coord St Jude Bike-Athon; Asst Supervisor 1st Chrstn Church Nursery; Asst Leader GSA; Carter Cty Ed 1974-; KEA Delegate 1984; KY Teacher Intnl Prgm Resource Teacher 1987-90; *home:* PO Box 805 Grayson KY 41143

PORTER, MYRA WADE, English Teacher/Chair; *b:* Mc Allister, OK; *c:* Ryan E., Clint M.; *ed:* (BFA) Speech/Drama, Univ of OK 1971; *cr:* Eng/Drama Teacher Cyril HS 1973-74; Speech/Drama Teacher 1979-83, Eng Teacher 1983-, Eng Dept Chairperson 1989 Jarman Jr HS; *office:* Jarman Jr HS 5 Mac Arthur Dr Midwest City OK 73110

PORTER, NANCY LEFGREN, First Grade Teacher; *b:* Council Bluffs, IA; *m:* Eugene D.; *c:* Theresa, Tracy; *ed:* (BS) Ed, Univ of IA 1976; Sci Ed; *cr:* Teachers Aid 1970-76, 1st/2nd Grade Teacher Sabin Elem 1976-79, 1st/2nd Grade Teacher Hills Elem 1979-; *ai:* Team Leader; Mentor Teacher; Building Rep; Piloted New Rdng Prgm; Press Release Coord; Cnslr Laision; E Cntrl Uniserve Unit Exec Bd 1987-; IA City Ed Assn (Pres 1984-85, VP Governmental Affairs 1983-); Intnl Rdng Assn, ASCD, Phi Delta Kappa 1990; League of Women Voters Exec Bd 1988-; Johnson Cty Democrats Precinct Chairperson Corporation Bd 1986-; Alpha XI Delta Alumnae Pres; Iowa City Ed Assn Negotiation Team; IA St Ed Assn PAC Cntrl Comm; Co-Authored Dist Outdoor Ed Book; *home:* 2519 Potomac Dr Iowa City IA 52245

PORTER, ROBERT CHRIS, 5th/6th Grade Math Teacher; *b:* Knoxville, TN; *m:* Sherry Lynn; *c:* Karen L., Robert B.; *ed:* (BS) Bus Ed, TN Wesleyan Coll 1970; (MA) Elem Ed, Tusculum Coll 1989; Math/Elem Course Work, Univ of TN; *cr:* 7th/8th Grade Math Teacher Taylor Elem 1970-74; Math/Algebra Teacher Cleveland Day Sch 1974-77; 7th/8th Grade Math Teacher 1977-89, 5th/6th Grade Math Teacher 1989- Northview Elem; *ai:* Honor Club Adv; TEA, NEA 1970-; SCEA 1977-; Teacher of Yr 1987; Northview Optimist Club Service Awd 1986; Career Leader III 1985; *home:* 1001 Walnut Ln Sevierville TN 37862

PORTER, ROGER JAMES, Fourth Grade Science Teacher; *b:* Minneapolis, MN; *c:* Steven, Fredrick, Susan Porter Powell; *ed:* (BS) Ed, Univ of MN 1960; (BS) Ed, Mankato St Univ 1967; *cr:* 4th Grade Teacher 1967-71, 6th Grade High Achievers 1971-77, 4th Grade Teacher 1977- Bloomington Public Schls; *ai:* Plan & Direct Extended Field Trips Elem Stu; Bloomington Fed of Teachers; Masons, Scottish, Rite, Shriner, Stephen Minister; Pack 464 Den Leader Coach; Nom Ashland Oil Teacher Achievement Awd; Nom MN Assn of Commerce & Industry Excl in Ed; Invited to Lennigrad USSR by Intnl Technology Exchange 1990; Advisory Bd Career Ed for Dist 287; *office:* Hubert Olson Elem Sch 4501 W 102nd St Bloomington MN 55437

PORTER, VALERIE A., 7th/8th Grade Teacher; *b:* Berkeley, CA; *m:* Kim R.; *c:* Kelly, Ian; *ed:* (BA) His, Santa Clara Univ 1971; (MA) Rdng, Fresno Pacific Coll 1990; *cr:* Substitute Teacher 1972-75, 5th Grade Teacher 1975-76 Los Angeles Unified; 8th Grade Eng Teacher Maderia Unified 1979-81; 8th Grade Eng/Math/His Teacher Coarsegold Union Sch Dist 1981-; *ai:* Rdng Comm Fresno Pacific Coll; Mentor Teacher 1987-89; NCTE; *office:* Coarsegold Sch PO Box 338 Coarsegold CA 93614

PORTERFIELD, ANITA LA VERNE, Reading Teacher; *b:* Ardmore, OK; *m:* Roger M.; *c:* Sara, Brent; *ed:* (BA) Span, 1965, (MED) Rdng Specialist, 1978 E Cntrl Univ; *cr:* Span Teacher Beverly Hills Intermediate 1966-69; Classroom Teacher Douglass TX 1969-70, 1972-73; Span Teacher Healdton HS 1974-77; Rdng Teacher Healdton Public Schls 1977-; *ai:* NEA 1966-; OK Ed Assn 1974-; Teacher of Yr 1977, 1987.

PORTERFIELD, COX, English Teacher; *b:* Holly Springs, MS; *m:* Terry D.; *c:* Ryan, Carrie; *ed:* (BS) Bus Ed, Lincoln Univ 1977; *cr:* Substitute Teacher 1977-78, 1981-83 Jefferson City HS; Eng Teacher California R-1 HS 1983-; *ai:* Jr HS Cheerleading & Stu Cncl Spon; MO St Teachers Assn 1983-89; MO Assn Teachers of Eng 1989-; Beta Sigma Phi (VP, Secy) 1979-; *office:* California R-1 HS 205 S Owen St California MO 65018

PORTO, CAROLYN J., 5th Grade Teacher; *b:* Evergreen Park, IL; *ed:* (BA) Elem Ed/His, North Cntrl Coll 1985; *cr:* Kndgtn Teacher Daybridge Learnlng Center 1985-86; 6th/7th/8th Grade His/Eng Teacher 1986-87, 4th Grade Teacher 1987-89, 5th Grade Teacher 1989- St Rita of Cascia Sch; *ai:* Stu Cncl Adv; Intermediate Wing Coord; NCEA 1985-; Bishop ONeil Awd in CathechticS 1989; *home:* 1034 Langley Cir Naperville IL 60563

PORTO, LOUISE C., Counselor; *b:* Fall River, MA; *m:* George T. Jr.; *ed:* (BA) Sociology, 1974, (MA) Ed/Counseling, 1976 Univ of CT; Psych, Univ of Hartford, S CT St Univ; *cr:* Cnslr Post Coll 1976-81; Cnslr/Ed Asst Univ of CT 1981-83; Cnslr Torrington HS 1983-; *ai:* Sub Comm Chairperson Yr Evaluation; Dept Rep Leadership Team; Pi Lambda Theta (Secy 1977) 1975-; Outstanding Young Women of America 1979, 1988; Torrington Ed Assn 1983-; MS Greater Waterbury Schlsp (Secy, Producer-Dir) 1988-; Planned Parenthood of Waterbury Advisory Mem 1980; MS CT Bus Mgrs Assn Secy 1985-; Article Published 1984; *office:* Torrington HS Major Besse Dr Torrington CT 06790

PORTREY, LEON PAUL, Business Teacher; *b:* Falls City, NE; *m:* Kathleen Ann Krutz; *c:* Paul, Douglas, Matthew, Jennifer; *ed:* (BS) Bus Ed, Peru St Coll 1969; *cr:* Bus Teacher Weeping Water HS 1969-70, Stanton HS 1970-74, Lake City HS 1979-84, Scotus Cntrl Cath HS 1984-86, Aquinas HS 1986-; *ai:* Head Boys Bsktbl Coach; Coach of Yr 1970-71; Teacher of Yr 1985-86; Prarie Fire Comm on Ed St of NE 1985-86; *office:* Aquinas HS P O Box 149 David City NE 68632

POSEY, KRIS KIBLER, Teacher & Counselor; *b:* Ft Sill, OK; *m:* Thomas D.; *c:* Matthew T., Nathan K.; *ed:* (BS) Elem Ed, 1974, (MS) Guidance/Counseling, 1978 Youngstown St; Tribes & Cmmty Intervention Drug & Alcohol Prevention Trng; *cr:* 1st Grade Teacher Beaver Local Schls 1974-78; 1st/2nd Grade Teacher Cincinnati City Schls 1978-80; Elem Cnslr Westerville City Schls 1986-89; *ai:* AACD, OSCA 1986-89; *home:* 3503 Cypressdale Dr Spring TX 77388

POSEY-HOOPER, BETTYE MC CULLOUGH, Mathematics & Religion Teacher; *b:* Rock Hill, SC; *c:* Stephanie K. Posey, John A. Posey III, Derrick M. Posey; *ed:* (BA) Elem Ed, Johnson C Smith Univ 1960; (MED) Guidance Instruction, Winthrop Coll 1972; Univ of SC; *cr:* Teacher Rock Hill Sch Dist 3 1960-82, Rosa Parks Cath Mid 1983; *ai:* SCEA, NEA 1960-82; Elem Teacher Assn Building Rep 1983-; Alpha Kappa Alpha; BSA Advisory Bd 1970-79; Red Cross Volunteer 1982-85; Order of Eastern Star; All St Roman Cath Church (Eucharist Minister, Lector, Church Choir, Networker); Guidance Instruction Grant Winthrop Coll 1970-72; *office:* Rosa Parks Cath Mid Sch 3510 Eldorado Ave Baltimore MD 21207

POSS, ALLISON MAUGHON, Fourth Grade Teacher; *b:* Good Hope, GA; *m:* Milton M. (dec); *c:* Lisa Schicho, Nan Smith, Celia Thompson, John; *ed:* (BS) Ed, Univ of GA 1953; Univ of GA 1962-73; *cr:* Teacher Walton Cty 1946-53 & 1961-65 & 1973-; *ai:* GAE Secy 1963-64; *office:* Monroe Elem Sch 203 Bold Springs Ave Monroe GA 30655

POSS, ELAYNE KNOX, Guidance Counselor; *b:* Greenwood, MS; *m:* Gregory A.; *c:* Shannon, Jake; *ed:* (BA) Eng, Delta St Univ 1971; (MED) Eng, William Carey Coll 1977; (MED) Guidance & Counseling, Univ of S MS 1983; *cr:* Eng Teacher St Martin HS 1971-83; Guidance Cnslr St Martin Mid Sch 1983-87, St Martin HS 1987-; *ai:* Scholars Bowl Coach; MS Cnslrs Assn 1983-; Gulf Coast Counseling Assn (Secy, Treas) 1989-; *office:* St Martin HS 10800 Yellowjacket Blvd Ocean Springs MS 39564

POSS, FREDERICK MAURICE, Dept Chair of Language Arts; *b:* Sparta, WI; *m:* Cheryl A.; *c:* Nicholas, Cheri A.; *ed:* (BS) Eng, Oshkosh St Univ 1970; (MA) Eng/Ed, Univ of WI Madison 1975; (MST) Rdng, Univ of WI Eau Claire 1978; Writing Fellow, Univ of WI Eau Claire 1980; Voc Study Skills, Free Lance Writer; *cr:* Teacher Central Jr HS 1970-82; Teacher/Dept Chm South Jr HS 1982-; Teacher Memorial Sr HS 1990-; *ai:* Forensics Coach; Bargaining Comm Mem; Drama Coach; Ftbl Referee; WI St Rdng Assn Pres 1978-80; WI Cncl Teachers of Eng Lucille Pooley Awd 1988/1989; Cub Scouts of America Asst Park Leader 1987-89; Articles How to Evaluate Writing & How to Write Publication Published USRA & UCTE Journals; *home:* 1139 E Tyler Ave Eau Claire WI 54701

POST, CLAIRE BENNETT, Kindergarten Teacher; *b:* El Dorado, AR; *m:* Gerald Randal; *c:* Ashley, Miranda, Justin; *ed:* (BS) Home Ec, LA Tech Univ 1974; *cr:* Kndgtn Teacher Linville HS 1974-75; Kndgtn Teacher 1984- Spearsville HS; *office:* Spearsville HS P O Box 18 Spearsville LA 71277

POST, KATHY ANGELA, Mathematics Teacher; *b:* Tunnelton, WV; *m:* Dana T.; *c:* Tessa, Jeremy; *ed:* (BS) Bus Ed, WV Univ 1971; (MS) Voc Tech Ed, Marshall Univ 1979; Math, E KY Univ 1983; *cr:* Bus Teacher Newburg HS 1971-74; Curr Writer Preston Cty Ed Center 1974-75; Bus Teacher United Career Center 1975-78, Preston Cty Ed Center 1978-79; Math Teacher Pulaski Cty HS 1983-; *ai:* Stu Government; Sonshine Club; Pulaski Cty Ed Assn Treas 1983-; KCTM, NCTM 1990; 5th Dist Math/Sci Alliance 1988-; Stenograph Shorthand Grant 1977-78; KY 5th Congressional Dist Excl in Teaching Awd 1990.

POSTELL, AURELIA TILLMAN, Lang Art & Reading Teacher; *b:* Adel, GA; *m:* Lamar; *c:* Debbie Buckholts, Donna Campbell, Sheri, Eric; *ed:* (BS) Elem Ed, 1969, (BS) Mid Sch, 1980, (MS) Rdng, 1981 Valdosta St Coll; *cr:* Teacher Adel Elem Sch 1969-71; Lead Teacher 1977-, Dept Head/Rdng Teacher 1986- Cook Mid Sch; *ai:* Team Leader; Intra Faculty, System

Media Advisory Comm; Stu Support Team; Stars; S GA Rdng Cncl of IRA (Building Rep, VP) 1979-80; Prof Assn of GA Educators Bldg Rep 1980-; Alpha Delta Kappa (Sargent at Arms 1985-86, Recording Secy 1989-); Adel United Meth (Cncl of Ministries, Admin Bd, Sunday Sch Teacher, Childrens Dept Head) 1962-; Meth Womens Chrstn Society Chm 1955-, Outstanding Meth Woman 1967; *home:* Rt 3 Box 577 Adel GA 31620

POSTELL-GEE, JOY M., English & German Teacher; *b:* Andrews, NC; *m:* Robert F. Gee; *ed:* (BA) Eng, Augusta Coll 1987; Role of Collegiate Chrldr Adv, Memphis St Univ; *cr:* HS Eng/German Teacher George P Butler Comprehensive 1987-; *ai:* Var Chrldr Coach & Coord; Y-Club Adv; Teacher Acad; Chrldr Organizational Forum of America Comm Mem; Natl Educators of America, AATG 1987-; NCTE, Phi Kappa Phi, Kappa Delta Pi, Natl Chrldr Coaches Assn; Arthritis Fnd; WCU Big Cat Club; Natl Fed Interscholastic Spirit Assn; Outstanding Young Woman of America; YMCA Outstanding Service Awd; GA Delegate to TPAI Revision Comm; *office:* G P Butler Comprehensive HS 2011 Lumpkin Rd Augusta GA 30906

POSTEN, KERMITT LEE, Science Dept Chair/Bio Teacher; *b:* Clarinda, IA; *m:* Susan Ann Jacobsen; *c:* Nichole A., Angela L.; *ed:* (BS) Bio, 1972, (MS) Bio, 1980 NW MO St Univ; *cr:* Sci Teacher West Nodaway RI 1972-74, Maryville R-II 1974-; *ai:* Bio Olympaid Coach; Teams Coach; MO St Teachers Assn 1972-; NSTA 1987-; *office:* Maryville R-II HS 1514 S Munn Ave Maryville MO 64468

POSTON, DIANN NEAL, Third Grade Teacher; *b:* Cookeville, TN; *w:* Beecher Lee (dec); *c:* Steve; *ed:* (BS) Bus Ed, 1970, (MA) Elem Ed, 1985 TN Tech; *cr:* 3rd/4th Grade Teacher Alpine Elem 1974-75; 3rd Grade Teacher Rickman Elem 1975-76; *ai:* Sch Newspaper Spon; Cty In-Service Comm; Cty Study Cncl; TTU, Intnl Rdng Assn Contact Person 1987-88; Delta Kappa Gamma Nominations Comm 1985-; OCEA, TEA, NEA 1974-; Okolona Meth Church (Treas, Teacher) 1975-; Overton Cty Teacher of Yr 1986; Ed Center Freelance Writer & Artist; *home:* R 1 Box 55 Rickman TN 38580

POTEAT, CAROLYN SENTER, First Grade Teacher; *b:* Centerville, TN; *m:* Billy Chandler; *c:* Kimberly D., Tonya R.; *ed:* (BA) Elem Ed, Mars Hill Coll 1966; *cr:* 1st Grade Teacher Glen Echo Elem 1966-67, Jacob Adams Elem 1967-69; 1st/3rd Grade Teacher Kings Fork Elem 1969-71; 1st Grade Teacher Suffolk Chrstn 1976-83, Alliance Chrstn 1983-; *ai:* Cheerleading Spon; VA Ed Assn 1966-71; Assn of Chrstn Schls Intnl 1983-; *home:* 1801 Kings Fork Rd Suffolk VA 23434

POTEAT, KATHRYN MARLOU JOYNER, Mathematics Teacher; *b:* Shelby, NC; *m:* William; *c:* Jonathan D., Rebekah M., Timothy P.; *ed:* (BA) Bible Ed, Columbia Bible Coll 1965; Grad Stud William & Mary Williamsburg VA; *cr:* 1st/2nd/4th-6th Grade Elem Rdng Teacher Botetourt Elem 1965-70; Kndgtn Teacher Danville Chrstn Sch 1977-80; Kndgtn/3rd Grade/Jr HS Math Teacher Cedar Grove Chrstn Acad 1980-; *ai:* Church & Childrens Ministries (Sunday Sch Teacher, VBS, Camps, Etc); *office:* Cedar Grove Chrstn Acad Tabor Rd & Rising Sun Philadelphia PA 19120

POTEAT, SHIRLEY PAGE, 4th Grade Teacher; *b:* Spartanburg, SC; *m:* Calvin Douglas; *c:* Brian, Neil, Holly; *ed:* (BA) Elem Ed, Univ of SC 1976; (MED) Elem Ed Converse Coll; *cr:* 4th Grade Teacher Hendrix Elem 1977-; *ai:* Spartanburg Dist 2 Incentive Pay Selection Comm; *home:* 2009 Evergreen Dr Inman SC 29349

POTEETE, DARRYL, Physical Education Teacher; *b:* Tahlequah, OK; *m:* Ruth Ann; *c:* Asa, Ana J.; *ed:* (BA) Phys Ed, 1978, (MS) Sch Admin, 1981 Northeastern St Univ; *cr:* Phys Ed Teacher Sequoyah Elem Sch 1978-; *ai:* Stu Cncl & 4-H Club Spon; Tahlequah Jr HS Spec Olympics Coach; Tahlequah Public Schls Drug Free Schls Comm Elem Rep; Title IV Parent Comm Past Mem; NEA, OK Ed Assn, Tahlequah Ed Assn Mem 1978-; OK Ofcls Assn 1977-; Tahlequah Ftbl Ofcls Assn (Mem 1978-, Past Pres); Tahlequah Bsktbl Ofcls Assn (Mem 1977-, Past Secy); Tahlequah Sertoma Club Teacher of Month 1987; *office:* Sequoyah Elem Sch 425 S College Ave Tahlequah OK 74464

POTEMPA, ROMAN PAUL, 5th Grade Teacher; *b:* Blue Island, IL; *m:* Sarah T. Robinson; *c:* Traci R.; *ed:* (BSED) Elem Ed, IL St Univ 1971; Numerous Classes; *cr:* 3rd-6th Grade Teacher Markham Park Sch 1971-; *ai:* Various Curr Writing; Summer Sch Enrichment Prgm; Gifted Art Ed; Unit Leader-Intermediate Grades; Safety Patrol Supervisor; Stu Drama Prgms, Inservice Comm; Report Card Dev; Dist 144 Ed Assn Building Rep, Working Conditions Comm, Negotiations Team; BSA (Dist Mem At Large 1985-, Merit Badge Cnslr, Local Troop Comm Mem, Presentor of Eagle Scout Awds); St Christopher Church Part of Ministry Team; *office:* Markham Park Sch 16239 Lawndale Ave Markham IL 60426

POTHIER, BERNADETTE ANN, Mathematics Teacher; *b:* Providence, RI; *ed:* (BA) Elem Ed/Eng, 1967, (MA) Eng, 1972 RI Coll; Math & Cmptr Sci Courses for Scndry Prof Cert; Cooperating Teacher & Adult Ed Courses for Cert; *cr:* Math Teacher Coventry Jr HS West 1967-78, Coventry Jr HS 1979-; *ai:* Math Club & Natl Jr Honor Society Adv; Kids Quiz, Mathcounts, Future Problem Solving, Natl All Star Academeic Team, Academic Decathlon Coach; Math & Cmptr Curr Comm; NCTM, RI Math Teachers Assn 1972-; Chi Alpha Mu Newsletter Ed 1984-85; ASCD 1987-; Smithsonian Mem 1977-; Natl Geographic Mem 1975-; RI St Finalist Excl in Math 1985; Wrkshps Presenter Problem Solving through Excl in Teaching Math RI Coll 1988; Whos Who in Amer Ed 1987-88; *home:* PO Box 406 Coventry RI 02816

POTLUNAS, JOHN FRANCIS, Instrumental Music Teacher; *b:* Pottsville, PA; *m:* Michelle Joan Horan; *c:* Michquelena; *ed:* (BS) Music Ed, W Chester Univ 1974; (MED) Music Ed, St of PA Dept of Ed 1985; *cr:* Music Teacher Nativity BVM HS 1974-78, Catasauqua HS 1978-79, Williams Valley HS 1980-; *ai:* HS Marching Concert, Jazz Bands, Percussion Ensembles; Asst Drama Dir; Fine & Practical Art Dept Chm; Soph Class Adv; MENC, PMEA (Secy, Pres, VP) 1978-; A F of Musicians Trustee 1985-87; NEA, PSEA 1980-; Cressona Band Dir 1979-; Sch Symphony Orch Asst Conductor 1987-88; St Patrick Church Choir Asst Conductor 1980-; *home:* 217 N George St Pottsville PA 17901

POTOCKI, KATHLEEN PENSON, Art Teacher; *b:* Jamaica, Queens, NY; *m:* Peter T.; *c:* Danny; *ed:* (BA) Fine Arts/Art Ed, 1977, (MA) Fine Arts, 1980 Adelphi Univ; *cr:* Art Teacher Northern Parkway Elem Sch 1978-88, Post Road Sch & Mamoroneck Ave Sch 1988-; *ai:* Art Curr Comm; Staff Dev Muralist; Faculty Club; Art Gallery & Art Club; Drama & Mural Club; NY St Art Teachers Assn 1977-; NY St United Teachers 1977-; NY St Teachers Retiremant System 1977-; White Plains Teachers Assn 1988-; Uniondale Parent Teacher Assn 1977-88; PTA Exec Bd Publicity & Advertisement 1979-88; Faculty Club Treas 1979-80; Cntrl Ed Cncl Mem 1981-82; White Plains Parent Teacher Assn 1988-; Illustrator for Bide-A-Wee Magazine; *office:* Post Road Sch 175 W Post Rd White Plains NY 10606

POTRIKUS, SUSAN FRANCES, Mathematics Teacher; *b:* Little Falls, NY; *ed:* (BA) Scndry Ed, SUNY Oswego 1973; Grad Stud Oswego St, Coll of St Rose; *cr:* Math Teacher Liverpool HS 1973-; *ai:* Pre-Calculus & Calculus Textbook Review Comm; Calculus Sch Awds Contest Chm; United Liverpool Faculty Assn, NY St United Teachers, AFT 1973-; *office:* Liverpool HS 4338 Wetzel Rd Liverpool NY 13090

POTTER, CRAIG EDWARD, English Teacher/Coach; *b:* Indianapolis, IN; *c:* Amanda C.; *ed:* (BA) Eng/Ed, W KY Univ 1972; (MS) Scndry Ed, IN Univ 1977; *cr:* Teacher/Coach Franklin HS 1972-73, Perry Meridian HS 1973-87, Greenfield-Cntrl 1988-; *ai:* Head Ftbl & Asst Wrestling Coach; NEA, ISTA 1972-; Greenfield Teacher of Yr 1989; *office:* Greenfield Cntrl HS 810 N Broadway Greenfield IN 46140

POTTER, JIM RUSSELL, Speech & Drama Teacher; *b:* Chicago, IL; *m:* Yvonne Lee Jensen; *c:* James R., Alyssa G.; *ed:* (BS) Speech Ed, Bob Jones Univ 1975; (MA) Dramatic Production, Pensacola Chrstn Coll 1980; *cr:* Speech/Drama Teacher Faithway Baptist HS 1975-77; Drama Seminar Dir The Acad of Arts of SC 1977-85; Speech/Drama Teacher Faith Baptist Sch 1985-; *ai:* Faith Drama Guild Spon; Dir Annual Speech & Drama Camp; *office:* Faith Baptist Schls 7306 E Atherton Rd Davison MI 48423

POTTER, JULIE A., English/Humanities Teacher; *b:* Highland Falls, NY; *ed:* (BA) Classical Civilizations, 1981, (BA) Eng Ed, 1985 FL St Univ; *cr:* 7th Grade Eng Teacher Bellevue Mid Sch 1985-86; 10th-12th Grade Eng/Hum Teacher Melbourne HS 1986-; *ai:* Co-Spon Stu Cncl; FL Assn of Stu Cncl Adv 1989-; *office:* Melbourne H S 74 Bulldog Blvd Melbourne FL 32901

POTTER, MARY ANN ANN SIKKEMA, English Teacher; *b:* Tullahoma, TN; *m:* Victor E.; *c:* Allan; *ed:* (BA) Eng, MI St Univ 1967; *cr:* Eng Teacher Pontiac Northern HS 1967-68; Eng/Soc Stud Teacher Zimmerman Jr HS 1968-69; Eng Teacher Carman Sr HS 1969-72; Eng/Soc Stud Teacher Utley Mid Sch 1973-78; Eng Teacher Athens Sr HS 1978-83, Millbrook Sr HS 1984-; *home:* 3412 Horseshoe Bend Raleigh NC 27613

POTTER, NANCY MOUDY, Fourth Grade Teacher; *b:* Mc Minnville, TN; *m:* Thomas H.; *c:* Sarah, Anna; *ed:* (BS) Elem Ed, Memphis St Univ 1972; *cr:* 2nd Grade Teacher Fayette Cty 1972-76; 4th Grade Teacher Reeves Rogers 1976-; *ai:* In-Service, Rdng Textbook, Fall Festival, Sch Prgm Comm; Memphis Ed Assn 1976-; TN Ed Assn 1972-; FCEA 1972-76; *office:* Reeves Rogers Elem Sch 1807 Greenland Dr Murfreesboro TN 37130

POTTER, PRESTON W., History Teacher; *b:* Roanoke, VA; *m:* Sheryl Lugene Giles; *c:* Melissa L., Chad P.; *ed:* (BS) Ed, Cumberland Coll 1975; *cr:* His Teacher Powell Valley HS 1978-; *ai:* Sr Class Spon; Key Club Adv; Wise Cty Ed Assn, VA Ed Assn, NEA; Lions Club, PTA; Outstanding Young Man of America 1988.

POTTER, ROSE M., Spanish Teacher/Dept Chair; *b:* Daggat, MI; *ed:* (BA) Span, Auburn Univ 1972; (MS) Span, Univ of N IA 1982; Oral Proficiency Tester Cert; *cr:* Teacher North Star Bourough Sch Dist 1979-81; Instr Tanana Valley Comm Coll 1981, Austin Comm Coll 1988-89; Teacher/Dept Chair/Dist Foreign Lang Coord Westlake HS 1982-; *ai:* Pan Amer Stu Forum Spon; Project Excel; Salamanca Coll Credit Prgm Summer Study; Coord & Travel Spon; AATSP VP 1984-; ATPE 1986-; TFLA 1982-; SW Rotary Club Teacher of Yr 1987; *office:* Westlake HS 4100 Westbank Dr Austin TX 78746

POTTER, ROSEMARY LEE, Reading Teacher; *b:* Miami, FL; *m:* Robert Ellis; *c:* Robert E. II, Kenyon D.; *ed:* (BS) Elem Ed, Maryville Coll 1960; (MS) Elem Ed, Univ of TN 1963; (EDD) Elem Ed, Univ of Miami 1973; Post Doctoral Rdng Stud, FL Intnl Univ & Atlantic Univ; *cr:* Swimming Instr Southwest YMCA 1956-62; Teacher Dade Cty Schls 1960-62, Hudson Sch Dist 1963-65, Dade Cty Schls 1965-77, Pinellas Cty Schls 1977-; *ai:* Cmptr Club & Drama Club Co-Spon; Performing & Visual Arts Improvement Comm; Natl Cncl for Children & Families; Pinellas Rdng Cncl Dir of Research & Legislation 1988-; Phi Delta Kappa; St Pauls United Meth Church Scout Coord 1979-86; St Petersburg Dist Scout 1986-; United Meth Church Coord; Pioneer-Televison Worth Teaching Awd; CBS/Univ of Boston Sch of Comm Natl Press Club Washington DC 1987; Pinellas cty Schls Teacher of Yr 1984; Teacher of Yr Semi-Finalist Suncoast Chamber of Commerce Equicor 1990; Consultant Jim Hensons Fraggle Rock TV Prgm & Rdng Rainbow TV Prgm; Books Published 1975, 1984, 1989; *office:* Safety Harbor Mid Sch 125 7th St N Safety Harbor FL 34695

POTTER, WENDY IRELAND, 10th/11th Grade Eng Teacher; *b:* Lowland, NC; *m:* Johnnie Wayne; *c:* Jon; *ed:* (BS) Eng/Scndry Ed, E Carolina Univ 1977; *cr:* 8th-12th Grade Eng Teacher Columbia HS 1977-78; Eng Teacher S Alamance Cty HS 1979-80, N Shore Sr HS 1980-81, 1982, Nimitz Sr HS 1982-83, Pamlico Cty HS 1984-; *ai:* Beta Club Spon Pamlico Cty HS 1984-; NC Assn of Educators Building Rep 1988-89; NC Eng Teachers Assn 1988-89; Wardens Grove Free Will Baptist Young Womens Circle Mem 1989-; NC Center for Advancement of Teaching 1989; Pamlico Cty HS Faculty Teacher of Yr 1989-; *office:* Pamlico Cty HS PO Box 699 Bayboro NC 28515

POTTER, WILLIAM T., II, Science Teacher; *b:* Beaver, OK; *c:* Angelia M., Audra L.; *ed:* (BSED) Natural Sci, NW OK St Univ 1967; (MED) Natural Sci, SW OK St Univ 1973; TX A&M Univ; *cr:* Sci Teacher Corn HS 1967-68, Shamrock HS 1968-; *ai:* TX Univ Interscholastic League Dist Sci Dir; Sci Dist UIL & Sr Spon; TX St Teachers Assn, Wheeler Cty Teachers Assn, NEA 1968-; Dist 16 Teachers Assn Secy 1968-; Natl Sci Fnd Grant TX A&I Univ 1969, Southwestern 1972.

POTTHAST, PATRICIA VAREL, Fifth/Sixth Grade Teacher; *b:* Breese, IL; *m:* Dennis L.; *c:* Jennifer, Stephanie; *ed:* (BS) Elem/Spec Ed, Eastern IL Univ 1971; (MS) Spec Ed, SIU Edwardsville 1975; Ed Math/Geography/Govt; *cr:* EMH Teacher 1971-77, 5th/6th Grade Teacher 1977- Greenville Elem; *ai:* IL ST Bd of Ed Consultant on Drug Ed; IL ST Bd of Ed Curr Dev of Occupant Restraints; Adv Sch Competitions Ie Geography Bee/IL Math League/Spelling Bee; NEA; IL Ed Assn; Greenville Ed Assn Secy/VP/Pres 1972-75; Bond Cty Ladies Democrat Club 1975-; Utlaut Memorial Hospital Auxiliary; Math/Cmptr Stud Fellowship Univ of IL 1985; Robert Taft Institute of Government Sangamon ST 1989; Natl Geographic Society Grant at SIU Edwardsville 1989; ISBE Occupant Restraint Safety Grant 1990; *office:* Greenville Elem Sch 800 N Dewey Greenville IL 62246

POTTS, BECKY ANN, Gifted Teacher; *b:* Great Falls, MT; *ed:* (BA) Psych/Elem Ed, Muhlenberg Coll 1975; (MS) Educl Admin, Bowling Green St Univ 1982; Gifted Certificate/PHD Prgm, OH St UNIV 1989; *cr:* 6th Grade Teacher 1978-81, 1981-89 Buckeye West Elem; Gifted Teacher Worthington Park Elem 1989-; *ai:* Nom OH Teacher of Yr 1988; Jaycess Outstanding Young Educator of Yr 1986; Graduate Asst Bowling Green St Univ 1982; *home:* 4999 Kingshill Dr Apt 104 Columbus OH 43229

POTTS, CHARLOTTE JEFFERS, First Grade Teacher; *b:* Millington, MD; *m:* Garvin W. Sr.; *c:* Schree, Garvin Jr.; *ed:* (BA) Elem Ed, Bowie St Coll 1961; 30 Hrs Temple Univ; Univ of MD; *cr:* 3rd Grade Teacher Garnett Elem Sch 1961-62; 1st Grade Teacher, Galena Elem Sch 1962-82; Millington Elem Sch 1982-; *ai:* Txtbk Comm; Equity Comm; Drug Curr Dev; Report Card Comm; Child Abuse Comm; Curr Dev Comm; MSTA 1961-; NEA 1961-; KCTA 1961-; Emmanuel U M Church Supt of Sunday Schl 1985-88;TBPOE of W Daughter Ruler 1985-; NAACP Mem; Teacher in Charge when Princ Absent; *office:* Millington Elem School Sassafras Millington MD 21651

POTTS, JOE VAUGHN, History Teacher; *b:* Dora, AL; *m:* Rebecca Campbell; *c:* Joe V. Jr., Lora A.; *ed:* (BS) Scndry Ed His, 1976, (MA) Scndry Ed, 1983 Univ of AL Birmington; Cert Ed Leadership; *cr:* Teacher Dora HS 1977-, Wallace St Comm Coll 1988-; *ai:* SGA Spon; Soc Stud Comm; AEA, NEA 1977-; DAR His Teacher of Yr 1987; *office:* Dora HS Rt 3 Box 42 Dora AL 35062

POTTS, JOSEPH PATRICK, English Teacher; *b:* Dubuque, IA; *ed:* (BA) Eng, Loras Coll 1987; Univ of IA; *cr:* Eng Teacher Dubuque Sr HS 1987-; *ai:* Writing Center Dir; Head Frosh Ftbl & Soph Bsbl Coach; NCTE, IA Cncl Teachers of Eng 1987-; Kappa Delta Pi Intnl Honor; Delta Epsilon Sigma Natl Scholastic Honor Society; IA Writers Project Participant; *office:* Dubuque Sr HS 1800 Clarke Dr Dubuque IA 52001

POTTS, NANCY TENNANT, Eng/Lang Arts Dept Chairperson; *b:* Colusa, CA; *m:* Lewis; *c:* Randolph, Debby, Cindy, Kevin; *ed:* (BA) Eng, Univ of the Pacific 1963; *cr:* 3rd Grade Teacher Erma Reese Elem 1963-64; Lakewood Elem 1964-65; 8th Grade Teacher Woodbridge Elem 1965-66; Eng/Rdng Teacher 7th/8th Grade Woodbridge Mid Sch 1966-; *ai:* Lang Arts Task Force Lodi Unified; Lodi Unified Dist Mentor Selection Comm; Woodbridge Promo/Retention Comm; Adv Sch Lit Magazine; Lodi Ed Assn VP 1967-68; Natl NCTE 1975-; CA Assn Teachers of Eng 1975-; CA Rdng Assn 1980-; Lodi HS Band Review Comm Secy 1978-84 Grand Marshal Lodi-Tokay Band Review 1986; Lodi Unified Sch Dist Teacher of Yr 1986.

POVERO, MARY BORROMEO, Latin Teacher/Lang Dept Chair; *b:* Geneva, NY; *ed:* (BA) Latin/Italian, Nazareth Coll 1942; (MA) Fr, Villanova Univ 1962; NDEA Fr Grant Notre Dame Univ 1963, Latin Grant St Univ of NY Albany 1967; *cr:* Teacher Aquinas Inst 1944-46; Prin/9th Grade Teacher St Anna 1951-53; Teacher Holy Family HS 1953-56, Notre Dame HS 1956-65, Our Lady of Mercy HS 1942-43, 1946-51, 1965-; *ai:*

Lang Dept Chm; Classical Assn Empire St 1965-; Rochester Area Foreign Lang Assn of Teachers 1965-; NY St Assn of Foreign Lang Teachers 1970-; Mercy Alumni Assn Moderator 1986-; Chaperoned Stus on Study/Cultural Tours W Europe & Quebec 1969-87; *home:* 1437 Blossom Rd Rochester NY 14610

POWDERLY, ROSEMARY SHEERAN, 5th Grade Teacher; *b:* St Louis, MO; *m:* Clyde A.; *c:* Patricia, John, James, Thomas; *ed:* (BS) Elem Ed, Fontbonne Coll 1967; *cr:* Teacher Sacred Heart 1956, Epiphany Sch 1967-72, Blue Ridge Sch 1976-; *ai:* Spon Young Astronauts Club; Mem of Building Leadership Comm; IRRA 1989-; *home:* Rt 7 3126 CB Lewis Rd Columbia MO 65202

POWE, JUDY PATE, Mid Sch Mathematics Teacher; *b:* Evergreen, AL; *m:* Mack Dare; *c:* Micheal B.; *ed:* (BS) Elem Ed, Troy St Univ 1965; Grad Classes Elem Ed, Cmptr Sci; *cr:* 6th Grade Teacher Wilcox Cty HS 1966-72; 4th-6th Grade Elem Teacher Catherine Acad 1972-75; Mid Sch Math Teacher Wilcox Acad 1975-; *ai:* Wilcox Acad Jr HS Beta Club Chrldrs Spon; Wilcox Acad Scholars Bowl Co-Spon; Honors Day Comm; Delta Kappa Gamma Pres, Outstanding Mem; NCTM 1989-; Camden Prepared City Team 1986-; Amer Legion Auxiliary; *office:* Wilcox Acad PO Box 1149 Camden AL 36726

POWEL, M. BETH, Biology Teacher; *b:* Fort Mc Clellan, AL; *ed:* (BS) Bio/Chem, 1975, (BS) Medical Technology, 1976 Memphis St Univ; (MAE) Scndry Ed/Bio, Univ of AL Birmingham 1983; ASCP Medical Technology Trng; IBM Prof Wordstar; *cr:* Medical Technologist Guadelupe Regional Medical Center 1976-77, Univ Hospitals Birmingham 1978-85; Sci Teacher/Medical Technologist Grissom HS 1985-, Huntsville Hospital 1987-; *ai:* Sci Club Adv; Sci Olympiad Coach; Chem Human Anatomy; Huntsville Cncl of Sci Teachers, NSTA, Huntsville Ed Assn, AL Ed Assn 1985-; Kappa Delta Pi 1984; Kappa Delta Epsilon 1983; TN Valley Jazz Society Secy 1990; Articles Published, Bibliography on Metrication for US Army Missile Command 1989; Summer Associateship Prgm for HS Sci & Math Faculty 1986-; Grissom PTSA Outstanding Teacher Appreciation 1989; *office:* Grissom HS 7901 Bailey Cove Rd SE Huntsville AL 35802

POWELL, A. ELWIN, Social Studies Chairman; *b:* Steamboat Springs, CO; *ed:* Grad Stud Towards PhD Speech, Univ of KS, Emporia Univ; *cr:* Soc Stud Teacher Cuba City HS 1964; His Teacher Roseburg HS 1965; Forensics Dir/Speech Teacher Cntrl MO St Univ 1965-66; Speech/Soc Stud Teacher CO Alpine Coll 1966-69; Soc Stud Teacher Revere HS 1969-71, Northern Heights HS 1972-; *ai:* NHS; Jr Class Dist Curr Cncl; Faculty Advisory Comm; North Lyon Cty Teachers Assn Pres; NEA 1973-; KS Ed Assn (Constitution & By-Laws Comm, Negotiations Teams Chief Spokesman) 1973-; Farm Bureau, Natl Rifle Assn; *office:* Northern Heights HS Allen KS 66883

POWELL, BEN C., English Teacher; *b:* Lynch, KY; *m:* Wandaleen Jenkins; *c:* Carleen, Darin; *ed:* (BA) Eng, 1964, (MED) Ed, 1982 Cumberland Coll; *cr:* Teacher/Coach Boone Cty HS 1964-65, Beechwood HS 1970-74, Boone Cty HS 1974-77, Ockerman Jr HS 1965-70, 1977-; *ai:* Ftbl Coach; Athletic Dir; BCEA 1974-; KEA, NEA 1964-; *office:* Ockerman Mid Sch 8300 Hwy 42 Florence KY 41042

POWELL, CAROL DAVIS, 5th Grade Teacher; *b:* South Bend, IN; *m:* Henry L.; *c:* Christopher, Corey; *ed:* (BS) Elem Ed, Univ of AR Pine Bluff 1964; (MS) Elem Ed, IN Univ South Bend 1977; *cr:* 1st Grade Teacher Goldstein Elem 1963-64; 2nd Grade Teacher Franklin Elem 1964-70; 3rd Grade Teacher Kennedy Elem 1972-73, Oliver Elem 1977-80; 7th/8th Grade Teacher Jackson Mid 1980-85; 5th Grade Teacher Hay Elem 1980-; 7th/8th Grade Teacher At Risk Stus; *ai:* 5th Grade Quiz Bowl Spon; Soc Comm; NEA Minority Affairs Comm Co Chairperson 1982-88; IN St Teacher Assn; Delta Sigma Theta; NAACP.

POWELL, CLARK ALBRIGHT, Eng/Creative Writing Teacher; *b:* Mobile, AL; *m:* Catherine Elizabeth Lemon; *c:* Mary, William; *ed:* (BA) Aesthetics & Persuasion, Univ of AL 1976; (ME) Spec Ed/High Potential, Univ of S AL 1990; Grad Stud Poetry; *cr:* Freelance Writer 1978-88; PACE Teacher Scarborough Mid Sch 1988, Murphy HS 1988-; *ai:* Publishing; Currently Writing a Weekly Column for the Mobile Press-Register; *office:* S S Murphy H S 100 S Carlen St Mobile AL 36606

POWELL, DIANA SPIVA, Kindergarten Teacher; *b:* Fredericksburg, TX; *m:* Edwin Erle Jr.; *c:* Dina, Ryan; *ed:* (BS) Elem Ed, Univ of TX Austin 1970; Kndgtn Cert, Baylor Univ; *cr:* 3rd Grade Teacher Allison Elem 1970-71; Kndgtn Teacher Gatesville Primary 1971-; *ai:* Girl Scout Leader; Church Act; TX St Teachers Local Comm 1970-; Delta Kappa Gamma Secy 1978-; PTA (Pres 1980, VP, Secy), TX Teacher Terrific 1984, Life Membership 1981; *office:* Gatesville Primary Sch 308 S 26th St Gatesville TX 76528

POWELL, DONALD K., Math Teacher/Dept Chairman; *b:* Lenexa, KS; *m:* Kay J. Smith; *c:* Marc A., Tim A., Danny D.; *ed:* (BS) Math/Sci, 1955, (MS) Admin/Supervision, 1958 Emporia St Univ; Post Grad KS Univ; KS St Univ; Wichita St Univ; San Jose St Univ; Univ of South FL; *cr:* Teacher/Asst Prin Abe Hubert Mid Sch 1955-; *ai:* NEA 1955-; KNEA 1955-; GCEA (Legislative Chm 1960-61/Negotiator 1963-65); NDEA Math Grant San Jose St 1968; NDEA Math Grant Univ of South FL 1971; *home:* 2006 Parkwood Ln Garden City KS 67846

POWELL, ELIZABETH PEARL, Mathematics Dept Chair; *b:* Kopperston, WV; *ed:* (BS) Math, Concord Coll 1974; (MA) Comm Stud, WV Univ 1982; Natl Registry Emergency Medical Technician 1981; WV St Certified Emergency Medical Technician 1981; *cr:* Adult Basic Ed Teacher WY Cty Schls 1982-83; Math Teacher Oceana Mid Sch 1974-; *ai:* Math Field Day, Cty Math Textbook Adoption Comm; NEA; WV Ed Assn Emerging Leader 1990; WY Cty Ed Assn (Treas 1987, Membership Chairperson 1988); WV Cncl Teacher of Math; Toneda Baptist Church (Sunday Sch Teacher, Bible Study Teacher, Youth Leader, Budget Comm, Advisory Bd, Nominating Comm); Selected Natl Math Project; WV Legislature Outstanding Teacher Citationl Regional Task Force Exception Children; Outstanding Young Women of America 1985; *home:* Box 213 Kopperston WV 24854

POWELL, ELSIE HALL, Fifth Grade Teacher; *b:* Ahoskie, NC; *m:* Eugene; *c:* Gregory, Nikki; *ed:* (BS) Health Ed, NC Cntrl Univ 1966; *cr:* 9th Grade Teacher Brawley HS 1966-68; Sci Teacher Bundy Elem Sch 1968-69; 4th Grade Teacher Incirlik Elem Sch 1969-70; 5th/6th Grade Combination Teacher Wanamaker Elem Sch 1970-72; 5th Grade Teacher C S Brown Elem Sch 1972-; *ai:* NCAE, NEA, HCNCAE; C S Brown Teacher of Yr 1987-88; *home:* Rt 2 Box 273-F Ahoskie NC 27910

POWELL, GERALD KING, Counselor; *b:* Tulsa, OK; *m:* Betty Jean Niklaus; *c:* Julie, Vicki, Marcia, Connie; *ed:* (AA) General, Belleville Area Coll 1969; (BS) Soc Stud/Ed, Tulsa Univ 1973; (ME) Ed/Counseling, NE OK St Univ 1975; (EDD) Adult/Occupational Ed, OK St Univ Stillwater 1981; *cr:* Musician USAF 1952-72; Teacher Union HS 1972-; *ai:* Key Club Faculty Adv; Coll & Careers Cnslr; Coll/Career Night Open House Public Relations; NEA, OEA 1987-89; AFT Pres 1983-87; Kiwanis of Tulsa SE Key Club Adv 1979-; *home:* 5649 S 84th E Ave Tulsa OK 74145

POWELL, GERTRUDE, Third Grade Teacher; *b:* Thomasville, AL; *ed:* (BA) Elem Ed, Talladega Coll 1977; (MS) Elem Ed, AL St Univ 1981; Working on Cert in Admin & Supervision; *cr:* Teacher Asst Holingers Island Sch 1978; Basic Skills Teacher 1978-80, Chapter I/4th/5th Grade Teacher 1980-88, 3rd Grade Teacher 1988- Mertz Elem; *ai:* MCEA, AEA, NEA; Memorial Presbyn Church (Presbyn Women Pres, Youth Adv, Sunday Sch Seccy, Adult Choir Mem); S AL Synod of Living Waters Historian; Mertz Elem Sch Teacher of Yr 1988-89; *office:* Mertz Elem Sch 950 Mc Rae Ave Mobile AL 36606

POWELL, GLORIA J., Assistant Principal; *b:* New York, NY; *c:* Kelli J., Anthony M.; *ed:* (BA) Span/Ed, Queens Coll 1974; (MA) Teaching Eng to Speakers Other Langs, Hunter 1977; (PHD) Teaching Eng to Speakers Others Langs/Bi-ling Ed, NY Univ; *cr:* Teacher 1974-88, Asst Prin 1988- Oliver Wendell Holmes Jr HS; *ai:* Organized Peer Tutoring Prgm & Sch Clubs; Liaision to La Guardia Comm Coll; Talent Search Prgm at J204; Coord Schlsps for Summer Study Prestigious Preparatory Schls; NAACP Mem 1974-; Amer Society Latin America Mem 1985-; Fulbright Scholar Participant to Argentina Fellow 1985; Amer Assn Span Mem 1974, Schlsp Spain; Contributing Author 1987; *office:* Oliver Wendell Holmes Jr HS 36-41 28th St Long Island City NY 11106

POWELL, JENNIFER ANNE, 7th Grade Soc Stud Teacher; *b:* Xenia, OH; *m:* Philip J.; *c:* Philip Andrew; *ed:* (BS) Soc Sci, Penn St Univ 1982; Sch Admin, Western MD; *cr:* Teacher Brunswick Mid Sch 1983-; *ai:* 7th Grade Team Leader; NEA 1983-; MSTA 1983-; FCTA 1983-; Frederick Presbyn Church 1989-; Innovative Teaching Awd 1987; *office:* Brunswick Mid Sch 301 Cummings Dr Brunswick MD 21716

POWELL, JENNIFER S. (THOMAS), English Teacher; *b:* Washington, DC; *m:* H. Grant; *ed:* (AA) Speech Comm, Prince Georges Comm Coll 1982; (BA) Ed/Speech/Drama, Anderson Univ 1984; (MS) Educl Leadership, Nova Univ 1990; *cr:* Eng Teacher Vero Beach Sr HS 1985-; *ai:* First Church of God Chrstn Ed Dir 1988-; Outstanding Young Women in America Awd 1988; Co-Authored Article.

POWELL, JUDITH MAC AVOY, Band Director; *b:* Kingston, PA; *m:* Richard Wayne; *ed:* (BS) Music Ed, Gettysburg Coll 1976; Grad Work Towards Masters William & Mary Coll; *cr:* Band Dir Newport News City Schls 1978-89, Poquoson City Schls 1989-; *ai:* Band Dir; Music Educators Natl Conference 1978-; NEA, VA Ed Assn, VA Band & Orch Dir Assn 1978-; Women Band Dirs Natl Assn 1986-; Amer Sch Band Dirs Assn 1988; Phi Beta Mu (St Secy, Treas) 1989; Kappa Delta Pi 1986-; VA Congress of Parents & Teachers; VA Awd for Distinguished Service 1988; *home:* 41 Dawn Ln Hampton VA 23666

POWELL, LARRY D., Science Teacher; *b:* Roswell, NM; *m:* Lana Wade; *ed:* (BS) Forest Sci, TX A&M Univ 1974; (MS) Arid & Semi Arid Land Use, TX Tech Univ 1980; (MS) Ed/Sci, E NM Univ 1984; Ed Admin Certificate; *cr:* Continuing Ed Coord E NM Univ 1974-75; Chem Teacher Roswell HS 1976-79; 7th-12th Grade Sci Teacher Dora Consolidated Sch Dist 1983-; Sci Instr E NM Univ 1989-; *ai:* Math Sci Club Spon; Sci Fair Judge & Spon; Chem, Anatomy, Bio Instr E NM Univ Clovis; Assn of Presidential Awardees Sci Teaching, NSTA, Earth Sci Teachers Assn; Presidential Awd Excl Sci Teaching 1987; US West Outstanding Teacher Awd Finalist 1988; Shell Oil Fellowship for Arid & Semi Arid Land Stu TX Tech Univ; *home:* Rt 3 Box 748-M Portales NM 88130

POWELL, LINDA LEDFORD, Sixth Grade Teacher; *b:* Gaffney, SC; *m:* Ronnie W.; *c:* Jeffrey; *ed:* (BS) Intermediate Ed, Gardner-Webb Coll 1973; Cert in Spec Ed, Appalachian St Univ 1976; (MS) Gardner-Webb 1981; *cr:* Spec Ed Teacher 1973-81, 4th/5th Grade Teacher 1981-89 Ellenboro Elem; 6th Grade Teacher Cliffside Elem 1989-; *ai:* Dir of Mid Grades Musical; *home:* 2739 Wood Rd Mooresboro NC 28114

POWELL, MARILYN ASH, Chapter I Reading Teacher; *b:* Lebanon, KY; *m:* John Allen; *c:* Brent L.; *ed:* (BS) Elem Ed, E KY Univ 1973; *cr:* 2nd Grade Teacher 1973-74, 1st Grade Teacher 1974-87, Chapter I Rdng Teacher 1987- Dublin Elem; *ai:* Kappa Delta Alumnae Assn Pledge Adv 1988-; *office:* Dublin Elem Sch PO Box 1106 Dublin VA 24084

POWELL, MARION S., 3rd Grade Teacher; *b:* Hammond, IN; *m:* Richard L.; *c:* Margaret C., Elizabeth Piekarczyk, Victoria Seitz, Richard; *ed:* (BA) Elem Ed, (MS) Elem Ed, 1968 IN Univ; Spec Ed Courses IN Univ 1979-81; *cr:* 3rd/4th Grade Teacher Arlington Elem 1959; 1st Grade Teacher Ellettsville Elem 1959-60; 2nd Grade Teacher Trafalgar Elem 1967-69; 3rd-5th Grade Teacher Unionville Elem 1969-; *ai:* Cmptr Coord Unionville Elem; NEA (Life Mem 1970) 1969-; ISTA, MCEA 1969-; *office:* Unionville Elem Sch 8144 East St RD 45 Unionville IN 47468

POWELL, MARTHA ARMSTRONG, Kindergarten Teacher; *b:* Montgomery, AL; *c:* Jonathan R., David A., Nancy E. Conner; *ed:* (BA) Elem Ed, 1979, (MS) Elem Ed, 1986 Univ of N FL; *cr:* 3rd Grade Teacher Mac Clenny Elem Sch 1980-81; 6th Grade Teacher Lake Butler Mid Sch 1981-85; 3rd Grade Teacher Lake Butler Elem Sch 1985-87; Instr Union Cty Adult Sch 1983-; Kndgtn Teacher Lake Butler Elem Sch 1987-; *ai:* Project Choice Drug Prgm Comm Mem; Lake Butler Elem Sch Safety Patrol Spon; Laubach Adult Literacy 1988-; Lake Butler Church of Christ (Mem, Sunday Sch Teacher); Lake Butler Elem Sch PTO Prgm Chm; *office:* Lake Butler Elem Sch 600 SW 6th St Lake Butler FL 32054

POWELL, MARTON LEE, JR., Math/Computer Science Teacher; *b:* Woodward, OK; *m:* Virginia Gale Atterly; *c:* Larissa D.; *ed:* (BS) Math, Southwestern OK St Univ 1975; (MS) Math Ed, Emporia St Univ 1980; *cr:* Platoon Leader US Army Signal Corps 1975-77; Math Teacher Eureka Jr-Sr HS 1977-; *ai:* Head Ftbl & Bstkbl, Asst Track Coach; NCTM, KS Assn Teachers of Math, NEA, Natl Strength & Conditioning Assn; Fellowship of Chrstn Athletes; Eureka Jaycees Outstanding Young Educator; *office:* Eureka Jr Sr HS Rt 2 Box 250 Eureka KS 67045

POWELL, MARY, English Teacher; *b:* Haskell, TX; *c:* Richard A. Craney; *ed:* (BA) His/Eng, Huston-Tillotson 1968; TX Womens Univ; TX Chrstn Univ; *cr:* Rdng Teacher Como HS 1969-71; Eng Teacher Southwest HS 1971-; *ai:* Assn of TX Prof Ed 1985-; TX Joint Cncl Eng Teachers 1980-; Phi Delta Kappa 1987-; Amer Airlines Apple II Cmptr 1990; *office:* Southwest H S 4100 Alta Mesa Blvd Fort Worth TX 76133

POWELL, NANCY ANN, 6th Grade Teacher; *b:* San Francisco, CA; *m:* James; *c:* Nathan J., Bryan J.; *ed:* (BA) Eng, CA St Univ Chico 1972; (MS) Sch Admin, CA St Univ Bakersfield 1989; *cr:* 6th Grade Teacher Orland Elem 1973-75; Teacher Denair Mid Sch 1975-78, Fairview 1978-80, Crestwood 1980-; *ai:* Academic Olympic Team Coach; Sch Chorus & Yr Round Sch Comm Chm; Mentor Teacher 1987-.

POWELL, RUTH ANN, 5th/6th Grade Teacher; *b:* Oneida, KY; *ed:* (BS) His/Eng, Cumberland Coll 1972; (MA) Elem Ed, Union Coll 1980; *cr:* 8th Grade Teacher Laurel Creek Elem 1972-73; 3rd-6th Grade Teacher Oneida Elem 1975-; *home:* Rt 1 Box 3-B Oneida KY 40972

POWELL, WANDA LEE, Fifth Grade Teacher; *b:* Chattanooga, TN; *ed:* (BS) Voc Home Economics Ed, Mid TN St Univ 1965; (MED) Elem Ed, Berry Coll 1976; Mid Grades Ed, West GA Coll 1986; *cr:* 2nd Grade Teacher Varnell Elem 1969-70; 3rd-5th Grade Teacher Valley Point Elem 1970-; *ai:* Lead Soc Stud Coord Valley Point; WEA; GAE; NEA; Pairs N Spares; Cherokee Hiking Club; Valley Point Elem Teacher of Yr 1980; *home:* 16 Oak Court Ringgold GA 30736

POWELL, WILLOWDEAN WIMS, Fifth Grade Teacher; *b:* Blakely, GA; *c:* De-Vicki K. Willis, Patrick J.; *ed:* (BS) Elem Ed, Albany St Coll 1955; (MED) Elem Ed, Mercer Univ 1974; *cr:* 5th Grade Teacher Carter Elem Sch 1955-60, Amer Dependent Sch 1961-62, Johnsonville Elem Sch 1962-67, Henderson Elem Sch 1967-79, Early Cty Elem 1979-; *ai:* Early Cty Teacher Assn; Governors Special Womens GA Cncl of Arts; Albany St Alumni; Mercer Univ Alumni; Ebernezar AME Church; Early Cty Drug Awareness; Early Cty Lib Comm; Early Cty 4-H Club Comm; Early Cty Insurance Comm; Butte Cty Teacher of Yr Awd; Outstanding GA Teacher Awd; Governors Special Attendance & Service Awd; Special Service Awd GA Cncl of Arts; *home:* P O Box 293 Blakely GA 31723

POWER, DONALD ROBERT, 4th Grade Teacher; *b:* Chicago, IL; *m:* Joann; *c:* Kelli, Karyn; *ed:* (BA) Ed, 1970, (MS) Ed Admin, 1978 N IL; Coll & Dist Approved Classes; *cr:* Phys Ed Instr 1970-73, 4th-6th Grade Classroom Teacher 1973- Elmhurst Schls; *ai:* Staff Dev Comm; Building Writing Specialist; Summer Sch Staff; AFT 1975-; Elmhurst Sch Dist 205 1988-89, Honorarium 1989; *home:* 377 S West Ave Elmhurst IL 60126

POWER, PAUL F., English Department Chairperson; *b:* Providence, RI; *m:* Anna J. Be; *c:* Brian, Denise A. Belmont, Marie A. Lowe, Kathleen, Paul C.; *ed:* (BA) Eng, Providence Coll 1956; Scndry Ed, RI Coll of Ed 1960-64; Scndry Eng Ed, SUC Oneonta 1964-68; *cr:* Eng Teacher La Salle Acad 1961-64; Eng Teacher/Chm Afton Cntrl Sch 1964-; *ai:* Asst Ftbl; Var Girls Vlybl; Jr Class Spring Track Asst Adv; Bldg Rep; ATA Negotiating Team;

Afton Fire Dept Emergency Squad 1967-83; Ordained to Permanent Diaconate Diocese of Syracuse 1981.

POWER, SAMUEL EUGENE, Science Dept Chairperson; *b:* Austell, GA; *m:* Karen Cason; *c:* Michael, Waylon, Dylan; *ed:* (BA) Liberal Art, CA St Univ 1976; *cr:* Sci Teacher Herschel Jones 1978-; *ai:* PAGE Mem 1989-.

POWERS, ALLEN WESTON, Mathematics Teacher; *b:* Bonnye Blue, VA; *m:* Nita B.; *c:* Philip, Arthur; *ed:* (BS) Math, Emory & Henry Coll 1959; (MED) Math/Ed, Univ of FL 1964; *cr:* Teacher Bell HS 1960-64, Trenton HS 1964-65, Lake-Sumter Comm Coll 1965-68, Bell HS 1968-; *ai:* NCTM, FCTM, MAA; *office:* Bell HS PO Box 130 Bell FL 32619

POWERS, BEVERLY KOS, Mathematics Department Chair; *b:* Chicago, IL; *m:* Marshall K.; *c:* Jennifer, Christopher; *ed:* (BED) Ed/Math, Chicago St Univ 1957; (MS) Math, Univ of IL 1959; Natl Sci Fnd Grant Northwestern Univ 1961-62; Advanced Placement Calculus, Oglethorpe Univ 1986; *cr:* Teacher Chicago Teachers Coll 1961-62, Embry Riddle Aeronautical Inst 1965-66; 4th-6th Grade Teacher/Dept Chairperson Fairview Elem 1976-80; Teacher Stockbridge Jr HS 1980-84, Teacher/Dept Chairperson Stockbridge Sr HS 1984-; *ai:* Math Team Spon; Advisory Comm; Staff Dev Coord; GCTM 1980-89; GCTM Changing Your Negatives to Positives 1989; Teacher of Yr 1976, 1982, 1985-86; STAR Teacher 1984, 1986, 1988; *office:* Stockbridge Sr HS 109 Lee St Stockbridge GA 30281

POWERS, BRINA SNYDER, 3rd Grade Teacher; *b:* Chicago, IL; *m:* David; *c:* Patrick, Julie; *ed:* (AA) General Ed, Univ of MN; (MS) Elem Ed, Mankato St Univ 1966; *cr:* 3rd Grade Teacher Fuller Elem Sch 1966-67, 3rd Grade Teacher 1967-68, Chapter I Teacher 1972-73 Park Elm Sch; 3rd Grade Teacher Sch of St Anne 1973-; *ai:* Rdng Curr Dev; HAVE Facult Rep; Environmental Comm; Career Day Chairperson; 4-H Leader; Church Lector 1970-; Communion Minister 1987-; *office:* Sch of St Anne 511 N 4th St Le Sueur MN 56058

POWERS, CHARLES ANDREW, 5th Grade Teacher; *b:* Gouverneur, NY; *m:* Janet B.; *c:* Scott, Jeffrey; *ed:* (BA) Ed, SUC Oneonta 1966; (MS) Ed, SUC New Paltz 1976; Mechanical Engineering & Design; Toolmaking; *cr:* 4th Grade Teacher 1966-70, 5th Grade Teacher 1970- Fishkill Elem Sch; *ai:* HUGS Comm; Project Team Mem; NY St United Teachers, Wappingers Congress of Teachers 1966-; Wappingers Little League Coach 1987-; Wappingers Soccer Club Mgr 1986-; Video Production Rep; *office:* Fishkill Elem Sch Church St Fishkill NY 12524

POWERS, IMOGENE SKEEN, First Grade Teacher; *b:* Corbin, KY; *m:* John L.; *c:* M. Susan Boehmer; *ed:* (BA) Elem Ed, Cumberland Jr Coll 1950; (BA) Elem Ed, Univ of KY 1960; *cr:* Teacher Whitly Cty 1950-52, Newport Ind Schls 1952-60, 1964, Bellevue Ind Schls 1964-68, Boone Cty 1968-; *ai:* NKEA, KEA, NEA 1950-60, 1964-; PTA Lifetime Membership; Commonwealth of KY Teacher Ockerman Elem; Honored at Founders Day Kelly PTA; *home:* 10034 Country Hills Ct Union KY 41091

POWERS, LINDA WALTERMIRE, Dept Chairman/Eng Instructor; *b:* Perry, OK; *m:* Ben Jack Jr.; *c:* Leah, B.J., *ed:* (BS) Language Arts Ed, Oklahoma State Univ 1971; Grad Work at Northeastern OK St Univ, Univ of Tulsa; Completed 36 Hrs Towards (MA) Eng, OK St Univ 1985-; *cr:* Bus Eng Instructor Southwestern Bus Coll 1971-72; Eng Instructor Billings HS 1972-74, 1979-80, Ft Gibson HS 1974-79, Blackwell HS 1980-81; Eng Instructor & Dept Chair Ponca City HS 1981-;; *ai:* Academic Cncl Ponca City HS; Sr Class Spon; OEA 1972-; NEA 1972-; NCTA, Treasurer, President (2 yrs); MCTA Pres Elect 1979-80; Ponca City Assn of Classroom Tchrs OEA Delegate 1987-91; Sec 1987-89, Pres 1990-92; ACT Building Rep, Negotiation Team; Curriculum Comm, Exec Comm 1986-88, Exec Comm Chm 1987-88 Ponca City HS; Kappa Kappa Iota, Sec, VP, Pres 1982-; Delta Kappa Gamma 1985-; OSU Educ Alumni Assn Bd of Dir 1989-91; OK Fnd for Excl in Educ; Outstanding Secondary Teacher 1988; Curr Consultant NEH Medieval Studies Inst 1985; Outstanding Young Women of Amer 1984; *home:* 600 Talmer Road Ponca City OK 74604

POWERS, MARGARET SWAIM, Mathematics Department Chair; *b:* High Point, NC; *m:* David Alton; *c:* Andrew, Jason; *ed:* (BS) Mid Grades Ed, E Carolina Univ 1971; *cr:* Teacher Roanoke Rapids City Schls 1971-74, Greenville City Schls 1974-75, Tuscaloosa City Schls 1975-76, Pitt Cty Schls 1978-; *ai:* Mathcounts Asst Coach; Differentiated Pay System Steering Comm; E B Aycock Jr HS Leadership Team; NCAE; NCCTM Mid Grades VP 1978-; Delta Kappa Gamma 1988-; NC Math & Sci Schlsp 1985, 1986; *office:* E B Aycock Jr HS 1325 Red Banks Rd Greenville NC 27858

POWERS, MARY ELLEN, 5th Grade Teacher; *b:* Chicago, IL; *ed:* (BS) Elem Ed/Eng, Stephen F Austin St Univ 1966; Lamar Univ, Univ of TX; *cr:* 5th Grade Teacher Pease Elem 1966-; *ai:* ATPE; Pease PTA (Treas, Pres 1989-, Lifetime Mem); Teacher of Yr; *office:* Pease Elem Sch 5924 Jade Ave Port Acres TX 77640

POWERS, MARY PATRICIA, Third Grade Teacher; *b:* Boston, MA; *ed:* (BSED) Ed, St Coll of Boston 1962; (MSED) Ed, Boston Coll 1970; Rdng & Psych Courses; *cr:* Elem Teacher City of Boston 1962-; *ai:* Grant Writing Comm; Sch Newspaper Co-Ed; Delta Kappa Gamma Secy; Impact II & Office of Technology Cmptr Grant; *office:* James A. Garfield Sch 95 Beechcroft St Boston MA 02135

POWERS, NANCY JOHNSON, 4th Grade Teacher; *b:* Washington, DC; *m:* Gilbert H. Jr.; *c:* Shad, Ryan; *ed:* (BA) Speech/Lang Pathology, 1968, (MA) Speech/Lang Pathology, 1969 Cntrl MI Univ; *cr:* Speech Therapist Clare Intermediate SD 1969-72; Elem Teacher Shepherd Public Schls 1974-; *ai:* Chairperson K-6 Sci & Mem K-12 Sci Curr Comm; MI Ed Assn, MI Sci Teachers Assn; *office:* Shepherd Elem Sch 168 E Maple Shepherd MI 48883

POWERS, RENITA ELAINE, Vocational Home Ec Educator; *b:* Winner, SD; *ed:* (AS) Home Ec, Rose St Coll 1977; (BS) Home Ec Ed, OK St Univ 1979; (MS) Home Ec Ed, Cntrl St Univ 1986; *cr:* Voc Home Ec Teacher Holdenville HS 1979-83; Retail Mgr Fabri Centers of Amer 1983-84; Voc Home Ec Teacher Hammon HS 1984-; *ai:* FHA & Young Homemakers of Amer Adv; Class Spon; AVA, OK Voc Assn, Amer Home Ec Assn, OK Home Ec Assn, NEA, OK Ed Assn 1979-; Certified Home Economist, *office:* Hammon HS Box 279 Hammon OK 73650

POWERS, SUE L., Teacher; *b:* Oahu, HI; *m:* Don Benton; *c:* Shelley, Beau, Ben; *ed:* (BS) Eng, Univ of S MS 1987; *cr:* Teacher Biloxi HS 1987-; *ai:* Frosh Class 1989- & Interact Club Spon; Phi Kappa Phi, Phi Delta Kappa 1987-; First Baptist (Teacher, Choir, Pres, Mem) 1984-85; *office:* Biloxi HS 1424 Father Ryan Av Biloxi MS 39530

POWERS-LOTSON, FRANCINE, Counselor; *b:* New York City, NY; *m:* Edward Joseph; *ed:* (BA) Ed, Morgan St Univ; (MA) Curr/Supervision/Admin, Antioch Univ; Endorsement in Counseling George Mason Univ; Grad Work Univ of VA, VA Polytech Inst; *cr:* Teacher Westchester Cty; Teacher of Gifted/Talented, Cnslr 1988, Teacher 1975- Fairfax Cty Public Schls; *ai:* SCA Spon; Just Say No Prgm; Fairfax Ed Assn Rep; VA Ed Assn, NEA Delegate; *home:* 6714 Quander Rd Alexandria VA 22307

POZSGAI, BILL, Health/Phys Ed/Psych Teacher; *b:* East Cleveland, OH; *ed:* (BA) Soc Psych, Heidelberg Coll 1977; Ed/Health Phys Ed, Akron Univ 1983; Grad Stud Akron Univ; *cr:* St Teacher/Coach Woodridge Local Schls 1983; Teacher/Coach Windham Exempted Village Schls 1984-; *ai:* Asst Var Bsktbl, Head Frosh Bsktbl, Head Var Bsbl, Asst Var Ftbl Coach; OAHPERD, NEA, OEA 1984-; OHSBCA 1986-; *office:* Windham HS 9530 Bauer Ave Windham OH 44288

PRACHT, WILLIS CHARLES, Principal; *b:* Belleville, KS; *m:* Connie Diane Koerner; *c:* Cahlib, Lara E.; *ed:* Pre Vet Med, Cloud Cty Comm Coll 1972; (BS) Elem Ed, Fort Hays KS St Coll 1974; (MS) Elem Admin, Fort Hays St Univ 1985; *cr:* 6th Grade Teacher Unified Sch Dist 457 Georgia Matthews 1975-86; Prin Jennie Barker Elem 1986-88, Friend Elem 1987-88, Theoni Elem 1987-89, Garfield Elem 1988-; *ai:* Phi Delta Kappa (VP, Membership, Pres, Delegate, Treas) 1987-; KS Assn Teachers of Math Pres 1986; *office:* Garfield Elem Sch 121 W Walnut Garden City KS 67846

PRADO, DONNA (PUFFINBURGER), Mathematics Instructor; *b:* Cumberland, MD; *m:* Ricardo L.; *c:* Tirra S., Dax L.; *ed:* (BSED) Math, 1974, (MA) Scndry Math, 1982 WV Univ; Measurement Wkshp Conductor RESA VIII; Spec Trng & Workbook Compiler Tech Math; *cr:* Math/Cmptr Instr Romney Jr HS 1981-; *ai:* Mathcounts & Asst Girls Bsktbl Coach; Sch Reporter Local Newspaper; Cheerleading Judge; Planning Comm Math Field Day; Sch Dance Team Coord; Sch Discipline Comm; NEA 1981-; NCTM, WV Cncl Teachers of Math; Math Assn of America 1989-; PTO Secy 1990; BSA (Cub Master 1986-, Webelo Leader 1989-, Den Leader 1986-), Cub Scouter of Yr 1987; Little League Team Mother 1989; Trip Chaperone 1985-; Nom Presidential Awd for Excl Math, Teacher of Yr Hampshire Cty WV, WV Inst for Sch Success; Wrote Hampshire Cty Pre-Algebra Curr Guide & Sch Cmptr Lab Proposal; *office:* Romney Jr HS School St Romney WV 26757

PRAGER, LINDA M., HS English Teacher; *b:* Jersey City, NJ; *c:* Lacey, Josh; *ed:* (BS) Scndry Ed/Eng, Univ TX Austin 1972; (MLA) Eng, Southern Meth Univ 1985; *cr:* Eng Teacher Gaston Jr HS 1972-77, Skyline HS 1977-82, Richland Jr Coll 1985-87, Skyline HS 1987-; *ai:* NCTE, Dallas Cncl of Teachers of Eng; *office:* Skyline HS 7777 Forney Rd Dallas TX 75227

PRAHL, RONALD H., English Teacher; *b:* Davenport, IA; *m:* Carlene Kay Nelson; *c:* Emily K.; *ed:* (BS) Bio, Sul Ross St Univ 1965; (MA) Eng, IA St Univ 1971; Eng, Drake Univ; *cr:* 8th/9th Grade Eng Teacher Cntrl Jr HS 1971-72, Berg Jr HS 1972-73; 10th-12th Grade Eng Teacher Newton HS 1973-; *ai:* Mentor Teacher 1988-; Co-Faculty Adv HS Literary Magazine; Sigma Tau Delta; Carnegie Scholar; Magazine Articles Published; Teaching Aids; Belin Fellowship for Teachers of Gifted & Talented Stus Univ of IA; *office:* Newton HS E 4th St S Newton IA 50208

PRANGE, GREGORY VERNOR, Science Teacher; *b:* Seymour, IN; *m:* Joyce Jean Greger; *ed:* (BS) Health/Safety Ed, 1983, (MS) Scndry Ed, 1987 IN Univ; Scndry Admin, Butler Univ 1987-; *cr:* Sci Teacher Seymour HS 1984-; *ai:* Hi-Y Club Spon 1984-87; Elem, Jr HS, Frosh Bsktbl Coach 1984-; Jr HS, Frosh, Var Ftbl Coach 1984-; IN St Teachers Assn, NEA, Seymour Ed Assn 1984-; IN Ftbl Coaches Assn, Hoosier Assn of Sci Teachers Incorporated; Elks Club, Amer Legion 1987-; *office:* Seymour HS 1350 W 2nd St Seymour IN 47274

PRATER, ROBERTA LOUISE (COOKE), Industrial Technology Teacher; *b:* Lincoln, England; *m:* Tracy Jones; *ed:* (BS) Industrial Ed, TX A&M Univ 1978; Univ of TX Tyler 1988 & UT Cambidge Univ 1987; *cr:* Industrial Technology Teacher John Foster Dulles HS 1979-; *ai:* Campus Action Team 1989-; Nom Teacher of Yr Campus Level 1989-; Finalist Teacher of Yr 1988-89; *office:* John Foster Dulles H S 500 Dulles Ave Sugar Land TX 77487

PRATHER, ELLA FRANCES DODSON, Third Grade Teacher; *b:* Somerset, KY; *m:* Wendell; *ed:* (BS) Elem Ed, (MS) Rdng Specialist, Spalding Univ; *cr:* 1st-8th Grade Teacher Slate Branch Sch 1959-60; 3rd Grade Teacher Lincoln Trail Sch 1960-61, St Jerome Sch 1965-; *office:* St Jerome Sch 901 Fairdale Rd Fairdale KY 40118

PRATHER, NORMA JO, Kindergarten Teacher; *b:* Carter, OK; *m:* Donald; *c:* Joe D., Kay L. Prather Brantley; *ed:* (BA) Elem Ed, Southwestern St Univ 1957; Kndgtn Endorsement; Eng as Second Lang, Wayland Baptist Univ; *cr:* 1st Grade Teacher Lubbock Public Schls 1957-58; 2nd Grade Teacher 1958-62, 1st Grade Teacher 1963-64, 1965-69, Kndgtn Teacher 1969- Muleshoe Public Schls; *ai:* NEA, TX St Teachers Assn; Delta Kappa Gamma Treas 1988-; PTA Life Membership; *home:* Rt 2 Box 1370 Muleshoe TX 79347

PRATLEY, MICHAEL B., English/Social Studies Teacher; *b:* Marshall, MI; *m:* Wendy S. Nevins; *c:* Anthony, Andrew, Rebecca; *ed:* (BA) Eng, Spring Arbor Coll 1976; (MA) Eng, W MI Univ 1981; Working Towards Ed Specialist Cntrl MI Univ; *cr:* Teacher/Coach Litchfield Cmmty Schls 1976-79, Frankfort Area Schls 1979-; *ai:* Var Ftbl Asst Coach; Frankfort Ed Assn Pres 1986-88, Teacher of Yr 1987; Lions Club Pres 1989, Distinguished Service 1989; Frankfort City Cncl Mem 1984-86; Frankfort United Meth Church Admin Bd Chm 1988-; Jr Achievement of Manistee Bd of Dir Mem 1986-; *office:* Frankfort HS 534 11th St Frankfort MI 49635

PRATO, MARILYN LEAH, 6th Grade Math Teacher; *b:* Wadsworth, OH; *m:* Gary Michael; *c:* Kerri A., Jonathan M.; *ed:* (BS) Elem Ed, Kent St Univ 1971; (MS) Competency Ed, Coll of Mt St Joseph 1986; *cr:* 3rd Grade Teacher Lake Cable Elem 1971-83; 5th Grade Teacher Jackson Memorial Mid Sch 1983-85, Lake Cable Elem 1985-87; 6th Grade Teacher Jackson Memorial Mid Sch 1987-; *ai:* 6th Grade Team Leader; JMEA, JCPA Recognition; Math Tournament Coach; Levy Comm Mem; Dinner Chairperson; JMEA (Bldg Rep 1983-88, Corresponding Secy 1989-), 15 Yr Service Awd; OEA, NEA 1971-; Jackson Girls Sftbl Bd Mem 1990; Corporate Cup Vlybl/Sftbl Team Mem 1988-; *office:* Jackson Memorial Mid Sch 7355 Mudbrook St N W Massillon OH 44646

PRATT, ANNE SMITH, Chemistry Teacher; *b:* Roanoke Rapids, NC; *m:* Samuel N.; *c:* Paige Pratt Stambler, Samuel N. Jr, Georgeanne; *ed:* (BS) Chem, Limestone Coll 1954; (MAT) Sci Ed, Winthrop Coll 1986; AP Chem Accreditation Furman Univ 1986; *cr:* Sr Chemist Celanese Corp 1954-55; Scndry Sci Teacher Sullivan HS 1959-62, York Rd Elem 1974-75, Rawlinson Rd Jr HS 1975-80, Northwestern HS 1980-; *ai:* Spon SADD & Hoofbeats; Textbook Approval Comm; Amer Chemical Society, SC Sci Cncl 1984-; Amer Saddlehorse Assn; NEA, SCEA Area Rep 1979-; Jr Welfare League 1964-; Fleur De Lis Garden Club, 1st Presbyn Church, Limestone Alumni Assn, Winthrop Alumni Assn; Fellowship Dreyfus Chem Wkshp Woodrow Wilson Fnd; Presenter SC Sci Cncl Convention 1986; *office:* Northwestern HS 2502 W Main St Rock Hill SC 29732

PRATT, BEVERLY DORITY, Social Studies Teacher; *b:* Gary, IN; *m:* Roy; *c:* Jamal, Giovanni; *ed:* (BS) Poly Sci/His, Grinnell Coll 1967; (MAT) His, IN Univ 1970; Advanced Placement US His Seminar, W KY Univ Bowling Green 1985, Earlham Coll 1987; *cr:* Soc Stud Teacher Horace Mann Sch 1967-71, Wirt HS 1974-80, Horace Mann HS 1980-; *ai:* Andrew Mellon Grant 1987.

PRATT, CAROLYN K., Sixth Grade Teacher/Dept Head; *b:* Madison, WV; *ed:* (BS) Elem Ed, Concord Coll 1964; Grad Work WV Univ & WV Coll of Grad Stud; *cr:* 6th Grade Teacher Madison Elem Sch 1964-69; 5th Grade Teacher Cumberland Heights Elem Sch 1969-70; 4th-6th Grade Teacher Lashmeet Elem Sch 1970-; *ai:* 4th-6th Grade Interdisciplinary Team Leader; Speaker Bureau, Pre-Referral Management Intervention Techniques, Princeton Partner-in-Ed Planning, 4th-6th Grade Scheduling Coord; Mercer Cty Rdng Textbook, Continuing Ed Advisory, Report Card Comms; Lashmeet Elem New Sch Facility Comm Mem; Sch Photographer; Mercer Cty Rdng Cncl (Corresponding Secy 1988-, Newsletter Ed/Publisher, Book Fair Comm Chairperson, Catch Them in the Cradle Comm Chairperson, Nominating Comm Chairperson, Membership Comm Chairperson), Rdng Teacher of Yr 1989, Cynthia Lorentz-Cook Memorial Awd; WV Mid Sch Assn, WV St Rdng Cncl; Intnl Rdng Assn Honor Cncl Chairperson; Developed Rdng Vocabulary Reinforcement Cmptr Prgms; Initiated Lashmeet Elem Shadow Day; Lashmeet Elem Teacher of Yr 1984-85; Cynthia Lorentz-Cook Memorial Awd;Golden Poet Awd 1987, 1988; Poems Published; *office:* Lashmeet Elem Sch PO Box 280 Lashmeet WV 24733

PRATT, ELEANOR M.(KOKE), Chapter I Teacher; *b:* Omaha, NE; *m:* Harlow E.; *ed:* Elem Ed, 1953; (BS) Elem Ed, 1963 Coll of St Mary; *cr:* 3rd Grade Teacher St Patricks Sch 1953-57; 2nd Grade Teacher Elkhorn Public Sch 1958-59; 3rd Grade Teacher 1959-87; Chapter I Teacher 1987- Gretna Public Sch; *ai:* Hobby Day Chairperson; Rdng Comm; NE St Ed Assn; NEA; Gretna Ed Assn Treas 1982-83/1985-86; Metropolitan Rdng Cncl Nominations Comm Chairperson; NE St Rdng Cncl; Intnl Rdng Cncl; St Patricks Church (Treas, CCD Inst, Bible Sch Instr); PTO Awd Guest of Optimist Organization; *home:* 19807 Buffalo Rd Gretna NE 68028

PRATT, ELLEN, Math & Algebra Teacher; *b:* Ashland, KY; *m:* Phil; *c:* John, Stacy; *ed:* (BS) Math, Lander Coll 1974; (MA) Phys Ed, E KY Univ 1975; (Rank I) Scndry Ed, Morehead St Univ 1978; *cr:* Teacher Breathitt Cty HS 1976-78, Lees Jr Coll 1976-78, Summit Jr HS 1978-; *ai:* KEA 1978-; Rose Hill Baptist Church Sunday Sch Teacher 1989-; *office:* Summit Jr HS 1226 Summit Rd Ashland KY 41101

PRATT, JOANNE PHILLIPS, Math Dept Chairperson; *b:* Salisbury, MD; *c:* Laura Donoway, Georgianne Hicks; *ed:* (BA) Math, Univ of DE 1961; (MED) Scndry Ed/Math, Salisbury St Univ 1976; Grad Stud Salisbury St Univ, Univ of MD Eastern Shore; *cr:* Math Teacher Dickinson HS 1961-62; Cmptr Programmer E I Dupont 1962-64; Math Teacher Bennett Jr HS 1970-75, James M Bennett HS 1975-86; Lecturer in Math 1983-, Math Dept Chairperson 1986- Salisbury St Univ; *ai:* Var Math Team Coach; Faculty Spon; Sch Improvement & Awds Comms; Wicomico Cty Ed Assn 1970-, Scndry Teacher of Yr 1989; MD St Teachers Assn 1970-; MD Cncl of Teachers of Math 1980-; NCTM 1978-; Phi Beta Kappa, Phi Kappa Phi, Kappa Delta Pi; Articles Published; *office:* James M Bennett HS E College Ave Salisbury MD 21801

PRATT, MARCIE BEARDAIN, 5th Grade Teacher; *b:* Memphis, TN; *m:* Michael; *c:* Jeffrey Douglas, Gina Rochelle; *ed:* (BE) Elem Ed, Memphis St Univ 1972; *cr:* 4th Grade Teacher 1972-74, 5th Grade Teacher 1981- Harding Acad; Teacher Brownsville Road Nursery Sch 1978-81; *ai:* Brownsville Road Church of Christ Ed Supervisor 1981-87; *office:* Harding Acad 3213 Raleigh Millington Rd Memphis TN 38128

PRATT, MARILYN KELLER, Gifted/Talented Teacher; *b:* Montclair, NJ; *m:* Jeffrey Scott; *c:* Amy E., Jonathan R.; *ed:* (BA) Ed, Westminster Coll 1981; Teaching Gifted & Talented; Grad Stud TCU; Advanced Curr Design for High Achieving & Gifted Strategies Teaching Elem Gifted; *cr:* 5th Grade Teacher 1981-82, 3rd-6th Grade Gifted Teacher 1983-84, 1988-89, 3rd-6th Gifted Teacher 1989- James A Arthur Elem; *ai:* TX Future Problem Solving, Chess Club, Oral Rdng Coach; St Judes Fundraiser Coord; Play Production 1987, 1989; TX St Teachers Assn 1981-; PTA (Patriotic, Cultural Arts) 1981-; TX Alliance for Geographic Ed 1988-; Friends of Lib Sorting Books 1989; Teacher of Yr Awd 1987; *office:* James A Arthur Sch 100 Mistletoe Kennedale TX 76060

PRATT, MARY SANBORN, Sixth Grade Teacher; *b:* Traverse City, MI; *m:* Samuel A.; *c:* Jason, Marcus; *ed:* (BAED) Sociology, Central MI Univ 1973; *cr:* 7th/8th Grade Teacher Immaculate Conception Mid Sch 1973-76; 7th-9th Grade Teacher T G Glover Jr HS 1976-78; 7th-9th Alternate Ed Teacher Traverse City Jr HS 1978-82; 6th Grade Teacher Central Grade Sch 1983-; *ai:* Contact Person for Gifted & Talented Mainstreaming Comm; MI Ed Assn, Traverse City Ed Assn, NEA; *office:* Central Grade Sch PO Box 32 Traverse City MI 49684

PRATT, PAUL EDWARD, Phys Ed Teacher/Coach; *b:* Oklahoma City, OK; *m:* Ellen B. Collin Pratt; *c:* Shannon, Shane; *ed:* (BS) Phys Ed, Cameron Univ 1975; Cmmnty & Recreational Leadership; WSI/First Aid Instr Amer Red Cross; Emergency Medical Technician; *cr:* Instr YMCA 1972-74; Phys Ed Teacher/Coach Ninnekah Public Schs 1975-78; Western Heights Schs 1978-; *ai:* Fellowship Chrstn Athletes Club Spon; Track Coach; TAC Ofcl Track; AAHPERD 1984-; OK-AAHPERD 1984-; FCA 1964-; Amer Red Cross 20 Yr Pin 1967-; APOSI 1984-; Coach Pratt-Recognition Awd for Dedication & Guidance for Pole Vaulters 1982-83; Cert of Appreciation-Phys Ed MSO Comm; *home:* 2825 SW 79th St Oklahoma City OK 73159

PRATT, RITA HAMILTON, 7th-8th Grade English Teacher; *b:* Fort Wayne, IN; *m:* Robert C.; *c:* Debra, Carl, Jonathan; *ed:* (BA) Soc Stud, MI St Univ 1963; *cr:* Soc Stud/Eng Teacher Lowell Area Schls 1963-; *ai:* Eng Dept Head; *office:* Lowell Area Sch 12675 Foreman Rd Lowell MI 49331

PRATT, SANDRA K., Bible Teacher/Acad Counselor; *b:* Flint, MI; *ed:* (BS) Scndry Ed, N MI Univ 1967; (MRE) Theology, Grand Rapids Baptist Seminary 1975; Scndry Sch Admin, MI St Univ; Working towards PhD Biblical Stud, Pensacola Chrstn Coll; *cr:* Teacher Oxford Jr HS 1967-70, Poza Rica Veracruz Mission Sch 1971-72; Teacher/Admin/Cnslr Grand Rapids Baptist Acad 1973-; *ai:* Arranging & Conducting Awds Ceremony; Helping Graduation Preliminaries; Planning & Helping Conduct Orientation Prgms; Written Bible Courses for Sch; *home:* 5082 Kalamazoo SE Kentwood MI 49508

PRATT, SHIRLEY LEONARD, Kindergarten Teacher; *b:* Marion, VA; *m:* Charles Walter; *c:* Jason, Sara; *ed:* (BS) Early Chldhd Ed, 1975, (MS) Early Chldhd Ed, 1981 Radford Univ; *cr:* 3rd Grade Teacher 1975-76, Chapter I Summer Sch Remediation Teacher 1978-80, Kndgtn Teacher 1976- Atkins Elem; *ai:* Child Study, Audit, Family Life Kndgtn Comm; Kndgtn Orientation Coord; NEA, VA Ed Assn, Smyth Cty Ed Assn 1975-83; SW VA Math Assn 1985-; SW Rdng Cncl 1989-; PTO (Adv, Reporter); Amer Angus Assn, VA Angus Assn, SW VA Angus Assn, VA Beef Cattle Improvement Assn, Amer Gelbrieh Assn; Smyth Cty Chamber of Commerce; GSA Leader 1976-83; Church of God (Sunday Sch Teacher 1975-, Bible Sch Dir 1984-89, Bd of Chrstn Ed 1983-89, Family Life Center Bd of Dir 1989-); Teacher of Yr 1990; *home:* Rt 1 Box 1205 Atkins VA 24311

PRAVE, KAREN FAIRCHILD, Science Teacher; *b:* Syracuse, NY; *m:* John; *c:* Kathleen M., Michelle C., John P.; *ed:* (BS) Scndry Sci, SUNY Oswego 1963; Perm Cert NYS Scndry Ed, SUNY Cortland 1970; *cr:* Sci Teacher Romulus Cntrl Sch 1963-69, 1976-; *ai:* Sci Club Adv; Romulus Faculty Assn Pres; Romulus Cntrl Sch Class Adv 1967, 1970, 1988; Prin Advisory Comm Mem; Sunshine Comm Chairperson; Delta Kappa Gamma Pres 1984-86, 1990; Romulus Cntrl Sch Parent Support Group Teacher of Yr 1988; *office:* Romulus Cntrl Sch Main St Romulus NY 14541

PRAVIDICA, SUSAN SHANLEY, First Grade Teacher; *b:* Chicago, IL; *m:* Martin; *c:* Eric; *ed:* (BS) Elem Ed/Child Dev, Rockford Coll 1973; (MS) Outdoor Ed, Northern IL Univ 1989; *cr:* 3rd Grade Teacher St Edwards Sch 1975-76; 2nd Grade Teacher 1976-78, 1st Grade Teacher 1978- Oregon Cmmty Unit Sch Dist; *office:* Jefferson Sch 1100 W Jefferson St Oregon IL 61061

PRAY, TONI HANSEN, Library Media Teacher; *b:* Logan, UT; *m:* Roger T.; *c:* Christopher, Catherine; *ed:* (BA) Eng, UT St Univ 1969; *cr:* Eng Teacher Kennedy Jr HS 1969-76, Brockton HS 1976-78; Eng/Rdng Teacher Copperton Mid Sch 1979-; Lib Media Teacher Bennion Jr HS 1979-; *ai:* Dist Book Selection Comm; ALA, AASL; PTA Sch Rep; UT St Poetry Society 1986-; Articles & Poems Published; *office:* Bennion Jr HS 6055 S 2700 W Salt Lake City UT 84118

PRAYTOR, BETH LYON, Business Teacher; *b:* Lindale, TX; *m:* Homer Charles; *c:* Renee; *ed:* (BBA) Bus, Tyler Jr Coll 1960; (BA) Bus, Stephen F Austin 1964; E TX St Univ, Univ of TX Austin, Univ of TX Tyler; *cr:* Bus Teacher Crosby HS 1964-66, Van HS 1966-; *ai:* UIL Shorthand & Keyboarding; Jr/Sr Spon; Several Comm; TX Bus Ed Assn (Secy, Dist Rep) 1984-, Outstanding Bus Teacher 1981; Delta Kappa Gamma New Mem 1990; NBEA; Lindale 1st Meth Church Sunday Sch Supt 1988-; Dist 7 Outstanding Bus Teacher 1981; *home:* 13036 FM Rd 2710 Lindale TX 75771

PRECOPIA, PENNY ANDERSON, Fourth Grade Teacher; *b:* Jacksonville, TX; *m:* David E.; *c:* David, Kimberly, Kari; *ed:* (BS) Elem Ed, 1974, (MED) Elem Ed, 1990 Univ of N TX; *cr:* Kndgtn Teacher Timbercreek Early Learning Center 1977; 3rd/4th Grade Teacher Word of Faith Chrstn Acad 1981-82; 3rd-6th Grade Teacher Chrstn Life Acad 1982-87; 3rd/4th Grade Teacher Eaglemount Chrstn Sch 1987-88; 4th Grade Teacher Stewarts Creek Elem Sch 1989-; *home:* 565 Auburn Lewisville TX 75067

PREHEIM, JOYCE RICHERT, 1st Grade Teacher; *b:* Freeman, SD; *c:* Robert, David, Eric; *ed:* (BA) Elem Ed, Northern St 1970; *cr:* 3rd/4th Grade Teacher Roslyn Grade Sch; Chapter I Math/1st/5th Grade Teacher Marion Elem; *ai:* Active in Church; *home:* 202 E Wagner Marion SD 57043

PRELESNIK, BARBARA COOPER, Fourth Grade Teacher; *b:* Detroit, MI; *m:* Kenneth Alan; *c:* Theresa A. Prelesnik Van Leeuwen, Sherryl A.; *ed:* (BA) Elem Ed, (MA) Curr/Teaching, MI St Univ; Math Stud, Grand Valley St Univ, Center Grad Coll; Ed, Marygrove Coll; Elem Teaching British Style, Hope Coll London England; *cr:* 2nd/3rd Grade Teacher 1964-72, 4th Grade Teacher 1972-85, 3rd Grade Teacher 1985-88, 4th Grade Teacher 1988- Grand Haven Public Schls.

PREMOSHIS, GREGORY FRANCIS, Chaplain/Religion Instr; *b:* Mount Pleasant, PA; *ed:* (BS) His, St Vincent Coll 1962; (MA) Religious Stud, Univ of Dayton 1979; *cr:* Chaplain/Religion Faculty Greensburg Cntrl Cath 1968-80; Chaplain/Religion Faculty/Dept Chm Geibel HS 1980-; *ai:* Chaplain of Sch; Youth Ministry, Pep Club Adv; Chaplain Ftbl & Bsktbl Teams; Homecoming & Sr Recognition Comm; NCEA; Seton Hill Coll & St Vincent Coll Teacher Excl Awds; *office:* Geibel HS 611 E Crawford Ave Connellsville PA 15425

PREROST, PATRICIA L. (MILNES), 7th & 8th Grade Math Teacher; *b:* Chicago, IL; *m:* James M.; *c:* Jennifer, Mary, Amy; *ed:* (BA) Ed/Home Ec, St Xavier Coll 1968; Univ CA Irvine; *cr:* Jr HS Teacher St John Fisher Sch 1968-74, St Edwards Sch 1985-; *ai:* Coord Jr HS Elective Prgm; Graduation Comm Chm; Math Dept Coord; Orange Cty Rdng Assn; *home:* 26752 Estanciero Dr Mission Viejo CA 92691

PRESCOTT, EDWIN WILLIAM, II, Math/Phys Ed Teacher/Coach; *b:* St Petersburg, FL; *m:* Peggy Collins; *c:* Will, Collins, Brett; *ed:* (BS) Phys Ed, 1971, (MAED) Ed, 1973 W Carolina Univ; *cr:* Teacher/Coach Ruffing HS 1971-72; Grad Asst W Carolina Univ 1972-73; Teacher/Coach Northwestern HS 1973-78, Laurens Dist 55 HS 1978-; *ai:* Asst Ftbl & Head Bsbl Coach; Natl HS Athletic Coaches Assn Region 3 Bsbl Comm Vice-Chm 1989-; SC Athletic Coaches Assn Bsbl Chm 1989-; SC Bsbl Coaches Assn All-Star Game Chm Region 3 Coach of Yr 1989; *home:* 114 Sherwood Forest Laurens SC 29360

PRESLEY, JEANNE HALE, Teacher; *b:* Birmingham, AL; *m:* Kenneth G.; *c:* Kenneth G. Jr., Charles W.; *ed:* (BA) Scndry Eng, NE OK St Univ; (MA) Scndry Supervision, E TX St Univ; Grad Work Counseling, N TX St Univ; *cr:* Teacher Dallas Ind Sch Dist 1966-84, Brownsboro Ind Sch Dist 1984-85, Athens Ind Sch Dist 1985-; *ai:* Phi Delta Kappa, TX Classroom Teachers Assn, TAIR, ASCD, Eng Teacher Organization; Classroom Teachers (VP, Rep); Base Line Document Scndry Eng Writer; Seminar Conductor; *home:* Box 169 Poynor TX 75782

PRESLEY, JUDENE C., 5th Grade Teacher; *b:* Emmett, ID; *c:* Jeremy; *ed:* (BA) Elem Ed, 1973, (MA) Elem Ed/Curr Dev, 1980 Boise St Univ; *cr:* 6th Grade Teacher Cntrl Mesa 1973-75; 5th Grade Teacher Butte View Elem 1975-88, Emmett Mid Sch 1988-; *ai:* Dist Comm Developing Instructional Model for Gem Cty Schls; Chairperson Lang Arts Evaluation Comm for Dist Accreditation Evaluation 1986-87; Alpha Delta Kappa Local Secy 1988-; PTA Bd Mem 1983-85, Life Merit Awd 1986; PTSA Bd Mem 1989-; Cmmty Bible Church Childrens Church Dir 1976-; Gem Cty Ed Assn Teacher of Month 1983; Teacher of Yr Nom Gem Cty Ed Assn 1987; Cooperating Teacher Boise St Univ Stu Teachers 1987-89; Lang Arts Evaluation Comm Chairperson Dist Accreditation Evaluation 1986-87; *office:* Emmett Mid Sch 301 E 4th St Emmett ID 83617

PRESNELL, JOHN, Social Studies Teacher; *b:* Detroit, MI; *m:* Patsy J. Schell; *c:* Joshua; *ed:* (BSED) His, Cntrl MI 1970; (MA) Rdng, Oakland Univ 1980; *cr:* Teacher/Coach Yale 1970-; Coach Peck Cmmty Schls 1986-, Saint Clair Comm Coll 1987; *ai:* Girls Bsktbl, Boys Bsktbl, Ftbl, Track Coach; BCAM 1986-, Coach of Yr 1986; Thumb Meet of Champs VP 1985-; Semi-Finalist Princeton Univ Hum Research; Yale Teacher of Yr 1974-75, 1975-76, 1978-79; Girls Bsktbl Coach of Yr 1986; Area Coach of Yr 1986, 1987; *office:* Yale Public Schls 198 School Dr Yale MI 48097

PRESSLER, LINDA HOOTON, Interim 1st Grade Teacher; *b:* Toledo, OH; *m:* John Thomas; *c:* Katherine Williams; John Addisn; *ed:* (AS) Psych, Dyersburg St 1975; (BS) Elem Ed, Univ TN 1977; Rdng/Art/Cmptr Sci; *cr:* 2nd Grade Teacher Cntrl Elem 1977-82; Pre-Sch Teacher 1st UMC 1986-88; 1st Grade Teacher Dyersburg Primary Interim 1989-; *ai:* Annual Staff 1980-81; PTO Secy 1989-; Sunday Sch Teacher Kndgtn 1989-; Vacation Bible Sch Chairperson 1989-; Dyersburg Ed Assn 1978-82; Bapt Stu Union Pres 1973-75 Pres Awd 1975; Bapt Stu West TN St Rep 1975; Stu Gov Sec 1974-75; Coalition Club 1982-86; Dyersburg Garden Club 1985-86; *home:* 316 Tucker Dyersburg TN 38024

PRESSON, ANITA MYRACLE, 1st Grade Teacher/Asst Prin; *b:* Decaturville, TN; *m:* Dwayne T.; *c:* Michael, Annie; *ed:* (BS) Voc Home Ec, Univ of TN Martin 1968; Elem Teacher Trng; *cr:* Home Ec Teacher Bruceton-Hollow Rock Cntrl HS 1968-69; 1st Grade Teacher 1972-, 1st Grade Teacher/Asst Prin 1 76- Camden Elem Sch; *ai:* NEA, TN Ed Assn, Benton Cty Ed Assn; Univ of TN Alumni Assn; Briarwood PTO; Post Oak Meth Church; Univ of TN Martin Center of Excl Enrichment of Sci & Math Ed 1987; *office:* Camden Elem Sch 208 Washington Ave Camden TN 38320

PREST, MARYELLEN (YANK), Guidance Counselor; *b:* Youngstown, OH; *c:* Stephen R.; *ed:* (BSED) Elem Ed, 1976, (MSED) Guidance/Counseling, 1982 Youngstown St Univ; Educators in Industry, Cleveland St Univ; Grad Stud Youngstown St Univ; Regional Cncl on Alcoholism Youth, Drugs & You; *cr:* Kndgtn Tutor Boardman Local Schls 1976-77; 1st Grade Instr Stow City Schls 1977-78; 5th/7th/8th Grade Math Instr Columbiana Exempted Village Schls 1978-85; Guidance Cnslr E Cleveland City Schls 1986-; *ai:* NEA, OH Ed Assn, E Cleveland Ed Assn, OH Sch Cnslrs Assn; Phi Kappa Phi, Kappa Delta Pi 1976-; BSA Treas Pack 105 1989-; *office:* Shaw HS 15320 Euclid Ave East Cleveland OH 44112

PRESTIA, LAURETTE RIGGIO, English Teacher; *b:* Newark, NJ; *m:* Joseph; *c:* Joseph D.; *ed:* (BA) Engl/Span, Carlow Coll 1968; (MA) Engl, Univ of Texas 1979; *cr:* Elem Teacher American Fnd Sch 1968-69; 2nd Grade Teacher Edinburg HS 1969-72; St Matthews Episcopal Sch 1976-79; 2nd Grade Teacher UT at Pan American 1978-79/89; *ai:* Edinburg HS Natl Honor Soc; TX Classroom Tachers Assn; Hidalgo Cty Foster Children Assn 1987-.

PRESTON, SANDRA UMBANHOWAR, 5th Grade Teacher; *b:* Hoopeston, IL; *m:* Dale Jr.; *c:* Julie, Scott; *ed:* (BS) Elem Ed, 1956, (MS) Elem Ed, 1979 IL St Univ; Post Grad Stud E IL Univ; *cr:* 3rd Grade Teacher Honeywell Grade Sch 1956-61; 6th Grade Teacher Lincoln Grade Sch 1966-67 & 1969; 5th Grade Teacher Maple Grade Sch 1970-84, John Greer Grade Sch 1984-; *ai:* Gifted Coord for Building; Spelling Pronouncer for Area Contests; Educl Television Coord; Delta Kappa Gamma (Parlimentarian 1975, Prgm Chairperson 1976-78) 1967-; Hoopeston Ed Assn, IL Ed Assn, NEA 1968-; Hoopeston Public Lib Bd (Mem, Treas 1970-76) 1970-; Danville Area Bd of Realtors 1979-89; IL Migrant Educators Assn 1988-; DAR Outstanding His Teacher Awd 1985; *office:* John Greer Grade Sch 609 W Main St Hoopeston IL 60942

PRESTON, THOMAS WILLIAM, 8th Grade Science Teacher; *b:* Neptune, NJ; *ed:* (BA) Elem Ed, Univ of Pittsburgh 1983; Working Towards Masters Sci Ed, Clarion Univ; *cr:* Mid Sch Sci Teacher Frick Intnl Stud Acad 1983-; *ai:* PA Jr Acad of Sci, Superbowl of Problem Solving & Sci Olympiad of PA Spon; NSTA 1986-; Univ of Pittsburgh Nationality Rooms Grant to Study in Germany; Leonard Schugar Awd for Photography in Pittsburgh; 3 Rivers Arts Festival; Documentary Video Chosen to Air Public TV Pittsburgh; *office:* Frick Intnl Stud Acad 107 Thackeray Pittsburgh PA 15213

PRETTY, SUSAN KAMALAY, 8th Grade Science Teacher; *b:* Detroit, MI; *m:* R. Douglas; *c:* Lisa, Todd; *ed:* (BA) Elem Ed/Math/Sci, MI St Univ 1972; (MA) Remedial Rdng, E MI Univ 1975; *cr:* 6th Grade Teacher Bates Elem 1972-75, Patrick Henry Mid Sch 1975-79; Remedial Rdng Teacher Henry Ford Comm Coll 1980-82; 8th Grade Rdng/Sci Teacher Patrick Henry Mid Sch 1982-; *ai:* Stu Cncl Adv; Sch Crisis & Mini-Grant Review Comm; St Frances Cabrini Church (Parish Cncl, VP, Secy) 1980-84; *office:* Patrick Henry Mid Sch 24825 Hall Rd Woodhaven MI 48183

PREUSS, LINDA SMITH, Teacher of Gifted & Talented; *b:* Evansville, IN; *m:* Donald L.; *c:* Gregory; *ed:* (BA) Ed, KY Wesleyan Coll 1966; (MA) Ed, 1976, (Rank I) Supervision/Gifted & Talented, 1987 W KY Univ; *cr:* 4th Grade Teacher Tamarack Elem 1966-87; Teacher of Gifted & Talented Daviess Cty Mid 1987-; *ai:* Academic Coach; HS Coord ADAPT Acad for Young Leaders; Daviess Cty Ed Assn, KY Ed AssN, NEA 1966-; KY

Assn Gifted Ed 1986-; Jr League Chm 1974-, Golden Rose Awd 1989; Champions Against Drugs Secy 1986-; *office:* Daviess Cty Mid Sch 1415 E 4th St Owensboro KY 42303

PREVOST, GERALD H., Business Teacher; *b:* Granville, NY; *m:* Rebecca Jean Bushey; *c:* Troy; *ed:* (AAS) Bus Management, St Univ of NY Delhi 1969; (BS) Bus Ed/Accounting/Retailing, Castleton St Coll 1971; (MA) Industrial Relations/Personnel, St Francis Coll 1972; Basic Cmptr Operation, Sign Lang I; *cr:* Bus Teacher Homer Cntrl 1972-80, Lyndon Inst 1980-; *ai:* Sr Class Dir & Adv; Drama Coach; Project Graduation; Track Statistician; Sch Accreditation Co-Chairperson; Salute to Teens Coord; Red Cross Blood Donor; Calidonia Fair Volunteer; VT Foster Parents Father of Yr 1987; *home:* Box 205 Lyndon Center VT 05850

PREYSS, LEONARD THOR, English Department Chair; *b:* Bronx, NY; *m:* Sandra Joy Murdaugh; *c:* Nicole M.; *ed:* (BA) Poly Sci, Kent St 1971; Ed & Curr Design 1990; *cr:* His Dept Chm San Luis Rey Acad 1975-77; Eng Dept Chm San Marcos Jr HS 1979-; *ai:* Boys & Girls Bsktbl Coach; Drama Adv; Gifted & Talented Ed Coord; Amer Youth Soccer Organization Coach 1988-89, 1st Place; Lang Art Curr, Soc Stud Curr, Writing Mentor Teacher; *office:* San Marcos Jr HS 650 W Mission Rd San Marcos CA 92069

PREYSZ, CLAUDIA KARPOWITZ, English Teacher; *b:* Milwaukee, WI; *m:* Louis R. F. III; *c:* Louis, Christine, Mike, Laura, Daniel; *ed:* (BS) Speech Ed, Univ of WI 1968; Trng in Positive Reinforcement Techniques; *cr:* Eng Teacher John Burroughs Jr HS 1968-69; Sci Teacher St James Cathedral Sch 1981-82; Eng Teacher Bishop Moore HS 1982-83, St Augustine HS 1984-; *ai:* General Problem Solving Comm; Supervision of FSU Intern Teacher; SJEA 1988-; NCTE, Alpha Delta Kappa 1990; Cathedral Basilica of St Augustine (Lector, Spec Minister) 1984-87; Coordinated Sr Mentors for Creative Stus Under Chevron Grant; *home:* 42 Southwind Cir Saint Augustine FL 32084

PREZIOSO, ARLENE GORMAN, Mathematics Teacher; *b:* Bronx, NY; *m:* Alfred Edward; *c:* Michael, Lisa Prezioso Ultan; *ed:* (BS) Ed, 1982, (MS) Ed, 1990 S CT St Univ; *cr:* Math Teacher Amity Jr HS 1982-; *ai:* NCTM 1983-; Math Activity Published in Newsletter of New England Piaget Conference Inc 1986; Presidential Awd for Excl in Teaching Math 1987; Amity Gold Pen Awd 1987-88; Letter Published in Natl Cncl of Teachers Math Magazine 1988; *office:* Amity Jr HS 20 Luke Hill Rd Bethany CT 06525

PRIBRAM, JOHN G., Social Studies Teacher; *b:* Prague, Czechoslovakia; *m:* Agnete Husfeldt; *ed:* (BA) Government/His, Harvard 1947; Ed Classes Univ of OK 1970-71; *cr:* Soc Stud Teacher/Dept Chm Sing Out Sch Germany 1966-69; Vice Prin Up With People HS 1969-71; Dean of Stu Monte Cassino HS 1971-83; Soc Stud Instr Union Jr HS 1984-; *ai:* Natl Jr Honor Society Spon Awd Received from Stus; OK Cncl of Soc Stud 1971-; United Nations Assn of E OK (Dir 1974-, Pres 1989-91); Horizons of Hope Autobiography Todd & Honeywell 1990; Today Cath Teacher 1989; A Living Civic Course; Articles in Momentum, Soc Stud Prof, OK Mid Sch Educl Journal; TV Interviews; 1st Class Teacher; Teacher of Month 1990.

PRIBYL, RICK R., English Teacher; *b:* Omaha, NE; *c:* Skip, Scott, Sean, Shea; *ed:* (BA) Eng, St Louis Univ 1970; Aviation, USAF 1971; (MA) Ed Admin, SD St Univ 1974; Soccer Natl B License; *cr:* Instr USAF 1971-77; Teacher Blue Valley North HS 1988-; *ai:* Var Boys & Girls Soccer, Asst Boys Wrestling Coach; NCA Steering Comm; NFLCA, NEA; *office:* Blue Valley North HS 12200 Lamar Overland Park KS 66209

PRIBYL, STEVEN DOUGLAS, 5th Grade Teacher; *b:* Ft Meade, MD; *m:* Sharon Lee Eichelberger; *ed:* (BA) Elem Ed, Univ of N IA 1980; *cr:* Resource Room Teacher White Mountain Jr HS 1980-82; 5th Grade Teacher Roosevelt Elem 1982-89, Overland Elem 1989-; *ai:* NEA 1980-; *office:* Overland Elem Sch 3400 Foothill Blvd Rock Springs WY 82901

PRICE, ALMA M., Teacher; *b:* Kearney, NJ; *m:* David W.; *c:* Karen, David, Tammy J., Lori B.; *ed:* (BS) Scndry Ed/Math, SUNY Oneonta 1963; Grad Work, SUNY Potsdam, SUNY Oneonta, SUNY Oswego, OH St Univ 1970-72; *cr:* Math Teacher Watertown HS 1963-65, Carthage Cntrl Sch 1968-; *ai:* NHS Selection Comm; Amer Legion Auxiliary 1963-; Natl Sci Fnd Grant OH St Univ 1970-72; *office:* Carthage Cntrl Sch Martin Street Rd Carthage NY 13619

PRICE, BRENDA RAWLS, Teacher; *b:* Columbia, SC; *m:* Reginald L.; *c:* D Etta; *ed:* (BS) Elem Ed, Winthrop Coll 1964; Univ of SC Studies; *cr:* Teacher Mossy Oaks Elem 1964-65, Lambs Elem 1965-66, Crestview & Clinton Elem 1966-67, Pelion Elem 1973-74, Springdale Elem 1974-; *ai:* PTA Pres 1986-88; PTA Mem Chm 1988-; Sch Adv Cncl 1989-; Delta Kappa Gamma Teaching Society VP 1977-; PSTA 1975-; Girl Scouts Svc Unit Dir Leader Consultant 1972-; Outstanding Volunteer Thanks Badge 1983 & 1986; Elca Church Camp Lutheridge Bd of Dir 1986-; Faith Lutheran Church Teacher Sunday Sch/Supt/Chm Ch Ed Comm/Youth En Abler/Property Dev Comm 1972-; Lamb Awd 1990; Springdale Teacher of Yr 1977-78; Springdale Distinguished Teacher of Rdng 1983; Lexington Sch Dist #2 Distinguished Teacher Rdng 1986; *home:* 1958 Nazareth Rd Lexington SC 29072

PRICE, DOUGLAS, Science Teacher; *b:* Detroit, MI; *m:* Sandra C.; *c:* Douglas, Laurie, Jennifer; *ed:* (BA) Soc Stud, Univ of TX 1968; (MA) Admin Mid Management, 1976, (MA) Composite Sci 1985 Univ of TX San Antonio; *cr:* Classroom Teacher Harlandale Ind Sch Dist 1968-73; Elem Prin Oakwood Ind Sch Dist 1974-76; Classroom Teacher Judson Ind Sch Dist 1985-; *ai:* UIL Chaperone; TX Prof Educators Assn; San Antonio Zoological Society; US Naval Inst; Amer Historical Soc; Curr Dev Oakwood Ind Sch Dist Awd; SWTSU Veterans Assn Secy; Harlandale Baptist Church Scoutmasters Awd; Viet nam Service Medal; *office:* Judson HS/ Gray Campus HS 9695 SCHAEFER Road Converse TX 78109

PRICE, ETHEL MAY (HOLCOMB), Retired; *b:* Coffey, MO; *w:* W. L. (dec); *c:* Janis Robinson; *ed:* (BS) Elem Ed, Maryville St 1963; *cr:* Bookkeeper MFA Produce Co 1937-47/1952-54; Teacher Rural Ford 1948-50; Teacher Gallatin 1950-51; Ed Secy 1st Baptist Church 1951; Teacher Gilman City 1956-63; Teacher Coffey R1 1964-81; *ai:* MSTA; Harrison Baptist Assn SS Dir/ UBS Dir; *home:* Box 14 Coffey MO 64636

PRICE, JERRY LYNN, Social Studies Teacher; *b:* Ewing, KY; *m:* G. Diane Vertrees; *ed:* (BA) His, 1971, (MA) His, 1974, Elem Endorsement, 1975 Eastern KY Univ; *cr:* 5th-6th Grade Teacher North Middletown Elem 1972-78; Soc Stud Teacher Bourbon Cty Mid Sch 1978-; *ai:* Academic Team & Sftbl Coach; Bourbon Cty Ed Assn Pres 1976-78; Cntrl KY Ed Assn Pres 1981-82; KY Ed Assn Bd Mem 1983-89; NEA Resolutions Comm Mem 1988-; KY Mid Sch Assn, Natl Assn of Soc Stud Teachers, Sftbl Assn; Grad Asst E KY Univ; KY Prin Internship Comm; KY Ed Television Forum on Ed; *office:* Bourbon Cty Mid Sch 3343 Lexington Rd Paris KY 40361

PRICE, JOHN A., 6th Grade English/Soc Teacher; *b:* Shell Lake, WI; *m:* Nancy; *c:* Ian; *ed:* (BA) Elem Ed, Univ of WI River Falls 1976; Ed, St Marys Coll 1991; *cr:* Core 6/Eng/Soc Teacher Rosemount Mid Sch 1976-; *ai:* Learners at Risk Coord; Mid-Day Activity, Adv/Advisee, Dist Assurance of Mastery Comm; Midwest Regional Conference Team Mem; MN Ed Assn, NEA 1976-; Rosemount Mid Sch Dist Cncl Quest for Excl Awd 1989; *office:* Rosemount Mid Sch 3135 143rd St W Rosemount MN 55068

PRICE, JOHN G., 6th Grade Teacher/Ath Director; *b:* East Chicago, IN; *m:* Debra Ann Bright; *c:* David, Laura; *ed:* (BS) Elem Ed, 1979, (MS) Elem Ed, 1983 IUPUI; Drivers Ed Endorsement 1988; Soc Stud Endorsement K-9th Grade 1990; *cr:* Teacher Clark Pleasant Sch Corp 1979-; *ai:* Athletic Dir 1984-; Bsktbl & Track Coach; ISTA/NEA Local VP 1986; *office:* Clark Pleasant Mid Sch 222 Tracy St Whiteland IN 46184

PRICE, JOHNNIE ANDREW, 6th-8th Grade Coach; *b:* Fort Worth, TX; *m:* Patricia Ann Thomas; *c:* Nicole A.; *ed:* (BS) Health/Phys Ed, Prairie View A&M Univ 1981; Cert Univ of Houston; *cr:* 6th Grade Sci Teacher Galena Park Mid Sch 1981-88; Drivers Ed Teacher Gulf Driving Sch 1982-; 6th-8th Grade Phys Ed Teacher Galena Park Mid Sch 1988-; *ai:* Boys Bsktbl, Ftbl, Track Coach; TX HS Coaches Assn General Mem 1981-; *home:* 198 Blackrock Rd Houston TX 77019

PRICE, JOSEPH WILLIAM, 7th/8th Grade Phys Sci Teacher; *b:* St Louis, MO; *ed:* (BA) Eng Lit/Bio/Ed, Morehouse Coll 1970; (MS) Pre-Medicine/Biophysics, Howard Univ; Working Toward Masters Cmptr Ed, Trinity Coll 1991; Cert Lit, Theatre Art, Univ of Ghana W Africa; Analytical Chem, Physics, Anthropometry, Smithsonian Inst; Clinical Chem Cert, Natl Health Labs; Cert Chem, Physics, Trng Inst Prince George Comm Coll; *cr:* Sci/Eng Teacher Hughes-Quinn Jr HS 1970-73; Sci/Rdng Teacher Charles Cty Comm Coll 1985-88; Sci/Math/Cmptrs Teacher Andrew Jackson Mid Sch 1984-89; Sci Teacher Nicholas Orem Sci-Math-Technology Magnet 1989-; *ai:* Spon & Instr Girls Drill Team Hughes Quinn Jr HS 1972-73; Sci Fair Coord & Club Adv Andrew Jackson Mid Sch 1987-88; Natl Jr Tennis League Supvr & Coach 1975-89;Odyssey of Mind 1989-; Natl Regis EMT 1978-, Lic 1979; Sigma Chi Honorary Physics Society Local Secy 1976; NSTA 1989-; WA Area Tennis (Supvr, Coach), Coaching Awd 1972, 1987; Chas Merrill Grant for Over-Seas Stud W Africa 1969; Bio-Medical Research Grant Natl Inst of Health & Howard Univ 1973-75; Woodrow Wilson Fellowship-Smithsonian Inst 1975; Nom by Peers for Outstanding Sci Teacher 1987; Research Fellow US Dept of Ag Summer Project 1989-; *office:* Nicholas Orem Sci-Math-Tech 6100 Editors Pkwy Hyattsville MD 20782

PRICE, KAREN STOKES, Sophomore English Teacher; *b:* Joplin, MO; *m:* James R.; *ed:* (BA) Eng/His/Sociology, Univ of TX Austin 1979; Ed, Corpus Christi St Univ 1985-87; *cr:* Stu Teacher Truman Mid Sch 1984; Eng Teacher Sinton HS 1985-; *ai:* Drill Team Spon 1985-87; Literary Magazine Spon 1987-; Prin Advisory Comm 1988; Problem-Solving Coach 1985-; Building Leadership Team 1989-; Prom Advisory Comm 1987; TX St Teachers Assn, NEA Mem 1985-; NCTE Mem 1986-; Excel Trng; Teacher Expectation, Stu Achievement Trng; Sinton HS Teacher of Yr 1988-89; Effective Schls Trng; *office:* Sinton HS 400 N Pirate Blvd Sinton TX 78387

PRICE, KATHLEEN KRISCENSKI, 6th-8th Grade Teacher; *b:* Bristol, CT; *m:* Walter E.; *c:* Zachary; *ed:* (BA) Eng, Univ of CT 1970; *cr:* 7th/8th Grade Teacher St Stanislaus Sch 1973-76; Spec Ed Aide Charter Oak Sch 1983-86; Math/Eng Teacher St Brigid Sch 1986-; *ai:* Yrbk Adv; Graduation Coord; Helped Author Drug Curr Guidelines; *office:* St Brigid Sch 100 Mayflower St West Hartford CT 06110

PRICE, MARIAN DUNAWAY, Third Grade Teacher; *b:* Stanford, KY; *m:* George Thomas; *ed:* (BS) Elem Ed, Campbellsville 1967; (MA) Elem Ed, Union 1970; (Rank I) E KY Univ; *cr:* Teacher Somerset Ind Sch Dist 1967-70, Memorial 1970-87, Hopkins 1987-; *ai:* Bridge, Golf, Tennis, Acts; SEA Treas 1972-73; KEA, NEA, Somerset PTA, Alpha Delta Kappa; Eastern Star, Beacon Hill Church; KY PTA Teacher Awd 1987; *home:* 6106 Lakeview Dr Somerset KY 42501

PRICE, MAXINE RODGERS, Business Education Teacher; *b:* Casey Cty, KY; *d:* John E.; *c:* John R.; *ed:* (BS) Commerce, 1945, (MA) Bus Ed, 1958 Univ KY; *cr:* Secy To VP Univ of KY 1945-46; Exec Secy General Electric 1952; Bus Teacher Liberty HS 1946-51, 1953-68, Casey Cty HS 1968-; *ai:* Chess Club Spon; Delta Kappa Gamma 1990; NEA, KY Ed Assn, Mid-Cumberland Dist Ed Assn, Casey Cty Teachers Assn; KY Colonel 1975, 1988, Contributions Awd; Campbellsville Coll Excl in Teaching Awd Meritorius Service to Ed 1990; *home:* Rt 4 Box 10 Middleburg St Liberty KY 42539

PRICE, MICHAEL EDWARD, History Teacher; *b:* San Antonio, TX; *m:* Vivian Rogers; *c:* Jessica, John, Amanda; *ed:* (BA) His, KS St Univ 1977; (MA) His, 1980, (EDD) 1987, Univ Of GA; *cr:* His Instr Cedar Shoals HS 1984-; Course Devloper/ Instr/Amer His Univ of GA 1988-; *ai:* His Club; Academic Bowl; Newsletter Editor; Various Comm; Natl His Day; NEA, NCSS, GA Ed Assn, GA His Society, Cncl for Soc Stud; Articles Published; STAR Teacher Clarke Cty Sch Dist 1988; Grad Asst Univ GA 1977-79, 1983-84; Co-Dir Life on the Land Project GA Environment Hum 1984-85; *office:* Cedar Shoals HS 1300 Cedar Shoals Dr Athens GA 30610

PRICE, MICHAEL J. (PRICE), Principal/Vocational Director; *b:* Jamestown, TN; *m:* Melissa A. Tinch; *c:* Jason, Joshua; *ed:* (BS) Ed/Ag, Mid TN St Univ 1974; (MS) Ed/Admin, TN St Univ 1985; Working Towards Doctoral TN St Univ; *cr:* Teacher Pickett Cty Sch System 1977-80, Wayne Cty Sch System 1980-86; Prin/ Voc Dir Wayne Cty Sch System 1986-; *ai:* Wayne Cty Ed Assn Pres 1984-85; Parks & Recreation Bd Mem 1988-89; Dixie Youth Bsbl Little League Coach 1983-88; Pickett Cty Schls Teacher of Yr 1978; Waynesboro City Commissioner 1988-; Whos Who Outstanding Young Men 1983; *home:* 104 Pope St Waynesboro TN 38485

PRICE, MICHAEL WILLIAM, HS Citizenship Teacher; *b:* Landstuhl, West Germany; *m:* Jill Banks; *ed:* (BS) Poly Sci, N GA Coll 1987; US Army Officer Basic Signal Sch; *cr:* Asst Instr Augusta Coll 1987-88; Soc Stud Teacher Glenn Hills HS 1988-; *ai:* Jr Var Ftbl & Golf Coach; Ecology Club & Just Say No Club Spon; Prof Assn of GA Educators 1988-; Natl Rifle Assn 1984-; Outstanding Young Men of America; *home:* 1612 Sandalwood Dr Augusta GA 30909

PRICE, NANCY L., French Teacher; *b:* Milwaukee, WI; *m:* Jerry; *c:* Jason, Aaron; *ed:* (BSE) Fr, Univ of WI Whitewater 1971; Georgetown Univ, Univ of Dijon France 1975; Grad Work in Fr, Univ of WI Milwaukee; *cr:* Fr Teacher Ft Atkinson Jr HS 1971-77, Ft Atkinson Sr HS 1985-, MATC Ft Atkinson 1975-; Fr/ Youngs Scholars Prgm Teacher Univ of WI Whitewater 1990; *ai:* Foreign Lang Dept Chairperson; Fr Club Adv; Various Faculty Comms; WI Assn of Foreign Lang Teachers, AATF, WI Ed Assn 1985-; Ft Atkinson Jr Womans Club Pres 1981-83; WI Fed of Womans Clubs Dist Pres 1984-86; Ft Atkinson Arts Cncl Pres 1990; Fed Grant to Study Fr & Ed Methods Foreign Lang Teaching Inst, Fr for the 21st Century 1989; Nationwide Finalist Fraternalist of Yr 1986; Grant/Schlsp to Attend Bus World Seminar 1989; *office:* Ft Atkinson Sr HS 310 S 4th St E Fort Atkinson WI 53538

PRICE, PATRICK SHANNON, Health Education Teacher; *b:* Sault Ste Marie, MI; *m:* Carrie Van Wieren; *c:* Kelly, Dustin, Courtney; *ed:* (BS) Soc Sci, 1962, (MA) His, 1963-, (MA) Health Ed, 1990 Cntrl MI Univ; Holistic Health Specialty Certificate, Western MI Univ 1988; *cr:* Teacher Lakeview Public Schls 1963-68; Health Ed Teacher 1969-, Stu at Risk, Crisis Intervention/Prevention Specialist 1990 Fennsville Public Schls; *ai:* Amer Fitness/Running Assn 1978-; Lions Club; *office:* Anna Michen Elem Sch N Maple Fennville MI 49408

PRICE, PEGGY REAVIS, Kindergarten Teacher; *b:* Henderson, NC; *m:* John Irven Jr.; *c:* Kecia, Karmen, Kamron; *ed:* (BS) Early Chldhd, East Carolina Univ 1969; *cr:* Kndgtn Teacher Goldsboro City Schls 1969-70; 2nd Grade Teacher 1970-71, Kndgtn Teacher 1971-73 Pitt Cty Schls; Kndgtn Teacher Vance Cty Schls 1973-89; *ai:* Calendar Comm; Sch Health, Phys Ed & Dental Coord; Curr Planning Comm; Pre K-3 Sch Support Team Rep; NC Assn of Educators (Faculty Rep, Secy) 1988-; NEA; Women of Church; Alpha Delta Kappa (Chaplin 1989-, Treas 1990-); Teacher of Yr; Teenline Volunteer for Coalition on Adolescent Pregnancy; *home:* Rt 3 Box 562 Henderson NC 27536

PRICE, RONALD GORDON, Math Teacher; *b:* Providence, RI; *m:* Rita Maria Clement; *c:* Sandra L., Rose M., Carol A., Robin J.; *ed:* (BS) Ind Arts, 1967, (MS) Ed, 1973, Math Cert, 1977 RI Coll; *cr:* Teacher Coventry Mid Sch 1967-77; Math Cmptr Teacher 1977-87; Math Teacher Coventry HS 1987-; *ai:* NCTE 1977-; RI Math Teachers 1986-; *office:* Coventry H S Reservoir Rd Coventry RI 02816

PRICE, SANDRA SMITH, English Teacher; *b:* Pecos, TX; *m:* Douglas; *c:* Dougas, Laurie, Jennifer; *ed:* (BSED) Elem Ed/Eng, Southwest TX St Univ 1965; Addtl Studies Eng, His; *cr:* 7th Grade Teacher Vestal Elem 1965-66; 7th/8th Grade Teacher Terrell Wells Mid Sch 1966-74; 8th-12th Eng Teacher Oakwood HS 1975; 7th/8th Eng/His Teacher Terrell Wells Mid Sch 1976-; *ai:* Univ

Interscholastic Leag Sch Dir; Mem Curr Research & Dev Team; Gifted & Talented Advisory Comm; Natl Jr Honor Society Advisory Cncl; UIL Coach-Writing, Spelling; Chm Sch Contest Comm; Spon Sch TX Future Problem Solving Teams; Terrell Wells PTA Spiritual Chm 1986-88; Assn TX Prof Educators; Order of Eastern Star; San Antonio Zoological Society; Project 90 Mini-Grant Student-Written Childrens Books; Awd Recognition; Certificate of Honor; *office:* Terrell Wells Mid Sch 422 W Hutchins San Antonio TX 78221

PRICE, THOMAS FREDRICK, 2nd Grade Teacher; *b:* Shelby, NC; *m:* Julia Lee Tiddy; *c:* Lea, Bonney, Garrett; *ed:* (BSED) Early Chldhd Ed, 1975, (MAED) Early Chldhd Ed, 1981 W Carolina Univ; *cr:* Teacher Elizabeth Sch 1975-; *ai:* K-3rd Grade Talent Show; Grade Chm; Planning Comm; Math Teacher of Yr 1985; *office:* Elizabeth Elem Sch 220 S Post Rd Shelby NC 28150

PRICE, WILLIE J., Mathematics/Computer Teacher; *b:* St Louis, MO; *ed:* (BS) Ed, Lindenwood Coll 1976; Advanced Trng in Educl Software Design, Cmptr Repair, Robotic Technologies; *cr:* Teacher St Louis Univ Elem Sch 1972-74, Brentwood Schls 1976-78, St Edwards 1978-79, Carlsbad Schls 1980-; *ai:* Cmptr Club Spon; At-Risk Cnslr; Mentor Mid Sch Stus; Carlsbad Ed Assn, NM Cncl of Cmptr Users, Intnl Robotic Cncl Mem 1989-; Apple Mem 1982-; Eddy Cty Cncl on Alcoholism Treas 1987-88; Mc Graw/Hill Research Grant; Software Publisher; *office:* Eisenhower Mid Sch 500 W Church St Carlsbad NM 88220

PRICHARD, LEONA ADKINS, Physical Science Teacher; *b:* Wayne, WV; *m:* Belvard Gillette; *c:* Mary P. Laverty, Belvard A., Karen P. Mills; *ed:* (AB) Home Ec/Sci/Eng, Marshall Univ 1955; Grad Work Marshall Univ; *cr:* Home Ec Teacher Appalachian Power 1955-62; Teacher Wayne Elem 1967-69, Wayne Jr HS 1969-80, Wayne Mid Sch 1980-84, Wayne HS 1984-; *ai:* FHA, Majorette, Chrldr Spon; 4-H Leader; Womens Club; Kappa Omicron Phi 1955-; Alpha Delta Kappa Secy 1988-; Home Ec Alumni 1955-; Mu Alumni Assn; *home:* 7041 Wilson Ck Rd Box 2101 Wayne WV 25570

PRICKETT, HARVARD PITTMAN, JR., Social Studies Teacher; *b:* Atlanta, GA; *m:* Linda Ray Williams; *c:* Kelli L. (dec); *ed:* (BA) Ed, 1965, (MED) Ed, 1970, (EDS) Ed, 1972 W GA Coll; *cr:* Soc Stud Teacher Douglas Cty HS 1965-; *ai:* GA Assn of Educators 1965-; NCSS, NEA; Kiwanis Key Club Spon 1970-75; Douglas Cty Media Comm 1990; Whos Who Southeast Marquee; *home:* 1541 Patricia Ln Douglasville GA 30134

PRICKETT, JEFFERSON BOLTON, History Teacher; *b:* Commerce, GA; *m:* Judy Wood; *c:* Christy, Shannon; *ed:* (BS) Soc Sci Ed, GA S Coll 1968; *cr:* Teacher Commerce Mid Sch 1968-; *ai:* Jr Var Girls Bsktbl & Var Golf Coach; Prof Assn of GA Educators 1980-; Gideons 1983-; Region 8A Golf Coach of Yr 1982-83, Var Girls Asst Coach of Yr 1988-89; Commerce Mid Sch Teacher of Yr 1982, 1984; Researched & Published HS Ftbl Statistics 1940-88; *home:* Rt 6 Box 443 Commerce GA 30529

PRIDDY, JERRY, Mathematics Department Chair; *b:* Albany, GA; *m:* Elaina Wilcox; *c:* Maxxon, Jeremy, Joshua; *ed:* (BS) Math/Ed, Youngstown St Univ 1987; Univ of Pittsburgh Sch of Pharmacy; *cr:* Math Instr Cerro Cosa Coll 1987-; Math Dept Chm Kern Valley HS 1987-; *ai:* Curr Comm; CSF Adv; Jr Var Ftbl & Var Bsbl Coach; Math Dept Chm; Jr Var Vlybl; VFW 1984-87; Nom Mentor Teacher Kern HS Dist; Kern Valley HS was Recipient of CA Distinguished Sch Awd 1988-89; *office:* Kern Valley HS Box 1027 Erskine Creek Rd Lake Isabella CA 93240

PRIEST, JOE ELLEN, HS Counselor; *b:* Mount Pleasant, MI; *ed:* (BS) His, Evangel Coll 1975; (Med) Pupil Personnel Services, Azusa Pacific Univ 1986; *cr:* His/Government Teacher 1977-85, Cnslr 1986 Modesto Chrstn Sch; *ai:* CSF Adv; Staff Rep Parent-Teacher Fellowship; Part-Time Guidance Instr Modesto Jr Coll; Mem Sch Accreditation Team; Pi Gamma Mu 1975-.

PRIEST, JOHN MICHAEL, History Teacher; *b:* Georgetown, DC; *m:* Rhonda C. Whitacre; *c:* M. Douglas, Jennifer M., Kimberly A.; *ed:* (BA) His, Loyola Univ 1972; (MA) Soc Sci, Hood Univ 1985; Cert Admin & Supervision; *cr:* Teacher Washington Cty Bd of Ed 1980-; *ai:* Supervise Civil War His Research Projects; Wrote Various Articles 1985, 1990; *office:* South Hagerstown HS 1101 S Potomac St Hagerstown MD 21740

PRIEST, RHONDA CAROL, Fourth Grade Teacher; *b:* Pittsfield, IL; *m:* Don; *ed:* (BS) Elem Ed/Spec Ed, E IL Univ 1971; Grad Stud S IL Univ; *cr:* Teacher of Educable Mentally Handicapped 1971-74, 2nd Grade Teacher 1974-82, Developmental 1st Grade Teacher 1982-84, 3rd Grade Teacher 1984-89, 4th Grade Teacher 1989- South Sch; *ai:* Evaluation of Emerging Prgms Comm Chairperson 1989-; Dist Cooperative Learning Wkshp Presenter 1989-; Cty Problem Solving Through Cooperative Learning Wkshp Presenter 1989-; NEA, IEA 1971-; CEA Secy 1971-; Dialogue in Methods of Ed 1988-; St Josephs Cath Church; Carlinville Schls Fnd Grant 1989; *office:* South Sch 218 S Broad Carlinville IL 62626

PRIMEAU, RUTH ANNE, 2nd Grade Teacher; *b:* St Louis, MO; *m:* Gerald Paul; *c:* Monica L., Brett A.; *ed:* (BA) Elem Ed, Harris Teachers Coll 1966; *cr:* 1st-3rd Grade/Transition Teacher New Overland 1966-67, De Hart 1967-71, Ireland 1972; 1st/3rd Grade Teacher Hawk Point 1972-76; 2nd Grade Teacher Moscow Mills 1976-; *ai:* MO St Teachers Assn 1972-; Alpha Sigma Tau Pledge Chm; Alpha Delta Kappa 1989-; *office:* Moscow Mills Sch Box 137 Moscow Mills MO 63362

PRIMM, JOHN THOMAS, Social Studies Teacher; *b:* Athens, IL; *m:* Sonia Kay Lovell; *c:* Dennis, David; *ed:* (BA) Ed, Univ of Tampa 1962; (MED) Supervision/Ed, FL A&M 1978; *cr:* Teacher Dunedin Highland Jr HS 1962-66, Ocala HS 1966-67, Fort King Jr HS 1967-69, Lombard Jr HS 1969-70, Vernon HS & Mid Sch 1971-; *ai:* Small Games & Puzzles Club Spon; FTP, WCEA Pres 1971-; FL Ed Assn 1962-; Lions Club 1972-79; Vernon City Cncl Pres 1974-76; *home:* PO Box 341 Vernon FL 32462

PRIMUS, IRMA BRITT, Counselor; *b:* Birmingham, AL; *c:* Ra Shawn S.; *ed:* (BS) Poly Sci, Tuskegee Inst 1971; (MA) Guidance/Counseling, CA Luth 1985; *cr:* Teacher Gage Jr HS 1978-79; Teacher 1980-88, Cnslr 1988- Bret Harte Intermediate Sch; *ai:* Stu Government & 8th Grade Class Spon; Los Angeles Sch Cnslrs Assn 1989-; *office:* Bret Harte Intermediate Sch 9301 S Hoover Ave Los Angeles CA 90044

PRIMUTH, ANDREA L., Counselor; *b:* Rockford, IL; *m:* Daniel; *c:* Chad, Kent; *ed:* (BS) Elem Ed/Phys Ed, Rockford Coll 1975; (MS) Counseling/Guidance N IL Univ 1988; *cr:* Dental Asst 1967-68; Phys Ed Teacher 1975-87, Track/Vlybl Coach 1975- Franklin Jr HS; Cnslr Harlem HS 1987-; *ai:* Jr HS Girls Track Coach; Stu for Stu Tutoring & Mentoring Assisted Stu at Harlem Spon; Career Speakers for Harlem; N IL Cnslrs Assn (Secy, Treas) 1987-; Aacd 1987-89; Harlem Fans Club; *office:* Harlem HS 9229 N Alpine Rd Rockford IL 61111

PRINCE, BETTY JO WOODSON, Fifth Grade Teacher; *b:* Dallas, TX; *m:* Mikel A.; *c:* Pam Merryman, Mark, Debra Mc Ewen, Cindy; *ed:* (BS) Bus Admin, Univ of TN 1962; (MAT) Teaching, E TN St Univ 1976; *cr:* Intern Teacher Van Pelt 1975-76, 2nd-4th/5th Grade Teacher Cedar Grove 1976-; *ai:* Just Say No Spon; Teacher Parents in Ed; Cedar Grove Teacher of Yr 1984, 1989; *office:* Cedar Grove Elem Sch 100 Coley St Kingsport TN 37660

PRINCE, KATHY S., Mathematics Teacher; *b:* Wedowee, AL; *ed:* (BS) Math, 1983, (MS) Math, 1988 Jacksonville St Univ; *cr:* 7th-9th Grade Math Teacher De Armanville Jr HS 1984-; *ai:* Math Team Spon; Vlybl & Sftbl Coach; *home:* Rt 2 Box 409 Woodland AL 36280

PRINCE, RACHELLA STANLEY, Sixth Grade Teacher; *b:* Beckley, WV; *m:* Robert Jackson Jr.; *c:* Tyler L., Scott E.; *ed:* (AA) Elem Ed, Beckley Coll 1978; (BS) Elem Ed, Concord Coll 1979; (MA) Mid Chldhd Ed, WV Coll of Grad Stud 1985; *cr:* 6th Grade Teacher Shady Spring Elem Sch 1980-; *ai:* Math Field Day & Soc Stud Fair Coord; WV Ed Assn 1980-; Kappa Delta Pi, Gamma Beta Phi 1979-; Stone & Thomas Teen Bd (Coord, Leader) 1983-84; Natl Deans List 1978-79; *home:* 2 Lynn Ave Daniels WV 25832

PRINCE, ROBERT M., English Teacher; *b:* Cleveland, OH; *m:* Donna M. Rudar; *c:* Lauren, Lisa; *ed:* (BA) Eng/Speech, Denison Univ 1969; Post Grad Stud, OH Univ; Lake Erie Coll; Cleveland St Univ; *cr:* Eng Teacher J F Kennedy Jr HS 1970-83, North HS 1983-; *ai:* Var Asst Ftbl Coach; Jr Var Head Ftbl Coach; Eng Curr Dev Comm Mem; NCTA Mem; *office:* North H S 34041 Stevens Blvd Eastlake OH 44095

PRINCE, SUZANNE ATTAWAY, Second Grade Teacher; *b:* Wrightsville, GA; *m:* John Wesley; *c:* Wesley, Parissa; *ed:* (BS) Elem Ed, GA Coll 1961; (MED) Elem Ed, W GA Coll 1975; Supervising Stu Teacher Cert, W GA Coll 1977-78; Master Teacher Data Collection, Univ of GA 1975; *cr:* 3rd Grade Teacher Newton Estates Elem Sch 1960-62; 4th Grade Teacher Eastern Elem Sch 1963; 2nd Grade Teacher Beaverbrook Elem 1965-; Asst Professor of Ed Mercer Univ 1981-; *ai:* Griffin-Spalding Federal Credit Union Bd of Dir 1986-89; Credit Comm (Chairperson, Secy 1988-, Vice Chairperson); 2nd Grade Adv Comm Chairperson; Griffin-Spalding Assn of Educators (Recording Secy 1983, 1985-86, Corresponding Secy 1982-83, 1985-86, 1988-89, Assn Rep 1977-); Henry Cty Democratic Exec Comm (Mem 1982-, Vice Chm 1982-89); Griffin-Spalding Assn of Educators (Legislative & PAC Chm 1984-); GA Art of Teaching Fair Judge & Winner; Presenter Wkshps St & Natl 1980; Myself & Class Featured in Magazine 1983; Article Published in Magazine; *home:* 140 Circle Dr Lake Talmadge Hampton GA 30228

PRINDLE, KATHRYN, Mathematics Dept Chair; *b:* Schenectady, NY; *m:* J. Richard Goodell; *ed:* (BA) Psych, SUNY Binghamton 1980; (MS) Math Ed, SUC Fredonia 1987; *cr:* Math Teacher Cassadaga Valley Cntrl Sch 1983-84; Math Dept Chairperson Maple Grove HS 1984-; *ai:* Honors Comm; *office:* Maple Grove HS Dutch Hollow Rd Bemus Point NY 14712

PRIOLO, CHARLENE SANGIUOLO, 8th Grade Teacher; *b:* New York, NY; *m:* Joseph; *c:* Joseph C.; *ed:* (BA) Soc Sci, John Jay Coll of Criminal Justice 1974; (MA) Forensic Psych, CUNY 1985; NJ Dept of Ed Alternate Route Prgm Kean Coll; *cr:* Drug/Alcohol Cnslr/Tutor Long Branch Outreach Center 1974-76; Probation Officer Monmouth Cty Probation Dept 1976-77; Cnslr/Tutor FDM Dormitory 1980-83; Teacher Frances Place Sch 1986-; *ai:* Prins Advisory & Mid Sch Steering Comm Mem; Stu Assistance Team; 8th Grade Schlsp Fund Adv; NEA, NJEA, Keansburg Teachers Assn 1986-; Anastasia Sch PTO (VP 1984-85, Pres 1985-86); Ad Hoc Comm 1985-86; Long Branch Soccer Assn Coach 1982-86; Teacher of Month 1988-89; *office:* Frances Place Sch Frances Pl Keansburg NJ 07734

PRIOR, RICHARD EDMON, Latin/Teaching Assistant; *b:* Syracuse, NY; *ed:* (BA) Classics, Univ NC Greensboro 1984; (MA) Classics, Univ of MD 1991; *cr:* Latin Teacher Greensboro City Schls 1985, Hampton City Schls 1985-87, Virginia Beach City Schls 1987-88, Chesapeake City Schls 1988-89; Latin Teaching Asst Univ of MD College Park 1989-; *ai:* Classical Assn of Mid-Western & Southern Sts 1984-; Vergilian Society 1983; Classical Assn of Atlantic Sts 1985-; Amnesty Intnl 1987-; NEH Fellowship 1987; *home:* 7715 Adelphi Rd Adelphi MD 20783

PRISKORN, GARY J., 6th-8th Grade Science Teacher; *b:* Trenton, MI; *m:* Pamela Florian; *c:* Jeffrey S., David J.; *ed:* (AA) Elem Ed, Concordia Coll 1966; (BA) Elem Ed, Concordia Univ 1968; (MED) Admin-Elem Ed, Wayne St Univ 1975; *cr:* Prin/7th/8th Grade Teacher Zion Luth Sch 1968-71; 6th-8th Grade Sci Teacher Our Shepherd Luth Sch 1971-; *ai:* Coaching; Family Life Dir; Luth Ed Assn 1968-; *office:* Our Shepherd Luth Sch 1658 E Lincoln Birmingham MI 48008

PRITCHARD, BETTY JO ANN (FRENCH), Teacher; *b:* Tuxedo, TX; *m:* Bill; *c:* Gregg, Cathy Smith; *ed:* (BA) Math/Eng/Ed, Hardin Simmons 1966; *cr:* Teacher Stamford Ind Sch Dist 1966-67, 1970-89; *ai:* Spon Univ I League of Mid Sch Math & Sci; TX St Teachers Assn Life Mem 1966-.

PRITCHARD, DAVID IVAN, English Teacher; *b:* E Cleveland, OH; *ed:* (BS) Eng/Speech, IA St Univ 1964; (MED) Remedial Rdng, Kent St Univ 1972; *cr:* Teacher Thomas Jefferson Jr HS 1967-87, Thomas Jefferson Intermediate Sch 1987-; *office:* Thomas Jefferson Sch 3145 W 46th St Cleveland OH 44102

PRITCHARD, LORI WILLIAMS, 8th Grade Reading Teacher; *b:* Buffalo, NY; *m:* Mark D.; *ed:* (BA) Eng/Ed, 1985, (MS) Elem ED, 1986 Potsdam Coll; *cr:* 8th Grade Rdng Teacher Newark Mid Sch 1987-; *ai:* Video Club Co-Adv; Building Planning Team Mem; *office:* Newark Mid Sch 316 W Miller St Newark NY 14513

PRITCHETT, BEVERLY BACON, Guidance Counselor; *b:* Birmingham, AL; *m:* William Gary; *c:* Marsha Pritchett Mc Farlane, Brenda Pritchett Doster, Millie A.; *ed:* (BS) Ed, Samford Univ 1964; (MA) Counseling/Human Dev, Troy St Univ 1988; *cr:* Math Teacher Mt Pisgah Mid Sch 1979-81; Math Teacher 1981-86, Guidance Cnslr 1986-88 Gulf Breeze Mid Sch; Math/Cnslr Leon HS 1988-89; Guidance Cnslr Gulf Breeze HS 1989-; *ai:* Keyette Club Spon; Jr Var Sftbl Coach; NCTM, MACTM 1979-81; WFGCA 1987-88; Gulf Breeze United Meth 1980-; Jr League Mini Grant 1988, 1990; FL Visual Ed Seminar 1987; *office:* Gulf Breeze HS 675 Gulf Breeze Pkwy Gulf Breeze FL 32561

PRITCHETT, LYNNE GHEESLING, Home Economics Teacher; *b:* Marietta, GA; *m:* Douglas R.; *c:* Kevin, David; *ed:* (BS) Home Ec, Berry Coll 1977; (MS) Home Ec, Univ of GA 1979; *cr:* Teacher Gilmer HS 1979-; *ai:* FHA Club Adv; GA Voc Assn, GA Educl Assn 1979-; *office:* Gilmer HS 500 S Main St Ellijay GA 30540

PRIVITT, JAMES STEPHEN, Algebra Teacher; *b:* Heber Springs, AR; *ed:* (BSE) Math, Univ Cntrl AR 1987; *cr:* Teacher Southwest Jr HS 1987-; *ai:* Stu Cncl & Math Spon; Sch Assessment Team; Personnel Services Comm; JTPA Tutoring Supvr; LRCTA Faculty Rep 1987-; AEA, NEA, ACTM, NCTM 1987-; *office:* Southwest Jr HS 3301 S Bryant St Little Rock AR 72204

PRIZLER, MARY LOU, Second Grade Teacher; *b:* Iowa City, IA; *c:* Marsha Elder, De Anna Nicholson; *ed:* (BA) Elem Ed, 1972; (MA) Elem Ed, 1978 Univ of IA; *cr:* Elem Teacher Rural Schls 1946-49; 2nd/3rd Grade Teacher Blue Grass IA 1956-60; 1st Grade Teacher Muscatine IA 1960-61; 1st/6th Grade Teacher Lone Tree IA 1966-90; *ai:* NEA; IA St Ed Assn; Lone Tree Ed Assn Educator of Yr 1975; Lone Tree PTO; Music Boosters; *home:* 204 E Jayne St Lone Tree IA 52755

PROBERT, EDWIN NIGHTINGALE, II, English Teacher; *b:* Newark, NJ; *ed:* (BA) Ed, Edinboro St Coll 1965; (MA) Admin, Univ of PA 1990; Art His, St Cathrines Coll; Lit, Villanova Univ; *cr:* Teacher Germantown Acad 1969-; *ai:* Stu Government Adv; United Way Coord; MAIS; Eng Speaking Union Philadelphia Branch VP 1970-; Co-Founder of British Fair Philadelphia; E-SU Study Travel Scholar 1978; Kast Grant Scholar 1990; *office:* Germantown Acad P O Box 287 Fort Washington PA 19034

PROBY, ERNESTINE GRIFFIN, Third Grade Teacher; *b:* Jonestown, MS; *m:* Robert L. (dec); *c:* Justina R., Cynthia M., Shannon O.; *ed:* (BS) Elem Ed, MS Valley St Univ 1960; *cr:* 3rd Grade Teacher Humphreys Cty Lower Elem 1960-; *ai:* Cub Scout Den Mother; Girls Scout Leader; MAE; NEA; Elks Lodge; *home:* 815 Cohn St Belzoni MS 39038

PROCK, JO ASHWORTH, Math Teacher; *b:* Custer County, OK; *m:* William J.; *c:* Dannie B.; *ed:* (BS) Math Ed, West TX St Univ 1972; *cr:* 8th Grade Math Teacher Pampa Mid Sch 1972-; *ai:* Alpha Chi 1972; Delta Kappa Gamma Society 1980-84; Kappa Kappa Iota 1984-89; Pres VP & Treas Local TSTA-NEA.

PROCKO, GRACE SMILNAK, Fourth Grade Teacher; *b:* New Britain, CT; *m:* William Jr.; *c:* Kendrick Hall, John Boich, David Swan, William D.; *ed:* (BS) Elem Ed, Cntrl CT St Univ 1951; *cr:* 1st Grade Teacher Northwest-Jones Sch 1951-53; 5th Grade Teacher Hartford/Enfield Cty Home 1953-54; 2nd/5th Grade Teacher Old Saybrook/Old Lyme Elem Schls 1960-64; 2nd Grade Teacher Flanders Elem Sch 1970-74; 4th Grade Teacher Cypress Elem/Calusa Elem 1975-; *ai:* Prin Advisory Comm; Drama Coach; Pasco Cty Teacher of Yr 1976-77, 1981-82, 1986-87; *home:* 7005 Parrott Dr Port Richey FL 34668

PROCTOR, CINDY ANN (BLACKBURN), 7th & 8th Grade Teacher; *b:* Durant, OK; *m:* Mark; *c:* Derek; *ed:* (BA) Health/Phys Ed, 1976, (MS) Health/Phys Ed, 1978 S OK St Univ; *cr:* Coach Wylie Mid Sch 1976-77; Coach/Teacher 1978-87, Teacher 1987- Yuba Sch; *ai:* 7th-8th Grade Spon; Coach of Yr; OK Girls Coaching Assn 1979-87; Nida Baptist; Epsilon Sigma Alpha 1989-; *home:* 118 Kimber Ln Durant OK 74701

PROCTOR, EDNA JACKSON, 5th Grade Teacher; *b:* Nanjemoy, MD; *m:* Anthony; *c:* Anthony Jr., Courtney; *ed:* (BS) Elem Ed, Bowie St Univ 1967; (MSED) Elem Ed, Univ of S Al 1979; *cr:* 2nd Grade Teacher Patapsco Neck Elem 1967-68, J C Parks Elem 1968-69; 3rd Grade Teacher Fred Smith Elem 1970-71; 5th Grade Teacher Eastlawn Elem 1972-; *ai:* MAE, NEA 1972-; PFO 1989-; *home:* 5778 Eastwood Dr Moss Point MS 39563

PROCTOR, JOANNA W., Kindergarten Teacher; *b:* Cape Girardeau, MO; *m:* Joe E.; *c:* Daniel, David; *ed:* (BS) Elem Ed, S IL Univ 1964; Various Wkshps & Spec Courses; *cr:* Teacher One Room Rural Sch MO 1953-57; Kndgtn Teacher Raytown MO 1957-58, Amer Dependent Schls Germany 1958-59, South Side Sch 1964-65, 1969-; *ai:* Delta Kappa Gamma (VP, Mem) 1976-; 1st Baptist Church (Sunday Sch Teacher, Choir Mem) 1969-; *home:* 822 Hilldale Herrin IL 62948

PROCTOR, KATHY HOLDEN, 8th Grade Reading Teacher; *b:* Hickory, NC; *m:* William T.; *c:* Tyler; *ed:* (BA) Mid Grade Rdng/Soc Stud, 1974, (MA) Rdng, 1976 W Carolina; *cr:* Teacher Fairview Elem 1974-76, W Carolina Univ 1974-81, Alarka Elem 1976-83, Swain HS 1983-; *ai:* Communications & Flexibility Comm; 8th Grade Publications; *office:* Swain HS 8 Fontana Rd Bryson City NC 28713

PROCTOR, LINDA JEAN, Science Teacher/Coach; *b:* Pine Bluff, AR; *ed:* (BS) Phys Ed/Sci, Univ AR Pine Bluff 1975; (MED) Ed Admin, Univ New Orleans 1986; Earth Sci; *cr:* Phys Ed Specialist Nicholls St Univ 1985; Teacher Livingston Mid Sch 1986-89; Enrichment Dir Southern Univ New Orleans 1990; Teacher/Coach Capdau Jr HS 1980-; *ai:* Asst Stu Cncl Spon; SACS Comm; Dept Chairperson; Chrldr, Vlybl, Track, Jr Var Girls Bsktbl Coach; NSTA 1983-; LA Earth Sci Teachers 1989-; LA Fed Teachers 1980-; UTNO Building Rep; LESTA 1989-; Earth Sci Teacher Grant; Natl Ftbl League Players Assn Awd; Outstanding 8th Grade Teacher.

PROESTOPOULOS, ELLEN CHAMBERS, 11th Grade English Teacher; *b:* Middletown, NY; *m:* Evan; *c:* Maria, Georgia, Demetra; *ed:* (BA) Scndry Ed/Eng, St Univ of NY Oneonta 1978; (MS) Scndry Ed/Eng, St Univ of NY New Paltz 1985; *cr:* Eng Teacher Strategakis Schls Greece 1978-79, Pine Bush HS 1979-; *ai:* Charity Fund Drive; NY St Eng Cncl Teacher of Excl 1989; Natl Greek Ladies Philoptochos VP 1989-; Greek Sch Chairperson 1986-; *office:* Pine Bush HS Rt 302 Pine Bush NY 12566

PROFFITT, JAN S., Seventh Grade Teacher; *b:* Morristown, TN; *m:* Chris; *ed:* (BS) Elem Ed, Univ of TN Knoxville 1979; Curr & Instruction, E TN St Univ; *cr:* 5th/7th Grade Teacher Newport Grammar Sch; *ai:* 5th/6th Grade Bsktbl & All-Star Academic Team Coach; Jr Beta Club & NGS Players Spon; Tip & Tag Coord; Republican Women of Cocke Cty 1988-; 1st United Meth Church 1981-; *office:* Newport Grammar Sch 202 College St Newport TN 37821

PROKOP, DEBRA L. RETHMEIER, 4th Grade Teacher; *b:* Lincoln, NE; *m:* James Jr.; *c:* Scott, Michael; *ed:* (BS) Elem Ed, Univ of NE 1974; Doane Coll; Kearney St Coll; Univ of NE; *cr:* 6th Grade Teacher 1977-78; 4th Grade Teacher 1979- Crete Elem; *ai:* Mem Stu Assistance Team; Spon Big Read Club; Mem Sci Curr Comm; Delta Kappa Gamma 1983-; NEA 1974-; Crete Ed Assn 1974-; Plymouth Congregational Church UCC Sunday School Supt 1985-; *office:* Crete Elem Sch 920 Linden Ave Crete NE 68333

PROPERT, SUE ANN SCIMENES, English Teacher; *b:* Dover, NJ; *m:* Jamed Edward; *c:* Zachary; *ed:* (BA) Eng/Liberal Art, Rider Coll 1975; (MAT) Eng/Scndry Ed, Trenton St Coll 1976; *cr:* Eng Adjunct Instr Rider Coll 1975-78; Eng Adjunct Instr/Grad Asst Trenton St Coll 1975-79; Eng/Soc Stud Teacher Pennington Sch 1976-80; Eng Instr Mercer Cty Comm Coll 1980-82; Eng Teacher Upper Freehold Regional Schls 1980-82; Eng Instr Edison Comm Coll 1982-; Eng Teacher Cape Coral HS 1983-; *ai:* Dual Enrollment Instr Contemporary Lit Edison Comm Coll; FL Cncl Teachers of Eng 1987-; Poe Society 1985-; Grade Level Eng Coord; NHS Nominations Team; Lee Cty Schls Fnd Mini Grant 1989; Golden Apple Teacher Awd Nom 1987, 1989; *home:* 1235 Burtwood Dr Fort Myers FL 33901

PROPST, ANGELA, Jr HS Language Arts Teacher; *b:* Harrisonburg, VA; *ed:* (BA) Eng, Shepherd Coll 1980; (MS) Speech Comm, WV Univ 1987; *cr:* Lang Arts Teacher Petersburg HS 1980-; *ai:* HS Nwspr Adv; Varsity Chrldr Adv; GCEA; WVEA; NEA; 4-H Asst Leader; Calvary Luth Eran Church; *office:* Petersburg H S Jefferson Ave Petersburg WV 26847

PROPST, ELLEN FARLEY, Mathematics Teacher; *b:* Princeton, WV; *m:* George Artennis; *c:* Amy, Joseph; *ed:* (BA) Elem Ed, Alderson-Broaddus Coll 1975; (MA) Elem Ed, WV Univ 1981; *cr:* Classroom Aide/Houseparent WV Sch for the Deaf 1973-74; 6th Grade Sci Teacher 1975-78, Math Teacher 1978- Philippi Mid Sch; *ai:* Philippi Mid Sch Asst Girls Bsktbl Coach; WVEA 1975-; Rebekah Lodge #275, Ladys Auxiliary of the Patriarch Militant, Ladys Encampment Auxiliary 1975-; Outstanding Young Woman of America 1982; Barbour Cty Teacher of Yr 1989-; *home:* Cherry St Philippi WV 26416

PROPST, KAREN TACKETT, Business Teacher; *b:* Charleston, WV; *m:* Dwayne Alan; *c:* Corey; *ed:* (BA) Bus Ed, Marshall Univ 1986; *cr:* Bus Teacher Franklin & Circleville HS 1986-; *office:* Franklin & Circleville HS PO Box 40 Franklin WV 26807

PROPST, MARILYN LEWIS, Math Dept Chair/Instructor; *b:* Decatur, IL; *m:* Thomas D.; *c:* Brad E., Erika L.; *ed:* (BS) Math, IL St Univ; *cr:* Math Instr Eisenhower HS 1966-69; Dept Chairperson/Instr Thomas Jefferson Mid Sch 1970-; *ai:* Math Task Force Decatur Public Schls #61; Math Club Adv & Mathcounts Coach Thomas Jefferson Mid Sch; Prgm Dir Section Cncl Decatur Schls #61; DEA, NEA, IEA 1966-; Those Who Excel Teacher Rep 1986; *office:* Thomas Jefferson Mid Sch 4735 E Cantrell St Decatur IL 62521

PROROK, JOHN R., Social Studies Teacher; *b:* Chicago, IL; *m:* Beth Munson; *c:* Mandy, Kyle; *ed:* (BA) Phys Ed, Luther Coll 1973; (BA) His, 1976, (MS) His, 1979 Winona St Univ; *cr:* Amer His Teacher North Jr HS 1975-76; Amer His/Soc Stud Teacher South Jr HS & Fair Oaks Mid Sch 1976-; Math/Soc Stud Teacher Phillips Mid Sch 1990; *ai:* 8TH Grade Ftbl, 7th/8th Grade Wrestling, Girls Track Coach; Amer Red Cross (Volunteer Instr, CPR) 1983-; *home:* 2726 17th Ave N Fort Dodge IA 50501

PROUDFOOT, DANA EVANS, Language Art Teacher; *b:* Pittsburgh, PA; *m:* George L.; *c:* Tori D., Kylie B., Lindy B.; *ed:* (BA) Ed/Eng/Soc Stud, Alderson Broaddus Coll 1971; (MA) Rdng Specialist, WV Univ 1982; Project TESA; *cr:* Teacher Coalton 12 Yr Sch 1974-76, Kasson Mid Sch 1979, Belington Mid Sch 1979-; *ai:* Yrbk/Newspaper Adv; N Cntrl Acceditation Steering Comm; Cty Spelling Bee Chm; Academic Games Teacher Coord; Delta Kappa Gamma; WV Ed Assn Newsletter Ed 1988-; Kiwanis; *home:* 306 Bradshaw St Belington WV 26250

PROUDFOOT, HAROLD B., Teacher; *b:* Parkersburg, WV; *m:* Mary Selchow; *c:* Kevin, Elizabeth, Michael, Jeffrey; *office:* Rogers Park Jr HS Rogers Park Dr Danbury CT 06810

PROULX, BEVERLY SUE, English Teacher; *b:* St Cloud, MN; *m:* Ronald James; *c:* Guy, John; *ed:* (BS) Speech/Theatre, Univ of WI River Falls 1964; (MED) Eng, Univ of MN 1980; Advanced Placement Eng Lit, Art in Curr, Hamline Univ; Creative Writing, St Cloud St Univ; Composition, Amer Lit, Creative Writing, Univ of MN; *cr:* Eng Teacher Hudson HS 1963-64; Eng/Speech Teacher North Branch HS 1964-72, Rush City HS 1972-; Eng/Theatre Art Teacher Cambridge Comm Coll 1986-; *ai:* Speech Team Coach, Sr Class Adv; MN St HS League 1974-77; Speech Advisory Comm 1985-87; Fine Art Coord 1988-; Rush City Ed Assn Secy 1986-88; Speech Assn of MN Secy 1979-83; MN Cncl Teachers of Eng; NCTE; Speech Coaches Assn; Natl Fed of Speech & Debate Coaches; Amer Assn of Univ Women Pres 1969-73; Ashland Oil Company Golden Apple Awd St of MN 1989; How to Coach Wkshp 1986-; *home:* Box 451 North Branch MN 55056

PROVANCE, SUSAN ELIN, Kindergarten Teacher; *b:* Trenton, MO; *ed:* (AA) Trenton Jr Coll 1970; (BSE) Elem Ed, Northeast MO St Univ 1973; *cr:* Kndgtn Teacher S M Rissler Sch R-9 Sch Dist 1973-; *ai:* Prof Dev Comm Chm; Delta Kappa Gamma (St Comm Chm1987-89); Pres 1974-75; 1986-87 Trenton Teachers Assn; Trenton Acting Guild (Pres 1985-87 Treas 1987-); Outstanding Young Women of Amer-1981; *office:* S.M. Rissler Elem School 801 W 4th Terr Trenton MO 64683

PROVENCHER, JANE BRYANT, Second Grade Teacher; *b:* Needham, MA; *m:* James E.; *ed:* (BS) Elem Ed, 1974, (MS) Elem Ed, 1982 Plymouth St Coll; Governors Cmptr For Teachers Advanced Summer Inst 1988; *cr:* 1st/2nd Grade Teacher 1974-75, 1st Grade Teacher 1975-76, 2nd Grade Teacher 1976- Bartlett Sch; *ai:* Head Teacher; Grade Level Chairperson; Co-Chairperson Act Comm; Boys Biddy League Bsktbl Coach, Sch Evaluation Visiting, Lang Art Curr Comm; NEA, Berlin Ed Assn 1974-; New England Rdng Assn 1988-89; New England Assn of Schls & Colls Public Elem Schls Comm; United Church of Christ Deaconess 1986-87; *office:* Bartlett Sch 56 Mt Forist St Berlin NH 03570

PROVENZA, SAM JAMES, Physical Education Teacher; *b:* Pueblo, CO; *m:* Karen Elizabeth Rush; *c:* Michael P., Nicholas J.; *ed:* (BA) Phys Ed, Univ of S CO 1976; (MA) Health/Phys Ed/Recreation, Adams St Coll 1988; *cr:* Phys Ed Teacher Tope Elem 1977-; *ai:* Phys Ed Curr Standing Comm, Asst Coach Girls Bsktbl, Track & Field, Ftbl Ofcl; Amer Assn of Health, Phys Ed, Recreation & Dance 1989-; Co Assn of Health, Phys Ed, Recreation & Dance 1989-; US Olympic Society 1984-; *office:* Tope Elem Sch 2220 N 7th St Grand Junction CO 81501

PROVINSAL, JOHN STEPHEN, Cooperative Work Experience; *b:* Wendall, ID; *m:* Elke; *c:* Mark S., Erika A.; *ed:* (BA) Psych/Child Dev, E WA St 1972; (MED) Spec Ed, Univ of OR 1976; *cr:* Spec Ed Teacher Marshfield HS 1972-75, Moss Jr HS 1977-78, Dodds Japan 1978-81; Special Ed/Cooperative Work Experience Teacher Dodds Nuernberg W Ger 1981-; *ai:* Cross Cntry, Track & Soccer Coach; Stu Advisory Comm Spon; Cncl Exceptional Children 1975-; ASCD 1989-; Assn for Mentally Retarded Citizens; NEH, OEA (Faculty Rep 1981-84) 1972-; Toastmaster Intnl Pres 1972-76; Misawa Runners Pres 1978-81; Ger Amer Club Pres 1988-; Coos Bay Teachers Assn Outstanding Teacher 1975; Rotary Interaction Teacher of Handicap Awd 1976.

PROVOST, SUSAN M., Spanish Teacher; *b:* Westwood, NJ; *ed:* (BA) Span/His, Franklin & Marshall Coll 1987; *cr:* Span Teacher Immaculate Heart Acad 1987-; *ai:* Sch Play, Christmas Show Supvr; Amer Assn of Teachers of Span & Portuguese 1988-; Foreign Lang Educators of NJ 1989-; NCEA 1990; *office:* Immaculate Heart Acad 500 Van Emburgh Ave Washington Townshp NJ 07675

PROW, ANNA D., English Teacher; *b:* LAFB Hampton, VA; *ed:* (BA) Eng Ed, Longwood Coll 1988; *cr:* Eng Teacher Smithfield HS 1988-; *ai:* Drama Team Spon & Coach, Warascoyak Wisdom Newspaper Spon; NCTE 1988-; 5 Mem Comm Adapted Materials & Techniques to Promote Learning & Mastery of Eng; *office:* Smithfield HS Rt 4 Box 115 Smithfield VA 23430

PRUCE, GLORIA FORSHLAGER, Teacher; *b:* Baltimore, MD; *m:* Irving Morton; *c:* Susan P. Davis, Steven P., Sally P. Schramm; *ed:* (BS) Ed/His, Towson St Univ 1951; (MED) Psych, 1965, Certificate of Advanced Study Ed/Psych, 1969 Johns Hopkins Univ; Psych, John Hopkins Univ 1972-76; *cr:* Teacher Benjamin Franklin Elem Jr HS 1952, Milford Mill Jr Sr HS 1953-54, Robert E Lee Jr HS 1954-55, Pimlico Jr HS 1957-60, Roland Park Elem Jr HS 1960-68, Western HS 1968-; *ai:* General Class Adv; Western HS Grad & Faculty Fund Comm; Youth Peace Alliance Spon; ASCD; Baltimore City Public Schls Book Selection Comm; Johns Hopkins Univ Alumni Assn; MD Cncl for Soc Stud; NCSS; NHS for Women in Ed; Towson St Univ Alumni Assn, Western HS Alumni Assn; MD Amer Lung Assn; Amer Museum of Natural His; Greenspring Valley Synagogue; John Hopkins Club; Levindale Geriatric Center Auxiliary; Smithsonian Institution; Pikesville Volunteer Fire Dept Honorary Mem; Baltimore City Public Schls Cooperating Teacher Certificate of Achievement; Baltimore City Public Schls & Western HS Dedicated Service Certificate Awd; Morgan St Univ Sch of Ed & Urban Stud Cooperating Classroom Teacher; Towson St Univ Teacher Ed Prgm Cooperatinv Classroom Teacher; Article Published.

PRUDEN, MARY A., English Teacher; *b:* Toledo, OH; *m:* Thomas W.; *c:* Bridget, Michelle Snyder, Amy; *ed:* (BED) Eng, Univ of Toledo 1976; Working Towards Masters; *cr:* Eng/Govt Teacher Bedford Adult Ed 1976-78; Eng Teacher Monroe Cty Co mm Coll 1978-79, Evergreen HS 1980-81, Univ of Toledo Comm Tech Coll 1981-82, Bowsher HS 1983-84, Waite HS 1984-; *ai:* Class of 1988 Adv; Dress Code Comm; Phi Kappa Phi 1976-; *office:* Waite HS 301 Morrison Dr Toledo OH 43605

PRUETT, DALE ALDEN, Computer Literacy Teacher; *b:* Okemah, OK; *m:* Jill Lynn Madole; *c:* Tiffany, Chad, Cheri; *ed:* (BS) Bus Ed, East Central St Coll 1965; OK Univ; Rose St Jr Coll; Cntrl St Univ; *cr:* Classroom Teacher 1965-; Bsbl/Bsktbl Coach 1968-83 Choctaw-Nicoma Park Publ Schls; *ai:* Bus Dept Chm for Choctaw-Nicoma Park Schls; Practical Arts Dept-Chm at Choctaw Jr HS; Mem-Policy and Procedures Comm; Mem-ACT Executive Comm; Bldg Rep to Choctaw Act; NEA 1965-; OK Ed Assn 1965-; Choctaw ACT 1965-; Tip-In Club 1986-; Choctaw Jr HS-Teacher of Yr 1982-83; Soc Stud Dept Chm 1975-89; *office:* Choctaw Jr HS 14667 3rd Choctaw OK 73020

PRUETT, NANCY CURTIS, First Grade Teacher; *b:* Chattanooga, TN; *m:* Charles Jefferson Jr.; *c:* Charles J. III, Robert T., John M.; *ed:* (BA) Eng, Carson Newman Coll 1953; (MA) Elem Ed, George Peabody Coll 1958; Univ of TN, GA Southern; *cr:* 1st Grade Teacher Chattanooga City 1953-61; Headstart Teacher/Consultant Univ of TN 1968-69; 1st Grade Teacher Sidney Lanier & Ristey Elem 1970-76; 3rd Grade Teacher 1976-85, 1st Grade Teacher 1985- St Simons Elem; *ai:* NEA 1960-; Prof Assn GA Educators 1985-; 1st Baptist Church of St Simons Island Teacher 1970-; Delta Kappa Gamma Educl Schlsp; 3rd Grade Team Leader 1976-85; *home:* 103 Ingham St Saint Simons Isl GA 31522

PRUITT, JAMES DONALD, JR., Biology Teacher/Football Coach; *b:* Lake Charles, LA; *m:* Kathleen L. Holley; *c:* Matthew, Chelsea; *ed:* (BS) Health & Phys Ed, TX A & M Univ 1982; Working Towards Masters Educl Admin, E TX St Univ; *cr:* Teacher/Coach Mc Donald Mid Sch 1982-84, Mesquite HS 1984-; *ai:* Var Asst Ftbl, Head Cross Cntry, Head Boys Track Coach; TX HS Coaches Assn; 1st Baptist Church of Mesquite Youth 12 Sunday Sch Dir 1989-; *office:* Mesquite HS 300 E Davis Mesquite TX 75150

PRUITT, LEWIS WILSON, Biology Teacher; *b:* Redding, CA; *m:* Margaret Ann Collins; *c:* Katie, Kevin; *ed:* (BA) Biologiacl Sci, Chico St Coll 1968; (MED) Counseling, St Marys Coll 1990; Teaching Credential, St Marys Coll 1987; Teacher Trng Biotechnology & Recombinant DNA, San Francisco St Coll 1989; *cr:* Stu Teacher Miramonte HS 1987; Bio Teacher Alhambra HS 1987-; *ai:* Ftbl & Golf Coach; Stu Asst Team Chm; NABT 1987-; NSTA 1987-; CA Assn of Bio Teachers 1987-; CA Sci Teacher Assn 1987-; Martinez Boy & Girls Club VP 1974-; Rotary Club of Martinez 1976-82; Martinez Ed Fnd 1984-88; *office:* Alhambra HS 150 E St Martinez CA 94553

PRUITT, MIKE DAN, Math Department Chairperson; *b:* Duncan, OK; *m:* Jeanette L.; *c:* Tina Dunn, Jeff, Ashlie; *ed:* (BS) Math, OK Baptist Univ 1967; (MS) Cnslng & Guidance, East Cntrl St Univ 1978; *cr:* Classroom Teacher Eisenhower HS 1967-68 & 1970-72, Velma-Alma Ha 1973-; *ai:* Coach; Senior Class Spon; DEA Delegate 1978-82; Article Cmptr Today 1984.

PRUITT, NANCY SHELTON, Reading Department Chair; *b:* Sugar Land, TX; *c:* Melinda Manfra, Sarah J.; *ed:* (BS) Elem Ed, Stephen F Austin Univ 1973; (MS) Elem Ed, Prairie View A&M Univ 1976; Rdng Specialist Certificate; *cr:* Teacher Dulles Jr HS 1973-74; Teacher/Dept Chairperson Sugar Land Jr HS 1975-79; Teacher Campbell Jr HS 1980-81, Quail Valley Jr HS 1982-83; Teacher/Dept Chairperson Sugar Land Mid Sch 1984-; *ai:* Dept Chairperson; Chrldr & Yrbk Spon; Tutor; Stu Mentorship; TX St Rdng Assn 1989-; Presbyn Church Bible Sch Teacher 1988; Dulles

HS Secy 1969, Miss Dulles & Head Chrldr 1969; Teacher of Yr Nominee; Blue Ribbon Task Force; Instructional Cncl; *office:* Sugar Land Mid Sch PO Box 1004 Sugar Land TX 77478

PRUITT, PAMELA HAYS, 2nd Grade Teacher; *b:* Russellville, AR; *m:* Rickey Lynn; *c:* Robert; *ed:* (BA) Elem Ed, AR Tech Univ 1981; *cr:* Elem Teacher Hector Public Schls 1981-; *office:* Hector Public Sch Rt 1 Box 24 Hector AR 72843

PRUITT, PEGGY P., Enrichment Teacher; *b:* Ocean City, MD; *m:* William Homer; *c:* Michael, Patrick, Jane P. Bradford; *ed:* (BS) Elem Ed, 1971; (MS) Elem Ed, 1975 Salisbury St Univ; K-12th Grade Rdng Teacher; Admins & Supvrs Certificate; *cr:* 5th Grade Teacher 1971-73, 6th Grade S S Teacher 1973-88, Enrichment Lab Teacher 1988-90, Sch Gifted/Talented Coord 1980- Snow Hill Mid Sch; *ai:* Yrbk Adv; MD Thinking Cap Quiz Bowl Spon; Odyssey of Mind Coach; St Regional Dir; Worcester Cty Teachers Assn, MD St Teachers Assn, Natl Teachers Assn 1971-; MD Mid Schls Assn; Bd of Dirs Julia Purnell Museum; Snow Hill Economic Dev Comm; *office:* Snow Hill Mid Sch Rt 3 Box 307 Snow Hill MD 21863

PRUNTY, LEE ANN SIBLEY, Third Grade Teacher; *b:* Shreveport, LA; *m:* Roy E.; *c:* David, Kevin; *ed:* (BA) Elem Ed, 1980, (MA) Elem Ed, 1986 LA Tech Univ; *cr:* 3rd Grade Teacher Platt Elem Sch 1981-83; Gifted Ed Teacher Platt Elem, Greenacres Jr HS, Kerr Elem, Princeton Jr HS 1983-88; 3rd Grade Teacher Platt Elem 1988-; *ai:* Bossier Schls Showcase Comm Mem 1990; NEA, LA Assn of Educators, Bossier Assn of Educators; St Vincents Acad Alumnae Assn Pres 1986-88; Bossier City Jaycee Jaynes New Jayne of Yr Awd 1973, 1974; Holiday in Dixie Diplomats; Bossier Parish Outstanding Young Woman 1981; LA Young Mother of Yr Runner-Up 1983; *office:* Platt Elem Sch 4680 Hwy 80 E Haughton LA 71037

PRUSA, MARLA MC COY, Home Economics Teacher; *b:* Oxford, NE; *m:* James; *c:* Danielle; *ed:* (BS) Home Ec 1981, (MS) Home Ec 1989 Univ of NE; *cr:* Home Ec Teacher Howells Public Schls 1981-; *ai:* FHA Adv; Soph Class Spon; Amer Vocational Assn; NE Vocational Home Ec Teachers Assn; Colfax Cty Ed Assn; NE St Ed Assn; *home:* 321 S 4th St Howells NE 68641

PRY, DANIEL ELVIN, Health/Science Teacher; *b:* Breckenridge, MN; *m:* Sandra Jeanne Chambers; *c:* Amber, Shannon; *ed:* (BS) Phys Ed, 1970, (MS) Phys Ed/Health, 1973 CA Poly SLC; Driver Ed/Driver Trng; Family Life Ed; *cr:* Teacher/Coach Royal HS 1973-74; Teacher/Coach/Dept Chm Newbury Park HS 1974-83; Teacher/Coach Atascadero HS 1983-; *ai:* Head Wrestling, Asst Ftbl & Asst Tennis Coach; SADD & Class Adv; Dir of Coaching Cert; Natl HS Coaches Assn, Tri Counties Wrestling Coaches Assn, CA Coaches Assn, NEA, CTA; Atascadero HS Boosters; TCWA Coach of Yr; Atascadero HS Co-Teacher of Yr; CIF SS Wrestling Team Champions; Franklin Coaches Awd; *office:* Atascadero HS 1 High School Hill Atascadero CA 93422

PRYOR, J. E., Mathematics Tutor; *b:* Gary, IN; *c:* Matthew E., Brian T.; *cr:* Teachers Aide Beckman Jr HS 1980-81, Spaulding Elem 1982-83, Norton Elem 1984-86; Tutor Tolleston Jr HS 1986-; *office:* Tolleston Jr HS 2700 W 19th Ave Gary IN 46404

PRYOR, LAVERNE HILL, English Teacher; *b:* Memphis, TN; *m:* Gabriel; *c:* Gabriel Jr., Brandon, Sheena; *ed:* (BA) Scndry Eng, Lemoyne-Owen Coll 1976; *cr:* 11th Grade Eng Teacher Southaven HS 1978-; *ai:* Co-Spon Whitehaven Forty-Niners Cheering Squad; NEA 1978-; MS Ed Assn 1978-; Rotary Club Teacher of Month 1988; *office:* Southaven HS 899 Rasco Rd Southaven MS 38671

PRZILAS, CATHERINE CLARA (KOCH), 5th & 6th Grade Teacher; *b:* Umbarger, TX; *m:* Oscar Otto; *c:* Mark, Maureen Childress, Kevin, Keith; *ed:* (BS) Elem Ed, 1961, (MS) Elem Ed, 1963 Our Lady of the Lake; Teaching Certificate, St of KS 1959; Continuing Ed, Amarillo Coll 1984; *cr:* 3rd/4th Grade Teacher St Vincents 1958-59; 1st Grade Teacher St Anns 1959-60; K/5th/6th Grade Teacher 1974-78, 5th/6th Grade Teacher 1978- St Anthonys; *ai:* Free Tutoring of Children; NCEA 1980-; Zeta Chi 1980-; Pilot Club; *home:* PO Box 428 Dalhart TX 79022

PTASNIK, GREGORY D., Business Education Teacher; *b:* Cheboygan, MI; *m:* Martha Clark; *c:* Ryan; *ed:* (BS) Bus Admin, Cntrl MI Univ 1970; Teaching Cert Mrktg/Distributive Ed, MI St Univ 1973; Certificate Paralegal, Univ of NM Law Sch 1976-; Educl Admin, Univ of WY; *cr:* Bus Ed Teacher Pinedale HS 1976-; *ai:* Mid Sch Ftbl Coach; Stu Cncl Adv; Sch Improvement Model, Peer Coaching & Dev, Curr Dev Comm; Pinedale Ed Assn (Pres 1985-86, Treas 1989-); NEA, WY Ed Assn 1976-; Wapiti Investment Club (Pres 1987-89, Financial Partner 1989-); Fulbright Teacher Exch Prgm; *home:* PO Box 923 Pinedale WY 82941

PUCKETT, A., Science Teacher; *b:* Atlanta, GA; *ed:* (BS) Home Ec, Berry Coll 1975; *ai:* Class & Honor Society Spon; Vlybl, Bsktbl, Sftbl Teams Coach; US & Atlanta Lawn Tennis Assn; *office:* Stone Mountain Chrstn Sch 5950 Shadow Rock Dr Lithonia GA 30085

PUCKETT, ANNE DUKES, Second Grade Teacher; *b:* Columbia, SC; *m:* Lawrence Jackson; *c:* Anne L. Puckett-Bednar, David L.; *ed:* (BS) Home Ec, Winthrop Coll 1960; Grad Work Early Chldhd Ed; *cr:* Kndgtn Teacher 1969-75, 1st Grade Teacher 1975-82, 2nd Grade Teacher 1982- Churchville Elem; *ai:* Citizenship-Discipline, Gifted & Talented Comm; PTA Faculty Rep 1988-; *office:* Churchville Elem Sch 2935 Level Rd Churchville MD 21028

PUCKETT, BEVERLY KLEIN, High School English Teacher; *b:* Passaic, NJ; *m:* George Albert; *c:* Scott J. Stofregen, Lance M. Stofregen, Keith G. Stofregen, Linda L.; *ed:* (BA) Eng Ed, 1984, (ME) Public Sch Admin, 1986 SE OR St Univ; *cr:* GED Instr Idabel Cmmty Ed Satellite 1985-; HS Eng Teacher Eagletown Schls 1986-; Coll Instr S AR Univ 1990; *ai:* NCTE, OK Ed Assn 1986-; *home:* Rt 1 Box 10 Broken Bow OK 74728

PUDERBAUGH, JOYCE BALDWIN, 5th Grade Teacher; *b:* Abilene, KS; *m:* Cecil; *c:* Heather, Morgan; *ed:* (BA) Elem, Washburn Univ 1967; (MS) Elem Curr, KS St Univ 1980; *cr:* 1st & 4th Grade Teacher Rossville Grad Sch 1967-69; 4th Grade Teacher Lawrence-Pinckney Grade Sch 1969-70; 2nd Grade Teacher Wakefield Grade Sch 1975-77; Chapter I Teacher Wilroads Garden Sch Dodge City Area 1978-79; 5th Grade Teacher Protection Grade Sch 1981-; *ai:* K-6 Quiz Bowl Coach; Jr HS Pep Club and Chrldr, Math Contest Spon; Spelling Bee Coord; Dist Curr Dev Comm; Phi Delta Kappa (Secy 1979-81) 1979-; Delta Kappa Gamma Xi Chapter (VP 1988-) 1981-; KNEA, NEA, Comanche Cty Teacher ASSN 1967-; Intl Rdng Assn 1978-; *home:* Box 566 Coldwater KS 67029

PUDLAS, CHARLES FLOYD, Marketing Ed Coordinator; *b:* Greenwood, AR; *m:* Carolyn Yadou; *c:* Sabrina, Jon; *ed:* (BSE) Industrial Ed, 1964, (MED) Voc Ed, 1967 Univ of AR Fayetteville; *cr:* ICT Coord 1964-66, Mktg Ed Coord 1966-69, Dean of Stu 1969-71, Mktg Ed Coord 1971- Fayetteville HS; *ai:* DECA Spon; Co-Spon 1988; FHS Leadership Seminar Dir; Supvr/Mgr Royal Dog Bookstore; North Cntrl Evaluation Steering Comm; Fay Ed Assn Pres 1969-70; AR Assn ME Teacher; Teacher of Yr 1976; Amer Voc Assn 1964-; Sequoyea Kiwanis (Pres 1978-79, Treas 1983-), Kiwanian of Yr 1976; AR Mktg Ed Teacher of Yr 1976; *office:* Fayetteville HS 1001 Stone Fayetteville AR 72701

PUGH, JUDY MILLER, First Grade Teacher; *b:* Martinsburg, WV; *m:* Bill; *c:* Justin W.; *ed:* (BA) Elem Ed, Shepherd Coll 1972; Grad Stud WV Univ; *cr:* 1st Grade Teacher Rosemont Elem 1972-; *ai:* WVEA Mem 1972-; *office:* Rosemont Elem Sch 301 S Alabama Ave Martinsburg WV 25401

PUGH, LUCIA ANN, Spanish Teacher; *b:* Coatesville, PA; *m:* Cecil Richard; *c:* Richard, John; *ed:* (BA) Span, Villa Maria Coll 1971; Millersville St Univ, Marywood Coll; *cr:* Span Teacher Abraham Lincoln Jr HS 1971-; *ai:* Honor Society, Booster Club, 9th Grade Party Adv; Rainbow Elem Sch Secy 1989-; PTO Rep; Lancaster Outstanding Teacher 1977; *office:* Abraham Lincoln Jr HS 1001 Lehigh Ave Lancaster PA 17602

PUGH, NANCY LEE, Science Chair/Physics Teacher; *b:* New Berlin, NY; *ed:* (BS) Bio, Coll of Env Sci & Forestry 1980; Masters Prgm Cortland St; *cr:* Math/Physics/Earth Sci/Chem/Bio Teacher Brookfield 1986; *ai:* Sci Club; Odyssey of the Mind; Frosh Class Adv; Var Girls Soccer & Boys Vlybl Coach; Prom Comm & Frosh Class Adv; NY St Challenger Fellowship; *office:* Brookfield Cntrl Sch Fairground Rd Brookfield NY 13314

PUGLIESE, DOMENICK, 8th Grade Teacher; *b:* Trenton, NJ; *m:* Paula Verdi; *c:* Joseph, Gina; *ed:* (BA) Ed, OK City Univ 1968; Trenton St Coll; *cr:* 5th Grade Teacher Grant Sch 1970-72; 6th Grade Teacher Jr #5 1968-70; 6th Grade Teacher 1972-89; 8th Grade Teacher 1989 Franklin Sch; *ai:* Head Sch Safety Patrol; Head Discipline Comm; TEA Mem 1968-; *office:* Franklin Sch William And Liberty St Trenton NJ 08611

PUGLISI, SUSAN, Science Dept Chair; *b:* Bridgeport, CT; *ed:* (BA) Bio, 1973, (MS) Bio, 1975 Univ Bridgeport; (PHD) Neurobio, Clark Univ 1979; Neuroanatomy, Univ MA Medical Sch 1979-81; Univ CT; *cr:* Asst Bio Prof Baruch Coll CUNY 1981-83, Univ of Bridgeport 1983-, Sacred Heart Univ 1983-; Sci Chm Sacred Heart Acad 1983-; *ai:* NHS Adv; Advanced Placement Course Coord; Class Adv; Amer Assn for Advancement of Sci 1975-; Society for Neuro-Sci 1981-; NY Acad of Sci, NABT 1982-; Amer Society of Zoologists 1979-; Amer Microscopical Society 1980-; Amer Inst of Biological Sci 1982-; Amer Museum of Natural His 1973-; CT Sci Teachers Assn 1987-; NSTA 1986-; Italian Grad Schlsp Comm at Univ of Bridgeport Recording Secy 1987-89; Published Article J Comparative Neurology 1981, Abstracts Anatomical Record 1980-81; *office:* Sacred Heart Acad 200 Strawberry Hill Ave Stamford CT 06902

PUGLISI, TERESA MARIE, School Counselor; *b:* Rochester, NY; *ed:* (BA) Eng, Notre Dame Coll 1968; (ME) Guidance/Counseling, 1980, Ed Spec Guidance/Counseling, 1988 Univ of Toledo; *cr:* Teacher Holy Cross Parochial 1968-69, St Johns Parochial 1970-71, Spencer Sharples HS 1971-78; Cnslr Byrnedale Jr HS 1978-; *ai:* Natl Jr Honor Society Adv; NOWACD, AACD; Toledo Opera (Chorus, Mem); *office:* Byrnedale Jr HS 3645 Glendale Ave Toledo OH 43614

PULATTIE, JO ANN BOYD, Journalism/English Teacher; *b:* Abilene, TX; *m:* Francis Frank Wynn; *c:* Pattie, Mike, Danny, Jay Roye, Janice Roye; *ed:* (BS) Ed, Univ of TX Austin 1975; (MA) Mass Comm/Ed, Univ of TX Permian Basin 1983; Baylor Univ, TX Tech, Univ of CA Davis; *cr:* Rdng/Eng Teacher Mildred HS 1975-76; Journalism/Eng Teacher Richfield HS 1976-77, Uvalde HS 1977-79; 9th-12th Grade Eng Teacher Cross Plains HS 1979-8, Munday HS 1980-81; 6th-8th Grade Eng/Rdng Teacher Rule Jr HS 1981-82; Eng/Journalism Teacher Coahoma HS 1982-83; 9th-12th Grade Eng Teacher Riesel HS 1983-84; Eng/Journalism Teacher Robinson HS 1984-; *ai:* Yrbk/Newspaper Spon; Robinson Classroom Teachers (Treas 1988-89, Schlrsp Chm 1989-); TX Assn HS Photography Teachers; Interscholastic League Press Conference; Alpha Delta Kappa; Outstanding Teacher 1975-76; Published in Hooray Natl Journalism Magazine; 1st Woman Sports Ed in Northern CA; Hosted Weekly Radio Prgm; *office:* Robinson H S 500 Lyndale Waco TX 76706

PULCINI, BARBARA, 7th Grade Teacher; *b:* Easton, PA; *ed:* (BS) Elem Ed, East Stroudsburg Univ 1979; Addl Studies, Elem Ed; *cr:* 7th Grade Teacher Sacred Heart Sch 1980-; Spec Ed Teacher Wiley House 1984-87; *ai:* Sch Newspaper Asst to Faculty Adv & Bus Mgr; Steering Comm Mem Mid States Assoc Self-Study; Facilitator Rainbows for All Gods Children Support Group; Sci Curr Coord; Oratoricals Coach; Teacher Rep PTA Bd; Catechetical Convention Planning Comm Mem; NCEA 1980-; St Catherine of Sienna Womens Alliance Mem 1989-; *office:* Sacred Heart Sch 1814 2nd St Bethlehem PA 18017

PULCINI, DIANE MARY, Fourth Grade Teacher; *b:* Sewickley, PA; *ed:* (BS) Ed, Clarion Univ 1980; Grad Stud; *cr:* 4th Grade Teacher St Titus Sch 1980-; *ai:* Intermediate Dept Coord; Talent Show Comm; NCEA; *office:* St Titus Sch 107 Sycamore St Aliquippa PA 15001

PULCINI, ELINOR DE LANCEY, Science Teacher; *b:* Dayton, OH; *m:* Ronald P.; *c:* Rafaella, Marcelina; *ed:* (BS) Bio/Chem, Chapman Coll 1974; Grad Stud Liminology, Univ of MT; *cr:* Sci Teacher Mc Nally Continuation HS 1974-75; Eng as a Second Lang Teacher Cambria Eng Inst Rancho Santiago-Cmmty Coll 1980-84; Sci Consultant 1976-80; Asst Fisheries Biologist MT Dept of Fish & Game 1985-87; Sci Teacher Bifork HS 1985-; *ai:* Career Prgm Coord; Sci Club Spon; NSTA, MT Sci Teachers Assn; *office:* Big Fork HS Commerce St Bigfork MT 59911

PULLAM, ROY N., Social Studies Teacher; *b:* Providence, KY; *m:* Velma; *ed:* (BA) His/Govt, 1968, (MA) His/Ed, 1972, (Rank I) His/Ed, 1973 Murray St Univ; Natl Sci Fnd Fellow Univ of IN 1977; *cr:* Teacher Dixon Jr HS 1968-69, Henderson HS 1969-71; Project Dir Henderson Union Webster Dev Cncl 1971-72; Teacher Henderson City HS 1972-77, North Jr HS 1976-; *ai:* Head Bonnet Film; Jr Optimist Club Dir; NCSS 1984-, Teacher Excl 1985; Phi Delta Kappa 1972-; NEA, KY Ed Assn, Henderson Cty Ed Assn Public Relations Chm 1968-; Optimist Intnl (Club Pres 1982-83, Dist VP 1990), Excl in Ed Awd 1989, Pride Awd 1984, Distinguished Pres; Immanuel Temple Deacon 1975-; Jaycees Star Teacher 1975; Teacher of Yr 1987; Heritage Cup 1985; Excl in Ed; *office:* North Jr HS 1707 2nd St Henderson KY 42420

PULLEN, CARL W., German Teacher; *b:* Storm Lake, IA; *m:* Norma Mc Bride; *c:* Kirsten, Heidi; *ed:* (BA) His/Ger, Simpson Coll 1965; (MA) Ger, Middlebury Coll 1971; Ger Stud Albright Coll 1965; *cr:* Ger Teacher Indianola HS 1965-; *ai:* Theater Mgr; Play Dir; Play Writer; Music Composer; Cmptr Programmer; AATG, NEA; Articles on Salt.

PULLEN, CAROL VAYDA, French Teacher; *b:* Trenton, NJ; *m:* Ronny G.; *c:* Melissa; *ed:* (BA) Fr/Sociology, Georgian Court Coll 1982; *cr:* Fr Teacher St Rose HS 1982-; *ai:* Soph Class Co-Moderator; NHS Moderator; AATF 1982-; *office:* St Rose HS 607 7th Ave Belmar NJ 07719

PULLEN, ELIZABETH BUSH, Spanish/Communications Teacher; *b:* Grand Rapids, MI; *m:* Richard Lee; *c:* Erica, Andrea; *ed:* (BS) Eng, Cntrl MI Univ 1968; (MA) Scndry Ed, MI St Univ 1972; *cr:* Span Teacher S Kent Cmmty Ed 1969-75, Eng/Span Teacher Coopersville Cmmty Ed 1974-75, Jenison Cmmty Ed 1978-79; Span Comm Teacher Godwin Hts Public Schls 1968-; *ai:* Sch Improvement Comm; NEA, MI Educl Assn, Godwin Hts Educl Assn; Beverly Womens Guild Secy 1985-86; Jenison Athletic Boosters Treas 1989-; WY Jaycees Outstanding Young Educator; *home:* 0-31 Brookside Dr Grandville MI 49418

PULLEY, PAULA JEAN, Math Teacher; *b:* Effingham, IL; *m:* Marty J.; *c:* Eric, Amy; *ed:* (BA) Elem Ed/Math, Eastern IL Univ 1981; (MS) Math, Southern IL Univ 1988; *cr:* Math Teacher Mt Vernon Township HS 1982-; *ai:* Careteam Drug Prevention, Teen Assistance Prgm Mem; CLOWN; Drug & Alcohol Awareness in Elem Grade; ICTM; *office:* Mt Vernon Township HS 320 S 7th St Mount Vernon IL 62864

PULLIAM, DOLORES ANNA SWIGGETT, Third Grade Teacher; *b:* Chester, PA; *m:* Sidnor R.; *c:* Taren, Karen D. Puckham; *ed:* (BS) Elem Ed, DE St Coll 1958; (MS) Elem Ed, Cheyney Univ 1983; Grad Courses St Josephs Univ, Univ of DE; Christina Dist Inservice Courses; *cr:* Elem Teacher Phyllis Wheatly Elem Sch 1958-62, George Gray Elem Sch 1962-78, Mc Vey Elem Sch 1978-; *ai:* Nom Christina Sch Dist Teacher of Yr 1978-79; *home:* 833 Broadfield Dr Newark DE 19713

PULLIAM, LINDA D., English Teacher; *b:* Mobile, AL; *m:* Allen W.; *c:* Amber, Ashley; *ed:* (BS) Eng, Univ of Southern MS 1970; *cr:* Eng Teacher Leakesville Jr HS 1970-; *ai:* Beta Club Spon; Chrldr Spon; Ladies Variety Club Mem; Leakesville First United Meth Church Mem; Chi Omega; USM Assn; Local Young Woman of Yr Prgm; *home:* Box 956 Leakesville MS 39451

PULLIAM, REBECCA SIMMS, Mathematics Teacher; *b:* American Falls, ID; *m:* Kenneth; *c:* Spencer, Joshua; *ed:* Assoc General Ed, Ricks Coll 1981; (BS) Eng/Math, ID St Univ 1985; *cr:* Eng Teacher Amer Falls Sch Dist 381 1985-87; Math Teacher Aberdeen Sch Dist 58 1987-89; *ai:* Jr Class & Academic Decathlon Adv; ID Ed Assn, NEA 1985-87; Jr Miss Co-Chairperson 1987-88; Elks Teacher of Month 1989.

PULLIAM, SHELIA DUKE, First Grade Teacher; *b:* Cullman, AL; *m:* Gwen Dolen; *c:* Melda Garrison Thornton, Derrick Garrison; *ed:* (BA) Elem Ed, Univ of AL Huntsville 1983; *cr:* 1st Grade Teacher Cold Springs Elem 1983-; *ai:* Talent Search Comm;

Spon & Dir Annual Christmas Prgm; Cullman Cty Ed Assn, AL Ed Assn, NEA 1983-; *home:* Rt 4 Box 158 Jasper AL 35501

PUNTER, ROBERT ALAN, Math Teacher; *b:* Valparaiso, IN; *m:* Barbara Miller; *c:* Erin K., Jeffrey, Laura A.; *ed:* (BS) Math, IN St 1969; (MALS) Ed, Valparaiso 1974; *cr:* Teacher Valparaiso IN 1969-; *ai:* Head Bsktbl Coach; ISTA, NEA, VTA 1969-; Teacher of Yr 1985-86; *home:* 108 Calhoun Ct Valparaiso IN 46383

PURCELL, JOHN CHRISTOPHER, Reading Specialist; *b:* Seattle, WA; *m:* Barbara Anne; *c:* Sheila, Mary, Liam, John, Beth; *ed:* (BA) Psych/Philosophy, Seattle Univ 1978; (MA) Elem Ed, Univ of AK 1981; Instr Leadership Acad; *cr:* Teacher/Cnslr Seattle Youth Services-Outward Bound 1977-78; Teacher/Dir St Josephs 1978-80; Teacher 1982-89; Rdng Specialist 1989- Nordale Elem; Teacher/Instr Univ of AK 1989-; *ai:* Intermural Act Dir; Dist Wide Assessment Team; NCTE 1982-84; NCTM 1985-83; *office:* Nardale Elem Sch 20 Eureka Fairbanks AK 99701

PURCELL, MICHAEL JAMES, Science Teacher/Coach; *b:* Casper, WY; *ed:* Associates Ed, Northwest Comm Coll 1984; (BS) Ed/Psych, Univ of WY 1987; Admin Degree, SD St Univ; SD AIDS Prgm; *cr:* Sci Teacher Vanderberg Mid Sch; Coach Douglas Sch System 1987-; Sci Teacher Natl Coll 1990; *ai:* Vandenberg Stu of Month Comm; 8th Grade Ftbl & Bsktbl Coach; 9th-12th Grade Track Coach; 5th/6th Grade Intramural Ftbl & Bsktbl; Douglas Ed Assn Rep 1987-; NSTA 1986-; SD Assn of Mid Level Educators 1988-; *office:* Vandenbrg Mid Sch 1 Patriot Dr Rapid City SD 57706

PURCELL, MILDRED M., Second Grade Teacher; *b:* Garrard County, KY; *m:* Joseph G.; *c:* Sherry J., Christy Purcell Denny; *ed:* (BA) Elem Ed, 1961, (Rank II) Elem Ed, 1989 E KY Univ; *cr:* 1st/2nd Grade Teacher Wrens View Elem Sch 1957-61; 1st Grade Teacher Junction City Elem Sch 1963-64; 1st Grade Teacher 1964-76, 2nd Grade Teacher 1976- Camp Dick Robinson Elem; *ai:* Mem Various Comm; NTA Mem 1957-; KY Teachers Assn 1957-; Garrard Cty Teachers Assn 1957-; Delta Kappa Gamma Intnl Society Treas; St William Altar Society Co-Pres 1989-; Outstanding Teacher of America; *home:* 720 Crab Orchard Rd Lancaster KY 40444

PURCELL, RON A., Biology Department Head; *b:* Chehalis, WA; *ed:* (BA) Sci Ed, OR St Univ 1984; Marine Bio, Oceanography, Cooperative Learning, Aviation Electronics Sch; *cr:* Machine Operator Freightliner 1972-79; Dept Service Reynolds Aluminum 1979-81; Field Technician OR St Univ 1982-84; Teacher Creswell HS 1984-; *ai:* Ftbl Coach; Environmental Club Organizer; Safety Comm; Class Adv; OR Ed Assn 1984-; *office:* Creswell HS 33390 Nieblock Ln Eugene OR 97405

PURCELL, RONALD ROY, Science Teacher/Dept Chair; *b:* Terre Haute, IN; *m:* Barbara Ann Bonham; *c:* Angela Ponto, Cindy Yates; *ed:* (BS) Phys Sci, 1958, (MS) Scndry Sci Ed, 1967 IN St Univ; *cr:* Teacher Cloverdale Sch Corporation 1958-72, Benton Cmmty Schls 1972-; *ai:* HS Drama Dir 1976-86; Sci Club Spon 1958-72; IN Classroom Teachers Assn Pres 1958-72; NEA 1972-; Lions Club Pres 1971, Jaycees Outstanding Young Educator 1972; Natl Sci Fnd Grants 1966, 1967; *office:* Benton Cntrl Jr/Sr HS R R 1 Oxford IN 47971

PURCELL, VIRGINIA M. ROBERSON, Music Teacher; *b:* Festus, MO; *c:* Paul J. Jr., Christopher A.; *ed:* (BSED) Music Ed, 1962, (MSED) Music Ed, 1971 NE MO St Univ; *cr:* Music Teacher Northwest Schls 1962-63, Fox C-6 Sch 1965, Jefferson R-VII Sch 1965-; *ai:* 8th Grade Class & Stu Cncl Spon; Elem Chorus; Jr HS Band; MO St Teachers Assn, Music Educators Natl Conference; *office:* Jefferson R-VII Sch Rt 4 Festus MO 63028

PURCELLA, LES ALLEN, Agriculture Education Teacher; *b:* Durango, CO; *m:* Linda L Prude; *c:* Carrie A., Micah; *ed:* Post Grad Courses; *cr:* Ag Teacher Hobbs Sch Dist 1975-76, Hagerman Schls 1976-79, Roswell Ind Sch Dist 1979-; *ai:* FFA & Jr Class Spon; NM Ag Ed Teachers Assn Pres 1979-80, Outstanding Young Teacher 1977-78; Natl Ag Teachers Assn Outstanding Teacher 1982-83; Jaycees 1977-79; 4-H Volunteer Leader 1976-, Honarary Mem 1988; NM DisT VI Area Planning Bd Governor Appointee 1979-80; Cmptr Instruction Systems & Meats Cutting Curr Dev Grants; *office:* Robert H Goddard HS 701 E Country Club Rd Roswell NM 88201

PURCIELLO, TERRI MICH, 2nd Grade Teacher; *b:* Bridgeport, CT; *m:* Robert Vincent; *c:* Angela, Alena; *ed:* (BS) Elem Ed, S CT St Univ 1977; *cr:* 6th Grade Teacher Holy Rosary Sch 1978-79; 2nd Grade Teacher St Lawrence Sch 1979-; *office:* St Lawrence Sch 505 Shelton Ave Huntington CT 06484

PURDY, DOUGLAS E., 6th Grade Math/Science Teacher; *b:* Oak Ridge, TN; *m:* Patricia K. Hamilton; *c:* Heather Lean; *ed:* (BS) Health & Phys Ed/Elem Ed, TN Wesleyan Coll 1974; (MA) Curr Instruction, Univ TN Knoxville 1980; Admin/Supervision, Univ TN Chattanooga 1981; Tims St Trng; *cr:* Health/Phys Ed Teacher Mc Minn Cntrl HS 1975; Math/Sci Teacher Riceville Elem Sch 1975-; *ai:* Coached Elem Bsktbl & Sftbl; Sch Yrbk Adv; Post Sch Enrichment Prgm Spon & Coord; *home:* Rt 2 Box 434 Englewood TN 37329

PURNELL, MICHAEL, Math/Sci/Soc Stud Teacher; *b:* Andalusia, AL; *m:* Kathryn Ann Murphy; *c:* Michelle; *ed:* (BA) Speech, La Grange Coll 1972; (MED) Ed Admin, Auburn Univ 1981; Univ of GA, George Peabody Coll for Teachers, Vanderbilt Univ, Univ of Montevallo; *cr:* 4th Grade Classroom Teacher Luthersville Elem 1971-73; Ford Fnd Southeastern US 1973-74; Speech Therapist Butler Cty 1974-78, Covington 1978-81; 5th/6th Grade Classroom Teacher Red Level Sch 1981-; *ai:* Boys 6th Grade 4-H Club Spon; AL Ed Assn 1974-; AL Assn Retarded Citizens 1979-81; Red Level Town Cncl Mem 1978-79; Covington Cty Bd of Ed Mem 1988; Fellow Ford Fnd Leadership Dev 1973; *home:* PO Box 53 312 Deens St Red Level AL 36474

PURSLEY, STEVEN NEALE, Third Grade Teacher; *b:* Milan, MI; *m:* Barbara; *ed:* (BA) Eng/Soc Stud, Grand Valley Univ 1969; (MA) Elem Admin, E MI Univ 1972; *cr:* Teacher Kent City Schls 1970-71, Hall of Devine Child 1971-73, Monore Public Schls 1973-; *ai:* Phi Delta Kappa 1973-; CYO Pres 1974-78; *office:* Custer Elem Sch 5003 W Albain Monroe MI 48161

PURTLE, JAMES CARROLL, Principal; *b:* Malvern, AR; *m:* Linda Gayle Brown; *ed:* (BSE) Soc Stud, Henderson St Univ 1975; (MSE) Scndry Admin, Univ of Cntrl AR 1988; Admin Cert for Superintendency; *cr:* Soc Stud Teacher Sheridan HS 1976-80; Soc Stud Teacher 1980-86, Asst Prin 1986-89, Prin 1989- Spring Hill HS; *ai:* AAEA, ASCD 1989-; AR Admin Ed Admin; Lions Club (Secy 1989-, Dist Chm for Drug Awareness SW AR 1989-); Justice of Peace Nevada Cty; SW AR Solid Waste Comission Bd of Dir; *home:* Rt 2 Box 18A Prescott AR 71801

PURVES, NORMAN DUANE, Lang Arts/Soc Stud Teacher; *b:* Chicago, IL; *ed:* (BSED) Soc Stud, 1960, (MSED) Guidance & Counseling 1965, Northern IL Univ; Grad Trng Univ of IL, Natl Coll of Ed, Western IL Univ, Univ of HI; *cr:* Teacher Schaumburg Sch Dist, Arlington Hts Public Schls; *ai:* Past Adv Stu Cncl; Strategic Action Curr Planning Comm; Jr HS Spec Act Mini Grants Comm Spon; NEA; IL Ed Assn; Arlington Teachers Assn; IL Cncl For Soc Stud; *office:* Thomas Jr H S 303 E Thomas St Arlington Heights IL 60004

PURVIS, EDGAR LEE, 8th Grade Soc Stud Teacher; *b:* Madden, MS; *m:* Dorothy Lewis; *c:* Tara Lee, Matthew Lewis; *ed:* (BS) Ed, 1972, (MS) Guidance/Ed, 1976, (MS) His, 1980, MS Coll; Amer Stud Prgm, MS Coll; *cr:* Teacher/Cnslr Lake HS 1972-81; Teacher Bettye Mae Jack Mid Sch 1981-; *ai:* Mem Ftbl Booster Club; Chrldr Co Spon Mid Sch; Bus Driver HS Band; Star Teacher Lake HS 1980; Sch Yrbk Dedication 1988; *home:* Star Rt Box 203A Morton MS 39117

PURVIS, MARCIA BEARD, 2nd Grade Teacher; *b:* Jackson, MS; *m:* Lewis Lavon; *c:* Mark, Alicia; *ed:* (AA) E Cntrl Comm Coll 1970; (BSED) Elem Ed, 1972, (MAED) Elem Ed, 1974 MS Coll; Working on Specialist Degree in Elem Ed & Cert in Admin; *cr:* 1st Grade Teacher 1972-84, 2nd Grade Teacher 1984- Morton Elem Sch; *ai:* Delta Kappa Gamma; MS Prof Educators (Bd Mem 1984) 1978-; MS Assn for Women in Educl Leadership 1989-; PTO; Polkville 1st Baptist Church Organist 1972-; Friends of Lib; MS Educl Admin Leadership Inst for Women; *office:* Morton Elem Sch Drawer L Morton MS 39117

PURYEAR, HILDA JONES, Fifth Grade Teacher; *b:* Mecklenburg Cty, VA; *m:* James E.; *c:* Chandler, Misty; *ed:* (BS) Home Ec/Bio, 1967, (MS) Supervision/Admin, 1983 Longwood Coll; *cr:* 6th Grade Teacher 1967-71, 1979-80, 5th Grade Teacher 1980- Chase City Elem; *ai:* NEA, VA Ed Assn, Mecklenburg Ed Assn 1967-71, 1989-; Southside Cncl Rdng Educators 1986-87, 1989-; Mt Horeb Baptist Church; Chase City Elem Sch Outstanding Teacher of Yr 1990; *home:* Rt 3 Box 870 Chase City VA 23924

PUSATORY, KATHERINE ANN, English/Drama Teacher; *b:* Pueblo, CO; *c:* Riley; *ed:* (BA) Theatre/Speech, Univ of S CO 1969; (MA) Theatre/Eng, Western St Coll 1971; (PHD) Lit, Univ of AL 1976; Graduate Work Western St Coll, Univ of CO Denver; *cr:* Theatre Speech Instr Clatsop Comm Coll 1971-73, Univ of AZ 1973-76; Theatre Dir Pearl Street Theatre 1976-83; Teacher East HS 1985-; *ai:* Stage Mgr, Theatre Dir East HS; Forensics Team; Grant Sangre de Cristo Arts Center; Writing Awds; One Cabaret Show Produced New York City, Producing Another; *home:* 1046 Carteret Pueblo CO 81004

PUSCHNIG, ANNE EBERHARDY, Third Grade Teacher; *b:* Milwaukee, WI; *m:* Gene; *c:* Joseph Eberhardy, John Eberhardy, Shawn; *ed:* (BSED) Elem Ed, Alverno 1971; Math; Gifted & Talented; Speculative Thinking; *cr:* 3rd/5th/6th Grade Teacher St Marys Hales Corners 1967-; *office:* St Marys Parish Sch 9553 W Edgerton Ave Hales Corners WI 53130

PUSKAS, DEBORAH DENISE, Choir Teacher; *b:* San Bernardino, CA; *m:* Terry L.; *ed:* (BME) Music Ed/Vocal, Univ of Redlands 1979; (MA) Music Ed/Vocal, ID St Univ 1984; San Bernardino Valley Coll; CA St Univ San Bernardino; *cr:* Choir Teacher Eagle Rock Jr HS 1983-83, North & South Bonneville Jr HS 1986-; *ai:* Mens & Show Choir; Sch Musical; Sch Improvement Comm; Clinician/Festival Schlsp Judge; Private Vocal Instr; MENC All-State Convention Performer 1982, 1990; Idaho Falls Jr Musical Club Vocal Chm 1987-.

PUTNAM, CAROLE ANN, Learning Disability Teacher; *b:* Dayton, OH; *c:* Greg, Michele; *ed:* (BA) Elem Ed, 1969, (MS) Learning Disability Rdng Instr, 1978 Univ of Dayton; Substance Abuse, Chemical Intervention Specialist; *cr:* Rdng Teacher Center City Sch 1978-81; Learning Disability Teacher 1982-, Learning Disability Coord 1988- Patterson Career Center; *ai:* Intnl Rdng Assn Mem 1979-; Cncl for Exceptional Children Mem 1985-; Kettering Rdng Assn Pres 1982; Kettering Assn of Children With Learning Disabilities Pres 1981; Grant Delta Theta Tau for 2nd Masters Degree Sch Counseling; *office:* Patterson Career Center 118 E 1st St Dayton OH 45402

PUTNAM, JOSEPH HECTOR, Cnslr/Chm Soc Stud Dept; *b:* Ogdensburg, NY; *m:* Nancy Louise Hunter; *c:* Christopher, Jeremy, Brett, Amy; *ed:* (BS) Poly Sci, Walsh Coll 1969; His Kent St Univ; *cr:* 7th Grade Soc Stud Teacher 1969-73, Track Coach 1969-71, Head Ftbl Coach 1969-76, 8th Grade His Teacher 1973-87, Cnslr 1988- Robert A Taft Mid Sch; *ai:* Peer Listening Adv; Plain Local Teachers Assn Rep 1982-84; ECOEA; OEA, NEA 1969-; *home:* 4024 E Lynn Ave N W Massillon OH 44646

PUTNAM, KEITH LEE, Science Teacher; *b:* Pigua, OH; *m:* Jean Ann Pulfer; *c:* Jodi, Jay; *ed:* (BS) Health/Phys Ed, OH St Univ 1971; (MS) Recreation, W FL Univ 1977; (MS) Educl Admin, Univ of Dayton 1982; *cr:* Navy Flight Officer US Navy 1971-77; Sci Teacher Anna Local Schls 1978-; *ai:* Jr Class Adv; Sci Fair Coord; US Navy Reserve Commander 1971-; Sch Bd Mem 1981-; Governors Awd for Educl Excl 1989; Outstanding Teacher 1989; 5 Yr St Schlsp Test Winner; *home:* 20800 Suber Rd Conover OH 45317

PYLANT, JUDY P., 1st Grade Teacher; *b:* Winnfield, LA; *m:* Roderick M.; *ed:* (BA) Elem Ed, 1975, (MA) Elem Ed, LA Tech Univ 1983; *cr:* 2nd Grade Teacher Glenbrook Acad 1975-76; 1st Grade Teacher Hico Elem Sch 1976-; *ai:* Beta Beta Conclave Kappa Kappa Iota Sec 1989-; Hico Elem Teacher of Yr 1987-88; *home:* 5035 Daniel Dr Ruston LA 71270

PYLE, ANITA LORAINE, Mathematics/Physics Teacher; *b:* Springfield, IL; *m:* J. Charles; *c:* Amy C., Jody C.; *ed:* (BS) Math, Ottawa Univ 1967; (MSED) Cnslr Ed, W IL Univ 1982; *cr:* Math/Sci Teacher Landon Jr HS 1967-68; Math Teacher Collingdale Jr/Sr HS 1968-71; Math/Physics/Pascal Teacher Bushnell-Prairie City HS 1980-; *ai:* Stu Cncl & JETS Adv; Drug-Free Grant Prgms Coord; NEA 1980-; Bushnell-Prairie City Teacher of Yr 1982; Finalist Governors Master Teacher Prgm 1984; W IL Univ Distinguished Teaching Awd 1989.

PYLE, CELIA CONWELL, Biology Teacher; *b:* Azle, TX; *m:* David Ross; *c:* Craig, Vince; *ed:* (BA) Health/Phys Ed, Ouachita Baptist Univ 1962; (MS) Natural Sci, Stephen F Austin St Univ 1985; *cr:* Health/Phys Ed Teacher Bowie Ind Sch Dist 1962-64, Klein Ind Sch Dist 1964-65, Midlothian Ind Sch Dist 1966-67; Bio/Health/Phys Ed Teacher Alvarado Ind Sch Dist 1967-71; Bio/Health Teacher Hubbard Ind Sch Dist 1971-72; Life Sci Teacher Klein Ind Sch Dist 1972-73; Bio/Health/Phys Ed Teacher Magnolia Ind Sch Dist 1973-80; Bio/Chem/Physics Teacher Tenaha Ind Sch Dist 1980-82; Life/Earth Sci Teacher Carlisle Ind Sch Dist 1982-84; Bio Teacher Henderson Ind Sch Dist 1984-; *ai:* JETS Spon.

PYLE, LARRY WAYNE, Science Teacher; *b:* Crawfordsville, IN; *m:* Joyce Snoeberger; *c:* Marci Huckstep, Marc, Ryan Pyle; *ed:* (BS) Bio, 1964, (MS) Bio, 1967 IN St Univ; *cr:* Teacher Warren Cmmty Schls 1964-66, Crawfordsville Cmmty Sch Corp 1966-; *ai:* Youth to Youth Key Club Spon; Crawfordsville Ed Assn, Hoosier Assn of Sci Teachers; *home:* 5810 S 400 W Crawfordsville IN 47933

PYLE, PAUL WILLIAM, Bible Dept Chair; *b:* Denton, TX; *m:* Nanette Louise Smart; *c:* Sarah, Nathan; *ed:* (BS) Eng, Evangel Coll 1977; Working Toward Masters, Dallas Theological Seminary; *cr:* Eng Teacher 1977-85, Bible/HS Teacher 1985- Dayton Chrstn HS; *ai:* Sr Class Adv; Pep Band & Small Group Ministries Dir; Soccer Game PA Announcer; Articles Published 1981, 1984; Contributed to Teacher Guide of Bible Curr Published 1989; *office:* Dayton Chrstn HS 325 Homewood Ave Dayton OH 45405

PYLES, MARIA MC ALISTER, 10th Grade Government Teacher; *b:* Florence, SC; *m:* Putesy Lafayette; *c:* Byron Mc Alister; *ed:* (BA) Soc Stud, Benedict Coll 1963; (MA) Black Stud, Southern Univ 1971; Southern His, LA St Univ 1972; Univ of MD, Kearney St Coll, Norfolk St Coll, Univ of Southwestern LA, Emory Univ, Clemson Univ; *cr:* Teacher Brewer HS 1963-68, Greenwood HS 1968-70, 1972-75, Clinton HS 1975-76, Greenwood HS 1976-; *ai:* Adv Natl Beta Club; Spon Youth in Government Club; Prin Advisory Comm; NCSS, Natl SC & Greenwood Ed Assn; Sigma Gamma Rho; Natl Assn for the Advancement of Colored People; Natl Cncl of Negro Women; Phi Delta Kappa Kappa; Fulbright Fellowship to Travel & Study in Egypt & Israel; SC Teacher of Yr; Natl Finalist Women of Achievement of Yr Awd; Recognition by The Aga Khan Ed Fnd; *home:* 105 Stage Coach Rd Laurens SC 29360

PYZIK, GLENNA MAGEE, Cooperative Education Coord; *b:* Joliet, IL; *m:* Robert H.; *ed:* (AS) Accounting, Joliet Jr Coll 1970; (BS) Bus Ed, 1972; (MS) Bus Ed, 1973 Eastern IL Univ; Certificate of Study Microcomputer Ed, Governors St Univ 1989; Dacum Facilitator; *cr:* Bus Ed Teacher J Sterling Morton East HS 1973-; *ai:* Bus Profs of America Club Adv, Bd Mem, Facilities Dir; Inservice Comm Bus Ed Rep; Educl Cncl Rep Secy for Cncl; Prgm Adv Bus Ed Regional Delivery System; Delta Pi Epsilon; Alpha Omicron Pi (Public Relations 1972-72, Pres 1972-73); Grad Asst Eastern IL Univ 1972-73; Bus Profs of America IL Merit Scholar; *office:* J Sterling Morton East HS 2423 S Austin Blvd Cicero IL 60650

Q

QUACKENBUSH, BARBARA BARLOW, 5th Grade Teacher; *b:* Jamestown, NY; *m:* Charles; *c:* Melissa, Julie; *ed:* (AA) Liberal Arts, Jamestown Comm Coll 1966; (BA) Ed, 1970, (MS) Ed, 1972 St Univ of NY Fredonia; *cr:* 4th Grade Teacher Persell Elem 1970; 6th Grade Teacher Rogers Elem 1970-88; 5th Grade Teacher Jefferson Mid Sch 1988-; *ai:* Jamestown Public Schls Mid Grades Comm; Jefferson Advisory Cncl; Gifted & Talented Comm; Jamestown Teachers Assn (VP 1986-88, Membership 1984-85, Soc Chairperson 1989-, Prof Negotiations 1984, 1986); Delta Kappa Gamma; St Lukes Episcopal Church Curr Comm 1989-; *home:* 220 Chautauqua Jamestown NY 14701

QUACKENBUSH, CAROL ANN, Math Department Chairperson; *b:* Kansas City, MO; *m:* Douglas; *c:* Beth Ann, Neal, Stuart; *ed:* (BS) Math/Home Ec, Emporia St Univ 1966; (MS) Cmptr in Ed, Lesley Coll 1987; *cr:* Math Teacher Raytown South Jr HS 1966-70, Blue Springs Schls 1978-, Longview Comm Coll 1988-; *ai:* Math Club Spon; Math Team Coach; Kansas City Teachers of Math (Pres) Mem 1980-; NCTM/MCTM; BSA Mothers Cncl 1982-; Campfire Girls Leader 1976-82; Blue Springs Jr HS Teacher of Yr; Jr HS Contest Coord for KCATM 1986-88; Executive Cncl MO Cncl of Teachers of Math 1988-; *office:* Blue Sprgs Butler Dwyer Jr H S 1200 Taylor Rd Blue Springs MO 64014

QUALEY, BARBARA WYCHE, 1st Grade Teacher; *b:* New Iberia, LA; *m:* Paul J.; *c:* Mary Malone, Jon King; *ed:* (BA) Lower Elem Ed, U of Southwestern LA 1958; *cr:* 1st Grade Teacher Eliz Forgy 1958-61, Barcelona 1961-63; 2nd Grade Teacher Enngland AFB 1963-65, Agnew Day Sch1973-77; 1st Grade Teacher St Marks Day Sch 1977-; *ai:* After Sch Rdng Prgm St Marks after Sch Enrichment Prgm; Northwestern Rdng Cncl; LA Rdng Assn 1987-; DAR 1957-; USL Alumni Assn 1958-; *home:* 4916 Longstreet Pl Bossier City LA 71112

QUARLES, RODNEY DEANE, Soc Stud Dept Chair/Teacher; *b:* Camden, AR; *m:* Debra Ann Marshall; *ed:* (BSE) Soc Stud, S AR Univ 1981; Gifted & Talented Ed, Univ of AR Little Rock; *cr:* Soc Stud Teacher Hampton HS 1983-87; Teacher of Gifted & Talented/Coord Hampton Public Schls 1985-87; Amer His Teacher Fairview HS 1987-; *ai:* NHS & Teenage Republican Spon; Quiz Bowl & Knowledge Master Open Teams Coach; AR Ed Assn, NEA 1988-; Republican Cty Comm Chm 1988-; Cty Election Commission 1990; *office:* Fairview HS 2708 Mt Holly Rd Camden AR 71701

QUATTROCCHI, CIRO ANTHONY, Italian & Spanish Teacher; *b:* Brooklyn, NY; *m:* Angela Taormina; *c:* Maria A.; *ed:* (BA) Italian/Span Lang, 1981, (MA) Italian Lang/Culture, 1987 NY Univ; *cr:* Foreign Lang Teacher Bishop Ford Cntrl Cath HS 1981-; *ai:* Foreign Lang Club Moderator; Amer Cncl Teaching of Foreign Lang, Amer Assn of Teachers of Italian Lang, Italian Acad Fnd, NY St Assn of Foreign Lang Teachers 1981-; St Fortunata Society Public Events Coord 1981-; *office:* Bishop Ford Cntrl Cath HS 500 19th St Brooklyn NY 11215

QUEEN, DIANE SUTTON, Fifth Grade Teacher; *b:* Pitt County, NC; *m:* Clyde B.; *c:* Laura Carol, John William; *ed:* (BS) Elem Ed, 1971, (MA) Elem Ed, 1979 East Carolina Univ; *cr:* 5th Grade Teacher F R Danyus Elem Sch 1971-77/1979-, Oak Road Elem Sch 1977-79; *ai:* Sci Dept Chm; Comm Mem of Math/Sci Eisenhower Title II for New Bern/Craven Co Schls; Cmptr Club Spon; Team Leader; New Bern Assn of Ed Pres 1977-80; NC Basketmakers Assn.

QUEEN, H. EUGENE, Math Teacher; *b:* Baton Rouge, LA; *m:* Opalee Lockhart Queen; *c:* Jennifer K., Susan G.Gass, Mark Graves; *ed:* (BA) Music Ed, Carson-Newman Coll 1974; (MS) Ed, Union Coll 1978; Math Cert; Grad Courses; *cr:* Eng/Chorus Teacher Cosby HS 1974-75; General Music Teacher 1975-80; Math 1980- Jefferson Mid Sch; *ai:* Track Field Events-Asst Coach; Beta Club Spon; TMTA;JCEA (Pub Rel Chm 1986; Assn Rep 1987-88; Research Chm 1977 & 1988); Jefferson Cty Teacher of Yr 1988; Exemplary Teacher of Yr Jefferson Cty 1989; *home:* Rt 2 Box 373 New Market TN 37820

QUEENER, MARY JULIAN, Fifth Grade Teacher; *b:* Knoxville, TN; *m:* George Clinton; *c:* Russell, Sara Twombly; *ed:* (BS) Home Ec/Ed, Univ of TN 1954; Grad Courses E IL Univ & S IL Univ; *cr:* 4th Grade Teacher Smithwood Sch 1955-56; 5th Grade Teacher Anderson Sch 1957-63, Jefferson Sch 1964-66; 1st-3rd/5th Grade Teacher Merriam Sch 1966-; *ai:* Head Teacher Merriam Sch; Curr & Evaluation Comm; Chrldr Co-Spon; Lyceum & Cmmty Resource Comm Chm; IL Ed Assn, NEA 1980-; Merriam Ed Assn (Pres, Secy, Treas) 1980-; Epsilon Sigma Alpha Intnl IL Wkshp Coord 1973-, Outstanding IL Woman 1979, IL Outstanding Educl Dir 1979, 1988, Top Ten Educl Awd 1979; *home:* RR 3 Fairfield IL 62837

QUEER, LINDA CARUSO, First Grade Teacher; *b:* Pittsburgh, PA; *m:* Michael Dennis; *c:* Jyllian, Michael; *ed:* (BA) Elem Ed, CA St 1971; Masters Equivilancy Elem Ed; *cr:* Kndgtn Teacher Blairesville Elem 1971-72; Spec Rdng Teacher Mt Pleasant Sch Dist 1972-73; Kndgtn Teacher Second Ward Sch 1973-79; 1st Grade Teacher Ramsey Elem 1979-; *ai:* PSEA Building Rep; *office:* Ramsay Elem Schl Eagle St Mount Pleasant PA 15666

QUESENBERRY, CONNIE JACKSON, Teacher; *b:* Pulaski, VA; *m:* Linda Woodward; *c:* Heather, Bryan; *ed:* (AA) His, Ferrum Coll 1967; (BA) His, 1969, (MA) Scndry Admin Ed, 1974 VA Tech; *cr:* Teacher Ft Chiswell HS 1970-; *ai:* Soc Stud Acad Coach for Competition; Wythe Cty Ed Assn Pres 1973-74; VA Ed Assn, NEA 1970-; Ruritan Club Pres 1972-74; Endowment for Hum Participant Inst Hollins Coll; *office:* Ft Chiswell HS Rt 3 Box 255 Max Meadows VA 24360

QUICK, KEVIN FOSTER, Biology Teacher; *b:* Utica, NY; *ed:* (BS) Phys Ed, AZ St Univ 1987; *cr:* Bio Teacher Mesa HS 1987-; *ai:* Certified Athletic Trainer ATC; NEA, AEA, MEA 1989-; NATA 1987-; *office:* Mesa HS 1630 E Southern Ave Mesa AZ 85204

QUICK, WAYNE S., 3rd Grade Teacher; *b:* Valley City, ND; *ed:* (BA) Elem/Early Chldhd Ed, 1977, (MS) Spec Ed/Pre-sch Handicapped, 1986 Univ of ND; Project Charlie Wkshp Trng Edina MN; *cr:* 3rd Grade Teacher Emerado Sch 1979-85, 1986-; *ai:* Project Charlie Sch Coord, Rdng Math Curr Comm Emerado Sch; Emerado Ed Assn (Negotiator 198-81, Pres 1984), Teacher of Yr 1986-87; Sharon Luth Church (Church Sch Teacher 1983-87, Choir Mem 1983-86); *home:* 1426 10th Ave N Grand Forks ND 58201

QUICK-GUNTHER, KATHLEEN ANN, 5th Grade Teacher; *b:* Detroit, MI; *m:* Kenneth; *ed:* (BS) Ed, Northern MI Univ 1978; (MS) Curr/Instruction, Seattle Pacific Univ 1987; Cooperative Learning, Learning Styles & Instructional Theory; *cr:* Spec Ed Teacher Riverview Sch 1979-81; 5th Grade Teacher Shining Mountain Elem 1981-85; 3rd Grade Teacher Rocky Ridge Elem 1985-89; 5th/6th Grade Teacher Centennial Elem 1989-; *ai:* Coll Lecturer & Staff Dev Trainer Cooperative Learning; Instructional Theory & Learning Styles; Delta Kappa Gamma, Phi Delta Kappa, WSASCD 1988-; *office:* Centennial Elem Sch 24323 E 54th Ave Graham WA 98338

QUIGLEY, DOROTHY LORRAINE ROBB, Jr HS Social Studies Teacher; *b:* Unionville, MO; *m:* Edwin R.; *c:* Judy Klinginsmith, Jerry; *ed:* (BS) Elem Ed, 1960, (MA) Elem Ed, 1976 Northeast St Univ; Grad Stud Soc Sci; *cr:* 1st-8th Grade Teacher Hand Houston 1953-55, Dodson 1956-56, Burns 1956-60, Douglas 1960-62; 7th/8th Grade Soc Stud Teacher Putnam Cty R-1 1962-; *ai:* 7th Grade Spon; MO St Teachers Assn, Cmmty Teachers Assn Mem 1962-; Rebekah Lodge Warden; *office:* Putnam Cty R-1 HS 801 S 20th Unionville MO 63565

QUIGLEY, SUSAN DIANNE, Chapter I Jr HS Tutor; *b:* Kalispell, MT; *m:* Emmett M.; *c:* Melissa, Paul; *ed:* (BA) Elem Ed, E Mt Coll Billings 1974; Grad Stud; *cr:* 2nd-3rd Grade Teacher Elder Grove Sch 1974-76; 1st-2nd Grade Teacher Cayuse Prairie Sch 1976-79; Substitute Teacher Various Sch Dist Kalispell Area 1981-87; 2nd Grade Job-sharing Teacher 1987-88, Chapter I Tutor 1988- Evergreen Sch Dist; *ai:* PTA Treas 1989-; Church Cantor 1986-; *home:* 211 Sullivan Crossroads Columbia Falls MT 59912

QUIGLEY, WILLIAM RICHARD, Physical Education Teacher; *b:* St Louis, MO; *m:* Jo Ann Coyle; *c:* Tim, Mike; *ed:* (BS) Phys Ed, Cntrl MO St Univ 1961; (MS) Scndry Admin, S IL Univ 1966; Grad Stud; *cr:* Teacher Mc Clauer Jr HS 1961-62; Intermural Dir 1962-65, Head Ftbl Coach 1966-75, 1978-81, Athletic Dir 1966-81, Teacher 1962- Ferguson Jr HS; *ai:* Intramural Flag Fleetball Spon; Help Spon Sch Bike-A-Thon; Jr HS Pres 1972-73; Athletic Dir of St Louis Cty; USS Swim Club of Bridgeton Pres 1979-80; *office:* Ferguson Mid Sch 701 January Ave Ferguson MO 63135

QUILLEN, CHARLES CASE, Mathematics Teacher/Coach; *b:* Kingsport, TN; *ed:* (BA) Ec/Bus, Emory & Henry Coll 1972; (MA) Ed, Union Coll 1975; *cr:* 7th Grade Teacher 1972-82, 5th Grade Teacher 1982-87 Shoemaker Elem; 8th Grade Math Teacher Shoemaker Jr HS 1987-88; Geometry/Algebra Teacher Gate City HS 1988-; *ai:* Coach Frosh Boys Bsktbl, Jr Var Boys Bsktbl, Head Girls Bsktbl 1989-, Asst Boys Bsktbl 1976-, Asst Girls Bsktbl 1980-88; NCTM, SW VA Cncl Teachers of Math, Mathematical Assn of America, Amer Mathematical Society, Natl HS Athletic Coaches Assn, VA HS Athletic Coaches Assn; *home:* PO Box 456 Gate City VA 24251

QUILLIN, LOIS GILMER, Principal; *b:* Nickelsville, VA; *m:* Charles T.; *c:* Susan R., Charles T., Sara J.; *ed:* (BS) Math/Chem, Radford Coll 1964; (MA) Admin, VA Polytechnic Inst & St Univ 1975; *cr:* Teacher Shoemaker Jr HS, Gate City Mid Sch; Prin Ft Blackmore Elem; *ai:* VPI Assessment Center Participant; Interim Evaluation Comm for Elem Sch; Math Counts Competition Team & 8th Grade Class Spon; NCTM, NAESP, SW VA Teachers of Math, NEA, VA Ed Assn, Scott Cty Teachers Assn, VA Assn of Elem Sch Prins; Jaycettes Secy 1966; Thelma Nickels Circle (Treas 1986-88, Secy 1986-87, Pres 1988-89); Natl Sci Fnd Grant in Math & Sci Curr 1973; St Teachers Schlsp 1960, 1964; *home:* PO Box 338 Gate City VA 24251

QUINBY, LUCY SANTINO, Spanish Teacher; *b:* San Diego, CA; *m:* Lewis Ward; *ed:* (BA) Ed, Humboldt St Univ 1964; (MA) Ed/Span, Humboldt St Univ & Univ of Madrid & San Francisco St Univ 1982; Various Classes & Wkshps; *cr:* Span Teacher Zane Jr HS 1965-68; 6th Grade Teacher Mark Twain Elem 1970-71, Alice Birney Elem 1971-72; Eng Teacher Zane Jr HS 1972-83; Eng/Span Eureka HS 1983-; *ai:* Foreign Lang Dept Chairperson; CA Schlsp Fed Adv; Self Study WASC Co-Chairperson 1989-; Staff Dev Co-Leader 1990; Phi Delta Kappa (Pres, VP, Secy) 1975-; Delta Kappa Gamma Secy 1973-; CA Foreign Lang Teachers Assn 1987-; CA Teacher Assn 1965-; Humboldt Cty Lib, Humboldt Cty Resource Center Advisory Comm; Pi Gamma Mu 1982-; Natl Rdng Assn; CA St Dept of Ed 1978-86 Appointed Curr Dev & Supply Materials Commission; Eng, Bi-ling, Foreign Lang, Fine Art Comm Chairperson; Eng/Lang Art Framework Chairperson St of CA; Excl in Teaching Awd Humboldt Cty Schls 1987, 1989; *office:* Eureka HS 1915 J St Eureka CA 95501

QUINN, AGNES GRIMES, Guidance Counselor; *b:* Denmark, TN; *c:* Kenneth, Karla, Terre Quinn-Martin; *ed:* (BA) Eng, Lane Coll 1957; (MS) Ed, WA Univ 1963; (MS) Guidance, Univ of MO St Louis 1973; *cr:* Teacher/Bsktbl Coach Denmark HS 1957-60; Teacher/Bsktbl Coach/Cnslr Soldan HS 1960-81; Cnslr Southwest HS 1981-83, Soldan Sr Classical Acad 1983-; *ai:* Scndry Schls Schlsp, Teacher & Employee Advisory Comm; NHS; St Louis Assn 1975-; St Louis Teachers Union 1984-; Antioch Baptist Church (Trustee Bd 1975, Sunday Sch Supt 1985).

QUINN, ELLEN ELLIS, Second Grade Teacher; *b:* Greenville, MS; *c:* Sonya L., Tonya L. Quinn Moore; *ed:* (BS) Elem Ed, 1971, (MS) Elem Ed, 1979 MS Valley St Univ; *cr:* Teacher Leland Elem 1971-; *ai:* 2nd Chairperson for Instructional Management; MS Assn of Educators 1974-; Good Apple Awd; *home:* 499 Redbud St Greenville MS 38701

QUINN, JAMES C., Elementary Teacher; *b:* Steubenville, OH; *c:* Robert, Jaclyn, Traci; *ed:* (BA) Soc Sci, West Liberty St Coll 1970; (MA) Guidance/Counseling, Western NM Univ 1972; Educl Diagnostician; Admin License; Cmptr Ed; *cr:* Cnslr 1973-75, Educl Diagnostician 1975-79 Grants Cibola Cty Schls; Teacher ME Taylor Elem 1981-, Mesa View Elem 1990; *ai:* Rdng Curr Guide Comm; Title II Math/Sci/Cmptr Trng; Lang Arts Festival; Video Microscope Trng; NM Math Cncl 1988-; NM Soc Sci 1988-; Cncl For Exceptional Children 1977-85; Cibola Cty Bsbl Assn VP 1976-77; Jump Rope for Heart Co-Chm 1983-87; *office:* Mesa View Elem 401 E Washington Grants NM 87020

QUINN, JUDY CAVALIER, First Grade Teacher; *b:* Bristol, CT; *m:* Bernard; *c:* Laurie, Nancy, Blair; *ed:* (BS) Nursing, St Joseph Coll 1953; (MA) Early Chldhd, S CT St Univ 1968; Cooperating Teacher, Mentor; Math Their Way Instr; *cr:* 1st Grade Teacher Deep River Elem 1967-68; 2nd Grade Teacher Center Sch 1968-76; 1st Grade Teacher John Lyman Sch 1976-89; *ai:* NEA, CEA, Region 13 Assn; Emblem Club; AARP; *office:* John Lyman Sch 106 Way Rd Middlefield CT 06455

QUINN, RHONDA CONDER, 8 Grade Math/Drama/Spl Teacher; *b:* Lexington, TN; *c:* Carisa; *ed:* (BS) Elem Ed, UT-Martin 1984; (MS) Admin & Supervision, Trevecca 1988; *cr:* 7th Grade Eng & Rdng Teacher 1984-86, 8th Grade Math/Drama & Spelling Teacher 1986- Parsons Jr HS; *ai:* Drama Club Adv; Stock Market Club; Decatur Cty Ed Assn Pres 1988-; Decatur Cty Homemakers 1974- Woman of Yr 1978; Order of Eastern Star Pianist 1973-.

QUINN, SUSAN BRANDT, 3rd Grade Teacher; *b:* Savannah, GA; *c:* Christopher, Michael, Francis; *ed:* (BS) Primary Ed, Campbell Univ 1972; (BS) Intermediate Ed, Methodist Coll 1975; *cr:* Kndgtn Teacher Bladen Cty 1972-74; 4th-6th Grade Teacher Columbus Cty 1976-79; 3rd-6th Grade Teacher Pender Cty 1979-; *ai:* Southern Assn Accreditation Steering Comm Chm 1985; Senate Bill 2 Chm 1990; *office:* Long Creek Grady Elem Sch Rt 1 Box 360 Rocky Point NC 28457

QUINN, SUSAN JOAN, Theology Dept Chairperson; *b:* Chicago, IL; *m:* Edward J.; *c:* David; *ed:* (BA) Ed, Univ of Dayton 1963; (MA) Religious Ed, La Salle Univ 1985; Inst Underpriveledged Youth; Youth Ministry; *cr:* Teacher Cath Schls 1956-69, Haddonfield Public Schls 1969-79; Dept Chairperson Camden Cath HS 1984-; *ai:* Future Teachers & Respect Life Clubs; Underpriveledged Youth Grant; Multi-Media Publication; *office:* Camden Cath HS Rt 38 & Cuthbert Rd Cherry Hill NJ 08002

QUINNEY, CAROL A., 7th/8th Grade English Teacher; *b:* St Davids, Bermuda; *m:* Glenn G.; *c:* Andrew; *ed:* (BA) Eng Literature-Magna Cum Ld, Emmanuel Coll 1974; (MED) Psycholinguistics, Boston Univ 1976; Boston Univ/Univ of Lowell/ Salem St Coll; *cr:* Spec Ed Teacher 1975-77; Eng Teacher 1977- Haverhill Public Schls; Eng Instr Fitchburg St Coll 1982-88; Reviewer/Analyst Silver Burdett & Ginn Publishers 1987-; *ai:* Yrbk Adv; NCTE 1987-; NEA 1975-; MA Teachers Assn 1975-; Haverhill Ed Assn 1975; *office:* John G Whittier Sch 265 Concord St Haverhill MA 01830

QUINTANA, LEO GENARO, Pre-Calculus Teacher; *b:* Santa Cruz, NM; *m:* Loyola Martinez; *c:* Sandra S., Leonard, James Mercedes; *ed:* (BS) Chem, 1958, (MS) Combined Math Sci, 1965 NMHU; Grad Stud Various Colls; *cr:* Math Teacher/Dept Chm Espanola Valley HS; *ai:* Knights of Columbus Chancelor.

QUINTANA-MIER, THERESE, 5th Grade Teacher; *b:* Green Bay, WI; *m:* John; *ed:* (BA) Ed, Dominican Coll 1961; Grad Courses & Wkshps in Counseling, Math, Lang Art, Cmptr, Geography, Lit, Fr, Theology; *cr:* Teacher Sisters of St Dominic 1954-67, Santa Fe Public Schls 1967-; *ai:* Camera Club; Sch Improvement Promoter for Matsushita Fnd; Chorus; Stu Cnslr; Math Comm 1981-82, 1987-88; NEA; Church Choir Dir; Boys Club of America 1967-69; St Elizabeths Shelter Volunteer 1988-; Delta Kappa Gamma 1973-79; Elks Club Assoc 1986-; Univ of TX Grant; *home:* Rt 6 Box 32B Santa Fe NM 87501

QUINTERO, BARBARA MARIA, Computer Teacher; *b:* Miami, FL; *ed:* (BS) Cmptr Sci, FL Intnl Univ 1988; Grad Stud FL Intnl & Nova Univ; *cr:* Substitute Teacher 1987-88, Cmptr Teacher 1988 Miami Sr HS; *ai:* Asst Act Dir; Cmptr Club Adv; Schlsp, Steering & Awds Comm; Jr Var Chldr Adv; Volunteer

Asst Girls Bsktbl Coach; Teaching Magnet Prgm Advisory Comm; Miami Sr Alumni Assn Secy 1988-; FL Assn Cmptr in Ed 1988-; Phi Kappa Phi, Miami HS Parent Teacher Stu Organization 1988-; Sallie Mae Beginning Teacher Awd Nom Teacher of Month 1990; Beta Club Honorary Membership; *office:* Miami Sr HS 2450 S W 1st St Miami FL 33135

QUINTERO, SOCORRO GOMEZ, Counselor; *b:* Jalisco, Mexico; *m:* Alfonso; *c:* Beatriz, Nadia; *ed:* (BA) Span, 1973, (MA) Ed Counseling, 1979 CA St Univ San Bernardino; Admin Credential Prgm, Asuza Pacific; Drug Prevention Facilitaros Trng; *cr:* 1st-6th Grade Bi-ling Teacher Coachella Valley Unified Sch Dist 1973-77, San Bernardino City Schls 1977-79; Resource Teacher 1979-84, Elem Cnslr 1984-86, Mid Sch Cnslr 1986- San Bernardino City Schls; *ai:* Spon Convalescent Hospital Trips; Spon High Risk Stu Camping Trips; San Bernardino Teachers Assn 1977-; Church Act Dir 1989-; *office:* Curtis Mid Sch 1472 E 6th St San Bernardino CA 92410

R

RAASCH, MICHAEL DEAN, English Teacher/Dept Chair; *b:* Fremont, NE; *m:* Lynda Sharlene Wilkinson; *c:* Christopher, Nicholas; *ed:* (BA) Eng, Midland Luth Coll 1980; Working Towards Masters Degree; *cr:* Eng Teacher Fremont Sr HS 1986-88, Fremont Learning Center 1989-; *ai:* Fellowship of Chrstn Athletes; Var Wrestling Asst Coach; Crisis Response Team Mem; *office:* Fremont Learning Center 957 N Pierce Fremont NE 68025

RABALAIS, ROBERT PAUL, Music Department Chair; *b:* Morgan City, LA; *m:* ALecia Duplantis; *c:* Aimee; *ed:* (BME) Instrumental Music, Nicholls St Univ 1980; Working on Masters Univ of SW LA; *cr:* 5th-8th Grade Band Dir Patterson Jr HS 1980-; *ai:* St Joseph Church Choir; Bayou Brass Performance Group Mem; LA Music Educators Assn 1980-; Prof Educators of LA 1984-; Natl Band Assn 1986-; St Mary Parish Teacher of Yr 1986; Conductor Dist 7 All-Youth Honor Band, Dist 8 Jr HS Honor Band, St Mary Parish Jr HS Honor Band; Adjudicator Small & Large Ensemble Festivals LA; *office:* Patterson Jr HS 1101 1st St Patterson LA 70392

RABATA, JOHN J., 5th Grade Teacher; *b:* Hillsboro, WI; *m:* Joyce Nevin; *c:* Randall, Diana, John; *ed:* (BS) Elem Ed, 1965, (MS) Elem Ed, 1967 UW-Whitewater; *cr:* 4th Grade Teacher 1965-66, 6th Grade Teacher 1966-68 East View Sch; 5th Grade Teacher Washington Sch 1968-; *ai:* Grade Level Leader; Boys Bsktbl Coach; Beaver Dam Assn Mem 1968-; Toastmasters VP 1971-72; Amer Legion Mem 1960-; *home:* N7622 N Crystal Lake Rd Beaver Dam WI 53916

RABATIN, MILDRED BRUCE, Seventh Grade Teacher; *b:* Philadelphia, PA; *m:* Edward F.; *c:* Regina M. Foresta, Teresa A.; *ed:* (BS) Elem Ed, St Josephs Univ 1975; *cr:* 5th Grade Teacher 1969-77, 7th Grade Teacher 1977-80 St Eugene Sch; 7th Grade Teacher St Louis Sch 1980-; *ai:* Soc Stud, Sci, Safety Patrol Coord; NCEA 1980-; Alpha Sigma Lambda St Josephs Univ; Deans List; *office:* St Louis Sch 801 W Cobbs Creek Pkwy Yeadon PA 19050

RABB, ANN COLEMAN, Science Department Chair; *b:* Crossnore, NC; *m:* J. Michael; *ed:* (AA) Lees Mc Rae Coll 1967; (BS) Bio, Appalachian St Univ 1969; (MA) Bio, 1985, (MA) Curr Specialist, W Carolina Univ; Mentor & Academically Gifted Cert; *cr:* Sci Dept Chairperson Mc Dowell Cty Schls 1969-; Anatomy Instr W Piedmont Comm Coll & Mc Dowell Tech Comm Coll 1989-; *ai:* Schlsp Comm; NC Assn of Educators, NC Sci Teachers Assn, Phi Delta Kappa, ASCD; Amer Red Cross; Mc Dowell Hospital Auxiliary; Mc Dowell Chamber of Commerce Ed Task Force; *home:* 305 S Garden St Marion NC 28752

RABBERMAN, ANNA MARIA LEHNER, Social Studies Teacher; *b:* Gyor, Hungary; *m:* Robert C. Sr.; *c:* Jeffrey, Brian, Kerri; *ed:* (BA) Soc Stud, 1974, (MED) Stu Personnel Services, 1978 Trenton St Coll; *cr:* Teacher Cncl Rock HS 1974-; Guidance Cncl Rock HS 1984-85; *ai:* Girls Cross Cntry Asst Coach.

RABE, RICHARD WAYNE, Agriculture Science Teacher; *b:* Beeville, TX; *m:* Peggy Jean; *c:* Wayne, Shyla; *ed:* (BA) Ag Ed, 1974, (MS) Ag Ed, 1978 TX A&I; *cr:* Teacher Pettus Ind Sch Dist 1974-; *ai:* Class Spon; FFA Adv; TX Voc Teachers Assn 1974-; N Bee Cty Fire Dist Dir 1989-; TX Sheriffs Assn Assoc Mem 1990; *office:* Pettus HS Box D Pettus TX 78146

RABOURN, NANCY ANN, Computer Teacher/Counselor; *b:* Everett, WA; *ed:* (BA) His, WWU 1963; Grad Stud Ed, Counseling & Cmptrs; *cr:* Teacher/Cnslr Hoquiam Mid Sch 1963-; *ai:* HTA, WEA, NEA; Delta Kappa Gamma; Eagles; *office:* Hoquiam Mid Sch 203 W Eklund Hoquiam WA 98550

RACHEFF, KATHRYN FOLEY, Third Grade Teacher; *b:* Decatur, GA; *m:* Tony; *c:* Stephen, Patrick; *ed:* (BS) Early Chldhd, Univ of GA 1978; *cr:* 3rd Grade Teacher 1978-81, 2nd Grade Teacher 1981-82, 4th/5th Grade Teacher 1982-83, 3rd Grade Teacher 1983- Livingston Elem; *office:* Livingston Elem Sch 3657 Hwy 81 S Covington GA 30209

RACHLISBERGER, RUSSELL NEIL, Band Teacher; *b:* Worthington, MN; *m:* Janice Marie Fiedler; *c:* Michael; *ed:* (BA) Music Ed, Univ of WI River Falls 1979; *cr:* Musician 392nd Army Band 1972-75, 451st Army Reserve Band 1975-; Band Dir Le Roy-Ostrander HS 1979-; *ai:* Le Roy-Ostrander Ed Assn Pres 1985-87; Army Commendtion Medal; Army Achievement Medals; *office:* Le Roy-Ostrander HS Hwy 56 Le Roy MN 55951

RACKOW, RUSSEL J., Fifth Grade Teacher; *b:* Cleveland, OH; *ed:* (BS) Elem Ed, Bowling Green Univ 1964; (MA) Elem Ed, CA St Univ Los Angeles 1966; *cr:* Teacher Alcott Sch 1964-70, Mt Diablo Elem 1970-; *ai:* Mt Diablo Ed Assn Pres 1986-; CA Teachers Assn WHO Awd; *office:* Mt Diablo Elem 5880 Mt Zion Dr Clayton CA 94517

RADA, EILEEN GLICKLEY, Religion Teacher; *b:* Chicago, IL; *m:* James H.; *c:* Chad, Douglas, Stephen, Megan, Margaret; *ed:* (BA) Religious Stud, 1986, (MA) Religious Stud, 1988 Mundelein Coll; Peoria Diocese Coord Cert 1986; *cr:* Pre-Sch Catechist St Vincent DePaul Church 1972-75; Catechist RCIC 1982-83, Catechist 1983-85, Confirmation Coord 1985-86 Holy Family Church; Religion Teacher Bergan HS Notre Dame 1986-; *ai:* Preparation Stu Eucharistic Ministers; RCIA Presenter Holy Family Church; NCEA 1986-; WTVP Public Broadcasting 3rd VP Friends Bd of Channel 47 1981-84; *office:* Peoria Notre Dame HS 5105 N Sheridan Peoria IL 61614

RADA, ROSE ANN, Art Teacher; *b:* Wyandotte, MI; *ed:* (BA) Art Ed, 1979, (MA) Art Ed, 1986 E MI Univ; *cr:* Art Teacher Camp Tanuga 1980-, Garden City Cmmty Ed 1980-87, Ladywood HS 1987-; *ai:* Jr Class Level Moderator; Ladywood HS Theatre Dir; Perform Volunteer Work at Sr Citizen Center; Ladywood HS Thespian Spon; Painted Murals at Sr Citizen Center Dearborn Heights MI 1987; *home:* 7370 Central Apt 11 Westland MI 48185

RADCLIFF, EVELYN DEBORAH LAWRENCE, 7th Grade History/Fr Teacher; *b:* Hertford, NC; *m:* Chyma Jr.; *c:* Rochelle C., Valerie M.; *ed:* (BA) His, Andrews Univ 1959; Grad Courses Ed, Chicago St Univ; Poly Sci, De Paul Univ; *cr:* 3rd Grade/HS Fr Teacher Shiloh Acad 1959-62; His/Fr Teacher Chicago Public Schls 1963-65, Montgomery Cty Schls 1975-77; 7th Grade His/Fr Teacher Hinsdale Jr Acad 1983-; *ai:* Curr Comm; ASCD.

RADCLIFFE, MERRI ANN BAKER, English Teacher/Dept Chair; *b:* Muskegon, MI; *m:* John; *ed:* (BS) Ed, 1975, (MA) Ed, 1980, (MA) His, 1983 Cntrl MI Univ; *cr:* Teacher Corunna Public Schls 1975-; *ai:* Gifted & Talented Ed Comm; Curr Cncl; Cheerleading Coach; Owosso Cmmty Theatre Bd of Dirs 1983-; Gifted & Talented Curr Publication; *office:* Corunna Public Schls 400 N Comstock Corunna MI 48817

RADDIN, PHILLIP THOMAS, Director of Choirs; *b:* Monticello, AR; *ed:* (BMusED) Music Ed, Mc Neese St Univ 1981; (MS) Music, Sam Houston St Univ 1984; Post Grad Work Univ of AZ Tucson 1986; *cr:* Choral Music Dir Alfred M Barbe HS 1981-82; Grad Asst 1983-84, Asst Choral Dir 1987-88 Sam Houston St Univ; Choral Music Dir Huntsville HS 1984-89; Choir Dir Klein HS 1989-; *ai:* TX Music Educators Assn; Region IX Vocal Chm; All Region Choir Organizer; AAT Clinic Coord; TX Choral Dirs Assn; Amer Choral Dirs Assn; Pi Kappa Lambda; Outstanding Young Men of America; *office:* Klein HS 16715 Stuebner-Airline Klein TX 77379

RADEBAUGH, CHARLENE SALLEE, Second Grade Teacher; *b:* Oklahoma City, OK; *m:* Mendell David; *c:* Julie Ferguson, Jeffrey, Jennifer; *ed:* (BA) Spec Ed, Northeastern St Univ 1968; (BA) Elem Ed, Bvllle Wesleyan Coll 1978 79; *cr:* Speech Therapist Salina Public Schls 1968; 2nd Grade Teacher Schulter Public Schls 1969-70; Spec Ed Teacher West Jr HS 1970-73; Spec Ed Teacher 1974-78, 2nd Grade Teacher 1978- Copan Public Schls; *ai:* Local OEA Pres; PTO Advisory Bd; Copan Ed Assn Pres 1989-; NEA 1974-; *home:* Box 318 Copan OK 74022

RADEMACHER, CAROL BOGARD, Business/Journalism Teacher; *b:* Cadillac, MI; *m:* Lonnie J.; *c:* Kyle, Cory; *ed:* (BA) Cmmty Sch Ed, Ferris St Univ 1977; (MS) Classroom Learning/Guidance, MI St Univ 1984; Various Wkshps Math, Bus, Journalism; *cr:* Cmmty Sch Dir McBain & Lake City Schls 1977-78; Teacher/Coach Pewamo-Westphalia Schls 1978-; *ai:* Math & Sci Comms; MI Bus Ed Assn 1988-; Bsktbl Coaches of MI 1981-, Coach of Yr 1984; MI Interscholastic Press Assn 1988-; *office:* Pewamo-Westphalia HS Rt 1 Clintonia Rd Pewamo MI 48873

RADEMACHER, MARY JANE, Fourth Grade Teacher; *b:* Kalamazoo, MI; *ed:* (BA) His, W MI Univ 1971; Grad Stud Elem Ed; *cr:* 4th Grade Teacher 1971-74, 3rd Grade Teacher 1974-77, 4th Grade Teacher 1977-84, 4th/5th Grade Teacher 1984-85, 4th Grade Teacher 1985- Hopkins Elem Sch; *ai:* Gifted & Talented Coord; Sch Improvement Comm; Hopkins Ed Assn VP 1979-80, Teacher of Yr 1983; MI Grant Japanese Stud; *office:* Hopkins Public Schls 400 Clark St Hopkins MI 49328

RADER, JOHN EDWARD, Mathematics/Computer Teacher; *b:* Findlay, OH; *m:* Rachel Marie Oman; *c:* John M.; *ed:* (BA) Math, OH Northern Univ 1980; (MS) Cmptrs in Ed, Univ of Dayton 1986; Guidance Cnslr Certificate Bowling Green St Univ 1989; *cr:* Math/Cmptr Teacher Van Buren HS 1980-; *ai:* Ftbl, Wrestling, Track; Cmptr Team; *office:* Van Buren Local Schls Main St Van Buren OH 45889

RADER, RACHEL OMAN, Mathematics/Computer Teacher; *b:* Findlay, OH; *m:* John Edward; *c:* John M.; *ed:* (BS) Scndry Math/Elem Ed, Bowling Green St Univ 1982; *cr:* Math Teacher Mohawk Local Schls 1984-85; Math/Cmptr Teacher Arlington Local Sch 1986-; *ai:* Var Vlybl & Track Coach; Jr HS Bsktbl Coach; Cmptr Programming Team Adv; *office:* Arlington Local Sch 336 S Main St Arlington OH 45814

RADFORD, DOROTHY L., Math Teacher; *b:* Cumberland, KY; *m:* Norman; *c:* Jimmie, Steve; *ed:* (AA) Elem Ed, Lindsey Wilson 1947; (BS) Elem Ed, 1960, (MA) Elem Ed, 1968, (Rank I) Rdng Specialist, 1974 Western KY Univ; *cr:* Classroom Teacher Cumberland Cty Sch System; *ai:* Governors Cup; Math Coord St Judes Hospital Mathathon; Various Comms; CCEA (Treas, Pres); KEA, NEA; United Meth Women (Pres, Secy); Homemakers Club Pres; CCMS Teacher of Yr 1988; *home:* Box 608 Burkesville KY 42717

RADFORD, GALE S., Biology Teacher; *b:* Burkesville, KY; *m:* David Michael; *c:* Dan S., Emily C.; *ed:* (BA) Bio, 1968, (MA) Ed/Bio, 1971, (Rank I) Guidance/Counseling, 1983 W KY Univ; Various Continuing Ed Trng; *cr:* Teacher Glasgow HS 1967-68, Hart Memorial HS 1969, Summersville Elem 1969-72, Green Cty Mid Sch 1972-75; Instr/Assoc Professor Somerset Comm Coll 1975-82; Teacher Monticello HS 1982-83, Wayne Cty Mid Sch 1983-84, Wayne Cty HS 1984-; *ai:* Sci Club & Sr Spon; Academic Team Coach; NSTA 1984-; KY Sci Teacher Assn (Bd Mem 1990-92) 1984-; NEA, KY Ed Assn 1983-; Nom Presidential Awd for Excl Sci & Math Teaching 1989; Outstanding Bio Teacher KY 1989; *home:* Rt 5 Box 355 Monticello KY 42633

RADFORD, MARIE RHODES, Business Education Teacher; *b:* Oviedo, FL; *c:* Eric; *ed:* (BS) Bus Admin, FL A & M Univ 1971; (MS) Bus Ed, FL Technological Univ 1976; (EDS) Admin/Supervision, Rollins Coll 1981; Trainee for Staff Dev Clinical Ed II; Word Processing Trng IBM Cmptr; *cr:* Clerical/Data Walt Disney World 1971-72; Bus Teacher Crooms Jr HS 1972-83; Bus Ed Teacher Seminole HS 1983-; *ai:* FBLA Co-Spon & Former Club Adv; Phi Delta Kappa; Alpha Kappa (Alpha Grammateus, Anti-Grammateus); Kappa Delta Phi; Antioch Gospel Choir Musician Plaque for Leadership; Antioch M B ChurcH (Organist, Pianist), Dedicated & Faithful Service; Seminole Cty Asst Prins Pool Mem; Teach Typing on Cmptr as Pilot Prgm; *office:* Seminole HS 2701 Georgia Ave Sanford FL 32771

RADICK, GREGORY JOSEPH, Refugee ESL Teacher; *b:* Minneapolis, MN; *m:* Janet Eilleen; *c:* Meghan C., Zachary J.; *ed:* (BS) Art, Univ of MN 1976; TESOL Certificate Eng as a Second Lang, Portland St Univ 1982; *cr:* Eng as a Second Lang Teacher Lewis Jr HS 1982-85; Mc Loughlin Mid Sch 1985-89; Refugee Eng as a Second Lang Teacher Portland Comm Coll 1989-; *home:* 4416 NE 20th Ave Portland OR 97211

RADIE, KEN NEAL, Sixth Grade Teacher; *b:* Cleveland, OH; *m:* Kathleen Logan; *c:* Kyle, Kara; *ed:* (BA) Elem Ed, Marietta Coll 1975; *cr:* 6th Grade Teacher Ellenwood Sch 1975-79, Hudson Mid Sch 1980-; *ai:* Head Ftbl Coach; Head Wrestling Coach; Stu Assistance Team Chem Intervention; NEA; OH Educl Assn; Hudson Educl Assn; Jennings Scholar; OH Dept Ed Grant Pollution Stud; Garden Club OH Citation Pollution Stud; *office:* Hudson Mid Sch 77 N Oviatt St Hudson OH 44236

RADLEY, MARILYN YVONNE (KOUNTER), 7th/8th Grade Teacher; *b:* Coffeyville, KS; *m:* G. Daniel; *c:* Kristen, Jayme; *ed:* (BA) Liberal Stu, CA St Univ Bakersfield 1985; Grad Work in Scndry Math Ed; Eng Curr/Instruction/Environmental Sci; *cr:* Math/Algebra/Oceanography Teacher Norris Mid Sch 1985-; *ai:* Local Sch Math Field Day Chairperson; Sch Site Comm Mem; Math/Algebra Curr Dev & Local Prgm Quality Review Comm; Chrstn Womens Sftbl League Pitcher; Norris Teachers Assn Rep 1988-; Mem CA Teachers Assn 1985-; Olive Knolls Church of the Nazarene Active Mem 1969-, Soloist & Organist Awd; *office:* Norris Mid Sch 6940 Calloway Bakersfield CA 93308

RADOSEVICH, LINDA LONG, English Teacher; *b:* Jersey City, NJ; *m:* James D.; *c:* David, Cynthia, Steven; *ed:* (BA) Scndry Ed, Longwood Coll 1969; Grad Stud Amer Lit, Ed; *cr:* Eng Teacher Fairfax HS 1969-73, St Marys HS 1987-; *ai:* Literary Jr Class Adv; NCTE 1988-; *office:* Saint Marys HS Duke Of Gloucester St Annapolis MD 21401

RADSHEID, JOHN E., Mathematics/Science Chair; *b:* Cleveland, OH; *m:* Mary Ann; *ed:* (BS) Physics, Bowling Green St Univ 1969; Grad Stud; *cr:* Technician L O F Glass Co 1968-69; Teacher Ida HS 1969-; *ai:* Division Math & Sci Chm; JETS Team Coach; NCTM 1988-; Univ of MI Frontiers in Sci Participant; *office:* Ida HS 3145 Prairie St Ida MI 48140

RADTKE, DELORES MC KEETH, 8th Grade Teacher; *b:* Eau Claire, WI; *m:* Herbert A.; *c:* Gregor; *ed:* (BS) Elem Ed, WI St Univ Eau Claire 1962; Univ of WI Stout; Univ of WI River Falls; *cr:* 8th Grade/Self-Contained Classroom Teacher Elmwood Sch Dist; *ai:* Pom Pon Adv & Dir; Cheerleading Adv; Sch Dist Prof Steering Comm; WCEA, NEA 1962-; Elem Ed Assn Pres 1970-71; Pierce Cty Ec Dev Corp (Pres 1989, VP 1988); Heritage of Elmwood Bd of Dir 1980-; West Cap Bd of Dir 1980-89; Elmwood Plan Comm Chm 1986-88; Univ Women Secy 1985-86; *office:* Elmwood Schls Wilson Ave Elmwood WI 54740

RADTKE, NANCY B., French Teacher; *b:* Longview, WA; *c:* Elisabeth; *ed:* (BA) Fr, 1966, (MA) Elem Ed, 1974, (MA) Fr, 1986 MI St Univ; *cr:* Fr/Eng Teacher Dwight Rich Jr HS 1967-79, Eastern HS 1979-; *ai:* Fr Club Spon; Effective Schls; ITIP; PTSA; Curr Cncl; FL Steering Comm; MEA, NEA, LSEA

1967-; AATF, MFLA 1971-; Peoples Church Stephen Minister 1989-; *office:* Eastern HS 220 N Pennsylvania Lansing MI 48912

RADZA, JOSEPH EDWARD, 5th Grade Sci/Hlth/Gft Teacher; *b:* Warren, OH; *ed:* (AS) General Stud, Kent St Univ 1977; (MS) Health Ed/general Sci, Youngstown St Univ 1980; Gifted & Talented Ed Specialist, Youngstown St Univ; Aids Ed/Childrens Support Group Trng; *cr:* 7th-8th Grade Life/Earth Sci Teacher Turner Jr HS 1980-81; Substitute Teacher/Home Instr Warren City Schls 1981-86; 7th-8th Grade Life/Earth Sci/Health Teacher Prospect Jr HS 1986-89; 5th Grade Sci/Health/Gifted Teacher Tod Woods Intermediate Sch 1989-; Wkshp Coord/Teacher Trumbull Cty Schls 1989-; *ai:* Coach Sci Olympiad Team 1986-; Coach Odyssey of Mind Team 1990-; Coord 4th/5th Grade Health Fair; Support Group, Homework, Gifted & Talented Comm; OH Ed Assn 1986-; Prospect PTSA 1986-89; Tod Woods PTSA 1989-; Sci Olympiad Regional Competition Outstanding Coach Awds 1st Place 1989, 3rd Place 1990; Girard City Schls Awd of Distinction for Outstanding Service 1987; PTSA Certificates of Appreciation for Valuable Contribution 1988-89; Ashland Oil Teacher Achievement Awd Nominee 1989; *office:* Tod Woods Intermediate Sch 443 Trumbull Ave Girard OH 44420

RAE, BRUCE A., Art Teacher; *b:* Ann Arbor, MI; *m:* Millie E. Smith; *c:* Brendnt A., Bronwen L.; *ed:* (BS) Fisheries/ Wildlife, 1963, (BA) Art/Ed, 1967, (MA) Art, 1968 MSU; Amateur & Prof Theatre; *cr:* Art Teacher Eaton Rapids Mid Sch 1967-68; Art/Theater Teacher Waverly East Mid Sch 1968-72; Art Teacher Okemos HS 1972-; *ai:* Art Club Spon; Fine Arts Area Coord; MI Art Ed Assn 1967-, Purchase Awd 1970; BSA Scoutmaster 1984-89; Art Work in Individual & Prof Collections; *office:* Okemos HS 4400 Okemos Rd Okemos MI 48864

RAEBEL, MARTIN GLEN, Mathematics Dept Chair; *b:* Yuma, AZ; *m:* Janice Kay Shipp; *c:* Cathryn S., Martin B.; *ed:* (BSED) Math, 1967, (MAT) Math, 1973 N AZ Univ; *cr:* Teacher Casa Grande HS 1966-67; Teacher 1967-, Math Dept Chm 1989- Yuma HS; *ai:* AEA, NEA 1967-; AATM 1989-; NCTM 1978-; Tandy Technology Scholars Outstanding Teacher Awd 1989-; *office:* Yuma HS 400 6th Ave Yuma AZ 85364

RAFA, MICHAEL JOSEPH, Biology Teacher; *b:* Wheeling, WV; *m:* Mary A. Mercer; *c:* Matt, Marie, Mickey; *ed:* (BS) Bio Ed, WV Univ 1976; Technology Ed, Natl Sci FND Summer Inst 1977; *cr:* Sci Teacher Wheeling Central Catholic HS 1976-81; Bio Teacher Brooke HS 1981-, Bethany Coll for Natl Sci Fnd Summer Prgm 1989; *ai:* Vlybl & Sftbl Coach; NSTA 1977-; BSA Leader 1989-; Finalist in WV Teacher in Space Prgm; Help Develop Test Questions for WV Teachers Cert Test in Bio; Published in Coaches Corner & North Amer Fisherman; *office:* Brooke H S Bruin Dr Wellsburg WV 26070

RAFAL, SAM ALLEN, Social Studies Teacher; *b:* Sarasota, FL; *ed:* (ABJ) Public Relations, Univ of GA 1982; Certified Emergency Medical Technician 1986; Amer Heart Assn CPR Instr; *cr:* Teacher Cedar Shoals HS 1988-; *ai:* Ftbl, Bsktbl, Soccer & Bsbl Athletic Trainer; Published in 1983 Spec Bsbl Issue & 1988 Issue of Magazines; *home:* 100 E Whitehall Rd Athens GA 30605

RAFFAY, CHARLES V., Physics Teacher; *b:* Orange, NJ; *m:* Deanna Darress; *c:* Charles, Russell; *ed:* (BA) Geology, Lafayette Coll 1960; NSF Insts; NJ Inst Tech; Worster Poly Inst; Dickinson Coll; Knox Coll; *cr:* Sci Teacher Mine Hill Twp Schls 1960-63, Roxbury HS 1963-; Adjunct Insstr NJ Inst Tech 1966-76; *ai:* Jr Boys Bsktbl Coach; Mem Gifted & Talented Dist Comm; Treas Schlsp Fund HS; NEA, NJ Ed Assn, Morris Co Ed Assn 1960-; Roxbury Ed Assn 1963-; NJ Sci Teachers Assn Northern Reg VP 1986-88 Participant Prgm Comm 1989; West Morris Area YMCA Bd of Dir (Pres 1985-86, VP 1983-84); *home:* 8 White Birch Rd Stanhope NJ 07874

RAFFERTY, LARRY DEAN, Mathematics Teacher; *b:* Hettinger Cty, ND; *m:* Lynette Hassel; *c:* Larry Jr., Edwin, Lene, Carmen Cain, Bryan Jacobs, Denise Jacobs; *ed:* (BS) Composite Sci, Dickinson St Univ 1959; (MS) Math, Univ of ND 1964; (MSNS) Natural Sci, Highlands Univ; *cr:* Math/Sci Teacher Elgin Public Schls 1959-64; Math Teacher Dickinson Public Schls 1965-; *ai:* Ftbl & Track Coach; NDEA 1959-88; DEA 1965-88; NEA 1978-88; Jaycees Pres 1969-73, Teacher of Yr 1972; Eagles 1979-; Elks 1976-; Sci Fellowship Grant 1964-65; Secy ND Math Teachers; ND Coach of Yr In Track 1975-79.

RAFFETY, CYNTHIA (KIRBY), Math Teacher/Dept Chairperson; *b:* Baltimore, MD; *m:* Jay C.; *c:* Jennifer L., Robert E.; *ed:* (BA) Math, Univ of MD 1970; WV Wesleyan Coll; Univ of VA George Mason Univ/WV Univ/WV Wesleyan Coll; *cr:* Math Teacher Suitland HS 1970-71, Sterling HS 1971-72, Jefferson HS 1981-83, B U Mid Sch 1983-; *ai:* Delta Kappa Gamma Honorary Intnl Ed Society; Buckhannon Jr Women Pres/Treas 1989-; Buckhannon Welcome Club Pres 1985-87; Chapel Hill United Meth Church Lay Leader 1987-; *office:* Buckhannon Upshur Middle Schl PO Box 250 Buckhannon WV 26201

RAFFONE, RUDY, JR., Mathematics Teacher; *b:* New Haven, CT; *m:* Patricia Mc Manus; *c:* Rudy III, Keith, Krisanne, Scott; *ed:* (BS) Accounting, Quinnipiac Coll 1966; (BS) Math Ed, Univ of Bridgeport; Grad Stud; *cr:* Asst Athletic Dir Quinnipiac Coll 1966-68; Athletic Dir/Math Teacher Kingsley Hall Sch 1968-69; Math Teacher New Haven Hebrew Day Sch 1970-78; Soccer Coach/Math Teacher Westbrook HS 1980-89, Notre Dame HS 1989-; *ai:* Math Club Adv; Soccer Coach; Long Term Planning & Alumni Exec Bd; Drug & Alcohol Comm; Greater New Haven Umpires Assn Pres 1980-84, Umpire of Yr 1986; Comm Coll Bsbl Umpires Interpreter 1988-; Natl Soccer Coaches Assn of America; Exchange Club 1987-; *home:* 21 Oak Vale Rd Westbrook CT 06498

RAFTER, JOSEPH PATRICK, 6th Grade Teacher; *b:* Hoboken, NJ; *m:* Joan Christine Aluotto; *c:* Brendan, Casey; *ed:* (BA) Psych, Fairfield Univ 1967; (MA) Psych, New Sch for Soc Research 1971; (MST) Ed, Fordham Univ 1972; Working Towards PhD, NY Univ; *cr:* Volunteer US Peace Corps 1967-69; Adjunct Professor Psych Hudson Cty Cmmty Coll 1975-80; Teacher New York City Bd of Ed 1970-; *ai:* UFT, AFT 1970-; Hoboken Bd of Ed (Pres 1988-89) 1986-89; Assn of Teachers NY Teacher of Yr 1985; *home:* 1023 Bloomfield St Hoboken NJ 07030

RAFTERY, MICHAEL PATRICK, English Teacher; *b:* Chicago, IL; *m:* Virginia Marie Wall; *c:* Matthew, Anne, Maureen, Erin, Daniel; *ed:* (BA) Eng, Iona Coll 1966; (MA) Lit/His, The Univ of Chicago 1980; Grad Course Governors St Univ; Inst for Teachers of Talented/Gifted Stud Carleton Coll 1982-, 1989, Albion Coll 1987; *cr:* 5th Grade Teacher Iona Grammar Sch 1964-65; 6th Grade Teacher St Albert The Great Grammar Sch 1965-67; Eng Teacher Brother Rice HS 1967-74, Rich East HS 1974-; *ai:* Newspaper Adv; Soph Eng Teachers Chm; IEA, NEA; NDEA Inst for Teachers St Univ of NY Albany 1967; NEH Ind Study Fellowship 1983; NEH Seminar on Tolstoi & Dostovsky OH St Univ 1988; *office:* Rich East HS 300 Sauk Trl Park Forest IL 60466

RAGAN, ARLYNE STOKES, Mathematics Teacher; *b:* Lubbock, TX; *ed:* (BA) Math/Phys Ed, Hardin-Simmons Univ 1958; (MED) Ed, N TX St Univ 1971; Odessa Jr Coll; *cr:* Teacher Ector Jr/Sr HS 1958-64, Hood Jr HS 1964-65, Ector HS 1965-82, Ector Jr HS 1982-; *ai:* Dept Chairperson; Algebra Textbook Comm; Revision of 8th Grade Math Curr; Prin Advisory Comm; W TX Frontier Cncl of Math 1987-; OCTA, TCTA 1965-; TSTA 1958-; Permian Basin Road Runners Club 1985-; *office:* Ector Jr HS Box 3912 Odessa TX 79760

RAGAN, KIM MONDAY, Second Grade Teacher; *b:* Chattanooga, TN; *m:* Ray L.; *c:* Rayna E., Sanra B.; *ed:* (BS) Elem Ed, Belmont Coll 1980; Working on Masters Austin Peay St Univ; *cr:* Teacher Vanleer Elem 1981-; *ai:* TN Ed Assn, NEA Mem.

RAGAZZO, ROBERT, Industrial Art/Voc Ed Coord; *b:* Rockville Center, NY; *m:* Ann Jane Quintoni; *c:* Robert, Rebecca, Jennifer; *ed:* (BS) Industrial Art Ed, St Univ Coll Oswego 1975; (MS) Ed & Human Services, New England Coll 1987; *cr:* Industrial Art Teacher Kearsarge Mid Sch 1975-79; Industrial Art Dept Coord Kearsarge HS 1980-; *ai:* Boys Var Soccer & Tennis Coach; NEA, NH Ed Assn 1975-; Kearsarge Ed Negotiations Chm 1984-; New London Lions Club Treas 1982-84; *office:* Kearsarge Regional Hs North Rd North Sutton NH 03260

RAGLAND, SANDRA HORTON, Art Teacher/Department Head; *b:* Tulare, CA; *m:* Davey Lynn; *ed:* (BSE) Eng/Art, Univ Cntrl AR Conway 1981; AR Writers Wkshp 1984; Wkshp Trng Gifted & Talented Prgm; PET & Mid Sch teaching Trng; *cr:* HS Art Teacher Vilonia HS 1983-; 7th Grade Eng Teacher Vilonia Jr HS 1983-; *ai:* Span Club Co-Spon; Art Club, All-Stars, 7th & 8th Grade Class Spon; In-Service Comm; Vilonia Ed Assn Exec Bd 1987-; AR Ed Assn, NEA 1986-; *office:* Vilonia HS PO Box 160 Vilonia AR 72173

RAGON, JUDITH ANN, English Department Chairperson; *b:* Rossville, GA; *m:* Ronald R.; *c:* Ronald, Gina; *ed:* (MED) Eng, 1988, (BS) Ed/Eng, 1962 Univ of TN; Data Collector Teacher Evaluator; *cr:* Eng Teacher Walker Cty 1962-63, Russell HS 1964-65, Trion HS 1969-71; Dept Chairperson/Eng Teacher Rossville HS 1976-88, Ridgeland HS 1989-; *ai:* Walker Cty Curr Study Comm; Future Teacher America Co-Spon Ridgeland HS; NEA, Walker Cty Ed, GA Assn of Educators, Intnl Rdng Assn; Delta Kappa Gamma (Membership Chairperson 1988-, Secy 1986-88); Teacher of Yr Beta Club, Sage Club, Faculty Rossville HS; *office:* Ridgeland HS Happy Valley Rd Rossville GA 30741

RAGSDALE, SONJA GUFFEE, Third Grade Teacher; *b:* Floydada, TX; *m:* Robert Russell; *c:* Rhett, Richard; *ed:* (BS) Elem Ed, W TX St Univ 1963; Elem Ed, Sci, Drama, Cmptrs, Spelling Summer Classes; *cr:* 3rd Grade Teacher 1963-64, 3rd Grade 1967-68 Mary Allen Elem; 1st Grade Teacher Spearman Elem 1968-69; 3rd Grade Teacher Mary Allen Elem 1981-; *ai:* UIL Spelling Coach; Bill Martin Schlsp Comm; ATPE 1981-; TSTA 1963-64, 1967-68; Better Homes Home Demonstration (Secy, Pres) 1974-80, Club Woman of Yr 1979; United Meth Women Treas 1980-82; Cub Scouts Past Den Mother 1973, 1978; *home:* HCR 2 Box 7 Stratford TX 79084

RAHILLY, IRENE PATRICIA, Third Grade Teacher; *b:* Holyoke, MA; *ed:* (BA) Eng, Elms 1964, (MED) Ed, Springfield Coll 1971; *cr:* 3rd Grade Teacher Patrick E Bowe 1964-71, Streiber 1971-; *office:* Hugh Scott Streiber Memorial Telegraph Ave Chicopee MA 01020

RAHN, PATRICIA ROBERTS, 5th Grade Teacher; *b:* Belen, NM; *m:* David L.; *c:* Clinton M., Terry L.; *ed:* (BA) Elem Ed, W NM Univ 1970; Grad Stud Spec Ed, E NM Univ; *cr:* 3rd Grade Teacher Hollaman AFB 1970-71; Spec Ed Teacher Melrose Elem 1972-74; 7th Grade Sci/9th Grade Math Teacher Taylor Elem 1979-85; 1st/2nd/5th Grade Teacher Taylor Elem 1979-85; 5th Grade Teacher Denver City Intermediate 1985-; *ai:* Promotion & Retention Policy, Text Book Adoption, Drug Curr Comms; NEA Building Rep 1983-84; ATPE 1987-88; Delta Kappa Gamma 1987-; TX Study Club 1988-; Order of Eastern Star Musician 1966-; *office:* Denver City Intermediate Sch 1003 N Avenue F Denver City TX 79323

RAICHE, CYNTHIA CLARK, 4th Grade Teacher; *b:* Detroit, MI; *m:* Ronald Michael; *c:* Renee, Danielle, Ryan; *ed:* (BS) Elem Ed/math, Western MI Univ 1975; *cr:* 1st 3rd Grade Teacher 1976-77, 3rd Grade Teacher 1977-80, 5th Grade Teacher 1981-87, 4th Grade Teacher 1988- Littlefield Public Sch; *ai:* Health Curr Comm; Building Improvement Team; Natl Ski Patrol 1972-79 Bravo 1975, Outstanding Service 1974.

RAIKES, SARAH MINOR, Home Economics Teacher; *b:* Lebanon, KY; *m:* Darrell Lynn; *ed:* (BA) Home Ec, 1987, (MS) Home Ec Ed, 1990 Univ of KY; *cr:* Home Ec Teacher Campbellsville HS 1987-; *ai:* Drill Team, Frosh Class Spon; FHA Adv; Entreprenuer Dir; KHEA, AHEA Dist Teacher of Yr 1988; KAVHET VP 1988-89; AVA; Younger Womens Club Fund Raising Chm 1988-; Young Baptist Women Missions Dir 1989-; Teen Parenting, Entrepreneurship Grant; *office:* Campbellsville HS 230 W Main St Campbellsville KY 42718

RAIMANN, LINDA J., Fifth Grade Teacher; *b:* Wells, MN; *m:* Richard D.; *c:* Christina, Lesley-Anne, Misty, Joshua, Ann; *ed:* (BS) Elem Ed, Mankato St Univ 1975; *cr:* 4th-6th Grade Teacher St Casimir 1975-; *ai:* Little Tykes Playsch Bd 1980-; Outstanding Young Educator Awd Wells Jaycees 1986; *office:* St Casimir Cath Sch 330 2nd Ave SW Wells MN 56097

RAINBOLT, LEISA W., Geography Teacher; *b:* Pineville, KY; *m:* Donnie Allen; *c:* Joshua; *ed:* (AS) Scndry Ed, Cleveland St Comm Coll 1976; (BS) Soc Sci, E TN St Univ 1978; *cr:* Teacher Honaker HS 1979-88, Lebanon HS 1988-; *ai:* Var Sftbl 1979-86; Var Vlybl 1979-82; Cheerleading 1979-86; BETA & Pep Club; Future Teachers; Hi-Y; SADD; SCA; Russell Cty Ed Assn, VA Ed Assn, NEA 1979-; Commonwealth Alliance for Drug Rehabilitation & Ed 1988-; *office:* Lebanon HS P O Box 217 Lebanon VA 24266

RAINER, PATRICIA C., Instrumental Music Teacher; *b:* Louisville, KY; *ed:* (BME) Music Ed, Morehead St Univ 1970; Working Toward Masters Various Schls; *cr:* Elem Music Teacher Saddleback Unified Sch Dist 1972-76; Jr HS Music Dir Serrand Intnl Sch 1976-80; HS Music Dir El Toro HS 1980-; *ai:* HS Marching & Jazz Band, Orch, Color Guard; Intnl Assn of Jazz Educators 1988-; S CA Sch Band & Orch Assn 1973-; Sigma Alpha Iota 1966-; Parent Stu Teacher Organization; Tournament of Roses Parade 1985; Portland Rose Parade 1986; US Rep to Brisbane Australia for Expo 1988; Halftime Performer NFL Game Wombley Stadium 1990; Festival of Music Geneva Switzerland 1990; Teacher of Yr 1983; Judge Portland Rose Parade 1987, 1989, Hula Bowl 1990; *home:* 19031 Wildwood Cir Trabuco Canyon CA 92679

RAINES, BETTY JANE, 8th Grade History Teacher; *b:* Glasgow, KY; *m:* John D.; *c:* Paul, Mark; *ed:* (BA) His, Sociology, 1975, (MA) Scndry Ed, 1982 Western KY Univ; Western KY Univ; *cr:* 8th Grade His Teacher Franklin-Simpson Mid Sch 1978-; *ai:* Pep Club Spon; Newspaper Adv; Sch Rep Bd of Academic Booster Club; Mem Bd of Ed Public Speaking Group; Mem Sch Cmmty Partnership Org; Simpson Cty Educ Assn (Secy 1985-86 Secy 1988-89); Lions Club 1987 Outstanding Teacher 1987; Outstanding Soc Stud Teacher KY 1984.

RAINEY, ANNE THOMPSON, Third Grade Teacher; *b:* Athens, GA; *m:* Alexander B.; *c:* Alex, Meg; *ed:* (BS) Elem Ed, 1971, (MED) Elem Ed, 1972 Univ of GA; *cr:* 3rd Grade Teacher Perny Elem 1972-73, Alps Road Elem 1973-74; Villa Rica Primary 1974-75; 1st/3rd Grade Teacher Ellijay Primary 1975-; *ai:* Literary Journal; Annual Staff; Prof Assn of GA Educators; *office:* Ellijay Primary 500 Library St Ellijay GA 30540

RAINEY, DIANE B., 1st Grade Teacher; *b:* Clearfield, PA; *m:* William; *c:* Gretta E.; *ed:* (BS) Elem 1973; (MS) Early Chldhd 1977 Indiana Univ of PA; *cr:* 5th Grade Teacher 1973-75; 2nd Grade Teacher 1975-76; 1st Grade Teacher 1976-; Glendale Sch Dist; *ai:* Chrldr Adv 1977-79; Nike Adv 1978-79; BPW Pres 1978-80; Whos Who Among Young Prof Women 1982; PTA 1988-; Brownie Leader 1977; *office:* Glendale Elem Sch Rd Flinton PA 16640

RAINEY, NANCY JEAN CALDWELL, First Grade Teacher; *b:* Shelbing, MO; *m:* Harold Nathan; *ed:* (BS) Elem Ed, NE MO St Teachers Coll 1951; (ME) Elem Ed, OK Univ 1967; *cr:* 1st/2nd Grade Teacher Shelbyville MO 1951-54; 1st Grade Teacher Grace v Wilson Sch 1954-55, Garfield/Hays Schls 1955-57, Shelbina MO 1957-59, Rancho Village/Hillcrest Schls 1959-; *ai:* Cooperating Teacher; Permitted Stus & Numerous Educators To Observe Classroom; Given Numerous Demonstrations Since 1974 on Creative Storywriting in Primary One; NEA, OEA, Delta Kappa Gamma Society 1959-; OK Rdng Cncl, OCCEA; Published Article in Town Review a Coll of Ed Publication 1987; Project Challenge Oklahomas Best Honor Roll 1989; Article Published in Daily Oklahoman 1989; *home:* 6608 S Villa Ave Oklahoma City OK 73159

RAINEY, PATRICIA ASTON, Social Studies Dept Chairman; *b:* Birmingham, AL; *m:* Ronald Lewis; *c:* Courtney M., Grant R.; *ed:* (BA) Speech, AL Coll 1961-65; Elem Ed, LA St Univ 1974; *cr:* Teacher Noble Street Elem 1966-67, Lake Harbin Elem 1967-68, Alexandria HS 1968-69, Southside Elem 1969-82, Southside Mid 1982-85, Scotland Mid 1985-; *ai:* Exxon Adoption, Faculty Advisory Comm; Dial-A-Teacher Rep; Broadcasting Club, Stu Cncl, Soc Stud Club Spon; 4-H Leader; Kappa Kappa Iota Pres 1986-87; Delta Kappa Gamma Prgms Dir 1981-86; NEA; Edna

Gladney Parkview Civic Organization Assn VP 1976-78; *home:* 5908 Parkforest Dr Baton Rouge LA 70816

RAINGE, THELMA GILLIAM, 6th Grade Reading Teacher; *b:* Essex, MO; *m:* Rudolph L.; *c:* Althea, Terri, Rainge; *ed:* (BS) Elem Ed, IN Univ 1969; (MS) Elem Ed, Roosevelt Univ 1973; *cr:* 5th Grade Reading Teacher Froebel Mid Sch 1969-71; 6th/7th/8th Grade Reading Teacher Edison Mid Sch 1971-; *ai:* Mid Grades Assessment Prgrm 1987-88; Performance Based Accreditation Comm 1989; Very Involved Parents Comm; Smart Start Comm; Interdisciplinary Comm 6th Grade; Gary Rdg Cncl Mid Sch Rep 1988-; IRA; Gary Eng Cncl; AFT Local #4; YWCA Bd Mem 1982-84; NAACP; Toured 13 European Countries & Sch As Guest Moorhead St Univ June 1987; *office:* Edison Mid Sch 5th Ave & Burr St Gary IN 46406

RAINGRUBER, ROBERT JOHN, Math Teacher; *b:* Eureka, CA; *c:* Eric; *ed:* (BA) Span/Math, Univ of CA Berkeley 1966; *cr:* Span Teacher La Loma Jr HS 1966-67; Math Teacher Grace Davis HS 1967-; *ai:* Chess Club Adv & Coach; Modesto Chess Club Pres; Co Author 2 Books.

RAINS, DIANNE DOBBINS, Readiness Teacher; *b:* Fort Payne, AL; *c:* Andy; *ed:* (BS) Early Chldhd Ed, Jacksonville St Univ 1977; Early Chldhd Ed, Univ of AL Gadsden Center 1990; *cr:* Chapter 1 Rdng Teacher Norwood Elem Sch 1977-80; 6th Grade Teacher Ashville Mid Sch 1981-84; 4th Grade Teacher W Cntrl Elem Sch 1984-85; Readiness Teacher Johnston Elem Sch 1985-87, 10th St Elem Sch 1987-; *ai:* Phi Theta Kappa 1974-75; Kappa Delta Epsilon Pres 1975-77; AL Assn Young Children Certificate of Recognition for Excl; Outstanding Young Women of America 1982; *home:* Rt 4 Box 409 Gadsden AL 35904

RAINS, MARTHA M., 5th Grade Teacher; *b:* Cincinnati, OH; *ed:* (BS) Elem Ed, Coll of Mt St Joseph 1964; Inst of Sacred Theology Aquinas Coll 1966-68 & Archdiocese of Cincinnati Cert; *cr:* 5th Grade Teacher St Francis Xavier Sch 1961-65; 5th-6th Grade Teacher St Martin De Porres Sch 1965-67; 6th Grade Teacher St Josephs Sch 1967; 5th Grade Teacher Holy Angels Sch 1968; 4th Grade Teacher Clifton Sch 1969; 5th Grade Teacher St Margaret Mary Sch 1969-; *ai:* PTA (Treas, Financial Secy, Membership Comm); Childrens Raffle Chairperson; NCEA; OCEA; PTA Lifetime Membership Awd 1981; Parish Festival Booth Chairperson; *office:* St Margaret Mary Sch 1830 W Galbraith Rd Cincinnati OH 45239

RAINVILLE, KATHLEEN (SULLIVAN), Latin/French Teacher; *b:* Kew Gardens, NY; *m:* Gerard A. Jr.; *c:* Thomas Harmon, Robert Harmon; *ed:* (BA) Latin, Marywood Coll 1962; Numerous Univs; *cr:* Latin/Fr Teacher Bay Shore HS 1962-66, Bowie HS 1972-; *ai:* Spon Natl Latin Honor Society; Faculty Awds & Fund Comms; Natl Classical Assn 1987-; Church (Parish Cncl Chairperson, Lector Society Chairperson); Foreign Lang Syllabus Comm; Arts & Hum Grant Univ of MD; *office:* Bowie HS 15200 Annapolis Rd Bowie MD 20715

RAKAY, MATHILDE MILLER, Retired 5th Grade Teacher; *b:* Brooklyn, NY; *w:* Al (dec); *c:* Peter, Bruce, Jane Rakay Nelson; *ed:* (BS) Ed, OH Univ 1963; (MA) Ed, WV Univ 1972; *cr:* Headstart Teacher Mc Mechen 1965-70; 5th Grade Teacher Center Mc Mechen Sch 1963-88; *ai:* NEA, WV Ed Assn, MCEA 1963-88; 648 Mental Health Bd Chairperson 1975-83; Tri Cty Womens Help Center Chairperson 1983-86; Belmont Cty Childrens Service Bd Chairperson; E OH Arts Cncl; Bellaire Clinic-HMO Bd of Trustees Mem 1958-80; *home:* 560 W 48th St Shadyside OH 43947

RAKOW, URSULA H., Science Department Head; *b:* New York, NY; *m:* Donald E.; *c:* Donald, David, Christina; *ed:* (BA) Ger/Eng, Valparaiso Univ 1963; (MS) Earth Sci, East TX St Univ 1981; *cr:* Ger Teacher Reitz HS 1964-65, NORTH HS 1966-68, BASSE HS 1970-71; Sci Teacher/Dept Head J W WILLIAMS 1976-; *ai:* Natl Jr Honor Society Spon; Adressing Behavioral Concerns Facilator; Dist Steering Comm Mem; We Help Ourselves Facilator; Discipline Comm; Facilities Comm; NEA 1976-; TSTA 1976-; NSTA 1976-; *office:* J W Williams 1050 Williams Rockwall TX 75087

RALEIGH, SUSAN CORDELL, 6th Grade Teacher; *b:* Little River, KS; *m:* Michael G. D.; *c:* Hilarie, Lucas, Fletcher; *ed:* (BA) Ed, Mc Pherson 1978; *cr:* 6th-8th Grade Teacher Marquette Elem; 5th-8th Grade Teacher Windom Mid Sch; *ai:* Vlybl & Bsktbl Coach; Pep Club Spon; *office:* Windom Mid Sch Box 67 Windom KS 67491

RALEIGH, WILLIAM PATRICK, 4th & 5th Grade Teacher; *b:* Jersey City, NJ; *m:* Linda Jane Modafferi; *c:* Jonathan, Jill; *ed:* (BA) Elem Ed, Jersey City St Coll 1968; (MA) Rdng, Seton Hall Univ 1973; Credits at Various NY Colleges; *cr:* 5th Grade Teacher Waldwick Mid Sch 1968-73; 4th Grade Teacher 1973-74, 5th Grade Teacher 1974-89, 4th & 5th Grade Teacher 1989- Traphagen Sch; *ai:* Head Coach-Waldwick HS Girls Tennis Team; Waldwick Ed Assn 1968-; NJ Ed Assn 1973-; NEA 1973-; *home:* 8 The Loop Ringwood NJ 07456

RALPH, DANIEL THOMAS, Counselor; *b:* Erwin, NC; *m:* Lauren Whittington; *c:* Morgan; *ed:* (BS) Bus Ed/Admin, Campbell Univ 1970; (MAE) Guidance, East Carolina Univ 1977; Media Stud CUNY 1974; *cr:* Cnslr Midway HS 1970-; *ai:* SADD & Peer Cnslrs Adv; Sampson Comm Coll Citizens Advisory Bd; Curr Dev Comm; Stu Information Management Coord; NC Sch Counselors Assn 1977-; Amer Personnel & Guidance Assn, NC Scndry Sch Counselors Assn; Y-Indian Princesses 1989-; Miss Erwin Denim Pageant Assn Chm 1980-; St Stephens Episcopal Church Vestry Secy 1980-84, 1986-88; *home:* 109 Pandora Cir Erwin NC 28339

RALSTON, MARGARET LOUISE, English Teacher; *b:* Kenton, OH; *c:* Erin M., Katherine L., Dennis E. Jr.; *ed:* (BS) Ed/Journalism, OH St Univ 1970; (MA) Psych, Univ of WV 1990; *cr:* Eng Teacher Kenton Jr HS 1970-73; Sr Eng Teacher/Dept Chairperson Ridgemont HS 1973-77; Technical Eng Teacher Carver Career Center 1977-81; Eng Instr Cabell Alternative Sch 1981-84; Public Relations Dir Goodwill Industries 1985-86; Graduate Asst Univ of WV 1989-; *ai:* Prom Spon; OH St Univ Womens Golf Team Mem 1966-69, Competition Honors Stu 1966-67; Television Talk Show 1987; *office:* Sherman HS Box AB Seth WV 25181

RAMBEAU, JANIE CULBRETH, French Teacher; *b:* Albany, GA; *m:* Ralph; *c:* Melvin, Lillian, Marvin; *ed:* (BA) Fr, Albany St Coll 1964; (MED) Eng, GA St Univ 1977; (MED) Fr, Valdolsta St Coll 1985; (MED) Fr, Valdosta Coll 1986; Ft Valley St Coll; Univ of GA Athens; *cr:* Teacher Southside Mid Sch 1964-69, Merry Acres Mid Sch 1969-74, Westover HS 1974-; *ai:* Foreign Lang Dept Chairperson; Fr Club Spon; Dougherty Cty Ed Assn, GA Assn of Educators 1964-; Foreign Lang Assn of GA 1985-; 1st Bethesda Baptist Church (Newspaper Ed 1979, Mem 1950), Service Awd 1988; Westover HS Yrbk Dedication 1986-87; Article Published 1977; *home:* 918 Whitney Ave Albany GA 31701

RAMBO, BETTY BURNER, Language Arts Teacher; *b:* Harrisonburg, VA; *c:* Alicia M.; *ed:* (BA) Eng/Bible, Catawba Coll 1965; (MA) James Madison Univ 1971; Academically Gifted Certificate; *cr:* Teacher Halifax Cty HS 1965-67, Spencer Elem 1967-69, N Rowan Jr HS 1969-; *ai:* Coach Public Speaking Contests; Yrbk Coord; Weekly Newsletter Ed & Publisher; Sch Improvement & Sch Based Comm; Awds Comm Chairperson; NEA 1965-80; NC Educators Assn 1967-80; Prof Educators of NC 1980-; N Rowan Boosters Club Treas 1989-; N Mid PTA 1969-; Kappa Delta Pi 1989-; *home:* PO Box 752 Salisbury NC 28145

RAMBO, JEAN ADELE (CAVANAUGH), Math/Sci/Soc Stud Teacher; *b:* St Louis, MI; *m:* Leo D.; *c:* Anthony M., John P., Paul D; *ed:* (BA) Elem Ed/Span - Cum Laude, Marygrove Coll 1951; (MA) Ed, Univ of MI 1957; Teaching of Sci, MI St Univ 1973; *cr:* 3rd Grade Teacher St Louis Grade Sch 1951-52; 3rd/4th Grade Teacher Lindemann Sch 1952-55; 2nd Grade Teacher St Marys Redford Sch 1955-56; Research Asst Univ of MI Engineering Research Inst 1957-58; 3rd/4th Grade Teacher Grand River Sch 1958-60; 4th Grade Teacher St Thomas Aquinas Sch 1970-; *ai:* Sch Testing Coord; Research, Recommendations, Dev Curr Comm; Presentations of Curr to Parent & Sch Groups; Sch Evaluations Comms; MI Ed Assn, NEA 1958-60; NCEA 1970-; MI Cncl for Teaching of Math 1974-77; Conservation Club 1956-59; Article Published.

RAMER, FAITH ELLEN, French/Psych/Math Teacher; *b:* Fredericksburg, VA; *ed:* (BA) Psych, Randolph-Macon Coll 1977; Fr, Mary Washington Coll; *cr:* Math Teacher Stafford HS 1978-83; Math/Fr Teacher North Stafford HS 1983-88; Pshcy/Fr/Math Teacher Richlands HS 1988-; *ai:* Coach Drama Guild; Forensics Team; Debate Team; Spon Soph Cncl; AATF 1987-; NEA, VEA, SEA Public Relations Comm 1985-86; TEA Secy 1990-91; Rappahannock Regional Area Teachers of Math 1980-88; Natl Forensics Fed of Interschlastic Speech & Debate Assn 1989-; Cedar Bluff United Meth Church Youth Cnslr 1988-; *office:* Richlands H S Rt 460 Richlands VA 24641

RAMETTA, SAMUEL JOHN, JR., Latin Teacher/Team Leader; *b:* Altoona, PA; *m:* Juanita Martin; *c:* Michelle; *ed:* (BA) Latin/Eng, St Vincent Coll 1962; (MA) Classics, Kent St Univ 1970; (MS) Ed Ad, Univ of Dayton 1980; *cr:* Latin/Eng Teacher Cntrl Cath HS 1962-67, Plain Local Schls 1967-; *ai:* Latin Club Adv; Lang Art Team Leader; Boys Var Tennis; Girls Jr Var Tennis; Stark Cty Latin Assn 1967-; Stark Cty Coaches 1987-; Glen Oak HS Teacher of Yr 1988; *office:* Glen Oak HS 2300 Schneider St NE Canton OH 44721

RAMEY, KATHY, Chapter Reading/Math Teacher; *b:* Oak Ridge, TN; *ed:* (BS) Elem Ed, TN Tech 1972; Rdng TN Tech; *cr:* Rdng Teacher Mullins Jr HS 1972-73; 4th/5th Grade Teacher Crossville Elem 1973-77; Cumberland Elem 1977-80; *ai:* Art 4th/5th/6th Grade Teacher South Cumberland Elem 1980-; Honor Awds Comm Co Chm; Five-Yr Base Plan Comm; Cumberland Cty Ed Assn 1973-89 South Cumberland Teacher of Yr 1986; TN Ed Assn 1973-89; NEA 1973-89; *office:* S Cumberland Elem Sch Rt 11 Box 316D Lantana Rd Crossville TN 38555

RAMIREZ, AMELDA S., 4th Grade Elementary Teacher; *b:* Laredo, TX; *m:* Alonzo L.; *c:* Alonzo Jr., David, Lourdes; *ed:* (BS) Sociology, 1956, (MA) Sociology, 1961 TWU Denton; *cr:* 2nd Grade Teacher Buenos Aires Elem Sch 1956-57; 4th Grade Teacher K Tarver Elem Sch 1957-59; 4th-6th Grade Teacher Hermelinda Ochoa Elem Sch 1959-72; 4th Grade Teacher M S Ryan Elem Sch 1972-; *ai:* 4th Grade Head Teacher; UIL Coach; LISD Textbook Comm Mem; TSTA 1956-72; Althea Society, Las Damas de la Republica Del Rio Grande, Princess Pocahontas Cncl Past Mem; Maemoc Club for Women Mem; *office:* M S Ryan Elem Sch 2401 Clark Blvd Laredo TX 78043

RAMIREZ, ANGELA CASTORIA, 8th Grade English Teacher; *b:* Albuquerque, NM; *m:* Larry Simon; *ed:* (BA) Comm Arts, 1970, (MA) Educl Admin, 1983 Univ of NM; *cr:* Teacher Taft Mid Sch 1972-; *ai:* Racewalker Club Spon; Foster Positive Attitudes Among Stus Comm Co-Chm; NM Cncl of Teachers of Eng 1988-; Phi Delta Kappa 1986-89; Marriage Enrichment Speaker 1980; St Thomas Aquinas Cath Church Parishioner 1980-; Taft Teacher of Yr Awd 1989; Wrote & Presented Positive Attitude Wkshp Taft Staff Sites Albuquerque Public Schl Sites; *office:* Taft Mid Sch 620 Schulte Rd NW Albuquerque NM 87107

RAMIREZ, BERNADINE DE LA CRUZ, 5th Grade At Risk Teacher; *b:* San Antonio, TX; *c:* Lawrence G.; *ed:* (AA) Ed, San Antonio Coll 1963; (BSE) Ed, Our Lady of the Lake Univ 1965; Wkshps, Inservices, Pilot Prgm, Seminars; *cr:* 2nd/3rd Grade Teacher Winston Elem 1965-69; 3rd Grade Teacher Valley HS Elem 1969-73; 3rd/4th Grade Bi-ling Teacher 1973-87, 5th Grade Advance Teacher 1987- Adams Elem; *ai:* Chess Club Spon; Advance Adv; Cultural Arts Chairperson; Sci Fair & Soc Stud Fair Chm; CDA Regent; TX Advisory Comm for Long Range Planning 1990; NS Classroom Teachers Assn Rep 1971-72; HTA, TSTA MEM 1973-; EDTA, TSTA, MEM 1965-69; NEA Mem 1965-69, 1973-; PTA (VP, Secy); Delta Kappa Gamma Soc Chairperson, Key Woman Educator 1989; Amer Legion Schlsp; Prin Awd 1989; UTSA Cooperating Teacher; Adams Elem Teacher of Yr 1982-83, 1987-88, Outstanding Elem Teacher of America 1974; *office:* Adams Elem Sch 135 E Southcross San Antonio TX 78214

RAMIREZ, GERARDO, First Grade Teacher; *b:* Weslaco, TX; *m:* Maria Medrano; *ed:* (BA) Elem Ed, Pan American Coll 1964; (MED) Elem Ed, Sul Ross St Univ 1970; *cr:* Teacher Weslaco Ind Sch Dist 1964-79, Progreso Ind Sch Dist 1979-; *ai:* Safety Patrol; *home:* PO Box 1471 Weslaco TX 78596

RAMIREZ, INOCENTE, JR., 6th Grade Teacher; *b:* Garciasville, TX; *m:* San Juanita Martinez; *c:* Jessica, Cassandra, Inocente III; *ed:* (BA) Span, SW TX St Univ 1971; (MA) Ed Rdng, Univ of TX Pan Amer 1988; Bi-ling Ed, Migrant Ed, Gifted/Talented Ed In-Services; *cr:* Teacher Edcouch Elsa Ind Sch Dist 1971-81, Weslaco Ind Sch Dist 1982-; *ai:* PTA Coord; Parent Partnership Prgm Comm Mem; *home:* Rt 1 Box 71 S Victoria Rd Donna TX 78357

RAMIREZ, JOSE JESUS, 5th Grade Teacher; *b:* Harlingen, TX; *m:* Diana A.; *c:* Jose J. Jr., Veronica V., Kristina D.; *cr:* 4th Grade Teacher 1980-88, 5th Grade Teacher 1989- Santa Rosa Elem; *ai:* Math Curr Writing, Gifted & Talented, Book, Fund Raising Comm; Dept Chairperson; TX St Teachers Assn Pres 1987-; City of Primera Alderman 1987-; Rio Grandy Valley Youth Soccer Assn Pres 1989-; TX St Teachers Assn Pres 1988-; Teacher of Month 1990; Nom Most Prominent Educators of TX 1983; *home:* Rt 1 Box 130-A Primera TX 78552

RAMIREZ, KENNETH WILLIAM, Science Teacher/Coach; *b:* San Francisco, CA; *m:* Julie Lyn Bair; *ed:* (BS) Mariculture, 1981, (BA) Bio, Humboldt St Univ 1983; *cr:* Sci/Math Teacher Colusa HS 1983-84; Sci Teacher NV Joint Union HS 1984-; *ai:* Water-Polo, Weight Trng, Swim Coach; TECC 4 Sci-Com Sci Conference (Organizer, Speaker) 1986-87; Church of Christ Preacher 1987-; Staff Mem of Yr 1984; Private Sci Curr Consultant 1986-87; NV Cty Sci Articulator 1985; *office:* Nevada Joint Union HS 11761 Ridge Rd Grass Valley CA 95945

RAMIREZ, RENE GEORGE, Assistant Professor; *b:* New York, NY; *c:* Renee; *ed:* (BA) Eng, CCNY 1966; (MA) Ed, NY Univ 1977; Doctoral Prgm Applied Linguistics, Teachers Coll Columbia Univ; *cr:* Case Aide Cath Charities 1968; Case Worker Soc Security Admin 1970; Teacher Span Amer Inst 1977-79; Instr/Professor Boricua Coll 1979-; *ai:* Asst Ed Journal of Educl Facliitalion; Tennis Player & Jogger; Modern Lang Assn; Martin Luther King Jr Fellowship Awd NY Univ 1980; Articles Published; *home:* 12 Seaman Ave New York NY 10034

RAMIREZ, ROSALINDA SAENZ, Fifth Grade Teacher; *b:* Robstown, TX; *m:* Jose A.; *c:* Rowena, Tony; *ed:* (BS) Ed, TX A&I Univ 1977; (MA) Guidance/Counseling, Corpus Christi St Univ 1988; *cr:* Teacher Dave Odem Elem Sch 1978-; *ai:* TEA Mem 1987-; TSTA Mem 1978-86; *home:* 11913 Hearn Rd Corpus Christi TX 78410

RAMLOSE, HERBERT V., JR., English Instructor; *b:* Chicago, IL; *m:* Theresa Vogt; *ed:* (BA) Eng, 1969, (BA) Speech/Drama, 1971 North Park Coll; (MAT) Eng, NE IL Univ 1975; Type 75 Admin Certificate; IL Writing Project Leadership Trng; *cr:* Eng Instr Alvernia HS 1969-78; Part-Time Eng Instr Coll of Lake Cty; Part-Time Speech Instr Mc Henry Cmmty Coll; Eng Instr Zion-Benton HS 1978-; *ai:* NCTE; IL Assn Teachers of Eng North Lakes Dist Leader 1987-; ASCD; Zion-Benton HS Teacher of Yr 1986; Articles Published; *home:* 230 Allanson Rd Mundelein IL 60060

RAMOLT, RONALD CHARLES, II, Communication Arts Teacher; *b:* Pittsburgh, PA; *m:* Germaine Ratkiewicz; *c:* Joshua, Sarah; *ed:* (BS) Comm/Eng, Univ of PA Edinboro 1986; *cr:* Substitute Teacher Keystone Oaks Sch Dist 1987-88; Teacher Brookville Area HS 1988-; *ai:* Stu Cncl & Drama Club Adv; NEA, PA St Ed Assn Mem 1987-; Brookville Cmmty Theatre 1988-.

RAMOS, ANTOINETTE TOSCANO, Kindergarten Teacher; *b:* Floresville, TX; *c:* Manuel A. Jr., Irene Ramos Rodriguez; *ed:* (AA) Elem Ed, San Antonio Coll 1961; (BA) Elem Ed/Span, Our Lady of Lake Univ 1972; *cr:* 4th Grade Teacher St James Cath Sch 1963-67; Teachers Aide San Antonio Sch Dist 1967-68; Pre-K Teacher Edgewood Ind Sch Dist 1968-77; Kndgtn Teacher San Antonio Ind Sch Dist 1977-87; *ai:* TX Retired Teacher Assn Mem 1987-; AARP Mem NRTA Division 1978-; Natl Comm to Preserve Soc Security & Medicare Mem 1988-; Humana Metro & Baptist Memorial Hospital Volunteer 1988-; *home:* 5047 Prince Valiant San Antonio TX 78218

RAMOS, JOSUE, Spanish Teacher; *b:* Cabo Rojo, PR; *ed:* (BA) Eng, Univ of N TX 1987; *cr:* Span Teacher Lincoln HS 1987-; *ai:* Edward J Olmos Chapter Spon; Natl Span Honor Society; Amer Assn of Teachers of Span & Portuguese 1989-; *office:* Lincoln HS 2826 Hatcher St Dallas TX 75215

RAMOS, ROBERT PEDRO, Spanish Teacher; *b:* Canton, OH; *m:* Sue C.; *c:* Christopher R., Michael P.; *ed:* (BS) Span, 1965, (MA) Foreign Lang Ed, 1968 OH St; Univ of Akron & Univ of Dayton; *cr:* Span Teacher Plain Local Schls 1965-66; Span/Math Teacher New Albany HS 1966-67; Span Teacher Dublin HS 1967-69, Glen Oak HS 1969-; *ai:* Stark Cty Curr Comm; Span Club Asst Adv; PLTA Dist Rep 1976-78; Canton Police Boys Club Bsktbl Coach 1984-85; NDEA Inst Grant 1966; NHS Teacher of Yr 1986-87 & Sr Class Teacher of Yr 1988-89; Jennings Scholar 1987-88; *office:* Glen Oak HS 901 44th St NW Canton OH 44709

RAMSAY, COLIN M., Asst Headmaster/Chm Soc Stud; *b:* Buffalo, NY; *m:* Marion Priestly; *c:* Colin C., Susan H.; *ed:* (BA) Hist/Govt/Intr Stud, 1976, (MAT) Hist, 1978 Norwich Univ; Ed Admin; *cr:* Soc Stud Teacher 1978-, Soc Stud Dept Chm 1984-, Asst Headmaster 1985- NY Military Acad; *ai:* Chm/Curr Comm; NASSP; NCSS; NY St Cncl of Soc Stud Supervisors; NSCD; *office:* New York Military Acad 96 Academy Ave Cornwall on Hudson NY 12520

RAMSAY, MILLICENT E., 4th Grade Teacher; *b:* Hyattsville, MD; *m:* David B.; *c:* Mary K. Mc Innis; *ed:* (BS) Elem Ed, Wilson Teachers Coll 1953; (MAT) Elem Ed, Rollins Coll 1977; Univ of VA, CLemson Univ, Univ of SC, FL Atlantic; *cr:* 3rd-5th Grade Teacher Kingsman Elem & Simon ELem 1953-56; 6th-8th Grade Teacher Calhoun-Clemson Elem 1958-62; 5th Grade Teacher East Lincoln Elem 1963-66; 4th-6th Grade Teacher Surfside Elem 1967-; *ai:* Patrol Coord; Rdng Cncl 1968-70; Math Club 1968-72; Kappa Delta Pi 1977-87; Surfside Elem Teacher of Yr 1981; Wrote Birds of FL Study & Life on Prairie Grants; Nom Soc Teacher of Yr; *home:* 249 Ellwood Ave Satellite Beach FL 32937

RAMSDALE, PORTIA RISSLER, Sixth Grade Reading Teacher; *b:* Roswell, NM; *m:* Dan Jerry; *c:* Jerry, Elizabeth, Stuart, Edward; *ed:* (BS) Elem Ed, TX Tech Univ 1968; Univ of Southern MS 1980-81; *cr:* 2nd Grade Teacher McWhorter Elem 1968; Burnet Elem 1968-71; 7th Grade Teacher Picayune Jr Hs 1978-79; 3rd Grade Teacher 1979-80, 5th Grade Teacher 1980-87 Eastside Elem; 5th Grade Teacher 1987-89, 6th Grade Rdg Teacher 1989- Southside Elem; *ai:* Chm Staff Dev Comm; Southside Teacher Cncl; Spon Geography Club; Coord Natl Geography Bee Southside Elem; Teacher in Charge; Intnl Rdng Assn; ASCD; Dist Nom Christa McAuliffe Fellowship; Supt Appointee Elem Curr Cncl; 5th Grade Chm Dist Math Curr Cncl; Pilot Teacher Critical Thinking Prgm; *office:* Southside Elem Sch 400 S Beech St Picayune MS 39466

RAMSER, BARBARA JUDITH, Geography & Science Teacher; *b:* Wheeling, WV; *ed:* (BA) Elem Ed, W Liberty Coll 1956; (MA) Elem Ed, Drury Coll 1968; Various Wkshps & Schls; Grad Stud Drury Coll 1969, WV Univ 1970-71; *cr:* 6th-8th Grade Teacher 1939-57, 7th/8th Grade Teacher 1957-58, 6th Grade Teacher 1958-61 Belmont Cty Schls; 6th Grade Teacher 1961-66, 4th-6th Grade Sci/Soc Stud Teacher 1966-73, 7th Grade Sci/ Geography Teacher 1973- Martins Ferry Schls; *ai:* Martins Ferry Ed Assn 1961-; OH Ed Assn 1939-; NEA; Natl Audubon Society, Wilderness Society, Natl Wildlife Fed, Natl Parks Assn, Save-The-Redwoods League, Appalachian Trail Conference Mem 1966-; Sierra Club Mem 1988; Selected Conservation Teacher of Yr Belmont Cty 1987; *office:* Steeple Valley Sch 3105 Colerain Pke Martins Ferry OH 43935

RAMSEY, CAROL J. (WARD), Mathematics Teacher; *b:* Arkansas City, KS; *m:* Johnny S.; *c:* Wesley S., Nikki D.; *ed:* (BA) Math, Univ of Permian Basin 1980; *cr:* Bookkeeper Teacher Odessa HS 1978-80; 5th Grade Teacher Lamar Elem 1980-81; Math Teacher Bowie Jr HS 1981-; *ai:* UIL Number Sense & Math; Odessa Classroom Teachers Assn 1980-; TX Math & Sci Assn 1983-; W TX Frontier Cncl of Math 1988-; 4-H Club Leader 1976-; *office:* Bowie Jr HS PO Box 3912 Odessa TX 79760

RAMSEY, CYNTHIA BURCH, Band Director; *b:* Lexington, VA; *m:* Kenneth Irvin; *ed:* (BMED) Music/Instrumental, James Madison Univ 1985; *cr:* Band Dir Liberty HS 1985-; *ai:* Marching, Jazz, Concert Symphonic Band; Music Educators Natl Conference, VA Music Educators Natl Conference, VA Band & Orch Dirs Assn (Mem, Exec Bd) 1985; *office:* Liberty HS R R 7 Box 208 Bedford VA 24523

RAMSEY, DEBRA TOWNSEND, Second Grade Teacher; *b:* Fort Scott, KS; *c:* Steven; *ed:* (BSED) Elem Ed, 1974, (MSED) Elem Ed, 1978 Pittsburg St Univ; Grad Stud; *cr:* Teacher of Emotionally Disturbed Winfield Scott Elem 1975-76; 2nd Grade Teacher W Bourbon Elem 1976-; *ai:* Captain Womens Bowling Team; NEA, KS Ed Assn 1982-.

RAMSEY, DONNA SCOTT, Sixth Grade Teacher; *b:* Kansas City, KS; *m:* Brian C.; *c:* Laura B., Lisa P.; *ed:* (BS) Ed, Univ of KS 1977; Grad Stud; *cr:* 6th Grade Teacher 1978-80, 5th Grade Teacher 1980-89 Junction Elem; 6th Grade Teacher Highland Mid Sch 1989-; *ai:* Building Advisory Cncl; Motivation Comm; KNEA 1989-; *office:* Highland Mid Sch 3101 S 51st St Kansas City KS 66106

RAMSEY, ELIZABETH COURTNEY, United States History Teacher; *b:* Pinehurst, NC; *ed:* (BA) His, 1969, (MA) His, 1977 Coll of William & Mary; *cr:* US His Teacher Lexington HS; *ai:* Jr Class Spon; Honor Comm; Forensics Coach; NEA (Local Pres 1982-83) 1969-; Amer Historical Assn 1985-; Lexington Presbyn Church Mem 1969-; Amer Cancer Society (Volunteer 1969) 1989-; League of Women Voters Mem 1977; Grant VA Military Inst 1987; Fellow NEH Seminar 1986; Rockbridge Jaycees Outstanding Young Educator 1971; *office:* Lexington HS 600 Waddell St Lexington VA 24450

RAMSEY, GAYLE RICHARDSON, Physical Ed/Driver Ed Teacher; *b:* Rome, GA; *m:* Lloyd Jr.; *c:* Lloyd A. III; *ed:* (BS) Phys Ed, Chicago St Univ 1970; Safety Ed, Driver Ed, Chicago St Univ 1986; *cr:* Phys Ed Crane HS 1970-77; Phys Ed/Driver Ed Teacher Lane Tech HS 1977-; *ai:* Crane HS Chrldr, Modern Dance, Sr Class Spon 1970-77; Gym Aides Spon 1980-; Lane Tech BSU Dance Coord 1979-87; IAPHER 1970-88; *office:* Albert G Lane Tech HS 1819 W Pershing Rd Chicago IL 60636

RAMSEY, GORDON EDWARD, 7th Grade Soc Stud Teacher; *b:* Ft Eustis, VA; *ed:* (BA) His/Military Sci - Cum Laude 1976, (MAED) Scndry Ed/His, 1982 Austin Peay St Univ; *cr:* 7th Grade Soc Stud Teacher Richview Mid Sch 1982-; *ai:* Yrbk Spon; Stamp Club Co-Spon; Jr Civitan Adv; Phi Alpha Theta 1974-; TN Ed Assn, NEA 1984-; *office:* Richview Mid Sch 2350 Memorial Dr Clarksville TN 37043

RAMSEY, KATHRYN BRADLEY, 4th Grade Teacher; *b:* Toledo, OH; *m:* Richard E.; *ed:* (BS) Ed, Univ of Toledo 1973; (MED) Curr & Supervision, Wright St Univ 1978; *cr:* 6th Grade Teacher 1973-86; 4th Grade Teacher 1986- Bellefontaine Cit Y Schls; *ai:* Elem Soc Stud Resource Teacher Bellefontaine City Schls; Teacher Saturday Enrichment Acad Logan Cty Schls 1978-; NEA OEA COTA BEA Building Rep 1973-; La Cultura Pres 1981-86; Martha Holden Jennings Scholar 1980-81; *home:* 211 Miami Ave Bellefontaine OH 43311

RAMSEY, LOUIS G., 7th-8th Grade Science Teacher; *b:* Jackson, NC; *c:* Jerron Greene, Teresa Greene, Je Cisken, Crystal; *ed:* (BS) Phys Ed & Health, Eliz City St Univ 1975; Elem Ed 4-8 & Sci 7-8, Wesleyan Coll 1981; *cr:* 6-8th Grade Lang Arts Teacher Garysburg Elem 1975-78; 4-6th Grade Lang Arts/Soc Stud Teacher Squire Elem 1981-83; 7&8th Grade Cci Teacher Gaston Jr HS 1983-; *ai:* Sci Club; Northampton Cty NCAE Sch Rep 1988-; Northampton Cty NCAE Delegate St Convention 1989; Teacher of Yr 86-87; Gaston Jr HS Outstanding Sci Teacher 1989-; *office:* Northampton Co Sch Drawer J Gaston NC 27832

RAMSEY, MARY JETER, Mathematics Department Chair; *b:* Prattville, TX; *m:* Morris D.; *c:* Richard L., Nancy Ramsey Atnip; *ed:* (BA) Eng, TX Womans Univ 1949; Religious Ed, SW Seminary; Math, Stephen F Austin Univ & St Thomas Univ; *cr:* Math Teacher Hefner Jr HS 1969-73, Moss Elem 1973-75, Hambrick Jr HS 1975-77; Math Dept Chairperson, Shotwell Mid Sch 1977-; *ai:* Math Team Coach; NCTM, TSTA, NEA, TCTM 1976-; PTA 1976-89; Oak Creek Village Womens Club, RTAT; Teacher of Yr 1988.

RAMSEY, PATSY HAINLINE, Social Studies Teacher; *b:* Dallas, TX; *m:* Billy Joe; *c:* Craig, Teresa Ramsey Le Fevre; *ed:* (BS) His, Midwestern Univ 1955; Various Colls; *cr:* Teacher Playhouse Kndgtn 1961-62, Ft Caroline Jr HS 1970-81, Vernon Intermediate 1983-; *ai:* Spirit Team Spon; Building Rep; Insurance Comm; Faculty Advisory Comm Mem; Assn of TX Prof Educators Mem 1984-; Teacher Stu Humanitarian Awd 1974; *office:* Vernon Intermediate Sch 2201 Yamparika Vernon TX 76384

RAMSTACK, KATHLEEN KLEIN, Third Grade Teacher; *b:* Milwaukee, WI; *m:* Douglas Allen; *c:* Beckie M., Amy M., Christy A.; *ed:* (BA) Psych, Marquette Univ 1971; *cr:* 3rd Grade Teacher Oak Creek Public Schls 1971-; *ai:* SJV Sch Bd Mem; Vlybl Coach; NEA, WEA, OCEA 1971-; Brownie Leader; *office:* Shepard Hills Sch 9701 S Shepard Hills Dr Oak Creek WI 53154

RAND, MICHAEL GENE, Visual Arts Teacher; *b:* Canton, OH; *m:* Kyong Ye Chue; *c:* Kimberlynn, Melissa; *ed:* (BS) Art Ed, Kent St Univ 1973; (MS) Supervision, Univ of Akron 1990; *cr:* Art Teacher Mapleton Jr HS 1973-76; Indian River Sch 1976-79; Louisville HS 1979-; *ai:* Louisville HS Art Club; Louisville HS Chrstn Youth in Action; Co-ChairPerson N Cntrl Self-Study Steering Comm; NEA 1980-; OH Art Ed Assn 1980-; High Mill Chrstn Center Mem 1985-; Outstanding Work with Youth & Exceptional Job Performance 1978; Outstanding Contribution to Dev of Prgm Guidelines for Youth 1978; Nom for Canton Chamber of Commerce Teacher of Yr 1989; *office:* Louisville City Schls 1201 S Nickelplate St Louisville OH 44641

RANDALL, DANIEL LEE, American History Teacher; *b:* Pt Comfort, TX; *m:* Katherine Ellen; *c:* Cameron L.; *ed:* (BA) Phys Ed, 1981, (BA) Scndry Ed/His, 1985 TX Luth Coll; *cr:* Asst Bsktbl Coach TX Luth Coll 1982-85; Head Bsktbl Coach Rosebud-Lott HS 1986-; *ai:* Head Bsktbl Coach; 2A All St & 2A Region IV Selection Comm; TX Assn of Prof Ed, TX Assn of Bsktbl Coaches, TX HS Coaches Assn 1986-; *office:* Rosebud-Lott HS Box 638 Rosebud TX 76570

RANDALL, ELIZABETH JO, Second Grade Teacher; *b:* Washington, DC; *ed:* (BS) Elem Ed, Univ of S MS 1978; Several Rdng Wkshps; *cr:* 1st-4th Grade Teacher Pass Road Elem 1978-; *ai:* Stu Assistance Team Chm; Insurance & Staff Dev Comm; Seashore Rdng Cncl 1985-; MS Rdng Assn 1987-; MAE 1987-88; PTA (VP 1986, Mem 1978-, Secy 1987); *home:* Sugar Mill Marina Apts Apt 238 Gulfport MS 39507

RANDALL, JOHN A., English Teacher; *b:* Piqua, OH; *m:* Lu Ann Highman; *ed:* (BS) Eng/His, Ashland Coll 1968; Grad Work Cleveland St, Oberlin Coll, OH St Univ, Akron Univ; *cr:* Eng Teacher Oberlin HS 1968-; *ai:* Yrbk Adv; Lang Art Curr Comm; NEA, Oh Ed Assn, NCTE, Oberlin Ed Assn; Martha Holden Jennings Scholar 1987-88; *home:* 111 Pyle Rd Oberlin OH 44074

RANDAZZO, ELISA GELICES, Foreign Lang Chair; *b:* Brooklyn, NY; *m:* Paul; *c:* Paul, Mark, Lisa; *ed:* (BSED) Span, St Johns Univ 1958; Grad Stud Span/Fr, Brooklyn Coll 1958-63; *cr:* Span Teacher Hunter Coll HS 1958; Span/Fr Teacher New Utrecht HS 1958-59; Span Teacher St Josephs Regional HS 1971-72; Span/Fr Teacher Immaculate Heart Acad 1973-; *ai:* Soph Class Coord; Spon Span Honor Society; European Trip Coord; AATSP 1986-; *office:* Emmaculate Heart Acad PO Box 300 Westwood NJ 07675

RANDECKER, CHARLES HENRY, Fifth Grade Teacher; *b:* Lock Haven, PA; *ed:* (BS) Elem Ed, Lock Haven Univ 1960; (MS) Elem Ed, Shippensburg Univ 1980; *cr:* Teacher Woolrich Elem 1960-74; Head Teacher Castonen Elem 1974-75; Head Teacher 1976-, Teacher 1988- Mill Hall Elem; *ai:* ACCE Pres 1968-69; PSEA, NEA; *office:* Mill Hall Elem Sch Kyler Ave Mill Hall PA 17751

RANDLE, LADONIA CAROLYN, Transition Teacher; *b:* Bay City, TX; *m:* Charles Fredrick; *c:* Kyle, Carrielynn; *ed:* (BA) Elem Ed, Huston-Tillotson Coll 1966; (MS) Elem Ed, Prairie View A&M Univ 1970; Spec Ed; *cr:* Teacher Austin Ind Sch Dist 1966-68, Cypress-Fairbanks Ind Sch Dist 1975-; *ai:* TX St Teachers Assn 1966- Teacher of Yr 1983-84; TX Elem & Kndgtn Teachers Assn 1980-86; *home:* PO Box 2823 Prairie View TX 77446

RANDLES, DORTHIE A., Sixth Grade Teacher; *b:* Laneville, TX; *m:* Wm. C.; *c:* Andy, Anne; *ed:* (BA) Elem Ed, Sterling 1974; (MS) Ed/Psych Ed, Wichita St 1981; Certified to Teach Gifted Ed; *cr:* Teacher Morgan Elem 1975-; *ai:* Head Teacher Morgan Sch; Phi Delta Kappa; Thinking Skills Math Grant 1990; *office:* Morgan Elem Sch 100 W 27th Hutchinson KS 67502

RANDLES, OLAND, Guidance Director; *b:* Knoxville, TN; *c:* Leigh Randles Defreitas; *ed:* (BA) Eng, Univ of TN 1955; (MS) Guidance/Cnslr, VA Commonwealth Univ 1979; Seminary Religion; *cr:* Teacher Holston HS 1958-64; Cnslr Chester Mid Sch 1964-; *ai:* AACD, VEA; *office:* Chester Mid Sch 3900 W Hundred Rd Chester VA 23831

RANDO, JANE OLSON, High School English Teacher; *b:* Brockton, MA; *m:* Carl; *c:* Chris, Catelyn; *ed:* (BA) Eng/Drama, Hartwick Coll 1973; Various Courses at Harvard, NY Univ; Grad Work in Creative Critical Thinking, Univ of MA; *cr:* Eng Teacher Brockton HS 1985-; *ai:* Ed The Brockton Teacher 1985-89; NEATE 1985-; NCTE 1989-; Lakeville Arts Cncl 1987-; New England Assn for Teachers of Eng Poet of Yr 1985; *office:* Brockton HS 470 Forest Ave Brockton MA 02401

RANDOLPH, EUNICE SPROUL, Teacher; *b:* Ohiopyle, PA; *m:* William E.; *c:* Randy T., Marcy Mc Clymonds, Rayne; *ed:* (BS) Biological Sci, CA St Teachers Coll 1948; (BS) Elem Ed, Slippery Rock Coll 1961; *cr:* Teacher Henry Clay Township Sch 1948-49, Mt Jackson Elem 1949-50, Mohawk Elem 1956-; *ai:* PA St Ed Assn, NEA 1956-; Bessemer Womens Club 1952-58; Sunday Sch Teacher 1980-82; *home:* RD 1 Box 153 Enon Valley PA 16120

RANDOLPH, GLORIA J., Life Management Skills Teacher; *b:* Tallahassee, FL; *c:* Michelle Campbell; *ed:* (BS) Home Ec Ed, FL A&M Univ 1971; (MS) Home Ec Ed, FL St Univ 1979; *cr:* Teacher Zephyrhills HS 1972-73, Howard Bishop Mid Sch 1973-75; Life Management Skills Teacher Santa Fe HS 1975-; *ai:* FL FHA; AVA 1988-89; Alachua Cty Assn 1975-86; Santa Fe HS Best All Around Teacher Awd; Sears-Roebuck Schlsp Awd; Whos Who Among Chrstn Women; *home:* 1325 NW 40th Terr Gainesville FL 32605

RANDOLPH, KATHLEEN PATRICIA, Third Grade Teacher; *b:* Mt Pleasant, PA; *m:* Frederick L. Jr.; *ed:* (BS) Elem Ed, Indiana Univ of PA 1971; Drug, Alcohol, Curr Dev Wkshps, St Vincent Coll; Staff Dev Wkshp, Prgm More Prevention Effective Teaching; Ed Courses Cert, Penn St Univ; *cr:* Rdng Teacher Federal Rdng Prgm Mt Pleasant Sch Dist 1971-72; 1st Grade Teacher Donegal & Norvelt Elem 1972-81; 5th Grade Teacher 1981-85, 3rd Grade Teacher 1985- Norvelt Elem; *ai:* PSEA, NEA 1971-; *home:* 617 Stamford Dr Greensburg PA 15601

RANDOLPH, KEVIN WILLIAM, Social Studies Teacher; *b:* Boston, MA; *m:* Donna Marie Cardano; *ed:* (BA) His, 1978, (MED) Soc Stud, 1983 Univ of VA; *cr:* Teacher Robert Goddard Mid Sch 1983-; *ai:* Environmental Ed Coord; *office:* Robert Goddard Mid Sch 9850 Goodluck Rd Lanham Seabrook MD 20706

RANEY, CHARLOTTE QUEENER, Reading Teacher; *b:* Pineville, KY; *m:* Danny; *c:* Larry, Charlisa, Amberly; *ed:* (BS) Elem Ed, Cumberland Coll 1976; (MA) Elem Ed, Eastern KY Univ 1982; *cr:* Teacher Broughtontown Elem 1977-78, Mc Kinney Elem 1978-; *ai:* Academic Coach 1986-89; Just Say No Club Spon 1988-; KY Academic Governors Cup Certified Evaluator FPS 1988-; Certified Resource Teacher for Internship Prgm 1988-; NEA; KY Ed Assn; Lincoln Cty Ed Assn; KY State Compensatory Ed Mini Session Leader 1987; *home:* 137 Edgewood Dr Stanford KY 40484

RANEY, PAULA SCHMITTGENS, Fourth Grade Teacher; *b:* Yoakum, TX; *m:* Roger S.; *c:* Ryan M., Melissa K.; *ed:* (BS) Home Ec, Southwest TX St Univ 1976; Cert Elem Ed, 1978, (MED) Curr/Instruction, 1987 Univ of Houston Victoria; *cr:* 5th Grade Teacher 1979-88, 4th Grade Teacher 1988- Yoakum Ind Sch Dist Intermediate Sch; Part-Time Lecturer Univ of Houston Victoria 1988 ; *ai:* Camp Fire Leader; Mem United Meth Church; Memorial Chm Amer Cancer Society; Delta Kappa Gamma (Corresponding Secy 1988-, 1st VP 1990-92); Phi Kappa Phi 1987-; Midcoast Rdng Cncl 1989-; Bluebonnet Youth Ranch Bd of Dirs 1988-; Yoakum Public Lib Bd of Dirs 1988-; San Antonio Cystic Fibrosis Fnd Speakers Bureau 1982-; Coll Lecturer Childrens Lit; Civic Groups Childrens Lit, Public Groups Cystic Fibrosis Wkshp Presenter; *home:* 906 Carroll Yoakum TX 77995

RANHART, JOHN DAVID, Instrumental Music Teacher; *b:* Pittsburgh, PA; *m:* Kathy Kuckuck; *ed:* Working Towards Masters Technology in Ed, WV Univ; *cr:* Asst Band Dir Jefferson Union HS 1980-82; Band Dir New Cumberland Jr HS 1982-; *ai:* Jazz Ensemble; NENC, WVBMA, NEA; *office:* New Cumberland Jr HS Court St New Cumberland WV 26047

RANHOFER, JOAN B., Science Instructor; *b:* Cranford, NJ; *ed:* (RN) Prof Nursing, Muhlenberg Hospital Sch of Nursing 1951; (MS) Nursing, Cath Univ of America 1956; (BSNED) Nursing/Sci Ed, Seton Hall Univ 1961; (MA) Ed/Admin, Kean Coll of NJ 1985; Various Courses & Schls; *cr:* Asst Chief Nurse/Aeromedical Sci Captain USAF Res 1958-62; Nursing Instr Newark Beth Israel Hospital 1963-64; Sci Instr Yeshiva Jewish Educl Center 1973-76, Elizabeth HS 1967-; *ai:* Sci Club & Class Adv; Curr Comm; Prins & Negotiation Comm; Kean Coll of NJ Search Comm, Dean, Sch of Ed; Promotion & Tenure Sch of Nursing & Sci Technology; Tri Cncl & Grad Dismissal Appeals Comm; Grad Curr in Ed; ASCD 1985-; NSTA, NJ Sci Teachers Assn 1968-; NABT, NJ Bio Teachers Assn, Recognition Awd 1968-; Assn for Ed of Teachers in Sci 1988-; Kean Coll of NJ Grad Stu Cncl (VP 1988-89, Treas 1989-91), Recognition Awd 1984-; Phi Delta Kappa (Treas 1988-91) 1986-; Kappa Delta Pi, (Secy 1987-88) 1986-; Natl Bio Teachers Assn NJ Dir, Outstanding Bio Teacher Awd 1988; Key Club Intnl Certificate of Recognition in Teaching 1988-89.

RANIERI, RONALD DAVID, Reading Teacher; *b:* Manila, Philippines; *m:* Lynn D. Thomas; *c:* Jennifer, Robert; *ed:* (BS) Ed, West Chester Univ 1973; Grad Work Ed, Penn St 1974-75, Marywood Coll 1976-79; *cr:* Rdng Teacher Oley Valley Sch Dist 1973-; *ai:* Stu Cncl Adv; Sftbl, Vlybl, Wrestling Coach; PA St Ed Assn; Coventry Little League Exec Bd 1988-, Volunteer Awd 1989; *home:* 437 Kemp Rd Pottstown PA 19464

RANK, SHERILYN SMITH, Drama Coach/Dir of Guidance; *b:* Warsaw, IN; *m:* David H.; *c:* Ashton; *ed:* (BA) Speech/Psych, Grace Coll 1979; *cr:* Speech Instr Lakeland Chrstn Acad 1979-81; Drama Coach/Dir of Guidance Grace Chrstn Sch 1981-; *ai:* Drama Dir; Outstanding Young Women of Amer 1989; Service Awd; Drama Awd 1979; *office:* Grace Chrstn Sch 430 E Lincoln Ave Myerstown PA 17067

RANKIN, LINDA KAY, 7th Grade Life Science Teacher; *b:* Ft Worth, TX; *ed:* (BS) Health/Phys Ed, 1973, (MED) Ed/Kinesiology, 1981 TX Chrstn Univ; *cr:* Bio Teacher Western Hills HS 1973-80; Phys Ed Teacher Morningside Mid Sch 1980-81; Teacher/Coach 1981-85, Teacher 1985- Wedgwood Mid Sch; *ai:* Spirit Club, Youth, Government & Sr Class Spon W Hills HS; 7th Grade Girls Bsktbl, Vlybl, & Track Coach Wedgewood Mid Sch; Stu Cncl Spon Wedgewood Mid Sch; Kappa Delta Pi 1972-73; Delta Psi Kappa Charter Pres 1972-73; Alpha Delta Kappa (Corresponding & Recording Secy) 1982-; Assn of TX Prof Ed 1988-; TCU Women Executives 1975-; TCU Ed Alumni Assn (Charter Mem, Bd Mem 1988-); *office:* Wedgwood Mid Sch 3909 Wilkie Way Fort Worth TX 76133

RANKIN, LINDA LOU (PETERSON), High School English Instructor; *b:* Rockford, IL; *m:* Richard Lee; *c:* Jacob A., Kimberly S.; *ed:* (BA) Eng, W IL Univ 1972; Numerous Courses; *cr:* Eng Instr Stockton Jr/Sr HS 1987-; *ai:* Soph Class Adv; IL Ed Assn, NEA 1987-; Meth Church (Sunday Sch Teacher, Church Comm Mem); Compiled & Edited Stockton Stu Booklet Selections; Write & Edit for Town Newspaper; *home:* 707 Water St Warren IL 61087

RANKIN, MARQUETIA FISHER, Art Teacher I & III; *b:* Aiken, SC; *m:* James Dallas; *ed:* (AS) Art Ed - Magna Cum Laude, Roane St Comm Coll 1977; (BS) Ed, Univ of TN Knoxville 1978; Eng, Bryan Coll of Dayton, Roane St Comm Coll; *cr:* Elem Teacher Spring City Elem Sch 1979-80; Voc Eng Teacher 1981-83, Academic Eng Teacher 1984-89, Art Teacher 1988- Rhea Cty HS; *ai:* Natl Art Honor Society Spon; NAEA 1988-; NCTE 1987-89; NEA 1984-; Gamma Beta Phi Society; Kappa Delta Pi; *office:* Rhea Cty HS Rt 2 Box 63 Evensville TN 37332

RANKIN, NEIL F., 5th Grade Teacher; *b:* Jersey City, NJ; *m:* Georgia K. Poulton; *c:* Tracy, Kelly, Shaun; *ed:* (BS) Elem Ed, Trenton St Coll 1972; Acad for Advancement of Teaching & Management 1989-; *cr:* Classroom Teacher Silver Bay Elem 1972-; *ai:* Bsktbl, Track Coach; Latch Key Prgm Dir; Brick Town Jaycees (Treas 1976, Secy 1975), Spoke of Yr 1974, Jaycee of Yr 1975; Staff Dev Instr; *office:* Silver Bay Sch Silver Bay Rd Toms River NJ 08753

RANSOM, MARGUERITE MITCHELL, English Teacher; *b:* Washington, DC; *m:* Randel Tomas; *ed:* (BA) Eng/Amer Lit/Poly Sci, Univ of CA 1984; Proficiency in Span, Span Lit; *cr:* Eng Teacher Damien HS 1985-; *ai:* Academic & Club Adv; Culture, Ethnicity, Expulsion Review Comm; Yrbk Ed & Adv; *office:* Damien HS 1124 Bonita Ave La Verne CA 91750

RANSOM, ROGER LYLE, 4th Grade Teacher; *b:* Bucyrus, OH; *m:* Deborah Jean; *c:* Laura, Kirk, Tricia; *ed:* (BA) Elem Ed, Heidelberg Coll 1973; Grad Work Wright St Univ, Heidelberg Coll, Bowling Green St Univ; *cr:* 6th Grade Teacher Wynford Mid Sch 1972-82; 4th Grade Teacher Wynford Intermediate Sch 1982-; *ai:* Summer Bsktbl Camp for Girls; Wayside Chapel Co-Youth Leader 1988-; *home:* 4896 Zeigler Rd Bucyrus OH 44820

RANSON, STEVEN ROBERT, English Department Chairman; *b:* Reno, NV; *m:* Sylvia E. White; *c:* Thomas, David; *ed:* (BA) Journalism, 1974; (MED) Ed Admin, 1980 Univ of NV; Eng Brighman Young Univ; Univ of TN; *cr:* Eng Teacher/Chm Wells HS 1976-84; Plt Eng Instr Northern NV Comm Coll 1979-84; Eng Teacher Balboa HS 1984-86; Eng Teacher/Chm/Pres Churchill Cty HS 1986-; *ai:* Newspaper Adv; Freshman Ftbl Coach; Shakespeare Festival Team; Eng Dept Chm; Curr & Textbook Comm; Prof Dev Ctr Level III; Natl Guard Assn 1986-; NV Teachers of Eng 1979-84/1989-; Phi Delta Kappa 1984-86; Optimists Newsletter Editor 1987-; Lions Club (Sec/Treas/VP 1979-84); Shakespeare Inst 1988 Univ of NV; City Cnclmn Wells NV; Whos Who in Amer Coll & Univ; Wrote Articles WY Wildlife/Western Outdoorsman; Special Recognition As Military Journalist Rep Korea & Panama; Bay Area Writing Project; *office:* Churchill County H S 1222 S Taylor St Fallon NV 89406

RAO, SARA S., Sixth Grade Teacher; *b:* Hyd, India; *m:* Satyanarayan S.; *c:* Shon S., Dana S.; *ed:* (BA) Poly Sci, Steubenville Coll 1968; (MS) Poly Sci, Villanova Univ 1970; Elem Cert, Rosemont Coll 1980; *cr:* 6th Grade Teacher Downingtown Sch Dist; *ai:* Research Fellowship; *office:* Dowiningtown Sch Dist 122 Wallace Ave Downingtown PA 19073

RAONICK, PATRICIA A., Fifth Grade Teacher; *b:* Dayton, OH; *m:* T. Jere; *c:* Jenny; *ed:* (BS) Ed, Univ of Dayton 1965; Grad Courses Master Teacher Ed; *cr:* Teacher J M Holt 1965-77, Southdale 1977-; *ai:* KCTA Teacher Rep; St Charles Cheerleading Adv; Southdale Choir Dir; Red Cross, Safety Patrol, Alter High Ball Girl Adv; Curr Dev, Competency Base Ed, Soc, Math & Rdng & Kndgtn Study Comms; Homeroom Mom; Kettering Classroom Teachers, NEA, WOEA; Twig 6 Secy; St Charles Church (Choir, Funeral Choir, Cantor); St Charles PTA; Excl in Teacher Semi-Finalist; Excl in Teacher Initiative Grants; Shakespeare & Dev of Big & Little Friend Prgm; *office:* Southdale Elem Sch 1200 W Dorothy Ln Kettering OH 45409

RAPLEY, GAY MAIRSON, English Teacher; *b:* Berwyn, IL; *c:* Sarah; *ed:* (BA) Zoology - Magna Cum Laude, Univ MN 1960; (MED) Eng Ed - Magna Cum Laude, Univ GA 1973; Endorsement Gifted Ed 1988; Rank I Gifted Ed 1987; *cr:* Research Asst Univ MN Med Sch 1960-64; Substitute Teacher DOD Schls 1964-68; Eng Teacher Athens HS 1969-71, Woerner Jr HS 1973-75, KY Governors Scholars Prgm 1984-85, 1987-88, Brown Sch 1975-; *ai:* Beta Club & Trivial Pursuit Club; Carnival Chairperson; KCTE, KAGE; Phi Beta Kappa, Phi Kappa Phi; KCLU; Smith Coll Under-Grad Schlsp; Presentations KAGE, KCTE; KY Ec Assn Schlsp; Louisville Writing Project; Lesson Plan Published; *office:* The Brown Sch 546 S 1st St Louisville KY 40202

RAPOSA, DANIEL GEORGE, JR., Civics Teacher/Athletic Dir; *b:* Attleboro, MA; *m:* Jamie M. Comey; *c:* Jenna, Jesse; *ed:* (BS) Admin, 1983, (MPA) Poly Sci, 1987 Univ of NH; *cr:* 6th-8th Grade Soc Stud Teacher 1985-89, 8th Grade Civics Teacher/Athletic Dir 1989- Berwick Acad; *ai:* Hockey & Bsbl Coach; 8th Grade Adv; Summer Sports Clinic Dir; NCSS; Amer Society of Public Admin; *office:* Berwick Acad Academy St South Berwick ME 03908

RARICK, CRAIG ALAN, Social Studies Teacher; *b:* Bucyrus, OH; *m:* Karen Sue; *c:* Stephanie, Amber; *ed:* (BS) Amer Stud, Bowling Green St Univ 1978; Soc Stud Comprehensive Cert Bowling Green St Univ & OH St Univ; Working Towards Masters in Admin, Ashland Univ; *cr:* Substitute Teacher Crawford Cty Schls 1978-79; Teacher of Learning Disabilities 1979-86, Soc Stud Teacher 1986- Buckeye Cntrl HS; *ai:* Asst Athletic Dir; Jr Var Girls Bsktbl Coach; 7th Grade Class Adv & Attendance Officer; OH Cncl for Soc Stud 1986-; *home:* 131 E Main St PO Box 174 New Washington OH 44854

RASBERRY, L. DARLENE, Mathematics Teacher; *b:* Mobile, AL; *m:* Kerry; *ed:* (BS) Elem Ed/Math, SW OK St Univ 1975; (MED) Adult Ed/Gerontology, Cntrl St Univ 1988; *cr:* Math Teacher Hoover Mid Sch 1975-79, Kerr Jr HS 1979-; *ai:* Honor Society Spon; OK Ed Assn.

RASCH, KELLY LYNN, HS Principal/Business Teacher; *b:* Garrison, ND; *ed:* (BS) Bus Ed/Phys Ed, Dickinson St Univ 1984; (MS) Educl Admin, ND St Univ 1989; Educl Leadership I, II, III, Educl Exec I, II; *cr:* Bus/Cmptr Teacher 1984-88, Bus Teacher/HS Prin 1988- Trenton Public Sch Dist; *ai:* Head Var Ftbl Coach; Phi Kappa Phi 1989-, Top 10 Per Cent Masters Graduating Class 1989; NBEA 1984-; ASCD 1988-; Natl Eagle Scout Assn Eagle Scout; ND Cncl of Sch Admin 1988-; Article Published 1989; Whos Who in Amer Ed 1989; *office:* Trenton HS Box 239 Trenton ND 58853

RASCOE, CAMILLE HOLMES, Business Education Teacher; *b:* Emporia, VA; *c:* Courtnee A.; *ed:* (BSC) Bus Ed, NC Cntrl Univ 1977; *cr:* Secy/Admin Asst US Dept of St 1977-80; Tech Information Specialist US Environmental Protection Agency 1980-82; Bus Teacher Bertie HS 1984-; *ai:* Cheerleading Coach; Cmptr Coord for HS Staff; NCAE, NEA 1984-; NC Bus Educators Assn 1987 & 1989; Delta Sigma Theta Parliamentarian 1988-; Zion Bethlehem Baptist Church (Sr Usher, Youth Leader, Pastors Aide) 1984-; *office:* Bertie HS Rt 3 Hwy 13 Windsor NC 27983

RASH, DEBORAH JOLLY, Spanish Teacher; *b:* Athens, TX; *m:* Stephen Charles; *c:* Scott, Steve, Kim; *ed:* (AA) Navarro Coll 1973; (BA) Eng/Span, Sam Houston St Univ 1975; *cr:* Eng/Span Teacher Mabank HS 1975-78; Span Teacher Mexia HS 1983-; *ai:* Span Club; UIL Debate Coach; Assn of TX Prof Educators; United Meth Women.

RASINSKI, KATHLEEN STUNDICK, Mathematics Teacher; *b:* Baltimore, MD; *m:* William; *c:* William J., Walter J.; *ed:* (BS) Scndry Ed/Math, Towson St Univ 1975; (MS) Scndry Ed/Math, Loyola Coll 1985; *cr:* Math Teacher Herring Run Jr HS 1975-79, Lake Clifton Sr HS 1979-80, Roland Park Elem & Mid Sch 1985-; *ai:* Morgan Math & Sci Fair Spon; Odyssey of Mind Participant 1989-; Algebra I Private Tutoring Prgm; General Math, Pre-Algebra, Algebra I Coaching Prgm; St Casimir Church (CCD, Religion Instr) 1989-; *office:* Roland Park Elem & Mid Sch 5207 Roland Ave Baltimore MD 21210

RASMUSSEN, CONNI CALHOON, Science Teacher; *b:* Norfolk, VA; *m:* Ian; *ed:* (BS) Bio, 1984, (MS) Admin, 1990 Old Dominicon Univ; *cr:* Naturalist Natl Audubon Society 1984-85; Teacher Norfolk Collegiate 1985-87, Norfolk Acad 1987-; *ai:* Varsity Sftbl Coach; Adventure Camps; Summer Prgm Dir; Natl Sci Teacher Assn; Natl Audubon; Fellowship with Natl Audubon Society 1984-85; *office:* Norfolk Academy 1585 Wesleyan Dr Norfolk VA 23502

RASMUSSEN, GARY L., Computer/OH History Teacher; *b:* Port Clinton, OH; *m:* Susan E. Fulkert; *c:* Brooke E., Leighanne, Jill M.; *ed:* (BSED) His/Poly Sci, OH Northern Univ 1969; Cmptr Lit Trng, Bowling Green St Univ, Ashland Coll; OH Peace Officer Trng Terra Tech Coll; Suicide Intervention Trng Ottawa Cty Sheriffs Dept; *cr:* Teacher 1969-, Dean of Stus 1977- Port Clinton Jr HS; *ai:* Cmptr Club Adv & Curr Comm; Bus Advisory Cncl; Staff Advisory Bd; Ftbl, Bsktbl, Track Coach; Athletic Dir; PC Fed of Teachers Treas 1974-75; OH Fed of Teachers; *office:* Port Clinton Jr HS 110 E 4th St Port Clinton OH 43452

RASMUSSEN, HARRY, Mathematics & Science Teacher; *b:* Spokane, WA; *m:* Susan Rene Lyon; *c:* Briana N., Denby Jens; *ed:* (BS) Bio, 1976, (MS) Bio, 1980 Walla Walla Coll; *cr:* Research Asst Loma Linda Univ 1976-78; Teacher Emerald Jr Acad 1981-; *ai:* ASB Spon; Yrbk Adv; Bsktbl Coach; Vice Prin; OR Sci Teachers 1987-; *office:* Emerald Jr Acad 35582 Zephyr Way Pleasant Hill OR 97455

RASMUSSEN, JOYCE PORTER, 6th Grade Teacher; *b:* Preston, ID; *m:* Robin Kemp; *c:* Krista Groll, Mark, Tanya, Jill; *ed:* (BA) Elem Ed, Weber St Univ 1979; Gifted & Talented Endorsement; *cr:* 3rd-6th Grade Teacher Vae View Elem 1979-; *ai:* Gifted & Talented Sch Implementor; SEM Vae View Elem; Peer Evaluator & Mentor Teacher/Trainer Davis Dist; UT Assn for Gifted Children Elem Commissioner 1990; *home:* 2496 N 400 W Sunset UT 84041

RASMUSSEN, RANDALL JAY, Youth in Custody Teacher; *b:* Long Beach, CA; *m:* Vivian Elaine Gottenbos; *c:* Matthew, Nathan; *ed:* General Phys Ed, Long Beach City Coll 1971; (BA) Phys Ed, CA St Univ Long Beach 1974; CA St Univ Northridge 1971-74; *cr:* Phys Ed Teacher Ashmont Scndry Sch 1975-87; Youth In Custody Teacher Bingham HS 1988-; *ai:* Var Girls BsktbL Head Coach, St Champions 1989-; Var Boys Bsbl Asst Coach 1987-89; New York Yankees Assoc Scout 1985; Seattle Mariners Assoc Scout 1990; Canadian Olympic Comm Athletics Advisory Cncl Mem 1981-85; St Paul Athletic Assn Mem; UT AAAA Girls Bsktbl Coach of Yr 1989-; Alberta Winter Games Bsktbl Coord 1985; AA Girls St Bsktbl Championships Tech Dir; *office:* Bingham HS 10400 S 2200 W South Jordan UT 84065

RASNAKE, JANE LLOYD, Fourth & Fifth Grade Teacher; *b:* Pearisburg, VA; *m:* George W.; *c:* Letina, Laura; *ed:* (AA) General Stud, Hiwassee Coll 1966; (BA) Bus Ed/Eng, TN Wesleyan Coll 1968; (MS) Upper Elem Ed, Radford Univ 1981; *cr:* 4th Grade Teacher Honaker Elem 1968-70; 5th Grade Teacher Swords Creek Elem 1970-; *ai:* 4-H Club Talent Show Coord; Kndgtn-5th Grade Sci Fair Chairperson; 4th-5th Grade Academic Competition Coord; Remedial Summer Sch Prgm Teacher Russell Cty; Adult Basic Ed Instr; NEA, VEA, Russell Cty Ed Assn; Honaker United Meth Church (Ed Newsletter, Vacation Bible Sch Dir 1988-); *office:* Swords Creek Elem Sch General Delivery Swords Creek VA 24649

RASNAKE, JOHN SAMUEL, II, English Teacher; *b:* Buxton, NC; *m:* Mary Russell; *c:* Jordannah L., Ryan J. Russell; *ed:* (BS) Eng/Philosophy/Hum, 1979, (MA) Eng, 1985 E TN St Univ; *cr:* Eng Teacher Sullivan East HS 1980-; *ai:* Acad Team Spon; NEA, TN Ed Assn; Sullivan Cty Ed Assn Exec Bd 1984-88; J R Bob Smith Oil Company Grants; *office:* Sullivan East HS 4180 Weaver Pike Bluff City TN 37618

RASPBERRY, JAMES ROLAND, Choral Director/Dept Chair; *b:* Kennett, MO; *m:* Judith G. Hicks; *c:* James R. Jr., Mark R.; *ed:* (BS) Music Ed, SE MO St Univ 1963; (MMED) Music Ed, St Louis Inst of Music 1968; (EDD) Music Ed, Washington Univ 1985; *cr:* Teacher Hillsboro HS 1963-; *ai:* MSTA, ACDA, MENC 1963-; Educl Grant Washington Univ 1976-77.

RASTEDE, MARCIA STAMP, English/Social Studies Teacher; *b:* Cushing, IA; *m:* Allan H.; *c:* Greg, Kelli, Carla; *ed:* (BAE) Soc Stud/Eng, Wayne St Coll 1969; Soc Stud & Eng; *cr:* Eng/Soc Stud Teacher Ponca Public Sch 1971-75, Allen Consolidated Sch 1975-; *ai:* Yrbk Publications Spon; 8th Grade Spon; Sch Coord Cty Spelling Bee/Geography Bee & NE His Day; Delta Kappa Gamma Secy/VP/Pres 1982-88;NE St Ed Assn; Allen Ed Assn (Sec 1978 Pres 1982-1989); Amer Legion Auxiliary; St Paul Luth Church SS Supt 1984-; Allen Centennial Exec Bd Secy 1989-; *home:* R R 1 Box 125 Allen NE 68710

RATAICZAK, THOMAS EDWARD, Engish Teacher & Dept Chm; *b:* Bellaire, OH; *m:* Linda S. Kahl; *c:* Sheri L., Terry E.; *ed:* (BA) Eng, Soc Stud, West Liberty St Coll 1968; (MA) Scndry Sch Admin, WV Univ 1974; Post Masters Studies Univ Dayton; *cr:* Teacher Bridgeport HS 1967-68; Bellaire HS 1968-; *ai:* Dept Chm; Historian Sch Records; Bsktbl Scorekeeper/Statistician-Boys/Girls; Newspaper Adv; Faculty Advisory Comm; Arena Scheduling Comm; Competency Test Comm; NEA 1985-; OH Ed Assn 1985-; Pres 1975; Building Rep 1974-77; Negotiations 1974-78 Bellaire Ed Assn; Claire Cribbs Memorial Schlsp Trustee 1985-; Z E Rataiczak Schlsp Fund Trustee 1988-; Hall of Fame Comm Chm 1988-; Bellaire HS Sports Fnd Trustee 1988-; St Task Force Proficiency Testing 1988-; Publish 5 Articles Natl Magazines; Own 2 Copyrights Bsktbl Scorebks/Stat Systems; Printed Book Motivational Messages; *home:* 64960 Breezy Point Ln Bellaire OH 43906

RATAJCZAK, JOHN MICHAEL, Industrial Arts Teacher; *b:* Tucson, AZ; *m:* Mary Rebecca; *c:* Amber, Kayce; *ed:* (BS) Ed - Summa Cum Laude, N AZ Univ 1985; Working Toward Masters Counseling; *cr:* Industrial Arts Teacher Emily Gray Jr HS 1986-.

RATAU, SYLVIANE LUBELSKI, French Teacher; *b:* Les Sables DOlonne, France; *c:* Aline, Michelle; *ed:* (MS) Ed Fr, SUNY New Paltz 1981; *cr:* Bi-ling Secy/Translator Permanent Mission of Tunisia to the United Nations 1963-64; Bi-ling Secy Belgian Chamber of Commerce 1964; Fr Teacher Newburgh Free Acad 1978-79, Marlboro Mid Sch 1979-; *ai:* NY St Assn of Foreign Lang Teachers Mem, NY St United Teachers Mem.

RATAY, GREGORY W., Psychology/Sociology Teacher; *b:* Chicago, IL; *m:* Marilyn Pray; *c:* Michele, Brett, Alicia; *ed:* (BA) Psych/Sociology, Wichita St Univ 1971; (MS) Soc Psych, OK Univ 1972; (PSYD) Clinical Psych, Forest Inst of Prof Psych 1986; *cr:* Math Teacher Holy Trinity HS 1972-73; Civics Teacher Gordon Tech HS 1973-74; Psych/Sociology Teacher Rolling Meadows HS 1974-78, Wheeling HS 1978-; *ai:* Substance Abuse Prevention Coord; *office:* Wheeling HS 900 S Elmhurst Rd Wheeling IL 60090

RATCLIFFE, BRUCE ALLEN, Science Teacher; *b:* Boston, MA; *m:* Gloria Burrola; *ed:* (BA) Bio, Univ of CA Berkeley 1972; *cr:* Sci Teacher Briggs HS 1976-79, Lodi HS 1979-83, Edison HS 1983-; *ai:* SE Asian Stus Club Spon; *office:* Edison Computech HS 540 E California Ave Fresno CA 93706

RATH, WILLIAM EDWARD, Government Teacher/Dept Chair; *b:* Chicago, IL; *m:* Rachel Margaret Culp; *c:* William, Jason; *ed:* (BA) Soc Sci, 1970, (MA) Soc Sci, 1974 San Jose St; US His, Inst Chico CA 1985; Washington DC Seminar 1988; *cr:* US His/Government Teacher Roseville HS 1975-; *ai:* Golf & Past Bsbl Coach; Various Comm; RSEA Pres 1977; Mentor Teacher 1986-89; *office:* Roseville HS 601 Tahoe Ave Roseville CA 95678

RATHBUN, DONNA LOUISE HESTER, 1st Grade Teacher; *b:* Cleveland, OH; *c:* Jessica Williams, R. Keaney, Laura Depas; *ed:* (BS) Elem Ed - Summa Cum Laude, Coll of Steubenville 1971-72; OH St Univ, OH Univ; *cr:* 1st Grade Teacher Harmony Elem 1971-85, Wintersville Elem 1985-; *ai:* Odyssey of Mind; Sch Adv; PTA Parliamentarian 1971-, Life Membership 1973; OEA, NEA (Dist Pres, OEA Convention Planning) 1970-; GSA (Leader, Asst Leader) 1960-, Woman of Achievement 1987; Womens League (Pres, Mem); Wintersville Demo Women; Teacher in Space Candidate; Outstanding Elem Sch Teacher of America 1973; Jefferson Cty Bd of Ed Sci Mini Grant Recipient 1989; Outstanding Stu of Ed Dept 1971-72 Coll of Steubenville; *office:* Wintersville Elem Sch 125 Fernwood Rd Wintersville OH 43952

RATHSACK, STEVEN ANGELO, 5th Grade Teacher; *b:* Manitowoc, WI; *m:* Anita Kay Pilon; *c:* John; *ed:* (BS) Ed/Math, Univ of WI Oshk Osh 1976; Math/Sci/Cmptr Ed; *cr:* 7th/8th Grade Teacher St Paul Sch 1971-1975; 5th Grade Teacher Omro Junction Sch 1976-; *home:* 1909 Ashland St Oshkosh WI 54901

RATLEDGE, JOHN ERIC, Mathematics Teacher; *b:* Sacramento, CA; *ed:* (BA) Math, Univ of CO 1985; Working Towards Master Math, CA St Univ Hayward; *cr:* HS Math Teacher Dallas Ind Sch Dist 1985-86; Jr HS Math Teacher Fremont Unified Sch Dist 1986-; *ai:* Girls & Boys Bsktbl Coach; *office:* Centerville Jr HS 37720 Fremont Blvd Fremont CA 94536

RATLIFF, LELA H., Second Grade Teacher; *b:* Little Rock, AR; *w:* Vernon T. Sr. (dec); *c:* Vernon T. Jr., Elizabeth A.; *ed:* (BA) Eng, TX Coll 1948; (MS) Elem Ed, Univ of AR 1953; Yearly In Service Trng for Teachers; *cr:* 1st Grade Teacher Little Rock Public Schls 1948-54; 1st/2nd Grade Teacher Temple Ind Sch Dist 1956-; *ai:* TX St Teachers Assn, TX Classroom Teachers Assn, NEA; PTO; Church Sch (Supt, Asst Supt) 1966-; Recipient Service Pin Awds 5 Yr Intervals; 30 Yr Pin from Temple Local TX St Teachers Assn 1987-88; Nom Golden Apple Awd Spon Temple Daily Telegram 1986, 1990; *home:* 502 East Avenue C Temple TX 76501

RATLIFF, PHYLLIS KNIGHTEN, Sixth Grade Teacher; *b:* Lake Charles, LA; *m:* David A.; *c:* Phillip J.; *ed:* (BA) Elem Ed, Mc Neese St Univ 1968; *cr:* 3rd Grade Teacher Western Heights Elem 1968-70; Summer Pilot Prgm Presch Teacher Westlake HS 1968-69; 2nd Grade Teacher Poland HS 1970-72; 1st Grade Teacher Lakeside Elem 1972-73, Peabody Elem 1973-75; Kndgtn Teacher Private Sch Memphis TN 1977-78; 2nd Grade Teacher Our Lady of Lake 1979; 3rd Grade Teacher Hollywood Elem 1980-81; 6th Grade Teacher 1981-82, 6Th-8th Grade Teacher 1982-83, Rdng/Bible Teacher 1983-85, 6th Grade Teacher 1985-88, 5th-6th Grade Teacher 1988- Parkview Baptist; *ai:* Faculty Liaison Comm; Assist Elem Choir; 3rd, 7th Spelling Contests Spon; Jaycee Jaynes Pres; Support ARC, Respite Care Assn, Church; *office:* Parkview Baptist Sch 5750 Parkview Rd Baton Rouge LA 70816

RATLIFFE, PHYLLIS, English Teacher; *b:* Dickenson Cty, VA; *ed:* (BA) Eng, John B Stetson Univ 1959; *cr:* Eng Teacher John S Battle HS 1959-; *ai:* NHS & Stu Cncl Adv; Forensics Coach; NEA, VA Ed Assn 1959-; Outstanding Young Educator Washington Cty 1973.

RATTIGAN, MARY ELIZABETH, Latin Teacher; *b:* Shenandoah, PA; *ed:* (BA) Soc Stud, Coll Misericordia 1951; (MED) Remedial Rdng, Lehigh Univ 1969; Masters Degree PA St Univ & Univ of Scranton; *cr:* Eng/Latin Teacher H F Grebey Jr HS 1959-66; Remedial Rdng Teacher Hazleton Area 1966-70; Eng/Latin Teacher Hazleton HS 1970-; *ai:* Sr Citizens Bd of Trustess 1980-; *office:* Hazelton HS 700 N Wyoming St Hazleton PA 18201

RAUBE, DEE DEE CARLS, 6th Grade Teacher/Asst Prin; *b:* Streator, IL; *m:* George Jr.; *ed:* (BS) Elem, 1966, (MS) Phys Ed/Health/Parks & Recreation, 1973 IL St Univ; Grad Stud Admin; *cr:* 5th-8th Grade All Subjects/Art/Girls Phys Ed Teacher Graymont Grade Sch 1964-68; 1st-12th Grade Phys Ed Teacher Odell Grade & HS 1968-69; 3rd/5th/6th Grade Teacher/Asst Prin Pontiac Elem Schls 1969-; *ai:* Safety Patrol, Chrldrs Adv; Pep Club & GAA Founder; Sr Class Spon; Health, Spec Events, Lincoln Sch New Prin Selection Comm 1989-; IEA, NEA 1964-; Pontiac Elem Assn (Secy 1970-75, Negotiation Comm, Chm) 1969-; Delta Kappa Gamma 1975-; PTO 1964-; NAASP, IL Prins Assn 1987-; St James Hospital Auxiliary 1980-; 1st Luth Church Sunday Sch Teacher 1964-71; Livingston Cty Gifted Coord Lincoln Sch; *home:* RR 4 Billet Rd Pontiac IL 61764

RAUCH, ELIZABETH MONTS, 8th Grade Mathematics Teacher; *b:* Columbia, SC; *m:* C. Mc Ray Sr.; *c:* C. Mc Ray Jr., Robert W., Christopher M., Elizabeth C.; *ed:* (BA) Ed, 1962, (BA) Music/Vocal Performance, 1963 Columbia Coll; (MED) Ed, Univ of SC 1981; Licensed Real Estate Broker St of SC; *cr:* Teacher Richland Dist II 1962-71, Private Piano 1962-73; Choral Teacher Richland Dist II 1962-70; Choir Dir/Organist Trinity Luth Church 1969-78; Teacher Lexington Dist V 1981-; *ai:* Beta Club; SC Cncl Teachers of Math, NCTM 1982-; SC Ed Assn, NEA 1962-; Kappa Kappa Iota (Natl Secy 1970-, Natl Bd of Dir), Schlsp Awd; Southern Assn of Schls & Colls Evaluator; Luth Women Pres 1960-; Columbia Coll Club Pres 1980-82; Temple Univ Rdng Prgm Fellowship 1968; *office:* Irmo Mid Sch Campus 6949 St Andrews Rd Columbia SC 29212

RAUCH, SHARON SHINKLE, Mathematics Teacher; *b:* Cincinnati, OH; *m:* John M. III; *c:* Stephanie, Brian, John D., Julie, Andrew; *ed:* (BA) Elem Ed, Coll of Mt St Joseph 1971; Wkshps & Classes in Math, Sci, Cmptrs; Space Camp for Educators 1988; *cr:* Math Teacher Shrine 1969-71, Little Flower 1971-73, Queen of Martyrs 1973-74; Math/Sci Teacher Sacred Heart Sch 1985-89; Math Teacher The Donoho Sch 1989-; *ai:* Jaycettes Pres 1976-77, Outstanding Jaycette 1975; Jr Service League 1985-; Assn for Retarded Citizens Bd Mem 1977-79; Sch Bd Sacred Heart Sch 1990; Educators in Space Grant Study 1988; *home:* 2301 Hathaway Hts Anniston AL 36201

RAUGHTON, CINDY ANN, Language Art Teacher; *b:* Stamford, TX; *m:* Rudy; *c:* Craig, Julie, Jill; *ed:* (BS) Phys Ed/Eng, Hardin Simmons Univ 1963; *cr:* Teacher Rosce Jr HS 1963-65, 1968-75; Lang Art Teacher Roscoe Jr HS 1977-; *ai:* 8th Grade Spon; ATPE.

RAULSTON, DOROTHY DRIVER, Math Teacher; *b:* Rome, GA; *m:* James Webster; *c:* John D., Cricket Raulston Terrell; *ed:* (BS) Elem Ed, 1971, (MED) Curr/Supervision, 1976 Univ of TN; Apple Cmptr Educl Consultant; *cr:* Math Teacher Girls Preparatory Sch 1971-83, Soddy-Daisy Mid Sch 1983-; *ai:* Mindbenders Club Spon; Chairperson Academic Contests; NCTM 1972-; ASCD 1976-; TN Mid Sch Assn 1987-; Chattanooga Area Math Teachers Assn 1985-; Public Ed Fnd Bd Mem 1989; Hamilton Cty Teacher of Yr Runner-up 1989; Career Level III Teacher 1988; *office:* Soddy-Daisy Mid Sch 200 Turner Rd Soddy-Daisy TN 37379

RAUPE, RUTH REEVES, English Teacher; *b:* Wichita, KS; *m:* Richard; *c:* Geoff, April; *ed:* (BA) Eng, OK East Cntrl Univ 1963; (MA) Eng, OK Southeastern Univ 1980; *cr:* Eng Teacher Mulhall HS 1963-65; Nicoma Park Jr HS 1965-66; 3rd Grade Teacher Cameron Elem 1977-78; Eng Teacher Calera HS 1978-81; Mulhall Orlando HS 1981-; *ai:* Natl Honor Society; SADD Chap; Speech Club; OEA/NEA 1963-; OK Cncl Teachers of Eng 1984-88; Cncl of Basic Ed Independent Study Grant 1989; OK Inst of Arts Quartz MT Schlsp 1989; *office:* Mulhall-Orlando H S Box 8 Orlando OK 73073

RAUTH, VIRGINIA A., 4th Grade Teacher; *b:* Plainfield, NJ; *ed:* (BS) Elem Ed, Trenton St 1956; *cr:* 3rd Grade Teacher 1956-57, 4th Grade Teacher 1957-59 Ella G Clarke Sch; 5th Grade Teacher Ella G Clarke Sch 1959-73, Princeton Avenue Sch 1973-74; 3rd Grade Teacher 1974-75, 4th Grade Teacher 1975- Clifton Avenue Grade Sch; *ai:* Ad Hoc Comm; NJEA Local Teacher of Yr 1979; LEA Teacher of Yr 1987; NEA, OCEA; Presbyn Church Elder; PTA (VP, Secy); *office:* Clifton Avenue Grade Sch Clifton Ave Lakewood NJ 08701

RAVERT, CHRISTIE ALLEN, Third Grade Teacher; *b:* Reading, PA; *m:* John T.; *c:* Allison E., John A.; *ed:* (BS) Elem Ed, Penn St 1973; Grad Work Elem Ed; *cr:* 5th Grade Teacher 1973-77, 3rd Grade Teacher 1977- Tulpehocken Area Schls; *ai:* Red Cross Rep; Rdng with Partners Coord; Career Ed Comm; NEA, PA Ed Assn, Tulpehocken Ed Assn 1973-; Myerstown Grace Brethren Church Mem 1982-; *office:* Bethel Sch RD 1 Bernville PA 19506

RAWHOUSER, JAMES AUSTIN, Mathematics Teacher; *b:* Bellingham, WA; *c:* Joshua, Nicholas; *ed:* (BS) Zoology, CA St Univ Long Beach 1971; (MA) Ed Admin, US Intnl Univ 1990; *cr:* Intern Teacher 1971-72, Teacher 1972-76 Mesa View Sch; Teacher Vista View Sch 1976-; *ai:* Mentor Teacher Ocean View Sch Dist 1987; *office:* Vista View Sch 16250 Hickory St Fountain Valley CA 92708

RAWIS, SHARON GAVIN, Fifth Grade Teacher; *b:* Chicago, IL; *m:* Lucas Shawntell; *c:* Shayne; *ed:* (BS) Phys Ed, 1972, (MS) Elem Ed, 1985 Chicago St Univ; *cr:* George T Donoghue 1972-75; Teacher Geothe 1975-76, John Farren 1976-79, Ralph J Bunche 1979-; *ai:* Cheerleading Coach; Drama Teacher; Tutoring; Chicago Teachers Union, AFT 1973-.

RAWLEY, DEBRA CRAWFORD, Kindergarten Teacher; *b:* Reidsville, NC; *m:* Albert Keesee Jr.; *c:* Adam Hunter; *ed:* (BS) Elem Ed, Averett Coll 1979; *cr:* Rdng Resource Teacher 1979-80, 3rd Grade Teacher 1980-83, Kndgtn Teacher 1983-88, G L H Johnson Elem Sch; Kndgtn Teacher Glenwood Elem Sch 1988-; *ai:* Kndgtn Task Force; Teachers Chorus; Weekday Early Ed Center Chm 1989-; Jr Wednesday Club 1988-; *office:* Glenwood Elem Sch Halifax Rd Danville VA 24540

RAWLINS, DARRYL LEE, Mathematics Teacher; *b:* Spokane, WA; *m:* June Ludwick; *ed:* (BS) Math, WA St Univ 1986; (MA) Curr Dev, E WA Univ 1988; *cr:* Math Teacher Kennewick HS 1986-; *ai:* Presidential Academic Fitness Awd; *office:* Kennewick HS 500 S Dayton Kennewick WA 99336

RAWLINS, JEFFERY ALAN, English Teacher; *b:* Toledo, OH; *ed:* (BS) Eng, Franklin Coll 1986; *cr:* Eng Teacher East Noble HS 1986-; *ai:* Var Ftbl; Girls Gymnastics Asst; Head Coach Kendallville Cntrl Track Mid Sch; *office:* East Noble HS S Garden St Kendallville IN 46755

RAWN, KENNETH H., Social Studies Teacher; *b:* Stamford, CT; *m:* Nancy L.; *c:* Emily; *ed:* (BS) Scndry Ed/US His, S CT St Univ 1967; (MED) Scndry Ed, RI Coll 1975; CT Coop Teacher Core Trng, Design for Effective Instruction Levels 1, 2 & Peer Coaching; *cr:* Teacher Montville HS 1968-; *ai:* Class Adv 1968-71, 1980-83; Asst Ftbl Coach 1968-75; Head Track Coach 1974-87; Asst Womens Cross Cntry Coach 1976-83; Head Womens Cross Cntry Coach 1984-; Montville Ed Assn (VP 1972-74, Legislative Chm 1989-); CT Cncl for Soc Stud Mem 1980-; Mohegan Striders Membership Secy 1988-; CT Cncl for Hum Inst 1989; E CT Conference Track Coach of Yr 1976-77; E CT Conference Cross Cntry Coach of Yr 1984-85; *office:* Montville HS Old Colchester Rd Oakdale CT 06380

RAWSKI, BARBARA ANNE, 2nd Grade Teacher; *b:* Hartford, CT; *ed:* (BS) Elem Ed, Univ of CT 1973; (MA) Early Chldhd, Cntrl CT St Univ 1979; Cert Soc Sci, Wesleyan Univ, Middletown CT; *cr:* Kndgtn Teacher 1974-76, 1st Grade Teacher 1976-77, 2nd Grade Teacher 1977 Myrtle H Stevens Elem Sch; *ai:* Unit Leader 13 Yrs; Mem Numerous Curr Comm; Chaired 2 Curr Comm/Co-Chaired Others; Mem Teachers Union Contract Negotiations Team; CT Writing Project 1986-; Rock Hill Teachers Assn, NEA 1973-; Nom Teacher of Yr Myrtle H Stevens Elem Sch; *office:* Myrtle H Stevens Elem Sch 322 Orchard St Rocky Hill CT 06067

RAWSON, TERESA A. (VENTURA), Adaptive Physical Ed Teacher; *b:* Greenville, MS; *m:* Richard D.; *c:* Anthony; *ed:* (BS) Phys Ed, Univ MS 1981; M R Endorsement Prairie View A&M 1989; *cr:* 3rd Grade Teacher St Ambrose Cath Sch 1981-83; Phys Ed Teacher Hobby Elem Sch 1983-85; Adaptive Phys Ed Teacher Cypress Fairbanks Sch Dist 1985-; *ai:* Jr HS Bsktbl & Sftbl Coach; Little Coord Sftbl; Chrldr Spon; Spec Olympics; TAPHER 1988-89; *office:* Cypress Fairbanks Sch Dist 12630 Windfern Rd Box 40040 Houston TX 77240

RAY, BARBARA MORAN, Fourth Grade Teacher; *b:* Washington, DC; *m:* William F.; *c:* Mark; *ed:* (BS) Elem Ed, Bob Jones Univ 1966; Grad Work Clemson Univ; *cr:* 2nd Grade Teacher Jefferson Elem 1966-68; 1st Grade Teacher Duke Street 1969-72, Faith Chrstn 1972-73; 4th Grade Teacher Sheets Memorial 1973-77, Shannon Forest Chrstn 1977-; *ai:* Soc Comm & Text Book Selection Chm; *office:* Shannon Forest Chrstn Sch 829 Garlington Rd Greenville SC 29615

RAY, DARLA DUNLAP, Drama Teacher/Director; *b:* Houston, TX; *m:* Dirk Anthony; *ed:* (BFA) Drama Ed, Univ of TX Austin 1983; Drama & Ed, Univ of Houston Clear Lake; *cr:* Drama/Eng Teacher Klein Oak HS 1983-84; Drama Teacher/Dir Clear Creek HS 1984-88, Clear Brook HS 1988-; *ai:* Drama Club Spon; Tech

Dir; TX Classroom Teachers Assn 1989-; UIL Dist Play Champion 1989; Produced & Directed Plays; *office:* Clearbrook HS 4607 F M 2351 Friendswood TX 77546

RAY, DENNIS ROBERT, Mathematics Teacher; *b:* Canton, OH; *ed:* (BA) Math, Coll of Wooster 1978; (MED) Math/Ed, OH Univ 1982; *cr:* Math/Cmptr Sci Teacher Chillicothe HS 1978-; *ai:* Girls Var Bsktbl Coach 1981-87; NCTM, OH Cncl Teachers of Math, NEA 1978-; MENSA 1988-; Amnesty Intnl 1989-; Martha Holden Jennings Scholar 1979; *office:* Chillicothe HS 385 Yoctangee Pkwy Chillicothe OH 45601

RAY, DIANA PROVIDENCE, First Grade Teacher; *b:* Indianapolis, IN; *ed:* (BA) Elem Ed, Marian Coll 1972; (MS) Elem Ed, IN Univ & Purdue Univ 1975; *cr:* 2nd Grade Teacher 1972-73, 1st Grade Teacher 1973- Our Lady of the Greenwood; *ai:* Intnl Rdng Assn (Pres 1985-86, VP 1984-85); Johnson Cty Cncl (VP Elect 1983-84, Mem) 1981-; Outstanding Young Educator Johnson Cty Jaycees Awd 1977; *office:* Our Lady of the Greenwood 399 S Meridian Greenwood IN 46143

RAY, EMILY CAMILLE, Kindergarten Teacher; *b:* Nashville, TN; *ed:* (AA) Elem Ed, Freed-Hardeman Coll 1972; (BS) Elem Ed, MTSU 1974; *cr:* 1st Grade Teacher West Elem 1974-79; Central AK Chrstn Sch 1979; Spec Ed Teacher 1980-81; 1st Grade Teacher 1981-82; Kndgtn Teacher Mt Juliet Elem 1982-83; West Elem 1983-; *home:* 3612-A Quail Dr Hermitage TN 37076

RAY, HOMA LEE (CHILDRESS), Retired Third Grade Teacher; *b:* Miles, TX; *m:* Charles Harvey; *c:* Clifford H., Alyce Kromer; *ed:* Bus Admin/Stenotype, San Angelo Bus Coll 1930; (BS) Elem Ed, Sul Ross Coll 1963; Many Wkshps & Seminars; *cr:* Elem Teacher Ray Sch 1931-33; 1st Grade Teacher Miles Ind Sch Dist 1933-35; Elem Teacher Norton Sch 1935-37; Life Insurance Secy Jefferson Standard Life 1940-41; Clerk Stenographer Goodfellow AFB 1942-44; Stenotypist N Amer Aviation 1945; Private Piano & Voice Teacher Miles Sch 1946-56; Substitute Teacher San Angelo Public Schls 1958-59; Private Music Class Teacher Veribest Sch 1959-60; Elem Teacher Fairview CSD 1960-71; 3rd Grade Teacher Water Valley Ind Sch Dist 1980-89; *ai:* Musical Events Pianist Fairview CSD 1960-71; Alpha Chi Mem 1961-; Kappa Delta Pi Mem 1961-64; TX St Teachers Assn 1971; TX Assn of Cmmty Schls 1980-85; Intnl Rdng Assn 1967-71; Amer Assn of Univ Women 1965-71; TX A&M Coll Mother Club (Pres 1958-61) 1957-65; PTA Teacher of Yr 1989; Miles Meth Church Pianist 1928-41, 1945-61; Sunday Sch Teacher 1945-61; Lakeview Meth (Church Pianist 1962-72, Sunday Sch Teacher 1971-72); Womans Society of Chrstn Service Meth Pres 1948-50; Open-Door Chrstn Fellowship Organist 1974-86; *home:* 2657 Parkview Dr San Angelo TX 76904

RAY, KATE LEE, Fourth Grade Teacher; *b:* Maynardville, TN; *m:* Edward R.; *c:* Richard, Barry, Renee Dalton; *ed:* (BA) Elem Ed, Univ of TN/Lincoln Memorial Univ 1972; *cr:* Teacher Powell Elem; 1st Grade Teacher Big Ridge Elem; 6th Grade Teacher Luttrell Elem; 4th Grade Teacher Maynardville Elem; *ai:* Bsktbl Coach; 4-H Leader; Union Cty Ed Assn Secy/Leadership Conferences/Rep Assembly Mem 1980-82; *home:* 5923 Atkin Rd Knoxville TN 37917

RAY, LYNDA TURNER, 3rd Grade Teacher; *b:* Maben, MS; *w:* Joe (dec); *c:* Lynn Russell, Joel; *ed:* (BS) Elem Ed 1973; (MS) Elem Ed, 1983 MS St Univ; Admin Courses; *cr:* 3rd Grade Teacher East Webster Elem 1973-; *ai:* Webster Cty Pres Teachers Assn 1984-85; Eupora Leadership Comm 1989-; *home:* 603 S Dunn Eupora MS 39744

RAY, MICHAEL HOYAL, Mathematics Teacher; *b:* Mineola, TX; *m:* Patricia Ann Davis; *ed:* (BS) Math, N TX St Univ 1972; *cr:* Math Teacher Richardson Jr HS 1973, R L Turner HS 1973-77, Northwood Jr HS 1978-87, Richardson HS 1987-; *ai:* TX St Teachers Assn 1973-; *office:* Richardson HS 1250 W Beltline Rd Richardson TX 75080

RAY, NANCY ROBERTA (HELTON), 8th Grade Soc Stud Teacher; *b:* Kansas City, MO; *m:* William D.; *ed:* (BS) Soc Stud, Cntrl MO St Univ 1973; Grad Stud Univ of MO Kansas City Rockhurst; *cr:* 8th Grade Soc Stud Teacher Bridger Jr HS 1975-; *ai:* His Club Bridger Jr HS, Environmental Animal Welfare Club Asst Spon; NEA, NCSS; Independence Teacher of Yr Nom; Neighborhood Cncl of Independence We the People Awd 1987; *office:* James Bridger Jr HS 2110 Speck Rd Independence MO 64050

RAY, RUBEN L., Electronics Instructor; *b:* Pineville, LA; *m:* Betty J. Vickers; *c:* Jon, Sallie, Jason, Olivia, Leigh, Stacy; *ed:* (MS) Electronic, 1981, (BS) Electronic, UTT 1979; (AS) Electronic, TJC 1972; Cert in Microprocessor Control Technology, TX A&M Univ; Cert in Foremanship, TEU; Cert in Control Systems; USN Electronic 1965-68; *cr:* Owner Electronic Servicing Center 1972-78; Instr US Navy Reserve 1972-86; Teacher TJC 1986-87, Ind Sch Dist Robert E Lee 1979-; *ai:* VICA Electronics Products Servicing 2144; TSTA Mem 1979-; VICA Teacher 1979-, Silver & Bronze Natl Winners 1982 & 1988; Alumni Assn Exec Comm 1982-84, UTT 1982-84; Naval Citation for Exceptionally Meritorious Service in Vietnam 1967-68; Sigma Tau Epsilon Charter Mem UTT; Chi Gamma Iota Charter Mem TJC; Advisory Comm for Curr Dev; Microcmptr Repaired Maintenance TJC; Advisory Comm for Industrial Electronic Prgm TJC; *home:* PO Box 1054 Van TX 75790

RAY, SANDRA R., Physical Education Teacher; *b:* St Louis, MO; *m:* Earl D.; *c:* Teresa, Christina; *ed:* (BS) Ed/Phys Ed, SE MO St Univ 1967; *cr:* Elem Phys Ed Teacher Ft Leonard Wood/Waynesville Dist 1967-68; Jr/Sr HS Phys Ed Teacher St James Sch Dist 1968-70; Phys Ed Teacher Mehlville Sr HS 1970-74; Phys Ed Teacher Oakville Jr HS 1978-81; 7th-8th Grade Lang Arts Teacher Buerkle Jr HS 1981-88; Phys Ed Teacher Oakville Jr HS 1988-; *ai:* Cross Cntry, Girls Vlybl & Jr HS Track Team Coach; Jr HS Newspaper Spon; Amer Alliance for Health, Phys Ed, Recreation & Dance 1988-; NEA, MO Natl Ed Assn 1978-; Mehlville Cmmty Teacher Assn Jr HS (VP 1986-88, Mem) 1978-.

RAYBUCK, ANNIE FARRELL, 7th Grade Teacher; *b:* Pittsburgh, PA; *m:* David Edward; *c:* David E., James F.; *ed:* (BS) Elem Ed, Edinboro Univ 1973; Accreditation Penn St Univ; *cr:* 6th Grade Teacher Laurenceville Cath Mid Sch 1973-74; 2nd Grade Teacher Ambridge Area Cath Sch 1974-77; 7th/8th Grade Teacher St Marys Sch 1977-; *ai:* Drama, Religious Presentations Teach Fr Academically Talented Prgm; St Agatha Secy for Worship Comm 1982-; BSA Cnslr Citizenship Merit Badges 1989-; *office:* St Mary Sch 609 10th St Beaver Falls PA 15010

RAYBURN, BETTY BECK, English Department Chairperson; *b:* Statesboro, GA; *m:* Thomas H.; *c:* Julie, Laura; *ed:* (BS) Elem Ed, GA Coll 1969; (MS) Elem Ed, GA St 1976; *cr:* Teacher Clayton Cty 1969-; *ai:* PAGE; *office:* Pointe South Jr HS 626 Flint River Rd Jonesboro GA 30236

RAYHILL, SUSAN CAROLINE MUELLER, Life Planning Skills Coord; *b:* Granite City, IL; *m:* Stephen Robert; *c:* Cynthia D., Elizabeth A.; *ed:* (BSED) Botany/Zoology, 1968, (MSED) Admin, 1983 E IL Univ; *cr:* Bio/Zoology Teacher Lakeview HS 1969-71; 7th/8th Grade Sci Teacher Roosevelt Mid Sch 1973-76, Thomas Jefferson Mid Sch 1976-87; Life Planning Skills/Drug Free Schls Coord Decatur Public Schls 1987-; *ai:* Richland Comm Coll Sci Fair Co-Chairperson; Making the Grade Public Forum; Fighting Back to Win Drug Free Macon Cty Public; Red Ribbon Week Activity Chairperson; Macon Cty Snowball Co-Organizer; Drug Free Schl Parochial Schls Consultant; Dist Sci Task Force Elem, Mid Sch, Steering Comm; Teen Mom Prgm Mid Sch Pilot Coord; NEA, IL Ed Assn, IL Sci Teachers Assn, NSTA 1969-; Decatur Ed Assn (Bd of Dirs, Building Rep, Consultants Rep); Phi Delta Kappa Secy 1983-; Delta Kappa Gamma 1987-; Natl Mid Sch Assn; ASCD; DARE Advisory Comm; Regional Prevention Group Chairperson 1985-89; 4-H Youth Cncl 1985-89; Born Free Substance Abuse Task Force 1985-89; Kids on Block Bd of Dirs; High Risk Infant Registry, Teen Parent Advisory Bd; Life Planning Skills/Drug Free Schls Advisory Comm Chairperson; AIDS Task Force (Ed Comm, Exec Comm); Mt Zion Booster Club Mem; Mt Zion Cmmty Awareness & Prevention Prgm; BABES Substance Abuse Prevention Prgm, Rock Springs TRUST Course, 708 Needs Identification Day Participant; Decatur Public Schls Those Who Excel Awd; *office:* Decatur Public Schls 1101 W Sunset St Decatur IL 62522

RAYMER, ANDREA A. COLEMAN, 4th Grade Teacher; *b:* Pittsburgh, PA; *m:* Dennis D.; *ed:* (BUS) Elem Ed, Clarion Univ 1966; *cr:* 4th Grade Teacher Hubert Street Sch 1966; Kndgtn Teacher Muse & Cecil Elem 1966-68; 2nd Grade Teacher 1968-71; 5th/6th Grade Teacher 1971-89 Hills-Hendersonville; 4th Grade Teacher Cecil Elem 1989-; *ai:* Girls & Boys 4th & 5th Grade Bsktbl Coach; Spon Natl Bicentennial Map Contest 1990; Spon Natl Geographics Geography Bee 1990; NEA; PA St Educl Assn; Canon Mc Millan Educl Assn; Conferternity of Chrstn Mothers Treas 1988-; Cannon Mc Millan Teacher of Yr 1986-87; *office:* Canon Mc Millan Sch Dist R D#1 Box 510 Cecil PA 15321

RAYMOND, JEANNE WARREN, 7th Grade Mathematics Teacher; *b:* Waco, TX; *c:* Daniel A. III, Martha I.; *ed:* (MS) Elem Ed, Baptist Coll of Charleston 1984; Grad Stud Toward Math Cert; *cr:* Math/Soc Stud Teacher Drayton Hall Mid Sch 1985-; *ai:* Drug & Alcohol Abuse Prevention Drayton Hall Mid Sch Adv; Civian (Pres, Chaplain) 1984-86; Toastmasters 1985-87; Charleston Republican Womens Club 1984-; SC Grant for Cert in Math; *office:* Drayton Hall Mid Sch 3183 Ashley River Rd Charleston SC 29414

RAYMOND, MAX EDWIN, Science Teacher; *b:* San Antonio, TX; *m:* Priscilla Elaine Langston; *c:* Christopher, Sarah, Rebekah, Gabriel; *ed:* (BS) Bio, Univ of N TX 1976; (MA) Ed, Stephen F Austin 1990; Nuclear Chem & Geography Prgm TX Utilities Summer Inst; *cr:* Sci Teacher Tupou HS 1977-79, Hubbard HS 1980-; *ai:* UIL Sci & Debate Coach; Assn of TX Prof Educators 1980-; Hubbard City Cncl Alderman 1985-87; Hubbard Cmmty Ed Prgm Charter Chm 1983-84; 1st United Meth Church (Chm, Bd Trustees) 1988-; Peace Corps 1977-79; Cmptr Graphics Book Author; Magazine Articles Published; *home:* 307 NW 2nd Hubbard TX 76648

RAYNER, KENNETH C., Technology Instructor; *b:* Buffalo, NY; *m:* Connie; *c:* Carrie, Laura; *ed:* (BS) Industrial Art Ed, 1972, (MS) Industrial Art Ed, 1975 Buffalo St; *cr:* Industrial Art Instr W Seneca West Sr HS 1972-; *ai:* Yrbk Adv; CSIP Comm Leader; Cmptr Advisory Team Mem; W NY Technology Ed 1974-; NY St Technology Ed (Newsletter Ed 1984-89) 1984-; *office:* W Seneca W Sr HS 3330 Seneca Street West Seneca NY 14224

RAYNOR, DOLORES LANIER, English/Reading Teacher; *b:* Jacksonville, NC; *m:* Willie Carroll; *c:* Mark S., Stephen L., Brian C., Carol F.; *ed:* (BA) Early Chldhd Ed, Univ of NC Wilmington 1974; Grad Work & Cert Soc Stud, Jr/Sr HS Eng, Rdng, Univ of NC Wilmington & E Carolina Univ; *cr:* Elem Ed Teacher Blue Creek Elem 1974-83, Morton Elem 1974-83; Rdng Teacher 1977-83, Eng Teacher 1984-89, Rdng Teacher 1989- Southwest HS; *ai:* Jr & Frosh Class Adv; Miss Southwest Pageant & Sr Project Graduation Asst; NEA, NCAE 1972-; Rdng Assn 1975-85; Pineland Presbyn Church Womens Circle 1960-; *office:* Southwest HS 500 Burgaw Hwy Jacksonville NC 28540

RAYNOR, PATRICIA D. ASTORQUIA, Spanish Teacher; *b:* Gooding, ID; *m:* Jack D.; *c:* James, Jeffery; *ed:* (BA) Span Ed, ID St Univ 1967; Grad Stud Boise St Univ, Coll of ID, Univ of ID; *cr:* Span Teacher Jerome HS 1967-70; Span Teacher 1970-, World Culture Teaccher 1985-87, 1989- Payette HS; *ai:* Class Adv All Levels; European Club Adv; ID Foreign Lang & Culture Assn, ID Ed Assn, NEA; Payette Ed Assn Building Rep 1985-88; Cath Womens League; Amer Assn of Univ Women VP Membership 1985-87; Bus & Prof Women Awd 1983; Foreign Lang Teacher of ID Plaque 1980; Milbrook Awd 1987; Golden Apple Awd & Plaque 1987; *office:* Payette HS 1500 6th Ave S Payette ID 83661

RAYON, MARSHALL SINGLETON, English Teacher; *b:* Montgomery, AL; *m:* Kenneth William Sr.; *c:* Kenneth W. Jr., Nicholas L.; *ed:* (BS) Eng, AL St Univ 1971; *cr:* Teacher Chicago Public Schls 1971-72, Prairie St Jr Coll 1972-73, Bloom HS 1973-; *ai:* Frosh Class Spon; Delta Sigma Theta 1969-; *office:* Bloom HS 101 10th St Chicago Heights IL 60411

RAYSOR, ROSA M., Classroom Teacher; *b:* Sumter, SC; *m:* Willie B.; *c:* Marsha; *ed:* (BS) Bus Ed, Allen Univ 1966; Univ of SC; *cr:* Teacher Richard Carroll HS 1966-68, Barnwell Cty Public Sch 1968-71; Librarian Voorhees Coll 1972-77; Adult Ed Coord Bamberg Cty Schls 1987-89; Teacher Bamberg-Ehrhardt HS 1977-; *ai:* FBLA Adv; Bamberg Ed Assn, SC Ed Assn, NEA, Bamberg Cty Ed Assn; Thankful Baptist Church Missionary Society Prgm Chm & Ed Day Comm Mem; Order of Eastern Star; Bamberg Cty Bd of Registration 1975-85, Volunteer Outstanding Service; Ladies Auxiliary of Post #10595; Outstanding Young Women of Amer; Volunteer Worker Veterans of Foreign War Campaign; *home:* PO Box 172 Bamberg SC 29003

REA, JERRY CREE, Fourth Grade Teacher; *b:* New Kensington, PA; *m:* Anna C. Hohos; *c:* Aaron; *ed:* (BS) Elem Ed, Clarion Univ 1968; Masters Equivalent Elem Ed, Penn St 1975; *cr:* 6th Grade Teacher Buffalo Elem Sch 1968-80; 4th Grade Teacher Freeport Elem Sch 1980-84, S Buffalo Elem Sch 1984-; *ai:* PA St Ed Assn 1968-; Freeport Ed Assn Pres 1972-73; NEA 1968-; Nom Thanks to Teachers Excl Recognition Univ of Pittsburgh; *office:* S Buffalo Elem Sch 562 Freeport Rd Freeport PA 16229

REA, MICHAEL L., Asst Prin/Eng Teacher; *b:* Mt Pleasant, MI; *m:* Shelda Henderson; *c:* John, Andrea; *ed:* (BS) Eng/Phys Ed, E MI Univ 1971; (MA) Admin, Cntrl MI Univ 1985; *cr:* Eng/Phys Ed Teacher Southfield Chrstn Sch 1971-73; Eng Teacher Marmion Military Acad 1973-79; Eng Teacher/Asst Prin/Coach Kingston HS 1979-; *ai:* Academic Games, Eng, Head Ftbl, Jr Var Bsktbl, Jr HS Track Coach; MASSP, NASSP 1985-; *office:* Kingston HS 5790 State St Kingston MI 48741

READ, HARRY WILSON, Health Coordinator/Educator; *b:* Neptune, NJ; *m:* Patricia Headley; *c:* Hannah, Isaac; *ed:* (BA) Health/Phys Ed, Morehead St Univ 1976; Family Life & Sexuality, Aids, Alcohol & Drug Ed; Teaching Admin, Springfield Coll; *cr:* Asst Phys Dir Princeton YMCA 1976-78; Grad Asst Springfield Coll 1978-79; Health Educator Rockland Dist HS 1979-86; Health Coord Camden/Rockport HS 1986-; *ai:* Health Ed Curr Comm Chm; ME Assn of Health, Phys Ed, Recreation & Dance VP Elect in Health 1989-; Nom Health Educator of Yr 1989; Teaching Fellowship Springfield Coll 1978-79.

READ, JENNIFER JONES, ESL/PALS Teacher; *b:* Portland, OR; *m:* R. Michael; *c:* Catherine, Patrick, Erin, Jeff; *ed:* (BA) His/Eng, Univ of Houston 1975; (MED) Curr/Instruction, Univ of TX 1987; *ai:* Spon TX Alliance for Minorities in Engrng; Phi Delta Kappa; NEA; Teacher of Eng to Speakers Other Lang; *office:* Georgetown Jr HS 1601 Leander Rd Georgetown TX 78628

READ, RICHARD M., Mathematics Instructor; *b:* Spirit Lake, IA; *m:* Lola Lee Matthews; *c:* Bruce M., Bryan H.; *ed:* (BA) Math, IA St Teachers Coll 1959; (MA) Math, Univ of SD 1971; *cr:* HS Math Teacher Lake Park Cmmty Sch 1959-63; Mid Sch Math Teacher Estherville Cmmty Sch 1963-65; Jr HS Math Teacher Spirit Lake Cmmty Sch 1965-66; 8th-12th Grade Math Teacher Harris-Lake Park Cmmty Sch 1966-; *ai:* Stu Cncl Adv; Harris-Lake Park Ed Assn Pres, IA St Ed Assn, NEA, IA Math Teachers 1959-; Dickinson Cty Fairboard VP 1984-; Lake Park City Cncl 1987-; United Meth Church (Chm Admin Bd 1985-87, Finance Chm 1986-89); Nom by Supt for Teacher of Yr St Competition; 4-H Alumni Awd Dickinson Cty; *home:* 502 E Railroad St Lake Park IA 51347

READ, SHARON LOCKWOOD, Music Teacher; *b:* Hampton, VA; *ed:* (BA) Music Ed, NC Wesleyan Coll 1976; (MM) Music Ed, E Carolina Univ 1981; *cr:* 7th Grade Music Teacher Parker Mid Sch 1976-; *ai:* Music Educators Natl Conference; NC Music Educators Assn; *office:* Parker Mid Sch 1500 E Virginia St Rocky Mount NC 27801

REAGAN, MICHAEL L., Middle School English Teacher; *b:* Bloomington, IN; *m:* Janine K. Ford; *c:* Kathleen, David; *ed:* (BS) Elem Ed, 1978, (MS) Elem Ed, 1983 IN Univ; Write More Learn More Seminar; *cr:* 4th/5th Grade Teacher Stinesville Elem Sch 1979-83; Eng Teacher Edgewood Jr HS 1983-; *ai:* 8th Grade Ftbl, Asst HS Wrestling, Hoosier Spell Bowl Team Coach; Athletic Cncl Mem; 8th Grade & Class Trip Spon; IN St Teachers Assn, NEA 1979-; Clear Creek Chrstn Church Elder 1982-; *office:* Edgewood Jr HS Reeves Rd Ellettsville IN 47429

REALER, WENDY, 4th Grade Teacher; *b:* Philadelphia, PA; *ed:* (BA) Elem Ed, Cheyney St Univ; *cr:* 4th Grade Teacher Evans Cmptr Magnet Sch; *ai:* PSEA/NEA; *office:* Evans Cmptr Magnet Sch Church Ln And Bailey Rd Yeadon PA 19050

REALL, JUDITH SPURGEON, 6th Grade Teacher; *b:* Columbus, OH; *m:* Robert R.; *c:* Jennifer, R. Ronald; *ed:* (BS) Elem Ed 1961, (MA) Early & Mid Childhood 1985 Oh St Univ; OH Univ; *cr:* 4th/5th Grade Teacher Ohio Avenue Elem 1964-64; 4th/6th Grade Teacher Medill Elem 1969-84; 6th Grade Teacher West Elem 1984-87; Cedar Heights Elem 1987-; *ai:* Lancaster Ed Assn Pres 1969-; OH Ed Assn Resolutions Commission; NEA Delegate to Re Assem; *home:* 1661 George Rd NE Lancaster OH 43130

REAMES, SPENCER EUGENE, Science Department Chair; *b:* Bellefontaine, OH; *m:* Anne Marie Nicolosi; *c:* Aaron S.; *ed:* (BS) Comprehensive Sci, Bowling Green St Univ 1968; (MS) Bio, Ball St Univ 1978; Recombinant DNA IN Univ; Natl Sci Fnd Honors Wkshps & Summer Inst; *cr:* Teacher Benjamin Logan HS 1968-73; Asst Biotechnology Project Dir OH Acad of Sci 1989; Teacher/Dept Chm Benjamin Logan HS 1973-; *ai:* Local Sci Fair Dir; Sci Club Adv; St Sci Day Judging Co-Chm 1980-; NABT Outstanding Bio Teacher of OH 1984; Assn of Presidential Awardees in Sci Teaching Treas 1989-; OH Acad of Sci (Sci Ed VP 1983-84, Exec Bd Mem 1985-89), Acker Outstanding Teacher 1986; Amer Society for Microbio, Amer Assn Advancement of Sci, Entomological Society of America, NSTA, Phi Delta Kappa, Sci Ed Cncl of OH, Society for Invertebrate Pathology, Benjamin Logan Ed Assn, OH Ed Assn, NEA; Hi-Point Bsbl Assn Treas 1985-86; Logan Cty Solid Waste Management Policy Comm 1989-; Logan Cty Litter Prevention & Recycling Comm 1989-; W Cntrl Sci Day Cncl Pres 1979-; Presidential Awd Excl in Sci Teaching 1986; Amer Society of Biological Chem Biochemical Research Fellowship 1987; Dept of Energy Research Assoc Appointment 1990; *office:* Benjamin Logan HS Rt 47 E Bellefontaine OH 43311

REAMY, ANN HINES, English/Social Studies Teacher; *b:* Lynchburg, VA; *m:* Charles Pitt Ramsdell; *c:* Ann Dobyns Reamy Butts, Martha Pitt; *ed:* (BA) Elem Ed/His/Eng, Westhampton Coll 1957; (MS) Admin, Longwood Coll 1982; *cr:* Classroom Teacher Dumbarton Elem Sch 1957-59, S Hill Elem Sch 1965-67, Boydton Elem Sch 1967-80, Bluestone Mid Sch 1980-; *ai:* Eng Dept Chm; Forensic Team Chm Spon; 7th Grade Team of Teachers Leader; Trainer in Project Teach-Staff Dev Prgm; Mecklenburg Ed Assn Sch Rep; Delta Kappa Gamma Recording Secy; Daughters of Amer Revolution Mem; Boydton Meth Church Choir Mem.

REARDON, PATRICIA MILLER, Physical Education Teacher; *b:* Charlottesville, VA; *m:* Kevin Scott; *c:* Patrick M., Kathleen Scott; *ed:* (BS) Phys Ed, Longwood Coll 1977; *cr:* Phys Ed Teacher Stone-Robinson Elem Sch 1977-; *ai:* VAHPERD 1977-80, 1985-; AAHPERD 1977-79, 1988-; GSA Leader 1981-84; PTO Advisory Bd 1977, 1981; YMCA Bsktbl Coach 1981; Co-Chm Comm Developing Elem Phys Ed Curr Guide for Albemarle Cty 1984; Co-Presented Guide at St Phys Ed Convention 1985; *office:* Stone-Robinson Elem Sch Rt 9 Box 413 Charlottesville VA 22901

REARDON, R. PURVES, Principal; *b:* Holyoke, MA; *m:* Ellen D.; *c:* Jamie, Jan-Anne; *ed:* Liberal Arts, Holyoke Jr Coll 1964; (BA) Ed, Amer Intnl Coll 1966, (MA) Educl Psych, Amer Intnl Coll 1974; US Army 1968-70; Elem Sch Admi; *cr:* 6th Grade Teacher Chicopee Public Schls 1966-68 & 1970-87; VP Bowie/ Selser Sch 1987-88; Prin Anna E Barry Sch 1988-; *ai:* NEA; MTA; CEA; Disabled Amer Veterans 1970-; Veterans of Foreign Wars 1970-; *office:* Anna E Barry Sch Lagadia St Chicopee MA 01020

REAS, JOYCE HILL, Health Teacher; *b:* Allen, NE; *m:* Charles P.; *c:* Mike, Mark; *ed:* (BA) Phys Ed, Coll of ID 1957; Health Endorsement Certificate; *cr:* Sci/Phys Ed Teacher Siletz HS 1957-58; Phys Ed Teacher Baker HS 1958-59, Washington Jr HS 1959-63; Phys Ed/Health Teacher Burley Jr HS 1972-; *ai:* Vlybl Coach; Chrldr Adv; Building Advisory Comm; Knife & Fork Club; Delta Kappa Gamma (Pres 1972-74) 1988-; NEA, ID Ed Assn, Cassia Cty Ed Assn; PEO Pres; Womens Intnl Bowling Congress Life Mem.

REASER, JAMES ROBERT, Vocal Music/Choral Director; *b:* Muncy, PA; *m:* Janice Sue Reed; *c:* Amy J. Reaser Diggan, Michael B.; *ed:* (BA) Music Ed, Susquehanna Univ 1968; SUNY New Paltz, Westminster Choir Coll, Susquehanna Univ; *cr:* General Music/Choral Dir M J M Jr HS 1968-69; General Music/Voice/Choral Dir J W Bailey 1969-72; Elem/Sr HS Vocal/Choral Teacher Shikellamy Sch Dist 1972-74; Choral Dir/ Music Theory/Voice/Electronic Music Teacher Shikellamy HS 1974-; *ai:* Choir, Chorus, Jubilation Singers Choral Dir; MENC, PMEA Scndry Rep; ACDA, NEA, PSFA; Cub Scouts Father of Yr; *office:* Shikellamy HS 6th And Walnut Sts Sunbury PA 17801

REASNER, ANN L., English Department Chairperson; *b:* Clare, MI; *m:* Robert C.; *c:* Julia A. Gracik, Gerald J. Nivlson, James J. Nivison; *ed:* (BA) Eng/Fr, Cntrl MI UniV 1962; MI St Univ; *cr:* Teacher John Glenn HS 1962-66, Tawas Area HS 1972-; *ai:* Dept Chairperson Eng 1972; Forensic Coach-Dir 1977-87; NCTF 1962-; MI Cncl Teachers of Eng 1962-; Tawas Ed Assn Treas 1971-74; Delta Kappa Gamma 1st/2nd VP 1987-; MSU Teacher Roundtable 1987-; Teacher of Yr St of MI 1989; Distinguished Teacher Awd Northwood Inst 1990; *office:* Tawas Area H S 255 W M55 Tawas City MI 48763

REASNER, SUSAN LAMPHIER, Teacher; *b:* L Anse, MI; *m:* Raymond L.; *ed:* (BA) Soc Sci, 1973, (MA) General Classroom, 1980 MI St Univ; Instr Theory into Practice, Math Their Way; *cr:* Stu Teacher Amer Sch 1972; Intern Teacher Winans Elem 1972-73; Classroom Teacher Midway Elem 1973-75, Hale Elem 1975-; *ai:* Adult & Cmmty Ed Dir 1981-87; Hale Elem Stu Cncl Adv 1988-; Discipline Comm Chm 1988-; Iosco Rdng Cncl Membership Chm 1975-, Educator of Yr 1983; Delta Kappa Gamma Schlsp Chm 1981-; Phi Delta Kappa 1982-; Safari Club Intnl Sables 1989-; Cntrl MI Univ Supvr of Stu Teachers 1978-86; Nom MI Teacher of Yr 1984; Safari Club Intnl Amer Wilderness Leadership Sch Grant 1990; *office:* Hale Elem Sch 204 W Esmond Rd Hale MI 48739

REASON, DAVID VERLE, Math Department Chairman; *b:* Muncie, IN; *m:* Sharon Elaine Applegate; *c:* Darren, Angela; *ed:* (BS) Math, 1969, (MS) Math Ed,1974 Ball St Univ; *cr:* Math Teacher Wilson Mid Sch 1969-; *ai:* Academic Coach; Spon Young Astronauts, Chess Club; Drama Coach; Charge Variety Show; Muncie Teachers Assn Building Rep 1970; BSA Scoutmaster 1967 Silver Beaver Dist Awd of Merit 1976-82; Childrens Clothing Center Pres 1986-; Resource for Math Teachers Book; Muncie Jaycees Outstanding Service to Youth Awd; *office:* Wilson Mid Sch 2000 Franklin Muncie IN 47302

REASOR, KEVIN ARTHUR, 7th/8th Grade Teacher/Prin; *b:* Elmira, NY; *m:* Lynn Elizabeth Ballard; *c:* Arthur S., Stephen L.; *ed:* (BA) Soc Stud Composite, SW Union Coll 1971; (MED) Sch Admin, Cntrl St Univ of OK 1983; Scndry Soc Stud Composite TX; Prof/Scndry/Elem/Admin, N Amer Division 7th Day Adv; *cr:* Elem Teacher Beaver Memorial Jr Acad 1971-75; Prin/ Teacher Shattuck Jr Acad 1975-80; Jr HS/HS Teacher Parkview Adv Acad 1980-89; Prin/Teacher Crestview Adv Elem 1989-.

REAVIS, LO ETTA BATES, Second Grade Teacher; *b:* Ivenhoe, TX; *m:* M. R.; *c:* David B., Christopher T.; *ed:* (BS) Elem Ed, SE St Univ 1958; (MED) Elem Ed, E TX St Univ 1981; Numerous Wkshps; *cr:* 2nd Grade Teacher Fairview Elem 1958-59; 3rd Grade Teacher Midwest City OK 1959-63; 4th Grade Teacher L B Barton 1963-64; 2nd Grade Teacher Tatum Elem 1977-; *ai:* Kids Under Construction Spon; TX St Teachers Assn 1958-59, 1977-; Delta Kappa Gamma 1986-; PTO 1985-; 1st United Meth Church (Mem, Choir); *office:* Tatum Elem Sch 501 N Washington Farmersville TX 75031

REBBER, MARY LEE, English Teacher; *b:* New Harmony, IN; *m:* William; *c:* Jennifer, Julie; *ed:* (BS) Soc Stud/Eng, 1968, (MS) Psych, IN St Univ 1969; *cr:* Eng Teacher Lawrenceville HS 1969-70, Southport HS 1970-73, Perry Meridian HS 1973-; *ai:* Textbook Adoption Comm; Prof Assn Involvement; Perry Ed Assn (VP, Exec Bd); IN St Teacher Assn, NEA; *home:* 3917 Hilton Dr Indianapolis IN 46237

REBECK, DIANA POWELL, First Grade Teacher; *b:* Los Angeles, CA; *m:* Theodore Walter; *c:* Cynthia, Kathleen Young, Karen, Christina Heimann, Curtis, Kenneth; *ed:* (BA) Ed, CA St Univ Los Angeles 1952; Grad Work; *cr:* Teacher Jefferson Cty Schls 1952, Valle Vista Elem Sch 1962-; *home:* 2480 N Euclid Upland CA 91786

REBENSKY, RAYMOND A., JR., Journalism Teacher; *b:* Syracuse, NY; *ed:* (BA) Scndry Ed/Eng, St Univ of NY Geneseo 1974; *cr:* Behavior Assn Hillsbooough Assn for Retarded Citizens 1975-76; Teacher Montanarie Clinical Sch 1976-77, Gulf HS 1977-; *ai:* Yrbk & Newspaper Adv; Cmptr Teacher Adult Ed; United Sch Employees of Pasco Cty Rep 1979-; Cmptr Software Evaluations Published FL Center for Instructional Computing Review Magazine 1986; *office:* Gulf HS 5355 School Rd New Port Richey FL 34652

REBHAN, DOTTIE ANN, 6th Grade Teacher; *b:* Salisbury, NC; *ed:* (AB) Elem Ed, Lenoir Rhyne Coll 1968; *cr:* 6th Grade Teacher Clear Creek Sch 1968-69, Jackson Park Elem 1969-89, Woodrow Wilson Elem 1989-; *ai:* Co-Authored Sixth Grade Resource Curr Notebook Kannapolis City Schls; NC Assn of Educators 1968-; Intl Rdng Assn 1969-; Sacred Heart Cath Church Cncl Pres 1989-; Rowan Rose Society Pres 1984-86; Nom Teacher of Yr 1971-73; *home:* 209 Hillcrest Pl Salisbury NC 28144

REBISCHKE, M. JILL VOGLER, Physical Education Teacher; *b:* Platteville, WI; *m:* James; *c:* Travis, Cody; *ed:* (BA) Phys Ed, Univ of WY 1979; Grad Work Towards Masters; *cr:* 10th-12th Grade Phys Ed Teacher D C Everest Sr HS 1979-; *ai:* Head Girls Tennis Coach; Stu-Athlete Resource Prgm; Schlsp Comm; US Tennis Assn 1984-; D C Everest Teachers Assn, WI Ed Assn 1979-; Church Sunday Sch Teacher 1988-; Nom Teacher of Yr 1989 Everest Sch Dist; *office:* D C Everest Sr HS 6500 Alderson St Schofield WI 54476

REBUCK, RICHARD HUGH, Physics Teacher; *b:* Chambersburg, PA; *m:* Carol Graham; *c:* David, Richard, Sherri; *ed:* (BSED) Physics/Math, 1963, (MED) Physics, 1968 Shippensburg Univ 1968; Millersville Univ, West Chester Univ, Miami Univ of FL, PA St Univ; *cr:* Physics Teacher John Dickinson HS 1964-66, Shippensburg Area Sr HS 1966-; *ai:* Chess Club Spon; Assembly Comm; NEA, PSEA, SAEA 1966-; AAPT 1968-; Grace United Church of Christ (Consistory 1970-76, Mem) 1953-; Red Cross Drive Co-Chm; Electro-Optics Test Engr AMP Cor; *home:* 11173 Spring Ridge Rd Shippensburg PA 17257

RECESKI, STANLEY JOSEPH, Fourth Grade Teacher; *b:* Indiana, PA; *m:* Nancy L.; *c:* Mitchell; *ed:* (BA) Elem Ed, 1970, (MS) Elem Ed, 1971 Indiana Univ of PA; *cr:* 4th-6th Grade Teacher Marion Center Area Schs 1971-; *ai:* Stu Cncl Spon; PSEA, NEA (Building Rep 1987-, Chief Negotiator 1988-89); *home:* Rd 6 Box 348-A Indiana PA 15701

RECK, NANCY JANE, 5th Grade Teacher; *b:* Greenville, OH; *m:* John K.; *c:* Jessica, Jenna; *ed:* (BS) Elem Ed, Olivet Nazarene Univ 1973; Miami Univ; *cr:* 6th Grade Teacher 1973-86, 5th Grade Teacher 1986- C R Coblentz Mid Sch; *ai:* NEA & CCTA 1973-; Greenville Music Club 1983-; Presbyn Church Mem 1985-; Honored at Eaton Childrens Home on Teacher Appreciation Day by Former Stu; *office:* C R Coblentz Mid Sch 9088 Monroe-Central Rd West Manchester OH 45382

RECKER, MARY A., High School English Teacher; *b:* West Union, IA; *m:* Loran C.; *c:* Valerie K., Sarah M., Elizabeth A.; *ed:* (BA) Eng, Coll of St Teresa 1973; (MSE) Effective Teaching, Drake Univ 1989; *cr:* 7th/8th Grade Eng Teacher Oelwein Jr HS 1973-77; Substitute Eng Teacher 1985-86, 10th Grade Eng Teacher 1986-87 Charles City HS; 9th/11th Grade Eng Teacher Riceville HS 1987-; *ai:* NHS Riceville Chapter Adv; Soph Class Spon; Riceville Ed Assn, IA St Ed Assn, NEA 1973-77, 1987-; Amer Assn of Univ Women (EFP Fund Chm 1988, 1989) 1985-; Gourmet Club Group Chm 1985-.

RECKIN, GENE, Science Teacher/Dept Chair; *b:* La Jolla, CA; *m:* Lenora Spencer; *c:* Kara, Rachel; *ed:* (BS) Wildlife Bio, 1977, (BA) Botany, 1979 Univ of MT; *cr:* Sci Teacher Libby Jr HS 1980-; *ai:* Jr HS Boys Bsktbl Coach; NEA, MT Sci Teachers Assn; *office:* Libby Jr HS 101 Ski Rd Libby MT 59923

RECKNER, RAYMOND E., JR., Sixth Grade Teacher; *b:* Johnstown, PA; *m:* Pamela R. Gindlesperger; *c:* Krista, Mitchell; *ed:* (BS) Elem Ed, 1971, (MS) Elem Ed, 1974 Clarion St Coll; ITEC Cmptr Course; *cr:* Elem Teacher Brockway Area Sch Dist 1971-; *ai:* Head Ftbl Coach 1985-; Jr HS Ftbl Coach 1973-85; Asst Var Wrestling Coach 1973-; Jim Kellys Celebrity Ftbl Camp 1989-; Brookway Area Ed Assn (VP 1984-85) 1971-; PA St Ed Assn, NEA 1971-; PA Ftbl Coaches Assn 1987-; Little 12 Ftbl Conference Coach of Yr 1986; *office:* Brockway Area Sch Dist 95 North St Brockway PA 15824

RECORD, LINDA MARLENE, First Grade Teacher; *b:* Marion, IN; *m:* Jack M.; *c:* Laurie M., Kelly R., Amy M.; *ed:* (BS) Elem Ed, 1972, (MA) Elem Ed, Ball St 1977; Wkshps Trng Seminar TESA Austin IN Univ; Wkshp Way Week Trng Session; Assertive Discipline Wkshp; *cr:* 2nd Grade Teacher 1972-76, 1st Grade Teacher 1977- Riverview Elem; *ai:* Writer Rdng Curr Comm; Co-Authored 1st Grade Rdng Prgm; Delta Kappa Gamma Beta Iota Chapter 1985-; Marion Teachers Assn Building Rep 1972-; NEA/ISTA; Grant United Meth Church Asst Supt 1975-; PTO Park Elem 1977-; *home:* 10436 S 350 E Fairmount IN 46928

RECORD, LUCI LAGARTO, English Teacher; *b:* Pawtucket, RI; *m:* James E.; *c:* James, Stephen, Lauren; *ed:* (BS) Eng/Scndry Ed, Boston Univ 1965; Working Towards Masters Eng, Bridgewater Coll; *cr:* Eng Teacher Bristol HS 1965-71, Silver Lake HS 1982-; *ai:* Cable Broadcast Club Adv; Steering Comm, NEASC; Sr Class Adv; Delta Kappa Gamma VP 1990; MTA 1982-, MTA-DEL 1988-; NCTE Silver Lake Ed Assn; Horace Mann Grant 1989-; *office:* Silver Lake Regional HS 32 Pembroke St Kingston MA 02364

RECTOR, GERRY TOMLINSON, 4th-6th Grade Teacher; *b:* Crocker, MO; *m:* James E. Jr.; *c:* Dorothy, James III, Howard, Jason, Benjamin; *cr:* Teacher Immaculate Conception Sch 1968-70; Substitute Teacher Camdenton RIII Schls 1970-78; Legal Secy Janice P Noland Atty 1978-81; Teacher Camden Chrstn Sch 1981-; *ai:* Childrens Church; Choir; Dramatics Dir; Yrbk Adv; Vlybl Coach; Remedial Rdng & Math Instruction; *office:* Camden Chrstn Sch P O Box 341 Hwy 5 South Camdenton MO 65020

RECTOR, MELODY HERMAN, Marketing Teacher; *b:* Gastonia, NC; *m:* Timothy Mark; *ed:* (BS) Mrktg Ed, Winthrop Coll 1986; *cr:* Teacher Orange HS 1986-; *ai:* DECA Adv; NCAE, Mrktg Educators Assn; *office:* Orange HS 500 Orange High Rd Hillsborough NC 27278

REDD, BETTY JO (MILLER), Kindergarten Teacher; *b:* Elk City, OK; *c:* Tana Jo; *ed:* (BS) Bus/Home Ec, 1966; (MS) Elem Ed, 1968 SWSC; *cr:* 5th Grade Teacher Cheyenne OK; Handicapped Teacher Albuquerque NM; Kndgtn Teacher Butler OK; Hammon OK; *ai:* FHA Mother; Class Parent; OEA Mem; NEA Mem; HEA; YHO Pres; HEA VP; *home:* Box 135 Hammon OK 73650

REDD, PATRICIA MOORE, Assistant Principal; *b:* De Kalb, MS; *m:* James Cecil Jr.; *c:* Summer R.; *ed:* (BA) Elem Ed, MS Univ for Women 1972; (MS) Elem Ed, Univ of Montevallo 1976; EDS Sch Admin, Univ of Montevallo 1990; *cr:* 4th Grade Teacher 1973-77, 3rd Grade Teacher 1979-86 Southside Elem; 4th Grade Teacher/Asst Prin Brantley Mid Sch 1986-88; Asst Prin Southside Elem 1988-; *ai:* Delta Kappa Gamma 1985-; Kappa Delta Phi 1989-; *office:* Southside Elem Sch 3104 Old Montgomery Hwy Selma AL 36701

REDDEMANN, SANDRA LEE (SOBEL), 9th-12th Grade English Teacher; *b:* Milwaukee, WI; *m:* James; *c:* Andrew Karsh, Elizabeth Karsh Brown; *ed:* (BS) Eng/His, Univ WI Madison 1960; (MS) Ed, Natl Coll of Ed 1988; *cr:* 7th/8th Grade His/Eng Teacher Hillel Acad 1966-71; 8th Grade His/Eng Teacher Bayside

Elem Sch 1971-72; 9th Grade His/Eng Teacher WI Hills Mid Sch 1972-77; 9th-12th Grade Eng Teacher Brookfield E HS 1977-; *ai:* Yrbk Adv; Group Facilitator of Stu Assistance Group on Drug Usage; Phi Beta Kappa; Menomonee Falls Pre-Sch Cooperative (Co-Founder, Pres) 1964-65; Creativity in Teaching Awd for Teachers of Eng WI Schls 1977; Articles Published; *office:* Brookfield E HS 3305 N Lilly Rd Brookfield WI 53005

REDDEN, BOYD J., Fourth Grade Teacher; *b:* Upalco, UT; *m:* Arva M. Tanner; *c:* Lyle B., Frances P. Beckstrom, Gary J., Rashelle Richardson; *ed:* (BA) Voc Ag, 1957, (BA) Smith Hughes Voc Certificate, 1957, (BA) Elem Ed, 1960 UT St Univ; Working Towards Masters; *cr:* Voc Ag Instr Jordan HS 1957-59; Ag Chemist Jensen Sandberg Inc 1959-62; 5th/6th Grade Teacher Davis Sch Dist 1962-67; 4th-6th Grade Teacher Uintah Sch Dist 1968-; *ai:* Sci & Soc Stud Clubs; Festival of The Arts; Cnty Fair Comm; Square Dancing Teacher; UT Ed Assn Various Local Offices 1957-; LDS Church Various Offices 1957-; Dinah Square Dancers (Dist III Pres 1989-, Dist III VP 1988-89, Various Local Offices 1968-); US Army 1953-55; Sears Roebuck Ag Schlsp 1950; *office:* Naples Elem Sch 1971 S 1500 E Vernal UT 84078

REDDICK, BRENDA CAROL LIGON, Fourth Grade Teacher; *b:* Bells, TN; *m:* James Elvin; *c:* Melissa A. Reddick Washington; *ed:* (BA) Elem Ed, Lambuth 1982; *cr:* Teacher Crockett Cty Elem 1971-83, Alamo Elem 1983-; *ai:* Crockett Cty Ed Assn, NEA 1971-; Teachers Welfare Comm 1988-; W TN Ed Assn Advisory Cncl VP 1982-84; PTA Reporter 1988-; Foster Care Review Bd 1988-; Alamo Elem Sch Teacher of Yr 1986; *home:* Rt 2 Box 56 Alamo TN 38001

REDDICK, DONALD, Band Dir/Fine Art Dept Chair; *b:* Nashville, TN; *m:* Dena Owen; *c:* Britney L., Blake O.; *ed:* (BS) Music Ed, Olivet Nazarene Univ 1979; (MS) Music Ed, Univ of IL 1988; *cr:* Band Dir RUCE Dist #3 1979-82, Kankakee Dist #111 1982-; *ai:* MENC 1984-; Kankakee Municipal Band 1988-; *office:* Kankakee Dist #111 240 Warren Ave Kankakee IL 60901

REDDICK, GLADYS THOMPSON, Sixth Grade Teacher; *b:* Camilla, GA; *m:* James A.; *c:* Jerome A., Adrienne D.; *ed:* (BS) Elem Ed, 1965, (MS) Mid Grade Ed, 1985 Albany St Coll; *cr:* Home Sch Visitor Clover Park Sch Dist 1973-75; 6th Grade Teacher Dougherty Cty Bd of Ed 1978-; *ai:* SECME & Invent America Building Coord; Sci & Engineering Club Spon; Intnl Rdng Assn Comm Chairperson; Natl Assn of Educators 1978-; GA Assn of Educators 1978-; DEAE 1978-.

REDDICK, IRIS LODGE, Fourth Grade Teacher; *b:* Washington, NC; *m:* Matthew E.; *c:* Bryan; *ed:* (BS) Elem Ed, Elizabeth City St Univ 1970; Rdng Cert/Ecu; *cr:* 6th Grade Teacher John Small Elem Sch 1970-75; 3rd Grade Teacher John Cotten Tayloe Elem Sch 1975-82; 4th Grade Teacher John Cotten Tayloe Elem Sch 1982-; *ai:* Lead Teacher 4th Grade, Screening Comm, Discipline Comm, John Cotten Taloe Sch; Task Force Rep Washington City Sch; NEA 1970-; NCAE Bldg Rep 1970-; Diamondnetts Civic Club Pres 1980-84 Mem of Yr 1982; Washington City Sch Teacher of Yr 1986; *office:* Washington City Schools 102 E 2nd St Washington NC 27889

REDDING, HELEN ALFORD, Choral Director; *b:* Monroe, LA; *m:* Robert V.; *c:* Daniel, Kate, Jenny; *ed:* (BM) Sch Music, SW at Memphis 1971; *cr:* Choral Dir Southern HS 1971-74, Mc Nairy Cntrl 1984-; *ai:* Soph Class Spon; Fine Arts Dept Chm; Selmer Mid Sch Choral Dir; Academic Decathlon Team Coach 1988-; Selmer Jr Civic League Ways & Means Chm 1980; Stephen Foster Music Club; 1st Meth Church Organist 1979-; TN Art Commission Grants Awarded 1989, 1990; Stu TN Ed Assn Outstanding Service Awd; *home:* 281 Mollie Dr Selmer TN 38375

REDDING, JOSEPH DWAYNE, Band Director/Music Teacher; *b:* Breckenridge, TX; *m:* Dorothy Ann Vogel; *c:* Kathryn D., Eric D.; *ed:* (BME) Music, Sam Houston St Univ 1970, (MM) Music, Midwestern St Univ 1979; *cr:* Band Dir/Music Teacher City View ISD 1974-; *ai:* Band Dir; TX Music Educators Assn 1975-; Several Yrs As Instr Midwestern St Univ Summer Band Camp; 2 Yrs Volunteering for The Wichita Falls Cmmty Band; Adult Volunteer with Boy Scouts Many Years; *office:* City View I.S.D. 1023 City View Dr Wichita Falls TX 76305

REDER, CONSTANCE KLEINDORFER, 5th Grade Teacher; *b:* Indianapolis, IN; *m:* Michael L.; *c:* Curt, Anne; *ed:* (BS) Elem Ed, IN Univ 1973; (MS) Elem Ed, IN Univ/Purdue Univ 1977; *cr:* 4th Grade Teacher Culver Elem 1973-74; 6th Grade Teacher Greenfield Mid Sch 1974-75; 5th Grade Teacher Harris Elem 1975-89; *ai:* ISTA 1973-89; Greenfield Classroom Teachers 1974-89; Bradley Meth Church Choir 1977-89; Cub Scout Leader 1988-89; Pi Lambda Theta; *office:* Harris Elem Sch 200 W Park Ave Greenfield IN 46140

REDGRAVE, PAT B., 2nd Grade Teacher; *b:* St Cloud, FL; *c:* Patti; *ed:* (BA) Elem Ed, FL St Univ 1951; *cr:* 3rd Grade Teacher Apopka Elem 1951; 1st-3rd Grade Teacher Osceola Cty; 2nd Grade Teacher Ft Pierce Elem, Thacker Avenue Elem; *ai:* OCTA, FTP; Delta Kappa Gamma, PTO; Silver Spurs Secy; Jr Womans Club, Beta Sigma Phi Pres; *office:* Thacker Avenue Elem Sch 301 Thacker Ave Kissimmee FL 34741

REDLIN, ROBERT P., Junior High Teacher; *b:* Sidney, MT; *m:* Lois Tweed; *c:* Kelsey Redlin Kintner, Tim, Mark, Kathy Hermanson, Kristi, Joel, David; *ed:* (BS) His, Minot St 1954; (MS) Elem Ed, Univ of ND Grand Forks 1973; Ed Courses; *cr:* Jr HS Sci Teacher 1957-67, Jr HS Teacher/Prin 1967-78, Jr HS Soc Stud Teacher/Basic Skills 1978- Divide Cty Dist 1; *ai:* Quarterback Club Membership Chm; NEA, NDEA 1957-; Jaycees 1955-60; Luth Brotherhood Mens Club; Concordia Luth Church Cncl; *home:* 6 NE 4th St Crosby ND 58730

REDLINGER, LAURIE FELGENHAUER, 7th Grade Soc Stud Teacher; *b:* Blue Island, IL; *m:* John E.; *c:* Kristin, Ryan; *ed:* (BA) His/Ed, W IL Univ 1968; (MS) Regional Stud, Augustana Coll 1985; Post Grad Stud N IL Univ, W IL Univ; *cr:* 7th Grade Soc Stud Teacher Rockridge Jr HS 1968-; *ai:* Cheerleading Spon; Asst HS Girls Track & Vlybl Coach; NEA, IEA; *office:* Rockridge Jr HS 14110 134th Ave W Taylor Ridge IL 61284

REDMAN, AMANDA SCHOEB, Kindergartn/Elem Music Teacher; *b:* Cherokee, OK; *m:* L. H.; *c:* Alyssa, Miles; *ed:* (BS) Elem Ed, OK St Univ 1973; *cr:* Kndgtn/Elem Music Teacher Helena-Goltry Schls 1973-; *ai:* OEA 1973-; Alfalfa Cty Ed Assn (VP 1976-77 Sec/Treas 1978-79); Delta Kappa Gamma Recording Secy 1988-; Helena Meth Church Organist 1973-; Jr Homemakers Pres 1983; OK St Univ Alumni Assn Cty (Secy/Treas 1988); Helena-Goltry Ed Assn Teacher of Yr 1983.

REDMON, ALICE PRESSGROVE, 8th Grade Lang Arts Teacher; *b:* Shelbyville, TN; *m:* Larry; *c:* Randi R.; *ed:* (BS) Elem Ed, 1970, (ME) Curr/Instruction, 1979, Ed Specialist Curr/Instruction, 1986 Mid TN Univ; *cr:* Sch Secy 1958-61, Teachers Aide 1964-67, 5th Grade Teacher 1968-69 Eagleville Sch; Title I Rdng/2nd-6th Grade Teacher Coll Grove Sch 1970-83; Eng/Rdng/Sci Teacher Page Mid Sch 1983-; *ai:* Williamson Cty Ed Assn, TN Ed Assn, NEA 1970-; Eagleville Church of Christ 1957-; Williamson Cty Mid Sch Teacher of Yr 1990; *office:* Page Mid Sch 6262 Arno Rd Franklin TN 37064

REDMOND, ALAN D., General Science Teacher; *b:* Roanoke, VA; *ed:* (EDS) Ed Admin, 1981, (MA) Ed Admin, 1977, (BS) Sci Ed, 1975 E TN St Univ; *cr:* Sci Teacher/Coach 1975-80, Asst Prin 1980-81, General Sci Teacher/Soccer Coach 1981- John Sevier Mid Sch; *ai:* Head Soccer Coach; Co-Dir Kingsport Summer Sci Challenge Prgm; Leader of 10 Environmental Trips; Sci Assn of TN (Exec Bd, Exec Comm) 1990; NSTA 1975-, Star Awd 1981; KEA, TEA, NEA Local Exec Bd 1975-; Kingsport Youth Soccer 1981-; Bays Mountain Park Naturalist Volunteer 1982-; Kingsport Fun Fest Organizer Sci Funshops 1985-; St Winner Presidential Awd for Excl in Sci Teaching 1987; TN Level III Teacher 1986; Sigma Xi Scientific Research Society Teacher of Yr 1986; Personalities of America 1984; TN Outstanding Achievement Awd Nashville 1984; *office:* John Sevier Mid Sch 1200 Wateree St Kingsport TN 37660

REDOLPHY, LENORE JACOBSON, 6th Grade Teacher; *b:* Utica, NY; *c:* Lisa Siegel; *ed:* (BA) Elem Ed, St Univ of NY Plattsburg 1956; Post Grad Work SUNY Binghamton; *cr:* 5th Grade Teacher Baldwinsville Cntrl Schls 1956-58; 3rd/5th-6th Grade Teacher Binghamton Sch Dist 1958-61; 6th Grade Teacher Vestal Cntrl Schls 1962-; *ai:* Mem Asst Supt Interview Comm; Athletic Team Supvr Var Girls Soccer; Scorekeeping Boys/Girls Bsktbl, Sftbl; Curr Dev Comm; Dir Class Trips NY City; Vestal Teachers Assn; NEA, NYEA: Tioga Hills PTA Honoree Cncl Dist Schlsp 1979; Natl Geographic Society Summer Inst SUNY Binghamton 1989; *home:* 608 June St Endicott NY 13760

REECE, FRONCELL, Ag-Science Technology Teacher; *b:* Willis, TX; *m:* Dorothy A. Weaver; *c:* Garry F., Yolanda D. Reece Montez; *ed:* (BS) Ag Ed, 1949, (MS) Ag Ec, 1950 Prairie View A&M Univ; Prairie View A&M Univ, TX A&M Univ, Sam Houston St Univ, TX Tech Univ; *cr:* Ag Teacher/Coach Willis Ind Sch Dist 1957, Cameron Ind Sch Dist 1957-59; Athletic Dir/Coach Crosby Ind Sch Dist 1959; Coach/Math Teacher 1960-63, Ag-Sci Teacher 1963- Conroe Ind Sch Dist; *ai:* Conroe FFA Adv; Conroe Young Farmers Dairy, Meat, Forestry Judging Teams; Jr/Sr Chapter Conducting Leadership Teams; Dist Chm Amer Farmer Degree Comm; TX Voc Ag Teachers Assn 1953-, Service Awd 1967, 1972, 1977, 1982, 1987; Natl Voc Ag Teachers Assn 1953-, Minute Club Awd 1979, Teaching Conservation Citation 1973, Honary Membership 1969, St Farmer Awd 1969; Prof Ag Workers of TX 1959-; TX St Teachers Assn 1952-; Assn of TX Prof Educators 1990; Metropolitan Day Care Inc (Bd of Dirs, Treas) 1968-, Appreciation 1988; Kiwanis Club Friendly City Conroe Charter Mem, Citation 1990; Montgomery Cty Fair Assn 1969, Life Mem; Conroe Area Youth Bsbl 1954-84; BSA 1948-70; Won St Sr Chapter Conduct in Leadership 1975, 2nd Place 1973, 3rd Place 1972; Ag Ed Magazine Publication 1979; TX Assn of FFA Leadership Citation 1977, Adv Honor Awd 1978; Natl FFA Honorary Amer Farmer Degree 1987; Prairie View A&M Distinguished Agriculture Alumni Signal Service Awd 1989; Coach St Champs Ftbl & Bsbl 1960, 1963, Boys & Girls Track 1958; *office:* Conroe HS 1712 Wilson Rd Conroe TX 77304

REECE, JAMES RANDALL, Asst to the Deputy Supt; *b:* Marietta, GA; *m:* Jessica Green; *ed:* (BS) His/Ed, 1975, (MS) Admin/Supervision, 1982, (EDS) Admin/Supervision, 1983 Univ of GA; *cr:* Soc Stud Teacher Garrett Mid Sch 1975-82; 6th-7th Grade Target Teacher 1982-85, Admin Asst 1985-86 J J Daniell Mid Sch; Asst Prin E Cobb Mid Sch 1986-88; Asst to the Deputy Supt Cobb Cty Sch Dist 1988-; *ai:* Phi Delta Kappa 1983-; Cobb Cty Admin Assn 1985-; GA Assn of Sch Personnel Admin 1988-; Cobb Cty Chamber of Commerce Ed Steering Comm 1988; Natl Sci Fnd Grant Emory Univ 1978; *office:* Cobb Cty Sch Dist 514 Glover St PO Box 1088 Marietta GA 30061

REECE, MARTHA BRACKEEN, First Grade Teacher; *b:* Athens, AL; *m:* James Milburn;; *c:* Sherry Schrimsher, Terry, Ramona Foster; *ed:* Assoc Elem Ed, Calhoun Coll 1975; (BS) Elem Ed, Athens St Coll 1976; (MA) Elem Ed, UNA 1978; *cr:* Rdng Aide West Limestone Sch 1971-75; 5th Grade Teacher Mooresville-Belle Mina 1976; 1st Grade Teacher West Limestone Sch 1977-; *ai:* LCEA, AEA 1976-; NEA 1977-; Amer Legion Ladies Aux 1987-; Amer Arthritis Fnd Cmmty Chairperson 1987-89; Limestone Cty Elem Teacher of Yr 1988-89; *office:* West Limestone Sch Rt 1 Box 99 Lester AL 35647

REECE, SHIRLEY JOHNSON, Fifth Grade Teacher; *b:* Columbia, TN; *m:* William Henry Sr.; *ed:* (BS) Elem Ed, 1969, (ME) Admin/Supervision 1979, Admin/Supervision 1983 TN St Univ; *cr:* 4th Grade Teacher Stanford Elem 1969-83, Pennington Elem 1983-89; 5th Grade Teacher Tulip Grove 1989-; *ai:* 4-H Club Leader; Spec Events Comm & Faculty Advisory Comm Recorder; Teacher of Yr Pennington Elem 1985; Natl Sci Fnd Grant Vanderbilt Univ 1988-89; *office:* Tulip Grove 441 Tyler Dr Nashville TN 37076

REECE, TONI BERNHEIM, Band Director; *b:* Far Rockaway, NY; *m:* Earnest R. Jr.; *c:* Adrienne N.; *ed:* (BME) Music Ed, Univ of MS 1985; *cr:* Band Dir Hunt Jr HS, Joe Cook Jr HS, Stephen D Lee HS 1985-; *ai:* Flag & Rifle Instr & Coord; Sch Improvement Comm; Academic Decathalon Coach; Jazz Band Dir; Color Guard Instr Coll Band Camps; MS Band Masters 1985-, A E Mc Clain 1988; NE MS HS Assn 1985-; NE Jr HS (Treas, Secy) 1990; Natl Womens Band Dir Assn 1986-; Outstanding Young Women of America 1989; Outstanding Young Band Dir Awd 1988; *office:* Stephen D Lee HS 1815 Military Rd Columbus MS 39701

REED, BOB, English Department Chair; *b:* Dallas, TX; *m:* Gaye Herring; *ed:* (BA) Eng, 1971, (MA) Eng, 1976 N TX St Univ; Grad Stud Phys Ed; *cr:* Teacher Dunbar Mid Sch 1971-76, Paschal HS 1976-; *ai:* Outdoor Adventure & Awareness Class; Creative Writing; Literary Magazine Spon; Ft Worth Area Cncl Teachers of Eng Teacher of Yr 1984; N TX St Univ Outstanding Alumnus 1985; NCTE Natl Center for Excl Awd; Article Published 1982; Ft Worth Star-Telegraph Frequent Book Reviewer; *office:* R L Paschal HS 3001 Forest Pk Blvd Fort Worth TX 76110

REED, CAROLYN WISE, Fifth Grade Teacher; *b:* Yuma, AZ; *m:* James Cabell; *c:* Gregory, Jonathan; *ed:* (BA) Elem Ed, Univ of AZ 1983; *cr:* 5th Grade Teacher Flowing Wells Sch Dist 1983-88, Catalina Foothills Sch Dist 1988-; *ai:* NEA 1983-88; AZ Ed Assn 1983-88; Flowing Wells Ed Assn Bldg Rep 1984-86; AZ Prof Ed 1988-89; Exemplary Teacher Status 1988-89; Catalina Foothills Prgm Stu Store Selected for AZ Quality Prgms; Practices System 1987; *office:* Catalina Foothills Sch Dist 2101 E River Rd Tucson AZ 85718

REED, CARREL JOSEY, English/Journalism Teacher; *b:* Camden, TX; *m:* Charles Ray; *c:* Earl R. Hudson; *ed:* (BA) Scndry Ed, E TX Baptist Univ 1978; (MA) Eng, Sam Houston St Univ 1982; *cr:* Teacher Corrigan-Camden Ind Sch Dist 1979-; *ai:* NHS Adv; UIL Spon; HS Coord; NCTE; TX Joint Cncl Teachers of Eng; Order of Eastern Star (Worthy Matron 1973, Membership) 1970-; TX Excl Awd for Outstanding HS Teachers; *office:* Corrigan-Camden HS S Home St Box 01060 Corrigan TX 75939

REED, CONNIE JEANETTE, Chapter I Reading Lab Teacher; *b:* Elizabeth, WV; *m:* Timothy Paul; *ed:* (BA) Early Chldhd Ed, Glenville St Coll 1977; (MA) Rdng, WV Univ 1983; APL, Effective Schls, ECRI; *cr:* 3rd/4th Grade Teacher 1977-78, 1st/2nd Grade Teacher 1978-79 Newark Elem Sch; 1st Grade Teacher 1979-86, Chapter I Rdng Lab Teacher 1986- Elizabeth Elem Sch; *ai:* Odyssey of The Mind Coach; Literacy Volunteer; Delta Kappa Gamma Membership Comm 1982-; NHS VP; OES 1982-; White Shrine 1984-; Brownie Leader Co-Leader 1981-84, 15 Yr Pin 1983; WV Schlsp; Best Performance in A Childrens Play Awd; *office:* Elizabeth Elem Sch PO Box 220 Elizabeth WV 26143

REED, CONSTANCE LORRAINE, Sixth Grade Teacher; *b:* Long Branch, NJ; *m:* David Allen; *c:* Kimberly, Natalee, David; *ed:* (BS) Elem Ed, Monmouth Coll 1970; *cr:* 4th Grade Teacher 1970-71, 2nd Grade Teacher 1971-73 Bangs Avenue Sch; 6th Grade Teacher Lakewood Bd of Ed Mid Sch 1973-76, Princeton Avenue Sch 1976-; *ai:* Home Tutoring; Lakewood Ed Assn 1973-; NJ Ed Assn 1970-; Ocean Cty Chapter Jack & Jill (Teen Adv 1988-89, Treas 1987-); Ladies of Alpha Phi Alpha (Sunshine Chm 1987-89, Secy 1989-), Cmmty Service 1989; Governor Keans Teacher Recognition Awd 1988-89; Lakewood Bd of Ed Certificate of Appreciation 1989; *office:* Princeton Avenue Sch Princeton Ave Lakewood NJ 08701

REED, DIANE THOMPSON, 4th Grade Teacher; *b:* Paducah, KY; *m:* Wesley Gene; *c:* Johnna; *ed:* (BS) Elem Ed, 1979, (MA) Elem Ed, 1983, (Rank I) Guidance, 1987 Murray St Univ; *cr:* 4th Grade Teacher Reidland Elem 1980-; *ai:* Yrbk Ed 1980-86; Ec Ed Consultant 1987-; Mc Cracken Cty Ed Assn Rep, Intl Rdng Assn Mem, KY Ed Assn, NEA, KY Cncl Soc Stud KY Ec Educators 1980-; Joint Cncl Ec Ed 1987-, 1st Place Winner, St Level Honorable Awd; *office:* Reidland Elem Sch 5741 Benton Rd Paducah KY 42003

REED, DIANNE ECKLER, Science Department Chair; *b:* Cincinnati, OH; *m:* Clifford A.; *ed:* (BA) Scndry Ed/Bio, Univ of KY 1972; (MA) Scndry Ed/Bio, N KY Univ 1979; *cr:* Sci Teacher Grant Cty HS 1972-; *ai:* Sci Club, A Team, Jr Soil Conservation Adv; Sr Class Spon; Academic Coach; NABT, NSTA, PDK; *office:* Grant Cty HS US 25 Dry Ridge KY 41035

REED, ELLA JEANNETTA WOOLSEY, Sixth Grade Teacher; *b:* Lone Wolf, OK; *m:* Vernon E.; *c:* Vicki L. Abbott, Karen B. Doudy, Dana A. Fosmire, Mark E.; *ed:* (BA) Elem Ed, 1971, (MA) Elem Ed, 1980 Adams St Coll; Post Grad Work Several Univ; Certified Spalding Teacher Instr 1988; *cr:* Chapter I Teacher Antonito Elem 1971-72; 6th Grade Math Teacher Evans Elem 1972-73; 4th Grade Teacher East Elem 1973-75; 4th/6th

Grade Teacher Lewis-Arriola 1975-; Teacher Trainer Spalding Ed Fnd 1988-; *ai:* Dist Rdng, Steering Comm; Tutoring in Lang Art; NHS Pres 1970-71, Cum Laude 1971; Phi Delta Kappa 1979-84; M-C Intnl Rdng Assn (VP, Pres); GSA (Leader, Trainer) 1961-69; Primitive Baptist Church Mem 1949-; Academic Schlsp ASC 1969-71; Climax Molybdenum Summer Study Fellowship 1979; CO Teacher Honorable Mention 1988; *home:* 13106 CR 21 Cortez CO 81321

REED, EMILY FOORE, Mathematics/Gifted Instructor; *b:* Huntingdon, PA; *m:* Jay; *c:* Bradley, Eric, Miranda; *ed:* (BS) Math, Shippensburg Univ 1963; Math & Ed Courses for Cert; Transactional Analysis; Teaching Through Learning Channels; Patterns for IDEAS; *cr:* Teacher Spring Cove Dist 1963-64, N Bedford Cty Dist 1964-66, Everett Area Sch Dist 1967-; *ai:* Dir Saturday Satellite Gifted Ed Prgm for Frostburg St Coll; Teach GED Classes to Adults for Altoona Area Sch Dist; PA Assn Gifted Ed; Gifted & Talented Ed 1982-84; Lead Teacher 1989-; PA Reflexology Assn VP 1988; Play Piano & Sing with Joyland Singers 1986-; Nom for Educator of Yr; Published Study Prgm in Basic Math; *office:* Everett Area HS North River Ln Everett PA 15537

REED, EULLALEE, Sixth Grade Teacher; *b:* Petersburg, MI; *m:* Carlos R.; *c:* David, Randy, John; *ed:* (BS) Soc Sci - Cum Laude, 1970; (MA) Elem Ed, 1974 E MI Univ; *cr:* 6th Grade Teacher Custer Elem 1970-; *ai:* STOIC.

REED, FREDA E., English Teacher; *b:* Hobbs, NM; *ed:* (BBA) Bus Ed, TX Tech Univ 1958; TX Chrstn Univ, Coll of Santa Fe, Univ of CO; *cr:* 7th/8th Grade Eng Teacher Young Jr HS 1962-66; 8th Grade Eng Teacher Nimitz Jr HS 1966-; *ai:* Basic Homeroom Tutoring; TX St Teachers Assn, TX Classroom Teachers Assn, TX Joint Cncl Teachers of Eng; *office:* Nimitz Jr HS PO Box 3912 Odessa TX 79760

REED, GRETCHEN KEEFER, Third Grade Teacher; *b:* Youngstown, OH; *m:* John R.; *c:* Beth Mc Clain, Wendy Szakacs; *ed:* (BSED) Elem Ed, Baldwin-Wallace Coll 1955; (MS) Rdng Specialist, Youngstown St 1980; Kent St Learning Inst; *cr:* 3rd Grade Teacher Liberty Sch 1955-59; 6th Grade Teacher Girard City 1966-67; 3rd Grade Teacher Liberty Schls 1967-; *ai:* Citizenship Comm Chairperson; Arbor Earth Peace Day Observances; Delta Kappa Gamma 1st VP 1990; Phi Delta Kappa 1985-; NEA, OEA, LEA, NEOTA; Church Hill United Meth Church Missions Chairperson 1986-, Mission Awd 1989; Leef, Math, Career Grants; Rotary Teacher of Month 1985; Jennings Scholar 1984-85; Outstanding Elem Teacher 1972; *office:* E J Blott Elem Sch 4003 Shady Rd Youngstown OH 44505

REED, GWENDOLYN HARTFORD, 6-8th Grade Lang Arts Teacher; *b:* Harrington, ME; *m:* Clarence Berton; *c:* Wendy; *ed:* (BS) Ed, WA St Teachers Coll 1956; Several Classes & Wkshps; *cr:* 5th/6th Grade Teacher Oceanville Sch 1956-57; 4th Grade Teacher Emma Hart Willard Sch 1957-59; 7th Grade Lang Arts Teacher Hodgkins Sch 1959-60; 9th-12th Grade Soc Stud Teacher Jonesport HS 1959-60; 8th Grade Rdng Teacher Brewer Jr HS 1961-75; 6th-8th Grade Lang Arts Teacher Jonesport Cove/ Jonesport Elem Sch 1975-; *ai:* Coached Plays for 32 Years; Past Chrldr Coach; ME Teachers Assn & NEA Mem 1989-; Jonesport Literary Club; Secy Local Teachers Club Brewer Sch System; *home:* Masons Bay Rd Jonesport ME 04649

REED, JERRY LEWIS, Head of Science Department; *b:* Hope, AR; *m:* Mary Ellen; *c:* Rebecca J., Jennifer L., William C.; *ed:* (BSED) Sci, S AR Univ 1976; Ed, Stephen F Austin St Univ 1984; *cr:* Sci Chm Shelbyville HS 1988-; *ai:* Head Ftbl & Bsktbl Coach; ATPE 1989-; TX HS Bsbl 1988-89, St Champs 1988, Runner Up 1989; Breakfast Lions Club 1989-; *office:* Shelbyville Ind Sch Dist P O Box 325 Shelbyville TX 75973

REED, JERRY RAY, Mathematics/Science Teacher; *b:* Guymon, OK; *m:* Mary Hathaway; *c:* Byron, Kerrie, Blake; *ed:* (BS) Math, Panhandle St Univ 1969; (MS) Math, SW OK St Univ 1979; W TX St Univ; TX Tech; OK St Univ; *cr:* Teacher/ Coach Hart TX HS 1972-74, Loop TX HS 1974-76, Darrouzett TX HS 1976-77; Teacher Tyrone HS 1977-; *ai:* Curr Contest Coord; Scholastic Team Coach; OEA-Panhandle Pres 1979-80; OEA, NEA; TX Coaches Assn (Dist Bsbl Coach of Yr 1976-77, Dist Ftbl Coach of Yr 1974-75); Math Today Article; Math Teachers Article; Tyrone Teacher of Yr 1985-86; *office:* Tyrone HS 6th & Beatrice Tyrone OK 73951

REED, JUANITA VIRGINIA, French Teacher; *b:* Texarkana, TX; *c:* Vanessa Wickes, Roderick, Kenneth; *ed:* (BA) Ec/SS/Fr, Prairie View A&M 1958; Grad Stud Fr; *cr:* Teacher John H Brown 1960-62, Pearl C Jr HS 1963-71, Samuell HS 1971-; *ai:* Fr Club; Tutoring Comm; NHS; Team Leader; Dept Head; Public Sch Week; AATF; Church Clerk; W W Samuell Teacher Perfect Attendance Plaque 1985-87; Nursing Home Volunteer Certificiate 1988-89; Dept Leader 1985-; Dallas Fellowship 7th Day Adv Chm Service Certificate; Textbook Comm Recognition; *home:* 1927 Danube Dr Dallas TX 75203

REED, L. RAY, Marketing Education Teacher; *b:* Littlefield, TX; *m:* D. Ann Williams; *c:* Lori A. Reed Smith; *ed:* Assoc Bus, S Plains Coll 1961; Assoc Bus Mortuary Sci, Dallas Inst 1964; (BBA) Bus Ed, W TX St Univ 1969; Mrktg Ed Advanced Teacher Trng; Comprehensive Master Teacher Trng; Management, Mrktg Ed Curr Dev; *cr:* Staff Consultant George C Price Incorporated 1959-67; Staff Office Mgr/Showroom Display Consultant/Sales Trng Amarillo Wholesale Furniture 1971-75; Staff Consultant Hammons Incorporated 1975-76; Mrktg Ed Teacher Granbury Public Schls 1976-; Bus Management Consultant Courtesy S B Consultation 1982-; *ai:* TX St Chapter 75 Curr Dev Comm; Distributive Ed Clubs of America Adv; Sr Class Adv & Fund Raising Chm; Hood Cty TSTA Pres 1980-81; Assn of TX Prof Educators 1981-; Mrktg Ed Teachers of TX 1976-; Amer Voc Assn 1976-; Amarillo Jaycees Bd of Dir 1972-73; FGBMFI (Treas, VP, Pres) 1983-89; DECA Mrktg Competive Events Adv; Mrktg Ed Teachers of TX Spec Awd for Curr Dev; *office:* Granbury HS 2000 W Pearl Granbury TX 76048

REED, NANCY C., Teacher/Lang Art Dept Chair; *b:* Detroit, MI; *m:* Gary A.; *ed:* (BSE) Ed, St John Coll 1970; (MAT) Ed, Saginaw Valley 1980; Wkshps in Instructional Theory into Practice, The Thematic Approach to Teaching, Asertive Discipline, MI New Definition of Rdng; *cr:* 4th-5th Grade Elem Teacher Macomb Park 1971-79; 5th Grade Elem Teacher Mc Kinley 1979-80; Jr HS Teacher Lincoln Jr HS 1980-; *ai:* MI Ed Assessment Prgm; Rdng, Writing, Mid Sch, Various Textbook Comms; Delta Kappa Gamma 1980-; MI Cncl Teachers of Eng, NCTE, MI Assn of Mid Sch Educators, MI Rdng Assn, MI Assn of Sch Curr Dev; Chosen Outstanding Teacher of Yr 1988; *office:* Lincoln Jr HS 22500 Federal Warren MI 48089

REED, PETER MARTIN, Special Education Teacher; *b:* Mount Kisco, NY; *m:* Elizabeth Carey; *c:* Carey, Stephen, Kevin; *ed:* (BA) Ed/His, Cntrl CT St Univ 1971; (MS) Ed/His, City Univ of NY 1973; *cr:* Crisis Intervention/Spec Ed Teacher Spankill Union Free Sch Dist 1973-77; Spec Ed Teacher Brewster Cntrl Sch Dist 1977-; *ai:* Girls Var Gymnastics Coach & Section I Coord; W Ct Supts Assn & Union Carbide Corporations Outstanding Teacher Awd 1986; NY St Coach of Yr 1989; *home:* 7 West St Pawling NY 12564

REEDER, DANIEL M., 6th Grade Teacher Team Coord; *b:* Salem, OH; *m:* Carole Moorefield; *c:* Andy Blair, Amy; *ed:* (BA) Elem Ed, 1971, (MA) Elem Ed, 1977 Morehead St Univ; *cr:* Teacher Montgomery Cty Schls 1972-; *ai:* KEA; Outstanding Elem Teacher 1980 Cmmty Awd; Sch Cmmty Awd 1986; *office:* Mc Nabb Mid Sch 3570 Indian Mound Dr Mount Sterling KY 40353

REEDER, ELOISE JENNINGS, Third Grade Teacher; *b:* Charlotte, NC; *m:* Vermoyn Donald; *c:* Daniel E., Charles A.; *ed:* (BS) Elem Ed, Bob Jones Univ 1961; (ME) Early Chldhd Ed, Stephen F Austin 1984; Kndgtn Endorsement Univ of Miami 1973; TX Math Teacher Trng; *cr:* 2nd/3rd Grade Teacher Northside Chrstn Day Sch 1961-62; 2nd Grade Teacher Thomasboro Elem 1964-66; 2nd/3rd Grade Teacher Great Falls Elem 1966-71; 3rd Grade Teacher Midway Chrstn Acad 1971-73; 3rd/4th Grade Teacher Dade Cty Public Sch 1973-77; Kndgtn/3rd Grade Teacher Carthage Ind Sch Dist 1978-; *ai:* TX Classroom Teachers (Corresponding Secy 1987-88, Building Rep 1981, 1985); 1st Baptist Church (Sunbeam Dir 1978-80, Girls Missionary Auxiliary Dir 1981-84, 1986-88, Sunday Sch Teacher 1982-85); Red Cross Rep 1975-77; PTA Officer 1968-69; *office:* Libby Elem Sch 1 Bulldog Dr Carthage TX 75633

REEDER, JAMES RONDELL, Chemistry Teacher; *b:* San Jose, CA; *m:* Merlene Corless; *c:* Diane, David; *ed:* (BS) Animal Sci, Brigham Young Univ 1959; (MS) Ed Admin, CA St Univ 1977; Life Sci, Phys Sci, CA St Univ 1965; *cr:* Sci Teacher 1965-71, Sci Dept Chm 1971-76, Admin 1976-78 Lincoln HS; Sci Teacher Amer Fork Jr HS & Orem HS 1978-88; *ai:* Jr Class Adv; NSTA 1978-; *office:* Orem HS 175 S 400 E Orem UT 84058

REEDER, JESSIE LA RUTH HOLLEY, 4th-12th Grade Music Teacher; *b:* Detroit, MI; *m:* Ray O.; *c:* Terry D., Leah H.; *ed:* Chrstn Ed/Music Tyndale Coll 1956; (BA) Music Ed, 1971, (MAED) Supervision/Admin, 1980 Baldwin Wallace Coll; Chemical Awareness & Children of Divorce; Music Cmptrs; Choral Conducting; *cr:* Vocal Music Teacher Murray Ridge Sch 1964-70, Oberlin Sch Dist 1971-; *ai:* Chemical Abuse Awareness Prgm; Oberlin HS Stu Cncl Adv; Music Curr, Gifted & Talented, North Cntrl Evaluation Comm; Amer Choral Dirs Assn 1971-; OH Music Ed Assn Mem 1971-; Natl Black Music Caucus 1979-; United Conference for Women; Music Educators Natl Conference 1971-; Oberlin OH Ed Assn; Allen Memorial Hospital Bd of Dir 1972-73; Lorain Cty Cncl for Retarded; Lorain Cty Art Cncl; Oberlin Sch Dist Teacher of Yr 1978, Recognition for Excl 1985; Stu Cncl Adv Recognition for Excl 1986; Nom Martha Holden Jennings Awd 1988; Baldwin Wallace Coll Outstanding Alumnus 1988; Natl Assn Negro Bus & Prof Womens Club Sojourner Truth Awd 1989; *home:* 133 Smith St Oberlin OH 44074

REEDY, CHARLOTTE EDWARDS, Spanish Teacher; *b:* Liberal, KS; *m:* Karl C. Jr.; *c:* Sara K., Mary M.; *ed:* (BA) Eng/ Foreign Lang, Emory & Henry Coll 1966; (MA) Eng, George Peabody Coll for Teachers 1970; Ed, Austin Peay St Univ; Jane Stallings Classroom Management Trng; TN Instructional Model TIMS Trng; *cr:* Eng Teacher Holston HS 1966-68, 1974-75, Patrick Henry HS 1970-72; Eng/Span Teacher Abingdon HS 1972-74, Springfield HS 1975-; *ai:* Cty Foreign Lang Group Chm; Span Club Spon; CIA Club; Press Reporter for Local Ed Assn 1990; Phi Delta Kappa, ACTFL, TFLTA, AATSP; Twentieth Century Club 1989-; Hum Fellowship 1969-70; Articles Published; *office:* Springfield HS 5240 Hwy 76 E Springfield TN 37172

REEDY, DAVID J., Physics Teacher; *b:* Summit, NJ; *ed:* (BA) Chem, Hamilton Coll 1968; (MS) Geology, Stanford Univ 1970; *cr:* Geologist Hanna Mining Company 1970-77; Teacher Brockport HS 1980-; *ai:* AAPT 1987-; Society of Ec Geologists 1974-79; BSA 1968-88, Silver Beaver Awd 1986; Camp Good Days & Spec Times 1986-, Teddi Awd 1987; BPO Elks Exalted Ruler 1982-83; *home:* 2407 S Union St Spencerport NY 14559

REEL, KENNETH ALAN, American History Teacher; *b:* Lawton, OK; *m:* Mary Ann Purnell; *c:* Matthew, Amy; *ed:* (BS) Soc Stud Comp, 1968, (MA) Amer His, 1973 Youngstown St Univ; Grad Stud Youngstown St Univ; *cr:* Teacher Canfield Mid Sch 1968-; *ai:* Past Track Coach & Intramural Dir; 8th Grade Girls Bsktbl Coach; Civil War Round Table (Bd Mem, Chaplain 1986-, VP 1989); NEA, OEA, CEA Building Rep; Smith Corners Church Chm Admin Bd 1975-; Dublin Grange Master 1970-74; Mahoning Cty Grange Master 1974-76; Canfield Teacher of Yr; Martha Holden Jennings Scholar; *office:* Canfield Mid Sch 42 Wadsworth St Canfield OH 44406

REEP, LINDA COOK, 7th Grade Lang Art Teacher; *b:* Charlotte, NC; *m:* Larry Richard; *c:* Amber A., Adam A.; *ed:* (BS) Elem Ed, Appalachian St 1968; Cert Lang Arts/Music; Working on Masters Rdng, UNC Charlotte; *cr:* 4th Grade Teacher Granite Quarry Sch 1968-79; 7th/8th Grade Lang Art Teacher E Iredell Sch 1979-; *ai:* Builders Club Adv; In-Service Wkshps for Cty Teachers; Mentor Teacher; Soc Comm Chm; NCAE, NEA, ACT 1968-; Outstanding Young Educator Rowan Cty 1976; Iredell Cty Teacher of Yr 1986; Teacher of Yr 1984-87; *home:* Rt 10 Box 281 Statesville NC 28677

REEP, VINCENT SCOTT, 6th Grade Teacher; *b:* Stanley, ND; *m:* Pamela D.; *c:* Anthony, Emily; *ed:* (BS) Elem Ed/Math, Dickinson St Univ 1976; (MED) Ed Admin, Univ of ND 1987; *cr:* 5th/6th Grade Teacher Gladstone Elem 1976-80; 5th Grade Teacher 1981, 6th Grade Teacher 1982- Lincoln Elem; *ai:* Elem Boys Bsktbl Coach 1976-85; Elem Boys Bsktbl Coord 1986-; Dickinson HS Cross Cntry Coach 1978-; Dickinson HS Girls Track Coach 1980-; Dickinson Public Schls Technology, Critical Thinking Skills, Gifted Ed, Reduction in Force, Health Insurance Study, Math, Sci, Extra Curr, Bus Ed, Teacher Supt Advisory Comm; Dickinson Ed Assn (Pres 1985, Mem) 1976-; ND HS Coaches Assn Mem 1983-; Blue Hawk Booster Bd of Dirs 1987-; Cub Scouts (Asst Pack Leader, Den Leader) 1988-; WDA Cross Cntry Coach of Yr 1986, 1989; *office:* Lincoln Elem Sch 102 10th St W Dickinson ND 58601

REES, DOROTHY JUNE, Fifth Grade Teacher; *b:* Vandalia, IL; *m:* John W. Sr.; *c:* John, Michael, David, Allen; *ed:* (BS) Elem Ed, Southern IL Univ Edwardsville 1975; Writing, Rdng, Cmptr Sci; Cert Gifted Ed; *cr:* 3rd Grade Teacher Troy Grade Sch 1976-79; 5th Grade Teacher Molden Elem Sch 1979-; *ai:* Comm Mem Annual Dist Wide Writers Rally; Gifted Ed Prgm Written Proposal for Local Dist St of IL; NEA, TEA 1976-; Troy U Meth Church Sec of Brd Admin 1990; Lay Speaker of U Meth Church 1987-; *office:* Molden Elem Sch 209 N Dewey Troy IL 62294

REES, GORDON T., English Teacher; *b:* Moroni, UT; *m:* Judy C.; *c:* Jennifer, Natalie, Christopher; *ed:* (BA) Eng, Brigham Young Univ 1965; Grad Stud Univ of UT; *cr:* Teacher Glendale Jr HS 1965-75, Highland HS 1975-; *ai:* UEA, SLTA, NEA 1965-85; AFT 1985-86; High Risk Stus Appeals, Curr Dev, Discrimination Comm Mem; Grant UT St Bd of Ed; Train Teachers to Teach Higher Order Thinking Skills Through Writing Process Using Cmptrs; *office:* Highland HS 2166 S 1700 E Salt Lake City UT 84106

REESE, ALAN CARROLL, English Teacher; *b:* Sayre, PA; *m:* Alberta E. Di Marino; *c:* Camille J., Jesse A., Joshua G.; *ed:* (BA) Eng, Towson St Univ 1976; *cr:* Eng Teacher Woodlawn Mid 1976-80, Perry Hall Mid 1980-84; Resource Teacher of Gifted & Talented 1984-86, Eng Teacher 1986- Dumbarton Mid; *ai:* Scrabble, Chess, Drama Club Spon; Faculty Cncl Chm; Yrbk Adv; *home:* 3115 Harview Ave Baltimore MD 21234

REESE, E. ANNETTE ROBERTSON, Band Director; *b:* Waynesville, NC; *m:* Mark A.; *c:* Caitlan A.; *ed:* (BMED) Instrumental/Vocal Music, Mars Hill Coll 1980; *cr:* Elem Music Teacher Marlboro Cty Schls 1980-81; Elem/Vocal Music Teacher N Gaston HS 1981-85; Instrumental Music Teacher Stanley Jr HS & E Gaston Sr HS 1985-; *ai:* Delta Omicron, Music Educators Natl Conference, NC Bandmasters Assn, NC Ed Assn & NEA; *office:* Stanley Jr HS/E Gaston Sr HS 317 Hovis Rd Stanley NC 28164

REESE, IDELLA KEELEY, Third Grade Teacher; *b:* White Springs, FL; *m:* Robert Lee Sr.; *c:* Paul R. Reed Jr., Robert L. Jr., Andre De Luv Keeley, Maurice A. Keeley; *ed:* (BS) Elem Ed, Bethune-Cookman Coll 1975; *cr:* Teacher Edith I Starke Elem 1976-78, George Marks Elem 1978-; *ai:* Ward Chapel AME Church; Young People Dir; Trustee Bd & Choirs Secy; VEA, FTP, NEA 1976-; Crescent City Womens Civic Assn 1988-; *home:* 1850 Wilson St Seville FL 32190

REESE, JAMIE L., Special Education Teacher; *b:* Pocatello, ID; *c:* Brent; *ed:* (BA) Home Ec Ed, 1971, (MA) Learning Disabilities, 1983 Marycrest Coll; Learning Strategies Thru Local AEA; Participant Wkshps; *cr:* Teacher Adult HS 1971-75, TAPP 1983-84, Sudlow Jr HS 1975-; *ai:* Stu Cncl Spon; Pi Lambda Theta 1983-; *office:* Sudlow Jr HS 1414 E Locust St Davenport IA 52803

REESE, JASPER BERNIE, Math Department Teacher; *b:* Hot Springs, NC; *m:* Helen Whisnant; *c:* John B., Brian D., Scott K., Eric L.; *ed:* (BA) Soc Stud, Lenoir Rhyne 1957; (MA) Jr Coll Ed, Appalachian St U Niv 1960; Scndry Admin; *cr:* Teacher Appalachian St Univ 1959-60; South Caldwell HS 1989-; Prin Patterson Schl for Boys 1963-67; Collettsville Elem 1968-70; *ai:* NEA; NCAE; PACE Chm 1971; Caldwell-NCAE Pres 1972; Teaching Fellowship-Assistantssip Appalachian St Univ 1959-60; Articles Publ NCAE Journal; *office:* South Caldwell HS 143 Cedar Valley Rd Hudson NC 28638

REESE, LORELLE LEONARD, Fourth Grade Teacher; *b:* Newark, NJ; *m:* William D.; *c:* Jean Reese Harvill, Christine Reese Proctor, William L., David C.; *ed:* (BS) Elem Ed, Towson St Univ 1950; (MED) Elem Ed/Eng, Univ of SW LA 1971; Prof Imp Prgm Classes & Seminars; LTIP-LTEP Assessor; *cr:* 1st Grade Teacher Owings Mills Elem Sch 1950-51; 3rd Grade Teacher Ascension Day Sch 1963-66; 3rd/4th Grade Teacher Edgar Martin Elem 1966-78; 4th Grade Teacher Broadmoor Elem 1978-; *home:* 320 Burdin Rd Lafayette LA 70508

REESE, MARJORIE WILSON, Fourth Grade Teacher; *b:* Ft Meade, MD; *m:* Anthony S.; *c:* Eric, Beth; *ed:* (BSED) Elem Ed, 1968, (MED) Elem Ed, 1984 OH Univ; *cr:* 4th Grade Teacher Hopewell Elem 1966-71, Madison Elem 1971-72; Learning Disability Tutor 1975-77, 3rd-5th Grade Teacher 1977- Nashport Elem; *ai:* Tri Valley Math Competency, Cmptr Curr, Spelling Bee Comm; Tri Valley Ed Assn, OH Ed Assn.

REESE, MARK ALLEN, Band Director; *b:* Emporia, KS; *m:* Annette Robertson; *c:* Caitlan A.; *ed:* (BMED) Music, Mars Hill Coll 1978; *cr:* Band Dir Parkwood HS & Mid Sch 1978-80, Rockingham Jr HS & Richmond Sr HS 1980-81, N Gaston Sr HS 1981-85, E Gaston Sr HS & Stanley Jr HS 1985-; *ai:* Phi Mu Alpha, Music Educators Natl Conference; Amer Sch Band Dir Assn, NC Bandmasters Assn, NEA, NC Educators Assn; NC Grade IV Contest Music List, S Cntrl Dist Solo, Ensemble Festival Chm; *office:* E Gaston Sr HS/Stanley Jr HS 710 S Lane Rd Mount Holly NC 28120

REESE, MINESUE WRIGHT, Kindergarten Teacher; *b:* Brownwood, TX; *m:* Bobby Charles Sr.; *c:* Randy, Gerry Sr., Bobby Jr., Donna Davison, Diane Hope; *ed:* (BS) Elem Ed, Mary Hardin Baylor Univ 1972; *cr:* Kndgtn Teacher Midway Ind Sch Dist 1973-; *ai:* Grade Level Chm; Grade Level Comm Person; Dist Grade Level Coord; ATPE, TEA, NEA Local Secy 1975; Kndgtn Teachers of TX 1988-; Baylor Univ Kndgtn Cncl 1985-; PTA (Secy, VP, Pres) 1967-70; BSA, GSA Leader 1960-69; *office:* Midway Ind Sch Dist 9101 Woodway Dr Waco TX 76712

REESE, OKEY LEONARD, Mathematics Teacher; *b:* St Marys, WV; *m:* Nina Loise Moschett; *c:* Okey M., Natalie M., Rebecca A.; *ed:* (BS) Scndry Ed/Math, Penn St 1966; Grad Work Pernament Cert Penn St; *cr:* Math Teacher Franklin Regional Jr HS 1966-72; Math Dept Head Franklin Regional Intermediate HS 1972-88; Math Teacher Franklin Regional Jr/Sr HS 1988-; *office:* Franklin Regional Jr/Sr HS 3200 School Rd Murrysville PA 15668

REESE, RANDY, Teacher/Football Coach; *b:* Cincinnati, OH; *m:* Janie Anderson; *c:* Jeff, Jason, Julie; *ed:* (BA) Ed, Marietta Coll 1970; (MED) Health/Phys Ed, OH Univ 1971; *cr:* Teacher/Coach Deer Park HS 1974-75; Teacher/Ftbl Coach Ludlow HS 1975-79, Paris HS 1979-87, Henderson Cty HS 1987-; *ai:* Head Ftbl Coach & Coord; Strength Coach; FCA Adv; St Coaches Assn, Natl Ftbl Coaches Assn; Coached St Championships 1975, 1981, 1982; Coach of Yr; Paris Citizen of Yr 1981, 1982.

REESING, JO CHRISTIAN, Second Grade Teacher; *b:* Trinity, TX; *m:* Ernest O. Jr.; *c:* Susan Carroll, Mike, Dan; *ed:* (BA) Elem Ed, Sam Houston St Univ 1963; Grad Stud; *cr:* 2nd Grade Teacher Trinity Ind Sch Dist 1968-76, Alpine Ind Sch Dist 1976-; *ai:* UIL Sponsorship; Assn TX Prof Educators 1977-; Alpine Volunteer Fire Dept Auxiliary 1976-; PTA Terrific Teacher 1983; *office:* Alpine Ind Sch Dist 200 West Ave A Alpine TX 79830

REETZ, MICHAEL LEON, Sixth Grade Teacher; *b:* Eau Claire, WI; *m:* Judith Marie Buchholz; *c:* Tamara, Amber; *ed:* (BS) Elem Ed, Univ WI Eau Claire 1973; (MS) Educl Admin, Winona St 1980; *cr:* 6th Grade Teacher Randall Sch 1973-80, Longfellow Sch 1981-87, De Long Mid Sch 1988-; *ai:* Head Coach Girls Bsktbl Eau Claire Memorial HS; Eau Claire Coaches Assn Pres 1987-88; Conference Coach of Yr 1987-90.

REEVES, BOYD ARRINGTON, English Teacher; *b:* Washington, GA; *m:* Kay Maddox; *ed:* (BA) Eng, Mercer Univ 1961; S Baptist Theological Seminary 1966-67; *cr:* Teacher Thomson HS 1961-71, Glascock Cty Consolidated Sch 1975-; *ai:* Glascock Cty Sr & Jr Beta Club Spon; Glascock Cty Annual Staff Adv; Sch Teacher Support Team Mem; Prof Assn of GA Educators 1984-; Fort Creek Baptist Church (Teacher, Mem) 1984-; STAR Teacher Glascock Cty 1980, 1983, 1987, 1989; *home:* Rt 1 Box 481 Dearing GA 30808

REEVES, DAVID MICHAEL, Social Studies Teacher; *b:* Ownesboro, KY; *m:* Kimberly Ann Frashure; *ed:* (BA) His, KY Wesleyan 1971; (MAT) His, Univ of Louisville 1974; *cr:* Teacher Mc Lean Cty HS 1975-77, Estes Mid Sch 1978-80, Owensboro Cath 1980-; *ai:* Girls Bsktbl & Sftbl Coach; Fellowship of Chrstn Athletes Spon; Phi Alpha Theta Pres 1970-71; Ky Colonel 1985; Outstanding Young Men 1985; WVJS-WSTO Coach of Yr 1984-86; Big 8 Conference Coach of Yr 1984.

REEVES, DEVOTA JEAN, English Teacher; *b:* Indianapolis, IN; *ed:* (BS) Eng, Ball St Univ 1983; *cr:* Teacher Monrovia Jr-Sr HS 1983-; *ai:* Drama Club & Stu Government Assn Spon; Dir of Sch Plays; NHS Faculty Cncl Mem; Sch Improvement & Stu Handbook Comm; *office:* Monrovia Jr-Sr HS State Rd 39 S Monrovia IN 46157

REEVES, GERALD ARCHIE, JR., Industrial Tech Teacher; *b:* Columbia, SC; *m:* Jeannie P. Burns; *ed:* (BS) Industrial Ed, Clemson Univ 1982; Masters Prgm for Industrial Technology, Clemson Univ; *cr:* Teacher Hillcrest HS 1983-; *ai:* Industrial Technology Club Adv; SC Industrial Technology Assn 1987-; SC Voc Ed Assn 1985-; Pine Grove Fire Dept 1983-; Blaney Fire Dept 1989-; Kershaw Cty Arson Control Team Investigator 1987-; SC Ed Improvement Act Grant; *office:* Hillcrest HS P O Box 151 Dalzell SC 29040

REEVES, JOAN, Teacher; *b:* Ft Payne, AL; *m:* John L.; *c:* Jonathan, Jason, Jessica; *ed:* (AS) Eng, NE AL Jr Coll 1972; (BS) Eng/His, Florence St Univ 1974; (MED) Eng Ed, Univ of TN Chattanooga 1977; Eng, Univ of AL; *cr:* Teacher Bryant 1974-81, N Sand Mountain 1981-; Instr NE St Jr Coll 1986-; *ai:* Prom Jr Class Spon; AEA; JCEA Secy 1988; NCTE; ADK Secy 1988-; PTO Secy 1986-; *office:* N Sand Mountain HS P O Box 129 Higdon AL 35979

REEVES, KITTY HANSON, Fifth Grade Teacher; *b:* Madison, GA; *c:* Jamey; *ed:* (BS) Ed, GA Coll 1967; (MS) Ed, 1977 (EDS) Ed Mid Grades, 1988 GA St Univ; *cr:* Teacher Union City Elem 1967-71; Teacher/Asst Prin Marion Smith Elem 1974-87; Teacher Oak Knoll Elem 1987-; *ai:* Leadership Team; Grade Chairperson; Chm Janus His Project; Mem of Ful Cty Math Curr Writing Comm; Co-Chm for Southern Assn Accreditation Assn; Fulton Cty Assn of Educators 1980-; GA Assn of Educators 1980-; NEA 1980-; Assn of GA Sci Teachers; PTO Prgm Chm 1967-; Band Booster Club 1988-89; Kappa Delta Pi; Houghton Mifflin Advisory Cncl; Lifetime Mem of PTAF Teacher Yr 1986; Fulton Cty Mini Grant-Correspondence with Kenya; *office:* Oak Knoll Elem 2626 Hogan Rd East Point GA 30344

REEVES, RHONDA LA FOLLETTE, 7th-12th Grade Spec Ed Teacher; *b:* Covington, KY; *m:* John Ralph; *ed:* (BS) Sch Health/Educable Mentally Handicapped, E KY Univ 1974; (MA) Ed, N KY Univ 1980; Working Towards Rank I Cert N KY Univ; *cr:* Teacher of Educable Mentally Handicapped Simon Kenton HS 1975-79, Grant Cty HS 1979-80; Teacher of Educable Mentally Handicapped/Learning Disabilities Henry Cty HS 1980-85, Walton Verona HS 1985-; *ai:* Chrldr Coach; Pep Club, Sr Class, Soph Class Spon; Gifted & Talented Prgm Summer Teacher; KY Ed Assn, NEA; Kenton Cty Fair Bd Beauty Pageant Coord 1987-; Spec Olympics; Nom A D Albright Awd 1989; Nom KY Teacher of Yr 1989; *office:* Walton-Verona HS School Rd Walton KY 41094

REEVES, SHARON KAY, 8th Grade English Teacher; *b:* Union City, TN; *m:* Terry; *c:* Kelly; *ed:* (BS) Elem Ed, 1981, (MS) Ed Psych/Guidance, 1986 Univ of TN Martin; *cr:* 5th Grade Teacher Hornbeck Elem 1981-82; 6th/7th/8th Grade Eng Teacher Woodland Mills Elem 1982-84; 8th Grade Eng Teacher Lake Road Elem 1984-88; Long Oak Mid Sch 1988; *ai:* Coach 7th Grade Girls Bsktbl; NEA 1981-; KY Ed Assn 1988-; Mc Cracken Cty Ed Assn 1988-.

REFF, STEVEN M., Economics Instructor; *b:* Elmhurst, IL; *m:* Cyndi Lynn; *ed:* (BS) Bus Ed, 1977, (MA) Scndry Ed, 1981 Univ of AZ; Grad Stud Ed; *cr:* Ec Instr Rincon/University HS 1985-; *ai:* Golf Coach; FBLA & Ski Club Adv; HS Hockey Team Coach 1989-; Mt Lemmon Ski Sch Dir 1989-; Royal Order of TANSTAAFL Mem 1987-; 2nd Runner-Up US West Outstanding Teacher of Yr in AZ 1989; Jr Achievement Tucson Teacher of Yr 1987, 1990; *office:* Rincon/University HS 422 N Arcadia Tucson AZ 85711

REGA, GEORGENE ROBERTA, Second Grade Teacher; *b:* Rochester, PA; *m:* James Philip; *c:* James P. II, Sheree L.; *ed:* (BA) Elem, Edinboro St 1970; (MA) Elem, Penn St 1976; *cr:* Kndgtn Teacher Ambridge Sch Dist 1970-71; 1st Grade Teacher 1971-73, 3rd Grade Teacher 1973-86, 2nd Grade Teacher 1986- Mt Pleasant Sch Dist; *home:* 100 College Ave Mount Pleasant PA 15666

REGAN, DAVID LEE, Health/Sci/Basic Skill Teacher; *b:* Denver, CO; *m:* Rolene; *c:* Joshua, Andrew, Caleb; *ed:* (BS) Phys Ed/Health, Pittsburg St Univ 1973; *cr:* 7th Grade Health/6th Grade Sci/8th Grade Basic Skills Teacher Fort Scott Mid Sch 1983-; *ai:* Ftbl, Bsktbl, Bsbl Coach; Sch Improvement Team Comm; Bsktbl & Bsbl Cards Club Adv; Fellowship of Chrstn Athletes; St Marys Cath Church; Outstanding Young Educator Pittsburg St Univ 1990; *home:* Rt 1 Bronson KS 66716

REGAS, MARY, First Grade Teacher; *b:* Cleveland, OH; *m:* Michael; *c:* Lauren; *ed:* (AS) Early Ed, Cuyahoga Comm Coll 1973; (BA) Elem Ed, Kent St Univ 1975; Outdoor Ed, Akron Univ; Ec, Ashland Coll; *cr:* Kndgtn Teacher Crestview Elem 1975-79; 1st Grade Teacher Memorial Elem 1979-81; Kndgtn Teacher Hickory Ridge Elem 1984-88; 2nd Grade Teacher 1988-89, 1st Grade Teacher 1989- Memorial Elem; *ai:* Young Authors Books Judge; Supv to Coll Stu; Staff Soc Comms; Brunswick Ed Assn, OH Ed Assn, NEA 1975-; Rdng Materials Grant.

REGINA, FRED ANTHONY, 6th Grade Teacher; *b:* Jersey City, NJ; *ed:* (BA) Italian Lang, Seton Hall Univ 1963; Elem Ed, Trenton St 1964-65; *cr:* 6th Grade Teacher Holmes Marshall Elem Sch 1963-69, Schor Mid Sch 1969-; *office:* Schor Mid Sch Norht Randolphville Rd Piscataway NJ 08854

REGISTER, CYNTHIA LEWIS, First Grade Teacher; *b:* Richmond, VA; *m:* John David Jr.; *c:* David L., Michael E., Meredith L.; *ed:* (BS) Elem Ed, E Carolina Univ 1977; *cr:* Classroom Teacher 1977-84, 1986-; *ai:* Lee-Jackson Primary Sch PTA Nominating Comm Vice-Chairperson; Jr Womens Club (VP, Educl Chairperson); *office:* Lee-Jackson Primary Sch Box 219 Mathews VA 23109

REGISTER, MARTHA H., Science Dept Chair/Teacher; *b:* Donalsonville, GA; *m:* G. Ashley Sr.; *c:* Ashley Jr., Mark E., H. Brinson; *ed:* (BS) Chem, Valdosta St Coll 1962; (MS) Sci Ed, Troy St Univ 1986; *cr:* Teacher Valdosta HS 1962-63; Chemist GA Dept of Ag 1963-64; Teacher Seminole Cty HS 1973-; *ai:* Gifted Stu Teacher; Sci Act Spon; Delta Kappa Gamma 1986-; Presbyn Church Elder 1988-; STAR Teacher; *office:* Seminole County HS 800 Marianna Hwy Donalsonville GA 31745

REGISTER, VICTORIA RICH, 8th Grade Mathematics Teacher; *b:* Tompkinsville, KY; *m:* Larry H.; *c:* Ryan L., Lindsey A.; *ed:* (BS) Math Ed, FL St Univ 1978; *cr:* Math Teacher Cobb Mid Sch 1978-79; Math Teacher 1979-80, Math/Sci Teacher 1983- Belle Vue Mid Sch; *ai:* Mathcounts Coach; Leon Cty Teachers of Math Exec Bd Mem 1989-; FL Cncl Teachers of Math, NCTM, FL Assn for Cmptrs in Ed, Leon Cty Rdng Cncl; Winner of Better Ed for Stu Tomorrow Fund Mini-Grant for Innovative Teaching Ideas for Living Skills 1989; 1st Place Winner of N FL Region Mid Sch Div, Ec Ed Teacher Awds 1989; 2nd Place Winner Mid Sch Div St of FL Ec Ed Teacher Awds 1989; Winner of St of FL Ec Mini-Grant for Ec Ed 1989-; Winner Natl Level the Natl Mid Sch Assn Selected Project to be Published in Visions of Teaching & Learning 80 Exemplary Mid Level Projects 1989.

REHG, ROBERT L., Biology Teacher; *b:* Highland, IL; *m:* Marie; *c:* Peggy Knebel, Deborah; *ed:* (BA) Chem, Mc Kendree Coll 1960; (MA) Bio, N AZ Univ 1966; Advanced Trng In Bio W MI Univ, S IL Univ Carbondale; *cr:* Bio Teacher Wilbur Trimpe Jr HS 1960-64, Coolidge Jr HS 1964-73, Granite City HS 1973-83, Granite City Sr HS 1983-; *ai:* Sci Club; NABT 1973-82, NSTA 1985-86; Lions Club (3rd VP 1967-68, 2nd VP 1968-69, 1st VP 1969-70, Bd Mem 1970-); Lion of Yr 1978-79; Natl Sci Fnd 1964, 1969, 1984; *office:* Granite City Sr HS 3101 Madison Ave Granite City IL 62040

REHRL-RUGGIO, CARMEN ANTOINETTE, German/French Teacher; *b:* New York, NY; *m:* Edward James Ruggio; *c:* Cyrina A., Nicolas G.; *ed:* (BA) Ger/Intnl Trade, SUNY Oswego 1977; (MS) Foreign Lang Ed, 1981, (MA) Ger Lang/Lit, 1982 Syracuse Univ; Germanistic Study Abroad Prgm, Univ Wurzburg 1976; *cr:* Grad Teaching Asst Syracuse Univ 1979-81; Substitute Teacher W Genesee Schls 1982-83; Permanent Substitute Ger Teacher Liverpool HS 1983; Data Production/Tech/Admin Support General Electric Co 1985-87; Instr Onondaga Comm Coll 1987; Teacher Skaneateles HS 1987-; *ai:* Ger/Foreign Lang Clubs Adv; SHS Intnl Festival, Chaperone After The Prom/Ball Festivities Comm; AATG 1988-; NUS Assn Foreign Lang Teachers 1980-; Foreign Lang Assn of Cntrl NY 1987-; Phi Sigma Iota (Secy 1981-82) 1981-; Delta Phi Alpha 1976; Two-Yr Grad Teaching Assistantship Syracuse Univ 1979-81 & Book Awd Consulate for Outstanding Teaching; Bronze Medal for Achievement in Ger SUNY 1977; Dist Grant 1990; *office:* Skaneateles Sr HS 49 E Elizabeth St Skaneateles NY 13152

REICH, SHIRLEY ANN, American History Teacher; *b:* Brownwood, TX; *ed:* (BA) Comm, TX Luth Coll 1983; (MED) Educl Psych, Univ of TX 1991; *cr:* Teacher Hays HS 1985-; *ai:* Jr Class & Speech Spon; Cheerleading Coach; Assn of TX Prof Educators 1985-; Kappa Delta Pi 1990; *office:* Hays HS Rt 2 Box 20 Buda TX 78610

REICH, STEVE, Social Studies Teacher; *b:* Bronxville, NY; *m:* Linda; *ed:* (BA) His/Eng, 1982, (MAT) Ed, 1983 Colgate Univ; *cr:* Teacher Mt Vernon Alternative Sch 1983-84, Valhalla HS 1984-; *ai:* Asst Ftbl & Track Coach; Asst Sr Class Adv; Sr Usher Adv; Stu Mentor Prgm; NCSS; Valhalla Teachers Assn Building Rep 1988-; Teacher Center St Univ of NY Policy Bd Mem 1989-; *office:* Valhalla HS 300 Columbus Ave Valhalla NY 10595

REICHEL, MARGARET GRANT, Mathematics Teacher; *b:* Chicago, IL; *m:* Robert M.; *c:* Margaret Koth, Fred Welfare, Catherine Welfare, Virginia Welfare, Richard Welfare, Barbara Welfare; *ed:* (BA) Music/Math, St Xavier Coll 1951; (MS) Ed/HS Curr, Chicago St Univ 1980; Grad Stud Cmptr Sci, IL Inst of Technology; *cr:* Teacher Fenger HS 1966-78, Kenwood Acad 1978-81, Bogan HS 1981-; *ai:* Bridge Club Spon; NCTM; MENSA; *office:* Bogan HS 3939 W 79th St Chicago IL 60653

REICHENBACH, DEBRA SUE, Mathematics Teacher; *b:* Rhinelander, WI; *ed:* (BS) Math, Univ of WI Oshkosh 1975; Grad Ed Courses; *cr:* Math Teacher J F Luther Jr HS 1975-78, Riverside Jr HS 1978-79, Smithson Valley HS 1980-81, Kitty Hawk Jr HS 1981-87, Judson HS 1987-; *ai:* Soph Class Spon; Assn of TX Prof Educators 1981-; Boysville Tutor 1984-; *office:* Judson HS Schaefer Rd Converse TX 78109

REICHENBAUGH, THOMAS MERLE, Social Studies Teacher; *b:* Spring Church, PA; *m:* Patricia Ann Wood; *c:* Teresa M.; *ed:* (BS) Geography, Clarion Univ 1972; (ME) Ed, WV Univ 1983; Gifted & Talented Ed, Cooperative Learning, Interdisciplinary Ed; *cr:* World Stud Teacher Poolesville Jr/Sr HS 1972-; *ai:* NEA, Mont Cty Ed Assn 1972-; Mont Cty Soc Stud Teachers Organization; Natl Rifle Assn 1980-; N Amer Hunting Club 1985-.

REICHERT, CELESTE MARIE, Fourth Grade Teacher; *b:* Saint Louis, MO; *ed:* (BA) Ed, Webster Coll 1958; (MA) Classical Latin, St Louis Univ 1964; (MA) Religious Stud, Providence Coll 1973; *cr:* 1st Grade Teacher St James Sch 1951-58; 1st Grade/HS Teacher Holy Rosary 1958-65; Eng/Latin/Religion Teacher/Dept Head St Edmund HS 1965-72; Eng/Religion Teacher/Dept Head St Dominic HS 1972-81; 7th/8th Grade Teacher Epiphany of Our Lord 1981-89; *ai:* Newspaper & Stu Cncl Moderator; NCEA 1981-; Italy Antiquities Fulbright Schlsp; US Eng Grant; NY St

Latin Grant; *office:* Epiphany of Our Lord 6576 Smiley Ave Saint Louis MO 63139

REICHMAN, DAVID MICHAEL, Music Department Chair; *b:* Linz, Austria; *m:* Karen Simons; *ed:* (BS) Violin Performance, IN Univ 1973;(MM) Violin Performance, Univ of The Arts 1975; Grad Stud Various Insts; *cr:* Music/Dept Chm Srpingside Sch 1988-; *ai:* Jr Lead Adv; A F of M, MENC, ASOL, Conductors Guild; *office:* Springside Sch 8000 Cherokee St Philadelphia PA 19118

REID, ALFREDA VINES, Language Arts Teacher; *b:* Canalou, MO; *m:* William J.; *c:* Robin; *ed:* (BS) Music/Eng, Oakland City Coll 1967; Eng; *cr:* Teacher Lilbourn HS 1967-69; Mgr Migrant Div Southeast MO Univ 1970-72; Teacher Egyptian Unit #5 1972-; *ai:* Initiated Jr HS Beta Club Into System/Spon; IATE; SIAET; MSTA; IEA.

REID, BENJAMIN DAVID, Target 2000 Teacher; *b:* Walterboro, SC; *m:* Carolyn A.; *c:* Daniel; *ed:* (BS) Math, Claflin Coll 1972; Furman Univ, Univ of SC Spartanburg; *cr:* Teacher Slater Marietta HS 1972-73; Teacher/Coach Mauldin HS 1973-; *ai:* Jr Var Bsktbl Coach; CEC Co-Adv; SCEA, NEA, Natl Fed of HS Ofcls; Phi Beta Sigma; *office:* Mauldin HS 701 E Butler Rd Mauldin SC 29662

REID, HARRIET (SLACK), Kindergarten Teacher; *b:* Stevens Point, WI; *m:* George W.; *c:* Matthew, Peter; *ed:* (BS) Kndgtn/Primary Ed, Univ of WI Stevens Point 1962; *cr:* Kndgtn Teacher Shady Lane Sch 1962-64; 1st Grade Teacher Elemendorf AFB 1964-65; Kndgtn Teacher Calvary Baptist Chrstn 1973-; *ai:* Patriotism Day Coord; Sch Display & Decoration Adv; WI Assn of Chrstn Schls 1980-; Amer Assn of Chrstn Schls 1975-; Military Wife of Yr Rep WI & Upper MI 1976; Certificate of Recognition for Volunteer Services to Sch Children Watertown Bd of Ed 1973; *home:* W 6246 Apple Rd Watertown WI 53094

REID, JACQUELINE HOPE, French Teacher; *b:* Tulsa, OK; *m:* Harlan G.; *c:* Roger, Debra Witt; *ed:* (BS) Fr, Univ of Tulsa 1974; *cr:* Fr Teacher Union HS 1974-; *ai:* Fr Club & Sr Class Spon; OK Educl Assn, NEA, AATF, Ok Foreign Lang Teachers Assn; *office:* Union HS 6636 S Mingo Rd Tulsa OK 74135

REID, JANA JONES, English Teacher/Drill Team Dir; *b:* Starkville, MS; *m:* Daniel J.; *ed:* (BS) Ed/Eng/His, Baylor Univ 1984; Grad Stud Eng & Ed, Tarleton St Univ; *cr:* Eng Teacher Weatherford HS 1984-86, Granbury HS 1986-; *ai:* Newspaper, Chrldr, Future Teachers of America, UIL Spon; Drill Team Dir; Project Graduation Steering Comm Mem & Decorations Chm 1989; Yrbk Adv; TX St Teachers Assn Pres 1989-; NCTE 1988-; 1st Baptist Church (Sunday Sch Teacher 1987-89, Choir 1986-, Choir Pres 1988-89, Comm Mem 1989-); *home:* 311 Spanish Trail Dr Granbury TX 76048

REID, JOANNE CAMERON, French Teacher; *b:* Pinehurst, NC; *m:* John William; *c:* Jim, Jeff; *ed:* (BSED) Fr, West Carolina Univ 1968; *cr:* Fr Teacher Henderson HS 1968-71; Eng/Soc Stud Teacher W Millbrook Jr HS 1977-78; Fr Teacher E Cary Jr HS 1978-89, E Cary Mid Sch 1989-; *ai:* Fr Club; Stu Cncl Adv; Attendance Comm; West Carolina Univ Alumni Assn Secy 1982-82; Cary HS Booster Club Secy 1986-88; *home:* 103 Coronado Way Cary NC 27511

REID, MARJORIE FOLLIS, Literature Librarian Teacher; *b:* Long Beach, CA; *m:* Fred M.; *c:* Richard, Gary, Thomas; *ed:* (BA) Ed, Long Beach St Univ 1960; (MA) Behavioral Sci, Sacramento St Univ 1973; *cr:* Elem Teacher Orange Unified Sch Dist 1960-65, Elem Teacher 1965-85, Lib Lit Consultant 1985-, Lodi Unified Sch Dist; *ai:* Delta Kappa Gamma 1981-; CTA, NEA 1960-85; Lodi Ed Assn Area Rep 1965-85; AAUW 1980-; PEO (Pres, Secy) 1950-; *home:* 1168 Northwood Dr Lodi CA 95240

REID, PAMELA B., German Teacher; *b:* Salem, OH; *m:* Richard W.; *c:* David, Benjamin; *ed:* (BA) Ger/Comm, Hiram Coll 1974; Ger, Johannes Gutenberg Universitat Mainz Germany 1974-75; *cr:* Ger Teacher Canfield HS 1975-80, Tinora HS 1985-; *ai:* Ger Club; AATG; First Presbyn Church Chrstn Ed Comm Secy 1989-; Fulbright Hayes Fellowship to Germany 1974-75.

REID, RICHARD WILLIAMS, Chemistry Teacher; *b:* Macon, GA; *m:* Mary Ann Spencer; *c:* Samuel; *ed:* (AA) Bio, Oxford Coll 1973; (BS) Bio, Emory Univ 1975; (MSED) Sci, GA St Univ 1981; *cr:* Teacher Gordon HS 1976-87, Redan HS 1987-; *ai:* City of Stone Mountain Zoning Bd 1985-; *office:* Redan HS 5247 Redan Rd Stone Mountain GA 30088

REID, ROBBIE VANCE, 5th Grade/Adjunct Eng Coll Ins; *b:* Fayetteville, TN; *m:* Merwyn Loyde; *c:* Erika, Jesse, Stacey; *ed:* (BA) Eng, Mid TN St Univ 1968; (MED) Supervision/Admin, Trevecca Nazarene Coll 1987; Eng; *cr:* Graduate Asst Eng Mid Tn St Univ 1968-70; Aide Amer Lang Skills Southwest MN St Coll 1970-71; 7th-11th Grade Eng Teacher Lincoln Consolidated Schls 1972-78; 1st/2nd/4th Grade Rdng Teacher Elora Elem Sch 1978-79; 6th Grade Teacher Flintville Elem Sch 1979-; *ai:* Faculty Sec; Mentor for New Teachers; Partners in Ed Adv; In-Service Comm; NEA; TEA; ICEA Rep; Girl Scouts Boy Scouts Day Camp Helper; 4-H Clubs Spon 1979-; Deans List Throughout Coll Graduate Assistantship MTSU; *office:* Flintville Elem Sch Rural Route 01 Flintville TN 37335

REID, RODNEY STEPHEN, Mathematics Teacher; *b:* Bluefield, WV; *m:* Patricia Gail Smith; *c:* Kelly, Joshua; *ed:* (BS) His, 1977, (BS) Scndry Ed, 1985 Bluefield Coll; *cr:* Math Teacher Tazewell Mid Sch 1985-; *ai:* Girls Var Bsktbl Head Coach Tazewell HS; Boys Var Bsktbl Asst Coach Tazewel HS; VEA, NEA, TEA Mem 1985-; Listed Whos Who Among Stus in Amer Univs & Colls 1976-77; Outstanding Young Men of Amer 1985; *office:* Tazewell Mid Sch 100 Bulldog Ln Tazewell VA 24651

REID, SANDRA GRAYSON, Senior English Teacher; *b:* Yazoo City, MS; *ed:* (BSED) Comm 1975, (MED) Speech, 1978 MS Coll; (AA) Eng, Univ S MS 1987; Grad of MEAL Inst MS Assn of Women in Educl Leadership 1989; *cr:* Eng Teacher Greenville HS 1978-79; Media Buyer The Agency Incorporated 1979-81; Speech/Eng Teacher Hancock North Cntrl 1981-87, Yazoo City HS 1987-; *ai:* Yrbk, Forensic Club, Sr Trip, Drama Club, Chrldr Spon; Sr Play Dir; Prom & Project Graduation Comm; Assn of Curr & Dev 1989-; NCTE, MS Assn of Educators; MS Ec Cncl STAR Teacher 1987.

REID, SUSAN QUARTERMAN, 7th/8th Grade Algebra Teacher; *b:* New Orleans, LA; *m:* Kenneth H.; *c:* Natalie, Samantha; *ed:* (BA) Speech/Scndry, 1972, (BE) Elem Ed, 1973 Univ of MS; *cr:* 7th-8th Grade Pre-Algebra/Algebra Teacher Olive Branch Mid Sch 1973-; *ai:* Natl Jr Honor Society Spon; Math Chm Olive Branch Mid Sch; Textbook Comm Mem 1989-; MS Assn of Educators; De Soto Cty Assn of Ed Faculty Rep 1973-; Awd of Excl from MS Educl Television 1982; Teacher of Yr 1989-; *office:* Olive Branch Mid Sch 8631 Pigeon Roost Rd Olive Branch MS 38654

REIDER, JUNE KERNS, Chapter I Teacher; *b:* Glendale, AZ; *m:* Howard; *c:* Monna Adams, Frank, Twila; *ed:* (BA) Elem Ed, Ft Lewis 1975; (MA) Elem Ed, NM St Univ Coll 1980; *cr:* 2nd Grade Teacher 1975-80, Chapter I Teacher 1980- Cntrl Elem; *ai:* Phi Delta Kappa 1988-89; Intnl Rdng Assn Schlsp Chairperson 1982-; NM Quality Ed Awd 1987-88; US Dept of Ed Secys Initiative Awd 1988; Dist, St, Natl Conference Presenter; *home:* 609 N Jordan Bloomfield NM 87413

REIDY, GEORGE HUGHES, Mathematics Department Chair; *b:* Baltimore, MD; *ed:* (BA) His, Wheeling Coll 1972; (MA) Intnl Ed/Human Resource Dev, George Washington Univ 1986; *cr:* Math Teacher Backus Jr HS 1974-80; Math Dept Chm Sch Without Walls 1980-; *ai:* Swimming; Sr Class Spon.

REIF, BARBARA ANN (COTTINGHAM), Kindergarten Teacher; *b:* Cincinnati, OH; *m:* R. Daniel; *c:* Mark D.; *ed:* (BA) Art Ed, 1958, (BS) Art, Univ of Cincinnati; (MS) Early Chldhd, 1872 Univ of Cincinnati; Courses to Complete Kndgtn Cert; Miami Univ; *cr:* K-6th Grade Art Teacher Concord Elem 1958-60; Pre-Sch Teacher Happy Hour Nursery Sch 1966-68; Kndgtn Teacher C O Harrison Elem 1968-; *ai:* 4th-6th Grade Music Prgms Dir; Grandparents Day Prgm; 4th Grade Christmas Prgm; 5th/6th Grade Spring Musical; C O Harrison Elem Soc Comm Mem; NEA, OH Ed Assn Mem 1968-; Oak Hills Ed Assn (Mem, Sch Rep); Cincinnati Zoo Mem; Friend of Shakertown Mem; Westwood Meth Church (Admin Bd Mem 1983-86, Missions Comm Mem 1983-86); Oak Hills Sch Dist Employee of Month 1990; Wrote & Composed 4th Grade Musical Story.

REIF, JODY ANN, Spanish Teacher; *b:* Oshkosh, WI; *ed:* (BS) Span Ed, Univ of WI Oshkosh 1979; Span Ed, Univ of WI 1985-86; *cr:* Span Teacher Butte Des Morts & Maplewood Jr HS 1979-80, Berlin HS 1980-85; Span Teaching Asst Univ of WI 1985-86; Span Teacher Berlin HS 1986-; *ai:* Span Club Adv 1979-; Berlin HS Pom Pon Squad Adv 1981-; WI Assn of Foreign Lang Teachers; WI Ed Assn Building Rep 1989; NEA, Kappa Delta Pi; Muscular Dystrophy Assn Cmmty Service Awd 1987-89; Berlin Jaycees (St Dir 1988-89, Pres 1989-, Management Dev VP 1990-), Jaycee of the Quarter 1987, Jaycee of Yr 1987-88, Pres Awd 1988-89; Outstanding Jaycee of Region 1989-; Organized, Chaperoned, Guided 8 Stu Trips to Mexico; *office:* Berlin HS 289 E Huron Berlin WI 54923

REIFF, LINDA SUE (CHERRY), 4th Grade Teacher; *b:* Charlotte, MI; *m:* Anthony Franklin; *c:* Benjamin, Christopher; *cr:* Elem Teacher Southern Wells Cmmty Schls 1971-; *ai:* Math Comm; Ducks Unlimited Area Chm 1990; Tri Kappa 1989-; Calvary Luth Church (Organist 1974-, Church Cncl 1974-); *home:* 125 W Wabash Bluffton IN 46714

REILLY, BARBARA COHEN, Fourth Grade Teacher; *b:* Wilkes-Barre, PA; *m:* Kevin M.; *ed:* (BA) Elem Ed, 1972, (MS) Elem Ed, 1975 Wilkes Coll; Grad Level Ed Courses PA St Univ, Wilkes Univ; *cr:* 4th Grade Teacher Dallas Elem Sch 1972-; *ai:* Act 178, Report Card, Writing Comm; Dallas Ed Assn Secy 1973-75; Delta Kappa Gamma Society Intnl 1986-; Excl in Ed 1989.

REILLY, THOMAS EUGENE, Psychology Teacher; *b:* Bronx, NY; *m:* Deborah Ann; *c:* Jared, Brendan; *ed:* (BS) Phys Ed, 1967, (MA) Spec Ed, 1970 George Washington Univ; (MAT) Admin/Supervision, The Citadel 1972; Spec Ed/Psych, Univ of S CA 1974; *cr:* Spec Ed Teacher Golden HS 1975-78, Evergreen HS 1978-79; Consultant Charleston Cty Sch Dist 1979-80; Psych/Teacher Wando HS 1980-; *ai:* Soccer Coach; Amer Psychological Assn, AFT; Phi Delta Kappa; Region 6 AAAA Conference 1983, 1985-86, Coach of Yr; Low Cntry Coaches Assn 1985-86, Coach of Yr; Fellowship Grad Stud; Ftbl Athletic Schlsp; *office:* Wando HS 1560 Mathis Ferry Rd Mount Pleasant SC 29464

REIM, GEORGE DAVID, Social Studies Department Chm; *b:* Philadelphia, PA; *m:* Ruth Wible; *c:* David, Jeffrey, Diane; *ed:* (AB) Liberal Arts, Cntrl 1964; (BS) Soc Stud, W Chester Univ 1968; (MED) Soc Stud Ed, Temple Univ 1973; Soc Stud Supervisory Certificate 1975; Scndry Prin Certificate 1976; *cr:* Teacher 1968-75, Housemaster 1975-76, Soc Stud Dept Chm 1977- Cheltenham HS; *ai:* Var Soccer & Girls Sftbl Coach; Intramural Bowling, Dev Ec Ed Prgm, Natl Bicentennial Competition on the Constitution & Bill of Rights Dir; Stu Mock Trial Coord; Phila Alpha Theta, Pi Gamma Mu; E Montgomery Cncl for Soc Stud (Pres 1974-75) 1971; Phi Delta Kappa 1973; PA Cncl for Soc Stud 1971; NCSS 1971; Cncl Rock Northampton Little League (Commissioner 1984-87, Treas 1987-), Service Awd 1988; Whos Who in Amer Ed Recognition; Developmental Ec Educator Awd; *office:* Cheltenham HS Rices Mill Rd & Carlton Ave Wyncote PA 19095

REIMANN, ROBERT HENRY, Fifth Grade Teacher; *b:* West Bend, WI; *m:* Patricia Schall; *c:* Patricia; *ed:* Elem Ed, Dodge Cty Teachers Coll 1964; (BS) Elem Ed, Univ of WI Oshkosh 1968; (MS) Admin, Univ of WI Superior 1972; Madeline Hunter Trng, Cooperative Learning; *cr:* 8th Grade Teacher/Prin Fremont Elem 1964-68; 7th/8th Grade Sci/Math Teacher Marion Sch Dist 1969-70; 5th Grade Teacher 1970-85, Prin 1985- Weyauwega-Fremont Schls; 5th Grade Teacher Weyauwega-Fremont Sch Dist; *ai:* CWRC, WEA, WI Math Cncl Mem; *office:* Weyauwega-Fremont Sch 615 Wolf River Dr Weyauwega WI 54983

REIMER, ARLENE E. (JOHNSON), 5-6th Grade Reading Teacher; *b:* Elkader, IA; *m:* Gerald L.; *c:* Cindy J. Mueller, Lesa J. Moose; *ed:* (BA) Elem Ed, Upper IA Univ 1971; Various Universities 1989; *cr:* Headstart Teacher NEIA Cmnty Action 1971-73; 5th Grade Teacher 1973-74, Remedial Math Teacher 1974-75 St Marys; Rdng Teacher 1975-76, Remedial Rdng/4th-6th Grade Teacher Cntrl Comm; *ai:* Phase 3 Projects Mid Sch Rep; Staff Dev Comm; Exec Bd of Cntrl Ed Assn; Steering Comm; NEA 1976-; IA St Ed Assn 1976-; Cntrl Ed Assn 1976-; GFWC Proteus Club Pres 1986-; Clayton Cty GFWC Pres 1990; Peace United Church of Christ Church Cncl Secy/Treas 1987-; Clayton Cty Cattlewoman of Yr 1987; *office:* Cntrl Comm Sch Volga Mid Sch Elkader IA 52043

REIMER, PATRICIA ALICE, Home Economics Teacher; *b:* Albany, GA; *ed:* (BS) Home Ec, GA Southern Coll 1984; Childcare Trng, GA St Univ; Home Ec Staff Dev Wrkshps; *cr:* Kndgtn Teacher Kindercare Daycare 1984-85; Home Ec/Occupational Childcare Teacher Troup Cty Comprehensive HS 1986-; *ai:* Home Ec Related Occupations Organization Adv; Prof Assn of GA Educators 1986-87; FHA Alumni 1988-89; Troup Cty Cncl on Child Abuse Educator 1988-89; *office:* Troup Cty Comprehensive HS 1920 Hamilton Rd La Grange GA 30240

REIMERS, FAYE NEIL, Second Grade Teacher; *b:* Ellendale, ND; *m:* Charles R.; *c:* Michelle; *ed:* (BS) Elem Ed/Bus, Ellendale St Teachers Coll 1963; (MS) Elem Ed, Univ of ND 1986; *cr:* 2nd Grade Teacher Northridge 1963-67, Winship 1968-69, Creek Valley 1970-71, Rita Murphy 1971-; *ai:* Bismarck Public Schls Health Comm; NEA 1963-; Grand Forks Ed Assn 1968-69; Bismarck Ed Assn 1963-67, 1971-; Natl Rdng Assn 1987-88; Grant From ND Lung Assn; Certified Natl Trainer for Growing Healthy Grade 2.

REIMINK, RONALD L., Biology Teacher; *b:* South Haven, MI; *m:* Linda; *c:* Jessee, Kelsey; *ed:* (BA) Bio, Hope Coll 1980; (MA) Bio, Univ of MI 1990; Chem, Grand Valley St Univ; Bio, MI St Univ; *cr:* Sci Teacher Hudsonville Public Schls 1982-; *ai:* Bsktbl Coach; Technology Comm Mem; MI Acad Sci 1990; MI Sci Teacher Assn 1987-89; NABT 1988-89; City Parks Commission Mem 1988-89; Biological Research During Summer Months 1982-; 6 Articles Published Scientific Journals; *office:* Hudsonville HS 5037 32nd Ave Hudsonville MI 49426

REINBOLD, MARIAN, 5th Grade Teacher; *b:* Farrell, PA; *m:* David G.; *c:* Margaret Trusa, David; *ed:* (BS) Elem Ed, Penn St Univ 1956; Lehigh Univ; *cr:* 4th Grade Elem Teacher Montclair NJ; 5th/6th Grade Teacher Lehighton PA; Kndgtn/4th/5th Grade Teacher Panther Valley Mid Sch; *ai:* Cty Envirothon; Schl Plays; Graduation Prgms; NEA, PSEA; Womens Club Pres; GSA Leader; BSA Den Mother; Sunday Sch Teacher; *office:* Panther Valley Mid Sch 11 E Bertsch St Lansford PA 18232

REINBOLD, PHILIP ALAN, Chemistry/Physics Teacher; *b:* Robinson, IL; *m:* Linda Klatt; *ed:* (BS) Chem, E IL Univ 1968; (MED) Curr/Instruction, Univ of WY 1974; *cr:* Sci Teacher Farmer City HS 1968-69, Riverton Jr HS 1969-70, Hanna Elk Mt HS 1970-; *ai:* Soph Class Spon; Amer Chem Soc, Amer Assn Physics Teachers, NSTA; Sons of Amer Revolution; Hanna Basin Historical Society Pres 1988-; IN Historical Society, KY Historical Society; *office:* Hanna Elk Mountain HS Hwy 72 Box 810 Hanna WY 82327

REINERT, PHYLLIS DOROTHY GALIKOWSKI, Teacher; *b:* Sobieski, WI; *m:* William T.; *c:* Gary, Ann Duebner; *ed:* (BS) Upper Elem, Oshkosh St 1960; *cr:* Teacher Waukesha Public Schls 1960-61, Thiensville Public Sch 1961-62, Grafton Public Schls 1962-64, Manitowoc Public Schls 1978-; *ai:* Unit Leader; Patrol Prgm; Building Rep Local Union; NEA, WI Ed Assn, Manitowoc Ed Assn; *office:* Stangel Elem Sch 1002 E Cedar Ave Manitowoc WI 54220

REINHARD, DEBORAH (BETZ), Kindergarten Teacher; *b:* Bluffton, IN; *m:* Rodney Wayne; *c:* Julie, Danielle; *ed:* (BA) Elem Ed, Huntington Coll 1974; (MS) Elem Ed, IN Univ 1978; *cr:* 3rd Grade Teacher Tunnel Hill Sch 1974-75; 2nd Grade Teacher Dawnville Elem 1975-76; 4th-6th Grade Spec Rdng Teacher 1976-77, 2nd Grade Teacher 1977-79, 4th Grade Teacher 1979-89, Kndgtn Teacher 1989- S Wells; *ai:* Prin Advisory, Math, Purchasing & Progress Reports Comms; Delta Kappa Gamma Mem; Park United Brethren in Christ Church (Mem, Former

Admin Bd Mem, Past WMF Pres, Childrens Choir Dir); *office:* Southern Wells Elem Sch 9120 S 300 W Poneto IN 46781

REINHARDT, JENNIFER ROBIN TAYLOR, 3rd/4th Grade Teacher; *b:* Lincolnton, NC; *c:* Shana B.; *ed:* (BA) Primary Ed, Mars Hill Coll 1978; *cr:* Teacher Southwest Elem 1978-; *ai:* Mentor & Math Wkshp Teacher; Nom Southwest Elem Terry Sandford Awd; *home:* Rt 3 Box 518 Newton NC 28658

REINHART, CHARLES PHILLIP, Mathematics Teacher; *b:* Urbana, IL; *m:* Elizabeth Sleeter; *c:* Ann, David, Mary Jo, Amy; *ed:* (BSED) Math Ed, E IL Univ 1962; (MAT) Math Ed, Rockford Coll 1968; Univ of MO, Univ of IN, N IL Univ, Parkland Comm Coll, Univ of IL; *cr:* Math Teacher Oregon Cmmty HS 1962-68; Part-Time Math Teacher Parkland Cmmty Coll 1968-; Math Teacher Monticello HS 1969-; *ai:* Math Curr Co-Chm; NEA, IL Ed Assn 1962-; Monticello Ed Assn 1969-; NCTM, IL Cncl Teachers of Math 1974-; *office:* Monticello HS 101 E William Monticello IL 61856

REINHART, KATRINA SCHUMACHER, Reading Teacher; *b:* Hazleton, PA; *m:* William E. Wilson, Jr.; *ed:* (BA) Psych, Beaver Coll 1973; (MED) Scndry Ed, Lehigh Univ 1974; Post Masters Studies Cmptrs in Writing, Reality Theory, Cooperative Learning, Portfolio Assessment, Developing Higher Order Thinking Skills, Curr Dev for Gifted & Talented Child; *cr:* Social Restoration Specialist Nitschmann Jr HS 1973-77; Rdng Specialist/Corrective Rdng Lab 1977-82; Dev Rdng Teacher 1982-Celia Snyder Mid Sch; *ai:* Faculty Advisory Comm to Princ; Mid Sch Advisory Comm to Asst Supt; Natl Mid Sch Assn 1989-; Bucks Cty Rdng Assn 1977-81; Intl Rdng Assn 1977-79; Greater Hazleton Judge 1985/86/89; Jr Chamber of Commerce; Pilots License 1983; Applicant Teacher in Space Prgm 1986; *office:* Cecelia Snyder Mid Sch 3330 Hulmeville Rd Bensalem PA 19020

REINHOLZ, JEANNE L., 4th Grade Teacher; *b:* Shawano, WI; *ed:* (BS) Elem Ed, Univ of WI Oshkosh 1972; Madeline Hunter Trng; Great Books Jr Division Facilitator; *cr:* 1st-4th Grade Teacher Keshena Elem Sch 1973-76; 4th Grade Teacher Lincoln Elem Sch 1976-; Summer Sch Supvr Shawano/Gresham Schl Dist 1988-; *ai:* Prof Trng, Ed for Employment Comm; Delta Kappa Gamma Society; Wolf River Rdng Cncl; Shawano Area Bus & Prof Women; Richard Jefferies Dedicated Teacher Awd 1988; *home:* 317 E Richmond Shawano WI 54166

REINITZ, JANE ANN, Foreign Lang Chair/Cnslr; *b:* Owensboro, KY; *ed:* (BA) Latin, IN St Univ 1967; (MAT) Latin, Loyola & IN St Univ 1969; (MS) Counseling, IN St Univ & Univ of Evansville 1971; Grad Work; *cr:* Teacher/Cnslr Warrick Cty Sch Corp; Counseling Instr Univ of Evansville 1974-75; *ai:* Curr Cncl Dept Chm; Jr Classical League Spon; IN Classical Conference; NEA, ISTA, WCCTA; Delta Kappa Gamma Treas 1984-88; IN Sch Cnslr Assn; AACA; Alpha Sigma Alpha Alum Assn; IN Jr Classical League Exec Bd; Philharmonic Guild Contributor; Museum Assn Mem; Chosen From Latin Teachers to Escort Honors Abroad Prgm 1974; *office:* Boonville HS N 1st St Box 649 Boonville IN 47601

REINKE, FRANCES KASPEREK, Science Dept Chairperson; *b:* Gary, IN; *w:* Leonard (dec); *ed:* (BA) Bio/Eng/Lib Sci, IN Univ 1963; (MA) Counseling/Guidance, Univ of MI 1965; (MS) Specialist/Geology, Univ of Notre Dame 1972; Natl Sci Fnd Inst, Bscs Trng, Biochem & Cytology, Ball St Univ 1964; Microbio & Genetics, Cath Univ of Puerto Rico 1967; Geology & Appalachia Field Stud Notre Dame Univ 1968; Geology Field Stud, Mt St Univ 1971; Sabbatical Working Toward Chem & Physics Cert, IN Univ 1979-80; Several Expeditions; Various Wkshps; Post Grad Stud Prevention of Drug & Alcohol Abuse, Concordia Coll 1988-; *cr:* Sci Educator Redford HS 1963-64; Bio/Anatomy Teacher to Phy Handicapped Hammond Public Schls 1965-73; Sci Educator Gavit HS 1965-79; Sci Teacher Homebound Tutorial Prgm Hammond Public Schls 1965-88; Sci Educator/Sci Dept Chairperson Clark HS 1980-; *ai:* Stu Act Dir; Coach Jr HS & HS Academic Decathlon, Sci Olympiad; Sci Fair Spon; Cmptr Trainer of Colleagues 1987; United Nations Medical Symposium 1987; IN Book Adoption Comm 1986-87; Labor/Management Conf 1988; Inland Steel Jets Prgm; Sierra Club; Sci & Engineering Competition; Sci & Chess Club Spon; Hoosiers Sci & Super Bowl; NCA Comm; Teacher in Space Prgm; Sci Fair Judge Organizer; Winter Formal, Prom & Graduation Comms; NHS Advisory Bd; NCA Comm; AFT, HFT, NSTA, NABT 1965-; HASTI 1984-; NEA, ISTA, CAST, IN Acad Of Sci Mem; Teacher Expectation Stu Achievement (Sch Improvement Prgm 1986-88, Lead Teacher 1988); Parent Stu Teacher Assn; Save the Dunes Cncl; Hammond Ed Cncl Awd 1987; Inland Steel Outstanding Teacher Awd 1986; Semi-Finalist St of IN Presidential Awds Excl in Sci & Math 1987; Outstanding Bio Teacher Nom 1988; *office:* George Rogers Clark HS 1921 Davis Ave Hammond IN 46327

REINKE, MARY ELLEN MARCELLUS, English/Journalism Teacher; *b:* Defiance, OH; *m:* David K.; *c:* Steven, D. Bradley, Kurt, Gregg; *ed:* (BS) Eng/Government, Miami OH Univ 1966; Grad Work Curr E MI Univ, Journalism Cntrl MI Univ, MI St Univ, Univ of Houston; *cr:* Jr HS Eng Teacher Howell Public Schls 1967-71; 10th Grade Eng Teacher Howell HS 1975-78; 10th Grade Eng/Journalism I/Newspaper Teacher Howell HS 1979-; *ai:* Main 4 Howell HS Weekly Page, Main 4 Attraction, Sr Edition Magazine, Charisma Lit & Art Magazine Adv; Mem of Sch Improvement Comm; Save our Schls Millage Comm; MI Interscholastic Press Assn (Secy, Bd Trustee) 1985-89, Golden Pen 1985; NCTE, GUPA; Grace Luth Church Chm of Vietnamese Resettlement Comm 1976-78; Freedom Fnd Schlsp to Attend Liberals Conservative Thought Course Valley Forge, PA 1984; Speaker at Various Conferences; MI Interscholastic Press Assn Summer Journalism Wkshp 1985- IN Univ; Publications have Won Top Honors in St & Natl Competition; MI Publication Adv of Yr; *office:* Howell HS 1200 W Grand River Howell MI 48843

REINWALD, SHERRI RITZ, Coord of Commonwealth Classrm; *b:* Cumberland, MD; *m:* Thomas P.; *ed:* (BS) Scndry Ed, Eng, Speech, 1970; (MS) Comm, 1975 Shippensburg St Coll; (MED) Scndry Sch Counseling, Shippensburg Univ 1987; *cr:* Eng/Speech Teacher Midpark HS 1970-72; Eng Teacher McConnelsburg HS 1973-76; Greencastle-Antrim HS 1976-89; Coord-Commonwealth Classroom Greencastle-Antrim HS 1989-; *ai:* Co-Adv, Peer Listeners; Mem, Stu Assistance Team; Co-Chairperson, Greencastle-Antrim Prof Dev Comm; PA St Ed Assn 1973-; NEA 1973-; Greencastle-Antrim Ed Assn 1975-Educator of Yr 1988-89; Central Fulton Ed Assn Treas 1973-76; Amer Assn of Counseling and Dev 1985-; Co-Authored NEA Drop-Out Prevention Project-Project Rescue; *office:* Greencastle Antrim H S 300 S Ridge Ave Greencastle PA 17225

REISCH, MARY LOU, Third-Fourth Grade Teacher; *b:* Dubuque, IA; *ed:* (BA) Elem Ed, Briar Cliff Coll 1966; *cr:* 4th-6th Grade Teacher Pocahontas Cath Sch 1958-61; 7th/8th Grade Teacher Holy Rosary Sch 1962-69, H T R Sch 1976-78, St John Sch 1969-76, 1978-79; 6th-8th Grade Teacher Aquin Sch 1979-89; 3rd/4th Grade Teacher Visitation Sch 1989-; *ai:* Safety Patrols, Lunch-Playground Supvr; Aquin Parent Teacher Group Mem 1982-89; Religion Comm Co Chairperson 1988-89; Interim Prin St John Sch Bancroft 1978-79; *office:* Visitation Sch 603 N Broad Stacyville IA 50476

REISENBICHLER, NANCY MIESNER, Business/Mathematics Teacher; *b:* Perryville, MO; *m:* Ralph W.; *c:* Amy, Steven; *ed:* (BS) Math, SE MO St Univ 1973; Working Towards Masters Bus Ed, SE MO St Univ; *cr:* Teacher Meadow Heights HS 1973-76, Perryville HS 1981-; *ai:* FBLA Club Adv; MO Bus Ed Assn, SE MO Bus Ed Assn 1981-; Alpha Delta Kappa 1984-; Golden Apple Awd Perryville HS 1989; *office:* Perryville HS College & Edwards Perryville MO 63775

REISER, CAROL KEPNER, Grammar/Literature Teacher; *b:* Springfield, IL; *m:* Norman James; *c:* Craig J., Amy L.; *ed:* (BA) Elem Ed, IL St Univ 1969; Cert Lang Art, St of IL 1970; *cr:* Elem Teacher Coal City Grade Sch 1964, 1966; HS Teacher St Joseph-Ogden HS 1970-71; Elem Teacher Blessed Sacrament Grade Sch 1974-79, Lettie Brown Grade Sch 1979-84; HS Teacher Morton HS 1984-; *ai:* Dist CRT Test Writer & Evaluator; Amer Assn of Univ Women; Jr Womens Club; *home:* 1208 S Lee Morton IL 61550

REISER-ANTONUK, RUTH ANN, Spanish Teacher; *b:* Rhinelander, WI; *m:* John W. Jr.; *ed:* Certificate Span, Univ of Barcelona 1966; (BA) Span, Univ of WI Oshkosh 1968; (MA) Ibero-Amer Stud, Univ of WI 1973; Jareriana Bogota Columbia; Forester Inst, San Jose Costa Rica; *cr:* Elem Teacher St Peters Grade Sch 1969-71; Span Teacher The Mercersburg Acad 1973-77, Rhinelander HS 1979-; *ai:* Span Club; WI Assn of Foreign Lang Teachers; *office:* Rhinelander HS Coolidge Ave Rhinelander WI 54501

REISIG, JERRY L., Mathematics/Physics Instructor; *b:* Billings, MT; *m:* Terri L. Shoquist; *c:* Jake, Lee, Ali; *ed:* (BS) Civil Engineering, 1978, (MS) Math, 1988 MT St Univ; *cr:* Math/Physics Teacher Bozeman Sr HS 1979-; *ai:* Ftbl & Track Coach; Intramural Bsktbl Dir; MT Ed Assn 1979-; *office:* Bozeman Sr HS 205 N 11th Ave Bozeman MT 59715

REITER, MARJORIE ANN, Fifth Grade Teacher; *b:* New York, NY; *m:* Herbert D.; *c:* Adam, Joshua, Daniel; *ed:* (BA) Ed, Queens Coll 1966; (MA) Ed, Stony Brook Univ 1975; Grad Stud; *cr:* Teacher Kings Park Schls 1966-71, 1981, S Huntington Schls 1984-; *ai:* Stu Cncl Adv 1984-87; Thinking Skills Prgm Trainer; Teacher Consultant; S Huntington Teachers Assn 1984-; Suffolk Rdng Cncl, NYSUT; Wrote Dist Curr Study Skills & Thinking Skills; *office:* Countrywood Elem Sch Old Country Rd South Huntington NY 11746

REITER, RICHARD WILLIAM, HS History Teacher; *b:* Detroit, MI; *m:* Linda Joy; *c:* Jonathan, Nathan; *ed:* (BRE) Bible, Midwestern Baptist Coll 1978; Teachers Certificate Pensacola Chrstn Coll; *cr:* HS His Teacher Liberty Chrstn Acad 1988-; *ai:* Bsktbl Coach; Chess Club Adv.

REITH, KAY T., Science Teacher; *b:* Raleigh, NC; *c:* Katherine L.; *ed:* (BS) Sci Teaching/Bio, Univ of NC Chapel Hill 1964; Courses in Cmptr Sci, Teaching Skills Sci & Adolescent Behavior; *cr:* Teacher Raleigh City Public Schls 1964-68; Research Supvr NC St Univ 1968-70; Teacher Brookville Mid Sch 1974-76, Linkhorne Mid Sch 1976-; Dept Chairperson Linkhorne Mid Sch 1985; *ai:* Staff Dev, Soc, Intramural & Teacher Advisory Comms; Sci Dept Chairperson; LEA, NEA 1988-; Career Ladder For Merit with Lynchburg Schls; *office:* Linkhorne Mid Sch 2525 Linkhorne Dr Lynchburg VA 24501

REITH, SANDRA ISABEL, English Teacher; *b:* Elmira, NY; *m:* Donald Arthur; *c:* Brian Naylor, Rich Naylor; *ed:* (BS) Eng, Mansfield Univ 1972; Grad Courses Mansfield Univ; *cr:* Eng Teacher Williamsport Area Sch Dist 1973, Liberty Jr/Sr HS 1974-; *ai:* Jr Class Adv; Faculty & Staff Group Chairperson; PA St Ed Assn, NEA 1973-; Southern Tioga Ed Assn 1974-; Blossburg Fire & Ambulance Dept EMT 1982-87; Tioga Cty Emergency Medical Technician Instrs Secy 1981-, Trainer 1989; Amer Heart Assn CPR Instr 1983-; Wellsboro Fire Dept & Ambulance Assn EMT 1988-; Trinity Luth Church Youth Group Adv 1989-; *office:* Liberty Jr/Sr HS PO Box 135 Liberty PA 16930

REITZ, MARGARET L., Third Grade Teacher; *b:* Brookville, PA; *ed:* (BS) Elem Ed, Clarion Univ 1976; Completed Micro-Cmptr Courses, Clarion Univ; *cr:* 1st Grade Teacher 1977-82, 2nd Grade Teacher 1978-79, 3rd Grade Teacher 1982-Punxsutawney Area Schls; *ai:* PA St Ed Assn 1977-; Amer Red Cross Bd Mem 1986-; Worthville Borough Cncl 1987-; *home:* PO Box 3 Worthville PA 15784

REITZ, PAMELA CRIBB, 6th Grade Math/Cmptr Teacher; *b:* West Point, GA; *m:* John David; *c:* John; *ed:* (BA) Elem Ed/Math/Eng, Univ of AL 1972; (MA) Ed/Math, Union Coll 1976; (MA) Supervision, Univ of TN 1989; *cr:* Teacher Kaiserslaughtern Elem Sch, West View Mid Sch; *ai:* Chrldr Spon; Long Range Planning & Inservice Comm; Hamblen Cty Ed Assn Pres 1976-77; Girls Club Cmmty Advisory Bd 1990; Keep America Beautiful Comm Mem 1987-; *office:* West View Mid Sch 555 W Economy Rd Morristown TN 37814

REITZNER, COLLEEN LOCY, K-12th Grade Art Teacher; *b:* Appleton, WI; *m:* Richard E.; *c:* Bradley, Shane; *ed:* (BS) Interior Design, Univ of WI Madison 1977; (BS) Art Ed, Univ of WI PLatteville 1980; *cr:* Interior Designer Donohoos 1977-80; Art Teacher Shullsburg Schls 1980-; *ai:* Fine Art Club Adv; Gifted & Talented Comm; NAEA 1981-, Outstanding Youth Art Month 1987; NEA; St Augustine Parish CCD Teacher 1989; Sch Art Grant 1981; Art World Teacher & Participant 1987; *office:* Shullsburg Public Schls 444 N Judgement Shullsburg WI 53586

REKTORIK-SPRINKLE, PATRICIA JEAN, Latin Teacher; *b:* Robstown, TX; *m:* Edgar E. Sprinkle III; *c:* Julie, Mark; *ed:* (BA) Eng/Latin, 1963, (MA) Eng/Latin, 1967 Our Lady of the Lake Coll 1967; (PHD) Linguistics, Univ of N TX 1990; *cr:* Latin/Eng Teacher Eastwood HS 1963-64; Latin Teacher Austin HS 1964-65; Eng as Second Lang Teacher Our Lady of the Lake Coll 1965-66; Rhetoric/Composition Teacher TX A&M Univ 1968-69, 1972-74, Harford Comm Coll 1970-72; Latin Teacher Denton Ind Sch Dist 1974-; *ai:* Denton Jr Classical League Spon; Classics Assn of SW US Pres 1987-88; TX Foreign Lang Assn Honorary Membership Chairperson 1979; Metroplex Classics Assn Charter Mem; Amer Classical League Sight Rdng Competition Chairperson 1986-; TX Classics Assn; Mc Kinley Schlsp of Amer Classical League 1987; Resident Advisory Bd TX Acad of Sci & Math 1988-89; Regional Advisory Bd TX Textbook Adoption Comm 1989; Wkshp Presentor Various Organizations 1985, 1987-; Latin Club of Yr for TX 4 Time Winner; *office:* Denton HS 1007 Fulton Denton TX 76201

REMBERT, ERROLE DONNARD, Discipline Teacher; *b:* Birmingham, AL; *m:* Brigid Moriarty; *c:* Kim, Joe; *ed:* (BA) Elem Ed, OH St Univ 1973; *cr:* 5th Grade Teacher Winterset Elem 1973-80; 6th Grade Teacher Everett Mid Sch 1980-89; Discipline Teacher Whets One HS 1989-; *ai:* Head Boys & Girls Vlybl Coach; Columbus Ed Assn 1986-; Columbus Bd Ed Teacher 1973-; Teacher of Yr 1978-79/1979-80; Columbus Prof Teachers Assn Treas 1986-88; Northwest Optimist Bd of Dir-1976-; Excl Grant 1987-88 to Write New Prgm 6th Grade; *office:* Whetstone H S 4405 Scenic Dr Columbus OH 43214

REMICK, KAREN NOREEN, Horticulture Instructor; *b:* Latrobe, PA; *m:* John E.; *c:* Darren, Tracy, Noreen; *cr:* Paraprofessional Horticulture Instr Greater Johnstown Voc Tech; *ai:* FFA & VSO Adv; Johnstown Mum Society; *office:* Johnstown Area Voc Tech Sch 445 Schoolhouse Rd Johnstown PA 15904

REMIEN, ROGER ALLEN, Soc Sci/Phys Ed Teacher/Coach; *b:* Aberdeen, SD; *m:* Kristine Engelhart; *c:* Ashley, Tyler; *ed:* (BA) Soc Sci/Coaching, Huron Coll 1983; *cr:* Teacher/Coach Waverly HS 1983-87, Florence HS 1987-; *ai:* Asst Ftbl, Head Boys Bsktbl, Grade Boys Bsktbl Coach; Athletic Dir; Pi Gamma Mu, SD HS Coaches Assn, SD Bsktbl Coaches Assn 1983-; *home:* 1280 3rd St NW Watertown SD 57201

REMIREZ, ELLEN SCADDEN, Foreign Lang Chm/Span Teacher; *b:* Waterbury, CT; *m:* Claudio I. Jr.; *c:* Kathleen Scadden; *ed:* (BS) Span, 1969, (MS) Span, 1972 Cntrl CT St Univ; Grad Stud Cmptr Ed; Span, Cntrl CT St Univ; *cr:* Foreign Lang Dept Lead Teacher 1971-89, Span Teacher 1969-, Foreign Lang Dept Chm 1989- J A De Paolo Jr HS; *ai:* Girls Vlybl, Co-Ed Tennis Team Coach; CT Cncl Foreign Lang Teachers 1975-; Amer Assn Teachers of Span & Portuguese 1990; Alpha Mu Gamma Mem; Jr Womans Club of Cheshire Philanthropy Chm 1975-84; *office:* Joseph A De Paolo Jr HS 385 Pleasant St Southington CT 06489

REMPE, DORIS, English Teacher; *b:* Kansas City, MO; *m:* Vernon F.; *c:* Christopher, Nicholas, Kevin; *ed:* (BS) Eng, Univ of NE 1970; *cr:* Eng Teacher Superior HS 1970-73; Proof and Transit Dept Dir Securty Natl Bank 1973-75; Trust Dept Bookkeeper 1st Natl Bank of Grand Island 1975-76; Eng Teacher Central Cath HS 1975-; *ai:* Freshman Class Spon; Boys Tennis Spon; Search Comm; NE Cncl Teachers of Eng 1970-73/1990; Superior Assn 1970-73; St Rep 1971-72; NE St Ed Assn 1970-73; NEA 1970-73; NE Writers Organization 1980-; Beta Sigma Phi 1970-75 (Sec 1973-74, Treas 1974-75); Superior Mrs Jaycees 1973-75 (1st Vp 1974-75, Awds Chm 1975-76); Grand Island Jaycettes 1975-84; Individual Dev Dir 1977-79/Adv 1979-80/VP 1981-82; NE Jayceettes 1973-84 (Regl Chm 1976-77, Future Directions 1981-82, St Kennedy Couple Chm 1982-83, Presidential Asst 1983-84); YMCA- 1989-; CNACLD Pres 1989-.

REMSBURG, CHARLES DOUG, English Teacher; *b:* Woodbury, NJ; *m:* Madelyn; *c:* Tuesday, Jay, Guy, Heidi, Kip, Ian, Dru; *ed:* (BA) Eng/Speech/Journalism Marietta OH 1958; (MA) Admin, Univ of DE 1978; Grad Stud Eng; *cr:* Teacher Pennsville HS 1958-60, De La Warr HS 1960-73; Asst Prin De La

Warr HS 1973-78, Gunning Bedford Jr HS 1978-80; Prin Groves Adult HS 1978-80; Teacher Glasgow HS 1980-, Groves Adult HS 1967-78, 1980-; GED Examiner Groves Adult HS 1978-; Teacher Newark Summer HS 1982-; *ai:* Newspaper Spon; Head Bsbl, Asst Bsktbl Coach; Sch Plays & Past Athletic Dir; NEA, DSEA 1960-; Natl Journalism Honorary, Natl Honorary; Whos Who In Amer Coll & Univs 1958; Travel in Russia & Iron Curtain Countries 1959; Published Article; Won St Bsktbl Titles as Head Coach 1969, 1970; *home:* 2 Georgian Cir Newark DE 19711

RENAKER, LORETTA HARTUNG, 3rd Grade Teacher; *b:* Dayton, OH; *c:* Deborah E. Montgomery, Sharon L. Lackey; *ed:* (BS) Elem Ed, Univ of Dayton 1962; (ME) Elem Ed/Diagnostic Remedial Rdng, Miami Univ 1972; Jr Great Books Trng 1982; Cmptr Literacy; *cr:* 3rd Grade Teacher Meadowlawn Elem 1957-59, Brookville Elem 1965-; *ai:* Sch Soc Comm; Textbook Reviewer; Supporting Mem Local SADD Comm; Delta Kappa Gamma 1980-; ISTA 1965-; United Meth Women Leader 1980-; Tri-Kappa Inactive Corresponding Secy 1973-83; Franklin Cty Fine Art Assn 1989-; *home:* 6155 Riley Rd Brookville IN 47012

RENDLEMAN, BILLIE DEAN, Social Studies Teacher; *b:* Cobden, IL; *m:* Juanita Mae Barrow; *c:* Charlotte A. Hill, Linda M. Smith; *ed:* (BS) Soc Stud, 1957, (MS) Admin, 1962 S IL Univ; *cr:* Teacher/Coach White Hall HS 1957-62; Elem Prin White Hall Jr HS 1962-63, North Green Jr HS 1963-66; Asst Prin 1966-69, Soc Stud Teacher 1969, N Greene HS; *ai:* Stu Cncl, Jr & Sr Class Spon; N Greene Ed Assn; IL Fed of Teachers, AFT; Masonic Lodge 466; 1st Baptist Church Bd of Trustees 1975-78; Taught Summer Sch in Mankato MN 1968; 2 Yrbks Dedicated to Me; *home:* 374 King St White Hall IL 62092

RENEAU, HELEN OWENS, Office Admin Teacher; *b:* Folsom, OK; *m:* Wayne K.; *c:* Shane, Shawn, Karen, Keith; *ed:* (BS) Bus Ed, 1970, (MA) Bus, TX Womens Univ Denton 1972; *cr:* Teacher Cooke Cty Coll, Denton HS, Keller HS; *ai:* Bus Prof of America Club Adv; Instructional Leader Voc Dept; Voc Office Ed Teachers Assn of TX 1970-88, 15 Yr Mem 1986; Delta Kappa Gamma Treas 1987-88; Mothers of Twins Club; *office:* Keller HS 101 Indian Trail Dr Keller TX 76248

RENEGAR, LINDA KAY, Gifted Program Developer; *b:* Wichita Falls, TX; *m:* Don Leird; *c:* Dona K., Dana D., Todd M.; *ed:* (BS) Elem Ed, Univ of South MS 1964; (MED) Spec Ed/Gifted, Northwestern St Univ 1982; Rdng Specialist; Grad Stud Northwestern St Univ 1985; *cr:* 3rd Grade Teacher St Martin Cty Sch 1964-65; 5th Grade Teacher Hancock Cty Sch 1967-68; 3rd Grade Teacher Green Park Elem 1970; 3rd-6th Grade Teacher Rosenthal Elem 1977-79; K-6th Grade Gifted Teacher Martin Park Elem 1979-88; K-12th Grade Gifted Prgm Dev J B Lafargue Spec Ed Center 1988-; *ai:* LA St Task Force of Gifted Ed; Liaison Between Admins, Teachers, Parents, Stu; Young Authors Writing Contest Spon; Jr Great Books Leader; Assn for Gifted & Talented Stus Bd of Mgrs, Rapides Parish Assn for Gifted & Talented Stus 1980-; Rapides Admin Assn 1989-; Prof Assn for Teachers of Gifted & Talented 1987-; LA Supt Writing Awds Prgm, LA St Jr HS Speech Tournament Judge; *office:* J B Lafargue Spec Ed Center 4515 New York Ave Alexandria LA 71301

RENFREW, WILLIAM HOWARD, Biology Teacher; *b:* Chambersburg, PA; *m:* Joy Bonsall; *c:* Carol; *ed:* (MED) Admin, Univ of PA 1962; (MS) Bio; Grad Stud Temple Univ; Univ of CA Berkeley; North Carolina St Univ of Ri; Univ of MD; Villanova Univ; West Chester Univ; *cr:* Bio Teacher 1956-60, 1961-89 Coatesville HS; *ai:* Ski Club & Fishing Club Spon; Cross Cntry, Track, Swimming, Indoor Track, Sftbl & Tennis Coach; Sponsored Pep & Sportsmenship Club; NEA, PA St Ed Assn 1961-89; Coatesville Area Teachers Assn Pres 1974; Greater Philadelphia Track Pres 1970-74, Green Jacket 1973; Coaches Assn Pres; Meth Men Wagontown Swim Club Pres; Fellowship Ford Fnd to PA; NSF Yr for Doctorial Study at Temple; NSF Yr West Chester Univ; NSF Summer Univ of MD; RIU Univ of CA; Univ of NC St; Service Awd CATA; Great Philadelphia Coaches Assn; *office:* Scott Intermediate HS 8th & Olive St Coatesville PA 19320

RENFROE, JANE VINCENT, 11th Grade English Teacher; *b:* Millington, TN; *m:* Clyde R. Jr.; *c:* Jason; *ed:* (MA) Eng, 1983, (BA) Eng, 1978 Univ of Cntrl FL; Univ of S FL 1984-86; *cr:* Eng Teacher Riverdale HS 1983-84, Ft Myers HS 1984-; *ai:* Spon Stu Cncl; Omega Club Spon 1985-87; Faculty Rep; Leadershp Conference; Graduation Comm Chairperson 1989-; Sigma Tau Delta 1981-; Phi Delta Kappa 1989-; FL Cncl Teachers of Eng 1984-; Lee Cncl Teachers of Eng (VP, Writing Contest Chairperson 1985-86, 1990); Ft Myers Womens Cmmty Club 1988-; Kappa Delta Alumni Assn 1986-; A&E Network Natl Teacher Grant Competition 1st Place; Semi Finalist Golden Apple Teacher Recognition Prgm; Mimi-Grant Lee Cty Public Schls Fnd; Inst for Advancement of Teaching 1990; Inst FL St Univ S Women Writers 1989; *office:* Ft Myers HS 2645 Cortez Blvd Fort Myers FL 33901

RENICKER, JOHN L., Industrial Art Teacher; *b:* Wichita, KS; *m:* Janice I. Weaver; *c:* Brian; *ed:* (BS) Industrial Art, Metropolitan St Coll 1976; (MS) Industrial Sci, CO St Univ 1983; *cr:* Industrial Art Teacher Oberon Jr HS 1977, Jefferson HS 1978, Huron Jr HS 1978-; *ai:* Intnl Tech Ed Assn 1977-; CO Tech Assn 1976-; NEA 1978-; *office:* Huron Jr HS 10900 Huron St Northglenn CO 80234

RENKENBERGER, LINDA HENDRICKS, Business Teacher; *b:* Salem, OH; *m:* Jeffrey L.; *c:* Susan Martz, Beth; *ed:* (BS) Comprehensive Bus, Kent St Univ 1964; Voc Bus Cert, Kent St Univ 1972; *cr:* Bus Instr Austintown Fitch HS 1964-68, Salem Sr HS 1972-73, Boardman HS 1978-83, Columbiana HS 1985-; *ai:* Bus Prof of America Adv; Sch System Communications Comm; NEA, OH Ed Assn, OH Bus Teachers Assn; Region II Bus Prof Adv 1985-86; *office:* Columbiana HS 28 Pittsburgh St Columbiana OH 44408

RENNELS, V. BETH, Sixth Grade Teacher; *b:* Danville, IL; *ed:* (BA) Eng/Bio, Austin Coll 1966; (MA) Eng/His, Sul Ross St 1967; *cr:* Elem Teacher Warder Elem 1975-; *ai:* Liaison; Building Cabinet; Intervention Team; JCEA; Mentor Teacher Prgm; *office:* Warder Elem Sch 7840 Carr Dr Arvada CO 80005

RENNER, BIFF GREGORY, Math Teacher; *b:* Cedar Rapids, IA; *m:* Cynthia Kirvin; *c:* Nicholas, Emily, Megan; *ed:* (AS) Marshalltown Cmmty Coll 1976; (BA) Math, 1978, (MA) Teaching, Univ of N IA; *cr:* Math Teacher Parkview Jr HS 1978-85, Ankeny HS 1987-; *ai:* 8th Grade Boys Bsktbl Coach; NCTM, ICTM; Article Published in IA Cncl Teachers of Math Newsletter; *office:* Ankeny HS 1302 N Ankeny Blvd Ankeny IA 50021

RENNER, COOPER BRYAN, 9th Grade Librarian; *b:* Dallas, TX; *ed:* (BA) Eng - Summa Cum Laude, Univ of TX Arlington 1974; (MA) His - Summa Cum Laude, Univ of TX Austin 1983; Lib Certificate 1976; Doctoral Hum, Univ of TX Arlington 1984-86; *cr:* Teacher Chrstn Acad Oak Cliff 1974-75; Librarian Alexander Elem Sch 1977-82; Teacher Duncanville HS 1983-87; Librarian Fairmeadows Elem Sch 1988-89, Duncanville 9th Grade Sch 1989-; *ai:* Frosh Class Spon; TX Lib Assn; Acad of Amer Poets; Univ of TX Austin Fellow 1982; Poetry Published Pseudonymously; *office:* Duncanville 9th Grade Sch 7101 W Wheatland Dallas TX 75249

RENNINGER, LILLIAN MARIE (LANCE), 4th Grade Teacher; *b:* Sterling, OH; *m:* Richard; *c:* Rochelle, Ron; *ed:* (BS) Ed, 1960, (MSED) Ed, 1980 Ashland Univ; *cr:* 2nd Grade Teacher Shreve Elem 1954-63; 1st Grade Teacher Smithville Elem 1964-65; 4th Grade Teacher Sterling Elem 1974-; *ai:* Principals Advisory Cncl; NEA, OH Ed Assn; PTA Secy 1990; Laura Frick Geography Items Grant 1990; *home:* 7487 Pleasant Home Rd Sterling OH 44276

RENO, JANET SCOTT (WILES), Kindergarten Teacher; *b:* Bay City, MI; *m:* Orville Joseph Jr.; *c:* O.J.; *ed:* (BS) Ed 1967, (MA) Elem Ed 197O Cntrl MI Univ; Current Improvement Classes in Early Elem Ed; *cr:* Kngdtn Teacher Bay City Public Schls 1967-; *ai:* Kndgtn Task Force Comm Mem; Outcome Based Ed Dist Core Comm Mem; Kndgtn Christmas Prgm & Mothers Day Tea; Bay City Ed Assn 1967-; MEA 1967-; NEA 1967-; Kinderfun Booklet Form-Quotes Heard in My Kndgtn Classroom Distributed to Parents Staff & Other Employees Yearly.

RENOE, N. LAWRENCE, Math/Sci/His Teacher; *b:* Philipsburg, PA; *m:* Donna L. Butler; *c:* Larry A., Lori S. Biggar; *ed:* (BS) Elem Ed, St Univ of NY Oswego 1974; (MED) Educl Admin, Penn St 1977; Working Toward PhD Educl Admin, Faith Baptist Bible Coll; *cr:* Journalist USAF 1960-80; Admin Faith Baptist Acad 1980-85; Teacher Mt Calvary Chrstn 1985-; *ai:* Bible Quiz Team Adv; Youth Group Leader; Air Force Assn, PA St Alumni Assn; Air Force Commendations & Recruiting Awds; Published Articles; *office:* Mt Calvary Chrstn 629 N Holly St Elizabethtown PA 17022

RENSEL, AILEEN MC ELHATTAN, English Teacher; *b:* Vandergrift, PA; *m:* William Donald; *c:* Susan Rensel Shaffner, Eric M.; *ed:* (BA) Eng, Waynesburg PA 1958; Courses at Penn St & Clarion Univ; *cr:* Eng Teacher Du Bois Area Sr HS 1959; Psych/Speech/Eng I-II Teacher Du Bois Bus Coll 1967-73; Eng Du Bois Area Jr/Sr HS 1974-; *ai:* Free Lance Writer; Writer, Dir & Producer of Jr HS Play; 7th-8th Grade Bible Study Leader; Teach Writing for Interested Stu; Prof Dev & Curr Comms; Du Bois Area Cultural Bd 1989-; Arts Assn; Home Camp Meth Church Teach Sunday Sch 1970-; Free Lance Writer Poems Published; PA Industrial Chemical Company Organization Schlsp from Clairton PA 1954; *home:* RD 1 Rockton PA 15856

RENTZ, HELEN (HARTMAN), First Grade Teacher; *b:* Altoona, PA; *m:* Gerald O.; *c:* Stacey, Eric; *ed:* (BS) Elem Ed, IN Univ of Pa 1973; (MED) Developmental/Remedial Rdng, PA St Univ 1976; *cr:* Kndgtn Teacher 1973-75, 1st Grade Teacher 1975-80 Mc Kinley Sch; 1st Grade Teacher Juniata Elem 1980-; *ai:* Public Relations Comm; Pres of Coalition of Altoona Prof; Asst Soccer Coach; PA St Ed Assn 1973-; Altoona Area Ed Assn 1973-; Religion Teacher 1989-; Chosen for Local TV Interview to Rep 1st Grade Teachers in Altoona Area Sch Dist; *office:* Juniata Elem Sch 7th Ave 4th St Juniata Altoona PA 16601

RENTZ, JEAN MAGEE, First Grade Teacher; *b:* Lemoyne, PA; *m:* Robert I.; *c:* Jacqueline Rentz Henry, Judy Rentz Garrett, John T., Joann Rentz Rowe; *ed:* (BS) Soc Sci, Albright Coll 1951; PA St Univ, W Chester Univ, Millersville Univ; *cr:* HS Soc Stud Teacher Christiana HS 1951-53; 1st Grade Teacher Octorara Elem Sch 1969-; *ai:* NEA; PA St Ed Assn 1986-88; Octorara Area Ed Assn Building Rep; Moore Memorial Lib Secy 1960-70; 4-H Club Sewing Leader 1965-71; BSA Den Mother 1957-59, 1967-69.

RENWICK, MARLENE A. (GUTOWSKI), 11th Grade English Teacher; *b:* Sharon, PA; *m:* Walter J.; *ed:* (BSED) Eng, 1964, (MED) Eng, 1970 Slippery Rock St Coll; Numerous Courses PA Intermediate Unit IV; *cr:* Eng Teacher Greenville HS 1964-; *ai:* Stus Entering Writing Contests Adv; GEA, PSEA, NEA, NCTE 1964-; ALAN; Coll Club of Sharon; *office:* Greenville HS 9 Donation Rd Greenville PA 16125

RENZ, HEATHER REEKIE, Mathematics Teacher; *b:* Cleveland, OH; *m:* Michael M.; *ed:* (BA) Elem Ed/Lang Art, OR St Univ 1980; (MAT) Ed, Lewis & Clark Coll 1990; *cr:* 1st Grade Teacher Brownsville Elem 1980-82; 4th/6th Grade Cmptr Teacher Summer Trng & Ed Prgm 1982-86; 7th/8th Grade Math/Algebra/Journalism Teacher Gordon Russell Mid Sch 1986-; *ai:* Math & Sci Dept Chairperson 1987-; 7th Grade Sch Newspaper Adv 1986-; Sch Improvement Team 1987-; Career Day Coord 1987-; OR Cncl Teachers of Math 1986-; GETA Secy Local Assn 1984-85; OEA, NEA; *office:* Gordon Russell Mid Sch 3625 E Powell Blvd Gresham OR 97080

REPKO, SHERRY LYNN, Sixth & Seventh Grade Teacher; *b:* Shamokin, PA; *c:* Jason Albert; *ed:* (BS) Elem Ed, Bloomsburg Univ 1978; Bloomsburg Graduate Degree Prgm; *cr:* Permanent Substitute Mount Carmel Area Sch Dist 1978-80; 7th Grade Teacher 1981-84, 5th/6th Grade Teacher 1984-86, 7th & 8th Grade Teacher 1986-89, 6th & 7th Grade Teacher 1989- St Casimir Sch; *ai:* Stu Cncl Adv; 8th Grade Graduation Breakfast/Ceremony; 8th Grade Yrbk; Sci Fair; Cath Sch Week Comm; Kappa Delta Pi Natl Honor Society; Natl Cath Ed Assn; Whos Who of Young Prof 1987-88; *home:* 349 W 3rd St Mount Carmel PA 17851

REPPERT, NELDA G., English & Music Teacher; *b:* Pottstown, PA; *m:* Stuart C.; *c:* Owen J., Todd C., Jolene K., Jocelyn L.; *ed:* (BS) Music Ed, West Chester Univ 1955; Eng, Scndry Ed, Washington Coll; *cr:* Music Teacher Nether-Providence Township 1955-58; Pre-Sch Teacher Powells Nursery 1960-61; Tome Sch & Faith City Chrstn Sch 1980-81; Eng/Music Teacher Mt Aviat Acad 1983-; *ai:* Piano Teacher; Tutor Learning Disabled Children & Teenagers; NCTE 1988-; Cecil Cty Music Teachers Assn Pres 1978-79; *office:* Mt Aviat Acad 399 Childs Rd Childs MD 21916

RESENDEZ, MARGARET THELMA, 6th Grade Teacher; *b:* Los Ebanos, TX; *m:* Joe Sr.; *c:* Dina A., Joe Jr., Javier K.; *ed:* (BA) Elem Ed, Pan Amer Univ 1965; Advanced Academic Trng Region I, Edinburg; *cr:* 5th Grade Teacher Hargill Elem 1956-74; 6th Grade Teacher Whitney Elem 1974-; *ai:* Safety Patrol Spon; Textbook Comm; 6th Grade Chairperson; Bi-ling Teachers Assn 1974-; TX Classroom Teachers Assn 1956-88; NCTM 1980-; Assn of TX Prof Educators, NSTA 1988-; Friends of Pharr Lib Secy 1980-85; Art League 1977-; *home:* 214 W Hawk Pharr TX 78577

RESINOL, MARSHA M., Physical Education Teacher; *b:* Pittsburgh, PA; *ed:* (BS) Health/Phys Ed, 1973, (MED) Health Ed, 1979 Slippery Rock Univ; (PHD) Higher Ed, Univ of Pittsburgh 1988; *cr:* Phys Ed Teacher Canon Mc Millaan Sch Dist 1973-; *ai:* Delta Psi Kappa 1971-; AAHPERD, PSAHPERD; Appalachian Trail Conference, Sierra Club 1988-; Whos Who Among Stu Amer Coll & Univ 1973; Mem Addvisory Panel NEA Publications 1982, 1989; *office:* Canonsburg Mid Sch 25 E College St Canonsburg PA 15317

RESLER, SUSANNA NATION, 5th Grade/Math/Science Teacher; *b:* Marion, IN; *m:* Rex L.; *ed:* (BS) Elem Ed, Manchester Coll 1968; (MA) Elem Ed, Ball St Univ 1973; *cr:* Pre Sch/1st-4th/6th Grade Elem Teacher Lincoln Elem 1968-83; 5th Grade Math/Sci/Soc Stud Teacher Jones Mid Sch 1983-; *ai:* Prin Adv Cncl; Craft Club, Invent America Coord; Delta Kappa Gamma; Alpha Delta Kappa (VP, Pres 1980-82); IN St Teachers Assn, NEA, Marion Teacher Assn; Teacher of Yr Jones Mid Sch 1986-87; *home:* 1409 Marlin Dr Marion IN 46952

RESTA, BARRY A., English Teacher; *ed:* (BS) Mid Chldhd Ed, Valdosta St Coll 1983; *cr:* Sci Teacher Cook Mid Sch 1983-85; Lang Art Teacher Fitzgerald Jr HS 1986-; *ai:* Phi Delta Pi Co-Ed Y Club & St YMCA of GA Adv; Fitzgerald Assn Ed (VP 1989-, Pres 1990-91); *office:* Fitzgerald Jr HS PO Drawer 190 Fitzgerald GA 31750

RESTIVO, EVELYN DARLENE BRANDT, Science Teacher; *b:* Enid, OK; *m:* Joe H.; *c:* Angela; *ed:* (BSE) Natural Sci, Cntrl St Univ 1969; Numerous Colls & Univs; *cr:* 10th-12th Grade Bio/Chem/Physics Teacher John Marshall HS 1969; 8th Grade Phys Sci Teacher Hoover Jr HS 1969; 8th-12th Grade Phys Sci/Bio Teacher Huntington Ind Sch Dist 1969-70; 8th-12th Grade Phys Sci/Health/Bio/Chem/Physics Teacher Zavalla Ind Sch Dist 1970-71; 5th-8th Grade Life Sci/Phys Sci/Earth Sci Teacher Cedar Bluff Mid Sch 1971-75; 8th Grade General Sci Bartlett Jr HS 1975-76; 9th-12th Grade Physics/Chem/Phys Sci/Bio/Ecology Teacher Savannah Chrstn Prep Sch 1976-83; 11th-12th Grade Physics/Advanced Placement Teacher John Marshall HS & Northside Ind Sch Dist 1984-86; 8th-12th Grade Sci/Chem/Physics Teacher Maypearl HS 1986-; *ai:* Academic Stu Senate & Awds; Sci Club & Fair; Jr Class; AAPT; Physics Teaching Resource Agent 1986; TX Assn Physics Teachers; Earth Sci Teachers Assn; Southern Assn Colls & Schls Comm Mem 1977; TX Chem Assn; Sci Teachers Assn of TX; Assn of TX Prof Educators; Natl Sci Fnd Prin Investigator; St Sci Curr Comm Mem 1990; Amer Inst Biological Sci Meetings 1972; Outstanding Young Women of America Awd 1978; NSF Physics Inst GA Southern Coll 1979; GA Chamber of Commerce STAR Teacher 1980; Nom James Bryant Conant Awd for Excl in Chem; Excl Sci & Math Teaching 1983, 1986; Governors Honors Sci Teacher 1980, 1982; Jr Engineering Tech Society Wkshps & Testing Prgms 1984-86; *office:* Maypearl HS 1 Panther Ln Maypearl TX 76064

RESUTKO, LARRY, Jr HS Teacher; *b:* Chicago, IL; *m:* Patricia L.; *ed:* (BS) Geography, Bradley Univ 1970; Joliet Jr Coll; IL Cntrl Coll; Eureka Coll; IL St Univ; *cr:* 6th Grade Teacher Lincoln Sch 1970-82; Bolin Sch 1982-86; Jr HS Teacher Central Jr HS 1986-; *ai:* Dist Soc Stud Comm; Leadership Comm; Ed Comm; Heartland Water Resources Cncl; Natl Cncl for Geographic Ed; IL Geographical Soc; Assn of Amer Geographers; NCSS;

Environmental Ed Assn of IL; NEA; *office:* Central Jr HS 601 E Washington Rd East Peoria IL 61611

RETALIS, CHRISTINA F., First Grade Teacher; *b:* Paterson, NJ; *ed:* (BA) Elem Ed, William Paterson 1970; Grad Stud Rdng, In-Service Apple Cmptr Courses, Fnd for Free Enterprise Certificate of Merit; *cr:* Eng/Span Substitute Teacher Anthony Wayne Jr HS 1970-71; 1st Grade Teacher 1971-73, 1975-78, 3rd Grade Teacher 1973-75, 1978-79, 4th Grade Teacher 1979-83, 1st Grade Teacher 1984- Sch 9; *ai:* Annual Sch Holiday Prgm; 1971-; Clifton Advisory Cncl Mem 1990-91; Math, Sci, Gifted & Talented, Cultural, 1st Aid, Soc, Affirmative Action Comm; Union Delegate; Sch 9 PTO (Mem 1971-, VP 1976-77); Clifton Teachers Assn (Mem 1971-, Delegate 1979-81, 1986-88); Passaic Cty Ed Assn Mem 1979-; NJ Ed Assn, NEA 1979-; Passaic Cty Bd of Elections; Ridgewood Ski Club Mem 1977-78; Maids of Athena Mem; Amer Hellenic Educl Progressive Assn Scholastic Achievement Awd 1966; Governors Teacher Recognition Awd 1990; Building Gifted & Talented Chairperson; Sci Rep; *office:* Sch 9 25 Brighton Rd Clifton NJ 07012

RETANO, VIVIEN MAITA, Third Grade Teacher; *b:* Bayonne, NJ; *m:* John J.; *c:* Angela, Jonathan; *ed:* (BA) Ed, Jersey City St Coll 1964; *cr:* Title I Comp Ed Boonton Bd of Ed 1979-80; Librarian 1980-81, 6th Grade Teacher 1981-87, 3rd Grade Teacher 1987- Our Lady of Mt Carmel Sch; *ai:* Educl Cncl; Steering Comm; CCD Teacher; Adv Alumni Comm; NCEA 1990; Girl Scouts of Amer Brownie Leader 1973-74; *home:* 506 Hillside Ave Boonton NJ 07005

RETORICK, MARY E. STERLING, First Grade Teacher; *b:* Morris Run, PA; *w:* George (dec); *c:* Stephen M.; *ed:* (BS) Elem/Early Chldhd Ed, Mansfield Univ 1951; Grad Stud Mansfield Univ, Elmira Coll, Oneonta Univ; *cr:* 3rd Grade Teacher Spring Valley NY 1951-53; 1st Grade Teacher Johnson City NY 1953-59, Blossburg PA 1962-; *ai:* NEA 1951-; PA St Ed Assn, S Tioga Ed Assn 1962-; *office:* Blossburg Elem Sch 132 Hanibal St Blossburg PA 16912

REUBISH, GARY RICHARD, 7th Grade Lang Arts Teacher; *b:* Breckenridge, MN; *ed:* (AA) Liberal Arts, ND St Coll of Sci 1969; (BS) Eng, Valley City St Coll 1971; *cr:* 9th-12th Grade Teacher Wolford Public Sch 1971-72; 7th-10th Grade Eng Teacher Lake Benton Public Sch 1972-76; 7th Grade Eng Teacher Wahpeton Public Schls 1976-; *ai:* MM Ed Assn; ND Ed Assn; Wahpeton Ed Assn; NCTE; Lake Benton Teacher of Yr 1976; *office:* Wahpeton Mid Sch 1209 Loy Ave Wahpeton ND 58075

REUSCHEL, SUSAN E., Mathematics Teacher; *b:* Quincy, IL; *ed:* (BS) Math, IL Coll Jacksonville 1982; *cr:* Math Teacher Nokomis HS 1982-; *ai:* Spon HS Scholastic Bowl; Asst Girls Bsktbl Coach; *office:* Nokomis HS Nokomis IL 62075

REUTER, RONALD EDWARD, Soc Stud Teacher/Dept Chair; *b:* Catskill, NY; *m:* Barbara A. Thibodeau; *c:* Matthew E.; *ed:* (BA) Sociology/His, Siena Coll 1970; (MA) Ed, Coll of St Rose 1974; *cr:* Teacher/Soc Stud Dept Chm St Marys Acad HS 1970-71, Vincentian Inst HS 1971-76, Tamarac HS 1976-; *ai:* Effective Schls Comm Tamarac HS; Yearly Voter Registration Prgm Coord; NY St Cncl of Soc Stud Teachers; NY St United Teachers Co-Rep Tamarac HS 1988-; Scholars Recognition Prgm; *office:* Tamarac HS RD 3 Box 200A Troy NY 12180

REVELLE, KATHLEEN ANN, Fourth Grade Teacher; *b:* Drexel Hill, PA; *m:* James Howard; *c:* Teri L., James Jr.; *ed:* (BA) General Elem, Glassboro 1972; *cr:* 2nd Grade Teacher Brigantine Cntrl Sch 1972089; 4th Grade Teacher Brigantine N Sch 1989-; *ai:* Brigantine Ed Assn Secy 1984; PTA Pres 1985; Citizen Advocate for Ed 1987; Brigantine Teacher of Yr 1987; Technology Teacher of Yr 1985; Governors Awd Recepient 1988; *home:* 410 E Cresson Ave Absecon NJ 08201

REVELS, KATHERINE JONES, Sixth Grade Teacher; *b:* Zirconia, NC; *m:* Vincent; *c:* Craig; *ed:* (BS) Lang Art, E Carolina Univ 1966; (MA) Ed/Curr Specialist, Pembroke St Univ 1988; His Seminary Lesley Coll; *cr:* 5th Grade Teacher Jasper Sch 1966-67, Swift Creek Sch 1967-68; 4th Grade Teacher Hickory Grove Sch 1968-69; 6th Grade Teacher Dublin Sch 1969-; *ai:* Sch Geography Bee Coord; Staff Dev Comm; NCEA, NEA Past Faculty Rep 1979-; Delta Kappa Gamma VP 1988-; Phi Delta Kappa, NC Center for Advancement of Teaching; Gideons Auxiliary Pres 1986-88; Natl Geographic Kids Network (Charter Mem, Coord) 1988-; Dublin Sch Teacher of Yr 1976, 1984; Outstanding Conservation Teacher 1987; NC Soil & Water Conservation Schlsp 1986; St Finalist NC Teacher of World Awd 1989; *home:* PO Box 6 Dublin NC 28332

REVERE, RONALD WILLIAM, Physics Teacher; *b:* Roanoke, VA; *m:* Sandra Lynn Cox; *c:* Amanda G.; *ed:* (BS) Bio, Coll of William & Mary 1972; (MAT) Natural Scis, Colgate Univ 1973; Working Towards EdD Univ of S CA & Univ of Houston; Marymount Univ, Univ of VA, Univ of MN; *cr:* Sci Teacher Fries HS 1973-76; Physics Teacher Frankfurt Amer HS 1976-79, Alief-Hastings HS 1979-80, Wakefield HS 1982-89, Washington-Lee HS 1989-; *ai:* AAPT, VA Sci Teachers 1985-; VA Physics Teachers Pres 1985-; N VA Sci Teachers VP 1988-; Mt Arrarat Baptist Church Teacher 1984-; DODDS Superior Teaching Awd 1976; Woodrow Wilson Natl Fnd 1990; Article Published 1985; *office:* Washington-Lee HS 1300 N Quincy St Arlington VA 22201

REVINSKAS, DIANE D., Mathematics Teacher; *b:* Brooklyn, NY; *ed:* (BA) Math, 1970, (MS) Math, 1973 Adelphi Univ; *cr:* Math Teacher Hillcrest HS 1972-73, Jamaica HS 1973-76, John Dewey HS 1976-; Cmptr Coord John Dewey HS 1988-; *ai:* Jr Math Team Coach; AMTNYS, NCTM; Brooklyn HS Recognition Day Awd Outstanding Prof Service; *office:* John Dewey HS 50 Avenue X Brooklyn NY 11223

REVOLINSKI, CHARLENE RUTH, First Grade Teacher; *b:* Milwaukee, WI; *ed:* (AA) Elem, Racine Kenosha Cty Teachers Coll 1970; (BA) Sci Ed, Univ of WI Whitewater 1976; Lesley Coll; Aurora Univ; Interdistrict Inservice Nework; *cr:* 4th Grade Teacher St Thomas Aqt 1970-73; 1st-2nd Grade Teacher Drought Elem Sch 1978-; *ai:* Mentor Beginner Teachers; Math/Rdng/Lang Art/Sci Curr Comm; NEA 1979-; WI Ed Assn 1979-; Drought Ed Assn 1979-; Racine Cty Sch Office Handicapped Awd 1979-80; No 1 Teacher Parents/Students Drought Awd 1981-82; Cmptr Programming Awd 1984; Cline/Fay Institute; Discipline with Love & Logic Awd 1985; *home:* 4408 Raynor Ave Union Grove WI 53182

REY, NANCY SPURLIN, Third Grade Teacher; *b:* Doylestown, PA; *c:* Christine, Thomas; *ed:* (BS) Elem Ed, 1969, (MED) Curr/Instruction, 1971 FL Atlantic Univ; *cr:* 2nd Grade Teacher Charles R Drew Elem Sch 1969-70; 1st-3rd Grade Teacher Lothian Elem Sch 1970-73; 2nd/3rd Grade Teacher W Meade Elem Sch 1977-; *ai:* MD Intnl Rdng Assn Cncl 1988-; Anne Arundel Cty Teachers Assn 1970-73, 1977-; Coll Park Boys & Girls Club 1981-; *office:* W Meade Elem Sch 2644 Riva Rd Annapolis MD 21401

REYNOLDS, BEVERLY ANN HANDY, 8th Grade Eng/Rdng Teacher; *b:* Opelousas, LA; *m:* Henry James; *c:* Courtney D.; *ed:* (BS) Eng, Grambling St Univ 1971; Eng as Second Lang to Minority Stus; Working Towards Masters; *cr:* Eng Teacher Palmetto HS 1974-75; Eng/Rdng Teacher Opelousas Cath 1976-78, Opelousas Jr HS 1978-; *ai:* Chrldr & Natl Jr Honor Society Past Spon; NEA, LA Assn of Ed; St Landry Assn of Educators (Pres 1988-89, VP 1985-88, Secy 1983-85), Outstanding Jr HS Teacher 1984-85; NCTE; *office:* Opelousas Jr HS 721 S Market St PO Box 112 Opelousas LA 70570

REYNOLDS, DEANA NIMMO, Speech & Debate Instructor; *b:* Marshfield, MO; *c:* Ashley N.; *ed:* (BS) Speech & Theatre/Eng, S MO St Univ 1984; Working Towards Masters Comm, S MO St Univ; *cr:* Speech/Debate/Drama/Eng Teacher Willard HS 1985-86; Speech/Debate/Eng Teacher Hillcrest HS 1986-; *ai:* Speech & Debate Coach; Speech Tournament Host; Natl Forensics League 1979-, Diamond Coach 1989; Speech & Theatre Assn of MO 1984-; Southwest Dist Speech Teachers Assn 1985-; *office:* Hillcrest HS 3319 N Grant Springfield MO 65803

REYNOLDS, DELPHA ANN, Fifth Grade Teacher; *b:* Dodge City, KS; *m:* Mark Leslie; *c:* Jeffery, Matthew, Jason; *ed:* (BA) Ed, Mid-America Nazarene 1977; (MS) Curr/Instruction, Emporia St Univ 1984; *cr:* 4th Grade Teacher 1977-80, 3rd/4th Grade Teacher 1980-82, 3rd Grade Teacher 1982-87, 5th Grade Teacher 1987- Cntrl Elem; *ai:* Cntrl Elem Social Fund Activity; Olathe Natl Ed Assn (Building Rep 1987-, Prof Cncl Negotiating Team 1988-); Alpha Delta Kappa (Teachers Recording Secy 1988-, Pres Elect 1990; First United Meth Church Womens Groups 1974-; Olathe Welcome Wagon Organization Pres 1974-75; Soc Stud Comm Rewriting Curr Goals, Objectives 1988-; Wrote 5th Grade Model Lesson Plans; Curr for Teach ing KS His.

REYNOLDS, ELLEN CLARISSA, English Teacher; *b:* Nashville, TN; *ed:* (BA) Eng, 1986, (MED) Eng, 1989 Belmont Coll; *cr:* Substitute Teacher Metropolitan Sch System 1987; Writing Lab Instr Belmont Coll 1988; Eng Teacher Davidson Acad 1989-; *ai:* Pep Club Adv, 7th & 8th Grade Cheerleading, Soph Class Spon, Chapel & Dress Code Comm; Kappa Delta Pi VP 1987-; Belmont Alumni Bd 1989-; *office:* Davidson Acad 1414 Old Hickory Blvd Nashville TN 37207

REYNOLDS, HELEN FIELDS, Retired Teacher; *b:* Granville, TN; *m:* Arnold; *c:* Patrick A., Michael D.; *ed:* (BS) Soc Sci, TN Technological Univ 1948; *cr:* Prin/Teacher Corinth Elem Sch 1944-46; Classroom Teacher Granville Elem Sch 1946-49, 1952-54, New Mid Elem Sch 1956-57, Gordonsville Sch 1957-86; *ai:* NEA, TN Ed Assn 1944-80; NRTA 1986-; Granville Cmmty Club Secy 1987-; Extension Homemakers Club Reporter 1988-; *home:* Rt 1 Box 108 Hwy 53 Granville TN 38564

REYNOLDS, HELEN PATE, English Teacher; *b:* Groves, TX; *c:* Mark; *ed:* (BA) Eng, Lamar Univ 1967; (MA) Eng, Univ of AR 1968; *cr:* Eng Asst Professor Texarkana Jr Coll 1968-69; Eng Teacher Hamilton HS 1969-73, Nederland HS 1978-; *ai:* TSTA, NEA, Nederland Teachers Assn; Delta Kappa Gamma Corresponding Secy 1988-; *office:* Nederland HS 220 17th St Nederland TX 77627

REYNOLDS, JERRY ROBERT, Social Studies Teacher; *b:* Philadelphia, MS; *m:* Diane Freeman; *c:* Kelly E.; *ed:* (BS) His Ed, MS Coll 1965; (MED) Ed, MS St Univ 1976; *cr:* Government Teacher Northwest Jr HS 1976-; *ai:* Assn of Meridian Educators Legislative Chm; Natl Jr Honor Society Advisory Cncl; Phi Delta Kappa 1989-; Assn of Meridian Educators, MS Assn of Educators, NEA 1976-; Cntrl United Meth Church 1972-; Meridian Chamber of Commerce 1985-; PTA Pres 1989-; Teachers Inaugural Expericence Appointment 1989; *office:* Northwest Jr H S 4400 32nd St Meridian MS 39305

REYNOLDS, JOHN DENNIS, Social Studies Teacher; *b:* Boston, MA; *m:* Judith Ann Connors; *c:* Joshua T., John D., Joanna L.; *ed:* (BA) Poly Sci, Univ of MA 1965; (MED) Scndry Sch Admin, Boston Univ 1975; Cmptr Ed, Univ of Lowell; *cr:* 1st Lieutenant US Army Dept of Intelligence 1966-68; Soc Stud Teacher Bedford HS 1968-; *ai:* Var Golf & Jr Var Bsbl Coach; Facilities Comm Chm; Discipline Comm Mem; Billerica Youth Bsktbl Coach; Billerica Advisory Comm Children with Spec Needs Mem; NEA, MA Teachers Assn, Bedford Ed Assn 1968-; Bedford Ed Assn Negotiations Team Mem; Prof Rights & Respobsibilities Comm Chm; Bicentennial Commission MA Constitution Delegate; Merit Research Comm Chm; Billerica Youth Bsktbl Coach; Billerica Advisory Comm Children with Spec Needs Mem; *office:* Bedford HS Mudge Way Bedford MA 01730

REYNOLDS, JOHN MICHAEL, 8th Grade Core Teacher; *b:* St Louis, MO; *m:* Karen Erickson; *c:* Brian, Jennifer; *ed:* (BS) Scndry Ed, Univ of NE Lincoln 1972; (MS) Educl Admin, Univ of NE Omaha 1981; *cr:* Teacher Morton Jr HS 1973-; *ai:* Staff Dev Advisory; Stu Cncl; Washington DC Trip; Omaha Ed Assn, NEA 1973-; NE St Ed Assn 1973-, Life Membership; NAASP In-Sch Suspension; Countryside Church Deacon 1987-; *office:* Morton Jr HS 4606 Terrace Dr Omaha NE 68134

REYNOLDS, JOHN WILLIAM, History Teacher/Asst Admin; *b:* Kansas City, KS; *m:* Susan Margret Lay; *c:* Emily, Rebekah; *ed:* (BGS) His, Pittsburg St Univ 1974; (MA) Bible, Pensacola Chrstn Coll 1983; *cr:* Teacher/Asst Prin Open Door Baptist Sch 1974-83, Shawnee Mission Chrstn Sch 1983-86, Bethesda Chrstn Sch 1986-; *ai:* Var Soccer & Bsbl; Jr HS Girls Bsktbl; Sr Class Spon & Trip Dir; Discipleship Dir & Chapel; *office:* Bethesda Chrstn Sch 7950 N 650 E Brownsburg IN 46112

REYNOLDS, JUDITH M., English Teacher; *b:* Washington, DC; *m:* Darden Jr.; *c:* Judd, Enley; *ed:* (BA) Eng, Univ of MS 1968; (MED) Eng, MS Coll 1971; *cr:* Teacher Callaway HS 1968-71, Woodland Hills Baptist Acad 1973-80, Clinton HS 1980-, Hinds Comm Coll 1989; *ai:* Head of Eng Dept; NCTE 1985-; MCTE 1985-; MAE NAE 1985-89; Star Teacher-1979/1983/1988; MS All-Star Teacher 1988; *home:* 1701 Midway Rd Clinton MS 39056

REYNOLDS, JUDY KAY, 2nd Grade Teacher/Asst Prin; *b:* Fort Atkinson, WI; *m:* Jack Guerndt; *ed:* (BA) Elem Ed, 1975; (MSE) Elem Ed, 1989 Univ of WI; *cr:* 6th Grade Teacher 1975-78; 2nd Grade Teacher 1978-83; 4th Grade Teacher 1983-84; 3rd Grade Teacher 1984-86; Asst Prin 1984-; 2nd Grade Teacher 1986- Summit Sch; *ai:* NEA 1975-; WI Ed Assn 1975-; Oconomowoc Ed Assn 1975-; *office:* Summit Sch 36316 Valley Rd Oconomowoc WI 53066

REYNOLDS, KATHLYN ROBERTS, Vocal Music Teacher; *b:* Shawnee, OK; *m:* Charles Robert; *c:* Denise L. Reynolds Leonard, Jeffrey A.; *ed:* (BM) Vocal Music, 1950, (BMED) Vocal Music, 1968 Univ of OK; Vocal Trng, OK City Univ 1965-67; *cr:* Music Teacher Cntrl Elem 1968-69, Tulakes Elem 1969-72, Wiley Post Elem 1972-; *ai:* Singing Blue Angels Chorus; Jr Police Spon; Hospitality, Arts in Ed Comm; OK Music Educators Assn VP/Elem 1978-80; Music Educators Natl Conf 1968-; Amer Choral Dir 1968-, Dir of Distinction 1987-88; Sigma Alpa Iota 1947-; Natl St Teacher of Yr 1982-; Delta Kappa Gamma 1980-; OK Kodaly Music Teachers 1978-; Homa-OK Orff Music Teachers 1975-; Chi Omega Alumni Outstanding Alumni 1967; United Meth Church of the Servant (Adult Choir Mem, 1971- Childrens Choir Dir 1957-); Jr Hospitality (Chairperson of Comm, Chaplain, Parliemantarians); OK Teacher of Yr 1981-82; PC Dist Teacher of Yr 1981; Composer of Music & Sch Materials; Outstanding Music Alumni Univ of OK 1982; Women in the News Awd 1982; *home:* 11612 Western View Oklahoma City OK 73162

REYNOLDS, LOIS A., Third Grade Teacher; *b:* Havre, MT; *c:* Jamie L.; *ed:* (BS) Elem Ed/Psych, Rocky Mountain Coll 1976; Ed/Psych, Univ of WY & Spearfish SD; *cr:* 1st Grade Teacher 1976-80, 3rd Grade Teacher 1980- Wagonwheel; *ai:* Stu Cncl Adv; Rdng Cncl & Liaison Mem; Sunshine Comm; Stu Cncl Pres 1975-76; Campbell Cty Ed Assn Secy 1985; Rdng Cncl Secy; Liaison Sch Comm; Meth Church Mem; Whos Who Among Stu/Teachers in Coll; Nom Teacher of Yr; *office:* Wagonwheel Elem Sch 800 Hemlock Gillette WY 82716

REYNOLDS, MARILYN DIANE, Business Education Instructor; *b:* Moscow, ID; *m:* Lyman Gallup; *ed:* (MS) Bus Ed, 1971, (MED) Bus Ed, 1974 OR St Univ; *cr:* Bus Ed Instr Cal Young Jr HS 1973-78; Full Time Substitute Teacher Meridian HS 1979; Substitute Boise HS 1980-85; Bus Ed Instr Meridian HS 1985-; *ai:* Bus Prof of America Adv; Meridian Ed Assn Treas; NBEA 1985-; ID Bus Ed Assn Treas 1988-; NW Women in Ed Ad 1989-; *office:* Meridian HS 1900 W Pine Meridian ID 83642

REYNOLDS, MARY WALLACE BYRD, English & Drama Teacher; *b:* Birmingham, AL; *m:* Putnam C.; *c:* Spencer P. B., Hunter C.; *ed:* (BA) Eng, Univ of AL 1973; (MAT) Eng, Univ of W FL 1982; Teaching Advanced Placement Eng, Univ of AL 1985; *cr:* Eng/Music Teacher Freeport Sch 1980-82; Adjunct Professor of Eng St Leo Coll, Jefferson St Jr Coll, Univ of Montevallo, Univ of Birmingham 1983-85; Eng/Drama Teacher Pelham HS 1985-; *ai:* Drama Club Adv; Kappa Delta Pi Mem 1982-; AL Cncl Teachers of Eng 1985-; MTNA 1980-; *office:* Pelham HS Bearden Rd Pelham AL 35124

REYNOLDS, NORMA (JENNINGS), Mathematics Department Chair; *b:* Washington, DC; *m:* Melvin Lee; *c:* Stephen L., Jennifer L.; *ed:* (BS) Math, Lynchburg Coll 1962; (MS) Math, Univ of TN 1977; *cr:* Teacher Keuka Coll 1966-70, Mc Minn Cty HS 1971-80; Teacher/Math Division Chairperson Spraybarry HS

1980-; *ai:* Math Team Spon; NCTM, GA Cncl Teachers of Math; *office:* Sprayberry HS 2525 Sandy Plains Rd Marietta GA 30066

REYNOLDS, PAT MATHEWS, Sixth Grade Teacher; *b:* Oak Park, IL; *m:* Tommy; *c:* Janet L., Lori A., Matt; *ed:* (BA) Elem Ed, Mid TN St Univ 1970; (MA) Admin/Supervision, TN St Univ 1984; Quest Intnl; *cr:* 1st Grade Teacher Hillsboro Elem Sch 1970; Homebound Teacher Franklin Cty Bd of Ed 1970-71; 2nd Grade Teacher 1971-80, 6th Grade Teacher 1980- Huntland Sch; *ai:* 6th Grade Extra Curr Math Contestants Coord; NEA, TEA 1970-; FCEA Huntland Sch Rep 1973; Herald Chronicle Distinguished Female Educator 1989; Teacher Center Advisory Bd 1988-; *home:* Rt 2 Box 34 Belvidere TN 37306

REYNOLDS, PAULETTE ANGRICK, Fifth Grade Teacher; *b:* Michigan City, IN; *m:* Jeffery Earl; *c:* Tracy L., Sheli A., Kili M.; *ed:* (BA) Elem Ed, Purdue Univ 1972; Univ of Evansville, IN St Univ; *cr:* 8th Grade Teacher 1978-82, St Joseph Sch; 7th Grade Teacher 1985-88, 5th Grade Teacher 1988- Resurrection Sch; *ai:* Organize Cath Schls Week; Coord Field Day Act; 5th-8th Grade Phys Ed Dir; Evansville Area Rdng Cncl, NCEA 1978-; Natl Cncl of Rdng Teachers 1985-; *home:* 8499 Lancaster Dr Newburgh IN 47630

REYNOLDS, PHYLLIS E., Health/Physical Ed Teacher; *b:* Mc Minnville, TN; *ed:* (BS) HPER, 1972, (MS) HPERS, 1979 Mid TN St Univ; *cr:* Teacher Whitwell HS 1973-74; Teacher/Coach Gordon Cntrl Complex 1974-; *ai:* HS Sftbl, Mid Sch Girls Bsktbl & Track Coach; Olympic in Schls Coord; AAHPER, GAHPER, NEA, GAE 1974-; Calhoun Church of Christ; *home:* 232 Owens Cir NE Calhoun GA 30701

REYNOLDS, RICHARD DUANE, Retired Math/His Teacher; *b:* Shamrock, TX; *m:* Shirley Beth Mullins; *c:* Jerry D., Janice D. Reynolds Williams; *ed:* (BS) Ed, Clarendon Jr Coll & TX Technological Coll 1955; W TX St Univ, Southwestern St Coll; *cr:* Teacher/Coach Lela Elem 1959-65, Hedley Ind Sch Dist 1965-67, Masterson Ind Sch Dist 1967-68, Hedley Ind Sch Dist 1968-70, Silverton Ind Sch Dist 1971-89; *ai:* TX St Teacher Assn; Assn TX Prof Ed Pres Local Unit 1985-86, 1989; First Baptist Church Deacon 1964-, Father of Yr Awd 1978; Silverton Ind Sch Dist Coach 1978, Dist Champ Bsktbl Coach; Natl Sci Fnd Grant; *home:* Box 664 Silverton TX 79257

REYNOLDS, RICHARD R., Chemistry Teacher; *b:* Passaic, NJ; *m:* Norma Christophel; *c:* Richard J., Patricia A.; *ed:* (ACSBS) Chem, Fordham Univ 1957; Ed, Montclair St; Cmptr Courses; *cr:* Teacher Marist HS & St Peters Coll 1957-59, Northern Valley Regional 1960-65; Sr Supervising Team Leader Anti-Poverty Prgm 1965-66; Teacher Waldwick HS 1966-; *ai:* Retired Ftbl & Wrestling Coach; Fairleigh Dickinson Univ Cooperative Mid Coll Prgm Advanced Chem Stus Leader; NEA, WEA, BCEA, NJ Ed Assn, Amer Chemical Society; Governors Teacher of Yr Princeton Awd 1986; *office:* Waldwick HS Wyckoff Ave Waldwick NJ 07463

REYNOLDS, SALLY GENOVINO, First Grade Teacher; *b:* Newark, NJ; *m:* William; *c:* Frank; *ed:* (BA) Elem Ed, Felician Coll 1970; *cr:* 3rd Grade Teacher St Josephs 1970-72; 4th Grade Teacher 1972-73, 3rd Grade Teacher 1973-83, 1st Grade Teacher 1985- Silver Bay Elem; *office:* Silver Bay Elem Sch Silver Bay Rd Toms River NJ 08753

REYNOLDS, SIMMIE COLENE, Chapter I Math Teacher; *b:* Brownwood, TX; *m:* Nathan Clyde; *c:* Travis, Laura; *ed:* (BS) Phys Ed/Bus Ed, Howard Payne 1969; Elem Ed; *cr:* Teacher Brownwood Jr HS 1980-; *ai:* Parent-Cncl Mem; TCTA; Brownwood HS Ex Stus; *home:* 3404 Vincent Brownwood TX 76801

REYNOLDS, SUSAN STANGE, Fourth Grade Teacher; *b:* New Hyde Park, NY; *m:* J. Carey; *c:* Matthew, Brendan, Amanda; *ed:* (BS) Elem Ed, Cabrini Coll 1971; (MS) Rdng/Learning Disabilities, Adelphi Univ 1976; *cr:* 2nd Grade Teacher 1971-74, 5th Grade Teacher 1974-79, 3rd Grade Teacher 1980, 5th Grade Teacher 1980-84, 4th Grade Teacher 1984- Sachem Sch Dist; *ai:* NYSUT, AFT.

REYNOLDS, VICTORIA ANNE, Social Studies Teacher; *b:* New Orleans, LA; *ed:* (BA) His, 1976, (MA) His, 1978, (BA) Ed, 1980 SE LA Univ; Grad Stud SE LA Univ 1984; *cr:* Teacher Folsom Jr HS 1980-83; Soc Stud Teacher Mandeville HS 1983-; *ai:* Teenage Republicans Spon; Mandeville Sesquicentennial Comm Chm; Self-Study Comm Mem; Jefferson Parish Historical Assn 1977-; SE LA Historical Assn 1978-; Articles Published; *office:* Mandeville HS #1 Skipper Dr Mandeville LA 70448

REYNOLDS, WILLIAM TAYLOR, Biology Teacher; *b:* Corpus Christi, TX; *ed:* (BA) Bio, Otterbein 1985; Grad Stud Ed; NSTA Conventions; *cr:* Bio Teacher W Jefferson HS 1985-; *ai:* Ftbl, Indoor & Outdoor Track, Wrestling Coach; Ski Club; NSTA 1990; OAT, CCC 1985-; Columbus Ftbl Coaches Assn 1987-; W Jefferson T D Club 1985-88; Beechcroft Booster 1988-; Otterbein Stu Teacher of Yr; *home:* 480 Foxtrail Cir W Westerville OH 43081

RHEEL, RUTH ANN ROSS, Language Arts Teacher; *b:* Halstead, PA; *m:* Robert P. Sr.; *c:* Robert P. Jr., Tracie A.; *ed:* (BS) Ed/Scndry Eng, Bloomsburg Univ 1965; (MS) Ed/Scndry Eng, Kutztown Univ 1969; Villanova Univ; *cr:* 11th/12th Grade Eng Teacher Pottsgrove HS 1965-70; 6th Grade Lang Art Teacher Pottsgrove Intermediate Sch 1980-; *ai:* 6A Team Coord; Peer Leaders Spon; Crisis Intervention Team Mem; Pottsgrove Ed Assn (Pres 1982-87, Mem); PA St Ed Assn, NEA Mem 1965-70, 1980-; Helping Hands Prgm Comm Chm 1985-; *office:* Pottsgrove Intermediate Sch Buchert Rd Pottstown PA 19464

RHEM-TITTLE, YVONNE SHIRLEY, 7th/8th Math & Science Teacher; *b:* New York, NY; *m:* James Esworth; *c:* Darlene Rhem, Deborah Jackson, Joseph Rhem, Olga V. Thomas, Augustine V. Rhem, Elizabeth V. Francis, Nathaniel Rhem; *ed:* (BS) Ed, Antioch Coll 1976; (MS) Teacher Ed, Bank St Coll 1983; Spec Ed, Coll of New Rochelle; *cr:* Paraprofessional 1972-75, Teacher 1976- St Augustine Sch; *ai:* 4th-8th Grade Young Astronauts Chapter Leader; St Augustine Sch Sci Chairperson; Natl Sci Mem 1985-; Sigma Gamma Rho Rhoer Adv 1988-; Fed of Cath Teachers Mem 1976-; Morrisania Ed Cncl 2nd VP 1971-76, Teacher of Yr 1980; Parent Assn Pres 1964-68; Featured on 60 Minutes CBS 1988; Outstanding Cmmty Service MEC 1976; Excl & Recognition in Teaching SASA 1990; *office:* St Augustine Sch of the Arts 1176 Franklin Ave Bronx NY 10456

RHINEHART, JO ANN, Mathematics/Computer Teacher; *b:* Ottumwa, IA; *ed:* (AA) Cmptr Maintenance, Indian Hills Comm Coll 1976; (BA) Elem/Scndry Math Ed, Wm Penn Coll 1984; *cr:* Cmptr Maintenance Engr Collins/Rockwell Intnl 1976-80; 8th-12th Grade Math/Cmptr Teacher Morning Sun Cmmty Sch 1984-; *ai:* Sr Class Spon; Cooperative Learning Coord; Phase III Chm; At Risk Comm Mem; IA Cncl of Teachers of Math, NCTM; Whos Who Among Young Amer Prof 1988; *home:* 110 N Blair Morning Sun IA 52640

RHINEHART, LAURA CLEO, English Teacher; *b:* Kenilworth, UT; *ed:* (BS) Ed, UT St Univ 1958; Univ of NV Reno, CA St Univ Irvine, San Bernardino, Redlands Univ; *cr:* Eng Teacher Bean River Jr HS 1960-62, J D Smith Jr HS 1962-63, Rancho HS 1963-68; Drama-GATE Eng Teacher Raney Jr HS 1970-89; Eng Teacher Norco HS 1989-; *ai:* Frosh Adv 1989-; Drama & Field Day Coach; Creative Writing Adv; NEA, Corona-Norco Teachers Assn; Inland Theatre League Playwriting Excl Awd 1976; Federal Grant Lang Inst Dedicated Service Awd; Spec Recognition Excl In Stu Writing CA St Univ Contest 1987-89; PTA Reflctions Prgm Recognition 1988; Outstanding Instructional Prgm St of CA 1984; *office:* Norco HS 2065 Temescal Ave Norco CA 91760

RHOADES, CATHIE BOLEN, Mathematics Teacher; *b:* Fostoria, OH; *m:* Russell L.; *c:* Bethany L., Robyn B.; *ed:* (BSED) Math, OH Univ 1971; (MED) Inst/Supervision in Cmptr Ed, Ashland Coll 1987; Coursework Bowling Green St Univ; *cr:* Math Teacher Northmont Jr HS 1971-72, Taft Mid Sch 1973-79, River Valley HS 1983-; *ai:* Class Adv; Competency Prgm Coord; Phi Delta Kappa 1988-; River Valley Teachers Assn, OEA, OH Cncl Teachers of Math, NEA; GSA Brownie Leader 1988-; Marion Cty Teachers Grant; *office:* River Valley HS 1267 Columbus Sandusky Rd N Marion OH 43302

RHOADES, GAIL WILLIAMS, Fifth Grade Teacher; *b:* Haworth, OK; *m:* Frank; *c:* Wesley; *ed:* (BS) Elem Ed, SE OK St Univ 1962; Grad Work NE TX Comm Coll, E TX St Univ; *cr:* Secretarial Subjects Teacher OK St Tech 1962-67; 2nd/3rd Grade Teacher Lukfata 1968-71; 5th Grade Teacher Detroit Ind Sch Dist 1971-84, Prairiland CISD 1984-; *ai:* UIL Ready Writing Spon; ATPE 1984-; 1st Baptist Church Mem; *home:* PO Box 159 N Jeffus St Deport TX 75435

RHOADES, SHIRLEY FIELDS, Fourth Grade Teacher; *b:* Stuarts Draft, VA; *m:* Wallace Edward; *ed:* (BS) Elem Ed, Norfolk St Univ 1974; Univ VA; James Madison Univ; *cr:* Secy/Bookkeeper Cntrl Augusta HS 1962-65; Secy/Dir Coll Unions Norfolk St 1968-73; Asst Secy/Dean Academic Affairs 1968-73, Secy 1973-74 Norfolk St Univ; Records Clerk VA Highway Dept 1974; Teacher Ladd Elem Sch 1974-77, Beverley Manor Elem Sch 1977-; *ai:* Va Ed, NEA Mem 1974-; Augusta Cty Ed (Mem, Faculty Rep 1989-) 1974-; Staunton Cmmty Action Comm Secy 1968-69; Coll Union Intnl Rep Norfolk St Univ 1973-74; Behavioral Sci Grant W K Kellogg; *home:* Rt 1 Box 24 Staunton VA 24401

RHOADS, SARAH GROSS, Retired 3rd Grade Teacher; *b:* Quentin, PA; *m:* Paul C.; *ed:* (BS) Rural Elem, Millersville Univ 1942; *cr:* 1st-8th Grade Teacher Rural Sch 1942-43; 1st-3rd Grade Teacher Palmer Township 1943-46; 2nd-3rd Grade Teacher Millbach Elem Sch 1948-49; 3rd-5th Grade Teacher Quentin Elem Sch 1949-72; 3rd Grade Teacher Cornwall Elem Sch 1972-81; *ai:* Lebanon Cty Honor Society, PASR, Lebanon Cty Retired Sch Employees Assn.

RHODEN, D. C., Music Teacher; *b:* Batesburg, SC; *m:* Jane O.; *c:* Tommy, Jenny; *ed:* (AB) Music, Univ of SC 1956; (MSM) Sacred Music, Southern Baptist Theoligical Seminary 1958; (CHM) Choral/Organ, Amer Guild Organists 1964; (PHD) Music Ed, FL St 1970; Summers Study, Union Theological Seminary NY; Univ of GA; Conductors Symposia, FL St Univ; Spec Ed, Columbia Univ NY; *cr:* Church Music Organist GA 1958-67; Grad Asst FL St Univ 1967-70; Music Teacher Athens Acad 1972-74; Choral Dir/Music Teacher Oconee Cty Schls 1974-; *ai:* Founder & Dir Oconee Cty Boys Chorus; Choral Dir Oconee Cty HS & Intermediate Sch; Organist 1st Baptist Church Athens; Pi Kappa Lambda, Omicron Delta Kappa, Phi Alpha Kappa, MTNA, Amer Choral Dir Assn; Amer Guild of Organists Academic Mem; Amer Boys & Childrens Choir Assn Natl Secy; Music Educators Natl Conference Standing Comm; Prof Assn of GA Educators; Athens & Macon AGO Dean 1959, 1962, Lewis Elmer Awd; Milledgeville Arts Assn Pres 1960; Macon SPEBSQSA Dir 1960; Athens Oratorio (Secy, Dir); Articles Published; *office:* Oconee Cty Schls Mars Hill Rd Watkinsville GA 30677

RHODEN, LINDA DONOHOE, Sixth Grade Teacher; *b:* Hamilton, OH; *c:* Shannon Rhoden Steele; *ed:* (BS) Ed, 1962, (MED) Curr/Supervision, 1974 Miami Univ; *cr:* 7th Grade Soc Stud Teacher Dayton City Schls 1962-67; 6th Grade Remedial Rdng/8th Grade Math Teacher Eaton City Schls 1967-; *ai:* Delta Kappa Gamma Secy 1978-; NEA; Camden Town Cncl Mem 1986-; Fire Bd VP 1988-; Preble Cty Lib Bd 1970- 0; Camden Archives 1980-; *home:* 1 Joy Ln Camden OH 45311

RHODES, BETTY BLAIR, 3rd Grade Teacher; *b:* Farmville, VA; *ed:* (BA) Sociology, Westhampton Coll Univ of Richmond 1958; (MRE) Religious Ed, Southern Bapt Theological Seminary 1960; Univ of VA; George Mason Univ; James Madison Univ; *cr:* Minister of Ed Warrenton Bapt Church 1960-65; Ginter Park Bapt Church 1965-67; 2nd Bapt Church 1967-70; Teacher Fauquier Cty Weekday Religious Ed 1970-71; Elem Teacher P B Smith Elem Sch 1971-; *ai:* Delta Kappa Gamma Comm Chm/Mem 1979-; Deacon/Active Mem Warrenton Bapt Church; Former Mem Warrenton Chorale; Personalities of the South 1969-70; *home:* 33 Calhoun St Warrenton VA 22186

RHODES, EUGENE, Social Studies Teacher; *b:* Toccoa, GA; *m:* Diane Wilson; *c:* Eugene Jr., Audrene; *ed:* (BA) Soc Stud, Clark Coll 1968; (MA) Ed, GA St Univ 1975; *cr:* Teacher 1970-85, Dept Chm 1975-85 Smith HS; Teacher/Dept Chm 1985-; Athletic Dir 1988- Southside HS; *ai:* Girls Track & Bsktbl Coach; Sch Athletic Dir; NEA 1970-; ASCD 1983-; Track Coach of Yr 1975; Masters Track Meet, High Point Man 1980-83; *office:* Southside HS 801 Glenwood Ave SE Atlanta GA 30312

RHODES, JANET MARIE, Science Teacher & Dept. Chair; *b:* Gallipolis, OH; *ed:* (AB) General/Biological Sci, Marshall Univ 1977; Grad Stud; *cr:* Teacher Hillcrest Baptist Church Sch 1977-78, Jefferson Jr HS 1978-80; Teacher/Dept Chairperson Langley-Bath-Clearwater Mid Sch 1980-; Teacher Midland Valley Adult Ed 1986-; *ai:* Beta Club Spon 1981-83; Sci Club Spon 1984-85; S Assn of Colls & Schls; Chairperson of Steering Comm Langley-Bath-Clearwater Mid Sch 1989-; Drama Dir 1982-84; SEED Cmptr Software Evaluator; Assessments of Performance in Teaching Observer; High Flyers Awd Aiken Cty Area 3 1988-89; Mentor Teacher 1989-; *home:* 704 Vincent Ave Aiken SC 29801

RHODES, JANET WILCOXEN, US His/Amer Government Teacher; *b:* Canton, IL; *m:* Gerald; *ed:* (BS) Soc Sci, IL St 1969; *cr:* Teacher Lewistown HS 1969-; *ai:* Stu Senate Adv; Soc Sci Dept Chairperson; Daughters of Amer Revolution (Historian, Librarian); Natl Rifle Assn; City of Lewistown Chamber of Commerce Citizen of Month 1989.

RHODES, JENNIE RICHARDSON, Third Grade Teacher; *b:* Glynn Cty, GA; *m:* King Edward; *c:* H. Preston, King E. Jr., Hubert B., Janice Casey, Joyce; *ed:* (BS) Elem Ed, Albany St Coll 1959; Valdosta St Coll, Univ of GA; Item Writer GA Criterion Reference Test; *cr:* Teacher Brantley Cty 1945-47; Adult Ed Coord 1947-48, Classroom Teacher/Rdng Coord 1949- Camden Cty; *ai:* Dir Taraboro Youth Patrol Group; Adult Ed Teacher; Dir Summer Rdng & Math Prgm; 3rd Grade Lead Teacher; NEA, GA Assn Educators, Camden Assn of Educators 1960-; Waycross Dist Laiety Secy 1979-, Plaque; Browns Chapel African Meth Secy 1968-, Plaque; Episcopal; Teacher of Yr; Outstanding Cmmty Service Awd; Certificate of Merit.

RHODES, JIMMY LEE, History Teacher; *b:* Houston, TX; *m:* Beverly Mc Clure; *c:* Micah, Joel; *ed:* (BAT) His/Sociology, Sam Houston Univ 1970; (MS) His, Univ Houston Clear Lake 1986; *cr:* Teacher North Shore Mid Sch 1970-; *ai:* Honor Society Sponsorship; Kappa Delta Pi 1986-; *office:* North Shore Mid Sch 13801 Holly Park Houston TX 77015

RHODES, MARJORIE L., Sixth Grade Teacher; *b:* Celina, OH; *m:* Sam Jr.; *c:* Mark, Timothy, Stephen, Jeffrey; *ed:* (BA) Elem Ed, Bowling Green St Univ 1972; (MS) Elem Ed/Rdng, IN Univ 1982; *cr:* 5th Grade Teacher 1968-84, 6th Grade Teacher 1985- Sherwood Elem; *ai:* Rdng/Math/Sci/Health Textbook Comm; NEA; OEA; TACLS Teachers Assoc Cntrl Local Schls (Exec Sec) 1982-87; Bus Professional Women 1985-87; Jennings Scholar; *office:* Sherwood Elem Sch Box 4506 Harrison Sherwood OH 43556

RHODES, RICHARD G., 6th Grade Teacher; *b:* Pampa, TX; *m:* Sarah Jeanne Savage; *c:* Samuel, Timothy, Elizabeth; *ed:* (AA) General Ed, Westark Comm Coll 1967; (BSE) Elem Ed, Univ AR 1971; 6 Yrs Military Comm; *cr:* 6th Grade Teacher 1971-, 5th/6th Grade Teacher 1988-89 Raymond F Orr; *ai:* JROTC Southside HS Pres; Church & Little League Bsbl; Lead Teacher 1988-; PTA Life Mem 1985; *home:* 3401 S Louisville Fort Smith AR 72903

RHODES, ROBERT JOSEPH, Special Education Teacher; *b:* Fayetteville, NC; *m:* Barbara Gail Stevens; *c:* Nicholas A.; *ed:* (BA) Sociology/Bio, Meth Coll 1969; (MED) Spec Ed/Mental Retardation, 1974, (MED) Learning Disabilities/Behavior Disorders, 1978 Valdosta St Coll; *cr:* Spec Ed Teacher Wacona Elem Sch 1973-78, Ware Cty Jr HS 1978-; *office:* Ware Cty Jr HS 1428 Gorman Rd Waycross GA 31501

RHODES, SOLVEIG HAUGSJAA, World Geography Teacher; *b:* Seattle, WA; *m:* Ike S.; *c:* Pam Rhodes Small, Tammy; *ed:* (BS) Art/Ed, Concordia Coll 1967; (MED) Counseling/Guidance, Univ of AZ 1975; *cr:* 5th Grade Teacher Ocean View Sch Dist 1967-69, Dept of Defense Okinawa & W Germany 1969-72; Art/His/World Geography Teacher Amphitheater Sch Dist 1972-; *ai:* Yrbk Adv; Nations Day Coord; Site Base Management Comm; *office:* L W Cross Mid Sch 1000 W Chapala Tucson AZ 85704

RHODES, STANLEY WILLIAMS, Sci/Industrial Arts Coord; *b:* Syracuse, NY; *m:* Hilda Tylston Wright; *c:* Robin E., Ellen T., Heather W.; *ed:* (BA) Psych, Amherst Coll 1960; (MS) Sci Ed, Syracuse Univ 1961; Educl Admin, Fairfield Univ 1977; Natl Sci Fnd Inst; Rutgers 1963; Temple 1965; CO 1966; Taft Ed Wkshp 1989; *cr:* Sci Teacher Lewis S Mills Regional 10 1961-66; Sci Teacher 1966-72, Asst Headmaster 1972-80, Admin Asst 1980-81, Division Coord 1981- Staples HS; *ai:* Chess Club Adv; Staples Governing Bd; Tri Town Sci/Technology; Participant CT Teacher/Mentor Prgm; Westport Think Tank; Natl Sci Teachers Assn 1961-; AAPT 1961-; CT Industrial Technology Assn 1975-; Natl Sci Supvrs Assn 1978-; CT Sci Supvrs Assn 1978-; NEA, CT Ed Assn 1961-; Easton/Redding AFS 1985-87; Redding Land Trust 1975-; Staples Governing Bd (Chm, Vice Chm, Whip, Treas); Certifcate of Support CT Bus & Industry Assn Ed Fnd; Whos Who Amer Ed 1988-89; *office:* Staples H S 70 North Ave Westport CT 06880

RHODES, VIKKI CHERYL, Latin Teacher/Act Dir; *b:* Anchorage, AK; *ed:* (BA) Eng/Latin, TX Tech Univ 1973; Drug Awareness, Refusal Skills Wkshps; *cr:* Surgical Asst Oral Surgeons Office 1978-80; Sales Rep Southwestern Bell 1980-82; Stock Broker Dean Witter & Prudential-Bache 1982-85; Teacher All Saints Episcopal Sch 1985-; *ai:* Act Dir; Chrldr & Patriot Ambassador Spon; Tennis Coach; Drug Comm; St Christophers Episcopal Church Women Pres 1987-88; Diocesan Episcopal Church Women Soc Relations Chairperson 1988; *office:* All Saints Episcopal Sch P O Box 64545 Lubbock TX 79464

RHODES, WILLIAM DON, Science Department Chair; *b:* Overton, TX; *m:* Kay Carol France; *c:* Katherine, Donna; *ed:* (BS) Chem, Stephen F Austin St Univ 1962; Grad Stud Univ of Houston; *cr:* Teacher Tyler Ind Sch Dist 1962-66; Chemical Engr 1966-86; Sci Dept Chm Westwood Ind Sch Dist 1987-; *ai:* Sci Club Adv; Univ Interscholastic League Sci Coach; Assn of TX Prof Educators 1989-; TX St Teachers Assn, NEA 1962-66, 1987-; Amer Inst of Chemical Engrs 1968-; *home:* 301 Larkspur Palestine TX 75801

RHODES-PRYOR, EUNICE LEVY, Fifth Grade Teacher; *b:* Savannah, GA; *m:* John E. III; *c:* Charles Rhodes II, Evette Rhodes, Craig Rhodes; *ed:* (BS) Elem Ed, Savannah St Coll 1975; (MED) Elem Ed, Armstrong-Savannah St Grad Prgm 1983; *cr:* Teacher Barnard Street Sch 1974-79, Haven Elem Sch 1979-; *ai:* Safety Patrol Adv; 5th Grade Chairperson; Soc Stud Curr Revision Writer; GA Assn of Educators, NEA, Chatham Assn of Educators Mem 1974-; Haven Elem Teacher of Yr 1983; *office:* Gilbert O Haven Elem Sch 5111 Dillon Ave Savannah GA 31405

RHOTEN, LINDA DUTTON, Fifth Grade Teacher; *b:* Findlay, OH; *m:* James Alan; *c:* Robert D., James L., Alisha L.; *ed:* (BS) Elem Ed, OH Northern Univ 1969; (MS) Lib Sci, Bowling Green St Univ 1978; Elem Guidance/Counseling; *cr:* 3rd Grade Teacher 1969-78, 4th Grade Teacher 1979-87, 5th Grade Teacher 1988- Van Buren; *ai:* Elem Lib & Mary Ann Baird Schlsp Comms; Delta Kappa Gamma Membership Chairperson 1986-88; OH Northern Univ Stambaugh Schlsp 1968-69; Tau Beta Sigma VP 1968-69; Experimental Aircraft Assn 1990; Van Buren Ed Assn, OH Ed Assn, NEA 1970-88; *office:* Van Buren Sch Main St Van Buren OH 45889

RHOTON, PATRICIA RUDD, 6th Grade Science Teacher; *b:* Brownwood, TX; *m:* David A.; *c:* Rhonda Pollard, Craig, Kevin; *ed:* (BA) Eng, Univ of TX Permian Basin 1975; Advanced Trng in Sci, TX Tech; *cr:* 6th Grade Teacher Cedar Crest Elem 1975-77; 6th Grade Sci Teacher Goliad Mid Sch 1977-.

RHOTON, PATRICIA T., Band Director; *b:* Rogersville, TN; *ed:* (BSME) Music Ed, E TN St Univ 1976; Working Towards Masters in Music Ed, Univ of TN; Grad Stud Accounting & Pre-Law; *cr:* Band Dir Hawkins Cty Schls 1977-79, DeKalb Cty Schls 1980-81, Hawkins Cty Schls 1982-85, Gaston Cty Schls 1985-; *ai:* Jazz Ensemble; HS Colorguard Instr; Spring Musical Spon; Winterguard Act; Christmas Madrigal Dinner; MENC 1977-; NC Band Dir Assn (Jr HS Honor Band Chm 1990) 1985-; *office:* Southwest Jr HS 1 Roadrunner Dr Gastonia NC 28052

RHYE, PATSY CROWLEY, Gifted Coord & Lang Arts; *b:* Madisonville, KY; *ed:* (BA) Scndry Ed/Eng, KY Wesleyan 1972; (MA) Scndry Ed/Eng, Murray Univ 1975; Scndry Ed/Supervision/Rdng, Murray Univ 1978; *cr:* Teacher 1972-; Gifted Coord 1976- Browning Springs Mid Sch; Parttime Teacher Madisonville Comm Coll; Parttime Teacher Murray Univ; *ai:* Chldr Spon; Governors Cup Academic Team; Scholastic Bowl Academic Team; KY Ed Assn 1972-; Hopkins Cty Ed Assn 1972-; NEA 1972-; Teacher of Yr Awd 1987-88; Grants for Gifted Prgrms; Whos Who of Women in Southwest; *home:* P O Box 62 Providence KY 42450

RIALS, BILLIE JUNE, Vocational Business Teacher; *b:* Samson, AL; *m:* Tommy; *c:* Wade, Ashley; *ed:* (BS) Voc Bus Ed, Auburn Univ 1976; (MS) Scndry/Bus Ed, Troy St Univ 1978; *cr:* Voc Bus Teacher Samson HS 1976-; *ai:* Sr HS Stu Cncl Spon; NEA, AEA, GCEA 1976-; Delta Kappa Gamma 1977-; AVA 1989-; Young Womens Organization (VP 1988) 1987-88; First Meth Church Treas 1988-; Samson HS Scndry Teacher of Yr 1987-88, Outstanding Teacher 1986; *office:* Samson HS 209 N Broad St Samson AL 36477

RIALS, JACKIE S., 8th Grade Matematics Teacher; *b:* Americus, GA; *c:* Heather; *ed:* (BS) Elem Ed, 1964, (MAED) Mid Grades, Ed Specialist Mid Grades, 1984 GA Southwestern Coll; *cr:* Teacher Lee Cty Elem 1968-70, Teacher 1973, Math Dept Chairperson 1982-87, Team Leader 1988- Lee Cty Mid Sch; *ai:* GA Cncl Teachers of Math 1984-; Lee Educl Assn, GA Ed Assn, NEA 1973-; Jr HS Dept of Math Team Leader; *office:* Lee Cty Mid Sch Rt 2 Box 385 Leesburg GA 31763

RIBAUDO, CATHERINE MARTINE, English Teacher; *b:* New York City, NY; *m:* Frank J.; *c:* Frank Jr., Paul, Lisa; *ed:* (BA) Eng, St Josephs Coll for Women 1958; (MA) Eng, NY Univ 1961; Eng, Dramatics, Ed, Brooklyn Coll 1982, NY Univ 1986-, Kingsborough Comm Coll 1985-87, New Sch 1987; *cr:* Eng/Dramatics Teacher Andries Hudde Jr HS 1958-60; Eng Teacher New Utrecht HS 1960-61; Eng/Creative Writing Teacher/Advanced Placement Coord Lafayette HS 1961-; *ai:* Sch Literary Magazine Faculty Adv; Marquis Club Adv; Intnl Club; Amer Film Inst 1985-; Drama Musical Works Mem 1987-; NY Times Schlsp 1986, 1987; NY Univ Writers Grant 1988; Published Poetry Amer Poetry Annual 1988; *office:* Lafayette HS 2630 Benson Ave Brooklyn NY 11214

RICCI, MICHAEL, English Teacher; *b:* Jersey City, NJ; *ed:* (BA) Eng, St Peters Coll 1967; (MA) Guidance, Jersey City St 1971; *cr:* Eng Teacher Academic HS 1985-, Ferris HS 1975-85; *ai:* Class Adv; Swimming Coach; *home:* 118 Sunset Key Secaucus NJ 07094

RICE, DEBRA ANN, 7th Grade English Teacher; *b:* Williamsport, PA; *m:* Raymond Allan; *c:* Ashley, Allan, Adam; *ed:* (BS) Soc Sci Ed, Lock Haven St Univ 1976; (MS) Eng Ed, FL St Univ 1989; Certified in Gifted Ed; *cr:* His Teacher Nims Mid Sch 1978-82; Teacher of Gifted Griffin Mid Sch 1982-87; Cmptr Programming II Instr Nova Univ 1985; Coord for Mid Sch Eng/Soc Stud 1987-88; Eng Teacher Griffin Mid Sch 1988-; *ai:* Soccer Coach; Cheerleading Adv; Yrbk Spon; NCTE; Natl Writing Project; ASCD; Natl Rdng Cncl; FL Dept of Ed Grant Marine Summer Sci Inst for Kids; Works Published 1987, 1989; *home:* 2633 Nez Perce Trl Tallahassee FL 32303

RICE, FLORETTA L., 6th/7th/8th Grade Math Teacher; *b:* Ironton, OH; *m:* Lanny B. I;; *c:* Lanny II; *ed:* (BA) Elem Ed, Morehead St Univ 1969; (MA) Ed, Morehead St Univ 1978; *cr:* 1st/2nd Grade Teacher Wurtland Elem 1969-86; Greysbranch Elem; Sunshine Elem; 7th/8th Grade Math Teacher Sunshine Elem 1986-89; 7th/8th Grade Math Teacher 1989 6th/7th Grade Accounting Teacher 1989 Mc Kell Elem; *ai:* Spon Jr Beta Club Mc Kell Mid Sch; NEA Mem 1969-; KY Ed Assn Mem 1969-; Greenup Cty Ed Assn Mem 1969; Alpha Belta Kappa Sgt at Arms 1988-; Sunshine United Meth Choir Dir Secy 1982-84; *office:* Mc Kell Mid Sch Rt 1 South Shore KY 41175

RICE, G. RANDALL, Science & English Teacher; *b:* Fowler, KS; *c:* Heather M.; *ed:* (BS) Elem Ed, KS St Univ 1980; *cr:* Teacher Stillwater Twp Sch 1980-; *ai:* Cmptr Technician Sch Cmptrs; Sci Comm Mem; Lang Arts Comm Mem; NJEA/SEA VP 1986-87; BSA Asst Scout Master 1987-; Governors Teacher Recognition Awd 1989; *office:* Stillwater Twp Sch PO Box 12 Stillwater NJ 07875

RICE, GARY L., Fifth Grade Teacher; *b:* Columbus, OH; *m:* Adelaide Fisher; *c:* Brian; *ed:* (BS) Speech/Journalism/Scndry Ed, Bowling Green St Univ 1966; Elem Cert; Gifted & Talented Certificate; *cr:* Speech/Journalism Teacher Columbus East HS 1966-70; 6th Grade Teacher Como Elem Sch 1970-79; 5th Grade Teacher Hudson Elem Sch 1979-87, Mc Guffey Elem Sch 1987-; *ai:* Instr Gifted/Talented Prgm; Just Say No Club & Sch Safety Patrol Adv; Prin Adv Comm & Intervention At-Risk Stu Team Mem; NEA, OH Ed Assn, Columbus Ed Assn 1980-; Re-Established Journalism Prgm & Sch Newspaper at Cty East HS; Instituted Ability Grouping Concept Como Elem 1972-78; Instituted After Sch Study Prgm for At-Risk Stu at Both Como & Hudson Elem Schls; *home:* 96 Belpre Pl E Westerville OH 43081

RICE, JERRY KEN, Foreign Language Dept Chair; *b:* Bloomington, IN; *m:* Susan Jane Brashaber; *ed:* (AB) Span, 1972, (MAT) Span, 1976 IN Univ; *cr:* Span Instr Binford Mid Sch 1972-74, IN Univ 1974-76, Bloomington HS N 1976-77, Shelbyville HS 1977-; *ai:* Foreign Lang Dept Coord; Amer Assn of Teachers of Span/Portuguese; IN Foreign Lang Teachers Assn; NEA; Fee Remission Fellowship, Grad Teaching Assistantship, Grad Preceptorship IN Univ; *office:* Shelbyville HS 2003 S Miller St Shelbyville IN 46176

RICE, KARYN S. MC CASLIN, First Grade Teacher; *b:* Ashland, KY; *m:* Chester Milton; *c:* Michael Mc Caslin, Shanna L. Mc Caslin; *ed:* (AB) Elem, Univ of KY 1968; *cr:* 2nd Grade Teacher Lincoln Elem 1968-69; Head Start Teacher Lexington KY 1969-73; 3rd Grade Teacher Johnson Elem 1973-74; 1st Grade Teacher Shearer Elem 1975-; *ai:* Sftbl Coach; Fraternal Order of Police Treas 1983-; Deputy Jailer, Lt Chief Deputy; *office:* Shearer Elem Sch 244 E Broadway Winchester KY 40391

RICE, LYNN V., English Teacher; *b:* Newark, NJ; *m:* Peter H.; *ed:* (BA) Eng, Kean Coll 1967; (MA) Eng, Univ of RI 1970; Gifted & Talented Teacher Trng St of NJ; Affirmative Action Prgms Rutgers; Writing Seminars; *cr:* Eng Asst Teacher Univ RI 1967-69; Eng Teacher Lake Taylor HS 1969-71, Franklin HS 1972-; *ai:* NHS Selection Comm; HS Literary Magazine Adv; NJEA, NCTE; Published Model Lesson on Affirmative Action; *home:* RD 1 Box 522 Princeton NJ 08540

RICE, MELVA POWELL, Retired; *b:* Celeste, TX; *m:* Clarence P.; *c:* Anna Cleary; *ed:* (BS) Elem Educ, 1955; (ME) Elem Educ, 1958 East TX Univ; *cr:* Teacher Tidwell Ind Sch Dist 1938-39; Prin/Teacher Merrick Ind Sch Dist 1942-44; Teacher Center Point Ind Sch Dist 1944-45; Greenville Ind Schls 1955-; Asst Prof East TX St Univ 1955-85; *ai:* Summer Enrichment Prgm Supv and Teacher; Tutoring Elem Stu in Summer; Supv of Stu Teachers Greenville Elem and East TX St Univ Office Field Experiences; TX Teachers Assn 1955-; Greenville Classroom Teachers Pres 1955-84; Greenville Local TSTA 1955-84; NEA 1955-84; Delta Kappa Gamma Society Pres 1959-; Greenville & Hunt Cty Bus & Professional Womens Club Pres 1942- Women of Yr 1989; Honorary Life Time Membership PTA; Deans List East TX St Univ; *home:* 14 Mulloney Rd Greenville TX 75401

RICE, MICHAEL DE LEON, Band Director; *b:* Mobile, AL; *m:* Veronica Kidd; *c:* Alandus Lamont, Donnisia Shantel, Michael E. De Leon; *ed:* (BS) Music Ed, AL A&M Univ 1977; Grad Studs Univ of MI; *cr:* Band Dir J F Shields HS 1977-83, Ed White Mid Sch 1983-; *ai:* AL Band Masters Assn; 1st Baptist Church (Evangelistic Team, Sr HS Bible Class Teacher); Superior Ratings Local Levels Band 1985; All Amer Music Festival & Smokey Mountain Music Festival Superior Ratings 1986-88; *home:* 2815 Crenshaw Dr Huntsville AL 35810

RICE, SANDRA DUNN, Homemaker; *b:* Birmingham, AL; *m:* Willie J.; *c:* La Sandra Y., Willie Jr., David V.; *ed:* Cmptr Programing, Career Trng Inst; *cr:* Long Distance Oper South Central Bell 1969-71; Kndgtn Teacher Mrs Rice Kndgtn 1975-85; *ai:* Bible Study Instr Youth & Adults; Freelance Writer; Title One Secy 1978-79.

RICE, SHIRLEY EXUM, 4th Grade Teacher; *b:* Kinston, NC; *m:* Otis L.; *c:* Charlinese Abbott; *ed:* (BA) Elem Ed, Fayetteville St Univ 1963; *cr:* 4th Grade Teacher Wayne Cty Schls 1963-64; 2nd Grade Teacher Kinston City Schls 1964-67; 2nd/4th Grade Teacher Pitt Cty Schls 1967-; *ai:* NCAE 1989-.

RICE, SUSAN POE, 5th Grade Teacher; *b:* Pikeville, KY; *ed:* (BS) Elem/Spec Ed, E KY Univ 1976; 5th Yr Degree Elem Ed, Morehead St Univ 1981; Working Toward Rank I Degree in Elem Ed; *cr:* Spec Ed Learning Disability Teacher Johns Creek HS 1977-78; 5th Grade Teacher Mullins HS 1978-; *ai:* Various Comms at Local Bd of Ed; Spec Ed Comm; Book Comms; *office:* Mullins HS 1265 N Mayo Trl Pikeville KY 41501

RICE, SUSAN ROWLAND, Business/Science Teacher; *b:* Gary, IN; *m:* B. Michael; *ed:* (BS) Scndry Ed, TX A&M Univ 1988; *ai:* Accounting UIL, Debate UIL Coach; Class Spon; Sci Fair; Twirler Coach; TX Phys Sci Teachers 1989-; Americas Outstanding Young Women Awd 1988; *home:* 411A Manuel College Station TX 77840

RICE, WALLACE WILLIAM, Earth Science Teacher; *b:* Basin, WY; *m:* Rozella P.; *c:* Steven C., Kevin E.; *ed:* (BS) Geology, 1959, (MS) Natural Sci, 1967 Univ of WY; Mining Inst; Weather Inst; *cr:* Asst Personnel Sch Dist 1 1962-63; HS Sci Teacher Johnson Jr HS 1963-66; Earth Sci Teacher Central HS 1966-; *ai:* Jr Class Spon; Chm Athletic Tickets; Wrestling Coach; Sci Club Spon; AFT (Pres 1974-76, Bd 1976-); Phi Delta Kappa 1977-; NSTA 1965-; Rheumatic Fever Prevention Secy/Treas 1962-; BSA 1946-, Silver Beaver 1984; Nom Teacher of Yr; *office:* Central HS 5500 Eucation Dr Cheyenne WY 82001

RICH, DONALD F., 6th Grade Teacher; *b:* Buffalo, NY; *m:* Kathleen D. Dahl; *c:* Kaelyn, Kellee; *ed:* (BA) Elem Ed, 1970, (MS) Ed, 1975 St Univ of NY Fredonia; *cr:* Elem Teacher Cassadaga Valley Cntrl Sch 1970-; *ai:* Cassadaga Valley Faculty Assn Pres 1984-; NY St United Teachers; *home:* 2747 Main Rd Sheridan NY 14135

RICH, JANE (BILES), Calculus/Physics/Math Teacher; *b:* Chandler, OK; *m:* Floyd L.; *c:* Jeramy S., Timothy R., John R.; *ed:* (BS) Pharmacy, Univ of OK 1971; Teaching Cert 1983, (MSED) Scndry Ed, 1988 East Cntrl Univ; *cr:* Sci Teacher 1983-84, Sci/Math Teacher 1984- Shawnee HS; *ai:* Scholastic Team & Sci Club Spon; Academic Bowl Coach; OK Sci Teachers Assn 1984-; OEA, SACT 1983-; AAPT 1986-, Physics Teaching Resource Agent 1986; Shawnee Teacher of Yr 1987-88; Shawnee Chamber of Commerce Educator Awd 1988; *office:* Shawnee HS 1001 N Kennedy Shawnee OK 74801

RICH, JANET L., 7th Grade Language Art Teacher; *b:* Kenova, WV; *m:* W. H.; *c:* Kimberly Rich Evans, Chip, Mark S.; *ed:* (BA) Ed, E KY Univ 1959; Grad Stud Memphis St; *cr:* Teacher Miamisburg Elem 1960-62; Owner/Teacher Private Kndgtn 1968-72; Teacher Germantown Elem 1976-82, Germantown Mid 1982-; *office:* Germantown Mid Sch 2734 Cross Country Ln Germantown TN 38138

RICH, LUCILLE H., Lang Art Teacher/Dept Chair; *b:* Ball Ground, GA; *m:* James H.; *c:* Randy, Sandra Rich Elrod, Gary, Tammie Rich Roper, Kirk; *ed:* (AA) Early Chldhd Ed - Cum Laude, 1973; (BS) Early Chldhd Ed/Elem Ed - Magna Cum Laude, 1974, (MA) Mid Grades Ed, 1981 Brenau Coll; GA Mountains Writing Project; Grad Work W GA Coll; Cert Endorsement as Data Collector to Evaluate Classroom Teachers; *cr:* Resource Teacher Pickens Cty Headstart 1969-73; Asst Prin/Teacher Ball Ground Elem 1976-83; Classroom Teacher Clayton Elem Sch 1983-86; Teacher/Coord Cherokee Cty Elem Summer Sch Prgm 1986; Classroom Teacher Marie Archer Teasley Mid Sch 1986-; *ai:* Young Authors Fair Teasley Mid Sch Coord; Faculty Advisory Comm; Drama Club Spon; Cherokee Ed Assn Budget Comm 1980-81, Local Sch Teacher of Yr 1984; GA Assn Educators Delegate to St Convention 1980; NEA; Delta Kappa Gamma Intnl Research Comm 1977-; Ball Ground Cmmty Assn Prgm 1977-80; PTA, PTSA 1963-; Bethesda Baptist Church Mem 1965-; Natl Delegate to Review, Select Headstart Models for GA 1968; Served On 9th Dist Advisory Bd for Headstart, Follow Through Prgms 1972-76; Cherokee Cty Teacher of Yr 1978;

Cherokee Cty Curr Comm, Textbook Comm; *office:* Marie Archer Teasley Mid Sch Rt 7 Hwy 20 W Canton GA 30114

RICH, PEARL M., Art Education Teacher; *b:* Portland, ME; *c:* Holly E. Clark, Leslie M. Clark, Linda A. Peterson, David S. Clark; *ed:* (BFA) Fashion Design/Illustration, MA Coll of Art 1951; (MED) Ed/Art, Notre Dame Coll 1987; Numerous Courses, Univs; *cr:* Art Educator Sunapee Sch Dist 1970-; *ai:* NH St Dept of Ed (Examining Bd, Teacher Cert Dept, Consultant) Alternative III 1980-; NH Elem Art Ed Curr; Alliance for Arts Ed Exec Bd 1979-81; NH Art Educators Assn (Cert Standards Comm, Exec Bd, Pres, Treas) 1980, Conference Planning, Financial Consultant 1990-; New England Art Ed Conference Incorporated (Co-Founder 1973, Financial Dir 1975-), Outstanding Contributions to Art Ed 1980; Publications St Dept of Ed 1980, Univ of NH, NAEA; Art Exhibits NH & TX; *office:* Sunapee Dist Schls North Rd Sunapee NH 03782

RICH, SHIRLEY FREEMAN, Second & Third Grade Teacher; *b:* Scottsville, KY; *m:* Fred Sr.; *c:* Elizabeth Gregory, Fred Jr., Mark A., Edward P.; *ed:* (BS) Elem Ed; (MA) Elem Ed; *cr:* 7th/8th Grade Sci/Math/Health Teacher 1977-78, 3rd Grade Teacher 1978-84, Rdng Teacher 1984-85, Transition Teacher 1985-86, 1st Grade Teacher 1986-87, 2nd Grade Teacher 1987- Chandlers Elem; *ai:* Sch Philosophy Comm; Lang Art, Art, Evaluation Comm; Logan Cty Ed Assn Rep; *office:* Chandlers Elem Sch 7815 Chandlers Chapel Rd Auburn KY 42206

RICHARD, DUDY STELLY, Business Teacher/Voc Coord; *b:* Sunset, LA; *m:* Duayne F.; *c:* Mason, Nicholas, Jonathan; *ed:* (BS) Bus Ed, 1973, (MED) Ed, 1976 Univ of SW LA; *cr:* Bus Teacher Sunset Elem Sch 1972-74, Sunset HS 1974-; *ai:* Class Spon; FBLA Adv; Honor Club, Homecoming Court, Open House, Prom, Graduation Act; Accreditation Review Comm; Stu Handbook Revision; St Landry Bus Ed Teachers Assn 1989-; NEA, LA Assn of Educators 1972-; St Landry Assn of Educators 1986-; NBEA 1972-76; St Ignatius PTC Secy 1988-; FBLA Prof Division 1989-; *office:* Sunset HS PO Box G Sunset LA 70584

RICHARD, KATHLEEN S. MAFFUCCI, Volunteer Teacher; *b:* Torrington, CT; *m:* Noel F.; *c:* Kaitlin M., Nevan M.; *ed:* (BS) Human Dev/Family Stud, Univ of CT 1978; Grad Courses St Joseph Coll, West Hartford, Univ of Hartford; *cr:* Teacher West Hartford Public Schls 1979-81, St Rose Parochial Sch 1981-83, Scooter Sch 1988-89; Volunteer Teacher St Bridget Sunday Pre-Sch 1986-; *home:* 90 Forest Ln Cheshire CT 06410

RICHARD, LARRY ANDRE, English Teacher; *b:* Nashville, TN; *m:* Tonie Seabrooks; *ed:* (BA) Eng, Univ of Louisville 1972; (MED) Scndry Ed, Temple Univ 1974; *cr:* Eng Teacher Chester HS 1972-75; Eng Instr Jefferson Comm Coll 1975-77; Pan-African Stud Lecturer Univ of Louisville 1976-78; Eng Teacher Belmont HS 1980-85, Walton HS 1985-; *ai:* Ftbl Coach Walton HS 1985-89; *office:* Walton HS 1590 Bill Murdock Rd Marietta GA 30062

RICHARD, LEE TWAROG, English Teacher; *b:* New Bedford, MA; *m:* George; *c:* Jessica, Amanda; *ed:* (BS) Ed, Fitchburg St 1969; *cr:* Eng Teacher Ashby HS 1969-71, N Middlesex Regional HS 1971-72 1978-; *home:* 92 Wilder Rd Lunenburg MA 01462

RICHARDS, BETTY JEAN (VAN RIPER), Gifted/Talented Coord/Teacher; *b:* Newton, NJ; *m:* Stephen D.; *c:* Stephen D. H.; *ed:* (BA) Elem Ed, 1973, (MA) Elem Ed/Soc Stud, 1978 William Paterson; Great Books Wkshps; Rdng; Apple Cmptr Introduction I & II; *cr:* 3rd Grade Teacher 1973; 4th Grade Teacher 1980; Coord of Gifted/Talented 1983; *ai:* NJ Gifted; Hardyston Bd of Ed Teacher/Educator of Yr 1977; Order of Eastern Star Worthy Matron 1980-81; *home:* 2 High Pt Cr Franklin NJ 07416

RICHARDS, CARL ANN (FLECK), K-6 Remedial Math Teacher; *b:* Philadelphia, PA; *m:* James T.; *c:* James H., John R.; *ed:* (BS) Elem/Eng Ed, St Univ of NY Geneseo 1964; Classroom Management; Elements of Instruction; *cr:* K-12th Grade Remedial Rdng Teacher Kendall Cntrl Sch 1978-79; 9th-12th Math Teacher 1984-85, 7th-12th Grade Eng Teacher 1986 Kendall HS; K-6th Grade Remedial Math Teacher Kendall Elem 1979-; *ai:* Sr Night Master of Ceremonies; Jr Var & Var Cheerleading; Soccer, Bsktbl, Wrestling Coach; Pep Club Adv; Dist Advisory Cncl; Blue & White Day Organizer; Genesee League Rep; Elem Math Comm; Sec V Sports; Genesee League Rep 1983-; KCS Learning Team Math Rep 1980-; Western Eagles Volunteer Cheer Coach 1986-, 1st Pl 1987-89; *office:* Kendall Elem Sch 1932 Kendall Rd Kendall NY 14476

RICHARDS, CHRISTIE CRAIS, 5th Grade Teacher; *b:* Baltimore, MD; *m:* Robert A. Jr.; *c:* Susan Richards Acker, Robert A. III; *ed:* (BS) Elem Ed, Jacksonville St Univ 1966; TABA Course; Values Clarification; Sci Course, Natl Sci Fnd; *cr:* 5th Grade Teacher Saks Elem 1965-66, Hewitt Trussville 1966-67; 4th Grade Teacher/4th-6th Non Graded Teacher Pennypacker 1967-71; 4th/5th Grade Teacher Twin Hills 1971-88; *ai:* Safety Adv; Cmptr, Math, Soc Stud, Sci, Spelling, Sexism, Bi-Centennial Comm; Wrote 4th Level Sci Curr 1974; Willingboro Teachers Assn Building Rep 1967-; Delta Kappa Gamma (Membership Chm 1987-, Recording Secy 1989-); W Jersey Rdng Cncl; PTA Teacher Liason 1967-; Willingboro Teachers Assn Building Rep 1967-; Nom Outstanding Elem Teacher of America 1973; Governors Teacher Recognition Prgm Outstanding Teacher 1981-83; *office:* Twin Hills Elem Sch Twin Hill Dr Willingboro NJ 08046

RICHARDS, JANET FISCHER, Chemistry Teacher; *b:* Philadelphia, PA; *m:* Kevin A.; *c:* Thomas; *ed:* (BA) Chem, Shippensburg Univ 1981; Scndry Ed, W Chester Univ 1986; *cr:* Research Asst Wistar Research Inst; Chemist Witco Chemical Company; Teacher Highland Regional HS 1986-; *ai:* Amer Chemical Society Ed Division, S Jersey Section Teachers Affiliate 1987-; NJ Sci Teachers Assn; Co-Author Company Paper; Teacher in Industry Hoechst-Celanese Research Labs 1988; *home:* 1545 W High St Haddon Heights NJ 08035

RICHARDS, JANET LAUDANO, Marketing Teacher; *b:* New Haven, CT; *m:* Jason Lee; *ed:* (AA) Liberal Arts/Bus, Manattee Comm Coll 1983; (BA) Mrktg Ed, Univ of S FL 1985; Working Towards Masters Educl Leadership, Univ of S FL; *cr:* Bus Teacher Mc Lane Jr HS 1985-86, Burns Jr HS 1986-87; Mrktg Teacher East Bay HS 1987-; *ai:* Distributive Ed Clubs of America, Tribe Spon; Dist Co-Adv for Mrktg Ed; TAP, Curr Dev, Test Writing Comms; FL Assn of Mrktg Educators Region IV Teacher of Yr; Hillsborough Voc Assn Rookie Teacher of Yr 1987-88; Nom AT&T in Search of Excl Awd for Mrktg Prgm Hillsboro Cty 1989-; Supervising Instr USF Interns; *office:* East Bay HS 7710 Big Bend Rd Gibsonton FL 33534

RICHARDS, JANICE, Mathematics Teacher; *b:* Clovis, NM; *ed:* (BS) Math/Phys Ed, Mc Murry Coll 1963; (MED) Math Ed, W TX St Univ 1976; *cr:* Math Teacher/Coach Haskell Ind Sch Dist 1963-68, Danbury Ind Sch Dist 1968-69, Smyer Ind Sch Dist 1969-71; Math Teacher Friona Ind Sch Dist 1971-; *ai:* NHS Adv; TSTA; *home:* 1208 Columbia Friona TX 79035

RICHARDS, JEANETTE M. (WILLIS), 5th Grade Teacher; *b:* Salem, OH; *m:* Carl E.; *c:* Thomas L., Susan L. Wearsch, Allen C.; *ed:* (BS) Provisional Certificate Elem Ed - Magna Cum Laude, Kent St Univ 1973; Prof Certificate Tenure; *cr:* 1st Grade Teacher 1973; 3rd Grade Teacher Hartville Elem 1976; 4th Grade Teacher 1979, 5th Grade Teacher 1983- Lake Elem; *ai:* Yrbk Ed 1985-; Washington DC Field Trip Comm 1984-; Lake Elem Ed Assn 1974-; OEA, NEA, ECOEA; Greater Canton Cncl Teachers of Math 1989-; PTO 1974-; Greater Canton Chamber of Commerce Teacher of Yr 1987; *office:* Lake Elem Sch 225 Lincoln St S W Hartville OH 44632

RICHARDS, JOAN SHRODEK, 2nd Grade Teacher; *b:* Warren, OH; *m:* David; *c:* Trevor, Tyler; *ed:* (BS) Elem Ed, Kent St Univ 1974; *cr:* 1st Grade Teacher 1976-78, 2nd Grade Teacher 1978- Bristol Local Sch; *ai:* Trumbull Cty Soc Stud Course of Study Revision Comm; OEA 1980-; Natl Arbor Day Fnd 1988-; Natl Parks & Conservation Assn 1990; *office:* Bristol Local Sch 1845 Greenville Rd Bristolville OH 44402

RICHARDS, LUCILLE SAWYER, Special Needs Teacher; *b:* Lowell, MA; *m:* Peter John; *c:* Elizabeth, Paul; *ed:* (BS) Spec Ed, Fitchburg St Coll 1981; (MED) Spec Ed, Boston Coll 1986; *cr:* Special Needs Teacher Hajjar Elem Sch 1982-83, Locke Mid Sch 1983-; *ai:* Lowell Assn For Retarded Citizens Distinguished Service Awd 1977.

RICHARDS, REBECCA WATSON, English Teacher; *b:* Cincinnati, OH; *m:* Theodore E. II; *c:* Rhys, Jake; *ed:* (BA) Eng, Bowling Green St Univ 1974; (MA) Eng/Lang/Lit, Univ of MI 1975; Cert Eng/Scndry, Bowling Green St Univ 1976; *cr:* Eng Teacher Forest Park HS 1977-; *office:* Forest Park HS 1231 W Kmper Rd Cincinnati OH 45240

RICHARDS, ROLEEN USSATIS, Fourth Grade Teacher; *b:* Valley City, ND; *m:* Robert W.; *c:* Kelly J.; *ed:* (BS) Elem Ed, Valley City St Coll 1969; *cr:* 2nd Grade Teacher Lisbon Elem Sch 1969-75; 4th Grade Teacher Wimbledon-Courtenay Sch 1977-; *ai:* Pep Club Adv; Cheerleading Coach; Wimbledon-Courtenay Ed Assn 1977-; ND Ed Assn, NEA 1969-; Wimbleton-Courtenay Alumni Assn VP 1980-; *office:* Wimbledon-Courtenay Sch Box 255 Wimbledon ND 58492

RICHARDS, SHARI, English Teacher & Dept Chair; *b:* Wichita, KS; *m:* Ross; *ed:* (BSE) Eng/Soc Sci, Emporia St Univ 1967; (MSE) Scndry Teaching, Pittsburg St Univ 1981; *cr:* Speech/Eng Teacher Roosevelt Jr HS 1967-68; Eng Teacher Field Kindley HS 1968-; *ai:* NCTE, KS Assn Teachers of Eng (bd of Dir, St Treas) 1980-; NEA Life Mem, Coffyville Ed Assn Pres; PEO 1985-; Meth Church Trustee 1986-88; Master Teacher of Unified Sch Dist #445; *office:* Field Kindley HS 8th & Roosevelt Coffeyville KS 67337

RICHARDS, VIRGINIA FRY, Home Economics Teacher; *b:* Dallas, TX; *m:* Donnie; *c:* Mary A.; *ed:* (BS) Clothing Design, 1967, (MS) Home Ec Ed, 1970 TX Tech Univ; Grad Work Ed, E KY Univ; *cr:* Merchandise Trainee Sanger Harris Dept Store 1967-69; Home Ec Teacher Thousand Oaks HS 1970-71, Dunbar HS 1971-73; Asst Prof E KY Univ 1973-77; Home Ec Teacher Huntsville HS 1977-82, Roosevelt HS 1982-; *ai:* FHA, Phi Upsilon Omicron Spon; Faculty Rep Comm Chairperson; Voc Home Ec Teachers of TX 1977-; TX St Teachers Assn 1977-; *office:* Roosevelt Ind Sch Dist Rt 1 Box 402 Lubbock TX 79401

RICHARDSON, ADA KATHERINE, 5th Grade Teacher; *b:* Tallahassee, FL; *ed:* (BS) Elem Ed, FL A&M Univ 1962; Further Study, FL A&M Univ 1967-72; FL St Univ 1973-78; Univ of FL 1975-80; Advanced Courses, Wkshps Orange Cty Sch Syst; *cr:* 1st Grade Teacher Callahan Elem 1962-63; 2nd Grade Teacher Eccleston Elem 1963-64; 2nd Grade Teacher 1965-77; 5th Grade Teacher 1977- Richmond Heights Elem; *ai:* Richmond Heights Elem Math Chairperson; Grade Level Chairperson; Guidance Comm; Peer-Teacher; Orange Cty Classroom Teachers Assn Faculty Rep 1980-; NEA Mem; Orange Cty Rdng Cncl Mem; Carter Tabernacle CME Church; Debonnaires Civic & Social Clubs (Sec, Pres, Historian) ; Richmond Heights Teacher of Yr 1972, 1973, 1987; *office:* Richmond Heights Elem Sch 2500 Bruton Blvd Orlando FL 32805

RICHARDSON, ARTHUR PATRICK, History Department Chairman; *b:* Pittsburgh, PA; *m:* Susan Marie Allen; *c:* Rachael, Erik, Lorinda; *ed:* (BA) His/Geography, 1967, (MED) His/Geography, 1975 Univ of Pittsburgh; *cr:* Teacher 1967-, Advanced Placement Coord 1972- Trinity HS; *ai:* PA Soccer Coaches Assn Pres 1986-88; Kiwanis; *home:* RD 1 Box 119A Prosperity PA 15329

RICHARDSON, CARITA JONES, Mathematics Teacher; *b:* West Jefferson, NC; *m:* Llewellyn Bentley Jr.; *c:* L. B. III; *ed:* (BS) Math/Span, Radford Univ 1970; *cr:* Math/Span Teacher Windsor HS 1970-; *ai:* Mathcounts Coach; Windsor HS Self Study Steering Comm; Cty Curr Math Dev Comm; IWEA, VEA, NEA 1970-; Windsor Chrstn Church Womens Fellowship Pres 1987-; Windsor Jaycees Teacher of Yr Awd 1978; *home:* Rt 2 Box 7 Windsor VA 23487

RICHARDSON, CAROL ANN, Second Grade Teacher; *b:* Rochester, NY; *ed:* (BS) Elem Ed, Roberts Wesleyan Coll 1988; Scndry Ed/Soc Sci, SUNY Oswego 1969-73; Ministerial Bible, Elem Bible Inst 1979-81; *cr:* 6th Grade Teacher New Covenant Chrstn 1984-87; Tutor Rochester Public Sch 1989; 2nd Grade Teacher New Covenant Chrstn 1989-; *home:* P O Box 187 North Chili NY 14514

RICHARDSON, CAROL DENISE, 7th Grade Teacher/Coach; *b:* Mc Alester, OK; *ed:* (ME) Elem Ed, East Cntrl Univ 1984; (BS) Psych/Sociology, Southeastern St Univ 1978; *cr:* LD/EMH 1979-84, 7th Grade Teacher 1984-, 7th & 8th Girls Bsktbl Coach 1983- Krebs Public Sch; *ai:* 7th & 8th Girls Bsktbl Coach; Girls Club Bsktbl; Camp Girls Club Sftbl; Licensed Bsktbl Referee; Volunteer at Olympic Festival 1989; Krebs Assn of Teachers Pres 1987-88; Victory Park & 2nd Baptist Churches (Cnslr, Dir Youth Camp, Kiamichi Baptist Assemblys Youth Leader 1979-); Selected by Rotary Club Intnl Exch Teacher from SE OK; *home:* Rt 5 Box 595 Mc Alester OK 74501

RICHARDSON, CAROLYN DANIEL, Vocational Home Ec Teacher; *b:* Fairmont, WV; *m:* Mitchell Lee; *c:* Mitchell, Mary K.; *ed:* (BA) Voc Home Ec Comprehensive, Fairmont St Coll 1975; (MS) Home Ec Ed, WV Univ 1979; Cert Pre Voc Career Exploration, Marshall Univ 1980; *cr:* Food Service Supvr Fairmont General Hospital 1975-76, WV Univ Hospital 1976-77; Voc Home Ec Teacher Marion Cty Bd of Ed 1977-; Part Time Home Ec Instr Fairmont St Coll 1990; *ai:* Fairmont Sr HS FHA Adv; Homebound Teacher for Ill Stu; Womans Club Reporter 1979-80; Ladies of Moose 1987-; *office:* Fairmont Sr HS Loop Park Fairmont WV 26554

RICHARDSON, DALE FOLSOM, Social Studies Teacher; *b:* Sumter, SC; *m:* Arthur Gregg; *ed:* (BS) Psych Ed, Univ of SC 1980; Grad Work Clemson Univ & Univ of SC; *cr:* Soc Stud Teacher Wilson Hall Sch 1980-81, Furman HS 1981-85, Ebenezer Jr HS 1985-86, Mayewood HS 1986-87, Ebenezer Jr HS 1987-; *ai:* Operate Sch Canteen; Teacher Adv Group Advisement Prgm; NCSS 1984-88; SC Palmetto Cncl for Soc Stud 1984-88; Strom Thurmond Fellow 1984; *office:* Ebenezer Jr HS 3440 Ebenezer Rd Sumter SC 29150

RICHARDSON, DAN LYNN, Fifth Grade Teacher; *b:* Martins Ferry, OH; *m:* Deborah Lee Ullom; *c:* Theodor; *ed:* (BA) Elem Ed, West Liberty St 1974; (BA) Speech Comm, WV Coll Univ 1985; *cr:* 5th Grade Teacher Fulton Elem 1974-75, Woodsdale Elem 1975-; *ai:* Lang Art & Math Cncl; WVEA, NEA Buidling Rep 1976-82; PTA Spelling Bee Chm 1979-82, Life Mem 1980; *office:* Woodsdale Elem Sch Bethany Pike & Maple Ave Wheeling WV 26003

RICHARDSON, DEBORAH JOY, 5th Grade Teacher/Math Teacher; *b:* Brooklyn, NY; *m:* James David Jr.; *c:* Frederick Jr., Jamie; *ed:* (BA) Elem Ed, Kean Coll of NJ 1990; *cr:* Dir Refuge Church Day Care Center 1978-79; 2nd Grade Teacher 1979-81, 4th Grade Teacher 1982-87, 5th Grade Teacher 1988- Calvary Chrstn Sch; *ai:* Calvary Chrstn Sch Elem Dept Chairperson 1979-Teacher of Yr; Church of Our Lord Jesus Christ Dir of Childrens Ministry Outstanding Service; *office:* Calvary Chrstn Sch 17 Lyons Ave Newark NJ 07112

RICHARDSON, DOROTHY JEAN LAUDERDALE, Dept Chair/Science Teacher; *b:* Ft Myers, FL; *c:* Joel A.; *ed:* (BA) Bio, Huntingdon Coll 1951; FL St Univ; Univ of W FL; In-Service Prgms; *cr:* Teacher Crestview HS 1947-49, Marbury HS 1949-51, Niceville HS 1951-52; Teacher/Dept Chairperson Ruckel Jr HS 1967-70, Niceville HS 1970-; *ai:* Sci Club; Stu Advisory Prgm; Okaloosa Cty Teachers Assn, FL Assn Sci Teachers, NSTA; *office:* Niceville Sr HS 800 E John Sims Pkwy Niceville FL 32578

RICHARDSON, DORTHY SMITH, 8th Grade Soc Stud Teacher; *b:* Troy, AL; *m:* David Napoleon; *c:* David N. Jr., Rosalyn M., Earl L. Goldsby; *ed:* (BS) His, AL St Univ 1973; (MA) His, Atlanta Univ 1975; Grad Stud His; *cr:* Teacher Banks Mid Sch 1974-75, Elizabeth S Chastang 1977-; *ai:* Soc Stud Fair & Staff Teachers Appreciation Day Coord; NEA, AL Ed Assn, Mobile Cty Ed Assn; PTA (AL Life Mem, Sch Fund Raising Chairperson); Mt Olive AME Zion Church (Mem, Dir of Children) 1985-; E S Chastang Teacher of Yr 1984-86; E S Chastang Mid Sch Teacher of Month 1989; Founder Church Based Free Tutoring Rdng/Math Prgm; *office:* Elizabeth S Chastang Sch 2800 Berkley Ave Mobile AL 36617

RICHARDSON, EMILY HAYDEN, Voc Dept Chair/Home Ec Teacher; *b:* Danville, VA; *m:* Thomas E.; *ed:* (BS) Voc Home Ec Ed, Radford Coll 1967; (MA) Home Ec Ed, Hampton Univ 1977; William & Mary, VPI, SU, Old Dominion Univ, Christopher Newport Coll; Adv Stud Prgm Supervision & Admin, ODU; *cr:* Home Ec Teacher Yorktown Intermediate Sch 1967-68, Queens Lake Intermediate Sch 1968-76; Home Ec Teacher/Voc Dept Chairperson Bruton HS 1976-; *ai:* FHA Hero Adv; VA Home Ec Assn (Elem Chairperson, Secy) St Teacher of Yr 1989-; VA Home Ec Assn Adult Ed Section 1974, 1976; VA Home Ec Teachers Assn (Pres-Elect, Pres, Past-Pres) 1974-77, Outstanding Teacher 1984; VA Voc Assn, Amer Voc Assn St VP 1975-76; York, VA, NEA St VP 1975-76; Delta Kappa Gamma (Secy 1988-, VP 1990-); Certified Home Economist Amer Home Ec Assn; Teacher of Yr 1987, 1990; York Cty Teacher of Yr 1990; *office:* Bruton HS 185 Rochambeau Dr Williamsburg VA 23185

RICHARDSON, GAIL ROUTZAHN, Kindergarten Teacher; *b:* Carlinville, IL; *m:* David; *c:* Carrie, Jeff; *ed:* (BS) Elem Ed, Greenville Coll 1976; (MSED) Rdng, W IL Univ 1985; *cr:* 2nd Grade Teacher 1976-89, Kndgtn Teacher 1989- Pawnee Grade Sch; *office:* Pawnee Grade Sch 810 4th St Pawnee IL 62558

RICHARDSON, GARY A., Principal; *b:* Cedar Falls, IA; *m:* Sue Kuehl; *c:* Tyler, Mallory; *ed:* (BA) Poly Sci, Univ of N IA 1978; (MSE) Admin, Drake Univ 1988; *cr:* Teacher Danville Cmmty Schls 1978-81; Teacher 1981-89, Prin 1989- Harris-Lake Park Cmmty Schls; *ai:* Boys Bsktbl, Golf, Ftbl, Girls Vlybl Coach; IBCA Bd of Dir 1981-, Coach of Yr 1988; ISEA 1978-89; NWICO 1981-89; Silver Lake Cntry Club (Pres, Bd of Dir) 1988-; *office:* Harris Lake Park Cmmty Sch 105 Avenue A West Lake Park IA 51347

RICHARDSON, GLORIA ELAINE SAVAGE, Science Teacher; *b:* Jackson, TN; *m:* Albert Earl; *c:* Mark A., Brian K., Waymon K., John L.; *ed:* (BS) Bio/Chem, Lane Coll 1973; Educl Admin, Marygrove Coll; Sci Ed, Univ of MI; *cr:* Sci Teacher Highland Park HS 1976-, Univ of MI 1987-88, Marygrove Coll 1986-; *ai:* Sci Club; Sci Fair Coord 1985-; Crisis Team 1989-; Union Local 684 Building Rep 1988-; Ed Forum Local 684 Mem 1986-; NSTA, MI Ed Assn of Sci Teachers 1986-; Gave Works on Black Scientists & Inventors MI Dept of Ed Lansing 1990; *office:* Highland Park HS 15900 Woodward Ave Highland Park MI 48203

RICHARDSON, GLORIA HENDERSON, Retired Teacher; *b:* Story City, IA; *m:* Charles A.; *c:* Susan Clark, Charles, Julie Lehman, John; *ed:* (BA) Ed/Eng/Speech/Fr, Univ of N IA 1945; Numerous Univ; *cr:* K-8th Grade Teacher Harrison Township 1942-43; Teacher Selah HS 119 1945-47, Omaha HS 1 1947; K-8th Grade Teacher Cedar Falls Elem 1951-52; Teacher Rosen Heights HS 1954-55, Martha HS 1958-59; K-8th Grade Teacher El Nido Sch Dist 1958-68, St Anthony Sch 1978-87; *ai:* Speech, Chorus, Drama, Violin, Debate, Viola; Amer Assn of Univ Women, N IA Alumni Assn 1945-; CA Teachers Assn 1968-; Gold Star Mother 1970-; Officers Wives Club 1953-; Veterans Foreign Wars Auxiliary 1978-; Kappa Delta 1955-; El Nido Sch Woman of Yr Awd 1970-72, 1975-76; *home:* 895 Juniper Ave Atwater CA 95301

RICHARDSON, IRVING ROOSEVELT, Sixth Grade Teacher; *b:* Leesburg, FL; *m:* Lucy Morris; *c:* Semarian Robinson, Darryl, Lorinda, Devan; *ed:* (BS) Phys Ed, NC A&T 1951; Chicago St Coll; *cr:* 7th/8th Grade Math Teacher William Cullen Bryant 1961-71; 6th Grade Teacher Hans Christian Andersen 1971-; *ai:* Math Comm; Poster Bd Chm; St Paul AME Church 1947-; Amer Legion 1964-; *office:* Hans Christian Andersen Sch 1148 N Honore Chicago IL 60622

RICHARDSON, JAMES MILAM, Social Studies Teacher; *b:* Odessa, TX; *m:* Stephanie Ogas; *c:* Daniele, Amber; *ed:* (BS) Ed/His/Eng/Sci, 1969, (MA) Ed/Admin, 1979 NM St Univ; *cr:* Teacher Dulce NM Schls 1969-70, Heights Jr HS 1973-; *ai:* Frosh Girls & Boys Bsktbl; Phi Delta Kappa 1987-; *office:* Heights Jr HS 3700 College Blvd Farmington NM 87401

RICHARDSON, JANE WINDERS, Fourth Grade Teacher; *b:* Wichita, KS; *m:* Peter Shane; *c:* Travis Shane; *ed:* (BA) Eng, KS St Teacher Coll 1972; (BSE) Elem Ed Emporia KS St Coll 1975; (MS) Elem Ed, KS St Univ 1980; Elem Ed; *cr:* 3rd Grade Teacher 1975-78, 6th Grade Teacher 1978-81, 4th Grade Teacher 1981- Buffalo Jones Elem; *ai:* Dept Head Sci/Soc Stud; NEA 1975-; KS NEA 1975-; Garden City Educator Assn Treasurer/Bldg Rep 1975-; *office:* Buffalo Jones Elem Sch 708 Taylor Ave Garden City KS 67846

RICHARDSON, JANET KETZ, Science Teacher; *b:* Beckley, WV; *m:* Douglas Ray; *ed:* (BS) Scndry Ed, WV Univ 1987; *cr:* Physics/Phys Sci Teacher Apex HS 1988-; *ai:* Sci Club; Fellowship of Chrstn Athletes; Sci Olympiad; Prof Educators of NC, NC Sci Teacher Assn; Sallie Mae Outstanding 1st Yr Teacher.

RICHARDSON, JEFFREY TRENT, 8th Grade Teacher; *b:* Marion, VA; *m:* Lynn Hartwig; *c:* Trent; *ed:* (BA) His, Emory & Henry Coll 1978; His, Radford Univ; *cr:* 8th Grade Teacher Marion Mid Sch 1978-; Adult Ed Teacher Smyth Cty Voc Sch 1989-; *ai:* NEA; VA Law & Government Project VA Commonwealth Univ 1990; Participated Dev VA St Dept of Ed Standards of Learning 1985; *office:* Marion Mid Sch 134 Wilden St Marion VA 24354

RICHARDSON, JOCQUELINE KILLINGS, Choral Music Teacher; *b:* Holt, AL; *m:* John William; *c:* John F., Aida; *ed:* (BA) Music Ed/Voice, Stillman Coll 1971; (MA) Music Ed/Voice, 1972, AA Certificate Spec Ed, 1976 Univ of AL; *cr:* Grad Asst Univ of AL 1971-72; Elem Spec Ed Teacher Oakdale Elem 1972-73; Choral Music Teacher Westlawn Jr HS 1973-80, Stillman Coll 1982-89, Cntrl HS 1980-; *ai:* Cntrl W Admin Advisory Comm; Music Dept, Assembly Prgms & Banquets Chairperson; NEA, Parent Teacher Stu Assn, Music Educators Assn, AL Vocal Assn 1972-; Bethel Baptist Church Minister of Music; AL Baptist St Convention (Dir, Musician); Crusade for Christ (Bd of Dir, Choral Dir); Alpha Kappa Kappa Under Grad Pres 1971, Mary Slone Outstanding Under Grad Awd 1971; Les Ouse Omies Federated Womens Club of America (Chaplin, Music Comm Chairperson); Natl Assn of Colored Women Girls & Boys Club of America (Dir, Musician); Mary Shane Outstanding Under Grad Awd; Highest Academic Average in Music; Cum Laude in Art & Sci; Grad Asst in Music Univ of AL; Sch Choirs 1st in Dist & St Choral Festival; Sch Choirs Performed AL Educators Assn Delegate Assembly & AL Educators Teachers Assn St Convention 1989; Sch Choral Group Represented the City of Tuscaloosa Performing for & Chor Dream Choir of Japan 1990; Outstanding Young Educator in Tuscaloosa City Schls.

RICHARDSON, KARLYN ANDERSON, 7th/8th Grade Lang Art Teacher; *b:* Spokane, WA; *m:* Mike; *ed:* (BA) Eng, WA St Univ 1973; Certificate Multnomah Sch of Bible; *cr:* 7th-12th Grade Lang Art Teacher Columbia Sch Dist 1973-79; 7th/8th Grade Lang Art Teacher Richland Sch Dist 1980-; *ai:* Grand Comm 1990; ASB Adv 1981-85; Chrldr Adv 1980-81; Dance Comm Chairperson 1985-86; *office:* Carmichael Jr HS 620 Thayer Dr Richland WA 99352

RICHARDSON, KATIE JONES, Mathematics Teacher; *b:* Raleigh, NC; *m:* Bobby L.; *c:* Bobbie K. Richardson Campbell, Barry L.; *ed:* (BS) Math, NC Cntrl Univ 1968; Early Chldhd Ed, Kean Coll; *cr:* Tutor/Instr NC Cntrl Univ 1968-69; Substitute Teacher Orange Bd of Ed 1972; Pre-Sch/Kndgtn Teacher Clinton Avenue Elem 1972-74; Math Teacher Clay Cty Sch Bd 1975-; *ai:* Math Field Day Coach; NEA 1986-; Delta Kappa Gamma 1988-; Ridgeview Sch & Clay Cty Teacher of Yr 1985; Clay Cty Citizens Advisory Comm 1984-85; Excl Awd Ridgeview Jr HS 1988; *office:* Ridgeview Jr HS 466 Madison Ave Orange Park FL 32065

RICHARDSON, KIM A., Math Teacher; *b:* Watford City, ND; *ed:* (BA) Phys Ed, Univ of S FL 1978; (MA) Curr/Instruction, SD St Univ 1990; *cr:* Phys Ed Teacher Hayden Elem Sch 1978-81, Vanderburg Mid Sch 1983-84; Math Teacher Dakota Jr HS 1984-87, Rapid City Cntrl HS 1987-; *ai:* Asst Cross Cntry, Boys & Girls Track; *office:* Rapid City Central HS 433 Mt Rushmore Rd Rapid City SD 57701

RICHARDSON, LINDA DIANE, Health Teacher; *b:* St Louis, MO; *ed:* (BS) Scndry Ed - Cum Laude, Southeast MO St Univ 1980; Several Seminars & Wkshps; *cr:* Substitute Teacher Pattonville HS & Florissant Jr HS 1980-82; Phys Ed/Health Teacher Pattonville HS 1982-; *ai:* Frosh Vlybl & Asst Swim Diving Coach; CARE Team; Phys Ed Curr, Health curr, Grading Policy Comm; Teenage Health Consultant & Health Fair Spon; MO Assn Health Phys Ed 1980-; NEA; Vlybl Coaches Assn 1988-; Sheltered Wkshp Benefit Entertainment 1986-; Clay West Hospital Alzheimers Benefit Entertainment 1990; Mahperd & Pattonville Teacher of Yr Nom; Dist AIDS Curr Co-Author; Article Published 1981; *office:* Pattonville HS 2497 Creve Cover Mill Rd Maryland Heights MO 63043

RICHARDSON, LINDA POWERS, Business Education Teacher; *b:* Alexandria, LA; *m:* Ronald Glen; *c:* Danielle, Blake; *ed:* (BS) Bus Ed, 1975, (MS) Bus Ed, 1977, Bus Ed, 1978 Northwestern St Univ; LA Prof Improvement Plan; *cr:* Grad Asst Bus Dept Northwestern St Univ 1976-77; 2nd/4th Grade Teacher 1977-78, Bus Teacher 1978- Converse HS; *ai:* Bus Ed Textbook Selection Comm Mem; Southern Assn Accreditation Team Chm; Climate-chm; Athletic Banquet; Christmas Pageant; Homecoming Coord; Class, FBLA, Stu Cncl Spon; Building Level Comm Mem; Phi Beta Lambda 1978-; 1st Baptist Church (Sunday Sch, Trng Union Teacher) 1988-; CHS Booster Club Reporter 1988-; Vacation Bible Sch (Dir, Teacher) 1980-; Selected CHS Teacher of Yr; Featured Teacher of Week by Sabine Index; Dept Head Bus Ed Converse HS; *office:* Converse HS P O Drawer 10 Converse LA 71419

RICHARDSON, LORENZO, Fourth Grade Teacher; *b:* Fairfield, AL; *m:* Evelyn Moore; *c:* Alastrina, Lonzie, La Crystal, Amber; *ed:* (BS) Elem Ed, Daniel Payne Coll; Working Toward Masters in Elem Ed; *cr:* File Clerk US Army 1972-74; ABE Teacher Bessemer Bd of Ed 1976-77, Miles Coll 1977-79; *ai:* BASE, Effective Schls Comms; NEA, AEA 1977-; PTA 1977-; Tutoring Services; Amer Legion Post 344; *home:* 3024 7th Ave N Bessemer AL 35020

RICHARDSON, MAGALENE ALLEN, Third Grade Teacher; *b:* Albany, GA; *m:* Morrice; *c:* Mashanika L., Marcie L., Morrice L.; *ed:* (BA) Sociology Albany St Coll 1969; (MED) Early Chldhd Ed, Georgia St Univ 1975; *cr:* 3rd Grade Teacher Locust Grove Primary 1969-78; Peachtree City Elem 1978-; *ai:* Fayette Cty Assn of Educators 1978-; GA Assn of Educators 1969-; Natl Assn of Educators 1969; Sr Usher 1982-; Willing Worker Pres 1985 & 86; Teacher of Yr Locust Grove Primary; *office:* Peachtree City Elem Sch Wisdom Rd Peachtree City GA 30269

RICHARDSON, RAY, Law Studies Teacher; *b:* Brooklyn, NY; *m:* Karen; *c:* Amber, Jessica, Adam; *ed:* (BA) His, Hofstra Univ 1969; (MA) His, Stony Brook Univ 1972; Law Courses, Criminal Justice; *cr:* Teacher Bay Shore Public Schls 1969-; *ai:* Most Court & Mock Trial Teams Adv; NY St Bar Assn Grant; *office:* Bay Shore Public Schls 155 3rd Ave Bay Shore NY 11706

RICHARDSON, ROBERT, Mathematics Teacher; *b:* Atlanta, GA; *m:* Nellie Andrews; *c:* Tony C.; *ed:* (BA) Math, Morehouse Coll 1961; (MA) Scndry Admin, Atlanta Univ 1969; Natl Sci Fnd 1962/1963; UCLA; *cr:* Teacher Atlanta Public Sch 1961-; Admin Asst B T Washington Evening Sch 1981-.

RICHARDSON, RONALD D., Mass Communication Teacher; *b:* Indianapolis, IN; *m:* Judith A. Pershing; *c:* Vikki L., Ronald D.; *ed:* (BA) Soc Stud/Eng, Butler Univ 1963; (MS) Mass Comm/His/Eng, IN Univ 1966; TESA; CEI; Learning Styles; Cooperative Learning; *cr:* Assoc Prin/Eng/Soc Stud Teacher W Newton Elem; Coach/Eng Teacher/AV Dir Decatur Cntrl Jr HS; AV Dir/Auditorium Dir/Teacher/Television Stud Teacher Decatur Cntrl HS; *ai:* Sports Taping; Auditorium Dir; Mass Comm; TV Projectionist Club; IN Ed Television Cooperative; Quaker Church Elder; *office:* Decatur Cntrl HS 5251 Kentucky Ave Indianapolis IN 46241

RICHARDSON, SHIRLEY MC INTOSH, Second Grade Teacher; *b:* Irvine, KY; *m:* Arnell; *c:* Carolyn S. Richardson Hohenboken; *ed:* (BS) Elem Ed, 1976, (MA) Curr/Supervision, 1983 Miami Univ; Post Masters Work Curr/Advanced Educl Stud; *cr:* Teacher Lee Cty Schls 1958-60, Miami Valley Child Dev 1970-74; Admin Miami Valley Child Dev 1975-76; Teacher Carlisle Schls 1976-; *ai:* Spelling Curr; ASCD; PTO Treas 1970-72; Meth Church Treas 1987-; Co-Authored Grant to Begin Instructional Materials Center & Good Apple Parent Volunteer Prgm; *office:* Carlisle Primary Sch 310 Jamaica Rd Carlisle OH 45005

RICHARDSON, STEVEN PAUL, Fourth Grade Teacher; *b:* Willmar, MN; *m:* Teresa Renee Lungstrom; *c:* Peter, Angela, Julie Anna; *ed:* (BA) Art Ed, Buena Vista Coll 1970; Elem Ed, Univ of AK 1980; AK St Math Consortium, Univ of AK Fairbanks 1988; *cr:* 4th Grade Teacher Nome City Schls 1970-72; 5th Grade Teacher Ft Yukon Sch 1972-73; Art Teacher Chugiak Jr-Sr HS 1973-75; Sr HS Supervisor Abbott Loop Chrstn Sch 1975-78; 4th Grade Teacher Valdez City Schls & Hermon Hutchens Elem 1980-; *ai:* Natl Assn Chrstn Educators 1986-; Intnl Rdng Assn 1983-87; AK & Valdez Rdng Assn 1983-; *office:* Hermon Hutchens Sch 1009 W Klutina PO Box 398 Valdez AK 99686

RICHARDSON, TED ROBERT, Middle School Principal; *b:* Scranton, PA; *m:* Florence Mc Bride; *c:* Terry R., King Yiu, King Ying; *ed:* Accounting/Finance, Wharton Sch Univ of PA 1950; (BA) Ed, 1973, (MA) Ed, 1975 Goddard Coll; Numerous Univs; *cr:* Athletic Dept Teacher St Pauls Cath HS 1950-54; Teacher 1954-56, Teacher/Admin 1956-87, Admin 1987- Porter-Gaud Sch; *ai:* Athletic Moderator; Sch Steering Comm; Sch Dept Chairperson; Natl Assn of Ind Schls 1967-; Notre Dame Club of Charleston 1980-; Presidential Classroom Young Amer 1983, Intntl Stud Grants 1981; Published in US Naval Proceedings; Consultant Project Charles River Counseling Center; *office:* Porter-Gaud Sch Albemarle Point Charleston SC 29407

RICHAU, DEBORAH L., Sixth Grade Teacher; *b:* Havre, MT; *m:* Gregory A.; *c:* Sienna, Ben; *ed:* (BA) Elem Ed, 1976, (MS) Sci Ed, 1990 E MT Coll; Ethnic, Cultural Heritage; Wild, Aquatic, Learning Tree Projects; *cr:* Environmental Ed Specialist Bureau of Land Management 1975-76; Dir/Ah-Nei Special Classroom 1976-83; 6th Grade Teacher Poly Dr 1983-89, Garfield Elem 1989-; *ai:* Sci Curr Comm Dist Wide; Project Wild Facilitator for MT; Alpha Delta Kappa Secy 1988, Schlsp 1989; Billings Ed Assn, MEA, NEA, 1976; Grant to Temple Univ, E MT Coll; Introducing Stus to Sci Using Book; *office:* Garfield Elem Sch 3212 1st Ave S Billings MT 59102

RICHBOURG, JOHN ALLEN, JR., Math Teacher; *b:* Orlando, FL; *m:* Anita; *c:* Sarah M., John A.; *ed:* (BS) Bio, the Citadel 1974; Working on Masters Ed; TX St Cert (Secndry Math & Bio); *cr:* Math Teacher St Pauls Sch 1985-.

RICHER, PATRICIA CASEY, 8th Grade English Teacher; *b:* Brooklyn, NY; *m:* Philip Neil; *c:* Jennifer, Lorraine, Aimee, Kevin; *ed:* (BA) Eng, Coll of Notre Dame 1963; (BS) Ed, FL Atlantic Univ; Legal Secy Pompano Bus Coll; Tet Barry Coll; *cr:* Payroll/Secy Lummus Constructin Company 1963-64; Manager/Secy Gill Hotel Chain 1964-66; Lawyer/Secy 1966-68; Manager/Secy Gill Hotel Chain 1968-72; Teacher St Mark Palm Bch Cty Sch 1990; *ai:* CCD Teacher/Dir; Coach Sftbl; Jr HS Society Asst/Team Leader/Merit Sch Comm/Bd of Dirs/Vlybl Club/Hurricane Hugo Relief 1989; Amer Bus Women Pres 1965; Phi Kappa Phi Mem Magna Cum Laude 1983; NCTE 1985; Kellys Heroes-Recognition for Hugo Relief.

RICHERS, LOIS JACK, First Grade Teacher; *b:* Donnellson, IA; *m:* Robert; *c:* Roger, Patty Hardin, Sandra Bozarth; *ed:* Elem Cert Elem Ed, IA Teachers Coll 1953; (BA) Elem Ed, IA Wesleyan 1976; *cr:* 3rd Grade Teacher Denmark Comm 1953-56; Cntry Sch Teacher Lee Cty Rural 1956-58; 2nd Grade Teacher Denmark Comm Sch 1958-59; Kndgtn Teacher Morning Sun Comm Sch 1960-62; 3rd Grade Teacher Yarmouth Sch 1962-64; 1st Grade Teacher Wapello Elem Sch 1964-; *ai:* ISEA, NEA 1974-; IA Rdng Cncl 1990; Louisa Cty 4-H Leader, 4-H Awd 1983; Photography Leader; United Meth Church, Mission Leader 1988; United Meth Church Mem; Wapello Bell Choir; *office:* Wapello Elem Sch Cedar St Wapello IA 52653

RICHMOND, CAMM HALLADAY, Social Studies Teacher; *b:* Columbus, OH; *m:* Linda Carol; *c:* Katherine; *ed:* (BS) Health/Phys Ed, Wilmington Coll 1969; (MS) Admin, Univ of Dayton 1976; Univ of Dayton; *cr:* Teacher Mechanicsburg HS 1964-70; Teacher/Head Ftbl Coach Madison South HS 1970-71, Vinton Cty HS 1971-72; Teacher Mechanicsburg HS 1974-75; Teacher/Coach Univ of Dayton 1976-77; Teacher Amelia Mid Sch 1977-; *ai:* Wilmington Coll Asst Ftbl Coach 1978-; Univ of Dayton Asst Ftbl Coach 1976-77; HS Coach; OH Ed Assn, Amer Ftbl Coaches Assn 1969-; W Clarmont Ed Assn Building Rep 1988-89; Sons of Amer Legion 1986-; London Jaycees 1970-76; Natl Championship Ftbl Game Coach 1980; OH St Teacher 1969-; *home:* 11980 Selsor Moon Rd South Solon OH 43153

RICHMOND, J. C., Social Studies Teacher; *b:* Finley, OK; *m:* Clairetta E. Tegart; *c:* Donna Rocha, Deberah Mora; *ed:* (BA) Soc Sci, West TX St Univ 1967; (MA) Sch Admin, Western NM Univ 1974; Rdng; Driver Ed; *cr:* Soc Stud Teacher Lordsburg NM Jr HS 1968-76; Carrizozo Mid Sch 1978; *ai:* Sch Geography Bee Coord; Soc Stud Textbook Comm; NEA NM Local Pres 1970-71/1979-80; Governors Sch Evaluation Comm Local Dir 1972-73; Teacher of Yr Awds 1970-72/1974-75; *home:* PO Box 671 Carrizozo NM 88301

RICHMOND, KATHRYN A., English Teacher; *b:* San Bernardino, CA; *m:* Donald L.; *ed:* (BS) Eng/Psych, W MI Univ 1964; Grad Stud W MI Univ, MI St Univ; Quest Trng, Cooperative Learning; *cr:* Fr/Eng Teacher Marcellus HS 1964-66, Grosse Ile Jr HS 1966-70; Eng Teacher Lakeview Jr HS 1970-; *ai:* K-12th Grade Lang Art Curr Comm Chm; Mid Cities Sch Improvement Team; MEA, NEA; Local LEA (Assn Rep 1980-85, 1988-); W K Kellogg Fnd Prof Dev Awd 1990; *office:* Lakeview Jr HS 20 S Woodrow Battle Creek MI 49015

RICHMOND, KIM ANN CRAGO, English Teacher; *b:* Crystal Falls, MI; *m:* Kent R.; *c:* Rachael; *ed:* (AA) Liberal Stud, Bay de Noc Comm Coll 1976; (BSED) Eng/Sociology, Northern MI Univ 1978; *cr:* Eng Teacher Westwood HS 1979; Alternative Ed Teacher Dickinson Cty Cmmty Schls 1980-83; Eng Teacher Kingsford HS 1987-; *ai:* Rockslide Keyboardist, Singer; Crisis Intervention Comm; NCTE Mem 1987-; Peninsula Singers Mem 1988-.

RICHMOND, KIM L. (MILLER), Lang/Music/Band Teacher; *b:* Oklahoma City, OK; *m:* Albert; *c:* Jeffrey Crisp, Jason Crisp; *ed:* (BME) Musc Ed, 1973, (me) Ed, 1979 Central St Univ; *cr:* Mid Sch Lang/Primary Music/Mid Sch Instrumental Music Teacher Schwartz Sch 1977-; *ai:* Bus Driver; Chrldr & 8th Grade Class Spon; Negotation Team Mem; OK Ed Assn, NEA 1977-; *office:* Schwartz Sch 12001 SE 104th Oklahoma City OK 73165

RICHMOND, NANCY LEE, Reading/English Teacher; *b:* New Martinsville, WV; *m:* Gregory W.; *ed:* (AB) Eng Ed, West Liberty St Coll 1978; (MA) Rdng Specialist, WV Univ 1985; Classroom Management, Cmptr Operation Evaluation of Stu Writing; WV Writing Assessment Scorers Mem; Cooperative Learning Johns Hopkins Univ Conference; Teacher Expectations & Stu Achievement Wkshp; *cr:* Eng Teacher Valley HS 1978-81 ; Eng Teacher, 1981, Rdng Teacher 1987- Magnolia HS; *ai:* Sr Class Adv; Alpha Delta Kappa VP 1985-89; Literacy Volunteers Bd of Dir 1987-88; *office:* Magnolia HS 601 Maple Ave New Martinsvlle WV 26155

RICHMOND, PLUMIE SHANNON, Elementary Guidance Counselor; *b:* Ridgeway, SC; *m:* Clifton G. Sr.; *c:* Veronica, Clifton Jr., VaShondra; *ed:* (BA) Early Chldhd Ed, 1978, (MED) Elem Guidance, 1982 Univ of SC; *cr:* Teachers Aide 1969-78, 1st Grade Teacher Gordon Elem Sch 1978-81; Guidance Cnslr Gordon Elem/Fairfield Primary 1981-; *ai:* NEA/SC Assn 1978-; SC Assn of Counseling & Dev 1981-; Girl Scouts of Amer Troop Leader 1987-; Lebanon Presby Church Mem/Elder; Lebanon Young Womens Auxiliary Mem/Former VP 1983-; *office:* Fairfield Primary Sch Rt 2 Box 9 E Winnsboro SC 29180

RICHMOND, ROBERTA THOMPSON, 4th Grade Teacher; *b:* Tampa, FL; *m:* Jim; *c:* Austin L., Ramsey T.; *ed:* (BSED) Elem Ed, Univ of GA 1968; (MAT) Curr in Elem Sch, Emory Univ 1973; Water Safety Instr 1990; Camp Horseman Assn Instrs Certificate 1987-; Interpretative Dance Instr 1977-; *cr:* 6th-7th Grade Drama Instr Mather Heights Elem 1969; 6th Grade Teacher Rehoboth Elem/Kincaid 1970-74; 7th-8th Grade Teacher Branford HS 1976; 4th Grade Teacher Suwannee Elem West 1977-; *ai:* Adv West Elem Stu Cncl 1989-; Grade Level Chm 4th Grade 1989-; Advisory Comm Mem West Elem Sch 1989-; ADK Chaplain 1990-91; Alpha Delta Kappa Alturistic Chm 1988-; Chrstn Camping Intnl Dovewood Pres 1977-; Sunday Sch Instr Ages 12-15 1989-; Womans Club VP 1974-78; Jr League of Atlanta Placement Cnslr 1971-74; Full Schlsp for Masters Degree Prgm at Emory Univ; Teacher of Yr West Elem Sch 1981; Secy/Treas Emory Alumni 1975-76; Sci-Math Instr for Elem Staff Grades 4-6 Teaching Teachers New Techniques in Math & Sci 1990; Public Relations Officer Rdng Cncl Suwannee Co 1989-; *home:* PO Box 606 Branford FL 32008

RICHMOND, VELMAR SINGLETON, Biology Teacher; *b:* Jacksonville, FL; *m:* Mossie J. Jr.; *c:* Deryle L., Reche A.; *ed:* (BS) Natural Sci Ed, Philander Smith Coll 1964; Wichita St Univ, Butler Univ, Ball St Univ; *cr:* Sci Teacher Lincoln HS 1964-65, Wabbaseka Elem Sch 1965-69, Childress HS 1969-70; Bio Teacher Wynne HS 1970-71, Southside HS 1971-73, Jonesboro HS 1973-; *ai:* Future Medical Careers Club, Photography Club, Sr Class 1989, Soph Class 1987 Spon; Curr & Textbook Selection Comm Mem 1990; AFT, Jonesboro Prof Teachers Organization, Amer Assn of Coll & Univ Women, Alpha Delta Kappa; Alpha Kappa Alpha; Natl Sci Fnd Fellowship Radiation Bio Cert 1965, 1967, 1969; *home:* 1704 Loberg Ln Jonesboro AR 72401

RICHTER, ERMA LEE PERRY, Reading Resource; *b:* Piggott, AR; *m:* George M.; *c:* Ginger M. Anderson, Gregory M.; *ed:* (BA) Education, Northeastern Univ 1972; *cr:* 4th Grade Teacher 1973-83; Reading Resource 1983- R Nathaniel Dett; *ai:* Spelling Bee Chairperson;; Hall Monitor; Den Mother for Boy Scouts 1968-69; Teacher Ed Schlsp Prgm; *home:* 5326 N Lockwood Ave Chicago IL 60630

RICHTER, NANCY J., Sr English Teacher/Dept Chair; *b:* Evanston, IL; *c:* Thomas M. Debrey, Lisa K. Debrey; *ed:* (BA) Eng, 1972, (MA) Comparative Lit, 1973 Sangamon St Univ; His, Augustana Coll 1952; His & Eng Courses, Sangamon St Univ 1975-89; Advanced Placement Seminars 1980-86; *cr:* Eng Teacher Griffin HS 1971-88; Eng Techer/Dept Chairperson Griffin Sacred Heart 1976-; Eng Teacher Lincoln Land Comm Coll 1981, Sacred Heart & Griffin HS 1988; *ai:* Natl Honor Society Moderator 1974; Literary Journal Griffin 1974 & Sacred Heart 1989-; Accompanist Glee Club & Sch Musical 1989-; NCEA, NCTE 1972-; Phi Alpha Theta His 1952; St Johns Hospital Guild Pres 1963-65, Service Awd 1965; St Louise De Marillac Guild Pres 1962-63, Service Awd 1963; St Johns Samaritans Hospital Escort Service 1988; Red Cross Youth Dir 1969-72; Short Stories & Poetry Published; *office:* Sacred Heart-Griffin HS 1200 W Washington Springfield IL 62702

RICHWINE, HARRY THOMAS, III, 5th Grade Teacher; *b:* Lebanon, PA; *c:* Todd, Harry T. IV; *ed:* (BS) Elem Ed, Millersville Univ 1969; Several Wkshps & Courses; *cr:* 3rd Grade Teacher S Lebanon Elem Sch 1969-; 5th Grade Teacher Union Canal Elem Sch 1990; *ai:* Odyssey of Mind Coach; Rdng Comm; Prin Cabinet; NEA, PSEA 1969-; *office:* Union Canal Elem Sch 400 Narrows Dr Lebanon PA 17042

RICK, NORMAN RUSSELL, Mathematics Instructor; *b:* Evergreen Park, IL; *m:* Patricia Ann Duffy; *c:* James, Colleen; *ed:* (BS) Math, Chicago St Univ 1970; *cr:* Math Teacher Harlan Cmmty Acad 1970-81, Lindblom Tech HS 1981-87, Whitney Young Magnet HS 1987-; *ai:* Sr Fees Collector; Kappa Mu Epsilon; *home:* 16653 S Parliament Tinley Park IL 60477

RICKARD, BILLIE LOU (SHARKEY), Language Arts Teacher; *b:* Kremlin, OK; *m:* Bruce E.; *c:* Ricki Percifield, Bruce II, Tonya Taylor, Dirk; *ed:* (BS) Home Ec, OK St Univ 1955; Cert of Career Enhancement Numerous Univs; *cr:* Home Ec Teacher Medicine Lodge HS 1955-57; Home Ec Agent Haskell Cty 1957-60; Home Ec Teacher Morrison/Covington 1960-63; Home Ec/Lang Art Hardtner & Agenda & Larned KS 1963-67; Medicine Lodge HS 1967-; *ai:* Eng & Home Ec Curr Comm; Yrbk Adv; Dir All Sch Play; Speech, Drama, Debate Coach; Sch Newspaper Adv; Pep Club, Chrldr, Frosh, Soph, Jr, Sr Classes, Stu Cncl Spon; NEA Delegate 1982-; KS Ed Assn (Constitution By-Laws Commission 1988-, Assemblies Delegate, Poly Action Interview Team, Membership Contact Comm); Ark Valley Uniserv Dist (Admin Bd, Treas 1990); OK Ed Assn 1960-63; Gyp Hills Ed Assn (Pres, Secy, Delegate To Coordinating Cncl, Prof Negotiations Comm); GSA Troop Leader 1970-75; United Meth Church; Kodak Company St Grant; Project Published; *home:* 213 N Cherry Medicine Lodge KS 67104

RICKE, MARY GALLES, 7th/8th Grade Teacher; *b:* Le Mars, IA; *m:* Patrick; *c:* Matthew, Michael, Maria; *ed:* (BA) Eng, Briar Cliff Coll 1971; Church Ministries; Tribes Cooperative Learning; *cr:* HS Eng Teacher St Marys HS 1971-72; 7th/8th Grade Teacher Spalding Elem 1982-; *ai:* Jr HS Speech; Camp Cnslr Cath Youth Camp; Retreat Leader; St Joseph Guild (VP, Pres, CDA, Chrstn Mothers) 1988-89; *home:* RR 2 Box 75 Granville IA 51022

RICKENBACH, KRISTINE, 4th Grade Classroom Teacher; *b:* Richfield, UT; *ed:* (BA) Elem Ed, Coll of ID 1976; *cr:* 1st Grade Teacher 1978-79, 4th Grade Teacher 1979- W Canyon Elem; *ai:* Vallivue Dist 139 Eng & Soc Stud Curr Comm, P R Comm Mem, 4th Grade Teacher Leader; Vallivue Ed Assn VP 1989-; ID Ed Assn Region 8 Delegate 1984-; Coll of ID Alumni Assn 1982-87; YWCA 1988-; Vallivue Sch Dist 139 Teacher of Yr 1989-; *office:* W Canyon Elem Sch 19548 Ustick Caldwell ID 83605

RICKER, GERALDINE MARGARET, Fourth Grade Teacher; *b:* Lewiston, ME; *ed:* (BSEE) Elem Ed, St Josephs Coll 1953; (MED) Advanced Elem, Univ of ME 1964; *cr:* 4th Grade Teacher Merrill Hill Elem 1953-54, Oakland Terrace Elem 1954-60; 3rd Grade Teacher Chisholm Sch 1960-65, Martel Sch 1966-74; 4th Grade Teacher Mc Mahon Elem 1975-; *ai:* Awds Comm Chm; Lewiston Teachers Assn (Secy 1967-70, Chm Membership 1970-73, Elem Rep); ME Teachers Assn NEA Delegate 1968-70; NEA; Cmmty Concert Assn General Chm 1968-71; Red Cross Volunteer 1960-68; Beta Sigma Phi Secy 1967, 1980, 1984; Delta Kappa Gamma Prof Assn; Church Womens Sodality Pres 1979-81; Coll Club 1970-; *office:* Mc Mahon Elem Sch N Temple St Lewiston ME 04240

RICKER, VIOLA MAE WILLOUGHBY, Fourth Grade Teacher; *b:* Mt Sterling, KY; *m:* Bennie Jay; *c:* Geoffery Burgess, Veronica Burgess-Wilson, Bennie, Paul; *ed:* (BS) Ed, Campbellsville 1965; (MA) Ed, Morehead 1979; *ai:* Montgomery Cty Ed Pres; Local Teacher Organization Pres Honor Awd; KY Colonel Awd; First Baptist Church Youth Leader; KEA Cntrl Dist Awd; KET Awd; *home:* 405 N Sycamore St Mount Sterling KY 40353

RICKETS, PEGGY ORT, Physics/Earth Science Teacher; *b:* Coral Gables, FL; *c:* Ben; *ed:* (BS) Geology, Univ of OK 1974; Grad Stud Educl Leadership/Policy Stud, 1988-; *cr:* Geological Technician Gulf Oil Co 1978-80; Teacher Norman Public Schls 1982, Moore Public Schls 1982-; *ai:* NCA Accreditation Comms; Sci Project Mentor & Consultant; Univ of OK Research Asst; OK Ed Assn 1985-; BSA Comm Mem 1988-89; Sierra Club Regional Exec Comm Mem 1990; Amer Society of Trng Dev Mem 1989-; Moore Schls Teacher of Yr 1988; *office:* Highland East Jr HS 1200 SE 4th St Moore OK 73160

RICKETTS, DAVID C., English Dept Chair; *b:* Shelbyville, KY; *ed:* (BA) Speech/Theatre, Asbury Coll 1967; (MS) Eng, E KY Univ 1974; *cr:* Teacher Ballard HS 1968-; *ai:* NEA, KEA, JCTA, NCTE, KCTE 1968-; *office:* Ballard HS 6000 Brownsboro Rd Louisville KY 40222

RICKMAN, JUDY GREEN, First Grade Teacher; *b:* Meredian, MS; *m:* James Lillard; *c:* Julie A., Jillian L. Jessica Ryan; *ed:* (BS) Elem Ed, 1975, (MA) Supervision/Instruction, 1985 Mid TN St Univ; *cr:* 1st Grade Teacher Marshall Elem 1975-; *ai:* Marshall Elem Sch Coordinating Comm; Marshall Cty Ed Assn 1975-, Teacher of Yr 1989-; TN Ed Assn, NEA 1975-; Delta Kappa Gamma 1988-; Church Street Church of Christ Teacher 1989-; Dept of Human Services Review Bd 1985-; *home:* 827 Mc Bride Rd Lewosburg TN 37091

RICKMAN, SAMUEL EUGENE, Band Master; *b:* Switchback, WV; *c:* Susan Smith, Scott, Samantha Bishop, Stephanie Shrewsbury; *ed:* (BS) Music Ed, Bluefield St Coll 1979; Grad Stud, WV Coll *cr:* Instr Armed Forces US Navy Sch of Music 1960-70; Asst Mgr Red Top Cab Company 1970-75; Stu Bluefield St Coll 1975-79; Band Master Bradshaw JR HS 1980-; *ai:* Flag Corps, Majorettes, Riffle Corp Spon Bradshaw JR HS; Mc Dowell Cty Music Educators Assn (Pres 1984-85, JR HS Division Chm) 1982-84; WV Band Masters Assn Mem 1980-; NEA, WVEA, MCEA Mem 1980-89; Amer Legion Post 178 Mem 1983-; VFW Mem 1984-; Lions Intnl Mem 1981-85; Whos Who In Amer Colls & Univs 1977-79; Numerous Musical Arrangements & Compositions Published; *office:* Bradshaw JR HS PO Box 40 Bradshaw WV 24817

RICKS, ANNIE ECHOLS, 6th Grade Science Teacher; *m:* Columbus B.; *c:* Angie Baromietta, Florence, Burgess; *ed:* (BS) Home Ec/Clothing & Textiles/Ed, MI St Univ 1955; (MED) Elem Ed, Tuskegee Inst 1965; Elem Ed for Teaching Cert, Jackson St Univ 1958-59; Elem Ed, Univ of MO Columbia; Psych & Intelligent Testing Trng, Tuskegee Inst & Univ of MO; Speedwriting & Bookkeeping Cert, Lansing Bus Univ; Sci Curr Improvement Study, Temple Univ 1971; *cr:* Clothing/Ed Instr Oakwood Coll 1957-58; Substitute Elem Sch Teacher Jackson Public Sch System 1958-60; Clothing/Food/Ed Instr Jarvis Chrstn Coll 1960-63; 5th Grade Sci/Rdng/Math Teacher 1971-72, 6th Grade Sci/Rdng/Math Teacher 1973- Capital Sch Dist; *ai:* NEA, NSTA, Natl Society for Study of Ed, NCTE, Natl Home Ec Assn, Amer Assn for Univ Professors; Teacher of Yr William Henry Mid Sch 1985; Stu Outstanding Teacher Trophy 1981-82.

RICKS, EDNA (HINSON), 6th Grade Lang Art Teacher; *b:* Conway, SC; *m:* Larry Michael; *c:* Justin, Stuart; *ed:* (BA) Elem Ed, Univ of SC 1973; Grad Stud; *cr:* 6th Grade Teacher Homewood Elem 1973-76, W Conway Mid Sch 1976-; *ai:* Served on Numerous Textbook Adoption Comms for Rdng, Lang & Soc Stud Books; Mid Sch Lang Art Curr Comm for Several Yrs; PTO Active Mem; *home:* 392 Heritage Ln Myrtle Beach SC 29577

RICKS, MARY HEFLIN, First Grade Teacher; *b:* Union, MO; *m:* Beverly Lee; *c:* Barry, Billy; *ed:* (BS) Elem Ed, 1953, (MED) Elem Ed, 1967 MO St Univ; Supvr of Stu Teachers N LA Univ; *cr:* Teacher West Point MO 1953-56, Greenwood MO 1956-65, Union MO 1968-69, Monroe LA 1966-68, 1970-; *ai:* NE Regional Rdng Assn 1965-; Alpha Delta Kappa 1973-89; Phi Delta Kappa 1989-; *office:* Jack Hayes Elem Sch 22 Old Sterlington Rd Monroe LA 71203

RICKSGER, DARRELL L., Vocational Agriculture Teacher; *b:* Oregon City, OR; *m:* Sandra Lea Roberts; *c:* Trent, Todd; *ed:* (BS) Ag Ed, OR St Univ 1972; Grad Stud, OR St; Portland St; *cr:* Teacher Cottage Grove HS 1971-72, North Clockamas 1972-77, Molalla HS 1977-81; Private Bus 1981-85; Teacher Canby HS 1985-; *ai:* FFA Adv; Grade Sch Bd Mem; Local/St Organization; Brade Sch Rd Mem 1989-; Canby HS Exec & Greivance Comms OEA/NEA/OVATA/OVA; Natl FFA; OR Opsba Post Pres; Amer Hampshire Sheep Assn; Amer Immentol Assn; *office:* Canby Union HS 721 SW 4th Canby OR 97013

RIDDELL, WILMA QUINONES, Spanish/Foreign Lang Teacher; *b:* Jacksonville, FL; *m:* Robert Lee; *ed:* (BA) Span/His, Old Dominion Univ 1978; Grad Stud Span; *cr:* Span Teacher Granby HS 1979-80, Norview HS 1980-83; Span/Foreign Lang Teacher Campostella Mid Sch 1983-; *ai:* Span Club; ACTFL, Span Heritage Assn, FLAVA 1979-; PETA, Doris Day Animal League, VA Animal Rights Assn 1987-; *office:* Campostella Mid Sch 1106 Campostella Rd Norfolk VA 23523

RIDDER, JANE BERGER, Third Grade Teacher; *b:* Washington, MO; *m:* Carl E.; *c:* Marcia, Julie, Jon; *ed:* (BS) Elem Ed, Cntrl MD State Univ 1964; (MS) Curr/Instruction Univ of MO 1988; *cr:* 3rd Grade Teacher 1964-67, Substitute Teacher 1967-72 Stanberry Public Schls; Substitute Teacher 1972-79, 3rd Grade Teacher 1979- Union RXI; *ai:* MNEA; UEA Building Rep 1987-; Delta Kappa Gamma Treas 1988-; 4-H Adult Leader 1978-; MU Extension Honor Roll 1990; Wrote & Received Grant Union Fnd; *office:* Central Elem Schl PO Box 440 Union MO 63084

RIDDICK, LYNNE RUSSELL, 5th Grade Teacher; *b:* Greensboro, NC; *m:* Patrick Henry Jr.; *ed:* (BA) Elem Ed, 1980, (MED) Educl Admin, 1989 Univ of SC; *cr:* 6th Grade Teacher Irmo Mid Sch 1981-82, 6th Grade Teacher 1982-89, 5th Grade Teacher 1989- Nursery Road Elem Sch; *ai:* SC Sci Cncl, ASCD, SC Rdng Cncl; Outstanding Young Women of America Awd; *office:* Nursery Rd Elem Sch 6706 Nursery Rd Columbia SC 29212

RIDDLE, CAROL LINTON, TELLS Remedial/Cmptr Teacher; *b:* Waynesburg, PA; *m:* John F.; *ed:* (BS) Elem Ed, CA Univ 1973; Grad Classes Penn St, Univ of Pittsburgh; *cr:* 5th Grade Teacher N Franklin Trinity Area 1975-87; TELLS Remedial Teacher 1987-89, Cmptr/TELLS Teacher 1989-Trinity Area; *ai:* Alpha Delta Kappa 1986-; *office:* Trinity Area Laboratory 99 Manse St Washington PA 15301

RIDDLE, CAROLE GOODE, Fifth Grade Teacher; *b:* Owensboro, KY; *m:* James Ellis; *c:* Chip, Susan; *ed:* (BA) Elem Ed, KY Wesleyan 1970; (MA) Elem Ed, W KY Univ 1980; *cr:* 4th Grade Teacher Tamarack Elem 1970-72; 6th Grade Teacher Sutherland Elem 1973-75; 4th/5th Grade Teacher Burns Elem 1975-76; 5th Grade Teacher Tamarack Elem 1977-; *ai:* Cncl for After Sch Care; Drop Out Prevention Mem; Academic Showcase Comm 1990; KEA, NEA, DCEA 1970-89; March of Dimes Volunteer 1978-; Optimist Club Assn 1974-; Church Organist 1968-; *home:* 605 Ben Ford Rd Utica KY 42376

RIDDLE, DOUGLAS STEPHEN, Choral Music Instructor; *b:* Vallejo, CA; *m:* Gabrielle Hurler; *ed:* (BM) Music Ed, Univ of Pacific 1973; Music Ed, UOP 1987-89; Choral Music, Crane Sch of Music, SUNY Potsdam 1985; Working Towards MS in Choral Conducting, N AZ Univ; *cr:* Choral Music Teacher Manteca Unified Schls 1973-77, Lodi HS 1977-89, E Flagstaff Jr HS/Coconino HS 1989-; *ai:* E Flagstaff & Cocoino HS Vocal Music Coach; Amer Choral Dir Assn 1979-; CA Music Educators Assn (Bay Area Rep 1987-89) 1974-89; AZ Music Educators Assn 1989-; Lodi Arts Commission Bd Mem 1984-87; Phi Mu Alpha 1970-; Lodi HS Teacher of Yr Awd 1988-89; Lodi HS Unanimous Superior Ratings Awd 1985-89; St Music Educators Convention Performances 1982, 1984, 1987; Western Division Music Educators Convention Performance 1987.

RIDDLE, MARY MORGAN, Teacher; *b:* Ashland, AL; *m:* Donald E.; *c:* Karen, Sharon, Jonathan; *ed:* (BS) Math, 1963, (MS) Guidance, 1972 Jacksonville St Univ; Teacher Talladega HS 1963-66, Clay Cty HS 1967-; *ai:* Math Club, Usher Club, Sr Class Spon; AEA, NEA 1963-; Delta Kappa Gamma Secy 1990; Modern Culture Club VP 1986-; *home:* Rt 2 Box 425-A Ashland AL 36251

RIDDLE, MICHAEL H., Mathematics/Writing Teacher; *b:* Linton, IN; *m:* Patricia C.; *c:* Chad; *ed:* (BS) Elem Ed, 1967, (MS) Admin, 1973 IN St Univ; (MS) Elem Ed, De Pauw Univ 1973; *cr:* 5th Grade Teacher Bloomfield Sch Dist 1969-73; Prin Worthington-Jefferson Sch 1973-74, Eastern Sch Dist 1974-78; 4th Grade Teacher Bloomfield Sch Dist 1978-; *ai:* Textbook Adoption Chm; Bloomfied Teachers Assn Pres 1986-87.

RIDDLES, HOWARD CARLTON, English Instructor; *b:* Pensacola, FL; *ed:* (AA) Liberal Arts, Pensacola Jr Coll 1971; (BA) Eng, 1973, (MA) Rdng, 1978 Univ of W FL; *cr:* 5th Grade Teacher St Thomas More Sch 1974-78, W Clayton Elem 1979-80; 4th Grade Teacher Tilson Sch 1984-85; Eng Instr Pace HS 1985-; *ai:* Newspaper Adv; Pride Awds Judge; Teachers as Advs Steering & St Journalism Cert Comms; Santa Rosa Cncl of Teachers of Eng 1987-, Distinguished Teaching Awd 1988-89; Journalism Educators Assn Pres 1989-; Pace HS Teacher of Yr 1990; *office:* Pace HS 407 Norris Rd Pace FL 32571

RIDENOUR, DAVID LEE, Physics Teacher; *b:* Cleveland, OH; *ed:* (BS) Mechanical Engineering, Case Inst of Technology 1963; (MA) Ed, NY Univ 1969; Summer Physics Inst Univ of VA 1988; *cr:* Math & Sci Teacher North Branch Sch 1983-86; Physics Teacher Albemarle HS 1986-; *ai:* SADD Spon; Assn of Physics Teachers; *office:* Albemarle HS 2775 Hydraulic Rd Charlottesville VA 22901

RIDENOUR, MICHAEL W., Secondary Teacher; *b:* Jellico, TN; *m:* Linda Owens; *c:* Abby E.; *ed:* (BA) Chem, Berea Coll 1975; (MA) Admin/Supervision Ed, Lincoln Memorial Univ 1985; Grad Stud Chem, Univ of TN Knoxville, Lincoln Memorial Univ; *cr:* Scndry Teacher Campbell Cty HS 1976-; *ai:* Beta Club Spon; Textbook Adoption Sci & Math Comm; S Campbell Cty Rotary Club Interact Club Spon 1982-85, Outstanding Service 1983; Natl Beta Club Spon 1976-, Outstanding Service Certificate 1987; Campbell Cty HS Teacher of Yr 1983-84; Articles Published 1975, 1985; *office:* Campbell County HS Rt 3 Box 61 Jacksboro TN 37757

RIDER, CAROL FLEMING, 1st Grade Teacher; *b:* Bayminette, AL; *m:* B.T.; *c:* Amity, Jonathan; *ed:* (BS) Elem Ed, Univ of South AL 1980; *cr:* 1st Grade Teacher Bay Minette Elem 1980-; *ai:* Chm Beautification Comm Bay Minette Elem; Comm of Cmnty & Sch; Aide Bay Minette Elem After-Sch Prgm; Mentor New Teachers in Sch Sys; AL Ed Assn; Baldwin Cty Prof Ed Assn; NEA; Bay Minette Public Lib (Bd Mem Treas 1989-); *home:* 715 E 9th St Bayminette AL 36507

RIDER, WILLIAM SCOTT, Guidance Counselor; *b:* Bloomsburg, PA; *m:* Ann E. Weitz; *c:* Nicole, Jordan, Jonathan; *ed:* (BS) Health/Phys Ed, Findley Coll 1972; (MA) Guidance, Western St Coll 1974; E Stroudsburg Univ 1973; *cr:* Health/Phys Ed Instr Shull Jr HS 1977-76; Guidance Cnslr Easton Area Mid Sch 1976-83, Easton Area HS 1983-; *ai:* Easton Area HS Ftbl Coach & Defensive Coord 1974-; Cnslr Adult Base Ed 1978-; PA St Ed Assn, Easton Area Ed Assn 1974-; PA Coaches Assn; *office:* Easton Area HS 25th St & Wm Penn Hwy Easton PA 18042

RIDGLEY, GARY MICHAEL, Math Teacher; *b:* Hammond, IN; *m:* Wanda M.; *c:* Ryan, Randy; *ed:* (BS) Math, 1973; (MS) Math, 1976 Purdue Univ; *cr:* Math Teacher George Rogers Clark HS 1973-; Purdue Univ 1978-83; *ai:* Head Ftbl Coach; IFCA 1989-90; TN Girls Sports Assn 1986-89; Adult Booster Club Pres 1987-89; Purdue Univ Calumet Alumni Coach of Yr 1989; "Teacher You Should Know" Hammond Ed Fdn 1988; *office:* George Rogers Clark Sch 1921 Davis Ave Whiting IN 46394

RIEDEL-MATTHEWS, HOLLY, English Teacher; *b:* Cedar Rapids, IA; *m:* James H.; *c:* John; *ed:* (BA) Eng Lit, Eckerd Coll 1976; (MA) Eng/Ed, Univ of South FL 1981; Puget Sound Writers Wkshp; *cr:* Eng Teacher Tampa Prep Sch 1976 77; Berkeley Prep Sch 1978-80; Sedro Woolley Mid Sch & HS 1985-87, Lake Stevens Mid Sch 1987-88, Wichita HS Southeast 1988-; *ai:* Thespian Troupe Asst; KS Dressage & Combined Trng Assn Bd 1988-; Rdng Comm Chairperson Sedro Woolley HS; *home:* 328 Colonial Pl Wichita KS 67206

RIEGEL, MARY CHRISTMAN, Second Grade Teacher; *m:* Mark Lee; *c:* Tyson L., Tara A.; *ed:* (BA) Elem Ed, OH Univ 1976; Cmptr, Sci Classes; *cr:* 2nd-6th Grade Teacher Scioto Sch 1976-; *ai:* 4-H Adv; PTO; JCEA; Jackson City Ed Assn, NEA, OEA 1977-; 4-H (Adv, Advisory Cncl) 1972-; Grange 1968-; PTO, Grace United Meth Church; *office:* Scioto Sch 4701 St Rt 776 Jackson OH 45640

RIEKEN, MARGARET WAGES, 7th/8th Grade Math Teacher; *b:* Lubbock, TX; *m:* Gray Wayne; *c:* Cheyenne, Levi; *ed:* (BS) Elem Ed/Math, TX Tech Univ 1970; *cr:* 5th Grade Teacher Abernathy Ind Sch Dist 1970-76; 5th Grade Teacher 1978-80, Mid Sch Math Teacher 1980- Arp Ind Sch Dist; *ai:* UIL Number Sense Coach Mid Sch; *home:* 22058 CR 2321 Arp TX 75750

RIEMER, MARTHA HELEN, Fifth Grade Teacher; *b:* Beloit, WI; *m:* Peter Lawrence; *ed:* (BA) Eng Lit, Beloit Coll 1975; (MAT) Rdng, Rockford Coll 1986; Grad Stud, Univ of WI Whitewater; Gifted Ed, N IL Univ De Kalb & IL St Univ Normal; *cr:* 6th-7th Grade Teacher 1975-76, 5th Grade Teacher 1976- Kinnikinnick Sch; *ai:* Comm for Writing Sci Curr; Kinnikinnick Ed Assn 1975-; BA Obtained Phi Beta Kappa with Academic Honors; *office:* Kinnikinnick Sch 5410 Pine Ln Roscoe IL 61073

RIES, HILMA ELIZABETH, French/German Teacher; *b:* Concord, NH; *m:* Hugh H.; *c:* Seth I.; *ed:* (BA) Fr, Georgetown Coll 1974; Ger, Bowling Green Univ 1987; (MA) Ed, Coll of Mount St Joseph 1986; *cr:* Fr Teacher 1976- ; Ger Teacher 1977 Upper Scioto Valley HS; *ai:* Soph Class Adv 2 Yr; Stu Cncl Adv 1 Yr; Chrldr Adv 1 Yr; Teacher Concerns Comm 1 Yr; OH Foreign Lang Assn; Univ Club II Treas 1989-; *home:* 12701 Tr 205 Kenton OH 43326

RIESENBERGER, DAVID ANTHONY, Mathematics Teacher; *b:* Rochester, NY; *ed:* (BA) Math, St John Fisher 1970; *cr:* 7th/8th Grade Math Teacher St Marys Jr HS 1970-71; 9th-12th Grade Math Teacher Cardinal Mooney HS 1974-76, St Agnes HS 1976-78, Bishop Kearney HS 1979-; *ai:* Soph Class Adv; Dept Chairperson St Agnes HS; *office:* Bishop Kearney HS 125 Kings Hwy S Rochester NY 14617

RIESTER, CONNIE AINSLEE, 2nd Grade Teacher; *b:* Mt Union, PA; *m:* William Charles Jr.; *c:* Jared, Sarah; *ed:* (BA) Elem Ed/Lib Sci, 1972, (MS) Early Chldhd, 1978 Shippensburg St Coll 1978; *cr:* Kndgtn Teacher 1973-76, 2nd Grade Teacher 1976- Shippensburg Area Sch Dist; *ai:* Elem Sch Craft Club Asst; Big Brothers & Big Sisters Bd Mem 1974; *office:* Shippensburg Areas Sch Dist N Morris St Shippensburg PA 17257

RIET, BRENDA YORGASON, 5th Grade Teacher; *b:* Salt Lake City, UT; *m:* H. J.; *ed:* (BA) Elem Ed, Univ of UT 1972; Post Grad Health Ed Gifted Ed ; *cr:* 3rd Grade Teacher 1975-87; 4th Grade Teacher 1987-88; 5th Grade Teacher 1989- Taylorsville Elem; *ai:* Teacher Affectiveness Team; Teacher Morale Team; Granite Sch Dist Writing Comm; Stu Recognition Career Ladder; Granite Ed Faculty Rep; Assn UT NEA/NEA 1975-.

RIEVES, JOYCE SHEFFIELD, First Grade Teacher; *b:* Mantachie, MS; *m:* Robert Samuel; *c:* Hannah J., Hayley P. J.; *ed:* (AA) Soc Work/Sociology, Itawamba Comm Coll 1969; (BS) Soc Work/Sociology/Soc Stud Ed, MS Univ for Women 1971; (BS) Elem Ed, Univ of MS 1973; *cr:* Remedial Rdng Teacher 1971-72, 1st Grade Teacher 1972- Mantachie HS; *ai:* Itawamba Ed Assn, MS Assn of Ed, NEA 1971-; GSA; Yrbk Dedication Awd; *home:* PO Box 208 Mantachie MS 38855

RIFE, ELAINE MOYER, Sixth Grade Teacher; *b:* Pottsville, PA; *m:* Richard P.; *c:* Cori, Erin; *ed:* (BED) Elem Ed, PA St Univ 1975; (MED) Elem Ed, Millersville St Univ 1981; Rdng Specialist; *cr:* Teacher Lebanon Sch Dist 1975-; *ai:* Drug Abuse Act Coord; Just Say No Club Adv; Bd Dir Lebanon Sch Dist Drug Free Schools Comm; Lebanon Cty Ed Honor Society; Leb Chem People Task Force Sch Liason 1988-; Penn St Alumni Assn 1975-; Lebanon Cty Ed Honor Society; *office:* Lebanon Sch Dist 1000 S 8th St Lebanon PA 17042

RIFFEE, BILLY JACKSON, Math Dept Key Teacher; *b:* Akron, OH; *m:* Betty Ruth Hoover; *c:* Belinda R., Brenda R., Beverly R.; *ed:* (BD) Bible, Bible Baptist Seminary 1972; (BA) Bible, Arlington Baptist Coll 1977; OH St Univ Coll of Engineering, Tarrant Cty Jr Coll, Dallas Baptist Coll, Univ of TX Arlington; *cr:* Math Dept Teacher Temple Chrstn Sch 1979-; *ai:* Amer Chrstn Honor Society Spon; Fairpark Baptist Church Assoc Pastor 1972-; *office:* Temple Chrstn Sch 6824 Randol Mill Rd PO Box 8499 Fort Worth TX 76124

RIFFLE, MARGARET JEAN, Elem Teacher of Gifted; *b:* Massillon, OH; *m:* Roger W.; *ed:* (BS) Elem Ed, Malone Coll 1967; Gifted Ed Akron Univ/Malone/Ashland; Gifted Stu Wkshp Malone/Ashland; *cr:* 4th Grade Teacher 1967-83; 4th/5th Grade Teacher 1983-84; 5th Grade Teacher 1984-86 L E York Sch; 3rd-6th Grade Gifted Resource Rm Teacher E G Bowers Sch 1986-; *ai:* Handwriting/Lang/Rdng/Sci/Spelling/Writing & Massillons Gifted Prgm Comm; City Spelling Bee Co-Chairperso N; NEA; OH Ed Assn; Massillon Ed Assn; OH Assn Gifted Children; Natl Assn Gifted Children; Massillon Museum; Malone Alumni Women; Wilderness Ctr; Natl Wildlife Fed; Coll Club of Canton; Support for Talented Stu; Nom Greater Canton Chamber of Commerce; Nom Teacher of Yr 1990; *home:* 602 Charldon S W Massillon OH 44646

RIFNER, PHILIP J., English Teacher/Department Chm; *b:* Lafayette, IN; *m:* Norma Miral Bautista; *c:* Donna M., Pamela J.; *ed:* (BA) Eng, Wabash Coll 1971; (MA) British Lit, Purdue Univ 1974; Educl Psych; *cr:* 7th Grade Eng Teacher Frankfort Jr Hs 1972-74, Sunnyside Jr HS 1974-84; K-12th Grade Teacher of Gifted & Talented Hahn Amer Schls 1984-86; 9th Grade Eng Teacher Tecumseh Jr HS 1986-87; 7th/8th Grade Eng Teacher Sunnyside Mid Sch 187-; *ai:* Chess Team & Eng Coach; Academic Competitions & Building Coord; Gifted & Talented; NAGC 1984-; Co-Authored Article 1989; Presentation 5th World Conference on Gifted & Talented Ed Hamburg FRG; *office:* Sunnyside Mid Sch 2500 Cason St Lafayette IN 47904

RIGGERT, KEVIN LYNN, Elementary Principal; *b:* Marysville, KS; *m:* Judy Ann Schaefer; *c:* Laura R.; *ed:* (BA) Elem Ed, Hastings Coll 1980; (MS) Educl Admin, Kearney St Coll 1983; Ombudsman Trng; Skills for Growing; Clinical Supervision; Ventures for Excl-The Best in Selection & Dev of People; Sch Improvement Prgm; *cr:* 6th Grade Teacher Howard Elem 1980-83; Asst Prin Barr Jr HS 1983-87; Elem Prin Lincoln Elem 1987, Seedling Mile Elem 1987-; *ai:* Chapter I Rdng Coord GIPS; Staff Dev Comm Mem GIPS; Co-Chm North Cntrl Accreditation GIPS; Mem Neighborhood Schls Comm-Pro Planning Time Comm; NCSA 1983-; NAESP 1987-; ASCD 1983-; Grand Island Area United Way Pres 1990; Grand Island Cmmty Dev 1986-; Grand Island Family Preservation Team 1987-; Grand Island Chamber of Commerce 1989; Governors Summit Children and Families; Recognized By St Dept Social Svcs Youth 2000; Phi Delta Kappa Mem; *office:* Seedling Mile Elem Sch 3208 E Seedling Mile Rd Grand Island NE 68801

RIGGS, BESSIE BARNES, 6th Grade ESL Teacher; *b:* Sapulpa, OK; *m:* Bobby Joe; *ed:* (BS) Elem Ed/Early Chldhd, Northeastern Univ 1978; (BA) Lib Sci, OK St Stillwater 1986; (MS) Ed, Natl Univ San Diego 1990; Grad Stud; *cr:* Librarian/2nd/6th Grade Teacher Wynona Public Schls 1977-86; 6th Grade ESL Teacher Coachella Unified Sch Dist 1986-; *ai:* 4-H Club & Stu Cncl Spon; Adventurers Lit Club & PTA Adv; Girls Bsktbl & ESL Coach; Osage Cty Teachers Assn (Pres 1985-86, VP 1984-85, Teacher of Yr 1984; Chamber of Commerce Mem 1982-86; AFT Mem 1986-; Outstanding Young Women of America 1979; Learning Magazine Article 1987-88; *office:* Coachella Valley Unified Dist 87-163 Center Thermal CA 92274

RIGGS, RICHARD E., Social Studies Teacher; *b:* Bradford, PA; *m:* Daneen Krupinski; *c:* R. Kent, Kelly C.; *ed:* (BS) His/Eng, Geneva Coll 1960; (MS) Scndry Guidance, Westminster Coll 1968; Grad Courses Ec, Univ of Pittsburgh; *cr:* Teacher Beaver Area Sch Dist 1960-; *ai:* BAEA VP 1975-76; PSEA, NEA; *office:* Beaver Area HS 855 2nd St Beaver PA 15009

RIGGS, ROBERT JOSEPH, Seventh Grade Teacher; *b:* Portsmouth, OH; *ed:* (BS) Ed, OH St Univ 1964; *cr:* 4th Grade Teacher Hartzler Elem 1964-66; 5th/6th Grade Teacher Weinland Park Elem 1966-79; 6th Grade Teacher Kingswood Elem 1979-80; 6th/7th Grade Teacher Dominion Mid Sch 1980-; Rdng Instr Columbus St Comm Coll 1988-; *ai:* Columbus Public Schls Spelling Bee Comm; Columbus Ed Assn (Awds Comm 1976-) 1966-, Dedicated Service 1978-80, Outstanding Building Rep 1978, Outstanding Mem 1980; Educator of Yr Dominion Mid Sch 1987; Nom for Ashland Oil Company Teaching Excl Awd 1990; *office:* Dominion Mid Sch 330 E Dominion Blvd Columbus OH 43214

RIGGS, STEVEN WAYNE, Phys Ed/Health Teacher; *b:* El Paso, TX; *m:* Gerre Ann Noble; *ed:* (AS) Bus Admin, N OK Coll 1974; (BS) Health/Phys Ed/Dance, OK St Univ 1977; *cr:* Health/Phys Ed Teacher Sequoyah Mid Sch 1977-89, John Ross Elem 1989-; Swimming Coach Edmond Memorial HS 1977-; *ai:* Head Swimming Coach Edmond HS 1977-; NISCA, ASCA, OK Coaches Assn Mem 1977-88; Kerr Mc Gee Swim Club Coach 1985-; Edmond YMCA Volunteer 1977-; OK Boys Swimming Coach of Yr 1979, 1981, 1984; OK Girls Swimming Coach of Yr 1979, 1983, 1986, 1987; OK Coaches Assn Coach of Yr 1983-1984; *office:* John Ross Elem & Edmond HS 1901 N Thomas Edmond OK 73034

RIGO, BARBARA HENKEL, 5th Grade Teacher; *b:* East Orange, NJ; *m:* Raymond Sr.; *c:* Raymond; *ed:* (BS) Elem Ed, Trenton St Coll 1972; *cr:* 7th/8th Grade Teacher 1972-73, 3rd Grade Teacher 1973-75, 1977-83, Remedial Math Teacher 1983-86, 5th Grade Teacher 1986- Frankford Township Sch; *ai:* FTEA Membership Chairperson; NJ Ed Assn 1972-; Christ Church Sch Teacher 1985-; *office:* Frankford Township Sch PO Box 430 Branchville NJ 07826

RIGSBY, SALLYE JOHNSON, English Teacher; *b:* Memphis, TN; *m:* Dean; *c:* Sheryl; *ed:* (BSE) Speech, Henderson St 1966; (MA) Speech, Univ of AR 1968; Educl Leadership UAB 1985; *cr:* Teacher Univ of Montevallo 1967-71, Pelham HS 1974-; *ai:* Yrbk Spon; Beauty Pageant Dir; Kappa Delta Epsilon 1989-; AEA, NEA 1974-; *home:* 1359 Whirlaway Cir Helena AL 35080

RIHA, JOAN (JOHNSON), English Department Chairperson; *b:* Cleveland, OH; *w:* James J. (dec); *ed:* (BA) Eng/Speech, Heidelberg Coll 1964; (MA) Comm/Rhetoric, Univ of Akron 1985; Several Wkshps & Seminars; *cr:* Eng Teacher Parma Sr HS 1964-68; Eng/Speech Teacher/Eng Dept Chairperson Normandy HS 1968-; *ai:* Adv Esprit De Corps; Stu of Month Comm Chairperson; NCTE 1968-; Parma Ed Assn (Chairperson, Instructional, Prof Dev); NEA, OEA 1970-; Martha Holden Jennings Lecture Scholar; John W Vaughn Excl Ed Awd; *office:* Normandy HS 2500 W Pleasant Valley Rd Parma OH 44134

RIHERD, SHIRLEY BENEDICT, Spanish Teacher/Dept Chair; *b:* New York, NY; *m:* James Michael Riherd; *c:* Michael C., David J., Peter A.; *ed:* (BA) Span, 1958, General Scndry Ed, 1959 Univ of CA Los Angeles; (MA) Scndry Curr, CA St Univ Los Angeles 1982; Trng of Trainers Inst for Foreign Lang Instrs, Foreign Lang Curr Implementation Center 1985; *cr:* Span/Eng Teacher Eliot Jr HS 1959-63; Span/Eng/Soc Sci Teacher Marshall Jr HS 1963-68; Mentor Teacher Pasadena Unified Schls 1985-88; Consultant Ed Testing Service Profieciency Exam CA Univ 1987-88; Span IV Teacher/Dept Chairperson Marshall Scndry 1974-; *ai:* Span Club Adv; Debate Team Coach; AIDS Educator, Translator, Volunteer Hospice Visitor; CA Foreign Lang; Altadena Little League Pres 1978-80; Babe Ruth (VP 1982-83, Player Agent 1981-82).

RIKER, CAROL WHERLEY, Kindergarten Teacher; *b:* Cleveland, OH; *m:* David Michael; *c:* John C., David C.; *ed:* (BA) Elem Ed, Heidelberg Coll 1965; (MED) Admin/Supervision, Xavier Univ 1974; Grad Stud Akron Univ, Kent St, Steubenville Univ, Dayton; *cr:* 2nd/3rd Grade Teacher John A Sutter 1964-65; 5th Grade Teacher Tuscarawas Avenue Elem 1965-66, East New Philadelphia 1966-70; 1st Grade Teacher 1971-84, Kndgtn Teacher 1984- East New Philadelphia; *ai:* NEA, OEA, ECOEA 1965-; NPEA Building Rep 1965-; VFW Womens Auxiliary Trustee 1988-89; Tuscaloosa Coll Club 1974-; *home:* 1035 4th St NW New Philadelphia OH 44663

RILEY, BEVERLY HAMRIC, Business Teacher; *b:* Charleton Heights, WV; *m:* Wesley L.; *ed:* (BA) Bus Ed Comprehensive, 1980, (BS) Secretarial Sci, 1980 Glenville St Coll; Working Towards Master, Ashland Coll; *cr:* Bus Teacher Westfall HS 1981-; *ai:* Dist Newsletter Coord; Homecoming Comm; Bus & Prof Women 1989-; *office:* Westfall HS 19463 Pherson Pike Williamsport OH 43164

RILEY, BRENDA JOYCE (FERGUSON), 4th Grade Teacher; *b:* Detroit, MI; *m:* William Scott; *c:* Colleen E., Kimberley D.; *ed:* (BA) Greenville Coll 1962; (BA) Wayne St; Grad Stid Wayne St; *cr:* Teacher Webster Sch 1962-; *ai:* Service Squad Spon; Faculty Teachers Rep; Alpha Delta Kappa Teachers Secy; Bus & Prof Womans Club 1970-76; PTA Teacher VP; Ferndale Free Meth Church Mem; *office:* Daniel Webster 431 W Jarvis Hazel Park MI 48030

RILEY, DENNIS PAUL, Principal; *b:* San Francisco, CA; *m:* Cheryl; *c:* Kristi, Kerri, Brian; *ed:* Cnslrs Credential; *cr:* Teacher Royal HS 1968-74, Fall River HS 1974-81; Cnslr Fall River HS 1981-89; Prin Mt View HS 1989-; *ai:* Ftbl, Bsktbl, Bsbl, Track Coach; Athletic Dir; Class Adv; ASCA 1989-; NEA, CTA 1968-89; Lions; Inter Mountain Handicapped Center Bd Mem 1989-; *office:* Mt View HS Mt View Rd Burney CA 96013

RILEY, DIXIE D., Elem Visual Art Consultant; *b:* Herington, KS; *ed:* (BSE) Elem Ed, Emporia St Univ 1974; Working Towards Masters Curr & Instruction, ESU; *cr:* 1st/2nd Grade Teacher Rolling Ridge Elem 1974-79; 1st/3rd Grade Teacher Prairie Center Elem 1979-84; Elem Art Consultant Olathe Schls 1984-; *ai:* NAEA Model Elem Curr Guide 1987; KS Art Ed Assn; NEA, KNEA, ONEA 1974-80; St of KS Prgm Educl Excl Awd 1987; ABET Awd Emporia KS Chamber of Commerce; Article Published 1989; *office:* Olathe Unified Sch Dist 233 1005 S Pitt Olathe KS 66061

RILEY, DON ALAN, Athletic Coordinator; *b:* San Antonio, TX; *m:* Dolores; *c:* Kristen, Clint; *ed:* (BS) Phys Ed, SW TX St 1982; *cr:* Athletic Coord/Head 8th Grade Coach Goodnight Jr HS 1984-; *ai:* 8th Grade Head Ftbl & Bsktbl Coach; Summer Bsktbl Camp Coach; TX HS Coaches Assn 1984-; Outstanding Achievement Awd Health Dept; *office:* Goodnight Jr HS 607 Peter Garza San Marcos TX 78666

RILEY, JOAN LORRAINE (KIDWELL), Retired; *b:* Frostburg, MD; *m:* Neal M.; *c:* Robin N., Joseph W.; *ed:* (BS) Elem Ed, Frostburg St Coll 1957; (MA) Elem Ed, WV Univ 1974; *cr:* Teacher Northeast Elem Sch 1957-64; Westernport Elem Sch 1964-89; *ai:* Retired June 1989, 32 Yrs Service in Allegany Cty; NEA; MSTA; ACTA 1988-89; Western MD Rdng Cncl & Bldg Rep; Beta Sigma Phi (Mem 1965-81 VP 1970 Girl of Yr Awd 1972; Westernport Elem Sch Bldg Comm; *home:* Rt 2 Thousand Acres Deep Creek Lake Swanton MD 21561

RILEY, MARCIA GALE, Fifth Grade Teacher; *b:* Kansas City, KS; *m:* Steven R.; *c:* Justin, Matthew; *ed:* (BS) Elem Ed, Univ of KS 1974; (MS) Curr & Instruction, Emporia St Univ 1990; *cr:* 4th-6th Grade Teacher Pinckney Grade Sch 1975; 5th/6th Grade Teacher 1975-87, 4th/5th Grade Teacher 1987- Williamstown Elem; *ai:* Dist Sch Improvement Team; *office:* Williamstown Grade Sch Rt 1 Perry KS 66073

RILEY, MARY ANN (ROE), Fifth Grade Teacher; *b:* Ventura, CA; *m:* Marion Robert; *c:* Melanie Riley Henderson, Michael R., Jeffrey S.; *ed:* (BA) Ed, Occidental Coll 1958; Fresno Pacific Coll, Univ of WY, UC Berkeley, Univ of Pacific, CA St Univ, Stanislaus; *cr:* 3rd/4th Grade Teacher Stamford Sch 1958-59; Eng Reader Scottsbluff HS 1963-67; 5th Grade Teacher Sherwood Sch 1977-; *ai:* Pilot Teacher for Math, Eng, Rdng, Soc Stud; CA Text Adoptions; Master Teacher Stu Teachers CSU & Stanislaus; Dist Wide Comm Mem; Gifted & Talented, Math, Soc Stud Dist Wide Comm Mem; NEA, CA Teacher Assn; Sylvan Dist Ed Assn Strategies Officer 1984-85; 4-H (Club Leader, Project Leader) 1968-79, 10 Yr Service Awd 1978; Magazine Article Published; *office:* Sherwood Sch 819 E Rumble Rd Modesto CA 95350

RILEY, PEGGY (ADAMS), Social Studies Teacher; *b:* Springfield, IL; *m:* Dean; *c:* Brad, Robin Kerckhove, Reggi, Christa Krenz; *ed:* (BA) Elem Ed, IL St Univ 1979; *cr:* 5th Grade Home Room/Soc Stud Teacher Milton Pope Sch 1979-; *ai:* Gifted Class.

RILEY, SHARI BAHLMAN, Choral Music Director; *b:* San Angelo, TX; *m:* Donald H. Jr.; *ed:* (BMED) Music Ed, Angelo St Univ 1984; *cr:* K-6th Grade Music Teacher Hays Elem 1984-85, Maplewood Elem 1985-86; General Music/Choral Asst San Angelo Ind Sch Dist 1986-87; Choral Dir Robert E Lee Jr HS 1987-; *ai:* TX Music Educators Assn, TX Choral Dir Assn 1984-; Amer Choral Dir Assn 1987-; San Angelo Symphony Chorale (Asst Dir 1989-) 1988-; *home:* 2009 Juanita San Angelo TX 76901

RILEY, VIRGINIA ANN (HAMRIC), English Teacher; *b:* Charlton Heights, WV; *m:* Mick; *ed:* Eng, Glenville St Coll 1977; *cr:* Eng Teacher Westfall HS 1977-; *ai:* Stus Active in Ed, Mustang Cntry Newspaper Staff, Homecoming Dance Adv; NCTE, OH Cncl Teachers of Lang Art; Bus & Prof Women 1989-; *office:* Westfall HS 19463 Pherson Pike Williamsport OH 43164

RIMBACH, LINDA M., Biology Teacher; *b:* Crane, TX; *c:* Deidre Stroosma, Heidi, Amy; *ed:* (BA) Bio, Univ of TX 1961; (MS) General Sci, Syracuse Univ 1963; *cr:* General Sci Teacher Patti Welder Jr HS 1961; Bio Teacher Victoria HS 1961-62; General Sci Euclid Jr HS 1962-63; Life Sci Teacher Jason Lee Jr HS 1969-85; Bio/Chem Teacher Wilson HS 1985-; *ai:* Math Engineering Sci Achievement Adv; NEA, WA Ed Assn, Tacoma Ed Assn; Outstanding Educator Math Engineering Sci Achievement Prgm 1988; *office:* Woodrow Wilson HS 1202 N Orchard Tacoma WA 98406

RINALDI, MARGARET HUSSEY, Mathematics Teacher; *b:* Waukegan, IL; *m:* Roger E.; *c:* Steven, Karyn, Robert; *ed:* (BS) Math, IA St Univ 1955; Ed Grad Courses; Accounting Assoc Certificate; *cr:* Math Teacher Grinnell HS 1955-56; Part-Time Instr Tulsa Jr Coll 1978-82; Math Teacher Monte Cassino Sch 1982-86, Catoosa HS 1986-; *ai:* OCTM, OEA, NEA; HS Teacher of Yr 1989-; *office:* Catoosa HS 2000 S Cherokee Catoosa OK 74015

RINALDO, ANGIE RAICEVICH, Social Studies Teacher; *b:* Colorado Springs, CO; *c:* Stephen; David; *ed:* (BA) His, Poly Sci, 1956 Univ Northern CO; *cr:* 5th Grade Teacher Cherry Hill Elem 1956-57; 7th/8th Soc Stud Teacher St Vincent De Paul 1963-67; St Marys of Littleton 1968-78; Laredo Mid Sch 1980- *ai:* Soc Stud Coord; Washington DC Tour Spon; K-12 Soc Stud Curr Review Comm; Co Cncl for Soc Stud Treas 1985-87; NCSS Outstanding Scndry Soc Stud Teacher 1987; Listen Fnd Brd of Dir 1971-81; CO St Bd of Ed Commitment to Excel Awd 1986; Laredo Mid Schl Teacher of Yr 1986; Cherry Creek Schl Dist Distinguished Teacher 1986; Runner-Up CO Teacher of Yr 1987; James Madison Project 87 Fellowship Univ of CA Berkeley; Taft Seminar Fellow 1985; a Teachers Inaugural Experience 1989; Several Articles & Curr Guides Published *office:* Laredo Mid Sch 5000 S Laredo Aurora CO 80015

RINAS, MICHELLE JANE, Principal/Science Teacher; *b:* Sisseton, SD; *ed:* (BS) Bio/Health, St Cloud St Univ 1983; Certified Laboratory Technician Medical Institute of MN; *cr:* Cert Lab Tech Granite Falls Municipal Hosp 1975-76, St Cloud Hospital 1976-83; Sci Teacher 1983-89, Prin/Teacher 1989- Petersburg Public Schl; *ai:* Jr Class Spon 1983; Sr Class Spon 1984; Asst Vlybll Coach 1984-1988; Pep Club/ Chrldr Spon 1984; Stud Cncl Spon 1989-; NEA/NSEA Secy 1985-86; NEA/NSEA Pres 1986-89; Petersburg Booster Club VP 1986-; Cmmty Against Substance Abuse VP/Sec 1988-; Luth Womens Missionary League VP 1985-89.

RINDERKNECHT, PRICILLA ANNE, Fourth Grade Teacher; *b:* Cedar Rapids, IA; *m:* Donald G.; *ed:* (BA) Elem Ed, Univ of IA 1967; (MA) Elem Ed, Northeast MO St 1971; Marycrest Coll; *cr:* 3rd/4th Grade Teacher Buchanan Elem 1967-71; 2nd-5th Grade Teacher Madison Elem 1971-; *ai:* Chm Writing Comm; Phase III Comm; Cadre Madison Sch; Cedar Wood Univ Unit Sch Rep; NEA 1967-; ISEA 1967-; Alpha Delta Kappa Corresponding Secy 1985-88.

RINDLISBACHER, ROBERT FRED, Science Teacher/ Chairman; *b:* Amalga, UT; *m:* Anita Zollinger; *c:* Teri Loveland, Tina Warren, Traci, Robert J., Christian, Tasha, Cody, Aaron; *ed:* (BS) Sec Ed Sci, 1963, (MED) Sci Ed, 1967 UT St Univ; *cr:* Teacher Valley Jr HS 1963-; Dir Metro Sci Fair 1988-; *ai:* Dir Salt Lake Metro Sci Fair; Instr Mill Hollow Sci Ctr; Gifted and Talented Comm; Chm of Sch Honor Society; UT Sci Teachers 1963- Awd for Excl in Sci Teaching 1979; Boy Scout Leader 1978; LDS Church Leader 1965-; Dev Successful Summer Sci Prgm; Wrote Dist Curr Materials; Dev Gifted Prgm; *home:* 3351 W 4200 S West Valley City UT 84119

RINEDOLLAR, THALIA NUNGEZER, Elementary Teacher; *b:* Ithaca, NY; *c:* Anne Burich, Molly; *ed:* (AB) Art His, Cornell Univ 1957; (MSED) Elem Ed, N IL Univ 1978; Ed, Cornell Univ 1958-59; *cr:* 4th Grade Teacher Greene Avenue Sch 1959-62, Rock River Sch 1962-63; 2nd Grade Teacher Ellis Sch 1969-71; 1st-6th Grade Teacher Welsh Sch 1972-; *ai:* Invent America Comm; Pi Lambda Theta Honorary 1959; IASCD Treas 1985-87; Rockford Ed Assn Excl Comm 1987-89; IEA, NEA 1987-89; Welsh of WI (Dir 1985-, Mgr 1989); Midwest Welsh Breeders Incorporated High Point Chm 1989-; Welsh Pony & Cob Society of America; Rockton Township Historical Society Tour Brochure Author; Equine Market (Columnist, Feature Writer) 1985-; Rockford Gifted Prgm Grant Literary Magazine Teacher/Adv 1980-82; *office:* Welsh Sch 2100 Huffman Blvd Rockford IL 61103

RINEHART, ELIZABETH ANN, Principal; *b:* La Harpe, IL; *ed:* (BS) Elem Ed, 1965, (MS) Educl Admin, 1978 Western IL Univ; *cr:* 2nd/3rd Grade Teacher Avon Elem 1962-64; 3rd Grade Teacher Stronghurst Elem 1964-67; 3rd Grade Teacher Mary Ellen West Sch 1967-69; 4th-6th Grade Teacher Gale Mid Sch 1969-71; 4th Grade Teacher Nielson Mid & Silas Willard Schls 1971-78; 5th GGrade Teacher Nielson Sch 1978-86; Prin Silas Willard 1986-; *ai:* Affirmative Action Comm Dist 205 Mem; Public Relations Comm Mem; Textbook Selection Comm 1988-89; Discipline Comm 1987-88; Developed Adapt-A-Sch Spon; Phi Delta Kappa VP 1988-89; ASCD 1988-; IL Prin Assn 1989-; NEA 1963-69; Henderson Cty Women Teachers Assn Treas 1966; Cable TV Comm VP 1988-; Sesquicentennial Comm Co-Chm Ed Comm 1987; Published Article Prairie Journal; *office:* Silas Willard Sch 495 E Fremont Galesburg IL 61401

RINEHART, JANET KLINGENSMITH, 6th Grade Teacher; *b:* Goshen, IN; *m:* Donald; *c:* Melissa Rinehart Acuna, Melinda Rinehart Ward, J. Todd; *ed:* (BSED) Elem Ed, 1959, (MAED) Curr, 1979 Ashland Univ; Grad Stud; *cr:* 6th Grade Teacher Tucson Public Schls 1959-61; Kndgtn/6th Grade Teacher Ashland City Schls 1961-63; *ai:* Intervention Assistance Team; Grant Elem Sch Yrbk Ed; Youth Choir Dir; Sunday Sch Teacher; ACTA, OCEA, NEA; Jennings Scholar & Grant; Ashland City Teacher of Yrl; *office:* Grant Street Elem Sch 730 Grant St Ashland OH 44805

RINEHART, SHARON JONES, Fourth Grade Teacher; *b:* Moultrie, GA; *m:* Thomas James; *ed:* (AS) Home Ec, Abraham Baldwin Ag Coll 1977; (BSHE) Early Chldhd Ed/Child Dev, 1979, (MED) Early Chldhd Ed, 1980 Univ of GA; (EDS) Early Chldhd Ed, Valdosta St Coll 1985; *cr:* 4th Grade Teacher Cox Elem 1980-; *ai:* 4th Grade Group Chm 1985-; NEA, GA Assn of Educators, Colquitt Cty Assn of Educators 1980-; Moultrie Jr Womans Club (Treas 1990, Ed Dept Chm 1987-88) 1985-; *office:* Cox Elem Sch 12th St SE Moultrie GA 31768

RINELLA, A. JAMES, Fifth Grade Teacher; *b:* Weymouth, MA; *m:* Rebecca Grant; *c:* Robin Hansen, James, Matthew; *ed:* (BS) Elem Ed, Boston Coll 1963; Grad Stud Bridgewater St; *cr:* 5th Grade Teacher Cushing Sch 1963-; *ai:* Winter & Spring Track Coach; Teacher for a Day, Salary, Track Coaches Salary Comm; Plymouth Cty Ed 1963-, Citation 1989; MTA, Sci Teachers Assn, NEA 1963-; Track Coaches Assn 1970-; N Weymouth Civic Assn 1974-; Scituate Teachers Assn Former Rep; St Coaches Hall of Fame 1987; Coach of Yr 1978; *home:* 36 Davids Island Rd Weymouth MA 02191

RINER, SUSAN MASON, 1st Grade Teacher; *b:* Durant, OK; *m:* Kenneth; *c:* Monica, Cody; *ed:* (BA) Elem Ed, Southern OK St Univ 1972; *cr:* 1st Grade Teacher Mannsville Elem 1972-74; 1st/2nd Grade Teacher Will Rogers Elem Sch 1976-; *ai:* Negotiation Packet Comm; Calendar Comm; Art Ed Comm; OEA/NEA/ACTA.

RING, BOB, English Teacher; *b:* Jacksonville, IL; *m:* Anne; *ed:* (BA) His, IL Coll 1978; *cr:* Feature Writer Illinoian Star 1979-82; Managing Ed Triopia Tribune 1983-86; Eng I/II/III Teacher Pittsfield HS 1987-; *ai:* Scholastic Bowl Coach; Phi Betta Kappa 1987-; Sons of Amer Legion 1985-; *home:* Mac Murray Coll Box 1148 Jacksonville IL 62650

RING, LUCY M., Spanish Teacher; *b:* New Brunswick, NJ; *m:* David L.; *c:* Kathy; *ed:* (BA) Span, OH Univ 1968; (MAED) Scndry Prin, Baldwin-Wallace Coll 1987; *cr:* Span Teacher Highland HS 1968-71; Strongsville Sr HS 1974-; *ai:* Acad Challenge; Prin Advisory Comm; NEA 1968-; OEA 1968-; Strongsville Ed Assn 1974-; OH Foreign Lang Teachers Assn 1968-; *office:* Strongsville Sr HS 20025 Lunn Rd Strongsville OH 44136

RINGER, SHERRY L., Physical Education Teacher; *b:* Redbank, NJ; *ed:* (BS) Phys Ed/Life Sci, Cal Poly Pomona 1976; (MS) Sport Psych, Azusa Pacific Univ 1986; *cr:* Spec Ed Teacher Fullerton Sch Dist 1977-82; Sci Teacher 1982-83, Phys Ed Teacher 1983- Parks Jr HS; *ai:* Health Week, Dare To Care Day Coord; 8th Grade Washington DC Trip Chaperone; Head Vlybl Coach; Parks Panther Awd 1987; Coach of Yr 1987; *office:* Parks Jr HS 1710 Rosearans Fullerton CA 92633

RINGS, DIANA ST. JOHN, Fifth Grade Teacher; *b:* Manhattan, KS; *c:* Eric; *ed:* (BS) Elem Ed, W IL Univ 1964; *cr:* 1st Grade Teacher of Gifted Vae View Elem 1963-64; 1st Grade Teacher 1965-69, 4th Grade Teacher 1975-89, 5th Grade Teacher

1989- Colchester Elem; *ai:* Chm Elem Sci Dept; Curr & Textbook Comm; NEA, IEA 1965-; *office:* Colchester Grade Sch Box 261 Colchester IL 62326

RINGSTED, NANCY HOYLE, 5th Grade Teacher; *b:* Turlock, CA; *m:* Larry; *c:* Karina K., Bryan B.; *ed:* (BA) Eng/Ed, Westmont Coll 1969; *cr:* 4th-6th Grade Teacher Daves Avenue Sch 1970-; *ai:* 5th/6th Grade Sch Choir Dir; Sci Coord Daves Avenue; Sip Comm; Sci Head; Wrestling Coach; CTA, NEA; Masons Teacher of Yr 1983; Church (Sunday Sch Teacher 1980-83, Choir 1980-83); Mentor 1988-89; PG&E Grant 1987; Hewlett-Packard 1988; Loral Rolm Mil-Spec Cmptrs 1989; *office:* Daves Avenue Sch 17770 Daves Ave Los Gatos CA 95030

RINGWALD, EDWARD CHARLES, Social Studies Teacher; *b:* Boonville, NY; *:* Karen Mayer; *ed:* (BA) Soc Stu, 1966, (MA) Soc Stud, 1967 SUNY Albany; *cr:* 8th Grade Soc Stud Teacher Case Jr HS 1967-; *ai:* NY St Rdng Assn, Intnl Rdng Assn Conference Presenter 1987-88; *home:* 1 Stafford Dr Black River NY 13612

RINKER, MARY E., 5th/6th Grade Teacher; *b:* Hanna, OK; *w:* Dannie C. (dec); *c:* Dana M. Cardoso, David C.; *ed:* Elem Ed, Northeastern St 1956-58; (BS) Elem Ed, Fresno St Univ 1965; *cr:* 2nd Grade Teacher, 1959-60, 4th Grade Teacher, 1960-62 Waukena Union Sch; 5th-6th Grade Teacher Buena Vista Sch 1963-; *ai:* Spelling Coach; Girls Sports Coach; Geography Coach; Mid Grade Math Coach; Parents Club Womens Missionary Group; Craft Group; *home:* 1345 William St Tulare CA 93274

RIORDAN, MARY MURPHY, Principal; *b:* Worcester, MA; *m:* Paul; *c:* Kevin; *ed:* (BA) Bio, Elms Coll 1960; (MED) Bio Ed, Framingham St 1976; (MA) Bio, Anna Marin Coll 1978; NSF Grant Univ of CT 1962; Regents Grant Univ of MA 1986; Cath Sch Leadership Boston Coll 1987-; *cr:* Bio/Chem Teacher West Boylston HS 1960-65, Yeshiva Acad 1978-80, Holy Name HS 1980-87; Prin Holy Name HS 1987-; *ai:* Elms Coll Trustee 1988-; Auburn Conservation Comm 1972-; Cntrl MA Reg Planning Commission Chm 1979-80; Regents Grant Univ of MA 1986; NSF Grant Univ of CT 1962; Anna Maria Grad Prgm, Advisory Bd in Bio; *office:* Holy Name HS 144 Granite St Worcester MA 01604

RIORDAN, MICHAEL J., JR., 5th Grade Teacher; *b:* New Haven, CT; *m:* Patricia A. Serfilippi; *c:* Christopher, Elizabeth Papadopoulus, Michael III; *ed:* (BA) US His, 1961, (MS) US His, 1966 S CT St Univ; *cr:* 7th/8th Grade Teacher Mathewson Sch 1961-66; 6th Grade Teacher Mary L Tracy Sch 1966-70; 5th Grade Teacher Yew Tree Sch England 1970-71; 5th/6th Grade Teacher Turkey Hill Sch 1971-; *ai:* Bsktbl Coach; Curr, Prof Dev, Gifted Comm; Orange Teachers League Pres 1968-70; BSA Agency Rep 1974-77; Fulbright Exch Teacher England 1970-71; *office:* Turkey Hill Sch Turkey Hill Rd Orange CT 06477

RIORDON, ANN MARIE BARBARA, Kindergarten Teacher; *b:* Staten Island, NY; *ed:* (BA) Soc Sci/Elem Ed, 1954, (MA) Soc Sci/Elem Ed, Notre Dame Coll; *cr:* Teacher Washington Sch 1954-55, PS 41 Sch 1955-; *ai:* Group Leader for Lang Group; Grade Leader; Subject Coord; Teacher Trainer; Cath Teachers Assn 1965-68; Staten Island Rdng Assn 1955-; Staten Island Early Chldhd Assn, United Fed of Teachers; NY St Teachers Assn; Richmond Cultural & Literary Society 1988-; *office:* PS 41 Sch Clawson St & Locust Ave Staten Island NY 10306

RIPA, RONALD ANTHONY, Theology Department Chair; *b:* Hazleton, PA; *ed:* (BA) Theology/Philosophy, Univ of Scranton 1981; (MED) Scndry Ed, E Nazarene Coll 1987; *cr:* Theology Teacher Monsignor Bonner HS 1981-82; Theology/His Teacher Matignon HS 1984-87; Theology/His Teacher/Dept Chm St Thomas Aquinas HS 1987-; *ai:* St Thomas Yrbk Adv 1987-; St Thomas Boys Tennis Coach 1989-; Matignon Girls Track Coach 1984-87; Matignon NewsPaper Adv 1984-85; *office:* St Thomas Aquinas HS 197 Dover Point Rd Dover NH 03820

RIPPEE, LINDA LOU (SMITH), English/Speech Teacher; *b:* Belen, NM; *m:* Noel; *c:* Christy, Chek; *ed:* (BS) Speech/Eng, 1971, (MA) Scndry Ed, 1984 E NM Univ; *cr:* Eng Teacher/Librarian Elida HS 1971, 1979-84; Eng Teacher Floyd HS 1984-; *ai:* Sr Play Dir; Pronouncer Roosevelt Cty Spelling Bee; Frosh Class Spon; Stu Cncl Adv; NM Textbook Evaluation Comm; NM Cncl of Teachers of Eng Treas 1979-82; *home:* Rt 1 Box 1 Floyd NM 88118

RIPPEL, PATRICIA BLACK, Fifth Grade Teacher; *b:* Derry, PA; *m:* Jerry M.; *c:* Laura Maxwell, Daniel; *ed:* (BA) Eng, Westminster Coll 1955; Elem Teaching Cert; *cr:* Secy Westinghouse Electric Corporation 1955-59; Elem Teacher Blairsville-Saltsburg 1970-; *ai:* PSEA/NEA; Century Club 1963-; *office:* Blairsville-Saltsburg Sch 4098 Indiana Hwy Blairsville PA 15717

RIPPEY, BETTY THOMPSON, Advanced Mathematics Teacher; *b:* Gary, WV; *m:* Will Neeley Jr.; *c:* Will N. III, George F., Robert D.; *ed:* (BS) Ed/Math, WV Univ 1951; (MA) Admin, Dayton Univ 1981; Wheeling Coll, OH Univ; *cr:* Math Teacher Coalwood Jr HS 1951-53, Gary HS 1954-55, St Clairsville 1966-67, Bellaire HS 1964-66, 1967-68, John Yeates HS 1968-70, Martins Ferry HS 1971-; *ai:* Math Dept Chm; Sr Class Adv; NEA, OEA 1971-; MFEA Treas 1971-; Delta Kappa Gamma Society IntnL (Pres, 1st VP, 2nd VP) 1973-; *home:* Rt 6 Spring Park St Clairsville OH 43950

RIPPEY, SANDRA N., Second Grade Teacher; *b:* Buffalo, NY; *m:* Will N.; *c:* Alison, Billy; *ed:* (BS) Elem Ed, Kent St Univ 1976; Madeline Hunter EEI Trng & Peer Coaching; *cr:* Substitute Teacher Portage Cty Schs 1976-77; 1st Grade Teacher 1977-83, 2nd Grade Teacher 1983- Cntrl Elem Sch; *office:* Cntrl Elem Sch N Manuta St And Park Ave Kent OH 44240

RIPPLE, KAREN HOELSCHER, Texas History/English Teacher; *b:* San Angelo, TX; *m:* Rodney W.; *c:* Kevin, Brandon; *ed:* (BA) His, Angelo St Univ 1976; *cr:* 6th-8th Grade Eng/Soc Stud Teacher Veribest Sch 1976-77; TX His/Eng Teacher Edison Jr HS 1985-; *ai:* Edison PRIDE Club Spon; Support Group Leader Edisons Stu Assistance Prgm; Assn of TX Prof Educators 1985-; *home:* 7849 Ripple Rd San Angelo TX 76904

RISER, JAMILA Q., Mathematics Teacher; *b:* Kabul, Afghanistan; *m:* Donald William; *c:* David M.; *ed:* (AS) Math, Wesley Meth Coll 1984; (BS) Math Ed, DE St Coll 1986; *cr:* Teacher W T Chipman 1986-; *ai:* Youth to Eliminate Lost Lives Spon; DSEA, NEA, NCTM, OCTM 1986-; NHS 1980-82; Honor Society in Coll 1982-84; PTA Phoebe Hearst Awd Excl in Teaching; Teacher of Yr Nom 1989; *office:* W T Chapman Jr HS Dorman St Hartly DE 19953

RISHER, DEANNE PHILLIPS, 2nd Grade Teacher; *b:* Biloxi, MS; *m:* Jerry H.; *c:* Kristy Risher Summer, Rusty; *ed:* (BS) Bus, Winthrop Coll 1963; (MED) Early Chldhd Univ of SC 1987; *cr:* Teacher Jackson Elem 1968-86; 2nd Grade Teacher Redcliffe Elem 1986-; *ai:* Outdoor Classroom Steering Comm; Teacher of Yr 1989-; Grade Level Chairperson 2 Yrs; *office:* Redcliffe Elem Sch 2880 Atomic Rd Jackson SC 29831

RISHOR, PATRICK F., JROTC Instructor; *b:* Midway, MT; *m:* Thelma J.; *ed:* (BBA) Bus Admin, Mc Kendree 1978; *cr:* Soldier US Army 1953-80; Teacher Bullitt Cntrl HS 1980-; *ai:* Drill Teams; Color Guard; Masons; *office:* Bullitt Cntrl HS Box 159 Hwy 44 E Shepherdsville KY 40165

RISHOVD, PAULA DE SHAW, Industrial Art Teacher; *b:* Minneapolis, MN; *m:* Larry; *ed:* (BA) Industrial Art/Phys Ed, Bemidji St Univ 1979; (MS) Cmptr Literacy/Applications, Nova Univ 1987; Grad Stud Technology Ed; *cr:* Woodshop Teacher J D Smith Jr HS 1979-83; Woodshop/Technology/Cmptr Teacher Brown Jr HS 1983-; *ai:* NV Ed Assn, Clark Cty Classroom Teachers Assn 1979-; Clark Cty Voc Assn (Officer 1989-) 1979-; NV St Task Force Technology Ed; St Curr for Technology Published; Pilot Technology Ed in Clark Cty; *office:* Brown Jr HS 307 Cannes Henderson NV 89015

RISK, DIANNA SCOTT, Elementary Teacher; *b:* Madison, IN; *m:* Carl William; *c:* Carl W., Joseph M., Jennifer K.; *ed:* (BS) Elem Ed, Eastern KY Univ 1971; (MS) Elem Ed, IN Univ 1976; Spec Ed Eastern KY Univ; Rdng Endorsement IN Univ; *cr:* Spec Ed Teacher Madison Cons Jr HS 1971-76; Rdng Teacher Elem Schls 1978-80; Gifted/Talented Teacher Eggleston Elem Sch 1980-84; 3rd/6th Grade Teacher Lydia Middleton Elem Sch 1984-; *ai:* Chi Omega Rush Adv, Hanover Coll & Natl Rush Team; Delta Kappa Gamma 1980-; Tri Kappa Treas 1974-; Chamber Commerce Cmmty Service 1986; Wrote Summer Sch Prgm; *home:* 2231 Taylor St Madison IN 47250

RISK, LARRY E., Assistant Superintendent; *b:* Madison, IN; *m:* D. Elaine Gray; *c:* James R., Rhonda, Larry A.; *ed:* (BS) Ed, Purdue Univ 1969; (MS) Sch Admin, 1874, (EDS) Sch Admin, 1979 IN Univ; *cr:* Teacher/Attendance Officer/Asst Prin Switzerland Cty Schls 1972-75; Asst Prin/Athletic Dir 1975-79, Elem Prin 1979-88, Asst Supt 1988- West Clark Cmmty Schls; *ai:* Substance Abuse, AIDS/HIV, Gifted & Talented, Staff Dev, Curr Coord; ASCD 1987-; NAESP, IN Assn Elem & Mid Sch Prin, Phi Delta Kappa 1979-; Kiwanis 1978-, Kiwanian of Yr 1987; Tri-Cty Substance Abuse Task Force, Cty Aids Cmmty Action Group 1988-; Natl Prin Fellowship 1985; IN Prin Leadership Acad 1986-88; *office:* West Clark Cmmty Schls 601 Renz Ave Sellersburg IN 47172

RISKE, JOYCE MEYER, Semi-Retired 1st Grade Teacher; *b:* Moulton, TX; *m:* Arnold W. Sr.; *c:* J. B. Bednar, Curtis, Arnold W. Jr.; *ed:* (AA) His/Sci, TX Luth Coll 1934; (BS) Elem Ed, SW TX Univ 1951; (MED) Elem Ed, Prairie View A&M Univ 1972; Grad Stud Sul Ross Coll, Our Lady of the Lake Coll; *cr:* Elem Teacher Bachelor Hill Sch 1934-35, Nickel HS 1935-38; Prin Michna Sch 1938-43, Green Sch 1943-51; Elem Teacher Shiner Elem 1951-85, St Ludmila Acad 1986-87; Substitute Teacher Shiner Elem 1987-; *ai:* Vlybl & Bsbl Coaching Michna & Green Schls; Stu Cncl Spon Shiner Elem Sch; Alpha Phi & Delta Kappa Gamma Past Secy 1972-; TX St Teachers Assn Mem; Shiner Elem PTA (Secy 1954) 1951-; United Dr Martin Luther Church Organist 1970-; Luth Ladies Aid (VP, Pianist) 1985-; Waelder OES Past Grand Matron 1951-; Post 201 Amer Legion Auxiliary; VFW Mem; Federal Schlshp Sch Without Walls Grant 1970-72; SW TX Univ Shift of Emphasis Project 1970-71; Shiner Elem Sch Service Pins; Career Ladder; Presented Music Wkshps; Outstanding Elem Teachers of America 1974; *home:* 512 N Avenue F Box 501 Shiner TX 77984

RISLEY, CATHY H., 2nd Grade Teacher/Team Leader; *b:* Erie, PA; *m:* John F.; *c:* Jon; *ed:* (BA) Elem Ed, Grove City Coll 1961; *cr:* Teacher Addison Mizner Sch 1968-70, Gocio Elem Sch 1971-; *ai:* Team Leader; PTA Liaison; Alpha Delta Kappa 1987-; Gocio Teacher of Yr 1983-84; *office:* Gocio Elem Sch 3450 Gocio Rd Sarasota FL 34235

RISLOV, GEORGE RAY, History Teacher; *b:* Oklahoma City, OK; *c:* Jill; *ed:* (BA) His, Univ of TX Dallas 1978; (MED) Scndry Ed, Univ of N TX 1985; Working Towards PhD Curr & Instruction, Univ of N TX; *cr:* His Teacher Wilson Mid Sch 1981-85, Shepton HS 1985-; *ai:* Club Adv Amnesty Intnl; Academic Coach Whiz Quiz, Octathlon; Campus Improvement Plan Chm; Critical Thinking Comm; TX Cncl for Soc Stud (Conference Prgm Presenter 1988-89) 1988-; NCSS 1988-89; Honoree Outstanding HS Teachers Southern Univ 1990; Mem Academic Freedom Comm; *office:* Shepton HS 5505 Plano Pkwy Plano TX 75093

RITACCO, JOSEPH SYLVESTER, Middle School Principal; *b:* Pittsburgh, PA; *m:* Kristine Stofan; *c:* Kari Jo, Joseph; *ed:* (BS) Elem Ed, 1970, (MED) Elem Ed, 1976 CA Univ PA; Elem Prin Cert 1985; *cr:* Teacher Fallowfield Elem Sch 1970-; Prin Charleroi Mid Sch 1988-; *ai:* In-Sch Scouting-Coord; Charleroi Area Teachers Assn 2nd VP 1974; PA Mid Sch Assn 1988-; PTA Parliamentarian 1975 Honorary St Life Mem 1976; Charleroi Amer Legion-Commander 1980 & 1990; PTA Honorary Natl Life Mem 1988; Holy Name Society Pres 1980-87; *office:* Charleroi Mid Sch Fecsen Dr Charleroi PA 15022

RITCHIE, LARRY ROSS, Chemistry/Physics Teacher; *b:* Big Spring, TX; *ed:* (BS) Bio, 1978, (BA) Chem, 1980 Univ of TX Arlington; Grad Stud Univ of TX Austin, Univ of TX Arlington, Univ of Houston, SWTSU, TCU, TCJC; *cr:* Teacher Everman HS 1981-; *ai:* Sci Club, UIL Calculator/Sci Spon; Sci Fair Coord; TSTA, Amer Chemical Society 1981-; Biological Society 1974-80; Mohn Educl Schlshp Author Univ of TX Arlington; FWRSF Teacher of Yr 1987; *office:* Everman HS 1000 S Race St Everman TX 76140

RITCHIE, SUZANNE, Eng/Speech/Journalism Teacher; *b:* Little Rock, AR; *c:* Matthew Marshall; *ed:* (BSE) Eng/Speech/Drama, 1971, (MS) Scndry Admin, 1985 Univ of AR; Gifted & Talented Ed Prgm for Effective Teaching; *cr:* Eng Teacher Immaculate Conception Sch 1979-82; Eng/Speech/Journalism Teacher Ridgeroad Jr HS 1982-; *ai:* Soccer Coach; Cheerleading Spon; N Little Rock Sch Dist Communications & Reorganization Comm; NCTE; March of Dimes Volunteer 1986-; Nom N Little Rock Teacher of Yr 1986; Original Poems, Scripts & Readers Theaters Presented & Produced Performing Art; *office:* Ridgeland Jr HS 4601 Ridgeroad North Little Rock AR 72116

RITCHIE, THOMAS JOSEPH, JR., Electrical Shop Teacher; *b:* Medford, MA; *m:* Catherine M. Lynch; *c:* Thomas, Joseph; *ed:* (ASCE) Cmptr Field Engineering, Control Data Inst 1972; (BSED) Voc Ed, Fitchburg St Coll 1984; Missle/Launcher Technician US Army; MA Journeyman Electrician; MA Master Electrician; *cr:* Electrical Shop Teacher Medford Voc Tech HS; Atlantic Gelitin Winchester MA; Foreman Electrician W B Stockwood Inc; *ai:* MTA, NEA; *office:* Medford Voc Tech HS 489 Winthrop St Medford MA 02155

RITENOUR, JAY K., Fifth Grade Teacher; *b:* Latrobe, PA; *m:* Barbara Hanson; *c:* Kristin, Kyle, Casey, Carrie; *ed:* (BS) Elem Ed, Slippery Rock Univ 1972; Recreation Supervision Certificate; Penn St Elem Ed; *cr:* 6th Grade/Head Teacher Seward Elem 1972-77; 6th Grade Teacher 1977-79; 4th Grade Teacher 1979-80, 5TH Grade Teacher Laurel Valley Elem; *ai:* Intramural Dir; Yrbk Adv; PSEA 1972-; LVEA 1972-; *office:* Laurel Valley Elem Sch Rd 1 New Florence PA 15944

RITER, CONSTANCE, Math Teacher/Department Chair; *b:* Weirton, WV; *d:* David; *c:* James; *ed:* (BA) Eng, Marygrove Coll 1962; (MATM) Math, Univ of Detroit 1967; Cmptr Wkshps, ITIP 1989; *cr:* Math Teacher Roxboro Jr HS 1967-69; Adjunct Math Professor Columbia Coll 1982-87; Math Teacher Cicero-N Syracuse HS 1969-; *ai:* Academic Decathlon Coach; Dist Math Comm Mem; Amer HS Math Exam Coach; Dept Chairperson; SAT Prep Course Teacher; Onondaga Cty Math Teachers Assn (VP, Pres) 1974-78; Assn of Math Teachers of NY St Cty Rep 1990; NCTM; N Syracuse Ed Assn 1967-; N Syracuse Federal Credit Union Supervisory Comm; BSA Troop Comm Mem; Natl Sci Fnd Grant 1962-67; Newmast Grant NASA Educl Wkshp 1990; *office:* Cicero-N Syracuse HS Rt 31 Cicero NY 13039

RITTENHOUSE, DEBORAH BOBLIT, Sixth Grade Teacher; *b:* Albany, GA; *m:* Bradley K.; *c:* Jaime N., Christopher R., Lindsey K.; *ed:* (BA) Elem Ed, OH Northern Univ 1976; *cr:* 6th-8th Grade Teacher Northwood Sch 1978-; *ai:* Spelling Bee Co-Chairperson; Sidney Ed Assn Secy 1988-89; OH Ed Assn, NEA; OH PTA, Natl PTA; Zeta Tau Alpha Life Mem; Piqua Youth Soccer Parents Assn; *home:* 1300 Nicklin Ave Piqua OH 45356

RITTER, JOAN ANTLE, English Department Chair; *b:* Jamestown, KY; *m:* Greg; *c:* Stephanie; *ed:* (BA) Eng, 1970, (MA) Cnslr Ed, 1980 (Rank I) Cnslr Ed, 1984 W KY Univ; *cr:* Eng Teacher Park City Sch 1970-71, Russell Cty HS 1971-73, Hiseville Sch 1976-77, Barren Cty HS 1977-; *ai:* Barren Cty Ed Assn, KY Ed Assn, NEA; *office:* Barren Cty HS 507 Trojan Trl Glasgow KY 42141

RITTER, STACEY GEORGES, First Grade Teacher; *b:* Bellaire, OH; *m:* Eric Beu;; *c:* Maria, Daniel; *ed:* (BS) Elem Ed, Univ of Steubenville 1974; (MS) Guidance/Human Services Counseling, Univ of Dayton OH 1979; *cr:* 1st Grade Teacher St Clairsville Elem 1974-; *ai:* OH Ed Assn, St Clairsville Ed Assn 1974-; *office:* Saint Clairsville Elem Sch 120 Norris St Saint Clairsville OH 43950

RITZ, VERONICA TOOLE, Mathematics Teacher; *b:* Rochester, NY; *m:* Franklin James; *ed:* (BA) Math, Nazareth Coll of Rochester 1984; (MA) Math, St Univ Coll Brockport 1989; *cr:* Math Teacher Wilson Magnet HS 1984-; *ai:* Career Day & Sch Assembly Awds Comm; Math Team Spon; Amer Math Society 1987-88; NY St United Teachers; Nom Dept of Math & Cmptr Sci for Membership to Amer Mathematical Society; *office:* Wilson Magnet HS 501 Genesee St Rochester NY 14611

RIVA, JEFFREY FRANCIS, Social Studies Teacher; *b:* Washington, DC; *m:* Nancy Jane Cutten; *c:* Jennifer, Jeffrey B., Brian; *ed:* (BA) Bus Admin, Marist Coll 1969; (MAT) Ed, SUNY New Paltz 1974; Natl Sci Fnd Geology Grant, NE US Vassar 1970; Certificate SUNY New Platz 1975; *cr:* Teacher/Coach Our Lady of Lourdes 1969-74, Millbrook HS 1974-85; Coach F D Roosevelt 1986-; Teacher Millbrook HS 1986-; *ai:* F D Roosevelt Asst Var Ftbl Coach; CHVOBB; Cntrl Hudson Valley Bd of Ofcls 1985-; Bsktbl Coach of Yr 1981-82; Sftbl Coach of Yr 1983-85; Teacher of Yr 1984; *office:* Millbrook HS Alden Pl Box AA Millbrook NY 12545

RIVERA, JOSEPH MANUEL, Assistant Principal; *b:* San Lorenzo, PR; *m:* Martha Barton; *ed:* (BA) Elem Ed, Cleveland St Univ 1974; (MA) Ed, Baldwin-Wallace Coll 1977; Educl Research, Dissemenation Prgm; *cr:* Teacher Walton Elem 1974-75; Teacher Intern Orchard Elem 1975-77; Teacher 1977-86, Asst Prin 1986- J T Brackenridge Elem; *ai:* Honors Club Spon; YBA Coach; Grade Level Chairperson; TEPSA 1987-; ASCD 1989-; Habitat for Humanity 1988-; *office:* J T Brackenridge Elem Sch 1214 Guadalupe St San Antonio TX 78207

RIVERS, CONSTANCE WILLIAMS, 4th Grade Teacher; *b:* Webster, FL; *m:* Roosevelt; *c:* Rodger C., Rhonda C., Reginald C.; *ed:* (BA) Elem Ed, 1956, (MED) Ed, 1961 FL A&M Univ; Rdng Specialist; *cr:* 5th Grade Teacher Holden Street Elem 1956-57; 5th Grade Teacher 1957-67, Rdng Teacher 1967-77, 4th Grade Teacher 1977- Washington Shores Elem; *ai:* Sch Safety Patrol Adv; ARMS Teacher; CTA 1960-; FSTA, NEA; New Bethel AME Sunday Sch (Supt 1986-88, Teacher 1970-87); Teacher of Yr Washington Shores Elem; *office:* Washington Shores Elem Sch 944 W Lake Mann Dr Orlando FL 32805

RIVERS, MARY FRANCIS WHITE, 6th Grade Teacher; *b:* Boston, MA; *m:* John A.; *c:* Robert, Julie, Christopher; *ed:* (BS) Ed, Boston Coll 1960; Working towards Masters Elem Ed, Bridgewater St; *cr:* Latin/Eng Teacher Stoughton HS 1960-63; Latin Teacher Chapel Hill Sch 1963-65; L D Tutor North Elem Sch 1970-75; Substitute/Resource Teacher Stoughton Jr HS 1975-78; 6th-7th Grade Teacher St Gregory Elem Sch 1978-; *ai:* Jr HS Level Coord; NCEA; West PTA Pres; *office:* St Gregory Elem Sch 2214 Dorchester Ave Dorchester MA 02124

RIVERS, NANCY L., 4th Grade Teacher; *b:* Bridgeport, CT; *ed:* (BA) Religion/Music/Elem Ed, Olivet Coll 1965; (MS) Elem Ed, Univ Bridgeport 1972; *cr:* 2nd Grade Teacher Fairfield Woods 1965-67; 1st-4th Grade Teacher Jennings 1967-75; 2nd/4th/6th Grade Teacher Mill Hill 1975-80; 4th Grade Teacher Riverfield 1980-; *ai:* Math Curr Comm; Eng Think Tank; Sch Improvement Adv Comm Chm; FEA; CEA; NEA; Delta Kappa Gamma; Eastern Star; White Shrine Church Choir; High Priestess 1975-76; Church Bd of Music; *office:* Riverfield Elem Sch Mill Plain Rd Fairfield CT 06430

RIVERS, SHIRLEY LE DUFF, English Teacher; *b:* Baton Rouge, LA; *m:* Joseph D.; *c:* Braden D.; *ed:* (BA) Fr, 1979, (MED) Scndry Rdng, 1985 Northwestern St Univ; *cr:* Eng Teacher Negreet HS 1979-84; Frosh Eng Teacher Northwestern St 1984; Eng Teacher Converse HS 1985-; *ai:* Jr HS & HS Quiz Bowl Coach; Foreign Exch Stu Coord; APEL 1987-; Northwestern St Univ Curia Grant Awd 1985; *office:* Converse HS PO Drawer 10 Converse LA 71419

RIVERSIDE, INEZ THORNBERRY/PETERSON, 3rd Grade Teacher; *ed:* (BS) Ed, N MI Univ 1969; Working Towards Masters Ed & Admin; *cr:* 3rd Grade Teacher Breitung Township Schls 1969-; *ai:* Curr, Personnel, Sch Improvement, Building Comm; Delta Kappa Gamma Secy 1979-; Phi Delta Kappa 1975-; Upper Peninsula Rdng Assn Secy 1972-76; Dickinson Cty Rdng Assn Secy 1977-78; Beta Sigma Nu Secy 1960-75; Delta Phi Pres; Breitung Township PTO (VP, Cncl 1960-65); *office:* Woodland Sch 2000 Pyle Dr Kingsford MI 49801

RIVET, KATHERINE ZIMMER, 5th Grade Teacher; *b:* Dallas, TX; *m:* Ronald P.; *c:* Catherine, Danielle; *ed:* (BA) Elem Ed, 1972; (MS) Elem Ed, 1977 Old Dominion Univ; *cr:* K-8th Sub Teacher VA Beach Public Schls 1972-73; 1st Grade Teacher Town and Country Day Sch 1973-74; 4th Grade Teacher 1974-87; 5th Grade Teacher 1987 St Matthews Cath Sch; *ai:* Coord St Judes Math-A-Thon; Soc Stud Coord; Intermediate Grade Level Coord; NCEA 1974-; *office:* St Matthews Cath Sch 3316 Sandra Ln Virginia Beach VA 23464

RIVETTE, MIRIAM SNYDER, 4th Grade Teacher; *b:* Kingston, NY; *c:* Edward W. Jr., Kevin M.; *ed:* (BS) Early Chldhd Ed, Univ of NY 1952; *cr:* Kndgtn Teacher Broadalbin Central Sch 1952-54; Kndgtn Teacher 1961-62; 3rd Grade Teacher 1962-67; 4th Grade Teacher 1967- Corinth Central Sch; *ai:* Activity Admissions Adv 1983-; Corinth Teachers Assn Treas 1975-; Corinth Cmmty Ctr 1988-; *office:* Corinth Cntrl Sch 105 Oak St Corinth NY 12822

RIVIERE, BARBARA SCANLON, Social Studies Teacher; *b:* Auburn, NY; *ed:* (BA) Liberal Arts, 1966, (MA) Soc Stud Ed, 1969 Syracuse Univ; (CAS) Educl Admin, SUNY Brockport 1976; *cr:* Teacher 1967-75, Dept Chairperson 1976-83, Teacher 1984- Eastridge HS; *ai:* ATAD Exch Stu Organization Adv; NYSUT Building Rep; Dist Travel, Building Report Card Comms; RACSS, NYSCSS; Gamma Phi Beta Philanthropy Chairperson 1980-; ROCLA; NDEA Grant; Ford Fnd Grant; Natl Endowment for Hum Grant; Travel Throughout Europe, Asia, Siberia, Latin Amer; *office:* Eastridge HS 2350 Ridge Rd E Rochester NY 14526

RIVLIN, TIMOTHY BENNETT, History Teacher; *b:* New York, NY; *ed:* (BA) Government, St Lawrence Univ 1975; *cr:* His Teacher Convent of Sacred Heart 1981-84, Cardinal Spellman HS 1984-; Head Eng Teacher Horizons Summer Prgm 1979-; Citizenship Teacher Stamford Public Schls 1985-; *ai:* Var & Jr Var Bowling Coach 1989-; Global Stud II Curr Coord; 10th-11th Grade Regents Review Bd; NCSS 1989-; *office:* Cardinal Spellman HS 1 Cardinal Spellman Pl Bronx NY 10466

RIZOS, ELEANOR CACHIONA, Spanish Teacher; *b:* Nashua, NH; *c:* STAR; *ed:* (BA) Lang, Univ of NH 1948; (MA) Ed, Rivier 1959; *cr:* Teacher Nashua Sr HS 1951-63; Span Instr Daniel Webster Coll 1966-67, 1972-73; Teacher Elm St Jr HS 1967-68, 1975-; *ai:* Yrbk Adv; NH of Foreign Lang Teachers; Daughters of Penelope; Elpis Society Secy.

ROACH, BARBARA BRUNNER, Science Teacher/Dept Chair; *b:* Fairfax, MN; *m:* Don D.; *c:* Jeremy D., Jennifer; *ed:* (BA) Bio, Whitman Coll 1963; (MA) Ed, Lindenwood Coll 1985; *cr:* Teacher A C Davis HS 1964-69, Hollenbeck Jr HS 1980-; *ai:* Amer Assn of Univ Women; Phi Delta Kappa; Delta Kappa Gamma; *office:* Hollenbeck Jr HS 4555 Central School Rd Saint Charles MO 63303

ROACH, JACQUELYN BOUTOT, Kindergarten Teacher; *b:* Kingman, ME; *c:* Jan Davis; *ed:* (BS) Ed, Univ of ME 1978; *cr:* 1st Grade Teacher Medway Elem Sch 1956-57; Kndgtn Teacher 1957-60, 4th Grade Teacher 1960-62, Kndgtn Teacher 1967-63 Mattawan Keag Elem Sch; K-3rd Grade Teacher Kingman Elem & Benedicta Elem 1965-; *ai:* ME St Employees Assn (Local Secy 1977-79, Local Pres 1988-); *home:* 200 Hancock St Apt 209 Bangor ME 04401

ROACH, KATHY RICHINS, English/Reading Teacher; *b:* Brigham City, UT; *m:* Floyd B.; *c:* Kristin, Michael; *ed:* (BA) Eng/ Rdng, Univ of UT 1981; (MED) Westminster Coll 1989; *cr:* Teacher Kennedy Jr HS 1982-; *ai:* Granite Sch Dist Writing Festival Chairperson; Intnl Rdng Assn Salt Lake Cncl (VP 1988-89, Pres 1989-); *office:* Kennedy Jr HS 4495 S 4800 W West Valley City UT 84119

ROACH, NANCY CAUBLE, English Teacher; *b:* Orleans, IN; *m:* George E.; *c:* Radford, Hal; *ed:* (BA) Lang Art, IN St Univ 1956; (MA) Lang Art/Ed, San Jose St Univ 1965; *cr:* Eng Teacher Clarksville HS 1956-57, Salinas HS 1957-60, 1965-; *ai:* Foreign Exch Club Adv; AFT, CA Assn Teachers of Eng, NCTE; AFS Sch Adv; *office:* Salinas HS 726 S Main St Salinas CA 93901

ROACH, PATSY WILLIAMS, English Teacher/Dept Chairman; *b:* Lake Providence, LA; *m:* Randy Lynn; *c:* Dustin, Kimberly; *ed:* (BS) Ed, Univ of West Fl 1984; *cr:* Substitute Teacher Benton AR Schls 1985; Teacher Escambia Chrstn 1986-; *ai:* Homecoming Organization Head; Newspaper Staff Spon; NCTE 1990; LACE 1986-90; Graduated Magna Cum Laude; *office:* Escambia Chrstn Sch 3311 W Moreno St Pensacola FL 32505

ROACH, RALPH ANN EBLEN, Third Grade Teacher; *b:* Loudon, TN; *m:* Ronald A.; *c:* Alex, Ronnie; *ed:* (BA) Elem Ed, TN Tech 1973; *cr:* Teacher Beech Elem 1974-; *ai:* Sci Festival Rep; Phys Sci Curr Chm; NEA, TEA, SCEA, Career Ladder; *office:* Beech Elem Sch Long Hollow Pike Hendersonville TN 37075

ROACH, WILLIAM RUSSELL, 7th Grade Teacher; *b:* Columbia, KY; *m:* Nancy Fredrickson; *c:* Annie L., William A.; *ed:* (AA) Sci, Lindsey Wilson Jr Coll 1974; (BS) Voc Ag, Univ of KY 1976; *cr:* Rem Math Teacher John Adair Mid Sch 1977-78; 7th Grade Teacher Knifley Grade Center 1978-82, Sparksville Grade Center 1982-; *ai:* KY GED Prgm Teacher; 7th/8th Grade Coach; *home:* 2091 Toria Rd Columbia KY 42728

ROANE, BONNIE CAMPBELL, English Teacher/Drama Advisor; *b:* Burlington, NC; *m:* Ernest Lee; *c:* Christopher B. Painter, James O. Painter, Derek Adams; *ed:* (BS) Eng, Fayetteville St Univ 1981; Effective Teacher Trng; Public Sch Law; Shakespeare Drama Wkshp; Cmptr Trng; Performance Appraisal Trng; Thinking Tactics Trng; IDEA Sch Improvement Trng; *cr:* Eng Teacher JEJ Moore Jr HS 1981-82, JFK Schuhe W Berlin Germany 1984-85, Williams HS 1985-; *ai:* Drama Club Adv; IMPACT Team Mem; BCAE Building Rep; Facilitator for Williams HS Sch Improvement Team; NEA, NCAE, BCAE NCTE Mem; Womens Poly Caucas of Alamance Cty; Alamance Cty Coalition for Peace; *office:* Williams HS 1307 S Church St Burlington NC 27215

ROARK, BRENDA SPANGER, Third Grade Teacher; *b:* Vincennes, IN; *m:* Dan R.; *c:* Lori; *ed:* (BA) Elem Ed, Univ of Evansville 1975; (MS) Elem Ed, Indiana St Univ 1980; *cr:* 4th Grade Teacher Summer Elem Sch 1975-79; 6th Grade Teacher 1979-83, 5th Grade Teacher 1983-86, 1st Grade Teacher 1986-89, 3rd Grade Teacher 1989- Franklin Elem Sch; *ai:* NEA 1975-; IN St Teachers Assn, Vincennes Ed Assn 1979-; IN Rdng Assn, Knox Cty Rdng Assn 1981-; St John United Church of Christ Mem; *home:* 1501 Franklin Dr Vincennes IN 47591

ROATEN, DIANE L., Third Grade Teacher; *b:* Hackensack, NJ; *m:* Teddy L.; *ed:* (BA) Elem Ed, Jersey City St Coll 1971; (MS) Cmptrs Elem Sch, Lesley Coll 1985; *cr:* 6th Grade Teacher New Egypt Elem Sch 1971-73, Ash Grove Elem 1974-76; 2nd/3rd Grade Teacher Aurora Public Schls 1977-; *ai:* Building Cncl Comm 1987-88; Curr Comm 1988-; Stu Advisory Comm 1983-85; Parent Advisory Comm 1985-86; Aurora Educl Assn, CO Ed Assn, NEA 1977-; 1st Baptist Church (Dir of Youth 1982-83, Stewardship Comm 1981-84); Butterfield Architect & Environmental Comm 1984-86; Higher Level Thinking Skills Master Teacher; *home:* 8500 N Sundown Trl Parker CO 80134

ROBB, DON G., Mathematics Teacher; *b:* Douglas, WY; *m:* Mertie L. Mackey; *c:* Sandra K. Robb Gale, Donald G. Jr. (dec); *ed:* (BS) Math, Bethany Nazarene Coll 1960; (MA) Scndry Ed/ Admin, Univ of N CO; *cr:* Math Teacher Greybull HS 1960-63, Skyview HS 1963-; *ai:* Wrestling Coach; Dist Task Force on Athletics; Math Dept Chairperson; CO Wrestling Ofcls Assn, Mapleton Ed Assn, CO Ed Assn, Drivers Ed Assn of CO; Recognition Awds HS Ftbl, HS Wrestling; *office:* Skyview HS 9000 York St Thornton CO 80229

ROBB, DONALD GEORGE, Sixth Grade Teacher; *b:* Estevan SK, Canada; *m:* Mary S. Haddock; *c:* Karen, Kenneth, David; *ed:* (BS) Elem, Byu 1970; (MS) Ed, Weber St Coll 1984; Supervisory/ Admin Certificate, UT St Univ 1988; *cr:* Math/His Teacher Union Park Jr HS 1970-71; 6th Grade Teacher Lincoln Elem 1971-72; Refrigeration Suprv Trans Amer Trailer 1972-74; 6th Grade Teacher Farmington Elem 1974-; *ai:* City Ftbl, Jr Jazz Bsktbl, Church Bsktbl Coach; Improvement & Prof Dev Comm Chm 1978-79; Davis Ed Assn Exec Bd Mem 1976-78; BSA (Scouting Coord 1978-83, Comm Chm 1984-88, Comm Mem 1988-); Acting Prin 1983-; *office:* Farmington Elem Sch 50 W 200 S Farmington UT 84025

ROBBINS, CAROL ALLEN, English Department Chair; *b:* Putnam, CT; *m:* Franklyn A.; *c:* Kristin, Jonathan; *ed:* (BS) Eng, 1972, (MA) Ed Psych, 1973, Counseling, 1979, (PHD) Higher Ed Admin, 1989 Univ of CT; *cr:* Psych Instr Comm Coll of RI 1974-77; Eng Instr Quinebaug Valley Comm Coll 1988-89; Chairperson/Eng Teacher Plainfield HS 1971-; *ai:* Scholars; Panther Prints; NHS Adv; Academic Decathlon Coach; Canterbury Bd of Ed, Vice-Chairperson 1976-88; Coll Frosh Composition Instr; *office:* Plainfield HS 87 Putnam Rd Central Village CT 06332

ROBBINS, CLAUDIA WILSON, English Department Chair; *b:* Columbia, SC; *m:* Richard B.; *c:* Katherine, Matthew; *ed:* (BA) Eng, Columbia Coll 1974; *cr:* Teacher St Johns HS 1974-; *ai:* Dist Eng Curr & Dept Chairperson; Alpha Delta Kappa Corresponding Secy 1987-; Palmetto St Teachers Assn Cty Chapter VP 1986-; *office:* St Johns HS 545 Spring St Darlington SC 29532

ROBBINS, DAVID G., Literature/Composition Teacher; *b:* St Helens, OR; *m:* Jennifer Ann Sacia; *c:* Amber, Brianna; *ed:* (BA) Eng, Portland St Univ 1970; (MAT) Ed, Lewis & Clark Coll 1976; *cr:* Eng Teacher/Coach Sunset HS 1971-; *ai:* Head Boys Cross Cntry Coach 1971-; Head Track Coach Boys & Girls; Head Ski Coach 1977-79; Beaverton Ed Assn Assembly Rep OR Ed Assn 1989-; OR HS Cross Cntry Coach of Yr 1980, 1982, 1984; Nom Natl HS Cross Cntry Coach of Yr 1984; *office:* Sunset HS PO Box 200 Beaverton OR 97075

ROBBINS, KARIN LESLIE, Physical Education Teacher; *b:* Springfield, VT; *ed:* (BA) Phys Ed, 1969, (MED) Phys Ed, 1977 Harding Coll; *cr:* Phys Ed Teacher Riverside Jr HS 1969-; *ai:* Girls Tennis Team Coach Springfield HS; AAHPEPD; *office:* Riverside Jr HS Fairground Rd Springfield VT 05156

ROBBINS, KATHLEEN L., 2nd/3rd Grade Lang Art Teacher; *b:* Ft Wayne, IN; *c:* Kimberley A., Kristine L.; *ed:* (BS) Elem Ed, IN Univ 1975; (MS) Elem Ed, IUPUI 1981; TESA Trainer & Trainee; *cr:* Pre-Sch Teacher Fall Creek Co-Lp Pre-Sch 1972-74; Teacher MSD Washington Twp 1976-; *ai:* Manage Adopted Grandparent Prgm with Stus at Hoosier Village Health Care; Teach & Manage Summer Enrichment Prgm for Grades K-5; Drama & Dance Presentation Dir; Tour with Prgm; IN Rdng Assn 1986-; Alpha Delta Kappa 1990; IN St Grant Awd 1989; *office:* Greenbriar Elem Sch 8201 N Ditch Rd Indianapolis IN 46260

ROBBINS, LINDA DE WITT, Counselor; *b:* Jackson, AL; *m:* Steve L.; *c:* Lee A.; *ed:* (BA) Eng/Scndry Ed, Univ of Montevallo 1970; (MA) Cnslr Ed, Univ of S AL 1974; *cr:* Teacher Hillsdale Mid Sch 1970-74, Satsuma HS 1974-78; Cnslr R H Watkins HS 1978-81, C F Vigor HS 1981-; *ai:* SE Consortium of Minority Engrs; AL Assn of Counseling & Dev Chapter 8 Pres 1988-89; AL Vocation Assn Secy of Guidance Div 1987-88; Alpha Delta Kappa 1987-; Amer Assn of Curr Supervision 1988-; *office:* C F Vigor HS 913 N Wilson Ave Prichard AL 36610

ROBBINS, MARJORIE GILMARTIN, Second & Third Grade Teacher; *b:* Newton, MA; *m:* Maurice Edward; *c:* John, Greg, Kris; *ed:* (BSED) Elem Ed, Gordon Coll 1962; Grad Stud Univ of S ME, Univ of ME Orono; *cr:* 2nd/4th Grade Teacher Center Sch 1962-64; 2nd Grade Teacher Israel Loring Sch 1965-66; 1st Grade Teacher Cheney Sch 1967-69; 2nd-4th Grade Teacher Palermo Consolidated 1975-; *ai:* ME Sch Union Steering & Gifted/ Talented Comms; Drama Club Coach; Educl Fair Judge; Supervising Teacher for Stu Teacher 1989; Wkshp Presenter; NEA, ME Teachers Assn; Palermo Teachers Assn Pres 1980-82; ME Educators of Gifted & Talented; Palermo Sch Club Exec Bd 1984-87; St Andrews Society 1987-; 2nd Baptist Church 1958-; Winter Street Baptist Church 1990; ME Sch Union Secy; Support Teams (Mem, Chairperson); *home:* 204 Dresden Ave Gardiner ME 04345

ROBBINS, MARY ANN, Fourth Grade Teacher; *b:* Hartford, CT; *m:* Theodore Frederick; *c:* Bonnie A., Todd F.; *ed:* (BA) Liberal Arts, Univ of Hartford 1959; (MA) Religious Ed, Hartford Seminary Fnd 1961; Elem Ed, Univ of NH 1963-68; Ec Ed, Whittemore Sch of Bus Univ of NH; Writing Process, Univ of NH; *cr:* Dir of Religious Ed 1st Baptist Church 1961-63; 4th Grade

Teacher Portsmouth Sch System 1963-66, 1968-; *ai:* Enrichment Comm Mem; Earth Day Coord New Franklin Sch; Alpha Delta Kappa St Chaplain 1990; NEA, NH Educl Assn, Portsmouth Teachers Assn; Amer Baptist Churches Ministers Cncl 1980-; Seacoast Area Clergy; Amer Baptist Women in Ministry; Asst to Minister Mid St Baptist Church 1980-90; Church World Service, Crop Walk For Hunger Participant & Comm 1981-90; Ordained Amer Baptist Minister; Curr Writer for Amer Baptist Educl Ministries; Sears Roebuck Fnd Fellowship Awd; *home:* 115 Piscataqua St Box 169 New Castle NH 03854

ROBBINS, MEGAN PRICE, Art/Physical Ed Teacher; *b:* East Chicago, IN; *m:* R. M.; *ed:* (BS) Elem Art, Univ of Indianapolis 1975; (MS) Elem Ed, IN Univ 1980; *cr:* (1) Art Lawrence MSD Elem 1976-79; (2) Spencer Elem 1979-81; (3) Art/Phys Ed/Music Teacher Patricksburg/Gosport Elem 1982-89; (4) Art/Phys Ed Teacher Patricksburg/Spencer Elem 1989-; *ai:* AHA Jump Rope for Heart Coord; Art Club; IN Assn for Gifted; IN Assn for Health/Phys Ed/Dance; Delta Kappa Gamma Gamma Nu; *office:* Patricksburg/Spencer Elem Sch PO Box 212 Patricksburg IN 47455

ROBBINS, MIACHEL L., Fifth Grade Teacher; *b:* Brodhead, KY; *m:* Peggy Diann Cash; *c:* Christopher; *ed:* (BS) Bus, W KY Univ 1977; (MS) Elem Ed, 1980, Sch Admin/Supervision, 1982 E KY Univ; *cr:* Teacher Livingston Elem 1977-; *ai:* Jr Beta, 4-H Club; NEA, KY Educl Assn 1977-; Lions Club Pres 1989-; Cty 4-H Cncl Pres 1980-; *office:* Livingston Elem Sch PO Box 190 Main St Livingston KY 40445

ROBBINS, NANCY (PHILLIPS), Developmental Teacher; *b:* Miami, OK; *m:* Rance; *c:* Mandy, Kade, Clay; *ed:* (BA) Elem Ed, NSU Tahlequah 1975; Assoc Elem Ed/Child Dev, NEO A&M 1977; (MS) Elem Ed, NSU Tahlequah 1984; Early Chldhd, NSU Tahlequah 1986; Gesell Developmental Testing; *cr:* 3rd Grade Title Teacher 1979-80, 4th Grade Teacher 1980-81, 2nd Grade Teacher 1981-83; Pre 1st Grade Teacher 1983-84, Elem/Early Chldhd Teacher 1979- Jay Public Schls; *ai:* Jay Livestock Booster Club; 4-H Leader; OEA, NEA, Chrstn Educators Assn, Assn of Chldhd Ed Intnl; Bus & Prof Women, Dist Career Woman of Yr 1990; Assembly of God Church; Jay Livestock Booster Club Past Officer; Idea Published in Book 1989; Elem Teacher of Yr 1986; *office:* Jay Grade Sch Drawer C-I Jay OK 74346

ROBBINS, NANCY TAYLOR, Teacher of Gifted & Talented; *b:* Houston, TX; *c:* Jason D., Adam G., Mark S.; *ed:* (BA) Elem Ed, Baylor Univ 1965; (MED) Elem Ed, Stephen F Austin St Univ 1990; Various Wkshps & Seminars; *cr:* 5th Grade Teacher Victoria Public Schls 1965-67; 3rd Grade Teacher 1967, Teacher of Trainable Mentally Retarded Children 1967-68 Beeville Public Schls; 2nd/3rd Grade Teacher Independence Public Schls 1968-69; Pre-Sch Ed Dir Memorial Hospital Systems 1970-71; 4th Grade Soc Stud Teacher New Caney Ind Sch Dist 1971-72; 3rd Grade Teacher Huffman Ind Sch Dist 1972-73; Pre-Sch Ed Dir Little Red Schoolhouse 1973-74; 1st Grade Teacher Crosby Ind Sch Dist 1977-79; 5th Grade Teacher Alvarado Ind Sch Dist 1979-82; 4th Grade Teacher 1982-83, 6th Grade Lang Art/Gifted & Talented Teacher 1983-88, K-8th Grade Gifted & Talented/AIM Prgm Teacher 1988- Fairfield Ind Sch Dist; *ai:* Gifted & Talented Super Saturday Coord Fairfield Ind Sch Dist 1984-86; Eng/Lang Art/Journalism Textbook Selection Comm Fairfield Ind Sch Dist 1984; Fairfield Ind Sch Dist Living Classroom Coord 1988-, Staff Dev Presenter 1985-86; Fairfield Ind Sch Dist UIL Prose Judge 1989, Contest Dir 1990; Delta Kappa Gamma Ceremonial Chm 1989-; TX St Teachers Assn Local VP 1983-84; TX Assn For Gifted & Talented; Mary Moody Northern Lib Childrens Fund Raiser Coord; Project Graduation Comm Mem 1989; 1st United Meth Church Choir; Baylor Stu Teacher of Yr 1965; Career Ladder Level 2 Fairfield Ind Sch Dist; Instructional Leader Eng/Lang Art Fairfield Ind Sch Dist 1983-85; Fairfield Ind Sch Dist Staff Dev Presenter Living Classroom 1985-86, K-12th Teacher on Gifted Ed 1988; Fairfield Ind Sch Dist Ed Conference Presenter 1985; TAIR Conference Facilitator 1989; *office:* Fairfield Ind Sch Dist 615 Post Oak Rd Fairfield TX 75840

ROBBINS, PAMELA S., Parenting/Mathematics Teacher; *b:* Mt Vernon, IL; *m:* William; *c:* Emily, Curt; *ed:* (AA) General Stud, Rend Lake Coll 1973; (BS) Home Ec Ed, Murray St Univ 1975; (MSED) Guidance/Counseling, E IL Univ 1990; *cr:* Home Ec/Math Teacher Fairfield Cmmty HS 1980-; *ai:* Stu Cncl Spon; IL Home Ec Assn Dist VI Treas 1975-; Amer Home Ec Assn 1975-; IL Voc Home Ec Assn 1980-; S Cntrl IL Teachers of Math 1988-; *office:* Fairfield Cmmty HS 300 W King Fairfield IL 62837

ROBBINS, PETER, Science Department Chairman; *b:* Cleveland, OH; *m:* Helen Lois Weeks; *c:* Mark, Amy; *ed:* (BS) Bio, Mansfield Univ 1967; (MS) Earth Sci, VA St Univ 1970; Edinboro Univ Natl Sci Fnd Geology Summer Grant; *cr:* Sci Teacher 1967-, Sci Dept Chm 1984- Haverling Cntrl Sch; *ai:* Sci Club & Acad All Star Adv; Soccer Referee; VA St Univ Natl Sci Fnd Grants 1969-70; *office:* Haverling Cntrl Sch 25 Ellas Ave Bath NY 14810

ROBBINS, ROGER LEO, 6th Grade Teacher/Elem Prin; *b:* Bozeman, MT; *m:* M. Joann Baker; *c:* Sarah, Nicholas; *ed:* (BS) Elem Ed, E Mt Coll 1976; (MS) Elem Ed, N Mt Coll 1985; Admin Courses, Spec Ed Endorsement; *cr:* 4th-5th Grade Teacher Winifred Public Sch 1976-77; 1st Grade Teacher 1977-78, 5th Grade Teacher 1978-84, 6th Grade Teacher 1985- Cascade Public Sch; *ai:* Mid Sch Vlybl Coach; NEA, MT Ed Assn 1977-; Natl Assn of Elem Sch Prins 1989-; Gideons 1983-84; Triumph Luth Church (Trustee, Chm) 1983-85; *office:* Cascade Elem Sch West End of Central Ave Cascade MT 59421

ROBBINS, SANDRA KAY STANLEY, Science Teacher; *b:* Shelby, NC; *m:* Ray Marshall Jr.; *c:* Melissa Margaret, Mary Elizabeth, Meredith Christine; *ed:* (BS) Sci Ed, Gardner-Webb Coll 1988; Converse Coll; *cr:* Teacher R-S Cntrl 1988; *ai:* Civinettes Spon United Way Rep for Sch; Acadmc Letter Comm; Sci Dept Comm; Womens Tennis Coach; Sci Fair Chairperson; NSTA 1987-; NCSTA 1987-; Uptown Revitialization Comm Rutherford Town Fair Co-Chairperson Civinette Plaque for Leadership 1989-;Youth Group Leader 1st Bap Rutherfordton 1988-; Mission Friends Dir 1987-88; Pres Sunday Sch Class 1988-89; Gardner Webb Coll Ed Dept Awd; *office:* R S Central HS 1 Laurel Dr Rutherfordton NC 28139

ROBBINS, SUSAN MEYERS, Mathematics Teacher/Dept Chair; *b:* Buffalo, NY; *m:* Martin; *c:* Zachary, Andrew; *ed:* (BS) Math Ed, NC St Univ 1978; *cr:* Math Teacher Wake Cty Public Schls 1979-83, Pender Cty Public Schls 1983-; *ai:* Math Fair Coord; NCCTM 1983-; NCTM 1988-; *office:* Pender HS Rt 2 Burgaw NC 28425

ROBBINS, WAYNE RUSSELL, Scndry Social Studies Teacher; *b:* Elmira, NY; *ed:* (BS) Scndry Soc Stud Ed, Suny Geneseo 1969; *cr:* 12th Grade Soc Stud Teacher Frankfort HS 1972-74; Scndry Soc Stud Teacher Letchworth Cntrl Sch 1974-; *ai:* Sr/Jr Class, Closeup Fnd Adv; Var & Jr Var Wrestling, Ftbl, Bsbl Coach; Letchworth Cntrl Teachers Assn (Pres 1988-, Chief Negotiator 1986-); *office:* Letchworth Cntrl Sch 5550 School Rd Gainesville NY 14066

ROBEAU, SALLY GARWOOD, History Dept Chair; *b:* Corpus Christi, TX; *m:* J. Ruel Jr.; *c:* James, Stephen, David, Catherine Campbell, Cheri Mc Cormick; *ed:* (BS) Ed His, 1973, (MS) Ed, 1979 TX A&I Univ; Historical Research Course, Univ of TX; Cmptr Trng Courses; *cr:* Teacher Calallen Ind Sch Dist 1973-; *ai:* Jr-Sr HS Historians Spon; Curr Comm; NCSS 1989-; TX Cncl of Soc Stud 1989; Assn of Teachers & Prof Educators 1982-; Nueces Cty Historical Society; Nueces Cty Historical Commission Chm 1981-82; TX Oral His Assn; Nuecestown Schoolhouse Historical Center (Pres, 1984-, Coord); Daughters of Amer Revolution Outstanding Amer Hist Teacher for TX 1988; Daughters of the Republic of TX Regional Winner Outstanding TX Teacher 1986; TX St Historical Assn Leadership in Ed 1989; *office:* Calallen Mid Sch 4602 Cornett Corpus Christi TX 78410

ROBERSON, ANNE H., Media Specialist; *b:* Thomasville, NC; *m:* Paul M.; *c:* Kenneth; *ed:* (BS) Primary Ed, Appalachian St Univ 1959; (MSLS) Lib Sci, Univ of NC 1968; *cr:* 3rd Grade Teacher Hartsell Sch 1959-62; Media Specialist Tuckasegee Sch 1962-73; Devonshire Sch 1970-73; Berryhill Sch 1976-; *ai:* Univ NC Alumni Assn Treas 1977-79; Amer Lib Assn 1976-; NC Lib Assn 1976-; Beta Sigma Phi 1968-; *office:* Berryhill Elem Sch 10501 Walkers Ferry Rd Charlotte NC 28208

ROBERSON, BEBE HAYDEN, Fifth/Sixth Soc Stud Teacher; *b:* Brooksville, MS; *m:* Jackie; *c:* Cindy Mitchell, Jerry W.; *ed:* (BA) Elem Ed, Livingston Univ 1974; (MED) Elem Ed, MS St Univ 1980; *cr:* Soc Stud Teacher Clarkdale Sch 1974-; *ai:* Phi Kappa Phi Honor Society; MS Cncl for Soc Stud; Lauderdale Cty Schls Teacher of Yr 1988; Clarkdale PTA; Author of World Regions; *home:* Rt 1 Box 573 Meridian MS 39301

ROBERSON, BETTY MOORE, 4th Grade Teacher; *b:* Lamesa, TX; *m:* Scott; *c:* Scotty, Gordon; *ed:* (BS) Elem Ed, TX Technological 1969; (MED) Rdng, Sam Houston Univ 1970; *cr:* 1st Grade Teacher Cleveland Elem 1972-73; 8th Grade Teacher Seminole Jr HS 1980-87; 4th Grade Teacher Seminole Elem 1987-; *ai:* Communications Comm; Refusal Skills Team; Keyboarder; Delta Kappa Gamma 1982-; TX Classroom Teachers Assn Pres 1980-; Seminole Music Club 1983-; *office:* Seminole Ind Sch Dist 600 SW Avenue B Seminole TX 79360

ROBERSON, JANICE HOOPER, Third Grade Teacher; *b:* Dyersburg, TN; *m:* Gene; *c:* Danny, Terry, Teresa Roberson Wiggins; *ed:* (BS) Early Chldhd Ed, Univ of TN Martin 1972; *cr:* 6th Grade Teacher Obion Elem 1960-61; 3rd Grade Teacher Black Oak Elem 1961-; *ai:* Obion Cty Ed Assn, West TN Ed Assn, NEA 1960-; Troy United Meth Church 1949-; PTA 1960-; Rep Obion Cty WTEA 1970; *office:* Black Oak Elem Sch Shawtown Rd Hornbeak TN 38232

ROBERSON, JODY DODD, Mathematics Teacher; *b:* Big Spring, TX; *m:* David W. Jr.; *c:* Melissa Denney, Barbra; *ed:* (BS) Scndry Ed, TX Tech Univ 1973; Conference Advancement Math Teaching; TX Math Staff Dev Module #23; Strategies Enhancing Self-Esteem in Classroom; Using Calculators Math Curr; Implementation of NCTM Strategies; Personel Cmptr Classroom Management; Math Prgm; Several Wkshps; *cr:* Mid Sch Math Teacher Lubbock Cooper 1973-74; Mid Sch/HS Math Teacher New Home 1974-78, Tahoka 1978-82, Sands 1982-84; HS Eng Teacher Rankin 1984-85; HS Math Teacher Crane 1985-; *ai:* Stu Cncl; Textbook, Test & Measurements Correlate Comms; Delta Kappa Gamma VP 1989-; Univ Women, TX Classroom Teachers Assn VP 1987-; NCTM 1989-; Teacher of Yr Lubbock Cooper & New Home; TX Ed Career Ladder II; *home:* Box 756 Crane TX 79731

ROBERSON, MARY GRACE, Band Director; *b:* Ft Stockton, TX; *m:* James Paul; *ed:* (BM) Music Ed, Hardin-Simmons Univ 1979; Working Towards Masters Music Ed, Hardin-Simmons Univ; *cr:* Band Dir Robert Lee Ind Sch DiSt 1979-84, Highland Jr HS 1984-; *ai:* Hobbs HS Band Asst; MENC 1984-; Phi Beta Mu 1985-; Sigma Alpha Iota (VP 1978-79) 1975-, Sword of Honor 1979; SW Symphony Hobbs 2nd Clarinet 1985-; *office:* Highland Jr HS 2500 N Jefferson Hobbs NM 88240

ROBERT, EARLENE MILLER, Mathematics Teacher; *b:* Attleboro, MA; *m:* Victor Jr.; *c:* Keri, Kristin; *ed:* (BA) Math, Bridgewater St Coll 1972; Grad Courses Worcester Polytech Inst; *cr:* Math Teacher N Attleboro HS 1972-; *ai:* Sch Improvement Cncl; NATA, MTA 1972-; Norton Cntry Club 1989-; *office:* N Attleboro HS Landry Ave North Attleboro MA 02760

ROBERT, VICTOR PAUL, JR., Social Studies Dept Chair; *b:* Pawtucket, RI; *m:* Earlene Miller; *c:* Keri, Kristin; *ed:* (BS) Ed, 1969, (MS) His, Providence Coll 1972; *cr:* His Teacher 1971-87, Soc Stud Dept Chm Tolman HS 1987-; *ai:* Century III Leadership Schlsp; Basic Ed Prgm Comm; Pawtuckets Rep for RI Sch Dist Teacher of Yr 1986; *office:* Tolman HS 150 Exchange St Pawtucket RI 02860

ROBERTA, M., SDR, Jr HS Religion Teacher; *b:* Buffalo, NY; *ed:* (BSE) Ed, Carlow Coll 1960; (MA) Theology, Univ of Windsor 1972; Duquesne Univ, Seton Hill Coll, St John Coll, Notre Dame Univ; *cr:* HS Teacher Divine Redeemer Acad & Duquesne Univ 1953-60; Art/Religion Teacher Boyle HS 1962-68, Serra HS 1972-75, Elyria Cath HS & Borromeo Coll 1975-82: Religion Teacher St Bartholomew Sch 1960-62, 1982-; *ai:* Sch Evaluation Teams for Diocese; Illustrated 4 Religion HS Textbooks; Planned & Designed Stained Glass Windows for 3 Churches; Professor at Duquesne Univ & Borromeo Coll; Art Articles Published; *home:* 141 Erhardt Dr Pittsburgh PA 15235

ROBERTS, ALICE JACKSON, 6th Grade Teacher; *b:* Dunn, NC; *w:* Harry B. (dec); *c:* Alice A., Harriett E.; *ed:* (AA) Elem Ed, Campbell Coll 1959; (BS) Elem Ed, Atlantic Chrstn 1961; Mentor Teacher Trng; *cr:* Classroom Teacher Coats Sch 1961-72, Lafayette 1972-73, Coats Sch 1973-; *ai:* Chrldr Spon/Coach; Head Spring Fund Raiser, Math Comm for Re Accrediation; Comm Long Range Goals; Ticket Comm NCAE Banquet; Supts Advisory Cncl Rep; Annual Staff; NEA 1961-; NCAE 1961-; Coats Womans Club 1961-73; Sunday Sch Teacher 1970; Democratic Women 1990; Benevolence Comm 1988-; *home:* Box 398 Coats NC 27521

ROBERTS, ANNE TINSLEY, Computer Applications Teacher; *b:* Richmond, VA; *m:* Michael Allen; *c:* Michael Allen Jr., John Samuel; *ed:* (BS) Bus Ed, Longwood Coll 1983; Guidance & Cnslng ; *cr:* Teacher Isle of Wight Acad 1983-85; Prince George HS 1985-; *ai:* FBLA Spon; *office:* Prince George H S 7801 Laurel Spring Rd Prince George VA 23875

ROBERTS, BARBARA BLUM, Fifth Grade Teacher; *b:* Temple, TX; *ed:* (BS) Ed, SW TX St Univ 1968; Certificate Elem Ed, Art, Lang, Learning Disabilities; *cr:* 4th Grade Teacher 1968-70, 5th Grade Teacher 1970-79, Whitcomb Elem; 5th Grade Teachedr Landolt Elem 1979-; *ai:* Sch Spelling Bee & Sch Talent Show Coord; Sch Sci Fair Co-Coord; Clear Creek Ind Sch Dist Textbook Adoption Mem; PTA 1968-, TX Lifetime Mem 1988; TX St Teachers Assn Life Mem 1968-; TX Classroom Teachers Assn 1968-74, 1989-; CTA Secy 1968-69; Nassau Bay Volunteer Fire Dept 1979-82, Medic of Yr 1980; Clear Creek Ind Sch Dist Gifted Dept Comm Mem; Natl Rdng Conference Co-Speaker; Clear Creek Ind Sch Dist First Aid for Classroom Co-Speaker; *office:* Landolt Elem Sch 2401 Pilgrims Point Friendswood TX 77546

ROBERTS, BEATRICE HESS, Fourth Grade Teacher; *b:* Benton, PA; *m:* Earnest L.; *c:* Thomas L. Fought, Jr., Tracey L. Fought, Ravis; *ed:* (BS) Elem Ed, Bloomsburg ST Coll 1961; Addl Studies Graduate Courses Bloomsburg Univ; *cr:* 1st Grade Teacher 1962-88; 4th Grade Teacher 1988- L Ray Appleman Elem Sch; *ai:* Chairwomen Benton Area HS Schlsp Comm; NEA 1962-; PSEA 1962-; BAEA 1962-; PACE 1980-; Columbia Co Democratic Comm Woman for Benton Boro 1986-; Chairwoman of Benton Recreation Comm; Pres & Sec Benton Area Alumni Assn; *home:* Box J Third St Benton PA 17814

ROBERTS, BILLIE CROOKS, 5th Grade Teacher; *b:* Gustine, CA; *m:* James L.; *c:* Allison Sweeney, Sean Sweeney, Kelli; *ed:* (BS) Elem Ed, Fitchburg St Coll 1963; Univ of NV; *cr:* 4th Grade Teacher Shawsheen Sch 1963-64; Winthrop Schls 1964-65/1973-77; Owyhee Sch 1977-82; 5th Grade Teacher Jackpot Combined Sch 1982-; *ai:* Assn Bd 1978-80; (VP 1983-87 Pres 1987-); Elko Cty Classroom Teachers Assn; NV St Ed Assn; NEA; *office:* Jackpot Combined Sch P O Box 463 Jackpot NV 89825

ROBERTS, CARLENE COPELAND, 6th Grade Teacher; *b:* Tuscaloosa, AL; *m:* Bruce Lee; *c:* Bruce L., Destry; *ed:* (BS) Elem Ed, 1976, (MS) Rdng/Elem Ed, 1983 USM Gulf Park; *cr:* Lang Art Teacher Woolmarket Elem 1976-80; *ai:* 6th Grade Honor Roll & Public Relations Chairperson; Intnl Rdng Assn, MS Rdng Assn NIE Chairperson, Seashore Rdng Cncl (VP 1989-, Pres); TOPS MS 190 1986-, St KOPS Beauty Awd 1987; Teacher of Yr Woolmarket Elem 1989, Teacher of Month Orange Grove Kiwanis Intnl 1988; Nom MS Power Fnd Teacher of Excl; Harrison Cty Staff Dev Plaques 1987-89; *office:* Woolmarket Elem Sch 12513 John Lee Rd Biloxi MS 39532

ROBERTS, CHARLENE FELTEN, First Grade Teacher; *b:* Chicago, IL; *m:* Ron; *c:* James; *ed:* (BS) Elem Ed, FL Intnl Univ 1974; *cr:* Teacher Carol City Chrstn Acad 1971-73; Asst Teacher Scott Lake Elem 1974-75; Teacher Northwest Chrstn Acad 1975-; *ai:* Jr HS Vlybl Coach; Girls in Action Dir 1976-; *office:* NW Chrstn Acad 951 Nw 136th St Miami FL 33168

ROBERTS, DIANE (BURDEN), 7th/8th Grade Math Teacher; *b:* Ryan, OK; *m:* Charles D.; *ed:* (BS) Ed, SE OK St Univ 1969; *cr:* 7th/8th Grade Math/8th Grade Algebra Teacher Burkburnett Ind Sch Dist 1969-; *ai:* Campus Improvement Team & Effective

Schls Team Mem; Local TSTA (Secy 1975-76, Treas 1974-75, 1989-); TCTM, NCTM, TMSCA, NEA, TSTA; *home:* 600 Mimosa Box 973 Burkburnett TX 76354

ROBERTS, DONNA RAINEY, English Teacher; *b:* Quincy, MA; *m:* Dallas Melvyn; *c:* Stuart, Rainey Roberts Perry, Heather; *ed:* (BS) Eng Ed, Liberty Univ 1977; (MED) Eng Ed, Lynchburg Coll 1989; *cr:* Eng Teacher Brookville HS 1977-79; Eng Teacher Lynchburg Christian Acad 1977-; Eng Instr Liberty Univ 1989; *ai:* Drama/Forensics/Chrldng/Stu Cncl Yrbk/Class Spon; Natl Honor Soc 1961; Natl Thespian Soc 1960-61; Traveled with Students to Europe 3 Times; *home:* PO Box 20 Lynch Station VA 24571

ROBERTS, FAIMON AUSTIN, Middle Sch Science Instructor; *b:* Scranton, PA; *m:* Elizabeth Simmons; *c:* Faimon, Laura, Anna; *ed:* (BA) Math, Univ of Montevallo 1964; (MED) Sch Admin, LA St Univ 1978; *cr:* Teacher E Baton Rouge Parish Schls 1969-78, Univ Lab Sch 1980-; *ai:* Ftbl Coach; Stu Cncl Spon; NSTA (Mid Level Comm, Teacher Ed Comm) 1984-; LA Sci Teachers Assn (Pres 1985-87) 1984-, Mid Sch Teacher of Yr 1985; Camp Fire Youth Leg Dir 1982-, Service Awd 1983; Presidential Awd Sch Teaching St Winner 1985, 1987; Gulf Sts Utilities Grant Energy Wkshp; *office:* Univ Laboratory Sch LSU Baton Rouge LA 70803

ROBERTS, GARY GRAY, 5th Grade Teacher; *b:* Kansas City, KS; *m:* Arlene Robinette; *c:* Amy A,, Abby J.; *ed:* (BS) Elem Ed, Phillips Univ 1972; Skills for Adolescence Instr; *cr:* 4th Grade Teacher Chisholm Elem Sch 1972-74; 5th-6th Grade Teacher Pioneer Pleasant Vale Sch 1974-; *ai:* Asst Bsktbl & Track Coach; Pioneer Pleasant Vale Assn Classroom Teachers Pres 1977-78; NEA, OEA 1972-; Cherokee Strip Rdng Cncl VP 1988-89; *office:* Pioneer Pleasant Vale Sch 6020 E Willow Enid OK 73701

ROBERTS, GEORGAN GRADY, Mid Sch Lang Art Dept Chairman; *b:* Lakeland, FL; *m:* Charles A.; *c:* Carrie A. Roberts Barnes, Kellie L. Roberts Rendek; *ed:* (BAE) Early Chldhd/Elem Ed/Mid Sch Lang Art, Univ of FL 1965; (MS) Supervision/Admin, Nova Univ; Inservice Trng; *cr:* Teacher High Springs Elem 1965, Newberry Elem 1969, Newberry Jr/Sr HS 1985; *ai:* Mid Sch Lang Art Dept Chm; 6th Grade Team Leader; Delta Kappa Gamma 1978; City Commissioner Mayor Pro Tem 1987-; High Springs Historical Society Treas 1986-; *home:* 210 NE 4th Ave PO Box 746 High Springs FL 32643

ROBERTS, GEORGE ALBERT, Writing & English Lit Teacher; *b:* Chicago, IL; *m:* Beverly Ann Dornier; *c:* Andrew, Juliet; *ed:* (BA) Eng Lit/Fr Lit, St Johns Univ 1965; (MA) Teaching, Coll of St Thomas 1970; Fr Lit, Sorbonne Paris France 1965-66; Amer Lit, Univ of MN 1968-69; *cr:* Eng Teacher Stillwater Public Schls 1969-70; Eng/Fr Teacher Minneapolis Public Schls 1970-; *ai:* Adv Lunchboy Theater; Dir Writing as Performance; NEH Fellow Yale 1982, Harvard 1986; Poetry Books Published 1976, 1981, 1986; St Arts Bd Grants 1976, 1981; *office:* North Cmmty HS 1500 James Ave N Minneapolis MN 55411

ROBERTS, HATTIE WETUSKI, 4th Grade Mathematics Teacher; *b:* Houston, TX; *m:* Dennis Lane; *c:* Copie D., Lane D., Brant D.; *ed:* (BS) Elem Ed, E TX St Univ 1975; *cr:* 3rd/4th Grade Math Teacher 1975-76; 4th Grade Math/Sci Teacher 1976-85; 4th Grade Math/Sci/Soc Stud Teacher 1985-89; 4th Grade Math Teacher 1989-; *ai:* TX St Teachers Assn Pres 1984-85; PTA Pres 1984-85; United Meth Women Pres 1988-; St Judes Math-A-Thon Chairperson.

ROBERTS, J. BERRY, Math Dept Chair/Teacher; *b:* Clinton, IA; *c:* James B. V; *ed:* (BA) Math, Western WA Univ 1966; Western WA Univ; *cr:* Teacher Shuksan Mid Sch 1966-71, Utterback Mid Sch 1971-; *ai:* Natl Jr Honor Society Adv; Audio-visual, Testing Coord; NEA; Tucson Ed Assn Building Rep 1972-77; Tucson Ftbl Ofcls 1971-; Tucson Bsktbl Ofcls (Pres 1985-86, Secy 1978-) 1971-; Tucson Pop Warner F B Ofcls Commissioner 1981-; Natl Sci Fnd Fellow 1968-69; *office:* Utterback Mid Sch 3233 S Pinal Vista Tucson AZ 85713

ROBERTS, JEAN HITCHCOCK, Fourth Grade Teacher; *b:* Macon, GA; *m:* George W.; *c:* Glen, Karen, David; *ed:* (BAE) Elem Ed, 1952, (MED) Elem Ed, 1957 Univ of FL; Grad Courses in Gifted Ed; *cr:* Teacher, Alachua Sch Dist 1952-53, Jacksonville Sch Dist 1953-55, Gainesville Sch Dist 1955-57, Louisville Sch Dist 1957-60, Jacksonville Sch Dist 1961-64, Brooksville Sch Dist 1964-65, Fernandina Beach Sch Dist 1965-66, Perry Sch Dist 1966-67, Denton Sch Dist 1967-68, Gerrish-Higgins Sch Dist 1968-69; Tri Cty Sch Dist 1969-; *ai:* Prof Dev & Partners in Ed Comm; Negotiating Team Rep; MI Ed Assn 1969-; NEA Life Membership; Tri Cty Ed Secy 1969-; First Baptist Church Mem; Intnl Conference of Meteorological & Oceanographic Society Grant 1989; Teacher of Yr Awd 1990; Co-Author of Ed Handbook on Cooperating Teachers for St of FL 1963; *home:* 635 Park St Box 96 Howard City MI 49329

ROBERTS, JOAN CAROL (SMITH), High School English Teacher; *b:* Lyons, NY; *m:* Kenneth L.; *ed:* (AA) General Ed, Auburn Comm Coll 1965; (BS) Ed, 1967, (MS) Ed, 1971 St Univ Coll Buffalo; *cr:* Eng Teacher Kenmore East Sr HS 1967-; *ai:* Youth & Adult Yoga Instr; Natl Assn of HS Eng Teachers 1982-; Golden Poet Awd 1989; Poem to be Published 1990; *office:* Kenmore East Sr HS 350 Fries Rd Tonawanda NY 14150

ROBERTS, JOHN JOSEPH, Social Studies Teacher; *b:* Chicago, IL; *ed:* (BS) Elem Ed, Chicago St Univ 1976; *cr:* 4th-6th Grade Teacher St Philip Neri Sch 1976-79; 5th Grade Teacher Metcalfe Magnet 1979-81; 7th/8th Grade Teacher St Paul Sch 1981-83; Soc Stud Teacher Metcalfe Magnet 1983-; *ai:* Soc Stud Dept Chm; Hockey & Bsbl Coach; CTU 1983-; AEA 1976-; PTA 1976-; *office:* Metcalfe Magnet Sch 12339 S Normal Chicago IL 60628

ROBERTS, JOHN W., Mathematics Teacher; *b:* Salem, IL; *m:* Judith Leekrone; *c:* Don, Doug, Kim; *ed:* (BS) Biological Sci, S IL Univ 1964; *cr:* Math Instr Salem Elem Sch Dist III 1964-; *ai:* Bsktbl Coach 1964-74, 1987-88; Mathcounts Coach 1984-; IEA, NEA; *office:* Franklin Park Sch 1325 N Franklin Salem IL 62881

ROBERTS, JUDY POYNER, Second Grade Teacher; *b:* Danville, IL; *m:* C. Geren; *c:* Heather, Dustin, Ashley; *ed:* (BA) Elem Ed, IL St Univ 1976; (MS) Ed/Rdng, Univ of IL Champaign Urbana 1985; *cr:* Chapter I Rdng/Kndgtn Teacher 1977-88, 2nd Grade Teacher 1988- Gifford Grade Sch; *ai:* Kappa Delta Pi Mem 1977-; IL Ed Assn Mem 1984-; Outstanding Teacher Awd 1988-89; *home:* 322 N West St Box 535 Gifford IL 61847

ROBERTS, LINDA CAROL (BRADY), First Grade Teacher; *b:* Amba, KY; *m:* Bertchel; *ed:* (BA) Ed, Pikeville Coll 1968; Continuing Ed, Miami Univ OH; *cr:* 1st Grade Teacher West Elkton Elem; *ai:* Administrative Staff Comm; NEA, OEA; PSLEA 20 Yr Service 1988; Tutoring Indigent Children; *office:* W Elkton Elem Sch State Rt 503 Box 97 West Elkton OH 45070

ROBERTS, MARIAN RUTH, Jr/Sr HS Trigonometry Teacher; *b:* Picher, OK; *m:* Thomas Paul; *c:* Melinda, Stephanie; *ed:* (BSED) Elem Ed, KS St Coll 1966; (MS) Ed/Math, SW OK St Univ Weatherford 1987; *cr:* 4th Grade Teacher Lamar Public Sch 1965-66; 1st/4th Grade Remedial Teacher Baxter Springs KS 1966-72; Elem Teacher Dewey OK 1977-83; K-5th Grade Jr/Sr HS Math Teacher Butler OK 1983-; *ai:* Jr/Sr Class Spon; NEA, OEA 1977-; Meth Church; *home:* 133 Sandra Rd Clinton OK 73601

ROBERTS, MARLENE B., Business Education Teacher; *b:* Johnstown, PA; *m:* W. Richard; *c:* Justin, Scott, Christopher; *ed:* Assoc Exec Secretarial, Mt Aloysius Jr Coll 1969; (BS) Bus Ed, Shippensburg Univ 1972; Teacher Cert PA St Univ; *cr:* Bus Teacher Cambria Rowe Bus Coll 1972, Richland Area HS 1974-75, Conemaugh Valley HS 1975-79, Greater Johnstown HS 1982-; *office:* Greater Johnstown HS 222 Central Ave Johnstown PA 15902

ROBERTS, MELINDA JANE, Third Grade Teacher; *b:* Noblesville, IN; *m:* Edward O. Jr.; *c:* Betsi, Sara; *ed:* (BS) Elem Ed, 1979, (MS) Elem Ed, 1983 IN Univ; *cr:* 5th Grade Teacher 1980-85, 2nd Grade Teacher 1986-87 Fall Creek Elem; 3rd Grade Teacher Fishers Elem 1988-; *ai:* Chm of Evaluation Comm for Sch Accreditation Process; White River Chrstn Church Mem; Developed & Presented Wkshp Ec Ed IN Prof Educators Fall Conference 1986; *home:* 604 Tulip Ct Noblesville IN 46060

ROBERTS, MICHAEL DON, Bible Teacher; *b:* Lubbock, TX; *m:* Cynthia Clarke; *c:* James; *ed:* (BA) Religion, OK Baptist Univ 1979; Working Towards Masters Divinity, SW Baptist Theological Seminary 1979-85; *cr:* Pastor New Hope Baptist Church 1982-85; Teacher Castle Hills 1st Baptist Sch 1985-; *ai:* Sr Class Spon; Tennis & Asst Var Girls Vlybl Coach; OBU Pres 1989-; *home:* 6975 Sunset Vlg San Antonio TX 78249

ROBERTS, PATRICIA HANCOCK, 1st Grade Teacher; *b:* Sparta, TN; *m:* Billy Carl; *c:* Tiffany J. Campbell; *ed:* (BS) Elem Ed, 1967, (MA) Ed/Rdng, 1976, (EDs) Ed Admin/Supervision, 1986 TN Technological Univ; *cr:* Librarian Bondecroft/Doyle/Findlay/Cassville/Central View 1967-75; 1st/2nd Grade Teacher Findlay Elem Sch 1975-; *ai:* Alpha Delta Kappa Pres 1978-; Phi Delta Kappa 1986-; Intnl Rdng Assn 1980-; Cty Lib Bd; *home:* Rt 3 Box 293 A Sparta TN 38583

ROBERTS, PATRICIA MORRIS, 3rd Grade Teacher; *b:* Lexington, KY; *m:* Owen L.; *c:* Shawn Morris, Shannon Morris; *ed:* (AB) Elem Ed, Morehead St Univ 1969; Elem Ed, E KY Univ 1978; *cr:* 4th Grade Teacher N Middletown Elem Sch 1969-73; 3rd Grade Teacher Huntertown Elem 1976-; *ai:* KEA 1969-; Glens Creek Church Recording Secy 1989-; *office:* Huntertown Elem Sch Rt 6 Huntertown Rd Versailles KY 40383

ROBERTS, PATTI PALMER, Mathematics Teacher; *b:* Port Arthur, TX; *m:* Alvin E. Jr.; *c:* Matthew, Joel; *ed:* (BS) Scndry Ed, Lamar Univ 1981; Grad Stud Ed; Numerous Wkshps Through Region V Service Center; *cr:* Math Teacher Lumberton HS 1981-; *ai:* NHS Spon; *office:* Lumberton HS PO Box 8123 Lumberton TX 77625

ROBERTS, RITA CAROL, 6th-8th Grade Reading Teacher; *b:* Hundred, WV; *m:* David E.; *c:* Chris; *ed:* (BS) Elem Ed, 1970, (MA) Rdng, 1979 WV Univ; Effective Schls, TESA, Cooperative Learning; *cr:* Remedial Rdng Teacher Hundred Elem 1970-73; Remedial Rdng Teacher 1978-84, 6th-8th Grade Eng Teacher 1985-86, 6th-8th Grade Rdng Teacher 1986- Long Drain Sch; *ai:* Academic Coach; Cultural Arts Co-Chairperson; FFA Speech Competition Adv; Mid Sch Task Force; Wetzel Cty Ed Assn (Building Rep 1987-) 1978-; WVEA, NEA 1978-; Hundred Public Lib Bd Mem 1983-; Cmmty Clinic (Bd Secy 1980) 1978-; Alpha Rho; WV Ed Fnd Grant Recipient 1986, 1989-; Wetzel Cty Rdng Teacher of Yr 1981; *home:* PO Box 247 Littleton WV 26581

ROBERTS, ROBERT WILLIAM, English Teacher/Dept Chair; *b:* Houtzdale, PA; *ed:* (BS) Eng/His, Murray St Univ 1968; PA St Univ & Harrisburg Comm Coll; *cr:* Eng Teacher Lawrenceburg Consolidated HS, Schuylkill Haven Area Sch Dist; *ai:* Jr Adv; 7th-12th Grade Lead Teacher; Schuylkill Writer Magazine Dir; Prins Advisory Comm; NEA, PSEA, SHEA.

ROBERTS, ROBIN LOUIS, Social Studies/Phys Ed Teacher; *b:* Bloomington, IL; *m:* Cynthia Lynn Rock; *c:* Courtney; *ed:* (AS) Sociology, Danville Jr Coll 1977; (BS) Phys Ed, IL Wesleyan Univ 1979; Sports Medicine, Geography, His, IL St Univ; *cr:* Asst Track/Head Cross Cntry Coach IL Wesleyan Univ 1979-80; Phys Ed Teacher St Marys Sch 1980; Mgr Omni Phys Fitness 1980-83; Soc Stud/Phys Ed Teacher/Head Track/Asst Cross Cntry Coach Tri-Valley Schls 1984-; *ai:* His Fair Spon & Coord; Phi Theta Kappa 1977; NEA 1984-; IL Ed Assn 1984-; IL HS Assn (Officiating Bsktbl/Ftbl) 1979-; IL Bsktbl Ofcl Assn Exec Mem 1987-; Bloomington-Normal Ofcl Assn VP 1982-; IL St Univ His Dept Teacher & Advisory Bd Mem; Boston Marathon 1980-86; *office:* Tri-Valley Jr/Sr HS 503 E Washington Downs IL 61736

ROBERTS, ROLAND D., Language/Soc Stud Teacher; *b:* Taft, TX; *m:* Edith Juanita Rice; *c:* Rachel Corlew, Kevin, Kippie, Leigh Lakes; *ed:* (BA) Speech, David Lipscomb Coll 1955; (MA) Religious Ed, Harding Coll 1958; *cr:* 7th/8th Grade Teacher Benham Sch 1955-56; HS Teacher Kensett Sch 1956-57; 8th Grade Teacher Harding Acad 1957-58; HS Teacher Madison Acad 1963-65; 7th/8th Grade Teacher Owens Cross Roads Sch 1967-; *ai:* Reinstated Yrbk; Yrbk Adv; Fall Festival, Southern Assn Accreditation Self Study, Interim Report Chm; Cty Wide Soc Stud Textbook Comm Chm; AL Ed Assn, Madison Cty Ed Assn 1967-; NEA 1973-; AFC Farming News Assn Ed; Farmers Cooperative House Organizer 1971-; Prof Journalist & Photographer; *office:* Owens Cross Roads School 161 Wilson Mann Rd Owens Cross Roads AL 35763

ROBERTS, ROSA LUMPKIN, Mathematics/Cmptr Sci Teacher; *b:* Sylvester, GA; *ed:* (BS) Industrial Management, GA Inst of Technology 1985; Cert Scndry Math, Albany St Coll 1987; *cr:* Quality Control Analyst Miller Brewing Company 1984; Cnslr Office of Minority Educl Dev GA Tech 1985; Night Math Laboratory Dir Albany Jr Coll 1986-87; Teacher Dougherty Cty Bd of Ed 1987-; *ai:* Dougherty Cty Assn of Educators, GA Assn of Ed, NEA 1987-; Alpha Kappa Alpha 1985-; Worth Cty of NAACP 1980-; *office:* Dougherty Cty Alternative Sch 600 S Madison Ave Albany GA 31701

ROBERTS, SANDRA BELL, 6th-8th Grade Lang Art Teacher; *b:* Humboldt, TN; *m:* Janes Ray; *c:* Penny, Holly, Mitzi; *ed:* (BA) Eng, 1969, Elem, 1983 Union Univ; *cr:* Span Teacher Coffee Cty Schls 1969-72; Eng Teacher Gibson 1972-75, Medina HS 1976-80; Lang Art Teacher Median Elem 1985-; *ai:* Sch Annual & Librarian; Beta Club Adv; NEA, TN Ed Assn, Gibson Cty Ed Assn; PTO; 1st Baptist Pianist 1972-; Career Ladder I 1985, Career Ladder II 1986; *office:* Medina Elem Sch 117 College Ave Medina TN 38355

ROBERTS, SHERI HURD, 9/10th Grade Engish Teacher; *b:* Fulton, KY; *m:* Tommy; *c:* Laurel Little, N. B. Little, Kelly; *ed:* (BS) Home Ec/Eng, 1970; (MA) Scndry Ed, 1976; Scndry Ed/Gifted Ed, 1983 Murray St Univ; *cr:* Eng Teacher Fulgham Sch 1970-72; Eng/Gifted Teacher Hickman Cty HS 1972-; Gifted Teacher Murray St Univ; *ai:* Acad Coach Club Spon; Jr Class Spon; Stu Cncl Spon; KAGE 1983-89; Outstanding Mem Plaque 1986; Hickman Cty Ed Assn Treas 1983-; KEA; NEA; Cty Fairs Contest Judge 1971-87; Hickman Cty Homemaker Pres 1984-85; 1st Methodist Church (Chmn Cncl on Ministries 1990 Chmn Nominations Comm 1988); Poems Published in Jesse Stuarts Fourth Summer; Outstanding Young Amer Woman 1970; Mem Kappa Omicron Phi Kappa Delta Pi; Prof Honorary; *office:* Hickman County HS Cresap St Clinton KY 42031

ROBERTS, SHIRLEY ADAMS, Teacher; *b:* Chicago, IL; *m:* William H.; *c:* Linda R. Menius; *ed:* (BS) His, Purdue Univ 1948; (MS) His, TX A&I Univ; Various Grad Courses His, Government, Psych; *cr:* Teacher Carroll HS 1959-; *ai:* NCSS, TSTA, CC Classroom Teachers Assn 1960-; AAUW 1970-89.

ROBERTS, SONJA RAMONA (DAVIS), Fourth Grade Teacher; *b:* Duncan, OK; *m:* Monty R.; *c:* Gaila M. Roberts Ford; *ed:* (BS) Elem Ed, Central St Univ 1965; (AA) Elem Ed, SW Assembly of God Coll 1962; Alphabetic Phonics, Vision Therapy, Cmptr Lit, Day Care Dirs Trng; *cr:* 2nd Grade Teacher Perley Sch 1965-66; 3rd Grade Teacher Westwood Sch 1966-67; Dir 1st Chrstn Church Day Care 1967-75, Small World Day Care Center 1975-76; 5th Grade Teacher 1976-83, 4th Grade Teacher 1983- OK Chrstn Schls; *ai:* Supvr of Intermediate Dept; *home:* PO Box 1129 Edmond OK 73083

ROBERTS, STEVEN ERNEST, Food Service Teacher; *b:* Springfield, MA; *m:* Deborah Jeanne Dunton; *c:* Kate L.; *ed:* Hotel/Restaurant Management, Holyoke; Voc Tech Ed, Cntrl CT St Univ; *cr:* Exec Chef Ellington Ridge Cntry Club 1983-84; Restaurant Mgr Mr Steak Restaurant 1984-89; Teacher Somers HS 1983-; Restaurant Mgr Neptunes Sea Fare Restaurant 1989-; *ai:* FHA/Hero, HS Restaurant Adv; CEA Building Rep; FHA/Hero Skill Events Co-Coord; Sftbl & Bsbl Umpire; Bsktbl & Track Ofcl; Vernon Bd of Umpires, ASA Sftbl Umpires 1989-; *office:* Somers HS 9th District Rd Somers CT 06071

ROBERTS, STEVEN PAUL, 6th Grade Soc Stud/Sci Teacher; *b:* Belton, TX; *m:* Patricia Marion Savoie; *c:* Kerri, Kristin, Katrina; *ed:* (BA) Elem Ed, Johnson St Coll 1978; *cr:* 7th-12th Grade Teacher Craftsbury Acad 1978-83; 6th Grade Teacher Leander Jr HS 1984-; *ai:* 6th Grade Team Leader; Just Say No Club Spon; *office:* Leander Jr HS 501 S Hwy 183 Leander TX 78641

ROBERTS, SUSAN MARIE, Mathematics/Science Teacher; *b:* Mansfield, OH; *m:* Richard J.; *ed:* (BS) Math Ed, Grace Coll 1984; *cr:* Math/Sci Teacher Heritage Chrstn Sch 1984-88; Math Teacher Omaha Chrstn Acad 1988-89; Math/Sci Teacher Heritage Chrstn Sch 1989-; *ai:* Cheerleading Adv; *home:* 1090 Walnut St Cadillac MI 49601

ROBERTS, SYLVIA L. REED, Art Teacher; *b:* Coventry, RI; *c:* L. Willis, Stuart M.; *ed:* (BS) Ed/Art, RI Coll 1969; Mat Prgm Art, RI Coll, RI Sch of Design 1955-57, Boston Museum Sch of Fine Arts 1958, Univ of RI 1964; *cr:* Textile Designer Appanaug Company 1956-58; Costume/Catalog Design Geo E Mousley Company 1958-60; Set Painter Theater by Sea 1976; Graphic Arts Vosburg Printers 1981; Art Teacher Coventry Jr HS 1969-; Part Time Art Teacher RI Coll 1969-; *ai:* Supervise Sch Newspaper; RI Sch of Design 1985-; Mystic CT Art Assn 1981-; Curr Dev & Writer; 1st Place Narragansett Art Festival 1966; Art Exhibits; *office:* Coventry Jr HS Foster Dr Coventry RI 02816

ROBERTS, TAUJUANNA LYNN, 8th Grade Lang Arts Teacher; *b:* Ardmore, OK; *m:* David Larry; *c:* Court, Libby, Clay; *ed:* (BA) Eng Ed/Pshych/Sociology, Southeastern OK St Univ 1974; *cr:* 7th-9th Grade Eng Teacher Madill Mid Sch 1977-79; 7th Grade Soc Stud Teacher 1980-84; 8th Grade Eng Teacher 1985 Ardmore Mid Sch; *ai:* YMCA Act; NEA; OEA; Lang Arts Curr Comm; *office:* Ardmora Middle Sch 21 Nh Washington Ardmore OK 73401

ROBERTS, VIVIAN FREEMAN, Fifth Grade Teacher; *b:* Riverton, WY; *m:* Laverne D.; *c:* Michael; *ed:* (BS) Elem Ed, Black Hills St Univ 1968; Advanced Trng in Elem Ed; *cr:* 1st Grade Teacher East Elem 1956-64; 5th Grade Teacher North Elem 1969-; *ai:* Stu Management Team, Math Book Adoption Comm, Budget Comm Mem; NEA, ID Ed Assn, Mountain Home Ed Assn 1956-64, 1969-; *office:* North Elem Sch 209 E 12th St N Mountain Home ID 83647

ROBERTS, WILMA JUANITA MITCHELL, Choral Music Teacher; *b:* Thomasville, GA; *c:* Elijah E. Jr., William E.; *ed:* (BA) Choral/General Music, St Augustines Coll 1952; Opera, CO Coll; General Music, CO St Univ; Ed/Child Abuse, Univ of CO Colorado Springs; *cr:* Music Teacher Brooks HS 1952-53, Rosenwald HS 1953-56; Choral Music Teacher Irving Sch 1959-64, Holmes Jr HS 1964-; *ai:* Music Ed Natl Conference; Alpha Delta Kappa (Music, St Chairperson); Alpha Kappa Alpha Music Dir; Payne Chapel AME Church (Choir Dir, Organist).

ROBERTS, Y. ANN, Pre-Kindergarten Teacher; *b:* Corpus Christi, TX; *m:* James E.; *c:* Raschel R., Brandi N., Russel R.; *ed:* (BS) Elem Ed/Eng, SW TX St Univ 1975; (MS) Ed, A&I Univ 1984; *cr:* 5th Grade Teacher Freer Elem 1975-78; 3rd-5th Grade Teacher Derry Elem 1978-81; 5th Grade/Pre-Kndgtn Teacher Norman Thomas Elem 1981-; *ai:* Coaching UIL Events Storytelling & Oral Rdng; TX St Teachers Assn 1975-; Teacher of Yr Derry Elem Port Isabel 1981; *home:* PO Box 407 504 Carle Freer TX 78357

ROBERTSHAW, RICK, Mathematics/Science Teacher; *b:* Chicago, IL; *m:* Beverly Jean Busse; *ed:* (BS) Bio, NE IL Univ 1977; *cr:* Teacher Carl Sandburg Jr HS 1977-; *ai:* Track Coach; Math Club & Sci Olympiad Spon; Pre Algebra/Algebra Text Adoption Comm; Presidential Awd for Excl Nom 1990; IL Recipient Awd of Excl 1988; Math Sci Acad; *office:* Carl Sandburg Jr HS 2600 Martin Ln Rolling Meadows IL 60008

ROBERTSON, ANN, 5th/6th Grade English Teacher; *b:* Long Island, NY; *m:* Walter Sellitto;; *c:* Walter Jr.; *ed:* (BA) Ed, Hofstra Univ 1970; (MA) LS/Ed, Stonybrook Univ 1973; *cr:* NY Telephone Company 1950-56; Secy Farmingdale HS 1965-70; Teacher St Patrick Sch 1970-; *ai:* Massapequa Civic Assn; *office:* St Patrick Sch Montauk Hwy Bay Shore NY 11706

ROBERTSON, BERNIE TAYLOR, Mathematics Teacher; *b:* Childress, TX; *m:* Velva Dale Leininger; *c:* Gary, Gregory; *ed:* (BS) Phys Ed, TX Chrstn Univ 1952; Grad Work NSF Math, San Jose St, Santa Clara; Correspondence, Univ of CA; *cr:* Math/Soc Stud Teacher Everman HS 1952-53; Math Teacher Bowie HS 1956-57; 8th Grade Teacher Freedom Elem 1957-58; 7th/8th Grade Teacher King City Elem 1958-60; Soc Stud/Math Teacher Russell Jr HS 1960-67; Math Teacher Rancho Jr HS 1967-83; 7th Grade Teacher Weller Elem 1983-85; Math Teacher Milpitas HS 1985-; *ai:* Soph Class Spon; CA Teachers Assn 1960-; PTA Life Membership; *office:* Milpitas HS 1285 Escuela Pkwy Milpitas CA 95035

ROBERTSON, BETTYE SNEAD, 7th Grade English Teacher; *b:* Birmingham, AL; *m:* Russell Daniel Jr.; *c:* R. Daniel III, Thomas M., Benjamin A.; *ed:* (BA) Psych/Eng, 1974, (MS) Guidance/Counseling, 1987 Jackson St Univ; Various Wkshps & Classes in Eng & Counseling; *cr:* Rdng Teacher Johnston Elem Sch 1974-77; Rdng/Eng Teacher Cobb Jr HS 1977-87; Rdng Teacher Randolph Elem Sch 1983-84; Eng Teacher/Cluster Leader Anniston Mid Sch 1987-; *ai:* Cobb Jr HS Drama Club; Johnston & Cobb Courtesy Comms; Anniston Mid Sch STEER, Textbook, Eng Comm, Scholars Bowl & Time Keeper; Cobb & Anniston Mid Sch Evaluation Comm; NEA, AL Ed Assn, Anniston Ed Assn 1974-; Amer Rdng Assn 1974-82; St Andrews Society 1980-; PTA 1968-; Anniston & Oxford Ftbl & Bsbl for Youth Team-Mother 1967-86.

ROBERTSON, CHARMAINE (BROWN), Mathematics/Phys Ed Teacher; *b:* Amarillo, TX; *m:* Jerry Don; *c:* Wade, Krista Robertson Courson; *ed:* (BS) Elem Ed, Panhandle St Univ 1970; *cr:* 2nd/3rd Grade Teacher 1965-66, 2nd Grade Elem Phys Ed Teacher 1966-69, 4th Grade Elem Phys Ed Teacher 1970-81, 4th-6th Grade Math/Elem Phys Ed Teacher 1981- Darrouzatt Sch; *ai:* 7th-8th Grade, Number Sense, Picture Memory Teams Coach; Delta Kappa Gamma Pres 1985-86; Assn of TX Prof Educators; Village Improvement Prgm; *office:* Darrouzett Sch 102 W Kansas Darrouzett TX 79024

ROBERTSON, DOLORES ECKERT, Fourth Grade Teacher; *b:* Kearny, NJ; *m:* George C.; *c:* Steven, David; *ed:* (BS) Elem Ed, Coll of St Elizabeth 1961; Weekly Seminars for Continued Ed 1959-69; *cr:* Teacher St Francis 1956-68, Harrison Bd of Ed 1968-70, Kearny Bd of Ed 1974-; *ai:* Sch Newspaper, Yrbk, Soc, Curr, Liaison Comm; NJEA, KEA, NEA, PTA; *office:* Garfield Sch 360 Belgrove Dr Kearny NJ 07032

ROBERTSON, EARL THOMAS, Biology Teacher-Sci Dept Chair; *b:* Frederick Cty, MD; *m:* Alice M. Fogle; *c:* Valerie L.; *ed:* (BS) Bio, Univ of MD 1965; (MED) Rdng, Shippensburg Univ 1975; *cr:* Cryptographic Operator US Army/Signal Corps 1953-56; Research Asst Ft Detrick 1960-65; Bio Teacher Hancock Sr HS 1965-66, Smithsburg Sr HS 1966-; *ai:* Sci Dept Chm; MD Assn of Bio Teachers 1970-; Amer Legion Post 11 1986-.

ROBERTSON, FRANCINE WATKINS, Sixth Grade Teacher; *b:* Richmond, VA; *c:* Victor, Pamela; *ed:* (BS) Elem Ed, VA Commonwealth Univ 1975; Math Instutitute for Teachers; Mentoring; Cmptr Math; Soft; *cr:* Teachers Aid Richmond Public Sch 1970-75; Teacher Petersburg Public Schls 1975-; *ai:* 6th Grade Team Leader; Teacher Adv; Mentor; Amer Bus Women Assn; 1st Bapt Church; Teacher of Month 1984; *office:* Peabody Mid Sch 125 Wesley St Petersburg VA 23805

ROBERTSON, GARY P., Social Studies Teacher; *b:* Baton Rouge, LA; *ed:* (BA) Poly Sci, Brigham Young Univ 1979; Grad Work Southern Univ & LA St Univ Baton Rouge; *cr:* Teacher Rougon HS 1979-83, Rosenwald HS 1983-88, Rougon HS 1988-; *ai:* Spon Beta Club; Adv Parish Stu Advisory Cncl; Coach St & Dist Literary Rally; Pointe Coupee Assn of Educators (Pres 1986-88, VP 1985-86, Exec Bd 1984-); LA Assn of Educators Bd of Dir 1985-; NEA Resolutions Comm Alternate 1989-; NCTE, Organization of Amer Historians; Rougon HS Teacher of Yr 1989- & Pointe Coupee Parish 1990; Outstanding Young Men of America 1987; *home:* 11519 Lazy Lake Dr Baton Rouge LA 70818

ROBERTSON, JACQUELYN DAVIS, 7th & 8th Grade Rdng Teacher; *b:* Austin, TX; *m:* Ronald Joel; *c:* Alaric; *ed:* (BS) Elem Ed, Prairie View A&M Univ 1972; (MA) Mid-Management, SW TX St Univ 1978; *cr:* 6th Grade Teacher Casis Elem 1972-1973, Baker 6th Grade Center 1971-76; 7th/8th Grade Rdng Teacher O Henry Mid Sch 1977-; *ai:* Stu Assistance Prgm Comm Mem; Rdng Dept Chm; Austin Assn of Teachers, TX St Teachers Assn, NEA 1972-; Cmmty Advocates for Teens & Parents Acting Bd Pres 1990; Natl Missionary Baptist Convention of America Mission II Auxiliary Recording Secy 1989-; City-Wide Mission II Auxiliary Asst Recording Secy 1989-, Woman of Yr 1989; New Lincoln Baptist Church Mission II Pres 1988-; Outstanding Young Woman of America 1983; New Lincoln Baptist Church Woman of Year 1980; Outstanding Jr Mission Austin Area Pres 1986; House of Hope Bd Mem 1988-; *home:* 9606 Monmouth Cir Austin TX 78753

ROBERTSON, JAMES H., Principal; *b:* San Bernardino, CA; *m:* Jeanne Tisdale; *c:* Rebecca; *ed:* (AA) Psych, San Bernardino Valley Coll 1966; (BA) Sociology, CA St Univ San Bernardino 1971; (MA) Sch Admin/Supvr CA St Univ Northridge 1976; Los Angeles Cty Management Trng Prgm 1988; CA Sch Leadership Acad 1990; *cr:* 2nd-5th Grade Teacher Yerba Buena 1972-76; Asst Prin Willow Sch & White Oak Sch 1976-89; Prin White Oak Sch 1989-; *ai:* Dir of Outdoor Ed 1976-81; Summer Sch Prin 1976-81; CA Sch Improvement Trainer & Reviewer 1981-; Las Virgenes Educators Assn (VP 1977-78, Treas 1976-77), Outstanding Teacher of Yr 1979; Assn of CA Sch Admin; *office:* White Oak Elem Sch 31761 W Village Sch Rd Westlake Village CA 91361

ROBERTSON, JOHN W., Science Teacher; *b:* Macon Cty, MO; *m:* Alice Rose Huskey; *c:* Janet C. Robertson White, June E., Jill A.; *ed:* (BSED) Bio, Northeast MO St Univ 1959; (MS) Zoology, Univ of SD 1964; *cr:* 7th/9th Grade Sci Teacher De Soto Jr HS 1959-63; 8th Grade Sci Teacher Shawano Jr HS 1964-66; 7th/8th Grade Sci Teacher Cy Jr HS 1966-; *ai:* Sci Chm; Girls Vlybl, Bsktbl, Boys & Girls Track Coach; NEA Life Mem 1959-; WY Ed Assn, Natrona Cty Ed Assn 1966-; Chrstn Church Sunday Sch Teacher 1959-; NSF AYI Univ of SD 1963-64; NSF Summer Inst CO St Univ 1963; NSF Summer Inst S IL Univ 1967; *home:* 5024 Alcova Rt Box 23 Casper WY 82604

ROBERTSON, JON C., English Teacher; *b:* Lynwood, CA; *m:* Nance S. Johns; *c:* Hayley; *ed:* (BA) Eng, San Diego St Univ 1973; (MA) Ed, USIU 1981; *cr:* Eng Teacher Torrey Pines HS 1975-; *ai:* Golf Coach; SAS Stu Cnslr; Newcomers & Video Club; *office:* Torrey Pines HS 710 Encinitas Blvd Encinitas CA 92024

ROBERTSON, JOSEPHINE ANGELA, English/Reading Teacher; *b:* Kingston, Jamaica; *m:* Kaestner; *c:* Martin; *ed:* Teachers Cert Eng/Geography, Mico Teachers Coll 1969; (BA) Geography/Ec, 1974, Geography, 1979 Univ of West Indies; Working Towards MAT Elem Ed, Andrews Univ 1990; Writing Prgm, Center for Effective Comm 1989; *cr:* Eng Teacher Tivoli Gardens Comprehensive Sch 1969-71, 1974-76; Geography/Ec Teacher Merl Grove HS 1976-80; 8th Grade Teacher Berea 7th Day Adv Acad 1980-87; Bi-ling Eng Tutor Worcester Sch System 1987-89; Eng/Rdng Teacher Berea 7th Day Adv Acad 1989-; *ai:* Graduating Class Spon; Coord for Developing Writing Prgm K-8th Grade & Staff Dev Berea 7th Day Adv Acad; E Jamaica Conference of 7th Day Adv Bd Mem 1977-78; Merl Grove HS Fine Art Chorale (Staff Bd Rep 1979-80, Mem 1970-); Best of Yr Ed Eng Magazine Berea Acad; *office:* Berea 7th Day Adv Acad 800 Morton St Mattapan MA 02126

ROBERTSON, MARYLEE BASKIN, Gifted Science Teacher; *b:* New York, NY; *m:* Glenn William; *c:* Jason, Mandy; *ed:* (BA) Eng, Eckerd Coll 1966; Certified in Sci, Gifted; *cr:* Eng Teacher Wilson Jr HS 1966-70; Sci/Gifted Teacher Cobb Mid 1982-; *ai:* Sci Fair Organizer; Sch Improvement Team; Head of Gifted Dept; *office:* Cobb Mid Sch 915 Hillcrest St Tallahassee FL 32308

ROBERTSON, NEAL ALONZO, Teacher; *b:* Quinlan, OK; *c:* Tracy Winchell, Jill, Adam; *ed:* (BS) Phys Ed/Math, OK St Univ 1954; (MA) Math Ed, CA St Northridge 1977; Designated Special Subjects, Driver Trng, CA St Univ Los Angeles 1986; *cr:* Teacher Keppel Union Sch Dist 1964-69, John Muir Jr HS 1969-; *ai:* Facutly Treas 1975-80; Faculty Chm 1980-81, 1989-; NCTM Mem 1964-; CA Math Cncl Mem 1969-; CA Teachers Assn; NEA Mem 1964-; Burbank Teachers Assn (Faculty Rep 1979-80, Treas 1981-85); BPO Elks Mem 1955; Natl Sci Fnd Space Sci 1966; *office:* John Muir Jr HS 1111 N Kenneth Rd Burbank CA 91504

ROBERTSON, TONI TRAYLOR, Mathematics Teacher; *b:* Jackson, MS; *m:* Robert David; *c:* Russell, Wendy; *ed:* (BS) Elem Ed/Math, Murray St Univ 1970; *cr:* Math Teacher Gar-Field Sr HS 1985-; *ai:* Alternative Ed for Math, SAT Preparation.

ROBEY, JOHN SAMUEL, Mathematics Teacher; *b:* Martinsville, IN; *m:* Beth Sadler; *c:* Amy B. Robey Johnson, Thomas M.; *ed:* (AB) His, Franklin Coll 1963; (MS) Educl Admin, Univ of Dayton 1985; *cr:* Teacher Brown Cty IN 1963-64, Lebanon IN 1965-69, Yellow Springs OH 1969-; *ai:* Prins Cncl; Faculty Advisory Comm; Phi Delta Kappa 1986-; OEA, NEA; North-South Skirmish Assn (Inspector 1975-76, Deputy Commander 1977-78, 1983-84, Commander 1985-88), Awd of Merit 1979; Knights of Columbus 1978-; *office:* Yellow Springs Jr/Sr HS 420 E Enon Rd Yellow Springs OH 45387

ROBICHAUD, CAROLYN WOMMACK, English Teacher; *b:* Gilbertsville, KY; *m:* John; *c:* Nicole Fann, Shawn; *ed:* (BA) Eng, David Lipscomb Univ 1963; (MA) Scndry Ed, Murray St Univ 1983; Rank I Cert; *cr:* Eng Teacher, Sharpe Elem 1964-74; North Marshall Jr HS 1974-88; Marshall Cty HS 1988-; *ai:* Co-Spon of Speech Team; NEA; Teacher Rep 1967-68; Negotiating Team 1976-84 Marshall Cty Ed Assn; KY Cncl of Teachers Eng; NCTE; Alpha Delta Kappa; Served on St Mid Sch/JR HS Indicators Comm;Selected Partcpnt Purch Area Writing Proj - Murray St Univ; KY Cncl Teachers of Eng Conf 1989; Mem St Sndry Sch Rcgntn Prgm.

ROBIN, AARON JAMES, Band Director; *b:* Breaux Bridge, LA; *m:* Diane Bila; *c:* Lori, Jennifer, Jeremy, Jeffrey; *ed:* (BA) Applied Music, 1971, (BME) Instrumental Music, 1973, (MA) Instrumental Music Ed, 1975 Univ of SW LA; Navy Sch of Music; *cr:* Band Dir Vandebilt Cath HS 1968-69, Northside HS 1973-76, Comeaux HS 1976-; *ai:* SW LA Band Dir Assn Past Pres 1975; Natl Assn of Jazz Educators LA Past VP 1976; LA Music Ed Assn Bd of Dirs 1986-; Broadmoor Swim Club Bd Dirs 1989; Acadiana Symphony Orch 1987; Lafayette Cmmty Concert Band 88; Lafayette Mardi Assn Bd Dirs 1989; *office:* Comeaux HS 100 W Bluebird Dr Lafayette LA 70508

ROBINETTE-BOUCHARD, ELEANORE T., Third Grade Teacher; *b:* Alpena, MI; *m:* Daniel P.; *c:* Marsha Rabiteau, Jo Ann Doule, Gary Robinette, Christine Klein, Michael Robinette, Katherine Froggett, Phillip, Randy, Brenda Williams, Lynn, Amy; *ed:* (BA) Soc Sci/Elem Ed, Cntrl MI Univ Mt Pleasant 1980; Certificate 1984; *cr:* K-8th Grade Teacher Maple Ridge Schls 1948-50; Long Distance Operator Bell Telephone Company 1950-51; K-8th Grade Teacher Alpena Twp Sch 1954-55, Maple Ridge Sch 1957-62, Alpena Cooperative Nursery 1962-63, St Anne Cath Sch 1967-; *ai:* Thunder Bay Rdng Cncl 1979-; Thunder Bay Cncl for Arts 1980-; St Anne Long Range Planning Comm Secy 1985-86; St Anne Church (Eucharistic Minister 1976-, Lector 1976); Hinks Sch PTA 1970-71; St Anne Sch Bd 1971-74, Home & Sch Assn Secy 1972-73; Outstndng Teacher 1986; *home:* 112 Glenridge Alpena MI 49707

ROBINS, GREGORY J., Fourth Grade Teacher; *b:* Wenatchee, WA; *m:* Joan Medved; *c:* Christine; *ed:* (BA) Hist/Elem Ed, Portland St Univ 1975; Portland St Univ; OR Writing Project 1983; *cr:* 3rd/4th Grade Teacher Howard Eccles Elem Sch 1976-; *ai:* Soccer Referee; Columbia Assn of Puppeteers; Teacher Incentive Grant of Puppetry in Classroom; Teacher Incentive Grant for Writing; OR Eng Sp 85; Howard Eccles Teacher Yr 1987; *office:* Howards Eccles Elem Sch 562 NW 5th Ave Canby OR 97013

ROBINSON, AMY LYNN, History/Science Teacher; *b:* Pensacola, FL; *m:* Hossein Abdollahi; *c:* Amir-Ahmad Abdollahi; *ed:* (BA) His, AZ St Univ 1980; *cr:* Sci Teacher Valley HS 1981-82; Lang Art/Sci/His Teacher Queen Creek Scndry Sch 1982-; *ai:* Natl Jr Honor Society & Film Club Spon; NEA; Queen Creek Ed Assn VP 1988-89; Amnesty Intnl; Natl Organization for Women; *office:* Queen Creek Scndry Sch 20435 S Ellsworth Queen Creek AZ 85242

ROBINSON, ARTHUR MC GUE, 6th Grade Teacher/Chair; *b:* Quincy, FL; *m:* Hurschel L. Sr.; *c:* Patricia Rumlin, Alma R. West, Hurschel Jr. (dec); *ed:* (AA) Elem Ed, Jackson Jr Coll 1962; (BS) Elem Ed, 1965, (MA) Elem Ed, 1975 FL A&M Univ; *cr:* Teacher Stewart Street Elem 1965-66, Attapulgus HS 1966-72, St John Elem 1972-; *ai:* 6th Grade Chairperson; Hospitality Asst Chairperson; Assist GSA Act; Sch Comprehensive Plan Mem;

Turnkey Ed Prgm Participant; Gadsden Models Prgm; Sch Advisory Comm; FTP, NEA, FAMU Alumni Organization; Gadsden Cty Rdng Cncl; Gadsden Cty Teachers Organization, 1st Elizabeth Missionary Baptist Church Mem; Pastors Aide Auxillary Secy; Class of 45 Organized Membership Mem; St John Elem Sch Teacher of Yr & Certificate Plaque; *home:* 218 S Shadow St Quincy FL 32351

ROBINSON, BARBARA CHAMBERLAIN, Kindergarten Teacher; *b:* Staten Island, NY; *w:* Roland James (dec); *c:* Bethany J., Alissa J.; *ed:* (BA) Geography/Geology, Hunter Coll CUNY 1968; (MED) Spec Ed, Univ of ME Orono 1983; *cr:* 1st Grade Teacher Rose Gaffney Sch 1968-70, W Jonesport Sch 1970-72; Kndgtn Teacher Jonesport Elem Sch 1972-; *ai:* Playground Equipment, Negotiations, Peer Coaching Comms; Girl Scouts Leader 1987-89; United Pentecostal Church Sunday Sch Teacher 1975-; Un Pent Church Jr Choir Dir 1985-; *office:* Jonesport Elem Sch PO Box 209 Jonesport ME 04649

ROBINSON, BONNIE LENDERMAN, Fourth Grade Teacher; *b:* Dallas, TX; *m:* Charles David; *c:* Jennifer, Forrest; *ed:* (BS) Elem Ed, 1974, (ME) Elem Ed, 1976, Stephen F Austin Univ; Effective Teaching Practices Inst Stephen F Austin Univ 1986; Cooperative Learning Facilitator Trng, Lufkin Ind Sch Dist 1989; Mamie Mc Cullough 1989; Reality Therapy Trng Wkshp; *cr:* Elem Teacher Herty Elem 1974-75, Redland Elem 1975-79, Herty Elem 1979-88, Kurth Elem 1988-; *ai:* Textbook Comm Rep Herty Elem 1986-86; Communication Comm Rep Herty Elem & Kurth Elem 1988-89; Supervising Teacher for Stu Teacher/Observers 1988-89; Presenter Creative Writing LISD In-Service 1988-89; Chm Publicity Comm Kurth Elem 1989-; TX Classroom Teachers 1974-; Lufkin Classroom Teachers (Reporter 1975-6, 1st VP 1988-89); Herty Elem PTA 1974-75; Redland Elem PTA 1975-79; Herty Elem PTA 1979-88 Recognition for Outstanding Service 1984; Kurth Elem PTA 1988-; Recipient 15 Yr Service Pin Lufkin Ind Sch Dist Awd Banquet; *office:* Kurth Elem 521 York St Lufkin TX 75901

ROBINSON, CAROL DIERKES, Spanish Teacher; *b:* St Louis, MO; *c:* John C., Benjamin T., Shanus L.; *ed:* (BS) Span/Eng, SE MO St Univ 1971; Mentor Trng; *cr:* Eng Teacher Jefferson Jr HS 1971-77; Span Teacher Oakville Sr HS 1979-; *ai:* Sr Prom, Sr Breakfast, Sr Trip Spon; NHS Selection Comm; NEA 1971-77, 1979-; MNEA, MCTA 1979-; FLTA 1988-; ACTFL 1987-; Yrbk Dedicatee 1990; *office:* Oakville Sr HS 5557 Milburn Rd Saint Louis MO 63129

ROBINSON, DARLENE FAYE, Kindergarten Teacher; *b:* Independence, MO; *ed:* (BA) Elem Ed, William Jewell Coll 1963; (MS) Elem Ed & Remedial Rdng, Cntrl MO St Univ 1971; Post Masters Studies/His & Sci/Univ MO; *cr:* 4th/5th Grade Teacher Spring Branch Sch 1958; Kndgtn/1st Grade Teacher Ott Elem Sch 1958; *ai:* Kndgtn Grade Level Chairperson Ott Sch 1988-; MO Dept of Elem & Scndry Ed Comm on Early Chldhd Parent Resources & Ed 1988-; Delta Kappa Gamma VP 1960-70; NEA; MO Ed Assn; Ind Ed Assn VP 1960-70; Friends of Historic MO Town Bd of Dir/Pres/VP 1976-; Heritage Commission Commsnr 1989-93; Jackson Cty His Society 1970-80; Heritage Leag of Kansas City MO 1980; Nom Teacher of Yr Excl Teaching; Researched/Wrote Ed Guide to Historic MO Town 1855; Rsrch/Writing Ind Queen City of Trails; *office:* Ott Elem Sch 1525 N Noland Rd Independence MO 64050

ROBINSON, DENNIS S., Physical Education Instructor; *b:* Peekskill, NY; *m:* Dorothy Crowell; *c:* Dennis, Kristine, Daniel; *ed:* (BA) Phys Ed/Health, Bethany Coll 1971; Grad Work NY Univ; *cr:* Teacher Lakeland Schls; *ai:* Head Bsbl Coach; Ski Club Adv; Sr Class Adv 1989; NY Daily News Coach of Yr 1984; SE Coaches Assn Pres 1985; *office:* Lakeland HS Old Rt 6 Shrub Oak NY 10588

ROBINSON, DIANNE Y., Fourth Grade Teacher; *b:* Bremen, GA; *c:* Kenny R., Charles W.; *ed:* (BS) Mid Grades Ed 1979; (MED) Mid Grades Ed 1984 West GA Coll; *cr:* 4th Grade Teacher Bowdon Elem Sch 1979-; *ai:* NEA 1979-; GAE 1979-; Phi Kappa Phi 1979-82; Alpha Lambda Delta 1975-76; Indian Creek Baptist Church 1988-; Presidential Scholar West GA Coll 1975-78; *office:* Bowdon Elem Sch 223 Kent Ave Bowdon GA 30108

ROBINSON, EARLEAN WILLIAMS, Third Grade Teacher; *b:* Orange, TX; *m:* Peter Joe; *c:* Danita Jones, La Juan Jones; *ed:* (BS) Elem Ed, Bishop Coll 1968; (MS) Elem Ed, East TX St Univ 1973; *cr:* 3rd Grade Teacher Pittsburg Ind Sch Dist 1968-; *ai:* Academic Awd Comm Mem; ASCD 1986-; Assn of TX Prof Educators 1989-; City of Pittsburg Main St Advisory Bd 1988-; Tea Direct Line Published Article I Wrote 1989; *home:* 202 Daphne St Pittsburg TX 75686

ROBINSON, EDWARD A., JR., Teacher; *b:* Mineola, NY; *m:* Kimberlie B. Robinson; *c:* Ashley, Hayley; *ed:* (BS) His & Geography, Murray St Univ 1969; (MS) Sch Managment & Admin, Pepperdine Univ 1977; Teaching Credentials, CA St Univ-Fresno 1971-72; *cr:* Teacher Tulane Western HS 1972-; Coll of the Sequoias 1984-; *ai:* Frosh Soph Jr Sr Classes 1972-83; Ftbl Bsbl 1974-84; Sch Play 1979-86; CA Cncl for Soc Stud Mem 1986-; Mentor Teacher 1986-; *home:* 5631 W Seeger Visalia CA 93277

ROBINSON, ELIZABETH ANN, Third Grade Teacher; *b:* Winchester, VA; *ed:* (BS) Elem Ed, VA Union Univ 1976; *cr:* Title I Teacher Berryville Primary Sch & D G Cooley Elem 1976-77; Title I Teacher 1977-78, 3rd Grade Teacher 1978- D G Cooley Elem Sch; *ai:* Grade Level Chm; Effective Schls Comm; Clarke Cty Ed Assn, VA Ed Assn, NEA 1976-; ASCD 1987-; Outstanding Young Women of America 1983; *office:* D G Cooley Elem Sch Rt 3 Box 5640 Berryville VA 22611

ROBINSON, ESTHER MARTIN, Social Studies Dept Chair; *b:* Buffalo, NY; *m:* Stephen Mark; *c:* Rachel A., Sarah E.; *ed:* (BA) His, Oral Roberts Univ 1978; (MA) His, Univ of Tulsa 1983; *cr:* Scndry Teacher Tulsa Public Schls 1978-80, Jenks Public Schls 1980-; Soc Stud Dept Chairperson Jenks HS 1989-; *ai:* Natl His Day, WA Close Up, Close Up Citizen Bee Spon; Prin Selection & 5 Yr Plan Comm; JCTA, OEA, NEA (Rep, Delegate) 1981-; OK Cncl Soc Stud, NCSS 1981-; Jenks Classroom Teachers Assn, OK Ed Assn; Kappa Kappa Iota (Secy 1986-88, Pres 1988-89); Rep Supt Prof Cncl; Meet & Confer, OK Bar Assn; Cradle Teacher 1990; *office:* Jenks HS 1st & B Sts Jenks OK 74037

ROBINSON, FAYE JOHNSON, 2nd Grade Teacher/Grade Leader; *b:* Chestnut, LA; *m:* Shelton H.; *c:* Donna Johnston, Allen, Melody Stephens; *ed:* (BA) Elem Ed, Northwestern St Univ 1954; Gifted & Talented Trng; *cr:* 6th Grade Teacher Parkview Elem 1954-55; Kndgtn Teacher Boulevard King 1964-65, 1st Baptist 1970-72; 2nd Grade Teacher Harris Elem 1972-; *ai:* UIL Spon; Assn for TX Prof Educators Mem 1987-88; PTA Life Membership Awd; *office:* C J Harris Elem Sch 2319 N Grand Pearland TX 77581

ROBINSON, GAIL MORGAN, Vocational Business Teacher; *b:* Warren, AR; *m:* Kenneth C.; *c:* Stephanie R. Vetrano, Clifford R. Evans; *ed:* (BS) Bus Admin, Centenary Coll 1968; (ED) Bus Ed, LA St 1975; Grad Voc Bus, Univ of AR Fayetteville; *cr:* Bus Teacher Junction City HS 1974-78, Ross Van Ness HS 1978-83; Voc Bus Teacher Lakeside HS 1983-; *ai:* FBLA Adv; Voc Bus Advisory Comm; AVA, AR Voc Assn 1987-; AR Bus Ed Assn 1989-; Delta Kappa Gamma Treas 1985-; Lake Village Festival Choir 1988-; Bayou Macon Baptist Church Music Dir 1982-; Recorded Gospel Tape; *home:* PO Box 172 Airport Rd Lake Village AR 71653

ROBINSON, GLENYCE LANDERS, Mathematics Teacher; *b:* Albertville, AL; *c:* Eric; *ed:* (BS) Arts/Sci, Samford Univ 1965; Cert Scndry Ed, 1967; (MS) Math, 1980 Univ of AL; Post Masters Studies, GA St Univ 1972-74; *cr:* Teacher Boaz HS 1965-67; Albertville HS 1967-70; Guntersville HS 1971-74; Oakhaven Acad 1975-77; Arab HS 1977-78; Guntersville HS 1978-; *ai:* Class Spon; Club Adv; Activity Sponshp; NEA/AEA/GEA Assnl Rep 1988-; AL Classroom Teachers Treas 1979-80; Kappa Kappa Iota Pres/Treas 1967-; Boy Scouts of Amer Explorer Ldr 1980-; Kappa Kappa Iota-Theta St Schlsp; Guntersville HS Outstanding Teacher; System Nom Jacksonville St Univ Teacher Hall of Fame; Nom Guntersville Chamber of Commerce Outstanding Teacher; *home:* 602 W Mc Kinney Ave Albertville AL 35950

ROBINSON, GLORIA MC CRARY, Mathematics Teacher; *b:* Griffin, GA; *m:* Gary Ricky; *ed:* (BS) Elem Ed, Albany St Coll 1969; (MA) Curr/Instruction, Univ of N CO 1978; Elem Ed, Mid Sch, Math; *cr:* Teacher Beaverbrook Elem Sch 1970-73, Charles R Drew Mid Sch 1973-; *ai:* Jr Honor Society Club Spon 1975-84; Future Teachers of America Club Spon; United Teachers of Dade 1973-; Certificate of Appreciation 1982-83; Teacher of Yr 1983-84; Teacher of Math 1983-84; Certificate of Appreciation 1988; Sch Uniform Proposal 1989-; *office:* Charles R Drew Mid Sch 1801 N W 60th St Miami FL 33142

ROBINSON, HARLAN PATRICK, 5th/6th Grade Soc Stud Teacher; *b:* Wild Rose, WI; *m:* Rita Joan Tubbs; *c:* Stephanie, Cavan; *ed:* (BA) Elem Ed, Univ of WI Stevens Point 1976; *cr:* 7th Grade Teacher White Lake HS 1976-78; 5th/6th Grade Soc Stud Teacher Tri-Cty Mid Sch 1979-; *ai:* Soc Stud, His Curr Comm; *office:* Tri-cty Mid Sch 409 West St Plainfield WI 54966

ROBINSON, HELEN S., Second Grade Teacher; *b:* Anderson, SC; *c:* Andrew; *ed:* (BA) Elem Ed, Clemson Univ 1969; (MED) Elem Ed, Clemson Univ 1974; *cr:* 2nd Grade Teacher Morrison Elem Sch 1969-; *ai:* Childrens Church Wesleyan Church; Sub Sunday Sch Teacher; Phi Delta Kappa; Delta Kappa Gamma; Alpha Psi; SC Ed Assn; NEA; 1975 Teacher of Yr/Morrison Elem; *office:* Morrison Elem Sch Frontage Rd Clemson SC 29631

ROBINSON, JAMES BERNARD, Math Teacher/Basketball Coach; *b:* Memphis, TN; *m:* Myrtle Zinn; *c:* Oliver; *ed:* (BS) Math, Rust Coll 1972; Memphis St Univ 1972-74; *cr:* Math Teacher 1972-, Bsktbl Coach 1973- Holly Springs HS; Bsktbl Coach Rust Coll 1978-; *ai:* HS Boys & Girls Bsktbl Coach; Jr Class Spon; Phi Beta Sigma VP 1987-89, Sigma of Yr 1986; MS Ed Assn, NAACP 1972-; Teacher of Yr; STAR Teacher; C *office:* Holly Springs HS 165 N Walthall St Holly Springs MS 38635

ROBINSON, JAMES WADE, History Dept Chairman; *b:* Houston, TX; *ed:* (BA) Amer His, 1975, (MA) Amer His, 1976 Austin Coll; North TX Univ; Collin Cty Comm Coll; *cr:* Intern 1975-76, Team Leader 1976-84 Wilson Mid Sch; Dept Chm Shepton HS 1984-; *ai:* Amnesty Intnl Spon; Citizens Bee Coord; Plano Sesquicentennial Comm Mem 1985-86; Ross Perot Awd Outstanding Mid Sch Teacher Plano Ind Sch Dist 1981; Outstanding Young Educator Plano Jaycees 1982; *office:* Shepton Scndry Sch 5505 Plano Pkwy Plano TX 75075

ROBINSON, JANET MAYBERRY, Secretarial Instructor; *b:* St Louis, MO; *m:* Keith; *c:* Brett, Karole; *ed:* (BS) Bus, E IL Univ 1963; (MED) Bus Ed, Univ of IL 1968; N IL Univ; *cr:* Polo Cmmty HS 1963-67; Maine South HS 1967-68, Lake Cty Voc Center 1977-; *ai:* Bus Prof of America Adv; Delta Pi Epsilon, IL Bus Ed Assn, AVA; N IL Univ Ed for Technology Grant; *office:* Lake Cty Area Voc Center 19525 W Washington Grayslake IL 60030

ROBINSON, JOHN PHILIP, Coll Amer His/Psych Teacher; *b:* Granite City, IL; *m:* Bonnie Mae Nistler; *c:* John C., Benjamin, Shanus L.; *ed:* (BS) Soc Stud, 1971, (MAT) His, 1975 SE MO St Univ; Working Towards Advanced Degree; *cr:* Soc Stud Teacher Mehlville Sr HS 1971-82; Zone Mgr Henco Inc 1982-83; Psych/Global His Teacher St Louis Univ HS 1983-85; His Instr Mehlville Sr HS 1985-; Adjunct His Teacher St Louis Univ 1979-82, 1986-; Instr Univ of MO St Louis 1989-; *ai:* Mehlville-Oakville Sch Dist Fnd Comm; Stu Cncl, Pep Club, Class Exec Cncl, Youth/Government, Close-up Spon; St Louis Regional Cncl for Self-Esteem Exec Comm 1986-89; Natl Cncl for Self-Esteem 1986-; NCSS 1989-; St Louis Assn For Counseling & Dev 1989-; NEA 1971-; MO Ed Assn 1973-; Mehlville Cmmty Teacher Assn 1971-; Johnny Mac Bsbl Assn Coach 1981-; Affton Athletic Assn Bsbl Coach 1985-88; YMCA Athletic Assn; Articles Published; Mehlville Sch Dist Teacher of Yr 1989; Nom MO Soc Stud Teacher of Yr 1990; *home:* 2729 Chalet Forest Dr Saint Louis MO 63129

ROBINSON, JOSEPH ALLEN, Mathematics Teacher; *b:* Neponset, IL; *m:* Jean Doherty; *c:* Jason, Jacqueline, Jennifer, Jeffery; *ed:* (BS) Phys Ed/Math/Health, E IL Univ 1970; Grad Stud Educl Courses; *cr:* 7th Grade Math Teacher Cntrl Jr HS 1970-74; Math Teacher Seneca Township HS 1974-; *ai:* Sr Class Adv; Head Soph Ftbl & Bsktbl Coach; In Service Comm; Seneca Ed Assn (Treas 1986-88, Pres 1988-); Jaycees Treas 1979-80; IL Cncl Teachers of Math, IL Coaches Assn; Village of Seneca Plan Commission; *office:* Seneca Township HS 307 E Scott St Seneca IL 61360

ROBINSON, JOYCE VINSON, First Grade Teacher; *b:* Swansboro, NC; *m:* Donald Thomas; *c:* Brenda Robinson Wooten, Susan Robinson de Beaumont; *ed:* (BS) Primary Ed, East Carolina Univ 1958; Grad Work Marshall Univ, East Carolina Univ; *cr:* 1st Grade Teacher Swansboro Elem Sch 1958-59, Park Elem Sch 1961-63, Sigsbee Park Elem Sch 1964-65, San Matio Elem Sch 1965-68, White Oak Elem Sch 1968-69, Holy Trinity Elem Sch 1970-72, Hannan Elem Sch 1972-74; 1st/3rd/5th Grade Teacher White Oak Elem 1974-; *ai:* Mentor Teacher; Mem Carteret Cty System Leadership Team; Chairperson White Oak Elem System Leadership Team; Steering, SACS Steering, Media Comms; Grade Level Chairperson; Helped Write Curr Cmptr Technology Carteret Cty; NC Assn of Educators, NEA, Carteret Cty Classroom Teachers Assn 1974-; Peletier Baptist Church Financial Secy 1985-, Sunday Sch Teacher; Teacher of Yr 1986-87; Carteret Cty Chamber of Commerce Teacher of Mont 1987; Educl Excl Awd 1989; VFW Patrio tism Awd 1985; *office:* White Oak Elem Sch Hwy 24 E Swansboro NC 28584

ROBINSON, KATHLEEN ANNE, Computer Lab Teacher; *b:* Neptune, NJ; *ed:* (BS) Ed, Monmouth Coll 1975; *cr:* Math Teacher John Witherspoon Mid Sch 1975-76; Elem Teacher Marlboro Township 1976-; *ai:* NJ Ed Assn 1975-; Marlboro Township Ed Assn Head Building Delegate 1988-; Governors Teacher Recognition Prgm 1989; *office:* Marlboro Mid Sch Rt 520 Marlboro NJ 07748

ROBINSON, LINDA GAY GRAYBEAL, Fifth Grade Teacher; *b:* Johnson City, TN; *m:* Michael Lynn; *c:* Bradley H.; *ed:* (BA) Elem Ed, Milligan Coll 1981; (MS) Admin/Supervision, E TN St Univ 1988; *cr:* Teacher West View Elem 1982-85, Gray Elem Sch 1985-; *ai:* WCEA 1982-88; Gray Elem Sch & WA Cty Teacher of Yr 1989-; Most Outstanding Stu Teacher 1981; I Dare You Awd for Leadership Qualities; Outstanding Young Women of America; *home:* Rt 9 Box 369BB Johnson City TN 37601

ROBINSON, LINDA KAY, 4th Grade Teacher; *b:* Fairmont, WV; *ed:* (BA) Elem Ed, Fairmont St Coll 1970; (MS) Elem Ed, WV Univ 1977; *cr:* 2nd Grade Teacher J Ralph Mc Elvane Elem 1970-71; 4th Grade Teacher Mannington Elem 1971-75, E Dale Elem 1975-; *ai:* Chm for Lang Art Curr Dev 1987-; Step Ahead Rdng Prgm 1990; Lead Teacher 1984, 1986, 1988; Supvr of Stu Teachers; MCEA, WVEA, Marion Cty Rdng Cncl 1971-; Joint Cncl of Ec Ed 1977-78, St Monetary Awd; Bethesda Baptist Church (Bible Sch Worker, Sunday Sch Teacher 1989-); WV Exemplary Elem Sch 1987; Natl Exemplary Elem Sch 1988-89; *office:* E Dale Elem Rt 3 Fairmont WV 26554

ROBINSON, LOU ANN (WILDER), 5th/6th Grade English Teacher; *b:* Philadelphia, MS; *m:* Slater Kenneth; *c:* Brooke; *ed:* (BS) Elem Ed, Univ of Southern 1982; *cr:* 5th/6th Grade Eng Teacher Taylorsville Elem 1982-; *office:* Taylorsville Elem Sch PO Box 8 Taylorsville MS 39168

ROBINSON, LOVIE VINSON, Fourth Grade Teacher; *b:* Bolton, MS; *c:* Benardytte F.; *ed:* (BS) Elem Ed, Tougaloo Coll 1968; (MED) Ed, MS Coll 1976; Further Study Jackson St Univ; *cr:* 3rd Grade Teacher Bolton Attendance Center 1968-70; 4th Grade Teacher Woodville Hgts Elem Sch 1970-; *ai:* Tougaloo Coll Natl Alumni Assn 1988-; United Meth Women 1985-; Woodville Hgts PTA Secy 1988-; *home:* PO Box 93 Bolton MS 39041

ROBINSON, LUCRETIA METZ, Eng/Hum/Journalism Teacher; *b:* Huntington, WV; *m:* David Harrison; *c:* Julianna; *ed:* (BA) Scndry Ed/Eng/His, Marshall Univ 1965; Post Grad Stud Marshall Univ, Univ of WA, Univ of Puget Sound, Seattle Univ, Univ of OR; *cr:* Eng Teacher Bath Jr HS 1965-66; Eng/Drama/Media Teacher 1966-70, Eng/Journalism/Career Ed Teacher 1978-81 Sharples Jr HS; His Teacher Garfield HS 1981-82; Eng/Hum/Journalism Teacher Chief Sealth HS 1982-; *ai:* Southwestern Newspaper Adv; NEA, WEA, SEA; Outstanding Service Awd Sharples Jr HS 1981; NEH Inst Fellowship Post World War II Japanese Lit 1987; Seattle Bus Comm Excl in Ed Awd 1990; *office:* Chief Sealth HS 2600 SW Thistle St Seattle WA 98126

ROBINSON, LYNDA K., Mathematics Teacher; *b:* Charleroi, PA; *ed:* (BS) Math, CA St Coll 1978; (MA) Math/Cmptr Sci, California Univ of PA 1986; Univ of Pittsburgh; *cr:* Teacher Ringgold Sch Dist 1980-; Professor California Univ of PA 1988-; *ai:* Peer Tutoring Spon; SAT Classes; Costumes for Musicals; PSEA, NEA 1983-; Natl Math Teachers of America 1987-; Campfire Incorporated 1970-; Internship Awd Univ of Pittsburgh; *office:* Ringgold HS Rd 4 Box 604 A Monongahela PA 15063

ROBINSON, MARTHA ALLIE MOE, 4th Grade Teacher; *b:* Rockingham, NC; *m:* Paul L. Jr.; *c:* Paul L. III, Melanie B.; *ed:* (BA) Elem Ed, Fayetteville St Teachers Coll 1951; (MS) DC Teachers Coll 1973; A&T Univ 1955; George Washington Univ 1962; Cmptr Literacy & Substance Abuse 1986; *cr:* 2nd Grade Teacher Waynesboro GA 1951-55, Moten Elem 1959-63; 2nd-6th Grade/Resource Teacher Harrison Elem 1964-; *ai:* Patrol Leader 1965-88; WA Teachers Union Citation for Service 1961; Outstanding Service Awd 1975-79; Perfect Attendance Awd 1985, 1988; Excl in Achievement 1978-86; Ward I Outstanding Teacher of Yr 1982; *home:* 6301 Kansas Ave NE Washington DC 20011

ROBINSON, MARY BOITNOTT, Retired Teacher; *b:* Princeton, KY; *m:* Noble Reed; *ed:* (BS) Elem Ed, Austin Peay St Coll & W KY St Coll 1958; *cr:* Teacher Cty Bd St Charles Sch 1941-43, Crofton Elem 1946-84; *ai:* TV Prgm Math Cntry Chairperson Ky Ed TV; Sch Comm; Channel 35 1964; NEA, KY Ed Assn, 2nd Dist Assn 1948-84; Eastern Star 1950-; Volunteer Worker Nursing Home 1984-; Retired Teachers KY Farm Bureau 1984-; *home:* 1098 Terry-Coal Rd Crofton KY 42217

ROBINSON, MICHAEL CHARLES, 5th Grade Teacher; *b:* Baltimore, MD; *m:* Venezuela; *ed:* (BS) Elem Ed, VA Union Univ 1979; (MS) Counseling, Kent St Univ 1986; *cr:* Teacher/Wrestling Coach Prospect Elem & Shaw HS 1979-83; Teacher Superior Elem 1984-; *ai:* Sci, Conflict Mgmt, Career Ed Clubs; Sch Guard Adv; PTA 1983-; Dorothy N Cowling Citizenship, Career Ed Awd; *office:* Superior Elem Sch 1865 Garfield East Cleveland OH 44112

ROBINSON, MILDRED SPEARMAN, English Teacher; *b:* Greenwood, SC; *m:* Jonathan; *c:* Jonathan, Felicia S.; *ed:* (BA) Eng, SC St Coll 1969; (MED) Ed, Clemson Univ 1983; Numerous Courses; *cr:* Teacher Edgewood HS 1969-70, Ninety Six HS 1970-73, 1975-; *ai:* Sr Class Spon; Advisory & Discipline Comm; SC Ed Assn, NEA, Greenwood Cty Ed Assn 1969-; Old Abbeville Highway Cmmty Club Pres 1984-86; SC St Coll Alumni Assn; Teacher of Yr Ninety Six HS; *home:* Rt 4 Box 97 Greenwood SC 29646

ROBINSON, NANCY L., Third Grade Teacher; *b:* Lynn, MS; *m:* Briard M.; *ed:* (BS) Elem Ed, Univ of ME 1963; (MS) Elem Ed, CA St San Bernardino 1985; *cr:* K-4th Grade Teacher Alvord Unified Sch Dist 1963-; *ai:* Discipline Comm & Incentive Assembly Chairperson; CA Alvord Unified Sch Dist Leadership Awd 1982; Nom Teacher of Yr 1979, 1981; Terrace Teacher of Yr 1985; Project Disseminator CA St Dept of Ed; Conference Presenter; Demonstration Teacher; *office:* Terrace Elem Sch 6601 Rutland Ave Riverside CA 92503

ROBINSON, NANCY ZWART, Principal; *b:* Middletown, NY; *c:* Sheryl Robinson Egner, Jodi Robinson Ruhl, William; *ed:* (BA) Citizenship Ed, The Kings Coll 1961; Grad Stud NY St Teachers Coll New Paltz; *cr:* 7th/8th Grade Soc Stud Teacher 1961-62, 7th/8th Grade Eng Teacher 1961-63 Drum Hill Jr HS; Prin/5th-8th Grade Teacher Bowen Sch 1963-64; 4th Grade Teacher 1978-89, Prin 1989- Atlantic Chrstn Sch; *ai:* Mid-Atlantic Chrstn Assn; Ocean City Baptist Church Choir 1981-; *home:* 1453 Old Stagecoach Rd Ocean View NJ 08230

ROBINSON, RONALD, Mathematics Department Chair; *b:* Paintsville, KY; *m:* Rheda; *c:* Traci, Kristi; *ed:* (BS) Math, E Ky Univ 1967; (MA) Ed, 1984, (BS) Geology 1989 Morehead St Univ; *cr:* Math Teacher 1967-, Guidance Cnslr 1989- Prestonsburg HS; *ai:* Floyd Cty Curr Comm; Math Advisory Chairperson; NCTM 1986-; KY STAR Teacher Awd 1975; *home:* HC 72 Box 63 East Point KY 41216

ROBINSON, ROSALINE JANET, Teacher; *b:* Longview, TX; *ed:* (BS) Math, 1975; (MS) Scndry Ed, 1977 Stephen F. Austin; *cr:* Math Teacher Henderson ISD 1976-; *ai:* Campus Leadership Comm 1989-; Textbook Comm; TSTA; NCTM.

ROBINSON, SARA LUCAS, Business Education Teacher; *b:* Union, SC; *c:* Calvin; *ed:* (BS) Bus Ed, Barber-Scotia Coll 1970; *ai:* FBLA Adv; NEA, NJ Ed Assn, NJ Bus Ed Assn; NJ Barber-Scotia Coll Alumni Assn Secy; *office:* Hillside HS 1085 Liberty Ave Hillside NJ 07205

ROBINSON, SARAH RAGIN, Third Grade Teacher; *b:* Atlanta, GA; *m:* Robert Lee Sr.; *c:* Robbie L., Rhonda L., Robert L. Jr.; *ed:* (BS) Elem Ed, Morris Brown Coll 1971; (MA) Elem Ed, Atlanta Univ 1976; *cr:* Teacher John Carey Elem 1971, Huntley Hills Elem 1974-77, Redan Elem 1977-80, Brockett Elem 1981-; *ai:* Brockett Sch Drill Team Co-Spon; Brockett Sch Instruction Comm; Lynn Owens Schlsp Comm Mem; Vlybl Team Brockett Staff Mem; GA Assn of Educators 1986-; DeKalb Cty Youth Assistance Prgm; *office:* Brockett Elem Sch 1855 Brockett Rd Tucker GA 30084

ROBINSON, STEPHEN EDWARD, HS English/Soc Stud Teacher; *b:* New York, NY; *m:* Kathleen Mary Donohue; *c:* Grace N., Thomas I.; *ed:* (BA) Sociology, St Univ of NY Geneseo 1977; (MSED) Cmptr Literacy, Nazareth Coll of Rochester 1990; Teaching Certificates, St Univ of NY Brockport, St Univ of Geneseo, Nazareth Coll Rochester; *cr:* 10th/12th Grade Eng/9th-11th Grade Soc Stud Teacher Cohocton Cntrl Sch 1985-; *ai:* Academic All-Stars Coach; 11th Grade Adv; Appointed Dist Cmptr Coord; *office:* Cohocton Cntrl Sch 30 Park Ave Cohocton NY 14826

ROBINSON, TY S., Science Department Chairman; *b:* Provo, UT; *m:* Jamie Dutton; *c:* Gary, Sheri, Stevie; *ed:* (BS) Earth Sci Composite, Brigham Young Univ 1987; Mid Sch Endorsement UT St Univ 1987; Scndry Level Math Endorsement 1988; *cr:* Sci Teacher 1987-88, Sci Dept Chm 1988-, Teacher of Gifted & Talented 1989- Spanish Fork Jr HS; *ai:* Sci Club Chm; Egg-Drop Contests, Sci Fairs, Engineering Contests Organizer; Bsktbl Coach; USTA, NSTA 1987-; UEA Faculty Rep 1988-; Helped Brigham Young Univ Launch Help Save Eart Sci Museum; *office:* Spanish Fork Jr HS 600 S 820 E Spanish Fork UT 84660

ROBINSON, VIRGINIA FEIDER, 6th Grade Teacher; *b:* Pomeroy, WA; *m:* Jame H.; *c:* Krystala, J. T.; *ed:* (BA) Ed, ID St Univ 1978; *cr:* 6th Grade Teacher Downey Elem 1979-80; 5th/6th Grade Combination Teacher 1980-82, 5th Grade Teacher 1982-89, 6th Grade Teacher 1989- Inkom Elem; *ai:* Church Volunteer Religious Ed Teacher; Campfire Sftbl Teams Volunteer Coach; *office:* Inkom Elem Sch Box 430 Inkom ID 83245

ROBINSON, WALTER, Social Studies Teacher/Coach; *b:* Bolton, MS; *m:* Debra White; *c:* Christian H., Faith, Chadrick; *ed:* (BS) Soc Sci, Jackson St Univ 1969; Grad Stud MS St Univ & MS Coll; *cr:* Soc Stud Teacher Forest Hill HS 1970-; *ai:* Head Sftbl, Vlybl, Girls Bsktbl Coach; United Way 1970-; Sunday Sch Teacher 1975-; Teacher of Month 1989; Forest Hill Outstanding Teacher 1971; Good Apple Awd 1989; *office:* Forest Hill HS 2607 Raymond Rd Jackson MS 39212

ROBISCH, NATALIE LEMOINE, English Teacher; *b:* N Adams, MA; *m:* Edwin; *ed:* (BA) Eng, St Univ of NY Albany 1959; (MA) Eng, Middlebury Coll 1965; Gifted Ed, Columbia Univ & Coll of St Rose; Inst on Civic Ed, Harvard Grad Sch of Ed; *cr:* 7th-9th Grade Eng Teacher 1959-, Eng Teacher in Charge 1965- Wappingers Cntrl Sch Dist; *ai:* Drama Club Adv; NY St Cncl of Eng 1983-, Teacher of Yr 1985; NCTE 1980-; Amer Society for Curr Dev 1985-; *office:* Van Wyck Jr H S Hillside Lake Rd Wappingers Falls NY 12590

ROBISON, BEVERLY ANN, Phys Ed Teacher/Coach; *b:* Sallisaw, OK; *ed:* (BS) Phys Ed/Health, 1983, (MS) Phys Ed, 1990 Northeastern St Univ; Instr, Air Force Reserve; *cr:* Teacher/Coach Crystal City HS 1984-85, Poth HS 1985-86, Van Alstyne HS 1986-88; Sftbl/Bsktbl/Track Coach Salina HS 1988-; *ai:* Sr Class Spon; Athletic Programming; NEA, OK Ed Assn, OK Coaches Assn; Coach of Yr 1987, 1988; *home:* PO Box 813 Salina OK 74365

ROBISON, MARY GILLAND, Second Grade Teacher; *b:* Franklin, TX; *m:* Fred L.; *c:* Jerry, Rhea; *ed:* (BS) Elem Ed, Sam Houston Univ 1956; A&M Univ Stud 1956; *cr:* Kindergarden Anahuac ISD 1956-57; 1st Grade Teacher 1961-72, ESAA 1972-75, 2nd Grade Teacher 1975- Bryan ISD; *ai:* Pilot Program in Elem Keyboarding & Word Processing; ATPE 1977-; Apple II Bug Pres 1990; Masonic Chalkboard Awd Outstanding Teacher BISD 1986.

ROBISON, SARA (FRANCIS), 5th Grade Teacher; *b:* Bakersfield, CA; *m:* Thomas M.; *c:* Kristen K. Ansted; *ed:* (BS) Sociology, CA St Univ Northridge 1973; Certified Family Life Educator; Completing Lib/Media Specialist & Masters Fresno Pacific Coll 1991; *cr:* 7th/8th Grade Lang Art Teacher Oakhurst Elem 1975-88; 5th Grade Teacher Oak Creek Intermediate Sch 1988-89; *ai:* Yrbk; Oral Interpretation/Speech Coach; Dist Family Life Ed; Staff Dev; Odyssey of Mind; Academic Pentathlon; NEA Local, CA Rdng Assn; American Assn of Univ Women, Muscular Dystrophy Assn; Mentor Teacher 1984-85; Fellow San Joaquin Valley Writing Project; *office:* Oak Creek Intermediate Sch 40094 Indian Springs Rd Rd 427 Oakhurst CA 93644

ROBOTIN, BARBARA ZIELINSKI, First Grade Teacher; *b:* Trenton, NJ; *m:* Robert John; *ed:* (BS) Elem Ed, Trenton St Coll 1972; *cr:* 1st Grade Teacher Holy Cross Parochial Sch 1973-; *ai:* Var Cheerleading, Girls Sftbl Past Asst Coach; Cath War Veterans Auxiliary; *office:* Holy Cross Sch Arch & Grand Sts Trenton NJ 08611

ROBSON, CAROL GARNAAS, Fourth Grade Teacher; *b:* Missoula, MT; *m:* Michael Richard; *c:* Jeremy, Shannon, Kylee; *ed:* (BA) Elem Ed, Univ of NE Lincoln 1973; *cr:* 3rd Grade Teacher 1973-76, Pre-Kndgtn/Kndgtn Teacher 1977-80, 4th Grade Teacher 1981- Omaha Publics Schls; *ai:* Omaha Public Schls Rdng Study Curr Comm; NEA, NE St Ed Assn 1973-; Omaha Ed Assn Building Rep 1973-; *office:* Ponca Elem Sch 11300 N Post Rd Omaha NE 68112

ROBSON, WILLIAM THURMAN, JR., Sixth Grade Teacher; *b:* Staunton, VA; *m:* Teresa Ann Hammer; *c:* William Thurman III; *ed:* (BS) Speech/Public Speaking/Elem Ed, James Madison Univ 1967; Grad Stud Univ of VA, James Madison Univ, East Mennonite Coll; *cr:* 5th/6th Grade Teacher Shenandoah Heights Elem 1967-; *ai:* Steering & TLC Comm; Prins Advisory Cncl; Mary Baldwin Coll Head of Cooperative Teachers; Waynesboro Schls 6 Yr Planning Comm on Ed; Waynesboro Ed Assn, VA Ed Assn, NEA 1967-; United Way Ed Co-Chm 1986-, Top Sch 1987-; Waynesboro Players Pres 1980-; Waynesboro Public Sch Employee Credit Union Ed Officer 1972-; Clinical Faculty of Mid-Valley Consortium for Teachers Ed; *home:* 827 High St Staunton VA 24401

ROBY, PEGGY MAY, Mathematics Teacher; *b:* Anderson, IN; *m:* James; *c:* Joshua, Carrie; *ed:* (BA) Math, Anderson Univ 1972; (MA) Math, Ball St 1982; *cr:* Algebra Teacher Knightstown HS 1972-73, Madison Heights HS 1980-81; Geometry/Algebra Teacher Highland HS 1982-88; 7th/8th Grade Math Teacher E Side Mid Sch 1988-89-; 7th/8th Grade Albebra Teacher N Side Mid Sch 1989-; *ai:* Highland HS SADD Spon; N Side HS Peer Tutoring Co Spon; Knightstown Chrldr & Class Spon; *office:* North Side Mid Sch 1815 Indiana Ave Anderson IN 46012

ROCAP, JOAN MARIE, Mathematics Teacher; *b:* Indianapolis, IN; *ed:* (BS) Math, Univ of Notre Dame 1978; (MAT) Ed, Northwestern Univ 1979; *cr:* Teacher Maine South HS 1978-79, Brebeuf Preporatory Sch 1979-; *ai:* Co-Moderator Math Club; Frosh Cheerleading Spon; Faculty Assn VP; NCTM Mem 1979-; *office:* Brebeuf Preparatory Sch 2801 W 86th St Indianapolis IN 46268

ROCHE, LYNNE ANN, 7/8th Grade Lang Arts Teacher; *b:* Chicago, IL; *m:* Terry; *c:* Tony, Laura; *ed:* (BA) English, Eureka Coll 1975; *cr:* 6th Grade Lang Arts Teacher Jordan Catholic Sch 1978-80; 6th & 7th Grade Eng Teacher St Patrick Sch 1982-83; 7th & 8th Grade Eng Teacher Cathedral Grade Sch 1983-84; 7th & 8th Lang Arts Teacher Nuttall Mid Sch 1986-; *ai:* Speech/Literary Team; IL ED Assn 1986-; NEA 1986-; *office:* Nuttall Mid Sch 400 W Rustic St Robinson IL 62454

ROCHE, MARGARET ANN STORER, 7th Grade Soc Stud Teacher; *b:* Chicago, IL; *ed:* (BS) Ed Emphaisi Art, Northern IL Univ 1969; Summer 1986 Teacher Inst; Oriental Inst Univ Chicago; 1984 Outdoor Ed Seminar Austria; *cr:* 7th Grade Teacher Sycamore Jr HS 1969-; *ai:* Pompon Squad Spon; Girls Vlybl Asst Coach; Yrbk Spon; NEA IEA Sycamore Ed Assn 1969-; Delta Kappa Gamma Society Intnl (Pres Gamma Chi Chapter of Lambda St 1979-82/Literary Arts 1986) 1976-; Kishwaukee Valley Art League 1984-; Prof Picture Framers Assn 1987-; Soc Stud Dept Chairperson Sycamore Jr HS 1978-84; Women in the Arts St Level Comm 1984; Delta Kappa Gamma Society Intnl Lambda St 1980-84; *office:* Sycamore Jr H S 150 Maplewood Dr Sycamore IL 60178

ROCHE, MICHAEL TERENCE, HS Sci Teacher/AV Coord; *b:* New York, NY; *m:* Jeanne Kohrman; *c:* Christian, Michelle; *ed:* (BS) Environmental Sci, Coll of Ag & Environmental Sci Rutgers Univ 1976; (MA) Environmental Stud, Montclair St Coll 1978; *cr:* Sci Teacher Manchester Township HS 1976-80; Summer Staff NJ Sch of Conservation 1976-77, 1982; Summer Consultat/Master Teacher Princeton Univ 1988-; *ai:* Sci Club Adv; NHS Co-Adv; Boys Girls Tennis Coach; Cmptr Curr Comm AV Coord; Stu Guides Author; Grants Recipient; Ocean Cty Teacher of Yr 1986; *office:* Manchester Township HS 101 So Colonial Dr Lakehurst NJ 08733

ROCHESTER, CLARE BLAGG, Magnet 6th Grade Teacher; *b:* Spokane, WA; *m:* Timothy Reed; *c:* Lacey; *ed:* (BS) ELem, 1979, (MED) Rdng, 1980 LA St Univ; *cr:* 4th/5th Grade Teacher of Gifted Greenville Elem 1980-83; Teacher of Gifted Sci/Math 1984-87, Magnet Soc Stud/Research/Stud Skills Teacher 1988- Mc Kinley Mid Magnet; *ai:* Beta Club Spon; EBRP Audit Team Mem; Soc Stud Fair Chairperson; NEA, LA Assn of Educators 1980-; *office:* Mc Kinley Mid Magnet Sch 1557 Mc Calop St Baton Rouge LA 70802

ROCK, HELEN DENNIS, Elementary Music Teacher; *b:* Columbus, OH; *m:* Donald F. Sr.; *c:* Donald F. Jr., Dennis F.; *ed:* (BS) Music Ed, FL Southern Coll 1951; Univ South FL; *cr:* Music Teacher Campbell HS 1951-52; 4th Grade Teacher Taylorsville Elem -HS 1952-53; Music Teacher Boylan-Haven Private Sch 1956-57; Band-Gen Music Teacher Alva HS 1960-69; Band Dir Pahokee HS 1969-74; Music Teacher Lehigh Elem 1974-; *ai:* Music Educators Natl Conference 1961-; FL Music Educators Assn 1961- Service Awd 1990; FL Elem Music Educators Assn 1974-; Lehigh Concert Band Dir 1980-; *home:* 17770 Caloosa Rd Alva FL 33920

ROCKEL, STEPHANIE C., Second Grade Teacher; *b:* Saint Louis, MO; *m:* Christopher M.; *c:* Jake D.; *ed:* (BS) Ed, MO Univ Columbia 1977; *cr:* 5th Grade Teacher 1978-79, 4th Grade Teacher 1979-82 Beasley Elem Sch; 1st Grade Teacher Catoosa Elem Sch 1984-85, Point Elem Sch 1986-88; 2nd Grade Teacher Point Elem Sch 1988-; *ai:* Elem Arithmetic Textbook Selection Comm for Mehlville Sch Dist; MO Ed Assn, NEA, Mehlville Cmmty Teachers Assn; *office:* Point Elem Sch 6790 Telegraph Rd Saint Louis MO 63129

ROCKETT, JULIA ELIZABETH, English Teacher; *b:* Atlanta, GA; *ed:* Eng, US Intnl Univ; (BSED) Eng Ed - Cum Laude, Univ of GA 1977; (MED) Eng Ed, GA St Univ 1983; Natl Endowment for Hum Summer Inst 1988; *cr:* Eng Teacher Dunwoody HS 1977-; *ai:* Annual Spring Literary Meet Coord; Cty Eng Textbook Adoption Comm Mem 1985, 1990; NCTE 1989-; Southern Company 1987-88, Educator Service Awd; Womens Resource Center of De Kalb Cty Volunteer 1987-; *office:* Dunwoody HS 5035 Vermack Rd Dunwoody GA 30338

ROCKETT, ROBERT CARL, Fourth Grade Teacher; *b:* Longview, WA; *m:* Sharon Case; *c:* Robert Jr., Tawnya, Eric; *ed:* (BA) Phys Ed, 1966, (MA) Phys Ed, 1972, Cntrl WA Univ; *cr:* Elem Teacher Willapa Valley 1966-; *ai:* Valley Booster Club 1966-; March of Dimes Co-Chairperson 1973-78; *home:* Rt 2 Box 163 Raymond WA 98577

ROCKEY, SUSAN MAY, Latin Teacher; *b:* Harrisburg, PA; *ed:* (BA) Classics/Latin/Greek, Wilson Coll 1977; Grad Courses Messiah Coll, Lebanon Valley Coll, Penn St Univ; *cr:* Latin Teacher Lower Paxton Jr HS 1977-79, Swatara Jr HS 1979-82, Cntrl Dauphin E HS 1986-87, Linglestown Jr HS 1977-86, 1988-; *ai:* Foreign Lang Curr Comm; Latin & Intnl Club; Capital Area Classical Assn (Secy 1982-83, Pres 1985-87); PA Classical Assn, Classical Assn of Atlantic Sts; Wilson Coll Alumnae Club Treas 1980-82; Presbyn Church Deacon 1982-86; Cntrl Dauphin Sch Dist Distinguished Service Awd 1990; *office:* Linglestown Jr HS 1200 N Mountain Rd Harrisburg PA 17112

ROCKWELL, JOHN W., Social Studies Teacher; *b:* Lehi, UT; *m:* Kathie Lee Walker; *c:* Genevieve (dec), Orrin P., John D., Don H., David S.; *ed:* (BA) His/Span, Brigham Young Univ 1973; *cr:* His/Span Teacher Duchesne HS 1973-75, Eisenhower Jr HS 1975-84; His Teacher Taylorsville HS 1984-; *ai:* Sons of UT Pioneers Chapter Pres 1988-89; *office:* Taylorsville HS 5225 S Redwood Rd Salt Lake City UT 84123

RODDY, PAULA MERRICK, Mathematics Teacher; *b:* Baton Rouge, LA; *m:* James Edward; *c:* Jamie J.; *ed:* (BA) His/Cmptr Sci, LA St Univ 1985; *cr:* Math Teacher Robert E Lee HS 1987-, LA St Univ 1988-; *ai:* Hi Stepper Dance Line Spon; *home:* 6706 Garland Ave Baker LA 70714

RODDY, ROBERT CONLIN, English Teacher; *b:* Baltimore, MD; *m:* Jacquelyn Szymecki; *c:* Rob, Becky, Jim, Zachary; *ed:* (BSED) Eng Ed, Slippery Rock Univ 1964; (MED) Eng Ed, Indiana Univ of PA 1969; Various Leadership & Advanced Placement Classes; *cr:* 7th/8th Grade Teacher Richland Township Jr HS 1964-68; 11th/12th Grade Mc Dowell HS 1968-; LE 111-112 Teacher Gannon Univ 1983-; *ai:* Academic Challenge Coach; Literary Magazine Adv; PSEA, MEA.

RODEFER, JAN SHETLER (FILLMORE), G/T Resource Teacher; *b:* Massillon, OH; *m:* Charles W.; *c:* Randy Fillmore, Robin Chapin, Russ Fillmore; *ed:* (BS) Elem Ed, Kent St Univ 1964; Univ of CT; Clarion Univ of PA; Univ of Akron; Ashland Univ; OH ST Univ; *cr:* 4th Grade Teacher Preston Sch 1959-60; 3rd-6th Grades Teacher Bode & Price Schls 1964-80; 6th Grade Sci Teacher Roberts Mid Sch 1980-85; G/T Resource Teacher Cuyahoga Falls Schls 1985-; *ai:* Acad Challenge Team Coach; Teams Coord & Coach; Odyssey of the Mind Coord; Sci Internship Prgm; Chuch Choir; ASCD; COCG; OAGC; Kappa Kappa Iota Pres Elect 1989-; Jaycees Cmmty Service 1985; Outstanding Conservation Teacher of Yr 1979; Jennings Scholar 1981-82; Roberts Teacher of Yr 1984-; Cuyahoga Falls Teacher of Yr 1984; *office:* Guyahoga Falls City Sch 431 Stow St P O Box 396 Cuyahoga Falls OH 44222

RODEN, KEITH T., Jr/Sr HS Music Teacher; *b:* Harrisburg, PA; *ed:* (BS) Music Ed, Lebanon Valley Coll 1983; Several Wkshps; PA Dept of Ed Masters Equivelency Certificate 1990; *cr:* Elem Vocal/Music Teacher W Shore Area Sch Dist 1983-84; K-12th Grade Vocal/Music Teacher Fannett-Metal Sch Dist 1986-88; 7th-12th Grade Vocal/Music Teacher/Choral Dir S Middleton Sch Dist 1988-; *ai:* Concert Choir, Girls Quartet, Mens Trio, Stu Assistance Team; Music Educators Natl Conference, PA Music Educators Assn 1983-; Amer Guild of Eng Handbell Ringers 1989-; Choristers Guild 1984-; 2nd United Church of Christ (Deacon 1985-87, 1990, Handbell Dir 1989-); *office:* S Middleton Sch Dist 4 Forge Rd Boiling Springs PA 17007

RODENBERG, BARBARA REID, Jr HS Sci/Math Teacher; *b:* Banff AB, Canada; *m:* William Lee; *c:* Karen, Mindy, Andrea; *ed:* (BA) Bio, Andrews Univ 1968; Teacher Cert Classes; Working Towards Masters Sci Ed, Univ of MD; *cr:* 5th-9th Grade Head Teacher Richmond Jr Acad 1979-81; Librarian Edmonton Jr Acad 1982-84; 5th-9th Grade Head Teacher Desmond T Doss Sch 1984-87; 6th Grade Teacher 1987-88, 7th-8th Grade Math/Sci Teacher 1988- John Nevins Andrews Sch; *ai:* Sci Academic Challenge & Stu Cncl Spon; NCTM 1987-89; NSTA 1988-; *office:* John Nevins Andrews Sch 117 Elm Ave Takoma Park MD 20912

RODEY, ROBERT ALAN, History Teacher; *b:* Shelby, OH; *m:* Pamela Ann Lowry; *c:* Laura, Elaine; *ed:* (BSED) His/Poly Sci, Bowling Green St Univ 1964; (MA) Soc Stud, Univ of IL 1971; Macalester Coll, Rutgers Univ, Fordham Univ, Johns Hopkins Univ, Univ of IL Chicago, Governors St Univ; *cr:* Teacher Rich East HS 1964-; *ai:* Scholastic Bowl Adv; Gifted Prgm Coord; NCSS; Comm for Amer Stud Ed; IL St Bd of Ed Master Teacher 1983; Cncl for Basic Ed Ind Study Grant 1989; Woodrow Wilson Fellowship 1990; *office:* Rich East HS 300 Sauk Trl Park Forest IL 60466

RODGERS, DEBBIE HAWKINS, Fifth Grade Home Ec Teacher; *b:* Charleston, IL; *m:* Ron; *c:* Lauren, Lindsey; *ed:* (BA) Elem Ed, E IL Univ 1978; Working Towards Masters S IL Univ; *cr:* 5th Grade Teacher Potomac Grade Sch 1978-79, Pinckneyville Jr HS 1979-; *ai:* HS Graduation Speaker; *office:* Pinckneyville Jr HS RR 4 Hwy 154 E Pinckneyville IL 62274

RODGERS, HELEN BYRNE, English Teacher; *b:* Osaka, Japan; *m:* David C.; *c:* Curtis, Valerie; *ed:* (BS) Eng Ed - Summa Cum Laude, 1982, (MED) Eng, 1987 Columbus Coll; *cr:* Teacher Shaw HS 1983-; *ai:* Newspaper Spon; Sr News Bulletin; Jr Class Cncl; Phi Kappa Phi, Lambda Iota Tau, Kappa Delta Pi 1982; NCTE (GA Writing Competition Judge, Regional Conference Presenter); Columbus Coll Outstanding Scndry Grad 1983; GA Governors Honor Prgm Judge; Columbus Coll Curr Review Comm Mem; Shaw Sail Teacher 1989-; *office:* Shaw HS 7601 Schomburg Rd Columbus GA 31909

RODGERS, JANICE DUKE, Social Studies Teacher; *b:* Chattahoochee, FL; *m:* Russell Mc Leod; *c:* Rusty, Robin, Ryan; *ed:* (BS) His, FL St Univ 1961; *cr:* Teacher Chattahoochee HS 1962-68, 1971-; *ai:* Soc Stud Dept Chairperson; Co-Spon & Adv NHS; SACS Steering Comm; Sr Class Co-Spon 1988-; Delta Kappa Gamma Mem 1972-; NCSS Mem 1986-; Chattahoochee Presbyn Church Chrstn Ed Comm 1988-; St of FL Prof Ethics Reviewer 1989-; Gadsden Cty Teacher of Yr 1987; Chattahoochee Hs Teacher of Yr Nom 1989; Nom FL Cncl Soc Stud Outstanding Soc Stud Teacher 1989; *office:* Chattahoochee HS Drawer #7 613 Chattahoochee St Chattahoochee FL 32324

RODGERS, KEN, Fifth Grade Teacher; *b:* Galesburg, IL; *ed:* (BS) Bus, 1969, (MS) Elem Ed, 1988 W IL Univ; IL Cert Teaching Gifted; *cr:* 3rd-6th Grade Teacher Rockridge Sch Dist 1969-.

RODGERS, LARRY JOE, Intermediate Math Teacher; *b:* Mason City, IL; *m:* Nancy Diann; *c:* Dewey P., Joel L., Mary T.; *ed:* (AA) General Ed, Canton Jr Coll 1968; (BS) Elem Ed, Murray St Univ 1970; (MA) Sch Admin, Sangamon St Univ 1984; *cr:* Intermediate Ed Teacher Greenview Sch Dist 1970-; *ai:* Frosh Class Spon; Teacher Evaluation Chm; Teacher Welfare Comm; Greenview Ed Assn (Pres 1979-80, VP 1981-83); IL Ed Assn, NEA 1970-; Mason City HS Alumni Pres 1980, 1990; United Meth (Marriage Encounter Team 1980-88, Engaged Encounter Exec Lay Couple 1990); *home:* 211 S Indiana Mason City IL 62664

RODGERS, MARTHA RACKLEY, Third Grade Teacher; *b:* Pontotoc, MS; *m:* Paul O.; *c:* Michael O., Bryan P.; *ed:* (BA) Eng, MS Coll Clinton 1949; *cr:* Teacher Pontotoc Sch System 1949-51, Amory City Schls 1951-52, Memphis City Schls 1952-54, De Soto Cty Schls 1972-; *ai:* MS Prof Educators; Shelby Cty PTA Cncl (Pres 1966-68, Volunteer 1954-72), St & Natl Life Membership; TN Congress PTA VP 1970-72; *office:* Hope P Sullivan Sch 7985 Southave Circle West Southaven MS 38671

RODGERS, SHARON L., Chemistry Teacher; *b:* Philadelphia, PA; *ed:* (BA) Chem, Univ of Rochester 1968; (MA) Chem, Boston Univ 1970; NSF Inst Chem Teachers, Beaver Coll 1971; *cr:* Chem Teacher Hingham HS 1969-72; Phys Sci Teacher Lincoln Jr HS 1973-83; Chem/Physics Teacher Junction City HS 1983-84; Chem Teacher Sheldon HS 1984-; *ai:* NSTA, NEA, OEA, EEA; Co-Author Glencoe Publishing Company 1989; *office:* Henry D Sheldon HS 2455 Willakenzie Rd Eugene OR 97401

RODGERS, VIOLA GAMBLE, 4th Grade Teacher; *b:* Buffalo, NY; *m:* Owen Jr.; *c:* Susan Fuhrmann, Barbara Mlynarski, Owen III; *ed:* (BS) Elem Ed, 1962, (MS) Rdng, 1974 Buffalo St Teachers Coll; *cr:* 4th Grade Teacher West Seneca Cntrl Sch System 1962-; *ai:* NY St Teachers 1962-; Order of Eastern Star 1953-; Daughters of Nile; Ladies Oriental Shrine; *office:* Potters Road Elem 675 Potters Rd West Seneca NY 14224

RODI, LINDA M., Fourth Grade Teacher; *b:* New Orleans, LA; *ed:* (BS) Elem Ed, Our Lady of Holy Cross Coll 1976; (MS) Admin, Loyola Univ 1982; Loyola Univ 1982; *cr:* Mgr Hayes Dairy 1962-73; Teacher Archdiocese of New Orleans 1973-74, St Bernard Sch System 1976-; *ai:* Volunteer Tutor Operatiom Mainstream 1986-87, 1990-; Volunteer Tutor for Deficient Readers 1978-; Delta Kappa Gamma (Correspondent Secy 1986-88), 1986-; Intnl Rdng Assn 1978-; LA Rdng Assn 1978-; Intnl Convention Comm 1984-85, 1988-89; St Bernard Cncl of Intnl Rdng Assn (Pres 1984-85, Various Comm 1985-) 1978-; St Bernard Parish Literacy Rep 1986; NEA, LA Assn of Educator 1978-; St Bernard Assn of Educator (Sch Rep 1982-85, Membership Rep 1990-) 1978-; St Bernard Bus Prof 1978-; Operation Mainstream Volunteer 1986-87, 1990-; St Bernard Cncl of Intnl Rdng Assn Wkshps 1984-87.

RODMAN, LORETTA FRATTZOLINO, Special Education Teacher; *b:* Cleveland, OH; *m:* Richard Wesley; *c:* Amanda L., Tyler J.W.; *ed:* (BS) Behavior Disorders/Learning Disabilities/ Elem Ed, 1977; (MED) Admin/Supervision, John Carroll Univ 1983; (BS) Scndry Ed/Soc Sci, 1985; *cr:* SBH Teacher Bellefaire Sch 1977-; *ai:* Review Bds; Parent-Teacher Conference Planner; Fund Raising Projects; Washington Trips Coord; CEC; Cath War Veterans Women; Alzheimers Assn Volunteer; John Carroll Alumni Assn; Child Welfare League of America Speaker; *office:* Bellefaire Sch 22001 Fairmount Ave University Heights OH 44118

RODMAN-DOWNING, MARY ANN, Media Specialist; *b:* Washington, DC; *m:* Craig Lawrence Downing; *ed:* (BA) Theater, Lenoir-Rhyne Coll 1976; (MLS) Lib Sci, Univ of TN Knoxville 1977; *cr:* Media Specialist Adamsville Jr/Sr HS 1982; *ai:* Lib Club Adv; Chrldr Spon; Draa Dir; NEA 1982-; TN Ed Assn 1985-; TN Assn of Athletic Coaches 1984-; Adamsville HS Teacher of Yr 1988.

RODRIGUES, ROBERT MANUEL, Civic Education Teacher; *b:* Pittsburgh, PA; *m:* Eleanor Anne Srooch; *c:* Robert A., Matthew J., Justin P., Nicole M., Annmarie E.; *ed:* (BSED) Scndry Ed, 1969, (MA) Modern European His, 1974, (MED) Scndry Admin, 1985 Duquesne Univ; Curr Dev, Civic Ed, Carnegie-Mellon Univ 1977-81; *cr:* Teacher Bishops Latin Sch 1969-73, W PA Sch for Deaf 1973-74; Consultant Carnegie Mellon Univ 1977-81, March of Dimes 1981; Teacher Chartiers Valley HS 1974-; Admin Comm Coll of Allegheny Cty 1985-, Woodville St Hospital 1989-; Sub-Comm Chm Cncl for Basic Ed 1989-; *ai:* Head Bsbl Coach; NHS Adv; Long Range Planning-Self Esteem Comm; Cncl for Basic Ed Network Sub-Comm Chairperson, Historical Society of W PA 1989-; Smithsonian 1987; St Maurice PTG Ed Comm 1983-84; BSA Asst Den Leader 1989-; Churchill Area Bsbl Assn Coach 1987-, Pres Awd; Natl Endowment for Hum & Cncl for Basic Ed Fellowship 1985; Gift of Time Service Awd 1990; Articles 1978, 1989; *office:* Chartiers Valley HS 50 Thoms Run Rd Bridgeville PA 15017

RODRIGUEZ, CAROL SCHUETZ, Journalism Teacher; *b:* Hollister, CA; *m:* Philip; *ed:* (BS) Ed, Univ of TX Austin 1968; (MS) Curr/Instruction, Univ of TX San Antonio 1982; *cr:* Teacher/Publications Adv Stroman HS 1968-70; Teacher Palo Alto Elem 1970-71, Harlandale Mid Sch 1971-76; Teacher/ Publications Adv Harlandale HS 1976-; *ai:* Sch Newspaper, Yrbk, UIL Journalism Team Spon; TX St Teachers Assn, Journalism Educators Assn; TX Assn of Journalism Educators; TX HS Photography Instr; *office:* Harlandale HS 114 E Gerald San Antonio TX 78214

RODRIGUEZ, ERNEST ANTHONY, Guidance Cnslr/Phys Ed Teacher; *b:* Santa Fe, NM; *m:* Gerardine Antoinette Martinez; *c:* Amanda R., Miguel A.; *ed:* (AA) General Stud, NM Military Inst 1982; (BS) Scndry Ed, Coll of Santa Fe 1984; Grad Stud in Counseling, NM Highlands; *cr:* Phys Ed Teacher/Coach Santa Fe HS 1984-88; Cnslr/Coach Mesa Vista HS 1988-; *ai:* Head Coach Boys Var Bsktbl, Track & Cross Cntry; Head Coach Girls Var Track & Cross Cntry; NM Coaches Assn 1984-; *home:* 1322 Lujan St Santa Fe NM 87501

RODRIGUEZ, JAMES ERNEST, 8th Grade English Teacher; *b:* Columbus, OH; *m:* Sharon Lynn Moon; *c:* Jennifer L., James R.; ; *ed:* (BA) Psych, SW TX St Univ 1978; *cr:* Lang Art Teacher Southside Mid Sch 1981-; *ai:* Stu Cncl Spon; TV 201; Natl Jr Honor Society Faculty Adv; ATPE 1981-88; *home:* 125 E Norwood San Antonio TX 78212

RODRIGUEZ, LEONOR A. LARA, 10th Grade English Teacher; *b:* San Antonio, TX; *m:* Louis; *c:* Anna L., Angela; *ed:* (BA) Speech, 1965, (MED) Scndry Ed, 1967 Our Lady of the Lake Univ; *cr:* 9th-12th Grade Eng/Speech Teacher Lanier HS 1965-68; 6th-8th Eng/Speech/Rdng Teacher Whittier Mid Sch 1969-88; Teacher of Gifted & Talented/10th Grade Eng Brackenridge HS 1988; *ai:* Curr Dev Comm for Gifted & Talented 1990; TX Assn of Gifted & Talented 1989-; NEA, TX St Teachers Assn, San Antonio Teachers Cncl 1965-; Whittier PTA (VP 1977-78, Treas 1987-88, Mem), Outstanding Teacher of Yr 1978, 1988, 1984-85; Outstanding Teacher Whittier Mid Sch 1984-85; Mem of Several TX Ed St Comms on Stu & Prof Assessment; *office:* Brackenridge HS 400 Temple St San Antonio TX 78210

RODRIGUEZ, MANUEL ROBERT, Mathematics Instructor; *b:* Charleroi, PA; *ed:* (BS) Math/Ed, 1970, (MED) Spec Ed, 1974, (MS) Psych, 1989 CA Univ of PA; Cert as Sch Psychologist; *cr:* Instr Ringgold Sch Dist 1970-; *ai:* Natl Assn of Sch Psychologist 1989-; PA Interscholastic Athletic Assn Referee 1972-; *office:* Ringgold Sch Dist 1200 Chess St Monongahela PA 15063

RODRIGUEZ, OLIVIA, English Teacher; *b:* Brownsville, TX; *ed:* (BS) Ed, 1977, (MA) Admin, 1980 SW TX St Univ; NJ Writing Inst; *cr:* 6th Grade Teacher Lamar Mid Sch 1977-84; Eng Teacher San Marcos HS 1984-; *ai:* Stu Cncl, Frosh Class, Jr Class Spon; Planning Our Future & Adopt-a-Sch Comms; TSTA; TCTA Rep 1983-84; Published Articles; *office:* San Marcos HS 1301 Hwy 123 San Marcos TX 78666

RODRIGUEZ, ORLANDO ANDREW, Band Director; *b:* Carlsbad, NM; *m:* Kathleen April Gallaway; *c:* Andrew G.; *ed:* (BMED) Instrumental, 1977, (MMED) Instrumental, 1980 E NM Univ; *cr:* Grad Asst E NM Univ 1978-79; Jr HS Band Dir Roswell Ind Sch Dist 1979-80; Band Dir Alamogordo Mid & HS 1980-86, Hobbs Municipal Sch 1986-; *ai:* Taskervitch Bsktbl Pep Band; Solo & Ensembles; SE NM Music Educators Assn Pres 1989-; NEA, Kappa Kappa Psi, Phi Mu Alpha, Phi Beta Mu, Music Educators Natl Confernce; Southwest Symphony Orch 1986-; Hobbs HS & Martin Rockwell Teacher of Yr 1987-88; Hobbs Jaycees Outstanding Educator Awd 1988; Outstanding Hispanic Citizen 1989; *home:* 400 W Rojo Dr Hobbs NM 88240

RODRIGUEZ, PATRICIA ANN (GUTIERREZ), Office Admin Lab Teacher; *b:* San Antonio, TX; *m:* Phillip C. Jr.; *c:* Phillip C. III, Lisa M.; *ed:* (BS) Bus Admin, 1973, (MED) Sch Admin, 1985 Our Lady of Lake Univ; Voc Office Ed Certificate, Univ of Houston & SW TX St Univ 1978-79; *cr:* Bus Teacher L W Fox Tech HS 1973-76, Luther Burbank HS 1976-77, L W Fox Tech HS 1977-78; Voc Office Ed/Pre-Employment Lab Teacher L W Fox Tech HS 1978-; *ai:* Co-Spon Bus Prof of America 1978-; San Antonio Teachers Cncl, TSTA, NEA Mem 1973-; St Matthews Cath Church Mem 1979-; Fox Tech HS PTA Mem 1973-; Colonies North Elem Sch PTA Mem 1982-; Hobby Mid Sch PTA Mem 1987-; St Marys Oyster Bake Volunteer 1983-; *office:* L W Fox Tech HS 637 N Main Ave San Antonio TX 78205

RODRIGUEZ, SYLVIA MARIA, Social Studies Teacher; *b:* Miami, FL; *m:* Ruben Godoy; *ed:* (BA) Poly Sci, 1981, (MS) Counseling, 1990 Barry Univ; *cr:* 7th/8th Grade Soc Stud Teacher St James Cath Sch 1981-84, Belen Jesuit Prep Sch 1984-86; 10th/ 11th Grade Soc Stud Teacher/11th/12th Grade Bus Teacher Monsignor Edward Pace HS 1986-; *ai:* Phi Alpha Theta VP 1980; NCEA Membership 1981-; Natl Deans List.

RODRIGUEZ, WILLIAM A., Instrumental Music Teacher; *b:* Tampa, FL; *m:* Eveline Mellor; *c:* William D., Eveline Henderson, Rebecca; *ed:* (BS) Music Ed, Univ of Tampa 1961; (MA) Music Ed, Univ of S FL 1974; *cr:* Teacher Ruskin Elem Sch 1961-66, Jefferson HS 1966-67, Van Buren Jr HS 1967-; *ai:* MENC, FMEA, FBA; *home:* 10401 N 22nd St Tampa FL 33612

ROE, MICHEL M., Attendance Counselor; *b:* Quincy, IL; *ed:* (BA) Elem Ed, CA Univ 1966; (MA) Ed, Pepperdine Univ 1975; Pupil Personnel Services Credential K-12, CA St Univ. 1987; *cr:* Elem Teacher 1966-88; Attendance Cnslr Elem & Jr HS 1988-; Los Angeles Unified; *ai:* Phi Delta Kappa; *office:* Los Angeles Unified Sch 915 E Century Blvd Los Angeles CA 90002

ROE, YVONNE HEATH, Senior High English Teacher; *b:* Mc Keesport, PA; *m:* Donald V.; *c:* Ward V.; *ed:* (BA) Eng/Speech, Muskingum Coll 1956; (MSED) Psych, Edinboro Univ 1985; Various Wkshps & Related Grad Courses; *cr:* Eng/Speech Teacher Bay Village HS 1956-57, Beaver Area HS 1957-60; Eng Teacher Rochester HS 1967-70, Beaver Area Jr/Sr HS 1973-; *ai:* Debate Coach 1967-70, 1974-80; Play Dir 1956-57, 1959-60; Sr Class Spon 1969-70, 1976-84; NCTC 1974-80; BAEA 1959-; PSEA, NEA 1957-; Parent Self-Help Group for Drug Usage in Children Organizer 1980-84; *home:* 1320 2nd St Beaver PA 15009

ROEDER, KENDRA LEIGH, Science Teacher; *b:* Kearney, NE; *ed:* (BS) Bio, Kearney St Coll 1979; Univ of NE, Kearney St Coll, Univ of WY; *cr:* Sci Teacher Ashland-Greenwood HS 1980-82, Overton HS 1982-88, Pine Bluffs HS 1988-; *ai:* Class Spon; Asst Vlybl, Head Track Coach; NEA 1978-; WY Ed Assn 1988-; E Laramie Cty Arts Cncl; *home:* 4th & Miller Pine Bluffs WY 82082

ROEHL, TERRY LEE, Jr HS Teacher/Athletic Dir; *b:* San Diego, CA; *m:* Kathleen N. Driscoll; *c:* Tiffany, Travis; *ed:* (BA) Ed - Cum Laude, Point Loma Coll 1978; (MA) Ed, Azusa Pacific Univ 1981; *cr:* 4th Grade Teacher/Coach Chrstn Unified Schls 1978-81; Jr HS Teacher/Coach Grace Chrstn Sch 1981-; *ai:* Athletic Dir, Prin Admin Comm, Newsletter Ed, Writer, Photographer; Yrbk Adv & Ed; 1st Baptist Church (Sound Technician, Lighting Technician) 1982-; Whos Who Among Amer HS Stu 1973; *office:* Grace Chrstn Sch 649 Crater Lake Ave Medford OR 97504

ROEMMELT, JOSEPHINE PASTIRIK, Third Grade Teacher; *b:* Horseheads, NY; *m:* Robert A. Sr.; *c:* Kathleen A. Tobey, Kristine A. Sigwald, Robert A. Jr., Bruce A.; *ed:* (BA) Sociology, 1951, (MS) Ed, 1976 Elmira Coll; Grad Stud Elmira Coll; In-Service Courses; *cr:* Soc Caseworker Chemung Cty 1951-52; Substitute Teacher 1964-69, 4th Grade Teacher 1969-76, Kndgtn Teacher 1976-83, 3rd Grade Teacher 1983- Horseheads Sch Dist; *ai:* Alpha Delta Kappa Pres 1983-85; Chemung Cty Fair Assn Dir 1984-; Veteran Grange Secy 1965-; *home:* 2282 Roemmelt Rd Horseheads NY 14845

ROENKER, PATRICIA HOPKINS, Business & Office Teacher; *b:* Covington, KY; *m:* Richard A. Sr.; *c:* Rob Arrasmith; *ed:* (AAS) Bus Admin, 1972, (BS) Bus Ed, 1975 Morehead St Univ; (ME) Scndry Ed, N KY Univ; Curr, Ed, N KY Univ 1990; *cr:* Bus Teacher Dixie Heights HS 1975-79, Scott HS 1979-; *home:* 14 Sidney Dr Independence KY 41051

ROESLER, LYNDA I., Sixth Grade Teacher; *b:* Burlington, IA; *m:* Brian; *c:* Cristine, Cathleen; *ed:* (BA) Elem Ed, Univ of Northern IA 1967; Cmptr Literacy; Whole Lang; Cooperative Learning; ABC Math; Gifted Ed; TESA; *cr:* 4th Grade Teacher Mark Twain Elem 1967-70; Substitute Teacher Bettendorf & North Scott Sch Dist 1971-76; 6th Grade Teacher Ed White Elem/North Scott Schls 1976-; *ai:* Coach 6th Grade Math Team; Stu Cncl Adv; Dist Math Curr Comm; NSEA Mem Chairperson 1967-; ISEA NEA 1967-; ITCM 1985-89; PTA 1967-70 & 1987-; *office:* Edward White Elem Sch 121 S 5th St Eldridge IA 52748

ROESNER, STEPHEN JOSEPH, Social Studies Teacher; *b:* Bronx, NY; *ed:* (BA) His, Concordia Coll 1981; *cr:* Soc Stud Teacher Mt St Michael Acad 1981-82; 6th Grade Teacher Grace Luth Sch 1983-84; 7th/8th Grade Teacher St Ann Sch 1984-86; Soc Stud Teacher Cardinal Spellman HS 1986-; *ai:* Ger Club & St Anns Chess Club Moderator; Spiritual Act Comm Mem; Co-Founder St Anns Players; Mount Players Producer; ASCD Mem 1989-; *office:* Cardinal Spellman HS 1991 Needham Ave Bronx NY 10466

ROETMAN, LOIS MAE ROMBERG, Second Grade Teacher; *b:* Hospers, IA; *m:* Robert Ray; *c:* Kendall, Linda (dec), Bradly; *ed:* (BS) Elem Ed, Northwestern Coll 1971; Grad Work Ed; *cr:* 1st Grade Teacher 1957-58, 3rd Grade Teacher 1958-60 Paullina Public Sch; 1st Grade Teacher 1969-70, 2nd Grade Teacher 1970- Ellsworth Elem; *ai:* MN Ed Assn (Pres 1974-76, Secy/Treas 1978-87); 1st Reformed Church (Youth Spon 1989-, Sunday Sch Teacher 1963-89, Co-Chm Lydia Circle 1988-); *office:* Ellsworth Public Sch Box 8 Ellsworth MN 56129

ROGERS, ANN H., Teacher of Academically Gifted; *b:* Norfolk, VA; *c:* Matt, Alex, Forrest; *ed:* (BA) Eng, Univ of AR 1983; Working Towards Masters Gifted & Talented Ed; *cr:* Teacher St Albans Sch 1979-81, Stuttgart Jr & Sr HS 1984-89, Northside HS 1989-; *ai:* Yrbk, Newspaper, Literary Magazine Adv; Quiz Bowl Coach; Schlsp Comm; Sr Class Adv; NCTE, NC Gifted & Talented, AGATE; Episcopal Church Vestry 1989-; Governors Advisory Cncl for Gifted & Talented Ed; Articles Published; *office:* Northside HS Rt 1 Box 177 Pinetown NC 27865

ROGERS, ANN HANLON, Social Studies Teacher; *b:* Quincy, MA; *m:* Edward James; *c:* Ann M. J., Judith L., Francine C.; *ed:* (BS) His, Boston Coll 1958; (MED) Ed, Boston St Coll 1962; *cr:* 4th Grade Teacher St Richards 1958-59; Soc Stud Teacher Whitman Public Schls 1959-62; 5th-6th Grade Teacher Quincy Public Schls 1962-69; Soc Stud Teacher St Clare HS 1984-; *ai:* Moderator St Clare SADD Chapter; Coord Close Up Prgm 1987; Partivipated in Substance Abuse Prevention Trng Prgms; NE Assn Soc Stud Teachers 1984-; *office:* St Clare HS 190 Cummins Hwy Roslindale MA 02131

ROGERS, BARBARA BERGERON, Third Grade Teacher; *b:* Houma, LA; *m:* Edgar G.; *c:* Mary Thomas, Janice Yantis, Lori; *ed:* (BA) Elem Ed, Nicholls St 1969; Terrebonne Parish Inservice Wkshps; *cr:* Teacher Boudreaux Canal 1954-58, Lisa Park Elem 1968-; *home:* 2436 Coteau Rd Houma LA 70364

ROGERS, BETTY ATZENWEILER, Biology Teacher; *b:* Atchison, KS; *ed:* (BSE) Bio, 1964, (MS) Bacteriology, 1967 KS St Teachers Coll; Grad Stud; *cr:* Teaching Asst KS St Teachers Coll 1964-67; Teacher Ocean City HS 1967-; *ai:* Yrbk Adv; NJ Ed Assn, NEA 1967-; Zoological Society Bd Dir 1989-; Zoo Ed Dir 1987-, Do Prgm within Dist & Cty in Zoo & Sci Ed; *office:* Ocean City HS 5th & Atlantic Ave Ocean City NJ 08226

ROGERS, CAROLYN MC DANIEL, Child Care Instructor; *b:* Baltimore, MD; *m:* Darrel; *c:* Nicolas; *ed:* (BS) Home Ec/Ed, Berea Coll 1969; (MED) Early Chldhd Ed, Univ of MD 1975; Supervision & Admin, Geo Washington Univ, Trinity Coll; Staff Dev Leadership, Cmptrs, Spec Ed; *cr:* 5th Grade Teacher T C Martin Elem Sch 1969; Head Start Teacher Walter J Mitchell Elem 1969; EDEL Instr Charles Cty Comm Coll 1982; Child Care Teacher Charles Cty Voc Tech Center 1969-; *ai:* Acting Prin Charles Cty Voc Tech Center; Yrbk Adv; Voc Industrial Clubs of America Spon; Effective Sch Comm; Crises Intervention Team; Soc, Open House, Sch Objectives Comm; Southern MD Assn for Ed Young Children Pres 1989-; EACC, MSTA, NEA, Amer Home Ec Assn 1969-; ASCD, Voc Industrial Clubs of America Membership; Advisory Comm Tri Cty Cmmty Action Comm Headstart; 4-H Clubs (Proj Adv, Teacher) 1986-; United Meth Church (Sunday Sch Teacher, Bible Sch Dir) 1985-; Little League Mother 1986-; Western Jaycees Outstanding Educators Awd 1974; Charles Cty Bd of Ed Exemplary Teacher 1989; Admin Internship 1990; *office:* Charles Cty Voc Tech Center R R 2 Box 75 Pomfret MD 20675

ROGERS, CAROLYN RECTOR, Drivers Ed/Health Teacher; *b:* Jonesborough, TN; *m:* R. Larry; *c:* Deborah, Larry B.; *ed:* (BS) Phys Ed/Health/Drivers Ed, E TN St Univ 1962; *cr:* Phys Ed Cloudland HS 1962-63; Phys Ed/Health/Drivers Ed/Sociology Teacher Happy Valley HS 1963-; *ai:* Sr Class Spon; *office:* Happy Valley HS Rt 11 Box 3500 Elizabethton TN 37643

ROGERS, CHARLOTTE A., Mathematics Teacher; *b:* Lexington, VA; *ed:* (BS) Elem Ed, Radford Coll 1971; (MS) Scndry Admin/Supervision, Radford Univ 1980; *cr:* Eng/Rdng/Spelling Teacher Parry Mc Cluer Elem 1971-76; Math Teacher Parry Mc Clue Mid 1976-79, Potomac HS 1980-81, Carver Mid Sch 1981-; *ai:* Chester Ed Assn 1982-; VA Ed Assn, NEA 1971-; VA Mid Sch Forum 1976-80; *office:* Carver Mid Sch 12400 Branders Bridge Rd Chester VA 23831

ROGERS, DEBRA BLANC, Vocal Music Teacher; *b:* Bismarck, ND; *m:* Kenneth V.; *ed:* (BS) Choral Music/Theatre Arts, Dickinson St Univ; *cr:* Music Instr Christ The King Sch 1976-78, Mandan Public Schls 1978-; *ai:* Swing Choir; ND Ed Assn, NEA 1978-; MENC 1978-80; ND Commission on Status of Women (Pres, Mem); Hit Inc Secy; Dakota Stage Ltd (Secy, Mem); Shade Tree Players Bd Mem; Bismarck Mandon Civic Chorus; *home:* 704 6th Ave NW Mandan ND 58554

ROGERS, DEBRA T., Marketing Teacher/Coordinator; *b:* Anchorage, AK; *m:* Michael D.; *c:* Shannon, Erin; *ed:* (BS) Mrktg Management, 1978, (MED) Mrktg Ed, 1983 Univ of S MS; *cr:* Teacher/Coord Harrison Cty Voc-Tech 1980-; *ai:* Coop Club Co-Adv; DECA Prof Division (Adv, MS St Newsletter Spon) 1980-, Placed Top 10 Nationally 1986-87; MS Assn of Distributive Ed Teacher 1980; MS Assn of Cooperative Voc Ed Teachers; Original Field Developer Mark Ed Learning Activity Questioning in the Selling Series; *office:* Harrison Cty Voc-Tech 15600 School Rd Gulfport MS 39503

ROGERS, DENNIS EDWIN, Teacher; *b:* Mt Victory, OH; *ed:* (BA) Eng/Philosophy, OH Univ 1974; (MA) Eng, Miami Univ 1976; Eng Ed, OH St Univ, OH Wesleyan Univ; *cr:* Teaching Asst Miami Univ 1975-76; Substitute Teacher Columbus Public Schls 1980-83; Teacher Dublin HS 1983-; *ai:* Dublin Quiz Team & Yrbk Adv; Greater Columbus In-The-Know League Mem; Dublin Shamrock 1984-87; OH St Univ Cooperating Teacher Excl Ed Awd; *office:* Dublin HS 6780 Coffman Rd Dublin OH 43017

ROGERS, EMILY WARNER, 4th-6th Grade Lead Teacher; *b:* Dallas, TX; *m:* Max Jerry; *c:* Laura Rogers Carroll, Carrie Rogers Smith, Jeffery S.; *ed:* (BS) Elem Ed, 1959, (MED) Elem Ed, 1970 N TX St Univ; Philosophy of Chrstn Ed; *cr:* 5th Grade Lang Art Teacher Jefferson Davis Elem 1959-61; 5th Grade Teacher Lamar Elem 1962-64; 6th-8th Grade Eng Teacher Dallas Chrstn Acad 1973-85; 6th-8th Grade Eng Teacher 1985-89, 4th-6th Grade Lead Teacher 1989- 1st Baptist Acad; 4th-6th Lang Art Teacher; *ai:* Officer Parent Teacher Fellowship; Spelling Bee Spon; Speech Meet Coach; Lead Teacher Coord; ACSI Convention Seminar Leader & Speaker; Kappa Kappa Gamma 1957-; Teacher of Yr Awd FBA East Campus 1988-89; ACSI Sch Evaluation Team; UIL Speech Judge; Outstanding Teacher of America Nominee 1975; Cnslr & Testing Coord K-12th Grade; *office:* 1st Baptist Acad 2380 Dunloe Dr Dallas TX 75228

ROGERS, HARL F., Phys Ed/Health Teacher; *b:* Roswell, NM; *m:* Beverly Jean Blackey; *ed:* (BS) Phys Ed, E NM Univ 1966; Health Ed, Drug Ed, HIV Cert; *cr:* 7th-12th Grade Teacher/Coach Cimarron Public Schls 1966-74; Teacher NM Boys Sch 1975-77; Mgr Oil Field Construction Company 1978-82; Teacher/Coach Cimarron Public Schls 1982-; *ai:* Jr Var & Var Vlybl, Jr HS Girls Bsktbl & Jr HS Vlybl Team Coach; NM Acts Assn Mem 1982-, Coach of North 1988, South All Star Vlybl Team; City Councilman & Police Commissioner; *home:* PO Box 583 Cimarron NM 87714

ROGERS, HELEN GEORGIANA, 9th-12th Biology/Sci Teacher; *b:* Selma, AL; *c:* Tony Fitzgerald, La Tonya C., Le Trell A., Mar Sell S.; *ed:* General Ed, Selma Univ 1971-72; (BS/BA) Bio Sci, AL St Univ 1976; (MED) Admin Supervision, 1989, Ed Doctorate 1986-89 Univ of MA Amherst; Bio Sci Ed, Troy St Univ 1979-82; Spec Ed, Sch Law, Brooklyn Coll 1988-89; EDd Univ of MA Amhurst; *cr:* Teacher Dallas Cty Bd of Ed 1976-81, Perry Cty Bd of Ed 1982, Concordia Coll 1977-82; Upward Bound Teacher Hofstra Univ 1985; Teacher Roosevelt HS 1984-; *ai:* FHA & Sci Club Adv; Tutor Attendance Drop Out Preventon Prgm; Liaison Faculty Comm; Drug Awareness Prgm Dir & Producer; Mid St Evaluation Comm Mem; Women in Sci Mem 1979; NY St United Teachers Mem 1984-; Roosevelt Teacher Assn Mem 1984-; Epiphany Church Choir Mem 1989-; Cath Church Mem; Roosevelt Bowling League Mem 1988-; Home Bound Stu Tutor 1984-; Volunteer Cmmty Service Worker; Hofstra Univ Upward Bound Curr Writer; Schlsp Pres Essay Oratorical Contest Winner; Honor Stu; *home:* 923 Elton St Brooklyn NY 11208

ROGERS, JAMES ROBERT, Mathematics Teacher/Chair; *b:* Shreveport, LA; *m:* Frances Ramsey Gardner; *c:* Amy E., Benjamin Gardner; *ed:* (BS) Math Ed, NE LA Univ 1969; (MED) Scndry Ed, 1975, (MA) Math, 1977 Univ of MS; *cr:* Math/Sci Teacher Carroll HS 1969-76; Teaching Asst Univ of MS 1976-77; Part-Time Instr NE LA Univ 1977-80; Math Teacher Neville HS 1977-; *ai:* NHS Adv; Sr Class Spon; Math Dept Chm; Phi Delta Kappa, Math Assn of America, NCTM, NEA; Amer MENSA Ltd, Univ of MS Alumni Assn, NE LA Univ Alumni Assn, Phi Kappa Phi; Univ of MS Math Fellowship 1977; Publications 1989; Monroe Jaycees Outstanding Young Educator 1974; Monroe Sertoma Club Service to Mankind Awd 1989; Teacher Recognition Awd; Scholars Banquet 1989; *office:* Neville HS 600 Forsythe Ave Monroe LA 71201

ROGERS, JOSEPH LEROY, Third Grade Teacher; *b:* Brunswick, GA; *m:* Valerie Carter; *c:* Josheika; *ed:* (BS) Elem Ed, Savannah St Coll 1979; GA Southern Coll Grad Stud; Management and Trng Corp; Just Say Know Drug Seminar; *cr:* Cnslr Savannah St Coll 1976-79; Orientation Specialist Brunswick Job Corps Center 1982-; Teacher Todd-Grant Elem 1979-; *ai:* Big Brothers Prgm; Mc Intosh Cty Youth Club; 4-H Volunteer Leader; Muscular Dystrophy, Easter Seals, Race Relations Comms; Alpha Phi Alpha Secy 1985-; Kappa Delta Phi 1978-; GA Sci Teachers Assn 1982-; Grace Baptist Church Jr Deacon 1979-; BSA Scout Master 1979-85; Concerned Citizens 1988-; Outstanding Young Men in America; Whos Who in Coll & Univ; *home:* 83 Chatford Dr Brunswick GA 31520

ROGERS, JUDITH DIANNE, American History Teacher; *b:* Gauley Bridge, WV; *ed:* (BA) Soc Stud, WV Inst of Technology 1969; *cr:* Math Teacher 1969-70, Math/Geography Teacher 1970-71, WV His Teacher 1971-80, Amer His Teacher 1980- Logan Jr HS; *ai:* Drill Team, Yrbk, Chrldrs, Pep Club, Beta Club Spon; Stu Cncl & Honor Society Co-Spon; Logan Jr HS Soc Stud Dept Head; *office:* Logan Jr HS 500 University Ave Logan WV 25601

ROGERS, KATHLEEN KELLY, Mathematics Department Chair; *b:* Canandaigua, NY; *ed:* (BS) Math Ed, Oral Roberts Univ 1985; *cr:* 4th Grade Teacher 1985-86, Math Dept Chairperson/Sci Teacher 1986- New Covenant Chrstn; *ai:* Jr HS Soccer Coach; Var Vlybl Girls Coach; Class of 1990 & 1992 & Ski Club Adv; Fellowship to Math Inst Brockport Univ; *office:* New Covenant Chrstn Sch 2070 Five Mile Line Rd Penfield NY 14526

ROGERS, KEITH RODNEY, Director of Speech Activities; *b:* Fort Knox, KY; *m:* Judith Marie Kirkland; *c:* Keith R., Karl R., Kurtis R.; *ed:* (BA) Speech/Drama, ID St Univ 1968; Higher Ed Admin, Univ of OK, OK St Univ Comm, Northwestern Univ; *cr:* Debate/Drama Teacher Shawnee HS 1976-81; Debate Teacher Booker T Washington HS 1981-83; Debate/Eng/Drama Teacher Ponca City HS 1983-88; Debate/Speech Teacher Jenks HS 1988-; *ai:* Natl Forensic League; Debate & Competitive Speech Coach; Lighthouse Sch Comm; NEA 1968-; OK Ed Assn, Natl Forensic League 1976-; 1988 Ponca City Teacher of Yr; Northwestern Univ Summer Speech Fellow 1985; Coach of 1979 Natl Extemp Champion; Natl Lincoln Douglas Debate Champion Coach 1983; *home:* 4125 E 22nd Pl Tulsa OK 74114

ROGERS, LILE ELLIS, Psychology/Sociology Teacher; *b:* Decatur, AL; *m:* C. L.; *c:* Mary K.; *ed:* (BS) Amer His/Sociology, Mid TN St Univ 1973; *cr:* Teacher Southaven HS 1973-76, Hendersonville HS 1976-; *ai:* Annual, Stu Cncl Spon; Homecoming, Prom Comm; Talent Show Chm; Alpha Delta Kappa; *office:* Hendersonville HS 201 E Main St Hendersonville TN 37075

ROGERS, LYNN WILLNER, Honors Biology/Psych Teacher; *b:* Albert Lea, MN; *m:* Maurice Lee Jr.; *c:* Mercedes L.; *ed:* (BS) Bio/Psych, E TX St Univ 1978; Grad Stud Psych; *cr:* Bio Teacher 1978-82, Bio/Psych Teacher 1982-88, Honors Bio/Psych Teacher 1988- Grand Prairie HS; *ai:* TSTA, NEA 1980-89; TCTA 1989-; Ex-Stu Assn & Coll of Ed; Univ of TX Austin; TX Excl Awd for Outstanding HS Teachers 1988; *home:* 6100 Amicable Ct Arlington TX 76016

ROGERS, MARSHA ANNE (BRITTON), 7th Grade Lang Arts Teacher; *b:* Brazil, IN; *m:* David E.; *ed:* (BA) Elem Ed, Olivet Nazarene Univ 1970; Spec Ed Developmentally Handicapped Grades K-12th; Cmptr Ed; Intervention Counseling for Drug/Substance Abuse; *cr:* Primary Spec Ed Teacher 1972-74, Interm Spec Ed Teacher 1974-76, 7th Grade Lang Art Teacher 1976- East Muskingum Schls; *ai:* Head Track Coach Grades 7th, 8th; Outdoor Ed Grade 6th; Chrldr Adv Grades 7th & 8th; Dist Lang Art Comm Curr; OH Mid Sch Assn; Learning Disability Wkshps & camps; *office:* E Muskingum Mid Sch 13125 John Glenn Rd New Concord OH 43762

ROGERS, MARY ANN PISECK, Teacher of Gifted & Talented; *b:* Herkimer, NY; *c:* Patricia Warren, Suzanne Strand, Michelle; *ed:* (BS) Ed, St Univ of NY Plattsburg 1960; (MS) Sch Counseling, 1981, (MA) Sch Management, 1984 Univ of La Verne; Upper Division & Grad Courses CA St Univ, Northridge, Univ of CA Los Angeles, Pepperdine Univ; *cr:* Home Ec Teacher Westbury Jr HS 1960-61, Yonkers Public Schls 1961-63; Career Ed Resource Teacher Lancaster Sch Dist 1971-83; Soc Stud/GATE Teacher Park View Sch 1968-; *ai:* Gifted & Talented Ed Contact Teacher; Coord Washington DC Trip for Honor Stu; Chairperson Academic Olympics; Teachers Assn Negotiation Team; Co-Chairperson Disaster & Yr Round Ed Comm; Phi Delta Kappa Pres 1990; NEA, CTA, Teachers Assn of Lancaster, CA Assn for the Gifted, Yr Round Ed Assn, NCSS; *office:* Park View Intermediate Sch 808 W Avenue J Lancaster CA 93534

ROGERS, MARY TERESA, Seventh-Eighth Grade Teacher; *b:* Philadelphia, PA; *ed:* (BS) Elm Ed, Gwynedd Mercy Coll 1983; 5th Grade Teacher St Veronica 1969-; 4th Grade Teacher 1971-85; 7th/8th Grade Teacher 1985- Assumption BVM; *ai:* Stu Cncl Adv; Soc Stud Coord; NCEA 1971-; *office:* Assumption BVM Sch 55 Bristol Rd Feasterville PA 19047

ROGERS, MICHAEL CARTER, 8th/9th Grade Band Director; *b:* Oxford, MS; *ed:* (BS) Music Ed/Music Therapy, E Carolina Univ 1984; *cr:* Band Dir Creswell HS & Elem 1984-85, Elizabeth City Jr HS 1985-; *ai:* Jr HS Fine Arts Prgm Coord; Music Ed of NC Dist 15 Pres 1980-; Phi Mu Alpha Music Dir 1980-; Pi Kappa Lambda 1983-; Lions Club Lion Tamer 1987-; *office:* Elizabeth City Jr HS 360 N Road St Elizabeth City NC 27909

ROGERS, PAT J., Co-Chair, English Department; *b:* Cottonwood, ID; *m:* Carol G. Chirgwin; *c:* Erica, Stewart, Katie; *ed:* (BA) Biblical Stud, Spokane Bible Coll 1981; (BA) Eng, Whitworth Coll 1983; *cr:* Lang Art/Soc Stud Teacher LakeLand Jr HS 1984-; *ai:* Co-Chairperson Eng Dept; Driver Ed Instr; Nom Teacher of Yr 1990; *office:* Lakeland Jr HS P O Box 98 Rathdrum ID 83858

ROGERS, PATRICIA ANN, English Teacher; *b:* Bloomsburg, PA; *m:* Scott S.; *c:* Gretchen, Zachary; *ed:* (BS) Eng, Bloomsburg St Coll 1971; *cr:* 7th Grade Eng Teacher E Lycoming Sch Dist 1971-72; 9th Grade Eng Teacher Troy Jr HS 1972-82, Troy Sr HS 1982-; *ai:* Adv NHS; Boys & Girls Var Track Head Coach; NCTE 1989-; *home:* RD 2 Box 19 Troy PA 16947

ROGERS, PATRICIA BUSBY, Business Education Teacher; *b:* San Antonio, TX; *m:* Roy C.; *c:* Brett, Trey, Trisha; *ed:* (BS) Bus Ed, SW TX St 1959; Voc Office Ed Cert; *cr:* Bus Teacher Runge HS 1959-60, Kenedy HS 1961-62; Eng Teacher Karnes City Jr HS 1963-65; Bus Teacher Bartlett HS 1965-70; Eng Teacher Taylor Mid Sch 1975-81; Bus Teacher Taylor HS 1981-; *ai:* NHS Spon; Bus Profs of America Club Adv; UIL Accounting Coach; ATPE Treas 1975-; Aggie Moms 1985-; *office:* Taylor HS 3101 N Main St Taylor TX 76574

ROGERS, PATRICIA REED, 4th Grade Teacher; *b:* Walnut Ridge, AR; *m:* Bennie Mack; *c:* Michael A.; *ed:* (AA) Elem Ed, Hinds Jr Coll 1963; (BAE) Elem Ed, Univ of MS 1965; (MED) Elem Ed, MS St Univ 1979; *cr:* 1st/2nd Grade Teacher Bearss Acad 1966-67; 3rd Grade Teacher Rankin Cty Schls 1967-71; Kndgtn Teacher Alta Woods Kndgtn 1972-74; 4th Grade Teacher Pearl Public Schls 1974-; *ai:* Stu Cncl Spon; Publicity, Spelling Bee, 4th Grade Instruction Management Chm; Annual Staff; Alpha Delta Kappa (Chaplain, Secy); MS Prof Educators; Pearl Band Boosters Secy 1988-89; South Jackson Music Club Pres; Pearl Public Schls Teacher of Yr 1987; *office:* Pearl Upper ELem Sch 180 Mary Ann Dr Pearl MS 39208

ROGERS, PAUL W., US History/Psychology Teacher; *b:* Tacoma, WA; *c:* Angela, Brett, Brad; *ed:* (BA) Phys Ed/His/Psych/Geography, Cntrl WA Univ 1971; Drug & Alcohol Trng; Suicide Awareness Prgm; *cr:* Teacher/Coach Franklin Jr HS 1971-77, Eisenhower HS 1977-; *ai:* Asst Ftbl Coach; Natural Helpers Intervention Group; Stu Assistance for Everyone Comm; Comm AD HOC Comm; Yakima Ed Assn, WA Ed Assn, NEA 1971-; *home:* 914 S 31st Ave Yakima WA 98902

ROGERS, REBECCA WALLACE, Mathematics Teacher; *b:* Birmingham, AL; *c:* Amie, Leslie; *ed:* (BS) Math, 1981, (MAT) Math, 1987 GA St Univ; *cr:* Teacher Woodward Acad 1981-; *ai:* Jr Var Math Team; NCTM 1981-; *office:* Woodward Acad PO Box 87190 College Park GA 30337

ROGERS, RENA (PERREAULT), Fourth Grade Teacher; *b:* Willimantic, CT; *m:* Ronald W.; *c:* David R., Kevin D., Michelle E., Julie M.; *ed:* (BS) Elem Ed, Fitchburg St Coll 1959; Rdng Update, Worcester St Coll; Sci Inst, Regional Educl Center; Project WRITE; Substance Abuse, Fitchburg St; Learning Disabilities; Nutrition; *cr:* 3rd Grade Teacher White St Sch 1959-60, Dolly Whitney Adams Sch 1960-62; 1st/3rd/4th Grade Teacher John R Briggs Sch 1970-; *ai:* Sci Curr Comm; Ashburnham Teachers Assn Recording Secy 1960-61; MA Teacher Recording Secy 1959-62, 1970; NEA 1970-; Beta Sigma Phi Intnl Order of Rose, Woman of Yr.

ROGERS, ROBERT WOODROW, III, Social Studies Teacher; *b:* Charleston, SC; *m:* Julie A. Cornwell; *c:* Haley A.; *ed:* (BA) His, Winthrop Coll 1983; (MSA) Scndry Admin, Citadel 1990; Prgm for Effective Teaching; Teacher Expectations of Student Achievement; Skills for Adolescence; *cr:* Teacher Westview Mid Sch 1983-89; Coach/Bsbl Goose Creek HS 1983-88; Berkeley HS 1989-; *ai:* HS Bsbl Coach-Berkeley HS; Intramural Co-Dir Westview Mid Sch 1986-89; Soc Stud Dept Chairperson Westview Mid Sch 1986-89; Dixieland Bassmasters Pres 1988-; *office:* Westview Mid Sch 101 Westview Blvd Goose Creek SC 29445

ROGERS, SHEILA BRYANT, HS Social Studies Teacher; *b:* Midwest City, OK; *m:* Anthony B.; *c:* Leslie K.; *ed:* (BA) Ed/Soc Stud, Cntrl St Univ 1987; *cr:* Soc Stud Teacher Wellston HS 1987-; *ai:* Wellston Public Schls NHS & Natl Jr Honor Society Spon; Wellston HS Citizen Bee Coord; Quiz Bowl Spon & Coord; Wellston Ed Assn Pres 1988-89; *home:* 9314 NE 50th Spencer OK 73084

ROGERS, VICKI MOORE, Data Processing Coordinator; *b:* Atlanta, GA; *m:* Daniel N.; *c:* Matthew L.; *ed:* (AS) Bus Admin 1975, (BS) Bus Ed, 1982, (MED) Bus Ed, 1984 GA Coll; *cr:* Teacher 1982-84, Data Processing Coord 1984- Jones Cty HS; *ai:* FBLA & St Officer Adv; Literary & FBLA Competitive Coach; GA Voc Assn 1982-; GA Bus Ed Assn 1982-, Nom Dist 10 Teacher of Yr 1987; Prof Assn GA Educators 1985-; *office:* Jones Cty HS Clinton St PO Box 609 Gray GA 31032

ROGERS, VIRGINIA FAYE, Second Grade Teacher; *b:* Laurel, MS; *ed:* (BA) Elem Ed, Univ of MS 1960; Univ of S MS, William Carey Coll, MS St Univ; *cr:* 5th Grade Teacher Bayou View Elem 1960-63, Harmon AFB Newfoundland 1963-64; 6th Grade Teacher Laon AFB France 1964-65, Cntrl Elem 1965-66, Trist Mid 1966-69; 4th Grade Teacher McDonald Sch 1969-71; 4th-5th Grade Teacher Laurel City Schls 1971-73; Coord Neighborhood Youth Corps 1973-74; 2nd-3rd Grade Teacher St Johns Day Sch 1974-; *ai:* Intnl Rdng Assn 1989-; Presbyn Church Circle Chm 1989-; *office:* St Johns Day Sch 520 N 5th Ave Laurel MS 39440

ROGERS, W. R., Math Dept Chairman/Teacher; *b:* Coffeyville, KS; *m:* Marilyn Weiland; *ed:* (BA) Elem Ed, 1973, (MED) Admin/Super 1980 Mc Neese Univ; *cr:* Teacher/Math Dept Chm S J Welsh Mid Sch 1973-; *ai:* LA Assn of Classroom Teachers Pres 1978-80; Masons Calcasieu Lodge 400, Scottish Rite Bodies, Habibi Shrine Temple; SW LA Coin & LA Fathomeer Scuba Club Pres; *office:* S J Welsh Mid Sch 1500 W Mc Neese St Lake Charles LA 70605

ROGERS, WARREN C., Principal; *b:* Eaton Rapids, MI; *m:* Janice Clark; *c:* Jordan; *ed:* (BS) Soc Sci Ed, MI St Univ 1972; (MS) Safety & Driver Ed, NC A&T St Univ 1978; *cr:* HS Teacher Emmanuel Baptist Schls 1980-82; Prin Portville Baptist Chrstn Sch 1983-85; 6th Grade Teacher Horseheads Chrstn Sch 1985-88; Prin Tioga Center Chrstn Sch 1988-; *home:* RR 1 Box 359 Ellis Creek Rd Barton NY 13734

ROGGIE, BERTHA, 6th Grade Reading Teacher; *b:* Croghan, NY; *ed:* (BS) Ed, E Mennonite Coll 1963; (MS) Ed, St Univ Coll Oswego 1974; *cr:* 4th Grade Teacher General Brown Sch Dist 1964-65, S Jefferson Sch Dist 1966-69; 4th Grade Teacher 1970-72, Rdng Specialist 1973-74, 6th Grade Rdng 1975- Warwick Sch Dist; *ai:* Drama Club Asst; LLRA, Keystone Rdng Assn 1975-; IRA 1970-; March of Dimes Volunteer 1983; *office:* Warwick Mid Sch 401 Maple St Lititz PA 17543

ROGNRUD, GORDON ALLEN, Marketing Education Teacher; *b:* Missoula, MT; *ed:* (BA) Hardware Retailing, IN Univ 1977; (BS) Bus/Mrktg Ed, MT St Univ 1982; Working Towards Masters US Army Combined Arms & Services Staff Sch; US Army Quartermaster Officer Basic Course 1983 & Officer Advanced Course 1989 Ft Lee Va; *cr:* Salesman/Store Mgr Hanson OK Hardware 1974-77; Residence Hall Adv/Head Resident MT St Univ 1978-82; Health Club Mgr Exec Health Club for Men 1984-85; Mrktg Ed Teacher/DECA Adv Bozeman Sr HS 1985-; *ai:* Spon Athletic Concessions, Graduation Announcements, Underclass Pictures; NEA, MT Ed Assn, Bozeman Ed Assn, AVA; MT Voc Assn Exec Bd 1986-; MT Assn of Mrktg Educators Pres 1986-; GTO Assn of America 1977-; Reserve Officers Assn, Assn of US Army Quartermaster Officers 1986-; US Army Commendation Medal; US Army Acheivement Medal-2 Awds; US Army Airborne Sch Grad; Mrktg Teacher of Yr St of MT 1989-; Outstanding Young Men of America 1982, 1985; *office:* Bozeman Sr HS 205 No 11th Ave Bozeman MT 59715

ROHDE, CHARLOTTE SCHETTLER, Second Grade Teacher; *b:* Dickinson, ND; *m:* Paul; *c:* Shila, John; *ed:* (BS) Elem, Dickinson St Coll 1974; Early Chldhd, 1986; *cr:* 3rd/4th Grade Teacher 1976-78, 1st/2nd Grade Teacher 1978-84 Golden Valley Public Sch; 1st Grade Teacher Dodge Elem Sch 1985-86; 2nd Grade Teacher Hazen Elem Sch 1986-; *ai:* NDEA 1976-80; ND Rdng Cncl 1988-89; Bizon Boosters 1989-; Town & Cntry Homemakers Pres 1983-87; Hazen Parent Communications Steering Comm 1989-; *office:* Hazen Elem Sch 520 1st Ave NE Hazen ND 58545

ROHE, CINDY DORRELL, Choir Teacher; *b:* Conroe, TX; *m:* Roark S.; *c:* Seth, Scott; *ed:* (BME) Music Ed, Sam Houston St Univ 1971; Grad Trng Kodaly Pedagogy, Grad Study Tour Hungary & Austria; *cr:* Elem Music Teacher Ben Franklin Elem 1971-72; 5th/6th Grade Elem Music Teacher 1972-78, 6th-8th Jr HS Choir Teacher 1978-89, 9th-12th Grade HS Choir Teacher 1989- Huntsville Ind Sch Dist; *ai:* Performing Choirs Spon; Choir Cncl; Contest, Solo Contest & All-St Choir Tryouts Coach; TX Music Educators Assn 1971-; TX Choral Dir Assn 1979-; Sigma Alpha Iota; Beta Sigma Phi 1978-; Concouristers-A Madrigal Society 1989-; Teacher of Yr Awd by Pizza Inn Corporation; *office:* Huntsville HS 441 FM 2821 E Huntsville TX 77340

ROHE, PATTI JANE (BROWN), 8th Grade English Teacher; *b:* Jersey Shore, PA; *m:* George G.; *c:* Kelly A.; *ed:* (BS) Comprehensive Eng, Lock Haven Univ 1964; Continuing Ed Penn St Univ, Mansfield Univ & Carlow Coll; *cr:* Eng/Rdng Teacher Roosevelt Jr HS 1964-65; Eng Teacher Bedford Jr HS 1965-66, Jersey Shore Area Jr HS 1971-; *ai:* Pen Pal Club Adv; Stu Assistance Prgm Team Mem; PSEA, NEA; *office:* Jersey Shore Area Jr HS Thompson St Jersey Shore PA 17740

ROHLEDER, LINDA LOU, 7th/8th Grade Math Teacher; *b:* Jasper, IN; *ed:* (BS) Elem Ed, St Benedicts Coll 1961; (MS) Elem Ed, IN St Univ 1963; IN Statewide Testing for Educl Progress Remediation Teacher; *cr:* 5th Grade Teacher St Anthony Sch 1961-63; Lang Art/Sci/Math Teacher Ireland Elem 1963-78; Math Teacher Jasper Mid Sch 1978-; *ai:* Jasper Mid Sch Chapter & Title I Coord; Academic & Hoosier Bowl Competition Coach; St Judes Childrens Research Hospital Marathon Chairperson; Local & St Textbook Adoption Comm; Jasper Classroom Teachers Assn (Secy, Treas), Nom Presidential Awd for Excl Math Teaching 1989; IN St Teachers Assn 1961-78; NEA 1961-78; NCTM 1987-88; St Joseph Cath Church (Stephen Minister, Eucharistic Minister); St Anns Society (Vocation Advisory Bd 1989-) 1978-; Jasper Mid Sch Teacher of Yr 1984, 1987 & Most Influential Teacher in Stu Life 1986, 1990; Summer ISTEP Exceptional Service Appreciation Awd 1989; *office:* Jasper Mid Sch 340 W 6th St Jasper IN 47546

ROHLFING, ALBERT F., Social Studies Teacher; *b:* St Louis, MO; *m:* Mary Lou Bohn; *c:* Scot, Gregg; *ed:* (BA) His, Cntrl Meth Coll 1957; (MA) His, St Louis Univ 1966; *cr:* Teacher/Coach Maplewood Richmond Heights Sr HS 1958-; *ai:* Coaching Ftbl, Wrestling, Track; Lettermans Club Spon; Athletic Dir; Stu Discipline Comm; Cmmty Teachers Assn (Welfare Comm Chm, VP, Pres); NEA 1958-; NIAAA 1984-; MIAAA, NFICA 1982-.

ROHLFING, TRACY DOLORES, English Teacher; *b:* Vandalia, IL; *ed:* (BS) Ed Eng, Greenville Coll 1980; *cr:* Eng Teacher Brownstown Jr/Sr HS 1982-; Presenter Educl Service Center 15 1988-; *ai:* Sch Newspaper & Sr Class Spon; Dir of All Sch Play; Curr Steering Comm Mem; Beta Sigma Phi 1987-; Sparkplug Awd IL Dept of Transportation & Office of Substance Abuse Prevention 1989; Awd of Recognition IL St Bd of Ed 1989; *home:* 1905 W Fillmore St Vandalia IL 62471

ROHLOFF, ARNOLD JAMES, Sixth Grade Teacher; *b:* Mayville, ND; *m:* Patricia Giles; *c:* Scott, Valerie, Elizabeth; *ed:* (BS) Elem Ed, Mayville St Univ 1979; CPR Instr; EMT/ECT Technician; *cr:* US Customs Inspector Pembina Border Station 1981-85; 6th Grade Teacher Pembina Public Sch 1979-; *ai:* Organized Noon Hour Bsktbl Prgm; Licensed Bus Driver; Jr HS Girls & 5th/6th Grade Bsktbl Coach; BSA 1990; West Trail Ambulance Service 1977-79; Pembina Ambulance Service 1979-84; *home:* 273 W Ramsey Box 262 Pembina ND 58271

ROHNER, EMMA LOU NEWMAN, Kindergarten Teacher/Chair; *b:* Wilmington, NC; *m:* John D.; *c:* Jonathan, Jason; *ed:* (BS) Primary Ed, E Carolina Univ 1967; Gussell Dev Wkshp; *cr:* 2nd Grade Teacher Blue Creek Sch 1966-69; 1st Grade Teacher North Branch 1969-70; 1st Grade Readiness Teacher 1970-75, Kndgtn Teacher 1976- Blue Creek Sch; *ai:* Big Buddy; Kndgtn Lead Teacher; NEA, NCAE, OCAE, NCAYC Gold; Teacher of Yr Blue Creek 1987; Sch Bd Recognition 1988; *office:* Blue Creek Sch 400 Burgaw Hwy Jacksonville NC 28540

ROHR, CAROL ANN (HUDSON), First Grade Teacher; *b:* St Louis, MO; *c:* Teri L. Wieduwitt, Tamara R. Walchshauser; *ed:* (BS) Ed, SE MO St Univ 1966; (MS) Ed, S IL Univ Edwardsville 1985; *cr:* 4th Grade Teacher Garrett Elem Hazelwood Sch Dist 1966-68, McCurdy Elem 1968-72; Kndgtn Teacher 1972-77, 1st Grade Teacher 1977- Jana Elem; *ai:* NEA, MNEA, Hazelwood Teachers Assn; Kappa Delta Pi; Alpha Chi Omega Secy 1958; Outstanding Elem Teachers of America 1972; *office:* Jana Sch 405 Jana Dr Florissant MO 63031

ROHR, RICHARD JOSEPH, Adv Composition/Eng XI Teacher; *b:* Massillon, OH; *m:* Janice Irene Anderson; *c:* Lisa A. Rohr Argabrite, Craig; *ed:* (BA) Eng, Walsh Coll 1974; *cr:* 9th-12th Grade Eng Teacher Strasburg HS 1974-79; Comp/Eng XI Teacher Dalton HS 1979-; *ai:* Sr Class Adv; Jr Var Bsbl Coach; Prin Advisory Cncl; NCTE 1975-; *office:* Dalton HS 177 N Mill St Dalton OH 44618

ROJO, VIOLA, First Grade Teacher; *b:* Marfa, TX; *ed:* (BA) Elem Ed, 1971, (MED) Ed, 1976 Sul Ross St Univ; Advanced Academic Trng Toward Placement on Career Ladder; *cr:* Teacher Headstart Prgm 1971-75; Eng as Second Lang/GED Teacher Adult Ed Prgm 1980-85; 1st Grade Teacher Marfa Elem Sch 1972-; *ai:* Sul Ross St Univ TAIR Rdng Conference Coord; NEA 1972-; TX St Teachers Assn (Presidio Cty Secy 1980, VP 1981); TX Assn for Improvement of Rdng 1985-; Notable Amer 1976-77; St Marys Cath Church Mem; Career Ladder 1984-; *office:* Marfa Elem Sch 413 W Columbia PO Box T Marfa TX 79843

ROLAND, CONNIE BOSTICK, Lead 8th Grade Math Teacher; *b:* Camilla, GA; *m:* Donald Russell; *c:* James, Donald C.; *ed:* (BS) Early Childhood Ed, 1981; (MS) Mid Grades Ed, 1987 GA Sputhwestern; Specialist Mid Grades Ed Ga Southwestern 1990; TPAI Data Collector; *cr:* Math Teacher A S Staley Mid ScH 1981-; *ai:* Teacher Advisory Comm; Beta Club Adv 1983-89; Lead Teacher; GA Assn of Educators 1981-; NEA 1981-; ASCD 1990; Staley Mid Sch Teacher of Yr 1983-84, VIP Awd 1984-85, Service Awd 1983-84; *home:* Rt 3 Box 54 Mockingbird Dr Americus GA 31709

ROLAND, JUNE HARDIN, Algebra Teacher/Math Dept Chm; *b:* Arbyrd, MO; *m:* Isaac N.; *c:* Richard, Anne R. England, Linda R. Franklin; *ed:* (BA) His, David Lipscomb Univ 1954; *cr:* Math Teacher East HS 1954-55, Rocky Hill Sch 1958-59; Algebra 1/ Pre-Algebra Teacher Parkway Jr HS 1974-; *ai:* Beta & Math Club Spon; Jackson Ed Assn Secy 1980-81; Alpha Delta Kappa 1984-.

ROLAND, SHIRLEY BRYANT, Special Education Teacher; *b:* England, AR; *c:* Karen Gosby; *ed:* (BA) Eng, Philander Smith Coll 1970; (BSE) Spec Ed, Univ Cntrl AR 1972; Cert Emotional Disturbed 1977; *cr:* Teacher Cntrl HS 1972-75, D A Hulcy Mid 1975-79, D W Carter HS 1979-; *ai:* 9th Grade Chrldr/Pep Squad Spon; Stu Cncl Spon; NEA, TEA 1977-; PTA Carter HS 1979-, Life Membership 1987; Advisory Bd; Singing Hills Recording Center Pres 1987-, Service 1989; Sigma Gamma Rho (Secy, VP, Pres) 1976-, Yellow Service Tea Rose 1986; Philander Smith Coll Alumni Chapter (Secy, VP, Pres) 1980-; Dallas Oak Cliff Chamber of Commerce Golden Oak Awd 1989; St of TX Stu Cncl Spons Pen 1989; *home:* 222 Davis Dr Desoto TX 75115

ROLING, DUANE JOSEPH, 7th & 8th Grade Teacher; *b:* Manchester, IA; *m:* Angie Maria Fernandez; *c:* Andrew; *ed:* (MS) Math, IA St Univ 1974; Apple Cmptr; *cr:* 7th/8th Grade Teacher RHCL 1975-; *ai:* Sci, Math, Cmptr Comms; *office:* Rhcl Holy Cross 791 Church St Holy Cross IA 52053

ROLLE, JOSEPHINE DAVIS, Sixth Grade Teacher; *b:* Miami, FL; *m:* Haston M.; *c:* Michael D., Mark A., Marci S.; *ed:* (BS) Elem Ed, a & T Univ 1955; (MS) Elem Ed, Nova Univ 1982; *cr:* Teacher Poinciana Park Elem 1956-66; Teacher Lorah Park Elem 1967-; *ai:* Spelling Bee Comm; Chairperson Global Awareness; Episcopal Churchwomen Pres 1985-87, Service Plaque 1987; Vestry Clerk 1985-87; Torchlighter's Parent Club Treas 1987, Service Plaque 1987; Teacher of Yr 1978, 1988; Global Teacher of Yr 1985.

ROLLERSON, MARY HOWARD, Language Arts Teacher; *b:* Sumter, SC; *m:* Alfred Leon; *ed:* (BA) Span/Eng, Bennett Coll 1976; (MA) Eng/Ed, Univ of SC 1984; Eng Ed, Univ of SC; *cr:* Rdng Teacher Warrensville Heights HS 1976-77; Beg Span/Eng Teacher Williams Jr HS 1977-78; Literature/Lang Arts Teacher R E Davis Mid Sch 1978-; *ai:* Lt Governors Excl in Writing Coord; NCTE; SC Intnl Rdng Assn; Delta Sigma Theta Alumni Chairperson Schlsp Comm 1984-; *office:* R E Davis Mid Sch Rt 5 Sumter SC 29150

ROLLINGER, MARY ELIZABETH, Secondary English Teacher; *b:* Jamestown, NY; *m:* William Francis; *c:* Keli A., Amy L.; *ed:* (BS) Scndry Eng Ed, Edinboro Univ 1974; Elem Ed, Scndry Eng Permanent Cert Penn St, Coll of St Rose, SUNY Fredonia; Working Towards Masters in Counseling St Bonaventure Univ Olean; *cr:* Tutor/Part-Time Eng Instr NY St Division for Youth 1976-78; Part-Time GED Instr/Teacher BOCES Fredonia 1978-83; Eng Teacher Maple Grove HS & Bemus Point Cntrl 1974-; Summer Enrich/Creative Writing Instr Chautuaqua Cty Sch Bds Assn 1985-; Writing Instr Chautauqua Cty Teachers Center 1987-; *ai:* Calligarphy Club & 7th Grade Class Adv; PTSA Teacher Rep; Bemus Point Faculty Assn Newsletter Chairperson; Delta Kappa Gamma Publicity Chairperson 1984-; NCTE, NY Ed Assn Alternate 1974; Lakewood Womens Club 1985-; Fortnightly 1986-; Open Minds Book Club 1989-; Delta Kappa Gamma Intnl Ed Schlsp; Nom Natl Teacher of Yr; Intnl Rdng Assn Featured Speaker 1990; *office:* Maple Grove HS Dutch Hollow Rd Bemus Point NY 14712

ROLLINS, ANN JOHNSTON, Vocal Music Teacher; *b:* Hattiesburg, MS; *m:* Lloyd; *c:* Jay, Benjamin; *ed:* (BME) Music Ed, Univ of S MS 1973; *cr:* Private Music Instr 1973-89; Choral Dir Gulfport HS 1988-89; Vocal Music Teacher Bartle Sch 1989-; *ai:* 5th & 6th Grade Chorus; Sch Spirit Comm; MS Music Teachers Assn Mem at Large 1986-88; Gulf Coast Music Teachers Pres 1684-86, 1988, Teacher of Yr 1988-89; NJEA 1989-; Gulf Coast Jr Womans Club 1987-89; United Methodist Women Circle Chairperson 1982-, Missions 1986; *office:* Bartle Sch 435 Mansfield Highland NJ 08904

ROLLINS, CHRISTOLYN TURNER, 6th-8th Grade Choral Director; *b:* Shreveport, LA; *m:* Edwill II; *c:* Edwill III, Giva A., Quiana E., Jarrell C.; *ed:* (BMED) Vocal Music Ed, Northwestern St Univ 1980; (MED) Music Ed, Univ of N TX 1984; Grad Stud Spec Ed, Univ of TX Tyler; *cr:* Asst Choral Dir Robert E Lee HS 1982-84; Choral Dir A T Stewart Mid Sch 1984-; *ai:* Sch Talent Show Spon; Music Dept Chairperson; TX Music Ed Assn, TX Choral Dir Assn, TX St Teacher Assn, NEA 1982-; Delta Sigma Theta 1978-; Chorale-Coll Baptist Church (Pres 1986-87) 1982-; *home:* 1500 W 1st Tyler TX 75701

ROLLINS, JENNIE BROWN, Choral Director; *b:* Norfolk, VA; *m:* David Sidwell; *c:* Brooks K.; *ed:* (BA) Music Ed, Hope Coll 1968; (MME) Choral Music Ed, FL St Univ 1976; *cr:* Elem Music Teacher Kenowa Hills Public Sch 1968-71, Mt Pleasant Public Sch 1971-75, Pineview Elem 1976-78; Chorus Dir Belle Vue Mid Sch 1978-; *ai:* Solo & Ensemble Coach; Delta Kappa Gamma (Corresponding Secy 1981-83) 1974; Fl Vocal Assn (Mid Sch Chm Dist 2 1987-) 1978; Sigma Alpha Lota 1969; FL Master Teacher Awd 1985; *office:* Belle Vue Mid Sch 2214 Belle Vue Way Tallahassee FL 32304

ROLLINS, MARILYN THOMPSON, Math/Accounting Teacher; *b:* Gorman, TX; *m:* John W.; *c:* Amy, Jennifer; *ed:* (BA) Eng/Math, Tarleton St Univ 1975; Accounting, Univ of TX Permian Basin; *cr:* Math Teacher Cisco HS 1976-77, Breckenridge Jr HS 1977-78, Joshua Mid Sch 1978-80, Goddard Jr HS 1980-81; Math/Accounting Teacher Midlothian HS 1983-; *ai:* NHS, Math Club, Just Say No Spon; UIL Accounting, Number Sense, Calculator Coach; TSTA, NEA; TX Mid-Continent Oil & Gas Assn Oil Information Comm; Participant in 24th Annual Petroleum Inst for Educators; *office:* Midlothian HS 925 S 9th St Midlothian TX 76065

ROMAGNOLI, DONNA GRANT, English Teacher; *b:* New Albany, IN; *m:* Robert Norman; *c:* Amy, Sara J.; *ed:* (BA) Eng/ His, W KY Univ 1972; (MED) Ed/Rdng, Univ of Louisville 1975; Counseling, Supervision W KY Univ; *cr:* Teacher Valley HS 1972-80, Bullitt Cntrl HS 1980-82, Warren Cntrl HS 1982-; *ai:* Teacher Comm Selection of Teachers; Faculty Rep Warren Cty Teachers Organization; Credentials Comm 3rd Dist Teachers Organizaion Chm; Warren Cty Teachers Organization VP 1988-89; *office:* Warren Cntrl HS 559 Morgantown Rd Bowling Green KY 42103

ROMAN, STEPHEN JAMES, 5th-8th Grade Science Instr; *b:* Long Prairie, MN; *m:* Karen Morgan; *c:* Sarah; *ed:* (BS) Ed, St Johns Univ 1982; (MS) Ed Research/Evaluation Univ of ND 1989; Cert Ed Admin, NW MO St Univ 1990; *cr:* 5th-8th Grade Sci Teacher New Market IA 1982-; *ai:* Ftbl, Track, Bsktbl Coach; Jr Great Books Instr; Various Curr Comms; New Market Ed Assn Pres 1986, 1989; Article in Multiple Regression Viewpoints 1988; *home:* Box 31 New Market IA 51646

ROMANO, CHARLES ANTHONY, Biology Teacher; *b:* Kenosha, WI; *m:* Francesca Morrone; *c:* Gina M.; *ed:* (BS) Life Sci/Chem, Univ of WI Parkside 1980; Working Towards Masters in Instructional Technology & Ed; *cr:* Teacher Washington Jr HS 1981-; *ai:* Stu Cncl Adv; Outdoor Ed Coord; Yrbk Photographer; Variety Show Dir.

ROMANO, CHRISTOPHER J., US History Teacher; *b:* Toledo, OH; *m:* Marilyn R. Nathanson; *c:* Jacqueline; *ed:* (BE) Soc Stud/Ed, Univ of Toledo 1986; *cr:* Educator Piper HS 1986-; *ai:* Ftbl Asst Coach/Def Coord; Golf Head Coach; *office:* Piper HS 8000 Nw 44th St Sunrise FL 33321

ROMANO, EDNA M., Principal; *b:* Helper, UT; *m:* Frank; *c:* Frank Jr., Kevin Patrick; *ed:* (BS) Elem Ed, 1951, (MA) Instrl Media, 1968 Univ of Ut; (MA) Educl Admin, BYU 1982; *cr:* Teacher Fresno Cty 1948-50, Soldier Summit 1951-52, Sally Mauro Elem 1952-87, Prin Castle Valley Ctr Sch for The Handicapped 1987-; *ai:* AARF Legislative Comm; Rep Southeast UT; CCEA/UEA/NEA 1950-; Delta Kappa Gamma Pres/Treas 1967-89; Helper City Cncl Councilwomen 1982-; Chamber of Commerce Bd of Gvernors Awd 1985; Delta Kappa Gamma St Treas; Helper His UT Historical Society; Salt Lake Tribune Beautification Cmmty Worker Awd 1988; Carbon Cty Woman of Yr 1983; Rural Teacher of Yr 1986-87; Conservation Teacher of Yr 1979; *home:* 105 W 2 N Helper UT 84526

ROMANO, MARY GRACE FIORE, Fourth Grade Teacher; *b:* Syracuse, NY; *m:* Lawrence D.; *c:* Lawrence D.; *ed:* (AA) Hum, Onondaga Comm Coll 1970; (BA) Elem Ed/Interdisciplinary/Soc Sci, Potsdam St 1972; (MS) Elem Ed/Interdisciplinary/Soc Sci, Syracuse Univ 1976; *cr:* 8th Grade Teacher St James Sch 1973-74; Sci Teacher 1974-85, 4th Grade Teacher 1986- St Rose of Lima; *ai:* Soccer Coach; Teacher of Religious Ed; Longbranch Gardening Club Pres 1981-84; *home:* 5094 Cliffton Dr North Syracuse NY 13212

ROMANO, SANDRA A., Teacher-Language Arts Dept; *b:* Pittsburgh, PA; *ed:* (BS) Eng, Clarion Univ 1969; Additional Credits for Cert; *cr:* Teacher Sto-Rox Sch Dist 1969-72, Holy Family Sch 1972-; *ai:* Yrbk, Sch Newspaper, Sch Store Adv; Class Play Dir; Sch Evaluation Team Mem 1989-; *office:* Holy Family Sch 323 Chestnut St Latrobe PA 15650

ROMANOWSKI, MICHAEL H., Social Studies Dept Chair; *b:* Kingston, PA; *m:* Janet K. Fenninger; *ed:* (MS) Soc Stud Ed, IN Univ 1985; (BS) Soc Stud Ed, Indiana Univ of PA 1984; *cr:* Soc Stud Teacher 1986- Soc Stud Dept Chm 1988- Elizabethtown Area HS; *ai:* Fellowship Educl Leadership Miami of OH Univ 1990; *office:* Elizabeth Area HS 600 E High St Elizabethtown PA 17022

ROMANS, PAUL BERNARD, Science Department Chair; *b:* Danbury, CT; *m:* Diane Christine Mc Donald; *c:* Rebecca A.; *ed:* (BS) General Sci, 1958; (MS) Sci Ed, 1970 OR St Univ; *cr:* Sci Teacher U S Grant HS 1962-66, Jackson HS 1966-82, Wilson HS 1982-89, Sci Dept Chm 1989- Wilson HS; *ai:* Coord City Sci Net; Mem Grievance & Wilson HS Comm; NSTA, OR Sci Teachers Assn, NEA; Portland Assn Teachers Exec Bd 1985-89; Natl Sci Fnd Grant 1967-70; Chm Bargaining Team 1986; *office:* Wilson HS 1151 SW Vermont Portland OR 97219

ROMAY, MARY HURST, 5th Grade Teacher; *b:* Cairo, GA; *w:* Donald Q. (dec); *c:* Donald Jr., Lisa; *ed:* (BS) Ed, Univ of GA 1951; *cr:* 6th Grade Teacher Southside Elem 1949-55; 5th Grade Teacher Atlanta Public Schls 1955-63; 4th Grade Teacher Nashville Public Schls 1968-69; 5th Grade Teacher Putnam Cty Schls 1977-; *ai:* Alpha Delta Kappa (Historian 1980-82, Secy 1958-59); Gideon Auxiliary Secy 1980-82; Baptist Sunday Sch Adult Teacher 1978-; Teacher of Yr Kelley Smith Sch 1989-; *home:* 2107 Golf Dr Palatka FL 32177

ROMEO, VEOLA TAYLOR, Chapter 1 Teacher; *b:* Buena Vista, GA; *m:* Gerald H.; *c:* Derrick Usher, Corliss Usher Brown; *ed:* (BA) Elem Ed, Clark Coll 1975; (MA) Elem Ed, Atlanta Univ 1982; *cr:* Chapter 1 Teacher Lena J Campbell Elem Sch 1975-76; Classroom Teacher 1976-89, Chapter 1 Teacher 1989- Lakewood Heights Elem Sch; *ai:* Hospitality Comm Support Teacher & Treas; TPAI Data Collector Sch System Server; Leadership Team; Atlanta Fed of Teachers Building Rep 1976-, Certificate of Recognition 1988-89; Atlanta Public Schls Teacher of Yr 1989; Stu Progress in Rdng & Math Certificate of Achievement; Several Academic Wkshps; Univ of GA Extension Service Outstanding Contribution to Young People & R J Research Certificate of Recognition 1987-89; *home:* 2266 Crestknoll Cir Decatur GA 30032

ROMERO, CHARLOTTE MARIE (AGUILAR), Counselor; *b:* Vaughn, NM; *m:* Robert John; *c:* John R., Contessa P.; *ed:* (BA) His/Rdng, 1979, (MA) Guidance/Counseling, 1985 NM Highlands Univ; *cr:* 7th/8th Grade Rdng Teacher 1979-, 8th Grade Girls Head Coach 1981- Alderson Jr HS; Cnslr Estacado HS 1990; *ai:* 8th Grade Girls Head Vlybl, Track, Asst Bsktbl Coach; Natl Jr Honor Society Faculty Cncl; Hospitality Comm Head; Phi Kappa Phi Mem 1985-, Pin 1985; PTA Mem 1979-; Christ The King Cath Church Mem 1979-; Alderson Jr HS Perfect Attendance 1979-82, 1985-86, 1987-88; Vlybl City Championship 1985; Track City Championship 1981-89; *office:* Estacado HS 1504 E Itasca Lubbock TX 79403

ROMERO, DONALD E., Music Instructor; *b:* Las Vegas, NM; *m:* Josephine Frances Griego; *c:* Dawn J., Kris H., Samantha J.; *ed:* (BA) Music Ed, 1973, (MA) Music Ed, 1975 NM Highlands Univ; *cr:* Music Instr Penasco HS 1973-76, Memorial Mid Sch 1977-; *ai:* Memorial Mid Sch Marching & Concert Band; NM Music Educators Assn VP 1985-86; Immaculate Conception Brass Choir 1988-; US Marine Corps Band 1969; *office:* Memorial Mid Sch 901 Douglas Ave Las Vegas NM 87701

ROMINE, JOANNE, HS Social Studies Teacher; *b:* Duncan, OK; *ed:* (BA) Ed/His/Phys Ed, 1980, (MA) Ed/His, 1981 E Cntrl Univ; *cr:* His Teacher Graham Public Sch 1981-82, Velma-Alma Public Sch 1982-; *ai:* Jr Class Spon; Assn of Velma-Alma Educators, OK Ed Assn, NEA; *office:* Velma-Alma HS Box 8 Velma OK 73091

ROMINES, ELIZABETH COURTNEY, Language Arts Teacher; *b:* Houston, TX; *m:* Richard Leroy; *c:* Taylor, Jennifer R., Jana L.; *ed:* (BS) Ed, Sam Houston St Univ 1964; (MED) Rdng, Stephen F Austin St Univ 1977; Gifted/Talented, Span, Cmptrs; *cr:* Elem Teacher Houston Ind Sch Dist, Liberty Ind Sch Dist, Hemphill Ind Sch Dist 1963-67; 3rd Grade Spec Ed/Kndgtn Teacher Henderson Ind Sch Dist 1969-71; 3rd Grade Teacher Barbers Hill Ind Sch Dist 1972-77; 6th-8th Grade Teacher Longview Ind Sch Dist 1978-; *ai:* Yrbk Adv; 6th-8th Grade Gifted & Talented; TX Assn of Gifted & Talented, TX Assn of Prof Ed, Eng Teachers of TX 1978-; Alpha Delta Kappa VP 1980-; *home:* 514 Richfield Longview TX 75601

RONALD, PAULINE CAROL, Art Department Head; *b:* York, England; *c:* Alexia; *ed:* (NDD) Art, Harrogate Sch of Art England 1965; (ATD) Art Ed, Univ of Newcastle Upon Tyne 1966; (MA) Art Ed, Ball St Univ 1977; *cr:* Art Teacher Knightstown IN 19 6-67, Dunkirk IN 1967-68, IN Univ East 1974-84, Richmond HS 1968-; *ai:* Academic Fine Arts Team Coach;Winner of St Competition 1988; Runner Up1989; RACT 1968-; NEA, ISTA 1966-; Richmond Art Museum Bd Mem 1985-; Richmond Civil Theatre 1968-, 4 Times Best Set Painting; Several Art Awds Paintings & Drawings 1966; Drawing Published; *office:* Richmond HS 380 Hub Etchison Pkwy Richmond IN 47374

RONAN, JOAN SMITH, First Grade Teacher; *b:* Newark, NJ; *m:* Harold Robert Jr.; *c:* Debbie Haughwout, Scott, David, Tracey, Steven (dec); *ed:* (BS) Elem Ed, Union St Teachers Coll 1952; *cr:* 1st Grade Teacher Demerest Sch 1952-53, Fairview Elem 1977-; *ai:* Cheerleading Coach.

RONAN, MARY MICHAEL, Director of Religious Ed; *b:* Waterbury, CT; *ed:* (BED) Eng, Duquesne Univ 1956; (MA) Fr Lit, Univ of Notre Dame 1967; Cert Lib Sci, Marshall Univ; Cert Religious Stud, St Charles Borromeo Seminary; *cr:* St Vincent Pallotti HS 1955-66; Rosary HS 1966-68; St Joseph Cntrl HS 1970-79; Our Lady of Fatima Jr HS 1980-88; Our Lady of Fatima Parish 1988-; *ai:* Eng & Fr Lit Tutor; Full Time Dir Religious Ed; Fr Spon, Creative Writing & Red Cross Club; NCTE 1960-65; Parish Cncl 1986-; Amer Hospital for Rehabilitation; *home:* 2900 1st Ave Huntington WV 25702

RONE, THETA KELLEY, 7th Grade Mathematics Teacher; *b:* Covington, TN; *m:* James Walter; *c:* Stephen K., Deanna Rone Nabors; *ed:* (BS) Math, Memphis St Univ 1961; (MS) Sci, Univ of TN Chattanooga 1976; Univ of IL, Univ of TN Martin, Memphis St; *cr:* Math Teacher Byars Hall HS 1961; Algebra/ Geometry Teacher Rantoul Township HS 1961-62; Sci Teacher Signal Mountain Jr HS 1970-76; Math Teacher Covington Elem Sch 1976-86; St Chairperson TN Teachers Study Cncl TN St Dept Ed 1986-87; Math Teacher Covington Elem Sch 1987-; *ai:* Jr Beta Club Spon; Southern Assn of Colls & Schls Steering, TN Teachers Study Cncl St Exec, Positive Attitudes in TN Schls Covington Elem Comms; NCTM 1987-; TN Assn of Mid Schls (St of TN Comm) 1988-; NEA, TN Ed Assn 1976-; Covington City Ed Assn (Pres 1978-79) 1976-; Alpha Delta Kappa (Mem, Pres); TN

Teachers Study Cncl Intnl Teachers Honorary St Chm 1986-87; Covington Elem PTO; Garland Baptist Church.

RONEY, BARBARA HOLIFIELD, Teacher; *b:* Laurel, MS; *m:* Larry H.; *c:* Tracy K., Tara J., Natalie M.; *ed:* (MS) Eng, Univ of S MS 1969; MS Teacher Assessment Evaluator 1988; *cr:* Teacher South Jones HS 1969-73, Taylorsville HS 1982-; *office:* Taylorsville HS P O Box 8 Taylorsville MS 39168

RONGEY, MARILYN FRANCIS, Fifth Grade Teacher; *b:* Granite City, IL; *c:* Deborah Epperson, Angela Epperson, Robert, Walter, Laura Marie; *ed:* (BS) Ed/Home Ec, Southern IL Univ 1958; Southern Il Univ; *cr:* Home Ec Teacher Central Jr HS 1958-59; 5th Grade Teacher Maryville Elem Sch 1967-70; 5th Grade Teacher Frohardt Elem Sch 1970-; *ai:* Volunteer Amer Cancer Society & Amer Heart Assn; Frohardt Sch Drug Coord; Work for Greenpeace; Citizens Utility Bd; Arbor Society; Delta Kappa Gamma Society Intnl; Aft Executive Bd 1989-; PTA Executive Bd 1986-88; Il Home Economics Assn 86-887; Honor Service Awd 1951; First Presbyn Church Trustee 1989-; Citizens Comm for Ed 1985-86; Articles Granite City Press-Record/ Journal; St Louis Post-Dispatch Newspaper; Weekly Reader; *office:* Frohardt Elem Sch 2040 Johnson Rd Granite City IL 62040

RONNING, KENNETH MICHAEL, Economics & History Teacher; *b:* Butte, MT; *c:* Carrie A., Kathleen M.; *ed:* (BA) His/ Economics/Poly Sci, Univ of MT 1969; (MS) Ed/Admin, 1971, (BS) Elem Ed, 1977 W MT Coll; *cr:* Teacher Blaine Elem 1969-72, Butte HS 1972-; *ai:* Class Adv; Butte Teachers Union Exec Cncl 1970-78; MT ASCD; Lions Club (VP, Pres) 1978-86; BSA Adv 1960-68; Longfellow Recreation Center (Pres, Treas) 1971-76; *office:* Butte HS 401 S Wyoming Butte MT 59701

RONZONI, ARNOLD DAVID, English Teacher; *b:* Philadelphia, PA; *ed:* (BS) Eng, La Salle Coll 1971; *cr:* Eng Teacher St John Neumann HS 1971-82, Little Flower HS 1982-; *ai:* Sch Newspaper Moderator; Union Rep; Sch Publicity Dir; SAT Verbal Prep Course Teacher; NACST 1971-; Temple Univ HS Journalism Teacher of Yr & Cath Teachers Assn Nominee Teacher of Yr 1989; *office:* Little Flower Cath HS 10th & Lycoming St Philadelphia PA 19140

ROOD, MARY A., English Teacher; *b:* Chicago, IL; *ed:* (BA) Eng, De Paul Univ 1965; *cr:* Eng Teacher Amundsen HS 1965-66, Austin HS 1966-79; Teacher/Tutor Austin HS 1979-83; Eng Teacher Mather HS 1983-; *ai:* Pom Pon & Russian Club Spon; Sr Class & Newspaper Adv; NCTE 1966-; ASCD 1989-; Chicago Archdiocese Sch System Bd Mem 1973; Fry Fnd Fellowship Univ of Chicago; *office:* Mather HS 5835 N Lincoln Chicago IL 60659

ROOKS, BARBARA JEAN, English Teacher; *b:* Newnan, GA; *ed:* (BS) Home Ed Ed, Bob Jones Univ 1979; Teaching Eng Bob Jones Univ 1981; *cr:* Home Ec/Eng Teacher Faith Chrstn Acad 1981-88; Eng Teacher Indiana Chrstn Acad 1988-; *ai:* Spring Play; *office:* Indiana Chrstn Acad 432 W 300 N Anderson IN 46012

ROOKS, BRENDA HAMBY, Teacher; *b:* Wilkesboro, NC; *m:* Larry Earl; *c:* Terri Hamby, Austin S.; *ed:* (BS) Elem Ed, 1970; (MA) Mid Sch Cir 1988; (MA) Rdng 1988 ASU; *cr:* Teacher Mountain View Elem 1970-74, Yadkinville 1974-; *ai:* Annual & Newspaper Staff; Teacher of Yr 1988; Delta Kappa Gamma Secy 1989.

ROOP, MARY MC DANIEL, Printing Instructor; *b:* Dublin, VA; *c:* Mark S.; *ed:* Certificate VA Poly Inst & VA St Univ & Univ of VA; Graphic Arts Tech Fnd, Pittsburgh 1980, 1987; *cr:* Printing Instr Pulaski Cty HS 1977-; *ai:* Voc Industrial Clubs of America Adv; Pulaski Cty Ed Assn, VA Ed Assn, NEA, Printing Industries of VA; Intnl Graphic Art Ed Assn Incorporated; Beta Sigma Phi 1965-, Order of the Rose 1980; Graphic Art Tech Fnd Advanced Teacher Awd; *office:* Pulaski Cty HS PO Box 518 Dublin VA 24084

ROOSA, MARK EDWARD, Earth Science Teacher; *b:* Amsterdam, NY; *m:* Maria Manna; *c:* Heather, Shannon, Melissa, Rachael; *ed:* (BS) Ed, 1970, (MS) Ed, 1974, (CAS) Ed/Admin, 1986 SUNY New Paltz; NYS DSAS Voc Trng; TCA Certified Drug Cnslr; *cr:* 6th Grade Teacher Kingston City Schls 1970-76; 1st Grade Teacher Ellenville Cntrl Sch 1977-79; Math/Rdng Teacher/Dir of Ed/Voc Ed Samaritan Village Inc 1979-86;Sci Teacher Ellenville HS 1986-; *ai:* Sr Class Adv; Var Ftbl Coach; STANYS; NYS Judo Incorporated Treas 1980-; *office:* Ellenville HS 28 Maple Ave Ellenville NY 12428

ROOT, MAURICE RICHARD, 4th Grade Teacher; *b:* San Jose, IL; *m:* Sandra L.; *c:* Bryan D.; *ed:* (BS) Ed, Quincy Col 1974; Univ of IL; Northeast Univ; *cr:* 4th Grade Teacher Mark Twain Elem 1974-; *ai:* Curr Comm; Spelling Bee Chm; MSTA VP 1976.

ROPER, RODDY LEE, Retired; *b:* Harrell, AR; *m:* Josephine Huntsman; *c:* Roddy L. Jr., Charmaine, John B., Theresa D. Roper Amos; *ed:* (BA) Lang Art/Soc Stud, ASC Conway 1950; (MAED) Ed/Supervision/Admin, N AZ Univ 1958; Ed Trng, Brigham Young Univ, Univ of UT Salt Lake City, UT St Univ Logan; *cr:* Soc Stud Teacher Gentry HS 1950; 1st-6th Grade Teacher Moccasin Elem 1950-53; Eng Lit/Soc Stud Teacher Fredonia HS 1953-57; 4th Grade Teacher Fredonia Elem 1957-58; K-12th Grade Prin Enterprise Schls 1958-81; 4th Grade Teacher Enterprise Elem 1981-84; *ai:* Coordinating & Scheduling Extracurricular Act K-12th Grades; Speech & Drama Act Adv & Coach; Responsible for Elem & HS Accreditation; UT Assn Scndry Sch Prins, NASSP, UT Assn Elem Sch Prins, NAESP 1958-81; UT Ed Assn, NEA, UT Rural Schls Assn 1975-81; *home:* 20 S 100 W PO Box 206 Enterprise UT 84725

ROPER, RONALD WAYNE, Language Art Teacher; *b:* Riverside, CA; *m:* Debra Denise Schroder; *c:* Thad, Trevor, Brian, Erin; *ed:* (BA) Eng, S UT St Coll 1980; *cr:* 4th-12th Grade Generalist Glacier View Sch 1981-; *ai:* Sr Class Adv; Hockey & Drama Coach; AK St Writing Consortium; Mensa; *home:* Box 1011 Palmer AK 99645

ROS, EVA VONCILE (LIVAUDAIS), Substitute Teacher; *b:* Moss Point, MS; *m:* Pol Mikel; *c:* John F., Linda M. Ros Savell, Charles M.; *ed:* (BA) Early Chldhd Ed, Tougaloo Coll 1979; Remedial Rdng 1979-80, Rdng Skills Dev 1981-82, Univ S MS; *cr:* Head Teacher/Soc Service Aide Dev Project Head Start; Teacher Aide/Teacher Jackson Cty Citizens for Child 1970-79; Teacher Our Lady of Victories Elem Sch 1979-86; Substitute Teacher Pascagoula Municipal Separate Sch Dist 1986-; *ai:* MS Rdng Assn 1983-; Amer Natl Red Cross Gray Lady in Elem Sch 1965-67; GSA (Volunteer, Troop Leader) 1962-70; Writers Unlimited Charter Mem 1967-; MS Poetry Society Inc (South Branch Secy 1982-) 1980-; *home:* 3020 Frederic St Pascagoula MS 39567

ROSA, SUSAN FREDERICK, Third Grade Teacher; *b:* Brockton, MA; *m:* Antone T.; *ed:* (BS) Elem Ed, Framingham St Coll 1982; British Primary Ed, Oxfordshire England; *cr:* 7th/8th Grade Teacher Hillsboro/Deering Mid Sch 1982-83; 1st/2nd Combined Teacher 1983-85, 1st-8th Grade Rdng Teacher 1985, 7th/8th Grade Combined Self Contained Teacher 1985-88 St Marys Sch; 8th Grade Rdng/Eng/Health Teacher Varnum Brook Mid Sch 1988-89; 3rd Grade Self Contained Teacher Townsend MA 1989-; *ai:* Yrbk Adv Varnum Brook Mid Sch; Spelling Bee Coord 1984-88; Sci Fair Coord St Marys Sch 1985-88; MTA, NEA 1988-; N Worcester Cncl Intnl Rdng Assn 1989-; *office:* Squannacook Elem Sch PO Box 642 66 Brookline Rd Townsend MA 01469

ROSALEZ, ALEX L., Computer Teacher; *b:* Ajo, AZ; *m:* Grace Tarango; *c:* Alex T., Erica R.; *ed:* (BS) Bus/Quantitative Sys, AZ St Univ 1975; Cert Ed, Grand Canyon Univ 1981; Cert Voc Ed, AZ St Univ 1990; Masters Prgm Media, Ed, Cmptr Sci; *cr:* Cmptr Operator 1974-75, Programmer 1975-77, Systems/Programmer Analyst 1978-80 Honeywell Info System; Cmptr Teacher 1981-; *ai:* Cmptr Club Spon; Head Sftbl Coach; Grant Writing; Support Group Facilitator; Valley Big Brothers 1976-.

ROSANDER, DEAN LEROY, Science Teacher; *b:* Fresno, CA; *m:* Karen Pettebone; *c:* Samuel, Jacob, Sarah; *ed:* (AS) Horticulture, Reedley Coll 1977; (BS) Ed, OK Baptist Coll 1981; *cr:* 5th Grad Teacher 1981-86, Jr/Sr HS Sci Teacher 1986- Windsor Baptist Sch; Bio/General Sci Teacher OK Baptist Coll 1986-; *ai:* Yr Adv; Sr Class Spon 1990; *office:* Windsor Hills Baptist Sch 5517 NW 23rd Oklahoma City OK 73127

ROSAS, DAVID A., Fifth Grade Teacher; *b:* Scottsbluff, NE; *m:* Sylvia M.; *c:* Angelica, Agustin, Daniel; *ed:* (BA) Ed, St Marys Univ 1977; (MA) Ed, Univ of TX San Antonio 1989; *cr:* 4th Grade Teacher Gates Elem Sch 1977-79; 5th Grade Teacher B T Washington Elem Sch 1979-89, Hillcrest Elem Sch 1989-; *ai:* Dir Span Translation Ministry; *office:* Hillcrest Elem Sch 211 W Malone San Antonio TX 78202

ROSBOROUGH, ROBERT, English Teacher; *b:* Flint, MI; *ed:* (BA) Soc Sci/Eng, W MI Univ 1965; (MA) Educl Admin, E MI Univ 1972; *cr:* Teacher Bryant Cmmty Jr HS 1965-75; Staff Specialist 1975-80, Teacher 1980- Northern Cmmty HS; *ai:* City-Wide Eng Advisory Comm; MEA, NEA, AFT, Phi Delta Kappa; Urban League, NAACP; Church of God in Christ Ordained Minister; Outstanding Scndry Educator 1974; *home:* 1707 Marlowe Dr Flint MI 48504

ROSCHMANN, DENNIS E., Teacher of Gifted Coordinator; *b:* Chicago, IL; *m:* Joanne Goldberg; *c:* Peg, Mary, Kathleen, Wendy, Joseph; *ed:* (BA) His, 1964, (MSE) Ed, 1969 N IL Univ; *cr:* 7th Grade His Teacher Stanley Field Sch 1964-79; Teacher of Gifted Coord W Northfield Dist 31 1979-; *ai:* Bsktbl Coach; Local Ed Assn Pres 1982-; IL Cncl for Gifted; Coached IL Future Problem Solving St Championship Teams 1981-84, 3rd Place Team Natl 1981, 1st Place Individual 1984; *office:* W Northfield Dist 31 1919 Landwehr Rd Glenview IL 60025

ROSCHMANN, JOANNE GOLDBERG, 6th Grade Reading Teacher; *b:* Chicago, IL; *m:* Dennis E.; *c:* Stacy A. Koch, Jeffrey A. Koch; *ed:* (BS) Ed, Northwestern Univ 1964; (MA) Eng Lang/ Lit, Univ of Chicago 1966; Rdng, Natl Coll of Ed; *cr:* 6th-8th Grade Rdng Teacher Emerson Sch 1964-68; 7th-8th Grade Rdng Teacher Springman Jr HS 1977-78; 6th Grade Rdng Teacher Field Sch 1978-; *ai:* Building Leadership Team; Report to Parents, Rdng Curr Comms; Intnl Rdng Assn, SCIRA Mem 1978-; Deerfield Park Civic Assn Pres 1972-76; *office:* Field Sch 2055 Landwehr Rd Northbrook IL 60062

ROSE, BARBARA L., Third Grade Teacher; *b:* Rugby, ND; *c:* Stefanie, Justin; *ed:* Speech Pathology/Audiology, 1972, Elem Ed, 1978 Univ of ND; Grad Stud Univ of ND; *cr:* Speech Pathologist Grand Forks Cty 1972-74, Thompson Sch 1974-79; Classroom Teacher Manvel Sch 1980-; *ai:* Manvel Ed Assn (Secy, Treas) 1982-; ND Ed Assn 1975-.

ROSE, CATHY CAROL, Fifth Grade Teacher; *b:* Carthage, TN; *m:* Jimmy W.; *ed:* (BS) Elem Ed, TN Technological Univ 1972; (MED) Supervision/Instruction, Univ of TN Chattanooga 1989; *cr:* Kndgtn/Sci Teacher Mt Juliet Jr HS & Elem 1971-73; Kndgtn Teacher Southside Elem 1973-75; Rdng Readiness Teacher Ninth Street Sch 1975-76; 2nd Grade Teacher Ninth & O Baptist Sch 1976-78, A B Hill Elem 1978-79; Jr HS Sci/Soc Stud Teacher Briarcrest Baptist Schls 1979-81; 5th Grade Teacher Blue Springs Elem 1981-; *ai:* NEA, Kappa Delta Pi; Freedoms Fnd Awd Blue Springs 1985; *office:* Blue Springs Elem Sch Rt 1 Blue Springs Rd Cleveland TN 37311

ROSE, CHARLES FREDERICK, 6th-8th Grade Math Teacher; *b:* Salmon, ID; *m:* Jean Carol Martinson; *c:* Sarah, Chris, Emily; *ed:* (BS) Ed, Brigham Young Univ 1978; Emergency Medical Technician & Advanced Trauma/Triage Care Combat Naval Reserves; *cr:* Substitute Teacher 3 Sch Dists 1978-80; Contract Teacher N Kitsap Sch Dist 1980-; *ai:* Natural Helpers Co-Coord; Cmmty Drug Awareness Week Mem Comm; Cross Cntry & Track Coach; US Naval Reserve Chiefs Assn (VP 1989-, 3rd Recon Okinawa 1974), Letter Commendation 1974; Toastmasters Mem 1980-82; LDS Church Seminary Teacher; Teacher of Yr Candidate N Kitsap Sch Dist 1988; Letter of Appreciation Cty Commissioner 1989; *home:* PO Box 622 Suquamish WA 98392

ROSE, DANIEL ALAN, Spanish Teacher; *b:* Clarksville, TX; *m:* Shirley Hosier; *c:* Daniel M., Edward M.; *ed:* (AA) General Ed, Paris Jr Coll 1957; (BA) His, 1959, (MED) Sch Admin, 1964 E TX St Univ; (EDD) Sch Admin, Nova Univ 1975; *cr:* Teacher 1959-67, Asst Prin 1967-70 South Oak Cliff HS; Prin John Heely Bryan Elem 1970-74; Asst Dir Instructional Services Cntrl Office Dallas Ind Sch Dist 1974-78; Prin T G Terry 1978-82; Span Teacher W H Atwell 1982-; *ai:* Honor Club Spon; Assn TX Prof Educators 1982-; Classroom Teachers of Dallas Honor Awd 1973; PTA Life Membership 1972; Wynnewood Kiwanis 1967-70; Oak Cliff Lions 1973-75; Teacher of Yr Atwell Mid Sch 1990; *home:* 436 Longridge Dallas TX 75232

ROSE, DEBBIE KARLSON, Fourth Grade Teacher; *b:* Spokane, WA; *m:* James A.; *c:* Marc; *ed:* (BA) Rdng, Eastern WA Univ 1978; (MA) Ed, Whitworth Coll 89; Gifted Ed; Self-Concept Research; *cr:* 3rd Grade Teacher Whitworth Elem 1978-80; 4th Grade Teacher Colbert Elem 1980-; *ai:* Rdng Comm Rep; Non-Athletic Rep; CAC Comm; Mead Ed Assn Exec Bd; Wash Ed Assn, NEA; Spokane Bus Gifted Ed Schlsp; Odyssey of Mind Coach 1984/1989; *office:* Colbert Elem Sch E 4526 Greenbluff Rd Colbert WA 99005

ROSE, HARVEY FRANKLIN, Mathematics Teacher; *b:* Marshall, AR; *m:* Joyce Ann Brisco; *c:* Guy, Roy; *ed:* (BSE) Math, Univ of Cntrl AR 1966; (MED) Scndry Ed, Univ of AR 1977; *cr:* Jr HS Math/Sci Teacher Marshall Sch 1961-63; Math Teacher Alpena Sch 1963-69, Green Forest HS 1969-76, Cotter HS 1976-77, Green Forest HS 1977-; *ai:* Sr Class Co-Spon; *home:* 501 Rainbow Dr PO Box 462 Green Forest AR 72638

ROSE, IVA MESSICK, Second Grade Teacher; *b:* Beech Grove, TN; *m:* Lee; *c:* Brent, Bradley; *ed:* (BS) Elem Ed, Mid TN St Univ 1963; *cr:* Teacher Coffee Cty Schls 1953-; *ai:* Asst Prin; Coffee Cty Ed Assn (Secy 1955-56) 1953-; TN Ed Assn, NEA 1953-; *home:* Rt 2 Box 3 Beech Grove TN 37018

ROSE, LINDA J., Eighth Grade Math Teacher; *b:* Jersey City, NJ; *c:* Whitney; *ed:* (BA) Elem Ed, Jersey City St Coll 1967-; Spec Ed Cert; *cr:* 3rd Grade Teacher Alexander D Sullivan 1967-68; 5th Grade Teacher 1969-75, 8th Grade Teacher 1975- Martin Luther King Jr; *ai:* Cheerleading Squad Asst Coach; Lincoln Center Inst Prgm; Joint Act Prgm; NEA, NJ Ed Assn, JC Ed Assn; Coll Women Inc Secy 1982-85; NAACP; Governors Recognition Awd 1986; Nom Teacher of Yr 1986, 1987; *home:* 23 Wade St Jersey City NJ 07305

ROSE, LINDA JAMISON, 7th/8th Grade Science Teacher; *b:* Albany, NY; *m:* Jim W.; *c:* Brian, Steven; *ed:* (BS) Psych, William Smith Coll 1982; (MS) Educl Psych, Suny Albany 1990; *cr:* Sci Teacher Acad of the Holy Names 1983-; *ai:* Sci Fair Coord; Chairperson Sci Dept; Phi Beta Kappa Society 1982-, Membership 1982; Unpublished Research Manuscript on Childrens Attitudes on Punishment SUNY Albany 1990; *home:* 482 Kenwood Ave Delmar NY 12054

ROSE, LOIS ANN, Secondary English Teacher; *b:* Mankato, MN; *m:* John; *c:* Laurie, Edward; *ed:* (BS) Eng/Speech/Theatre Arts, Mankato St Univ 1970; Working Towards Masters; *cr:* Eng Teacher Clearfield Cmmty Sch 1981-86, E Union HS 1987-; *ai:* Spring Play & Drama Dir; Jr & Sr Class Spon; ISEA Mem 1987-; 1st-3rd Place Awds & Poems Published; *office:* E Union HS 1000 Eagle Dr Afton IA 50830

ROSE, MARY ETTA, Director; *b:* Indianapolis, IN; *ed:* (BS) Ed, Ball St Univ 1937; (MS) Ed, Butler Univ 1947; Various Univs & Colls; *cr:* Teacher Indianapolis Public Schls 1943-88; Dir Witherspoon Performing Art Center 1988-; *ai:* IN Retired Teachers Assn, Intnl Society of Music Ed, Intnl Cncl for Traditional Music, Natl Alliance of Black Sch Educators, US-China Peoples Friendship Assn, Amer Assn of Univ Women, Natl Assn for Advancement of Colored People, Indianapolis Ed Assn Leadership in Ed Awd 1985; Phi Delta Kappa Open Fellowship 1984, Outstanding Educator of Yr 1987; Indianapolis Museum of Art, Urban League, Natl Cncl of Negro Women, Indianapolis Music Promoters, Bridgette Club; Ladies of Note Dir; Indianapolis Public Schls Above & Beyond Call of Duty 1987, Teacher of Yr 1981-82, Fnd Grants 1985, 1987; Purdue Univ Black Women in Midwest 1986; Whos Who in Midwest 1984; Whos Who of Amer Women 1983; Whos Who in World 1984; Lilly Endowment Fellowship 1964, 1984; Intnl Biographe Whos Who in Music 1987; Pres Ronald W Reagan Letter of Recognition 1987; Senator Richard G Lugar Letter of Recognition 1987; Citation Congressional Record 1987, 1989; *office:* Witherspoon Performing Art Ctr 5136 N Michigan Rd Indianapolis IN 46208

ROSE, NANCY SILVIA, French Teacher; *b:* Fall River, MA; *m:* Michael; *c:* Mark, Neal; *ed:* (BA) Fr, Bridgewater St Coll 1969; Univ of Pau France Summer Session 1970; *cr:* Fr Teacher Spec Abilities Prgm 1969-70, Talbot Mid Sch 1970-; *ai:* MA Teachers Assn 1969-; MA Foreign Lang Assn 1988-; *office:* Edmond P Talbot Mid Sch 124 Melrose St Fall River MA 02723

ROSE, PATRICA STALLINGS, Head Middle School Teacher; *b:* Burlington, NC; *m:* J. Evans Jr.; *c:* Henry L. Clement III, Jennifer C. Clement; *ed:* (BA) Eng, Univ of NC Chapel Hill 1961; Various Colls & Seminars; *cr:* 12th Grade Eng Teacher Peabody HS 1962-64; Eng Teacher/Volunteer to Vietnamese Refugees 1975-77; 9th Grade Eng Teacher 1975-, Head of Mid Sch 1988- Sewickley Acad; *ai:* 8th Grade Girls Club Adv; Natl Assn of Ind Sch, Natl Assn Teachers of Eng, Natl Assn of Mid Sch; Sewickley Presbyn Church Elder; Yrbk Dedication for Teacher of Yr; Natl Anthology of Poetry & Cathedral Poets; Travel Articles; *office:* Sewickley Acad Academy Ave Sewickley PA 15143

ROSE, PATRICIA ANN (GALEA), English Teacher; *b:* Queens, NY; *m:* George A.; *c:* Allison, Matthew; *ed:* (BS) Eng Ed, St Francis Coll 1973; (MS) Gifted Ed, Dowling Coll 1981; (CAS) Ed Admin, NY Univ 1988; *cr:* Eng Teacher Longwood HS, Our Lady of Mercy Acad, Maria Regina Sch; *ai:* Effective Schls Facilitator 1987-88; Long Island Sch Press Assn Bd Mem 1982-84; Longwood Teachers Assn Bd Trustee 1986-88; *office:* Longwood Sr H S Longwood Rd Middle Island NY 11953

ROSE, PAUL FREDERICK, Physics/Calculus Teacher; *b:* Erie, PA; *m:* Patricia Ann Meade; *c:* Mark D., Sharon K.; *ed:* (BS) Math/Physics, Edinboro St Coll 1962; (MA) Math, Univ of IL 1966; Project Physics, Bemidji St Coll 1970; *cr:* Math/Physics Teacher Harbor Creek HS 1962-; *ai:* HCEA (Pres), PSEA, NEA 1971-72, 1981-82, 1984-85; AAPT 1971-; *office:* Harbor Creek HS 6375 Buffalo Rd Harborcreek PA 16421

ROSE, TERESE ANN, First Grade Teacher; *b:* Lincoln, NE; *ed:* (BA) Elem Ed, 1978, (BS) Improvement of Instruction, 1986 Univ of NE Omah; *cr:* Chapter I Bryan Elem 1978-79; 1st Grade Teacher Rockwell Elem 1979-89,Ezra Millard Elem 1989-; *ai:* SAT Team; PAYBAC Liason; Cultural Arts Iniator; *home:* 1336 S 121 Plaza Omaha NE 68144

ROSE-BAXLEY, PEGGY C., Social Studies Teacher; *b:* Gorgas, AL; *m:* William; *c:* Esta Rose Pettis; *ed:* (BA) His Ed, Univ of W FL 1971; (MS) Ed/Supervision Troy St Univ 1978; *cr:* Scndry Teacher Sneads HS 1971-; *ai:* Sneads HS & Jackson Ctys Academic Team Coach; Sneads HS Yrbk Adv; Soph Class Spon & Teacher Advisory Prgm; Stu Cncl Adv 1978-88; Beta Club Spon 1976-83; Chrldr Spon 1983-84; Various Classes Spon 1972-; JCEA Building Rep, NEA 1971-; 1st Baptist Church (Librarian, Sunday Sch Teacher, Acteens) 1971-; Cystic Fibrosis Bike-A-Thon Chm 1970-82; Amer Cancer Society Volunteer 1976-86; Sneads HS Teacher of Yr 1976, 1982; Young Educator of Yr Sneads Jaycees 1974; Jackson Ctys Young Woman of Yr Dir & Producer; Miss Sneads & Little Miss Sneads Beauty Pageants Dir & Producer; *office:* Sneads HS P O Box 219 Sneads FL 32460

ROSEBROCK, GENIE B., 8th Grade English Teacher; *b:* Toledo, OH; *ed:* (BA) Comm, Amer Univ 1964; Univ VA, George Mason Univ; *cr:* Instr Public & Private Schls 1965-67; Professor Eurhythmics Gallandet Univ 1967-72; Teacher/Curr Specialist/ Area I Project Coord Fairfax Cty Schls 1973-; *ai:* Chairperson of Care Comm; Mid Sch Comm; Supt Advisory Meetings Rep; VA Theatre Assn, CEC; NAEA; Smithsonian Assocs, VA Assn of Teachers of Eng, NCTE; *office:* Washington Irving Intermediate 8100 Old Keene Mill Rd Springfield VA 22152

ROSELLE, DEBORAH MUHLENBERG, English Teacher; *b:* Wilmington, DE; *m:* Robert C.; *c:* Ernest Muhlenberg; *ed:* (BA) Eng, 1970, (MA) Eng, 1972 Univ of DE; Writing Process, Rdng, Teaching Writing, West Chester Univ; Eng, Villanova & St Josephs Univ; *cr:* Grad Asst Writing Center Univ of DE 1970-71; Grad Asst/Frosh Composition Instr 1971-72; Eng Teacher/Dorm Adv St Andrews Sch 1972-75; Eng Teacher Kennett HS 1975-; *ai:* Frosh Class Spon Kennett HS; De Valley Writing Assn; PA Writing Project (Consultant, West Chester PRCP Comm) 1981-; PSEA, NEA, NCTE; Articles Published; PA Writing Project Fellowship; *office:* Kennett HS S Union St Kennett Square PA 19348

ROSENBALM, JAN DURAN, Math Teacher; *b:* Henderson, TX; *m:* James A.; *c:* Breanna Lee, James Brady; *ed:* (BBA) Economics/Finance, East TX St Univ 1976; TX St Univ; *cr:* Math Teacher Greenville HS 1984-; *ai:* Gifted & Talented Comm HS Implementation; *office:* Greenville HS 3515 Lions Lair Greenville TX 75401

ROSENBAUM, LINDA, 2nd Grade Teacher; *b:* Peoria, IL; *ed:* (BS) Elem Ed, 1974, (MS) Elem Ed, 1984 IL St Univ; Classes Taken Through N IL UniV; Wkshps on Cooperative Learning to Teachers; *cr:* 4th Grade Teacher Dwight Elem Sch 1974-77; Unit Leader/Asst Dir/Cnslr in Trng Dir/Camp Dir Kickapoo Cncl of Girl Scouts 1975-77, 1978-80, 1981-82; Camp Dir Centrillio Cncl of Girl Scouts 1988; 2nd Grade Teacher Dwight Elem Sch 1977-; *ai:* Staff Dev Comm; Local Inst Planning; Cntrl Advisory Comm Chm Dwight Sch 1988-89; Dwight Ed Assn Pres 1983, 1986; IL Ed Assn, NEA Mem 1974-; IL Cncl Teachers of Math, NCTM, NSTA Mem; Delta Kappa Gamma Mem 1981-; GSA (Leader 1975-, Neighborhood Chm 1986-); Centrillio Cncl GSA Bd Mem 1988-, Thanks Badge 1989; Articles Published.

ROSENBAUM, MARY LOUISE (QUAM), Second Grade Teacher; *b:* Wayzata, MN; *m:* Mitchell D.; *c:* Shauna, Brent; *ed:* (BS) Elem Ed, Univ of MN 1965; *cr:* 1st Grade Teacher Aurora Sch 1965-67, Ramey AFB 1967-68; 1st/3rd Grade Teacher Kadena AFB 1968-71; 3rd Grade Teacher Illesheim Germany 1971-72; 2nd/5th Grade Teacher Dysart Unified Schls 1973-; *ai:* NEA 1965-.

ROSENBAUM, MITCHELL D., Social Studes Department Chair; *b:* Phoenix, AZ; *m:* Mary L.; *c:* Shauna, Brent; *ed:* (BA) Ed/Poly Sci/Geography, AZ St Univ 1971; (MA) Ed/Counseling, N AZ Univ 1989; Working Towards EdD N AZ Univ; *cr:* Teacher Paterdell Sch 1971; Head Teacher Morristown Unified Sch Dist 1972-74; Teacher Dysart Sch Dist 1974-, Lamson Jr Coll 1986; *ai:* Builders Club Spon; Dysart Ed Assn (Secy, Pres, Negotiations Chm); AZ Ed Assn, ASCD; Phoenix Metro Lions Dir 1987-89; Paradise Valley Jaycees; Co-Author Daily Test for Thinking; *office:* Dysart Jr HS 11405 Dysart Rd Peoria AZ 85345

ROSENBAUM, WILLIAM LEOPOLD, Counselor & Psychology Teacher; *b:* New Orleans, LA; *ed:* (MED) Counseling, Loyola Univ 1973; (BS) Psych, LA St Univ 1968; *cr:* Soc Stud Teacher St Thomas Moore 1967-69; Soc Stud Teacher 1971-, Cnslr 1985- St Martins Episcopal; *ai:* Academic Affairs Comm; Sr Adv; Peer Support Groups; Life Skills Curr; Amer Assn for Counseling & Dev, Amer Sch Cnslr Assn, Assn for Specialists Group Work.

ROSENBERGER, NANCY LOUISE, High School English Teacher; *b:* Philadelphia, PA; *m:* Rudy D.; *c:* Charles P. Boinske, Stefanie A. Boinske, Paul T. Boinske; *ed:* (BS) Eng, Penn St Univ 1958; (MA) Eng, West Chester Univ 1982; Grad Stud; *cr:* 7th Grade Eng Teacher Keith Jr HS 1958-61; 7th-9th Grade Eng Teacher Lionville Jr HS 1971-74; 9th-12th Grade Eng/Challenge Teacher Valley Forge Jr HS & Tredyffrin Jr HS & Conestoga HS 1975-; *ai:* Amnesty Intnl Spon; Schlsp & Multicultural Comms; Critical & Creative Thinking Teacher Wkshps Leader; Tredyffrin/ Easttown Assn, PA Ed Assn 1975-; Superior Service Awd; PA Commonwealth Partnership Fellow; NEH Grants Toni Horrison Ind Study 1989, Womens Lit Seminar 1990; Nom PA Teacher of Yr 1990; KYW-TV Teacher Excl 1990; *office:* Conestoga HS Irish & Conestoga Rds Berwyn PA 19312

ROSENBLATT, INA BARBARA, Spanish Teacher; *b:* Brooklyn, NY; *m:* Theodore; *c:* Gregory, Megan; *ed:* (BA) Span, Long Island Univ 1968; (MA) Span, Adelphi Univ 1971; *cr:* Span Teacher G W Hewelt HS 1968-; *ai:* Natl Honor Society Adv; Chairperson PTA/Faculty Human Relations Comm; Prof Advisory Group Mem; AATSP 1968-; NYSAFLT 1968-; LILT 1986-; HWFA Union Secy 1980-; Wrote Curr Textbook for Teaching Span to CSE Learning Disabled Emotionally Disabled Stu 1990; *office:* G W Hewlett H S 60 Everit Ave Hewlett NY 11571

ROSENBLATT, MARJORIE BAKER, Reading Specialist; *b:* Baltimore, MD; *m:* Richard David; *c:* Karen, Jon; *ed:* (BS) Elem Ed, Univ of MD 1964; (MA) Rdng, Trinity Coll 1983; *cr:* Classroom Teacher Baltimore City Public Schls 1964-65; Classroom Teacher 1965-68, 1979-86, Rdng Specialist 1986- Prince Georges Cty Public Schls; *ai:* Test Coord; NEA, MD St Teachers Assn 1964-68, 1979-; Prince Georges Cty Educators Assn 1965-68, 1979-; *home:* 508 Pine Rd Ft Washington MD 20744

ROSENBLUM, HOPE CAROL (LISELL), Teacher; *b:* Brooklyn, NY; *m:* Leroy; *c:* Tammy Hasenzahl, Wayne; *ed:* (BA) Ed, Brooklyn Coll 1957; (MS) Ed, C W Post 1975; Ed Courses At Southampton Univ & Long Island Univ; *cr:* Nursery Sch Teacher JCH Cmmty House 1956-57; Kndgtn Teacher PS 47 1958-60; Elem Substitute Teacher 1971-74; Elem Teacher 1974-; *ai:* Theater Clubs; Intnl Rdng Assn 1989-; PTA (Cncl 1972-74) 1969-82; *home:* 12 Thomas St Coram NY 11727

ROSENBLUTH, HELEN OLIVER, Science Teacher; *b:* Richmond, VA; *m:* Lennie; *c:* Beth Webster, Steven; *ed:* (BA) Sci/ Eng, Univ of NC Chapel Hill 1956; Grad Stud Univ of NC; *cr:* Teacher Wilson Schls 1964-65, Dade Cty Schls 1966-; *ai:* Act Dir; Yrbk, Leadership, Faculty Cncl; UTD 1968-; Society for Prof Journalism 1980-; NASAA 1970-; FSPA 1980-, 1st Place; SIPA 1985-, 1st Place; NSPA 1st Place; NASC; CSPA Judge 1980-, Medalist, Gold Circles; Teacher of Yr 1984, 1986; *office:* Glades Mid Sch 9451 SW 64 St Miami FL 33173

ROSENE, HAROLD LAWRENCE, 5th & 6th Grade Teacher; *b:* San Francisco, CA; *m:* Anna Bell; *c:* Cynthia, Daniel; *ed:* (BA) Elem Ed, Portland St Univ 1967; (MED) Elem Ed, Univ of Portland 1972; Cmptr Sci, Portland Univ 1987-88; Creative Writing, Lewis & Clark Coll 1980; Environmental Ed, Cntrl WA Univ 1984; *cr:* 7th Grade Teacher 1967-70, 5th Grade Teacher 1970-76, 6th Grade Teacher 1976-89 Menlo Park Schls; 5th/6th Grade Teacher Gilbert Heights Sch 1989-; *ai:* Coach Boys Bsktbl; OR Ed Assn 1967-; David Douglas Ed Assn 1967-; Radio Emergency Associated Communications Team Trng Officer 1987-; OR Electric Rail Historical Society 1987- Service 1988; *office:* Gilbert Heights Elem Sch 12839 SE Holgate Blvd Portland OR 97236

ROSENFELD, MARCIA, Spanish Teacher; *b:* Bronx, NY; *m:* Alan; *ed:* (BA) Span, Queens Coll 1972; (MA) Scndry Ed, Hofstra Univ 1975; Grad Stud 1976; *cr:* Span Teacher Lawrence Jr HS 1972-74, Sommers Jr HS 1974-76, Wilson Jr HS 211 1976-77, Nathaniel Hawthorne Ind Sch 74 1977-.

ROSENGARTEN, HENRY ALAN, Language Arts Teacher; *b:* Jamaica, NY; *m:* Robert Toback; *c:* Mark, Daniel; *ed:* (BS) Elem Ed, 1967, (MS) Elem Ed, 1971 SUNY New Platz; *cr:* 4th Grade Teacher Port Ewen Elem 1967-69; 6th Grade Teacher Marlboro Mid Sch 1970-; *ai:* Chess Club, Stage Crew Adv; Adult Ed SAT; New Paltz Rescue Squad Pres 1979-84; New Paltz Planning Bd 1986-88; NeW Paltz Village Trustee 1988-89; Gardens for Nutrition (Pres 1986-89) 1979-; Weekly Newspaper Columnist 1986-89; *office:* Marlboro Mid Sch Birdsal Ave Marlboro NY 12542

ROSENKRANZ, JOSEPHINE, OSF, 4th Grade Teacher; *b:* La Salle, IL; *ed:* (BA) His, Coll of St Francis 1970; (MS) Ed, St Francis Coll 1979; Accounting; *cr:* 3rd/4th Grade Teacher St Joseph Sch 1958-61; 1st/5th Grade Teacher Sacred Heart 1961-64; 4th Grade Teacher St Joseph Peru 1964-65; 2nd Grade Teacher St Joseph Lockport 1965-66; 4th/5th Grade Teacher Immaculate Conception 1966-68; 6th Grade Teacher Sacred Heart 1968-71; 2nd/4th-6th Grade Teacher Peru Cath 1971-87; *ai:* NCEA 1958-; Government Grant Lewis Univ; Field Bio/Ecology 1968; Natl Sci Fnd Grant N IL Univ De Kalb Math 1978, 1979; *office:* Peru Cath Sch 900 Schuyler St Peru IL 61354

ROSENMAN, DEBORAH BOHM, 4th Grade Teacher; *b:* Detroit, MI; *m:* Alon; *c:* Adam, Joseph; *ed:* (BA) Soc Sci, Univ of MI 1978; (MA) Classroom Teaching, MI St Univ 1986; Post Masters Stud Assertive Discipline, AIMS Math & Sci Ed, Lit & Critical Thinking; *cr:* 5th Grade Teacher Barnard Elem 1981-82; 6th Grade Teacher Smith Mid Sch 1984; 4th Grade Teacher Barnard Elem 1983-; *ai:* Barnard Comm Chairperson & Self-Esteem Comm; Dist Marketing Team Mem, PACE Review Comm, Teacher of Yr Comm; NEA, MEA, TEA 1981-; Intnl Rdng Assn, MI Rdng Assn 1989-; Attention Deficit Disorder Assn Secy 1989-; Meadowlake Farms #1 Assn (VP 1988-89, Secy 1987-88); MI St Bd of Ed Pilot Teacher 1988-89; MI Rdng Assn St Conference Informan Assessment Rdng Prgm Presenter 1990; MI St Univ Outstanding Academic Achievement Awd 1986; *office:* Barnard Elem Sch 3601 Forge Troy MI 48083

ROSENTHAL, MILTON EUGENE, 7th Grade Science Teacher; *b:* Boston, MA; *m:* Willa Ruth Meyerhoff; *c:* Matthew M., Jamie L.; *ed:* (BA) Bio, 1955, (MA) Bio/Chem, 1956 Boston Univ; Newton Math Prgm, Harvard Coll; *cr:* Exp Research Asst/ Cytology Instr Boston Univ Researh Laboratory 1956-58; Bio/ Chem Instr/Sci Dept Chm New England Hebrew Acad 1958-60; 7th-9th Grade Math/Sci Teacher Bigelow Jr HS 1957-86; Visiting Bio/Math Instr Huntington Preparatory Sch 1960-66, 1968, 1970; Bio Instr Newton HS 1972-75; Math Instr Stoughton HS 1976; 7th Grade Sci Teacher Day Jr HS 1986-; *ai:* Stu & Teachers Group Team Leader; Tennis Coach; Report Card Comm Mem; Mid Sch Gifted Prgm Chem & Meteorology Instr; Newton HS Voc Ed Prgm Bio Instr; Newton Teachers Assn, MA Teachers Assn 1957-; NEA Life Mem 1957-; NSTA STAR Prgm Sci Teaching Achievement Recognition 1970; Blue Hills Weather Organization Charter Mem 1980-; BSA Merit Badge Cnslr 1960-; John Gunthers High Road Regional Awd; Articles Published; *office:* Day Jr HS 21 Minot Pl Newtonville MA 02160

ROSETTE, LOTTIE STIERS, Retired 2nd Grade Teacher; *b:* Aspen, CO; *m:* Walter E.; *c:* Walter E., Paul R.; *ed:* (BA) Elem Ed, Univ of N CO 1967; *cr:* 2nd Grade Teacher Esma Lewis Elem Sch 1960-82; *home:* 302 Hutton Ave Rifle CO 81650

ROSHOLT, RICHARD M., Social Studies Teacher; *b:* Minneapolis, MN; *m:* Linda; *c:* Katharine; *ed:* (BA) His/Ed, St Olaf Coll 1968; (MA) His, IA St Univ 1970; Admin Certificate, Univ of IL 1982; *cr:* Soc Stud Teacher Thomas Jr HS 1970-74, Buffalo Grove HS 1974-82, Glenbrook North HS 1982-; *ai:* Model United Nations Club Spon; NHS Co-Spon; Natl Cncl of Soc Stud 1974-88; Chicago Hisotrical Society 1983; Outstanding Amer His Teacher Nom; Daughters of Amer Revolution Skokie Chapter 1989-; Coll Bd Advanced Placement Reader & Consultant 1984-; *office:* Glenbrook North H S 2300 Shermer Rd Northbrook IL 60062

ROSIN, MARY ANN, Math Teacher/Math Dept Chair; *b:* Green Bay, WI; *ed:* (BS) Math, Univ of WI Green Bay 1975; (MEPD) Curr, Univ of WI Stevens Point 1985; *cr:* Math Teacher West Jr HS Wisconsin Rapids 1975-78, Lincoln HS 1975-; *ai:* Dept Chairperson; Dist Math Coord; Scndry Math Comm Chairperson; Developmental Guidance, Gender Equity, Able Learner, Olympiad Awds Comms; NCTM, ASCD 1988-; WI Math Cncl 1986-; WI Ed Assn Cncl 1975-; UWGB Alumni Assn 1975-; Natl Sci Fnd Participant; MAPCO Teacher Achievement Awd; Mentor Teacher.

ROSS, B. GEORGE, Health Teacher/Dept Head/Coach; *b:* Albuquerque, NM; *m:* Teresa Darlene; *c:* Tami; *ed:* (BS) Health/ Phys Ed, 1969, (MS) Health/Phys Ed, 1976 E NM Univ; *cr:* Teacher/Coach Gattis Jr HS 1969-73, Clovis HS 1973-79, John Jay HS 1979-; *ai:* Boys & Girls Cross Cntry, Girls Track Head Coach; Girls Bsktbl Asst Coach; TEA 1969-85; ATPE 1985-; NM Girls Bsktbl Coach of Yr 1977, Track 1975, San Antonio Girls Track 1983, 1988; *office:* John Jay HS 7611 Marbach Rd San Antonio TX 75227

ROSS, BETTE ELAINE, Fifth Grade Teacher; *b:* S Charleston, OH; *ed:* (BSED) Elem Ed, Bowling Green St Univ 1967; (MSED) Elem Classroom Teacher, Wright St Univ 1971; Wkshps & Seminars; *cr:* 5th Grade Teacher Park Layne Elem 1967-70; 6th Grade Lang Art Teacher Graham S Elem 1970-71; 5th Grade Teacher Park Layne Elem 1971-; *ai:* Dist Lib Skills Curr Comm; 5th Grade Play Co-Dir; NEA, OEA, TEA, COTA; *office:* Park Layne Elem Sch 620 Cliffside Dr New Carlisle OH 45344

ROSS, BRENDA J., 6th Grade Teacher; *b:* Portola, CA; *c:* Randi Collier, Justin Williams; *ed:* (BS) Ed, Univ of NV 1970; Masters Equivalency at Univ of CA Chico, San Francisco, Univ of ID, Univ of NV Reno; *cr:* Teacher Gooding Elem Sch, Portola Elem Sch; *ai:* Yearly Shakespearean Play; 4-H Leader 1972-79; Theta Lambda (Secy, Treas) 1972-; *office:* Portola Elem Schl 425 Nevada St Portola CA 96122

ROSS, CAROLYN HENSON, 8th Grade Mathematics Teacher; *b:* Sayre, OK; *m:* John Michael; *c:* Ashley E., Kyle B., Chad M.; *ed:* (BS) Elem Ed, 1968, (ME) Elem Math, 1972 SW OK St Univ; *cr:* 3rd/5th/6th Grade Teacher Sentinel Ind Sch Dist 1968-72; 5th Grade Teacher Carnegie Ind Sch Dist 1972-73, Burns Flat Ind Sch Dist 1974-75; 7th/8th Grade Soc Stud Teacher Mustang Ind Sch Dist 1975-76; 8th Grade Math Teacher Plainview Ind Sch Dist 1976-81, 1986-; *ai:* TX Classroom Teachers Assn, TX S Plains Cncl Teachers of Math; Plainview PTA, 1st United Meth Church; *office:* Estacado Jr HS 2200 W 20th Plainview TX 79072

ROSS, CHARLES DANIEL, 6th Grade Elementary Teacher; *b:* Uniontown, PA; *m:* Christine T. Hrisoulas; *c:* Matthew Davis; *ed:* (BS) Elem Ed, Univ of CA 1973; Grad Work Penn St Univ; *cr:* 6th Grade Teacher Kerr Elem Sch 1973-; *ai:* Asst Var Boys Bsktbl, Jr HS Track & Field, 9th Grade Girls Bsktbl Coach; PSEA Mem 1973-; Amer Family Inst Gift of Time Tribute 1990; *office:* Kerr Elem Sch 341 Kittanning Pike Pittsburgh PA 15215

ROSS, DAVID MICHAEL, Social Studies Teacher; *b:* Biloxi, MS; *m:* Pamela Jean Wells; *c:* Michael J., Kyle D.; *ed:* (BS) His, S IL Univ Carbondale 1977; *cr:* Teacher Winola HS 1978-79, Silvis Jr HS 1980-; *ai:* 7th Grade Boys Bsktbl, 6th-8th Grade Girls Vlybl Coach; Twin Rivers Bass Assn (Pres 1988-89, Secy, Treas 1990); *office:* Silvis Jr HS 1305 5th Ave Silvis IL 61282

ROSS, DON L., English Teacher; *b:* Port Arthur, TX; *m:* Becky; *c:* Ellanda, Lauren, Nathan; *ed:* (BA) General Stud/Eng Core, Ambassador Coll 1978; (BGS) Liberal Arts, Lamar Univ 1985; *cr:* Soc Stud Teacher Thomas Edison Mid Sch 1986-87; Eng Teacher Nederland HS 1987-; *ai:* Campus Communications Comm 1989-; Project Celebration 1987-88; Helped Bulldog Believers 1988-89; NEA, TSTA 1987-; Youth Educl Services (Girls Track Coach, Mini-Camp Field Sports Dir) 1982-.

ROSS, GLENDA DAVIS, Fifth Grade Teacher; *b:* Huntington, WV; *m:* Robert Louis; *c:* Bobbi L.; *ed:* (AB) Elem Ed, 1963, (MA) Elem Ed, 1969 Marshall Univ; *cr:* 5th Grade Teacher Ona Elem Sch 1963-72; 5th/6th Grade Teacher Milton Elem Sch 1972-; *ai:* Summer Sci Camp Instr; Alpha Delta Kappa Mem; WV Sci Teachers Assn Mem; Cabell Cty Teacher of Yr 1977; *home:* 1028 Ponderosa Dr Culloden WV 25510

ROSS, HARRY JOHN, Teacher of Eng/Dir Stu Act; *b:* Chicago, IL; *ed:* (BSED) Eng/Speech/Play Production, Northeast MO St 1960; (MED) Admin/Ed/Supervision, Loyola Univ Chicago 1977; *cr:* Prom Moderator/Eng Teacher/Speech/Debate Coach Mendel Cath 1961-66; Loyola Acad; Speech/Debate Coach Brother Rice HS 1969-; *ai:* Dir of Stu Act; Prom Moderator; Ed Teacher Awd; Moderator of Stu Cncl; NCEA; Kiwanis; Educator Teacher USAF/US Navy; Pres Chicago Cath Forensic Society; Debate Coaches; *office:* Brother Rice H S 10001 S Pulaski Rd Chicago IL 60642

ROSS, JANETTE CIPOLLA, 5th Grade Teacher; *b:* Kansas City, MO; *m:* William Russell; *c:* Shane A., Ian J.; *ed:* (BS) Elem Ed, 1975, (MS) Elem Ed, 1979 Cntrl MO St Univ; Advanced Trng Courses; *cr:* 5th Grade Teacher Peculiar Elem Sch 1975-; *ai:* Peculiar Elem Prin Advisory Bd & Mentor Teacher; NEA Pres Raymore-Peculiar Sch Dist 1988-; Peculiar PTA (Advisory Bd 1988-, Admin 1989-) MO Assn for Supervision & Curr 1987-; Lambda Tau Delta MO Pres 1979-80; Candidate MO Teacher of Yr 1987-88; *office:* Peculiar Elem Sch E Broadway St Peculiar MO 64078

ROSS, JOAN HEITZ, Science Teacher; *b:* Delphos, OH; *m:* George A.; *c:* John P., Amy E.; *ed:* (BA) Soc Stud, Coll of St Teresa 1955; Univ of AZ, OH St Univ; *cr:* Bio/Soc Stud Teacher Ross HS 1955-61; Government/His Teacher Sycamore HS 1961-63; Sci/Soc Stud Teacher OLSH 1964-68; Sci Teacher St Margaret Mary 1978-; *ai:* Textbook Selection & Stu Handbook Comm; HS & Univ Regional Sci Fair Judge; Sci Ed Cncl of OH 1980-; NSTA 1986-; OH Acad of Sci 1988-; Coll Club of Cincinnati Comm Mem 1980-; Various Teacher Educl Grants; Presentation at SECO Convention 1987; US Cath Teacher of Yr Awd 1987; Presider NSTA Convention 1988; Project Sharing in Todays Cath Teacher 1988; Governors Awd for Excl Sci 1989; *home:* 88 Silverwood Cir Cincinnati OH 45246

ROSS, JOHN, Reading Teacher; *b:* Belzoni, MS; *m:* Gester Dean; *c:* Mona P.; *ed:* (BS) Elem Ed, MS Valley St Univ 1964; (MA) Elem Ed, Jackson St Univ 1978; *cr:* Head of Lang Art Dept 1962-65, Asst Prin 1966-70 Tepper Elem; Head of Rdng Lab Humphreys Cty Voc Complex 1971-78; Rdng Teacher Humphreys Mid Sch 1978-88; Humphreys Cty Jr HS 1988-; *ai:* Humphreys Cty Teachers Assn; MS Ed Assn; NAACP; Out Reach Club; Humphr Eys Cty Laman Choir; *home:* 106 Piper St Belzoni MS 39038

ROSS, JUDY L., 7th/8th Grade Teacher; *b:* Van Wert, OH; *ed:* (BA) Elem Ed, Defiance Coll 1969; (MA) Counseling, N AZ Univ 1989; *cr:* 5th-7th Grade Teacher Ayersvil;e Local 1969-83; 7th-8th Grade Teacher Litchfield Sch Dist 1983-; *ai:* Stu Cncl Adv; *office:* Scott L Libby Elem Sch 553 Plaza Cir Ste A Litchfield Park AZ 85340

ROSS, L. PATRICK, Social Studies Teacher; *b:* Greenville, SC; *m:* Joan Cerra; *c:* Ashley, Clifford; *ed:* (BA) Soc Stud, E Stroudsburg Univ 1966; *cr:* Teacher Nitschmann Jr HS 1966-82, East Hills Mid Sch 1982-; *ai:* Debate; Scrabble; Earth Day; Tannersville Lions Club Pres 1970-; Masons 1982-; PA Assn Township Supvrs 1978-; PA St Public Relations Comm; Monroe CT Elected Ofcls Pres; PA St Historical Society; Pocono Township Park Bd & Planning Comm; Pocono Mt Realtors Mem; *home:* Box 161 Tannersville PA 18372

ROSS, LINDA COCHRAN, Biology/Earth Science Teacher; *b:* Phillips, TX; *m:* Robert N.; *c:* Rebecca L.; *ed:* (BA) Bio/Eng, Sam Houston St 1970; (MSIS) Bio, Univ of TX Tyler 1985; *cr:* Bio Teacher Tomball HS 1970-72; 6th Grade Teacher Crockett Int Sch 1972-73; 6th Grade Teacher Collins Cath Sch 1975-82; Grad Teacher Asst Univ TX Tyler 1982-84;Bio/Earth Sci Teacher Blooming Grove Jr/Sr HS 1984-; *ai:* HS UIL Sci Coach; Jr HS UIL Dir; Gifted & Talented Teacher; TSTA & NEA HS Rep 1989-; Amer Bus (Pres & VP) 1976-83 Woman of Yr 1979; 1st Womens Assn United Meth Church 1985-; *home:* 716 Northwood Blvd Corsicana TX 75110

ROSS, NANCY S., 7th Grade Lang Arts Teacher; *b:* Louisville, KY; *ed:* (BS) Eng, IN Univ 1969; *cr:* 7th Grade Lang Arts Teacher Linderman Sch 1969-; *ai:* Facilitor for Alcohol/Drug Abuse Group; Writing Study Comm; NCTE 1985; IN Univ Alumni Assn 1975-; Northwest Humane Society 1990-; Spotlight on Excl Teaching 1985; Article Published in Eng Journal Supplement Notes Plus; Article Published in Devotional Magazine Upper Room; *office:* Linderman Schl 124 Third Ave E Kalispell MT 59901

ROSS, REBECCA HARRELL, Fifth Grade Teacher; *b:* Cincinnati, OH; *w:* Robert R. (dec); *c:* Damita C. Ross Morton, Naekomi D.; *ed:* (BS) Ed, Wilberforce Univ 1961; (MA) Urban Ed, Governor St Univ 1979; *cr:* 4th-6th Grade Teacher 12th Street Sch 1961-64; 5th Grade Teacher Keefe Avenue Sch 1964-66; 2nd/6th Grade Teacher Riley Sch 1966-76; 6th Grade Teacher Whittier Sch 1976-79; 4th-6th Grade Teacher 24th Street Sch 1980-89; 5th Grade Teacher Mc Nair Sch 1989-; *ai:* Cmmty Advisory Cncl for Service Delivery Area II Milwaukee Public Schls; Teacher Rep 1989-; Milwaukee Teacher Ed Assn 1980-; Pilgrim Rest Cmmty Center Bd Mem 1989-; WI Gospel Music Wkshp Bd Mem 1987-; Pilgrim Rest Missionary Baptist Church (Musician, Dir) 1983-.

ROSS, RUTH A., POD/Economics Teacher; *b:* Spring Run, PA; *m:* John R.; *c:* Lyle, Lisa; *ed:* (BA) His, Shippensburg Univ 1965; Penn St; *cr:* His Teacher 1965-, Soc Stud Dept Chairperson 1986- Bellwood Antis HS; *ai:* NCSS; Eastern Star.

ROSS, SHARON LYNN, Second Grade Teacher; *b:* Melrose Park, IL; *ed:* (BA) Ed, Concordia Teachers Coll 1969; (MA) Ed/Curr, Concordia Coll 1979; *cr:* 2nd-4th Grade Teacher 1969-, Rdng Asst 1986 Jane Addams Sch; *ai:* Stu Cncl Spon; PTO Teacher Rep; Assn for Supervision & Curr Dev; *office:* Jane Addams School 910 Division Melrose Park IL 60160

ROSS, SHERRY DUPLECHAIN, Mathematics Teacher; *b:* Mamou, LA; *m:* William James; *c:* Kyle J., Candice A.; *ed:* (BS) Math Ed, 1974, (MED) Supervision, 1982 Mc Neese St Univ; Cmptr Sci; *cr:* Teacher Hackberry HS 1975-; *ai:* Academic Comm & Parent Nights Comm; 9th Grade Homeroom Spon; *office:* Hackberry HS 1390 School St Hackberry LA 70645

ROSS, THELMA WILLIAMS, Remedial Reading Teacher; *b:* Orange, TX; *m:* Willie Emmitt; *ed:* (BA) Bus Ed, TX Coll 1957; TX Southern Univ & Stephen F Austin Univ; *cr:* Secy TX Coll 1957; Teacher H G Temple HS 1957-63, Lufkin Ind Sch Dist 1963-; *ai:* Intnl Rdng Assn, Stone Fort Rdng Cncl; TX Classroom Teachers Assn Local Secy; TX St Teachers Assn, NEA; Long Chapel CME Church, Natl Cncl of Negro Women, Natl Assn Advancement of Colored People, Amer Assn of Univ Women, TX HS Coaches Wives Assn, Top Ladies of Distinction Incorporated, AARP.

ROSSET, EMILY JEAN JEFFRIES, High School Supervisor; *b:* Barrington, NJ; *m:* George A.; *c:* Penni J. Caldwell, James A., SAndi L. James; *ed:* (BS) Elem Ed, Bob Jones Univ 1957; *cr:* 2nd Grade Teachere Maple Shade Sch 1957-58; 3rd Grade Teacher Linwood Elem 1958-59; 2nd Grade Teacher Miami East Schls 1968-78; 3rd-6th Grade Teacher Maranatha Chrstn Acad 1979-87; HS Teacher Grace Baptist Sch 1987-; *ai:* Jr Class Adv.

ROSSI, THERESA ROSE, Teacher/Performing Arts Dept; *b:* San Francisco, CA; *ed:* (AA) His, City Coll of San Francisco 1968; (BA) His/Theatre 1970-, (MA) Scndry Ed, 1974 San Francisco St Univ; Video Production; Photography; Tech Theatre; Extensive Trng Womens His; *cr:* Teacher Antioch HS 1974-; *ai:* Drama Club, Thespian Troupe, Comedy Club Spon; His Day Competitive Team Coach; CA Educl Theatre Assn; NCSS; Natl Womens His Project; Fnd for Cable Television 1985-89, TV Production Grant 1986; Natl Org for Women Secy 1986; Antioch Unifed Sch Dist Teacher of Yr; *office:* Antioch HS 700 W 18th St Antioch CA 94509

ROSSITER, DAPHNE ANNE, Mathematics Teacher; *b:* Fremont, NE; *m:* David Lawrence; *c:* Kelli M.; *ed:* (BA) Math, AZ St Univ 1985; (MA) Scndry Admin, N AZ Univ 1990; *cr:* Math Teacher Chandler HS 1986-; *ai:* St Math Contest & Aquatics Club Spon; *home:* 2437 E Pebble Beach Tempe AZ 85282

ROSSLER, MARY LOUISE, 8th Grade Teacher; *b:* Sealy, TX; *m:* Louis G. Jr.; *c:* Jon W.; *ed:* (BS) Elem Ed, Sam Houston St 1961; *cr:* 6th Grade Teacher Landrum Jr HS 1962-63; 8th Grade Teacher Sealy Jr HS 1966-; *ai:* UIL Coord; United Meth Church Music Dir 1988-; *office:* Sealy Ind Sch Dist 901 West St Sealy TX 77474

ROSSMAN, TERRY MICHAEL, 8th Grade Social Stud Teacher; *b:* Watertown, NY; *m:* Janet Guthrie; *c:* Joshua, Eric, Melissa; *ed:* (BS) Scndry Ed/Soc Sci, St Univ of NY Oswego 1974; RSST, Individualized Lang Art, Assertive Discipline; Grad Stud St Univ of NY Oswego; *cr:* US/World His Teacher Pulaski Jr/Sr HS 1974-75; Teacher Asst Mexico HS 1978-79; World/US/Afro Asia Inys His Teacher Sackets Harbor HS 1979-85; US His Teacher Mexico Mid Sch 1985-; *ai:* Class Adv; Head Ftbl & Bsbl, Soccer, Bsktbl, Bowling, Sftbl Coach; 5th-8th Grade Soc Stud Dept Leader; NY St Cncl Soc Stud, NY St Teachers Assn; *office:* Mexico Mid Sch Fravor Rd Mexico NY 13114

ROSSON, SUSAN COLEMAN, English IV Teacher; *b:* Cameron, TX; *ed:* (BA) Ed/Eng, Southwestern Univ 1952; (MA) Ed/Eng, Baylor Univ 1956; (MA) Eng, TX A&M 1968-75; Hum/Arts, Columbia Univ; Instrumental Music, Univ of Mary Hardin Baylor & Baylor Univ; Adv Academic Trng; *cr:* 2nd Grade Teacher Marlin TX 1952-54, Cameron TX 1954-59; 4th Grade Teacher Richardson TX 1959-68; Scndry Eng Teacher Cameron TX 1968-; *ai:* Sr Class Spon; NHS Adv; Literary Criticism UIL Event Spon; Cameron Educators Assn (Secy, Bldg Rep 1968-); TX St Teachers Assn, NEA 1952-; *office:* C H Yoe HS 300 E 10th Cameron TX 76520

ROST, LOREE POLANSKY, 6th Grade English Teacher; *b:* Dime Box, TX; *m:* O Barr W.; *c:* Helen C., Paul D., Carl S., Mari L. Rost Budde; *ed:* (BS) Home Ec, Univ of Tx 1948; (ME) Elem Ed, TX A&M 1976; *cr:* 6th Grade Eng/Lang Art Teacher Giddings Mid Sch 1971-; *ai:* UIL Spon; Career Ladder, Dist Improvement Goals, Curr, Textbook Comms; R Y K Public Lib Secy 1970-85; St Margarets Cath Church Organist 1960-; Nom TX Teacher of Yr 1987; *office:* Giddings Mid Sch PO Box 389 Hwy 77 Giddings TX 78942

ROSVALL, PATRICIA, Biology Teacher; *b:* Salt Lake City, UT; *m:* Gene Howard; *c:* Robert, Todd, Jennifer; *ed:* (ASN) Registered Nursing, Weber St Coll 1983; (BS) Bio Composite, Westminster Coll 1986; *cr:* Teacher John F Kennedy Jr HS 1987-; *ai:* Granite Sch Dist Partners in Ed, Citizenship Comms; Chm Emergency Preparedness; Building Comm Mem; Granite Ed Assn Rep 1988-; UT Ed Assn House of Delegates 1988-; Governors Panel on Teaching Sex Ed in Public Schls Mem 1987; People to People Stu Ambassador Prgm Delegation Leader 1990; Listed in Academic All Amer Collegiate Directory 1987; *office:* John F Kennedy Jr HS 4495 S 4800 W West Valley City UT 84120

ROTH, AUDREY STANEK, 6th Grade Teacher; *b:* Washington, MO; *m:* Frank III; *c:* Frankie, Danny; *ed:* (BS) Ed, Northeast MO St 1973; *cr:* 3rd Grade Teacher 1973-80; 6th Grade Teacher 1985- Claude Brown Elem; *ai:* MSTA Mem 1973-80/1985-; Cub Scout Den Leader 1988; Khoury League 1986-; *office:* Claude Brown Elem Sch 711 W College Troy MO 63379

ROTH, DUANE, 6th Grade Teacher; *b:* Richardton, ND; *ed:* (BS) Math/Elem Ed, Mayville St 1970; (MS) Elem Ed, Northern St 1976; (EDD) Elem Ed, Univ of Northern CO 1982; *cr:* 6th Grade Teacher Pioneer Elem 1974-; *ai:* Wellness Comm; Bismarck Ed Assn, ND Ed Assn, NEA 1974-; Amer Legion 1972-; YMCA 1978-; ND Alternate Teacher Space Prgm; *office:* Pioneer Elem Sch 14th & Braman Bismarck ND 58501

ROTH, JAMES H., Third Grade Teacher; *b:* Perryville, MO; *m:* Sally Guettler; *c:* Christopher, Benjamin, Daniel; *ed:* (BA) Elem Ed, Concordia Teachers Coll 1972; *cr:* 3rd-5th Grade Teacher St Peter Luth Sch 1972-73; 3rd Grade Teacher Hilltop 1973-87, Edgebrook 1987-89, Riverwood 1989-; *ai:* IEA, NEA (Building Rep 1973-79, Liaison Rep 1986-); Kiwanis (Bd Dir 1988-, 1st VP 1990); Church (Youth Dir 1972-73, Church Cncl, Head of Evangelism 1982-84); Nom Those Who Excel; *office:* Riverwood Sch 300 S Driftwood Mc Henry IL 60050

ROTH, NANCY ANN, Sixth Grade Teacher; *b:* Rockport, IN; *m:* James Robert; *c:* Jeffrey S., Tina L., Todd R. (dec); *ed:* (BA) Ed, Univ of Evansville 1969; (MA) Curr/Instruction, Univ of N CO 1982; *cr:* Teacher Stanley Hall 1969-71, Stringtown 1971-74, Guild 1976-78, Rucker-Stewart 1979-; *ai:* Discover Prgm; Tutoring; Sumner Cty Ed Assn Comm Chairperson 1980-85; NEA, TEA; Delta Kappa Gamma (VP, Comm Chairperson) 1985-87; Career Ladder III Governors Writing Acad; WPLN Radio Reader for Blind; Adult Ed Night Sch GED Classes; *home:* 370 Sunset Island Trl Gallatin TN 37066

ROTH, PATRICIA ANN, Principal; *b:* Bremerton, WA; *m:* Carl Andrew; *c:* Craig, Shelley, Jill, Kristen; *ed:* (BA) Liberal Stud, 1977, (MA) Curr/Instruction, 1981 San Diego St Univ; Grad San Diego Area Writing Project 1986; Grad CA Schls Leadership Acad 1989; Admin Services Credential 1985; Multiple Subjects Credential 1978; Cooperative Learning Trainer 1987; Tribes Peer Interactive Model Trainer 1985; *cr:* 1st-6th Grade Teacher 1978-87, Mentor Teacher 1984-87, Prin 1987- Chula Vista City Schls; *ai:* Sftbl Mgr Tierrasanta Girls Little League 1975-87; Delta Kappa Gamma (Schlsp Comm 1988-89) 1986-; CA Assn For Gifted 1983-87; Assn of CA Sch Admin 1987-; ASCD 1986-; PTA 1978-, Honorary Service Awd 1975, Life Membership 1986; Chula Vista Chamber of Commerce 1984; *office:* Hazel Goes Cook Elem 875 Cuyamaca Ave Chula Vista CA 92011

ROTHENBERGER, GWENDOLYN OLENE, Elem Prin/Kndgtn Teacher; *b:* Mitchell, SD; *ed:* (BA) Elem Ed/His/Poly Sci, Dakota Wesleyan Univ 1969; (MA) Elem Admin, Northern St Univ 1975; *cr:* Kndgtn Teacher/Elem Prin Stickney Public Sch 1971-79; Elem Prin Kimball Public Sch 1979-83; Elem/Mid Sch Prin Corsica Elem Sch 1983-89; Elem Prin/Kndgtn Teacher Letcher Public Sch 1989-; *ai:* Sch Admin of SD 1979-; SD Assn of Elem Sch Prins 1979-; Zion Luth Church (Choir, Bd of Ed) 1989-; Outstanding Young Educator Stickney SD 1973; *office:* Letcher Elem Sch PO Box 68 Letcher SD 57359

ROTHER, RONALD ANTHONY, Vocal Music Teacher Dept Chm; *b:* Northfield, MN; *m:* Lynnette Everetts; *c:* Tony, Shannon Peiper, Sarah, Shane Peiper; *ed:* (BS) Music Ed, 1973, Drivers Ed, 1975 Mankato St Univ; *cr:* 7th-12th Grade Vocal Music Teacher 1973-, 9th-12th Grade Drivers Ed Teacher 1975- Adrian HS; *ai:* Stu Cncl & Class Adv; MN Fed of Teachers 1973-; MN Music Ed Assn 1975-; *home:* 504 Connecticut Ave Adrian MN 56110

ROTHFUS, LAURA LOWTHER, 2nd Grade Teacher; *b:* Morgantown, WV; *m:* Rodger A.; *c:* Randy, Lovelle; *ed:* (BA) Elem Ed, Northwest MO Univ 1965; *cr:* 4th Grade Teacher Moore Elem Sch 1966-68; 3rd Grade Teacher Oakpark E Lem Sch 1969-72; 5th Grade Teacher Studebaker Elem Sch 1972-75; 2nd Grade Teacher Carlisle Elem Sch 1977-; *ai:* High Potential Comm; Adv Comm; Lang/Math/Spelling Curr Comm; NEA 1966-; IA St Ed Assn 1966-; Des Moines Ed Assn 1966-75; Carlisle Cmmty Ed Assn 1977-.

ROTHLISBURGER, RODNEY JOHN, Music Instructor; *b:* Bottineau, ND; *ed:* (BA) Music - Cum Laude, St Olaf Coll 1962; (MA) Musicology, Eastman Sch of Music 1967; (DMA) Choral Music, Univ of CO Boulder 1978; *cr:* Choral Music Instr Anacortes WA Public Schls 1962-64; Organist/Choirmaster US Military Acad West Point 1965-67; Choral Music Instr Bowdoin Coll 1967-70; Choral Music Instr Melbourne Australia HS 1973-75, Berea Coll Berea Ky 1976-77, Concordia Coll 1979-81; Keyboard/Voice Instr Mayville St Univ 1981-88; Choral Music Instr Moorhead Public Schls 1989-; *ai:* Chamber Ensembles; Carolers & Renaissance Singers; Sch Musical; Amer Guild of Organists Dean 1986-88; Coll Music Society, Amer Choral Dirs Assn, Music Educators Natl Conference; Lake Agassiz Arts Cncl Exec Bd 1986-, Citation 1989; St Olaf Coll Honor Society; NDEA Grad Fellowship Univ of CO Boulder; Founder Melbourne Australia Youth Choir; *office:* Moorhead Sr H S 2300 4th Ave S Moorhead MN 56560

ROTONDE, ALBERT ROBERT, Music Teacher; *b:* Gloversville, NY; *c:* Ross, Robert; *ed:* (BS) Music Ed, 1958, (MS) Music Ed, 1968 Potsdam St Univ; Naval Sch of Music 1950-52; *cr:* Music Teacher J W Leary Jr HS 1958-; *home:* RD 2 Box 45 Winthrop NY 13697

ROTONDO, MICHAEL DENNIS, Reading Teacher; *b:* Bethlehem, PA; *m:* Candy J. Mc Fetridge; *c:* Michael J., Scott A.; *ed:* (BA) Eng, Moravian Coll 1970; (MED) Rdng, Lehigh Univ 1974; Rdng Specialist; *cr:* Teacher Broughal Jr HS 1970-81, East Hills Mid Sch 1981-; *ai:* Ftbl, Archery, Track, Debate Coach; Eng Dept Chm; *home:* 3862 Devonshire Rd Bethlehem PA 18017

ROTTMAN, MARY ROSE, Fourth Grade Teacher; *b:* Chicago, IL; *ed:* (BSED) Elem Ed, Chicago St Univ 1968; *cr:* 4th Grade Teacher St Denis Sch 1968-; *office:* St Denis Sch 8300 S St Louis Chicago IL 60652

ROTTMANN, BARBARA BEHRMANN, Third Grade Teacher; *b:* Indianapolis, IN; *m:* Robert P.; *c:* Mark, Todd; *ed:* (BS) Elem Ed, Valparaiso Univ 1963; (MS) Elem Ed, Butler Univ 1972; *cr:* 4th Grade Teacher George Myers Sch 1963-65; 2nd/3rd Grade Teacher Moorhead Elem Sch 1965-66; Owner/Teacher Hi-Ho Nursery Sch 1971-77; 1st Grade Teacher Cntrl Lyon Sch 1977-78; 3rd Grade Teacher Chapelwood 1979-; *ai:* Human Relations, Awds Day, Chapelwood Action Plan Comms; Delta Kappa Gamma Corresponding Secy 1988-; PTA (Secy, Treas, Devotion Leader); Church Ladies Guild Pres 1982-84; Church Bd of Ed Pres 1986; Volunteer Childrens Museum 1987-; Project Compassion Chm 1988-; Teacher who Influenced Lives; *office:* Chapelwood Elem Sch 1129 N Girls Sch Rd Indianapolis IN 46214

ROTTO, JUDY CAROL (ERICKSON), Kindergarten Teacher; *b:* Mankato, MN; *m:* Luther Isaac; *c:* Isaac D., Karl L.; *ed:* (BS) Elem Ed, Concordia Coll Moorhead 1972; (MS) Elem Ed, St Cloud St Univ 1981; Grad Stud Various Areas of Elem Ed; *cr:* 3rd Grade Teacher 1972-80, Kndgtn Teacher 1981- Dist 742 Public Schls; Interim Instr St Cloud St Univ 1987-88; *ai:* Grade Level Chairperson 1975-80; Soc Stud Curr Comm 1974-80; Phi Delta Kappa 1986-; MN Ed Assn, NEA, St Cloud Ed Assn 1972-; Building Rep; Bethlehem Luth Church Music Teacher 1988-; Co-Published Story Lessons; Published Young Children Story Hrs & Presentations Around St for Title I Educators & Teachers.

ROTZ, DUANE L., English Teacher; *b:* Waynesboro, PA; *m:* Carolyn Deavers; *c:* Lindsey; *ed:* (BA) Geography, Towson St Univ 1980; Geography, Towson St Univ; Eng, Shippensburg St Univ; *cr:* Teacher Grace Acad 1983-; *ai:* Chrstn Service Club Adv; *office:* Grace Acad 530 N Locust St Hagerstown MD 21740

ROTZ, GLENN ELDON, Fifth Grade Teacher; *b:* Colorado Springs, CO; *m:* Mary Alice Herring; *c:* Katie, Molly, Zachary; *ed:* (BA) Elem Ed, NW Nazarene Coll 1972; (MA) Elem Ed, Boise St Univ 1976; Learning Styles, NLP; *cr:* 4th/5th Grade Teacher Sunny Ridge Elem 1972-76; 5th Grade Teacher Whitman Elem 1976-78; 4th/5th Grade Teacher Highland Elem 1978-87; 5th Grade Teacher Grantham Elem 1987-; *ai:* WEA 1978-; IEA 1972-76; NEA 1972-76, 1978-; Mem St of ID Mobile Lab 1976-78; Article Concerning Mail System Written about Ed Weekly & in Learning Magazine1983; *home:* 3522 8th St E Lewiston ID 83501

ROUGHEAD, ROSALIE VALERIA, English Department Chair; *b:* Chicago, IL; *m:* William G.; *c:* William A., David M., Paula C., Rosalie L. Rice, Marie T. Thompson, Ruth A. Burrell; *ed:* (BA) Fr, 1974, (MED) Eng, 1977 N GA Coll; (EDS) Lang Art, Univ of GA 1981; Course Work & Residence Completed for PhD Lang Art, Univ of GA 1983; Fr, Laval Univ; *cr:* Fr/Eng Instr Dawson Cty HS 1976-83; Eng Instr GA Inst of Technology 1983-84; Fr/Eng Instr Rabun Cty HS 1984-85, Forsyth Cntrl HS 1985-89; Eng Dept Chm S Forsyth HS 1989-; *ai:* Curr Comm; Kappa Delta Pi, Nu Gamma 1974; Nom for Teacher of Yr 1982; STAR Teacher 1989; *office:* South Forsyth HS 585 Peachtree Pkwy Cumming GA 30130

ROULO, SHERRY TANGUAY, Principal; *b:* Trenton, MI; *m:* Rick; *ed:* (BS) Elem Ed, 1968, (MS) Elem Admin, 1981 Eastern MI Univ; *cr:* 1st Grade Teacher 1968-72, Kndgtn Teacher 1972-75, 2nd Grade Teacher 1975-83 Lafayette Elem Sch; Prin Keppen Elem Sch 1983-87; James a Foote Elem Sch 1988-; *ai:* Stu Code of Conduct Comm; Dist Spelling Bee Chm; Teacher Inservice Comm; Eastern MI Adv Bd; Report Card Comm; Lincoln Park Admin Assn; PTA (Teacher/VP) Distinguished Service Awd 1982; Youth Asst Prgm Sch Laison 1988-; Service Awd Lafayette PTA 1980; Service Awd Lincoln Park PTA Cncl 1983; *office:* James A Foote Elem Sch 3250 Abbott Lincoln Park MI 48146

ROUNDTREE, CAROLYN, 7th Grade Teacher; *b:* Suffolk, VA; *c:* Antoine; *ed:* (BS) Elem Ed, Norfolk St Univ 1975; Grad Stud Gerontology; *cr:* Substitute Laborer B T Washington; Classroom Teacher St Marys Acad; *ai:* Supvr of Sci Fair; Dept Chm; *home:* 2517 Rush St Norfolk VA 23513

ROUNTREE, JANE DANIELS, Second Grade Teacher; *b:* Raleigh, NC; *m:* Frank S.; *c:* Sarah, Daniel; *ed:* (MAED) Early Chldhd, Atlantic Chrstn Coll 1972; (BS) Elem Ed, E Carolina Univ 1990; Elem Mentor Trng; *cr:* 1st Grade Teacher Lucama Elem Sch 1972; 4th Grade Teacher Creswell Elem Sch 1972; 2nd-4th Grade Teacher Sunbury Elem Sch 1972-; *ai:* Steering Comm Chm for Sch & Southern Assn of Colleges & Schls; NC Assn of Educators (Secy/Treas 1974-75); NEA; Gates Cty Jaycettes Secy 1973-77; Mid Swamp Baptist Church (Sunday Sch Teacher, Choir Dir) 1973-; Sunbury Elem Sch Teacher of Yr 1988-89; *office:* Sunbury Elem Sch PO Box 180 Sunbury NC 27979

ROUNTREE, SHERRY HILL, Second Grade Teacher; *b:* Augusta, GA; *m:* Michael Y.; *c:* Morgan, Kathleen; *ed:* (BS) Early Chldhd Ed, E Carolina Univ 1977; *cr:* 1st/2nd Grade Teacher Moss Street Elem Sch 1978-; *ai:* Wellness Comm; Sch Improvement Team; United Meth Women (Sch Play Comm, Pres 1987-88); *office:* Reidsville City Schls 419 Moss St Reidsville NC 27320

ROUPP, GARY WAYNE, Sixth Grade Teacher; *b:* Shelbyville, IN; *ed:* (BA) Elem Ed, Franklin Coll 1976; (MS) Elem Ed, IN Univ 1981; *cr:* Elem Teacher Hendricks Township Sch 1976-77, Southwestern Elem 1977-; *ai:* Jr HS Boys Track Coach; Gideons Intnl; *office:* Southwestern Elem Sch RR 4 Box 245-A Shelbyville IN 46176

ROUSE, DORETHA STIRGUS, Elementary Mathematics Teacher; *b:* Memphis, TN; *m:* Frahn V.; *c:* Keli, Frahn V. Jr.; *ed:* (BS) Elem Ed, TN St Univ 1962; (MS) Elem Ed/AV, IN Univ 1969; *cr:* Teacher Beveridge Sch 1963-66, 103 St Sch 1966-67, Beveridge Sch 1967-69, Froebel Sch 1969-74, Nobel Sch 1974-; *ai:* Mentor & STAR Prgm; Amer Childhood Ed Assn; Gary Rdng Cncl; Gary Teachers Union 1963-; St Timothy Cmmty Church Choir Pres 1979-85; Joy Vocal Ensemble Dir 1980; Alpha Kappa Alpha; NAACP; Educators for Christ VP 1987-89; *office:* Nobel Sch 8837 Pottawatomie Tr Gary IN 46403

ROUSE, MILTON B., English Teacher; *b:* Lynwood, CA; *m:* Susan R.; *c:* Hobie, Christopher; *ed:* (BA) Philosophy/Eng, Whittier Coll 1972; Grad Work Eng Ed, Natl Endowment for Hum Inst; *cr:* Eng Teacher San Clemente HS 1975-76, Capistrano Valley HS 1976-78, Dana Hills HS 1985-; *ai:* NEA, CA Teachers Assn; Educators for Soc Responsibility; Natl Endowment for Hum; *office:* Dana Hills HS 33333 Golden Lantern Dana Point CA 92629

ROUSE, RENARD R., 4th Grade Teacher; *b:* Tacoma, WA; *m:* Janette Louise Cobb; *c:* Sarah, Jonathan, Kara; *ed:* (BA) Elem Ed, Univ of Puget Sound 1970; *cr:* 5th Grade Teacher Peter G Schmidt Elem 1970-81; 6th Grade Teacher Tumwater Mid Sch 1981-84; 4th-5th Grade Teacher Black Lake Elem Sch 1984-89; 4th Grade Teacher E Olympia Elem Sch 1989-; *ai:* Neighborhood Chrstn Center Supt of Ed 1986-87; WA St 4-H Club Leader 1987-88; Yelm Prairie Chrstn Center (Youth Cnslr, Bd Mem) 1989-; *home:* 8519 83rd Ave SE Olympia WA 98503

ROUSE, RUTH DENNIS, Fourth Grade Teacher; *b:* Kewanee, IL; *m:* Maynard R.; *c:* Larry, Steve Cornaghie, Nicole Cornaghie, Sarah; *ed:* (BA) Elem Ed, Western IL Univ 1967; Several Wrkshp-Elem Math, Great Books Fnd & Teaching Chem Elem Studs; *cr:* Teacher Harrison Sch 1967-71 & 1972-73; Tyng Sch 1974-76 & 1978-80; Hines Sch 1980-83; Thomas Jefferson 1983-; *ai:* Scholars Cup Coach; Drama Club; *office:* Thomas Jefferson Elem Schl 918 W Florence Peoria IL 61604

ROUSE, THERESA ELAINE (MURPHY), Fifth Grade Teacher; *b:* Camp Atterbury, IN; *m:* Michial Wayne; *c:* Carmeleta E., Sabrina M., Zebulon W.; *ed:* (BS) Elem Ed, IN St Univ 1975; (MS) Elem Ed, IN Univ Purdue 1979; Gifted & Talented Course; Teacher Conservation Camp; *cr:* 1st-2nd Grade Teacher Crawford Elem 1975; 3rd Grade Teacher 1975, 1st Grade Teacher 1975-76 Wayne Elem; 1st Grade Teacher Mc Dowell Elem 1976-77; Kndgtn Teacher Remedial Rdng Vallonia Elem 1978; 5th Grade Teacher Freetown Elem 1978-; *ai:* Arbor Day 1978-, Sch Field Day Prgm 1977-88; NEA, ISTA 1975-; Purdue Jackson Cty Extension Homemakers Pres 1988-; Freetown PTO 1978-; Freetown Meth Church Bible Sch Various Comm 1985-; In Red Star Cloggers Participant 1989-; *home:* R 1 Box 225 Freetown IN 47235

ROUSE, VELMA SPATES, Math Teacher; *b:* Rockford, IL; *m:* Milton Eugene; *c:* David, Sharon; *ed:* (BS) Ed, Chicago St Univ 1971; (MS) Admin, Roosevelt Univ 1990; *cr:* Teacher Dewitt Clinton 1971-; *ai:* ASCD; Church Musician Schlsp 1984-; Ship Guild Chairperson; *office:* Clinton Sch 6110 N Fairfield Ave Chicago IL 60659

ROUSER, SANDRA MAE (BAKER), Business Education Teacher; *b:* Fremont, OH; *m:* Donald Edward; *ed:* (BA) Comprehensive Bus, Heidelberg Coll 1964; *cr:* Bus Ed Teacher Hopewell-Loudon Sch 1964-; *ai:* NHS, Jr, Sr Class Adv; Sch & Cmmty Newsletter; Delta Kappa Gamma Past Secy 1975-; NEA, OEA 1964-; Hopewell-Loudon Ed Assn Treas 1964-; Martha Holden Jennings Scholar; *home:* 104 Monroe St Box 413 Bettsville OH 44815

ROUTSON, JAMES L., Mathematics Teacher; *b:* Toledo, OH; *m:* Janet Marie Jaquilland; *c:* Cynthia Roth, Pamela Pinelli, David, Mark; *ed:* (BED) Math, Bowling Green St Univ 1961; (MM) Math, Univ of SC 1968; *cr:* Math Teacher Oregon Clay HS 1961-; *ai:* Math Club; Math Dept Chm; OH Cncl Teachers of Math, Toledo Cncl Teachers of Math 1961-; AFT 1965-; *home:* 124 N Goodyear Oregon OH 43616

ROVARIS, KATIE MOORE, English Teacher; *b:* Alexandria, LA; *c:* Robbie L.; *ed:* (MED) Curr/Instruction, Univ of New Orleans 1989; (BA) Eng Ed, Southern Univ 1971; Prof Improvement Prgm Loyola Univ 1982-85; *cr:* Eng Instr Carver Sr HS 1971, Walter L Cohen Sr HS 1971-72, Marion Abramson Sr HS 1972-; *ai:* NHS Spon; Natl Assn of Stu Activity Advs; Abramson HS Advance Placement Admissions Advisory Bd Mem; Phi Delta Kappa 1990; NCTE 1975-; St Marys PTA 1988-; AFT Educl Research & Dissemination 1988-; Outstanding Educator Awd 1987-88; *office:* Marion Abramson HS 5552 Read Blvd New Orleans LA 70127

ROVESTI, RANDY, Physical Ed & Science Teacher; *b:* Wilkinsburg, PA; *m:* Debra L.; *c:* Randy, Kelly, Chelsey; *ed:* (BS) Phys Ed, William & Mary 1974; (MA) Phys Ed, Brigham Young 1976; Advanced First Aid, CPR, Life Guard Instr; *cr:* Teacher Plum Borough Sch Dist 1979-84, Norwin Sch Dist 1984-; *ai:* Head Ftbl Coach; NEA, PA Ftbl Coaches Assn 1979-; Westmoreland Ftbl Coaches Assn 1984-; *office:* Norwin HS 251 Mc Mahon Dr North Huntingdon PA 15642

ROVITO, EILEEN BUEHLER, 7th-12th Grade Phys Ed Coach; *b:* Schenectady, NY; *m:* Kevin A.; *c:* Ryan A., Mitchell F.; *ed:* (AA) Liberal Arts, Adirondack Comm Coll 1983; (BA) Phys Ed, SUNY Coll Cortland 1985; Working Towards Masters Ed Theory/Practice SUNY Albany; *cr:* Phys Ed Teacher/Coach Mayfield Cntrl Sch 1985-; *ai:* Jr Var Vlybl & Var Sftbl Coach; *office:* Mayfield Jr Sr HS School St Mayfield NY 12117

ROWANS, DAVID LEE, 7th Grade Language Art Teacher; *b:* Central City, KY; *ed:* (BA) Eng, 1971, (MA) Eng/Ed, 1975 W KY Univ; *cr:* Eng Teacher Seminary Mid Sch 1971-80, Madisonville Comm Coll 1984-86, Browning Springs Mid Sch 1980-; *ai:* Pops Comm, Advice Guidance Comm Adv; KEA, NEA, KMSA; *office:* Browning Springs Mid Sch 357 W Arch St Madisonville KY 42431

ROWBERRY, CONNIE LYNN, Geography Teacher; *b:* Mora, MN; *m:* Hal C.; *c:* Kristopher, Raegan, Tyler, Ky; *ed:* (BA) Speech/Drama, Brigham Young Univ 1975; *cr:* Speech/Debate Teacher Spanish Fork HS 1975-76; 7th Grade Geography Teacher South Bonneville Jr HS 1985-; *ai:* Debate Team, Young Amer, Voice of Democracy, Intnl Club, Boys Soccer Team, Chrldr Adv; Amer Freedom Tour 1976; Prins Awd for Excl 1985-86; Teacher Trainer for Stu Teacher 1977; *office:* South Bonneville Jr HS 2955 E Owen Idaho Falls ID 83406

ROWBOTHAM, ROGER KIM, Health Education Teacher; *m:* Betsy Amekland; *c:* Scott, Katie; *ed:* (BA) Health/Phys Ed, Bemidji St Univ 1976; (MA) Curr Ed, St Thomas Coll 1985; *cr:* Teacher/Coach Fred Moore Jr HS 1976-85, Anoka Sr HS 1986-; *ai:* Var Ftbl & Wrestling Asst; *office:* Anoka Sr HS 3939 7th Ave N Anoka MN 55303

ROWE, GLENDA RAYMOND, Math Teacher; *b:* Jonesboro, LA; *m:* Gilbert W.; *c:* Michelle Mc Kernan, Melissa, Melanie, Wayne; *ed:* (BA) Math Ed/Soc Stud Ed, Mc Neese St Univ 1961; Grad Work Math at Univ of Houston Clear Lake; *cr:* 7th Grade Math/Sci Teacher La Grange Jr HS 1962-63; Algebra I/II Teacher Belair HS 1963-64; Algebra I/Geometry 1978-80, Algebra I/II/III/Geometry/Precalculus 1980- Clear Lake HS; *ai:* NHS; SADD; NCTM Standards Study Comm; TCTA 1984-; Math Assn of America 1988-; NCTM 1987-; Nom Outstanding Math Teacher TX; *office:* Clear Lake H S 2929 Bay Area Blvd Houston TX 77058

ROWE, LA VERNE MARCY, Retired Elementary Teacher; *b:* Lincoln, NE; *c:* Stephen T.; *ed:* (BS) Eng/Ed, Univ of NE 1938; Grad Work Univ of NE, Univ of AZ, AZ St Univ, Pepperdine Coll; *cr:* Kndgtn Teacher Coolidge Elem 1943-47; 1st Grade Teacher Eloy Elem 1947-52; 1st/3rd Grade Teacher Casa Grande Elem 1952-80; *ai:* OES 1944-; Girls St Staff 1973-85; Amer Legion Auxiliary Dept Chairmanships; AAUW 1987-, Outstanding Mem 1990; Alpha Delta Kappa Book; *home:* 728 E Brenda Dr Casa Grande AZ 85222

ROWE, MARK ANTHONY, Physical Education Teacher; *b:* Owensboro, KY; *m:* Pamela Henderson; *c:* Mark C., Matthew L.; *ed:* (BA) Phys Ed, E KY Univ 1976; (MA) Scndry Ed, W KY Univ 1984; *cr:* Phys Ed Teacher Macco & Highland Elem 1977-83; Coach Daviess Cty HS 1977-; Phys Ed Teacher Daviess Cty Mid Sch 1983-; *ai:* KY St Champs Cross Cntry Coach 1982; Track Coach; *home:* 5626 Graham Ln Owensbow KY 42303

ROWE, XANDRA KAY, Third Grade Teacher; *b:* Pottstown, PA; *m:* Raymond J.; *c:* Kimberly, Lisa; *ed:* (BS) Elem, Millersville Univ 1967; *cr:* 4th Grade Teacher Oaks Elem Sch 1967-68; 4th Grade Teacher 1976-77, 3rd Grade Teacher 1977 Limerick Elem Sch; *ai:* Staff Dev Cadre Mem; Spring Ford Ed Assn, PA St Ed Assn, NEA 1976-; *office:* Limerick Elem Sch 81 Limerick Ctr Rd Royersford PA 19468

ROWEKAMP, CHERYL L. (FOSS), 5th-6th Grade Teacher; *b:* Garrett, IN; *m:* J. Thomas; *c:* Kelli, Kraig, Kristi; *ed:* (BS) Ed, Valley City St 1968; *cr:* Sr HS Teacher Sanborn HS 1968-71; Jr HS Eng Teacher 1978-88, Cmptr/Librarian 1988-89, 5th-6th Grade Teacher 1989- St Catherine Sch; *ai:* Jr HS Religion Coord; PEO Sisterhood St Pres 1987-88.

ROWH, JAY ALLEN, Mathematics Instructor/Coach; *b:* Norton, KS; *m:* Rita Rasmussen; *c:* Grant, Brett, Greg; *ed:* (BS) Phys Ed/Math, 1969, (MS) Ed/Phys Ed, 1975 Ft Hays St Univ; KS St Univ, Washburn Univ, Benedictine Coll, Ft Hays St Univ; *cr:* Math Instr/Coach Beloit HS 1969-79; Automotive Implement Dealer IH Farm Equipment 1979-85; Math Instr/Coach Beloit HS 1985-; *ai:* Beloit HS Head Girls Bsktbl Coach; Jr HS Asst Ftbl Coach; Lettermens Club Spon; NCTM, KS Assn Teachers of Math, KS Coaches Assn, KS Bsktbl Coaches Assn; Beloit Optimist Club Bd Mem 1987-; *office:* Beloit HS 1711 N Walnut Beloit KS 67420

ROWLAND, EMMA LEE, Guidance Counselor; *b:* Clinton, KY; *m:* Richard Otis; *c:* Richard Jr.; *ed:* (BS) Eng/Sociology, 1973, (MS) Guidance/Counseling, 1977, Psychometry, 1978 Murray St Univ; *cr:* Eng Teacher Murray St 1973-74; Eng Teacher 1973-88, Cnslr 1981- Mayfield Mid Sch; *ai:* Grooming Club; Drug & Alcohol, Sex Ed, Future Directions, Attendance Comm; Stu of Month Spon; Sch & Bus Partnerships; KY Ed Assn, Mayfield Ed Assn, KY Mid Sch Assn, NEA, Natl Mid Sch Assn 1973-; KY Assn of Cnslrs 1988-; Mayfield Housing Commissioner Chm 1983-; 2nd Chrstn Church (Choir Dir, Adult Sunday Sch Teacher); Washington PTA 1989-; *office:* Mayfield Mid Sch 112 W College Mayfield KY 42066

ROWLAND, GERALDINE SCHMITTER, English Teacher; *b:* Queen City, MO; *m:* Loyal D.; *ed:* (BS) Eng, 1967, (MA) Eng, 1969 Northeast MO St Univ; *cr:* Part-Time Lbrn 1967-69; Lbrn/Teacher 1970-74; Teacher 1975- Schuyler R-1 Sch; *ai:* Prof Dev Comm VP; MO St Teachers Assn; NCTE; CTA/PTO; *office:* Schuyler R-1 Sch Hwy 63 Queen City MO 63561

ROWLAND, RHONDA STOCKTON, Mathematics Teacher; *b:* Farmville, VA; *m:* Michael Alan; *ed:* (BS) Math, Longwood Coll 1976; *cr:* Math Teacher Cntrl Jr HS 1976-79; Randolph-Henry HS 1979-; *ai:* SCA, Beta Club, Algebra Plus Club Spon/Co-Spon; CCEA/VEA/NEA; Piedmont Cncl Teacher of Math; VA Cncl Teachers of Math; Bethpeor Baptist Chruch (Treas 1988-, Sunday Sch Dir 1987-); Article Published 1990; *home:* HC L Box 980 Farmville VA 23901

ROWLETT, BARBARA RUSSELL, Kindergarten Teacher; *b:* Norlina, NC; *ed:* (BA) Sociology/Soc Welfare, 1972, (BA) Early Chldhd, 1973 St Augustines Coll; *cr:* Kndgtn Teacher Everetts Elem Sch 1972-73, Vaughan Elem Sch 1973-; *ai:* 4-H Organizational Leader; Chrldrs Spec Olympics Adv; Dir Vacation Bible Sch; Missionary Society Pres; Warren Cty Ushers VP; NC Assn of Young Children, NC Assn of Ed, NC Assn of Supervision; Univ Women Secy; Warren Cty Chapter of Les Gemmes Pres 1984-85; Mentor Teacher 1984-; Outstanding Math Teacher NC Awds 1988-89; Regional Nominee Leadership Team Mem 1990; *home:* PO Box 23 Ridgeway NC 27570

ROWLETT, HERMAN ELLIOTT, JR., Principal; *b:* Louisville, KY; *ed:* (BME) Voice/Music Ed, Georgetown Coll 1967; (MM) Opera/Voice Pedagogy, IN Univ 1971; (MA) Principalship/ Supervision of Instr, Spalding Univ 1979; (Rank I) Cert Music Ed/Elem Ed, Eastern KY Univ 1972; *cr:* 4th & 6th Grade Teacher Lebanon Elem Sch 1969-77; Prin/5th-6th Grade Teacher Holy Cross Elem Sch 1977-80; Prin/Music Teacher St Charles Elem Sch 1980-84; Prin St Charles Mid Sch 1984-88, West Marion Elem Sch 1989-; *ai:* Mem Cty Discipline Code Comm; Mem Cty Health/Safety Comm; Mem Cty Fine Arts Cncl; KY Assn Elem Sch Prins 1977-; KY Ed Assn 1969-; Marion Cty Ed Assn Delegate 1969-; KY Mid Sch Assn 1984-88; KY Assn Sch Admin 1977-; Hustonville Baptist Church Minister of Music 1972-; Stephen Foster Story Drama Dir 1972-80; Lebanon Chamber of Commerce Ed Comm 1988-; Fellowship in Univ Opera Company; Outstanding Young Men of America 1979; *office:* West Marion Elem Sch Rt 2 Box 886 Loretto KY 40037

ROWLEY, GENINE MARY, Mathematics/Computer Teacher; *b:* Carson City, NV; *m:* Derek G.; *c:* Glenn S.; *ed:* (BS) Scndry Ed/ Math, Univ of NV Reno 1987; Ed in Correctional Setting, Cmptr Basic Lang; *cr:* Teacher Carson City HS 1987-; *ai:* Drill Team Adv 1985-; Jr & Soph Class Adv; Choreographer Drama Presentation; OCEA, NSEA 1987; Latter Day Saints Church Laurel Adv 1989-; *office:* Carson City HS 1111 Saliman Carson City NV 89701

ROY, ANGELIKA A., Foreign Language Dept Chair; *b:* Erfenbach, Germany; *m:* Philip A.; *c:* Eileen C. Johns, Michael L., Christine A.; *ed:* (BA) His/Ger, Univ of Marry Hardin Baylor 1980; St Foreign Lang Wkshp; *cr:* Teacher 1981-85, Foreign Lang Dept Chm 1985- Copperas Cove Ind Sch Dist; *ai:* Ger Club Adv; Sr Class, Positive Peer Pressure Group Spon; Faculty, Campus Planning Advisory Comm; Foreign Lang Competition Coach; Curr Dev; Assn of TX Ger Teachers, TX Assn of Foreign Lang Teachers; 4-H Adult Leader 1982-; *office:* Copperas Cove HS 400 Sth 25th Box 580 Copperas Cove TX 76522

ROY, DEBORAH COUTURE, Spanish Teacher/Dept Chair; *b:* Waterville, ME; *m:* Thomas S.; *c:* Mariel; *ed:* (BA) Span, Univ of ME Orono 1975; *cr:* Teacher Gorham HS 1975-; *ai:* Span Club & Sociedad Honoraria Hispanica Adv; Amer Assn of Teachers of Span & Portuguese Pres 1989-; FLAME Advisory Bd 1989-; AATSP Natl Exam Coord 1986-; Staff Dev Chm 1980-86; Gorham HS Yrbk Dedication 1988, Teacher of Yr 1985; *office:* Gorham HS 41 Morrill Ave Gorham ME 04038

ROY, JOHN DENNIS, III, Adjunct Prof/Soc Stud Teacher; *b:* Willimantic, CT; *m:* Martha Ellen Miller; *c:* Michael, Patrick; *ed:* (BA) His, Mc Kendree Coll 1966; (MA) European His, E IL Univ 1971; Greek Culture, Vanderbilt Univ 1984; Psych, Belleville Jr Coll 1984-85; *cr:* USAF 1966-70; Inspector Victor-Dana Corporation 1971; Curator Mascoutah Areospace Museum 1989-; Teacher Mascoutah HS 1972-; *ai:* Homebound Consultant & Adv; Project Catch-Up; Museum Dir; Murals Artist; Phi Mu Gamma Treas 1965-66; Monumental Brass Society 1970-; Natl Hum Endowment Awd 1984; Founded Mascoutah Aerospace Museum; *home:* 611 Mary Jane St Lebanon IL 62254

ROY, LU ANN JACKSON, Science Teacher; *b:* Birmingham, AL; *m:* Derrick; *ed:* (BS) Scndry Ed, Jacksonville St Univ 1986; Mid Sch Cert Samford Univ 1988; Lions Quest Skills Adolescence Prgm; *cr:* Teacher Rutledge Mid Sch 1987-; *ai:* Rutledge Mid Sch Natl Jr Honor Society Spon; AL Ed Assn 1988-; AL Sci Teachers Assn 1987-; *office:* Rutledge Mid Sch 1221 8th St Midfield AL 35228

ROY, LYNNE ELIZABETH, English Teacher; *b:* Lake City, FL; *ed:* (MAED) Eng, 1975, (BAED) Scndry Eng, 1970 Univ of FL; *cr:* Eng Dept Chm 1982-83, 1988-89, Eng Teacher 1970- Suwannee HS; *ai:* Peer Teacher Beginning Teacher Prgm St of FL 1982; Schlsp Comm; Advisory Cncl 1982-83; NCTE, FL Cncl Teachers of Eng 1970-; ASCD 1986-; March of Dimes Walkathon Chm 1977, 1979; Friends of Suwanee River Regional Lib; St of FL Teachers Schlsp 1968; Master Teacher 1987; Eng Comm Writing St Course Objectives; *office:* Suwannee HS 1314 SW Pine Ave Live Oak FL 32060

ROYAL, BRENDA C., Science Department Chair; *b:* Cookeville, TN; *m:* Mike; *c:* Julie; *ed:* (BS) Chem/Bio, 1980, (MS) Bio, 1982, Teaching Cert Sci, 1987 Mid TN St Univ; *cr:* 9th Grade Phys Sci Thurman Francis Jr HS 1987-88; Physics/Chem/Bio Teacher La Vergne HS 1988-; *ai:* Fellowship of Chrstn Athletes Spon; Rines Against Drugs; Frosh Clas s Sci Dept Chm; Faculty Cncl Secy & Mem; NABT 1988-; AAPT 1989-; NEA, TEA, REA 1987-; Rutherford Cty Drug Alliance Treas 1989-; Parent-to-Parent Trng Facilitator; South Gate Baptist Church.

ROYALS, RAYMOND JOHN, Vocational Trade Instructor; *b:* Torrington, CT; *m:* Sharri Ann Graziani; *c:* Jennifer, Michelle; *cr:* Voc Trade Instr Oliver Wolcott Tech Sch 1987-; *ai:* Auto Club Adv & Chm; Inlands & Wetlands Comm Commissioner 1988-; *office:* Oliver Wolcott Tech Sch 75 Oliver St Torrington CT 06790

ROYBAL, STEVEN E., Art/Photography Teacher; *b:* Pueblo, CO; *m:* Colleen M.; *c:* Melissa, Stephanie; *ed:* (BA) Art Ed, Univ of Southern CO 1972; (MA) Art Ed, Univ of CO 1975; Univ of NM; *cr:* Art Teacher Mc Kinley Mid Schl 1975-84; Art Teacher West Mesa HS 1984-; Photo Teacher TVI 1987-; *ai:* Dept Chm Fine Arts West Mesa HS; NM Art Ed Assn 1978-82; Art Posters Hispanic His Accepted By St Dept of Ed NM Used in Public Schls in NM; *office:* West Mesa HS 6701 Fortuna Rd N W Albuquerque NM 87121

ROYER, WILLIAM M., Fourth Grade Teacher; *b:* Lancaster, PA; *m:* Susan Rial; *c:* Timothy; *ed:* (BS) Elem Ed, 1973, (MA) Instructional Comm, 1978 Shippensburg Univ; *cr:* Elem Teacher Claysburg-Kimmel Sch Dist 1973-; *ai:* Head Jr HS Ftbl Coach Claysburg-Kimmel Sch Dist; NEA, PA St Ed Assn 1973-; Claysburg-Kimmel Educl Assn; Dist Lead Teacher 1989; *office:* Claysburg-Kimmel Sch Dist R D 1 Bedford St Claysburg PA 16625

ROYSTER, MARY COLLIS, Biology Teacher; *b:* Richmond, VA; *m:* Elgie Thomas; *c:* Mark, Janet R. Bishop, Matthew; *ed:* (AA) Pre Nursing, Mars Hill Coll 1956; (BA) Bio, Averett Coll 1971; Univ VA, Radford Univ, NC St; *cr:* Bank Bookkeeper Bank of Chatham 1958-68; Teacher Aide Chatham HS 1968-69; Bio Teacher Dan River 1971-72, Gretna HS 1972-; *ai:* NABT 1985-; *office:* Gretna HS Box 398 Gretna VA 24557

ROYSTON, COLLEEN CONWAY, 7th-12th Grade Span/Fr Teacher; *b:* St Louis, MO; *m:* Randy; *ed:* (BA) Foreign Lang Fr/ Span, Drury Coll 1984; Cert Span, SW MO St Univ; Drury Coll; *cr:* Teacher Strafford HS 1987-; *ai:* Beta Club; FIFA, USSF Soccer Ofcl; SW MO Soccer Ofcls Assn Mem Bd of Dir 1989-; *home:* Rt 3 Box 576 Rogersville MO 65742

ROYUK, BRENT RONALD, Advanced Placement Teacher; *b:* Cleveland, OH; *m:* Sandra J. Muehler; *ed:* (BSED) Physics/Math, Concordia Coll 1988; *cr:* Teacher Metro-East Luth HS 1988-; *ai:* Asst Coach Ftbl; Head Coach Girls Bsktbl; *office:* Metro-East Luth HS 1001 Center Grove Rd Edwardsville IL 62025

ROZAK, KATHLEEN MARIE, Jr HS Teacher; *b:* Chicago, IL; *ed:* (BA) Ed, St Xavier 1972; (MA) Multi Cultural Ed, Concordia River Forest 1983; *cr:* 4th Grade Teacher 1972-73, 5th/6th Grade Combined Teacher 1973-76, 7th/8th Grade Combined Teacher 1976-; Holy Trinity; *ai:* Acting Prin; Stu Cncl Adv; Standardized Test Coord; Yrbk Ed; Asst Cmptr Coord; *office:* Holy Trinity Sch 1900 W Taylor St Chicago IL 60612

ROZANSKI, NORBERT ANTHONY, Religion/Music Teacher; *b:* Chicago, IL; *m:* Rebecca Krogull; *c:* Christopher, Bryan, Nicole, Aaron, Kathryn; *ed:* (BA) Music Ed, NE IL St Coll 1969; (MRE) Religious Ed, Loyola Univ 1989; Study Skills Seminars, Consultant Coll Racine 1972; *cr:* Music Teacher/Prin Freeport Cath Schls 1970-78; Music/Religion Teacher/Alumni Dir/Tennis Coach Aurora Cntrl Cath HS 1978-; *ai:* Dir/Producer Sch Musical; Alumni Dir; ASCD 1988-; *office:* Aurora Cntrl Cath HS 157 N Root St Aurora IL 60505

ROZNOWSKI, MARIE DE CAIRE, Junior High Teacher; *b:* Alpena, MI; *m:* Joseph N.; *c:* Becci, Amy; *ed:* (BA) Sociology/His, Aquinas Coll; MI St, Cntrl MI Univ; *cr:* San Ignacio 1964-66; Holy Redeemer 1966-69; Pierson Jr HS 1969-71; St Anne 1971-; *ai:* Quiz, Jr Knowledge Bowl, Natl His Day, Natl Geographic Geography Bee, Safety Patrol, Girls Sftbl Coach/Adv; NCEA, Mi Ed Assn, Natl Trust for Historic Preservation, Thunder Bay Rdng Cncl; Greenpeace; Outstanding Educator 1986; *home:* 1024 River Alpena MI 49707

RUANE, JAMES JOSEPH, English Teacher; *b:* San Francisco, CA; *m:* Diana Korpa; *c:* Pamela, Denise, Michael, Kenneth; *ed:* (BS) Eng, 1954, (MA) Eng, 1967 Univ of San Francisco; *cr:* Asst Ftbl Coach 1954-74, Head Ftbl Coach 1974-86, 9th-12th Grade Teacher 1958- George Washington HS; *ai:* Letter Society Spon; Athletic Hall of Fame Bd Mem; San Francisco Coaches Assn 1959-86; San Francisco Fed Teachers 1986-; AXT Memorial & CIF Section Coach of Yr 1982; *office:* George Washington HS 600 32nd Ave San Francisco CA 94121

RUBEL, NOMAN RAY, Biology Teacher; *b:* Hillsdale, MI; *m:* Judith A. Wisman; *c:* Randall R., Mark S., Lance E., Jeffery S.; *ed:* (BS) Bio, Hillsdale Coll 1958; (MA) Traffic Safety, MI St Univ 1965; Bio, W MI Univ 1959; Bio, Univ of Detroit 1960-62; Bio, Univ of OR 1963; Traffic Safety, MI St Univ 1964-65; *cr:* Sci/Bio Teacher Lakeview HS 1958-; *ai:* Lakeview Sch Cadre Teach Other Teachers; ITIP Methods; Teach in Cty Gifted & Talented Prgm & After Sch Advanced Placement Prgm in Bio; Var Ftbl Photographer; MI Educl Assn, NEA, MI Sci Teachers Assn Outstanding Sci Teacher of Yr 1979; NSF Fnd Grants 1959-63; MI Alternate Most Influential Sci Teacher for Natl Inst of Healths Centennial Scholars & Teachers Prgm 1987; Master Teacher Awd Lakeview Schls 1976, Lakeview Adult HS 1977; Kiwanis Club Citizen of Month 1979; Commencement Speaker Lakeview HS 1979; Outstanding Educator by W K Kellogg Fnd 1984-89; Chr Lakeview HS Sci Dept 1965-75, Driver Ed Dept 1967-; Math & Sci Comm Chm Battle Creek Area Schls 1984; *office:* Lakeview HS 300 S 28th St Battle Creek MI 49015

RUBENSTEIN, DAVID MILES, English Teacher; *b:* Manhattan, NY; *m:* Bonita Blount; *c:* Jennifer, Rebekah, Dov; *ed:* (AA) Liberal Art, Sullivan Cty Comm Coll 1965; (BS) Ed/Eng, 1967, (MS) Ed/Elem, 1986 SUNY New Paltz; *cr:* Eng Teacher Middletown HS 1967-69, Plainview Old Bethpage 4 1969-71, Saugerties Jr HS 1971-; *ai:* Group II Schlsp & Needs Assessment Comms; Staff Newsletter; Lip Sync Tryout Panel; Sch Newspaper & Stu Government Adv; Saugerties Teachers Assn (Building Rep 1978-81, Treas 1981-83, Public Relations Social 1979-83); *office:* Saugerties Jr HS Washington Ave Ext Saugerties NY 12457

RUBIN, BRENDA, Judaic Studies Teacher; *b:* Washington, DC; *ed:* (BS) Bus Management-Summa Cum Laude, Towson St Univ 1988; Certified Judaic Stud Teacher; Beth Jacob Teachers Seminary of Jerusalem 1985; *cr:* 8th-11th Grade Teacher 1985-, Guidance Cnslr 1988- Bais Yaakov Baltimore; *ai:* Jr HS Guidance Cnslr; *office:* Bais Yaakov Baltimore 11111 Park Hts Ave Owings Mills MD 21117

RUBIN, MARCIA ORWICK, Spanish Teacher; *b:* Canton, OH; *m:* Jeffrey L.; *c:* Michael, Diane; *ed:* (BA) Span, Muskingum 1971; Ashland Coll, Univ of Akron, Kent St; *cr:* Teacher Perry-Edison Jr HS 1971-; *ai:* Club Adv Modern Lang Club; OFLA 1971-; Outstanding Teacher Edison 1979-80; *office:* Perry-Edison Jr HS 4201 Harsh Ave Massillon OH 44646

RUBIN, MICHAEL SCOTT, Social Studies Teacher; *b:* Cleveland, OH; *ed:* Grad Stud Poly Sci; *cr:* His Teacher Edgewater HS 1987-; *ai:* Head Jr Var Ftbl Coach; Asst Weightlifting Coach; Model United Nations Adv; Likud-Herut USA 1989-; Holocaust Resource & Ed Center Volunteer 1987-89, Certificate of Recognition 1988; Featured in Article; Selected to Evaluate FL Soc Stud Exam for New Teachers; Attended & Taught

Cooperative Learning Techniques Seminars; *office:* Edgewater HS 3100 Edgewater Dr Orlando FL 32804

RUBINO, MICHAEL JOHN, Music Teacher; *b:* San Francisco, CA; *m:* Janice Hathaway; *c:* Brandi, Michael; *ed:* (AA) Music, Cabrillo Coll 1964; (BA) Music, San Jose Univ 1967; *cr:* Music Teacher Watsonville HS 1968-70; Oakgrove HS 1970-71; Live Oak HS 1971-; *ai:* Marching & Symphonic Band; Color Guard; Jazz Ensemble; Choir; Morgan Teachers Assn 1971-78, Teacher of Yr 1975; WSMBC Pres 1986-; Citizen of Yr 1984; Marching Bands of America Natl Champs 1976, 1978; 1st HS Band to Perform in China 1987; 1st HS Marching Band to Perform in Soviet Union.

RUBIS, WILLIAM M., Language Art Teacher; *b:* Benson, MN; *m:* Loretta Fenske; *c:* Daniel, Jessica; *ed:* (BA) Radio & TV Speech, 1962, (BS) Lang Art Ed, 1963 Univ of MN; Grad Stud Eng, Soc Stud, Counseling, Admin; *cr:* Eng/Soc Stud Teacher Minneapolis Public Schls 1963-66; Eng/Speech/Drama Teacher Grove City HS 1966-85; Eng/Speech Teacher Atwater & Grove City HS 1985; *ai:* Speech, Drama, Knowledge Bowl, Academic Decathlon Coach; MEA 1963-; Meeker Cty Land Owners Pres 1982-86; *home:* Rt 2 Box 137 Grove City MN 56243

RUBLEY, TODD STEPHEN, Marketing Ed Teacher; *b:* Davenport, IA; *s:* John M., Lauren, Jill;; *ed:* (BS) Voc Distributive Ed, Auburn Univ 1984; Human Resource Management, Troy St Univ 1990; *ai:* DECA Club Spon; Support Team Comms; Voc Transition for Spec Needs Stus; Jr Achievement Adv; Lee Cty Voc Assn; Cusillo, Kairos.

RUBY, NANCY EDDLEMAN, 6th Grade Teacher; *b:* Pauls Valley, OK; *m:* Patrick A.; *ed:* (BS) Elem Ed, OK St Univ 1979; Guidance/Counseling; *cr:* 5th/6th Grade Teacher James L Dennis Elem 1979-; *ai:* Stu Cncl Spon; Lang Arts Vertical Comm; North Cntrl Evaluation Steering Comm; Pre-Referral Comm for Learning Disabled or Emotionally Disturbed; PC Rdng Cncl Newsletter 1982-; OK Ed Assn 1979-; NEA 1979; Kappa Kappa Gamma OSU Ref Bd Chm 1979; Beta Sigma Phi 1988-; James L Dennis Teacher of Yr 1984; Sch Dist Drug Prevention & Intervention; Spoken on St & Local Levels Using Novels to Teach Rdng; *home:* 8732 Raven Oklahoma City OK 73132

RUCKER, POLLY GRIGG, Asst Principal/Lang Art Coord; *b:* Mitchell, SD; *m:* James F.; *c:* Rebecca Edmondson, Deborah Maloch, David; *ed:* (BS) Eng, OH Univ 1946; Dakota Wesleyan Univ; *cr:* HS Eng Teacher Shelby HS 1946-50; Wheat Ridge HS 1950-54; HS Homebound Teacher Midland HS 1957-60; 7th/8th Grade Lang Art Teacher St Thomas More 1964-; *ai:* Sch Newspaper Spon; Yrbk Spon; Spelling Bee Spon; NCEA; NCTE; NCTE of TX; PEO Pres 1965/1968/1971; Miriam Joseph Farrell Region 10 Awd from NAEA; Distinguished Service Cath Sch Awd; *office:* St Thomas More Sch 5927 Wigton Houston TX 77096

RUDDER, BENNIE JACK, Industrial Arts Teacher; *b:* Pueblo, CO; *m:* Theresa Savala; *c:* Robert T.; *ed:* (BA) Industrial Art 1979, (MA) Scndry Ed, 1985 Adams St Coll; *cr:* Teacher Sanford Public Schls 1979-; *ai:* Prom Spon; CO Industrial Arts/Technology Ed Assn 1979-; Sanford Teachers Organization Past Chm 1986-88; Beaver Creek Youth Commission (Chm 1981-) 1977-; Amer Legion (Commander 1990) 1985-; San Luis Valley 4-H Fnd (Chm 1986-88) 1979-88; Alamosa Emergency Medical Service Volunteer Emergency Medical Technician; CO Division of Wildlife Master Hunter Ed Instr; American Red Cross Standard 1st Aid/CPR Instr; US Dept of Ag, US Dept of Interior-US Fish, Wildlife Service Natl Recognition Natural Resources Volunteer Leader for 4-H 1984; *home:* 115 Alamosa Ave Alamosa CO 81101

RUDE, DEBBIE MIRICH, Third Grade Teacher; *b:* Rock Springs, WY; *m:* Harvey; *c:* Jessica, Daniel, Benjamin, Jenna; *ed:* (BA) Elem Ed, 1976, (MA) Elem Ed, 1986 Univ of N CO; *cr:* 1st Grade Teacher Weld Migrant Sch 1976; 1st Grade Transitional Teacher Tozer Elem Sch 1976-78; 1st Grade Teacher W Ward Elem Sch 1978-80; 3rd Grade Teacher Berthoud Elem Sch 1980-; *ai:* Building Advisory Comm, Thompson Ed Negotation Comm Mem; Thompson Ed Assn Exec Bd 1987-89; CO Ed Assn St Delegate 1990; NEA; Loveland City Human Relations Commission Chairperson 1987-89, Service Awd 1989; Larimer Cty Human Resource Comm 1988-89; *office:* Berthoud Elem Sch 560 Bunyan Ave Berthoud CO 80513

RUDISILL, LINDA HARRILL, Healthful Living Teacher; *b:* Lincolnton, NC; *m:* Kenneth R.; *ed:* (BS) Health Ed/Phys Ed, ASU 1960-63; (MS) Health Ed, Gardner-Webb Coll 1982-83; Health Ed Teachers Wkshp & AIDS Wkshp Guest Panelist 1987; *cr:* Wray Jr HS 1963-70; 8th Grade Health Ed/Phys Ed Teacher Ashley Jr HS 1970-87; Visiting Teacher Lincoln Arts-Sci Day Camp 1983-86; 8th Grade Health Ed/Phys Ed Teacher York Chester Jr HS 1987; Recreation Supvr Lincoln Cty Summer Recreation Prgm Massey Sch 1973-; Adjunct Professor Gardner-Webb Coll 1985-; *ai:* NC Legislative Health & Fitness Day Comm; Accreditation & Southern Assn Visiting Comm Mem; Prentice Hall Textbook Reviewer 1987-; NEA, NCAE, ACT 1963-; NCAHPERD; AAHPERD 1984-; Reebok Prof Alliance Instr 1984-; Bus Prof Women 1986-88; SDAHPERD Sch Division Chm 1989; Gaston Cty Adolescent Pregnancy Cncl Advisory Bd 1989; Commissioners Sch of Excl Asst Dir 1988-; Articles Published; NC Health Educator of Yr 1985-86; Southern Dist Health Educator of Yr Awd 1986; Ashley Jr HS Teacher of Yr 1986-87; Gaston Cty NCAE Human Relations Awd 1978; Gaston Cty Bd of Commissioners Commendation 1986; Spotlight on Women Conference Nom St Career Woman of Yr 1987, 1988; Lincoln Cty Woman of Yr 1986; NCAE Certificate of Service 1984; *office:* York Chester Jr HS 601 S Clay St Gastonia NC 28092

RUDOLPH, BECKY J., Eng Speech/Debate Teacher; *b:* Twin Falls, ID; *m:* Rod L.; *c:* Kelli, Joshua; *ed:* (AA) Sociology, Coll of S ID 1971; (BA) Comm/Soc Sci, Boise St Univ 1977; *cr:* Teacher Castleford Sch Dist 1977-78, Valley Sch Dist 1978-; *ai:* Debate Coach; Soph Class Adv; 4th Dist ID Speech Arts Teacher Assn (VP 1989-, Secy 1986-87); Whos Who in Amer Jr Coll 1970-71; ID Debate Coach of Yr 1989-; *office:* Valley HS 882 Valley Rd S Hazelton ID 83335

RUDOLPH, JAN COCKERILL, Second Grade Teacher; *b:* Paducah, KY; *m:* Larry; *ed:* (BS) Elem Ed, Murray St Univ 1973; *cr:* Phys Ed Teacher 1973-74, 4th Grade Teacher 1974-76 Metropolis City Schls; Kndgtn Teacher 1976-87, 2nd Grade Teacher 1987- Massac Unit 1; *ai:* Curr Advisory Cncl Mem 1985-; Math Grant Exxon Oil Company 1988-; *office:* Cntrl Elem Sch 103 W 11th St Metropolis IL 62960

RUDOLPH, MARK HELMUT, 5th Grade Teacher; *b:* Celle, Germany; *m:* Laura M. Roy; *c:* Eric M., David P.; *ed:* (BA) Ed, Curry Coll 1971; *cr:* Research/Dev Teacher Chief of Naval Ed & Trng USN 1971-75; Math/His Teacher Union 96 E Sullivan 1976-81; 5th-8th Grade Teacher Winter Harbor Grammar 1983-; *ai:* US Navy 1971-75, Navy Commendation Awd 1975; Warrington FL Volunteer Fire Dept Firefighter 1973-75, Life Saving Awds 1975; Sullivan Volunteer Fire Dept Deputy Chief 1976-; *office:* Winter Harbor Grammar Sch Box 99 School St Winter Harbor ME 04693

RUE, KARON S., English Instructor; *b:* Holdrege, NE; *m:* Thomas D.; *c:* Shane, Kelly; *ed:* (BS) Eng, Univ of WY 1967; (MS) Speech, Kearney St 1985; *cr:* Eng Teacher Dean Morgan 1967-68, Laramie Jr HS 1968-70, Farnam Public Sch 1973-82, Medicine Valley 1982-; *ai:* All Sch Play; Weekly Cable TV News Prgm; NSEA, NCTE; CEA Pres; PEO, Little Theatre; Parenting Classes Leader; *office:* Medicine Valley Sch Box 9 Curtis NE 69025

RUELA, KATHLEEN A., Business/Marketing Teacher; *b:* Perth Amboy, NJ; *m:* Benito; *c:* Anthony, Ben J.; *ed:* (BS) Bus/Marketing Ed, 1979, (MA) Bus/Marketing Ed, 1983 Trenton St; Berkeley Schls Diploma, Exec Secretarial Stud; *cr:* Admin Asst/Secretarial Continental Ins Co 1965-66; Secy Amerada-Hess 1966-69; Admin Asst Trans-Am Consultants 1974-77; Bus Teacher Carteret Public Schls 1980-84, Spotswood Public Schls 1984-; Instr Berkeley Schls 1987-; *ai:* Carteret & Spotswood Class & DECA Adv; Careret FBLA Adv; Mid Sts Self Evaluation Appeals Comm, Preventive Discipline; Kappa Delta Pi, Delta Pi Epsilon, NJBEA, NKEA, NEA, DECA, NJAMTC; BSA Merit Badge Cnslr; Conducted Wkshp at Spotswood; NJBEA Conference Presentor; *office:* Spotswood HS Summerhill Rd Spotswood NJ 08884

RUENZ, CARMA HOINES, English/Journalism Teacher; *b:* Britton, SD; *m:* Stewart Lynn Jr.; *c:* Jacob, Joshua, Lyndse; *ed:* (BA) Eng, Northern St Univ 1977; *cr:* Eng/Journ Teacher Hecla HS 1978-; *ai:* Jr/Sr Play, Torch, Sr Class, Yrbk Adv; Declam Coach; NEA, SD Ed Assn 1978-; Hecla Ed Assn (Pres 1983-84) 1978-; *office:* Hecla HS Box 185 Hecla SD 57446

RUETHER, MICHAEL KEITH, Music Director; *b:* Independence, MO; *m:* Laura; *ed:* (BME) Music Ed, Cntrl Meth Coll 1986; *cr:* Music Dir Steelville R-3 Schls 1986-; *ai:* Jazz Band; Jr HS Bsktbl; Soph Class Spon; Schlsp Comm; CTA, MSTA, MBA, MENC, MMEA, NFIOA; *office:* Steelville R-3 Schls Box 339 Steelville MO 65565

RUFF, SHARON THIEGE, English Department Chair; *b:* Vancouver, WA; *m:* Wesley L.; *c:* Steven, Karl; *ed:* (BA) Eng, WA St Univ 1967; (MA) Curr/Instruction, Seattle Univ 1985; Seattle Pacific Univ, W WA Univ, Univ of WA, Seattle Univ; *cr:* Eng Teacher W Valley HS 1967-72; Eng Teacher/Dept Chairperson Mariner HS 1973-; *ai:* Adv ARGO Magazine; Prin Cabinet; Schlsp, Honor Society Comm; NCTE Writing Achievement Awd Coord; Steering Comm for Lang Art Adoption 1991; NCTE Mem 1968-; WA Cncl Teachers of Eng Mem 1988-; Educl Excl Network Mem 1989-; Seattle Art Museum, WA St Univ Alumni Club Mem 1985; Smithsonian Inst Mem 1981; Received Cncl for Basic Ed Grant for Independent Study in Hum 1989; Appointed Eng Dept Chairperson 1988; Illustrated K-12th Grade Ed Manual 1982; Contributed Cartoon Illustrations to WA Ed Assn Public Clip Art 1978; *office:* Mariner HS 200 120th SW Everett WA 98204

RUGGLES, MARY FREDERICK, Kindergarten Teacher; *b:* Clifton Springs, NY; *m:* Clayton Robert; *ed:* (BS) Biological Sci/Ed, St Univ of NY Brockport 1971; Cmmty Intervention; Jr Great Books; Talents Unlimited; *cr:* 1st Grade Teacher Oriskany Falls Union Free Dist 1972-74; 2nd Grade Teacher 1974-75, 3rd Grade Teacher 1975-78 Clifton Springs Elem; 3rd Grade Teacher Phelps Elem 1978-81; Remedial Math Teacher 1981-82, 4th Grade Teacher 1982-83, Kndgtn Teacher 1983- Clifton Elem; *ai:* Supts Advisory Comm; Sch Improvement Team; PTA Pres 1987-89; Amer Field Service Pres 1982-84; NYSUT, AFT Treas 1974-75; United Meth Women 1975-76; Wrote NY St Sci Curr; Certified NY St Metric Teacher Leader Trainer; *office:* Phelps Clifton Spgs Cntrl Sch Banta St Phelps NY 14532

RUGH, MATTHEW SHEALY, Health & Pre-Algebra Teacher; *b:* Springfield, OH; *m:* Sheila J. Boswell; *c:* Jessica, Jamie; *ed:* (BA) Elem Ed, Wittenberg Univ 1981; (MS) Admin/Supervision, Univ of Dayton 1985; Drug Intervention & Child Abuse Referrals; *cr:* Clerk Gold Circle Department Stores 1975-81; Teacher Springfield City Schs 1981-; *ai:* Substance Abuse Comm Co-Chm; Phi Delta Kappa Mem 1986-; *office:* Roosevelt Mid Sch 1600 N Limestone Springfield OH 45503

RUHE, MARY ANN GALLAGHER, Biology Teacher; *b:* Dalton, PA; *m:* Bruce; *ed:* (BS) Biological Sci, Barry Univ 1972; (MST) Bio, Rutgers Univ 1986; Project Teach, Monmouth Coll 1978; Spec Problems Teacher Ed, Rutgers 1981; *cr:* Bio Teacher Madonna Acad 1973-74, St John Vianney HS 1974-77, Cedar Ridge HS 1977-; *ai:* Developed Cedar Ridge Environmental Organization; Bio I, II Teams Competition NJ St Sci League Coach; Future Physicians Club Adv; *office:* Cedar Ridge HS Rt 516 Matawan NJ 07747

RUHL, RANDALL WAYNE, Mathematics Teacher; *b:* Jersey Shore, PA; *m:* Lois J. Raub; *ed:* (BS) Math Ed, Lock Haven Univ 1980; *cr:* Math Teacher Sullivan Cty HS 1981-; *ai:* Builders Club Adv; Math Tells Tutor; *home:* Box 68 Laporte PA 18626

RUHLMAN, SUSAN LYNN, Mathematics Teacher; *b:* Hammonton, NJ; *ed:* (BS) Math Ed, FL St Univ 1973; *cr:* Math Teacher Coconut Creek HS 1973-75, South Plantation HS 1975-82, Ft Lauderdale HS 1982-; *ai:* Math Club Spon; Math Competitions Coord; NEA 1974-; *office:* Fort Lauderdale HS 1600 NE 4th Ave Fort Lauderdale FL 33305

RUIZ, JUAN CARLOS, Band Director; *b:* Falfurrias, TX; *m:* Suzette Ana; *c:* Victor, Marlynda, Judyth M.; *ed:* (BMED) Music, TX Luth Coll 1973; Clinics/Seminars TX Music Educators Assn, TX Bandmasters Assn; Grad Sch SW TX St Univ; *cr:* Band Dir Fannin Jr HS 1973-75, Dilley HS 1975-76, Rio Grande City Jr HS 1977-83, Zapata Jr HS 1983-84, Mission HS 1984-85, Southside HS 1985-; *ai:* Marching Band, Concert Band, Wind Ensemble Dir; Solo & Ensemble Spon; TX Music Educators Assn, TX Bandmasters Assn; Southside HS Band Sweepstakes Awds; *home:* 2002 Pale Valley San Antonio TX 78227

RUMBOLD, PAULA LATHROP, Second Grade Teacher; *b:* Stockton, CA; *m:* David R.; *c:* Jennifer; *ed:* (BA) His, Concordia Teachers Coll 1975; (MS) Elem Ed, St Univ of NY Oneonta 1983; *cr:* Kndgtn Teacher Suburban Bethlehem Luth Sch 1975-76, St Matthew Luth Sch 1976-78 Crossand Crown Day Sch 1978-79 St Matthew Luth Sch 1979-80 & 1983-87; 2nd Grade Teacher Teacher River Roads Luth Sch 1987-; *ai:* Choir Accompanist; United Way Campaign; Luth Ed Assn; *home:* 2929 Wisconsin Saint Louis MO 63118

RUMMEL, ALVIS JAY, 8th Grade Science Teacher; *b:* Uvalde, TX; *m:* Jane Patton; *c:* Julie, John; *ed:* (AA) Ag, Southwest TX Jr Coll 1968; (BS) Ag Ed, SWT 1970; SWT; UTSA; *cr:* Teacher Bay City ISD 1971-75, UCISD 1975-; *ai:* ATPE Mem 1975-; Uvalde Volunteer Fire Dept Pres Chaplin; *office:* Uvalde Jr H S 1000 N Getty Uvalde TX 78801

RUMP, ROBERT ERWIN, Science Department Chairman; *b:* Tipton, IN; *m:* Valerie Sue Wheeler; *c:* Joshua, David; *ed:* (BS) Earth Sci, Ball St Univ 1976; (MED) Ed, GA S Coll 1982; GA SW Coll 1986; *cr:* Sci Teacher/Dept Chm Appling Cty Comprehensive HS 1976-; Evening Coll Instr Brewton-Parker Coll 1983-; *ai:* SACS Sci Comm Chm, SACS Steering Comm Mem, ACCHS Media Comm Mem 1989-; PAGE 1987-; GSTA 1989-; Appling Cty Civil Defense Radiological Monitoring Volunteer 1982-; *office:* Appling Cty Comprehensive HS Rt 7 Box 45 Baxley GA 31513

RUMSEY, CHERYL RUDD, Spanish Teacher; *b:* Idaho Falls, ID; *m:* Philip G.; *c:* Anne, Elaine Rumsey Wagner, Lisa; *ed:* (AA) Eng, Ricks Coll 1964; (BA) Eng/Span, Brigham Young Univ 1966; Centro de Mexico de Idiomas Morelia, Mexico; *cr:* Span Teacher Irving Jr HS 1973-76; Span Teacher/Foreign Lang Dept Chm Marsh Valley HS 1980-; *ai:* Girls League Adv; Trainer Natural Helpers Prgm; Adv Young Woman of Yr Comm; Schlsp Comm Mem; ID Teachers of Foreign Lang & Culture 1982-; Mem Natl Stu Act Assn 1987-; Jr Miss Comm, Girls St Comm 1986-; 4-H Club Leader 1982-; Marsh Valley Sch Dist Teacher of Yr, Runner Up St of ID Teacher of Yr 1989-; ID Span Teachers Grant 1989-; *office:* Marsh Valley HS 12655 S Hwy 91 Arimo ID 83214

RUMSEY, ROBERT CHARLES, Technology Teacher; *b:* Philadelphia, PA; *m:* Myrle Esther Heim; *c:* Kimberly, Christopher, Jennifer; *ed:* (BA) Industrial Arts/Technology Ed, Pittsburg St Univ 1964; (MS) Technology Admin, Glassboro St Coll 1973; Foundrymans Seminar, NC St; Leadership Conference Ripley WV; *cr:* Industrial Art Ed Teacher Corvallas Intermediate Sch 1964-67, Cntrl Jr HS & Mid Sch 1967-71; Gauger Chapter Technology Stu Assn & Asst St Adv; *ai:* Technology Stu Assn Adv Gauger Chapter & Asst St Adv; Phi Delta Kappa 1964-; Industrial Technology Ed Assn 1989-; DE Technology Ed Assn 1989-; Our Redeemer Luth Church (Property Bd Chm 1981-83, VP 1984-85, Elder of Evangelism 1986-88); Technology Adv of Yr 1988, 1989-; Christina Mid Sch Teaher of Yr 1988; *office:* Gauger Mid Sch 50 Gender Rd Newark DE 19713

RUMSEY, ROSELLA FRANCA, Math/Computer Teacher; *b:* Kew Gardens, NY; *m:* Dion Paul; *c:* Christina; *ed:* (BA) Math, Fordham Univ 1981; Cmptr Sci & General Ed Wkshps; *cr:* Student Teacher Martin Luther King HS 1980-81; Math Teacher Bishop Kearney HS 1981-83, Mary Louis Acad Summer 1981-83; Math/Cmptr Sci Teacher Msgr McClancy Memorial HS 1984-; *ai:* Eucharistic Minister; Prof Tutor; 8th Grade Teacher Lang Art for Cooperative Entrance Exam; Womens Club of Forest Hills Mem 1986-87; Math Club Fordham Univ VP 1981; Partial Schlsp Fordham Univ; Natl Teacher Exam.

RUNDELL, JUDY L., Instructor; *b:* Alexandria, LA; *m:* Edward E.; *c:* Martha, Sarah; *ed:* (BA) Elem Ed, LA Tech Univ 1966; (BA) Elem Ed, Univ of TX 1972; (EDD) Elem Ed, Northwestern St Univ 1983; *cr:* Elem Teacher Austin Ind Sch Dist, Rapides Parish Sch Bd, Alexandria Cty Day; Coll Instr LA St Univ 1989-; *ai:* Debate Coach; Phi Delta Kappa, NCTM, ASCD; *office:* LA St Univ Sr Coll Alexandria LA 71302

RUNION, SALLY CHAPMAN, Language Arts Teacher; *b:* Jackson, KY; *ed:* Scndry Ed, 1974, (MA) Scndry Ed, 1978, (BS) Literature & Composition, 1980 Morehead St Univ; *cr:* Teacher Sebastian Mid Sch; *ai:* Coach-Lang Arts & Composition; Governors Cup Academic Competition; KEA; NEA; KAGE; *office:* Sebastain Mid Sch Box 766 Jackson KY 41339

RUNNELS, PEGGY JOYCE (ROTH), Basic Skills Math Teacher; *b:* La Grange, TX; *m:* Harold Wayne; *c:* Elizabeth C. Moore, Suzanne Roth; *ed:* (BA) Elem Ed, Baylor Univ 1955; *cr:* 4th Grade Teacher Ft Worth Ind Sch Dist 1955-56; Girls Phys Ed Teacher 1959-62, 4th Grade Teacher 1960-62 Killeen Ind Sch Dist; 3rd Grade Teacher Edna Ind Sch Dist 1969-70; 4th Grade/3rd-5th Grade Basic Skills Math Teacher 1979- Killeen Ind Sch Dist; *ai:* Assn of TX Prof Educators 1979-; TX St Teachers Assn 1955-56, 1969-70; US Army Commissary Advisory Cncl Zueibruecken W Germany Pres 1977-79; Killeen Daily Heralds Excl in Teaching Awd 1988; *office:* Mt View Elem Sch 500 Stagecoach Rd Harker Heights TX 76543

RUNNING, JOLENE, English/Mathematics Teacher; *b:* Pipestone, MN; *ed:* (AA) Music, Cypress Coll 1970; (BA) Ger, CA St Univ Long Beach 1973; *cr:* Teacher/Vice Prin, St Cecilia Sch 1975-84; Teacher St Bruno Sch 1984-; *ai:* Stu Cncl Moderator; Choir Dir; Yrbk Adv; NCEA 1976-85; OCRA 1979-87; Ed Grant for Use of Cmptr in Critical Thinking 1989-; *office:* St Bruno Sch 15700 Citrustree Rd Whittier CA 90603

RUPERT, BARBARA JEAN, Spanish Teacher; *b:* Seattle, WA; *m:* David A.; *c:* Megan; *ed:* (BA) Speech, W WA Univ 1984; Working Towards Masters Pacific Luth Univ; *cr:* Span/Speech Teacher Sandy Union HS 1984-88; Span Teacher Washington HS 1988-; *ai:* Past Chrldr, Ski Club Dance Team, Class Adv; Past Speech Team Coach; Phi Kappa Delta Highest Distinction Mem 1984; Sandy Ed Assn Secy 1987-88; WA Assn of Foreign Lang Teachers 1988-; Sandy HS Teacher of Month 1985; *home:* 3308 Louise St W Tacoma WA 98466

RUPERT, JOYCE O'NEILL, Third Grade Teacher; *b:* Brookville, PA; *m:* Richard L.; *c:* Carrie, Matthew, Erin, Andrew; *ed:* (BS) Elem Ed/Geography, Clarion Univ 1968; *cr:* 4th Grade Teacher 1968-71, 3rd Grade Teacher 1972-76 Sugarcreek Elem Sch; 3rd Grade Teacher Cooperstown Elem Sch 1976-; *ai:* Valley Grove Ed Assn, NEA, PA Ed Assn 1968-; PTA Treas 1989-; Sch Improvement Grant 1987; *office:* Cooperstown Elem Sch 2 Church St Cooperstown PA 16317

RUPERT, LOUIS C., Junior ROTC Commander; *b:* Grayson, KY; *m:* Pheba Ann Rucker; *c:* Louis Jr., Jeffrey S.; *ed:* (BS) Sci, Morehead Univ 1963; (MA) Bus Admin, Webster Univ 1976; *cr:* Lt/Col USAF; JROTC Teacher Russell HS, Niceville HS; *ai:* Drill, Saber & Rifle Team; Color Guard; Rocket & Model Club; NEA; FL Okaloosa Cty Teachers Assn; Shriners; Scottish Rite; Amer Legion; *office:* Niceville HS 800 E John Sims Pkwy Niceville FL 32578

RUPERT, NANCY GOTTSHALL, Developmental Reading Teacher; *b:* Altoona, PA; *m:* Robert; *c:* Robert, Amy; *ed:* (BS) Elem Ed, Lock Haven Univ 1958; Courses for Permanent Cert Penn St; *cr:* Elem Grade Teacher Garfield 1958-62; Teacher Keith Jr HS 1963-64; Mid Sch Teacher Bellwood-Antis 1967-; *ai:* Jr Class, Sr Class, Future Teachers of America Adv; Ladies Golf Assn SVCC VP 1967-70; PSEA, NEA; Nom Outstanding Educator in America 1973-74; *office:* Bellwood-Antis Sch Dist Martin St Bellwood PA 16617

RUPINSKI, MARILYN JOYCE (HOLLAND), 6th Grade Teacher; *b:* Grand Rapids, MI; *m:* Edward Dale; *c:* Anthony E., Matthew J.; *ed:* (BA) Elem Ed, 1972, (MS) ClassRoom Ed, 1986 MI St Univ; Assertive Discipline; Instructional Theory Into Practice; *cr:* 6th/7th Grade Teacher Kenowa Hills Jr HS 1973-; *ai:* Lang Art Dept Chairperson; Academic Track; Develop Thematic Units 6th Grade Level & N Cntrl Accreditation Comm; NCTE 1989-; North Park Presbyn Church Deacon 1979-82; *office:* Kenowa Hills Public Schls 4252 3 Mile Rd NW Grand Rapids MI 49504

RUPP, LINDA (HIMELHAN), First Grade Teacher; *b:* Wauseon, OH; *m:* Edward D.; *c:* John, Andrew, Mark, Matthew; *ed:* (BA) Elem Ed, Bowling Green St Univ 1974; *cr:* 1st Grade Teacher Evergreen Local Schls 1975-; *ai:* Evergreen Ed Assn 1975-; Mini-Youth Church Group Youth Dir 1986-88; *home:* 14608 Cty Rd S T Lyons OH 43533

RUPP, SHERRY L., Third Grade Teacher; *b:* Dayton, OH; *d:* David Randall; *c:* Heather L., Joshua A.; *ed:* (BS) Elem Ed/Eng, Bowling Green St Univ 1970; Ed Miami Univ, Wright St Univ; *cr:* 4th Grade Teacher Main Sch 1971-71; 3rd Grade Teacher Smith Place 1971-81; Sci Seminar Instr Wilmington Coll 1989; 3rd Grade Teacher Denver Sch 1981-; *ai:* Sci Comm Chm 1981-83; Wilmington Coll Guest Speaker 1980-; Inservice Comm Plays & Musicals; WEA, SEOEA 1971-; OEA, NEA, ECE, OCTELA; First Church of Christ Scientist (Pres, Reader, Organist, Sunday Sch Teacher) 1970-; Outstanding Young Educator Jaycees 1979; Produced Musicals & Plays; *office:* Denver Sch 291 Lorish Ave Wilmington OH 45177

RUSCETTI-KAY, NANCY HAGARMAN, Teacher of Gifted; *b:* Sharon, PA; *m:* Lawrence; *c:* Tracy Ruscetti; *ed:* (BS) Elem Ed, 1972, (MA) Spec Ed/Gifted, 1984 Univ of NM; ASCP Histology Tech Clinical & Research 1959-71; *cr:* 5th Grade Teacher John Baker Elem 1972-79; Professor Highlands Univ 1985; 4th/5th Grade Teacher Sunset 1986; 4th/5th Grade Teacher of Gifted John Baker Elem 1979-; *ai:* Sci Fair Organizer; Astronomy Comm; John Baker Art Rep; Talented & Gifted Teachers of NM (VP 1983-84, Pres 1985-86); Cncl for Exceptional Children of NM Outstanding Service Awd 1986; DAR His Teacher of Yr 1990; *home:* 1923 Snow Ct NE Albuquerque NM 87112

RUSCHEWSKI, WOODSON EARLE, Mathematics Dept Chairman; *b:* Lexington, MS; *m:* Bruce; *ed:* (BSED) Math, Delta St Univ 1983; *cr:* Teacher Knoxville City Schls 1986-87, Benton Acad 1987-; *ai:* Jr HS Chrldr & Stu Cncl Spon; Star Teacher 1989; *office:* Benton Acad PO Drawer D Benton MS 39039

RUSELL, DOUGLAS THOMAS, 8th Grade US History Teacher; *b:* Ft Fairfield, ME; *c:* Elizabeth, Douglas F.; *ed:* (BS) Elem Ed, Cntrl CT St Coll 1966; (MS) Ed, Univ of Hartford 1970; Media Admin Degree Univ of CT 1972; *cr:* 6th Grade Teacher Hooker Sch 1966-71; Media Specialist Weaver HS/Bulkeley HS 1971-76; 8th Grade Teacher Naylor Sch 1976-; *ai:* Hartford Fed of Teachers 1st VP 1973-75; *office:* Naylor Sch Franklin Ave Hartford CT 06114

RUSEN, GARY VLADIMIR, Visual Arts Teacher; *b:* Scranton, PA; *m:* Susan Jesikiewicz; *c:* Bethany, Lauren; *ed:* (BS) Art Ed, Kutztown Univ 1976; Working Towards MEQ Art Ed, Millersville Univ 1990; *cr:* Visual Art Teacher N Lebanon Sr HS 1976-; *ai:* Fencing Coach; NAEA Mem 1980-; US Fencing Assn Secy 1983-; *office:* N Lebanon Jr/Sr HS RD 1 Fredericksburg PA 17026

RUSH, JUDY DUNCAN, English Teacher; *b:* Wamego, KS; *m:* John Marvin; *c:* Janiece, Jon M., Jennifer; *ed:* (BSE) Speech/Eng, 1962, (MSE) Ed/Journalism, 1971 Emporia St Univ; Journalism, KS St Univ 1975-85; Licensed Financial Planner; *cr:* Eng/Speech/Debate Teacher St Marys HS 1962-67; Eng/Journalism/Debate Teacher Wamego HS 1969-; *ai:* NHS & Yrk Adv; Delta Kappa Gamma 1975-; Newspaper & Educl Journals Publications; *home:* Rt 3 Box 37 Wamego KS 66547

RUSHING, LAURA ELLIS, 6th Grade Reading Teacher; *b:* Tahoka, TX; *c:* James M., Cecil J., Terri A.; *ed:* Baylor Univ 1951; (BS) Ed, TX Tech Univ 1956; Spec Ed, Sul Ross 1974; Gifted Talented Incarnate Word San Antonio; Classroom Management 1985; Gifted Talented, Univ of TX 1986; *cr:* 2nd Grade Teacher Lubbock & Post & Smyer TX 1957-60; 4th-8th Grade Rdng/Spelling Teacher Smyer TX 1967-68; Kndgtn Teacher Lamar CISD 1968-69, Calallen TX 1970-73; LLD Teacher Ingram TX 1973-74; Kndgtn Teacher Kerrville 1974-88; Rdng/JLC Cmptr Rdng Teacher Peterson Mid Sch 1988-; *ai:* TX St Teachers Assn, NEA; *office:* Peterson Mid Sch 1010 Barnett Kerrville TX 78028

RUSHING, MURLINE ROBINSON, 7th/8th Grade Teacher; *b:* Ruston, LA; *m:* J. E.; *c:* David Bissic, Walter Bissic; *ed:* (BA) Elem Ed, Grambling St Univ 1951; (MA) Elem Ed, LA Tech Univ 1970; LA Tech Univ 1981; *cr:* Postal Clerk Grambling Post Office 1947-62; Teacher Bienville Parish 1962-; *ai:* Sch Building Level Comm Chm; Disciplinary Comm; LAE, NEA 1970-; Bienville HS Teachers Assn 1967-, Teacher of Yr 1987; *office:* Bienville HS P O Box 106 Bienville LA 71008

RUSHING, NAN SHEALY, Seventh Language Art Teacher; *b:* Shellman, GA; *m:* Delmas Jr.; *c:* Delmas III; *ed:* Home Ec, Abraham Baldwin Coll 1948; (BSED) Ed, 1971, (MED) Ed/Lang Art, 1985 GA Southern Coll; *cr:* Teacher Swainsboro HS 1948-50; Supply Teacher Claxton HS 1951; Teacher Nevils Elem 1951-52, 1971-; *ai:* Bulloch Cty Jr HS Write-Off Dir; Bulloch Cty Assn Educators Pres 1976-77, Trip to Natl Educators Assn 1975; Prof Assn of GA Educators Sch Rep 1985-; GA Cncl Teachers of Eng 1985-, Presenter at Conferences 1989-; New Castle Homemakers Club (Pres, SE Dir); 1956-57; GA Homemakers Cncl Pres 1972-73, GA Homemaker 1972, Farm Journal Test Family 1965-72, St Peanut Cooking Contest 1968; Teacher of Yr 1978, 1986; Bulloch Cty Teacher of Yr 1987; SE Bulloch Star Teacher 1980; Bulloch Cty Instructional Grant; *home:* Rt 1 Box 71 Register GA 30452

RUSHING, SANDRA SPLAWN, Third Grade Teacher; *b:* Greenville, SC; *m:* Robert E.; *c:* Kellie, Brant; *ed:* (BA) Elem Ed, 1972, (MED) EarlY Chldhd Ed, 1982 Armstrong St Coll; S-5 Data Collector, Savannah-CHatham Public Sch 1984; Rdng Specialist Degree 1982; *cr:* 2nd Grade Teacher Butler Elem 1971, Memorial Day Sch 1971-73; Behavior Disorders Teacher Pulaski Elem 1973-74; 2nd/3rd Grade Teacher Calvary Day Sch 1979-; *ai:* Accrediting Comm Chm; Intnl Rdng Assn 1982-83; TETI Grant; *office:* Calvary Day Sch 4625 Waters Ave Savannah GA 31404

RUSHING, SHIRLEY ANN, HPER Coach; *b:* Jasper, TX; *ed:* (BA) HPRE, TX Southern Univ 1963; NY Univ, St Thomas Univ; *cr:* Phys Ed Teacher Union Tree Sch Dist 1964-70; Cnslr Encampment for Citizenship 1965; Phys Ed Instr Schenectady Comm Coll 1970-72; Prgm Admin Harlem Hospital 1972-75; Cnslr/Recruiter New York City Sch 1975-79; Phys Ed Teacher Houston Ind Sch Systems 1979-; *ai:* Coach Girls Bsktbl, Vlybl, Track; Dance Teacher & Spon; NEA, HTE, TEA 1979-; Teacher of Month 1985; 1st in Dist 4 Girls Bsktbl; *office:* Woodson Mid Sch 10720 Southview Houston TX 77047

RUSHING, VIRGINIA MINOR, Social Studies Teacher; *b:* Parrish, AL; *m:* Jim E.; *c:* Cortney, Keri; *ed:* (BS) Elem Ed, North AL Univ 1967; (MED) Mid Grades, Berry Coll 1978; *cr:* 5th Grade Teacher Kate Duncan Smith DAR Sch 1966-67; 6th Grade Teacher Howell Graves Elem 1967-68; 6th-8th Grade Teacher Naomi Elem 1968-76; 8th Grade Teacher La Fayette HS 1977-79, La Fayette Mid Sch 1979-; *ai:* Spon GA Hist Bowl; Prof Assn of GA Educators Building Coord 1984-90; Delta Kappa Gamma Treas 1986-; La Fayette Mid Sch Teacher of Yr 1982 & 1986; Co Editor of Teacher Hndbk that Accompanies GA in Amer Society; *office:* La Fayette Mid Sch P O Box 359 La Fayette GA 30728

RUSK, FRANCES CAESAR, 7th Grade Teacher; *b:* Cleveland, OH; *m:* Walter F.; *c:* W. Thomas; *ed:* (BA) Elem Ed, St John Coll 1969; Cmptr Ed & Cmptr Repair; Sci Wkshp, Ursuline Coll; *cr:* 5th Grade Teacher Cath Diocese of Cleveland 1957-69; Berea City Schls 1969-74; 5th & 6th Grade Teacher St Jude Cath 1980-85; 7th Grade Teacher St Martin of Tours 1985-; *ai:* Plain Dealer Spelling Bee Chairperson; Sch Acad Challenge; Field Trips Coord; NCEA Mem 1980-; 1990 Bicentennial Map Contest 1st Place 20th Congressional Dist Winner; *office:* St Martin of Tours Schl 14600 Turney Rd Maple Heights OH 44137

RUSNAK, MARY LISKA, K-6th Grade Substitute Teacher; *b:* Mala Cerna, Czechoslovakia; *m:* John Joseph; *c:* John C., Joseph R.; *ed:* (BA) Eng, Seton Hill Coll 1975; PA St Univ Grad Sch; IN Univ of PA Grad Sch; *cr:* 5th Grade Teacher St Gertrude Sch 1963-67, St James Sch 1968-87; K-6th Grade Substitute Teacher Kiski Area Sch Dist 1987-; *ai:* Creative Article Published; Art Teacher of Month Greensburg Diocese; *home:* 410 Harrison Ave Vandergrift PA 15690

RUSS, BARBARA HESTER, 4th Grade Mathematics Teacher; *b:* Washington, DC; *m:* Ronald Thomas; *c:* Ron, Jennifer; *ed:* (BA) Bus Admin, 1969, (BS) Bus Ed, 1969, (BS) Elem Ed, 1975 Pembroke St Univ; Bladen Cty Cert Teaching Gifted & Talented; *cr:* 6th Grade Teacher Rose Hill NC 1970-72; 7th Grade/Lang Art Teacher Clarkton NC 1972-76; 4th Grade/Math Teacher Bladenboro NC 1976-; *ai:* NC Math Teachers Assn 1989-; Delta Kappa Gamma Secy 1989-; First Baptist Church; *office:* Bladenboro Elem Sch PO Box 459 Bladenboro NC 28320

RUSS, FAYE R., English Department Chairman; *b:* Atlanta, GA; *m:* James S.; *ed:* (BA) Eng, 1968, (MED) Scndry Guidance, 1970 GA St Univ; *cr:* Guidance Cnslr Wills HS 1969-72; Eng Teacher Hunter-Kinard-Tyler HS 1983-; *ai:* Stu Cncl & Sr Class Adv; Sch Improvement Cncl Mem; NCTE, SC Cncl Teachers of Eng 1989-; Amer Legion Auxiliary 1989-; Exch Auxiliary 1975-; Eng Dept Chm; *office:* Hunter-Kinard-Tyler HS PO Box 158 Norway SC 29113

RUSS, JOHN ROBERT, Assistant Principal; *b:* Avon Park, FL; *ed:* (AA) S FL Jr Coll 1969; (BA) His Ed, Univ of W FL 1971; (MA) Admin/Supervision, Nova Univ 1985; *cr:* Soc Stud Teacher Avon Park Mid Sch 1971-; Asst Prin Sebring Mid Sch 1990-; *ai:* Stu Government Spon & Natl Jr Honor Society Co-Spon; NEA, FTP; Avon Park Mid Sch Teacher of Yr 1987; *office:* Sebring Mid Sch 500 E Center St Sebring FL 33870

RUSS, LAURENCE STARR, 6th Grade Teacher; *b:* Cleveland, OH; *m:* Ruth Louise Rothacker; *c:* Scott A., Jason M., April M.; *ed:* (BS) Elem Ed, Kent St Univ 1968; (MED) Curr/Instruction, Cleveland St Univ 1974; *cr:* Teacher Cleveland Public Schls 1968-77, Midview Mid Sch 1977-78, Open Door Chrstn Sch 1978-; *ai:* Girls Bsktbl, Var, Jr Var, Soccer, Jr HS, Jr Var Wrestling Coach; Jennings Scholar; Martha Holden Jennings Fnd 1972-73; *office:* Open Door Christn Sch 8287 W Ridge Rd Elyria OH 44035

RUSSELL, ANN MARTIN, 6th Grade Soc Stud Teacher; *b:* Memphis, TN; *m:* Robert Dennis; *c:* Ed White, Rhonda A. White; *ed:* (BA) Elem Ed, Blue Mountain Coll 1966; (MED) Elem Ed, Univ of MS 1977; *cr:* 2nd-3rd Grade Teacher New Site Sch 1966-68; 5th Grade Teacher Booneville Mid Sch 1973-79; 2nd/5th Grade Teacher Germantown Elem Sch 1979-85; 5th-6th Grade Teacher Germantown Mid Sch 1985-; *ai:* TN Ed Assn, NEA 1980-; Elected by Peers as Heart Person; *office:* Germantown Mid Sch 2734 Cross Country Ln Germantown TN 38138

RUSSELL, BARBARA A., English Teacher; *b:* Clarksville, TN; *m:* Gordon F.; *c:* Shannon L., Shawn D.; *ed:* (BA) Eng/Fr, Coe Coll 1961; Working Towards Masters Univ of MD, Cath Univ; *cr:* Fr Teacher Bladensburg Jr HS 1961-64, Rollingcrest Jr HS 1965-72; Eng/Fr Teacher Bladensburg Jr HS 1973-83; Eng Teacher Bladensburg HS 1983-; *ai:* Faculty Advisory, Black His, Amer Ed Week, Testing Comm; Writing & Scoring Team Chairperson; NEA, MD St Teachers Assn, Prince Georges Cty Educators Assn, NCTE; *office:* Bladensburg HS 5610 Tilden Rd Bladensburg MD 20710

RUSSELL, BARBARA BAIRD, 7th Grade Lang Art Teacher; *b:* Excelsior Springs, MO; *m:* Dean E.; *c:* Lori Russell Holliday, Amy K., Julie N., Megan S.; *ed:* (BS) Elem Ed, Emporia St Univ 1969; *cr:* Lang Art Teacher Eureka Jr/Sr HS; *ai:* 7th Grade Class Spon; Jr HS Kayette Spon; KNEA, NEA, NCTE; KATE Exec Bd 1989-; Eureka Teacher of Yr 1989; *home:* 301 Mission Rd Eureka KS 67045

RUSSELL, GAIL ROBERTS, 7th Grade Eng/Rdng Teacher; *b:* Wilkes Barre, PA; *m:* Leonard; *c:* Beth, Sara; *ed:* (BS) Ed/Scndry Ed/Eng, E Stroudsburg St Univ 1965; (MS) Ed/Soc Scis, W CT St Univ 1990; *cr:* 7th-8th Grade Eng/Span Teacher Abington Heights Schls 1965-66; Clerk Office of Governor Cheyenne 1966; Asst Dir of Teacher Cert St Dept of Ed Cheyenne 1967; Eng/Rdng Teacher New Fairfield Mid Sch 1982-; *ai:* NCTE, CT Cncl

Teachers of Eng, NEA, CEA, NFEA 1982-; New Fairfield United Meth Church (Secy, Staff, Parish Relations Comm) 1988-; Recipient of Outstanding Service Awd New Fairfield Bd of Ed 1988; Prof Educator Recognition by Union Carbide Corp 1988; Recipient of Awd for Prof Dedications & Academic Excl Delta Kappa Gamma W CT St Univ 1989; *office:* New Fairfield Mid Sch Gillotti Rd New Fairfield CT 06812

RUSSELL, GREGORY D., History Dept Chair/Teacher; *b:* Neenah, WI; *m:* Elizabeth Weaver; *c:* Hannah, Andy; *ed:* (BS) Asian Stud, Univ of WI Stevens Point 1974; (MA) His/Ed, St Univ of NY Brockport 1985; Asian Stud, Univ of WA; *cr:* Peace Corps Volunteer South Korea 1976-78; His Teacher John F Kennedy Preparatory Sch 1978-79, Port Byron HS 1980-82; Dept Chm/Teacher Palmyra-Macedon HS 1982-; *ai:* Class Adv 1987; Vlybl Coach 1983-84; Dept Chm 1988; Fox Fire Outreach Mem 1986-; Univ of Rochester Teacher of Yr 1987.

RUSSELL, HELEN BULL, Soc Stud Teacher/Dept Chair; *b:* Burksville, KY; *w:* Charles G. (dec); *c:* Rick, Eddie; *ed:* (BA) His/ Geography, 1971, (MA) His, 1974 W KY Univ; Wkshps & Seminars in Soc Stud; *cr:* 7th Grade Teacher Red Cross Elem 1971-73; Teacher Barren Cty HS 1973-; Part-Time Teacher W KY Univ 1986-; *ai:* Jr Class Spon; Soc Stud Dept Chairperson; Barren Cty Ed Assn, KY Ed Assn, NEA; Excl in Teaching Soc Stud KY Cncl for Soc Stud 1975 & 1981; Meritorious Teaching Awd Natl Cncl for Geographic Ed 1980; Teacher of Yr Dist Winner KY Dept of Ed 1989; *office:* Barren Cty HS 507 Trojan Trail Glasgow KY 42141

RUSSELL, HELEN HELM, HECE Teacher/Coord; *b:* Java, SD; *m:* Joel Tracy; *c:* Mark, Timothy; *ed:* (BS) Ed/Home Ec, Stout Inst 1950; Grad Stud Mankota St, Univ of TX Austin, SW TX St Univ; *cr:* Home Ec Teacher Lancaster WI 1950-51, Mobridge SD 1951-53; Home Ec Teacher 1968-69, 1973-89, Home Ec Cooperative Ed Teacher 1989- Austin Ind Sch Dist; *ai:* FHA Adv; FHA HERO; AAT, TEA, NEA 1973-; Faculty Rep 1988-; Voc Homemaking Teachers of TX (Bd Mem 1975-79, Mem 1973-86); League of Women Voters (Pres 1964, Bd Mem, VP 1969, Mem 1957-73); Article Published 1950; *office:* L C Anderson HS 8403 Mesa Dr Austin TX 78759

RUSSELL, JO ANN, Business Education Teacher; *b:* Speedwell, TN; *ed:* (BS) Bus Ed, Lincoln Mem Univ 1969; Extra OR Re-Cert Trng Union Coll, UT Knoxville; *cr:* 8th Grade Teacher Powell Valley Elem 1974-81; Eng Teacher 1981-87, Bus Ed Teacher 1987 Powell Valley HS; *ai:* Academic Honors Prgm, Yrbk, Sch Newspaper Spon; Pi Omega Pi Pres 1968-69; NEA, TEA 1974-; CCEA Secy 1974; Outstanding Young Woman Awd 1971; LMU Alumnus of Month; *office:* Powell Valley HS Rt 1 Box 275 A Speedwell TN 37870

RUSSELL, JUDITH ANN, Third Grade Teacher; *b:* St Louis, MO; *ed:* (BS) Elem Ed, SW MO St Univ 1968; (MAT) Elem Ed, Webster Univ 1978; Post Grad Stud NE MO St Univ, SE MO St Univ, Univ of MO, Webster Univ; *cr:* 2nd Grade Teacher Lincoln Cty R-III Sch Dist 1968-69; 3rd Grade Teacher Meramec Valley R-III Sch Dist 1969-; *ai:* Rdng Curr, Prof Rights & Responsibilities Comm; NEA, PTO, MO St Teachers Assn, Kappa Delta Pi; Natl Wildlife Fed 1987-; Greenpeace 1990; MADD 1989-; *office:* Zitzman Elem Sch Payne St Pacific MO 63069

RUSSELL, JULIA THOMAS (JACKSON), Middle School Teacher; *b:* Millen, GA; *m:* James H.; *c:* Phabien Jackson, Jennifer Jackson; *ed:* (BS) Lang Art, Savannah St Coll 1971; (MA) Mid Grades, GA St Univ 1986; *cr:* Teacher Sharp Mid Sch 1975-; *ai:* Yrbk Spon 1977-78; Good Grooming Girls Club 1986-88; Media Center Comm; Dept Chairperson 1979-82; Team Leader 1981-85, 1988-89; New Teachers Mentor; GA Assn of Educators 1975-; Newton Cty Assn of Educators 1975-; Bethlehem Baptist Church (Enrichment Prgm Instr 1984-88, Asst Sunday Sch Supt 1990, Newsletter Editor 1985-, Sunday Sch Teacher 1981-86), Trophy 1988; *home:* 35 Otelia Ln Covington GA 30209

RUSSELL, KRISTINE LOUISE, First Grade Teacher; *b:* Bellingham, WA; *c:* Charisse Chandra; *ed:* (BS) Elem Ed/Lib Sci, James Madison Univ 1972; Grad Stud Shenandoah Conservatory of Music, Univ of VA, W VA Univ; *cr:* Lib Technician Lib of Congress 1972-73; Media Specialist Rolling Valley Elem 1973-75; 4th/5th Grade Teacher Valley View Elem 1975-77; Media Specialist/Teacher Apple Pie Ridge Elem 1977-; *ai:* 4-H Club, Lib Club & Stu Cncl Assn Spon; Frederick Cty Ed Assn 1977-89; *office:* Apple Pie Ridge Elem Sch Rt 8 Box 1093 Winchester VA 22601

RUSSELL, LAWRENCE P., Mathematics Department Chair; *b:* St Louis, MO; *m:* Margaret; *c:* Anna, Kathleen; *ed:* (BA) Physics, Bellarmine Coll 1970; (MS) Physics, St Louis Univ 1972; *cr:* St Louis Prep Seminary 1975-; Asst Professor St Louis Comm Coll 1976-; *ai:* Intramurals, Set Crew Dir; Bookstore Mgr; Sigma Xi 1972-74; Natl Sci Fnd Traineeship; *office:* Saint Louis Prep Seminary 5200 Shrewsbury Ave Saint Louis MO 63119

RUSSELL, LEE TALBOTT, First Grade Teacher; *b:* Monroe, LA; *m:* David L.; *c:* David, Kaley Russell Walker; *ed:* (BS) Elem Ed, SUCO Oswego 1976; Trng in Essential Elements, Whole Lang, SUCO, Oswego 1980; *cr:* 2nd Grade Teacher 1977-82, Kndgtn Teacher 1982-89, 1st Grade Teacher 1989- Cato Meridian Cntrl Sch; *ai:* Lang Art Cncl; Young Authors Day, Parents as Rdng Partners Comm; Summer Rdng Prgm; Cato Meridian Teachers Assn Newsletter Ed 1987-; Cato Lib (Bd of Trustees, Pres) 1987-88; PTO; Awarded Master Teacher Status 1987, & 3 Minigrants from Cayuga Orondaga Teachers Center in Teaching, Rdng. Writing, Lit; *home:* 2357 Veley Rd Cato NY 13033

RUSSELL, LOIS ANN, Second Grade Teacher; *b:* Burton, TX; *m:* Thomas R.; *c:* Brad, Linda Case; *ed:* (BS) Eng/Elem Ed, Univ of Mary Hardin Baylor 1967; (MA) Prairie View A&M 1980; Several Wkshps; Gifted & Talented Conferences; *cr:* Teacher Academy Elem Sch 1967-; *ai:* Gifted & Talented Curr; Univ Interscholastic League Judge; UIL Story Telling Spon; Area Service Center Summer Wkshp Teacher; PTO 1967-; Delta Kappa Gamma Secy 1978-89; Assn of TX Prof Educators; *office:* Academy Ind Sch Dist Rt 2 Temple TX 76502

RUSSELL, MARSHA K., English/Social Studies Teacher; *b:* San Benito, TX; *ed:* (BM) Vocal Performance, Southwestern Univ 1978; (MA) Eng, Univ of TX 1982; Teacher Cert Univ of TX 1984; Honors Cert Austin ISD 1989; Stu Asst Prgm Core Team Cert Natl Trng Assocs 1989; *cr:* Eng/Soc Stud Teachers Martin Jr HS 1984-86, Fulmore Jr HS 1986 87, Mendez Mid Sch 1987-; *ai:* Natl Jr Honor Society Spon; Stu Asst Prgm Core Team Mem; Assn of TX Prof Educators 1985-89; Cntrl TX Cncl Teachers of Eng 1988-89; Tracor Teacher of Yr 1988; Mendez Mid Sch Above & Beyond the Call of Duty Awd 1989; *office:* Mendez Mid Sch 5106 Village Sq Austin TX 78704

RUSSELL, MARY LOUISE SMITH, 3rd Grade Teacher; *b:* Tyndall, MD; *M:* Frederick Sr.; *c:* Rhea L., Frederick E. Jr.; *ed:* (BA) His, Howard Univ 1949; Ed, Wayne St; *cr:* Teacher Kansas City MO 1949-68; St Louis MO 1968-73; Des Moines IA 19 3-74; Detroit MI 1974-; *ai:* Participated Dev and Pilot Prgm-Central-St Louis MO Sch Sys.

RUSSELL, MICHELE TAF, Mathematics Teacher; *b:* Waterbury, CT; *m:* Paul Thomas; *ed:* (BA) Math, Regis Coll 1983; (MAT) Ed, Sacred Heart Univ 1990; *cr:* Math Teacher Kolbe Cathedral HS 1983-; *ai:* Stu Cncl, Cheerleading, Dress Code Adv; ATOMIC 1983-; Rotary Club Bridgeport Service Above Self Awd 1988; *home:* 43 Country Hill Rd Naugatuck CT 06770

RUSSELL, NELDA ROARK, Kindergarten Teacher; *b:* Jena, LA; *m:* Donald W.; *c:* Karen, Susan Whitehead, Rhonda Robertson; *ed:* (BS) Home Ec Ed, N LA Univ 1961; Working Toward Masters Supervision Admin; Additional Prof Improvement; *cr:* Home Ec Ed Teacher LaSalle HS 1961-64, Fountain Hill Sch 1965; Kndgtn Teacher Trout-Goodpine Kndgtn 1973-; *ai:* NEA 1973-; LAE (Local Secy 1976-77) 1973-; *home:* PO Box 763 Jena LA 71342

RUSSELL, PEGGY BOGGESS, Social Studies Dept Chairman; *b:* Ft Meade, FL; *m:* Edward E.; *c:* Edward, Ann Craven, Linda Brett, Douglas, Pamela; *ed:* (BA) Soc Stud, Tift Coll 1958; Addl Studies Western Carolina, Univ of South FL, Univ of FL; *cr:* Teacher Chamberlain HS 1958-61; West Elem 1961-62; Colonial HS 1962-63; Key West HS 1963-65; DeSoto Cty HS 1968-; *ai:* Spon of Classes, Omegas (Serv Club), Stu Cncl; Chairperson Soc Stud Dept, Comprehensive Planning Comm; FL Cncl Soc Stud; Pianist Sunday Sch Dept; Ladies of the Elks Have Held All Offices; Written & Recd Grants for Law Stud, Soc Stud Dept; *home:* Rt 1 Box 420 Arcadia FL 33821

RUSSELL, THEODORE EDWARD, Lang Art Coord/Eng Teacher; *b:* Hornell, NY; *ed:* (BS) Elem Ed, 1958, (MED) Eng, 1969 Geneseo St; *cr:* 5th Grade Teacher 1958-64, 7th-12th Grade Eng Teacher 1964-70 Bloomfield Cntrl; 5th/6th Grade Eng Teacher 1970-80, 7th/8th Grade Eng Teacher 1980- St Michael Sch; *ai:* Drama Dir; Cheerleading Coach; Oratory Club; NCEA; St Michaels Teacher of Yr & Cheerleading Coach of Yr 1989; *office:* St Michael Sch 320 S Main St Newark NY 14513

RUSSELL, THOMAS DAVID, Mathematics Teacher; *b:* Louisville, MS; *ed:* (BS) Scndry Ed/Math, 1968, (MED) Admin/ Supervision, 1972 Livingston Univ; Cmptr Ed, Brewer St Jr Coll; *cr:* Teacher/Asst Prin Aliceville Mid Sch 1968-89, Teacher Aliceville HS 1989-; *ai:* Jr HS Boys & Girls Bstkbl Head Coach; Aliceville Mid Sch Athletic Dir; Mu Alpha Theta Adv; Math Team Spon; Pickens Ed Assn, AL Ed Assn, NEA 1968-; *office:* Aliceville HS 300 Eutaw Rd Aliceville AL 35442

RUSSELL, TONY F., 8th Grade Amer His Teacher; *b:* Gadsden, AL; *ed:* (BS) His/Poly Sci, 1979, (MS) His, 1981 Jacksonville St Univ; Working Towards Masters His; *cr:* Teacher Centre Mid Sch 1980-; *ai:* Yrbk Adv; AL Ed Assn, NEA 1980-; Centre Mid Sch Teacher of Yr 1987; *office:* Centre Mid Sch 350 E Main St Centre AL 35960

RUSSO, DANIEL M., Social Studies Teacher; *b:* Staten Island, NY; *c:* Nancy; *ed:* (BA) His, 1969, (MA) Scndry Ed, 1971, (MA) Sch Admin, 1973 City Univ of NY; *cr:* Teacher Rothchild Jr HS 1969-70, Prall Intermediate Sch 1970-77; Rocco Laurie Intermediate Sch 1977-; *ai:* Bus Adv; Yrbk; United Fed of Teachers 1969-; *office:* Rocco Laurie IS 72 33 Ferndale Ave Staten Island NY 10314

RUSSO, DEBORAH MARIE, Fifth Grade Teacher; *b:* Philadelphia, PA; *ed:* (BSED) Soc Stud/His, Millersville St Coll 1976; (MED) Rdng, Beaver Coll 1983; Numerous Courses; *cr:* Substitute Teacher Chelthenham Sch Dist, Cncl Rock Sch Dist, Abington Sch Dist 1976-77; Departmentalized Teacher 1977-79, 5th Grade Teacher 1979- Redeemer Luth Sch; *ai:* Environmental Ed Coord; Faculty Secy; Intnl Rdng Assn 1983-; Philadelphia Cncl of IRA 1985-; NCSS 1987-; *office:* Redeemer Luth Sch 3212 Ryan Ave Philadelphia PA 19136

RUSSO, LILA AMMEEN, Third Grade Teacher; *b:* Ellwood City, PA; *m:* Vincent; *ed:* (BA) Fr, Carlow Coll 1967; Univ of Besancon France 1964-65; Grad Stud Temple Univ & Univ of Arts; *cr:* Adult Evening Fr Teacher Bartram HS 1967-70; Teacher Chester A Arthur Sch 1967-; *ai:* Fr Club; PATHS Writing Team; Schoolwide Project Writing Comm; Columbus Forum Educators Organization, Philadelphia Fed of Teachers, AFT; *office:* Chester A Arthur Sch 20th & Catherine Sts Philadelphia PA 19146

RUSSO, NUBE CABEZAL, 6th-8th Grade Math Teacher; *b:* Brooklyn, NY; *m:* Peter; *ed:* (BA) Ec/Math, Brooklyn Coll 1974; (MS) Bi-ling Ed, Long Island Univ 1976; Grad Stud Math at Brooklyn Coll, CCNY Columbia, Long Island Univ, Kungshouroug, NY Univ 1976-88; *cr:* Store Mgr 1950-52, Jewelery Buyer 1952-54 Franklin Simon; Dress Designer/Owner Nubes Designes 1955-60; Dress Designer Love & Florelee Designs 1960-72; Teacher Bi-ling Center & Public Sch 189 1972-; *ai:* After Sch & Summers Math Tutoring; *office:* Public Sch 189 1100 E New York Ave Brooklyn NY 11212

RUSSO, PAULETTE CARRO, Fourth Grade Teacher; *b:* Methuen, MA; *m:* Kenneth J.; *ed:* (BS) Elem Ed, Lowell Univ 1970; *cr:* 4th Grade Teacher 1970-79, 3rd Grade Teacher 1979-89, 4th Grade Teacher 1989- William T Barron Elem Sch; *ai:* Teacher Cncl; NEA, NHEA 1970-; Jaycee Women 1977-79; *home:* 5 Lansing Dr Salem NH 03079

RUSSOCK, HELEN LODOR, Sixth Grade Teacher; *b:* Hamilton, NY; *m:* Frank L.; *c:* Deborah Heslop, Deidre Simmons; *ed:* (BA) Eng Ed, Keuka Coll 1949; (MS) Elem Ed, SUNY Cortland 1957; Ed Courses at Colgate Univ & Syracuse Univ; *cr:* 9th-12th Grade Eng Teacher De Ruyter Cntrl Sch 1949-52; 6th Grade Teacher Morrisville Eaton Cntrl Sch 1952-53, 1955-89; *ai:* Delta Kappa Gamma 1978-; Pi Gamma Mu 1947-; NEA 1949-; Eaton Public Lib Bd 1955-80; RLC Auxiliary Pres 1980-; NY Eng Teachers Recognition Certificate; Employee of Yr MECS 1988-89; *office:* Morrisville-Eaton Cntrl Sch Eaton St Morrisville NY 13408

RUST, ELIZABETH ANNIE MOORHEAD, Home Economics Teacher; *b:* Denver, CO; *m:* Stanley Richard; *c:* Adrienne, Stephanie; *ed:* (BS) Voc Home Ec, OK Univ 1971; (MS) Home Ec Compentencies, Cntrl St Univ 1985; *cr:* Voc Home Ec Teacher Bartlesville HS 1971-72, Blanchard HS 1981-89; Home Ec Teacher West MHS 1989-; *ai:* Red Ribbon Week Comm; Dinner Theater Production; FHA & Young Homemakers of OK Adv; OK Voc Assn, AVA, OK Ed Assn; Blanchard Teachers Assn (Secy, Treas); PEO.

RUST, JAMES EUGENE, Fifth Grade Teacher; *b:* Nashville, TN; *m:* Susan Christine Knapp; *c:* Jennifer, Melanie; *ed:* (BSED) Elem, 1970, (MAED) Ed Media/Technology, 1981 Kent St Univ; Cmptr Sci, Gifted Ed, Classroom Management, Reality Therapy, Fundamentals of Supervision; *cr:* 6th Grade Teacher 1970-71, 1974-82, 4th Grade Teacher 1982-88, 5th Grade Teacher 1988-89 Buckeye Local Schls; *ai:* OH Future Problem Solving Coach; Kingsville Elem Sch Newspaper Ed; Buckeye Ed Assn (Pres 1979-81, Negotiation Team, EPAC Comm Chairperson); OH Ed Assn, NEA, OH Assn for Gifted Children; Ashtabula Little League; Ashtabula HS Music Boosters (VP 1988-, Pres 1990); Ashtabula Cty Gifted Advisory Cncl; *office:* Kingsville Elem Sch 5875 Rt 193 Kingsville OH 44048

RUST, MELVA GORRELL, Home Economics Teacher; *b:* Elkton, KY; *m:* Robert O.; *c:* Mark, Scot; *ed:* (BS) Voc Home Ec, 1957, (Rank I) Ed, 1981 Murray St Univ; Univ of Louisville, Vanderbilt Univ; *cr:* Home Ec Teacher Utica HS 1957-59, Daviess Cty HS 1959-63; Soc Service Worker Dept Human Resources 1963-64; Home Ec Teacher 1968-88, Child Care/Parenthood Ed Teacher 1988- Christian Cty HS; *ai:* FHA, HERO Adv; Day Care Dir; Am Home Ec Assn KHEA (Regional Pres, VP, Treas); KY Assn Children Under Six; St John United Meth Church; *office:* Christian Cty HS 731 E 2nd St Hopkinsville KY 42240

RUSTON, MARY NELL OLFERS, Fifth Grade Teacher; *b:* Fredericksburg, TX; *m:* Charles L.; *ed:* (BS) Ed, Southwestern Univ 1966; (MA) Ed, Univ of TX San Antonio 1976; *cr:* 4th Grade Teacher Westside Elem 1966-67, Thomas Withe Elem 1967-68; 4th/5th Grades Teacher 1971- Ogden Elem; *ai:* Spon Cotton Eyed Kids-Dance Group; TSTA; NEA; *office:* Ogden Elem Sch 2215 Leal San Antonio TX 78207

RUTAN, LAWRENCE RICHARD, Mathematics Instructor; *b:* Baltimore, MD; *m:* Joanne M.; *c:* Chip, Jeneen; *ed:* (BS) Electrical Engineering, GA Tech 1966; (MA) Ed, Glassboro St 1977; Rutgers Math Inst 1988; *cr:* Teacher Maple Shade HS 1972-; *ai:* Bible Club Adv; Yrbk Bus Mgr; Bowling Coach; MSEA Treas 1980-81; NJ Math Teachers 1988-; Phi Delta Kappa 1978; *office:* Maple Shade HS Frederick & Clinton Ave Maple Shade NJ 08052

RUTH, THOMAS GRISWOLD, History Instructor; *b:* Benton Harbor, MI; *ed:* (BA) His, Univ of MI 1963; (MA) His, Univ of TX Austin 1968; *cr:* Prof Escuela Americana-Nicaraguense 1965-67; Instr Hill Sch 1968-; *ai:* 3rd Form Adv; Head of Dormitory; Exec Comm & Numerous Comm; Organization of Amer Historians Life Mem; Independence Fnd Academic Chm; *office:* The Hill Schl High St Pottstown PA 19464

RUTHERFORD, ELAINE BLACKBURN, Business Education Teacher; *b:* Williamson, WV; *m:* Michael Keith; *ed:* (AS) Exec Secretarial Sci, S WV Comm Coll 1979; (BS) Scndry Ed/Bus Ed, Pikeville Coll 1981; (MBE) Bus Ed, Morehead St Univ 1983; Working Toward Rank I & Ed Specialist Degree; Teacher Expectation Stu Achievement Prgm Mem; *cr:* Bus Ed Teacher Belfry HS 1981-; *ai:* Mock Trial Team Spon; Phi Delta Kappa 1987; FBLA Adv 1981-; Eastern Star Worthy Matron 1984-85; Selected KY Colonel; Nom Teacher Individual Excellent Awd; Whos Who Amer Ed 1990; *home:* PO Box 27 Huddy KY 41535

RUTHERFORD, JOSEPH DOUGLAS, English/Health Teacher; *b:* Maryville, TN; *m:* Brenda Grindle; *c:* Benjamin; *ed:* (BS) Eng Ed, 1975, (MS) Health Ed, 1980, (EDD) Ed, 1986 Univ of TN Knoxville; *cr:* Teacher Porter HS 1976-79, Heritage HS 1979-; Adjunct Prof Lincoln Memorial Univ 1986-; *ai:* Asst Girls Bsktbl Coach; Southeastern Accrediatation of Schls & Colls; Health Ed Comm Chm; Curr & Textbook Comm; NEA, TN Ed Assn, Local Ed Assn; *home:* Rt 6 Box 368 Lenoir City TN 37771

RUTHERFORD, KATHLEEN A., Retired; *b:* Boston, MA; *w:* Frederick J. Moran (dec); *c:* Linda A. (Dec); *ed:* (BED) Elem Ed, 1945, (EDM) Elem Ed, 1953 Boston Univ; Drug Seminar Yale Univ Sch of Medicine; *cr:* Teacher Henry L Higginson 1947-48, Julia Ward Howe 1949-54, Florence Roche Sch 1954-85; *ai:* Substitute Teaching K-12; MTA; NEA; Groton-Dunstable Teachers Assn; Wrote A Childrens Book; *home:* West Shore Dr PO Box 547 Bristol NH 03222

RUTLAND, PATRICIA MOODY, Science Teacher; *b:* Sheffield, AL; *m:* Warren Hovater; *c:* Andrea W., Paige L., Warren B.; *ed:* (BS) Elem Ed, 1973, (MA) Elem Ed, 1985 Univ of N Al; *cr:* 4th Grade Teacher 1974, 5th Grade Teacher 1974-75, 6th Grade Teacher 1975-77, Title I Teacher 1977-82, 8th Grade Sci Teacher 1982 Cherokee Mid Sch; *ai:* Newspaper & Yrbk Co-Spon; Southern Assn of Geographers & Educators 1986-; NEA, AEA 1974-; Cherokee Study Club 1975-; Alpha Delta Kappa 1989-; *home:* Rt 4 Box 38 Cherokee AL 35616

RUTLAND, PEGGY BLENIS, Science Department Chairman; *b:* Boston, MA; *m:* Charles W.; *c:* Kristy, Tony, Rett; *ed:* (BS) Mid Grades, Kennesaw Coll 1981; (MED) Mid Grades, Berry Coll 1984; *cr:* 4th Grade Sci Teacher 1981-82, 5th Grade Sci Teacher 1983-84 Cloverleaf Elem; 6th Grade Sci Teacher Cass Elem 1985-86; 5th/6th Grade Sci Teacher Hamilton Crossing 1986-88; 6th Grade Sci Teacher S Cntrl Mid Sch 1989-; *ai:* GAE, NEA 1989-; Teacher of Yr Candidate 1988.

RUTLEDGE, CURTIS E., Social Studies/Reading Teacher; *b:* Berwyn, IL; *m:* Maureen Werner; *c:* Wayne, Brett, Scott; *ed:* (BA) Soc Sci, Blackburn Coll 1971; (MA) Ed, Concordia Coll 1978; Grad Work; *cr:* Enlisted Marine NCO US Marine Corps 1964-67; Soc Stud Teacher West Mid Sch 1971-79; Soc Stud/Rdng Teacher B J Ward Mid Sch 1979-; *ai:* Natl Geographic Geography Bee Spon; Admin Cncl B J Ward Mid Sch; Soc Stud Assessment Comm; NCSS, AFT 1971-; Joliet Bicycle Club 1975-; Prairie St Road Runners 1978-, Runners Runner 1984; Outstanding Young Educator Certificate Romeoville Jaycees 1973, 1975; Nominee Distinguished Service Awd Bolingbrook Jaycees 1988; Article Published 1983; *office:* B J Ward Mid Sch 200 Recreation Dr Bolingbrook IL 60440

RUTLEDGE, EUGENE, 4th/5th Language Arts Teacher; *b:* Gary, IN; *ed:* (BA) Eng Comm, MI St Univ 1967; (MA) Rdng Instruction, MI St Univ 1975; Oakland Univ; *cr:* Teacher Flint Bd of Ed Sobey 1967-; *ai:* Upper Elem Chairperson; Lang Art Cncl Rep; Staff Dev Policy Bd Mem; Elem Curr Writing Comm; *office:* Sobey Comm Sch 3701 N Averill Flint MI 48506

RUTLEDGE, JAMES JOSEPH, Mathematics Teacher; *b:* West Pittston, PA; *m:* Joyce Irene Thompson; *c:* Justin, Nathan; *ed:* (SB) Hum/Sci, MA Inst of Technology 1970; (MA) Math Ed, Univ Of S FL 1989; PHD Prgm Math, Univ of S FL; *cr:* Building Contractor 1971-83; Mgr/Salesman Jo Marie Designs 1983-84; Math/Cmptr Depts Head Naples Chrstn Acad 1984-89; Math Instr Lely HS 1989-; *ai:* Academic Scholar Coach; Mathematics Assn of America, NCTM, FL Cncl Teacher of Math, Lee Cncl Teacher of Math 1987-; FL Assn Cmptrs in Ed 1986-; Collier Cty Ed Assn 1989-; Amer Mensa 1989-; Grad Scholar Awd Univ of South FL 1989; Phi Kappa Phi Membership Invitation; Nom Presidential Awd Excl in Sci & Math Teaching Natl Sci Fnd; Univ Grad Fellowship Awd Univ of S FL 1990; Whos Who in Southwest 1990; *office:* Lely HS 324 Lely Blvd Naples FL 33962

RUTLEDGE, JANICE GAYLE, English Teacher; *b:* Mooreland, OK; *ed:* (BS) Bus Ed, 1969; (ME) Ed, 1978 Southwestern OK St Univ; Fort Hays St Univ; *cr:* Eng Teacher Scott City Mid Sch 1969-90; *ai:* Stu Cncl Spon; Delta Kappa Gamma Society Intl 1974-90; Jennabelle Watson Schlsp 1978; KS Natl Ed Assn 1969-90; Scott Cty Teachs Assn 1969-; Outstanding Young Educator 1979-80; KS Fed Music Club Northwest Dist Vp 1984-88; Scott City Music Club Pres & Reporter 1978-90; Meth Chancel Choir 1972-90; Chime a Leers Hand Bell Choir 1977-90; Intl Youth in Achievement 1981; Delta Kappa Gamma Soc Intl Beta Chapter Past Schlsp Chm; *home:* 608 Russell St Scott City KS 67871

RUTSTEIN, BARBARA LERNER, Mathematics Department Teacher; *ed:* (BSED) Jr HS Math/Sci Ed, Salem St Coll 1965; (MED) Ed, Cambridge Coll 1991; *cr:* Math Teacher Roberts Jr HS 1978-; *ai:* Medford Teachers Assn, MA Teachers Assn, NEA, NCTM; Medford League of Women Voters Pres 1977-80; MA League of Women Voters Field Service Adv 1982; Medford Recycling Comm Founder; *office:* Milton F Roberts Jr HS 35 Court St Medford MA 02155

RUTTER, JEANNE BARRON, Physical Ed Teacher/Coach; *b:* E St Louis, IL; *ed:* (BS) Phys Ed, 1973; (MS) Safety Ed, IL St Univ 1978; Admin Certification in Ed; *cr:* Teacher/Coach Pontiac Township HS 1974-; *ai:* Head Girls Vlybl Coach; Head Girls Sftbl Coach; IL HS Assn IL Coaches Assn for Girls & Womens Sport; IL Assn for Heal Th Phys Ed & Recreationf Amer Vlybl Coaches Assn; US Army Reserves 1979-85; Amer VLybl Coaches Assn Recogntion; Certificate for Coaching Career; *office:* Pontiac Twnshp H S 1100 Indian Ave Pontiac IL 61764

RUTTER, KAREN LORD, Home Economics Teacher; *b:* Dublin, GA; *m:* David Michael; *c:* David C., Mikella K.; *ed:* (BSED) Home Ec Ed, GA Southern Univ 1979; (MED) Home Ec Ed, 1981, (EDS) Home Ec Ed, 1982 Univ of GA; *cr:* Home Ec Teacher Forsyth Cty HS 1979-81, Loganville HS 1982-; *ai:* FHA Spon; Quality Enrichment Team Comm; Stu Home Ec Assn Pres 1977-79; GA Home Ec Assn Chairperson of Work Comm 1985-86; AVA 1979-; Phi Kappa Phi 1979-; Phi Upsilon Omicron 1976-; Walton Cty Teacher of Yr; *office:* Loganville HS Hwy 81 Loganville GA 30249

RUWERSMA, VIVIANN BUCHANAN, Sixth Grade Teacher; *b:* La Fayette, IN; *c:* Tad; *ed:* (BS) Scndry Ed/Soc Stud, 1970, (MS) Elem Ed, 1976 IN St Univ; Quest; Grad Stud Purdue Univ, IN St Univ, Manchester Coll 1990; *cr:* Teacher Lincoln Elem Sch 1970-; *ai:* Inter-Sch Comms; Quest Parent Meeting Facillitator; N Newton Ed Assn Co-Pres 1990; Citizens United for the Right Ed; *office:* Lincoln Elem Sch Roselawn Dr Roselawn IN 46372

RUX, JEAN DIXON, Fifth Grade Teacher; *b:* Cheyenne, WY; *m:* Russell Dean; *c:* Benjamin, Abigail, Clinton; *ed:* (BA) Elem Ed, Univ of WY 1983; *cr:* 6th Grade Teacher 1984-87, 5th Grade Teacher 1987- St Laurence Sch; *ai:* Cmmty Drug Advisory Comm Chairperson; Parenting as Prevention Team Mem; Dist WY Centennial Comm Mem; Intnl Rdng Assn (Local Cncl Building Rep 1985-88, VP 1988-89, Pres 1989-), NCTE 1988-; NCEA 1984-; Phi Delta Kappa; Intnl Rdng Cncl Snowy Range Cncl (Building Rep 1985-88, VP 1988-, Pres 1988-); St Laurence Church Choir Mem 1984-; Peer Proof Group Facilitator 1990; Article Submitted for Publication; Nom Intnl Rdng Assn Elem Teacher of Yr; *office:* St Laurence Sch 608 S 4th St Laramie WY 82070

RYAN, ANGELA UDOVICH, Spanish/French Teacher; *b:* Waynesburg, PA; *m:* Duane A.; *ed:* (BS) Fr/Span, California Univ of PA 1977; (MA) Span, Kutztown Univ of PA 1982; *cr:* Span/Fr Teacher Millersburg Area HS 1977-; *ai:* Yrbk, 10th Grade Class, NHS, Foreign Lang Club Adv; Prof Dev Comm; Amer Assn of Teachers Span/Portuguese 1977-; PA Sch Press Assn 1987-; PA St Modern Lang Assn 1989-; PSEA, NEA Local Secy 1977-; Meals on Wheels Voluneteer 1990; *office:* Millersburg Area HS 799 Center St Millersburg PA 17061

RYAN, ANNE B., 4th Grade Teacher; *b:* Buffalo, NY; *m:* Patrick T.; *ed:* (BA) Elem Ed, SUC Brockport 1973; *cr:* 4th Grade Teacher Geneva Public Schls 1973-; *ai:* Local Literary Publication for Children; Geneva Historical Society Project African-Amer; NEA 1973-; Ansley Schoolhouse Preservation Society 1984-; Geneva Schlsp Assocs VP 1989-; NAACP 1982-; Article XII Grants; Develop Gifted & Talented Prgm; Curr Comm; *office:* West St School 30 West St Geneva NY 14456

RYAN, BARBARA (BOYD), Social Studies Teacher; *b:* Detroit, MI; *m:* Charles G.; *c:* Rhonda Burnett, Regina Sparks, Gordon A.; *ed:* (BS) Speech/His, Sam Houston St Univ 1953; (MED) Ed/Counseling, Univ Houston Victoria 1980; Grad Stud Law, Psych; *cr:* Instr Sam Houston St 1956-58; Speech Teacher Wharton HS & Jr HS 1960-65, Boling HS & Wharton Jr Coll 1965-69; Teacher Bay City HS & Jr HS 1969-; *ai:* Intern Counseling; Soc Stud Dept Chairperson; Curr Comm; TCTA, TSTA, TCSS; DAR, Assn Chrstn Cnslrs 1988-.

RYAN, CONNIE M., 6th Grade Lang Art Teacher; *b:* Harlan, IA; *m:* Daniel L.; *c:* Timothy L., Taressa L.; *ed:* (AA) Elem Ed, IA St Teachers Coll 1960; (BA) Elem Ed, St Coll of IA 1962; (MS) Educl Admin, Univ of NE 1970; Elem Sch Curr Dev, Techniques of Supervision, Teaching of Writing, Clemson Writing Project, Clemson Univ; *cr:* Teacher Cedar Falls Cmmty Sch 1961-63, Alliston-Bristow Cmmty Sch 1963, Council Bluffs Cmmty Sch 1965-67; Substitute Teacher Council Bluffs Cmmty Sch 1968-74. Underwood Cmmty Sch 1968-74; Teacher Brownell-Talbott Ind Sch 1975-77; Professor Cntrl Wesleyan Cntrl Coll 1985-88; Teacher Pickens Cty Sch Dist 1978-; *ai:* NEA, SCEA, IRA; Breadloaf Rural Writing Project Grant 1986-89; EIA Writing Sci 1988-89; *office:* Morrison Elem Sch Frontage Rd Clemson SC 29631

RYAN, CORINNE ENGLISH, Home Economics Teacher/Coord; *b:* St Paul, MN; *m:* Michael E.; *ed:* (BA) Home Ec Ed, Univ of WI Stout 1969; (MA) Home Ec Ed, Ball St Univ 1970; Teacher Ed 1972; Elem Ed Cert 1983; *cr:* Home Ec Teacher/Coord Park Sr HS 1970-; *ai:* Home Ec Related Occupations Adv; AVA; Home Ec Ed Assn; MN Bus Industry Internship 1988; *office:* Park Sr HS 8040 80th St S Cottage Grove MN 55016

RYAN, DOROTHY ANN, French Teacher; *b:* Allentown, PA; *c:* Jacqueline, Laura; *ed:* (AB) Fr, 1971, (MS) Ed, 1977 IN Univ; *cr:* Fr Teacher Brown Cty HS 1973-; *ai:* Fr Honor Society; Trefle Francais Fr Club; Frosh Class Spon; AATF; St Marks Meth Church Sunday Sch Teacher; *office:* Brown County HS P O Box 68 Nashville IN 47448

RYAN, JANE F., 6th-8th Grade Soc Stud Teacher; *b:* Zanesville, OH; *ed:* (BS) Speech/Scndry Ed/Poly Sci, Rio Grande Coll 1972-; Elem Ed Cert Grad Courses OH Univ; *cr:* Substitute Teacher Morgan Local Schls 1972-75; 6th-8th Grade Soc Stud Teacher Windsor Elem 1975-; *ai:* NEA, OH Ed Assn, Morgan Local Ed Assn; Morgan Cty OH Historical Society; Morgan Camera Club Prgm Chm 1987, Numerous Photo Awds 1987-; Howard Chandler Christy Art Guild; Morgan Cty Republic Women; Grant Photo His Prgm; Fed Grant Money 1989-; *home:* 370 N Kennebec Ave Mc Connelsville OH 43756

RYAN, JOYE MOORMAN, Mathematics Teacher; *b:* Fayetteville, AR; *m:* Charlie Ray; *ed:* (BED) Math/Scndry Ed, Univ of AR 1985; Admin 1988; *cr:* 9th Grade Math/Advanced Placement Geometry/Algebra/Pre-Algebra Teacher Central Jr HS 1985-; *ai:* 7th & 8th Grade Girls Bsktbl Coach; Impact Comm Mem; ACTM Mem 1985-89; NEA Mem 1985-88; Nom Jaycee Young Educator Awd 1987-88; Nom Teacher of Yr 1989; *office:* Central Jr HS 2811 W Huntsville Springdale AR 72764

RYAN, JUDITH BELKNAP, Third Grade Teacher; *b:* Detroit, MI; *ed:* (BA) His, Marygrove Coll 1958; *cr:* Teacher Detroit Public Schls 1964-66, Our Lady Queen of Martyrs 1958-64, 1966-; *ai:* In Charge of Educl Supply Orders Our Lady Queen of Martyrs; Mem of Survey Comm at Our Lady Queen of Martyrs; NCEA Mem; The Joe Lynch Memorial Honor Roll Awd 1986; Participation Awd in Athletic Prgms; *office:* Our Lady Queen Of Martyrs 323460 Pierce Birmingham MI 48009

RYAN, KATHLEEN A., Social Studies Teacher; *b:* Chicago, IL; *ed:* (BA) Ed, Northeastern IL Univ 1974; *cr:* Soc Stud Teacher Dunbar Vocational HS 1976-82, Farragut Career Acad 1982-88, Dunbar Vocational HS 1988-; *office:* Dunbar Voe H S 3000 S King Dr Chicago IL 60616

RYAN, LORNA L., Resource/Program Specialist; *b:* Monterey Park, Los Angeles Cty; *ed:* (BA) Psych, CA St Long Beach 1974; (MA) Ed, CA St Los Angeles 1976; Resource Specialist Certificate, CA Luth; *cr:* Teacher 1st Luth Elem Sch 1976-79; LH Teacher El Monte Elem Schls 1979-81; Rsp/Prgm Specialist Lompoc Unified Shls 1981-; *ai:* Math, Lang Art, Soc Sci Task Force; Project Mentor; Staff Dev Liaison Comm; Lompoc Federated Teachers Temp Rep 1986-89; Impact II 1989, Grant Awd; Kappa Delta Pi Assn Mem 1977-; Impact II Teacher Grant; Panelist Teachers Convention 1989 Washington DC; Mentor Teacher 1988-; Lompoc Unified Sch Spec Ed Math Curr; Lang Art Task Force Mem; Soc Sci Task Force Mem; *office:* Lompoc Unified Sch Dist 1301 North A Street Vandenburg Village Lompoc CA 93436

RYAN, MAUREEN HOLMAN, 5th-8th Grade Science Teacher; *b:* New Haven, CT; *c:* Erin, Christopher; *ed:* (BS) IU Ed, 1972, (MS) Spec Ed, 1977 S Ct St Univ; *cr:* 5th-8th Grade Sci Teacher St Vincent De Paul Sch 1974-; *ai:* NHS Adv; Sci Fair Coord; *office:* St Vincent De Paul Sch 35 Bishop St East Haven CT 06512

RYAN, RICHARD D., Principal/Mathematics Teacher; *b:* Redondo Beach, CA; *m:* Joan L. Scott; *ed:* (BA) Phys Ed/Bio, CA St Univ Long Beach 1966; Grad Work Ed & Religion, Union Coll & Loma Linda Univ; *cr:* Teacher La Vida Mission Sch 1975-86, Intermountain Jr Acad 1986-89; Prin/Teacher Las Vegas Jr Acad 1989-; *ai:* 10th Grade Spon; Improving Quality of Ed for Native Amers Navajo Reservation; *office:* Las Vegas Jr Acad 6059 W Oakey Las Vegas NV 89102

RYAN, SUSAN ANDERSON, Third Grade Teacher; *b:* Jackson, MI; *m:* Bruce K.; *c:* Scott K.; *ed:* (BS) Ed, Miami Univ 1961; Grad Stud OH St Univ; *cr:* 4th Grade Teacher, Kndgtn Teacher 1970-80, 3rd Grade Teacher, Substitute Teacher Heath City Schls; *ai:* Building Chm of Retired Citizens Day; OH Ed Assn, NEA, Cntrl OH Teachers Assn, Heath Ed Assn Building Rep; 2nd Presbyn Church Session 1984-86; Alpha Phi Alumnae (Pres, Secy); *office:* Garfield Elem Sch 680 S 30th St Heath OH 43056

RYAN, SUZANNE POLMEAR, English Teacher; *b:* Pontiac, MI; *m:* Richard E.; *c:* Michael P., Martin J., Daniel E., Rebecca N.; *ed:* (BA) His/Eng, Margrove Coll 1967; (MS) Sociology, IL Inst Technology 1971; *cr:* Dept Chairperson/Teacher Providence St Mel HS 1971-74; Teacher De Paul Univ 1974-, Rosary Coll 1982-85, St Ignatius Coll Prep 1987-; *ai:* Chairperson N Cntrl Outcomes Assessment 1989-; Citizen Involvement Comm 1978; Cmmty Relations Comm 1979-81; League of Women Voters Chairperson 1979-83; Whos Who in Amer Ed 1972-74; Teacher of Yr De Paul Univ 1985; Teaching About our Pluralist Society; Curr Design De Paul Univ, Providence, St Mel HS, SICP; Natl Sci Fnd Grants Univ Co, N IL Univ, De Paul Univ; *office:* St Ignatius Coll Prep 1076 W Roosevelt Rd Chicago IL 60608

RYCOMBEL, THOMAS JAMES, 7th Grade English Teacher; *b:* Buffalo, NY; *ed:* (BA) Eng, Univ of Buffalo 1962; (EDM) Scndry Eng, St Univ of NY Buffalo 1966; Curr Dev Prgm; *cr:* Eng Teacher Niagara-Wheatfield Cntrl Schls 1962-79, Lauderdale Lakes Mid Sch 1979-80; Eng Teacher/Dept Chm Niagara-Wheatfield Cntrl Schls 1980-; *ai:* Sch Newspaper, Span Club, Poetry Contest Adv; Ski Club & Play Dir; Staff Dev Lang Art Project Coord; NY Eng Cncl, ASCD 1970; Buffalo Area Eng Teachers Assn 1960-70; Poetry Published 1988; Golden Poet Awd 1988; Consultant for Dist Video Public Relations Tape for Niagara-Wheatfield Schls; Project CUE NY St; *home:* 400 Getzville Rd Snyder NY 14226

RYDESKI, DONALD A., Science Teacher/Sci Dept Chair; *b:* Silver City, NM; *ed:* (BA) Scndry Ed, 1980; (MA) Sch Admin, 1990 W NM Univ 1990; *cr:* Teacher C C Snell Jr HS 1980-81, La Plata Mid Sch 1981-; *ai:* Stu Cncl Spon; Yrbk Adv; Sci Dept Chairperson; Dist Discipline Comm; Dist Family Life Ed Comm; NASSP, Phi Delta Kappa, NM Acts Assn; Silver City Main Street Project; Silver City Ofcls Assn Group Leader 1984-86; Amer Museum of Natural His; Nom NM Teacher of Yr 1984, 1985; Nom Presidential Awds for Excl Sci & Math 1985-; *office:* La Plata Mid Sch 2810 N Swan St Silver City NM 88061

RYE, JUDY CELINE, Fifth Grade Teacher; *b:* Phoenix, AZ; *m:* Leon O.; *c:* Scott, Leanne; *ed:* (BA) Elem Ed, 1976, (MA) Elem Ed, 1983 AZ St Univ; Grad Stud Gifted Ed, Curr, Future Problem Solving; *cr:* 3rd Grade Teacher 1976-84, 5th Grade Teacher 1984-85 Four Peaks Sch; 5th Grade Teacher Gold Canyon Elem Sch 1985-; *ai:* Stu Cncl Spon; Young Astronauts; Prins Advisory Comm; North Cntrl Accreditation; *home:* 2032 E Libra Tempe AZ 85283

RYHERD, ANN COLLINS, Computer/Science Teacher; *b:* Philadelphia, PA; *m:* Brian D.; *c:* Jonathan; *ed:* (BA) Scndry Ed, Concordia Coll 1984; *cr:* 5th Grade Teacher 1984-85, 5th-8th Grade Sci/Cmptr Teacher 1985- Pilgrim Luth; *ai:* Cmptr Club Spon; Cmptr Contest Coord; Spelling Bee Co-Spon; TCEA 1986-; *office:* Pilgrim Luth Sch 8601 Chimney Rock Rd Houston TX 77096

RYKOSKEY, CAROL KLEBER, Third Grade Teacher; *b:* Pittsburgh, PA; *c:* Ronald, Michael, Mark; *ed:* (BS) Ed, Duquesne Univ 1958; (MS) Counseling, Univ of Dayton 1979; *cr:* Learning Disability Tutor Kettering Schls 1974-75; 3rd Grade Teacher Croftshire & JF Kennedy Elem 1976-; *office:* John F Kennedy Elem Sch 5030 Polen Dr Kettering OH 45440

RYLANDER, JANET F., English Dept Chair; *b:* Brooklyn, NY; *m:* Thomas R. Sr.; *c:* Thomas Jr., Jennifer; *ed:* (BA) Eng, Coll of Chestnut Hill 1961; (MA) Hum, Hofstra Univ 1988; Admin, Supervision, S CT St Univ 1989; San Jose St Univ 1963; TESA Trng 1987; Hunter Model, 4-Mat Bernice Mc Carthy 1988; Columbia Univ Writing Inst 1990; *cr:* Eng Teacher South HS 1961-66, R H Brown Sch 1977-; *ai:* Self Evaluation Comm; Curr Co-Chairperson; Dist CORE Trng Stu Teacher, Mentor Prgm Interview Comm Chairperson; Literary Magazine Ed; ASCD, NCTE, NEATE; Scranton Public Lib Treas 1987-; Chestnut Hill Concerts Secy 1987-; CT St Grant Co-Writer Hum Course R H Brown Sch; S CT St Univ Grant Cty Revised Stu Teacher Course; Madison Ed Assn Negotiating Team; Coord Eng Dept; *office:* R H Brown Mid Sch 980 Durham Rd Madison CT 06443

RYMER, VICTORIA ANNETTE (BEEM), 5th Grade Teacher; *b:* Waukegan, IL; *m:* Richard Alan; *c:* Matthew, Michael, Mark; *ed:* (BSED) Elem Ed, N IL Univ 1968; Various Wkshps, Grad Courses, Seminars; *cr:* 5th Grade Teacher Beach Park Sch 1968-69, Mc Call Sch 1969-70, Lafe Nelson Elem 1970-71, Beach Park Sch 1978-; *ai:* Beach Park Educators; *home:* 1619 27th St Zion IL 60099

RYOR, RITA MILLSOM, 6-8th Grade Rdng/Lit Teacher; *b:* Saginaw, MI; *m:* George A.; *c:* Kathleen M., Amy E. Evans, Timothy A.; *ed:* (BS) Biological Sci, MI St Univ 1958; (MA) Rdng, Kean Coll of NJ 1975; Univ of CT; Natl Sci Fnd Fellowship Summer 1959; Supervision & Curr Dev Kean Coll 1980-81; Courses in Lib Sci/Information Stud Rutgers Univ 1987-; *cr:* Bio/Chem & General Sci Teacher Springfield HS 1958-60; 8th Grade Sci/Soc Stud Teacher Stafford HS 1960-61; Title I Rdng Teacher Fairmount Elem 1975-76; Rdng Teacher Eisenhower Mid Sch 1976-82, Hillside Mid Sch 1982-; *ai:* Asst to Drama Club Teacher; Coach for Knowledge Master Contest 1989-; Self-Esteem Comm in Building; Dist Comm for Evaluation of Enrichment Prgm; NEA/NJEA 1976-; Intnl Rdng Assn 1976-; Cntrl Jersey Cncl of IRA 1980-, Rdng Teacher of Yr 1988; NJ Rdng Teachers Assn 1980-; NJ Teachers of Gifted and Talented 1983-; Educl Media Assn of NJ 1987; Church of the Assumption Chm of Lectors 1975-; Cntrl Jersey Cncl of Intnl Rdng Assn; Teacher of Yr Rdng 1988; 8th Grade Stu Travel to Washington Dc Folger Lib Shakespeare Festival 1988; *office:* Hillside Mid Sch 844 Brown Rd Bridgewater NJ 08807

RYPKA, STEPHANIE G., Teacher of Academically Gifted; *b:* Baltimore, MD; *m:* Jay Michael; *c:* Birch R., Brook E.; *ed:* (BA) Elem Ed, W CT St Univ 1970; Trng in Gifted Ed & ITIP Coach; *cr:* 3rd Grade Teacher 1970-86, Teacher of Gifted & Talented 1987- Meeting House Hill Sch; *ai:* Dist & Building Staff Dev Cncl Mem; Peer Coach; Mentor for Best Prgm; W CT Assn of Gifted & Talented 1987-; ASCD 1989-; Celebration of Excl Awd 1986; *office:* Meeting House Hill Sch 24 Gillotti Rd New Fairfield CT 06812

RYSCAVAGE, MARY MC CLESKEY, Language Arts/Soc Stud Teacher; *b:* Americus, GA; *m:* Jerome James; *c:* Jeff, Kathryn, Susan; *ed:* (BA) Ed, Mercer Univ 1956; (MED) Ed, Auburn Univ 1959; *cr:* 6th Grade Teacher Arco Elem 1956-57; 7th Grade Teacher Paxton Jr HS 1957-59; Dean of Girls Escambia HS 1959-60; *ai:* NEA; *office:* Southern Mid Sch Broad Ford Rd Oakland MD 21550

RYTERSKI, CAMELLA (PARRETT), Middle School Science Teacher; *b:* Urbana, IL; *m:* Larry T.; *c:* Erin, Korrin, Lindsay; *ed:* (BS) Ed, IL St Univ 1969; (MED) Ed, Univ of IL 1972; *cr:* Sci Teacher Warrensburg-Latham Mid Sch 1969-; *ai:* Natl Jr Honor Society Spon; Warrensburg-Latham Ed Assn 1988-89; *home:* RR 8 Box 380A Decatur IL 62522

S

SABADAY, JOSEPH ANDREW, 7th/8th Grade Math/Sci Teacher; *b:* Pottsville, PA; *m:* Gail Arlene Yost; *ed:* (BS) Elem Ed, Kutztown St Univ 1977; Rdng Specialist Cert Bloomsburg St Univ 1980; *cr:* Substitute/4th Grade Teacher Minersville Area Sch Dist 1978-79; Rdng Specialist Saint Clair Area Sch Dist 1979-81; 7th-8th Grade Math/Rdng/Sci Teacher Holy Redeemer Sch 1984-; *ai:* Stu Preparation for Natl & Pottsville Republican Local Spelling Bee; Matheletes; Sci Fair Coord; Allentown Diocesan Lay Teachers Assn 1990; St Clair Lions 1977-78; Rescue Hook & Ladder 1972-80; *home:* 106 Broad St Saint Clair PA 17970

SABAN, JO ANN LOUISE, First Grade Teacher; *b:* Fairmont, WV; *ed:* (BA) Elem Ed, Fairmont St Coll 1969; (MS) Ed, WV Univ 1976; Grad Stud; *cr:* 1st-3rd Grade Teacher Burton Grade Sch 1969-79; 1st/2nd Grade Teacher Long Drain Sch 1979-; *ai:* NEA 1969-; WV Ed Assn (Building Rep 1979-80, Mem); WV Univ Alumni Assn, WV Sheriffs Assn; Parent Teacher Stu Assn (VP 1973, Mem); Croatian Union Life Mem; Polka Ambassadors 1988-; Burton Homemakers VP 1975-; St Marys Cath Church; *home:* 7th St Carolina WV 26563

SABATKA, CARRIE MORTELL, Math/Social Science Teacher; *b:* Appleton, WI; *m:* Tim; *c:* Rebecca; *ed:* (BA) Psych, E IL Univ 1984; *cr:* Teacher Ombudsman Educl Service 1985-86, Mc Henry HS East 1986-; *ai:* Frosh Vlybl & Boys & Girls Track Coach; *office:* Mc Henry East HS 1012 N Green St Mc Henry IL 60050

SABATO, MICHAEL JOSEPH, 7th Grade Science Teacher; *b:* Philadelphia, PA; *m:* Debra Lee Ingram; *c:* Rita M., Michael A., Andrea B.; *ed:* (BA) Elem Ed, Concordia Coll 1976; (MA) Soc Stud, Glassboro St Coll 1981; *cr:* 7th-8th Grade Sci/Math Teacher Edgewood Jr HS 1976-81; 9th-12th Grade Teacher/Prin Venetie HS 1981-82; 9th-12th Grade Teacher Arctic Village HS 1982-83; 7th-8th Grade Sci/Soc Stud Teacher Wendler Jr HS 1983-; *ai:* Wrestling, Track, Sftbl, Ftbl Coach; NSTA 1988-; Anchorage Ed Assn (Building Rep, Rep at Large 1987-, Faculty Rep & Bargaining Comm 1987-88); Amer Society for Microbiology 1986, Certificate of Commendation 1986; AK Sci & Engineering Fair Comm Organizing Comm 1986-89; Nuwaka Valley Little League Bd of Dir 1985-88; Jr Achievement Project Bus Teacher 1984-85, Citation of Merit 1984-85; Anchorage Sch Dist Certificates of Appreciation 1987-; *home:* 2351 Paxson Dr Anchorage AK 99504

SABBATINI, TONI ELEN, Spanish Tutor; *b:* Rome, Italy; *ed:* (BA) Span - Cum Laude, 1980, (MED) Scndry Ed, 1985 Valdosta St Coll; Univ of Madrid 1984 & Univ of Salamanca 1978; *cr:* Span Teacher Westfield Schls 1985-88; Span Tutor All About Learning 1990; *ai:* Sigma Alpha Chi, Alpha Chi, Sigma Delta Pi, Cardinal Key; Amer Assn Teachers of Span & Portuguese 1987-; *home:* 3400G Chelsea Park Ln Norcross GA 30092

SABINA, FRANK JAMES, English/French Teacher; *b:* Scranton, PA; *m:* Veronica Griebel; *c:* Jeffrey, Lauren, Gregory; *ed:* (BS) Fr, E Stroudsburg Univ 1973; (BS) Eng, Marywood Coll 1975; Grad Stud Eng, Fr; Masters Equivalency; *cr:* Fr/Eng Teacher Carbondale Area Sch Dist 1973-; *ai:* Adv Fr Club, Newspaper, Drama Club 1990; NE Writing Cncl (Secy, Newsletter Ed) 1988; NCTE, PSEA; NE PA Writing Project Fellowship; Published Author; Whos Whos Among Amer Writers, Editors & Poets; *office:* Carbondale Area Jr-Sr HS Rt 6 Carbondale PA 18407

SABO, CYNTHIA L., Art Teacher; *b:* Wilmington, DE; *c:* Thomas A., Jennifer E.; *ed:* (BA) Art Ed, 1984, Elem Ed, 1984 Wright St Univ; Grad Stud Art Ed; *cr:* 8th Grade Math/Rdng Teacher 1984-85, 8th Grade Rdng Teacher 1985-89, 6Th-8th Grade Art Teacher 1989- New Carlisle Mid Sch; *ai:* Stu Cncl Adv; *office:* New Carlisle Mid Sch 1203 S Kennison Dr New Carlisle OH 45344

SABO, JUDITY M. (BURGER), Biology Teacher; *b:* Allentown, PA; *m:* James M.; *c:* Jenine, Mary K.; *ed:* (BS) Eng, Kent St Univ 1971; Sci, Univ of Akron; *cr:* Eng/Bio Teacher 1972-77, Bio Teacher 1988- Rittman HS; *ai:* Stu Cncl Adv; Three Art Club Pres 1984-85; Northeast OH Dance Ensemble Bd of Trustees 1988-; *office:* Rittman HS 100 Saurer St Rittman OH 44270

SABOL, DAVID, Mathematics Dept Chair; *b:* Beaver Meadows, PA; *m:* Lynn Ann Lechleitner; *c:* Stephanie; *ed:* (BS) Math, Kings Coll 1978; *cr:* Math Teacher Nativity BVM HS 1978-; *ai:* Athletic Dir; PA St Athletic Dirs Assn; *office:* Nativity BVM HS Lawtons Hill Pottsville PA 17901

SABOL, LUCINDA MAHOLICK, First Grade Teacher; *b:* Palmerton, PA; *m:* Joseph P.; *ed:* (BS) Elem Ed, E Stroudsburg Univ 1973; (MED) Elem Ed, Lehigh Univ 1976; Writing Process Courses; Primary Ed Wkshps; Whole Lang Courses & Wkshps; *cr:* 1st Grade Teacher Lehighton Area Sch Dist; *ai:* 6th Grade Scholastic Scrimmage Adv, Area Winner; Lehighton Area Ed Assn Building Rep 1973-; PA St Ed Assn, NEA 1973-; Bus & Prof Womans Club (Secy 1976, 1987-89, 1st VP 1989-, Dist Secy 1981-83), Dist Young Careetist Awd; PTO Teacher Rep; Experimental Pre-1st Grade Summer Sch Prgm Grant Temple Univ; *office:* Franklin Sch 1122 Fairyland Rd Lehighton PA 18235

SACCOMAN, STEFANIE ANN, Science Teacher/Dept Chair; *b:* San Francisco, CA; *ed:* (BS) Bio, 1976, (MA) Ed, 1980 CA Polytechnic Univ Pomona; *cr:* Environmental Scientist Engineering Sci Incorporated 1977-82; Sci Teacher 1983-, Mentor Teacher/Dept Chairperson 1987- Pasadena HS; *ai:* Class Adv 1983-87; CA Schlsp Fed Co-Adv 1988-; 10th Grade Restructuring Comm 1989-; Phi Delta Kappa Mem 1987-; St of CA Grant Inst for Cellular Molecular Bio CA Polytechnic Univ Pomona; Outstanding Young Woman of America 1981; Verdugo Hills Hospital Distinguished Teacher Awd 1988; *office:* Pasadena HS 2925 E Sierra Madre Blvd Pasadena CA 91107

SACHITANO, SHELIA LOUVIERE, English/French Teacher; *b:* Austin, TX; *m:* Fred C. Jr.; *c:* Derek; *ed:* (BA) Fr/Eng, Univ of TX Austin 1970; (MA) Eng, Lamar Univ 1975; *cr:* Teacher Anahvac HS 1970-76, Hamshire-Fannett HS 1978-; *ai:* Fr Club Spon; UIL Prose; Career Ladder Comm; TSTA Pres 1985-87; Assn of Curr & Supervision; Daughters of Amer Revolution; the Damours De Louvieres in France/Canada/LA; Pres Modern Electric Company of Beaumont Incorporated.

SACHLIS, CONSTANCE KOGER, Reading Specialist; *b:* Bassett, VA; *m:* Richard C.; *c:* Tommy Kraus; *ed:* (BS) Elem Ed/Psych, Carson-Newman Coll 1963; (MA) Curr/Instruction, Memphis St Univ 1967; Post Grad Rdng, Memphis St Univ 1968; *cr:* 3rd Grade Teacher South Park Elem 1963-67; Rdng Teacher Colonial Heights Jr HS 1967-68; Asst Professor Gulf Coast Comm Coll 1968-70; 2nd Grade Teacher S Bryan Jennings Sch 1970-71; Asst Professor Gulf Coast Comm Coll 1971-73; Rdng Specialist Waynesboro HS 1973-; *ai:* NHS Adv; VA St Rdng Assn, Natl Rdng Assn 1973-; NEA 1980-; *office:* Waynesboro HS 1200 W Main St Waynesboro VA 22980

SACK, RONALD P., Marketing/Co-Op Teacher; *b:* Flint, MI; *m:* Barbara Lynn; *c:* Stephannie, Ryan; *ed:* (BBE) Mrktg Ed, E MI Univ 1970; (MA) Scndry Ed, Univ of MI 1976; *cr:* Mrktg Ed Teacher Flint Northern HS 1970-76, Flint Southwestern HS 1976-88, Flint Southwestern Acad 1988-; *ai:* Distributive Ed Clubs of America Adv; Wrote Music & Lyrics for Sch Fight Song; Youth Bsbl Coach; *home:* 3233 Norwood Dr Flint MI 48503

SACKET, BILLY RAY, JR., 6th/7th Grade Science Teacher; *b:* Alva, OK; *m:* Barbara Ann Burkes; *c:* Michael, Jeremy, Sherry; *ed:* (BAED) Soc Sci, NW OK St Univ 1975; *cr:* 6th Grade Sci Teacher Abilene Mid Sch 1975-77; 5th Grade Contained Teacher 1977-79, 6th/7th Grade Teacher 1979- Chamberlain Mid Sch; *ai:* St of OK Curr Test Review Comm; Tri-Sch Sci Telecommunications Cooperative Spon; OK St Dept of Ed Post-Scndry Teacher Ed Prgms Evaluators Mem; Abilene Ed Assn 1975-77; KS Ed Assn Delegate 1975-77; Fairview Teachers Assn (Pres 1980) 1977-83; Major Cty Ed Assn (Pres Elect 1981, Pres 1982) 1977-83; OK Ed Assn Mem 1977-; NEA Mem 1975-; Fairview Ed Assn Mem 1984-; OK Sci Teachers Assn Mem 1986-; Aline City Cncl Bd Mem 1972-75; Aline Volunteer Fire Dept Mem 1973-75; Fairview Breakfast Lion Club (Secy, Treas) 1978-79; Fairview BSA Webelos Leader 1979; Aline Lions Club (Pres 1986) 1985-; Aline Public Works Authority Water & Waste Water Operator 1984-; Aline-Cleo T-Ball Summer Prgm Coach 1986-89; Aline Chrstn Church (Elder 1988-, Sunday Sch Supt 1985-89, Asst Sunday Sch Supt 1989-, Ed Comm Chm 1988); Aline Alumni Assn (Pres 1989) 1971-; Nom Fairview Teacher of Yr 1980; Fairview Teacher of Yr 1981, 1988; Major Cty Teacher of Yr 1981; Finalist OK Presidential Awds Excl in Sci Teaching 1985; Nom OK Fnd for Excl Gold Medal Excl in Teaching 1987; Dissemination of Information Grant 1987; Finalist OK St Teacher of Yr 1988; Nom Presidential Awd Excl in Sci Teaching 1989; Outstanding Ed Grad NW OK St Univ 1990; Named to KOCO-TV5 Project Challenge 1990; *home:* PO Box 134 Aline OK 73716

SACKETT, BEVERLY A. STEVENS, Sixth Grade Teacher; *b:* Meadville, PA; *m:* Gary T.; *c:* Todd; *ed:* (BS) Elem Ed, Edinboro St Coll 1969; *cr:* 4th Grade Teacher Conneaut Sch Dist 1969-70; Bus Teacher Randolph HS 1972-73; 5th-6th Grade Teacher Randolph Elem 1973-84; 6th Grade Teacher Maplewood Mid 1984-; *ai:* PAEA, NEA 1969-; Amer Diabetes Assn 1969-; *office:* Penncrest Sch Dist Maplewood Sch RD 1 Townville PA 16360

SACKMAN, JOAN V., Third Grade Teacher; *b:* Glens Falls, NY; *m:* Edward James; *c:* Barbara Graham, E. J. III; *ed:* (BS) Elem Ed, SUNY Plattsburgh 1953; Comparative Ed Stud in Russia/Kenya; *cr:* 2nd Grade Teacher North Colonie Cntrl Sch 1954-59; 3rd Grade Teacher Schuylerville Cntrl Sch 1967-; *ai:* Schuylerville Teacher Assn Secy 1957-58; NYS United Teachers; America Assn of Univ Women Corresponding Secy 1980-82; I Touch the Future I Teacher Awd Girl Scouts in Memory of Christa Mc Auliffe; *home:* 550 Rt 32 Schuylerville NY 12871

SACOMAN, PATRICIA J. GONZALES, Math Teacher; *b:* Alamosa, CO; *m:* Guadalupe A.; *c:* Ernest, Angela; *ed:* (BA) Math/Span/Scndry Ed, Adams St 1964; (MS) Math/Span/Scndry Ed, Univ of NM 1972-; Ed Admin, San Diego St Univ 1981; *cr:* Math/Span Teacher Pojoaque Valley Schls 1964-69; Math Teacher Seattle Schls 69-70; Los Lunas Consolidated Schls 70-71; Calexico Unified 71-81; Albuquerque Public Schls 81-; *ai:* Drama; Pep; Student Council; FTA; Chrldrs Class; Sr Spon; Math/Span Club; Dir of Stu Store and Acad Decath Coach; NTCM; Albuq Cncl Math Teachers; Teacher Fed; *home:* 13508 Witcher NE Albuquerque NM 87112

SACRE, IDA BUPPERT, Lang Art Teacher/Vice Prin; *b:* Hobson, VA; *w:* Emil A. (dec); *c:* Karen Sacre Al-Bahloly, Gail Sacre Rodriguez, Sam E.; *ed:* (BA) Eng, Incarnate Word Coll 1969; Prospective Cath Admin Prgm 1988-; *cr:* Substitute Teacher 1962-63, 5th Grade Teacher 1964-67, 8th Grade Teacher 1967-70,

7th Grade Teacher 1970-72, 8th Grade Teacher 1972-, Vice Prin 1985- St Gregory the Great; *ai:* Spon Stu Cncl; Moderator Speech Club; NCEA Mem 1990; PTA 2nd VP 1960-61; PTC Club (2nd VP 1961-62, Treas 1963-64).

SADEGHPOUR, MARGARET PLATTENBERGER, 4th-6th Grade Science Teacher; *b:* Cedar Rapids, IA; *c:* Mitra, Cameron; *ed:* (BSED) Bio/General Sci, NE MO St Univ 1965; Elem Cert Elem Ed, Univ of IA 1980; (MSED) Sci/Writing, Marycrest Coll 1988; PHD Prgm Sci Ed, Univ of IA; *cr:* Eng Teacher Iran Amer Society 1968-69; Jr HS Sci Teacher 1969-70, Elem Music Teacher 1970-71, 5th Grade Self-Contained Teacher 1971-72 Tehran Amer Sch; Teacher Tokyo Union Pre-Sch 1974-76; 1st/3rd Grade Teacher Iran Zamin Intnl 1977-79; Sci Teacher Lincoln Elem 1980-; *ai:* Young Astronauts Club; Performance-Based Pay, Wellness, ISEA-LEA Grievance, Sch Advisory Comms; Delta Kappa Gamma Research Chairperson 1984-; Jones Cty Conservation Ed Comm VP 1988-, Schlsps 1986-87; Century Club Conservation Chairperson 1982-, Conservation Awds 1984-89, 1st in St 1990; Cedar Cty Soil Conservation Comm 1982-; IA Acad of Sci 1987-; Church 1979-; Cub Scouts 1982-87; Brownies 1976-79; IA Wildlife Fed; Rainforest Alliance; Jones Cty Resource Enhancement & Protection Comm Secy; Cmmty Theater (VP, Dept Chairperson, Production Asst); IA Writers Project Conference Papers Presenter; IA Acad of Sci & IA Math/Sci Teacher Conference; Nom Presidential Awd Excl in Teaching Sci; IA Conservation Teacher of Yr; Outstanding Conservation Teacher of IA & Cty 1983; Cedar Cty Conservation Teacher of Yr; Allis Chalmers Conservation Awd Nominee; *office:* Lincoln Elem Sch Mechanicsville IA 52306

SADLER, JOHN WAVLEY, JR., Teacher of Academically Gifted; *b:* Henderson, NC; *m:* Jane Powell; *c:* John-Caleb W., Michael D.; *ed:* (AB) Eng Ed, Univ of NC Chapel Hill 1973; Pursuing Masters Degree in Mid Grades Ed, NC St Univ Raleigh; *cr:* Teacher of Academically Gifted Henderson Jr HS 1973-; *ai:* Exceptional Childrens Dept Head; Sch Based Comm Chairperson; Raising Stu Aspirations Comm; Phi Delta Kappa Newsletter Ed 1986-87; Peaces Chapel Baptist Church Deacon 1979-; Vance Cty Teacher of Yr 1978; Dist 11 Teacher of Yr 1978; NC St Teacher of Yr Competition 1978; Outstanding Young Educator Vancy Cty Jaycees 1978; Vance Cty Mini Grant 1989; Capital Area Writing Project Fellow 1989; *office:* Henderson Jr HS 219 Charles St Henderson NC 27536

SADLER, REBECCA MC AFEE, Chemistry Teacher; *b:* Nashville, AR; *m:* Henry Davis Jr.; *c:* Kristen, Kaitlin; *ed:* (BA) Chem, Univ of AR Fayetteville 1980; *cr:* Research Asst Natl Center for Toxicological Research 1979; Dir SE AR Medical Information Center 1980-83; Sci Teacher White Hall Jr HS 1986-87; Chem Teacher Pine Bluff HS 1987-; *ai:* Odyssey of Mind Coach; Sci Fair Adv; Secy Sci Dept; Interdisciplinary Team of Teachers Mem; AR Sci Teachers Assn 1988-; Arts Center for SE AR Performing Arts Comm 1986-; Lakeside Meth Church Youth Cnslr 1981-; Center Stage Players (Secy 1988) 1987-; *office:* Pine Bluff HS 711 W 11th Ave Pine Bluff AR 71601

SADLER, SHEILA HUDSPETH, First Grade Teacher; *b:* Jacksonville, TX; *m:* Robert E.; *c:* Ryan, Kirk; *ed:* (AA) Lon Morris Coll 1971; (BS) Elem Ed/Rdng, Stephen F Austin 1972; (MS) Rdng, Univ of TX Tyler 1983; *cr:* 1st Grade Teacher East Side Elem 1973-; *ai:* Phi Theta Kappa 1970-71; Kappa Delta Pi 1971-72; Alpha Chi 1972-74; Delta Kappa Gamma Corresponding Secy 1986; *office:* East Side Elem Sch 711 Ft Worth Jacksonville TX 75766

SADLER, SHERARD MICHAEL, 8th Grade History Teacher; *b:* Pecos, TX; *m:* Helen; *ed:* Health/Phys Ed/His, 1979, Driver Ed, 1989 Sul Ross St Univ; *cr:* 9th Grade Asst Ector Jr HS 1979-82; 8th Grade Head Ftbl/9th Grade Head Bsktbl Coach 1982-89, 9th Grade Head Ftbl Coach 1990 Hood Jr HS; *ai:* Hood Jr HS Fellowship Chrstn Athletes Spon; TSTA 1988-; THSCA 1979-; Omega Psi Phi Mem 1984-; ECISD 10 Yr Service Awd; *office:* Hood Jr HS PO Box 3912 Odessa TX 79762

SADLO, MARY HEMKER, 4th Grade Teacher; *b:* Richmond Heights, MO; *m:* Edward G.; *ed:* (BSED) Ed/Eng, St Thomas Aquinas Coll 1967; (MAED) Ed/Soc Stud, WA Univ 1973; Grad Work Counseling Psych, Lindenwood Coll; *cr:* 6th Grade Teacher Manchester & Parkway 1967-70; 4th-6th Grade Teacher Clayton Woods & Parkway 1970-77; 6th Grade Teacher Warren Cty R-222 1977-79; 4th/5th Grade Teacher Winfield Intermediate 1979-; *ai:* Winfield CTA, MO Ed Assn; *office:* Winfield Intermediate Sch 6th & Elm * Winfield MO 63389

SADOWSKI, KEN J., Teacher; *b:* Milwaukee, WI; *m:* Jane Marie Murphy; *c:* Lara, Lisa, Lynn, Luke; *ed:* (BA) His/Eng, Dominion Coll 1972; (MA) Ed, Univ of WI Whitewater 1981; *cr:* Teacher/Coach St Catherines 1972-73, Marquette University HS 1973-75, St John Military Acad 1977-78, Waterford Union HS 1978-89; *ai:* St Coaches Assn 1980-84; *home:* W 327 S 6774 Westgate Dr Mukwonago WI 53149

SAFFORD, EUNICE A., 5th Grade Teacher; *b:* Berlin, WI; *ed:* (BSE) Ed, Mt Mary Coll 1958; (MED) Ed, Cardinal Stritch Coll 1988; *cr:* 2nd Grade Teacher St Alphonsus 1948-50, St Elizabeth 1951-55; 1st-3rd Grade Teacher St Josephs 1955-58; 3rd Grade Teacher St Aloysius 1958-60; 6th Grade Teacher Rudolph WI 1960-62; 4th/6th Grade Teacher Elm Grove WI 1962-63; 4th-6th Grade Teacher Port Washington WI 1963-68; 6th-8th Grade Teacher Fredonia WI 1968-72; 5th Grade Teacher West Bend WI 1972-; *ai:* Dist Rdng Curr Comm; Assn for Curr Dev, Intnl Rdng Assn 1982-; NEA 1972-; WI Ozaukee Rdng Cncl 1980-; West Bend Ed Assn Secy 1978-80; YMCA 1985-; Implementation Grant; *office:* Barton Elem Sch 614 School Pl West Bend WI 53095

SAGE, LINDA MARY, Spanish Teacher; *b:* Chicago, IL; *m:* Victor; *c:* Jennifer, Jacquelyn, Adam; *ed:* (BA) Span, Univ IL 1973; Completing Masters in Educl ADmin; Pursuing Type 75 Cert; *cr:* Span & Eng Teacher Cntrl Comm Unit Dist #4 1973-78; Span Teacher Crete-Monee Dist 201-U 1978-; *ai:* IFLTA Mem; Honored Natl Jr Honor Society Deer Creek Jr HS *home:* 3642 Elm Ct Flossmoor IL 60422

SAGEN, JUDY, Vocal Music Teacher; *b:* Virginia, MN; *m:* Michael Atherton; *c:* Brent Atherton, Amy Atherton; *ed:* (BME) Music Ed, Drake Univ 1975; (MME) Music Ed, Univ of MN 1990; *cr:* Vocal Music Dir Valley Mid Sch 1975-80, Rosemount HS 1980-89, Eagan HS 1989-; *ai:* Dir ENCORE; Music Dir Sch Musicals & Summer Cmmty Productions; Mu Phi Epsilon (VP 1974) 1975-89; Outstanding Mu Phi 1975; Phi Kappa Lambda 1971-75; Amer Choral Dirs Assn; MN Music Educators Assn; Nom Teacher of Yr Valley Mid Sch 1978-79; *office:* Eagan HS 4185 Braddock Tr Eagan MN 55123

SAGER, DONNA L., French Teacher; *b:* St Louis, MO; *ed:* (BA) Eng/Fr, Univ of TX San Antonio 1980; Working Towards Masters Modern Lang, SW Tx St Univ; WIN Writing Inst; Fr Summer Inst 1988, 1989; *cr:* Fr/Eng Teacher West Campus HS 1984-85; Eng/Dance Teacher Roosevelt HS 1985-86; Fr/Eng Teacher John Marshall HS 1986-; *ai:* Fr Club Asst Spon; Cooperative Learning Seminar; Eng II Curr Writer; John Marshall HS Action Planning Comm; TFLA Convention Presenter 1989-; TFLA, AATF 1986-; San Antonio Little Theatre Performer 19845-85; Alamo city Theatre Performer 1989-; NSISD Certificate of Recognition 1989-; Roosevelt HS Certificate of Recognition 1985-86; Fr Summer Inst Grant 1988, 1989; *office:* John Marshall HS 8000 Lobo Ln San Antonio TX 78240

SAGER, NORMAN EUDEAN, Science Teacher; *b:* Sewal, IA; *m:* Pamela Lynne Woods; *c:* Sarah, Anne, Martha, David; *ed:* (GE) General, Trenton Jr Coll 1968; (AB) Zoology, Univ of MO Columbia 1971; (MS) Bio, NW MO St Univ 1972; *cr:* Sci Teacher W Nodaway Schls 1972-73, Princeton Schls 1973-74, Winston Schls 1974-76, Trenton R-9 Schls 1976-; Part-Time Bio Instr N Cntrl MO Coll 1981-; *ai:* NSTA, MSTA, MACJC; Trenton Ball Assn (Pres 1988-, VP 1987-88); Masonic Lodge; Interface Steering Comm; *office:* Trenton R-IX Schls 1312 E 9th Trenton MO 64683

SAGER, RENA, 4th Grade Teacher; *b:* Newark, NJ; *cr:* Elem Teacher Dennis B O Brien Sch 1970-; *ai:* NJEA, NEA, Morris Cty Ed Assn; *home:* 100 Vail Rd E11 Parsippany NJ 07054

SAGONA, BARBARA JOAN SEPASHE, 6th Grade Mathematics Teacher; *b:* Pricedale, PA; *m:* Andrew L.; *c:* Lisa L., Ellen S.; *ed:* Grad Certificate Advanced Stenographic, Robert Morris Coll 1959; (BS) Elem Ed, California Univ of PA 1970; Grad Courses WV Univ 1973 & California Univ of PA; Undergrad Courses California Univ of PA; *cr:* Draft Bd Clerk US Selective Service System 1958-66; Teacher Clark Sch & WA Park Mid Sch 1970-; *ai:* Delta Kappa Gamma (Historical Records Chm, Membership) 1978-; WA Ed Assn PACE 1971-; Confraternity of Chrstn Mothers 1986-; Colleg Club 1982-84; Selective Service System Certificate of Appreciation 1960, 1964.

SAGRAVES, MARY ANNE (BOKAN), Language Art Teacher; *b:* Toledo, OH; *m:* Allan Todd; *c:* Scott G., Ann D.; *ed:* (BA) Elem Ed, Univ of N CO Greeley 1959; (MS) Elem Ed, Cntrl CT St Univ 1970; *cr:* Teacher A Leo Weil Sch 1960-61, Substitute Teacher New Britain Public Schls 1961-76; Teacher Stanley Campus Sch 1974-77, St Francis of Assisi Sch 1977-; *ai:* Natl Jr Honor Society Adv; Faculty Rep; Exec Bd; St Francis Home Sch Assn; CT Ed Assn, NEA Mem; YWCA (Mem 1969-, Bd of Dir) 1973-75; YMCA (Mem, Bd of Dir) 1982-84; Numerous Cmmty Organizations Mem; *office:* St Francis of Assisi Sch 30 Pendleton Rd New Britain CT 06053

SAHAGIAN, JANET HELEN, Vocal/Choral Music Director; *b:* Milwaukee, WI; *ed:* (BFA) Music Ed, Univ of WI-Milw 1979; (MEDP) Ed, Univ of WI-La Crosse 1989; Reality Therapy Cert, Univ of WI-La Crosse 1988; *cr:* Music Dir Irving Elem 1980; Choir Dir South St Paul Jr HS 1981-82; Vocal/Choral Music Dir Longfellow Mid Sch; *ai:* Show Choir Dir; Curr Comm; Dist Act Cncl; MENC 1979-; ACDA 1979-; *office:* Longfellow Mid Sch 1900 Denton St La Crosse WI 54601

SAILE, ROBERTA CHARLTON, Special Education Teacher; *b:* Philadelphia, PA; *ed:* (BS) Spec Ed, Penn St Univ 1976; *cr:* Sp 1 Teacher Woodhaven Center 1977-79; L & A Teacher Indian Crest Jr HS 1979-86; Learning Disabilities Teacher Souderton HS 1986-; *ai:* Class Spon & Adv 1987-; Stu Government Adv 1984-87; CEC 1990; *office:* Souderton Area HS 41 N School Ln Souderton PA 18964

SAILER, PHILIP PATRICK, Social Studies Teacher; *b:* St Augustine, IL; *m:* Margaret Frances Tornabane; *c:* Mary J. Marriott, Lisa A. Wilkens, Christine C. Nurenburg, Patricia J.; *ed:* (BS) Phys Ed/His, 1959, (MSED) Counseling/Guidance, 1974 W IL Univ; *cr:* Teacher/Coach St Edmond HS 1959-63; Ftbl Coach St Ambrose Coll 1980-84; Teacher/Coach Alleman HS 1963-; *ai:* Frosh Ftbl & Girls Track Head Coach; *home:* 2544 28th Ave Rock Island IL 61201

SAILES, MICHEAL EDWARD, Business Department Chairman; *b:* Chicago, IL; *m:* Rosa M. Jordan; *ed:* (BS) Bus Ed, Chicago St Univ 1968; (MS) Accounting, Roosevelt Univ 1976; Bus Technology, N IL Univ; *cr:* Cnslr 1974-77, Teacher 1969- Carver Area HS; *ai:* Stu Cnsl & Honors Spon; Var Ftbl & Bsktbl Asst Coach; Var Bowling Head Coach; Steering Comm Chm; Bus Prof of America-IL Bd of Dirs; Chicago Bus Ed Assn Treas 1988-89; Bus Prof of Amer-Chicago Comptroller 1986-; St John Baptist Church Finance Secy 1985-; Kate Maremont Dedicated Teacher Awd Chicago Region PTA 1983; Blum Kovler Outstanding Teacher Awd Univ of Chicago 1984; Outstanding Teacher Waste Management of IL 1985; *office:* G W Carver Area HS 13100 S Doty Rd Chicago IL 60627

SAILLER, ROBERT J., English Teacher; *b:* Kansas City, KS; *ed:* (BA) Eng, Rockhurst Coll; Ed, Univ of KS; *cr:* Eng Teacher Immaculata HS 1980-84, Mission Valley HS 1984-86, Eudora HS 1986-; *ai:* Head Boys Bsktbl Coach; Images Adv; 8th Grade Spon; KS Bsktbl Coaches, NEA, Fellowship of Chrstn Athletes; NCTE; Founding Father of Cardinal Shooting Clinic; Foul Tips Weekly Column Author; Awarded Title of The Stus Friend; *home:* 736 Acorn Eudora KS 66025

SAIN, LLOYD, 7th Grade English Teacher; *b:* Forrest City, AR; *ed:* (BSE) Eng, 1985, (MSE) Eng, 1990 Univ of Central AR; *cr:* Eng Forrest City Mid Sch 1985-; *ai:* Jr Beta Club, Head Spon; Dist Evaluation Mem; Pet Classroom Mgmt Trainer; FCEA/NEA Bldg Rep 1985-88; Spirit Awd 1989; FCMS Favorite Teacher 1988-; Nu Alpha Phi Spon Outstanding Young Men of America 1986; *home:* 630 Christian St Forrest City AR 72335

SAIN, PAUL E., Sixth Grade Teacher; *b:* Salt Lake City, UT; *m:* Sheryl Ann Woodward; *c:* Christopher P., Melody A.; *ed:* (BA) Sociology, Univ of UT 1970; (MED) Ed, Westminster Coll 1981; *cr:* Teaching Fellow Univ of UT 1973-77; Sch Dist Consultant Jordan Sch Dist 1975, 1977-78; In Service Instr Salt Lake Sch Dist 1977, 1981-83; 5th Grade Teacher Parkview Elem 1978-83; Sch Dist Consultant Various Sch Dist 1980-83; 5th Grade Teacher Rose Park Elem Sch 1983-84; 6th Grade Teacher Nibley Park Elem Sch 1984-85, Rose Park Elem Sch 1985-; *ai:* Traffic Patrol, Math & Sci Club Adv; Sight-Based & Dist Maturation Comm Mem; Instr of Advanced Parenting Class for Children at Risk; Conductor of Nutty Band; NEA, UT Ed Assn Mem 1978-; Salt Lake Teachers Assn (Sch Rep 1987-88, Mem 1978-); UT St Republican Convention Delegate 1986; Teaching Fellowship Univ of UT 1973-77; Co-Authored Elem Ed Art Methods Text for Univ of UT; Written Math & Health Curr for Salt Lake Sch Dist; Ethics & Math Specialist for Salt Lake Sch Dist; *home:* 1524 E 3900 S Salt Lake City UT 84124

SAINER, PAUL ANTHONY, Director of Bands; *b:* Blue Island, IL; *m:* Karen Marie Eidman; *ed:* (BS) Music Ed, Univ of IL Champaign/Urbana 1982; *cr:* Dir of Instr Music Acad of Art/Music/Dance & Theatre of Chicago 1982-83; Dir of Bands Hillsboro HS 1983-85, Harrison HS 1985-; *ai:* Dept Head, Fine Arts Dept; Marching & Jazz Band; Building Accountability Comm; Electronic Music Sound Production; Phi Mu Alpha Prof 1979-83; Pikes Peak Music Educators Assn Pres 1988-; Harrison Band CO Rep Natl Independence Day Parade Washington DC 1989; Several Compositions Published; *office:* Harrison HS 2755 Janitell Rd Colorado Springs CO 80906

ST. AUBIN, SHEILA KATHERINE, Principal; *b:* Temple, TX; *m:* Donald; *ed:* (BA) Fr, W IL Univ 1967; (MSED) Admin, N IL Univ 1978; (MS) Management/Dev of Human Resources, Natl Coll of Ed 1989; *cr:* 3rd Grade Teacher Fairview Elem 1967-70; 2nd Grade Teacher 1973-81, Asst Prin 1981-83 Ellis Elem; Prin W J Murphy Elem 1983-; *ai:* IL Prin Assn 1990; Delta Kappa Gamma 1986-; Lake Cty Resource Cncl; Articles Published; *office:* W J Murphy Elem Sch 220 N Greenwood Round Lake IL 60073

ST.CLAIR, ALBERT LEE, Math Teacher; *b:* Williamstown, MO; *m:* Louise June Harvey; *c:* Heather L., Melanie K; *ed:* (BSE) Math, Northeast MO St Univ 1969; *cr:* 8th-12th Grade Math Teacher Linn Cty 1971-72; 7th-8th Grade Math Teacher Lewis Cty C-1 Schls 1972-76; 8th-10th Grade Math Teacher Clark Cty R-1 Schls 1976-; *ai:* MO St Teachers Assn; Clark Cty Teachers Assn; Amer Simmental Assn; MO CattleMens Assn; *office:* Clark County R-1 H S 427 W Chestnut St Kahoka MO 63445

ST. CLAIR, GERRI GILBERT, Chemistry Teacher; *b:* Kingsport, TN; *m:* Robert Alan; *ed:* (BS) Sci Ed, Univ of TN Knoxville 1983; (MED) Educl Policy/Leadership, E TN St Univ 1990; *cr:* Chem Teacher Sullian South HS 1984-; *ai:* Sci Honor Society Spon; NSTA 1988-; ACS Ed Division 1986-, Certificates for Placing Candidates in Natls of ACS Olympiad 1988-; Jazzercise Franchisee 1987-; *office:* Sullivan South HS Rt 17 Moreland Dr Kingsport TN 37664

ST. CLAIR, JO (DIAZ), 8th Grade English Teacher; *b:* Dayton, OH; *c:* Shawn L., Matthew S.; *ed:* (BS) Eng, Bowling Green St Univ 1977; Working Towards Masters Elem Ed, Bowling Green St Univ 1991; *cr:* Eng Teacher Bowling Green Jr HS 1979-82, Otsego Jr HS 1982-83, Bowling Green Jr HS 1983-; *ai:* Bowling Green City Schls Cmptr Comm 1989; 7th Grade Vlybl Coach 1980, 1981, 1985; NEA, OH Cncl Teachers of Eng & Lang Art 1990; Bowling Green Ed Assn Jr HS Rep; *office:* Bowling Green Jr HS 215 W Wooster Bowling Green OH 43402

ST. CLAIR, MARY ALICE, 2nd Grade Elementary Teacher; *b:* Marshall, MO; *m:* M. Franklin; *c:* Andy, Will; *ed:* (MA) Elem Ed, 1989, (BSE) Elem Ed, 1977 NE MO St Univ; *cr:* 2nd Grade Teacher New Florence Elem Sch 1978-81, Brookfield R-III Elem 1981-; *ai:* Elem Sci Club Co-Spon; MO St Teachers Assn, Brookfield Cmmty Teachers Assn; Beta Sigma Phi City Cncl Pres 1989-; Trinity United Meth Church Admin Cncl 1989-; Presenter Early Educl Conference; *office:* Brookfield Elem Sch Rt 3 Box 230-B Brookfield MO 64628

ST. CLAIR, THOMAS ARTHUR, Second Grade Teacher; *b:* Somerset, PA; *m:* Deborah Joy Lazier; *c:* Ciminy A., Aimee A., Kelcy Lazier; *ed:* (BS) Elem Ed, CA St Coll 1974; Military Police US Army; *cr:* 3rd Grade Teacher Meyersdale Area Sch Dist 1975; 2nd/3rd/5th Grade Teacher North Star Sch Dist 1975-; *ai:* North Star Elem Wrestling Coach; North Star Ed Assn Building Rep 1975-; PA St Ed Assn, NEA 1975-; North Star Wrestling Boosters Club VP 1980-, Work & Dedication Awd 1989; Friends of Somerset Cty Lib Pres 1985-; *home:* 218 Main St Boswell PA 15531

ST. JOHN, GAYLE MULLEN, English Teacher; *b:* Moberly, MO; *m:* Craig Allen; *c:* Andrew; *ed:* (BS) Ed, Univ of MO 1976; (MA) Eng Lit, Univ of NC 1978; *cr:* Frosh Eng Teaching Asst Univ of NC Chapel Hill 1978-79; Eng Teacher Chapel Hill HS 1979-80, Norman HS 1982-; *ai:* Head Sr Class Spon; Lang Art Advisory Bd Rep; NCTE, NEA, OK Ed Assn, Prof Educators of Norman (Dist Advisory BD, Building Rep); Mc Farlin United Meth Church Society & Church Commission; Decisions for Excl Cadre Mem; SW Region of Coll Bd Advanced Placement Spec Recognition Awd; Natl Hum Center Summer Eng Inst 1987; Challenges to Hum Conference 1984; Norman HS & Dist Teacher of Yr Nominee; Presidents Natl Sch Recognition Awd 1989; Lighthouse Project 1989; *office:* Norman HS 911 W Main St Norman OK 73069

SAITO, NORA ISHIDA, Fourth Grade Teacher; *b:* Lihue, HI; *m:* Reynold M.; *c:* Dean M., Rae Ann M.; *ed:* (BED) Elem Ed, 1966; Prof Certfct Ed, 1967 Univ of HI; *cr:* 4th/5th Grade Teacher Eleele Sch 1967-69; 4th/5th/6th Grade Teacher Waipahu Elem 1969-; *ai:* HSTA Grievance Rep; APC Mem; Grade Level Chm; Lang Arts Comm Mem; PTSA Bd Mem; Fundraiser Comm; Fclty Rep 1986-87; Fclty Rep - APC 1987-88; Grievance Rep - APC 1988- HSTA; PTSA Newsltr 1988-.

SAIZ, MICHELE LOBAN, Junior HS Science Teacher; *b:* Rockville Centre, NY; *m:* Stephen G.; *c:* Andrew; *ed:* (BS) Elem Ed, IA St Univ 1972; *cr:* Teacher Vista Volunteer Alternative Ed 1972-75, 1976-77, Our Lady of Lourdes Sch 1975-76, 1977-80, Immaculate Conception Sch 1980-; *ai:* Jr HS Coord; Earth Day Comm Head; NSTA Mem 1982-; NCEA Mem 1980-; Jr HS Outdoor Ed Grant 1986, 1990; Nom Presidential Outstanding Sci Teacher Awd 1988-89; *office:* Immaculate Conception Sch 715 Monroe St Fairbanks AK 99701

SAKAL, WAYNE, Physics Teacher; *b:* Bridgeport, CT; *ed:* (BS) Bio/Chem, Tarleton St Univ 1981; (MAT) Ed, Sacred Heart Univ 1984; (CAS) Cmptr Sci, Fairfield Univ 1988; US Space Acad Level I & II; Emergency Medical Technician; *cr:* Teacher Notre Dame Cath HS 1981-; Lecturer Museum of Art, Sci & Industry 1989-; Educator Sacred Heart Univ 1990; *ai:* Videovation Faculty Adv; Soph Class Moderator; Newmast Aerospace Resource Agent 1986-, Honors Teacher 1986; Physics Spectrum Editorial Advisory Bd 1984-86; Natl Geographic Society Mem 1981-; Sacred Heart Univ (Alumni Relations 1984-, Challenge 90 1989-), Undergrad Recruitment 1989; BSA Asst Scoutmaster 1971-84, Eagle Scout Awd 1976; CRAF/Cassini Pilot Educl Project, Voyager Neptune Project; St of CT Educator Talent Pool; *office:* Notre Dame Cath HS 220 Jefferson St Fairfield CT 06432

SAKOWICZ, EDWARD F., Science Teacher; *b:* Elizabeth, NJ; *c:* Julie E., Edward F.; *ed:* (BA) Elem Ed, Newark St Coll 1968; (MA) Admin/Supervision, Kean Coll 1972; *cr:* Teacher Hamilton Mid Sch 1970-; *ai:* Alternate Route NJ; Civic Involvement; Governor Teacher Awd; *office:* A Hamilton Mid Sch 310 Cherry St Elizabeth NJ 07208

SALARY, GEORGIA, Reading Teacher; *b:* Montgomery, AL; *ed:* (BS) Elem Ed, 1969; (MS) Elem Ed, 1973 AL St Univ; Data Collector K-8th; *cr:* Teacher Clay Cty Elem Sch 1969-; *ai:* Girls Drill Squad Adv; GA Assn of Educators 1969; NEA 1969; Ebonnaires Civic Club Secy 1969-; ETA Rhoi Chapter of Alpha Pi Chi; Old Elam Missionary Bapt Church; Outstanding Service Awd & Spec Recognition Awd for Special Service in Youth Dept Springfield Missionary Bapt Church 1989; *office:* Clay Cty Elem Sch Rt 1 Box 50 Fort Gaines GA 31751

SALAS, LUCIA M., English Teacher; *b:* Passaic, NJ; *ed:* (BA) Eng, Univ of Miami 1983; (MS) Eng Ed, FL Intnl Univ 1987; *cr:* Eng Teacher Coral Gables Sr HS 1983-; *ai:* Honor Rolls & Honor Roll Luncheon Coord; Delta Kappa Gamma 1989-; NCTE 1984-89; Southern Assn of Colls & Schls Evaluating Comm; Missionaries of Charity Co-Worker 1986-; Legion of Mary Pres 1989-; Mellon Fellow Advanced Placement Inst 1989; *office:* Coral Gables Sr HS 450 Bird Rd Coral Gables FL 33146

SALAS, MARY (NEUFELDER), Fourth Grade Teacher; *b:* Haubstadt, IN; *m:* Cruz; *c:* Mark, Stephanie, Teresa; *ed:* (BA) Elem Ed, 1965, (MS) Elem Ed, 1968 IN St; Admin, Notre Dame Univ; *cr:* 4th Grade Teacher Parochial Schls in IN 1956-67; Prin Our Mother of Sorrows Sch 1968-74; 4th Grade Teacher Globe Unified Dist #1 1975-; *ai:* Delta Kappa Gamma, NEA, Globe Classroom Teachers Assn 1977-; *office:* Copper Rim Sch 501 Ash St Globe AZ 85501

SALAZAR, IRMA TERAN, 7th-12th Grade Counselor; *b:* Crystal City, TX; *m:* Ernesto G.; *c:* Peter A., Yuracy I.; *ed:* (BS) Elem Ed, 1976, (MS) Biling Ed, 1978 A&I Univ; Advanced Trng Counseling; Several Wkshps; *cr:* Pre-K Teacher Crystal City Ind Sch Dist 1976-77; Adult Basic Ed Instruction SW TJC 1977-79; 3rd Grade Lang Art Teacher 1977-81, Jr/Sr HS Cnslr 1981-88, 4th/5th Grade Elem Cnslr 1988-89 Crystal City Ind Sch Dist; 7th-12th Grade Cnslr La Pryor Ind Sch Dist 1989-; *ai:* Local Schlsp Chairperson; SW Area Cnslrs Assn 1987-89; TSTA Treas; Lib Bd 1977-78; CASH Advisory Bd 1987-88; TX Assn of Cnslrs 1984-85; Teacher of Month; Adult Basic Teacher 1977-79; *home:* PO Box 111 La Pryor TX 78872

SALAZAR, ROZAN CRUZ, Social Science Teacher; *b:* Stockton, CA; *m:* Elias Jr.; *c:* Jerry A., Angela A.; *ed:* (BS) Social Sci, 1981, (MS) Poly Sci, 1982 E NM Univ; NM Law Related Ed Project, Univ of NM; *cr:* Teaching Asst E NM Univ 1981-82; Teacher Dexter HS 1982-; *ai:* Close Up, Mock Trial, Class Spon; NHS Adv; Natl Inst for Citizenship in Law St Rep 1987; NM Law Related Ed Project SE Regional Rep & Trainer, Center for Research St Rep 1989-; *home:* 700 S Plaza Dr Roswell NM 88201

SALBERG, JEFF A., Social Studies Teacher; *b:* Omaha, NE; *c:* Samantha J., Clayton A.; *ed:* (BS) Soc Sci, 1979, (BS) His, Peru St Coll 1979; (MS) Admin, Creighton Univ 1984; *cr:* Soc Stud Teacher Fairmont NE 1980-82, Millard North HS 1983-; *ai:* 9th Grade Ftlb & Wrestling; Millard Ed Assn, NE Ed Assn 1983-; *office:* Millard North HS 1010 S Pacific St Omaha NE 68154

SALCIDO, DELORES JONES, 6th Grade Teacher; *b:* Birkburnette, TX; *m:* Henry; *c:* Ryan; *ed:* (BA) Elem Ed, Pepperdine 1964; (MS) Counseling, CA St Los Angeles 1974; *cr:* 5th-8th Grade Elem Teacher Monterey Highlands Sch 1965-76; Elem Teacher Northrup Sch 1977-; *ai:* 6th Grade CAP Sci & Field Tester 1990; Alhambra Teachers Assn Bargaining Team Mem 1986; Monterey Hills Corporation Treas 1981-89; USA Teachers to Japan 1975.

SALDANA, GENARO ALONZO, Spanish Teacher; *b:* Kingsville, TX; *m:* Maria Guadalupe Rodriguez; *c:* Andres; *ed:* (BA) Span, TX A&I Univ 1970; Grad Stud; *cr:* Span Teacher Asherton HS 1970-71, Gonzales HS 1971-; *ai:* Span Club & Span Honor Society Adv; TX St Teachers Assn 1970-; TX Classroom Teachers Assn 1971-; Amer Assn Teachers of Span & Portuguese 1975-; Optimist Club 1982-87; St James Cath Church Eucharistic Minister 1979-; *home:* 1304 St Paul Gonzales TX 78629

SALDINO, MARGOT LUCE, Jr HS Math & Science Teacher; *b:* Grand Rapids, MI; *m:* Joseph A.; *c:* Thomas, Michael, Lorna, Robert; *ed:* (BA) Phys Ed, MI St Univ 1964; (BA) Health Sci, Grand Valley St Univ 1983; Working Towards Masters Scndry Admin, Grand Valley St Univ; *cr:* Teacher Grand Rapids South HS 1964-66, St Thomas the Apostle 1978-80, St Louis the King 1980-82, St Thomas the Apostle 1983-; *ai:* East Kentwood Pom Squad Var Coach; Grandville & Hudsonville HS Drama Dir; Kentwood Sch Bd Secy 1974-78; Natl Sci Fnd Grant Manipulative Math Stud in Mid Sch; *office:* St Thomas the Apostle Sch 1429 Wilcox Park Dr Grand Rapids MI 49506

SALE, MARGARET LEE HYDE, Kindergarten Teacher Retired; *b:* Niangua, MO; *m:* Onal Carter (dec); *c:* Sara L.; *ed:* (BSED) Art, Southwest MO St Univ 1946; Grad Stud, Pittsburg St Univ/Southwest MO St Univ; *cr:* 1st Grade Teacher Niangua Public Schls 1939-43, Marshfield Public Schls 1943-46, Cntrl Elem Sch 1946-50; Kndgtn Teacher Cntrl Elem Sch 1962-87; *ai:* MO Retired Teachers Assn 1987-; MO St Teacher Assn 1946-87; PTO Life Mem 1976-; Beta Sigma Phi Intnl Chapter Dir 1963-; Neosho Chamber of Commerce Teacher of Yr Awd 1984; *office:* Central School Hickory St Neosho MO 64850

SALEWSKI, ROBERT JOSEPH, Mathematics Department Chair; *b:* New York City, NY; *m:* Kathleen L. Gosselin; *c:* Michael, Lynn, Craig; *ed:* (BS) Math, FL Southern 1970; (MA) Bus/Management, Univ of NE 1976; Teacher Cert, George Mason Univ 1984; *cr:* USAF Officer 1963-83; Math Teacher Paul VI HS 1984-; *ai:* Math Team; NHS Faculty Rep; Planning/Steering Comm Mem; NCTM, VCTM, FCTM 1984-; USAF Lt Col 1963-83, Total-25 Plus Awd; DOD Wkshp for Math Teachers; *office:* Paul VI HS 10675 Lee Hwy Fairfax VA 22030

SALGADO, EMMA EUGENIA, Spanish Teacher; *b:* Mexico City, Mexico; *c:* Hector Villalobos, Ivonne Villalobos; *ed:* (BA) Elem Ed, Escuela Normal Para Maestros 1960; (MA) Span Lit, Universidad Nacioual de Mexico Mexico City 1960; *cr:* Bi-ling Teacher Instituto Zumarraga 1965-70; Foreign Lang Chairperson Instituto Simon Bolivar 1970-72; Educl Service Chairperson Mexico City Museum of Natural His 1972-78; Superior Ed/Eng as 2nd Lang Teacher Natl Polytechnic Inst CENLEX 1978-80; Eng as 2nd Lang/Amnesty Teacher El Rancho Adult Sch 1984-; *ai:* Natl Sch For Blind Children Diploma 1976; Mexico City Museum of Natural His Public Service AWds 1977; Honorary Mention on Thesis; *office:* Daniel Murphy HS 241 S Detroit Los Angeles CA 90036

SALIBA, LINDA GUARIN, Spanish Teacher; *b:* Boavita Boyaca, Colombia; *w:* Alexy E. (dec); *c:* Frank, Gary, Van; *ed:* (BA) His/Span, Troy St Univ 1980; Span - Cum Laude, Univ of AL 1984; *cr:* Span Teacher Enterprise HS 1985-; *ai:* Span Club Spon; Translator for TV Interviews & Legal Documents Mem of Cmmty; Natl Assn of Span Teachers, AL Assn of Span Teachers, AL Ed Assn; PTA Treas 1967-68, Lifetime Membership Awd 1968; Given Grant AL Commission of Higher Ed Trained as Oral Proficiency Evaluator Univ of NY Albany 1988; *home:* 110 Gibson St Apt 8 Enterprise AL 36330

SALINAS, DOMINIC, Assistant Principal; *b:* Birtingwood AFB, England; *ed:* (BS) Biological Sci, LA St Univ Shreveport 1977; (MS) Sci Ed, LA Tech Univ 1982; NEWMAST 1988; NSF 1987-88; *cr:* Teacher Captain Shreve HS 1977-79, Bossier HS 1979-89; Asst Prin Parkway HS 1989-; *ai:* Write Grants, Curr; NEA, LEA, BAE Building Rep 1989-; NSTA, LSTA 1985-; LA Acad of Sci 1986-, Achievement Awd 1988; Lions Club VP 1981-; Boys Club Bd of Dir 1985-88; Bossier Cty Jaycees 1985-87, Outstanding Young Educator 1985-86; Teacher Module on Aids 1988; Parish Sex Ed Curr Guide 1989; *office:* Parkway HS 4301 Panther Dr Bossier City LA 71112

SALINAS, JOE, JR., Spanish Teacher; *b:* Premont, TX; *m:* Laura Garza; *c:* Jose III, Pedro L.; *ed:* Phys Ed/Health/Span, TX A&I 1976; *cr:* 6th/7th/8th Grade Phys Ed/Health Teacher Jim Hogg Ind Sch Dist 1976-79; Phys Ed/Health Teacher 1979-84, Span Teacher 1984- Benavides HS; *ai:* Jr Var & Var Ftbl, Track Boys & Girls Field Events Coach; TSTA, NEA; Democrat Precinct Chm 1976-78; *home:* Rt 1 Box 112 Concepcion TX 78349

SALK, HARVEY LEON, Fourth Grade Teacher; *b:* New Bedford, MA; *m:* Saralee Mazur; *c:* Abrah J.; *ed:* (BA) Psych, Rider Coll 1965; (MED) Guidance/Counseling, Bridgewater St 1969; *cr:* 5th Grade Teacher Sarah D Ottiwell Sch 1965-71; Asst Prin Mt Pleasant Sch 1971-75, Keith Jr HS 1975-76; 4th Grade Teacher Elwyn G Campbell Sch 1976-77, Alfred J Gomes Sch 1977-; *ai:* NBEA, MTA, NEA 1965-.

SALKIN, JOAN CHERYL, 6th Grade Teacher; *b:* Cleveland, OH; *ed:* (BS) Elem Ed, OH St Univ 1968; (MED) Guidance/Counseling, Kent St Univ 1973; *cr:* 4th Grade Teacher 1968-73, 6th Grade Teacher 1973-87 Ludlow Elem; 6th Grade Teacher Woodbury Elem 1987-; *ai:* Drama Club Spon; USSR Exch Comm; Shaker Hts Teachers Assn Building Rep 1985-; Martha Holding Jennings Fnd Fellowship Finalist; Shaker Heights Teachers/PTA Fellowships; *office:* Woodbury Elem Sch 15400 S Woodland Rd Shaker Heights OH 44120

SALLADE, SUSAN JANE, English Teacher; *b:* Wilkes Barre, PA; *m:* Donald R.; *c:* Laurel A.; *ed:* (MED) Eng, Loras Coll 1976; (BS) Elem Ed, Bloomsburg Univ 1969; Grad Stud West Chester St Coll, Drake Univ, Univ of IA, Marycrest Coll; *cr:* 6th Grade Team/Eng Teacher W Bradford Elem 1969-72; 4th-6th Grade Lang Art/Math/Phys Ed Instr Stowe Elem 1972-74; 6th-8th Grade Lang Art/Art/Phys Ed Instr St Marys Sch 1974-76; 7th-12th Grade Lang Art/Eng Teacher Cascade Jr Sr HS 1976-89; 9th/12th Grade Eng Teacher/Coord of Talented/Gifted Cascade HS 1989-; *ai:* Large Group Speech Coach; Sch Newspaper Adv; Eng Standing Comm Chairperson; Talented & Gifted Comm; Stu Assistance Team; NEA 1969-; WDEA Exec Bd 1988-; Delta Kappa Gamma (charter Mem, Chairperson Various Comm) 1982-; Poetry Published Leadstone Review; *office:* Cascade Jr Sr HS 505 Johnson St NW Cascade IA 52033

SALLAS, AMELIA STEFANOS, Fifth Grade Teacher; *b:* Chicago, IL; *m:* Dean A.; *c:* Thomas D., Paulette; *ed:* (BA) Ed, Univ of IL Champaign 1963; Coursework Grad Prgm of NW Univ Sch of Ed 1964-66; Recipient of Certificate for Completion of Teacher Trng Prgm of Inst for Psychoanalysis Chicago 1969-71; *cr:* 3rd Grade Teacher Southeast Sch 1963-68; 4th-5th Grade Teacher Rutledge Hall 1968-71; 3rd/5th Grade Teacher Joseph Sears Sch 1979-; *ai:* Ongoing Dist Curr Study/Revisions Comm; Reporting to Parents Comm System Update; NEA 1968-; KEA 1979-; Annunciation Greek Orthodox Cathedral of Chicago Dir of Religious Ed 1975-; Greek Orthodox Diocese of Chicago (Religious Ed Commission, Mem, Wkshp Leader) 1984-; Sch Dist 68 Parent Rep to Admin Cncl 1984-88; Niles N HS Dist 219 HS Parents Volunteer Assn Officer 1986-89; *office:* Joseph Sears Sch 542 Abbotsford Rd Kenilworth IL 60043

SALLEE, CLAUDE DOUGLAS, Phys Ed, Health Teacher; *b:* Dayton, OH; *m:* Jane Hisle; *ed:* (BA) Scndry Phys Ed, 1979, (MA) Ed/Phys Ed, 1981, (Rank I) Scndry Admin, 1984 E KY Univ; Health & History; *cr:* Teacher George Rogers Clark HS 1980-; *ai:* Asst Var & Head Jr Var Boys Bsktbl Coach; Head Boys Tennis Coach; Clark Cty Ed Assn, KY Ed Assn, KY Coaches Assn 1980-; Var Boys Bsktbl St Tournament Appearances; Jr Var Dist Championships in Boys Bsktbl; Doubles Tennis Team & Regional Championship; *office:* George Rogers Clark HS 620 Boone Ave Winchester KY 40391

SALLEE, VIVIAN G. (SANDERS), Special Education Teacher; *b:* Moline, IL; *c:* James J.; *ed:* (BSED) Spec Ed/Elem Ed, IL St Univ 1970; La Verne Coll, IL Cntrl Coll, N IL Univ, IL St Univ; *cr:* Spec Ed Teacher Peoria Public Schls 1969-; *ai:* Supvr Teacher Candidates from IL St Univ & Bradley Univ; Cncl for Exceptional Children 1970-72; Peoria Fed of Teachers 1985-; Singles Together Pres 1981-86; Cnslr/Tutor for At Risk Stus; *office:* Peoria Public Schls 1419 S Folkers Peoria IL 61605

SALLEY, GLENDA GRITTMAN, 8th Grade English Teacher; *b:* Greenville, MS; *c:* David, Boyce; *ed:* (BA) Eng, Delta St Coll 1964; Grad Work Delta St Univ & Univ of Cntrl FL; *cr:* 7th Grade Eng Teacher Indianola Separate Sch Dist 1967-69; 11th/12th Grade Eng Teacher Riverside HS 1970-71; 9th/10th Grade Eng/Speech Teacher Leland Acad 1971-73; 6th-8th Grade Teacher Jackson Heights Mid Sch 1973-78; 9th-11th Grade Journalism/Eng Teacher Oviedo HS 1978-79; 6th-8th Grade Eng Teacher Milwee Mid Sch 1980-; *office:* Milwee Mid Sch St Rd 427 Longwood FL 32750

SALMI, NANCY PETERSON, Social Studies Teacher; *b:* Willmar, MN; *m:* Robert W.; *c:* Virginia Salmi Cran, Robert J.; *ed:* (BA) His, Augsburg Coll 1968-; Macalaster Coll & Stanford Univ; *cr:* Soc Stud Teacher Virginia HS 1968-89; *ai:* Close-Up Adv; League of Women Voters; Stanford Univ COE Fellowship 1986; Macalster Coll Taft Inst Fellowship 1978; *office:* Virginia Scndry Sch Technical Bldg 5th Ave S Virginia MN 55792

SALMONS, VICTORIA ANN, Business Teacher; *b:* West Hamlin, WV; *m:* Daniel Scott; *c:* Danielle N., Brett A.; *ed:* (BS) Bus Ed, Univ of Charleston 1980; (MA) Bus Ed, Marshall Univ 1984; *cr:* Bus Teacher Hamlin HS 1980-; *ai:* Stu Cncl & SADD

Spon; Harveys Creek Church Pre-Sch Sunday Sch Teacher; *office:* Hamlin HS Gen Del Hamlin WV 25523

SALQUERO, ARTHUR RAYMOND, IV, Sixth Grade Teacher; *b:* El Paso, TX; *c:* Jennifer K. Harp; *ed:* (BA) Poly Sci, Univ of TX El Paso 1973; Teacher Cert Univ of TX El Paso 1981; *cr:* US Army Captain Air Defense Artillery 1974-79; 6th Grade Teacher Valley View Mid Sch 1981-84, Lancaster Elem Sch 1984-; *ai:* Assn of TX Prof Educators Faculty Rep 1984-; Lions Intnl VP 1990; Natl Geographic Society 1974; NASA & Park Seed Company Project Seeds Teacher-Dir; *office:* Lancaster Elem Sch 9230 Elgin El Paso TX 79907

SALSI, BONNIE CHAPPELL, 5th Grade Teacher; *b:* Lewisburg, PA; *m:* John James; *c:* Joshua, Nathan, Noah; *ed:* (BS) Elem Ed, Edinboro Univ 1971; (MED) Elem Ed, Univ of Pittsburgh 1974; *cr:* 2nd/4th-6th Grade Teacher Norwin Sch Dist 1972-; *ai:* Ski Club; Prof Dev Comm; Sci Comm; *office:* Scull Elem Sch 780 Brush Hill Rd North Huntingdon PA 15642

SALSMAN, ROBERT L., Industrial Arts Teacher; *b:* Brighton, MO; *m:* Nancy N. Youngblood; *c:* Larry D., Sandra M.; *ed:* (BSED) Industrial Ed, SW MO St 1959; (MSED) Industrial Ed, MO Univ 1965; *cr:* Industrial Art Teacher Niangua Schls 1959-62, Strafford Schls 1962-66; Purchasing Mgr Eagle Picher Industries 1966-70; Industrial Arts Teacher Walnut Grove HS 1970-71, Jasper R-5 Schls 1971-; *ai:* Epislon Pitau 1958-60; Phi BetA Kappa 1964-65; *office:* Jasper R-5 Schls 113 W Mercer Jasper MO 64755

SALTAR, MARY M. ROBERT, 6th Grade Soc Stud Teacher; *b:* Omaha, NE; *m:* Richard A.; *c:* Tyanna J., Kassidy K.; *ed:* (BA) Spec Ed, Loretto Heights Coll 1971; (MA) Creative Arts Ed/Curr Dev Lesley Coll 1987; Grad Stud Psych & Ed; Meology Spec Trng, Mendez Fnd FL; *cr:* Spec Ed/2nd/5th/6th Grade Teacher Denver Public Schls; 6th Grade Soc Stud Teacher Kunsmiller Mid Sch; *ai:* Teacher Spon for Cenikor Drug Assn Children; Money for Cenikor Cty Teacher Charge of Cincode Mayo Act; CEA, NEA, Denver Classroom Teacher Assn; Received Grant for Public Ed Coalition for Cincode Mayo Mini Mercado 1987; *office:* Kunsmiller Mid Sch 2250 S Quitman St Denver CO 80219

SALTERIO, PAUL WILLIAM, Department Head-Classics; *b:* Boston, MA; *ed:* (BA) Philosophy, Mary Knoll Coll 1962; (MED) Admin/Psych, St Coll Boston 1965; Post Grad Stud Classics & Theology, Boston Coll; *cr:* Teacher Roslindale HS 1963, Archbishop Williams HS 1963-65, Brighton HS 1965-66, Boston Latin Sch 1966-; Dept Head Boston Latin Sch 1986-; *ai:* Dir Public Declamation; Classical Assn of New England; Black Stu Assn Past Adv; Book Published 1987; *office:* Boston Latin Sch 78 Ave Louis Pasteur Boston MA 02115

SALVADGE, GAY EVANS, Sixth Grade Teacher; *b:* Wellsboro, PA; *m:* Michael R.; *c:* Michael, Wade; *ed:* (BS) Ed, 1974, (MA) Elem Ed, 1977 Mansfield St Coll; *cr:* 6th Grade Teacher 1975-78, 7th/8th Grade Rdng Teacher 1980, 6th Grade Teacher 1980-86, 2nd Grade Teacher 1986-87, 6th Grade Teacher 1987- Galeton Area Sch; *ai:* Cub Scouts Den Leader 1987-; Awd for Superior Teaching & Overall Performance 1988; *home:* 240 Clinton St Ext Galeton PA 16922

SALVATERRA, RICHARD J., Physical Education Teacher; *b:* Bronx, NY; *m:* Tirzah Kingsbury; *c:* Christopher; *ed:* (BS) Phys Ed, Manhattan Coll 1968; (MS) Health Ed, Herbert H Lehman Coll 1970; Cert Learning Disabilities, Manhattanville 1975; *cr:* Phys Ed Teacher Windward Sch 1968-72; Kndgtn-6th Grade Phys Ed Teacher Fox Meadow Sch 1972-; *ai:* Dist Health & Scarsdale Public Schls Safety Comm; Fox Meadow Health Comm Chm; NY St Assn of Health, Phys Ed, Recreation, Dance (Elem Section Pres 1981-82) 1978-; John Jay HS Booster Club (Pres 1982-84) 1980-86; Katonah Memorial Park Assn Bd of Dirs 1980-; Katonah Little League Incorporated (Pres 1981) 1979-83; Book Published 1978; *office:* Fox Meadow Sch Brewster Rd Scarsdale NY 10583

SALYER, BRENDA EVERMAN, 2nd Grade Teacher; *b:* Lexington, KY; *m:* John; *c:* Glenn, Julie, Whitney; *ed:* (BA) Elem Ed, 1967, (MA) Elem Ed, 1976, (Rank I) Elem Ed, 1989 E KY Univ; Powell Cty Sch Dist Distinguished Intern Teacher Resource Leader Rep 1985; *cr:* 2nd Grade Teacher Fairdale Elem Sch 1967-69, Wheeler Elem Sch 1969-70; 1st Grade Teacher Clay Elem Sch 1978-79; MIgrant Ed Teacher Powell Cty Bd of Ed 1979-81; *ai:* Chrldr Spon; Clay City Elem Sch KY Dept of Ed Comm for Excl Ed Rep; KY Ed Assn Membership 1967-68; Home Makers Pres 1972-73, Outstanding Homemaker 1973; Younger Womens Club Membership 1976-78; Actors Theater Distinguished Chef 1975-78; *home:* 573 Pompeii Rd Clay City KY 40312

SALYER, LAURA L., Mathematics Teacher; *b:* Louisa, KY; *ed:* (BS) Math, 1973, (MA) Ed, 1979 Morehead St Univ; *cr:* Math Teacher Scott Cty HS 1973-75; 7th-8th Grade Math Teacher Louisa HS 1975-77; Math Teacher Lawrence Cty HS 1977-; *ai:* Academic Team Coach; NHS Spon; KY Ed Assn; *office:* Lawrence Cty HS Hwy 644 Bulldog Ln Louisa KY 41230

SALZER, DEBORAH DAVIS, 8th Grade English Teacher; *b:* Lumberton, NC; *m:* Leo IV; *c:* Courtney, Eric; *ed:* (BS) Elem Ed, Pembroke St Univ 1977; (MS) Intermediate Ed, E Caroline Univ 1982; Mentor & QUEST Trng 1989; *cr:* 4th-7th Grade Sci Teacher Merry Hill & J P Law Elem 1977-78; 6th-8th Grade Title I Rdng Teacher Hillcrest Mid Sch 1978-81; Self Contained 4th Grade Teacher Howard L Hall Elem 1981-83; 7th/8th Grade Eng Teacher Upchurch Mid Sch 1983-87; 8th Grade Eng Teacher Carver Mid Sch 1987-; *ai:* QUEST Leader; Discipline Comm; Sounding Bd Rep; NC Intnl Rdng Assn 1977-; Mother of Twins 1986-87.

SAMA, FRANCIS BRUNO, Assistant Principal; *b:* Woodbury, NJ; *m:* Judith A.; *c:* Christopher, Abbie; *ed:* (BA) Math, Lowell Univ 1969; (MS) Scndry Admin, Glassboro St Coll 1977; Cmptr Ed, Gloucester Comm Coll; *cr:* Teacher 1969-88, Asst Prin 1988- Penns Grove Mid Sch; *ai:* Head of Discipline Comm; Parents in Ed Mem; Work with Local Clergy to Help Parents Become More Involved in Educl Process; NEA, NJEA Mem 1969-; Prof Picture Framers Assn Mem 1986-; Pres List for Outstanding Academic Achievement Gloucester Cty Coll; Educl Testing Service, Math Consultant; Gloucester Cty Voc Sch Math Advisory Comm; Effective Schls Comm Chm; *office:* Penns Grove Mid Sch Virginia & Maple Ave Penns Grove NJ 08069

SAMANIEGO, ROBERT JERRY, Sixth Grade Teacher; *b:* San Francisco, CA; *m:* Jill Ann Church; *c:* Anthony; *ed:* (BS) Chem, 1971, (MA) Spec Ed, 1972 CA St Univ Northridge; Admin Stud; *cr:* Chemist Hyland Labs 1967-69; Teacher Sherwoods Oaks HS 1969-70; 4th-6th Grade Spec Ed Teacher 1972-77, 4th/6th Grade Regular Classroom Teacher 1978- Mark Keppel Elem; *ai:* Bsktbl Coach Asst; CA PTA Service Awd 1976; *office:* Mark Keppel Elem Sch 730 Glenwood Rd Glendale CA 91206

SAMBALL, LORETTA, Grade 8 Social Studies Teacher; *b:* Sharon, PA; *ed:* (BA) Soc Stud/His/Eng, Slippery Rock St Coll 1965; (MS) Guidance, Westminster 1978; *cr:* 7th/8th Grade Eng Teacher 1965-79, 7th/8th Grade Soc Stud Teacher 1979-87 Vernon Elem; 8th Grade Soc Stud Teacher Badger Mid Sch 1987-; *office:* Badger Mid Sch 6144 Youngstown Conneaut Rd Kinsman OH 44428

SAMEC, JAYNE MILLER, 9th/10th Grade English Teacher; *b:* Niles, MI; *m:* James Michael; *c:* Jamie Samee Saroli, Brooke; *ed:* (BA) Eng/Speech, Cntrl MI Univ 1961; *cr:* Eng Dept Chairperson 1984-89; *ai:* Adv NHS; MEA; NEA; Girls Athletic Boosters Pres 1985-87; Girls Sftbl Boosters Treas 1985-; *office:* Kearsley HS 4302 Underhill Dr Flint MI 48506

SAMELA, LORRAINE ANN, 5th Grade Teacher; *b:* Waterbury, CT; *ed:* (BS) Elem Ed, Southern CT St Univ 1969; (MS) Inner City Ed, Cntrl CT ST Univ 1970; Supplementary Courses, Post Coll; *cr:* 3rd/5th Grade Teacher Webster Grammar Sch 1970-78; 5th Grade Teacher Regan Elem Sch 1978-; *ai:* Waterbury Teacher Assn, Ct Ed Assn, NEA 1970-; Waterbury Symphony Orch Mem 1970-89; Ellis Island Fnd & Statue of Liberty Mem 1983-; PTA of Amer Mem 1970-; *office:* Regan Elem Sch 2780 N Main St Waterbury CT 06704

SAMMONS, MARTHA L., Biology/Anatomy Teacher; *b:* Fulton, KY; *c:* Mary P.; *ed:* (BS) Chem/Bio, 1960, (MA) Ed, 1967, (MA) Ed, Murray St Univ; Grad Stud Ed, Murray St Univ; Scndry Admin Cert; *cr:* Life Sci/Math Teacher Sharpe Mid 1960-62; Life Sci Teacher Long Beach CA 1962-63; Chem Teacher Byars Hall HS 1963-65; Life Sci Teacher Calvert Mid Sch 1965-66; Chem/Bio Teacher S Marshall HS 1966-67; Life Sci Teacher Murray HS 1967-70; Bio Teacher Marshall Cty HS 1980-; *ai:* Preparing Public Relations Video; Marshall Cty Ed Assn Building Rep PN, KY Ed Assn, NEA, KY Sci Teachers Assn, NSTA; Fellowship Univ KY Physiology Wkshp; Cty Cncl Elected Mem 1976-78.

SAMPLE, BETTE JEAN HART, Second Grade Teacher; *b:* Long Beach, CA; *m:* Ronald C.; *c:* Jennifer, Leah; *ed:* (BS) Elem Ed/Speech and Drama, Augustana Coll 1966; 50 Hrs Univ of WY; CO St Univ; Black Hills St Univ; SD St Univ; Chadron St Univ; *cr:* 3rd Grade Teacher Whittier Sch 1966-67; 4th Grade Teacher North Park Elem Sch 1967-68; 1st Grade Teacher Gertrude Burns Elem Sch 1976-88; 8th Grade English Teacher Newcastle Mid Sch 1988-89; 2nd Grade Teacher Gertrude Burns Elem Sch 1989-; *ai:* Mentor for New 1st Grade Teacher; Supervising Teacher for Stud Teacher; Lib Bd Adv; Part Time Instr for Eastern WY Coll Childrens Literature; NEA; Christ the King Luth Church; *office:* Gertrude Burns Elem Schl 116 Casper Ave Newcastle WY 82701

SAMPLE, PATTY LOU, Science Teacher; *b:* Wynne, AR; *ed:* (BSE) Bio/Geology, AR St Univ 1971; Various Classes, Seminars & Projects; *cr:* Teacher Weiner HS 1971-73, Mc Geehee HS 1973-74, Evening Shade HS 1976-; *ai:* Class & Beta Club Spon; Dir Sch Play; GED Teacher; Drama Coach & Adv Cmmty Theatre; AR Sci Teachers Assn; NE AR Astronomical Society; Evening Shade Town Cncl Alderperson 1984-; Ambulance Bd (Mem, Rep) 1988-; *office:* Evening Shade HS P O Box 240 Evening Shade AR 72532

SAMPLE, ROBERTA KLINGEL, 2nd Grade Teacher; *b:* Marion, OH; *m:* Gerald H.; *c:* Ebben, Aaron, Ian; *ed:* (BS) Elem Ed, OH St Univ 1974; Liberal Arts, Robert Morris Coll; Various Wkshps Ashland Coll; OSU; *cr:* 3rd-4th Grade Teacher Dublin Local Schls 1975-78; 2nd Grade Teacher Mt Gilead Exempted Village Schls 1978-; *ai:* NEA, OH Ed Assn, Mt Gilead Teachers Assn 1978-; Intnl Teachers Assn 1987-; *office:* Edison Elem Sch St Rt 95 Edison OH 43320

SAMPLER, DEBRA BASS, Third Grade Teacher; *b:* Carrollton, GA; *m:* Nathan Steven Sr.; *c:* Nathan S. Jr., Emily S.; *ed:* (BS) Early Chldhd Ed, 1975, (MED) Early Chldhd Ed, 1980 W GA Coll; *cr:* 1st Grade Teacher Sand Hill Elem 1975-76; Kndgtn Teacher Heard Cty Elem 1977; 2nd Grade Teacher 1977-80, Kndgtn Teacher 1980-83, 4th Grade Teacher 1983-84, 3rd Grade Teacher 1984- H A Jones Elem; *ai:* Grade Level Lead Teacher & Budget Rep 1986; Textbook Selection, Social Stud Rep; Attendance Review Comm; NEA, GA Assn of Ed 1977-84; Prof Assn of GA Educators 1985-; Carrollton Jr Womans Club (Ed Dir 1984) 1979-85; W GA Coll Alumni C ncl 1983-; Southern Assn of Colls & Schls (Sch Chairperson, Cmmty Chairperson); *office:* H A Jones Elem Sch Lakeview Dr Bremen GA 30110

SAMPLES, BRENDA DARLENE, 6th Grade Science Teacher; *b:* Boaz, AL; *m:* Robert Earl; *c:* Stephanie M., Stanfield, Nathan; *ed:* (BA) Elem Ed, Jacksonville St 1980; (MA) Elem Ed, Univ of AL 1988; Working Towards Masters; *cr:* Teacher Etowah Mid Sch 1981-; *ai:* Drug Awareness Educator; Just Say No Club, Stu of the Week, Sci Fair Spon; NEA, AEA 1981-; Foster Parent Dept of Human Resources 1979-; Foster Parent Assn Pres 1981-82; Honorary Lieutenant Colonel Aide-de-Camp AL St Militia Drug Awareness Prgm; *home:* Rt 7 Box 249 Boaz AL 35957

SAMPLES, EDITH LEONA, 6th Grade Math/English Teacher; *b:* Cleveland, TN; *ed:* (BS) Elem Ed, TN Wesleyn 1959; (MED) Curr/Instruction, MTSU 1974; *cr:* 6th Grade Teacher Waterville Elem 1955-56, Oak Grove 1956-59; 7th-9th Grade Teacher Arnold Jr HS 1959-61; 6th Grade Teacher George R Stuart Sch 1961-; *ai:* Math Dept Comm Chm; Academic Olympic Team Coach; Bradley Cty Ed Assn (Secy 1957-58) 1955-59; Cleveland Teachers Assn 1959-; TEA, NEA 1955-; *office:* George R Stuart Sch 902 20th St Cleveland TN 37311

SAMPSON, ANDREW JAMES, Science Teacher; *b:* Jacksonville, FL; *m:* Eva Marie Noisette; *c:* Andretta Hampton, Ly Cynthia, Andrew Jr.; *ed:* (BS) Elem Ed, Morris Brown Coll 1969; (MS) Admin & Supervision, GA St Univ 1977; Constitutional Law, Univ of Chicago Law Sch; Sci, GA St Univ; *cr:* Sci Teacher Atlanta Public Schls 1970-; *ai:* Coach Girls & Boys Bsktbl; Stu Government Assn Adv; Safety Patrol Supvr; Fire Safety Chm; NEA, GA Assn of Educators; Teacher of Yr 1989-; *office:* Dean Rusk Elem Sch 433 Peeples St Atlanta GA 30310

SAMPSON, GARY DAVID, English Department Chair; *b:* Canastota, NY; *m:* Karla Johnson; *c:* Anna, John; *ed:* (BA) Hum, Fort Lewis Coll 1976; (MA) Eng, NM Highlands Univ 1981; Chinese Mandarin, Defense Lang Inst; *cr:* Soc Stud Teacher 1981-84, Eng Teacher 1984- Robertson HS; *ai:* Stu Cncl Anthropology Club Spon; Literary Magazine Adv; NMCTE NE Regional Coord 1987-; Public Safety Commission Mem 1986-88; Published Poetry; *office:* Robertson HS 901 Douglas Ave Las Vegas NM 87701

SAMPSON, JAMES EDWARD, 8th Grade Teacher; *b:* Natchez, MS; *ed:* (BA) Liberal Art, Chicago St Univ 1969; (MS) Ed, Natl Coll 1983; *cr:* Teacher W Q Greshem Elem 1970-73, Marcus Garvey Elem 1973-77, Bateman 1977-78, Beard & Edison 1978-; *ai:* Schlsp Comm AFC; *office:* Edison Gifted Sch 6220 N Olcott Ave Chicago IL 60631

SAMPSON, JEANNETTE WASZNICKY, Fourth Grade Teacher; *b:* Leominster, MA; *m:* John A.; *c:* Jennifer, June; *ed:* (BA) Ed, Rivier Coll 1969; (MS) Educl Technology, Fitchburg St Coll 1990; *cr:* 2nd Grade Teacher St Leos Sch 1969-70; Teachers Aide N Middlesex Regional Sch 1977-79; 4th Grade Teacher Varnum Brook Mid Sch 1979-; *ai:* Educl Technology Cncl; NMRSDTA Treas & Building Rep; Soc Stud Comm; Network Admin; *office:* Varnum Brook Mid Sch Hollis St Pepperell MA 01463

SAMPSON, MARY CATHERINE (MOORE), First Grade Teacher; *b:* Helena, AR; *m:* Danny; *ed:* (BSE) Elem/Eng, 1966, (MSE) Counseling/Elem, 1988 Henderson Univ; *cr:* 2nd/3rd Grade Teacher Paron Elem 1966-67; 1st Grade Teacher Glen Rose Elem 1967-; *ai:* AEA, NEA; Glen Rose Teachers Assn Pres; *home:* PO Box 212 Donaldson AR 71941

SAMPSON, SALLY ANN SWEESY, French/English Teacher; *b:* Akron, OH; *m:* Donald Thomas Jr.; *c:* Donald III, Rhys; *ed:* (BA) Fr/Eng, Mt Union Coll 1967; (MA) Eng, Kent St Univ 1982; N MI Univ, Cntrl MI Univ, Laval Univ; *cr:* Fr Instr Marlington HS 1967-69, Minerva HS 1971-73, Republic Michigamme HS 1973-76; Eng/Fr Instr Boardman HS 1976-; *ai:* Fr Club; AATF, NEA, OEA; BSA Comm Chairperson 1979-89, Scouter of Yr 1983; United Meth Church (Organist, Choir Dir) 1976-; Laval Univ Grant 1984; *home:* 2071 Bonner Rd Deerfield OH 44411

SAMS, SUE WILLIAMSON, Mathematics Dept Chair; *b:* Franklin, NC; *m:* Clay E.; *ed:* (BS) Math, W Carolina Univ 1965; (MS) Math, Univ NC Charlotte 1982; *cr:* Math Teacher Grier Jr HS 1966-67, Myers Park HS 1967-72; Math Dept Chairperson E Mecklenburg HS 1973-89, Providence Sr HS 1989-; *ai:* Keyette Club & Sr Class Adv; Faculty Cncl Rep; Math Contest Coach; Academically Gifted & Minority Achievement Comm; NC Cncl of Teachers of Math 1975-, W W Rankin Awd 1989; Math Assn of America 1980-; Classroom Teachers Assn 1970-; NC Assn of Gifted Teachers; Alpha Delta Kappa (Treas, Pres) 1970-; Phi Delta Kappa 1987-; Carmel Cntry Gardeners Pres 1989-; St Presidential Awd Winner 1983, 1985, 1986; Teacher of Yr 1982, 1990; *office:* Providence Sr HS 1800 Pineville-Matthews Rd Charlotte NC 28226

SAMSON, TAMMINA O., 1st Grade Teacher; *b:* Hatch, NM; *m:* Robert G.; *ed:* (BA) Elem Ed, Western NM Univ 1971; (MA) Ed, Western NM Univ 1976; *cr:* 3rd Grade Teacher Trailor Elem 1971-72; Rdng Teacher Reserve Elem Jr HS 1972-74; 1st Grade Teacher Reserve Elem 1974-80; Valley View Elem 1980-; *ai:* Teacher Adv Comm; Sch Improvement Comm; Intnl Rdng Assn; NEA; Commencement Speaker Reserve HS 1989; *office:* Valley View Elem Sch 1400 S Washington Ave Roswell NM 88201

SAMUEL, DORIS L., Chapter Reading Teacher; *b:* Wiergate, Newton; *m:* J. W.; *ed:* (BS) Elem Ed/Music/Art Ed, 1956, (BS) Elem Ed/Music/Art Ed, 1966 Prairie View A&M Univ; *cr:* 3rd-4th Grade Teacher 1958-66, 3rd Grade Teacher 1967-71 Nome Elem; 5th Grade Teacher 1971-89, Kndgtn-3rd Grade Teacher 1989- Sour Lake Elem; *ai:* TX St Teachers Assn, NEA, Hardin-Jefferson CIA Mem; *home:* 4030 Procter St Beaumont TX 77705

SAMUEL, RAY GYORA, English/Reading Co-Chair; *b:* Cincinnati, OH; *ed:* (BS) Elem Ed, Univ of Cincinnati 1976; Ed Admin; *cr:* Dir of Jewish Ed Dayton OH 1979-82; Teacher/Consultant Testing/Curr Cincinnati 1982-86; Eng Teacher/Dir 1986- 9, Teacher 1980- Peoples Mid Sch; *ai:* Eng Adv Cncl 1987-; Outstanding Teachers of Jewish Ed 1976-80; CFT 1976-; NEA 1976-; Articles Published; Awds for Jewish Ed Service & Involvement of OWA Dept Head Eng; *home:* 2502 Vera Ave #3 Cincinnati OH 45237

SAMUELS, LYNNE STONE, Teacher of Gifted & Reading; *b:* Chicago, IL; *m:* Neil; *c:* Anne D., Craig S.; *ed:* (BA) Poly Sci, Northwestern Univ 1958; Liberal Stud Degree, Lake Forest Coll; Courses Related to Rdng & Gifted Ed; *cr:* 7th/8th Grade Lang Art/Soc Stud Teacher Wilmot Jr HS 1960-61; 6th Grade Lang Art/Soc Stud/Rdng Teacher Briarwood Elem Sch 1972-76; 7th/8th Grade Teacher of Gifted & Rdng Shepard Jr HS 1977-; *ai:* Sch Newspaper Adv; Sch Musical Stage Mgr; Dist Rdng & Gifted Comm; Phi Beta Kappa 1957; League of Women Voters Bd Mem 1967-; Deerfield Youth Cncl 1981-89; Dist 109 Caucus Chairperson 1970-71.

SAMUELSON, SAHNI WEINHARDT, Theatre Arts Teacher; *b:* Cleveland, OH; *c:* Dan, Shawn, Jesika; *ed:* (BA) Speech Pathology/Audiology, Kent St Univ 1963; (MS) Speech Pathology/Audiology, San Jose St 1965; (MA) Theatre Arts, Portland St Univ 1983; *cr:* Speech/Lang Specialist Elyria Public Schls 1963-64, Shasta Cty Schls 1966-74, Redland Schls 1979-81; Grad Asst Portland St Univ 1981-83; Theatre Arts Teacher Lake Oswego Public Schls 1985-; *ai:* Thespian Club & Assemblies Adv; Play & Musical Dir; NEA, OR Ed Assn; Amer Alliance for Theatre & Ed 1986-; 1st Congregational Church Choir 1975-; Portland Civic Theatre Performer 1975-; Lake Oswego Cmmty Theatre Performer 1976-; Nom Irene Ryan Awd for Acting Excl 1983; *office:* Lakeridge HS 1235 Overlook Dr Lake Oswego OR 97034

SANBORN, CYNDI M., 2nd Grade Teacher; *b:* Staten Island, NY; *m:* J. Ross; *c:* Slade, Clint; *ed:* (BA) Elem Ed, MI St Univ 1971; Grad Work, Rndg & Math; *cr:* 1st Grade Teacher Mt View Elem 1971-79; 4th Grade Teacher 1979-81, 3rd Grade Teacher 1981-86 Ely Grade Sch; 2nd Grade Teacher Mt View Elem 1986-; *ai:* Supervising Concerts; White Pine Cty Classroom Teachers Assn Exec Bd 1988-89; NV Ed Assn, NV St Ed Assn; 4-H 1988-; Delta Kappa Gamma 1988-; Ely Volunteer Fire Dept Womens Auxilliary Treas 1975; Helped Set Up AIDS Curr for K-3rd Grade W P Cty; Served on Soc Stud, Lang Art Curr; *office:* Mountain View Elem Sch 11th St East Ely NV 89315

SANBORN, ROBERT LAURENT, Spanish Teacher; *b:* Paris, France; *m:* Dayle E. Darrough; *c:* Margot, Bobby, Grayson; *ed:* (BA) Span/Hispanic Civilization, Univ of CA Santa Barbara 1973; (MA) Scndry Admin, E WA Univ 1989; Univ of CA Berkeley; *cr:* Span/His/Eng Teacher Imbler Schls 1975-77, Cashmere Schls 1977-79; Span Teacher Wenatclee Valley Coll 1977-, Corvallis Schls 1980-84; Span/Eng Teacher Auburn WA 1984-85, Okanogan Schls 1985-; *ai:* Sr Class Adv; Wrestling Coach; Jr HS Curr Comm; 7th Day Adv Church Sch Bd Chm 1985-88; Lead Consortium Selection for Admin Trng; *office:* Okanogan HS 244 5th St S Okanogan WA 98840

SANCHES, CLEMENTE VAZ, Spanish/Portuguese Teacher; *b:* Chaves, Portugal; *ed:* (BA) Span/Fr, 1974, (MS) Linguistics, 1980 S CT St Univ; *cr:* Span/Portugese Teacher Berlitz 1977-80, Danbury Bd of Ed 1981-; *ai:* Captain & Mem of New Haven Soccer Team; *home:* 129 Cedar St New Haven CT 06519

SANCHES, MARGARET LIVINGSTON, Fourth Grade Teacher; *b:* Fredericksburg, VA; *m:* Gary Anthony; *c:* Kelly, Kyle; *ed:* (BA) Art/Eng, Univ of SC Rock Hill 1965; Grad Stud Various Univs; *cr:* 4th Grade Teacher Pukalani Elem Sch 1987-; *ai:* Stu Government; Campus Patrol; Cub Scout Den Mother; Ftbl, Soccer, Track; Taxi Driver; Natl Teachers Assn 1966-; HI St Teachers Assn 1970-; HI Ed Assn 1973-; *office:* Pukalani Elem Sch 2945 Iolani St Pukalani HI 96768

SANCHEZ, ANGELA R., Third Grade Teacher; *b:* Las Vegas, NM; *m:* Paul; *c:* Roseann Connell, Geno; *ed:* (BA) Elem Ed, NM Highlands Univ 1978; Endorsement in Rdng & Bi-ling; *cr:* Chapter I Rdng Teacher 1978-80, 2nd Grade Teacher 1980-81 Wagon Mound NM; Chapter I Rdng Teacher 1981-82, 3rd Grade Teacher 1982-83 Santa Fe Schls; Chapter I Rdng Teacher 1983-86, 3rd Grade Teacher 1986- Las Vegas City Sch; *ai:* Drill Team Spon; *office:* Legion Park Mid Sch 901 Douglas Ave Las Vegas NM 87701

SANCHEZ, CLARA CASTILLO, English Honors Teacher; *b:* Albuquerque, NM; *m:* Joseph P.; *c:* Joseph M., Paul A.; *ed:* (BS) His/Eng, Univ of NM 1968; Grad Stud; *cr:* Teacher Rio Grande HS 1968-70, Polk Mid Sch 1972-73; Instr Univ of AZ Medical Sch 1975-76; Teacher Tucson HS 1976, Manzano HS 1979-; *ai:* Soph Curr Team Leader 1980-83; Amer Lit Curr Team Leader 1988-; Asst Academic Decathlon; Albuquerque Chamber of Commerce Blue-Ribbon Teacher 1990; Nom Teacher of Yr; Co-Author Publication 1983; *office:* Manzano HS 12200 Lomas Blvd NE Albuquerque NM 87112

SANCHEZ, GUS MICHAEL, Teacher; *b:* Santa Clara, Cuba; *m:* Desiree Elizabeth; *c:* Michael, Victoria; *ed:* (BS) Mechanical Engineering, FL Intnl Univ 1975; (MDIV) Theology, SW Baptist Seminary 1982; Commercial Pilots License & Instrument Rating; *cr:* Teacher Alice HS 1984-85, Freer Jr HS 1985-; *ai:* Lieutenant Jr Grade Chaplain USNR; *office:* Freer Jr HS Rt 1 Box 170-P Alice TX 78332

SANCHEZ, MILTON, 5th Grade Bilingual Ed Teacher; *b:* El Paso, TX; *m:* Armida Cuellar; *c:* Robert L., Cristobal M.; *ed:* (AA) Liberal Arts, El Paso Comm Coll 1976; (BS) Elem Ed, Univ TX El Paso 1978; *cr:* 5th Grade Teacher Fannin Elem Sch 1978-82; 6th Grade Teacher Clendenin Elem Sch 1982-86; Instr Adult Basic Ed Rusk Elem Evening Sch 1979-; 5th Grade Bi-ling Ed Teacher Clendenin Elem Sch 1986-; *ai:* Span Spelling Bee Co-Chm; Newspaper in Ed, 5th Grade Math Chm; El Paso Boys Bsbl Coach 1989, Sportsmanship 1989.

SANCHEZ, NICOLE GERAUD, French & Gifted Ed Teacher; *b:* Marseille, France; *m:* Henry; *c:* John, Linda Sanchez Holt; *ed:* (BS) Bus/Lang, Aix-Marseille Univ 1955; (MS) Adult Ed, 1974, (MS) Spec Ed, 1980 KS St Univ; Gifted Ed, Bi-ling & Multicultural Ed, Eng as Second Lang; *cr:* Fr/Bus Teacher Coll De Wassy France 1956-60; Fr Teacher KS St Univ 1963-64, Fort Riley Adult Ed Center 1965-66, St Xavier HS 1967-73; Fr/Gifted Ed Teacher Fort Riley Jr HS 1974-; *ai:* Natl Jr Honor Society Spon; Effective Sch Panel, Prof Dev Cncl, Parent-Stu-Teacher Alliance Mem; KS Foreign Lang Assn Mem 1968-; AATF (Pres 1978-79, Mem 1968); NEA (Public Relations 1979-80, Mem 1968); Disabled Amer Veterans Auxiliary Past Historian 1970; Intnl Club Chairperson of Bicentennial Celebrations 1976; Intl Rdng Assn; Dev of Fr Course 5th Army Lang Sch; Implementation of Lang Cadet Prgm; Master Teacher Awd 1980; *home:* 327 S Webster Box 519 Junction City KS 66441

SANCHEZ, ROBERT A., 8th Grade US His, Span Teacher; *b:* Las Vegas, NM; *m:* Mary Ann Baca; *c:* Carlos, Alicia, Tomas; *ed:* (BA) Poly Sci, Univ of NM 1975; Bi-ling Ed; *cr:* Teacher Albuquerque Public Schls 1977-; *ai:* Leadership Team; Cinco De Mayo Comm; Soc Stud Dept Chm; Albuquerque Teachers Fed Rep 1986-; NM Assn for Bi-ling Ed 1987-; Translated His Curr into Span.

SANCHEZ, RUBY JUDY, Third Grade Teacher; *b:* Laramie, WY; *ed:* (BA) Elem Ed, Univ of WY 1975; Rdng & Lib Sci; *cr:* Bi-ling Teacher Lincoln Elem 1975-76; 2nd Grade Teacher 1979-81, 1st Grade Teacher 1981-85, 3rd Grade Teacher 1985- Hanna Elem; *ai:* Curr, North Cntrl Accreditation Teacher Center Comm; Stu Teacher Supvr; NEA, WEA, Intnl Rdng Assn, Delta Kappa Gamma Mem; PTO Mem.

SANDBURG, JO ELLEN MAURER, French Teacher; *b:* Fairbury, IL; *m:* Jeffrey Martin; *c:* Jori M.; *ed:* (BA) Fr, Knox Coll 1966; (MA) Guidance Counseling, NE IL Univ 1972; U of Lausanne Switzerland/Univ of Brest/Univ of Rennes/Univ of Quimper France; *cr:* Fr/Eng Teacher Wheeling HS 1966-68; Fr/Amer His Teacher Merrill 1970-71; Fr/Eng Teacher John Hersey HS 1969-79; Fr Teacher Barrington Mid Sch 1979-; *ai:* L'Aventure Francaise Weekend Cnslr for Fr Immersion Camp; Mem Core Team of BMS; Global Fest Commission Mem; ACIS Mem Take Study Groups to France in Summer; AATF Mem Exec Cncl; IL Forg Lang Teachers Assn 1980-; IL Cncl of Teachers of Forg Lang 1988-; Barrington Youth Services Advisory Bd 1984-; United Meth Church Ed Commission Plus Confirmation Teacher; Dept Chairperson 3 Times; 1 of 25 Mem of Strategic Plan Commission; Semi-Finalist Golden Apple Awds; 1st St Master Teacher Awd By Gov Thompson; St Consultant in Forg Lang; Textbook Writer for Scott Foresman; *home:* 5 Hickory Ln Barrington Hills IL 60010

SANDE, SANDRA LEE (NORTON), 8th Eng Teacher & Dept Chair; *b:* Williston, ND; *m:* Dean A.; *c:* Brent, Alesha; *ed:* (BS) Eng, Minot St Univ 1969; *cr:* 9th Grade Eng Teacher 1969-70, 8th/9th Grade Eng Teacher 1971- Jim Hill Jr HS; *ai:* Eng Curr & Teacher Travel Comm; Eng Dept Chairperson; ND Ed Assn 1971-; Phi Delta Kappa, Assn of Teacher Educators 1986-; Political Action Comm for Ed Mem 1984-; PTA Mem 1971-; Minot Zoological Society Mem 1983-; Nom City of Minot Outstanding Young Educator 1981-82; Nom ND Teacher of Yr 1986-87; *home:* 514 20th St SE Minot ND 58701

SANDER, STEPHANIE ANN, 5th Grade & Ranking Teacher; *b:* New Orleans, LA; *cr:* 1st/5th Grade Teacher Our Lady Star of the Sea Sch 1972-; *ai:* Yrbk Ed; Composer; Coach Boys Flag Ftbl, Bsktbl & Boys/Girls Indoor Ball; Stu Newspaper Adv; Art Dir; Numerous Sch/Church Comms; 4-H Organizatonal Leader; Eucharistic Minister; Sch Bd Mem 1977-; Natl Cath Educl Assn Mem 1980-; Parish Cncl Mem 1987-; Teacher of Yr Awds; Coaching Awds; *office:* Our Lady Star of The Sea Sch 1927 St Roch Ave New Orleans LA 70117

SANDERS, ADRIAN LIONEL, Gifted & Talented Ed Teacher; *b:* Paragould, AR; *m:* Molly Jean Zecher; *ed:* (AA) Ed, Bakersfield Coll 1959; (BA) Elem Ed, San Francisco St Univ 1961; (MA) Sci Ed, San Jose St Univ 1967; Grad Stud; *cr:* 7th Grade Teacher Sharp Park Sch 1961-62; 5th Grade Teacher Mowry Sch 1962-64; Sci Teacher Blacow Sch 1964-76; 5th Grade Teacher Warm Springs Sch 1977-; *ai:* CA Teachers Assn 1961-; Fremont Unified Dist Teachers Assn, NEA 1965-; San Jose Historical Society 1980-; Hayward Dance Club 1987-; Natl Geographic Society 1976-; Outstanding Young Educator Finalist 1965; Sabbatical 1986-87; *office:* Warm Springs Sch 47370 Warm Springs Blvd Fremont CA 94539

SANDERS, BARBARA BROWN, Science Teacher; *b:* Tulia, TX; *m:* John A.; *c:* Hatcher J., Detrick A.; *ed:* (BS) Engl/Sci, West TX St Univ 1962; (MS) Human Anatomy/Growth, Univ of OR 1967; Educ Admin, Central St Univ; Educ Courses Secndry Admin Cert; *cr:* Math/Sci/PE Whittier Elem 1962-64; PE/Coaching Seminole Jr-Sr HS 1965-66; PE/Anatomy Lab Univ of OR 1966-67; Phy Ed Central St Univ 1967-75; PE/Coaching Salina Elem Jr HS 1975-76; Sci Teacher Choctaw Jr HS 1979-; *ai:* Natl Jr Honor Society Spon; Stu Cncl Spon; Academic Teams Coach; NSTA; NEA/OEA/CCTA Pres 1981-82; Choctaw Schls Teacher of Yr 1982-83; Laubauch Literacy 1985-; Natl Sci Fnd Scholar Prgm 1988; *office:* Choctaw Jr H S 3rd & Main Choctaw OK 73020

SANDERS, BEA BETTY GARVER, English Teacher; *b:* Fessenden, ND; *m:* Forrest S.; *c:* Alen Gardner (Dec) *ed:* (BA) Eng/Latin, Jamestown Coll 1946; (MA) Dramatic Theory Lit, Univ of IA 1963; Univ; Temple Univ; Univ of IA; Cornell Univ; Suny Buffalo; *cr:* Lecturer in Speech Southern IL Univ 1962-63; Asst Prof Speech Elmira Coll 1963-70; Social Worker Southern Tier Assn for Blind 1970-74 Eng Teacher Horseheads HS 1974-; *ai:* NCTE 1963-87; NYSEC 1964-86; Arnot Art Museum; Friends of Steele Memorial Lib; Tri-Cities Opera Guild; Tanglewood Nature Center; Clemons Art Center; HHDS HS Teacher of Yr 1985; *office:* Horseheads H S Fletcher St Horseheads NY 14845

SANDERS, BEVERLY ISIDORE, Rdng/Math Laboratory Teacher; *b:* New Orleans, LA; *c:* Lauren, Kelly; *ed:* (BA) Eng Ed, LA St Univ New Orleans 1971; Elem Rdng & Math, Chicago St, Coll of Natl Ed; *cr:* 7th Grade Teacher D H Williams 1975-80; 5th Grade Teacher 1980-84, Math/Rdng/Cmptr Lab 1984- James Wadsworth; *office:* James Wadsworth Elem Sch 6434 S University Ave Chicago IL 60637

SANDERS, BEVERLY RUTH, Language Arts Chair; *b:* Bryan, TX; *ed:* (BSE) Phys Ed/Eng, Midwestern St Univ 1974; (MSE) Phys Ed, Univ of OK 1975; Academic Trng Gifted Ed; *cr:* Teacher Richardson West Jr HS 1975-79; Teacher/Chairperson Wilkinson Mid Sch 1980-; *ai:* Natl Jr Honor Society & Chrldrs Spon; Mid Sch Task Force & Poly Action Comm Mem; TX Assn Gifted/Talented 1984-; TX Joint Cncl Teacher of Eng 1984-; *office:* Wilkinson Mid Sch 2100 Crest Park Mesquite TX 75149

SANDERS, BRENDA GRAHAM, Fourth Grade Teacher; *b:* Silsbee, TX; *m:* John Edison Sr.; *c:* John E. Jr.; *ed:* (BS) Elem Ed, 1970, (MED) Elem Ed, 1973 TX Southern Univ; Eng as Second Lang, Cmptr Technology; *cr:* 3rd Grade Teacher Walnut Bend Elem 1970-71; 4th Grade Teacher Hartsfield Elem 1971-; *ai:* Black His Comm; San Jacinto Cncl & Troop Leader GSA; Houston Teachers Assn, TX St Teachers 1970-; NCTE 1980-82; Delta Sigma Theta Historian 1982-; Iota Phi Lambda Regional Journalist 1979, Local Spon of Yr 1988; Hartsfield Elem Outstanding Young Educator, Teacher of Yr; *home:* 6615 Glen Rock Houston TX 77087

SANDERS, CONNIE FAY (CALL), Fourth Grade Teacher; *b:* Windsor, MO; *m:* Elliott Jacob; *c:* Justin, Ashlea, Nicholas; *ed:* (BS) Elem Ed, Cntrl MO St Univ 1981; Minor in Health Ed K-9; *cr:* 4th Grade Teacher Lone Jack Elem 1981-83; 4th Grade Teacher 1983-84, 5th Grade Teacher 1984-86, 4th Grade Teacher 1986-87, 5th Grade Teacher 1987-88, 4th Grade Teacher 1988- Windsor Elem; *ai:* HS Cheerleading Spon; Spring Banquet Comm; Cmmty Teachers Assn Secy 1985-86; MO St Teachers Assn 1981-; First Chrstn Church (Evangelism Comm Chm 1984-85, Bd Secy 1985-87, Membership Comm Chm 1988-89, Deacon Chm 1989-); *office:* Henry Cty R-1 Elem Sch S Main Windsor MO 65360

SANDERS, CYNTHIA CASSELMANN, First Grade Teacher; *b:* Eunice, LA; *m:* Charles Gardner; *c:* Teri L. Brown; Mark W. Brown; Tracy A. Brown; Michael L., Katherine M. Sanders Smith; *ed:* (BA) Elem Ed, LA Coll 1966; Working Toward Masters; *cr:* 1st Grade Teacher Cherokee Elem 1966-67; 2nd Grade Teacher Lessie Moore Elem 1968-70; 3rd Grade Teacher Silver City Elem 1970, Peabody Elem 1971-72; 2nd Grade Teacher Expressway Elem 1972-73; 1st/4th-6th Grade Teacher J S Slocum Elem 1974-; *ai:* Prof Faculty Study; Study for Accreditation; Parish Rdng & Writing Comm; *home:* 509 Hiawatha Trl Pineville LA 71360

SANDERS, DICKIE DEE, Mathematics Teacher; *b:* M, Shawnee; *m:* Connie Sue Tarrant; *c:* Todd, Matt; *ed:* (BSED) Math, 1973, (MED) Math, 1976 East Cntrl Univ; *cr:* Math Classroom Teacher Wanette HS 1973-74, Amber-Pocasset HS 1974-; *ai:* OEA 1973-75; 1st Baptist Church Deacon 1985-; *office:* Amber-Pocasset HS Box 38 Amber OK 73004

SANDERS, DORIS JACKSON, Third Grade Teacher; *b:* Lumberton, NC; *m:* Alger Joseph Jr.; *ed:* (BS) Elem Ed, Fayetteville St Univ 1966; *cr:* Teacher Proctorville Sch 1966-; *ai:* K-6th Grade Math, Sch Improvement, Comm Skills, Comprehensive Ed Plan, Screening, Budget Comms; PTA Treas; NEA, NC Assn of Educators, Robeson Assn of Educators 1968-; Proctorville Sch Teacher of Yr 1989-; *home:* 201 Front St PO Box 64 Lumberton NC 28358

SANDERS, GERALD DAVID, Teacher/Principal; *b:* Sunbury, PA; *m:* Patricia A. James; *c:* Devin M., Gavin K.; *ed:* (BS) Elem Ed, Mansfield Univ 1969; (MSED) Curr Specilist, 1973; Elem/Scndry Prin Cert, 1979 Bucknell Univ; Drug Curr, Penn St; Sci Prgm, Clarion Univ; *cr:* ESEA Title I 1970-72; 5th Grade Teacher 1972-83; Prin/Teacher 1983-Shirellamy Sch Dist; Consultant Susquehanna Univ 1986-88; *ai:* Flag Ftbl; Outdoor Ed-Week Long Stu Resident Prgm; SVEPA 1986-; Lewisbrg R & P Pres 1986-88; NPTSSA 1970-; Gama Theta Upsilon Published Ed Study-1972; *office:* Oaklyn Elem Sch Rd 2 Sunbury PA 17801

SANDERS, JESSIE, Kindergarten Teacher; *b:* Bayou Current, LA; *c:* Jouselyn, Joseph, Martin; *ed:* (BA) Elem/Kndgtn, Southern 1973; Spec Ed; *cr:* Teacher 1970-73, Dir 1973-76 Melville Headstart; Adult Teacher St Landry Parish Sch Bd 1976-78; Eng/Sci Teacher Melville Mid Sch 1978-84; Kndgtn Teacher Melville Elem 1984-; *ai:* Stu Cncl; Spelling & Writing Adv; Writing to Read Planner; NEA & SLAE Booster; Southern Univ Magna Cum Laude 1973; *home:* PO Box 418 Melville LA 71353

SANDERS, JO MC CONNELL, German/Russian Teacher; *b:* Cedar Rapids, IA; *m:* Robert B.; *c:* Ross, Stefan, *ed:* (BA) Ger, Univ of IA 1964; (MA) Ger, Univ of OK 1968; (ABD) Ger Lit, Penn St 1972; Gothic & Old High Ger, Univ of Nottingham; Middlebury Coll Summer Inst; *cr:* Ger Teacher Univ of OK 1962-63, Brighton HS 1971-72, West HS 1972-73; Ger/Russian Teacher/Dept Chairperson Bartlett HS 1973-; *ai:* Ger/Amer Partner Sch Prgm Exch & USSR-USA Academic Sch Exch Spon; Ger Club, Russian Club, NHS, Natl Russian Honor Society Adv; AATG Pres 1983-, Outstanding Ger Teacher 1982; AK Foreign Lang Assn Pres 1988-; Amer Cncl Teachers of Russian; NEA Teacher of Yr 1988; Pacific NW Cncl on Foreign Lang Exec Bd 1988-; Anchorage Womens Ice Hockey Assn Goalie 1980-, Rookie of Yr 1980, Most Inspirational 1989-; Fullbright Exch Teacher West Germany 1987-88; Rockefeller Grant East Germany 1990; Disney Salute to Amer Teacher Natl Winner 1990; Dir & Founder St Lang Camps 1976-; *home:* 11661 Rockridge Dr Anchorage AK 99516

SANDERS, LENA MARBRA, Government/Economics Teacher; *b:* Port Gibson, MS; *m:* Nathaniel Jr.; *c:* Damien D., Daniel D.; *ed:* (BS) Soc Stud, Alcorn St Univ 1968; Grad Stud Delta St Univ, MS StUniv, Univ of S MS, MS Coll; *cr:* Instr/His Teacher Humphrey Cty Schls 1968-69, Leland Public Schls 1969-75; Eligibility Worker St Dept of Public Welfare 1976-79; Government Teacher Our Lady of Victories Sch 1979-87; Teacher/Act Coord Moss Point HS 1987-; *ai:* Youth Legislature; Free Enterprise Competition; Law Day Prgm; Stu Cncl Adv; Interact Co-Spon; Homecoming Act Coord; Carnival Ball; Assist in Planning Jr/Sr Prom; St Textbook Adoption Comm Mem; NCSS; Common Cause; STAR Teacher Awd; Moss Point HS Teacher of Yr Awd; Yrbk Dedication; *office:* Moss Point HS 4924 Church St Moss Point MS 39563

SANDERS, LYNN CATLETTE, Teacher; *b:* Greenwood, MS; *m:* Harry Sargent; *c:* Hilah White Sanders, Gordon C.; *ed:* (BS) Math, MS Univ for Women 1969; *cr:* Teacher Westpoint HS 1969-71, Caldwell HS 1971-; *ai:* Sr Class Spon; Staff Dev Comm; Math & Sci Competition Coach; Columbus Classroom Teachers 1971-; Columbus Jr Auxiliary 1984-89; *office:* Caldwell HS 820 Browder St Columbus MS 39703

SANDERS, MARTHA L., Second Grade Teacher; *b:* Noxapater, MS; *c:* Tonya M. Lyons, Theadore Lyons II; *ed:* (BS) Bus Admin, MS Valley St Univ 1968; (MA) Elem Ed, SE MO St Univ 1975; Grad Work Educl Admin, Elem Ed; *cr:* 5th Grade Teacher Charleston Sch Dist 1968-72; Curr Coord 1975-77, 2nd Grade Teacher 1973- Cairo Sch Dist 1; *ai:* Cairo Assn of Teachers Pres 1974-77, Plaque 1982; Guardianship & Advocacy Commission, Certificate of Appreciation 1989; *home:* 205 33rd Cairo IL 62914

SANDERS, MARY J., Junior High Teacher; *b:* Lucerne, MO; *c:* Larry A.; *ed:* (MS) Elem, Northeast Univ 1975; *ai:* 8th Grade Spon; BPW Pres 1982-84; Beta Chi Pres 1988-; *home:* 620 N 21st Unionville MO 63565

SANDERS, MERTHA RANKIN, Social Studies Chairman; *b:* Magee, MS; *m:* Doril; *c:* Marquez, Jacquez; *ed:* (BS) Soc Sci, MS Valley St 1970; (MS) Soc Sci, 1979, (EDS) Soc Sci, 1990 MS Coll; *cr:* Teacher Magee Mid Sch; *ai:* Co-Ed Y Club Spon, Church Youth Group; AFT.

SANDERS, PATRICIA (MUEHRER), Span Teacher/Foreign Lang Head; *b:* Hammond, IN; *m:* David; *c:* Nicholas, Moreno; *ed:* (BA) Span/Theology, Valparaiso Univ 1975; (MA) Span, Wayne St Univ 1985; Minor Eng; ITIP; Deaconess-Prof Church Worker; *cr:* Youth Worker Calexico CA, Faith Luth Church/St Paul Luth 1976-77, Trinity Luth Church 1977-78; Teacher/Vlybl Coach Luth HS 1978-; *ai:* Intnl Club Adv; Foreign Lang Dept Head; MI Foreign Lang Assn, Oakland Foreign Lang Assn 1987-; Families of Latin Children On-Going Organizer 1988-; Presentation at Prof Conferences MI Assn of Non-Public Sch Study Skills; *office:* Lutheran HS North 16825 24 Mile Mount Clemens MI 48044

SANDERS, PATRICIA SMITH, English Teacher; *b:* Andalusia, AL; *m:* Michael R.; *c:* Rebecca, Allison; *ed:* (BS) Eng Ed, Auburn Univ 1974; *cr:* Eng Teacher S Girard HS 1975-78; Alexandria Sr HS 1977-78; Eng/Fr Teacher Tioga HS 1978-; *ai:* Class & Homecoming Court Spon; Stu of Week Comm; NCTE 1978-89; NEA 1975-89; Teacher of Yr; *office:* Tioga HS P O Box 1030 Tioga LA 71477

SANDERS, PEARLIE ORR, Teacher; *b:* Toccoa, GA; *m:* Henry Osborn; *c:* Tony, Michael; *ed:* (BA) Psych, Spelman Coll 1964; (MA) Guidance Counseling, Atlanta Univ 1975; (EDS) Early Chldhd Ed, GA St Univ 1988; Cert Early Chldhd Ed, Atlanta Univ 1978; *cr:* Teacher Grove Park Elem 1964-66, Garden Hills Elem 1969-76, John Hope Elem 1977-; *ai:* Leadership Team Chairperson 5 Yrs; Young Authors Coord 1985-; Writers Roundup Coord 1985-; Lang Arts Coord 1990; Adopt a Sch Liason Grady Hospital; AAE, NEA 1964-77, AFT, GFT 1978; St Mark AME Church Class Leader 1989-; Spelman Coll Alumnae Assn 1964-; GA St Alumnus Assn 1988-; Academic Achievement Awd; Area III Atlanta Public Schls 1985-86; Teacher of Yr 1987; Teacher of Sci Excl 1988; Whos Who Among Prof/Exec Women 1989; *office:* John Hope Elem 112 Blvd NE Atlanta GA 30312

SANDERS, RALPH LEE, Mathematics Department Chair; *b:* Greenville, TX; *m:* Doris Bennett; *c:* Knikole, Cavyn, Caryn; *ed:* (BS) Elem Ed, 1980, (MED) Ed Admin, 1989 E TX St Univ; *cr:* Teacher Travis Elem 1980-82; Teacher 1982-, Math Chm 1986- Greenville Intermediate; *ai:* Stu Cncl Spon; Math Therapist; Sunshine Comm Chm; TX Classroom Teachers Assn Faculty Rep 1988-; Deans List & Pres Honor Roll E TX St Univ; *office:* Greenville Intermediate Sch 3201 Stanford Greenville TX 75401

SANDERS, RICHARD J., 4th Grade Teacher; *b:* Toledo, OH; *m:* Patricia Beazley; *c:* Bethany, Benjamin, Laura; *ed:* (BA) Creative Drama/Theatre, Univ of Toledo 1975; *cr:* 4th Grade Teacher Clay Elem 1975-80, Olney Elem 1980-; *ai:* Drama Coach; Eng Curr Update Chm; Talking about Whale Lang Mem; NRA 1975-; *office:* Olney Elem Sch 1512 Lemoyne Rd Northwood OH 43619

SANDERS, ROSA ANNE, Science Teacher; *b:* Louisville, MS; *c:* Theresa M.; *ed:* (BS) Bio, Alcorn St Univ 1967; (MS) Bio Sci Ed, 1977; (EDS) Bio Sci Ed, 1985 MS St Univ; Scndry Admin Prgm; *cr:* Sci Teacher Harris HS 1967-68; Roosevelt Att Ctr 1968-69; Boler HS 1969-70; Beulah Hubbard HS 1970-; *ai:* Co-Spon Sci Club; Y-Team; Girl Scout Co-Leader; Dean of Dist Congress; Pres Missionary Society; S S Teacher; Secy State Dean; NEA/MAE 1970-; NSTA 1980-; NCAE 1970-; MSTA 1986-; New Ed St Conv State Dir 1981-; Heroines of Jericho Mem 1986-; NAACP Mem 1983-; NSF Grant Chem Summers 1973 & 1974; Grant from Amer Chem Society Summer 1989; Article Publ Focus Journal MS Assn for Supervision & Curr Dev 1987; *home:* Rt 1 Box 106 Noxagater MS 39346

SANDERS, RUBY COWAND, English IV Teacher; *b:* Colerain, NC; *m:* Frank Cranford; *c:* Andrew, Elizabeth; *ed:* (BA) Eng, Campbell Univ 1968; *cr:* Eng Teacher W Montgomery HS 1968-; *ai:* Sr Spon; Sr Grade Chm; Mentor Teacher; NC Assn of Educators, NEA 1968-; NCTE; *office:* W Montgomery HS Rt 3 Mount Gilead NC 27306

SANDERS, THOMAS WILLIAM, Fifth Grade Teacher; *b:* Petoskey, MI; *c:* Thomas R., Levi S., Daniel W., Theodore L., Anthony L., Jason Q., Henrietta L.; *ed:* (BS) Bio, 1961, (BA) Ed, 1961, (MA) Elem Ed, 1971 Cntrl MI Univ; Real Estate Broker; Tae Kwon Do; Tae Chi Kwan; Shiatsu; *cr:* 6th Grade Teacher Mt Pleasant Public Schls 1961-63, Escondido Union Schls 1963-64; Elem Mid Sch Teacher Cntrl Montcalm Public Schls 1964-; *ai:* Class Adv; Golf, Track, Bsktbl, Ftbl Coaching Comm; Rdng, Math, Sci, Soc Stud, Lang, Phys Ed, Curr Dev; Cntrl Montcalm Ed Assn VP 1968-70; Natl Defense Act Grant; *home:* 2590 S Sheridan Rd Stanton MI 48888

SANDERS, WAYNE, II, Sixth Grade Teacher; *b:* Akron, OH; *m:* Linda G. Rininger; *ed:* (BS) Elem Ed, 1978, (BA) His, 1978, (BS) Cmptr/Soc Stud/Scndry Ed, 1979, (MS) Elem Ed, 1982 Univ of Akron; *cr:* 6th Grade Teacher Manchester Local Schls 1978-; *ai:* Var Boys & Girls Head Tennis Coach; Public Lib Film Courier; Kappa Delta Pi, Gamma Theta Upsilon 1977-; Phi Alpha Theta 1975-; Alpha Kappa Delta, Pi Sigma Alpha 1976-; OH Tennis Coaches Assn 1982-, Awd; *office:* Manchester Mid Sch 760 W Nimisila Rd Akron OH 44319

SANDERS, YVETTE LA LONDE, Guidance Counselor; *b:* El Paso, TX; *m:* Thomas O. III; *c:* Thomas O. IV, Shannon C., Yvette L.; *ed:* (BS) Scndry Ed/His, Univ of TX at El Paso 1963; (MS) Scndry Ed/Soc Stud, Univ of SC; Grad Work Counseling; Teacher Cadet Prgm Trng; *cr:* Eng Teacher Barnwell Jr HS 1964-65; US His/Government Teacher Barnwell HS 1965-66; Prin Barnwell Cty Headstart Prgm 1968; US His Teacher Gainyard-Butler Mid Sch 1984-85; Guidance Cnslr/Teacher of Talented & Gifted 1985-87, Guidance Cnslr/Cadet Prgm Teacher 1987- Barnwell HS; *ai:* NHS; Trivia Bowl Team; Mentorship Prgm; Public Relations for Honors Sch; SC Assn for Counseling & Dev, SC Scndry Sch Cnslr Assn; Barnwell United Meth Church Bd of Trustees 1983-; Steve Thurmond Inst Fellowship; *office:* Barnwell HS Jackson St Ext Barnwell SC 29812

SANDFORD, JANICE MAYFIELD, Jr HS Social Studies Teacher; *b:* Lake Charles, LA; *m:* Leroy Joseph; *c:* Lyle J., Lisa C.; *ed:* (BA) Elem Ed, Xavier Univ 1955; (MA) Admin/Supervision, Mc Nesse St Univ 1978; Univ of CA, North East Univ; Gifted & Talented, Mc Neese St Univ; *cr:* 4th Grade Teacher Mill Street Elem 1955-70, Nelson Elem 1970-77; Gifted Prgm Teacher Ralph Wilson Elem 1978-79; 6th Grade Teacher Sacred Heart 1980-85; *ai:* Religious Instr for Adults Dir; Delta Sigma Theta Chairperson UNCF 1986-87, Delta of Yr 1980; Writing Book; Poems & Choral Rdngs to be Published; *home:* 736 Esplanade Lake Charles LA 70605

SANDIFORD, ANDERSON PATRICK, English Teacher/Assoc Prin; *b:* St James, Barbados; *m:* Lynette Merilyn Edwards; *c:* Givona, Lemar, Devan; *ed:* (BA) Eng, 1981, (BS) Behavioral Sci, 1981 Atlantic Union Coll; (MA) Ed, Loma Linda Univ 1984; *cr:* Eng Teacher Loma Linda Acad 1981-87; Eng Teacher/Asst Prin 1987-89, Eng Teacher/Assoc Prin 1989- Miami Union Acad; *ai:* Stu Assn & Knights of Honor Spon; Discipline Comm Chm; Southeastern Conference Teachers Assn (VP 1988-89, Pres 1989-90); *office:* Miami Union Acad 12051 W Okeechobee Rd Hialeah FL 33016

SANDKNOP, JANE K., 9th Grade English Teacher; *b:* Kirksville, MO; *m:* Bob; *c:* Jennifer, Erin; *ed:* (BSE) Eng NE MO St Univ 1979; (MA) Sch Admin, 1980 NE MO St Univ; *cr:* 8th/9th Grade Eng Teacher Kirksville Jr HS 1979-86; 9th/10th Grade Teacher of Gifted Terrell Ind Sch Dist 1986-88; 9th/10th Grade Eng Teacher Rockwall Ind Sch Dist 1988-; *ai:* Assn of TX Prof Educators 1986-88; *office:* Rockwall Ind Sch Dist 1201 High School Rd Rockwall TX 75087

SANDLIN, CHERYL WATSON, Third Grade Teacher; *b:* Ardmore, OK; *m:* Earl; *ed:* (BS) Elem Ed, SE OK St Univ 1978; Early Chldhd Trng & Counseling; *cr:* Head Start Teacher Big Five Cmmty Services 1978-80; 3rd Grade Teacher Velma-Alma Sch 1980-; *ai:* 6th/7th Grade Cheerleading Spon 1988-; Staff Dev Comm; OEA Building Rep; OK Ed Assn, Velma-Alma Educators Assn, NEA 1988-; OK Rdng Cncl 1987-89; Epsilon Sigma Alpha (Secy, VP) 1983-; Immanuel Baptist Adult II Welcome Comm 1989-; S OK St Univ Senate Mem 1977-78; Entelechy (VP. Pledge Trainer) 1975-78; Whos Who Among Young Professionals 1990; *home:* 212 North N Duncan OK 73533

SANDMAN, SUSAN RICHARDS, Third Grade Teacher; *b:* Cincinnati, OH; *m:* Lawrence William; *c:* Ben, Andrew, Daniel, William *ed:* (BS) Elem Ed, Univ of Cincinnati 1975; *cr:* 5th Grade Teacher Our Lady of Lourdes 1975-76; 6th Grade Teacher St Helen 1976-77; 5th Grade Teacher 1977-78, 4th Grade Teacher 1978-87, 3rd Grade Teacher 1898- St John the Baptist; *ai:* Co-Wrote & Co-Directed 4th Grade Plays; Mission Coord; Taught Vietnamese Children Rdng & Eng Grammer 1975; *office:* St John the Baptist 110 Hill St Harrison OH 45030

SANDMEIER, KATHERINE K., Social Studies Teacher; *b:* Boston, MA; *c:* Kirk, Kathy, Heidi; *ed:* (BS) Ed, Butler Univ 1969; Grad Work Geographic Ed, Univ of CO; *cr:* Teacher Niwot HS 1984-; Teacher/Consultant Natl Geographic Summer Inst 1989-; *ai:* Close Up Club; NCSS, CO Cncl Soc Stud, Natl Cncl for Geographic Ed, CO Geographic Alliance; NCSS Japan Keizai Koho Fellowship; Natl Geographic Summer Geographic Inst 1986.

SANDOMIR, LAWRENCE PHILIP, 6th Grade Teacher/Writing Adv; *b:* Bronx, NY; *m:* Mindy Stilman; *c:* Rachel, Justin, Chelsea; *ed:* (BA) Elem Ed, 1972, (MA) Urban Stud/Admin, 1973 Queens Coll; *cr:* 6th-8th Grade Teacher Leonardo Da Vinci Jr HS 1972-75; 8th Grade Teacher Elizabeth Barrett Browning Jr HS 1975-76; Head Teacher/Faculty Adv/Curr Coord Ramaz Sch 1976-; *ai:* Yrbk & Literary Magazine Faculty Adv; Photography Coord; General Stud Lang Art Curr Coord; *office:* Ramaz Sch 125 E 85th St New York NY 10028

SANDOVAL, ANTHONY JOSEPH, GATE Algebra/Science Teacher; *b:* Los Angeles, CA; *m:* Sharon J.; *c:* Maria Pryor, Anthony D., Kathie Sanjorjo, Nicole; *ed:* (BS) Geology, 1960, (MAED) Guidance Counseling, 1964 AZ St Univ; Admin Credential, Whittier Coll; Renewed Innovations in Sci Ed, UCLA; *cr:* Sci/Math Teacher Superior Schls 1960-63, El Rancho Unified 1963-66; Cnslr 1966-72, Admin 1972-83, Sci/Math Teacher 1983- El Rancho Unified; *ai:* Mathcounts Coach; after Sch Gate Sci Teacher; Sci Olympiad Coach; Sci Club; Ecology Team Coach; CA Sch Cnslrs Assn Area VI Dir 1970-73; CA Personnel & Guid Assn Chicano Caucus Pres 1972-73 Presidents Gavel 1973; ERA/CTA/NEA; Acad of Amer Educators Outstanding Educator in Amer 1973-74; UCLA/Sacnas Presenter Natl Conv of Sci Teachers 1988; *office:* Rivera Mid Sch 7200 Citronell St Pico Rivera CA 90660

SANDOVAL, BERTHA V., Spanish Teacher; *b:* Santa Fe, NM; *c:* Rita Sanchez; *ed:* (BA) Span Ed, 1965, (MA) Span, 1973 Univ of NM; *cr:* Teacher 1965-, Foreign Lang Dept Chairperson 1970- Pojoaque HS; *ai:* El Circulo Espanol, Class of 1988, Class of 1993 Spon; Numerous Comms; HS Advisory Comm 1987-; Foreign Lang Assn of N NM (VP 1989-, Pres 1987-88); Organization of Lang Educators 1987-; NM Modern & Classical Lang Task Force Mem 1988-; *office:* Pojoaque HS Rt 1 Box 207 Santa Fe NM 87501

SANDOVAL, JANETTE GRAHAM, Spec Projects Resource Teacher; *b:* Brawley, CA; *m:* Juan Jose; *c:* Juan J. Jr., Jennifer M.; *ed:* (BA) His/Soc Sci, San Diego St Univ 1971; Sch Admin, San Diego St Univ; *cr:* 5th Grade Teacher J W Oakley & Myron D Witter Schls 1971-74; 6th Grade Teacher 1975-77, 2nd Grade Teacher 1977-78 Myron D Witter Sch; 3rd Grade Teacher J W Oakley & Myron D Witter Schls 1978-81; 4th Grade Teacher Myron D Witter Sch 1981-82; 1st Grade Teacher 1982-86, Spec Projects Resource Teacher 1986- J W Oakley Sch; *ai:* Sacred Heart Cath Sch Bd Mem 1980-82; Imperial Cty Teacher Ed & Cmptr Center Bd Rep 1980-82; Brawley Elem Teachers Assn (Secy, Faculty Rep, Mem) 1972-86; CA Teachers Assn, NEA Mem 1971-; Certificated Pupil Personnel Assn (Mem, Negotiator) 1986-; Westmoreland 4-H Club (Adv, Leader) 1984-; Imperial Valley Horse Exhibitors Assn (Secy, Mem) 1985-; *office:* J W Oakley Sch 261 D Street Brawley CA 92227

SANDOVAL, NANCY WILSON, Spanish/ESL Teacher; *b:* Houston, TX; *c:* Ana Luisa; *ed:* (BA) Span, 1975, (MA) ESL, 1982 Univ of North TX; *cr:* Teaching Fellow 1975-78, ESL Instr 1979-88, Asst Dir 1981-83 Univ of North TX; Span Teacher Manor HS 1988-; *ai:* Intnl Club Spon; Textesol III 1979-; Tesol 1979-; Sierra Club, Natl Parks & Recreation, World Wildlife Fund 1988-; Literacy Volunteer 1990; TX Excl Awd for Outstanding HS Teachers-Manor HS Recipient & St Nominee; Presenter Intnl Tesol NY 1985; *office:* Manor H S Box 679 Manor TX 78653

SANDOW, DEBORAH RANAE BILLINGSLEY, Mathematics Department Chair; *b:* Midland, MI; *m:* Patrick James; *ed:* (BA) Math, Spring Arbor 1988; *cr:* Math Teacher/Dept Chairperson All Saints 1988-; *ai:* Stu Cncl Adv; Var Vlybl Coach; *office:* All Saints Central Schl 217 S Monroe Bay City MI 48708

SANDS, DAN J., English Teacher; *b:* Viroqua, WI; *m:* Iso Gutierrez; *c:* Jesse, Laura; *ed:* (BS) Eng, Univ of WI La Crosse 1974; Grad Work Northern AZ Univ; ESL Certified 1988; *cr:* Eng Teacher St of New South Wales 1975-77, Santa Cruz Cooperative Sch 1978-82, Escuela Americana 1982-84, Holbrook HS 1984-; *ai:* Head Cross Cntry, Asst Wrestling Coach; Detention Supvr; NEA; AEA; AZ-TESOL; Regional Cross Cntry Coach of Yr 1989-; *office:* Holbrook H S PO Box 640 Holbrook AZ 86025

SANER, ELIZABETH LESLEY, Second Grade Teacher; *b:* Scarborough, England; *m:* Edward Cotton; *c:* Jeremy Rentschlar, Mark Rentschlar, Diana; *ed:* Eng/Elem Ed, Cheshire Cty Coll England 1957; (BSC) Elem Ed 1977; (MED) Elem Ed 1981 Coll of Charleston; *cr:* 3rd Grade Teacher Pownall Green Elem Sch Cheshire England 1957-58; 5th/6th/7th/8th Grade Teacher His/ Eng 1969-70, 3rd Grade Teacher 1970-71 Divine Redeemer Sch;2nd Grade Teacher Yeamans Park Sch 1971-75; 2nd Grade Teacher George R Fishburne Elem Sch 1977-; *ai:* Teacher Rep PTA Bd; Mem Cty Sci Advisory Comm; Produce-Dio-Choral Speaking Puppet Shows; SCEA Faculty Rep 1978-81; SCEA Poly Action Chairperson 1979-80; Teacher of Yr 1980; Article Published Eng Paper; *office:* G R Fishburne Elem Sch 6215 N Murray Ave Dr Hanahan SC 29406

SANFORD, DORRIS ORENE, English Teacher; *b:* Ellijay, GA; *m:* Emuel; *c:* Eric, Jennifer; *ed:* (AA) Ed, Truett Mc Connell Coll 1983; (BA) Scndry Eng Ed, N GA Coll 1985; *cr:* Clerk Huff Drugs 1974-75; Substitute Teacher 1978-83, Eng Teacher 1985- Gilmer HS; *ai:* PAGE; WMU Secy 1987-; *office:* Gilmer HS 500 S Main Ellijay GA 30540

SANFORD, L. G. G., Biology Professor; *b:* Walker Cty, AL; *m:* Marilyn Virginia Henderson; *c:* David W., Nancy L.; *ed:* (BS) Bio, Univ of N AL 1957; (MS) Zoology, 1963, (PHD) Entomology, 1966 Auburn Univ; *cr:* Bio Aide TN Valley Authority 1956-58; Bio Teacher W Jefferson HS 1958-60; Zoology Instr 1960-63, Research Asst 1963-65 Auburn Univ; Assoc Prof Bio 1965-69, Bio Prof 1969- Jacksonville St Univ; *ai:* Beta Beta Beta Spon; AL Acad of Sci, AL Ed Assn 1965-; NEA 1972-; *office:* Jacksonville St Univ N Peleham Rd Jacksonville AL 36265

SANFORD, PATRICIA BULLOCK, Fifth Grade Teacher; *b:* Collins, MS; *m:* Steven Louis; *c:* Brett, Jonathan; *ed:* (BA) Elem Ed, Univ of S MS 1979; (MS) Elem Ed, William Carey Coll; JTPA Summer Sch Trng; *cr:* 5th Grade Teacher Seminary Attendance Center 1979-; *ai:* Chrldr & Jr/Sr Prom Spon; Homecoming Reception & Hospitality Club Chm; Covington Cty Teachers Assn Secy 1988-89; Covington Cty Chamber of Commerce 1989-; *home:* Rt 2 Box 265 Collins MS 39428

SANGER, THERESA LUKENICH, Phys Sci/Physics Teacher; *b:* Honolulu, HI; *ed:* (BA) Eng, CO St Univ 1966; (PD) Teachers Cert, 1967, Sci Cert, 1976 Univ of HI; Prof Teacher Reclassification, Univ of HI 1968-76; Grad Stud in Physics, Univ of N IA 1988-89; *cr:* Sci/Eng Teacher Kaimuki Intermediate 1968-84; Phys Sci/Physics Teacher Mc Kinley HS 1984-; *ai:* Physics Club Co-Adv; Mc Kinley Staff Dev Comm Co-Chairperson; Mc Kinley HS Coordinating Comm Rep; Amer Assn of Physics Teachers 1988-; HI Sci Teachers Assn 1980-; HI St Teachers Assn 1974-; Woodrow Wilson Fellowship Phys Sci Univ Princeton; Honolulu Dist Teacher of Yr 1989; Dr Shiro Amioka Awd Excl in Teaching 1989; NSF Grant Prisms Univ of N IA; *office:* Mc Kinley HS 1039 S King St Honolulu HI 96814

SAN MIGUEL, MARY L., Business Instructor; *b:* Waukesha, WI; *c:* Emilio; *ed:* (BBA) Bus Admin, Coll of Sante Fe 1987; *ai:* Jr Class Adv 1989-; Jr Class Prom Coord 1989- & Prom Asst 1988-89; *home:* 131 Alamo Dr Santa Fe NM 87501

SANN, DEBORAH J. BALENTINE, English Teacher; *b:* Greenburg, PA; *m:* Harry James; *c:* Nathaniel J., Bethany M.; *ed:* (BA) Comm, 1972, (MED) Eng, 1977 CA St Univ of PA; (BS) Soc Sci, Seton Hill Coll 1984; *cr:* Yough Sch Dist 1972-; *ai:* Stu Cncl Adv; Amer Cncl of Eng Teachers 1972-; Stanwood Elem PTO (Secy, VP) 1986-89; Greensburg Coll Club; Adult Group St Lukes Luth Church 1986-; *office:* Yough Sr HS 99 Lowber Rd Herminie PA 15637

SANSON, RICK G., History Teacher/Athletic Dir; *b:* Glen Cove, NY; *m:* Kathleen Marie Cupit; *ed:* (BA) Writing, Houghton Coll 1982; Teachers Cert Courses 1984, His Cert Courses 1989 FL Intnl Univ; *cr:* Eng/His Teacher 1982-86, His/Bible Teacher 1986- Miami Chrstn Sch; *ai:* Athletic Dir; Var Bsktbl Head Coach; Sr Class Spon; *office:* Miami Chrstn Sch 200 N W 109th Ave Miami FL 33172

SANTA CRUZ, OSCAR ROBERTO, Computer Science Teacher; *b:* Cochabamba, Bolivia; *m:* Mary Faye Witt; *c:* Monica, Michelle, Melisa, Melanie; *ed:* (BA) Span Ed, 1972, (MED) Sch Admin, 1989 Cntrl St Univ; *cr:* Bio Teacher Del Crest Jr HS 1972-73; Span/Fr Teacher 1973-75, Span Teacher 1975-85, Cmptr Sci Teacher 1985- Keu Jr HS; *ai:* Var Golf Coach; OEA, NEA, ACT 1972-89; ASCD 1990; *home:* 1401 Hampton Dr Del City OK 73115

SANTAFERRARA, JAMES PHILLIP, Sixth Grade Teacher; *b:* Solvay, NY; *m:* Nora I. Bridges; *c:* Dedra Clark, James P. Jr., Lorraine; *ed:* (BA) Soc Sci, Syracuse Univ 1968; (MS) Management, SUNY Binghamton 1979; Masters Prgm Educl Courses Syracuse Univ 1971-72; *cr:* Elem Teacher St Peters 1980-; *ai:* Girls Bsktbl Coach St Peters; Diocese of Syracuse Outstanding Teacher Awd 1989; *home:* 709 Floyd Ave Rome NY 13440

SANTAGATE-SUTTON, CHERYL, Science Teacher; *b:* Groton, CT; *m:* Brian Paul; *ed:* (BA) Chem, Elms Coll 1986; (MED) Ed, Univ of MA 1987; *cr:* Sci Coord Oliver Jr HS 1986-87; Sci Teacher Nashoba Regional HS 1987-; *ai:* Stu Cncl Adv; Nashoba Teachers Assn Grant Comm; Girls Track Asst; Kappa Gamma Pi 1986-, St Catherine Medal 1986; NEA, MA Teachers Assn 1987-; NE Cath Peace Fellowship 1985-; Molecular Genetics Research Univ of MA Medical Center; *home:* 6 S Ward St Worcester MA 01610

SANTEE, GLADYS (SNYDER), Kindergarten Teacher; *b:* Allentown, PA; *m:* Kenneth William; *c:* Todd A., Scott K.; *ed:* (BS) Medical Technology, Cedar Crest Coll 1948; Elem Ed, Kutztown Univ, PA St Univ, Lehigh Cty Comm Coll; *cr:* Medical Technologist Allentown General Hospital 1948-51, St Lukes Hospital 1952-55, Laboratory of Clinical Pathology 1957-64; Kndgtn Teacher Schuylkill Haven Area Sch Dist 1969-; *ai:* Prin Advisory, Rdng, Act 178, Soc Stud Comms; Schuylkill Haven Ed Assn (Treas 1978-81, Soc Chm 1986-87, Welfare Chm 1987-); Cub Scouts of America Den Mother 1958-62; Luth Church Women Treas 1962-64; Lionettes (Treas 1967, 1975-77, VP 1968, Pres 1969); St Pauls Luth Church Cncl (Secy 1987-, Stewardship Comm 1987-, Evangelism 1989-); *office:* Schuylkill Haven Area Sch Dist Haven St Schuylkill Haven PA 17972

SANTEE, LESLIE R., 8th Grade Social Stud Teacher; *b:* Oskaloosa, IA; *m:* Diane E. Hoyka; *c:* Joey M., Frank J.; *ed:* (BA) Liberal Art/Poly Sci, Drake Univ 1967; (MA) Scndry Admin, Univ of IA 1973; Pride Drake; Mastery Teaching Madeline Hunter; Child Abuse; Cmptr Courses; *cr:* 8th Grade Teacher Taft Mid Sch 1967-69; 11th-12th Grade Teacher Jefferson HS 1969-70; 8th-9th Grade Teacher Taft Mid Sch 1970-85, Harding Mid Sch 1985-; *ai:* Asst Bsbl Coach Taft 1967-69; Mid Sch Boys Swim Coach 1973-; Jefferson HS Asst Boys Swim Coach 1973-; Jefferson HS Asst Girls Swim Coach 1975-; NEA, ISEA, Cedar Rapids Ed Assn 1967-69, 1973-; Cedar Rapids Fed of Teachers 1969-73; IA Swim Coaches Assn E IA Dist Rep 1973-; *office:* Harding Mid Sch 4801 Golf St NE Cedar Rapids IA 52402

SANTIAGO, EDNA, 7th/8th Grade English Teacher; *b:* Aguadilla, PA; *c:* Edna, Rene, Cedys; *ed:* (BA) Span/Psych/Eng, Univ of PR 1973; Nurse Aid, Ward Clerk; *cr:* Teacher Acad Primaria Adventista 1970-72; Ward Clerk/Nurse Aid Bella Vista Hospital 1972-74; Teacher Acad Primana Adventista 1974-77; Account Asst Itel Pas 1977-79; Teacher Acad Primaria Adventista 1979-85, Acad Adventista Metropolitana 1985-; *ai:* PA Secy; Sr Class Adv; Yrs Teacher 1986-87; *home:* San Fernando #93 Ext Comandante Rio Piedras PR 00924

SANTIAGO, MARIE GONZALEZ, High School Geology Teacher; *b:* San Juan, TX; *c:* Gina V.; *ed:* (BS) Bio, Pan American Univ 1971; (MED) Adult Ed, TX A&I Univ 1982; *cr:* Teacher Lyndon Baines Johnson Jr HS 1973-86, Pharr San Juan Alamo HS 1986-; *ai:* Geological Society Spon; *office:* Pharr-San Juan Alamo HS 1229 South I Road Pharr TX 78577

SANTINE, ANN (DONNELLY), 7th/8th Grade Math Teacher; *b:* Hastings-On-Hudson, NY; *m:* Vincent Lee; *c:* Christopher, Elizabeth, Collette; *ed:* (BA) Math, Coll of Mt St Vincent 1961; Stan Cert Teaching, KS St Univ, OK St Univ, Bartlesville Wesleyan Coll; *cr:* 1st Grade Teacher Freehold Sch 1962-63, Seven Dolores Sch 1963-68, St Johns Sch 1976-82; Math Teacher Dewey Jr HS 1982-; *ai:* Mathcounts Team Coach; Kappa Kappa Iota 1987-; OK Teachers of Math 1986-89; Pilot Club of Dewey Corresponding Secy 1986-; *office:* Dewey Jr HS 1 Bulldogger Rd Dewey OK 74029

SANTINI, MARTIN EDWARD, Social Studies/Cmptr Teacher; *b:* Cleveland, OH; *m:* Kimberly Ross; *ed:* (BA) Soc Stud Comp, 1978, (MALL) Amer Stud, 1988 Marietta Coll; *cr:* Soc Stud Teacher Warren HS 1978-79; Soc Stud/Cmptr Teacher Warren Elem 1979-; *ai:* Head Wrestling, Asst Ftbl Coach Vincent Warren HS; WLEA, OEA, NEA 1978-; SEOWCO 1988-, Coach of Yr 1990; OHSWCO 1987-; *office:* Warren Elem Rt 2 Box 138 Marietta OH 45750

SANTISTEBAN, MARIA CRISTINA, Math/Computer Teacher; *b:* Havana, Cuba; *ed:* (AA) Math/Chem, Univ of S FL 1978; (BA) Elem/Math, 1986, (MS) Elem Ed, 1990 St Univ of NY New Paltz; *cr:* Math/Cmptr Teacher Wappingers Falls Jr HS 1986-; *ai:* Co-Adv Quill & Ink; Project Adventure Team Mem; Math Dept Curr Comm; NYSHRSC Fellowship for MS Degree 1986-; *office:* Wappingers Falls Jr HS Remsen Ave Wappingers Falls NY 12590

SANTOS, KATHLEEN JOAN (RYAN), 6th-8th Grade Soc Stud Teacher; *b:* Puritan, MI; *m:* Tomas; *ed:* (BA) His, Alverno Coll 1960; Strategies in Teaching 1990; Cmptr Use in Classroom 1984, 1989; *cr:* 7th/8th Grade Soc Stud/Sci Teacher St Ann 1960-67; 7th/8th Grade Sci/Lang Art Teacher Blessed Sacrament 1967-76; 6th-8th Grade Soc Stud/sci Teacher St Vincent De Paul 1976-79; 6th-8th Grade Lang Art Teacher Blessed Sacrament 1978-80; 6th-8th Grade Soc Stud/Sci Teacher St Thomas More 1980-; *ai:* NCEA 1960-; Marine Corps League Auxiliary St Pres 1977-79; Diocesan Planning Comm 1986-88; *office:* St Thomas More Sch 20th & Weston La Crosse WI 54601

SANTOS, REBECCA BASIL, English Teacher; *b:* Beaumont, TX; *m:* Allan R.; *c:* Mark A., Michael A.; *ed:* Supvr Cert Stephen F Austin Univ; *cr:* Eng Teacher Anahuac HS 1965-68, Westchester HS 1968-73, Memorial HS 1976-78, Northbrook HS 1978-81, Woodville HS 1981-; *ai:* UIL Literary Criticism Spon; TX Joint Cncl Teachers of Eng; Our Lady of Pines Catholic Church Liturgy Dir 1987-; *office:* Woodville HS 505 N Charlton Woodville TX 75979

SANTOS, SALLY ROSS, 8th Grade Mathematics Teacher; *b:* Portland, OR; *m:* August G.; *c:* Gregory, Michael, Peter; *ed:* (AB) Math, Emmanuel Coll 1973; *cr:* Math Teacher Ford Mid Sch 1973-; *ai:* Cmptr Problem Solving; Sch Evaluation Study Comm Chm; MTA, NEA, ATA 1973-; Fairhaven Historical Society 1983-; Fairhaven Improvement Assn Bd of Dirs 1989-; Rogers Sch PTA VP 1989-; Horace-Mann Grants 1987-88, 1988-89; *office:* Ford Mid Sch 708 Middle Rd Acushnet MA 02743

SANTOS, YAKELIN D., History Teacher; *b:* San Juan, PR; *ed:* (BA) Drama Theatre, 1987, (BA) His, 1988, (BA) Ed, 1989 Univ of PR; *cr:* His Teacher Disciples of Christ Acad 1987-89; *ai:* NHS Cnslr; Evaluation Comm; Close Up Teacher; Disciples of Christ Church (Rules Comm 1988, Programation Comm 1989, Communications Comm 1989); *home:* Box 3357 Bayamon Gardens Bayamon PR 00620

SANTUOSO, MADELINE CLAIRE, First Grade Teacher; *b:* Jersey City, NJ; *ed:* (BA) Elem Ed, 1979, (MA) Rdng Specialist, 1983 Jersey City St Coll; Admin, Supervision Certificate; *cr:* 2nd Grade Teacher St Aloysius Elem Sch 1978-80; 1st Grade Teacher 1980-, Acting Prin 1988-89, Asst Prin 1987- Acad of St Aloysius; *ai:* Extended Care Prgm Coord; Stu Cncl & Cheerleading Moderator; JCSC Alumni Pres 1988-; ASCD, NCEA, Phi Delta Kappa; Jersey City Bus & Prof Women VP 1990; Outstanding Young Woman of America 1986; Dist Woman of Achievement NJ Fed Bus & Prof Women 1989; *home:* 226 Neptune Ave Jersey City NJ 07305

SANTYMIRE, EARL B., History Teacher; *b:* Cumberland, MD; *m:* Elizabeth Sindorf; *c:* James, David; *ed:* (BA) Speech, David Lipscomb Univ 1976; (MED) Admin Supv, TN St Univ 1988; *cr:* Teacher/Coach David Lipscomb Hs 1976-77; Nashville Chrstn Sch 1977-79, Ezell Harding Sch 1979-80; Teacher/AD/Coach Columbia Acad 1980-82; Teacher/Coach Fred J Page HS 1984-; *ai:* Parking Lot Supervisor; Detention Coord; SADD Sponsor; Asst Ftbl Coach; Asst Boys Bsktbl Coach; Head Bsbl Coach; Awds Comm/Academic Bsktbl Comm; Policy Comm; Phi Delta Kappa TSU Comm Editor 1989-91; NEA; TEA; WCEA Convention Rep 1985-89; Grant for The Taft Inst 1986; *office:* Fred J Page H S 6281 Arno Rd Franklin TN 37064

SAPALA, LAURENE JANE, Kindergarten Teacher; *b:* New York, NY; *m:* Richard; *c:* Jennifer, Stefanie; *ed:* (BA) Early Chldhd, Trenton St Coll 1970; *cr:* 1st Grade Teacher Mac Afee Road Sch 1970-79; Kndgtn Teacher Elizabeth Avenue 1982-; *ai:* NEA, NJ Educl Assn, Franklin Township Educl Assn; S Brunswick Jaycettes VP 1975-84; *office:* Elizabeth Avenue Sch Elizabeth Ave Somerset NJ 08873

SAPP, ANNA MAE, Remedial Reading Teacher; *b:* Powell, WY; *ed:* (AAS) Ed, Northwest Comm Coll 1978; (BA) Ed, 1980, (MED) Ed Admin, 1985 Univ of WY; Various Courses in Curr Dev; Jr Great Books Leader Trng; *cr:* Rural Sch Teacher Niobrara Cty Sch Dist 1 1980; K-6th Grade Remedial Rdng Teacher Campbell Cty Sch Dist 1 1980-83; 6th-8th Grade Rdng Teacher Park Cty Sch Dist 1 1983-; Cmmty Coord/Adult Basic Ed/Eng 2nd Lang Northwest Coll 1986-; *ai:* North Cntrl Assn Steering Comm; Rdng Curr, Effective Schls Planning Comm; Faculty Senate; Powell Ed Assn Pres 1986-87; WY Ed Assn 1980-; Delta Kappa Gamma (Treas 1988-, 2nd VP 1990); WY Lib Assn; Literary Volunteers Cmmty Coord 1986-; Intnl Rdng Assn; Powell Rdng Cncl Exec Comm 1983-88; Very Spec Arts Festival Planning Comm 1983; Park Cty Lib Bd of Dirs, Secy 1988-; Presenter WY Mid Sch Conference 1987, Western Regional Mid Sch Conference 1989; 17th Plains Regional Intnl Rdng Assn Conference 1989, NCTE Western Regional Conference 1990; *office:* Powell Mid Sch 160 N Evarts Powell WY 82435

SAPP, PAULA RICHEY, 6th Grade Teacher; *b:* Glasgow, KY; *m:* Louis Ray; *c:* Patrick D., Tamara L.; *ed:* (BA) Elem Ed, Wesleyan Coll 1973; (MA) Elem Ed, W KY Univ 1978; *cr:* Teacher Wayland Alexander Elem 1973-; *ai:* Sci Fair Coord; Stu Written Articles Published Cty Paper Adv; KY Environmental Educators Netkork, KY Assn of Environmental Educators 1989-; KY Academic Assn 1986-; GSA Troop Leader 1985-87; 4-H Horse Club Adv 1980-86; 4-H Area Cncl Secy 1982-86; Youth Bowling Assn Coach 1979-82; Sci, Eng Composition, Quick Recall Coach Governors Cup; *office:* Wayland Alexander Elem Sch 100 Render St Hartford KY 42347

SARAKOS, JOANNE ESPOSITO, Mathematics/Computer Teacher; *b:* Brooklyn, NY; *m:* Joseph; *c:* Nicholas, Lauren; *ed:* (AA) Liberal Art, Suffolk Comm Coll 1973; (BA) Scndry Math, St Univ Coll Oneonta 1975; (MA) Liberal Stud, St Univ Stony Brook 1980; *cr:* 7th-9th Grade Math Teacher Samoset Jr HS 1976-79; 7th/8th Grade Math/Cmptr Teacher Seneca Jr HS 1979-; *ai:* Math Team Adv; Improvement of Academic Instruction Comm Mem; Long Island Math Fair Judge; Dev New 8th Grade Cmptr Class Curr & 7th Grade Accelerated Prgm Enriched Curr; *office:* Seneca Jr HS 850 Main St Holbrook NY 11741

SARGENT, HELEN ASHER, Retired Teacher; *m:* Loren C. (dec); *c:* Linda B., Sylvia O., Paul; *ed:* (BS) Elem Ed, 1955, (MS) Rdng/Sp 1966 IN Univ; Elem Ed Rdng Sp Cert; *cr:* Columbia Twp Fayette Cty 1939-41, Aurora City 1941-43; Greensburg City 1943-46, Gunnison MS 1947, Elnora Twp Daviess Cty 1953-60; Loogootee Cmmty Schls 1960-85; *ai:* Tutoring Learning Disability Stus; Loogootee Classroom Teachers 1960-85; IN St Teachers Assn, Natl Teachers Assn 1939-85; Intnl Rdng Assn 1965-75; PTAS, ME Church, OES; *home:* R 1 Box 259 Odon IN 47562

SARGENT, KATHRYN MARIE, 8th Grade Earth Sci Teacher; *b:* Neosho, MO; *ed:* (BSED) Phys Ed, SW MO St Univ 1985; *cr:* Teacher Hermann Mid Sch 1986-; *ai:* 7th/8th Grade Girls Bsktbl

Coach; MO St Teachers Assn 1986-; Kappa Delta Pi 1985-; *office:* Hermann Mid Sch 808 Washington Hermann MO 65041

SARGENT, LLOYD LIONEL, 7th/8th Grade Science Teacher; *b:* Thibodaux, LA; *m:* Iola Martha Warren; *c:* Lloyd L. Jr., Robin S. Joseph, Brian R., Travis W.; *ed:* (BA) Elem Grades, 1961, (MS) Admin/Supvr, 1974 Southern Univ Baton Rouge; Sci, Clark Coll; Sci, Dillard Univ; General Ed, Nicholls St Univ; *cr:* Teacher Greenwood Elem 1961-62, C M Washington HS 1962-68, S Thibodaux Jr HS 1968-78, E Thibodaux Jr HS 1978-; *ai:* Bsktbl Coach Greenwood Elem 1961; Bsktbl Coach C M Washington HS Intramural; Asst Supvr for Summer Rec Kent Hadley Elem; Lafourche Assn of Educators 1978-80; LAFEDA Credit Union Chm 1981-; BSA Scoutmaster 1980-82; Allen Chapel Meth Church (Pres, Trustee) 1982; Lafourche Cmmty Action Agency Chm, 15 Yrs Awd 1988; Natl Sci Fnd Schlsp Clark Coll 1967, Dillard Univ 1968.

SARGENT, SANDRA OWENS, Fifth Grade Teacher; *b:* Grays Knob, KY; *m:* Charles M.; *c:* Gina Sizemore, Charles G.; *ed:* (BS) Elem Ed, Cumberland Coll 1964; (MA) Elem Ed, Union Coll 1970; *cr:* Teacher Liggett Elem Sch 1960-99, Elzo Guthrie Elem Sch 1966-; *office:* Elzo Guthrie Elem Sch HC 78 Box 559 Harlan KY 40831

SARGENT, TERRI CREECH, Fourth Grade Teacher; *b:* Seymour, IN; *m:* Terry R.; *c:* Andrew, Laura; *ed:* (BS) Elem Ed, 1974, (MSE) Elem Ed, 1978 Ind Univ; *cr:* 5th Grade Teacher 1974-75, 4th Grade Teacher 1975- Hayden Elem; *ai:* Mem First United Meth Church; IN St Teachers Assn 1975-; NEA 1975-; Jennings Cty Classroom Teachers Assn 1975-; First United Meth Church North Vernon; *home:* 526 Summit St North Vernon IN 47265

SARGI, TERRIE ANDERSON, Fifth Grade Teacher; *b:* Youngstown, OH; *m:* Thomas L.; *c:* Trisha, Tiffani; *ed:* (BA) Elem Ed 1970, (MS) Master Teacher 1979 Kent St Univ; *cr:* 6th Grade Teacher 1970-75, 5th Grade Teacher 1975- Longcoy Elem Schl; *ai:* Longcoy Sch Safety Patrol Adv; EEI Peer Coach; Delta Kappa Gamma 1986; *office:* Longcoy Elem Sch 1069 Elno Ave Kent OH 44240

SARINANA, CECILIA, 5th Grade Teacher; *b:* Mission, TX; *m:* Martin; *c:* Abel, Sofia; *ed:* (BA) Ed, Pan American Univ 1974; (MA) Ed, TX A&I Univ 1984; Creative Writing, Univ of Sam Houston 1986; Literature, Pan American Univ 1988; *cr:* 4th Grade Teacher Wilson Elem 1974-75; 5th Grade Teacher 1975-76; 6th Grade Teacher 1976-86; 5th Grade Teacher 1986- Marcell Elem; *ai:* Coached UIL Duet Acting 1986-87; Coached UIL Oral Rdng 1987-89; Mentor Teacher 1987-89; ATPE Mem 1976-; Marcell PTO Treas 1982-84; United in Faith Mem 1986-89; *home:* 807 Rankin Mission TX 78572

SARR, CLARENCE ARTHUR, Mathematics-Science Head; *b:* Syracuse, NY; *m:* Royce Irene Peterson; *c:* Charles A., Claryce J. Caviness; *ed:* (BA) Chem/Fr/Math, 1942, (MAT) Chem/Math 1970 Andrews Univ; Bio, Univ NC Ashville; Phys Sci, W Carolina; *cr:* 7th-9th Grade Teacher Clear Lake 1942-43; 5th-8th Grade Teacher Syracuse Church Sch 1945-47, 1947-49; Chemist Dow Chemical Company 1949-62; 5th-8th Grade Teacher Union Springs 1962-64; Teacher Newfoundland 1964-70, Fletcher Acad 1943-45, 1970-78, Laurelbrook Sch 1980-; *ai:* Stu Transportation; Lib Comm Treas 1971-73; GA Cumberland Conference Teacher Zapara Awd; Cncl Grads Comm at Andrews 1990; *office:* Laurelbrook Sch Rt 3 Dayton TN 37321

SARRAFF, MERCEDES AYALA, Third Grade Teacher; *b:* Guines, Cuba; *m:* Osvaldo; *c:* Lexie, Lilliane; *ed:* (BA) Scndry Ed/Span, 1973, (MA) Span, 1974 CA St Univ Fullerton; Cert Elem Ed, Mercy Coll 1977; *cr:* Span Dept CA St Univ 1973; Span Teacher Santiago Jr HS 1973-74; ESOL/Eng Teacher 1974-80, 3rd Grade Teacher 1980- Seminole Elem; *ai:* Amer Hispanic Educators of Dade; Teacher of Yr 1985-86; Appeared in Television Segment Showing Techniques Used to Teach Critical Thinking Skills 1988-89; *home:* 2951 SW 77th Pl Miami FL 33155

SARRATORE, ANTHONY A., 6th/7th Grade Elem Teacher; *b:* Wheeling, WV; *ed:* (BS) Elem Ed, OH Univ 1974; (MS) Admin, Dayton Univ 1981; *cr:* Laborer City of Martins Ferry 1966-69, Picoma Industries 1969-70; Dir 1970-74, Elem Teacher 1974- North Elem; *ai:* Sch Adv 7th Grade Annual Trip To Washington DC; Martins Ferry Civics 1967-; Fraternal Order of Eagles Aerie #995 1989-; North PTO Pres 1980-81, Plaque 1981; Martins Ferry Volunteer Fireman (Secy, Treas) 1971-83, Plaque 1987; Italian Amer Citizens Club (Pres, Treas) 1967-; Martins Ferry City Councilman 1983-; Belmont Cty Democrat Committeeman 1989-; *home:* 719 N Zane Hwy Martins Ferry OH 43935

SARTAIN, KERRY L., Science Department Chair; *b:* Jasper, AL; *m:* Diane; *c:* Holly, Misty; *ed:* (BS) Composite Sci, 1972, (MA) Ed/Sci, 1974, (AA) Ed, Univ of AL 1976; *cr:* Teacher Boldo Jr HS 1972-74, Curry HS 1974-; *ai:* Sci Dept Chm; Sci Club; Textbook Comm; Walker Cty Sci Teachers Assn Pres; AL Sci Teachers Assn 1980-; Church; Natl Sci Fnd Summer Prgm Auburn Univ; MESC Marine Prgm in MS; NASA Space Acad for Teachers; *office:* Curry HS Rt 13 Box 65 Jasper AL 35501

SARTHER, DAVID J., Jr HS Literature/Rdng Teacher; *b:* Chicago, IL; *m:* Constance Lally; *c:* Catherine F., David D.; *ed:* (BA) His, Loras Coll 1967; (MSED) Curr/Instruction/Amer Lit, Chicago St Univ 1979; Creative Writing & Cmptr Ed Wkshps; *cr:* Jr HS Lit/Rdng Teacher Burbank Sch Dist III 1967-; *ai:* Spon Safety Patrol 1967-87 & Yrbk 1975-79; Asst Teaching Prin 1986-87; Interscholastic Sports 1968-86; Amer Fed of Teachers Mem 1969-; PTA (Adv, Mem) 1967-; Palos Heights Public Lib (Pres, Treas) 1979-88; Burlington Route Historical Society (Dir 1986- Officer 1983-89); AFT Cncl III Schlshp Comm Chm 1984-86; Sch Dist 118 Parent Advisory Comm 1986-87; Mary Jean Kill Pena Memorial Schlsp Fund Bd of Dirs 1985-86; Sch Dist III Eng Textbook Selection Comm 1984-85, Perfect Attendance 1987-88; *office:* Rosa G Maddock Sch 83rd & Sayre Sts Burbank IL 60459

SARTIN, ANITA JOYCE, 4th-6th Grade Teacher; *b:* Hopkinsville, KY; *ed:* (BS) Elem Ed, 1966, (MA) Elem Ed, 1971, Elem Ed, 1982 Western KY Univ; *cr:* 4th Grade Teacher Franklin Elem 1966-69; Rockfield Elem 1969-70; 6th Grade Teacher Eleventh St Sch 1970-71; 4th/5th/6th Grade Teacher T C Cherry 1971-; *ai:* Alpha Delta Kappa Sec 1973; T C Cherry PTA (Sec 1972/Treas 1982); Outstanding Young Educator T C Cherry Elem Sch 1972-74.

SARTIN, CHARLOTTE STAFFORD, Kindergarten Teacher; *b:* Trigg, VA; *m:* Calvin H.; *c:* Jonathan P., Melissa Sartin Conley; *ed:* (BS) Elem Ed, Radford Univ 1952; (MA) Elem Ed, VPI 1978; *cr:* 1st Grade Teacher Newport Elem 1951-62; Spec Rdng Teacher Giles Cty 1965-66; 1st-3rd Grade Teacher 1966-69, Kndgtn Teacher 1969- Rich Creek Elem; *ai:* GEA, VA Ed Assn, NEA 1953-; PTA, PTO; Rich Creek Meth Church; *office:* Rich Creek Elem Sch Box J Rich Creek VA 24147

SARTOR, LINDA NIXON, Mathematics Teacher; *b:* Kilgore, TX; *m:* Thomas Wayne; *c:* Heather A., Holly E.; *ed:* (AS) Kilgore Coll 1972; (BS) Math/Scndry Ed, Stephen F Austin Univ 1973; (MED) Curr/Instruction, Univ of TX Tyler 1976; Advanced Academic Trng; *cr:* 7th/8th Grade Math Teacher Foster Mid Sch 1974-76; Math Teacher Longview HS 1976-84; Algebra/Math Teacher Kilgore HS 1984-; *ai:* Future Teachers of America Club Adv; NCTM 1973-; NEA, TSTA 1974-89; PTSA 1973-, Life Membership 1989; Alpha Delta Kappa Secy 1986-; *home:* 1 Pine Manor Cir Kilgore TX 75662

SARTY, MARY JANE (LOPARO), Second Grade Teacher; *b:* Bellevue, OH; *m:* August Thomas; *c:* Kimberlie J., Thomas A.; *ed:* (BA) Elem Ed, OH Dominican 1966; Remedial Rdng/Elem Ed, Bowling Green St Univ & Ashland Univ; *cr:* 3rd Grade Teacher St Peters Sch 1966-67; Remedial Rdng Teacher York Sch 1967-77; 2nd Grade Teacher Shumaker 1977-; *ai:* Soc Chm Shumaker Sch; Health Course Study & Rdng Competency Comm Mem; Bellevue Ed Assn, NEA 1967-; Club Amer-Italian Auxiliary 1978-; Daughters of Isabella 1982-; *office:* Shumaker Elem Sch Castalia Rd Bellevue OH 44811

SARVER, VICKI BOST, 1st Grade Teacher; *b:* Akron, OH; *m:* Randall L.; *ed:* (BS) Elem Ed, Western IL Univ 1971; *cr:* 1st Grade Teacher 1971-76, 2nd/3rd Grade Teacher 1977-80, 2nd Grade Teacher 1981-84, 1st Grade Teacher 1985-89 Southeast Primary Sch; *ai:* Southeast Local Dist Teachers Assn Pres 1982-85; Northeast Organization of Teachers Assn 1971-89; OH Ed Assn Teacher Rep 1980-88; NEA 1971-89; Cuyahoga Falls Bapt Church 1976-89; Ravenna Cmmty Choir 1980-85; Jennings Grant Whole Lang Approach to Rdng 1988; *office:* Southeast Primary Sch 8301 Tallmadge Rd Ravenna OH 44266

SASAKI, MICHAEL DUAINE, Sixth Grade Teacher; *b:* Ontario, OR; *m:* Susan Alice Moore; *c:* Teresa, Jon, Brent; *ed:* (BA) Elem Ed, 1972, (MED) Elem Ed, 1980 Coll of ID; *cr:* 6th Grade Teacher West Canyon Elem 1972-80; 6th Grade Teacher/Coach Wilson Elem 1980-81, West Canyon Elem 1981-; *ai:* Asst Varisty Bsbl Coach; Chm Elem Sci Curr; NEA 1972-; Vallivue Ed Fnd Comm 1987-; Vallivue Cmmty Memorial Schlsp Comm Chm 1979-; Vallivue Sch Dist Teacher of Yr 1989; *office:* West Canyon Elem Sch 19548 Ustick Rd Caldwell ID 83605

SASS, MELINDA TUTTLE, Social Studies Teacher; *b:* Elizabeth City, NC; *m:* Ronald Paul; *c:* Corinne; *ed:* (AA) Pre-Law, Coastal Carolina Comm Coll 1982; (BA) Poly Sci, Univ of NC Wilmington 1984; *cr:* Teacher Northeastern HS 1987-; *ai:* Girls Vlybl Coach; Jr/Sr Prom Spon; Citizen Bee Adv; NCAE 1988-; *home:* 1007 Oak Dr Elizabeth City NC 27909

SASSENBERG, GARY R., English Teacher; *b:* New Ulm, MN; *ed:* (BA) Speech/Drama, 1973, (BS) Eng/Speech/Drama, 1974, (MS) Eng, 1989 Mankato St Univ; Grad Word Eng, Speech, Drama, Curr/Instruction, Various Univ; *cr:* Instr Gibbon HS 1975-76, New Prague HS 1976-80, Winona HS 1980-81, Clark Cty Sch Dist 1981-; *ai:* Frosh Class Adv; Drama Assistance; NCTE; Cmmty & Educl Theatre Participant; *office:* Bonanza HS 6665 Del Rey Ave Las Vegas NV 89102

SASSO, PATRICIA ANN VALENTE, Eng as Second Lang Teacher; *b:* Stoneham, MA; *c:* Armanda; *ed:* (BS) Ed, Boston St 1975; *cr:* Elem Teacher Malden 1978-81, St Jeans 1982-85; End as Second Lang Teacher 1985-; *office:* Malden Sch 77 Salem St Malden MA 02148

SASSOON, INGRID ANNY VON SIEMERING, Kindergarten Teacher; *b:* Hamburg, Germany; *c:* Robert S.; *ed:* (BA) Elem Ed/Art, Hunter Coll 1966; (MA) Educl Admin, 1974, NY St Certificate Internship Educl Admin, 1975 NY Univ; Fashion Illustration, Parsons Sch of Design 1947; Acting Television Commercials, Weist Barron Sch of Television 1976; *cr:* Educator/Painter/Graphic Artist/Illustrator/Writer/Ford Agency High Fashion Model Harpers Bazaar & Modern Bride 1947-65; Teacher Hunter Coll Elem Sch for Gifted 1966; Kndgtn/1st Grade Lang Arts Teacher PS 57 M 1966-74; Admin Asst/Art Coord Dist 4 Manhattan 1974-76; Kndgtn Lang Arts/Math Coord PS 181 K 1976-78; Kndgtn Teacher PS 26 Manhattan 1978-; *ai:* Navy League of US Mem 1967-; Natl Assn of Women Artists 1959-; Intnl Assn Iranian Art & Archeology 4th Congress 1960-; Natl Platform Assn 1970-; Natl Study Society for Study of Ed 1978-; Written up Art Digest, La Revue, NY Post 1950-60; Designer/Creator Semi-Animated Film 1950; Painting Exhibits Feragil Gallery 1950, Argent Gallery 1959, Natl Acad Gallery 1960, 1961, 1963, Lever House 1968, Liberty Music Shops 1950-55, Elinor Lewenthal Group 1960; *home:* 160 E 89th St Apt 7B New York NY 10128

SATTERFIELD, JAMES ALBERT, Mathematics Teacher/Dept Chair; *b:* Six Mile Run, PA; *m:* Joyce Elaine Putt; *c:* Keith M., Trisha M. Tenley; *ed:* (BS) Math, Shippensburg Coll 1957; Masters Equivalent, Penn St & Univ of NM; *cr:* Math Teacher Gettysburg HS 1957-59, Tussey Mountain HS 1959-; *ai:* Natl Sci Fnd Grant Penn St & Univ of NM; *home:* R D 1 Box 91 Saxton PA 16678

SATTERTHWAITE, KAREN LYNN MC ILVAINE, 5th Grade Teacher; *b:* New Brunswick, NJ; *m:* Richard A.; *ed:* (BS) Elem Ed, Fairleigh Dickinson Univ 1968; Grad Work Jersey City Coll, Rutgers; *cr:* 3rd Grade Teacher 1968-72, 4th/6th Grade Teacher 1972-78, 5th Grade Teacher Lincoln 1978-82; 5th Grade Teacher Campbell 1982-; *ai:* Co-Ed Rambler Bd of Ed Newsletter; Safety Patrol Adv; Bell Comm; Bedside Tutor; South River Ed Assn 1968-; Middlesex Cty Ed Assn 1968-; NJ Ed Assn, NEA 1968-; NJ Plate Collectors VP 1985-87; Ricker Bartlett Club; Goebel Club; Precious Moments Club; Opened Business Teachers Touch; *office:* Campbell Schl David St South River NJ 08882

SATTERWHITE, DEBORAH CONNER, Speech Therapist; *b:* Jacksonville, TX; *m:* Eugene Smith Jr.; *c:* Mary, Katherine; *ed:* (BS) Speech/Hearing Therapy, Hardin-Simmons Univ 1973; (MED) Elem, E TX St Univ 1978; Working on Kndgtn Endorsement, Univ of TX Tyler; *cr:* Speech Therapist Jacksonville Ind Sch Dist 1973-74, Winnsboro Ind Sch Dist 1974-; *ai:* Delta Kappa Gamma 1979; Quitman Univ Women 1989; *home:* 408 Elaine Quitman TX 75783

SATTERWHITE, DIANA MC CLEAD, History Teacher/Tennis Coach; *b:* Seminole, TX; *m:* Gary Lloyd; *c:* Mandy D.; *ed:* (BS) Elem/His, TX Tech Univ 1976; Working Toward Masters TX Tech Univ; *cr:* 1st Grade Teacher Mc Whorter Elem 1977-82; 4th Grade Teacher Parsons Elem 1982-83; 4th/5th Grade Teacher Waters Elem 1983-89; 7th-9th Grade Teacher Irons Jr HS 1989-; *ai:* 7th-9th Grade Tennis Coach; Delta Kappa Gamma 1986-89; *office:* Irons Jr HS 5214 79th St Lubbock TX 79424

SATTON, SARALOU (COMBS), Second Grade Teacher; *b:* Dayton, OH; *m:* Raymond E.; *c:* Stephanie; *ed:* (BA) Elem Ed, 1966, (MA) Elem Ed, 1970 AZ St Univ; *cr:* 2nd/3rd Grade Teacher Squaw Peak Elem Sch 1966; 2nd Grade Teacher Solano Elem Sch 1968-; *ai:* Sci Adoption Comm 1989-; Chi Omega Valley Alumnae Pres 1987-88; Osborn Ed Fnd Mini-Grant Recipient 1988; *office:* Solano Elem Sch 1526 W Missouri Ave Phoenix AZ 85015

SATURDAY, JANICE MORGAN, Lead Teacher; *b:* Savannah, GA; *m:* James M. Jr.; *ed:* (BS) Elem Ed, GA Southern Coll 1977; (MED) Early Chldhd Ed, Armstrong St Coll 1987; (EDS) Early Chldhd Ed, GA Southern Coll 1990; Working on Cert in Leadership, Admin/Supervision; *cr:* 4th Grade Teacher Marlow Elem Sch 1977-84, S Effingham Elem Sch 1985-87; Lead Teacher S Effingham Elem Sch 1987-; *ai:* Prof Assn of GA Educators; *home:* 1 Starboard Ct Savannah GA 31419

SAUCIER, LINDA ALLEN, Second Grade Teacher; *b:* Winona, MS; *m:* Ronald L.; *c:* Kim, Katie; *ed:* (BS) Elem, 1970, (MS) Elem, 1975 Delta St Univ; MS St Univ; *cr:* 2nd Grade Teacher Greenville Chrstn Sch 1970, Matty Akin Elem 1971; 1st Grade Teacher Nailor Elem 1972-75; Elem Teacher/Supvr Stu Teachers MS St Univ 1975-76; 2nd Grade Teacher Starkville Acad 1978-; *ai:* MS Ed Assn, Dept of Classroom Teachers 1972-75; MS Private Sch Assn 1978-; STAR Teacher 1989; *office:* Starkville Acad Academy Rd Starkville MS 39759

SAUL, MARK E., Computer Coordinator; *b:* New York, NY; *m:* Carol P.; *c:* Susanna, Michael, Peter; *ed:* (BA) Math/Slavic Lang, Columbia Univ 1969; (MS) Math, 1974, (PhD) Math, 1987 NY Univ; Admin & Supervision, Hunter Coll 1988-; Music Ed, Kodaly Center of America 1975; *cr:* Grade Adv/Math Teacher Bronx HS of Sci 1969-85; Cmptr Coord Bronxville Sch 1985-; Dir Research Sci Inst Center for Excl in Ed 1987-; *ai:* Math Advisory Bd; Quantum Magazine; Pres Amer Regions Math League; Mathematical Assn of America; HS Contests Comm; NCTM, Math Assn of America 1975-; Teachers of Math Assn Excl Bd Mem 1979-85; La Guardia HS of Performing Arts Admissions Panel 1979-86; Natl Sci Fnd Presidential Awd for Excl in Teaching Math 1984; Admiral H G Rickover Fnd Fellowship 1985; Sigma XI Recognition Awd 1981; Author 1986; *office:* Bronxville Sch Pondfield Rd Bronxville NY 10708

SAUL, SUSAN POWELL, 4th Grade Teacher; *b:* Covington, VA; *c:* John D.; *ed:* (BS) Elem Ed, Radford Univ 1972; *cr:* 5th Grade Teacher Cntrl Elem Sch 1972-74; 4th/5th Grade Teacher Critzer Elem Sch 1974-; *ai:* Stu Act; 4-H Club Spon; Critzer Sch PTA Secy 1988-89; Pulaski Cty Ed Assn, VA Ed Assn, NEA 1972-; Jr Womans Club Pulaski Inc (Corresponding Secy 1989, 1st VP 1990); *office:* Critzer Elem Sch 100 Critzer Dr Pulaski VA 24301

SAULET, BOBBIE JEAN (GRAYSON), Fifth Grade Teacher; *b:* Kansas City, KS; *m:* Harold Antoine; *c:* Mark A., Patrick, Linda A., Emile A.; *ed:* (BS) Elem Ed, Tuskegee Inst 1956; (MA) Teaching, Webster Univ; Grad Stud Univ of MO Kansas City; Rdng Instructions & Mentor Trng; *cr:* 2nd Grade Teacher Dunbar S Elem Sch 1956-59; 3rd Grade Teacher Ladd Elem Sch 1961-69, Chick Elem Sch 1970-73; 5th/6th Grade Teacher 1973-87, 5th Grade Teacher 1987- W C Bryant Sch; *ai:* MO St Teachers 1961-85; Intnl Rdng Assn 1961-66; Kansas City Teachers Assn 1960-65; Alpha Kappa Alpha 1954-, Pres Basilus 1970; Drifters Incorporate 1957-, 25 Yrs Awd 1979; Mayme J Ewing #95 OES 1954-, 25 Yrs Awd 1979; St Andrew United Meth Church (Usher, Adult Sunday Sch Teacher, Chm of Ed) Service Awd; MO West Conference United Meth Women (Publicity Secy, Human Relations Secy); Kansas City Sch Dist Volunteer Awd.

SAULSBERRY, WILLIE LOUIS, JR., 7th/8th Grade Soc Stud Teacher; *b:* Gary, IN; *c:* Lisa; *ed:* (BS) Scndry Ed/Sociology, Lincoln Univ 1971; (MS) Scndry Ed, IN Univ 1975; *cr:* Teacher Roosevelt HS 1971-84, Kennedy-King Mid Sch 1984-; *ai:* Kennedy-King Sch Union Building Comm Mem; AFT Mem 1971-; Meth Hospital Volunteers Group Mem 1988-; St Timothys Church Missionary Group Mem 1987-; *office:* Kennedy-King Mid Sch 301 Parke St Gary IN 46403

SAULSBURY, SAMMIE FOWLER, Guidance Counselor; *b:* Winn Parish, LA; *m:* Olin B.; *ed:* (BS) Voc Home Ec Ed, TX Tech Univ 1958; (MA) Ed, St Xavier of Chicago 1974; Guidance Cert NE LA Univ 1978; Grad Work Univ of Louisville, NE LA Univ; *cr:* Teacher Crockett Jr HS 1958-65, Evans Jr HS 1965-67, Seneca HS 1967-69; Teacher/Coord Evergreen Park Cmmty HS 1969-75; Teacher/Cnslr West Monroe HS 1975-; *ai:* Homecoming Comm & Substance Abuse Prevention Ed Chm; Interact Club & Jr Class Spon; Jr/Sr Prom & NHS Adv; West Monroe HS Booster Club; Delta Kappa Gamma St Secy 1989-; Phi Delta Kappa 1989-; LA Assn of Counseling & Dev 1986-; Amer Assn of Counseling & Dev 1986-; LA Sch Cnslrs 1986-; Guidance Assn Pres; West Monroe Chamber of Commerce Ed VP 1990; Adopt-A-Sch Task Force 1988-; Little Theatre of Monroe Pres 1988; Monroe Beautification Bd 1989-; Pi Beta Phi Alumnae Club Treas; NE LA Arts Cncl Bd Mem 1989-; Ouachita Pastoral Counseling Organization; Monroe Garden Club; Friends of Civic Center Theater; Drug-Free Sch & Chamber of Commerce Scholars Banquet Task Force; Supts Advisory & Inservice Comm.

SAULSGIVER, DANIEL SCOTT, Science Teacher; *b:* Falconer, NY; *m:* Carol Dianne Sandquist; *c:* Heather, Matthew, Melissa; *ed:* (AS) Liberal Arts, Jamestown Comm Coll 1972; (BS) Bio, SUNY Cortland 1974; (MAT) Teaching, Colgate Univ 1976; Sci; *cr:* Bio Teacher Madison Cntrl Sch 1974-; *ai:* Class Adv; Var Soccer & Bsbl Coach; NABT, NSTA; Dir Oneida Madison Electric Cooperative Secy 1982-; Bd of Chrstn Ed Chm 1983-; Nucleonics Course PA St Univ, Biotechnology Prgm Univ of Rochester, Cmptr Sci Prgm Ithaca Coll Grants; *office:* Madison Cntrl Sch Rt 20 Madison NY 13402

SAUNDERS, DAVID ALLEN, Mathematics Teacher; *b:* Wyoming General, WV; *m:* Lisa; *ed:* (BS) Math/Sci/Scndry Ed, Alderson Broaddos 1986; *cr:* Math Teacher Liberty HS 1987-; *ai:* Head Var Bsbl, Asst Var Ftbl Head Frosh Bsktbl Coach; *home:* 202 Bolton Dr Rt 2 Beckley WV 25801

SAUNDERS, GERALDINE BARBARA, School Librarian; *b:* Detroit, MI; *m:* Robert; *c:* Stephanie L.; *ed:* (BA) Elem Ed, MI St Univ 1969; (MS) Early Chldhd, Oakland Univ 1974; Supervision, NJ; NJ Ed Media Assoc Degree; *cr:* Teacher Ferndale MI 1969-77; Teacher 1978-89, Ed Media Specialist 1989- Mt Laurel NJ; *ai:* Cmptr Turnkey; W Jersey Rdng Cncl 1980-; Burlington Cty Media Assn 1987-; Delta Kappa Gamma 1990; NJ Governors Teacher Recognition Awd 1988; *home:* 12 Eastwood Dr West Berlin NJ 08091

SAUNDERS, PEGGY J., English Teacher; *b:* Anchorage, AK; *ed:* (BA) Eng, Weber St Coll 1977; *cr:* Dorm Cnslr UT Sch for the Deaf 1977-80; Eng Teacher Kaysville Jr HS 1981-82; Eng Teacher/Journalism Sunset Jr HS 1982-; *ai:* Girls Bsktbl Coach; Natl Jr Honor Society Adv; Honors Prgm Chm; NASSP Stu Act 1988-; NCTE 1983-87; Amer Guild of Eng Handbell Ringers (UT St Chm) 1981-86, 1988-; Honorable Mention Ogden Stan Examiner Apple for Teacher Awd; *office:* Sunset Jr HS 1610 N 250 W Sunset UT 84015

SAUNDERS, STEPHEN DOUGLAS, Science Teacher; *b:* Huntington, WV; *m:* Kathy Gragg; *c:* James, Stephen Jr.; *ed:* (BS) Bio, Centre Coll 1977; (MS) Recreation, E KY Univ 1978; Teaching Cert, N KY Univ 1986; *cr:* Recreation Dir 1979-84, Juvenile Cnslr 1984-86 N KY Treatment Center; Teacher Dixie Heights HS 1986-; *ai:* Boys Track & 6th Grade Boys Bsktbl Head Coach; Stu Asst Team Mem; Teacher of Month 1988; *office:* Dixie Heights HS 3010 Dixie Hwy Fort Mitchell KY 41017

SAUTER, CINDY ELISSA (BERG), Spanish Teacher; *b:* Bronx, NY; *m:* Joseph; *ed:* (BA) Span/Ed, Cedar Crest Coll 1974; (MA) Span/Scndry Ed, NY Univ 1977; Undergraduate Stud Univ of Valencia, Spain 1973; Grad Stud Univ of Madrid, Spain 1977; *cr:* Span Teacher Middletown HS 1979-; *ai:* Spon Stu Trip to Spain; Span Club Adv; Chm Stud Comm Mid States Accredidation; Amer Assn Teachers of Span & Portuguese 1978-84; Natl Fed of Foreign Lang Teachers 1984-; NY St United Teachers 1979-; Middletown Teachers Assn 1979-; Mentor Middletown Mentor/Intern Prgm Funded by NY St Grant 1988-89; *office:* Middletown H S Gardner Ave Extension Middletown NY 10940

SAVACHECK, MARY GATES, Sixth Grade Teacher; *b:* Loveland, CO; *c:* Laura Holley; *ed:* (BA) Elem Ed, Univ of N CO 1960; Branch Grants, NMSU, Univ of New Mexico Albuquerque; *cr:* 2nd-3rd Grade Teacher Mt Taylor Elem 1960-70; 6th Grade Teacher Mesa View Elem 1970-; *ai:* Chm Elem Sci Fairs; 6th Grade Chm, Coord; Delta Kappa Gamma Pres 1982-84; Intnl Rdng Assn Secy 1985-86, Literary Awd 1988-89; NEA Pres 1987-89; Grants Cibola Cty Sch Health Employee 1989; Outstanding Leadership Awd NM Ed Assn of NEA 1989; *office:* Mesa View Elem Sch 400 Washington Ave Grants NM 87020

SAVAGE, EDGAR OSBORNE, Physical Education Teacher; *b:* Framingham, MA; *ed:* (BS) Phys Ed, Univ of NH 1970; *cr:* Instr Hampton Academy Jr HS 1970-; *ai:* Phys Ed & Athletic Dir; Girls Jr HS Sftbl Coach; Seacoast Ed Assn, NH Ed Assn, NEA 1970-; New England Lacrosse Ofcls Assn, NH Soccer Ofcls Assn 1986-; E MS Soccer Ofcls Assn 1989-; *office:* Hampton Academy Jr HS 29 Academy Ave Hampton NH 03842

SAVAGE, FRANCES BUCHAN, Volunteer Teacher; *b:* Baxley, GA; *m:* Leonard A (dec); *c:* George, Joseph, Kathryn Hegstad, John; *ed:* (AA) Fine Art, Gainesville Coll 1970; (BA) Elem Ed, Brenau Coll 1972; Grad Courses Brenau Coll; *cr:* Teacher Flowery Branch Sch 1971-76, Chestnut Mtn 1976-77, Nahunta Elem 1977-80, Brunswick Chrstn Acad 1981-85; Volunteer Teacher Chrstn Renewal Acad 1987-; *home:* 167 Nottingham Dr Brunswick GA 31520

SAVAGE, LINDA JUANENE PHELPS, English Teacher; *b:* Concord, NC; *ed:* (BA) Eng/Span, Lenoir-Rhyne Coll 1966; (MA) Eng/Ed, Appalachian St Univ 1976; *cr:* Eng Teacher Cntrl Cabarrus HS 1966-; *ai:* Sr Class Adv; FTA-SAE Spon; Eng Dept Chairmanship 1990; Sch Guidance Cncl Mem; NEA, NCTE, NCETA; NCAE Secy Cabarrus Cty; Delta Kappa Gamma 2nd VP 1983-85; Kimball Memorial Luth Church (Mem, Church Cncl, Church Women & Various Comms); Cabarrus Cty Teacher of Yr Finalist 1987; *office:* Central Cabarus HS 505 Hwy 49 S Concord NC 28025

SAVAGE, PATRICIA ANN, Mathematics Teacher; *b:* Elizabeth, NJ; *ed:* (BA) Math, Douglass Coll & Rutgers Univ 1984; (MA) Educl Admin, Kean Coll 1987; Grad Stud Cmptr Courses; *cr:* Math Teacher Marquis De Lafayette Mid Sch 1984-85, David Brearley Regional HS 1985-; *ai:* Sr Class Adv 1989; Basic Skills Improvement Summer Schl Prgm Instr 1987-; NJ Cncl Teachers of Math 1984-; AFT 1985-; *office:* David Brearley Regional HS Monroe Ave Kenilworth NJ 07033

SAVAGE, PATRICK JOSEPH, Teacher/Head Coach; *b:* Brooklyn, NY; *m:* Nancy Ann Sullivan; *c:* Patrick G., Julie K., Daniel J.; *ed:* (BSBE) Bus Ed, 1967, (MSBE) Ec, 1971 De Paul Univ; Grad Work Northwestern Univ, N IL Univ, ND St, Azusa Pacific Coll; *cr:* Teacher/Head Coach De Paul Acad 1966-68, St George HS 1968-69, Niles West HS 1969-; *ai:* Head Cross Cntry, Asst Track Coach 1969-; Many Sch Comm; IL Track Coaches Assn Pres 1981-83; NBEA, IL Consumer Ed Assn, Amer Voc Ed Assn; Niles West/Oakton Track Club Head Coach 1969-; IL Track Hall of Fame 1989; St Mel HS Man of Yr 1989; Articles Published; *office:* Niles West HS Oakton & Edens Expressway Skokie IL 60077

SAVELLA, KAREN NOELLE, English Teacher; *b:* Rochester, NY; *m:* Fernando; *c:* Jonathan, Aaron; *ed:* (BA) Eng, St Univ NY Brockport 1985; Mastery Learning Seminars; *cr:* 10th-12th Grade Eng Teacher Nazareth Acad 1987-; *ai:* Alateen Spon; Spectrum Literary Magazine Adv; *home:* 21 Menlo Pl Rochester NY 14620

SAVICH, JULIE HACKMAN, 6th Grade Science Teacher; *b:* Seymour, IN; *m:* Stevan; *ed:* (BS) Elem Ed, Univ of IN 1981; (MS) Elem Ed, Purdue Univ 1985; Lang Arts & Soc Stud 1981; *cr:* 8th Grade Lang Arts Teacher 1985-89; 6th Grade Sci Teacher 1989-Kankakee Vly Mid Sch; *ai:* Track Coach Mid Sch 1987-; Co Chm North Cntrl Comm 1988-89; Beta Gamma Upsilon 1989-.

SAVILLE, SHIRLEY D., Sixth Grade Teacher; *b:* Covington, VA; *m:* Calvin C.; *c:* David, Donna; *ed:* (BS) Ed, James Madison Univ 1972; Methods, Philosophy & Lit; *cr:* 7th Grade Teacher Eagle Rock Elem Sch 1956-63; 5th & 6th Grade Teacher Callaghan Elem Sch 1967-; *ai:* Eagle Rock HS Productions Williamsburg Trip, Fund Raising, Planning, Conducting, Art Assistance; AEA, VEA, NEA; Delta Kappa Gamma Pres 1982-84, Pin 1984; 4-H Spon 1954, All-Star Key; GSA Leader; PTA Teacher of Yr 1988-89; *office:* Callaghan Elem Sch Rt 3 Covington VA 24426

SAVITZ, PHILIP BARTH, Physical Education Teacher; *b:* Columbia, SC; *m:* Jan H.; *c:* Zack, Erin; *ed:* (BS) Phys Ed, 1978, (MAT) Phys Ed, 1979 Univ of SC; US Soccer Fed License; *cr:* Grad Asst/Soccer Coach Univ of SC 1978-79; Soccer Coach Irmo HS 1979-; Phys Ed Teacher Irmo Mid Campus I 1979-; *ai:* Var Soccer Coach Irmo HS; St Soccer Assn Staff Coach; St Classic Team Head Coach; US Soccer Fed Evaluator 1975-, A License 1987; Natl Soccer Coaches Assn of America 1985-, Region Coach of Yr 1989; SC Ed Assn 1980-; SC St Soccer Coach of Yr; SE Region Coach of Yr 1989; *office:* Irmo Mid Sch Campus I 6949 St Andrews Rd Columbia SC 29210

SAVOY, DORIS JEAN HURD, Spanish Teacher; *b:* Mobile, AL; *m:* Rodney Purcell III; *c:* Sean P., Scott P., Courtney M.; *ed:* (BA) Span, Morris Brown Coll 1967; Grad Stud Trinity Coll, Howard Univ, Georgetown Univ; *cr:* Span Teacher Calvin Coolidge Sr HS 1968-71, Hine Jr HS 1971-73, Rabaut Jr HS 1973-88, Calvin Coolidge Sr HS 1988-; *ai:* Writing to Learn Comm; Span Club Spon; Liason Youth for Understanding Exch Prgm; Amer Assn Teachers of Span & Portuguese 1976-; Alpha Kappa Alpha; Jack & Jill of America Incorporated; Natl Endowment of Hum Grant Study Child in Hispanic Literature 1986, Study Teaching of Advanced Placement Span Lit 1989; *office:* Calvin Coolidge Sr HS 5th & Tuckerman Sts Washington DC 20011

SAWYER, CARMEN SANCHEZ, Jr HS English Teacher; *b:* Alvin, TX; *m:* James Barney; *c:* Carl E., Kimberly L., Carmen E.; *ed:* (AA) Liberal Art, Alvin Comm Coll 1968; (BA) Scndry Eng, Sam Houston St 1970; (MA) Ed/Counseling, Univ of Houston Clear Lake 1983; Future Problem Solving Evaluation Trng 1989; *cr:* Eng I/Eng I Basic Ed/Eng Advanced/Eng II/Eng IV Teacher 1970-85, Creative Writing Teacher 1983-85 Alvin Independent Schls; Eng III/Advanced Eng Teacher Ingram Tom Moore 1985-; *ai:* NHS & Jr Honor Society 1986-, Sr Class 1988-89, Jr Class 1988-89, Drill Team 1987-89 HS Literary Magazine Spon 1982-85; 9th Grade Eng Chairperson 1982-85; NHS 1966; Quill & Scroll 1966; Phi Theta Kappa 1966-68; Kappa Delta Pi 1970; Future Teachers of America 1966; TX Joint Teachers of Eng 1990; NEA 1970-85; TX St Teachers Assn 1970-85; Future Teachers of America Schlsp 1966-68; Fellowship in Eng TX Chrstn Univ 1970; Administered SAT at ITM & Helped Conduct SAT Clinic 1987-89; *office:* Ingram Tom Moore HS 700 Hwy 39 Ingram TX 78025

SAWYER, EARLINE JORDAN, English Department Chair; *b:* Washington Cty, AL; *c:* Leah A. Sawyer Breland, Libye J.; *ed:* (BS) Eng Ed, 1971, (MA) Scndry Ed, 1979 Univ of S AL; *cr:* Teacher/Adv Murphy HS 1971-; *ai:* Yrbk Adv; Spon of Quill & Scroll; Dir of Panther Spirit Night; Chm of Spec Prgm Comm; CSPA Judge 1974-, Gold Crowns 1986-89; NSPA 1974-, All Amer; Hector Awd Outstanding Journalist 1982; *office:* Murphy HS 100 S Carlen St Mobile AL 36606

SAWYER, MARY ELLEN KEEFFE, Social Studies Teacher/Chair; *b:* Elmira, NY; *m:* Stephen Leslie; *c:* Anna M., Patrick S.; *ed:* (BA) His, Mt St Agnes/Loyola 1964; Numerous Grad Courses; *cr:* Teacher Immaculate Heart of Mary 1964-66, Mt Mercy Boys Sch 1966-67, St Francis de Sales 1967-68, St Jerome 1968-77; Asst Prin 1988-89, Teacher 1977- St Luke; *ai:* Stu Cncl Spon; Soc Stud Chairperson; Educators Against Apartheid; Global Ed Assocs; NCEA; Global Horizons; St Luke Sch 10 Yr Awd for Excl in Teaching 1987; Amer Univ Educating Global Citizenship Grant 1989; *office:* St Luke Sch 7005 Georgetown Pike Mc Lean VA 22101

SAWYER, POLLY KENTFIELD, Retired Elem Teacher; *b:* Beaver City, NE; *c:* Louise (dec), Kathy Tegtman, Mary, Polly Richter; *ed:* (BA) Ed, Kearney St 1971; Grad Stud Spec Ed; *cr:* K-8th Grade Elem Teacher Rural Dist 23 1936-38, Rural Dist 35 1954-56, Rural Dist 60 1656-58; Elem Teacher Edison Public Schls 1959-83; *ai:* Furnos Cty Teachers Assn VP 1971-72, Outstanding Teacher 1974; NE St Ed Assn 1959-83; NRTA, AARP 1983-: Prsbyn Church; Beaver Cty Lib Bd Mem 1967-75; US Humane Society 1989-; Wrote Monthly Columns for Various NSEA Newspapers; *home:* 722 M Street Beaver City NE 68926

SAWYERS, LYNN LEWIS, 3rd Grade Teacher; *b:* Waco, TX; *m:* Ronnie E.; *c:* Jay, Bryan; *ed:* (BS) Ed, Sam Houston St Univ 1968; *cr:* 3rd Grade Teacher Groesbeck Elem 1968-75; 4th/5th Grade Teacher 1975-76, 3rd Grade Teacher 1976- Mart Elem.

SAXON, BEN L., Social Studies Teacher; *b:* Winter Haven, FL; *c:* Meredith J., Robert T.; *ed:* (BA) His/Ed, FL Southern Coll 1969; (MEd) His, Univ of FL 1980; *cr:* Intern Lakeland Jr HS 1968; Teacher Howard HS 1969, Forest HS 1969, FOrt King Mid Sch 1969-; *ai:* Marion Ed Assn (Building Rep 1976-78, Building Comm 1990); Ocala Jaycees Outstanding Young Educator 1982; Daughters of Amer Revolution Outstanding Amer His Teacher 1984; Jr Achievement Prgm 1988; Project Bus Teacher 1986-89; Job Trng Partnership Act Worksite Supvr 1981-; *office:* Fort King Mid Sch 545 NE 17th Ave Ocala FL 32670

SAXON, VICKI KIDWELL, COE/Business Education Teacher; *b:* Seattle, WA; *m:* Robert; *c:* Robyn; *ed:* (BS) Bus Ed, 1973, (MED) Bus Ed, 1983 Univ of AZ; Advanced Cmptr Sci Courses; *cr:* COE/Bus Ed Tucson Unified Sch Dist 1973-75; Assoc Faculty Pima Comm Coll 1976-85; COE/Bus Ed Tucson Unified Sch Dist 1978-; *ai:* COE Club Spon; Faculty Cncl; Applications Technologies Task Force Dist Chairperson; Tucson COE Coords Assn; AZ Bus Ed Assn 1982-; AZ COE Coords Assn 1989-; MADD 1985-; Greenpeace 1989-; Co-Writer Article; *office:* Palo Verde HS 1302 S Avenida Vega Tucson AZ 85710

SAXTON, JOSEPH JAMES, JR., English Teacher; *b:* Elizabeth, NJ; *m:* Wendy Lee Horn; *c:* Marlee F.; *ed:* (BA) Eng, 1983, (MED) Admin/Supervision, 1990 Rutgers Univ; Five Day Writing Inst; Writing Prgm That Works & Improving Rdng Comprehension Seminars, YA Literature; Cmptrs in Classroom; *cr:* Teacher Lacey Township HS 1983-; *ai:* Proposal for Extra Curricular Writing Club; Organize Informal Athletic Act; ASCD, NCTE Mem 1988-; Luth Church Sunday Sch Teacher 1988-; Co-Lead Chrstn Fellowship Group 1985-; Ocean Cty Guidance Assn Forum Speaker 1986-89; Ocean Cty at Risk Comm Mem 1990; *office:* Lacey Township HS PO Box 206 Haines St Lanoka Harbor NJ 08734

SAYEGH, ROBERT, English Teacher; *b:* Brooklyn, NY; *m:* Jo Ann Boron; *c:* Tracy Sayegh Funcheon, Robert; *ed:* (BA) Eng, William Paterson Coll 1965; (MA) Eng, Montclair St Coll 1968; *cr:* Eng Adjunct Professor William Paterson Coll 1970-73; Eng Teacher Passaic Valley HS 1965-; *ai:* Audio Visual Production; Film Club, Ski Club, Editing & Publishing Class Adv; Passaic Valley Ed Assn (Pres, VP, Grievance Chm); NJ Ed Assn; Passaic

Valley HS Teacher of Yr 1985; 2 NJ St Mini-Grants 1973; *office:* Passaic Valley Regional HS E Main St Little Falls NJ 07424

SAYERS, BILLYE BURROUGH, Mathematics Teacher; *b:* Pittsburg, OK; *m:* Stanley E.; *c:* Elayne Weger, James; *ed:* (BSED) Math, 1954, (MT) Ed, 1964 E Cntrl Univ; OK St Univ, Univ of OK; *cr:* Teacher Stuart HS 1962-63, Roff HS 1963-68, Duncan Jr HS 1971-; *ai:* Mathcounts Coach 1983-; Natl Jr Honor Society 1974-85; NEA, OEA 1973-75; ADE (Secy, Treas, VP) 1981-83, Teacher of Yr 1985; NCTM Mem 1971-; OK Cncl Teachers of Math Jr HS VP 1980-82; Delta Kappa Gamma (Pres 1990, 1st VP 1988-, Treas 1983-88); Duncan Chamber of Commerce Certificate 1988; St Mathcounts Team Coach 1988; Mathcounts Team 1st Place St of OK 1988; *home:* 2207 Chisholm Dr Duncan OK 73533

SAYERS, JOHN WALLACE, 1st-3rd Grade Phys Ed Teacher; *b:* Cleveland, OH; *m:* Beverly Joyce; *c:* Abby L.; *ed:* (BAED) Health/Phys Ed, Bowling Green St Univ 1972; Cert Elem Ed, Cleveland St Univ 1976; Certified Teacher Adventures in Movement for Handicapped 1978; *cr:* Visiting Teacher 1973-76, Phys Ed Teacher 1976- Olmsted Falls Schls; *ai:* Health Curr Comm; Jump Rope for Heart St Task Force; NEA Local Rep; OH Ed Assn Local Rep 1974-; OH Assn of Health, Phys Recreation & Dance 1976-; Kiwanis Intnl 1983-88; Rotary Intnl Teacher Exch to France 1977; Amer Leadership Study Groups Cnslr 1978; Cultural Heritage Alliance Cnslr 1979; *home:* 10444 E River Rd Columbia Stn OH 44028

SAYLES, KENNETH LYNN, Social Science Teacher; *b:* South Gate, CA; *c:* Kristen, Ryan; *ed:* (BA) Poly Sci, CA St Long Beach 1972; (MA) Poly Sci, Univ S CA 1975; Substance Abuse Ed; *cr:* Teacher Long Beach Sch for Adults 1977-79, Capistrano Valley HS 1979-, Saddleback Coll 1985-86; *ai:* Academic Decathlon Cross Cntry & Track Coach; Mentor Teacher; Soc Sci Curr & Soc Sci Textbook Selection Comm; Amer Poly Sci Assn; Mentor Teacher 1986-87, 1989-; Teacher of Yr 1982; CTIIP Grant Recepient 1985; Go For It Grant 1990; Natl Endowment for Hum Summer Inst Mentor Teacher 1987; *office:* Capistrano Valley HS 26301 Via Escolar Mission Viejo CA 92691

SAYLOR, JACKIE L., 7/8th Grade Rdng/Eng Teacher; *b:* Peach Creek, WV; *m:* David; *c:* Sandy Meeks, Steve, Stacey; *ed:* (BS) Elem Ed, Defiance Coll 1972; (MA) Rdng, St Francis Coll 1987; Numerous Classes, Univ of Toledo; *cr:* Teacher Defiance City Schls 1973-; *ai:* Adv Jr HS SADD Club; Delta Kappa Gamma/Phi Delta Kappa 1988-; Jennings Scholar 1979-80; *home:* 1031 Latty St Defiance OH 43512

SAYLORS, MICHAEL EVAN, Social Studies Dept Chairman; *b:* Tyler, TX; *ed:* (BS) His/Phys Ed, Univ TX Tyl er 1975; Teaching Gifted/Talented Stu; Advanced Academic Trng; *cr:* Teacher/Coach Alvin Jr HS 1975-78; Soc Stud Teacher Athens Mid Sch 1978-; *ai:* Soc Stud Dept Chm; TX HS Coaches Assn 1975-85; Teacher of Six Weeks 1985-89; Level II Career Ladder; Head Ftbl Coach Dist Champs 1977; Head Bsktbl Coach Dist Champs 1980; *home:* 807 A Windmill Ln Athens TX 75751

SAYRE, CATHY, Third Grade Teacher; *b:* Sarnia ON, Canada; *ed:* (BA) Bio, W MD 1966; (MA) Equivalent Ed, Towson St; *cr:* 1st Grade Teacher Back River Neck Elem 1967-68; 1st Grade Teacher 1968-73, 4th Grade Teacher 1973-74, 3rd Grade Teacher 1974-80, 4th Grade Teacher 1980-82, 2nd/3rd Grade Teacher 1982-83 Solley Elem; *ai:* Math & United Way Chairperson; TAAAC (Rep, Membership Comm 1968-81); MSTA, NEA; *office:* Solley Elem Sch 7608 Solley Rd Glen Burnie MD 21061

SAZAMA, NOMA LARSON, Middle School Teacher; *b:* Mission, SD; *m:* George; *c:* Susie Larson, Nancy, Barbara Kuxhaus, George, Mary, Beth; *ed:* (BS) Elem Ed, Northern Univ 1968; Grad Stud Black Hills Univ & Univ of SD; *cr:* 7th/8th Grade Teacher 1950-52, 6th Grade Teacher 1955-56, 4th Grade Teacher 1964-70, 7th/8th Grade Teacher 1972- Mission; *ai:* TC Jr NHS Bd; Team Leader; Building Rep; SDEA IP&D Comm Mem; Todd Cty Ed Assn, SD Ed Assn, NEA, SD Sci Assn, Natl Sci Assn, SD Math Assn, Natl Math Assn; Aid Assn for Luths (Branch VP 1980-, Legicator 1984-); *office:* Todd Cty Mid Sch P O Box 726 Mission SD 57555

SBORAY, STEPHEN CHARLES, III, Chemistry Teacher; *b:* Roanoke, VA; *m:* Sarah Robinson; *c:* Karen M., Stephen C. IV; *ed:* (BS) Chem, VA Military Inst 1967; (MS) Sci Ed, Radford Univ 1982; Pilot Trng USAF; *cr:* Pilot USAF 1967-73; Teacher Prince George Cty HS 1974-76, Cave Spring HS 1976-78, William Byrd HS 1978-; *ai:* Sci Club Spon; Schlsp Selection & Guidance Advisory Comms; Amer Chemical Society Blue Ridge Section; NEA, VA Ed Assn; William Byrd HS Teacher of Yr 1987-89; *office:* William Byrd HS 2902 Washington Ave Vinton VA 24179

SBRISCIA, DONNA PIZANO, 5th Grade Teacher; *b:* Kingston, PA; *m:* Duane; *c:* Dean, David; *ed:* (BA) Elem Ed, Moravian Coll 1977; Educl Technology, Lehigh Univ; *cr:* Compensatory Ed Teacher Harmony Township Sch 1978-80; Adult Ed Instruction Phillipsburg HS 1977-81; 6th 7th & 8th Grades Eng Teacher 1978-80, 5th Grade Teacher 1980- Harmony Township Sch; *ai:* Cheerleading Adv 1980-81; Gifted & Talented Comm 1983-85; Cultural Arts Comm 1984; *office:* Harmony Twp Schl 2551 Belvidere Rd Phillipsburg NJ 08865

SCAGNELLI, ELAINE FITCH, Science Teacher; *b:* Asheville, NC; *m:* Paul; *ed:* (BA) Elem, Newton Coll 1964; (MAT) Bio, Univ of NC 1970; Mentor Trng; Grad Stud; *cr:* Teacher St Genevieves 1964-71, Holt Elem 1971-87, Northern HS 1987-; *ai:* Teacher Recruiter; Future Teachers Club; NC Educator Assn 1971-; NASTA 1987-; Delta Kappa Gamma VP 1986-88; Neighborhood Assn Bd Mem 1989-; Durham Cty Teacher of Yr 1989-; *home:* 1408 Virginia Ave Durham NC 27705

SCALES, FRANCES WILLIAMS, Fifth Grade Teacher; *b:* Bennettsville, SC; *c:* Stephanie A.; *ed:* (BA) Elem Ed, 1973, (MS) Elem Ed, 1978 Francis Marion Coll; *cr:* 5th Grade Teacher Greenwood Elem 1973-; *ai:* NEA, SC Educators Assn 1973-; Church of God St Youth Choir Dir 1984-; Observer Assessments Performance in Teaching Teacher of Yr 1981-82 ; *office:* Greenwood Elem Sch 2300 E Howe Springs Rd Florence SC 29505

SCALES, LINDA KAY, 4th Grade Teacher; *b:* Atlanta, TX; *ed:* (BS) Elem Ed, Southern Nazarene Univ 1968; (MED) Ed, East TX St Univ 1974; Summer Wkshps; *cr:* Teacher Redwater ISD 1968-; *ai:* UIL Picture Memory; Soil & Water Conservation; Yearly Poster Contest; TSTA 1968-; Church of Nazarene Mem; Bowie Cty Soil & Water Conservation Dist; 1987 Outstanding Conservation Teacher; Career Ladder Teacher; *office:* Redwater Elem Sch P O Box 347 Redwater TX 75573

SCALES, LOIS L., 1st Grade Teacher; *b:* Greenwood, MS; *m:* Eddie B.; *c:* Eddie, Eric; *ed:* (BS) Elem Ed, MVSU 1968; (MS) Elem Ed, MSU 1977; Workshop Trng-Leflore Cty Sch; Mthi Trng; *cr:* Teacher Leflore Cty Schls 1969-; *ai:* Faculty Rep; Political Action Chm; Mem Federated Womens Club; Mem PTA; MAE/NEA/LCAE; Outstanding Teacher 1972; Outstanding Participation 1978; Task Force Comm Certificate of Meritorius Service 1979; Leflore Cty Assn of Educators Certificate of Appreciation 1981; Centrl Delta Uni-Serve Region Bldg Rep Awd 1982; Follow Through Teacher of Yr Awd 1982; Outstanding Young Women of America Awd 1979; Leflore Cty Assn of Educators Membership Promotion Awd 1986; Outstanding Membership Promotion Awd 1985; St Membership Comm MAE; Staff Dev Leflore Cty Schls.

SCALZI, LOUISE HERRERA, 6th/7th Grade Science Teacher; *b:* Winchester, MA; *m:* Michael David; *ed:* (BA) Bio, 1981, (MLA) Hum, 1989 W MD Coll; *cr:* 6th/7th Grade Sci/General/ Life Sci Teacher Mt Airy Mid Sch 1982-; *ai:* Intramural Girls Soccer, Field Hockey, Vlybl Coach; Volunteer Prgms Liason; Sch Earth Week & Sci Fair Coord; Cty Drug Alcohol Task Force; Amer Assn Univ Women (Secy 1990-) 1989-; Hashawa Environmental Center Trustees Bd Mem 1988-; Church of the Brethren Witness Comm; Potomac Appalachian Trail Club; AAUW Secy; *home:* 2200 Ridge Rd Westminster MD 21157

SCANDROLI, LYNN ESSINGTON, 2nd Grade Teacher; *b:* Rockford, IL; *m:* Carl; *c:* Kelly Childs; *ed:* (BA) Elem Ed, 1968, (MS) Elem Ed, 1976 N IL Univ; Grad Stud; *cr:* Teacher R K Welsh Elem 1968-71, Richmond Sch 1971-72, R K Welsh Elem 1973-; *ai:* Rockford Ed Assn Act; *office:* R K Welsh Elem Sch 2100 Huffman Blvd Rockford IL 61103

SCANLON, MARY (HARRIS), Third Grade Teacher; *b:* Silverton, OR; *c:* Carrie E. Starks, Richard L., John M.; *ed:* (BS) Elem Ed, W OR St Coll 1965; OR Div of Continuing Ed; *cr:* 4th Grade Teacher Roosevelt Elem 1965-76; 5th Grade Teacher Peterson Elem Sch 1977-79; 4th Grade Teacher Altamont Elem 1979-86; 3rd/4th Grade Teacher Shasta Elem 1986-89; 3rd Grade Teacher Fairhaven Elem 1989-; *ai:* Amer Cancer Society & Fairhaven Elem Sch Art Show Comm; Delta Kappa Gamma 1970-; Klamath Falls Ed Assn Secy 1965-; Amer Bus Women 1987-; Klamath Luth Church Pres 1970-; *office:* Fairhaven Elem Sch 5400 Hwy 66 Klamath Falls OR 97601

SCANTLIN, EUPHEMIA E., English Teacher; *b:* Boston, MA; *c:* Emilie; *ed:* (BA) Eng Ed, Univ of FL 1981; Grad Stud Middlebury Coll & Bread Loaf Sch of Eng 1983-84; Univ of NH Durham 1987, 1989; *cr:* 7th Grade Eng Teacher Beasley Mid Sch 1984-84; Sr HS Eng Teacher Londonderry HS 1984-85, Raymond HS 1986-; *ai:* Grading Comm; Discipline Comm; Curr Dev Comm; NH Assn Teachers of Eng 1987-; *office:* Raymond HS 45 Harriman Hill Rd Raymond NH 03077

SCANZANI, FRANK R., Science Teacher; *b:* Beverly, MA; *m:* Phyllis Morency; *c:* Kristina, Nicole; *ed:* (BA) Urban Stud, St Anselms Coll 1968; (MA) Ed, Salem St Coll 1978; Media, Salem St Coll 1978-80; *ai:* MA Teachers Assn 1972-87/1989-; Sch Comm Delegate; Girl Scouts, I Touch the Future, I Teach 1989; Yrbk Adv 1980-81; Conducted Sci Club 6th Grade 1975-86; Gifted/Talented Prgm 1985-89; Schl Comm Mem 1980-85; *home:* 48 Lakemans Ln Ipswich MA 01938

SCANZILLO, JANET PACKO, Third Grade Teacher; *b:* Union City, PA; *ed:* (BS) Elem Ed, 1968, (MS) Elem Ed, 1971, Rdng Specialist, 1975 Edinboro St; Elem Ed 1990; *cr:* 2nd Grade Teacher Waterford Elem 1968-69; 3rd Grade Teacher Robison Elem 1969-75, Summit Cntrl 1975-; *ai:* Ft Leboeuf Sch Dist Youth Empowering Comm; PA St Ed Assn, NEA, Ft Leboeuf Ed Assn 1982-; Keystone St Rdng Assn, Intnl Rdng Assn 1980-; PTA 1968-; *office:* Summit Cntrl Elem Sch RD 4 Townhall Rd Erie PA 16509

SCARBERRY, TIMOTHY LEE, Social Studies Chairman; *b:* Huntington, WV; *m:* Millie Florence Thompson; *c:* Timothy II; *ed:* (BA) Soc Stud, 1972, (MS) Geography, 1975 Marshall Univ; (PHD) Ed Admin, CPU 1986; Dayton Univ Classes; Wesley Theo Seminary Classes; *cr:* Instr Head of Dept Hannan Trace HS 1972-; *ai:* Sr Class Adv; Beta Spon; Past Bsbl Coach; NEA, OEA; Councilman at Large 1987-; Mem Trinity United Meth Church Lay Leader; *home:* 11 Wakefield Point Pleasant WV 25550

SCARBORO, DOLORES ALFORD, Fifth Grade Teacher; *b:* Raleigh, NC; *m:* C. Glenn; *c:* Scott H., Bradford L.; *ed:* (BS) Elem Ed, E Carolina Univ 1970; *cr:* 4th Grade Teacher 1970-71, 5th Grade Teacher 1971- Rolesville Elem; *ai:* Stu Cncl Adv; NC Assn of Educators 1971-; Rolesville Jaycettes Pres 1978-84; Rolesville Womens Club 1984-; *home:* 209 W Young St Box 209 Rolesville NC 27571

SCARBOROUGH, DELORES (BARBER), Secondary Math Teacher; *b:* Stantonville, TN; *m:* Truman Denton; *c:* Aletha, Hannah; *ed:* (AA) Math, NE MS Jr Coll 1961; (BS) Math, Bethel Coll 1962; (MRE) Religious Ed, SW Baptist Theological Seminary 1967; (MED) Math, Delta St Univ 1975; Addl Stud, Murray St Univ, MS St Univ; *cr:* Math Teacher Huntingdon HS 1962-65, Tupelo HS 1968-70, Quitman Cty Schls 1977-81, Philadelphia HS 1981-86, Grenada HS 1986-; *ai:* Coach Academic Competition Team; Math Club Spon; MS Prof Educators; MS Cncl of Teachers of Math; NCTM; Progressive Ladies Club 1986-; *home:* PO Box 241 Coffeeville MS 38922

SCARBOROUGH, KAROL ANDREA, Soc Stud Teacher & Dept Chair; *b:* Athens, GA; *ed:* (BSED) Soc Sci Ed, 1980, (MED) Soc Sci Ed, 1985 Univ of GA; *cr:* Teacher 1980-, Soc Stud Dept Chm 1986- Madison Cty HS; *ai:* Sr Spon; *office:* Madison Cty HS PO Box 7 Old Comer Rd Danielsville GA 30633

SCARDINA, PHILIP A., History Teacher; *b:* Milwaukee, WI; *m:* Aralee Dudley; *c:* Laura D'Amato, Rita Baxter; *ed:* (BS) Ed, Univ of WI 1957; Masters Equivalency Univ of WI Whitewater 1964; *cr:* 8th Grade Teacher La Follette Grade Sch 1957-60; His/ Eng Teacher Bell Jr HS 1960-84; His Teacher Roosevelt Mid Sch 1984-; *ai:* Bi Monthly Variety Sch Producer *home:* 8108 S Mona Ct Oak Creek WI 53154

SCARFIA, JAMES MICHAEL, Soc Stud/Theology Teacher; *b:* Rochester, NY; *m:* Shirley Bean; *c:* Matthew, Jillian; *ed:* (BA) Religious Stud, St John Fisher 1978; (MA) Theology/His, St Michaels Univ 1982; Theological Sch; Participated in Mid St Evaluation; Working Toward Masters in His; *cr:* Theology Teacher Andrean HS 1978-79; Soc Stud/His Teacher Aquinas Inst Rochester 1982-; *ai:* Ftbl Mgr; Head Var Bowling Coach; Rochester Area Cncl of Soc Stud Mem 1985-; Keryama Awd Teaching of Theology 1990, Keryama 1990; Rochester Cath Diocese 1982-, Keryama 1990; Elected to Faculty Advisory Cncl 1986; Teacher Rep to Admin; *home:* 8151 Morley Rd Sodus Point NY 14555

SCARLETT, ANNIE BROWN, 2nd Grade Teacher; *b:* Clinton, OK; *c:* Mary, Kaye, Mike, Rhonda, Stacy, Leon Jr.; *ed:* (BA) Elem Ed, 1980; (MS) Rdng Spec, 1987 SWOSU; Adm Certfct SWOSU 1990; *cr:* 2nd Grade Teacher Nance Elem 1980-; *ai:* BSU Spon Black Stud Union; Bibleclass Teacher (2nd Grade); Clinton Ed Assn VP 1989-; NEA Mem 1980-; Klahoma Ed Assn Mem 1980-; Bus & Prof Women Mem 1987-; Clinton Woman of Yr 1987; Assaulton Illiteracy VP 1990-92; Nom for Athena Awd 1988; Sophia Awd Best Character 1987; *home:* 901 Glenn Smith Rd Clinton OK 73601

SCARTOZZI, CHERYL CEVOLI, 8th Grade Teacher; *b:* Yeadon, PA; *m:* Thomas A.; *c:* Sandy, Tommy, Melissa; *ed:* (BS) Elem Ed, St Josephs Univ 1971; Post Grad Work West Chester Univ, Villanova Univ; *cr:* 2nd Grade Teacher St Colmans Sch 1968-72; 6th Grade Teacher 1972-74, Remedial Math Teacher 1974-75, 6th Grade Teacher 1981-89, 8th Grade Teacher 1990 Our Lady of Loreto; *ai:* Lang Art Coord; Safety Patrol Moderator; Talent Shows Producer & Dir; *home:* 7333 Lindbergh Blvd Philadelphia PA 19153

SCECINA, PATRICIA A., Nursery School Teacher; *b:* Cold Spring, NY; *m:* Andrew; *ed:* (AA) Liberal Arts, Dutchess Comm Coll 1971; (BS) Elem Ed, SUNY Plattsburgh 1973; (MS) Theatre Ed, Emerson Coll 1979; *cr:* 5th-6th Grade Teacher Garrison Union Free Sch 1973-78; 4th Grade TeachEr Weston Elem Sch Dist 1978-79; Pre-Sch Teacher Cmmty Nursery Sch 1989-; *ai:* Childrens Drama Teacher Garrison Art Center Bd of Dir Philipstown Cmmty Cncl; PTA 1988-; Emerson Coll Fellowship 1979; Delta Kappa Gamma Mem; Educators Honor Society.

SCHAAF, KAREN ANNE, Jr High Language Arts Teacher; *b:* Dayton, OH; *ed:* (BA) Elem Ed, Walsh Coll 1973; (MA) Rdng Specialist, Univ of Akron 1983; Learning Disabilities & Behavior Disorders Honorary Degree, Walsh Coll; *cr:* 5th Grade Teacher St Marys 1968-69; 6th/8th Grade Teacher St Paul 1969-79; GED Instr Mc Kinley Sr HS 1972-73; 4th Grade Teacher Sauder Elem 1979-83; 6th/7th Grade Teacher Jackson Mid Sch 1983-; *ai:* Faculty Team Leader; Prins Advisory Cncl Mem; Schls Soc Comm Rep; NEA, OH Educators Assn, E Cntrl OH Educators Assn 1979-; *home:* 152 36th St NE Canton OH 44714

SCHAAF, MARY LOU (AMOLE), English/Speech Teacher; *b:* Coatesville, PA; *m:* Steven J.; *c:* Lauren; *ed:* (BSED) Comm Art/ Speech, Shippensburg St 1980; (MED) Scndry Counseling, Shippensburg Univ 1990; *cr:* Step Cnslr Chester Cty Intermediate Unit 1980-81; CETA Cnslr Susquehanna Intermediate Unit 1982-83; Teacher Juniata Cty Sch Dist 1980-; *ai:* Newspaper Adv; Television Studio Adv; Career Club Adv; Amer Assn of Counseling & Dev 1989-; PA Interscholstic Athletic Assn Hockey Secy 1987-, Sftbl 1980-; *office:* Juniata H S Rd 2 Mifflintown PA 17059

SCHACH, ANN WILCOX, Science Teacher; *b:* Ottumwa, IA; *m:* Kim A.; *c:* Brady; *ed:* (BA) Bio, Monmouth Coll 1976; (MSED) Educl Foundations, W IL Univ 1990; Grad Stud Cmptrs, Marycrest; Physics, Univ of IA; Writing Across the Curr, Univ of IA Iowa City; *cr:* Bio Teacher Aquinas HS 1976-78; Sci Teacher

Arnold HS 1978-; *ai:* Jr Class & Sci Club Spon; Stu Adv; Sci Curr, Substance Abuse Curr, Dist-Wide Curr Steering Comms; NSTA, IA Acad of Sci, IA Ed Assn, Phi Kappa Phi; Grade A Plus 1987-89; *office:* Arnold HS 408 Van Weiss West Burlington IA 52655

SCHACHTER, LINDA (ZEMON), Business Education Teacher; *b:* Miami, FL; *m:* Howard; *c:* Brian; *ed:* (BA) Bus Ed, Univ of S FL 1972; (MS) Cmptr Ed, Nova Univ 1984; *cr:* Bus Ed Teacher Leto Sr HS 1972-73, North Miami Sr HS 1974, Palmetto Sr HS 1974-75, Miami Cntrl 1975-78, Miami Sunset Sr HS 1978-; *ai:* Dept Head; Dade Cty Bus Ed Assn; Delta Kappa Gamma; *office:* Miami Sunset Sr HS 13125 SW 72nd St Miami FL 33183

SCHAEFER, CAROL RAMMING, Biology Teacher; *b:* St Louis, MO; *c:* Vickie, Cindy Fults, Gerald; *ed:* (BA) Elem Ed, 1975, (MAT) Bio, 1978 Webster Univ; Individually Guided Ed Seminar; *cr:* Teacher Our Lady of Sorrows Holy Innocents 1960-; K-8th Teacher St Bartholomew 1977; 7th-8th Grade Teacher Wade IGE 1977-81; Bio Teacher Beaumont HS 1981-; *ai:* Teacher Adv for Drug Ed Prgm; NSTA 1981-; Assn for Individually Guided Ed 1977-, MO Delegate 1977-80; MO St Teachers Assn 1975-; *office:* Beaumont H S 3836 Natural Bridge Saint Louis MO 63107

SCHAEFER, JAMES JOHN, English Teacher; *b:* Beaver Dam, WI; *m:* Barbara Bryn; *c:* Laura; *ed:* (BS) Bio, St Norbert Coll 1961; (MS) Eng Ed, Univ of WI Whitewater 1972; Various Univs; *cr:* Bio/Eng Teacher Mayville HS 1962-68; Eng Teacher Arrowhead HS 1968-; *ai:* Ftbl, Bsktbl, Track, Forensics Coach; NCTE 1963-; WI Cncl Teachers of Eng 1968-; Phi Delta Kappa 1978-; St Charles Mens Club Secy 1971-; Simmons Coll NDEA Schlsp Grant 1968; *office:* Arrowhead HS 700 North Ave Hartland WI 53029

SCHAEFER, JOSEPH M., Assistant Principal; *b:* Anna, IL; *m:* Paula Wilson; *c:* Brian; *ed:* (BS) Ag, Sin Carbondale 1974; (MED) Ed Univ of IL 1977; Admin Cert Univ of IL 1980: *cr:* Ag Teacher 1974-80, Asst Prin 1980-Highland HS; *ai:* Stu Act Dir; IL Prin Assn 1989-; VFW 1980-; *office:* Highland H S 1500 Troxler Highland IL 62249

SCHAEFER, KAREN KOSTER, 4th Grade Teacher; *b:* New Orleans, LA; *m:* David John; *c:* Kelli; *ed:* (BA) Elem Ed, Univ of New Orleans 1979; *cr:* 5th & 6th Grade Teacher St James Major Sch 1979-82; 4th & 5th Grade St Christopher Sch 1984-; *ai:* Co-Moderator Jr Beta Club; Co-Moderator Corners Literary Mag; Grade Level Coord; NCEA 1984-.

SCHAEFER, LYLE LOREN, History Department Chairman; *b:* Guide Rock, NE; *m:* Wanda Lee Kemmerer; *c:* Linda, Valerie, Gloria Schaefer Rybkowski; *ed:* (AB) His/Eng, Kearney St Coll 1957; (MA) His, 1963, (PHD) His/Geography, 1976 Univ of Denver; His Inst of Nationalism, Univ of Denver 1965, Taft Inst for Two Party Govt, Univ of N CO 1985; *cr:* Rural Teacher Nuckols Cty Schls 1950-53; Elem Teacher Eckley Consolidated 1953-56; Scndry Teacher/Dept Chm Luth HS 1957-; *ai:* Chief Statistician Luth HS 1957-; Metro League Statistician 1971-; Archivist CO Luth Church MO Synod 1969-; Organization of Amer Historians 1976-; West His Assn 1970-; Concordia His Society 1969-; Metropolitan League Hall of Fame 1982; Wrote Book 1969; Articles Published; Book Reviewer; *office:* Lutheran HS 3201 W Arizona Ave Denver CO 80219

SCHAEFER, SHERRY WILLIFORD, Fourth Grade Teacher; *b:* Carbondale, IL; *m:* Gregory A.; *c:* Jeremy C.; *ed:* (BS) Elem Ed, S IL Univ 1973; Grad Stud; *cr:* 4th Grade Teacher Carterville Grade Sch 1973-; *ai:* Building Rep; Carterville Ed Assn, IL Ed Assn, NEA; Delta Zeta Alumni; *office:* Carterville Unit #5-Cambria PO Box 98 Cambria IL 62915

SCHAFF, DEANNA K., Mathematics/Science Teacher; *b:* Cheyenne Wells, CO; *m:* Robert A.; *c:* Monte N., Dean A.; *ed:* (BA) Math, St Mary of the Plains Coll 1969; Miscellaneous In-Services, Wkshps & Summer Courses; *cr:* Teacher St Francis De Sales HS 1969-72, Bethune Public Schls 1985-; *ai:* Mathcounts Coach; Triangle Fair Comm Chm; NCTM, CCTM 1985-; BOCES Hi-Plains Educator Awd; Bethune HS Teacher of Yr 1987, 1988; *office:* Bethune Public Schls 145 W 3rd Bethune CO 80805

SCHAFFER, HANNAH LOEB, Second Grade Teacher; *b:* Akron, Israel; *m:* Jack; *c:* Kyla; *ed:* (BS) Elem Ed, Univ of IL 1963; Fingermath; *cr:* 2nd/3rd Grade Teacher Ray Sch 1964-70, 1977-; *ai:* Local Sch Cncl Finance; Univ of Chicago Sch Math Project; Piloting; Chicago Teachers Union; Womens Amer ORT Hadassah (Pres 1983-84, VP 1988-); *office:* William H Ray Sch 5631 S Kimbark Chicago IL 60637

SCHAFFSTALL, ROBERT DALE, 5th Grade Teacher; *b:* Harrisburg, PA; *m:* Susan D.; *c:* Stacy, Kimberly; *ed:* (BA) His, Messiah Coll 1967; (MS) Elem Ed, Shippensburg Univ 1968; *cr:* 5th Grade Teacher Mechanicsburg Sch Dist 1968-; *ai:* Soc Stud Comm; Coached Sftbl; Cumberland Valley Sftbl Assn; MEA Bldg Rep 1968-; PSEA 1968-; NEA 1968-; *office:* Upper Allen Elem Sch 1790 S Market St Mechanicsburg PA 17055

SCHALK, JOYBELL DIE, Algebra Teacher; *b:* Nacogdoches, TX; *m:* Thomas E.; *c:* Trey, Joyann; *ed:* (BA) Music/Math, TX Chrstn Univ 1967; *cr:* Math Teacher Lake Charles LA 1967; Eng Teacher Era TX 1968; Math Teacher Gainesville Mid Sch & HS 1971-; *ai:* NHS & Jr Class Spon; Textbook Comm; Jubilee Co-Chm; Delta Kappa Gamma 1985-; Beta Sigma Phi; *office:* Gainesville HS 1201 Lindsay St Gainesville TX 76240

SCHALLERT, GARY T., Director of Bands; *b:* St Petersburg, FL; *ed:* (BME) Music Ed, NM St 1987; Working Toward Master Music Ed, Univ of NM; *cr:* Band Asst Dir Del Norte HS 1987-88; Band Dir Manzano HS 1988-; *ai:* Marching Band; Pep Band; MENC 1985-; NAJE 1989-; Asst Dir Albuquerque Concert Band 1989-; NM St Marching Band Championships 1989; *office:* Manzano HS 12200 Lomas Blvd NE Albuquerque NM 87112

SCHANEL, MARY J., Mathematics Department Chair; *b:* Chicago, IL; *ed:* (BA) Math, 1980, (MAMED) Math Ed, 1989 De Paul Univ; *cr:* Math Dept Chairperson Resurrection HS 1981-; Instr Loyola Univ 1986-; *ai:* Sr & Jr Class Moderator; Cmptr Lab Coord; TMPB Facilitator; Curr Comm; Academic Cncl; Procedural Concerns; Adult Ed Instr; NCTM, ICTM, NIME, MTA 1981-; Natl Sci Fnd Awd 1988; Nom Presidential Awd Excl in Teaching; Univ of IL Summer Inst Participant; *office:* Resurrection HS 7500 W Talcott Ave Chicago IL 60631

SCHANKWEILER, ROBERT DANIEL, Bus Ed Dept Chairperson; *b:* Danville, PA; *m:* Karen Shuck; *ed:* (MED) Bus Ed, 1965 Bloomsburg Univ; Grad Stud Temple, Shippensburg, Penn St Univ; *cr:* Bus Ed Teacher 1961-; Dept Chairperson 1983- Lower Dauphin HS; *ai:* Staff Dev & Cmptr Technologies Comm; NEA 1961-; PA St Ed Assn Life Mem 1961; Lower Dauphin Ed Assn Pres 1965-66; Hummelston Lions Club 1987-; *office:* Lower Dauphin HS 201 S Hanover St Hummelstown PA 17036

SCHAPER, LAUREL T., Reading/Spelling Teacher; *b:* San Diego, CA; *ed:* (BS) Eng/Journalism, Sam Houston St Univ 1967; Scndry Ed & Lang Art; *cr:* 8th Grade Rdng/Spelling Teacher Blocker Mid Sch 1982-; *ai:* Co-Spon Blocker 8th Grade Class Day Variety Show; Blocker Memory Book & Sch Newspaper Spon; Faculty Advisory Comm Sch Rep; TX Classroom Teachers Assn Membership VP 1989-; Alpha Delta Kappa 1986-; *office:* Blocker Mid Sch 500 14th Ave N Texas City TX 77590

SCHAPKER, THOMAS JOSEPH, 5th Grade Teacher; *b:* Evansville, IN; *m:* Kathy Jayne; *c:* Brian, Andrea, Nicholas; *ed:* (BA) Elem Ed, 1974, (MA) Elem Ed/Drivers Ed, 1976 IN St; Elem Ed Admin; *cr:* 5th Grade Teacher S Terrace Elem Sch 1974-; *ai:* 5th Grade Bsktbl Coach; Advisory Comm Supt; NEA, N Posey Ed Assn, IN Sci Teachers Assn, N Posey Sci Teachers Assn Mem 1974-; N Posey Teacher Assn Pres 1983-84; Little League Mgr 1984-; Easter Seals Coord 1988-; *office:* S Terrace Elem 8427 Haines Rd Wadesville IN 47638

SCHARER, JULEY ANN, 6th Grade Teacher; *b:* Hollywood, CA; *m:* Jon Walter; *c:* Glendon, Darin; *ed:* (BA) Music, Univ of Redlands & Whittier Coll 1957; Various Coll Courses & Wkshps in Elem Ed; Consortium Planning Directorship, Scndry & Elem Ed Teachers, Math 1987; Drug Abuse Ed Trainer Redlands Unified Schls; *cr:* Teacher Monroe Elem Sch 1957-61, Arcadia Unified Schls 1964-65, Clement Jr HS 1967; Crafton Elem 1970-; *ai:* Drug Abuse Ed Trainer of Teachers; Textbook Selection, Report Cards, Proficiency Test Planning & Grading, Assessment Instruments Comm Redlands Unified Schls; ASCD 1985-; City of Redlands Drug Task Force Mem 1988-; PTA Mem 1970-; Honorary Service Awd 1974; Redlands Educl Partnership Fnd Outstanding Teacher of Yr 1988; Masonic Lodge Outstanding Teacher Drug Abuse Ed 1990.

SCHARRINGHAUSEN, JULIE, German Teacher; *b:* Oelwein, IA; *m:* Ernst; *c:* Britt, Gretchen; *ed:* (BA) Ger, Wartburg Coll 1970; Grad Work at Bonn Univ, Univ of N IA; *cr:* Ger Teacher Divine Word Coll 1971-72, Andrew HS 1971-77, Dubuque Sr HS 1978-; *ai:* Ger Club, Delta Epsilon Phi Spon; AATG, DEA, ISEA, NEA; JDC Uniserv Unit VP 1989-; Univ of N IA Project HS Coll Collaboratives; Uni Doe Project; *office:* Dubuque Sr HS 1800 Clarke Dr Dubuque IA 52001

SCHATH, IMOLEE JOY BROWN, Fourth Grade Teacher; *b:* Macksville, KS; *m:* Robert Ferdinand; *c:* Jeffrey, Debra June, Huddleston, Peggy Marie Baumgardner, Michael Luchen; *ed:* (BA) Elem Ed, Univ of MO Kansas City 1974; *cr:* Elem Teacher Blessed Sacrement 1974-77; 3rd Grade Teacher Dixon R1 Public Sch 1977-78; Elem Teacher Rolla Dist 31 Public Sch 1978-; *home:* Rt 5 Box 675 Rolla MO 65401

SCHATZ, GERENE AIKO, Third Grade Teacher; *b:* Tachikowa, Japan; *m:* Tom; *c:* Tim; *ed:* (BA) Elem Ed, Univ of Cincinnati 1974; Spec Ed, Cooperative Learning; *cr:* 4th/5th Grade Teacher Nicolet Elem Sch 1979, Clovis Elem Sch 1979-81, Jefferson Elem Sch 1981-83; 5th Grade Teacher 1983-89, 3rd Grade Teacher 1989- Banta Elem Sch; *ai:* Cooperative Learning Trainers Team Mem; WFT K-12 Cncl Mem 1986-87; Article Published; *office:* Banta Elem Sch 6th St Menasha WI 54952

SCHATZLEY, BILL, Boys Basketball Coach; *b:* Pontiac, MI; *m:* Dawna J Wilborn; *c:* Andy, Caseey; *ed:* (BSE) Phys Ed, Southeast MO St 1979; *cr:* Teacher/Coach Southland HS 1979-82, Knobel HS 1982-84, Senath-Hornersville HS 1984-86, Corning HS 1986-; *ai:* Jr High Boys Bsktbl Coach; Sr High Boys Bsktbl Coach; Asst Bsbl Coach; *home:* 305 N 12th Paragould AR 724

SCHAUER, LARRY D., Teacher/Assistant Dept Head; *b:* Massillon, OH; *m:* Gail Lantzer; *c:* Heather, Kimberly; *ed:* (BA) Comprehensive Sci, Univ of Akron 1978; Cntrl St Univ Ada, Univ of IA; *cr:* Sci Teacher Mc Alester HS 1978-84; Temporary Staff Univ of IA 1983; Sci Teacher Bixby Jr HS 1984-; *ai:* Asst Dept Head; OK Ed Assn, Bixby Ed Assn, NEA; Whitey Ford Bsktbl League Coach 1989-; *home:* 12502 S Florence Jenks OK 74037

SCHAUFLER, MARY RUTH (MURR), Media Specialist; *b:* Pendleton, OR; *m:* John D.; *c:* Arlyn J., Rick W.; *ed:* (BS) Elem Ed, 1972, (MS) Geographical Ed, 1976 Univ of OR; Media Endorsement W OR 1986; *cr:* 5th Grade Teacher Centennial Elem 1972-80, Yolanda Elem 1980-81, Ridgeview Elem 1981-86; *ai:* Young Authors, Lib Curr, Wellness Comm; Alpha Delta Kappa Historian 1988-; OR Lib Assn; *office:* Moffitt Elem 1544 N 5th St Springfield OR 97477

SCHEARER, MIRIAM J., Third Grade Teacher; *b:* Reading, PA; *m:* Frederic C.; *c:* Timothy, Christine; *ed:* (BS) Elem Ed, Kutztown Univ 1960; *cr:* 1st Grade Teacher Reading Sch Dist 1960-61; 2nd Grade Teacher 1961-63, 3rd Grade Teacher 1963-64, 1st Grade Teacher 1977-78 Kutztown Ares Sch Dist; 2nd Grade Teacher Albany Elem Sch 1978-79; 3rd Grade Teacher Maxatawny Elem Sch 1979-; *ai:* NEA, PA St Ed Assn 1960-64, 1977-; Kutztown Area Teachers Assn 1961-64, 1978-; Womans Club of Kutztown (Recording Secy 1970-72, Stu Loan Comm 1978-82, Chm 1981-82) 1967-; Brownie Girl Scout Troop Leader 1974-76; Church Choir 1960-64, 1988-; *office:* Kutztown Area Sch Dist Maxatawny Elem Sch RD 1 Box 444 Kutztown PA 19530

SCHEDLEY, HOLLY JEAN, 7th Grade Lang Art Teacher; *b:* Cleveland, OH; *ed:* (BS) Eng, 1971, (MS) Rdng Supervision, 1982 Ashland Coll; Quest Certified; Grad Stud in Admin, Curr, Instruction; *cr:* 7th/8th Grade Lang Art Teacher 1971-73, 7th Grade Librarian 1973-76, 7th Grade Lang Art Teacher 1976- Western Reserve Schls; *ai:* Huron Cty Young Authors, Spelling Bee Comms; NEA, OEA; Delta Kappa Gamma Recording Secy 1988-; Natl Spelling Bee 1987; *home:* 6201 Darrow Rd Huron OH 44839

SCHEEL, LEONARD G., Science Department Chairman; *b:* Chicago, IL; *m:* Catherine E. Smith; *c:* Kenneth, Stephan, Deborah; *ed:* (BS) Bio, 1957, (MS) Bio, 1962 N IL Univ; Bio, Univ of NM 1966, Bemidji St Coll 1967, AR St 1969, Univ of CO 1970; Admin, N IL Univ 1978-84; *cr:* Teacher Sch Dist 155 1967-; *ai:* NHS Adv; NEA, IEA 1967-; NSTA 1967-; Nabt 1967-80; IL Assn Bio Teachers VP 1972; BSA Scoutmaster 1970-, Dist Awd of Merit 1979, Silver Beaver 1982, Wood Badge 1978; Natl Sci Fnd Grants 1966, 1967. 1969, 1970; NSTA OHANS Awd 1984; St of IL Master Teacher Awd 1985; Presidents Awd of Excl 1989; Outstanding Educator Awd 1979; *office:* Crystal Lake S HS 1200 S Mc Henry Ave Crystal Lake IL 60014

SCHEER, CATHERINE MARIE, Science Teacher; *b:* Whittier, CA; *m:* Gerald Dan Jr.; *c:* Valerie, Erica, Celeste; *ed:* (BA) Biological Sci, CA St Fullerton 1974; Granted Sabbatical Leave to Earn MS Degree 1990; GESA Trng; Care & Prevention of Athletic Injuries; Qualities of Good Instr; Outdoor Ed, Teton Sci Sch; Assertive Discipline; Tactics in Thinking Skills; Cooperative Learning; TESA Trng; Metacognitive Skill; *cr:* Teacher Rock Springs Cath Sch 1977-79, Monroe Sch 1981-84, Lincoln Mid Sch 1984-; *ai:* Sci Fair Coord; Stu Cncl Adv; Dist Mid Sch Task Force Chairperson; Dist Budget Comm; Gifted & Talented Stu Selection Comm Mem; Dist Sci Curr Comm; Core Leader; NSTA 1984-; Natl Mid Sch Assn 1986; WY Ed Assn, NEA, Green River Ed Assn 1981-; City of Green River Parks & Recreation Advisory Bd 1989-; Young Womens Chrstn Assn; US Dept of Energy Teacher Research Assoc 1990; Natl Mid Sch Conference Presenter 1986; Nominee Outstanding Young Educator Awd Jaycees 1978; Teacher of Month Lincoln Mid Sch; *office:* Lincoln Mid Sch 600 W 3rd N Green River WY 82935

SCHEFFER, CHERYL ANN, Mathematics Department Chair; *b:* Winamac, IN; *ed:* (BA) Math, 1968, (MS) Math, 1972 IN St Univ; Acceleration Prgms, Earlham Coll 1984; Math for Gifted & Talented, Purdue Univ 1986; *cr:* Math Teacher Twin Lakes Sr HS 1968-72; Math Teacher/Dept Chairperson Pioneer Jr-Sr HS 1972-; *ai:* NHS, Sr Class Spon; Fund Raising Comm; Academic Super Bowl Invitational Coord; Math Team Coach; IN Cncl Teachers of Math 1980-; NCTM 1976-; Mathematical Assn of America 1982-; Delta Kappa Gamma 1989-; *home:* RR 2 Box 59 Star City IN 46985

SCHEFFER, JAMES DAVID, Mathematics Teacher; *b:* Salina, KS; *m:* Kathryn Ann York; *ed:* (BA) Math, 1967, (MS) Math, 1969 KS St Univ; *cr:* Asst Math Prof Wayne St Coll 1969-73; Math Instr Cursicana HS 1973-78; Insurance Agent Wenger-York Ins 1978-83; Math Instr Salina HS 1983-; *ai:* Head Golf & Asst Bsktbl Coach; NHS & Sch Pride Comm; NCTM; Salina Noon Optimist Club (Secy 1978-81, Pres 1981-82); Salina Mens Golf Assn Pres 1988-89; Math, Sci Teacher of Yr Wayne St Coll 1972; *office:* Salina HS South 730 E Magnolia Rd Salina KS 67401

SCHEFFT, WALTER ROBERT, Principal; *b:* Cleveland, OH; *m:* Georgia Seitz; *c:* Mark, Paul; *ed:* (BA) Elem Ed, Concordia Univ 1965; (MSED) Elem Ed, IN Univ SE New Albany 1974; Natl Luth Prin Acad; Natl Assn of Scndry Sch Prins Assessor Trng, S IL Univ Edwardsville; Ed Admin Prgm; *cr:* Teacher/Prin Grace Luth Sch 1965-68; 5th/6th Grade Teacher St John Luth Sch 1968-75; 8th Grade Teacher Wyneken Memorial Luth Sch 1975-79, Holy Cross Luth Sch 1979-87; Prin Holy Cross Luth Sch 1987-; *ai:* Luth Ed Assn 1965-; ASCD 1987-; *office:* Holy Cross Lutheran Sch South & Seminary Collinsville IL 62234

SCHEIBLE, STEVEN A., 7th Grade Geography Teacher; *b:* Racine, WI; *m:* Pamela Susan Stewart; *c:* Mark, Lindsey, Jacob; *ed:* (BS) His-Geography, 1974, (MST) Mid Level Ed, 1977 Univ WI-Eau Claire; *cr:* 9th Grade His Teacher 1974-, 7th Grade Eastern Hemisphere Geography Teacher 1990 Delong Jr HS; *ai:* Head Coach Boys/Girls Interschlastic Swimming/Diving Teams; UW-Eau Claire Alumni Assn (Pres 1984 Bd of Dir 1977-85); WI Assn of Educators 1980-; WI Fed of Teachers 1974-; Univ WI-Eau

Claire Fnd Bd of Dir 1983-85; Eau Claire Coaches Assn Bd Mem 1989-; *office:* Delong Jr HS 2000 Vine St Eau Claire WI 54703

SCHEICK, EVYONNE LIVESAY, First Grade Teacher; *b:* Kyles Ford, TN; *m:* Louis R.; *c:* Robin Schieck Coffey, Karen Schieck Underwood; *ed:* (BS) Elem Ed, Carson Newman Coll 1957; Rdng, ETSU; Walter St Coll; N VA Comm Coll; *cr:* 2nd Grade Teacher Glengary Sch 1957-58; 1st Grade Teacher Woodlynne Elem 1958-62, Surgoinsville Elem 1968-69; Kndgtn Teacher Bean Station Elem 1974-75; 1st Grade Teacher Berkshire Sch 1975-78, Washburn Elem 1978-79; 1st-2nd Grade Taecher Bean Station Elem 1979-; *ai:* NEA, Grainger Cty Ed Assn, TN Ed Assn 1978-; Our Savior Luth Church; Whole Lang Conference 1990; Presentor for Inservice 1987, 1988; Creative Writing Wkshp Presentation & Display 1987; Art Wkshp Knoxville 1988; 1st Grade Conference MTSU 1989; *home:* Rt 2 Box 5425 Bean Station TN 37708

SCHEIN, EILEEN HOFFMAN, Spanish Teacher; *b:* Philadelphia, PA; *m:* Joseph; *c:* Samantha J.; *ed:* (AB) Span, Long Island Univ 1969; (MA) Span, NY Univ Prgm at Univ of Madrid Spain 1970; Adelphi Univ Natl Trng Inst 1980-84; *cr:* Chairperson/Foreign Lang Teacher Woodrow Wilson HS 1974-81; Span Teacher Woodrow Wilson HS & Harry S Truman HS 1970-; Chairperson/Foreign Lang Teacher Harry S Truman HS 1988-; *ai:* Span Club Adv 1990; Var Sftbl Coach 1970-80, Championships 1973-76; Var Cheerleading Coach 1970-80; Bristol Twp Ed Assn, PA St Ed Assn, NEA 1970-; Long Island Univ Semper Vigilante Alumnae Awd, Optimates & Modern Lang Honor Society 1969; Woodrow Wilson HS Teacher of Yr 1975, Yrbk Dedication 1978; *office:* Harry S Truman HS 3001 Green Ln Levittown PA 19057

SCHELICH, ROBERT DEAN, Eighth Grade English Teacher; *b:* Celina, OH; *m:* Jane E.; *c:* Amy, Nina, Elena, Andrea, Jennifer; *ed:* (BA) Scndry Eng, Wright St Univ 1971; *cr:* Eng Teacher Celina Jr HS 1971-; *ai:* CEA; NEA; OEA; *office:* Celina Jr H S E585 E Livingston St Celina OH 45822

SCHELL, ROBERT, 4th Grade Teacher; *b:* Lead, SD; *m:* Sally Anderson; *c:* Bobbi, Dustin; *ed:* (BS) Soc Sci Composite, Black Hills St 1967; Grad Stud Various Courses at Various Insts; *cr:* 11th/12th Grade Soc Stud Teacher Sheboygan South HS 1967-68; 4th-8th Grade Teacher Wyodak Sch 1968-72; 5th-8th Grade Teacher 1972-87, 4th Grade Teacher 1987- Rozet Sch; *ai:* Boys & Girls Bsktbl Coach; HS Rodeo Club Spon; Campbell Cty Ed Assn, WY Ed Assn, NEA 1968-; *office:* Rozet Elem Sch Rozet Way Rozet WY 82727

SCHENCK, THERESA YOUNG, Foreign Language Dept Head; *b:* San Diego, CA; *m:* Alonzo Leo; *ed:* (BA) Fr/Philosphy, Mt St Marys Coll 1963; (MA) Fr/Span, Cath Univ of AM 1965; Grad Stud Fr, Span, Univ of CO Boulder, Columbis Middlebury Coll, Univ of AZ, Univ of San Diego; Anthropology, Rutgers Univ; *cr:* Teacher Grover Cleveland Jr HS 1968-69, Roselle Cath Boys HS 1969-73, Colonia Sr HS 1973-76; Dept Chairperson Parsippany Hills HS 1976-; *ai:* Foreign Lang Forensics Team; Cooperative Relations, Hum, Cultural Awareness Comm; Foreign Lang Educators of NJ (Secy 1972-76, Mem 1971-); AATF 1988-; Amer Assn of Teacher of Span & Portuguese 1978-81; Fnd for Intnl Cooperation Pres 1986-; MI Historical Society & MN Historical Society, St Historical Society of WI, Tekakwitha Conference of Cath Indians; French-Canadian Inst of Lang & Culture Grant 1988; Article Published 1988; *office:* Parsippany Hills HS 20 Rita Dr Parsippany NJ 07054

SCHENK, JUDY FISHER, Teacher/Vice Principal; *b:* Los Angeles, CA; *m:* Jim; *c:* Christopher, Sarabeth; *ed:* (BA) Ger/Ed, Holy Names Coll 1964; *cr:* Teacher Edward Kimble Sch 1964-67, Town & Cntry Pre-Sch 1971-76; Teacher 1977-, Vice Prin 1988- Presentation Sch; *ai:* Stu Cncl, Sci & Quest Moderator; NCEA; Jr League Chm of Provisionals; Cerebral Palsy Guild; *office:* Presentation Sch 3100 Norris Ave Sacramento CA 95821

SCHENK, SANDRA BOUSMAN, 9th Grade Mathematics Teacher; *b:* New Burn, NC; *m:* David R.; *c:* Melanie Maisel; *ed:* (BA) Math, Queens Coll 1969; *cr:* Teacher Needham Broughton HS 1969-70, J T Barber Sch 1973-79, China Grove Jr HS 1979-; *ai:* Pep Club Adv; Sch Improvement Comm; NCAE 1969-; NC Teachers of Math 1969-; *office:* China Grove Jr HS 1013 N Main St China Grove NC 28023

SCHENKEL, THOMAS FRANCIS, Mathematics Teacher; *b:* Jamaica, NY; *m:* Regina Kraus; *c:* Christian, Heidi, Oliver; *ed:* (BA) Eng, Queens Coll 1971; (MS) Scndry Ed, Hofstra Univ 1973; *cr:* Museum Intern Nassau Cty Historical Museums 1969-73; Eng Teacher Garden City Jr HS 1973-80; Math Teacher Garden Cty Mid Sch 1980-; *ai:* Boys Soccer Coach 1973-; Garden City Athletic Assn Soccer Coach 1983-89; Centennial Soccer Coach 1983-89; BSA Weblos Leader 1988-89; *office:* Garden City Mid Sch Cherry Valley & Stewart Ave Garden City NY 11530

SCHER, NANCY EARLLEY, Kindergarten Teacher; *b:* Carthage, NY; *m:* Mark L.; *ed:* (BS) Elem Ed, Edinboro St Coll 1965; Various Univs; *cr:* Kndgtn Teacher Mount Lebanon Schls 1965-68; Pre K-2nd Grade Teacher Penn Yan Cntrl Schls 1968-; *ai:* Dist Philosophy Comm 1988-89; Drug Free Schls Team 1988-89; Primary Workload Comm 1987-88; Pi Lambda Eta 1967; PYTA, NYSTA, NEA 1968-; Meth Church Choir 1972-89; Faculty Mem Continuing Ed Prgm Elmira Coll 1975-76; *office:* Penn Yan Elem Sch Maple Ave Penn Yan NY 14527

SCHERMAN, TERRY R., Principal; *b:* Chicago, IL; *m:* Janet L. Lesniak; *c:* James, Christine; *ed:* (BS) Phys Ed, 1970, (MS) Ed, 1979 NIU DeKalb; Admin Acad, Coll of Lake Cty; *cr:* Teacher 1970-, Asst Prin 1983-, Prin 1990 Westfield Jr HS; *ai:* Boys Bsktbl Coach; Athletic & Boys Intramural Dir; Stu Cncl Adv; Yrbk Ed; IL Prin Assn 1986-; IL Coaches Assn 1982-; Zion Lions Club (Pres 1983-84, 1986-87, Secy 1980-83) Lion of Yr 1984; Winthrop Harbor Lions Treas 1989-; Coalition of Citizens with Disabilities; Winthrop Harbors 1st Teacher of Yr 1987-88; *office:* Westfield Jr HS 2309 9th St Winthrop Harbor IL 60096

SCHERSCHEL, PEGGY JO, Sixth Grade Teacher; *b:* Bedford, IN; *m:* Gregory Lee; *c:* Dana L., Gretchen Ottilia, Joshua K., Joseph P.; *ed:* Assoc Cmptr Programming, Vincennes Univ 1971; (BA) Elem Ed, IN Univ 1982; (MS) Elem Ed, IUPUI Indianapolis 1989; *cr:* Teacher All Saints Cath Sch 1982-; *ai:* Cheerleading Spon 1984-86; Bartholomew Rdng Cncl (Secy, Treas) 1983-; Psi Iota Xi 1969-; *home:* 1612 Franklin St Columbus IN 47201

SCHETZSLE, BARBARA ANN, World His/Civics/Rdng Teacher; *b:* Tiffin, OH; *m:* John A.; *c:* Erin, Laura, Holly; *ed:* (BA) His & Govt, OH Univ 1970; (MA) Rdng Supervision, Ashland Coll 1985; *cr:* World His/Civics/Rdng Teacher North Fork Local Schls 1970-; *ai:* Chrldr Class Adv; Curr Comm; OH Ed Assn; Northfork Teachers Assn; *home:* 164 Hillgail Rd Pataskala OH 43062

SCHEU, GRACE MARIE, Third Grade Teacher; *b:* New York, NY; *m:* George A.; *c:* Virginia Suntum, Gregory; *ed:* (BS) Elem Ed, Salisbury St 1958; Advanced Certificate for Catechist, Diocese of Wilmington; *cr:* 3rd Grade Teacher Thomas Addison Elem 1958-59; Homebound Teacher St of DE 1963-70; 3rd Grade Teacher Ursuline Acad 1970-; *ai:* Catechist for Communion Prgm; Cath Charities Bd Mem 1985-; Cath Church Eucharistic Minister 1985-; Nom Cath Teacher of Yr Awd 1985; *home:* 900 N Broom St Wilmington DE 19806

SCHEUERMANN, KENNETH LEE, Teacher; *b:* Carthage, IL; *m:* Ruth Maxine Harker; *c:* Dennis, Arthur, Pamala Sheffler; *ed:* (BS) Math, W IL Univ 1958; (MS) Math, IL St Univ 1964; Washington Univ; *cr:* Teacher Rock Ridge HS 1958-59, Amboy HS 1959-64, Mt Pleasant HS 1965-67, Carthage HS 1967-; *ai:* Contest Coach Academic; IEA, NEA, ICTM St Contest Comm; Natl Sci Fnd Grant; *home:* RR 1 Nauvoo IL 62354

SCHIAVO, SUSAN G., Activities Director; *b:* Elizabeth, NJ; *m:* Chris; *ed:* (BA) Eng, Rutgers Univ 1986; *cr:* Eng Teacher 1987-89, Act Dir 1989- San Benito HS; *ai:* Stu Cncl, Congress; Rally Club Adv; CADA 1989-; CASC Reg Adv 1989-; *home:* 170 Gibson Dr #24 Hollister CA 95023

SCHIBIG, JAMES MICHAEL, Principal; *b:* St Louis, MO; *m:* Jeanne Ann Timmer; *c:* Christine, Scott; *ed:* (BA) Elem Ed, Harris Teachers Coll 1967; (MA) Elem Admin, Univ of MO St Louis 1977; *cr:* 6th Grade Teacher St Louis Public Sch 1967-72; 4th Grade Teacher 1972-75, 6th Grade Teacher 1975-79, Asst Prin 1979-81, 6th Grade Teacher 1981-83, Asst Prin 1983-85, Prin 1985- Mehlville Sch Dist; *ai:* ASCD; *office:* Beasley Elem Sch 3131 Koch Rd Saint Louis MO 63125

SCHIDDELL, BETTY L., Dean of Instruction Math/Sci; *b:* Chicago, IL; *ed:* (BA) Bio/Scndry Ed, 1969; (MS) Bio, 1973 NE IL Univ; PhD Pgrm Curr & Instr, Univ IL Chicago; *cr:* Math/Sci Teacher Morton East HS 1969-89; Bio Teacher Triton Comm Coll 1980-89; Dean of Instruction Math/Sci Morton East HS 1989-; *ai:* Co-Coord of Gifted Prgm Morton East; Chm Morton Township Math Comm; Co-Chm Sci Literacy Grant Dist 201; NABT, NSTA, IL Assn Bio Teachers, IL St Teachers Assn, ASCD, IL Assn for Supervision & Curr Dev, NCTM, IL Cncl Teachers of Math, NCSM; Des Plaines ESDA; Nom Presidents Awd for Excl in Teaching Sci; *office:* Morton East HS 2423 S Austin Blvd Cicero IL 60650

SCHIEBER, CRAIG EVAN, Gifted/Talented Prgm Coord; *b:* Mexico City, Mexico; *m:* Leeann Hittenberger; *ed:* (BA) Elem Ed, OH St Univ 1978; (MA) Child Dev, Univ of WA 1981; Numerous Stud; *cr:* 3rd Grade Teacher Horizon Elem Sch 1978-79; 4th Grade Teacher Manchester Elem Sch 1979-80; 4th-8th Grade Teacher Issaquah Sch Dist 1980-; *ai:* Act Coord; Drama Coach/Dir; Odyssey of the Mind Coach; New Mid Sch Ed Specs Comm; Pi Lamda Theta Mem 1978; PTA Golden Acorn 1989; *office:* Issaquah Mid Sch 565 NW Holly Issaquah WA 98027

SCHIEL, JOSEPH BERNARD, JR., Biology Teacher; *b:* Wilkes-Barre, PA; *m:* Charlotte Thomas; *c:* Joseph, Joyce, Holly, Jean; *ed:* (BS) Bio Sci/Geography/Ed, Penn St 1962; (MAT) Geography/Ed, OR Coll of Ed 1967; (PHD) Medical Geography/Biogeography, Univ of IL Urbana 1971; PA Dept of Health 1963; Millersville St Coll 1965; Bowling Green St Univ 1966; E NM Univ 1981; TX Tech Univ 1985; NM St Univ 1985; E NM Univ 1985-86; NASA Human Physiology Wkshp 1990; *cr:* 7th/8th Grade Teacher Dallastown Area Schls 1963-64; 8th-12th Grade Teacher Wilkes-Barre City Schls 1964-66; Teaching Asst Univ of IL Urbana 1967-70; Asst Geography Professor Univ of OK Norman 1970-75; Mgr TX Testing Laboratories 1976-79; Production/Drilling Supvr Latch Operations 1979-85; Assoc Faculty E NM Univ Roswell 1985, NM St Univ Carlsbad 1986-88; Bio Teacher/Sci Dept Head Carlsbad City Schls 1985-; *ai:* Chrldr Spon; NABT NM Rep 1987-, Outstanding Bio Teacher 1989-; NSTA, NM Sci Teachers Assn, NEA, NM Ed Assn, Carlsbad Ed Assn, Sigma Xi; Natl Wildlife Fed, NM Wildlife Fed, Smithsonian Assoc, Amer Museum of Natural His Mem, Natl Geographic Society, Audubon Society; BSA (Scoutmaster 1979-85, Camp Wehinahpay Staff 1986) Dist Awd 1983; Natl Sci Fnd Grants 1965-66, 1970, 1985; Experienced Teacher Fellowship Grant 1966-67; *office:* Carlsbad HS 3000 W Church Carlsbad NM 88220

SCHIFF, ALISON GOODWIN, Art Teacher; *b:* New York, NY; *m:* John Charles; *c:* Corinne, Anthony; *ed:* (BA) Art, 1962, (MA) Art, 1967 Hunter Coll; Art, Teachers Coll Columbia, Metropolitan Museum of Art; *cr:* Art Teacher/Grade Guide/Admin Asst Jr HS 13 1962-64, 1975-80; Art Teacher Dacca Amer Society Sch 1964-65; Art Teacher Sports Sch 1980-85, Manhattan E Center for Arts & Academics 1985-87, Hunter Coll HS 1987-; Art Ed Instr New York Univ 1988-; *ai:* Womens Issues, Photo, Human Rights Watch Clubs; NY St Art Teachers Assn 1985-; NAEA 1989-; Show of Hands Crafts Collective 1972-79; HRA Grant; Impact II Grant 1981; Nom Kappa Delta Pi Teachers Coll 1982; Art Honor Society Hunter Coll 1962; *office:* Hunter College HS 71 E 94th St New York NY 10128

SCHIFFER, MARK R., Science Department Chairman; *b:* New York, NY; *ed:* (BA) Bio, Columbia Univ 1969; (MAT) Bio, Rollins Coll 1976; *cr:* Teacher US Peace Corps Fiji Islands 1970-71, Teague Mid Sch 1973-74; Teacher/Dept Chm Crooms HS 1974-81, Lake Mary HS 1981-; *ai:* Chess Club Spon; Amer Assn for Advancement of Sci, NSTA 1976-; NABT, FL Assn of Sci Teachers 1975-; Author FL St Honors Sci Symposium; FL Bio Parting Score Task Force; F L Assoc Merit Teacher; Seminole Cty Gifted Advisory Comm; Elected to Kappa Delta Pi; *office:* Lake Mary HS 655 Longwood Lake Mary Rd Lake Mary FL 32746

SCHIFINI, PATRICIA MARIE, Religion Teacher; *b:* New York, NY; *ed:* (BA) His, Coll of New Rochelle 1982; (MS) Religious Ed, Fordham Univ 1985; *cr:* 1st/4th Grade Teacher Our Lady of Angels Sch 1982-85; Religion Teacher Acad of Mt St Ursula 1986-; *ai:* Athletic Assn Moderator; Youth Ministry, Retreat Team & Liturgy Group; Volunteer Providence House Shelter; *office:* Acad Of Mt St Ursula 330 Bedfod Park Blvd Bronx NY 10458

SCHIFO, NANCY VESELY, Gifted Education Coordinator; *b:* Chicago, IL; *m:* Ross; *c:* Kristy, Brett; *ed:* (AA) General, Morton Coll 1975; (BS) Elem Ed, N IL Univ 1977; *cr:* Classroom Teacher Cicero Sch DIst #99 1978-81, Brookfield-La Grange Park Dist #95 1984-89; Gifted Ed Coord Forest Park Sch Dist #91 1989-; *ai:* Faculty Spon; Math Olympiad Team & Sci Olympiad Team Coach; IEA, NEA 1983-; *office:* Forest Park Sch Dist 925 Beloit Ave Forest Park IL 60130

SCHILDBERG, PEGGY SUE (GOSSETT), 5th Grade Science Teacher; *b:* Mexico, MO; *m:* William Dulaney; *c:* Michael W. (dec), Kristen A.; *ed:* (BS) Elem Ed, 1966, (MS) Curr / Instruction, 1978 Univ of KS; Cert Gifted & Talented K-9, Univ of KS 1986; *cr:* 4th Grade Teacher East Antioch Grade Sch 1966-67, Pinckney Elem Sch 1967-69; 5th Grade Teacher Martin City Elem Sch 1973-74; 3rd/4th Grade Teacher Meadowmere Elem Sch 1974-77; 3rd Grade Teacher/Lang Art Coord Conn-West Elem Sch 1977-81; 5th Grade Sci Teacher High Grove Elem Sch 1981-; *ai:* PTA Fund Raising Act; 5th Grade Literary Rdng Club; Exch City of Learning Exch-High Grove Chairperson; Grandview Chapter Intnl Rdng Assn (Charter Mem 1975-, VP 1984-85/1990, Pres 1985-86); MO St Chapter IRA Asst TTreas 1987-88; IRA Grandview Chapter 2nd VP 1990-91 Celebrate Literacy Awd; Luth Church Women Pres 1984-85; Together Grandview Ed Curr Comm 1988-; KS Assn Teachers of Sci Cmmty Drug & Alcohol Prgm 1985-; FOCUS Gifted & Talented Organization Grandview 1987; NEA Amer Ed Week Chairperson 1987-; MO Assn for Teachers of Eng & MO Dept Elem & Scndry Ed Spring Conference Presenter 1987; Excl in Teaching Awd Nom 1986-87; *office:* High Grove Elem Sch 2500 High Grove Rd Grandview MO 64030

SCHILDKAMP, R. JOSEPH, Secondary Art Teacher; *b:* Greensburg, PA; *m:* Patricia Lynn Lovell; *c:* Corey J., Katie E.; *ed:* (BS) Fine Arts/Ed, 1975, (MA) Drawing, 1984- IN Univ of PA; Prgm in Layout & Production Art, Art Inst of Pittsburgh; *cr:* Scndry Art Ed Teacher Hempfield Area Sch Dist 1977-; Con Ed Art Instruction Teacher Greensburg Art Club 1977-; *ai:* Former Dir of Drama Group 1980-88; Educl Support Team Mem 1989-; NAEA, PAEA 1978-; PSEA, HAEA 1977-; Phi Kappa Psi 1973-; Greensburg Art Club (VP 1987-88, Treas 1985) 1976-; NAEA Logo Design Awd in Natl Contest 1986; *office:* Hempfield Area Sch Dist RD 6 Box 76 W Newton Rd Greensburg PA 15601

SCHILLACI, PATRICIA ANN, Mathematics Teacher; *b:* Pittston, PA; *ed:* (BA) Math/Span, Wilkes Coll 1976; (MS) Scndry/Math, Univ of Scranton 1979; Mid Sts Evaluator 1988; *cr:* Permanent Substitute Teacher WY Area Hs 1976-79; Math/Span Teacher Martin/Mattei Jr HS 1979-84; Math Teacher Pittston Area HS 1984-; *ai:* Key Club & Sr Class Adv 1987-; NCTM Mem 1976-; *office:* Pittston Area HS 5 Stout St Yatesville PA 18640

SCHILLING, ALICE MARIE (FOUST), 5th Grade Teacher; *b:* Dayton, OH; *m:* Rex M.; *c:* Kathee J. Schilling Reed, Kim Schilling Kesler, Thomas L.; *ed:* (BS) Bus, 1955, (BS) Elem Ed, 1967 Manchester Coll; (MS) Ed, St Francis Coll 1975; *cr:* 3rd Grade Teacher Claypool Elem 1967-71; 5th Grade Teacher Silver Lake Elem 1972-; *ai:* Eng Adoption, Chapter II Grant, Crisis Team Comms; Building Base Team; Elem Task Force; IN St Teachers Assn, Warsaw Cmmty Sch Teachers Assn, Rdng Cncl, NEA 1989-; Parent-Teacher Cncl; *office:* Warsaw Sch Corporation Box 188 Silver Lake IN 46982

SCHILLING, DAWN DIANE, English Teacher; *b:* Valley City, ND; *ed:* (BSE) Eng, Minot St Univ 1987; *cr:* Eng Teacher Agua Fria Union HS 1988-; *ai:* Wickiup Publications Yrbk; Wrestlerettes; Class Adv; NCTE 1987-; Minot Women of Today

Bd of Dir 1985-87; *office:* Agua Fria Union HS 530 E Riley Dr Avondale-Goodyear AZ 85323

SCHIMMER, DEBORAH ANN (HART), 5th Grade Teacher; *b:* Oklahoma City, OK; *m:* Michael Roy; *c:* Michael J., Paul A.; *ed:* (BS) Elem Ed, Southwestern St Univ 1973; Cmptr Technology; *cr:* 5th Grade Sci Teacher 1973-76, 5th Grade Lang Art Educator 1977- Shedeck Elem; Adult Ed/Cmptr Night Class Instr Canadian Voc Tech 1988-; *ai:* Dist Curr Technology & Josten Learning Corporation Proposal Comm; Cmptr Technology Staff Dev Presenter; Stu At-Risk Apple Cmptr Instr; 5th-8th Grade Dist Spelling Bee Meet Spon & Rep 1985-89; Delta Kappa Gamma Historian 1977-, Beta Beta Teaching Excl 1988; Yukon Prof Educators Assn 2nd VP 1972-, Shedeck 1987-88, Teacher of Yr 1990; Kappa Kappa Iota (Pres, VP, Treas) 1972-85; Yukons Best Fundraiser Volunteer; BSA Asst 1986-87; Connections 90 St Art Cncl of OK; Homeland Stores & Apple Cmptr Incorporated OK Top Teacher 1990; Mid-Amer Regional Teacher of Yr 11988; IBM OK Teacher of Yr 1988; Cmptr Technology Grant 1988; Featured in Magazine 1988; *office:* Shedeck Elem Sch 2100 S Holly Ave Yukon OK 73099

SCHINDEL, RICHARD H., Bus Ed Dept Chair; *b:* Aurora, IL; *m:* Susan Roadruck; *c:* Laura, Joanne; *ed:* (BS) Mrktg, Univ of IL 1970; (MA) Ed, Natl Coll 1989; *cr:* 7th Grade Teacher Holy Angels Sch 1970-73; 7th-9th Grade Teacher Waldo Jr HS 1973-79; 10th-12th Grade Teacher E Aurora HS 1979-; *ai:* Soph Bsbl; VAr Head Ftbl; ME & DECA Adv; IAME 1979-; Educator of Yr East HS 1987-89; Those Who Excel in Ed 1989; *office:* E Aurora HS 500 Tomcat Ln Aurora IL 60505

SCHINDLBECK, DAVID JOHN, Principal; *b:* Aurora, IL; *m:* Lynn M.; *c:* Scott, Heidi, Mark; *ed:* (BS) Biological Sci, 1961, (MS) Ed Admin, 1969 IL St Univ; (CAS) Ed Admin, N IL Univ 1973; *cr:* Sci Teacher Winston Churchill Coll 1968-69; Phys Ed Teacher Freeport Jr HS 1961; Rdng Teacher 1977-87, Sci Teacher 1977-87 Yorkville Circle Center Sch; Prin Momence IL & Kirksville MO & Yorkville IL & Pontiac IL 1973-; *ai:* ASCD Mem 1986-; IL Prins Assn Mem 1982-; BSA Dist Chm 1988-, Awd of Merit 1990; Whos Who in MO Admin Recognition 1972-74; *office:* Pontiac Jr HS Morrow St Pontiac IL 61764

SCHIPPER, ELIS-BARBARA WOESCHKA, German Teacher; *b:* Rossbach, Czechoslovakia; *m:* Harold L. Jr.; *c:* Lynnette M. Muncey; *ed:* (BA) Ger, CO Univ 1974; (AA), Coll of the Canyons; *cr:* Ger Teacher Broomfield HS 1976-; *ai:* Sch Improvement Team 1984-85; Stu Act Comm North Cntrl Evaluation 1988-89; Jr Class & Ger Club Spon; Boulder Valley Teachers Assn Mem 1976-; CO Congress of Foreign Lang Teacher Mem 1976- CO Teacher of Ger 1989; Presbyn Church Choir Dir 1972-; Civic Chorus Choir Dir 1988-; Alpha Mu Gamma 1970; Delta Phi Alpha 1973; Alpha Gamma Sigma 1970-71; Yrbk Dedicated By Broomfield HS Stu 1980; *office:* Broomfield H S 1000 Daphne St Broomfield CO 80020

SCHIPPER, WILLIAM ROBERT, History Teacher; *b:* Kalamazoo, MI; *m:* Clarissa L. Lauffer; *c:* William Jr., Christine Flynn; *ed:* (BED) Music, W MI Univ 1958; Univ of MI, E MI Univ; *cr:* Instrumental Music, 1958-82, His, 1982- Clio Carter Mid Sch; *ai:* MEA, NEA Life Mem; Clio Lions Club Pres 1979-80, 100 Percent Pres Awd 1980; Genesee Lions Club (Secy 1985-87, Pres 1989-), 100 Percent Secy 1985-87, 100 Percent Pres Awd 1990; Clio Amphitheater Bd Pres 1988-89; *home:* 13142 N Center Rd PO Box 361 Clio MI 48420

SCHIPPERS, ROBERT JOHN, 5th Grade Teacher; *b:* Plainwell, MI; *m:* Francine; *c:* Shari, Carrie, Ben; *ed:* (BA) Soc Stud, Calvin Coll 1971; (MA) Line Admin, W MI Univ 1975; *cr:* 4th Grade Teacher Blain Elem 1971-86; 5th Grade Teacher Brown Elem 1986-; *ai:* MI Ed Assn Delegate 1980-; Coalition for Excl Grant Sci & Math Ed 1990; *office:* Byron Public Schls 8064 Byron Center Ave SW Byron Center MI 49315

SCHIRF, MARTHA, First Grade Teacher; *b:* Latrobe, PA; *ed:* (BA) European His/Elem Ed, Seton Hill Coll 1971; (MED) Elem Ed, IN Univ of PA 1978; *cr:* 1st Grade Teacher Saltsburg Elem Sch 1971-; *ai:* Delta Kappa Gamma Ch World Fellowship 1989-; NEA, PSEA, BSEA 1971-; Daughters of Amer Revolution (Secy, VP); PTA Cultural Prgms Chairperson; Friends of Saltsburg Lib Secy; Saltsbburg Drama Club (Pres, VP, Secy); *office:* Saltsburg Elem Sch 250 3rd St Saltsburg PA 15681

SCHIRO, EDGAR LOUIS, Instrumental Music Teacher; *b:* New Orleans, LA; *m:* Deborah A.; *c:* Kelie, Edgar L. Jr.; *ed:* (BMED) Instrumental Music, Nicholls St Univ 1981; (MM) Performance-Conducting, Univ of Southwestern 1989; Post Masters Studies Nicholls St Univ; *cr:* Music Dir Berwick Elem 1981-87; Berwick Jr HS 1981-87; Grad Asst Univ of Southwestern 1987-88; Music Dir Berwick HS 198-89; H L Bourgeois HS 1989-90; *ai:* 1st Vice Pres 1983-84; 2nd Vice Pres 1980-90 LA Music Educators Assn; Associated Prof Educators of LA 1987-90; Music Educators Natl Conf 1981-90; *home:* 114 W 54th St Cut Off LA 70345

SCHLAGETER, ROBERT LEO, Math Teacher/Math Dept Chair; *b:* Rochester, NY; *m:* Karen Ann Leydecker; *c:* Ronald, Robert T., Linda, Sharon; *ed:* (BA) Math, Ithaca Coll 1959; Grad Hours at Various Univ; *cr:* Teacher Springville-Griffith Inst 1959-; *ai:* Ftbl & Bsktbl Coaching; NCTM 1971-83; NEA 1967-; NYSUT 1973-; SASC Treas 1976-; Natl Sci Fnd Grants; NY St Dept of Ed Approved Curr Guides Teaching FORTRAN; *office:* Springville-Griffith Inst 290 N Buffalo St Springville NY 14141

SCHLAGLE, DONALD E., Business Teacher; *b:* Independence, MO; *m:* Kay Zumwalt; *c:* Kelli, Jamie, William; *ed:* (AA) Liberal Art, Longview Comm Coll 1988; Naval Trng Center, San Diego Cmptr Programming; Kessler Air Force Base, Biloxi MS WWMCCS Cmptr; Voc Cert, Univ of MO Columbia; *cr:* Software Engineer Management Resources Inc 1979-82; Data Processing Mgr Intnl Graphics Industries 1983; Pres Viscom Inc 1983-86; Bus Teacher Fort Osage Area Voc-Tech Sch 1986-; *ai:* FBLA Adv; Gifted & Talented Prgm Spon; MO St Teacher Assn Local VP 1986-, Awd of Merit 1990; MO Voc Assn, MO Bus Ed Assn 1986-; Independence Plan for Neighborhood Cncls (VP, Bd Mem 1986-89) Top 10 Achievers Awd 1988; St Marys Church Vice Chm of Finance Comm 1986; Fort Osage Art Teacher of Yr 1987-88; Fort Osage Sch Dist Employee of Month 1990; Whos Who in the Cmptr Industry 1990; Published Introduction to the IBM System 34/36 Utilities; *office:* Fort Osage Area Voc-Tech Sch 2101 N Twyman Rd Independence MO 64058

SCHLATTER, JOHN WAYNE, Drama Teacher; *b:* Buffalo, NY; *ed:* (BA) Speech/Drama, Pepperdine Univ 1957; CA St Fullerton, Long Beach St; *cr:* Drama Teacher/Stu Government Adv Sycamore Jr HS 1962-67; Drama Teacher Katella HS 1967-70, Oak Jr HS 1971-86, Mc Auliff Mid Sch 1986-; *ai:* God Love Ya Productions Dir & Producer; CTA, NEA 1980-; Presidential Task Force Mem 1980-; PTA Lifetime Membership 1977; Orange Cty Supt Outstanding Contributions to Ed 1986; Kiwanis Club Outstanding Teacher Awd 1980; Honored by Cmmty Los Alamitos Testimonial Pinne; *home:* PO Box 577 Cypress CA 90630

SCHLATTER, JUDITH BAHR, Substitute Elementary Teacher; *b:* Ft Scott, KS; *m:* Philip A.; *ed:* (AA) General Basics, Ft Scott Comm Coll 1978; (BS) Elem Ed, KS St Univ 1980; (MS) Elem Ed, Pittsburg St Univ 1985; *cr:* 1st Grade Teacher 1980-89; Substitute Teacher Sarasota Sch System 1990; *ai:* KS Ed Assn 1981-86; Alpha Delta Kappa (Treas 1986-88, Pres 1988-89); Bourbon Cty Bus Prof Women Outstanding Young Educator 1985-86; Young Careerist 1989; Pittsburg St Univ Outstanding Young Women of America 1986; *home:* 2304 Ringling Blvd #209 Sarasota FL 34237

SCHLATTMANN, JANET L. (LIBAL), Middle School Math Teacher; *b:* Lexington, NE; *m:* Ronald; *c:* Annette, Michael; *ed:* (BS) Math, Univ of NE 1973; *cr:* 7th-9th Grade Math Teacher McCook Jr HS 1973-75; 7th-12th Grade Math Teacher Bladen Schls 1982-83; 8th-12th Grade Math Teacher St Agnes Acad 1985-88; 6th-9th Grade Math Teacher Alliance Mid Sch 1989-; *ai:* Quiz Bowl Spon; 4-H Leader 1983-, Outstanding Alumni 1986; Presbyn Church (Youth Choir Asst Dir, Accompanist) 1985-; *home:* 1225 Grand Alliance NE 69301

SCHLEGEL, LAURIE SHERIDAN, 6th Grade Teacher; *b:* Portland, OR; *m:* William E.; *c:* Sheridan A.; *ed:* (BS) Rec & Park Mgmt, Univ of OR 1974; Elem Ed, Portland St Univ 1979; *cr:* 6th Grade Teacher Ladd Acres Elem 1980-88; Reedville Elem 1988-; *ai:* OR Ed Assn 1980-; Reedville Ed Assn 1980-; *office:* Reedville Elem Sch 2695 SW 209th Aloha OR 97006

SCHLEICHER, ANN W., Scndry English/Speech Teacher; *b:* Bradford, PA; *m:* Earl A.; *c:* Timothy, Scott, Luke; *ed:* (BA) Comprehensive Eng/Speech Ed, LA St Univ 1968; (MED) Comm, Univ of Pittsburgh 1983; Cmptr, Univ of Pittsburgh; Madeline Hunter Staff Dev Allegheny Intermediate Unit; Eng & Ed, Penn St Univ; *cr:* Eng/Speech Teacher Avonworth Sch Dist 1969-; *ai:* Leon Owoc Schlsp Comm; Fragments Literary Magazine; Sr HS Stu Cncl; Jr HS Newspaper; NCTE 1981-86; W PA Cncl Teachers of Eng 1986-; St Joseph Parent Teacher Group (Bd Mem 1989-, Active Mem 1983-); WPCTE Distinguished Teacher Awd 1988; WPCTE Convention Wkshp Presenter 1985; Leon Owoc Schlsp Chairperson 1983-88; *office:* Avonworth HS 250 Josephs Ln Pittsburgh PA 15237

SCHLEIFER, NEAL H., English Teacher/Lab Admin; *b:* New York, NY; *m:* Tricia; *c:* Ian, Jessica; *ed:* (BA) Eng, Brooklyn Coll 1970; (MED) Admin & Supervision, Univ of S FL 1982; Working Towards EDD in Cmptr Ed, Nova Univ; *cr:* Teacher Brookside Jr HS 1974-82; Teacher/Lab Admin Riverview HS 1982-; *ai:* Cmptr Lab Admin; Cmptr Advisory, Sarasota Cty Telecommunications Comm; Phi Kappa Phi 1982-; FL Assn for Cmptr Ed 1989-; FL Ed Assn 1974-; Articles Published; Cmptr Learning Fnd 1989 2nd Place Awd; Prgm of Excl FL Dept of Ed 1989; Certificate of Recognition 1989, Sarasota Cty Sch Bd; 3rd Annual Teleconference for Technology in Ed 1988; Natl Endowment for Hum 1986; *office:* Riverview HS 1 Ram Way Sarasota FL 34231

SCHLELEWAY, NORMA JEAN HANSEN, Third Grade Teacher; *b:* Aberdeen, SD; *m:* Eugene John; *c:* Jack, Bryan, Jeanne Heimes, Gary, Karen; *ed:* (BS) Elem Ed, Black Hills St Univ 1972; *cr:* Teacher Rural Sch 1955-56, West Elem 1972-; *ai:* SEA, SDEA, NEA; SD Grant Ed 1972; Spearfish Teacher of Yr 1979; *home:* 606 8th St Spearfish SD 57783

SCHLENTNER, ELIZA CALDERWOOD, English & History Teacher; *b:* Johnstown, PA; *m:* Karl L.; *c:* Sandra Mc Cleary, Scott; *ed:* (BA) His, Thiel Coll 1962; (MED) Ed, Indiana Univ of PA 1966; *cr:* 7th Grade His Teacher Richland Twp HS 1962-65; Substitute Teacher North Clarion 1972-86; 7th/9th/10th Grade Teacher West Forest HS 1988-; *ai:* Band Front; PA St Ed Assn, Forest Area Ed Assn, NEA 1988-; GSA Troop (Organizer, Leader) 1974-74, 10 Yr Service 1984; PTO VP 1980-82; *office:* West Forest HS SR 2 Box 15 Tionesta PA 16353

SCHLESINGER, BARBARA GROVEMAN, First Grade Teacher; *b:* Brooklyn, NY; *c:* Iris, Mark; *ed:* (BA) Span, Syracuse Univ 1949; Working Towards Masters Span, Middlebury Coll; Ed, Brooklyn Coll & Adelphi Univ; *cr:* Kndgtn Teacher Public Sch 63 Queens 1963-65; Kndgtn Teacher 1965-67, Early Chldhd Sci Teacher 1967-98; 5th/6th Grade Span Teacher for Gifted 1968-75, 1st Grade Teacher 1968- Public Sch 207 Queens; *office:* Public Sch 207 159-15 88th St Jamaica NY 11414

SCHLEYER, JOHANNA WEISSINGER, Second Grade Teacher; *b:* Esslingen, Germany; *m:* Heinz; *c:* Anneliese M.; *ed:* (AS) Early Chldhd Ed; Harcum Jr Coll 1974; (BS) Elem Ed, 1976, (BA) Sociology, 1976 Univ of PA; *cr:* Kndgtn Asst 1977-78, 2nd Grade Teacher 1978- the Baldwin Sch; *ai:* Phi Theta Kappa 1974; Pi Lambola Theta 1976; *home:* 335 Oxford Rd Havertown PA 19083

SCHLICK, JEROME FRANCIS, Language Arts/Health Teacher; *b:* Cleveland, OH; *m:* Barbara Ellen Moyer; *c:* Amanda, Kourtney; *ed:* (BA) Scndry Ed, Bellarmine Coll 1970; (MED) Intermediate Ed, Bowling Green St Univ 1987; *cr:* Elem Teacher St Marys 1970-83, Republic Elem 1983-85; 7th-8th Grade Lang Teacher Seneca East Jr HS 1985-; *ai:* Var Ftbl Coach & Defensive Coord 1984-; 8th Grade Bsktbl 1985-, 7th-8 th Grade Boys Track 1989- Coach; OEA Building Rep 1984-; OH HS Ftbl Coaches Assn 1984-; NW OH Ftbl Coaches Assn 1984-; Seneca Cty Bd of Ed Minigrant 1988; Seneca Cty Schls Co-Authored Cty Health Course 1989-; *office:* Seneca East Jr HS PO Box 39 Republic OH 44867

SCHLIEF, DAN RAY, HS Math & Science Teacher; *b:* Doniphan, MO; *ed:* (BS) Geology/Math, SE MO St 1984; Grad Stud Natural Sci; *cr:* Teacher Woodland R-IV; *ai:* Stu Cncl Spon; Satellite Network Coord; MSTA; Planetary Society; BSA Comm Chm 1989-; Wrote 2 HS Sci Ed Grants; *office:* Woodland R-IV Hwy 34 W Marble Hill MO 63762

SCHLIMPERT, THOMAS LEE, Assistant Principal; *b:* St Louis, MO; *m:* Sherrill Roof; *c:* Ryan, Lyndsey; *ed:* (BS) Earth Sci, 1975, (MS) Scndry Admin, 1984, Specialist Scndry Admin, 1990 SE MO St Univ; *cr:* Teacher 1975-87, Asst Prin 1987- Poplar Bluff Jr HS; *ai:* MO St Teachers Assn 1975-; NASSP 1988-; *office:* Poplar Bluff Jr HS Hwy 67 N Poplar Bluff MO 63901

SCHLITT, DAVID ALAN, Creative Dramatics Instructor; *b:* Pomona, CA; *ed:* (AA) Bus, Mt San Antonio Coll 1968; (BA) Soc Sci, 1970, (MA) Clinical Psych 1974, (MA) Educl Admin, 1980 Azusa Pacific Univ; *cr:* Instr Ruddock Intermediate Sch 1972-85, Royal Oak Intermediate Sch 1985-; *ai:* Comedy Road Show Dir; COEA, PTA Mem 1972-, HSA 1990; *office:* Royal Intermediate Sch 303 S Glendora Ave Covina CA 91723

SCHLITZKUS, JOLLY MADDOX, Instructional Facilitator; *b:* Seguin, TX; *c:* Jean L.; *ed:* (AA) Eng, Kilgore Jr Coll 1968; (BS) Scndry Ed/Eng/His, TX A&I Univ 1970; (MA) Eng, SW TX Univ 1982; Working on Supervision Cert Univ of Houston Victoria; Instructional Leadership, IMPACT Trng; *cr:* Teacher Pettus HS 1970-75, Skidmore Tynan HS 1975-81; Part-Time Instr Bee Cty Coll 1982-89; Instructional Facilitator Skidmore Tynan Ind Sch Dist 1982-; *ai:* NHS Spon; Univ Interscholastic League Literary Act Coach; Delta Kappa Gamma 1978-; TSTA, NEA, ASCD; Sierra Club; Whos Who Amer Ed 1989-; UIL Regional Advisory Comm Mem; *office:* Skidmore-Tynan Ind Sch Dist PO Box 409 Skidmore TX 78389

SCHLOMER, THELMA, Sixth Grade Teacher; *b:* Cincinnati, OH; *ed:* (BS) Ed, 1972, (MED) Ed, 1978 Xavier Univ; *cr:* 5th Grade Teacher St William 1966-68; 7th-8th Grade Teacher St Augustine 1968-70; 5th-8th Grade Teacher St Lawrence 1970-77; Remedial Math Teacher Cincinnati Public Schs 1978-82; 4th Grade Teacher St Dominic Sch 1983-85; 6th Grade Teacher Price Hill Cath Sch 1985-; *office:* Price Hill Cath Sch 3001 Price Ave Cincinnati OH 45205

SCHLOSSER, DEBRA STUART, Spec Ed/Resource Room Teacher; *b:* Philadelphia, PA; *m:* Joseph; *c:* Drew S.; *ed:* (BS) Early Chldhd/Infancy, 1976, (MED) Spec Ed, 1981 Temple Univ; *cr:* Substitute Teacher Philadelphia Sch System 1976-77; 1st Grade Teacher St Timothys Sch 1977; 3rd Grade Teacher Strawbridge Sch 1977-83; Resource Room Teacher Van Sciver Sch 1983-; *ai:* Rdng Comm; Spec Ed Summer Prgm Coord; Rdng & Math Curr Co-Writer; Completed & Published Sch Dist Spec Ed Spelling Curr; CEC 1981-; Developed Rdng Prgms 1987.

SCHLOSSER, RUTHE PALMER, Fifth Grade Teacher; *b:* Akron, OH; *m:* Larry E.; *c:* Kim Schlosser Mc Fadden, Larry T., Raymond L.; *ed:* Jr Drafting, Goodyear Industrial Univ 1955; (BA) Elem Ed, OH Univ 1976; Grad Stud; *cr:* Tutor Lancaster Sch 1976-77; 4th Grade Teacher 1977-87, 5th Grade Teacher 1987- Berne Union Elem Sch; *ai:* Supvr Sch Patrol; Outstanding Elem Stu Awd Sponsored Columbia Gas; Kappa Delta Pi 1977-; Grant Psycholinquistic Style Teaching Rdng; Jennings Scholar 1985-86; *home:* 1470 Lynn Dr Lancaster OH 43130

SCHMALE, LEIGH A., Social Studies Teacher; *b:* Schuyler, NE; *m:* Julie Luther; *ed:* (BA) Soc Sci/Scndry Ed, Midland Lutheran Coll 1980; (MS) Scndry Admin, Univ of NE Omaha 1986; Grad Level Courses in Ed; *cr:* Soc Stud Instr Clarkson HS 1980-81, Bergan HS 1981-88, Sidney HS 1988-; *ai:* Head Ftbl & Asst Track Coach; Strength Trng Coord; Jr HS Stu Cncl Spon; IA St Ed Assn, NE Coaches Assn, IA Ftbl Coaches Assn; *office:* Sidney HS 1002 Illinois St Sidney IA 51652

SCHMALE, RUBY MAE WENDE, First Grade Teacher; *b:* Axtell, KS; *m:* Harold A.; *ed:* (BA) Elem Ed, Univ of Northern CO 1979; CO Real Estate License; *cr:* 1st Grade Teacher Plateau Dist RE-5 1979-; *ai:* CO Cncl Intnl Rdng Assn 1985-; Church Choir; Health Fair Volunteer; Peetz Plateau Ed Assn Pres, Secy, Treas; *home:* 23939 Road 46 Iliff CO 80736

SCHMEISING, SAM A., 4th Grade Teacher; *b:* Maria Stein, OH; *m:* Sue Kaiser; *c:* Jeff, Sheri, Whitney; *ed:* (BS) Elem Ed, 1971; (MED) Spec Ed-Elem Ed, 1975 Wright St Univ; Cmptrs; *cr:* 4th Grade Teacher Coldwater Sch; *ai:* Jr HS Coach Ftbl & Track; Church Cncl; *office:* Coldwater Schls 220 N 1st St Coldwater OH 45828

SCHMEITS, SHEILA ANN, Mid Sch Math/Sci Teacher; *b:* Spalding, NE; *ed:* (BS) Elem Ed, St Mary Coll 1970; Grad Work Various Univs; *cr:* Teacher Spalding Acad 1970-80, St Agnes Acad 1981-; *ai:* 7th Grade Homeroom & 5th-8th Grade Stu Cncl Spon; NE Assn Teachers of Math, Natl Assn Teachers of Math; Amer Assn of Univ Women Pres 1984-86, 1988-; Alliance Art Cncl Secy 1988-; Alliance Literacy Cncl Secy 1988-; Box Butte Unit of Natl Assn of Parliamentarians; Whos Who in Midwest 1989-; Whos Who in Amer Ed 1989-; *office:* St Agnes Acad 1104 Cheyenne Ave Alliance NE 69301

SCHMIDGALL, CARY PRINCE, Kindergarten Teacher; *b:* Portland, OR; *m:* Michael Robert; *c:* Matthew R.; *ed:* (BA) Elem Ed, Univ of N CO 1983; (MA) Management, Webster Univ 1990; Essential Elements of Instruction & Cooperative Learning; *cr:* 5th Grade Teacher Rancho Viejo Elem 1985-87; 5th Grade Teacher 1987-89, Kndgtn Teacher 1989- H L Suverkrup Elem; *ai:* Cub Reporter Adv for The Bear Essential News for Kids; Crane Ed Assn Mem 1985-; *office:* H L Suverkrup 1590 S Ave C Yuma AZ 85364

SCHMIDT, AARON L., 6th Grade Teacher; *b:* Clinton, IA; *m:* Jeannine K. Lawson; *c:* Luke, Jessica; *ed:* (BA) Elem Ed, Luther Coll 1975; (MA) Elem Ed, Univ of IA 1979; *cr:* Teacher Alan Shepard Elem & N Scott Sch Dist 1975-; *ai:* Sch Store Mgr; Math Bee Coach; Educl Technology & Math Curr Comm; Parkview Luth Church Pre-Sch (Bd, Vp 1988-89, Pres 1990); Scott Cty Outstanding Teacher Awd 1989; *office:* Alan Shepard Elem Sch 220 W Grove St Long Grove IA 52756

SCHMIDT, ALAN LEE, High School Science Teacher; *b:* Ida Grove, IA; *m:* Kim Jean Friedrichsen; *c:* Matthew A., Aaron L., Micah J., Isaac N., Audra J.; *ed:* (BA) Phys Ed, Buena Vista Coll 1974; Drake, IA, Marycrest; *cr:* Instr Miford Cmmty 1974-76; Coord NW IA Tech 1976-78; Instr Odebolt-Arthur Cmmty 1978-; *ai:* Head HS Wrestling Coach; Head HS Academic Dept; Arthur City Cncl Mayor Pro-Term 1985-; *home:* 209 S Maple Arthur IA 51431

SCHMIDT, ANNE KATHRYN, Health/Phys Ed Coordinator; *b:* Somerville, NJ; *ed:* (BS) Phys Ed, Douglass Coll 1954; (EDM) Phys Ed, Rutgers Univ 1960; *cr:* Kndgtn-8th Grade Health/phys Ed Teacher Plainfield Public Schls 1954-; *ai:* Intramural Coord; Bsktbl, Sftbl Coach; NEA 1954-; NJ Ed Assn 1954-; NJ Assn for Health, Phys Ed, Recreation, Dance 1954-, 25 Yr Service 1980; Kappa Delta Pi Grad Honor Society Rutgers Univ 1960; Outstanding Scndry Educators of America 1974; Teacher of Yr; Governors Teacher Recognition Prgm 1989-; *home:* Southwyck Vlg 39 Wareham Ct Scotch Plains NJ 07076

SCHMIDT, CAROL ANN (CULLEY), Science Teacher/Dept Chairman; *b:* Indianapolis, IN; *m:* Stephen P.; *c:* Wendy L., Stephen L.; *ed:* (BS) Phys Ed/Bio, 1971; (MST) Bio 1973 Tarleton Univ; Post Masters Studies, Geology, San Antonio Coll, Trinity Univ, Univ TX; Cmptrs Univ TX; *cr:* Sci Teacher Memorial HS 1972-73; Gymnastics Coach Churchill HS 1974-76; Sci Teacher/Coach Alamo Hts JR HS 1976-80; Sci Teacher Corbett JR HS 1984-; *ai:* Sci Club/Spon; Dist Insurance Comm; Dist Cmptr Tech Comm; Gifted/Talented Prgm; Natl Earth Sci Teachers Assn 1985-; TX Earth Sci Teachers Assn 1985-; NSTA 1984-; Aggie Wives Club (VP 1983) 1980-; Natl Sci Fnd Grant Study Geology Trinity Univ; Lower Co River Authority Grant Electricity Enviroment Univ TX; *office:* Ray D Corbett Jr H S 301 Main St Schertz TX 78154

SCHMIDT, DIANE KAY, 3rd Grade Teacher; *b:* Excelsior Springs, MO; *m:* Gary; *c:* Kelly, Ryan, Stephani; *ed:* (BA) Elem Ed, CMSU; (MA) Elem Ed, Webster Univ; *cr:* 1st Grade Teacher Elkhorn 1973,1975; 1st-4th Grade Teacher 1976-, 3rd Grade Teacher 1990 Westview Elem; *ai:* Outdoor Classroom, Prgm Playground, Homework Comm; 3rd Grade Dist Coord; Norco Cncl of Intnl Rdng Assn; *office:* Westview Elem Sch Wornall/Jesse James Excelsior Springs MO 64024

SCHMIDT, GERALD JOSEPH, English Teacher; *b:* Kankakee, IL; *m:* Lisa Johnson; *ed:* (BA) Eng, Loras Coll 1972; *cr:* Teacher W Dubuque HS 1972-; *ai:* Girls Bsktbl Coach.

SCHMIDT, HERBERT E., Civics/US History Teacher; *b:* Potlatch, ID; *m:* Glenda C.; *ed:* Grad Work Cntrl Univ, Eastern Univ, WA St Univ; *cr:* Teacher Prosser HS 1965-; *ai:* Sr Class Adv; Ftbl Time-Keeper & Scoreboard; Bsktbl Ofcl Book; Masonic Lodge (Master 1978) 1971-; City Of Prosser Councilman 1988-; Stus to Europe Tour Leader 1970, 1976, 1980, 1986, 1990; *office:* Prosser HS 1203 Prosser Ave Prosser WA 99350

SCHMIDT, JAN A., 6th Grade Teacher; *b:* Bryam, TX; *m:* Richard A.; *c:* Erik R.; *ed:* (BED) Eng/Span, Univ of AK Fairbanks 1968; (MED) Elem Ed, Univ of AK Anchorange 1976; Grad Hours Elem Ed; *cr:* 7th/8th Grade Teacher Moscow Jr HS 1968-69; 4th-6th Grade Teacher Rabbit Creek Elem 1969-76; 5th/6th Grade Combination Teacher Huffman Elem 1976-80; 4th/5th Grade Combination Teacher Susitna Elem 1980-88; 6th Grade Teacher Tudor Elem 1988-; *ai:* Stu Asst Team Tudor; Whole Child Educl Task Force; *home:* 11601 Wagner St Anchorage AK 99516

SCHMIDT, JEANETTE PRICE, Language Arts Teacher; *b:* Chardon, OH; *m:* James R.; *c:* Jessamyn, Kate; *ed:* (BFA) Theatre Art, Denison Univ 1972; (MA) Ed, IN Univ 1983; Kent St Univ, Amer Acad of Dramatic Art; *cr:* Teacher Paul Harding HS 1976-; *ai:* East Allen Cty Schls Center Stage Theater (Artistic & Drama Dir, Bd); *office:* Paul Harding HS 6501 Wayne Trace Fort Wayne IN 46816

SCHMIDT, JO ANN IRENE, LD Teacher; *b:* Flasher, ND; *m:* Leo Joseph; *c:* Kyle; *ed:* (BS) Elem Ed, Valley City St Univ 1963; (MS) Rdng, Moorhead ST Univ 1985; NDSU/UND/Minot St Univ; *cr:* Teacher Fort Yates Public Schls 1960-61, Bismarck Public Schls 1961-62, St Catherine Sch 1963-89; LD/Teacher Sheyenne Valley Spec Ed Unit 1989-; *ai:* Rdng Curr Chm; Chemical Health Guide; ND Ed Assn 1960-; NEA 1960-; Intnl Rdng Assn 1989-; Delta Kappa Gamma Personal Growth & Services 1980-81; Kappa Delta Pi 1962-80; St Catherines Awd Winner for Diocese of Fargos Excl in Teaching Awd; St Catherines Awd Winner for Miriam Joseph Farrell Awd for Distinguished Teaching; *home:* 936 Riverview Dr Valley City ND 58072

SCHMIDT, KATHLEEN LOUISE TURNER, 5th Grade Teacher; *b:* Cleveland, OH; *m:* Tom Jeffrey; *c:* Jason W., Jeffrey T.; *ed:* (BS) Ed, Ashland Coll 1971; (MS) Guidance/Counseling, John Carroll Univ 1979; Designing Effective Instruction; Glassers Sch Without Failure; Teacher Effertiveness Trng; A Fellowship Lake Erie Garfield Sr Coll Concepts of Economics; Trng Teletype Cmptrs Programming; Achvievement Motivation for Educators; Transactional Analysis in the Classroom; *cr:* Teacher Shoregate Elem 1971-81; Summer Rdng Teacher Shoregate Elem Roosevelt Elem 1972-74; Teacher Royalview Elem 1981-; *ai:* Sch Store; Taught Bell Choir; Sch Photographer; Photography Club Adv; Jennings Scholar for Outstanding Teachers 1975-76; *office:* Royalview Elem Sch 31500 Royalview Dr Willoughby OH 44094

SCHMIDT, LARRY LEE, Band Director; *b:* San Antonio, TX; *m:* Cheryl Le Mae Behrends; *c:* Kara M., Sean Larson; *ed:* (BSME) Music, 1970, (MAED) Music Specilization, 1974 SW TX St; Admin Cert, Counseling & Guidance, Supervisory Cert, SW TX St 1974; *cr:* Asst Band Dir San Marcos Baptist Acad 1968-70; 4th/5th Grade US Army Bands 1971-73; Asst Band Dir 1974-76, Head Dir 1976-82 Eisenhower Mid Sch; Private Instrumental Instr 1968-; Head Dir Bradley Mid Sch 1983-; *ai:* TX Band Masters Assn, TX Music Educators Assn, Natl Jury Educators Assn Mem 1967-; *office:* Bradley Mid Sch 14819 Heimer Rd San Antonio TX 78232

SCHMIDT, MARY KOTHMANN, Science Teacher; *b:* Fredericksburg, TX; *m:* Harold Reagan; *c:* Scott, Sabyn Park, Sid; *ed:* (BS) Elem Ed, Angelo St Univ 1973; Grad Courses TX Tech Univ; Cmptr Courses SW TX St Univ; *cr:* 5th/6th Grade Sci Teacher Mason Elem Sch 1973-; *ai:* Drug Ed Liaison; Elem Sci Fair Spon; TSTA, NEA Mem 1973-; TX Sci Teachers Assn Mem 1980-; TX Cncl Elem Sci Mem 1985-; St Paul Luth Church Mem 1964-; Delta Kappa Gamma Mem 1982-; Natl Geographic Society, Cousteau Society, Nature Conservancy, Natl Wildlife Fnd; *office:* Mason Elem Sch Drawer I Mason TX 76856

SCHMIDT, MICHELLE MARIE, Mathematics Teacher; *b:* Monticello, IA; *ed:* (BSE) Math Ed, NE MO St Univ 1986; *cr:* Math Teacher Adair Cty R-I Sch 1986-; *ai:* Academic Team & Class Spon; Weighted Grade Comm Chairperson; MO St Teachers Assn NE Dist Public Relations Comm 1987-; Cmmty Teachers Assn (Pres 1990, VP 1989-); NCTM; MO Cncl Teachers of Math; Alpha Sigma Tau Nominations Chm 1989-; *office:* Adair Cty R-I Sch Hwy 149 N Novinger MO 63559

SCHMIDT, MILDRED WESTRUP, Sixth Grade Teacher; *b:* Plentywood, MT; *m:* Karl; *c:* Karl, Paula Weglarz; *ed:* (BA) Elem Ed, Wayne St Univ 1960; (MA) Teaching, Saginaw Valley St 1976; Grad Stud; *cr:* Teacher Cleveland Sch, Frankenmuth Luth, Mt Clemens Cmmty Schls, Roseville Cmmty Schls; *office:* Huron Park Elem Sch 18530 Marquette Roseville MI 48066

SCHMIDT, SANDRA SMITH, English Teacher; *b:* Cameron, TX; *c:* Amy, William; *ed:* (BA) Eng/Government, Univ of TX 1963; *cr:* Eng Teacher Mac Arthur HS 1964-68; Teacher/Coord on Site Classroom Childrens Hospital 1969-71; Eng Teacher Krueger Mid Sch 1983-; *ai:* Academic Pentathalon Coach 1989-; TESA Presenter at UTSA 1989-; Textbook Adoption Comm 1989-; Curr Design Team 1990; NCTE; Northern Hills Cntry Club Chm of Bd of Governors 1988-, Recognition Awd 1983 & 1987; San Antonio Tennis Assn Dir 1988-; Law in Action Chm 1975; San Antonio Bar Assn Womens Auxiliary Pres 1976; Law in a Changing Society Chm 1977; San Antonio Jr Forum Bd of Dir 1978-79; Howard Sch PTO Pres 1980; NEA Coraut for Study of Linguistics at Univ of TX 1966; *office:* Krueger Mid Sch 438 Lanark Dr San Antonio TX 78218

SCHMIDT, SHIRLEY A. SIEBRASSE, Fifth Grade Teacher; *b:* Humphrey, NE; *m:* Willard; *c:* Anthony, Patrick, Gretchen; *ed:* (BA) Elem Ed, Cntrl MI Univ 1966; Grad Stud; *cr:* 5th Grade Teacher Buena Vista 1955-60, Bangor Township Schls 1962-66, Bay City Sch Dist 1967-; *ai:* Dist Wide 6th Grade Spelling Bee Spon; Alpha Delta Kappa Treas 1985-87; Chrstn Bd of Ed Supt 1987-89; GSA Leader 1955-57; *office:* Auburn Sch 301 E Midland Rd Auburn MI 48611

SCHMIDT, STEPHEN, Science Teacher/Dept Chair; *b:* Rockford, IL; *ed:* (BS) Botany, N AZ Univ 1977; Ed, Bio, Univ of AZ; *cr:* Sci Teacher Tuba City HS 1981-; *ai:* NAU Upward Bound Spon; Sci Club 1984-88 Spon; NEA, AEA 1981-; MACY Fnd Bio Preparatory Prgm.

SCHMIDT, SUZANNE FARNSWORTH, Second Grade Teacher; *b:* Detroit, MI; *m:* Thomas M.; *c:* Paul G., Ryan T.; *ed:* (BS) Interdepartmental Sci/Math, Cntrl MI Univ 1969; *cr:* 6th Grade Teacher 1970-78, 2nd Grade Teacher 1978- Pinery Park Elem; *ai:* Effective Schls Prgm Core Team Mem; Wellness Prgm Rep; WY Ed Assn, MI Ed Assn, NEA; Womens Auxilliary Knights of Columbus Family of Yr 1985; *office:* Pinery Park Elem Sch 2550 Rogers Ln Wyoming MI 49509

SCHMIDTKNECHT, RAMONA ANN, Home Economics/Math Teacher; *b:* Galesville, WI; *ed:* (BSHEC) Home Ec, Alverno Coll 1958; (MED) Home Ec, St Louis Univ 1968; *cr:* 5th-6th Grade/Home Ec Teacher St Boniface Sch 1958-60; Home Ec/Math Teacher Bishop Bergan HS 1960-62; Home Ec Teacher St Benedict HS 1962-63; Home Ec/Math Teacher St Marys HS 1963-69, Cadet HS & Jr HS 1969-; *ai:* Parent Act; Coord of Annual Bazaar; Cadet Child Care Center (ChairPerson, Vice Chairperson); Craft Comm Holly Springs Voc HS 1989-; Established Cadet Child Care Center 1974; Amer Legion Citation for Meritorious Service for Dedication to Improvement of Standards of Living; *office:* Cadet Sch 395 N West St Holly Springs MS 38635

SCHMIEDESKAMP, ROGER WILLIAM, Mathematics Teacher; *b:* Mapleton, IA; *m:* Dian Kay Eckerman; *c:* Ragan, Micaela; *ed:* (BAE) Phys Ed/Math, Wayne St Coll 1973; *cr:* Teacher/Coach Washington Jr HS 1973-76, Interstate 35 Schls 1976-80, Saydel HS 1980-86, Linn HS 1987-; *ai:* Var & Frosh Boys Bsktbl Asst; Amnesty Intnl & Frosh Class Spon; MNEA 1989-; NEA, ISEA 1973-86; MCTM 1988-89; *home:* 2011 Meadow Ln Jefferson City MO 65109

SCHMITT, CLAUDIA K. (GALUSHA), English Teacher/Dept Head; *b:* Enid, OK; *m:* Thomas Anthony; *c:* Christopher; *ed:* (BA) Sociology/Eng, 1970, (MS) Eng Ed, 1977 Phillips Univ; Post Grad Stud OK Univ & Northeastern St Univ; *cr:* Stu Union Dir 1975-77, Eng Instr 1976-77 Phillips Univ; Sociology/Psych Teacher Broken Arrow Public Schls 1979; 9th Grade Eng Teacher/Jr HS Dept Head Bixby Public Schls 1979-87; Cmptr Instr Tulsa Jr Coll 1987; *ai:* Stu Senate & Natl Jr Honor Society Spon; North Cntrl Accreditation Comm Chairperson; Staff Dev Comm; Bixby Ed Assn Secy 1990; OK Cncl Teachers of Eng, NCTE, NEA 1990; Walk for Mankind; 1st Chrstn Church UBS Dir 1990; Bixby Public Schls Teacher of Yr 1987-88 & Class Act Awd 1987; MAPCO Teachers Achievement Awd 1988; *office:* Bixby Jr HS Box 160 Bixby OK 74008

SCHMITT, LINDA SUE, Fifth Grade Teacher; *b:* Evansville, IN; *ed:* (BA) Elem Ed, Harris Teachers Coll 1970; Religious Cert Cath Schls; *cr:* Teacher St Martin of Tours 1970-; *ai:* Upper Grade Coord; NCEA 1970-; *office:* St Martin of Tours Sch 618 W Ripa Saint Louis MO 63125

SCHMITT, RANDAL L., Lang Art/Foreign Lang Teacher; *b:* Le Mars, IA; *m:* Mairlyn Tamm Schmitt; *ed:* (BA) Eng/Ger/Speech, Westmar Coll 1972; Working Toward Masters Educl Admin, Drake Univ; *cr:* Eng/Ger/Speech/Lang Art Teacher Fonda Cmmty Schls 1972-; *ai:* Phase III & Curr Coord; Ger Club; NCTE 1972-; OLGC Parish Church Organist 1966-; Cmmty Theater Dir 1978-; Cmmty Choir Organist 1972-; Fonda Cmmty Sch Teachers Organization Past Pres; Univ of MN Overseas Prgm Univ of Erlangen Germany; Overseas Educl Stu Trips Spon; *home:* 505 Franklin Fonda IA 50540

SCHMITT, ROSEMARY WHITE, Fourth Grade Teacher; *b:* Geneva, IL; *m:* David R.; *ed:* (BS) Elem Ed, WI St Univ La Crosse 1968; *cr:* 2nd-4th Grade Teacher Shady Lane Elem Sch 1968-; *ai:* Soc Stud Comm Secy; Sch Advisory & Staff Dev Comms; *office:* Shady Lane Elem Sch W172 N8959 Shady Lane Blvd Menomonee Falls WI 53051

SCHMITZ, ELIZABETH ANN (ZYDERVELT), Principal; *b:* Los Angeles, CA; *m:* Dr. Charles Dale; *c:* Kristina; *ed:* (MED) Ed/Curr, 1970, (EDD) Educl Admin, 1980 Univ of MO; Leadership Acad Grad St of MO; *cr:* Cost Analyst Instr Univ of MO 1967-70; Teacher 1970-80, Instructional Materials Center Dir 1980-83 Columbia Public Schls; Elem Prin Midway Heights Elem 1983-; *ai:* Natl Assn of Elem Prins, MO Assn of Elem Prins 1980-; Intnl Rdng Assn 1987-; Outstanding Young Women of America 1980; Co-Authored Book; Conducted over 40 Wkshps on Ed; Presenter at Natl, St & Regional Meetings; *office:* Midway Heights Elem Sch 8130 W Hwy 40 Columbia MO 65202

SCHMOEKEL, JERRY LEE, Science Teacher; *b:* Seguin, TX; *m:* Monima Jo Long; *c:* Kristina Monima, Brian E.; *ed:* (BA) Eng, 1970, (MA) Physics, 1982 SW TX St Univ; Univ of TX Nuclear Symposium 1978, Energy Symposium 1985, 1987; *cr:* Teacher SW TX St Univ 1975-77, Nixon Ind Sch Dist 1977-79, SW TX St Univ 1979-82, Nixon-Smiley CISD 1983-; *ai:* Sci Club; UIL Sci Dir; Gifted/Talented & Grading Comm; Society of Physics Stu 1980-; TX Classroom Teachers Assn 1988-; *home:* Rt 1 Box 672 Seguin TX 78155

SCHMOLDT, CLIFFORD JAMES, Program Director; *b:* Watertown, WI; *ed:* (BSE) Ed, Univ of WI Whitewater 1977; Natl Wildlife Fed Nature Quest Instr; *cr:* Teacher of Gifted Sullivan Public Schls 1978; 3rd-8th Grade Teacher/Choir/Organist St Paul Luth Sch 1978-84; 5Th/6th Grade Teacher Christ Luth Sch

1984-89; *ai:* Teach Nature Classes; *office:* Camp Phillip Rt 3 Box 190-4 Wautoma WI 54982

SCHMUCK, JUDY KUERGELEIS, First Grade Teacher; *b:* St Louis, MO; *m:* James; *ed:* (BA) Elem Ed, William Woods Coll 1972; (MS) Early Childhood Ed, Southern IL Univ 1974; Additional Hrs Early Childhood Ed; *cr:* 1st Grade Teacher W S Zahnow Elem 1972-; *ai:* Waterloo Classroom Teachers Assn 1972-; Friends of St Pauls Cathedral London 1986-; Friends of St George Windsor 1984-; Alpha Chi Omega; Outstanding Young Women of America 1986; *office:* W J Zahnow Elem Sch 301 Hamacher St Waterloo IL 62298

SCHNAKE, PHYLLIS STEWART, Fifth Grade Teacher; *b:* Deerfield, MO; *w:* Ivan E. (dec); *c:* Richard L., Michael B.; *ed:* (BS) Ed, SW MO St Univ 1979; *cr:* 1st-8th Grade Teacher Rural Sch Lawrence Cty 1951-53; 5th Grade Teacher Pierce City Cntrl Sch 1979-; *ai:* Mem Prof Rights & Responsibilities Comm; Textbook Selection Comm; MO St Teachers Assn Mem, Cmmty Teachers Assn 1979-; *home:* 1319 Kevin Dr Mount Vernon MO 65712

SCHNEEHAGEN, RUTH GOREY, Second Grade Teacher; *b:* Springfield, MA; *m:* William H.; *c:* Carol Evans, Colleen Reeb, Cynthia Kisamore; *ed:* (BS) Ed, Towson St Univ 1973; (MED) Supv & Admin, Western MD Coll 1982; Loyola Univ; George Washington Univ; Johns Hopkins Univ; Gesell Inst of Child Dev; *cr:* Teacher Mechanicsville Elem 1970-71, Sandymount Elem 1971-75, Freedom Elem 1975-; *ai:* Founder & Dir CATS; Coach Odyssey Mind Teams; St & Natl Judge Odyssey of Mind; MS St Teachers Assn 1970-89; Natl Assn Gifted Children 1982-; Odyssey Mind (Western Regnl Dir 1987 Bd of Dir 1988-); Nom Recognition As Teacher Yr 1987; St of MD Gov Awd 1989; Salute to Excl Awd; Awarded Cert of Appreciation Sch Bd Carroll Cty 1988; *home:* 5238 Braddock Rd Woodbine MD 21797

SCHNEIDER, ANN LENORE, Teacher; *b:* Charleston, WV; *ed:* (BA) His, 1970, (MAT) His, 1971 Duke Univ; (DA) His, Carnegie-Mellon Univ 1981; *cr:* Teacher Coleytown Jr HS 1970-71, Saxe Mid Sch 1971-79, 1982-86, Wheaton Coll 1981-82; Part Time Professor Kings Coll 1983-; Teacher New Canaan HS 1986-; *ai:* Soc Stud Review, Faculty Cncl, NHS Comms; Girls TracK Coach; CT Cncl for Soc Stud, NEA, CEA, NCEA, NCSS; Spec Grant to Develop Stu Tour New Canaan Historical Society; Mock Constitutional Convention US His Stu; Units for Teaching USSR; Developed European His Course & Advanced Placement European His Course; Study in E Africa Colonino Awd; Duke Univ & Carnegie-Mellon Univ Grad Fellowships; Outstanding Young Woman of America; Fulbright to China & Netherlands; Distinguished Teacher; *office:* New Canaan HS Farm Rd New Canaan CT 06840

SCHNEIDER, BARBARA BAUMGART, 7th Grade Reading Teacher; *b:* Mount Pleasant, MI; *m:* Charles C.; *c:* Nicole, Julia; *ed:* (BA) Eng, 1970, (MA) Rdng, 1975 MI St Univ; Counseling Endorsement-Central MI Univ; *cr:* Eng Teacher De Witt HS 1970-74; Rdng Teacher Reed City Sch 1974-; *ai:* Theater Dir; Stu Cncl; Yrbk Ski Club; MI Rdng Assn 1980-; United Meth Church; *office:* Reed City Mid Sch 238 W Lincoln Reed City MI 49677

SCHNEIDER, DENNIS RAY, Band Director; *b:* Shattuck, OK; *m:* Eva Gladys; *c:* Clay B., Zane C. (dec); *ed:* (BME) Music, Pan Handle St Univ 1963; (MA) Music, E NM Univ 1967; *cr:* Music Dir Cimarron Municipal Schls 1963-65, Shiprock HS 1966-69, Dulce Public Schls 1970, Cimarron Municipal Schls 1971-; *ai:* Teach Band Segment; NENMMEA Treas 1975-; Church of Christ Minister 1981-; Cimarron Ambulance Service EMB-B 1978-; Masonic Lodge Secy 1987-, Twice Master; *home:* Rt 1 Box 8 Cimarron NM 87714

SCHNEIDER, DUANE LE ROY, Science Teacher; *b:* Mobridge, SD; *m:* Diana Lee Stull; *c:* Scott E., Karri L., Dustin J.; *ed:* (BS) Phys Ed, Dickinson St Univ 1969; *cr:* Sci Teacher Golva HS 1969-72, Herried HS 1972-73, Pollock HS 1977-81, Garrison HS 1981-; *ai:* NEA, NDEA, GEA Mem; Garrison Boosters Pres 1984; *home:* 132 6th Ave NE Garrison ND 58540

SCHNEIDER, ELAINE ROSE, OSF, Eighth Grade Teacher; *b:* Columbus, OH; *ed:* (BA) Math, 1957; (MA) Theology, 1968 Coll of St Francis; Ed, Miami of OH 1972; *cr:* 5th-8th Grade Math Teacher St Marys 1960-66; 7th-8th Grade Math Teacher Immaculate 1966-68; GED Teacher Joliet Jr Coll 1968-76; 8th Grade Teacher St Matthew 1976-; *ai:* Vice Prin; Stu Cncl Moderator; NCEA 1966-; NCTM 1966-68; Modern Math Course for Adults.

SCHNEIDER, JOAN A., Kindergarten Teacher; *b:* Newark, NJ; *ed:* Eng Lit, Drew Univ; (BA) Elem Ed, Kean 1965; Kent St, Monmouth Coll, Brookdale, Kean; *cr:* Kndgtn Teacher Manasquan Public Schls 1957, Keyport Cntrl 1958-; *ai:* HS NHS; NEA; NJ Ed Assn Mem; Monmouth Cty Teachers Assn; NDEA Eng Inst Advanced Study of Eng Kent St Fellowship 1968l Drew Univ Kappi Pi.

SCHNEIDER, LEROY PAUL, Science & Chemistry Teacher; *b:* Fairbank, IA; *m:* Betty Ann Basche; *c:* Sue Thompson, Keith, Rod, Jerry; *ed:* (BA) Bio/General Sci, Wartburg Coll 1959; (MA) General Sci Ed, NE MO St 1965; Grad Stud, IA St Univ, Univ IA, Univ Northern IA, Drake, Bowling Green & NE MO St; *cr:* Sci Teacher Roosevelt Jr HS 1959-62, Grinnell Cmnty Mid Sch 1962-81; Chem/Health/environmental Teacher Grinnell Cmnty HS 1981-; *ai:* Sch Dist Phase III Comm; IA Acad of Sci; Grinnel; Newburg Ed Assn (VP, Pres 1965-68) 25 Yr Service 1987; IA & Natl Ed Assn; Jaycees 1964-72 Outstanding Young Educator 1970; St Johns Luth Church (Church Sunday Sch Teacher, Supt Youth Group Leader 1962-); Several NSF Grants Ed; IA Lottery Grants Environmental Sci; Supt Advisory Comm, Dist Advisory Comm; *home:* 1822 Spring St Grinnell IA 50112

SCHNEIDER, LINDA M., 6th Grade Teacher; *b:* Ithaca, NY; *m:* Frederick R. Jr.; *c:* Heather D.; *ed:* (BS) Elem Ed, Bloomsburg St Univ 1969; Masters Equiv; *cr:* K-6th Grade Teacher Lincoln Elem 1969-; *ai:* Rdng Pilot Prgm; Morning Announcements; Bristol Twp Ed Assn, PA St Ed Assn, NEA 1969-; *office:* Lincoln Elem Sch 10 Plumtree Pl Levittown PA 19056

SCHNEIDER, MARY JO KELLY, Chapter I Teacher; *b:* Sioux Falls, SD; *m:* Frank; *ed:* (BS) Elem Ed, Mankato St Univ 1968; (MA) Elem Curr, Univ of IA Iowa City 1980; (EDS) Elem Admin, Univ of IA 1988; *cr:* Pre 1st/1st/4th Grade Teacher Cedar Rapids Cmmty Schls 1968-89; Chapter I Teacher Pequot Lakes Ind Sch Dist 186 1989-; *ai:* Phi Delta Kappa, ASCD, MEA, NEA, Univ of IA Alumni Assn; PEO; *home:* Rt 1 Box 187 Pequot Lakes MN 56472

SCHNEIDER, WILLIAM LEE, Mathematics Department Chair; *b:* Chicago, IL; *m:* Renata Vivian Weythman; *c:* Bryan, Kathleen, Michelle, Sean; *ed:* (BA) Math, Benedictine Coll 1961; *cr:* Math Instr Troy HS 1961-62, MO St Hosp 1962-64, Sts Peter & Paul HS 1964-74, Sidney HS 1974-79, Nevada HS 1979-; *ai:* Head Girls Vlybl & Bsktbl; Asst Boys Track; ICTM 1979-; Coach of Yr 1988; *office:* Nevada HS 1001 15th St Nevada IA 50201

SCHNEIDERMAN, ETTA M., Mathematics Teacher; *b:* New York, NY; *m:* Samuel; *c:* Ari, Steven, Celia, Debra; *ed:* (MS) Cmptr Technology, CW Post 1986; Cmptr Programming; *cr:* Sci Teacher Sands Point Acad 1966-69, Great Neck Public Schls 1969-72; Math/Sci Teacher Port Washington Sch Dist 1976-84; Math Teacher Sewanhaka CHS Dist 1984-; *ai:* Teacher Professionalism Comm; Mid States Steering Comm Chairperson; Dist Teacher Center Facilitator; SAT Prep Course; SFT, NEA 1986-; Sisterhood Temple Beth Israel Pres; NSF Grant 1987; Published Cmptr Assisted Instruction Software; *home:* 39 Sandy Ct Port Washington NY 11050

SCHNELL, ARNOLD HAMILTON, Sixth Grade Teacher; *b:* Hominy, OK; *m:* L. Joyce Stephens; *c:* Carol Graff, Jeanie Pond, Sharon Tyler, Timothy; *ed:* (AAS) Industrial Tech Elect, Rochester Inst Tech 1963; (BS) Elem Ed, Atlantic Union Coll 1970; Prof Cert 1978, (MED) Elem Admin, 1979 Walla Walla Coll; *cr:* 5th-10th Grade Sci/Phys Ed Teacher Houston Jr Acad 1970-71; 1st-8th Grade Teacher Killeen 7th Day Adv Sch 1971-73; 5th-10th Grade Math/Sci/Phys Ed Teacher Culver Sch of 7th Day Adv 1973-76; 6th-8th Grade Math/Sci Teacher Portland Adv Elem 1976-; *ai:* NSTA 1977-; Natl Assn Teachers of Math 1980-; *office:* Portland Adventist Elem Sch 3990 NW 1st Gresham OR 97030

SCHNELL, PAMELA JANE, Science Teacher; *b:* St Paul, MN; *m:* Larry P.; *c:* Michael, Rebecca, Cathy; *ed:* (BS) Bio, Chadron St Coll 1969; *cr:* Sci Teacher Hay Springs HS 1969-70, Alliance HS 1985-; *ai:* Class Spon 1991; Stu Asst Team Mem; NEA 1986-; ADK 1988-; 4-H Leader 1980-, Outstanding Leader 1985.

SCHNITZER, ROBERT JAY, English/Drama/ESL Teacher; *b:* Newark, NJ; *ed:* (BAS) Eng/Drama, OH Univ 1972; Teaching Credential, San Francisco St Univ 1984; *cr:* Eng/Drama Teacher Lowell HS 1984; Eng Teacher Francisco Mid Sch 1985; Eng/Drama/Eng as 2nd Lang Teacher Galileo HS 1985-; *ai:* Class of 1990 Spon; Dir Schls Annual Spring Production; Coached Wrestling & Bsbl; Co-Spon Chinese Culture Club; After Sch Tutoring Prgm; Phi Delta Kappa 1984-; Young Life Volunteer 1979-, 10 Yr Service Awd 1989; *office:* Galileo HS 1150 Francisco St San Francisco CA 94109

SCHNURBUSCH, VIRGINIA (LINEBARGER), Teacher/Counselor; *b:* Perryville, MO; *m:* Jerome; *c:* Patricia Fausz, Steven, Nancy Mc Millian, Larry; *ed:* (BS) Elem Ed, 1969, (MA) Scndry Cnslr Ed, 1973 Semo Univ; *cr:* Teacher Layton Sch 1949-52, St Vincent Elem Sch 1958-62, Sim Layton Sch 1962-64, St Vincent Mid Sch 1964-; *ai:* Lang Art Dept Chairperson; Chrldr Moderator; Self Study Steering Comm Chairperson; Semo Cnslrs Assn, MO Cnslrs Assn 1973-; Alpha Delta Kappa, Beta Lambda (Pres 1987-88) 1974-; Amer Legion Auxiliary (St Pres 1983-84) 1961-; Perry Cty Cmmty Counseling (Bd of Trustees, VP); Semo Alumni Perry & St Genevieve Ctys Pres 1976; Outstanding Elem Teachers of America 1975; Natl Amer Legion Outstanding Teacher 1989; *home:* 2109 W St Joseph St Perryville MO 63775

SCHOBER, ALBERT GUSTAV, Chemistry Teacher; *b:* St Louis, MO; *m:* Carole; *c:* James, Laurie Westin, Steve, Jonathon; *ed:* (BA) Chem, Augsburg Coll 1963; (MS) Organic Chem, Purdue Univ 1966; Natl Sci Fnd Insts Univ of WI; *cr:* Teacher Robbinsdale Dist 281 1966-; *ai:* Gifted & Talented Comm; MN Sci Teachers Assn Comm Mem 1970-75; Regional Sci Fair Judge; *home:* 5016 40th Ave N Robbinsdale MN 55422

SCHOCH, RAY, Social Studies Teacher; *b:* Buffalo, NY; *c:* Jason; *ed:* (BSED) His, NE MO St Univ 1966; WA Univ, Univ of MO St Louis, Univ of MO Columbia, NE MO St Univ, Webster Univ, Univ of CA Davis; *cr:* Teacher Mc Cluer HS 1966-70, Mc Cluer North HS 1971-; *ai:* Head Varsity Sftbl Coach; Drama, Thespian Asst; N Cntrl Evaluation Steering & Curr Comm; Dist Salary Advancement Appeals Comm; MO Ed Assn 1966-; OR-CA Trails Assn Charter Mem 1983-; Awarded Grant Natl Endowment for Hum 1984; Book Reviews Published; *office:* Mc Cluer North HS 705 Waterford Dr Florissant MO 63033

SCHOEN, ALLIE B. (LANDERS), 7-12th Grade Science Teacher; *b:* Abilene, TX; *m:* Willie D.; *c:* Derek, Mitsy; *ed:* (BS) Bio, Tarleton St Univ 1976; Advanced Academic Trng 1988; Advanced Bio 1987; *cr:* 7th-12th Grade Sci Teacher Gordon CISD 1978-79, Blanket CISD 1979-80; Spec Ed Teacher Throckmorton CISD 1981; 7th-12th Grade Sci Teacher Blackwell CISD 1981-; *ai:* Jr Class Spon; UIL Sci; Blackwell VFD 1984- EMT; Nom TX Excl Awd Outstanding HS Teachers Level III Career Ladder 1990; *office:* Blackwell H S P O Box 505 Blackwell TX 79506

SCHOEN, WILLIAM JOSEPH, Chemistry Teacher; *b:* Brooklyn, NY; *m:* Linda A.; *c:* Christopher, Nancy; *ed:* (BS) Pharmacy, 1961, (MS) Chem Ed, 1964 St Johns Univ; *cr:* Chem/Bio Teacher St Johns Preparatory 1962-68; Chem Teacher 1968-, Chem Teacher/Sci Dept Chm 1979- John Jay HS; *ai:* Stu Cncl & Sci Olympiad Adv; Natl Assn of Scndry Act Advs, NY St Assn of Act Advs; Nom Presidential Awd Excl in Sci Teaching 1985; *office:* John Jay HS Rt 52 Hopewell Junction NY 12533

SCHOENEGGE, PAUL WILLIAM, Spanish Teacher; *b:* Athens, OH; *m:* Christine Cullen; *ed:* (BA) Eng/Span/His, Kenyon Coll 1979; Akron Univ; *cr:* Span/His Teacher Margaretta HS 1982-; *ai:* Bsktbl Coach; Drama Dir; Foreign Lang Club Adv; *home:* 209 Main St Castalia OH 44824

SCHOENHALS, RUTH FAYE, Jr HS Language Art Teacher; *b:* Reydon, OK; *m:* Clarence; *c:* Clarissa, Kimberly; *ed:* (BS) Bus, Panhandle St Univ 1966; Grad Stud W TX ST Univ Canyon; *cr:* Bus/Eng Teacher Guymon HS 1966, Lakin HS 1966-68, Springfield HS 1968-69, Darrouzett HS 1969-74, Follett HS 1980-81, Darrouzett HS 1981-; *ai:* Yrbk; Drama Coach; UIL Spon; NCTE 1985-86; Delta Kappa Gamma Corresponding Secy: Assn of TX Prof Educators; VIP; Darrouzett Industrial & Dev Bd; Career Ladder.

SCHOENLAUB, ELIZABETH CORNMAN, Remedial Reading Teacher; *b:* Newport News, VA; *c:* Jeanette A. Schoenlaub Carter, Susan L. Schoenlaub Alden, Paul E., Judith L., Deborah M. Schoenlaub Schaaf; *ed:* (BSED) Elem, 1974, Learning Disablities/EMH, 1980 MO Western St Coll; (MS) Diagnosing/Remediating Rdng, NW MO Univ 1985; *cr:* 6th Grade Elem Ed Teacher 1974-80, 5th Grade Elem Ed Teacher 1980-86, Teacher of Learning Disabilities 1986-87 Buchanan City R IV Sch Dist; Chapter I Remedial Rdng Teacher St Joseph Sch Dist 1987-; *ai:* Tutoring; MO St Teachers Assn, Cmmty Teacher Assn 1974-; Delta Kappa Gamma 1989-; Faith UCC Church (Ministry Comm Secy 1989-); *home:* 2802 Frederick Ave Saint Joseph MO 64506

SCHOENLEIN, KAREN KLEMENCIC, Fourth Grade Teacher; *b:* Cleveland, OH; *m:* David E.; *c:* Kristin L., Christopher D.; *ed:* (BS) Elem Ed, Bowling Green St Univ 1968; Grad Work & Wkshps Baldwin-Wallace Coll, John Carroll Univ, Univ of Dayton, Kent St Univ; *cr:* 5th Grade Teacher Parma City Schls 1968-69; 4th/6th Grade Teacher Brecksville-Broadview Heights City Schls 1969-; *ai:* Competency Based Ed Comm 1983-; Brecksville Ed Assn (Building Rep, Comm Chairperson) 1976, 1978; Martha Holden Jennings Awd 1985.

SCHOEPF, LOREAN O., English Teacher; *b:* Bonesteel, SD; *m:* Glen L.; *c:* James, Mary, Lori; *ed:* (BSE) Eng/Math, Southern St Coll 1964; Various Courses Univ of SD Vermillion, Black Hills Univ Spearfish, Univ of CO Greeley, SD St Univ Brookings; *cr:* Eng Teacher Philip Ind Sch 1964-69, Wagner Cmmty Sch 1969-; *ai:* Oral Interpretation Adv; Soph Class Spon; Argus Leader Spelling Contest Adv; Wagner Ed Assn (Secy 1988-, Pres); SD Ed Assn 1964-; St Johns Luth (Ed Chm 1984-87, Circle Chm 1987-, Sunday Sch Teacher); Jaycette Mem; Teacher of Yr; *home:* PO Box 2 Wagner SD 57380

SCHOESS, SANDRA MARIE, 6th Grade Teacher; *b:* St Paul, MN; *m:* Mark; *ed:* (BS) Elem Ed, 1981, (MS) Rdng, 1989 Univ of WI River Falls; *cr:* 6th Grade Teacher Unity Mid Sch 1982-; *ai:* St Croix Valley Rdng Cncl Mem 1984-; *office:* Unity Mid Sch Box 307 Balsam Lake WI 54810

SCHOFIELD, JAMES THOMAS, English/Communications Teacher; *b:* Pasadena, CA; *m:* Lisa Perkins; *c:* Dustin, De Anna, Michelle; *ed:* (BA) Eng, CA St Univ Los Angeles 1988; *cr:* Eng/Comm Teacher Mark Keppel HS 1988-; *ai:* Drama, Stage, TV Productions Dir; Drama Club Adv; *office:* Mark Keppel HS 502 E Hellman Ave Alhambra CA 91801

SCHOFIELD, THOMAS PATRICK, 7th/8th Grade Math Teacher; *b:* Chicago, IL; *m:* Michol M.; *c:* Colleen, Mickey, Tammy; *ed:* (BA) Philosophy, St Mary of the Lake 1967; (BS) Elem Ed, 1976, (MST) Elem Ed, 1978 Univ of WI Eau Claire; (MSE) Elem Admin, Univ of WI Superior 1988; *cr:* 7th Grade Math Teacher Queen of Martyrs 1968-72; Jr-Sr Religion Teacher Regis HS 1973-75; 4th-5th Grade Teacher Pederson Elem 1976-81; 7th-8th Grade Math Teacher Altoona Mid Sch 1981-; *ai:* Mathcounts & Bantam Hockey Coach; NCTM Mem 1988-; Altoona Hockey Assn Coach 1976-; Regis Sch Bd Mem 1977-78; Natl Sci Fnd Grant Cmptr Sci 1970-71; *office:* Altoona Mid Sch 1903 Bartlett Ave Altoona WI 54720

SCHOLL, LINDA LEE (WENZELMAN), Physical Education Teacher; *b:* Kankakee, IL; *m:* Robert L.; *c:* Kerri, Heather, David; *ed:* (BS) Phys Ed, Easter IL Univ 1970; *cr:* Teacher Bonfield Grade Sch 1970-; Reddick Grade Sch 1988-; *ai:* Coaching Boys & Girls Track & Cross Cntry; Baseline II Core Team; *home:* RR 1 Box 94 Bonfield IL 60913

SCHOLTEN, BECKY TREUR, German Teacher; *b:* Grand Rapids, MI; *m:* David W.; *ed:* (BA) Ger, Calvin Coll 1987; Educl Psych, MI St Univ; *cr:* Ger/Sociology Teacher Lansing Chrstn HS 1988-89; Ger Teacher South Chrstn HS 1989-; *office:* South Christian H S 160 68th St Grand Rapids MI 49508

SCHOLTEN, JAMES KENT, Mathematics Teacher; *b:* Grand Rapids, MI; *m:* Teresa Ellen Burkholder; *c:* Jeff, Philip, David; *ed:* (BS) Math/Phys Ed, 1975; (MA) Ed Leadership, 1990 Grand Valley St Univ; *cr:* Math Teacher Tri Cty Area Schls 1975-; *ai:* Jr HS Track Coach; Prof Dev Comm; Tri Cty Ed Assn (Pres, VP) 1985-87; Rockford Reformed Church Treas 1985-87; *office:* Tri Cty Intermediate Sch 412 E Edgerton Howard City MI 49329

SCHOLZ, MARY B., English Teacher; *b:* Roanoke, VA; *ed:* (BA) Eng, Mary Baldwin Coll 1960; (MED) Ed/Eng, Univ of VA 1971; *cr:* Eng Teacher Madison HS 1968-; *ai:* Faculty Advisory & Basics Comm; 12th Grade Chairperson; AFT; Delta Kappa Gamma; *office:* James Madison HS 2500 Madison Dr Vienna VA 22181

SCHOMAKER, ANNE MARIE, 5th Grade Teacher; *b:* Brooklyn, NY; *ed:* (BS) Ed, SUNY Oneonta 1964; (MA) Liberal Stud, SUNY Stony Brook 1970; (MS) Ed/Learning Disabilities, Hofstra 1975; *cr:* 3rd/5th Grade Teacher Whiporwil & Bretton Woods Elem Schls 1964; 3rd Grade Teacher 1964-71, 5th Grade Teacher 1971-; *ai:* PTA (Teacher Rep 1980-81) Mem 1964-; Jenkins Memorial Awd 1981; NYSUT; Democratic Party Town Comm Women 1988-89; NY St United Teachers Delegate Representing Hauppauge; Secy, Treas Hauppauge Teachers Assn; Building Rep; *office:* Bretton Woods Elem Sch Club Ln Hauppauge NY 11788

SCHOOLER, JOHN, Band Director; *b:* Buhl, ID; *m:* Joan Coker; *ed:* (BA) Music Ed, 1976; (MA) Music Ed, 1977 Univ of ID; Berklee Coll of Music; ID St Univ; *cr:* Band Dir Eagle Rock JR HS 1977-; Elem Schls 1977-85; *ai:* Photographer Eagle Rock J H Annual Staff/Newspaper; Pep/Jazz Band Dir; Intl Clarinet Society 1972-; Music Educators Natl Conf 1972-; Natl Assn of Jazz Educators St Sec/Treas 1979-84; Bands Performances ID Music Educators Convention 1982-90; Command Performances Gov Evans & Andrus 1980-81/83; NAJE Natl Chapter Awds 1982-83; Published Articles ID Music Educators Journal 1987-89; Published Booklet Recommend St Solo/Ensemble List Competition 1977-79; *office:* Eagle Rock Jr H S 2020 Pancheri Dr Idaho Falls ID 83402

SCHOON, STEVEN RAY, Mathematics/Physics Teacher; *b:* Wadena, MN; *m:* Pamela Carr; *c:* Carrie, Sarah; *ed:* (BS) Math/Physics, Bemidji St 1975; *cr:* Math Teacher Sebeka HS 1975; Math/Physics Teacher/Coach Holdingford HS 1976-; *ai:* Boys & Girls Var Bsktbl & Boys Jr Var Bsbl Coach; Holdingford Fed of Teachers 1979-; Holdingford Ed Assn 1976-78; Holdingford Jaycees 1977-78; *office:* Holdingford HS Holdingford MN 56340

SCHOONOVER, BARBARA BENNETT, Science-Mathematics Teacher; *b:* Mason City, IA; *m:* Craig A.; *c:* Jamie L., Cory A.; *ed:* (BS) Math Ed, Univ of IL Champaign/Urbana 1973; *cr:* Math Teacher Hinsdale S HS 1973-74, Willow Springs Sch 1974-76; Substitute Teacher Canton Dist 66 1977-81; Sci/Math Teacher Cuba Jr-Sr HS 1981-; *ai:* Jr HS Yrbk & Cheerleading Spon; IL Fed of Teachers Local Secy 1989-; St Marys Cath Church 1977-; Canton YMCA 1986-; *office:* Cuba Jr-Sr HS 652 E Main Cuba IL 61427

SCHOONOVER, MARY ELLEN ELLEN ROSEBOOM, English Department Head; *b:* Oklahoma City, OK; *m:* Dennis Edwin; *c:* Rachel Ward, Robin, Jesse; *ed:* (BA) Eng, Univ of N CO 1969; (MLA) Liberal Art, S Meth Univ 1987; *cr:* 12th Grade Eng Teacher Wyandotte HS 1969-70; 7th-12th Grade Eng Teacher Agate Jr/Sr HS 1980-85, Elbert Jr/Sr HS 1988-; *ai:* Speech Coach; Sch Play Dir; Stu Cncl Adv; Soph Class Spon; NCTE; Univ of CO Natl Endowment for Hum Grant 1984; *home:* PO Box 795 Bennett CO 80102

SCHOONOVER, WAYNE KEITH, JR., Sixth Grade Teacher; *b:* Vinton, IA; *m:* Judy Kay Roberts; *c:* Caleb, Billie J.; *ed:* (BS) Ed, N IL Univ 1977; (MS) Counseling, SW OK St Univ 1983; Elem Sch Admin, Univ of OK; *cr:* 6th Grade Teacher Jackson Elem 1977-83, Woodland Hills Elem 1983-; *ai:* Outdoor Ed Camp Co-Dir; Prof Planning, Dev, Policy Comm; Lawton Area Rdng Cncl Pres 1986-87; OK Sci Teacher Assn, ASCD, NSTA; *office:* Woodland Hills Elem Sch 405 N W Woodland Dr Lawton OK 73505

SCHORPP, JANICE FINKEY, Fourth Grade Teacher; *b:* Carlisle, PA; *m:* Edward L.; *ed:* (BS) Elem Ed/Spec Ed, Slippery Rock Univ 1971; (MS) Elem Counseling, Shippensburg Univ 1973; (DED) Elem Ed, Temple Univ 1986; Admin Courses; Madeline Hunter Trng; *cr:* Spec Ed Teacher Carlisle Jr HS 1971-73; 4th Grade Teacher Hamilton Elem 1973-77, Stevens Elem 1977-82, Crestview Elem 1982-; *ai:* Delta Zeta Secy 1967-; *office:* Crestview Elem Sch 623 W Penn St Carlisle PA 17013

SCHOTTLE, BRAD LEE, Mathematics Teacher; *b:* Mountain Lake, MN; *m:* Kerrie; *c:* Anne; *ed:* (BA) Math, CA St Univ Sacramento 1987; *cr:* Math Teacher Elk Grove HS 1987-; *ai:* Math Club & Frosh Class Adv; *office:* Elk Grove HS 9800 Elk Grove-Florin Rd Elk Grove CA 95624

SCHOWENGERDT, JANET C., Lang Art Dept Chairperson; *b:* Houston, TX; *m:* George C.; *c:* Gwen M., David K., Summer D.; *ed:* (BS) Latin/Fr/Scndry Ed, Univ MO Columbia 1987; Coursework at Center for Linguistic Study Abroad Avignon France 1989; *cr:* Fr/Latin/Gifted Teacher Laquey R-V 1987-; *ai:* Fr & Latin Club & Class Spon; NHS Advsory Cncl Chairperson; Rdng & Social Comm VP; Local Cmmty Teachers Assn; MSTA, CTA VP 1987-; MOJCL, NJCL Classics Mem 1987-; Phi Delta Kappa 1989-, Young Educator Awd 1990; Gifted Grant 1988-89; *office:* Laquey R-V Sch P O Box 130 Laquey MO 65534

SCHRACK, NORMA JEAN (MOORS), 2nd Grade Teacher; *b:* Worcester, MA; *m:* Ward E.; *c:* Susan Kincaid, Ward B., Stacy Peterson, Bradley; *ed:* (BA) Elem Ed/Early Chldhd, Kearney St Coll 1972; Grad Stud; *cr:* 2nd Grade Teacher Northeast Elem 1972-; *ai:* NE St Ed Assn, Kearney Ed Assn 1972-; Delta Kappa Gamma Honorary Teaching 1982-; Campfire Girls Pres 1972; 1st United Meth Church; Teacher of Yr 1983 Kearney Public Schls Northeast Elem.

SCHRADER, DIANA LEE, 8th Grade Teacher; *b:* New York, NY; *ed:* (BA) Ed, Concordia Univ 1968; *cr:* 1st Grade Teacher Emmanuel Luth Sch 1968-69; 3rd/4th Grade Teacher 1969-70, 1st/2nd Grade Teacher 1970-74 Grace Luth; 3rd-5th Grade Teacher Queens Sch 1974-76; 8th Grade Teacher St Matthew Luth 1979-; *ai:* Stu Cncl, Cmptr Room Adv; Bell Choir Dir; Chapel Comm; ASCD; Articles Written for Ebony Jr, Jack & Jill, Instr, Teacher, Learning, Crof-Nei Teaching Publications; Books Published Take My Hands; *office:* St Matthew Luth Sch 200 Sherman Ave New York NY 10034

SCHRADER, RITA J. (ZELLER), Kindergarten Teacher; *b:* Salem, OH; *m:* Robert W.; *c:* Lori Koch, Julie Hilderbrand, William, John, Tim; *ed:* (BS) Elem Ed, Bowling Green St Univ 1953; Post Grad Stud; *cr:* 1st Grade Teacher Sandusky City Schls 1951-54; Kndgtn Teacher Perkins Local Schls 1959-61; 5th Grade Teacher 1974-75, Kndgtn Teacher 1975- Sandusky Cty Schls; *ai:* Delta Kappa Gamma, OH Ed Assn, NEA; *office:* Hancock Sch 2314 Hancock Sandusky OH 44870

SCHRAG, ARNOLD LEE, 6th Grade Teacher; *b:* Hutchinson, KS; *ed:* (BA) Elem Ed, Sterling Coll 1975; *cr:* 6th Grade Teacher USD 352 1975-; *ai:* Timekeeping Colby Public Schls; Timekeeping Colby Comm Coll; Colby Teachers Assn; KS Sci Teachers Assn.

SCHRAMKA, LAWRENCE P., Social Studies Teacher; *b:* Chicago, IL; *m:* Carolyn J. Dintelman; *c:* Ryan D., Nathan K.; *ed:* (BSED) His, E IL Univ 1972; (MAT) His, SE MO St Univ 1977; *cr:* Jr HS Soc Stud Teacher Jonesboro Cmmty Cons Dist 43 1972-; *ai:* 8th Grade Class Spon; IL Cncl for Soc Stud, S IL Cncl for Soc Stud 1984-; Phi Alpha Theta 1971-; Anna Kiwanis Club 1983-; Anna 1st Baptist Church (Deacon, Chm 1977-, Trustee, Secy 1987-); *office:* Jonesboro Cmmty Cons Dist 43 PO Box 69 Cook St Jonesboro IL 62952

SCHRANZ, BONNIE SIMONTON, English/Journalism Teacher; *b:* Youngstown, OH; *m:* Paul R.; *c:* Jordon M., Justin P.; *ed:* (BSC) Speech Comm, 1969, (MA) Speech Comm, 1970 OH Univ; Eng, Media Stud, Governors St Univ; *cr:* Teacher Rich E HS 1970-75, Peotone HS 1976-; *ai:* Dir Fall Tour Show & Spring Musical; Devils Advocate, Thespians Spon; IL Theater Assn, IL Journalism Ed Assn; 1st Presbyn Church Choir Dir 1990; Peotone Womans Club Publicity Chairperson 1990; Potential Teacher Fellowship 1969; Talent Schlsp Governors St Univ 1978; Natl Endowment for Hum Shakespeare Fellowship 1984; Ed Newspaper 1978-; *office:* Peotone HS 1 Blue Devil Dr Peotone IL 60468

SCHRAUBEN, ALAN JAMES, Social Studies Teacher; *b:* Portland, MI; *m:* Karla Osborn; *c:* Adam, Kyle, Alex; *ed:* (BSED) Phys Ed, Cntrl MI Univ 1977; Grad Stud MI St Univ; *cr:* Jr HS Soc Stud Teacher 1979-87, HS Soc Stud Teacher 1988- Portland St Pats; *ai:* Frosh Class Adv; Var Girls Bsktbl & Var Boys Bsbl Coach; Bsktbl Coaches Assn of MI 1984-.

SCHRAUFNAGEL, PATRICIA LOUISE, 5th Grade Teacher; *b:* Ashland, WI; *m:* Stephen Gerald; *c:* Jessica, Blake, Jacob, Luke, Thomas; *ed:* (BS) Elem Ed, Coll of St Scholastica 1973; (MS) Rdng, Univ of WI Superior 1980; Grad Courses Univ of WI Superior, Northland Coll; *cr:* Chapter I Teacher Superior Public Schls 1976-81; Rdng Spec/Chapter I Teacher 1985-89, 5th Grade Teacher 1989- Mellen Sch; *ai:* Safety Patrol Coord; Lib Curr Comm; WI St Rdng Assn 1987-.

SCHRECKENGOST, FRANK JAMES, JR., Mathematics Teacher; *b:* Ypsilanti, MI; *m:* Judith Woolard; *ed:* (BA) Ed/Math, 1971, (MED) Ed Admin, 1977 Univ of WY; *cr:* Math Teacher 1971-77, Asst Prin 1977-79 Laramie Jr HS; Prin Rock River Sch 1979-83; Math Teacher Laramie Sr HS 1983-; *ai:* Head Track Coach; Head Math Dept; NEA, WEA 1971-; *home:* 10 Knoll Dr Laramie WY 82070

SCHREFFLER, PAMELA HICKS, Second Grade Teacher; *b:* Orlando, FL; *m:* Mike; *c:* Lindsey, Ty; *ed:* (BA) Elem Ed, 1977, (MA) Mental Retardation, 1982 Univ of Cntrl FL; *cr:* Teacher Altamonte Chrstn 1975-77, Longwood Elem 1977-; *ai:* Soc Comm; Sch Anthology; In Charge of Speakers for 2nd Grade; Semiole Cty Rdng Cncl; Schls Teacher of Yr; *office:* Longwood Elem Sch Orange Ave Longwood FL 32750

SCHREIDER, JAMES QUINT, Mathematics Teacher; *b:* Boston, MA; *m:* Judith Friedman; *c:* Lauren, Jill; *ed:* (BA) Math, 1972, (MED) Scndry Math Ed, 1973 Boston Univ; *cr:* Math Teacher Newton N HS 1972-; *ai:* SAT Achievement Test Coord; Fun with Math Presenter; NEA, MTA, NTA 1972-; Horace Mann Grant 1987, Newton Schools Fnd Awd Winner 1990; *office:* Newton North HS 360 Lowell Ave Newtonville MA 02160

SCHREITER, RHONDA REPPERT, Third Grade Teacher; *b:* Danville, PA; *m:* Barry Kevin; *c:* Ryan, Brielle, Brooke; *ed:* (BS) Elem, 1979, Rdng Specialist, 1983, (MS) Elem Ed, 1986 Mansfield Univ; *cr:* Adult Ed Teacher Danville St Hospital 1979; 3rd Grade Teacher Loyalsock Valley Elem 1979-; *home:* 725 4th Ave Williamsport PA 17701

SCHREMPH, HOWARD R., JR., Math Department Chairperson; *b:* Fulton, NY; *m:* Darice Van Wie; *c:* Kelly L.; *ed:* (BA) Psych, SUNY Potsdam 1974; Grad Hrs Various Colleges; *cr:* Teacher of Emotionaly Distrubed Rochester Mental Health Center 1974; Teacher Camden Mid Sch 1974-; *ai:* Prin Advisory & Prin Advisory Group Plus Submitted Application for Challenge Project for Excl Mid Level Ed; AMTOC 1990; *office:* Camden Mid Sch 32 Union St Camden NY 13316

SCHRIEFER, MICHAEL CARL, Mathematics Teacher; *b:* Tell City, IN; *m:* Mary Elizabeth; *c:* Matthew, Maria; *ed:* (BS) Math/Ed, 1972, (MS) Math/Ed, 1977 IN Univ; *cr:* Teacher Heritage Hills HS 1972-; *ai:* Jr HS Stu Cncl Spon; Asst Var Ftbl & Head 7th Grade Bsktbl Coach; North Spencer Ed Assn Pres 1975-77; IN Cncl Teachers of Math; Dale Park Bd; St Joseph Parish Cncl Pres 1984; St Joseph Maintenance & Finance Bd Chm 1989; Phi Delta Kappa Maintaining TeAcher Effectiveness; North Spencer Gifted & Talented Planning Grant Steering Comm Mem; *home:* RR 1 Box 321 Dale IN 47523

SCHROEDER, CAROL (STUDT), Mathematics Teacher; *b:* Chicago, IL; *m:* Dennis William; *c:* Elizabeth, Michael; *ed:* (BA) Math, NE IL Univ 1969; *cr:* Teacher Austin HS 1969-82, Hyde Park Career Acad 1982-; *ai:* Developed System to Monitor & Cncl Stu; *office:* Hyde Park Career Acad 6620 S Stony Island Chicago IL 60637

SCHROEDER, DAVE J., 7-8th Grade Soc Stud Dept Chm; *b:* Newton, KS; *M:* Marlene K. Wilkerson; *c:* Jeffrey; *ed:* (BS) His, Bethel Coll 1979; *cr:* 8th Grade His Teacher Union Valley Grade Sch 1979-80; 7th-8th Grade Soc Stud/His Teacher Prairie Hills Mid Sch 1980-; *ai:* Head Girls Vlybl Coach; Asst Track Coach; MC Rel Bldg Leadership; Team Leader; Soc Stud Dept Chm; Buhler Mennonik Church (Adult Sunday Sch Teacher 1989-; Ushers 1986-; Youth Comm 1987-89); Published Article KS Heritage Magazine Emporia St Univ 1989; *office:* Prairie Hills Mid Sch 3200 Lucille Dr Hutchinson KS 67502

SCHROEDER, EDWARD MARSHALL, English Department Chair; *b:* Granite City, IL; *m:* Ruth A. Thomas; *c:* Deidra Hughes, Neil; *ed:* (BA) Ger/Eng, S IL Univ Edwardsville 1963; Grad Work S IL Univ Edwardsville, Univ of MO St Louis; Project Teach Instr; *cr:* Eng/Ger Teacher Pekin Cmmty HS 1963-65, Granite City Cmmty HS 1965-66; Eng/Ger Teacher 1966-83, Eng/Gifted Teacher 1983-, Eng Dept Chairperson 1986- Coolidge Jr HS; *ai:* Dist Curr, Project Teach, Those Who Excel Comms; Adv Honors Prgm & Talent Show; ASCD, NCTE, Granite City Gifted Cncl, IL Teachers of Gifted Assn; Masonic Temple #877, Ainad Shrine, Scottish Rite Bodies, York Rite Bodies; Amer Cancer Society (Past Chm, Bd of Dir); Lewis & Clark Lung Assn (Past VP, Bd of Dir); Animal Protection Assn Bd of Dir; Granite City Public Lib Bd Pres; IL Distinguished Educator Awd 1988; Granite City Ambassadors Club Citizen Awd 1989; *home:* 1300 27th St Granite City IL 62040

SCHROEDER, GAIL LYNN, Third Grade Teacher; *b:* La Porte, IN; *c:* Jason, Jeremie, Jessica; *ed:* (BS) Elem Ed, 1972, (MS) Elem Ed, 1978 IN Univ South Bend; *cr:* 3rd Grade Teacher Olive Township Elem 1979-; *ai:* Soccer Coach; Spelling Bee Chm; Pres of Olive Twp Elem Building Cncl; NEA 1985-; IN St Teachers Assn 1985-; Ninety-Nines Inc Intnl Org of Women Pilots Vice-Chm 1986 Amelia Earhart Mem Schlsp 1989; LaPorte Aero Club Secy 1990; First United Meth Church Ministry Coord 1990; Private Pilot License with Instrument Rating; Aviation Ground Sch Instr HS Stu & Adults; Written Test Examinerfor Fed Aviation Admin; *home:* 2555 N 450 E Rolling Prairie IN 46371

SCHROEDER, GLENDA RENICK, Math/Computer Literacy Teacher; *b:* Kirkwood, MO; *m:* Raymond J.; *c:* Shannon, Stacey; *ed:* (AA) Pre-Math, E Cntrl Coll 1978; (BS) Math/Physics, SW MO St Univ 1980; (MAT) Math/Cmptr Ed, Webster Univ 1986; *cr:* Math/Cmptr Teacher Washington Jr HS 1980-; *ai:* WTA, MSTA 1980-; AAUW Treas 1986-; *office:* Washington Jr HS 401 E 14th St Washington MO 63090

SCHROEDER, JAMES ANTHONY, Mathematics/History Teacher; *b:* Jasper, IN; *m:* Donna Pfister; *c:* Kim, Evan, Kevin, Kurt, Keith; *ed:* (AS) Scndry Ed, Vincennes Univ 1967; (BS) Math/Soc Stud, 1969, (MS) Math/Soc Stud, 1973 IN St; *cr:* Teacher NE Dubois Cty Schls 1969-; *home:* 189 Meridian Rd Jasper IN 47546

SCHROEDER, JANICE ELLENBERGER, Language Arts Teacher/Chair; *b:* Windber, PA; *c:* Carla Schroeder Hiob; *ed:* (BA) Eng, Otterbein Coll 1958; (MA) Ed, Pepperdine Univ 1976; *cr:* Teacher Worthington Jr HS 1958-61, Wyoming Jr HS 1961-63; Teacher/Chairperson Laton HS 1963-66, Pomolita Jr HS 1966-67, Rea Jr HS 1967-81, Te Winkle Jr HS 1981-; *ai:* Site Improvement Prgm, Teacher Credential, Assignment Coord; Master Teacher; CA Teachers Assn, Natl Teachers Assn 1967-; United Meth Church (Lay Leader 1985-88, Lay Speaker 1985-); Mentor Teacher; *home:* 3139 Sumatra Pl Costa Mesa CA 92626

SCHROEDER, JUNE FAULK, 8th Grade Eng Teacher; *b:* Samson, AL; *m:* Gene Mc Donald; *c:* Traci Schroeder Simpson, Vikki A., Gene M. II, *ed:* (BS) Elem Ed/Eng, 1971, (MS) Elem Ed, 1972 Troy St Univ; *cr:* 2nd Grade Teacher Robinson Springs

Elem 1959-60; 5th Grade Teacher Stringer Elem 1968-69; 6th-8th Grade Teacher D A Smith Mid Sch 1971-; *ai:* NEA, AL Ed Assn, Ozark Ed Assn 1971-; NCTE 1985-88; Pres of Troy St Univ Grad Sch 1971-72; Stu/Faculty Grad Sch Rep 1971-72; *home:* 202 Shadow Ln Troy AL 36081

SCHROEDER, MARY ELIZABETH, Biology Instructor; *b:* Dubuque, IA; *ed:* (BS) Health/Phys Ed/Recreation, Briar Cliff Coll 1981; *cr:* Bio Teacher Wakefield Cmmty Sch 1981-85, Hartington Cedar Cath 1985-; *ai:* Head Vlybl Coach Hartington Cedar Cath; Asst Bsktbl Coach; NCEA 1985-89; NE Ed Assn 1981-85; USA Today Achviever of Yr-Coaching Category 1989; Mary Schroeder Vlybl Schlsp Briar Cliff Coll; *office:* Hartington Cedar Cath HS 401 S Broadway Hartington NE 68739

SCHROEDER, MARY MC DOUGAL, 5th Grade Teacher; *b:* Salem, IL; *m:* David Harrison; *c:* Jonathan; *ed:* (BA) Elem Ed 1976; (MS) Elem Ed 1978 Northern IL Univ; Gifted Ed/Lang Arts; *cr:* 1st-5th Grade Teacher IL Park Sch 1976-87; 5th Grade Teacher Eastview Elem Sch 1987-; *ai:* Rainbows Group Leader; Gifted Teacher; Jr Great Books; Playground Supervisor; Aerobics Instr; ETA Sch Rep 1976-; IEA 1976-; NEA 1976-; Newcomers Club 1989-; Parent/Teachers of Eastview 1987-89; Northern ILlinois Rdng Cncl 1987-; Fellowship Prgm; *office:* Eastview Elem Sch 321 North Oak St Bartlett IL 60103

SCHROEDER, MAXINE A. (PASCHEN), 1st & 2nd Grade Teacher; *b:* Staunton, IL; *m:* Gary E.; *c:* James, Linda; *ed:* (BS) Elem Ed, Concordia Coll 1962; *cr:* 1st/2nd Grade Teacher Faith Luth Sch 1962-67; Kndgtn Teacher Immanuel Luth 1967-68; 1st/2nd Grade Teacher Clover Trinity Luth 1976-85, 1989-; *ai:* Church Organist; Adult & Youth Chime Choir Dir; 1st-8th Grade Musicals Music Dir; Bethel Bible Teacher; ID Cncl IRA 1989-; LWML 1968-76; Good Shepherd Auxiliary Project Chm 1985-89; Luth HS Assn Treas 1978-83; *home:* 1364A E 3500 N Buhl ID 83316

SCHROEDER, ROSE STURDEVANT, Kindergarten Teacher; *b:* Wellsville, NY; *m:* Michael; *c:* Aaron P., Nathan K.; *ed:* (BS) Elem Ed, Mansfield Univ 1974; Addl Studies Elem Ed Alfred Univ 1979; *cr:* 4th Grade Teacher Belmont Central Sch 1974-76; 4th Grade Teacher 1976-89; Kndgtn 1989- Scio Central Sch; *ai:* Ski Club Adv; Asst Girls & Boys Track Coach; Scio Teachers Assn VP 1987-; Kanakadea Rdng Cncl Mem 1986-; *office:* Scio Central Sch S Washington St Scio NY 14880

SCHROER, MICHAEL ALLEN, Science Teacher/Biology Instr; *b:* Kansas City, MO; *m:* Linda Marie R.; *c:* Julie, Amy, Robert; *ed:* Bio, Univ of MO Columbia 1966; (MA) Bio/Educl Admin, 1977, (EDS) Educl Admin/Curr, 1980-Univ of MO Kansas City; *cr:* Sci Teacher Raytown JR HS 1966-68, Raytown S Mid Sch 1972-; Bio Instr Longview Comm Coll 1989-; *ai:* NCTA, Raytown Cmmty Teachers Assn, MO ST Teachers Assn 1966-; BSA Cubmaster 1988-; Blue Ridge Presbyn Elder 1980-; *office:* Raytown S Mid Sch 8401 E 83rd Raytown MO 64133

SCHROLL, BEVERLY LOHR, English Teacher; *b:* Mt Pleasant, PA; *m:* Carl Jacob Jr.; *c:* Jamey B., Carl J. III; *ed:* (BA) Ed, Alderson Broaddus Coll 1971; Grad Stud Univ of Pittsburgh, PA Univ; *cr:* Eng Instr Mt Pleasant Area Sch Dist 1971-; *ai:* Stu SADD Chapter Spon; Commencement Speakers Adv; PSEA, NEA 1971-; *office:* Mt Pleasant Scndry Facility RD 4 Mount Pleasant PA 15666

SCHRUPP, THOMAS DANA, 9th Grade Phys Ed Teacher; *b:* Glasgow, MT; *m:* Ann Robertson; *c:* Kim, Amy, Tracy; *ed:* (BS) Phys Ed, MT St Univ 1976; *cr:* Phys Ed Teacher Campbell Cty Schls 1976-; *ai:* HS Ftbl Assn Defensive Coord; HS Girls Bsktbl Asst Coach; *home:* 3501 Crestline Gillette WY 82716

SCHUBERT, BARBARA EMILY, 5th Grade Teacher; *b:* Bay Shore, NY; *ed:* (BA) Elem Ed, SUNY Plattsburgh 1969; (MA) Elem Ed, SUNY Stony Brook 1974; Grad Work; *cr:* 5th Grade Teacher 1969-74, 4th Grade Teacher 1974-88, 5th Grade Teacher 1988- Merrimac Elem Sch; *home:* 196 Cambridge Dr Port Jefferson Sta NY 11776

SCHUBERT, BLYTHE GALLAWAY, English Teacher; *b:* Elizabeth, NJ; *m:* Robert L. II; *c:* Rod, Amy; *ed:* (BA) Eng, Denison Univ 1968/Oberlin Coll 1964-66; Kent St Univ/OH Univ Marietta Coll; *cr:* Instr Adult Basic Ed Mid East OH Joint Voc Sch 1979-86; Teacher Morgan HS 1977-; *ai:* Volunteer Writing Tutor; Basic Ed Classes; Morgan Literacy Tutor; Morgan Local Ed Assn 1974-; Chesterhill Meth Church; Childrens Conservation Club 1974-; Martha Holding Jennings Scholar; Steering Comm Co-Chairperson for North Cntrl Evaluation Team; Valedictorian Choice for Educator of Yr; *office:* Morgan H S 800 Raider Dr Mc Connelsville OH 43756

SCHUEDER, JEAN, 4th Grade Teacher; *b:* Aurelia, IA; *m:* Jack; *c:* Michael, Tom, Cindy Koenig, MiChele Nutty; *ed:* (BA) Elem, Buena Vista Coll 1973; Affective & Gifted Ed, Teaching Strategies; *cr:* Elem Teacher O Brien Cty Cntry Sch 1952-53; 2nd Grade Teacher 1969-70, 5th Grade Teacher 1971-76 Spalding Elem; 6th Grade Teacher Sutherland Elem 1976-77; 4th Grade Teacher Spalding Elem 1978-; *ai:* Head Teacher; St Anns Church Guild Pres 1965, 1983; Natl Campers & Hikers Field Dirs 1979-; Calumet Betterment Cncl Pres 1987; *home:* 107 N Morse Calumet IA 51009

SCHUELER, MARIA CAVALIERI, French Teacher; *b:* Bridgeport, CT; *m:* Richard Joseph; *c:* Christopher, Keith; *ed:* (BS) Fr/Scndry Ed, 1968, Foreign Lang, 1977 S CT St; Alliance Francaise Paris 1969; Design for Effective Instruction Prgm 1989; Working Towards Span Cert; *cr:* Fr Teacher Stratford HS 1968-69, Johnson Jr HS 1970-79; Fr/Eng Teacher Wooster Jr HS 1980-81; Fr Teacher Stratford HS 1981-82, 1984-, Bunnell HS 1982-84 /1989-; *ai:* Societe Honoraire de Francais; Ct Cncl of Lang Teachers, Amer Assn Teachers of Fr, Stratford Ed Assn, Ct Ed Assn, NEA; Cath Guild, PTA; *home:* 663 Broadview Rd Orange CT 06477

SCHUELER, MARY ELLEN BECKMAN, Gifted Resource Teacher; *b:* Dieterich, IL; *m:* Dennis R.; *c:* Cheryl Baran, Lisa Baran; *ed:* (BA) Ed/His, Loyola Univ 1974; (MED) Gifted Ed, Natl Coll of Ed 1978; Critical Thinking, Math Problem Solving, Methods for Teaching Gifted Children; *cr:* Primary Teacher Sch Dist #30 1959-60; 2nd Grade Teacher St Ferdinands Sch 1960-62; 3rd Grade Teacher High Ridge Knolls 1974-76; 1st Grade Teacher Brentwood Sch 1976-84; Gifted Resource Teacher Devonshire Sch 1984-; *ai:* Organize & Coach After Sch Academic Club; Conduct Dist & Classroom Model Teaching Demonstrations; Phi Delta Kappa 1987-; ASCD; Nom Golden Apple Awd by Fnd for Excl in Teaching; *office:* Devonshire Sch Dist 59 1401 S Pennsylvania Ave Des Plaines IL 60018

SCHUESLER, MARY M., Science/Math Teacher; *b:* Spring Glenn, UT; *m:* John Richard; *c:* John T., Janet S., Jeffrey M.; *ed:* (BA) Phys Sci, CA St Univ Fresno 1949; (MA) Ed, Pepperdine Univ 1975; Service Credential Admin, 1982; Sci Ed, UCI Irvine 1985-87; Curr Dev, Fresno Pacific Coll 1986-88; Doctoral Candidate, Pepperdine Univ 1990; *cr:* 3rd Grade Teacher Pershing Sch 1949-51; 4th/7th Grade Teacher Fairmead Sch 1951-53; 6th Grade Teacher Del Monte Sch 1953-54; 4th/6th Grade Teacher US Dependent Schls Japan 1954-55; 5th Grade Teacher Indianapolis City Sch Dist 1955-57; Kndgtn Teacher Indianapolis City Sch 22 1961-64; 7th/8th Sci/Math Teacher Marine View Sch 1968-; *ai:* Wkshp Teacher UCI Irvine Summer Sci Inst; Ocean View Sch Dist Admin, Natl Sci Fnd Mentor Teacher; Sci Fair, CTIIP/AB803 Grants Coord; Drama, Stu Cncl, Stu Academic Competition, Chrldr, Environmental Ed, Sch Dances, Athletic Events Spon; Curr Coord; NHS; NEA, CA Teachers Assn 1975-; NSTA 1986-; Orange Cty Sci & Engineering Fair Bd Pres 1978-; CA St Sci Fair Advisory Bd Judge Coord 1976-84; Teacher Educl Cmptr Center Policy Bd Mem 1983-84; Museum of Natural Sci (Mem, Bd of Dir) 1982-84; Bird Migrations Grant; Outdoor Ed; HS Salutatorian; Outstanding Teacher Awd Orange Cty Sci Fair; AIMS Integrated Math & Sci Books Writer; Amer Learning Corporation Writer.

SCHUETT, ARTHUR GEORGE, Social Science Teacher; *b:* Oak Park, IL; *m:* Crystal K.; *c:* Kurt, Kenneth; *ed:* (BA) Ger, His, IL St Univ 1969; (MA) Ger, Univ of IL 1974; (MA) Sch Admin, Roosevelt Univ 1979; Span Coll of Du Page; Ed Lewis Univ; Ger Goethe Inst; *cr:* Instr Morton Coll 1971-1984; Morton HS 1969-; *ai:* Ftbl; Track; Ger Club; Model United Nation Club; Martial Arts Club; Weight Lifting Club; Ed Cncl; AATG 1969-; NCSS 1984-; ASCD 1988-; LA Grange Park Fire Dept Firemen/Paramedic 1980-; Outstanding Young Men Amer; *office:* J Sterling Morton East HS 2423 S Austin Blvd Cicero IL 60650

SCHUETTE, RICHARD C., 4th Grade Teacher; *b:* Staunton, IL; *m:* Kay Korte; *c:* Thomas R., Daniel G.; *ed:* (BS) Elem Ed, S IL Univ 1975; *cr:* 4th-6th Grade Sci/Health Teacher Muddy Sch 1975-76; 4th Grade Teacher Marine Grade Sch 1976-; *ai:* Bsktbl & Vlybl Coach; Optimist Club Schlsp Chm 1983-; *office:* Marine Grade Sch W Division St Marine IL 62061

SCHUETZ, ALAN LEE, 5th-8th Grade Science Teacher; *b:* Somerville, NJ; *m:* Eileen Bentz; *c:* Alan, Michael, Karen, Jennifer; *ed:* (BS) Horticulture, Delaware Valley Coll Sci & Ag 1970; Trenton St Coll; *cr:* Sci Teacher Califon Public Sch 1970-; *ai:* 8th Grade Adv; Bsktbl Coach; Teacher in Charge; Right to Know Comm; Califon Teacher Assn Pres 1989-; NEA, NJEA, HCEA; Elks; Califon PTA; High Bridge PTO; Calfion Teacher of Yr 1988; *home:* 51 Thomas St High Bridge NJ 08829

SCHUG, JOHN RUSSELL, English Teacher; *b:* Easton, PA; *m:* Jeanne Marsh Krause; *c:* Jonathan, Adam, Noah; *ed:* (AB) Eng, Muhlenberg Coll 1952; Eng, Lehigh Univ; *cr:* Grad Asst Lehigh Univ 1953-55, 1957-58; Teacher Lancaster Cntry Day Sch 1958-62, William Penn Charter Sch 1962-; *office:* William Penn Charter Sch 3000 Schoolhouse Ln Philadelphia PA 19144

SCHUG, MAUREEN DALY, 6th-8th Grade Teacher; *b:* Greenwich, CT; *m:* Alan; *c:* Julie, Susan, Lori, Meredith, Stephen, Elizabeth, Michael; *ed:* (BA) Soc Stud, Niagara Univ 1970; Drug & Alcohol Intervention Trng with Cmmty Intervention 1989; *cr:* ESP Rdng/Eng/Religion/Soc Teacher Stella Niagara Ed Park 1974-; *ai:* We-Can Public Relations 1986-89; Renew Diocese of Buffalo Small Group Coord 1986-88; *office:* Stella Niagara Ed Park Sch 4421 Lower River Rd Stella Niagara NY 14144

SCHULER, JANET KAY (ROSSON), Elementary Vocal Music Teacher; *b:* Tulsa, OK; *m:* Richard D.; *c:* Cindy Schuler Brown, Michael D., Julie Schuler Williams; *ed:* (BME) Music, OK St Univ 1966; Many Seminars & Wkshps in Music; *cr:* 1st-12th Grade Teacher Harper Schls 1966-68; 1st-6th Grade Teacher Unified Sch Dist 443 1968-; *ai:* MENC 1966-72, 1988-; Prof Educators of KS; Dodge City Educators Chairperson 1987-; Sweet Adelines Dir 1971-, Sweet Adeline of Yr; PTA 1966-, Life Membership Awd; Elem Music Teacher of Dodge City Chm; *office:* Lincoln Sch 613 W Cedar Dodge City KS 67801

SCHULTHEIS, EUGENE RICHARD, Teacher; *b:* Ransom, PA; *m:* Eleanor Marshalek; *c:* Daniel; *ed:* (BS) Math, Bloomsburg Univ 1956; Masters Equivalency Ed, PA Dept of Ed 1966; Univ of Scranton, Lehigh Univ, Marywood Coll, Wilkes Coll, E Stroudsburg Coll; *cr:* Teacher Abington Heights Sch Dist 1956-; *ai:* Sch Locker Assignments; NCTM 1971-; PA Cncl Teachers of Math 1987-; NEA, PA St Ed Assn 1956-; Abington Heights Ed Assn Past Pres; Lehigh Univ Natl Sci Fnd Schlsp 1967-68; Elected Township Auditor; *home:* 1322 Gravel Pond Rd Clarks Summit PA 18411

SCHULTHEISS, KAREN, Teacher and Coach; *b:* Topeka, KS; *ed:* (AA) Teacher Ed, Independence Comm Coll 1973; (BS) Health/Phys Ed, KS St Univ 1975; (MS) Phys Ed, Pittsburg St Univ 1988; Health Ed; *cr:* Teacher/Coach Caney Valley Jr Sr HS 1975-; Teacher Coffeyville Comm Coll 1989-; *ai:* 7th Grade Class; Girls Athletic Assn; Fellowship of Chrstn Athletes; Coaching Jr Hs Girls Bsktbl; Head Track Coach Jr-Sr HS; Core Team Drug Awareness & Prevention 1986-; Caney Valley Teachers Assn Schlsp Comm 1975-; NEA 1971-; Delta Psi Kappa 1973-; Natl Fed of Intercollegiate Athletics 1975-; Fellowship of Chrstn Athletes-Spon 1985-; Red Cross Instr 1975-76; Outstanding Young Women of America 1988; *home:* Rt 1 Box 295 Caney KS 67333

SCHULTZ, ANDREW NATHAN, 6th-8th Grade Teacher; *b:* Porterville, CA; *m:* Yolanda Ilene Tritch; *c:* Ashlee, Aaron, Alexander; *ed:* (AA) General Ed, Porterville Jr Coll 1972; (BA) Liberal Stud, CA St Univ Chico 1974; (MA) Educl Admin, CA St Univ Bakersfield 1990; *cr:* 4th-8th Grade Teacher St Isidors 1976; 5th-8th Grade Teacher 1976-89, 6th-8th Grade Teacher/Vice Prin 1989 Rockford Elem Sch; Summer Sch Teacher/Migrant Prgm Porterville & Terra Bella Schls 1980-; *ai:* Rockford Sch Athletic Dir; Haloween Carnival Chm; Zion Luth Church Life Mem; Zion Luth Sch Bd Mem 1978-82; Rockford Sch Mentor Teacher; Porterville Jaycees Teacher of Yr 1988; *office:* Rockford Elem Sch 14983 RD 208 Porterville CA 93257

SCHULTZ, DARLENE LINDSETH, Third Grade Teacher; *b:* Bemidji, MN; *m:* Howard Charles; *ed:* (BA) Elem Ed, Bemidji St Univ 1962; Elem Ed; *cr:* 4th Grade Teacher Bagley Elem Sch 1962-64; 2nd Grade Teacher Bemidji St Univ Lab Sch 1964-66; Title V/Adults Teacher Bemidji Dist 31 1966-67; 4th/5th Grade Teacher 1967-69, 4th Grade Teacher 1969-87, 3rd Grade Teacher 1987- Northern Elem; *ai:* Delta Kappa Gamma Secy 1987-89; Salem Luth Church Choir Dir 1980-; 4-H Co-Leader 1967-69; *home:* 12932 Wildwood Rd NE Bemidji MN 56601

SCHULTZ, DIANE OBERSHEIMER, English Teacher; *b:* Buffalo, NY; *m:* David; *c:* Eric, Andrew; *ed:* (BA) Eng, Dickinson Coll 1968; (MS) Ed, Buffalo St Coll 1982; *cr:* Eng Teacher Hamburg Jr HS 1968-; *ai:* Literary Magazine; Whole Lang Resource Team; Hamburg Fredonia Liaison; Phi Delta Kappa; WNY Writers Project; Hamburg Service Awd; *office:* Hamburg Jr HS 360 Division St Hamburg NY 14075

SCHULTZ, FRANK A., Social Studies Teacher; *b:* Orlando, FL; *m:* Linda Jean French; *c:* Erica J.; *ed:* (BA) His, Sch of the Ozarks 1968; (MA) His, SE MO St 1973; Grad Stud in Soc Stud & Ed; *cr:* Teacher Hillsboro HS 1968-; *ai:* Gate Worker Dist Blue Ribbon; Act & Curr Comm; Track Starter-Official; NEA 1984-; NCSS 1986-; MO Historical Society 1984-; Optimist Club VP 1989; Civic Club; Hillsboro Planning & Zoning; Natl Endowment Hum Naval War Coll 1984; Taft Inst for Government; Denver Univ Sociology Forum 1976; *home:* 43 Pearl Dr Hillsboro MO 63050

SCHULTZ, GEOFFREY ALLEN, Jr/Sr HS Band Teacher; *b:* Oskaloosa, IA; *ed:* (BA/BM) Music Ed, Simpson Coll 1974; (MA) Music Ed, NE MO St 1987; *cr:* 4th-6th Grade Vocal/7th-12th Grade Band Instr Knoxville Cmmty Schls 1974-; Choir Dir 1st United Meth Church 1976-; *ai:* Wedding Accompanist; Percussive Arts Society Mem 1983-; *office:* Knoxville Cmmty Schls 308 W Marion Knoxville IA 50138

SCHULTZ, GERALD LEE, Industrial Technology Teacher; *b:* Fort Dodge, IA; *m:* Jean A. Ransom; *c:* Jesse J., Jeremy L.; *ed:* (BA) Industrial Arts Ed, Univ of Northern IA 1971; Vocational Ed, IA St Univ; *cr:* Teacher Roosevelt Mid Sch 1971-; *ai:* 7th-8th Grade Boys & Girls Track & Fld Coach; 6th Grade Boys Intermural Bsktbl; Odyssey of the Mind Coach; Industrial Technology Club; IA Industrial Technology Ed Assn; Natl Industrial Technology Ed Assn; Christ Church Presbyn Deacon 1988-; Presentor Mid Sch Industrial Technology Curr St Convention 1988; *office:* Theodore Roosevelt Mid Sch 300 13th St Nw Cedar Rapids IA 52405

SCHULTZ, GREG WYNNE, History/Speech/Comm Teacher; *b:* Spokane, WA; *m:* Cheryl Ann Esser; *c:* Garrett W., Ashleigh P.; *ed:* (BA) His/Speech, 1975, (MED) Ed, 1977 Gonzaga Univ; (MA) His, Univ of WA 1982; *cr:* Teacher/Coach St Josephs Elem 1975, All Saints Mid Sch 1975-76, Medford HS 1976-79, Mead HS 1979-; *ai:* Asst Ftbl Coach; WA St Coaches Assn 1980-; Natl Forensic League Dist Chm 1977-, Double Diamond Key 1984; WA St Debate Coaches Assn VP 1979-85, Local Coach of Yr 1981, 1983; *office:* Mead HS 302 W Hastings Rd Spokane WA 99218

SCHULTZ, JEANNE DEMICK, Principal; *b:* Pittsfield, MA; *m:* Frank L.; *c:* Ethan J. Coulson, Aaron L. Coulson, Seth F.; *ed:* (BS) Ed Elem, St Univ Coll Oneonta 1969; (MS) Ed Counseling, Univ of S CA 1979; Admin, N Adams St Coll 1990; Numerous Classes; *cr:* Adult Ed Instr Army Ed Center 1970-72, Big Bend Comm Coll Baumholder Germany 1977-79; Elem Teacher Berlin Cntrl Sch Dist 1979-87; Prin Berlin Elem Sch 1987-; *ai:* Berlin PTO, Playground Comm Active Mem; 4-H Leader; NY St Rdng Assn 1988-; Berlin Cntrl Sch Dist (Planning Comm, Chairperson of Nominating Comm) 1989-; Teacher Center Grant 1986; *office:* Berlin Elem Sch Box 259 School St Berlin NY 12040

SCHULTZ, JUDITH ANN, 5th Grade Teacher; *b:* Wisconsin Rapids, WI; *ed:* (BS) Elem Ed, UW Eau Claire 1971; *cr:* 3rd Grade Teacher West Ridge Elem 1971-1972; 5th Grade Teacher McKinley Elem 1972-1981: 5th Grade Teacher Gifford Elem 1981-; *ai:* Cmptr Sch Comm Volunteer 5th Grade Camp; Amer Assn Univ Women 1984-; *office:* Gifford Elem Sch 8332 Northwestern Ave Racine WI 53406

SCHULTZ, KAREN (WHITNEY), 6th Grade Teacher; *b:* Waupaca, WI; *m:* Russell D.; *c:* Janette, Joyce Singer; *ed:* Teaching Cert Waushara Cty Teachers Coll 1960; (BS) Ed, Univ of WI Stevens Point 1972; *cr:* Teacher Elm Valley Sch 1960-61, Forest Lane Elem Sch 1964-; *ai:* Town of Douglas Clerk 1980-87; *office:* Montello Schls 222 Forest Ln Montello WI 53949

SCHULTZ, NANCY E., 5th Grade Teacher; *b:* Chicago, IL; *m:* Gary; *c:* David, Cindy; *ed:* (AB) His, Loyola Univ of Chicago 1973; (MA) Rdng, NE IL Univ 1989; *cr:* 5th Grade Teacher/Asst Prin St Viator Sch 1978-; *office:* St Viator Sch 4140 W Addison St Chicago IL 60641

SCHULTZ, RONALD MATTHEW, Science Department Chairman; *b:* Hanover, IL; *m:* Janice Marie Erickson; *c:* Jon M., Kirk M., Jason M., Kristin M.; *ed:* (BA) Life Sci/Bio, Luther Coll 1965; (MA) Life Sci/Bio, Univ of WI Platteville 1976; Grad Stud Univ of WI PlattevilLe, Univ of WI Green Bay; *cr:* Life Sci Instr Cuba City Public Schls 1965-; Sci Instr Univ of WI Platteville 1988-; *ai:* Track Clerk of Course Home Meets 1979-; Class, Prom, Trip Adv 1966-; Head Wrestling Coach 1967-; Asst Ftbl 1965-, Asst Track 1965, 1974, 1976, Coach; Tournament Mgr Conference & Regional Wrestling; Sci Dept Head; Bio Club 1978-; WI Interscholastic Athletic Assn (Ofcl 1981-86, Bd of Cntrl Wrestling Ofcl 1983-86); US Wrestling Fed SW Chm 1976; NABT 1976; SWEA (Legislative Comm, CC Delegate 1981-85, 1987-89) 1976-; NSA (Delegate 1981-85) 1976-; WEA (CC Delegate 1981-85) 1976-; Lions Club 1974-85; Church Cncl 1974-77, 1987-89; Cub Scouts (Cubmaster 1975-85, 1987-88), Bridge Builder Awd 1987; Governor Appointee N Cntrl Regional Ed Lab 1984; WI St Advisory Cncl; Elected to Bd of Dir NCREL 1990; Certificate of Commendation Governor of WI 1989, NSA Pres 1985, SWEA Pres 1981; *office:* Cuba City Public Schls 101 N School St Cuba City WI 53807

SCHULTZ, WARREN THOMAS, Assistant Principal; *b:* Brooklyn, NY; *m:* Ruth; *c:* Richard, James; *ed:* (BA) His, Queens Coll 1966; (MS) Elem Ed/Curr, St Johns Univ 1972; Admin & Supervision, Queens Coll 1984; *cr:* Teacher P S 123 Queens 1966-77, P S 90 Queens 1977-88; Asst Prin P S 56 Queens 1988-; *ai:* Instr of Graduate Level Courses for Teachers; Fall Semester Art Experiences for Young Children New Rochelle Coll; Spring Semester Art Across the Curr Brooklyn Coll & Wkshps in Childrens Art for Teachers of Dist 27 Queens; Outstanding Teacher of Yr 1986 NY Alliance of Public Schls; *home:* 422 Lumur Dr, Sayville New York NY 11782

SCHULZ, JANICE COX, 5th Grade Teacher; *b:* Great Falls, MT; *m:* Steven; *ed:* (BS) Elem Ed, MT St Univ 1966; (BA) Soc Sci, CA Univ 1970; *cr:* Teacher Amy Blanc Sch 1966-68; Stewardess Seaboard Airlines 1968-69; Substitute Teacher Los Altos, Fairfield & Amy Blanc 1970-75; Teacher Amy Blanc 1978-; *ai:* Yr Around Sch Track Leader; Teacher-In-Charge; Curr & Lib Selection Comms; Phi Delta Kappa 1979-; *office:* Amy Blanc Sch 230 Atlantic Ave Fairfield CA 94533

SCHULZE, HOWARD DEAN, Science Department Chair; *b:* Buckeye, TX; *m:* Martha Gliddon; *c:* Cristopher, Todd; *ed:* (BS) Bio/Ed, 1950, (MA) Ed/Bio, 1957 SW TX St Univ; *cr:* Mid Sch His Teacher Edcouch-Elsa Ind Sch Dist 1950; HS Eng Teacher Calallen Ind Sch Dist 1952; HS Sci Teacher San Marcos Acad 1952-56; US Army 1950-52, 1957-85; HS Sci Teacher Acad Ind Sch Dist 1986-; *ai:* Sci & Class Spon; Textbook Selection & Schlsp Comm; Associated Chem Teachers of TX, Chem Teachers Assn of TX 1989-; Sci Teacher Assn of TX 1990; *office:* Acad HS Rt 2 Temple TX 76502

SCHULZE, LESA A., 5-6 Grade Soc Stud Teacher; *b:* Abilene, TX; *M:* Ronald C.; *c:* Corrie J., Mindy J.; *ed:* (AA) Cicsco Jr Coll 1967; (BS) Elem Ed, Tarleton St Univ 1969; Robert a Taft Institute of Govt Abilene Christian Univ; *cr:* 2nd Grade Teacher Godley ISD 1970-73, 2nd/3rd Grade Teacher Gorden ISD 1973-74; 5th/6th Grade Soc Stud Teacher San Saba ISD 1974-; *ai:* UILL Dictionary Skills; Taft Seminar for Teachers-Grant.

SCHULZE, RONALD C., Social Studies Teacher/Coach; *b:* Fredricksburg, TX; *m:* Lesa A. Self; *c:* Corrie J., Mindy J.; *ed:* (BA) His, Tarleton St Univ 1971; *cr:* Teacher/Coach San Saba HS 1977-; *ai:* 8th Grade Ftbl, 7th & 8th Grade Boys Bsktbl, 7th & 8th Grade Var Boys & Girls Golf Coach; Textbook Comm; Effective Sch Campus Rep; Jr HS Athletic Dir; Jr HS Soc Stud Chairperson; TX HS Coaches Assn 1977-; TX HS Golf Coaches Assn 1988-; Assn of TX Prof Educators; TX St Hostorical Assn 1987-; Taft Inst of Teachers Assoc Mem 1988-; 7 Times Dist Jr HS Ftbl Champions; 3 Champions in Bsktbl; Var Boys Golf Regional Qualifers 1979-, Dist, Regional & St Championships; Girls Golf Regional Qualifers 1979-, Dist & Regional Championships & St Qualifiers; *office:* San Saba Jr HS 601 W Storey San Saba TX 76877

SCHULZE, SHIRLEY GAIL, Business Teacher; *b:* Floresville, TX; *ed:* (BA) Bus Composite, TX Luth Coll 1978; *cr:* Teacher Randolph HS 1978-; *ai:* Jr Class Adv; UIL Typing & Accounting Teams; Assn of TX Prof Educators (Pres 1985, Mem 1978-); Nom TX Excl Awd 1989; Teacher of Month 1989; Finalist N San Antonio Chamber of Commerce Key Educator 1988.

SCHUMACHER, BETH ANN, Soc Stud Teacher & Dept Chair; *b:* Des Moines, IA; *m:* Mark; *c:* Abigail; *ed:* (BA) His/Poly Sci, 1976, (MA) HS, 1985 Univ of Northern IA; Grad Work Eng & Sociology Univ of IA; *cr:* Soc Stud/Eng Teacher Clarence-Lowden HS 1977-79, Southeast Polk HS 1979-80; Eng/ESL Teacher 1980-85, Soc Stud Teacher/Dept Chairperson 1985- Clear Lake HS; *ai:* Mock Trial & Quiz Bowl Coach; Model United Nations & NHS Adv; Chairperson Staff Dev, K-12th Grade Soc Stud Curr, Sch Improvement Comm; Phi Alpha Theta 1975-; NCSS, ASCD 1985-; OR-CA Trails Assn, Spinal Bifida Assn of IA 1985-; Order of Eastern Star 1973-; Book Published 1976; Thesis Published 1985; Law Related Ed Curr Published Through ERIC 1990; *office:* Clear Lake HS 125 N 20th St Clear Lake IA 50428

SCHUSTER, BARBARA ENTERS, 6th Grade Teacher; *b:* Oconomowoc, WI; *c:* Mary, Kathryn, Patrick, Margaret; *ed:* (BA) Elem Ed/Sociology, U of W-Milwaukee 1973; Quest Prgm; *cr:* 6th Grade Teacher Summit Sch 1973-; *ai:* Dist Soc Stud Comm; NEA; WEA; *office:* Summit Sch 36316 Valley Rd Oconomowoc WI 53066

SCHUSTER, JOHN PAUL, Athletic Director/Math Teacher; *b:* Corpus Christi, TX; *m:* Glenda Ann Watson; *c:* John M.; *ed:* (BA) Math, Union Univ 1978; (MDIV) Pastoral Care, S Baptist Theological Seminary 1982; *cr:* Math Teacher Howardville Mid Sch 1978-79; Scndry Math Teacher 1980-, Athletic Dir 1985- Ninth & O Baptist Acad; *ai:* Var Soccer & Bsktbl Coach; Natl Interscholastic Athletic Admin Assn 1985-; *office:* Ninth & O Baptist Acad 2921 Taylor Blvd Louisville KY 40208

SCHUSTER, LORY ZEIDEL, 4th Grade Teacher; *b:* Brooklyn, NY; *m:* Arnie; *c:* David, Robert, Lori, Lessette; *ed:* (BA) Early Chldhd-Magna Cum Laude, Newark St Coll 1972; (MA) Guidance & Counseling/Sch Social Work/Summa Cum Laude, Kean Coll 1982; Post Masters Studies Admin & Supervision; *cr:* Teacher Elmora Sch 12 1972- ; *ai:* NJ Ed Assn 1972- ; Elizabeth Ed Assn 1972-; NEA 1972-; Jewish Family Services Bd of Dir 1989-; Union Cty Volunteer Probation Officer 1980-82; Natl Honor Society; Phi Beta Kappa; *home:* 301 Elizabeth Ave Cranford NJ 07016

SCHUTT, MICHELE CAMILLE, 3rd Grade Teacher; *b:* Pontiac, MI; *ed:* (BS) Elem Ed, N MI Univ 1965; *cr:* 2nd Grade Teacher Attleboro MA 1966-68; 3rd-4th Grade Teacher Bahia Brazil 1968-70; 2nd-5th Grade Teacher Los Angeles CA 1970-; *ai:* Co-Chairperson Shared Decision Cncl; NEA 1970-; United Teacher of Los Angeles (House of Rep, Chapter Chairperson); *office:* Heliotrope Elem Sch 5911 Woodlawn Ave Maywood CA 90270

SCHWAB, NANCY ANN, First Grade Teacher; *b:* Chicago, IL; *ed:* (BED) Primary Ed, Chicago Teachers Coll 1955; (MED) Admin & Supervision, Loyola Univ 1961; *cr:* Teacher Chicago Public Schls 1955-56; 1st Grade Teacher Nathan Hale Sch 1956-; *ai:* Head Teacher & Lead Teacher of Primary Dept; Book Selection Comm; Prof Problems Comm; Chicago Teachers Union Delegate 1985-87; Local Sch Cnci 1989-; Congressman Wm Lipinskis Teacher Merit Awd 1988; *office:* Nathan Hale Sch 6140 S Melvina Chicago IL 60638

SCHWAB, RICHARD ALAN, Mathematics Teacher; *b:* Syracuse, NY; *m:* Barbara Jean; *c:* Robyn L., Kristin E., Kathryn D.; *ed:* (BS) Scndry Math, 1972, (MS) Scndry Math, 1977 SUC Cortland; *cr:* Teacher E Syracuse Minoa Sch Dist 1972-; *ai:* Coach ESM Math Team; Participate Writing of Onondagu Cty Math Contest & Symposium; AMTNYS (Cty Chm 1980-, Jr HS Level Rep 1987-89); NYSUT; ESMUT Treas 1989-; OCMTA VP; Lions Club 1989-; Jr HS Level Rep for Assn of Math Teachers of NY St; *office:* Pine Grove Jr HS Fremont Rd East Syracuse NY 13057

SCHWABAUER, JOHN ANTHONY, Mathematics Teacher; *b:* Oxnard, CA; *m:* Sheryl Ann; *c:* Shelby, John; *ed:* (BA) Math, Chico St Univ 1985; *cr:* Math Teacher Red Bluff Union HS 1986-; *ai:* Ftbl & Wrestling Coach; NCTM; *office:* Red Bluff Union HS 1260 Union St Red Bluff CA 96080

SCHWAMBERGER, JACK ALLEN, Phys Science/Health Teacher; *b:* Toledo, OH; *m:* Rosemary A. Riley; *c:* Ty A., Sue A.; *ed:* (BS) Ed/His/Government, OH Northern Univ 1969; (MS) Sch Admin, Univ of Dayton 1980; Cert in Sci, Bowling Green St Univ 1970-72; *cr:* Teacher/Coach Allen E Local Schls 1969-70, Covington Village Schls 1970-; *ai:* Sci Olympiad, Ftbl, Wrestling, Bsbl Coach; CEA, OH Sci Teachers Assn Pres 1988-; OEA, NEA; BUCC Boosters 1970-; Masons Lodge 168 Jr Warden 1987-88; Wright St Sci Schlsp; Teacher of Yr 1970; *home:* 39 Wenrick Covington OH 45318

SCHWARTZ, EVELYN NOON, Eng/Accounting/Psych Teacher; *b:* Cambridge, MA; *m:* Michael; *c:* Nathan, Kylie; *ed:* (BS) Sci, E NM Univ 1987; Grad Stud Univ of NM Albuquerque; *cr:* Eng/Accounting/Psych/Typing Teacher Carrizozo HS 1988-; *ai:* Bd Revision & Budget Comms 1989; Spon Stu Cncl 1988-, Frosh Class 1989-; Phi Kappa Phi 1986-; NM Teacher of Eng 1989-; *home:* PO Box 772 Carrizozo NM 88301

SCHWARTZ, GLORIA JEAN (RINGWALD), 5th Grade Teacher; *b:* Van Wert, OH; *m:* Larry E.; *c:* Larry E. Jr., Jeffery L.; *ed:* (BA) Elem Ed, 1974; (MS) Edctnl Leadership, 1989 Wright St Univ; *cr:* 3rd Grade Teacher 1974-84; 5th Grade Teacher 1984- Mendon Union Local Schls; *ai:* 3 Yrs Umpire HS Bsbl & Sftbl 1986-88; NEA/OEA/MURA Sec/Treas 1987-89; *office:* Mendon Union Sch P O Box 98 Mendon OH 45862

SCHWARTZ, HELEN JEANNE LACELL, Mathematics Teacher; *b:* Rome, NY; *m:* Steven H.; *c:* Daniel J., Catherine S. M.; *ed:* (BS) Ed, SUNY Oswego 1977; *cr:* 5th Grade Teacher 1977-80, Mid Sch Math Teacher 1983-83 Stafford Mid Sch; HS Math Teacher North Stafford HS 1983-; *ai:* Yrbk Adv; Asst Sr Spon; Rappahannock Regional Area Teachers of Math 1983-; Stafford Ed Assn 1977-83; VA Ed Assn 1977-83; *office:* North Stafford HS 839 Garrisonville Rd Stafford VA 22445

SCHWARTZ, KATHRYN ANN, Social Studies Chairman; *b:* Monterey Park, CA; *ed:* (BA) His, 1968; (MS) Ed, 1970 Univ of Southern CA; Post Masters Studies CSUN; CSLA; *cr:* Teacher Granada Elem 1970; *ai:* Stu Body Adv; Leadership Team; Dist Textbook Selection Comm; Coord Peer Guidance Counseling Prgm; ATA 1970-; CTA 1970-; NEA 1970-; PTA Life Memshp; *office:* Granada Elem Sch 100 S Granada Ave Alhambra CA 91801

SCHWARTZ, LOUISE WARNS, Health/Phys Ed Teacher; *b:* Toledo, OH; *m:* James Allen; *c:* Chad A., Cortny R.; *ed:* (BA) Health/Phys Ed, Bowling Green St Univ 1974; Quest, ADELPHI Natl Drug Inst; Project Charlie; Additional Work Health Ed, Bowling Green St Univ 1974-; *cr:* DECA Merchandising Toledo Public Schls 1976-77; Substitute Teacher Gibsonburg Woodmere 1977-78; Learning Disibilities/Phys Ed Teacher Woodmore 1978-83; Health/Phys Ed Teacher Oregon City Schls 1984-; *ai:* Vlybl & Track Coach; Youth-To-Youth Adv; Var Blybl Ofcl; Health & Phys Ed Curr Comm; Greater Toledo Vlybl Offcl Assn VP 1979-; Kappa Delta Phi 1973-80; OH HS Ofcls Assn 1979-; St Johns Luth Church 1990; Fremont Messenger Good Neighbor Awd 1978; *home:* 9287 Oak Harbor SE Rd Oak Harbor OH 43449

SCHWARTZ, NANCY S., Marketing Instructor; *b:* Flint, MI; *c:* Eric J.; *ed:* (BA) Marketing Ed/Bus Ed, Western MI Univ 1973; Western MI Univ, MI St, Univ oF MI; *cr:* Admin Clerk-Great Lakes Cmptr Center 1973; Marketing Instr 1974-; *ai:* Adv DECA Club; Building Rep Bd of Dirs; BSA Comm; MOEA; MI Marketing Educators.

SCHWARTZ, PATRICIA B., Fourth Grade Teacher; *b:* New York, NY; *m:* Harris A.; *c:* Jason T., Jonathan C., Jennifer R.; *ed:* (BA) Fr, Barnard Coll 1962; (MA) Teaching Fr, 1963, (MED) Educl Admin, 1981, (EDD) Educl Admin, 1986 Teachers Coll Columbia; Several Wkshps; *cr:* Elem Fr Teacher Teaneck Public Schls 1962-66; 5th Grade Teacher Belmont Public Schls 1966-69; 4th-6th Grade Teacher Teaneck Public Schls 1969-; *ai:* Staff Dev for Teaching Essentials, Styles & Strategies Prgm; ASCD 1978-; NCTE 1984-; Citizens Educl Advisory Comm to Maywood Bd of Ed Secy 1977-84; Spec Salary Awd 1969; Minigrant NJ St Dept Of Ed 1973; Strategies for Thoughtful Teaching 1988; Author Elements of Thoughtful Teaching; FL Challenge Grant for Gifted & Talented 1990; Curr Dev NJ Provisional Teacher Trng Grant; *office:* Hawthorne Sch Fycke Ln Teaneck NJ 07666

SCHWARTZ, PAULA FIELDS (VARCO), 7th-8th Eng/Rdng/Quest Teacher; *b:* Yakima, WA; *m:* William C.; *c:* Scott C., Laural A., Robert W.; *ed:* (BA) Ed, 1969, Ed, 1975 Central WA Univ; Life Skills for Adolescents Quest/Quest Advanced Trng; *cr:* 5th Grade Teacher 1969-71, 5th/7th/8th Grade Coach Summitview Elem Sch 1971-72; 3rd Grade Teacher 1972-75, 4th Grade Teacher 1975-76, 4th Grade 1976-77, 3rd Grade Teacher 1977-85, 9th Grade Lit/8th Grade Eng Teacher 1985-86, 9th Grade Lit/8th Grade Rdng Teacher 1986-87, 8th Grade Eng/Rdng/7th Grade Eng Teacher/Quest 7th-8th Grade Teacher 1987-88, 8th Grade Eng/Rdng/7th Grade Rdng/Quest 7th-8th Grade Teacher 1988- UnioN Gap Sch; *ai:* ASB Dance Coord; Quest Activity Dir; Drug & Alcohol Dir; Cncl Eng Teachers Mem 1987-; Cmptr Comm Mem 1989-; Staff Dev Comm Participant 1988-; Curr Comm West Valley Participant 1970-71; Curr Comm Union Gap Participant 1987-88; West Valley Ed Assn Secy 1971-72; Union Gap Ed Assn Mem 1972-; Wa Ed Assn Mem 1969-; NEA Mem 1969-; Union Gap Ed Assn (Secy 1974-72, Pres 1975-76, Negotiations Team 1976-86, Grievance 1988-); Dept Chairperson/5th Grade Teachers West Valley 1971-72; Lions Quest Intl Facilitator/Act Coord 1987-; Lions Quest Intl Parenting Class Teacher 1987-88; Bel Canto Vocalist/Big Sister 1985-; Sanctuary Singers Vocalist 1987-; Outstanding Elem Teachers of America 1972; Christa Mc Auliff Awd St of WA 1988; West Valley Ed Assn Secy 1971-72; *office:* Union Gap M S 3200 S 2nd St Union Gap WA 98903

SCHWARTZ, RICHARD HENRY, Sixth Grade Teacher; *b:* Starbuck, MN; *m:* Jean Ellingson; *c:* Benjamin, Megan; *ed:* (BS) Elem Ed, Moorhead St Coll 1971; *cr:* 6th Grade Teacher Blooming Prairie Elem 1975-77, Long Prairie Elem 1977-78, Blooming Prairie Elem 1978-; *ai:* Asst Ftbl & Head Bstbl Coach; Blooming Prairie Teachers Assn (Pres 1975-, Negotiator 1989); MN Ed Assn 1975-; Lions (Pres 1978-, Secy 1980-82); Blooming Prairie Teacher of Yr 1976-77; *office:* Blooming Prairie Elem Sch 110 1st St NW Blooming Prairie MN 55917

SCHWARTZ, ROBERTA HELLERMAN, Biology Teacher; *b:* New York, NY; *m:* Michael D.; *c:* Janet, Daniel; *ed:* (BS) Bio, Brooklyn Coll 1961; (MAT) Sci Ed, Fairleigh Dickenson 1981; *cr:* Research Asst Univ Hospital 1961-62; Clinical Bacteriologist Bellevue Hospital 1962-69; Teacher Dwight-Englewood Sch 1979-; *ai:* Lead Environmental Awareness Field Trip to Cape Cod; Adv Dwight-Englewood Against Drunk Driving Club; NABT 1975-; New York St Cecilia Choir Mem 1982-; *office:* Dwight-Englewood Sch 315 E Palisades Ave Englewood NJ 07631

SCHWARTZ, SHIRLEY ANN, First Grade Teacher; *b:* Appleton, WI; *m:* Harland; *c:* David, Pamela, Brenda, Michael; *ed:* Cert Ed, Oshkosh St Coll 1956; (BS) Ed, Univ WI Oshkosh 1972; *cr:* 1st/8th Grade Teacher Rural Brothertown Sch 1956-59; 3rd/4th Grade Teacher Forest Junction Elem Sch 1959-61; 3rd/

7th-8th Grade Teacher 1972-73; 1st Grade Teacher 1973- Brillion Public Sch; *ai:* At Risk Comm; Brillion Womens Club Dir 1986-88; *home:* Rt 2 Sunnyslope Rd Brillion WI 54110

SCHWARZ, CATHERINE E., HS Writing/Literature Teacher; *b:* Flint, MI; *m:* John C.; *ed:* (BA) His, Marygrove Coll; (MA) His, Univ of Detroit; (MA) Counseling, Univ of MI Ann Arbor 1977; Grad Stud Various Colls; *cr:* 5th-8th Grade Teacher 1950-56; HS Teacher 1957-; *ai:* Student Advocate; ASCD; Phi Delta Kappa; Appointed to Editorial Bd the Ed Digest; NDEA Grants; Honored by Supt, Bd of Ed, Teachers, Parents & Stus Upon Retirement June 1990; Author; *home:* 2777 Colony Rd Ann Arbor MI 48104

SCHWARZ, JANET, 8th Grade Science Teacher; *b:* Hollywood, CA; *ed:* (BA) Philosophy/Theology, Univ of San Francisco 1970; Teaching Credential Ed, 1978, Rdng Specialist Credential Ed, 1979 San Francisco St Univ; St Patricks Seminary Theological Update; Numerous Classes & Wkshps; *cr:* 1st Grade Teacher St Annes 1964-66; 1st-3rd Grade Teacher St Teresas 1966-74; 2nd Grade Teacher Epiphany 1974-75; 1st/8th Grade Teacher/Asst Prin Nativity 1975-; *ai:* Asst Prin; Sch Ecology Recycling Prgm; San Mateo Sci Camp, Yosemite Inst Sci Camp; Sci Fair; Christmas Play; NCEA Mem 1964-; CJSF Moderator 1981-88; Project Bus Mem 1981-; CA Acad of Sci Mem 1985-; Archdiocese of San Francisco Educl Curr Bd; WASC Evaluation Comm of Cath Schls; Master-Teacher; Given Curr Wkshps to Teachers for Archdiocese of San Francisco; *office:* Nativity Sch 1250 Laurel St Menlo Park CA 94025

SCHWARZ, SHARON ANN, Mathematics Teacher; *b:* Chicago, IL; *ed:* (BS) Math, Univ of IL Chicago 1971; (MAT) Math, SE MO St Univ 1979; *cr:* Instr SE MO St Univ 1980-81; Math Teacher Marquand-Zion RVI 1986-; *ai:* Beta Club Spon; CTA Treas; Sci Fair Coord; NCTM; MO Cncl Teachers of Math; Girardot Rose Chapter Sweet Adelines Inc Treas 1980-; Natl Sci Fnd Inst for HS Math Teachers on Mathematical Applications Univ of MO St Louis; *office:* Marquand-Zion RVI HS PO Box A Marquand MO 63655

SCHWARZKOPF, GLORIA GROSSENBACHER, Former Teacher; *b:* Chicago, IL; *m:* Alfred E.; *ed:* (BE) Chicago Teachers Coll 1949; (ME) Lib/Sci, Chicago St Univ 1956; Drug Ed; Reality Therapy Level II; Attended 22 Universities & Coll Since with IIT for Chem Most Recent Jan; *cr:* Instr Gov St Univ 1985 & 87; Teacher Clay Sch 1951-; *ai:* Alateen Spon; Seminarist on Drugs; Drug Resource Person; Operation Snowball Speaker; NEA Life Mem 1949-; ILADA; IACA; Women of Medinah Auxiliary; Chicago Bd of Ed Supt Awd for Excl 1976; IL Math & Sci Acad Awd/Recognition 1988; Innovative Program Grant Feeling Good a Good Feeling 1981; *office:* Henry Clay Schl 13231 S Burley Rd Chicago IL 60627

SCHWEHR, HAROLD JOHN, 7th/8th Grade Soc Stud Teacher; *b:* Highland, IL; *m:* Mary Ellen Heuberger; *c:* Susan L. Knight, Terry D. Meyer, Wendy J. Porter, Christie A., Greg A.; *ed:* (BA) Soc Stud, S IL Univ Carbondale 1956; Ed Admin, S IL Univ Edwardsville; *cr:* 6th Grade Teacher Brush Sch 1956-57, Troy Elem 1958-60; 7th/8th Grade Soc Stud Teacher Mc Cray Dewey Jr HS 1960-; *ai:* Triad HS Jr Var Soccer Coach; Mc Cray Dewey Jr HS 8th Grade Bsktbl & 7th/8th Grade Track Coach; Triad Ed Assn (Building Rep, Pres, VP); NEA, IL Ed Assn; Troy Jaycees (Secy 1964-65, Dir 1967-68, Pres 1966-67, VP 1965-66), Jaycee Man of Yr 1968; Troy PTA (Pres, VP); Troy Khoury League Pres, Umpire in Chief, Dir, Commissioner; Tri-Township Park Dist Planning Bd Mem; *home:* 111 W Henderson Troy IL 62294

SCHWEIGER, DAVID FRANK, Science Teacher; *b:* Hibbing, MN; *m:* Christine Anderson; *ed:* (BS) Bio/Chem, Winona St Univ 1979; (BS) Life Sci/Earth Sci, 1985, (MA) Sci Ed, 1989 Univ of MN; *cr:* Teacher Osseo Jr HS 1985-; *ai:* Boys Track Coach; MN Sci Teachers Assn 1985-.

SCHWEITZER, DEBRA ANN (PERRY), Teacher of Gifted & Talented; *b:* Cleveland, OH; *m:* John H. Jr.; *c:* Brian, Brad; *ed:* (MED) Gifted & Talented, Kent St Univ 1990; (BS) Elem Ed, Miami Univ 1973; Cmptr Sci; *cr:* 6th Grade Teacher Parma City Schls 1973-77; 5th/7th Grade Teacher St Charles Cleve Diocese 1984-87; Teacher of Gifted & Talented University Hts Schls 1989-; *ai:* Gifted & Talented Curr Prgm; OAGC, AFT 1989-; *office:* Cleve Hts-Univ Hts Schls 2155 Miramar Blvd University Heights OH 44118

SCHWEITZER, JOHN H., Social Studies Teacher; *b:* Cleveland, OH; *m:* Debra Ann Perry; *c:* Brian, Brad; *ed:* (BSED) Comp Soc Stud, Miami Univ 1973; (MED) Educl Admin, Kent St Univ 1978; Coll of Mt St Joseph; Cleveland St Univ; *cr:* Cross Cntry/Bsbl Coach Parma Schls 1976-81; Sftbl Coach Parma Sr HS 1984-86; Teacher Parma Schls 1973; *ai:* Key Club Adv; Academic Coach; Parma Ed Assn, OH Ed Assn, NEA 1973-; Greater Cleveland Cncl for Soc Stud 1986-; Parma Amateur Athletic Fed Coach 1984-89; Kiwanis Outstanding Service Awd 1988; Curr Writing & Criterion Test Guide 1975; Jr Achievement Project Bus Awd 1977-81; *office:* Parma Sr HS 6285 W 54th Parma OH 44129

SCHWEMM, STEVEN JAMES, Social Studies Teacher; *b:* Sumner, IA; *m:* Kathryn Jo Buss; *c:* Michael, Ann; *ed:* (BA) His, Univ of Northern IA 1972; Grad Work at Univ of IA/Univ of Northern IA; *cr:* 7th-8th Grade Soc Stud Teacher Oelwein Jr HS 1972-; *ai:* IA Cncl for The Soc Stud 1980-; Church Cncl VP 1988; Cmmty Chest Bd Mem 1987-; Oelwein Jaycees-Outstanding Young Educator-1982; *office:* Oelwein Jr H S 300-12th Ave SE Oelwein IA 50662

SCHWENDY, DONNA MERRILL, English Teacher; *b:* Cortland, NY; *m:* Bruce R.; *c:* Caroline L., Susan E., Nancy A.; *ed:* (BS) Ed/Eng, SUNY Potsdam 1961; *cr:* Eng Teacher Gates Chili HS 1961-62, Long Branch HS 1962-64; Tutor/Substitute Teacher Gates-Chili HS 1974-76; Eng Teacher Hoover Drive Mid Sch 1977-; *ai:* At-Risk Stu Comm; Delta Kappa Gamma 1987-; Kappa Delta Pi; Back to the Classics Sch Dist Presentation.

SCHWENK, ARTHUR, German Teacher; *b:* New Castle, IN; *m:* Marcia Finke; *c:* Laura E., John A., Ingrid K.; *ed:* (BAED) Ger, 1968, (MA) Ger, 1971 Ball St Univ; Univ of Scranton 1969, Goethe Inst Munich W Germany 1970, IN Univ, Purdue Univ 1969-86, De Pauw Univ 1978, IN Univ 1975-87; *cr:* Ger Teacher Rochester HS 1968-70; IUPUI 1972-73, 1983-84, 1989-; Ger/Math Teacher Columbus North HS & Northside Mid Sch & Cntrl Mid Sch & Mc Dowell Adult Ed Center 1970-; Research Asst Oldenburg Universitat & IN Ger Heritage Society 1986-; *ai:* Ethnic Expo Cultural Fair 1974; Ger Textbook Selection Comm Chm 1984, 1990; Columbus Educators Assn Rep 1971-78; IN St Teachers Assn, NEA, IN Ger Heritage Society, IN Foreign Lang Teachers Assn; Columbus Chippers Woodcarvers Club Pres 1973-74; Bar-Cons Credit Union Bd Mem 1974-79; BSA Troop Bd Mem 1975-78; Bartholomew Cty Historical Society Bd 1986-88; St Peters Luth Church Elder 1984-; Pro Musica Symphony Consultant 1990-; Natl Defence Ed Act Fellowship Ger Univ of Scranton 1969; Fulbright Fellowship Ger Stud in Germany 1970; IN Heritage Research Grant Ger Settlement Patterns IN St 1987; Grant IN Comm for Hum The Lilly Endowment Incorporated Teacher Creativity Fellowship 1988; Local His Grant Bartholomew Cty Historical Society 1988; Bartholomew Consolidated Sch Fnd to Develop Teaching Materials Grants 1982, 1990; *home:* 10990 N 900 E Hope Hope IN 47246

SCHWENK, MARGIE MAUD, Teacher of Gifted & Talented; *b:* Carroll, IA; *m:* Larry; *c:* Brianna; *ed:* (BS) Respiratory Therapy, Coll of St Mary 1975; (BS) Elem Ed, IA St Univ 1977; Grad Classes in Ed; *cr:* Respiratory Therapist Cass Cty Cmmty Hospital 1975-76; 5th/6th Grade Teacher Coon Rapids Cmmty Sch 1977-85; Teacher of Gifted & Talented Coon Rapids-Bayard Cmmty Sch 1986-; *ai:* Human Growth, Dev, Drug-Free Sch, Gifted & Talented Ed Comm; K-2 Regional Curr Writing & Gifted Ed; NSTA; Coon Rapids-Bayard Ed Assn 1989-; IA Talented & Gifted Assn 1986-; PEO, Alpha Lambda Delta; *office:* Coon Rapids-Bayard Sch PO Box 297 Coon Rapids IA 50058

SCHWERMANN, BETTY KNUTSON, Teacher of Gifted; *b:* Cottonwood, MN; *m:* Manfred; *ed:* (BA) Eng, St Cloud St Univ 1966; (MA) Gifted, St Thomas 1984; *cr:* 9th-11th Grade Eng/His Teacher St Charles HS 1966-69; 7th/8th Grade Eng Teacher 1969-86, Resource Teacher of 6th-8th Grade Gifted/Coord of K-12th Grade Gifted 1986- Chaska Mid Sch; *ai:* Future Problem Solving Coach 1984-88; MA Ed Gifted & Talented Bd of Dirs 1982-; Natl Assn of Gifted Children 1985-; MN Assn of Mid Level Educators (Bd of Dirs 1982-85, Treas 1983-84); MEA, MN Cncl Teachers of Eng, MCLU; Nom MN Teacher of Yr 1971, 1986; Nom Ashland Oil Awd 1990; Articles Published 1988; *office:* Chaska Mid Sch 1600 Park Ridge Dr Chaska MN 55318

SCHWINN, MYRON E., Zoology/Botany Teacher; *b:* Easton, KS; *m:* Joretta Lindt; *c:* Scott; *ed:* (BS) Bio, 1960, (MS) Bio, 1964 KS St Teachers Coll Emporia; Earth Sci, Nuclear Eng for Sci Teachers, KS State, NSF Inst; *cr:* Sci Teacher Everest Rural HS 1961-64; Bio Teacher Manhattan Jr HS/Mid Sch 1964-81; Botany/Zoology Teacher 1981-, Wide Horizons Nature Prgm Dir 1982- Manhattan HS; *ai:* Environmental Club Spon; Sch Dst Hazardous & Toxic Chemicals Coord; Sci Dept Chairperson; Sch Improvement Comm Mem; KABT Pres 1969, Outstanding Bio Teacher 1987; Manhattan Ed Assn Pres 1971-72; NEA, KNEA, NABT; Riley Cty Fish & Game Pres 1982; KS Wildlife Fed VP 1980, Educator of Yr 1969; KS Assn of Taxidermists Pres 1981-82; Natl Sci Fnd Grants for Summer Inst 1964-66; Sigma XI Scientific Research Society Outstanding Sci Teacher 1980; *office:* Manhattan HS 2100 Poyntz Ave Manhattan KS 66502

SCIACCA, ANNA DEGLIOMINI, Seventh Grade Teacher; *b:* Passaic, NJ; *m:* Frank R.; *c:* Joanna; *ed:* (BA) Elem Ed, Felician Coll 1975; (MA) Admin/Supervision, Jersey City St Coll 1985; *cr:* Title I Teacher 1976-78, Basic Skills Teacher 1978-79, 3rd Grade Teacher 1979-81, 7th/8th Grade Teacher 1981- Garfield Sch System; *ai:* Woodrow Wilson Girls Bsktbl Team 1984-; Woodrow Wilson Home & Sch Assn Treas 1986-; NJ Governors Teachers Recognition Awd 1989; *office:* Woodrow Wilson Sch #5 205 Outwater Ln Garfield NJ 07026

SCIEGAJ, ROBERT ALLEN, Mathematics Dept Chair; *b:* Derby, CT; *m:* Cathy L. Loar; *ed:* (BS) Bus Admin, WV Univ 1976; (AB) Ed/Math, Fairmont St Coll 1978; (MS) Mid Sch Admin, VA Tech 1987; *cr:* Math Teacher Daniel Morgan Mid Sch 1978-; *ai:* Admin Dean; Daniel Morgan Mid Sch NHS & Math Teams Spon; NEA, VEA, WEA 1978-; Natl Mid Sch Assn 1989-; VA Con Teachers of Math 1988; Friends of Handley Lib Bd Mem 1989-; Potomac Edison Power Companies Cmptr Grant; Article Published 1990; *office:* Daniel Morgan Mid Sch 48 S Percell Ave Winchester VA 22601

SCIENEAUX, DELORIS JACKSON, English Teacher; *b:* New Orleans, LA; *m:* Bearl P.; *c:* Karl, Terry L., Kenneth, Lawrence; *ed:* (BS) Eng, 1964, (MS) Scndry Ed, 1977 S Univ Baton Rouge; *cr:* Eng Teacher Magnolia HS 1965-68, St James HS 1969-; *ai:* Yrbk Staff Adv; Paperwork Comm; Eng Dept Chairperson; NTCE, NEA, LEA; New Home Missionary Assn Mt Triumph BC Secy 1986-; Poems Published 1989; St James HS Teacher of Yr 1986-87.

SCILINGO, WILLIAM JAMES, Physics Teacher; *b:* Ridgway, PA; *m:* Sharon Ann Pennington; *c:* Michele Steudler, William J. Jr.; *ed:* (BSED) Chem, Clarion Univ PA 1966; (MS) Physics, Syracuse Univ 1971; Modern Physics, Univ of WA; Cmptr Skills, Intermediate Unit IV; *cr:* Math/Sci Kane Area Schls 1966-67; Physics/Cmptr St Marys Area Schls 1967-; *ai:* NHS Adv; AAPT 1989; PSEA, NEA 1966-; A Kaul Memorial Hospital Mem Bd of Trustees 1987-; Bd of Ed Johnsonburg Area Sch Dist Mem; *office:* St Marys Area HS 977 S St Marys Rd Saint Marys PA 15857

SCIORTINO, MARIA, Jr High Math Teacher; *b:* Attard, Malta; *ed:* (BA) Fr/Elem Ed, 1973; Working Towards Masters Math Ed; *cr:* Jr HS Math Teacher Holy Name of Jesus 1972-78, St Mary Magdalen 1978-80, Acad of Holy Names 1980-81, St Mary Magdalen 1981-; *ai:* Organize Field & European Trips for Stus; Fund-Raising Act; Sacristan at Church Weekday & Sunday Masses; *office:* St Mary Magdalen Sch 869 Maitland Ave Altamonte Springs FL 32701

SCOGIN, HELEN L., Fourth Grade Teacher; *b:* Doniphan, MO; *m:* Louis; *c:* John Wheeler, Bob Wheeler, Linda Sietz, Larry Wheeler, Susan Stroder; *ed:* SE MO St Teachers Coll; *cr:* 1st-4th Grade Teacher Ripley Cty Rural; Substitute Teacher Granite City & Venice Schls; 4th Grade Teacher St Paul Elem; *ai:* Numerous Comms; *home:* 722 Troy Rd Collinsville IL 62234

SCOTT, ALLEN WAYNE, Math/Computer Teacher; *b:* Roscoe, TX; *m:* Betty Sue Cole; *c:* Kevin R., James F., Tanya R.; *ed:* (BSED) Scndry Ed/Math, 1963, (MED) Scndry Ed/Math, 1968, (END) Scndry Ed/Research, 1969 North TX St Univ; Grad Study Cmptr Sci/Physics/Gifted Ed; *cr:* Math Teacher Blocker Jr HS 1963-65, Denton Jr HS 1965-66; Research Admin Dallas Ind Sch Dist 1969-82; Math/CS Teacher Talented & Gifted Magnet HS 1982-; *ai:* Spon Math Club/Cmptr Club; Coach Cmptr Competition Team; TX Cmptr Ed Assn 1984-; Classroom Teachers of Dallas 1982-; TX St Teacher Assn 1982-; NEA 1982-; Title IV Research Trainee Grant 1965-69; Nom Teacher of Yr; Chosen Most Influential Teacher SMU; Numerous Research/Evaluation Reports; *home:* 6169 Berwyn Ln Dallas TX 75214

SCOTT, ANITA KNIPLING, Writing Skills Teacher; *b:* Menard, TX; *m:* Fred C.; *c:* Craig, Kimberly, Brian, Kathryn; *ed:* (BA) Eng, Westhampton Coll 1959; (MA) Hum, Marymount Univ 1988; Various Grad Level Courses; *cr:* Teacher 1959-63, Part Time Teacher 1968-72, Teacher 1972- Arlington Cty Schls; *ai:* Stu Cncl Assn Co-Spon; Arlington Oratorical Contest Spon; 1990 Williamsburg Writers Fair Coord; Delta Kappa Gamma (Secy, Various Comm Chairmanships) 1978-; Arlington Outdoor Ed Assn Bd Mem 1968-; Sabbatical Fellowship 1987-88; Awarded Honorary Lifetime Mem Natl PTA 1987; *office:* Williamsburg Intermediate Sch 3600 N Harrison St Arlington VA 22207

SCOTT, BENJAMIN, JR., Math Teacher; *b:* Lobeco, SC; *m:* Claudia Brown; *c:* Nakia V., Benjamin J. III; *ed:* (BS) Elem Ed, SC St Coll 1977; (MS) Early Chldhd Ed, Univ of SC 1984; Enrolled in Ed Specialist Degree Prgm; *cr:* Teacher James J Davis Elem Sch 1977-89, Robert Smalls Mid Sch 1989-; *ai:* 6th Grade Acad Challenge Math Team Coach; Weightlifting Club Spon; Orientation Comm Mem; Beauford Cty Ed Assn, SC Ed Assn, NEA 1977-; Alpha Phi Alpha Inc Treas 1989-; *home:* PO Box 4021 Burton SC 29903

SCOTT, BERNARD JAMES, Agriscience Instructor; *b:* Zanesville, OH; *m:* Jean Ellen; *c:* Selenel, Gary, Alan, Joyce, Jill, Dasa, Sara; *ed:* (BS) Ag Ed, 1961, (MS) Supervision, 1977 OH St; Inservice Wkshps; *cr:* Instr Otsego HS 1962-; *ai:* FFA & Jr Fair Adv; AVA, OH Voc Assn; OVATA St Secy 1976-77, Outstanding Teacher 1978; NVATA, NEA, OEA; Fire Dept VP 1988-; Park Dev Coord 1985-; Spirit of Wood Cty 1989; St & Amer Honorary FFA Degrees; *home:* 18577 Tontogany Rd Tontogany OH 43565

SCOTT, BEVERLY JEAN, Science Teacher; *b:* Denver, CO; *m:* Richard Walter; *c:* Suzanne E., Kevin R.; *ed:* (BS) Scndry Sci Ed, Univ of WY 1979; *cr:* Title IV Aide 1979-80, Substitute Teacher 1980-81 Sch Dist 25; Sci Teacher Wind River HS 1981-; *ai:* Stu Cncl Spon; Wind River Ed Assn (Pres 1990, VP 1986-87, 1988-, Chm Reduction in Force Comm 1988-); Phi Kappa Phi 1979-; North Central Evaluation Team 1986, 1988; Cntrl WY Coll Faculty Womens Assn Pres 1979-81; Certified Emergency Medical Technician (WY 1977-80, 1972-75); Nom Presidential Awd Excl in Sci Teaching 1990; *office:* Wind River HS Kinnear WY 82516

SCOTT, BOBBY RAY, Fifth Grade Teacher; *b:* Columbia, KY; *m:* Edwanna Garmon; *c:* Tracey L. Kessler, Tabitha A.; *ed:* (BA) Elem Ed, Campbellsville 1962; (MA) Principalship, 1965, (Rank I) Leadership Cert 1967 W KY Univ; Cmptr Trng; Math Wkshps; Bible Courses; *cr:* Elem Teacher Lincoln Trial Elem 1959-69; Asst Prin North Hardin Jr HS 1969-70; Elem Prin Parkway Elem 1970-78; 5th Grade Teacher G C Burkhead Elem 1978-; *ai:* Teaching Whiz Kiz Math & Governors Cup Stus Math; Phys Ed Comm Chm; Family Life Comm Dist Rep; KEA, NEA 1959-; Hardin Cty Ed Assn Pres 1964-65; Prof Rights & Responsibilities Commission (4th Dist Chm 1964-65, St Comm); Lincoln Trail PTA Pres 1966; Gideon Secy 1987-; St Fact Finding Comm; Outstanding Young Educator Awd 1965; St Outstanding Teacher 1985; *home:* 2681 Locust Grove Rd Elizabethtown KY 42701

SCOTT, BRENDA FOSTER, English Teacher; *b:* Moultrie, GA; *m:* Bernard; *c:* Jason, Marcus; *ed:* (BA) Eng, Fisk Univ 1975; (MA) Eng, Clark-Atlanta Univ 1986; *cr:* Admin Asst PP&T Engineering Co 1976-77; Teacher Lakeside HS 1977-; *ai:* Jr Civitan Club Adv; Awds Comm Mem; Writing Across the Curr Consultant; GAE, NEA.

SCOTT, CHARLES R., HPER Teacher & Coach; *b:* Portsmouth, OH; *m:* Barbara J. Spies; *c:* Amy M., Janna E.; *ed:* (AB) HPER, Fairmont 1972; (MAED) Scndry Sch Principalship, WV Univ 1975; *cr:* Teacher/Coach Martinsburg North Jr HS 1972-76, Hedgesville HS 1976-78, Jefferson HS 1978-86, Hedgesville HS 1986-; *ai:* Var Club Adv; Attendance Policy Comm; Var Bsktbl Coach; WV Ed Assn, WV Coaches Assn; *office:* Hedgesville HS Rt 1 Box 89 Hedgesville WV 25427

SCOTT, CHESTER EUGENE, Instructional Mgr Auto Service; *b:* Fremont, MI; *m:* Norma Jean Dickinson; *c:* Ronald C., Dennis L., Melany L. Goetsch; *ed:* (BS) 7th-12th Auto Service, Ferris St Coll 1979; MI Voc Teaching Certificate; MI 5 Yr Provisional Teaching Certificate Gen Ed 7th-12th Grade; MI Master Mechanic Automotive, ASE; MI Master Truck Mechanic; MI Certificate Driver Ed & Traffic Safety; *cr:* General Mechanic MaGee Motor Sales/Service 1956-58; Head Mechanic/Trans Supt 1958-69, Auto/Small Engine Instr 1969-72 Fremont Public Schls; Auto Serv Instructional Mgr NCAVC 1972-; *ai:* Youth Leader; Bible Quiz Coach & Master; Local Baptist Church Youth Dir, Deacon, Chm of Bd; State Baptist Camp Dir & on St Bds; Inst in Basic Youth Conflicts Seminar Area Coord; Awana Youth Group Leader & Commander; MI Ed Prof Dev Comm; Republican Party St Delegate; Honorary Chapter FFA; Fremont Public Sch Outstanding Teacher; Ferris St Univ Certificate for Outstanding Work with Stu Teachers; Newaygo Cty Area Voc Center I Care About Kids Employee of Yr; *home:* 451 E Elm St Fremont MI 49412

SCOTT, DIANE M., Kindergarten Teacher; *b:* Princeton, MN; *m:* Robinson I.; *c:* Sarah, Lucas; *ed:* (AA) Elem Ed, Anoka Ramsey Comm Coll 1970; (BA) Elem Ed, St Cloud Univ 1972; (MS) Curr/Instruction, St Thomas Coll 1986; *cr:* 1st Grade Teacher St Francis Elem 1972-82, E Bethel Elem 1982-87; Kndgtn Teacher St Francis Elem 1988-; *ai:* Dist Steering Act Rdng, Art & Soc Stud; GSA Co-Leader 1988-; PTA Treas 1986-87; Whos Who in Amer Jr Coll 1970; Living Sch Yr 1987-88 in Sweden doing Observations & Research on Swedish Sch System & Curr; *home:* 5020 184th Ave NW Anoka MN 55303

SCOTT, DONALD MARK, Social Studies Teacher; *b:* New Castle, IN; *m:* Deborah Jayne Wallace; *c:* David, Chely, Tara, Cameron; *ed:* (BS) Eng/Speech/Theatre, 1957, (MS) Ed, 1968 Ball St Univ; Peace Corps Trng, Columbia Univ; *cr:* Teacher New Castle Cmmty Schls 1957-65, Cameroon Africa Peace Corps 1965-67, New Castle Cmmty Schls 1967-; *ai:* Tennis, Track, Vlybl, Speech Coach; Sch Paper Adv; NEA, IN St Teachers Assn, Classroom Teacher Assn 1957-65; 1st Nighters Civic Theatre 1961-, Best Actor 1973, 1978, 1981, 1983, 1988; *home:* 704 S Main St New Castle IN 47362

SCOTT, DONNELL LYNN, Third Grade Teacher; *b:* Perry, IA; *ed:* (BS) Elem Ed, IA St Univ 1981; IA Writing Project, Univ of IA; *cr:* 3rd Grade Teacher Dysart-Geneseo Elem 1981-; *ai:* Phase 3 Comm; Prgm of Autonomous Learners Task Force; Black Hawk Cncl IA Rdng Assn 1989-; Rebekah Circle Dysart United Meth Church Mem; Dysart Ambulance Service EMT; *office:* Dysart-Geneseo Elem Sch 411 Lincoln Dysart IA 52224

SCOTT, DORETHA HOLLINS, Math/Sci Mentor Teacher; *b:* Baton Rouge, LA; *m:* Benjamin Sr.; *c:* Benjamin E. Jr, Daryl D.; *ed:* (BA) Elem Ed, Southern Univ 1954; (MA) Admin/Supervision, 1980, (MA) Counseling, 1981 Point Loma Coll; *cr:* 6th/8th Grade Teacher Upper Maringouin Sch 1954-59; 3rd/6th-8th Grade Teacher 1973-, 6th Grade Math/Sci/Mentor Teacher 1990 John Marshall Scndry; *ai:* Lincoln Avenue Church Youth Club Adv 1988-89; 7th Grade Adv 1990; Math, Gifted & Talented Comms 1989-; Daughters of Amer Revolution Awd 1984; Star News Design Ad Awd 1983; Pasadena Masonic Bodies Awd 1984-85; Supt Public Instruction Mentor Teachers Awd 1989; John Marshall Fundamental Sch Certificate of Appreciation 1989-.

SCOTT, DORETHA JACKSON, 4th Grade Teacher; *b:* Warner Robins, GA; *m:* Willie Frank; *c:* Durrell B.; *ed:* (BA) Elem Ed, 1978, (MS) Mid Grade Ed, 1981, Ft Valley St Coll; *cr:* 5th Grade Teacher Ft Valley Mid Sch 1978-79; 4th Grade Teacher Bonaire Elem Sch 1979-; *ai:* Stu Support Team & Grade Level Chairperson; 4th Grade Media Comm Chairperson; NEA, GAE, Houston Assn of Educators 1978-; Alpha Kappa 1985-; Church Women United Assn Secy 1988-; Warner Robins Hospitality Circle 1985-; Alpha Kappa Alpha Nom Comm 1985-; World Changers on the Move 1988-; Mattie E. Coleman Circle for Missionary Ladies 1985-; *office:* Bonaire Elem Sch 201 Elm St Bonaire GA 31005

SCOTT, DOROTHY PERSON, Third Grade Teacher; *b:* Chicago, IL; *m:* Michael Joseph; *c:* Michelle Haizel, Marianne; *ed:* (BA) Ed, Chicago Teachers Coll 1948; (MA) Ed, Northwestern Univ 1953; Grad Stud Various Univs; *cr:* 4th-6th Grade Teacher Southside Sch 1948-61; 3rd/4th Grade Teacher Harnew Sch 1971-; *ai:* Southwest Symphony Orch Spon; AFT, NEA; Friends of Oak Lawn Lib; PTA 1971-; *office:* Harnew Sch 9100 Austin Ave Oak Lawn IL 60453

SCOTT, DWIGHT LEWIS, Phys Ed Chair/Athletic Dir; *b:* Washington, DC; *m:* Helen Miller; *c:* Susan, Mark, Jean S. Brookman, John, Mike, Regina M. Costlow, James, Matthew; *ed:* (BA) Phys Ed, W MD 1953; (MA) Phys Ed, Univ of MD 1965; Grad Stud Drivers Ed; *cr:* Private/1st Lieutenant US Army 1953-57; Ftbl/Bsktbl/Bsbl Coach/Phys Ed Teacher Lewis-Palmer HS 1957-58; His Teacher Washington-Lee HS 1958-59; Ftbl Coach/Phys Ed Teacher/Track & Field Coach 1959-, Cross Cntry Coach 1976-, Athletic Dir 1978- Boonsboro HS; *ai:* Head Coach Boys & Girls Cross Cntry, Indoor & Outdoor Track & Field; Athletic Dir; MD Athletic Dirs, Natl Track/Field Coaches, MD Teachers Assn, Washington Cty Teachers Assn; MD Health, Phys Ed, Recreation Assn; Amer Legion 1974-; MD Natl Fed HS Coach of Yr 1985; *office:* Boonsboro HS 10 Campus Ave Boonsboro MD 21713

SCOTT, EVELYN M., Teacher; *b:* Grady, AR; *c:* Tiffinie D. Bell; *ed:* General Ed, Kennedy HS 1964; (BA) Home Ec, AM & N Coll 1969; (MA) Educl Leadership MI St 1982; Sex Ed; *cr:* Beauty Cosmetics Mary Kay Cosmetics; *ai:* Church Choir Dir; Sch Schlsp; *home:* 167 Hastings St Benton Harbor MI 49022

SCOTT, FLORETTA P., Mathematics Department Chm; *b:* Mobile, AL; *c:* Carlos J. Phillips, Carletta J. Franks, Carmen J. Franks; *ed:* (BA) Math, Talladega Coll 1968; Cert Mobile Coll; *cr:* Benefits Examiner Soc Security Admin 1968-69; Teacher Magnolia 1969-71, Mobile Cty Trng Sch 1978-79, K J Clark Mid Sch 1979-; *ai:* SECME Organization Coord; SACS Comm; AEA, NEA, MCEA 1978-; 3rd Baptist Church; Teacher of Yr 1984-85; Heart of Gold Awd 1989-; *office:* K J Clark Mid Sch 50 12th Ave Chickasaw AL 36611

SCOTT, GEORGIA PERRY, 8th Grade Mathematics Teacher; *b:* Vance Cty, NC; *m:* James Oliver; *c:* Kari E.; *ed:* (BS) Math, Norfolk St Univ 1967; (MA) Math, Hampton Univ 1972; *cr:* 7th Grade Math/Algebra Teacher Buckroe Jr HS 1967-76, Jones Jr HS 1976-80; 7th/8th Grade Math/Algebra Teacher Eaton Fundamental Mid Sch 1980-; *ai:* Cmptr Club Spon; Cmptr Activity Club Adv; Natl Cncl of Math 1980-; VA Ed Assn, NEA 1967-; *office:* Eaton Fundamental Mid Sch 2108 Cunningham Dr Hampton VA 23666

SCOTT, GLADYS SUITOR, Third Grade Teacher; *b:* Corinth, MS; *m:* Robert Albert III; *c:* Robert A. IV, Benjamin A., Lelia Kelly, Mae E. Wright, John C.; *ed:* (BS) Elem Ed, 1947, (BS) Scndry Ed, 1947 MS St Univ; Grad Study Elem Ed; *cr:* Teacher Mc Allen Bus Coll, Mc Allen City Public Sch System, Corinth City Public Sch System, NEM Jr Coll, Alcorn Cty Public Sch Sys; *ai:* HS Sr Spon; 4-H Leader; HS Annual Adv; Missionary Society Pres; Gideons Auxiliary Intnl Pres; Sunday Sch Teacher; Gideons Auxiliary Chaplain; NEA, MEA; Pta (Pres, Secy); Summa Cum Laude; Outstanding Elem Teacher of America 1975; *home:* Rt 1 Box 305 Corinth MS 38834

SCOTT, JEFFRIE GLENN, Mathematics Teacher; *b:* Birmingham, AL; *m:* Beverly Watts; *ed:* (BS) Bus Admin, Tuskegee Inst 1976; (MBA) Finance, Atlanta Univ 1980; *cr:* Math Teacher Green Pastures Chrstn Acad 1986-; *ai:* Track & Field Coach; Sch Newspaper Adv; Spring Olympics Coord; *office:* Green Pastures Chrstn Acad 5455 Flat Shoals Rd Decatur GA 30034

SCOTT, JULIA ARLENE, Junior High School Teacher; *b:* Celina, OH; *ed:* (BS) Elem, 1978, (MA) Ed/Learning Disabilities/Behavioral Disabilities, 1984 Wright St Univ; *cr:* EMR Teacher 1978-79, Jr HS/Teacher of Learning Disabilities 1979- Mendon-Union Schls; *ai:* Spec Projects & Grants & Local Sch Dist Gifted Coord; Former Yrbk Adv; Mendon-Union Ed Assn (Pres 1979-83, VP 1983-85); Kappa Delta Pi Mem 1984; Zoning Appeals Bd Secy 1989-; Martha Holden Jennings Scholar 1983-84; *home:* 6688 Coldwater Beach Rd Celina OH 45822

SCOTT, JULIA MC INTYRE, Principal; *b:* Filter, MS; *m:* William Frederick; *c:* Jada, Joseph, Joy; *ed:* (BS) Eng, MS Valley St Univ 1963; (MED) Eng, Tuskegee Univ 1975; Eng Wkshps, Rugers St Univ, Atlanta Univ, Univ of S MS, MS St Univ; *cr:* Teacher Simmons HS 1963-64, Leland Attendance Center 1964-65, Shirley Owens HS 1965-69, Moss Point HS 1970-82, Eastside Mid Sch 1983-88; Coord Selma City Schl 1988-89; Prin Eastside Mid Sch 1989-; *ai:* SEA, AEA 1983-; AAMLA 1989-; AATE 1990; ASCD 1989-; SCLC 1989; Sripend Rutgers & Tuskegee Univ; Teacher of Yr 1972, 1985; STAR Teacher 1978-; Personalities of Youth; *home:* 1209 Kings Bend Rd Selma AL 36701

SCOTT, KATHLYN JANE, Spanish Teacher; *b:* Eau Claire, WI; *m:* Brian John; *c:* Megan L., Adam J., Kelly E.; *ed:* (BA) Span/Eng, Univ of Dubuque 1972; Univ of Madrid Spain 1969; *cr:* Span/Eng Teacher Lisle Jr/Sr 1972-76; Span Teacher Oak Grove HS 1986-; *ai:* Span Club; Newspaper Adv; Flarr Speaker 1986-; AATSP 1972-76; *home:* 1826 S 23rd St Fargo ND 58103

SCOTT, KAY KELLER, English Teacher; *b:* Omaha, NE; *m:* William Gordon; *c:* Jessica E., Dylan B.; *ed:* (BS) Ed, Univ of Tn 1971; (MA) Media Stud, Antioch Coll 1975; Grad Work Eng Lit & Cmptr Sci, Alfred Univ, Empire St Coll, Univ of KY; *cr:* Lang Art/Eng/Film & Video Teacher Canisteo Cntrl Sch 1971-74, 1979-84; 7th-12th Grade Comm/Rdng/Writing Teacher Arkport Cntrl Sch 1976-79; 9th-12th Grade Eng/Writing Coord Teacher Western Hills HS 1984-89; 6th-7th Grade Lang Art/Soc Stud Teacher Midlakes Mid Sch 1989-; *ai:* Teachers as Writers Group; Instructional Leadership & Public Relations Comm; Directed Musicals; KY Cncl Teachers of Eng 1985-89; NCTE 1987-; NY St Union of Teachers 1971-84, 1989-; Hornell Area Arts Cncl Exec Dir, Hornell Little Theatre Secy 1972-75; Womens Sharing Group Canisteo Cncl of Churches 1977-84; Mortar Bd Schlsp Univ of TN; Kappa Delta Pi Honorary Society; Natl Endowment Summer Study Fellowship; NY St RACET Awds; Wrote & Received Prjoect Grants; All-Academic Faculty 1988-; Books Published; *home:* 6169 Hunters Dr Farmington NY 14425

SCOTT, LINDA BROWN, Sixth Grade Teacher; *b:* Greensboro, NC; *m:* Daniel B.; *c:* Celeste, Doug; *ed:* (BA) Elem Ed, Baptist Coll of Charleston 1971; (MA) Elem Ed, Coll of Charleston 1976; *cr:* 4th Grade Teacher Albert R Lewis Elem 1972, Riverland Terrace Elem 1972-73; 4th/5th Grade Teacher Stiles Point Elem 1973-88; 6th/8th Grade Teacher Drayton Hall Mid Sch 1988-; *ai:* James Island Opti-Mrs (Secy 1983-84, Membership Chairperson 1985-87); Teacher of Month 1987; *home:* 2408 Pristine View Charleston SC 29414

SCOTT, LINDA HALL, Math Teacher/Level Leader; *b:* Blooming Grove, TX; *m:* J. Sam Jr.; *c:* Cristin, Jeff; *ed:* (BA) Eng/Speech, E TX St Univ 1969; (BS) Math, Univ of TX Arlington 1982; Grad Work at Univ of TX Dallas; *cr:* Eng Teacher Thomas Edison Jr HS 1969-70; Pre-Kndgtn Teacher Fielder Road Early Chldhd 1976-82; Algebra Teacher Young Jr HS 1982-; *ai:* TX St Teachers Assn (Secy, NEA Delegate) 1989; Faculty Liaison Comm Chm 1987-89; St Advisory Cncl Early Chldhd 1978-82; Young Jr HS Teacher of Yr; *office:* Young Jr HS 3200 Woodside Dr Arlington TX 76016

SCOTT, LINDA HILSABECK, 3rd Grade Teacher; *b:* Maryville, MO; *m:* Jerry C.; *c:* Eric Myers; *ed:* (BS) Elem Ed, Northwest MO St Univ 1971; Addl Studies Elem Ed Northwest MO St Univ; *cr:* 2nd Grade Teacher 1971-76; Kdgtn Teacher 1976-77; 3rd Grade Teacher 1977- South Nodaway R-IV; *ai:* Elem Supv K-6 South Nodaway R-IV; MO St Teachers Assn 1971-; Intl Rdng Assn 1988-; ASCD 1989-; *home:* Rr 3 Box 95 Maryville MO 64468

SCOTT, LINDA JORDAN, 6th Grade Teacher; *b:* Blackshere, GA; *m:* Richard W.; *c:* Eric; *ed:* (BS) Elem Ed, 1969, (MS) Elem Ed, 1973 GA Coll; Data Collector; Stu Teacher Supervision; *cr:* Teacher Mattie Wells Sch 1969-72, 1974-; *ai:* Natl Teachers Assn, GA Assn of Teachers, PAGE; Tattnall Square Baptist Church Sunday Sch Mem; Whos Who in Sports Bsktbl; *office:* Mattie Wells Sch Rt 14 Box 100 Macon GA 31211

SCOTT, LINDA L., 6th-8th Remedial Rdng Teacher; *b:* Olean, NY; *m:* Theodore L.; *c:* Jeffrey, Christopher; *ed:* (MS) Ed, SUNY Geneseo 1972; (BS) Ed, St Bonaventure 1976; Working on Masters, Counseling; *cr:* 4th-6th Grade Elem Teacher/Jr HS Remedial Rdng Teacher Portville Cntrl; *ai:* Dir PSEN Prgm; Stu Cncl Adv; ACE 1989-; NY St Rdng Assn, NY St Teachers Assn; PTA, BSA; FAC Assn Secy; 6th Grade Ecology Prgm & Camp; *office:* Portville Cntrl Sch Elm St Portville NY 14770

SCOTT, LINDA SIMKINS, 2nd Grade Teacher; *b:* Columbia, SC; *m:* Robert H.; *c:* Ashley, Brandon; *ed:* (BA) Elem Ed, Benedict Coll 1969; Elem Ed; *cr:* Elem Teacher Janna Elem Sch 1970-; *ai:* Math Tutor; Mentor for Students; Phila Fed of Teachers 1970-; Han H & S Assn; Fitler H & S Assn 1982-; Jenks H & S Assn; Paths Grant for Cultural Backgrounds Soc Stud.

SCOTT, MADELYN COHEN, 6th Grade Teacher; *b:* Luthersville, GA; *m:* Theo C.; *c:* Karen Rouse, Kevin Rouse; *ed:* (AA) Truett-Mc Connell Coll 1957; (BS) Elem Ed, Tift Coll 1969; Staff Dev Courses; *cr:* Teacher Luthersville Elem 1958-60; Crawford Cty Elem; Humphries Elem 1964-74; East Clayton Elem 1976-; *ai:* Vacation Bible Sch Dir; Dept Dir Childrens Sunday Sch Dept; Childrens Choir Dir/Coord; Clayton Cty Intnl Rdng Assn VP 1989; Clayton Cty Eng Lang Arts Cncl Treas; GA Cncl Teacher of Eng 1984-; NEA; GA Assn of Edctrs; Clayton Cty Ed Assn 1976-; Natl Teachers of Eng 1980-; GA Cncl Intnl Rdng Assn 1986-; Intnl Rdng Assn 1986-; ASCD; Alpha Delta Kappa 1986-; Strategic Planning Comm Clayton Cty Comm Mem 1989-; PTA Teacher of Yr; Mount Zion Chrstn Acad (Chairperson Bd of Ed, Steering Comm Chairperson) Svc Plaque; Designed & Taught Staff Dev Prgm; Writing Inservices Jackson Cty GA Teachers; Presented Writing Prgm Land Arts Conf GA St Univ; Southern Assn Comm Reaccreditation Process 10 Yr Study; *office:* East Clayton Elem 2750 Ellenwood Rd Ellenwood GA 30049

SCOTT, MARK STONEWALL, Theology/Art Teacher; *b:* Chicago, IL; *ed:* (BA) Art, Loyola Univ 1972; St Mary of The Lake Univ, Univ of Notre Dame, Xavier Coll; *cr:* Teacher St Juliana Elem 1975-76, Quigley S HS 1977, St Laurence HS 1978-; *ai:* Dir of Stu Act; *office:* St Laurence HS 5556 W 77th St Burbank IL 60459

SCOTT, MARTHA S., 8th Grade Soc Stud Teacher; *b:* Columbus, MS; *c:* Yale, Thor; *ed:* (BS) Elem Ed, MS St Coll for Women 1968; (MED) Mid Grades, Columbus Coll 1983; Working Towards Ed Specialist; *cr:* 5th Grade Rdng/Eng Teacher St Marys Elem Sch 1968-69; 7th/8th Grade Math/Eng Teacher Talbotton Rd Jr HS 1971-73; 8th Grade Math/Soc Stud Teacher Marshall Jr HS 1978-80; 4th-6th Grade Rdng Teacher Rosemont Elem Sch 1980-81; 7th/8th Grade Eng/Soc Stud Teacher Fort Jr HS 1981-; *ai:* Quiz Bowl Founder; Academic Team Spon; Teacher Innovator, Teacher/Employee Public Relations Comms Mem; Prof Assn of GA Educators (Pres 1985-87, System Rep 1988-, Division I Dir 1988-); Alpha Delta Kappa (Chaplin 1988-, Dist Historian 1990, Mem 1987-); Kappa Delta Pi 1990; *office:* Fort Jr HS 2900 Woodruff Farm Rd Columbus GA 31907

SCOTT, MARY JANE, 8th Grade English Teacher; *b:* Humboldt, TN; *m:* Robert H.; *c:* Keith, Kathy S. Pruitt, Kent, Kevin; *ed:* (BA) Elem Ed, UT at Martin 1982; *cr:* 2nd Grade Teacher Trenton Elem Sch 1982; 7th Grade Eng Teacher 1982-84, 8th Grade Eng Teacher 1984- Trenton Mid Sch; *ai:* Beta Club Spon; Odyssey of the Mind; West Tn Cncl Teachers of Eng 1989-; Tn Cncl Teachers of Eng 1989-; NCTE 1984-; *office:* Trenton Mid Sch 2nd St Trenton TN 38382

SCOTT, MICHELLE WILLIAMS, Sixth Grade Teacher; *b:* Daytona Beach, FL; *m:* William Randolph; *c:* Maury D., Natalya C., Trenton D.; *ed:* (BS) Elem Ed, FL Ag & Mechanical Univ 1978; Indian River Cty Peer Teacher Trng; Cmptr Trng; FL

Writing Project; *ai:* Sebastian River Mid Jr HS Rdng Club; Teachers-Parents Helping Their Child Make the Grade; FL Ed Assn 1978-; Alpha Kappa Alpha 1976-; FL A&M Univ Alumni 1978-; Golden Apple Awd; Lang Art Blue Ribbon Task Force; Sebastian River Mid Jr HS Finalist Teacher of Yr; Progressive Civic League; Elem & Scndry Tutor; *office:* Sebastian River Mid Jr HS 9400 State Rd 512 Sebastian FL 32958

SCOTT, NANCY KEETON, 7th Grade Soc Stud Teacher; *b:* Huntsville, AL; *m:* Warren L.; *c:* Lori S. Stanfield, Robert J., Susan E., Benjamin C.; *ed:* (BS) Home Ec, Univ of Montevallo 1961; Cert Scndry Soc Stud, Huntingdon Coll 1964; *cr:* 4th/5th Grade Soc Stud Teacher Prattville Elem & Intermediate 1964-70, 1973-78; 7th Grade Soc Stud Teacher Prattville Jr HS 1978-; *ai:* Natl Teachers Assn, AL Ed Assn, Autauga Cty Teachers Assn 1964-; AL Soc Stud Cncl & NCSS 1978-; Intnl Pilot Club (Recording Secy 1990) 1988-; Spinners Service Organization Club Corresponding Secy 1973-; Amer Assn Univ Women 1964-68; *office:* Prattville Jr HS N Chestnut St Prattville AL 36067

SCOTT, NICHOLAS, History & Journalism Teacher; *b:* Toledo, OH; *m:* Patricia E. Mc Guire; *c:* Nicholas III, Karen M., Michael, Eileen; *ed:* (BED) Comprehensive Soc Stud, 1967, (MA) Amer His, 1973, Spec Ed Admin/Supervision 1976 Univ of Toledo; Working Towards PhD Amer His, Univ of Toledo; *cr:* Teacher/Asst Prin Whiteford HS; *ai:* Sr Class Adv; Yrbk & Newspaper; NEA, MI Ed Assn, NCSS; Knights of Columbus; *office:* Whiteford HS 6655 Consear Rd Ottawa Lake MI 49267

SCOTT, PEARL ROBERTS, Third Grade Teacher; *b:* Quincy, FL; *m:* Simon Lamar; *c:* Tyrone; *ed:* (BS) Elem Ed, FL A&M 1956; *cr:* Teacher Pine Park Elem 1956-66, St John Elem 1967-; *ai:* Gadsden Cty Classroom Teachers Assn, Rdng Cncl, FL Teaching Profession; Heroines of J Secy 1973-; Womens Missionary S Pres 1977-78, Trophy 1986; St Hebron Choir Treas 1979-.

SCOTT, PHYLLIS JEAN, Sixth Grade Teacher; *b:* Oneida, KY; *m:* Jasper; *c:* E. Scott Arnett; *ed:* (BA) Elem Ed, Cumberland Coll 1976; (MS) Elem Ed, Union Coll 1978; (Rank I) Supervision, E KY Univ 1983; KY Internship Prgm; *cr:* 2nd/3rd Grade Teacher Oneida Elem 1977-84; 6th Grade Teacher London Elem 1984-; *ai:* KEA, NEA; KY Internship Prgm Resource Teacher; Cumberland Coll & E KY Univ Supervising Teacher; *home:* Rt 3 Box 94-B Corbin KY 40701

SCOTT, RANDALL JAY, Science/Computer Teacher; *b:* Detroit, MI; *m:* Kathleen Ann; *c:* Zachary, Justin, Mac Kenzie; *ed:* (BS) Bio, Cntrl MI Univ 1974; Grad Work Educl Cmptrs, Wayne St Univ; *cr:* Sci Teacher Clawson HS 1974-76, Cheboygan Jr HS 1979-; Educl Cmptrs Teacher Cntrl MI Univ 1986-; *ai:* Ski & Cmptr Club; Stu Assistance Comm; MI Assn for Cmptr Users in Learning 1986-; Cntrl MI Univ Off-Campus Faculty Mem; Cheboygan Hockey Assn 1979-87; Cheboygan Soccer Assn 1980-; Teach Classes in Educl Computing & Logo; *office:* Cheboygan Jr HS 504 Division Cheboygan MI 49721

SCOTT, ROGER DALE, 8th Grade Science Teacher; *b:* Sweetwater, TN; *m:* Twila Dearlene Crye; *c:* John M.; *ed:* (BS) Ag Ed, 1973, (MS) Ed/Admin/Supervision, 1978 Univ of TN Knoxville; *cr:* Voc Ag Teacher Huntland Public Sch 1973-74; 7th-8th Grade Sci Teacher Elem Sch 1974-78; 8th Grade Sci Teacher North Mid Sch 1978-; *ai:* Chess Club Spon; Grade Level & Dept Chm; Dance Dir; Loudon Cty Ed Assn (Pres 1978-79, 1987-89); TEA, NEA; ASCD 1986-; Mountain View Lodge #519 F&AM (Worshipful Master 1984, Secy & Dist Chm 1989-); *office:* North Mid Sch Rt 1 Hickory Creek Rd Lenoir City TN 37771

SCOTT, ROGER WILKINS, SR., 7th Grade Teacher; *b:* Dixie, GA; *m:* Willie Mae Williams; *ed:* (BS) Soc Stud, Savannah St 1958; *cr:* 6th/7th Grade Elem Teacher Morven Elem; *ai:* 7th Grade & Math Club Adv; NAE, GAE; Morven PTO; Brooks Cty Credit Union Loan Officer; Morven Elem STAR Teacher 1967 & Teacher of Yr 1988, 1990.

SCOTT, ROSE MISURACA, Physical Education Teacher; *b:* New Orleans, LA; *m:* Charles E.; *ed:* (BS) Phys Ed, Northwestern St 1966; (MED) Guidance & Counseling Loyola Univ 1974; Grad Work USM, UNO 1980; *cr:* Teacher/Coach Chalmette HS 1966; Teacher/Coach/Athletic Dir Andrew Jackson HS 1967-; *ai:* Dept Chm; Natl HS Athletic Coaches Assn (Sftbl Vice Chm, Natl Convention Sftbl Chm 1986), Natl Sftbl Coach of Yr 1985, Regional Sftbl Coach of Yr 1979; NEA, LA Ed Assn, St Bernard Ed Assn; LA Health & Phys Ed Assn Mem 1966-; Amer All Health & Phys Ed Assn; Amer Red Cross (First Aid/CPR Instr 1966-, Swim Instr 1966-84), 20 Yr Awd 1987; LA HS Coaches Assn Exec Comm; Articles Published; *office:* Andrew Jackson HS Chalmette Ave at 8th St Chalmette LA 70043

SCOTT, SHARON TERRY, Kindergarten Teacher; *b:* Oneida, TN; *m:* Daniel L.; *ed:* (BA) Scndry Ed/Eng, Cumberland Coll 1972; Elem Ed Endorsement, TN Tech Univ; *cr:* Remedial Rdng Teacher 1972, Kndgtn Teacher 1973- Oneida Elem; *ai:* Oneida Ed Assn (Secy 1976) 1972-; TN Ed Assn, NEA 1972-; Delta Kappa Gamma (Corresponding Secy 1984-86, 2nd VP 1986-, Mem 1978-); *office:* Oneida Elem Sch PO Box 1015 Main St Oneida TN 37841

SCOTT, SHEILA E., Marketing Education Teacher; *b:* Columbus, OH; *m:* Wendell; *c:* Jeriah Scurry, Alison; *ed:* (BS) Ed, OH St Univ 1978; (MBA) Public Admin, Cntrl MI Univ 1988; *cr:* Mrktg Coord Columbus Public Schls 1978-; *ai:* Distributive Ed Clubs of America Adv; Columbus Ed Assn Building Rep 1990; OH Ed Assn, NEA; Alpha Kappa Alpha 1986; Jack & Jill of American Public Relations 1988; OH Ed Assn Delegate; *office:* Eastmoor HS 417 Weyant St Columbus OH 43213

SCOTT, SHIRLEY CARROLL, Business Education Teacher; *b:* Daphne, AL; *m:* Willie C.; *c:* Derek L.; *ed:* (BS) Commerce, AL St 1960; (ME) Scndry Ed, Univ of S AL 1975; Several Certificates for Participation in Wkshps and Seminars; Visiting Comm for Self-Study Mem; *cr:* Teacher Douglasville HS 1961-67, Baldwin Cty HS 1967-; *ai:* NHS Spon; Ten-Yr Self-Study Evaluation Report Chm; Bus Ed Dept Chm; Secy Local Teachers Assn; Faculty Cncl Mem; Baldwin Cty Ed Assn Secy 1978-79, 1989-; Key Club Teacher of Yr 1980; Mt Aid Baptist Church Secy 1965-; Port City United Voices Finance Secy 1983-, Outstanding Service Awd 1984, Extra Mile Awd 1990; Numerous Original Poems; Wrote & Submitted First Gospel Song to Gospel Music Wkshp of America; Supervised Layout & Typing of Cookbook for Church Group; Woman of Yr Awd 1989; *home:* PO Box 76 Spanish Fork AL 36527

SCOTT, SUZANNE DE TURK, 5th Grade Teacher; *b:* Champaign, IL; *c:* Ellen Scott Fodge, Katherine Scott Smith, Jennifer L.; *ed:* (BA) Elem Ed, 1980, (MA) Curr/Instruction/Gifted Ed, 1986 MI St Univ; *cr:* Coord/Trainer Volunteer Prgms 1974-78; 5th Grade Teacher Elliott Elem 1981-83, Dimondale Elem 1983-; *ai:* Mem Gifted & Talented Comm, Learning Task Force, Sci Curr Improvement Wkshp; Holt Ed Assn Cncl Rep 1980-; Lansing Area Assn Academically Talented 1990; GSA (Secy, Capitol Area Cncl Bd Dir) 1976-78; Teacher Summer Gifted Prgms Intermediate Sch Dist; *home:* 4 Cedarwoods Mason MI 48854

SCOTT, T. MICHAEL, English Teacher; *b:* Des Moines, IA; *m:* Barbara Gwynne; *ed:* (BA) Eng, Univ of CA 1970; (MS) Ed, CA St Fullerton 1983; Learning Handicapped, Resource Specialist Credentials; *cr:* Teacher Garey HS 1977-83, Patrick Henry HS 1983-87, Morse HS 1987-; *ai:* Race/Human Relations Comm; Collaboration Team; 9th Grade Curr Comm Chm; NCTE, Peer Counseling Assn; Mentor Teacher 1989-; *office:* Morse HS 6905 Skyline Dr San Diego CA 92114

SCOTT, TONYA PENDERGRAFT, Math Teacher; *b:* Durham, NC; *m:* John B.; *c:* Heather, Jonathan E., Beth; *ed:* (BS) Ed Math/Sci, Appalachian St Univ 1977; *cr:* Math Teacher Lowes Grove Jr HS 1978-88; Math Sci Teacher Apex Mid Sch 1988-89; Math Teacher Lowes Grove Mid Sch 1989-; *ai:* Mathcounts Co-Spon; Project Ride Reg Ed Teacher Rep; Co-Chr Self-Study Comm; Telecomm Comm Rep; NC Assn of Educators 1979-; NEA; NC Cncl Teachers Math; NCTM; Team Grant Mitsubishi 1989-; *office:* Lowes Grove Mid Sch 4418 S Alston Ave Durham NC 27713

SCOTT, VERA SARGENT, Counselor; *b:* Oldtown, KY; *m:* Conard; *c:* Michael, Chanda; *ed:* (BA) Elem Ed, 1968; (MA) Ed, 1971; Rank I Cnslng, 1981 Morehead St Univ; KY Intern-Resource Teacher; *cr:* 3rd Grade Teacher Russell Central Elem 1968-69; 4th Grade Teacher 1969-74; 7th Grade Teacher 1974-89 Argillite Elem; Mid Sch Cnslr Wurtland Mid Sch 1989-; *ai:* Resource Teacher for Beginning Interns; KEA; NEA; KACD; PTSA; *office:* Wurtland Mid Sch 700 Center St Wurtland KY 41144

SCOTT, WALTER LEE, Dean of Students; *b:* E St Louis, IL; *m:* Carolyn J. Manfredi; *c:* Walter L. II, Jeffrey A.; *ed:* (BSED) Industrial Ed, E IL Univ 1965; (MSED) Educl Admin, Sangamon St Univ 1981; *cr:* Ind Ed Instr Danville Cmmty HS 1965-66; Ind Ed/Building Trades Teacher Mc Henry Cmmty HS 1966-77; Ind Ed Teacher Lakeview HS 1978-82; Ind Ed Instr Stephen Decatur HS 1982-83; Dean of Stu Eisenhower HS 1983-; *ai:* Track & Field Ofcl; IL HS Assoc; IL Deans Assn 1984-85; *office:* Dwight D Eisenhower HS 1200 S 16th St Decatur IL 62521

SCOTT, WILBUR WINSTON, JR., 6th Grade Teacher; *b:* Memphis, TN; *m:* Betty Rainey; *c:* Stanley, Elisabeth; *ed:* (BA) Bio, Univ AR Pine Bluff 1969; (MA) Educl Leadership, Western MI Univ 1987; *cr:* 6th Grade Teacher Benton Harbor Area Schls 1969-; *ai:* 4-H 6th Grade Bsktbl Coach 1978-84; Chm of Sci Fair 1989-; 2nd Baptist Church (Sunday Sch Supt 1971-87, Deacon 1979-) Service 1981/1987; Elem Teacher of Yr Benton Harbor Area Schls 1988-89; *home:* 557 Waverly Benton Harbor MI 49022

SCOTT, WILLIAM CONWAY, Social Studies Chair; *b:* Philadelphia, PA; *m:* Jeanene Bricker; *c:* Sherene Toebe, Darin; *ed:* (BSE) Soc Stud, West Chester Univ 1960; (MA) His/Poly Sci, Villanova Univ 1964; *cr:* Teacher 1960-, Dept Chm 1987- Marple Newtown HS; *ai:* Ftbl, Bsbl, Sftbl, Girls Vlybl Coach; PA Cncl for Soc Stud, Mid States Cncl for Soc Stud, NCSS; *office:* Marple Newtown HS 120 Media Line Rd Newtown Square PA 19073

SCOVILLE, ROBERT CHARLES, Social Science Teacher; *b:* Glendale, CA; *ed:* (AA) Eng, Glendale Jr Coll 1965; (BA) Eng, CA St Univ Northridge 1967; Grad Sch CA St Univ Northridge; *cr:* Substitute Teacher Long Beach Schls 1969-71; Home Study Teacher Fresno Unified Schls 1971-76; Teacher Bullard HS 1976-80, Wawona Mid Sch 1980-83, Bullard HS 1983-; *ai:* Model United Nations Coach; Class Spon; Sch Building Comm Chm; Amer Government & Ec Curr Comm Chm; NCSS; YMCA Fundraiser 1985-86; GreenPeace Mem 1988- ; Fresno Metropolitan Museum 1989; Teacher of Yr Bullard HS 1986; *office:* Bullard H S 5445 N Palm Fresno CA 93704

SCRANTON, WALTER M., Head Counselor; *b:* San Diego, CA; *m:* Catherine Erkl; *ed:* (AS) Fire Sci, Mesa Jr Coll 1975; (BS) Psych, 1978, (MS) Counseling, 1979 San Diego St; MS in Admin; *cr:* Dist Counseling Riley Sch 1980-83; Head Counseling Ernstein Jr HS 1983-85, San Diego HS 1985-; *ai:* Jr Var Bsbl Coach; HS Diploma Prgm; Club Adv; Help Publish Article; *office:* San Diego HS 1405 Park Blvd San Diego CA 92101

SCREEN, ELIZABETH JAMES, Science Department Chairperson; *b:* Dawson, GA; *m:* Arnold; *c:* Curtis Cheeks Jr., Erica Y. Cheeks, Arnold III, Arlando J.; *ed:* (BS) Bio, Fort Valley St Coll 1973; (MAT) Earth Sci, Univ of SC 1982; Proj Wild SC Wildlife Svc; Earth Sci Inst; Cmptr Trng; *cr:* Operator Southern Bell 1970; Secy/Rearcher Ft Valley St Coll 1970-73; Sci Teacher Northside Jr HS 1974-76; Sci Teacher 1972-90; Chairperson Sci Dept 1988- Gilbert HS; *ai:* Jr Sci Club; Textbook Comm; Acad Quiz Bowl; Comphnsv Hlth Comm; NEA 1974-; Lexington I Ed Assn Pres 1977; SC Earth Sci Assn 1980-; NSTA 1980-; PTA 1976-; 4-H Ldr 1980-; Girl Scout Ldr 1976-82; Little League Chrldr Coach 1976-82; Little League Ftbl Bd 1976-84; *home:* 927 Hendrix St Lexington SC 29072

SCREWS, DONALD G., JR., 8th Grade Science Teacher; *b:* Dublin, GA; *m:* Cindy Douglas; *c:* Christopher; *ed:* (AA) Ed, Mid GA Coll 1978; (BS) Ed, 1980, (MA) Ed, 1985, (SPED) Ed 1988 GA Southwestern; *cr:* 7th/8th Grade Teacher Chester Elem 1980-81; 8th Grade Sci Teacher Dodge Mid Sch 1981-; *ai:* NEA Pres 1979-80; GA Ornithological Society Nature Conservancy; Audubon; *office:* Dodge Mid Sch Herman Ave Eastman GA 31023

SCRIBNER, JANE ANN, English Dept Chairperson; *b:* Ft Worth, TX; *m:* Walter Glen; *c:* Bryan, Marty; *ed:* (BS) Phys Ed, 1971, (MED) Phys Ed, 1977 Pan Amer; *cr:* Eng/Phys Ed Teacher/Coach McAllen Ind Sch Dist 1972, 1975; Eng/Phys Ed/Health Teacher Pflugerville Ind Sch Dist 1977-80; Eng Teacher Gunn Jr HS 1983-; *ai:* Textbook & Curr Writing Comm; Honor Society; Kappa Delta Pi; Kappa Delta (Pres, VP) 1969-70; PTA Life Membership; *office:* Gunn Jr HS 3000 F Fielder Rd Arlington TX 76015

SCRIBNER, SUSAN ANN, 6th Grade Teacher/Team Leader; *b:* Mason City, IA; *ed:* (BA) Elem Ed, Rollins Coll 1961; (MED) Admin Careers, Lesley Coll 1978; Certificate Classtoom Application in Cmptr Technology, Cntrl New England Coll of Technology; *cr:* 4th Grade Teacher Catalina Elem Sch 1961-63; 3rd Grade Teacher Blue Hill Elem Sch 1963-64; 2nd/4th-6th Grade Teacher Westwood Public Schls 1967-; *ai:* Asst to Prin; Chairperson Sci Prgm Review Comm; Mem Prgm Dev Cncl; Liaison Prof Performance Appraisal System; Coord Outdoor Sci Ed Prgm; Harvard Prins Center 1988-; MA Teachers Assn 1967-; ASCD 1988-; Westwood Teachers Assn (VP, Pres) 1980-84; *office:* Sheehan Sch 549 Pond St Westwood MA 02090

SCROBACK, JO ANN KOPP, Mathematics Teacher; *b:* Wales, NY; *m:* Theodore A.; *c:* Jill Seward, Todd Seward, Amber, Caleb; *ed:* (BA) Scndry Math Ed, Houghton Coll 1966; Grad Stud Math & Ed Courses; *cr:* Math Teacher Perry Cntrl Sch 1966, Arcade Cntrl Sch 1967-68, Pioneer Cntrl Sch 1970-75, TMI Acad 1976-80, Anderson Cty Schls 1984-; *ai:* TN Collaborative for Educl Excl; Task Force Mem; Anchor Club Asst & Frosh Class Adv; Anderson Cty Ed Assn, TN Ed Assn, NEA, Math Assn of America; Teacher of Yr Levels 6th-8th in Anderson Cty Sch System 1986; TN Career Level III Teacher 1985-; *office:* Anderson Cty HS 100 Maverick Dr Clinton TN 37716

SCUDDER, CATHERINE PATRICIA GENTHNER, Teacher of Gifted/Talented; *b:* Nobleboro, ME; *m:* Rowlett George; *c:* Pamela Goguen, Paula Meany, Peter Goguen, Nancy Holmes; *ed:* (BA) Government/His, Tufts Univ 1954; (MA) Ed, Univ of San Francisco 1978; Grad Stud Various Univ; *cr:* 4th-6th Grade Teacher Village View 1963-67; 4th-6th Grade Gifted/Talented Teacher Ocean View 1967-; *ai:* Teachers Advisory Comm & Supt; Ocean View Teacher Assn VP 1981; CA Gifted Assn 1970-80; Outstanding Teacher Awd; Teacher of Month Awd; *office:* Circle View Sch 6761 Hooker Dr Huntington Beach CA 92647

SCUITTE, LORENE MICHELLE, English Teacher; *b:* Salina, KS; *ed:* (BA) Engl/Speech Comm, KS Wesleyan Univ 1984; *cr:* Substitute Teacher Salina Jr HS South 1984; Teacher Ell Saline Jr/Sr HS 1984-; *ai:* 8th Grade Class Spon; Jr HS Chrldng Spon; HS Forensics Spon; KATE 1990; NCTE 1990; St Johns Luth Church 1961-; Salina Cmmty Theatre Pres 1988-89; Players Organization; Two Gold Star Awds from Bd Ed for Efforts in & Out of Classroom 1988-89; *office:* Ell-Saline H S PO Box 97 Brookville KS 67425

SCULLY, DAVID JOHN, French/Spanish/Chinese Teacher; *b:* Exeter, NH; *m:* Estela Lopez Varela; *c:* Anita T. D Ermes, Joseph, Adam, John, Edward; *ed:* (BA) Fr, Univ of NH 1955; (MA) Fr, Amer Univ 1973; Sch of Advanced Intnl Stud John Hopkins Univ; *cr:* Teacher Bishop Ireton HS 1979-; *ai:* Critical Lang Prgm Coord; Fr NHS & Fr Club Moderator; Phi Kappa Phi 1973; *office:* Bishop Ireton HS 201 Cambridge Rd Alexandria VA 22314

SCURRY, BETTY JO, 1st Grade Teacher; *b:* Williamsburg, VA; *m:* William Mc Farland; *c:* Dale S. Richardson, Jo Ellen, Ann Curtis; *ed:* (BS) Elem Ed, Lander Coll 1961; *cr:* 3rd Grade Teacher Cleo Bailey 1961-62; 1st Grade Teacher Ninety Six Elem 1968-; *ai:* Church Organist & Choir Dir; Served on SACS Comm; *office:* Ninety Six Elem Sch 121 S Cambridge St Ninety Six SC 29666

SCUTTI, PAUL N., Mathematics Teacher; *b:* Elmira, NY; *m:* Denise Decker; *c:* Erin; *ed:* (BS) Elem Ed/Environmental Ed, Glassboro St Coll 1977; *cr:* 6th Grade Teacher 1977-86, 7th/8th Grade Math Teacher 1988- Martin J Ryerson Mid Sch; *ai:* 7th & 8th Grade Boys Bsktbl 1988-, 7th & 8th Grade Girls Bsktbl 1978-86 Coach; Co-Coord 6th Grade Environmentaal Ed Prgm

1980-86; *office:* Martin J Ryerson Mid Sch Valley Rd Ringwood NJ 07456

SEACORD, MARGARET ANNE, Teacher of Grade 8; *b:* Detroit, MI; *ed:* (BS) Eng, Mercy Coll of Detroit 1963; Masters Courses Rdng, Marygrove Coll; *cr:* 6th Grade Teacher 1963-64, 8th Grade Teacher 1965- St Scholastica Grade Sch; *ai:* Cheerleading Coach 1967-68; Eng Dept Head 1967-; NEA 1979-80; Favorite Teacher Contest Sponsored by the Detroit News Sch Winner 1968; *office:* St Scholastica Grade Sch 17351 Southfield Rd Detroit MI 48235

SEACRIST, MARILYN HUBER, Language Arts/Computer Teacher; *b:* Easton, IL; *m:* G. R. Jr.; *c:* Michael, Donald, Anne; *ed:* (BS) Math, ISNU 1957; *cr:* Math Teacher Havana Cmmty HS 1957-60; Jr HS Teacher Sacre Coeur Grade Sch 1969-89; Lang Art/Cmptr Teacher Father Sweeney Sch 1989-; *ai:* Scholastic Team Assoc Coach; Altar & Rosary 1970-89; Timberlake Bd Golf Gov 1989-; *office:* Father Sweeney Sch 401 Ne Madison Ave Peoria IL 61603

SEAGLUND, SHARON TRADER, French Teacher; *b:* Detroit, MI; *c:* Eric, Brian, Kenneth; *ed:* Lang Cert Inst of Europena Stud Paris France 1967; (BA) Fr, Barat Coll 1968; Continuing Ed Theater, Oakland Univ 1972; Working on Foreign Lang Ed Degree, Wayne St Univ; *cr:* Fr Teacher Mercey HS 1968-69, St Francis of Assisu 1969-70, Benedictine HS 1979-81, Lamphere Schls 1982-; *ai:* Intnl Club & Frosh Class Moderator; AATF, Oakland Cty Assn of Teachers of Fr, Fr Inst Alliance Francaise; Lamphere HS Teacher of Yr 1985; *office:* Lamphere HS 610 W 13th Mile Rd Madison Heights MI 48071

SEAGO, ANITA RENEE, English Teacher; *b:* Texas City, TX; *m:* Robert H.; *c:* Julia Brayton, Joel; *ed:* (BA) Eng, Stephen F Austin 1979; Grad Stud Counseling; *cr:* Eng Teacher Lufkin HS 1979-84, Corrigan-Camden HS 1985-; *ai:* Sr Class Spon; Poetry & Prose UIL Coach.

SEALE, JERRY NELLE (WARD), 8th Grade English Teacher; *b:* El Paso, TX; *c:* Raymond U.; *ed:* (BA) Eng, Washington Univ St Louis 1958; Grad Stud E NM Univ; *cr:* Eng Teacher Washburn HS 1959-62; 8th Grade Eng/Lang Art Teacher Mesa Mid Sch 1973-; *ai:* Spelling Bee & Speech Contests Spon & Coach; Delta Kappa Gamma (Pres 1988-, Secy, 1st VP 1984-88); Roswell Ed Assn 1973-; NMEA, NEA; 1st Baptist Church (Childrens Divisional Dir 1981-84, Teacher 1975-80, Cnslr 1985-); *office:* Mesa Mid Sch 1601 E Bland Roswell NM 88201

SEALS, BILLIE ANN, First Grade Teacher; *b:* Lawrence Cty, IL; *m:* Donald L.; *c:* Donald L., Leslie A.; *ed:* (BS) Elem Ed, 1960, (MS) Elem Ed, 1986 E IL Univ; *cr:* 3rd/4th Grade Teacher Fillmore Elem 1956-57; 4th Grade Teacher Robinson Elem 1957-59; 1st Grade Teacher Redmon Elem 1965-88, Mayo Elem 1962-63, Memorial Elem 1988-; *ai:* Phi Delta Kappa; *home:* 201 Grandview Paris IL 61944

SEALS, ERNEST R., II, 6th Grade Teacher; *b:* Danville, IL; *m:* Nan Puckette; *c:* Nanette, Chad, Kristie, Robbin, Sandi; *ed:* (BA) Phys Ed, 1967, (MED) Ed-Mid Sch 1969 Lynchburg Coll; *cr:* Phys Ed/Math/Sci Teacher Holy Cross Sch 1967-73; Phys Ed Teacher Amherst Elem Sch 1973-77; Rdng/Math/Sci Teacher Gadys Elem Sch 1977-86; Math/Sci/Soc Stud Teacher William Campbell Mid Sch 1986-; *ai:* Coaching; *office:* William Campbell Mid Sch PO Box 120 Naruna VA 24576

SEAMAN, DEBORAH LOUISE, Second Grade Teacher; *b:* Kittery, ME; *ed:* (BSE) Elem Ed, 1975, (ME) Rdng Supervision, 1983 Ashland Coll; *cr:* K/Remedial Rdng Teacher Bronson Elem Sch 1975-76; 1st Grade Teacher Benedict Elem Sch 1976-80; 2nd Grade Teacher Maplehurst Elem Sch 1980-; *ai:* Young Authors Conference; Curr Cncl; Math Course of Study; Intl Rdng Assn 1975-; Norwalk Teachers Assn Secy 1976-77/1987-88; Lefty Grove Youth Bsbl Media Liason 1987-; Martha Holden Jennings Scholar 1985-86; *office:* Maplehurst Elem Sch 195 St Marys St Norwalk OH 44857

SEAMAN, RUTH E., Sixth Grade Teacher; *b:* Watertown, NY; *ed:* (AA) Liberal Arts, Jefferson Comm Coll 1968; (BA) Elem Ed/Eng, SUNY Fredonia 1970; (MS) Ed Admin, SUNY Oswego 1986; *cr:* Elem Teacher Watertown City Sch Dist 1970-85; Curr Coord Cayuga-Onondaga BOCES 1985-86; Elem Teacher Watertown City Sch Dist 1986-; *ai:* Educl Comm; Curr Dev; Stu Act; Watertown Ed Assn, NYSUT 1970-; Alpha Zeta, Alpha Delta Kappa 1978-; Miss NY St Schlsp Pageant Chm of Hostesses 1980-85; *office:* Harold T Wiley Sch 1351 Washington St Watertown NY 13601

SEARING, KATHLEEN CARDEN, English Teacher; *b:* Binghamton, NY; *m:* Robert John; *c:* Robert, Thomas, Matthew; *ed:* (BA) Eng/His, 1980, (MAT) Ed/Scndry Eng, SUNY Binghamton 1984; *cr:* Substitute Teacher Johnson City Cntrl Schls 1982-85; Eng Teacher Susquehanna Valley Jr HS 1985-; *ai:* Jr HS Yrbk Adv; Mem SVJH Sch Improvement Team; *office:* Susquehanna Valley Jr HS 1040 Conklin Rd Conklin NY 13748

SEARING, VIRGINIA MARY, Mathematics/Computer Teacher; *b:* New Rochellen, NY; *ed:* (BA) Math, Coll of Mt St Vincent 1972; (MA) Math, Manhattan Coll 1975; Cmptr Sci Wkshps; NY St Technology Wkshps; Cert CEMREL Math Instr; *cr:* 1st Grade Teacher 1963-67, 7th Grade Math Teacher 1967-71 St Barnabas Sch; 4th-8th Grade Math Teacher Nativity of Our Blessed Lady 1971-81, St Joseph Sch 1981-; *ai:* HS & Gifted Stu Instr SAT Preparation; 7th-8th Grade NY St Mathcounts Coach; 4th-8th Grade Math League & Mid-Hudson Math League; Cmptr Club Moderator; Athletic Commission Teacher Rep; Choir Moderator; Parish & Sch Folk Group Guitarist; Archdiocesan Curr Dev Planning Group Comm Mem 1988-; Substance Abuse Awareness Cncl (Chairperson 1981-, Coord) 1981-; Natl Sci Fnd Grant; *office:* St Joseph Parochial Sch 21 Glenmere Ave Florida NY 10921

SEARLE, C. DAVID, Retired Teacher; *b:* Irumu, Zaire; *m:* Mary Jane Armerding; *c:* Douglas, Stephen, Andrew; *ed:* (BS) His, Wheaton Coll 1949; (MA) Ed Admin, Wayne St 1952; *cr:* Teacher Sakeji Sch 1953-58, Merriewood Sch 1959; Advanced Academic Placement/Teacher of Gifted Lafayette Sch Dist 1960-89; *ai:* Phi Delta Kappa Mem 1952; CTA, NEA, LEA Exec Comm; *office:* Burton Valley Elem Sch 561 Merriewood Dr Lafayette CA 94549

SEARLES, JEFFREY, High School English Teacher; *b:* Rochester, MN; *m:* Kathleen M. Fjelstad; *c:* Delana, Jonathan, Thomas; *ed:* (BS) Lang Art, Bemidi St Coll 1974; Various Wkshps & Seminars; *cr:* Lang Art Teacher Isle HS 1974-; *ai:* Golf Coach; *home:* Box 364 Isle MN 56342

SEARS, CHARLOTTE BOWEN, English Teacher; *b:* Crossroads, SC; *c:* Mark Anthony, Teleatha A.; *ed:* (BA) Eng/Liberal Arts, Clemson Univ 1976; *cr:* Eng Teacher Seneca HS 1977-; *ai:* Weight Loss Club; Lounge Comm; Learning Areas Comm; Learning Media Comm; *home:* Rt 2 Westminster SC 29693

SEARS, JUDY E. GRIBLER, First Grade Teacher; *b:* Breese, IL; *m:* Ralph Mallory; *ed:* (BA) Elem Ed, Bob Jones Univ 1967; (MA) Rdng, E MI Univ 1970; *cr:* 3rd Grade Teacher L Anse Creuse Public Schls 1967-70; 3rd Grade Teacher 1970-71, 4th Grade Teacher 1971-72, Transition Teacher 1972-75 Traverse City Area Public Schls; Resource Teacher MI Migrant Projects 1970-; 1st Grade Teacher Traverse Bay Intermediate Sch Dist 1975-; *ai:* Delta Kappa Gamma Treas 1983-86; Natl Assn of St Migrant Dirs Outstanding Educator Awd; *office:* Willow Hill Sch 1250 Hill St Traverse City MI 49684

SEARS, NAOMI SMITH, 2nd/4th & 5th Grade Teacher; *b:* Eagan, TN; *m:* Lee E.; *c:* Leshia, Lee E. Jr., Lori A., Lloyd; *ed:* (BS) Elem Ed, Cumberland Coll 1967; (MA) Elem Ed, Eastern KY Univ 1978; *cr:* 5th/7th/8th Grade Teacher Newtonsville OH 1962-64; Bethel Local 1965-68; 7th Grade Teacher Twenhoffel 1968-69; 4th Grade Teacher Eastview 1970-74; 2nd/4th/5th Grade Teacher Poplar Creek 1974-; *ai:* Whitley Cty Ed Assn Sec 1988- ; WCEA Schl Rep 1978 ; KY Ed Assn Deligate to Conv 1978-85/1988-89; 4-H Club (Adv Bd Mem 1975-78 Rcgntn Cert 1986-88 Chaperone-Trips 1975-88); Farm-Homemakers Club Pres 1978-80 Cert; Whitley Cty Soil Conservation Assn Teacher of Yr 1989; *home:* HC 89 Box 381 Williamsburg KY 40769

SEARS, RUSSELL TODD, Physical Education Teacher; *b:* Long Beach, CA; *m:* Constance Marye Lyman; *c:* Jennifer N., Samantha M.; *ed:* (AA) Long Beach Comm Coll 1974; (BA) Phys Ed, CA St Univ Long Beach 1978; *cr:* Teacher/Coach Downey Unified Sch Dist 1982-83, Riverside Unified Sch Dist 1983-84, Bellflower Unified Sch Dist 1984-; *ai:* Asst Var Boys Bksktbl; Boys Girls Track; Soccer Head Coach; CA Teachers Assn, NEA 1982-; *office:* Bellflower HS 15301 Mc Nab Bellflower CA 90706

SEARS, WILLIAM RUSSELL, 7 & 8 Grade Ind Arts Teacher; *b:* Salina, KS; *m:* Joyce Elaine Reese; *c:* John C., Jennifer M. Walker, Leilani E. Love, Jason D.; *ed:* (AA) Industrial Arts, Coll of Sequoias Visalia 1971; (BA) Industrial Arts, CA St Univ Fresno 1973; *cr:* Metalshop Teacher Lemoore HS 1974-75; Woodshop Teacher Roosevelt Jr HS 1976-; *ai:* Epsilon Pi Tau 1973-; Alpha Lambda Chapter; BSA Cncl Comm 1956- (Scouters Key 1978, Sequoia Medal for Leadership 179, Silver Beaver 1984); *office:* Roosevelt Jr HS 10th & Draper Sts Kingsburg CA 93631

SEAT, MARLENE STATON, 9th Grade Mathematics Teacher; *b:* Shattuck, OK; *m:* Stanley F.; *c:* Paula L., Neel S., Mary E.; *ed:* (BS) Scndry Ed/Math/Art, Dallas Baptist Univ 1985; Working towards Masters; *cr:* 9th Grade Math Teacher Richardson Jr HS 1985-; *ai:* Advisee Comm Adv; Richardson Ed Assn, TX Prof Educators Assn, N TX Cncl Teachers of Math 1985-; *home:* 1900 Harvard Richardson TX 75081

SEATON, JUDY HEFFNER (ELMORE), 1st Grade Teacher; *b:* Charleston, WV; *m:* James L.; *c:* Bane S. Mc Cracken, Tana L. Pardue; *ed:* (BA) Elem Ed, 1971, (MA) Early Chldhd Ed, 1977 Marshall Univ; Inservice Trng, Beginning Teachers Prgm, Grad Stud Marshall Univ; *cr:* 1st Grade Teacher Ona Elem 1971-88; 3rd Grade Teacher Larkdale Elem 1988-89; 1st Grade Teacher Ona Elem 1989-; *ai:* In-Service Presenter; Soc Stud Curr Comm 1982-85; NEA, WV Ed Assn, Cabell Cty Ed Assn (Sch Rep, Membership Chm) 1980-; Cabell Cty Rdng Cncl Mem 1987-; K-1 Society Mem 1989-; Beta Sigma Phi 1979-, Girl of Yr 1985-87; Xi Upsilon; Misty Glade Garden Club (Secy, Pres, Co-Founder) 1977-; Kappa Delta Pi; *office:* Ona Elem Sch US Rt 60E Ona WV 25545

SEAVER, DANNY WADE, Mathematics Teacher; *b:* Kingsport, TN; *m:* Teresa Elaine Dula; *c:* Emily B., Charlton E., Errol K.; *ed:* (BS) Math/Scndry Ed, Applachian St Univ 1976; (MA) Mid Sch Ed/Ag, Lenoir-Rhyne Coll 1987; Math Ed; *cr:* Math Teacher Gamewell-Collettsville HS 1976-77, West caldwell HS 1977-; *ai:* Key Club Adv; World Future Society; Caldwell Comm Coll & Tech Inst Part-Time Instr; NCTM 1985-; NC Cncl Teachers of Math 1987-; Math Assn of Amer 1989-; Hickory Bd of Ed Mem, Hickory Lions Club Mem 1989-; Rotary Club Group Stud Uruguay Exch Team Mem 1987; Natl Sci Fnd Teching Fellow Appalachian St Univ 1987-89; NC St Dept of Public Instruction Schlsp 1985, 1988-89; NC Math & Sci Ed Network Grant 1988; Teaching Unit Published; *office:* West Caldwell HS 300 W Caldwell Dr Lenoir NC 28645

SEAVERT, KATHLEEN E., 1st Grade Teacher; *b:* Lisbon, ND; *m:* Larry; *c:* Lindsey, Allyson; *ed:* (BS) Elem Ed, Valley City St Coll 1969; (MS) Elem Ed, Univ of MN 1975; Grad Stud; *cr:* Elem Dir Staff Dev 1983-84, K/1st/2nd/4th Grade Teacher 1969- Ind Sch Dist 279; *ai:* Continuing Ed Comm, Career Ed, Elem Affairs; OFT Building Rep; Sch Patrol Adv; Summer Sch Teacher; Team Leader; Family Life Presentor; Osseo Fed of Teachers 1969-; MN Fed of Teachers (Building Rep 1975-) 1969-; Womens Sorority 1975-; Cmmty Ed Instr 1987-89; Family Life Writer; Illustrator Sports Guide; Script Writer Video Kidshow; *office:* Rice Lake Elem Sch 13755 89th Ave N Maple Grove MN 55369

SEAY, CAROL ROSE, Psychology Teacher; *b:* Louisville, KY; *m:* Will E.; *c:* Stacy, Will E. Jr.; *ed:* (BA) Psych/Sociology, Western KY Univ 1969; (MS) Urban Stud, Univ of Louisville 1976; Advanced Cmptr Trng; *cr:* Teacher Ballard HS 1971-; *ai:* Sr Class, Psych Club, Mentor Teacher Spon; Soc Stud Curr Writer; Amer Psychological Assn AFATE Mem 1980-; KY Soc Stud Teachers Mem 1980-, Soc Stud Awd 1980-82; Jefferson Cty Teachers Assn Mem 1975-85; Jr League of Louisville Mem, Young Life Mem 1987-; Green Castle Baptist Church Youth Adv 1982-; New Fnd Grant; *office:* Ballard HS 6000 Brownsboro Rd Louisville KY 40222

SEBRING, GWENDOLYN ALLEN, 5th Grade Teacher; *b:* Montgomery, AL; *m:* Daryel E.; *c:* Lisa, LeAnn; *ed:* (BS) Elem Ed, Troy St Univ 1968; (MED) Elem Ed, Auburn Univ 1976; *cr:* 3rd Grade Teacher Carver Elem 1968-72; 4th Grade Teacher Southlawn Elem 1972-79; 4th/5th Grade Teacher Wares Ferry Elem 1979-; *ai:* Faculty Spon Law Awareness Prgm; Faculty Spon Soc Stud Fair; NEA 1980-; AL Ed Assn 1980-; Delta Kappa Gamma 1985-; Montgomery Ed Assn 1980-; Beta Sigma Phi (Secy 1987-) Pledge of Yr 1987; *home:* 3116 Overlook Dr Montgomery AL 36109

SECHLER, LOUISE BRUSCA, Mathematics Teacher; *b:* Abington, PA; *m:* J. Wilbur Jr.; *c:* Cynthia Sechler Aiken, David L.; *ed:* (BS) Math, Chestnut Hill Coll 1957; *cr:* Logical Designer Univac 1957-58; Math Teacher Sanford Sch 1969-81, Salesianum Sch 1981-; *ai:* NCTM, AACST; GSA Asst Leader 1969-73.

SECHRIST, CAROLYN, Psychology Teacher; *b:* Elkhart, IN; *ed:* (BA) Psych, Olivet Nazarene Univ 1968; (MA) Psych, 1972, (PHD) Psych, 1975 Rosemead Sch of Psych Biola Univ; *cr:* Full Professor Olivet Nazarene Univ 1977-86; Self-Employed Renaissance Enterprises 1987-; Teacher Oak Ridge HS 1987-; Adjunct Professor St Leo Coll 1989-; *ai:* Chrstn Assn For Psychological Stud, Amer Psychological Assn Affiliate, Chrstn Educators Assn Intnl; Phi Delta Lamba 1968; Faculty Mem of Yr 1983-84; Outstanding Young Women of Amer 1977-78, 1980, 1982; Merit Schlsp Awd 1968; Whos Who Among Stus in Amer Colls & Univs 1968; Whos Who Among Human Service Profs 1986-89; *office:* Oak Ridge HS PO Box 4208 Winter Park FL 32793

SECHRIST, DOROTHY MC DONALD, Fourth Grade Teacher; *b:* Detroit, MI; *w:* Howard W. Jr. (dec); *c:* Vivian Sechrist Kuhn, Regina; *ed:* (BA) His, Marygrove Coll 1951; (MED) Educl Psych, Wayne St Univ 1957; Polishing Teaching & Instructional Skills 1982-; Teaching & Instructional Conferencing 1983-; Strategic Ongoing Application of Rdng Research 1986-; Cert to Teach CSMP Math 1988-; Integrating Math & Sci Project 1988; *cr:* 2nd & 3rd Grade Teacher Henry Ford Sch 1951-59; 1st-3rd Grade Teacher Salina Sch 1960-63; 2nd-4th Grade Teacher Lowrey Sch 1966-; *ai:* City Beautiful, Sch Wide Positive Reward Comm; PTA Upper Elem Rep 1981-83; Wayne Cty Rdng Cncl; Fairlane Music Guild Mailing Chm 1979-82; Dearborn Cmmty Arts Cncl, Dearborn Historical Society; Prepared Workbook & Inservice on Metric System 1975-78; Present Wkshps on Teacher Skills 1984-87; *office:* Lowrey Elem Sch 6601 Jonathon Dearborn MI 48126

SECHRIST, LONNIE R., Principal; *b:* Leaksville, NC; *m:* Ethel Adkins; *c:* Heather A.; *ed:* (BS) Elem Ed, W Carolina Univ 1969; (MED) Ed Admin, Univ of NC 1973; (EDS) Advanced Admin, Applachian St Univ 1989; *cr:* Teacher Fines Creek Elem 1969-70, Leaksville-Spray Intermediate 1970-83; Prin Lakeside Elem 1983-85, Douglass Elem 1985-; *ai:* ASCD 1989-; NC Assn of Prins & Asst Prins 1988-; NC Assn of Educators 1969-85, Teacher of Yr 1978; *home:* Rt 2 Box 392A Stoneville NC 27048

SECOR, MARILYN M., Spanish & Lang Art Teacher; *b:* Luxemburg, WI; *m:* Kenneth J.; *c:* Nathan, Jonathan; *ed:* (BA) Eng, Carroll Coll 1976; *cr:* Eng/Span Teacher Luxemburg-Casco Jr HS 1977-; *ai:* Forensics Coach; Iberoamerican Cultural Exch Prgm Rep; WI Assn of Foreign Lang Teachers 1988-; Mensa, Philanthropic Educal Assn Mem 1988-; Amer Intercultura; Stu Exch Host Parent 1985-86; *office:* Luxemburg-Casco Jr HS 619 Church Ave Casco WI 54205

SECRATT, SHARON EILEENE, 8th Grade Science Teacher; *b:* Tahlequah, OK; *m:* Haskell Dean; *c:* Deena Secratt Wright, Laura Secratt Reasnor; *ed:* (BS) Elem Ed 1973, (MA) Elem ED, 1983- NE OK Univ; Grad Stud Sci; *cr:* 2nd Grade Teacher Kinta Public Sch 1974-80; 8th Grade Sci Teacher 1984-, Teacher of Gifted/Talented 1984- Muldrow Mid Sch; *ai:* Sci Dept, N Cntrl Accreditation, Title VII Chairperson; 8th Grade Class Spon; MCTA, OEA, NEA Mem 1984-; N Cntrl Assn Steering Comm Chairperson; 4th of July Celebration Chairperson 1977-79, Outstanding Citizen 1977; Red Ribbon Chairperson 1989-; *home:* PO Box 372 Muldrow OK 74948

SECULOFF, FLORENCE ANN, 6th-8th Departmental Teacher; *b:* Fort Wayne, IN; *ed:* (BS) Ed, St Francis Coll 1954; (MA) Ed, Ball St 1958; US His, Marquette Univ 1965-66; *cr:* 2nd-4th Grade Teacher Lincoln Sch 1954-59; 5th Grade Teacher Pima Sch 1959-61; Instr St Francis Coll 1961-62; 1st/5th/6th Grade Teacher St Barbara 1962-64; Teacher/Prin St Marys 1964-65; Departmental Teacher Queen of Angels Sch 1966-; *ai:* Sch Co-Chm Festival of Art & Music Elem; Delta Epsilon Sigma 1954; Pi Lambda Theta 1957-; Allen Cty Fort Wayne Historical Society 1970-; Historical Society Ed Comm 1970-; Co-Chm Pioneer Wkshp 1973; *office:* Queen of Angels Sch 1600 W State Blvd Fort Wayne IN 46808

SEDDON, KAREN CULLINANE, 5th Grade Teacher; *b:* Elizabeth, NJ; *m:* John Michael; *c:* Jacquelyn, Kelly; *ed:* (BS) Elem Ed, Trenton St Coll 1974; *cr:* 3rd/5th Grade Teacher 1974-79, 7th-8th Grade Teacher 1980-88 Woodbine Elem Sch; 5th Grade Teacher Highlands Elem Sch 1988-; *ai:* Spokesmans Club Dir; NJ Teacher of Yr 1988; Osceola Cty Soc Stud Teacher of Yr 1989; Lit Prgms Grants; *office:* Highlands Elem Sch 800 W Donegan Ave Kissimmee FL 34741

SEDLACEK, ROBERT C., English Teacher; *b:* Glen Carbon, IL; *c:* Elyse, Ryan, Ross, Camille; *ed:* (BA) Eng, MO Valley Coll 1964; (MA) Eng, Emporia St Univ 1967; Grad Stud S IL Univ, Coll of Santa Fe; *cr:* Eng Teacher Napa HS 1965-66, Los Alamos HS 1966-67, Institute 1967-68, Waukegan HS 1968-69; Eng Instr S IL Univ 1969-75; Eng Teacher St Paul HS 1984-86, Belleville Area Coll, Lewis & Clark Comm Coll, Mater Dei HS 1987-; *ai:* Mater Dei HS Yrbk Spon 1988-89; *office:* Mater Dei HS 9th & Plum Sts Breese IL 62230

SEDLAK, ROSE MARIE ASSAD, New Direction At Risk Teacher; *b:* Cleveland, OH; *m:* Dennis R.; *c:* Adeena, Michael; *ed:* (BS) Elem Ed, Cleveland St Univ 1973; (MED) Educl Media, Kent St Univ 1977; (JD) Law, Cleveland Marshall Coll of Law 1986; Chemical Dependency & Cmmty Intervention Trng & Group Facilitator Trng Glenbeigh Hospital; Chemical Dependency Relapse Trng St John Westshore Hospital; *cr:* Elem Teacher John Glenn Elem Parma Schls 1973-76; Media Specialist Green Valley Elem Parma Schls 1976-81; Public Relations Librarian Cleveland-Marshall Law Lib 1982-83; Rdng Teacher Hillside Jr HS Parma Schls 1985-; Instr Cleveland St Univ 1989-; *ai:* Hillside Jr HS I Say No Club Adv; Chemical Dependency Group Facilitator; Children at Risk Prgm Coord; OH Assn for Supervision & Curr Dev; NEA, OH Ed Assn, NE OH Teacher Assn; PTA Awd St Honorary Life Membership 1988; St Elias Church; Alpha Delta Kappa; Parma Cncl of PTAs Fellowship Awd; Grant for Children at Risk Prgm; Martha Holden Jennings Scholar 1990; *home:* 1345 Simich Dr Seven Hills OH 44131

SEE, ROBERT HAROLD, Science Teacher; *b:* Grand Rapids, MI; *m:* Sata B. (Savage); *c:* Robert I., Julie L.; *ed:* (BT) Theology, OR Bible Coll 1961; (BS) Spec Ed, 1964, (MS) Ed, 1965 St Cloud St Univ; *cr:* Spec Ed Teacher 1965-82, Rdng Teacher 1982-83, Eng/Soc Stud Teacher 1983-85, Sci/Math Teacher 1985-88, Sci Teacher 1988- South Whittier Sch Dist; *ai:* Yrbk Photography Staff & Adv; Sch Improvement Prgm; Administrative Intern; South Whittier Teacher Assn Pres 1968-70, 1978, WHO Awd 1979; Whittier Area Fed Credit Union (Chm of Bd 1989-, Dir 1985-), 5 Yr Pin 1990; Academic Insurance Company Dir 1987-; *office:* S Whittier Intermediate Sch 13243 E Los Nietos Rd Whittier CA 90605

SEEL, NANCY KOUBIK, Choral Director; *b:* St Paul, MN; *m:* Donald W.; *ed:* (BA) Eng, Mt Mary Coll 1969; (ME) Ed, Buffalo St Coll 1979; Wkshps With Robertshaw, Westminster 1982-87; Choral Wkshps With Sir David Willocks Choir Coll Princeton NJ 1988-89; *cr:* Jr HS Instr Parochial Sch 1960-70; Instr Basic Rdng Skills St Paul MN 1970-74; General Music Teacher Northwood Elem 1975-76; Choral Dir W Seneca West Jr HS 1976-86, W Seneca East Sr HS 1986-; *ai:* Producer/Dir of HS Musical; Always Ready & Available Person Mem; Support Group for Stus; Sch Improvement Comm Mem; Amer Choral Dir Assn, MENC, NYSSMA; Amer Cancer Society Collector 1986-; Co Authored Article for Journal of Creative Behavior; W Seneca Dist Teacher of Yr 1990; *office:* W Seneca E Sr HS 4760 Seneca St West Seneca NY 14224

SEELAND, THOMAS WILLIAM, Instrumental Music Teacher; *b:* New Brunswick, NJ; *m:* Rene Ann Kammeyer; *ed:* (BA) Music Ed, 1981, (MA) Music Performance, 1988 Trenton St Coll; *cr:* Music Teacher S Hunterdon Regional HS 1981-82, Cecil S Collins Sch 1982-83, Arbor Sch & Schor Mid Sch 1983-; *ai:* All Township Band & Jazz Rock Ensemble Dir; Superchief Band Staff; Govenors Teacher Recognition Prgm Outstanding Teacher; *office:* Arbor Sch & Schor Mid Sch 7th & Rock Ave Piscataway NJ 08854

SEELEY, JAMES LEO, English Teacher; *b:* Leominster, MA; *m:* Linda D.; *c:* Gretel, Amy; *ed:* (BA) His/Ed, Worcester St Coll 1967; (MED) Eng, Fitchburg St Coll 1971; Creative Writing, Lit, Univ of MA; *cr:* Jr HS Teacher Groton Jr HS 1967-69; 8th Grade Teacher Salem Mid Sch 1969-82; HS Teacher Salem HS 1982-; *ai:* Chairperson Creation of Summer Rdng List for HS Stu; 1st Baptist Church Beverly Youth Fellowship Adv 1985-88; *home:* 23 Sargent Ave Beverly MA 01915

SEELOFF, ROBERT CARL, 4th Grade Teacher; *b:* Lockport, NY; *m:* Colleen Marie Kerr; *c:* Robert C. II, Rhett C.; *ed:* (BA) His/Ec, St Univ of NY Potsdam 1972; (MS) Rdng Ed, St Univ of NY Oswego 1979; *cr:* 4th Grade Teacher Park Hill Elem 1972-79; 5th Grade Teacher 1980-89, Modified 4th Grade Teacher 1990 Kinne Street Elem; *ai:* Jr HS Soccer & Bsbl Coach; East Syracuse-Minoa Technology Adv Comm Sch Rep; NYSUT; Corrective Rdng Summer Sch Project Mini-Grant Onondoga Cty BOCES 1978; *office:* Kinne Street Elem Sch 230 Kinne St East Syracuse NY 13057

SEELY, ANNA M. ERICKSON, Kindergarten Teacher; *b:* Canova, SD; *m:* J. Craig; *c:* Scott, Brad; *ed:* (BS) Home Ec/Child Dev, SD St Univ 1951; Various Courses & Wkshps; *cr:* Home Ec Teacher Estelline Public Sch 1951-53; Nursery Sch Teacher All Saint Epis Sch 1961-66; Kndgtn Teacher 1966-68, Kndgtn/Home Ec Teacher 1968-75, Kndgtn Teacher 1975- Baltic Public Sch; *ai:* Jr Class & FHA Adv; SDEA, NEA 1951-; FHA SD 1st Pres 1945-46; HHU Meth Church Trustees-COM 1958-; Extension Work Ext Home Makers 4-H Leader; Amer Legion Auxiliary 1962-; *home:* RR Box 71 Baltic SD 57003

SEELY, STEVEN A., English Teacher; *b:* Mineola, NY; *m:* Linda Martin; *c:* Kristin L., Eric A.; *ed:* (BA) Eng, 1969, (MAE) Eng, 1970 Allegheny Coll; In-Service Courses Cmptr Literacy & Teaching Methodology, Sewanhaka Cntrl; *cr:* Stu Eng Teacher 1968-69; Eng Teacher South HS 1969-70, Cold Spring Harbor HS 1970-72, Alva T Stanforth Jr HS 1972-75, Sewanhaka HS 1975-; *ai:* SAT Preparation Tutor; Jr Var Soccer & Bsbl Sewanhaka Sch Dist; St Hughes-St Elizabeth Little League (Mgr, Coach) 1989-; *office:* Sewanhaka HS 500 Tulip Ave Floral Park NY 11001

SEEVER, SHIRLEY MILLER, Fifth Grade Teacher; *b:* Alexandria, KY; *m:* George Dennis; *c:* Melanie; *ed:* (BA) Elem Ed, Univ of KY 1971; Morehead Univ 1974; *cr:* 6th Grade Math Teacher Campbell Cty Mid Sch 1971-72; 5th Grade Teacher Southern Elem 1972-; *ai:* Curr Incentive Comm Chm; 3rd-6th Grade Cheerleading Coord; NEA, KY Ed Assn, PCEA 1971-; Town & Country Homemakers 1980-; Fairlane Baptist Church 1965-; *home:* Rt 4 Falmouth KY 41040

SEEWER, MICHAEL L., AP His & Lit Teacher; *b:* Lima, OH; *m:* Judy L. Smith; *ed:* His, OH Wesleyan Univ 1963-64; (BSED) His/Eng, OH St Univ 1967; (MA) His, Wright St Univ 1971; (PHD) His/Lit, Columbia Pacific Univ 1983; *cr:* His/Eng Teacher Fairborn HS 1967-71; His/Lit Teacher Fairborn Park Hills HS 1971-82; His/Adjunct Instr Wright St Univ 1972; His/Lit Teacher Fairborn HS 1982-; *ai:* Advanced Placement Coord 1981-85; Fairborn City Schl Academic Cncl, Scndry Standards Comm 1986-89; Soc Stud Dept Chm 1977-81; Fairborn Ed Assn, OH Ed Assn, NEA, W OH Ed Assn 1967-; Assn of Amer Historians 1971-; NCTE 1980-; Presbyn Church (Session Mem, Ordained Elder) 1987-; Chrstn Ed Comm Chm 1988-89; Amer Civil Liberties Union; DAR Outstanding His Teacher St of OH 1984; Daughters of Colonial Wars Natl Outstanding Teacher 1984; Recognition OH Legislature for Teaching Excl 1984; Wright St Dept of Ed for Teaching Excl 1986; OH Univ Recognition for Teaching Excl 1988; *office:* Fairborn HS 900 E Dayton-Yellow Springs Rd Fairborn OH 45324

SEFCIK, JAMES RICHARD, GED Teacher; *b:* Joliet, IL; *ed:* (BA) Biological Sci, Lewis Univ 1969; (MA) Health Public Ed, George Williams 1979; Chemical Dependency Counseling; *cr:* Bio Teacher St Francis Acad 1969-70; Sci Teacher Fairmont Jr HS 1970; All Sci Teacher Channahon Jr HS 1970-84; Health/Sci Teacher St Josephs 1984-85; Tutor Joliet Public Schls 1987-89; Private Tutor 1969-; *ai:* Officer St Francis Lodge 29 KSKJ; NEA, IEA Life Mem; NSTA Mem 1987-88; Multiple Sclerosis Bd of Dirs Outstanding Service 1974, 1976; *home:* 1217 Hosmer Joliet IL 60435

SEGARS, COOPER LEE, JR., Soc Studies Teacher/Ftbl Coach; *b:* Columbia, SC; *m:* Karen Lia Boner; *ed:* (BA) His, Guilford Coll 1983; *cr:* In-School Suspension Teacher Pine Forest HS 1983-84; Soc Stud Teacher Hartsville HS 1984-; Athletic Dir/Soc Stud Teacher Dillon HS 1990; *ai:* Ftbl Coach Dillon HS 1990; Weight & Conditioning Coach Hatsville HS 1984-; Asst Ftbl & Track Coach Pine Forest HS 1986-84; SC Athletic Coaches Assn 1984-; *office:* Hartsville Sr HS Clyburn Cir Hartsville SC 29550

SEGER, SUSAN WAGNER, Second Grade Teacher; *b:* Jasper, IN; *m:* Bruce A.; *c:* Adam, Joseph, Jonathan; *ed:* (BS) Elem Ed, 1975, (MS) Elem Ed, 1978 IN St Univ; *cr:* 3rd Grade Teacher 1975-80, 2nd Grade Teacher 1980- Tenth Street Sch; *ai:* Eng & Spelling Comm; ISTA, NEA 1975-; Beta Sigma Phi 1981-; Vacation Bible Sch Teacher 1986-87, 1989; Positive Educator Awd 1987-89; *home:* R 3 Box 251K Jasper IN 47546

SEGERT, RICHARD RAY, Jr High School Teacher; *b:* Gary, IN; *ed:* (BA) Elem Ed, Concordia Univ 1975; *cr:* Teacher St Pauls Luth 1975-; *ai:* Athletic Dir; Var Bsktbl & Bsbl Coach; Jr HS Choir Dir; Spring Musical Dir; 8th Grade Spon; Kankakee Jaycees Little League Coach 1988-; Kankakee Girls Sftbl League Coach 1985-; Playmakers Cmmty Theatre Crown Point IN; Accredidation Team-Luth Schls; Church Organist; Bible Class Teacher; Adult Choir; Youth Bd; *office:* St Pauls Lutheran Sch 240 S Dearborn Kankakee IL 60901

SEGUIN, JAMES WILLIAM, English Teacher; *b:* San Antonio, TX; *m:* Lillian Angelin Preston; *ed:* (BS) Eng/Speech, SW Adventist Coll 1977; (MA) Sch Admin, TX A&I Univ 1984; Write For Life, Curr Writing, Critical Thinking Seminar; Cert in Scndry Ed, Eng, Speech; *cr:* Eng Teacher San Benito Sch Dist 1977-79, Catholic HS 1978-80; Eng/Speech Teacher Gladys Porter HS 1980-; *ai:* Stu Cncl Spon; Univ Interscholastic League Spelling Spon; Staff Dev & Textbook Comm; NCTE Mem; TX Eng Teachers 1982-84; Muscular Dystrophy Rep 1979-80; *office:* Gladys Porter HS 3500 International Blvd Brownsville TX 78520

SEGULJI, ANN H., IHM, Math Teacher; *b:* Brooklyn, NY; *ed:* (BA) Math, St Joseph Coll 1953; (MA) Math, St Johns Univ 1967; Del Mod Project Sci, Environmental, Math Ed; Applied Math for Scndry Teachers, Univ of DE Natl Sci Fnd; Marywood Coll; *cr:* Math/Sci Teacher St Joseph; Math Teacher Marywood 1967-69; Math Dept Chairperson/Teacher St Marks HS 1969-79; Math Teacher St Marys Girls HS 1979-; *ai:* NCTM, NCEA.

SEHLINGER, CAROL ANN (CASPER), 5th-8th Grade Math Teacher; *b:* Chicago, IL; *m:* Ralph J.; *ed:* (BA) Eng, Siena Heights Coll 1966; (MA) Spec Ed, NE IL 1974; Grad Stud Math, NE IL, Univ of IL; *cr:* 4th Grade Teacher St Bridgets 1958-59; 2nd/3rd/5th/6th Grade Teacher St Carthage 1959-63; 4th Grade Teacher St Albert the Great 1963-65; 2nd/5th/6th Grade Teacher St Columbanus 1965-68; 4th Grade Teacher Christ the King 1968-71; 6th Grade Teacher St Columbanus 1971-75; 6th/8th Grade Teacher Sacred Heart 1975-76; 5th-8th Grade Teacher St Columbanus 1976-; *ai:* Sewing Teacher; Mercy Boys Home Big Sister; St Columbanus Stu Cncl & Safety Patrol Facilitator; Math Dept Chairperson; 5th-8th Grade Unit Leader; IL Teachers of Math Recognition Awd 1989; *office:* St Columbanus Sch 7120 S Calumet Ave Chicago IL 60619

SEIBERT, CATHY MALONE, Fourth Grade Teacher; *b:* Athens, AL; *m:* Henry D.; *ed:* (BA) Elem Ed, Athens St Coll 1977; (MS) Elem Ed, A&M Univ 1987; *cr:* 6th Grade Teacher 1977-89, 4th Grade Teacher 1989- E Limestone; *ai:* AL Ed Assn, NEA 1977-; Kappa Delta Pi 1986-; *office:* E Limestone Sch Rt 3 Box 190 Athens AL 35611

SEIDEL, DON, Staff Development Coordinator; *b:* Rochester, NY; *m:* Marie Peters; *c:* Peter, Ann Ash; *ed:* (BS) Ed, Brockport St Teachers 1961; (MA) Soc Stud Ed, Univ of Rochester 1965; Grad Stud Supervision & Admin; Bd of Ed Cooperative Services Trng Effective Teaching, Supervision & Related Areas; *cr:* 7th/8th Grade Soc Stud Teacher East Irondequoit Sch Dist 1961-67; 7th-12th Grade Soc Stud Teacher Rochester City Sch Dist 1967-70; 7th/8th Grade Soc Stud Teacher/Soc Stud/Eng Dept Head 1970-88, Dist Staff Dev Coord 1988- Churchville-Chili Schls; *ai:* Yrbk, AV Club, Stu Cncl, Newspaper Adv; Golf, Track, Cross Cntry Coach; Officiate Bsktbl & Bsbl Games; Rochester Area Cncl Soc Stud, NY St Cncl Soc Stud 1965-; NY St Staff Dev Cncl 1988-; Genesee Golf Club Secy 1980-; Democratic Party Comm Person 1978-; Henrietta Planning Bd 1978-81; *office:* Churchville-Chili Sch Dist 139 Fairbanks Rd Churchville NY 14678

SEIDEL, KATHERINE VUKELIC, Eng Teacher/Honors Pgrm Coord; *b:* Benld, IL; *m:* Milton Joseph; *c:* Joseph L.; *ed:* (BS) Eng, St Louis Univ 1956; (MS) Ed, S IL Univ 1972; (PHD) Spec Ed, Univ of MD 1989; *cr:* Eng Teacher Roxanna Jr HS 1968-71, Wood Jr HS 1972-81; Eng Teacher 1982-, Honors Prgm Coord 1984- Rockville HS; *ai:* CEC, AAUW; *office:* Rockville HS 2100 Baltimore Rd Rockville MD 20851

SEIDENBERGER, SYLVIA TUPA, Third Grade Teacher; *b:* Moulton, TX; *m:* Max E.; *c:* Mike, Pat; *ed:* (BS) Elem Ed, 1950, (MED) Elem Ed, 1959 SW TX Univ; Wkshp Career Ladder Level II; *cr:* Teacher Pine Spring 1943-44, Evergreen 1945-46, Shiner Public Sch 1945-; *ai:* Shiner Centennial Comm; Delta Kappa Gamma Pres, 25 Yr Certificate; Classroom Teachers Pres; PTO Pres; Cath Daughters Grand Regent; Chrstn Mothers Pres; Cooperating Teacher Univ of Houston 1990.

SEIER, MARK JEROME, Biology Teacher; *b:* Neligh, NE; *m:* Beverly Ann Foss; *c:* Lisa, Jill, Michelle, Daniel; *ed:* (BS) Bio Ed, 1975, (MS) Bio Ed, 1982 Kearney St Coll; *cr:* Bio Teacher Newman Grove Public Schls 1975-; *ai:* Yrbk Spon; NHS Adv; Phi Delta Kappa 1970-; Newman Grove Ed Assn (Pres, Negotiation Chm) 1975-; NE Ed Assn, NEA 1975-; Greater NE Area Teachers of Sci 1980-; NABT 1983-; Newman Grove Lions Club (Pres, Secy, Zone Chm) 1978-; Newman Grove Fire & Rescue 1989-; Newman Grove Civil Defense 1990; KOLN/KGIN Teacher of Day Awd; *home:* Box 445 Newman Grove NE 68758

SEIGEL, JOYCE BRATTER, English Teacher; *b:* Brooklyn, NY; *m:* Harold; *c:* Jessica Bratter, Brittany; *ed:* (BA) Art/Eng, Brooklyn Coll CUNY 1978; Correspondence Course Inst of Childrens Lit; Ed, Nova Univ & FIU; *cr:* Journalism Teacher 1984-85, Lang Art/Creative Writing Teacher 1984- Hammocks Mid Sch; *ai:* Act Comm Mem; Newspaper Adv; O M Coach; Poetry Published 1989-; Nom Career Teacher of Yr 1990; *office:* Hammocks Mid Sch 9889 Hammocks Blvd Miami FL 33196

SEITER, BONNIE WULBER, Fifth Grade Teacher; *b:* Batesville, IN; *c:* Kenneth, Allen; *ed:* (BS) Elem Ed, IN Univ 1978; (MA) Elem Ed, Ball St 1981; Gifted/Talented Endorsement 1990; *cr:* 2nd Grade Teacher Mt Carmel Sch 1978-80, Brookville Elem 1980-82; 5th Grade Teacher Brookville Elem 1982-89, Brookville Mid Sch 1989-; *ai:* 5th Grade Girls Bsktbl Coach 1988-89; PTC Teacher Rep 1988-89; PACA Bd Mem 1987-89.

SEITER, CLAUDIA COLLIER, Social Studies Dept Chair; *b:* Colorado Springs, CO; *m:* David M.; *c:* Cathleen Schroader; *ed:* (BS) His, 1978, (MED) His/Ec, 1980 Weber St Univ; *cr:* Teacher/Dept Chairperson Millcreek Jr HS 1978-83; Assoc Professor UT St Univ 1987-88; Teacher/Dept Chairperson Layton HS 1983-; *ai:* NHS Adv; Delta Kappa Gamma VP 1988-; UT Cncl Soc Stud 1989-, Teacher of Yr 1989; Citzenship Bee Regional Dir 1989-; NCSS Intnl Ed Comm; UT Historical Society 1986-, Teacher of Yr 1987; Layton-Kaysville Historical Society Acts Chairperson 1987-; Intnl Ed Consortium; Bill of Rights Ed Collaborative Natl Governmnet Bd; Natl Sci Fnd Fellowship 1981; Atlantic Cncl for Soc Stud, Natl Cncl for Soc Stud 1987; *office:* Layton HS 440 Lancer Ln Layton UT 84041

SEITER, PATRICIA RAGLEY, English Teacher; *b:* Painesville, OH; *m:* Richard D.; *c:* Molly B., Jennifer N.; *ed:* (BS) Eng, Bowling Green St Univ 1965; (MA) Lib Sci, Cntrl MI Univ 1975; *cr:* Eng Teacher Defiance Public Schls 1966-67, Bowling Green Public Schls 1967-69; Journalism Teacher Cntrl MI Univ 1985; Eng Teacher Mt Pleasant Public Schls 1976-; *ai:* Class of 1990 Adv; North Cntrl Accreditation Steering Comm; Cmptr Usage Comm; Eng Dept Head; Lang Art Task Force; NCTE, MI Cncl Teachers of Eng; Phi Delta Kappa Fnds Rep 1990; Mt Pleasant Public Schls Scndry Teacher of Yr; MI Interscholastic Press Assn Asst Exec Dir; Articles Published in Newletters; *office:* Mt Pleasant HS 1155 S Elizabeth Mount Pleasant MI 48858

SEITZ, SANDRA STUMP, Kindergarten Teacher; *b:* York, PA; *m:* Lonny La Mont; *ed:* (BA) Elem Ed, Millersville 1966; (MA) Elem Ed, PA St 1976; *cr:* 4th Grade Teacher 1966-69, Kndgtn Teacher 1969- A D Goode Sch; *ai:* PSEA, YCEA 1966-; *home:* 5210 Harmony Grove Rd Dover PA 17315

SEKULA, DOLORES LA CHEPELLE, World Geography Teacher; *b:* San Antonio, TX; *m:* Edmund Peter; *c:* Emily; *ed:* (BA) His, Our Lady of Lake Univ 1971; Grad Stud Dynamics of Human Behavior, Our Lady of Lake Univ; Advanced Methods, Rdng, Writing, Univ of TX San Antonio; TX Ed Agency Advanced Academic Trng; *cr:* Eng/His Teacher S San Antonio HS 1971-76, 1977-80; His/Geography Teacher Cntrl Cath Marianist HS 1986-; *ai:* Soc Stud Dept Chairperson; Mem Academic Cncl Cntrl Cath Marianist HS; World His Assn 1990; Intnl Rdng Assn, NCSS 1987-; TX Cncl for Soc Stud 1989-; NCEA 1986-; Amer Assn of Univ Women 1987-; Mem of Soc Stud Curr Guide Comm for Archdiocese of San Antonio 1987-88; Summer Assembly for Global Ed TX A&M Univ 1990; *office:* Cntrl Cath Marianist HS 1403 N St Marys St San Antonio TX 78215

SELBY, STEVEN GAIL, Mathematics Dept Chairman; *b:* Hillsboro, OR; *m:* Terri L.; *c:* Shannon, Scott; *ed:* (BS) Math Ed, 1973, (MS) Counseling, 1977 OR St Univ; *cr:* Math Teacher Monticello Mid Sch 1973-; *ai:* 8th Grade Vlybl Coach; Self Study Act Chm; Math Curr & Advisory Comm; WEA, NEA, NCTM; Co-Author Math Books; *office:* Monticello Mid Sch 28th & Hemlock Longview WA 98632

SELDEN, MONICA SCHUFTAN, Seventh Grade Math Teacher; *b:* New York, NY; *m:* Joel; *c:* David; *ed:* (BS) Elem Ed, Monmouth Coll 1973; *cr:* Math Teacher Copeland Mid Sch 1974-; *ai:* AMTNJ; *office:* Copeland Mid Sch 1 Lake Shore Dr Rockaway NJ 07866

SELF, CANDACE CARMEAN, Spanish & English Teacher; *b:* Chillicothe, OH; *c:* Jennifer, Catherine; *ed:* Span Stud, Univ of Madrid Spain 1966; (AB) Span/Eng. Ashland Univ 1966-67; Grad Stud Eng, OH St 1987-88; Scndry Counseling, Univ of Dayton; *cr:* Eng Teacher Dayton City Schls 1968-69; Span Teacher Lexington Local Schls 1969-71; Eng Teacher Bellefontaine City Schls 1972-73, Cntrl Local Schls 1977-79; Span/Eng Teacher Milton-Union Schls 1979-86, Northmont City Schls 1986-; *ai:* Great Books Leader; Quest Teaching Instr; Organized 8 Wk European Trip for Lang Studs; Gifted Prgm Teacher Defiance Cty OH St Teen Inst Kenyon Coll; TASC Team Mem Northmont HS; Faculty Advisory Cncl; NEA; OH Ed Assn; Northmont Dist Ed Assn; Wrote Curr for Milton-Union Schls While Serving on Supts Comm; Twice Received Supts Awd of Merit from Milton-Union Schls; *office:* Northmont Sr H S 4916 National Rd Clayton OH 45315

SELF, CLYDE CRAIG, Sixth Grade Teacher; *b:* Mt Vernon, IL; *m:* Martha Ann Boner; *c:* Whitney A., Ethan C.; *ed:* (BA) Elem Ed, IL St Univ 1978; (MS) Elem Ed, 1984, Type 75 Educl Admin, 1987 E IL Univ; Assertive Discipline for Parents & Teachers & Homework Without Tears for Teachers & Parents Prgm Trng Lee Carter & Assoc; *cr:* 3rd Grade Teacher 1979-80, 6th Grade Teacher 1980-89 Bennett Elem; 6th Grade Teacher Hawthorne Elem 1989-; *ai:* Childrens Welfare Fund for Underprivileged Stus Dir; Sci Comm Adv; Mattoon Educl Assn 1979-; Phi Delta Kappa 1984-; United Way of Mattoon (Sch Division Chairperson, Bd Mem 1985-); Cntrl Cemetery Comm Bd Mem 1975-; Arbor Day Society 1978-, Small Sch Outstanding Awd Tree Conservation 1983; Recognition of Excl Awd St of IL 1986; Those Who Excel Awd of Merit St of IL 1989; *office:* Hawthorne Elem Sch 2405 Champaign Mattoon IL 61938

SELF, DANNY MACK, Math Department Chair; *b:* Holly Grove, AR; *c:* Steven, Christopher, Jason, Matthew; *ed:* (BS) Math, 1967, (MS) Math, 1968 AR St Univ; *cr:* Teacher Pocohontas HS 1968-72, Piggott HS 1973-; *ai:* Math Honor Society & Jr Class Spon; PDEA, AEA, NEA; *home:* 644 E Locust Piggott AR 72454

SELF, NORMA J., English & History Teacher; *b:* Toledo, OH; *m:* Robert K.; *ed:* (BS) Soc Sci/Eng, E MI Univ 1969; (MA) Scndry Sch Curr, E MI 1973; *cr:* 7th-9th Grade Teacher Bedford Jr HS 1969-; *home:* 2015 Stoneybrook Ln Temperance MI 48182

SELFE, ROBERT WILSON, Senior English Teacher; *b:* Richmond, VA; *m:* Carolyn Swahn; *c:* Michael C.; *ed:* (BA) Ed, Univ of S FL 1975; *cr:* Eng Teacher Hudson HS 1977-78, Ridgewood Jr HS 1978-83, Ridgewood HS 1983-; *ai:* Literary Corner Founder & Spon 1979-86; Girls Tennis Team Coach 1980-85, 1987-; Gulf Coast Conference Coach of Yr 1984-85, 1987 & 1989; *office:* Ridgewood HS 7650 Orchid Lake Rd New Port Richey FL 34653

SELICH, JUDITH ANN (JEFFERS), English & Amer History Teacher; *b:* Glendale, CA; *m:* Edward D.; *c:* Adrienne, Alexandra; *ed:* (BA) Soclgy, Whittier Coll 1969; Addl Studies Univ of CA; *cr:* Gifted Eng/Soc Stud/Sci Teacher Hisamatsu Tamura Sch 1969-79; Sci/Gifted Eng/Soc Stud Gisler Sch 1979-84; Harry C Fulton Sch 1984-85; Harry C Fulton Middle Sch 1985-89; *ai:* Stu Cncl Adv; Chrldg Adv & Yrbk Adv; CTA/NEA 1969-; FVEA 1989- ; CA Leag Mid Schls 1984-89; Girl Scouts of Amer Leader 1986-88; Harbor View Parent Faclty Orgnztn 1983-89; Fountain Valley PTO 1969-89; Corona Del Mar HS PTA 1989-; Golden Galleon Awd Jostens Printers Jrnlstc Excl 1984-88; Presentor at Mentally Gifted Minors Conf 1978; Presentor at CA Leag of Mid Schls Con 1986; *home:* 201 Milford Dr Covena Del Mar CA 92625

SELKING, BARBARA WHARTON, Teacher of Three Year Olds; *b:* Hampton, IA; *m:* Andrew; *c:* Mark; *ed:* (BS) Elem Ed, Concordia Teachers Coll 1978; *cr:* 5th Grade Teacher 1978-85, 5th-8th Grade Math Teacher 1985-89, Teacher of 3 Yr Olds 1989- St Paul Luth Sch.

SELL, DAVID ALAN, Fourth Grade Teacher; *b:* Fort Wayne, IN; *m:* Valarie Sue Nyenhuis; *c:* Ciara Lyn, Nathaniel Ray; *ed:* (BS) Elem Ed, Fort Wayne Bible Coll 1981; (MS) Elem Ed, IN Univ 1989; *cr:* 3rd Grade Teacher Lincoln Elem Sch 1979-80; 5th Grade Teacher 1981-83, 6th Grade Teacher 1983-84, 4th Grade Teacher 1984- North Decatur Elem Sch; *ai:* 5th/6th Grade Bsktbl Coach 1981-; Young Astronaut Cncl Spon 1988-; Cmptr Comm Chairperson 1985-; *home:* RR 1 Box 390 Fairland IN 46126

SELLA, JOSEPH J., Math Teacher; *b:* New York, NY; *m:* Linda M. Crugnale; *c:* Guy J., Eric P.; *ed:* (BA) Math, Adelphi Univ 1953; (MS) Ed, Hofstra Univ 1971; *cr:* Mgr Industrial Engineering Republic Aviation 1953-65; Dir of Manufacturing Kollsman Instrument 1965-70; Teacher Massapequa HS 1970-78; Self Employed Marida 1978-84; Teacher St Anthonys HS 1985-; *office:* St Anthonys HS 275 Wolf Hill Rd South Huntington NY 11747

SELLARS, CINDY HOLMES, Math Teacher; *b:* Conroe, TX; *m:* Thomas W.; *c:* John T., Ginger A.; *ed:* (BA) Psych, TX A&M Univ 1979 ; *cr:* Math Teacher 1978-81, 1983 Booker T Washington Jr HS; *ai:* Math Club Spon; Fellowship Comm; OM Coach 1987-89; Curr for Conroe 7th Gifted Prgm; TX St Teacher Assn 1983-89; NEA 1983-89; Conroe Ed Assn 1983-89; 1960 Area Math Cncl 1983-89; NETM 1987-89; *office:* Booker T Washington Jr H S 507 Ave K Conroe TX 77301

SELLERS, ARLENE SELTENRIGHT, Second Grade Teacher; *b:* Plymouth, IN; *m:* Paul Marion; *c:* Cynthia, Timothy, Sandra; *ed:* (BS) Ed, Ball St 1961; (MS) Ed, Purdue North Cntrl 1972; *cr:* 3rd Grade Teacher Bremen Elem 1961-62, Culver Elem 1962-63; 2nd/3rd Grade Teacher Washington Elem 1965-; *ai:* Dev of Math Curr; PTA Treas 1981-; Gleaner Ober Arbor 477 (Assoc Mem, Prgm Chm) 1987-; Goodtime Singers 1985-; Candidate Knox Cmmty Sch Corporation Teacher of Yr 1989; *office:* Washington Elem Sch RR 3 Box 385 Knox IN 46534

SELLERS, BRENT LEE, Elementary Principal; *b:* Sidney, OH; *m:* Ann B.; *c:* Wesley, Megan; *ed:* (BA) Elem Ed, 1978, (MA) Elem Admin, 1982 Bowling Green St Univ; *cr:* Teacher 1978-84, Asst Prin 1984-86 New London Local Elem; Prin League Elem 1986-; *ai:* Dollars for Scholars Bd of Dir; Prin Top 40 Rdng Prgm; Rdng Is Fundamental Building; PEGASUS Enrichment Prgm Teacher & Prgm Coord; OH Assn Elem Sch Admin 1982-; Phi Delta Kappa 1985-; Project Leadership; North Cntrl Review Team Comm Chm; *office:* League Elem Sch 16 E League St Norwalk OH 44857

SELLERS, JO ANN COXWELL, US History/Journalism Teacher; *b:* George Cty, MS; *m:* Louie Rudolph; *c:* Lori; *ed:* (BS) Journalism/Scndry Ed, Univ of S MS 1969; (ME) His, William Carey Coll 1984; *cr:* Reporter/Photographer George Cty Times 1965-77; Journalism/Eng Teacher George Cty HS 1967-73; Owner Childrens Retail Store 1975-78; Eng Teacher Cntrl Elem Sch 1978-85; Journalism/His Teacher George Cty HS 1985-; *ai:* Newspaper, Quill & Scroll Adv; Photography & Jr Class Spon; Five-Yr Planning Comm; Academic Boosters Club Officer; George Cty Ed Assn Pres 1986-88, Teacher of Yr 1987-88; MS Assn of Educators Bd of Trustees 1989-, Mem of Yr 1986, Leadership Grant; MS Press Women Past Treas 1970-, HS Adv of Yr 1990; Lucedale Fine Arts Club Historian 1975-88; George Cty Jr Miss Prgm (Dir, Chm) 1980-88; George Cty HS Boosters Club Publicity 1978-; Horace Mann Insurance Service in Ed Awd; George Cty Sch Dist Teacher of Yr 1987-88; MS Soc Stud Comm 1990; *home:* PO Box 802 Lucedale MS 39452

SELLERS, JUDITH ANNE PARK, Language Arts Teacher; *b:* Pensacola, FL; *m:* James Edward; *c:* Kimberly L., James M.; *ed:* (AA) Eng Ed, Faulkner St Jr Coll 1974; (BA) Speech Comm/Eng Ed, Univ of S FL 1976; (MED) Admin/Supervision, Univ of W FL 1984; *cr:* Lang Art Teacher Pensacola HS 1976-81, Brownsville Mid Sch 1981-; *ai:* 7th Grade Team Leader; Sch Newspaper Spon; Intnl Rdng Assn, Escambia Cty Cncl Teachers of Eng, Escambia Ed Assn; Brownsville Mid Sch Parent Teacher Stu Assn (Pres 1986-88, VP 1988-89); GSA Leader 1987-89; Book Published; *office:* Brownsville Mid Sch 1800 N Kirk St Pensacola FL 32505

SELLERS, LINDA BAYSDON, 5th Grade Teacher; *b:* Columbus County, NC; *m:* Tommie James; *c:* Lana Ellen Formy Duval Bryson; *ed:* (BA) Primary Elem Ed, Univ NC 1965; *cr:* 3rd Grade Teacher Hallsboro Sch 1965-66; 4th Grade Teacher Old Dock Elem 1966-70; 5th Grade Teacher Hallsboro Elem 1970-; *ai:* 5th Grade Chairperson Halloween Carnival Comm; Honors Prgm Comm; Amer Ed Week Comm; Cty Instructional Supply & Materials Comm Chairperson; Public Relations Comm; Supplementary Book Comm; NC Assn of Educators; PTA; *home:* Rt 1 Box 268 Hallsboro NC 28442

SELLNER, ELAINE DOUTHITT, Former Teacher; *b:* Douglas, AZ; *m:* William Thomas; *c:* Kyle, Amy; *ed:* (BS) Elem Ed, Southwestern Bible Coll 1979; *cr:* 3rd Grade Teacher Western Chrstn Sch 1979-81; 4th Grade Teacher Grace Cmmty Chrstn Sch 1981-85; *ai:* Faith Evangelical Free Church Womens Ministries 1989-; *home:* 4814 E Pearce Rd Phoenix AZ 85044

SELLS, BARBARA HOLT, English Teacher; *b:* Albermarle, NC; *c:* Kelly Baker Jones, Bob Baker, Scotty, Stacy; *ed:* (BA) Eng, UNC Greensboro 1960; *cr:* 7th/9th Grade Eng/Soc Stud Teacher Wiley Jr HS 1960-61, 7th/8th Grade Eng/Soc Stud Teacher Albemarle HS 1963-70; 1969-70; Eng I/II W Montgomery HS 1974-; *ai:* Beta Club Spon; Eng Dept Secy; Media Advisory & Sch Based Comm; NCAE 1974-; Delta Kappa Gamma 1988-; *office:* W Montgomery HS Rt 3 Mount Gilead NC 27306

SELLS, D. RANDALL, Asst Dir Learning Skills Lab; *b:* Steubenville, OH; *m:* Debra Marie Carmichael Sells; *c:* Matthew, Andrew; *ed:* (BS) Recreation Admin, Kent St Univ 1978; Univ of Steubenville; *cr:* Prin Wintersville Chrstn Acad 1979-88; Instr WV Northern Comm Coll 1986/89; Dir Dret Sch 1989-; Asst Dir Jefferson Tech Coll 1989-; *ai:* Athletic Dir; Coached Bsktbl/Vlybl & Bsbl; Fine Arts Dir; Natl Right-To-Life Mem 1986-; Natl Republican Party Mem & Candidate 1985-; 18th Dists Nom for US House of Reps 1990; *home:* 148 Beechwood Dr Wintersville OH 43952

SELMAN, CAROL, High School History Teacher; *b:* New York, NY; *m:* Jules L. Schneider; *c:* Karen Schneider, Nancy Schneider; *ed:* (BA) His, Cornell Univ 1968; (MA) Amer Stud, SUNY Stony Brook 1981; Grad Stud Amer His, SUNY Stony Brook 1982-83; *cr:* Teaching Asst SUNY Stony Brook 1982-83; Teacher Millburn Sr HS 1969-; *ai:* Amnesty Intnl Club Adv; NJ Ed Assn Legislative Liaison; Organization of Amer Historians; Natl Endownent for Hum Fellow; *office:* Millburn Sr HS 462 Millburn Ave Millburn NJ 07041

SELPH, RHONDA KAY, 8th Grade Soc Stud/Eng Teacher; *b:* Valdosta, GA; *ed:* (AA) Ed, North FL Jr HS 1971; (BS) ED, FL Atlantic Univ 1973; *cr:* Teacher Hamilton Mid Sch 1973-; *ai:* 8th Grade Teacher Leader; Hamilton Cty Ed Assn (Secy 1979-80 Pres 1980-81 VP 1981-82).

SELVIG, LINDA KAY (SIPILA), Earth Science Teacher; *b:* Wallace, ID; *m:* Wayne; *c:* Cynthia, Bradley; *ed:* (BS) Scndry Phys Ed, Boise St Univ 1978; Earth Sci, Sci; *cr:* Teacher Aide Spec Ed Sch 1975-77; Earth Sci/Phys Ed Teacher Lowell Scott Jr HS 1979-87; Earth Sci/Honors Earth Sci Teacher Centennial HS 1987-; *ai:* Jr Var Vlybl, Sftbl Coach Girls; Jr Class Adv; ID Earth Sci Teacher Assn (Pres 1990-92, Pres Elect 1990-91); Lowell Scott Jr HS Teacher of Yr 1985; Mount St Helens Project; Fellowship NSF 1988; Fellowship Marine Resource Dev Fnd 1989; Fellowship NSF Boise St Univ 1985 & 88; Publications NSTA, SCOPE 1985-87; *office:* Centennial 4600 Mc Millian Rd Meridian ID 83642

SEMERANO, RONALD J., Health Teacher; *b:* Port Jervis, NY; *m:* Doreen Winters; *c:* Matthew; *ed:* (AA) Phys Ed, Wesley Coll 1975; (BS) Health/Phys Ed, Lock Haven St Coll 1978; (MS) Phys Ed, E Stroudsburg Univ 1983; *cr:* Health Teacher Port Jervis HS; *ai:* Girls Var Bsktbl Coach; Var Ftbl Offensive Coord; Youth-At-Risk Comm; Supt of Recreation City of Port Jervis; Times Herald Record Bsktbl Coach of Yr 1985; *office:* Port Jervis HS Rt 209 Port Jervis NY 12771

SEMON, CARL WILLIAM, Aerospace Science Instructor; *b:* Waterford, OH; *m:* Sharon Sue Roberts; *c:* Kristin A., Craig W.; *ed:* (BA) Bus, Park Coll 1976; *cr:* Field Trng Instr USAF 1969-77; 12th Grade Aerospace Sci Instr R B Hayes HS 1977-; *ai:* Drill Team & Color Guard Adv; Amer Legion Commander 1980-85; DE Red Cross (Dir, Bd) 1987-; Veterans Service Commission Dir 1989-; Outstanding Instr Awd 1981, 1987; *office:* Rutherford B Hayes HS 289 Euclid St Delaware OH 43015

SEMONE, ELZURAH BRASHEAR, 3rd Grade Teacher; *b:* Hazard, KY; *c:* Ethan B; *ed:* (BS) Elem Ed 1967, (MS) Elem Sch Lib 1974, (Rank 1) Kndgtn 1975 Eastern KY Univ; KY Intern Resrce Teacher; *cr:* Elem Teacher, McAfee Sch 1967-68; Elem Teacher, Eli Brown,II Sch 1968-69; Lib,New Haven Sch 1969-70; Elem Teacher, Mercer Cnty Elem Sch 1970-90; *ai:* Textbk Comm, Intern Resrce Comm, Mercer Cnty Elem Sch; Mercer Cnty Ed Assoc 1970-90; KY Ed Assoc 1967-90; Natl Ed Assoc 1967-90; Order of KY Colnls; *home:* Box 335 Burgin KY 40310

SEMPLE, DEBORAH OSLYN, Mathematics Teacher; *b:* Georgetown, Guyana; *ed:* (BS) Bio/General Sci, Fordham Univ 1982; Re-Cert Math, Long Island Univ & Hellmans Inst; Working Towards Masters Lehman Coll 1991; *cr:* Math Teacher Acad of Mt St Ursula 1983-86; Sci Teacher 1986-87, Math Teacher 1987- William Niles Jr HS 118; *ai:* Niles Jr HS 118 NHS; NY St United Teachers Assn, United Fed Teachers Assn; Church of Our Savior Organist 1989-; Asbury United Meth Church Choir Mem; Achievers Fellowship (Musician 1988-, Devotional Leader 1989); NAACP 1978-79; *home:* 29 S 12th Ave Mount Vernon NY 10550

SEMROCK, HAROLD REYNOLD, Bible Teacher/Principal; *b:* Graytown, OH; *m:* Carol Elizabeth Puls; *c:* Christopher, Carly, Jennifer; *ed:* (BA) Phys Ed, Valparaiso Univ 1967; *cr:* Elem Teacher Tucson Tabernacle Chrstn Sch 1979-84; Prin/Teacher Bible Believers Chrstn Sch 1984-89, Rapid City Chrstn Acad

1989-; *ai:* Drama Adv, Outdoor Ed; *home:* 1702 E Hwy 44 Lot 156 Rapid City SD 57701

SENDELBACH, NOVA MADELINE (HAUGH), Art Teacher; *b:* Bascom, OH; *m:* Roland F.; *c:* Rolanda Williams, Micheal, Tonja Moreno, Thaddeus, Thedore, Adonica; *ed:* (BS) Elem Ed, Bowling Green 1970; Math & Art, Artist Sch MA; *cr:* 7th/8th Grade Math Teacher St Marys 1965-64; 2nd Grade Teacher 1966-71, Elem Art Teacher 1971-77 Seneca E; 7th/8th Grade Math Teacher E Jr HS 1980-82; Art Teacher Canton Elem 1982-83; 7th/8th Grade Math Teacher 1983-85, Jr/Sr HS Art Teacher 1983- Hopewell-Loudon; *ai:* Yrbk Adv; 11th Grade Teacher Competency Math; OEA; Clinton Township Volunteer Fire Dept Ladies Auxiliary 1961-; *office:* Hopewell-Loudon Box 400 Bascom OH 44809

SENDERLING, SUSAN G., Fifth Grade Teacher; *b:* Darby, PA; *ed:* (BA) Math, Montclair St Coll 1966; Elem Cert Trenton St Coll; *cr:* 4th-6th Grade Teacher Tinicum Elem Sch 1966-; *ai:* UNICEF & Spelling Bee Chairperson; Home & Sch Assn Rep; Soc & Prin Advisory Comm; In Charge of Ron Bozzuto Memorial Schlsp Fund Comm; NEA, PA St Ed Assn 1966-; Palisades Ed Assn (Building Rep, Treas) 1966-; *home:* 577 Milford Warren Glen Rd Milford NJ 08848

SENER, SCOTT T., Sixth Grade Teacher; *b:* Columbia, PA; *m:* Carol A. Houseal; *c:* Abby; *ed:* (BS) Elem Ed, Lebanon Valley Coll 1973; *cr:* 5th Grade Teacher H C Burgard Elem 1973-80; Head Teacher Elm Tree Elem 1981-; *ai:* Asst Girls Sftbl Coach; NEA; PA St Ed Assn; Manheim Cntrl Ed Assn Building Rep 1973-80; 1st United Meth Church Finance Chairperson 1987-; Society for Preservation & Encouragement of Barbershop Quartet Singing in America Inc; Taught Dist Teachers Prescriptive Math Approach; *office:* Elm Tree Elem Sch 1360 Strickler Rd Mount Joy PA 17552

SENFTLEBER, JANA LYNNE, French Teacher; *b:* Hobart, OK; *m:* Albert; *c:* Michael De Chellis, Matthew De Chellis; *ed:* (BA) Fr, TX Tech Univ 1978; Fr Lit; *cr:* Teacher Webster Intermediate Sch 1980-82, League City Intermediate Sch 1982-84, Clear Creek HS 1985-; *ai:* Fr Club & Paws Spon; Spon & Organizer of Clear Creek Stud Group in France 1981, 1986-; NEA, TSTA (Faculty Rep 1981-82) 1980-; *office:* Clear Creek HS 2305 E Main League City TX 77573

SENKA, FRANK MICHAEL, JTPA-Tutorial Representative; *b:* Chicago, IL; *ed:* (BS) Soc Stud, Southern IL Univ Carbondale 1970; *cr:* 7th/8th Grade Soc Stud/Lang/Rdng/Spelling Teacher Christopher Elem Sch 1980-86; Jr Trng Partnership Act Tutorial Rep Christopher Comm HS 1988-; *ai:* Stu Cncl 1989-; St Andrew Cath Church Trustee 1987-; Christopher Comm Public Lib Bd Mem 1987-; Shawnee Dist Lib Bd Mem 1987-89; Knights Of Columbus; Christopher Chamber of Commerce Comm Service Awd 1989; Dist Coord IL Assn of Jr High Stu Cncls 1985-86; Stu Cncl Christopher Elem Sch 1980-86; *office:* Christopher HS 901 Ernestine Christopher IL 62822

SENOR, VIRGINIA L., Spanish Teacher; *b:* Cleveland, OH; *c:* Kyle S.; *ed:* (AB) Span, Cleveland St Univ 1968; (MED) Admin, John Carroll Univ 1980; Various Univ; Grad Hrs Span & Teaching Foreign Lang; *cr:* Teacher West Geauya Schls 1968-75, 1978-; E Cleveland City Schls 1980-; *ai:* Drama & Span Club; Talent Show; Prin Advisory; OH Foreign Lang Assn Exec Rec 1986-89; Cntrl Sts Amer Cncl on Teaching of Foreign Lang, NEA, OEA, NEOTA, ECEA; Rockefeller Grant 1986; NEH Grant 1985; Fulbright Exch Teacher Argentina 1987-88; E Cleveland Teacher of Yr 1989-; *home:* 1496 Parkhill Rd Cleveland OH 44121

SENSEMAN, DOUGLAS CHARLES, Social Studies Teacher; *b:* Warren, OH; *ed:* (BA) Poly Sci, Kent St Univ 1979; (MED) Ed, Youngstown St 1989; *cr:* Teacher Brown Mid Sch 1981-; *ai:* OH Cncl of Soc Stud; NEA, Ravenna Ed Assn; *home:* 445 Scott NE Warren OH 44483

SENSKE, HOWARD VICTOR, Science Teacher; *b:* Gaylord, MN; *m:* Charlotte J. Peterson; *c:* Peter, Heather; *ed:* (BA) Bio, Gustavus Adolphos Coll 1966; Grad Work San Diego St Coll; *cr:* Teacher Hector Public Schls 1966-69, Seeley Public Schls 1969-70, Jordan Public Schls 1971-; *ai:* Hope Luth Church Pres 1972-76; Jordan Jaycees Dir 1973-78; Jordan Lions Dir 1980-81; Jordan St Bsbl Tourney Dir of Food 1981-82; *office:* Jordan Public Schls 500 Sunset Dr Jordan MN 55352

SENTENO, SYLVIA, History Teacher; *b:* Brownsville, TX; *ed:* (BFA) Studio Art, Univ of TX 1980; *cr:* San Benito HS 1980-; *ai:* Acad Spon; Masterminds, TX Academic Decathlon, TX Academic Octathlon Coach; Faculty Advisory Comm; TX Classroom Teachers Assn Secy 1988-; TX St Teachers Assn 1988-; Delta Kappa Gamma Society IntlResearch Chm; *office:* San Benito HS 450 S Williams Rd San Benito TX 78586

SENUTA, SUZANNE, Level 6 Teacher; *b:* Akron, OH; *m:* Robert; *c:* Anne, Julie, Peter, Beth; *ed:* (BAED) His/Government, 1960, (MAED) Rdng, 1980 Univ of Akron; Retraining Elem Ed, Univ of Akron 1973-74; *cr:* World His/Health Teacher Garfield HS 1960-62; Level 6 Teacher Riverview Elem 1975-88, Stow Public Schls 1975-, Lakeview Elem 1988-; *ai:* Rdng Curr, Textbook Selection, Right to Read, Soc Stud Comm; Rdng Auction Chm; Intnl Rdng Assn 1990; NEA, OH Ed Assn, Stow Teachers Assn 1975-83; Hudson Garden Club (Publicity Chm 1987-, Hospitality Chm 1985-87); Hudson Chamber of Commerce 1987-; Pres Perfect Answer Incorporated; *home:* 7303 Marblehead Dr Hudson OH 44236

SEPELYAK, CAROL WALLACE, Spanish Teacher; *b:* Philadelphia, PA; *ed:* (BA) Span/Eng as Second Lang, Montclair St Coll 1979; (MA) Educal Admin, Kean Coll 1990; *cr:* 6th-8th Grade Span Teacher Hart Ed Complex 1979-; *ai:* Natl Jr Honor Society Adv; John L Costley Sch Peer Coach; ASCD, NJ Foreign Lang Educators, NJ Ed Assn, Phi Delta Kappa; *office:* John L Costley Sch 116 Hamilton St East Orange NJ 07017

SEPUTIS, THOMAS JOHN, Business Department Chair; *b:* Berwyn, IL; *m:* Grace J. Gatewood; *c:* Andrew T.; *ed:* (BS) Management, N IL Univ 1969; (MBA) Management, Governors St Univ 1978; *cr:* Management Trainee Jewel Foods Incorporated 1969; Teacher Bishop Mc Namara HS 1969-71; Dept Chm/ Teacher Marist HS 1971-; *ai:* Intramural Dir; Natl Assn of Tax Preparers 1987-; NBEA 1988-; *office:* Marist HS 4200 W 115th St Chicago IL 60655

SERATT, NANCY WHITE, Biology Teacher; *b:* Bells, TN; *m:* Harry E.; *c:* Claire E., Joseph E.; *ed:* (BS) Bio/His/Scndry Ed, 1964, (MST) Biological Sci, 1973- Memphis St Univ; Numerous Coll & Wkshps; *cr:* Sci Teacher Memphis City Schls 1966-71; Bio Teacher/Sci Dept Chairperson Harding Acad 1973-; *ai:* Elem Sci Coord; NABT; Highland St Church of Christ (Primary Dept/ Supervisor/Sunday Sch Teacher) 1979-; *office:* Memphis Harding Acad 1100 Cherry Rd Memphis TN 38117

SERENE, JOYCE E. MC MAHON, Senior High School Art Teacher; *b:* Apollo, PA; *m:* Donald D.; *c:* Lisa Koroly, Christine Muchnok, Mari-Beth Pratkanis, Joseph Pratkanis; *ed:* (BFA) Teaching Cert Fine Art Studio/Eng, Univ of PA 1984; Various Courses at Numerous Univs; Working Towards Masters in Fine Arts, Univ of PA; *cr:* Freelance Artist 1960-; Prof Exhibition Juror 1983-; Art Research Writer/Consultant Univ of PA 1984-87; Grad Asst Univ of PA 1985-87; Sr Hs Art Teacher Ford City Hs 1987-; *ai:* Sr Art Club Spon; Ford City Stu Assistance Team Mem; Art Portflio Consultant; Indiana Univ of PA Womens Stud 1986-87, Womens Leadership Awd 1986; Indiana Univ of PA Grad Stu Assn (Art Delegate 1985-87, Pres 1986-87, VP 1985-86), Grad Merit Awd 1986, Jurors Awd of Distinction 1987; NEA 1987-; Kappa Delta Pi 1985-; Sigma Tau Delta; Arts Assoc of Johnstown Exhibiting Artist 1984-90, Merit Awd 1987; Allied Artists of Johnstown Exhibiting Artist 1984-90, Purchase Awd 1987; Pittsburgh Society of Artists Exhibiting Artist 1984-90, Purchase Awd 1985; Intnl Presentation Convergence 1986-87; Invited Solo Exhibition of Art Cote St Lue 1987; Womens Advisory Bd Stu Orientation Panel, PA Art Ed Assn Region 3 1986;Invited Exhibition Coord Natl Endowment of Hum Shakespeare Inst Exhibition 1986-87; Invited Solo Exhibition in Univ of PA Armstrong Campus E Room Gallery 1989; IUP Armstrong Campus Lecture Series 1989; Westmoreland Art Assn, Ford City Art Assn 1988; Invitd Exhibiting Artist IUP Womens Symposium Art Exhibition 1987; *office:* Ford City HS 4th St & 11th Ave Ford City PA 16226

SERGEANT, ROBERT STEWART, English Teacher/Admin Asst; *b:* Stauton, VA; *m:* Dianne Busby; *ed:* (BA) Eng, Mary Baldwin Coll 1975; (MA) Eng, James Madison Univ 1977; *cr:* Grad Teaching Asst James Madison Univ 1975-77; Eng Dept Head/Academic Dean Staunton Military Acad 1977-78; Instr/ Admin Asst Norfolk Acad 1978-; Adjunct Professor St Leos Coll 1988-; *ai:* Sch Renewal Climate Comm Chm; Luminary Ed; Poetry Book Ed & Spon; Elem Sch Forensics Prgm Dir; Chess Club Spon; Jr HS Bsktbl Coach; Lib Study Comm Mem; VA Beach Fnd Contributor 1989-; Norfolk Sister City Assn Judge 1989; VA Assn of Ind Schls Convention, Mid Atlantic Teacher Conference, VA Assn Ind Schls Dist Conference Presenter; Norfolk Acad James B Massey Distinguished Teacher Awd 1982; *office:* Norfolk Acad 1585 Wesleyan Dr Norfolk VA 23502

SERGENT, RONALD LEE, 8th Grade Amer His Teacher; *b:* Ventura, CA; *m:* Marsha Twitty; *c:* Scott, Jason; *ed:* (BS) Soc Stud, 1969, (MED) Educl Admin, 1974 Univ of MO Columbia; *cr:* Soc Stud Teacher Ritenour Sr HS 1970-74; Field Mgr St Louis Cty Office of Drug Abuse Prevention 1974-77; Soc Stud Teacher Columbia Public Schls 1977-; *ai:* Spon of Drug Free Group; Coord of Stu Assistance Prgm; Tennis Coach; NSCC 1989-; Columbia Teachers Assn 1968-89; Columbia Jaycees Bd Mem 1981-82; MO Alumni Assn 1988-; MO Alumni of Delta Upsilon Bd Mem 1969-, Outstanding Alumni 1988; Chm Comm on Staff Parish Relations MO United Meth Church; *office:* Jefferson Jr HS 713 Rogers St Columbia MO 65201

SERRA, MICHAEL G., Social Studies Teacher; *b:* Covina, CA; *ed:* (AA) General Ed, Los Angeles City Coll 1981; (BA) Poly Sci, Univ of CA Los Angeles 1983; *cr:* His Teacher Schurr HS 1986-; *ai:* Jr Statesmen Chapter Spon; Class of 1990 Adv; CTA 1986-; NEA 1986-; Univ of CA Los Angeles Alumni 1985-; *office:* Schurr HS 820 N Wilcox Ave Montebello CA 90640

SERRA, PAUL THOMAS, Mathematics Teacher; *b:* Baltimore, MD; *ed:* (BS) Math, Kent St Univ 1962; *cr:* Math/Phys Ed Teacher Shore Jr HS 1962-; Math Teacher Euclid Sr HS 1972-; *ai:* Head Bsbl Coach 1977-; Euclid Teachers Assn 1962-, Teacher of Yr 1982; OEA, NEA 1962-; Euclid ELks Club 1976-; *home:* 19770 Monterey Ave Euclid OH 44119

SERROS, CHARLES, Math Department Chairperson; *b:* Oxnard, CA; *m:* Elizabeth Mary Perrotto; *c:* Charles L., Patrick E., Rebecca J., Manuel C.; *ed:* (AA) General Stud, Oscar Rose Jr Coll 1979; (BS) Ed, 1981, (ME) Ed, 1986 Univ TX El Paso; *cr:* Math Teacher J M Hanks HS 1981-88, Loretto Acad 1988-, El Paso Comm Coll 1988-; *ai:* Soph Class Spon; NCTM; *office:* Loretto Acad 1300 Hardaway El Paso TX 79903

SERROTT, BEVERLY MANN, Sixth Grade Teacher; *b:* Schnectady, NY; *m:* Clyde A.; *c:* Stephen P., Stanley C., Stuart R., Sherryl Curnutte; *ed:* (BA) Elem Ed, Asbury Coll 1954; Miami-Dade Comm Coll, Broward Comm Coll, FL Intnl Univ; *cr:* 2nd Grade Teacher Greenlawn Elem Sch 1954-55, Burdette Avenue Sch 1955-56, Eisenhower-Nova Elem 1966-76, Princeton Chrstn Sch 1976-80, Westwood Chrstn 1980-83; 6th Grade Teacher Princeton Chrstn 1983-; *ai:* FL Assn Chrstn Schls 1976-, Dedicated Servant Awd 1989; Princeton Chrstn Sch Teacher of Yr 1979, 1986; *home:* 10220 SW 28th St Miami FL 33165

SERVIS, MARY CARMICHAEL, Science Teacher; *b:* Shattuck, OK; *m:* Darris; *c:* Cole, Caley; *ed:* (BSE) Natural Sci/ Health/Phys Ed, NW OK St Univ 1981; Grad Stud SW OK St Univ, OK St Univ; *cr:* Sci Teacher Freedom HS 1983-87; Sci Dept Chairperson/Teacher Deer Creek-Edmond HS 1987-88; Sci Teacher Vici HS 1988-89, Woodward HS 1989-; *ai:* Pep Club & Cheerleading Spon; AAHPERD 1980-84; NW Domestic Violence Crisis Center Bd Mem 1989-; Alva Womens Athletic Assn Bd of Governors 1978-81; Freedom Public Schls Teacher of Yr 1983; Woods Cty Teacher of Yr 1983; NWOSU Outstanding Alumni 1984; *office:* Woodward HS 10th And Downs Woodward OK 73801

SESNIE, THOMAS CHARLES, Social Studies Teacher; *b:* Jamestown, NY; *m:* Dorothy Reed; *c:* Ronald, Carolyn, Cathryn; *ed:* (BS) Elem Ed, SUC Fredonia 1961; (MS) Scndry Soc Stud, St Univ Buffalo 1966; *cr:* Teacher Sherman Cntrl Schls 1961-62, Maryvale Sch System 1962-; *ai:* Maryvale Mid Sch Effective Schls Comm Mem; NY St United Teachers, NEA 1961-; *office:* Maryvale Sch System 1050 Maryvale Dr Cheektowaga NY 14225

SESSIONS, BILLIE PALMER, Art Teacher/Fine Arts Head; *b:* Tacoma, WA; *m:* Alan J.; *c:* Aaron J., Andrew P., Neil P.; *ed:* (BFA) Art, Art Ed, 1970, (MED) Instruction Technology/Art, 1985 UT St Univ; Multi-Projector Media Presentations; Photography; Serigraph; Ceramics; *cr:* Art Instr Western WY Coll 1975-; Art Teacher Star Valley Jr HS 1980-84; Silkscreen Consultant Utah St Univ 1984; Art/Ceramics Star Valley HS 1985-; *ai:* Spon Natl Art Honor Society WY Sr Adv; Sch Play Scenery Dir; Graduation Design Dir; WY Scndry Art Educators (Pres Elect 1988-89) Pres 1989-); Intnl Society for Ed Through Art St Rep 1988-; Natl Art Ed 1988-; WY Alliance for Arts-Bd Mem 1988-; WY Cncl of Arts Slide Registry 198-; 1990 Fulbright Seminar Finalist; 1986 Schlsp Recipient for Art Educators Honors Seminar; RI Sch of Design; Grant Recipient-Natl Endowment for Arts; Painting-Vermon Studio Sch 1987; Natl Winner Cameras in Curr 1985; *home:* Box 98 Afton WY 83110

SESSIONS, ZENOBIA DELIYANNI, French Teacher; *b:* Athens, Greece; *m:* William A.; *c:* Andrew, Eric; *ed:* (BA) Fr, Academie Franconse d Athenes Greece; (BA) Fr, GA St Univ 197 ; (MA) Fr, Emory Univ 1972; *cr:* Exec Secy La Baloise Compagnie D Assurane 1949-61; Fr Instr GA St Univ 1973-74; Fr Teacher Tucker HS 1974-; *ai:* Fr Club Spon; AATF, Foreign Lang Assn of GA 1974-; Deans List; PTA Study Grant; NHS Teacher of Yr 1986; STAR Teacher 1989-; GA St Univ Best Teacher 1973; Translated Chapters AMS Press Book; *office:* Tucker HS 5036 La Vista Rd Tucker GA 30084

SESSO, CAROL ANN, Jr HS Teacher; *b:* Bedford, OH; *ed:* (BSE) Ed, 1971, (MSED) Counseling, 1985 Cleveland St Univ; Numerous Seminars & Wkshps; *cr:* 3rd/4th Grade Teacher St Ann 1958-62; 4th Grade Teacher Nativity 1962-1963; 5th/6th Grade Teacher St Benedict Sch 1963-65; 5th-7th Grade Teacher St Pius X Sch 1963-80; 6th-8th Grade Jr HS Teacher St Catherine Sch 1980-; *ai:* Asst Prin; Stu Cncl Moderator; Liturgical Music Dir; Cnslr; NCEA 1980-; NCTE 1977-87; Amer Alliance for Theater in Ed 1987-88, 1989-; Amer Theater Assn; Bedford/Solon Independence Theaters (Founder, Dir); Cleveland Cath Schls Master Teacher Outstanding Teacher Awd 1990; *office:* St Catherine Sch 3443 E 93rd St Cleveland OH 44104

SESSOMS, MARGARET JOHNSON, Science Teacher; *b:* Fayetteville, NC; *m:* Timothy Wayne; *c:* Joshua, Brian; *ed:* (BS) Bio, Pembroke St Univ 1980; *cr:* Sci Teacher Flora Mac Donald Acad 1980-84, Hoke Cty HS 1984-86, Cumberland Hospital 1986-88, Red Springs HS 1988-; *ai:* Sci Club; Cheerleading, Sci Fair, Sr Class, Beta Club, Quiz Bowl Spon; NEA, NCAE, NCSTA, NSTA 1984-; NC Network for Animals 1989-; *office:* Red Springs HS N Vance St Red Springs NC 28377

SETHASANG, VERONICA DIRECTO, Bilingual Teacher-Dept Chair; *b:* Manila, Philippines; *m:* Pume; *c:* Sam, Philip, Jennifer; *ed:* (BSE) Span/Industrial Arts, Philippine Coll of Arts/Trade 1966; (MA) Ed, Adamson Univ 1968; (AA) San Joaquin Delta Coll 1972-73; (MAED) Arts in Ed/Curr Instruction, Univ of Pacific 1973-76; MA Curr Instr, Bi-ling Specialist/Pilipino/Span, Univ of Pacific; *cr:* Epifanio De Los Santos Elem 1966-68; Genevieve Horton Sch Dist 1971-73; Substitute Teacher Stockton Unified Sch Dist 1973-75; Teacher 1975-79, Bi-ling Teacher 1979- Marshall Mid Sch; Instr San Joaquin Delta Coll 1987-; *ai:* Bi-ling Dept Chairperson; Multicultural Club Spon Adv; John Marshall Sch Leadership Team Mem; Parents Bi-ling Advisory Comm Adv; Bi-Ling Dept Chairperson; Filipino Amer Educators Secy 1972-88, Dedicated Mem Awd; CA Bi-ling Assn Mem 1985, 1987-88; Filipino Cmmty Assn Mem 1988-; Fresno Teacher Assn Mem 1975-; Marharlika Dance Troupe VP 1982-84; Armed Forces Retirees Assn 1980-89; *office:* John Marshall Mid Sch 1141 Lever Blvd Stockton CA 95206

SETSER, SHERRY LYNN, Social Studies Teacher; *b:* Clothier, WV; *m:* Larry R.; *c:* Larry A., Kevin B., Brian K.; *ed:* Assoc General Stud, S WV Comm Coll 1984; (BS) Scndry Ed/Soc Stud, WV St Coll 1985; Mid Chldhd Certificate, WV Coll; *cr:* Soc Stud Teacher Madison Mid Sch 1986; Rdng Teacher Wharton Mid Sch 1986-87; Soc Stud Teacher Madison Mid Sch 1987-88; Soc Stud Teacher Van Jr/Sr HS 1988-; *ai:* Stu Cncl Spon; WV His Club Spon; Phi Alpha Theta 1985-; Kappa Delta Pi Secy 1985-, Delegate to Regional Convention 1985; PTA Secy 1974-87; *office:* Van Jr Sr HS Box 453 Van WV 25206

SETTER, ALAN MICHAEL, Physical Science Teacher; *b:* Pueblo, CO; *m:* Sharon Cooper; *c:* Shawna, Melissa; *ed:* (BA) Bio, Western St 1969; (MA) Scndry Ed, Adams St 1989; *cr:* Math Teacher Granada Jr-Sr HS 1969-76, Lamar Jr-Sr HS 1976-80; Sci Teacher Lamar Mid Sch 1980-; *ai:* Lamar Mid Sch Ftbl Coach; Lamar Ed Assn Negotiating Team 1986-88; CO Ed Assn Lions Awd 1988; Optimist Club 1983-84.

SETTLE, LINDA K., French Teacher; *b:* Salt Lake City, UT; *c:* Courtney A., Dana R.; *ed:* Fr Culture, Univ of Grenobus 1963, Sorbonne 1964; (BA) Fr, Univ of WA 1966; (MBA) Finance, Univ of Puget Sound 1986; *cr:* Fr Teacher UPS Extension Prgm 1970-71; Client Exec Asst Frank Russell Company 1981-84; Fr Teacher Wilson HS 1983-84, Pensinsula HS 1984-; *ai:* Fr Club Adv; Exch Prgm Coord; 2001 Comm; WAFLT 1984-87; Free Lance Writer; *office:* Peninsula HS 14105 Purdy Dr N W Gig Harbor WA 98335

SETTLE, MARSHA HUNTER, Fourth/Fifth Grade Teacher; *b:* Louisville, KY; *m:* David Gates; *c:* Sarah, Julia, Emily; *ed:* (BS) Elem Ed, 1972, (MA) Elem Ed, 1976 Western KY Univ; KY Teacher Intern Prgm; *cr:* 6th Grade Teacher Wayland Alexander Elem 1973-75; Daviess Cty Mid Sch 1976-77;3rd-5th Grade Teacher Thurston Elem 1977-; *ai:* VP PTA Thruston Sch; Spelling Bee Cty Chm; Sch Sci Comm & Amer Ed Comm; PTA VP 1988-; DCEA; KEA; NEA; Owensboro Daviess Cty Youth Ftbl 1989-; Chrldr Co Commissioner; Settle Memorial Kndgtn Bd 1979-80; *office:* Thruston Elem Sch 5620 KY Hwy 144 Owensboro KY 42303

SETTLE, VIRGINIA MARTINEZ, English/Spanish Teacher; *b:* Canon City, CO; *m:* Edward J.; *c:* Jason, Joe; *ed:* (BA) Eng, Univ of CO 1969; Various Courses; *cr:* Teacher Denver Public Schls 1969-72; Volunteer/Clerk Mesa St Coll 1976-84; Volunteer 1972-84, Substitute Teacher 1983- Sch Dist #51; *ai:* Palisade HS Accountability Comm; Eng & Foreign Lang Dept Chm; Span Club & Frosh Class Spon; CCFLT 1987-; CLAS 1990; St Matthews Episcopal Church Adult Ed Coord 1986-87; Chamber of Commerce Outstanding Educator Awd 1990; Palisade HS Teacher of Yr Awd 1988; *office:* Palisade HS 711 Iowa Palisade CO 81526

SETTOON, KATHY R., Elementary Teacher; *b:* Baton Rouge, LA; *ed:* (BA) Elem Ed, 1971, (MED) Admin/Supervision, 1974 SE LA Univ; Prof Improvement Prgm; Grad Stud LA St Univ 1979; *cr:* Teacher Targipahoa Parish Sch Bd & Tucker Elem Sch; *ai:* S Assn & Rdng Grade Level Co-Chairperson; Fine Arts & Phys Ed Comm; Arbor Day Chairperson; SE LA Rdng Cncl Corresponding Secy 1978-79; LA Assn of Educators, Tangipahoa Assn of Educators Tucker Rep 1980; March of Dimes Hammond Area Steering Comm 1990; March of Dimes Captain Tucker Elem, 12 1/2 Mile Walker 1989-; Quad Area Alt Bd of Dir 1990; Ponchatoula Jaycees 1989-; Teacher of Month 1990; Conducted Wkshps for Teachers; *office:* Tucker Elem Sch 310 South 3rd St Ponchatoula LA 70454

SEVERIN, ARLENE M., English Teacher/Dept Chair; *ed:* (BA) Eng, Seton Hill Coll 1970; (MA) Eng, WV Univ 1971; Prof II Scndry Level; *ai:* Literary Magazine Spon; *office:* Geibel HS 611 E Crawford Ave Connellsville PA 15425

SEVERIN, ESTHER MC DONALD, Third Grade Teacher; *b:* Des Moines, IA; *m:* Walter M.; *c:* Lorilyn Schultes, Sherilyn Karamitros; *ed:* (BS) Elem Ed, 1962;(MS) Curr Elem Sch, Drake Univ 1968; *cr:* Elem Teacher Exira Comm Sch 1951-54, Audobon Comm Sch 1960-; *ai:* IPD Comm; PRR Comm; Church Officer; ISEA; NEA Lifetime Mem; *office:* Audubon Elem Sch 600 Tracy Audubon IA 50025

SEVERO, TOM, English Teacher; *b:* New York, NY; *m:* Maureen; *c:* Thomas, Stephen, Elaine; *ed:* (BS) Eng, Salem St Coll 1971; (MED) Ed, Antioch Univ 1976; Working Beyond Masters; *cr:* Eng Teacher Marshall Mid Sch 1971-; *ai:* Billerica Memorial HS Girls Var Soccer, Jr Var La Crosse, Intramural Bsktbl Coach; Marshall Mid Sch Stu Cncl Adv; NCTE, EMSOA; Lowell Sun Coach of Yr 1984, 1987; *office:* Marshall Mid Sch Floyd St Billerica MA 01821

SEVERSON, JOHN BYRON, Science Instructor; *b:* Minneapolis, MN; *m:* Cynthia Jensen; *c:* Sam, Max; *ed:* (BS) Bio, Univ of MN St Paul 1980; (BS) Ed, Univ of MN Minneapolis 1987; Working Toward Masters in Biochem, Univ of MN St Paul; *cr:* Sci Instr Cannon Falls HS 1987-; *ai:* Sci Club, Sr Class, Chess Club Adv; MN Sci Teachers Assn, Area Chem Teachers 1987-; *office:* Cannon Falls HS 820 E Minnesota St Cannon Falls MN 55009

SEVERSON, ROBERT KEITH, 7th & 8th Math Teacher; *b:* Hudson, SD; *m:* June Kay Grotewold; *c:* Michael, Michelle Hons, Melinda; *ed:* (BA) Phys Ed, Sioux Falls Coll 1965; Sci, Math, UNI; Phys Ed, Ed; *cr:* Phys Ed Teacher & Coach 1965-72; Math Teacher 1972- West Liberty Cmmty Schls; *ai:* West Liberty Golf & Country Club Pres & Club Champion 1989; Coach 7th Grade Boys Bsktbl & Jr HS Boys & Girls Track; ISEA; NEA; WLEA; West Liberty Golf & Country Club (Pres 1989- VP 1979-81 Bd Mem); Math Grant UNI; Sci Grant IA; Young Educator Yr 1973; West Liberty Jaycees; *home:* 615 N Clay West Liberty IA 52776

SEVERSON, SHERRY ANNE, Science Teacher/Coach; *b:* Ft Wayne, IN; *ed:* (BS) Bio, MI St Univ 1987; Working Towards Masters Sci Ed Arts, W MI Univ Kalamazoo; *cr:* Sci Teacher/Coach Lakeland HS 1987-; *ai:* Lakeland HS Girls Sftbl Head Coach 1988-, Girls Bsktbl Head Coach 1989-; Staff Dev Comm 1989-; Golden Key Natl Honor Society Mem 1986-; IN St Teachers Assn Mem 1987-; Trinity Luth Church Mem 1969-; Ft Wayne News Sentinel Area Coach of Week 1989.

SEVERT, MARILYN ANN, Third Grade Teacher; *b:* Coldwater, OH; *ed:* (BS) Elem Ed, 1974; (MED) Teacher Leadership Curr & Supervision, 1979 Wright St Univ; Post Grad Classes Bowling Green St Univ, Univ of Dayton & Ashland Coll; *cr:* 3rd Grade Teacher Coldwater Exempted Village Schls 1974-; *ai:* Grade Level Chairperson; Sci Curr Study; Supt Advisory Comm; Home Instruction; NEA 1976-; OEA 1976-; Coldwater Teachers Organization (Secy 1983-84/1987-89, Building Rep 1976-77/1981-82, Negotiations Team 1989-;) Service Awd 1989; Alpha Delta Kappa Corresponding Secy 1988-; Jr Great Books Leader; Curr for Gifted & Talented Children; Conducted Wkshp For K-5th Grade Teachers; Martha Holdings Jennings Conference; Teacher Grant from St Dept; Evaluator 2 Yrs Teacher Grants for St Dept; *office:* Coldwater Exempt Village Sch 220 N 1st St Coldwater OH 45828

SEWELL, BETH LOCKE, 8th Grade US History Teacher; *b:* Corpus Christi, TX; *m:* Sam B.; *c:* Cheri Sewell Caddenhead, Tony L.; *ed:* (BA) His, 1982, (MA) Early Amer His, 1987 Sam Houston St Univ; *cr:* 7th Grade Teacher Shepherd Jr HS 1982-83; 8th Grade Amer His Teacher Lincoln Jr HS 1983-; *ai:* Girls Vlybl, Bsktbl, Track Coach; Mem Dist Improvement Comm; Stu Cncl Spon; Jr NHS Co-Adv; TX Cncl for Soc Stud 1988-; Miss San Jacinto Cty Pageant Comm Mem 1980-; San Jacinto Cty Fair Assn Parade Chm 1978-80; Lincoln Jr HS Teacher of Yr 1990; Sam Houston St Univ Outstanding Scndry Ed Stu Awd 1982; *office:* Lincoln Jr HS P O Box 39 Coldspring TX 77331

SEWELL, CAROLYN HUGHES, Mathematics Teacher; *b:* Center, TX; *m:* Gary L.; *c:* Cody, David; *ed:* (BA) Math, Lamar Univ 1986; *cr:* Adjunct Instr Lamar Univ 1986-87; Teacher Thomas Jefferson HS 1987-; *home:* 2329 6th Ave Port Arthur TX 77642

SEWELL, JOANNA COMPTON, Language Arts Teacher; *b:* Somerset, KY; *m:* Fitch Cagle; *c:* Gary R.; *ed:* (BS) Bus Ed, E KY Univ 1961; *cr:* Teacher Sci Hill Elem 1961-68, Meece Mid Sch 1968-; *ai:* Curr & Calendar Comm; Cmptr Instr; Beacon Hill Church Organist 1980-; KEA, NEA 1961-; *office:* Meece Mid Sch 219 Barnett St Somerset KY 42501

SEWELL, MARIE FINLEY, 4th Grade Lang Arts Teacher; *b:* Drew, MS; *m:* James Lamar; *c:* Kevin, Kerry, Kyle; *ed:* (BA) Elem Ed, MS Univ for Women 1965; *cr:* 5th Grade Teacher Aurora Gardens Acad 1968-69; 4th Grade Teacher Jefferson Parish Schls 1969-71; 4th Grade Teacher Olive Branch Schls 1984-; *office:* Olive Branch Elem Sch 8631 Pigeon Roost Rd Olive Branch MS 38654

SEXTON, COLLEEN LINDA, English Teacher; *b:* Pittsburgh, PA; *m:* Jimmy Dale; *c:* Heather M.; *ed:* (MA) Speech Ed, (AB) Speech Ed/Eng 1975 Marshall Univ; *cr:* Speech Teacher Marshall Univ 1976; Eng Teacher Chesapeake Mid Sch 1982-; *ai:* Right to Read Comm Chairperson 1983; Drama Club & Writer of Month Spon; Joint Eng Comm Chairperson 1988-89; Newspaper Staff Adv; Dist Literary Magazine Coord 1985; Sch Aerobic Writing Prgm Creator; OEA Mem 1987-88; Teacher Excl Prgm; Huntington Track Club 1987; New Teacher Proficiency Testing St Selection Comm; Dist Magazine Coord; Nom Ashland Oil Teacher Achievement Awd; Stus Published Nationally; *office:* Chesapeake Mid Sch PO Box 10 Chesapeake OH 45619

SEYBOLD, JOHN FRANCIS, 7th Grade Teacher/Vice Prin; *b:* New York, NY; *ed:* (BA) Soc Sci, CSU Sacramento 1979; Grad Stud Eng as Second Lang Instr; *cr:* Teacher St Joachims Sch 1979-, Madera Adult Ed/Alternative Ed 1988-; Vice Prin St Joachims Sch 1989-; *ai:* Yrbk Ed; WASC Review Chairperson 1991; *home:* PO Box 902 Madera CA 93639

SEYMOUR, ASHLEIGH MOOD, Drafting Teacher; *b:* Durham, NC; *m:* Virginia Mc Donald; *c:* Maria Medlin, Scott Medlin; *ed:* Assoc Mechanical Technology, Richmond Comm Coll 1975; (BA) Technology, Appalachian St Univ 1977; Cmptr-Aided Drafting Courses, Apprentice Sch Seaboard Railroad; *cr:* Car Man Seaboard Railroad 1961-72; Teacher Richmond Sr HS 1977-, Richmond Comm Coll 1982-; *ai:* Tennis Coach; Pep Club Adv; Marks Creek Presbyn Deacon 1985-87; Natl Grant Winner; *office:* Richmond Sr HS Rt 1 N Rockingham NC 28379

SEYMOUR, CHARLES O., Band Director; *b:* Nyack, NY; *m:* Donna Maria Piotrowski; *c:* Emily J., Jay A.; *ed:* (BMUS) Music Ed, St Univ NY Fredonia 1970; (MS) Curr/Instruction, St Univ NY Albany 1975; Fine Art Dir Certificate, Fitchburg St Coll 1988; *cr:* General Music Teacher Saratoga Springs Jr HS 1970-71; Instrumental Music Teacher Shenendehowa Mid Sch 1971-76, Camden-Rockport Schls 1976-; *ai:* MSAD 28 Music Curr Coord & Fine Arts Dir; Dist Building, Assembly, In-Service, Gifted & Talented Comm; Meguniticook Teachers Assn (Pres 1987-89, Treas 1989-); ME Music Ed Assn Dist III Chm 1989-; Trout Unlimited 1988-; ME Teacher of Yr 1986; *office:* Mary E Taylor Mid Sch 34 Knowlton St Camden ME 04843

SEYMOUR, CHRISTINE GRAFF, Kindergarten Teacher; *b:* Ft Lauderdale, FL; *c:* Chad; *ed:* (BS) Elem Ed, Edinboro Univ of PA 1973; *cr:* 1st Grade Teacher Waterford Elem 1974-87; Grad Asst Edinboro Univ of PA 1987-88; Kndgtn Teacher Waterford Elem 1988-; *ai:* Ft Le Boeuf Ed Assn; Whole Lang Networking Group; Ft Le Boeuf Historical Society; Waterford Elem PTO; *office:* Waterford Elem Sch 323 Cherry St Waterford PA 16441

SEYMOUR, DONNA CAROL, Fourth Grade Teacher; *b:* New York, NY; *ed:* (BA) Sociology, Jackson Coll Tufts Univ 1966; MA Equivalency Ed, Univ of VA 1975; Various In-Service Courses; *cr:* 3rd Grade Teacher Adams Sch 1966-69; 4th-6th Grade Teacher Barnsley Sch 1969-; *ai:* MCEA, MSJA, NEA; *office:* Barnsley Elem 14516 Nadine Dr Rockville MD 20853

SEYMOUR, ELPHREDA BRITTENUM, Sixth Grade Teacher; *b:* Rossville, TN; *m:* James A. Sr.; *c:* Nathan Jones III, Natalie Jones Catchings; *ed:* (BS) Elem Ed, Le Moyne Owen Coll 1953; (MED) Elem Ed, Memphis St Univ 1973; Ed, Memphis St Univ; *cr:* 4th-6th Grade Teacher Grant Elem, Melrose Elem, Alcy Elem 1953-74; Team Leader Teacher Corps Memphis St Univ, Memphis City Sch 1974-81; 6th Grade Teacher Hamilton Elem 1981-; *ai:* Grade Chm; MEA, TEA, NEA; *home:* 1986 Quinn Memphis TN 38114

SEYMOUR, SHARON ANNE, Sixth Grade Teacher; *b:* Syracuse, NY; *ed:* (BA) Math/Elem Ed, Roberts Wesleyan Coll 1974; Cert NY St 1978; *cr:* Teacher Faith Heritage Sch 1977-; *office:* Faith Heritage Sch 3740 Midland Ave Syracuse NY 13205

SEYMOUR, STEPHEN FRANKLIN, Science Educator; *b:* Detroit Lakes, MN; *m:* Claudia Kay Madison; *c:* Suzanna M., Rebecca G., Victoria R.; *ed:* (BS) Bio/Pscyh, Moorhead St Univ 1973; *cr:* 7th-12th Grade Sci Teacher Gackle Public Sch 1973-; *ai:* Soph Class, Sci Fair Adv; NEA, ND Ed Assn 1973-; NSTA 1985-; Gackle Lions Club (Pres 1980-81) 1973-; ND Presidential Awd Excl in Sci Teaching 1986; ND St Awd for Conservation Ed 1986-87, 1989; *office:* Gackle Public Sch Box 375 Gackle ND 58442

SEYMOUR, STEVEN PAUL, Sixth Grade Teacher; *b:* Waverly, NY; *m:* Meredith Rose Nestle; *c:* (BS) Elem Ed, 1972, (MS) Elem Ed, 1975, (CAS) Ed Admin, 1988 St Univ of NY Fredonia; *cr:* Intermediate Grade Teacher Westfield Cntrl Sch 1972-; *ai:* Westfield Cntrl Sch Gifted & Talented Comm; Elem Sci Comm 1979-84; Elem Soc Stud Comm 1985; Grade Level Chairperson 1981, 1984, 1987; St Univ of NY Fredonia Stu Teachers Advisory Bd 1985-88; Sci Teachers of NY Bd of Dir 1980-82; Westfield Teachers Assn, NY Ed Assn VP 1987-; Loyal Order of Moose 1984-; United Meth Church (Cncl on Ministries 1977-81, Admin Bd 1977-81, Staff Parish Relations Comm 1975, Pres 1988); Westfield Day Care Center Bd of Dir; BOCES Project Appollo Advisory Comm; *office:* Westfield Cntrl Sch E Main St Westfield NY 14787

SEYON, PATRICK L. N., US History Teacher; *b:* Sasstown, Liberia; *m:* Marina Dundas; *c:* Donald, Tuan, Juah, Gwyn, Florence, Marina; *ed:* (BA) Eng Lit/African His, Univ of Liberia 1962; (MS) Scndry Sch Admin, KS St Univ 1967; (MA) Poly Sci/Amer His, 1975, (PHD) Higher Ed Admin, 1977 Stanford Univ; Ed Admin, Univ of MI Ann Arbor 1967-69; *cr:* Dir/Dev 1977-80, VP 1980-84 Univ of Liberia; Visiting Scholar/Lecturer Center/Intnl Affairs Harvard Univ 1984-86; Instr Boston Latin Acad 1986-; *ai:* Chm Geography Curr Comm; Coord of Geography Project; African Stud Assn 1982-; Liberian Stud Assn 1972-; Amer Educl Research Assn; Mem Constitution Commission that Wrote Liberias Constitution; Fulbright Scholar Stanford Univ 1972-77; Carnegie Corporation, Ford Fnd, Boston Plan of Excl in Public Schls Research Grants; *home:* 49 Summer St 2B Arlington MA 02174

SFARNAS, EVANGELINE LITSA, Sixth Grade Teacher; *b:* Philadelphia, PA; *ed:* (BA) Ed/Eng, 1973, (MED) Elem Ed, 1974 Beaver Coll 1974; Educl Leadership Prgm, Beaver Coll; Several Wkshps; *cr:* Eng Teacher 1974-86, Eng Dept Chairperson 1977-85 Holland Jr HS; 6th Grade Eng/Lang Arts Teacher Churchville Elem Sch 1985-; *ai:* Mid Sch Eng Dept Coord; Produced Sch Newspaper, Booklet Stu Poem & Short Stories; Organized Natl Spelling Bee Contest; Talent Shows & Plays Dir; Contributed to Curr Groups; Phi Delta Kappa 1974-; Cncl Rock Ed Assn 1974-; NEA 1974-; Hellenic Univ Club 1983-; Amer Hellenic Educl Progressive Assn; Amer Hellenic League 1983-88; Society for Preservation of Greek Heritage 1987-; PTO 1985-; Thanks to Teachers Excl Awd Nom 1990; Beaver Coll Grad Assistantship 1973-74; Greek Orthodox Church Recognition of Prominent Educators 1986; *office:* Churchville Elem 100 New Road Churchville PA 18966

SHABAZZ, DORIS BLACKWELL, Guidance Counselor; *b:* Anderson, SC; *m:* Ahmad Faheem; *c:* Chieoma; *ed:* (BS) Health/Phys Ed, SC St Coll 1968; (MED) Personnel Services, Clemson Univ 1978; Emotionally Handicapped Trng; *cr:* Phys Ed Teacher McDuffie HS 1968-69; Health/Phys Ed/Sci Teacher Pendleton Mid & Jr HS 1970-80; Health/Guidance Teacher Riverside Mid 1980-81; Guidance Cnslr Teacher Pendleton Jr HS 1981-; *ai:* SC Ed Assn; ACEA Pres 1982-83; NEA, SCGA; NAACP 1976-; Partnership for Academic & Career Ed 1989-; Local Teacher of Yr 1978; Designed & Implemented Career Ed Prgm; *home:* Rt 2 Box 454 Charles Reed Rd Starr SC 29684

SHADLEY, LORRI EBERT, French/Physical Ed Teacher; *b:* Traverse City, MI; *c:* Bobbie, Matthew; *ed:* (BSED) Phys Ed, Cntrl MI Univ 1977; Grad Study Cntrl MI Univ 1977-87; *cr:* Fr/Phys Ed Teacher Marlette HS 1978-; *ai:* Marlette Jr Var Girls Bsktbl Coach; Stu Groups Trips to France; Bsktbl Coaches Assn of

MI 1979-, 100 Club 1987; *office:* Marlette HS 3051 Moore St Marlette MI 48453

SHADOW, MARCELYN HELLBUSCH, IPP Teacher/Team Leader; *b:* San Diego, CA; *c:* Christian J. Morton; *ed:* (BA) Philosophy, CA St Univ Long Beach 1969; Philosophy Ed, Univ of IL; (MED) Curr/Instruction, Univ of WA 1988; Prins Cert Univ of WA 1987-88; Philosophy for Children 1986; *cr:* Teacher Clinton Sch 1970-73, Leal Sch 1973-74; Resource/Substitute Teacher Whitworth Elem, Madrona Elem, Wash Mid Sch 1987-89; Teacher Seattle Public Schls 1974-; *ai:* Dist Mid Sch Interdisciplinary Curr Writing Comm Chairperson; Team Leader WA Mid Sch Individual Progress Prgm Interdisciplinary Gifted Team; WA Assn Educators of Talented & Gifted 1986-; NW Gifted Child Assn Bd of Dir 1980-86, Speaker Bureau 1989; NW Gifted Child Assn Seattle Pres 1982-86; Natl Philosophy Honor Society 1969; Peace Luth Church Choir 1981-; IPP Curr Model Trainer; St of WA Annual Christa Mc Auliffe Excl in Ed Awd 1988; Nom Seattle Excl in Ed 1985-86; Articles Published; *home:* 8449D 25th Ave SW Seattle WA 98106

SHAEFFER, BRENT H., Social Studies Teacher; *b:* Lander, WY; *m:* Kerry; *c:* Ryan, Helen, Ross; *ed:* (BA) Scndry Ed/Soc Sci, Univ of WY 1982; *cr:* Teacher/Coach East Jr HS 1982-; *ai:* Ftbl, Bsktbl, Wrestling Coach; Stu Cncl Spon; WY Cncl for Soc Stud 1989-; Natl Cty Ed Assn 1982-; *office:* East Jr HS 900 S Beverly St Casper WY 82601

SHAFER, JAMES W., 4th Grade Teacher; *b:* Pittsburgh, PA; *m:* Andrea La Bella; *c:* Alison, Michael; *ed:* (BS) Ed, Edinboro St Coll 1970; (MS) Ed, Duquesne Univ 1974; *cr:* 6th Grade Teacher 1970-80, 4th Grade Teacher 1980- Ramsey Elem Sch; *ai:* NEA Mem 1970-; PA St Ed Assn Mem 1970-; Plum Boro Athletic Assn Coach 1986-; YMCA Youth Bsktbl Coach 1988-; *office:* Ramsey Elem Sch 2200 Ramsey Rd Monroeville PA 15146

SHAFER, JOSEPH FRANCIS, Social Studies Teacher; *b:* Wilkes Barre, PA; *ed:* (BA) Soc Stud, 1976, (MS) His/Ed, 1980 Wilkes Coll; *cr:* ESEA Title I Teacher Wilkes Barre Township Jr HS 1976-84; Soc Stud Teacher GAR Memorial 1984-; *ai:* Head Sftbl Coach; NEA, PA St Ed Assn, Wilkes-Barre Area Ed Assn 1984-; *office:* GAR Memorial HS 250 S Grant St Wilkes-Barre PA 18702

SHAFER, THOMAS RUSSELL, English/Literature Teacher; *b:* Dayton, OH; *m:* Jane Elizabeth Seifried; *ed:* (BS) Eng Ed, Wright St Univ 1984; *cr:* 7th Grade Eng Teacher 1984-85, 7th/8th Grde Eng Teacher 1985-88 West Carrollton Jr HS; 10th-12th Eng Teacher West Carrollton Sr HS 1988-; *ai:* Dir of HS Intramural Prgm; West Carrollton Earth Day Club; Faculty Adv Class 1992; Faculty Adv-After Prom Comm; Co-Ed of WCEA News; West Carrollton Ed Assn Building Rep 1984-88; West Carrollton Recognition Assn Significant Teacher Awd 1984-89; NEA, OEA Mem 1984-; Natl Parks Assn Mem 1988-; Natl Geogrpahic Society Mem 1984-; *office:* West Carrollton H S 5833 Student St West Carrollton OH 45449

SHAFFER, BONNIE J., Music Teacher; *b:* Tampa, FL; *m:* Edward O.; *c:* Edward, David, Philip; *ed:* (BA) Music Ed, Univ of S FL 1964; (MA) Music Ed, Governors St Univ 1983; *cr:* Elem Music Teacher Hillsborough Cty Public Schls 1964-75; Jr HS Music Teacher Southwood Jr HS 1976-; *ai:* Chorus; Musical Play Productions; IMEA, MENC, IEA, NEA; *office:* Southwood Jr HS 18635 S Lee St Country Club Hills IL 60478

SHAFFER, DON, Activities Director; *b:* Orange, CA; *m:* Annette Parks; *c:* Lindsay, Jillian; *ed:* (BA) Phys Ed, Point Loma Coll 1974; (MA) Sch Admin, Azusa Pacific Univ 1986; *cr:* Sports Information Dir Point Loma Coll 1974-76; Phys Ed Teacher Brookhaven Elem Sch 1976-78; Phys Ed Teacher 1978-86, Act Dir 1986- Kraemer Jr HS; *ai:* Stu Cncl Spon; Ftbl, Bsktbl & Track Coach; CA Assn of Dir of Act, Leadership Assn of S CA 1986-; Bd Mem 1990; Honorary Service Awd 1990; *office:* Kraemer Jr HS 645 Angelina Placentia CA 92670

SHAFFER, FRANKIE WATKINS, Business Education Instructor; *b:* Fayette, AL; *m:* Richard A.; *c:* Lance Alan, Brian Richard, John Edward; *ed:* (BS) Bus Ed, Florence St Coll 1960-63; (MA) Ed, OH Univ 1963-65; OH St Univ; *cr:* Bus Math Teacher Lee HS 1965-66; Res Hall Dir OH St Univ Columbus 1966-69; Intensive Office Ed Teacher North Union HS 1973-75; Bus Ed Instr OH Hi Point Joint Voc-Sch 1975-; *ai:* Chm-Calendar Comm Mem-Supt Advisory Comm; in Service Comm; Natl Voc Assn; OH Voc Assn; OH Bus Teachers Assn; United Meth Women Missions Comm; Emmaus Cmmty Modern Mothers Treas 1981-82; OCCL Historian 1980-81; *office:* Ohio Hi-Point Jvs 2280 SR 540 Bellefontaine OH 43311

SHAFFER, JAMES LANTY, Mathematics Teacher; *b:* Richwood, WV; *m:* Peggy Jean Osborne; *c:* Peter; *ed:* (BS) Math Comprehensive, WV Inst of Tech 1978; Grad Stud; *cr:* Math/ Cmptr Teacher Fayetteville Mid Sch 1979-; *ai:* Cmptr Lab Coord; Sch Improvement Team Mem; WVEA 1979-88; Mt Pleasant Baptist Church (Deacon, Clerk) 1963-; Fayetteville Mid Sch Teacher of Yr 1987; Leaders of Learning Conference 1989; Ashland Oil Teacher Achievement Awd Nom 1990; Presidential Awds for Excl Sci & Math Teaching Nom 1990; *office:* Fayetteville Mid Sch 135 High St Fayetteville WV 25840

SHAFFER, JANET EILEEN, Mathematics Teacher; *b:* Corona, CA; *ed:* (BS) Elem Ed, Univ of Tulsa 1975; Grad Stud Univ of Tulsa, OK St Univ, OK St Univ Tech Inst, Univ N CO; Lions Quest Skill for Adolenscences Trng; Various Wkshps; *cr:* Math Teacher Union Jr HS 1975-; *ai:* Dept Head; Academic Team Competitions; Math Curr Comm; Walk for Mankind; OK Ed Assn 1975-, Zone Teacher of Yr 1986; NEA, Union Classroom Teachers Assn (Mem 1975-, Mem & Chairperson Teacher of Yr Comm 1982-840; NEA 1975-; NCTM Mem 1975-80, 1984-; OK Cncl Teachers of Math Mem 1985; Fellowship of Chrstn Athletics (Mem 1977-; OK Bd of Rep 1986-, Jr HS Huddle Spon 1977-0, OK Spon of Yr Awd 1983; Concerned Women of Amer (Mem, Spon); Emmaus Wall Cmmty Mem 1989-; Will Rogers United Meth Church (Mem 1971-, Several Comm, Dist & Conference Church Camps); Compassion Intnl Child Spon; Union Jr HS Teacher of Yr 1984, 1986; UCTA Dist Teacher of Yr 1986; *office:* Union Jr HS 7616 S Garnett Tulsa OK 74133

SHAFFER, KATHY ELAINE GOLDRING, Eng/Hist/Spanish Dept Chair; *b:* Fort Worth, TX; *m:* Harry Charles III.; *c:* Jay Hamilton, Hollyanna M.; *ed:* (BA) Foreign Lang/Span 1971, 2nd Teaching Major Eng, (3rd Minor) His, Univ TX Arlington 1975; OK Univ Coursework; Creative Writing/Screenwriting; Shirley Mckee Creative Writing Course; Writers Digest Grad of Short Story Course & Novel Writing Wkshp; *cr:* Clsnlr Bauder Fashion Coll 1969-70; Substitute Teacher Various Ft Worth Schls 1971-73; Span Dept Chairperson 1978-, Eng Dept Chairperson 1979 Alvarado Inter Sch Dist; *ai:* Attendance Comm Chairperson; Hospitality Comm; Jr Class Spon; Sr Class Spon; Prin Adv Bd; Span Club Spon; TX St Teachers Assn; NCTE; United Meth Women VP/Secy 1978; JCCW-Johnson Cty Creative Writers Contest Coord 1989-; JCCW Secy 1988-89; Article Published in Womans Day; Writing Awd 1st, 2nd, 3rds & Honorable Mentions; Author of Two Mystery Novels; *office:* Alvarado H S 1100 Cummings Dr Alvarado TX 76009

SHAFFER, PAULA LYNN, English Teacher; *b:* Muskegon, MI; *m:* Bruce Douglas; *c:* Dustin; *ed:* (AA) Engl, Muskegon Comm Coll 1974; (BA) Engl Western MI Univ 1976; Additional Studies Eng and Educ Western MI Univ; *cr:* Eng & Span Teacher Dowagiac Union Schls 1977-90; *ai:* Delta Kappa Gamma 1985-88; Dowagiac Educ Assn - Assn Rep 1983-85; *office:* Dowagiac Central Mid Sch 206 Main St Dowagiac MI 49047

SHAFFIER, CAROLYN HOWARD, 8th Grade Teacher/Vice Prin; *b:* Dayton, OH; *m:* Dennis Ray; *c:* Kimberly Howard, Kristen Howard, Kevin Howard, Aaron, David; *ed:* (BA) His, Loma Linda Univ 1970; (JD) Law, Univ of La Verne 1986; *cr:* Teacher Fairview Acad 1971-72; Teacher 1972-74, Teacher/Vice Prin 1989- San Fernando Valley Acad; *ai:* Talented & Gifted Comm; Pacific Union Conference of 7th day Adv; Writing Curr; *office:* San Fernando Valley Elem Sch 17601 Lassen St Northridge CA 91325

SHAFRAN, AVI, Religious Studies/His Teacher; *b:* Baltimore, MD; *m:* Gita; *ed:* Talmudic Law, 1975, (MS) Talmudic Law, 1977 Ner Israel Rabbinical Coll; *cr:* Instr Hebrew Inst of CA 1979-82; Dean of Religion Stud Midrasha Kerem of CA 1982-84; Religious Stud/His Instr New England Acad of Torah 1984-; *ai:* Cnslr; Adult Ed Instr; Yrbk Adv; Author; Articles Published; *office:* New England Acad of Torah 450 Elmgrove Ave Providence RI 02906

SHAHAN, GARY B., Social Studies Teacher; *b:* Denver, CO; *ed:* (BAED) Scndry Ed-His, 1969, (MAED) Scndry Ed, 1972 AZ St Univ; Extensive Travel; Advamced Placement His Semimard Univ of OR & San Jose St; *cr:* Soc Stud Teacher Tempe Union HS 1970-; *ai:* Girls Tennis Coach; Teacher of Yr Tempe HS 1987; *office:* Tempe HS 1730 Mill Ave Tempe AZ 85281

SHAHEED, STANLEY F. H., Mathematics Department Teacher; *b:* Atlanta, GA; *m:* Sherrie Towns; *c:* Taji; *ed:* (AA) Philosophy/Math, 1983, (AS) Cmptr Sci/Engineering Technology, 1983 Atlanta Jr Coll; (BS) Math, 1985, (MED) Math Ed, 1989 GA St Univ; *cr:* Math Teacher Sequoyah HS 1985-89, Cross Keys HS 1989-; *ai:* Study Table & Homework Helpline Tutor; Jr Var Math Team Coach; Strategic Planning Comm Mem; Sequoyah HS Teacher of Yr 1988-89; Staff Mem of Month 1989; Finalist Cross Keys HS Teacher of Yr 1990; *office:* Cross Keys HS 1626 N Druid Hills Rd Atlanta GA 30319

SHAMBERG, ROBERT A., 5th Grade Teacher; *b:* Los Angeles, CA; *m:* Kathleen L.; *c:* Katie, Tessa, Michael; *ed:* (BSED) Elem/ Spec Ed, N AZ Univ 1976; (MAADM) Elem Admin, Univ of ID 1984; *cr:* 6th Grade Teacher Murphy Elem 1976-78; 4th Grade Teacher 1978-83, 3rd Grade Teacher 1983-84, 5th Grade Teacher 1984- Hayden Lake Elem; *ai:* Coeur D Alene Ed Assn; *home:* 3225 York Ct Hayden Lake ID 83835

SHAMBRY, GERALDINE MORGAN, English/Spanish Teacher; *b:* Millport, AL; *m:* Hugh L.; *c:* Heather; *ed:* (BA) Eng, Stillman Coll 1968; (MA) Eng, MS Univ for Women 1974; Grad Stud Ed; *cr:* Eng Teacher Todd HS 1968-69; Eng/Rdng Teacher Sulligent HS 1969-72; Eng/Span Teacher Millport HS 1972-86, South Lamar HS 1986-; *ai:* Span Club Adv; Prom Spon; Knowledge Bowl Team Eng Coach; AL Ed Assn, NEA; LEA (Pres, VP, Secy); Millport Public Library, Holly Grove Baptist Church; Millport Area Chamber of Commerce Treas; *home:* PO Box 185 Millport AL 35576

SHAMDANI, ROSA NELSON, French/Spanish Teacher; *b:* Albany, NY; *m:* Esmaeel; *ed:* (BA) Fr, Marist Coll 1979; (MA) Univ of ME 1981; Laval Univ 1976-77; MD Advanced Prof Certificate 1988; *cr:* Teacher Univ of ME 1979-81, Newfound Memorial HS 1983-84; Greenville HS 1984-86; Mc Donough HS 1987-; *ai:* Fr Club Adv; Fr Sr Awd Schlsp Founder; St James Church Organist; VFW His Awd 1975; Univ of ME Foreign Stu Assn Secy 1980-81; Undergrad Presidential Schlsp; Univ of ME Grad Fellowship; NY St Teacher Schlsp; *office:* Maurice Mc Donough HS Box 74 Q Rt 2 Pomfret MD 20675

SHAMMO, LEAH M., Third Grade Teacher; *b:* Dalton, OH; *ed:* (BS) Elem Ed, Malone Coll 1966; *cr:* 5th Grade Teacher 1966-81, 3rd Grade Teacher 1981- Dalton Elem Sch; *ai:* Dalton Local Assn (Secy 1968-69, Treas 1973-74); *home:* 2542 SW Lebanon Rd Dalton OH 44618

SHANAHAN, RICHARD STEPHEN, 6th Grade Teacher of Gifted; *b:* Evanston, IL; *ed:* (BS) Ed of Socially & Emotionally Maladjusted Children/Elem Ed, St Marys Coll & NE IL Univ 1975; Working Towards Masters Sch Admin & Supervision; *cr:* Teacher of Emotionally Disturbed/Socially maladjusted Joseph Brennemann Sch 1975-77; Teacher of Educably Mentahlly Handicapped Perkins Bass Sch 1977-78; Dramatic/Creative Arts Teacher Joyce Kilmer Sch 1978-87; Teacher of Gifted Alexander Graham Bell Sch 1987-; *ai:* Jr His Fair Chairperson; 5th/6th Grade Sci Fair; SAT Preparation; Sch Cncl Curr & Building/ Maintenance Comm Mem 1989-; Chicago Teachers Union Building Delegate 1976-77, 1986-87; PTA VP 1978-87; Dist 2 Ed Cncl (Kilmer Sch 1987-, Curr Chairperson 1985-87); Partner in Sci Grant 1990; Named Schlsp 1975; *office:* Alexander Graham Bell Sch 3730 N Oakley Chicago IL 60618

SHANDERA, JOE R., Physical Education Teacher; *b:* Lincoln, NE; *m:* Linda J. Cox; *c:* Michelle R., Jill L.; *ed:* (BA) Phys Ed, Univ of NE Lincoln 1969; (MS) Phys Ed, Univ of N CO 1972; Grad Stud, Kearney St Coll; *cr:* Teacher/Coach Medicine Valley HS 1969-78; Teacher/Coach N Platte HS 1978-; *ai:* Asst Var Ftbl & Track Coach; Bsktbl Referee; Amer Assn of Health Phys Ed & Recreation, NE Ed Assn 1969-; East/West All Star Game Asst Coach 1990; Nom Distinguished Teaching Awd 1972; *office:* North Platte HS 1000 W 2nd St North Platte NE 69101

SHANDS, MARY JANE (HALE), Science Department Chair; *b:* Brownwood, TX; *m:* John C.; *c:* Tracy, Allison, Jeanne; *ed:* (BS) Bio, Pan Amer Univ 1972; *cr:* 7th Grade Teacher Immaculate Comception Sch 1971; Bio/Eng Teacher Hanna HS 1971-73; Sci Dept Chairperson St Joseph Acad 1981-; *ai:* Brownsville Jr Service League Sustaining Mem 1975-; SCUBA Certified NAUI 1981; Established M J Shands Art Studio Incorporated 1987; Sold Limited Edition Lithographs; *office:* St Joseph Acad 101 St Joseph Dr Brownsville TX 78520

SHANE, PENNY FROHNAPFEL, Business Education Teacher; *b:* Martins Ferry, OH; *m:* Robert Bruce; *c:* Jason, Kellen; *ed:* (AS) Secretarial Sci, Belmont Tech Coll 1973; (BS) Scndry Ed, OH Univ 1981; (MS) Sch Counseling, Univ of Dayton 1987; Intensive Office Ed, Kent St Univ; Born Free Cnslrs, Drug & Alcohol Inervention for Sch Cnslrs, OH Univ; *cr:* Bus Teacher Belmont Harrison Voc Sch 1980-, Belmont Tech Coll 1983-; *ai:* Bus Prof of America Adv; Sch Christmas & Halloween Dances, Challenge Days & Sch Picnics Spon; OEA-NEA Secy 1990-; Martins Ferry Child Study Club Treas 1984-85; North Cntrl Evaluation Team Mem; *home:* 716 Springhaven Dr Martins Ferry OH 43935

SHANHOLTZ, SHIRLEY DAY, First Grade Teacher; *b:* Harrisonburg, VA; *m:* Ronald W.; *c:* Julie A.; *ed:* (BA) Elem Ed, 1972; (MS) Elem Ed, 1976 Frostburg St; *cr:* 2nd Grade Teacher Mt Lena Elem 1963-65; 3rd Grade Teacher Broadway 1965-66; Spec Ed Teacher Quincy 1966-67; 1st Grade Teacher Smithsburg Elem 1967-; *ai:* Teacher Rep; Citizen Adv Comm; Math & Spelling Comm; MSTA 1963-; WCTA 1970-; NEA 1970-; "Hands On" Sci Curr 1st Grade Stu Washington Cty; *office:* Smithsburg Elem School 67 N Main St Smithsburg MD 21783

SHANK, ELIZABETH A., 5th Grade Teacher; *b:* Winamac, IN; *ed:* (BA) Fr, Rosary Coll 1954; (MA) Ed, St Francis Coll 1966; Rosarys Branch, Villa des Fougeres, Univ of Fribourg Switzerland; *cr:* 3rd Grade Teacher Visitation Sch 1954-56; 4th Grade Teacher St William Sch 1956-61; 3rd/4th Grade Teacher St Peter Sch 1961-65; 5th Grade Teacher Palmer Elem 1966-; *ai:* Prin Designee; Beginning Teacher Mentor; Spelling Bee Coach; Delta Kappa Gamma Pres 1978-80; NEA, IN St Teachers Assn, Knox Classroom Teachers Assn Pres 1974-76.

SHANK, JOHN F., 5th Grade Teacher/Asst Prin; *b:* Rensselaer, IN; *m:* Linda Sue Odle; *ed:* (BS) Elem Ed, St Josephs Coll 1972; (MED) Elem Ed, Valparaiso Univ 1976; Elem Admin & Supervision, IN St Univ 1979; *cr:* 6th Grade Teacher 1972-78, 5th Grade Teacher 1978-, Asst Prin 1979- De Motte Elem Sch; *ai:* ASCD; Knights of Columbus; *office:* De Motte Elem Sch PO Box 340 Demotte IN 46310

SHANK, NANCY TROJANOSKI, 4th Grade Teacher; *b:* Jacksonville, FL; *ed:* (BS) Elem Ed, FL St Univ 1972; (MED) Curr/Inst, Univ of TX 1977; Specialized Trng Gifted & Talented Stus; *cr:* Kndgtn Teacher Pinedale Elem Sch 1972-73. Seoul-Amer Elem Sch 1973-74; 4th Grade Teacher Sevemty-First Elem Sch 1974-75; Elem Teacher Austin Ind Sch Dist 1975-; *ai:* Austin Ind Sch Dist IBM Initiative Project; Empowerment Momentum Team Mem; Assn of TX Prof Educators 1986-; Kappa Delta Pi Mem; Co-Authored Sr Citizens Volunteer Prgm 1981-82; Conducted Wkshps for Teachers in Austin Area; TX Ed Agency Elem Math Curr Guide Dev 1986; *home:* 5716 Penny Creek Dr Austin TX 78759

SHANK, WALTER GLENN, JR., 7th Grade Mathematics Teacher; *b:* Johnstown, PA; *m:* Susan B. Malarich; *c:* Angela M., Jacob W.; *ed:* (BS) Elem Ed, Salem Coll 1974; Shippensburg Univ, Univ of Pittsburgh Johnstown, Millersville Univ; *cr:* Day Care Teacher Somerset Cty Day Care & Child Dev Prgm 1977-82; 6th-8th Grade Math Teacher North Star Mid Sch 1984-; *ai:* Jr HS & Jr Var Bsktbl Asst Coach; Mid Sch Fund Raising Chairperson; NEA, PA St Ed Assn, N Star Ed Assn 1984-; PA Cncl of Teachers of Math, ASCD, NCTM 1990; *office:* North Star Mid Sch Kantner PA 15548

SHANKS, MARY ELLA (FORE), Second Grade Teacher; *b:* Plainview, TX; *m:* Howard Carroll; *c:* Mike, Chris; *ed:* (BSE) Elem, Abilene Chrstn Univ 1967; (ME) Elem, E NM Univ 1981; Postive Discipline, Project Learning Tree, Project Wild Wkshps; *cr:* 1st Grade Teacher Valley View Elem 1967-69; 2nd Grade Teacher Sunshine Elem 1969-70, Capitan Elem 1978-; *ai:* Teaching & In-Service to Promote Project Soil; Promote & Spon Dev Outdoor Classroom Capitan Elem; Alpha Delta Kappa (Secy 1986-88, VP 1990); Earth Team Volunteer 1987-, Volunteer of Yr 1988-89; Intnl Rdng Assn 1989-; Auxiliary Soil & Water Conservation Dist Teacher of Yr 1989; Outstanding Conservation Teacher of Yr 1989; Deutz Allis Conservation Teacher of Yr 1987; Wrote Environmental Prgm; *home:* Box 711 Capitan NM 88316

SHANLEY, DEANNA GENUA, European/World History Teacher; *b:* Washington, DC; *m:* Peter J.; *c:* Elissa, Johanna; *ed:* (BA) Modern European His, Dumbarton of Holy Cross 1970; *cr:* Advanced Placement Modern European His/World His Teacher 1987-88; World His Teacher Salesianum HS 1988-; *ai:* NCSS; *office:* Salesianum HS 18th & Broom Sts Wilmington DE 19802

SHANNON, FLEETA CARTHEL, Jr HS English Teacher; *b:* Plainview, TX; *m:* Hugh M. II; *c:* Leeta Prather, Kyle Adams, Lon Adams, Hugh, Aaron; *ed:* (BA) Elem Ed, Wayland Bapt Coll 1976; TX Tech; West TX Univ; *cr:* 6th Grade Math Teacher Lockney ISD 1976-77; 4th Sci/Rdng Teacher Floydada ISD 1977-79; 4th Grade Elem Teacher 1979-87; Jr HS Eng Teacher 1987- Shamrock ISD; *ai:* UIL Coach 6th Thru 8th Grade Spelling & Ready Writing; TX Classroom Assn 1980-; *home:* 410 S Nebraska Shamrock TX 79079

SHANNON, JERRY WAYNE, Mathematics Department Chair; *b:* Hixson, TN; *m:* Donna Ruth Lively; *c:* Daniel; *ed:* (BS) Math, Mid TN St Univ 1968; (MS) Admin/Supervision, Trevecca Nazarene Coll 1990; Various Stud at Various Colls & Univs; *cr:* Teacher Red Bank Jr HS 1968-80; Teacher/Math Chm Red Bank HS 1980-; *ai:* Math Club Spon; Academic Contest Coach; Hamilton Cty Ed Assn (Prof Rights & Responsibility Chm, Assn Rep) Teacher of Yr; TN Math Teachers Assn; Chattanooga Area Math Teachers Assn Newsletter Comm; NCTM; Chattanooga Area Math Assn, TN Ed Assn, NEA 1968-; Southern Assn of Schls & Colls Objectives Comm Chm; PTA Life Mem; St Teacher of Yr Nom; Hamilton Cty Curr Guide Author; Co-Author of Hamilton Cty Basic Skills 7th-8th Grade 1st Test; St Forum on Paperwork Cutting Mem; Hamilton Cty Teacher of Yr; Kappa Delta Pi Charles Hyder Awd; Laura Handly Brock Memorial Awd; Teacher Outstanding Performance Awd; Natl Sci Fnd Presidential Awd for Sci & Math Teaching Nom; Hamilton Cty Ed Assn Distinguished Classroom Teacher of Yr Nom; *office:* Red Bank HS 640 Morrison Springs Rd Chattanooga TN 37415

SHANNON, JUANITA BILLUPS, 8th Grade Mathematics Teacher; *b:* Elizabeth City, NC; *m:* S. Glover; *c:* William Mc Caffity Jr., Glovette O.; *ed:* (BA) Intermediate Ed, Elizabeth City St Univ 1973; (MS) Ed, E Carolina Univ 1989; *cr:* Math Teacher Sterling Mid Sch 1973, J P Knapp Sch 1974-81, P W Moore Sch 1982-86, Elizabeth City Jr HS 1987-89; *ai:* Math Sci Ed Network Teacher; NC Assn of Educators; *office:* Elizabeth City Jr HS 306 N Road St Elizabeth City NC 27909

SHANNON, LORI ANN (HEKTER), English Teacher; *b:* Council, IA; *m:* Jack; *ed:* (BA) Eng, Univ of N IA Cedar Falls 1976; *cr:* Eng/Speech Teacher Ar-We-Ba HS 1976-80; Eng Teacher Harlan Jr HS 1980-81; Eng/Speech/Span Teacher Manning HS 1982-; *ai:* Speech Coach; NEA; Outstanding HS Teacher Awd Univ of Chicago 1987; *office:* Manning Cmmty Sch 208 10th St Manning IA 51455

SHANNON, MARSHA K. RICE, Mathematics Dept/Art Teacher; *b:* Louisa, KY; *m:* James Anthony; *ed:* (MA) Scndry Ed, Morehead St 1987; *cr:* 6th Grade Math Teacher 1981-84, 8th Grade Algebra/Math Teacher 1984-85, 6th-8th Grade Remedial Math Teacher 1985-87, 8th Grade Math/Algebra/5th Grade Art Teacher 1987- Louisa Mid Sch; *ai:* Math Team Coach 1984-85, 1987-89; Spon 8th Grade Dance 1987-, Graduation 1989-; Myrtle Chapel Church (Sunday Sch Teacher 1977-, Secy 1989-); *office:* Louisa Mid Sch PO Box 507 Louisa KY 41230

SHANNON, MICHIAL SCOTT, 6th Grade Teacher; *b:* Lake Charles, LA; *m:* Gwendolyn K. Windecker; *c:* Scott L., Cameron C.; *ed:* (BA) Elem Ed, TX Luth Coll 1976; (MS) Elem Ed, Univ of Houston Clark Lake 1987; *cr:* 3rd Grade Teacher 1976-79; 5th Grade Teacher 1979-86 Clear Lake City Elem; 4th Grade Teacher 1986-87; 6th Grade Teacher 1987- Walter Hall Elem; *ai:* Grade Level Chm; TX St Teachers Assoc 1976-; Clear Creek Educators Assoc (Treas 1978-79) 1976-; Outstndg Young Men of Amer 1988; *office:* Walter Hall Elem Sch 5931 Meadowside League City TX 77573

SHANNON, STEVE O., Teacher; *b:* Beebe, AR; *m:* Judy Robbins; *c:* Steve Jr., Richard, Laura, John; *ed:* (BA) Math, Harding Univ 1966; (MAT) Math, W MI Univ 1974; *cr:* Teacher Bald Knob Public Schls 1966-67; Teacher/Coach S Haven Public Schls 1968-78, Pasadena Ind Sch 1982-89; *ai:* Univ Interscholastic League; Number Sense & Calculator Spon; Houston Math & Sci Improvement Consortium Grad Assoc; Outstanding Teacher of Yr 1990.

SHANNON, SYLVIA HENCE, Fourth Grade Teacher; *b:* Memphis, TN; *m:* Billy J. Sr.; *c:* Billy J. Jr., Malik J., Cozetta D.; *ed:* (BS) Elem Ed, Le Moyne-Owen Coll 1973; (MA) Elem Ed, Memphis St Univ 1978; Univ of MS 1978, 1981; *cr:* Teacher Horn Lake Elem Sch 1973-; *ai:* Sci Fair Coord; Grade Chairperson; AL-LA-MS Math Contest Coord; Public Relations Comm; St Jude Math-A-Thon Coord; MTAI Trained Evaluator; MEA 1973-; Memphis Bd of Realtors 1985-; *home:* 1265 Oakwood Memphis TN 38116

SHANTZ, SALLY COPPER, Fourth Grade Teacher; *b:* Buffalo, MO; *w:* Donald G. (dec); *c:* Joseph B., Wm. R.; *ed:* (AB) Ed, Drury Coll 1954; Grad Stud; *cr:* 4th Grade Teacher Buffalo Elem 1953-83, Westport Sch 1983-; *ai:* Westport Sch Soc Comm Chm & Talent Show Comm; Buffalo PTA Life Membership Awd 1981; Buffalo Teachers Assn VP 1976-79; MO St Teachers Assn Life Mem 1953-; Springfield Teachers Assn Building Rep 1983-; Amer Chldhd Ed Assn Soc Chm 1983-; Delta Kappa Gamma Schlsp Comm 1965-; Teacher of Yr 1987-88; Textbook Selection, Writing of Curr, Building Planning Comm.

SHAPPEE, DONNA JONES, Sixth Grade Teacher; *b:* Utica, NY; *m:* James W.; *c:* Michael; *ed:* (BA) Elem Ed, SUC Cortland 1967; (MA) Ed, Syracuse Univ 1972; *cr:* 4th Grade Teacher Rush-Henrietta 1967-70; 5th/6th Grade Teacher Phelps-Clifton Springs Sch Dist 1970-; *home:* 419 N Main St Canandaigua NY 14424

SHARIT, DIANNE JOHNSTON, Third Grade Teacher; *b:* Bessemer, AL; *m:* Ronald Lee; *c:* Shannon Leigh, Steven G.; *ed:* (BA) Eng, Univ of Montevallo 1968; (MA) Early Chldhd Ed, Univ of AL 1983; *cr:* 7th Grade Eng Teacher West Mastin Lake Sch 1968-69, Hewitt-Trussville Jr HS 1969-71; K/2nd/3rd Grades Teacher Guntersville Elem 1979-; *ai:* Sch Textbook Selection Rep; Coord Lit Fair; GAMA BELL Prgm; Conducted In-Service Sessions Process Writing; NEA 1979-; AEA 1979-; GEA 1979-, Sch Rep 1986-87; 1st United Meth Church (Cnslr 1978-/Youth Fellowship 1987-); Long-Range Planning Comm 1987-88; Needs Assessment Comm 1989-; Nominee Jacksonville Teacher Hall of Fame; Adoptors Golden Apple Awd; *home:* 803 Travis St Albertville AL 35950

SHARKEY, ELLEN M., Physical Education Teacher; *b:* Detroit, MI; *ed:* (BS) Phys Ed, 1968; (MA) Guidance & Counseling, 1980; (LDS) Spec Ed, 1980 Eastern MI Univ; Teacher Effective Trng Thomas Gordan 1974; *cr:* Phys Ed Allen Park Mid Sch; *ai:* Allen Park Mid Sch Cheerleading Coach 1988-89; Sch Improvement Allen Park Mid Sch; Dept Head Phys Ed 88-89; Allen Park Curr Comm Phys Ed 1988-89; NASSP Stu Act 1987-89; Aahperd 1990; PTA Teacher/Stu Rep 1986-88 Teacher of Yr 1986; PTA Teacher of Yr; *office:* Allen Park Mid Sch 8401 Vine Allen Park MI 48101

SHARKEY, MARCIA GOULET, Fifth Grade Teacher; *b:* Brockton, MA; *m:* Roy James; *c:* Justin T.; *ed:* (BS) Elem Ed/His, RI Coll 1966; Grad Credits RI Coll, Univ of RI & Special Trng Prgm; Trng in Gifted-Talented Area & Talents Unlimited; *cr:* 2nd/3rd Grade Teacher 1966-78, Remedial Rdng Teacher 1968-69 Knotty Oak Sch; 4th/5th Grade Teacher Western Coventry Sch 1979-; *ai:* Newspaper Club Adv; Curr & Sch Routine Comm, Townwide Rdng Curr Comm; Bicentennial Sch Coord; Coventry Teachers Alliance Negotiating Team 1970-71; RI Rdng Assn 1978-85; PTA Teacher Rep 1967-; *office:* W Coventry Sch 4588 Flat River Rd Coventry RI 02816

SHARKEY, PETER MICHAEL, Mathematics Teacher; *b:* New York, NY; *m:* Maureen Fitzsimmons; *c:* Eilise, Kathleen, Kevin; *ed:* (BA) His, Quinnipiac Coll 1974; (BA) Ed, Fresno Pacific 1978; (MS) Psych/Counseling, Univ of LaVerne 1984; Admin Trng Prgm, Fresno Unified Sch Dist; *cr:* Teacher/AD St Therese 1976-84; Teacher Winchell Elem 1984-85; Teacher/Coach Hoover HS 1985-; *ai:* Womens Bsktbl Coach; Athletic Dir; Class Adv; Sch Sight, Self Esteem Comm; All League Coach of Yr 1986, 1987, 1989; All Star Coach 1986-89; Article Published.

SHARP, ALLENA H., Third Grade Teacher; *b:* Sharps Chapel, TN; *m:* C. B.; *c:* Wayne E., Ralph L., Warren L.; *ed:* (BS) Ed, Lincoln Memorial Univ 1975; Masters Prgm Elem Ed; *cr:* 1st-4th Grade Teacher Big Sinks Elem Sch 1951-53, Oak Grove Elem Sch 1953-56; 4th-8th Grade Teacher Big Sinks Elem Sch 1964-65; 2nd-4th Grade Teacher Sharps Chapel Elem Sch 1968-; *ai:* East TN Ed Assn Secy 1977-79; TN Ed Assn; NEA; Delta Kappa Gamma (Pres, Secy) 1981-; Baptist Church; PTA Secy 1979-80; *home:* RR 1 Box 12 Sharps Chapel TN 37866

SHARP, BETTY BURKART, High School French Teacher; *b:* Portland, OR; *m:* James Steven; *c:* Elisabeth; *ed:* (BA) Fr, 1980, (MA) Curr/Instruction, 1987 Univ of OR; *cr:* Teacher Dunn Elem Sch 1979-80, Springfield Sch Dist 1980-; Coord Relais Universitaries 1989-; *ai:* NHS & Fr Club Adv; Foreign Lang Curr Advisory Comm; Confederation of OR Sch Admins 1989-; Confederation of OR Foreign Lang Teachers 1980-; Pacific Northwest Cncl on Foreign Lang 1985-; Amer Assn of Foreign Lang 1982-; Quebec Fellowship 1988; Univ of OR & NEH Grant 1986; *office:* Springfield HS 875 N 7th St Springfield OR 97477

SHARP, BRUCE WILLIAM, Mathematics Teacher; *b:* Des Moines, IA; *m:* Susan M. Strothers; *c:* Kelli Sharp McGinty, Lori Sharp-Fisher, Jeri L.; *ed:* (BS) Math, 1966, (MS) Ed/Counseling/Guidance, 1968 SW TX St Univ; *cr:* Adult Ed Teachers Aide 1969-74, Adult Ed Teacher 1974-79 Phoenix Union HS; Teacher Trevor G Browne HS 1979-; *ai:* Black Stu Union, Wrestlerettes Cheer Squad, Tennis Club Spon Trevor G Browne; Var Girls Tennis Coach Trevor G Browne; *office:* Trevor G Browne HS 7402 W Catalina Phoenix AZ 85033

SHARP, CHARLES K. (KIRKWOOD), Honors Biology Instructor; *b:* Milwaukee, WI; *m:* Marilyn Rose Taggart; *c:* Charles Taggart Jr., Victoria Dalton, Thomas, Anne Mac Donald, Matthew, Margaret Ross, David, Mary Buzzard, Andrew, Philip, James (Dec); *ed:* (BA) Ger, Baldwin Wallace Coll 1953; OH St Univ; Western Reserve Univ; PA St Univ; Albright Coll; Celveland St Univ; Univ of Guam; MI St Univ; Baldwin Wallace Coll; *cr:* Teacher St Edward HS 1956-60, Chas F Brush HS 1960-72; Teacher Dept Chm Luth HS 1974-76, St Ignatius HS 1976-80; Teacher Holy Name HS 1980-; *ai:* Natl Honor Soc Advisory Comm; Worked with Stu on Sci Fair Projects; Amer Assn Advancement of Sci; Cleveland Reg Cncl of Sci Teachers; Cleveland Natural His Museum; Amer Assn of Bio Teachers; Greenpeace; 3 NSF Fellowships to Western Reserve; 1 NSF Fellowship to PA St; 1 NDEA Fellowship to Albright Coll; 3 NSF Fellowships to MI St Univ; *office:* Holy Name H S 6000 Queens Hwy Parma Heights OH 44130

SHARP, DONNA JEAN, Design Research Specialist; *b:* Oak Park, IL; *m:* Terry G.; *c:* Ryan A.; *ed:* (BSED) Elem Ed, IL St Univ 1979; (MED) Educl Technology, Univ of OK 1988; *cr:* Kndgtn Teacher Paul Bolin Elem Sch 1979; 2nd Grade Teacher 1979-82, 3rd Grade Teacher 1982-85 Marquette Elem Sch; Design Research Specialist MN Educl Computing Corporation 1988; *ai:* Marquette Elem Sch Cmptr Club Co-Spon; Marquette Elem Sch Young Astronauts Club Spon; ASCD 1990; Educl Technology Club Mem; Articles Published; ASCD Teaching Thinking Network & Cooperative Learning Network; NASA Teacher in Space Applicant.

SHARP, EDNA HAWKINS, Retired Kindergarten Teacher; *b:* Cresaptown, MD; *m:* Robert B.; *c:* Mary A. Mourc, Leslie D. Smith; *ed:* (BS) Elem Ed, Muskingum Coll 1973; Early Chldhd Ed, Univ of Dayton; *cr:* Elem Teacher Green Local 1948-50, Stanton Local 1952-54, J U Sch Dist 1960-61, Edison Local Sch Dist 1963-84; *ai:* OH Retired Teachers Assn, Jefferson Cty Retired Teachers Assn; Annapolis Prebyn Church; *home:* RD 2 Bloomingdale OH 43910

SHARP, JEAN STEWART, Math Teacher/Math Dept Chair; *b:* Decatur, IL; *m:* Karl F.; *c:* Joseph, Cynthia White; *ed:* (BS) Math, Univ of IL 1957; (MS) Scndry Ed, N IL Univ 1969; Admin Certificate; *cr:* Math Teacher/Dept Head 1971-78, Asst Prin 1978-83, Math Teacher 1983-85 Eisenhower Mid Sch; Math Teacher/Dept Head Guilford HS 1985-; *ai:* Sabre n Spurs Adv; Cmptr Lab Dir; Phi Delta Kappa Research Dir 1981-82; *office:* Guilford HS 5620 Spring Creek Rd Rockford IL 61111

SHARP, JOYCE COOK, First Grade Teacher; *b:* Cynthiana, KY; *c:* Jeremy T., Jonathan H.; *ed:* (BS) Elem Ed, Campbellsville Coll 1974; (MAED) General Elem Ed, E KY Univ 1979; *cr:* 1st Grade Teacher Mercer Cty Elem 1975-; *ai:* Summer Enrichment Camp Teacher; KY Ed Assn, NEA 1986-; *office:* Mercer Cty Elem Sch Tapp Rd Harrodsburg KY 40330

SHARP, KAREN WHITLOW, Mathematics Teacher; *b:* Jacksonville, FL; *m:* Randy Ray; *c:* Todd, Lindsey; *ed:* (AS) Andrew Coll 1972; (BS) Scndry Math Ed, FL St Univ 1974; *cr:* Math Teacher Fayette Cty HS 1980-89, Bishop Kenny HS 1990; *ai:* Spon Class of 1990 Fayette Cty; Jr Civitans; *office:* Bishop Kenny HS 1055 Kingman Ave Jacksonville FL 32207

SHARP, LISA ANN, English Department Chair; *b:* Chamberlain, SD; *ed:* (BS) Speech/Theatre/Vocal Music, Black Hills St 1978; *cr:* Rdng Teacher Mc Laughlin HS 1978-80; Eng/Vocal Teacher Madelia HS 1980-81, Harmony HS 1981-82; Eng Teacher White River HS 1982-; *ai:* Declam Coach; Drill Team; Class Spon; Theatre; Voice Lessons; Swing Choir; Musicals; SDEA, NEA, MENC, MTNA; General Fed of Womens Clubs Pres 1984; United Meth Women Pres 1983; *home:* 106 S 1st St White River SD 57579

SHARP, MARY A., Science Teacher; *b:* Lasalle, IL; *ed:* (BS) Elem Ed, 1980, (MS) Elem Ed, 1982 IL St Univ; *cr:* Sci Teacher Bradley Cntrl Jr HS 1980-; *ai:* Stu Cncl Spon; Yrbk Adv; IL Assn Jr HS St Cncls Dist Dir 1988-; *office:* Bradley Central Jr HS 235 N Michigan Ave Bradley IL 60915

SHARP, NEIL F., Guidance Counselor; *b:* Mt Vernon, NY; *m:* Greta K.; *c:* William A., Douglas B.; *ed:* (BA) Economics, Cornell Arts & Sci 1955; (MA) Guidance, SUNY Albany 1959; (EDD) Ed Admin, Columbia Tech Coll 1974; Financial Planning, Adelphi Univ 1983; *cr:* Jr HS Math Teacher Freeport Public Schls 1959-62; Sr HS Math Teacher 1962-65, Guidance 1966- N Babylon Public Schls; *ai:* Honor Society; Prof & Testing Comm; Jr HS Bowling, Sr HS Var Bowling, Jr HS Soccer, Sftbl Coach; Phi Delta Kappa 1972-; Article Published on Dissertation; *office:* Robert Moses Mid Sch N Babylon Public Schls North Babylon NY 11703

SHARP, PAMELA ANN (CORBELL), Teacher; *b:* Texarkana, TX; *m:* Ronald D.; *c:* Alexander M., Grace A.; *ed:* (AS) General Jr Coll, Jacksonville Coll 1980; (BS) Phys Ed, Univ of TX Tyler 1982; Grad Stud; *cr:* Teacher 1982-84, Teacher/Coach 1984-86 Jacksonville Ind Sch Dist; Teacher Joe Wright Elem 1987-; *ai:* Coached Girls Bsktbl & Track Mid Sch Level; ATPE.

SHARP, SUSAN WARREN, 11th Grade English Teacher; *b:* Dublin, TX; *m:* Michael Dean; *c:* Nicholas, Sasha; *ed:* (BS) Phys Ed/Eng, 1976, (MED) Ed/Eng, 1982 Tarleton St Univ; *cr:* Coach/Teacher Weslaco Ind Sch Dist 1976-77, Brownwood Ind Sch Dist 1977-78, Lometa Ind Sch Dist 1978-79, Albany Ind Sch Dist 1979-82, Big Spring Ind Sch Dist 1982-86, Comanche Ind Sch Dist 1986-; *ai:* UIL Journalism, HS Girls Cross Cntry, Bskbtl,

Track Coach; Literary Criticism; ACADEC Team; Natl Joint Cncl Teachers of Eng, Assn of TX Prof Educators, TX Girls Coaches Assn 1976-; Beta Sigma Phi VP 1979-; *office:* Comanche HS N Hwy 16 Comanche TX 76442

SHARP, TONYA, Secondary Math/Science Teacher; *b:* Pueblo, CO; *ed:* (BS) Scndry Sci/Wildlife Bio, Univ of WY 1984; *cr:* Substitute Teacher Pueblo Sch Dist 60 1985-87; GED Instr Bueno-HEP-GED 1987-89; Math/Sci Teacher John Mall HS 1989-; *ai:* Frosh Class Spon; *office:* John Mall HS 355 Pine St Walsenburg CO 81089

SHARPALISKY, REBECCA WILLIAMS, Learning Disabilities Teacher; *b:* Beckley, WV; *m:* James Michael; *ed:* (BA) Elem/Spec, 1983, (MS) Learning Disabilities, 1988 WV Univ; Guidance & Counseling; *cr:* Spec Ed Teacher Alderson Elem Sch 1983-85; Learning Disabilities Teacher Buckhannon-Upshur HS 1985-; Part Time Instr WV Wesleyan Coll 1990; *ai:* Nom for Comm Keep Stu from Dropping Out of Sch; Stu Cncl Co-Adv; 1st United Meth (Youth Coord 1985-86, Pastor Parish Relations 1990); Buckhannon Cmmty Theatre 1990; Buckhannon Arts Alliance; *home:* 12 E Victoria St Buckhannon WV 26201

SHARPE, ALFRANCES LYMAN, English Teacher; *b:* Chicago, IL; *c:* Hosac W. III, Haqumai W.; *ed:* (BS) Speech/Drama, TN St Univ 1960; Addl Studies Writing Wkshps; *cr:* Eng Teacher Marshall H S 1960-71; Kelly H S 1972-73; Curie H S 1973-82; Whitney M. Young H S 1982-; *ai:* Pep Squad Spon; Disciplinarian Red/Blue; Sr Snow Ball Co-Spon; Speech Coach; Voice of Democracy Oratory; Academic Decathalon Team; Alpha Kappa Alpha Sorority 1958-; Ladies Auxiliary of Peter Claver Court 200 1986-; Natl Cncl of Negro Women 1989-; Golden Apple Semi-Finalist; Teacher Rep Local Sch Cncl; Holy Angels Sch Adv Bd; Holy Angels Church/Mass Lector; *home:* 5050 S. Lake Shore Dr. #3409 Chicago IL 60615

SHARPE, BETTY DELBRIDGE, Chemistry & Biology Teacher; *b:* Littleton, NC; *c:* Joseph G.; *ed:* (BS) Bio, Greensboro Coll 1960; (MTS) Bio/Chem, Coll of William & Mary 1966; Scndry Admin & Supervision; *cr:* Teacher Newport News HS 1960-62, 1964-66, 1968-71, Athens HS 1966-67; Dept Head Newport News HS 1970-71; Teacher 1971-, Dept Head 1977-Ferguson HS; *ai:* NHS Spon; Steering, Governors Sch Selection, Schlsp Selection Comm; Chairperson Sch Evaluation, Commencement Comm; Sch Bus Partnership Co-Coord; VA Acad of Sci Teacher of Yr 1979; Delta Kappa Gamma (Pres 1982-84, Treas 1978-82, 1984-); Contact Peninsula 1989-; Natl Sci Fnd Schlsp 1964-66; Teacher of Yr 1979; Outstanding Teacher oF Yr Warwick Ruritan Club 1986; Chem Teacher of Yr; Hampton Roads Section Amer Chemical Society 1987; PTSA Service Awd 1989; *office:* Homer L Ferguson HS 11 Shoe Ln Newport News VA 23606

SHARPE, BEVERLY ADAMS, Mathematics Teacher; *b:* Monterey, TN; *m:* William L.; *ed:* (BS) Math, 1984, (MED) Admin/Supervision, 1987 Trevecca Nazarene Coll; *cr:* Teacher Mt Juliet HS 1984-; *ai:* Youth in Government & Future Teachers of America Spon; Stu Staying Straight Core Team Mem; TEA, NEA 1984-; Church of the Nazarene (Bd Secy 1989-, Choir Mem); *office:* Mt Juliet HS Mt Juliet Rd Mount Juliet TN 37122

SHARPE, GWENDOLYN H., Mathematics Teacher; *b:* Thomaston, GA; *m:* Gary E.; *c:* Christopher, Adam; *ed:* (BA) Math Ed, Tift Coll 1974; (MED) Math Ed, 1978, Spec Ed Math Ed, 1989 Columbus Coll; Advanced Placement Calculus; *cr:* Math Teacher Woodland Acad 1973-74, Worthy Jr HS 1974-75, Upson HS 1975-76, Worthy Jr HS 1976-77, Upson HS 1977-; *ai:* Jr Class Spon; Chattahoochee Cncl Teachers of Math 1987-89; *home:* 1624 Jeff Davis Rd Thomaston GA 30286

SHARPE, LINDA STEVENS, Language Art Teacher; *b:* Louisville, KY; *m:* Donald M.; *c:* Camille Sharpe Smith, Donna L.; *ed:* (BA) Eng, Univ of Louisville 1967; Grad Study Ed; *cr:* Volunteer Tutoring Amer Sch & Harringswell 1967-69, Amer Schls in Kuala Lumpur, Malaysia & Singapore 1970-71; Jr HS Lang Art Teacher Our Lady of Fatima Sch 1974-; *ai:* Dir of Jr HS Play; Coord Creative Writing Booklet; Lang Art, Curr, Courtsey Comm Mem; NCTE, NCEA Mem; *office:* Our Lady of Fatima Sch 2315 Johnston St Lafayette LA 70506

SHARPING, ALICE RAYETTE, English Teacher; *b:* Chamberlain, SD; *ed:* (BA) Eng/His/Elem Ed, Dakota Wesleyan Univ 1977; Cert Trng Massage Therapy 1988; *cr:* Eng Teacher Bloomfield Public Sch 1978-80; 1st Grade Teacher Church of Acts Acad 1982-83; Eng Teacher Calvary Assembly Acad 1984-85, Maranatha Chrstn Acad 1985-; *ai:* Yrbk Adv; Foodshelf Coord; Speech Coach.

SHARPLESS, BEVERLY J., 5th & 6th Grade Math Teacher; *b:* Wilmington, DE; *ed:* (BS) Ed, Univ of DE 1954; *cr:* Gifted & Talented/6th Grade Teacher David W Harlan 1954-59; 4th/6th Grade Teacher Saunder Sch 1959-63; 4th-9th Grade Math/Phys Ed Teacher Pinecrest 1963-66; 5th/6th Grade Teacher Wilburn 1966-78, Pangburn Elem Sch 1978-; *ai:* Elem Math N Cntrl AccrediationChm; Personnel Policy & Textbook Adoption Comm; Youth Cncl; Cath Youth Organization; Y-Teens; *office:* Pangburn Elem Sch PO Box 68 Pangburn AR 72121

SHARPTON, JUDY SASSER, Fourth Grade Lang Art Teacher; *b:* Lyons, GA; *m:* William Glenn; *c:* William Jr., Robert; *ed:* (BSED) Elem Ed, Univ of GA 1976; *cr:* 5th Grade Teacher Lyons Elem 1977-79; 4th Grade Teacher Vidalia City 1982-; *ai:* Young Authors Conference Comm; Stans Comm Chairperson; Alpha Delta Kappa Altruistic Chairperson 1988-; Southern Assn of Colls & Schls Visiting Comm Mem; Beta Sigma Phi Secy 1984-, Pledge Awd 1986; Pilot Club VP 1982-84, Prgm Awd 1982; Spokesperson Amer Heart Assn; Local Coord Cancer Society Collections; United Way Coord of Sch; *office:* Sally D Meadows Elem Sch Waters Dr Vidalia GA 30474

SHASTEEN, LYNDA CLARK, 6th Grade Teacher; *b:* Winchester, TN; *m:* A L Jr.; *c:* Mark A., Holli L. Counts; *ed:* (AS) Elem Ed, Motlow St 1975; (BS) Elem Ed, 1977, (MED) Admin/Supervision, 1985 Mid TN St Univ; *cr:* Teacher Rock Creek Elem 1977-; *ai:* Tutorial Prgm after Sch; 4-H Club Adv; Cattlewomen Dir 1989-; *office:* Rock Creek Elem Sch R 3 Box 350 Estill Springs TN 37330

SHAUVER, ANNETTE HANNULA, English & Reading Teacher; *b:* Lansing, MI; *m:* Dennis; *ed:* (BS) Phys Ed/Eng, MI St Univ 1982; Scndry Eng, MI St Univ; *cr:* Substitute Teacher Lansing Sch Dist 1983-85; Eng/Rdng Teacher Most Holy Trinity Sch 1985-; *ai:* Trinity Tribune Adv; NCTE, MI Rdng Assn, Clinton Rdng Cncl, Teacher Roundtables, Inst For Democracy in Ed 1988-; *home:* 512 S Holmes St Lansing MI 48912

SHAVERS, SUZANNE RICHTER, Second Grade Teacher; *b:* Cullman, AL; *m:* James Cecil Jr.; *c:* Amanda H., Megan M.; *ed:* (BS) Elem Ed, Florence St Univ 1970; *cr:* Music Teacher West Point Sch & Jones Chapel Sch 1970-71; 2nd Grade Teacher Fairview Elem Sch 1971-; *ai:* Faculty Rep, In-Service Comm; NEA, AL Ed Assn, Cullman Cty Ed Assn 1970-; Outstanding Young Women of America 1981; *home:* 308 Schwann Ave NE Cullman AL 35055

SHAW, ANDREW DWIGHT, Science Department Chair; *b:* Baltimore, MD; *m:* Pamela Murphy; *c:* Melissa, Matthew, Mark, Michael; *ed:* (BA) Natural Sci/Physics, Covenant Coll 1974; (MA) Sci Ed, Univ of TN Chattanooga 1977; Maryville Coll, Hope Coll, Univ of MO St Louis, Univ of MO Columbia; *cr:* Physics/Bio Teacher Tiner HS 1974-77; Teacher/Coach/Sci Dept Head Westminster Chrstn Acad 1977-; Honors Physics/Honors Chem/Coll Chem/Adjunct Astronomy Teacher Maryville Coll 1990; *ai:* Area Teachers & Home Schooling Parents Wkshps; Local Grade Schls Sci Shows; Chm Sci Dept; Facul;ty Salary & Cmptr Comm; NSTA 1985-; Westminster Reformed Presbyn Church Elder 1989-; NSF Grad Chem Prgm 1987; Westminster Teacher of Yr Awd 1985; Tri-St Chrstn Athletic Conference Soccer Coach of Yr 1983; *office:* Westminster Chrstn Acad 10900 Ladue Rd Saint Louis MO 63141

SHAW, ANDREWETTA ANDERSON, 7th Grade Science Teacher; *b:* Charlotte, NC; *m:* James M; *c:* Earl A. Vaughn, Shawn A.; *ed:* (BS) Bio, Bennett Coll 1967; Med Temple Univ; Rdng VA Union; Admin Univ DE; *cr:* Chem Teacher Celanese Corp 1967-68; Bio Instr Warner Mid Sch 1970-71; Bayard Mid Sch 1972-78; Brandywine Spri Ngs Mid Sch 1978-80; Wilmer E Shue Mid Sch 1980-; *ai:* Coach DE Sci Olympiad; DE Assn (Supv/Curr Dev) 1989-; DE Sci Assn 1980-; DE Ed Assn 1987-; DE Fed of Teachers 1972-80; Enlightened Women in Christ Intercessary 1987-; Jack & Jill of Amer Inc 1975-; Teacher of Yr-Christina Dist 1984; Teacher of Summer-Forum Summer Prgm; Stud in Mech Engrg 1984; *home:* 1119 Flint Hill Rd Wilmington DE 19808

SHAW, ANNA ELIZABETH, Retired Teacher; *b:* Omaha, TX; *ed:* (ME) Elem Ed, E TX St Univ 1956; *cr:* 2nd/3rd Grade Teacher S F Austin Elem 1952-68; Spec Ed Coord Jefferson Ind Sch Dist 1968-70; 2nd Grade Teacher Jefferson Elem Sch 1970-81; *home:* 401 W Douglas Jefferson TX 75657

SHAW, DONNA LYNNE (BECKMAN), Second Grade Teacher; *b:* San Francisco, CA; *m:* Bill D.; *c:* Dawn Scorggins, Shawn, Shannon; *ed:* (BA) Elem Ed, 1963, (MA) Creative Arts Ed, 1971 CA St Univ San Francisco; Wright St Univ; Univ of Dayton; *cr:* 2nd Grade Teacher Travis Unified Sch Dist 1964-66; 3rd Grade Teacher San Francisco Unified Sch Dist 1966-67; 2nd Grade Teacher Dept Defense Dep Schls 1967-68; 5th Grade Teacher San Francisco Unified Sch Dist 1968-70, Dept of Defense Schls 1971-73; Consultant/Research Asst Addison Wesley Publishing 1974-76; Consultant Harcourt Brace Jovanovich Inc 1976-78; 2nd/5th/6th Grade Teacher Northmont City Schls 1978-; *ai:* NEA; League of Women Voters; Guild of Dayton Art Institute; OH Historical Society; Aullwood Audabon Society; *office:* Northwood Elem Sch 6200 Noranda Dr Dayton OH 45415

SHAW, GISELE JACKSON, Secondary Math Teacher; *b:* Gulfport, MS; *m:* R. S.; *ed:* (BS) Psych, Univ of Southern MS 1984; Cert Scndry Ed Math, Southern MS 1984-86; *cr:* Prescription Learning Lab Coord 1987; Alg I-II Teacher 1987 Gulfport HS; *ai:* Co-Spon for Gulfport HS Cncl 1989-; GHS Stud Assistance Team 1989; NCTM Mem 1989-; *home:* 1419 32nd Ave Gulfport MS 39501

SHAW, J. MICHAEL, Mathematics Teacher; *b:* Camden, NJ; *m:* Judith L. Hayes; *c:* Kaitlyn; *ed:* (BS) Elem Ed, St Francis Coll 1980; *cr:* 3rd Grade Teacher 1980-82, 5th Grade Teacher 1983-89 Bells Elem; 7th Grade Math Teacher Chestnut Ridge Mid Sch 1989-; *ai:* WA Township HS Var Sftbl Coach; WTEA Rep; *office:* Chestnut Ridge Mid Sch Hurfville & Crosskey Rd Sewell NJ 08080

SHAW, JOAN STROUD, English/Speech Teacher; *b:* Batesville, AR; *m:* Billy G.; *c:* Bart, Robert; *ed:* (BSE) Speech/Eng, Univ of Cntrl AR 1973; *cr:* Eng Teacher Mt Vernon HS 1974; Eng/Speech Teacher Brinkley HS 1974-76; Eng Teacher Heber Springs Mid Sch 1976-82; Eng/Speech Teacher Quitman HS 1982-; *ai:* Heber Springs Stu Cncl; Brinkley & Quitman Chrldrs Spon; AEA, NEA 1974-; ACTE 1990; *office:* Quitman HS P O Box 178 Quitman AR 72131

SHAW, KATHIE SCHRAEDER, First Grade Teacher; *b:* Clifton, TX; *c:* Kelli R.; *ed:* (BS) Elem Ed, Tarleton Elem 1972; Working Towards Masters in Fine Art, Lang Art, Math, Sci, Soc Stud; *cr:* Kndgtn Teacher James Bowie Elem 1972-75, Jonesboro Elem 1978-81; 1st Grade Teacher Jonesboro Elem 1981-; *ai:* PTA Treas; TX Assn of Cmmty Schls; Organize & Write Resource Math /Writing Books; *office:* Jonesboro Ind Sch Dist PO Box 125 Hwy 36 Jonesboro TX 76538

SHAW, MARTHA AMANDA, Fourth Grade Teacher; *b:* West, TX; *ed:* (BS) Elem Ed, Prairie View A&M 1967; *cr:* 4th Grade Teacher St Marys 1968-; *ai:* St Marys Stu Cncl Spon; UIL Spon; NCEA; West Cmmty Hosp Bd Mem 1990; Bold Spg Baptist Church (Youth Spon 1985- & Secy 1975-; *home:* 612 Spruce West TX 76691

SHAW, MARY JEAN, Elem Administrative Intern; *b:* Macon, MS; *ed:* (BA) Elem Ed, Harris Teachers Coll 1974; (MS) Ed Admin, Univ of MO St Louis 1979; Ed Admin/Specialist Advanced Cert, Univ of MO NCATE Accredited 1988; *cr:* 4th-8th Grade Lang Art Teacher Compton Heights Cath 1974-77; Title I Math Teacher Blue Hills Home Corporation 1977-79; 5th Grade Teacher/Facilitator 1979-89, Elem Admin Intern 1989- Jennings Sch Dist; *ai:* NEA 1979-; ASCD 1989-; *office:* Jennings Sch Dist 8888 Clifton Jennings MO 63136

SHAW, MICHAEL IRVING, Science Teacher; *b:* Mt Airy, NC; *m:* Lisa Parries; *ed:* (BS) Bio, E Carolina Univ 1978; (AAS) Cmptr Programming, Forsyth Tech Coll 1984; (MAED) Bio, Wake Forest Univ 1986; Certificate of Advanced Study Sci Ed, Univ of NC Greensboro; *cr:* Sci Teacher East Surry HS 1978-79, Chestnut Grove Jr HS 1979-; *ai:* Mem Chestnut Grove Teacher Recognition Comm 1990; NEA, NC Assn of Educators 1979-; NC Sci Teachers Assn 1984-; Amer Chemical Society 1987-; NC Math & Sci Teachers Schlsp Prgm 1986-88; Chestnut Grove Techer of Yr Awd 1980-82, 1988; Stokes Cty Outstanding Sci Teacher 1988; *office:* Chestnut Grove Jr HS Rt 4 Box 185 King NC 27021

SHAW, NANCY SEXTON, Health Occupations Teacher; *b:* Independence, VA; *m:* William Cecil; *ed:* (RN) Nursing, VA Baptist Hospital Sch of Nursing 1941; Health Occupations Coll Courses; *cr:* Private Duty Nurse VA Baptist Hospital 1941; General Duty Nurse Mary Washington Hospital 1942-45; Industrial Nursing Glen L Martin Cty 1945-47; Dental Asst Dr Charles Bryan 1947-49; Dental Receptionist Dr Marvin T Jones 1947-49; Private Duty Nurse Rex Hospital 1950; Office Nursing Dr John S Rhodes 1950-68; Urologist Dr Tom B Daniel 1950-68; General Duty Nurse Yancey Hospital 1968-70; Title I ESEA Sch Nurse 1970-73, Health Occupations Adv 1973- Yancey Cty Sch; *ai:* Health Occupations Stu of America Chapter Adv; Mountain Heritage Vocational Dept Chairperson; Prepared Stus for Competition & Received Many Honors; Worked Amer Red Cross Bloodmobile with Stus; NC Nurses Assn; NC Health Occupations Teachers Assn (Secy, Newsletter Editor); NC Voc Assn, AVA; Higgin Memorial United Meth Church, Order of Eastern Star; Yancey Cty Teacher of Yr 1982 & Outstanding Educator Achievement Awd 1984.

SHAW, RICHARD ELLIS, Teacher; *b:* Greenfield, MA; *m:* Valerie Moses; *ed:* (BA) His/Psych, Elmhurst 1970; (MS) Ed, 1981, (EDS) Counseling, 1990 N IL Univ; Doctorate Applied for 1990; *cr:* Teacher Chicago Public Sch 1970-71, Vallew View Public Sch 1973-; Therapist Child Sexual Abuse Trng & Clinic 1987-89, Chrysallis Family Therapy 1989-; *ai:* Good Samaritan Hospital; Youth Eating Sensibly; Phi Delta Kappa 1987-; Amer Assn Marriage & Family Therapist 1989-; Outstanding Educator Nom 1989; *office:* B J Ward Mid Sch 200 Recreation Dr Bolingbrook IL 60439

SHAW, SCOTT O., 7th Grade Geography Teacher; *b:* Clearfield, PA; *m:* Laura Allen; *c:* Carol, Christopher; *ed:* (BS) Soc Stud, 1971, (ME) Soc Stud, 1976 EDINBORO UNIV; Cert Elem Ed, Edinboro Univ 1982; *cr:* Soc Stud Teacher Ridgeway Sch Dist 1972-89; *ai:* Asst Ftbl Coach; Asst Track Coach; NEA 1972-89; *home:* 120 Tyler Ave Ridgway PA 15853

SHAWGO, KATE WALLMAN, 2nd Grade Teacher; *b:* Lima, OH; *M:* Roger; *ed:* (BA) Child Dev, 1980, Elem Ed, 1984 Eastern WA Univ; Winning at Teaching Summer Institute in Discipline; *cr:* 3rd Grade Teacher 1980-85, 2nd Grade Teacher 1986 Sadie Halstead Elem; *ai:* Yrbk Comm; Elem Drug/Alcohol Ed Coord; Self-Study Parent/Teacher Comm; Discipline Policy Comm; Past Asst Coach of Jump-Rope Demo Team; Inservice Instr; WA Ed Assn Mem 1980-; Newport Ed Assn Mem 1980-; Balloon Fed of Amer Mem 1988; Inland Empire Aeronaut Society (Mem, Secy) 1988-; Sch Bd Cert of Merit Teaching Excl & Inservice Ed & Discipline; Private Pilot License Hot Air Balloon; *office:* Sadie Halstead Elem Sch PO Box 70 Newport WA 99156

SHEA, GERALD J., Language Art Teacher; *b:* Galesburg, IL; *c:* Colin, Brynn; *ed:* (MSED) Rdng, 1975, (BA) Eng, 1971 W IL Univ; Prof Photographer Winnona Sch; *cr:* Photography Teacher Mc Henry Comm Coll 1980-88; Eng Teacher Sch Dist 47 1975-; *ai:* Freelance Writing; Newspaper Work; IEA, NEA, PP of A; Mc Henry Comm Coll Photographer of Yr 1979; Poems & Articles Published; Founding Ed Crystal Lake Times 1989-; *office:* Sch Dist 47 Commerce Rd Crystal Lake IL 60014

SHEA, SANDRA BARNES, Social Studies Dept Chair; *b:* Austin, TX; *m:* Alan William; *c:* Kelly A.; *ed:* (BA) His, Univ of TX 1960; Grad Work Univ of TX & PA St; *cr:* Teacher Austin Public Schls 1961-62, Overseas Schls Madrid & Spain 1962-65, Cleghorn Schl 1965-66, Pennsburg Schls 1967-; *ai:* Soc Stud Dept Chm; World Affairs Club, Mock Trial Team, Environmental Club Spon; Delta Kappa Gamma VP 1990; NCSS, NEA, PSEA, PEA; Delta Gamma (Alumnae Pres 1986-88, Province Chairperson 1988-89); Top 20 Teachers PA 1989; *home:* 124 Woodstock Dr Newtown PA 18940

SHEA, SANDRA THOMPSON, First Grade Teacher; *b:* Springfield, MA; *m:* William; *c:* Katherine, Michael; *ed:* (BS) Cmmty Ed, Springfield Coll 1973; Working Toward Masters Ed/Curr/Instruction/Cmptrs, Lesley Coll 1991; Effective Teaching Wkshp Research Based Instruction Trng; *cr:* Remedial Math Teacher Park Avenue Sch & Memorial Sch 1973-74; *ai:* MA Teachers Assn, HCTA, WSEA 1973-; Falcon Swim Club Secy; *office:* Memorial Sch 201 Norman St West Springfield MA 01089

SHEAFFER, JOHN CLARENCE, Middle School Science Teacher; *b:* Ephrata, PA; *m:* Shelly A. Lafferty; *c:* Jared Brent, Caleb Patrick; *ed:* (BS) Bio Ed, Millersville Univ 1981; Millersville U/Penn St Univ; *cr:* Bio Teacher Upper Dauph Area HS 1981-82; Life & Earth Sci Teacher Millersburg Area Mid Sch 1982-; *ai:* Asst Track Coach; NSTA 1981-; MAEA/PSEA/NEA Pres-Elect of Local 1988-; BSA Asst Scout Master; Stu Teaching Awd Millersville Univ 1981; *office:* Millersburg Area Mid Sch 799 Center St Millersburg PA 17061

SHEAFFER, WILLIAM A., HS Science/Psychology Teacher; *b:* Lansdale, PA; *ed:* (BS) Bio, Millersville Univ 1976; Masters Equivalent Health Ed, Penn St Univ 1984; *cr:* HS Sci Teacher Middletown Area Sch Dist 1976-77; HS Sci/Health/Psych Teacher Millersburg Area Sch Dist 1977-; *ai:* Chess Club; Athletic Trainer; Red Cross 1979-; *office:* Millersburg Area Sch Dist 799 Center St Millersburg PA 17061

SHEAHAN, ANNA L., Spanish Teacher; *b:* Moline, IL; *m:* Joseph; *c:* Natalie; *ed:* (BA) Span, Marycrest Coll 1982; Grad Stud N IL Univ, San Jose Costa Rica; *cr:* Span Teacher Kewanee HS 1984-; *ai:* Swing Choir Dir; *office:* Kewanee HS 1101 E 3rd St Kewanee IL 61443

SHEALY, BETTYE TYLEE, 2nd Grade Teacher; *b:* Charleston, SC; *m:* David J.; *c:* Jonathan D.; *ed:* (BS) Elem Ed, Winthrop Coll 1967; *cr:* 1st Grade Teacher Lambs Elem 1967-68; St Stephen Elem 1968-70; 1st & 2nd Grade Teacher 1970-89; Headmistress 1988-89 St Stephen Acad; 2nd Grade Teacher Andrews Acad 1989; *ai:* Annual Spon; Chrldr Spon; Garden Club Fed Pres 1980-82/ 86-; Church Music Dir 1985-; *home:* 105 Pitt PO Box 397 St Stephen SC 29479

SHEALY, KAREN SUSAN, Fifth Grade Teacher; *b:* Columbia, SC; *ed:* (BS) Elem Ed, Winthrop Coll 1972; (MED) Elem Ed, Converse Coll 1989; Specialists Certificate, SC St Dept of Ed; *cr:* 5th Grade Teacher Ridge Spring-Monetta Elem 1972-75, New Prospect Elem 1975-; *ai:* Stu Cncl Spon; NEA, SC Ed Assn; Thermal Belt Bus & Prof Women (Pres 1987-89), Woman of Yr 1990; Friends of Lib Landrum Branch VP 1989-; *office:* New Prospect Elem Sch 9251 Hwy 9 Inman SC 29349

SHEALY, KELLY, Mathematics Teacher/Coord; *b:* Prosperity, SC; *ed:* (BA) Math, Newberry Coll 1979; Advanced Placement Endorsement St of SC; *cr:* Math Teacher Barnwell HS 1979-; *ai:* NHS Adv; Palmetto St Teachers Assn, SC Cncl Teachers of Math, SC Assn for Advanced Placement Math Teachers; *office:* Barnwell HS Jackson St Barnwell SC 29812

SHEARER, G. MICHAEL, Guidance Counselor; *b:* Chambersburg, PA; *m:* Karen Ehrlichman; *c:* Thomas, Todd; *ed:* (BS) Elem Ed, Shippensburg Univ 1966; (MS) Spec Ed, Millersville Univ 1971; (MS) Guidance/Counseling Shippensburg Univ 1977; *cr:* Spec Ed Teacher Eastern St Sch & Hospital 1966-71, Antietam Jr HS 1971-80; Guidance Cnslr Waynesboro Mid Sch 1980-; *ai:* Waynesboro Area Ed Assn, PA St Ed Assn, NEA, PA Sch Cnslrs Assn 1971-; Natl Rifle Assn 1980-; Chambersburg Elks Club 1978-; Chambersburg Pistol & Rifle Club, Chambersburg Club 1985-; Chambersburg YMCA.

SHEARER, MARILYN RUTH (DAVIS), 5th Grade Teacher; *b:* Clare, MI; *m:* Francis; *c:* Kimberly Ziccarelli, Jonathan; *ed:* (BA) Ed, MI St Univ 1961; *cr:* 5th Grade Teacher Waupaca Elem Sch 1970; *ai:* Waupaca Teachers Assn; Occasional Singers 1986; *office:* Waupaca Schls 425 School St Waupaca WI 54981

SHEARER, PATRICIA WATSON, Reading Specialist; *b:* New Haven, CT; *m:* Charles K. Jr.; *c:* C. Justin; *ed:* (BSE) Ed, 1975, (MS) Ed/Rdng, 1980 Westfield St Coll; Chadron St 1989-; Univ of Ma 1978; ND St 1986; Univ of NH 1976; SD St Univ 1982-87; *cr:* Rdng Specialist Easthampton Sch System 1978-81, Pathfinder Vo-Tech HS 1982, Douglas Sch System 1982-; Instr SD St Univ 1984-87; *ai:* Public Relations Person for Sch; Dist Rdng Comm, Building Cncl, Sch Cmnty Cncl Mem; Intnl Rdng Assn 1979-; SD Rdng Assn 1982-; Black Hills Rdng Cncl 1982- Sd Sch of Mines & Technology Womens Club (Treas 1984-85, Secy 1988-89); Amer Assn of Univ Women Coord for RIF Prgm 1982-86; SD Assn for Mid Level Ed 1989-; Natl & St Mid Sch Conferences & Regional St & Rdng Conferences 1979-; Publications the MS Rdng Journal, AZ J Ournal of Rdng & MA Primer; Grant from MA Rdng Assn for Research; Grad Assistanceship from Westfield St Coll; Grant from Division of Elem/Scndry Ed St of SD; Grant from Douglas Sch Dist; Awarded 3 Red White & Blue Awds from DougLas Sch Dist; *home:* 6499 S Canyon Rd Rapid City SD 57702

SHEARER, PEGGY YOUNG, English Teacher; *b:* Cooper, KY; *m:* Gordon; *c:* Aaron, Whitney; *ed:* (BA) Ed, 1977, (MS) Ed, 1979 Univ of KY; (Rank I) Ed, E KY Univ 1989; *cr:* Shelby Cty HS 1979-82; Wayne Cty HS 1982-; *ai:* Academic Team Coach; Stu Cncl & Class Adv; Project Graduation Chm; Homemakers VP 1988; *office:* Wayne Cty HS Rt 4 Monticello KY 42633

SHEAROUSE, MARGARET MC KNIGHT, Fine Arts Dept. Head & Teacher; *b:* Augusta, GA; *m:* John Chapman; *c:* Chapman, Clinton; *ed:* (BFA) Art Ed, Univ of GA 1977; Journalism, Univ of SC; Grad Courses Art & Curr, Augusta Coll; Mac Intosh Cmptr Wkshp, Walsworth Publishing Company Apple Cmptr Incorporated; *cr:* Art Teacher Mc Cormick Mid Sch 1977-78; Career Ed Consultant Columbia Cty Bd Of Ed 1978-79; Art Teacher Harlem HS 1979-; *ai:* Yrbk, Art Club, NHS, Natl Art Honor Society, Frosh Class Spon; Staff Dev Instr; Media & Fine Art Curr Revision Comms; S Interscholastic Press Assn (Advisory Cncl 1988-92, Secy 1990-92, Exec Bd 1989-); GA Art Ed Assn Pres Cntrl Savannah River Dist 1987-; Delta Kappa Gamma Scrapbook Comm Chairperson; Academic Booster Club Teacher Rep 1988-89; Westmont PTO; Fairview Presbyn Church Bible Sch Coord 1987-; Yrbk Ratings Excl & Superior SIPA, 1st Place Taylor Publishing Company 1984, 1st Place Delmar Publishing Company 1985; STAR Teacher 1985, 1989; Harlem HS Outstanding Teacher 1982; Sch Art Symposium Regional Coord; Greater Augusta Art Cncl Grant 1990; *office:* Harlem High School Box 699 Hwy 221 Harlem GA 30814

SHEEHAN, HELEN (FULLER), Counselor/Teacher; *b:* Fort Worth, TX; *m:* Richard Martin; *c:* James M., Bruce F.; *ed:* (BA) Psych/Eng, Baylor Univ 1945; (MS) Educl Personnel, IN Univ 1947; Central MO St Univ, Lamar St Coll Beaumont, North TX St Univ, TX Tech Univ, Univ of MO; *cr:* 10th Grade Cnslr Irving HS 1962-65; HS Cnslr 1965-85, Cnslr/Teacher 1985- Lafayette Cty HS; *ai:* Curr Dev & Principals Adv Comm; Future Teacher of America 1965-80, Class Spon; Cntrl MO Guidance Pres 1983; Mo Sch Cnslrs Assn; C-1 Teachers Assn; MO Natl Ed Assn; 1st Presbyn Church (Elder, Deacon, Choir Mem, SS Teacher); Wrote & Co-Chaired Two Yr Grant for Career Ed; *home:* 202 W 21st St Higginsville MO 64037

SHEEHAN, KEVIN PATRICK, Director of Student Projects; *b:* Brooklyn, NY; *m:* Irene Vogel; *c:* Ryan; *ed:* (BA) His, 1971, (MA) Ed, 1972 Albany St; (PD) Admin, C W Post 1979; Coaches Cert, Adelphi Univ; *cr:* Soc Stud Teacher Oceanside Mid Sch 1972-80; Teacher of Gifted Oceanside Schls 1981-88; Dir of Stu Projects Oceanside Mid Sch 1988-; *ai:* Assoc Head Lacrosse Coach, Adelphi Univ; Ftbl, Girls Soccer, Wrestling, Bsktbl, Lacrosse Coach; Stu Cncl Club Adv; Future Problem Solving Club Adv; PTA Lifetime Membership; Published Articles on Gifted Ed & Coaching Lacrosse; *office:* Oceanside Mid Sch Alice & Beatrice Aves Oceanside NY 11572

SHEEHAN, NANCY PALASZEWSKI, Health/Physical Ed Teacher; *b:* Norfolk, VA; *m:* William Michael; *c:* Kellie A.; *ed:* (BS) Health/Phys Ed, Old Dominion Univ 1979; *cr:* 9th Grade Health/Phys Ed Teacher 1980-81, 10th Grade Driver Ed/Bio Teacher 1981-82, 10th Grade Bio Teacher 1982-83 Norfolk Cath HS; Pre K-8th Grade Health/Phys Ed Teacher Holy Trinity Sch/Blessed Sacrament Sch 1984-88; 5th-7th Grade Sci Teacher Holy Trinity Sch 1988-89; Pre K-8th Grade Health/Phys Ed Teacher Holy Trinity Sch/Norfolk Cath Mid Sch 1989-; *ai:* Jr Var Sftbl Coach Norfolk Cath HS; 8th Grade Yrbk 1988-89; Sci Fair Admin 1988-89; Organized 8th Grade Grad; Delta Psi Kappa 1978-; *home:* 6449 Grimes Ave Norfolk VA 23518

SHEEHY, VIRGINIA CADAN, 8th Grade Teacher; *b:* Brooklyn, NY; *m:* William B.; *c:* Catherine Dempsey, Virginia, Barbara Donovan; *ed:* (BS) Ed, Coll Misericordia Dallas 1948; *cr:* Teacher St Clare Sch 1961-; *ai:* Yrbk Moderator; Sch Sci Fair; Staten Island Rdng Assn, Staten Island Sci Teachers Assn, Kappa Gamma Pi; Woman Who Cares Awd Staten Island Fed of Cath Sch Parents 1984; Educator of Yr Awd Staten Island Continuum of Ed 1988; *office:* St Clare Sch 151 Lindenwood Rd Staten Island NY 10308

SHEELEY, SHARON K. (GRUNDEN), Second Grade Teacher; *b:* Kenton, OH; *m:* Charles E.; *ed:* (BS) Elem Ed, Bowling Green St Univ 1974; (MED) Ed Curr/Supervision, Wright St Univ 1986; Various Seminars & Wkshps; *cr:* 1st-2nd Grade Teacher Huntsville Elem 1970-72; 2nd Grade Teacher Belle Center Elem 1976-; *ai:* Right to Read Coord; Young Authors Spon; Building Curr/Whole Learning Team; Back to Sch Participant; Future Teachers Supvr; OH Ed Assn, NEA; Ben Logan Ed Assn (Bldg Rep 1984-87, VP 1987-89); Faculty Administrative Cncl Secy 1986-88; Logan Cty Rdng Cncl Secy 1985-88; Intnl Rdng Cncl, OH Rdng Cncl; The Kings Daughters & Sons (Secy 1984-, Treas 1978-83); Weekday Religious Ed Assn Voting Delegate 1987-; Teacher Spotlight Awd from Excl in Ed Comm; Ed Mini-Grants; Right-To-Rad Ideas Cty Presenter; *office:* Belle Center Elem Sch 107 School St Belle Center OH 43310

SHEER, RODNEY NATHAN, Mathematics Teacher; *b:* Wellsboro, PA; *m:* Eva J. Cortez; *c:* Quinton, Rebecca; *ed:* (BS) Math, Mansfield St Coll 1968; (MS) Math, Elmira Coll 1971; St Marys Univ; Elmira Coll; *cr:* Math Teacher Emira City Sch DiSt 1968-; Tax Consultant Sharon Enterprises 1979-; *ai:* Sch Act Cntrl Treas; Chemung Cty Schl Dist Federal Credit Union Supervisory Comm 1986-89; *home:* 1627 Rolling Acres Pine City NY 14871

SHEERMAN, JOYCE JOHNSTON, Third Grade Teacher; *b:* Moberly, MO; *m:* James Clyde; *c:* James T., John M.; *ed:* (BS) Elem Ed, Univ of MO 1967; (MA) Elem Ed, NE MO St Univ 1982; *cr:* Eng/Spelling Teacher New Haven Elem 1067-69; 5th Grade Teacher 1969-70, 1975-89, 3rd Grade Teacher 1989- Marceline R-5; *ai:* Prof Dev; Soc Stud Curr; Policies; CTA Schlsp; Volunteers; Co-Spon Dist Math Contests; Marceline Cmmty Teachers Assn (Pres 1978-79, Secy 1989-); MO St Teachers Assn; Lydia Group 1st Chrstn Church (Secy 1985-87, Pres 1989-); Tiger Booster Club; *office:* Marceline R-5 Sch 314 E Santa Fe Marceline MO 64658

SHEESLEY, BETTY JO, 8th Grade Science Teacher; *b:* Mexico, MO; *m:* William B.; *c:* Daphne J. Szezuka, Rebecca L.; *ed:* (BS) Elem Ed, Memphis St Univ 1960; Earth Sci/Phys Labs/Cmptrs Shelby Cty Bd of Ed; *cr:* 6th Grade Teacher Scenic Hills Elem 1960-61, 1963-64, Elmore Park Elem 1962-63; 7th & 8th Grade Sci Teacher Shadowlawn Mid Sch 1976-; *ai:* Sunshine Faculty Chm; Stu Assistance Prgm; Band Chaperone; NEA, TEA; SCEA Heart Person 1985-86; PTA (Pres, VP), Life Mem 1970-; Ellendale United Meth Church (PPR Chairperson 1974, Bd Chairperson 1975); Church Choir & Bell Choir; *office:* Shadowlawn Mid Sch 4734 E Shadowlawn Rd Arlington TN 38002

SHEESLEY, CONNIE RAY, Fourth Grade Teacher; *b:* Temple, TX; *m:* Terry Lee; *ed:* (BA) Elem Ed, Penn Coll 1968; *cr:* 3rd Grade Teacher Eddyville Elem 1968-71; Pre-Sch Head Teacher Day Care CO 1971-72; 4th Grade Teacher Eddyville Elem 1972-; *ai:* 2nd/4th Grade Peer Tutoring Project; Young Writers Conference Facilitator; Planning Comm AEA Teachers Inservice; I Read Assn (Treas 1980-81, VP 1981-82); Local, St, NEA mem 1968-83, 1988-; Church (Teacher, Supvr) 1970-82; Teen Summer Camp Cnslr 1974-78; Outstanding Young Women of America 1970, 1979; IA St Teacher of Yr Honors 1979-81; *office:* Eddyville Elem Sch Berdan Rd Eddyville IA 52553

SHEETS, DANIEL D., Mathematics & Computer Teacher; *b:* Marion, MI; *m:* Camilla Louise Bachi; *c:* Jenelle, Carrie; *ed:* (BSED) Soc Sci, Cntrl MI Univ 1967; (MA) Curr Dev, Univ of MI 1972; MI St Univ, W MI Univ, Cntrl MI Univ; *cr:* Teacher Riverside Jr HS & Mid Sch 1967-; *ai:* Stu & Intramural Act Dir; Textbook Selection Comm; Mid Sch Task Force; Grand Rapids Ed Assn Mid Sch Rep 1988-89; MI Cncl Teachers of Math 1983-; Cntrl MI Univ Alumni Assn (Natl Bd of Dir 1972-77, Grand Rapids Pres 1974-76); Natl Sci Fnd for Soc Stud Curr Dev 1971-72; Univ of MI Grant Improvement of Mid Sch Math & Cmptr Teachers 1983; *office:* Riverside Mid Sch 265 Eleanor NE Grand Rapids MI 49505

SHEETS, GEORGE WILLIAM, Language Art Teacher; *b:* Celina, OH; *m:* Kathleen S.; *c:* Brannon; *ed:* (BS) Eng/Ed, Bowling Green St Univ 1972; Grad Stud Bowling Green St Univ; *cr:* 7th/8th Grade Lang Art Teacher Lykens Jr HS 1972-75; 11th/12th Grade Lang Art Teacher Ridgedale HS 1975-; *ai:* Jr & Sr HS Ftbl, Jr Var Bsbl & Girls Bsktbl Coach; Stu Cncl Adv; Act Coord; NCTE, OH Ed Assn, NEA, OH Cncl Teacher of Eng; United Commercial Travelers, Bowling Green Alumni Assn; Ridgedale Schls Teacher of Yr 1983-84; *home:* PO Box 74 St Rt 98 Sulphur Springs OH 44881

SHEETS, NEDRA ELLEN (JACOBS), 1st Grade Teacher; *b:* Luckey, OH; *m:* Richard J.; *c:* Todd A., Landry L.; *ed:* (BSED) Elem Ed, 1962, (MED) Spec Ed, 1966 Bowling Green St Univ; *cr:* Elem Teacher Eastwood Schls 1962-; *office:* Webster Elem Sch 17345 Rt 199 Pemberville OH 43450

SHEETZ, JANE HERNLEY, Kindergarten Teacher; *b:* Manheim, PA; *m:* Jesse F.; *c:* Robin S. Heim; *ed:* (BS) Elem Ed, Elizabethtown Coll 1949; Grad Stud Temple Univ, PA St Univ, Millersville Univ; *cr:* 2nd Grade Teacher Manheim Cntrl 1949-51; 1st Grade Teacher Greenwood Joint 1951-53, Wilson Joint 1953-57; Kndgtn Teacher Wyomissing Area 1964-; *ai:* PA St Ed Assn, NEA 1949-; Wyomissing Area Teachers Assn 1964-; Friends of the Rdng Berks Public Libraries 1988-; Delta Kappa Gamma Mem 1976-80; CEC Awd 1984; Amer Family Inst Gift of Time 1989; *office:* Wyomissing Hills Elem Sch Woodland Rd Wyomissing PA 19610

SHEFFER, WILLIAM ALBERT, Vocational Agriculture Teacher; *b:* Maysville, MO; *c:* William L., Jon D.; *ed:* (BS) Botany, Univ of AZ 1963; Grad Work Ag Ed; *cr:* Voc Ag Teacher Young Public Sch; *ai:* FFA; ASCD, AVTA, NVTA; Cmmty Cncl Mem 1990; Volunteer Fire Dept Mem 1989-; *home:* PO Box 405 Young AZ 85554

SHEFFIELD, LUCILLE LEMONS, Third Grade Teacher; *b:* Atlanta, GA; *c:* Sherri Tisdell, Shelley Lamar Stewart; *ed:* (BS) Elem Ed, Ft Valley St Coll 1958; (MA) Elem Ed, Columbus Coll 1978; Certified in Bi-ling Ed; *cr:* 3rd Grade Teacher Carver Elem Sch 1958-60; Librarian 5th Avenue Elem Sch 1965-71; 3rd Grade Teacher Gentian Elem 1971-; *ai:* Tutoring; MEA (Sch Rep 1980-81) 1965-71; GEA, NEA 1965-71; Brownie Troup Adv; Church Dir of Chrstn Ed; Ft Valley St Coll Alumni Assn 1958-; Columbus Coll Alumni Assn 1978-; Modernistic Soc/Civic Club (Pres, Treas) 1965-; *office:* Gentian Elem Sch 4201 Primrose Rd Columbus GA 31907

SHEKOSKI, NAOMI, CSA, Fourth Grade Teacher; *b:* Two Rivers, WI; *ed:* (BS) Ed, Marian Coll 1955; (MS) Ed, Marygrove 1973; *cr:* Prin/Teacher St Charles 1961-67; 1st Grade Teacher Presentation Sch 1970-80; 5th Grade Teacher St Marys 1980-88; 4th-6th Grade Teacher S S Peter & Paul 1988-; *ai:* Outstanding Teacher Awd Archdiocese of Milwaukee.

SHELBURNE, CAROLYN JANE, Sixth Grade Teacher; *b:* Radford, VA; *ed:* (BS) Elem Ed, 1972, (MS) Elem Ed, 1977 Radford Univ; Cert in Elem Admin 1980; *cr:* 3rd Grade Teacher 1972-73, 4th Grade Teacher 1973-74 Northwood Elem Sch; 6th Grade Teacher Pulaski Mid Sch 1974-83, Dublin Mid Sch 1983-; *ai:* Pep Club Spon; Spec Olympics, Career Day, Morning Activity Comm; NEA, VEA, PCEA 1972-78, 1985-; Phi Delta Kappa 1977-; *home:* PO Box 1192 Radford VA 24141

SHELLENBARGER, NELSON LYLE, Secondary Science Teacher; *b:* West Branch, CO; *m:* Jacquelyn Maltis; *c:* Barry, Jennifer; *ed:* (BA) Bio, Sociology, Phys Ed, 1966 N MI Univ; *cr:* Teacher Hale HS; *ai:* Bsbl, Bsktbl, Ftbl Coach; Class Adv; Originated Sports Boosters; Class Field Trips Pistons; *home:* 8690 W Riley Rd Hale MI 48739

SHELLMAN, WILLIS, Guidance Counselor; *b:* Savannah, GA; *m:* Mary Grant; *c:* Kevin, Kalandra; *ed:* (BS) His, Savannah St Coll 1974; (MED) His Ed, Armstrong/Savannah St 1976; Guidance/Counseling, GA Southern Coll 1978-80; *cr:* Teacher Aide Greenbriar of Savannah 1974-76; Teacher 1976-78, Counselor 1978- Effingham Cty HS; *ai:* Whos Who Among Amer HS Stus, Society of Distinguished Amer HS Stus, GA Governors Honors Spon; Adult Bsktbl Coach; NEA, GAE 1976-; EAE Building Rep 1976-; BSA (Scout Master 1966-74, Asst Cubmaster 1967-69); *office:* Effingham County HS Rt 1 Box 154 Springfield GA 31329

SHELLNUTT, JACK G., Athletic Director/Teacher; *b:* Mc Kinney, TX; *m:* Neta Kay; *c:* Misty M.; *ed:* (BS) Math/Health/Phys Ed, 1972, (MS) Ed, 1979 E TX St Univ; *cr:* Coach/Teacher Italy HS 1973-76, Ore City HS 1976-77, Liberty Eylau HS 1977-78; Athletic Dir/Coach/Teacher Edgewood HS 1978-; *ai:* Athletic Directing; Coaching Var Boys Bsktbl; THSCA 1972-89; TABC 1979-89; *home:* PO Box 459 Edgewood TX 75117

SHELLY, JOHN BENJAMIN, 4th Grade Teacher; *b:* Galesburg, IL; *m:* Sarah Beth Hoben; *c:* Andrew, Ellen; *ed:* (BA) Russian Area Stud Knox Coll 1973; *cr:* 4th Grade Teacher Mable Woolsey Elem Sch 1976-; *ai:* Patrol Spon; Phi Beta Kappa Outstanding Knoxville Educator; Outstanding Area Educator Knox Coll; *office:* Mable Woolsey Elem Sch Pleasant Ave Knoxville IL 61448

SHELLY, SUE V., 3rd/4th Grade Teacher; *b:* Middleton, TN; *m:* Robert; *c:* Tanya; *ed:* (BS) Elem Ed, 1973, (MS) Curr/Instruction, 1985 Memphis St Univ; Grad Stud; *cr:* Teacher Middleton Elem 1971-; *ai:* Sch Extend Day-Care; Hardeman Cty Ed Assn, TN Ed Assn, NEA 1971-; Delta Kappa Gamma 1981-; Kappa Delta Pi 1984-; TN Career Ladder III 1986; Chamber of Commerce Hardeman Cty Teacher Awd 1989; *office:* Middleton Elem Sch 180 Robin Cir Middleton TN 38052

SHELMAN, MICHAEL DAVID, Sixth Grade Teacher; *b:* Mt Pleasant, IA; *m:* Molly Ann Rich; *c:* Spencer; *ed:* (BSE) Elem Ed, NE MO St Univ 1984; Grad Stud Elem Ed; *cr:* 6th Grade Teacher Marceline R-5 Sch 1984-; *ai:* Head Girls Bsktbl & HS Asst Ftbl Coach; MSTA 1984-; *office:* Marceline R-5 Sch 314 E Santa Fe Marceline MO 64658

SHELTON, CAROL LOUDEN, English Teacher; *b:* Henry County, KY; *m:* Robert Clyde; *c:* Sheree S. Richter, Shawn, Shannon; *ed:* (BA) Eng/Health/Phys Ed, E KY Univ 1959; (MA) Scndry Ed, 1972, (Rank I) Scndry Ed, 1988 Georgetown Coll; *ai:* Speech Coach; Chrldr, Prom, Golf Team Spon; KY Cncl of Eng Teachers; *office:* Carroll Cty HS Highland Ave Carrollton KY 41008

SHELTON, CHARLES W., Retired 6th Grade Teacher; *b:* Watauga, KY; *m:* Leta Kay Campbell; *c:* Janet L.; *ed:* (BS) Elem Ed, E KY Univ 1961; *cr:* Head Teacher Pine Grove Elem Sch 1959-66; His/Soc Stud Teacher Clinton Cty Jr HS 1966-76; 6th Grade Teacher Clinton Cty Elem Sch 1976-85; *ai:* 7th Grade Bsktbl Coach; 4-H Leader; KEA, NEA 1959-85; *home:* HC 71 Box 469 Alpha KY 42603

SHELTON, CHERYL ANN, English Teacher; *b:* Denver, CO; *ed:* (BA) Elem Ed, Denver Baptist Bible Coll 1977; (MS) Educl Admin, Pensacola Chrstn Coll 1985; *cr:* Elem Ed Teacher Temple Baptist Acad 1977-86; Eng/Scndry Teacher Beth Eden Baptist Sch 1987-; *ai:* Drama Dir; Academic Cnslr; Jr & Sr Class Spon; Yrbk Adv; Admin Duties; *office:* Beth Eden Baptist Sch 2600 Wadsworth Blvd Denver CO 80215

SHELTON, CLAUDIA PROVINCE, Fourth Grade Teacher; *b:* Jonesboro, AR; *m:* Mickey; *c:* Whitney A. Thigpen, Amy M.; *ed:* (BS) Sociology, AR St Univ 1962; Post Grad Continuing Ed & Updating 1967, 1973, 1985, 1986; *cr:* 4th-6th Grade Teacher Blytheville Public Schls 1962-74; Soc Worker St of AR 1975-76; 3rd/4th Grade Teacher Brookland Elem 1977-; *ai:* Phi Delta Kappa; Blytheville Ed Assn; *office:* Brookland Elem Sch PO Box 35 Brookland AR 72417

SHELTON, JOHN ANTONIO, Gifted Ed/Soc Stud Teacher; *b:* Barstow, CA; *m:* Julie Jones; *ed:* (BA) His/Political Sci, 1979, Ed, 1981- Univ Puget Sound; Certified Health Fitness; Instr, Amer Coll of Sports Medicine; Licensed Realtor, St of WA; *cr:* Soc Stud Teacher Lakes HS 1981, Hudtloff Jr HS 1982; Gifted Ed Teacher Mann Jr HS/Various Elem Schs 1982-86; Gifted Ed/Soc Stud Teacher Mann Jr HS 1986-; *ai:* Tennis, Girls Track Coach; Knowledge Master Open Coach; Academic Team; Clover Park Ed Assn Mem 1981-; Amer Coll of Sports Medicine Mem 1986-; Health/Fitness Cert 1986; Clover Park Sch Dist Minority Recruitment Comm 1989-; Natl Assn of Realtors 1990; Fort Steilaroom Running Club Mem 1980-; Resolution Run Series Winner 1987-90; Pacific Northwest Tennis Assn Mem 1978-82; Mens Singles Alphabetical Ranking 1982; Clover Park Sch Bd Recognition 1989; Knowledge Master Open Team; CPSD Fnd Awd, Schlsp to St Seminar Gifted Ed; Finisher of Boston Marathon 1987; *home:* 489 Alameda Ave Tacoma WA 98466

SHELTON, LESTER THOMAS, Science Teacher; *b:* Paducah, KY; *m:* Sharon Rhew; *c:* Matt, Melissa; *ed:* (BS) Chem, 1973, (MA) Ed, 1980 Murray St Univ; *cr:* Sci Teacher Sikeston Jr HS 1974, Heath HS 1974-76, Ballard Memorial 1976-84, Marshall Cty HS 1984-; *ai:* Asst Ftbl Coach; Sci Curr Comm; *home:* Rt 1 Box 152B Calvert City KY 42029

SHELTON, SAMMIE LEE, 4th Grade Teacher/Chairman; *b:* Mc Beth, TX, *m:* Gloria Jean Bass; *c:* La Jeanna L., Samantha L., Karla N.; *ed:* (BA) Elem Ed, AZ St Univ 1972; Span Trng Amer Grad Sch Intnl Management; *cr:* 7th/8th Grade Soc Stud Teacher Roosevelt Sch 1973; 7th/8th Grade Sci Teacher John F Kennedy Sch 1973-76; 6th Grade Teacher 1976-80, 4th/5th Grade Self Contained Teacher 1980- Martin L King Elem Sch; *ai:* Ftbl, Bsktbl, Floor Hockey Coach City of Phoenix Jr League; Boys Club Adv Hayden Park Boys in Action; NEA 1973-; Roosevelt Classroom Teachers Assn (Executive Bd 1975-76, Building Rep 1984-89); Martin L King Peace Awd 1987; Roosevelt Sch Dist Scholastic Achievement Awd 1988; *office:* Martin Luther King Elem Sch 4615 S 22nd St Phoenix AZ 85040

SHELTON, WILLIAM ALLEN, History Department Chairman; *b:* Lexington, KY; *ed:* (BA) His, TX Chrstn Univ 1967; (MA) Amer His, Univ of KY 1969; (MDIV) Church His, Brite Divinity Sch TCU 1971; (PHD) Amer His, Univ of KY 1978; *cr:* Instr Evening Coll TCU 1970-71, Atlantic Chrstn Coll 1975-76, Univ of KY 1976-78; Teacher KY Cntry Day Sch 1979-84; *ai:* Var Track & Bsktbl Coach; Advanced Placement Coord; KY Historical Society, Southern Historical Society; Daughters of Amer Revolution Amer His Teacher of Yr 1989; Advanced Placement Recognition Awd SW Region of Coll Bd 1990.

SHENASSA, ANN J., Assistant Principal; *b:* Chicago, IL; *m:* John; *c:* Jeffrey, Katie; *ed:* (BA) Adult Ed, Univ Of IL 1975; (MS) Ed Admin, Univ of Chicago 1978; *cr:* Teacher, Cont Ed Cntr 1975-79; Asst Prin, Ben Franklin Mid Sch 1980-; *ai:* Curr Dev; Phi Kappa Phi; Travel Stud, Ed Admin, Western Europe; *office:* Ben Franklin Mid Sch 423 Foster Wauconda IL 60084

SHENK, WARREN R., Social Studies Dept Chair; *b:* Connersville, IN; *m:* Mary Elen Crandall; *c:* Marye J.; *ed:* (BA) Poly Sci, IN Univ 1974; (MED) Curr Dev, Brigham Young Univ 1983; (EDS) Educl Admin, Univ of UT 1987; Geography for Teachers, George Washington Univ; *cr:* Soc Stud Teacher Batesville Mid Sch 1975-78; Soc Stud Dept Chm Payson Jr HS 1979-; *ai:* UT Geographic Alliance 1982-; NCSS 1980-; Natl Cncl of Geographic Educators 1988-; AFT 1976-; UT Cty Republican Party Area Chm 1983-; Natl Geographic Society Summer Geography Inst UT Rep 1988; *office:* Payson Jr HS 1025 S Hwy 91 Payson UT 84651

SHEPALAVY, JULIE NOWADLY, Chemistry Teacher; *b:* Buffalo, NY; *m:* Taras; *c:* Danylo; *ed:* (BA) Chem, SUNY Buffalo 1964; (MS) Scndry Sci Ed, Syracuse Univ 1971; Chem; *cr:* Chem Teacher Jordan-Elbridge HS 1979-80, Manlius Pebble Hill Sch 1980-84, Ballston Spa HS 1984-; *ai:* BSEA Building Rep & Schlsp Comm; ACS Div Chem Ed 1980-; GE Stu & Teacher Achievement & Recognition Awd 1984; Golub Fnd Scholar; Teacher Recognition Awd 1987-; Amer Chemical Soc; Excl in Teaching Chem 1990; *office:* Ballston Spa HS Garrett Rd Ballston Spa NY 12020

SHEPARD, CARLA (EASTMAN), Third Grade Teacher; *b:* Janesville, WI; *c:* Torrie A.; *ed:* (BS) Elem Ed, Univ of WI La Crosse 1975; Assertive Discipline Trng for Teachers, Individually Guided Ed Prgm; *cr:* 3rd Grade Teacher Beach Elem Sch 1975-; *ai:* Curr Dev & Math Curr Dev Comm; Natl Assn for Prof Educators Mem 1975-; *office:* Beach Elem Sch 1421 N Ardmore Dr Round Lake IL 60073

SHEPARD, DOROTHY HARTENSE, English Teacher; *b:* Tyler, TX; *m:* John Edward; *c:* Von Gretchen Shepard Mc Alpin, Chiquita R., Cassandra P. Shepard Young; *ed:* (BA) Eng, TX Coll 1950; E TX St Univ; TX Southern Univ; San Diego St Univ; Univ of CA San Diego; *cr:* English Teacher Emmett Scott HS 1957-70, Robert E Lee HS 1970-71, Morse HS 1971-78, Patrick Henry HS 1978-; *ai:* Educal Cultural Stu Union & Fashion Image Coca Cola Adv; Human Relations & Restructuring Comm Mem; TX Teachers Assn 1957-71; Zeta Phi Beta VP Certificate; CA Teachers Assn, San Diego Teacher Assn 1971-; NEA; Las Munecas Ebony Fashion Show Spon 1971-; Women Extraordinaire Civic Club Secy; Key Club Intnl Certificate of Recognition; Joan Rivers Talk Show Participant; *home:* 8628 Renown Dr San Diego CA 92119

SHEPARD, JAN PRICE, 2nd Grade Teacher; *b:* Lubbock, TX; *m:* Glenn; *c:* Tanner, Brooke; *ed:* (BA) Art Ed, TX Tech Univ 1971; Elem Ed, TX Chrstn Univ 1977; (MS) Elem Ed, N TX St Univ 1987; *ai:* 2nd Grade Teacher Stafford Elem 1978-; Italy HS Tennis Coach

SHEPARD, R. JEAN, First Grade Teacher; *b:* Bryan, OH; *m:* William C.; *c:* Beth E. Studebaker, David E., Steven E.; *ed:* (BS) Elem Ed, Defiance Coll 1965; Wright St, OH Northern; *cr:* 1st Grade Teacher Swanton Local 1956-57, Defiance Cntry 1957-58, Defiance City 1958-59, Swanton Local 1959-65, Greenville City 1965-; *ai:* Greenville Ed Assn (Treas, Negotiations) 1974-76, 1987-89; NHS Honorary Mem 1989; *office:* Gettysburg Elem Sch 260 E Main St Gettysburg OH 45328

SHEPEARD, ANNA PALM, Texas History Teacher; *b:* Houston, TX; *c:* William J., Martin Palm; *ed:* (BS) Elem Ed, Sam Houston St 1962; (MED) Ed, 1984, Supvr Certificate Ed, 1985 Stephen F Austin; *cr:* Teacher Aldine Ind Sch Dist 1962-65, New Caney Ind Sch Dist 1974-82, Humble Ind Sch Dist 1982-; *ai:* Jr Historian; Odyssey of Mind; Natl His Day Contestants; Assn of Prof Educators; TX St Historical Assn Leadership Awd; TX Historical Fnd, Phi Delta Kappa; PTA Life Membership; Montgomery Cty Historical Commission; E Montgomery Cty Lib Bd Treas; Univ of Houston His Fair Bd Dir; St of TX Leadership Awd; Creekwood Mid Sch Teacher of Yr 1987; Outstanding TX His Teacher 1990; *home:* PO Box 808 New Caney TX 77357

SHEPHERD, BILLY HUGH, JR., Phys Ed Teacher/Coach; *b:* Greenwood, MS; *m:* Denise Henkel; *c:* Kenlyn M., Zachary C.; *ed:* (BS) Phys Ed, Mars Hill Coll 1983; *cr:* Phys Ed Teacher/Coach Canton Jr HS 1983-88, Andrews HS 1988-; *ai:* Ftbl Defensive Coord; Boys Bsktbl Coach; NC Coaches Assn 1984-; Andrews United Meth Church (Pastor, Parish Relations) 1989-; *home:* PO Box 1095 Andrews NC 28901

SHEPHERD, GREG, Physical Education Teacher; *b:* Chillicothe, OH; *m:* Sherry Lynn Moore; *c:* Joel W., Erica L.; *ed:* (AA) General Ed, OH Valley Coll 1976; (BA) Phys Ed, 1978, (MED) Phys Ed, 1979 Harding Univ; *cr:* EMR/Spec Ed Teacher Western Local Sch Dist 1979-80; Phys Dev Specialist Pike Cty Sch for Child Advancement 1980-82; K-12th Grade Phys Ed Teacher Scioto Valley Local Schls 1982-; *ai:* Boys Head Cross Cntry & Track Coach 1982-; Pee Wee Bsktbl Coord; *home:* 275 Zahn St Waverly OH 45690

SHEPHERD, PHYLLIS CAROL, English Teacher; *b:* Ary, KY; *m:* Willard Ray; *ed:* (BA) Eng, 1981, (MA) Scndry Ed, 1986, (Rank I) Cert Curr & Instruction, 1988 Univ of KY; *cr:* Eng Teacher Dike Combs Mem HS 1986-; *ai:* Ballroom Dancing Coach; NCTE, KY Cncl of Teachers of Eng, Lang Art 1986-; *office:* Dilce Combs Memorial HS P O Box 159 Jeff KY 41751

SHEPP, CLAIRE CANNY, 6-8th Grade Math Teacher; *b:* Cleveland, OH; *m:* Dale Bernard; *c:* Dawn Cartwright, Dale P., Kathleen E.; *ed:* (BSE) Elem Ed, St. John Coll of Cleveland 1963; (MEE) Elem Ed (Eng, Rdng, Math),AR St Univ 1970; (For Mid Sch Math & Sci), AZ Teachers Acad-Summer 1988, Univ of AZ; *cr:* Sci,Eng, Apache Junction Elem Sch 1968-70; Eng,Math, Queen of Peace Elem Sch 1970-81; Rdng,Eng,Math, St Theresa Elem Sch 1981-85; Math, St Francis Xavier Elem Sch 1985-90; *ai:* Natl Cncl of Teachers of Math 1988-89; AZ Assoc of Teachers of Math; *office:* St Francis Xavier Elem Sch 4715 N Central Ave Phoenix AZ 85012

SHEPPARD, DIANE ROBERTSON, 2nd Grade Teacher; *b:* Hamlet, NC; *m:* John Reese III; *c:* John IV, Robert J.; *ed:* (BA) Eng, Berea Coll 1961; (MED) Ed/Rdng, 1975, (MS) Lang Art, 1989 Univ of SC Columbia; Grad Stud Lang Art, Univ of SC Columbia & Citadel; SC St Dept of Ed Certificate Awd; *cr:* 1st Grade Teacher Williston-Elko Elem 1965-68; Rdng Consultant Williston-Elko Sch Dist 1971-78; Undergrad Lang Art Instr Univ of SC Allendale 1980-84; Eng Teacher Williston-Elko HS 1984-89; 2nd Grade Teacher Kelly Edwards Elem 1989-; *ai:* Say No To Drugs & Drop Out Prevention Comm; HS Lang Art Remedial Stu Tutor; Phi Kappa Phi 1960-; Intnl Rdng Assn 1970-; Delta Kappa Gamma 1989-; First Baptist Church Sunday Sch Teacher 1960-, Recognition; Door to Door Amer Cancer Drive Co-Chm 1963-88, Banquet Recognition 1986-88; Barnwell Cty Commission on Alcohol & Drug Abuse (Chm 1988-) 1982-; Berea Coll Schlsp 1958-61; Outstanding Young Woman of America 1967-; Newspaper Article Published 1985; *office:* Kelly Edwards Elem Sch 808 Elko St Williston SC 29853

SHEPPARD, JOHNNIE FRANK, Unit Head/Teacher; *b:* Detroit, MI; *ed:* (BS) His/Speech, 1973, (MSED) Ed Admin, 1975 Wayne St Univ; Quest & EEEI Trng; *cr:* Teacher Cerveny Mid Sch 1974-; Unit Head Emerson Mid Sch 1990; *ai:* Mem of the Dads Club at Emerson Mid; Tutorial Prgm Teacher at Cerveny & Emerson; LSCO Mem-Cerveny & Emerson; Natl Cncl for Rdng 1987; Metropolitan Cncl for Rdng 1987; NAACP 1980-.

SHEPPARD, MARCIA (WYCHE), Kindergarten Teacher; *b:* Brewton, AL; *m:* Daniel P.; *c:* Mary Libb, Shana, Dayon; *ed:* (BA) Elem, FL St Univ 1963; (MA) Early Chldhd, Univ of W FL 1986; *cr:* 2nd Grade Teacher Pace Elem 1963-64; Headstart Teacher Santa Rosa Sch Bd 1965-66; Teacher Jay HS 1969-71; Kndgtn Teacher Jay Elem 1971-; *ai:* Sch Contact Volunteer Prgm; Rdng/Lang Art; Environment, Career Ed; Teacher Inservice; Kndgtn Grade Level Chm; Spring Talent Show Producer; NEA, FL Teaching Profession, Santa Rosa Prof Educators 1963-; Intnl Rdng Assn 1976-; Santa Rosa Cty Rdng Assn Pres 1976-; Delta Kappa Gamma Music Chm 1980-; Phi Delta Kappa 1986-89; Pine Level Baptist Church (Pianist, Choir, Teacher); Beta Sigma Phi Pres 1967-, Girl of Yr 1971, 1988; Jay Quarterback Club Ways & Means 1987-89; Jay Concerned Citizens Spokesperson 1972-78; Jay Elem Teacher of Yr 1987; Environmental Ed Grant, FL Dept of Ed; Pensacola Jr League Rdng Grant; *office:* Jay Elem Sch 702 S Alabama St Jay FL 32565

SHEPTOCK, COLLEEN COLLINS, Guidance Counselor; *b:* Pittsburgh, PA; *M:* Neal P.; *ed:* (MED) Elem Guidance/Psych, Univ of Edinboro 1979; (BS) Elem Ed, Univ of Slippery Rock 1974; Certified Red Cross Instr on AIDS; Adult Basic Ed Cnslr/Muncy Correctional Inst; Admin, Univ Nova; *cr:* Elem Teacher Pittsburgh Parochial Schls 1974-80; ABE Cnslr Muncy Correctional Inst 1983-86; Elem Guidance W L Myers Elem Schl

1980-; *ai:* Chairperson/Author Dist Staff Dev Plan; Play (School) Make Up Artist; Permanant Record Comm (Designed); Retention Comm (Designed Policy-Chairperson); Pres 1987-89; VP 1986-87 Muncy Ed Assn; PA Schl Counselors Assn Mem 1980-; New Comers Club Mem 1981-83; Lib Assn Public Relations Coord 1978-80; Ed of Homeless/Children & Youth Assn Resource Person 1989-; Elem/Mid Sch Idea Booklet (Articles); Anthology of Contempory Poetry (Poem Published); Indian Artifact Magazine Column Written Monthly; *office:* Ward L Myers Elem Sch New Street Muncy PA 17756

SHERBO, JOHN WILLARD, JR., Science Department Chairman; *b:* Tampa, FL; *m:* Jacqueline June Stegink; *c:* Cheryl A. Haines, Michelle L. Mellor; *ed:* (BS) Ed/Phys Ed/General Sci, 1966, (MS) Sci Ed/Earth Sci, 1972 NW MO St Univ; (EDD) Curr/Instruction Sci Ed, Univ of KS 1978; Prin Cert, Univ of MO Kansas City; *cr:* Sci Teacher Northgate Jr HS 1966-80; Bio Teacher/Sci Dept Chm N Kansas City HS 1980-; *ai:* Track Coach; Prin Advisory Comm; Dist Teacher Recognition Comm; NSTA (Publications Comm, Jr HS Comm) 1966-; Phi Delta Kappa 1983-; NEA Rep 1966-; Campfire Inc Bd of Dir 1973-80, Sebago 1979; Ind Halfway House Inc Bd Pres 1980-84, Distinguished Service 1984; Midwest Diving Cncl Bd Pres 1968-, Distinguished Service 1985; Fellowship Sci Pioneers Jr Acad of Sci 1989; MO Scholars Acad Teacher 1988; Master Teacher Mentor Prgm 1988; Chamber of Commerce Excl in Ed Awd 1990; *office:* N Kansas City HS 2300 Gentry North Kansas City MO 64116

SHERCK, LINDA CAROL, Mathematics Teacher; *b:* Charleston, IL; *m:* Michael M.; *c:* Lauri, Steven; *ed:* (BS) Math/Physics, 1973, (MS) Math/Ed 1975 IN St Univ; (CAS) Math/Ed, Univ of NC 1987; Academically Gifted Ed; *cr:* Math Teacher 1973-77, Math Dept Chairperson 1975-77 Connersville Jr HS; Math Teacher Southmont HS 1978-84, Wiredell HS 1985-; *ai:* Amer Bus Womens Assn D-Team Membership Chairperson 1986-; E Side Baptist Church (Secy-Sunday Sch Teacher 1984-); Federal Grants Awd Supplemental Enrichment Prgm 1976; Remedial Math Prgm 1974; Accepted to NC Center for the Advancement of Teaching; Southmont HS Teacher of Yr 1987.

SHERER, JANE SCOTT, Math Teacher; *b:* York, SC; *m:* Richard L.; *c:* Leigh Boyd, Elizabeth Jane; *ed:* (MS) Elem Ed, 1963, (MAT) 1974 Winthrop; *cr:* 1st Grade Teacher Mc Celvey Elem 1963-64; 2nd Grade Teacher Westminster Elem 1964-65; 6th Grade Teacher Mc Celvey Elem 1965-66; 7th/8th Grade Teacher York Jr HS 1967-; *ai:* Natl Jr Honor Society; Phi Kappa Phi; York ARP Church; *home:* 2017 Creekwood York SC 29745

SHERFEY, GERALDINE RICHARDS, Sci Teacher/Stu-At-Risk Coord; *b:* Pontiac, MI; *c:* Emily J., Laura A. Manning, Susan, William Jr.; *ed:* (BS) Biological Sci, 1963, (MS) Biological Sci, 1965 IN St Univ; (EDS) Supervision/Ed, 1972, (EDS) Curr, 1978 Univ of GA; *cr:* Teacher Hammond Public Schls 1963-65; Sci Teacher/Sci Coord Griffith Public Schls 1965-70; Instr Purdue Calumet 1973-75; Teacher 1975-78, Mid Sch Prin 1978-80, Curr Asst to Asst Supt 1980-82 City of Hammond Schls; Voc Ed/Adult Ed Coord 1984; HS Sci Teacher 1986-; *ai:* Mid Sch Sci Fair Coord; ASCD 1970; World Cncl Curr & Instruction 1978; Phi Delta Kappa 1990; Natl Mid Sch Assn 1975; Natl Sci TeachersAssn Presenter; IN Assn of Adult Ed (Newsletter Co-Ed 1984-89) 1980-, Outstanding Service Awd 1984; Articles Published; *office:* Donald E Gavit Mid Sch & HS 1670 175th St Hammond IN 46324

SHERICK, PHILIP LYLE, German/English Teacher; *b:* Fremont, OH; *ed:* (BSED) Ger/Eng, 1981, (MA) Ger, 1983 Bowling Green St Univ; Univ of Salzburg Austria; West Berlin Goethe-Institut Seminar; *cr:* Eng/Ger Teacher Westland HS 1983-85, Port Clinton HS 1985-; *ai:* Ger Club Adv; AATG 1982-; AFT 1985-; Martha Jennings Lecture Series Scholar 1988-89; *office:* Port Clinton HS 821 S Jefferson St Port Clinton OH 43452

SHERIDAN, DOROTHY FAYE, Retired Teacher; *b:* Etna, UT; *m:* James; *c:* Marcia Carrell (dec), Sherry Spencer, Cordell, Marlon; *ed:* (BA) Elem Ed, NW Nazarene Coll 1970; Spec Ed Certificate, Brigham Young Univ 1981; *cr:* 1st-4th Grade Combination Teacher Snowville Elem 1945-46; 4th-6th Grade Combination Teacher Grouse Creek Elem 1946-47; 6th Grade Teacher Malta Elem 1963-68; 5th-8th Grade Combination Teacher Almo Elem 1969-74; Remedial Rdng Teacher/Librarian Malta Elem 1975-80; 1st-6th Grade Combination Teacher Almo Elem 1981-83; Spec Ed Teacher Malta Elem & Raft River HS 1984-89; *ai:* Cassia Cty Ed Assn 1970-88; Delta Kappa Gamma 1981-85; *home:* PO Box 198 Almo ID 83312

SHERIDAN, ELAINE S. (FISHER), Spanish Teacher; *b:* Lima, OH; *m:* Ray E.; *ed:* (BS) Scndry Ed/Span/His, 1976, (MA) Span, 1980 Bowling Green St Univ; Grad Courses & Wkshp Univ of Dayton & Wright St Univ; *cr:* Span/His Teacher Riverdale HS 1976-78; Grad Asst Bowling Green St Univ 1978-79; Span Teacher Greenon HS 1980-; *ai:* Mad River-Green Pres 1984-86; Local Ed Assn VP 1983-84.

SHERIFF, VIVIAN SHARP, Fourth Grade Teacher; *b:* Liberty, KY; *m:* Alfred J.; *c:* Sherry Ponder, Leane Schisler; *ed:* (BS) Elem Ed, Miami Univ 1966; Miami Univ; Eastern KY Univ; *cr:* 4th Grade Teacher, Jefferson Elem 1966-68; Buchanan Elem 1968-; *ai:* NEA; OEA; HCTA; Sr Citizens Inc Vlntr Svcs; *office:* Buchanan Elem School Hancock & Harmon Aves Hamilton OH 45011

SHERLINSKI, MARK, 5th Grade Teacher; *b:* Wilkes-Barre, PA; *m:* Carol Lynn Booth; *ed:* (BS) Elem Ed, Bloomsburg St Coll 1975; *cr:* 4th/5th Grade Teacher Millville 1975-; *ai:* Environmental Ed, Drug & Alcohol Curr Head; Millville Ed Assn VP 1979-; NRA; Prof Rodeo; St Johns Luth Church; Natl Wild Turkey Fed; Columbia Cty Conservation Teacher of Yr; *office:* Millville Elem Sch Box 300 Millville PA 17846

SHERLOCK, BETTY WILKINSON, 5th Grade Teacher; *b:* Headland, AL; *c:* Diane S. Tunstall; *ed:* (BS) Elem Ed, 1968, (MA) Elem Ed, 1973 Livingston AL; Cert in Admin 1976; *cr:* Teacher Alba Elem Sch 1968-; *ai:* NEA, AEA, MCEA 1968; *home:* 10830 Paul Warden Rd Grand Bay AL 36541

SHERMAN, CAROL SIMPSON, Mathematics Dept Chair; *b:* Cambridge, MA; *m:* John D.; *c:* John C., Robert D.; *ed:* (AB) Math, Mt Holyoke 1958; Cmptr Related Courses; MAT Prgm Harvard; *cr:* Math Teacher Muzzey Jr HS 1958-62, Westfield Sr HS 1962-64; Math Dept Chairperson John F Kennedy HS 1980-; *ai:* SAT Prep Course; DuPont Fellowship for MAT; *office:* John F Kennedy HS Rt 138 Somers NY 10589

SHERMAN, DARYL EDITH, 6th Grade Teacher; *b:* New York, NY; *m:* Stephan; *c:* Danielle, Angelo; *ed:* (BS) Elem Ed, City Coll of NY 1971; (MS) Curr/Instruction, CA St Univ Fullerton 1977; *cr:* 4th/5th Grade Teacher Alessandro Elem 1973-78; 6th Grade Teacher Kimbark Elem 1978-; *ai:* CTA, NEA 1978-; Mentor Teacher St of CA; *office:* Kimbark Elem Sch 18021 Kenwood Ave San Bernardino CA 92407

SHERMAN, DOUGLAS ALLEN, Sixth Grade Teacher; *b:* Sodus, NY; *m:* Veronica O'Toole; *ed:* (BS) Behavioral Sci/Ed, St Univ of NY New Paltz 1966; St Univ NY New Paltz, Syracuse Univ; *cr:* 6th Grade Teacher Wallkill Cntrl Sch 1966-67; 4th Grade Teacher Spackenkill Union Free Sch 1967-68; 5th Grade Teacher Islip Public Schls 1968-71; 5th/6th Grade Teacher Wappingers Cntrl Sch Dist 1971-; *ai:* NY St Eng Cncl, NYSUT; Hudson Valley Writers Assn VP 1986-87; *home:* RD 1 Box 10 Salt Point NY 12578

SHERMAN, ELEANOR O. (STONE), Kindergarten/1st Grade Teacher; *b:* Indianola, IA; *m:* James F.; *c:* Dian L. Saito, Tobi J. Brown, James D.; *ed:* (BA) Sci/Bio, Univ of N Ia 1951; *cr:* Sci/Eng/Math Teacher Hartford HS 1951-52; Kndgtn Teacher San Antonio Elem Sch 1970-75; Kndgtn/1st Grade Teacher W Valley Elem Sch 1975-; *ai:* NEA, CTA, CEA 1970-.

SHERMAN, MARY E., Math Teacher; *b:* Warsaw, NY; *ed:* (MS) Math Ed, 1967, (BS) Early Scndry Ed, 1962- SUNY Geneseo; Several Wkshps & Mini Courses Rochester Inst of Technology & Comm Coll of the Finger Lakes; *cr:* Jr HS Math Teacher Penn Yan Cntrl 1962-65, Greece Schls 1965-66; HS Math Teacher Hammondsport Cntrl Sch 1966; Visiting Lecturer I Corning Comm Coll 1988; *ai:* Scndry Schlsp Comm & Class A Pass System Chairperson; Class Adv; Hammondsport Teachers Assn Treas 1972-75, NY St Assn Math Teachers, Kappa Delta Pi, NY Ed Assn; Yates Performing Arts Series Patron; Rochester Philharmonic Orch Mem; *office:* Hammondsport Cntrl Sch Main St Ext Hammondsport NY 14840

SHERMAN, MARY JO, Reading Teacher; *b:* Pontiac, IL; *m:* John R.; *ed:* (AB) Eng/Theatre, Millikin Univ 1963; (MA) Speech, S IL Univ 1967; *cr:* Teacher Eisenhower HS 1963-66, Warren Sch 1970-71, South HS 1971-77; Heaton Mid Sch 1978-; *ai:* Sch Newspaper Spon; Intnl Rdng Assn (Comm Chairperson 1990, Mid Sch Interest Group Pres 1990, Fiction Reviewer), Nila Banton Smith Awd 1987; Womens Life Festival Outstanding Woman in Ed 1988; Sch Dist 60 Outstanding Employee 1986; Article Published; Dist & Natl Rdng Stud Skills Consultant; Local, St, Regional, St Conference Presentations in Rdng & Mid Level Ed; *home:* 38 Robertson Rd Pueblo CO 81001

SHERMAN, RAMONA (PREWITT), Parent Educator; *b:* Pleasant Hill, MO; *m:* William Elmore; *c:* Jim, Cathy Sherman Spencer; *ed:* (BS) Bus Ed, 1955, (BS) Elem Ed, 1969 Cntrl MO St Univ; Early Chldhd Ed, Univ of MO Kansas City; Parent-Educator Trng MO Parents Prgm; *cr:* 1st Grade Classroom Teacher 1962-64, Kndgtn Classroom Teacher 1965-85, Parent Educator 1985- Pleasant Hill Sch; *ai:* Building Planning Comm 1988-; PTA 1962-, Lifetime Membership 1972; Alpha Delta Kappa 1984-; *office:* Pleasant Hill R-III Sch Eklund Dr Pleasant Hill MO 64080

SHERMER, RUTH DOBBINS, 7th & 8th Grade Math Teacher; *b:* Yadkinville, NC; *c:* Allen V. Jr., William P., David Nolson; *ed:* (BA) Primary Ed, Guilford Coll 1955; (MA) Mid Sch Ed, ASU 1983; NC Effective Teaching; Mentor Trng, TPAI Trng; *cr:* 3rd Grade Teacher Yadkinville Elem Sch 1955-56; Resource Teacher Raleigh City Schls 1957-59; 4th/5th Grade Teacher 1972-82, 6th-8th Grade Math/Sci Teacher 1982- Yadkinville Elem Sch; *ai:* Prins Advisory & Hospitality Comm; Math Counts Coach; Amer Math Competitions; Surry Comm Coll Area Coord 1979-85; Phys Fitness Instr SCC 1982-; NCAE Hospitality Comm; NEA; Yadkin Cty Bd of Adjustments 1979-; Yadkinville Presbyn Church Mem; Teacher of Yr 1988-89; Nominee for Presidential Awd Excl in Math 1988-89; Whos Who Amer Ed; Natl Reference Inst 1989-; *office:* Yadkinville Elem Sch PO Box 518 Yadkinville NC 27055

SHERMETTA, KATHLEEN E. (BARNA), 5th Grade Teacher; *b:* Allentown, PA; *m:* Steven C.; *c:* Steven M.; *ed:* (BS) Elem Ed, E Stroudsburg St Univ 1980; (MED) Elem Ed, Lehigh Univ 1985; *cr:* 4th-6th Grade Intermediate Teacher Fountain Hill Elem 1980-82; 5th Grade Teacher Governor Wolf Elem 1983-; *ai:* Safety Patrol Club Adv; Bethlehem Ed Assn, PA Ed Assn, NEA; *office:* Governor Wolf Elem Sch 1920 Butztown Rd Bethlehem PA 18017

SHERRARD, EDITH RANDAL, English Teacher/Director; *b:* Port Angelos, WA; *m:* Donald J.; *c:* Jean R., Kael G., Nathan K.; *ed:* (BA) Eng, 1958, (MA) Eng, 1969 Univ of WA; Fine Arts; Child Psych; *cr:* Classroom Teacher Public & Private Schls 1958-69; Founder/Dir/Eng Teacher Hillside Stu Cmmty 1969-; *ai:* Cmmty Service Projects; Writers Club; Conflict Resolutions; Creator of Values Centered Curr.

SHERRARD, JAMES GLEASON, Calculus/Physics Teacher; *b:* Waynesboro, VA; *ed:* (BA) Math, UMI 1965; (MAED) Phys Ed, UPI & SU 1990; *cr:* Teacher Hampton City Schls 1968-; *ai:* Math Honor Society; Odyssey of Mind; VA Cncl Teachers of Math 1980-; US Army Research Schlsp; NSF Grant for Excl in Teaching Physics; *office:* Phoebus HS 100 Ireland St Hampton VA 23663

SHERRILL, JEAN W. (WILLIAMS), Jr HS Teacher; *b:* Cleveland, OH; *m:* Thomas C.; *c:* Katrina, Nikki J.; *ed:* (BA) Eng/Ed, Upsala Coll 1970; (MA) Bus Management, Univ of Phoenix 1983; *cr:* 3rd-4th Grade Teacher Trinity Luth 1970-72; 7th Grade Teacher Dist 38 1972-73; 7th-8th Grade Teacher Christ Luth 1978-; *ai:* Vlybl & Sftbl Coach; St Mark Bd of Ed 1985-88; *office:* Christ Luth Sch 3901 E Indian Sch Rd Phoenix AZ 85018

SHERRILL, NANCY GOUCHER, Teaching Principal; *b:* Oklahoma City, OK; *m:* Don W.; *c:* Chris, Martha Sherrill Burge, Steve; *ed:* (BS) Elem Ed, OK St Univ 1955; *cr:* Teacher 1962-87, Teaching Prin 1987- Burbank Sch.

SHERRY, ELAINE CLAUDETTE, Sixth Grade Teacher; *b:* Los Angeles, CA; *c:* Joanne; *ed:* (BA) Speech/Music Minor-Cum Laude, Fresno St Coll 1971; Supplimentary Authorization Credential in Math 1990; *cr:* 5th/6th Grade Teacher/Highly Gifted Germain Street Sch 1972-73; CETA Teacher Delevan Drive Sch 1973-74, Atwater Avenue Sch 1974-75; CETA/ESL Teacher Lockwood Avenue Sch 1975-77; 5th/6th Grade Teacher Winchell Elem 1977-82, Robinson Elem 1982-; *ai:* Math Coach; Traffic Patrol Spon; Math Awd CA Math Cncl 1985; Session Speaker CA Math Cncl Conference 1984; Session Speaker Teachers Helping Teachers Conference 1990; RSP Assessor Panel Mem Master Plan Office 1984-85/1988-; *home:* 6192 N Benedict Ave Fresno CA 93711

SHERWOOD, LORNA JOYCE, 8th Grade Lit/Rdng Teacher; *b:* Chicago, IL; *m:* David G.; *c:* Natalie A., Lauren L.; *ed:* (BA) Elem Ed, AZ St Univ 1974; (MA) Rdng Ed, IL St Univ 1989; Jr Great Books Leader Trng 1985; Cooperative Learning Trng 1990; Becoming a Sch of Readers Trng at Center for Study of Rdng Univ of IL 1990; *cr:* 6th Grade Rdng/Sci Teacher Smith Mid Sch 1974-77; 5th-6th Grade Teacher Taylor Hicks Elem Sch 1977-78; 8th Grade Lit/Lang Art/Cmptr Prose/Phys Ed Teacher Georgetowne Mid Sch 1979-; *ai:* Young Author Coord; Natl Jr Honor Society Spon; Lang Art/Rdng Curr Dev; Vlybl Coach; At-Risk Prgm Dev; Summer Sch Teacher; IL Rdng Cncl 1980-82, 1989-; Beta Sigma Phi 1982-84; *office:* Georgetowne Mid Sch 51 Yates Rd Marquette Heights IL 61554

SHERWOOD, WILLIAM CURTIS, Fifth Grade Teacher; *b:* East Liverpool, OH; *m:* Narbirda Lynn Osborne; *c:* Bill, Brian; *ed:* Assoc Criminal Justice/General Stud, 1974, (BS) Elem Ed, 1977 Kent St Univ; (MS) Elem Ed/Rdng Specialist, Youngstown St Univ 1980; Working Towards EdS at Kent St Univ; *cr:* Infantry US Army 1966-68; General Laborer General Motors 1971-73, Amer Standard 1973-75; Park Ranger Cape Hatteras Natl Seashore Natl Parks 1988; Claims Examiner OH Bureau of Employment Services 1975-77; 5th Grade Teacher Orchard Hill Elem 1977-; *ai:* Jr HS Track Coach 1987-; Salem Cougars Bsktbl Coach Salem Parks & Recreation 1981-; NEA, OEA 1977-.

SHESTAK, JOAN CAROLE, 5th Grade Teacher; *b:* Brooklyn, NY; *ed:* (BSED) Elem Ed, Wagner Coll 1965; (MSED) Guidance/Counseling, Fordham Univ 1968; Grad Stud; *cr:* Teacher Public Sch 214 1965-68; Teacher 1969-, Mentor 1989-, Public Sch 26; *ai:* Stu Cncl Adv; Kappa Delta Pi 1968-; *office:* Billard Public Sch 26 Bldg 711 Governors Island NY 10004

SHEW, JANET BURKE, 2nd Grade Teacher; *b:* Cairo, IL; *m:* Robert Alan; *c:* Christopher A., Amy R.; *ed:* (BA) Elem Ed, SE MO St Univ 1958; (MA) Elem Ed, NE MO St Univ 1987; Grad Stud Math Ed with Piaget; *cr:* 2nd Grade Teacher, Kndgtn Teacher, Pre-Sch Teacher Ferguson-Florissant; 1st Grade Teacher Ladue; *ai:* NCTM, ASCD, Kappa Gamma Delta; United Meth; Teacher of Yr 1987.

SHEWMAKER, JOYCE A., Sci Dept Chm/Chemistry Teacher; *b:* Saint Joseph, MO; *ed:* (AA) Sci, Yavapai Coll 1974; (BS) Bio/Chem, Northern AZ Univ 1981; (MS) Botany, Northern AZ Univ 1987; Research in Cooperative Learn Ng; Wrkshps Assertive Discipline & READS; *cr:* Chem/Gen Sci Teacher Ashfork Public Schls 1979-80; Greenhouse Technician Northern AZ Univ 1980-83; Chem/Bio Teacher Red Mesa Unified Sch Dist 1983-85; Dept Chm/Chem Teacher Kayenta Unified Sch Dist 1985-; *ai:* Spon Natl Honor Society; Sch Improvement Comm; Phi Kappa Phi 1981-; Alpha Delta Kappa Historian 1986-; Nsta 1983-; Red Mesa Ed Assn Pres 1982-83; Kayenta Ed Assn Negotiator 1983-85; Navajo Reservation Teacher of Yr Awd 1983-84; Masters Thesis Fungal Consumption By the AZ Gray Squirrel 1987; *office:* Monument Valley H S Box 337 Kayenta AZ 86033

SHIBA, KATHERIN LYNN, Chapter I Teacher; *b:* Bay City, TX; *m:* William; *c:* Aaron, Ryan, Jeremy; *cr:* 4th Grade Teacher 1981-82, 4th/5th Grade Combination Teacher 1982-83 Sahuarita Elem; 3rd Grade Teacher Sopori Elem 1983-85; 3rd Grade Teacher 1985-87, Developmental 1st Grade Teacher 1987-

Sahurita Elem; *ai:* K-3rd Grade Target Teacher; Sci Curr Comm; NEA, Sahuarita Ed Assn 1988-; *office:* Sahuarita Elem Sch PO Box 26 Sahuarita AZ 85629

SHIBATA, KIRK MICHAEL, Mathematics Teacher; *b:* Basin, WY; *ed:* (BS) Math/Ed, Univ of WY 1984; *cr:* Math Teacher Nye Cty Sch Dist 1985-86; Advanced Placement Calc Teacher Victor Valley HS 1986-; *ai:* Golf & Jr Var Girls Vlybl Coach; *office:* Victor Valley HS 16500 Mojave Dr Victorville CA 92392

SHICKLE, LOUISE MARIE (GRUBE), Mathematics Teacher; *b:* Lancaster, PA; *m:* Richard C. Sr.; *c:* Denise J., Lisa M., Richard C. Jr., Martha F.; *ed:* (BA) Math, Dana Coll 1969; (MAT) Math, Univ of NE Lincoln 1975; Grad Stud; *cr:* Teacher US Army Ed Center 1970-73, Waynesboro Area HS 1976-80, James Wood HS 1982-; *ai:* Class Spon 1990; NCTM 1975-; VCTM, V2CTM; 1st United Meth Church; *office:* James Wood HS Rt 5 Box 700 Winchester VA 22601

SHIECK, ADRIENNE GRIFFIN, Science/Social Studies Teacher; *b:* Saginaw, MI; *m:* Gordon W.; *c:* Victoria, Valerie Machain, Jennifer; *ed:* (BA) Bio/Soc Sci, Univ of MI 1969; (MA) Sci Ed, Eastern MI Univ 1975; Curr/Admin, MI St Univ 1988; *cr:* Teacher Mt Morris Schls 1969-81; Prin Westfield Jr Acad 1982, Cedar Lake Elem 1983; Teacher E A Johnson HS 1983-; *ai:* NHS Adv, Amer Red Cross Adv, Project Outreach Adv; Close Up Washington/Europe Coord; ASCD 1986-88; Close Up Fnd 1983-Service Awd 1990; Amer Red Cross 1982- Service Awd 1987-89; Political Awareness Prgms for HS Stu Local, St, Natl & Intnl Levels Through Close Up Fnd; *office:* E A Johnsn Mem H S 8041 Neff Rd Mount Morris MI 48458

SHIELDS, ARBERTA EVELYN, Retired Teacher; *b:* Hillsboro, WV; *ed:* (BS) Elem Ed, Concord Coll 1960; *cr:* Classroom Teacher Buckeye, Frust, Huntersville; 1st Grade Teacher Hillsboro Elem; *ai:* WVEA 1954-.

SHIELDS, CHARLOTTE ANN, Fourth Grade Teacher; *b:* Wilmington, DE; *m:* Ron; *c:* Sean, Cornett; *ed:* (BA) Elem Ed, Univ Puget Sound 1964; *cr:* 1st Grade Teacher Westhill Elem 1964-66; 1st Grade Teacher Adak AK 1966-67; 1st Grade Teacher Crystal Springs Elem 1967-68; 1st-4th Grade Teacher Woodin Elem 1970-; *ai:* Dept Head/Grade Rep.

SHIELDS, ELNORA JOYNER, English Dept Chm/Teacher; *b:* Durham, NC; *c:* James, Jacqueline S. Griffin, Joy; *ed:* (BA) Eng, NC Central Univ 1958; (MED) Eng Ed, Duke Univ 1972; Univ of NC 1986; *cr:* Eng/Fr Teacher Hargrove HS 1958-59; Whitted Jr HS 1959-60; Eng Teacher Norfolk City Schls 1965-72; Jordan HS 1973-; *ai:* Spon Math-Sci Pre-College Prgm; Honor Society Advisory Comm; NC Eng Teachers Assn Pres 1986-87; NCTE 1958; NC Assn of Educators Pres Durham Cty 1977; Delta Sigma Theta Service 1954; Mellom Fellowship Teach Eng Univ of NC 1987; Natl Ctr for Humanities Grant Study at Humaniaties Inst 1987; Selected to Teach Governors Sch for Gifted and Talented 1976-85; *office:* C E Jordan H S 6806 Garrett Rd Durham NC 27707

SHIELDS, JOHN J., Teacher; *b:* Drexel Hill, PA; *c:* Katie, Sean; *ed:* (BS) Soc Sci, 1966, (MED) Soc Sci, 1971 Westchester St Coll; (MFA) Fine Art/Photography, Univ of DE 1981; Temple Univ Sch of Law; Oxford Univ; *cr:* Unionville Chaddsford Sch System 1966-70; Teacher Univ of DE 1979-81; Studio 53 Photography Studio 1979-83; Mainland Regional HS 1971-; *ai:* Stu Cncl; Surfing Team; Photography, Drama Clubs; Sch Newsletter; Gifted & Talented Prgm; Philosophy; Outstanding Young Educator Chester Cty 1968; Numerous Publications of Photographs & Awds Work on Display in NY Galleries; *office:* Mainland Regional HS Oak Ave Linwood NJ 08221

SHIELDS, KAREN KAY (SMITH), Elementary Principal; *b:* Roscoe, TX; *m:* William Francis; *c:* Robert D., Kari L., Wray F.; *ed:* (BS) Elem Ed, 1967, (MS) Elem Guidance/Counseling, 1971 Univ of NE Omaha; *cr:* 1st Grade Teacher Ralston Public Schls 1967-72; Pre-Sch Dir Plattsmouth Baptist Church 1976-88; 6th Grade Teacher 1980-88, Elem Prin 1988- Conestoga Public Schls; *ai:* Chapter I Dir; ASCD 1980-; NAEYC 1976-; NAESP 1988-; Conestoga Ed Assn (Past Pres, Negotiator); Joslyn Art Museum Artward Bound Speaker.

SHIERK, WILSON ANDREW, Principal; *b:* Kenosha, WI; *m:* Sylvia M. Schoettler; *c:* Rose Shierk Martin, Wilson A. III; *ed:* (BA) His/Scndry Ed, Dominican Coll 1960; (MS) Curr & Instruction, Univ of WI Milwaukee 1979; Admin License, Univ of WI Milwaukee; *cr:* Teacher Greenbay Road Sch 1960-74, Lance Jr HS 1975-87; Asst Prin Mc Kinley Jr HS 1987-88; Prin Whittier Elem Sch 1988-; *ai:* PDK 1984-; ASCD 1988-; Civic Parade Comm 1985-; Religious Ed Coord/Teacher 1983-; Church Cncl 1990-; Jr HS Teacher of Yr, KUSD No 1 Distinguished Service Awd 1986; *office:* Whittier Elem Sch 8542-31st Ave Kenosha WI 53142

SHIFFLETTE, MARJORIE JOAN B., 7th Grade English Teacher; *b:* Aiken, SC; *m:* Larry D.; *c:* Melissa, Laura; *ed:* (BS) Eng, Coll of Charleston 1961; Grad Work Univ of Ky, The Citadel, Coll of Charleston; *cr:* Teacher St Johns HS 1961-64, Harbor View Elem 1964-68, 1972-83, Fort Johnson Mid 1983-; *ai:* 7th Grade Essay & Speech Contests Spon; Palmetto St Teachers Organization 1987-; NEA 1964-86; Tri Delta Kappa 1987-; NCTE 1984-; Ft Johnson Mid Sch Teacher of Yr; Optimist Appreciation Awd; *office:* Fort Johnson Mid Sch 1825 Camp Rd Charleston SC 29412

SHIFLETT, BERNICE MC EACHERN, First Grade Teacher; *b:* Ellenton, GA; *m:* Wilburn Thomas; *c:* George, Vickie Parker; *ed:* (AA) Elem Ed, Norman Coll 1950; (BS) Elem Ed, Valdosta St Coll 1969; *cr:* 3rd Grade Teacher Ellenton Elem Sch 1951-57; 1st Grade Teacher Adel Elem Sch 1969-; *ai:* GAE 1969-80; PAGE 1982-; Adel Elem Teacher of Yr 1981; *office:* Adel Elem Sch 216 E 8th St Adel GA 31620

SHILAKES, CAROL H., Sixth Grade Teacher; *b:* Detroit, MI; *m:* J. Ronald; *c:* Christopher, Jessica; *ed:* (BA) Ed, Wayne St 1963; (MA) Ed Psych, Univ of MI 1965; *cr:* Teacher 1963-77, Acting Prin 1977-78 Livonia Public Schls; Teacher St Michael Sch 1978-63, St Joseph Sch 1963-; *ai:* Forensic Team Moderator; Academic Team Coach; W Morris Cty Gifted & Talented Consortium Mem; NJ Sci Teacher Assn, Cncl For Elem Sci Inter 1987-; NCEA 1980-; NJ Cncl on Ec Ed 1st Pl Elem Division 1988; St Elizabeth Seaton Awd 1987; Lions Club Grant Quest Drug Ed; *office:* St Joseph Sch 8 West Main St Mendham NJ 07945

SHIMABUKURO, GRACE KUO, 7th Grade Mathematics Teacher; *b:* Taipei, Taiwan; *m:* Donald T.; *c:* Kendall; *ed:* (BSEd) Scndry Math, NE MO St Teachers Coll 1967; Grad Stud Several Univs; *cr:* Math Teacher Scotland Cty RI Sch 1967-69, Paia Sch 1970, IAO Intermediate Sch 1970-; *ai:* Mathcount & Bridge Building Coach; Math Enrichment; *office:* IAO Intermediate Sch 1910 Kaohu St Wailuku HI 96793

SHIMKUS, MARJORIE MONSON, Retired Teacher; *b:* Nicollet, MN; *m:* Frank S.; *c:* Frank S., William M., Robert B.; *ed:* (BS) Elem, Mankato Univ 1973; Credits Toward Spec Ed Cert; *cr:* 1st-8th Grade Teacher Dist #32 Rural Sch 1940-43; 1st/2nd Grade Teacher St Peter Public Sch 1943-46; 1st Grade Teacher Hutchinson Public Sch 1946; Spec Ed Teacher 1967-72, 1st/4th Grade Teacher 1972-86 Richfield Public Sch; *ai:* Active in Cmmty Affairs, Church, Local Food Shelf VEAP; REA; *home:* 6845 Bloomington Ave Richfield MN 55423

SHIMODA-JUNG, ELAINE, Fifth Grade Teacher; *b:* Los Angeles, CA; *m:* Dennis; *c:* Corbin T.; *ed:* (BA) Child Dev, 1979, (MA) Elem Ed, 1983 CA St Univ Los Angeles; *cr:* 4th/5th Grade Teacher 1980-84, 5th Grade Teacher 1984- C C Carpenter Elem Sch; *ai:* Stu Cncl Adv; Spelling Bee Coach; Kappa Delta Pi 1983-; *office:* C C Carpenter Elem Sch 9439 Foster Rd Downey CA 90242

SHINHOLSTER, JAMES EDWARD, Science Teacher; *b:* Gordon, GA; *m:* Francis Z. Strange; *c:* James Jr.; *ed:* (BA) Elem Ed, KY St Univ 1980; *cr:* Teacher Twiggs Cty 1980-; *office:* Danville Elem Rt 1 Danville GA 31017

SHINKMAN, KAREN L., Math Teacher/Dept Chair; *b:* Scranton, PA; *ed:* (BS) Math, Mansfield Univ 1974; (MS) Research/Management, S CT St Univ 1980; Continuing Ed Prgms Design for Effective Instruction, Teacher Effectiveness, Stu Achievement, Clinical Supervision; Applications of Math Scndry Classroom Wkshp; *cr:* Teacher 1974-, Dept Chairperson 1985-Amity Regional Sr HS; *ai:* Advisory Comm on Teacher Evaluation; Curr Work in Applied Math, Cmptrs, Algebra II, Statistics; NCTM 1974-; Natl Cncl of Supvrs Math 1988-; CT Cncl of Supvrs Math 1989-; CT Assn of Teacers of Math 1985-; Assn of Supervision & Curr Dev 1985-; NEA 1974-, CT Ed Assn 1974-; Commission on Instruction, Prof Dev 1989-; Resolutions Comm 1989-; Nominee For Quinnipiac Coll Teacher of Yr 1987, Presidential Awd Excl in Sci & Math Teaching 1987; Coordinating K-12th Grade Implementation of New Math Curr Standards With Math Supvrs of 4 Sch Dists; *office:* Amity Regional Sr HS 20 Newton Rd Woodbridge CT 06525

SHINKO, ROSEMARY ELLEN, European History Teacher; *b:* Pittsburgh, PA; *m:* Kevin M. Bavolar; *c:* Nicholas A. Bavolar; *ed:* (BA) Speech/Poly Sci, Duquesne Univ 1977; (MA) Poly Sci, Duquesne Univ 1983, Seminars on Critical Thinking, Preparation of His Teaching, Advanced Placement European His 1989; *cr:* 7th/8th Grade Soc Stud/Lang Art Teacher St John The Baptist 1982-83; 5th-8th Grade Soc Stud/Geography Teacher St Francis 1983-84; Global Stud/European Cultures Teacher Good Counsel HS 1984-87; European His Teacher Sacred Heart Acad HS 1988-; *ai:* Academic Advisement Comm; Amer Poly Sci Assn 1980-; *office:* Sacred Heart Acad HS 265 Benham St Hamden CT 06514

SHINNERS, PAULA ELIZABETH BARNES, Jr HS Exceptional Ed Teacher; *b:* Buffalo, NY; *m:* Sean M.; *ed:* (BSED) Exceptional Ed, 1969, (MSED) Exceptional Ed, 1974 St Univ Coll of NY Buffalo; Certified Instr, Technologies for Creating DMA Inc; Working Towards Masters; *cr:* 3rd-6th Grade Exceptional Ed Teacher 1969-76, Resource Room Teacher 1976-78 Ford Fnd Demonstration Sch; Exceptional Ed Component to Teacher Corps 1976-78; Exceptional Ed Teacher Buffalo Acad for Visual/Performing Arts 1978-; *ai:* Buffalo Acad for Visual & Performing Arts Integration Concerns Comm Rep; NEA Mem, NY Ed Assn Mem 1969-; Buffalo Teachers Fed (Mem 1969-, Delegate 1975); Comm on Spec Ed Teacher Rep 1976-78; Childrens Hospital of Buffalo Volunteer Service 1980-84; Holy Angels Acad Alumnae Assn Mem Bd of Dir 1984-; Fellowship from St Univ Coll of NY; Study of Communication Problems of Mentally Retarded Awd 1970; *office:* Buffalo Acad 333 Clinton St Buffalo NY 14204

SHIPLETT, SUSAN TILLMAN, Chorus Teacher; *b:* Augusta, GA; *m:* David Wayne; *c:* Rachel, Brian Smith; *ed:* (BM) Music Performance, Augusta Coll 1974; Grad Work Univ of SC; *cr:* Organist Lake Park Baptist Church 1965-70, Crawford Avenue Baptist Church 1970-76; Chorus Teacher Glenn Hills HS 1974-76; Organist 1976-88, Trinity on the Hill United Meth Church Youth Choir Dir 1981-86; Chorus Teacher Evans HS 1986-; *ai:* Literary Competition Coord; Musical Dir for Yearly Spring Musicals; Coordinate & Prepare All Extra-Curricular Musical Act; GA Music Educators Assn, Prof Assn of GA Educators 1986-; MTNA 1989-; GA HS Assn 1987-; 1st Baptist Church Orch Pianist 1988-; *office:* Evans HS 4550 Cox Rd Evans GA 30809

SHIPLEY, CAROL MC NABNEY, Physical Education Teacher; *b:* Effingham, IL; *m:* John; *c:* Greg, Carla; *ed:* (BA) Phys Ed, 1965, (MS) Phys Ed, 1970 Ball St Univ; *cr:* Teacher Lowell HS 1965-66, Taft Jr HS 1966-; *office:* Taft Jr HS 1000 S Main St Crown Point IN 46307

SHIPLEY, CHRISTOPHER JON, 7-12th Grade Soc Stud Teacher; *b:* St Louis, MO; *m:* Marie Addudell; *c:* Joe Dee Whitaker, Hollie Whitaker, Nicholas, Anastasia, Nichol; *ed:* (BA) Soc Sci, CO St Univ 1972; (MA) Curr & Instruction, Univ of N CO 1978; *cr:* Soc Stud Teacher Strasburg Jr/Sr HS 1972-; *ai:* Soccer Ofcls Assn of CO HS VP 1988-; US Soccer Fed 1983-, St 1 Referee 1986-; *office:* Strasburg Jr/Sr HS Box 207 Strasburg CO 80136

SHIPLEY, MELODY LEA JACKSON, HS Mathematics Instructor; *b:* Endicott, NY; *m:* Jerry K.; *c:* Savannah, Jacob; *ed:* (BA) Math Ed, 1983, (MED) Ed, 1990 Mid-America Nazarene Coll; *cr:* Math Instr Gallatin HS 1983-84, Copeland HS 1985-86, Grundy R-V HS 1986-; *ai:* Sr Spon; Sr Class Play Dir; CTA 1986-; NCTM 1989-; Nazarene Church (Song Dir, Teen Dir, Bd Mem); Increased Stu Interest in Upper Level Math Courses; Successful Sr Plays; *office:* Grundy R-V HS P O Box 6 Galt MO 64641

SHIPLEY, PATRICIA K., Jr HS Language Arts Teacher; *b:* Corning, IA; *m:* Thomas A.; *c:* Kate; *ed:* (BS) Speech/Phys Ed, IA St Univ 1975; Grad Towards Masters NW MO St Univ Maryville; *cr:* Elem Phys Ed/Scndry Teacher Farragut Cmmty Schls 1975-80; Jr HS Lang Art Teacher Corning Cmmty Jr HS 1980-; *ai:* Jr HS Bsktbl, Track, Vlybl Coach; Inservice & Phase III Comms; IA St Ed Assn Exec Bd 1975-; NEA Bd of Dirs 1987-; PEO Sisterhood Guard 1983-; Villisca Theatre Inc Pres/Secy 1981-; Delta Kappa Gamma 1979-; NEA Dir for IA 1987-; Nom by Dist IA Teacher of Yr 1985; *office:* Corning Jr HS 10th & Washington Corning IA 50841

SHIPMAN, JUDY CAPEHART, High School Counselor; *b:* Tulsa, OK; *m:* Dale R.; *c:* Gregory; *ed:* (BS) Bus Ed, OK St Univ 1966; (MA) Prof Stud, Univ of Tulsa 1979; Numerous Courses; *cr:* Bus Teacher Broken Arrow HS 1967-68, Bixby HS; *ai:* Jr Class Spon; Bixby Ed Assn 1971-; OK Ed Assn, NEA 1967-; OK Sch Cncl Assn 1977-85; Phi Kappa Delta 1979-83; Pilot Club Secy 1980; 1st Baptist Church (Sunday Sch Teacher 1988-89, Bible Sch Teacher 1987-); *office:* Bixby HS P O Box 160 Bixby OK 74008

SHIPMAN, VERLA SUE, First Grade Teacher; *b:* Wister, OK; *c:* Karen Hasting, Kristie Morris, Billy; *ed:* (BA) Elem, Northeastern Coll 1959; Teaching.

SHIPP, FRANCUS RUTH, Biology/Physiology Teacher; *b:* Albertville, AL; *ed:* (AS) Phys Ed/Bio, Snead St Jr Coll 1980; (BS) Phys Ed/Bio, 1982, (MS) Phys Ed/Bio, 1986 Jacksonville St Univ; *cr:* Teacher Weaver HS 1982-; *ai:* Jr & Sr HS Vlybl, Sftbl Coach; Jr Class Spon; Peer Cnslr; SADD; Academic Letter Comm; Health Ed Assn of AL 1988-; ASAHPERD 1987-, AL Public Sch Health Educator of Yr 1988-89; AAHPERD 1988-; Outstanding Young Women of America 1984, 1985, 1988; Honorary Attorney General 1985; NE AL EMS Service Awd 1986; Teacher of Month Weaver HS 1988-; *office:* Weaver HS 917 Clairmont Dr Weaver AL 36277

SHIPP, NADINE H., Home Economics Teacher; *b:* Crossville, AL; *m:* Robert Byron; *c:* Gail Mc Callie, Stanley B.; *ed:* (BS) Voc Home Ec, Jacksonville Univ 1962; (MS) Family Living/Housing, Auburn Univ 1967; Univ of AL; *cr:* Home Ec Teacher Fyffe HS 1962-67; Home Service Adv S M Electric Cooperative 1967-70; Sci Teacher Fyffe Elem 1970-72; Home Ec Teacher Fyffe HS 1972-; *ai:* FHA Adv; DeKalb Cty Teachers Assn Delegate 1986-; Voc Teachers Assn Pres 1984-85; AL Home Ec Teachers Assn Pres 1985-86; Alpha Delta Kappa (Chaplain, Historian) 1984-86; Rainsville Sr Citizen Bd Mem 1989-; *home:* 131 Marhsall Rd NE Rainsville AL 35986

SHIPTON, SHARON MICHELLE, Business Teacher; *b:* Covina, CA; *m:* Russell; *c:* Sarah; *ed:* (BS) Bus Ed, UT St Univ 1986; *cr:* Bus Teacher Uintah HS 1986-; *ai:* FBLA Adv; Asst Vlybl Coach; PTSA Teacher Rep 1989; NBEA Mem, UT Bus Ed Assn Mem 1984-; AVA Mem 1989-; *office:* Uintah HS 1880 W 500 N Vernal UT 84078

SHIREY, MICHAEL R., Business Education Teacher; *b:* Coudersport, PA; *m:* Jill E. Stahlman; *c:* Lindsey, Jay, Nicholas; *ed:* (BS) Bus Ed/Accntng, Bloomsburg St Coll 1976; Grad Work Clarion Univ; *cr:* Bus Ed Teacher North Clarion HS 1976-; *ai:* Girls Var Track & Field & Girls Jr HS Bsktbl Coach; North Clarion Ed Assn Treas 1976-; PA St Ed Assn Chm Cty Bargaining 1976-; NEA 1976-; Clarion Lions Club 1983-89; Immaculate Conception Church Lector 1981-; North Clarion HS Initial Lead Teacher Rep; Nom Thanks to Teachers Natl Recognition Prgm; Franklin Life Insurance & Scholastic Coach Magazine Select Circle of Coaches Honoree; *office:* North Clarion Cty Jr/Sr HS RD 1 Box 194 Tionesta PA 16353

SHIRING, MARK A., Fifth Grade Teacher; *b:* Butler, PA; *m:* Debra Taggart; *c:* Kristyn, Adam; *ed:* (BS) Elem Ed, Slippery Rock Univ 1976; (MA) Curr Ed, Univ of S FL 1981; *cr:* Remedial Rdng Instr Grove City Schls 1977-78; 5th Grade Teacher Wauchula Elem Sch 1978-82, Enterprise Elem Sch 1982-; *ai:* Stu Cncl Assn & Sch Newspaper Spon; Grade Level Chm; Enterprise

Advisory Cncl Mem; VEA Mem 1982-; VA Adv Stu Cncl Assm Mem 1984-; 5th Grade Presentation Taming of Shrew Dir 1987; *office:* Enterprise Elem Sch 13900 Lindendale Rd Woodbridge VA 22193

SHIRLEY, ANN CERRA, 6th Grade Teacher; *b:* Wichita Falls, TX; *c:* Charlie; *ed:* (AS) Elem Ed, MS Gulf Coast Comm Coll 1970; (BS) Elem Ed, 1972, (MS) Rdng, 1973 Univ of S MS; Additional Coursework Higher Cert, Univ of GA; *cr:* 6th Grade Teacher Biloxi Sch Dist 1973-75; Rdng Specialist Newton Cty Schls 1975-80; 6th-7th Grade Teacher Biloxi Sch Dist 1980-; *ai:* SADD Spon; 7th Grade Stus Fundraising Drive Vietnam Veterans Memorial; Phi Theta Kappa Alumni 1988-; Cub Scouts Asst Den Leader 1981-, Participation 1983; Ocean Springs Little League Treas 1989-; Univ S MS Fellowship for Grad Stud 1973; *home:* 234 Woodland Cir Ocean Springs MS 39564

SHIRLEY, GEORGE RUSSELL, JR., Teacher; *b:* Atlanta, GA; *m:* Jessica Yvette Good; *ed:* (BA) Inter Disciplinary Stud/ Sociology/His/Bible, Covenant Coll 1977; Teaching Cert Scndry Ed/Math, 1983, (MED) Math, 1989 GA St Univ; *cr:* Teacher Morrow HS 1983-, Eagles Landing HS 1990; *ai:* Spon Jr Var Math Team; GA Cncl of Teachers of Math, NCTM 1983-; Clayton Cmmty Church Choir 1990; Morrow HS Teacher of Month Crystal Apple Awd 1990.

SHIRLEY, JO ANNE COAKLEY, Fourth Grade Teacher; *b:* Arlington, VA; *m:* Brian Douglas; *c:* Tanner F., Brian M., Anna E.; *ed:* (BA) Elem Ed, James Madison Univ 1968; Grad Work in Rdng Ed; *cr:* 1st Grade Teacher Middlebrook Elem Sch 1968-70; 2nd Grade Teacher Riverheads Elem Sch 1970-73; 4th Grade Teacher Ladd Elem Sch 1976-; Interpreter Museum of Amer Frontier Culture 1987-; *ai:* Teacher for Pilot LIFT Prgm; Bethany Luth Church Dir of Chrstn Ed 1987-; Museum of Amer Frontier Culture Founding Mem 1985-; *home:* 609 Meadowview Cove Waynesboro VA 22980

SHIRLEY, RUBY THOMAS, Fourth Grade Teacher; *b:* Glasgow, KY; *w:* Morris Lane (dec); *c:* Thomas Lane, Joey J.; *ed:* (BS) Elem Ed, 1969, (MA) Elem Ed, 1974 W KY Univ; Rank I W KY Univ; *cr:* Teacher Edmonton Elem Sch; *ai:* NEA, KY Ed Assn, Metcalfe Cty Ed Assn; *home:* 202 Rogers St Edmonton KY 42129

SHIRLEY, SHARON ELIZABETH, Math Department Chair; *b:* Salt Lake City, UT; *m:* Thomas Bernard; *c:* David, Jeffery; *ed:* (BA) Elem Ed, W NM Univ 1971; Bi-ling TESOL Prgm; *cr:* 1st/ 2nd/4th/6th Grade Teacher Jordan Sch Dist 1973-81; Mid Sch Core Teacher 1981-82, Math Teacher 1982-84, Math Dept Chairperson 1984- Oquirrh Hills Mid Sch; *ai:* VIE Chm; Faculty Advisory, Career Ladder, 9th Grade Spec Awds Comm; UEA, JEA, NEA 1973-83; Cmmty Cncl Educl Officer 1987-88; Teacher of Yr 1988-89; *office:* Oquirrh Hills Mid Sch 12949 S 2700 W Riverton UT 84065

SHIROMA, JOEL ISAMI, 8th Grade Teacher; *b:* Kula, HI; *m:* Crystal; *ed:* (BED) Scndry Ed/Math, 1985, (PD) Scndry Ed/ Math, 1987 Univ of HI; *cr:* 8th Grade Math Teacher Aliamanu Intermediate 1985-; *ai:* Bsktbl & Vlybl Coach; Math Club Adv; *office:* Aliamanu Intermediate Sch 3271 Salt Lake Blvd Honolulu HI 96818

SHISLER, RICHARD LEE, Eighth Grade Teacher; *b:* Delaware, OH; *ed:* (BA) Philosophy/Latin, Carroll Coll 1958; (MS) Elem Ed, Univ of Dayton 1982; *cr:* Instr Carroll Coll 1976-81; Teacher St Mary Sch 1964-; Prin St Anthony Sch 1990; *ai:* Sch Newspaper the Action, Sch Safety Patrol; Sch & City Spelling Bee Adv; Organist for All-Sch Liturgies; NCEA 1964-; Selected Leaders of Amer Elem & Scndry Ed 1971; *office:* St Mary Schl 66 E William St Delaware OH 43015

SHIVE, JANICE MONGER, 6th Grade Teacher; *b:* Tulsa, OK; *m:* Frank; *c:* Matthew Creason; *ed:* (BA) Elem/Spec Ed, NEOSU 1977; Admin, Central St Univ; *cr:* HS EMH/LD Teacher Gentry HS 1977-78; Spec Ed EMH Teacher 1978-80, 2nd Grade Teacher 1980-88, 6th Grade Teacher Mc Loud Intermediate Sch 1988-; *ai:* OK Ed Assn; OK Rdng Cncl; *office:* Mc Loud Intermediate Sch P O Box 40 Mc Loud OK 74851

SHIVELEY, M. SCOTT, Biology Teacher; *b:* Rochester, PA; *ed:* (BS) Bio, Geneva Coll 1965; (MAT) Zoology/Physiology, Miami Univ of OH 1971; Univ of Pittsburgh, Kent St Univ; *cr:* Bio Teacher Sandusky HS 1965-66; Bio I/II Teacher Boardman HS 1966-; *ai:* NEA, OEA; Local Showings Sculpture Artist; *office:* Boardman HS 7777 Glenwood Ave Boardman OH 44512

SHIVELY, ANN HAWKINS, Assistant Principal; *b:* Louisville, KY; *m:* Walter B.; *c:* Christian; *ed:* (BA) Eng, W KY 1976; (MA) Scndry Ed, IN Univ 1983; *cr:* Teacher Evangel HS 1979-82/ 1986-88; Asst Prin/Cnslr Evangel Chrstn Sch 1988-; *ai:* Alumni Dir; Stu Cncl, Yrbk, Sr Class Spon; NCTE 1975-; *office:* Evangel Chrstn Sch 5400 Minors Ln Louisville KY 40219

SHIVER, MISSY CHESTER, Business Teacher; *b:* Boonton, NJ; *m:* Michael Lamar; *ed:* (BBA) Bus Ed, Valdosta St Coll 1980; (MED) Bus Ed, Albany St Coll 1989; *cr:* Bus Teacher Irwin Cty HS 1980-81, Washington-Wilkes Comprehensive HS 1981-84; Bus Instr James Coll 1984-85; Bus Ed Teacher Middleburg HS 1985-86, Lee Cty HS 1987-; *ai:* FBLA & Sr Class Spon; Grievance Comm Mem; Soc Comm Mem; GA Bus Ed Assn Dist Dir 1989-; NEA, GAE; LAE Secy 1988-89; Lee Cty Assn of Ed; FBLA Region I Adv of Yr 1990; *home:* 2030 W Broad Ave #80 Albany GA 31707

SHIVERS, JANICE POLK, High School Principal; *b:* Biloxi, MS; *m:* James Harold; *c:* Jamey, Veronica; *ed:* (BS) Elem Ed, 1967; (MS) Elem Ed/Remedial Rdg, 1968 USM; Specialist Elem Ed/Scndry Admin/Elem Admin, William Carey Coll 1975; Above Specialist Degree in Advanced Ed; *cr:* Elem Teacher Prentiss 1970-76; Instr Jones Cty Comm Coll 1969; 9th Grade Teacher Bassfield HS 1976-; Elem Teacher Sumrall Elem 1977-83; Teacher 1984-85, Prin 1985-86 Sumrall Jr HS; Prin Sumrall HS 1986-; *ai:* Spon HS Chrldr; Staff Dev Comm; Cty 5 Yr Plan Comm; Cty Discipline Comm; Delta Kappa Gamma, MS Assn of Scndry Admin; MS Assn of Scndry Sch Prin; Bassfield Baptist Church Organist 1970-; *home:* Rt 2 Box 232 Bassfield MS 39421

SHOAF, JOSEPH BERNARD, Soc Studies Teacher/Dept Head; *b:* Connellsville, PA; *m:* Dolores Jean Zagursky; *c:* Joseph M., Michael G.; *ed:* (BS) Ed, CA St Univ 1957; (MA) Ed, WV Univ 1961; *cr:* 7th-8th Grade Teacher/Prin Colebrook Elem 1957-62; Soc Stud Teacher/Coach Grand Valley Local 1962-67; Prin HS Ledgemont Local 1967-72; Soc Stud Teacher Grand Valley Local 1972-; *ai:* Sr Class Adv; NEA, OEA; Grand Valley Ed Assn (Pres, Pres Elect); Church Act; Chamber of Commerce; *office:* Grand Valley H S 44 N School St Orwell OH 44076

SHOAT, WILLIAM RICHARD, Junior High Sci/P E Teacher; *b:* St Louis, MO; *m:* Carol Ballard; *c:* Alan Wade, Richard Lynn; *ed:* (BSE) Phys Ed, AR St Univ 1961; Bio/Health/Recreation/ Drivers Ed; *cr:* Class Room Teacher 1967-, Jr HS Bsktbl Coach EasT Carter R-2 Sch 1967--78; Jr/Sr HS Coach Risco R-2 Sch 1960-67; *ai:* Drug Ed Comm; Jr HS/Sr HS Bus Driver & Chaperone for Athletics; Career Ed Ladder; MO ST Teachers Assn 1960-; Class Room Teachers Assn 1980-; Risco Kiwanis Club 1960-67; BSA Pack Leader 1960-65; 4-H Troop Leader 1972-75; *home:* Rt 1 Box 49 Ellsinore MO 63937

SHOBE, CHARLES LEE, JR., 7th Grade Lang Art Teacher; *b:* Hampton, VA; *m:* Carol Ann Butzher; *ed:* (BS) Eng, E Carolina Univ 1963; *cr:* Teacher Hampton City Schls 1963-; *ai:* HEA, VEA, NEA Mem; 1st Series of Fiction Published.

SHOCK, CHERYL HOLT, Sixth Grade Teacher; *b:* Helena, AR; *m:* Bobby Jr.; *c:* Jonathan Bradley; *ed:* (BSE) Early Chldhd Ed, Univ of Cntrl AR 1978; *cr:* Kndgtn Teacher Little Rock AFB Elem 1978-79; 5th Grade Teacher 1979-83; 6th Grade Teacher 1988- Mt Vernon; *ai:* AR Ed Assn, NEA 1988-; *office:* Mt Vernon Sch P O Box 118 Mount Vernon AR 72111

SHOCKEY, MARK BRUCE, American Cultures Teacher; *b:* Waynesboro, PA; *m:* Bonnie Lee Hess; *c:* Lisa, Matthew; *ed:* (BS) Soc Stud, 1962, (MS) Soc Stud, 1967 Shippensburg Univ; *cr:* Soc Stud Teacher Palmyra Area Sch Dist 1962-63, Waynesboro Area Sch Dist 1963-; *ai:* NEA, PA St Ed Assn, Waynesboro Area Ed Assn; Held Local Elected Office within Democratic Party; *office:* Waynesboro Mid Sch 702 E 2nd St Waynesboro PA 17268

SHOCKEY, RITA LYNNE SMITH, Second Grade Teacher; *b:* Hugo, OK; *m:* Jerry Dewayne; *c:* Chay D., Clacy L.; *ed:* (BA) Elem Ed, 1977, (MS) Stan/Rdng Specialist, 1982 SE OK St Univ; *cr:* 2nd Grade Teacher Rattan Elem 1977-; *ai:* Booster Club; Summer League Ball; OK Educl Assn, NEA 1977-; Rattan Assn Classroom Teacher; DKG 1982-85.

SHOEMAKER, A. T., JR., 6th Grade Teacher; *b:* Breckenridge, TX; *m:* Joy Dale Ritchie; *c:* Sharon K. Tischer, Randy; *ed:* (BA) Elem Ed, 1955, (MED) Elem Ed, 1963 Northeast LA Univ; Cert Guidance Cnslr, Auburn Univ; *cr:* 5th-7th Grade Teacher Winnsboro LA 1955-66; 6th Grade Teacher/Cnslr/Prin Vidalia LA 1966-70; 6th Grade Teacher Spring Valley Elem 1970-78, Bowie Elem 1978-; *ai:* Math Team Coach; RATPE Secy 1978-79; TX St Teacher Assn 1970-; PTA Teacher Rep Life Mem 1984-85; *office:* Bowie Elem Sch 7643 La Manga Dr Dallas TX 75248

SHOEMAKER, CANDACE L., 4th/5th Grades Gifted Teacher; *b:* Allentown, PA; *m:* Scott E.; *c:* Tracey, Cristian, Adam; *ed:* (BS) Elem Ed, VCU 1979; *cr:* Teacher Greenfield Elem 1980-83, Swift Creek Elem 1983-89; Gifted Prgm Teacher Hening Elem 1989-; *ai:* Gifted Prgm Planning Comm; Gifted Rep Cty Meetings; VA Assn for Ed of Gifted 1980-; VA St Rdng Assn 1989-; Whos Who in Amer Ed 1989-; *home:* 14203 Long Gate Rd Midlothian VA 23112

SHOEMAKER, LINDA L., Director of Bands; *b:* Bell, CA; *ed:* (BS) Music, Univ NV-Reno 1965; (MS) Music Ed, CW Post Center of Long Island Univ 1973; Sch Admin CW Post; *cr:* Elem Band Woodbury Ave & Flower Hill Schls 1967-71; Asst Dir Huntington HS 1969-79; Dir of Bands J Taylor Finley Jr HS 1971-82, Huntington HS 1982-; *ai:* Marching Band; Jazz Ensemble; Wind Ensemble; Pit Orch; MENC 1967-; NYSSMA 1967-; SCMEA 1967-; Long Island Sunrisers Sr Drum & Bugle Corp 1979-; The Huntington HS Blue Devil Band Won Long Island Championship Tournament of Bands; Rep NY St Tournament of Roses Parade 1989; *office:* Huntington H S Oakwood And Mckay Rds Huntington NY 11743

SHOEMAKER, MATTHEW L., 5th-12th Grade Band Director; *b:* Cincinnati, OH; *m:* Diane L. Owen; *c:* Jennifer, Jeff; *ed:* (BM) Music Ed, Miami Univ 1980; Summer Classes, Univ of Dayton; *cr:* 5th-12th Grade Asst Band Dir Middletown City Schls 1980; 5th-12th Grade Band Dir Perry Local Schls 1980-85, Preble Shawnee Local Schls 1985-; *ai:* Marching & Pep Bands; Asst Musical Dir; OMEA, MENC 1980-; Masonic Lodge, Scottish Rite 1989-; *office:* Preble Schawnee Local Schls 5495 Somers-Gratis Rd Camden OH 45311

SHOEMAKER, RACHEL JOANN, Art Teacher; *b:* Hagerstown, MD; *c:* Ashley; *ed:* (BA) Art Ed, Shepherd Coll 1983; *cr:* Itinient Art Teacher Paw Paw Elem/Jr/Sr HS & Gt Cacapon Elem Sch & Greenwood Elem Sch & Pleasant View Elem Sch 1984-87; Art Teacher Natural Bridge Mid/HS 1987-; *ai:* Art Club, Jr Class & Jr Var Cheerleading Spon; *home:* Rt 1 Box 196A Buena Vista VA 24416

SHOEMAKER, THOMAS DAVID, Math Teacher/Computer Coord; *b:* Plainwell, MI; *m:* Tonda Sue Boothby; *c:* Jesse R., Lexis P., Wyatt A.; *ed:* (BA) Bus Ed, Western MI Univ 1970; Math Reserve Teacher-Trng Through Mid Sch Math Project & Western MI Unv; *cr:* Math Teacher Hartford Pub Schls 1971-; Classroom Teacher-1978-83, Career Exploration Prgm Instr 1984- Van Buren Inst Sch Dist; *ai:* Mid Sch Ftbl Coach; Dist Rep RCCMCREG; Mid Sch Math Club; Hartford HS/Mid Sch Ski Club Spon; Chm Prgm & Personnel Evaluation Comm Dist Citizens; MCTM 1981-; NCTM 1989-; Presbyterian Church (Deacon Elder) 1986-88 & 1980; Explorer Post #195; *office:* Hartford Mid Sch 141 School St Hartford MI 49057

SHOEMAN, DIANE WALLSCHLAG, Science Teacher; *b:* Newark, NJ; *m:* Larry P.; *c:* Christopher, David; *ed:* (BS) Ag, Univ of FL 1978; Physics, FL Atlantic Univ, Univ of Cntrl FL; *cr:* Ag Teacher Lake Weir Mid Sch 1978-80; Sci Teacher John I Leonard HS 1981-85, Palatka HS 1985-; *ai:* Stu Cncl Spon; SAC Steering Comm; FL Assn Sci Teachers 1981-; Putnam Cty Recycling Educl Consultant; FL Doe Summer Honors Sci Symposium; *office:* Palatka HS 302 Mellon Rd Palatka FL 32177

SHOFNER, REBECCA LEE, Choral Teacher/Music Chair; *b:* New Orleans, LA; *m:* Cecil Monroe; *c:* Michael, Del, Laura; *ed:* (BMED) Music Ed, Univ of S MS 1967; (MS) Music Ed, Troy St Univ 1987; Cert Admin, Troy St Univ; *cr:* Choral Teacher Theodore HS 1968, John Shaw HS 1969, Bellingrath Jr HS 1970-71; Music Teacher Head Elem 1980-84; Choral Teacher Brewbaker Jr HS 1984-; *ai:* Music Appreciation Club Spon; Music Dept Chm; Inservice Comm; AL PTA Mem 1987-88, St Teacher of Yr 1987-88, Outstanding Teacher of Yr 1987; AL Vocal Assn Mem, MENC Mem 1984-; 2 Coll Review Teams St Dept of Ed; *office:* Brewbaker Jr HS 4425 Brewbaker Dr Montgomery AL 36116

SHOOK, BRUCIE ANNE PARCELL, Media Specialist; *b:* Statesville, NC; *m:* David H.; *c:* Alex D., Amy K.; *ed:* (BA) His, 1966, (MLS) Lib Sci, 1981 Univ of NC Greensboro; *cr:* Eng/Soc Stud Teacher Summerfield Sch 1966-67, Mendenhall Jr HS 1967-68; Walhalla Jr HS 1968-69; Civics/US His Teacher Walhalla Sr HS 1969-70; Eng/Soc Stud Teacher Mendenhall Jr HS 1970-71; 4th-6th Grade Media Specialist Mt Zion Sch 1982-84; 7th/8th Grade Lang Art/Soc Stud/Teacher of Gifted & Talented Aycock Jr HS 1984-86; 6th-8th Grade Media Specialist Mendenhall Mid Sch 1986-; *ai:* Sch Amer Ed Week & Sch Media Advisory Comm Chairperson; Readers Academy Club Co-Adv; ALA, AASL, NEA, NCAE, NCLA, Greensboro Assn of Sch Librarians Secy 1990; Habitat for Hum Chm Family Selection Comm 1987-; *office:* Mendenhall Mid Sch 205 Willoughby Dr Greensboro NC 27408

SHOOK, DENISE EGGLESTON, Assistant Principal; *b:* New York City, NY; *c:* Tamiko, Keisha; *ed:* (BS) Sociology/Ed, Lehman Coll NYC 1974; (MS) Elem Ed, Hunter Coll NYC 1979; Mem of Super Center NYC; *cr:* K-6th Grade Teacher 1974-, 3rd-6th Grade Admin Resource Teacher, 3rd-5th Grade Teacher Asst Prin 1974- P S 9 Sch; *ai:* Mem of Plan to Read Center for Educl Leadership & CSIP; Bronx Rdng Cncl, NYC Assn of Asst Prin; Mem of Super Center NYC 1988-; NYC Admin Women in Ed Certificate of Merit 1990; *office:* PS 9 Sch E 183rd & Ryer Ave Bronx NY 10458

SHOOP, SCOTT LANE, English Department Chair; *b:* Riverton, WY; *m:* Carma Milliner; *c:* Madison C., Carson J.; *ed:* (BA) Scndry Eng Ed, AZ St Univ 1985; *cr:* 9th-12th Grade Eng Teacher New Castle HS 1985-89; Eng Dept Chair Chino Valley HS 1989-; *ai:* NCA Steering Comm; Stu Cncl Adv; Speech & Drama Coach; Asst Bsktbl Coach; Curr Comm Chair; WY Assn of Eng Teachers, NCTE 1985-89; AZ Assn of Eng 1989-; NAASP 1985-; *office:* Chino Valley HS Box 225 Chino Valley AZ 86323

SHOPE, GLORIA DZIEWIATEK, Foreign Language Teacher; *b:* Passaic, NJ; *m:* Randolph; *c:* David, Ryan; *ed:* (BA) Fr/Scndry Ed, Caldwell Coll 1970; Certificat D Etudes Francaises, Universite De Poitiers Tours France; *cr:* Fr Teacher Paterson Cath Regional HS 1970-74; Fr/Span Teacher Pope John XXIII Regional HS 1983-; *ai:* Peer Leader Coord; BSA Career Awareness Exploring Unit Adv; *office:* Pope John XXIII Regional HS 28 Andover Rd Sparta NJ 07871

SHORES, ELAINE MARIE, Phys Ed Teacher/Coach; *b:* Pensacola, FL; *ed:* (BS) Sports Sci, Univ of W FL 1983; *cr:* Teacher/Coach Booker T Washington HS 1985-; *ai:* Girls Jr Var Bsktbl Coach; Girls Var Bsktbl & Girls Track Asst; Potential Academic Winners Spon; Drop Out Prevention Teacher; FL Athletic Coaches Assn 1987-; Asst Coach Girls Bsktbl St Championship Team, Twice 2nd Place Finishers; *office:* Booker T Washington HS 6000 College Pkwy Pensacola FL 32504

SHORT, CARLEEN LUCKE, Seventh & Eighth Grade Teacher; *b:* Lima, OH; *m:* George S.; *c:* Daniel; *ed:* (BS) Elem Ed, OH St Univ 1974; *cr:* 5th/6th Grade Teacher St Rose Sch 1974-77; 4th-6th Grade Teacher St Catherine Sch 1977-80; 3rd Grade Teacher St Joseph Sch 1980-83; 4th/7th/8th Grade Teacher St Mary Sch 1984-; *ai:* Stu Cncl Adv; Curr Dev; Sci Fair Comm; Lib Coord; *office:* St Mary Sch 34516 Michigan Ave Wayne MI 48184

SHORT, JAMES B., Science Teacher; *b:* Defiance, OH; *ed:* (BS) Ag/Fisheries Mgmt, OH St Univ 1973; Teacher Cert Defiance Coll; Continuing Ed OH St Univ/Univ of Toledo; Basic & Facilitator Trng From Cmmty Intervention; *cr:* Sci/Cmptr Teacher Gorham Fayette HS 1974-; *ai:* Chm of Local Sci Fair; Cmptr Challenge Team Coach; Class Adv; Sci Ed Cncl Of OH; OH Acad of Sci; North Dist OH Cncl Mem, Chm Of Special Awds 1980-; US Jaycees Bryan Chapter VP, Treas, Dir; Fayette Care Team Chm 1988; OH Teacher Grant 1981; 4 Eisenhower Sci/Math Grants 1989; Governors Awd for Outstanding Youth Opportunities In Sci 1985-89; Tandy Technology Scholar/Teacher Awd 1985-89; *office:* Gorham-Fayette HS Eagle St Fayette OH 43521

SHORT, JAMES LESTER, Mathematics Teacher; *b:* Bulawayo, Zimbabwe; *m:* Carol Stein; *c:* Aidan, Kathryn; *ed:* (BA) Math, 1973, (MS) Math, 1975 S IL Univ; Educl Admin, Univ of CA Santa Barbara; *cr:* Chm Math Dept Marlborough HS Zimbabwe 1979-81, Villanova Preparatory Sch 1982-87; Math Teacher Hueneme HS 1987-; *ai:* Stu Achievement & Peer Networking Comm; Boys Var Soccer Coach; NCTM Mem 1979-84; AFT Mem 1987-; ASCD Mem 1989-; Church of Christ Minister 1972-; Church Youth Camps Dir 1980-82; Asst Examiner, ZCE Exam Zimbabwe 1981; Math Fellowship, SIU-C 1973-75; UC Regents Schlsp, UCSB 1987-88; *office:* Hueneme HS 500 Bard Rd Oxnard CA 93033

SHORT, KAREN LEE (GUNTER), Third Grade Teacher; *b:* Welch, WV; *m:* Bert III; *c:* Kristy, Rachelle; *ed:* (BS) Elem Ed, Concord Coll 1980; (MA) Speech Comm, WV Univ 1983; Working Towards Masters; *cr:* 1st Grade Teacher Coal Mountain Grade Sch; 3rd Grade Teacher Berlin Mc Kinney Grade Sch; *ai:* WVEA (Mem, Building Rep); NEA.

SHORT, LINDA BLACKWOOD, Social Studies Teacher; *b:* Quincy, IL; *m:* Ed; *c:* Sarah, Jim; *ed:* (BA) Soc Stud Ed, Univ of IL Urbana-Champaign 1969; Ed, Univ of IL 1970; His, 1971; Music, 1974 Western IL Univ; Math, Carl Sandburg Coll 1986; *cr:* Jr & Sr HS Soc Stud Teacher Payson HS 1969-70; 7-8th Grade Soc Stud Teacher Warsaw Elem Sch 1970-; *ai:* Warsaw Classroom Pres 1981-82; Teachers Assn 1989-; IEA-NEA; Order of Eastern Star; Trinity United Meth Church Choir Dir 1970-; *office:* Warsaw Jr HS S 11th St Warsaw IL 62379

SHORT, MARGARET CAROL, English Teacher; *b:* Milford, DE; *ed:* (MA) Ed, DE St Coll 1987; (BA) Eng, Univ of SC 1968; *cr:* Eng Teacher Milford HS 1979-; *ai:* Milford HS Class of 1993 Adv; DE Assn Teachers of Eng, Natl Assn Teachers of Eng Mem 1989-; Univ of SC Alumni Assn 1989-; *office:* Milford HS 1019 N Walnut St Milford DE 19963

SHORT, PEGGY MINGLE, Jr High Reading Teacher; *b:* Ridgely, TN; *m:* Olen; *c:* Shannon Hogg, Robert D.; *ed:* (BS) Ed, Univ of TN 1969; *cr:* Jr HS Lang Arts Teacher 1969-84; 5th Grade Jr HS Teacher 1984-85 Hornbeak Elem; Rdng Teacher Black Oak Elem 1985-; *ai:* Scorekeeper Bsktbl; Delta Kappa Gamma Society 1989; Obion Cty Ed Assn 1989-; West TN Rdng Assn 1989-; Outstndg Teacher of Yr 1989; *home:* Rt 1 Box 232 C Hornbeak TN 38232

SHORT, ROBERT CHARLES, 7th/8th Grade Health Teacher; *b:* Cleveland, OH; *m:* Joyce June Deuel; *c:* Robert Jr., Shari; *ed:* (BS) Phys Ed, W MI Univ 1977; *cr:* Teacher Dowagiac Union Schls 1977-; *ai:* Veterans of Foreign Wars Trustee; *office:* Central Mid Sch 206 Main St Dowagiac MI 49047

SHORTHAIR, BETTY BARLOW, Business Teacher; *b:* Tuba City, AZ; *m:* Norman; *c:* Vanessa, Lynn, Amy, Warren, Norma; *ed:* (BS) Bus Ed, Coll of Ozarks 1973; (MA) Voc Ed, N AZ Univ 1984; *cr:* Bus Teacher Tuba City HS 1973-74, 1975-84, Shonto Boarding Sch 1985-87, Page HS 1987-; *ai:* Page Intercultural Club Spon 1988-; Page FBLA Spon 1989-; Tuba City Commerce Club, Chrldr, Upward Bound Spon; 9th-11th Grade Spon 1974-84; *office:* Page HS PO Box 1927 Page AZ 86040

SHORTT-ROSS, ANN BURNETTE, Spanish Teacher; *b:* Maysville, KY; *m:* Kenneth Forman; *c:* Joshua Shortt; *ed:* (AA) Liberal Arts Stephens CoIL 1966; (BA) Span/Eng, 1968, (MA) Span Lang/Lit 1972 E KY Univ; Teacher Cert, Brescia Coll 1975; Grad Stud Rdng, W KY Univ 1985; *cr:* Eng/Rdng Instr Univ of KY 1972-74; Span Teacher Owensboro HS 1975-77; Lit/Eng Instr Owensboro Jr Coll 1979-84; Span/Eng Teacher Owensboro Cath HS 1984-88; Span Teacher Mason Cty HS 1988-; *ai:* Yrbk Adv Owensboro Cath HS 19884-87, Mason Cty HS 1989; Pep Club Spon Owensboro Cath HS 1988; Faculty Adv to Stu Government & Act Owensboro Jr Coll 1981-84; Foreign Lang Club Spon Owensboro HS 1975-77, Mason Cty HS 1988-; KY Ed Assn 1975-77, 1988; NEA 1975-77, 1988; Natl Cncl of Foreign Lang Teachers 1988-; Prof Bus Womens Assn 1982-84; Limestone Jaycees 1988-; Outstndng Spon Stu E KY Univ 1968; Teaching Fellowship E KY Univ 1970-72; Sigma Delta Pi; Natl Span Honorary; *home:* 415 Forest Ave Maysville KY 41056

SHOTTS, STEVEN LANDIS, Amer/TX History Teacher/ Coach; *b:* Abilene, TX; *ed:* (BS) Phys Ed, Angelo St Univ 1983; *cr:* Teacher/Coach Grape Creek Ind Sch Dist 1985-; *ai:* Ftbl, Boys Bsktbl, Boys & Girls Tennis Coach; *office:* Grape Creek Ind Sch Dist 9633 Grape Creek Rd San Angelo TX 76901

SHOTZBERGER, GEORGE LEE, Art Teacher; *b:* Richmond, VA; *m:* Colleen T. Hogan; *c:* Shawn; *ed:* (BS) Art Ed, 1974, (MS) Ed, 1985 DE St Coll; *cr:* Art Teacher Smyrna HS 1975-; *ai:* Art Club Adv; Odyssey of Mind Coach; DE St Ed Assn, Smyrna Educators Assn, NEA 1975-; Smyrna HS Teacher of Yr 1982, 1986, Dist Teacher of Yr 1986; DE St Art Ed Stu Performance Comm; *home:* 405 Main St PO Box 310 Clayton DE 19938

SHOWALTER, CATHERINE LYNN (WHITE), 1st Grade Teacher; *b:* Richmond, TX; *m:* David R.; *c:* David R., Krista A.; *ed:* (BS) Elem Ed, 1977; (MS) Elem , 1980 Ball St; *cr:* 2nd Grade Teacher Rose Hamilton 1976-77; 5th Grade Teacher 1977-88; 1st Grade Teacher 1988- Northeastern Elem; *ai:* Drug Advisory; Richmond Area Rdng Cncl Bldg Rep 1984-87 Mem 1978-; BSA Den Leader 1988-; Semi Finalist in Top 10 for 1986 Teacher of Yr; *office:* Northeastern Elem Sch 534 W Wallace Rd Fountain City IN 47341

SHOWALTER, DIANA MC KINNEY, Principal; *b:* Peru, IN; *m:* Randy J.; *c:* Kelli C., Aron C.; *ed:* (BA) Elem Ed, Purdue Univ 1972; (MS) Elem Ed, IN Univ 1974; *cr:* Teacher Brown Cty Sch Corporation 1972-77; Teacher 1979-86, Prin 1986- Wabash City Schls; *ai:* Testing, TESA, K/Grade 1 Coord; Summer Sch Admin; Direct Instruction/Madeline Hunter Trainer; ASCD 1988-; IN Assn of Elem & Mid Sch Prins 1986-; Trinity Luth Church Pres 1990; IN Prins Leadership Acad; Madeline Hunter Trng; *office:* West Ward Elem Sch 277 N Thorne St Wabash IN 46992

SHOWERS, NADINE TOLBERT, Mathematics Teacher; *b:* Grand Bay, AL; *m:* William E. III; *ed:* (BS) Sci/Math, 1962, (MA) Admin, 1977 AL St Univ; Human Relations; *cr:* Teacher Williamson HS 1962-69, C F Vigor HS 1969-; *ai:* Faculty Relations Comm; SECME Team Mem; MCEA, AEA, NEA; Providence Baptist Church Financial Secy 1989-; NSF Grant.

SHOWS, NANCY LINDLEY, 4th Grade Teacher; *b:* Hattiesburg, MS; *m:* Danny R.; *c:* Jonathan, Nathan, Anthony; *ed:* (BS) Elem Ed, 1971, (MS) Elem Ed, 1975, Ed Specialist Elem Ed, 1979 William Carey Coll; *cr:* Remedial Rdng Teacher 1971, 2nd Grade Teacher 1972-78, 1st Grade Teacher 1978-82, 5th/6th Grade Teacher 1982-84, 6th/7th Grade Teacher 1985-88, 4th Grade Teacher 1988- Moselle Elem; *ai:* JCEA, MAE, NEA; Moselle Baptist Church (Sunday School Teacher, Youth Comm, Adult Choir Mem, Children Choir Co-Dir); *home:* Rt 2 Box 263 Moselle MS 39459

SHRADER, JAN MUNN, Medicine/Allied Health Coord; *b:* Portsmouth, OH; *c:* Rob, Rebecca; *ed:* (AS) Nursing, W KY Univ 1972; Health Occupations Ed, Univ of Louisville; Grad Stud Voc & Spec Needs Ed; *cr:* Instr Lyndon Voc Center 1976-85; Staff Nurse Louisville Veterans Admin Medical Center 1984-89, Medical Careers Teacher Cntrl HS 1985-86; Staff Nurse Norton Hospital 1972-; Medicine/Allied Health Magnet Coord/Instr Cntrl HS 1986-; *ai:* Class of 1991 Spon; Var Chrldr Coach; Magnet Schlshp Steering & Sch Plan Comm; Jefferson Cty Teachers Assn 1976-; Oncology Nursing Society 1989-; *office:* Cntrl HS 1130 W Chestnut St Louisville KY 40203

SHRADER, KURK VANN, Business Teacher; *b:* Lincoln, NE; *m:* Kristyn Ann Meyer; *c:* Mikaela D.; *ed:* (BS) Bus Ed, 1983, (MA) Bus Ed, 1988 Univ of NE Lincoln; *cr:* Bus Teacher/FBLA Adv Fairbury HS 1983-86, Elmwood HS 1986-; *ai:* FBLA Adv; Soph Class Spon; NE St Bus Ed Assn Dist Rep 1984-; NBEA 1988-89, 2nd Place Share An Idea 1988, 1st Place Share An Idea 1989; Elmwood Chrstn Church Bd Pres, FBLA Bd of Dir 1986-; Articles Published; *office:* Elmwood Public Schls 400 West F Street Elmwood NE 68349

SHRADER, MARY HEARN, Fourth Grade Teacher; *b:* Monticello, MS; *m:* Andrew J.; *c:* Melanie Thomas, Gracie; *ed:* (BSE) Elem Ed, Univ of AR 1969; Grad Stud Univ of AR; *cr:* Exec Secy Voc Rehab MS Baptist Hospital 1949-56; Classroom Teacher Springdale Schls 1969-; *ai:* Springdale Ed Assn Publica Relations Comm 1969-; NEA 1969-; NW AR Rdng Cncl 1980-; PTA 1969-; Nom Teacher of Yr 1989; AR Dept of Ed Teacher Recognition Grant 1988, Exemplary Prgm Dissemination Grant 1989; Youth 2000 Prgm AR Legislatures 1989; *home:* 1601 Greenbriar Springdale AR 72764

SHRAGG, MIKE SIDNEY, Director of Activities; *b:* Minneapolis, MN; *c:* Diane, Jamie; *ed:* (BS) Engineering Physics, Morningside Coll 1952; (MS) Industrial Arts, Bradley Univ 1953; *cr:* Math/Algebra Teacher Arcadia HS 1953-54; Industrial Crafts Teacher Whittier HS 1954-55, Santa Fe HS 1955-57; Industrial Crafts Teacher 1957-71, Activity Dir 1971- Montebello Intermediate Sch; *ai:* Bsktbl Coach; Bsktbl & Water Polo Referee; Yrbk Spon; Leadership Teacher/Adv; Industrial Arts Morningside Coll (Mem 1953-57, Pres Stu Body 1954, Mem of Intrafraternity Cncl 1954, Pledgemaster Gamma Iota Alpha 1954); Montebello Intermediate Teachers Club Pres 1959-61; Parents Without Partners (Pres 1970-72, Mem 1968-), Best Prgm for Youths 1971, Outstanding Mem Organization 1972; Athletic Journal 1968; Sch Shop 1961; Responsible & Implementing a Quad Like a Park Setting; Cooperative Achievement Awd Excl in Ed by Pres of US.

SHRAWDER, ANTOINETTE FIERRO, First Grade Teacher; *b:* Wilkes-Barre, PA; *m:* Myron C.; *c:* Jeremy; *ed:* (BS) Elem Ed, Bloomsburg Univ 1975; (BC) Religion, Diocese of Harrisburg 1989; *cr:* 1st Grade Teacher St Boniface Sch 1976-77; 5th/6th Grade Teacher 1979, 1st Grade Teacher 1979- Holy Spirit Sch; *ai:* Elem Cmptr Coord; Summer Bible Sch Elem Teacher; NCEA Mem 1979-; Rainbow for All Gods Children Coord 1988-; Human Life Center Mem 1988-; Easter Seals Coffee Day for Crippled Children Fund Raiser 1978; Lenten Appeal Chm 1981-82; *office:* Holy Spirit Sch 250 West Ave Mount Carmel PA 17851

SHREEVE, DAVID WILLIAM, Activities Director; *b:* Missoula, MT; *m:* Wendy Bogar; *c:* Scott, Daniel; *ed:* (BS) Industrial Ed, MT St Univ 1980; T & I Voc Cert; *cr:* Instr Hot Springs Public Schls 1980-82; Instr 1982-87, Act Dir 1987- Colstrip Public Schls; *ai:* Dist Wide Boys & Girls Act Dir; Natl Interscholastic Athletic Admin Assn St Liaison 1989-; MT St Athletic Admin Assn 1987-; MT St Liaison to Natl Fed of Athletics; *office:* Colstrip Public Schls PO Box 159 Colstrip MT 59323

SHREVE, DONNA SWAGERTY, Math Specialist; *b:* Vallejo, CA; *m:* John C.; *c:* Aaron, Brad; *ed:* (BA) Eng/Speech, 1967, Teaching Credential, 1968 Univ of the Pacific; Admin Cert; *cr:* Elem Teacher East Lyme Sch Dist 1968-72, Escalon Sch Dist 1972-73; Sci Specialist 1988-89; Math Specialist 1989 Lodi Unified Sch Dist; *ai:* NCTM; Mentor Teacher 1984-86; San Joaquin Math Teacher of Yr 1988; Mem of CA Math Project 1989; *office:* Lodi Unified Sch Dist 1300 Lodi Ave W Lodi CA 95242

SHRIVER, LOUIS MARSH, Geometry Teacher/Athletic Dir; *b:* Pittsburgh, PA; *m:* Priscilla Ann Ambrose; *c:* Pamela, Patricia; *ed:* (BA) His, St Bonaventure Univ 1958; US Army Field Artillery Sch Advanced Course; US Army Command & General Staff Coll; Dept of Army Inspector General Sch; *cr:* Military Sci Professor Duquesne Univ 1967-69; Prin 1978-84, Athletic Dir 1985- Hampton Chrstn HS; *ai:* Womens Bsktbl Coach; Sr Class Adv; *office:* Hampton Chrstn HS 2419 N Armistead Ave Hampton VA 23666

SHRIVER, TERESA BURNSIDE, Bio/Sci Teacher/Dept Chair; *b:* Clarksburg, WV; *m:* Donald L.; *ed:* (BS) Bio, 1982, (MS) Curr/Instruction, 1988 Salem Coll; WV Univ, Marshall Univ, Alderson-Broaddus Coll, WV Teachers Acad 1987; *cr:* Bio/Sci Teacher/Dept Chairperson Flemington HS 1982-; *ai:* Project BASICS Building Coord; Jr Class & Prom Spon; Sch Promotion & Retention Comm Co-Chairperson; Taylor Cty Rdng Cncl 1988-; WV Teachers Acad Grads 1987-; WV Sci Teachers Assn 1987-; NSTA 1990; Salem Bus & Prof Womens Club Pres 1987-89; Lighthouse Baptist Church Clerk 1989-; Nom Christa Mc Auliffe Fellowship 1989; Presidential Awd Excl in Sci & Math Teaching 1990; Taylor Cty Honor Teacher 1987-89; Taylor Cty Rep for Acad Sci & Math Teachers 1988 & WV Teachers Acad 1987; *home:* Rt 1 Box 266 Salem WV 26426

SHROUDER, JANICE M., Mathematics Teacher; *b:* Douglas, GA; *m:* Billy J.; *c:* Kelly; *ed:* (BBA) Comprehensive Bus Ed, 1975, (MED) Bus Ed, 1979 Valdosta St Coll; Grad Stud; *cr:* Teacher Citizens Chrstn Acad 1975-; *ai:* Pep Club Adv; Homecoming Comm; 4-H Club Spon; Honors Banquet Chairperson; Adult Literacy Instr Basic Rdng Classes in Douglas; *office:* Citizens Chrstn Acad PO Box 1064 Douglas GA 31533

SHRUM, LOIS I., Jr HS Language Arts Teacher; *b:* Lutesville, MO; *m:* Robert; *ed:* (BS) Voc Home Ec Ed/Eng SE MO Univ 1967; *cr:* Home Ec Teacher Zalma Public Sch 1969-73, Marquard Public Sch 1974-78; Eng/Home Ec Teacher Woodland R-4 Sch 1978-; *ai:* 7th Grade Spon; CTA, MSTA; New Bethel Church Sunday Sch Teacher 1964-; Marble Hill Lutesville Jr Womens Club (Treas 1990) 1980-; *home:* Rt 2 Box 139AA Lutesville MO 63762

SHUBIN, JOANNA T., Science Dept Chm & Teacher; *b:* Long Island, New York; *m:* Jonathan; *ed:* (BA) His, 1967; (MS) His/ Ed, 1972 Queens Coll; Post Masters Studies Sci Courses St Rose Coll; Bank Street Coll of Ed; CCNY; Hofstra Univ; Univ of AL; South Eastern MA Univ; *cr:* 5th Grade Teacher Most Precious Blood Sch 1970-81; Sci Coord K-7th Grade Garden Sch 1981-85; SR Staff Instr Sci Museum of Long Island 1985-86; Sci Chairperson Garden Sch 1986-; *ai:* Young Astronauts Club Spon & Adv; Rocketry Club Spon & Adv; NSTA; Astronomical Socty of the Pacific; Planetary Socty; Okeanos Fnd; Greenpeace the Nature Conservancy; Challenger Center - Fndg Spon; Natly Certfd in Sci By NSTA, Article Publ Learning Magzn for Creatv Tchg 1974; NSTA/NSF Inst for Mid Sch Sci Teachers; Volunteer-Schneider Childrens Hosp; *office:* Garden Sch 33-16 79th St Jackson Heights NY 11372

SHUGART, THERESA LIVELY, English/Latin Teacher; *b:* Corsicana, TX; *c:* David N., Peter G.; *ed:* (BS) Scndry Ed, North TX St Univ 1957; (MA) Eng, Northeast LA Univ 1979; Univ of TX Austin Memphis St Univ; Univ of MS; Stephen F Austin St Univ; Univ of GA; *cr:* Teacher Public Evening Sch 1967-68, Coumbia LA HS 1975-76, Memphis City Schls 1980-81, Corsicana Ind Sch Dist 1981-; *ai:* Latin Club Spon; Jr Classical League Spon; Amer Classical League 1985-; TX Classical Assn 1987-; TX Joint Cncl of Teachers of Eng 1981-; Phi Delta Kappa 1988-; Natl Endowment Humanities Fellowship US Study Classics at Univ of GA 1986-87.

SHULL, KENNETH H., Mathematics Teacher; *b:* Allentown, PA; *m:* Mary Anne Frazer; *c:* Kate, Allyson, Natalie; *ed:* (BA) Math, Millersville Univ 1975; (MS) Counseling, Shippensburg Univ 1985; *cr:* Math Teacher Holicong Jr HS 1975-80; Guidance Cnslr 1987-89; Math Teacher 1980- Faust Jr HS; *office:* Faust Jr HS 1957 Scotland Ave Chambersburg PA 17201

SHULL, SHARON MC MECHAN, French Teacher; *b:* Effingham, IL; *m:* Donald Steven; *c:* Brent A., Brian S.; *ed:* (BS) Fr/Eng, E IL Univ 1969; Grad Stud Eng; Seminar in Avignon, France Univ of Avignon; *cr:* Eng Teacher Lincoln HS 1969-70, Oblong HS 1970-80; Eng/Fr Teacher Newton Hs 1980-85; Fr Teacher Charleston HS 1985-86; Eng/Fr Teacher Effingham HS 1986-; *ai:* European Travel Group Spon; AATF, ACTFL; IL Nacel Rep; *office:* Effingham HS 700 S Henrietta Effingham IL 62401

SHULTZ, ELLEN L., English Teacher/Drama Director; *b:* Jamestown, NY; *m:* Charles H.; *c:* David, Christina; *ed:* (BA) Eng, 1958, (MA) Rdng Ed 1978 Alfred Univ; Theatre Ed, Syracuse Univ; *cr:* Teacher Jamestown HS 1958-63; Librarian Southern Tier Lib System 1966-68; Act Dir Hornell Nursing Home 1973-78; Teacher Alfred Almond Cntrl Sch 1978-; *ai:* Drama Prgm Dir; Drama Club & Stage Crew Adv; NCTE, ITS; Union Univ Church; *office:* Alfred Almond Cntrl Sch Rt 21 Almond NY 14804

SHULTZ, ROBERT MICHAEL, Mathematics Dept Chair; *b:* Oklahoma City, OK; *m:* Diann Gaye Elzo; *c:* Marsie, Chad; *ed:* (BS) Math, 1971, (MA) Guidance/Counseling, 1979 Univ of OK; Cmptr Trng & Self Esteem Class; *cr:* Teacher Tecumseh HS 1971-75, Yukon HS 1975-; *ai:* NHS, Sr Class, JETS Spon; Cmptr & Curr Comm; Academic Coach; COTM, OTM 1980-; NCTM 1977-; NEA, YPEA, OEA Negotiator 1975-; Teacher of Yr 1975-78, 1985-86, 1987-88; Distinguished Teacher 1990; Adjunct Professor OK City Comm Coll; *home:* 305 Vickie Dr Yukon OK 73099

SHUMAKER, BETTY RICHARDSON, English Teacher; *b:* Cairo, IL; *m:* David Leon; *c:* Susan Baugher, Stacey Parker; *ed:* (BS) Bus Ed, 1960, (MS) Curr/Gifted, 1989 S IL Univ; *cr:* 1st/2nd/4th-6th/9th/10th Grade Jr HS Eng Teacher Century 1966-89; *ai:* Speech Coach; Magazine Co-Ed; NCTE 1987-; Century Booster Club 1980-; Century Teacher of Yr; Gifted Fellowship 1987; *office:* Century HS Rt 1 Ullin IL 62992

SHUMAKER, LINDA MC CAIN, High School Science Teacher; *b:* Cape Girardeau, MO; *m:* Gerald Dale; *c:* Jarod, Jessica; *ed:* (AS) Shawnee Comm Coll 1975; (BS) Ed/Bio, S IL Univ 1977; *cr:* HS Sci Teacher Egyptian Cmmty Sch 1979-; *ai:* Sci Club, Stu Cncl, Class Spon; St Marys Cath Church; Teacher Sunshine 1982; *office:* Egyptian Cmmty Sch Rt 1 Tamms IL 62988

SHUMAN, JULIE ANN (LUMLEY), Cty Coordinator of Gifted Ed; *b:* Canton, OH; *ed:* (BS) Elem Ed/Spec Ed, 1976, (MED) Math, 1982 Kent St Univ; Doctoral Candidate, Spec Ed, Kent St Univ; *cr:* Bank Teller Society Bank; Teacher/Coord of Gifted Ed Carrollton Exempted Village Sch; *ai:* NHS Co Adv; Chairperson Classroom of Future Steering Comm; Partcipating Institutions St Level for Classroom of Future Cncl Mem; St Leadership Team Mem for Math Curr Study; OH Assn of Gifted Children, Coord of Creative & Gifted Children, ASCD; Kiwanis 1988-; Bus Prof Women VP 1990-; Carroll Cty Chamber Commerce 1989-; Carrollton Recreation Bd Adv 1988-; Author of Sci Mentorship Grant; Major Grant for Classroom of Future; 2 Journal Articles; *home:* 331 2nd St SE Carrollton OH 44615

SHUMAN-RILEY, BRENDA BARTON, Assistant Principal; *b:* Marietta, GA; *m:* Charles Alexander Riley; *c:* Brooka Paige Shuman, Blair Alexandra Riley; *ed:* (BSED) Eng Ed, GA Southern Coll 1972; (MED) Eng Ed, Univ of GA 1979; Half Completed Add On Certificate in Sch Counseling, Working on Ed Specialist in Admin & Supervision, Data Collector; *cr:* Eng Teacher St Angela Acad 1972-74, Aquiras HS 1974-76, Samuel Elbert Acad/Elbert Cty HS 1977; Developmental Stud GA Southern Coll 1979-80; Eng Teacher Telfair Cty HS 1984-89; Asst Prin Cntrl Elem Sch 1988-89, Telfair Cty Mid Sch 1989-; *ai:* FGE Club Spon; Sr Class & Span Club Adv: Discipline Handbook Comm; Chm Textbook Adoption, Staff Dev, Alternative Sch, Teacher Supplement Comm; Phi Delta Kappa, Kappa Delta Pi 1984-; Page 1985-; GAMSP, NAMSP Mid Sch Prin Assn 1988-; Delta Zeta Alumni Assn 1972-; GSA Leader of Troop 1983; ASCD 1988-; *office:* Telfair Cty Mid Sch Hwy 280 W Mc Rae GA 31055

SHUMARD, SALLY L., High School Art Teacher; *b:* Tulsa, OK; *m:* John C. Gibbs; *c:* Samuel T. Gibbs; *ed:* (BS) Fine Art, Miami Univ 1979; *cr:* Art Teacher Wellston HS 1979-; *ai:* Wellston HS Yrbk Coord; Delta Kappa Gamma 1989-; *office:* Wellston HS 600 S Pennsylvania Ave Wellston OH 45692

SHUMATE, EVELYN SMITH, English Teacher; *b:* Marion, AL; *m:* Claude Allen Jr.; *c:* Kimberly Smith, Claude A. III; *ed:* (MA) Eng, Judson Coll 1953; (MED) Eng Ed, Columbus Coll 1979; *cr:* 3rd Grade Teacher Demopolis Elem Sch 1953-56; 7th-9th Grade Eng Teacher Bryan Station Jr HS 1956-59; 7th/8th Grade Eng Teacher Columbus Jr HS 1973-78; 9th/12th Grade Eng Teacher Columbus HS 1978-83; 7th/8th Grade Eng Teacher Daniel Jr HS 1984-; *ai:* Natl Jr Honor Society Adv; Adopt-A-Sch Prgm Coord; Honors Day, Textbook, Faculty Soc Comm Mem; SAC & Sch Excl Comm Chm; Muscogee Assn of Educators, GA Assn of Educators, NEA 1973-; *home:* 5722 Nrassie St Columbus GA 31909

SHUMATE, O. HELEN HORTON, Third Grade Teacher; *b:* Surveyor, WV; *m:* Richard Milrid; *c:* Karen E. Hamilton, Barbara L. York, Sheila R. Mann, Cheryl A. Larkins, Richard W.; *ed:* (BA) Soc Stud/Lang Arts, Morris Harvey Coll 1971; (MA) Elem Ed, Coll of Graduate Stud 1975; Behaviorial Stud; Class B Status for Supervising Teacher; *cr:* 2nd & 3rd Teacher Ameagle Elem Sch 1944-45; 5th & 6th Teacher Sophia Elem Sch 1945-46; 3rd & 4th Grade Teacher Soak Creek Elem Sch 1965-67; 3rd Grade Teacher Crab Orchard Elem Sch 1968-; *ai:* Teacher Yr 1987-88; *home:* 303 Washington Ave Crab Orchard WV 25827

SHUPITA, HARLAN HARRY, Physics Teacher/Sci Dept Chair; *b:* Branch, WI; *m:* Janice Marie Sobeck; *c:* Bryan, Kevin; *ed:* (BS) Physics/Math, 1967, (MS) Physics/Ed, 1982 Univ of WI Oshkosh; Sci Enrichment Courses & Wkshps; *cr:* Teacher Preble HS 1967-70, Edison Jr HS 1970-75, West HS 1975-; *ai:* Academic Decathlon & Sci Academic Competition Coach; NSTA, WI Society of Sci Teachers, AAPT; Sigma XI Scientific Research Society Sci & Math Teaching Awd 1983; *office:* West HS 966 Shawano Ave Green Bay WI 54303

SHURNICKI, ROBERTA, Teacher of Gifted & Talented; *b:* Wilkes-Barre, PA; *ed:* (BS) Spec Ed/Elem Ed, Kings Coll 1975; Masters Equiv Psych, Marywood Coll 1986; Psych, Marywood Coll; *cr:* Pre-Sch Teacher Coll Misericordia 1975-76; Substitute Teacher Wyoming Valley 1976-77; Phys Handicapped Teacher Luzerne Intermediate Unit 1978-79; Gifted Teacher Luzerne Cty 1979-; *ai:* Lehigh Univ Stock Market Game for Elem Stus; PSEA, NEA; Delta Kappa Gamma Publicity Chm; Amer Heart Assn Bd Mem; Serve Your City Club Publicity Chm; Amer Red Cross Chm of Youth; *home:* 10 Bond Ave Denison Commons Swoyerville PA 18704

SHUTTERS, EDWARD EARL, Science Teacher; *b:* Chicago, IL; *m:* Faith Keren Langhoff; *c:* Diana, Jessica; *ed:* (BS) Biological Sci, Univ of IL Chicago 1975; (MEPD) Ed/Physics, Univ of WI Whitewater 1986; Inst for Chemical Ed 1988; *cr:* Instructer Dr Martin Luther Coll 1976-78; Teacher Lakeside Luth HS 1978-; *ai:* Class Adv; Track Coach; Academic Affairs Comm Chm; Sports Video Coord; AAPT, NAST; *office:* Lakeside Lutheran Hs Woodland Beach Rd Lake Mills WI 53551

SHUTTLESWORTH, NEWANA GOOLSBY, Business Teacher; *b:* Dallas, TX; *m:* Herschall; *c:* Mark, Pamela Shuttlesworth Roberts, Debbie Shuttlesworth Bates, Eddie; *ed:* (BBA) Bus Admin, Hardin-Simmons Univ 1953; (ME) Elem Ed, N TX St Univ 1969; Income Tax Preparation, H&R Block; Cmptr, Univ TX Tyler; *cr:* Bus Teacher Roby HS 1953-57; 6th Grade Teacher St Jo Elem 1964-65; Bus Teacher St Jo HS 1965-69; Bus Teacher Arp HS 1969-; *ai:* Jr, Sr, Chrldr Spon; Yrbk & Sch Newspaper Adv; TSTA (Treas, HS Rep 1980-); Church (Teacher, Dir); Arp HS Teacher of Yr 1986-87; *home:* Box 189 Arp TX 75750

SHY, MARY LOUISE, Fourth Grade Teacher; *b:* Sikeston, MO; *ed:* (BS) Elem Ed, 1979, (MA) Elem Ed, 1986 SE MO St Univ; *cr:* Teacher of Learning Disabilities 1979-81, 4th Grade Teacher 1981- New Madrid Elem; *ai:* Summer Sftbl Goach; Cmmty Teacher Assn VP 1986-88; Delta Kappa Gamma, MSTA; Beta Sigma Phi Pres 1987-88; *office:* New Madrid Elem Sch Hwy 61 N New Madrid MO 63869

SHY, TERRI RAWLS, Biology Teacher; *b:* Cleveland, OH; *m:* Philbert; *c:* Tiffany; *ed:* (BS) Bio, Univ of Cincinnati 1980; Teaching Cert Cleveland St 1986; *cr:* Bio Teacher Shaw HS 1986-; *ai:* Gave In-Service Wkshp Introducing the MBL Cmptr Prgm to Staff Mems in Sci; *office:* Shaw H S 15320 Euclid Ave East Cleveland OH 44112

SICH, ANN CATHERINE (DYE), Library-Media Teacher; *b:* Alton, IL; *m:* Ronald W.; *ed:* (BS) Ed, SIU Carbondale 1964; Lib-Media and Ed; *cr:* Geography/Civics Teacher Murphysboro HS 1964-65; History Teacher Roxana Jr HS 1966-68; Teacher & Soc Stud Dept Head/Lib Media Prof Grigsby Jr HS 1969-; *ai:* Spon Knowledge Master Cmptr Quiz Team; IL Sch Lib Medic Assn; DAR Corresponding Sec; *office:* Grigsby Jr H Sch 3801 Old Cargill Rd Granite City IL 62040

SIDERIS, KATHLEEN SHEEHAN, First Grade Teacher; *b:* Hartford, CT; *m:* Ven; *c:* Brian, Emily; *ed:* (BA) Elem Ed, 1971, (MA) Elem Ed, 1976 Univ of CT; *cr:* 1st Grade Teacher Thompson Memorial Elem Sch 1971-; *ai:* Thompson Ed Assn (VP 1982-84, Membership Chairperson 1984-); Ct Ed Assn, NEA 1971-; Latin Amer Parent Assn 1987-; *office:* Thompson Memorial Elem Sch 785 Riverside Dr North Grosvenordal CT 06255

SIDES, HARRIET HARTLEY, Fifth Grade Teacher; *b:* Lexington, NC; *m:* Larry W.; *c:* Scott, Salli; *ed:* (BA) Ed/Religion, Meredith Coll 1960; (MA) Mid Schls Ed, Appalachian St Univ 1988; *cr:* Teacher Welcome Elem Sch 1964-70, 1976-; *ai:* Grade Level Chm; NCEA, NEA; Welcome Baptist Church; Teacher of Yr 1990; NC Center for Advancement of Teaching; *home:* PO Box 485 Welcome NC 27374

SIDLIK, STAN A., Drama & Theater Arts Teacher; *b:* Chicago, IL; *ed:* (BS) Theatre, Loyola Univ 1957; Loyola Univ; Television, Purdue Univ; *cr:* Dir-Radio/TV Loyola Univ 1960-62; Drama Teacher Bateman HS 1962-67, Lourdes HS 1973-; *ai:* Drama Dir; Drama Festival; George Awds Show; Fall & Spring Prod; Blue Key Society; NCEA; *office:* Lourdes H S 4034 W 56th St Chicago IL 60629

SIDLIK, STEVEN RUDOLPH, Social Studies Department Chm; *b:* Cudahy, WI; *ed:* (BS) Soc Stud, Concordia Teachers Coll 1954; Rollins Coll; Concordia Teachers Coll; *cr:* Teacher 1954-64; Soc Stud Dept Head 1965 St Lukes Luth Schl; *ai:* In-Service Comm to Help Beginning Teachers; Audio-Visual Aids Chm; Faculty Rep on Sch Bd; Luth Ed Assoc; FL-GA Luth Teachers Conference 35 Yr Awd 1989; *home:* 1710 Rebel Run Oviedo FL 32765

SIDNER, ANNE C., English Teacher & Dept Chair; *b:* Springfield, OH; *ed:* (BA) Ed, Mary Manse Coll 1966; (MA) Eng, Univ of Toledo 1975; *cr:* Eng Teacher St Clare Acad 1968-69, Cardinal Stritch HS 1969-76, St Paul HS 1976-77, Bishop Ready HS 1977-; *ai:* Yrbk Adv; NCTE; *office:* Bishop Ready HS 707 Salisbury Rd Columbus OH 43204

SIDOROFF, DIANE DOREEN, Reading Teacher; *b:* Teaneck, NJ; *ed:* (BS) Elem Ed/Mid Sch Math, Bemidji St Univ 1986; Scndry Math Cert; Rdng Specialist Cert; *cr:* Math Teacher 1986-88, Rdng Teacher 1989- Gladys Porter HS; *ai:* Spirit Club Spon; TX Ed Assn 1990; NCTM 1987-89; *office:* Gladys Porter HS 3500 International Blvd Brownsville TX 78521

SIDWELL, MARLENE AHNER, Third Grade Teacher; *b:* Stillwater, OK; *w:* James Barry (dec); *ed:* (AA) Modesto Jr Coll 1965; (BA) Biological Sci, CA St Univ Fresno 1969; *cr:* 3rd/5th-8th Grade Teacher Rockford Elem Sch 1970-; *ai:* Strathmore Baptist Church Chrstn Ed Bd 1973-; Wrote Cmptr Lab Funding AB803 Grant 1986; Prgm Quality Review Coord & Reviewer 1988; *office:* Rockford Elem Sch 14983 Rd 208 Porterville CA 93257

SIEBEN, PATRICK TIMOTHY, Music Instructor; *b:* Pasadena, CA; *m:* Julie Clare Otteson; *c:* Ryan; *cr:* Music Instr Cajon HS 1981-83, Belleview Elem 1983-86, Sonora HS 1983-; *ai:* Choral & Instrumental Music Act Musical Show, Jazz Band, Marching Band; CA Band Dir Assn 1989-; Natl Assn Jazz Educators 1988-; Music Educators Natl Conferance 1989-; Readers Digest Heroes in Amer Ed 1989; *office:* Sonora Union HS 430 N Washington St Sonora CA 95370

SIEBERS, PERRY JAMES, English Department Chair; *b:* Kaukauna, WI; *m:* Amy Marie Weber; *c:* Jacqueline, Nicole; *ed:* (ba) Eng/Psych, Carroll Coll 1981; Working Towards Masters Curr & Instruction, Univ of WI Milwaukee 1990; *cr:* Eng Teacher St Johns Military Acad 1981-; *ai:* Soccer Coach; Sch Newspaper & Yrbk; NCTE 1981-84; *office:* St Johns Military Acad 1101 N Genesee St Delafield WI 53018

SIEFFERT, RONALD LEE, Sixth Grade Teacher; *b:* Traverse City, MI; *m:* Susan Marie Kreiger; *c:* Brian, Kevin; *ed:* (BA) Elem Ed, 1966, (MA) Elem Ed, 1972 Cntrl MI Univ; *cr:* 5th Grade Teacher 1966-70, 6th Grade Teacher 1970- Mt Pleasant Public Schls; *ai:* Safety Patrol; Lang Art Cmmty; MEA, NEA 1966-; Knights of Columbus 1966-72; *office:* Mt Pleasant Public Sch 3800 S Watson Mount Pleasant MI 48858

SIEG, ROSEMARY, First Grade Teacher; *b:* Newton, KS; *ed:* (BS) Ed, St Mary of The Plains 1968; (MS) Ed/Rdng, Pittsburgh St Univ 1978; Teachers Certificate; *cr:* Kndgtn Teacher St Anthonys Sch 1953-55; 3rd/4th Grade Teacher St Marys 1955-56; 1st/2nd Grade Teacher St Anthonys 1956-58; 1st Grade Teacher 1958-59, 5th Grade Teacher 1959-60, 7th Grade Teacher 1960-61, 7th/8th Grade Teacher 1961-62 Immaculate Conception; 1st Grade Teacher Cathedral Sch 1962-63; 5th Grade Teacher 1963-66, 6th Grade Teacher 1966-68 St Judes; 4th Grade Teacher St Marys 1968-72; 5th Grade Teacher 1972-73, 3rd Grade Teacher 1973-74, 5th Grade Teacher 1974-76, 6th Grade Teacher 1976-77 Blessed Sacrament; K/2nd Grade Teacher 1977, K/3rd Grade Teacher 1977-78, K/4th Grade Teacher 1978-81, 5th Grade Teacher 1981-82 St Marys; 1st Grade Teacher 1982-84, Kndgtn Teacher 1984-85, K/1st Grade Teacher 1985-86, 1st Grade Teacher 1986- St Marys; *ai:* Eucharistic Minister; Parish Cncl Mem; Childrens Choir Dir; Teach Eng to Foreign Stus; Rdng Tutor; *office:* St Marys Cath Sch 101 E 9th Newton KS 67114

SIEGEL, MARCELLA JEAN, Fourth Grade Teacher; *b:* Burlington, IA; *ed:* (BS) Elem Ed, 1962, (MA) Elem Ed/Eng, 1968 NE MO St Teachers Coll; *cr:* 2nd/3rd Grade Teacher Charlotte Sch 1957-61; 4th Grade Teacher Walcott Elem Sch 1961-; *ai:* NEA, IA St Ed Assn, Davenport Ed Assn; Cub Scouts (Den Mother, Den Leader Coach); *office:* Walcott Elem Sch 545 E James St Walcott IA 52773

SIEGELMAN, RICHARD JAY, Third Grade Teacher; *b:* New York City, NY; *m:* Laura Diamant; *ed:* (BA) Sociology, St Univ of NY Binghamton 1965; (MED) Elem Ed, Lehigh Univ 1966; *cr:* 4th Grade Teacher Bermingham Elem Sch 1966-76; 3rd Grade Teacher Bermingham & Roosevelt Schls 1976-82; 1st-6th Grade Teacher of Gifted Roosevelt Sch & Vernon Mid Sch 1982-89; 3rd Grade Teacher Theodore Roosevelt Elem Sch 1989-; *ai:* NYSUT, NEA 1966-; Articles Published in Gifted Children Monthly & Grade Teacher Magazine; Cover Story Subject in March 1989 Teaching K-8 Magazine; *office:* Roosevelt Elem Sch W Main St Oyster Bay NY 11771

SIEGLER, IRVING, 4th Grade Teacher; *b:* Mt Vernon, NY; *ed:* (BA) Lit, Antioch Coll 1968; (MS) Eng, Elmira Coll 1971; *cr:* 6th Grade Teacher Severn Sch 1968-71; 8th/9th Grade At Risk Teacher Corning Sch Dist 1971-73; 8th Grade Eng Teacher Northside Blodgett Jr HS 1973-74; 5th Grade Teacher Severn Sch 1975-77; Evening & Summer Instr Elmira Coll 1974-78; 4th Grade Teacher Severn Sch 1977-89; *ai:* Soc Stud Comm Mem; Teacher Designee; Corning Teachers Assn (VP, Negotiator) 1980-; Co-Authored 3 Books; *home:* 500 Victoria Hwy Painted Post NY 14870

SIEGMUND, WINONA S., English Teacher; *b:* Washington, DC; *m:* Donald F.; *ed:* (BA) Eng, 1978, (MALS) Eng, 1990 Mary Washington Coll; Teach Advanced Placement Eng Foxcroft Sch; *cr:* Eng Teacher 1978-, Advanced Placement Eng Teacher 1979- Stafford Sr HS; *ai:* Advanced Placement & Presidential Classroom Coord; Schlsp & Awds Comm Mem; Stafford Ed Assn (Mem 1978-. Building Rep 1979-81); VA Ed Assn, NEA 1978-; NCTE 1989-; VA Assn Teachers of Eng 1988-; Article Published 1989; Outstanding Teacher of Gifted N VA Cncl Gifted & Talented Ed 1989; Advanced Placement Examination Reader 1990; *office:* Stafford Sr HS 33 Stafford Indian Ln Falmouth VA 22405

SIEGRIST, EVELYN LOEPPKE, 2nd Grade Teacher; *b:* Garden City, KS; *m:* Richard G.; *c:* Jennifer Scofield, Janet Hilgers; *ed:* (BS) Elem Ed, Sterling Coll 1969; (MS) Psych, Emporia St Univ 1974; *cr:* 1st-8th Grade Teacher 1944-46, 1st-4th Grade Teacher 1946-48 Rural Schls; Teacher of Educable

Mentally Handicapped Level II 1969-77, 3rd-5th Grade Teacher 1977-79 North Reno Sch; 2nd Grade Teacher North Reno-Mitchell 1979-; *ai:* KS Ed Assn 1969-; CEC 1969-77; Assn for Retarded Citizens 1969-79; *office:* Mitchell Elem Sch 2804 W 56th Hutchinson KS 67502

SIEMS, STANLEY WAYNE, Vocational Drafting Teacher; *b:* Shelley, ID; *m:* Ann K. Robinson; *c:* Susan, Jason, Caleb, Lucas, Joshua, Rebekah; *ed:* (A) Psych, Ricks Coll 1968; (BS) Ed, 1970, (MS) Voc Ed, 1975 Brigham Young Univ; *cr:* Gen Shop Teacher Garside Jr HS 1970-73; Wood Shop Teacher Chapporal HS 1973-74; Voc Drafting Teacher Bonneville HS 1974-; *ai:* Drafting Section Adv for VICA; NEA; ID Ed Assn; East Bonneville Ed Assn; Among 1st in ID to Inst Computerized Drafting Instr As Part of Reg Drafting Curr; *office:* Bonneville H S 3165 E Iona Rd Idaho Falls ID 83401

SIENKO, JANET FERRIOL, 7th/8th Grade Science Teacher; *b:* Newark, NJ; *m:* Stephen S.; *c:* Laura, Andrea; *ed:* (BA) Fr, Montclair St Coll 1970; *cr:* Fr Teacher Belleville Jr HS 1972-76; Fr/Sci Teacher Our Lady of Victories Sch 1984-; *ai:* Sci Fair & Earth Day Chairperson; Yrbk Adv; Pi Delta Phi, Kappa Delta Pi Mem 1969; *office:* Our Lady of Victories Sch 36 Main St Sayreville NJ 08872

SIERK, JANICE A. (LOSEY), First Grade Teacher; *b:* Berlin, WI; *m:* John B.; *c:* Gretchen, Seth; *ed:* (BA) Ed, Univ of WI Stevens Point 1974; *cr:* 1st Grade Teacher Tri-Cty Area Schls 1974-76, Lanark Elem 1976-78, Tri-Cty Area Schls 1978-; *ai:* Church Comm; NEA 1974-; WI Ed Assn 1974-76, 1978; *home:* PO Box 182 Hancock WI 54943

SIERRA, ELSA, First Grade Teacher; *b:* Brownsville, TX; *ed:* (BS) Elem Ed/Bi-ling, 1979, (MED) Supervision/Bi-ling Ed, 1981 Pan Amer Univ; *cr:* 5th Grade Teacher 1979-, 2nd Grade Teacher 1980-87, 1st Grade Teacher 1987- R E Del Castillo Elem Sch; *ai:* Lead Teacher; Lang Proficiency Assessment Comm; *office:* R E Del Castillo Elem Sch 105 Morningside Rd Brownsville TX 78521

SIEVERS, CECIL NORMAN, Language Art Teacher; *b:* New York, NY; *m:* Marilyn Jeannette Huggins; *c:* Michael, Devin; *ed:* (BS) His, Lincoln Univ 1973; (MS) Rdng, 1977, Advanced Cert Admin/Supervision, 1988 City Coll of NY; *cr:* Teacher Dean of Boys Intermediate Sch 136 1973-77; Dist 6 Drug Prevention Prgm Teacher Intermediate Sch 134 1977-80; Ed Career Guidance Dir Sports Fnd 1980-; Lang Art Teacher/Group Guidance Coord Intermediate Sch 184 1983-; *ai:* Project Dir Adolescent Voc Exploration Prgm; Upper Manhattan Rdng Cncl Exec Comm; Sports Fnd Prgm Dir 1983-, Top Achiever 1989; *office:* Intermediate Sch 184 778 Forest Ave New York NY 10456

SIEWERT, MARY MARGARET, Third Grade Teacher; *b:* Henderson, KY; *m:* Mike; *c:* Emily, John; *ed:* (AA) Elem Ed, Henderson Comm Coll 1968; (BS) Elem Ed, 1970, (MS) Elem Ed, 1972 W KY Univ; Grad Work Elem Ed, Murray St Univ; *cr:* 2nd/3rd Grade Teacher 1970-73, Upper Grades Rdng Teacher 1973-79, 5th Grade Teacher 1980-84, 4th Grade Teacher 1985-86, 4th/5th Grade Teacher 1988-89, 3rd Grade Teacher 1989- Niagara Elem; *ai:* Meth Church (Youth Spon, Bible Sch Dir) 1980-89, Unison Civic Awd 1989; Volunteer Fire Dept Auxiliary; *home:* 16359 Hwy 136 E Robards KY 42452

SIEWERT, SANDRA K., Home & Career Skills Teacher; *b:* Astoria, NY; *ed:* (BS) Home Ec Ed, SUC Oneonta 1979; (MS) Rdng/Spec Ed, Adelphi Univ 1984; Sign Lang & Crafts; *cr:* Teacher Holland Patent Mid Sch 1979-80, Whitesboro Jr HS 1980, Baldwin Jr HS 1980-81, Bellmore-Merrick Schls 1981-82, Wisdom Lane Mid Sch 1982-; *ai:* Club Adv & Enrichment Teacher Home & Career Skills; Mid Sch Evaluation Comm; Phi Upsilon Omicron Mem 1978-; Departmental Honors Home Ec SUC Oneonta.

SIGLE, SUSAN VANCE, Counselor; *b:* Moorefield, WV; *m:* Kenneth Sigle; *c:* Kim, Shane; *ed:* (BA) Lang Art, Shepherd Coll 1970; (MS) Media, 1980, (MED) Counseling, West Chester Univ 1987; *cr:* Eng Teacher 1975-87, Counselor 1987- Downingtown Jr HS; *ai:* Past Hockey Coach; Lancer Leaders Play Dir; Downingtown Ed Assn; NEA Building Rep; *office:* Downingtown Jr HS 335 Manor Ave Downingtown PA 19335

SIGLER, GWEN LIGHT, Retired English Teacher; *b:* Martinsburg, WV; *m:* Curtis E.; *c:* Chuck Russler, Scott; *ed:* (BA) Eng/Phys Ed, Shepherd Coll 1953; *cr:* Eng Teacher Hedgesville HS 1953-58; Eng Teacher Marlowe Jr HS 1958-60; Eng/Phys Ed Teacher Martinsburg HS 1960-61; Eng Teacher North Mid Sch 1969-88; *ai:* Girls Bsktbl Coach; Cheerleading & Pep Club Adv; Drama Coach; Worked With Projects Charlie & Horizon Prgms; ACE Awd, A Caring Educator 1988; *home:* PO Box 353 Falling Waters WV 25419

SIGLIN, RALPH DWAINE, 6th Grade History Teacher; *b:* Elmira, NY; *m:* Lynne C. Guiles; *c:* Tim, Heidi, David; *ed:* (BA) Chrstn Ed, Baptist Bible Coll of PA 1967; (MS) Elem Ed, Pensacola Chrstn Coll 1982; Cmptr Applications Certificate York Tech Coll; *cr:* Teacher Aderondack Chrstn Sch 1970-77, Trinity Chrstn Sch 1977-; *ai:* 5th/6th Grade Soccer Coach; Rock Hill Area Chamber of Commerce 1989-, Teacher of Yr; Rock Hill Youth Sports Cncl; *home:* 649 Rabun Cir Rock Hill SC 29730

SIGMON, NANCY COUND, Spanish Teacher; *b:* Ft Leavenworth, KS; *m:* Paul Wayne; *c:* Erin E.; *ed:* (BSW) Soc Work, Univ of KS 1980; Certificate Scndry Span Ed 1987; *cr:* Teacher E Gaston HS 1987-; *ai:* Span Club Spon; NCAE 1989-; Sigma Delta Pi 1979-80; Gaston Cty Bar Auxiliary Soc Chm 1989-; *office:* E Gaston HS 710 S Lane Rd Mount Holly NC 28120

SIGNORE, RICHARD A., Spanish & Latin Teacher; *b:* Rochester, PA; *ed:* (BA) His, 1966, (MED) Scndry Ed, 1972 Duquesne Univ; Universidad Autunoma De Guadalajara Mexico, Universidad De Guadalajara Mexico, Westminster Coll, Washington Theological Coalition, Towson St Univ; *cr:* Soc Stud Teacher Beaver Sr HS 1968-73; Span/Latin Teacher Seton-La Salle HS 1976-; *ai:* SADD Spon; Classical Assn of Pittsburgh & Vicinity, PA Classical League, Classical Assn of Mid-Atlantic St, Amer Classical League; Fulbright Fellowship to Mexico; Natl Endowment for Hum Fellow; *office:* Seton-La Salle HS 1000 Mc Neilley Rd Pittsburgh PA 15226

SIGNORINI, DANIEL ALBERT, English/Language Arts Teacher; *b:* Martins Ferry, OH; *ed:* (BA) Elem Ed, OH Univ 1975; (MS) Admin, Dayton Univ 1978; *cr:* 6th Grade Math Teacher Dillonvale Elem 1975-77; 5th Grade Soc Stud Teacher Adena Elem 1977-84; 8th Grade Eng Teacher Buckeye South Jr HS 1984-; *ai:* Jr HS Dir of Athletics; 8th Grade Boys Bsktbl Coach; Holy Name; OH Ed Assn; NEA; *office:* Buckeye South Jr HS 209 Market St Yorkville OH 43971

SIHLER, CAMILLE CARSO, Third Grade Teacher; *b:* Monroe, LA; *m:* Kenneth H.; *ed:* (BA) Elem Ed, LA Tech Univ 1969; Teaching Credential CA St Univ Hayward; *cr:* 1st Grade Teacher New Orleans Public Sch System 1969-77; 3rd Grade Teacher St Joseph Cath Sch 1978-80, Christ the King Cath Sch 1980-; *ai:* Stu Cncl Moderator; SRA Testing Coord; *office:* Christ the King Cath Sch 195 Brandon Rd Pleasant Hill CA 94523

SIKARAS, HELENE, 4th Grade Teacher; *b:* Chicago, IL; *ed:* (BA) Ed, 1972; (MED) Ed, 1976 Univ of IL; *cr:* Teacher Koraes Elem Sch 1972-; *ai:* Cmptr Coord; IRA; NCTE; Art Institute Volunteer 1982-; Univ IL Alumni; Recipient of AHEPA Schlsp; *office:* Koraes Elem Sch 11025 S Roberts Rd Palos Hills IL 60465

SIKKEMA, WILMA BONNEMA, 3rd Grade Teacher; *b:* Garfield, NJ; *m:* Arthur J.; *c:* Jane E. Fricker, Marjory A. Brokaw; *ed:* (BS) Elem Ed, William Paterson Coll 1950; Monmouth Coll; Fairleigh Dickinson Univ; *cr:* 4th Grade Teacher Calvin Coolidge Sch 1950-54; 8th Grade Teacher Abraham Lincoln Sch 1954-56; 6th Grade Teacher 1957-59/1976-79; 3rd Grade Teacher 1979- Calvin Coolidge Sch; *ai:* Curr Cncl; Math Curr Comm; Wyckoff Ed Assn; Bergen Cty Ed Assn; NJ Ed Assn; Intnl Rdng Assn; Amer Legion Awd; Kappa Delta Pi Honor Ed Society; Wyckoff Bd of Ed Grant to Produce Resource Book/Handbook & Video Tape on Township; *office:* Calvin Coolidge Sch 420 Grandview Ave Wyckoff NJ 07481

SIKORA, JOHN H., Head Science Dept; *b:* Madison, IL; *m:* Sharon K. Nemeth; *c:* John, Michelle Hecimovich, Gary; *ed:* (BS) Sci/Bio, MO Valley Coll 1962; (MS) Educl Admin, SIUE 1974; *cr:* Teacher Ruskin HS 1962-63, Cntrl Jr HS 1963-70, Grigby Jr HS 1970-; *ai:* Head Ftbl, Girls Bsktbl, Track Coach; AFT; Awd of Excl Granted By the IL Math/Sci Acad 1988; *office:* Grigsby Jr H S 3801 Cargill Rd Granite City IL 62040

SILAS, KAYRON MILES, Fifth Grade Teacher; *b:* Fayette, AL; *m:* Wayne; *c:* Heather F., Chanda L.; *ed:* (BA) Scndry Math, 1971, (MA) Elem, 1977 Univ of AL; *cr:* 7th/8th Grade Math Teacher Marion Cty HS 1971-72; Elem Teacher Brilliant Elem 1972-; *ai:* 4-H Club, St Jude Math-A-Thon, Birmingham Post Herald Spelling Bee & AL-LA-MS Math League Spon; Southern Assn Comm Chairperson; Delta Kappa Gamma (Secy 1982-83, Treas 1990-91); Marion Cty Teachers Secy 1979-80; Church Group Ladies (Secy, Treas 1981-82, 1988-); Cmmty Pride Grant 1988-89, 1989-; *home:* Rt 4 Box 664 Winfield AL 35594

SILBER, MARCIA LIEPPER, 2nd Grade Teacher; *b:* Brooklyn, NY; *m:* Herbert J.; *c:* Lynn, Howard; *ed:* (BS) Nutrition, Pratt Inst 1948; (MS) Ed, Hofstra Univ 1967; Univ of Hartford, C W Post; *cr:* 2nd Grade Teacher Otsego Elem Sch 1967-; *ai:* Sci Coord; Nassau Rdng Cncl; HALH Hollow Hills Teachers Assn 1967-; Jericho Lib Bd Mem 1965-67; GSA Leader 1960-63; Otsego PTA 1967-, Teacher of Yr 1978; Robert Williams PTA VP 1959-61; Soc Stud Curr Guide Published W Hartford Schls.

SILBERMAN, BARBARA ANN, Kindergarten Teacher; *b:* Brooklyn, NY; *c:* Gail, Mark; *ed:* (BA) Early Chldhd Ed, 1965, (MS) Early Chldhd Ed, 1970 Brooklyn Coll; Admin & Supervision, City Coll of NY 1989; *cr:* Kndgtn Teacher PS 64 Queens 1965-67; Teacher/Lib/Metrics/Kndgtn/1st Grade PS 178 Queens 1978-; *ai:* Early Chldhd Rep Dist 26 Comm; Lincoln Center Prgm Coord; United Fed of Teachers Chapter Chairperson 1984-; Queens Early Chldhd Assn; Temple Israel of Jamaica Nursery Sch Chairperson 1988-; Danforth Scholar 1988-89; Asst Prins Internship Prgm NYC Bd of Ed; Research NY Teacher Centers Consortium 1988-89; Impact II Devloper Awd 1988; *office:* Public Sch 178 Queens 189-10 Radnor Rd Holliswood NY 11423

SILER, DAVID C., Math Teacher/Athletic Trainer; *b:* Winston Salem, NC; *m:* Donna Johnson; *ed:* (BS) Math Ed, NC St Univ 1986; *cr:* Math Teacher Havelock HS 1986-; *ai:* Certified Athletic Trainer; Wrestling Coach; *office:* Havelock HS 101 Webb Blvd Havelock NC 28532

SILER, DORIS GRIFFIN, Science Teacher; *b:* Birmingham, AL; *c:* Winifred, Florita; *ed:* Elem Ed, Miles Coll 1974; Working Towards Masters Univ Birmingham; *cr:* Classroom Teacher/Soc Stud Dept Head Kingston Elem Sch 1979-87; Sci Teacher Hayes Mid Sch 1989-; *ai:* Chrldr & Sewing Club Supvrs; Sch Philosophy Comm; Amer Ed Week & Black His Month Prgms; Birmingham Ed Assn (Mem 1974-, Rep 1988) Certificate; Classroom Teacher Assn 1985-; Citizen Participation Youth Supv (Secy 1987-88, Co-Chm 1987-88), Certificate of Appreciation; Awd for Excl Beyond call of Duty from Prin T L Jones; Awd from 4th Ave YMCA; Certificate from Sci Dept Birmingham Southern Coll for Activity Involvement; James Morris Memorial Awd; *home:* 4517 N 13th Ave Birmingham AL 35212

SILLARS, JOYCE ANN MARSHALL, 6th-8th Grade Teacher; *b:* Camden, NJ; *m:* Robert; *c:* Jeffrey, Kathryn; *ed:* (BS) Elem Ed/Spec Ed/MR, Millersville Univ 1972; *cr:* 3rd Grade Teacher Cntrl Sch 1972-74; 4th Grade Teacher St Margarets Sch 1974-76, Our Lady of Perpetual Help Sch 1976-79; Remedial Math Teacher Voorhees Mid Sch 1979-81; 6th-8th Grade Teacher St Matthew Regional Sch 1981-; *ai:* Safety Patrol; Yrbk Staff; Math Coord; NJ Math & Sci Teachers Assn 1987-; *office:* St Matthew Regional Sch Hessian Ave Verga NJ 08093

SILLAVAN, CHRISTINA, English Department Chair; *b:* Houston, TX; *m:* John D.; *c:* Karly; *ed:* (BA) Eng/His, 1969, (MA) Eng, 1973 Sam Houston St Univ; Advanced Credit Writing & Classroom Management Classes; *cr:* 7th/8th Grade Teacher Spring Branch Ind Sch Dist 1969-71; 11th Grade Eng Teacher Northbrook HS 1971-81; Fr/Eng Teacher Houston Comm Coll 1973-75; 11th Grade Eng Teacher Katy HS 1983-; *ai:* Sr Women Spon; W Houston Area Cncl Teachers of Eng Exec Bd 1989-; TX Joint Cncl Teachers of Eng, NCTE 1987-; *office:* Katy HS 6331 Highway Blvd Katy TX 77450

SILLIMAN, BENJAMIN D., GUIDANCE DIRECTOR; *b:* Des Moines, IA; *m:* Susie Welch; *c:* Amy J., Carrie L. Debnam; *ed:* (BS) Industrial Art, 1958, (MS) Guidance/Counseling, 1961 IA St Univ; (EDD) Counseling, Univ of KS 1973; *cr:* 6th-12th Grade Industrial Art Teacher Kansas City Public Schls 1958-64; 7th-9th Grade Math/Industrial Art/Cnslr Center Cmmty Sch #58 1964-70; Staff Cnslr Univ of KS 1970-73; Cnslr/Educator VA Tech 1976-80; Guidance Dir Fairfax Cty Public Schls 1980-; *ai:* 7 Period Day Transition Comm Co-Chm; Cty Level Admin Research Comm; Amer Assn for Counseling & Dev 1970-; Assn for Specialists in Group Work Editorial Bd 1973-; VA Assn for Specialists in Group Work Pres 1974-; N VA Cnslrs Assn Pres 1973-, Outstanding Chapter Mem 1978; Intermediate Guidance Directors Assn (Founder, Past Pres); Univ of KS Honors Grad; 2 Book Chapters & 8 Published Articles; *office:* Rocky Run Intermediate Sch 4400 Stringfellow Rd Chantilly VA 22021

SILLS, JANE HUBER, 7th Grade Lang Arts-Team Ldr; *b:* Summit, NJ; *m:* James R.; *c:* Amy; *ed:* (BA) Spec Ed, 1968; (BA) Elem, 1968 Murray St Univ; Mid Sch Curr; Supv of Teachers; Enhanced Instrtl Process Coaching Class; *cr:* Spec Ed Teacher Raritan Township Schls 1968-69; Ld Spec Ed Teacher Madison Township Schls 69-72; Fairfax Cnty Sch Sys 72-73; 6th Grade Teacher Manassas Park Sch Sys 76-81; 7th Grade Teacher Prince William Cty Schls 81-; *ai:* 7th Grade Dept Coord Team Leader/Pep Club Adv/Spelling Bee Sch Coord/Sch Rep to Supt/Coach in Enhanced Instrtl Process Tchg Teachers; Manassas Park Teachers Assoc Pres 1978; Teachers of Yr Manassa Park 1979; *home:* Box 24 Clifton VA 22024

SILVA, NEVA JANE MOORE, Fifth Grade Teacher; *b:* Miami Beach, FL; *m:* Bernard R.; *c:* Julia S. Howett, Bruce R., Brent R., Neva J., Melanie J.; *ed:* (BED) Elem Ed, Univ of Miami 1963; Grad Work FL Intl Univ; Elem Ed; *cr:* Substitute Teacher Dade Cty 1955-62; Elem Teacher Rockway Elem 1963-; 5th Grade Teacher Rockway; *ai:* FL Reading Assn 1963-; Dade Cty Reading Cncl 1963-; United Teachers of Dade 1963-; Order of Easter Star Worthy M Tron 1979-80; Order of Rainbow Girls (Mother Adv) 1973-80 Grand Cross Color 1975; Univ Baptist Church Sunday Sch Teacher 1985-; *home:* 7540 S Waterway Dr Miami FL 33155

SILVASI, LOUIS ALEX, Journalism/Economics Teacher; *b:* Whiting, IN; *m:* Connie Alfonso; *c:* Danie, Suzanne Deal; *ed:* (AA) Drafting/Technology, Purdue Univ 1948; (BS) Soc Stud, 1951, (MS) Guidance/Counseling, 1953 IN Univ; *cr:* Scndry Teacher Herrick House 1951-52; Elem Teacher Whiting Public Schls 1952-54; HS Teacher Hazel Park HS 1954-; *ai:* Sr Class Adv; NCSS; Knights of Columbus Ed 1960-72, Service 1966; Troy HS Boosters Club (Pres 1979-80, Past-Pres 1986); 2 Free Lance Articles; *office:* Hazel Park HS 23400 Hughes Hazel Park MI 48030

SILVER, STEWART H., JR., 6th Grade Teacher; *b:* Louisville, KY; *m:* Marsha K. Feller; *c:* Stephanie M., Stewart M.; *ed:* (BA) Phys Ed, William Penn Coll 1973; (MS) Elem Ed, IN Univ 1980; *cr:* Teacher Brown Elem 1976-; Coach Seymour HS 1976-; *ai:* Head Girls Cross Cntry & Track Coach; IN St Teachers Assn 1976-; *home:* 425 Schleter Ct Seymour IN 47274

SILVERIA, JOHN F., English Teacher; *b:* Lowell, MA; *m:* M. Sandra; *c:* John P., James A., Jennifer M., Jeffrey P.; *ed:* (AB) Eng 1967, (MED) Rdng Elem Level, 1971 Univ of Lowell; Rdng Scndry Level, Boston Univ 1972; *cr:* Eng Teacher Dr Paul Nettle Sch 1967-72; Rdng Specialist/Teacher Dr Paul Nettle Sch & C D Hunking Sch 1972-76; Eng Teacher J G Whittier Sch 1976-81, Haverhill HS 1981-; *ai:* Haverhill Ed Assn 1967-; MA Teachers Assn 1967-; MA Cncl Teachers of Eng 1981-; NTCE 1981-; Friends of Lowell HS VP 1989-; Belvidere Residents Assn Pres 1990; Horace Mann Grant Recipient; *office:* Haverhill HS 137 Monument St Haverhill MA 01830

SILVERS, JOAN RENEE, Social Science Teacher; *b:* Calhoun, GA; *ed:* (BA) European His, Berry Coll 1977; (MED) Soc Sci, Univ of S MS 1985; Cmptr Literacy; Mid Eastern His/Inst; *cr:* His Teacher Trion HS 1977-78, Soc Stud Teacher Adairsville HS

1978-; *ai:* Chrldr, Track, Sftbl Coach; Close-Up Teacher; One Act Play Co-Spon; GA Cncl for Soc Stud Presenter 1985; GA Assn of Educators, NEA; Welcome Gap Baptist Church Sunday Sch Teacher 1985-; Cmmty Volunteers 1980-; Berry Coll His Honor Society; Mid East Inst Emory Univ; Latin Amer Affairs Emory Univ; Global Ed Conference; FTA, VICA, Close-Up Certificates of Appreciation; *office:* Adairsville HS 100 College St Adairsville GA 30103

SILVERS, MARY LO, Social Studies Teacher; *b:* Burnsville, NC; *ed:* (BS) Soc Stud, 1953, (MA) Amer His, 1956, Educl Specialist/Admin/Supervision, 1982 E TN St Univ; *cr:* Teacher Lamar HS 1953-71, David Crockett HS 1971-; *ai:* Washington Cty Ed Assn, TN Ed Assn, NEA, Delta Kappa Gamma; Excel Teacher of Yr 1986; Outstanding Teacher Awd Franklin Cncl & TN Cncl for Soc Stud 1986; Outstanding Teacher Awd TN Hum Cncl 1986; Excel Grant 1986, First Place Awd Recognition for Outstanding Teaching of Ec by the TN Cncl on Ec Ed 1986; Whos Who in Amer Ed Natl Reference Inst 1989-; Washington Cty Teacher of Yr 1987; *home:* Rt 14 Box 430 Jonesboro TN 37659

SILVERSTEIN, JACLYN MARCIA, 7th Grade Math Teacher; *b:* Newark, NJ; *m:* Edward; *ed:* (BS) Elem/Mid Grades, Monmouth Coll 1975; *cr:* Math Teacher Chapel Hill Mid 1978-; *ai:* Math Dept Chm 1980-86; Cheerleading Spon 1978-79; Cmptr Club Co-Spon 1985; GA Assn of Educators Mem 1978-; NEA Mem 1978-; Whos Who Outstanding Young Women in America 1982; *home:* 5872 Oak Ct Douglasville GA 30135

SILVERTHORN, ERNEST KASBAUM, Mathematics/Science Teacher; *b:* New Orleans, LA; *m:* Marie Adams; *c:* Ernest E. E.; *ed:* (BA) Anthropology/Psych, Univ of TX 1952; (MED) Counseling Psych, Stephen F Austin Univ 1960; (EDS) Clinical Ed, Univ of Houston 1975; Bacculaureate Psych, Univ of TX 1954; *cr:* Elem Teacher East & Mt Houston Dist 1954-56; L D Teacher Ft Bend Sch Dist 1957-60; Stu Life Teacher TX Tech Univ 1960-61; Scndry Homebound Teacher Cmmty Services/Child Guidance Center 1961-; *ai:* Amer Psych Assn, NEA, Cncl for Exceptional Children 1966-; Amer Assn Cncl & Dev 1959-; Amer Legion 1988-; Arabia Shrine Temple 1975-; Natl Def Ed Act Grant; United Commercial Travelers of America & Houston Area Cncl for Retared Children Schlsps; *home:* 4110 Leeshire Houston TX 77025

SILVESTRI, VINCENT, English Teacher; *b:* Weehawken, NJ; *m:* Diane De Vito; *c:* Derek, Brad; *ed:* (BA) Eng, Montclair St Coll 1970; (MA) Stu Personnel Services, Jersey City St 1978; Seminars & Wkshps on Teaching, Writing in HS Curr; *cr:* Eng Teacher Memorial HS 1970-; *ai:* Chairperson Admin & Staff Comm for Mid Sts Accreditation Evaluation; Chairperson Memorial HS Faculty; Admin Laison Comm 1986-89; NCTE 1970-; Lincoln Center Film Society 1987-; NJ Citizens for Action 1987-; US Tennis Assn 1988-; NJ Ed Assn 1970-; Teachers Assn Representation 1978-; Fair Contract Co-Chairperson Comm 1988-89; NJ St Dept of Voc Ed; *office:* Memorial HS 5501 Park Ave West New York NJ 07093

SILVIA, THOMAS A., Government Teacher; *b:* Danbury, CT; *m:* Essonia Williams; *c:* Thomas, Robert; *ed:* (BA) His, Inter Amer Univ 1972; (MS) Human Resources Management, Gonzaga Univ 1976; (BS) Bus Ed, Lambuth Coll 1983; *cr:* Major/Nav USAF 1954-77; Math Teacher Cypress Jr HS 1983-84, TN AC 1984-85; Math/Government/His Teacher Haywood HS 1985-; *ai:* Scout Master; Stu Cncl Spon; Haywood Cty Ed Assn Pres 1989-; *office:* Haywood HS College St Brownsville TN 38012

SIMANDLE, STANTON ANTHONY, Principal; *b:* Lexington, KY; *m:* Lynn Mc Coy; *c:* Kessler Mc Coy, Chandler Mc Coy; *ed:* (BA) Elem Ed, Transylvania Univ 1974; (MA) Elem Ed, W KY Univ 1979; (EDD) Ed Admin/Supervision, Univ of KY 1985; *cr:* 2nd/4th Grade Teacher Russell Elem 1974-82; 4th/6th Grade Teacher Julius Marks Elem 1983-87; Admin Intern Fayette Cty Public Schls 1987-88; Prin Tates Creek Elem 1988-; *ai:* NEA 1974-; NAESP, Phi Delta Kappa, KY Assn of Sch Admin 1988-; *office:* Tates Creek Elem 1113 Centre Pkwy Lexington KY 40517

SIMBECK, DON K., Biology & German Teacher; *b:* Loretto, TN; *m:* Donna Neidert; *c:* Dana, Damien, Dawn, Danielle; *ed:* (BA) Bio/His, 1963, (MA) Bio, 1968 Univ of N AL; (EDS) Bio, George Peabody Coll 1974; NSF Inst Univ of IA 1972; *cr:* Bio Teacher Lawrence Cty HS 1963; Elem Teacher Liberty Grove Sch 1964; Bio/Ger Teacher Loretto HS 1964-; *ai:* Scholastic Bowl Coach; Ger Lang Club; Soph Spon; United Teaching Profession 1964-; NABT Regional Dir 1966-; Outstanding TN Bio Teacher Awd 1974; Tn Acad of Sci 1972-, Distinguished Teacher 1975; Loretto Lions Club (Secy, VP, Pres) 1967-77; Rotary Club Outstanding Young Educator Awd 1969; *office:* Loretto HS 525 2nd Ave Loretto TN 38469

SIMCIK, KAREN DYKOWSKI, 8th Grade Teacher; *b:* Taylor, TX; *m:* John R.; *c:* John Albin; *ed:* (AA) Temple Jr Coll 1973; (BS) Ed, Southwestern Univ 1976; *cr:* 2nd Grade Teacher 1973-75, 5th Grade Teacher 1976-77 SS Cyril & Methodius Sch; Kndgtn Teacher 1979-86, 2nd Grade Teacher 1986-87, 8th Grade Teacher/Building Coord 1987- St Marys Sch; *ai:* Building Coord; Choir Dir; NCEA 1980-; St Marys Parish Family of Yr Awd 1983; Parent Teachers Club; St Marys Folk Choir; Cath Youth Organization Youth Moderator 1980-89; Cath Daughters; Teacher of Yr Awd 1988; *home:* 2209 Gladnell Taylor TX 76574

SIMCIK, WILLIAM ANDREW, English Teacher/Team Leader; *b:* Hazelton, PA; *m:* Ann Marie DeHoff; *c:* Lisa A. Konopelski, Jennifer A., Terri A. Fritz; *ed:* (BS) Eng Ed, 1967, (MED) Counseling, 1973 Kutztown Univ; *cr:* Teacher Rdng Sch Dist 1967-; *ai:* Team Leader; *office:* Rdng Sch Dist 8th & Washington Sts Reading PA 19601

SIMERLY, JUDITH GAIL (PRICE), Second Grade Teacher; *b:* S Charleston, WV; *m:* Michael Anthony; *c:* Michael, Matthew; *ed:* (BA) Elem Ed, Anderson Coll 1969; (MA) Ed, Ball St Univ 1976; *cr:* Teacher South Elem Sch 1969-79, East Elem Sch 1979-; *ai:* Classroom Teacher Assn (Secy 1986-88, Building Exec 1988-89); East Side Church Bd of Ed & Ministries 1988-; Outstanding Young Woman 1979; Prof Dev Grant 1990; *office:* East Elem Sch 893 E U S 36 Pendleton IN 46064

SIMERLY, MARY ALICE BALDWIN, Cosmetology Instructor; *b:* Friendsville, TN; *m:* Benjamin; *c:* Bill D., John W., Richard (dec); *ed:* (BS) Voc Ed, Univ of TN; Cosmetology Seminars; *cr:* Cosmetologist TN Beauty Shop; Cosmetology Salon Mgr Millers Dept Store 1960-70; Cosmetology Instr Doyle HS 1970-; *ai:* Voc Industrial Clubs of Amer; Stu Participation with Nursing Home Residents Hair, Skin, Nail Care; Church Musician; Caring for Aged Relatives; TN Ed Assn, NEA, AVA; Natl Cosmetology Assn Blue Ribbon; Laurel Bank Missionary Baptist Church; Amer Assn of Retired People; Song Writer; *home:* Rt 15 Box 205 Maryville TN 37801

SIMICH, SUZANNE, Second Grade Teacher; *b:* Eldorado, IL; *ed:* (AA) SE IL Coll 1971; (BA) Elem Ed, Asbury Coll 1973; (MSED) Elem Ed, 1979, Certificate Admin Endorsement, 1987 S IL Univ; *cr:* K-12th Grade Substitute Teacher Eldorado Cmmty Unit #4 Schls 1973-74; 1st-8th Grade Remedial Rdng Teacher 1974-77, 3rd Grade Teacher 1977-82, 2nd Grade Teacher 1982- Hamilton Cty Unit #10 Schls; *ai:* Staff Dev & In-Service Comm; Primary Teacher Rep Dist Discipline Comm, Grade Level Rep Grade Card Evaluation Comm; Young Authors Dist & Dist Title TX Evaluation Coord; Fine Arts Grant Prgm; Write-on IL Trng Building Rep; Negotiations Team Rep 1985-87, 1987-89; Hamilton Cty Teachers Fed (Building Rep, 2nd VP); AFT, IFT (2nd VP 1989-, 1st VP 1990, Building Rep 1985-); *home:* 1705 Newton St Eldorado IL 62930

SIMIELE, CAROL A., 4th Grade Teacher; *b:* Syracuse, NY; *m:* John A. Jr.; *c:* Mary Beth, Linda, Karen; *ed:* (BS) Elem Ed, SUNY Oswego 1965; *cr:* 5th Grade Teacher Prospect Sch 1965-68; 1st Grade Teacher Lakeland Elem 1973-76; 4th Grade Teacher Solvay Elem 1976-; *ai:* Solvay Teachers Assn 1965-; NYSUT; AFT; Impact II Mini-Grants Co-Winner; Contributing Author Impact II Handbooks; *office:* Solvay Elem Sch Woods & Orchards Rds Solvay NY 13209

SIMMERMAN, JACK RAY, Agricultural Education Instr; *b:* Martin Cty, IN; *m:* Linda Moore; *c:* Mark, Chris, Suzan; *ed:* (BS) Ag Ed, 1962, (MS) Ag Ec, 1967 Purdue; *cr:* Ag Ed Instr Owen Cty Sch System 1964-; *ai:* FFA Adv; Variety of Teacher/Sch Comms; IN Voc Ag Teachers Pres 1988-89, Outstanding Dist Teacher 1987 & 1989; Cty Cncl (Mem, VP) 1987-; Ec Dev & Cncl Pres 1989-; Forestry Resources Assn, Cty Fair Bd, Farm Bureau Coop, Teachers Assn, Civil War Round Table Pres; IN FFA Honorary St Degree; Natl FFA Honorary Amer Degree; IN Assn of Cty & Dist Fairs Hall of Fame Mem; IN 4-H Assn Outstanding Alumni Awd; *office:* Owen Valley HS R 4 Box 13 Spencer IN 47460

SIMMONS, BARBARA B., English/Speech Teacher; *b:* Hazlehurst, MS; *ed:* (BS) Eng Ed, MS St Univ 1975; (MED) Scndry Ed, Univ of S MS 1980; *cr:* 8th Grade Eng Teacher Magnolia Jr HS 1975-76; Eng Teacher Columbia HS 1976-82; Eng/Speech Teacher Mc Comb HS 1982-; *ai:* NHS Adv; Forensics Coach; MS Speech Assn 1982-; Beta Sigma Phi 1986-; *office:* Mc Comb HS 310 7th St Mc Comb MS 39648

SIMMONS, CONSTANCE HILGA, 5th Grade Teacher; *b:* Hazlehurst, GA; *ed:* (AS) Elem Ed, South GA Coll 1967; (BS) Elem Ed, 1969; (MED) Elem Ed, 1975 GA Southern Coll; *cr:* Teacher Jeff Davis Mid Sch 1969-89; *ai:* GA Assn of Educators; NEA.

SIMMONS, DOUGLAS R., Science Teacher; *b:* Oneonta, NY; *c:* Brett, Kelly; *ed:* (BS) Forestry, SUNY Coll of Environmental Sci & Forestry 1963; (MS) Sci Ed, SUNY Oneonta 1970; Natl Sci Fnd Inst Univ of N CO; *cr:* Sci Teacher Fort Plain Cntrl Sch 1965-; *ai:* Jr HS Wrestling Coach; Chief Negotiator Fort Plain Teachers Assn; S Minden Fire Dept Treas 1986-; Town of Minden Councilman; *office:* Fort Plain Cntrl Sch West St Fort Plain NY 13339

SIMMONS, ELINOR MOUNT, 4th Grade Educator; *b:* Panama City, FL; *m:* Bernard Franklin; *c:* Bernard II, Brittney, Deanna; *ed:* (BA) Eng/Bus, FL St Univ 1979; *cr:* 5th Grade Teacher 1980, 3rd Grade Teacher 1980-84, 4th Grade Teacher 1984- Chapman Elem; *ai:* Stu Cncl Assn Adv, GED Tester; Write Column for Weekly Paper; FCTA, FTP, NEA VP 1986-; Democratic Comm Mem 1988-; City Lib Bd Mem 1989-; Apalachicola Club Bus Mgr 1985-; NAACP Mem 1990; Teacher of Yr 1988-89; *home:* 401 24th Ave Apt 4D Apalachicola FL 32320

SIMMONS, ELIZABETH HILL, Bio & Human Physiology Teacher; *b:* Kosciusko, MS; *m:* William C.; *c:* Vietta S. Lewis, Sandra S. Boyd, Audrea L.; *ed:* (BA) Bio, Rust Coll 1954; Advance Work Bio, MS Univ for Women; Advance Work Earth Sci, Univ Southern MS; Advance Work Human Anatomy, MS Valley St Univ; Intensive Study in Bio Sci, Delta St Univ; *cr:* Bio & Human Physiology Amanda Elzy HS 1986-89; *ai:* Sci Club Spon; Advisory Comm Mem Supt of Ed; Le Flore Cty Assn 1957- Outstanding Service 1987-89; Delta Region Assn VP 1989- Outstanding Local Assn 1988; MS Sci Assn VP 1987; Natl Teachers Assn 1957-; Kappa Alpha Omega Chapter 1978- Soror of Yr 1985, Outstanding Service 1987; Cotillion Federated Club 1960-; Teacher of Yr 1988; Intensive Study in Biological Sci 1988; Mem MS Bio Evaluating Testing 1987-.

SIMMONS, GILLIE GILMORE, Sixth Grade Teacher; *b:* Birmingham, AL; *ed:* (BA) Eng/Scndry Ed, Birmingham Southern Coll 1973; (MED) Elem Ed, AL A&M Univ 1984; *cr:* 3rd Grade Teacher Wagner Elem 1973-74; 7th-12th Grade His/Eng Teacher Woodville HS 1975-80; 5th Grade Teacher 1980-81, 6th Grade Teacher 1981- Woodville Sch; *ai:* 9th-12th Grade Drama Club, 6th-8th Grade Jr Beta Club Spon; AL Ed Assn, NEA 1973-; Jackson Cty Ed Assn 1975-; Huntsville Cmmty Chorus Assn (Secy 1986-87, Public Relation Chairperson 1982-86, Exec Comm & Bd of Dirs 1981-); Nom Jackson Cty Teacher of Yr 1989-; Woodville Elem Teacher of Yr 1989-; Teacher of Month 1977; *office:* Woodville Sch Rt 1 College St Woodville AL 35776

SIMMONS, JAMES WILLIAM, World/European History Teacher; *b:* Atlanta, GA; *m:* Lisa Burting; *ed:* (BSED) His, GA Southern 1987; *cr:* Teacher Effingham Cty HS 1987-; *ai:* Bsbl Coach; *office:* Effingham County HS Hwy 119 Springfield GA 31329

SIMMONS, JONN LOUIS, Principal; *b:* Columbus, OH; *m:* Sue Ellen Mechling; *c:* Katherine, Daniel; *ed:* (BS) Elem Ed, (MED) Admin, OH Univ; Working Towards PhD Admin; *cr:* Teacher Glenford Elem Sch 1974-84; Prin Somerset Elem Sch 1984-; *ai:* OAESA, NAESA; Lions Intnl, Gideons Intnl; Past Mayor Glenford OH; Past Chm Hopewell Township Fire Dept; Perry Cty Childrens Services Bd of Dir Mem; Hopewell Township Zoning Commission Chm; *office:* Somerset Elem Sch 100 High St Somerset OH 43783

SIMMONS, KIVIE MC RAY, 7/8th Grade Lang Arts Teacher; *b:* Whiteville, NC; *m:* Sonda Evans; *c:* Kevin Gene; *ed:* (AA) Coll Transfer, Southeastern Cmmty Coll 1970; (BA) Elem Ed, UNC-Wilmington 1972; (MED) Elem Ed, USC-Coastal Campus 1986; *cr:* Occupational Ed Teacher NakinaHS 1972-73; 7th/8th Grade Teacher Old Dock Sch 1973-; *ai:* Jr Beta Club Spon; Old Dock Jr Historians Club Spon; 8th Grade Class Act Spon; Field Day Comm; Cultural Arts Comm; NCAE; NEA; Fire Dept Aux Sec 1989; Lebanon Masonic Lodge Master 1980; Palmyra Baptist Church Deacon 1977-90; *home:* Rt 4 Box 223 Whiteville NC 28472

SIMMONS, LUCY BARKER, Fifth Grade Teacher; *b:* Wilkes Cty, NC; *m:* Rochelle F.; *c:* Keith, David; *ed:* (BS) Grammar Grade Ed/HS Eng, Appalachian St Teachers Coll 1956; (MA) Intermediate Grades, Pembroke St Univ 1989; Mentor/Support Team, Performance Appraisal Trng Prgm NC; *cr:* 5th Grade Teacher Benham Grammar Sch 1955-56, Joe P Moore Sch 1956-58, Tanglewood Sch 1958-76, Joe P Moore Sch 1976-81; Eng Teacher Robeson Comm Coll 1978-86; L Gilbert Carroll Mid Sch 1981-; *ai:* Sch Base & Philosophy Comm, 5th Grade Math Chm; 5th Grade Cafeteria Schedule; NEA, NC Assn of Educators 1956-; Lumberton City Assn of Educators (Treas 1966-67) 1956-89; Robeson Assn of Educators 1989-; Alpha Delta Kappa (Treas 1982-86) 1976-; Lumberton Civinette Club (Pres 1970-71, 1986-87, Secy 1978-79, Treas 1979-81) 1966-89, Lumberton Civinette of Yr Awd 1980-81; Plant & Pray Garden Club (Pres 1976-77) 1969-; Inquirers Book Club (Treas 1984-86, 1989-) 1984-; Outstanding Young Educator Awd Lumberton Jaycees 1969; Devoted Teacher Awd Hunts Photography 1969; *home:* 526 Roslyn Dr Lumberton NC 28358

SIMMONS, MARTI J. J., Coordinator of Gifted/Talented; *b:* Great Lakes, IL; *m:* Ernest L. Jr.; *c:* Scott E., Leah K.; *ed:* (BS) Eng, Pitzer Coll/Minot St Univ 1980; Elem Endorsement, Moorhead St Univ 1986; Specialist Degree Gifted & Talented, Moorhead St Univ 1980; *cr:* Tutor Agassiz Jr HS 1980-84; Teacher/Coord West Fargo Mid Sch 1984-; *ai:* Newspaper Ed; Valley Teachers of Gifted Organizer 1984-; Valley Rdng Cncl 1985-; NDEA, WFEA; Alpha Delta Kappa (Chapter Pres 1986-88, St Officer 1988-); Inservice Speaker Gifted Ed; Article Published; Curr Presented St Conferences ND & MN; Curr Bd ND Centennial Forum; *home:* 2714 Rivershore Dr Moorhead MN 56560

SIMMONS, MICHAEL LAWRENCE, Physical Education Teacher; *b:* Herkimer, NY; *c:* Matthew, Megan; *ed:* (BA) Phys Ed/Health, Ithaca Coll 1987; Provisional Driver Ed Trng; *cr:* Head Var Bsbl Coach Newfield HS 1987; Permanent Substitute Coach Whitesboro HS 1988; Phys Ed/Jr HS Health Teacher NY Mills HS 1989-; *ai:* Var Club, 9th Grade Adv; Asst Var Ftbl Coach; 7th & 8th Grade Bsktbl Head Coach; Jr HS Bsbl Head Coach; NY Mills Optimists Club 1989-; NY St Phys Ed & Dance 1987-; *home:* 83 W Clark St Ilion NY 13357

SIMMONS, NELL MEALING, Retired; *b:* North Augusta, NC; *m:* Marion R. Jr.; *c:* Marion III, Catherine Hines; *ed:* (BA) His & Eng, Winthrop Coll 1942; Univ of SC; *cr:* Teacher Iva Jr HS; Teacher Walterboro HS; Retired 1986; *ai:* Delta Kappa Gamma Society 1972; Bethel Presbyn Church Elder 1990; DAR Vice-Regent 1990; Colleston Cty His Society 1985; Chm Soc Stud Dept 1961-86; *home:* 103 Marion Ave Walterboro SC 29488

SIMMONS, PAMELA AUGER, Assistant Principal; *b:* South Bend, IN; *m:* Robert Franklin; *ed:* (BS) Elem Ed, Ball St Univ 1974; (MA) Elem Ed, Univ of S FL 1981; *cr:* Teacher Nocatee Elem 1974-80; Primary Specialist 1980-82, Asst Prin 1982- West Elem; *ai:* Delta Kappa Gamma 1982-; FL Assn of Sch Admin 1983-; NAESAP 1983-; ASCD 1989-; Spec Olympics Finance Officer 1980-; St Paul Church (Dir of Religious Ed 1989-, Youth

Dir 1989-); *office:* West Elem Sch 304 W Imogene Arcadia FL 33821

SIMMONS, PATRICIA REESE, Rdng Recovery-Remedial Teacher; *b:* Parkersburg, WV; *m:* Phillip L.; *c:* Shelee, David, Timothy; *ed:* (BS) Elem Ed, Univ of Akron 1972; Rdng Specialization, Univ of Akron 1986; Rdng Recovery, OH St Univ 1988; *cr:* 3rd Grade Teacher Kleckner Elem 1972-85; Remedial Rdng Teacher 1985-, Rdng Recovery Teacher 1987- Greenwood Primary; *ai:* Supts & Prin Advisory Cncls; Retention & In-Service Comms; Green Ed Assn, Intnl Rdng Assn; *home:* 2854 Long Rd Akron OH 44312

SIMMONS, PAULA RIGGI, Fourth Grade Teacher; *b:* Latrobe, PA; *ed:* (BS) Elem Ed, Edinboro Univ 1974; Master Equivalency Elem Ed; *cr:* Kndgtn/Rdng Teacher 1974-83, 4th Grade Teacher 1983- Jackson Elem; *ai:* Act 178 & Course of Study Comm; NEA, Intnl Rdng Assn; *home:* 829 Walnut St Latrobe PA 15650

SIMMONS, RAYMOND MICHAEL, Fifth Grade Teacher; *b:* Birmingham, AL; *ed:* (BA) His, Jacksonville St 1970; (MA) Elem Ed, Univ of AL Birmingham 1975; *cr:* 5th Grade Teacher Blountsville Elem 1971-; *ai:* Awds Comm Chm; Blount Cty In-Service, Insurance, Textbook Comm; AL Educl Assn, NEA, Blount Cty Ed Assn 1971-; 4-H Leader 1971-76, 1983-, Blount Cty Club of Yr; *home:* 2305 Reed Rd NE Birmingham AL 35215

SIMMONS, RICHARD LEE, History Teacher; *b:* Auburn, WA; *m:* Carol Ann Kercher; *c:* Michael, Larry; *ed:* (BS) Soc Stud, E MT Coll 1962; (MS) Amer His, MT St Univ 1971; *cr:* Teacher Pasco HS 1962-63; Teacher Billings Sr HS 1963-; *ai:* Billings Ed Assn VP 1970-71; MT Ed Assn; NEA; COE Fellowship; *office:* Billings Sr HS 425 Grand Ave Billings MT 59101

SIMMONS, ROBERT RANDOLPH, Elementary Principal; *b:* Philadelphia, PA; *m:* Patricia A.; *c:* Tricia M., Robby R.; *ed:* (BA) His, MI St Univ 1958; (MA) Cmmty Sch Leadership, 1967; Specialist Arts Educ Admin, 1976 Eastern MI Univ; (EDD) Ed Admin/Supv, Univ of MI 1978; Substance Abuse Stu Asst Prgm; Effective Schls Project; *cr:* Math Teacher Sch Dist City of Flint 1962-68; Elem Prin Sch Dist City of Flint 1970-; Lecturer Eastern MI Univ 1988-; *ai:* Consultant-Founder Stewart-Brennan Youth Club Inc 1987-; Phi Delta Kappa Treas 1986-88; ASCD 1988-; MAESP 1987-; NEA Consultant 1988-; Urban Leag; NAACP; Flint Jr Chamber of Commerce 1968-70; Dort-Oak Park Neighborhood Cncl Exec Bd 1970-78; Mini-Grants Awds 1973-75/1979-80; Spec Ed Awd 1985; Flint Teacher Golf Leag Champ Awds-1974/1984; Greater Flint Olympian Canusa Assn Golf Awds 1981/1984; Rsrch Job Satisfaction Elem Sch Prin 1978; Univ of MI 1978; *home:* 2262 Nolen Dr Flint MI 48504

SIMMONS, ROBERT THOMAS, High School English Teacher; *b:* Orange, NJ; *m:* Judith Diane Coppedge; *c:* Khadija, Janae, Serenity; *ed:* (BA) Ed, Hampton Inst 1976; *cr:* Per Diem Substitute Menchville HS 1976-77, Newark Sch System 1977; Teacher E Orange HS 1977-; *ai:* NHS; Newspaper Adv Mgr; Teen Arts Coord; Writing Lab Cooperating Teacher; E Orange HS Teacher of Yr 1988-89; *office:* E Orange HS 34 N Walnut St East Orange NJ 07017

SIMMS, TANYA ROBERTSON, Third Grade Teacher; *b:* Langdale, AL; *m:* Michael Scott; *c:* Scott, John, Ben; *ed:* (BS) Elem Ed, 1978, (MED) Elem Ed, 1980 Auburn Univ; *cr:* 3rd Grade Teacher Lanett Cntrl Elem 1978-; *office:* Lanett Cntrl Elem Sch 200 S 8th Ave Lanett AL 36863

SIMNETT, JOYCE LE CLAIRE, Third/Fourth Grade Teacher; *b:* Boston, MA; *m:* Robert Edwin; *c:* Theresa A. Le Claire; *ed:* (BS) Elem Ed, Bridgewater St Coll 1966; (MS) Integrated Art in Ed, Lesley Coll 1978; Adult Basic Ed Certificate; *cr:* 4th Grade Teacher Finberg Sch 1966-75; 3rd-5th Grade Teacher Hyman Fine Sch 1975-; *ai:* Gymnastics Show Ribbon Dancers Coach; Alpha Delta Kappa (Historian, Secy) 1980-; Attleboro Ed Assn, MA Ed Assn, NEA 1966-; GSA Leader 1966-67; Camp Shady Pines Dev Comm 1974; Project Art in Rdng; Horace Mann Grant; *home:* 445 Locust St Attleboro MA 02703

SIMON, BONNIE M., US History & Civics Teacher; *b:* Canton, OH; *m:* Dennis V.; *c:* Daniel E., Jessica A., Andrew V.; *ed:* (BS) Ed His/Poly Sci, OH Univ 1969; Coursework Akron Univ; Kent St Univ; Ashland Coll; *cr:* Teacher Perry Local Schls 1969-; *ai:* Stu/Teacher Tutoring Prgm; PCTA 1969-; OEA 1969-; NEA 1969-; Jr Achvt Teacher Adv 1987-; *office:* Edison Jr H S 4201 Harsh Ave S W Massillon OH 44646

SIMON, CYNTHIA MC MULLEN, Mathematics Teacher; *b:* Columbus, OH; *m:* George David; *ed:* (BS) Elem Ed, Bowling Green St Univ 1970; Grad Stud Univ of Toledo; *cr:* 3rd Grade Teacher Lake Elem 1970-73; Title I Rdng Teacher Maumee Youth Camp 1974-79; 6th Grade Teacher Nathan Hale Elem 1979-84; 7th/8th Grade Math Teacher Leverette Jr HS 1984-; *ai:* Asst Vlybl Coach; Cheerleading & Youth to Youth Adv; Toledo Fed of Teachers Mem 1979-; Toledo Cncl of Math Mem 1985-89; *office:* Leverette Jr HS 1111 Manhattan Blvd Toledo OH 43608

SIMON, MARGARET MILLER, 4th Grade Teacher; *b:* Waseca, MN; *m:* Roger C.; *ed:* (BA) Elem Ed, St Teresa Coll 1963; (ME) Elem Ed, Natl Univ 1983; Rdng Coord; *cr:* 1st/2nd Grade Team Leader 1970-79, Jr Great Books Leader 1978-80, 3rd Grade Team Leader 1980-84 Walker Sch; Soc Stud Rep 1980-87, Young Authors Under Prgm Writer Dist 65 1982-88; 4th Grade Team Leader Walker Sch 1988-; *ai:* Geography Day 1989 & Earth Day 1990 Yr Act Dir; IL Ed Assn, NEA, Dist 65 Teachers Cncl 1979-; Delta Kappa Gamma Comm Chm 1989-; Dist 65 Master Teacher 1988; *office:* David E Walker Elem Sch 3601 Church St Evanston IL 60203

SIMON, PAMELA S., Teacher/Consultant Grades K-6; *b:* Cleveland, OH; *ed:* (BS) Ed, CA Univ of PA 1972; (MED) Ed, Univ of Pittsburgh 1979; Curr/Supervision/Real Estate, Univ of Pittsburgh; Income Tax Preparer H&R Block; Modeling/Finishing, Earl Wheeler Sch; Private Vocal Trng; Modern Dance Tap/Ballet/Jazz; *cr:* 5th/6th Grade Teacher Kiski Area Sch Dist 1972-77; K-6th Consultant Gifted Prgm Teacher Arin Intermediate Unit 28 1977-; *ai:* Past Producer/Dir Elem Musicals; Instr Adult Ed; PSES/NEA/AEA 1972-; Page 1977-; New Kensington Civic Theater 1972-; Cast Mem 9 Musicals; Leading Roles 4 Musicals; Mini Grant Awd Artist in Residence; *home:* 1218 Dallas Ave Natrona Hts PA 15065

SIMON, WILLIAM, Music/Band Teacher; *b:* Toledo, OH; *m:* Ameena; *c:* Deborah, Karen, Lila; *ed:* (BS) Music, Wayne St 1955; *cr:* Teacher Livonia Bd of Ed, 1965-67, Toledo Bd of Ed 1967-; *ai:* OMEA 1980-; *office:* Byrnedale Jr HS 3645 Glendale Ave Toledo OH 43614

SIMONDS, BETTY LEE PRICE, Retired Teacher; *b:* Redbird, MO; *m:* Roy Edward; *c:* Roy E. Jr., P. James, Jill Lines, R. Michael, Lisa Kissell; *ed:* (BA) Elem Ed, ID St Univ 1971; Grad Stud; *cr:* 1st Grade Teacher Falls Valley Elem 1971-77; Kndgtn Teacher Ammon Elem 1977-78; 2nd Grade Teacher 1978-84, 1st Grade Teacher 1984-87 Falls Valley Elem; *ai:* Delta Kappa Gamma, PTO; Trinity United Meth Church (Parish Relations Comm, Chm Ed Comm, Chm Church & Society Comm, Mem & Treas Bd of Trustees); Honorable Mention Awd for Teacher of Yr 1984; Awarded ASISU Schlsps; *home:* 1302 Laurel Dr Idaho Falls ID 83404

SIMONDS, RICHARD BRUCE, Social Studies Teacher; *b:* Oakland, CA; *m:* Darcy Hough; *c:* Joel, Wes; *ed:* (AA) General Ed, Diablo Valley Jr Coll 1970; (BA) Industrial Arts/Soc Stud, 1972; (MA) Industrial Arts/Soc Stud, 1974- CA St Univ Fresno; High Performance Learning, Learning Methods Group, England Techology Leadership Acad; *cr:* Soc Stud Teacher/Chm Los Cerros Mid Sch 1973-; Dir Learning to Learn Wkshps 1985-; *ai:* Rocket Club Adv; Earth-Day, Yosemite Inst Coord; St of CA Technology Dist Curr Cncl Consultant; Dist Wellness Prgm; Mentor Teacher; Prgm of Excl Awd for Interdisciplinary Prgm in Soc Stud 1990; Phoebe Hearst Outstanding Educator Awd 1990; *office:* Los Cerros Mid Sch 968 Blemer Rd Danville CA 94521

SIMONE, ELIZABETH BUTTERWORTH, Retired Reading Specialist; *b:* New York, NY; *m:* Henry L.; *c:* Susan K. Burrows, Jayne K. Heckman; *ed:* (BA) Ec - Cum Laude, Tufts Coll 1944; (MA) Ed, Syracuse Univ 1959; ABD in Rdng Sch of Ed, Syracuse Univ; *cr:* 4th-5th Grade Elem Classroom Teacher 1957-65, Rdng Specialist 1965-83 Main St Elem Sch; 7th-12th Grade Rdng Dir Manlius Military Acad 1968; Rdng Specialist Roxboro Road Mid Sch 1983-88; *ai:* Teaching Teachers Rdng in Content in Service & Childrens Lit 1969-71; Oranized, Developed, Led Wkshp for Scndry Teachers 1973; Cntrl NY Rdng Cncl (VP in charge of Prgms 1975-76, Pres 1976-77) 1962-; Teacher of Excl NY 1986; N Syracuse Ed Assn VP 1963-64; Guest Speaker on Lang Art & Poetry Syracuse Univ in Dr Margaret Earlys Classes: Guest Speaker, Lecturer Univ SC; Summer Inst Rdng at Syracuse Univ 1965; Article Published 1960; Excl in Teaching Awd; Key-Note Speaker Dist Wide for Rdng in Content for Scndry Teachers; *home:* 126 Sun Harbor Dr Liverpool NY 13088

SIMONE, MARY JO, Elementary Vice Principal; *b:* Cleveland, OH; *m:* Raymond Pietz; *c:* Ryan Pietz; *ed:* (BS) Elem Ed, Kent St Univ 1970; (MSED) Curr/Instruction, Univ of OR 1980; Basic Prin Certificate 1988; *cr:* 1st/3rd Grade Teacher St Michael Sch 1970-74, Ten Mile Sch 1974-76; 1st Grade Teacher Laurel Elem 1977-80; 2nd Grade Teacher Territorial Elem 1981-87; 1st-4th Grade Cnslr/Vice Prin Laurel-Territorial Elem 1988-; *ai:* Counseling Groups; 1st-4th Grade Soc Skills Trng; Peer Conflict Mgr & Organized & Implemented Prgm; ASCD 1987-; NEA, OEA 1974-; Confederation of OR Sch Admin 1989-; NW Women in Educl Admin 1987-; NAESP 1988-; Soroptomist Intnl 1989-; OR Society of Individual Psych 1988-; Leadership on Site Comm; Coordinate Staff Dev; *office:* Laurel-Territorial Sch 1401 Laurel St Junction City OR 97448

SIMONES, MARIE DOLOROSA, Social Studies/Eng Lit Teacher; *b:* Dubuque, IA; *ed:* (BA) His, Loretto Heights Coll 1948; (MA) Ed, Notre Dame Univ 1967; *cr:* 3rd/4th Grade Teacher St Anns Normandy 1951-55; 5th Grade Teacher St Anns Arlington 1955-61; 7th/8th Grade Teacher St Augustine 1961-63; 8th Grade Teacher St Paul The Apostle 1963-67, St Vincent De Paul 1967-; *ai:* Jr HS Wits Clash Coach; Stu Cncl Adv; Natl Geographic; Focus-Geography; NCEA; *office:* St Vincent De Paul Sch 2401 E Arizona Denver CO 80210

SIMONETTA, STEFANIE GASBARRE, French Teacher; *b:* Buffalo, NY; *m:* Anthony John; *c:* Daniella; *ed:* (BA) Italian, 1985, (MAH) Hum, 1990 ST Univ of NY Buffalo; Study Abroad Univ St Ranieri; *cr:* Italian Teacher ST Univ of NY Buffalo 1983-85; Fr Teacher John F Kennedy HS 1985-; *ai:* Fr Club Adv; NYSFLT, NY St Assn of Fr Teachers; Teaching Assistantship St Univ of NY Buffalo; *office:* John F Kennedy Jr Sr H S 305 Cayuga Creek Rd Cheektowaga NY 14227

SIMONS, SUE LYNN, English Department Chair; *b:* Great Falls, MT; *ed:* (BA) Eng, CA St Univ Long Beach 1986; *cr:* Eng Teacher St Joseph HS 1986-; *ai:* Yrbk & 25th Anniversary Booklet Adv; Jongleur Adv 1989-; Eng Cncl of Long Beach Cath HS Rep 1989-; NCTE, CATE, SCTE Mem 1986-; Amer Schlolastic Press Assn 1st Place Awd.

SIMONSEN, RANDALL WAYNE, Director of Bands; *b:* Flint, MI; *m:* Betty Lucinda Lowell; *c:* Bethany, David, Stephen, Edward, Thomas; *ed:* (BME) Music Ed, N MI Univ 1977; Grad Work Music; *cr:* Band/Choir Dir 1977-78, Band Dir 1979-80 Ishpeming Public Schls; Band/Choir Dir Sch Dist of Crivitz 1983-85; Band Dir L Anse Area Schls 1985-; *ai:* Marching Band Oddessy of Mind; MI Band & Orch Assn Dist Secy 1985-; Keweenaw Music Educators Assn 1986-; *office:* L Anse Area Schls 201 N 4th St L'Anse MI 49946

SIMPSON, DELOISE LYSGAARD (PERRY), Classroom Teacher; *b:* Marion, ND; *m:* Melvin R.; *c:* Greg A. Perry, Judy Buntemeyer, Douglas, Bruce; *ed:* Elem Ed, Univ of N IA 1952; (BS) Elem Ed, Univ of NE 1971; Working on Masters in Rdng; *cr:* 6th Grade Teacher Rudd Public Schls 1952-54; 5th Grade Teacher W Fargo Public Schls 1954-55, Anoka Public Schls 1955-56, Sioux Falls Public Schls 1956-57; 3rd-4th Grade Team Teacher Lincoln Public Schls 1971-; *ai:* NEA, NSEA, Lincoln Ed Assn; PTA; *home:* 3520 Poplar Pl Lincoln NE 68506

SIMPSON, FREDA COX, 2nd Grade Teacher; *b:* Corbin, KY; *m:* Robert W.; *c:* Kelly R., Sarah C.; *ed:* (MA) Elem Ed/Rdng, Union Coll 1971; *cr:* Remedial Rdng Teacher Flat Lick Elem Sch 1969-70; 1st Grade Teacher 1970-72, 2nd Grade Teacher Lynn Camp Elem 1976-88 West Knox Elem 1989-; *ai:* KEA/NEA; Central Baptist Church; *office:* West Knox Elem Sch 4300 Poplar Grove Rd Corbin KY 40701

SIMPSON, JEANNE GILLETTE, Second Grade Teacher; *b:* Brooklyn, NY; *m:* Don; *c:* Richard, Brent, Brianne; *ed:* (AA) Ed, MI Chrstn Coll 1966; (BSE) Ed, Abilene Chrstn Univ 1968; Grad Stud Univ of MI, TX Womens Univ, TX Wesleyan Univ; *cr:* 4th Grade Teacher Ludington Public Schls 1968-69; 2nd Grade Teacher Coloma Cmmty Schls 1970-71; 5th Grade Teacher Southwest Chrstn Sch 1982-84; 2nd Grade Teacher Fort Worth Chrstn Sch 1984-; *ai:* TCTA; Church of Christ Bible Class Teacher; *office:* Ft Worth Chrstn Sch 7517 Bogart Dr Fort Worth TX 76180

SIMPSON, JOYCE ANN, Secondary Eng & Span Teacher; *b:* Henderson, NC; *ed:* Amer Exchange Stu Prgm Span Lang/Mexican Culture, Ibero Coll of Univ of Mexico 1972; (BA) Eng Lit/Scndry Span, SUNY Purchase NY 1974; (Teachers Cert) Eng Lit/Scndry Span, Manhattanville Coll 1974; Bronx Comm Coll 1965; Manhattan Bible Inst 1965-67; *cr:* Teacher Asst The Child Dev Center 1965-70; Substitute Eng Teacher Mt Vernon Mid Sch 1974-79; Scndry Eng/Primary Span/His Teacher/Head Teacher of Span Dept The Kings Acad 1980-; *ai:* Spon Periodic Plays Skits In Span; Spon Periodic Prgm Eng/His Depts; The True Church Of God Communicant 1970-; Thesis The Black Amer as Depicted in Amer Lit; *office:* The Kings Acad Sch 2341 Third Ave New York NY 10035

SIMPSON, LINDA BUNDREN, 5th Grade Teacher; *b:* Stonefort, IL; *m:* Jack; *c:* Richard, Robert, Rena, Rhett; *ed:* (AA) Southeastern IL Coll 1963; (BSE) Southern IL Univ 1965; Southern IL Univ 1966-89; *cr:* Adult Basic Ed 1966-68, Pre-Sch Coord 1968-73 Center For Adult Ed; Kndgtn/2nd/3rd/5th Grade Teacher Eldorado Elem Sch 1973-; *ai:* North Cntrl Accreditation Steering Comm Mem; Young Authors Coord 1983-; 5th Grade Drug Abuse Prevention Prgm Presentor; Eldorado Ed Assn (VP 1982-83, Pres 1984); IL Ed Assn Convention Delegate 1983-84 & 1990; NEA 1966-; 1st Chrstn Church Teacher & Missions Comm; Delta Alpha Chapter Delta Theta Tau Pres, Natl Conventions Delegate 1967/1985; Saline Cnty Coll Club Pres 1978-79; Saline Cnty Chairperson Southern IL Center Pastoral Counseling 1986-87; Personalities of the West & Midwest 1968; Dictionary of Intnl Biography 1977; Ed of Cmmty Leaders & Noteworthy Amers 1976-77; Book Honor 1979; Psi Chapter Delta Kappa Gamma Society Intnl for Women Educators 1987-.

SIMPSON, LYNDA SUE HARRIS, Fifth Grade Teacher; *b:* Wilson Cty, TN; *c:* Bobbie S., Melinda K.; *ed:* (BS) Bus Ed, Mid TN St Univ 1964; (CPS) Certified Prof Secy, 1973; Grad Work at Numerous Univs; *cr:* Bus Ed Teacher Cannon Cty HS 1964-68; Secy/House & Senate Judiciary Comms TN St Legislature 1971-73; Elem/Jr HS Teacher De Kalb Cty 1973-77; 5th Grade Teacher Watertown Elem 1977-; Adult Basic Ed/GED Instr Lebanon HS 1986-; *ai:* Benjamin Franklin Stamp Club Spon; 4-H Adult Leader; Wilson Cty Ed Assn (Building Rep 1986-88, Area Rep 1989-, Secy 1990-91); Teachers Negotiation Team Mem 1988-; 4-H Adult Leader 1980-, Florence Lester Memorial Awd 1989; Sound & Light Bd of Trustees 1985-, Richard Lawlor Awd 1989; Cmmty Theater Secy 1986-; *office:* Watertown Elem Sch W Main St Watertown TN 37184

SIMPSON, MARIE WEBBER, Sixth Grade Teacher; *b:* Gaston Cty, NC; *m:* James A.; *c:* Thomas Mc Cray, Steven; *ed:* (BA) Elem Ed, Barber-Scotia Coll 1956; Certified to Teach Academically Gifted Stus; *cr:* Teacher Dallas Elem 1956-60, Warlick Elem 1960-; *ai:* NCAE Sch Rep 1982-, Certificate 1989; NEA; *office:* Warlick Elem Sch 1316 Spencer Mountain Rd Gastonia NC 28054

SIMPSON, NANCY P. JEAN, 8th Grade Science Teacher; *b:* Ventura, CA; *m:* Charles R.; *c:* Charles G., Melvin B.; *ed:* (BS) Elem Ed, Murray St Univ 1965; *cr:* Math Plus Teacher Coral Ridge Elem Sch 1978-79; Kndgtn/5th Grade Teacher OK Elem Sch 1979-82; 4th Grade Teacher Blake Elem Sch 1982-84 Lang Art/Sci Teacher Newburg Mid Sch 1984-; *ai:* Stu Cncl 1984-86; 8th Grade Trip 1986-87; Jefferson Cty Teachers Ed, Bd Mem 1984-; KY Teachers Assn 1965-; NEA 1965-; Task Force on Lib in Jefferson Cty; St Teacher Recognition 1985; *office:* Newburg Mid Sch 5008 Indian Trl Louisville KY 40218

SIMPSON, PATRICIA WARNER, First Grade Teacher; *b:* Charlestown, SC; *c:* Chan D. Jr., Chad D.; *ed:* (AA) Elem Ed, North FL Jr Coll 1965; (BS) Elem Ed, FL ST Univ 1967; (MS) Admin Supervision, FL A&M Univ 1974; *cr:* 4th, 5th Grade Rdng Teacher Leonard Wesson Elem 1968-1978; 1st, 4th Teacher Gilchrist Elem Sch 1979-; *ai:* Teacher Ctr Rep; Sch Improvement Team; Grade Level Chairperson; L CTA, FTP NEA Convention Delegate 1968-; DKG-Beta Phi Mem Chairperson 1975-; IRA, Leon Rdng Cncl; Peer Teacher, Recommended for Leadership Master's Prgm FAMU; *home:* 2144 Shady Oaks Dr Tallahassee FL 32303

SIMPSON, ROBERTA JEAN, English Teacher; *b:* Chicago, IL; *c:* Margaret L. Grimshaw, Kathryn A. Guy, Suzanne J. Trapp; *ed:* (BA) Eng, San Jose St Univ 1966; Addl Studies Curr Dev/Psych/Counseling/Lit/Inter-Ethnic Stud; *cr:* 6th Grade Teacher Faria Elem Sch 1966-67; Meyerholz Elem Sch 1967-69; Eng Teacher Joaquin Miller Jr HS 1969-; *ai:* Stu Cncl Adv; Journalism Adv 1971-74; Chairperson/Faculty Advisory Comm; Cupertino Ed Assn-Rep; Dist Curr Dev Comm; Prin of Summer Sch Prgm; Eng Dept Chairperson 1972-75; CATE 1980-; Cupt Teachers Assn Newsletter Editor 1972-74 St Awd Best Assn Newsletter 1973-74; CTA; NEA; PTA 1966-; PTA Life Svc Awd 1981; *office:* Joaquin Miller Jr High 6151 Rainbow Dr San Jose CA 95129

SIMPSON, SHIRLEY ROLAND, Third Grade Teacher; *b:* Mason, KY; *m:* Lawson B.; *c:* Lawson B. Jr., Paul R.; *ed:* (BA) Elem Ed, Georgetown Coll 1971; Masters Rdng Specialist Xavier Univ 1980; (Rank I) Elem Ed, Georgetown Coll 1987; *cr:* 1st-3rd Grade Teacher Williamstown Ind Schls 1971-73; 2nd Grade Teacher Mason Elem Sch 1973-75, Calvary Chrstn Sch 1975-79; Rdng Teacher Crittenden Mt Zion Elem Sch 1979-81; 3rd Grade Teacher Mason Elem Sch 1981-; *ai:* Union Building Rep; New Sch Building Comm; Mason Baptist Church (Sunday Sch Teacher, Comm Work) 1980-89; *home:* R 1 Box 173C Williamstown KY 41097

SIMPSON, SONDRA RENEE (GARRISON), Mathematics Department Teacher; *b:* Tulsa, OK; *m:* Grove Lee; *c:* Devin L., Sarah R.; *ed:* (BS) Math Ed, OK St Univ 1982; *cr:* Teacher Sapulpa Jr HS 1982-; *ai:* Ftbl Cheerleading Spon; *office:* Sapulpa Jr HS 7 S Mission Sapulpa OK 74066

SIMPSON, WESLEY ALLEN, Social Studies Teacher; *b:* Houston, TX; *m:* Cynthia Diane; *c:* David A., Jennifer L.; *ed:* (BSED) Geography, SW TX St Univ 1973; (MSED) Scndry Ed, Stephen F Austin Univ 1988; Sch Admin, Supervision, Gifted & Talented Trng; *cr:* 8th-12th Grade Soc Stud Teacher C E King Jr HS 1974-79; 8th Grade Soc Stud Teacher Cleveland Jr HS 1979-80; 12th Grade Soc Stud Teacher Tarkington HS 1982-; *ai:* Stu Cncl Spon; Sr Class Adv; Voice of Democracy Citation; *office:* Tarkington HS Rt 6 Box 130 Cleveland TX 77327

SIMS, CARL WALKER, Fifth Grade Teacher; *b:* Youngstown, OH; *m:* Vicki Lynn Simmons; *c:* Carlton W.; *ed:* (BA) Psych, Adrian Coll 1977; Teaching Cert Youngstown St Univ 1978; *cr:* Substitute Teacher Youngstown Public Schls 1977-79; Teacher Calvary Chrstn Acad 1979-; *ai:* Athletic Dir Calvary Chrstn Acad; Head Bsktbl Coach; Math Olympic Coord; NE OH Chrstn Conf Pres 1989-; Articles Published; *office:* Calvary Chrstn Acad 1812 Oak Hill Ave Youngstown OH 44507

SIMS, DAMON ANDERSON, JR., Social Studies Teacher; *b:* Lexington, KY; *m:* Norma Jean Ritz; *c:* Susan L. Wilhoit, Damon Ritz, John Anderson; *ed:* (BA) His/Poly Sci, Transyvania Univ 1950; (MS) Ed, IN Univ 1964; *cr:* Teacher/Coach Millersburg Military Inst 1950-52, Erlanger Lloyd HS 1952-55, New Albany HS 1955-; *ai:* Square Dance Club Spon; NHS Comm; NEA, IN St Teachers Assn 1955-; IN Assn of Track Coaches (VP 1967) 1955-76; IN Track Coach of Yr 1964; *home:* 1437 Mc Cartin Dr New Albany IN 47150

SIMS, GAYLE A., Chapter I Reading Teacher; *b:* Terre Haute, IN; *m:* M. Randy; *c:* Katie; *ed:* (BS) Elem Ed, 1981, (MS) Elem Ed, 1989 IN St Univ; *cr:* Chapter I Rdng Teacher N Salem Elem 1982-; *ai:* Intnl Rdng Assn, IN Rdng Assn Mem; *office:* N Salem Elem Sch PO Box 69 North Salem IN 46165

SIMS, JEAN TYLER, Fourth Grade Teacher; *b:* Charlottesville, VA; *ed:* (BA) Elem Ed, Univ of NC 1966; Grad Stud GA St Univ; *cr:* 3rd Grade Teacher Brooks Sch 1966-69; 2nd/4th Grade Teacher Christ the King 1969-72; 3rd/4th Grade Teacher Westminster Schls 1972-; *ai:* GAIS, MAIS 1990; Atlanta Jr League 1972-.

SIMS, JOYCE MITCHELL, Third Grade Teacher; *b:* Selmer, TN; *m:* Lawrence O.; *c:* William E, Etta K. Johnson, Darryl E.; *ed:* (AA) Ed, Jackson St Comm Coll 1976; (BS) Elem Ed, Lambuth Coll 1979; (MS) Ed Admin & Supv, Trevecca Nazarene Coll 1989; Addl Studies Divinity & Memphis Theological Semnry; *cr:* Mach Oper Shirt Factory 1964-65; Recptnst/Typst Walker Monuments 1965-66; Clrcl Work/Tele Slsprsn Sears 1966-67; Recptnst/Bkkpr the Independent 1967-69; Recptnst/Bkkpr the Spring Co 1969-70; Ins Clerk Selmer Clinic 1970-71; Clrcl Work Conley Brothers Bldg Supply 1971-72; Recptnst/Bkkpr Whitehurst Lumber Co 1972-72; Bkkpng Townhouse Inc 1972-74; Mach Oper Clrcl General Electric 1974-74; Teacher Emr Selmer Mid Sch 1976-79; 2nd-4th Grade Teacher Adamsville Elem Sch 1979-; *ai:* Mc Nairy Cty Ld Assn Pres; Mc Nairy Cty Ed Assn Humn Rels 1988-89; TEA; NEA; The Order of Eastern Star Dixie Chapter 115 1969; Mc Nairy Cty Ed Grant; Full Schlsp Memphis Theological Seminary; Publc Article in the Cumberland Presbytrn Missionary Messenger Jan 1990; *home:* R 2 Box 780 Selmer TN 38375

SIMS, KENNETH, Second Grade Teacher; *b:* Cowen, WV; *m:* Evelyn Eveon Hedges Smith; *c:* Retta V.; *ed:* Elem, Beckley Jr Coll 1963-64; (BA) Elem, Sheppherd Coll 1964-73; (BA) WV Univ Morgantown 1976; *cr:* 1st-4th Grade Teacher/Prin Cherry Run Elem 1964-66; 2nd/3rd Grade Teacher Great Cacapon Elem 1966-70; 2nd Grade Teacher North Berkeley Sch 1970-; *ai:* WV Ed Assn 1964-; BSA Leader 1966-69; Church (Organist, Teacher, Trustee) 1965-; Pleasant View Cmmty Center Pres 1977-79; Intnl Cake Exploration Society 1984-, Gold Metal 1988; Teacher of America 1990; *office:* N Berkeley Sch 213 Harrison Ave Berkeley Springs WV 25411

SIMS, RICKY RHEA, Science Teacher; *b:* Ozark, MO; *ed:* (BA) Bio, Sch of the Ozarks 1976; Grad Stud SW MO St Univ; *cr:* Sci Teacher Hurley 1976-78, Galena 1978-81, Blue Eye R-V Schls 1981-; *ai:* Jr Class, Stu Cncl, Beta, Sci Quiz Bowl, Sr Class, Tournament of Knowledge Spon; MO St Teachers Assn & PTA Mem 1989-; Cmmty Teachers Assn Mem 1988-; Lampe First Baptist Deacon 1984-; New Teacher Mentor; Prof Dev Comm; Compilation of Invertebrate Life Forms of MS Sound 1981; *office:* Blue Eye R-V Schls P O Box 38 Blue Eye MO 65611

SIMS, SHEILA M., Science Teacher/Sci Dept Chair; *b:* Dallas, TX; *m:* Charles D.; *c:* Samantha, Cameron; *ed:* (BSED) Elem Ed, David Lipscomb Univ 1980; (MED) Elem Ed, Stephen F Austin St Univ 1986; Sci Essential Elements, Sci Fair Project; Anatomy & Psychology; *cr:* 6th Grade Teacher Greater Atlanta Chrtn Sch 1980-81; 6th Grade Math Teacher 1981-82, 7th Grade Sci Teacher 1982- Mexia Jr HS; *ai:* Sci Club, Regional Sci Fair, Media Fair Spon Local Sci & Media Fair Coord; Sci Dept Chairperson; Mem Accreditation Plan Writing, Courtesy, Supt Advisory, Textbook, Drug Awareness Comms; Assn of TX Prof Educators (Secy 1984-86, 1987-89, Pres 1989-, Mem 1981-, St Conv Delegate 1990); Church of Christ (Mem, Bible Class Teacher, Work with Youth); Leadership Fellowship Baylor Univ 1984; *office:* Mexia Jr HS 616 N Red River PO Box 2000 Mexia TX 76667

SIMS, SUSAN BLACKMAN, First Grade Teacher; *b:* Pulaski, TN; *c:* Jay; *ed:* (BS) Elem Ed, Athens Coll 1972; (MED) Rdng, MTSU 1985; Grad Stud TSU 1988; *cr:* 8th Grade Teacher Bridgeforth Mid Sch 1968-69; 5th Grade Teacher W Hill Elem 1969-70; 1st Grade Teacher Pulaskl Elem 1972-89; *ai:* Pulaski Elem Homecoming Chm 1986; Public Relations Comm TABS Chm 1988; Giles Cty Ed Assn, TN Ed Assn, NEA 1968-89; Phi Delta Kappa 1986-89; Friends of Childrens Hospital Mem 1982-; Mainstreet Craft Show Chm 1987-89; March of Dimes Volunteer 1990; Leukemia Volunteer 1990; Jaycees Outstanding Young Educator 1975-76; St Dept of Ed Giles Cty Nominee; K-4th Grade Teacher of Yr 1989-.

SIMS, YVONNE NICHOLS, Guidance Counselor; *b:* Little Rock, AR; *m:* Rufus; *c:* Kimili A., Khalida A.; *ed:* (BA) Elem Ed, Bowling Green St Univ 1973; (MED) Curr/Instruction, Cleveland St Univ 1978; *cr:* Elem Sch Teacher Carywood Elem Sch 1973-80; Elem Sch Guidance Cnslr Aurora & Cntrl Elem Sch 1980-84; HS Guidance Cnslr Bedford HS 1984-89, Cleveland Heights HS 1989-; *ai:* Chrldr Adv 1983-89; NEA, BEA, OEA Membership 1983-89; AFT Membership 1989-; *office:* Cleveland Heights HS 13623 Cedar Rd Cleveland OH 44118

SIMSARIAN, KAREN ANN, 6th Grade Teacher; *b:* Buffalo, NY; *ed:* (BS) Elem Ed, Medaille Coll 1970; (MS) Elem Ed, Canisius Coll 1976; *cr:* Teacher St Gregory the Great Sch 1969-81; P H Green Elem 1981-; *ai:* Stu Cncl Adv; Yrbk Adv; VP PTA; TEA Mem 1981-; CCEA Mem 1981-; NEA Mem 1981-; Life Mem TX PTA; *office:* P H Greene Sch 2903 Friendswood Link Rd Webster TX 77598

SINCLAIR, BRENDA ARNETT, Sixth Grade Teacher; *b:* Macon, MS; *m:* Ralph; *c:* Scarlet B.; *ed:* (BS) Elem Ed, MS St Univ 1969; *cr:* 2nd Grade Teacher Neshoba Cntrl 1969-70; 6th Grade Teacher 1970, Elem Supvr 1988 Winston Acad; *ai:* MPSEA Dist Spelling Chm 1987; Sunday Sch Teacher 1984-; Outstanding Young Women of America 1983; *home:* 117 St Charles Ave Louisville MS 39339

SINCLAIR, CECELIA ANN, Spanish/French Teacher; *b:* Rahway, NJ; *m:* Timothy Charles; *c:* Christopher, Kelli, Jodie; *ed:* (BA) Fr/Span, Carthage Coll 1975; *cr:* Fr Teacher 1975-76, Fr/Span Teacher 1976-77, Span Teacher 1977-78 Schaumburg HS; Span Teacher 1986-89, Fr/Span Teacher 1989- St Petersburg Cath HS; *ai:* Dept Head; Lang Club Moderator; Faculty Advisory Bd; NHS Selection Comm; Alpha Mu Gamma 1975-; Cub Scouts SE Area Song Dir 1987-; HS Stus Leader Educl Trips to Europe Through Cultural Heritage Alliance; *home:* 1706 Woodhaven Dr Bradenton Beach FL 33510

SINCLAIR, E. MARDELE (FIELD), Kindergarten Teacher; *b:* New Brighton, PA; *m:* Daniel R.; *c:* Michelle, Brian; *ed:* (BS) Elem, Indiana Univ of PA 1967; (MS) General Elem, Slippery Rock Univ of PA 1973; Dr Glassers Schls Without Failure; Staff Dev Prgm; Heres Looking at You Yr 2000; *cr:* 3rd Grade Teacher 1967-70, Kndgtn Teacher 1970-71, 3rd Grade Teacher 1971-73, 1st Grade Teacher 1973-83, Kndgtn Teacher 1983- New Brighton Elem; *ai:* Former Safety Patrol Adv; NEA; PSEA (Past Secy, Building Rep) 1967-; Eastern Star 173 Organist 1965-; Presbyn Women (Deacon, Bd Mem, Moderator 1986-88, Secy 1990); Nom Thanks to Teachers Prgm; *office:* New Brighton Elem Sch 3200 43rd St New Brighton PA 15066

SINCLAIR, MICKY MERCER, Fifth Grade Teacher; *b:* Eldorado, OK; *m:* Charles W.; *ed:* (BS) Elem Ed, Southwestern St Coll Weatherford 1958; (MS) Elem Ed, East TX St Univ 1970; Advanced Academic Trng Rdng Specialization; *cr:* 1st Grade Teacher Ector Cty Ind Sch Dist 1958-63; 1st-3rd Grade Teacher Old Union Sch 1963-64; 1st Grade Teacher 1964-70, 3rd Grade Teacher 1970-80, 5th Grade Rdng Teacher 1980- Mount Pleasant Ind Sch Dist; *ai:* TX St Teachers Assn Pres 1970-71; Classroom Teacher Assn; Oustanding Elem Educators of America; Coll of Ed Outstanding Teacher Awd East TX St Univ Centennial.

SINCLAIR, STEVE JAMES, English Teacher; *b:* Coronado, CA; *ed:* (BA) Eng Lit, Univ of CA Santa Cruz 1985; *cr:* Teacher Westmont HS 1986-88, Leigh HS 1988-; *ai:* NCTE 1989-; San Jose Area Writing Project Teacher Adv 1988-; Dorothy Wright Awd for Excl in Teaching Eng; *office:* Leigh HS 5210 Leigh Ave San Jose CA 95124

SINDA, ROBERTA MARTIN, American History Teacher; *b:* Detroit, MI; *m:* Donald P; *c:* Paul, Mary Anne; *ed:* (BSE) Elem Educ, St John Coll 1960; (MAT) Rdng, Lang Arts, Oakland Univ 1981; Post Masters Studies Lib Sci Western Reserve Univ; G Richard Basic Course; Cert Catechist in Archdiocese of Detroit; *cr:* Teacher Fitzgerald Public Sch 1964-65; Van Dyke Public Sch 1966-70; St Germaine Sch 1977-; *ai:* Hist Dept Head; St Germaine Sch Yrbk Staff, Educ Comm Mem, Publicity Chm, & Dev Coord Cmptr Pals Prgms; Spec Sch Prog Coord; Parish Bulletin Columnist; Coached & Spon Students for VFW; Voice Democracy Broadcast Scriptwriting Prgm; Catechist 20 Years; Organized & Co-Directed Summer Bible Sch Prgm 1988-89 St. Donald Parish; St Germaine Sch Forensics Spon Jr HS; Lector St Mark Parish; *office:* Saint Germaine Sch 28250 Rockwood Saint Clair Shores MI 48081

SINENI, FRANK JOSEPH, Sixth Grade Teacher; *b:* St Joseph, MI; *ed:* (BA) His/Soc Sci, W MI Univ 1978; Working Towards Masters Degree Spec Ed of Gifted Univ of CT; *cr:* 3rd Grade Teacher 1978-80, 5th Grade Teacher 1980-81, 6th Grade Teacher 1981-, Bronson Schls 1981-; *ai:* 5th-6th Grade Bsktbl Coach; Dist Gifted & Talented Coord; Sch Improvement Comm; Bronson Youth Recreation Assn Pres 1981-86; St Conference on Gifted & Summer Inst on Gifted Univ CT Presenter; *office:* Chicago Street Sch 501 E Chicago St Bronson MI 49028

SINGER, BARBARA J., English Teacher; *b:* Cincinnati, OH; *m:* Norman; *c:* Debra Harter, Todd; *ed:* (BED) Eng, Univ of Miami 1967; Grad Stud; *cr:* Eng Teacher Miami Killian Sr HS 1967-68, Vine Jr HS 1968-72, Mohawk Jr Sr HS 1972; Advanced Placement Eng Teacher Centennial Sr HS 1976-; *ai:* Dir Annual Shakespeare Festival Centennial HS; Yrbk Adv; NEA 1967-; Columbus Ed Assn 1972-; Worthington Cmmty Theatre 1980-, Worthy Awd 1986-88; 1st Yrbk Adv at Miami Killian Sr HS; Published Articles on Career Exploration Voc Educator; Columbus Public Schls Desegregation Team; Developed Multi-Disciplinary Team Teaching Scheme Mohawk Jr/Sr HS.

SINGER, GWENDOLYN KEIPER, Second Grade Teacher; *b:* Fountain Hill, PA; *ed:* (BS) Elem Ed, PA St Univ 1971; (MED) Ed, Lehigh Univ 1973; Grad Stud; *cr:* 1st Grade Teacher 1971-74; 2nd Grade Teacher Lower Saucon Elem Sch 1974-83; 2nd Grade Teacher Reinhard Elem Sch 1983-; *ai:* Delta Kappa Gamma (Chapter Pres 1988-, 1st VP 1984-88); E PA Cncl Teachers of Math Mem 1982-87; Saucon Valley Ed Assn Public Relations 1976-80; Delta Kappa Gamma; Saucon Valley Cmmty Center (Bd of Dirs, Secy 1987-); Nom PA Teacher of Yr 1980; Lehigh Univ Top Ten Educators 1981; Saucon Valley Sch Dist Teacher of Yr 1981; Prof Affairs Chairperson St of PA 1989-; *office:* Reinhard Sch 315 Northampton St 1050 Main St Hellertown PA 18055

SINGER, KARLA ANN, 8th Grade Lang Arts Teacher; *b:* New Bedford, MA; *ed:* (BA) Elem Ed, Univ of WY 1986; Curr & Instr; *cr:* 8th Grade/Lang Arts Teacher Panorama Mid Sch 1987-; *ai:* Writing Assessment Comm; Talent Show Coord; Kappa Delta Pi Mem 1986-; Animal Care Group Mem 1986-88; People for The Ethical Treatment of Animals Mem 1990; Greenpeace Mem 1990; *office:* Panorama Mid Sch 2145 S Chelton Rd Colorado Springs CO 80916

SINGER, MARY THERESA, Social Studies Teacher; *b:* Brooklyn, NY; *m:* Joel; *ed:* (BA) Child Study/His, St Joseph Coll 1971; (MS) Ed, Richmond Coll 1974; *cr:* Early Chldhd Teacher Public Sch 105K 1971-75; Soc Stud Teacher Visitation Acad 1977-79; Soc Stud/Kndgtn Teacher Annunciation Sch 1979-81; Soc Stud Teacher St Augustine Sch 1981-82; Soc Stud/Health Teacher Our Lady of Victory HS 1982-; *ai:* Animal Lovers Club Moderator; Yrbk Financial Mgr; West Chester Cncl for Soc Stud Mem 1988-; Assn of Teachers of NY Educator of Yr Awd 1984-85; Intnl Cat Assn (Show Mgr 1989-, Cat Show 1990); Bay Ridge Ambulance Volunteer Organization Charter Mem 1974-79; *home:* 808 Bronx River Rd Bronxville NY 10708

SINGER, SONNY MIRIAM (GORIN), Reading Specialist; *b:* Heidenheim, Germany; *m:* Max Edward; *c:* Jeff, Kurt, Eric Shecter, Missy R. Shechter; *ed:* (BA) Ed 1969, (MA) Rdng, 1974 Univ of MO Kansas City; Elem, Rdng Specialist, Soc Stud, Comp; *cr:* Elem Teacher Ridgeview Elem 1969-71; Pre-Sch Teacher 1975-78; Rdng Specialist Nike Mid Sch Dist 231 1979-; Johnson Cty Comm Coll 1989-; *ai:* Dist Rdng Comm Mem; Intnl Rdng Assn; Brandeis; Natl Cncl for Jewish Women; Menorah Medical Center Auxillary; *home:* 9708 W 103rd Terr Overland Park KS 66212

SINGER, SUSAN JACOBS, H S English Teacher; *b:* Murray, KY; *m:* Robert Bruce; *c:* Eric B.; *ed:* (BA) Eng/Speech/Drama/Journalism, Univ of KY 1970; Eng/Comm, IL St Univ, Eureka Coll, Governors St, Roosevelt, Univ of KY; *cr:* Eng Teacher East Peoria Cmmty HS 1970-73, Cntrl HS 1973-74, Acad/Spalding HS 1979-84; Eng/Speech Teacher Stevenson HS 1985-; *ai:* Sch Curr Comm; Jr Comm for Jr Eng Revision; AFT; IL Ed Assn; NEA; Assn of Teachers of Eng; Womens Symphony Guild Bd

Mem; Hadassah; ORT; Michael Reese Fund Raiser; Bus & Prof Womens Club Awd; IL Master Teacher Finalist Awd; *home:* 1745 Central Ave Deerfield IL 60015

SINGH, KABUL, Algebra Teacher; *b:* Dhapali, Punjab India; *m:* Amarjit Kaur Sidhu; *c:* Prabhlee K. B. Khaira, Rajpreet Singh Bhullar; *ed:* (BA) Physics/Math, 1954, (BSED) Math/Sci, 1956 Punjab Univ; (MAT) Math Univ of TX Dallas 1987; Advanced Physics/Physics, Univ of Punjab 1964; Eng Educl System/Ed/Teaching Practice, Univ of Nottingham Inst of Ed 1969; *cr:* Sci/Math Teacher Rede Scndry Sch England 1971-79; Algebra Teacher Bishop Dunne HS 1980-81; Math Teacher Cecil W Webb Mid Sch 1981-; Dev Math Part Time Instr Richland Coll 1988-; Dev Math Instr Collin Cty Coll 1989-; *ai:* Prepare Math Stus Various Contests; Responsible Organizing & Developing Sci In Lower Sch; Curr Comm; Staff Dev Leadership; Algebra Hons/Book Selection Sub-Comm; Natl Union of Teachers England 1971-79; Webb Sch Presidential Awd for Excl Teaching of Math Nom 1988; Cncl Suburban Teachers Schlsp Univ TX Dallas 1986, 1987; Dr Pepper Schlsp Univ TX Dallas 1987; *home:* 2558 Primrose Dr Richardson TX 75082

SINGLETARY, KATY ADKINS, 2nd Grade Teacher; *b:* Cordele, GA; *m:* Ralph; *ed:* (BS) Elem Ed, GA St Coll for Women 1962; *cr:* 3rd Grade Teacher Meigs Elem Sch 1950-54; 2nd Grade Teacher Norcrest Elem Sch 1963-70; 3rd Grade Teacher Lee Cty Elem 1971-86; 2nd Grade Teacher Lee Cty Primary 1986-; *ai:* Natl Assn of Educators, FL & GA Assn of Educators 1950-; Lee Assn of Educators 1971-, Teacher of Yr 1978; *home:* Rt 1 Box 91 Leesburg GA 31763

SINGLETARY, POLLY BAKER, School Social Worker; *b:* Thomasville, GA; *ed:* (BA) Psych, Converse Coll 1972; (MED) Elem Ed, 1974, (MSW) Clinical Soc Work, 1988 Univ of GA; *cr:* 2nd Grade Teacher Union Cty Schls 1972-73; Title I Rdng Instr 1975-78, 1st/2nd Grade Teacher 1978-80, Sch Soc Worker 1980- Fulton Cty Schls; *ai:* Facilitate Self Esteem Groups Mid Sch & HS Levels; Sch Soc Work Assn of GA 1980-; Fulton Cty Homeless Task Force 1990; *office:* Fulton Cty Schls 786 Cleveland Ave SW Atlanta GA 30315

SINGLETON, JOHN LEE, Science Teacher; *b:* Waynesville, NC; *m:* Lynn Perry; *ed:* (BS) Mid Sch Ed, 1986, (MA) Mid Sch Sci, 1989 Gardner-Webb Coll; *cr:* Teacher W P Grier Jr HS 1986-; *ai:* Coach 9th Grade Quiz Bowl & Odyssey of Mind; Adv Stu Booster Club & Sci Club; Drop-Out Prevention Comm; Instr Caston Cty Commissioners Sch of Excl; NEA, NCAE Faculty Rep 1987-; NCSTA 1986-; 1st Baptist Church Youth Dir 1989-; Project Graduation Finance Chm 1989; Habitat for Humanity Volunteer 1990; Spangler Fellowship Recipient Gardner-Webb Coll; *office:* W P Grier Jr HS 1622 E Garrison Blvd Gastonia NC 28054

SINGLETON, LYNDA KING, Sixth Grade Teacher; *b:* Gainesville, FL; *m:* Joseph A. Jr.; *c:* LaTanya, Brandilyn; *ed:* (BA) Elem Ed, Savannah St Coll 1975; (MS) Elem Ed, Fort Valley St Coll 1988; *cr:* 4th Grade Teacher 1975-84, 5th Grade Teacher 1984-88, 6th Grade Teacher 1988- Eugenia Hamilton; *ai:* Sch Safety Patrol Prgm, Stu Cncl, Dance Team Adv; Sch Drug & Testing Coord; Sixth Grade Lead Teacher; Peer Coach; Bibb Assn of Educators, GA Assn of Educators, NEA 1975-; Tampa Mendez Drug Prevention Prgm Trainer; *office:* Eugenia Hamilton Elem Sch 1870 Pionono Ave Macon GA 31201

SINGLETON, MAE JOYCE (BURKE), 6th Grade Social Stud Teacher; *b:* Greenville, SC; *m:* Edwin A.; *c:* Tashmonique S., Beverly, TananArive, Taylon; *ed:* (BA) His, Bennett Coll 1963; (MED) Elem Ed, Clemson Univ 1983; *cr:* His Teacher Westside HS 1963- 70; Civics Teacher Mccants Jr HS 1970-71; Elem Teacher Nevitt Forest Elem Sch 1972-85; Soc Stud Teacher Mc Cants Mid Sch 1985-; *ai:* Quest for Understanding Adv & Spon; NEA; SCEA; ACEA; Aspiring Writer of Novels for Children; *home:* 126 Leawood Ave. Anderson SC 29621

SINGLETON, RONALD KENNETH, Physical Ed Teacher/Coach; *b:* Graham, TX; *m:* Martha Luttrell; *c:* Shelley, Kara, Melissa, Jaron; *ed:* (BS) Phys Ed, Univ of NM 1966; (MA) Phys Ed, W NM Univ 1972; *cr:* Teacher/Coach Carlsbad Mid HS 1966-81, Carlsbad HS 1981-82, Eisenhower Mid Sch 1982-; *ai:* 9th Grade Asst Ftbl, HS Boys Track Coach; NEA Mem 1966-; NM Coaches Assn Mem 1980-; NM Phys Ed Assn VP Phys Ed 1967-83, Honor Awd 1977; AAHPERD Mem 1971-; Jaycees VP 1968-75, Outstanding Young Educator 1972; BSA Scoutmaster 1970-80, Silver Beaver 1978; *home:* 403 S Lake Carlsbad NM 88220

SINGLEY, MARION R., English Teacher; *b:* Columbia, SC; *m:* George Carlton Betenbaugh; *c:* Judy, Michael, Tim, Susan, Ann; *ed:* (BA) Ed, Univ of SC 1959; *cr:* His Teacher Eau Claire HS 1959, Hand Jr HS 1960-61; Eng/His Teacher J Mason Smith Jr HS 1964-70, Falls Church HS 1970-; *ai:* Eng Writing Team; Eng Coord; NEA; VA Ed Assn; Fairfax Ed Assn; NCTE; *office:* Falls Church H S 7521 Jaguer Trl Falls Church VA 22042

SINGTON, SHARON CRENSHAW, Mathematics Department Chair; *b:* Dothan, AL; *m:* Leonard Turner; *c:* Nancy S. Burton, Leonard Jr.; *ed:* (BA) Math/Scndry Ed, Auburn Univ 1971; (MS) Math/Scndry Ed, Univ of AL Birmingham 1978; *cr:* Teacher/Chairperson Midfield HS 1971-; *ai:* Geometry Math Team; Jr Class Spon; Textbook Comm; AL Cncl Teachers Math; All Amer Bowl Womens Comm 1983-; Salvation Army Womens Comm 1988-; *office:* Midfield HS 1600 High School Dr Midfield AL 35228

SINHA, DAVID KUMAR, Gifted Education Teacher; *b:* Abington, PA; *m:* Vonda Kay Nelson; *c:* Devin, Ariel; *ed:* (BS) Elem Ed, Univ of WI Madison 1977; (MA) Educl Psych, 1982, (EDD) Curr, 1985 Univ of GA; Numerous Wkshps; Staff Dev Act; *cr:* Classroom Teacher WI Rapids Public Schls 1978-81; Asst Professor Emporia St Univ 1985-87; Ad Hoc Professor Univ of KS 1988; Gifted Ed Teacher Shawnee Mission N HS 1989-; *ai:* Spec Ed Dist Curr Review Comm; Adv & Spon Astronomy, Philosophy Clubs Shawnee Mission N HS; KS Assn for Gifted (Exec Bd, Univ Liaison) 1988-; ASCD, Natl Assn for Gifted Children; Articles Published; Coll Mini Grant 1989-; Public Service Radio Interview on Gifted Prgms; Prof Conferences Presentations; *office:* Shawnee Mission N HS 7401 Johnson Dr Shawnee Mission KS 66202

SINIBALDI, CAROL CHASE, Fifth Grade Teacher; *b:* Lawrence, MA; *m:* Robert John; *c:* Gayle Sinibaldi Merrill, Robert S.; *ed:* (BED) Elem Ed, Keene St 1956; Grad Stud Math, Sci, Lang Art; *cr:* 5th Grade Teacher Salem Public Schls 1963-70, 1972-; *ai:* Strategic Planning Comm; Salem Ed Assn, NHEA, NEA 1963-; *home:* 218 North St Georgetown MA 01833

SINK, DIANE WILLIAMS, Kindergarten Teacher; *b:* Lexington, NC; *m:* Russell W.; *c:* Jeremy, Matthew, Wesley; *ed:* (BA) Early Childhood Elem, High Point Coll 1972; *cr:* 2nd Grade Teacher Pilot Elem 1974-76; 5th Grade Teacher 1979-86, Kndgtn TEACHER 1986- Wallburg Elem; *office:* Wallburg Elem Sch PO Box 65 Wallburg NC 27373

SINK, LEONA OWENS, Soc Stud/Phys Ed Teacher; *b:* Davidson County, NC; *m:* Fred C.; *c:* Susan Sink Wagner, Kimberly Fritts, Holly Sink Poarch, Jody Sink Davis; *ed:* (BA) Soc Stud/Health/Phys Ed, Lenair Rhyme Coll 1954; Several Wkshps; *cr:* Phys Ed Teacher N Davidson 1954-55; 8th Grade Phys Ed Teacher Stanly Cty 1955-56; Phys Ed Teacher Lexington Mid Sch 1957-58, Tyro Jr HS 1959-63, West HS 1965-; *ai:* Vlybl & Sftbl Coach; Pep Club Adv; NCAE PACE Comm 1980; Vlybl Co-Coach of Yr 1982; Bronze Awd Winning Sftbl Games 1989; Pres Davidson Cty Republican Women; Asst Sunday Sch Teacher St Lukes Luth Church; *office:* W Davidson HS Rt 5 W High Lexington NC 27292

SINKS, JO ANN, Third Grade Teacher; *b:* St Louis, MO; *ed:* (BA) Elem Ed, MO Baptist Coll 1981; *cr:* 3rd Grade Teacher Tower Grove Chrstn Sch 1980-; *ai:* St Louis Univ Hospital Volunteer 1974-87; II Corinthian Missionary Baptist Church (Sunday Sch Teacher, Treas) 1974-; Outstanding Young Women of America 1983; *home:* 2329 Hickory St Saint Louis MO 63104

SINNETT, TERRY BROOKS, English Teacher; *b:* New Bern, NC; *m:* Walter Drew; *c:* John, Sarah; *ed:* (BA) Eng, Meredith Coll 1976; *cr:* Teacher Newton-Conover Jr HS 1980-83, Walhalla HS 1983-; *ai:* NCTE; *office:* Walhalla HS Razorback Ln Walhalla SC 29691

SINNOTT, DANNA HINTZ, Spanish Teacher; *b:* Spokane, WA; *m:* Michael Lawrence; *c:* Cody; *ed:* (BA) Span/Eng, Carroll Coll 1973; Universidad Ibero Americana Mexico City; Univ of MT Missoula; *cr:* Span Teacher Wolf Point HS 1975-77; Span/Eng Teacher West Yellowstone HS 1977-79, Imbler HS 1979-82; Span Teacher Helena HS 1984-; *ai:* Span Club; MALT, NEA, HEA 1985-; PNCFL 1985-89; *office:* Helena HS 1300 Billings Ave Helena MT 59601

SINNOTT, EILEEN MARIE, Principal; *b:* Wexford, Ireland; *ed:* (BS) Ed, Duquesne Univ 1964; (MS) Admin/Supervision, St John Coll of Cleveland 1973; Theology & Religious Ed; *cr:* Prin St Mary Sch 1964-70, Corpus Christi 1970-77, St Patrick Sch 1978-; *ai:* Continuing Chrstn Dev Dir; NCEA, OH Cath Educl Assn; Diocesan Prins Assn Pres 1981-84; Articles Published; *office:* St Patrick Sch 224 Center Ave Weston WV 26452

SINOPULOS, ANN M., Third Grade Teacher; *b:* Campbell, OH; *m:* Louis S.; *c:* Steven, Sylvia; *ed:* (BS) Medical Technology, OH St Univ 1948; Farleigh Dickinson, William Paterson Coll, Columbia Univ, Teachers Coll, Youngstown Univ; *cr:* Medical Technologist Med Lab 1953-61; Teacher Lindbergh Sch 1968-; *ai:* Governors Teacher Recognition Prgm Teacher of Yr 1987; NEA, NJ Assn 1968-; *office:* Lindbergh Elem Sch Glenn Ave Palisades Park NJ 07650

SINQUEFIELD, JO ANN MARTIN, Business Teacher; *b:* Yazoo City, MS; *m:* Stephen Bruce; *c:* Stephanie A., Luther C.; *ed:* (BS) Bus Ed, MS Coll 1969; (MS) Bus Ed, Univ of MS 1981; Courses in Cmptr Literacy; *cr:* Bus Teacher Olive Branch HS 1969-73, Horn Lake HS 1980-87, Senatobia HS 1987-; *ai:* Sr Class & Bible Club Spon; Jr & Sr Banquet, Sr Breakfast, Graduation Comms; Alpha Delta Kappa 1989-; *home:* PO Box 492 Senatobia MS 38668

SIPE, LYNN GARRISON, Third Grade Teacher; *b:* Bridgeton, NJ; *m:* Ellsworth L.; *c:* Darin L.; *ed:* (BA) Elem Ed, Shepherd Coll 1965; Grad Stud; *cr:* 1st Grade Teacher Middleton Valley Elem 1965-67; 1st/2nd/5th Grade Teacher Crestview Elem 1969-83; 3rd Grade Teacher Arrowhead Elem 1980-; *ai:* Cluster Chairperson; Testing Comm; Prince George Cty Ed Assn, MD St Teachers Assn, NEA 1965-; Chesapeake Riding Masters; Alpha Delta Kappa Historian 1985-88; Eastern Amateur Arabian Horse Assn 1989-; PTA Lifetime Membership; *office:* Arrowhead Elem Sch 2300 Sansbury Rd Upper Marlboro MD 20772

SIPES, CAROL SCHRANTZ, Mathematics Teacher; *b:* Saint Paul, MN; *m:* Charles H. Jr.; *c:* Thomas, Daniel, Kristin; *ed:* (BA) Math, Coll St Catherine 1959; Addl Stud Univ of VA Falls Church; George Mason Univ; *cr:* 5th Grade Teacher St Lukes Sch 1961-64; 7th/8th Grade Teacher St Josephs 1966-69, Our Lady of Good Counsel 1979-86; Math Teacher Bishop Denis J O Connell 1986-; *ai:* Stu Cncl Act Asst Moderator; NCTM; *office:* Bishop Denis J O'Connell HS 6600 Little Falls Rd Arlington VA 22213

SIPES, STUART MICHAEL, Fourth Grade Teacher; *b:* Terre Haute, IN; *m:* Jodie Ann Wood; *ed:* (BS) Elem Ed, IN St Univ 1984; *cr:* 5th Grade Teacher 1984-87, 4th Grade Teacher 1987- Terre Town Elem; *ai:* Vigo Cty Teachers Assn 2nd VP 1987-89; Intnl Rdng Assn 1984-; Phi Lambda Phi 1981-; *office:* Terre Town Elem Sch 2121 Boston Ave Terre Haute IN 47805

SIPOS, JOHN F., JR., Math Teacher & Dept Chairman; *b:* Homer City, PA; *m:* Susan Washington; *ed:* (BS) Math Ed, SUNY Geneseo 1966; (MS) Math Ed, SUNY Fredonia 1982; *cr:* Math Teacher 1966-, Math Dept Chm 1983- Amsdell Heights Jr HS; *ai:* Yrbk Adv & Co-Adv; PTA Teacher Rep 1983-, Life Membership Awd 1988; Kiwanis Secy 1980-; *office:* Amsdell Heights Jr HS 2751 Amsdell Rd Hamburg NY 14075

SIPPEL, GEORGIA LOESCH, Kindergarten Teacher; *b:* Lohman, MO; *m:* William J.; *c:* Rodney, Karen Pace, Richard; *ed:* (BSED) Ed, Lincoln Univ 1969; (MAT) Tchng Lang Arts, Webster Univ 1973; *cr:* 6th Grade Teacher 1969-71; Open Clssrm Teacher 1971-78; 1st-3rd/5th Grade Teacher 1979-85; Kndgtn Teacher 1985 Webster Groves Sch Dist; *ai:* Early Chldhd-Dist; Sch Improvement; Staff Dev-Dist; Co-Chm-Success/Rdng Writing; NEA Secy 1984; Bridging the Gap 1988-; *office:* Clark Elem Sch 9130 Big Bend Webster Groves MO 63119

SIRAK, ANITA BOGUSKO, Math Dept Chairperson; *b:* Wilkes-Barre, PA; *m:* Richard M.; *ed:* (BS) Math, Coll Misericordia 1973; (MSED) Math Ed, Wilkes Univ 1976; Cmptr Literacy ITEC Prgm; Religious Ed Inst Prgm, REI Scranton Diocese; *cr:* Math Teacher 1973-, Math Dept Chairperson 1980- Bishop O Reilly HS; *ai:* Sr Class Moderator; Jr Acad of Sci Spon; Sr-Jr Prom Adv; Sch Play Soung Coord; NCTM 1974-; Scranton Diocese Assn of Cath Teacher Secy 1984-; Luzerne Cty Math Cncl 1974-87; Bishop O Reilly Ed Assn (Secy, Negotiator) 1979-; *office:* Bishop O Reilly HS 316 N Maple Ave Kingston PA 18704

SIREN, ANNE HANBY, Journalism/English Teacher; *b:* Pascagoula, MS; *m:* Edward D.; *c:* Beth, Edward, Catherine, Christopher; *ed:* (BA) Eng, FL Atlantic Univ 1975; Eng Ed, Journalism, Eng; *cr:* Teacher Ely HS 1985-; *ai:* Natl Academic Games; Jr Civitans Yrbk & Newspaper; Quill & Scroll Adv; Journalism Teachers of America Mem; *office:* Ely HS 1201 NW 6th Ave Pompano Beach FL 33060

SIRIANNI, FRANK JOSEPH, English Teacher; *b:* Long Branch, NJ; *m:* Kelly Nichols; *c:* Mark, Cortney, Erik; *ed:* (BA) Eng, Univ NC-Chapel Hill 1962; *cr:* 6th Grade Teacher N Dover Elem-Intermediate East 1962-65; 8th Grade Teacher Intermediate East 1965-79; HS Teacher Toms River HS South 1979-; *ai:* Meet Dir Jr St Indoor Track Championships; Coached 26 Years before Retiring 1989; NJSIAA St Meet Dir 1977- Track Coach 1984; Jr Ed Asst VP 1968-69; Jaycees Dir 1962-70; Brant Beach YC Commodore 1986-87; *office:* Toms River H S South Hyers St Toms River NJ 08753

SISCO, LINDA MARIE (RAY), 2nd Grade Teacher; *b:* Oklahoma City, OK; *m:* Jimmie Lee; *c:* Ryan H., Dean, Craig; *ed:* (BS) Elem Ed, OK St Univ 1970; (MED) Rdng, NE OK St Univ 1976; Grad Stud Lib Media Specialist; *cr:* 2nd Grade Teacher Tulsa Public Sch 1973-77; 6th-12th Grade Rdng Teacher Heritage Hall Schls 1978-83; 6th/7th Grade Remedial Teacher Jones Mid Sch 1983-85; 2nd Grade Teacher Jones Primary Sch 1985-; *ai:* 5th Grade Bsktbl Concessions Chm; Parents on Enriched & Gifted Stu Assn; Staff Dev Comm (Chm 1985-86) 1984-87; Cub Scouts Den Leader 1984-86; Teacher of Yr Jones Dist 1985-86; *office:* Jones Public Schls PO Box 790 Jones OK 73049

SISCO, PATTY TINGLEY, English Teacher; *b:* Vallejo, CA; *m:* Chandler; *c:* Amber, Adrienne, Chad; *ed:* (BS) Eng, 1970, (MED) Counseling, 1974 Univ of N TX; Spec Ed; *cr:* Teacher Irving HS 1970-77; Cnslr Crockett Jr HS 1977-82; Teacher Irving HS 1985-; *ai:* Sr Class Spon; Campus Improvement Plan Comm; Assn of TX Educators; Presbyn Church Elder; *home:* 2210 Ivanhoe Cr Grand Prairie TX 75050

SISK, DONNA CLARK, Second/Third Grade Teacher; *b:* Huntsville, AL; *m:* James Noel; *c:* Courtney L., Lauren M.; *ed:* (BS) Elem Ed, Univ of Montevallo 1973; *cr:* Title I Rdng Teacher Hayden Sch 1973-74; 2nd Grade Teacher New Hope Sch 1974-76; 5th Grade Teacher Walnut Grove Sch 1976-78; 2nd-4th Grade Teacher Owens Cross Roads Sch 1978-; *ai:* Alcohol & Drug Abuse Ed Prgm, Effective Sch, Hospitality, Amer Ed Planning, Clean Cmmty Planning Comms; AEA, NEA, MCEA Madison Cty, N AL Rdng Assn; *home:* 2300 Winnie Dr Huntsville AL 35803

SISSON, ESTHER, First Grade Teacher; *b:* Hurley, SD; *m:* Marlyn K.; *c:* Dain; *ed:* (BA) Elem Ed, Sioux Falls Coll 1969-70; Advanced Trng Wkshps & Coll Courses, Elem & Gifted Ed; *cr:* 1st-8th Grade Teacher Turner Cty Sch Dist 1944-58; 5th-8th Grade Teacher Chancellor Elem 1958-59; 1st Grade Teacher Parker Elem 1960-; *ai:* Parker Ed Assn (Secy, Pres); SDEA 1944-85; Presbyn Church Session 1981-89; Order of Eastern Star 2 Star Points Chaplain; *home:* Box 302 Parker SD 57053

SISSON, MARILYN JEAN, Second Grade Teacher; *b:* Burrows, IN; *m:* James Roger; *c:* Karen Bahler, Brenda Duttlinger, Richard; *ed:* (BS) Elem Ed, 1973, (MS) Elem Ed/Rdng, 1981 IN Univ; *cr:* 6th Grade Teacher 1973-74, 2nd Grade Teacher 1974-79 Galveston Elem Sch; 2nd Grade Teacher Meredith Thompson

Elem 1980-; *ai:* Pi Lambda Theta Educl Honorary Corresponding Secy; *office:* Meredith Thompson Elem Sch St Rd 218 W Walton IN 46994

SITES, MARY RAMSEY, Rdng & Performing Art Teacher; *ed:* (BA) Comm, Rio Grande Coll 1987; *cr:* Comm Instr Jackson HS 1987-; *ai:* Theatre Dir; Prin Advisory Comm; JCTA, OEA, Little Buckeye Theatre 1987-; Gallia Baptist Church, Womens Fire Dept Aux; Number One Teacher Spring-Jackson HS; *office:* Jackson HS Tropic And Vaughn St Jackson OH 45640

SITZLAR, DENISE ELAINE, 6th Grade Teacher; *b:* Akron, OH; *m:* Jeffrey Scott; *c:* Brett; *ed:* (BS) Elem Ed, Univ of Akron 1987; *cr:* 8th Grade Rdng/Sci Teacher 1987-88, 6th Grade Teacher 1988- U L Light Mid Sch; *office:* U L Light Mid Sch 292 Robinson Ave Barberton OH 44203

SIVELL, BRENDA MC CLURG, 5th Grade Teacher; *b:* La Grange, GA; *c:* Beth, Benji; *ed:* (BS) Ed, Univ of GA 1970; (MS) Ed, Columbus Coll 1976; *cr:* 4th Grade Teacher Brown Ave Sch 1970-75; 5th Grade Teacher Gentian Sch 1970-76; 4th/5th Grade Teacher Center Sch 1976-88; 5th Grade Teacher Long Cane Sch 1988-; *ai:* NEA, GAE 1970-78; PAGE 1985-89; Selected Teacher of Yr Center Elem Sch 1987-88; *office:* Long Cane Elem Sch 238 Long Cane Rd La Grange GA 30240

SIVERTS, ANN HARVEY, English Teacher; *b:* Corry, PA; *m:* Rod; *c:* Thomas, Scott; *ed:* (BS) Scndry Ed/Comprehensive Eng, Edinboro St 1970; *cr:* Eng Teacher Baldwin Whitehall Schls 1970-71, Bethel Park Sch Dist 1979-80, Faith Cmmty Chrstn Sch 1980-; *ai:* Drama Spon; Bible Dept; NCTE; Kappa Delta Pi; *office:* Faith Cmmty Chrstn Sch 35 Highland Rd Bethel Park PA 15102

SIVERTSEN, DAVID LAVERN, Chem/Cmptr Science Teacher; *b:* Miller, SD; *m:* Delores L. Smith; *c:* Shane, Shannon, Shawna; *ed:* (BS) Ag, SD St Univ 1965; (BS) Bio, Huron Univ 1970; US Army Command & General Staff Coll; *cr:* Sci Teacher Miller Jr HS 1970-72; Chem/Cmptr/Voc-Ag Instr Miller HS 1977-; *ai:* FFA, Photography Adv; Cmptr Sci Coord; SD Voc Ag Teachers Assn (Pres 1987) 1977-; AVA Mem 1977-; Amer Legion, Veterans of Foreign Wars; Hand Cty Memorial Hospital Bd of Dirs; Honorary SD FFA Degree; Huron Univ Bio Grad of Yr; 4-H Meritorious Service Awd; *home:* HCR 5 Box 6 Miller SD 57362

SIZEMORE, EMILIE J., Guidance Counselor; *b:* Widen, WV; *m:* Pete Dorsey; *c:* Chris, Todd; *ed:* Phys Ed, Marshall Coll; (BA) Phys Ed/Health, Glenville St Coll 1957; (MS) Phys Ed, WV Univ 1962; Guidance Cnslr of DE, Salisbury St Coll; *cr:* Teacher Clay HS 1957-62; Teacher/Coach Georgetown Spec Sch & Sussex Cntrl HS 1962-77; Guidance Cnslr Delmar Jr/Sr HS 1977-78, Laurel Sr HS 1978-; *ai:* AFS, Peer Cnclr Adv; DE Adolescent Prgm Inc Coord & Acad Challenge Prgm Coord; Advisory Bd; Faculty Advisory Comm; Class Spon; Laurel Ed Assn, DE Ed Assn, DE Sch Cnslrs Assn, NEA, DE Assn for Counseling & Dev; Parent Teacher Stu Organization; Sussex Cty Assn of Cnslrs Prof Recognition Awd 1989-; Grace United Meth Church (Numerous Comm, Chm of Official Bd) 1962-; DE St PTA Distinguished Service Awd 1988; Certificate of Appreciation USAF Recruiting; *office:* Laurel Sr HS 1133 S Central Ave Laurel DE 19956

SIZEMORE, GEORGIA MONTGOMERY, Fifth Grade Teacher; *b:* Greenville, SC; *m:* Mike; *c:* Adam, Kyle; *ed:* (BA) Elem Ed, 1972, (MA) Elem Ed, 1978 Clemson Univ; *cr:* 5th Grade Teacher Dunean Elem 1972-80, Greenview Elem 1980-; *ai:* Berea 1st Baptist Church (Sunday Sch Teacher 1985- /T-Ball Coach Sosn Team 1986-); Duncan Elem Teacher of Yr 1973; Greenview Elem Teacher of Yr 1987; *home:* 18 Gardenia Dr Greenville SC 29611

SIZEMORE, LLOYD WAYNE, Social Studies Chairperson; *b:* Oceanside, CA; *m:* Cheri L.; *c:* Melanie, Matthew, Michael; *ed:* (BS) Scndry Ed, Univ of N TX 1977; Critical Thinking Skills & Classroom Techniques & Management; *cr:* Teacher Watauga Jr HS 1977-83; Teacher 1983-86, Teacher/Dept Chm 1986- Haltom HS; *ai:* Youth in Government Spon; Citizen Bee Spon; Boys St Spon; Assn of TX Prof Ed VP 1988-; Certificate of Recognition Amer Legion; *office:* Haltom HS 5501 N Haltom Rd Fort Worth TX 76137

SKAGGS, JO LYNN, Bio/General Sci Teacher; *b:* Wichita, KS; *ed:* (BS) Bio HPER, SW Coll 1976; Grad Stud Emporia St Univ, Pittsburg St Univ; *cr:* Bio/Health/Phys Ed Teacher Unified Sch Dist 256 Marmaton Valley 1976-78; Bio/Gen Sci Teacher Erie HS 1978-; *ai:* Sci Club; SADD; KS Future Educators of America; NEA, KNEA; Delta Kappa Gamma 2nd VP; *office:* Erie HS PO Box 18 Erie KS 66733

SKAGGS, PATRICIA KARON (WARD), Business Education Teacher; *b:* Poplar Bluff, MO; *m:* Benny Alonzo; *c:* Shannon; *ed:* (BSE) Bus Ed, 1970, (MSE) Bus Ed, 1974 AR St Univ; *cr:* Teacher Neelyville HS 1971-; *ai:* Class of 1990 & FBLA Spon; NEA, MO Voc Assn 1986-; Neelyville Classroom Teachers Assn Pres 1985; Beta Sigma Phi (Secy, VP, Pres, Cncl Pres 1989) 1981-, Woman of Yr 1983, 1989.

SKALSKI, MARIE PAULINE, Reading Teacher; *b:* Jackson, MI; *ed:* (BA) Ed, Mount St Joseph Coll 1965; (med) Exceptional Children, Xavier Univ 1971; *cr:* Teacher St Dominic Elem 1964-67, St Joseph Orphanage 1967-71; Prin St Mary Elem 1971-81; Teacher Shrine Grade Sch 1981-; *ai:* Cncl For Prevention Of Child Abuse Bd Of Dir; Rainbow Support Groups Facilitator; *office:* Shrine Grade Sch Woodward at 12 Mile Rd Royal Oak MI 48067

SKAVRON, GEORGE JOSEPH, JR., Mathematics/Science Teacher; *b:* Bourne, MA; *m:* Deborah Shaddinger; *c:* Ryan M., Brooke L.; *ed:* (BS) Petroleum Engr, LA St Univ 1985; *cr:* Teacher Millerville Acad 1985-86, ITT Tech Inst 1989, Hillwood Comprehensive HS 1987-; *ai:* Univ of TN 1987-89, Outstanding Teacher 1987; Metropolitan Nashville Ed Fnd Mini-Grant; Comm on Presidential Scholars 1987-89; Distinguished Teacher 1987; *home:* 820 Cedar Pointe Pkwy Antioch TN 37013

SKAY, MARGARET NELSON, Third Grade Teacher; *b:* Willmar, MN; *c:* Summer; *ed:* (AA) 1954, (BA) Elem Ed, St Cloud Univ 1958; Hartnell Coll, San Jose St, Mankato Univ of Mn; *cr:* 1st Grade Teacher Johnson Elem 1954-55, Sherwood Elem 1955-56; 8th Grade Sci/Geography Teacher Univ of MD 1956-57: 1st Grade Teacher Garfield Elem 1958-60; 1st-3rd/6th Grade Teacher Eliot & Aquila Elem 1960-; *ai:* MEA, NEA, AFT 1955-; *office:* Aquila Elem Sch 8500 W 31st St Saint Louis Park MN 55426

SKEEN, REVA JEAN, 5th/6th Grade Teacher; *b:* Ansley, NE; *m:* Dale P.; *c:* Gary, John; *ed:* (BA) Elem Ed, Kearney St 1980; *cr:* Teacher Class 1 Schls 1945-47, 1956-63, Mason City Public 1979-; *ai:* NEA, NSEA, NE Ed Assn; *home:* Rt 2 Box 197 Broken Bow NE 68822

SKEEN, TERRI HEER, 5th Grade Soc Studies Teacher; *b:* Birmingham, AL; *m:* Jon P.; *c:* Jonathan, Stacey L.; *ed:* (BS) Elem Ed, Univ of AL Birmingham 1980; *cr:* 5th Grade Teacher Hayden Elem 1980-; *ai:* Elem Girls Sftbl Coach; AL Ed Assn, NEA 1980-; *office:* Hayden Elem Sch 160 Bracken Ln Hayden AL 35079

SKELLETT, LINDA MARLENE JENKINS, 3rd Grade Teacher; *b:* Beverly Hills, CA; *m:* Duane Paul; *c:* Sean, Dustin, Katherine, Nina; *ed:* (BA) Soc Sci/Ed, Univ of S CA 1962; (MA) Curr/Instruction, NM St Univ 1989; Various Courses at Various Univs; *cr:* Elem Teacher Los Angeles City Schls 1962-69, Ruidoso Municipal Schls 1971-; *ai:* Architectural Planning, Site Based Budget Comms; Soc Stud Curr; Emergency Crisis Team; Foster Parent; Ruidoso Ed Assn, NEA 1971-87; IRA 1990; Altrusa Episcopal Church 1978-87; HS Career Day Organizer & Chairperson 1986-87; Holy Mt Episcopal Pre-Sch Coord 1973-78; *home:* Box 1170 Ruidoso NM 88345

SKELLY, LINDA BRIGID O'KEEFE, English Teacher; *b:* New York City, NY; *m:* Thomas F. III; *c:* Bonnie J., Shamus, Brendan; *ed:* (BA) Eng/Scndry Ed, Herbert H Lehman Coll City Univ of NY 1971; (MA) Speech Comm, Western CT St Univ 1974; Admin Certificate in Supervision, Southern CT St Univ; *cr:* Eng Teacher New Fairfield HS 1971-; *ai:* Adv to New Fairfield HS; Sch & Cmnty Volunteer Service; Twice Recognized By Governor William ONeill for Outstanding Merits; Phi Delta Kappa 1974-; NEA Life Mem 1971-; CT Ed Assn 1971-; Univ of CT Alumni Assn Excl in Teaching 1989; 1st Runner Teacher Yr New Fairfield HS 1988; Plaque 16 Yrs of Service New Fairfield System 1987; *office:* New Fairfield H S Gillotti Rd Danbury CT 06812

SKELTON, DIANE JONES, 9th Grade Teacher of G/T ENG; *b:* Pascagoula, MS; *m:* Danny D.; *c:* Shannon, Colin, Nicholas; *ed:* (BS) Eng/Journalism, Univ of S MS 1969; Trng for Gifted & Talented Teachers TX Governors Sch; Cinematography, Univ TX Tyler; Continuing Ed Writing Fiction for Publication Tyler Jr Coll; *cr:* Teacher/Instruction Grace King HS 1970-72; Art Teacher 1979-85, 5th-6th Grade Teacher 1985-87 All Saints Episcopal Sch; Gifted & Talented 9th Grade Eng Teacher Robert E Lee HS 1987-; *ai:* UIL Spelling Team Coach; Soph Class Spon; Tyler Friends of Gifted, TX Assn for Gifted & Talented, NCTE; Natl Panhellenic Editors Assn Top Feature Article 1980; Delta Zeta (Natl Newsletter Chm 1986-, Tyler Area Alumna Pres 1982-84), Alumna Service Awd 1984; Outstanding Young Women of America; Wkshp Presenter TX Assn for Gifted & Talented St Convention 1989; Region VII Gifted & Talented Workout Presenter 1989; Whos Who in Amer Ed 1989; *office:* Robert E Lee HS 411 E Loop 323 Tyler TX 75701

SKELTON, SANDRA KAY (SUNBERG), Jr HS Mathematics Teacher; *b:* Hammond, IN; *m:* Bryan L.; *ed:* (BA) Cmptr Sci, Mid Amer Nazarene Coll 1985; Scndry Math Ed, S IL Univ Edwardsville 1987; *cr:* Math Teacher Roxana Jr HS 1987-; *ai:* Belleville 1st Church of Nazarene (Choir Dir, 1986-89, Compassionate Ministries Soc Dir 1989-, Secy of Bd 1986-); *office:* Roxana Jr HS N Chaffer Ave Roxana IL 62084

SKETEL, AMIE LYNN (NELMS), Mathematics Teacher; *b:* Wheeling, WV; *m:* Richard M. Jr.; *c:* Whitney L., Kelsey A.; *ed:* (BS) Elem Ed, OH Univ 1983; *cr:* Math Teacher Union Local HS 1983-; *ai:* Club Adv 1992; Delta Kappa Gamma 1989-.

SKIDMORE, JUDY L., Vocational Home Ec Teacher; *b:* Circleville, OH; *m:* J. Robert; *c:* John, Kelly; *ed:* (BA) Voc Home Ec Ed, Miami Univ 1976; Trng Akron Univ, Mt St Josephs, OH Univ, Franklin Univ; *cr:* Home Ec Teacher Circleville Jr HS 1976-82; Voc Home Ec Teacher Circleville HS 1982-; *ai:* Soph Class Adv; NEA, OEA 1976-; CEA Building Rep 1989-; Sigma Sigma Sigma Natl Officer 1976-82; AAUW Secy 1983-85; Cmmty United Meth Church (Various Comm, Music Dir); Teach Quilting Classes within Cmmty; *office:* Circleville HS 380 Clark Dr Circleville OH 43113

SKINNER, KATHY A., Spanish Teacher; *b:* Corydon, IN; *m:* Robert B.; *ed:* (BA) Eng, 1969-72; (MA) Eng/Span, 1973-75, Certificate Scndry Counseling, 1978 Univ of Evansville; Span, Purdue Univ 1975; Cmptr Wkshps Univ of Evansville 1978; *cr:* Teacher Castle HS 1973-; Crisis Line Cnslr Albion Fellows Bacon Center for Domestic Violence 1985-; *ai:* Chargerettes Pom Pon Squad; Speech Team; Alrise Support Groups; Kappa Kappa Iota (St Pres 1984-86, Local Pres 1978-81); Alpha Lambda Delta; Lambda Iota Tau; Natl Forensic League; Albion Fellows Bacon (Mem, Volunteer) 1988, 1990, Volunteer of Yr; Cerebral Palsy Volunteer 1990, Volunteer of Yr; WKDQ Radio Working Woman of Day 1990; Published Poem: *office:* Castle HS 3344 Hwy 261 Newburgh IN 47630

SKINNER, LAURENCE, 5th/6th Grade Teacher; *b:* Mobile, AL; *m:* Martha Parker; *c:* Karen Skinner Spellman, Sharon A., Laurence Jr.; *ed:* (BA) Ed, Univ of S CA 1972-73; Pupil Personnel Counseling, Pepperdine Univ 1973-74; (MS) Soc Sci/Ed, Azusa Univ 1976; *cr:* Cmmty Teacher Aide 1967-69, Instructional Teacher Aide 1969-71, Bd of Trustees Liason 1969-72 Compton Unified Schls; Cnslr/Teacher Lynwood Unified Schls 1973-; *ai:* Chm Black His Comm; Co-Chm Track Team; Co-Founder Compton Sounders Drill Team; Asst Coach Compton Little League Pop Warner; Lynwood Teacher Assn Rep 1974-75; CA Teacher Assn, NEA 1973; PTA VP 1968-69; *office:* Mark Twain Elem Sch 12315 Thorson Ave Lynwood CA 90262

SKINNER, MARGARET SWEENEY, Spanish Teacher; *b:* Mt Pleasant, MI; *m:* Robert A.; *c:* Robert, Elizabeth; *ed:* (MA) Eng, 1973, (BA) Span 1962 Cntrl MI Univ; *cr:* Span Teacher Marysville HS 1965-68; Latin Teacher Bay City Cntrl 1975-78; Eng Teacher Clio HS 1978-84; Span Teacher T L Handy 1984-; *ai:* Amnesty Intnl Spon; AATSP 1989-; BCEA Exec Bd 1990; Friends of Lib 1980-; Juan Carlos I Quincentennial Fellowship 1989; *home:* 1506 Borton Essexville MI 48732

SKINNER, PATRICK F., English Teacher; *b:* Tacoma, WA; *m:* Martha Spaulding; *c:* Lisa, Sara; *ed:* (BA) Eng, Univ WA 1965; (MA) Eng Lit, San Francisco St Univ 1973; Univ CA/Berkeley; Sonoma St Univ; Dominican Coll; *cr:* Teacher Davidson Jr HS 1966-68, Terra Linda HS 1968-; *ai:* Boys Bsktbl Coach; NCTE 1966-; Bay Area Writing Project Consultant 1975-; CA Lit Project Consultant 1988-; Mentor Teacher in Eng; 2 Articles Published; Frequent Graduation Speaker; Designer of Dist Curr for Coll Prep & Honors Eng; *office:* Terra Linda HS 320 Nova Albion Wy San Rafael CA 94903

SKIRVEN, SHIRLEY BERBERIAN, Math Department Chairperson; *b:* Arcadia, FL; *w:* George H. (dec); *c:* Kimberly, Andrea, Lindsay; *ed:* (BA) Math, Dickinson Coll 1964; (MS) Teaching of Scndry Math, Temple Univ 1968; IBM Programming Sch; H&R Block Tax; *cr:* Teacher Cheltenham HS 1964-68, 1970; Homebound Tutor Naperville IL 1973-79; Math Dept Chairperson Acad of Notre Dame 1981-; *ai:* Stu Handbook Comm; NCTM 1983-; *office:* Academy of Notre Dame 180 Middlesex Rd Tyngsboro MA 01879

SKLACK, ELIZABETH LAURETTA (MC CURDY), Kindergarten Teacher; *b:* Butler, PA; *m:* Peter; *c:* Michael, David, Dennis; *ed:* (BA) Elem Ed, Slippery Rock 1964; Grad Word Elem Field; Several Wkshps; *cr:* Kndgtn Teacher Freedom Area Sch Dist 1964-; *ai:* Wrestling, Chrldr Spon; Tamburigans Spon & Treas; PSEA, NEA, FAEA; Unionville PTA (Pres 1967-68, Big Knob PTA Treas 1970-71), Schlsp Awd 1989; *office:* Big Knob Elem Sch 200 Fezell Freedom PA 15042

SKLARSKY, THOMAS, Fourth Grade Teacher; *b:* Sewickley, PA; *m:* Raye Ann Yocca; *c:* Alexander; *ed:* (BS) Elem Ed, Edinboro St Coll 1974; (ME) Elem Ed, Univ of Pittsburgh 1980; *cr:* Tutor ACLD 1975-78; 3rd-6th Grade Teacher Edgeworth Elem Sch 1975-; *ai:* Quaker Valley Ed Assn (Building Rep 1978-89/ Executive Comm 1978-89); Sewickley Shooting & Fishing Club (Dir 1985-88/VP 1988-); *office:* Edgeworth Elem Meadow Ln Edgeworth PA 15143

SKOGEN, DANIEL LEE, Fifth & Sixth Grade Teacher; *b:* Blue Earth, MN; *m:* Susan Jean Kroeger; *c:* Aaron, Rebecca, Nathaniel; *ed:* (BA) Elem Ed, Augustana Coll 1973; (MS) Elem Ed/Gifted, Mankato St Univ 1984; *cr:* 5th-6th Grade Teacher Sioux Valley Schls 1973-; *ai:* Photography Club Adv; Calendar Comm; SD Ed Assn 1973-; Sioux Valley Ed Assn Pres 1975-76; NEA 1973-; Jaycees 1974-76, Outstanding Young Educator 1978; Beta Psi People Helping People Awd 1982; Jaycees Outstanding Young Man of Yr 1986; BSA Scoutmaster 1974-, Dist Scoutmaster of Yr 1983; Gideons Intnl Mem 1984-; *home:* 209 Washington Rd Volga SD 57071

SKOGEN, DARRELL LEE, Social Studies Chairperson; *b:* Minneapolis, MN; *m:* Ruth A. Elhard; *ed:* (BA) His/Eng, Augsburg Coll 1971; (MA) Liberal Stud, Hamline Univ 1988; *cr:* His Teacher Wabasso HS 1971-75; His Teacher/Dept Chairperson St Micha El-Albertville HS 1975-; *ai:* MN Fed of Teachers Newsletter/ Editor 1986-89 Awds for Newsletter Editing/Writing 1989; MN Cncl for Soc Stud 1972-75; Jaycees 1976-78; Taft Seminar Mac Alester Coll 1975; *home:* 9575 Glacier Ln Mapel Grove MN 55369

SKOKO, PAUL IVAN, English Teacher; *b:* Georgetown, SC; *ed:* (BS) Eng, Coll of Charleston 1965; *cr:* Eng Teacher Mc Clenaghan HS 1965-66, 1974-75, S Florence HS 1976-; *ai:* Stu Cncl Homecoming, Miss S Florence Pageant, Awds Night, Elections; Jr-Sr Prom; NEA, SCEA, FIEA, NCTE; Duncan Memorial United Meth Church Organist 1965-; *office:* S Florence HS 3200 S Irby St Florence SC 29501

SKOMP, LISA HASSFURDER, Third Grade Teacher; *b:* Newcastle, IN; *m:* Mark E.; *c:* Sarah E., Matthew W.; *ed:* (BS) Ed, 1973, (MS) Ed, 1977 IN Univ; Grad Stud Ed; *cr:* Substitute Teacher Kokomo Consolidated Schls 1973-75; Mgr Cole Natl 1975-78; Bus Owner Long Key FL 1978-79; Teacher Cherokee Cty

Schls 1979-; *ai:* Track Coach; Help with Midget-Mite Bsktbl 4th-8th Grade; *home:* 204 Valley River Ave Murphy NC 28906

SKOMRA, JEAN GEALY, Reading Teacher; *b:* Mc Keesport, PA; *m:* Gary L.; *c:* Shannon; *ed:* (ME) Rdng Specialist, 1989, (BS) Elem Ed, 1969 California Univ of PA; ADAPT, ITECI, Natl Geographic Society Mid Sch Curr; *cr:* 3rd Grade Elem Teacher Victory Sch 1969-72, William Penn Sch 1972-73; Rdng Teacher E F Jr HS 1973-; *ai:* Academic Games Coach; Natl Academic Games Project Mid Division Coord; E-F Ed Assn, PSEA, NEA (Bldg Rep 1978-79) 1969-; PA Geographic Alliance 1989-; PTA; Intnl Rdng Assn 1970-89; OES 1966-; Trout Unlimited 1972-; Jim Davis Outstanding Spon Awd; Natl Geographic Society Grant; Natl Academic Games Soc Stud Chm; *office:* Elizabeth Forward Jr HS 401 Rock Run Rd Elizabeth PA 15037

SKOOG, JUDITH STAHL, 4th Grade Teacher; *b:* Yonkers, NY; *m:* Richard John; *ed:* Liberal Arts, Barnard Coll 1962-63; (BA) Elem Ed, Potsdam Coll of SUNY 1963-66; (MS) Ed, Hunter Coll 1967; Admin & Supervision, Forham Univ; In-Service Credits & Courses, Yonkers Teacher Center; *cr:* 3rd Grade Teacher 1967-81, 4th Grade Teacher P S 8 1981-; *ai:* Rdng Comm; Cum Laude Society 1962; Potsdam Coll Alumni Assn 1966; PTA Rep on Exec Bd; Teacher Interest Comm; Sch Improvement Plan; Church Organist, Choir Dir, Recreational Leader for Disadvantaged Youth; *home:* 436 Pine Grove Ln Hartsdale NY 10530

SKORA, DENNIS JOHN, 8th Grade Soc Stud Teacher; *b:* Binghamton, NY; *m:* Maureen Murphy; *c:* Karen, Kevin; *ed:* (BS) Ed/Soc Stud, SU Coll CortLand 1965; (MS) Ed/Soc Stud, SU Coll New Paltz 1972; Certificate of Advanced Study, Admin; *cr:* 6th Grade Teacher 1965-66, Soc Stud Teacher 1966- Wappingers Falls Jr HS; *ai:* Sch Newspaper Adv; Intramural Supvr; NY St Cncl for Soc Stud 1966-; 3 Title IV Grants; *office:* Wappingers Falls Jr HS Remsen Ave Wappingers Falls NY 12590

SKORA, SHIRLEY JEANETTE, Instrumental Music Teacher; *b:* Oswego, NY; *ed:* (AAS) Music, Onondaga Comm Coll 1979; (BMUS) Music Ed, Syracuse Univ 1982; (MS) Ed, SUNY Oswego 1987; *cr:* Band Dir Mexico Mid Sch 1983-; *ai:* Winterguard & Field Band Dir; Marching Band Co-Dir; Oswego Cty Music Educators Assn (Secy 1986-88, VP 1988-89); Tubists Universal Brotherhood Assn, NY St Sch Music Educators; *office:* Mexico Mid Sch Fravor Rd Mexico NY 13114

SKRDLA, JEROME J., Biology Teacher; *b:* Atkinson, NE; *m:* Darcy A.; *c:* Stefanie, Morgan; *ed:* (BS) Bio, 1977, (MS) Math/Sci, 1984 Kearney St Coll; *cr:* Bio Teacher/Coach Kearney Cath HS 1977-87, Ft Calhoun HS 1987-; *ai:* Asst Ftbl Coach; Girls Bsktbl & Boys Track Head Coach; NE St Educl Assn 1989-; NE Coaches Assn 1977-; Knights of Columbus 1973-; *home:* 2512 N 121st Omaha NE 68164

SKROBAK, JOANNE SLIVKO, Third Grade Teacher; *b:* Bethlehem, PA; *m:* Donald J.; *c:* Nicholas; *ed:* (AAS) Early Chldhd Ed, Northampton Comm Coll 1978; (BS) Early Chldhd Ed, Lock Haven Univ 1980; Grad Stud Kutztown Univ; *cr:* Elem Teacher Rdng Area Sch Dist 1980; 2nd Grade Teacher Avona Elem 1981-82; Kndgtn Teacher Avona/Wilson Elem 1982-83; 3rd Grade Teacher 1983-84, Kndgtn Teacher 1984-86, 2nd Grade Teacher 1986-87 Williams Township Elem; 3rd Grade Teacher Avona Elem 1989-; *ai:* PA St Ed Assn, NEA 1980-.

SKROH, VANYA (CAROTHERS), 7th-12th Grade Math Teacher; *b:* Marshalltown, IA; *m:* Roger Neil; *c:* Sara, Karen, Bart; *ed:* (BSE) Elem Ed, 1970, (MS) Master Teacher, 1975 Emporia St Univ; Admin, Math, NW MO St Univ; Math, Spec Ed, Univ of Cntrl AR; Visually Impaired, Lindenwood Coll; *cr:* 3rd/5th Grade Elem Teacher Junction Elem 1970-75; K-2nd Grade Elem Teacher 1975-80, Elem Prin 1976-85, 7th-12th Grade Math Teacher 1980- Cainsville R-I Sch; *ai:* 7th-12th Grade Class Spon; Academic Coach; GSA Leader; KS Ed Assn Secy 1970-75; MSTA, Cainsville CTA (Pres, VP, Treas, Parliament) 1975-; NW MO Math Teacher 1987-; New Century Club (Secy, VP) 1975-83, Woman of Yr 1979; JC Wives Pres 1977-79; PEO (Chaplain, Guard, Treas) 1980-; Amer Legion Auxiliary 1975-; Nom Presidential Awds for Excl Math Teaching 1990.

SKWARCZYNSKI, NANCY A., Math Teacher; *b:* Lasalle, IL; *m:* Alan M.; *c:* Michael, Mark; *ed:* (BS) Math, IL St Univ 1973; (MS) Scndry Ed, Northern IL Univ 1990; *cr:* 6th/7th/8th Grade Math Teacher Gompers Jr HS 1973-77, Minooka Jr HS 1977-; *ai:* Math Club Spon; Dis Climate Comm; Math Contest Coach; St Item-Writing for Assessment Comm; Dist Curr Comm; Dist Articulation Comm; Math Cadre Tri Cty Ed Service Center; IL Cncl Teachers of Math; NCTM; ASCD; *office:* Minooka Jr H S Dist 201 305 Church St Minooka IL 60447

SKWERES, AUDREY CAROL (WARD), Third Grade Teacher; *b:* Albuquerque, NM; *m:* Mark A.; *c:* Ashley A., Britton L.; *ed:* (BAT) Elem Ed, Sam Houston St Univ 1980; *cr:* 2nd Grade Teacher St Jeromes Cath Schl 1980-81; 3rd Grade Teacher St Ambrose Cath Sch 1981-82; 1st Grade Teacher Berry Elem 1982-85; 6th-8th Grade Teacher Seton Cath Jr HS 1985-89; 3rd Grade Teacher Francis Elem 1989-; *ai:* Odyssey of Mind Natl Competition Judge; Festival of Arts Comm.

SKYLES, MARY, 5th Grade Teacher; *b:* Mason City, IA; *ed:* (BA) Eng, Clarke 1965; Courses in Math, Cmptr, Theology; *cr:* 1st Grade Teacher St Patrick 1952-62, Sacred Heart 1957-62; 3rd-5th Grade Teacher St Mary 1963-67; 4th Grade Teacher St Patrick 1969-70; 5th Grade Teacher Resurrection 1970-77, St Mary 1977-82; 5th/6th Grade Teacher St Joseph 1982-84; 5th Grade Teacher Seton 1984-; *ai:* IA Rdng Assn.

SLABY, KRISTI LYNN, Biology Teacher; *b:* Rensselaer, IN; *m:* Frank; *c:* Joy; *ed:* (BA) Bio, Ball St Univ 1971; (MLS) Sociology, Valparaiso Univ 1981; Human Genetics, Ball St; Advanced Placement Bio, Stanford; *cr:* Instr St Josephs Coll 1983-84; Teacher Kankakee Valley HS 1984-; *ai:* Girls & Boys Var Swimming; Sunshine Sr Class; N Cntrl Chairperson; Curr & Staff Dev; NSTA, IN St Teacher Assn, NABT, Kankakee Valley Teacher Assn 1985-; Sigma Phi Gamma Pres 1978-; St Sci Curr Comm; Teacher Cert Test Evaluator; *office:* Kankakee Valley HS R 3 Box 183 Wheatfield IN 46392

SLACK, EMILY FOX, 3rd Grade Teacher; *b:* Allentown, PA; *m:* Edward Lewis; *c:* Erin R., Rachel D.; *ed:* (BS) Elem Ed/Early Chldhd, East Stroudsburg St 1976; (MS) Elem Ed, Kutztown St Univ 1990; *cr:* 6th Grade Teacher Upper Perkiomen Mid Sch 1976-77; 4th Grade Teacher 1977-82, 2nd Grade Teacher 1982-84 Hereford Elem; 4th Grade Teacher Red Hill Elem 1985-86; Kndgtn Teacher 1987-88, 3rd Grade Teacher 1988- Hereford Elem; *ai:* Elem Liaison Comm; NEA 1976-; PA St Ed Assn 1976-; Intnl Rdng Assn 1988-; Welcome House Adoptive Parents Group Spokesperson 1986-87; Janus Palyers (Secy 1981-82, Pres 1983-84) 1980-84; New Goshenhoppen United Church of Christ Infant Nursery Dir 1989-; Upper Perkiomen Valley Jaycees Awd; Outstanding Young Educator 1989; *office:* Hereford Elem Sch Rt 29 Hereford PA 18056

SLADE, KENNETH LEE, History Teacher; *b:* Weatherford, TX; *ed:* (BS) Soc Stud, Univ of Southern MS 1974; (MED) Scndry Ed, Univ of North TX 1984; *cr:* His Teacher Weatherford Mid Sch 1974-75, Grapevine Mid Sch 1975-; *ai:* His Dept Chairperson; Pentathlon Coach; TX Cncl & Mid-Cities Cncl for Soc Stud 1982-; Assn of TX Prof Educators 1979-; Outstanding Young Men of Amer 1979; Grapevine Mid Sch Teacher of Yr 1979/1985; Grapevine-Colleyville Ind Sch Dist Teacher of Yr 1985; *home:* 1613 Chaparral Ct Grapevine TX 76051

SLAFKA, STEPHEN MICHAEL, 6th Grade Teacher; *b:* Mc Keesport, PA; *m:* Maryann Pranaitis; *c:* Matthew; *ed:* (BS) Elem Ed, 1971, (MS) Elem Ed, 1974 Indiana Univ of PA; *cr:* 5th Grade Teacher Myer Avenue Sch 1971-74; 5th Grade Teacher 1974-86, 6th Grade Teacher 1986- Port Vue Elem Sch; *ai:* Asst Track Coach 1977-79; S Allegheny Ed Assn Treas 1977-79; Liberty Boro VFD (Recording Secy 1988, Mem 1983-); *office:* Port Vue Elem Sch 1201 Romine Ave Port Vue PA 15133

SLAGLE, ELAINE SANDERSON, Second Grade Teacher; *b:* Nanty Glo, PA; *m:* Richard; *c:* Sherie Lukanen, Karen Cooney, Beth; *ed:* (BA) Elem Ed, Glassboro St 1975; *cr:* 6th Grade Teacher Edgewater Park Township 1975-78; 2nd Grade Teacher St Paul Sch 1978-; *ai:* CBTS Test Coord; Faculty Teacher Rep; Primary Dept Chairperson; *office:* St Paul Sch 16th & James Sts Burlington NJ 08016

SLAK, DANIEL JAMES, Mathematics Teacher; *b:* Milwaukee, WI; *cr:* Teacher Pius XI HS; *ai:* Young Republicans Moderator; Var Bsbl Coach; Greater Milwaukee Hall of Fame in Bowling Mem; *home:* S 98 W 12772 Loomis Muskego WI 53150

SLAKEY, STEPHEN LOUIS, Social Science Teacher; *b:* Oakland, CA; *m:* Sylvia A.; *c:* Andrew, Stephanie; *ed:* (BA) Soc Sci/His, CA St Univ Hayward 1967; (MA) Geography, CA St Univ Fullerton 1974; Ed Admin; *cr:* Teacher La Puente HS 1969-; Summer Geography Dir CA Polytechincal Univ Pomona 1990; Teacher/Consultant Natl Georgraphy Society 1986-; *ai:* Mentor Teacher; Staff Dev Coord; Academic Delathlon Coach; CA Geography Society Bd Mem 1973-, Outstanding Teacher 1973; CA PTA Local Pres 1983-, Honorary Service Awd 1985; Glendora Little League Coach 1983-84; Glendora Beautiful Pres 1982-85; CA Dev Grant; Innovative Teacher Grants; Several Articles; *office:* La Puente HS 15615 E Nelson Ave La Puente CA 91744

SLANE, JACQUELINE MARIE (GAGE), Second Grade Teacher; *b:* Caldwell, ID; *m:* George E.; *c:* Shannon Slane Murakami, Jeff; *ed:* (BA) Elem Ed, Boise St Univ 1970; ATV Safety Trng License; *cr:* Trans 1st Grade Teacher 1970-76, 2nd Grade Teacher 1977- Van Buren Elem; ATV Safety Trng Teacher Speciality Vehicle Inst of America 1988-; *ai:* NEA, IEA, CEA 1970-; *office:* Van Buren Elem Sch 516 N 11th N Caldwell ID 83605

SLANE, MICHAEL LEROY, Social Studies Teacher; *b:* Toledo, OH; *m:* Judith Thomas; *c:* Courtney; *ed:* (BA) Soc Stud, 1967, (MA) Educl Admin, 1972, (MA) Guidance/Counseling, 1975 Univ of Toledo; *cr:* Soc Stud Teacher Oakdale Elem 1970-76, Byrnedale Jr HS 1976-; *office:* Byrnedale Jr HS 3645 Glendale Ave Toledo OH 43614

SLATE, KAY LASATER, High School English Teacher; *b:* Longview, TX; *m:* Harold D. Jr.; *c:* Kristine, Amanda; *ed:* (BS) Phys Ed/Eng, E TX Baptist Coll 1980; *cr:* Teacher Trinity Episcopal Day Sch 1981-83, Hallsville HS 1983-; *ai:* At-Risk Advisory Team Dist Comm; TSTA Mem 1988-; *office:* Hallsville HS Bobcat Ln Hallsville TX 75650

SLATER, JACK JAMES, Reading & English Teacher; *b:* Fort Worth, TX; *m:* Helen Marie Clark; *c:* Mary; *ed:* Ed, Paul Quinn Coll; Ed Wiley Coll; (BA) Ed, TX Coll 1966; TX Chrstn Univ; *cr:* Teacher George Washington Carver Elem 1966-70, S T Stevens Elem 1970-72, Forest Oak Mid Sch 1972-; *ai:* Stu Adv, Stu Cncl Adv, At Risk Adv; BSA Spon; Sch Safety Comm, Campus Coordinating Comm; Ftbl, Track Coach; Fort Worth Classroom Teachers 1966-; TX St Teachers Assn Life Mem 1966-; Natl Teacher Assn Life Mem 1966-; Fort Worth Coaches 1972-; TX HS Coaches 1975-; Fort Worth Rdng Cncl 1970-; Fort Worth Eng Cncl 1980-; *office:* Forest Oak Mid Sch 3220 Pecos Fort Worth TX 76119

SLATER, PAMELA GUE, French/English Teacher; *b:* Jackson, MI; *ed:* (BA) Eng, 1983, (MA) Educl Admin, 1988 N MI Univ; Summer Inst Angers France Univ Catholique de l'Ouest 1985; *cr:* Eng Teacher Bangor HS 1984; Fr/Eng Teacher Forest Park HS 1984; Eng Teacher Lycee Maxence Vander Meersch 1988-89; Fr/Eng Teacher Forest Park HS 1989-; *ai:* Fr Prgm Act Organizer; Curr Comm; AATF 1986-88; Cmmty Concerts VP 1987-; Fulbright Teaching Assistantship to France 1988-89; Working on Grant for Developing Hypercard Computerized Fr Lang Prgm Through Intermediate Sch Dist; *office:* Forest Park HS 801 Forest Pkwy Crystal Falls MI 49920

SLATON, MARY LOIS, Teacher; *b:* Archer City, TX; *m:* Edwin; *c:* Eva Solomon; *ed:* (BS) Ed, North TX Univ 1955; *cr:* Teacher Fort Worth Sch Dist 1955-70, Northeast Ind Sch Dist 1970-78, Graham Ind Sch Dist 1978-; *ai:* Graham Womens Club Bd Mem 1989-; 1st United Meth Church Lifetime; Goals for Graham Comm.

SLAUGHTER, DANNY LEE, Reading/Soc Stud Teacher; *b:* Peru, IN; *m:* Patricia Lytle; *c:* Darren B., Curt A., Carie J.; *ed:* (BA) Mid Grades Soc Stud, GA Coll 1975; *cr:* 4th Grade Teacher Midway Elem 1975-76; 3rd Grade Teacher Bethel Elem 1976-80; 4th/5th Grade Teacher Morning Star Elem 1980-85; 7th/8th Grade Teacher Canton Jr HS 1985-; *ai:* Amer Legion Commander 1968; VFW Society 1st Infantry Div Aide De Camp 1967; *home:* R 4 Box 363 Canton NC 28716

SLAUGHTER, KEITH ALAN, Marketing Ed Teacher/Coord; *b:* Indianapolis, IN; *m:* Bonita Jean Yater; *c:* Mark, David; *ed:* (BS) Bus Ed, Univ of Indianapolis 1957; (MA) Bus Ed, Ball St Univ 1965; IN Univ 1960, 1969, 1971, 1974; Voc Ed, Ball St Univ 1969-71; Distributive Ed; *cr:* Bus Ed Teacher Northern Cmmty Schls 1957-63, Kokomo HS 1963-68; Distributive Ed Teacher/Coord Haworth HS 1968-84; Mrktg Ed Teacher/Coord Kokomo Area Career Center 1984-; *ai:* DECA Club, Youth Club, Mrktg Ed Prgm Adv; Mrktg Ed Dist Coord; Haworth HS Head Bsbl Coach 1969-79; AVA 1973-; IN Voc Assn Mem 1973-, Awd of Merit 1976; Distributive Ed Clubs of America; Natl Mrktg Ed Assn; Morning Star United Brethren Church 1972-; IN HS Bsbl Coaches Assn Hall of Fame 1986; IN Cntrl Coll Alumni Bsbl Coach of Yr 1970, 1978; *office:* Kokomo Area Career Center 303 E Superior Kokomo IN 46901

SLAUSON, SUSAN LE MASTER, 5th Grade Teacher; *b:* Philadelphia, PA; *m:* Paul R.; *c:* Robert; *ed:* (BA) Elem Ed/Spec Ed, Univ of WI Whitewater 1974; Gifted & Talented Ed; *cr:* 3rd Grade Teacher 1974-80, 5th Grade Teacher 1980- Lake Mills Sch Dist; *ai:* Gifted & Talented & Sci Curr Comm; WI Educators for Gifted & Talented; WI St Rdng Assn; PTA; *office:* Prospect Elem Sch 135 E Prospect St Lake Mills WI 53551

SLAWSON, CRAIG LEWIS, Teacher of Gifted & Talented; *b:* Galveston, TX; *ed:* (BA) Span, Univ of CA Santa Barbara 1969; (MA) Elem Ed, Univ of Redlands 1977; Certificate Ed for Gifted, Univ of CA Riverside; Counseling Certificate Prgm Univ of CA Riverside; *cr:* 3rd Grade Teacher Bakersfield Unified Sch Dist 1969-70; 3rd/4th Grade Teacher Redwood City Sch Dist 1970-74; 3rd-6th/Bi-ling/GATE Teacher Hemet Unified Sch Dist 1974-; Teach Eng as 2nd Lang Mt San Jacinto Coll; *ai:* Valle Vista Elem Schls Stu Study Team Mem; Hemet Teachers Assn Pres 1980-81, 1982-83; CA Assn for Gifted 1984-; Mentor Teacher 1983-86; Teacher of Yr Whittier Elem Sch & Hemet Unified Sch Dist 1985-86; Guest Speaker CA Assn for Gifted Conference 1987-88; *home:* PO Box 262 Idyllwild CA 92349

SLAYTON, LINDA LINDSEY, Advanced Math Teacher; *b:* Grove Hill, AL; *m:* Charles Edward Sr.; *c:* Carey, Scott, Andy; *ed:* (BS) Ed, 1971, (MS) Adm & Supv,1975 Livingston Univ; *cr:* Math Teacher Clarke Cty HS 1971-; *ai:* Spon Beta Club; Coach Scholars Bowl Team; Chairperson Steering Comm Southern Assn Accreditation; NEA 1980-89; AL Ed Assn 1980-89; Clarke Cty Ed Assn Chairperson Legislative Contact Team 1986-89; Grove Hill Baptist Church Clerk 1987-; Teacher of TEL Class 1980-; *office:* Clarke County H S PO Box 937 Grove Hill AL 36451

SLEEPER, JOYCE ELAINE, Fourth Grade Teacher; *b:* Philadelphia, PA; *m:* Bruce; *c:* Kristie Mac Neil, Michael; *ed:* (BA) Poly Sci, Grinnell Coll 1957; (MS) Elem Ed, Russell Sage 1962; Cmptr Ed Appleworks I & II; Teacher Expectation Stu Achievement; *cr:* 1st-2nd Grade Teacher Big Lagoon CA 1965-66; 3rd/4th/6th Grade Teacher Duanesburg Elem 1970-73, 1976-; *ai:* Channel 45 & 17 Dist Coord; Chm Sunshine Comm, Report Card Revision; Dist Safety Comm Mem; Pollworker Sch Voting; Duanesburg United Teacher VP 1988-; NY St United Teachers, AFT 1970-; Duanesburg Town Bd Councilperson 1980-85; Niskayuna Garden Club 1975-; Duanesburg Math Comm 1987-; Dedicated Service Awd 1985; *home:* Box 130 Delanson NY 12053

SLEMONS, SUELLA SWALES, English Department Chair; *b:* New Castle, IN; *c:* Michael, Elizabeth; *ed:* (BS) Soc Stud/Eng, IN Univ 1964; Working Towards MA Guidance, Counseling, Northeastern Univ; *cr:* Teacher Adirondicks Sch for Girls 1965-66; Substitute Teacher USAF Dependent Sch 1967-69; Eng Dept Chm Tulsa Chrstn Schls 1984-; *ai:* Tulsa Chrstn Schls Yrbk Adv 1984-; Guidance Office Asst; Mid-America Assn of Chrstn Schls Sch Affiliation; *office:* Tulsa Chrstn Schls 3434 S Garnett Rd Tulsa OK 74146

SLICER, GEORGE WILLIAM, Science Teacher, Dept Chair; *b:* Kennett, MO; *m:* Karen Sue; *c:* Raeann N., Brock D., Benjamin G., Lorilei M.; *cr:* 8th Grade Sci Teacher Paragould Mid Schls 1974; Chem/Physics Teacher Moberly Sr HS 1975; Sci Teacher/Chm E Carter R-2 1976-; *ai:* Jr Class Spon; SEMO Track Coach 1979-; Pres Three River Striders 1983-87; Mayor J C Allen Awd; *home:* Rt 7 Box 64-B Poplar Bluff MO 63901

SLICK, KIM JOEL, Chemistry/Computer Sci Teacher; *b:* Altoona, PA; *m:* Kathy Eileen Fegely; *c:* Jason; *ed:* (BS) Scndry Ed, PA St Univ 1978; (MS) Chem, Univ of Pittsburgh 1981; (EDD) Educl Technology, Lehigh Univ 1990; *cr:* Chem Teacher Brandywine Heights Area HS 1978-80; Grad Teaching Asst Univ of Pittsburgh 1980-81; Chem/Cmptr Sci Teacher Brandywine Heights Area HS 19810; Instructional Systems Teacher Penn St Continuing Ed 1988-; *ai:* Sr Class Adv; NEA 1978-; Brandywine Heights HS Yrbk Dedication 1984; *office:* Brandywine Heights Area HS Weiss St Topton PA 19562

SLIFKA, JIM ANTHONY, Industrial Arts Teacher; *b:* Cresco, IA; *m:* Charlotte Elaine Johnson; *c:* Todd, David, Kelly, Jennifer; *ed:* (BS) Industrial Arts, Winona St Coll 1961; Grad Stud Winona St & Bemidji St; *cr:* Teacher/Coach Medford Public Sch 1961-; *ai:* Asst Var Ftbl & Head Wrestling Coach; Elem Wrestling; Class Adv; Wrestling Boosters Club; MEA Ec Services; Dist IV Coaches Secy 1985-86, Dist Wrestling Coach of Yr 1982; St Wrestling Coaches Assn, St Coaches Assn 1962-89; Medford Ed Cncl 1990; Christ the King Presbyn Church Cncl 1987-88; Knights of Columbus Wardan 1989-, Knight of Month 1978, 1988, KC Family of Yr 1983; Medford Fire Dept Assn Chief 1990; Steele Cty Park & Recreation Bd 1979-83; Medford City Cncl 1975-78; *office:* Medford HS 104 2nd St N E Medford MN 55049

SLIGH, LOUISE BEAUDROT, 8th-9th Grade Algebra Teacher; *b:* Greenwood, SC; *m:* William Page; *c:* William P. Jr.; *ed:* (BS) Bus Admin, Erskine Coll 1975; *cr:* Sci Teacher Hillcrest HS 1978-80, Summerville Intermediate HS 1980-81; Math Teacher E Cooper Sch 1981-83; Sci Teacher Northside Jr HS 1983-84; Math Teacher Emerald Jr HS 1985-; *ai:* Beta Club Co-Spon; Mathcounts Team Spon; SC Math Teachers 1988-; *home:* 428 Cothran Ave Greenwood SC 29649

SLOAN, ANITA JOYCE, Mathematics/Chemistry Teacher; *b:* Birmingham, AL; *ed:* (BA) Math, 1970, (MED) Scndry Ed/Chem, 1974 Univ of Montevallo; *cr:* Math Teacher Columbiana Mid Sch 1970-71; Math/Chem Teacher Shelby Cty HS 1971-83, Freeport HS 1983-; *ai:* Stu Cncl Spon; FL Assn of Sci Teachers, Math Assn of America, Delta Kappa Gamma; Coastal Animal Protection Services VP 1988-; Teacher Adv Prgm Teacher of Yr Freeport HS; *office:* Freeport HS Kylea Laird Dr Freeport FL 32439

SLOAN, ANN HENDERSON, 6th-8th Grade Math/Sci Teacher; *b:* Piqua, OH; *m:* Lowell Glenn; *c:* Todd G., Susan M.; *ed:* (BS) Elem Ed, Capital Univ 1962; *cr:* 3rd Grade Teacher 1960-61, 1962-1965, 7th Grade Math/Sci Teacher 1965-66 Covington Exempted Village; Substitute Teacher Piqua City Schls 1976-82; Art Teacher 1982-84, 6th-8th Grade Math/Sci Teacher 1984-Troy Chrstn Sch; *ai:* Sci Fair, Olympiad; Odyssey of the Mind; Young Astronauts; OH Sci Ed 1986-; Geology Teachers of OH 1989-; Teacher Intern for Young Experimental Scientists; OH Excl in Sci Awd; *home:* 8220 N Lambert Dr Piqua OH 45356

SLOAN, LINDA (KLINGSTEDT), Vocational Home Ec Teacher; *b:* Dallas, TX; *m:* David B.; *ed:* (BS) Vocational Home Ec Ed, OK St Univ 1980; Guidance Counseling Central St Univ; *cr:* Gen Sci/Bio Teacher Comanche HS 1980-81; Voc Home Ec Teacher Pryor HS 1981-83; Choctaw HS 1983-; *ai:* Dist Vocational Home Ec/Home Ec Dept Head; FHA Spon; Natl Honor Society Review Comm; Adult Ed Coord Choctaw Voc Home Ec; OK Vocational Assn 1980-; Amer Vocational Assn 1980-; 1st Assembly of God Church Mem; Young Marrieds Sunday Sch Class Co-Teacher 1984-; Outstanding Svc Awd Pryor HS 1981-83; Teacher of Yr Finalist Choctaw HS 1989-; North Cntrl Evaluating Team Mem 1985/1988-; *home:* 837 Briarlane Rd Del City OK 73115

SLOAN, MARY JANE ENOCHS, Science Department Chair; *b:* Chicago, IL; *m:* Gary Lee; *c:* Emma L.; *ed:* (BA) Bio, Transylvania Univ 1986; *cr:* Sci Teacher Lexington Cath HS 1987-; Substitute Teacher Fayette Cty Public Schls 1986-87; Teacher/Instr Univ of KY 1988-; *ai:* Jr Class, Jr Var Cheerleading Spon; Curr Comm.

SLOAN, MARY PAGE T., English Teacher; *b:* Spartanburg, SC; *m:* Samuel Hardin Jr.; *c:* Trip, Mary E.; *ed:* (BA) Eng, Coll of Charleston 1972; (MED) Eng/Ed, Converse Coll 1988; *cr:* Eng Teacher Paul M Dorman HS 1984-; *ai:* Jr & Sr Prom, Sch Newspaper Spon; NEA, SCEA; *home:* 471 Mockingbird Ln Spartanburg SC 29302

SLOAN, NELLWYN DELORES LEE, Teacher; *b:* Shreveport, LA; *m:* Eddie Jr.; *c:* Darryl, Latonya, Latoya, Shadrick, Shadra; *ed:* (BA) Elem Ed, Southern Univ 1966; (MA) Elem Ed, 1974, (MA) Elem Ed/Rdng, 1978 LA Tech; *cr:* Teacher Eden Gardens Elem & Jr HS 1966-67, Eden Gardens Elem 1967-70, Atkins Elem 1970-71, Eden Gardens Elem 1971-81, W Shreveport Elem 1981-; *ai:* Caddo Parish Sch Bd Writing Comm Inservice Presenter; 5th Grade After Sch Cultural Act Spon; Caddo Parish Sch Bd Pupil Progression Plan Comm 1985; Caddo Parish Sch Bd Rdng Comm 1989; Lang Art Curr Guide Development Comm 1982; Delta Sigma Theta, Inc Secy 1979-81 Service Awd 1982; Caddo Assn of Educators Area 1 VP, Elem Educator of Yr 1982; LA Assn of Ed, NEA, W Shreveport Elem PTA; Allendale Branch YWMCA; NW Rdng Cncl Rdng Teacher of Yr 1981.

SLOAN, THELMA WILLIAMS, 5th Grade Teacher; *b:* Tallahassee, FL; *c:* Russell D., Richard R. II; *ed:* (BS) Home Ec Teacher, Fort Valley St Coll 1956; (MS) Admin & Supervision, Nova Univ; Elem Ed Cert Courses, FL A&M & Barry Coll; *cr:* Home Ec Teacher Carver Sr HS 1956-57; 6th Grade Teacher Douglas Elem Sch 1965-67, Phyllis Wheatley Elem Sch 1967-70; 5th Grade Teacher Kensington Park Elem Sch 1970-; *ai:* Future Educators of America Spon; Career Ed, Black His Comm; United Teachers of Dade Union Rep 1984-; Career Awareness Facilitator 1981- Service Awd; Delta Sigma Theta 1956-; Grade Group Chairperson; Nom Teacher of Yr 1976; Faculty Cncl Chairperson; *home:* 3015 NW 99th St Miami FL 33147

SLOAT, HAROLD WAYNE, Social Studies Teacher; *b:* Vera, OK; *m:* Patsy Loraine Chandler; *c:* Tony, Nicholas Whitney; *ed:* (BAED) His, NE OK St Univ 1968; (MS) Public Sch Admin, 1978, (BAED) Elem Ed, SE OK St Univ 1986; *cr:* Soc Stud Teacher Haskell City Schls 1969-73, Valliant Schls 1973-76; Soc Stud Teacher/Admin Eagletown Schls 1976-; *ai:* Staff Dev Comm; Textbook Selection; 8th Grade Class Spon; Mc Curtain Cty Ed Assn Pres 1979-80; Valliant Jaycees Pres 1975-76; *office:* Eagletown Schls PO Box 38 Eagletown OK 74734

SLOCUM, LORI SUE, English/Reading Teacher; *b:* Defiance, OH; *ed:* (BA) Comm Art, The Defiance Coll 1981; (MED) Scndry Ed, Bowling Green St Univ 1986; Teacher Expectations & Stu Achievement 1989; *cr:* Eng/Rdng Teacher Tiora Jr HS 1981-; *ai:* Stu Cncl, Newspaper Adv; Speech Cont Coord; Acad Boosters Organizational Comm; Summer Sch Instr; NE Local Teachers Assn, OH Ed Assn, NEA; OH Teacher Forum Delegate 1986; Careers in Comm Mini-Grant 1988; *home:* 1051 Ralston Ave Apt B-22 Defiance OH 43512

SLOMBACK, RONALD GEORGE, 8th Grade Science Teacher; *b:* Bronx, NY; *m:* Kathleen Ott; *c:* Scott, Stephanie; *ed:* (AA) Liberal Art, St Petersburg Jr Coll 1969; (BS) Scndry Ed, Univ of FL 1971; Working Towards Masters Ed; *cr:* Sci/Phys Ed Teacher Pasadena Acad 1972-73; Sci Teacher Riviera Mid Sch 1973-89; *ai:* Teachers of Riviera Organization Rep; PCSTA 1973-89; PCTA Rep 1974-89; Girls Sftbl League Pres; *home:* 6977 Duncansby Ave N Saint Petersburg FL 33709

SLONE, JOYCE M. WINGATE, Social Studies Teacher; *b:* Orange, TX; *m:* Arthur Ray; *c:* Ronda L., Robert R.; *ed:* (BS) His/Eng, Univ of TX Austin 1966; (MED) Curr/Instruction, Univ of Houston 1976; Mid-Management Cert 1990; Advanced Supervision; Working Towards Doctorate Univ of Houston; *cr:* 3rd Grade Teacher Mission Valley Elem Sch 1965-66; Teacher Victoria HS 1966-67, Stroman HS 1968-75, Howell Intermediate Sch 1976, Univ of Houston 1989, Stroman HS 1976-; *ai:* Victoria Ind Sch Dist Domain V Chairperson; Effective Teaching for Stroman HS Domain IV Chairperson Comm; Jr Class Spon; TSTA, NEA (Local Pres 1980, St Exec Comm Mem 1983-88, St & Natl Delegate 1980-88); ASCD 1990; Chamber of Commerce Ed Comm Chairperson 1985; Rotary Club Guest Speaker; Future Teachers of America Assn; FBLA; Pilot Club; FFA, Stu Cncl, Farmer & Ranchers Assn; Advanced Stud in Poly Sci & Sociology; Outstanding Scndry Educator of America & TX; Outstanding Young Women of America; Ran for St Rep of TX 1983; Written Curr Guides for Victoria Ind Sch Dist; *office:* Stroman HS 3002 North St Victoria TX 77901

SLONEKER, MARLENE GESELL, Kindergarten Teacher; *b:* Franklin, IN; *m:* Malcolm Lee; *c:* Wm. Tully Milders, Phillip T. Milders, Traci Milders Stevison; *ed:* (BSED) Elem Ed, Miami Univ Oxford 1955; 30 Hrs Grad Stud; *cr:* 2nd Grade Teacher Butler Cty Schls 1954-57; Kndgtn Teacher Hamilton City Schls 1970-; *ai:* NEA, OEA, BCAEYC; Delta Kappa Gamma; Presbyn Church Elder; Church Treas; *home:* 105 Tari Ct Hamilton OH 45013

SLOPER, LORRAINE OBATA, Math Teacher; *b:* Los Angeles, CA; *m:* Timothy Richard; *c:* Ashley, Courtney; *ed:* (BA) Sociology, Univ of CA Los Angeles 1981; *cr:* Math/Algebra Teacher Holland Jr HS 1983-; *ai:* NEA Mem 1984-; Intnl Stu Center UCLA (Teacher, Dir of ESL) 1979-81; *office:* Holland Jr HS 4733 N Landis Ave Baldwin Park CA 91706

SLOTTKE, GLORIA JANE, Teacher; *b:* Milwaukee, WI; *ed:* (BS) Elem Ed, St Norbert Coll 1966; Grad Courses Admin & Supervision; *cr:* Teacher La Crosse Diocese 1950-67; Prin St Pauls 1967-70; Teacher Milwaukee Archdiocese 1971-74; Prin St Pauls 1974-80; Teacher Blessed Sacrament 1981-; *ai:* Parish Organist; Mem Liturgy Comm; Volunteer Service; Schlshp Grant Saint Norbert Coll; Certificate of Prof Dev; Team Evaluator Elem Schls; Teacher Recognition Service; Outstanding Elem Teacher of Amer; *home:* 3020 S 17th St Milwaukee WI 53215

SLOUGH, ELAINE ANN (SONNICHSEN), German Teacher; *b:* Toledo, OH; *m:* Ronald J.; *c:* Ronald P., Tracie L.; *ed:* (BE) Ger, Univ of Toledo 1969; Working Towards Masters; *cr:* Ger Teacher Start HS 1970-72, Whitmer HS 1977-86, Springfield HS 1986-; *ai:* Ger Club; Natl Ger Honorary Society; Teacher Ed Prgm, Advisory Comm; Sch Improvement Advisory Comm; Human Relations Advisory Cncl; AATG 1986-; OH Modern Lang Assn 1980-; OH Ed Assn, NEA 1977-; *home:* 6622 Inglewood Holland OH 43528

SLUGA, CRAIG CHARLES, 6th Grade Mathematics Teacher; *b:* Kane, PA; *m:* Anne Marie Clark; *c:* Felicity, Rachel, Emily; *ed:* (BSED) Elem Ed/Early Chldhd Ed, 1972, (MED) Guidance/Counseling, 1975 Edinboro Coll; *cr:* 4th Grade Self-Contained Teacher 1972-73, 5th-6th Grade Health Teacher 1973-77, 5th-6th Grade Math Teacher 1977-86, 6th Grade Math/Spelling/Penmanship Teacher 1986- Lawrence Park Elem; *ai:* Var Track & Field Coach; Strength & Conditioning Club Adv; PA St Ed Assn, NEA 1972-; Iroquois Ed Assn Chm; PA Track & Field Coaches Assn; Natl Fed Interscholastic Coaches Assn; *office:* Lawrence Park Elem Sch 4231 Morse St Erie PA 16511

SLUYTER, REBECCA L., Health Occupations Coordinator; *b:* Corpus Christi, TX; *c:* Darren J., Victor M., Stephen S.; *ed:* (ADN) Nursing/RN, Pan American Univ 1975; Occupational Ed, TX A&M Univ 1981; *cr:* Public Health Nurse Cameron Cty Health Dept 1975-77; Staff Nurse Tanana Valley Clinic 1977-78; Health Occupations Coord/Instr Harlingen HS 1980-; *ai:* Spon Harlingen HOSA; Teachers Health Occ Assn 1989-90; AVA 1989-90; Heart Assn Bd Mem 1984-86; Beta Sigma Phi 1983-89; PTA 1986-; *office:* Harlingen H S 1201 E Marshall Harlingen TX 78550

SLY, JOHNNY RICHARD, Social Studies Teacher; *b:* Pryor, OK; *c:* Jimmy, Billy; *ed:* (BA) His, 1973, (MS) Counseling, 1985 NSU; Grad Work NSU; Outdoor Ed OSU 1985; *cr:* Soc Stud Teacher Katchum HS 1973-76; Indian Stud Teacher Catousa Jr HS 1976-78; Cnslr Northeastern St Univ 1979-83; Soc Stud/Indian Culture Teacher/Coach Hulbert HS 1985-; *ai:* Title IV & 8th Grade Spon; Ftbl, Bsktbl, Bsbl Coach; OEA, NEA 1990; Pres Honor Roll NSU 1970-73; NSU Bi-ling Ed Prgm Participant & Schlsp 1985; *home:* 106 Carol St Tahlequah OK 74464

SMAIL, SAMUEL JAMES, Head Teacher 6th Grade Teacher; *b:* Mt Pleasant, PA; *m:* Wanda A. Mc Cullough; *c:* Samuel D., Joshua J., Jack C.; *ed:* (BS) Elem Ed, 1972, (MS) Ed, 1979 California Univ of PA; *cr:* 5th Grade Teacher 1972-, Head Teacher 1983-, 6th Grade Teacher 1990 Ramsey Elem Sch; *ai:* Long Range Planning Comm; PSEA Mem; Hecla Volunteer Fire Dept Committeman 1972-; 4-H Sheep Leader 1989-; *office:* Ramsey Elem Sch Eagle & Walnut Sts Mount Pleasant PA 15666

SMAILA, JOHN, Athletic Director; *b:* Rupa, Yugoslavia; *m:* Cynthia Kay Bittner; *ed:* (BA) Span/Ed, Clarion St Coll 1970; Educl Credits 1972; *cr:* Span Teacher 1972-89, Soc Stud Teacher 1974-89, Athletic Dir/Tutorial Coord 1989- Meyersville Area HS; *ai:* Sftbl Coach; Var Club Adv; PA Athletic Dirs Assn 1989-; PA St Ed Assn 1972-; BPDE Elks 1973-; Sftbl Coach of Yr; *office:* Meyersdale Area HS RD 3 PO Box 60 Meyersdale PA 15552

SMALARA, ANN VALLA, Fourth Grade Teacher; *b:* Harwick, PA; *m:* Alfred A.; *c:* Frank, Regina, Mary Collins, David, Susan; *ed:* (BS) Elem Ed, Slippery Rock Univ of PA 1955; Graduate Work, Univ of Pittsburgh; *cr:* 4th Grade Teacher East Deer Elem 1955-56; 3rd Grade Teacher Cheswick ELem 1956-57; 2nd Grade Teacher All SaintS Elem 1957-58; Remedial Math Teacher 1977-82, 4th Grade Teacher 1982- Carmichaels Area Sch Dist; *ai:* NEA; PSEA; Carmichaels Lib Bd; *home:* 207 E Greene St Carmichaels PA 15320

SMALL, ANN LOUISE, 7-8th Grade Lang Arts Teacher; *b:* Phoenixville, PA; *ed:* (BSED) Scndry Eng, Millersville St Coll 1973; (MSED) Ed, Temple Univ 1980; Writing Process & Collins Writing Folder Approach; Cooperative Learning, Increasing Teacher Effectiveness; *cr:* Lang Art Teacher Cocalico Mid Sch 1973-; *ai:* Drama Club Adv; Induction Cncl Comm Mem; Mid Sch Lang Art Dept Chairperson; PA St Ed Assn, NEA 1973-; Cocalico Ed Assn (Secy, Parliamentarian); NCTE 1973-75/1988-; Mount Zion United Meth Church (Worship Comm Chairperson 1989-, Servic e Writer/liturgist 1985-); *office:* Cocalico Mid Sch S 4th St Denver PA 17517

SMALL, MICHELLE HOLCOMB, AP Eng Teacher/Dept Chair; *b:* Borger, TX; *m:* James C.; *c:* Jaime Gallagher, Jason; *ed:* (BA) Eng/Latin, N TX St Univ 1968; Eng/Latin, N TX St Univ; Ed, CO St Univ; *cr:* 7th Grade Eng Teacher Lewisville Mid Sch 1969-73; ESL-GED Teacher Adult Learning Center 1974-75; 9th Grade Eng Teacher Northeast Jr HS 1974-79; 11th-12th Grade Eng Teacher Skyline HS 1979-; *ai:* Gifted/Talented & Brown Bag Speakers Prgm; Odyssey of Mind Team; NEA, CEA; Honorable Mention CO Teacher of Yr 1984; Presenter CO St Curr Symposium 1988, TAG Conference Snowmass 1989; Instr Staff Dev Class; Co-Author Curr Incorporating Word Processing Into Eng Composition; *office:* Skyline HS 600 E Mountain View Longmont CO 80501

SMALL, PETER VAN, Science Department Chairman; *b:* Portland, ME; *m:* Jean M. Mc Farland; *c:* Laurie, Peter Jr., Cathleen; *ed:* (BA) Bio, Bowdoin Coll 1966; (MST) Sci, Univ of S ME 1974; Grad Stud Marine Bio, Natl Sci Fnd Inst; Advanced Bio, Summer Inst; *cr:* Sci Teacher 1966-, Sci Dept Chm 1988- S Portland HS; *ai:* NEA, ME Teachers Assn; *office:* S Portland HS 637 Highland Ave South Portland ME 04106

SMALL, RITA, Latin Teacher; *b:* Morrisville, PA; *ed:* (BA) Latin, Villanova Univ 1958; (MA) Latin, Cath Univ 1967; Scndry Ed Admin Courses; *cr:* Elem Ed Teacher Philadelphia Cath Schls 1948-56; Latin Teacher Archbisop Prendergast HS 1956-65, Walsingham Acad 1965-69; Dean of Stu Carroll HS 1969-78; Dean of Admissions Prendergast HS 1978-85; Latin Teacher Merion Mercy Acad 1985-; *ai:* Latin NHS, Latin Clubs, Kates Girls Adv; Philadelphia Classical Society, PA Classical Society.

SMALLEY, PAMELA DIANE, Mid Sch Rdng/Geography Teacher; *b:* Marshalltown, IA; *m:* Don Allen; *c:* Mark A., Jenna L.; *ed:* (BA) Elem Ed, Univ of N IA 1974; *cr:* Substitute Teacher Cedar Rapids Cmmty Schls 1974-75; 4th/5th Grade Teacher 1975-82, Mid Sch Rdng/Geography Teacher 1982- Mar-Mac Cmmty Schls; *ai:* Mid Sch Quiz Bowl; Technology & Wellness Comm; NEA, IA Ed Assn 1974-; Mar-Mac Ed Assn (Secy, Treas)

1975-; *office:* Mar-Mac Cmmty Sch 918 W Main Mc Gregor IA 52157

SMALLIGAN, CHARLES LEE, Science Teacher; *b:* Muskegon, MI; *m:* Sheryl Ann Barlow; *c:* Justin, Suzanne, Jeanna; *ed:* (BA) Bio, Calvin Coll 1968; (MS) Sci, W MI Univ 1971; *cr:* Sci Teacher Northeast Mid Sch; *ai:* 7th Grade Sci Class Camping Coord; GREA, MEA, NEA; Calvinist Cadet Core Cnslr 1989-; Natl Woodcarvers Assn 1982-; Intnl Woodcarving 1st Place Awds; Art Fair Awds; *home:* 2345 Ridgefield Dr NE Grand Rapids MI 49505

SMALLS, CURTIS MARIE FORTE, Social Studies Dept Chair; *b:* Aliceville, AL; *m:* Morris Jr.; *c:* Twana, Morris III; *ed:* (BS) His/Lib Sci, AL St Univ 1970; Lib Sci, The Citadel 1971-72; Admin/Supervision, Bowie St Coll 1986-; *cr:* Audio Visual Lib R E Hunt HS; Media Specialist Baxter Patrick Elem 1970-71; Audio Visual Lib R B Stall HS 1972-73; Media Specialist C C Blaney Elem 1975-79; *ai:* Odyssey of the Mind, Black His Club Spon; Staff Dev In-Service Coord; Stu of Talented & Gifted Stu; NEA 1979-; Prince Georges Cty Ed Assn 1983-, Outstanding Educator 1988; MD St Teachers Assn 1983-; Alpha Kappa Alpha 1975-, Prof Achievement 1987; Amer Librarian Assn 1972-79; NCSS 1984-; Prince Georges Cty Ed Support Advisory Cncl Mem; Published Soc Stud Mini Unit for Sci & Math Technology Prgm Prince Georges Cty; *home:* 609 Etna Dr Upper Marlboro MD 20772

SMARTSCHAN, CARL ERNEST, Biology Teacher; *b:* Allentown, PA; *m:* Nancy Louise Leinbach; *c:* Adam, Neil; *ed:* (BS) Scndry Ed/Bio, Millersville St Coll 1974; (MED) Bio, Kutztown Univ 1989; *cr:* Life Sci Bensalem Township Schls 1974-75; Bio Teacher Allentown Sch Dist 1975-88, Emmaus HS 1988-; *ai:* Asst Boys Var Bsktbl Coach; Reader for Addison-Wesley Publishing Co; *office:* Emmaus HS 851 North St Emmaus PA 18049

SMEDLEY, PATRICIA ZAVESON, Social Studies Teacher; *b:* Akron, OH; *m:* Dennis L.; *c:* Paula, Donovan, Dennis, Sabra; *ed:* (BA) His, Univ of Akron 1961; *cr:* Jr HS Soc Stud Teacher Southwestern City Sch Dist 1961-65; Soc Stud Teacher Kodiak Jr HS 1982-84, Kodiak HS 1984-; *ai:* AK Cncl for Soc Stud, NCSS 1987-; US Coast Guard Officers Wives Club 1968-.

SMELSTOR, THOMAS W., History Teacher; *b:* Norwood, MA; *m:* Pamela Anne Yost; *c:* Jeremy, Lindsay; *ed:* (BA) Ed, Norwich Univ 1969; *cr:* Teacher Norwood Jr HS 1969-88, Norwood Sr HS 1988-; *ai:* Boys & Girls Cross Cntry & Girls Spring Track Coach; MA Teachers Assn, NEA, Norwood Teachers Assn, Norfolk Cty Teachers Assn 1969-; Benevolent & Protective Order Elks 1983-; Friends of Hanover Hocky Secy 1990; *office:* Norwood Sr HS Nichols St Norwood MA 02062

SMIDDY, GLORIA HAWKINS, Business Teacher; *b:* Portland, TN; *m:* James L.; *c:* Pam Hannah, Judith Standifer, Mellissa Stakich, Kevin Kerr, Allison Montgomery; *ed:* (BS) Bus Ed, TN Tech 1955; (MS) Bus Ed, Univ of TN 1975; *cr:* Bus Teacher Bradley Cntrl HS 1956-; *ai:* Bradley Cty Teachers Ed Assn 1955-, Teacher of Yr 1987; TN Ed Assn, NEA 1955-; Bus Prof of America Spon; Alpha Delta Pi 1973-; Teachers Credit Union Bd Mem; *office:* Bradley Cntrl HS 1000 S Lee Hwy Cleveland TN 37311

SMIEJA, DEBRA ANNE, Mathematics Teacher; *b:* Whitehall, WI; *m:* James Patrick Roden; *ed:* (BS) Math/Cmptr Sci, 1977, (MS) Math, 1980 Univ WI Eau Claire; Post Grad Advanced Trng in Cooperative Learning; Stu Teachers Supvr; *cr:* Math Teacher Menomonie HS 1977-80, Delong Jr HS 1980-87; General Ed Teacher Chippewa Valley Tech Coll 1984; Math Teacher Memorial HS 1987-; *ai:* Eau Claire Sch Dist Cooperative Learning Skills Trainer; Eau Claire Sch Dist Comm for Instructional Use of Cmptr Technology Comm Mem; Univ of WI Eau Claire Sch of Ed Advisory Comm Mem; NY Acad of Sci Mem 1984-; Phi Delta Kappa Mem 1981-; Phi Kappa Phi Mem 1977-; NCTM Mem 1984-; WI Math Cncl Mem 1982-; Amer Assn of Univ Women, WI Women Leaders in Ed Awd 1987; Received Presidential Awd for Excl Teaching in Math from Pres Reagan 1986; Natl Sci Fnd Grant; Author of Complete Tutorial Course on IBM Cmptr; *home:* 1119 Jensen Rd Eau Claire WI 54701

SMIENS, DOYLE GENE, English/Drama/Speech Teacher; *b:* Waterloo, IA; *m:* Grace Bestebroer; *c:* Kyle, Krystal; *ed:* (BA) Drama/Speech, Dordt Coll 1979; (BA) Eng Ed, Univ of N IA 1984; *cr:* Eng/Speech/Drama Teacher Unity Chrstn HS 1984-; *ai:* Speech & Chapel Comm; Head Girls Bsktbl & Sftbl; NCTE 1988-; 2 Yrs Dir of Cmmty Theatre; Cooperative Learning Seminar Leader; *office:* Unity Chrstn HS 216 Michigan Ave SW Orange City IA 51041

SMIGALA, THEODORE FRANCIS, US History Teacher; *b:* Danbury, CT; *m:* Jean A Dumas; *c:* Robin Parisi, Glen, Maribeth; *ed:* (BS) Soc Sci, 1959, (MS) Scndry Soc Sci, 1965 W CT St Univ; Grad Stud; *cr:* Soc Sci Jr HS Teacher Hayestown Avenue Sch 1959-64, Danbury Jr HS 1964-67, Broadview Jr HS 1967-; *ai:* NEA 1959-; Owned & Operated Green Knoll Daycamp 1966-85; *home:* 3 Fieldstone Rd Brookfield CT 06804

SMIKLE, PATRICIA ANN, 4th Grade Teacher; *b:* Lynch, NE; *ed:* (BS) Elem Ed, SMS 1964; (MS) Elem Ed, Drury 1974; *cr:* Teacher Seymour R 2 Schls 1964-; *ai:* Arbor Day Chm R 2 Schls; Prof Dev Comm; MO Ed Assn (Secy 1982) 1980-; PTA (Secy 1979, Treas 1980, Hospitality Dir) 1964-; United Meth Church Adult Sunday Sch Teacher 1985-; L E Cox Auxiliary of Women 1987-; *home:* RR 3 Seymour MO 65746

SMILEY, BETTY SUE, Business Teacher; *b:* Princeton, KY; *ed:* (BS) Bus Ed, Western KY Univ 1961; (MS) Bus Ed, Murray St Univ 1965; *cr:* Bus Teacher Irvington HS 1961-65, Breckinridge Cty HS 1965-; *ai:* FBLA, Sch Paper, Chrldr Spon; BCEA, KEA, NEA, NBEA; *office:* Breckinridge Cty HS Rt 1 Box 130 Harned KY 40144

SMILEY, DIANA GAYLE, Fourth Grade Teacher; *b:* Mesa, AZ; *ed:* (BA) Elem Ed, 1971, (MA) Learning Disabilities, 1975 AZ St Univ; *cr:* Spec Ed Teacher 1971-79, 4th Grade Teacher 1979- Alta Vista Sch; *ai:* Alta Vista Stu Cncl Spon; NEA, AEA, WDEA 1971-; *office:* Alta Vista Sch 8710 N 31st Ave Phoenix AZ 85051

SMILEY, MARY ALICE DAWSON, Fourth Grade Teacher; *b:* Pontiac, MI; *m:* William E.; *c:* Kathlyn Smiley Spindler, Thomas G., Timothy W.; *ed:* (BA) Art/His/Sci, Cntrl MI Univ 1966; Sci/Math/Art; *cr:* 3rd/4th Grade Teacher Furgus Sch 1959-60; Teacher French Sch 1963-68; 7th/8th Grade Art Teacher Washington Sch 1968-69; 4th Grade Teacher Dorland Sch 1969-79; 3rd/4th Grade Teacher Auburn Sch 1979-; *ai:* Altar Guild-St Albans Episcopal Church; Officer SEMKC & MCKC Clubs; Mem Midland Art Cncl; Teach Puppy Training Classes; Res Artist for Natl Dog Publisher; Prof Artist; SE MI Keeshond Club Pres 1980-84; MCKE Officer 1982-86 & 1990; Illustrated Natl Dog Magazine & AKC Gazette; Made Awds Natl Dog Show; *home:* 960 N Meridian Rd Midland MI 48640

SMILIE, TADE LAMPLEY, History Teacher; *b:* Eufaula, AL; *m:* Luther Christman; *c:* Andrew, Merrill; *ed:* (BA) His, Univ of AL 1965; Advanced Coursework Auburn Univ; *cr:* Teacher Bellingrath Jr HS 1965-70, 1980-89, Lanier HS 1989-; *ai:* Scholars Bowl Spon 1986-88; His Club Spon 1980-81; Jr League 1970-; *office:* Sidney Lanier HS 1756 S Court St Montgomery AL 36104

SMILNAK, ANDREW JOSEPH, Mathematics/Quest Teacher; *b:* Detroit, MI; *m:* Susan Miller; *ed:* (BS) Elem Ed, Wayne St Univ 1972; (MS) Early Chldhd, Oakland Univ 1979; Quest Trng; *cr:* 1st-5th Grade Teacher Royal Oak Sch Dist 1971-79; HS Teacher Melbourne Australia 1975-76; 6th-8th Grade Math/Quest Teacher Troy Sch Dist 1979-; *ai:* Ftbl Coach; Act Dance, Run Dance, D J; *office:* Smith Mid Sch 5835 Donaldson Troy MI 48098

SMITH, AL JOSEPH, Social Studies Teacher; *b:* Saint Louis, MO; *m:* Patricia Kustra; *c:* Alicia, Jessica, Luke; *ed:* (BS) Ed/Poly Sci, Univ of MO St Louis 1969; Grad Work Univ of MO Columbia; *cr:* Teacher Affton Sr HS 1972-76; Educl Therapist Child Ctr of Our Lady 1977-88; Teacher Luth HS North 1988-; *ai:* Golf Coach; Recruitment Comm; Comm for Guidance & Counseling; NCSS 1988-; *office:* Lutheran H S North 5401 Lucas & Hunt Saint Louis MO 63121

SMITH, ALGIE RAY, Eighth Grade Reading Teacher; *b:* Russellville, KY; *m:* Betty Lou Wheat; *c:* Kip, Karol; *ed:* (AB) Eng 1963, (MA) Eng, 1964, Ed, 1969 W KY Univ; *cr:* 7th Grade Eng Teacher Koffman Jr HS 1964-66; 11th Grade Eng/Speech Teacher Todd Cty Cntrl 1967-69; 8th Grade Rdng Teacher Russellville Mid Sch 1970-; *ai:* Sch Newspaper & 8th Grade Spon; Sch Yrbk; Jr Achievement; Pep Club; Practical Arts Fair; Todd Cntrl 1969, STAR Teacher; *office:* Russellville Mid Sch 7th & Summer St Russellville KY 42276

SMITH, ALICE HARLAN, 4th Grade Teacher; *b:* Reagan, TX; *w:* Roy E. (dec); *c:* Roy A., Lydia C. Smith Justice; *ed:* (A) Ed, Henderson Cty Jr Coll 1978; (BA) Elem Ed, Univ of TX 1980; *cr:* Plan a Teacher North Mid Sch 1980-81; 4th Grade Teacher West Elem 1981-87; 4th Grade Teacher Intermediate 1987-; *office:* Athens Intermediate 307 Madole Athens TX 75751

SMITH, AMELIA MORRIS, Home Economics Teacher; *b:* Athens, AL; *m:* Lester Ray; *c:* Jason R., Matthew W.; *ed:* (BS) Home Ec, Univ of N AL 1970; (MED) Home Ec, A&M Univ 1978; *cr:* Home Ec Teacher Elkmont HS 1970-; *ai:* FHA Adv; Homecoming Chm; AEA, NEA 1970-; AVA 1970-, Most Outstanding Teacher Dist 1 1987; Delta Kappa Gamma 1983-89; *office:* Elkmont HS PO Box 248 Elkmont AL 35620

SMITH, ANDREW G., III, English Teacher; *b:* San Diego, CA; *m:* Karyn Joy Kann; *c:* Dinah L. Smith Stielau, Andrew IV; *ed:* (BA) Industrial Art, 1957, (MA) Industrial Art, 1967 San Diego St Univ; (PHD) Industrial/Tech Ed, AZ St Univ 1979; Automotive Air Pollution Control Inspector St of CA License; *cr:* Admin San Diego Cty Regional Occupational Ed 1976-80; Columnist Copley News Service Syndicate 1980-81; Consultant General Dynamics-Convair 1983-84; Teacher Grossmont Union HS Dist 1957-58, 1960-; *ai:* Class Advisorships; Spon Russian Lang Club; Founder El Cajon Valley HS Voc Fair; Career Days; Coach Natl Trophy Team Detroit 1963; Phi Delta Kappa Mem 1972-; NEA 1957-; CA Teachers Assn Chapter Pres 1963-64; Ramona Unified Sch Dist Governing Bd Pres 1975-77; San Diego Cty Traffic Safety Cncl 1955-63; E Cty ROP Coord Cncl 1976-80; Grossmont Dist Voc Ed Cncl Founding Mem 1966-74; Natl Assn of Broadcasters 1989-; Published Article in Magazine 1970; Speaker CA Assn Sch Bds Convention 1978-, CA Assn Teachers Eng Conventions 1978-82, 1987; *office:* El Cajon Valley HS 1035 E Madison Ave El Cajon CA 92021

SMITH, ANN MOSS, 2nd Grade Teacher; *b:* Charleston, WV; *m:* Huntington F.; *c:* Cynthia Smith Waugh, Matthew, Andrew; *ed:* (BA) Elem Ed, WV Wesleyan Coll 1955; Educl Courses Cert Renewal at WV Univ; *cr:* 2nd Grade Teacher Montgomery Cty Bd of Ed 1955-56, Webster Cty Bd of Ed 1956-57, Prince Georges Cty Bd of Ed 1958-60, Morgan Cty Bd of Ed 1977-; *ai:* NEA, WVEA, LEA; 4-H Club Leader 1974-84, Gold Clover Awd 1984; Teacher of Yr N Berkeley Elem 1987; *home:* PO Box 545 Horse Ridge Farm Berkeley Springs WV 25411

SMITH, ANNE MARIE BARNES, Sixth Grade Teacher; *b:* Hattiesburg, MS; *m:* Cary Arlen; *c:* Jerome; *ed:* (BSED) Elem Ed, OH Univ 1965; (MSED) Curr/Instruction, Case W Reserve Univ 1973; Chisanbop Math 1974; *cr:* Teacher Andrew Jackson Rickoff 1965-; *ai:* Chapter I Lead Teacher; Staff Led Team Chairperson; Project Perform Leader; Math Competency Comm 1981-; Delta Sigma Theta; Liberty Hill Baptist Church Trustee; Martha Holding Jennings Scholar; *office:* Andrew Jackson Rickoff Sch 3500 E 147th St Cleveland OH 44120

SMITH, ANNE WHITT, Teacher Visually Handicapped; *b:* Seneca, SC; *c:* Andrea; *ed:* (BS) Sociology, 1971, (MS) Visually Handicapped, 1977 Univ of SC; *cr:* Teacher of Visually Handicapped Georgetown Cty 1971-72, Lexington Sch Dist 2 1972-; *ai:* NEA, SCEA; BCEA Local Treas; CEC, Assn for Ed of Visually Handicapped ; *office:* Northside Mid Sch 1218 Batchelor St West Columbia SC 29169

SMITH, APRIL FLOWERS, 5th Grade Teacher; *b:* Darlington, SC; *w:* C. Bernard (dec); *c:* William B. II, Barry L.; *ed:* (BS) Elem Ed, Winthrop 1957; Art/Lib Sci; *cr:* 2nd Grade Teacher Randleman Elem 1957-59, St Johns Elem 1959-62; 1st Grade Teacher Woodruff Elem 1962-64, Delmae Heights Elem 1964-67; 3rd Grade Teacher Roebuck Elem 1967-70; 3rd-5th Grade Teacher Pauline Glenn Springs 1977-; *ai:* NEA/SCEA Local 1959-; Pauline Glenn Springs Teacher of Yr 1984-85; Delta Kappa Gamma 1962-; Church Work Teacher; *office:* Pauline Glenn Springs Elem Sch P O Box 195 Pauline SC 29374

SMITH, ARTHUR HERBERT, Social Studies Teacher; *b:* Clanton, AL; *m:* Frances May Hagen; *c:* Frederick A., Bruce M., Arthur A.; *ed:* (BA) Soc Sci, Univ of Montevallo 1978; *cr:* Soc Stud Teacher Adair Mid Sch 1978-; *ai:* Bsbl Coach Little League; Boy Scout Leader; Girls Sftbl Coach; NEA; *office:* Adair Mid Sch 504 1st Ave S Clanton AL 35045

SMITH, BARBARA J. NELSON, 8th Grade Amer His Teacher; *b:* Mound Bayou, MS; *ed:* (BA) Soc Sci, MS Valley St Univ 1967; *cr:* Teacher Lula Elem 1967-68, Alexander Jr HS 1968-; *ai:* NCSS 1988-; NEA, MS Assn of Educators 1967-; Brookhaven Assn of Educators Building Rep 1967-; Brookhaven Homemakers Club; Veterans of Foreign Wars Past Pres Ladies Auxiliary 1987-89; Natl Repository Catalog of Teacher Developed Lesson Plans in Law & Constitution 1989-; MS HS Handbook 1988-89; Teaching Law to HS Stu in MS 1988-89; *home:* 901 S Washington St Brookhaven MS 39601

SMITH, BESSIE JOHNSON, Second Grade Teacher; *b:* Brunswick Cty, VA; *m:* James A. Jr.; *c:* Janet S. C. Dugger, Janice S. Johnson, James A. III; *ed:* (BS) Elem Ed, St Pauls Coll 1965; (MSED) Primary Ed, Univ VA 1972; *cr:* Teacher Hicksford Elem, Meherrin-Powellton Elem; *ai:* Coord of Gifted & Talented 1984-86; Brunswick Ed Assn Building Rep 1979-81; VA Ed Assn, NEA 1965-; Delta Sigma Theta Inc Lawrenceville Alumnae Pres 1984-86; Natl Assn Advancement of Colored People 1970-; Natl Cncl of Negro Women 1986-; 1st Baptist Church (Pres, MS Society) 1964-; *home:* PO Box 427 Lawrenceville VA 23868

SMITH, BETTY HAMILTON, 5th Grade Teacher; *b:* Jayton, TX; *m:* Eldon Reese; *c:* Michael T., Terry W.; *ed:* (BS) Elem Ed, TX Tech Univ 1965; Numerous Courses; *cr:* 1st-4th Grade Teacher Bean Elem 1965-74; 1st-6th Grade Teacher Overton Elem 1974-; *ai:* Owned & Operated Boys & Girls Private Camp; Church Retreats at Camp; *office:* Overton Elem Sch 2902 Louisville Lubbock TX 79410

SMITH, BETTY S., Kindergarten Teacher; *b:* Celina, TN; *m:* Durell; *c:* Kim Richardson, Christopher, Taunee K.; *ed:* (BA) Elem Ed, 1975, (MA) Elem Ed, 1989 TN Technological Univ; *cr:* Classroom Teacher Hardys Chapel Elem Sch, Rickman Elem Sch; *ai:* NEA, TEA, OCEA Mem; Southern Baptist; *office:* Rickman Elem Sch General Delivery Rickman TN 38580

SMITH, BILLIE JUNE, Fourth Grade Teacher; *b:* Samson, AL; *m:* Donald James; *c:* James W., Jason D.; *ed:* (BS) Elem Ed, Troy St Univ 1962; *cr:* Jr HS Eng/Soc Stud Teacher Geneva HS 1963-72; Elem Teacher Samson Elem Sch 1974-; *ai:* DKG Chairperson Honoring Outstanding Young Sr Women; AL Ed Assn, NEA 1963-; Delta Kappa Gamma Recording Secy 1987-88; *office:* Samson Elem Sch 505 N Johnson St Samson AL 36477

SMITH, BLANCHE V. (LINVILLE), 8th Grade Teacher; *b:* Greensburg, IN; *W:* Daniel L. (dec); *ed:* (BS) Elem Ed Eng, Anderson Univ 1961; Spec Ed Advance Trng, Univ of Northern CO; Univ of CO; *cr:* Spec Ed Teacher Chaplin Special 1961-66; Hobbs NM 1967-69; Spec/Regular Ed Teacher Aurora Public Schls 1969-; *ai:* Adopt-A-Student Comm South Mid Sch Aurora Co; Saturday Sch Comm Chairperson & Stu Awds Comm South Mid Sch Aurora Co; Aurora Ed Assn Faculty Rep 1969/1970; Co Ed Assn; NEA; Assn for Supervision and Curr Dev; Mem Alpha Delta Kappa; Co Distinguished Teachers Awd Granted 1989; *office:* South Mid Sch 12310 E Parkview Dr Aurora CO 80012

SMITH, BONNIE (MAC AULAY), Fifth Grade Teacher; *b:* Middleboro, MA; *m:* Robert Richard; *c:* Wendy J., Rebecca L.; *ed:* (BS) Elem Ed, Cntrl CT St Coll 1969; *cr:* 6th Grade Teacher 1971-72, 5th Grade Teacher 1974- Henry B Burkland Sch; *office:* Henry B Burkland Sch 41 Mayflower Ave Middleboro MA 02346

SMITH, BONNIE BRACEWELL, English Teacher; *b:* Dublin, GA; *m:* Gerald Robert Jr.; *c:* Ranna, George R.; *ed:* (BA) Comm, Georgetown Coll 1973; (MED) Scndry Ed/Eng, GA Coll 1983; *cr:* Teacher W Laurens HS 1973-78, TX Chrstn Univ Upward Bound 1978-79, Dublin Jr HS 1979-80, W Laurens HS 1980-84, Berkmar HS 1984-; *ai:* Drama Dir; Literary Coord; Chrldr Coach; NEA, GA Assn of Educators 1984-; GA Cncl Teachers of Eng 1989-; NCTE 1987-; Atkinson Rd Baptist Kndgtn Comm Chm 1984-; STAR Teacher Lions Club Awd; *office:* Berkmar HS 405 Pleasant Hill Rd Lilburn GA 30247

SMITH, BONNIE DOUBERLEY, 8th Science Teacher/Dept Chm; *b:* Miami, FL; *m:* Gregg Alan; *c:* Abigail Marie; *ed:* (BA) Scndry Sci 1976, (MED) Scndry Sci 1980 Clemson Univ; (EDS) ScndrySci, Univ of GA; *cr:* 7th/8th Grade Sci Teacher Pendleton Jr HS 1978-83; 8th Grade Math Teacher Dacula Mid 1984-85; 8th Grade Sci Teacher/Dept Chairperson Lilburn Mid 1985-; *ai:* GSTA 1985-; GCSS 1985-; Norcross Jaycees VP 1984-; *office:* Lilburn Mid Sch 4994 Lawrenceville Hwy Lilburn GA 30247

SMITH, BONNIE M., English/Drama Teacher; *b:* Hettinger, ND; *m:* Norman A.; *c:* Steven A., Kristen M.; *ed:* Concordia Coll 1963-65; Drake Univ 1969; (BS) Eng/Ed - Magna Cum Laude, Dickinson St Coll 1969; ND St Univ, Univ N Augustana; *cr:* Eng/Drama Teacher/Yrbk Adv Hettinger Public Sch 1969-70, 1977-; *ai:* Drama Coach; Yrbk Adv; Asst Speech Coach; NEA, ND Ed Assn, Hettinger Ed Assn, NCTE, NDCTE; ND Speech & Theatre Assn Exec Bd, Teacher of Yr 1989; Prairie Arts & Hum Cncl (founder, Pres) 1970-; Festival of Amer Folklore Chairperson; Milwaukee Repertory Theatre Company, Commedia Theatre Company Coord; Dakota Concert Assn (Lighting, Tech Asst); Adams Cty Homemakers Centennial Cookbook Ed; Hettinger City Cncls Chairperson 1988; Beta Sigma Phi Art Show Chairperson 1970, 1971, 1973; Hettinger Luth Church (Choir, Soloist, Pres, Bd of Parish Ed, Deacon, Womens Group Secy); ND Drama, Region X Drama Coach of Yr 1989; Directed Plays, Won 2 St Championships, 2 St Runners-Up Titles, 7 Regional Championships; Yrbk Journalism Division IL Sweepstakes Trophy 1983, All-Northern Rating Several Yrs, Numerous Spec Recognition Trophies 1989-, Mellon Fnd Study Grant Hum 1987;St Fair Writing Contest Adult Division Honorable Mention; Whos Who in Amer Colls & Univs; Whos Who in Amer Women 1967-68.

SMITH, BRENDA BROWNING, Language Arts Teacher; *b:* Chicago, IL; *m:* Rick; *ed:* (BA) Bus Ed, WV Inst of Tech 1983; (MA) Counseling, WV Coll of Grad Stud 1987; *cr:* Teacher Road Branch Grade Sch; *ai:* 6th Grade Class Spon; WV Ed Assn, NEA 1983-; Lacoma Baptist Church Revival Chairperson 1989-; *home:* Box 444 Cyclone WV 24827

SMITH, BRENDA SCOTT, 9th Grade English Teacher; *b:* Yazoo City, MS; *m:* Johnny R.; *ed:* (BS) Eng Ed, Jackson St Univ 1969; (MA) Multicultural Ed, San Diego St Univ 1977; Eng, NE IL Univ Chicago; Rdng, Jackson St Univ; *cr:* Eng Teacher Hess Upper Grade Center 1970-74, Bell Jr HS 1974-80, Yazoo Cty Schls 1980-87, Yazoo City City HS 1987-88, Greenville HS 1988-89; *ai:* Faculty Spon; Scrabble Club Adv; Greenville Assn of Educators 1989-.

SMITH, BRETT KENDALL, Physical Education Head; *b:* Arkadelphia, AR; *m:* Karen E.; *ed:* (BS) Health Phys Ed, Oral Roberts Univ 1982; *cr:* Jr Ftbl Coach/8th Grade Sci Teacher 1982-85, HS Ftbl Coach 1984-85 Wagoner OK; Head Ftbl Coach/8th Grade Sci Teacher 1985-86, Head Ftbl Coach/HPE Dept Head K-12 Pulaski Acad 1986-; *ai:* Var Head Ftbl Coach; Health/Phys Ed Dept Head K-12; Impact Team Mem; AAPHRD 1985-; AR Act Assn 1985-; OK Act Assn 1982-85; FCA 1977-; Calvary Baptist Church 1986-88; Indian Springs Baptist Church 1989-; *office:* Pulaski Academy 12701 Hinson Rd Little Rock AR 72212

SMITH, CAROL ANN, Band/Orchestra Director; *b:* Denver, CO; *m:* Colin L. Jr.; *c:* Gwynth, Carrie; *ed:* (BA) Music Ed, Univ of AZ 1976; Grad Stud; *cr:* Band/Orch/General Music/Choir Teacher Grace Chrstn Sch 1976-80; Orch/General Music/Elem & Adaptive Ed Teacher Craycroft/Valencia Sch 1980-85; Band/Orch/General Music Teacher Sierra Mid Sch 1985-; *ai:* Sch Effectiveness Team Outstanding Sch Recognition Comm; MENC, ABODA Mem 1980-; SABODA Pres 1986-; Valencia Elem Teacher Outstanding Service Awd 1985; Sierra Mid Sch Teacher Outstanding Service to Stu Body 1988; *office:* Sierra Mid Sch 5801 S Del Moral Blvd P O Box 11280 Tucson AZ 85706

SMITH, CAROL ANN (KING), Second Grade Teacher; *b:* Clymer, PA; *m:* John E.; *c:* Dave, John; *ed:* (BS) Elem Ed, Miami Univ 1971; *cr:* 2nd Grade Teacher Purchase Line Schls 1961-62; 1st-6th Grade Music Teacher Indian Lake Schls 1967-68; 4th/6th Grade Teacher Edgewood Schls 1968-72; 2nd/5th/6th Grade Teacher Hamilton City Schls 1972-; *ai:* Sch Chorus Accompanist; Soc Stud Curr Comm; OH Ed Assn 1967-; NEA; Hamilton Classroom Teachers Assn Executive Comm 1983-; *home:* 111 N Washington Blvd Hamilton OH 45013

SMITH, CAROL C, Co-op Teacher/Coordinator; *b:* Siler City, NC; *m:* Albert Edward; *c:* Grant R., Lauren E., Hayley M.; *ed:* (BS) Comp Bus Ed, Campbell Univ 1977; Grad Sch at Univ of NC Greensboro; *cr:* Math/Bus Teacher W Lee Jr HS 1977-78; Bus Ed Teacher 1978-89, Admin Support Occupations Teacher/Coord 1989- Lee Cty Sr HS; *ai:* FBLA Club Co-Spon; Cntrl Carolina Comm Coll Adv; Lee Sr Voc Schlsp Comm Mem; NCBEA 1978-; Jaycees Outstanding Young Educator 1984; *office:* Lee Cty Sr HS 1708 Wash St Sanford NC 27330

SMITH, CAROLE L., English Teacher; *b:* Stamford, CT; *ed:* (BA) Scndry Ed/Eng, W CT St Univ 1972; (MS) Scndry Ed/Amer Studs, Fairfield Univ 1985; *cr:* Eng Teacher Brookfield HS 1972-; *ai:* Peer Counseling Adv; Brookfield Ed Assn Rep; BEA Schlsp, NHS Selection, Sr Schlsp, BEAPRR&E Comm; Brookfield Ed Assn 1972-; NCTE 1984-; Teachers & Writers Collaborative 1986-; *office:* Brookfield HS 45 Longmeadow Hill Rd Brookfield CT 06804

SMITH, CAROLE LYNN, 6th Grade Teacher; *b:* De Ruyter, NY; *ed:* (BA) Elem Ed/Soc Stud, Houghton Coll 1972; Grad Stud SUNY Cortland; *cr:* Elem Teacher De Ruyter Cntrl Sch 1972-; *ai:* Effective Schls Elem Team Mem; Asst Sftbl Coach; Phi Delta Kappa Educator of Yr 1983-84; 1st Baptist Church Youth Group Teacher 1980-; Concerned Women of America 1989-; Amer Quarter Horse Assn 1980-; *office:* De Ruyter Cntrl Sch 711 Railroad St De Ruyter NY 13052

SMITH, CAROLYN, Spanish Teacher; *b:* Evansville, IN; *m:* Curtis Edward; *c:* Charles E.; *ed:* (BA) Span, Georgetown Coll 1965; Morehead St Univ, Univ of KY; Seminar for Teaching Advanced Placement, W KY Univ; *cr:* Span Teacher 1965-, Dept Head 1989- Simon Kenton HS; *ai:* Foreign Lang Club Spon; Regional Foreign Lang Festival & Frosh Advisory Comms; Tour Cnslr for Trips Abroad E F Educl Tours; KY Cncl Teachers of Foreign Lang, Amer Assn Teachers of Span & Portuguese, NEA, KY Ed Assn; *office:* Simon Kenton HS 5545 Madison Pike Independence KY 41051

SMITH, CATHY G., English Teacher; *b:* West Memphis, AR; *m:* Billy Mack; *c:* Jason M.; *ed:* (BSE) Ed/Eng, Univ of AR Little Rock 1976; *cr:* Eng Teacher Hughes Jr HS 1977-79, Marion Mid Sch 1979-82, West Panola Acad 1982-86, West Memphis HS 1988-; *office:* West Memphis Sr HS 53 Judge Smith Dr West Memphis AR 72301

SMITH, CATHY SUZANNE, English Teacher; *b:* Jasper, AL; *ed:* (AS) Ed, Walker Coll; (BS) Ed, Univ of AL; Univ of AL Birmingham; *cr:* Eng Teacher Dora Jr HS, Oakman HS; *ai:* Sr Spon; Annual Staff Adv; Oakman HS Teacher of Yr 1985-86 & 1986-87; *office:* Oakman H S P O Box 286 Oakman AL 35579

SMITH, CECILIA SPOLETI, 5th & 6th Grade Teacher; *b:* Brooklyn, NY; *m:* Talmage D.; *c:* Talmage R., Cynthia A.; *ed:* (BS) Elem Ed, 1970, (MS) Elem Ed 1974 Eastern NM Univ; *cr:* 1st Thru 6th Grade Educator Alamogordo Public Sch 1970-; *ai:* Remediation Comm; Prin Pro-Temp; Sierra In-House Improvement Comm; Delta Kappa Gamma Intnl 2nd VP 1984-86; Kappa Kappa Iota; Amer Bus Women's Assn Treas 1978-79; *office:* Alamogordo Public Schls 2211 Porto Rico Ave Alamogordo NM 88310

SMITH, CHARLEN WYCOFF, Voc Home Economics Instr; *b:* Dodge City, KS; *m:* Douglas James; *ed:* (AA) Assoc Arts, Dodge City Coll 1968; (BS) Home Ec, 1970, (MS) Home Ec, 1987 KS St Univ; Teaching Educators to Design, Develop & Deliver Inservice Ed, KS Univ Food Sci Pilot Project, KS St Univ; *cr:* Home Ec Instr Sylvan Grove Unified Sch Dist #299 1971-74; Home Bound Instr Dodge City Spec Ed Coop 1974-75; Home Ec Instr Dodge City Sr HS/Area Voc Tech 1975-; *ai:* FHA Adv; Dist Dodge City Unified Sch Dist #443 Inservice Comm Officer & At Risk Comm; Dodge City Educators Assn Comm Chm; Dodge City Natl Assn, NEA; Delta Kappa Gamma Corresponding Secy 1989-; Phi Delta Kappa 1989-; ASCD 1980-; KS Assn Voc Home Ec Teachers (Inservice Chm, Exec Bd) 1975-, Master Voc Educator 1986; Amer Home Ec Assn, KS Voc Assn; Order Eastern Star Worthy Matron 1985; Soc Order of Beauseant Pres 1988; Daughters of Amer Revolution 1988-; KS Staff Leadership Dev Conference Presenter; KAVHET Mid Winter Conference Chm; KS St Advisory Bd for FHA; *office:* Dodge City Sr HS SW KS Area Voc Tech Comanche & 2nd Ave Dodge City KS 67801

SMITH, CHERLYN M., Earth Science Teacher; *b:* Springfield, MO; *m:* Terry Michael; *c:* Jody M., Toby W.; *ed:* (BSED) Earth Sci, 1969, (MSED) Earth Sci, 1980 SW MO St Coll; Field Geology, Univ of MO Columbia & SW MO St Univ 1990; NSF Grant, WY; *cr:* Zoo Sci Teacher 1989, Earth Sci/Bio Teacher 1969- Springfield Public Schls; *ai:* Sci Club Spon; Field Geology For HS Stus; Earth Sci Textbook Selection Comm; Co-Authored Curr Guide For Earth Sci Honor Courses; Natl Earth Sci Teachers Assn, Sci Teachers of MO, NEA; Collectors Club of Springfield Secy 1985-86; Presented Papers at NSTA Natl Meeting, MO St Meeting; Wrote Curr Guide, Textbook for Field Geology; *office:* Kickapoo HS 3710 S Jefferson Springfield MO 65807

SMITH, CHERYL ARMSTRONG, Assistant Principal; *b:* Chicago, IL; *m:* John L. Jr.; *c:* John, Gregory, Pamela, Michelle; *ed:* (BSED) Elem Ed, Loyola Univ 1967; (MBA) Human Resources, IL Inst of Technology 1985; *cr:* 5th Grade Teacher 1968-70, 6th Grade Teacher 1971-73, 8th Grade Teacher 1974-87, Asst Prin 1988- James Mc Cosh Elem Sch; *ai:* Mc Cosh Sch Local Sch Cncl Dedication to Youth Awd 1982; *office:* James Mc Cosh Elem Sch 6525-43 S Champlain Ave Chicago IL 60637

SMITH, CINDY MC MINN, Junior High Science Teacher; *b:* Lebanon, TN; *m:* Tommy G.; *c:* Ryan, Joanie D.; *ed:* (BS) Home Ec Ed, 1973, (BS) General Sci/Biological Sci, 1983 MS St Univ; *cr:* Teacher Winston Acad 1974-75, Ackerman HS 1975-76, Starkville Acad 1980-83, 1986-; *ai:* Co-Spon Sch Sci Fair; 9th Grade & Sci Club Spon; MS Private Sch Assn Dist Chm 1990-91; *office:* Starkville Acad Academy Rd Starkville MS 39759

SMITH, CLARA OWENS, First Grade Teacher; *b:* Prestonsburg, KY; *m:* Gaylor W.; *c:* Chason Smith II., Brittney; *ed:* (BS) (EE) Elem Ed, 1976, (MA) Elem Ed, 1984 Austin Peay St Univ; *cr:* Chapter Rdng Teacher West Huntsville Elem 1977-77; Mid Sch Drama Teacher Stone Mid 1977-78; 6th Grade Sci Teacher Mid Dependant Sch South 1978-79; 8th Grade Sci Teacher Fort Campbell Dependant Schls South 1979-87; 1st Grade Teacher CLarksville-Mont Cty Schls 1987-; *ai:* Clarksville Natl Bsbl League Candy Chm 1989; *office:* Barksdale Elem Sch Madison Clarksville TN 37043

SMITH, CLAUDETTE HENCE, Third Grade Teacher; *b:* Memphis, TN; *m:* Anthony C.; *c:* Anthony Jr., Bradley; *ed:* (BS) Ed, Le Moyne-Owen 1969; (MA) Rdng, Univ of MS; Working Towards Specialist Degree Supervision & Admin, Univ of MS Oxford; *cr:* 6th Grade Teacher Jerome Elem 1969-77; 3rd Grade Teacher Horn Lake Elem 1977-; *ai:* Horn Lake Elem Honor Club Adv; Miss World Pageant Spon Horn Lake Elem; Peer Evaluator for MS Teacher Assessement; Little League Bsbl Team Mother; Horn Lake Optimist Club; MS Incorporated Pres 1987-88; Delta Sigma Theta 1966-; Minority Fellowship Ole MS Univ; STAR Teacher 1985; Yrbk Dedication 1987; *office:* Horn Lake Elem Sch 6341 Ridgewood Horn Lake MS 38637

SMITH, CLYDE TIMOTHY, Health & Physical Ed Teacher; *b:* Ferrum, VA; *ed:* (BS) Health/Phys Ed, Carson-Newman Coll 1981; Public Sch Admin, Radford Univ & VPI & SU; *cr:* ISS Teacher Gretna HS 1981-83; Teacher/Coach Franklin Cty Mid Sch 1983-; *ai:* FCA Spon; Var Coach Asst Ftbl & Boys Tennis; *office:* Benjamin Franklin Mid Sch Rt 1 Box 3700 Rocky Mount VA 24151

SMITH, CONZELLA PRUDE, 8th Grade Math Teacher; *b:* Pontotac Cty, MS; *m:* O. B.; *c:* Keith O., Kertina L.; *ed:* (BS) Bus Ed, Rust Coll 1961; JTPA Trng & Certificate; *cr:* Bus Ed/Sch Secy Siggers HS 1961-65; Bus Ed/Math Teacher Carver HS 1965-69; Math Teacher Milam Jr HS 1969-; *ai:* MAE, NEA, MCMT, NMCMT 1987-89; CBS Reunion Secy; *office:* Milam Jr H S 720 W Jefferson St Tupelo MS 38801

SMITH, CRYSTAL PERRY, World Cultures Teacher; *b:* Coatesville, PA; *c:* Maya; *ed:* (BA) Psych/Scndry Ed, Eastern Coll 1979; Human Relations, Univ of OK; Ed, USC; *cr:* World Cultures Teacher Scott HS 1985-; *ai:* Stu Cncl Adv.

SMITH, CYNTHIA LEWIS, Music Director; *b:* Portsmouth, VA; *m:* Robert William; *c:* William; *ed:* (BA) Music, Old Dominion Univ 1982; *cr:* Music Ed Dir Colton Piano 1979-84; Music Dir Our Lady of Victory Sch 1985-87, Sacred Heart Sch 1989-; *ai:* Sacred Heart Choir & Handbell Choir Dir; Sigma Alpha Iota 1972-79; *home:* 43044 Fenner Ave Lancaster CA 93534

SMITH, CYNTHIA MC BRIDE, Home Economics Teacher; *b:* Franklin, LA; *m:* Kevin; *c:* Nisha, Courtney; *ed:* (BS) Home Econ, Northwestern St 1978; *cr:* Rdng Lab Teacher 1980; Home Ec Teacher 1980-; Phys Ed Teacher 1983- Evans HS; *ai:* Little Dribblers VP Coach 9-10 Yr Old Girls; FHA Adv; Chrldr Adv; Frosh Class Adv; LAE/NEA 1980-; Vernon Parish Home Ec Teachers 1980-; Evans Athletic Booster Club 1985-; Evans Alumni Assn 1981-; Evans Little Dribblers Assn Secy 1985-88; Evans Pioneer Day Assn 1986-; Evans Little Dribbler Coach (13-14 Yr Old Girls Dist Champ & Natl Champ 1984, 7-8 Yr Old Girls Dist Champ 1985-88, 9-10 Yr Old Girls Dist Champ 1989); Yrbk Adv 1984-87; Stu Cncl Adv 1980-84; Sftbl Coach HS Girls 1987-88; *home:* Rt 1 Box 89 Evans LA 70639

SMITH, D. BROOKS, Industrial Technology Teacher; *b:* North Augusta, SC; *m:* Laurie Emmette; *c:* Shanna; *ed:* (BS) Industrial Ed, Clemson Univ 1986; *cr:* Teacher East Jr HS 1986-; *ai:* Stu Cncl & Radio Controlled Car Club Spon; 9th Grade Girls Bsktbl.

SMITH, DAN R., Fourth Grade Teacher; *b:* Hickory, NC; *m:* Kathleen H.; *ed:* (BA) Intermediate Ed, Lenoir Rhyne Coll 1977; *cr:* Teacher Caldwell Cty Schls 1978-; *ai:* NCAE Sch Rep; Glaxo Fellowship in Sci; Sch Teacher of Yr; *office:* Granite Falls Elem Sch 60 N Highland Ave Granite Falls NC 28630

SMITH, DARALEA HARLOW, Second Grade Teacher; *b:* Terre Haute, IN; *m:* George Quentin; *c:* Kimberly Smith Plew, Jennifer, Quentin, megan; *ed:* (BA) Spec K-12, 1975; (BA) Elem K-9, 1975 IN St Univ; *cr:* 4th Grade Teacher Hutsonville Elem 1975; 2nd Grade Teacher Marshall Elem 1976-; *ai:* PR & Soc Comm; MEA Assn Rep 1989-; Marshallettes Co-Spon; Cub Cadettes Spon 1989-; Phi Upsilon Omicron 1974; Jr Womans Civic Club Pres 1978; PTA Pres 1974-75; *home:* 714 S 5th St Marshall IL 62441

SMITH, DARCI ANN, 4th-12th Grade Supervisor; *b:* Altoona, PA; *m:* James Jay; *ed:* (BA) Elem Ed, Liberty Univ 1989; *cr:* 4th-12th Grade Supervisor Gospel Light Chrstn Acad 1989-; *ai:* Kappa Delta Pi Secy 1987-89; *home:* 7131 Mt Vernon Rd Lithia Springs GA 30057

SMITH, DAVID G., English Teacher/Activities Adv; *b:* Waupaca, WI; *c:* Andrew; *ed:* (BA) Eng, 1971, (MA) Prof Dev, 1987 Univ of WI Whitewater; CPR; Ftbl, Bsktbl, Bsbl Coaching Clinics; Prof Dev Prgm; Mukwonago HS In-Service; *cr:* Teacher 1971-84; Teacher/Act Adv 1984- Mukwonago Area Sch Dist; *ai:* Soph Bsktbl & Frosh Bsbl Coach; Stu Government, Spirit Club, M Club, Yrbk Adv 1989-; Jr & Sr HS Scndry Fund Raising & Non-Athletic Extra-Curricular Prgms Coord 1989-; Coaches Assn 1979-; NASSP 1987-; WI Assn of Stu Cncls 1984-, Continuous Membership Awd 1989; WI Ed Assn, NEA 1971-; Friends of Volunteers 1988-, Service to Youth 1990; Waukesha Cty Volunteer

Center 1985-, Dirs Awd 1989; ASCD 1989-; Union (Pres, Negotiator, Grievance Chairperson); Braveland Conference Cncl Comm Chairperson 1988-; Whos Who Among Stus in Amer Colls & Univs 1987-88; Marine Corp Cnslr Command Visit 1987; Poems, Article, Essay Published 1970-85; *office:* Mukwonago HS 605 W School Rd Mukwonago WI 53149

SMITH, DAVID LAWRENCE, Sixth Grade Teacher; *b:* Canandaigua, NY; *ed:* (BA) Sociology, Coe Coll 1972; (MS) Elem Ed, Nazareth Coll of Rochester 1978; *cr:* 6th Grade Teacher Penn Yan Cntrl Schls 1972-; *ai:* Study Skills Comm; NEA; NEA/NY; Penn Yan Teachers Assn Pres 1983-85; *office:* Penn Yan Mid Sch Liberty St Penn Yan NY 14527

SMITH, DAVID PAUL, His/Civics/Geography Teacher; *b:* Burbonnais, IL; *ed:* (BA) Psych, Carson Newman Coll 1985; Teachers Cert, Univ of TN Chattanooga 1988; *cr:* Psych/His Teacher 1988-89, Geography/Civics Teacher 1989- Red Bank HS; *ai:* Asst Cross Cntry & Track Coach, Head Wrestling Coach; Key Club Spon; Banned Book Club Adv; *home:* 107 Mc Farland Ave Chattanooga TN 37405

SMITH, DAVID PAUL, History Teacher; *b:* Nacogdoches, TX; *m:* La Wanna Ruth Easley; *c:* Geoffrey, Audra, Madison; *ed:* (BS) Phys Ed, Baylor Univ 1971; (MED) Ed, 1973, (MA) Amer His, 1975 Stephen F Austin St Univ; (PHD) Amer His, Univ of N TX 1987; *cr:* His Teacher Rains Cty HS 1972-73, Highland Park HS 1975-; *ai:* Citizen Bee Spon; Phi Alpha Theta, Phi Delta Kappa; Teaching Fellowship Univ of N TX 1978-79; Historical Articles to be Published 1991; Historical Articles Published; *home:* 5038 Boca Raton Garland TX 75043

SMITH, DAVID WALTER, Freshman Science Teacher; *b:* Santa Ana, CA; *m:* Kerri Naifeh; *ed:* (BS) Phys Ed/Health Sci, CA St Fullerton 1981; Supplement Frosh Sci; *cr:* Teacher/Coach Garden Grove HS 1983-84, La Quinta HS 1984-; *ai:* Boys & Girls Tennis Team Head Coach; Coach of Yr Garden Grove HS 1983; *home:* 5727-13 E Stillwater Orange CA 92669

SMITH, DAVID WILEY, Choral Director; *b:* Jacksonville, FL; *m:* Linda King; *c:* Jennifer M., Matthew T., Laura E., Mallory S.; *ed:* (AA) Music, Andrew Coll 1967; (BA) Music Ed, Adams St Coll 1969; (MED) Admin/Supervision, Valdosta St Coll 1976; (MED) Music Ed, Columbus Coll 1979; *cr:* USAF 1969-73; General Music Teacher Seminole Cty 1973-77; Choral Dir Early Cty Mid & HS 1977-; Dir of Music 1st United Meth Church 1977-; *ai:* Early Cty Mid Sch Jr Beta Club Spon; Early Cty Mid Sch Pride Team Co-Spon; Prof Assn of GA Educators; GA Music Educators Assn, Music Educators Natl Conference, Dist Choral Chm 1986-88; Amer Choral Dir Assn; Choral Prgm & General Music Curr in Early Cty Sch System; *office:* Early Cty HS & Mid Sch 420 Columbia Hwy Blakely GA 31723

SMITH, DEBORAH B., Assistant Principal; *b:* Taylor, PA; *m:* Ronnie W.; *ed:* (BS) Elem Ed, 1976, (MED) Curr/Instruction, 1984 Univ of TN Chattanooga; Endorsement Admin & Supervision, Trevecca Coll 1986; *cr:* 2nd Grade Teacher Armuchee Valley Elem 1976-77; Spec Ed Teacher E Ridge Jr HS 1977-78; Resource Teacher 1978-79, 7th Grade Sci Teacher Ooltewah Mid Sch 1979-87;Asst Prin Brown Mid Sch 1987-; *ai:* Mentorship Prgm for Academically Talented Stus Spon; Academic Contest Teams & Outdoor Ed Prgm Chairperson; Kappa Delta Pi 1984-; Phi Delta Kappa 1987-; Sci Assn of Teachers 1980-; Hamilton Cty Ed Assn Chairperson Amer Ed Week 1977-; Hamilton Cty Ed Assn Amer Ed Week Chairperson 1977- (Distinguished Classroom Teacher Awd 1985-86, Pres Awd 1987-88); NEA, TEA 1977-; Kappa Delta Pi 1984-; Phi Delta Kappa 1987-; Sci Assn of Teachers 1980-; UTC Alumni Cncl Secy 1984-; Alpha Delta Pi (Alumni Pres 1987-88, Chapter Adv 1982-), Outstanding Alumni 1986; Better Schls Prgm Career Level III Teacher; Ooltewah Mid Sch Outstanding Teacher 1985-86; Nom Outstanding Sci Teacher & Pres Awd 1985; Hamilton Cty Teacher of Yr 1986; St of TN Mid Sch Teacher of Yr 1986; Prin Trainee 1987-88; *home:* 5415 Woody Trail Ooltewah TN 37363

SMITH, DEBORAH N., 7th/8th Grade Soc Stud Teacher; *b:* Canton, OH; *m:* Donald L. Jr.; *c:* Megan L., Carolyn E.; *ed:* (BSED) Elem Ed, Otterbein Coll 1970; *cr:* 1st Grade Teacher, 1970-72, 2nd Grade Teacher Columbus Public Schls 1970-72; LD Tutor 1979, 7th/8th Grade Soc Stud Teacher 1989- Plain Local; *ai:* Planning Team for Expansion of Local Dist; FADD Adv; Facilitator for Team Intervention; PLEA Treas 1985-86; New Albany Academic Boosters VP 1989-; Working on Comm for Grant to Begin Outdoor Ed Centers for Local Dist; *home:* 3755 Pine Meadow Rd New Albany OH 43054

SMITH, DELVER B., English Teacher; *b:* Weymouth, England; *m:* Jeanne Steele; *c:* Felicia, Tain, Melissa; *ed:* (BS) Eng, CA St Coll 1967; (MS) Eng, IN Univ of PA 1973; *cr:* Eng Teacher Hempfield Area Sch Dist 1967-; *ai:* Appleworks Cmptr Club; After-Sch Tutoring; PSEA, NEA, HAEA 1967-; Penn St Rhetoric Project Fellow 1982.

SMITH, DENISE (DAVIDSON), Business Teacher; *b:* Concordia, KS; *m:* Charles R.; *ed:* (BS) Bus Ed, KS St Univ 1985; Voc Ed 1988; *cr:* Bus Teacher Junction City HS 1987-; Adult Ed Night Sch Bus Teacher Alternative Ed Center 1988-; *ai:* Stu Cncl Spon; NEA, NBEA, KS Ed Assn, KS Bus Ed Assn; *office:* Junction City H S 9th & Eisenhower Junction City KS 66441

SMITH, DENNA LANTRIP, Fifth Grade Teacher; *b:* Houston, MS; *m:* Donny Ray; *c:* La Tessa R., John R.; *ed:* (BA) Elem Ed, MS St Univ 1978; MS St Univ; Univ of MS; *cr:* Jr HS Math/Soc Stud/Remedial Math/4th-6th Grade Math/5th Grade Rdng & Sci Teacher Woodland Attendance Center 1978-; *ai:* Math Supervision; Natl Sci Fnd Project; NEA, MS Assn of Educators 1979-; NCTM 1988-; Arbor Grove Baptist Church 5th/6th Grade Sunday Sch Teacher 1988-; Arbor Grove Baptist Church (Youth Comm 1989-, Childrens Comm 1979-89); Pilot Club Nominee 1988; Outstanding Young Educator Awd; *office:* Houston Mid Sch Thorn Rd Houston MS 38851

SMITH, DIANE MAC MILLAN, 1st Grade Teacher; *b:* Bloomington, IL; *m:* Merlin; *c:* Andrew; *ed:* (BS) Ed, IL St Univ 1969; *cr:* 2nd Grade Teacher Princeville Grade Sch 1969-75, Edelstein Grade Sch 1975-85; 1st Grade Teacher Princeville Grade Sch 1985-; *ai:* NEA, IL Ed Assn 1969-; Friends of Lillie M Evans Memorial Lib Treas 1987-; *home:* 416 N Walnut Princeville IL 61559

SMITH, DONALD RAY, 7-9 English Teacher; *b:* Bluefield, WV; *ed:* (BA) Eng, Concord Coll 1976; Grad Stud WV; *cr:* Teacher Bradshaw Jr 1978-; *ai:* Girls & Boys Bsktbl Coach; Stu Cncl & Drama Club Spon; Cty Textbook, SBAT, Stu Act Comm; WV Ed Assn 1978-; *home:* Rt 1 Box 426 Bluefield WV 24701

SMITH, DORAN EUGENE, Science Teacher; *b:* Coffeyville, KS; *m:* Julie Ann Lane; *c:* Amanda Prudhomme, Tara Prudhomme, Eli Prudhomme, Kessa, Jessica; *ed:* (BS) Natural Sci, Southwestern OK St Univ 1984; *cr:* Sci Teacher Chautauqua Cty Schls 1984-; *ai:* Jr Class Spon; Jaycees 1990; *home:* 410 S Chautaugua Sedan KS 67361

SMITH, DOROTHY SMALL, Music Teacher/Choral Director; *b:* Greensburg, IN; *m:* Damon L.; *c:* Scott E., Matthew L., Mark E.; *ed:* (BS) Music, Ball St Univ 1973; (MS) Ed, IN Univ 1988; *cr:* Music Choral Dir Edgewood Jr HS 1978-; *ai:* 7th/8th Grade Show Choirs; 6th/7th Grade Class Spon; Textbook Adoption General Music Comm Mem; Admin & Staff Comm Mem North Cntrl Assn Accreditation; Delta Delta Delta; Sigma Alpha Iota; IN Music Educators Assn; Music Assn; Music Educators Natl Conference; Consistent 1st Div Superior Awds Concert Choirs at Annual IN St Sch Music Assn; Keyboard Teacher Smith-Holden Music Bloomington IN; Show Choir Sullivan IL Contest; *home:* 5975 Matthews Dr Ellettsville IN 47429

SMITH, DORRIS ANN, 4th Grade Teacher; *b:* Waco, TX; *ed:* (BA) Ed, Mc Lennan Comm Coll 1970; (BA) Ed, Baylor Univ 1973; Region XII Advanced Trng Wkshps; Teachers Advanced Trng Baylor Univ; Free Enterprise Baylor & Mc Lennon Comm Coll; *cr:* Teacher Bosqueville Ind Sch Dist 1974-; *ai:* Plan & Book Comm; UIL Coord & Spon; Heart Assn Jump-A-Thon & RIF Rdng Prgm Coord; TSTA Treas 1974-; NEA; TX Classroom Assn 1987-88; PTA 1974-, Teacher of Month 1985.

SMITH, DORSEY WHETSIL, English/Oral Comm Teacher; *ed:* (BS) Speech/Drama, 1962, (MA) Eng/Theatre, 1978 E TN St Univ; *cr:* Eng/Speech Teacher Grundy Sr HS 1963-70; Eng/Drama Teacher Andrews Lewis HS 1970-75; Eng Teacher Grundy Sr HS 1979-; *ai:* Forensic Dir; NEA, VEA 1963-.

SMITH, DOUGLAS ROSS, Math/Science Teacher; *b:* Des Moines, IA; *m:* Paul A. Deitz; *c:* David, Penelope, Stephen; *ed:* (MS) Math Ed, MI St Univ 1978; (MAT) Math, Cntrl MI Univ 1989; Emergency Medical Technician Specialist Instr, Coord; *cr:* Math/Sci Teacher Plainfield Cons Schls 1979-81, Whitefish Twp Sch 1981-87; Emergency Medical Technician Instr Lake Superior Univ 1986-; Math/Sci Teacher Brimley HS 1987-; *ai:* Adv of Class of 1993; BEA Treas 1988-; Eastern Upper Emergency Medical Services (Adv Cncl Chm 1987-89, Medical Control Bd Mem 1987-); Whitefish Township EMS Emergency Medical Technican 1981-; *office:* Brimley H S Rt 221 Brimley MI 49715

SMITH, E. SHELDON, III, Science Dept Head; *b:* Flushing, NY; *m:* Alice Mc Nary; *c:* Shelley Mac Donald, Joseph, Jennifer; *ed:* (BS) Genral Sci, 1955, (MED) Scndry Ed, 1957 Bridgewater St Coll; (CGS) Physics, Boston Coll 1965; Certificate Prgms Math, Physics & Cmptr Sci, Rutgers, Univ of RI, Brown Univ, MIT, Southeastern MA Univ; *cr:* General Math I/II/Bio Teacher Attleboro HS 1955-57; General Sci/Physics/Chem Instr S Attleboro Jr HS 1957-61; Sci Dept Head/Physics Instr Joseph Case HS 1961-; *ai:* Photography Club Adv; NSTA 1957-; AAAS 1949-; Southeast MA Physics Alliance 1988-; BSA Weblos Leader 1968-71; Parents Cncl for Hard of Hearing 1955-; Amer Heart Assn CPR Instr 1976-84; Kappa Delta Phi Alpha Chm 1951-; Articles Published; Teacher of Yr Sigma XI; *office:* Joseph Case HS 70 School St Swansea MA 02777

SMITH, EARLDEEN ATWOOD, Third Grade Teacher; *b:* Franklin, KY; *m:* Tom H.; *c:* Tommi Smith Hamilton, Terri Smith Gabriel; *ed:* (BMED) Music, W KY St Coll 1961; Endorsement Elem Ed, 1975, (Rank II) Elem Ed, 1981 W KY Univ; *cr:* Elem Music/Chorus/Band Teacher Hughes-Kirk Sch 1961-62; Choral Dir Little Miami Jr/Sr HS 1965-71; Elem Music/Chorus/Band Teacher Dorton Sch 1972-73; 2nd/3rd Grade Teacher Taylor Cty Elem & Mannsville Elem 1976-; *ai:* E KY Teachers Network Mem 1989-; Campbellsville BPW Club Pres 1976-77; Campbellsville Taylor Cty Rescue Squad Mem; Campbellsville 1st United Meth (Mem, Chancel Choir); Outstanding Young Women of America 1976; Participant Mellon Seminar 1989; Certified Emergency Medical Technician; *home:* 3465 New Lebanon Rd Campbellsville KY 42718

SMITH, ELIZABETH ANN (HILL), 3rd Grade Teacher; *b:* Sparta, TN; *m:* William G.; *c:* William G., Gina S.; *ed:* (BS) Elem Ed, 1973; (MA) Admin Supv/Elem Prin, 1986 TN Tech Univ; *cr:* 7th-10th Grade/Eng Teacher Centertown Sch 1967-68; 4th Grade Teacher Dibrell Sch 1968-69; 3rd Grade Teacher Irving Coll 1969-70; Eastside 1970-; *ai:* Purchasing Comm; GED Inst Rest Homes; Alpha Delta Kappa, Chaplain 1983-84; TEA/NEA/Warren Cty Ed Assn Mem; Warren Cty Fair Bd 1987-; Warren Cty Alumni TN Tech Chapter 1973-; *home:* Rt 11 Box 159 Mc Minnville TN 37110

SMITH, ELIZABETH FAULKNER, Third Grade Teacher; *b:* Union County, NC; *m:* Tony Alexander; *c:* Mary E.; *ed:* (BS) Ed, Appalachian St Univ 1979; *cr:* Kndgtn Teacher 1979-80, 3rd Grade Teacher 1980- Marshville Elem; *ai:* Media Comm; Sci Textbook Comm; NCAE 1979-; Teacher of Yr Marshville Elem Sch 1987; *home:* Rt 2 Box 243-A Marshville NC 28103

SMITH, ELIZABETH R., 5th-8th Grade Lang Art Teacher; *b:* Auburn, NJ; *c:* Michael, Paul, Clement; *ed:* (AA) Liberal Art, Salem Comm Coll 1976; (BA) Elem Ed, Glassboro St Coll 1978; *cr:* S/Sargeant USAF/WAF Randolph AFB 1951-55; Civil Service/Clerk Typist Finance Dept Randolph AFB 1955; Invoice Clerk E I Dupont 1962-67; Lang Art Teacher St James Grammar Sch 1978-; *ai:* Lang Art & Rdng Coord; Spelling Bee & Essay Moderator; Choir Dir, Church Lector; Bingo Caller; Secular Franciscan Order Mem 1975-; Salem Countians Against Toxins Pres 1987-89; St James Regional Sch Bd Mem 1990; Drug & Alcohol Prgm 1988; Project Write 1989; Cmptr Trng Prgms 1990; *office:* St James Regional Grammar Sch Beach Ave Penns Grove NJ 08069

SMITH, ELSA AICHELER, High School Counselor; *b:* Brooklyn, NY; *m:* James F.; *c:* Kathleen Smith Wisniewski, Terrence M., James B., Cynthia Smith Frick, Timothy, Matthew, Patricia M.; *ed:* (BS) Home Ec/Sci, Marygrove Coll 1951; (MED) Family Life Ed, 1972, (MA) Guidance/Counseling, 1980 Wayne St Univ; Seminars; *cr:* Teacher Lincoln Jr Sr HS 1951-52, Highland Park Public Schls 1952; Teacher/Dept Chairperson Region HS 1967-86; Teacher Roseville & Brablec HS 1982-88; Adjunct Instr Marygrove Coll 1985-; Cnslr Regina HS 1986-; *ai:* Alumnae Adv; Career Cnslr; Job Placement; NHS Comm; Amer Home Ec Assn, Assn Counseling & Dev, Archiocesan Counseling Assn; Outstanding Leaders in Scndry Ed; *home:* 21100 Lakeland St Clair Shores MI 48081

SMITH, ELVIN ESTIL, JR., Fifth Grade Teacher; *b:* Liberty, KY; *m:* Kathryn Downing; *c:* Edward, Donald, Georganne; *ed:* (BS) Elem Ed, 1965, (MA) Elem Ed, 1968 W KY Univ; *cr:* Elem Teacher Daviess Cty Schls 1965-67; Jr HS Teacher 1968-, Elem Teacher 1990 Hardin Cty Schls; *ai:* Jr HS Boys & Girls Bsktbl Coach; Video Yrbk Spon; Sci Dept Chm; KY Ed Assn, NEA 1965-; Hardin Cty Ed Assn 1968-; BSA Scoutmaster 1967; Cub Scouts of America Asst Cub Master 1980; Optimist Club Stu Act Chm 1981; Hardin Cty Schls Sci Fair Chm; *home:* 617 Sportsman Lake Rd Elizabethtown KY 42701

SMITH, EMMETT RAY, English Teacher/Coach; *b:* Phoenix, AZ; *m:* Jacqueline Joan Hiland; *c:* Robin, Scott, Richard, Laurie Wilson; *ed:* (BA) Journalism Univ of AZ 1959; (MA) Eng, AZ St Univ 1970; *cr:* Eng Teacher/Coach Glendale HS 1959-60, Cortez HS 1960-70, Apollo HS 1970-73, AZ St Univ 1973-74, Apollo HS 1974-; Motivational Specialist Brigham Young Univ 1979-; *ai:* Head Cross Cntry Coach 1960-; Track Coach 1960-; NEA 1980-; Phoenix Teacher of Yr; AZ Teachre of Yr; Valley Forge Freedom Fnd Teachers Awd; Glendale Citizen of Yr; AZ Coach of Yr; Natl Coaches Awd; *office:* Apollo HS 80485 N 47th Ave Glendale AZ 85302

SMITH, ETTA EVANS, Principal; *b:* Rankin Cty, MS; *m:* Jim L.; *c:* Jim L. Jr., Dina S.; *ed:* (BA) Bio, 1967, (MS) Early Chldhd, 1972, Spec Ed Elem Ed, 1980 Jackson Univ; Rdng/Admin, Univ of MS; *cr:* Teacher St Joseph HS 1969-70; Early Ed Teacher 1972-76, Elem Teacher 1976-86, Elem Admin 1986- Jackson Public Schls; *ai:* Writing Curr Materials Dist Instructional Cncl; Booster Club Spon; Dist Shared Governance & Textbook Selection Comm, ASCD Mem 1984-86; MASCD Mem 1986-87; United Way Mem 1987-88, Outstanding Contribution Awd; Outstanding Service to Public Ed Awd Jackson Public Schls; NAASP Awd Certificate of Achievement MS Assessment Center; *office:* Clausell Elem Sch 3330 Harley St Jackson MS 39209

SMITH, FRANKLIN FOSTER, Sixth Grade Teacher; *b:* Rochester, NY; *m:* Elsie Sparks; *c:* Susan Sedlak, William, Debra Koenig; *ed:* (BS) Ed, George Washington Univ 1976; (MA) Ed, VA Polytechnic Inst 1984; *cr:* US Coast Guard 1949-75; Teacher Beechtree Elem 1976-79, Clearview Elem 1979-; *ai:* Lead Sci Teacher; Effective Sch Comm; US Coast Guard Natl Pres 1973-75 Alexander Hamilton 1974; Chief Petty Officers Assn; US Coast Guard Federal Credit Union Pres; PTA Clearview Pres 1979-81; BSA Veteran 1940- Eagle Scout 1948, Award of Merit, Silver Beaver, Woodbadge; Boy Scouts Order of Arrow Vigil Honor; Scottish Rite Mason & Master Mason; Teacher of Yr Nom 1987; Fairfax Cty Public Schls; *office:* Clearview Elem Sch 12635 Builders Rd Herndon VA 22070

SMITH, FRANKLIN LA VAUGHN, Student Activities Director; *b:* Jacksonville, FL; *m:* Reba Davis; *c:* Erica, Eric, Marche, Jayla, Jeneen, Jason; *ed:* (BA) Eng, Edward Waters Coll 1976; (BA) Journalism, Univ of FL 1977; (MED) Educl Leadership, Jacksonville Univ 1990; Mid Sch Cert & Trng for Consultation; Inservice Trng for Consultation; *cr:* Teacher Payon Jr HS 1977-87; Inservice Consultant Duval Cty Sch Bd 1987-89; Stu Act Dir William M Raines HS 1989-; *ai:* Jr, Sr & Soph Class Stu Cncl; Drama; NHS Yrbk; NCTE, NASSP, Natl Mid Sch Assn; NAACP, Emancipation Proclamation Assn; Teacher of Yr 1982, 1985, 1986, 1987; Most Valuable Teacher 1986; Phi Delta Kappa Educator of Yr 1989; *office:* William M Raines HS 3663 Raines Ave Jacksonville FL 32209

SMITH, FREDERICK DALE, History & English Teacher; *b:* Grand Rapids, MI; *m:* Ruby Nichols; *c:* Leonard D., Denise Smith-Calleja, John W.; *ed:* (BA) Elem Ed/His, Emmanuel Missionary Coll 1958; (MA) His, Andrews Univ 1967; *cr:* Teacher Gobles Jr Acad 1967-70; Teacher/Prin Glenwood Union Sch 1970-77, Eau Claire 7th Day Adv Sch 1981-84; His/Eng Teacher Little Creek Acad 1984-; *ai:* Building, Maintenance, Grounds Care; *home:* 1810 Little Creek Ln Knoxville TN 37922

SMITH, FREDERICK SAMUEL, Social Studies Teacher; *b:* Jamestown, RI; *m:* Barbara Mcleod; *c:* Frederick Jr., Deborah M. Hathaway, Brendan, Patrick; *ed:* (BA) Poly Sci, Univ of RI 1953; (MS) Ed, Southern CT ST Univ 1963; Post Masters Studies, Educl Admin, Univ of CT; *cr:* Soc Stud Teacher Guilford Jr HS 1959-70; Soc Stud Dept Head/Teacher Adams and Baldwin Mid Schls 1970-85; Dir of Adult Ed Guilford 1977-89; Soc Stud Teacher Adams & Baldwin Mid Sch 1985-; *ai:* NCSS 1960-; NEA 1970-; CEA 1959-; GEA Pres/VP 1959-; *office:* Elisabeth Adams Mid Sch Church St Guilford CT 06437

SMITH, FRIEDA SUE, 1st Grade Teacher; *b:* Columbus, OH; *m:* Jon I.; *c:* Tracy L., Troy A.; *ed:* (BS) Elem Ed, Miami Univ 1970; (MS) Admin Ed, Univ of Dayton 1989; *cr:* Teacher Anthony Wayne Sch 1970-71, Westerville OH 1971-80, Wellston OH 1981-; *ai:* Bundy Bldg Rep Adv Cncl; Delta Kappa Gamma 1982-; Mothers Club 1980-; Jr Study Club 1980-; Hope U M Church 1980-; *home:* 751 N Pennsylvania Wellston OH 45692

SMITH, GAIL EVANS, Second Grade Teacher; *b:* Washington, DC; *m:* Robert Franklin; *c:* Jim, Rob; *ed:* (BA) Early Chldhd Ed/Elem Ed, 1979, (MED) Ed/Rdng Specialist, 1984 Univ of SC; Additional Stud Sci, Psych of Young Children, Rdng; *cr:* Teacher Greenville Cty Sch System; *ai:* SAC Chairperson; St Certified APT Evaluator; Sci Coord; Dow Inst Grant; Alliance for Ed Grant; *office:* Mountain View Elem Sch 6350 Hwy 253 Taylors SC 29687

SMITH, GENE ANTHONY, World Cultures Teacher; *b:* Strausstown, PA; *c:* Leslie A. Boettcher, Burgess A., Craig E., Valerie Gene Hirsch; *ed:* (BA) His, Cedar Crest Coll 1947; Nursing, Reading Hospital Sch of Nursing, PA St Univ, Juniata Coll; *cr:* Soc Stud Teacher Upper Moreland HS 1947-49; 6th Grade Teacher Juniata Elem Sch 1967-69; World Cultures Teacher Juniata Valley HS 1982-; *ai:* Stu Cncl Adv; Juniata Valley Ed Assn (VP 1967-69) 1982-; Huntingdon Cty Bd of Realtors; Huntingdon Area Bd of Ed (Pres 1974-78) 1971-79; Bd of Trustees Lancaster Theological Seminary 1984-; Huntingdon Cty Medical Society Auxiliary Pres 1966-70; *office:* Juniata Valley HS R D 1 Alexandria PA 16611

SMITH, GENNET M. L., Fifth-Sixth Grade Teacher; *b:* Williston, ND; *m:* Richard L.; *c:* Douglas, Craig; *ed:* (BS) Elem Ed, Minot St Univ 1971; Grad Stud Elem Ed; *cr:* 5th/6th Grade Teacher Bainville Public Sch 1966-; *ai:* MEA, NEA 1966-71; MCTM 1978-87; MSRC 1988-; Bainville Cmmty Club Secy; Bainville Cmmty Dev Corporation (Secy, Treas) 1985-88; *home:* PO Box 164 Bainville MT 59212

SMITH, GEORGE FRANCIS, JR., Mathematics Teacher/Coach; *b:* Georgetown, TX; *m:* Margaret Ann Burk; *c:* George Kelly, James Walker; *ed:* (BAT) Math, Sam Houston St Univ 1974; Engr Lab Technician, USN Nuclear Power Submarines; *cr:* Sci Teacher Calvert Ind Sch Dist 1969-70; Math Teacher/Coach Sequin Ind Sch Dist 1974-77, Weimar Ind Sch Dist 1977-81, Sabinal Ind Sch Dist 1981-; *ai:* NHS & Jr HS Number Sense Spon; Defensive Coord; Ftbl Offensiveline & Head Bsktbl Coach; Gifted/Talented & Textbook Selection Comm; Math Dept Chm; TX HS Coaches Assn 1974-; Nom Math Teacher of Yr 1990; *office:* Sabinal Ind Sch Dist P O Box 338 Sabinal TX 78881

SMITH, GEORGE MICHAEL, 6th Grade Teacher; *b:* Los Angeles, CA; *m:* Marie Engledow; *c:* Mike Jr., Marty; *ed:* (BA) Geography, CA St Univ Los Angeles 1969; (MA) Early Chldhd Ed, USIU 1972; BA Equivalent Chinese, Defense Lang Inst 1968; *cr:* Switchman Union Pacific RR 1962-68; Pres Calmag Engineering 1968-72; 2nd Grade Teacher Rancho Santa Fe 1972-75; Pres/Owner Three Rivers Resort 1975-; Teacher Valley Elem 1984-; *ai:* IEA, NEA Mem; ID Travel Cncl Chm 1982-88; ID Centennial Commission Commissioner 1984-88; ID Outfitters & Guides Mem; ID St Senator 1980; ID Travel Industry Man of Yr 1988; *office:* Valley Elem Sch P O Box 100 Kooskia ID 83539

SMITH, GLENDA ROGENE, Social Studies Dept Chair; *b:* Fairbury, IL; *m:* Thomas C.; *ed:* (BS) His, 1975, (MS) His, 1980 IL St Univ; Working Towards DA in His; *cr:* His/Eng Teacher Minooka HS 1976-; His Teacher Joliet Jr Coll 1982-; *ai:* Fall Play Dir; Yrbk Adv; Intervention Team Mem; NCSS, IL Cncl for Soc Stud 1988-; Morris Theater Guild 1979-84, Best Dir 1983-84; Aux Sable Historical Society 1988-; Eco Lab Excl in Ed Awd 1990; *office:* Minooka HS Box 489 Wabena & Mc Evilly Minooka IL 60447

SMITH, GLENDA SCHALANSKY, First Grade Teacher; *b:* Norton, KS; *m:* Kelvin Le Roy; *c:* Rachelle L., Sheila R.; *ed:* (BA) Elem Ed, Fort Hays St Univ 1973; *cr:* 1st Grade Teacher Roosevelt Elem 1973-74; Rdng Tutor Unified Sch Dist 212 Valley Long Island & Almena 1974-75; 1st/2nd Grade Teacher Unified Sch Dist 212 Long Island 1975-78; 1st Grade Teacher Unified Sch Dist 212 Almena 1978-81; Kndgtn Teacher Unified Sch Dist 212 Long Island & Almena 1981-88; 1st Grade Teacher Unified Sch Dist 212 Almena 1988-; *ai:* Asst Girls Bsktbl Coach 1988-; KS Rdng Assn 1990; Delta Kappa Gamma 1984-; Northern Valley Educators Assn Past Pres; Prof Dev Cncl Pres 1988-; Athena Study Club Pres 1979-80; Amer Legion Auxiliary, Eastern Star; Outstanding Young Women of Amer Awd 1977-78, 1980; *office:* Northern Valley Elem Sch 512 W Bryant Almena KS 67622

SMITH, GLENDA WELLS, Elem Prin/6th Grade Teacher; *b:* Valdosta, GA; *m:* Billy Wayne; *c:* Brandon S.; *ed:* (BS) Elem Ed, Valdosta St Coll 1969; *cr:* 3rd Grade Teacher Lackawanna Elem 1969; 5th Grade Teacher Rufus E Payne Elem 1971-73; 6th Grade Teacher Greater Jacksonville Chrstn Sch 1973-; *ai:* Var, Jr Var, Jr HS Cheerleading, Safety Patrol Spon; Honor Society Adv; *office:* Greater Jacksonville Chrstn 3737 Collins Rd Jacksonville FL 32238

SMITH, GLENN GRAHAM, 5th Grade Teacher; *b:* Ann Arbor, MI; *m:* Jadine Duby; *c:* Rachel Duby, Joshua Duby; *ed:* (BA) Elem Ed, 1976, (MA) Rdng, 1983 MI St Univ; *cr:* 5th Grade Teacher Galewood Sch 1977-; *ai:* Co-Facilitator Dist Sch Improvement Team; Prof Negotiations Team & Gifted & Talented Comm Mem; *office:* Galewood Elem Sch 512 E Lovett Charlotte MI 48813

SMITH, GLORIA JOHNSON, Second Grade Teacher; *b:* Athens, GA; *m:* Leroy Jr.; *c:* Jonathan; *ed:* (BS) Elem Ed, Morris Brown Coll 1974; (MS) Early Chldhd Ed, Univ of GA 1975; *cr:* 3rd Grade Teacher Washington Wilkes Primary Sch 1975-77; 2nd Grade Teacher Nancy Creek Elem Sch 1977-; *ai:* Morris Brown Alumni 1975-, Outstanding Service 1980; Church of Christ Bible Sch Teacher 1975-; *office:* Nancy Creek Elem Sch 1663 E Nancy Creek Dr NE Atlanta GA 30019

SMITH, GLORIA SHARPE, Language Arts Teacher; *b:* Orlando, FL; *m:* Ernest T.; *c:* Vincent P., Anthony D.; *ed:* (BS) Eng, 1981, (MS) Scndry Ed, 1985 IN Univ; Rdng Endorsement; *cr:* Instr Davenport Bus Coll 1987-89; Teacher/Dept Chairperson Kennedy-King Mid Sch 1983-; Teacher/Instr IN Univ Northwest 1985-; *ai:* Natl Jr Honor Society Adv; Gary Eng Cncl Pres 1986-; IN Cncl Teachers Eng; NCTE; Alpha Kappa Alpha Pres 1979-81; *office:* Kennedy-King Mid Sch 301 S Parke Gary IN 46403

SMITH, HELAINE L., English Teacher; *b:* Cambridge, MA; *m:* Stuart A.; *ed:* (BA) Eng, Boston Univ 1965; (MA) Eng, Hunter Coll 1979; Univ of Birmingham Shakespeare Inst; Grad Stud Hunter Coll; *cr:* Eng Teacher Hunter Coll HS 1974-89, The Brearley Sch 1989-; *ai:* Advanced Placement Eng Exam & ECT Reader.

SMITH, HELEN FOX, Fifth Grade Teacher; *b:* Waco, TX; *m:* John Dodd; *c:* Bryan, Catherine; *ed:* (BA) Eng, Southern Meth Univ 1957; (MED) Elem Ed, P V A&M Univ 1974; Trng for Gifted-Talented & Law Related Educl Prgms; *cr:* Eng Teacher Rylie HS 1957-59, Giddings HS 1963-66; 3rd Grade Teacher 1971-84, 5th Grade Teacher 1984- Giddings Elem; *ai:* 5th Grade Gifted & Talented Teacher; Univ Interscholastic & UIL Spon; PTO; Career Ladder Comm 1989-; Lee Cty Opera Bd of Dir 1990; 1st United Meth Church; Rufus Young King Lib Bd Mem; Selected Teacher of Yr by Giddings Ind Sch Dist Admin 1989; Nom for TX St Teacher of Yr Awd 1989.

SMITH, HELEN GABRIEL, 7th Grade Math/Soc Std Teacher; *b:* Roxbury, PA; *ed:* (BA) His, Chestnut Hill Coll 1968; Graduate Courses-Johns Hopkins Univ/Trinity Coll/Towson St Coll; *cr:* 2nd-8th Grade Teacher Cath Schls PA/MD/VA 1948-; Math Teacher St Ritas Cath Sch 1978-85; Math/His Teacher St Anne Cath Sch 1987-; *ai:* Rdng Coord; NCEA.

SMITH, HERBERT JAMES, Fifth Grade Teacher; *b:* Glens Falls, NY; *m:* Ann Marie Prevost; *c:* Lara, Jinel; *ed:* (AA) Art, Adirondack Comm Coll 1969; (BS) Art/Ed, Brockport St Coll 1971; Grad Courses; Castleton St Coll, Brockport St Coll, St Joseph the Provider; *cr:* 5th Grade Teacher Granville Cntrl Sch 1971-; *ai:* Granville Summer Enrichment Prgm Art Instr; NY St United Teachers; Harrisena Cmmty Church 5th/6th Grade Instr.

SMITH, HILDA SMITH, 1st Grade Teacher; *b:* Leakesville, MS; *m:* Anthony C.; *c:* Leah S., Brewer, Anthony G.; *ed:* (BS) Elem Ed, William Carey Coll 1967; Phys Ed Recrection; Mobile Coll; Univ of Southern MS; *cr:* 2nd Grade Teacher Sand Hill Elem 1966-67; 3rd Grade Teacher Indian Springs 1967-68; 1st Grade Teacher Leakesville Elem 1971-; *ai:* Greene Cty Teachers Assn 1971-; MS Prof Educator; MAE; NEA 1967-; *office:* Leakesville Elem Sch PO Box Leakesville MS 39451

SMITH, HUGH DAVID, Science/Bible Teacher; *b:* Baltimore, MD; *ed:* (BA) Bio, Appalachian St Univ 1975; Bible Trng, New Tribes Bible Inst; Grad Trng in Scndry Ed, TN Temple Univ; *cr:* Jr/Sr HS Teacher SW VA Chrstn Acad 1979-80, Knoxville Baptist Chrstn Schls 1980-; *ai:* Photography Club Adv; Sunday Sch Teacher; Church Bus Driver; Teaching Awd Knoxville Baptist Chrstn Schls; *office:* Knoxville Baptist Chrstn Schls 2434 E 5th Ave Knoxville TN 37917

SMITH, J. FRANK, Science Dept Chair; *b:* Memphis, TN; *m:* Deanna Sue Mullen; *c:* Jason, Heather; *ed:* (BSA) Animal Sci, AR St Univ 1970; Grad Stud in Ed; *cr:* Sci Teacher Blytheville HS 1970-71, Piggott HS 1971-80, Clay Cty Cntrl HS 1981-; *ai:* Sci Club & Sr Class Spon; AR Ed Assn (Budget Prgm 1986-88/Prof Rights & Responsibilities Comm 1988-); Piggott Park Commission 1979-86; *office:* Clay Cty Cntrl HS W 5th Rector AR 72461

SMITH, JACQUELINE JONES, Mathematics Teacher; *b:* Memphis, TN; *m:* William Stanley; *c:* William G., Courtney E.; *ed:* (BS) Math Le Moyne-Owen Coll 1978; *cr:* Directory Asst Operator South Central Bell 1979-80; Sales Associate AT&T Phonecenter 1981-86; Math Teacher Westside HS 1985-; *ai:* Dancing Wildcat Spon; Southern Assn Mem; Co-Spon Stu Cncl; Memphis Ed Assn Faculty Rep 1986-88; *office:* Westside HS 3389 Dawn Dr Memphis TN 38127

SMITH, JACQUELINE KAY, 3rd Grade Teacher; *b:* Elizabeth City, NC; *ed:* (AS) Early Chldhd, Wingate Jr Coll 1974; (BS) Early Chldhd, Appalachian St Univ 1977; Effective Teacher Trng; Sci & Math Integrated Learning Experience; Teacher Perf Appraisal Instrument; *cr:* 3rd Grade Teacher W H Knuckles 1978-; *ai:* Testing Contact Person for W H Knuckles; NCAE Sch Rep 1987-89; Woodhaven Alzheimers Care Center Vol 1989; *office:* W H Knuckles Elem Sch M L King Drive Lumberton NC 28358

SMITH, JANE PEELE, Elementary Counselor; *b:* Goldsboro, NC; *m:* Billy R.; *c:* Roger; *ed:* (BS) Intermediate Ed, 1976, (MA) Intermediate Ed, 1984, (MA) Counseling, 1988 E Carolina Univ; *cr:* 4th Grade Teacer Nahunta Elem Sch 1976-78; 4th Grade Teacher 1978-88, Elem Cnslr 1988- Eastern Wayne Elem Sch; *ai:* Parent Volunteer, Eastern Wayne Elem Newsletter, Testing Coord; Sch Field Day, Guidance, Wayne Cty Schl Cnslrs Comm; NCAE 1976-88; NCSCA 1989-; Phi Kappa Phi 1976-; Alpha Delta Kappa 1983-; *home:* Rt 2 Box 360 Goldsboro NC 27534

SMITH, JANET MEYER, Ger Teacher/Foreign Lang Chair; *b:* Des Moines, IA; *m:* Douglas R.; *c:* Brennen, Ryan; *ed:* (BA) German/Eng, Morningside Coll 1968; (MA) Library Sci, Univ of IA 1970; *cr:* Eng Teacher Southeast Polk HS 1968, West Branch HS 1968-69; German Teacher Des Moines Schls 1987-; *ai:* Ger Club Adv; East HS Cntrl Campus Building Advisory Comm Rep; IA Foreign Lang Assn, AATG 1988-; Book Published 1981; *office:* Cntrl Campus HS 1800 Grand Ave Des Moines IA 50307

SMITH, JANET V., Sixth Grade Teacher; *b:* Chicago, IL; *ed:* (BA) Elem Ed/US His, NE IL St Univ 1968: (MED), Natl Coll of Ed 1987; *cr:* Classroom Teacher James Otis Elem Sch 1968-; *ai:* Prof Personnel Advisory Comm; IL Cncl for Soc Stud; Trng Tape for Chicago Public Schls; Chicago Public Schls Teacher of Yr 1987-88; Mini Grant Winner Chicago Fnd for Ed 1988, 1989; *office:* James Otis Elem Sch 525 N Armour Chicago IL 60622

SMITH, JANET WARLICK, Spanish/English Teacher; *b:* Atlanta, GA; *m:* Charles W. Jr.; *c:* Brian, Jana; *ed:* (BA) Span, Birmingham Southern Coll 1974; (MA) Scndry Ed, Univ of AL Birmingham 1980; *cr:* Span/Eng Teacher Pleasant Grove HS 1974-89, Bottenfield Jr HS 1989-; *ai:* Span Club Adv; Newsletter Coord; Recognitions Comm; Jefferson Cty Ed Assn, AL Ed Assn, NEA 1974-; Hispanic Conference of Birmingham, AL Assn Teachers of Span & Portuguese 1985-; Bottenfield Athletic Boosters Secy 1988-; Crumly Chapel United Meth Women 1987-; Outstanding Young Women of America 1982; Teacher of Yr Pleasant Grove HS 1985-86; Second Mile Teacher Awd 1989-; *office:* Bottenfield Jr HS 400 Hillcrest Rd Adamsville AL 35005

SMITH, JANICE M., Retired; *b:* Hallie, KY; *m:* Hassel; *c:* Scotty, Marsha; *ed:* (BS) Elem, Pikeville Coll 1965; *cr:* Jr HS Math Teacher Kingdome Come Settlement 1965-66; 5th Grade Teacher 1966-68, 1st & 2nd Grade Teacher 1968-83, 5th Grade Teacher 1983-85 Campbells Branch; *ai:* KY Ed Assn; Lethcer Cty Teachers Org.

SMITH, JANICE NELSON, Business Education Instructor; *b:* Green Cove Springs, FL; *m:* Randal Rei; *ed:* (BA) His, Elon Coll 1981; Bus Ed, Edison Comm Coll; *cr:* Asst Dir of Admissions Elon Coll 1981-83; Dir of Admissions Ft Myers Bus Acad 1983-86; His Teacher 1986-87, Bus Ed Teacher 1987- Riverdale HS; *ai:* FBLA 1986-; FBLA Dist Dir 1988-89; Project Invest Comm 1989-; Curr Comm 1989-; Lee Cty Voc Assn, FL Voc Assn, FL Bus Ed Assn 1987-; March of Dimes Coord Schls 1989-, Plaque 1989; *office:* Riverdale HS 2815 Buckingham Rd SE Fort Myers FL 33905

SMITH, JAYNE RUTH, English Teacher; *b:* Bristow, OK; *ed:* (BFA) Drama, 1954, (BA) Eng, 1955 Univ of OK; (MA) Eng, Univ of TX Austin 1968; Classes & Wkshps Numerous Univs; *cr:* Eng/Drama Teacher Raymondville HS 1955-57, Monahans HS 1957; Eng Teacher Jefferson HS 1957-; *ai:* Literary Magazine Spon; T J Ecology Club & Fine Art Festival Chm; SE TX Cncl Teachers of Eng Dir 1973-87; NCTE; PTA Life Membership 1988; Earth Day Comm 1989-; G & F L White Schlsp Comm 1975-; Cmmty Concert Bd Dir; Eng Journal Writing Awd 1983; Top 10 AP Teachers in SW 1988; Articles Published; 2 Books Published; *office:* Jefferson HS 2200 Stadium Rd Port Arthur TX 77642

SMITH, JERRIE LEAN, 7th Grade Soc Stud Teacher; *b:* Birmingham, AL; *m:* Ural Jr.; *c:* Ural III; *ed:* (BA) Elem Ed/Soc Stud, 1975, (MS) Rdng, 1980 Hofstra Univ; *ai:* 7th Grade Class Adv; Coord Black His Month; Head Debate Club; Negro Bus & Prof Womens Organization Mem; At Risk Kids Consultant; Teacher of Yr 1979; *home:* 100 Manhattan Ave Roosevelt NY 11575

SMITH, JILL WADE, 7th/8th Grade English Teacher; *b:* Glasgow, KY; *m:* Joseph Warren; *c:* Taylor D.; *ed:* (AB) Speech Comm, 1981, (MA) Ed, 1984 W KY Univ; *cr:* 7th/8th Grade Eng Teacher Edmonton Elem 1984-; *ai:* Jr Beta Spon; KY Ed Assn; Excl in Teaching Awd Campbellsville Coll 1989; *home:* 301 Wilson Cir Edmonton KY 42129

SMITH, JOAN BIDDLE, Kindergarten Teacher; *b:* Philadelphia, PA; *m:* Douglas Kendall; *c:* Douglas, Brian, Tracy; *ed:* (BA) Soc Sci (Geo), San Diego St Univ 1970; (MS) Early Childhood Ed, La Verne Univ 1976; Post Masters Studies San Diego St Univ; *cr:* Teacher 2nd/3rd Grades 1970-72; Teacher K 1972- Webster Acad of Life Sci; *ai:* San Diego Unified Sch Dist Mentor Teacher; Staff Inservicing; Curr Dev; CA K Assn 1988-; CA Elem Ed Assn 1988-; Excel Awd for Excellence in Public Ed 1988; *home:* 3033 Alcott Street San Diego CA 92106

SMITH, JOANN ARNOLD, English Teacher; *b:* Cedartown, GA; *m:* Jonathan Leonard; *c:* Allison E., Casey M.: *ed:* (BA) Eng, W GA Coll 1978; W GA Coll; *cr:* Eng Teacher Lithia Springs HS 1978-79, Eng Teacher Haralson Cty HS 1979-81, 1987-; *ai:* Beta Club Spon; PAGE 1987-; GAE 1978-81; *office:* Haralson Cty HS PO Box 547 Tallapoosa GA 30176

SMITH, JOANNE WATTS, Assistant Principal; *b:* Moultrie, GA; *ed:* (BS) Bio/Natural Sci, Paine Coll 1970; (MS) Admin/ Supervision, Nova Univ 1978; FL Atlantic Univ, Univ of GA, Valdosta St, Albany St, Univ of FL; *cr:* Classroom Teacher Pompano Beach Mid Sch 1970-79, Ramblewood Mid Sch 1979-83, Colquitt Cty Jr HS 1983-86; Asst Prin Colquitt Cty Sr HS 1987-; *ai:* Spec Ed Curr Comm; Schedule & Extracurricular Acts Admin; GA Assn of Scndry Sch Prins, NASSP, NEA, GA Assn of Educl Teachers 1970-; Delta Sigma Theta 1970-; Womens Federated Club 1989-; La Nouvelle Society; Whos Who Among Stu in Amer Univs & Colls 1970; GA Assessment Test Writer; Sci Teacher Spec Recognition Awd; *home:* 1000 3rd Ave SW Moultrie GA 31768

SMITH, JOHANNA (TERRY), 2nd Grade Teacher; *b:* Chatsworth, GA; *m:* Ward B. Jr.; *c:* Emily A.; *ed:* (AA) Liberal Art, Dalton Jr Coll 1973; (BA) Early Chldhd, 1975, (MS) Early Chldhd, 1979 W GA Coll; *cr:* 1st Grade Teacher Ranburne Elem Sch 1975-76, East Side Elem 1976-77, Franklin Elem 1977-79; 2nd/4th Grade Teacher Chatsworth Elem 1979-.

SMITH, JONATHAN KENNON THOMPSON, Curriculum Coordinator; *b:* Camden, TN; *ed:* (BS) His/Ed, George Peabody Coll 1960; (MA) Ed Admin/His, Memphis St Univ 1962; Grad Stud Cert in Educl Admin & Supervision, Memphis St Univ 1983; *cr:* Teacher/Curr Coord Shelby Cty Schls 1962-; *ai:* Writer of Local His; Benton Cty TN Historian/Emeritus; TN Ed Assn Shelby Cty Ed Assn 1962; TEA Convention Delegate; Committment to Children; AwardEd Life Membership in TN Congress of Parents & Teachers 1978; *home:* Box 18557 Memphis TN 38181

SMITH, JONEL RENE, Civics Teacher; *b:* Torrington, WY; *m:* Tony; *ed:* (BA) Phys Ed/Health, Western MT Coll 1985; *cr:* Civics Teacher West Jr HS 1986-; *ai:* Vlybl Coach; 8th Grade Girls Bsktbl Coach; Teacher Mentor; *office:* West Jr H S 1003 Soo San Drive Rapid City SD 57702

SMITH, JOYCE WATSON, 3rd Grade Teacher; *b:* Nashville, TN; *m:* William Russell; *c:* Gregory Erwin, Jeffrey Earl, Leann Smith Argo; *ed:* (BA) Elem Ed, 1957, (MED) Admin/Supervision, 1969 MTSU; *cr:* 3rd & 4th Grade Teacher Lincoln Sch 1957-60; Kndgtn Teacher Hardison Elem 1966-76; 4th Grade Teacher 1976-87, 3rd Grade Teacher 1988- Johnson Elem; *ai:* 4-H Club Leader; Sunday Sch Teacher; Franklin Ed Assn Pres 1985-86; Delta Kappa Gamma Pres 1986-88; Amer Cancer Society Pres 1988-89; Celebration of Life 1989; PTA Bd Mem 1989-; Sci Grant Vanderbuilt Univ.

SMITH, JUDITH HARDAWAY, Principal; *b:* Columbus, GA; *m:* Tyrone L.; *ed:* (BA) Ed, WV St 1963; (MA) Ed, John Carroll Univ 1978; Cert Admin & Supervision, Cleveland St Univ 1985, Kent St Univ 1988; *cr:* Teacher 1969-85, Asst Prin 1985-86, Teacher 1986-87, Prin 1987- Cleveland Public Schls; *ai:* Supervise & Coord after Sch Prgms; Ed Comm of Urban League; Phi Delta Kappa Natl; ASCD; Cleveland Cncl of Admin & Supvrs; Grants Motivating at Risk Stus; Jennings Awd Work with Gifted & Talented; *office:* Gracemount Elem Sch 16200 Glendale Ave Cleveland OH 44128

SMITH, JUDITH MURRELL, Lang Art Teacher/Curr Dir; *b:* Russellville, MO; *m:* Scott Jay; *c:* Barbara E. Carothers *ed:* (BA) Speech/Drama/Debate, 1961, Remedial & Dev Rdng 1972 Lincoln Univ; Lang Art, Winona St Univ 1978; Curr Auditing; *cr:* Speech/Drama/Debate Teacher Waynesville MO 1962-63; Speech/Drama Teacher Lanark HS 1964-65; Rdng/Speech Teacher Springville HS 1965-68; Rdng Teacher Linn-Marr Sch 1968-74; Rdng/Lang Art Teacher St Charles HS 1976-; *ai:* Jr Class Adv; Meet & Conference; Jr Var Vlybl; NCTE 1968-; AASA, ASCD 1988-; SCEA Pres; *office:* St Charles Public Schls Hwy 14 E Saint Charles MN 55972

SMITH, JUDY LEITH, 3rd/4th Grade Teacher; *b:* Breese, IL; *m:* Franklin D.; *c:* Franklin D. III, Cody W.; *ed:* (AA) Elem Ed, Kaskaskia Jr Coll 1973; (BS) Elem Ed, SIU-E 1975; *cr:* Aide in Learning Center 1975-76, 1st Grade Teacher 1976-86, 3rd & 4th Grade Teacher 1986- Breese Elem Dist #12; *ai:* Cheerleading Spon; *home:* 1490 Methodist Barlyle IL 62231

SMITH, JUDY THOMAS, English Teacher; *b:* Greenville, AL; *m:* Charles Howard; *c:* Jeremy, Jeffrey, Jason; *ed:* (BS) Scndry Ed/Eng, Auburn Univ 1977; (MS) Scndry Ed/Eng, Troy Univ 1988; (EDS) Scndry Ed/Eng, AL St Univ; *cr:* Eng Teacher Greenville Acad 1979-84, Greenville Jr HS 1984-; *ai:* Spon Jr Act; Coach Eng Team; Coord Spelling Bees; Delta Kappa Gamma Research Comm 1988-; AL Ed Assn St Public Relations Comm 1989-, 1st Place Awds; Butler Cty Ed Assn St Delegate 1990-; NCTE; Polling Clerk Crenshaw Cty AL 1988-; Presenter Gulf Coast Writing Conference; Ed Butler Cty Ed Newsletter; AL Ed Assn Best New Newsletter, Best Graphics, Best Editorial, Honorable Mention Best Local Coverage Awds; *office:* Greenville Jr HS Overlook Rd Greenville AL 36037

SMITH, KAREN KAYE, 2nd Grade Teacher; *b:* Springfield, MO; *m:* Steve N.; *c:* Sierra N.; *ed:* (BS) Elem Ed, Cntrl MO St Univ 1980; Lib Sci, Cntrl MO St Univ 1980; *cr:* 2nd/3rd Grade Teacher Benton Cty R II 1980-89.

SMITH, KAREN NEAL, English Teacher; *b:* De Queen, AR; *m:* Michael W.; *c:* Lee, Clay, Laura; *ed:* (MS) Eng/His, E TX St Univ 1980; Lib Sci, UCA 1991; *ai:* Jr Chrldr Spon; Phi Delta Kappa 1989-; *office:* Foreman HS Box 280 Foreman AR 71836

SMITH, KATHLEEN (CAFER), Third Grade Teacher; *b:* Cottonwood, AZ; *ed:* (AA) General Ed, Barstow Coll 1967; (BA) Psych, Chico St 1970; Grad Stud; *cr:* 6th-8th Grade Teacher Harmony Elem 1970-72; 7th/8th Grade Teacher Mc Kinleyville Elem Sch 1972-82; 5th/6th Grade Teacher 1982-89, 3rd Grade Teacher 1989- Morris Sch; *ai:* Lang Art, Health, Soc Stud Textbook Comm Mem; Sftbl, Bsktbl, Cheerleading Coach; Coord of Gifted & Talented Ed; Humboldt Cty Olympics of Mind Co-Chm; *office:* Morris Elem Sch 2395 Mc Kinleyville Ave Mc Kinleyville CA 95221

SMITH, KEITH ELLIOTT, Math Teacher; *b:* Colorado Springs, CO; *m:* Elizabeth Edwards; *ed:* (BS) Ed, Univ of North TX 1986; Working Towards MS in Math, TX Womens Univ; *cr:* Teacher Denton HS 1986-89; *ai:* Math Team Coach; Math Club Adv; NCTM Mem; *office:* Denton H S 1007 Fulton Denton TX 76201

SMITH, KENNETH EDWARD, II, Social Studies Teacher; *b:* Richlands, VA; *ed:* (BA) His/Soc Sci, Emory & Henry Coll 1980; Advanced Cmptr Software Univ of VA 1985; *cr:* Soc Stud Teacher Grundy Sr HS 1980-; Rock Climbing Instr SW VA Comm Coll 1985-; *ai:* Chess Club Spon 1981-; Ftbl Letterman Emory & Henry Coll 1980-82; NEA, VEA 1980-; BSA High Adventure Explorers Grundy Sr HS 1984-87; Civil Air Patrol (Supply Officer 1986-87, Squadron Trng Officer 1987-89, Squadron Commander 1989-, Region Staff Coll Grad 1989, Encampment Commander 1988-), Commanders Commendation 1988, 1989; Civil Air Patrol Aerospace Ed Awd; *home:* Rt 2 Box 68-A Grundy VA 24614

SMITH, KIMBERLY WALKER, Jr High Science Teacher; *b:* Paris, TX; *m:* David Wilson; *c:* Erin, Craig; *ed:* (BS) Phys Ed/ Health, 1978, (MS) Life Sci/Earth Sci, 1983 E TX St Univ; *cr:* Phys Ed Teacher/Coach Quinlan Jr HS 1978-80; Sci Teacher W Lamar Ind Sch Dist 1983-85, Chisum Jr HS 1985-; *ai:* Chrldr Co-Spon; Assn of TX Prof Educators 1983-89; *office:* Chisum Jr HS Rt 4 Paris TX 75460

SMITH, LANE DREW, English Teacher; *b:* Pocatello, ID; *m:* Mabel Jones; *c:* Jennifer, Lisa, Stacie, Carrie; *ed:* (BA) Phys Ed, UT St Univ 1967; *cr:* Eng Teacher Firth HS 1967-70; Phys Ed Teacher Firth HS & Elem Sch 1969-72; Eng Teacher Firth HS & Mid Sch 1972-80, Harding Gibbs Mid Sch 1980-; *ai:* Ski Club Adv; St Writing Assessment Grader; City Cncl Councilman 1969-71; ID Ed Assn Officer 1982; Firth Teachers Assn Officer 1986; Shell/Firth Credit Union Bd of Dir 1980-85; *office:* Harding Gibbs Jr HS PO Box 247 Firth ID 83236

SMITH, LARRY HUDSON, 5th Grade Head Teacher; *b:* Brookville, PA; *m:* Vicki T.; *c:* Nathan T.; *ed:* (BS) Elem Ed, Edinboro Univ 1970; (MS) Elem Ed, Clarion Univ 1973; *cr:* Teacher, Head Teacher Brookville Area Schls; *ai:* Brookville Area Ed Assn VP 1975-76; PA Ed Assn; NEA; Free & Accepted Masons; Ohnadagon Society Pres 1986-88; YMCA; *office:* Brookville Area Schls Jenks St Extension Brookville PA 15825

SMITH, LESLIE ANNE, Chemistry/Biology Teacher; *b:* Lebanon, MO; *m:* Kelly John; *c:* Meagan Kaeli, Savannah E.; *ed:* (BSED) Bio/Chem, 1986, (BS) Wildlife Ecology/Conservation, 1986 NW MO St Univ; Working Towards MSED Natural Sci, Math, SW MO St Univ 1991; *cr:* Chem/Bio Teacher Mansfield HS 1986-; *ai:* Sci Fair & Sci Club Spon; Intnl Sci & Engineering Fair 1988-89; Sci Teachers of MO 1987-; Sigma Xi Iota Honorary Mem, Sci Teacher of Yr 1990; NSTA Review Comm Mem 1986-; Tri Beta Bio (Secy, Treas) 1983-86; GSA Asst 1988-; Cmmty Recycling Comm Ed Consultant 1989-; Natl Wildlife Fnd Action Lobby 1986-; Paper Submitted for Publishing 1990; Mark B Robbins Wildlife Sch 1986; NWSUU Alumni Awd 1986; Young Explorers Sch 1984; Ed Research Sch 1984; Regents Schlsp 1982.

SMITH, LINDA KAY, Second Grade Teacher; *b:* Lamar, CO; *m:* Francis L.; *c:* Erik, David, Amber, Nicole; *ed:* (BA) Elem Ed, Western St Coll 1967; (MS) Elem Rdng, Cntrl MO St Univ 1984; Grad Stud; *cr:* 1st Grade Teacher Glen Avon Elem 1968-72; 1st/ 2nd/4th Grade Teacher Miami Elem 1973-77; 2nd Grade Teacher Butler Elem 1977-; *office:* Butler Elem Sch High St Butler MO 64730

SMITH, LINDA KNESEK, High School Counselor; *b:* San Antonio, TX; *m:* Robert E.; *c:* Charles R., Randal, Richard, Scott; *ed:* (BA) Eng/Poly Sci, SW TX St Univ 1970; (MS) Counseling, Corpus Christi St Univ 1977; *cr:* Eng Teacher Aransas Pass Jr HS 1970-78; Cnslr Kieberger Elem 1978-79, Aransas Pass HS 1979-; *ai:* TX Assn for Counseling & Dev, Gulf Coast Assn for Counseling & Dev 1986-; Aransas Pass Womans Club 1989-; *office:* Aransas Pass HS 450 S Avenue A Aransas Pass TX 78336

SMITH, LOTTIE LEE, Fourth Grade Teacher; *b:* Honea Path, SC; *m:* Robert Lionel; *c:* Karon Weldon, Cody; *ed:* (AA) Assoc Art, Anderson Coll 1968; (BA) Elem Ed, Lander Coll 1973; (MA) Elem Ed, Clemson 1979; Recertification Courses; *cr:* 6th Grade Teacher Estes Elem 1973-79; 4th Grade Teacher New Prospect Elem 1979-; *ai:* Local Sch Comms; *office:* New Prospect Elem Sch New Prospect Church Rd Anderson SC 29621

SMITH, M. SANDRA, Science Department Chair; *b:* Montgomery, AL; *ed:* (BA) Bio, Rice Univ 1960; (MED) Sci Ed, Univ of FL 1980; *cr:* Research Asst Bowman Gray Sch of Medicine 1960-65; Sci Teacher Dupont Jr HS 1965-72, Bradford HS 1972-; *ai:* Sr Class Spon; Peer Teacher; Sci Dept Chairperson; FL Assn Sci Teachers, NSTA 1970-; STAR Teacher of Yr 1976; Yrbk Dedications 1970, 1980; Bradford Cty Teacher of Yr; Master Teacher Cert FL; *office:* Bradford HS 581 N Temple Ave Starke FL 32091

SMITH, MADONNA TUCKER, English Teacher; *b:* Effingham, IL; *m:* Gregory Harold; *c:* Gretchen Marie; *ed:* (BS) Eng, IL St Univ 1973; (MA) Journalism, Northern IL Univ 1987; *cr:* Reporter Effingham Daily News 1973-74; Eng Teacher Tuscola HS 1974-79, Downers Grove HS North 1979-; *ai:* Yrbk & Newspaper Adv; Incorporated Bronte Society, Quill & Scroll, Journalism Ed Assn, NCTE, IL Assn Teachers of Eng, Kappa Tau Alpha.

SMITH, MARCIA BABCOCK, Business Education Teacher; *b:* Frostburg, MD; *m:* Harry P.; *c:* Kelly, Heather, Corey; *ed:* (BS) Bus Ed, Frostburg St Univ 1986; Working Towards Masters Admin & Supervision; *cr:* Bus Ed Teacher Westmar HS 1987-; *ai:* Sch Store; Cheerleading Adv; *office:* Westmar HS RR 36 Lonaconing MD 21539

SMITH, MARGARET S., Mathematics Dept Chairman; *b:* Dothan, AL; *m:* Thomas Owen; *c:* Sharon S., Kittie S., Thomas O. Jr.; *ed:* (ME) Math, Auburn Univ 1970; *cr:* Math Teacher Montgomery Cath HS 1963-70, Eclectic Acad 1970-76: Math Dept Chairperson Edgewood Acad 1976-; *ai:* Yrbk Adv; Auburn Univ Fellowship; *office:* Edgewood Acad P O Box 26 Elmore AL 36025

SMITH, MARIAN J., 5th Grade Lang Art Teacher; *b:* Kaplan, LA; *m:* James W. Jr.; *c:* Rodney J., Nicole R.; *ed:* (BA) Ed, 1971; (MED) Ed, 1978 Southern Univ; *cr:* Elem Teacher Eaton Park Elem Sch 1971, Gonzales Primary 1972-77, Gonzales Mid Sch 1978-; *ai:* LA Assn of Educators, NEA, LA Rdng Assn; *home:* 5509 Monmouth Ave Baton Rouge LA 70808

SMITH, MARILYN ELIZABETH, 7th Grade Teacher; *b:* Elmore, MN; *ed:* (BS) Elem, 1976; (MED) Guid Cnslr/Dir, 1979 Bridgewater St; *cr:* Guid Cnslr/Asst Prin Belmont Elem 1979-80; 7th Grade Teacher St Joseph 1980-; *ai:* Music Coord; Choir Dir; *home:* 24 Meadowlark Dr Wareham MA 02571

SMITH, MARILYN MOFFETT, 7th/8th Grade Typing Teacher; *b:* Dallas, TX; *m:* Orion Dwain; *c:* Scott S., Jill N.; *ed:* (BSED) Bus/Eng, Univ of N TX 1968; (MSED) Scndry Supervision, Stephen F Austin Univ 1976; *cr:* Classroom Teacher Reed Jr HS 1969-; *ai:* Co-Spon Chrldrs & Pep Club 1975-80; Annual Staff Spon 1972-75, 1980-; Assn of TX Prof Educators 1980-; TX St Teachers Assn 1969-80; Alpha Delta Kappa VP 1990; PTA Lifetime Awd; Reed Jr HS Annual Dedication 1980; Natl Jr Honor Society Honorary Awd Outstanding Teacher; *office:* Reed Jr HS 530 E Freeman Duncanville TX 75116

SMITH, MARK F., Choral Director; *b:* Huntington, NY; *m:* Suzanne Carter; *ed:* (BA) Music Ed, 1984, (MS) Music Ed/ Conducting, 1990 Bowling Green St Univ; *cr:* Choral Dir Bedford HS 1986-; *ai:* Dir & Producer Sch Musicals; Amer Choral Dir Assn, MI St Vocal Assn 1986-; Phi Mu Alpha Ritual Chm 1982-85; Toledo Repitoire Theatre Musical Dir 1988-; *office:* Bedford HS 8285 Jackman Rd Temperance MI 48182

SMITH, MARSHA KAY, Assistant Principal; *b:* Beckley, WV; *ed:* (BS) Elem Ed/4-8 Gen Sci, Concord Coll 1981; (MA) K-8 Admin, WV Coll of Graduate Stud 1986; FM WV Coll of Graduate Stud; *cr:* 6th Grade Teacher 1981-86; Guidance Cnslr 1986; Asst Prin 1986 Trap Hill Mid Schl; *ai:* Discipline Comm; WV Prof Treas 195-84; WV Educators Assn 1984-; WV Scndry Prinpls Assn 1986-; NEA 1984-; Crab Orchard Bapt Church Sunday Sch Teacher 1983-85; *home:* Box 62 Crab Orchard WV 25827

SMITH, MARTIN ROBERT, Sixth Grade Teacher; *b:* Philadelphia, PA; *m:* Tamar Anne Kucharsey; *c:* Martin S.; *ed:* (BS) Elem Ed, 1973, (MED) Educl Leadership, 1979 Univ of DE; Advanced Preparation Courses Towson St Univ, W MD Coll, Loyola Univ, Univ of DE; *cr:* Sergeant USAF 1961-65; Research Asst E I Dupont Company Incorporated 1965-69; Stu Univ of DE 1969-72; Teacher Cecil Cty Public Schls 1972-; *ai:* Faculty Advisory, Sch Budget, Sick Leave Book Comm; Initiator of Family Math Prgm; Cub Scout Parent Volunteer; Cecil Cty Teachers Assn Pres 1975-76, 1978-79; MD St Teachers Assn, NEA 1972-; Various Seminars & Prof Dev Symposiums; *office:* Calvert Elem Sch 79 Brick Meetinghouse Rd Rising Sun MD 21911

SMITH, MARY ANN TODORICH, 5th Grade Teacher; *b:* Bradys Bend, PA; *m:* James M.; *c:* James M. Jr., Jerry M.; *ed:* (BS) Elem Ed/Scndry Eng, Geneva Coll 1952; *cr:* Elem Teacher Union Sch Dist 1952-59; 5th Grade Teacher Mercer Elem 1967-; *ai:* Drama Club Adv; PSEA, NEA 1952-; Mercer Ed Assn (Faculty Rep 1979-81, VP 1982-83, Pres 1985-); Insurance Agent for Croatian Fraternal Union; Past Pres and Secy Sloga Jr Tamburitzans; Natl Secy Croatian Fraternal Union's Jr Cultural Tamburitzan Federation; Eleven yr Mem "Od Srca", Playing Second Brac; Mem Immaculate Heart of Mary Church; Past Mem Parish Cncl; Pres and Secy Altar-Rosary Society; Publisher Church Bulletin; Financial Secy Croatian Fraternal Union Lodge #126; Mem of Sports Comm; *home:* PO Box 331 Mercer PA 16137

SMITH, MARY DOBMEYER, Fourth Grade Teacher; *b:* Brooklyn Center, MN; *m:* William B.; *c:* Rachael, Matthew; *ed:* (BA) Elem Ed, Mankato St Univ 1981; *cr:* 4th Grade Teacher Waseca Public Schls 1981-82; Kndgtn Teacher Hartley Elem 1983; 4th Grade Teacher S Side Elem 1983-; *ai:* Chm Spring Fling Sch Carnival & Talent Show; Co-Chm Track & Field Day; Camp

Patterson Aids Curr, Wase Management, Sci, Teacher Assistance Team Comms; MEA, NEA; WEA Secy 1985-86; *office:* South Side Elem Sch 609 S State St Waseca MN 56093

SMITH, MARY LEWIS, English/Reading Teacher; *b:* Columbus, MS; *m:* Tazzell; *ed:* (Bs) Ed, Rust Coll 1955; Pepperdine Coll, Univ of CA Los Angeles, CA St Coll Advanced Trng; *cr:* Teacher CA Elem Sch 1964-68, Mesa Robles Jr HS 1968-; *ai:* Stu Government, Debating Teams; Stu Cncl & Stu Organizations Adv; Working Adult Literacy Prgms; Conducts Rdng/Writing Wkshps for Sch Dist; NEA Life Mem; CA Writing Projects; Reader of St Tests; Teacher of Yr 1976; Certificate of Recognition Univ of CA Santa Monica Coll; *office:* Mesa Robles Jr HS 16060 Mesa Robles Dr Hacienda Heights CA 91745

SMITH, MARY MILLER, Gifted/Talented Facilitator; *b:* Little Rock, AR; *m:* Kenneth Lee; *c:* Kyle, Jared; *ed:* (BA) Eng, S AR Univ 1974; (MA) Eng, AR St Univ 1976; (MSE) Gifted/Talented Ed, Univ of AR; Mid Southern Writing Project 1978; Writing Project 1985; *cr:* Eng/Adv Creative Writing Teacher Jonesboro 1976-78; Eng Teacher N Little Rock Ole Main 1978-79, Bryant HS 1979-86; Teacher Gifted/Talented Bryant Jr HS 1986-; *ai:* Odyssey of Mind Coach; Quiz Bowl; Knowledge Master; Alpha Delta Kappa; AR Ed Assn 1976-; AR Future Problem Solving (Evaluator, St Bd) 1988-; Ozark Society Nature Conservancy Conservation Co-Chm 1979-84; YMCA/SW Little Rock Young Mens Chrstn Assn Bd Mem; Outstanding Teacher of Composition Mid Southern Writing Project 1978; AR Ed Dept Outstanding Teacher Recognition Grant 1985; Intnl Future Problem Solving Coaches Competition 2nd Place 1986; *office:* Bryant Jr HS 200 NW 4th Bryant AR 72022

SMITH, MARYA BOOTH, French Teacher; *b:* Audubon, NJ; *m:* David Gyle; *c:* Gyle, Luke, Andrew; *ed:* (BS) Fr, IA St Univ 1969; *cr:* Fr/Math Teacher Collins Cmmty Schls 1969-71; Fr Teacher North Scott HS 1984-; *ai:* Foreign Lang Club; Phi Sigma Iota Mem 1969-.

SMITH, MELANIE MAXTED, 8-12 English/Theatre Teacher; *b:* Galveston, TX; *m:* Jesse Daley; *c:* Stephanie Smith Gillette (dec), Laura Smith Kennedy, Ronald P.; *ed:* (BA) Eng, Rice Univ 1962; (MA) Eng, Howard Payne Univ 1969; Theatre Arts, Rdng; *cr:* Teacher/Eng Dept Chairperson Richland Springs Ind Sch Dist 1966-; *ai:* Jr Class Spon; Drama Club; Dir of Contests in Writing, Spelling, Journalism, Speaking, Oral Interpretation & Theatre; Bsktbl Game Clock Ofcl; Excl in Schls Team Mem; Fr Club; NCTE; Delta Kappa Gamma 1979; TX Educl Theatre Assn (K-12 Bd Secy 1990, Mem 1980); TX Joint Cncl Teachers of Eng Consultant 1990; Creative Drama Network Consultant 1985; TX Educl Theatre Assn Scndry Section Educator of Yr 1990; *office:* Richland Springs Ind Sch Dist Box E Richland Springs TX 76871

SMITH, MERODEE BUCHANAN, Mathematics Teacher; *b:* Portland, OR; *m:* William R.; *ed:* (BS) Elem Ed, 1972, (MS) Ed, 1976 Portland St Univ; *cr:* Math/Sci Teacher Mt View Jr HS 1973-77; 5th Grade Teacher Hanford Elem 1977-83, Badger Mt Elem 1983-84; Math Teacher Richland HS 1984-; *ai:* Class Adv; W WA Univ Awd Prof Excl 1986; *office:* Richland HS 930 Long Ave Richland WA 99352

SMITH, MICHAEL GEORGE, Dept Chair, Cmptr Sci Teacher; *b:* Saginaw, MI; *c:* Kimberlee J.; *ed:* (AS) Earth Sci, Delta Coll 1970; (BS) Teaching Cert Earth Sci, Cntrl MI Univ 1972; (MAT) Ed/Teaching, Saginaw Valley St Coll 1986; (MAED) Ed/Admin, Saginaw Valley St Univ 1989; Specialist in Ed Admin/Supervision, Cntrl MI Univ 1990; *cr:* Chm/Teacher Ruben Daniels Lifelong Learning; Cmptr Teacher Center HS 1986-; *ai:* Presenter Adult Extended Learning Services Conference MI Dept of Ed 1990; *office:* R Daniels Lifelong Learning HS 115 W Genesse Saginaw MI 48602

SMITH, MICHAEL LEE, Math Teacher; *b:* Scottsbluff, NE; *m:* Rita Lavonne Sircin; *c:* Christopher, Rachel; *ed:* (AA) Math, Scottsbluff Jr Coll 1967; (BS) Math, 1970, (MS) Math/Sci, 1978 Chadron St Coll; Chadron St; Kearney St; *cr:* Math Teacher Mitchell HS 1970-75, Gering HS 1976-; *ai:* Wrestling & Weightlifting Coach; Fellowship of Chrstn Athletes & Jr Class Spon; Ftbl/Wrestling Official; Phi Delta Kappa Honorary (VP, Pres) 1990; Lambda Delta Lambda Sci Honorary 1969-70; 1st Baptist Church (Chm of Deacon Bd, Bd of Trustees, Bd Chrstn Ed); Outstanding Wrestling Ofcl NE Bestowed By National Fed Ofcls; NE Presidential Scholar Teacher 1989; Recipient Presidential Phys Fitness Awd Weightlifting; *home:* 2025 16th Gering NE 69341

SMITH, N. MARLIENE, 3rd Grade Teacher; *b:* Roswell, NM; *m:* Calvin; *c:* Wendy, Ginger; *ed:* (BA) Ed, 1964, (MA) Ed, 1986 E NM Univ; Natl Defense Summer Inst in Span 1964; Good Apple Summer Wkshp for Gifted TN 1964, St Louis MO 1983; *cr:* Elem Span Teacher 1964-66, 5th & 6th Grade Teacher 1966-70, 1972-76 Tucumcari Public Schls 1966-70, 1972-76; 2nd/3rd/6th Grade Teacher Aztec Public Schls 1977-; *ai:* Problem Solving Comm; NEA 1964-; Chrstn Writers Assn 1989-; Aztec Public Schls Service Awd 1987; *home:* 1115 Graceland PO Box 1041 Aztec NM 87410

SMITH, NANCY L (MC ELWRATH), Elementary Science Teacher; *b:* Holcomb, MO; *m:* Jerry R.; *c:* Jerry R. Jr.; *ed:* (AA) Gen, Belleville Jr Coll 1973; (BS) Biological Sci Ed, Southern IL Univ 1975; (ME) Sci Ed, IN Univ at Kokomo 1980; Gifted & Talented Trng; Cmptr Trng; Earth Sci Courses; *cr:* Sci Teacher Clarkton HS 1975-76; New Athens HS 1976-77; Maconaquah Mid Sch 1978-; *ai:* Natl Jr Honor Society Spon; Focus Public Relations Comm; Academic All Star Competition Coach; Focus Selection Comm; Broadbased Planning Comm Focus Gifted & Talented Prgm; North Central Steering Comm; NSTA 1987-; Delta Kappa Gamma 1987-; Phi Delta Kappa 1984-; HASTI 1987-; Outstanding Teacher Awd 1981-83; Natl Teacher of Yr Nom for Corporation 1986.

SMITH, NANCY L. (LEE), English Teacher; *b:* El Paso, TX; *m:* John Dollins; *c:* Kirk M., Stacy L.; *ed:* (BA) Eng/Choral Music, SW TX St 1959; *cr:* Choral Music Teacher San Marcos HS 1965-66; Eng Teacher New Braunfels HS 1967-68; Choral Music Teacher New Braunfels HS & Jr HS 1969-72; Eng Teacher Canyon Mid Sch 1974-79, Lee-Scott Acad 1985-; *ai:* Spon Sr Beta Club; Help Coach Jr HS Scholars Master Team 1989-; AAUW Pres 1977-78; Mentor Study Club Pres 1984-85; Delta Kappa Gamma 1978-79; Crescendo Music Club Pres.

SMITH, NATALIE R., English Teacher; *b:* Austin, TX; *m:* Barron Wayne; *c:* Paige, Nina K.; *ed:* (BA) Eng, SW TX St Univ 1980; *cr:* Eng III/IV Teacher Round Rock HS 1980-81; Eng III Teacher Westwood HS 1981-82; Eng IV Teacher Gregory-Portland HS 1982-86; Eng III Teacher Fredericksburg HS 1987-; *ai:* Stu Cncl Adv; TX Assn of Prof Educators; *office:* Fredericksburg HS 202 W Travis Fredericksburg TX 78624

SMITH, NELLIE MAE, HS Counselor; *b:* Ashford, AL; *ed:* (BS) Psych, Bethune-Cookman Coll 1974; (MS) Guidance Counseling, Univ of TN 1975; (AA) Sch Counseling, Troy St Univ 1988; Cert Psychometric Testing 1986; Working Toward Sch Admin Cert; *cr:* Outpatient Cnslr Cmmty Mental Health 1976-78; Minority Affairs Coord Univ of W FL 1978-79; Trng Instr Michelin Tire Corporation 1979-83; Cnslr Troy St Univ 1983-85; Psychometrist Dothan City HS 1985-86; Cnslr Dothan HS 1987-; *ai:* Sch Improvement Comm; YWCA Adv; ASCD 1989-; DNEA 1985-; ASC 1983-; Publication Univ of W FL Frosh Handbook; Cmmty Mental Health Volunteer Work Awd; *home:* PO Box 626 Ashford AL 36312

SMITH, NELLIE MANDA, Mathematics Teacher; *b:* W Palm Beach, FL; *m:* H. Frank; *c:* Nancy Griffith Lewis, Warren Griffith, Rhonda Eaddy, Sharon Eaddy; *ed:* (BA) Math, FL St Univ 1959; (MS) Math Ed, GA St Univ 1986; AP Calculus Certified, Oglethorpe Univ 1989; *cr:* Math Teacher Clayton Cty GA; *ai:* N Clayton HS Leadership Team; GMTC 1987-; *office:* N Clayton HS 1503 Norman Dr College Park GA 30236

SMITH, OCTAVIA HAWKINS, Business Teacher; *b:* Cleveland, OH; *m:* Johnnie B.; *c:* Thomas, Gregory, Jeffrey; *ed:* (BS) Bus Ed, Central St Univ 1965; Grad Courses, Cleveland St Univ, Duquesne Univ, Nazareth Coll, St Univ Coll of Arts & Sci Geneseo; *cr:* Teacher East Tech HS 1965-66, Glenville HS 1966-1970, Bratenahl HS 1971-1977, Charles H Roth 1977-80, Shaw HS 1980-81, Euclid Jr HS 1982; Instr Center for Secretarial Sci 1983-83; Teacher Strong Vincent & East HS 1983-85; St Benedict Acad 1985-87; Kirby HS 1987-; *ai:* Amer Ed Week Comm; NEA; AVA; Alpha Kappa Alpha (CorrespondiNg Secy 1984-86, Membership Chairperson 1985-87); *office:* Kirby H S 4080 Kirby Pkwy Memphis TN 38115

SMITH, PAGE A., Social Studies Instructor; *b:* St Marys, OH; *m:* Patricia A.; *c:* Adam B., Tara S.; *ed:* (BA) Soc Stud Comp, Wright St Univ 1978; (MS) Educl Admin, Univ of Dayton 1983; St of OH Apprentice Cncl 1976, Stationary Steam Engr 3rd Class 1984; *cr:* Instr/Dept Chm Celina Sr HS 1978-84; Ec Instr Wapakoneta Sr HS 1985-87; Instr Wright St Univ 1983-, Celina Sr HS 1987; *ai:* Mercer Cty Young Republicans & Teens for Life; NCSS 1978-; OH Cncl for Soc Stud Outstanding Stu Teacher of Yr Awd; Mercer Cty Republican Party Steering Mem 1990; Ed & Research Inst Washington DC; Natl Journalism Center Awarded Internship; *office:* Celina Sr HS 735 E Wayne St Celina OH 45822

SMITH, PAMELA MARIE, Band Director; *b:* Jasper, AL; *ed:* (BS) Music Ed, 1982, (MS) Music Ed, 1983 Jacksonville St Univ; Grad Stud Music Ed; *cr:* Band Dir Pleasant Valley HS 1983-; *ai:* Sole Responsibility all Act of Band Prgm 7th-12th Grade Including Outside Individual Competitions & Fundraising; MENC, ABA, NEA, AEA 1983-; Chm Calhoun Cty Honor Band; SeLection Comm Southerners Honor Band.

SMITH, PATRICIA A., Mathematics Teacher; *b:* Marshall, MO; *ed:* (BS) Elem Ed, 1973, (MS) Ed, 1975 Cntrl MO St Univ; *cr:* Elem Teacher Blue Springs Sch Dist 1973-78; Math Teacher Pleasant Lea Jr HS 1979-; *ai:* Mathcounts Coach; NCTM, Kansas City Area Teachers of Math, MO Aerospace Educators Assn; Civil Air Patrol, Dream Factory, Delta Kappa Gamma; Nom Lees Summit Chamber of Commerce Excl in Teaching Awd 1986; Recognition Sch Bd Outstanding Rep of Sch 1986; *office:* Pleasant Lea Jr HS 630 W Persel Lees Summit MO 64081

SMITH, PATRICIA ANN, 7th/8th Grade Science Teacher; *b:* Vineland, NJ; *ed:* (AS) Phys Ed, Cumberland Cty Coll 1976; Sci, Glassboro St Coll; *cr:* 5th-8th Grade Sci Teacher Sacred Heart Regional Sch 1976-; *ai:* Yrbk Co Adv; Young Astronauts Assn, Spelling Bee, Jump Rope for Heart, Spirit Club, Intramural Prgm Adv; Dept Chm Phys Ed; Girls Bsktbl Timer; Sci Fair Coord; Amer Assn for Advancement of Sci 1988-89; NCEA 1980-; Sacred Heart Church Parish Cncl Secy 1980-82; Cath Youth Organization Girls Bsktbl 1974-80, Cty Champion 1976-80; Sacred Heart Advisory Bd Mini-Grant 1989-; *office:* Sacred Heart Regional Sch 922 E Landis Ave Vineland NJ 08360

SMITH, PATRICIA FLEMING, First Grade Teacher; *b:* Mobile, AL; *m:* Stephens Gerald; *c:* Jeremy, Rebeka; *ed:* (BA) Elem Ed, Patrick Henry Jr Coll 1974; (BS) Elem Ed, Troy St Univ 1976; (MED) Elem Ed, Livingston Univ 1979; *cr:* 8th Grade His/Eng Teacher Wilson Hall Mid Sch 1976-77; 1st/2nd Grade Teacher 1977-78, 2nd Grade Teacher 1978-79, 1st/3rd Grade Teacher 1979-85 Fulton Elem; 1st Grade Teacher Grove Hill Elem 1985-; *ai:* PTA Secy 1990; NEA, AEA 1976-; *home:* Rt 3 Box 429 Grove Hill AL 36451

SMITH, PAUL M., 5th Grade Teacher; *b:* Meadville, PA; *m:* Anna Mendez; *c:* Michelle, Michael, David; *ed:* (BS) Elem Ed, 1972, (MS) Elem Ed, 1977 Edinboro Univ; *cr:* 5th Grade Teacher Neason Hill 1972-; *ai:* Intermural Bsktbl & Vlybl Coach; *office:* Neason Hill Elem Sch Williamson Rd Meadville PA 16335

SMITH, PAULINE CAMPANELLO, Business Teacher; *b:* Spanishburg, WV; *m:* Buster Jr.; *c:* Deanna L., Cynthia L.; *ed:* (BS) Bus Ed, Concord Coll 1958; WV Univ, Marshall Univ, Univ of VA; Cmptr & Word Processing Bluefield St Coll; *cr:* Teacher Mc Lains Bus Coll 1958-62, Pocahontas HS 1962-63; Substitute Teacher Bluefield HS 1965-81; Secy Mercer Cty Bd of Ed 1981-86; Teacher Bluefield HS 1986-; *ai:* Former FBLA Adv; Project Graduation Booklet; *office:* Bluefield HS 535 W Cumberland Rd Bluefield WV 24701

SMITH, PEGGY MAURER, First Grade Teacher; *b:* Morgantown, WV; *m:* Douglas W.; *c:* Nicole A.; *ed:* (BA) Elem Ed, Univ of WY 1974; *cr:* 1st Grade Teacher Wilson Elem 1974-; *ai:* Intnl Rdng Assn, Delta Kappa Gamma; PTO; *office:* Wilson Elem Sch 351 Monroe Ave Green River WY 82935

SMITH, PHILIP R., Math/Science Teacher; *b:* Russell Springs, KY; *m:* Patricia L. Rouse; *c:* Rhonda, Kevin; *ed:* (BS) Ag Ed, Gen Sci 1963, (MS)Ag Ed, 1966 Univ of KY Lexington; Scndry Principalship EKU Richmond 1983; *cr:* Vo Ag Teacher Hiseville HS 1963-69; Dir of Marketing KY Dept of Ag 1969-80; Vo Ag Teacher Lincoln Cty HS 1981-85; Math/Sci Teacher Hustonville Elem 1985-; *ai:* KEA 1963-69; NEA 1963-69; SCS Chm 1988-; Dix River CC Mem 184-; Hiseville FFA-Chapter Farmer Awd; Glasgow Jaycees-Outstanding Young Educator; Lincoln FFA-Chapter Farmer Awd; *office:* Hustonville Elem Sch PO Box 6 Hustonville KY 40437

SMITH, PHILLIP BALLARD, 5th Grade Science Teacher; *b:* Newman, GA; *m:* Susan Powers; *c:* Brian, Christy, Katie; *ed:* (BS) Bus Admin, 1969, (MED) Elem Ed, 1974, (EDS) Elem Ed, 1976 W GA Coll; *cr:* 5th Grade Teacher Heard Cty Elem 1969-; *ai:* HAE, GAE, NEA 1969-; GA Sci Teachers Assn 1987-; Teacher of Yr; *office:* Heard Cty Elem Sch Bevis Rd Franklin GA 30217

SMITH, PHILLIP LYN, Fifth Grade Teacher; *b:* Oklahoma City, OK; *m:* Andrea Yvonne Thomas; *c:* Solera Smith-Thomas; *ed:* (BA) Poly Sci, CA St Long Beach 1967; Grad Stud; CA Writing Project; *cr:* Scndry/Elem Ed US Peace Corps 1967-69; 3rd Grade Teacher Paramount Sch Dist 1970-71; Math Wkshps Teacher Trng US Peace Corps 1978-80; 4th/5th Grade Teacher Carmel Sch Dist 1972-; *ai:* Carmel Schls Lang Comm; CA Teachers Assn 1972-; CA Pirg 1986-; Several Watercolor Awds; Painting Used as Bookcover; *office:* Tularcitos Sch PO Box 966 Carmel Valley CA 93924

SMITH, RAYMOND KEVIN, English Teacher; *b:* Hartford, CT; *m:* Irene Wasik; *c:* R. Kevin, Siobhan, Deidre, Maura, Audra, Caitlin, Erin; *ed:* (BA) Eng, Univ of CT 1962; Cert Eng/Ed, Cntrl Univ of CT 1964; (MED) Scndry Ed, Univ of Hartford 1975; (MA) Counseling, 1979, (CAGS) Counseling, 1987 St Joseph Coll; *cr:* Adjunct Prof St Joseph Coll W Hartford 1979-88; Eng Teacher Granby Memorial HS 1964-; *ai:* Phase II Restructuring Comm; Phase III Steering Comm Chm; Cheer & Schlshp Comms; Graduation Coord; CT Drama Assn Treas 1970-75; NEA, CT Ed Assn, Granby Ed Assn, NCTE 1964-; Asylum Hill Inc Bd of Dir; St Francis Hospital Incorporator; Founder W Hartford Counseling Service; *office:* Granby Memorial HS 315 Salmon Brook St Granby CT 06035

SMITH, REBECCA-LYNN SWANSON, 8th Math Teacher; *b:* Murphy, NC; *m:* Bert; *c:* Rebecca S., John H.; *ed:* (BS) Mid Grades Math/Sci/Rdng, - Summa Cum Laude Western Carolina U 1977; Real Est Brokers License Haywood Comm Coll 1985; *cr:* Math Teacher Haywood Cty Schls 1977-; *ai:* Drama Club Spon; NCAE/NEA/IRA Sch Rep 1980-82; Waynesville Bus & Prof Womens Club 1980-81; *home:* 505 Ridgewood Dr Waynesville NC 28786

SMITH, REX ALAN, 8th Grade Earth Sci Teacher; *b:* Hiawassee, GA; *m:* Audrey Teresa; *c:* Tamara, Clifton, Tabitha; *ed:* (BS) Elem Ed, W Carolina Univ 1981; *cr:* 8th Grade Earth Sci Teacher Woodmont Mid Sch 1984-; *ai:* Jr Beta Club Spon; NSTA 1988-; SC Sci Cncl 1987-; NASA Newmast 1989; SC Prof Dev Prgm; Earth Sci Teacher Resource Agent; *office:* Woodmont Mid Sch Flat Rock Rd Piedmont SC 29673

SMITH, RICHARD L., English Teacher; *b:* Capac, MI; *m:* Judy; *c:* Jennifer Smith Goy, David, Todd, Nathan, Matthew; *ed:* (BA) Eng/Soc Stud, W MI Univ 1958; W MI Univ; *cr:* Teacher/Coach Kalamazoo Public Schls 1958-; *office:* Loy Norrix HS 606 E Kilgore Rd Kalamazoo MI 49001

SMITH, RICHARD LEONARD, HS Band Director; *b:* Joplin, MD; *M:* Karen Winking; *c:* Sean M., Erin M.; *ed:* (BA) Music Ed, SIU 1970; Music Performance Southern IL; *cr:* HS Band Dir Riverview Gardens HS 1970-; *ai:* Marching Band; Band Festivals Fall Months; Bingo Chmn Bingo Games Riverview Gardens Band Booster Club; Local 2-197 Amer Assn of MusicIANS 1967-; MO Teacher of Yr Finalist 1989-; NAJE 1989-; Performing Musician St Louis Municipal Theatre Assn 1969; Transposed Music Incoming Opera Presentations St Louis Area; Awd Winning Stu

Group; *office:* Riverview Gardens Sr H S 1218 Shepley Dr Saint Louis MO 63137

SMITH, RICK WALLACE, Mathematics Dept Chairman; *b:* Jacksonville, IL; *m:* Susan L. Turpin; *c:* Richard Seymour, Kyle, Phillip; *ed:* (BA) Math, IL Coll 1973; *cr:* Math Teacher/Coach Franklin Jr/Sr HS 1973-; *ai:* Coach Jr HS Bsktbl 1973- & HS Cross Cntry 1980-; AFL, CIO 1973-; IBCA 1980-; Morgan Cty Conference Pres 1975-; Fan Booster Club Treas 1973-; IL Bsktbl Coaches Assn Dist 17 Jr HS Coach of Yr 1988-; *office:* Franklin Jr Sr HS 110 State St Franklin IL 62638

SMITH, ROBERT PAUL, History/Spanish/Psych Teacher; *b:* Scranton, PA; *m:* Julianne M. Rosar; *c:* Robb, Christopher; *ed:* (BS) His, Univ of Scranton 1972; *cr:* His/Sci Teacher Nativity of Our Lord Sch 1975-77; His/Span/Psych Teacher Sacred Heart HS 1978-; *ai:* Stu Cncl, Sch Newspaper, Jr Class, Prom Moderator; NCSS, NASSP 1980-; *office:* Sacred Heart HS 44 S Church St Carbondale PA 18407

SMITH, ROBIN W., Secondary Business Teacher; *b:* Knoxville, TN; *m:* E. Franklin; *ed:* (BS) Bus Admin, Meredith Coll 1977; (MBA) Bus Admin, Wilmington Coll 1988; BASIC Programming; AppleWorks Prgms; IBM Wkshps; Numerous Cmptrs Wkshps; *cr:* Stu Aide Teacher Environmental Protection Agency 1975-77; Admin Asst Univ of DE 1977-79; Bus Teacher Appoquinimink Sch Dist 1979-80, Woodbridge Jr/Sr HS 1980-; *ai:* Dist Bus Advisory Cncl Coord; DE Bus Ed Assn, NBEA, NEA 1979-; DE St Ed Assn Building Rep 1980-89; Bus Prof of America Advisory Bd; Amer Assn Univ Women Secy 1978-; United Meth Women 1979-; Occupational Events BPA St Competition Coord 1990; Content Stans Writing Bus Ed Mem; *office:* Woodbridge Jr/Sr HS 307 Laws St Bridgeville DE 19933

SMITH, ROGER RAYMOND, 6th Grade Teacher; *b:* Fremont, MI; *m:* Jean Marilyn; *c:* Margie, Ray, Sue, Brian; *ed:* (BS) Elem/Spec Ed, Univ of MO 1970; (MA) Admin, Cntrl MI Univ 1978; Governmental Courses; Educl Wkshps from Rdng to Math, Cmptr Conferences to Rdng Spec; *cr:* Spec Ed Jerseyville Public Schls 1970-72; Elem Ed/Jr HS Teacher White Cloud Public Schls 1973-; *ai:* Have Sponsered Many Act; Ftbl, Bsbl, Bsktbl Coach; Sci MSTA All Mid Sch Rep Sch 1980; Township & Assessors Assn (Sup, Assessor) 1987-; Everett Township Officer (Clerk 1973-78, Supvr 1987-, Assessor 1987-); Cty Chm & Awd for Cty Party 1990; Received Grants for Sch & Government; *office:* White Cloud Public Schls 640 Pine St White Cloud MI 49349

SMITH, RONALD GENE, Music Teacher; *b:* Huntington, WV; *m:* Alice Jane Gardner; *c:* Ryan, Jason, Jeremy; *ed:* (AB) Music Ed, Marshall Univ 1976; (MM) Music Ed, Ithaca Coll 1978; Candidate DMA in Trombone Performance LA St Univ; Grad Study, Pensacola Chrstn Coll; *cr:* Music Teacher Huntington Chrstn Acad 1978-80, Pensacola Chrstn Sch & Coll 1980-; *ai:* Pensacola Symphony; Intnl Trombone Assn 1972-; FL Republican Party Mem 1987-; Grad Asst Music Ed Ithaca Coll 1978; Whos Who Among Stus in Amer Colls & Univs 1976; *home:* 217 St Eusebia St Pensacola FL 32503

SMITH, RONALD GEORGE, Mathematics Department Chair; *b:* Rochester, IN; *m:* Janet Elsie Metsker; *c:* Jeffrey S., Melinda S., Amy L.; *ed:* (BS) Math, Manchester Coll 1961; (MS) Math/Scndry Ed, Southeastern St Coll 1967; General Micro-Cmptrs; *cr:* Math Teacher Columbia Joint HS 1961-65, Triton Sch Corporation 1965-; *ai:* Cross Cntry & Golf Coach; Stu Cncl; TTA Pres; ISTA, NEA, NCTM; Golf Coaches Assn 1970-; Semifinalist IN Teacher of Yr Awd; Natl Sci Fnd Grant.

SMITH, ROSALEE REYNOLDS, Vocational Business Teacher; *b:* Pikeville, KY; *m:* Kenneth F.; *c:* Kenneth C., John W.; *ed:* (BS) Gen Bus, Pikeville Coll 1; *cr:* Teacher Mullins HS 1964-71; Johns Creek 1971-; *ai:* Pike Cty Ed Assn Mem Prof Negotations Comm 1968-69; KY Ed Assn Teachers United for Fairness 1988-; NEA; Pikeville Jr Womans Club Secy 1966-67; KY Star Teacher Awd 1975; *home:* 162 Burning Fork Rd Pikeville KY 41501

SMITH, ROSELYN MILLER, 5th Grade Reading Teacher; *b:* Kingstree, SC; *m:* Eugene; *c:* Theodore T., Daphne R.; *ed:* (BA) Art, Claflin Univ 1970; (MS) Ed, Troy St Univ 1987; Univ of SC, SC St Coll, Columbus Coll; *cr:* 3rd Grade Teacher Battery Park Elem Sch 1970-71; Art Coord Williamsburg Cty Art Assn 1972-74; 4th-5th Grade Teacher Manchester Elem Sch 1978-84; 5th Grade Teacher Manchester Mid Sch 1984-; *ai:* MAE Secy 1981-82; GAE, NAE 1978-; Delta Sigma Theta Asst Secy 1986-; Kappa Delta Pi 1989-; Claflin Univ Alumni Assn 1970-; *home:* 3311 Flintlock Dr Columbus GA 31907

SMITH, RUSSELL, English Teacher; *b:* Albany, NY; *m:* Donna Lynne Hannefield; *c:* Shannon E.; *ed:* (BA) His/Eng, CA St Los Angeles 1967; (MA) Eng, Univ of San Diego 1970; (MA) Bus Admin, 1975, (MA) Curr/Supervision, 1976 Point Loma Univ; Western St Coll of Law 1982; *cr:* Teacher/Coach William Workman HS 1967-; *ai:* Var Sftbl Head Coach; Litteratus Club, Newspaper/Journalism Adv; Sch Site Cncl; Curr & Staff Dev Comm; W Covina Chamber of Commerce Mem, W Covine Small Businessmens Assn 1979-; *office:* Workman HS 16303 E Temple Ave La Puente CA 91744

SMITH, SALLY L., Fifth Grade Teacher; *b:* Salem, NJ; *m:* James Dale; *c:* James D. Jr.; *ed:* (BA) Elem Ed, 1971, (MA) Stu Personnel Services, 1975 Glassboro St Coll; *cr:* 6th Grade Teacher Fairfield Township Sch 1967-70; 5th Grade Teacher Lowel Alloways Creek Elem Sch 1970-; *ai:* NJ Ed Assn, LACEA VP; LAC Mothers Circle Secy Teacher of Yr 1985; *home:* 717 Smick Rd Salem NJ 08079

SMITH, SANDRA HARGROVE, Guidance Counselor; *b:* Suffolk, VA; *m:* Roderick Isaiah; *c:* Rodrienne L.; *ed:* (BS) Elem Ed, VA St Coll 1968; (MA) Guidance/Counseling, Hampton Inst 1975; Old Dominion Univ, Norfolk St Univ, Coll of William & Mary, Univ of VA; *cr:* Elem Teacher Truxton Elem & Hodges Manor Elem 1968-76; Elem Guidance Cnslr Highland Biltmore & Brighton Elem & Emily Spong Elem & Douglas Park Elem & Lakeview Elem & Hodges Manor Elem 1976-81; Elem Teacher Port Norfolk Elem 1981-84; Scndry Guidance Cnslr Harry Hunt Jr HS 1984-; *ai:* Chrome Club Adv; Portsmouth Ed Assn, VA Ed Assn, NEA, Hampton Roads Guidance Assn, ASCA; Rehoboth Fellowship Church; Teacher of Yr Harry Hunt Jr HS 1989-; *home:* 3771 Towne Point Rd Portsmouth VA 23703

SMITH, SANDRA LEE (FRENCH), Librarian; *b:* Hinton, WV; *m:* Edward G.; *ed:* (BA) Elem/Lib Sci, Clarion Univ 1968; (MS) Elem, Univ of Pittsburgh 1970; Cmptrs Intermediate Unit; *cr:* 2nd Grade Teacher Clinton Elem Sch 1968-72; 2nd/3rd Grade Teacher 1972-79, Librarian 1979- Wilson Elem Sch; Cmptrs Teacher Comm Coll of Allegheny Cty 1986-; *ai:* Lib Helpers Spon; Log House Restoration Comm; NEA 1972-; PA St Ed Assn 1972-; Cncl of Sch Librarians Advisory Cncl 1989-; PA Sch Lib Assn St Conference Comm/Wkshp Moderator 1989-; Annual Achievement Awd Childrens Cncl of Western PA 1987; Amer Family Inst Gift of Time Awd 1990; Project Published Hands on His Inspiration Booklet Pittsburgh His & Landmarks; *office:* Wilson Elem Schl 67 B Boggs Rd Imperial PA 15126

SMITH, SCOTT, Social Studies Teacher; *b:* Buffalo, NY; *ed:* (BA) Soc Stud Ed, SUNY Fredonia 1983; (MED) Sch Admin/Supervision, Bowie St Univ 1990; *cr:* Soc Stud Teacher Largo HS 1984-; *ai:* Asst Coach Boys Soccer; Head Coach Boys Indoor & Outdoor Track; Largo Faculty Awd Comm Mem; AFT Mem 1990; *home:* 3403 Everette Dr Bowie MD 20716

SMITH, SHERYL JEANNE (CURRAN), HS Mathematics Teacher; *b:* Lancaster, PA; *m:* Larry E.; *c:* Rachel L., Kirby A.; *ed:* (BS) Math/Scndry Ed, Millersville Univ 1966; Grad Work Math;Additional Stud Beyond Masters; *cr:* Jr HS Math Teacher Milford Sch Dist 1966-68, West York Area Sch Dist 1968-69; Jr/Sr Title I Teacher West York Area Sch Dist 1978-81; Sr HS Math Teacher Dover Area Sch Dist 1981-; *ai:* NHS, Academic Quiz Bowl, Choir Candle Fund, Dover HS Class of 1988 Adv; SAT Coord; NEA, PA Ed Assn, Dover Area Ed Assn; York Hospital Auxilliary Mem 1970-; Faith UCC Deaconess 1978; Jobs Daughters Adv 1988-; Young Womens Club (Coresponding Secy, Monthly Newsletter Chm); *office:* Dover Area Sch Dist W Canal St Dover PA 17315

SMITH, SHIRLEY ANN, Chapter I Reading Teacher; *b:* Plainfield, NJ; *m:* Gordon A.; *c:* Susan Gerlick, Eric, Bradley; *ed:* (BS) Elem Ed, Cntrl MI Univ 1970; Grad Stud Cntrl MI Univ; *cr:* 1st Grade Teacher Wright Avenue Sch 1970-75; 1st Grade Teacher 1975-77, 3rd Grade Teacher 1977-81, Kndgtn Teacher 1981-82 Pine Avenue Sch; Chapter I Rdng Teacher Highland Elem Sch 1982-; *ai:* MI Rdng Assn, Intnl Rdng Assn Mem; *office:* Highland Elem Sch Downie St Alma MI 48801

SMITH, SHIRLEY HALL, Second Grade Teacher; *b:* Kensington, GA; *m:* Mack; *c:* Troy Stephen, Sanford Mark; *ed:* (BS) Elem Ed, GA Coll 1956; (MS) Early Chldhd Ed, Berry Coll 1987; *cr:* Teacher Graysville Elem Sch 1953-58; Fairview Elem Sch 1958-59; Rock Spring Elem Sch 1959-63; Cedar Grove Elem Sch 1963-64; Rock Spring Elem Sch 1964-; *ai:* NEA; GAE; WAE; *office:* Rock Spring Elem Sch Rock Spring GA 30739

SMITH, SHIRLEY LYNCH, Second Grade Teacher; *b:* Mesa, AZ; *m:* Jimmie Allen; *c:* Donna S. Cassity, Evan D., Debbie L. Lawson; *ed:* (BA) Elem Ed, 1977, (MED) Elem Ed, 1985 AZ St Univ; Rdng Endorsement; *ai:* Teach Folk Dancing; NEA, AZ Ed Assn 1977-; *office:* Florence Elem Sch 1709 S Orlando St Florence AZ 85232

SMITH, SHIRLEY WILSON, 7th-8th Grade English Teacher; *b:* Eldon, IA; *m:* Howard Nelson; *c:* Vicki Riegel, James H., Doug M.; *ed:* (BA) Elem Ed, Parsons Coll 1968; (MA) Elem Ed, N MO St Univ 1976; Elem Ed Admin 1978; *cr:* Elem Teacher Selma Consolidated Sch 1951-52, Cardinal Cmmty Schls 1964-76; Mid Sch Eng Teacher Cardinal Cmmty Schls 1976-; *ai:* 7th & 8th Grade Cheerleading & Drama; *home:* Rt 1 Box 22 Birmingham IA 52535

SMITH, STAN GORDON, Science & Math Instructor; *b:* Dallas, TX; *m:* Donna Carroll; *c:* Joshua Mc Crae, Timothy Matlock, Jonathon D.; *ed:* (BS) Civil Engineering, 1973, (MS) Physics, 1979 TX Tech Univ; *cr:* Teachers Asst TX Tech Univ 1977-79; Sci/Math Instr Christ The King HS 1979-81; Engineer Investigator TX Air Control Bd 1981-86; Sci/Math Instr Mesilla Valley Chrstn Schls 1986-; *ai:* Local Mission Speaking Comm; Tau Beta Pi 1971-73; Epsilon Phi Epsilon 1978-79; Creation Research Society 1978-; Article Published; *office:* Mesilla Valley Chrstn Schls 2001 Wisconsin Las Cruces NM 88001

SMITH, STEPHEN A., Social Studies Teacher; *b:* Kansas City, MO; *m:* Robin Lorie Johnson; *c:* Matthew S., David E.; *ed:* (BA) His, 1974, (MA) His, 1976 SW MO St Univ; *cr:* Soc Stud Teacher Bolivar HS 1977-80, Cntrl Mid Sch 1980-81, Sumner Acad of Arts & Sci 1981-; *ai:* CLOSE-UP Club & Fellowship of Chrstn Athletes Spon; Var Ftbl & Wrestling Coach; Effective Teaching Comm Mem; NCSS 1981-; MO Cncl of Soc Stud 1977-80; KS Univ Outstanding Teacher 1985; Kansas City Sch Dist Leadership Dev Awd; *office:* Sumner Acad of Arts & Sciences 800 Oakland Kansas City KS 66101

SMITH, STEVE A., Middle School Art Teacher; *b:* Albion, IN; *m:* Retha E. Engle; *c:* Phillip A., Gina M. Keeling, David L., Laureen K. Webb, Michael S., Rebecca I., Daniel R.; *ed:* (BS) Scndry Art Ed, Goshen Coll 1963; (MS) Scndry Art Ed, St Francis Coll 1972; *cr:* Art Teacher North Liberty HS 1963-67, John Glenn HS 1968-73; Art/Bible Teacher Trinity Chrstn Acad 1973-77; 6th-8th Grade Art Teacher Carter Mid Sch 1985-; *ai:* Art Club Adv Carter Mid Sch 1985-; NEA 1964-72, 1988-; TN Assn of Mid Schls 1989-; *office:* Carter Mid Sch 204 N Carter School Rd Strawberry Plains TN 37871

SMITH, STUART DAVIS, English Teacher; *b:* Lynchburg, VA; *m:* Richard Thomas; *c:* Megan, Richard Jr.; *ed:* (BA) Amer Stud, Meredith Coll 1974; Working Toward Masters in Guidance & Counseling, Campbell Univ; *cr:* 6th Grade Teacher Jonesboro Mid Sch 1974-77; 8th Grade Teacher E Lee Cty Jr HS 1977-; *ai:* Chm of Steering Comm Southern Assn Self Study Report; Discipline Comm; Tri-Cty Eng Alliance Cty Coord 1986-88; Amer Assn for Counseling & Dev; St Thomas Episcopal Church Chrstn Ed Comm, Sunday Sch Teacher; *home:* 535 Summit Dr Sanford NC 27330

SMITH, SUSAN D., 2nd Grade Teacher; *b:* Chicago, IL; *m:* Michael; *c:* Alicia, Josh; *ed:* (BS) Elem Ed, Univ of IL 1979; *cr:* 3rd Grade Teacher, Hancock Elem 1979-86; 2nd Grade Teacher, Ben Franklin Elem 1986-; *ai:* Staff Dev Comm; Txbk Comm; BSA, Den Leader/Comm Chair 1989-; *office:* Ben Franklin Elem Sch Box 7011 Long Grove IL 60060

SMITH, SUSAN ELISABETH (SCHMIDT), English/Journalism Teacher; *b:* St Joseph, MO; *m:* Richard L.; *ed:* (BS) Eng/Lang Art, Univ of KS 1966; Grad Stud Eng; *cr:* Lang Art Teacher St Joseph Sch Dist 1966-67; Eng Teacher Maysville R-1 Sch 1967-69; Lang Art Teacher St Joseph Co-Cathedral Sch 1971-77; Eng/Journalism/Speech Teacher Craig R-3 Sch 1977-78, Nodaway-Holt R-7 Sch 1978-; *ai:* All-Sch Play, All-Sch Variety Show, 6th Grade Variety Show Dir; Journalism Adv; Chrldr, Pep Club, Sr Spon; CTA Pres 1985-86; Delta Kappa Gamma Society; BJG Club Reporter 1988-; Record Album Folksongs Released 1976; 5 Original Folksongs Published 1975-76.

SMITH, SUSAN K., Athletic Dir/Phys Ed Teacher; *b:* Flint, MI; *ed:* (BA) Phys Ed/Health - Cum Laude, Seattle Pacific Univ 1984; *cr:* Substitute Teacher Lake Washington Sch Dist 1984-85; Phys Ed Teacher Edmons Sch Dist 1985-86; Summer Asst Athletic Admin City of Repmond 1980-; Spec Ed/Health/Phys Ed Teacher Kamiakin Jr HS 1986-; *ai:* Athletic Dir; Natural Helper; Vlbyl & Bsktbl Coach; Stu off Substances; WAHPERD, NEA; *home:* 8305 NE 158th St Bothell WA 98011

SMITH, SUSAN POWERS, Chemistry Teacher; *b:* Newnan, GA; *m:* Phillip Ballard; *c:* Brian, Christy, Katie; *ed:* (BA) Chem, 1974, (MED) Scndry Sci, 1979 West GA Coll; Advanced Placement Chem Inst; Woodrow Wilson Dreyfus Fnd Inst; Chem Ed 1989; Several Cmptr Wkshps; *cr:* Chem Teacher Newnan HS 1976-; *ai:* Beta Club, Sci Team Spon; Sci Olympiad Co-Spon; Dir Mid Sch Sci Bowl Teams; Chem Team Spon; Safety Comm Cowet a Cty; Chem Curr Comm; Item Review Comm Teacher Cert Test; HS Planning Comm Biennial Conference Chem Ed 1990; Judge Sci Fair & Invent America Competitions; Alpha Delta Kappa Mem 1987-; CAE, GAE, NEA Mem 1976-; GA Sci Teachers Assn 1986-; PTA (Pres 1986/1988, VP 1984/1985); Sunday Sch, Choir, Vacation Bible Sch Teacher 1978-; Star Teacher 1987; Article Published The Lattice Network; High Technology Sci Teacher Awd; *office:* Newman H S 190 LaGrange St Newnan GA 30263

SMITH, SYLVIA MC CALEB, 4th Grade Teacher; *b:* Bradford, TN; *m:* Robert Joseph Sr.; *c:* Rebecca Smith Howard, Robert J. Jr.; *ed:* (BS) Ed/Secretarial Sci, Memphis St 1954; Renew Cert Jackson St, Lambuth Coll, Univ of TN Martin; *cr:* Teacher Newburn HS 1955-56; 4th Grade Teacher Sherwood Elem 1956-57; 4th-5th Grade Teacher Bradford Elem 1969-85; 4th Grade Lang Art Teacher Anderson Mid Sch 1985-; *ai:* Sr Spon Newburn HS Local Haywood Cty Teachers Assn, TN Ed Assn, Nea; Newburn HS PTA Secy; Bradford Sch PTA Pres; Peabody HS Best Citizenship Awd 1950; *home:* 2428 Rudolph Rd Brownsville TN 38012

SMITH, TAMARA BENGE, Art Teacher; *b:* Manchester, KY; *m:* Gary Russell; *c:* Travis R.; *ed:* (BA) Art Ed, E KY Univ 1980; (MA) Art Ed, 1983, (Rank I) Admin, 1985 N KY Univ; *cr:* Art Teacher Hazard Ind Schls 1980-81, Ludlow Ind Schls 1981-; *ai:* Stu Cncl & Just Say No Club Spon; Prin Advisory Comm; KY Ed Assn, KY Art Ed Assn; KY Arts Cncl TIP Grant; N KY Golden Apple Winner Outstanding Teacher.

SMITH, TERI HELLMAN, English Teacher; *b:* Torrance, CA; *m:* Robert H; *c:* Robert E., Nicole, Jacqueline; *ed:* (BA) Eng, CA St Univ Long Beach 1977; Grad Stud in Eng/Media/Ed, CA St Univ Long Beach & Univ of CA Santa Cruz; *cr:* Teacher Ocean View HS 1977-80, Mission Viejo HS 1980-82, Mayfair HS 1982-; *ai:* Speech Adv/Coach; Literary Club & Class Adv; Quiz Bowl Coach; Bellflower Ed Assn 1978-; CTA, NEA; CA League of Mid Schls 1989-; Parent-Stu-Teacher Assn 1977-; Bellflower Unified Sch Dist Teacher of Yr 1988; Curr Awd for Gifted Ed from CA St Univ 1986; *office:* Mayfair HS 6000 N Woodruff Ave Lakewood CA 90713

SMITH, TERRI LEA, 5th Grade Teacher; *b:* Mullens, WV; *m:* Barry; *c:* Cassidy L.; *ed:* (BA) Elem Ed, Concord Coll 1981; (MA) Ed Admin, WV Coll 1985; *cr:* 5th Grade Teacher Mullens Mid Sch 1981-; *ai:* Mullens HS Var Cheerleading Spon 1984-86; WV Ed Assn 1981-87; AFT 1987-; Gamma Alpha; First Presbyn Church; *office:* Mullens Mid Sch Box 1025 Mullens WV 25882

SMITH, THOMAS GEORGE, Life Science Teacher; *b:* Gettysburg, PA; *m:* Shirley Mooney; *c:* Brittany N.; *ed:* (BSE) Bio, 1967, (MED) Bio, 1969 Shippensburg Univ; Bio Trng, PA St Univ; Wilks Coll; Millersville Univ; St Univ of NY; *cr:* Sci Teacher Big Spring Sch Dist 1967-; *ai:* Field Trips AZ-West Germany & Cape Cod; Wrestling Coach 1967-87; Prof Dev for Staff; Prof Induction for New Teachers; Asst Sci Dept Chairperson; Phi Delta Kappa; ASCD; Amer Assn for Advancement of Sci; Authored Booklet on Mid Sch Stu; Wrestling Coach 20 Yr Awd; Promoting High Standards of Teaching Profession Awd; *office:* Big Spring Mid Sch 47 Mount Rock Rd Newville PA 17241

SMITH, THOMAS JOSEPH, 6-7 Science/8th Grade Teacher; *b:* Detroit, MI; *m:* Barbara; *c:* Brian, Mike, Terry; *ed:* (BA) Phys Ed/His, Adrian 1971; Boston Univ; U of WI La Crosse; Amer Univ; U S Army Command & General Staff Coll; *cr:* Major Ret US Army 1963-83; Coach/6th Grade Sci Teacher St Patricks 1984; *ai:* Boys Varsity Line Ftbl, Asst Westling Coach; Military Order of Purple Heart 1973-; Amer Legion 1987; Knights of Columbus 1975-; 1st Cav Division 1988-; *office:* St Patricks Catholic Sch 318 W Dale Sparta WI 54656

SMITH, TRAVIS NEIL, Band Director; *b:* Jacksonville, TX; *m:* Sara Candace Gore; *c:* Candace M.; *ed:* (BM) Music, Stephen F Austin 1975; Working Toward Music Masters Univ of TX Tyler; *cr:* Jr HS & HS Asst Band Dir Chapel Hill TX 1975-77; All Level Band Dir Troup Ind Sch Dist 1977-79, 1984-; *ai:* Band Dir; Sr Class Spon; Phi Mu Alpha 1973-75; Spec Band Awd 1978; Sweepstakes Bands 1986-; Region 21 Exec Music Office; *office:* Troup Ind Sch Dist PO Box 578 Hwy 135 Troup TX 75789

SMITH, TREACIE BRADLEY, Spanish Instructor; *b:* Gary, IN; *m:* Lloyd Kenneth; *c:* Kenneth J., Erica C., Candace m.; *ed:* (BA) Fr/Span Ed, 1965, (MS) Ed, 1975 Purdue Univ; Endorsement Bi-ling Ed; *cr:* Laboratory Technicion Meth Hospital Gary 1959-64; Span Teacher 1965-81, Span/Fr Teacher 1981-83, Span Teacher 1983- Gary Public Schls; *ai:* Hi Y Spon; Span Club Co-Spon; NABE 1987-; AFT 1965-; MADD, Christ Temple Church; King Juan Carlos Fellowship; *office:* West Side HS 9th Ave & Gerry St Gary IN 46406

SMITH, TRUDY L., Language Art/French Teacher; *b:* Ogden, UT; *ed:* (BA) Scndry Ed, UT St Univ 1988; *cr:* Eng/Fr Teacher S Ogden Jr HS 1988-; *ai:* Cheerleading, Natl Jr Honor Society & Fr Club Adv; Stu Teacher of Yr Awd from UT St Univ 1987-88; *office:* S Ogden Jr HS 4300 Madison Ave Ogden UT 84403

SMITH, TYRONE WADE, Social Studies Teacher; *b:* Fairfield, AL; *m:* Harrilen G.; *c:* Ayanna E.; *ed:* (BS) Elem/Spec Ed, Tuskegee Univ 1981; *cr:* Teacher Hudson Mid Sch 1980-; Psychiatric Nursing Technician Childrens Hospital 1985-; *ai:* Tennis, Bsktbl & Sftbl; NEA; Gentleman of Distinction VP 1980-84; Teacher of Yr Monroeville Jr HS 1980-81.

SMITH, VALERIE LYNN, Instrumental & Vocal Instr; *b:* Saint Louis, MO; *ed:* (BS) Music Ed, Univ of MO Columbia 1982; Casa Sch of the Arts 1966-76; *cr:* Music Consultant City of St Louis Housing Authority 1982-83; Music Instr Long Mid & Scruggs Elem 1983-84, Humboldt Visual & Performing Arts Mid 1984-; Proprietor/Instr Val Lynns Sch of Music 1985-; *ai:* Co-Dir Clarence Haydn Wilson Music Guild Jr Division; Vocal Instr Natl Gospel Choirs & Choruses Covention; Natl Assn of Negro Musicians 1987-; Music Educators Natl Conference 1978-; St Marks Cath Church Minister of Music; Guest Conductor St Louis Mass Choir Rome 1990; *office:* Humboldt Visual/Performing Art 2516 S 9th Saint Louis MO 63104

SMITH, VALERIE MORITZ, English Teacher Dept Chair; *b:* Philadelphia, PA; *m:* Jay D.; *c:* Laura, Ian, Gregory; *ed:* (BA) Eng, Ursinus Coll 1965; (MA) Eng, Beaver Coll 1988; Additional Grad Courses, Writing & Ed; *cr:* Teacher Cntrl Bucks Sch Dist 1983-84; Teacher/Dept Chairperson Palisades Sch Dist 1984; *ai:* NEA 1984-; NCTE 1985-; SAT Coach & Teacher; Local Ed Assn (Pres, Treas, Membership Chairperson, Building Rep); Writing Teacher for other Teachers; *home:* 1017 Butler Ln Perkasie PA 18944

SMITH, VERNETTA L. T., Lang Art/Teacher of Gifted; *b:* Warrenton, NC; *m:* Melvin C. H.; *c:* Ashanti; *ed:* (AA) Elem Ed, Kittrell Jr Coll 1973; (BA) Intermediate Ed, Shaw Univ 1975; Academically Gifted Cert; *cr:* 5th Grade Teacher Montross Elem Sch 1975-77; 6th Grade Teacher Garner Jr HS 1977-78; 4th/5th Grade Teacher Cople Elem 1979-86; Jr HS Lang Art/Soc Stud/ Teacher of Academically Gifted Grantham Sch 1986-; *ai:* Beta Club Spon; Drill Squad Club Adv; Human Relations, Sch Base, 4-H Advisory Comm; NCEA, NEA 1986-; Bus & Prof Women Asst Secy 1985-.

SMITH, VERONICA ROSE, HS Mathematics/History Teacher; *b:* Saliba, CO; *m:* Richard; *c:* Micheal, Mark; *ed:* (BA) Fine Arts, Univ N CO 1968; *cr:* HS Teacher/Cnslr New Life Chrstn Sch 1981-; *ai:* Sr Trip Fund Raising, Annual Club, Stu Cncl Spon; Stu Cnslr; Pregnancy Resource Center Cnslr 1990; *home:* 600 Cypress Wood Ln Delta CO 81416

SMITH, VICTOR H., Fifth Grade Teacher; *b:* Clairton, PA; *m:* Amy Beth Sheffic; *c:* Megan, Marta, Claire, Lynne; *ed:* (BA) Elem Ed, CA St Coll 1968; *cr:* Teacher North Start West Elem; *ai:* Ftbl Var Asst 1968-76, Bsktbl Asst 1968-72; Head Coach 1972-77; Stu Cncl Adv; Intramural Instr; PSEA; *home:* 182 Front St Jenners PA 15546

SMITH, VIVIAN ANN, Science Teacher; *b:* Clarkesville, TN; *m:* Johnny R.; *c:* David Philips, Emily, Katie; *ed:* (BS) Bio/Chem, Berry Coll 1975; (MS) Physiology, 1978, (MS) Scndry Sci, 1980 Univ of Ga; Gifted Cert; Stu Teacher Supervision Cert; Ramp-alcohol & Drug Trng; Outdoor Classroom Project; *cr:* Sci Teacher Oconee Cty HS 1979-84; Oconee Cty Intermediate Sch 1984-; *ai:* Stu Cncl Spon; Sci Fair Comm; Comprehensive Staff Dev Comm; Honors Comm; Stu Support Team; Sci Curr Comm; PAGE 1984-; GA Sci Teachers Assn 1989-; NSTA 1989-; Sigma Xi 1978-; Gamma Sigma Delta 1978-; Reebok Prof Instrs Alliance 1985-; Published 2 Articles GA Sci Teacher; Teacher of Yr 1990; *home:* 1040 Riverhaven Ln Watkinsville GA 30677

SMITH, WANDA J., Mathematics Teacher; *b:* Luverne, AL; *ed:* (BS) Math Ed/Bio, 1973, (MED) Supervision/Admin, 1977 Auburn Univ; *cr:* Part-Time Admin 1984-87, Math Teacher 1973- Jefferson Davis HS; *ai:* Stu Cncl Spon; Mem Sch Improvement Team; Faculty Advisory Comm Chairperson; NEA, AEA, MCEA, AL Cncl Teachers of Math; Neighborhood Assn (Helped Write By Laws 1988, Exec Bd, Hospitality Comm); Sch Outstanding Teacher Finalist Jefferson Davis 1989.

SMITH, WARREN LEE, Instructor/Professor; *b:* La Plata, MD; *c:* Neale, Morgan, David; *ed:* (BS) Eng/Psych, Towson St Coll 1971; (MED) Rdng/Ed, Salisbury St Coll 1981; *cr:* Pres Palominx Limited Incorporated 1982-88; Instr Berlin Mid Sch 1971-; Professor Wor-Wic Tech Comm Coll 1988-; *ai:* Odyssey of Mind Coach; MCTELA 1985-; MSTA, NEA 1972-; SOMIRAC Presenter 1990; Dog Stories Published 1982; Towson St Coll 1st Coll-Wide Computerized Course; *office:* Berlin Mid Sch Wor-Wic Tech Comm Coll PO Box 117 Snow Hill MD 21863

SMITH, WILLIAM E., Bus Ed Teacher/Chair; *b:* Carol Bay, VI; *m:* Cecilia M Walters; *c:* William E. II; *ed:* (AA) Construction Technology, Univ of VI 1966; (MA) Bus Admin, Inter-Amer Univ 1969; (MA) Bus Admin, Univ of VI 1981; Programming Lang/ Software Applications, Memphis St Univ; Introduction to Cmptrs in Ed, Univ of VI; Sch Law/Educl His, Miami Univ; *cr:* Administrative Asst US Army 1969-70; Acting Asst Prin 1989, Bus Ed Teacher 1970-, Dept Chairperson 1989- Charlotte Amalie HS; *ai:* FBLA Chapter Adv 1980-; Male Var Vlybl Coach; Stu Information Processing Coord; NBEA; VI Vlybl Fed Pres 1975-79; VI Vlybl Assn VP 1972-74; St Thomas-St John Fed of Teachers Treas 1980-; Designed & Presented Bus Ed Teacher In-Service Trng Wkshp St Thomas-St John Dist; Disk Operating Systems Fundamentals/Applications 1989; *home:* 295 Hillside Dr Annas Retreat PO Box 8761 Saint Thomas VI 00801

SMITH, WILLIAM EDWARD, Mathematics Teacher; *b:* Quinter, KS; *m:* Andrea Louise Lorer; *c:* Bryce A., Darren E., Regan E., Rebecca J.; *ed:* (BAED) Math, W WA Univ 1962; Stan Cert 1965; Grad Stud 1975, 1985; *cr:* Math Teacher Castle Rock HS 1962-65; 7th Grade Teacher Pioneer Sch 1965-68; Jr HS Math Teacher Hood Canal Sch Dist 1968-80; Sr HS Math Teacher Shelton HS 1980-; *ai:* 7th Grade Head Ftbl & HS Asst Track Coach; *office:* Shelton HS 3737 N Shelton Springs Rd Shelton WA 98584

SMITH, WILLIAM STEPHEN, Language Art Teacher; *b:* Bremer Haven, Germany; *m:* Dorothea M.; *c:* Christopher, Erin, Kelly; *ed:* (BA) Eng/Philosophy, Univ of Scranton 1969; Coaching Cert Courses; Working Towards Masters Eng/Ed, SUNY Binghamton; *cr:* Lang Art/Soc Stud Teacher Bishop Hannon HS 1970; Lang Art Teacher Maine-Endwell Mid Sch 1971-; *ai:* Adv Mid Sch Memory Book; Spring Play & Fall Musical Dir; Girls Modified Soccer Coach; 4-H Volunteer; Prof Horse Trainer & Show Judge; Penn Jersey Horse Show Assn 1968-70; Empire St Quarter Horse Assn, Amer Quarter Horse Assn 1972-81; Article Published; *office:* Maine-Endwell Mid Sch 1119 Farm to Market Rd Endicott NY 13760

SMITH, WILLIAM TODD, History Teacher/Ftbl Coach; *b:* Jackson, MS; *m:* Deidre S; *c:* William Z., Kalee B., Bryant Z.; *ed:* (BS) Soc Stud Ed/Coaching, Univ Of S MS 1986; MS Teaching Assessment Instriment Evaluator; *cr:* His Teacher/Head Ftbl Coach Cntrl Hinds 1986-88; His Teacher/Coach Petal HS 1988-; *ai:* Asst Ftbl Coach Offensive Coord; Head Track Coach; MS Assn of Coaches Mem 1987-; MS Natl Guard Sergent 1980-, Army Achievement Medal 1984; *office:* Petal HS 1145 Hwy 42 E Petal MS 39465

SMITH, WILLIE B. WILLIS, 5th/6th Grade Science Teacher; *b:* Doddsville, MS; *m:* Reubin; *c:* Wilton R.; *ed:* (BS) Elem Ed, MS Valley St Univ 1961; (MED) Elem Ed/Elem Supervision, Delta St Univ 1969; (MED) Adult Ed, AL A&M 1976; *cr:* 4th Grade Teacher Ruleville Cntrl HS 1961-67, Friars Point Elem 1967-69; 6th Grade Teacher 1969-73, 5th/6th Grade Sci Teacher 1973- Friars Point Elem; *ai:* Friars Point Sch 5 Yr Study Comm Local Chairperson 1989; Friars Point Elem Sch Self-Study Evaluation Steering Comm 1975; Coahoma Cty Assn of Educators Faculty Rep 1967-, Service Certificate 1976; MS Assn of Educators, NEA 1967-; MS Valley St Univ Alumni Assn. Delta St Univ Alumni Assn 1961-69; Heroines of Jericho Jr Matron 1986-, Post Matron Degree 1977; New Bethel Baptist Church Deaconess 1976-; Friars Point PTA Treas 1986-88, Service Pin 1988; Irma Gambrell Early Chldhd Dev Center Craft Comm Mem 1989-; Outstanding Elem Teacher of America 1972, 1975; Valedictorian of Delta Industrials HS Class; Honor & Most Sch Spirit Medals 1958; Honor Grad MS Valley St Univ; *home:* PO Box 434 Clarksdale MS 38614

SMITH, WIN V., History Teacher; *b:* Poteau, OK; *m:* Lynn Mason; *ed:* (BA) Phys Ed, Southeastern Univ Durant 1965; (MS) Ed, Talequah Northeastern 1975; *cr:* Coach/Teacher Hartshorne HS 1965-68, Fairland HS 1968-; *ai:* OEA, NEA; *office:* Fairland HS 202 W Washington Fairland OK 74343

SMITHERMAN, BETTY CLARK, Sixth Grade Teacher; *b:* Chicago, IL; *w:* Albert T. (dec); *c:* Marsha Reid, Andre Smitherman, Keith; *ed:* (BA) Elem Ed/Psych, 1974, (MED) Educl Therapy, 1980 Natl Coll of Ed; Sci, Math, Cmptr, Univ of IL Chicago; Gifted Courses, Rosary Coll; Writing Courses, Natl Coll; *cr:* Pre-Sch Teacher Evanston Headstart Dist 65 1974-77; K-2nd/ 4th-6th Grade Teacher Dist 97 1977-; *ai:* Drama Club; Afro-Amer Dramatic Musical Writer & Producer; Yrbk Club; Spon 6th Grade Yrbk Comm; Phi Delta Kappa 1980-; ICSS General Mem 1989-; Fields Museum 1987-88; BAG Spon Girls Club 1974-78; Nom Fnd for Excl Teaching Awd 1988; Univ of IL Chicago Natl Sci Fnd Teacher Enhancement Prgm 1986; *office:* Lincoln Sch 1111 S Grove Oak Park IL 60304

SMITHERMAN, KAREN COACH, Coordinator of Partnerships; *b:* Seattle, WA; *m:* Bill; *c:* Pamela, Sharon; *ed:* (BA) Sociology, Univ of WA 1974; Cntrl WA Univ; Grad Work Univ of Puget Sound; *cr:* Teacher 1976-86, Cmmty Resources Specialist Tacoma Public Schls 1986-89; Coord of Partnerships Tacoma Public Schls, Tacoma-Pierce Cty Chamber of Commerce 1986-; *ai:* Managed Legislative Campaign for St House of Reps 1982-84, St Senate Campaign 1986; Admin Women in Ed Pres 1987-; NCEA; Natl Assn of Partners in Ed; Pierce Cty Cmmty Housing Resource Bd; Jr Achievement; United Way; Citizen Lifesaver Certificate; Featured Story US West Annual Report 1988; *office:* Tacoma Public Schls PO Box 1357 Tacoma WA 98401

SMITHERMAN, LYNDA COOPER, English Teacher; *b:* Selma, AL; *m:* John D. Jr.; *c:* Lara M., J. C.; *ed:* (BS) Eng - Suma Cum Laude, Auburn Univ 1976; (MED) Scndry Ed/Eng, Livingston Univ 1981; Grad Stud Auburn Univ, Livingston Univ, Univ of AL; Advanced Placement Seminar; *cr:* AP Eng/Sr Honors Eng Teacher Selma HS 1976-; Part Time Eng/Speech Teacher Wall Comm Coll 1981-; *ai:* Scholars Bowl Team Coach; Dance Line Creator Spon; Sch Play Stage Mgr; NEA Delegate 1987-89; AL Ed Assn (Delegate, Instruction Prof Dev Commission) 1988-; Selma Ed Assn Pres 1988-89; Selma Choral Society; Phi Alpha Theta; Prin Awd for Excl; *office:* Selma HS 2180 Broad St Selma AL 36701

SMITHERS, DELORES LORRAINE, Principal/French Teacher; *b:* Lynn, MA; *m:* Edward T.; *c:* John, Ronald, Debra Brown, Susan Beatty, Karen Thomas; *ed:* (BS) Elem Ed, 1978; (MA) Rdng, 1982; (MA) Admin, 1990 Salem St Coll; *cr:* 2nd Grade Teacher 1977-87; 1st Grade Teacher 1984-87; Prin 1987- St Jean Baptiste Sch; *ai:* NCEA 1977-; Assn for Supv/Curr Dev 1987-; Lynn Bus/Ed Fnd Bd Mem 1989-; *office:* St Jean-Baptiste Sch 7 Endicott St Lynn MA 01902

SMITHERS, JAMES R, District Computer Director; *b:* Berkeley, CA; *M:* Denise Hargreaves; *c:* Kristyn, Ashley; *ed:* (BA) Ed, Coll of ID 1976; Cmptr Sci, Univ of ID/Coll of ID Boise St Univ; *cr:* 4th Grade Teacher Washington Elem 1976-86; 8th & 9th Grade Cmptr Sci Jefferson Jr HS 1986-88; Cmptr Sci Dir Jefferson/Dist Office 1988-; *ai:* Ski Team Coach; Honor Society Adv; Cmptr Club Adv; Academic Cncl; Pres/Editor Cmptr Educators of ID; Dist Team Mem Effective Schls; Cmptr Educators of ID Pres 1989-; Outstanding Young Man in America 1989; Grants Appel Cmptr Inc 1988-; Hearing Impaired Grant 1988; Geography, Teacher Grant 1989; Outstanding Edicator 1990; *office:* Jefferson Jr H S/Caldwell Dist 3311 S 10th Ave Caldwell ID 83605

SMITHERS, JOYCE WANDA, Fourth Grade Teacher; *b:* Richmond, IN; *ed:* (BS) Elem Ed, Univ of KY 1968; (MA) Elem Ed, N KY Univ 1978; *cr:* 4th/5th Grade Teacher Ora L Roby Sch 1969-70; 4th Grade Teacher Grandview Elem 1970-; *ai:* After Sch Intramural Prgm; 4-H Club Spon; Spelling Bee Coord; Delta Kappa Zamma 1984-; BEA (Treas 1989-92, Secy 1984-85); *office:* Grandview Elem Sch 500 Grandview Bellevue KY 41073

SMITHSON, ROBERT GEORGE, JR., Health Instr/Head Bsbl Coach; *b:* Russelville, AR; *m:* Mary Joan Smith; *ed:* (BA) Health/Phys Ed/Recreation, St Ambrose Univ 1972; (MS) Phys Ed/Athletic Admin/Coaching, Univ of S MS 1973; *cr:* Prof Bsbl Player CA Angel Minor League System 1965-68; Health/Phys Ed/Head Bsbl Coach Enterprise St Jr Coll 1973-78, Everett Sch Dist 1985-; *office:* Cascade HS 801 E Casino Rd Everett WA 98203

SMITS, ANJEAN ELIZABETH, Kindergarten Teacher; *b:* Mason City, IA; *ed:* (BS) Elem Ed, Northwestern Coll 1972; *cr:* Kndgtn Teacher Temple Chrstn Acad 1972-79; 2nd-3rd Grade Teacher 1979-81, Kndgtn Teacher 1981- Walnut Ridge Baptist Acad; *ai:* IA Prof Bus Women 1988; *office:* Walnut Ridge Baptist Acad 1307 W Ridgeway Ave Waterloo IA 50701

SMOCK, THOMAS MAYNARD, Physics/Sci Research Teacher; *b:* Pompton Plains, NJ; *m:* Karla Sylvester; *c:* Hannah C., Daniel S.; *ed:* (BS) Sci Ed/Pysics, FL Inst of Technology 1986; Microcomputers, Sci, Technology, Society, Aerospace Wkshps for Teachers Summer Inst; *cr:* Bio/Math Teacher 1986-87, Bio Teacher 1987-88, Physics/Research Teacher 1988- Eau Gallie HS; *ai:* Eau Gallie HS Sci Research & Physics Olympics Team Spon; Eau Gallie HS Steering Comm Chairperson 1989-; CCTS Grant

Recipient Aerospace Wkshp; *office:* Eau Gallie HS 1400 Commodore Blvd Melbourne FL 32935

SMOLICK, DIANE MARIE (KRUELL), Kindergarten Teacher; *b:* N Charleroi, PA; *m:* Terry Lee Kruell; *c:* Tara M.; *ed:* (BS) Elem Ed, California Univ of PA 1967; *cr:* K-6th Grade Art Teacher 1967-71, Kndgtn Teacher 1971- Charleroi Area Sch Dist; *ai:* Local Teachers Organization Sick Bank Comm Chairperson; Mentor Teacher; Directing Teacher for Stu Teachers; PSEA, NEA 1967-; CAEA (Comm Chairperson, Building Rep, Exec Bd) 1967-; PTA (VP 1976-77, 1978-79, Pres 1977-78), Outstanding Local Unit St & Natl, Life Membership 1978-79; *office:* Crest Avenue Elem Sch 6th St & Crest Ave Charleroi PA 15022

SMOTHERMON, DEBBIE KAY, Third Grade Teacher; *b:* Dallas, TX; *m:* Gary P.; *c:* Kari, Michael Watkins; *ed:* (BA) Elem Ed, Univ of OK 1978; (MS) Educl Admin, E TX St 1985; *cr:* 2nd Grade Teacher Rochell Elem 1978-81; 4th Grade Teacher Rochell & Reinhardt Elem 1981-88; 3rd Grade Teacher Reinhardt Elem 1988-; Team Leader Reinhardt Elem & Rochell Elem 1980-; *ai:* Career Ladder Selection, Textbook, Concerned Citizens Comm; Assn of TX Prof Educators Pres 1982-83; *home:* 707 Lake Meadows Dr Rockwall TX 75087

SMRIGA, GAYLE (VINCENT), Third Grade Teacher; *b:* Shattuck, OK; *m:* Michael J.; *c:* Ginny Smriga Giambrone, Chad; *ed:* (BS) Bus Ed, Phillips Univ 1962; (MS) Elem Ed, Ball St Univ 1967; Involved in Sch Improvement Prgm for Township; *cr:* 4th/5th Grade Teacher Alexandria Cmmty Schls 1962-64; 3rd Grade Teacher Marion Cmmty Sch 1966-67; 4th Grade Teacher Hammond Public Sch 1967-69; 3rd Grade Teacher Hobart Township Cmmty Schls 1969-; *ai:* Supts Advisory Group; Building Prgm Comm; Teachers Assn Building Rep; PTA Secy; Hobart Township Teachers 1990, Teacher of Yr 1990; Quilt Guild Prgm Chm 1988; Amer Sewing Guild 1989-; Church Choir; *office:* River Forest Elem Sch Indiana St & Huber Blvd Hobart IN 46342

SMUZYNSKI-PENLAND, BONNIE LANE, 6th Grade Teacher; *b:* Cleveland, OH; *m:* David W. Penland; *c:* Aaron W. Smuzynski, Damon L. Smuzynski; *ed:* (BS) Elem Ed, Elon Coll 1970; (MED) Admin/Supervision, VA Polytechnic Inst 1988; *cr:* 4th Grade Teacher Occoquan Elem 1970-72; 4th/5th Grade Teacher Rockledge Elem 1972-84; 6th Grade Sci Teacher Woodbridge Mid Sch 1984-; *ai:* Dept Chairwomen Soc Stud/Budget Comm for Site Based Management; Sci Fair Coord; Phi Delta Kappa 1990-; Greater Newington Women (Pres, VP, Secy, Delegate) 1978-84; Greater Newington Jaycee Women Delegate 1979-80; *office:* Woodbridge Mid Sch 2201 York Dr Woodbridge VA 22191

SMYERS, DENNIS D., Language Art Dept Chairperson; *b:* Carlisle, PA; *ed:* (BS) Eng/Speech/Theatre, Clarion St Coll 1972; (MS) Instructional Comm, Shippensburg St Coll 1977; *cr:* Eng Teacher 1972-, Speech/Drama Teacher/Dept Chm 1986-Littlestown HS; *ai:* Dir of Plays; Speech Team Coach; Mock Trial Team Coach; PSEA, NEA 1972-; Hanover Cmmty Players (Dir, Actor) 1975-; *office:* Littlestown Sr HS 200 E Myrtle St Littlestown PA 17340

SMYRE, VELMA WHITLOW, Fourth Grade Teacher; *b:* Skelton, WV; *m:* Jerome Elphonso; *c:* Tiffany N., Tara J.; *ed:* (BS) Elem Ed, Bluefield St Coll 1977; (MA) Admin, WV Coll of Grad Stud 1987; Leaders of Learning Conferences 1989; *cr:* 6th Grade Teacher Bramwell Elem Sch 1977-78; 4th/6th Grade Teacher Mabscott Elem Sch 1978-; *ai:* Vlybl Coach 1978-79; WV Educl Assn 1978-; Alpha Kappa Alpha Mem 1975-, Queen 1975; NAACP Mem 1989-; *office:* Mabscott Elem Sch PO Box 174 Mabscott WV 25871

SNACK, RONALD, Teacher & Dept Chair Ind Ed; *b:* Passaic, NJ; *m:* Carol Ann; *c:* Christopher, Julianne, Tamara; *ed:* (BA) Industrial Art, 1961, (MA) Industrial Art, 1973 Montclair St; Media/Supervision, Jersey Cty St & Montclair St; *cr:* Coach De Paul HS 1959-88; Teacher 1961-, Dept Chm Ind Ed 1982- Orange HS; *ai:* Mid St Steering, Admin Cncl, Effective Schls Steering Comms; Adopt-A-Stu Prgm Mem; NJSIAA 1961-88, Coaches Hall of Fame 1983; PSA Mem 1982-; Pequannock Golf League Pres 1983-89; Passaic Cty Coaches Pres 1970-81, Honor Coach 1975; St & Federal Grant Writing for Career Ed Orange HS 1983-88; De Paul HS Athletic Hall of Fame 1989; *office:* Orange HS 400 Lincoln Ave Orange NJ 07050

SNADERS, ANN CREWS, English Teacher; *b:* Samson, AL; *m:* Nick R.; *c:* Tiffany, Crews; *ed:* (MS) Ed, 1980, (BS) Bus Ed, 1971 Troy St Univ; Eng Cert, Univ of Cntrl FL 1987; *cr:* Bus Teacher Charles Henderson HS 1971-73, Bullock Memorial HS 1978-79, Lake Brantley HS 1981-82, Bus/Eng Teacher Lake Mary HS 1982-84, 1986-; *ai:* NEA 1985-87; Seminole Voc Assn Rep 1981-84, 1987; Seminole Cty Teachers of Eng 1986-; *office:* Lake Mary HS 655 Longwood-Lake Mary Rd Lake Mary FL 32746

SNAPP, CLARISSA SUMNERS, Social Studies Teacher; *b:* Indianapolis, IN; *m:* Jeffery Carlton; *c:* Laura E., David J.; *ed:* (BS) Ed, IN Univ 1972; (MA) Ed, De Pauw Univ 1978; *cr:* Teacher Mooresville HS 1974-; *ai:* Grade, Corporation Gifted & Talented Comm; At-Risk Tutoring; Faculty Adv; NCSS, IN Cncl for Soc Stud 1982-; NEA, IN St Teachers Assn 1980-; Mooresville Classroom Teachers Assn (VP 1986-88, Discussion Comm Chm, Membership Chm) 1980-; Kappa Kappa Kappa (Secy, 1st & 2nd VP, Asst Treas) 1980-; Alpha Delta Kappa Secy; GSA Troop Leader 1983-; Phi Delta Kappa 1990; IN Bicentennial Fellowship 1988; Bill of Rights Fellowship 1990; Teacher of Month 1988; Mooresville HS Acad Excl 1987-88; *office:* Mooresville HS 550 N Indiana St Mooresville IN 46158

SNARR, DANIEL RAY, High School Teacher; *b:* Murray, UT; *m:* Rhonda Wyler; *c:* Jeffery, Steven, Wendy, Kristi, Devin, Kathryn, Jason; *ed:* (BA) Life Sci, Weber St 1976; (MED) Scndry Ed, UT St Univ 1986; *cr:* Teacher Roy HS 1975-76, S Ogden Jr HS 1976-78, Skyline HS 1978-79, Kennedy Sr HS 1979-80, Skyline HS 1981-; *ai:* Tennis Coach; Key Club Adv.

SNAVELY, ROBERT BRADLEY, Secondary Mathematics Teacher; *b:* Johnstown, PA; *m:* Helen Elaine Moore; *c:* Scott E.; *ed:* (BS) Math, Univ of CA St 1968; (MED) Lang Comm, Univ of Pittsburgh 1976; Prins Certificate, Univ of Pittsburgh 1985; Supt Letter of Eligibility; *cr:* Teacher Chartiers Valley Sch Dist 1968-71, Chartiers Valley HS 1972-; *ai:* HS Liaison Comm Mem; *office:* Chartiers Valley HS 50 Thoms Run Rd Bridgeville PA 15017

SNEED, BARARA FOLLINS, French/Spanish Teacher; *b:* New Orleans, LA; *m:* Felton; *c:* Brett P.; *ed:* (BS) Span/Fr, Southern Univ 1965; (MED) Guidance/Counseling, Univ of New Orleans 1977; Admin, Loyola & Univ of New Orleans 1982; Univ of Dijon 1978, Univ Catholique de l Ouest 1984, Univ de Poitier 1987; *cr:* Teacher Natl Cncl of Jewish Women 1965, Orleans Parish Public Schls 1965-; *office:* Warren Easton HS 3019 Canal St New Orleans LA 70119

SNELICK, GREGORY LEONARD, Mathematics Teacher; *b:* Dubois, PA; *m:* Charlene Stanish; *c:* Rebecca, Matthew; *ed:* (BS) Scndry Ed/Math, Clarion St Univ 1975; Instructional II Teaching Certificate, Clarion St Univ, Penn St Dubois & Gannon Univ; *cr:* Math Teacher N Harford HS 1975-79, Elk Cty Chrstn HS 1979-; *ai:* Asst Var Ftbl Off & Def Backs Coach; Asst Track, Sprint & Sprint Relays Coach; Co-Scheduler, Schedule Stu, Teachers; Faculty Senate Mem; St Marys Church Mass Commentator 1989-; *office:* Elk Cty Chrstn HS 600 Maurus St Saint Marys PA 15857

SNELL, MAMIE LA VONNA ADAMS, Fourth Grade Teacher; *b:* Oak Ridge, TN; *m:* David Henry; *c:* Danny, Carolyn Duguay; *ed:* (BS) Elem Ed, 1969, (MA) Rdng, (MA) Counseling, E KY Univ; *cr:* Teacher Hannah McClure 1969-; *home:* 505 Hutchison Rd Paris KY 40361

SNELLEN, SUSAN MOORE, 7th Grade Science Teacher; *b:* Covington, KY; *c:* David Jr., Kelly; *ed:* (BS) Elem Ed, E KY Univ 1973; (Rank II) N KY Univ 1985; Rank II Rdng, N KY Univ ; *cr:* 5th Grade Teacher Leesville Elem 1976-77; Substitute Teacher Kenton Cty Schls 1982-85; 7th Grade Sci Teacher Twenhofel Mid Sch 1985-; *ai:* 7th Grade Team Captain; Sci Fair Coord; Impact CORE Team; NEA, KEA 1985-; *office:* Twenhofel Mid Sch 6955 Taylor Mill Rd Independence KY 41051

SNIDER, CYNTHIA DENISTON, Senior HS English Teacher; *b:* Logansport, IN; *m:* Rick Stedman; *c:* Steven K., Timothy S.; *ed:* (BA) Eng, 1969, (MA) Comm, 1971 Purdue Univ; Working Towards PHD Eng Lit, GA St Univ; *cr:* Teacher Southeastern Jr HS 1969-70; Instr Purdue Univ 1971-73; Teacher East HS 1983-85, Fayette Cty Schls 1986-; *ai:* Class of 1993 Spon;Fayette Cty Lang Art Comm; Staff Liaison Comm Mc Intosh HS; GA Cncl Teachers of Eng 1986-; NCTE 1984-; The Jr League 1976-; Fellowship Awarded Natl Endowment for Hum & Univ of CO 1990; GA Cncl Teachers of Eng Awd 1988.

SNIDER, JAMES HENRY, Teacher & Team Leader; *b:* Franklin, KY; *ed:* (BS) His/Math/Admin Services Area/Government Emphasis, 1975, (MA) Guidance/Counseling, 1977 W KY Univ; (EDD) Sch Admin, George Peabody Coll of Vanderbilt Univ 1986; Space Orientation for Educators, Univ of AL Huntsville; Rimm UnderachiEvement Wkshp WI; Invent America Creativity Conference Washington DC; Comparative Poly & Ec Systems, Georgetown Univ Inst; Various Wkshps & Conferences Math Univ of London 1990; *cr:* Photographer 1972-; Substitute Teacher KY Sch Systems 1976 83; 7th/8th Grade Math Teacher/Dept Head Alvaton Elem Sch 1983-86; 7th/8th Grade Math Teacher East Mid Sch 1986-; *ai:* Mid Sch Team Leader; Math Team Coach; Math Contest Coord; Chm Pro Team Prof Dev Comm; Yrbk Photographer; Excel Comm Chm; Sch & Bus Partnership Comm; Teacher Study Cncl Dist Mem; Volunteer Scorekeeper, Timer Bsktbl & Ftbl; Curr Advisory Comm Mem; NCTM, NEA 1983-; TN Math Teachers Assn, TN Assn for the Gifted, TN Ed Assn, Metro Nashville Ed Assn 1986-; KY Assn for Gifted Ed 1984-; Mid TN Math Assn 1987-; European Cncl for High Ability 1988-; Cty Historical Society (Pres, VP, Dir) 1977-; 1st Baptist Church (Deacon, Bible Teacher, Youth Leader, Pianist) 1963-; Ella Hay Goodwright Music Club Mem 1970-; Cty Bd of Elections (Mem, Secy) 1973-; 4-H (Judge, Project Leader); HCA Teacher Awd Grant; Metro Nashville Public Ed Grant; George Newton Bullard Fnd Grant 1990; Honorable Mention Dist Distinguished Teacher; Honorable Order of KY Colonels; TN Governors Certificate of Achievement; Co-Authored Franklin & Simpson Cty 1819-75, Reflections of 1976; Designing Prgm for Gifted Math Stus in Jr HS, Mid Schls; Career Leader Teacher Received Outstanding Service Certificate from TN Governor, *home:* 507 E Madison St Franklin KY 42134

SNIDER, JO ELLEN STEWART, Fifth Grade Teacher; *b:* New Martinsville, WV; *m:* Robert Steven; *c:* Kristopher S., Mitchell J.; *ed:* (BS) Elem Ed/Music, WV Univ 1972; Cooperative Learning Trng, Johns Hopkins Univ; Music, WV Univ; *cr:* Music Teacher 1972-73, 3rd Grade Teacher 1973-77 William Barr Elem; 3rd Grade Teacher 1978-80, 5th Grade Teacher 1980- Wetzel Cty Bd of Ed; *ai:* Plays, Theater Booster Dir; Cheerleading Coach; Show Choir Dir; Spec Task Force Comm; WV Ed Assn, NEA 1978-; Hundred Pool Comm VP 1978-; Hawks Athletic Boosters Pres 1988-; PTA Co-Pres 1984-85; Rush Run Meth Church Teacher 1990; Competitive Grant; Project Title for Long Drain Sch; *office:* Long Drain Elem Sch Bx 108a Metz WV 26585

SNIDER, MARY BETH, 6th Grade Teacher; *b:* Defiance, OH; *ed:* (BSED) Elem Ed, Bowling Green St Univ 1975; Working Towards Masters in Mid Grades Ed, Toledo Univ; Drug Intervention Trng; *cr:* 7th/8th Grade Sci/His/Rdng Teacher St Augustine Sch 1975-76; 6th Grade Teacher Bryan Mid Sch 1978-; *ai:* Mid Sch Athletic Dir; 8th Grade Vlybl Coach; Bryan Ed Assn (Treas 1980-82, Corresponding Secy 1987-88); Delta Kappa Gamma; Williams Cty Playhouse Pres 1987-88; Maumee Valley GSA Cncl Field Aide 1976-77; *office:* Bryan Mid Sch 1301 Center St Bryan OH 43506

SNIDER, TONI ARNOLD, 2nd Grade Teacher; *b:* Boise, ID; *m:* Steven J.; *c:* Dennis, Darrin; *ed:* (AS) Elem Ed, Boise Coll 1966; (BA) Elem Ed, 1968, (MA) Elem Ed/Curr & Instruction 1975 Boise St Univ; Emergency Medical Technician; *cr:* 2nd Grade Teacher Marsing Grade Sch 1968-73; 5th Grade Teacher Kuna EZlem 1973-76; 2nd Grade Teacher Hubbard Elem 1976-; *ai:* Outdoor Bsktbl Court Fund Raiser; ID Sch Dist Centennial Chairperson; Leos Club Adv; Horizons Rdng Cncl; Kuna Ed Assn (Pres, Secy, Treas, Delegate, Membership Chm) 1973-; Kuna PTA 1973-; Kuna Lady Lions (Secy, Pres); Kuna Ambulance (Pres, Secy) 1975-82, Emergency Medical Technician of Yr 1978; Canyon Teachers Credit Union (Secy, VP, Pres) 1979-; Teacher of Yr 1980; Fire Dist Commissioner; Poems Published; Golden & Silver Poet Awds; *office:* Hubbard Elem Sch 311 Porter Rd Kuna ID 83634

SNIPES, JESSICA JOHNSON, Fifth Grade Teacher; *b:* Washington, DC; *m:* Wayne; *c:* Dionne; *ed:* (BS) Elem Ed, Morgan St Univ 1972; (MED) Elem Ed, OH Univ 1973; *cr:* 2nd-6th Grade Teacher Yorktown Elem 1973-85; 5th Grade Teacher Samuel Ogle Elem 1986-; *ai:* Stu Cncl Spon; Sch Improvement & Budget Comm Mem; NEA, MSTA Mem 1973-; Math Teachers Cncl of MD Mem 1988-; Prince George Public Schls Rep Outstanding Educator Awd 1983-84; Participate Math Inst Bowie St Univ; *office:* Samuel Ogle Elem Sch 4111 Chelmont Ln 411 Chelmont Ln Bowie MD 20715

SNOAD, GREGORY THOMAS, HS Social Studies Teacher; *b:* Atlanta, GA; *m:* Suzanne Lander; *ed:* (BA) Poly Sci, W IL Univ 1980; AP European His; *cr:* Teacher Mauldin HS 1985-; *ai:* Head Boys Var Soccer, Asst Head Boys Var Bsktbl Coach; Faculty Cncl; On Site Budget Comm; Earth Day Coord; Teacher of Yr 1989-; *office:* Mauldin HS 701 E Butler Rd Mauldin SC 29662

SNODGRASS, GERRI A. (MARLEY), 4th Grade Teacher; *b:* Gary, IN; *m:* Roy A.; *c:* Jeffrey, Scott, Timothy; *ed:* (BS) Elem Ed/Sociology, IN Univ 1975, (MS) Elem Ed, 1978 IN Univ NW 1978; *cr:* 4th Grade Teacher Boone Grove Elem 1976-77, Porter Lakes Elem 1978-79; 1st Grade Teacher 1985-86, 4th Grade Teacher 1987- Porter Lakes Elem; *ai:* Building Based Team; Teacher Expectation Stu Achievement; Sci Fair Judge; Drug Abuse, Hospitality Comm; Sch Improvement Plan St of IN; Project Homework Organization Planning for Ed; NEA, IN St Teachers Assn, Assn of Porter Township Educators; PTA (VP, Treas) 1972-74; Jr Womens Club Pres, Outstanding Club in IN 1976-78; 1st United Meth (Admin Bd, Contemporary Choir); *home:* 549 W 100 N Valparaiso IN 46383

SNODGRASS, SNOWE STILWELL, Visual Arts Teacher; *b:* Canton, OH; *m:* Thomas L.; *c:* Lance A., Sam, Cristin; *ed:* (BFA) Art Ed/Eng, OH Univ Athens 1974; (MS) Comm Stud, WV Univ 1988; *cr:* Art Teacher Buckeye Local Sch Dist 1975-; *ai:* Buckeye S Jr HS & Buckeye SW HS Art Club Adv, Dept Head; Progressive Artist League 1990; Alpha Delta Pi Alumni Assn; Buckeye Local Chrstn Assn 1989-; Rayland ME Church (Organist 1970-, Sunday Sch Song Dir, Family Ministries Dir, Wkshp Comm Mem); Lions Club Recognition for Fundraiser; *home:* PO Box 102 Rayland OH 43943

SNOKE, SHEILA HARDIE, 5th/6th Grade Teacher; *b:* Fairview Park, OH; *m:* Robert Lee; *c:* Brandi, Kyle, Christopher; *ed:* (BA) Psych, 1973, (BS) Elem Ed, 1976 OH Univ; Grad Stud Elem Ed, OH Univ; *cr:* Remedial Rdng Teacher 1976-77, 5th Grade Teacher 1977-79, 6th Grade Teacher 1980-85 Amanda Elem; 8th Grade Eng/Rdng Teacher Clearcreek Jr HS 1985-86; 5th Grade Teacher Amanda Elem 1986-; *ai:* Adv 5th & 6th Grades Musical Production; Awds & Attendance Comms; ACEA Pres 1982-83; OEA, NEA, ACEA Bldg Rep 1989-; TWIG 21 (Treas 1990, Co-Treas 1989-) 1987-; *home:* 466 Sells Rd Lancaster OH 43130

SNOW, AVIS CORDLE, Media Specialist; *b:* Rome, GA; *m:* David G.; *c:* Lindsay A., Thomas C.; *ed:* (BS) Art, Jacksonville St Univ 1981; (MED) Mid Grades, Berry Coll 1986; (MED) Media, Jacksonville St Univ 1989; *cr:* Carpet Designer Don Marlowe & Assoc 1981-83; Teachers Aide 1983-84, 5th Grade Teacher 1984-88, Media Specialist 1988- Chattooga Cty Bd of Ed.

SNOW, JOHN O., 7th/8th Grade Science Teacher; *b:* York, ME; *m:* Cynthia E. Haviland; *c:* Jill, Matthew; *ed:* (BS) Bio, Univ of ME 1970; Electronics Courses; *cr:* Sci Teacher Houlton Jr HS 1971-73, York Jr HS 1973-76, Wentworth Mid SCh 1976-; *ai:* Rockerfeller Grant for Art in Sci Prgm; Published Two Books; *office:* Wentworth Mid Sch Gorham Rd Scarborough ME 04074

SNOW, KENNETH, Biology Teacher; *b:* Kalamazoo, MI; *m:* Pamela Zinter; *ed:* (BA) Bio, 1976, (MA) Sci Ed, 1981 W MI Univ; *cr:* Bio Teacher Boone Grove HS 1979-; *ai:* Jr HS Sci Club Spon; Direct Students in Ind Research Projects; Sci Fair Co-Dir; *office:* Boone Grove HS 325 W 550 S Boone Grove IN 46302

SNOW, VERONICA DICKENSON, Computer Science Teacher; *b:* Clovis, NM; *m:* Joseph H. III; *c:* Amelia J.; *ed:* (AA) General Transfer, Yavapai Coll 1984; (BED) Phys Ed, Hardin Simmons Univ 1987; *cr:* Teacher/Coach Abilene HS 1987-; *ai:* Coach Jr Var Bsktbl, Vlybl & Frosh Vlybl & Bsktbl Asst Coach; TCEA 1987-; AAHPERD 1986-89, Outstanding Stu 1987; TCCA 1987-; TABC 1989-; *office:* Abilene HS 2800 N 6th Abilene TX 79603

SNOWDEN, ELAINE W., Lang Art Teacher/Consultant; *b:* Macon, GA; *m:* George W.; *c:* Wesley, Liz Snowden-Taylor, Carol Akamian; *ed:* (BS) Ed, Univ of Houston 1969; (MED) Rdng, Univ of AK Anchorage 1977; Trained in Anchorage Writing Project; Teacher Researcher; *cr:* Teacher 1970-85, Teacher Consultant 1985- Anchorage Sch Dist; *ai:* Teaching Coll Credit Courses Whole Lang; Teacher-Researcher Spelling; NCTE (Mem Exec Comm, Rep at Large 1981-83) 1980-; Intnl Rdng Assn 1980-; Phi Delta Kappa 1985-; AK Cncl Teachers of Eng Pres 1978, Meritous Service 1985; Anchorage Area Cncl Teachers of Eng Pres 1987, Distinguished Service 1988; Published NCTE Video Tape; *office:* Anchorage Sch Dist 4600 De Barr Ave Anchorage AK 99508

SNOWDEN, PAMELA ANN (EVANS), Business Education Teacher; *b:* Oakland, CA; *m:* Larry Edward; *c:* Elizabeth A., Jeffrey E.; *ed:* (BS) Bus Ed, Southeastern St Univ 1975; (MS) Sch Admin, Northeastern St Univ 1990; Minor in Accounting; *cr:* Bus Teacher DE HS 1975-76, Panola HS 1976-79, Preston HS 1979-, Ind Treas Preston HS 1981-; *ai:* Preston Sch Bus Class Adv; Preston Sch Photographer; AAUW Secy 1978-79; Pi Omega Pi Secy 1975; Bus Studs Won OSU Tech Bus Contest 4 Times; Bus Stus Place Top 3 132 Times Interscholastic Meets; General Bus Stud Won St General Bus Contest; *office:* Preston H S P O Box 418 Preston OK 74456

SNUFFER, LARRY PRESTON, Economics/Government Teacher; *b:* Bolt, WV; *m:* Connie Lee Foose Compston; *c:* Lynn M. Compston; *ed:* (BA) Soc Stud Comp, WV Inst of Technology 1968; (MA) Speech Comm, WV Univ 1980; (MA) Sports Medicine, Marshall Univ 1987; *cr:* Teacher Woodrow Wilson HS 1968-69, Cowen HS 1969-71, Eccles Jr HS 1972-73, Marsh Fork HS 1973-74, Clear Fork HS 1974-76, Shady Spring HS 1977-; *ai:* Asst Wrestling Coach; Ftbl Athletic Trainer; Boys Track Head Coach; NHS Spon; WV Trainers Assn 1987-; Phi Alpha Theta 1967-; WV Wrestling Coaches Assn 1977-; *office:* Shady Spring HS Drawer A Shady Spring WV 25918

SNYDER, ALICE (KLEINMAN), High School French Teacher; *b:* Ft Belvoir, VA; *m:* Norman W.; *c:* Aaron, Noelle; *ed:* (BS) Elem Ed, 1974, (MA) Early/Mid Chldhd Ed, 1985 OH St Univ; Fr Lang, Fr Culture; K-12 Supervision; *cr:* 1st Grade Teacher 1975-79, 4th Grade Teacher 1976-86 Leesville Elem; 5th Grade Teacher Whetstone Elem 1986; 9th-12th Grade Fr Teacher Colonel Crawford HS 1986-; *ai:* Fr Club Adv; HS Drama Dir & Adv; Fr Stu Trip to France Spon; OH Foreign Lang Assn 1983-; Crawford Cty Intnl Rdng Assn 1979-; Phi Delta Kappa 1985-; NEA, OEA, NCOEA, CCEA (Treas 1988-) 1975-; Women of Moose 1990; *office:* Colonel Crawford HS 2303 St Rt 602 North Robinson OH 44856

SNYDER, BRENDA SUE, Teacher of Gifted & Talented; *b:* Columbus, IN; *ed:* (BA) Elem Ed, Franklin Coll 1975; (MS) Elem Ed, IN Univ 1979; Endorsement Gifted & Talented Ed, IN Univ 1988; *cr:* 2nd Grade Teacher 1975-76, 4th Grade Teacher 1976-77, 3rd Grade Teacher 1977-81, 6th Grade Teacher 1981-84, 2nd/3rd Transition Teacher 1984-86, 3rd Grade Teacher 1986-88, Teacher of 3rd Grade Gifted & Talented 1988-89, Teacher of 6th Grade Gifted & Talented Lang Art/Lit 1989- East Side Elem; *ai:* Gifted & Talented Roundtable & Curr Writing; Eng Curr Writing & Textbook Adoption; 5th/6th Grade Chrldr Coach; Franklin Coll Teacher Advisory Bd; Study Skills Comm; Kappa Kappa Kappa 1978-80; Beta Sigma Pi 1981-83; Zeta Tau Alpha Alumnae 1975-; Edinburgh Teacher of Yr; Whos Who in Amer Ed; Nom Christa Mc Auliffe Fellowship; Weekly Newspaper Columnist; *home:* 307 E Park Dr Edinburgh IN 46124

SNYDER, CAROL LYNN, Language Art Teacher; *b:* Canton, OH; *ed:* (BS) Elem Ed, Malone Coll 1977; (MA) Spec Ed, Walsh Coll 1986; *cr:* 5th Grade Teacher Pleasantview Elem Plain Local 1977-80; Lang Art Teacher Louisville Jr HS 1980-; *ai:* Writing Coach Power of the Pen; Mid Sch Steering & Dist Writing Competency Comms; Westbrook Park United Meth Church (Lay Mem 1987-, Sanctuary Choir 1973-, Adult Bell Choir 1980-); *office:* Louisville Jr HS 300 E Gorgas St Louisville OH 44641

SNYDER, DOYAL B., Elementary Principal; *b:* Caldwell, ID; *m:* Gwen Davis; *c:* Bryan, Erin; *ed:* (BA) Elem Ed, NW Nazareth Coll 1970; (MS) Elem Ed, E OR St Coll 1987; Elem Prin Certificate; *cr:* 5th Grade Teacher Nyssa Elem Sch 1970-72; 5th-6th Grade Teacher Alameda Elem Sch 1972-88; Prin/Teacher Pioneer Elem Sch 1988-; *ai:* Elem Prin; COSA, NESPA 1988-; *office:* Pioneer Sch 4744 Pioneer Rd Ontario OR 97914

SNYDER, JANE HYDER, English Teacher; *b:* Maryville, MO; *m:* Dennis Lee; *c:* Mark; *ed:* (BSED) Concentrated Eng, 1971, (MSED) Scndry Admin, 1986 NW MO St Univ; *cr:* Eng Teacher Martinsville HS 1971-72, N Andrew HS 1972-; *ai:* NHS Spon; All-Sch Play Dir; N Andrew Career Ladder Participant; Admin Advisory & CTA Building Comms; N Andrew CTA, MO St Teachers Assn, NCTE, Kappa Delta Pi; Savannah Chrstn Church Chairperson of Church Schlsp Comm; Outstanding Educators in Scndry & Elem Ed 1976; *office:* North Andrew R VI Sch Box 128 Rosendale MO 64483

SNYDER, JANICE BUSSIE, Third Grade Teacher; *b:* Sylacauga, AL; *m:* Jerry W.; *c:* Tammy Fancher, Jamie, Jonathon Rodgers; *ed:* (BS) Elem Ed, Jacksonville St Univ 1972; (MA) Elem Ed, Univ of Montevalla 1977; *cr:* 4th Grade Teacher 1972-74, 3rd Grade Teacher 1974- Pinecrest Sch; *ai:* Faculty Rep; Grade Chm; Sylacauga Teachers Assn, AL Ed Assn, NEA; Delta Kappa Gamma Secy 1990; Periwinkle Garden Club Past Secy.

SNYDER, JEFFREY L., Music Teacher/Suprv of Music; *b:* York, PA; *m:* Lisa K. Leiphart Snyder; *ed:* (BS) Music Ed, West Chester Univ 1968; (MED) Music, Western MD Coll 1971; Supervision of Music Cert Western MD Coll 1984; Post Masters Studies East Stroudsburg Univ; Amer Univ; in Univ of PA; Penn St Univ; Towson St Univ; Wilkes Coll; *cr:* Vocal Music Dover Intermediate Sch 1968-71; Dover HS 1971-; Supv of Music Dover Area Sch Dist 1984-; *ai:* Renaissance-Select Choral Group; Music Educators Natl Conf 1968-; PA Music Educators Assn 1968-; ASCD 1984-; Dover Jaycees Outstanding Young Educator 1981; *office:* Dover Area Sch Dist West Canal St Dover PA 17315

SNYDER, JOHN H., Computer Science Instructor; *b:* Wichita, KS; *m:* Patricia J. Reilly; *c:* Matthew M. G.; *ed:* (BA) Eng, Speech, Human Relations Univ of KS 1970; (MS) Cmptr Ed, Nova Univ 1984; Post Masters Studies Cmptr Sci Univ NV; *cr:* Teacher South HS 1971-80; Wichita St Univ 1980-81; Hyde Park Jr HS 1981-86; Chaparral HS 1986-; *ai:* Cmptr Club Adv; Mem Instructional Technology Planning Comm Clark Cty Sch Dist; NEA St Comm Chm 1978-79; Phi Delta Kappa Newsletter Editor 1989-; Cmptr-Using Ed 1986-; Knights of Columbus (3rd & 4th Degree Secy 1989-) Family of Month 1989; Amer Legion 1977-; Clark Cty Teacher of Yr 1989-; NV Teacher Yr 1989-; Bus Week Magazine Awd Innovative Teaching 1990; Whos Who Cmptr Industry; Articles Published in Inforworld & ND Journal of Ed & Natl Poetry Anthology; *office:* Chaparral H S 3850 Annie Oakley Dr Las Vegas NV 89121

SNYDER, LEE ANN A, Music Teacher; *b:* Canton, OH; *ed:* (BME) Music Ed, IN Univ 1971; (MA) Psych, Ball St 1982; *cr:* Music Teacher Franklin-Monroe 1971-72, Miami East 1972-79, Mendon-Union 1982-; *ai:* Homecoming; Sftbl, Jr HS Bsktbl Coach; OH Music Ed Assn; Tau Beta Sigma; *office:* Mendon-Union Sch Box 98 Jefferson St Mendon OH 45862

SNYDER, LINDA BRADLEY, Fifth Grade Teacher; *b:* W Lafayette, IN; *m:* Charles Joseph; *c:* Matthew J.; *ed:* (BS) Elem Ed, Ball St Univ 1972; (MS) Elem Ed, Butler Univ 1976; Stu Asst Prgm; At Risk Trng Teenage Pregnancy, Death & Dying; Quest-Skills for Adolescene; Camp Tecumseh; *cr:* 5th/6th Grade Teacher 1972-85, Chapter I Rdng Consultant 1987-88, 5th/6th Grade Teacher 1988- Westfield Washington Mid Sch; *ai:* Lang Art Curr Dev, Textbook Adoption Comm; Performance Based Accreditation; Mentor; Adopt-A-Teacher; Hamilton Cty Intnl Rdng Assn 1990; Kappa Delta Pi 1976-; Westfield Classroom Teachers Assn, IN St Teachers Assn, NEA 1972-; Omega Phi Tau 1981-; Westfield Washington PTA 1972-; Nom WTNR Shining Star Awd 1990; *office:* Westfield Mid Sch 328 W Main St Westfield IN 46074

SNYDER, RAY A., Art Teacher/Department Chair; *b:* Loganville, PA; *m:* Ann Elizabeth Stanley; *c:* Matthew, Michael; *ed:* (BA) Art Ed, Davis & Elkins Coll 1969; (MED) Art Ed, PA St Univ 1972; Primitive Pottery, Univ of TN; Art His, Univ of Rome; *cr:* Eng Teacher Susquehannock Sr HS 1969-; Art Teacher Spring Grove Jr HS 1969-72, Spring Grove Sr HS 1972; *ai:* HS Mid St Evaluation Self Study Coord; NEA, PA St Ed Assn, Spring Grove Ed Assn 1969-; NAEA, PA Art Ed Assn 1972-; Hanover Area Art Guild 1972-; Fulbright Scholar Italy 1972; Numerous Photos in Natl Magazines; *office:* Spring Grove Area Sr HS Hanover & Jackson Sts Spring Grove PA 17362

SNYDER, SHANNON CLAIRE, English/Hum/Drama Teacher; *b:* Spanish Fork, UT; *ed:* (BA) Eng, Brigham Young Univ 1967; (MS) Eng Ed, Buffalo St Univ 1976; *cr:* Eng/Lang Art Teacher Lincoln Jr HS 1967-68; Eng Teacher Amherst Jr HS 1968-73; Eng/Hum/Drama Teacher Dixon Mid Sch 1978-; *ai:* Drama Coach; Dixon Mid Sch Comm; Performing Arts Night Chairperson; VEA, NEA, PEA, NCTE; Grant Coring & Hum 1986; Grant Hum Core II 1987; Grant Drama Act Mid Sch 1988; Most Remembered & Most Concerned Teacher Stu Voted Awds; Grant Folk Arts Public Sch Appreciation 1980; Curr Leader Mid Sch Provo Dist 1987; Guest Lecturer Folk Lore in Schls.

SNYDER, TRECA YOCUM, Fourth Grade Teacher; *b:* Kansas City, MO; *m:* Michael; *ed:* (BS) Elem Ed, Baker Univ 1982; *cr:* 5th/6th Grade Teacher 1982-89, 4th Grade Teacher 1989- Strasburg Elem; *ai:* Cmmty Teachers Assn Pres 1984-86; *home:* 7404 Crown Belton MO 64012

SNYDER, WAYNE, Physics Teacher; *b:* Plainfield, NJ; *m:* Sylvia Culver; *c:* Sabrina, Justin; *ed:* (BS) Bio, Grove City Coll 1974; (MS) Environmental Sci/Toxicology, Univ of Rochester 1977; *cr:* Adjunct Professor Physics Univ of NY Brockport; Teacher Wayne Cntrl HS 1977; *ai:* Stu Senate Adv; Stu Leadership Trng & Mentor for Gifted & Talented Prgms; AAPT, Sci Teachers Assn of NY, NSTA; Odyssey of the Mind Regional Coord 1987-; Rochester East Electric Teachers Advisory Group; Reader for AP Physics Exam; Teacher of Yr; Physics Teaching Resource Agent; Operation Physics Amer Physical Society; Nom for Presidential Awd for Excl in Sci Teaching.

SNYDER, WILLIAM BIRCH, 9th Grade Lang Arts Teacher; *b:* Philadelphia, PA; *m:* Jennifer Sue Sullivan; *ed:* (BA) Eng/Soc Stud, 1964, (MA) Eng, 1972 Millersville St Univ; *cr:* Lang Arts Teacher Palmyra Mid Sch; *ai:* Lebanon Cty Ed Honor Society 1988; PA St Ed Assn Life Mem; NEA 1964; PA Trappers Assn, Milton Hershey Alumni Assn, US Chess Fed Life Mem; PA Three Mem; *office:* Palmyra Mid Sch W Cherry St Palmyra PA 17078

SOBEL, JOY F., English/Communications Teacher; *b:* Chicago, IL; *m:* Burton C. Thompson; *c:* Benjamin, Rachel; *ed:* (BA) Eng, Univ of IL Urbana-Champaign 1970; UCSD, SDSU; *cr:* Eng Teacher Highland Park HS 1970, Evanston Township HS 1970-72; Eng/Speech Teacher Hilltop Jr HS 1973-86, Bonita Vista HS 1986-; *ai:* Mentor Teacher; Sch Contest Promoter; Speech Coach; Fine Arts Club Adv; Intnl Baccalaureate Instr; NEA, SEA, NCTE; Cited for Academic Excl 1989 & Most Inspirational Teacher 1988 Bonita Vista HS; *office:* Bonita Vista HS 751 Otay Lakes Rd Chula Vista CA 92013

SOBIERAJSKI, FRANK, Math Teacher; *b:* Yonkers, NY; *m:* Mickey Jo Cooper; *c:* Krysta, Mark; *ed:* (BA) Math, St Univ NY Potsdam 1974; Cmptr Engineering, Syracuse Univ; *cr:* Math Teacher Cato-Meridian Cntrl Sch 1977-84, N Rose-Wolcott Cntrl Schls 1984-; *ai:* Class Adv 1989; NEA Pres 1989-; Univ of Rochester Excl Teaching 1987; *office:* N Rose-Wolcott Cntrl Schls Salter-Colvin Rd Wolcott NY 14590

SOBIESIAK, JAMES JOHN, Counselor; *b:* Staten Island, NY; *m:* Joan Thompson; *c:* Katie, Andrew; *ed:* (BA) Eng, 1975, (MS) Ed, 1979 Geneseo St; (MS) Sch Counseling, Alfred Univ 1987; Project Intervention; *cr:* Eng Teacher 1975-86, Sch Cnslr 1987- Wayland Cntrl Sch; *ai:* Ski Club Adv; Advanced Placement Coord; Wayland Teachers Assn Pres 1982-86; Genesee Valley Teachers Assn Pres 1985-86; Genesee Valley Cnslrs Assn Secy 1988-89; Livingston Cty Youth Bd Mem 1989-; Teacher Resource Center Grant 1990; *office:* Wayland Cntrl Sch 2350 Rt 63 Wayland NY 14572

SOBKOVIAK, CAROL JO, English Dept Chair/Teacher; *b:* Chicago, IL; *m:* Dennis A. Chase; *c:* Preston Chase; *ed:* (BS) Speech/Eng, Univ of WI River Falls 1972; (MA) Eng, N AZ Univ Flagstaff 1978; Various Wkshps & Seminars Univ of AZ; *cr:* Teacher Coolidge Hs 1972-78, Flowing Wells HS 1978-81, Cntrl AZ Coll 1982-84, Mountain View HS 1984-; *ai:* Chrldrs & Speech Class Sponsorships; Builders Club; ASCD, NCTE; MEA, ASA, NEA (Rep, Treas) 1985-87; Dept Chairperson Appointed Several Comm; Mentor-Master & Supervising Teacher; *office:* Mountain View HS 3901 W Linda Vista Tucson AZ 85741

SOBOCIENSKI, PATRICIA SUE (SEARS), Mathematics Department Chair; *b:* Traverse City, MI; *m:* Charles Daniel; *ed:* (AA) Math, NW MI Univ 1962; (BA) Math, W MI Univ 1964; (MA) Math Ed, E MI Univ 1970; Working Towards Masters Cmptrs; *cr:* Teacher Madison Public Schls 1964-; *ai:* Math Dept Chairperson; Class of 1991 Spon; MI Ed Assn 1964-; Natl Sci Fnd Summer Math Inst; *office:* Madison HS 915 E 11 Mile Rd Madison Heights MI 48071

SOBOTKA, KATHLEEN HAVRILLA, 7th Grade English Teacher; *b:* Homestead, PA; *c:* Jennifer; *ed:* (BA) Eng, Univ of AL Huntsville 1972; Grad Level Courses Eng; *cr:* 7th/8th Eng Teacher Whitesburg Mid Sch 1973-79; 8th Grade Eng Teacher Mountain Gap Mid Sch 1979-83; 7th/8th Grade Eng Teacher Whitesburg Mid Sch 1983-; *ai:* Natl Jr Honor Society Spon; Birmingham Post Herald Spelling Bee Contest; Red Cross Volunteer 1988-; *office:* Whitesburg Mid Sch 107 Sanders Rd Huntsville AL 35802

SOBUCKI, ANDREW JOSEPH, Science Teacher; *b:* Chicago, IL; *ed:* (BA) Sci Ed, Calumet Coll of St Joseph; Working towards MS in Educl Admin, Purdue Univ; *cr:* Sci Instr/Physics/Chem Teacher St Francis de Sales HS 1981-; *ai:* Head Wrestling Coach 1980-; Alumni Dir 1989-; Mens Dir of Athletics 1988-; Recruiting Coord 1989-; Chicago Cath League Bd of Control Secy 1990; IN HS Assn of Sci Teachers 1981-; Amer Society of Metallurgists 1984-; Amer Coaches Effectiveness Prgm 1990; *office:* St Francis de Sales HS 10155 Ewing Ave Chicago IL 60617

SOCQUET, DIANNE FALARDEAU, Teacher; *b:* Putnam, CT; *c:* Kristen, Marc; *ed:* (BA) Sociology, Stonehill Coll 1969; (MS) Ed, Eastern CT St Univ 1977; Numerous Courses In Teaching & Learning; *cr:* Teacher 1971-73, Title I Math Teacher 1970-80 St James; Teacher Brooklyn Jr HS 1980-; *ai:* Stu Cncl Adv; Consultation Comm; BEA/CEA; *office:* Brooklyn Jr H S Gorman Rd Brooklyn CT 06234

SODERBERG, MARION COOK, Elementary Guidance Counselor; *b:* Washington, DC; *m:* Charles R.; *ed:* (BA) Ed, Radford Coll 1968; (MAED) Ed/Counseling, VA Tech 1990; *cr:* Classroom Teacher Yorkshire Elem 1969-89; Guidance Cnslr Loch Lomond Elem 1989; *ai:* Delta Kappa Gamma 1985-; Amer Assn Counseling & Dev, VA Counseling Assn.

SODOMA, KAREN J., Math Teacher; *b:* Rochester, NY; *m:* Ronald L.; *c:* Amanda, Rebeca; *ed:* (BS) Ed of Math, 1966; (MS) Math, 1971 St Univ NY; *cr:* 8th & 9th Grade Math Teacher Pittsford Cntrl Sch 1966-68; 7th Grade Math Teacher Albion Cntrl Sch 1968-; *ai:* Cheerleading Asst Adv; Building Courtesy Chairperson; Delta Kappa Gamma Pres 1982-84; Society Intnl; Girl Scouts Asst Leader 1980-; Purple Eagle Yrbk 1986-87; Delta Kappa Gamma Pi St Comm Awd 1983-87; Cert for 20 Yrs of Service to Albion Cntrl Sch; *office:* Albion Central Sch 325 East Ave Albion NY 14411

SOETE, BERNADINE PLEVIAK, 5th/6th Grade Math Teacher; *b:* Carbondale, PA; *m:* Frederick C.; *ed:* (BS) Elem Ed, Misericordia 1960; (ME) Elem Ed, 1973, (MS) Elem Ed, 1976 Marywood; Coll of St Francis 1963-64, La Salle Coll 1965-66, Univ of Scranton 1976-80; *cr:* Teacher Private Schls 1949-67;5th/6th Grade Math Teacher Forest City Regional 1968-; *ai:* NEIU

#19 Sch Improvement Prgm; PA Cncl Teachers of Math 1987-; Pro-Life 1983-; Nom Outstanding Elem Teachers of America 1973; Natl Deans List 1979-80; *office:* Forest City Regional 100 Susquehanna St Forest City PA 18421

SOFIANOS, JUDITH JACOBSON, Fourth Grade Teacher; *b:* Chicago, IL; *m:* Leo; *c:* Audrey, Dan, Craig Helfand, Mark Helfand; *ed:* (BED) Elem Ed, Natl Coll of Ed 1961; Grad Stud; *cr:* 1st Grade Teacher Kimball Hill Sch 1961-67; 1st/3rd/4th Grade Teacher Winston Churchill Sch 1972-; *ai:* Rdng & Report Card Comm; *office:* Winston Churchill Sch 120 Babcock Dr Palatine IL 60067

SOKOL, LEISA LYNN DU BECK, Third Grade Teacher; *b:* Cambridge, OH; *c:* Aarica; *ed:* (BS) Elem Ed/Eng, OH Univ 1981; *cr:* 5th-6th Grade Teacher Pleasant City Elem 1981-84; 3rd Grade Teacher Byesville Elem 1984-; *ai:* HS Cheerleading Adv 1981-84; Co-Adv Stu Cncl Byesville Elem 1989-; Rolling Hills Ed Assn Mem, NEA Mem 1981-; Jennings Scholar 1988; *home:* Sunrise Dr Byesville OH 43723

SOKOLOWSKI, TED S., Fifth Grade Teacher; *b:* Nanticoke, PA; *m:* Theresa Gurzynski; *c:* Kristen, Kelly, Erin; *ed:* (BA) Soc Stud/Elem Ed, Wilkes Univ 1972; (MS) Elem Ed, Scranton Univ 1976; Extra Credits Soc Stud, Discipline, Peer Coaching, Cmptrs; *cr:* Elem Phys Ed Teacher 1972-74, Elem Teacher Greater Nanticoke Area 1974-; *ai:* Elem Soc Stud Comm; In Charge Campbells Soup Label Prgm; PSEA, NEA; *office:* K M Smith Elem Sch Robert St Sheatown PA 18634

SOLANO, LOUIS EMIL, Fifth Grade Teacher; *b:* Cambridge, MA; *m:* Betty Joyce Dent; *c:* Michael; *ed:* (BS) Elem Ed, 1966, (MED) Elem Ed, 1969 MA St Coll at Bridgeport; Univ of MD; *cr:* 4th-6th Grade Teacher Perkins Elem 1966-68; 6th Grade Teacher Winthrop Elem 1968-69; 5th/6th Grade Teacher Fullerton Elem 1969-73; 4th/5th Grade Teacher Cape St Claire Elem 1973-; *ai:* Sci Dept Chairperson Cape St Claire Elem; Sci Fair Coord; Safety Patrol Supvr; NEA 1973-; MD St Teachers Assn, Teachers Assn of Anne Arundel Cty; PTA Anne Arundel Cty 1973-; *office:* Cape St Claire Elem Sch 931 Blue Ridge Rd Annapolis MD 21401

SOLBERG, BARBARA VARBERG, 7-8th Eng/9th Grade Teacher; *b:* Minot, ND; *m:* Richard; *c:* John Scott, Jessica; *ed:* (BS) Speech Comm, 1969, (MA) Speech Comm, 1972 Univ of ND; 2nd Lang Trng; Gen Aptitude T Est Battery Admin & Interpreter; *cr:* Eng Instr Stanley Cmmty Schls 1977-79 & 1985-; Free Lance Writer 1984-, Extension Div Instr Univ of ND Ext 1988-; *home:* 717 Horseshoe Dr Stanley ND 58784

SOLE, JIM L., English Teacher; *b:* Lindsborg, KS; *m:* Le Ann Nelson; *c:* Tony, Julie; *ed:* (BA) Eng/Ed, Bethany Coll 1959; (MA) Emporia St 1962; Grad Stud Denver Univ; *cr:* Hutchinson Public Schls 1959-63; Southwestern Coll 1963-66; Pacific Luth Univ 1967-69; Tacoma Public Schls 1969-; *ai:* NEA; Tacoma Ed Assn (Poly Action Chm 1979-84, Secy 1975-79), Spec TACT-PAC 1980, Cnslr Consortia Spec Service Awd 1979; Washington Ed Assn; Tacoma Cmmty Schls (Building Coord 1976-85, Secy 1975-79), Service to Others 1985, Cnslr Consortia Spec Service Awd 1979, 500 Hr Volunteer Pin 1984; Pacific Luth Univ Secy 1975-79, Cnslr Consortia Service Awd 1979; Tacoma PTA Golden Acorn 1977; Tacoma Comm Coll Part-Time Teacher; Seattle Pacific Univ Adjunct Faculty & Part-Time Teacher; Articles, Poem, Biographies, Free Lance Writing Published; *home:* 12226 Shady Wood Ln SW Tacoma WA 98498

SOLECKI, MARCY (KOZACKI), Sixth Grade Teacher; *b:* Chicago, IL; *M:* James E.; *c:* Steve, Sandra; *ed:* (BA) Elem Ed, ID St Univ 1982; *cr:* 5th Grade Teacher 1982-87, 6th Grade Teacher 1987 Ethel Boyes Elem; *ai:* 6th Grade Track Coach; Jump Rope Coach; Jump Rope for Heart Coord; Stu Cncl Adv; IFEA Sch Rep 1982-; Rdng Cncl 1989-; *office:* Ethel Boyes Elem Sch 1875 Brentwood Idaho Falls ID 83402

SOLEIMANI, LIANE HARDING, 4th Grade Teacher; *b:* Provo, UT; *c:* Benjamin; *ed:* (BA) Ger, Brigham Young Univ 1961; (MED) Curr, Univ of UT 1984; *cr:* Teacher Weber HS 1962-63; Eliot JR HS 1963-64; Elem Foreign Lang Teacher Caly 1966-71; Teacher Terra Linda Elem 1973-; *ai:* Amer Mensa Gifted Child Prgm Coord 1987-; NEA/VEA; *office:* Terra Linda Elem Sch 3400 South 8400 West West Jordan UT 84088

SOLES, LAVERNE TUFARELLI, 7th Grade Science Teacher; *b:* Newark, NJ; *m:* Alfred Joseph; *ed:* (BA) Bio, Coll of St Elizabeth 1968; (MS) Ed, Monmouth Coll 1978; Natl Sci Fnd Grant for Bio, Biochemistry, Cell Physiology, Biophysics, Molecular Bio Stevens Inst of Tech; *cr:* Sci Teacher Neptune 1968-; *ai:* Cert Life Guard; 7th/8th Grade Bsktbl Coach 1972-73; Curr Steering Comm; Sci Fair Judge DE Valley Regional; NSTA 1979-; Contributing author for NSTA Sci Scope 1979-89; Published 4 books on Teaching Slow Learners.

SOLINSKI, DAWN MARIE, 2nd Grade Teacher; *b:* Owasso, MI; *m:* Michael; *ed:* (BA) Elem Ed, MI St Univ 1972; *cr:* 3rd Grade Teacher 1973-80, 2nd-3rd Grade Split Teacher 1980-81, 2nd GrAde Teacher 1981- Birch Run Area Schls; *home:* 12044 Oak St Birch Run MI 48415

SOLIS, LINDA KATHLEEN, 8th Grade Eng Teacher; *b:* Lyons, KS; *m:* Juan Jesus; *c:* Jaime; *ed:* (BA) Eng, Univ of TX 1969; (MS) Curr/Instruction, National Univ 1990; Working Towards Admin Credential; *cr:* Teacher Del Rio Jr HS 1969-75, Pierce Jr HS 1975-85, Pease Mid Sch 1985-87, Twin Peaks Mid Sch 1988, Pierce Mid Sch 1988-; *ai:* Drama Adv; Writing & Lang Art Consultant; CAP Writing Resource Teacher; ASCD 1989-, Lang Art Teacher Awd 1987; PTSA of Romona 1988-; 8th Grade Eng Manuals; *office:* Olive Peirce Mid Sch 1521 Hanson Ln Ramona CA 92065

SOLIZ, YOLANDA, Spanish Teacher; *b:* Kingsville, TX; *ed:* (BA) Span/Geography, TX A&I Univ 1975; (MA) Span/Linguistic Lit/Methodology, Univ of Houston 1986; Oral Proficiency Inst I & II Univ of TX San Antonio 1987 & Morelia Michoacan Mexico 1989; *cr:* Span Teacher Brazosport Ind Sch Dist 1976-87, Stafford MSD 1987-; Eng as Second Lang/Adult Ed/HCC Teacher Region IV; *ai:* Jr Var Chrldr Spon; All Span Extracurricular Act; TX Foreign Lang Assn 1976-; Amer Assn Teachers of Span & Portuguese 1987-.

SOLLOSI, TOM R., HS Mathematics Teacher; *b:* Monongahela, PA; *m:* Evelyn G.; *c:* Tommy, Timmy; *ed:* (THB) Theology, Baptist Bible Coll 1971; (MS) Ed Admin, Pensacola Chrstn Coll 1982; (MA) Prof Counseling, Liberty Univ 1988; Ed Specialist GA St Univ; *cr:* Teacher Pinewood Chrstn Acad; *ai:* Career, Marriage & Family, Academic Counseling; Testing & Evaluation; Amer Assn for Counseling & Dev 1988-; ASCD 1989-; Amer Cancer Society Chm 1989-.

SOLOMON, ALLEN, Mathematics Department Chair; *b:* Patton, PA; *m:* Rose Marie Baldini; *c:* Jill M. Wysocki, Patrick; *ed:* (BS) Math, 1962, (MS) Math, 1964 Indiana Univ of PA; Cmptr Stud; *cr:* Math Teacher Warren Jr HS 1962-63, Cntrl Cambria HS 1963-; *ai:* Class of 1991 Adv; Math Dept Chairperson; *office:* Cntrl Cambria Sr HS Rt 422 W Box 800 Ebensburg PA 15931

SOLOMON, DEBBIE ENTZ, Fifth Grade Teacher; *b:* Newton, KS; *m:* Ron; *c:* Erin, Tara, Kelly; *ed:* (BS) Elem Ed, KS St Univ 1975; (MS) Curr/Instruction, Emporia St Univ 1981; *cr:* 5th Grade Teacher 1977-80, Yates Center Elem 1982-; *ai:* Soc Sci Curr Chm; Delta Kappa Gamma, Woodson Assn of Teachers; Woodson Cty Cattle Women (Secy 1977-79, VP 1984-85, Pres 1988); MRB 4-H Club Cmmty Leader 1989-; United Meth Church Mem 1977-; *office:* Yates Center Elem Sch S Main Yates Center KS 66783

SOLOMON, PAUL HAMPTON, English Teacher; *b:* Sumter, SC; *m:* Josie Alice Randolph; *ed:* (BA) Scndry Ed, Clemson Univ 1983; Working Towards MS Rdng, Psych; *cr:* Teacher Furman HS 1984-85, Andrews HS 1985-; *ai:* Drama Club; Prom & Southern Assn Comm; Fine Arts Demonstrator; NCTE 1986-89; Georgetown Rdng Cncl VP 1988; Georgetown Cty Arts Commission 1988-; *office:* Andrews HS Alder Andrews SC 29510

SOLOMONSON, BETTY RYDEEN, Retired Elementary Teacher; *b:* Minnapolis, MN; *m:* Ernest H.; *c:* Barbara J. Peterson, Mary A. Leonard; *ed:* (BA) Ed, River Falls WI 1964; *cr:* Elem Teacher Grantsburg Schls 1966-86; *home:* 357 W Wisonson Ave Grantsburg WI 54840

SOMERS, KATHLEEN SNYDER, Commercial Foods Teacher; *b:* Elkin, NC; *m:* Ronald H.; *ed:* (BS) Home Ec Ed, 1975, (MED) Home Ec Ed, 1976 Univ NC Greensboro; *cr:* Commercial Foods Teacher Weaver Center 1978-; *ai:* FHA Natl Consultant & Local Adv; Dept Chairperson Weaver & Team Leader NC Vocats Comm; Amer Voc Assn, NCVA Pres Elect 1989-; HERO Alumni 1988-; NC Voc Assn Home Ec Division Pres Elect; Amer Red Cross Disaster Action Team 1990; Greensboro Public Schls Teacher of Yr 1986; Natl Restaurant Assn Teacher Work Study Grant 1988; *office:* Weaver Ed Center 300 S Spring St Greensboro NC 27401

SOMERVILLE, BERTHA OLGETREE, Second Grade Teacher; *b:* Lagrange, GA; *m:* Nathaniel Jr.; *c:* Rosalyn S. Terry, Dwayne, Valerie D.; *ed:* (BS) Music, Morris Brown Coll 1962; (MA) Elem Ed, Atlanta Univ 1969; *cr:* Music Teacher Beacon Elem Schls 1962-69; Elementary Teacher Atlanta Public Schls 1970-84; TEA Coord APS/Clark Coll 1984-85; 2nd Grade Teacher Hutchinson Sch 1984-; *ai:* Technology Contact Person; Discipline Comm Chairperson; GA Teachers Assn; Atlanta Assn of Educators; NAACP; NEA; Mount Moriah Bapt Church Courtesy Guild Sec; Braemar Neighborhood Club Pres 1988-; Distinguished Teaching Performance Awd 1989; Amer Red Cross Awd; *office:* Hutchinson Elem 650 Cleveland Ave SW Atlanta GA 30315

SOMMARS, EDNA M., Fourth Grade Teacher; *b:* Mounds, IL; *m:* Louis E.; *c:* Donna, Wayne, Patricia, Michael, Teresa; *ed:* (BS) Elem Ed, Southern IL Univ Edwardsville 1973; Master Catechist Religious Ed; Cmptr Trng, Alton HS; *cr:* Teacher St Ambrose Sch 1973-; *ai:* SIUE Alumni Assn (Mem 1973-, Prgm Chm 1983-85, Act Chm 1985-88); SIUE Advocate Prgm Mem; NCEA Teacher Assoc 1973-; Knights of Columbus Auxiliary (Pres 1988-89, Trustee 1989-); Natl Arbor Day Fnd Mem 1988-; Ed Advantage Awd 1988; Cath Ed Awd; *office:* St Ambrose Cath Sch 820 Homer Adams Pky Godfrey IL 62035

SOMMER, DEBORAH KELLY, Spanish Teacher; *b:* Great Lakes, IL; *c:* Lauren; *ed:* (BA) Span/Scndry Ed, James Madison Univ 1974; Foreign Lang Methodology, Univ of VA; Gabriel Garcia Marquez, VA Commonwealth Univ; Oral Profiency in Foreign Lang, Univ of VA; *cr:* Substitute Teacher Edison HS 1974; Span Teacher Davis Jr HS 1974-85, Bethel HS 1985-; *ai:* Span Club Spon; NHS Advisory Bd; Schlsp Comm; Colonial Uniserv (Chairperson 1986-88, Vice Chairperson, Treas), Distinguished Service 1981-89; Foreign Lang Assn of VA; Assn of Teachers of Span & Portuguese 1990; Hampton Ed Assn (Pres 1983-85, VP), Distinguished Service 1981-88; PTA 1978-; Hum Fellowship; *office:* Bethel HS 1067 Big Bethel Rd Hampton VA 23666

SOMMER, ELFRIEDE, Host Nation Teacher; *b:* Regensburg, West Germany; *ed:* (MA) Eng, 1980, (MA) Ger 1980, Univ of Regensburg; Grad Stud Bus Ed; *cr:* Teacher German HS 1980-82; Host Nation Teacher Grafenwohr Elem Sch 1982-; *ai:* Public Relations, Soc Sunshine, TAG Comms; *home:* Kirchaeckerstr 14 B 8480 Weiden Opf West Germany

SONAGGERA, ALAN A, Teacher; *b:* Mc Alester, OK; *ed:* (BA) His, Cntrl St Univ; Univ of CA, San Francisco St; *cr:* Teacher Booker T Washington HS 1969, Juan Crespi Jr HS 1969-; *ai:* United Teachers of Richmond Mentor Selection Comm; NEA Chairperson; *home:* 1000 Judah St #202 San Francisco CA 94122

SONCRANT, ROBERT LEO, 7th Grade Math Teacher; *b:* Boston, MA; *m:* Doris M.; *c:* Kristin, Rob, Keith; *ed:* (BS) Elem Ed, 1971, (MED) Fnd of Ed, 1974 Suffolk Univ; Math & Admin, Boston St Coll 1975-81; Math, Univ of MA 1981; Teaching Gifted Stu Emmanuel Coll 1974-75; Teaching Gifted & Talented TX Chrstn Univ 1987-; *cr:* Teacher Roger Walcott Elem 1971-75; Math Teacher Wilson Mid Sch 1975-82, Young Jr HS 1982-; *ai:* Masonic Lodge; PTA Teacher of Yr 1986-87; Teacher of Yr 1987-88; *office:* Young Jr H S 3200 Woodside Dr Arlington TX 76016

SONDERGAARD, JOAN RUMBLE, 5th Grade Soc Stud Teacher; *b:* Bridgeport, CT; *m:* Philmore M.; *ed:* (BS) Elem Ed, Cntrl CT St Univ 1960; (MS) Elem Ed, Univ of Bridgeport 1964; Certified Trainer Talents Unlimited Model; *cr:* 5th Grade Teacher 1960-63, 1st Grade Teacher 1963-75, 2nd Grade Teacher 1975-79, 3rd Grade Teacher 1979-80, Talented & Gifted Teacher 1980-82, 4th Grade Teacher 1982-85, 5th Grade Teacher 1985- Monroe Public Schls; *ai:* Joint Curr Comm; Soc Concerns Rep; 5th Grade Adv; Monroe Ed Assn Secy 1961-63; Delta Kappa Gamma Pres 1988-; Monroe Historical Society Curator 1984-, Distinguished Service Awd 1987; Monroe Bd of Ed Teacher of Yr 1985-86; CT Bd of Ed Teacher of Yr Finalist 1985-86; Co-Author 2 Booklets Old Sturbridge Village; *office:* Fawn Hollow Sch 345 Fan Hill Rd Monroe CT 06468

SONTAG, VIVIAN C., 5th Grade Teacher; *b:* Chicago, IL; *ed:* (BA) Sociology/General Ed, CA St Los Angeles 1963; (MA) Family/Child Therapy, CA Family Study Center 1989; Grad Studs Soc Psych, CA St Los Angeles; *cr:* Teacher Normandie Avenue Sch 1963-73; 5th Grade Teacher Colfax Avenue Sch 1973-; *ai:* Health & Sci Coord; UTLA Sch Rep 1983-86; NEA; Sierra Club 1983-; Assn of Amer Family Therapists; *office:* Colfax Avenue Sch 11724 Addison St North Hollywood CA 91607

SOOJIAN, PAUL KRIKOR, Grade 7 Science Teacher; *b:* Worcester, MA; *m:* Rhonda J. Gorham; *c:* Paul K. II, Katherine J.; *ed:* (BA) Bio, 1975 (MED) Admin, 1989 Worcester St Coll; *cr:* Teacher Memorial Mid Sch 1975-; *ai:* Yrbk Adv 1983; Spon of Natl Sci Olympiad; Mem of Sch Improvement Comm; Educl Assn of Leicester VP 1985-87; MA Teachers Assn 1975-; NEA 1975-; ASCD 1988-; Worcester St Coll & Coop Schls Exemplary Teacher of Sci; *home:* 1676 Main St Leicester MA 01524

SORACE-THOMAS, KAREN KAYE, Art Department Chairman; *b:* Cleveland, OH; *m:* George Stanton; *ed:* (BSED) Art Ed, 1970, (MED) Art Ed, 1989 Kent St Univ; Stu Teaching The Amer Sch of Paris France; *cr:* Art Dept Chm Holy Name HS 1971-; *ai:* Sr Class, Yrbk, Cheerleading, Newspaper, Art Club & Yr Video Adv; CHALTA Pres 1976-78; OH Art Ed Assn; Partners Diocesan Art Teachers Assn Co-Founder 1988-; Cleveland Museum of Art Mem; Kent St Alumni Assn; Designed, Developed & Wrote Workbook for Basic Design Classes Holy Name HS; *office:* Holy Name HS 6000 Queens Hwy Parma OH 44130

SORBEN, GERALDINE A., English & Latin Teacher; *b:* Fergus Falls, MN; *ed:* (BA) Eng, 1960, (BA) Art, 1960 Moorhead St Univ; (MA) Eng, Univ of UT 1972; *cr:* Eng/Speech Teacher Evansville HS 1960-62; Art/Eng Teacher Appleton MN Schls 1962-64; Art/Eng/Latin Teacher South HS 1964-88; Eng Teacher East HS 1988-; *ai:* Curr Dev for High Risk Stu; Spon of Academic Decathlon Team; NEA, UT Ed Assn, Salt Lake Teachers Assn; *office:* East HS 8405 1300 E Salt Lake City UT 84102

SORBER, BARBARA ANN, Computer/Mathematics Teacher; *b:* Wilkes, PA; *ed:* (BS) Math/Scndry Ed, Bloomsburg Univ 1975; Masters Equivalency, Grad Work Cmptr Sci & Math; *cr:* Teacher 1975-, Cmptr Chairperson 1989- Northwest HS; *ai:* Yrbk Cmptr Entry; Video Club; NEA, PSEA; *office:* Northwest HS RR 2 Shickshinny PA 18655

SORENSON, BARBARA KAY, 3rd Grade Teacher; *b:* Lansing, MI; *m:* Geoffrey Beckett; *c:* Colin P. Beckett; *ed:* (BA) Comm, Univ of MI 1972; (MA) Prof Teacher, Univ of S ME 1985; *cr:* 1st-4th Grade Art/Music Teacher Carman & Ainsworth Schls 1972-08; 3rd Grade Teacher Yarmouth Schls 1980-87, Baltimore Cty Schls 1987-88, Yarmouth Intermediate Sch 1988-; *ai:* Staff Dev Comm; *office:* Yarmouth Intermediate Sch Mc Cartney St Yarmouth ME 04096

SORENSON, JANICE EKMAN, Language Art Teacher; *b:* Littlefork, MN; *m:* William A.; *ed:* (AA) General Ed, Rainy River Jr Coll 1969; (BS) Eng, Bemidji St Coll 1971; Grad Stud St Cloud Univ, Hamline Univ; *cr:* Teacher Milaca Jr HS & Milaca Mid Sch; *ai:* Lang Art Dept Chairperson; NEA, MN Ed Assn, MN Assn of Mid Level Educators, MN Rdng Cncl; Son of Norway, Salem Luth Church; Milaca Teacher of Yr 1987-88; MN Assn Mid Level Educators Regional Conference Presented Homeroom Curr; Personal Effectiveness & Reflective Leadership Trng; *office:* Milaca Mid Sch 500 S W 4th St Milaca MN 56353

SORICE, WILLIAM CHARLES, Asst Principal/Reading Teacher; *b:* Chicago, IL; *m:* Lisa Ann; *c:* Kyle; *ed:* (BA) Philosophy, Univ of Cntrl FL 1984; *cr:* Phys Ed Teacher Good Shepherd 1973-78, St Andrew 1978-84; Hum/Rdng Teacher St Andrew 1984-; *ai:* Athletic Dir & Girls Var Bsktbl Coach; Dir Stations of the Cross Shadow Play Jr HS Talent Show; Facilities Coord Fall Festival; NCEA; *office:* St Andrew Sch 877 Hastings St Orlando FL 32808

SORKIN, NEAL B., Social Studies Teacher; *b:* Syracuse, NY; *m:* Carol Mary; *c:* Andrew D.; *ed:* (BA) Liberal Arts/Poly Sci, 1963, (MS) Soc Stud Ed, 1965 Syracuse Univ; Grad Stud Syracuse Univ; *cr:* 7th/8th Grade Soc Stud Teacher Roxboro RD Jr HS 1964-65; 8th Grade Soc Stud Teacher Jamesville-Dewitt Mid Sch 1966-; *ai:* Jamesville-Dewitt Tenure Seniority Comm 1976-; Jamesville-Dewitt Dist Evaluation Comm 1989-; Jamesville-Dewitt Mid Sch Prin Cabinet 1980-; Jamesville-Dewitt Faculty Assn Exec Comm 1968-; Jamesville-Dewitt Faculty Assn Rep NY St United Teachers Rep Assembly 1974-; Jamesville-Dewitt Faculty Assn Rep to Amer Fed of Teachers 1973-; Onondaga Cty Democratic Labor Advisory Comm 1988-; Onondaga Cty Teachers Assn Exec Comm 1970-;Onondaga Cty Ed Reform Network Mem 1988-; Onondaga Historical Assn Mem 1987-; Cntrl NY Cncl for Soc Stud Mem 1980-; NY St United Teachers Dist Dir 1974-; NY St Ed Dept Tenure Panel Pool 1976-; NY St Cncl for Soc Stud Mem 1980-; Greater Syracuse Labor Cncl Dir 1989-; NY St Labor His Assn Mem 1989-; NY St United Teachers Cntrl NY Poly Action Rep 1980-; Amer Poly Items Collectors Mem 1978-; Natl Assn for Advancement of Colored People Mem 1984-; Jamesville-Dewitt Faculty Assn Pres 1969-70; Onondaga Cty Teacher Assn Pres 1974-75; Onondaga Cty Mental Health Task Force 1973; Greater Syracuse Labor Cncl Trustee 1982-88; Alternate Delegate to Democratic Natl Convention 32nd Congressional Dist 1980, 27th Congressional Dist 1984; *home:* 6305 Danbury Dr Jamesville NY 13078

SORKNESS, THOMAS JOHN, Secondary Soc Studies Teacher; *b:* Fort Benton, MT; *m:* Lois D. Kent; *c:* Elisabeth, Kristiana, Erik, Louisa; *ed:* (BA) His, Gordon Coll 1980; Theology Courses Westminster Theology Seminary; Scndry Soc Stud Cert Prgm Temple Univ; Grad Courses Poly Sci Villanova Univ; *cr:* Scndry Soc Stud Teacher Philadelphia-Montgomery Chrstn Acad 1983-; *ai:* Orthodox Presbyn Church Ruling Elder 1988-; *office:* Phila-Montgomery Chrstn Acad 35 Hillcrest Ave Erdenheim PA 19118

SORRELL, CHARLOTTE PRICHARD, History Teacher; *b:* Halls, TN; *m:* Billy; *c:* Kelly; *ed:* (AS) General, Dyersburg St Comm Coll 1978; (BS) Scndry Ed, Univ of TN Martin 1980; (MA) His, Memphis St Univ 1986; *cr:* Teacher Washington Jr HS 1981-; Parttime Instr Dyersburg St Comm Coll; *ai:* Prof Dev Comm-Curr; Chairman Soc Stud Dept; Founder Washington Jr HS Honor Society; NCSS; MO St Teachers Assn; Caruthersville Cmmty Teachers Assn Secy 1984; Friends of Lib Dyersburg St Cmmty Coll; Dyersburg Cmmty Concert Assn; Baptist Stu Union Chm/Steering Comm; *home:* 2108 Starlight Dr Dyersburg TN 38024

SORRELL, MARK STEPHEN, 8th Grade His Teacher/Coach; *b:* Erwin, TN; *c:* Josh B.; *ed:* (BS) His/Poly Sci, Univ of TN Chattanooga 1974; (MED) Mid Grades Ed, Univ of GA 1989; *cr:* Teacher/Coach Elbert Long Jr HS 1975-76, Tyner Jr HS 1976-81, Westside Mid 1981-; *ai:* Ftbl & Wrestling Coach; Y Club Spon; NEA 1975-85; AFT 1985-; Civic War Roundtable 1980-; Bsbl Coach of Yr 1977-78, 1980-81; Teacher of Yr 1981.

SORRENTO, CHARLES ROBERT, Art Teacher; *b:* Boston, MA; *m:* Margaret Ann Sarjeant; *c:* Leslie M., Kimberly A.; *ed:* (BS) Applied Art, Northeastern Univ 1974; (MED) Art Ed, MA Coll of Art 1976; Fine Arts, Vesper George Sch of Art 1967; *cr:* Art Teacher Silver Lake Reg Jr HS 1976-81; Silver Lake Reg HS 1981-; *ai:* Jr HS Ftbl Coach 1977-80; HS Ftbl Coach 1981-86; HS Track 1984; Jr HS Bsktbl Coach 1977-80; Yrbk Adv HS 1987-88; VP HS Teachers Assn 1986-87; Exec Bd Mem HS Teachers Assn 1988-89; Silver Lake Reg Jr HS Teacher of Yr 1978.

SOSA, GRACIE, Mathematics Teacher; *b:* Loving, NM; *m:* Fidel; *c:* Marcos, Mario; *ed:* (BA) Math/Span, 1971, (MA) Math, 1976 E NM Univ; *cr:* Teacher Causey Public Schls 1971-72, Hagerman Public Schls 1972-74, Carrizzo Public Schls 1974-75, Hobbs Municipal Schls 1975-; *ai:* Stu Cncl & Math Team Spon; Delta Kappa Gamma (Corresponding Secy 1979-81, VP 1981-83) Outstanding Mem 1985; Hobbs HS Teacher of Yr 1986; *office:* Hobbs Municipal Schls 800 N Jefferson Hobbs NM 88240

SOSKIN, LAURIE WECHTER, Language Art Resource Teacher; *b:* Chicago, IL; *m:* Larry; *c:* Elizabeth; *ed:* (BA) Sociology, Univ of CA Los Angeles 1969; Various Continuing Ed Classes 1973-; Masters Prgm Curr, CA Luth 1989-; *cr:* 1st-6th Grade Teacher Mitchell Elem Sch 1972-88; Lang Art Resource Spec Teacher Sulphur Springs Sch 1988-; *ai:* Stu Cncl Adv 1986-; Dist & Site Inservices 1987-89; Curr Comms; Testwiseness Consultant 2 Dists; Santa Clarita Valley Rdng Cncl 1986-; Dist Teachers Assn (Pres 1979-80, Pres Elect 1978-79, Secy 1977-78); Temple Ahavat Shalom Mem Bd of Trustees 1988-; Classroom Teacher Instructional Improvement Grant 1986-87; Mentor Teacher 1987-; *office:* Sulphur Springs Sch 16628 Lost Canyon Canyon Country CA 91351

SOTO, JOYCE ANN, Physical Education Teacher; *b:* Ann Arbor, MI; *m:* Juan Daniel; *c:* Gina M. Reed, Amy J. Reed, Michael J. Reed, Jennifer D.; *ed:* (BS) Phys Ed/Bio, Pan Amer Univ 1979; (MED) Educl Admin, Univ of TX 1990 *cr:* Teacher/Dance Team Dir Mc Allen HS 1979-81; Teacher/Coach Lamar Jr HS 1981-85, Morris Jr HS 1985-; *ai:* Girls Vlybl & Bsktbl Coach; TAPHER Mem 1975-84; TX Coaches Assn Mem Dist Championships Coaching Awd 1981-; Assn of TX Prof Educators (Mem, Building Contact) 1985-; Parent Teacher Stu Assn Mem 1985-89; Natl Youth Sports Prgm Mem Univ of TX 1985-87; Natl Deans List; Mc Allen Ind Sch Dist 5 Yr & 10 Yr Teaching Awd; *home:* 2909 Pelican Mc Allen TX 78504

SOUCIE, ELIZABETH ANN (FRANTZ), Spanish/Soc Stud Teacher; *b:* Lake Charles, LA; *m:* Dennis M.; *c:* Damon M., Denton T.; *ed:* (BA) His, CO St Coll 1970; Grad Stud, Univ N CO & Chadron St Coll; *cr:* Span/Soc Stud Teacher Lodgepole HS 1970-78, 1980-; *ai:* Concessions; Chrldrs; Phi Sigma Iota; *home:* HC 65 Box 108 Lodgepole NE 69149

SOUCY, BARBARA J. (STONE), Fourth Grade Teacher; *b:* Oneida, KS; *c:* Anne M. Soucy-Brinsmead, Alissa Soucy-Mc Bride; *ed:* (BA) Eng, Washburn Univ 1955; Grad Work Eng Composition, Univ of NH 1986; *cr:* 3rd Grade Teacher Central Park Sch 1955-57, Midview Sch Dist 1970-72; 3rd & 4th Grade Teacher Lake Ridge Acad 1972-; *ai:* Lower Sch Soc Stud Comm Chm.

SOUDERS, JAMES A., Band Director/Dept Head; *b:* Chattanooga, TN; *m:* Jensi Peck; *ed:* (BS) Instrumental Music, Mid TN St Univ 1969; *cr:* Band Dir Lakeview-Ft Oglethorpe HS 1969-; *ai:* GA Music Educators Assn Instrumental Chm 1988-; Natl Band Assn 1985-; Cty & Sch STAR Teacher 1983; Mid TN St Univ Band of Blue Hall of Fame 1988; *office:* Lakeview-Ft Oglethorpe HS Battlefield Pkwy. Fort Oglethorpe GA 30742

SOULES, BOBBY JEAN, 3rd Grade Teacher; *b:* Aledo, TX; *m:* Marion L.; *c:* Stephen, Timothy; *ed:* (BA) Ed, N TX Univ 1957; Bus Trng, Art; *cr:* Soc Stud/7th Grade Teacher Burleson HS; Eng Teacher Azle HS 1960, Quinlon HS; 4th Grade Teacher Hyde Park Elem; 5th Grade Teacher Thackerville OK; 3rd/4th Grade Teacher Lincoln Elem; *ai:* Personnel Comm; *office:* Lincoln Elem Sch P O Box 479 Lincoln AR 72744

SOUSA, MARIA, Fourth Grade Teacher; *b:* Azores, Portugal; *m:* Lino Correia; *c:* Lino Jr., Tony C.; *ed:* Ed Natl 1961; (BA) Fr - Cum Laude, Coll of Notre Dame 1972; Standard Teaching Credential K-9th Bi-ling Cross Cultural Institution; *cr:* Teacher Five Wounds Sch, Anne Darling Sch; *ai:* Five Wounds Sch Appreciation Awd 1984.

SOUTH, LUCINDA MARY, Sociology Teacher; *b:* Bradford, PA; *ed:* (BA) Soc Stud, Mansfield St UNiv 1970; (MED) Admin/Supervision, Univ of South FL 1984; Beginning Teacher Prgm, Learning Channels, Collegial Coaching; Teachers as Advisors Prgm; Southern Assoc of Coll & Schls; Sec Ed, PA St Univ; *cr:* Teacher Sch Street Jr HS 1970-74, Hudson Sr HS 1974-78, Dept Head/Teacher Hudson Sr HS 1976-78, Ridgewood HS 1978-86; *ai:* Foreign Study Adv, Coord & Chaperone Stu European Travel & Study Prgm for Coll Credit; Faculty Advisory & Rdng Comm; Pasco Cty Rep to Ec Ed Center; Pasco Ctys Outstanding Soc Stud Teacher of Yr; Outstanding Young Woman of America; DAR Outstanding Amer His Teacher; *office:* Ridgewood HS 2401 Orchid Lake Rd New Port Richey FL 34652

SOUTHER, DORIS HUNTER, Second Grade Teacher; *b:* Blairsville, GA; *w:* Warren R. (dec); *c:* William R., Roxanne Barrett, Christopher; *ed:* Elem Ed, Young Harris Coll 1945; (BA) Elem Ed, N GA Coll 1974; (MED) Elem Ed, N GA Coll & Univ of GA 1976; *cr:* Teacher Town Creek Elem 1945-50; Para Prof 1968-70, Teacher 1974- Union Cty Elem; *ai:* NEA, GAE (Pres 1979-80, Membership Comm 1984-88, Building Rep 1986-) 1974-; Delta Kappa Gamma (Personal Growth & Services Comm, Public Relations Comm 1988-; Alpha Delta Kappa Membership Comm 1988; Union General Hospital Authority Bd 1986-.

SOUTHER, NEIL CLIFFORD, Latin Teacher; *b:* Minot, ND; *ed:* (BA) Fr/Latin, Univ of ND 1961; (MA) Fr, Middlebury Coll 1968; Classical Stu Teresianum Rome Italy; *cr:* Fr/Latin Teacher Valley City HS 1961-63, Tabor Acad 1964-65; Fr/Latin/Span Teacher Bismarck Public Schls 1965-76, 1977-; *ai:* St Pres of Jr Classical League; Sch Latin Club Adv Bismarck; St Librarian Part Time St Penitentiary; Foreign Lang Assn of ND, Latin Liturgy Assn, AATF, Amer Classical League, NEA, NDEA, BEA 1966-; Phi Beta Kappa 1961; Classical Assn of Mid West & South Good Teaching Awd 1987; 1 of 2 Latin Teachers Geographical Area; Rockefeller F L Awd 1988; NEH Grant to Study Cicero ST Olaf 1989.

SOUTHERLAND, GINNY KITE, English Teacher; *b:* Greeneville, TN; *ed:* (BS) Eng, E TN St Univ 1967; Numerous Courses, Walters St Coll & Univ of TN; *cr:* Teacher Bulls Gap Elem Sch 1966-67, Witt Elem Sch 1967-68, Hawkins Elem Sch 1968-72, Bulls Gap Mid Sch 1972-; *ai:* Spon Sch Paper, Stu Cncl, Yrbk, Spring Fling, Scholastic Banquet, 8th Grade Night; Hawkins Cty Ed Assn 1967-; ETEA, NEA, TEA; Delta Kappa Gamma Parlimentarian 1988-; Trinity United Meth Church Pianist 1976-; Hamblen Cty Humane Society Mem, Phi Mu; TN Instructional Model Teacher; Effective Questioning Wkshp; *office:* Bulls Gap Mid Sch Allen Dr Bulls Gap TN 37711

SOUTHERLIN, CAROLYN ROSSI, English Dept Chair; *b:* Waterbury, CT; *m:* David M.; *ed:* (BA) Eng, Univ of CT 1968; (MA) Eng, W CT St Coll 1973; Several Wkshps Brigham Young Univ, Univ of UT, UT St Univ; *cr:* Eng Teacher Watertown HS 1968-75, Carl Winters Mid Sch 1977-80, Wasatch HS 1980-; *ai:* NHS & Sr Class Adv; Eng Dept Chairperson; Advanced Placement Coord; Academic Decathlon Coach; NCTE 1980-; UEA, NEA Faculty Rep 1980-; PC Fire Dist (Secy 1979-87, Commissioner 1987-89); UT Writing Project 1981; *office:* Wasatch HS 64 E 600 S Heber City UT 84032

SOUTHERN, ALAN RICHARD, Science Teacher/Dept Chair; *b:* Lewiston, ID; *ed:* (BS) Scndry Ed/Earth Sci, Univ of ID 1985; Grad Work ID St Univ, Boise St Univ; *cr:* 7th/8th Grade Sci Teacher 1985-, Dept Chm 1988- Mountain View Mid Sch; *ai:* Building Public Relations Comm Chairperson; Coordinating Cncl; Credit Review Comm; ID Sci Teachers Assn Outstanding Region Mid Sch Sci Teacher 1989; BlacKfoot Ed Assn St Delegate 1986-; Natl Earth Sci Teachers Assn; Elks Outstanding Teacher of Month 1987; Dist 55 Teacher of Month 1988; Building Teacher of Yr 1988-89; *office:* Mountain View Mid Sch Rt 3 Box 429 Blackfoot ID 83221

SOUTHERN, E.R., JR., Counselor; *b:* Middlesboro, KY; *m:* Dorothy Jean Seal; *c:* Adam W., Eve M., Leslie E.; *ed:* (BA) Sociology, Lincoln Memorial Univ 1971; (MA) Ed Curr/Inst, Univ of TN 1985; Trng for Career Ladder Teachers; *cr:* Classroom Teacher 1971-86, Sex Equity Coord 1986-87, Cnslr 1987- Hancock Cty HS; *ai:* Beta Club & Soph Class Spon; TN Cattlemen Assn 1980-; Hancock Livestock Assn Dir 1975-; Outstanding Young Men of America 1971; *home:* Rt 2 Box 173 Sneedville TN 37869

SOUTHERN, JAMES TERRY, English Teacher; *b:* Haleyville, AL; *m:* Brenda Gay Rice; *c:* Craig A., Jason L.; *ed:* (BS) Eng/His, Univ of N AL 1967; (MA) Eng, Univ of AL 1970; Information Officer Basic Course, Defense Information Sch Ft Benjamin 1972; *cr:* Eng Teacher NW AL St Jr Coll 1969-71; Writer/Ed US Army Missile Command Redstone Arsenal & US Army Aviation Systems Command 1971-74; Research Assoc/Ed Center for Bus & Ec Research Univ of AL 1975-80; Eng/Soc Stud Teacher Northside HS 1980-81; Eng Teacher Hale Cty HS 1981-82, Hillcrest HS 1982-; *ai:* Jr Class Spon; NEA, AL Ed Assn 1980-; Tuscaloosa Cty Ed Assn Rep 1982-89; Kappa Delta Pi 1982-; ASCD 1983-88; NEH Summer Inst 1988, 1990.

SOVA, JOYCE SPRAGUE, Fifth Grade Teacher; *b:* Malone, NY; *m:* Leon; *c:* Greg, Jeff, Alan, Kerry; *ed:* (BS) Elem Ed, SUNY Plattsburgh 1962; Grad Stud Russell Sage Troy NY; *cr:* 4th Grade Teacher N Syracuse NY 1962-63; 2nd Grade Teacher Salmon River Cntrl 1963-64; Kndgtn Teacher Malone NY 1966-67; 5th Grade Teacher Saratoga Springs NY 1968-; *ai:* Worked with Stu Teachers from Several Area Colls; *office:* Caroline Street Elem Sch 310 Caroline St Saratoga Springs NY 12866

SOWDEN, EILEEN L., 2nd Grade Teacher; *b:* Palmerton, PA; *m:* Ronald L.; *ed:* (BS) Elem Ed, Kutztown Univ 1964; *cr:* 2nd Grade Teacher Lehighton Area Sch Dist 1964-; *office:* Lehighton Area Schls 200 Beaver Run Rd Lehighton PA 18235

SOWELL, JOYCE BANKS, Social Studies/Reading Teacher; *b:* New Brockton, AL; *m:* Gary; *c:* Quinton A., Antonia R.; *ed:* (BS) Soc Sci/Soc Stud, Fayetteville St Univ 1980; *cr:* Pre-Sch/Kndgtn Teacher Kindercare Learning Center 1980; Employment Interviewer Employment Security Commission 1980-81; Substituete Teacher Dept of Defence Dependent Schls 1981-85; Teacher Morgan Road Mid Sch 1986-; *ai:* Morgan Road Mid Sch Yrbk Adv 1988-89; Current Event Ralley Sch Coord 1988-; PTA Rep; *office:* Morgan Road Mid Sch 3635 Hiers Rd Hephzibah GA 30815

SOWRI, AROKIADOSS, Science Teacher; *b:* Bhavanisagar, India; *m:* Patsy; *c:* Anand, Rakesh; *ed:* (BS) Physics, Univ of Madras India 1974; (MS) Physics, Annamalai Univ India 1977; (BED) Ed, Annamalai Univ India 1980; *cr:* Physics & Math Teacher Fatima & NLC High Schs Neyveli India 1979-80; Physics Teacher Holy Childhood HS Kingston Jamaica VI 80-81; Math & Science Teacher PiersonHS Turks & Caicos Islands VI 1981-86; Research Assistant F3X Chase Cancer Ctr 1986-87; Physics/Chem Teacher St Maria Goretti HS 1987-; *ai:* Soccer Coach; Judge Delaware Valley Sci Fairs; Research Work Published Journal of Biomolecular Structure & Dynamics; *office:* St Maria Goretti H S 10th & Moore St Philadelphia PA 19148

SPACHT, IRENE, OSB, 8th Grade Teacher; *b:* Erie, PA; *ed:* (BA) Elem Ed, Mercyhurst Coll 1970; (MED) Sch Counseling, Edinboro Univ 1985; *cr:* 5th Grade Teacher St Joseph Sch 1959-60; 2nd Grade Teacher Sacred Heart Sch 1960-61; 6th Grade Teacher Mt Calvary Sch 1961-62; 2nd Grade Teacher St Michael Sch 1962-63; 6th-8th Grade Teacher St Joseph Sch 1963-66; 7th Grade Teacher St Stephen Sch 1966-67; 9th/12th Grade Math Teacher Venango Chrstn HS 1967-77; 7th/8th Grade Teacher St Gregory Sch 1977-; *ai:* Amer Counseling & Dev, Intnl Rdng Assn; NE Cmmty Fair Assn; *home:* 6101 E Lake Rd Erie PA 16511

SPADA, RICHARD E., Social Studies/ESL Teacher; *b:* Port Jervis, NY; *c:* Ella M., Richard E. Jr.; *ed:* (BA) Ed, SUNY Brockport 1967; (MS) Ed Environmental Emphasis, SUNY New Paltz 1980; *cr:* Teacher Ellenville Elem 1967-68; Sales Various Companies 1968-77; Teacher Rondout Valley Cntrl Sch 1977-80, Ellenville HS 1980-; *ai:* Sr Class & Ski Club Adv; Advisory Cabinet 1982-86; Summer Curr Comm 1980-86, 1988-; NHS Induction Comm 1987-; *office:* Ellenville HS 28 Maple Ave Ellenville NY 12428

SPADE, LARRY EDWIN, Intermediate Math Teacher; *b:* Lewistown, PA; *m:* Vicki Diann Ritzman; *c:* Shelbee Guyer, Randy Guyer; *ed:* (BS) Scndry Ed, Penn St Univ 1970; *cr:* 4th-6th Grade Soc Stud/Math Teacher Fayette Elem Sch 1971-89; *ai:* Little League Bsbl Coach 1971-74; Juniata Cty Ed Assn 1974-; BSA Scoutmaster Troop 65 1973-; Fayette Lions Club (Secy 1974,

1977, Pres 1975) 1973-; *office:* Fayette Elem Sch Schl St Mc Alisterville PA 17049

SPAGNUOLO, JOHN RALPH, Biology Teacher; *b:* Wilkes Barre, PA; *m:* Marie Ellen Corcoran; *c:* John, Deborah; *ed:* (BS) Bio, Kings Coll 1964; (MS) Scndry Ed, Univ of Scranton 1969; Grad Stud Penn St Univ, Wilkes Univ, Bucknell Univ, Temple Univ, Univ of Rochester Sch of Medicine & Dentistry; *cr:* Sci Teacher High Bridge Jr/Sr HS 1964-65; Sci Teacher 1965-81, Bio Teacher 1981- E L Meyers HS; *ai:* Luzerne Cty Sci Teachers Assn; Wilkes Barre Ed Assn Membership Chm 1968-71; PA St Ed Assn, NEA; Knights of Columbus Cncl 302; *office:* Elmer L Meyers HS Carey Ave & Hanover Sts Wilkes-Barre PA 18702

SPAHN, ETHEL PARKLLAN, Cont. Family Studies Teacher; *b:* Detroit, MI; *c:* Richard, Karen, Elise B. Slaughter, William; *ed:* (BA) Family Stud/Consumer Sci, 1963, (MA) Ed, 1970 San Diego St Univ; *cr:* Educator San Diego Unified Sch Dist 1963-; *ai:* Hospitality Class; Amer Home Ec Assn (St, Local) 1961-; Intnl Fed of Home Economists, NEA, CA Teachers Assn, San Diego Teachers Assn 1963-; San Diego Zoological Society, Lambs Players, House of Pacific Relations; FHA HERO; Greater San Diego Cncl for Industry & Ed Awd for Outstanding Teacher; *home:* 3836 Vista Grande Dr San Diego CA 92115

SPAID, JOSEPH S., Government/Economics Teacher; *b:* Lyons, NY; *m:* Patricia; *c:* Joseph, John, Sarah; *ed:* (MS) Guidance, Syracuse Univ 1962; *cr:* Asst Prin G Ray Bodley HS 1974-78; Teacher Lakeside Jr HS & Mc Duffie HS 1969-; *ai:* NHS Adv; YMCA Model Stu Legislature; Mc Duffie Sch Improvement Cncl Mem; Anderson Ed Assn Pres; Habitat for Humanity Working Volunteer Carpenter 1985-; Mc Duffie HS Teacher of Yr 1988-89; *office:* Mc Duffie HS 1225 S Mc Duffie St Anderson SC 29624

SPAIN, MARIE ROBERTSON, Teacher of Gifted; *b:* Booneville, MS; *m:* Billy O.; *c:* William L., Laura Spain Harber, David A.; *ed:* (BAE) Eng, Univ of MS 1960; Gifted Ed Cert, MS St Univ 1979; *cr:* 9th-12th Grade Eng Teacher Marietta HS 1960-62; 6th-8th Grade Eng Teacher Hills Chapel Attendance Center 1962-64; Eng Teacher Booneville Jr HS 1964-79; Gifted Ed Teacher Anderson Jr HS 1979-83, Booneville HS 1983-; *ai:* Adv Sch Newspaper The Hi-Boone & Literary Magazine Touche; Future Problem Solving Club Spon; Intermediate & Sr Division Future Problem Solving Prgm Teams Coach; Prentiss Cty Teachers Assn Pres; MS Assn of Educators, NEA, MS Assn of Talented & Gifted; Delta Kappa Gamma Society Pres 1980-82; United Meth Women Spec Life Membership; 1st United Meth Church Teacher of Yr 1983; Runner-Up MS Teacher of Yr 1980; Booneville HS & Prentiss Cty Recipient Phi Delta Kappa Educator of Yr Awd 1986; Booneville HS STAR Teacher 1988; *home:* Rt 2 Box 140 Booneville MS 38829

SPAITH, KAREN CONKLIN, Facilitator Gifted Education; *b:* Kansas City, KS; *ed:* (BSE) Eng/Soc Sci, 1968, (MS) Soc Sci, 1975 Emporia St Univ; (MS) Spec Ed/Gifted, KS St Univ 1981; *cr:* Classroom Teacher 1968-80, Gifted Ed Teacher 1980-86 Trailridge Jr HS; Gifted Ed Teacher Shawnee Mission Northwest 1986-; *ai:* NEA Life Mem; KEA 1968-; Shawnee Mission Ed Assn 1968-; Phi Delta Kappa 1989-; KS Assn for Gifted/Talented 1988-; Shawnee Mission Assn for Gifted 1985-; PTA 1968-; Fellow Society of Antiquaries of Scotland 1988-; Amer MENSA Ltd Regional Coord for Gifted Children 1989-; Amer MENSA Ltd Annual Gathering Steering Comm 1989-; Mid America MENSA Pres 1990; Kansas City Saint Andrew Society 2nd VP 1989-; Kansas City Highland Games Bd of Dir 1988-89; Robert Burns Study Group Secy 1986-; Monticello Historical Society Charter Mem 1989-; Ed of Two Editions; Articles & Poetry Published; *office:* Shawnee Mission Northwest Sch 12701 W 67th St Shawnee Mission KS 66216

SPALDING, ALLEN CARL, 5th Grade Science Teacher; *b:* Detroit, MI; *c:* Kirsten, Tyler; *ed:* (BA) Math/Sci, N MI Univ 1973; (MA) Outdoor Recreation, Cntrl MI Univ 1988; Certified Hunter Safety Instr & Scuba Diver; Federal Bird Bander; *cr:* 6th Grade Sci Teacher Coleman Mid Sch 1973-82; 5th Grade Sci Teacher Coleman Elem Sch 1982-; *ai:* Elem Sci Coord; Hunter Safety Instr; Coleman Ed Assn (Grievance Chm 1982-, VP 1987-); Wildlife Recovery Assn 1988-; Inland Bird Bander Assn 1987-; Natl Rifle Assn 1986-; MI Bow Hunters 1978-; Safari Club Intnl Summer Outdoor Ed Seminar; *office:* Coleman Elem Sch Box W Coleman MI 48618

SPANG, JAMES CHARLES, English Teacher; *b:* Lancaster, PA; *m:* Barbara Fay Mc Lean; *c:* Stephen; *ed:* (BS) Eng, Millersville Univ 1967; MS Candidate, Cnslr Ed, W MD Coll; *cr:* 11th-12th Grade Eng Teacher Susquehannock Jr/Sr HS 1967-68; 7th-8th Grade Eng Teacher Southern Mid Sch 1968-; *ai:* Chess Club Spon; NEA 1967-; Amer Psychological Assn, Amer Assn for Counseling & Dev 1989-; Knights of Columbus Secy 1987-; Self Study Chm for Sch Evaluation 1986; *office:* Southern Mid Sch P O Box 128 Glen Rock PA 17327

SPANGLER, DANIEL LEROY, JR., History Teacher/Athletic Dir; *b:* Mt Vernon, IL; *m:* Melanie Duckworth; *c:* Elizabeth; *ed:* (AS) Bus, Rend Lake Coll 1985; (BS) Phys Ed, Southwest Baptist Univ 1988; *cr:* Teacher/Athletic Dir Englewood Chrstn Sch 1988-; *ai:* Girls Var Vlybl, Bsktbl, Bsbl Coach; *office:* Englewood Chrstn Sch 10628 Winner Rd Independence MO 64052

SPANGLER, HARRIET CALDWELL, Mathematics Teacher/ Dept Chair; *b:* Bristol, TN; *m:* Otto M.; *c:* Chuck, Victor, Elizabeth Grubbs; *ed:* (BS) Math, Carson-Newman 1958; (MS) Admin, Nova Univ 1978; *cr:* Math Teacher Western Jr HS 1958-59; Math/Physics Teacher Cntrl HS 1960-61; Math Teacher Ballard Cty HS 1966-67, Lone Oak HS 1967-72, Newberry HS 1972-; *ai:* Steering Comm; Delta Kappa Gamma (2nd VP 1988-, 1st VP 1990); First Baptist Church (Sunday Sch Teacher 1973-88, Deacon 1990); *office:* Newberry HS P O Box 339 Newberry FL 32669

SPANGLER, PAMELA KAREN, Spec Admin Assignment Teacher; *b:* Faribault, MN; *ed:* (BS) Health/Phys Ed, Moorhead St Univ 1971; (MED) Developmental Phys Ed, Univ of MN 1983; Ed Admin License, St Thomas Coll 1990; *cr:* Health Instr Rosemount Sr HS 1971-72; Health/Phys Ed Coach Valley Mid Sch 1972-78; Health/Adapted Phys Ed Coach Osseo Jr & Sr HS 1978-89; Admin Asst Osseo Sr HS 1989-; *ai:* MN Essential Learner Outcomes; MN Cmptr Assessment Comm; Intramurals Supvr; MN Assn of Health, Phys Ed VP Health 1982-86, Carl Knutson St Health Educator Awd 1989; St Prof Organization (VP, Secy), Presenter Various Wkshps; *office:* Osseo Sch Dist #279 317 2nd Ave NW Osseo MN 55369

SPANGLER, STEPHEN RAY, 6th Grade Teacher; *b:* Middlesboro, KY; *m:* Anita Lynn; *ed:* (BA) Phys Ed, 1981, (MA) Sports Admin, 1986 E Ky Univ; *cr:* Chapter 1 Math/Rdng Teacher West End Elem 1983-85; Chapter 1 Math Teacher Middlesboro Mid Sch 1985-86; Grad Asst E KY Univ 1986; 6th Grade Teacher Middlesboro Mid Sch 1986-; *ai:* 8th Grade Boys Bsktbl & Asst HS Bsbl Coach; KY Ed Assn, NEA, KY Coaches Assn; Outstanding Young Men of America; *home:* 610 1/2 S 24th St Middlesboro KY 40965

SPANN, SAMUEL CLEOTHO, Music/Art Teacher; *b:* Jackson, TN; *ed:* (BA) Music, Lane Coll 1955; (MS) Music, TN St Univ 1965; Univ of CA Los Angeles, Pepperdine, Cal Poly Pomond, La Verne Univ; European Ind Study in 13 Countries; *cr:* Music/Eng Teacher Barrets Chapel HS 1956-67; Vice Prin Victory Baptist Day Sch 1967; 6th Grade/Music Teacher 1967-74, Music/Art Teacher 1974- Garvey Int Sch; *ai:* Garvey Choir Dir; Recorder Players Guild; Mustang Singers Keyboardist; GTA VP 1969-70; NCTE 1970-; MENC 1974-; NEA 1956-; John Wood Masonic Lodge Secy 1970-; Most Worshipful Sons of Light Grand Lodge 1970-; Alpha Phi Alpha 1953-; PTA Awd 1989; Outstanding Elem Teacher of America Awd 1973; Garvey Dist Teacher of Yr 1988; Soroptimist Intnl of Monterey Park Awd 1989; *home:* 9116 5th Ave Inglewood CA 90305

SPARACCIO, KATHLEEN, English Teacher; *b:* Rockville Centre, NY; *m:* Salvatore Paul; *c:* Salvatore P., Nicholas D.; *ed:* (BA) 7th-12th Grade Eng Ed, Molloy Coll 1981; (MS) Rdng, Adelphi Univ 1988; *cr:* Eng Teacher Maria Regina Diocesan HS 1981-84, Holy Trinity Diocesan HS 1984-; Writing Teacher Nassau Comm Coll 1986-; *ai:* Literary Society; Phi Theta Kappa Active Mem 1977-79, Schlsp Money Awd 1979-81; Lambda Iota Tau Active Mem 1980-81; Deans List 1977-87.

SPARACCIO, KATHLEEN MALONE, English Teacher; *b:* Rockville Centre, NY; *m:* Salvatore Paul; *c:* Salvatore P., Nicholas D.; *ed:* (BA) Eng Ed, Molloy Coll 1981; (MS) Rdng, Adelphi Univ 1988; *cr:* Eng Teacher Maria Regina HS 1981-84, Holy Trinity 1984-; Writing Teacher Nassau Comm Coll 1986-; *ai:* Literary Society; Phi Theta Kappa Active Mem 1979, Natl Jr Coll Honor Society Schlsp 1977-79; Lambda Iota Tau Active Mem 1980-81; Deans List 1977-81.

SPARACIO, CELIA, Spanish Teacher; *b:* Camden, NJ; *m:* George; *c:* Melissa Pancari; *ed:* (BA) Span Ed, Douglass Coll of Rutgers 1967; (MA) Gifted Ed, Widener 1983; Span Advanced Placement, Bates Coll; Gifted Ed; *cr:* Span Teacher 1967-, Gifted/ Talented Coord 1983- Delsea Regional HS; *ai:* 1990 Class Adv; Academic Decathlon, Olympics of Mind Coach; City Sch of Excl, S Gloucester Cty Municipal Alliance Comm; Teen Arts Cty Coord; NJEA 1967-; NJE Gifted & Talented (Secy 1982) 1981-; NAGC 1987-; Delsea Regional Teacher of Yr 1989-; *office:* Delsea Regional HS Blackwoodtown Rd Franklinville NJ 08322

SPARE, PATRICIA KANIA, Fifth Grade Teacher; *b:* Stafford Springs, CT; *m:* Mark; *c:* Christine, Jennifer, William; *ed:* (BA) Elem Ed, 1974, (MS) Elem Ed, E CT Univ; Cooperative/Mentor Teacher Prgm; *cr:* 2nd/3rd/5th Grade Teacher Center Road Sch 1975-; *office:* Center Road Sch 20 Center Rd Vernon-Rockville CT 06066

SPARGUR, LORA REEVES, Grade 5/6 Academically/Talentd; *b:* Charlottesville, IN; *m:* Charles Erwin; *c:* Ramona; *ed:* (BS) Elem Ed, 1968, (MS) Elem Ed 1970 Butler Univ; *cr:* 2nd Grade Teacher MSD Wayne Township 1968-69; 4th-6th Grade Teacher Indpls Pub Schls 1969-; Soc Stud Methods Teacher IN/Purdue Univ Indianapolis 1987-; *ai:* Cmptr Resource Teacher; His Fair Act Local St Natl; St His Fair Judge; Partner in Ed; Project Enable; Academically Talented Screening Comm; IN Assn of Teacher Educators; Delta Kappa Gamma; IN Sch Women; Natl Cncl Teachers of Soc Stud; IN St Teachers Assn St Rep; IL Jamalie (Pres 1980, VP 1979, Sec 1978); Lilly Fellowship Intensive Study of Cmptrs; ABCD Awd; Teacher of Yr Finalist; Won Trip to Washington DC Pres Essay; Won Trip to Disney World Geography Video; *office:* Lew Wallace Schl 107 3307 Ashway Dr Indianapolis IN 46224

SPARKMAN, CAROLYN HOPKINS, 5th Grade Soc Stud Teacher; *b:* Texarkana, TX; *m:* Billy; *c:* Scott, Shannon, Sharon; *ed:* (BSE) Elem Ed - Cum Laude, S AR Univ 1970; (MED) Elem Ed, E TX St Univ Texarkana 1976; Post Grad Work E TX St Univ Texarkana; *cr:* 5th Grade Soc Stud Teacher Pleasant Grove Elem 1970-86, Pleasant Grove Mid Sch 1986-; Ed Dept Adjunct Faculty Mem E TX St Univ Texarkana 1986-; *ai:* UIL 5th Grade Listening Team Coach; Stu Store Spon; TX Classroom Teachers Assn 1985-; Delta Kappa Gamma Membership Chm 1988-; ASCD 1989-; Rose Hill Baptist Church (Bible Stud Teacher, Childrens Division Dir) 1953-; *office:* Pleasant Grove Mid Sch 5605 Cooks Ln Texarkana TX 75503

SPARKS, CAROLYN JEAN, Second Grade Teacher; *b:* Paintsville, KY; *ed:* (BA) Elem, 1967, (MA) Elem, 1977, Elem, MSU 1980; *cr:* Teacher Blaine 71-; *ai:* LCEA L Cty Teacher of Yr 1983-84; *home:* HC 81 Box 785 Blaine KY 41124

SPARKS, CATHERINE JANE, Kindergarten Teacher; *b:* Paintsville, KY; *ed:* (AB) Elem Ed, Berea Coll 1969; (MA) Early Chldhd Ed, E KY Univ 1977; *cr:* Spec Ed Teacher 1969-70, 3rd Grade Teacher 1970-73, 4th Grade Teacher 1973-76, Kndgtn Teacher 1977-78, 1st Grade Teacher 1978-79 Oil Springs Elem; Kndgtn Teacher Cntrl Elem 1979-80, Oil Springs Elem 1979-; *ai:* Co-Spon of Yrbk; KEA; PTA (Secy, Treas) 1989-; *office:* Oil Springs Elem Sch Rt 40 Oil Springs KY 41238

SPARKS, EDWIN CLAUDE, JR., 6th Grade Science Teacher; *b:* Nashville, TN; *m:* Jane May; *c:* Edwin C. III, Corey S.; *ed:* (BA) His, 1965, (MA) His, 1969 Mid TN St Univ; Post Grad Work Ed; *cr:* His/Poly Sci Teacher Martin Jr Coll 1968-69; Algebra/His Teacher Whitwall HS 1969; 8th Grade His Teacher Waverly Jr HS 1970-72; World His/Amer His/Eng Teacher Waverly Cntrl HS 1972-75; Homebound Instr Humphreys Cty 1975-81; 6th Grade Teacher Waverly Jr HS 1981-; *ai:* Statewide US His Day Act Stu Spon 1981-; Humphreys Cty Ed Assn (Pres Elect, Pres) 1971-72; Teacher Study Cncl 1974-75; Hunter Safety Instr for Gun 1981- & Bow 1983-; *home:* Cirlce Dr Mc Ewen TN 37101

SPARKS, GEORGIA THOMPSON, Kindergarten Teacher; *b:* Temple, TX; *m:* W. E.; *c:* Gene, John R., Terry, Jerry; *cr:* Teacher First Baptist Kndgtn 1971-; *ai:* Deaf Smith Cty C of C Womens Division Pres 1975-76, Women of Yr 1981; *home:* 506 Westhaven Hereford TX 79045

SPARKS, KATHERINE JACKSON, Third Grade Teacher; *b:* Smithfield, NC; *m:* Lowery Houston; *c:* Scooter, Kristi; *ed:* Elem Ed, Troy St Univ 1966-69; Elem Ed, LA St Univ New Orleans 1970; (BA) Elem Ed, Univ of W FL 1971; Working Towards Masters FSU; *cr:* 2nd Grade Teacher Christ The King 1968-69; 3rd Grade Teacher Little Flower 1969-70; Kndgtn/4th Grade Teacher Wewahitchka Elem 1970-72; 3rd Grade Teacher Tyndall Elem 1975-; *ai:* Cty Cheerleading Adv & Spon; Sci Assn, Rdng Assn Mem; Jaycettes Mem; Teacher of Yr 1976; *office:* Tyndall Elem Sch Tyndall Pkwy Tyndall AFB FL 32404

SPARKS, NANCY MUSTARD, Health Occupations Teacher; *b:* Richlands, VA; *m:* Lanny L. Sr.;; *c:* Blenna Patterson, Lanny L. Jr.; *ed:* (RN) Nursing, Lewis Gale Sch of Nursing 1963; Ed Courses, Univ VA, VPI, SU, Radford Univ; *cr:* Staff Nurse Lewis-Gale Hosp 1963-65; Office Nurse 1967-68; Staff Nurse R J Reynold Hosp 1968-70; RN Supvr St Albans Psychiatric Hospital 1970-72; Teacher Radford HS 1972-76, Pulaski Cty HS 1976-; *ai:* HOSA Spon; NEA 1989-; VA Ed Assn 1988-; Pulaski Cty Ed Assn 1989-; VA Vocational Assn 1989-; *home:* Rt 1 Box 232 Dublin VA 24084

SPARKS, WANDA HODGES, Sixth Grade Teacher; *b:* Bernie, MO; *ed:* (BS) Elem Ed, 1969, (MS) Admin, 1972 SEMO Univ; *cr:* 3rd/4th/5th Grade Teacher Dexter Elem Schls 1969-77; Remedial Math Teacher 1978-86, 6th Grade Teacher 1986- Bernie Elem; *ai:* Textbook Comm; DARE Drug Abuse Prgm; CARE Drug Abuse Prgm; MSTA 1969-85; *office:* Bernie R-13 Sch P O Box 470 Bernie MO 63822

SPARRE, MARY, Third Grade Teacher; *b:* Youngstown, OH; *ed:* (BSED) Elem Ed, Youngstown St 1973; *cr:* 3rd Grade Teacher Franklin Elem 1974-; *ai:* Lang Art & Health Curr Comm; OH Ed Assn, NEA; Co-Developed Grant Titled Intensive Map & Globe Study Grant; *office:* Franklin Elem Sch School St Summitville OH 43962

SPARROW, LORNA HAWES, Retired Elementary Teacher; *b:* Indianola, IA; *m:* George Jr.; *c:* Kathy J. Danielson, Cynthia A.; *ed:* (BS) Elem Ed, Culver Stockton Coll 1974; *cr:* Elem Teacher Argyle Grade Sch 1953-54, Warsaw Grade Sch 1954-86.

SPARROW, MARY ELLEN, Teacher of Gifted; *b:* Baltimore, MD; *c:* Jim, John; *ed:* (BS) Ed, 1981, (MED) Ed, 1985 GA St Univ; *cr:* Sci Teacher Otwell Sr HS 1981-83, Crabapple Mid Sch 1983-; *ai:* Coach Academic Bowl Team; GA Sci Teachers Assn Mid Grades Rep 1988-89; Kappa Kappa Gamma 1981-; Crabapple Teacher of Yr 1986; *office:* Crabapple Mid Sch 10700 Crabapple Rd Roswell GA 30075

SPAULDING, DAVID L., Science/Mathematics Teacher; *b:* McGregor, IA; *m:* Rosalie Bartolo; *c:* John, Stephen, Mark; *ed:* (BA) Sci, Univ of N IA 1951; Univ of AK, Carlton Coll, TX Tech Coll, Univ of WA; *cr:* Sci Teacher Calamus Consolidated Sch 1951-53; Sci/Math Teacher Twin Rivers Cmmty Sch 1953-64, Cook Cty Sch 1964-65, Rolfe Cmmty Sch 1965-83, Twin Rivers Cmmty Sch 1983-; *ai:* Quiz Bowl; Jr Class Spon; NEA, IA St Ed Assn 1953-; Twin Rivers Ed Assn 1983-; Amer Legion Post Commander 1953-; Natl Rifle Assn 1968-; Natl Sci Fnd Summer Inst; Rolfe Lions Club Teacher of Yr; Twin Rivers Cmmty Sch Teacher of Yr.

SPAULDING, DIANA LYNN, Math Teacher; *b:* Manchester, TN; *m:* Charles E.; *c:* Chase, Chelsea; *ed:* (BS) Mid TN 1980; (MS) TN St Univ 1986; *cr:* Teacher Huntland HS 1981-; *ai:* Org & Coord Homecoming Parade-Ceremonies-& Act; 1987-88 Nom Young Educator of Yr; 1988-89 Nom Teacher of Yr; 1988-89

Franklin Ctys Teacher of Yr; 1989- Comm to Select Teacher of Yr; *home:* Rt 1 Huntland TN 37345

SPAULDING, MARY JANE, Fourth Grade Teacher; *b:* Lebanon, KY; *m:* Nelson Reed III; *c:* Nelson IV, Robert Taylor; *ed:* (AA) Bus, St Catharine Coll 1972; (BS) Elem Ed, 1974, (MA) Elem Ed, 1981 E KY Univ; *cr:* 4th Grade Teacher St Dominic Sch 1974-; *ai:* NCEA 1988-; Washington Cty Homemakers Treas 1987-.

SPAULDING, MARY MC GLONE, 4th Grade Teacher; *b:* Frankfort, KY; *m:* Daryl Ralph; *c:* Scott, Jeanne; *ed:* (BA) Elem Ed, Morehead St 1972; (MA) Elem Ed, Georgetown Coll 1975; Rank I Rdng, N KY Univ; N KY Writing Project; *cr:* 2nd Grade Teacher Ryland Heights Elem 1969-72; 5th Grade Teacher A J Jolly Elem 1973-76; Classroom Teacher Crittenden Mt Zion Elem 1976-; *ai:* Young Authors Coord; Academic & Dist Evaluation Comms; Interns Resource Teacher; KY Ed Assn, NEA, IRA; *office:* Crittenden Mt Zion Elem Sch Rt 2 Dry Ridge KY 41035

SPAULDING, ROBERTA KLIMASKI, Teacher/Sci Department Head; *b:* Youngstown, OH; *c:* Jeremy; *ed:* (BA) Bio, Carlow Coll 1964; (MS) Biochemistry, NM Inst of Mining & Technology 1979; Engineering, Math & Ed Courses Univ NM & NM Inst of Mining & Technology; *cr:* Teacher San Miguel Sch 1984-86, Socorro HS 1986-89, G C Marshall 1989-; *ai:* Boys HS Soccer Coach; Elem Academic Act Spon; Sch Sci Fair Co-Spon; Curr Dev Comm Chairperson 1990-; Ankara Intnl Charities 1990; NM Regional Sci Fair Spon of Yr Jr Div 1985-86; NM Sci Olympiad Coach 1st Place Team 1987; NM St Dir Sci Olympiad 1987-89; *office:* George C Marshall Sch Ankara American Schls APO New York NY 09254

SPAZIANO, CAROL MURPHY, Mathematics Teacher; *b:* Warwick, RI; *m:* John G.; *c:* Carrie; *ed:* (BA) Math, 1974, (MED) Instructional Tech, 1979 RI Coll; *cr:* Math Tech Teacher Comm Coll RI 1974-77; Math Teacher Coventry HS 1977-; Math Instr Comm Coll RI 1980-; *ai:* Sch Climate Comm; GSA RI Leader 1983-89.

SPEAKMAN, J. DAVID, Mathematics Department Chair; *b:* Cushing, OK; *m:* Carol Lynne Champion; *ed:* (BA) Math, 1965, (MA) Scndry Ed, 1970 CA St Univ Los Angeles; Cmptr BASIC, Univ of CA Riverside; *cr:* Math Dept Chm Emerson Jr HS 1965-69; Math Dept 1970-79, Math Dept Chm 1980- Pomona HS; *ai:* Math, Engineering, Sci Achievement Sch Adv; Pomona HS Schslp Comm; NEA 1965-; CA Teachers Assn (Poly Action Comm Mem 1980-) 1965-; Associated Pomona Teachers (Sch Rep 1968-73) 1965-, Teacher of Yr 1980, 1988; Hewlett Packard Gift of Cmptrs & Software; *office:* Pomona HS 475 Bangor Pomona CA 91767

SPEAR, GAIL W., French Teacher; *b:* Herkimer, NY; *m:* Jeffrey T.; *c:* Amy, Alison; *ed:* Fr, Vassar Coll 1967-69; (BA) Fr, Univ of MA 1971; *cr:* Fr Teacher Mahar Regional HS 1971-75, Wilbraham Public Schls 1979-81, Monson Jr/Sr HS 1981-; *ai:* Project France & Fr Club Adv; Sch Improvement & Parent Advisory Cncl; MA Foreign Lang Assn, Amer Cncl for Teaching Foreign Lang, NEA, MTA, AATE; League of Women Voters (VP, Bd Mem) 1978-80, 1990; Horace Mann Grant for Dev of Foreign Lang Related Cmptr Software; *office:* Monson Jr/Sr HS 25 Thompson St Monson MA 01057

SPEAR, GEORGE GILBERT, 10th/12th Grade Eng Teacher; *b:* Butte, MT; *m:* Patricia A. Urmson; *c:* Ryan, Stephen, Staci; *ed:* (BA) Eng, Carroll Coll 1969; (MAT) Ed, Lewis & Clark Coll 1974; *cr:* Eng Teacher Mc Loughlin Jr HS 1969-80, Ft Vancouver HS 1980-; *ai:* Ft Vancouver HS Golf Coach; WEA 1969-; Vancouver Sch Dist Wrestling Coach of Yr 1976, 1978; *office:* Ft Vancouver HS 5700 E 18th St Vancouver WA 98661

SPEARMAN, TERESA FOLAND, Language Arts/Speech Teacher; *b:* Wilmington, OH; *m:* David Rogers; *ed:* (BS) Ed, OH Univ 1972; Working Towards Masters; *cr:* Eng Teacher Morgan Local HS 1972-73; Eng/Speech Teacher Ft Frye Local HS 1973-; *ai:* Future Teachers Club Adv; Ft Frye Teachers Assn, OH Cncl Teachers of Eng 1973-; NCTE 1973; Childrens Conservation League Pres 1989-; Marietta Chorale (Soloist, Bd of Dir Mem) 1978-; Outstanding Women of America Awd; Martha Holden Jennings Scholar; Freedoms Fnd Participant; Articles Published; *office:* Ft Frye Local HS 5th St Beverly OH 45715

SPEARS, DORIS ARNOLD, Fourth Grade Teacher; *b:* Dothan, AL; *m:* Philip Ben; *c:* Ben, Anna K.; *ed:* (BS) Elem Ed, Troy St Univ 1973; *cr:* 4th Grade Teacher Heard Elem Sch 1973-75, Montana Street Elem Sch 1975-; *ai:* NEA, AEA, DEA 1973-; Delta Delta Beta (VP 1985-86, Pres 1986-87, Corresponding Secy 1989-), Woman of Yr 1987; *office:* Montana Street Elem Sch 1001 Montana St Dothan AL 36303

SPEARS, LUCILLE COLEMAN, Health & Physcial Ed Teacher; *b:* Yazoo City, MI; *m:* Reginald M.; *c:* Shaintay D., Katrina; *ed:* (BS) Health/Phys Ed, TN A&I St & MS St Univ 1964; (MS) Elem Ed, Jackson & Delta St Univ 1966-73; Grad Stud Delta St Univ & Univ of S MS; *cr:* Phys Ed Teacher John F Kennedy 1964-65; Elem Teacher Wormack Hodge 1967-68; Sci Teacher Louise HS 1968-72; Phys Ed Teacher Grenada Jr HS 1972-; *ai:* Cmmty Appearance Campaign Comm; March of Dimes for Mother; Organized 1st City Sftbl League for Black Girls; Chairperson 1st MS Debutante; Playground Comm Marching Dance Group; Adult Ladies Club; Amer Alliance, Amer Assn of Univ Women, Natl Assn of Colored Womens Club 1990.

SPEARS, PAT (SITZ), Fourth Grade Teacher; *b:* Corum, OK; *m:* Jay A.; *c:* Randall, Jayme L. Branch, Lawrence D.; *ed:* (BS) Phy Ed/Elem, Cntrl St Univ 1954; (MAED) Elem Counseling, E Cntrl Univ 1990; Columbus Coll & Univ of OK Norman; *cr:* Phys Ed Teacher John Marshall HS 1954-59; Womens Phys Ed Teacher Univ of OK Norman 1957-58; Elem Phys Ed Teacher Schaumburg Sch Dist 1967-70; 5th/6th Grade Teacher Reese Road Elem 1974-76; 4th Grade Teacher Meridian 1980-; *ai:* Comanche Ed Assn Pres Elect 1989-; OK Assn for Counseling & Dev 1990; OK Ed Assn , NEA 1980-; *home:* Rt 1 Box 202 Comanche OK 73529

SPEASE, DEBORAH LYNN (RAY), Kindergarten Teacher; *b:* Cape Girardeau, MO; *m:* William Charles; *c:* Mark A., Barbara A.; *ed:* (AA) Elem Ed, Three Rivers Comm Coll 1975; (BS) Elem Ed, 1977, (MS) Early Chldhd Ed, 1983 SE MO St Univ; PAT Inst Univ of MO St Louis 1987; *cr:* Kndgtn Teacher 1977-, Parent Educator 1987- Naylor R-II; *ai:* GSA Daisy, Jr, Cadette, Sr Scouts Leader; Founder & Leader Ripley Cty Early Chldhd Educators Assn; MO St Teachers Assn Delegate; NAEYC 1987-; Beta Sigma Phi (Pres 1987, VP 1986) Woman of Yr Awd 1986; Career Ladder Comm 1988-89; Help Establish Incentive Grant Naylor R-II Sch 1986-87; *office:* Naylor R-II Elem Sch 101 School St Naylor MO 63953

SPECKMAN, JULIA A., Foreign Language Dept Chairman; *b:* Indianapolis, IN; *m:* George R.; *c:* George Jr., Mark, Gretchen, Michael; *ed:* (AB) Span/Fr, Marian 1953; (MS) Ed, Butler Univ 1973; Ed Prgm, Purdue Univ; *cr:* Span Teacher Roncalli HS; *home:* 804 Orchard Ln Greenwood IN 46142

SPEED, ORYAN RILEY, Fifth Grade Teacher; *b:* Port St Joe, FL; *ed:* (BS) Elem Ed, 1976, (MED) Admin/Supervision, 1984 FL A&M Univ; Univ of S FL Tampa; *cr:* 6th Grade Teacher Brown Elem Sch 1976-84; 5th Grade Teacher Sulphur Springs Elem Sch 1984-; *ai:* Sci & Math Resource Teacher; Prime Lead Teacher; Amer Red Cross Coord; Grade Level Chm; Peer Teacher Beginning Teachers Prgm; NEA 1976-; Hillsborough Cty Teachers Assn 1984-; Hillsborough Cty Elem Math Cncl 1987-; Sulphur Springs Teacher of Yr 1989-; *office:* Sulphur Springs Elem Sch 8412 N 13th St Tampa FL 33604

SPEED, WILHEMINA HAWKINS, Home Economics Teacher; *b:* Orlando, FL; *m:* Joseph; *ed:* (BS) Voc Home Ec, FL A&M Univ 1971; (MS) Home Ec Ed, FL St Univ 1977 Performance Learning System Teacher Trng Prgm; *cr:* Teacher Day Care Center 1971-72; Teacher/Coord Cty Prgm for Pregnant Teens Alachua Cty Schls 1972-75; Home Ec Teacher Howard Bishop Mid Sch 1975-; *ai:* FHA Chapter Adv; Alachua Cty Voc Assn; Home Ec Teachers Assn 1972-; Alpha Kappa Alpha; FL Assn FHA Hero 1981; Distinguished Service Awd; Alachua Cty Voc Assn Leaders; Certificate & Awd 1988-89; *office:* Howard Bishop Mid Sch 1901 NE 19th St Gainesville FL 32609

SPEER, JUDITH ANN, Fine Arts Dept Chair; *b:* Evanton, IL; *ed:* (BFA) Directing, 1961, (MFA) Directing, 1962 Goodman Sch of Drama; Theater, Univ of WI Madison; *cr:* Dean/Teacher the Faulkner Sch 1967-74; Eng Dept Chairperson Joliet Cath HS 1975-78; Division Chaiperson Providence St Mel HS 1978-81; Teacher/Fine Arts Chairperson Regina Dominican HS 1981-; *ai:* Directory Designer Producer Annual Musical Childrens Play Drama Productions; Forensics Coach; Individual Events; Moduator ITS; Auditorium Mgr; IL Speech Theater Assn; Chicago Cath Forensics League (Secy, Treas) 1984; IL Theater Assn; Natl Forensic League; *office:* Regina Dominican H S 701 Locust Rd Wilmette IL 60091

SPEER, TONY A., Mathematics Teacher; *b:* Tulsa, OK; *m:* Vickie A.; *c:* Leah N.; *ed:* (BS) Ed, OK Univ 1974; (MS) Spec Ed, Northeastern St 1984; *cr:* Phys Ed Teacher/Wrestling Coach Union HS 1976-78; Learning Disabilities Teacher/Wrestling Coach Mc Lain HS 1978-80, Central HS 1980-84, East Cntrl 1984-; *ai:* HS Wrestling Coach; OEA; *office:* Tulsa East Cntrl HS 12150 E 11th Tulsa OK 74128

SPEERS, JOHN KEITH, Math Dept Chairman/Teacher; *b:* Pontiac, IL; *m:* Carol Ann Grieff; *c:* Brian K., David J.; *ed:* (BS) Math, 1962, (MS) Math 1968 N IL Univ; Working Beyong Masters Various Univs; *cr:* Math/Cmptr Programming Teacher 1962-, Math Dept Chm/Math/Cmptr Programming Teacher 1990 Fenton HS Dist 100; *ai:* Ftbl, Wrestling, Bsktbl Timer & Scorer; IL St Wrestling Tournament Timer; NCTM, IL Cncl Teachers of Math, NEA, IL Ed Assn, Fenton Ed Assn 1962-; *office:* Fenton HS Dist 100 1000 W Green St Bensenville IL 60106

SPEIER, PATRICIA M., English Department Chairperson; *b:* San Antonio, TX; *m:* Charles M. Woodruff Jr.; *ed:* (BS) Eng Ed, 1970, (MA) Eng Ed, 1973 Univ of TX Austin; Writing Process, Gifted Ed; *cr:* Eng Teacher Furr Jr/Sr HS 1970-71; Eng Teacher/Dept Head Taylor HS 1973-82; Eng Teacher 1984-, Eng Dept Head 1989- Westlake HS; *ai:* Rdng Writing Spon; Lang Art Scope & Sequence Comm Mem; TX St Teachers Assn 1973-82, 1984-; NEA 1984-; NCTE 1985-; Laqua Gloria Art Museum Dir 1982-84; Named Distinguished Teacher Presidential Scholars Prgm 1988.

SPEIGHT, ROSEMARY CYNTHIA, 5th Grade Teacher; *b:* Anderson, SC; *ed:* (BA) Elem Ed, Univ of SC 1979; Ed, Clemson Univ; *cr:* 6th Grade Teacher 1980-85, 5th Grade Teacher 1985- New Prospect Elem; *office:* New Prospect Elem Sch Rt 12 Box 14 New Prospect Church Rd Anderson SC 29621

SPELL, AVA BARGMANN, Biology I & II Teacher; *b:* Yorktown, TX; *m:* Alvin; *c:* Bill, Rex; *ed:* (BAT) Bio, Sam Houston St Univ 1976; Grad Stud Phys Sci; *cr:* Bio Teacher Conroe HS 1976-; *ai:* ISEF Intnl Sci Fair Spon 1990; Conroe HS Sci Club Spon 1978-86; NSTA 1983-; NABT 1987-88; Greater Houston Math & Teachers of Sci 1986-88; NASA Cmmty Involvement Project Educl Comm 1988; Houston Sci Fair Teacher of Yr 1980; Conroe Ind Sch Dist Second Mile Awd 1988, Teacher of Yr 1989; *office:* Conroe HS 3200 W Davis Conroe TX 77304

SPELL, BETTY KNIGHT, Second Grade Teacher; *b:* Portsmouth, VA; *m:* James Andrew; *c:* Darren, Deidre Spell Fontenot, Donnie; *ed:* (BS) Bus Ed, Mc Neese St Univ 1964; (MED) Rdng, LA St Univ 1973; *cr:* Bus Teacher Evans HS 1964-65, Eunice HS 1966-70; Elem Teacher W W Stewart Elem 1973-79, Mid Way Elem 1979-81, W W Stewart Elem 1981-; *ai:* NEA, LAE; Elton Pentecostal Church Supvr of Teachers 1983-; *office:* W W Stewart Elem Sch P O Box 338 Basile LA 70515

SPELL, DANA C., High School English Teacher; *b:* Chicago, IL; *ed:* (BA) Eng, Rosary Coll 1988; *cr:* Eng Teacher Providence St Mel 1988-; *ai:* Girls Bsktbl Coach; Lambda Iota Tou 1987-; Holy Family Recognition of Cmmty Service 1983; Rosary Coll Distinguished Sr in Eng Awd 1988; *office:* Providence-St Mel HS 119 S Central Pk Chicago IL 60624

SPELL, GAY CAIN, Fifth Grade Teacher; *b:* Kosciusko, MS; *m:* Jerry R.; *c:* Jay; *ed:* (BA) Elem Ed, MS ST 1983; *cr:* 5th Grade Teacher 1983-85, 1st Grade Teacher 1985-87, 2nd Grade Teacher 1987-89, 5th Grade Teacher 1989- C B Murphy Elem Sch; *ai:* Beta Club Spon; *office:* C B Murphy Elem Sch Hwy 607 Gen Del Pearlington MS 39572

SPELLICY, JAMES PAUL, Social Studies Teacher; *b:* Wellsville, NY; *ed:* (BA) His, St Univ of NY 1976; (MA) His, Mc Gill Univ 1979; *cr:* Asst Mgr Suiro & Company Incorporated 1982-85; Teacher J Eugene Mc Ateer HS 1986-88, Phillip & Sala Burton HS 1988-; *ai:* Stu Government & Acad of Finance Spon; Amer His Assn; Keck Fnd Grant Pepperdine Univ; *office:* Phillip & Sala Burton Acad HS 45 Conkling San Francisco CA 94124

SPELLMAN, PEGGY PRICE, 3rd Grade Teacher; *b:* Massillon, OH; *c:* Andrew A., Amy J.; *ed:* (BS) Elem Ed, Ashland Coll 1966; (MED) Elem Admin, Ashland Univ 1983; *cr:* 6th Grade Teacher Greenwood Sch 1966-67; 6th Grade/Dev Handicapped Montgomery Sch 1967-69; 1st-3rd Grade Teacher Ashland City Taft Sch 1974-; *ai:* Curr Comm; PTO Rep; Sch Calender; Negotiation Team; Prin Adv; Taft Social; AHS Chrldr Adv; Aux Adv; Pres Ashland City Teacher Assn; Pres North Central OH Assn; Phil Delta Kappa 1986-; Alpha Delta Kappa Comm Chm 1983-; North Central OH Ed Pres Assn 1986-87; Lou Bach Tutor Adult Rdng Tutor 1985-; Back to Sch Prgm Ashland City Sch; Final Round Teacher of Yr; *home:* 2202 Lakewood Dr Mansfield OH 44905

SPELLMON, MERCEDES PHYTALION, Fifth Grade Teacher; *b:* Derry, LA; *m:* F. L.; *c:* Mercedes Singleton, Tonya, Terance; *ed:* (BA) Secretarial Sci, Morris Brown Coll 1958; (MED) Elem Ed, Univ of TX San Antonio 1977; *cr:* Typing/Shorthand Teacher USAF Inst Japan 1960-63; 2nd Grade Teacher Edgewood Ind Sch Dist 1966-67; Typing Teacher Kennedy HS 1968; 2nd Grade Teacher 1968-71, 5th Grade Teacher 1971- Lyndon B Johnson Elem; *ai:* Stu Cncl Spon; Awds Comm; NEA, TX St Teachers Assn, Edgewood Classroom Teachers Assn 1966-; TX Alliance Black Sch Educators 1990; Alamo City Debs Inc Bd Mem 1984-; Modernaires Civic & Social Club VP 1990; Cmmty Workers Cncl Mem 1971-; Sherman Chapel AME Church Secy 1963-.

SPELLS, SHERRY ROBINSON, Kindergarten Teacher; *b:* Camilla, GA; *m:* Alton W.; *c:* Alta D., Alton W. III; *ed:* (BS) Elem Ed, Albany St Coll 1973; Early Chldhd Ed, Milledgeville GA Coll; *cr:* Kndgtn Teacher Louisville Acad Elem 1973-; *ai:* GSA Troop Leader 49; St Paul Baptist Church Youth Adv; GA Assn of Educators 1989-; Alpha Kappa Alpha Ivy Leaf Reporter 1989-; Louisville Acad Teacher of Yr 1988-89; *home:* PO Box 525 Louisville GA 30434

SPENCE, BRENDA SUE ROMAINE, English Teacher; *b:* Gettysburg, PA; *ed:* (BS) Scndry Ed/Eng, Lock Haven Univ 1985; (MS) Developmental Strategies/Ed, Wilkes Coll 1989; *cr:* Eng Teacher Waynesboro Area Sr HS 1985-; *ai:* Fairfield Sr HS Field Hockey Coach; *home:* 2175 Mt Hope Rd Fairfield PA 17320

SPENCE, CHRISTOPHER LOWRY, Government & Economics Teacher; *b:* Elizabeth City, NC; *m:* Linda Johnson; *c:* Danyel, Byron; *ed:* (BS) Soc Sci, Elizabeth City St Univ 1974; Various Wkshps; *cr:* Teachers Aide P W Moore Jr HS 1974-75; General Math Teacher Weeksville Elem Sch 1975-76; Dean of Stu 1985-86, Soc Stud Teacher 1976-87 Elizabeth City Jr HS; Government Teacher Northeastern HS 1987-; *ai:* 8th/9th Grade Ftbl 1976-86, Bsktbl Girls 1978-81, Boys 1982-86, Girls Var Bsktbl Coach Northeastern HS 1986-; St Games of NC Asst Coach 1989, Head Coach 1990; NC Assn of Educators, NEA 1974-; NC HS Coaches Assn 1981-; Daughters of Amer Revolution & Fleet Reserve Assn Branch 293 Essay Contest Coord 1976-; Outstanding Young Man in America 1986; *office:* Northeastern HS 963 Oak Stump Rd Elizabeth City NC 27909

SPENCE, JADA SUE (COX), Kindergarten Teacher; *b:* Monticello, AR; *m:* Kenny; *c:* Jennifer, Chris; *ed:* (BA) Elem Ed, Univ of AR Monticello 1979; *cr:* Kndgtn Teacher Dermott Schls 1979-81; 3rd Grade Teacher 1981-82, Kndgtn Teacher 1982- Mc Gehee Schls; *home:* 1004 N 4th Mc Gehee AR 71654

SPENCE, PHILIP GARY, 5th Grade Teacher; *b:* Decaturville, TN; *m:* Mary C.; *c:* Beth, Jeanna, Susan; *ed:* (BS) Bus Admin/Phys Ed, Bethel Coll 1970; (MS) Ed Admin & Supervision, UT Martin 1973; *cr:* Teacher 1970-75; 1976-77; Prin 1976-77 Parsons Jr HS; Decatur Cty Riverside HS 1978-81; *ai:* TEA 1970-; NEA 1970-; Parsons Lions Club (Dir VP & Pres 1976); *home:* PO Box 334 Parsons TN 38363

SPENCE, STEVEN LAURENCE, 7th Grade Math Teacher; *b:* Guatanamo, Cuba; *m:* Kimberly Ann Mose; *c:* Robert, Brittany; *ed:* (BS) Elem Ed, Univ Cntrl FL 1984; *cr:* Teacher Silver Sands Jr HS 1984-; *ai:* Yrbk, Sch Paper, Debate Team Spon; Talent Show Dir & Producer; Phi Theta Kappa NHS; *office:* Silver Sands Jr HS 1300 Herbert St Port Orange FL 32119

SPENCER, ALICE SIMS, Eng/Speech Teacher/Dept Chair; *b:* Richmond, VA; *m:* Harold Harding Jr.; *c:* David H., Stephen L.; *ed:* (BA) Public Speaking, 1968, (MA) Platform Art, 1970 Bob Jones Univ; *cr:* Frosh Speech Teacher Bob Jones Univ 1971-72; HS Eng Teacher Peninsula Chrstn Sch 1984-86; HS Eng/Speech Teacher Denbigh Baptist Chrstn Sch 1986-; *ai:* Honor Society Adv 1987-; Grad Assistantship Bob Jones Univ 1968-70; *office:* Denbigh Baptist Chrstn Sch 13010 Mitchell Point Rd Newport News VA 23602

SPENCER, BARBARA HIGDON, English/Speech Teacher; *b:* Leon, IA; *m:* Steven Eldon; *c:* Trisha M.; *ed:* (AA) General Ed, Trenton Jr Coll 1972, (BSE) Eng Ed, 1974, (BS) Sociology, 1974, (MS) Eng Ed, 1979- Northeast St Univ; *cr:* Teacher Jameson HS 1974-75, Trenton HS 1975-; *ai:* Play Production; Forensics Coach; Grundy Cty Friends of Arts Treas 1987-; Speech Teachers Assn of MO; NCTE; Grundy Cty Historical Society; *office:* Trenton R-9 HS 1415 Oklahoma Ave Trenton MO 64683

SPENCER, BETTY JEAN SCOTT, 5th Grade Teacher of Gifted; *b:* Atlanta, GA; *m:* John W.; *c:* Deborah Spencer Harris, John C., Brian R.; *ed:* (BS) Elem Ed, TN St Univ 1963; (MS) Admin, Univ of Dayton 1983; *cr:* 1st Grade Teacher 1963-65, Lang Dev Teacher 1966-67 Fulton Elem Sch; 2nd Grade Teacher Watkins Elem Sch 1969-71; 5th Grade Gifted & Talented Teacher Stockbridge Elem Sch 1986-; *ai:* CEA Faculty Rep 1981-87; OH Ed Assn, Columbus OH Teacher Assn, NEA; United Negro Coll Fund Coord 1986, Meritorious Service Awd 1986; United Way Coord 1986, Certificate 1986; Jennings Scholar for Outstanding Teachers 1980-81; Educl Grant 1982; Teacher Assistance Master Teacher 1981-82; *home:* 314 Meditation Ln Worthington OH 43085

SPENCER, BRUCE EDWARD, Science Department Chairman; *b:* Chicago, IL; *m:* Carol Stevens; *c:* Edward, Steven, Anne, Maria, Matthew; *ed:* (BA) Chem, Knox Coll 1963; (MA) Chem, Bowling Green St Univ 1970; NSF Inst Knox Coll 1964/1969; NSF Inst Bowdoin Coll 1970; NSF Inst Hope Coll 1981; *cr:* Chem Teacher/Dept Chm Galesburg HS 1963-; Chem Teacher Carl Sandburg Coll 1975-; Chem Instr Bradley Univ 1985; Instr Coll for Kids Knox Coll 1985-; *ai:* Co-Spon Natl Honor Society; IL Assn of Chem Teachers 1963-; NEA; IL Ed Assn; Galesburg Ed Assn Pres 1980; Knox Cty YMCA Swim Team VP 1980-81; Galesburg Jr Hardball Bd Mem 1986-88; Knox Coll Founders Day Teacher Recognition Awd 1986-1988; *office:* Galesburg HS 1135 W Fremont Galesburg IL 61401

SPENCER, BUEL, 5th Grade Teacher; *b:* Muskogee, OK; *ed:* (BA) Health/Phys Ed/Elem Ed, UTEP 1961; Boise St Univ; ID St; *cr:* Teacher Oklahoma City 1963-64; Teacher/Coach Boise ID 1964-80; Teacher Meeker OK 1980-; *ai:* MEA Pres 1986-87; OEA; NEA Life Mem; Boise Boys Bsbl Pres 1970-71 Optimist of Yr 1972/1984; Optimist Club Pres 1966-67/1969-70/1988-89; *home:* 303 E 45th #3 Shawnee OK 74801

SPENCER, CONSTANCE EILEEN, Categorical Program Advisor; *b:* Los Angeles, CA; *ed:* (BA) Early Chldhd Dev, Whittier Coll 1976; (MA) Multicultural Ed, Univ San Francisco 1978; *cr:* Sub Teacher Rowland Unified Sch Dist 1976-78; Lynwood Unified Sch Dist 1976-78; Classroom Teacher 1978-89; Categ Prgm Adv 1989 Los Angeles Unified Sch Dist; *ai:* Dir Sci Fair; Coach Black His Speech Contest; Adv Creative/Multicultural Arts; NSTA 1987-89; *office:* West Athens Elem Sch 1110 W 119th St Los Angeles CA 90044

SPENCER, DIANA BLAKE, Biology Teacher; *b:* Wichita, KS; *m:* Mark; *c:* Jessica, Julia; *ed:* (BA) Bio Ed, Univ of Houston/Clear Lake 1978; *cr:* Teacher Clear Lake HS 1978-79, Jenks HS 1979-; *ai:* Great Organization for Environmental Restoration; NABT 1988-, OK Outstandeing Bio Teacher 1988-89; HS Teacher of Yr Jenks Public Schls 1989-; Natl Assn of Sci Teachers Area Convention Wkshp; Jenks Public Schls Fnd Grant Environmental Project; *office:* Jenks Public Schls 1st & B Street Jenks OK 74037

SPENCER, ESTHER FAULKNER, 5th/6th Grade Teacher; *b:* Roxboro, NC; *m:* Charles; *c:* Rosalyn; *ed:* (BS) Intermediate Ed, Winston-Salem St Univ 1973; Effective Teaching Trng, TESA Trng, Effective Schls Trng, Impact Trng, Mentor Trng; *cr:* 5th/6th Grade Teacher Bethel Hill Elem Sch 1973-; *ai:* 4th-6th Grade Level Rep; NCAE, NEA, PACE; WSSU Alumni Assn Person Cty Chapter Treas 1988-; Person Cty Arts Cncl 1981-82; *home:* 114 Shady Hill Dr Roxboro NC 27573

SPENCER, GLORIA KIRKMON, English Teacher & Dept Chair; *b:* Clarksdale, MS; *m:* Thomas Jr.; *c:* Patricia L. Vallot, Kerry D. Moore, Timothy D.; *ed:* (BA) Eng, Tougaloo Coll 1948; (ML) Eng, 1961, (ME) Cnslr Ed, 1971, Cnslr Ed, 1973, (PHD) Cnslr Ed, 1983 Univ of Pittsburgh; *cr:* Eng Teacher Cottage Hill Voc HS 1948-49, Mound Bayou HS 1950-51, W A Higgins HS 1956-60; Instructional Leader 1967-69, Eng Teacher 1960-, Dept Chairperson 1969- Westinghouse HS; *ai:* Annual Black His Poetry Contest Spon; Commencement Speakers Coach; Mem Instructional Cabinet; Cmmty Resources Comm Chairperson; NCTE; Conference for Scndry Sch Eng Dept Chairperson; Black Caucas; Pittsburgh Fed Teachers; Western PA Cncl Teachers of Eng; Westinghouse Faculty Assn; Monroeville Mall Ministry Volunteer 1975-, Service Pin 1988; Macedonia Baptist Church; NAACP, Urban League 1983-; Mid St Assn of Coll & Schls Evaluator 1979, 1989; Spec Ed Evaluator PA Dept of Ed; Scriptwriter, Poetess, Consultant, Spec Occasion Speaker; Nom Outstanding Citizen Awd; *office:* George A Westinghouse HS 1101 N Murtland Ave Pittsburgh PA 15208

SPENCER, HELEN M., Vocational Dept Chairperson; *b:* Washington, NC; *ed:* (BS) Bus Ed/Ec, St Pauls Coll 1951; (MS) Scndry Ed, VA St Coll 1958; Sch Law & Ec, Univ of PA 1963-65; Curr Dev, Univ of VA 1972-74; Management & Supervision, Paul D Camp Comm Coll 1989; Technological Inservice Wkshps & Seminars; *cr:* Teacher E Suffolk HS 1951-65, John F Kennedy HS 1965-; *ai:* John F Kennedy Faculty Rep; NHS & FBLA Adv; Voc Ed Chm; Prins Advisory Comm; EAS (Secy 1966-72, Treas 1966-72), Teacher of Yr 1975; VEA, NEA, VBEA; Alpha Kappa Alpha (Epistoleus 1970-72, VP 1974-76, Pres 1976-80); Suffolk City Employees Credit Union VP 1985-; St Marks Episcopal Church (ECW, Choir, Vestryman, Register); John F Kennedy HS Perfect Attendance Awd 1988-89; Energizers Awd of Excl 1988; Nansemond Count Ed Assn Teacher of Yr 1965; *office:* John F Kennedy HS 2325 E Washington St Suffolk VA 23434

SPENCER, JAMES HOWARD, Science/Math Teacher; *b:* Kingston, WV; *m:* Nila Jackson; *c:* Jim, Tina; *ed:* (BS) Education, Bluefield St Coll 1974; Addl Studies EPA, Abestos Inspecting, Management Control Beckley Mining Acad; Water Control Classes, St Spon Graduate Classes VPI & Radford Univ; *cr:* Teacher Narrows Elem Sch 1974-90; *ai:* Coach Ftbl; 7 & 8 Grade Spon; Sci Chm Narrows Elem Sch; NEA-GEA 1977-; Ballard Baptist Church Deacon 1975-; Glen Lyn Fire Dept Chaplin 1977-; Ruitian Club President 1988; Town of Glen Lyn Mayor; *home:* Rt 1, Box 45 Glen Lyn VA 24093

SPENCER, JANICE GREEN, Sixth Grade Teacher; *b:* Mobile, AL; *m:* Stephen Lynn; *c:* Bradford, G. Scott, Sidney; *ed:* (BS) Elem Ed, 1973, (MS) Elem Ed/Rdng, 1977 Troy St Univ; GA St Univ; *cr:* Teacher Talledega Cty Trng Sch 1973, George Washington Carver Elem Sch 1973-77, Riverside Elem Sch 1977-79, Mc Adory Elem Sch 1981-; *ai:* NEA, AEA 1973-; Kappa Kappa Iota 1975-78; Riverchase Presbyn Church (Session Mem, Elder) 1987-; Riverchase Cntry Club; Hoover Athletic Assn Womens Auxiliary; *home:* 2153 Bailey Brook Dr Birmingham AL 35244

SPENCER, JEWELENE SINGLETON, Third Grade Teacher; *b:* Jefferson, TX; *m:* Howard W.; *c:* Sabrina E., Tyrone R.; *ed:* (BS) Bus Ed/Soc Sci, Prairie View A&M 1960; (MA) Teaching/Elem Ed, Univ of Southern CA 1970; (EDS) Admin/Rdng, Cntrl MI Univ 1980; Advanced Classes in Human Ecology; Doctorial Prgm at MI St Univ; *cr:* Teacher Orange Ind Sch Dist 1960-65, Ilmir Amer Schls 1967-68, Athenia Amer Schls 1968-69, Oscoda Area Schls 1970-; *ai:* Organized Jr HS NHS; Mem Discpline Comm & Sch Improvement Team; Bus Profession Women 1974-; Oscoda Area Assn VP 1980-; Delta Kappa Gamma Pres 1988-Woman of Distinction 1988; Delta Sigma Thea 1974-; Lioness Parliamentarian 1987-88; Non-Commissioned Wives ParliamentariaN 1980-; Teacher & Educator of Yr; *home:* 6009 Norway Dr Oscoda MI 48750

SPENCER, JOYCE CAZAD, English Teacher; *b:* Barboursville, WV; *m:* Richard Lee; *c:* Jo A. Watson, Conde S., Robbyn Detring, Christi; *ed:* (AB) Eng/Bus Ed, 1964, (MA) Bus Ed, 1971 Marshall Univ; Grad Stud Marshall Univ; *cr:* Eng Teacher Barboursville Jr HS 1964-67; Eng/Bus Ed Teacher Barboursville HS 1967-; *ai:* Barboursville HS Advisory & Textbook Selection Comm Mem; NEA, WVEA 1964-; WVBEA St Officer 1970; Barboursville Jr Womans Club Mem 1971; Clubwoman of Yr; Barboursville First United Meth Church Adult Sunday Sch Teacher; *office:* Barboursville HS 1400 Central Ave Barboursville WV 25504

SPENCER, JUDITH K. (CRABTREE), English/Humanities Teacher; *b:* Butler, MO; *c:* Valerie L. Husted, David M.; *ed:* (AA) General, Northeastern OK A&M 1958; (BS) Ed/Lang Art, OK St Univ 1962; (MA) Ed/Lang Art, Univ of KS 1976-; Post Grad Stud; *cr:* 9th Grade Unified Stud Teacher Trailridge Jr HS 1970-76; 10th-12th Grade Eng/Hum Teacher Shawnee Mission N 1976-; *ai:* Categories Team Spon; Drama Productions Dir; Phi Delta Kappa 1985; Alpha Delta Kappa 1989; Phi Theta Kappa OK St Univ; Rep to Natl Convention NCTE 1983; *office:* Shawnee Mission N HS 740 Johnson Dr Overland Park KS 66202

SPENCER, KATHRYN CURRAN, Latin & World History Teacher; *b:* Waukegan, IL; *m:* Colin T. Sr.; *c:* Heather, Colin Jr.; *ed:* (BA) Teaching of Latin, Univ of IL 1965; *cr:* Latin Teacher United Township HS 1965-67; Latin/US His Teacher Geneva Cmmty HS 1967-70, Rosary HS 1987-; *ai:* Latin Club; Amer Classical League, IL Classical Conference, IL Cncl for Soc Stud; Amer Legion Auxiliary District Pres 1981; *office:* Rosary HS 901 N Edgelawn Aurora IL 60506

SPENCER, KIMBERLY LOWE, Computer Studies Teacher; *b:* Springfield, MO; *m:* Dwight Lee; *c:* Kaylee Ann; *ed:* (BA) Elem Ed/Math, Southwest MO St Univ 1981; Curr/Instr/Math, Univ of MO-Kansas City; *cr:* 7-9 Grade Math/Cmptr Teacher Highland Jr HS 1984-89; 6 & 7 Grades Cmptr Teacher Highland Mid Sch 1989-; *ai:* Track & Field Coach; Bsktbl & Vlybl Coach; *office:* Highland Jr H S 3101 S 51 Kansas City KS 66106

SPENCER, LONNIE L., Biology Teacher/Science Chair; *b:* Albion, MI; *m:* Barbara Anne Power; *c:* Grant A.; *ed:* (BS) Bio, 1975, Ed, 1978 Evangel Coll; *cr:* Teacher Walnut Grove HS 1978-80, Boyle Cty HS 1981-83, Jessamine Cty HS 1983-85; Teacher/Coach Maple Valley HS 1985-; *ai:* Sci Dept Chm; Sr Class Adv; Var Bsbl Coach; MI HS Bsbl Coaches Assn Dist Rep 1989-; MI HS Ofcls Assn 1986-; MI HS Coaches Assn 1990; *office:* Maple Valley HS 11090 Nashville Hwy Varmontville MI 49096

SPENCER, MADGE ANDERSON, Third Grade Teacher; *b:* Milwaukee, WI; *m:* Jack B.; *c:* David R. Boomhower, Debra B. Cossey; *ed:* (BA) General Sci, Univ of OR 1947; *cr:* 3rd Grade Teacher 1960-74, Remedial Rdng Teacher 1975-81 Harold Smith Sch; 4th Grade Teacher 1982-85, 3rd Grade Teacher 1986-William C Jack Sch; *home:* 5049 W Frier Dr Glendale AZ 85301

SPENCER, PAULA (HOLT), Social Studies Teacher/Chair; *b:* Summit, NJ; *m:* Richard O.; *c:* Richard, Kristen, Ryan; *ed:* (BA) His/Poly Sci, FL St Univ 1963; (MA) Guidance, Chapman Coll 1973; Various His & Ed Courses, Univ of VA; *cr:* Soc Stud Teacher 1969-80, Soc Stud Teacher/Dept Chairperson 1980- W T Woodson HS; *ai:* His Club & Citizen Bee Spon/Coach; Colleague Teacher Coord; WTW Mentor Prgm; Soc Stud Curr Advisory & VA St Textbook Comm; FEA, VEA, NEA, VA Cncl Soc Stud, NCSS 1970-; PTSA 1975-; Nom for Cty Teacher of Yr 1987; *office:* W T Woodson HS 9525 Main St Fairfax VA 22030

SPENCER, REX L., Soc Stud Teacher & Dept Chmn; *b:* Kendallville, IN; *m:* Diana Carole Land; *c:* Katie Jo, Emily Paige; *ed:* (BS) Soc Stud Comprehensive, Defiance Coll 1966; (MA) Amer His, 1970, (PhD) Amer His, 1988 Ball State Univ; *cr:* Classroom Teacher Ansonia HS 1966-80, Ansonia Mid Sch 1982-86, Edison State Comm Coll 1983-87, Ansonia HS 1986-, Defiance Coll 1988-; *ai:* Ftbl/BskblL & Track Coach; Stu Cncl & Sr Class Adv; Athletic Dir; Ansonia Ed Assn Pres 1961-; OH Ed Assn 1966-; NEA 1966-; OH Cncl for Soc Stud 1982-; Mercer Cty Historical Society 1985-; Doctoral Fellowship 2nd Place Excl in Economic Ed; 49th Place Natl Awards Prgm for Teaching Economics; Ansonia Dist Teacher of Yr; Published in Economics Ed; *home:* 303 N Mill St Celina OH 45822

SPENCER, ROSA LEAH (STORY), Business Teacher; *b:* West Plains, MO; *m:* Bobby Gene; *c:* Freddy, Darla, Susan; *ed:* (BS) Bus Ed, SMSU 1976; *cr:* Teacher Dora HS; *ai:* Jr Class Spon; Cheerleading Spon; Yrbk & Newspaper Adv; MBEA; *office:* Dora R-III Sch Gen Del Dora MO 65637

SPENCER, SALLY BAILEY, Senior HS English Chairperson; *b:* Memphis, TN; *m:* Kenneth C.; *c:* Stephanie Logan, Amy Cook, Piper; *ed:* (BA) Eng, Memphis St Univ 1972; *ai:* Drama Club Coach; Jr Class, Prom, Sr HS Academic Adv; Rossville Acad Beauty Review; Rossville Acad Literary Magazine; MPSA Eng Chairperson 1989-; Rossville Garden Club VP 1984-; Rossville Zoning Review Bd 1984-; MS Private Sch Assn Eng Chairperson; *office:* Rossville Acad 29 High St Rossville TN 38066

SPENCER, SHEILA FRANCES (WALSH), Dean of Students; *b:* Dallas, TX; *m:* Alan; *c:* Timothy, Lindsey; *ed:* (BA) Eng/Fr, TX Tech Univ 1975; (MED) Ed Admin, E TX Univ 1980; *cr:* Teacher Bishop Lynch HS 1975-77, Sequoyah Acad 1977-82, Edison Acad 1982-84, Wilson Mid Sch 1984-86; Staff Appraiser Plano Ind Sch Dist 1986-89; Dean of Stus Shepton HS 1989-; *ai:* Sch Paper Rampage, Sch Newspaper, Amer Ed Week, Sr Class Spon; Academic Emphasis Class, Rdng/Testing Taking Techniques, Staff Dev, Sch Tutorial, Hum Enrichment Prgms; Annual Field Investigation Trip Coord; 7th/8th Grade Eng Chairperson; Faculty Rep Classroom Teachers of Dallas; Faculty Advisory & Prin Comm; Phi Delta Kappa; *office:* Shepton HS 5505 W Plano Pkwy Plano TX 75093

SPERBER, CAROL HEFFNER, Media Specialist; *b:* Daytona Beach, FL; *m:* Perry R.; *c:* Bryan; *ed:* (BA) Elem Ed, Univ of Cntrl FL 1976; Media Specialist Cert Univ of Cntrl FL; *cr:* Teacher S Daytona Elem 1976-86; Media Specialist New Smyrna Beach Mid Sch 1987-89; *ai:* Media Advisory Bd; Dist Teacher Advisory Cncl; Youth Motivator; Volusia Cty Assn of Media in Ed (Pres Elect 1989-, Pres 1990-91); FL Assn of Media in Ed; Teacher of Yr S Daytona Elem 1985-86; Teacher of the Quarter 1989-; Certified Master Teacher; *home:* 809 Wells Dr South Daytona FL 32119

SPERCES, DELMER TROY, History Teacher; *b:* Whitewright, TX; *m:* Barbara; *c:* Anthony, Christopher; *ed:* (BS) His, E TX St Univ 1978; *cr:* His Teacher Edna Ind Sch Dist 1981-82, Callisburg Ind Sch Dist 1982-87, Cumby Ind Sch Dist 1988-89, St Jo Ind Sch Dist 1989-; *ai:* Head Coach Ftbl, Boys & Girls Track; TX Coaches Assn, TX St Teachers Assn 1979-89; *office:* St Jo Ind Sch Dist Drawer L Saint Jo TX 76265

SPEVACEK, DONNA MUNSON, Fifth Grade Teacher; *b:* La Grosse, WI; *m:* John E.; *c:* Michael, Jan Guehlstorf, Christine; *ed:* (BA) Elem Ed, Univ of WI La Crosse 1961; Courses Univ of WI Green Bay, Timberlake Stevens; *cr:* 4th Grade Grade Mc Kinely Sch 1961-64; 3rd-7th Grade Teacher Schultz Elem 1965-; *ai:* Authors Club; Vlybl; Delta Kappa Gamma Society Intnl Secy 1984-; MEA, WEA; Teacher of Yr 1986; *home:* 132 Barthels Rd Two Rivers WI 54241

SPICER, LINDA J., 5th/6th Grade Teacher; *b:* Cisne, IL; *m:* Steve K.; *c:* Ryan, Aron; *ed:* (BS) Ed, 1972, (MS) Admin 1982 Eastern IL Univ; Performance Lrng; *cr:* 4th Grade Teacher 1972-88, 5th/6th Grade Teacher 1988 Geff Grade Sch; 1988-90; Part Time Instr SIU 1987; *ai:* Delta Kappa Gamma 1976-89; *home:* PO Box 45 Cisne IL 62823

SPICER, SELMA GWENDOLYN, Alternative Education Teacher; *b:* Washington, DC; *ed:* (BA) Elem Ed, Shaw Univ 1966; Religious Ed, Richmond VA Theological Seminary; *cr:* Music/Lang Art Teacher Edgecombe Cty Sch System 1966-68; Rdng Teacher 1968-84, Alternative Ed Teacher 1984- Hampton City Schls; *ai:* Crocheting-Crafts Club; Accompanist Schls Concert Choir; HEA, VEA, NEA 1966-; *office:* Spratley Mid Sch 339 Woodland Rd Hampton VA 23663

SPIEGELHALTER, WILLIAM ROBERT, Band Director; *b:* Erie, PA; *m:* Mary Jo Edinger; *c:* Jennifer, Joseph; *ed:* (BMED) Music Ed, 1969, (MMED) Music Ed, 1973 Univ of Louisville; *cr:* Band Dir Western Jr HS 1969-75, Westport HS 1975-81, Westport Mid & Waggener HS 1981-87, Westport Mid Sch 1987-; *ai:* Prof Musician; Active Adjudicator for Marching & Concert Bands; Solo & Ensemble Festivals; Private Instr All-Cty Band & Jefferson Cty Inservice Planning Comm; Jefferson Dist Music Educators Assn Band Chm 1979, Teacher of Yr 1987; KY Music Educator Assn Asst All St Band 1980; Natl Band Assn 1977-; Holy Spirit Organ Comm 1990; Commonwealth Brass Band 1989-; Numerous Superior Ratings in St & Local Music Festivals Mid Sch & HS Level; HS Music Teacher of Yr 1987; Selected to Conduct Jefferson Cty All Cty Band 1982; *office:* Westport Mid Sch 8100 Westport Rd Louisville KY 40222

SPIEKER, JOSEPH, English Teacher/Coach; *b:* Queens, NY; *m:* Judy Marie Mc Almond; *c:* Keith B.; *ed:* (BA) Eng, Carroll Coll 1966; (MA) Spec Ed, E MT Coll 1979; 7th-12th Grade Scndry Sch Principalship; Reach America Drug & Alcohol Prevention; *cr:* Teacher Hobson Public Schls 1966-67; Teacher/Coach Helena Cntrl Cath HS 1967-69, Helena Public Schls 1969-; *ai:* Head Cross Cntry Coach; MT Tecn Inst Adv; MT Coaches Assn Coach of Yr Awd 1974, 1976, 1977, 1980; NEA, MT Ed Assn; Helena Ed Assn 1969-; *home:* 1101 Knight St Helena MT 59601

SPIERS, MARY CAROLYN, English Teacher/Dept Head; *b:* Vicksburg, MS; *m:* Edward E. Jr.; *c:* Wendy, Lawson; *ed:* (BS) Eng, MS St Coll for Women 1965; (MED) Scndry Ed, MS St Univ 1975; *cr:* Eng/Phys Ed Teacher Culkin Acad 1965-67; Eng Teacher Warren Cntrl Jr HS 1968-70, 1972-74; Eng/Bus Teacher Vicksburg Commercial Coll 1971-72; Eng Teacher 1974-, Dept Head 1984- Vidor HS; *ai:* UIL Literary Criticism Coach; VISD Writing Team Mem; Assn of TX Prof Educators 1986-; Alpha Delta Kappa (VP, Secy) 1984-; Daughters of Amer Revolution Secy 1965-.

SPIESMAN, JOHN MICHAEL, 6th Grade Teacher; *b:* Geneva, OH; *ed:* (BSED) Elem Ed, 1979, (MSED) Rdng/Supervision, 1981 Lake Erie Coll; Spec Ed, Cleveland St Univ; Instructional Technology, Kent St Univ; Educl Media, Univ of WY; Educl Admin, Drug & Alcohol Abuse Prevention, Youngstown St Univ; *cr:* Instr Lakeland Comm Coll 1980-82, Coll of Mt St Joseph 1982-89, Geneva Area City Schls 1978-, Performance Learning Systmes Incorporated 1980-; *ai:* Cork Elem Sch Head Teacher & Just Say No Club Adv; Phi Delta Kappa 1987-; Intnl Freelance Photographers Assn 1989-; Cleveland Press Club 1988-; Youth for Understanding Area Rep 1982-; Amer Red Cross Instr 1980-; Youth for Understanding Assoc Field Mgr 1990; Ashtabula City Soil & Water Conservation Teacher of Yr 1983; Martha Holden Jennings Fnd Grant 1985-88, Jennings Scholar 1986; Cleveland Electric Illuminating Company Grant 1986-87; Hannon Electric Company Grant 1986; Publication Contributor 1984; *office:* Geneva Area City Schls 341 Rt 534 Geneva OH 44041

SPIGNER, MARY FRANCES, Mathematics Teacher; *b:* Hope, AR; *m:* Harold; *c:* Mike, Steve; *ed:* (BSE) Math/Sci, Henderson St Univ 1959; *cr:* Math Teacher Jefferson Avenue Jr HS 1959-61, Nashville HS 1961-; *ai:* Soph Class Spon; NCTM; AR Cncl of Math Teachers; Twice Selected Teacher of Yr; *home:* Rt 4 Box 408 Nashville AR 71852

SPIKER, SHIRLEY F., Social Studies Teacher; *b:* Swanton, MD; *m:* Carl William; *c:* Jeffrey S.; *ed:* (BS) Elem Ed, Frostburg St 1978; Grad Stud Frostburg, Garrett Comm Coll, Univ of KY; *cr:* Teacher Southern Mid Sch 1978-; *ai:* Soc Stud Dept Chairperson; Stu Cncl Adv; Garrett Cty Teachers Assn Rep 1982-; MD St Teachers Assn, NEA Mem 1982-; Amer Legion Auxiliary Post 155 Mem 1985-; Republican Womens Club Mem 1990; *office:* Southern Mid Sch 903 Broad Ford Rd Oakland MD 21550

SPIKES, JAN EDWARDS, 2nd Grade Teacher; *b:* Hughes Springs, TX; *c:* Fertisha, Valerie; *ed:* (BA) Elem Ed, Javis Chrstn Coll 1965; Grad Stud Eng, E NM Univ; *cr:* Elem Ed Teacher E NM Univ Grad Sch; *ai:* Women Aglow Clovis Secy; Clovis Ed Assn Mem; Hugh O Brian Leadership Conference 1989, Cnslr Certificate 1989; *home:* 125 Manson Dr Clovis NM 88101

SPILLANE, MARGARET SCHMITZ, Third Grade Teacher; *b:* Richland Center, WI; *c:* Debbie Jackson, Mary, Dan, Theresa, Tom, Tim; *ed:* (BS) Elem Ed, Univ of Platteville 1968; Elem Ed, Platteville St Coll 1956; *cr:* 3rd Grade Teacher Shullsburg Public Sch 1968-; Rural Sch Teacher Silverthorne Sch 1960-61; 3rd/4th Grade Teacher Evansville Public Sch 1956-58; *ai:* Benjamin Franklin Stamp Club Organizer; Adv HS Group Friends Helping Friends; Facilator Stu Asst Prgm Drug/Alcohol Comm; Human Growth/Dev Comm; Lafayette Genealogy (Wrkshp Sec 1988-89 Wrkshp Bd 1989-90) Shullsburg Industrial Corp 1988-; Sesa III Teacher of Yr 1989-; *home:* 436 E Water St Shullsburg WI 53586

SPILLER, ANDREW, Social Studies Teacher; *b:* Mc Bride, MS; *m:* Betty M.; *c:* Andrea, Andre, Kristy; *ed:* (BS) Elem Ed, Alcorn St Univ 1966; Soc Stud Certificate; *cr:* Teacher Loyd Star HS 1975-; *ai:* Soc Stud Chm; MS Assn of Educators, NEA; Brookhaven Housing Authority Chm 1989; STAR Teacher of Yr; *home:* Rt 3 Box 883-A Brookhaven MS 39601

SPILLER, BETTY MC BETH, Home Economics Teacher; *b:* Brookhaven, MS; *m:* Andrew; *ed:* (BS) Home Ec, Alcorn St Univ 1967; MS St Univ, Univ of S MS; *cr:* Home Ec Teacher J E Johnson 1967-68; Elem Teacher Eva Harris 1968-70; Home Ec Teacher Enterprise HS 1970-76, Alexander Jr HS 1976-; *ai:* FHA & Bertharette Club Adv; Home Ec Assn, Natl Assn of Educators, MS Assn of Educator; Brookhaven Hum Auxiliary Socialities; Teacher of Yr 1980; Teacher Appreciation Grant; *office:* Alexander Jr HS Beaugard St Brookhaven MS 39601

SPILLER, CAROL ANN, Earth Science Teacher; *b:* Detroit, MI; *c:* Jonathon P.; *ed:* (BA) Elem Ed/Sci/Math, MI St Univ 1974; (MA) Scndry Ed/Geology, Univ of Houston/Clear Lake 1978; *cr:* 7th Grade Math/8th Grade Sci Teacher Baker Jr HS 1978-80; 6th/8th Grade Sci Teacher Cedar Bayou Jr HS 1980-85; Part-Time Lecturer/Lab Instr Univ of Houston/Clear Lake 1982-88; Earth Sci/Environmental Sci Teacher St Johns Sch 1985-; *ai:* Mid Sch Sci Club; Academic Competition Spon; Study Skills Comm; Food Coord; Field Camp in Big Bend Natl Park; NSTA, Earth Sci Teachers Assn, Marine Ed Assn; Earthwatch, Astronomical Society of the Pacific; Earthwatch Fellowship 1988; Houston Math & Sci Improvement Consortium 1986; Weeks Working Mentor Houston Natural Sci Museum; Inst for Chemical Ed 1989; Article Published by Good Apple in Challenge Magazine; *office:* St Johns Sch 2401 Claremont Houston TX 77019

SPILMAN, JAMES B., Science Department Chair; *b:* Marysville, CA; *ed:* (BA) Biological Sci, CA St Univ Chico 1969; *cr:* Sci Teacher/Sci Dept Chm Lompoc Valley Mid Sch 1970-85; Bio/Chem Teacher/Sci Dept Chair Lompoc HS 1985-; *ai:* Water Polo Asst Coach; CA Assn Chem Teachers; PTA Service Awd; Natl Sci Fnd Protozoology Research Grant; *office:* Lompoc HS 515 W College Ave Lompoc CA 93436

SPINDLER, DAVIDANNE M., SSCM 8th Grade Teacher; *b:* Gary, IN; *ed:* (BS) Bio, Alvernia Coll 1975; (MS) Scndry Sch Sci, Villanova PA 1983; *cr:* 7th Grade Teacher Holy Trinity Sch 1970-71; 7th-8th Grade Teacher St John 1971-73; 8th Grade Teacher St Joseph 1973-76, St Catherine La Boure 1976-79, Holy Trinity 1979-; *ai:* Sch & Parish Liturgy & Choir Dir; Parish Adult Rel Ed; Sch Sci Coord; Asst Track Coach; Lake Interfaith Families Together; *office:* Holy Trinity Sch 425 W 12th Ave Gary IN 46407

SPINETTA, VIRGINIA A., Kindergarten Teacher; *b:* Bronx, NY; *m:* Sylvester C. Jr.; *c:* Sylvester III, James; *ed:* (BA) Eng, Notre Dame Coll 1964; (MS) Early Chldhd, Wagner Coll 1974; *cr:* Teacher New York Bd of Ed 1965-, Public Sch 69 1976-; *ai:* Grade Leader 1976-87; Mainstream Comm 1980-84; Staff Consultation Comm 1989-; UFT (Mem 1965-, Delegate 1975); Impact II Developer Grant for Developing Educl Unit; *office:* Public Sch 69 144 Keating Pl Staten Island NY 10314

SPINNER, COZETTE REGENA (BELL), 5th Grade Language Arts; *b:* Carbondale, IL; *w:* Hezekiah Jr. (dec); *c:* Darla E. K., Harold O. T.; *ed:* (BS) Elem Ed, S IL Univ 1964; Grad Prgm S IL Univ; Post Grad Prgm Wayne St; *cr:* 1st Grade Teacher Washington Elem 1964-66, Attucks Elem 1966-68; Hum Teacher Mc Kerrow Elem 1968-70; Vocal Music Teacher Mc Kerrow Elem 1970-71, Mann/Weatherby 1971-72; Lang Art Teacher Parkman Elem 1973-; *ai:* Future Teacher Supv Service Squad; Black His, Martin L King Special Ceremonies; Stu Cncl Supvr; Girl Scout Leader; Glee Club Supvr; Sch Curr Planning Comm; Red Cross Volunteer 1968, Pin 1698; NEA, MEA, DFT, Detroit Rdng Cncl 1968; Order of Eastern Stars 1968; Eastern Progressive Dist Assn Bible Teacher 1970-85; Petra Dist Assn Bible Teacher 1986-; 2nd Chapel Hill MI Baptist Church (Sunday Sch Teacher, Supvr, Dir, Deaconess, Mission Pres, Vacation Bible Sch Dir, Supvr) 1985-, Distinguished Service Awds.

SPINOSI, BARBARA A., Sixth Grade Teacher; *b:* Scranton, PA; *m:* Mario; *c:* Todd, Kami; *ed:* (BS) Elem Ed, East Stroudsburg Univ 1966; Cooperative Learning Conference, John Hopkins Univ; Peer Coaching, Marywood Coll; Heres Looking at You 2000; *cr:* 1st Grade Teacher W Wayne Sch Dist 1966; 3rd/5th/6th Grade Teacher Mid Valley Sch Dist 1966-; *ai:* PSEA Rep 1970-; *office:* Mid Valley Elem Center Underwood Rd Throop PA 18512

SPIRES, DENISE TATE, Mathematics Teacher; *b:* Oxford, AL; *m:* Wesley D.; *ed:* (BS) Math, Auburn Univ 1979; Working Towards Masters Math Ed 1990; *cr:* Math Teacher Crisp Cty HS 1979-; *ai:* Stu Cncl Adv; Crisp Cty HS Teacher of Yr 1989-; Teacher of Yr 1989-; *office:* Crisp Cty HS E 24th Ave Cordele GA 31015

SPIRK, JAYNIE SUE (HANSEN), Mathematics Teacher; *b:* Wakefield, NE; *m:* James S.; *c:* Peter, Benjamin; *ed:* (BS) Math Ed, Univ of NE Lincoln 1972; Math Ed; *cr:* Math Teacher Nelson Public Schls 1972-; *ai:* Class Spon; NCTM; PEO (VP, Pres, Chaplain); *office:* Nelson Public Schls 380 S Maple Nelson NE 68961

SPIRO, JONATHAN PETER, Social Studies Teacher; *b:* Manchester, CT; *ed:* (BA) His, Univ of CA Los Angeles 1982; *cr:* Soc Stud Teacher 1983-, Athletic Dir 1984 El Camino Real HS; *ai:* Athletic Dir; Sch Based Management Cncl; Surfrider Fnd; *office:* El Camino Real HS 5440 Valley Circle Blvd Woodland Hills CA 91367

SPITZER, JOSEPH LAWRENCE, Third Grade Teacher; *b:* Washington, DC; *ed:* (BS) Elem Ed, Univ of MD 1972; Grad Stud Univ MD; *cr:* Classroom Teacher Longfields Elem 1972-; *ai:* Effective Schls Comm; Grade Level Chairperson; Taught Spec Ed, Highly Able & Gifted, TAG Pullout Prgm; Supvr Cty TAG Prgm; *office:* Longfields Elem Sch 3300 Newkirk Ave Forestville MD 20747

SPITZER, MARY ELIZABETH, Fifth Grade Teacher; *b:* Ann Arbor, MI; *ed:* (BA) His, CA St Univ Humboldt 1970; *cr:* Spec Ed Teacher 1977-80, 5th Grade Teacher 1980- Valley Springs Elem 1980-; *ai:* Delta Kappa Gamma (Pres, 1986-88, Secy 1983-86) 1983-; Mentor Teacher Calaveras Unified Sch Dist 1985-89.

SPIVEY, CHERYL SIMS, Second Grade Teacher; *b:* Williston, FL; *m:* Michael Lee; *c:* Jaime Leigh; *ed:* (AA) Cntrl FL Comm Coll 1980; (Ba) Elem Ed, Univ of FL 1982; (MS) Elem Ed, Univ of North FL 1986; *cr:* Teacher Bronson Elem 1982-; *ai:* Girls Varsity Bsktbl Coach Bronson HS from 1982-84; Girls Varsity Vlybl Coach Bronson HS 1982-84; Team Leader of BES 1987-88; Comm Mem Who Assisted in the Writing of the Counties Sci Curr Guide 1988; *office:* Bronson Elem Sch PO Box 220 Bronson FL 32621

SPLEAR, WANDA K., Business Education Teacher; *b:* Kankakee, IL; *m:* Duane D.; *c:* Grant E., Aaron H.; *ed:* (BA) Bus Ed, IL St Univ 1969; Cmptrs; *cr:* Phys Ed Teacher Bonfield Grade Sch 1969-70, Yuba City Intermediate Sch 1970-72; Bus Ed Teacher Herscher HS 1972-; *ai:* St Curr Asst Prgm Adv; Teacher Curr Advisory Comm; Bus Club & Ftbl Cheerleading Spon; Frosh Boys Bsktbl Score Keeper; NBEA 1974-; Limestone Little League Bd of Dir Uniform & Equipment Dir 1989-; *office:* Herscher HS 501 N Main St Herscher IL 60941

SPOFFORD, GREGORY BYRON, 1st Grade Teacher; *b:* St Cloud, MN; *m:* Vicki Lyseng; *c:* Beth, Andy, Erika; *ed:* (BA) Elem Ed/Phys Ed, Univ of MN Morris 1978; (MS) Curr/Instruction, St Cloud St Univ 1988; MN Educl Effectiveness Prgm; Project Charlie Trng; *cr:* 5th/6th Grade Teacher St Marys Sch 1978-80; 1st/3rd-5th Grade Teacher Ind Sch Dist #482 Little Falls 1980-; *ai:* 6th & 8th Grade Mid Sch Boys Tennis Coach; Little Falls Schls Writing Comm; MN Ed Assn 1980-; Oasis & Share-A-Meal Bd Mem 1987-; St Marys Parish Cncl Vice-Chm 1988-; *office:* Lindbergh Sch Broadway & SE 9th Little Falls MN 56345

SPOKAS, ROBERT ALEX, Counselor; *b:* Chicago, IL; *m:* Marsha Kirk; *c:* Ryan, Timothy; *ed:* (AA) Liberal Arts, YMCA Jr Coll 1968; (BA) Ed, Natl Coll of Ed 1971; (MA) Guidance/Counselling, Roosevelt Univ 1980; *cr:* 4th Grade Teacher Canterbury Sch 1971-72, Okinawa Japan US Army 1972-74; 3rd Grade Teacher Wildflecken Germany USAF 1974-75; 5th-6th Grade Teacher 1975-88, Cnslr 1988- Chateaux Sch; *ai:* Sports Club Adv; NEA 1971-; Boys Club Mgr 1988-; *office:* Chateaux Sch 3600 Chambord Ln Hazel Crest IL 60429

SPONAUGLE, DON LEE, Science Teacher; *b:* Cortland, NY; *ed:* (BS) Bio, VT 1968, (MS) Sec Ed Sci, 1976; Admin, 1987 Univ of Bridgeport; NSTA Grant Earth Sci, Western CT St Coll 1969; *cr:* Phys Sci Teacher Dolan Mid Sch 1968-; *ai:* Staff Dev & Magnet Mid Sch Comm Treas Sch/Parent/Stu Organization; NEA Mem 1969-; CT Ed Assn Mem 1969-; Stamford Ed Assn (Treas/Bd of Dir 1974-76) 1969-; NSTA Mem; *office:* Dolan Mid Schl 51 Toms Rd Stamford CT 06907

SPONAUGLE, ROBERT LLOYD, English Teacher; *b:* Columbus, OH; *c:* Matthew P.; *ed:* (BS) Eng/Humanities, OH St Univ 1975; *cr:* Teacher/Coach Barrett Jr HS 1975-80; Eastmoor Sr HS 1980-84; Teacher Whetstone Sr HS 1984-85; Teacher/Coach Marion-Franklin HS 1985-; *ai:* Bsktbl Coach & Lecturer; Speaker & Publisher on Bsktbl Coaching & Shooting; Speaker & Lecturer to 9th Grade Assem; Study Skills Comm Mem for Curr Change Columbus Public Sch; Columbus Ed Assn 1975-; Central OH Teachers Assn 1975-; Columbus Coach Assn 1980-; Speaker at Conf Teaching Poetry in Urban Setting; Selected Participant Supt Adv Cncl; Publ Poet OH St Lantern; Publ Poet Anthology Echoes of Unlocked Odyssey; *office:* Marion-Franklin HS 1265 Koebel Rd Columbus OH 43207

SPONHEIMER, ELIZABETH JOY, Language Art Teacher; *b:* Derby, CT; *m:* Paul F. Jr.; *c:* Callah E.; *ed:* (BS) Elem Ed, Univ of CT 1975; (MS) Ed/Rdng, 1980, Classroom Teacher Specialist, 1990 S CT St Univ; *cr:* Lang Art Teacher Great Oak Mid 1977-; *ai:* Natl Jr Honor Society & Debate Club Adv; Kids-on-Kids & Spelling Bee Comm; *office:* Great Oak Mid Sch 222 Governors Hill Rd Oxford CT 06483

SPOONER, JANICE SUE, Spanish Teacher; *b:* Ft Worth, TX; *m:* Phil Silvernail; *c:* Denise, Stephanie; *ed:* (BA) Span/Eng, N TX St Univ 1968; Grad Work N TX St Univ; *cr:* Teacher Grapevine Mid Sch 1968-69, Hurst Jr HS 1969-70, Harwood Jr HS 1978-79, Haltom Jr HS 1979-82, Richland Jr HS 1982-85, Richland HS 1985-; *ai:* Fiesta Dancers Spon; Assn of TX Prof Educators 1986-; TX Foreign Lang Assn 1976-; TX Flute Assn 1975-; Harmony Club 1986-; Local Orchs Guest Performer Masterworks Series; Prin Flutist Ft Worth Civic Orch & New Philharmonic Orch of Irving; *office:* Richland HS 5201 Holiday Ln Fort Worth TX 76180

SPORINSKY, SUSAN DONALDSON, English Teacher; *b:* Anderson, IN; *m:* Jack; *c:* Nick; *ed:* (BS) Eng, 1973, (MS) Scndry Ed, 1978 Ball St Univ; *cr:* Eng Teacher Pendleton Heights HS 1973-; *ai:* Chairperson Steering Comm North Cntrl Assn Evaluation; Dir All Sch Play; IN Cncl of Teachers of Eng 1971-; IN Cncl of Teachers of Writing 1989-; IN Assn for Gifted 1990;

First United Meth Church of Pendleton, Amer Cancer Society Volunteer; *office:* Pendleton Heights HS R 3 Jct St Rds 67 & 38 Pendleton IN 46064

SPORTSMAN, ROY, Mathematics Teacher; *b:* Rothville, MO; *m:* Denise B.; *c:* Michel, Patricia Blair, Marc; *ed:* (BA) Ed, 1973, (MA) Ed, 1976 Univ of MO Kansas City; *cr:* Teacher Raymore-Peculiar R-II 1973-89; *ai:* Phi Kappa Phi Mem 1973-; *office:* Raymore-Peculiar R-II 211th St & School Rd Peculiar MO 64078

SPOSATO, JOSEPH, Math Teacher/Athletic Dir; *b:* Geneva, NY; *m:* Laura; *c:* Mark, Joe; *ed:* (BA) Math, Cortland 1974; (MS) Ed, Elmira 1978; Admin 1985; *cr:* Teacher Waterloo HS 1974-; *ai:* Var Bsktbl & Bsbl Athletic Dir; NY St Coaches Assn, NY St Bsktl Coach Assn, NY St Athletic Assn; Knights of Columbus; Most Achievements in Coaching; Bsbl Coach of Yr; Bsktbl Section 5 Chm; *office:* Waterloo HS 65 Center St Waterloo NY 13165

SPOTTS, LARRY LEE, French Teacher; *b:* N Kansas City, MO; *ed:* (BSE) Fr, Cntrl MO St Univ 1977; (MA) Counseling/Guidance, Univ of MO Kansas City 1984; Univ of Paris XIII; Kansas Univ; *cr:* Span Teacher Bishop Kelley HS 1977-78; Span/Fr Teacher Benton HS 1978-80, Turner HS 1980-81; Fr Teacher Olathe S HS 1981-; *ai:* Asst Wrestling, Class of 1985 & AFS Spon; NEA 1979-; Olathe Natl Ed Assn Treas 1988-; AATF 1982-; Alliance Francaise Service Cultuel Schlsp Paris 1988; Poly Action Chair for Olathe, NEA; *office:* Olathe S HS 1640 E 151st St Olathe KS 66062

SPRAGUE, BELLE B., Language Art Teacher; *b:* San Diego, CA; *m:* Terry A.; *ed:* (BA) Eng, Chapman Coll 1974; *cr:* Lang Art/Soc Stud Teacher Wilshire Jr HS 1976-, Parks Jr HS 1980-; *ai:* CA Cncl for Soc Stud Outstanding Teacher 1983; John Hopkins Univ CA Teacher Recognition Prgm 1988; *office:* Parks Jr HS 1710 Rosecrans Ave Fullerton CA 92633

SPRAGUE, BETTY TEECE, English Teacher; *b:* Fort Valley, GA; *m:* Richard Morrison; *c:* Mark, Kent, Jonathan; *ed:* (BA) Eng, Asbury Coll 1956; (MAT) Elem, Rollins Coll 1981; *cr:* Eng Teacher Harrodsburg Jr HS 1956-58, Tavares Mid Sch 1980-; *ai:* Eng Dept Chairperson; Mastermind Spon; Asbury Covenant Church Pianist; Teacher of Yr 1987; *home:* 31026 Cove Rd Tavares FL 32778

SPRAGUE, JEANETTE (HILL), Vocational Business Teacher; *b:* Bethany, MO; *m:* Benny; *c:* Trisha L.; *ed:* (BSED) Bus Ed, 1977, (MSED) Bus, 1980 NW MO St Univ; *cr:* Voc Bus Teacher Gallatin R-V 1977-; *ai:* FBLA Adv; Asst Track Coach; CTA Career Ladder; MO Voc Assn 1977-; MO Bus Ed Assn 1988-; Cmmty Teachers Assn Treas 1984-85; *office:* Gallatin R-V HS 602 S Olive Gallatin MO 64640

SPRAGUE, SUSANNE FURTEK, Jr HS Science Teacher; *b:* Berwyn, IL; *m:* William T.; *c:* Karen, Andy, Scott; *ed:* (BS) Ed, W IL Univ 1974; Various Sci Classes; *cr:* Sci Teacher Sacred Heart Sch 1987-; *ai:* Ed Comm 1989-; Racine Cath Schls Sci Olympiad; Sci Fair Adv; NSTA, W WI Elem Sci Teachers; Sci Fellows I & II Univ of WI Parkside Regional Staff Dev.

SPRAYBERRY, MELVIN J., Science Teacher; *b:* Birmingham, AL; *m:* Mary Linda Stevens; *c:* Michael, Tracy; *ed:* (NA) Navy Nuclear Power Trng, US Navy 1963; (BS) HS Ed, Univ of AL Birmingham 1988; Working Towards MS in Sci Ed, Univ of Montevallo 1990; *cr:* Chem Teacher Hueytown HS 1988-89; Physics/Chem/Sci Teacher Mortimer Jordan HS 1989-; *ai:* Phi Kappa Phi Mem; Pineywoods Fire Dept Chm Bd of Dir 1987-88; Deans Awd Univ of AL Sch of Ed 1988; *home:* Rt 1 Box 408 Jasper AL 35501

SPRECHER, DORIS WERNER, Retired; *b:* Junction City, KS; *m:* Eldred Alvin; *c:* Ruth Alice Weingartner, Roger William; *ed:* (AB) Ed/Bio, Park Coll 1938; Ed, Emporia St Univ; Ed/Sci/Art, Pittsburg St Univ; *cr:* Rural Sch Teacher Half Acre Sch; Music/Sci/5th/6th Grade Teacher Kendall HS; Kndgtn/1st Grade Teacher Eugene Ware Sch; *ai:* NEA; NRTA; Delta Kappa Gamma; U M Church; U M Women.

SPRENG, DAVID L., Science Department Teacher; *b:* Ashland, OH; *m:* Diana J.; *c:* Bryan; *ed:* (MS) Teaching Competency, Coll of Mt St Josephs 1987; Martha Holding Jennings Fnd & OH Bd of Regents Sci is Fun Project Facilitator; *cr:* 7th Grade Sci Teacher Loudonville-Perrysville Jr HS 1983-; *ai:* Sci Fair Dir; Sci Club Adv; Mohican Area Sci Fair Comm; *office:* Loudonville-Perrysville Jr HS 155 W 3rd St Perrysville OH 44864

SPRIGGS, MARJETTA RAGAN, Fifth Grade Teacher; *b:* Corsicana, TX; *m:* Ricky; *c:* Stacy; *ed:* (BAT) Elem Ed, 1976, (MED) Spec Ed, 1979 Sam Houston St Univ; Marylin Burns Math Solutions; Power of Positive Stu; Writing as a Process Inst; *cr:* 4th Grade Teacher Ennis Ind Sch Dist 1976-78; 5th Grade Teacher Conroe Ind Sch Dist 1978-79; 5th Grade Teacher Huntsville Ind Sch Dist 1979-; *ai:* Cmptr Club Spon; Power of Positive Stu Leadership Team; Lang Art Dev Comm; Intnl Rdng Assn, TX Assn Gifted & Talented, TX Rdng Assn; Intnl Brangus Assn Auxiliary; *office:* Huntsville Ind Sch Dist 441 F M 2821 E Huntsville TX 77340

SPRING, JEFF S., Mathematics Teacher; *b:* Washington, DC; *ed:* (BA) Math/Chem, Penn St Univ 1969; (MS) Math, Univ of PA 1973; (MA) Math Educators, Rutgers Univ 1975; (MED) Admin, Kea Coll 1977; Doctoral Research Cmptr Sci, Princeton Univ; Cmptr Sci Research, Univ of PA; Math, LSU; SSCMCIS Prgm, Rutgers; *cr:* Teaching Fellow Penn St Univ 1973-75; Math Teacher Ternil Jr HS 1975-77, Scotch Plains HS 1977-; Math Adjunct Teacher Rutgers Univ & Middlesex Coll & Kea Coll & Montclair St Coll 1977-; *ai:* HS Head Cross Cntry & Head Track Coach; Quiz Bowl Adv; Jr HS Ftbl, Soccer, Swimmer, Wrestling Swimming, Wrestling & Girls Sftbl Coach; NEA, NJEA, NJCTM, MAA; YMCA Teach Handicapped Stu to Swim; Phi Beta Kappa; Teach Fellowship for Masters Degree; Math Teacher Articles Published; NSF Speaker Gifted & Talented Stu; Nom for Teacher of Yr Awd; *office:* Scotch Plains-Fanwood HS Westfield Rd Scotch Plains NJ 07076

SPRINGER, MARK A., 7th Grade Watershed Teacher; *b:* Bryn Mawr, PA; *m:* Allison Hooven; *c:* Colin, Lauren; *ed:* (BA) Eng, Haverford Coll 1974; (MAT) Eng, Univ of Chicago 1975; *cr:* Eng/Hum Teacher 1975-80, Teacher of Gifted 1981-86, Teacher of Watershed Prgm 1987- Radnor Mid Sch; Amer Stud Teacher Eastern Coll 1980-; GED Prgm Teacher Gaudenzia House Incorporated 1975-; *ai:* Wrestling, Ftbl, Track Coach; Worked Actively with Intramural Prgm & Drama Groups; NEH Fellowship 1979; Articles in Numerous Publications; Co-Created Watershed Alternative Learning Prgm; *office:* Radnor Mid Sch 131 S Wayne Ave Wayne PA 19087

SPRINGS, SYLVIA HOOKS, 12th Grade English Teacher; *b:* Mullins, SC; *m:* Sammy Dale; *c:* Kelly, Kara; *ed:* (BA) Scndry Eng, Lander Coll 1969; (MED) Scndry Sch Guidance, Univ of SC 1988; *cr:* Eng Teacher Loris HS 1970-75; West Florence HS 1967-77; Rdng Teacher Aynor HS 1977-78; Eng Teacher Loris HS 1979-; *ai:* SR Class Spon; Teachers Goodwill Comm; SR Adv; NCTE; NEA; SC Ed Assn; Horry Cty Ed Assn; 1st Bapt Church of Loris; Adult Choir Mem; Loris Elem Adv Bd; *office:* Loris HS Heritage Rd Loris SC 29569

SPRINKLE, MARY ELIZABETH CHANDLER, Biology Teacher; *b:* Marshall, NC; *m:* Jobie Fain; *c:* Jobie Fain Jr., William Tobie; *ed:* (BA) Bio, Tusculum Coll 1949; Western Carolina Univ; Univ of NC; *cr:* Bio Teacher Fairview HS 1949-51, Mars Hill HS L1951-56, Marshall HS 1963-; *ai:* Sponsorship Y-Teens; Beta ClubSch Newspaper Adv; Faculty Social Comm Bus Sci Club; NEA; NC Assn of Educators Sec 1976-77; Classroom Teachers Assn; Alpha Epsilom Delta Sec/Treas 1949; Order of Eastern Star Worth Matron 1956-57.

SPROUL, DIANNE PAYNE, Kindergarten Teacher; *b:* Asheville, NC; *m:* John Dandridge; *c:* Claire C.; *ed:* (BS) Elem Ed, Nyack Coll 1973; (MSED) Early Chldhd, W Carolina Univ 1982; *cr:* Kndgtn Teacher Candler Elem Sch 1973-; *ai:* Publicity & Public Relations Comm; Extra Duty & Pay Comm Chairperson; Phi Kappa Phi Honor Society 1983-; Intnl Rdng Assn 1985-; NC Assn of Educators, NEA; To Our Survival (Staff Artist 1980-, Drug Abuse Prevention Consultant), Volunteer Awd 1980-; Tarheel Family Album Collection of Sch Writing 1990; NC Center for Advancement of Teaching 1987; *office:* Candler Elem Sch Rt 3 Box 234 Candler NC 28715

SPROULL, BARBARA L., Mathematics Teacher; *b:* Tarentum, PA; *m:* James F.; *c:* Kevin, Jennifer; *ed:* (BS) Math Ed, IN St Coll 1965; (MED) Scndry Ed, Penn St Univ 1970; *cr:* Math Teacher Monroeville Jr HS 1965-67, St Coll Jr HS & HS 1967-71; Part-Time Instr Penn St New Kensington 1983; Math Teacher Freeport HS 1984-; *ai:* 7th Grade Bsktbl & Asst Sftbl Coachs; MCWP, PCTM, NCTM; *home:* 633 Sarver Rd Sarver PA 16055

SPRUEL, RICHARD OWEN, Mathematics Department Chair; *b:* Belmont, IL; *m:* Marilyn Miller; *c:* Stacey Roosevelt, Glennette; *ed:* (BSED) Math, E IL Univ 1961; (MA) Math, Univ of IL 1965; *cr:* Math Teacher Mt Carmel HS 1961-; *ai:* Math Coach; Dept Head; Curr Adv; IL Cncl Teachers of Math 1975-; South Cntrl Cncl Teachers of Math 1988-; *office:* Mt Carmel HS 201 Pear St Mount Carmel IL 62863

SPRUILL, SHIRLEY R., Social Studies Dept Teacher; *b:* Cleburne Cty, AL; *m:* Farris E.; *c:* Karol Higgins, Nancy Greiner; *ed:* (AB) His, 1968, (MED) Scndry ED, 1972 W GA Coll; Private Art Classes; Grad Work Ball St Univ 1979; *cr:* Teacher Mt Zion HS; *ai:* Sr & 4-H Club Spon; Dinner Theater Coach; NEA; GAE, CAE Treas 1970; PDK Historian 1970-, Innovative Teacher of Yr; Carroll Cty Art Alliance 1980; Carroll Cty Ed Task Force 1989; Carroll Cty Public Policy Comm 1988-89; Rep GA at Ball St Univ Natl Endowment for Hum; Presented Prgm for Governors Conference on Ed & SE Regional Soc Stud Conference Nashville 1989; *office:* Mt Zion HS 132 Eagle Dr Mount Zion GA 30150

SPRUNG, DELLA JOHNSON, Retired First Grade Teacher; *b:* Little Cedar, IA; *m:* Russell E.; *c:* Cheryl Pearson, Marilyn Waldschmidt, Alan; *ed:* (BA) Elem Ed, Upper IA Univ 1970; *cr:* 3rd Grade Teacher Stanley Elem 1948-50; 1st Grade Teacher Mc Intire Elem 1950-51; Rural All Grades Teacher Brownville 1956-59; Kndgtn/1st Grade Teacher Riceville Cmmty 1959-89; *home:* RR 2 Box 29 Osage IA 50461

SPUNGEN, ALBERT M., Social Studies Instructor; *b:* St Johns NF, Canada; *m:* Karen Chandler; *c:* Jennifer M., Amy J.; *ed:* (BA) Soc Stud, 1976, (MA) His, 1988 Univ of MO Kansas City; *cr:* His Instr Maize HS 1978-85; Soc Stud Instr Rockhurst HS 1985-; Amer His Instr Rockhurst Coll 1988-, Kansas Citt KS Comm Coll 1988-; *ai:* Stu Poly Action Founder & Spon; Faculty Dev Comm Mem; Intnl Relations Cncl 1985-; Cncl of Soc Stud 1985-; Maize Teachers Union Pres; NEA 1983-84; Fellowship Univ of MO Kansas City Art of Teaching Soc Stud Scndry Schls; *office:* Rockhurst HS 9301 Stateline Rd Kansas City MO 64131

SPURGEON, KENNETH WILLIAM, Soc Stud Teacher/Principal; *b:* Altamont, KS; *m:* Stacie Ann Wilson; *c:* Gabriel; *ed:* (BSED) His, 1977, (MSED) Scndry Sch Admin, 1986 Pittsburg St Univ; Specialist Work Pittsburg St Univ, MO Leadership Acad; *cr:* Soc Stud Teacher Bronaugh R-7 1977-79, Golden City R-3 1979-82; Soc Stud Teacher 1982-89, Prin 1989- Liberal R-2; *ai:* Bsktbl Coach 1977-; NAASP, MO Assn Scndry Sch Prin 1989-; Fellowship of Chrstn Athletes Spon 1988-; Liberal Booster Club; Published Article 1977; Midwest Conference Girls Bsktbl Coach of Yr 1988; Joplin Globe Dist Girls Bsktbl Coach of Yr 1989; *office:* Liberal R-2 HS P O Box 38 Liberal MO 64762

SPURGEON, LARRY DAYTON, Art Teacher; *b:* Beach City, OH; *m:* Sandra Kay; *c:* Christopher, Chad; *ed:* (BA) Art Ed, 1966, (MA) Painting, 1979 Kent St Univ; *cr:* Art Instr/Elem/Jr HS/HS Teacher Canton Local Schls 1966-; *ai:* Canton South Art Guild Club Adv; Painting Show at Kent St Univ & Work Displayed in Competitive Shows; *home:* 3233 Greenpark St Massillon OH 44646

SPURLIN, DAVID L., Consultant; *b:* Murfreesboro, TN; *m:* Connie; *c:* Kristi; *ed:* (BS) Bible, Cntrl Baptist Coll 1980; (MA) Counseling, Faith Chrstn Coll 1981; (DMIN) Pastoral Care, Covington Seminary 1984; Ed, Psych, Harding Univ Grad Ssh; Behavioral Analysis, Inst for Motivational Living; *cr:* Instr Cntrl Baptist Coll 1982; Pres Freedom Bible Coll & Acad 1986-; *ai:* United Assn of Chrstn Cnslrs 1981-; Chrstn Assn for Psychological Stud 1984-89; Guild of Clergy Cnslrs, Amer Assn of Chrstn Cnslrs 1988-; Articles Published; *home:* PO Box 2394 Batesville AR 72503

SPURLIN, GLENN E., Instrumental Music Teacher; *b:* Albertville, AL; *m:* Patricia Jane Harper; *c:* Juli, Corey, Joshua; *ed:* (BS) Music Ed, 1791, (MA) Music Ed, 1974 Univ of AL; *cr:* Band Dir Piscah HS 1971-72, Childersburg HS 1972-81, Joseph Saks HS 1981-; *ai:* Symphonic, Concert, Jr, Beginning, Jazz, Marching, Pep Band; AL Bandmasters Assn, Music Educators Natl Conference, Natl Band Dir Assn, Calhoun Cty Educators Assn, AL Educators Assn; Natl Music Festival (Music Festival Adv, Chm AL Festival); AL Unit Intnl Assn Jass Educators Pres; *office:* Joseph Saks HS 4401 Saks Rd Anniston AL 36206

SPURLOCK, REGINA L., Phys Ed Teacher/Coach; *b:* Corsicana, TX; *ed:* (BS) Phys Ed, Baylor Univ 1980; (MED) Counseling/Guidance, TX Womans Univ 1987; Wkshps on Teenage Suicide, Eating Disorders in Adolescence; *cr:* Phys Ed Teacher/Dept Head Keller Mid Sch 1980-83; Health Teacher/Dept Head Watauga Jr HS 1984-89; Phys Ed Teacher/Dept Head Watauga Mid Sch 1989-; *ai:* Coaching 1980-; Head Coach Keller 1981-83, Watauga 1987-; Dist Track Champions 1986-; Mid Sch Advisory Comm; City League Sftbl Coach; Care Team Watauga Mid Sch;Natl Jr Honor Society 1980-83; Assn of Teachers & Prof Educators, TX Girls Coaches Assn 1980-; Notable Women of TX 1984-85; Guest Lecturer Univ of N TX 1989; *home:* 5112 Nancy Ln Fort Worth TX 76180

SPYIES, GLADINE HUNTER, Teacher; *b:* Tennille, GA; *m:* James; *c:* Carla B., Jimmille R.; *ed:* (BS) Bus Ed, Fort Valley St Coll 1973; (MS) Mid Grade Ed, Ft Valley St 1976; Admin Supervision, Univ of GA 1988-; Working Towards EDS; *cr:* Coll Work Study Coord Fort Valley St Coll 1973-76; Teacher Ada Banks Elem 1976-81, Porter Elem 1981-; *ai:* Quiz Bowl, Math Bowl, Future Teachers Spon; Bibb Cty Assn of Educators Building Rep 1983-; GA Assn of Ed 1976-; Natl Alumni Secy 1973-80, Distinguished Alumni 1980; Fellowship Bible Baptist Church Clerk 1980-; Teacher of Yr 1981, 1983, 1986; Cty & St Data Collector, Master Teacher 1988-; *office:* James H Porter Elem Sch 5802 School Rd Macon GA 31206

SQUATRITO, FRANCIS PAUL, Assistant Director of Fine Art; *b:* Boston, MA; *m:* Marguerite Carol Sartini; *c:* Carl D., Glen M.; *ed:* (BSED) Ed, 1962, (MSED) Art Ed, 1973 MA Coll of Art; Grad Stud Salem St Coll, Tufts Univ; Extension Prgm Filene Center; Summer Inst & Inservice Faculty Dev Prgms; *cr:* Art/Crafts Teacher E Islip HS 1962, Melrose HS 1963-67; Art/Crafts/Photography Teacher Lexington HS 1967-70, Melrose HS 1970-; *ai:* Photography Club Adv; Art Festival Dir; Philosophy & Chm Evaluation Fine Arts Comm; Lexington Ed Assn 1967-70; Melrose Ed Assn 1963-67, 1970-; MA Ed Assn, NEA 1963-; Natl Art Ed Assn 1960-83; Pop Warner Ftbl Coach 1961; Little League Bsbl Coach 1981, Bsktbl Coach 1982-83; Art Lottery Cncl Bd 1985-88; Art Lottery Research Grant 1987-88; Area Art Competition Judge 1965-; *home:* 9 Sunset Rd Melrose MA 02176

SQUIRES, GEORGE WINSTON, Fr, Span, Latin Teacher; *b:* Bridgetown, Barbados; *c:* Ian, Sharon, Andre; *ed:* (BA) Fr, Univ of W Indies 1962; (BED) Ed, Univ of New Brunswick Canada 1968; (MA) Fr, NY Univ 1974; Cert Detudes Franchises Modernes, Univ De Strasbourg France 1982; Span, St Univ NY Stony Brook; Intnl Summer Sch, Univ of Salamanca Spain 1981; *cr:* Fr/Span Teacher Boys Scndry Sch 1962-65, Turks & Calcos Scndry Sch 1965-67, Park Jr HS 1968-71; Fr/Span/Latin Teacher Patchogue-Medford HS 1971-; *ai:* Amer Assn Teachers of Span & Portuguese, Amer Cncl on Teaching Foreign Langs 1968-; NY St Assn of Foreign Lang Teachers 1971-; Court Interpreter in Fr; Kingstown Dist Court St Vincent 1962; *office:* Patchogue-Medford HS Buffalo Ave Medford NY 11763

SQUIRES, ROBERT LARRY, Jr High Mathematics Teacher; *b:* Kooskia, ID; *m:* M. Felicia Jolley; *c:* Teresa, Cynthia; *ed:* (BS) Elem Ed, Univ of ID 1972; *cr:* Teacher Clearwater Valley Schls 1959-62; 6th Grade Teacher Amer Falls Elem 1962-64; Teacher Kamiah Jr HS 1964-; *ai:* Track Coach; ID Ed Assn, NEA 1964-; Dist II Coaches Assn Pres 1989-; ID St Coaches Assn Bd of Dir 1989-; Kamiah Ed Assn Pres 1971-73; Lions Club Pres 1972-73;

Boys St of ID Track Coach of Yr 1979-80; St of ID Nominee for Natl HS Coach of Yr 1981, 1988, 1989; Girls St of ID Track Coach of Yr 1987, 1988, 1989; ID Dist II Coach of Yr; *home:* Rt 2 Box 577 Kamiah ID 83536

SREMANIAK, MARY JEAN MUNARETTO, Spanish Teacher; *b:* Chicago, IL; *m:* Michael W.; *c:* Michael J., Matthew; *ed:* (BS) Ed/Foreign Lang, Rosary Coll 1977; *cr:* Span Teacher Sacred Heart of Mary HS 1980-82; Span/Eng as Second Lang Teacher Rhodes Sch 1983-86; Span Teacher West Leyden HS 1986-; *ai:* Sacred Heart of Mary HS Sr & NHS Adv; Rhodes Sch Stu Cncl Spon & Sch Interpreter; West Leyden Class of 1990 Spon, Operational Advisory & NHS Selection Comm; Amer Assn Teachers of Span & Portuguese 1980-; IL Foreign Lang Teachers Assn 1988-; River Grove Dist 85.5 Sch Bd Mem 1989-; *office:* West Leyden HS 1000 Wolf Rd Northlake IL 60164

SRODA, SOPHIE URBANICK, First Grade Teacher; *b:* Linesville, PA; *m:* Marion Joseph; *c:* Joseph, Janette Sroda Wilson, Joan; *ed:* (BS) Elem Ed, Edinboro St Univ 1961; Religion Certified Teaching Elem Religion, Ursuline Coll & Notre Dame Coll; Grade Courses Edinboro Univ & Penn St Coll; *cr:* 1st Grade Teacher Summit Sch 1961-63; 4th-6th Grade Phys Ed Teacher Linesville-Conncaut Summit HS 1961-63; 1st Grade Teacher Fullerton Sch 1963-66; Pre-Prof Young Adult Asst Cleveland Public Lib Fleet Branch 1963-66; 2nd Grade Teacher Fullerton Sch 1970-71; K-8th Grade Substitute Teacher Cleveland Public Schls & Parma Schls & Cleveland Cath Diocese Schls 1971-78; Beginning Swimmers Instr Independence Pool 1978-; 1st Grade Teacher St Columbkille Sch 1978-; *ai:* Liturgy & Sch Spirit Comm; NCEA 1978-; Cuyahoga-Summit Intnl Rdng Assn (Corresponding Secy, Sch Rep) 1981-; OH Rdng Assn, Intnl Rdng Assn 1981-; St Columbkille PTA 1986-; Seven Hills Homemakers II (VP 1973, Pres 1974-78); Cuyahoga Cty Homemakers Bd VP 1974-76; Seven Hills Garden Club Jr Adv 1973-78; Nom Ashland Oil Teacher Achievement Awds 1990.

STACEY, PAULA VICK, English Teacher; *b:* Dempolis, AL; *w:* Alex Wayne (dec); *c:* Marcus; *ed:* (BA) Eng, Judson Coll 1975; *cr:* Teacher Monroe Acad 1975-; *ai:* Sr Class, Beta Club, Anchor Club, Orange Aides Pep Club Spon; Cheerleading Coach; Monroeville Jr Womans Club; Cmmty Concert Assn Bd of Dir; Judson Alumnae Assn VP 1975-.

STACHO, LINDA S. NOTMAN, English Teacher; *b:* Massillon, OH; *m:* William R.; *ed:* (BS) Eng/Scndry, Kent St Univ 1973; (MED) Curr/Instruction, Cleveland St Univ 1978; *cr:* Eng Teacher Northwest HS 1974-75, John Hay HS 1975-; *ai:* Teen Club & Peer Counseling Adv 1988-; Greater Cleveland Cncl Teachers of Eng 1988-; John Hay Cleveland Teachers Union Secy 1989-; John Hay Union Conference Comm Mem 1989-; Co-Authored & Received Grant Thomas White Charitable Trust 1987-88 & Cuyahoga Cty Teen Pregnancy Prevention Project to Operate Teen Club 1989-; *office:* John Hay HS 2075 E 107th Cleveland OH 44106

STACK, EVELYN A., Language Arts Teacher; *b:* Johnson City, TN; *ed:* (BA) Eng Ed, FL Atlantic Univ 1968; Grad Stud; *cr:* Teacher Miami Shores Elem 1968-69, Palmview Elem 1969-71, Crystal Lake Mid 1971-; *ai:* Lang Art Dept Head; *office:* Crystal Lake Mid Sch 3551 NE 3rd Ave Pompano Beach FL 33064

STACKHOUSE, VIVIAN HAWTHORNE, Science Teacher; *b:* Due West, SC; *m:* Porter Lee; *c:* Deborah, Cedric, Larry, Victor, Omega, Alicia, Virgil; *ed:* (BS) Sci/Home Ec, Allen Univ 1960; Univ of SC, Clemson Univ, Lander Coll; *cr:* Teacher Due West Elem 1970-; *ai:* Adv Sci Club; Abbeville Cty Ed Assn (Building Rep, Mem) 1960-; SCEA, NEA Mem 1960-; PRC Mem 1986-; *home:* Rt Box 444 Donalds SC 29638

STACY, ESTHER CATTERTON, Guidance Counselor; *b:* Mc Kendrick, MD; *m:* Arnold Jr.; *c:* Jennifer, Jessica; *ed:* (BA) Ed, Univ of MD 1964; (MA) Guidance/Counseling, 1970, (Rank I) Guidance/Counseling, 1976 Morehead St Univ; *cr:* Teacher Southern HS 1964-69; Cnslr Menifee Cty HS 1970-71; Teacher 1973-76, Cnslr 1976- Bath Cty HS; *ai:* Beta & Academic Club Spon; Written Assessment & Quick Recall Coach; Bath Cty Ed Assn Treas 1986-; Delta Kappa Gamma (Chairperson & Office) 1986-; Bath Cty Ed Assn Corresponding Secy; Owingsville Baptist Church Womens Club Secy 1971-; *home:* PO Box 187 W Main St Owingsville KY 40360

STACY, GERALDINE PARCELL, Retired Teacher; *b:* Red Jacket, WV; *m:* Paul G.; *ed:* (BA) Elem, Marshall Univ 1968; *cr:* Teacher Westmoreland Elem Sch 1968-79, Kellogg Elem Sch 1979-83; *ai:* Alpha Delta Kappa (Corresponding Secy 1982-84, Chaplin 1984-86); Westmoreland Womens Club, Chrstn Womens Club, Meth Church, WV Retired Sch Employees.

STAFFORD, EDWIN CHARLES, Junior High Science Teacher; *b:* Pecos, TX; *m:* Lynda Jane; *c:* Sherri Locke, Stacae; *ed:* (BA) Bio, 1976, (MS) Ed, 1980 Tarleton St Univ; *cr:* Teacher 1976-79, Prin 1979-87, Teacher 1987- Dublin Ind Sch Dist; *ai:* UIL Sci; 8th Grade Class; ATPE Local Chm 1976-; Lions Club 1970-; *office:* Dublin Jr HS 405 N Camden Dublin TX 76446

STAFFORD, G. SUE ELDRIDGE, 2nd Grade Teacher; *b:* Eufaula, AL; *m:* Timothy M.; *c:* Scott, Mark, David; *ed:* (BS) Elem Ed, 1976, (MS) Rdng, 1982 USM; *cr:* 1st Grade Teacher D Iberville Elem 1976-82; Learning Lab Coord MS Gulf Coast Comm Coll 1982-85; 2nd Grade Teacher D Iberville Elem 1986-; *ai:* AFT; MS Gulf Coast Alumni Assn; Univ of Southern MS Alumni Assn; Billikens Carnival Assn; USM Graduate Highest Honors; MS Gulf Coast Jr Coll Highest Honors; *office:* Diberville Elem Sch 4540 Brodie Rd Biloxi MS 39532

STAFFORD, GARY LEE, Mathematics Dept Chairman; *b:* Brinkley, AR; *m:* Pamela Sue Guiltner; *ed:* (BSE) Math, Univ of Cntrl AR 1988; Math, SW MO St Univ; *cr:* Scndry Math Bradleyville Public Schls 1988-; *ai:* Math Club, Soph Class, Sign Lang Club Spon; MO Assn of Rural Educators Mem 1988-; *home:* 207 S Meadowview Springfield MO 65802

STAFFORD, MARY ANN ANN MULLINS, 7th Grade Lang Art Teacher; *b:* Williamson, WV; *m:* James R.; *c:* Rusty; *ed:* (BS) Eng, Pikeville Coll 1973; (AME) Scndry Ed, Morehead St 1982; (Rank I) Elem Ed, 1988; Elem Endorsement 1987; *cr:* Teacher Blackberry Elem 1980-84, Bevins Elem 1984-; *ai:* Schls Sports Prgms & Acts Volunteer; NEA, KY Ed Assn, Pike Cty Ed Assn Mem; *office:* Bevins Elem Sch Box 84 Sidney KY 41564

STAGGERS, MICHELLE GREEN, English Teacher; *b:* Georgetown, SC; *m:* Patrick Leroy; *c:* Aloysius L.; *ed:* (BA) Ed/ Eng, Allen Univ 1985; *ai:* Chrldr Coach Jr Var & Var 1987-; SC Cncl of Teachers, SC Teachers of Eng 1987-; Delta Sigma Theta 1982-; *home:* 402 Santee Dr Georgetown SC 29440

STAGGS, DIANA MEADOWS, Social Studies Department Chm; *b:* Maysville, KY; *m:* Jon; *c:* Laura E., Jon M.; *ed:* (BA) Geography/His, Univ of KY 1976; (MA) Scndry Ed, Morehead St Univ 1980; *cr:* 7th Grade Geography Teacher Maysville Jr HS 1976-87; 7th/10th Grade World Civilizations Teacher Maysville Jr/Sr HS 1987-; *office:* Maysville Jr/Sr HS Box 99 Limestone St Maysville KY 41056

STAHL, ALANA JUNE, Mathematics Teacher; *b:* Chicago, IL; *ed:* (BS) Math, 1972, (MS) Math Ed, 1974 Bradley Univ; Grad Stud; *cr:* Math Teacher/K-12th Grade Math Curr Dir Princeville HS 1972-; *ai:* Asst NHS Adv; *office:* Princeville HS 306 Cordis Ave Princeville IL 61559

STAHL, CARYL LYNN, Second Grade Teacher; *b:* Madison, WI; *ed:* (BS) Elem Ed, 1970, (MS) Elem Ed, 1975 Jacksonville St Univ; Grad Stud Gifted Ed, Univ of AL; *cr:* 5th Grade Teacher 1970, 1st Grade Teacher 1970-80 Saks Elem; Itinerant Teacher of Gifted Calhoun Cty Sch System 1980-82; 1st Grade Teacher 1982-88, 2nd Grade Teacher 1988- Saks Elem; *ai:* 2nd Grade Mastery Skills Dev Prgm Comm; Kappa Delta Phi, Delta Omicron; Pilot Club (Intnl Dir 1983-, Corresponding Secy 1985-86, Area Leader Intl Relations 1984-85, Area Leader Ed 1986-87); GSA Asst Leader; JSU Inservice Center Governing Bd Mem; Jacksonville St Univ Chamber Singers & Cmmty Chorus; Nom Sch & System Teacher Hall of Fame 1987-88, 1988-89; *office:* Saks Elem Sch 31 W Watson Anniston AL 36206

STAHL, GERALDINE ANN, 4th & 5th Grade Teacher; *b:* Langdon, ND; *m:* Russell Rayfield; *c:* Greta; *ed:* (BA) Elem Ed, Minot St Coll 1965; (MS) Instructional Design, Univ of IA 1979; *cr:* 4th Grade Teacher/Phys Ed Glasgow Elem; 5th Grade Teacher Carrington Elem 1966-68; 4th-6th Grade Teacher Madisson Elem 1969-89; *ai:* Dev Curr; NEA; Alpha Delta Kappa Secy Alturistic; Highland Womens Golf; *home:* 811 N Hampshire Mason City IA 50401

STAHL, KAREN E. (PEDERSEN), HS Physical Education Teacher; *b:* Yankton, SD; *m:* Waldo J.; *ed:* (BS) Phys Ed, CO St Univ 1960; Grad Stud; *cr:* Phys Ed Instr Delano HS 1960-; *ai:* Var Girls Vlybl Coach; Girls Bsktbl Ofcl Scorekeeper; NHS Club Adv; Mentor Teacher 1986-87; Girls Phys Ed Dept Chairperson 1986-88; Local Teachers Assn Secy; Alpha Delta Kappa Secy 1974-76; Womens Golf Assn Pres 1977-78, Top Women Golfer 1977-78, 1989-; *office:* Delano HS 1331 Cecil Ave Delano CA 93215

STAHLMAN, STEVE W., High School Science Teacher; *b:* Chicago, IL; *m:* Beth J. Sliuken; *c:* Michael, Sara; *ed:* (BS) Bio, Univ of IL 1973; Sci; *cr:* Sci Teacher Parkland Jr HS 1973-74, John L Nash Jr HS 1974-76, Cissna Park HS 1976-79; Bio Teacher Boscobel HS 1979-; *ai:* Environmental Ed Curr Comm Mem; Public Relations Rep Local Union; Officiate Bsbl, Bsktbl, Sftbl, Ftbl, Vllybl; Local Sportsmans Club 1980-, Conservation Service Awd 1988; Local Prairie Enthusiasts; Bird Banding Assn 1987-89; Natl Wildlife Fed 1980-; Natl TurkeyFed 1982-;Ducks Unlimited 1979-; Nom Presidential Awd of Excl Sci 1985, 1986; Selected Enroll Sci World Pigeon Lake 1990; *office:* Boscobel HS 300 Brindley St Boscobel WI 53805

STAHLY, MARLENE WILSON, English Teacher/Dept Chair; *b:* Pontiac, MI; *m:* Larry Dean; *c:* Thomas, Tracy; *ed:* (BA) Eng, CA St Univ 1971; Completed Course Work Masters Scndry Ed, Specialization in Rdng 1973; *cr:* Eng/His Teacher Bassett Unified Sch Dist 1973-81; Eng Teacher Los Angeles Unified Sch Dist 1983-; *ai:* Eng Dept Chairperson 1986-; Mentor Teacher 1985-; Gave 5 Staff Dev Inservices this Yr; Mem Budget Comm; Eng Cncl of Los Angeles Outstanding Teacher 1989; NEA 1987-; United Teachers of Los Angeles 1983-; Voted Best Teacher Sr Class 1988; Presented Plaque for Appreciation Homeroom Class 1985; Torch Intermediate Sch Teacher of Yr 1978, 1979, 1980; Lincoln HS Teacher of Yr; *office:* Abraham Lincoln HS 3501 N Broadway Los Angeles CA 90031

STALCUP, DONALD SOULE, Sixth Grade Teacher; *b:* Memphis, TN; *m:* Ann Ussery; *c:* Brenda, Donnie; *ed:* (BS) His, Memphis St Univ 1962; *cr:* Teacher Trenton Elem 1964-; *office:* Trenton Elem Sch 308 N Washington Trenton IL 62293

STALEY, LORRIE BELCHER, Reading/Mass Media Teacher; *b:* Delaware, OH; *m:* David J.; *c:* Adam; *ed:* (BS) Eng Comm, OH St Univ 1986; *cr:* Teacher Heath HS 1987-; *ai:* Producer of Weekly TV Magazine; Frosh Class Adv; NCTE; *office:* Heath HS 300 Licking View Dr Heath OH 43056

STALIS, RACHEL HELEN, Third Grade Teacher; *b:* Madera, CA; *m:* George Frank; *ed:* (AA) Coalinga Coll 1967; (BA) Soc Sci, Fresno St Coll 1970; *ai:* Fresno Teachers Assn, CA Teachers Assn, NEA 1970-; *office:* Viking Elem Sch 4251 N Winery Ave Fresno CA 93726

STALL, PATRICIA KELLY, Second Grade Teacher; *b:* Washington Court H, OH; *m:* Steven Paul; *c:* Steven E.; *ed:* (BSED) Elem Ed, OH Univ 1980; Currently Working On Elem Ed Masters Degree At OH Univ; *cr:* 4th Grade Teacher 1980-83, 2nd Grade Teacher 1983- Windsor Elem; *ai:* Career Resource Dev Comm; Hands-On Sci Resource Comm; OH Ed Assn 1980-; NEA 1980-; Morgan Local Ed Assn 1980-; NSTA 1989-; Amer Red Cross Water Safety Instr 1975-; Amer Red Cross CPR Instr, First Aid Instr 1990; Trinity United Meth Church Admin Cncl 1990-92; *office:* Windsor Elem Sch Box 288 Broadway St Stockport OH 43787

STALLARD, VINCENT A., Business Dept Chairperson; *b:* Tucumcari, NM; *c:* Marla; *ed:* (BS) Bus Ed, 1972, (MBE) Bus Ed, 1975 Eastern NM Univ; Ed & Guidance & Counseling; *cr:* Educator Gallup-Mc Kinley Cty Public Schls 1972-73, Deming Public Schls 1973-; *ai:* Spon Fellowship Chrstn Athletics; Jr Class; Dept Chairperson; Vlybl Coach; Bus Club; Master Teacher Prgm-Essential Elements of Instruction; Phi Delta Kappa, NM Bus Ed Assn, NEA, NM HS Coaches Assn, Amer Voc Assn; Teacher of Month; NM St Coach of Yr; NM All Star Vlybl Coach; Wrote Classroom Text for Cmptr; Nom for Local/St Educator of Yr; *office:* Deming H S 1100 S Nickel Deming NM 88030

STALLINGS, DEBBIE FINLEY, Kindergarten Teacher; *b:* Milan, TN; *m:* Richard Nile; *c:* Devon H., Dustin H.; *ed:* (BS) Elem Ed, Bethel Coll 1978; (MED) Curr/Instruction Early Chldhd Ed, Memphis St Univ 1983; *cr:* Kndgtn Teacher Huntingdon Primary Sch 1978-; *ai:* Jr Girl Scout & Tiger Cub Boy Scout Leader; T-Ball Girls Coach; Delta Kappa Gamma 1989-; TN Ed Assn, NEA, Huntingdon Ed Assn 1978-; TN Assn for Young Children 1983-; United Meth Women 1988-; Bus & Prof Women 1988; *home:* Rt 1 Box 183 Mc Kenzie TN 38201

STALLINGS, MERLE RIGBY, Fourth Grade Teacher; *b:* Rexburg, ID; *m:* Boyd Irvin; *c:* Nancy S. Coltrin, Judy K. S. Terry, Craig B., Richard Rigby, Ranae S. Black, Robyn S. Jensen; *ed:* (BS) Elem Ed, UT St Logan 1972; *ai:* Delta Kappa Gamma 1982-; BEA Sch Rep; NEA; ID Cncl of Intnl Rdng Assn 1989-; Elem Teacher of Yr 1982-83; *home:* 389 W 200 N Blackfoot ID 83221

STALLWORTH, BARBARIS MOORE, Fourth Grade Teacher; *b:* Mc Cool, MS; *c:* James M. Jr.; *ed:* (BS) Elem Ed, Memphis St Univ 1966; (MS) Admin/Supervision, Trevecca Nazarene Coll 1988; *cr:* 3rd Grade Teacher Hollywood Elem Sch 1966-70, Balmoral Elem Sch 1970-71; 3rd Grade Teacher 1971-79, 4th Grade Teacher 1979- Alton Elem Sch; *ai:* UTP 1966-; *office:* Alton Elem Schl 2020 Alton Ave Memphis TN 38106

STALLWORTH, JACQUELYN ANN (BLACKWELL), Language Arts Teacher; *b:* Gulfport, MS; *m:* Robert; *ed:* (BA) Elem Ed, Dillard Univ 1977; *cr:* 7th/8th Grade Lang Art Teacher Phoenix HS 1979-; *ai:* Spelling Bee Coach; Plaquemines Teachers Fed, LA Fed of Teachers 1979-.

STALNAKER, DENISE GOWER, Special Ed/Journalism Teacher; *b:* Buckhannon, WV; *m:* Joey D.; *ed:* (BA) Bus/ Journalism, Fairmont St Coll 1983; (MS) Learning Disabilities, WV Univ 1988; *cr:* Spec Ed Teacher Homestead Sch 1985-86; Spec Ed/Journalism Teacher Coalton 12 Yr Sch 1986-; *ai:* Yrbk Adv; Var Girls Asst & Jr HS Boys Bsktbl Coach; WV Press Assn 1989-; *home:* Star Rt Box 69-F Coalton WV 26257

STALZER, HILDEGARD, Ger/Fr/Span Language Teacher; *b:* Retz, Austria; *m:* John M. Bomer; *c:* Frances S. Bomer, Paula E. Bomer, Maxine A. Bomer; *ed:* 1st Faculty Degree Fr Lang, 1963, 2nd Faculty Degree Fr Lit, 1964 Sorbonne; (BA) Ger Lit, Univ of WI 1966; (MA) Counseling Psych, Univ of Notre Dame 1973; *cr:* Teaching Asst Univ of WI 1967-68; Therapist Family & Children Center 1973-75; Lang Teacher St Josephs HS 1978-; *ai:* Mentor Teacher; Ger Club Moderator; AATG 1979-; AATF 1986-; Amer Assn of Span & Portuguese 1987-; Womens Intnl League for Peace & Freedom Branch Chairperson 1986-88; Translation of Best Childrens Book Cath Press Assn 1985; Most Influential Teacher Academic All Star Scholar 1989; Prin Teaching Awd 1989; IN NEH Teacher Scholar Grant 1990; *office:* St Josephs HS 1441 N Michigan Ave South Bend IN 46617

STAMEY, BONNIE MATTHEWS, Reading Specialist; *b:* Buies Creek, NC; *m:* William Gregg Sr.; *c:* William G. Jr.; *ed:* (BS) Ed, 1960, (MA) Ed/Rdng, 1961 Appalachian St Univ; Grad Stud Wake Forest Univ; Rdng Cert Mars Hill Coll; W Carolina Univ Wkshps; *cr:* 3rd/4th Grade Teacher Appalachian Elem Demonstration Sch 1960-61; 4th Grade Teacher Morningstar Elem Sch 1961-62; Rdng Specialist/Eng/US His Teacher Tuscola Sr HS 1978-; *ai:* Soph Class Adv; Stu Referral Placement & Morale Comm; Eng & Remediation Dept Mem; NC Assn of Educators 1961-62, 1978-; Intnl Rdng Assn Sch Rep 1978-; Haywood Cty Teachers Assn; First Baptist Church (Childrens Sunday Sch Teacher, Adult Womens Sunday Sch Teacher, Sunbeam Leader, Girls Auxiliary Leader); YMCA Volunteer; Natl Trust for

Historic Preservation, Haywood Cty Friends of Lib, Haywood Cty Democratic Women; Haywood Cty Democratic Precinct (Secy, Treas, Delegate); Appalachian St Univ Teaching Fellowship; *office:* Tuscola Sr HS 350 Tuscola School Rd Waynesville NC 28786

STAMEY, EVA CAROLYN, Sixth Grade Teacher; *b:* Waynesville, NC; *ed:* (BA) Ed Music, Mars Hill Coll 1972; *cr:* Choir Dir W Canton Baptist Church 1973-81, Beulah Baptist Church 1982-84, Oak Grove Baptist Chruch 1985-89, Mt Zion Baptist Church 1989-; Classroom Teacher Bethel Sch 1972-; *ai:* 6th Grade Chorus Spon; Senate Bill 2 Comm; Care Comm Chairperson; Grade Level Chairperson 1980-85; NEA, NC Assn of Educators 1976-; Intnl Rdng Assn 1976-86; Amer Legion Auxiliary Local Unit #61 (Pres 1974-76) 1980-; Amer Legion Auxiliary NC 25th Dist Pres 1986-87; *office:* Bethel Sch Rt 3 Waynesville NC 28786

STAMMEYER, JACQUELYN WINTER, 7th Grade Soc Stud Teacher; *b:* Dubuque, IA; *m:* David W.; *c:* Magdalena, Nathan; *ed:* (BA) His, Mt Mercy Coll 1980; Working Toward Masters His, NE MO St Univ Kirksville; *cr:* Teachers Aide Revere C-3 Schls 1980-81; Soc Stud Teacher Clark Cty R-1 Schls 1981-; *ai:* Jr HS Stamp Club, Geography Bee & His Day Spon; MO St Teachers Assn 1980-; Cmmty Teachers Assn (Pres, VP, Secy, Treas) 1980-; Delta Kappa Gamma 1989-; MO Dept of Soc Stud 1985-; Amer Legion Auxiliary 1975-; Clark Cty Historical Society 1982-; Clark Cty R-1 Teacher of Yr 1989; MO Key Skills & MS Mastery Achievement Tests Dev Comms; *office:* Clark Cty R-1 Schls 384 N Jefferson Kahoka MO 63445

STAMMLER, JULIE ANN (JACKSON), Business Education Teacher; *b:* Minneapolis, MN; *m:* Charles; *c:* Grant, Garret; *ed:* Assoc Account Clerk, WI Indianhead Tech 1977; (BS) Univ WI Superior 1987; H&R Block Income Tax Course; *cr:* Jr Accountant Builders Supply Company 1977-79; Clerk/Treas Village of Lake Nebagamon 1980-81; Owner/Operator Von der Stammler Kennels 1984-; Bus Ed Teacher Lincoln HS 1987-; *ai:* Manitowoc Cty Youth Hockey Comm Mem; Branch Bsbl Peanuts Coach; Phi Beta Lambda 1986-87; NBEA 1986-, Merit for Outstanding Achievement 1987; Bus Prof of America (Natl & Local Secy 1986-87, Natl Pres 1987-88, Local Treas), Local Mem of Yr 1987; Keynote Speaker OH All Voc Ed Conference 1988; *office:* Lincoln HS 1433 S 8th St Manitowoc WI 54220

STAMPER, PATRICIA G., Counselor; *b:* Olive Hill, KY; *m:* Carl; *c:* Dana, Joshua, Elizabeth; *ed:* (BA) Eng/Sociology, 1969, (MA) Guidance/Counseling, 1974, (Rank I) Guidance/Counseling, 1987 Morehead St Univ; *cr:* Teacher Olive Hill HS 1969-71, W Carter HS 1971-; Cnslr W Carter HS 1988-; *ai:* Carter Cty Ed Assn (VP 1969-,) 1970-71; KY Ed Assn, NEA 1969-; PTSA; *office:* W Carter HS Box 479 Olive Hill KY 41164

STAN, TRUDY LOUISE (REILLY), Third Grade Teacher; *b:* Manitowoc, WI; *m:* Steven John; *c:* Carrie, Jordan; *ed:* (BA) Elem Ed, Silver Lake Coll 1977; *cr:* 3rd/4th Grade Teacher St Gregory Sch 1977-78; 1st/2nd Grade Summer Teacher Manitowoc Public Schls Title Prgm 1978-80; 3rd Grade Teacher St Francis de Sales 1978-; *ai:* Public Relations Comm; NCEA 1978-; *office:* St Francis de Sales Sch 1408 Waldo Blvd Manitowoc WI 54220

STANAWAY, BARBARA COLLEEN (SEARS), 5th/6th Grade Teacher; *b:* Bartlesville, OK; *c:* Amy L. Stanaway Hack, Gay D. Stanaway Knapp, Ian N., Tia (dec) *ed:* (BS) Elem Ed, Southern Coll of 7th Day Adv 1970; (MS) Elem Ed, Univ of TN Chattanooga 1975; Post Grad Courses Exceptional Child, Rdng Diagnosis & Teaching; *cr:* Voucher Room & Accounting Dept Clerk Phillips 66 Comptrollers Dept 1954-55; Patient Escort X-Ray Dept St Francis Hospital 1964-65; 1st-8th Grade Teacher Nowata 7th Day Adv Elem Sch 1968-69; 3rd/4th Grade Girls Phys Ed/Homeroom Teacher Oak Park Jr Acad 1970-72; Elem Ed Methods Contract Teacher Southern Coll 1978-83, 1987; 4th-6th Grade Teacher A W Spalding Elem 1972-; *ai:* Intnl Rdng Assn 1970, 1972-; GA Cumberland Conference Teachers Assn A W Spalding Teacher of Yr 1989-; Whos Who in Religion in America 1985; A W Spalding Sch Annual Dedication 1986; *home:* 4862 College Dr E Po Box 754 Collegedale TN 37315

STANCZAK, ALLAN MICHAEL, High School Science Teacher; *b:* Chicago, IL; *m:* Barbara Kay Swearingen; *c:* Junette M.; *ed:* (BA) Zoology, S IL Univ 1975; (MS) Bus Admin, Univ of N CO 1982; (BS) Scndry Ed/Math/Sci, Hyles Anderson Coll 1988; *cr:* Accounting & Finance Specialist E3 US Air Force 1975-77; Supply Corps Officer US Navy 1977-86; Bookkeeper Lakeshore Leasing Incorporated 1986-88; HS Sci Teacher Metropolitan Baptist Sch 1988-; *ai:* Asst Soccer Coach; 1st-12th Grade Cmptr Usage Teacher; Navy Reserve Assn Mem 1988-; S IL Univ Alumni Assn Life Mem 1975-; US Navy Reserve Lieutenant Commander 1986-; Chrstn Servicemans Fellowship Organization Bd of Trustees 1988-; Air Force Commendation Medal 1977; Navy Commendation Medal 1984; Navy Achievement Medal 1990; *office:* Metropolitan Baptist Sch 730 Neeleys Bend Rd Madison TN 37115

STANCZAK, DAVID JOHN, Mathematics Teacher; *b:* Chicago, IL; *m:* Sharon Kay Porter; *c:* Jonathan; *ed:* (BS) Aeronautical Engineering, Univ of IL 1982; (MS) Scndry Ed, Hyles-Anderson Coll 1988; *cr:* Aerospace Engr Naval Air Rework Facility 1983-86; Jr-Sr HS Math Teacher Franklin Road Christian Sch 1988-; *office:* Franklin Road Chrstn Sch RR 2 Box 60 Murfreesboro TN 37130

STANCZAK, RICHARD JOSEPH, Gifted Program Coordinator; *b:* Pittsburgh, PA; *m:* Nancy Bernhardt; *c:* Christopher J.; *ed:* (BA) Scndry Ed, 1973, (MED) Scndry Ed, 1976 Univ of Pittsburgh; Cmptr Sci, Univ of Pittsburgh, Allegheny Comm Coll; Psych Research Methods Cognitive Psych, Westminster Coll; *cr:* Soc Stud Coord/Instr Penn Circle Cmmty HS 1972-73; Soc Stud Instr Churchill Area Sch Dist 1973-81; Psych Instr Westminster Coll 1987-; Gifted Prgm Coord/Soc Stud Instr Woodland Hills Sch Dist 1981-; *ai:* APA HS Affiliate; PSEA; NEA; Delivered Paper at APA Convention 1989; Developed & Designed Ofcl Rules & Format for Westminster Coll HS Psych Fair; Conducted In-Service Prgms for HS Psych Teachers; Designed & Conducted In-Service Prgm Ethics for Teachers; *office:* Woodland Hills HS 2550 Greensburg Pike Pittsburgh PA 15221

STANDAFER, JUDY LYNN, 6th Grade Teacher; *b:* Lexington, KY; *ed:* (BS) Elem Ed, Univ of ND 1981; Addl Studies Teacher's Aid 1 Yr at ND Sch for The Blind in Multi-Handicap Class; *cr:* 5th Grade Teacher Eugene Field 1981-82; 6th & 8th Grade Sci 1982-83; 6th & 7th Grade Sci 1983-84 Hoover Mid Sch; 6th Grade Teacher Hoover Sch 1984-; *ai:* Sch Store Spon; YWCA Rape Crisis Ctr 1983-85; Spon Class Which Won "Best Over All" Project in Designing a Learning Ctr in Space; *office:* Hoover School 2401 N W 115 Ter Oklahoma City OK 73120

STANDS, SUSAN HOFFMAN, Language Arts Teacher; *b:* Dothan, AL; *m:* Gordon; *c:* Geoffrey, Susan C.; *ed:* (BA) Eng, NW Nazarene Coll 1966; Grad Stud NW Nazarene Coll, Boise St Univ; *cr:* Rdng/Eng Teacher South Jr HS 1980-85; Lang Art Teacher Greenleaf Friends Acad 1985-; *ai:* Academic Bowl & NHS Adv; Drama Coach; Intnl Rdng Assn 1981-84, 1989-; Valley Rdng, ID Rdng Cncl 1980-; *office:* Greenleaf Friends Acad PO Box 365 Greenleaf ID 83626

STANEVICH, LAURENT ROBERT, Eng/Fr/Cmptr Sci Teacher; *b:* Waterbury, CT; *ed:* (BA) Fr Lit, Yale Univ 1987; *cr:* Teacher Iolani Sch 1987-, Taft Educl Center 1988-; *ai:* Asst Wrestling Coach; *office:* Iolani Sch 563 Kamoku St Honolulu HI 96826

STANFORD, JUNE SMITH, Fourth Grade Teacher; *b:* Carrollton, GA; *m:* Stephen Tony; *c:* Stephanie, Staci; *ed:* (BA) Elem Ed, 1975, (MA) Mid Grades, (EDS) Mid Grades, W GA Coll; *cr:* 4th Grade Teacher Bowdon Elem Sch 1975-; *ai:* 4th Grade Service Team Leader; Phi Kappa Phi 1975; Phi Kappa Delta 1985; GA Assn of Educators; Carroll Cty Assn of Educators; NEA; KS Baptist Church; Bowdon Elem PTO; Bowdon Elem Teacher of Yr 1981; 1st Runner Up Carroll Cty Teacher of Yr 1981; *home:* 70 Dogwood Ln Bowdon GA 30108

STANFORD, MADONNA BOEHM, Substitute Teacher; *b:* Bismarck, ND; *m:* Dennis Earl; *c:* Morgan, Cole, Sarah; *ed:* (BS) His/Phys Ed/J S 1972, Elem Endorsement 1983 Valley City St Univ; *cr:* 5th Grade Teacher 1981-87, 2nd Grade Teacher 1987-88, 5th Grade Teacher 1988-89 St Catherine Sch; Substitute Teacher Valley City Public Schls 1989-; *home:* 1230 6th Ave NE Valley City ND 58072

STANGE, E. JEAN, Retired Teacher; *b:* Hazelcliff SK, Canada; *m:* Irving; *c:* Denise Stange Olmsted, Cheryl Duey, Kevin; *ed:* (BS) Elem Ed, Univ of NE 1968; Grad Stud; *cr:* Teacher Dist 102 NE 1943-44, Yutan Public Sch 1962-82, 1984-88; *ai:* NSEA, NEA; Amer Legion Auxiliary (Pres, Treas); *home:* 509 Oak St Yutan NE 68073

STANGE, JO ANN PAYTON, English & Commercial Teacher; *b:* Clanton, AL; *m:* Joseph Mitchell; *c:* Maranda, Brandi; *ed:* (BS) Secretarial Ed, Jacksonville St Univ 1970; *cr:* Teacher Isabella HS 1971-; *ai:* Yrbk Spon; Chilton Cty Teachers Assn Secy 1977-79; *office:* Isabella HS Rt 2 Box 239 Maplesville AL 36750

STANIEC, VICTOR G., Chemistry/Physics Teacher; *b:* Ancona, Italy; *m:* Joanne Monaco; *c:* Alycia, Rusty, Stephen, Christian; *ed:* (BS) Sci, Penn St Univ 1973; (MA) Scndry Sci, Trenton St Coll 1977; *cr:* Sci Dept Chm Archbishop Ryan HS 1974-86; Chem/Physics Teacher/Audio-Visual Dir Franklin Learning Center HS 1986-; *ai:* Asst Wrestling Coach; Sci Contest Spon; PA Sci Teachers Assn, NSTA, Philadelphia Scndry Sci Teachers; Wildwood Hotel/Motel Assn; Cape May Cty Visitors Bureau; Cape May Cty Chamber of Commerce; Patent Lipase & Protease Enzymes Added to Laundry Detergents; *office:* Franklin Learning Center HS 15th & Mt Vernon Sts Philadelphia PA 19130

STANKEWICZ, MARY CHRISTINE, 7th Grade Geography Teacher; *b:* Perth Amboy, NJ; *ed:* (BA) Soc Stud, Trenton St Coll 1971; Grad Stud Geography, Amer His; *cr:* Teacher Avenel Jr HS 1971-81, Woodbridge Mid Sch 1981-; *ai:* 7th Grade Vlybl Intramurals; Alpha Delta Kappa (Historian 1984-86, Corresponding Secy 1986-88, Pres 1988-); NJ Geographic Alliance, NJ Cncl for Soc Stud, Natl Cncl for Geographic Ed; Amer Legion Post 471 Teacher of Yr 1988; Governor Keans Teacher Recognition Awd Woodbridge Mid Sch 1988; *office:* Woodbridge Mid Sch 525 Barron Ave Woodbridge NJ 07095

STANLEY, BILLY RALPH, 4th Grade Teacher; *b:* Woodbine, KY; *m:* Sandra R.; *c:* Dana, Carlos; *ed:* (BS) Elem Ed, Cumberland Coll 1973; (MA) Elem Ed, Union Coll 1977; Rank I, Union Coll; *cr:* Remedial Math Teacher, Pleasent View Elem 1974-75; Rockholds Elem 1975-78; 4th Grade Teacher Rockholds Elem 1978-; *ai:* Elem Bsktbl Coach.

STANLEY, BRENDA CASH, Fifth Grade Teacher; *b:* Birmingham, AL; *m:* Jeffrey Lane; *c:* Layne; *ed:* (BS) Elem Ed, 1979, (MA) Elem Ed, 1980 Univ of AL; *cr:* 5th Grade Teacher Woodward Elem 1979-; *ai:* 4-H Club Leader; AL Ed Assn, NEA Mem 1979-; 2nd Mile Teacher Awd 1989-; *home:* 1101 12th Ct Pleasant Grove AL 35127

STANLEY, FREDERICK GUY, 6th-8th Grade Art Teacher; *b:* Salamanca, NY; *m:* Carmella Stanley Gionti; *c:* Steven; *ed:* (BA) Art, Allegheny Coll 1967; (MED) Art Ed, Edinboro Coll 1971; Grad Work Niagara Univ; *cr:* Auto/Drawing Teacher Arcade Jr Sr HS 1968-69; Pottery Niagara Cty Comm Coll 1981-82; Auto Teacher Emmet Belknap Mid Sch 1971-; *ai:* LEA, NYSUT 1971-; Hartland Fire Dept Volunteer; Middleport Meth Church Mens Club Pres; *office:* Emmet Belknap Mid Sch 491 High St Lockport NY 14094

STANLEY, JACQUELYN CHERYL, Third Grade Teacher; *b:* Detroit, MI; *ed:* (BA) Hum, Univ of Detroit 1973; (MS) Educl Psych, Wayne St Univ 1977; Health Ed; *cr:* Teacher Detroit Bd of Ed 1973-; *ai:* Future Teachers of Amer & Stu Cncl Spon; Grade Level Chairperson; Eta Phi Beta; Metropolitan Rdng Cncl; Writing Bonding Seminar; Academic Gaming; Perfect Attendance Awd; Clarion News Area B; Staff Dev Seminar; Writing Coords Inservice Presenter; Natl Writing Project; *home:* 8560 Sorrento Detroit MI 48228

STANLEY, JIMMY W., Sixth Grade Science Teacher; *b:* Birmingham, AL; *m:* Patricia A.; *c:* Kimberly Bane, Bruce, Mike; *ed:* (AA) Elem Ed, Walker Jr Coll 1966; (BA) Elem Ed, Univ AL Tuscaloosa 1970; (MA) Elem Ed, 1976, (AA) Elem Ed, 1979 Univ AL Birmingham; *cr:* 4th Grade Teacher Sipsey Jr HS 1967-70; 8th & 9th Grade Eng Teacher Cordova HS 1970-71; 4th Grade Teacher Cordova Elem 1971-89; 6th Grade Teacher Bankhead Mid Sch 1989-; *ai:* Spon 5th & 6th Grade Beta Club; Spon 7th & 8th Grade Bsktbl Chrldr; Choir Dir; Walker Cty Ed Assn Pres 1983-84 & 1987-88; AL Assn Classroom Teachers St Pres 1985-86 & 1990-91; Walker Cty Assn of Classroom Teachers Pres 1985-86; Cordova Lions Club Pres 1988-89 Citizen of Yr 1982; Long Memorial United Meth Church; BSA Scoutmaster/Cubmaster/Explorer Adv; Activity on Math Flowers to Be Published By Merrill Publishing; Chm of AEAS Legislative Commission; Pres Uniserve Cncl; NEA/AEA; *office:* Bankhead Mid Sch 500 School St Cordova AL 35550

STANLEY, KAREN HOUSMAN, Physical Education Teacher; *b:* Florence, AL; *m:* Edward T. Jr.; *c:* Chase, Tyler; *ed:* (BS) Phys Ed/Eng, Univ of N AL 1980; (MED) Phys Ed, Univ of S AL 1981; *cr:* Phys Ed/Rdng/Eng Teacher Peter F Alba Mid Sch 1981-; *ai:* Phys Ed Dept Head; Mid Sch Girls Vlybl, Track Coach; Coaches & Phy Educators 1989-; NEA, AL Ed Assn, Mobile Cty Ed Assn 1981-; Baptist Young Women Prayer Chm 1987-; *office:* Peter F Alba Mid Sch 288 S Wintzell St Bayou La Batre AL 36509

STANLEY, KATHY LAMBERT, Instructional Coordinator; *b:* Mobile, AL; *m:* Joe T.; *c:* Brian, David D.; *ed:* (BS) Ed, Univ of S AL 1970; (MED) Ed, GA Coll 1977; (EDS) Supervision/Admin, Univ of GA 1988; Course Work in Curr; *cr:* Teacher 1970-86, Instructional Coord 1986- Houston Cty Bd of Ed; *ai:* Early Intervention Prgm Coord Macon Coll; Phi Delta Kappa Fnd Rep 1989-; Kappa Delta Pi, ASCD; GACIS, GASCD; *office:* Northside HS 926 Green St Warner Robins GA 31093

STANLEY, RETHA THOMPSON, K-8th Grade Librarian; *b:* Waco, TX; *m:* Kerry L.; *c:* Molly K., Kerry R.; *ed:* (BS) Elem Ed, TX Womans Univ 1971; (MLS) Lib Sci, N TX St Univ 1980; *cr:* 6th Grade Math/Sci Teacher Lindale Jr HS 1974-87; K-8th Grade Librarian Lindale Ind Sch Dist 1987-; *ai:* Chrldr Spon; UIL Coord & Coach; Classroom Teachers Assn (Treas 1976-78, VP 1979-80, Pres 1980-81); Beta Sigma Phi 1976-84, Pledge of Yr 1976; *office:* Lindale Ind Sch Dist PO Box 370 Lindale TX 75771

STANLEY, SALLY SEAVER, Interdisciplinary Teacher; *b:* San Francisco, CA; *c:* Sally Mclean, Don Mclean, Elizabeth; *ed:* (MS) Curr & Instruction, Univ of OR 1984; *cr:* Classroom Teacher Sutherlin Sch Dist 1975-79; Classroom Teacher 1980-, Rdng Curr Coord 1984- Junction City Sch Dist; *ai:* 5th/6th Grade Rdng Curr Coord; Phi Delta Kappa 1965-; *office:* Oaklea Mid Sch 1515 Rose St Junction City OR 97404

STANLEY, SHARON, English/Drama Teacher; *b:* Harriman, TN; *m:* Llew; *c:* Travis; *ed:* (BS) Eng/Sociology, Cumberland Coll 1972; (MA) Eng/Psych, TN Tech Univ 1979; *cr:* Eng Teacher Oneida HS 1975-78, Mabank HS 1981-82; Eng/Drama Teacher Scott HS 1982-; Adjunct Eng Instr Roane St Comm Coll 1984-; *ai:* Drama Club Spon; Univ of TN Stu Teacher Supvr 1989-; NEA, TN Ed Assn 1975-78, 1982-86; Oneida Ed Assn (Pres 1977) 1975-78; ITS 1990; Scott Cty Youth League Little League Commissioner 1987-88; Cub Scouts Den Leader 1986-88; TN Tech Univ GA 1972-74; Univ of TN Fellowship 1980; TN Governors Acad 1990; *office:* Scott HS Scott High Dr Huntsville TN 37756

STANOSCH, SHARLENE RAMEY, Kindergarten Teacher; *b:* Spokane, WA; *m:* Joseph A.; *c:* Kurt; *ed:* (BA) Elem Ed/Speech Path Therapy, WA St Univ 1970; Grad Stud Various Univs; *cr:* Speech Therapist Medford OR 1970-71; Spec Ed Teacher Epton Sch 1972-73; 1st Grade Teacher Bovill Sch 1974-85; Kndgtn Teacher Discovery Sch 1986-; *ai:* Delta Kappa Gamma (VP 1983-, Officer 1985); Tamarack Rdng Cncl (Mem, VP 1983-84, Pres 1984-85) 1981-86; Panhandle Rdng Cncl 1986-88; BSA Den Leader 1987-89; PTO 1986-; Wrote Nutrition Grant Primary Stud; *home:* 12395 St James Hayden Lake ID 83835

STANSBERRY, DONALD WAYNE, English Teacher; *b:* Evansville, IN; *m:* Karen Clayton; *c:* Christopher, John-Matthew; *ed:* (MS) Eng/Ed, IN Univ Evansville 1975; Rdng Endorsement; *cr:* Eng/Journalis/Creative Writing Teacher Gibson Southern HS 1975-; *ai:* Class & Yrbk Spon; Newspaper; IN St Teachers Assn; Lib Bd Pres 1989-; Church Missions Family Ministries Chm 1988-; Poetry Published 1989; *office:* Gibson Southern HS R R 1 Fort Branch IN 47648

STANSBERRY, ELIZABETH RABY, Fifth Grade Teacher; *b:* Baton Rouge, LA; *m:* Alfred Charles; *c:* Donna L., Alfred C. III, Katia G.; *ed:* (BA) Spec Ed/Elem Ed, Southern Univ 1964; Spec Ed, LA St Univ; Elem Ed, CO Univ; *cr:* Teacher of Spec Ed Saginaw Public Schls 1964-65, E Baton Rouge Parish Schls 1965-66, Washington DC Public Schls 1966-74; Elem Teacher E Baton Rouge Parish Schls 1984-88; Elem Ed Teacher Denver Public Schls 1976-84, 1988-; *ai:* Oakland Elem Teacher of Yr 1989; *home:* 4565 Nepal St Denver CO 80249

STANSBURY, CLAUDINE, Biology Teacher/Sci Dept Chair; *b:* Memphis, TN; *ed:* (BS) Bio, 1966, (MST) Phys Sci/Chem, 1970, (MS) Cmmty Health, 1979 Memphis St Univ; *cr:* Teacher Lincoln Jr HS 1966-70; Teacher/Dept Chairperson Sheffield HS 1970-; *ai:* City-Wide Sci Chm & Sci Olympiad Comm; Sheffield Jr HS Sci Olympiad Coach; Memphis Ed Assn, TN Ed Assn, NEA 1966-; Natl Sci & Bio Teachers Assn; St Andrew AME Church Choir Pres 1981-85; St Andrew AME Church (Sunday Sch Teacher 1961-86, Supt 1980-86); Delta Sigma Theta Inc (Financial Secy, Treas) 1978-88, Service Awd 1982; Career Ladder III Teacher; Mellon Fnd Grant AP Bio Wkshp Univ of AL 1987; Rotary Awd for Teacher Excl 1989; *office:* Sheffield HS 4315 Sheffield Memphis TN 38118

STANSEL, HAROLD LUTHER, 5th Grade Teacher; *b:* St Augustine, FL; *m:* Mary Jo Whitehead; *ed:* (AA) General Ed, St Johns Riv R Comm Coll 1972, (BA) Elem Ed, 1974; (MED) Spec Ed M H, 1976 Univ of North FL; *cr:* 6th Grade Teacher Ponte Verda Palm Valley Elem Sch 1974-78, 4th Grade Teacher 1978-80; 5th Grade Teacher 1980 R B Hunt Elem Sch; *ai:* St Johns Cty Spec Olympics; FL Cncl on Elem Ed 1985-; NEA 1974; FL Teaching Prof 1974-; St Johns Cty Rdng Cncl St Johns Cty Ed Assn 1974; R B Hunt PTO 1978-; Young Educator of Yr 1980; *home:* 230 Queen Rd Saint Augustine FL 32008

STANTON, BEVERLY (SAY), Spanish & Computer Sci Teacher; *b:* Franklin, PA; *m:* David; *ed:* (BA) Span, Houghton Coll 1969; Essential Elements of Instruction, Alfred Univ; Foreign Lang Summer Wkshp Skidmore Coll; *cr:* Clerk/Teller/Asst Branch Mgr Key Bank Incorporated 1973-81; Substitute Teacher/Asst Librarian C Bolivar Cntrl Sch 1981-84; Span/Cmptr Teacher Friendship Cntrl Sch 1984-; *ai:* Span Club & NHS Adv; NY St Assn Foreign Lang Teachers 1984-, Teacher Incentive Grant 1987; Western NY Foreign Lang Educators Cncl 1984-; Friendship Teachers Assn Secy 1989-; Jones Memorial Hospital Secy 1975-77; Instr Adult Ed Cmptr Classes For Sch Dist; *office:* Friendship Cntrl Sch W Main St Friendship NY 14739

STANTON, VIRGINIA DLUGOS, Kindergarten Teacher; *b:* Woodside, NY; *m:* Donald J.; *c:* Andrew J., Peter J., Jenifer Stanton Fleury; *ed:* (BS) Elem Ed, Hofstra Univ 1956; (MA) Behavorial Sci, Stony Brook Univ 1982; *cr:* 3rd-5th Grade Teacher New Hyde Park Rd Elem Sch 1956-58; 4th Grade Teacher Village Green Elem Sch 1959; Kndgtn Teacher St James Elem Sch 1967-; *ai:* Smithtown Cntrl Sch Dist Elem Sci Curr Comm; Kndgtn Report to Parents Comm; Intl Rdng Assn 1980-; Assn of Chldhd Ed Intl 1980-; NCTM 1990; Nassau Early Chldhd Ed Cncl 1985-; Amer Assn Univ Women 1980-.

STAPLETON, PATRICK JOSEPH, 8th Grade Mathematics Teacher; *b:* Hartford, WI; *m:* Lois H. Heldt; *c:* Sean, Ryan; *ed:* (BS) Math, Univ of WI Oshkosh 1970; *cr:* Math Instr Washington HS 1970-71, L B Clarke Mid Sch 1971-; *ai:* HS Cross Cntry, HS Track, Mid Sch Track, Intramurals Coach; WI Math Cncl, WI Cross Cntry Coaches Assn; Men of Holy Redeemer Parish; *office:* L B Clarke Mid Sch 4608 Bellevue Pl Two Rivers WI 54241

STAPLETON, SHELIA LUCAS, Third Grade Teacher; *b:* Logan, WV; *m:* Louis Jacob; *ed:* (BA) Elem Ed, Marshall Univ 1976; Working on Masters in Elem Ed; *cr:* 3rd Grade Teacher Hamlin Elem 1976-; *ai:* Say No to Drugs Club Adv; Sch Advisory Cncl Comm; PTO; WV Ed Assn 1976-; Lincoln Cty Ed Assn (VP 1990) 1976-; Womans Club of Hamlin 1988-; *home:* 783 State St Hamlin WV 25523

STAR, DIANNE BARNES, Learning Disabilities Teacher; *b:* Donalsonville, GA; *m:* Robert E.; *c:* Pamela L. Star Fuller, Robert E. Jr., Kimberly A. Starr Bartlett; *ed:* (BS) Music/Eng, Troy St Univ 1956; (MS) Learning Disabilities, AL St Univ 1982; AL Career Incentive Prgm for Prof Dev; *cr:* Music Teacher Whitfield Sch 1968-78; Learning Disabilities Resource Eng Teacher Goodwyn Jr HS 1978-; *ai:* Montgomery Cty Learning Disabilities Prgm Curr Comm 1988-89; Inservice Speaker for Learning Disabilities Trng 1986-88; IEP Dev Comm 1988-89; AL Ed Assn 1980-; NEA 1985-; Alpha Delta Kappa 1985-88; *office:* Goodwyn Jr HS 209 Perry Hill Rd Montgomery AL 36109

STARBUCK, ROBERT WILLIAM, Audio-Visual Teacher; *b:* Washington, DC; *m:* Jennifer Lynn Davison; *ed:* (BA) Eng/Soc Stud, Whittier Coll 1965; (MA) Sch Management, Univ of La Verne 1986; USNR Commission Ensign-Lieutenant 1968-70; *cr:* MGM Prgm Teacher Hesperia Jr HS 1970-72; Coord Audio/Visual Teacher Apple Valley HS 1974-79; Dean of Stu Hesperia Jr HS 1984-86; Audio/Visual Teacher Hesperia Jr HS 1987-; *ai:* Stu Video Production Supvr for Sch Bd; Desert Cmmtys United Way 1983-84, Spec Pres Awd 1984; *office:* Hesperia Jr HS 10275 Cypress Ave Hesperia CA 92345

STARK, ANNE GREEN, Fourth Grade Teacher; *b:* Portland, OR; *m:* Carl L. Jr.; *c:* Beth, Kenneth, Jon; *ed:* (BS) Elem Ed, Lewis & Clark Coll 1958; Various Courses Ed; *cr:* K-6th Grade Substitute Teacher; 3rd Grade Teacher Del Norte Sch 1960-62; 1st Grade Teacher W Tualatin View Sch 1964-67; K/1st Grade Teacher Highland Sch 1967-70; 4th Grade Teacher Harrison Sch 1974-; *ai:* Dist Curr Comm; Green River Ed Assn (Parliamentarian, Secy) 1974-; WY Ed Assn 1974-; NEA 1960-; *office:* Harrison Sch 1825 Alabama St Green River WY 82935

STARK, MARGARET C., 4th Grade Teacher/Mentor; *b:* Los Angeles, CA; *ed:* (BA) Ed/Eng, Coll of Holy Names 1963; Rdng Specialist; Gen Elem Teaching Credential Coll of Holy Names; Cert Raskob Rdng Inst & Loyola Marymount Rdng Clinic; *cr:* 1st-2nd Grade Teacher Northern & Southern CA 1955-68; 1st-6th Grade Substitute Teacher Los Angeles Rosemead 1968-69; 3rd-4th Grade Teacher Shuey Sch 10-; 1st-7th Grade Teacher Shuey Sch 1970-; Mentor Teacher Rosemead Sch Dist 1989-; *ai:* Lang Art Lectures & Wkshps; Classroom Management & Positive Discipline Procedure, Motivation of Stu, Lang Art Instruction, Master Teacher Prgm, Prins Designee to New Staff Mems 1970-89; *office:* Emma W Shuey Sch 8472 E Wells St Rosemead CA 91770

STARK-OLSON, JEANIE CARROLL, Resource Teacher; *b:* Denver, CO; *ed:* (AA) General Ed, Long Beach City Coll 1974; (BA) Home Ec, Fresno St Univ 1977; Working Towards Masters Educl Admin, Univ of San Francisco; Human Dev Trng; CA Prgm Review Trng; San Joaquin Valley Project; CA Sch Leadership Acad; *cr:* Teacher Spring Valley Sch 1980-88; Resource Teacher Clovis Unified Sch Dist 1988-; *ai:* Asst Pep & Cheer Adv; Sci Fair, Child Study Team Coord; Oral Interpretation Coach; Assoc Sch Curr Dev; CA Sch Leadership Acad; CA AB 803 Technology Ed Grant; Demonstration Teacher-Demostration Summer Sch; *office:* Lincoln/Clovis USD 774 E Alluvial Fresno CA 93710

STARKEY, DANIEL EDWIN, Counselor/Phys Ed Teacher; *b:* Cincinnati, OH; *m:* Sarah Jane Drake; *c:* Robby, Maria; *ed:* (BS) Health/Phys Ed, Univ of Indianapolis 1975; (MS) Guidance, Xavier Univ 1977; His Teaching Certificate; Univ of Cincinnati; *cr:* Teacher/Cnslr Roger Bacon HS 1977-; *ai:* Var Ftbl & Wrestling Coach; Adv SADD; OH Coaches Assn 1977-; Southwestern OH Coaches Assn Pres 1984 Coach of Yr 1989-90; *office:* Roger Bacon HS 4320 Vine St Cincinnati OH 45217

STARKEY, PATRICIA SOUTH, English/Science Teacher; *b:* Mc Call, ID; *c:* Joshua E., Patrick L.; *ed:* (BS) Phys Ed, Boise St Univ 1976; Masters Course Work In Sport Physiology; *cr:* Eng Teacher Mountain Home Air Base Jr HS 1978-79; Eng/Sci Teacher Mountain Home Jr HS 1979-; *ai:* 8th Grade Girls Bsktbl Head Coach.

STARKIE, ILDA B., Business Teacher; *b:* New Bedford, MA; *m:* Fred; *c:* Daniel, Paul, Barbara; *ed:* (BS) Accounting, SE MA Univ 1970; (MS) Sch Admin, Bridgewater St Coll 1981; (MS) Bus Ed, Suffolk Univ 1981; *cr:* Statistical Office Worker New England Fire Insurance Rating Assn 1949-65; Bus Teacher Wareham HS 1970-; *ai:* Class of 1991 Adv; Wareham HS Awds Comm Asst Chairperson & Steering Comm Chairperson; Wareham Ed Assn Treas 1986-88; MA Teachers Assn, NEA, Plymouth Cty Teachers Assn, Bus Ed Assn of MA; *office:* Wareham HS Marion Rd Wareham MA 02571

STARKS, ROSALYN JUNE, Physical Education Teacher; *b:* Phoenix, AZ; *ed:* (BS) Ed, Univ of AZ 1974; Counseling/Human Relations, Northern AZ Univ; *cr:* Phys Ed Teacher Santa Cruz Valley Union HS 1975-84, Phoenix Union HS Dist 1985-; *ai:* Jr Var Vlybl Coach; Var Sftbl Coach; Chm South Mountain Wellness Comm; South Mountain Events Comm Mem; Chemical Awareness Prgm Group Facilitator; AZ Assn Health/Phys Ed/Recreation & Dance; Amer Alliance for Health/Phys Ed/Recreation & Dance; AZ Interscholastic Assn; 5a Sftbl Advisory Comm 1989-; AZ A Cntrl Division Sftbl Coach of Yr 1980; *office:* South Mountain H S 5401 S 7th St Phoenix AZ 85040

STARKS, VIVIAN MC CADNEY, 7th/8th Grade Lang Art Teacher; *b:* St Louis, MO; *m:* James Edward Jr.; *c:* Kevin C. Holliday; *ed:* (BA) Psych, Lincoln Univ 1970; (MA) Ed, Webster Coll 1983; *cr:* Spec Ed Teacher Clinton Elem, St Louis Public Schls 1971-80; 7th-8th Grade Lang Arts Teacher Academic & Athletic Acad 1980-; *ai:* Mentor Teachers Prgm St Louis Public Schls; 7th/8th Grade Public Relations Comm Spon; Building Rep Union Local 420; Soloist Free Lance; Delta Sigma Theta 1972-; *office:* Academic & Athletic Acad 5910 Clifton Ave Saint Louis MO 63109

STARMER, GENE D., Mathematics Teacher; *b:* Fremont, NE; *m:* Barbara D. Johnson; *c:* Jennifer, Jeffrey; *ed:* (BSED) Math, Midland Luth Coll 1971; (MSED) Scndry Ed, Univ of NE Omaha 1978; Undergraduate Stud in Cmptrs & Grad Stud in Instructional Improvement Taken at Various Univs; *cr:* 7th-9th Grade Math Teacher Cntrl Jr HS 1970-78; 9th-10th Grade Math Teacher Millard South HS 1980-; *ai:* Var Boys & Girls Tennis Coach; Saturday Sch Supvr; Effective Schls & Study Skills Comm; Metro Tennis Coaches Assn VP 1989-; MEA, NEA, NSEA 1970-78, 1980-; Kappa Alpha Lambda Alumni Pres 1984-86; Messiah Luth Church Cncl Pres 1986; *office:* Millard South HS 14905 Q Street Omaha NE 68137

STARN, NANCY GEIGER, Biology Teacher; *b:* Findlay, OH; *c:* Lori A., Eric A.; *ed:* (BS) Bio, Capital Univ 1970; (MA) Sci Ed, OSU 1973; *cr:* 7th Grade Sci Teacher Reynoldsburg Mid Sch 1971-76; 8th/9th Grade Sci/Bio I & II Teacher Liberty Union HS 1979-85; Bio I & II/Physiology Teacher Watkins Memorial HS 1985-; *ai:* Licking Cty Sci & Math Cncl; Sci Ed Cncl of OH 1985-; Dow Chemical Awd Excl in Sci Teaching 1986; *home:* 279 S Main St Box 259 Pataskala OH 43062

STARNES, DAVID EDGAR, Social Studies Teacher; *b:* Biltmore, NC; *m:* Kaye Keely; *c:* David Jr., Brian; *ed:* (BA) Soc Stud, Univ of MD 1969; (MA) Ed, Towson St 1973; *cr:* Teacher N Harford HS 1969-; *ai:* Cross Cntry & Track Coach 1969-; Sch Curr Comm 1989-; Supt Advisory Comm 1987-; Harford Cty Ed Assn 1983-; Renaissance All Sports Athletic Club Pres 1985-; *office:* N Harford HS 211 Pylesville Rd Pylesville MD 21132

STARNES, DEBRA HUDSPETH, Home School Teacher; *b:* Rock Hill, SC; *m:* E. J. Jr.; *c:* Alison, Hollie, Jason; *ed:* Chrstn Ed, Baptist Bible Coll; Advanced Trng in Accelerated Chrstn Ed, Alpha-Omega Curr, A Beka Curr; Cmptr Trng IBM Basics; *cr:* Teacher Fairhaven Chrstn Acad 1984-85; Teacher/Supvr Timothy Chrstn Acad 1986-88, Faith Chrstn Acad 1988-89, Faith Home Acad 1989-; *ai:* VA Home Educators Assn Mem; *home:* HC 62 Box 55-A Natural Bridge Stn VA 24579

STARR, EILEEN KAGAN, Elementary Teacher; *b:* Chicago, IL; *m:* M. Lee; *c:* Marianne, Lisa Starr Burns; *ed:* (BS) Speech/Elem Ed, Univ of Miami 1948; Post Grad Work Univ of AZ 1948-80; *cr:* Elem Classroom Teacher Robison 1970-75; Self Contained Classroom Teacher of Gifted Corbett Elem 1975-81; Resource Teacher of Gifted Roger Elem 1981-; 3rd-6th Grade Teacher of Gifted 1988-89; Spec Pre-Retirement Prgm 1989- Tucson Unified Sch Dist; *ai:* AZ Academic Decathlon; NEA, AZ Ed Assn, Tucson Ed Assn, Assoc Gifted & Talented, AZ Cncl Rdng 1950-89; Planned Parenthood Spec Events/Ed Comm; PTA; Amer Red Cross Schls Rep; Mission Ostomy Assn; *office:* Tucson Unified Sch Dist 1010 E 10th St Tucson AZ 85719

STARR, FAITH BRUMBERG, 2nd Grade Teacher; *b:* DuBois, PA; *M:* Michael A. Sr.; *c:* Toby; *ed:* (BA) Elem, West Liberty St Coll 1973; *cr:* 5th Grade Teacher 1973-74, 2nd Grade Teacher 1974- Brockway Elem Sch; *ai:* Brockway Area Ed Assn 1973-.

STARR, JOAN OF ARC, HM, Retired Teacher; *b:* Byerville, OH; *ed:* (BS) Teaching, Parochial Schls 1950; Enrichment Courses Dayton Univ; *cr:* Elem Ed Teacher Cleveland OH; *ai:* Cmmty Work for Sisters of Humility of Mary; Church Act at St Raphaels Cath Church; *home:* 525 Dover Center Rd Bay Village OH 44140

STARR, WILFRED EUGENE, English & Soc Stud Teacher; *b:* Chattanooga, TN; *m:* Dorothy Lorraine Hedrick; *c:* Lynnette; *ed:* (BS) Elem Ed, S Missionary Coll 1973; *cr:* 7th/8th Grade Teacher Jacksonville Jr Acad 1977-84; Prin Knoxville Adv Sch 1984-86, Duluth Jr Acad 1986-87; Eng/Soc Stud Teacher Beltsville Adv Sch 1987-; *ai:* Safety Patrol & Cmptr Club Spon; MD Cncl Teachers of Math Mem 1989-; Challenger Center Charter Mem 1988-; *home:* 14832 Belle Ami Laurel MD 20707

STARRETT, WILLIAM GRANT, Social Studies Teacher; *b:* Dayton, OH; *m:* Patricia A. Adcock; *c:* W. Grant, Trisha S., J. Matthew, Julie A.; *ed:* (BA) Soc Stud, Grace Coll 1964; (MED) Curr & Supervision, Miami Univ 1970; Audio-Visual Media Cert & Lib Cert; *cr:* Classroom Teacher Ferguson Jr HS 1964-; *ai:* Dayton Chrstn HS Wrestling Coach Asst; Beavercreek Ed Assn Building Rep 1966-67; Beavercreek Teachers Credit Union Loan Officer 1966-76; *office:* Ferguson Jr HS 2680 Dayton-Xenia Rd Beavercreek OH 45385

STARTUP, NANCY HANCOCK, Physical Education Teacher; *b:* Springfield, TN; *m:* William R. Jr.; *ed:* (BS) Health/Phys Ed, Mid TN St Univ 1977; (MS) Admin/Supervision, TN St Univ 1987; *cr:* Math Teacher Wright Jr HS 1978-81; Phys Ed Teacher Ewing Park Mid Sch 1981-; *ai:* Girls Vlybl, Track, Asst Bsktbl Coach; Faculty Advisory Comm Mem; Athletic Intramurals Coord; *office:* Ewing Park Mid Sch 3411 Knight Rd Nashville TN 37207

STASICHA, BARRY ROBERT, Middle School Math Teacher; *b:* N Charleroi, PA; *m:* Carole Faye Romansky; *c:* Briana F.; *ed:* (BS) Elem Ed, 1974, (BS) Drivers Ed, 1987, (BS) Scndry Math, 1986 California Univ of PA; *cr:* Teacher Charleroi Area Elem Schls 1975-84; Math Teacher Charleroi Area Jr HS 1984-88, Charleroi Area Mid Sch 1988-; *ai:* Charleroi Mid Sch Girls Bsktbl Coach; Charleroi HS Var Girls Bsktbl Asst Coach; PSEA, NEA, Charleroi Area Ed Assn 1975-; *home:* 520 Rear Railroad St Stockdale PA 15483

STATEN, BOBBY D., Science/Health Teacher; *b:* Waynesboro, MS; *m:* Ada Ward; *c:* Bradford, Brandilynn; *ed:* (BA) Health/Phys Ed, Alcorn Univ 1970; (MS) Sci, Southern Univ 1977; *cr:* Teacher Waynesboro Jr HS 1970-; *ai:* Sch Bus Driver; Jr HS Coach; Stu Adv; Prof Educators 1970-; MEA 1987-; *home:* Rt 6 Box HW-79 Waynesboro MS 39367

STATHOS, DONNA BOHLE, 7th & 8th Math Teacher; *b:* Exeter, NH; *m:* Charles George; *c:* Erica L., Christina L.; *ed:* (BS) Elem Ed, Plymouth St Coll 1975; Grad Courses in Cmptrs/Discipline/Creativity/Innovations of Math; *cr:* 7th-8th Grade Math Teacher Henry W Moore Sch 1975-; *ai:* Coaching Sftbl/Cheerleading/Vlybl/Bowling/Bsktbl; Yrbk Adv; 8th Grade Grad Adv; Sch Bus Driver; Math Grades R-8 Coord; Candia Fed of Teachers Pres 1980-84; Candia Ed Assn Secy/Treas 1984-; Nom

Presidential Excl of Math Teaching 1988 & 1990; *office:* Henry W Moore Sch Deerfield Rd Candia NH 03034

STATTLER, GARY L., Art Instructor; *b:* Keswick, IA; *m:* Mary E. Rupp; *c:* David; *ed:* (BA) Art, Univ N IA 1966; (MA) Art Ed, Univ of IA 1977; New Art Basics, IA St Univ; *cr:* Art Instr Miller Mid Sch 1964; *ai:* Stu Senate Adv; Gifted & Talented Coach; Art Ed of IA (Pres 1970-73, Curr Dir 1969-70); BSA Cncl Exec Bd 1988-, Silver Beaver 1980, Vigil Honor 1972; Univ of N IA & IA St Univ Stu Teacher Preparation Advisory Bd; *office:* Marshalltown Cmmty Schls S 11th St Marshalltown IA 50158

STAUB, LINDA GURTLER, Eng Journalism Speech Teacher; *b:* Cumberland, MD; *m:* Gregory; *ed:* (BA) Lang Arts 7-12, Shepherd Coll 1974; Graduate Courses, WV Univ/Shephard Coll/WV Coll of Graduate Stud/Univ TN Chattanooga; *cr:* Eng Teacher Hampshire HS 1974-75, Bryant Sch 1975-77; Office Mgr/Writer Church of Today 1977-79; Asst to Mrktg VP First Federal 1979-81; Eng Teacher Romney Jr HS 1981-86; Eng/Journ/Speech Teacher Hampshire HS 1986-; *ai:* Jr Class Spon/FEA Club/Trojanettes Drill Tm; Newspaper Yrbk Adv; Hampshire Cty Ed Assn Newsletter Ed; Literary Magazine Adv; NEA 1981-; WVEA 1981- Outstanding Newsletter Editor 1988/89; Hampshire Cty Ed Assn/Mem Executive Comm 1981-; Delta Kappa Gamma 1985-; Friends of Library 1988-; 1988 Hampshire Cty Teacher of Yr; Finalist WV Teacher of Yr; Free Lance Writer for Martinsburg Journal; Ed of Outstanding Teachers Assn Newsletter; *home:* Star Rt 1 Box 441 Fort Ashby WV 26719

STAUB, WILLIAM R., Humanities Teacher; *b:* Santiago, Chile; *m:* Renee Ito; *c:* Kevin; *ed:* (BA) His, 1967, (MAT) Ed, 1971 Lewis & Clark Coll; Numerous Colls; *cr:* 10th-12th Grade Teacher Hoquiam WA #28 1967-73; 8th Grade Teacher Vernon Sch 1973-78, George Sch 1979-85, George Mid Sch 1985-; *ai:* Sch Newspaper Adv; 8th Grade Unit Leader; Career Ed Coord; SS Textbook Adoption Comm for Dist Stu Teacher Supvr; Portland Assn of Teachers Exec Bd 1980-81; Portland Assn of Teachers Mem 1973-; Phi Beta Kappa; *office:* George Mid Sch 10000 N Burr Portland OR 97203

STAUDE, EDMUND DAVID, Mid Sch Eng/Math Teacher; *b:* St Joseph, MI; *m:* Claudia Ann Garchow; *c:* Gretchen, Katrina; *ed:* (BS) Ed, Concordia Teachers Coll 1976; (MED) Ed, Univ of MO St Louis 1987; Working Towards Educl Doctorate Univ of MO St Louis; *cr:* 3rd-8th Grade Lang Art Teacher Martin Luth Sch 1977-81; 6th-8th Grade Teacher/Prin Zion Luth Sch 1981-82; 6th-8th Grade Eng/Math Teacher Immanuel Luth Sch 1982-; *ai:* Boys Athletic Coord; Jr HS Boys Soccer Spon; 8th Grade Boys Bsktbl Coach; Jr HS Asst Drama Coach; Bsktbl Curr Comm; Luth Ed Assn, ASCD; Luth HS Bd of Dir 1983-88; *home:* 2809 Norwich Saint Charles MO 63301

STAUDENMAIER, ANDREA MEYER, Mathematics Teacher/Dept Chair; *b:* Leavenworth, KS; *m:* William A.; *c:* Rebecca, Judith; *ed:* (BA) Math, Benedictine Coll 1968; (MS) Ed, KS St 1977; *cr:* Teacher Lillis HS 1968-69, Alter HS 1969-70, Millbrook Jr HS 1973-76, Oregon Trail Jr HS 1976-; *ai:* Math Counts Team; Prins Advisory Comm; Pi Delta Kappa 1983-; NEA 1973-; NCTM 1980-; Church Circle Leader 1985-; *office:* Oregon Trail Jr HS 1800 W Dennis Ave Olathe KS 66061

STAUDER, PHILLIP J., Third Grade Teacher; *b:* Pana, IL; *m:* Cynthia; *c:* Melissa, Matt; *ed:* (BA) Elem Ed, IN St 1971; *cr:* Teacher Daniel Elem Sch & Danville Area Comm Coll 1990; *home:* 1511 Gernand Danville IL 61832

STAUDT, JOSEPH, Science Department Chair; *b:* Passaic, NJ; *m:* Carolyn Sue Elliott; *c:* Kim S. Ree, Holly J. Hee; *ed:* (BS) Bio, Coll of Emporia 1968; (MS) Sci Ed 1981, (EDS) Higher Ed, 1990 Pittsburg St Univ; *cr:* Teacher Unified Sch Dist 445 1971-; *ai:* NSTA 1980-; *home:* RR 4 Box 144-2A Coffeyville KS 67337

STAUDT, MARY M., Fourth Grade Teacher; *b:* Joliet, IL; *m:* David A.; *c:* Scott; *ed:* (BS) Elem Ed, W IL Univ 1977; Working on Masters Ed, Natl Coll of Ed Evanston IL; *cr:* 2nd Grade Teacher 1977-79, 4th Grade Teacher 1979-80, Kndgtn Teacher 1980-81, 3rd Grade Teacher 1981-82, Kndgtn/4th Grade Teacher 1985- Lemont Consolidated Dist 113; *ai:* Discipline Curr Comm; PTA Prgm Co Chairperson 1984; Lemont Elem Cncl Secy 1983.

STAUFENBIEL, DEBORAH MILLER, Sixth Grade Teacher; *b:* Vincenza, Italy; *m:* Eric Allen; *ed:* (BS) Elem Ed, Quincy Coll 1982; *cr:* Kndgtn Teacher 1982-83, 4th Grade Teacher 1983-84 Little Rock Chrstn Sch; 6th Grade Teacher Point Elem Sch 1984-; *ai:* Stu Cncl Spon; Lang Art Curr Comm; Cmptr Coord; Asst Vlybl Coach; MCTA; Mehlville Sch Dist Teacher of Yr Nom; *office:* Point Elem Sch 6790 Telegraph Rd Saint Louis MO 63129

STAUFFER, DAVID BRIAN, Music Instrumental Teacher; *b:* York, PA; *m:* Deborah A. Martin; *c:* Randi M.; *ed:* (BS) Music, Towson St Univ 1980; *cr:* Archbishop Curley 1981-; *ai:* Concert Band; Jazz Ensemble; *office:* Archbishop Curley HS 3701 Sinclair Ln Baltimore MD 21213

STAUFFER, JOHN DAVE, Science Teacher; *b:* San Antonio, TX; *m:* Janis Ann Noble; *c:* Kyle N., John D. Jr., Jacob P.; *ed:* (BSE) Sci/HPER, Tulsa Univ 1976; Video Specialist; Working on Masters in Admin; *cr:* Sci Teacher/Coach Tulsa E Cntrl HS 1977-78, Claremore Sequoyah HS 1978-79, Tulsa E Cntrl HS 1979-; *ai:* Bsbl & Sftbl Head Coach; Stu Cncl & Fellowship of Chrstn Athletes Spon; Tulsa Metro Sftbl 1981-, All St Coach 1986; Tulsa Metro Bsbl Pres 1987; Tulsa Sci Teachers Assn 1983-; Harvard Avenue Chrstn Church (Jr HS Dir, Deacon) 1989-; *office:* E Cntrl HS 12150 E 11th St Tulsa OK 74128

STAUFFER, RICK ALAN, Mathematics/Soc Stud Teacher; *b:* Omaha, NE; *ed:* (BA) Ec, Trinity Univ 1972; (MED) Ed, Univ of Houston 1984; Math Cert, Univ of Houston 1989; *cr:* Long Term Substitute Teacher 1982-84, Teacher 1984- Holub Mid Sch; *ai:* Mock Trial; Field Day Coord; *office:* Holub Mid Sch 9515 S Dairy-Ashford Houston TX 77099

STAUTZ, DANIEL F., English Teacher; *b:* Lakota, ND; *c:* Shay, Shari, Michel, Scott; *ed:* (BS) Phys Ed/Eng, Seattle Univ 1963; (MS) Phys Ed, Univ of WA 1966; Ed, AZ St Univ 1978; *cr:* Teaching Asst Univ of WA 1965-66; Instr Walla Walla Jr Coll 1967-69, Cntrl AZ Coll 1969-71; Teaching Asst AZ St Univ 1971-72; Instr Sahuarita HS 1973-; *ai:* Vlybl, Bsktbl, Golf Coach; NEA Life Mem; *office:* Sahuarita HS P O Box 26 Sahuarita AZ 85629

STAVER, JILL LEAHY, Third Grade Teacher; *b:* Shullsburg, WI; *m:* Kenneth Allen; *c:* Matthew, Ann; *cr:* Kndgtn Teacher 1976-80, 2nd Grade Teacher 1980-83, 1st Grade Teacher 1983-86, 3rd Grade Teacher 1986- Cuba City Public Sch; *ai:* Cuba City Dist Eng & Talented & Gifted Comm; Univ of WI Platteville Coll for Kids Comm; Holy Rosary Parish Sunday Sch Teacher 1989-; DFD Auxiliary 1988-; *home:* 300 Washington St Darlington WI 53530

STAVISH, DORIS J. MARTIN, 3rd Grade Teacher; *b:* Staples, MN; *w:* Richard (dec); *c:* Elizabeth Modsen, Eileen Schmidt, Paula Wolford, Michael (Dec), Patricia Schmidt, Pamela J.; *ed:* (BS) Elem, St Cloud St Univ 1952; St Cloud St Univ; *cr:* 5th Grade Teacher Nastwauk Elem Sch 1952-53; 5th Grade Teacher Charles Lindbergh Elem Sch 1953-59; 3rd/4th Grade Teacher 1961-63; 5th Grade Teacher 1966-71 Dr S G Knight Sch; 3rd/5th Grade Teacher Knight Sch 1971-; *ai:* Stu Cncl Adv; Memory Bk Adv; Drama Dir; Great Books Adv; Safety Patrol Chm; Dr Knight Teacher of Yr 1976; *home:* Randall MN 56475

STEADHAM, ZAN STALLINGS, Social Studies Dept Chair; *b:* Carrollton, GA; *m:* John Thomas; *ed:* (BA) His, 1977, (MA) His, 1981, (EDS) Scndry Soc Stud, 1985 W GA Coll; Teaching Advanced Placement European His; *cr:* Teacher J W Stewart Mid Sch 1979-85; Instr W GA Coll 1983; Teacher Douglas Cty HS 1985-86; Teacher/Dept Chairperson Robert S Alexander HS 1986-; *ai:* Oral Interpretation & Extemporaneous Speaking Literary Coach; Full Circle Bd Mem; Amer His Assn 1987-; NEA 1978-; *office:* Robert S Alexander HS 6500 Alexander Pkwy Douglasville GA 30135

STEADMAN, RICHARD JOHN, Head Counselor; *b:* Butte, MT; *m:* Betty J. Eagle; *c:* Staci R., Lisa M.; *ed:* (BS) Soc Stud, W MT Coll 1962; (MED) Counseling, 1968, (DED) Adult Ed, 1987 MT St Univ; *cr:* K-12th Grade Cnslr New S Wales Australia Sch 1966-68; Cnslr Billings West HS 1968-71; Asst Dir MT St Univ 1971-79; Elem Cnslr Dhahram Acad Saudia Arabia 1979-85; Head Cnslr Palo Verde HS 1987-; *ai:* Interact Service Club Adv; Riverside Cty Task Force to Promote Self Esteem & Responsibility Mem; *office:* Palo Verde HS 687 N Lovekin Blythe CA 92225

STEBBINS, BARRY STEVEN, Science Teacher; *b:* Dayton, OH; *m:* Cynthia K Shoutd; *c:* Christopher, Jenna; *ed:* (BS) Sci Ed, 1971, (MA) Sci Ed, 1976 OH St Univ; Voc Coord Course Work, OH St; Hyper Card & Multi-Media, Apple Cmptr Inc; *cr:* General Sci Teacher Roosevelt Jr HS 1971-78; Voc Coord Wedgewood Jr HS 1978-79; Voc Coord 1979-86, Bio/Physics Teacher 1986- West HS; *ai:* West HS Girls Jr Var Bsktbl Coach 1979-82; Vlybl Asst Coach 1980-82, Var Coach 1982-, City All-Star Team Coach 1987, St Coaches Drill Book Creator 1987-; Marine-Bio Study Trip Leader FL Keys 1973-88; Bio Textbook Review Comm 1981, Bio Course of Study Chm 1982; Cmptr Implementation into Voc Classroom 1983-86; Apple Classrooms of Tomorrow Project Start-Up Team Mem 1986; Organizer Dist HyperCard Educator User Group 1987-88; Wedgewood Jr HS Cheerleader Adv 1978-79; NEA, OEA Mem 1971-; Sigma XI Mem 1989-, Sci Teacher Awd 1989; Westerville Judo Club Black Belt Bd 1971-; West HS Athletic Booster Mem 1980-; OH HS Vlybl Coaches Assn 1982-; Testified Before Congress on Improving Sci Ed; Comm Hearing of Natl Acad of Sci; Lazarus Writing Awd; Articles Published; Sigma Xi Society Teacher of Yr Awd 1989; Nom Ashland Oil Teacher Achievement Awd 1990, West HS Educator of Yr 199); Presenter at Various Conferences 1987-; Team Mem Cornell Univ Multiple Representation in Math Research Project 1989-, Stanford Univ Sci for Living Technology Fair 1990; *office:* West HS 179 S Powell Ave Columbus OH 43204

STEBER, RONALD J., Power Technology Instructor; *b:* Hazleton, PA; *m:* Jacqueline L. Mc Govern; *c:* Melissa, Noelle, Jeffrey; *ed:* (BS) Industrial Art Ed, Penn St Univ 1974; Masters Equivalency Industrial Art Ed 1982; *cr:* Power Technology Instr Hazleton HS 1974-75; Wood Shop Instr Freeland HS 1975-76; Power Technology Instr Hazleton HS 1976-; *ai:* PSEA, NEA 1974-; TEAP 1983-; Hazleton Heights Vol Fire Dept Delegate 1971-; Mid Atlantic Air Museum 1987-; Instituted Aircraft Restoration Power Technology Curr Conjunction with Mid-Atlantic Air Museum 1987; 1st Place Stu Project Industrial Ed; Magazine For Restoring Aircraft Engine; Building Spirit of St Louis Replica; *office:* Hazleton HS 9th & Wyoming St Hazleton PA 18201

STECHMASSER, DIANE SCHOENHOFF, Third Grade Teacher; *b:* St Louis, MO; *m:* Arlin; *c:* Amy Elder; *ed:* (BS) Spec Ed, S IL Univ Edwardsville 1972; Learning Disabilities; *cr:* 3rd Grade Teacher Immaculate Conception Sch 1972-; *office:* Immaculate Conception Sch 321 S Metter Columbia IL 62236

STECK, BONNIE F., 8th Grade Math Teacher; *b:* Pittsfield, MA; *m:* Charles Gary; *c:* Mauralee Ramirez, Merry; *ed:* (BA) Art/Ed, Otterbein Coll 1959; Wright St Univ 1974-75; Palomar Coll 1980-; San Diego St Univ 1988-89; *cr:* 7th-8th Grade Teacher Clinton Jr HS 1959-60; Art Teacher Trotwood-Madison HS 1960-61; Substitute Teacher Chandler HS 1961-62, Falmouth HS 1962-63, Johnstown City Schls 1964-65, Trotwood-Madison City Schls 1975-78, San Marcos City Schls 1979-80, Escondido Chrstn Sch 1979-81; 8th Grade Teacher Escondido Chrstn Sch 1981-; *ai:* Yrbk Adv; United Meth Church (Pres United Meth Women 1970-72/Chm Worship Comm 1979-85); Teacher of Yr Awd Escondido Chrstn Sch 1990; *home:* 1020 Mac Mahr Rd San Marcos CA 92069

STECKEL, MARY CATHERINE, Third Grade Teacher; *b:* Jersey Shore, PA; *ed:* (BS) Elem Ed, Kutztown Univ 1971; (MED) Elem Ed, Lehigh Univ 1975; PA Dept of Ed Writing Consultant 1980; Basic & Advanced Levels of Process Writing at Teachers Coll, Columbia Univ 1989, 1990; *cr:* 5th Grade Teacher Fogelsville Sch 1971-73; 4th Grade Teacher Fogelsville & Kernsville Schls 1973-75; 3rd Grade Teacher Kernsville Sch 1975-76; 1st Grade Teacher 1976-87, 3rd Grade Teacher 1987- Fogelsville Sch; *ai:* Parkland Mentor 1989-; Dist Writing Curr Comm 1989-; Dist Rdng Curr Comm 1988-; Elected to Staff Dev Comm 1989-; Gifted Prgm Comm 1984-86; PTO Bd Mem 1984-; Phi Delta Kappa 1988-; Lehigh Cty Humane Society 1985-; PA Stage Company Theater Guild 1988-; Parkland Jaycees Outstanding Educator of Yr 1990; Developed & Lead Numerous Wkshps for Teachers, Intermediate Unit & Colls, Univs 1977-; Demonstration Site Leader 1990; *office:* Fogelsville Elem Sch Rd 6 Box 487 Allentown PA 18106

STEDENFELD, MICHELLE COURY, Art Teacher; *b:* Scranton, PA; *m:* Raymond Allen; *c:* Stephanie, Shelby E.; *ed:* (BA) Art Ed, Marywood Coll 1980; *cr:* Art Teacher Western Wayne HS 1989-; *ai:* Art Club Adv; NAEA; Pennsylvanians for Human Life; *office:* Western Wayne HS RD 2 Lake Ariel PA 18436

STEDILLIE, MICHAEL PATRICK, Theatre Director; *b:* Youngstown, OH; *m:* Ebba Marie Niegowski; *c:* Tony, Alaina; *ed:* (BSED) Theatre Ed, 1974, (MSED) Lit, 1986 Chadron St Coll; *cr:* Speech/Theatre Teacher Gering HS 1974-78; Speech/Debate Theatre Teacher Scottsbluff HS 1978-86; Theatre Dir Kelly Walsh HS 1986-; *ai:* Asst Forensics Dir; Auditorium Mgr; Drama Club Adv; Natrona Cty Ed Assn, WY Ed Assn, NEA; Jaycees Outstanding Young Educator 1978; Teacher in Space NE St Finalist; *office:* Kelly Walsh HS 3500 E 12th St Casper WY 82609

STEDMAN, MARK A., Science Department Chair; *b:* Ft Worth, TX; *ed:* (BS) Bio/Eng, 1980, (MS) Sci Ed/Admin, 1983 SW TX St; Leadership Trng TASC; Crisis Intervention Trng; *cr:* Teacher SW TX St 1983-85; Teacher/Chm Lockhart HS 1985-; *ai:* Stu Cncl Spon; Stu Act Dir; Tennis Coach; Sch Improvement Comm Mem 1987-; TCTA Pres Elect 1985-; STAT, NSTA Mem 1985-; Cmmty/Sch Action Team Mem 1988-; *office:* Lockhart HS 906 Center St Lockhart TX 78644

STEED, DENA BETH, Band Director; *b:* Nacogdoches, TX; *ed:* (BM) Music 1975, (MA) Music Ed, 1978 Stephen F Austin Univ; Grad Stud Mid-Management & Music Supervision; *cr:* Asst Band Teacher Clarksville Ind Sch Dist 1975-76; Band Dir Garrison Ind Sch Dist 1976-81, Humble Ind Sch Dist 1981-; *ai:* Marching Band; Drum Majors; Twirlers; Jazz Band; IOST; Concert Band; Bsktbl Pep Band; TX Music Educators Assn; 2000 Noteable Amer Women; United Cerebral Palsy Assn 1988-89; Women Band Dir Natl Assn; TX Bandmasters Assn; *office:* Humble HS 1700 Wilson Rd Humble TX 77338

STEED, HARRIET MOORE, 5th Grade Teacher; *b:* Warsaw, NC; *m:* Joe Jr.; *c:* Tyrone C., Timothy C.; *ed:* (BS) Elem Ed, Fayetteville St Univ 1967; (MED) Mid Grades Ed, Columbus Coll GA 1983; *cr:* 1st Grade Teacher Douglass HS 1967; Gifted Mid Grade Teacher Douglass HS 1967-69; 6th Grade Teacher Glendale Acres Elem 1970-77, Hillcrest Mid Sch 1977-80; 1st/4th/5th Grade Teacher South Columbus Elem 1980-; *ai:* Band Booster Pres; Parent Comm Mem HS Adoption; Sci, Math & Track Team Coach; Sch Math Coord; SACS Visiting Team Mem; NEA 1967-; NCTM 1989-; GMAE 1980-; Cub Scouts Den Mother 1978-80; Teacher of Yr S Columbus Elem 1984; Employee of Quarter 1989; *home:* 3916 Curry St Columbus GA 31907

STEEDLY, MAE T., First Grade Teacher; *b:* Sylvania, GA; *m:* Guinn R.; *c:* Gina, Karen; *ed:* (BS) Elem, GA Southern Coll 1965; Working Towards Masters; *cr:* 1st Grade Teacher Folkston Elem 1960-63, St Marys Elem 1960-; *ai:* Elem Chorus Helper; Assessment Trng; PAGE; Church Act; Local Sch Teacher of Yr 3 Times; *office:* St Marys Elem Sch 510 Osborne St Saint Marys GA 31558

STEEGE, DOROTHY SCHAEFER, Teacher of Gifted/Talented; *b:* Santa Monica, CA; *c:* Laura, Suzanne, Troy; *ed:* (BA) His, Mt St Marys 1959; Gifted & Talented Ed Trng; *cr:* Teacher Yokota Air Force Base Japan 1960-63, Las Vegas NV 1964-67; Teacher 1968-, Teacher of Gifted & Talented 1972- Garden Grove Unified Sch Dist; *ai:* SIP Comm Key Planner; Garden Grove Ed Assn (Mentor Teacher Selection Comm Chairperson 1984-, PAC Chairperson 1987-, Assoc Ed of Advocate 1989-), WHO 1990; Marymount Alumni Assn, Mt St Marys Alumni; Garden Grove Unified Sch Dist Team Consultant; *home:* 7402 Coho Dr #111 Huntington Bch CA 92648

STEEL, NARISSA, English Teacher; *b:* South River, NJ; *m:* Donald; *c:* Jane, James; *ed:* (BA) Eng/His, Trenton St Coll 1955; Grad Work Univ of MD, Trinity Coll, Bowie St Univ; *cr:* Core Teacher Bladensburg Jr HS 1955-62; Eng Teacher Pride HS 1963-64, Duval HS 1965-66, Forestville HS 1983-; *ai:* Literary Magazine Spon, Tennis Team Coach, Academic Athletic Adv Forestville HS; US Tennis Assn; NCTE, MD Cncl Teachers of Eng, MD St Teachers Assn, NEA; NHS Honorary Mem 1988; Teacher of Yr Awd 1989; *office:* Forestville HS 7001 Beltz Dr Forestville MD 20747

STEELE, ADA SHAFFER, Science Teacher; *b:* Grayson, KY; *m:* George F.; *c:* Travis; *ed:* (AB) Poly Sci, 1974, (MA) Ed, Morehead St Univ; Rank I Cert Scndry Prin 1982; *cr:* 7th/8th Grade Sci Teacher Prichard Elem; *ai:* Academic Team Coach; Beta Spon; NEA, KY Ed Assn; Grayson First Baptsit Church (Sunday Sch Teacher, Childrens Church Worker); Grayson Area Little League (Secy, Treas, Pres 1989); Teacher of Yr Grayson Chamber of Commerce 1989; *home:* PO Box 24 Grayson KY 41143

STEELE, ALICE LEE ROBBERSON, Orchestra & Fine Arts Teacher; *b:* Tucumcari, NM; *m:* Gail Frederick; *c:* Glen F., Kristin A. Wolf; *ed:* (BA) Music Ed, Univ of NM 1962; Grad Trng String Pedagogue Several Univs; Wkshps Amer Strings Teachers Assn; *cr:* Private Violin Instr 1968-89; Orch/Fine Art Teacher Clear Lake Intermediate 1974-; *ai:* Organize Soc Events Spon; Stu Coach; Participate in UIL Contests & Region Act; TX Music Educators Assn 1974-, Honor Dir 1984; TX St Teachers Assn 1980-; Amer String Teachers Assn 1974-; Clear Lake United Meth Church Mem 1968-; Sigma Alpha Iota Bay Area Alumni Chaplain 1978-; Clear Lake Symphony Concert Mistress 1978-; Concordia Trio Mem 1984-; TMEA Jr HS Honor Orch Dir 1983-84; TMEA & ASTA Jr HS Orch Performance & Clinic Orch Spon 1989; Runner-Up TMEA St Competition 1985-86, 1988-89, 1989-.

STEELE, ARCHIBALD FEATHERSTON, JR., Mathematics Teacher; *b:* Jackson, MS; *m:* Helen Sue Callahan; *c:* Archie F. III, Walter D. W., Tom W.; *ed:* (BS) Math, Univ of S MS 1957; (MA) Ed Admin, Azusa Pacific Univ 1978; Grad Semester Units Math, Ed Admin; *cr:* Math Teacher Enochs Jr HS 1961-63; Math Teacher/Math Dept Chm Tolleson Union HS 1963-68; Retired Lt Col US Marine Corps Reserve 1978; Math Teacher Moreno Valley HS 1968-; *ai:* Chm Three Strnd; Four Yr Plan & Electer Mem Sch Improvement Prgm Site Comm; Moreno Valley Ed Assn 1968-; NEA 1961-; CA Ed Assn 1968-; Natl Sci Fnd Grant 1963, 1966, 1967; *office:* Moreno Valley HS 23300 Cottonwood Ave Moreno Valley CA 92388

STEELE, CHARLES WALTER, History Teacher; *b:* Gary, IN; *m:* Petra Manning; *c:* Kevin, Andrew, Christopher, Nicholas; *ed:* (BS) Ed, Ball St Univ 1962; (MS) His, IN St Univ 1964; *cr:* Teacher Gary Cmmty Schls 1962-; *ai:* Crown Point Cmmty Lib Trustee 1980-; *office:* West Side HS 9th And Gerry St Gary IN 46406

STEELE, DARRELL GRANT, History Teacher; *b:* Salisbury, NC; *m:* Vicke S.; *c:* Marcia, Deryl; *ed:* (BS) His, Winston-Salem St Univ 1976; (MS) Intermediate Ed, NC A&T St Univ 1982; Rdng; *cr:* Teacher Mocksville Mid Sch 1979-80; Teacher/Coach NDJH 1980-; *ai:* Varsity Boys Bsktbl Coach; Girls Sftbl Coach; Davie Girls Sftbl Coach Comm Sch Coord; NCAE 1979-; Coaches Assn 1980-; Masonic Lodge 1986-; *office:* North Davie Jr H S Rt 2 Box 44 Mocksville NC 27028

STEELE, DERREK EUGENE, Teacher/Coach; *b:* Lawton, OK; *m:* Christina Devonne Prather; *c:* Dominique N., Deante Lamar; *ed:* (BA) Psych, James Madison Univ 1984; *cr:* Mgr Trainee Giant 1984; 1st Insructional Aid/2nd Grade Teacher/Bsktbl Head Coach Mt Vernon HS 1984-; *ai:* N VA Boys Bsktbl Coaches Assn Treas 1989-; *office:* Mt Vernon HS 8515 Old Mount Vernon Rd Alexandria VA 22309

STEELE, MARY KOPP, English/Computer Teacher; *b:* St Marys, PA; *m:* Stephen A.; *c:* Timothy J., Stephen Jr., Patrick J.; *ed:* (BS) Comm, Lock Haven Univ 1976; *cr:* Eng Teacher Spotsylvania HS 1977-84; Eng Teacher/Comp Coord Queen of World Sch 1984-; *ai:* Yrbk Adv, Cmptr Coord, Awesome Apple Club Spon; Parent Teacher Guild 1984-; Parish Cncl 1989-; Little League Team Mother 1990; Master Teacher 3 Yrs; *office:* Queen of the World Sch 134 Queens Rd Saint Marys PA 15857

STEELE, MICHAEL JAMES, Chem Teacher/Sci Dept Chairman; *b:* Lebanon, IN; *m:* Caroline Conolly; *ed:* (BA) Chem, Bridgewater Coll 1986; Working Towards Masters Univ of VA; *cr:* Permanent Substitute Teacher Hedgesville HS 1985-86; Lab Technician Diagnostic Assays Service Incorporated 1986-87; Chem Teacher Manassas Park HS 1987-; *ai:* Class Spon; Asst Var Ftbl & Head Var Boys Bsktbl Coach; Academic Advisory Comm; *office:* Manassas Park HS 140-A Kent Dr Manassas VA 22111

STEELE, SHARON KAY MC GHEE, Second Grade Teacher; *b:* Little Rock, AR; *m:* Darryl William; *c:* Jamie A., Jeffery W.; *ed:* (BA) Elem Ed, 1972, (MA) Elem Ed, 1987 AR Tech Univ; *cr:* 2nd Grade Teacher Louise Durham Elem 1972-; *ai:* Staff Dev Comm; Delta Kappa Gamma Music Chm 1980-; Phi Delta Kappa Secy 1986-; Grade Level Rep; *office:* Louise Durham Elem 106 N Reine Mena AR 71953

STEELE, THOMAS MICHAEL, Social Studies Chair; *b:* Moline, IL; *m:* Linda; *c:* Mark, Teresa, Jennifer; *ed:* (BA) His, Augustana Coll 1971; (MA) Soc Stud, Univ of IL 1975; *cr:* Teacher J D Darnall HS 1971-; *ai:* Soc Stud Chair; Prof Improvement & Curr Comm; Geneseo Ed Assn Pres 1985-91; IL Ed Assn Bd Dir 1983-91; NEA Lifetime Mem; Heney Cty Bd of Dir Mem 1989-; *office:* J D Darnall HS 700 N State St Geneseo IL 61254

STEELE, WALTER DANIEL, Mathematics Dept Chairman; *b:* Encino, CA; *m:* Robyn Lynn Pickrell; *ed:* (BA) Comm, Pepperdine Univ 1983; *cr:* Prof Athlete Milwaukee Brewers 1980-81; O & M Sash & Door Head of Sales 1981-82; Math Dept Chm Montclair Coll Prep 1983-; *ai:* Class & Math Club Spon; Class Adv; Asst Var Ftbl Coach; Head Var Girls Bsktbl & Boys Bsbl; *office:* Montclair Coll Prep Sch 8071 Sepulveda Blvd Van Nuys CA 91402

STEELMON, KENNETH MARTIN, 7th/8th Grade Science Teacher; *b:* Crossville, TN; *m:* Polly Sue Smith; *c:* Marty, Karen Steelmon Bunch, Paul R. Watts; *ed:* (BS) Ed/Phys Ed/Bio/ Sociology, Lincoln Memorial Univ 1959; *cr:* Bsktbl/Track Coach/ Teacher La Fontaine HS 1960-61; Phys Ed Teacher/Coach Oliver Springs Elem & Jr HS 1962; Bsktbl/Track Coach/Teacher Clinton HS 1963-64; Asst Dir of Recreation City of Oak Ridge 1964-74; Dir of Recreation CiTy of Oak Ridge 1974-77; Teacher/ Coach Union Chapel Jr HS 1978-79; Tech Worker Burton Manufacturing Company 1979; Sftbl Supvr Jasper Parks & Recreation Dept; Sci Teacher Valley Jr HS 1980-; *ai:* TN Recreation & Parks Assn (Mem, Pres Elect Nom); Natl Recreation & Parks Assn Mem; Amateur Sftbl Assn Dist Sftbl Commissioner St of TN; Amer Ed Assn Mem; Intnl Frisbee Assn Honorary Mem.

STEELMON, SUE SMITH, Mathematics Teacher; *b:* Birmingham, AL; *m:* Kenneth M.; *c:* Marty, Karen Bunch, Paul Watts; *ed:* (BS) Math, Univ of Montevallo 1965; *cr:* Teacher Valley Jr HS 1978-; *ai:* Beta Club, 4-H Club, Math Academic Team Spon; AL Ed Assn.

STEELY, ALLEN M., Science Teacher; *b:* Geneva, IL; *m:* Marcia A. Limkeman; *c:* Rachel, Joshua, Jonathan; *ed:* (BA) Psych, Wheaton Coll 1974; *cr:* Psych Teacher Igbaja Theological Seminary 1974; Sci Teacher Bingham Acad 1974-76, Rockford Chrstn Sch 1978-; *ai:* Soccer & Track Coach; Stu Cncl Spon; Natl Fed Interscholastic Ofcls Assn Soccer Referee 1979-, Recognized Level 1981-; 1st Evangelical Free Church Vice-Chm Soc Concerns Commission 1988-; Article Published 1975; IL Math & Sci Acad Academic Excl Awd 1988; *office:* Rockford Chrstn Sch 220 Hemlock Ln Rockford IL 61107

STEEN, KAREN SUE (KEISTER), Business Instructor; *b:* New Lexington, OH; *m:* John R.; *ed:* (AA) OH Valley Coll 1980; (BS) Comprehensive Bus Ed, 1982, (MS) Home Ec, 1989 OH Univ; Intensive Office Ed, 1983, Cooperative Office Ed, 1984 Kent St Univ; Word Processing Certificate, Hocking Tech Coll 1982; *cr:* Exec Secy New Lexington City Schls 1982-83; Teacher Guernsey Noble Voc Sch 1983-84; Teacher Sheridan HS 1984-; Business Instr Cntrl OH Tech Coll 1987-; *ai:* Bus Prof of America Adv 1983-; Parliamentary Procedure Team Adv 1986-; Delta Phi Epsilon, AVA, OH Voc Assn 1989-; OH Bus Teachers Assn 1982-; Amer Red Cross Water Safety Instr 1977-; Somerset Church of Christ 1988-; Perry Cty Bus & Prof Womens Club 1986-; Cancer Swim-A-Long Chm 1988-89; Cystic Fibrosis Swim-A-Long Chm 1989; *home:* 419 S Columbus St Somerset OH 43783

STEEVES, ROBERT BURNS, 5th Grade Teacher; *b:* Potsdam, NY; *m:* Patricia Harmon; *ed:* (AAS) Retail Bus Admin, Mohawk Valley Comm Coll 1955; (BS) Ed, 1963, (MS) Ed, 1972 St Univ of NY; Admin Cert; Metric System In-Service Staff Instr; Work with Gifted & Talented Prgm; *cr:* Teacher Bainbridge-Guilford Cntrl Sch 1963-65; Prin Bridgewater Summer Sch 1964; Teacher Chenango Valley Cntrl Sch Dist 1965-67; Stu Act Dir Broome Comm Coll 1967; Teacher Chenango Valley Cntrl Sch Dist 1967-; *ai:* Jr HS Bsktbl Coach; Stu Cncl Bainbridge & Hillcrest Schls; Reorganization & Textbook Selection Comms; NYSUT; Port Crane Civic Assn; *home:* RD 1 Box 62 Bainbridge NY 13733

STEFANICH, GEORGE MATTHEW, 4th Grade Teacher; *b:* Tower, MN; *ed:* (BS) Elem Ed, Bemidji St Univ 1968; *cr:* 3rd/4th Grade Teacher Washington Elem Sch 1968-; *ai:* MEA 1968-; St Martins Church Tower (Mens Club, Usher).

STEFFEN, CAROL MARIE, Fourth Grade Teacher; *b:* Ansonia, OH; *ed:* (BSED) Elem Ed, Miami Univ 1950; Various Summer Wkshps; *cr:* 3rd Grade Teacher 1950-82, 5th Grade Teacher 1982-85, 6th Grade Teacher 1985-87, 4th Grade Teacher 1987- South Elem Sch; *ai:* GEA, OEA, NEA; OES (Worthy Matron 1980-81/1983-84/1987, Gr Rep DE/OH 1985-86); *home:* 351 E Main St Versailles OH 45380

STEFKA, DEBORAH ANN, Mathematics Teacher; *b:* Caldwell, TX; *ed:* (BS) Curr/Instruction, 1982, (MSED) Curr/Instruction, 1988 TX A&M Univ; *cr:* Math Teacher Caldwell HS 1982-; *ai:* Natl Honor Society & Jr Class Spon; NCTM, TX St Teachers Assn, Assn of TX Prof Educators; Outstanding Young Women in America; *office:* Caldwell HS 203 N Gray Caldwell TX 77836

STEGALL, NANCY BLAKEMORE, 4th-6th Grade Teacher; *b:* Fayette, MO; *m:* Jerry F.; *c:* Lisa A., Jason F.; *ed:* (BA) Elem Ed, 1961, (MA) Elem Ed, 1964 Drury Coll; MO Univ, Univ of NM, Cntrl MO St Univ, Lincoln Univ; *cr:* 1st Grade Teacher Parkway Sch Dist 1961-65; Soc Stud Teacher 1978-80, 4th-6th Grade Teacher 1981- Jefferson City Public Schls; *ai:* Just Say No Club Co-Spon; Alpha Delta Kappa 1987-; NEA 1988-; NSTA-CTA Treas 1978-82; Phi Alpha Theta 1986-; Jaycee Jills Treas 1970-73, Outstanding Jill 1971; Little Theatre of Jefferson City 1970-78; Lioness Club Treas 1971-; Epsilon Sigma Alpha (Pres, VP, Secy & Treas) 1972-83; Educl Exch Prgm Soviet Union 1985; Teacher Exch Prgm United Kingdom 1989; *home:* 800 Geneva St Jefferson City MO 65109

STEGALL, PAMELA JANE, Jr High Science Teacher; *b:* Martinsville, VA; *ed:* (BA) Bible/Religon, King Coll Bristol 1982; (MA) General Theology, Covenant Seminary St Louis 1990; *cr:* HS Bible/Yrbk Teacher 1985-89, Jr HS Sci Teacher 1989- Westminster Chrstn Sch; *ai:* Columbia Scholastic Press Assn Yrbk, 2nd Pl 1988, 1st Pl 1989; FL Scholastic Press Assn Yrbk, 4th Pl 1986, 3rd 1987, 2nd 1988, 1st 1989; Taylor Publishing Co Nom for Yrbk Cover Design 1988.

STEGALL, RUBY WATERS, First Grade Teacher; *b:* Lincolnton, NC; *m:* Thomas Bruce; *c:* Tamara, Thomas B. Jr.; *ed:* (BS) Elem Ed, Appalachian St Univ 1961; *cr:* Teacher Idlewild Elem 1961-65, Marshville Elem 1965-68, 1978-; *ai:* Jaycees Educator of Yr 1983; *office:* Marshville Elem Sch N Elm St Marshville NC 28103

STEGER, JAN K., Choral Director; *b:* Dunkirk, NY; *ed:* (BMUS) Voice/Music Ed, NY St Univ Fredonia 1974; *cr:* Choral Dir Lockport Sr HS 1974-76, Warsaw Consolidated Schls 1976-77, West Seneca E Sr HS 1977-79, Ligon G T Mid Sch 1984-; *ai:* Music & Choral Dir for Sch Musicals; Music Educators Natl Conference; NC Music Educators Assn; *office:* Ligon Gifted/ Talented Mid Sch 706 E Lenoir St Raleigh NC 27601

STEGMAN, BERNADETTE, Kindergarten Teacher; *b:* Spearville, KS; *ed:* (BA) Elem Ed/Hum, Mary Mount Coll 1972; *cr:* 2nd Grade Teacher St Marys Grade Sch 1972-75; 3rd Grade Teacher 1975-84; Kndgtn Teacher 1984- St Mary Queen of Universe Grade Sch; *ai:* NCEA Mem 1972-; *office:* St Marys Grade Sch 304 E Cloud Salina KS 67401

STEGMAN, JOYCE LYNN (CRAMB), Special Education Teacher; *b:* Lamar, CO; *m:* Donald A.; *c:* Scott, Jeff, Kara; *ed:* (BS) Psych/Spec Ed, KS St Teachers Coll 1970; (MA) Spec Ed of Educationally Handicapped, Adams St Coll 1977; *cr:* Spec Ed Teacher Granada Elem 1971-72, Washington Elem 1972-78, Evans Elem 1979-80; Eng/Soc Stud Teacher 1985-87, Spec Ed Teacher 1987- Ortega Mid Sch; *ai:* Prin Advisory Comm; NEA, CO Ed Assn, Alamosa Educators 1986-; PEO 1979-; Outstanding Young Educator of Yr Lamar CO 1976; 2 Life Skills Act Projects Published; *office:* Ortega Mid Sch 1301 Main St Alamosa CO 81101

STEHENS, EDNA MITCHELL, Teacher; *b:* Maryville, TN; *m:* Issac Reed; *c:* Nancey Stephens Stinnett, Sherry Stephens Adcox, Donna Stpehens Trentham, Julia Spring; *ed:* (AA) Bus Ed, Hiwassee Coll 1961; (BS) Bus Ed/Elem Ed, TN Wesleyan 1973; Rdng Specialist, Univ of TN 1980-86; Adult Basic Ed & Teaching Illiterate Adult, TN Tech Univ; *cr:* Teacher Rural Vale Elem 1966-67, Coker Creek Elem 1967-70, Tellico Elem 1970-74, Coker Creek Elem 1974-; *ai:* Taught Music; Help with Prgms & Plays; Taught Inservice Teaching Rdng; TN Master Teacher Level II 1983-; Faculty Rep Chm 1984-; Rescue Sq Crewettes Captain; Eastern Star Worthy Matron 1989-; *home:* Hwy 68 Rt 4 Box 216A Tellico Plains TN 37385

STEHUR, PETER, Science Dept Chair; *b:* Wilkes-Barre, PA; *m:* Mary Nanorta; *c:* Suzanne, Diane, Peter, Julianne, Joanne, Michael, Marianne; *ed:* (BS) Chem, Wilkes Univ 1966; (MS) Chem, Univ of Scranton 1970; Grad Courses Math & Physics, Univ of Scranton; Summer Practucum Environmental Ed, Marywood Coll; *cr:* Chem/Physics/Math Teacher/Sci Dept Chm Hanover Area Jr/Sr HS 1966-; *ai:* JETS Team Coach; PA Jr Acad of Sci Stu Spon; NEA, PA Ed Assn, Local Ed Assn 1966-; Luzerne Cty Sci Teachers Assn Pres 1976-77; Church Cncl Pres 1984-; Received Luzerne-Lackawanna Cty Environmental Cncl Teachers Awd; *office:* Hanover Jr/Sr HS 1600 Sans Souci Pkwy Wilkes-Barre PA 18702

STEIDLE, LAURA STOCKER, 8th Grade Reading Teacher; *b:* Richmond, KY; *m:* David V.; *c:* James L.; *ed:* (BA) Elem Ed, Univ KY 1972; (MA) Elem Rdng, Northern KY Univ 1982; *cr:* 6th Grade Teacher Amelia Elem Sch 1972-78; 7th-8th Grade Lang Art/Rdngteacher Amelia Mid Sch 1978-; *ai:* Sch Play Co-Spon; Lang Art Curr Comm; Dist Comm Cncl; Faculty Advisory Cncl; IMPACT Trng; Faculty Study Group Critical Thinking Skills; NCTE 1990; Northern KY Cmmty Chorus Section Leader 1984-; St Josephs Choir 1976-; *home:* 230 Ft Mitchell Ave Fort Mitchell KY 41011

STEIGHORST, PAMELA WEISS, Phys Ed/Health Teacher; *b:* St Louis, MO; *m:* Mark E.; *c:* Blake, Brooke, Blair; *ed:* (BS) Phys Ed, SE MO St Univ 1976; (MA) Ed, Webster Univ 1984; *cr:* Phys Ed/Health Teacher Hillsboro Mid Sch 1978-; *ai:* Var Cheerleading Coach; NEA, MO Chrldr Coaches Assn; MO St HS Act Assn St Cheerleading Comm Mem; Article in MO St HS Act Assn Journal; *home:* Rt 4 Box 45B De Soto MO 63020

STEILL, LAUREL CARLSON, English Teacher/Dept Chair; *b:* Buchanan, MI; *m:* Nicholas J.; *ed:* (BA) Eng, 1963, (MS) Ed, 1968 Saint Francis Coll; Gifted/Talented Endorsement; *cr:* Eng Teacher Buchanan HS 1963-64; Lecturer Saint Francis Coll 1974-77; Eng Teacher Columbia City Joint HS 1964-; *ai:* NHS Adv; Advanced Placement Coord; NCTE; IN Cncl of Teachers of Eng Pres Elect 1989-, Hoosier Teacher of Eng 1981; Phi Delta Kappa; NEA; IN St Teachers Assn; Whitley Cty Teachers Assn; Modern Lang Assn, Conference of Scndry Sch Eng Dept Chairpersons; Outstanding Young Educator Awd; IN Univ Fnd Frosh Div Outstanding Teaching Awd; Natl Endowment for Hum Grant; *office:* Columbia City Joint HS 600 N Whitley St Columbia City IN 46725

STEIN, ALAN, Fourth Grade Teacher; *b:* Manhattan, NY; *c:* Andrew B., Matthew E.; *ed:* (MS) Elem Ed, IN Univ 1977; *cr:* Teacher Julian D Coleman 1973-83, Elder Diggs 1983-84, Julian D Coleman 1985-; *ai:* Julian D Coleman Sch 110 Ftbl Coach, Sch 37 Bsktbl Coach; Math Adoption Comm; IN Historical Society IN His Pilot Prgm; Wrote 5th Grade Math Curr Indianapolis Public Schls System; *office:* Julian D Coleman Sch 1740 E 30th St Indianapolis IN 46218

STEIN, ANN WEESE, 8Th Grade Reading Teacher; *b:* Akron, OH; *c:* Morgan A.; *ed:* (BS) Phys Ed/Health Ed Univ ofAkron 1974; (MED) Rdng Supervision, OH Univ 1976; Real Estate Research, OH Paralegal Inst 1979; Learning & Behavioral Disabilities; Cmptr Ed; *cr:* Teacher/Intern Meigs Local Teacher Corps 1974-76; Learning Disabilities Tutor/Substitute Teacher Wadsworth City Schls 1976-78; Learning Disabilities Teacher 1978-85;Rdng Teacher 1985- New Philadelphia Schls; *ai:* Athletic Aide; Dist Grad Card Comm; Yr of Reaching for Vision Comm; Corporate Recreation Dir; NEA/OEA/NPEA Building Rep 1984-86; Emmanuel Luth Choir Mem/Yth Chairperson 1983-; Meigs Local Teacher Corps Schlsp; *office:* Welty Mid Sch 315 4th St NW New Philadelphia OH 44663

STEIN, BARBARA LINDA, Sixth Grade Teacher; *b:* Brooklyn, NY; *m:* Jay Ira; *ed:* (BS) Elem Ed, AZ St Univ; (BS) Elem Ed, Univ of MD 1970; Grad Stud Music, Univ of MD; ; *cr:* 1st-3rd Grade Teacher Langley Park Elem 1970-73; 3rd-6th Grade Teacher James Mc Henry Elem 1974-; *ai:* Stu Cncl Spon & Adv; Honor Roll & Math Comm; NEA, MD Ed Assn, Lanham Ed Assn; PTA Exec Bd; Private Violin Teacher; *office:* James Mc Henry Elem Sch 8909 Mc Henry Ln Lanham Seabrook MD 20706

STEIN, JAMES WILLIAM, Mathematics Teacher; *b:* Sheboygan, WI; *m:* Jean; *c:* Valerie, Daniel; *ed:* (BS) Ed/Scndry Math, Univ of WI Oshkosh 1964; (MS) Ed/Math, N MI Univ 1975; *cr:* Teacher Stoughton Public Schls 1964-65, Norway-Vulcan Public Schls 1965-67, Green Bay Public Schls 1990; *ai:* 3rd-12th Grade Bsktbl Coach 1964-84; NEA, WEA 1964-; Green Bay Building Rep 1980-84; Meals on Wheels Volunteer; Red Cross (Firesis Donor, 10 Gallon Blood Donor); Phoenix Booster Club 1987-; Natl Sci Fnd Grant; Green Bay Teachers Apple Awd.

STEIN, SHIRLEY TATLEY, First Grade Teacher; *b:* Bismarck, ND; *m:* Ray; *c:* Bryan, Stacey Schuler, Jill, Steve; *ed:* (BS) Elem Ed, Minot St Univ 1967; (MS) Ed/Rdng, Univ of ND 1987; *cr:* 4th Grade Elem Teacher Surrey Public Sch 1967; 3rd Grade Elem Teacher Beulah Public 1967-68; 1st Grade Elem Teacher Devils Lake Public Sch Dist 1968-89; *ai:* NEA, ND Ed Assn 1963-89; Devils Lake Ed Assn Secy 1960-82; Intnl Rdng Assn 1987-89; Outstanding Educator Devils Lake Sch Dist; Author Articles Insights into Open Ed & Dept of Public Instruction ND Perspectives; *office:* Prairie View-Devils Lake Sch 12th Ave Devils Lake ND 58301

STEIN, SUE T., Office Technology Teacher; *b:* Lock Haven, PA; *m:* W. Forrest Jr.; *c:* Marc L.; *ed:* (BS) Bus Ed, PA St Univ 1972; (MBE) Bus Ed, Mid TN St Univ 1987; *cr:* Bus Teacher Quakertown HS 1972-73, Griffin Mid Sch 1978-84; Office Ed Teacher Beech HS 1984-; *ai:* Bus Profs of Amer & Stu Cncl Spon; Stu Taking A Right Stand Coreteam Mem; Parents Awareness Network Coord; Renaissance & Morale Comms; Class Spon; Delta Pi Epsilon Corresponding Secy 1987-89; TN Bus Ed Assn Schlshp Comm 1989-; Beautiful Hendersonville Recycling Volunteer 1988-; Beta Sigma Phi (Pres 1983-84, VP 1982-83), Woman of Yr 1983; *office:* Beech HS 3126 Long Hollow Pike Hendersonville TN 37075

STEINBACK, TIM J., Science Teacher; *b:* Clarksburg, WV; *m:* Barbara Joyce Shutt; *c:* Sonya; *ed:* (BS) Metallurgical Engineering, 1969, (MAT) Scndry Ed, 1971 Pitt; Metallurgical Engineering; *cr:* Metallurgical Engr NUMEC 1969-70; Chem/Physics Teacher Clairton Sr HS 1970-71; Chem Teacher Lenape Vo-Tech 1976-79; Chem/Physics Teacher Apollo-Ridge 1986-; *ai:* SADD Co-Spon; Entrepreneurs Club Spon; Washington Township Volunteer Fire Company VP 1971-81; Washington Township Rotary Club 1990; US & Canadian Patents Air Handling System for Indoor Swimming Pools Awd; Integrapool Systems Incorporated Pres; *home:* 666 Sportsman Dr Apollo PA 15613

STEINBERG, HAROLD SYLVAN, English Teacher; *b:* San Francisco, CA; *m:* Carol V. Hartgogian; *c:* Ann D., David G.; *ed:* (BA) Eng/Soc Sci, San Francisco St 1958; *cr:* Eng Teacher El Dorado Union HS 1962-64, Galileo HS 1964-78, Lowell HS 1978-; *ai:* United Educators of San Francisco 1964; CA Teachers Assn (Building Rep, Finance) 1961-; NEA (Comm 1968) 1964-; *office:* Lowell HS 1101 Eucalyptus Dr San Francisco CA 94132

STEINBROOK, RUSSETTA LYNN, Fourth Grade Teacher; *b:* Columbus, OH; *ed:* (BA) Practical Chrstn Trng, Bob Jones Univ 1977; Elem Ed, Pensacola Chrstn Coll 1991; *cr:* Teacher Dade Chrstn Sch 1978-80, Licking Cty Chrstn Acad 1980-; *ai:* Var Chrldrs Soccer, Jr Var Chrldrs Bsktbl, Elem Vlybl 4th-6th Grade Girls Coach; Outstanding Young Women of America 1987; *home:* 15A Licking View Dr Heath OH 43056

STEINER, DORIS SNYDER, Fourth Grade Teacher; *b:* Sunbury, PA; *m:* Louis; *c:* Marie D; *ed:* (BS) Elem Ed, E Nazarene Coll 1962; Grad Stud Ed; *cr:* 4th Grade Teacher 1962-81, 5th Grade Teacher 1981-82, 4th Grade Teacher 1983- Northampton Area Sch Dist; *ai:* Northampton Area Ed Assn, PA St Ed Assn 1963-; NEA 1967-; *home:* 1073 N Oaks Rd Danielsville PA 18038

STEINER, KATHERINE ELIZABETH (HASLETT), Cheerleading Coach; *b:* Bethlehem, PA; *m:* Jay Scott; *c:* Carey, Kim, Pamela; *ed:* (BA) Elem Ed, Upsala Coll 1965; Early Chldhd Ed, Kean Coll NJ; *cr:* 2nd Grade Teacher Allen W Roberts Sch 1965-67; Head Teacher Nursery Sch Livingston NJ 1970-72; Substitute Elem Teacher Randolph NJ 1980; Cheerleading Coach Randolph HS 1981-; *ai:* Head Cheerleading Coach; NJ Ed Assn 1965-72; PTA 1973-87; Randolph Recreation Cheerleading Coach 1978-80; Fresh Air Fund (Trip Chaperone, Comm Mem) 1977-87; Church Youth Choir Dir 1971-72; Welcome Wagon VP 1971-72; Amer Field Service 1985-87; *home:* 3 Drum Hill Ln Randolph NJ 07869

STEINERT, WILLIAM EDWARD, English Teacher/Dept Chair; *b:* Oshkosh, WI; *m:* Carol Ann Bowman; *ed:* (BS) Eng Ed, Univ of WI Oshkosh 1986; Eduol Psych, Univ of WI Milwaukee Grad Sch; Trained AOD Facilitator & Cnslr CASI Training Inst of Appleton WI; *cr:* Long Term Substitute Eng Teacher Oshkosh West HS 1987-88; Eng Teacher/Dept Chm Stockbridge Public Schls 1988-; *ai:* Drama Dir; SADD Coord; AOD & SAP Facilitator & Curr Developer; Soph Class Adv; Attendance/Truancy Comm; Union Secy; NCTE, NEA 1988-; Stockbridge Ed Assn Secy 1988-; AODA for Stockbridge Sch Dist Grant 1988-89; *office:* Stockbridge Public Schls 110 School St Stockbridge WI 53088

STEINGLEIN, BARBARA, Second Grade Teacher; *b:* Northampton, MA; *ed:* (BA) His, Smith Coll 1962; (MLS) Lib Sci, Simmons Coll 1963; *cr:* Librarian Boston Public Lib 1963-68; 2nd Grade Teacher Breor Elem 1971-; *ai:* MA Teachers Assn, Natl Ed Assn; Parish Cncl St Josephs Church.

STEINHAUSER, JUDITH WILKINSON, English Department Chair; *b:* Eldorado, IL; *m:* Jay R.; *c:* Brad, Grant, Anne; *ed:* (BA) Eng, Mac Murray Coll 1968; (MA) Lit, Sangamon St Univ 1975; *cr:* Instr Lincoln Land Comm Coll 1980-82; Eng Dept Chairperson Greenview HS 1968-; *ai:* Sr Class; JETS; Stu Cncl; NHS; IL Cncl Teachers of Eng 1970-; Greenview Ed Organization Pres 1980-81; IL Ed Assn, NEA 1968-80; *office:* Greenview HS PO Box 320 Greenview IL 62642

STEINHEISER, GLENN WAYNE LAMONT, 4th Grade Teacher; *b:* Butler, PA; *m:* Linda Lucille White; *c:* Adam W., Troy S.; *ed:* (BS) Ed, 1965, (MED) Ed, 1967 Slippery Rock St Coll; Grad Stud Univ of DE; Rdng, Univ of Pittsburgh; *cr:* 3rd/5th Grade Teacher Harford Cty Schls 1965-67; 4th Grade Teacher Mohawk Area Schls 1967-; *ai:* Mohawk Ed Assn (Pres, VP, Building Rep) 1967-; PA Ed Assn Convention Delegate 1967-; NEA Convention Delegate 1965-; 1st Wesleyan Church Sunday Sch Supt 1967-; Gideons Intnl (Pres, VP, Secy) 1984-; *home:* 101 Orange Dr New Castle PA 16101

STEININGER, PATRICIA PONITZ, Third Grade Teacher; *b:* Detroit, MI; *m:* James Anton; *c:* Jill S.; *ed:* (BA) Elem Ed/Sci/Math, 1969, (MA) Elem Ed, 1973 MI St Univ; Co-Operative Learning, Instructional Theory into Practice, Process Writing, Assertive Discipline; *cr:* 3rd Grade Teacher Grand Blanc Cmmty Schls 1969-; *ai:* Sch Improvement Project-Steering Comm; Sci Fair Coord; Quality of Work Life; NEA, MI Ed Assn, Grand Blanc Ed Assn 1969-; Mt Olive Luth Church 1983-; 20 Yr Service Awd Grand Blanc Cmmty Schls; *office:* Grand Blanc Cmmty Sch 11920 S Saginaw Grand Blanc MI 48439

STEINMETZ, KEVIN LEE, Mathematics Teacher/Dept Chair; *b:* Willard, OH; *m:* Dianne L. George; *c:* Kyle; *ed:* (BS) Elem Ed, OH St Univ 1983; *cr:* Mid Sch Teacher Shiloh Mid Sch 1983-; *ai:* St Jude Math-A-Thon Spon; Stu Cncl Adv; Head Bsbl, Asst Ftbl & Bsktbl Coach; Knights of Columbus 1980-; BPO Elks Club 1984-; *home:* 615 Dale Willard OH 44890

STELEVICH, ANN ELIZABETH, Home Economics Teacher; *b:* Wilkes Barre, PA; *m:* Douglas; *c:* Jennifer A.; *ed:* (BS) Home Ec/Ed, Coll Misericordia 1967; (MA) Curr Planning/Supervision, Georgian Court Coll 1979; Grad Stud; *cr:* Home Ec Teacher Thompson Jr HS 1967-68, Jackson Twp HS 1969-71, Jonas Salk Mid Sch 1971-; *ai:* Alpha Delta Kappa (Historian 1988-, Corresponding Secy 1990); NEA, NJEA, OBEA, PTA; Lakewood Jackson Jr Womens Club & MADD 1972-79; Jackson Women of Today 1988-; Strand Theater League 1986-87; NJ Competitive Grant for Ind Living 1986-87; *office:* Jonas Salk Mid Sch W Greystone Rd Old Bridge NJ 08857

STELLER, ROBERT EDWARD, History/Polticial Sci Instr; *b:* Spring Lake, NJ; *m:* Patricia Louise Gibson; *ed:* (BS) His/Ed, Villanova Univ 1969; *cr:* His/Poly Sci Instr Middletown HS South 1969-; *ai:* Moderator Cultural Affairs Club & Poly Sci CLub; Adv Georgetwon Intnl Relations Model United Nations & Monmouth Coll Stu Government Institute; Fall Poly Sci South Dir; NJ Ed Assn 1975-; Borough of Spring Lake (Mayor, Councilman) 1974-80; Spring Lake Planning Bd (Mem, Vice Chm) 1976-81; Spring Lake Historical Society (VP 1983, Pres 1982, Trustee 1984-87, Mem) 1975-; Fairway Mews Cmmty Assn Bd of Dirs 1989-; Architecture Comm Chm 1989-; Gov Keane Excl in Ed Teacher of Yr Awd & Grant 1988; *office:* Middletown HS South 501 Nutswamp Rd Middletown NJ 07748

STELLFOX, JEAN LOUISE, English Teacher; *b:* Danville, PA; *ed:* (BA) Eng, Dickinson Coll 1960; (MA) Eng, PA St Univ 1962; Natl Endowment for Hum Oberlin Coll; Amer Stud Prgm Eastern Coll; Religious Lit Prgm PA St Univ; *cr:* Eng Teacher Shamokin Area HS 1961-; *ai:* Delta Kappa Gamma, Phi Beta Kappa, Delta Phi Alpha, Shamokin Area Ed Assn; NEA Life Mem; *office:* Shamokin Area HS 2000 W State St Shamokin PA 17872

STELLY, NOELIE M., Mathematics/French Teacher; *b:* Iota, LA; *ed:* (BA) Math/Fr, 1958, (MED) Admin/Supervision, 1966 Our Lady of Lake Univ; Cert of Stud Fr, Laval Univ 1962, Univ d Angers 1973; Math, Modern Geometries Our Lady of Holy Cross 1990; Fr Schlshp Loyola Univ 1977; *cr:* Fr/Math Our Lady of Lake Univ & Our Lady of Holy Cross; Teacher/Admin Congregation of Divine Providence 1954-70; Math Teacher L W Higgins HS 1970-79; Math/Fr Teacher Gretna Jr HS 1984-; *ai:* Mathcounts; AL, LA, MS Math League Competitive Exams; Substance Abuse Prevention Ed; SADD; NCTM 1967-78, 1987-; Amer Assn of Fr 1961-68, 1989-; Cncl for Dev of Fr Adv 1973-; Assn of Classroom Teachers Pres 1975-76; Congregation of Divine Providence Advisory Cncl 1967-70; Mayors Cncl of Public Relations 1967-68; Food Bank 1984-; Modern Music Master Honoray Mem 1966; Natl Sci Fnd Grants 1959, 1973; Codofil Grant to France 1973 & Loyola Univ 1977.

STEMEN, JUDITH (BAHR), First Grade Teacher; *b:* Grosse Pointe, MI; *m:* Jerry L.; *c:* Jennifer; *ed:* (BS) Elem Ed, OH St 1969; (MS) Curr & Supervision, Univ of Dayton 1975; *cr:* 4th Grade Teacher 1969-71, 3rd Grade Teacher 1971-73, 2nd Grade Teacher 1973-76 Edison; Kindergarten Teacher 1976-82, 1st Grade Teacher 1982- Washington Mc Kinley; *ai:* Yrbk Photographer; Special Music Act; Piano Lessons; LEA/DEA/NEA 1969-; PTA (Secy 1970-72 VP 1972-74); Southside Christian Church Christian Womens Fellowship Pres 1977-79; St Peter Lutheran Choir Dir 1984-; Awarded 300 Dollars Lottery Grants for Classroom; Used to Set Up Learning Centers; *office:* Washington Mc Kinley Sch 681 Calumet Lima OH 45804

STENAL, JOHN L., Biology Teacher; *b:* Antigo, WI; *m:* Nancy E. Gralla; *c:* Matthew, Emily; *ed:* (BA) Bio, Univ WI Stevens Point 1970; Grad Stud Photography, Bus Ed, Environmental, Health; *cr:* Bio Teacher Kenai Cntrl HS 1970-80, Soldotna HS 1980-; Sci Dept Chm Kenai HS, Soldotna HS 1978-; *ai:* Cross Cntry Running Coach; Sci Club; Red Cross (1st Aid, CPR Instr) 1974-; NEA; Peninsola Flying Club 1975-, Outstanding Safety Awd 1983; Recyling Club 1971-; NSTA 1971-; Outstanding Teacher Awd 1983; Nom Outstanding Bio Awd 1984-85, 1987-; Krista Mc Cullaf Nomination 1988; *office:* Soldotna HS 425 W Marydale Soldotna AK 99669

STENDER, DIANE LYNN, Rdng/Social Studies Teacher; *b:* Bellaire, OH; *m:* John Francis; *c:* Mario F., Anarosa D., Hailee C.; *ed:* (BSED) Scndry Ed/Soc Stud, OH Univ 1975; (MS) Rdng Specialist, WV Univ 1980-; APL Summer Wkshp 1989-90; Teacher Expectations Stu Achivement 1989-90; Career Class, WV Univ 1990; *cr:* Teacher 1975-, Chrldr Adv 1976-79 Ellsworth Mid Sch; Chrldr Adv Tyler HS 1977-85; *ai:* Spec Ed Effectiveness Review System; Curr Facility Design Comm; Chm of Soc Stud Textbook Comm; Chm of Soc Stud Fair; St Fair Judge; WVEA 1975-88; NEA 1975-88; United Chrstn Church Mother of Yr 1986; Prof Best Leadership Awd 1990; Published Article His Book of Tyler Cty WV 1984; Soc Stud Awds; *office:* Ellsworth Mid Sch Park Ave Box 105 Middlebourne WV 26149

STENFTENAGEL, CLAUDIA ANN (ROTHRING), Third Grade Teacher; *b:* Indianapolis, IN; *m:* Dennis L.; *c:* Conrad; *ed:* (BS) Elem Ed, St Benedict Coll 1970; (MS) Ed, IN Univ 1974; *cr:* 3rd Grade Teacher Holland Elem Sch 1970-72; 6th Grade Teacher Holland Elem Sch 1972-73, Huntingburg Mid Sch 1973-74; 3rd Grade Teacher Holland Elem Sch 1974-; *ai:* NEA 1971-; Amer Legion Aux Chaplain 1972-74; *office:* Holland Elem Sch Holland IN 47541

STENGEL, ROBERTA ZUPAN, 5th Grade Teacher; *b:* Lander, WY; *m:* David L.; *c:* Kassi; *ed:* (BA) Ed, MT St 1977; *cr:* 4th Grade Teacher Lockwood 1977-78; 6th Grade Teacher Jefferson 1978-84; 6th Grade Teacher 1984-85; 6th Grade/8th; 8th Grade Lang Arts Teacher 1986-87 C S Porter; Job Sharing 5th Grade Teacher Lowell 1988-; *ai:* Sch Improvement Comm; MEEA (Secy) 1978-; *office:* Lowell Elem Sch 1200 Sherwood Missoula MT 59802

STENGLER, FAY M., Language Arts Dept Chair; *b:* Jackson, MS; *c:* Samuel, Susan; *ed:* (BS) Speech/Drama Sam Houston St Univ 1956; (MS) Eng/Rdng Univ of Houston Clear Lake 1978; *cr:* Teacher Woodrow Wilson Jr HS 1956-57, South Park HS 1957-58, Webster Intermediate Sch 1970-71; Teacher/Dept Chairperson League City Intermediate 1980-; *ai:* Literary Magazine; Bay Area Scrabblers Helpshop Founder; TX St Teachers, NEA, Clear Creek Teachers Assn, Delta Kappa Gamma; PTA Pres, Life Mem 1983; *office:* League City Intermediate Sch 2451 E Main St League City TX 77573

STENHOUSE, LINDA JACKSON, In-School Suspension Teacher; *b:* Hope Mills, NC; *m:* James Dewitte Jr.; *c:* Anne, James; *ed:* (BA) Poly Sci, Pembroke St Univ 1971; (MA) Poly Sci, Appalachian St Univ 1973; *cr:* 3rd Grade Soc Stud Teacher Gordon Elem 1971; Teacher White Oak HS 1971-72; Grad Asst Appalachian St Univ 1972-73; Teacher Mauldin HS 1973-76, Woodmont HS 1981-82, Woodmont Mid Sch 1982-; *ai:* Southern Assn of Colleges & Schls Steering Comm; Stu Cncl Spon; Soc Stu Dept Chairperson; Stu Recognition Comm; Sch Grievance Rep; Greenville Cty Cncl for Soc Stud; Strom Thurmond Seminar Schlsp; Wyff & Winn-Dixie Golden Apple Awd; *office:* Woodmont Mid Sch 325 Flat Rock Rd Piedmont SC 29673

STENNETTE, JANICE S., Soc Stud Teacher/Dept Chair; *b:* Lynchburg, VA; *c:* Tari, Coe, Stennette; *ed:* (BA) His, 1969, (MED) Ed/His, 1973 Lynchburg Coll; Post Grad Work Univ of VA; *cr:* Teacher Bedford Cty 1969-; *ai:* Co-Ed Hi-Y Club; Jr Class Spon; Sch Consultation Team; NEA Local Pres 1976; NCSS; Society Historical Archaeology; Natl Endowment for Hum Insts 1985, 1988; VA Ed Assn Mini-Grants 1988-; Teacher of Yr

Jefferson Forest 1989-; *office:* Bedford Cty Sch Jefferson Forest HS Forest VA 24551

STENSON, ED, English Teacher; *b:* Spokane, WA; *m:* Carol Mc Manaway; *ed:* (BA) Lang Art, E WA St Univ 1951; (BA) Journalism, Univ of MT 1955; Grad Stud Univ of MI, NE MO St, ID St Univ; *cr:* PR Writer MT Hwy Patrol 1955-56; Advertising Sales/Management The Missoulian & The Times & The Courier 1956-78; Eng Teacher Sch Dist 25 1982-; *ai:* Acts Supvr; Native Amer Stus Faculty Rep; Sigma Delta Chi; Missoula Cty Humane Society VP 1960-70; MT St Humane Society VP 1970; Missoula Cmmty Theatre 1960-70; Missoula Crippled Childrens Hospital 1960-70; Whos Who in Amer Colls & Univs; *office:* Highland HS 1800 Bench Rd Pocatello ID 83202

STENTIFORD, ALAN GEORGE, Social Studies Teacher; *b:* Evanston, IL; *m:* Anne C. Youngquist; *c:* Denise Ferchaud, Gregory, Kari, Mitch; *ed:* (BA) Ec, Ripon Coll 1958; Teacher Trng LA St Univ; *cr:* Teacher/Coach Cath HS of Pointe Coupee 1987-89; Teacher Our Lady of Mercy 1989-; *ai:* Bsktbl, Sftbl, Asst Ftbl Coach; Athletic Dir; Homecoming Parade Coord; LA Assn Bsktbl Coaches 1987-; Weekly Bsktbl Articles; *home:* 1524 S Marilyn Dr Baton Rouge LA 70815

STENZEL, HOWARD KARL, Mathematics Teacher; *b:* Hillsboro, KS; *m:* Evelyn F. Dyck; *c:* Eric R., Eugene L., Kevin H.; *ed:* (BS) Math/Ed, 1961, (MS) Math/His Ed, 1968 KS St Univ; Wichita St Univ, Emporia St Univ, KS St Univ, KS Univ; *cr:* Math Teacher Jr/Sr HS 1961; Math/His Teacher Eldorado Jr HS 1961-63; Math Teacher Allison Jr HS 1963-68; Math/His Teacher Marion HS 1968-70; Math Teacher Jr/Sr HS 1970-; *ai:* Math Contest Team Spon; Faculty Soc Comm; NEA, KNEA, NCTM, KATM 1961-; PHi Delta Kappa 1964-, 25 Yr Service 1986; Light Capital Singers (Treas 1974-81, Pres 1977, Membership Chm 1979), Achievement 1978; St Barbershop Quartet Contests 2nd Place 1978, 3rd Place 1979-80; NSF Inst KS Univ 1962; Article on Baptist Youth Involvement 1967; Building Rep Local Teachers Assn 1973-74, 1978, 1981, 1987-88; Church Youth Spon 1980-; *office:* Mc Pherson HS 801 E 1st Mc Pherson KS 67460

STEPHENS, BETTY LOUISE, Mathematics Teacher; *b:* Somerset, KY; *ed:* (BS) Math, 1971, (MA) Math, 1974 E KY Univ; Admin & Physics Cert; *cr:* Math Teacher Ludlow HS 1971-79, Newport HS 1979-; *ai:* Vlybl, Bsktbl, Track Coach; Chrldrs, Stu Cncl, Academic Team, Plays Spon; NTM; KY Cncl of Teachers of Math Treas 1987-; N KY Cncl of Teachers of Math 1989-; Taught Governors Sch Prgm; Nom Golden Apple Awd; *office:* Newport HS 900 E 6th St Newport KY 41071

STEPHENS, DELORIS K., Sixth Grade Teacher; *b:* Red Level, AL; *c:* Mark, Reginald; *ed:* (BS) Elem Ed, AL St Univ 1962; Additional Elem Ed, Various Colleges 1979; *cr:* 6th Grade Teacher Greensboro Elem Sch 1963-64/1966-67, Saraland Elem Sch 1968-70-71-73; Sp Ed Teacher East Cleveland Elem Sch 1970-71; 6th Grade Teacher Hamilton Elem Sch 1974-; *ai:* NEA; MVTA; Mount Vernon Teachers Assn; Church-Macedonia Corr Sec 1976-; Baptist Church Sr Usher Bd; Academic Schlsp Awd Frosh Yr Coll Highest Average; *home:* 40 E Sidney Ave Apt 17H Mount Vernon NY 10550

STEPHENS, DEXTER, 7th Grade Lang Art Teacher; *b:* Burlington, NC; *m:* Dorothy Wright; *c:* Di Nina, La Mesha, Sharon; *ed:* (BS) Elem Ed, Winston-Salem St Univ 1962; (MS) Soc Stud, 1974, (MS) Ed Admin, 1975 A&T St Univ; *cr:* Teacher Glen Raven Elem 1962-63, Vance Cty Schls 1963-69, Warren Cty Schls 1969-; *ai:* John Graham Leadership Comm Mem; NCAE; Shiloh Baptist Church Sunday Sch Teacher; *office:* John Graham Mid Sch 307 N Main St Warrenton NC 27589

STEPHENS, DOROTHY FOREACRE, Teacher; *b:* Dubuc, Canada; *c:* Kent, Gayle, Craig; *ed:* (AA) Eng Ed, CO Womans Coll 1950; (BA) Elem Ed, Univ of Denver 1958; Grad Stud Univ of CA Santa Barbara, Univ of Santa Clara, Chapman Coll, Univ of Boston; *cr:* 6th/8th/9th Grade Teacher Coll View Sch 1950-51, 1958-60; 6th Grade Teacher Miller Street Sch 1960-62; Teacher Orcutt Schls 1962-; *ai:* Sch Site Comm Rep; Soc Comm; Delta Kappa Gamma Mem; CA Teachers, NEA; Orcutt Elem Assn VP; Amer Red Cross 1959, Group Awd; BSA Womens Auxiliary Pres; Santa Maria Recreation Aqua Fins Mothers Group Pres 1960; Phi Sigma Alpha Cmptr Sweetheart 1990; Meth Church Ed Commission; *home:* 448 Chaparral Dr Santa Maria CA 93454

STEPHENS, ELAINE THOMAS, English/Journalism; *b:* Waycross, GA; *m:* John J.; *c:* Katie, Mark; *ed:* (BSED) Eng, 1969, (MED) Eng, 1972, (EDS) Eng, 1980 GA Southern Univ; Advanced Placement Oglethorpe Univ 1985; *cr:* Instr Waycross HS, Benedictine Military Acad, Claxton HS, South GA Coll, Brewton Parker Coll, Appling Cty Comprehensive HS; *ai:* Yrbk; Newspaper; Cheerleading; GA Assn of Educators Pres Elect; Meth Church Choir Mem/Sunday Sch Teacher; Campaign Chm Lt Gov 1990; GAE; Alpha Delta Pi; Beta Sigma Phi; Pilot Club; NCTE; 8th Dist Pres of Eng Teacher; Womens Young Careerist; Chm of Seven Cty Curr Revision Comm; Outstanding Young Women of America; Star Teacher 1973-75/1982; Teacher of Yr 1972/1976; Phi Delta Kappa Honorary Educl; Kappa Delta Pi Honorary Ed; Grant Comm Course 1990; Deal Most Outstanding Awd; Ten Best Dressed of Coll Newspaper; GA Collegiate Press Awd for Best Feature Story; Stu Government; Rotary Stu; House Cncl; Campus Life Enrichment Comm; Southern Singers; Miss GSC Contest; Miss Reflector Contest; *home:* PO Box 596 Baxley GA 31513

STEPHENS, JANET SUE, Mathematics Teacher; *b:* Bethesa, MD; *m:* Richard Lamar; *c:* Mary; *ed:* (BS) Math, FL St 1973; *cr:* Math Teacher Godby HS 1973-82; Teacher Lincoln HS 1983-; *ai:* Mu Alpha Theta; Math Teams Coach; Y-Club; Head of SACS Math; NCTM, FTM; *office:* Lincoln HS 3838 Trojan Trl Tallahassee FL 32301

STEPHENS, LAURA MARBLE, 6th Grade Teacher; *b:* Belle Glade, FL; *m:* Fred E.; *c:* Christopher, Sara; *ed:* (BA) Ed, Newberry Coll 1982; *cr:* 5th Grade Teacher 1982-85, 6th Grade Teacher 1985- Lee Cty Mid Sch; *ai:* Goals, Discipline, Literary & Soc Comms; NEA; *home:* 1313 5th Ave Albany GA 31707

STEPHENS, LINDA LANE, Second Grade Teacher; *b:* Dyer, TN; *m:* Joe C.; *c:* Allan R., Amye L., Abbye C.; *ed:* (BA) Elem Ed, Univ of TN 1966; *cr:* Classroom Teacher Obion Cty Bd of Ed 1966-; *ai:* Cheerleading Spon; TEA, OCEA, NEA; First Baptist Church Sunday Sch Teacher; *office:* Kenton Elem 300 W College Kenton TN 38233

STEPHENS, LORIE ANN, Home Ec Teacher; *b:* Loris, SC; *c:* Dana; *ed:* (BS) Home Ec Ed, NC A&T St Univ 1982; (PVA) Handicapped & Disadvantaged Ed, Pembroke St Univ 1986; *cr:* Voc Handicapped Teacher Hallsboro HS 1983-87; Adult Ed Instr Southeastern Comm Coll 1984-85; Home Ec Teacher East Columbus HS 1987-; *ai:* FHA Co-Adv; NC Assn of Educators 1983-; NEA 1983-; Kappa Omicron Phi Honor Society Alumni Chap 1983-85; United Holy Church Assn 1983-; Teacher of Yr Nom; *home:* 101 W 5th St Tabor City NC 28463

STEPHENS, MAXINE MILLER, Retired English Teacher; *b:* Stella, MO; *m:* Harold; *c:* Kendall, Shandra; *ed:* (BE) Eng, Humboldt St Univ 1959; Rdng Specialist, MMSC 1972; *cr:* Teacher Lone Dove MO 1946-47; Mc Donald Cty Fairview MO 1947-49; Prin Teacher Pepperwood CA 1949-51; Teacher Rio Del CA 1951-65; Teacher Seneca MO; *ai:* Chrldr Spon; Citizenship Instr for Foreign Stu & Adults; AAUW 1975-80; Delta Kappa Gamma 1980-; PTA 1947-87; CTA 1947-87; MSTA 1965-87; *home:* Box 605 Seneca MO 64865

STEPHENS, NORMAN CHASE, 7th/8th Grade Math Teacher; *b:* Charleston, WV; *m:* Carolyn Meeks; *ed:* (BS) Bus Admin, 1971, (BS) Scndry Ed/Math, 1986 WV St Coll; *cr:* 7th/8th Grade Teacher Clay Jr HS 1980-; *ai:* Performing Arts & Fishing Clubs; Mathcounts Coach; *home:* 378 Elk River Rd N Clendenin WV 25045

STEPHENS, RICHARD EUGENE, Anatomy & Physiology Teacher; *b:* Murphysboro, IL; *m:* Jane Ann Griffith; *c:* Daniel J., David B., Richard L., Katherine J.; *ed:* (BS) Biological Sci, 1964, (MS) Biological Sci, 1966, (AD) Biological Sci, 1990 IN St Univ; Medical Technician & Natl Cancer Instr; *cr:* Teacher Linton Jr HS 1964-66, Otter Creek Jr HS 1966-69, Gerstmeyer HS, Terre Naute North HS 1971-; *ai:* Exercise Physiology & Running Club; *office:* Terre Haute North HS 3434 Maple Ave Terre Haute IN 47804

STEPHENS, WILLIAM AVERA, JR., HS Math/Cmptrs/Physics Teacher; *b:* Dallas, TX; *M:* Susie Singleton Stephens; *c:* Connie; *ed:* (Bs) Scndry Ed, TX A&M Univ 1973; Theology, Perkins Sch of Theology SMU 1974-76 Cmptr Cert Corpus Christi St Univ 1986; *cr:* Mid Sch Math Teacher/Bus Driver Belton ISD 1977-80; Math/Physics Teacher/Bus Driver Gregory-Portland ISD 1980-82; Math/Physics/Cmptrs Teacher/Bus Driver Moody ISD 1983-; *ai:* Moffat Cemetery Assn Treas 1989-; Licensed Minister Southern Baptist Denomination; Preach in Nursing Homes; Participated Mission Trips to Haiti & Mexico; *home:* Rt 5 Box 270-B Moffat Temple TX 76501

STEPHENSON, DENISE (LACKEY), English Teacher; *b:* High Point, NC; *m:* Benjamin Martin; *ed:* (BA) Eng, High Point Coll 1973; (MA) Eng, NC A&T St Univ 1989; Academically Gifted Cert 1989; Mentor Teacher Cert 1990; Advanced Placement Eng 1988; *cr:* Eng Teacher East Davidson HS 1973-; Part-Time Eng Instr Davidson Cty Comm Coll 1989-; *ai:* Mentor Teacher; Club Spon; Cmmty Fund Chm; Goals, Incentive, Academic Honors, Steering, Senate Bill 2, SAT Comm Mem; NCAE, NEA 1980-; NTE 1978-; NC Assn Gifted & Talented 1988-; Colonial Cntry Club 1980-; Thomasville Service League 1988-; *home:* 806 Overbrook Dr Thomasville NC 27360

STEPHENSON, JOAN SADOWSKI, Fifth Grade Teacher; *b:* Bronx, NY; *m:* Roger Kent; *c:* Brian, Jeanne; *ed:* (BA) Elem Ed, Queens Coll 1969; Grad Sch, Russell Sage 1972; *cr:* 1st Grade Teacher 1969-80, 5th Grade Teacher 1980- Van Schaick; *ai:* Stu Cncl Adv; Calvary Church Sch Supt 1980-81; *office:* Van Schaick Island Elem Sch 150 Continental Ave Cohoes NY 12047

STEPHENSON, JOHN WM., Teacher; *b:* Memphis, TN; *c:* John T.; *ed:* (BS) His/Government, Univ of NE 1974; (MAE) Ed, Tusculum Coll 1989; *cr:* Teacher Kingsbury HS 1976-78, Melrose Jr HS 1978-81, Cypress Jr HS 1981-82, Kingsbury Jr HS 1982-; *ai:* TN Army Natl Guards Sargeant & Major; NEA 1976-; Career Ladder I; *office:* Kingsbury Jr HS 1276 N Graham Memphis TN 38122

STEPHENSON, JUDY A., Choral Director; *b:* Altus, OK; *m:* Stan; *c:* Julie, Susan; *ed:* (BM) Music, Univ of OK 1963; (MA) Music, Univ of HI 1973; *cr:* Music Teacher Valley HS, Lackland City, Meadow Village Elem 1976-77; Choral Dir Coke Stevenson Mid Sch 1977-83; John Marshall HS 1984-; *ai:* Academic Decathlon Team Coach; TX Music Educators Assn (Region VP 1988-, Region Chairperson, Area Chairperson) 1984-88; TX Music Adjudicators Assn Judge 1986-; Gamma Phi Beta Financial Adv 1989-; Served as Tabulations Chairperson for TX Music Ed Assn Contest; Served as Ajudicator for Solo/Ensemble Contests; UIL Concert, Sight Rdng Contests, Music Festivals; Choirs Consistant Sweepstakes Winners; TX All St Choir Mem; *office:* John Marshall HS 8000 Lobo Ln San Antonio TX 78240

STEPHENSON, KATHRYN CLASKA, Fourth Grade Teacher; *b:* Eugene, OR; *m:* Robert E.; *c:* Zachary; *ed:* (BAED) Eng, Seattle Univ 1969; (MED) Curr/Instruction, Univ of OR 1976; *cr:* 2nd Grade Teacher East Hill Elem Sch 1969-72; 1st-4th Grade Teacher Crest Drive Elem Sch 1974-78; 4th Grade Teacher Howard Elem Sch 1978-85; 3rd-5th Grade Teacher Westmoreland Elem Sch 1985-; *office:* Westmoreland Elem Sch 1717 City View Eugene OR 97402

STEPHENSON, MARY ANNA, English II Teacher; *b:* Chandler, TX; *m:* James Henry; *c:* Matt, Rheatia, Rhonda; *ed:* (ABA) Bus Admin, Tyler Jr Coll 1963; (BBA) Bus Admin, Sam Houston Univ 1965; (MS) Eng, Univ of TX Tyler 1990; Grad Stud Psych, Philosophy; *cr:* Eng III/Bus Teacher Chapel Hill HS 1965-68; Eng II/Teacher of Gifted & Talented/Coach Van HS 1976-; *ai:* Girls Bsktbl, Vlybl, Track Coach 1965-85; Jr Class Spon 1965-79, 1984-; Academic Excl Comm 1989; Textbook Comm 1983, 1988; Tyler Public Awareness Comm 1986-87; TSTA Local (Secy 1980-82) 1963-85; NEA Mem 1963-85; ATPE Mem 1985-; Novel Published; *home:* Rt 3 Box 3232 Ben Wheeler TX 75754

STEPHENSON, SUSAN M., English Teacher; *b:* Butler, PA; *ed:* (BS) Comm, Clarion St Coll 1976; (MS) Comm Media, Indiana Univ of PA 1989; *cr:* Eng/Drama/Journalism Teacher Amelia Cty HS 1976-80; Eng Teacher Seneca Valley Jr HS 1980-; *ai:* Academic Games Coord; Seneca Valley Ed Assn Prof Rights & Responsibilities Chairperson 1985-; Natl Academic Games Organization (Advisory Bd, Lang Art Coord), Outstanding Coord 1985; W PA Acad Games League VP; PA Academic Games Tournament Co-Chm Keystone Bowl; *office:* Seneca Valley Jr HS 124 Seneca School Rd Harmony PA 16037

STEPHENSON, YVONNE NEWTON, English Teacher; *b:* Toxey, AL; *m:* Danny J.; *ed:* (BS) Scndry Ed/Eng, 1970, (ME) Scndry Ed/Eng, 1977 Univ of S AL; *cr:* Teacher Wesleyan Chrstn Acad 1970-71, Blount HS 1971-77, Murphy HS 1977-; *ai:* Azalea Trail Maids Comm; NCTE Writing Awd Nominees Comm; Mobile Cty Educators Assn; *office:* Murphy HS 100 S Carlen St Mobile AL 36606

STERCHI, BRENDA S. (MC KNIGHT), Fifth Grade Teacher; *b:* Olney, IL; *ed:* (BS) Elem Ed, Olivet Nazarene Univ 1971; E IL Univ, S IL Univ, N IL Univ; *cr:* 4th-6th Grade Teacher E Richland Unit Dist 1 1971-; *ai:* E Richland Ed Assn Pres 1981-82; IEA, NEA Mem 1971-; IL Sci Teachers Assn 1989-.

STERLING, GARY C., English Teacher; *b:* Hollywood, CA; *m:* Shirley Carol Seip; *c:* Derek; *ed:* (BA) Eng, Univ CA Riverside 1965; (MA) Eng, CA St Univ Los Angeles 1975; Several Wkshps Univ CA Riverside, CA St Univ Los Angeles, Banff Sch of Fine Arts; *cr:* 5th Grade Teacher Washington Elem 1966-70; Teacher Longfellow Elem 1970-80, John Muir HS 1980-84, Marshall Fundamental Scndry 1984-; *ai:* Newspaper & Homeless Project Staff Adv; Academic Decathlon Coach; Founder Pasadena Project Socrates Teacher Recruitment Prgm; Rdng is Fundamental HS Prgm Coord; Staff Liason; Stu Literary Critic Prgm Public Libraries; Phi Delta Kappa; Pen Anti-Censorship Comm; Poets & Writers, United Teachers of Pasadena; Pasadena Fed of Teachers VP; Friends of Altadena Lib Newsletter Ed; Southwest Museum; Pasadena Literacy Action Network Newsletter Copywriter; Various Teacher of Yr & Month Awds; UCI Martin Luther King Awd; Numerous Publications; *office:* Marshall Fundamental Scndry HS 990 N Allen Ave Pasadena CA 91104

STERLING, SANDRA ELAINE, English Teacher; *b:* Lakeland, FL; *ed:* (BA) Eng, Univ of S FL 1971; Additional Courses Univ of Houston, Univ of S FL; *cr:* Eng Teacher Denison Jr HS 1971-73, Winter Haven HS 1973-75, Auburndale Jr HS 1975-89, Auburndale Sr HS 1989-; *ai:* Polk Ed Assn, FL Ed Assn, NEA, Polk Cty Cncl of Teachers of Eng; Greenpeace, Amnesty Intnl, Natl Organization of Women World Wide Fund; *office:* Auburndale Sr HS 1 Bloodhound Blvd Auburndale FL 33823

STERNBERG, MILTON H., US History Teacher; *b:* El Paso, TX; *m:* Elizabeth Whitworth; *c:* Michael B., Karla W.; *ed:* (BA) Poly Sci/His, Coll of Santa Fe 1963; N TX St Univ; Univ of NM; *cr:* Teacher/Librarian Santa Fe HS 1967-; *ai:* Previous Dept Chm, Soc Stud, Lib Spon; Stu Cncl, Honor Society Jr Class; NEA 1967-; Grant Attend His/Ourselves Brookline MS; *office:* Santa Fe HS 2100 Yucca Rd Santa Fe NM 87501

STERNFELS, LEONARD LEE, Science Teacher; *b:* St Louis, MO; *m:* Mary Ann Hebda; *ed:* (BS) Scndry Ed, Southern IL St Univ 1977; (MA) Sci Ed, Northeast MO St Univ 1985; *cr:* Sci Teacher The City of St Charles Sch Dist 1978-; *ai:* Team Leader; Floor Hockey Coach; Sci Fair Dir; NSTA 1978-; MO Mid Sch Assn 1987-; ASCD 1988-; St Charles Teachers Assn 2nd VP 1984-86; *office:* Hardin Mid Sch 1950 Elm St Saint Charles MO 63301

STERNOFF, DIANE MARKRACK, Mathematics Teacher; *b:* Bremerton, WA; *m:* Richard L.; *c:* Jeffrey, Jonathan; *ed:* (BA) Ed/Math, 1965, (MED) Curr/Instruction, 1970 Univ of WA; *cr:* 4th Grade Teacher Sunny Hills Elem Sch 1965-66; Math Teacher George Wythe HS 1966-67, Robert Gray Jr HS 1967-68, Newport HS 1968-69; Math Coord St Monica Sch 1978-80; Math Teacher Eastside Cath HS 1980-; *ai:* Academic Decathlon Coach; WA St Cncl Teachers of Math, NCTM; WA St & Eastside Cath Teacher of Yr Finalist; Eastside Cath HS Nom Tandy Technology Scholars; Outstanding Teacher of Math; *office:* Eastside Cath HS 11650 SE 60th Bellevue WA 98006

STERRETT, SUE L., Enrichment Resource Teacher; *b:* Joplin, MO; *ed:* (BS) Ed, 1966, (MS) Ed, 1969 KS St & Pittsburg; Various Wkshps; Gifted Ed Courses; *cr:* 3rd Grade Teacher Kelsey Norman Elem 1966-88; Enrichment Resource Teacher Washington Ed Center 1988-; *ai:* MSTA; Delta Kappa Gamma VP; Judge Clay Cowgill Blair Memorial Awd for Teaching Excl.

STERWERF, MARY PETER, Pastoral Minister; *b:* Hamilton, OH; *ed:* (BA) Ed, Marian Coll 1960; (MA) Admin, Clarke Coll 1982; *cr:* 5th-6th Grade Teacher St Peter Sch 1970-77; 1st-8th Grade Prin St Marys N Vernon 1977-80; 6th Grade Teacher St Mary New Albany 1980-86; Pastoral Minister St Peter Sch 1986-; *ai:* Ministerial Assn Secy 1989-; *home:* 126 Church St Chillicothe OH 45601

STETSON, ROBYN, Computer Middle/HS Teacher; *b:* Fergason, MO; *ed:* (BS) Scndry Ed/Math, Southeast MS St 1986; Introduction to Mac Intosh Hypercard I RCET; *cr:* 6th/8th Grade Sci Teacher Arch Diocese of St Louis 1986-; Math/Cmptr Teacher Wright City RII 1986-; *ai:* SADD Adv; Fashion/Makeup Club Spon; Dist Cmptr Comm; MSTA, CTA 1987-; Sigma Sigma Sigma Money-Making 1985 Pledge of Yr 1983; *office:* Wright City RII PO Box 198 Wright City MO 63390

STEVE, MICHAEL G., Mathematics Teacher; *b:* Clymer, PA; *m:* Nancy Newhouse; *c:* Michele L., Michael W., Matthew A.; *ed:* (BAED) Scndry Math, 1967, (MED) Scndry Guidance, 1973 IN Univ of PA; *cr:* Math Teacher Hempfield Area Sr HS 1967-; *home:* 624 Buckingham Dr Greensburg PA 15601

STEVEN, CHERYL BROOKS, Fourth Grade Teacher; *b:* Winnsboro, LA; *m:* James Burch; *c:* Samantha L.; *ed:* (BA) Elem Ed, Northeast LA Univ 1970; (MED) Elem Ed, Northeast LA Univ 1980; Northeast LA Univ 1985; *cr:* 2nd Grade Teacher Crowville HS 1968-69, Ward III HS 1970-71; Remedial Rdng Teacher 1972-74, Kndgtn Teacher 1974-81, 5th Grade Teacher 1981-89, 4th Grade Teacher 1989 Crowville HS; *ai:* Var Chrldr Spon; Var Pep Squad Co-spon; Associated Prof Educators of LA 1985-; Prof Educators of LA 1982-85; *office:* Crowville HS P O Box 128 Crowville LA 71230

STEVEN, SHARON SUE, 4th Grade Teacher; *b:* Dallas, TX; *ed:* (BS) Elem Ed, Univ of N TX 1970; Advanced Academic Trng; LEvel Class E TX St Univ; *cr:* 6th Grade Teacher 1970-74, 4th Grade Teacher 1974- J O Schulze Elem; *ai:* ATPE; Alpha Delta Kappa (Chaplain, Secy) 1974-; J O Schulze Elem Teacher of Yr 1988-89; *office:* J O Schulz Elem Sch 1200 S Irving Heights Irving TX 75060

STEVENS, CAROL, SSSF Music Director; *b:* Aurora, IL; *ed:* (BME) Music Ed/Liturgical Music, Alverno Coll 1969; (MS) Music Ed, Univ of IL 1974; *cr:* Teacher Holy Ghost Sch 1967-68; Music Dir Our Lady of Good Counsel 1969-; *ai:* Parish Choir Dir, Principle Organist, Parish Guitar Group Leader; Mem Parish Liturgical Commission; MENC, NPM; *office:* Our Lady of Good Counsel Sch 601 Talma Aurora IL 60505

STEVENS, CAROLYN B., French & Publications Teacher; *b:* Phoenix, AZ; *ed:* (BA) Fr, Fresno St Univ 1966; FSU for Teaching; *cr:* Teacher Kingsburg HS 1966-68, Carrell HS 1968-69, Westside HS 1969-75, Kingsburg HS 1987-; *ai:* Yrbk; Newspaper; Stu Speakers Contests; Phi Kappa Phi; CA Teachers Assn; NEA; Journalism Ed Assn; Bus & Prof Women; *office:* Kingsburg HS 1900 18th Ave Kingsburg CA 93631

STEVENS, DEBORAH CORNETT, First Grade Teacher; *b:* Barbourville, KY; *m:* M. Kent; *c:* Katherine, Ellen; *ed:* (BS) Elem Ed, Georgetown Coll 1974; (MS) Ed/Rdng Emphasis, Eastern KY Univ 1979; (Rank I) Ed, Georgetown Univ 1979; *cr:* 1st/2nd Grade Teacher 1974-75, 5th/8th Grade Lang Art Teacher Rutherford Elem 1975-77; Homebound Teacher Anderson Cty Bd of Ed 1977-79; 1st Grade Teacher Saffell Street Elem 1979-; *ai:* GSA Leader; KY Ed Assn 1974-; Anderson Cty Ed Assn Pres 1983-; Lawrenceburg Womans Club 1989-; Beta Sigma Phi VP 1986-87; Inservice, Cmmty Ed & Gifted & Talented Comm; *office:* Saffell St Elem Sch 210 Saffell St Lawrenceburg KY 40342

STEVENS, DOUGLAS ALAN, 8th Grade Science Teacher; *b:* Tipp City, OH; *m:* Marta Anne Moser; *c:* Nicole, Christian, Christopher, Alexi; *ed:* (BSED) Phys Ed, OH Univ 1973; *cr:* Phys Ed Teacher Miami Local Schls 1973-74; Industrial Arts Teacher Fairborn HS 1976; Sci Teacher Wellington Schls 1976-; *ai:* HS Bsktbl; Lorain Cty Coaches Assn 1976-; NEA, OEA, MNEA, WEA 1976-; Jaycees 1975-77; Penfield Cmmty Church (Trustee, Deacon) 1978-; *office:* Wellington Schls 201 S Main Wellington OH 44090

STEVENS, KATHRYN W., First-Second Grade Teacher; *b:* St Louis, MO; *m:* Thomas G.; *c:* John; *ed:* (BSEE) Elem Ed, SE MO St Univ 1961; (ME) Spec Ed/LD, Univ of AK Anchorage 1980; *cr:* 1st Grade Teacher Clarenceville Sch Dist 1961-65, Dept of Defense Germany 1963-64; 2nd-3rd Grade Teacher Montgomery Cty Sch Dist 1965-67; 1st Grade Teacher Du Pont & Clover Park Sch Dist 1967-72; 1st-3rd Grade Teacher Anchorage Sch Dist 1975-; *ai:* Anchorage Ed Assn 1975-; PEO (Recording Secy, Treas, Pres 1976-); Grant Teaching Rdng through Lang Experience; *office:* Russian Jack Elem Sch 4420 E 20th Ave Anchorage AK 99508

STEVENS, LOIS KATZ, Third Grade Teacher; *b:* Elizabeth, NJ; *m:* Gregory James; *c:* Melissa, Brian; *ed:* (BA) Elem Ed, Kean Coll 1970; Working Towards Masters Kean Coll; *cr:* 3rd Grade Teacher Clark Mills Sch 1970-72, Pine Street Sch 1972-74, Clark Mills Sch 1974-; *ai:* Curr Study Skills Comm; Liaison Comm Between Teachers & Prin; NJ Ed Assn, Manalapan Englishtown Ed Assn Mem 1970-; NJ Governors Recognition Awd & Grant 1986-87; *office:* Clark Mills Sch Gordon Corners Rd Manalapan NJ 07726

STEVENS, LYNDA HENDERSON, English Teacher; *b:* Winnfield, LA; *m:* J. Cheston Jr.; *c:* Jack; *ed:* (BA) Soc Sci Ed, Northwestern St 1970; (MA) Soc Stud Ed, LA Tech 1975; Reservation of Principles of Freedom, Summer Prgm Univ of Scranton 1978; Amer Politics Seminar, CT Coll 1979; *cr:* Eng Teacher Winnfield Sr HS 1971; Soc Stud Teacher Winnfield Mid Sch 1971-81; Eng/Soc Stud Teacher Prairie View Acad 1985-88; Eng Teacher Bastrop Hs 1988-; *ai:* Winnfield Assn of Educators (Secy 1980-81) 1971-81, Service Awd 1980; NEA, LA Ed Assn 1971-81; Kappa Kappa Iota 1988-; Sigma Sigma Sigma Alumni; Outstanding LA Educators 1980; *office:* Bastrop HS 401 Highland Ave Bastrop LA 71220

STEVENS, NANCY SMITH, Fourth Grade Teacher; *b:* Pecos, TX; *m:* Joseph Edward; *c:* Christina C. Stevens Curless, Gary E.; *ed:* (BA) Elem Ed, 1966, (MA) Teaching, 1976 W NM Univ; Grad Stud Educl Classes; Various In-Service Trngs & Wkshps; Drug Ed; *cr:* 4th Grade Teacher Stout Elem 1971-; *ai:* Stu Cncl Spon 1989-; Drug Free Schls & Cmmtys Ed Comm Mem 1987-; Yrbk Comm 1988-; Silver City Ed Assn Mem 1971-; Kappa Kappa Iota Pres 1981-82; Drug Ed (Coord 1987-, Comm 1988-); Junior 24 Club Pres 1979-80; Chamber of Commerce Act 1989-; Community Needs Co-Chairperson 1983-85; *office:* Stout Elem Sch 2810 N Swan Silver City NM 88061

STEVENS, PATRICIA, K-6th Grade Art Teacher; *b:* Jackson, TN; *c:* Denna Denton Siler; *ed:* (BS) Ed, 1965, (MS) Elem Ed, 1983, Elem Ed/Rdng 1983, Memphis St Univ; Airbrushing; *cr:* Soc Stud/Librarian Whiteville HS 1965-67; Phys Ed/Home Ec Teacher Cntrl HS 1967-68; 4th-6th Grade Rdng/Math Teacher 1976-86, K-6 Art Teacher 1986- Bolivar Elem; *ai:* Teach Private Art Lessons & Swimming Lessons; Design Clothing for Companies; Teach Sunday Sch; Parent Involvement in Ed; HCAC Pres; DKG (VP, Pres); TEA, NEA, HCEA; TN Arts Acad Nashville; *home:* Rt 1 Box 111 Clifft Rd Bolivar TN 38008

STEVENS, PENNY LYNN, Third Grade Teacher; *b:* Cut Bank, MT; *ed:* (BS) Elem Ed, Northern MT Coll 1976; MT St Univ/ Univ of MT; *cr:* 1st/4th Grade Teacher Shelby Elem Sch 1976-; *ai:* MT Ed Assn (Treas 1978-79/VP 1980-81); Jaycees 1977-80; Outstanding Educator Awd 1990; *home:* 815 7th St S Shelby MT 59474

STEVENS, RICHARD K., Chemistry Teacher; *b:* Pittsburgh, PA; *m:* Gloria Jeanne De Haven; *c:* Matthew; *ed:* (BA) Chem, 1970, (BS) Ed, 1971 Slippery Rock St; (MED) Sci Ed, Clarion Univ 1988; Wkshps & Seminars; *cr:* Cnslr Slippery Rock St Coll 1970; Teacher Oil City Area Sr HS 1970-; *ai:* SADD Adv; Sci Olympiad Coach; PSEA, NEA; PA St Sci Teachers, NSTA Conventions Presenter 1985-; NASTS 1989; Youth Alternative Bd of Dirs; Condust Inservice Prgms; *office:* Oil City Area Sr HS 10 Lynch Blvd Oil City PA 16301

STEVENS, SYLVIA BAILEY, 2nd Grade Teacher; *b:* Maysville, KY; *m:* Roger E.; *ed:* (BA) Elem Ed, 1972, (MA) Ed, 1980 Moreland St Univ; Rank I Elem Prin; *cr:* 2nd Grade Teacher Ewing Elem 1972-90; *ai:* Resource Teacher for Beginning Intern Teacher; KY Teacher Intern Prgm; NEA 1972-; KY Ed Assn 1972-; Fleming Cty Ed Assn 1972-.

STEVENS, TED, Art Dept Representative; *b:* Ft Carson, CO; *ed:* (BA) Art Ed, KS St Univ 1978; *cr:* Art Teacher Mitchell HS 1983-; *ai:* Mitchell Visions Comm; MA Mitchell Advocates for Stu Success; Dist II Gifted & Talented Advisory Cncl; Jr Var Ftbl & Bsktbl Coach; CO Art Educators Assn; Black Educators; *office:* Mitchell HS 1205 Potter Dr Colorado Springs CO 80909

STEVENS, TERESA RICE, Ag/Horticulture Teacher; *b:* Leesburg, VA; *m:* G. Douglas; *ed:* (BS) Ag Ed, Univ of MD College Park 1987; Working Towards Masters Ag; *cr:* Teacher Brunswick HS 1987-; *ai:* FFA Adv; MD Ag Teachers Assn 1987-, Outstanding 1st Yr Ag Teacher 1988; Magazine Article Published 1988; *office:* Brunswick HS 101 Cummings Dr Brunswick MD 21716

STEVENSON, DAVID ROY, Science Teacher/Dept Chair; *b:* Lebanon, OR; *m:* Barbara Sue Highful; *c:* Davy, Angela; *ed:* (BS) Wildlife Bio/Art, 1973, (BS) Biological Science/Math, 1982 SE OK St Univ; *cr:* Lake Ranger US Corporation of Engineering 1973-74; Quality Controller Weyerhauser Company 1974-79; Sci Teacher 1982-, Dept Chm 1986- Idabel Public Schls; *ai:* Little League Ftbl & Pony League Bsbl Coach; OK Ed Assn, NEA 1983-; OK Scndry Sch Athletic Assn, Natl Fed Interscholastic Ofcl Assn 1984-; OK Ofcl Assn 1984-; Masonic Lodge Secy 1980-81; *home:* 401 Kaye Dr Broken Bow OK 74728

STEVENSON, JAMES K., 8th Grade Lang Art Teacher; *b:* Dayton, OH; *m:* Ava Rayma Thomas; *c:* James K. III; *ed:* (BA)(AB) Eng, E KY Univ 1966; (MED) Scndry Ed/Eng, Univ of Cincinnati 972; Post Grad Stud Xavier Univ, Purdue, Ball St Univ; *cr:* Teacher Greendale Mid Sch 1966-; *ai:* Photography & Rdng Club; A-V Dir; In Sch Improvement & Technology Dev Comm; Various Church Projects; Vietnamese Boat People Sponsorship 1983; Phi Delta Kappa, Kappa Delta Pi 1972-; Dearborn Cty Clearing House 1986; Published in Mid Sch Prin; *office:* Greendale Mid Sch 200 Tiger Blvd Lawrenceburg IN 47025

STEVENSON, JIM, Science Teacher; *b:* Tallahassee, FL; *m:* Carol Marie Hokanson; *ed:* (BS) SOK, FL St Univ 1976; (MED) Bio, GA Southwest 1980; (ABD) Bio, FL St Univ 1986; *cr:* Teacher Whigham HS 1979-80, Apalachicola HS 1980-82, Leo HS 1982-; *ai:* Direct Sch Sci Fair; Regional Comm; Sci Club Spon; Amer Bio Teacher of Yr Finalist; *home:* 1815 Mayhew Dr Tallahassee FL 32304

STEVENSON, MARGARET MEAGHER, Retired Teacher; *b:* Detroit, MI; *w:* Stewart W. (dec); *c:* Stewart, Christopher, Brian, James, Thomas; *ed:* (BS) Poly Sci Ed, Mercy Coll of Detroit 1967; Advanced Trng Rdng; Sci, MI St Univ, Oakland Univ; *cr:* 5th/6th Grade Teacher 1967-70, 1st Grade Teacher 1971-76, 7th Grade Teacher 1976-87 Our Lady Queen of Martyrs; *ai:* Cath Teachers Assn 1967-87; MI Educators Assn; Beverly Home Owners Assn Secy 1950; Hillcrest Acres Assn Pres 1983-85; *home:* 25821 Lois LN Southfield MI 48075

STEVENSON, PHILLYS JANET (LEE), Fourth Grade Teacher; *b:* Winterhaven, CA; *m:* John Wesley; *c:* Janet K., Carol J.; *ed:* (BA) Elem Ed, 1960, (MS) Teaching, 1962 SW OK St Univ; *cr:* Kndgtn/3rd Grade Teacher Holbrook Public Schls 1960-61; 3rd Grade Teacher Geary Public Schls 1961-62; 2nd Grade Teacher El Reno Public Schls 1962-63; Kndgtn/3rd Grade Teacher OK Public Schls 1969-72; K-5th Grade Teacher Canton Public Schls 1972-; *ai:* Soc Stud Curr Textbook Comm; NEA 1960-63, 1969-; AZ Educl Assn 1960-62; OK Educl Assn 1962-; Canton Educl Assn 1972-; First Baptist Church 1948-, Baptist Stu Union Summer Missionary 1958; Canton City Cncl 1979-80; Services for Mentally Retarded St Advisory Mem 1987-; Parent Guardian Assn; Enid St Sch for the Mentally Retarded (Treas 1988-) 1972-; Wrote the First Kndgtn Handbook; *home:* RR 3 Box 216E Weatherford OK 73096

STEVENSON, ROBERT GEORGE, Social Studies Instructor; *b:* Del Rio, TX; *m:* Eileen Patricia Casey; *c:* Robert L., Sean C.; *ed:* (BA) His, Holy Cross Coll 1967; (MAT) Ed/His, Fairleigh Dickinson Univ 1968; (MA) Soc Sci, Montclair St Coll 1970; (EDD) Death Ed, Fairleigh Dickinson Univ 1984; Certified Guidance Cnslr, Supvr, Psych Instr, His Teacher; Natl Cert as Death Educator; *cr:* Teacher/AD Bergen Cath HS 1967-70; Teacher/Coach River Dell Regional Schls 1970-; Chm Columbia Univ Seminar on Death 1984-; *ai:* Head Cross Cntry & Bowling Coach; Assn of Death Ed & Cty Ed Task Force Chm 1986-; NJ Chess Assn St Treas 1970-87, Man of Yr 1987; Cty Coaches Assn Awds Chm 1978-, Coach of Yr 1984; Center for Help in Time of Loss Bd of Dir 1977-85; Fnd of Thanatology VP 1980-; Hall of Fame Inaugural Mem Bergen Cath HS 1990; Published Articles in Prof Journals; All-Suburban Coach of Yr; NY Road Runners Club Natl Coach of Yr 1984; *home:* 585 Hoover Ave Westwood NJ 07675

STEVER, DEBORAH JUNE, Teacher/Asst Prin; *b:* Hancock, NY; *ed:* (BA) Religious Ed, Valley Forge Chrstn Coll 1979; *cr:* Teacher/Asst Prin Deposit Chrstn Acad 1979-; *ai:* Yrbk Staff, Newspaper Staff, Youth Group Adv; Teen-Hi Teen Sunday Sch Teacher; Eng Tutor; *office:* Deposit Christian Acad PO Box 63 1 Maple Ln Deposit NY 13754

STEWARD, DONNA MARIE, Spanish Teacher; *b:* Amsterdam, NY; *ed:* (BS) Elem Ed, SUNY Oneonta 1973; (MS) ESL Eng, SUNY Albany 1976; *cr:* 4th/6th Grade Teacher East Main Street Sch 1973-75; 6th Grade Teacher Marie Curie Eastside Sch 1975-87; 8th Grade Span Teacher Wilbur Lynch Mid Sch 1987-; *ai:* AFT 1973; NY St United Teachers 1973; United Way Sch Div 1976-; Eastside PTO Life Mem 1981-82; *office:* Lynch Mid Sch Coolidge Rd Amsterdam NY 12010

STEWARD, LARRY DEAN, 6th Grade Sci/Health Teacher; *b:* Mansfield, OH; *m:* Sally Jean Gwirtz; *c:* Amanda, Anne; *ed:* (BA) Elem Ed, Fairmont St Coll 1972; *cr:* 6th Grade Teacher Olentangy Local Schls 1972-89; *ai:* Prin Advisory Comm; Mid Sch Sci Liason; Head 6th Grade Teacher; Gifted/Talented Facilitator; Sports Card Collectors Group Leader; Outdoor Ed Coord 6th Grade; Olentangy Teachers Assn (Pres 1977-78, Treas 1988-); *home:* 1727 Brookfield Sq N Columbus OH 43229

STEWART, ANDREA MAYS, Biology Teacher; *b:* Daytona Beach, FL; : Andrew B.; *ed:* (BS) Sci Ed, E TN St 1988; (AA) Assoc Arts, Daytona Beach Comm Coll 1984; *cr:* Bio Teacher Andrews HS 1989-; *ai:* Jr Class & Stus Against Drunk Driving Spon; Vlybl, Jr Var Bsktbl, Girls Track Coach; *office:* Andrews HS 6th & Walnut Sts Andrews NC 28901

STEWART, ANNE REYNOLDS, 5th-8th Grade English Teacher; *b:* Pinewood, SC; *m:* William Harley; *c:* William Reynolds; *ed:* (BA) Eng/His - Cum Laude, Columbia Coll 1951; Post Grad Work Univ of SC; *cr:* Eng Teacher Denmark HS 1951-58, Allendale HS 1959-67, Barnwell Jr HS 1967-73, Brunson Elem 1987-; *ai:* Literary Yrbk Spon & Producer; Sigma Tau Delta, Phi Alpha Theta 1949-; Outstanding Scndry Educators of America, Personalities of South 1974; Outstanding Leaders Elem & Scndry Ed in America 1980; Honorary Schlsp to Columbia Coll Based on Scholastic Achievement; Articles Published Local & St Newspaper, Coll Literary & Natl Magazines; Dedication of Yrbk.

STEWART, CAROLE KEYS, Fifth Grade Teacher; *b:* Calhoun, GA; *c:* Melanie E. Jr.; *ed:* (BA) Elem Ed, Berry Coll 1967; Working Toward Masters Univ of FL Jacksonville; *cr:* Teacher N Shore Elem 1969-70, Moncrief Elem 1970, Highlands Elem 1970-78, Hogan Spring Glen Elem 1978-; *ai:* Grade Level Chairperson; Steering Comm for Accreditation; Teacher of Yr Hogan, Finalist for Duval Cty 1985; *home:* 9645 Baymeadows Rd #775 Jacksonville FL 32256

STEWART, CAROLYN B., 2nd Grade Teacher; *b:* Richmond, IN; *m:* Robert G.; *c:* Cynthia, Kimberly; *ed:* (BS) Elem Ed/Kndgtn Spec, 1962; (MA) Elem Ed, 1964 Ball St Univ; *cr:* Kndgtn Teacher Fall Creek Sch 1962-67; 5th Grade Teacher Maplewood 1977-87; 2nd Grade Teacher Westlake 1988-; *ai:* Classroom Teachers Assn 1977-; Meth Hospital Volunteer 1985-; Speedway Chrstn Church (Church Deacon, Sunday Sch Teacher); Extra Mile Awd; Teacher of Yr Awd Maplewood; Sr Choice Awd 1990; *office:* Westlake Elem Sch 271 N Sigsbee Indianapolis IN 46214

STEWART, CHERYL LARSON, Math Teacher/Academic Advisor; *b:* Chicago, IL; *c:* Kristen, Craig; *ed:* (BA) Math, San Jose St Coll 1968; Post Grad Continuing Ed; *cr:* Math Resource Teacher 1982, Career Resource Teacher 1987-89, Math Teacher 1969- Fremont HS; Academic Adv 1990; *ai:* Math A/B Curr Comm; Academic Adv; Fremont Ed Assn, CA Teacher Assn, NEA 1969-; NCTM Life Membership 1969-; CA Math Cncl 1969-; Amer Heart Assn (Dist Chm, Area Chm) 1980-86; Natl Sci Fnd Inst San Jose St 1972-73, Mentor Teacher 1984-85; Teacher of Month Fremont HS 1986; N CA Semifinalst Presidential Awd for Excl in Teaching Math & Sci 1986; Inst of Cmptr Technology Summer Project Fellowship 1990; *office:* Fremont HS 1279 Sunnyvale-Saratoga Rd Sunnyvale CA 94087

STEWART, CLAIRE HUNOLD, Third Grade Teacher; *b:* Fond Du Lac, WI; *m:* James M.; *c:* J. Scott, Brenda K., Gregg M., Michael C., A. Tricia; *ed:* (BS) Elem Ed, Edgewood Coll 1959; (MS) Rdng, 1978, (MPD) Sch Admin, 1987 Univ WI Whitewater; Supervision of Stu Teachers Course; *cr:* 1st Grade Teacher Grafton Bethel Elem 1964-65, Mt Olive Sch 1967-68; 4th-5th Grade Teacher Little Fort Elem 1969; 3rd Grade Teacher St Johns Elem 1975-76, West & Sullivan Elem Schls 1976-; *ai:* Dist Staff Dev Comm; Dist Rdng Curr Comm; Teacher Negotiating Team Mem; DPI Strategies Trainer; WI Ed Assn Building Rep, S WI Ed/Inservice 1976-; Delta Kappa Gamma Society Intnl 1990; NHS; *home:* 745 Center St Whitewater WI 53190

STEWART, DENNIS MARSHALL, Biology Teacher; *b:* Danville, PA; *m:* Julia Ellen Dicken; *c:* Marshall, Aspen; *ed:* (BA) Zoology, Univ of KS 1970; (MS) Scndry Sci Ed, Cntrl MO St Univ 1977; *cr:* Teacher Lafayette Cty C-I HS 1970-78, Bridger Jr HS 1978-81, William Chrisman HS 1981-; *ai:* NHS Selection Comm; Distance Track Coach; Teacher Stu Adv; NEA Building Rep 1989-; Sci Teachers of MO; Highpointers Club, Kansas City Climbing Club; Univ of KS Athletic Hall of Fame; 2 Mile Relay & NCAA Indoor World Record Champion 1970; MO Valley AAU Most Outstanding Distance Runner 1973; *office:* William Chrisman HS 1223 N Noland Independence MO 64050

STEWART, DONNA F., Math & Science Teacher; *b:* Jellico, TN; *m:* David C.; *c:* Toby M., Adam D.; *ed:* (BA) Elem Ed, TN Tech Univ/Middle TN St Univ 1972; (MED) Ed Admin, Xavier Univ 1979; *cr:* Math/Sci Teacher Lockland HS 1972-; *ai:* Cheerleading Coach; LEA Treas & Secy; *office:* Lockland Jr HS 210 N Cooper Ave Lockland OH 45215

STEWART, DORIS M., Teacher; *b:* Crow Agency, MT; *c:* Aldean Good Luck, Delean, Dorcus, Joni, Tanner Plain Feather; *ed:* (BA) Elem Ed, E MT Coll 1975; Counseling, E MT Coll; AISES Teacher Trng 1986; *cr:* Bi-ling Curr Specialist Crow Tribe 1976-78; Health Worker/Asst Dir Crow Cmmty Health 1978-81; Teacher Lodge Grass Grade Sch 1981-84, Pretty Eagle Sch 1985-.

STEWART, FRANCES VALARIES WARD, Language & Science Teacher; *b:* Augusta, GA; *ed:* (BS) Educl Psych, Ft Valley St Coll 1981; (MS) Public Admin, Brenau Coll 1987; Behavior Modification/Interaction Pattern Trng; Psych Testing & Measurement; Natl Prgm Assisting Cmptr Trng; *cr:* Behavior Technician 1982-83, MH/MR Monitor 1988 Gracewood St Hospital; Teacher Immaculate Conception Sch 1984-; *ai:* Moderator IC Gospel Choir, CSRA Sci Fair, Beta Club, Red Cross Comm, Immaculate Conception Dev Cncl, CSRA Homework Cncl; Natl Eng Teachers Assn 1987-, Outstanding Service 1990; NCTA 1984-; NSTA 1989-; Delta Sigma Theta 1980-; *office:* Immaculate Conception Sch 1016 Laney Walker Blvd Augusta GA 30901

STEWART, GARY LYNDON, Math Teacher; *b:* Rotan, TX; *m:* Cynthia Gail Bright; *c:* Christopher, Scotty, Brindy; *ed:* (BS) Math Ed, Univ of AR 1976; *cr:* Math Teacher Foreman Public Schls 1976-79, Lewisville Public Schls 1980-81, Foreman Public Schls 1982-83, 1985-; *ai:* SADD Adv; Teacher of Yr Little River Cty 1990; *home:* Rt 2 Box 227 Foreman AR 71836

STEWART, GARY WAYNE, 5th Grade Teacher; *b:* Canonsburg, PA; *m:* Frances Bergman; *c:* Francesca L.; *ed:* (BA) Elem Ed, Waynesburg Coll 1973; Clarion Univ; Penn St; in Univof PA; Pitt Univ; *cr:* Sub Teacher 1973-74; Teacher 1974 Fort Cherry Sch Dist; *ai:* Fort Cherry Sch Dist Act 178 Comm New Elem Building Comm; Building Rep 1976-80; Treas; Pace Chairperson 1989; Fort Cherry Ed Assn; PA St Ed Assn; Center United Presbyn Church Elder 1979-81; Midway Volunteer Fire Dept (Treas 1979-81, Water Ofcr 1990); PTA 1974-; *office:* Fort Cherry Elem Center RD 4 Box 145E Mc Donald PA 15057

STEWART, GAYLE WASHINGTON, Mathematics/Computer Teacher; *b:* Linden, TX; *m:* Gary David; *c:* Lana G., David F.; *ed:* (BS) Elem Ed/Math, 1979; (MS) Elem Ed/Math, 1982 E TX St Univ Texarkana; AAT Credit in Gifted & Talented; *cr:* Teacher Linden Kildare Jr HS 1980-; *ai:* Chrldr Spon 1988-; NCTM 1988-; *office:* Linden Kildare Jr HS PO Box 840 Linden TX 75563

STEWART, HAROLD F., Principal; *b:* Houlton, ME; *m:* Marilyn; *c:* Scott, Amy; *ed:* (BA) Bus & Ec , Ricker Coll 1967; (MA) Admin, Univ of ME 1974; Supt Cert 1988; (7-12) Teach Gen Elem 501; (K-12) Prin Prof 502; *cr:* Jr H S, Union 114, Island Falls 1967-70; Math & Sci 6-8th, Caravel Jr H S 1970- 74; Prin & Math & Sci K-5th, Caravel Elem Sch 1974-78; Prin & Math K-8, Caravel Elem & Jr H S 1978-79; Prin, Caravel Jr H S; *ai:* Curr Comm Chm-MSAD #23; Penobscot Valley Jr H S Leaque-Bsktbl; MSAD #23, Teachers Assoc-Pres 1972-74; Hermon Meadows Golf Assoc-Pres 1972-78; Hermon Scout Trp, Asst Scout Master 1976-80; *office:* Caravel Jr H S Irish Rd Carmel ME 04419

STEWART, JAMES C., Mathematics Teacher; *b:* Pittsburgh, PA; *m:* Janice Hostler; *c:* Rachel, Brian; *ed:* (BS) Math, Grove City Coll 1972; Grad Stud PA St Univ; *cr:* Math Teacher Greensburg Cntrl Cath 1973-; *ai:* Athletic Dir; Head Boys Bsktbl & Asst Bsbl Coach; NCTM, PA Cncl Teachers of Math; *office:* Greensburg Cntrl Cath Sch 901 Armory Dr Greensburg PA 15601

STEWART, JANA (RICHARDSON), Reading Teacher; *b:* Pauls Valley, OK; *m:* Steve; *c:* Stacey, Scott; *ed:* (BS) Ed Eng Ed/Elem Ed, East Cntrl Univ 1974; (MED) Learning Disabili Ties, East Cntrl Univ 1976; *cr:* Learning Disabilities Teacher Hayes Elem 1974-; Lang Arts/Math Teacher Grades 6/7/8 1974-78; 8th Grade Teacher Rdng/Advanced Rdng 1978- Ada Mid Sch; *ai:* 8th Grade Stud of Month Chairperson 1990; 8th Grade Comm Mem; Ada Ed Assn 1974-; OK Ed Assn 1974-; NEA 1974-; Pontotoc Cty Rdng Cncl; 1989 KOCO-TV OK Best Teacher Honor Roll; *office:* Ada Mid Sch 223 W 18th Ada OK 74820

STEWART, JEROME LEX, History Teacher; *b:* Des Moines, IA; *m:* Raquel; *c:* Elliott, Gabriel; *ed:* (BA) Religion, Simpson Coll 1977; (MA) Spec Ed, Drake Univ 1986; *cr:* Teacher/Coach Caprock HS 1987-; *ai:* Wrestling & Soccer Coach; Wrestling Team 1st in St 1988; Natl Press Women 1st Place 1985, 1984; Simpson Coll Hall of Fame 1987; Danforth Fellow 1990; *office:* Caprock HS 3001 E 34th St Amarillo TX 79103

STEWART, JOAN N., 7th Grade Life Science Teacher; *b:* Hamilton, TX; *m:* Troy G.; *c:* Will V.; *ed:* (BS) Phys Ed/Bio, Howard Payne Univ 1968; *cr:* 9th Grade Phys Sci Teacher 1968-78, 7th Grade Life Sci Teacher 1980- Brownwood Jr HS; *ai:* NCTA, Sci Teachers Assn of TX; Natl Wildlife Fed; *office:* Brownwood Jr HS Calvert Rd Brownwood TX 76801

STEWART, JOANNE PATTERSON, Third Grade Teacher; *b:* New Market, AL; *m:* John Milton; *c:* Rosemary Stewart Kipreos, Ann; *ed:* (BS) Elem Ed, Florence St 1953; Grad Stud; *cr:* 1st/2nd Grade Teacher Austinville Sch 1953-54, Irondale Sch 1954-56, West Clinton Sch 1956-58, Lopez Sch 1958-60; 1st Grade Teacher Randall Sch 1970-71; 3rd Grade Teacher Caldwell Sch 1971-89; *ai:* NEA, AEA, SEA; Scottsboro 1st Meth Church.

STEWART, KATHARINE STRAUGHAN, 6th Grade Teacher; *b:* Bonne Terre, MO; *m:* Joe A.; *ed:* (BS) Elem Ed, SE MO St 1972; (MAT) Elem/Arts in Teaching, Webster Univ 1984; *cr:* 3rd-7th Grade Teacher 1967-, 6th Grade/6th-8th Grade Eng Teacher 1985- St Joseph Cath Sch; *ai:* Speech Team Adv; Missions Chairperson; NCEA 1968-; MO Rdng Teachers Assn 1986-87; Bus & Prof Women Secy 1972; United Meth Women Dist VP 1989-; *office:* St Joseph Cath Sch 501 St Genevieve Ave Farmington MO 63640

STEWART, LYNN EUGENE, Counselor; *b:* Wichita, KS; *m:* Kathleen Madison Stewart; *c:* Jaime L., Laura L.; *ed:* (BA) PE, Driver Ed, Wichita St Univ 1972; (MA) Guidance, Cnslng, SouthWestern St Univ 1987; *cr:* PE Teacher/Coach Eisenhower HS 1972-89; Counselor Tomlinson Jr HS 1989-; *ai:* Coached Girls Sftbl 1989; Cnslr Tomlinson Jr HS 1989; OK Sftbl Coaches Assn 1982-89 (Regional Coach 1984 Area Coach 1985); NEA 1972-89; OK Ed Assn 1972-89; OK Ofcls Assn 1980-89; Outstanding Young Man of Amer 1984; Deacon/Youth Spon Western Hills Chrstn Church 1980-89; OK Regional Sftbl Coach of Yr 1984; OK Area Sftbl Coach of Yr 1985; *home:* 7204 N W Maple Dr Lawton OK 73505

STEWART, MARGARET HARVEY, 8th Grade Soc Stud Teacher; *b:* Chicago, IL; *m:* Charles E. Sr.; *c:* Charles II, Lottye Stewart Wilkins, Dorothea B. Jones; *ed:* (BS) Ed, Natl Coll of Ed 1965; (MS) Ed, IN Univ 1972; Governors St Univ, N IL Univ; *cr:* 3rd Grade Teacher Hale Primary 1965-73; Admin/Curr Teacher Horace Mann & Whittier 1973-75; 6th Grade Teacher Hale Intermediate & Hale Mid 1975-82; 8th Grade Teacher Kerr Mid 1982-; *ai:* Natl Jr Honor Society, Soc Stud, Discipline Policy Comms; Blue Island Ed Assn VP 1981-83; IL Ed Assn Regional 28 Cncl Comms 1976-; Posen/Robbins (Sch Bd 1987-, VP 1989-); *office:* Dist 130 Kerr Mid Sch 12900 S Maple Blue Island IL 60406

STEWART, MARSHA DEVERE, Third Grade Teacher; *b:* Berea, KY; *m:* Les G.; *ed:* (BA) Elem Ed, Berea Coll 1973; (MA) Elem Ed, E KY Univ 1977; *cr:* 7th/8th Grade Math Teacher Kit Carson Elem Sch 1973-74; 3rd Grade Teacher Silver Creek Elem 1974-; *ai:* Drill Team Instr & Spon; Madison Cty Ed Assn Building Rep 1974-; Baptist Women 1984-; Acteens Leader 1988-; *home:* 9 Country Estates Dr Paint Lick KY 40461

STEWART, MARY N. (HAND), Fifth Grade Teacher; *b:* Dawson, GA; *m:* Bennie; *c:* Cheryl Hobbs, Shelia Meeks; *ed:* (BA) Early Chldhd/Elem Ed, Univ of N FL; Bus Trng, FL Comm Coll; *ai:* 5th Grade Level Chairperson; Supt Writing Prgm Chairperson; Safety Patrol Spon; Rachel Brooks Choir Pres 1980-89, Plaque 1985; Church (Young Adult Choir Dir 1979-, Planning Comm Pres 1990); Teacher of Yr 1989-; Perfect Attendance 1978-80; *office:* Northshore Elem Sch 5701 Silver Plz Jacksonville FL 32208

STEWART, NICOLE CHASE, Former Teacher; *b:* Amsterdam, NY; *m:* Daniel P.; *ed:* (BS) Psych/Sociology/Elem Ed, 1975, (MS) Health Ed, 1979 Russell Sage Coll; Ed Admin, SUNY Albany 1982; Admin Certificate, North Adams St Coll; *cr:* 1st/6th Grade Elem Ed Teacher Broadalbin Cntrl Sch 1975-85; *ai:* Past Comm of the Handicapped; Dev of Writing Prgm/Policy Review Update/Dev Career Guidance Curr K-6/Rdng Textbook Dir/Coord/Testing Evaluation/Gifted & TalentedAdv Primary Stu Cncl/Produced & Directed Several Christmas Pagents Committees; *home:* HC 1 Box 27 Gloucester Point VA 23062

STEWART, PATRICIA ROBINSON, Vocal Music Teacher; *b:* Perryville, MO; *m:* Ben Beaven; *c:* Benjamin L.; *ed:* (BS) Vocal/Instrumental Music, SE MO St Univ 1964; Grad Stud, WA Univ, Webster Univ; *cr:* Kndgtn-12th Grade Vocal/Instrumental Music Dir Bismarck MO Schls 1964-67; HS & Jr HS Vocal Music Dir Pacific MO Schls 1967-69; Kndgtn-12th Grade Vocal Music Dir Bismarck MO Schls 1969-73; 7th-9th Grade Vocal Music Dir 1973-81, 9th-12th Grade Vocal Music Dir 1981-85, 7th/8th Grade Vocal Music Dir 1985- De Soto MO; *ai:* Natl Jr Honor Society & Teachers Aid Society of Kids Spon; Jefferson Cty Music Educators Pres 1980-82, Membership 1973-; MO Music Educators 1964-; Amer Choral Dir MO Jr HS Vocal (Chairperson 1989-, Mem 1975-); MO St Teachers Assn 1964-; Article Amer Choral Dir JournaL; Choirs Perform MO Music Educators Conventions; Choirs Performed MO St & Dist Teachers Conventions; Choirs Invited to Perform Austria & England; George Awd Cmmty Involvement Bismarck MO 1971; *home:* Plum & Cedar 5 De Soto MO 63020

STEWART, PHOEBE, Mathematics Teacher; *b:* Memphis, TN; *m:* Thomas C.; *c:* LEA, Thomas M. II; *ed:* (BA) Ed/Math, 1974, (MS) Ed/Math, 1987 Univ of MS; *cr:* Math Teacher/Dept Chairperson Henry Jr HS 1974-79; Math Teacher Marshall Acad 1979-83, Holly Springs HS 1983-; *ai:* NCTM 1974-, Pres 68th Natl Convention 1990; Math Assn of America 1988-; ASCD 1989-; Fist United Presbyn Soc Chm 1988-; Belles & Books Literacy Treas 1988; Town & Cntry Garden Pres; Democratic Exec Comm 1988; MS Private Sch Assn Dist Chm; Teacher Assessment Instruments Evaluator 1988; STAR Teacher 1985, 1987; MS Stu Teacher Achievement Recognition.

STEWART, POLLY NORRIS, 4th Grade Teacher; *b:* Dunn, NC; *m:* Larry V.; *c:* Zachary; *ed:* (BS) Elem Ed, 1973, (MED) Ed, 1988 Campbell Univ; Ec Seminar; *cr:* 4th Grade Teacher Coats 1973-; *ai:* Soc Stud Lead Teacher; Media Comm; 4th-6th Grade Team Leader; NCAE, NEA; *office:* Coats Elem Sch P O Box 1029 Coats NC 27521

STEWART, ROBERT THOMAS, History/Civics Teacher; *b:* Akron, OH; *m:* Jill Albaugh; *c:* Tyler, Nathan; *ed:* (BS) Soc Stud, The Defiance Coll 1966; (MA) Soc Stud, W MI Univ 1972; Skills for Adolescence Quest Fnd; Civil War Wkshp Freedoms Fnd Valley Forge PA; Reproductive Health Inst MI Dept of Ed; *cr:* Teacher/Coach 1965-, Athletic Dir 1986- Quincy Mid Sch; *ai:* Athletic Dir; Jr Var Boys Bsktbl Coach; Soc Stud Dept Head; MI Ed Assn 1965-; Bsktbl Coaches Assn of MI 1980-; Outstanding Leaders in Elem, Scndry Ed 1976; Presentor MI Assn of Mid Sch Educators 1976-77; *office:* Quincy Mid Sch 41 E Jefferson St Quincy MI 49082

STEWART, SALLY, English Teacher; *b:* Miami Beach, FL; *m:* Stanley Hancock; *c:* Jennifer Annand; *ed:* (BA) Eng/Ed, Univ of FL 1960; (MA) Eng, 1965, (PHD) Eng, 1979 Univ of CO; Vassar Coll, Univ of Oslo; *cr:* Asst Professor Western St Coll 1972-74; Eng Teacher Sierra HS 1982-; *ai:* Yrbk; Sierra Club 1965-; CO Environmental Coalition 1988-; NY St Ed Grant; Excl in Teaching Univ of CO; Art & Hum Fellowship Univ of CO; Article Published 1984; *office:* Sierra HS 2250 Jet Wing Dr Colorado Springs CO 80916

STEWART, TIM EDWARD, French Teacher; *b:* Athens, GA; *ed:* (BA) Eng, GA Coll 1981; Scndry Cert Fr, GA St Univ; *cr:* Eng Teacher/Coach Cntrl Fellowship Chrstn Acad 1981-84; Eng/Drama Teacher/Coach Franklin Cty HS 1984-87; Eng Teacher/Coach Oglethorpe Cty HS 1987-88; Fr Teacher/Coach Franklin Cty HS 1988-; *ai:* Girls Bsktbl Coach; GAE 1987-; *office:* Franklin Cty HS P O Box 543 Carnesville GA 30521

STEWART, WILLIAM CHARLES, JR., Teacher/Math Department Head; *b:* Lexington, TN; *m:* Molly Caroline Chandler; *c:* William C. III, Carla M.; *ed:* (BA) His, Drury Coll 1958; (MED) Admin/Supervision, 1983, (EDS) Curr/Instruction, 1986 Mid TN St Univ; *cr:* Math/Ec Teacher Fairview HS 1980-81; His/Cmptr Teacher Fairview Mid Sch 1981-84; Cmptr Teacher Northside Mid Sch 1984-85; Math/Cmptr Teacher Fairview HS 1985-; *ai:* Beta Club Spon; Academic Excl Comm Banquet Chairperson; Mid TN Math Teachers Assn 1985-; TN Math Teachers Assn 1987-; Article TN Assn of Mid Schls Journal 1983; CTE Gift Fellowship 1990; *home:* PO Box 429 Fairview TN 37062

STEWART, ZELMA BROWN, Fifth Grade Teacher; *b:* St Louis, MO; *m:* James; *c:* James Jr., Gylnis M.; *ed:* (BS) Elem Ed, Cleveland St Univ 1975; Lib Skills, Childrens Lit; *cr:* 5th Grade Teacher St Agatha St Aloysius Sch 1987-89; *ai:* Cmmty Bus Service Awds; Group Spon; Drama, Dance & Jazz Appreciation Spon; NCEA, St Agatha St Aloysius Parent Teacher Union; Teacher of Yr Cath Sch Excl Awd 1989-; Book Published 1987; *office:* St Agatha-St Aloysius Sch 640 Lakeview Rd Cleveland OH 44108

STEYER, ROBERT EUGENE, Mathematics Teacher; *b:* Fostoria, OH; *m:* Donna Rae Kastner; *c:* Sara, Theresa, Jennifer, Mary; *ed:* (BS) Ed, 1963, (MA) Math, 1966 Bowling Green St Univ; Summer Inst Colby Coll 1970; Cmptr Sci, Bowling Green St Univ 1972; *cr:* Teacher Arcadia HS 1963-70, Fostoria HS 1970-78, Hopewell-Loudon HS 1978-; *ai:* 8th Grade Class Adv; Statistics Var Ftbl; Scorebook, Statistics Var Bsktbl; HLEA Pres 1989-; OEA, NEA, OCTM; Knights of Columbus 1197 Grand Knight 1976-78; Hopewell-Loudon HS Teacher of Yr 1987-88; *office:* Hopewell-Loudon HS P O Box 400 Bascom OH 44809

STICKLEY, BETTY WINDLE, Sixth Grade Teacher; *b:* Monroe, TN; *m:* W. Scott; *c:* Allen, Fred, Walter; *ed:* (BS) Home Ec, TN Tech Univ 1948; (MS) Elem Ed, Union Coll 1979; Grad Stud; *cr:* Extension Home Agent Univ of TN 1948-51; 6th Grade Teacher Avoca 1966-; *ai:* NEA, TEA, BTEA.

STICKNEY, PHYLLIS, Mathematics Teacher; *b:* Philadelphia, PA; *ed:* (AB) Math, Temple Univ 1961; (MA) Math Ed, Beaver Coll 1978; *cr:* Math Teacher Sch Dist of Philadelphia 1967-; *ai:* Frosh Class Spon; Supv Peer-Tutorial Prgm; Treas Human Relations Comm; IBM Grant Wrtng Comm; Math/Sci Collobrative Technology Comm; NCTM 1973; Presenter of Wkshps Use of Technology in Math Classroom Via Software Use; MA Inst Technology Outstanding Math Teacher; Received 3 Grants; Published in EDC Journal; *office:* Carver HS of Engineering & Sci 17th & Norris Sts Philadelphia PA 19121

STIDHAM, PAM HICKS, Math Teacher; *b:* Kingsport, TN; *m:* Michael J.; *ed:* (BS) Elem Ed/Math, 1983, (MED) Math Ed, 1986 East TN St Univ; *cr:* Math Teacher John Sevier Mid Sch 1985-; *ai:* 6th Grade Instr Math Counts Team; NCTM; TN Cncl of Teachers of Math; Upper East TN Cncl of Teachers of Math; Southwest VA Cncl of Teachers of Math; NEA; TN Ed Assn; Kingsport Ed Assn; Alpha Delta Kappa 1987-; Kingsport Ed Assn Mem Chm 1989-; KEA Public Relations Comm 1986-088 Chm 1988; *office:* John Sevier Mid Sch 1200 Wateree St Kingsport TN 37660

STIELER, BEVERLYANN, Elementary Teacher; *b:* Wyandotte, MI; *m:* Stephen; *ed:* (BA) Elem Ed, 1965, (MA) Elem Ed, 1967 Wayne St; *cr:* Elem Teacher Wyandotte Bd of Ed 1965-; *ai:* Eng, Math, Report Card Comm; WGH Auxiliary; *office:* Garfield Elem Sch 340 Superior Blvd Wyandotte MI 48192

STIERWALD, MARLENE LYDIA, Rdng, Eng, Soc Stud Teacher; *b:* New Orleans, LA; *ed:* (BA) Ed, Univ of New Orleans 1971; *cr:* Teacher St Raphael The Archangel Sch 1971-; *ai:* Audiovisual Coord; Sch in Cmmty Chairperson; NHS; Jr Achievement & Civic Beautification Coord; NCEA Mem 1971-.

STIFFLER, ELSIE MARSHALL, English Teacher; *b:* Chicago, IL; *m:* Paul Eugene; *c:* Cheryl Schultz, Jonathan; *ed:* (BA) Eng/Soc Stud/Ed, N Cntrl Coll 1950; (MA) Ed, Natl Coll of Ed 1982; Course Work Teaching Skills & Journalism; *cr:* Jr HS/Kndgtn Teacher Lisle Elem 1950-56; Teacher Eastridge HS 1964-70, Proviso Nest 1971-72, Willowbrook HS 1972-; *ai:* Centurion Yrbk Adv; Coord of Gifted Prgm; Consultant for The Thinking Connection; NEA, IEA 1975-; JEA 1980-; Mem of Exec Bd for KEMPA; Employee of Yr Awd Dist 88 1989; Whos Who in Amer Ed 1989; *home:* 405 S Cornell Villa Park IL 60181

STIGALL, RHODA MAYS, Kindergarten Department Chair; *b:* Memphis, TN; *m:* Charles Edward; *c:* Detric, Stephanie, Christopher; *ed:* (BS) Elem Ed, 1978, (BS) Early Chldhd Ed 1978, Memphis St Univ; (MED) Admin/Supervision, Trevecca Nazarene Coll 1989; *cr:* Teacher Asst Longview Elem 1973-76; Cmptr Assisted Instr Aide 1976-78; Kndgtn Teacher Humes Jr HS 1978; *ai:* RAPPERS Club Spon & Adv; Just Say No Club; My Buddy Club Spon; Drug Free Schls & Cmmty Team Chairperson; Adopt A Sch Mem; MEA, TEA, NEA 1978-; St Peter M B Church Sunday Sch Teacher 1980-, Loyal & Faithfull Service 1987; Leadership Trng Sch Dean 1987-; Drug Free Schls Cmmty Chairperson 1988-, Leadership 1989; Teacher Initiative Grant 1988-; *home:* 2236 Pratt St Memphis TN 38106

STIKELEATHER, LAVONNE BRUCE, Second Grade Teacher; *b:* Mc Coy, KY; *c:* Glen A.; *ed:* (Rank II) Elem Ed, Western KY Univ 1990-; Addl Studies Workshops and Adult Ed; *cr:* Elem Ed Leitchfield Independent & H.W. Wilkey 1956-; Adult Ed Grayson Cnty HS 1982-89; *ai:* Curr Comm; Ed Adv Comm; Grayson Cty Ed Assn 1972-; KEA 1956-; NEA 1956-; Leitchfield Woman's Club 1960-65; *home:* 116 School Street Leitchfield KY 42754

STILES, NANCY JO TENNANT, Fifth Grade Teacher; *b:* Odessa, TX; *c:* Sheldon T.; *ed:* (BS) Elem Ed, TX Tech Univ 1962; (MLA) Liberal Arts, S Meth Univ 1976; Gifted Ed Cert; *cr:* 4th Grade Self Contained Teacher Fruitdale Elem 1962-63; 2nd Grade Self Contained Teacher Harriet Bishop Elem 1963-64; 4th Grade Self Contained Teacher Hays Elem 1964-65, Parkway Elem 1965-67; Pre-Sch Teacher Lake Park Private Sch 1971; 5th Grade Lang Art/3rd Grade Art/Music/Lang Art Teacher Runyon Elem 1969-71; 7th Grade Lang Art/Soc Stud Teacher Gill Elem 1972-76; 4th-6th Grade Enrichment Gifted Prgm Teacher Reinhardt Elem 1976-80; 5th/6th Grade Gifted Prgm Teacher Lakewood Elem 1980-84; 6th Grade Self Contained Gifted Prgm Teacher K B Polk Gifted Vanguard 1984-87; Teacher Hoffman Elem 1987-89; Teacher/Team Leader Harrington Elem 1989-; *ai:* Stu Cncl, Sch Newspaper, Sch Yrbk Spon; Coord Sch Awds Prgm; Staff Dev, Classroom Teachers Rep: Prin Advisory Bd; Spelling Bee, Dept for Gifted Vanguard, Cultural Arts Chairperson; Delta Kappa Gamma Secy Achievement Awd 1988-89; H Ross Perot Outstanding Teacher Awd; Outstanding Teacher Nominee for Dallas Ind Sch; Consultant Values Clarification Text Materials; Judge Media Fair St Teacher Convention; Instr SMU Experimental Arts Prgm; Facilitator for Area Staff Dev, Success Motivation Seminar; Conducted Wkshps Teachers Staff Dev Several Dallas Ind Sch Dist Schls; Consultant Gifted Prgm Trng, Staff Dev, Region 10, Irving Ind Sch Dist.

STILES, ROBERT WILLIAM, Director of Music Education; *b:* Leroy, MI; *m:* Audrey Lee Woolworth; *c:* Denise R. Stiles Dickey, Cynthia L. Stiles Carpenter, Lisa M.; *ed:* (BS) Music Ed, Olivet Nazarene Univ 1961; (MA) Instrumental Music, Univ of MI 1969; Various Seminars on Vocal & Instrumental Music by MSVA & MSBOA; *cr:* Dir of Music Ed Sparta Area Schls 1961-79, Belding Area Schls 1979-; *ai:* Faculty Cncl Mem Belding HS; MSVA 1963-; MSBOA 1961-; Sparta Ed Assn Pres 1974-76, Teacher of Yr 1976; Belding Ed Assn (VP, Pres) 1983-85; Berkley Hills Wesleyan Church Minister of Music; Bob Stiles Day by Sparta Cmmty 1983; Helen Cusack Fine Arts Awd 1986; Labor Day Co-Grand Marshall with Asst Prin; Head Ftbl Coach Charles Barker from Belding Cmmty; *office:* Belding Area HS 850 Hall St Belding MI 48809

STILL, BEVERLY BRYAN, Eighth Grade English Teacher; *b:* Dothan, AL; *m:* Steven M.; *ed:* (BME) Choral Music Ed, Troy St Univ 1983; (BS) Scndry Eng Ed, Troy St Univ Dothan 1984; *cr:* 8th Grade Eng Teacher Beverlye Mid Sch 1984-; *ai:* Yrbk Pep Club, Newspaper, Stu Forum, Eng Team Spon; Adv TMR Big Brothers/Big Sisters Adv; Span Choir Dir; Shakespeare Day Coord; MENC Pres 1983; NCTE Mem 1989; *office:* Beverlye Mid Sch 427 S Beverlye Rd Dothan AL 36301

STILL, CANDACE TYSON, Choral/Assistant Band Director; *b:* Huntsville, AL; *m:* Glenn Leslie; *c:* Leslie, Jenny; *ed:* (BS) Music Ed, 1976, (MS) Music Ed, 1990 Jacksonville St Univ; *cr:* Choral Dir Cordova HS 1976-78; Private Instruction Teacher Powder Springs 1978-85; Choral/Asst Band Dir Paulding Cty HS 1985-; *ai:* Delta Omicron (Musicale Dir 1974-75, Secy 1975-76); Music Educators Natl Conference, GA Music Educators Assn, Prof Assn of GA Educators 1986-; *home:* 5528 Macland Rd Powder Springs GA 30073

STILL, ROSEMARY WOOLFOLK, 8th Grade American His Teacher; *b:* Jersey City, NJ; *c:* Ethel R., William J. Brown *ed:* (BA) His, Bethune-Cookman Coll 1970; Amer His Daytona Beach Comm Coll; Numerous Wkshps; *cr:* Teacher Campbell Jr HS 1971-; *ai:* 8th Grade Soc Stud Contact Teacher; Volusia Educators Assn, FL Teacher Profession, NEA; Bethune-Cookman Coll Alumni; Sang Solo Memorial Service for Dr Martin King Jr Bethune Comm Coll; Performed Solos for Various Churches in Cmmty; *home:* 239 Oak Tree Cir Daytona Beach FL 32114

STILLER, DAVID W., Chemistry Teacher; *b:* South Orange, NJ; *m:* Connie Keider; *c:* Erich P., Sonja R., Geoffrey D.; *ed:* (BA) Bio, Eastern Coll 1965; (MS) Biochemistry, 1970, (PHD) Animal Nutrition, 1976 Univ of ME; Microcmptrs, Cmptr Interfacing, Wilkes Univ; Advanced First Aid, Stan First Aid, CPR Instr; Emergency Medical Technician & Instr PA Certified; *cr:* Chem Teacher John Baptist HS 1973-78; Phys Sci Instr Penn St Univ 1986-89; Chem Teacher MMI Preparatory Sch 19878-; EMT Instr Luzerne Cty Trng Inst 1988-; *ai:* Mentor Ind Stu Research Projects; Sci Research Club & Sr Class Adv; After Sch First Aid & CPR Instr; Luzerne Cty Sci Teacher Assn (Pres 1984, Bd Mem) 1978-; PA Assn of Ind Schls Exec Bd Mem 1980-; PA Sci Teacher Assn (Presenter 1983, Mem 1982-); Natl Assn of Ind Schls; PA Jr Acad of Sci; PA Acad of Sci; Laurel Lodge F&AM Past Master 1983-84; Amer Red Cross (Health & Safety Comm, Instr) 1985-; White Haven Ambulance Assn EMT 1985-; Tandy Technology Scholar Finalist 1990; MIT Influential Teacher 1987; Nom Teacher of Yr 1986; Edison Mc Graw Oustanding Stu Research Dir 1985; Houdry-Sun Oil Company Industrial Ed Awd 1965-66; Merck Sharp & Dohme Academic Awd 1966-68; Northeast Region Research Project Awd 1968-70; Outstanding Sci Teacher New England Jr Sci Symposium 1974, 1976 & PA Jr Sci Symposium 1984, 1986, 1988, 1989; Information Technology in Ed Grant 1985, 1987-88 *home:* RD 1 Box 125 Sandy Valley White Haven PA 18661

STILLWELL, ELIZABETH NELL, 7th & 8th Grade Teacher; *b:* Sylva, NC; *ed:* (BS) Elem Ed, Western Carolina Univ 1965; *cr:* Teacher Aualla Elem Sch 1965-80, Smokey Mountain Elem 1980-; *ai:* Jr Beta Club Spon; Placement Comm for Spec Ed; Core Team; NEA 1965-; NCEA 1965-; JCEA 1965-; Teacher of Yr 1978-79; *home:* Rt 3 Box 212A Sylva NC 28779

STILLWELL, JAMES THOMAS, Soc Stud Teacher/Dept Chair; *b:* Mountain Grove, MO; *ed:* (BA) His/Ed, 1965, (MED) Soc Stud, 1982 Drury Coll; *cr:* Core Teacher Nathan Hale Jr HS 1965-70; Teacher/Prin Raymondville Elem 1970-73; Soc Worker MO Division of Family Services 1974-77; Teacher/Dept Chm Clinton Mid Sch 1977-; *ai:* NEA Local Treas 1965-73, 1980-; MO St Teachers Assn 1977-80; Masonic Lodge 1970-; Optimist VP 1977-82; Clinton Teacher of Yr; Clinton Featured Educator 1986, 1988; *home:* 1501 S 7th St Clinton MO 64735

STIMSON, SUSAN, English Teacher; *b:* Rutland, VT; *ed:* (BA) Eng, Whitworth Coll 1969; (MS) Ed, CA St Univ 1976; Rdng Specialist Credential; *cr:* Sch Improvement Resource Teacher 1983-89, Eng Teacher 1969- Cupertino HS; *ai:* Sch Site Cncl; Stu Teacher Supvr; Curr Dev; NEA, NCTE; Jr Honors, Sch Wide Rdng Prgm Author Coord; *office:* Cupertino HS 10100 Finch Ave Cupertino CA 95014

STINCHCOMB, MARIE CONTY, Social Studies Teacher; *b:* La Junta, CO; *m:* John L.; *c:* David; *ed:* (BA) Soc Stud, Univ of N CO 1957; *cr:* 6th-8th Grade Soc Stud Teacher Corwin Mid Sch 1957-; *ai:* Kappa Delta Pi 1957-; NEA, Pueblo Ed Assn 1957-; *office:* Corwin Mid Sch 1500 Lakeview Ave Pueblo CO 81004

STINE, JAMES M., JR., Social Studies Teacher; *b:* La Plata, MD; *ed:* (BS) His, Towson St Coll; (MA) Scndry Ed, George Washington Univ; *cr:* Soc Stud Teacher 1973-, Soc Stud Dept Chairperson 1987- General Smallwood Mid Sch; *ai:* Spon Sci Fiction Club; *office:* General Smallwood Mid Sch R R 210 Indian Head MD 20640

STINE, JOYCE TAYLOR, Math Dept Chair/Teacher; *b:* Jefferson, TX; *m:* Charles O; *c:* Christopher A., Shannon D., Carrisa N.; *ed:* (BS) Math, TX Coll Tyler 1964; (ME) Curr/Instruction, Univ of TX Tyler; *cr:* Math Teacher Bruce HS 1964-68, Gilmer HS 1968-69; Teacher/Dept Chm Jacksonville HS 1969-; *ai:* Math Dept Team Leader & Dept Head; TX St Teachers Assn, NEA 1964-89; NCTM 1987-; TX Cncl Math Teachers 1989-; TX Teaching Career Ladder Level III; *home:* 1106 Pierce Ln PO Box 1827 Jacksonville TX 75766

STINE, KATHY, Second Grade Teacher; *b:* Lynwood, CA; *ed:* (BA) Soc Sci/Elem Ed, Biola Univ 1973; Rdng Specialist; *cr:* Kndgtn Teacher Liberty Chrstn Sch 1973-75; 2nd Grade Teacher 1st Baptist Elem Sch 1975-76, Chrstn Acad 1976-78; Kndgtn Teacher Baldwin Park Chrstn 1978-79; 2nd Grade Teacher Santa Fe Chrstn Sch 1979-; *ai:* ACSI 1973-; Opencourt Publishing Company Consultant; *home:* 838 Mola Vista Way Solana Beach CA 92075

STINEHELFER, JAMES DANIEL, JR., 6th Grade Science Teacher; *b:* Lima, OH; *m:* Debra Jean Kyser; *c:* Jennifer, Jessica; *ed:* (BS) Elem Ed, The Defiance Coll 1972; (MS) Elem Ed, IN Univ 1983; *cr:* 5th Grade Teacher Squires Elem Sch 1971-73; 6th Grade Teacher Sherwood Elem Sch 1973-80; 6th Grade Sci Teacher Superior Mid Sch 1980-; *ai:* Sci Fair & Sherwood Homecoming Chm; Sci Curr, Prin Advisory, Wms Cty Entry Yr Comm; Wms Cty Mentoring Trainer; Montpelier Ed Assn Pres 1987-89; Negotiations Chief Negotiator 1984-88; OH Ed Assn, NEA VP 1988-89; St John Luth Church Pres 1987-; Sherwood Village Bd of Public Affairs 1984-85; Shawnee BSA Cncl Eagle Review Bd 1987-; Jennings Scholar 1982-83; Nom OH St Teacher of Yr 1984; Friends of 4-H Awd 1987; *office:* Superior Mid Sch Rt 3 St Rt 576 Montpelier OH 43543

STINES, SUSAN MUNN, Mathematics Teacher; *b:* Columbus, OH; *m:* Billy Joseph; *c:* Jeffrey M., Bryan T.; *ed:* (BS) Math Ed, NC St 1977; SC Prof Dev Prgm for Math/Sci Teachers; Working Toward Masters Pembroke Univ; *cr:* Teacher Bunn HS 1977-80, Aiken Cty 1980-85, Mc Cormick HS 1985-88, Hallsboro HS 1988-; *ai:* Math Club; NCTM 1984-; Baptist Church (Youth Teacher, Leader) 1974-; NC Math/Sci Teachers Grant; *office:* Hallsboro HS Hallsboro NC 28442

STIRZAKER, THOMAS DUNCAN, Scndry Instrumental Music Inst; *b:* Gallipolis, OH; *ed:* (BME) Music Ed, Univ of SC 1981; (MM) Applied Music, Univ of MS 1983; (PHD) Fine Arts, TX Tech Univ 1988; *cr:* Woodwind Instr Mc Murry Coll 1983-85, Wayland Baptist Univ 1986-88; Instru Music Instr Harlingen Consolidated Ind Sch Dist 1988-; *ai:* Marching Band; Symphonic & Concert Bands; TX Bandmasters Assn 1988-; Music Ed Assn 1983-; Phi Mu Alpha Sinfonia Pres Local Chapter 1977-; Schlsp Stu Univ of SC; Teaching Assistantship at Univ of MS & TX Tech Univ; *office:* Harlingen Public Sch 1202 E Marshall Harlingen TX 78550

STITT, NANCY SNEED, Science Teacher; *b:* New Orleans, LA; *m:* Richard Marks; *c:* Taylor M., Carson P.; *ed:* (AA) General, St Petersburg Jr Coll 1970; (BA) Bio Ed, 1972, (BS) Nursing, 1976 Univ of S FL; Grad Level Courses in Ed, Sci, Cmptr Sci; *cr:* 6th Grade Sci/Math Teacher Canterbury Sch of FL 1972-74; 6th Grade Sci Teacher Madeira Beach Mid Sch 1977-80; Asst Dir of Nursing Beverly Manor Convalescent Center 1980-82; 6th Grade Sci Teacher Meadowlawn Mid Sch 1982-; *ai:* Meadowlawn Mid Schls Sci Fair & Sci Competition Team Coord; 6th Grade Team Leader; Health & Safety Comm; Pinellas Cty Sci Teachers Assn 1982-; Pinellas Cty Teachers Assn, FL Teachers Assn; NEA 1977-80 & 1982-; St Petersburg Jr Womans Club 1983-84; Meadowlawn Mid Schls Teacher of Yr Nom 1986-87; *office:* Meadowlawn Mid Sch 5900 16th St N Saint Petersburg FL 33703

STITTSWORTH, MARIE ADELE, Second Grade Teacher; *b:* Ely, NV; *m:* David E.; *c:* Randall L., Valerie, Michelle S. Hobbs; *ed:* (BS) Elem Ed, Brigham Young Univ 1961; Grad Stud Various Univs; *cr:* 3rd Grade Teacher Arlington Sch 1962-63; 3rd-5th Grade Teacher Washington Sch 1967-76; 2nd Grade Teacher Browns Valley Sch 1976-; *ai:* Napa Valley Educators Assn Faculty Rep 1989-, Years of Membership 1977-; CA Teachers Assn, NEA, Napa Valley Rdng Assn; Church of Jesus Christ of Latter Day Saints (Childrens Organ, Choirster) 1990; *office:* Browns Valley Sch 1001 Buhman Ave Napa CA 94558

STOBAUGH, ANN SIEVER, Mathematics Teacher; *b:* Dermott, AR; *m:* John H.; *c:* John; *ed:* (BSE) Math, Univ of AR Monticello 1979; *cr:* Math Teacher Conner Jr HS 1980-; *ai:* Curr Comm; TWIGS Benefit of AR Childrens Hospital 1989-; *office:* Conner Jr HS PO Box 767 Mc Gehee AR 71654

STOCK, MALCOLM, Health Instructor/Dept Chair; *b:* New York, NY; *m:* Rosalyn L.; *c:* Mark L., Erinn M.; *ed:* (BS) Phys Ed, 1957, (MS) Phys Ed, 1961, (EDD) Ed, 1972 UCLA; Numerous Univs; *cr:* Instr/Coach Sierra HS 1958-59; Phys Ed Dept Chm/Sci/His Teacher Patrick Henry Jr HS 1959-85; Health Dept Chm/Coach Granada Hills HS 1985-; *ai:* Health Dept Chm; Amer Assn for Health, Phys Ed, Recreation; CA Assn for Health, Phys Ed, Recreation; United Teachers of Los Angeles; Phi Epsilon Kappa, Phi Epsilon Delta; Rotary Club; YMCA; Conejo Valley Bd of Realtors; SW Outdoor Writers Assn; Natl Fed of Interscholastic Coaches Assn; Nom Outstanding Teacher Awd 1988; Recorded the Highest Enrollment & Lowest Attrition Rate in Two US His Courses 1984; Delivered Keynote Address UCLA In-Service Inst; Recreational Services Employees in Pauley Pavilion 1977; Developed Pure Fishing Course 1975; Served as Teacher in a Panel Presentation on Teacher Trng 1975 Cahper Convention; Appointed Regional Writer of South Coast of CA 1990; *home:* 4031 Monterey Ct Newbury Park CA 91320

STOCK, MICHAEL ROBERT, Athletic Director/Teacher; *b:* Sycamore, IL; *m:* Judith Ann Hesemann; *c:* Kristin A., Jennifer L., Robert M., Joseph A.; *ed:* (AA) Concordia Ann Arbor 1970; (BA) His/Phys Ed Concordia River Forest 1973; Concordia Seminary 1973-74; *cr:* Teacher Rockford Luth HS 1973-77; New Luth HS 1977-; *ai:* Dean of Chapel; Coach Boys Soccer/Bsktbl/Bsbl; Athletic Dir; WADA 1989; Pilgrim Luth Church (Elder 1986-, Bd of Ed 1977-79); *office:* New Luth HS P O Box 33105 Green Bay WI 54303

STOCKARD, PAMELA D. HOPKINS, English Teacher; *b:* San Diego, CA; *m:* Jim; *c:* Kim, Jil; *ed:* (MA) Curr/Eng, OK St Univ 1978; *cr:* Eng Instr Joplin MO & Coffeyville KS 1964-75; Eng Teacher Sapulpa Jr HS 1975-89; Writing Instr Tulsa Jr Coll 1980-88; Eng Teacher San Bernardino Public Schls 1989-; *ai:* Chrldr Adv & Coach 1989-; Stu Cncl Spon 1980-88; Assembly Dir 1970-88; NEA 1964-; OK Ed Assn 1975-89; CA Ed Assn 1989-; *office:* San Bernardino HS 1850 E Street San Bernardino CA 92405

STOCKDILL, OWEN WAYNE, 5th Grade Teacher; *b:* Minot, ND; *m:* Carrie Joyce Bender; *c:* Deanna, Danielle; *ed:* (BS) Elem Ed/Phys Ed, Dickinson St Univ 1977; *cr:* 5th Grade Instr Divide Cty Public Schls 1977-79, Mandan Public Schls 1979-; *ai:* Asst Boys Bsktbl, Asst Girls Track, Amer Legion Bsbl Head Coach; *home:* 1032 Adobe Trl Mandan ND 58554

STOCKER, JOYCE ANN, English Teacher; *b:* Middlebourne, WV; *c:* Stephen, Sally; *ed:* (BS) Eng, WV Univ 1956; (MA) Scndry Ed, OH Univ 1968; *cr:* Eng Teacher Preston Cty 1956-57; 4th Grade Teacher Farmington MI 1957-59; Eng Teacher River View HS 1965-; *ai:* Jr Class, Future Teachers, NHS Adv; Delta Kappa Gamma; Rotary Club Teacher of Yr 1989; *home:* 1015 S 16th Coshocton OH 43812

STOCKER, JOYCE SAUNDERS, 8th Grade Teacher English Comp; *b:* West Wyoming, PA; *m:* Robert E.; *c:* Desiree Stackhouse, Rebecca Genelow, Joyce Scrobola; *ed:* (BM) Music, Coll Misericordia 1953; Addl Studies/Music/Writing/Eng/Humanities/Bucknell Univ/Wilkes Coll/Coll Misericordia/Mary Wood Coll/PA St Univ; *cr:* Music/Lang Teacher West Pittston Sch Dist 1953-60; 5th-8th Grades Music Teacher 1970-78; 8th Grade Eng Comp Teacher 1978-; Lang Arts Dept Chm of MS 1982- WY Area Sch Dist; *ai:* WY Area Sch Dist Prof Dev Plan Mem & Sec of Comm; WAEA/PSEA/NEA 1953-60 & 1970-; NCTE 1983-; NE PA Writing Cncl 1987-; Delta Kappa Gamma Intnl Music Chm 1983-; United Meth Church Choir Dir & Organist 1958-; Dir Centennial Choir Wyoming PA; Wyoming Area Faclty Writing Comm; Judge on St & Natl Lvl Natl His Day Act 1985-; *office:* Wyoming Area Sch Dist Memorial Street Exeter PA 18643

STOCKS, STEPHANIE ROSE, Science/Bible/Phys Ed Teacher; *b:* Huntsville, AL; *ed:* (BS) Sci/Sociology, Trevecca Nazarene Coll 1980; (MS) Scndry Sch Instr, TN St Univ 1986; *cr:* Bio/Phys Sci/Chem Teacher 1980-85, Life Sci/Earth Sci/Bible/Phys Ed Teacher 1985- Donelson Chrstn Acad: *ai:* Coach Cross Country 1983-, Track & Field 1984-; Jr HS Winterim Spon; 7th Grade Excursion Jekyll Island GA Sci Stud; NSTA 1987-; TN Scndry Schls Athletics Coaches Organization 1988-; Civitans 1987-89; 1st Church of Nazarene Teacher 1987-; NSTA Convention Atlanta GA 1990; Outstanding Young Women of America 1987; *office:* Donelson Chrstn Acad 3151 Stafford Dr Nashville TN 37214

STOCKTON, JOLENE HOGREFE, Third Grade Teacher; *b:* San Diego, CA; *m:* Santiago Jim; *c:* Santi; *ed:* General Degree Liberal Arts, Cottey Coll 1964; (BS) Elem Ed, 1966, (MA) Guidance/Counseling, 1968 Univ of NM; *cr:* Teacher Cochiti Elem Sch 1967-72; Elem Cnslr Carlas Rey & Chaparral & Stronghurst & Cochiti & Griegos 1972-77; Teacher Whittier Elem Sch 1977-; *ai:* Soccer & Little League Active Mom; Sch Improvement Team; Prgm Planning Comm; Phi Delta Kappa Mem, Elem Teacher Awd 1988; Delta Kappa Gamma, PEO Sisterhood Mem; *office:* Whittier Elem Sch 1110 Quincy SE Albuquerque NM 87108

STOCKTON, JUDITH BEELER, Sixth Grade Teacher; *b:* Nashville, TN; *m:* Kent F.; *c:* Grant, Bret; *ed:* (BS) Elem Ed, Mid TN St Univ 1960; (MS) Elem Ed, TN St Univ 1981; *cr:* 2nd Grade Teacher Donelson Elem Sch 1960-68; Adult Ed Teacher Metropolitan Nashville Schls 1970-74; Coord Gifted Ed 1978-79, 6th Grade Instr 1982-86 Scales Elem Sch; 6th Grade Instr Brentwood Mid Sch 1986-; *ai:* At-Risk Prgm Coord; 7th-8th Grade Boys Academic Skills & Classroom Behaviors; NEA. TN Ed Assn, Williamson Cty Ed Assn; Parent Volunteer Prgm COORD; *home:* 5112 Meadow Lake Rd Brentwood TN 37027

STODDARD, WESLEY D., Vocational Education Teacher; *b:* Woodland, CA; *m:* Letitia Wood; *c:* Gail, Sandra; *ed:* (AA) Liberal Art, Sierra Coll 1964; (BA) Industrial Art, 1967, (MA) Industrial Art, 1972 Fresno St Coll; *cr:* Teacher Merced Union HS 1968-82, Quincy Jr/Sr HS 1982-; *ai:* VICA Adv; Frosh Ftbl Coach; Ski Coach & Instr; CA Industrial Technology Ed Assn 1968-; *office:* Quincy Jr/Sr HS PO Box 10400 Quincy CA 95971

STOFFEL, WALLACE JAMES, Mathematics Department Teacher; *b:* Huntington, IN; *m:* Janet Gail Bowman; *c:* Kyle, Doug; *ed:* (BS) Math, Huntington Coll 1962; (MS) Counseling, St Francis Coll 1964; Cmptr Programing Endorsement, Notre Dame 1975; Driver Ed Cert 1965; *cr:* Teacher/Coach Lincoln Sch 1962-64, Central Sch 1964-67, S Campus HS 1967-69, Huntington N HS 1970-; *ai:* Bsktbl, Track, Ftbl, Bsbl Coach; Cmptr Club; Huntington Cty Classroom Teacher (Chm, Negotiator) 1963-; ISTA, NEA 1962-; Semi-St Bsbl & Bsktbl 1970-74; Huntington Recreation Dir 1963-67; Knights of Columbus Mem 1962-; Outstanding Educator Huntington Cty Cmmty Schls 1964-66, 1986; Natl Sci Fnd Grant Cmptr Sci 1974-75; *office:* Huntington North HS 450 Mc Gahn St Huntington IN 46750

STOKES, ALBERT B., III, 10th-12th Grade His Teacher; *b:* Columbia, SC; *ed:* (BA) His, Roanoke Coll 1971; (MED) Scndry Ed/His, Clemson Univ 1981; Advanced Placement Cert; *cr:* Teacher Starr Elem Sch 1971-73, Anderson Acad 1975-79, Crescent HS 1979-; Dept Chm Crescent HS 1981-; *ai:* Academic Competition Teams Spon; Peer Teacher Evaluator; Peer Coaching Building Coord; NEA, SC Ed Assn 1979-; SC Historical Society, SC Cncl of Soc Stud 1987-; Sons Confederate Veterans (Adjutant 1986-88, Paymaster 1989-, Historian 1984-86); Cresent Teacher of Yr 1987; Outstanding Amer His Teacher of SC 1988; *office:* Crescent HS P O Box 88 Iva SC 29655

STOKES, BOBBIE VAULX, Sixth Grade Chair; *b:* Brownsville, TN; *m:* John R. Sr.; *c:* Sherry C., John R. Sr.; *ed:* (BA) Elem Ed, Lane Coll 1958; Grad Stud Memphis St Univ; *cr:* 1st Grade Teacher Carnes Elem 1958-62, Georgia Ave Elem 1964-69, Goodlett 1970-73; 1st/6th Grade Teacher Knight Rd 1973-; *ai:* Grade Chm; Spelling Bee Coord; Memphis Ed Assn, TN Ed Assn, Nea 1958-; Jack & Jill of America Pres 1979-81; Shelby Cty Link Inc Champlain 1985-88; Foster Care Adoption Bd of Dirs 1988-; Task Force Mem.

STOKES, DANIEL C., Mathematics Teacher; *b:* Chicago, IL; *m:* Modena Sue Keeling; *c:* Kathleen, Jennifer, Emily; *ed:* (BA) Math/Theatre, Blackburn Coll 1973; (MAT) Comm, Webster Univ 1977; Cmptr Instruction; *cr:* Teacher Hancock Place Sch Dist 1974-79; Mgr Wagner Group 1979-81; Teacher Valley Park Sch Dist 1981-; *ai:* Mentor, Schlsp, Prof Dev Comm; Network for Educl Dev Cadre; MNEA, NEA VP 1987-88; NCTM 1988-; Educl Employees Credit Union Rep; Adjunct Faculty Webster Univ Math 1978-, Math Cmptr 1988-; *office:* Valley Park Sch Dist 356 Meramec Station Rd Valley Park MO 63088

STOKES, GLORIA BRYANT, Latin Teacher; *b:* Macon, GA; *m:* Franklin S.; *c:* Bryant F., Ginia C.; *ed:* (BA) Latin, 1965, (MED) Mid Grades/Latin, 1972 Mercer Univ; *cr:* Latin Teacher Northeast HS 1965-72; 6th-7th Grade Teacher Agnes Barden Elem 1972-84; Latin Teacher Southwest HS 1984-88, Jonesboro HS; *ai:* SW Chrldrs Coach; Latin & Beta Club Spon; Foreign Lang Assn of GA Flag Mem; Pine Forest Baptist Church Mem; St Beta Club Spon 1966; STAR Teacher 1989; *home:* 7941 King Henry Ct Jonesboro GA 30236

STOKES, LILLIE BALLARD, Teacher Math Dept Chairperson; *b:* Clinton, NC; *ed:* (BS) Elem Ed, Fayetteville St Univ 1972; (MS) Elem Ed, Campbell Univ 1983; *cr:* Math Teacher Bulter Ave Sch 1972-73; Rdng Teacher Tyrrell Elem Sch 1973-74; Soc Stud Teacher Columbia HS 1974-75; Elem Math Teacher Sampson Mid Sch 1975-; *ai:* Drama Club; Grade Level & Steering Comm Chairperson; Sex Ed, Child Abuse, Exceptional Children Comms; Sch Rep Southern Assn Team, Math Conference, Pegasus Rdng Prgm; NC Teachers of Math Assn, NCAE, NEA, PTA, Delta Sigma Theta Mem; ACT (Mem, Clinton City Schls Pres); Sunday Sch Teacher; Environmental Awareness Leader; Pastors Aid & Missionary Club; Vacation Bible Sch Teacher;Jr Choir Dir; Sr Choir Mem; Cape Fear Assembly 263 Loyal Lady Ruler; *home:* PO Box 24 Clinton NC 28328

STOKES, LOIS D. PENNY, ABE Teacher; *b:* Bessemer, AL; *m:* Cleve; *c:* Lebanian; *ed:* (BS) Elem Ed, 1954, (MED) Elem Ed, 1965 AL St Univ; *cr:* Teacher Oak Grove Jr HS 1954-61, Trinity Gardens & Brazier Elem Sch 1962-70, Thomas Elem Sch 1970-75, Stanton Rd Elem Sch 1975-80, Brazier Elem Sch 1980-86; ABE Teacher Davidson 1980-; *home:* 1073 Joy Ln Mobile AL 36617

STOKES, PEARL SHIPMAN, 7th-8th Grades Math Teacher; *b:* Elamville, AL; *m:* Vaughn, Jr.; *c:* Larry; *ed:* (BS) Sci/Math, AL St Univ 1963; (MS) Ed/Sci, Troy St Univ 1972; *cr:* Teacher Rebecca Comer HS 1963-67, Clio Public HS 1968-69, Clio HS 1969-80, Clio Jr HS 1980-; *ai:* Spon; Beta Club; Sr Class 4-H; Chairperson; Sch Testing Prgrm Sch Self Study; Performance Based Accreditation Prgm of Local Sch; Mem Barbour Cty Need Assessment Comm; Math/Sci Curr Comm of Barbour Cty Schls; AL Teachers Assn Faculty Rep 1978-80/Service 1979-80; Barbour Cty Teachers Assn Secy 1977-79; Eunita Taylor Chapter #867 Order of Eastern Star Secy 1967-; Ladies Aide Missionary Society VP 1988-; Teacher of Yr 1969 Clio Public Sch; Teacher of Yr 1989-; Clio K-8 Sch; Sci Teacher of Yr 1988-89 Clio K-8 Sch; *home:* PO Box 52 Clio AL 36017

STOKES, VICKI GRAHAM, Guidance Counselor; *b:* Batesville, AR; *m:* Tommy; *c:* Tonia; *ed:* (ASE) Ed, N AR Comm Coll 1978; (BSE) Math, 1979, (MSE) Spec Ed, 1981 Univ of Cntrl AR; Grad Trng & Cert Guidance/Counseling UCA; Cmptr Programming Various Institutions; *cr:* Spec Ed Teacher 1979-84, Math Teacher 1984-86, Spanish Teacher 1979-, K-12th Grade Guidance Cnslr 1986- Bruno-Pyatt Sch; Dist Testing Coord Marion Cty Rural Schls 1986-; *ai:* Sr Class, Span Club, Drug Prevention Club Spon; Delta Kappa Gamma Prof Affairs Chm 1989-; AR Sch Cncl Assn; AR Assn of Guidance Counseling Membership Aed 1987; AR Ed Assn, NEA Elections Comm 1988-; Mem AR Teacher Ed Cert & Evaluation Comm 1986-88; AR Power & Light Grant; AR Ed Assn Mini-Grant; *home:* Rt 1 Box 121 Everton AR 72633

STOLEN, HANNELORE M. A., Jr HS Teacher; *b:* Noiken, Germany; *m:* Derrick Wayne; *c:* Angelica; *ed:* BA Equivalent Ed, Teachers Coll Germany 1964; (BA) Ger, St Thomas Coll 1980; *cr:* Teacher Elly, Heuss, Knapp Schule Scndry Tech Sch 1964-66, Presentation of Mary Sch 1968-; *ai:* Stu Cncl Adv; Soc Stud & Foreign Lang Chairperson; Adult Ed Ger; *office:* Presentation of Mary Sch 1695 Kennard Maplewood MN 55109

STOLL, KEN, Latin Teacher; *b:* Cincinnati, OH; *m:* Johnette Mohn; *c:* Ken Jr., Rob, Andrew, Emily, Jacob; *ed:* (AB) Eng, 1963, (MED) Ed, 1965 Xavier Univ; *cr:* Eng/Latin Teacher Reading HS 1963-65, Milford HS 1965-83; Dist Foreign Lang Coord Milford HS 1972-83; Eng/Latin Teacher Mariemont HS 1983-; *ai:* Var Boys Soccer Coach; OH Classical Conference 1970-; OH Foreign Lang Teachers Assn 1963-; Conducted Wkshps on Bld Latin Prgms Twice OH Classic Conference 3 Times OH Foreign Lang Teachers Assn; Greater Cincinatti Fnd Grant Amer Classical League Conference at Miami Univ 1986; *office:* Mariemont HS 3812 Pocahontas Ave Cincinnati OH 45227

STOLL, WILLIAM DAVID, Mathematics Teacher; *b:* Royal Oak, MI; *m:* Karen Susan Reppenhagen; *c:* Jeffrey, Andrew; *ed:* (BS) Math, N MI Univ 1982; *cr:* Math Teacher Tawas Area Schls 1983-; *ai:* Math Competition Team & Girls Var Bsktbl Coach; MI Cncl Teachers of Math 1981-; Zion Luth Church (Bd of Elders, Chm) 1990; *office:* Tawas Jr HS 255 West M-55 Tawas City MI 48763

STOLTZ, SYLVIA A., 3rd Grade Teacher; *b:* Hammond, IN; *m:* Dennis W.; *c:* Steven, David, Karen; *ed:* (BA) Ed, Concordia 1962; *cr:* 2nd/3rd Grade Teacher Zion Luth 1962-64/79-85; Teacher Garfield 1985-1988; Black Hawk 1988-; *ai:* NEA; SDEA; RCEA; Presenter at SD Luth Teachers Conf 1989; Presenter at Math Conf Regional Oct 1989.

STOLZ, ANNA MAPLES, Kindergarten Teacher; *b:* Sugden, OK; *m:* William E.; *c:* Kathy Van Cleave, Mike, Steven; *ed:* (BS) Elem Ed, Central St Coll 1958; *cr:* 1st Grade Teacher Garfield 1958-59; Kndgtn Teacher United Meth Church 1965-68, Kingfisher Public Schls 1969-; *ai:* Staff Dev Comm; OEA/NEA 1969-85; AFT 1985-87; *office:* Gilmour Elem Sch Oak And Chisholm Kingfisher OK 73750

STONAKER, ASHLEY SHACKELFORD, Fifth Grade Teacher; *b:* Charlottesville, VA; *m:* David M.; *c:* L. Scott; *ed:* (BS) Spec Ed, Univ of VA 1966; N Harris Cty Coll, Sam Houston St Univ, TX Wesleyan Univ; Advancement on Career Ladder & Prof Growth; Completed Real Estate Trng & Received St License; *cr:* Primary Spec Ed Teacher Magruder Elem Sch 1967-68; 1st Grade Teacher Crimora Elem Sch 1968-69; LLD Teacher Rockaway Meadow Sch 1969; Gross Motor Teacher St Francis Episcopal Day Sch 1972-77; 4th/5th Grade Teacher Lemm Elem Sch 1977-; *ai:* Coached Odyssey of Mind Teams; Conducted In-Service Trng for Fellow Teachers in Sci & Composition; Sci Teachers Assn of TX 1988-; TX Assn for Gifted & Talented 1986-88; TX & Klein Ed Assn (Rep 1983) 1981-89; Houston Society Prevention of Cruelty to Animals Volunteer 1984-; TX Wildlife Rehabilition Coalition Volunteer 1989-; *office:* Lemm Elem Schl 19034 Joanleigh Dr Spring TX 77388

STONE, ALIEDA MAE, Second Grade Teacher; *b:* Miles City, MT; *m:* Thomas Walter Helm; *c:* Starre Y.; *ed:* (AA) Sci Miles Cmmty Coll 1978; (BS) Elem Ed Mt St Univ 1981; *cr:* 4th Grade Teacher 1981-82/1983-87; 3rd Grade Teacher 1982-83; GarfieldSch; 2nd Grade Teacher Highland Park Sch 1987-; *office:* Highland Park Sch 1604 Main St Miles City MT 59301

STONE, AMELIA PATRICIA, English Teacher; *b:* Boston, MA; *m:* Paul G.; *ed:* (BA) Elem Ed, New England Coll 1976; (MAT) Eng, Keene St Coll 1987; Project Adventure; Bread Loaf Sch of Eng 1990; *cr:* 6th-8th Grade Teacher Washington Center Sch 1979-81; 6th Grade Teacher Bernardston Elem 1981-82; 7th Grade Eng Teacher 1982-87, 8th Grade Writing Teacher 1988 Brattleboro Union Jr HS; Basic Writing Instr Comm Coll of VT 1988-89; 7th Grade Eng Teacher Brattleboro Union Jr HS 1988-; *ai:* Artists-in-Ed, Assemblies, Public Sch Approval Media Comm Chairperson; London Theatre Adventure Co-Leader; NCTE, NEA, ASCD; Storytelling Article Published; *home:* RR 2 Box 788 Dummerston VT 05346

STONE, BERNADETTE BARKOUSKIE, English I Teacher; *b:* Mexia, TX; *m:* W. N.; *c:* William R., Monette L.; *ed:* (BS) Elem Ed, 1960, (MA) Eng, 1963 Sam Houston St Univ; *cr:* 4th/5th/9th Grade Teacher Mexia Ind Sch Dist 1963-; *ai:* Sch Newspaper Adv-Teacher; Mexia HS Honors Chm; TSTA; *home:* Rt 2 Box 196A Mexia TX 76667

STONE, CAROLYN SPENCER, Third Grade Teacher; *b:* Tulsa, OK; *m:* Loye E.; *c:* Terri Campbell, Ronnie, Paul; *ed:* Music, Baptist Bible Coll 1970; *cr:* Kndgtn Teacher Victory Baptist Schls 1973-76; 3rd Grade Teacher Moody Chrstn Acad 1980-84, Tulsa Chrstn Schls 1984-; *ai:* Spelling Bee Spon; Claremore Baptist Temple 1984-; Soprano Soloist; MO Assn of Chrstn Schls Teacher Convention Speaker; *office:* Tulsa Chrstn Schls 3434 S Garnet Tulsa OK 74146

STONE, DONNA CHRISTINE, English/Leadership Teacher; *b:* Sealy, TX; *ed:* (BSED) Phys Ed, Abilene Chrstn Univ 1985; (MSED) Phys Ed, Baylor Univ 1986; *cr:* Teacher/Coach Friendswood HS 1986-; *ai:* Var Girls Bsktbl & Asst Girls Track Coach; FCA Spon; Campus Improvement Comm; TX St Teachers

Assn, TX Girls Coaches Assn 1986-; *office:* Friendswood HS 702 Greenbriar Dr Friendswood TX 77546

STONE, ELLEN WEAVER, Soc Stud Dept Chairperson; *b:* Mc Allen, TX; *m:* Larry G.; *c:* Clifford, Elizabeth; *ed:* (BA) Govt/His, 1972; (MA) His/Govt; *cr:* Teacher Donna HS 1972-75; Teacher Canterberry Sch 1980-83; Teacher Mc Allen HS 1984-90; *ai:* Mock Trial Team; Citizen Bee Team; Natl Bicentennial Competition Constitution & Bill of Rights; TX St Teachers Assn; TX NCSS; League of Women Voters; *office:* Mc Allen HS 2021 La Vista Mc Allen TX 78501

STONE, EMILY WALL, English Teacher; *b:* Quanah, TX; *m:* Greg; *c:* Justin; *ed:* (BS) Scndry Ed/Eng/Sociology, TX Tech Univ 1985; Span Cert; *cr:* Teacher Chillicothe HS 1985-; *ai:* NHS Adv; UIL Spelling Coach; TX St Teachers Assn; *office:* Chillicothe HS 1 Eagle St Chillicothe TX 79225

STONE, GAYLE KLOEPPEL, 5th Grade Teacher; *b:* Sioux City, IA; *m:* Robert K.; *c:* Rick, Mike, Chris; *ed:* (BAE) Elem Ed, Wayne St Coll 1970; Grad Courses Elem Ed; *cr:* 4th-6th Grade Elem Teacher Lincoln Elem Sch 1970-; *ai:* Lincoln Sch Red Cross Rep; NW IA Area Ed Agency Teacher; Advisory Comm Mem; Sioux City Ed Assn 1970-; *office:* Lincoln Elem Sch 115 Midvale Ave Sioux City IA 51104

STONE, GERALDINE MC CROSKEY, Third Grade Teacher; *b:* Washington Cty, VA; *m:* Curtis Mitchell Sr.; *c:* Curtis M. II; *ed:* (BS) Elem Ed, Radford Univ 1952; Grad Courses Ed, Univ of VA; *cr:* 4th Grade Teacher Valley Inst Elem 1952-67; 3rd Grade Teacher High Point Elem 1967-; *ai:* Stu At-Risk Comm; NEA, VEA, Washington Cty Ed Assn; Edgemont Presbyn Church; *home:* 23 Bramble Ln Bristol VA 24201

STONE, JOHN RANDALL, JR., Music Teacher/Band Director; *b:* Bloomsburg, PA; *m:* Letha Mary Payne; *c:* Bethany A., Matthew R.; *ed:* (BS) Music Ed, Mansfield Univ 1979; West Chester Univ, Bloomsburg Univ; *cr:* Band Dir Sayre Area Sch Dist 1979-86; Music Teacher/Band Dir Bloomsburg Area Sch Dist 1986-; *ai:* Band Dir Elem & Mid Sch; Brass Instr HS Marching Band; PA Music Educators Assn, PA St Educators Assn, Music Educators Natl Conference 1979-; *office:* Bloomsburg Area Sch Dist 12th & Railroad Sts Bloomsburg PA 17815

STONE, KATHIE DORMAN, Health Occupations Coordinator; *b:* Monmouth, IL; *m:* Paul W.; *c:* Gary, Kristy; *ed:* (RN) Nursing, Luth Hospital 1965; (BS) Voc Ed, Wayland Baptist 1985; Certified CPR Instr; Certified TPN Admin; *cr:* Moline Public Sch Dist Head Start 1980-82; Carbon Cliff-Barstow Sch Dist 1978-83; High Plains Baptist Hospital 1981-83; Caprock HS 1983-; *ai:* Health Occupations Stud of America Chapter 49 Adv; Univ of TX Curr & TEA Curr Comm; TX Health Occupations Teachers Pres of Area IV 1987-89, Service Awd 1989; Outstanding Caprock Teacher 1990; *home:* Rt 7 Box 3-6 Amarillo TX 79118

STONE, KAY S., English Teacher; *b:* Talladega, AL; *m:* Gordon P. Jr.; *c:* Gordon P. III, M. Brett; *ed:* (BA) Elem Ed, Univ of Montevallo 1967; *cr:* 6th Grade Teacher Sandtown Elem 67-70; 1st Grade Teacher Butts Rd Elem 73-79; 7th Grade Teacher Great Bridge Jr HS 83-; *ai:* 7th Grade Spon; NEA; VEA; CEA; VATE; PTA Life Mem Awd 1979; *home:* 413 Woodwards Ford Rd Chesapeake VA 23320

STONE, KRISTEN PATRICIA, 3rd/4th Grade Tag Teacher; *b:* Parkersburg, WV; *ed:* (BA) Elem Ed, Marietta Coll 1977; Ohio Univ; Ohio St *cr:* 2nd Grade Teacher North Hills Sch 1977-78; Teacher Aide Santa Rosa Schls 1978-79; 2nd/4th Grade Teacher 1979-89; 3rd/4th Split Tag Class Teacher 1989- Marietta City Schls; *ai:* Negotiating Comm for MEA 88-89; Curriculum Comms; Labor/Management Group; Delta Kappa Gamma; Alpha Delta Kappa; Aauw Bd Mem 1987-89; Marietta Ed Assn; Jennings Scholar 1988-89; *home:* 512 7th Marietta OH 45750

STONE, MARIANNE E., Second Grade Teacher; *b:* St Paul, MN; *m:* Ross A.; *c:* Kim, Sarah; *ed:* (BS) Elem Ed - Magna Cum Laude, Moorhead St 1973; Elem Ed, Mankato St Univ; *cr:* 4th Grade Long Term Substitute Teacher Freeborn Elem 1973; 2nd Grade Teacher Ellendale-Geneva Sch 1974-; *ai:* Comm Ed Aerobic Teacher; Continuing Ed Chairperson 1976-; Church (Chrstn Ed Chairperson 1989-, Chancel Choir 1974-, Faith Fitness Fellowship Group 1989-); *office:* Ellendale-Geneva Sch School St Ellendale MN 56026

STONE, MARY KOHNS, 2nd Grade Teacher; *b:* Fremont, MI; *m:* Ronald D.; *c:* Ellen M., Adam E.; *ed:* (BS) Elem Ed, IN Wesleyan Univ 1966; (MA) Elem Ed, Ball St Univ 1968; IN Univ Kokomo; *cr:* 1st Grade Teacher Park Elem 1966-68; Kndgtn Teacher 1969-79, 2nd Grade Teacher 1980 Hamilton Heights Elem; *ai:* Mid Cntrl Rdng Cncl VP 1988-89; IN St Teachers Assn; Red Cross Volunteer 1980-; Sheridan Wesleyan Youth Dir 1979-; Missionary Society Pres 1983-88; *office:* Hamitlon Heights Elem Sch 25150 State Rd 19 Arcadia IN 46030

STONE, MAZIE ANNE, English/His/Geography Teacher; *b:* Wrightsville, GA; *ed:* (BA) Eng, FL St Univ 1967; (MS) Eng, GA Southern Coll 1978; Cmptr Courses; Educl Testing & Evaluation; Teacher Effectiveness Trng I & II; *cr:* 7th-9th Grade Eng Teacher Fort Myers Jr HS & Dunbar Cntrl 7th Grade Center 1967-70; 9th-11th Grade Eng Teacher Early Cty Jr & Sr HS 1970-77; 8th-12th Grade Rdng Teacher Vidalia Comprehensive HS 1978-81; 7th-12th Grade Eng/Bible/Psych/Journalism Teacher Robert Toombs Chrstn Acad 1981-83; Teacher Paul Anderson Youth Home 1983-84; 7th-10th Eng/His/Geography Teacher Faith Chrstn Sch 1984-; *ai:* ECHS Bible Club; RTCA Debate Team; Sr Spon; Steering Comm to Develop Mid Sch; Eng Dept Head Dunbar Cntrl 7th Grade Center; Lee Cty Teachers Assn, FL Ed Assn, NEA, GA Ed Assn; Delta Kappa Gamma (Chapter Secy 1976-77, Chaplain 1990-92); United Meth Women Secy 1987-88; United Meth Church (Sunday Sch Secy, Mission Chm, Ofcl Bd) 1988-; Daughters of Amer Revolution, United Daughters of Confederacy,St Joseph Historical Society; *office:* Faith Chrstn Sch 801 20th St Port Saint Joe FL 32456

STONE, PEGGY R., Gifted/Talented Coord; *b:* Malakoff, TX; *c:* James G. III, Janell; *ed:* (BS) Elem Ed, Sam Houston St Univ 1964; Univ of Houston Victoria; *cr:* 5th Grade Teacher Jackson Elem Sch; 6th/8th Grade Teacher Industrial Jr HS; 5th Grade Teacher La Ward Elem Sch, Vanderbilt Elem Sch; K-8th Grade Teacher Industrial Elem Sch; *ai:* Assn of TX Prof Educators, TX Assn for Gifted & Talented; Industrial Assn for Gifted & Talented; *office:* Industrial Jr HS PO Box 208 Lolita TX 77971

STONE, SANDRA LOUISE, Assistant Principal; *b:* Ironwood, MI; *m:* David L.; *c:* David L., Christopher, Charles; *ed:* (BA) Soc Stud Ed, Univ of TX El Paso 1976; (MA) Educl Admin, Sul Ross Univ 1987; *cr:* 4th Grade Teacher Clardy Elem 1976-83; 5th/6th Grade Teacher Cielo Vista Elem 1983-85; 6th Grade Gifted Ed Teacher Mac Arthur Mid Sch 1985-86; Asst Prin Vilas Elem 1987-; *ai:* Phi Delta Kappa 1986-; Delta Kappa Gamma Secy 1989-; El Paso Admin Assn Secy 1987-; *office:* Vilas Elem Sch 220 Lawton Div For Administration El Paso TX 79902

STONE, SIDNEY P., 7th/8th Grade Lang Art Teacher; *b:* Decatur, IL; *m:* Cheryl Sue Devall; *c:* Parker, Mindy, Trey; *ed:* (BA) Eng, Millikin Univ 1971; *cr:* 7th/8th Grade Eng Teacher Cumberland Jr HS 1971-; *ai:* Literary Instr 1971-; Coached 6th Grade Bsktbl 1976-77, 7th Grade Bsktbl 1977-78; NEA, IL Ed Assn 1988-; *home:* RR 1 Box 39A Greenup IL 62428

STONE, VIRGINIA LEE, 6th Grade Teacher; *b:* Springfield, IL; *m:* Robert A.; *c:* Bradley, Mark, Bruce; *ed:* (BS) Eng/Elem, IL St 1952; Advanced Rdng Methods Certificate Millikin Univ 1960; Spec Math Wkshp 1970-72; Literary Coaches Clinics 1960-80; Cooperative Learning Courses 1988-; *cr:* Kndgtn Teacher Gibson City Grade Sch 1952-53; 1st Grade Teacher Rolla Elem 1953-54; Kndgtn Teacher Ft Leonard Wood Base Sch 1954-55; 1st Grade Teacher Illiopolis Grade Sch 1957-58; Eng Teacher Illiopolis Jr HS 1958-76; 4th Grade Teacher Riverton 1976-89; 6th Grade Teacher Riverton Mid Sch 1989-; *ai:* St Literary Comm Coach; Cooperative Learning Comm; IESA Comm Mem 1970-; IEA Secy 1959-61; NEA; Natl Rdng Cncl 1952-60; Natl Eng Teachers 1958-76; Catechism Teacher 1960-65; Jr Womens Club 1956-70; St Elizabeths Altar Society Secy 1960-64; Cancer Drive Chm 1965-70; *home:* RR 1 Box 233 Illiopolis IL 62539

STONECIPHER, BRENDA (VALLOWE), Family Support Specialist; *b:* Mt Vernon, IL; *m:* Larry D.; *c:* Andrea, Aaron; *ed:* (BSED) Soc Sci, E IL Univ 1974; Grad Stud Curr/Instruction/Media, S IL Univ; *cr:* Teacher Field Cmmty Consolidated Sch 1975-87, Blessed Sacrament Sch 1987-88; Family Support Specialist IL Dept of Public Aid 1988-; *ai:* Scholastic Bowl & Cheerleading Spon; Girls Bsktbl Coach; Dir Field Sch 5th-8th Grade Gifted Prgm; Delta Kappa Gamma, NCSS, Amer Assn of Univ Women; Memorial Hospital Orientation Prgm Sangamon Cty Schls Coord; *home:* 14 Penacook Dr Rochester IL 62563

STONEHOUSE, RICK B., English Teacher; *b:* Cody, WY; *m:* Jill Vannoy; *c:* Taylor, Ty; *ed:* (BS) Eng/Rdng Ed, 1982, (MA) Amer Stud, 1990 Univ of WY; *cr:* Eng/Rdng Teacher New Castle HS 1983-85; Eng Teacher Laramie Jr HS 1985-; *ai:* Coach Jr HS Ftbl, Bsktbl, Jr Sr HS Track, HS Skiing; PSIA Ski Instr 1986-; Phi Delta Kappa 1990; BPOE Elks 1983-; WY Cncl for Hum Activity Evaluator; *home:* 4317 Cheyenne Dr Laramie WY 82070

STONEKING, NANCY MARIE, Administrative Asst to Supt; *b:* Detroit, MI; *m:* Frank L.; *c:* Kathy; *ed:* (BA) Lang Art/Soc Stud, 1971, (MA) Elem Ed/Lang Art, 1974 Oakland Univ; Grad Stud; *cr:* Classroom Teacher 1971-80, Prgm STRIVE Teacher 1980-82, Chapter I Coord 1982-84 Utica Cmmty Schls; Acting Prin Ewell Elem 1983-84; Prin Burr Elem 1984-86; Coord of Elem Prgms 1986-89, Admin Asst Supt 1989- Utica Cmmty Schls; *ai:* Delegation Leader People to People Stu Ambassador Prgm; Supts Cabinet; Early Chldhd Ed Comm Mem; NAEYC, MI Assn of Sch Admins; Alpha Delta Kappa; Pres Macomb Assn of St & Federal Prgm Specialists 1987-88; *office:* Utica Cmmty Schls 51041 Shelby Rd Utica MI 48087

STONER, JAMES FREDERICK, JR., 6th-8th Grade Science Teacher; *b:* Lancaster, OH; *m:* Janet Louise Evans; *c:* James, Daniel, Sarah; *ed:* (BS) Elem Ed, OH Univ 1966; NFS, OH Dominican Coll; Micro-Cmptr, Hocking Tech Coll; *cr:* 5th Grade Teacher Logan Sch System; Sci Teacher St Mary Elem; *ai:* Sci Fair Mid Sch; Diocese of Columbus Sci Comm to Revise Sci Curr; OH Acad of Sci 1985-; Olive Dale Cmmty Band 1990; *office:* St Mary Elem Sch 309 E Chestnut St Lancaster OH 43130

STONNER, KATHY DODD, Kindergarten Teacher; *b:* Wichita Falls, TX; *m:* Brian; *ed:* (BSE) Elem Ed, Midwestern Univ 1973; (ME) Spec Ed/Diagnostician, Midwetern St Univ 1978; *cr:* Kndgtn Teacher Hardin Elem 1973-; *ai:* TX St Teachers Assn; Kndgtn Teachers of TX; Amateur Radio Emergency Service; Wichita Amateur Radio Society; Burkburnett Lib Bd (Bd Mem 1985-89 Pres 1988-89).

STOOKSBERRY, BARBARA ANN, Earth Science Teacher; *b:* El Paso, TX; *m:* Ronny Gilbert; *ed:* (BS) Geology/Earth Sci, Univ of TX Permion Basin 1974; (MA) Eng/Earth Sci, Sul Ross Univ 1986; *cr:* Sci Teacher Bowie Jr HS 1974-75, Kermit Jr HS 1975-; *ai:* Stu Cncl Spon; Honor Society Spon; ATPE 1977-; NSTA 1985-; Delta Kappa Gamma (Secy 1985-87 1st VP 1987-89); Delta Kappa Gamma Schlsp Recipient 1986.

STOOKSBERRY, MARY ELLEN NIELSEN, English/Drama Teacher; *b:* Martin, TN; *m:* Robert Michael; *c:* Eric, Patrick, Sarah B., Emily; *ed:* (BS) Eng Ed, Univ of TN 1976; *cr:* 7th/8th Grade Lang Art Teacher Waynesboro Mid Sch 1979-83; Adult Basic Teacher Weakley Cty Voc Center 1986-87; Eng/Drama Teacher Dresden HS 1987-; *ai:* Drama Club Spon & Adv; Soph Class Spon; Weakley Cty Ed Assn 1987-; TN Ed Assn, NEA 1979-; Wayne Cty Heart Assn Pres 1983-85; TN Performing Arts Acad 1990; *home:* 220 Oxford Martin TN 38237

STOPINSKI, PAMELA INGLE, Fourth Grade Teacher; *b:* Chattanooga, TN; *m:* Dean; *ed:* (BS) Elem Ed, 1978, (MED) Elem/Spec Ed, 1985 Mid TN St Univ; Cmptr Class, Motlow Coll; Sch Law, Assertive Discipline; *cr:* 4th Grade Teacher 1978-79, 3rd Grade Teacher 1979-86, 4th Grade Teacher 1986- R E Lee Elem; *ai:* Soc Stud & Textbook Comm; ASCD, TCEA Jr Rep; PTO Exec Comm Mem; Grant for Volunteer Prgm; *home:* 236 Motlow Coll Rd Normandy TN 37360

STOPPA, THOMAS M., History/Science Teacher; *b:* Alpena, MI; *ed:* (BSED) His, Cntrl MI Univ 1985; *cr:* His/Sci Teacher 1986-, Soc Stud Chm 1987- St Marys Preparatory; *ai:* Sr Class Adv & Substance Abuse Prgm Coord 1989-; Amer Historical Society, NSTA, NCSS; BSA (Troop Comm 1981-, Order of Arrow Vigil Adv 1987-), Vigil Honor & Founders Awd 1983; Outstanding Young Men of America 1988; *office:* St Marys Preparatory Sch 3535 Indian Trail Rd Orchard Lake MI 48033

STOPPER, VIRGINIA SWEET, Home Economics Teacher; *b:* Gardner, MA; *c:* Robert, Kathryn, Elizabeth; *ed:* (BS) Foods/Nutrition, Framingham Teachers 1951; (MS) Spec Ed, Cntrl CT St Univ; Intern, Mt Auburn Hospital Amer Dietetic Assn; *cr:* Home Ec Teacher Wolcott HS 1960-63; Teaching Dietitian Waterbury Hospital Sch on Nursing 1965-67; Diet Therapy Instr Practical Nurse Prgm Waterbury Hospital 1968-78; Nutrition & Diet Therapy/Home Ec/Bio Instr Warren F Kaynor Tech Sch 1976-78; Home Ec Teacher Great Oak Mid Sch 1978-; *ai:* Cheerleading & 8th Grade Class Adv; CT Ed Assn, Oxford Ed Assn; St Peters Parish Sunday Sch Supt 1967-79; Oxford Little League Mothers Pres 1968; Brownie Troop Leader 1969-71.

STOREY, JOHNNA VAUGHAN, 8th Grade Lang Arts Teacher; *b:* Albuquerque, NM; *c:* Jeanette, Bonnie; *ed:* (BA) Eng 1973, (MA) Eng, 1985 E NM Univ; Grad Stud Univ of NM; *cr:* Teachers Asst 1973-75, Instr 1975 E NM Univ; Eng Teacher Laguna-Acoma Jr/Sr HS 1976; Lang Arts Teacher Los Lunas Mid Sch 1979-; *ai:* Spon Conflict Resolution Prgm; Legends Team Leader; Los Lunas Mid Sch Tigerettes Spon & Choreographer 1989; NEA Membership Dir 1989-; Valencia Cty Arts Cncl All Arts Festival Comm 1989-; Los Lunas Effective Teaching Strategies (Presenter, Task Force) 1989-; Finalist Los Lunas Schls Distinguished Teacher Awd 1989; Los Lunas Mid Sch Yrbks Most Admired Teacher 1989-; Thanks to Teachers Excl Awd Finalist 1990; *office:* Los Lunas Mid Sch PO Box 1300 Los Lunas NM 87031

STOREY, PEGGY FULLER, 1st Grade Teacher; *b:* Elba, AL; *m:* Zackie L.; *c:* Zackary M.; *ed:* (BS) Elem Ed, Troy St Univ 1961; *cr:* 1st Grade Teacher Goodman Jr HS 1962-77, Zion Chapel Sch 1977-; *ai:* Southern Sch Accreditation Steering Comm for Re-Evaluation; Delta Kappa Gamma Corresponding Secy 1987-; AL Ed Assn Faculty Rep 1980-; *home:* Rt 1 Box 78L Elba AL 36323

STORINO, JOHN EDWARD, Social Studies Teacher; *b:* Tacoma, WA; *m:* Diana; *c:* Angela, Marie; *ed:* (BA) Bus Admin, Univ of Puget Sound 1962; (MA) Poly Sci, WA St Univ 1968; *cr:* Teacher Puyallup HS 1962-; *ai:* NEA, WA Ed Assn, Puyallup Ed 1962-; Sons of Italy Pres 1972-74; Amvets Post 5 Mem 1981-; Elks Lodge #174 Mem 1962-; Allenmore Mens Club, Golf Course Mem 1980-; *office:* Puyallup HS 105 7th St SW Puyallup WA 98371

STORK, JANICE A., English Teacher; *b:* Bluffton, IN; *m:* Ronald L.; *c:* Todd, Tammy Stork Denlinger; *ed:* (BA) Bio, Manchester Coll 1958; (MS) Scndry Ed, IN Univ 1974; *cr:* Eng Teacher Bluffton HS 1958-59, Concord Jr HS & Concord HS 1969-; *ai:* Fellowship of Christian Athletes Spon; Impact Core Team Mem; Kids Empowering Stu Co-Spon; Concord Teachers Assn VP 1983-84; IN St Teachers Assn, NEA, NCTE; Natl Questers VP 1987-88; Intnl Delta Kappa Gamma Recording Secy 1990-92; Republican Natl Comm; In Univ Var Club; *office:* Concord HS 59117 Minuteman Way Elkhart IN 46517

STORLIE, WILLARD STANLEY, Fifth Grade Teacher; *b:* Northfield, MN; *m:* Marietta Johnson; *c:* Heather L., Heidi M.; *ed:* (AA) General, Normandale Jr Coll 1970; (BS) Elem Ed, 1972, (MS) Elem Ed, 1977 Mankato St Univ; *cr:* 5th Grade Teacher Northview Elem 1972-79, Thomas Lake Elem 1979-84; 4th Grade Teacher Cedar Park Elem 1984-89; 5th Grade Teacher Echo Park Elem 1989-; *ai:* Yrbk Supvr; *office:* Echo Park Elem Sch 14100 Cty Rd 11 Burnsville MN 55337

STORMER, EUGENE E., APH English Instructor; *b:* Cincinnati, OH; *m:* Bette Jean Biederman; *c:* Patti J. Laws, Thomas S.; *ed:* (BA) Eng, Long Beach St Coll 1960; (MA) Eng, CA St Univ Long Beach 1967; Presentor Multiple Advanced Placement Seminars, CA St Comm for Gifted 1977; Lecturor Foreign Study League, European Stud Prgm 1970-74; *cr:* Eng Dept Chm 1967-87, Eng Instr 1961-, Coord of Gifted & Talented 1962-, APH Eng Instr 1987- Bolsa Grande HS; *ai:* Orange Cty

Academic Decathelon Coach; General Schlsp Adv; All Japan Kendo Fed Yudansha 1961-; Natl Teacher Hall of Fame Mem 1971; Dir Gifted & Talented Bolsa Grande 1962-88; *office:* Bolsa Grande HS 9401 Westminster Blvd Garden Grove CA 92644

STORTI, DANIEL ANTHONY, Mathematics Teacher/AV Coord; *b:* Providence, RI; *m:* Jane Kanaczet; *ed:* (BA) Liberal Art, Providence Coll 1971; (MA) Elem Ed, 1974, (MS) Instructional Technology, 1987 RI Coll; *cr:* Teacher Tyler Sch 1971-73; Math Teacher 1973-, AV Coord 1985- Coventry Jr HS; *ai:* AV Club; RIEMA, RI Math Teachers Assn; Natl Ski Patrol; *office:* Coventry Jr HS 19 Foster Dr Coventry RI 02816

STORTZ, G. BARRY, Mathematics/Computer Teacher; *b:* Ottawa, IL; *m:* Barbara A. Koll; *c:* Benji T., Bryan G., Brett F.; *ed:* (BA) Math, Bradley Univ 1968; Advanced Stud Ed, Math, Cmptr Sci; *cr:* Math Teacher Farmington East HS 1968-80; Math/Cmptr Teacher Dunlap HS 1986-; *ai:* Farmington HS Head Ftbl & Wrestling Coach; Dunlap HS Class Spon; NCTM, NEA, IL Ed Assn, Dunlap Ed Assn; Dunlap Recreation Bd VP 1985-; Farmington HS Excl in Ed 1980; Dulnap HS Teacher of Yr Awd 1988, 1989; *office:* Dunlap HS Shaw Rd Dunlap IL 61525

STORY, BILLIE DIANE TARKINGTON, Reading Specialist; *b:* Chesapeake, VA; *m:* William Joseph III; *c:* William J. IV, Warren H.; *ed:* (BS) Elem Ed, ODU 1974; (MS) Rdng, Univ of Va 1988; *cr:* Teacher 1974-88, Rdng Specialist 1988- Suffolk City Public Schls; *ai:* NEA, VEA, EAS 1974-; SRC 1974-, Teacher of Yr 1989-; Womans Club (Dist Head of Ed Dept 1965-66, VP, Treas, Secy 1965-); Waverly Baptist Church (Teacher, Dist Treas Asst) 1962-; Suffolk Rdng Teacher of Yr 1989; Stus Published Book; Article Published; *office:* Suffolk City Schls Suffolk City Sch Bd PO Box 582 Suffolk VA 23434

STORY, RAY C., Sixth Grade Teacher; *b:* Bremerton, WA; *m:* Kathleen A. Schultz-Story; *ed:* (BA) Elem Ed, W WA Univ 1978; Numerous Courses Seattle Pacific Univ; *cr:* 2nd-4th Grade Teacher Silver Lake Elem 1978-81; 5th Grade Teacher Liberty Elem 1981-82; 3rd Grade Teacher Emerson Elem 1982-83; 6th Grade Teacher Clear Creek Elem 1983-; *ai:* Stu Patrol Adv; Cmptr Specialist; Co-Adv Outdoor Ed Prgm; Intermediate Team Leader Building Mangement; WEA, NEA; PTA; *office:* Clear Creek Elem Sch 3999 Sunde Rd Silverdale WA 98383

STOUT, CAROL TOUCHTON, Math Teacher; *b:* Dade City, FL; *m:* James D.; *ed:* (BS) Math Ed, Cumberland Coll 1983; *cr:* Teacher Burgin HS 1983-84; Pasco Comprehensive HS 1984-; *ai:* Jr Class Spon; Geometry Mu Alpha Theta Coach & Spon; Comm Comm; Womens Ensemble 2nd Soprano 1989-; *office:* Pasco Comprehensive H S 1204 State Rd 52 Dade City FL 33525

STOUT, CHARLES ROBERT, 6th Grade Teacher; *b:* Elizabeth, NJ; *m:* Dolores Ann Sobozenski; *c:* Mark R., Scott R.; *ed:* (BS) Bus, Seton Hall Univ 1960; (MA) Admin/Supervision, Kean Coll 1968; Grad Work Fairleigh Dickinson Univ; *cr:* Teacher Toms River Sch Dist 1960-; *ai:* Teaching Gifted & Talented Children & Cmptr Literacy to Young Children; NJEA, NEA, TRTA Sch Rep 1960-; Thesis Cross Age Grouping on Dev of Self Concept; *office:* Cedar Grove Elem Sch Cedar Grove Rd Toms River NJ 08753

STOUT, GARNET J. (CAMPBELL), Fourth Grade Elem Teacher; *b:* La Farge, WI; *m:* John Joe; *c:* Carmen L.; *ed:* (BA) Elem Ed, La Crosse St Univ 1968; Vernon Cty Normal 1960; *cr:* 4th Grade Elem Teacher La Farge Area Sch 1960-; *ai:* NEA, WI Ed Assn 1968-; La Farge Ed Assn Treas 1968-; PTO 1986-88; *home:* RR 2 Box 20 La Farge WI 54639

STOUT, JAMES EDWARD, Retired; *b:* Salem, WV; *m:* Glenda Dennison; *c:* Angela Dawn Harkness, James Edward II; *ed:* (Ba) Eng/Soc Stud, Salem Coll 1958; *cr:* Soc Stud Teacher Daddridge Cty HS 1958-59; Eng Teacher Franklin Jr HS 1960-66; Eng Teacher Edison Jr HS 1966-88; *ai:* WCEA 1960-88; DCEA 1958-59; WVEA 1958-88; *home:* 1700 S Hills Dr Parkersburg WV 26101

STOUT, JERRY LYNN, Physical Science Teacher; *b:* Jellico, TN; *m:* Josephine Brooker Young; *ed:* (BS) Bio/Chem, Cumberland Coll 1966; (MA) Adm/Supervision, 1975, (EDS) Admin/Supervision, 1985, Union Coll; *cr:* Sci Techer Conniston Sch 1966-74, Lafollette Jr HS 1974-82, Campbell Cty Comp HS 1983-; *ai:* Spon Campbell Cty Comprehensive HS Amateur Radio Club; Sci Dept Chm; Amer Fed of Teachers VP 1985-87 Local 3847; TN Scndry Sci Assn; Campbell Cty Amateur Radio Club Pres 1987-89; Hunter Safety Instr TN Wildlife Resources Agency 1975-; Instr Amer Radio Relay League 1986-; Career Level III Teacher Awarded by St of TN; Nom for TN St Sci Teacher of Yr 1988; *home:* 125 Maple Dr La Follette TN 37766

STOUT, JOANNA WHEAT, Art Teacher/Historian; *b:* Alexanderia, LA; *m:* Donald M.; *c:* James M.; *ed:* (BFA) Art, Sam Houston St Univ 1989; Art Wkshps; Univ of NM, Southwest Inst, Southwestern Stud; Anthropology, Archaeology of Southwest US Univ of NM; *cr:* Teacher Our Lady of Assumption 1971-, New Caney HS 1989-, N Harris Cty Comm Coll 1989-; *ai:* Art Club, Choir Booster Club VP; Working to Establish a Discipline Based Art Ed Prgm; TX Art Ed Assn, Coll Art Assn; Kingwood Cmmty Theatre Pres Cncl 1986-89; Atascocita Cntry Club Bd of Dirs 1987-89; Outstanding Ed Stu Awd 1989 Sam Houston St; *home:* 18910 Oak Bower Ataceocita TX 77346

STOUT, JUDY WILSON, First Grade Teacher; *b:* Elizabethton, TN; *m:* Harlan Wayne; *c:* Michael; *ed:* (BS) Elem Ed, 1975, (MED) Educl Admin, 1988 E TN St Univ; *cr:* 1st Grade Teacher Unaka Elem 1975-76; 1st-2nd Grade Teacher Midway Elem 1977-80; 1st Grade Teacher Unaka Elem 1980-; *ai:* NEA, TN Ed Assn, Carter Cty Ed Assn 1988-; Gamma Beta Phi Society 1988-; PTA 1975-; Career Level 1 Teacher; *office:* Unaka Elem Sch Rt 10 Box 1150 Elizabethton TN 37643

STOUT, RUSSELL L., JR., English Teacher; *b:* Oskaloosa, IA; *ed:* (BA) Eng/Speech, Wake Forest Univ 1972; *cr:* Teacher Great Bridge HS 1972-78, Oskaloosa Jr HS 1979-; *ai:* Oskaloosa Ed Assn Pres 1983-89; Oskaloosa Cmmty Theatre Pres 1981-86; *home:* 806 9th Ave E Oskaloosa IA 52577

STOVALL, ELLEN HARTMAN, Kindergarten Teacher; *b:* Poplar Bluff, MO; *c:* Beverly, Suzanne, Bill, Matthew; *ed:* (BS) Ed, Southeast MO Univ 1966; (MA) Ed, Univ MO St Louis 1981; *cr:* 1st Grade Teacher 1966-71, Kndgtn Teacher 1972- Northwest R-1 Sch Dist; *ai:* Dist Soc Stud Comm; Dist Math Comm; Dist Prof Dev Comm; *office:* R-1 Northwest Sch Dist Box 500 House Springs MO 63051

STOVALL, ROBERT DANIEL, JR., US History Teacher; *b:* Stephenville, TX; *c:* Dana, Delight, Darby; *ed:* (BS) Phys Ed/Health, Tarleton St Univ 1974; Working Towards Masters Tarleton Tx Tech; *cr:* Teacher/Coach Junction Ind Sch Dist 1974-86, Llano Ind Sch Dist 1986-; *ai:* Var Ftbl, Frosh Girls Bsktbl, Var Boys & Girls Tennis Coach; Sr Class Spon; TX HS Coaches Assn, TX Tennis Coaches Assn Coach of Yr 1981; *office:* Llano HS Hwy 71 E Llano TX 78643

STOVER, BETTY JO FAINTER, Reading Specialist Teacher; *b:* Waynesboro, VA; *m:* Robert L. Jr.; *ed:* (BA) Psych, Mary Baldwin Coll 1972; (MED) Rdng-Ed Univ of VA 1977; Rdng, Univ of Va; *cr:* 1st Grade Teacher Berkley Glenn Elem 1972-85; Rdng Teacher Berkeley Glenn Elem/Wenonah Elem 1985-87; Berkeley Glenn Elem 1987-89; Berkeley Glenn Elem/Shenandoah Hts Elem 1989-; *ai:* SVRA Contact Person 1988-; VA St Rdng Assn; Waynsboro Ed Assn VA Assn; Presented Prgm Using Patterns to Get 1st Graders to Write for The Shenandoah Vly Rdng Cncl; *office:* Berkeley Glenn Elem Sch 1020 Jefferson Ave Waynesboro VA 22980

STOVER, EARL J., Retired Teacher; *b:* St Louis, MO; *ed:* (BS) Ec, Washington Univ 1959; *cr:* Teacher Clinton Sch 1961-71, Mallinckrodt Sch 1971-.

STOVER, KATHY ANDERSON, Mathematics Teacher; *b:* Sun Valley, ID; *m:* Paul E. Jr.; *c:* Rand, Niki; *ed:* (BS) Math Ed, 1971, (MM) Math, 1973 UT St Univ; Various Grad Credits from Area Univs; *cr:* Teaching Asst 1971-73, Instr 1973-74 UT St Univ; Eng Teacher 1974-76, Math Teacher 1976- Twin Falls HS; *ai:* NHS Head Adv 1984-; NEA, ID Ed Assn 1975-; Twin Falls Ed Assn (Building Rep, Delegate Assembly Rep) 1987, 1990; OR Math Teachers Assn, NCTM 1988-; ID Cncl Teachers of Math 1987-; Delta Kappa Gamma 1980-; PEO Guard 1978-; Teaching Excl Awd Univ of ID Alumni Assn 1990; *office:* Twin Falls HS 1615 Filer Ave E Twin Falls ID 83301

STOVER, LOUELLA MARIE (HALLEY), Business Education Teacher; *b:* Gallipolis, OH; *m:* Garry B. III; *ed:* (AA) Bus Admin, Rio Grande Coll 1978; (BS) Bookkeeping/Basic Bus Ed, OH Univ 1980; Voc Cert, OH St Univ; Becker CPA Review Course, Charleston WV; *cr:* Teacher Gallipolis Bus Coll 1980, Tri-Cty Joint Voc Sch Dist 1980-81, Gallia-Jackson-Vinton Joint Voc Sch Dist 1982-85; Vinton Cty Local Schl Dist 1985-; *ai:* Jr Class Tri-Advsor & CORE Team Mem; OH Bus Teacher Assn, Vinton Teacher Assn, NEA, OH Ed Assn 1985-; Phi Kappa Phi 1979-; Canaan Missionary Baptist Church Jr Teacher 1985-88; *home:* 672 Centerville Rd Thurman OH 45685

STOVER, RONNA LEE PRICE, Health & Physical Educator; *b:* Bedford, PA; *m:* Les C.; *c:* Seth A.; *ed:* (BS) Health/Phys Ed, West Chester Univ 1980; Athletic Trng; *cr:* Substitute Teacher Various Dist Cntrl Pa 1981-82; Health/Phys Ed Teacher Upper Adams Sch Dist 1982-84; Health/Phys Ed/Trainer Big Spring Sch Dist 1985-; *ai:* Athletic Trainer; Various Sch Comm; NEA; Natl Athletic Trainers Assn, PA Athletic Trainer Assn; *home:* PO Box 89 51 Greason Rd Plainfield PA 17081

STOW, JAMES WILLIAM, 9th Grade World His Teacher; *b:* Olympia, WA; *m:* Dorothy Bales; *ed:* (BA) Music/His, 1959, (MA) Music/his, 1964 W Wa St Coll 1964; Advanced Courses From Univ of WA, Santa Clara, Cntrl WA St Univ, S Il; *cr:* Music/His Instr Thorp HS 1959-60, Waitsburg HS 1960-62; Music/Eng Instr N Kitsap Jr HS 1962-67; Music/His Instr Olympic Jr HS 1967-; *ai:* Honor Society & Yrbk Adv; Drama; Knowledge Bowl & Track Meet Coord; Auburn Ed Assn Treas 1976; N KITSAP Ed Assn Pres 1964; NEA, WEA, WA St Cncl of Soc Stud Teachers; *office:* Olympic Jr HS 1825 K Street SE Auburn WA 98002

STOWELL, WILLIAM R., SR., 5th Grade Teacher; *b:* East Hampton, NY; *m:* Joan Stark; *c:* John D., Richard W., William R.; *ed:* (BA) Elem, Geneseo St 1963; *cr:* 6th Grade Teacher New Berlin Cntrl Sch 1963-65; 5th Grade Teacher Tuckahoe Common Sch 1965-68; Spec Ed Teacher Worcester Cntrl Sch 1968-70; 5th Grade Teacher New Berlin Cntrl Sch 1970-; *ai:* Morris Rotary Club Pres 1980-81, 1983-84, Paul Harris Awd 1987; *home:* Box 321 Morris NY 13808

STOWERS, LINDA L. (SCHEER), Administrative Assistant; *b:* Torrington, WY; *m:* Phillip T.; *c:* Shannon Girard, Bowdy, Shaun; *ed:* (BA) Elem Ed, Univ of WY 1974; *cr:* Teacher Sweetwater Cty Sch Dist 1974-86; Pres WY Ed Assn 1983-86; Elem/Fine Art Consultant 1986-88, Admin Asst 1988- WY Dept of Ed; *ai:* WY Ed Assn (Treas 1979-86, Pres 1983-86); Phi Delta Kappa 1983-; Green River Lioness 1976-79; Wy Profession Standards Bd 1979-86; St Drug/Alcohol Bd 1989-; Green River Teacher of Yr 1978; *home:* 1061 Everglade Cheyenne WY 82001

STOWERS, MARY KATHRYN, English Department Chair; *b:* Dehue, WV; *m:* Paul G.; *c:* Christopher, Lori; *ed:* (AB) Lang Art, Marshall Univ 1971; (MA) Comm Stud, WV Univ 1986; WV Mid Sch Endorsement, Lang Art 1982; *cr:* Teachers Aide Spruce Grade Sch 1968-70; Eng Teacher Oceana Mid Sch 1972-; *ai:* WV Task Force Mid Sch Lang Art; Young Writers Chairperson Oceana Mid Sch; Cty Textbook Adoption Comm for Eng; NEA, WV Ed Assn; Wyoming Cty Ed Assn Treas 1979; *home:* Box 271 Oceana WV 24870

STOWERS, PATRICIA JUSTICE, Third Grade Teacher; *b:* Landville, WV; *m:* Charles; *ed:* (BA) Elem Ed, Marshall Univ 1970; *cr:* Elem Teacher Lorado Grade Sch 1969-72; Earing Grade Sch 1972-74; South Man Grade Sch 1974-; *ai:* Teach Cmptr Literacy Classes 1st-3rd Grade; Mem Parent Adv Com South Man Grade; WV Ed Assn 1969-; Logan Cty Ed Assn 1969-; Logan Cty PTA Teacher of Yr 1979; Rotary Club Excl in Ed Awd 1989; *office:* South Man Grade Sch 301 E Mac Donald Ave Man WV 25635

STRAAYER, CAROLE KERR, Fourth Grade Teacher; *b:* Jackson, MI; *m:* Richard Lee; *c:* Steven J., Susan K.; *ed:* (BS) Elem Ed, 1957, (MA) Elem Ed, 1961 E MI Univ; Various Courses; *cr:* Teacher Napoleon Sch Dist 1954-56, Waterford Township Sch Dist 1957, Jackson Public Schls 1957-; *ai:* MEA, NEA, JEA Tenure Chairperson 1979-80; Delta Kappa Gamma (Pres 1986-88) 1980-; Amer Assn of Univ Women; Jackson Ed Assn Building Rep; First Presbyterian Choir Mem 1979-; Volunteer Adult Tutoring 1989-; MASCD Region 3 Rep; Newspaper Classroom Schlsp; Co-Author Teaching Booklet; Prof Staff Dev Chairperson; Jackson Hillsdale Prof Dev Consortium Jacksonville Public Schls Rep; *office:* Hunt Elem Sch 1143 N Brown Jackson MI 49202

STRACHAN, MARTHA VERONICA, Fourth Grade Teacher; *b:* Brighton, MA; *ed:* Elem Ed, Lesley Coll; (BSED) Elem Ed, 1969, (MAED) Guidance, 1971, (MAED) Rdng, 1982 Worcester St Coll; Open Classroom, John Clarke Univ England 1971; Montessori Stud, Worcester St Coll Italy 1977; Franco Amer/Canadian Stud, Univ of ME Orono 1979; *cr:* 3rd Grade Teacher Clara Barton Sch 1968-86; Rdng Specialist 1986-87, 5th Grade Teacher 1987-, 4th Grade Teacher 1988- Allen L Joslin Sch; *ai:* Cntrl MA Rdng Cncl Pres 1981-82, 1984-86, St Coord Awd 1986-87; MA Rdng Assn Celebrate Literacy Comm 1982-83, Sylvia Brown Schlsp 1986; Intnl Rdng Assn; Phi Delta Kappa (VP, Pres) 1989-; MA Teachers Assn Annual Convention Delegate 1981-; Oxford Ed Assn Bid of Dirs 1987-, Williamston Summer Leadership; French River Ed Center Incorporated (Secy, Treas, Bd of Dirs); PTO (Wkshp Presenter, Teacher Liason); Cath Alumni Club (Past Pres, Asst VP) 1989-; First Commonwealth of MA Classroom Management In-Service Grant; Natl Endowment for Hum New England Stud CT 1985; *office:* Allen L Joslin Maple Rd Oxford MA 01540

STRAIT, DARRELL L., 6th Grade Science Teacher; *b:* Carrolton, MO; *m:* Kathy Jenkins; *ed:* (BS) Ed, Cntrl MO St Univ 1974; Admin; *cr:* Teacher Pleasant Hill Mid Sch 1974-83, 1985-; *ai:* Staff Dev Leader; PTA Lifetime Membership 1987; CTA Pres 1978; Cmptr Lab Incentive Grant 1989-; *office:* Pleasant Hill Mid Sch 327 N Mc Kissock Pleasant Hill MO 64080

STRAIT, LARRY H., Biology Teacher; *b:* Tremont, PA; *m:* Joan I. Stephens; *c:* David Hoover, Jeffrey Hoover, Larry H. Jr., S. Jared, Shane J.; *ed:* (AA) Liberal Art, Hershey Jr Coll 1958; (BS) Bio Ed, Lebanon Valley Coll 1960; (MED) Bio Ed, Penn St 1967; *cr:* Teacher Derry Township Sch Dist 1961-62, Lower Dauphin Sch Dist 1962-63, Derry Township Sch Dist 1963-; *ai:* Boys & Girls Tennis Coach; Rod & Gun Club Adv; *office:* Hershey HS Homestead Rd Hershey PA 17033

STRAITON, WALTER JAMES, Director of Orchestras; *b:* Harrisburg, PA; *d:* Dorothy; *c:* Katherine; *ed:* (BS) Music Ed, Millersville Univ 1977; (MA) Music Ed, Eastman Sch of Music 1988; *cr:* Dir of Orchs Williamsport Area HS 1977-; *ai:* Millionaire Strolling Strings; Intnl Assn of Jazz Educators String Chm 1984-; PA Unit Natl Sch Orch Assn Pres 1987-88; John F Kennedy Center Fellowship for Teachers in Arts 1989; *office:* Williamsport Area HS 2990 W 4th St Williamsport PA 17701

STRAND, PATRICIA ANDERSON, Business Education Teacher; *b:* Canton, SD; *m:* Glenn O.; *c:* Simon, Adam, Elliott; *ed:* (BA) Bus Ed, Augustana Coll 1972; Grad Stud Cmptr Sci; *cr:* Bus Ed Teacher St James HS 1972-75, Sioux Falls Jr & Sr HS 1975-; Office Skills Teacher Kilian Comm Coll 1986-; *ai:* SD, Mountain Plains, NBEA Mem 1972-; Sioux Falls Ed Assn, SD Ed Assn, NEA 1972-; SD Bus & Office Ed Assn (Bus Ed Coord 1976-78, Co-Editor Magazine 1977-80); Amer Legion Post 307 (Mem, Americanism Officer, Service Officer); Naval Enlisted Reserve Assn Life Mem 1973-; Sioux Falls Blood Bank Mem; Mothers of Twins Club Mem; *home:* 6701 W Essex Dr Sioux Falls SD 57106

STRANDBERG, BERNIECE (KIRCH), 5th/6th Grade Music Teacher; *b:* Chandler, OK; *m:* Richard; *c:* Kristin; *ed:* (AA) Elem Ed, St Johns Luth Coll 1962; (BS) Elem Ed/Soc Sci, Concordia Teachers Coll 1964; Grad Stud Rdng & Music; *cr:* 5th/6th Grade Music/3rd-6th Grade Choir/Substitute Teacher Rolla Luth Sch;

ai: Childrens Choir Act; Dorcas Society Mem; Adult Church Choir Dir & Head Organists; Luth Ed Assn 1964-66; Amer Guild of Organists 1962-64; *office:* Rolla Luth Sch 807 W 11th St Rolla MO 65401

STRANG, M. JANICE GREEN, 6th Grade Teacher; *b:* Troy, NY; *m:* Joseph J.; *c:* Genevieve, Janice Denio, Katie, Joe, Bill, Eric; *ed:* (BA) Soc Stud, Coll of St Rose 1965; Rdng, Russell Sage Coll 1978; Sci A Process Approach, Positive Attitude Toward Learning, Assertiveness Trng, Ronzuli Gifted & Talented Approach; *cr:* 2nd Grade Teacher 1979-81, 4th Grade Teacher 1981-86 Sch #2; 6th Grade Teacher Sch #18 1986-; *ai:* Stu Cncl; Yrbk & Video Project Adv; Intnl Peace Balloon; 4-H, Cmmty Gardens Instr 1981-86; Excl Teaching Article in Dist Newspaper; *office:* School #18 412 Hoosick St Troy NY 12180

STRANGE, JAMES ESTLE, Retired Teacher; *b:* Hartford, TN; *m:* Deema Simmons; *c:* Steve; *ed:* (BS) Elem Ed, Carson Newman Coll 1975; E TN St Univ; Univ of TN; E TN St UNIV, UNIV of TN; *cr:* Teacher New Prospect, Bell Hill, Compton Memorial, Gulf 1945-63; Prin/7th-8th Grade Teacher Grassy Fork Elem Sch 1963-88; *ai:* NEA, TEA, CCEA 1945-; *home:* Rt 1 Hartford TN 37753

STRANGE, WANDA JACOBS, English & Journalism Teacher; *b:* Indianapolis, IN; *m:* Robert; *ed:* (BA) Eng, St Mary of the Woods Coll 1965; (MAT) Eng, IN Univ 1969; Grad Stud Various Univs; *cr:* Indianapolis Star City Room 1948; Teacher Our Lady of Mercy Sch 1952-54, St Angela Sch 1954-57, St Teresa of Avila Sch 1957-58, St Anthony Sch 1958-61; St Charles Sch 1961-65, Chartrand HS 1965-67, St Agnes Acad 1967-69; Cath Sch Office 1969-71; Teacher Lawrence Cntrl HS 1971, River Forest HS 1971-79, Perry Meridian HS 1979-; *ai:* Yrbk Adv; 9th Grade Gifted & Talented Teacher; NCTE, IN Cncl Teachers of Eng, Indianapolis Cncl Teachers of Eng; Academic Banquet Guest 1987-; Poems Published; Nom Outstanding Teacher by Township Supt 1973; *home:* 7217 N Tukedo Indianapolis IN 46240

STRASHEIM, PATRICIA ANN, 5th Grade Teacher; *b:* Norfolk, NE; *m:* Dwayne S.; *c:* Robyn, Sally, Jane; *ed:* (BA) Elem Ed, Hastings Coll 1972; (MA) Elem Ed, Kearney St Coll 1982; *cr:* Elem Teacher Stanton Public Schls 1961-62; Grant Elem Sch 1962-63; Trumbull Consolidated Schls 1972-; *ai:* Odyssey of Mind Coach; Future Problem Solving Coach; Gifted Prgm Coord; NEA/NSEA 1972-; Trumbull Ed Assn (Pres/VP/Secy/Treas) 1972-; NE Assn for Gifted; NCTE; Order of Eastern Star 1978-; BPO DOES 1972-; Alpha Delta Kappa 1976-89; *home:* 733 Valley Chase Ave Hastings NE 68901

STRASSBURG, JENNIFER AUDENTIA, Music Department Chairperson; *b:* Niagara Falls, NY; *ed:* (BME) Music Ed, Brigham Young Univ 1974; *cr:* Music Teacher West Lake Jr HS 1976-; *ai:* Dir Musicals 1976-; Girls Cncl 1978-88; Promotion Comm 1976-; Boys Var Vlybl Coach 1989; Athletic Events Scorer 1976-; Assembly Comm 1982-; Building Comm 1988-; NEA, UT Ed Assn, Granite Ed Assn (Rep 1989-) 1976-; Amer Fed of Musicians 1966-85; Church of Jesus Christ Latter Day Saints Lifetime Active Mem; Amer Cancer Society Patient Services 1988-89; Recipient of Excl Awd Honorable Mention Outstanding Service to Ed in UT 1989; *office:* West Lake Jr HS 3400 S 3450 W West Valley City UT 84119

STRASZHEIM, CINDY BLAKEMAN, 5th Grade Teacher; *b:* Madisonville, KY; *m:* James H. Jr.; *c:* Kristina, Carrie; *ed:* (BSED) Elem Ed, Miami Univ 1972; *cr:* 5th Grade Teacher 1972-73, 6th Grade Teacher 1973-74 East Elem; 5th Grade Teacher Dixon & Bruce Sch 1974-; *ai:* 2 Cty Grants 1989-.

STRATTON, DOROTHEA HESS, Chapter 1/Reading Teacher; *b:* Pipestone, MN; *m:* Harlan John; *c:* Jacqueline, Jolene Stratton Philo, John; *ed:* (BA) Ed, Westmar Coll 1961; (MA) Ed, Morningside Coll 1969; St of IA Writing Project; Various Teaching Courses; *cr:* 6th Grade Teacher Roland Ind Sch 1948-51; 4th Grade Teacher Nevada Ind Sch 1951-53; 3rd Grade Teacher Malvern Cmmty Sch 1958-60; 3rd/6th Grade/Chapter 1/Rdng Teacher Le Mars Cmmty Sch 1960-; *ai:* NEA, ISEA, Local Assn.

STRAUB, AARON JOHN, Athletic Director; *b:* St Marys, PA; *m:* Joanne Marie Gerg; *c:* Aaron J., Douglas J., Allison M.; *ed:* (BS) Health/Phys Ed, Indiana Univ of PA 1979; (MED) Ed, Gannon Univ 1990; *cr:* Health/Phys Ed Teacher Elk Cty Chrstn HS 1979-; *ai:* Golf Coach 1982-; Boys Bsktbl Coach 1979-; *office:* Elk Cty Chrstn HS 600 Maurus St Saint Marys PA 15857

STRAUB, MARYBOB HOGENKAMP, Spanish Teacher; *b:* Lima, OH; *m:* James Joseph; *c:* Kelly R., Lara R.; *ed:* (BA) Span, John Carroll Univ 1976; El Instituto Tecnologico Y de Estudios Superiores De Monterrey, Nuevo Leon Mexico; Bowling Green St Univ Stud Madrid Spain; Grad Work Geography, Bowling Green St Univ; *cr:* Span Teacher Leipsic HS 1979-80, Lima Cntrl Cath HS 1980-85, Ada HS 1986-; *ai:* Chemical Abuse & Stu Assistance Prgms Co-Chairperson; Instr Insight Classes & Lifeguides Prgm; NEA, OH Foreign Lang Assn, Natl Assn of Teachers of Span & Portuguese 1976-; Educl Fnd for Foreign Study Regional Coord 1985-; St Charles Advisory Bd Mem 1990; OH Right to Life 1981-; Heartbeat Hotline 1989-; Article Published; *office:* Ada HS 500 Grand Ave Ada OH 45810

STRAUGHN, LEO RICHARD ARNOLD, Math Teacher/Soccer Coach; *b:* Ft Ord, CA; *m:* Paula Sterghos; *c:* Alexandra N.; *ed:* (BS) Ed/Math, Univ of S AL 1986; *cr:* Math Teacher/Soccer Coach S S Murphy HS 1986-; *ai:* Coaching Soccer; Intervention Team 1989-.

STRAUSS, JOHN W., English Teacher; *b:* Chicago, IL; *m:* Teresa M. Houdek; *c:* Kathleen M.; *ed:* (ALA) Eng, Triton Coll 1980; (BA) Eng/Philosophy, Rosary Coll 1982; (MA) Eng, Loyola Univ 1985; *cr:* Eng Teacher Argo Cmmty HS 1983-87, W Leyden HS 1987-, Triton Coll 1987-; *ai:* Forensics Team Coach; NCTE; IL Teacher of Yr Nom 1990-; Univ of Chicago Recognition for Teaching Excl 1989; *office:* W Leyden HS 1000 Wolf Rd Northlake IL 60131

STRAUSS, THELMA HAUER, Sixth Grade Teacher; *b:* Lebanon, PA; *m:* David Stanley; *c:* Christopher, Rebecca, Bethanne; *ed:* (BS) Elem Ed, Lebanon Valley Coll 1958; Certified Elem Lib; Peer Coach/Mentor & Teach Critical Thinking; Cmptr Literacy, Effective Teaching & Assertive Discipline; *cr:* Teacher Annville Cleona Schls 1957-60, Lebanon Sch Dist 1960-; *ai:* Math Curr Comm; Teacher Assisting Teacher Team; Dist CATS Comm; Amer Ed Week Comm; Dist Mentor Prgm; Spring Concert Staff; Lebanon Ed Assn Secy 1966-68; PSEA; NEA; Jr Womans Club of Lebanon Pres 1966-68; Outstanding Young Women of Amer 1967; Lebanon Co Fed of Womens Clubs Pres 1978-80; Lebanon Co Emergency Management Agency Transportation Officer 1987-; Emergency Health Services Cncl Secy 1972-85; Lebanon Cty Ed Honor Society; Natl PA/Berks Cty Assn of Parliamentarians; *office:* Lebanon Sch Dist 1000 S 8th St Lebanon PA 17042

STRAVLO, WILLO DEAN, First Grade Teacher; *b:* Elk City, OK; *m:* Richard; *c:* Ron, Don; *ed:* Assoc General Ed - Summa Cum Laude, Sayre Jr Coll 1959; (BS) Elem Ed - Cum Laude, Southwestern St Univ 1962; (MS) Early Chldhd Ed, Cntrl St Univ 1976; Grad Work; *cr:* Kndgtn Teacher Western Heights Public Schls 1962-63; 1st Grade Teacher Harrah Public Schls 1963-66, Okarche Public Schls 1966-67; Kndgtn Teacher Harrah Public Schls 1967-79; 3rd/4th Grade Teacher 1979-80, Kndgtn Teacher 1980-81 White Rock Public Schls; 7th Grade Teacher 1981-82, 1st Grade Teacher 1982-83, Kndgtn Teacher 1983-88, 1st Grade Teacher 1988- Harrah Public Schls; *ai:* Elem Yrbk Ed 1989-; Awds Assembly Comm; NEA, OEA 1962-; OK Cty Ed Assn (VP, Pres); Harrah Act (Negotiation Team 1986-89, Pres, VP, Secy, Treas); Pres Honor Roll Cntrl St Univ; Dist Teacher of Yr 1975-76; *office:* Clara Reynolds Elem Sch 701 S Harrison Harrah OK 73045

STRAW, ROBERT EUGENE, Elem Art Teacher; *b:* York, PA; *m:* Brenda Lucille Schwirt; *c:* Lisa M., Lori J.; *ed:* (BFA) Art Teacher Ed, MD Coll of Art 1969; Grad Work Penn St York Campus, Millersville St Univ; *cr:* Elem Art Teacher West York Sch Dist 1969-; *ai:* Jr HS Girls Bsktbl & Intramural Sports Coach; Class of 1989 Float Adv; W York Ed Assn, PA St Ed Assn 1969-; *home:* 1815 Lilac Rd York PA 17404

STRAWN, CHARLOTTE EDWARDS, Retired; *b:* Coleman, TX; *c:* Anthony J.; *ed:* (BS) Elem Ed, 1954; (MED) Elem, 1959 Howard Payne Coll; *cr:* Teacher Whitt ISD 1943-44; Talpha ISD 1944-45; Echo ISD 1945-46; Coleman ISD 1954-; *ai:* Cub Scout Asst Den Mother-1955-58; Girl Scout Troop Ldr 1972-74/1980-82; Sunday Sch Teacher; ATPE 1980-89; TSTA 1954-79; Girl Scout Bicentennial Heroine 1975; Whos Who in TX Ed 1976; Most Prominent Educators of TX 1983; *home:* 402 Live Oak Coleman TX 76834

STREAGLE, JIMMI DINEEN, Earth Science Teacher/Mentor; *b:* Bangor, ME; *m:* Timothy Robin; *c:* Lauren A.; *ed:* (BS) Geology, James Madison Univ 1982; Grad Work Cert Earth Sci, Coll of William & Mary; Grad Work Geology Field Camp Radford Univ; *cr:* Collator/Inventory Smithsonian Institution Dept of Paleobiology 1982-84; Historical Interpreter Colonial Williamsburg Living Museum 1985; Earth Sci Teacher Denbigh HS 1985-86, Varina HS 1986-; *ai:* Sci Club, SCA Spon 1990; Kappa Delta Phi 1987-; *office:* Varina HS 7053 Messer Rd Richmond VA 23231

STREI, CLARICE HEIER, Retired; *b:* Williamsburg, VA; *m:* Alfred; *c:* Wayne; *ed:* (BS) Elem Educ, WI St Univ 1961; *cr:* 1st-8th Grade Teacher Frank Sch 1943-45; Linzy Brook Sch 1945-48; Sunny Lawn Sch 1948-54; 1st-4th Grade Teacher Mosling Sch 1956-59; 1st-2nd Grade Teacher Bonduel Sch Dist 1959-88; *home:* 6434 Settlement Rd Gillett WI 54124

STREIFEL, JO MARIE, Business Teacher; *b:* Eureka, SD; *ed:* (BS) Bus Ed, Northern St Univ 1981; *cr:* Bus Teacher Winner HS 1981-; *ai:* Girls Bsktbl & Track Coach; SD Ed Assn Mem; *office:* Winner HS E 7th Winner SD 57580

STREIT, CANDIS DERRIG, Reading Teacher; *b:* Fort Dodge, IA; *m:* Daniel M.; *ed:* (AA) IA Cntrl Comm Coll 1974; (BA) Elem Ed, Buena Vista Coll 1978; IA Endorsement 91, Rdng Endor ement, Marycrest Coll; *cr:* Teachers Aide Fort Dodge Cmnty Schls 1974-78; Substitute Teacher Fort Dodge Cmnty Sch & Fort Dodge Cath Schls 1978-79; Rdng Teacher Fort Dodge Cath Grade Schls 1979-; *ai:* Past-Spelling Bee Spon; Personnel Sub-Comm; Long Range Planning; Stu Orientation to Study Habits & Skill Dev; Intnl Rdng Assn; Beta Sigma Phi; Sacred Heart Church (Eucharistic Minister, Hospitality) 1988; *office:* Sacred Heart Sch 214 S 13 St Fort Dodge IA 50501

STREIT, NORMAN JOSEPH, Technical Teacher; *b:* Buffalo, NY; *m:* Angeline Dolce; *c:* Christopher; *ed:* (BSED) Voc Tech, 1970, (MSED) Voc Tech, 1973 St Univ NY Coll Buffalo; Machinist Mate Sch US Navy 1948; Cooperative Work Study Cert Coord 1974; *cr:* Designer E R Faelton PE 1955-57; Designer/Engr Aro Firewel Corporation 1957-62; Engineering Services Mgr Carleton Control Corporation 1962-67; Teacher Hutchinson Cntrl Tech HS 1968-; *ai:* Buffalo Teacher Fed Building Rep; Sch Advisory Cncl Mem; Buffalo Voc Tech Guild Secy 1987-; Red Cross (CPR Instr, Pheresis Donor); Futuring Occupational Ed Tech Comm Chm 1983; Created Final June Regents Exams in Mechanical Technology; *home:* 3710 Bowen Rd Lancaster NY 14086

STREITFERDT, CAROLYN CHESTNUT, Asst Principal-Teacher; *b:* Florence, SC; *m:* Thomas Jr.; *c:* Thomas III, Shawn-Anton; *ed:* (PBS) Bus Admin, Berkeley 1969; Assoc Early Chldhd Ed, True Witness Ministries 1974; *cr:* Transcriber True Witness Time 1969-74; Teacher Kings Chapel Assembly 1974-80; Section Mgr 1980-88, Asst Prin 1988- The Kings Acad; *ai:* Graduation Ceremony Coord; Skiing Instr; Bsbl Booster; True Church of God Trustee; *office:* The Kings Acad 2341 3rd Ave Manhattan NY 10035

STREITMATTER, REBECCA LYNN (RUPE), English Teacher; *b:* Gallipolis, OH; *m:* Mark; *c:* Bethany, Amy; *ed:* (BA) Eng, Cedarville Coll 1980; (MED) Ed, Natl Coll of Ed 1983; *cr:* Eng Teacher Tri Cty HS 1980-; *ai:* NHS Adv; Tri Cty Stus Teacher of Yr 1989; *office:* Tri County HS Rt 1 Box 130A Wolcott IN 47995

STRENNEN, JAMES, Elem Math Department Chairman; *b:* Darth, PA; *m:* Joanne C. Greene; *c:* Judith Ann Knott, Jay Calvin, Jody Stephen, Joni Gladys Schwenker, James J., Jerry Jon; *ed:* (BS) Elem Ed, 1964, (MA) Elem Ed, 1967 CA St Coll PA; Graduate Credits WV Univ/St Univ NY Buffalo/St Univ NY Albany/Morehead Univ KY; *cr:* Teacher Fair Chance-Georges Sch Dist 1964; Teacher/Math/Dept Chm 1964-; Adult Basic Ed Teacher 1965- Trinity Area Sch Dist; *ai:* Elem Math Dept Chairperson; PCTM 1987-; NCTM 1987-; *home:* RD 1 Box 264 Scenery Hill PA 15360

STRESMAN, DIANE K. (SCHULZ), English Teacher; *b:* Merrill, WI; *m:* Kevin D.; *ed:* (MA) Rdng, E MI Univ 1988; (BS) Eng/Sociology Ed, Concordia Teachers Coll 1980; *cr:* Teacher Luth HS N 1980-84; Accounts Payable Bookkeeper Wm Sell & Son 1984-85; Teacher Luth HS East 1985-89, Luth HS Westland 1989-; *ai:* Video Yrbk Spon & Adv; Jr Class Spon; Serve-A-Thon Comm; Sch Newspaper Adv; Girls Bsktbl Statistician; NCTE 1980-; Luth Church MO Synod; MI Dist Constitutional Review Comm 1990; St Matthews Womens Sftbl Team 1990; *office:* Luth HS Westland 333000 Cowan Rd Westland MI 48185

STRESMAN, SHIRLEY MARIE, 3rd/4th Grade Teacher; *b:* Saginaw, MI; *m:* Kenneth C.; *c:* Shelly, Kevin, Lori Farnum; *ed:* (AA) Music, Concorida 1955; (BS) Fine Arts, Eastern MI Univ 1971; *cr:* 1st/4th Grade Teacher St Matthew Luth Sch 1956-58; 1st/2nd Grade Teacher Mt Calvary Luth Sch 1956-58; 1st Grade Teacher St Mark the Evang Luth 1964-66; 1st/4th Grade Teacher Holy Ghost Luth 1966-; *ai:* Childrens Choir Dir; Handbell Choir Dir; Church Organist; Nrsg Home Vlntr; Luth Educ; *home:* 6447 E Dunbar 325 Monroe MI 48161

STRIBLING, VERNELL D., 4th Grade Teacher; *b:* Crockett, TX; *m:* Clifton Eugene; *c:* Gary D., Jonathan K.; *ed:* (BS) Elem Ed/Art, 1965, (MS) Ed, 1977 Prairie View A&M; Lamar Tech; *cr:* Teacher Orange Ind Sch Dist 1965-66, Dallas Ind Sch Dist 1968-; *ai:* Jr Cross Spon; TAG Advisory & Sch Improvement Plan Comm; Tutorial Prgm Teacher; PTA Mem 1968-, Life Membership Awd 1979; Metro Women Bus & Prof Financial Secy 1986-; Delta Sigma Theta 1986-; Church (Sch Teacher 1984-, Jr Choir Spon 1983-), Certificate 1988, Plaque 1985; Mt Tabor Matrons Secy 1967-, Certificate 1986; Jack Lowe Teacher of Yr 1985; Cabell Teacher of Yr 1986; *office:* T G Terry Elem Sch 6661 Greenspan Dallas TX 75232

STRICKLAND, CAROL ANN, Business Teacher; *b:* Pottsville, PA; *m:* Jack; *c:* Jacob, Corey, Lindsey; *ed:* (BS) Bus Ed, Bloomsburg St Coll 1973; (MA) Voc Ed, Northern AZ Univ 1983; Working Towards ESL Cert Through N AZ Univ; *cr:* Bus Teacher Kutztown HS 1974-, Kofa HS 1974-88, Cibola HS 1988-; *ai:* FBLA Adv 1974-; Alpha Delta Kappa Treas 1989-;Phi Delta Kappa 1983-; AZ Bus Ed Assn 1974-; *office:* Cibola HS 4100 20th St Yuma AZ 85364

STRICKLAND, CHARLOTTE D., Language Arts Teacher; *b:* Quincy, FL; *m:* Larry E.; *c:* Jonathan, Jason; *ed:* (AA) General Ed, Chipola Jr Coll 1969; (BS) Eng Ed, FL St Univ 1973; (MS) Eng Ed, Nova Univ 1987; Mid Sch Trng; Natl Resource Center for Mid Grades Ed; *cr:* Teacher Liberty Cty HS 1973-; *ai:* Asst to Mid Grades Coord; Jr Beta Club & Adv-Advisee Spon; *home:* Rt 1 Box 94-AA Bristol FL 32321

STRICKLAND, DEBRA GWEN, Language Arts Teacher; *b:* Loris, SC; *ed:* (BS) Elem Ed, 1974, (MA) Elem Ed, 1985, Specialist Cert Rdng, 1990 Univ of SC; *cr:* Teacher Green Sea Elem 1974-76, Green Sea Floyds Mid 1976-; *ai:* Jr Var Chrldr & 8th Grade Spon; NEA, Intnl Rdng Assn; *office:* Green Sea Floyds Mid Sch Green Sea Green Sea SC 29545

STRICKLAND, JUNE SMITH, 7th Grade Teacher/Lang Art Chm; *b:* Lumberton, NC; *m:* Aubrey Dale; *c:* Nadena C., Jonathan C.; *ed:* (BA) Eng, Pembroke St Univ 1973; (MED) Rdng, Univ of SC 1975; Addl Studies, Coastal Carolina Univ, Citadel Coll, Univ of GA; *cr:* Teacher Lower Richland HS 1973-75, E L Wright Mid 1976-77, Dora Jones/Gayle 1977-78, Latimer Mid 1985-; *ai:* Grantsmanship, Textbook, Jr HS Prom Comms; Sch Inservice Coord; Latta Drug Free Sch Cncl Dept Chm; Dee Dee & SC Intnl Rdng Assn 1988-; Lattas Womens Club Reporter 1988-; PTO 1985-; World Wildlife Fund 1988-; Grant to Work on Drug Abuse Problem in Latta Schls; *office:* Latimer Mid Sch 503 Willis St Latta SC 29565

STRICKLAND, MARY LOU, 5th Grade Teacher; *b:* Greenville, NC; *ed:* (BS) Elem Ed, Atlantic Chrstn Coll 1966; (MA) Intermediate Ed, Lenoir Rhyne Coll 1981; *cr:* Teacher Fairview Heights Sch 1966-70; Summer Sch Dir Iredell Cty Schls; Teacher E Iredell Elem 1970-; *ai:* Supt Advisory Southern Assn Accreditation Comm Chm; Teach In-Service Courses Iredell Cty Schls; NCEA, NEA Treas Local Unit 1975-76; ASCD, NCASCD 1988-; Womans Civic Club of Statesville (VP 1989, Pres 1976, 1990); Jaycees Teacher of Yr; E Iredell Teacher of Yr; *office:* E Iredell Elem Sch 400 E Elementary Rd Statesville NC 28677

STRICKLAND, PRISCILLA BURGESS, English Teacher; *b:* Birmingham, AL; *m:* Marlin Lee; *c:* Amelia J., Joshua L.; *ed:* (BS) Elem Ed, 1974, (MED) Elem Ed, 1978 Univ of Montevallo; *cr:* 1st Grade Rdng Teacher 1974-76, 1st Grade Self Contained Teacher 1977-81, 7th Grade Lang Art Teacher 1982-89, 7th Grade Eng Teacher 1989- Oak Grove Sch; *ai:* Lang Art Comm; AEA, NEA, UCEA 1974-.

STRICKLAND, SANDRA ELLSWORTH, Fourth Grade Teacher; *b:* Delaware Cty, IN; *m:* Kenneth Eugene; *c:* Kenneth R., Cynthia A. Van Gordon, Stephen E.; *ed:* (BS) Elem Ed, 1973, (MA) Elem Ed, 1978 Ball St Univ; *cr:* 4th Grade Teacher Montpelier Elem 1973-; *ai:* Kappa Kappa Kappa (Recording Secy 1988-, Pres 1980-83); Montpelier Chamber of Commerce Outstanding Teacher Awd 1987; *home:* 208 E Brice Montpelier IN 47359

STRICKLER, KAREN SUE (DE POY), English Dept Chairperson; *b:* Beloit, KS; *m:* William H.; *c:* Kristina, Matthew, Michael, Marshal; *ed:* (AA) Miltonvale Wesleyan Jr Coll 1966; (BSE) Eng, Emporia St Univ 1968; Working Towards Masters 1990; *cr:* Eng Teacher Onaga HS 1968-69, Tescott HS 1969-70; Eng/Journalism Teacher Jefferson Cty North HS 1970-; *ai:* Newspaper & Yrbk Adv; Sr Class Spon; JCNEA Pres 1989-; NCTE, JEA; *office:* Jefferson Cty North HS Drawer D Winchester KS 66097

STRICKLIN, PATRICIA NAPLES, English Teacher; *b:* Los Angeles, CA; *m:* David; *ed:* (BA) Eng Lit, 1973, (MA) Rdng Ed, 1983 Univ of CO Boulder; Type D Certificate Admin; Admin, Curr, Supervision Univ of CO Denver 1990; *cr:* Eng/Rdng/Speech Teacher Frederick Jr-SR HS 1979-86; Eng/Forensics Teacher Longmont HS 1986-; *ai:* Coach Forensics Team; Peer Coaching & Onward to Excl Comms; Child Study Team Chairperson; NCTE 1978-; ASCD 1987-; Phi Delta Kappa 1984-; Most Valuable Teacher Frederick Jr-Sr HS 1985-86; Communicating Through Careers Grant 1981; *office:* Longmont HS 1040 Sunset St Longmont CO 80501

STRICKLING, STELLA L., Fourth Grade Teacher; *b:* Clarksburg, WV; *ed:* (BA) Elem Ed, W Liberty St Coll 1975; (MA) Elem Ed, WV Univ 1980; Grad Stud WV Univ; *cr:* 5th Grade Teacher First Ward Elem 1975-78; 5th Grade Teacher 1978-80, 4th Grade Teacher 1980- Mc Ninch Elem; *ai:* Assertive Discipline Comm Mem 1988-89; Acad Comm 1989-; Sch Spelling Bee Coord 1990; WV Ed Assn 1975-; Glen Dale United Meth Church Financial Secy 1984-89; *office:* Mc Ninch Elem Sch 2600 4th St Moundsville WV 26041

STRIDACCHIO, DONNA MARIE, Mathematics Teacher; *b:* Newark, NJ; *ed:* (BS) Accounting, Seton Hall Univ 1979; (MA) Admin/Supervision, Montclair St Coll 1990; *cr:* Accountant 1st Natl Bank 1979-81; Math Teacher Livingston HS 1981-82, University HS 1982-; *office:* University HS 55 Clinton Pl Newark NJ 07108

STRIFLER, PETE, Social Studies Teacher; *b:* Kennenburg, W Germany; *ed:* (BSED) Soc Stud, IL St Univ 1971; *cr:* Teacher Tremont Cmmty 702 1973-; *ai:* Yrbk Spon; Sports Ticker Seller; Scholastic Bowl Moderator; *office:* Tremont Cmmty 702 400 W Pearl St Tremont IL 61568

STRILICH, WILLIAM THOMAS, Industrial Technology Teacher; *b:* Buhl, MN; *c:* Debi Marks, Wanda Olinyk, Donna, Marie, Carol; *ed:* (AS) Industrial Ed, VA Jr Coll 1954; (BA) Industrial Arts, 1957, (MA) Industrial Arts, 1965 CO St Coll of Ed; Univ of MD, Univ of N IL, IA St Univ, Drake Univ, SE MO St Univ; *cr:* Guest Instr Univ of N IA 1971, Cntrl MO St Univ 1972, IA St Univ 1973-75; Industrial Tech Teacher Cedar Rapids Cmmty Sch Dist 1957-; *ai:* Camera Club Adv; Odyssey of Mind Coach; NEA, IA St Ed Assn, Cedar Rapids Ed Assn, Intnl Technology Ed Assn Outstanding Teacher 1972; IA Industrial Ed Assn/IA St Univ Outstanding Teacher 1983; Presented at N Cntrl Accrediting Assn Conference Chicago; Textbook Revision Conference Mc Knight Publishing Co; Teaching Strategies; Authored Ed Articles; *office:* Harding Mid Sch 4801 Golf St NE Cedar Rapids IA 52402

STRIMPLE, CLYDE WILLIAM, Mathematics Teacher/Dept Chm; *b:* Rossville, KS; *m:* Martha Maxine Sutherland; *c:* Marcilyn E. Rust, Jerri K. Sitek, Cassie L. Sturegon; *ed:* (AB) Math, Washburn Univ 1952; (MS) Math, S IL Univ 1967; KS St Univ, Univ of KS, NW OK St, Univ of MO Kansas City, San Francisco Univ; *cr:* Teacher/Coach Waterville HS 1952-57, Anthony Rural HS 1957-62; Teacher/Coach 1962-81, Teacher 1981- Wyandotte HS; *ai:* NCTM 1965-82; NEA Mem 1952-; NEA KS City (VP 1986-89, Pres 1989-), Master Teacher Awd 1982; Lions Club 1952-62; Natl Sci Fnd Grant 1964-67; Wyandotte HS Hall of Fame 1986; Employee of Month Dist 500 1988; KS St Champion Track Coach Wyandotte HS 1987; Undefeated Ftbl Teams 1956, 1957, 1959; *office:* Wyandotte HS 25th & Minnesota Kansas City KS 66102

STRINGER, DELILAH ROARK, Librarian; *b:* Olla, LA; *m:* Gary Layne; *c:* Brittany L.; *ed:* (BA) Elem Ed, 1974, (MED) Elem Ed, 1980 NE LA Univ; *cr:* Teacher Robinson Elem 1975-77, S Shaver Elem 1977-78; Librarian/Teacher Mitchell Sch & A L Smith Sch 1978-89; Librarian George Welch Elem Sch 1989-; *ai:* Phi Delta Kappa 1984-; LA Lib Assn 1989-; Ouachita Assn of Sch Librarians 1978-; Mitchell Sch Teacher of Yr 1988-89; *office:* George Welch Elem Sch 199 Caldwell Rd West Monroe LA 71291

STRINGER, JAN WEBSTER, Amer History/English Teacher; *b:* Dutton, AL; *m:* Jim; *ed:* Assoc Sci, NE St Coll 1967; (BSED) Eng/His, Athens St Coll 1988; *cr:* Eng/His Teacher Section HS; *ai:* Phi Alpha Theta 1988-; Alpha Beta Lambda His Honor; Sigma Tau Delta Eng Honor 1987-; Order of Eastern Star Star Point 1970-; The Ladies Ducks Unlimited Pres 1988-; Pleasant View Baptist Church 1960-; *office:* Section HS Drawer A Section AL 35771

STRINGER, JO ANN HARPER, Honors Biology I & II Teacher; *b:* Maryville, MO; *m:* Donald L.; *c:* Pamela Thomspon, Janet Ramsdell, Mary, Linda Coyner; *ed:* (BAE) Ed/Bio Sci, NE St Teachers 1961; Marywood Coll; Stetson Univ; Univ of Houston Clear Lake; *cr:* Bio/Health/Girls Phys Ed Teacher Wayne HS 1961-62; Life Sci/Phys Sci Teacher/Gifted & Talented Dept Chairperson Edgewood Jr HS 1962-65, 1966-67; Life Sci/Bio Teacher East Jr HS 1966-65; Bio Teacher South Houston HS 1977-; *ai:* Homeroom & Class of 1991 Spon Courtesy Club Treas; Academic Achievement Task Force; Strategic Planning Action Team; Campus Improvement Comm 1990-; Delta Kappa Gamma 1984-; NEA, FEA 1967-77; Brevard Cty Teacher of Yr 1975; Pasadena Ind Sch Dist Golden Apple 1987; Contributing Writer Health Bio Ed 1991; *office:* South Houston HS 3820 S Shaver South Houston TX 77587

STRINGER, LOUISE SMITH, Secondary English Teacher; *b:* Columbus, GA; *m:* L. E.; *c:* Susan R., Kim S., Melissa Stringer Braddock; *ed:* (BS) Ed, MS St Univ 1954; Grad Stud Guidance Counseling; *cr:* Teacher Bibb Jr HS 1954-55, Bassfield HS 1958-61; Teacher/Cnslr Peeples Jr HS 1961-65, Brown Jr HS 1965-66; Teacher St Helena HS 1984-; *ai:* Beta Club & Jr Class Spon; Eng Dept Head; NEA, LEA; NCTE 1989-; *home:* PO Box 243 Greensburg LA 70441

STRINGFELLOW, RUTHIE H., Health Occupations Instructor; *b:* Yonkers, NY; *ed:* (BS) 1978, (MED) 1980 Univ of GA Athens; (AS) Dental Hygiene, Columbus Coll 1981; Dental Assisting Study Course Columbus GA 1966-67; Dental Hygiene Preceptorship Trng, Dr H Stanley Benson Jr 1966-68; *cr:* Part-Time Chairside Dental Asst Dr Alonzo L Rogers 1959-60; Sr Secy AL Cooperative Extension Service 1960-66; Chairside Dental Asst 1966-68, Registered Dental Hygenist 1968-77 Dr H Stanley Benson Jr; Health Occupations Ed Instr Bullock Cty Area Voc Center 1978-79; Health Occupations Ed Instr/Adult Dental Assisting Prgm Phenix City Area Voc Tech Center 1979-86; Registered Dental Hygenist Dr Malinda B Nix 1985-89; Health Occupations Ed Instr Russell Cty HS 1989-; *ai:* Health Occupations Stu of America Club Spon, AL & Russell Cty Mem; Dental Hygiene Advisory Comm Mem Columbus Coll 1982-83, Chattahoochee Valley Comm Coll 1982-85; Amer Dental Hygenists Assn, Western Dental Hygenists Assn Mem; GA Dental Hygenists Assn (Mem, Bd of Trustees 1973-75); Beta Kappa, Kappa Delta Pi Mem; Amer Dental Assts Assn (Mem, Annual Sessions Alternate Delegate 1972); GA Dental Assts Assn (Mem, Ed Comm Chairperson 1973-74, Keynote Speaker 1980, 1982); Western Dist Dental Assts Society (Mem, Pres 1974-75); Western Dist Hygenists Society Charter Pres 1974-75; Univ of GA Prof Health & Safety Educators Mem; Organized Health Occupations Stus of America Bullock Cty 1978 & Russell Cty 1989; Designed, Organized, Implemented Phenix Public Schls Dental Health Prgm 1980; Consultant St Dept of Ed Curr Dev 1984-85, Russell Cty HS Dev Comm 1987-, Dental Asst Curr Dev 1987-; Teacher of Yr Bullock Cty Area Voc Center 1979, AL Voc Assn 1984; Nom Teacher of Yr Phenix City Educl Assn 1983; Journal Article Published 1972; *office:* Russell Cty HS P O Box 38 Seale AL 36875

STRINGFIELD, JOANNABELLE HOLCOMB, 6th Grade Teacher; *b:* Alamogordo, NM; *m:* Herschel A.; *c:* Marykay Satterfield, Herschel A. Jr., Michael A.; *ed:* (BS) Elem Ed, NM St Univ 1970; Ed Courses, Univ Northern CO, Eastern NM Univ, NM St Univ; *cr:* 7th/8th Grade Teacher Sunbright Elem Sch 1954-55; 2nd/4th/6th Grade Teacher North Elem Sch 1970-; *ai:* Sch Improvement Team Comm Mem; Safety Patrol Spon; NEA, NM Ed Assn 1970-; NM Cncl for Soc Stud Inc 1989-; GSA Troop Leader 1962-70; PTA Comm Mem 1961-; Zeta Tau Alpha Mem 1952-; Alamogordo Chamber of Commerce Mem 1980-; *home:* 1506 Alaska Ave Alamogordo NM 88310

STRIPLING, CHARLES MITCHELL, Assistant Principal; *b:* Camilla, GA; *m:* Patricia Hackney; *c:* Mitch; *ed:* (BA) His, Eckerd Coll 1968; (MS) Educl Leadership, 1975, (EDS) Educl Leadership, 1979 Valdosta St Coll; (PHD) Educl Leadership, FL St Univ 1985; *cr:* 8th-9th Grade Teacher Mitchell Cty HS 1971-74; Fed Prgm Dir 1974-77, Supt 1977-84 Mitchell Cty Schls; HS Teacher 1986-87, Asst Prin 1987- Central Gwinnett HS; *ai:* Woodrow Wilson Designee 1968; Mc Arthur Alumni Awd Eckerd Coll 1984; *home:* 524 Windsor Ct Lawrenceville GA 30245

STRIPLING, MARGARET KOLLMANN, English Teacher; *b:* Royal, IA; *m:* Clement M.; *c:* Craig, Kerry, Jennifer; *ed:* (BS) Eng, Drake Univ 1969; *cr:* Jr HS Teacher Fonda Public Sch 1948-49; 3rd Grade Teacher Livermore Public Sch 1949-51; 2nd Grade Teacher Lu Verne Public Sch 1951-52; Jr HS Teacher Lu Verne Cmmty Sch 1953-89; *ai:* IA Ed Assn, NEA 1948-89; Local Lu Verne Assn (Secy, Treas) 1975-89; *home:* Lu Verne IA 50560

STROBEL, HAROLD C., Biology Teacher; *b:* Eureka, SD; *m:* Virginia Klos; *c:* Susan Strobel Sievert, Sharon M.; *ed:* (BA) Bio/Eng, Yankton Coll 1952; (MA) Zoology/Ed, Univ of NE Lincoln 1955; Bio, Univ of S IL Carbondale, 1959; Geology, SD Sch of Mines 1960; Bio, Rutgers Univ 1963; *cr:* Sci/Eng Teacher Roscoe Public Schls 1955-56; Bio Teacher N Platte Public Schls 1956-59; Sci Teacher Minneapolis SW HS 1960-81, Minneapolis Washburn HS 1981-89; *ai:* Chairperson Sci Dept; Chairperson & Mem Faculty Cncl; Team Coach of Sci Olympiad Team; NEA Life Mem 1956-; MN Fed of Teachers 1981-; MN Sci Teachers 1960-; United Church of Christ Congregational Church (Deacon, Sunday Sch Teacher, Confirmation Curr Consultant); Minneapolis Teacher of Yr 1967; MN Teacher of Yr 1967; MN Outstanding Bio Teacher 1968; Presented Yale Univ Distinguished Teacher Awd 1968; Selected Yankton Coll Alumni Achievement Awd 1977; Co-Author 2 Chronobiology Articles Presented at Chronobiology Conference 1971; *home:* 4217 Drew Ave S Minneapolis MN 55410

STROHMEYER, JUDITH BISHOP, Teacher; *b:* Litchfield, IL; *m:* Eric Richard; *c:* Sarah, Rachel; *ed:* (BS) Elem, E IL Univ 1963; Masters Elem, Univ of IL 1967; Univ of CO, MT St Univ; *cr:* 4th Grade Teacher Cherokee Sch 1963-66; 5th Grade Teacher Jackson Sch 1967-69; 7th/8th Grade Teacher Bozeman Jr HS 1975-; *ai:* Dist Rdng Comm; PR & R; BEA, MEA, NEA Building Rep 1975-; Delta Kappa Gamma Pres 1986-88; NCTE; Phi Delta Kappa Historian 1987-88; *home:* 1241 Tayabeshockup Bozeman MT 59715

STROM, LOIS ELEANOR, 1st Grade Teacher; *b:* Graceville, MN; *m:* John C.; *c:* Karen J., Jon M., Steven J.; *ed:* (AA) Early Chldhd, Stephens Coll 1948; (BA) Elem Ed, WI St U 1965; (MBA) MA Bus Admin, Azusa Pacific 1978; Natl Ldrshp Trng Inst 1988; *cr:* Kndgtn Teacher Hudson Public Sch 1948-1956; 1st Grade Teacher Stillwater Dist 834 1957-1960; 1st & 2nd Grade Teacher Desert Sands USD 1962-; *ai:* Aims Classes Taught Fresno Pacific Coll & San Bernardino St Coll; Staff Dev Classes Aimes Desert Sands USD; Chm Bd of Govt Hope Luth Pre-Sch; Church Cncl Hope Luth; Curr Cncl Desert Sands USD; Intnl Rdng Assn; Delta Kappa Gamma; NEA; WI/MN/CA Teachers Assn 1948-; WI Tchers Assn Secy 1949-; AAL (Sec/Treas 1976-/Lamplighter 1980-; Gold Star; Brownie & Girl Scouts Leader; Desert Sands Grant to Aims & Sci Fest; *home:* 75-410 Fairway Dr Indian Wells CA 92210

STROM, MICHAEL JOHN, 6th Grade Teacher; *b:* Ellenberg, WA; *m:* Carolyn; *ed:* (BA) Elem Ed, WA St 1982; *cr:* 6th Grade Teacher Jackpot Combined; *ai:* Asst Ftbl; Head Girls Bsktbl; NSF 1988 Summer Sci Inst; Boise St Univ Grant; Coach of Yr Girls Bsktbl 1988-89.

STRONG, EDWARD DICKERSON, JR., Math Teacher; *b:* Pearisburg, VA; *ed:* (BS) Math Ed, Bluefield St Coll 1964; (MS) Scndry Sch Adm, Radford Univ 1967; *cr:* Teacher Tazewell Cty Public Schls 1964-68; Asst Prin/Teacher 1968-76, Teacher 1976-83 Clifton Forge HS; Clifton Mid Sch 1983-; *ai:* NEA 1964; Phi Delta Kappa 1967-; *office:* Clifton Mid Sch Commericial Ave Clifton Forge VA 24422

STRONG, ELMINOR MORRIS, 5th Grade Teacher; *b:* Philadelphia, PA; *m:* James A.; *c:* Jill; *ed:* (BS) Elem Ed, Cheyney St Univ 1970; (EDM) Elem Ed, Temple Univ 1976; Prin Cert Prgm & Supervisory Cert Prgm Temple Univ; *cr:* 4th/5th/6th Grade Teacher Shawmont Public Sch 1970-; *ai:* Red Cross Club Spon; United Negro Coll Fund Shawmont Chairperson; 5th Grade Chairperson; Shawmont Sch Plan-Sci Curr Chairperson; Tells Test Shawmont Coord; AFT; PA Fed Teachers; Philadelphia Fed of Teachers; PA Conference on Black Basic Ed; Comm Outreach Sunday Sch Pgm 1964-; Service Awd, 1974; Women in Chrstn Service Treas 1985; Service Awd 1987; *office:* Shawmont Public Sch Shawmont Ave & Eva St Philadelphia PA 19128

STRONG, FLORENE SNIPES, Math Teacher; *b:* Moundville, AL; *m:* Charles William Jr.; *c:* Charles W. III, Thomas M.; *ed:* (BS) Math, Livingston Univ 1962; (MA) Scndry Ed, Troy St Univ 1975; *cr:* Math Teacher Baldwin Cty HS 1962-70, Bay Minette Mid Sch 1970-; *ai:* Yrbk, Newspaper Spon; Coord Academic Credit Card Prgm; Project Asset St of AL; NEA, AEA, BCEA 1962-; Natl Mid Sch Assn, Phi Delta Kappa 1986-; 1st Baptist Church Sunday Sch Dir 1988-; Pilot Club of Bay Minette Pres, Past Mem) 1972; Article Published Mid Sch Journal; *office:* Bay Minette Mid Sch 1000 Track St Bay Minette AL 36507

STRONG, LINDA DAVIDSON, 6TH Grade Teacher; *b:* Philipsburg, PA; *m:* Larry E.; *c:* Scott A.; *ed:* (BS) Elem, IN Univ Pa 1970; PA Permanent Cert; Essential Elements of Instruction Trng; *cr:* 3rd Grade Teacher Washington Sch 1970-71; 2nd Grade Teacher 1971-75; 6th Grade Teacher Adams Schl 1984-; 5th Grade Teacher Warriors Mark Sch 1976-84; *ai:* Tyrone Area Ed Assn Treas 1970-; PSEA 1970-; NEA 1970-; Womens Club of Tyrone Corresponding Secy 1987-; Tyrone Recyclers Inc Special Act 1987-; Christ United Meth Church Lay Speaker Chm 1984-; *home:* RD 1 Box 239 Tyrone PA 16686

STRONG, LINDA MAHAN, Elementary Guidance Counselor; *b:* Alhambra, CA; *m:* Mike G.; *c:* Michael, Angela; *ed:* (BS) Ed, Univ of MO St Louis 1980; (MA) Cnslng & Sch Psych, Wichita St Univ 1988; *cr:* 4th Grade Teacher 1981-88; K-6 Guidance Cnslr 1988- Buhler USD 313; *ai:* KS Assn for Cnslng & Dev 1988-; Phi Kappa Phi 1980-; Kappa Kappa Iota 1989-; NEA 1981-89; KNEA; ASCA 1988-; *office:* Union Valley/Prosperity 2501 E 30th Ave Hutchinson KS 67502

STRONG, LINDA N., 4th Grade Teacher; *b:* Celina, TN; *m:* Gerald L.; *c:* Dale, Daniel; *ed:* (BS) Elem Ed, 1975, (MA) Elem Ed, 1981 TN Tech Univ; *cr:* 4th Grade Teacher Celina K-8 Sch 1975-; *ai:* Clay Cty Ed Assn (Treas, Membership Chm) 1988-; TN Ed Assn, NEA 1975-; Delta Kappa Gamma 1985-; TN Rdng Assn 1982-; *home:* Clark Subdivision Celina TN 38551

STRONG, MARK CHRISTOPHER, Third Grade Teacher; *b:* Milwaukee, WI; *m:* Patty Hajinian; *c:* Courtney, Renee, Stuart; *ed:* (BS) Early Chldhd Ed-Magna Cum Laude, Univ WI 1980; *cr:* 3rd Grade Teacher Stone Bank Sch 1980-90; K-3 Sci Teacher Waukesha Montessori Sch 1980-89; *ai:* Teach K-3 Odyssey of Mind; Gifted & Talented Kndgtn Comm Mem; *home:* 269 Glenwood Rd Oconomowoc WI 53066

STRONG, MARY HELEN (HIX), Kindergarten Teacher; *b:* Tulsa, OK; *m:* Franklin D.; *c:* Scott; *ed:* (BSED) Elem Ed, 1971, (MSED) Elem Ed, 1977 Northeastern Univ; *cr:* Kndgtn Teacher Moseley Elem Sch 1971-72, Leach Elem Sch 1973-; *ai:* Staff Dev Chairperson; Volunteer 4-H Leader; Sch Yrbk Ed; Curr Improvement Comm; DE Cty Ed Assn, OK Ed Assn, NEA 1973-; *office:* Leach Elem Sch PO Box 211 Twin Oaks OK 74368

STRONG, PRISCILLA TULL, Second Grade Teacher; *b:* Salisbury, MD; *m:* James; *c:* Shannon M.; *ed:* (BS) Elem Ed, Bowie St Coll 1964; Elem Ed, Bowie Grad Sch 1975; *cr:* Elem Teacher Fairmount Heights Elem Sch 1964-70, Laurel Elem Sch 1970-71, Oaklands Elem Sch 1972-; *ai:* St Mark United Meth Church (Bd of Higher Ed Mem, Campus Ministries Mem, Sunday Sch Teacher); Nom Outstanding Educators Awds 1978-79; *home:* 1437 Evergreen Rd Severn MD 21144

STRONSTORFF, BERT H., Drug Education Instructor; *b:* Highland, IL; *c:* Melissa, Lee; *ed:* (BA) Elem Ed, Monmouth Coll 1969; *cr:* Teacher N Hanover Township Schls 1970-; *ai:* Family Life Curr Comm; Township Little League Coach 1981-88; Guitarist & Part Time Guitar Instr; Woodcraft Designs Creations 1990; N Hanover Township Ed Assn Building Rep 1975-77; Adult Ed Instr; Cmmty Ed Literary Skills.

STROTHER, PHYLLIS HELMS, English Teacher; *b:* Mexia, TX; *m:* Ralph T.; *c:* Rhett, Jack, Matt; *ed:* (BA) Eng/Ed, Baylor Univ 1964; (MA) Eng, Sam Houston St Univ 1967; Various Wkshps; *cr:* Teacher of 11th Grade Gifted Waco HS; *ai:* Elite Eng Society, Sch Newspaper, Sr Class, UIL Academic Act Spon; Project Graduation; Athletic Booster Club; Dept Chm; Nom Waco HS Outstanding Teacher; Waco Ind Sch Dist Drug Abuse/ Alcoholism Cncl Curr Writer.

STROUD, KAY HUMPHREY, Biology Teacher; *b:* Pasadena, TX; *m:* W. Lynn; *c:* Jamie, Tracy; *ed:* (BS) Psych, TX A&M Univ 1985; *cr:* Bio Teacher Palestine HS 1986-; *ai:* Future Problem Solving Prgm, Frosh & Jr Var Chldr Coach; TX Classroom Teachers Assn, Sci Teachers Assn of TX, TX Assn of Bio Teachers; Psi Chi, Phi Kappa Phi; *office:* Palestine HS 1600 Loop 256 Palestine TX 75801

STROUGH, CATHY FAYE (CARTER), Business Educator; *b:* Caldwell, ID; *m:* Kelly Lee; *c:* Carly F., Kirsten L.; *ed:* (BBA) Bus Ed, Boise St Univ 1976; *cr:* Bus Educator St Maries HS 1976-78, Fruitland HS 1979-; *ai:* Pres Reagan Distinguished Teacher 1986; Bus Prof of America ID Adv of Yr 1986; Book Author 1986; *office:* Fruitland HS PO Box 387 Fruitland ID 83619

STROUP, JAMES EARL, English Teacher; *b:* Gastonia, NC; *m:* Gracie Woolwine; *ed:* (BA) Eng-Speech/Religion, Carson-Newman Coll 1971; (MRE) Religious Ed, Southern Baptist Theological Seminary 1975; (MED) Supervision/Admin East TN St Univ 1985; *cr:* Teacher/Coach Rush Strong Sch 1971-73; Minister of Ed-Youth Manley Baptist Church 1975-82; Eng Teacher Morristown-Hamblen HS West 1982-; *ai:* Co-chairperson Eng Dept 1988-89; Accreditation Comm Philosophy, Objectives 1989-; Jr-Sr Prom Comm 1987-88; Hamblen Cty Ed Assn, TN Ed Assn, NEA 1982-; NCTE 1987-; Part Time Minister of Music Buffalo Trail Baptist Church 1982-; Douglas-Cherokee Economic Authority Bd of Dir Alternate 1986-; Cmmty Action Agency; Seminar Leader For TN Dept Ed 1990 & Lib-Classroom Cooperatives 1989; *office:* Morristown-Hamblen West H S 1025 Sulphur Springs Rd Morristown TN 37814

STRUBLE, KAREN (VANDECAR), 6th Grade Teacher; *b:* Ypsilanti, MI; *m:* Charles D.; *c:* Julie A., Lauren K.; *ed:* (BA) Vocal Music Ed, MI St Univ 1971; (MA) Elem Ed, E MI Univ 1979; *cr:* Elem Vocal Music Teacher Dearborn Heights 7 1972-73; 2nd/3rd Grade Teacher Quirk Elem Sch 1981-84; Elem Vocal Music Teacher Edgemont & Haggerty 1973-79, 1981-; 6th Grade Teacher Edgemont & North Mid Sch 1978-81, 1984-; Concert Choir Dir North Mid Sch 1989-; *ai:* Spelling Bee Spon; Concert Choir Dir; Prof Dev Advisory Cncl Mem; Alpha Delta Kappa St Music Chm 1980-; *office:* North Mid Sch 47097 Mc Bride St Belleville MI 48111

STRUBLE, RONALD RAY, Technology Education Teacher; *b:* Sigourney, IA; *m:* Deann Louise Johnson; *c:* Michael, Laura, Lindsay; *ed:* (BA) Industrial Art, 1973, (MA) Industrial Art, 1986 Univ N IA Cedar Falls; Assertive Discipline, Drake Univ; *cr:* Teacher 1973-, Dept Chm 1986- West Delaware HS; *ai:* Jr Class Spon & Chaperone; NHS Selection Comm; West Delaware Ed Assn (Mem 1973-, Pres 1987-88); Chamber of Commerce Mem 1990; 4-H (Adv, Teacher) 1978-87; IA Natl Guard NCO 1970-76, 1986-, Army Commendation Medal 1986; *home:* 704 Tanglewood Dr Manchester IA 52057

STRUEBING, DAVE DEAN, Physical Ed/History Teacher; *b:* David City, NE; *m:* Beverly Jo Lowery; *c:* Brett, Kyle, Sadie; *ed:* (BS) Phys Ed, NE Wesleyan Univ 1977; Grad Stud; *cr:* Teacher Sandhills HS 1977-78, East Butler 1979-; *ai:* Letterclub Spon; Head Ftbl & Girls Track; Jr HS Girls Bsktbl & Track; NE Ed Assn, NEA, NE Coaches Assn; Red Cross Instr 1982-; Volunteer Fire Dept Emergency Medical Tech 1981-; *office:* East Butler Sch 317 Madison St Brainard NE 68626

STRUEBING, DONNA GAIL (WAGNER), 1st/4th Grade Reading Teacher; *b:* Lincoln, IL; *m:* David Bruce; *c:* Derek, Sarah; *ed:* (BS) Spec Ed, IL St Univ 1974; *cr:* Remedial Rdng/Kndgtn Teacher 1975-79, 1st Grade Teacher 1976-80, Kndgtn-4th Grade Rdng Teacher 1987-, Math Tutoring 1988- Hartsburg-Emden Unit Sch Dist; *ai:* NEA 1975-80; Kappa Delta Phi; St Peters Luth Church (Childrens Choir, Fellowship Leader, Couples Club, Womens Bible Study Group); Amer Legion Auxiliary Unit 506; Cub Scout Pack 127 Comm Mem; *office:* Hartsburg-Emden Elem Sch Market St Emden IL 62635

STRUMEYER, ARLINE Z., Social Studies Teacher; *b:* New York City, NY; *m:* Joseph; *c:* Jeffrey M., Sheri L. Bayles, Donna G. Ratner; *ed:* (BA) His/Soc Stud, 1949, (MA) His, 1950 St Univ of NY Albany; *cr:* Substitute Teacher 1968-80, Soc Stud Teacher 1981- South Side Sr HS; *ai:* Key Club Faculty Adv; NCSS, NY St Cncl of Soc Stud, Long Island Cncl of Soc Stud 1980-; PTA Pres 1967-69, Life Membership 1968; Bd of Ed Valley Stream Dist #13 (Trustee, Pres 1975-79, 1984-85, 1987-88,) 1972-; *office:* South Side HS Shepherd St Rockville Centre NY 11570

STRUVE, RICHARD DALE, Scndry Math Mentor/Dept Chair; *b:* Pomona, CA; *m:* Constance Marie; *c:* Kevin, Krista, Tonya, Todd; *ed:* (BS) Bus, 1965, (BS) Accounting, 1967, (BS) Math, 1969 CA St Poltechnic Univ; *cr:* Temple City Unified Sch Dist 1972-74; Chino Unified Sch Dist 1975-; *ai:* Soccer & Bsbl Coach; Chino Unified Sch Dist Scndry Math Mentor & Math Chm; CA Math Cncl; Claremont Little League Treas 1983-85; Claremont Pony League Publicity 1985-86; Credit Union (Chm of Audit, Loan Comm); Chino Unified Sch Dist Teacher of Yr 1983, 1985; *home:* 2271 N Campus Ave Upland CA 91786

STRUWE, MERLE EUGENE, 8th United States His Teacher; *b:* Madison, SD; *m:* Elaine Shirley Merager; *c:* Gregg, Jeff, Todd; *ed:* (BA) His/Phys Ed, General Beadle St Coll 1951; SD St Univ; *cr:* 7th-8th Grade Teacher Chester Schls 1954-56; 8th Grade Teacher General Beadle Campus 1956-63, Lake Cntrl 1963-; *ai:* 8th Grade Ftbl Coach; Benevolent Protector Order of Elks Exalted Ruler 1978-79; *home:* 316 N Lee Madison SD 57042

STRZALKA, ALICE GLOWACKI, Mathematics Teacher; *b:* Chicago, IL; *m:* Chester R.; *c:* Mary B. Strzalka-Benham, Brian, Mary A., Mary T. Strzalka-Sobel; *ed:* (BA) Math, Coll of St Francis 1951; (MA) Math, Loyola Univ 1959; Grad Work in Ed, Admin, Supervision; *cr:* Teacher Chicago Public HS 1951-53, St Ann HS 1962-65, Acad of the Sacred Heart 1965-72; Prin St Matthias Elem 1974-78, St Joseph Elem 1978-81, St Gregory Elem 1981-83; Teacher Good Counsel HS 1983-; *ai:* Faculty Adv Educl Service Club; ASCD, IASCD, Assn of Math Teachers.

STUART, F. KAY STAPLES, Computer Science Teacher; *b:* Wellsboro, PA; *m:* Edward Wallace; *c:* Blaine E.; *ed:* (BS) Scndry Ed/Math, 1973, (MS) Ed, 1990 Mansfield Univ; *cr:* Math Teacher Troupsburg Cntrl Sch 1974-75; Continuing Ed Mansfield Univ 1983-86; Teacher/Stu Personnel Dir Cowanesque Valley HS 1975-; *ai:* Sch Musical Dir; Sr HS Stu Cncl Adv; Stu Asst Prgm Team Mem; Delta Kappa Gamma Mem 1990; PA Assn of Stud Cty Past Pres 1989-; Pack 22 Cub Scout BSA Comm Chm, Knoxville Yoked Churches Sunday Sch Supt 1989-; *office:* Cowanesque Valley HS Old Fairgrounds Rd Westfield PA 16950

STUART, LOIS GLOFF, Orchestra Teacher; *b:* Milwaukee, WI; *m:* Theodore M.; *c:* Ellyn Briggs, Theodore, Lynn, Carolyn; *ed:* (BS) Music Ed, Univ of WI Milwaukee 1952; Numerous Univ; *cr:* Band Dir Milwaukee Public Schls 1952-54; String Classes/Private Stus Teacher/Private Studio 1964-74; Orch Dir Prince William Public Schls 1974-; *ai:* Music Educators Natl Conference 1974-; NEA; Suzuki Organization 1974-77; Prince William Symphony (Founder, Bd Mem); Prince William Youth Symphony (Bd Mem 1983-87, Conductor 1988-89) Amer String Teachers VA Unit Outstanding Mid Sch Orch Prgm Awd 1988; *office:* Woodbridge Mid Sch 2201 York Dr Woodbridge VA 22191

STUART, MICHON MICHAEL, Fifth Grade Teacher; *b:* Endicott, NY; *m:* Elaine De Giovanni; *c:* Marissa; *ed:* (BA) Elem Ed, St Univ Fredonia 1970; Post Grad Stud SUNY Binghamton; *cr:* 6th Grade Teacher 1970-83, 5th Grade Teacher 1983- Vestal Sch System; *ai:* Soc Stud & Eng Curr Comm; Supt Interview Comm Mem 1990; Dir Grade Trips NYC 1972-; Dir 6th Grade Outdoor Ed Prgm 1979-88; After Sch Floor Hockey Prgm; 6th Grade Medieval Dinners Sch Dir 1979-88; Sch Colonial Dinner Dir 1990; Vestal Teachers Assn (Building Chm 1971-73, Building Rep 1973-76, 1986-); Vestal Democratic Comm Chm 1982-; Vestal Hills PTA Pres 1977-79, Honorary Life Mem 1983; Clayton Avenue PTA Mem 1983-87, Honoree Dist Cncl Schlsp 1987; Democratic Natl Convention Alternate Delegate 1980; 20 Yrs Teaching Honor Vestal Bd of Ed 1990; *home:* 409 Butternut Dr Vestal NY 13850

STUART, STEPHAN A., Counselor; *b:* Denver, CO; *m:* Carol L. Talafous; *c:* Heather, Colleen; *ed:* (BA) His/Ed, 1968, (MA) Counseling, 1970, (EDS) Admin, 1979 Univ of NM; *cr:* Teacher Mosquero Public Schls 1968-70; Cnslr 1970-74, Curr Specialist 1974-79 Albuquerque Public Schls; Prin Carrizozo Municipal Schls 1979-81; Prin/Asst Supt Jemez Springs Public Schls 1981-86; Cnslr Albuquerque Public Schls 1986-; *ai:* Ravens Against Drugs Stu Assn Core Team; Adult Intervention Team Drug Use & Abuse; *home:* Mt Rt Box 1E Jemez Springs NM 87025

STUBBLEFIELD, SANDRA C., Business Education Teacher; *b:* Madison, TN; *m:* Ronnie R.; *ed:* (AA) Bus Admin, Volunteer St Comm Coll 1976; (BS) Bus Ed, MTSU 1983; Voc Cert, MTSU; Working Towards Master Degree MTSU; *cr:* Teacher Sumner Cty Bd of Ed 1884-; *ai:* Anchor Club Spon; Renaissance & Bus Ed Textbook Renewal Comms; FBLA Spon; NEA, TN Ed Assn, Sumner Cty Ed Assn 1984-; Amer Voc Assn 1984-86; NBEA 1989-; TN Bus Ed Assn 1989-; Delta Pi Epsilon 1989-; Natl Arbor Day Fnd, Sumner Cty Farm Bureau 1988-; Upper Sumner Concerned Citizens Inc 1987-; Honorary FFA Mem; Nom for Renaissance Teacher 1989-; *office:* Beech Sr H S Long Hollow Pike Hendersonville TN 37075

STUBBS, GARY LE ROY, Business Teacher; *b:* Colorado Springs, CO; *m:* Sue Anne Stubbs Wilson; *c:* Kari Sue, Le Anne Kay, Kevin Le; *ed:* (BA) Bus Ed/Speech, 1974, (MS) Vocational Ed, 1983 Kearney ST Coll; Prof Dev in Bus and Office 1985;Prof Dev Techniques in Ed 1986; *cr:* Teacher Litchfield Public Schls 1975-82, Ravenna Public Schls 1982-; *ai:* FBLA 1975-; Jr/Sr HS Bsktbl Coach-1975-; Girls Sftbl Coach-1975-; NE ST Bus Ed Assn Mem 1975- Secy/Treas 1979-81; FBLA ST Bd 1986-89; Natl Bus Ed Assn Mem 1975-; Pleasant Hill Sch Pres 1986-89; FBLA St Bd 1979-82 Plaque 1982; NE Coaches Assn 1975-; NE ST Bus Ed Secy/Treas 1975-88; ST Bd 1975-88; FBLA ST Bd of Dir 1979-82; Wrote Curr for St Bus Comm 1986-87; *office:* Ravenna H S Rr 2 Box 84a Ravenna NE 68869

STUBBS, PATRICIA GIFFORD, French Teacher; *b:* Fort Collins, CO; *c:* Erin M., Collin R.; *ed:* (BA) Fr, 1973, (BA) Eng, 1973 Kearney St Coll; Learning Strategies; *cr:* Teacher Belleville HS 1975-76, Litchfield Cmmty Sch 1979-80; Owner Wholesale/ Retail Gift Bus 1980-84; Teacher Superior HS 1984-; *ai:* TAT Team Mem; Superior Ed Assn Building Rep 1984-; NEA; NE St Ed Assn; AATF 1988-; PEO (Guard, Pres); *office:* Superior HS W 8th St Superior NE 68978

STUBBS, THOMAS ALBERT, History/English Teacher; *b:* Shawneetown, IL; *w:* Wilma Jean Boling (dec); *c:* Thomas A. Jr.; *ed:* (BSED) Soc Stud/Eng, 1950, (MSED) Sch Admin, 1952 S IL Univ; Post Grad Stud Comm, Boston Univ 1960; *cr:* Officer USAF 1952-72; His Teacher Camp Springs Chrstn Schls 1975-89; Eng/ His Teacher Grace Brethren Chrstn Schls 1989-; *office:* Grace Brethren Chrstn Sch 6501 Surratts Rd Clinton MD 20735

STUBER, ISABELL A. (ZITTEL), Retired Teacher; *b:* Alma, WI; *m:* Norman G.; *c:* Ronald N., Gene A., Kathleen I. Stuber Crosby; *ed:* (BA) Elem Ed, Univ WI Eau Claire 1963; Continuing Ed Child Care, Northeast WI Tech Coll 1988; *cr:* Rural Sch 1st-8th Grade Teacher Bohris Valley Sch 1943-46 & 1949-50; Rural Sch 1st-6th Grade Teacher Beversdorf Sch 1955-56; Rural Sch 1st-8th Grade Teacher TX Sch 1956-65; Kndgtn Teacher Keshena Elem Sch 1965-76; 2nd Grade Teacher Lincoln Elem Sch 1976-86; *ai:* Shawano Gresham Ed Assn 1956-86; WI Ed Assn 1956-86; NEA 1956-86; PTA 1965-86; Shawano Cty Retired Teachers Assn 1986-; WI Retired Teachers Assn 1986-; AARP Natl 1986-.

STUBY, GORDON WILLIAM, Fifth Grade Teacher; *b:* Indiana, PA; *m:* Mary Ruth Mc Creight; *c:* Laura M., Eric W., Brian M.; *ed:* (BA) Elem Ed, Slippery Rock Univ 1970; Grad Work Indiana Univ of PA, Clarion Univ; *cr:* Teacher Punxsutawney Area Sch Dist 1970-; *ai:* 9th Grade Ftbl Coach; Punxsutawney Booster Club Bd of Dir; PA Ed Assn Pres 1978-80; NEA, PSEA; Reynoldsville Presbyn Church Elder 1980-84, 1989-; *home:* RD 3 Box 10A Reynoldsville PA 15851

STUCKEY, SHARI TAYLOR, English Teacher; *b:* Sewickley, PA; *m:* Jon Carl; *ed:* (BA) Scndry Eng/Psych Rdng, Malone Coll 1987; *cr:* Eng Teacher Orrville HS 1987-; *ai:* NHS Selection Comm; Jr Var Cheerleading Coach; Dist Policy Comm HS Rep; Grading & Right to Read Week Comms; NEA/OEA; OCTELA; Kappa Delta Pi; *office:* Orrville HS 841 N Ella St Orrville OH 44667

STUCKEY, VANESSA, English/Lit Teacher/Dept Chair; *b:* Bennettsville, SC; *ed:* (BA) Eng, SC St Coll 1981; (BA) Admin, Furman Univ; *cr:* Teacher Woodmont HS 1981-82; Teacher/Dept Chairperson Hillcrest Mid 1982-; *ai:* Sch Lit Magazine & Black His Comm Chairperson; Natl Jr Beta Club Spon; Natural Helpers Adv; Phi Delta Kappa, ASCD 1989-; Outstanding Young Women of America 1985; NEA 1981-; Delta Sigma Theta Pres 1988-; Natl Cncl of Negro Women; United Negro Coll Fund Pres 1989; Local Sickle Cell Anemia Fnd; Cryovac Schlsp; *office:* Hillcrest Mid Sch Rt 4 Garrison Rd Simpsonville SC 29681

STUCKEY, WANDA MC DEARIS, English Teacher; *b:* Manchester, GA; *m:* James M.; *c:* Sarah, Samantha, Rachel, Jamesan; *ed:* (BA) Eng, 1974, (MED) Eng Ed, 1978, (EDS) Eng Ed, 1984 Columbus Coll; Grad Work Communicative Art, GA St Univ Atlanta GA; *cr:* Eng Teacher Manchester Mid Sch 1974-87, Griffin HS 1987-; *ai:* Homecoming Act Faculty Adv; Spalding Cty Assn of Teachers of Eng, Griffin-Spalding Ed Assn, GA Ed Assn, NEA; Lambda Iota Tau Literary Honor Society; Outstanding Stu Amer Coll, Univs 1987; *home:* 130 Morning Mist Way Fayetteville GA 30214

STUCKWISCH, THOMAS JOE, Mathematics Department Chair; *b:* Seymour, IN; *m:* Vivian Larie Barkman; *c:* Sarah, Clayton; *ed:* (BA) Math, Hanover Coll 1973; (MAT) Math, IN Univ 1978; *cr:* Math Teacher Crothersville HS 1973-74, Paoli HS

1974-; *ai:* Var Bsbl & Asst Var Ftbl Coach; NEA, ISTA, NCTM, IFCA, IHSBCAA; *office:* Paoli Cmmty Schls 501 Elm St Paoli IN 47454

STUDDARD, CYNTHIA LYNNE, High School Science Teacher; *b:* Cleveland, TN; *m:* John Floyd; *c:* Greg; *ed:* (AS) Natural Sci, Cleveland St Comm Coll 1982; (BS) Scndry Ed/Bio, Univ of TN Chattanooga 1984; Chem in Cmmty Wkshp; *cr:* 8th Grade Earth Sci Teacher Hixson Jr HS 1984; 9th-12th Grade Physics/Chem/Bio/General Sci/Phys Sci Teacher Charleston HS 1985-; *ai:* Beta Club, BU Club, Frosh Class Spon; Prins Advisory, Grades, Title II Needs Comms; WTCI Programming Comm Mem; BCEA, TEA, NEA 1985-; March of Dimes Mothers March Volunteer 1988-; Delano Baptist Church Mem 1985-; Charleston Teacher of Month 1988; Cleveland Jaycees Outstanding Young Educator 1990; Charleston HS Teacher of Yr 1990; Bradley Cty Teacher of Yr 1990; Nom Presidential Merit Awd Excl in Sci Teaching 1990; *office:* Charleston HS Hwy 11 Charleston TN 37310

STUDNICKI, HENRY THOMAS, 7th/8th Grade Math Teacher; *b:* Fairhope, PA; *m:* Elma Louise Cekola; *c:* Lorraine Wilson, Joyce Smith, John; *ed:* (BS) Phys Sci, California Univ of PA 1957; *cr:* Math Teacher California Area Sch Dist 1960; Physic Teacher 1988, Math Teacher 1960- Belle Vernon Area Sch Dist; *ai:* NEA, PSEA, BVAEA 1960-; US Army E-4 1957-59; Natl Sci Fnd Grant 1961-62; *office:* Bellmar Mid Sch 500 Perry Ave Belle Vernon PA 15012

STUEFLOTEN, JERRY TELFORD, Science Department Chair; *b:* San Jose, CA; *c:* Tracey, Kari, Heather; *ed:* (BA) Ed, 1963, (MA) Life Sci Teaching, 1967 San Jose St Univ; Post Grad Work, Cal Poly St Univ; *cr:* 4th Grade Elem Teacher Fremont Elem Sch 1963-64; 7th/8th Grade Sci Teacher Wilson Intermediate Sch 1964-80; 7th-9th Grade Sci/Math Teacher Buchser Jr HS 1980-85; 9th-12th Grade Sci Teacher Santa Clara HS 1985-; *ai:* Dept Chm; Dist AIDS Task Force; Sci Club Adv; Stu Asst Prgm; Univ Master Teacher Prgm; CA Teachers Assn 1980-; Mono Lake Comm 1979-; PTA Honorary Life Mem, Service Awds; *office:* Santa Clara HS 3000 Benton St Santa Clara CA 95051

STUEVER, VICKI LESLIE, Honors Eng/Psych Teacher; *b:* Blackwell, OK; *m:* Charles E.; *c:* Jade, Jason; *ed:* (BAED) Eng Ed, NW OK St Univ Alva 1973; (MED) Ed, Phillips Univ 1990; Grad Stud Wichita St Univ 1974; *cr:* Eng Teacher Caldwell HS 1973-75, Frederick Jr HS 1975-76, Kremlin HS 1979-81, Chisholm HS 1981-; *ai:* NHS Faculty Cncl Sr Spon; Head Eng Dept; NEA; CEA Parliamentarian 1987-88; OEA; NW OK St Univ Dorm Cncl (Resident Asst 1971-73, Head Resident 1974); Chisholm HS Teacher of Yr 1990; *home:* 308 Candlewood Cr Enid OK 73701

STULKEN, SHARYL LEE, HS Social Studies Teacher; *b:* Monticello, IA; *m:* Stephen; *c:* Douglas, Stephanie; *ed:* (BA) Sociology/His, Univ of N IA 1969; Advanced Trng in Stu at Risk, Writers Wkshp Supervising Stu Teachers, Amer Political Behavior; World Politics & Other Soc Sci Courses; *cr:* Jr HS Soc Stud Tilford Jr HS 1971-76; HS Sociology/Ec Washington HS 1978; HS Soc Stud Teacher Urbana HS 1979-89, Center Point Urbana HS 1989-; *ai:* Adv to Model United Nations; Mem Stu Asst Team; Bd of Cty Mental Health Secy 1985-; *home:* RR 1 Box 36-1 Vinton IA 52349

STULL, FRANK WALTER, 8th Grade Soc Studies Teacher; *b:* Easton, PA; *m:* Darlene Joy Hunsicker; *c:* James, Ronald, Wendy; *ed:* (BS) Ed/Soc Stud, East Stroudsburg St Univ 1956; (ME) Ed Admin, Lehigh Univ 1966; Geogrpahy, PA St Univ; *cr:* 8th Grade Soc Stud Teacher Howell Twp Elem Sch 1958-59, Holland Twp Elem Sch 1959-; *ai:* Mem Soc Stud Curr Comm; NEA, NJEA, Holland Twp Ed Assn 1958-; Hunt Cty Ed Assn 1959-; NCSS 1990; Hunterdon Cty Sch Employees Fed Credit Union (Dir, Secy, Treas, Mgr 1969-87) Meritorius Service Awd 1988; Cubmaster-Cub Pack #54 1971-72; BSA Merit Badge Cnslr 1970-84; Phi Delta Kappa 1964; Experienced Teacher Fellowship; Geography PA St Univ 1967; Outstanding Elem Teacher of America 1972; St of NJ the Governors Teacher Recognition Prgm Winner 1987; Distinguished Achievement Awd Researching/Preserving His Holland Twp &Surrounding Areas 1989; *home:* 806 Rugby Rd Phillipsburg NJ 08865

STULMAKER, RICHARD M., Social Sciences Teacher; *b:* Brooklyn, NY; *c:* Alissa A., Jeffrey M., Kenneth L.; *ed:* (BA) & (MA) Soc Sci/Sociology/Psych SUNY Albany 1962-64; United States Army Reserves Officer Grad Prgm Civil Affairs & Public Admin, NY Univ 1964-67; Stud African Affairs NY Univ 1964-66; *cr:* Teacher/Coach/Adv Herkimer HS 1964-; Adjunct His/Sociology HCCCC 1971-80; Adjunct Sociology MVCC 1972-, Utica Coll of Syracuse Univ 1989-; *ai:* Class & United Nations Club Adv; VFW Annual Voice of Democracy Coord 1979-90; Hum Seminar Spon; Bsbl, Cross Cntry, Girls Sftbl & Coed Cross Cntry Coach; Kappa Phi Kappa Ed Honors Society 1962-; Cncl for the Soc Stud 1965-; Co-Founder of Narcotics Guidance Cncl 1967-72; Sole Dir of Summer Hum Film Discussion 1969-70; VFW Good Citizen of Yr Awd Winner 1986; Temple Beth Joseph (Trustee, Cultural Ed Chm) 1975-80; Parochial Sch Admin; Grants to Develop Data for Sociology Elective; Womens Rights; Political Participation Elective; Videotaped Clergy Interview on Marriage Counseling; Guest Lecturer Boces Honors Seminar; Speaker for Civic Organizations; Published Analysis of Antisemitism 1962; Developed Amer Stud Advanced Placement Course.

STULTS, DALLAS M., Biology Teacher; *b:* Wilder, TN; *m:* Carolyn Boswell; *c:* Andrea, Amber; *ed:* (BS) Health/Phys Ed, TN Tech 1968; (MS) Health Ed, Univ of TN 1973; *cr:* Teacher Tellico Plains HS 1968-70, Lake City HS 1971-74; Asst Prin Lake City HS 1975-79; Teacher Clinton Jr HS 1980-84, Anderson Cty HS 1985-; *ai:* Head Girls Bsktbl Coach; Breakaway Staff Mem; *home:* 106 Hillcrest Dr Clinton TN 37716

STULTS, GREGORY LEE, English Teacher/Dept Chair; *b:* Des Moines, IA; *m:* Nancy Lee Callen; *c:* T. K. Wignall (dec), Daniel Wignall, David Wignall, Nicole Wignall, Gregory, Michael; *ed:* (BS) Eng, IA St Univ 1970; *cr:* Teacher Knoxville Schls 1972-; *ai:* Jr HS Boys Track; Var Boys Cross-Cntry; HS Debate; IA Assn of Track Coaches St Track Coach of Yr 1980, Regional Coach of Yr 1981, 1989; Track Conference Team Champions; Cross-Cntry St Top 10, St Team Title 1980, Runner-Up 1981; Debate League Titles; *office:* Knoxville HS 102 N Lincoln Knoxville IA 50138

STULTZ, LUCY CAROLE, 5th Grade Teacher; *b:* Martinsville, VA; *ed:* (BS) Ed, 1966. (MS) Ed, 1969 James Madison Univ; *cr:* 4th Grade Teacher Druid Hills Elem 1966-67, Spottswood Elem 1967-69; 4th/6th Grade Teacher Shenandoah Heights Elem 1969-75; 6th Grade Teacher Jackson Wilson Elem 1975-77; 5th/6th Grade Teacher Westwood Hills Elem 1977-; *ai:* Virginia Valley Cncl Teachers of Math 1984-; Alpha Delta Kappa 1979-; 1st Presbyn Church Deacon 1989-; *office:* Westwood Hills Elem Sch 548 Rosser Ave Waynesboro VA 22980

STUM, LISA MICHELE, Spanish/Psych/Math Teacher; *b:* Glasgow, MT; *m:* Frank E.; *ed:* (BA) Soc Work, Evangel Coll 1987; Learning Disabilities, Purdue Univ; *cr:* 2nd Grade Teacher 1987-88, HS Teacher 1988- Heritage Chrstn Sch; *ai:* Sr Class Spon; Tutoring; *office:* Heritage Chrstn Sch 7350 Kennedy Hammond IN 46323

STUMP, KATHY GIBSON, 5th & 6th Grade HS Art Teacher; *b:* Guymon, OK; *m:* David L.; *c:* August, Piper, Katrina, Krista; *ed:* (BA) Fine Art, Cntrl St Univ 1973; (MS) Spec Ed, KS St Univ 1978; Elem Ed Cert; *cr:* Art Teacher/Spec Ed Teacher Topeka St Hospital 1974-76, Youth Center Topeka 1978-81; 5th/6th/HS Art Teacher Hadesty Sch 1981-; *ai:* OK Ed Assn; Apostalic Faith Church Youth Leader; *office:* Hardesty Public Sch P O Box 129 Hardesty OK 73944

STUPKE, SYLVIA ANN, 3rd-4th Grade Teacher; *b:* Cortland, NY; *ed:* (BS) Elem Ed, Cortland St Teachers Univ 1959; *cr:* 2nd-3rd Grade Teacher Rome NY Public Sch 1959-67; 2nd/4th Grade Teacher Dept of Defense Overseas Dependent Sch 1967-80; 4th Grade Teacher Warner Robins Chrstn Acad 1980-; *ai:* NYSTA 1959-67; OEA 1967-70; *office:* Warner Robins Chrstn Acad 2601 Watson Blvd Warner Robins GA 31088

STURDIVANT, BETTY MILLS, Team Leader/7th Grade Teacher; *b:* Jackson, MS; *m:* Robert V.; *c:* Robert M., Suzanne F., Mary V.; *ed:* (BA) Elem Ed, Belhaven Coll 1959; (MED) Elem Ed, Emory Univ 1961; Certificate Supervision I, NC St Univ Raleigh 1981; *cr:* Teacher DeKalb Cty GA 1959-68, Floyd Cty GA 1969-76, Wake Cty NC 1977-; *ai:* Team Leader; Sci Club; NEA 1959-; ACT, NCAE 1977-; Kappa Delta Gamma 1989-; Cty Mentor Trainer; *office:* W Millbrook Mid Sch 8115 Strickland Rd Raleigh NC 27615

STURDIVANT, BRENDA ADAMS, Fourth Grade Teacher; *b:* Houlton, ME; *m:* Barry Lee; *ed:* (BA) Elem Ed, Univ of S ME 1972; *cr:* 4th Grade Teacher Oxford Elem Sch 1972-82; 3rd Grade Teacher 1982-83, 4th Grade Teacher 1983- Perkins-Peaco Sch; *ai:* Delta Kappa Gamma Finance Chairperson 1983-; Delta Kappa Gamma 2nd VP 1990-; ME Rdng Teachers Assn 1989-; *office:* Perkins-Peaco Sch Pleasant St Oxford ME 04270

STURGEON, PATRICIA DOYLE, Home Economics Teacher; *b:* Horse Cave, KY; *m:* Robert Lewis; *c:* Robin Stacey, Jennifer Grant; *ed:* (BS) Home Ec, 1964, (Rank II) Health Ed, 1987 W KY Univ; *cr:* Jr HS Math/Health Teacher 1965-72, Home Ec Teacher 1973- Barren Cty Scl System; *ai:* FHA Adv; Natl Assn Voc Home Ec Teachers, KY Assn Voc Home Ec Teachers 1972-; Cave City Baptist Church Mem; *office:* Barren Cty HS 507 Trojan Trl Glasgow KY 42141

STURGES, CARL MARTIN, Assistant Principal; *b:* Salt Lake City, UT; *m:* Ruth Dillman; *c:* Philip C.; *ed:* (BA) His/Eng, Tulane Univ 1976; (PHD) European His, Claremont Grad Sch 1985; *cr:* Instr Harvey Mudd Coll 1980-82; His Teacher 1983-87, Academic Team 1987-88, Asst Prin 1988- Rowland Hall St Marks Sch; Adjunct Professor Westminster Coll 1989-; *ai:* Debate Coach & St Championships 1986, 1987, 1988; Advanced Placement Coord; NHS spon; Prefect Adv; Wasatch Front Intnl Ed Consortium (Mem, Steering Comm) 1989-; UT St Debate Coaches Assn Pres 1984-89; Patricia McCarthy Sumner Awd for Excl 1986; Haynes Fellowship Dissertation Research CGS 1982-83; *office:* Rowland Hall St Marks Sch 843 Lincoln St Salt Lake City UT 84102

STURIOLO, JANICE FIEDOR, Mathematics Teacher; *b:* Altoona, PA; *m:* Gary F.; *c:* Gregory S., Todd R.; *ed:* (BS) Scndry Ed/Math, PA St Univ 1972; Grad Work, Shippensburg Univ, WV Univ, W MD Coll; *cr:* Math Teacher Smithsburg HS 1972-76, Hagerstown Jr Coll 1981-89, Boonsboro HS 1987-; *ai:* NCTM 1972-74; *office:* Boonsboro HS 10 Campus Ave Boonsboro MD 21713

STURTZ, AGNES LEONARD, 6th Grade Teacher/Admin Asst; *b:* Cambridge, MD; *ed:* (BS) Elem Ed, Salisbury St Coll 1966; Working Towards Masters Ed/Rdng, Salisbury St Univ 1990; *cr:* 2nd Grade Teacher 1966-67, 4th-5th Grade Teacher 1967-68 Hurlock Elem Sch; 6th Grade Teacher Denton Elem Sch 168-69; 6th Grade Teacher 1969-85, 6th Grade Teacher/Admin Asst 1985- Preston Elem Sch; *office:* Preston Elem Sch Main St Preston MD 21655

STUTZMAN, RANDAL GRIER, Social Studies Teacher; *b:* Peoria, IL; *m:* Donna Driscoll; *c:* Nicole C., Danielle L.; *ed:* (BA) Poly Sci, Washburn Univ of Topeka 1969; Geography, His & Poly Sci; *cr:* Soc Stud Teacher Pueblo Cntrl HS 1969-; *ai:* Cntrl HS Soc Stud Dept Chm 1985-; Intnl Relations Club Spon; N Cntrl Accrediation Steering Comm; NCSS 1985-; CO Historical Society 1985-; Pueblo Historical Society 1983-; Dante Society; *office:* Pueblo Central HS 216 E Orman Pueblo CO 81004

STUTZMAN, RANDALL LYNN, Social Studies Dept Teacher; *b:* Oshkosh, WI; *m:* Loretta Magalske; *c:* Jed, Walker; *ed:* (BS) Soc Sci/His, 1975, (MA) His, 1984 Univ of WI Oshkosh 1984; *cr:* 7th/8th Grade Soc Stud Teacher St Marys 1975-77; Soc Stud Teacher Olson Jr HS 1977-82; Ed J J Keller Assn 1982-83; Sr HS Soc Stud Teacher Augusta HS 1983-; *ai:* Gifted/talented Coord; Asst Var Ftbl, Mock Trial, Jr HS Bsktbl Coach; Sr Class Adv; WI Cncl for Soc Stud 1983-; Amer His Organization 1985-; His Teachers Organization 1988-; NEH Fellowship 1985; WI Cncl fOr Hum Grant 1987; WI Cncl Soc Stud Sectional Presentation 1990; Published Article; *office:* Augusta HS Rt 2 Augusta WI 54722

SUBERS, STEPHEN EDWARD, Mathematics Teacher; *b:* Darby, PA; *ed:* (BS) Bio, West Chester Univ 1980; (MED) Math, Widener Univ 1986; Cmptr Ed, Philadelphia Coll of Textile & Sci; *cr:* Bio Teacher Devereux Fnd 1981-82, Garnet Valley Sch Dist 1982-83, William Penn Sch Dist 1983-86; Math Teacher Marple Newtown Sch Dist 1986-; *ai:* Indoor & Outdoor Track Coach; ATMOPAV 1986-; NCTM 1988-; *office:* Marple Newtown Sr HS 120 Media Line Rd Newtown Square PA 19073

SUBLETT, DAWNA (SPARKS), English Teacher; *b:* Great Bend, KS; *m:* Steven R.; *c:* Shane, Michael; *ed:* (BS) Home Ec, KS St Univ 1972; (MA) Counseling, Ft Hays St Univ 1978; Cert Lib Media Spec, Wichita St Univ 1990; *cr:* Home Ec Teacher Geneseo Jr/Sr HS 1973-76; Eng/Home Ec/Counseling Teacher Gorham HS 1977-80; Eng Teacher Holton Jr HS 1980-83; Eng/Speech/Drama Teacher Wellington Sr/Jr HS 1983-84; Eng Teacher Valley Center Jr HS 1984-; *ai:* Play Cast Dir; Eng Dept Head; Negotiator for Teachers; Valley Center Ed Assn Pres 1984-, Teacher of Yr 1988; KS Ed Assn Admin Bd 1973-, Most Active Mem Awd 1987; Plainskeeper 1987-; Greenpeace 1987-; *office:* Valley Center Jr HS 737 N Meridian Valley Center KS 67147

SUBLETT, MARY KATHERINE, History Teacher; *b:* San Diego, CA; *c:* Jacqui, Jarrard; *ed:* (BS) Soc Stud, Univ of TN Martin 1969; Recertification Memphis St Univ & Univ of MS; Natl Sci Fnd Seminar Univ of MS; *cr:* 2nd/3rd Grade Teacher Walls Elem Sch 1970-71; 8th/9th Grade Teacher Walls Jr HS 1971-77; 7th Grade Teacher Horn Lake Jr HS 1977-82; 8th Grade Teacher Horn Lake Mid Sch 1982-; *ai:* Natl Jr Beta Club Co-Spon; *office:* Horn Lake Mid Sch 6870 Center St Horn Lake MS 38637

SUDBURY, ALBERT LOUIS, Social Studies Teacher/Coach; *b:* Salt Lake, UT; *m:* Sherry Coon; *c:* Craig, Todd, Mary J.; *ed:* (BA) Phys Ed, S UT St Coll 1966; *cr:* Phys Ed Teacher/Coach Brockbank Jr HS 1966-67, S Summit HS 1967-69, Bingham HS 1969-76, Tooele HS 1976-81; Socl Stud Teacher/Coach Bingham HS 1981-; *ai:* Head Ftbl & Bsbl Coach; Asst Bsktbl Coach; Athletic Dir; Letterman Club Adv; Jordan Sch Dist Teacher of Month 1983; *home:* 7181 W 3800 S West Valley City UT 84120

SUDDUTH, ELIZABETH MUIRHEID, Third Grade Teacher; *b:* San Diego, CA; *m:* Ulysses D. Jr.; *ed:* (BA) Psych, Mary Washington Coll of Univ VA 1971; Post Grad Stud; *cr:* Instr/Cnslr VA Governors Sch for the Gifted 1973, 1975-76; 2nd Grade Teacher 1971-75, 3rd Grade Teacher 1975- Grafton Village Elem Sch; *ai:* Jr Great Books; Cmptr Coord; VA Assn for Ed of Gifted 1983-85; UTP, SEA, VEA, NEA 1971-; Mary Washington Coll (Natl Alumni Bd of Dir 1981-83, Chm, Regional Scholar Selection 1984, 1985); Potomac Estuaries Environmental Cncl Chm 189-; Belmont Memorial Gallery Docent 1973-83; Outstanding Teacher of Gifted N VA Cncl for Gifted & Talented Ed 1987; Mary Washington Coll Today Editorial Bd 1986-; *office:* Grafton Village Elem Sch 501 Deacon Rd Falmouth VA 22405

SUE, ELIZABETH, Spanish Teacher; *b:* Burlington, NC; *ed:* (BA) Span/Ed - Cum Laude, Elon Coll 1975; (MED) Ed/Span, Univ of NC Greensboro 1981; Span Immersion Wkshp Univ of NC Chapel Hill 1984; Spain 1974, Columbia & Ecuador 1979; Extensive Travel; *cr:* Eng Teacher Centro Colombo Americano Columbia South America 1981-82; Span Teacher Graham HS 1975-; Span Instr Alamance Comm Coll 1986-; *ai:* Span Club Adv; Budget Comm; Foreign Lang Chairperson; Sr Class Spon; Responsible for Graduation Reception; NEA, NCEA, ACAE, Foreign Lang Assn of NC 1975-; Haw River United Meth Church Choir Mem 1970-; Alamance Cty Teacher of Yr Finalist 1985-86; *office:* Graham HS 903 Trollinger Rd Graham NC 27253

SUFFIELD, JUDITH KREUTZ, English Teacher; *b:* Fargo, ND; *m:* Martin J.; *c:* Kristine, Peter; *ed:* (BA) Eng Ed, Univ of IL 1966; (MS) Scndry Ed, IN Univ 1987; *cr:* Teacher Burns L Darden Elem 1966-67, George Mason Jr/Sr HS 1967-69, Edgewood Jr HS 1969-71; Stu Teacher/Supvr Stephens Coll 1975-76; Teacher Western HS 1982-; Adjunct Faculty IN Univ Kokomo 1987-; *ai:* Battle of Books Coach; Midwest Talent Search

Coord; IN St Teachers Assn, NEA 1982-; IN Teachers of Writing 1987-; Kappa Kappa Kappa Inc Schlsp Chairperson 1982-; Grace United Meth Church Secy of Admin Bd 1983-; *home:* 812 Venetian Way Kokomo IN 46901

SUGAHARA, TEI ANN, 6th/7th Grade Teacher; *b:* Norman, OK; *m:* Kiyoshi; *c:* Allison; *ed:* (BA) Far East Area Stud/His, Sophia Univ Tokyo 1979; *cr:* Gate Teacher 1981-82; 6th-8th Grade Teacher 1982-; Mentor Teacher-Lang Art/Soc Stud 1988-89 Chualar Elem; *ai:* Speech and Drama Coach; Spelling Bee-Newspaper-Yrbk Adv; Girls Bskbl/Vlybl Coach; Txtbk Selection Comm; Sch Site Cncl; Curr & Instrtn Cncl; Lang Art Articulation Comm; Dist Curr Guides Comm; Minimum Proficency Comm; Monterey Cty Mid Sch Task Force; CA Rdng Assn 1985-; Monterey Bay Cncl for Soc Stud Bd Mem 1988-; Salinas-Kushikino Sister City Assn Bd Mem 1985-; Published Hitori Goto De EikaiWa Shufu No Tomo Press Tokyo 1979; *office:* Chualar Elem Sch PO Box 188 24285 Lincoln St Chualar CA 93925

SUGDEN, NANCY L., Music Dept Chair/Choral Dir; *b:* Camden, NJ; *ed:* (BS) Flute Performance, 1977, (BS) Choral General Music, 1979 Ball St Univ; Working Towards Masters Scndry Ed, Ball St Univ; *cr:* Choral Dir Frankton HS 1979-85, Shelbyville Sr HS 1985-; *ai:* HS Show Group; Sch Musical; Dept Coord; Gifted & Talented Comm; Building Comms; Amer Choral Dir Assn, Music Educators Natl Conference, IN Music Assn; *office:* Shelbyville Sr HS 2003 S Miller St Shelbyville IN 46176

SUGGS, NANCY J., Mathematics Teacher; *b:* Hartsville, SC; *ed:* (BA) Math, 1982, (MED) Sch Admin, 1989 Campbell Univ; *cr:* Teacher Douglas Byrd Sr HS 1982-; *ai:* Stu Government Adv.

SUGIMOTO, LILY OGAWA, Third Grade Teacher; *b:* Wahiawa, HI; *m:* Wallace Hiromitsu; *c:* Mark Y., Jon M., Nathan H., Joy M.; *ed:* (BS) Elem Ed, Bob John Univ 1956; (MA) Ed, Pepperdine Univ 1975; *cr:* 3rd Grade Teacher Hanalani Sch 1987-89; *office:* Hanalani Sch 94-294 Anania Dr Mililani HI 96789

SUHOVSKY, TRACY BARNETT, Chemistry Teacher; *b:* Oceanside, NY; *m:* Edward; *ed:* (BS) Bio, Marist Coll 1980; (MA) Ed, Adelphi Univ 1983; *cr:* Sci Teacher St Agnes Mid Sch 1980-81, Valley Stream Cntrl HS Dist 1981-; *ai:* Odyssey of Mind & Young Astronauts Club; *office:* Valley Stream North HS 750 Herman Ave Franklin Square NY 11010

SUITS, JOHN MICHAEL, English Teacher; *b:* Rockwood, TN; *m:* Patti Jo Fry; *ed:* (BS) Eng, Mid TN St Univ 1976; Grad Courses, Univ of TN; *cr:* Eng Teacher Roane Cty HS 1976-; *ai:* Spon Jr Class, Jr-Sr Prom; Eng Coach Academic Decathlon Team; Kingston Cmmty Theater (Bd Mem 1977-82, Play Dir/Producer 1977-82); Honored at Kingston Rotary Club Banquet 1989; *office:* Roane Cty HS Cumberland St Kingston TN 37763

SULLEN, JANET THOMAS, Language Arts Dept Chair; *b:* Tuskegee, AL; *m:* Lennon Sr.; *c:* Tiffany, Lennon Jr., Daniel; *ed:* (BS) Eng Ed, 1972, (MED) Lang Art, 1974 Tuskegee Inst; Auburn Univ; *cr:* Asst Mgr Smart & Classy 1984-89; Teacher D C Wolfe 1972-, Southern Voc Coll 1974-, Upward Bound 1974-, Tuskegee Univ Eng Dept 1987-; *ai:* NHS, Natl Jr Honor Society; NEA, AL Ed Assn, Ed Assn of Macon Cty 1972-; Delta Sigma Theta 1969-; Kappa Delta Pi, Lambda Iota Tau 1970-; Awarded Several Grants from St Arts Cncl; Teacher of Yr 1974; Textbook Selection Comm; Macon Cty Democratic Club Achievement Awd; *office:* Deborah Cannon Wolfe HS Rt 1 Box 6 Shorter AL 36075

SULLENGER, BEVERLY CANADAY, Spanish Teacher; *b:* Little Rock, AR; *m:* Robert Vernon; *c:* Robert V. Jr., Sandra Sullenger Register; *ed:* (BA) Sociology, Southern Meth Univ 1953; (MSE) Span, Univ Cntrl AR 1967; 30 hrs Spanish beyond M S E *cr:* Span Teacher Forest Heights Jr HS 1961-71, Pulaski Heights Jr HS 1971-72, Forest Heights Jr HS 1972-; *ai:* Span Club; Mem Care Comm; Past Stu Cncl, Chrldrs, Natl Jr Honor Society, Sch Newspaper; AR Foreign Lang Teachers Assn 1979-; L R Classroom Teachers Assn, AR Ed Assn, NEA 1961-; *office:* Forest Heights Jr H S 5901 Evergreen Little Rock AR 72205

SULLINGER, JOAN FOOS, Fourth Grade Teacher; *b:* Marion, OH; *m:* Rex; *c:* Holli; *ed:* (BSED) Elem Ed, Otterbein Coll 1973; (MED) Ed, Wright St Univ 1989; *cr:* 4th Grade Teacher Benjamin Logan Schls 1973-; *ai:* Teacher Leader; Benjamin Logan Ed Assn, OH Ed Assn, NEA 1973-; Kappa Delta Pi 1988-; Coord Meaning, Modes, Moods of Movement Grant 1978-79; *home:* 18945 CR 155 Ridgeway OH 43345

SULLIVAN, ANN MARTIN, Chemistry Teacher; *b:* Okolona, MS; *m:* James A.; *c:* Steven A.; *ed:* (BS) Home Ec Ed, 1968, (MS) Sci Ed, 1977, Specialist Curr/Instruction, 1988 Univ of S MS; *cr:* 6th Grade Teacher Improve Elem Sch 1968-69; Home Ec Teacher Runnelstown HS 1969-70; Sci Teacher Improve Jr HS 1970-72; General Sci Teacher 1972-84, Chem Teacher 1984- Oak Grove HS; *ai:* Oak Grove & MS St Beta Club Spon; MS Sci Teachers Assn, NSTA, Amer Chemical Society, SE MS Assn of Chem Teachers; Delta Kappa Gamma Secy 1974-; Kappa Omicron Phi 1968-; Immanuel Baptist Church; MS Power Fnd Grant 1988; Sigma Xi Scientific Research Society Awd & Grant 1987; Outstanding Young Educator 1971-72; Oustanding Scndry Educator 1973-74; *office:* Oak Grove HS 2543 Old Hwy 24 Hattiesburg MS 39402

SULLIVAN, BILLIE ANDERSON, Retired Second Grade Teacher; *b:* Las Cruces, NM; *m:* Paul; *c:* Paula Sullivan Moran, Susan Sullivan Upchurch; *ed:* (BS) Bus Admin, NM St Univ 1947; Scndry & Elem Ed Cert; *cr:* 2nd Grade Teacher Mesilla Park Elem Sch 1960-84; *home:* Box 236 Mesilla Park NM 88047

SULLIVAN, CHERYL PINTO, 1st-2nd Grade Teacher; *b:* Palo Alto, CA; *m:* Bill; *c:* Adam; *ed:* (AA) Liberal Arts, Foothill Jr Coll 1968; (BA) Sociology, Univ of CA Santa Barbara 1970; Various Wkshps Elem Ed; *cr:* 1st Grade Teacher 1971-78, 2nd Grade Teacher 1978-89, 1st-2nd Grade Teacher 1989- Burns Valley Sch; *ai:* Quality Review Leadership Team; Mentor Teacher Selection, Planning, Lib Advisory, Lib Site Selection Comm; CA Teachers Assn; PTO; *office:* Burns Valley Elem Sch Austin & Pine Clearlake CA 95422

SULLIVAN, CHRISTINE ANNE, Spanish Teacher; *b:* Albany, NY; *ed:* (BA) Span, Albertus Magnus Coll 1978; (MS) Span, Cntrl CT St Univ 1989; Immersion Prgm Span Teachers in Mexico Univ of CT; *cr:* Span Teacher Sacred Heart Acad 1978-79; St Marys HS 1983-; *ai:* Culture Vulture Club Soph Class Moderator; NHS Faculty Cncl; Trips Abroad Organizer-Chaperone; NCEA 1983-; Amer Assn Teachers of Span/Portuguese Advisory Bd St Level 1987-; St Lawrence Church Coord Elem CCD Prgm & Mass Lector 1987-; St Elizabeth Seton Grants 1986-88; Cntrl CT St Univ Awd Excl in Lang Study, Honor Schlsp 1987-88; *home:* 175 Elm St A21 West Haven CT 06516

SULLIVAN, CONNIE BETTS, Gate Teacher; *b:* Tacoma, WA; *m:* Jim; *c:* James; *ed:* (BA) Ed, Cntrl WA St Univ 1963; *cr:* 3rd/4th Grade Teacher Vineland Elem 1963-65; 4th Grade Teacher 1965-83, Teacher of Gifted & Talented 1984-89 Guadalupe Elem; Teacher of Gifted & Talented Ed Carlton Elem 1989-; *ai:* CA Assn for Gifted; *office:* Carlton Elem Sch 2421 Carlton Ave San Jose CA 95124

SULLIVAN, DOROTHY DECKER, Fourth Grade Teacher; *b:* Staten Island, NY; *m:* John F.; *c:* Kerry, Lisa; *ed:* (BS) Elem Ed, Wagner Coll; Grad Study Wagner/Richmond Coll in Elem Ed/Sch Supv; *cr:* Teacher Grades 3rd/4th/5th Public Sch 22; Teacher Grades 4th/5th Woodglen Sch 1978-; *ai:* NJ Rdng Assn; Voorhees HS FAA Secy 1988-89; *office:* Woodglen School R R 2 Box 295 Califon NJ 07830

SULLIVAN, EDWARD LAWRENCE, Guidance Counselor; *b:* Salem, OH; *m:* Nancy La Rue Justice; *c:* Tom, Cindy, Don; *ed:* (BSED) Elem Ed, Youngstown Coll 1955; (MAED) Elem Admin, WV Univ 1966; Completed Guidance Cert St of OH; *cr:* Elem Teacher Southside Elem Sch 1955-56; Math Teacher/Coach Canfield Jr/Sr HS 1956-61, Boardman Jr HS 1961-69; Math Teacher/Coach 1969-75, Guidance Cnslr 1975- Boardman Center Mid Sch; *ai:* 6th Grade Washington DC Tour; 7th-8th Grade Philadelphia, Gettysburg, Valley Forge Tour; Head Bsktbl Coach; Leetonia Teachers Assn VP 1955-56; Boardman Ed Assn 1961-; OH HS Bsktbl Coaches Assn 1955-; Natl Sci Fnd Summer Math Schlsp Bowling Green St Univ.

SULLIVAN, ELIZABETH E., 7th Grade Social Stud Teacher; *b:* Smyrna, TN; *m:* Walter T. Jr.; *c:* Wyatt, Todd; *ed:* (BS) Eng, 1966, (MED) Ed, 1976 Mid TN St Univ; *cr:* 5th Grade Teacher John Coleman Sch 1972-76; 6th Grade Teacher 1976-87, Jr HS Teacher 1987- Roy L Waldron Sch; *ai:* Faculty Advisory Comm; Spon of Annual Staff; UTP, NEA, TEA, REA; La Vergne HS Athletic Booster Club 1988-; Governors Acad; Waldron Sch Teacher of Yr; Selected as Best Representing the Esprit de Corpsi for Waldron Sch; *office:* Roy L Waldron Sch Stones River Rd La Vergne TN 37086

SULLIVAN, ELLEN BUTLER, Third Grade Teacher; *b:* Jackson, MS; *m:* Bert E.; *c:* Bert Jr., Pat, John; *ed:* (BS) Elem Ed, Belhaven Coll 1976; *cr:* 3rd Grade Teacher Richland Attendance Center 1976-; *home:* 190 Lowe Cir Richland MS 39218

SULLIVAN, JANENE COLLUM, French Teacher; *b:* Bogalusa, LA; *m:* Gene D.; *c:* Bruce, Shannon Sullivan Braselton, Lydia Sullivan Arnall, Troy D.; *ed:* (BS) Scndry Ed/Fr, LA St Univ 1962; (MAT) Fr, GA St Univ 1978; Working Toward Ed S Univ of GA; *cr:* Fr/Soc Stud Teacher Mt Carmel Chrstn Sch 1978-79; Fr/Eng Teacher Dekalb Cty Schls 1978-87, Dekalb Chrstn Acad 1980-84, Shiloh HS 1984-; *ai:* Fr Club Adv & Sr Class Homeroom Adv; Supervising Stu Teacher, Comm for Alternative Scheduling; AATF Secy 1976-; Flag Mem 1979-; ACTFL Mem 1985-; SCOLT Advisory Bd, Nom for Bd of Dir 1986; 1st Baptist Church Sanctuary Choir 1987-; Adult SS Class Secy 1985-; Mountain Shadow Civic Assn 1981-; Shiloh HS Teacher of Yr 1987; Project Comm for St Fr Immersion Weekend 1983-; Wkshp Fr Immersion Weekend 1990; Endowment for Hum Seminar 1984; Summer Inst in Fr 1986; Summer Schlsp in Avignon, France 1981.

SULLIVAN, JEAN STREAM, Retired Teacher; *b:* Kenosha County, WI; *m:* Robert I.; *c:* Kent A., Erin J.; *ed:* (BA) Elem Ed, 1956, (MA) Elem Ed, 1958 Univ of N CO; *cr:* 3rd Grade Supervising Teacher E Horn Elem 1956-58; 3rd Grade Teacher Denver Public Schls 1958-59; 2nd/3rd Grade Teacher Sheridan Public Schls 1967-72; 1st-3rd Grade Teacher Graland Cntry Day Sch 1973-88; *ai:* Intnl Rdng Assn 1985-88; Jobs Daughters Parent Cncl Treas 1978-79; CSCE Fellowship 1956-58; *home:* 1864 S Glencoe St Denver CO 80222

SULLIVAN, JEROME MICHAEL, Social Studies Teacher; *b:* Detroit, MI; *m:* Nancy; *c:* Amy, Kathleen; *ed:* (BS) Ed, Wayne St Univ 1968; *cr:* Teacher Highland Park Cmmty HS 1969-; *ai:* Youth in Government Spon; MI Week Comm Chm; Curr Cncl Mem & Chm; Wayne Cty Intermediate Sch Dist Software Comm; Gifted/Talented Coord; AFT 1969-; MI Assn of Cmptr Users in Ed, Metropolitan YMCA 1982-, Volunteer in Yr 1983, 1989; Natl Fnd for Improvement of Ed Christa Mc Auliffe Fellow 1989; *office:* Highland Park Cmmty HS 15900 Woodward Ave Highland Park MI 48203

SULLIVAN, JOHN THOMAS, Junior High Math Teacher; *b:* Manchester, CT; *m:* Jo Leanne Adams; *ed:* (BA) Math, CA St Univ Stanislaus 1974; *cr:* 6th Grade Teacher Denair Mid Sch 1975-79; 4th Grade Teacher Elmerwood Sch 1979-80; 6th Grade Teacher Mitchell K-6 Sch 1980-86; 7th/8th Grade Math Teacher Mitchell Sr Elem Sch 1986-; *ai:* Mitchell Sr Elem Sch 8th Grade Girls Bsktbl Coach 1986-; *office:* Mitchell Sr Elem Sch 1753 5th St Atwater CA 95301

SULLIVAN, JOY JEAN, Fourth Grade Teacher; *b:* Oklahoma City, OK; *ed:* (BS) Elem Ed, Southwestern OK St Univ 1962; (ME) Elem Ed, Central St Univ 1970; *cr:* Music/4th/6th Grade Teacher Rush Elem Sch 1962-67; 3rd/4th Grade Teacher Traub Elem Sch 1967-; *ai:* Mid-Del ACT, OEA, NEA 1967-; Intnl Rdng Assn 1982-86; PTA Parlimentarian; Kappa Kappa Iota (Local Pres 1971-72, 1979-80, St Secy 1971-72); Meadowood Baptist Church; *office:* Traub Elem Sch 6500 SE 15th St Midwest City OK 73110

SULLIVAN, LISA (HERROLD), Social Studies Teacher; *b:* Bremerton, WA; *c:* T. Ryan; *ed:* (AA) Arts, Olympic Coll 1981; (BA) Geography/SS Ed, W WA Univ 1984; Standard/Multi-Cultural Ed, Univ of WA 1987; Mid-Masters Curr, Univ of WA; *cr:* 8th/9th Grade Soc Stud Teacher Kalles Jr HS 1984-; *ai:* Honor Society Adv; Head Girls Bsktbl, Track & Field Coach; Fair Parking Fund Raiser for ASB Coord 1984-; Puyallup Ed Assn Minority Affairs Chairperson 1986-87; WA Ed Assn, NEA 1984-; Bible Study Fellowship 1985-89; Multicultural Advisory Cncl 1990; Natl Endowment of Hum Asian Stud Awd 1990; Co-Author St Publication; Presenter in Wkshps; *office:* Kalles Jr HS 515 3rd St S E Puyallup WA 98371

SULLIVAN, LORNA NYBAKKEN, Fourth Grade Teacher; *b:* Iowa City, IL; *c:* Sean, Beth Sullivan Levesque, Colleen; *ed:* (BS) Elem Ed, 1959, (MA) Elem Ed, 1976 Willimatic St Coll; Grad Stud; *cr:* 4th Grade Teacher Charles Wright 1959-60; 4th/5th Grade Teacher Windham Center 1960-61; 4th Grade Teacher S B Butler 1962-63; 3rd-5th Grade Transitional Elem Teacher Fair Oaks 1968-; *ai:* Evaluation of Staff & Prof Dev Comm; Montville Ed Assn Secy 1968-; CT Ed Assn, NEA 1959-; *office:* Fair Oaks Sch Old Colchester Rd Oakdale CT 06370

SULLIVAN, M. TRINITAS, OP, Associate Principal; *b:* Bronx, NY; *ed:* (BSED) Ed, St Thomas Aquinas Coll 1961; (BSM) Sacred Music, Manhattanville Coll 1971; (MA) Sacred Music, Villa Schifanoia-Florence Italy 1975; (MED) Admin/Supervision/Scndry Ed, Rutgers Univ 1989; *cr:* Teacher 1960-73, 1981-86; Admin Asst NY Sch Liturgical Music 1978-81; Math Teacher 1986-89, Assoc Prin 1989- St Pius X HS; *ai:* Opera Club; Steering & Homecoming Comm; Metuchen Diocese Festival Choir; NCEA 1975-; Natl Assn Pastoral Musicians 1977-; Metropolitan Opera Guild 1975-; Dominican Sister of Divine Providence Mid Sts Evaluation Teams 1988-; NY Archdiocese Commission Church Music 1972-81; Metuchen Diocese Commission Worship & Preaching 1990; Published Article Musart; Entries Cath Encylopedia Indexing Pastoral Music 1976-82; *home:* 137 Metlars Ln Piscataway NJ 08854

SULLIVAN, MARSHA CELESTE, 4th Grade Teacher; *b:* Nashville, TN; *m:* Gerald A.; *c:* Ryan, Stephanie; *ed:* (BS) Elem Ed, Mid TN St Univ 1970; Grad Courses TN St Univ, Belmont Coll & Trevecca Coll; *cr:* 2nd Grade Teacher Fehr Elem 1970-71; 2nd-3rd Grade Teacher Stanford Elem 1971-76, 1978; 4th Grade Teacher Haywood Elem 1979-; *ai:* TN Rdng Assn, MNEA, TEA, NEA; Career Ladder Teacher; *office:* Haywood Elem Sch 3790 Turley Dr Nashville TN 37211

SULLIVAN, MARY BRACKETT, Teacher of Gifted; *b:* Portland, ME; *m:* Robert J.; *ed:* (BS) Elem Ed, Univ of ME 1981; (MA) Educl Psych, 1983, 6th Yr Diploma Admin, 1990 Univ of CT; *cr:* Teacher Clover Street Sch 1983-; *ai:* Coach Future Problem Solving Prgm Coach; Windsor Public Schls Teachers of Gifted & Talented Unit Leader; Phi Delta Kappa 1983-; Natl Assn for Gifted Children 1988-; Ct Educators Network for the Talented & Gifted 1984-; Young Scholars Saturday Semester Coord & Presenter Confratate 1984-; Consultant Challenge Projects Houghton Mifflin Company; Author of Articles; Presenter NE Regional Conference for Parents of Gifted & Talented; *office:* Clover Street Sch 57 Clover St Windsor CT 06095

SULLIVAN, MARY DOOLITTLE, 6th Grade Sci & Rdng Teacher; *b:* Shreveport, LA; *m:* Billy Thomas; *c:* Edmond C. Henson Jr, Margaret Henson Alston, James P. II; *ed:* (BS) Elem Ed, 1981, (MED) Elem Ed/Admin, 1982 AL St Univ; Doctoral Stu Auburn Joint Prgm; *cr:* Teacher St Joseph 1961-62, Holy Family 1963-65; Office Mgr White Realty 1966-73; Acct Office Mgr/Agent Herman Maisel & Company 1976-79; Teacher Calcedeaver 1981-83, Kate Shepard 1983-84, Baker Elem Mid Sch 1984-; *ai:* Amer Society Women Accts (Bd Secy, Pres) 1970-79; Alpha Delta Kappa; BSA Pack Comm 1987-; PTA Treas 1990; Holy Family Sch Pres Sch Bd 1970-73; NASA Space Camp Teacher Orientation Grant; *home:* 3504 Shadowwood Ct Mobile AL 36693

SULLIVAN, MICHAEL JOHN, English Teacher; *b:* Buffalo, NY; *m:* Kathleen Mason; *c:* Benjamin, Colleen, Patrick, Timothy; *ed:* (BA) Eng, 1973, (BS) Scndry Ed/Eng, 1977 St Univ Coll Buffalo; Scndry Ed, St Univ Coll Geneseo 1983; Project Advance Eng, Syracuse Univ 1987; *cr:* Eng Teacher Phelps-Clifton Springs Schls 1977-87, Oswego HS 1987-; *ai:* Univ of Rochester Excl in

Scndry Teaching Awd 1987; *office:* Oswego HS 2 Buccaneer Blvd Oswego NY 13126

SULLIVAN, PATRICK L., Sixth Grade Teacher; *b:* Seymour, IN; *m:* Michele T. Mc Grath; *c:* Erin, Sean, Robert; *ed:* (BA) Elem Ed, Midland Luth Coll 1974; (MS) Elem Ed, IN Univ 1976; *cr:* 6th Grade Teacher Hayden Elem Sch 1974-; *ai:* Little Hoosier Historians Spon; Drama Coach; Jennings Cty Classroom Teachers Assn Pres 1977-78; IN St Teachers Assn/NEA; Hayden Alumni Assn Pres 1980-; *office:* Hayden Elem Sch 1 Main St Hayden IN 47245

SULLIVAN, PATRICK SHANNON, Sixth Grade Teacher; *b:* Pauls Valley, OK; *m:* Diana Sue Hobson; *c:* Scott; Philip; *ed:* (BA) Soc Stud, 1972, (BS) Elem, 1973, (ME) Elem, 1978 East Central St Coll; Conservation & Sci Wkshps; *cr:* 6th Grade Teacher Stratford Elem 1973-; *ai:* 6th Sci Fair Co-Dir; 6th Engineering Fair Dir; OK Ed Assn Pres 1979; NSTA 1989-; Chapter II Math & Sci Grant; Elected Delegate 10 Yrs OK Ed Assn; *home:* Rt 2 Box 124A Stratford OK 74872

SULLIVAN, PAUL M., SJ, History Teacher/Assoc Prin; *b:* Fall River, MA; *ed:* (AB) His, Coll of the Holy Cross 1973; (MED) Religious Ed, Boston Coll 1975; (MA) Philosophy, Gonzaga Univ 1977; (MDIV) Theology, 1984, (THM) Theology/His, 1984 Jesuit Sch of Theology; *cr:* Teacher 1977-80, Teacher/Dept Head 1984-88 Cheverus HS; Teacher 1988-89, Teacher/Assoc Prin/ Admissions Dir 1989- Bishop Connolly; *ai:* Stu Government & Sailing Club Moderator; Advanced Placement Prgm Coord; NCSS 1986-; US Cath Historical Society 1984-; ME Cncl for Soc Stud 1985-88; ME Historical Society 1985-; Freetown MA Historical Society 1988-; Alumni Assn Admin Rep; Sch Bd of Regents (Mem, Secy); John Hancock Fellow MA & ME Constitutional Bicentennial 1986-87; Vision 2000 Mem; Published Book 1988; *office:* Bishop Connolly HS 373 Elsbree St Fall River MA 02720

SULLIVAN, RANDALL JAY, Speech & Drama Teacher; *b:* Dickson, TN; *m:* Glenda Lee; *c:* Brian Wesley; *ed:* (BS) Speech Comm/Theatre Austin Peay St Univ 1982; *cr:* Teacher Dickson Cty HS 1984-; *ai:* Dramatics Club Spon; Forensics Coach; NEA, TN Ed Assn 1984-; *office:* Dickson Cty HS Henslee Dr Dickson TN 37055

SULLIVAN, REBECCA HAMMOCK, English/Latin Teacher; *b:* Carrollton, GA; *m:* Roderick B.; *c:* Robin K., Clifford F.; *ed:* (BA) Eng, 1971, (MED) Eng Ed, 1977 W GA Coll; Numerous Wrkshps & Conferences; *cr:* Eng Teacher Haralson Cty HS 1971-75, Villa Rica HS 1976-77, Haralson Cty HS 1977-81; Eng/ Latin Teacher Carrollton HS 1981-; *ai:* Graduation Speeches & Essay Contests Coord; Lang Art Curr, Media, Schlsp, Dept Heads Comm Membership; Carrollton Assn of Educators Building Rep 1981-; GA Assn of Educators 1971-; NEA 1975-; Teacher of Month 1988-; Outstanding Scndry Educator of America 1974; *office:* Carrollton HS 202 Trojan Dr Carrollton GA 30117

SULLIVAN, RICHARD WILLIAM, Elem/Phys Ed Teacher; *b:* Covington, KY; *m:* Toni Diane Townson; *c:* Amber, Brandee, Brent; *ed:* (BS) Elem Phys Ed/HS Eng, St Bernard Coll 1977; (MS) Ed, 1986, (Rank II) N KY Univ; *cr:* Frosh Phys Ed/Soph Eng Teacher Bishop Brossart HS 1977-78; K-5th Grade Phys Ed Teacher Florence Elem 1978-; *office:* Florence Elem Sch 103 Center St Florence KY 41042

SULLIVAN, SUE, American History Teacher; *b:* Pilot Point, TX; *m:* Charles G.; *c:* Paul, Steve, Karen Hoey; *ed:* (BS) His, Cntrl St Univ 1970; Grad Stud Penn St Univ; *cr:* Psych Teacher Putnam City HS 1970; Amer His Teacher 1971-78; Amer His/Honors Advanced Placement Putnam City North HS 1978; *ai:* Citizen Bee Spon; Close Up; Academic Bowl Comm; Soc Stud Chairperson; DAR OK Prairies Chapter Registrar 1986-; OK Cty Voter Registrar 1976-; *office:* Putnam City North HS 11800 N Rockwell Oklahoma City OK 73162

SULLIVAN, THOMAS E., Science Teacher; *b:* Brainerd, MN; *m:* Sheryl R. Lindteigen; *c:* Lisa, Daren; *ed:* (BA) Bio/Chem, Concordia Univ 1968; (MA) Ed, Moorhead St Univ 1975; Ed Adm; Master Instr Course Ft Belvoir VA; Realtor Lisc; Wkshp Valley City St, Minot St 1980-84; *cr:* Teacher/Coach Ben Franklin Jr HS 1969-; *ai:* Ftbl, Wrestling, Track Coach; Sci Club Adv; Jr Educators of Tomorrow Participant; Chm of Sci Dept; NEA, NDEA, FEA Prof Rights Chm 1976-80; FEA Negotiations Team 1985-87; NEA Life Mem 1970-; Fargo Public Schls Coaches Cncl 1975-89; Boulage Sci Ctr Adv Bd 1989-; Masonic Temple Ed 1969-; Church Cncl Bd 1984-; Reserve Officers Assn 1980-; Excl Awd in Ed; Fargo Forum; Outstanding Educator; North Cntrl Accreditation Teams 1987-89; *office:* Ben Franklin Jr HS 1420 N 8th St Fargo ND 58102

SULLIVAN, THOMAS WILLIAM, English Teacher; *b:* Highland Park, MI; *m:* Priscilla Ellen Pierce; *c:* Colleen E., Sean T.; *ed:* (BA) Eng Lit, DIT 1964; Grad Stud WSU; *cr:* Eng/Soc Stud Teacher Stout Jr HS 1968-73; Eng Teacher Woodworth Jr HS 1973-79, Maples Jr HS 1979-82, Fordson Sr HS 1982-; *ai:* Work with Young Writers; Speak to Educl Groups; MENSA 1965-73; Arcadia Mix 1986-; Lathrup Village Commissioner 1979-88; Articles Published; Pulitzer Prize Nom 1989; Numerous Literary Prizes & Awds; *office:* Fordson HS 13800 Ford Rd Dearborn MI 48126

SULLIVAN, TIMMERIE ROSE, Athletic Dir/Coach/Teacher; *b:* Long Beach, CA; *ed:* (AA) Phys Ed, Fullerton Coll 1974; (BS) Phys Ed, CA St Univ Fullerton 1976; CPR; First Aid; Womens Collegiate Bsktbl Ofcl; Trainer; *cr:* Teacher/Coach St Columban Jr HS 1972, Fullerton Coll 1974-77, Canyon HS 1976-77; Teacher/Coach/Athletic Dir Cornelia Connelly Sch 1977-; *ai:* Girls Athletic Assn; Trainer; Var Bsktbl & Sftbl Coach; Athletic Dir; CAHPERD 1973-; NCAA 1972; WBA 1985; NCAA Womens Collegiate Level Bsktbl Ofcl 1985-; Sch Admin Grant; Coaches Effectiveness Certificate; *office:* Cornelia Connelly Sch 2323 W Broadway Anaheim CA 92804

SUMMAR, SHARON KAY, 4th Grade Teacher/Cmptr Coord; *b:* Decatur, IL; *ed:* (BSED) Elem Ed, 1970, (MS) Math/Ed, 1988 IL St; *cr:* Teacher Green Valley Grade Sch 1970-; *ai:* Cmptr Coord; Gifted Prgm; NCTM, ICTM; *office:* Green Valley Grade Sch Box 224 Green Valley IL 61534

SUMMERFIELD, STEVEN LYLE, School Counselor; *b:* Portland, OR; *m:* Lucinda Ray Bennett; *c:* Jill, Deri, Anna, Adam; *ed:* (BS) Elem Ed, 1975, (MS) Counseling, 1989 Univ of OR; *cr:* 3rd/4th/6th/8th Grade Health Teacher 1977-85; K-8th Grade Cnslr Sisters Sch Dist 1986-; *ai:* Coach Cross Cntry & 8th Grade Girls Bsktbl; Stu Evaluation Team Comm; OR Cty Assn; Sisters Cmmty Action Group, Together for Children Advisory Role 1988-; John Mc Adams Schlsp Comm 1981-; *office:* Sisters Schl Dist PO Box 99 Sisters OR 97759

SUMMERS, BONNIE MANWILL, Fourth Grade Teacher; *b:* Salt Lake City, UT; *m:* Robert M.; *c:* Richard R., Stuart N.; *ed:* (BS) Elem Ed, UT St Univ 1966; ID St Univ; Brigham Young Univ; *cr:* 2nd Grade Teacher Ashton Elem Sch 1956-63; Spec Ed Teacher Lincoln Elem Sch 1963-64; 1st Grade Teacher Thirkill Elem Sch 1964-77; 4th Grade Teacher Hooper Elem Sch 1977-; *ai:* Soda Springs Ed Assn (VP & Pres 1976-77 Pres 1988- IEA Delegate Assembly Various Yrs; Amer Power Boat Assn (Secy & Scorekeeper) 1981-83; Campbell Soup Co Favorite Teacher 1989; ID Ed Assn Awd Membership Recruitment 1988-89; *home:* 2463 Hwy 30 W Soda Springs ID 83276

SUMMERS, CHARLES ALAN, Science Teacher; *b:* Dayton, OH; *m:* Vicki Jean Hoffman; *c:* Christopher A., Kimberly A., Kevin M.; *ed:* (BS) His/Government, Bowling Green St Univ 1971; (MS) Educl Admin, Univ of Dayton 1984; *cr:* Sci Teacher St Henry Local Schls 1972-; *ai:* Asst Bsktbl Coach 1980-; Head Golf Coach 1972-74; Asst Bsbl Coach 1975-; Asst Ftbl Coach 1972-83; St Henry Sci Day Dir; Mercer Cty Rep Dist 6 of OH Acad of Sci; Jennings Fnd Scholar 1985-86; NEA 1972-; Natl Assn of Bsktbl Coaches HS Comm Mem At-Large 1986-; Mercer Cty Elks 1982-; Articles Published; Governors Awd for Opportunities in Sci Ed; *office:* St Henry Mid Sch 381 E Columbus St Saint Henry OH 45883

SUMMERS, FREDIA WHITE, English Teacher; *b:* Taylor Cty, KY; *m:* Roy L.; *ed:* (BS) Eng, Campbellsville Coll 1969; (MED) Rdng, Wright St Univ 1978; Rdng Specialist Cert; OH Writing Project Grad, Advanced Seminar Grad; *cr:* Eng Techer Nelson Cty Schls 1969-70, Miami East Local Schls 1971-; Part-Time Eng Teacher Edison St Coll 1980-86; *ai:* Drama Club & Sr Class Adv; Musical Dir; Miami Cty Writing Competency & Curr Comms; North Cntrl Accreditation Chairperson; NCTE; *office:* Miami East HS 3825 N State Rte 589 Casstown OH 45312

SUMMERS, GRACE DAVIS, Math Teacher; *b:* Mccomb, MS; *m:* Hallie Lee III; *c:* Hallie IV, Shawn, Ouida; *ed:* (BA) Math Ed, Univ MI 1976; (MA) Math Ed, Wayne St Univ 1979; Scndry Math; *cr:* Teacher Campbell Elem Sch 1977-86, MacKenzie HS 1986-; *ai:* Spon/Coach; Academic Games Supervisor; Youth Ushers; Bible Study for Youth; DACTM, NCTM; Alpha Kappa Alpha; *office:* Mackenzie H S 9275 Wyoming Detroit MI 48204

SUMMERS, JAMES L., Social Studies Teacher; *b:* Ft Wayne, IN; *m:* Sonja R. Ballinger; *c:* Troy, Tori Homann; *ed:* (BSED) Soc Sci, 1958, (MSED) Soc Sci, 1959 E IL Univ; *cr:* 6th Grade Teacher Farmer City Elem 1959-61; 7th-8th Grade Soc Stud Teacher Farmer City Jr HS 1961-71, Farmer City-Mansfield Jr HS 1971-87, 1987, Blue Ridge Jr HS; *ai:* Jr HS Bsbl Coach; *office:* Blue Ridge Jr HS Mansfield IL 61854

SUMMERS, JANET LOUISE, Fourth Grade Teacher; *b:* Alexandria, LA; *ed:* (BA) Elem Ed, Newberry Coll 1966; Grad Classes Univ of VA, VA Commonwealth Univ, VA St Univ; *cr:* 5th Grade Teacher Unionville Elem 1966-67; 3rd Grade Teacher Keysville Elem 1967-68; 3rd Grade Teacher 1968-70, 4th Grade Teacher 1970- Rohoic Elem; *ai:* Self Study Comms; Sch Staff & Admin; Math Comm Chairperson; Hospitality Nomintaing Comm; SCA Spon; Dinwiddie Ed Assn 1968-82; Va Ed Assn 1966-82; NEA 1966-82; PTO Nominating Comm 1969-; Southside VA Equestrian Club (Pres 1986, Mem 1972-88), Outstanding Mem 1985; 4-H Club Leader 1976-; Whos Who in Ed 1974; *office:* Rohoic Elem Sch Rt 4 Box 335 Petersburg VA 23803

SUMMERS, LORETTA JUMP, Mathematics Teacher; *b:* Taylorsville, KY; *w:* Bruce (dec); *c:* Suzanne Cox, Edward; *ed:* (BS) Elem Ed, 1972, (MA) Cnslr Ed 1981 W KY Univ; Grad Stud W KY Univ; *cr:* 4th-6th Grade Teacher Upton Sch 1972-78; 1st-8th Grade Migrant Math Teacher Upton Sch & Sonora Sch 1978-87; Math/Cmptr Ed Elem Teacher Sonora Sch 1987-; *ai:* Hardin Cty Cmptr Comm; KY Ed Assn, NEA 1974-; *office:* Sonora Sch PO Box 98 Sonora KY 42776

SUMMERS, OREN CHARLES, Advanced Math/Physics Teacher; *b:* Bunkie, LA; *m:* Rhoda Marson; *c:* Jamie D.; *ed:* (BS) Math/Physics Ed, LA Coll 1966; Cmptr Programming, La Salle Univ 1970; Math Courses, USL; Voc Ed, LA St Univ; *cr:* Math Teacher Oak Hill HS 1966-70, Hayden HS 1970-72, Morrow HS 1972-73, Palmetto HS 1973-79, Electronics Instr T H Harris Voc/ Tech Sch 1979-86; Advanced Math/Physics Teacher Opelousas Sr HS 1986-; *ai:* Opelousas Sr HS Pressbox Co-Mgr; St Landry Parish Sci Textbook Adoption Comm Mem; LA Teachers Assn, NEA 1966-80, 1986-; Electronic Instrs Assn 1980-86; Future Teachers Assn (LA St Spon 1978-79, 1988-89) 1966-80, 1986-; Morrow Baptist Church Musician 1980-; *home:* Rt 1 Box 26 Morrow LA 71356

SUMNER, CATHY JONES, Mathematics/Science Teacher; *b:* Galay, VA; *m:* Blake Duane Jr.; *c:* Jessica C., Terri L.; *ed:* (BS) Elem Ed, 1973, Minor Sociology, 1973 Radford Univ; *cr:* Head Start Aide Sumner Prgm Grayson Cty Sch 1968, 1969; 1st/ 4th-7th Grade Teacher Providence Sch 1973-88; 6th/7th Grade Remedial/Math/Lang Art Teacher Independence & Fries 1988-89; 6th/7th Grade Teacher Fries Mid Sch 1989-; 6th/7th Grade Teacher Sumner Sch Remedial 1988, 1989; *ai:* Cheerleading Spon; 4H Leader & Adv Bd Pres; Lib Club, Wildcat Monogram Club & Dramatics Co-Spon; NEA, UEA 1976-; GCEA (Faculty Rep 1987-, Convention Delegate 1989-); Fries Baptist Church (Youth Leader 1980-, Sunday Sch Supt 1985-87); PTO Membership Chm 1979-87; Outstanding 4-H Leader 1986; Supts Trophy Phys Ed 1987; *office:* Fries Mid Sch PO Box 446 Fries VA 24330

SUMNER, DONNA CELLUCCI, Mathematics Department Chair; *b:* Newton, MA; *m:* G. Laurence; *ed:* (BA) Math/Ec, Regis Coll 1977; Accounting, Bentley Coll; *cr:* Math Teacher 1977-82, Math Dept Chairperson 1983- Matignon HS; *ai:* Math Club & Newspaper Moderator; Acad & NHS Faculty Cncl Mem; SAT Prep Course Teacher; Sr Act, Fundraising Auction Volunteer, Advanced Placement Calculus Coord; Boston Archdiocese Teachers Assn 1979-; NCTM 1978-; NHS Most Exemplary Teacher Awd.

SUMNER, JENNETTE C., Third Grade Teacher; *b:* Adel, GA; *m:* John Floyd Jr.; *c:* John III, Jennifer Sumner Probst; *ed:* (BA) Elem Ed, Wm Carey Coll 1968; Working Towards Masters USM Hattiesburg, William Carey Coll; *cr:* Private Secy Goodwill Store 1953-64; Elem Teacher Poplarville Attendance Center 1968-69, Powers Attendance Center 1969-78, Moselle Attendance Center 1978-; *ai:* Lambda Iota Tau Secy 1968; NEA, MAE 1969-; *office:* Moselle Elem Sch Rt 2 Attendence Cntr Moselle MS 39459

SUMNERS, PENNY LENOIR, History Teacher/Dept Chairman; *b:* Memphis, TN; *m:* Steven L.; *c:* Stacy, Shelly; *ed:* (BS) His/Scndry Ed, Univ of AL 1972; (MS) Scndry Ed Admin & Supervision, AL A&M 1987; Admin Trng, Univ AL, Vanderbilt Univ 1987-89; Advanced Placement US His Trng 1988; *ai:* Honor Society & Academic Booster Club Spon; Seven Period Day Supvr; Cmmty & Parent Coord; Huntsville Cncl Soc Stud (Pres, VP) 1978-82; Alpha Delta Kappa Secy 1979-86; Jr League of Huntsville Bd Mem 1972-89; Panoply of Arts 1984-88; Freedom Fnd George Washington Awd of Honor 1988; Outstanding Young Educator for Huntsville-Molim Cty 1985; Outstanding Teacher of Amer His 1984; Amer Awd Scottish Rite 1983; *office:* Lee HS 606 Forrest Cir Huntsville AL 35811

SUMNERS, ROBERT DEAN, 7th-9th Grade Math Teacher; *b:* Manhattan, KS; *m:* Frankie Blair; *c:* John Q., Megan R., Robert A.,; *ed:* (BS) Phys Ed, Emporia St Univ 1969; (MS) Curr/ Instruction, KS St Univ 1983; Math Inst, Washburn Univ 1970; *cr:* 8th Grade Teacher Hoyt & Mayetta 1969-72; 5th-8th Grade Math Teacher Westmoreland Grade Sch 1973-86; 7th-9th Grade Math Teacher Westmoreland Jr Sr HS 1986-; *ai:* 7th Grade Spon, Prof Dev & Stu at Risk Comm; Local Building Rep for Teacher Organization; KATM, NCTM 1983-; KNEA 1969-, NEA 1969-, Life Membership; WPCTA Local Teachers 1969-81; FFA Alumni 1983-; Westmoreland Service Club; *home:* Box 68 Westmoreland KS 66549

SUMPTER, ANNE GRAHAM, English Teacher; *b:* Roanoke, VA; *m:* James H. III;; *c:* Hardee, Graham; *ed:* (BA) Eng, James Madison Univ 1972; Univ of VA, Univ of Richmond, VA Commonwealth Univ; *cr:* Eng Teacher William Fleming HS 1972-74, William Ruffner Jr HS 1976-81; Eng/Journalism Teacher Clover Hill HS 1986-; *ai:* REA, CEA, VEA, NEA Mem; CATE, VATE Mem 1986-; PTA, Church Affiliated Groups; Spon of Cavalierian HS Newspaper 1986-89; Chesterfield Cty CORE Curr Journalism Comm 1989; Helped Revise/Rewrite Ctys Journalism Curr Guide; Eng Dept Chairperson Wm Ruffner Jr HS; *office:* Clover Hill HS 13900 Hull Street Rd Midlothian VA 23112

SUMPTER, SARAH DAVIS, English Teacher; *b:* Pittsburgh, PA; *m:* Thomas Jr.; *c:* Crystal, Caryn; *ed:* (BA) Eng Ed, 1972, (MA) Scndry Ed, 1978 Univ of Pittsburgh; *cr:* Eng Teacher Pittsburgh Bd of Ed 1972-; *ai:* Chrldrs, Stu Cncl, Bowling League, New Future Fashion, Talent Spon; NCTE 1980-; ASCD 1988-; Schenley Heights Civic Survive Schlsps; Pittsburgh Bd of Ed New Teacher Inductees 1988; Schenley Teacher Center Cooperative Learning Prgm; Centers of Excl Published Statement & Picture; *office:* Carrick HS 125 Parkvield St Pittsburgh PA 15210

SUNDERMAN, JOEL THOMAS, Band Dir/Fine Art Dept Head; *b:* Lincoln, NE; *m:* Nancy Sue Kroger; *c:* Julie; *ed:* (BME) Music Ed, 1978, (MM) Music Theory/Trumpet Performance, 1980 Univ of NE; *cr:* Band Dir Nebraska City Public Schls 1982-; *ai:* Fine Art Dept Head; NE St Bandmasters Assn Elem Jr HS Chm 1982-; Nebraska City Ed Assn Past Pres 1982-; NE Music Educators Assn 1982-; Nebraska City Municipal Band Dir 1982-; Apple Corps Barbershop Chorus Dir 1984-86; 1st Luth Church Choir Dir 1982-86; NE St Ed Assn Schlsp Selection Comm 1987-; *office:* Nebraska City Jr HS 217 S 9th St Nebraska City NE 68410

SUNDERMAN, MAX BRYAN, Secondary Science Teacher; *b:* Canyon, TX; *m:* Anna Beth Line; *c:* Bryan, Holly; *ed:* (BS) Bio/Psych, W TX St Univ 1972; Grad Work Bio & Ed; Lab X-Ray Technician Trng Panhandle Rule Health Coor 1982; Effective Sch Trng Region XVI ESC 1986; *cr:* 7th Grade Sci Teacher Floydata Mid Sch 1976-77; Phys Sci/Earth Sci/Chem/Physics/Anatomy/Physiology Teacher Vega HS 1977-; *ai:* Chrldr Spon; Organizer of Alcohol Drug Free Act; Textbook Comm; TX Classroom Teacher Assn, TX Assn of Sci Teachers 1984-; Nom Presidential Awd Excl Sci & Math Teaching 1986-88, St Finalist 19886-87; Nom TX Excl Awd Outstanding HS Teachers 1987-88; Teacher of Yr 1977-79, 1985-89; *home:* Box 253 Vega TX 79092

SUNDQUIST, SUZANNE KATHLEEN, Fifth Grade Teacher; *b:* Cudahy, WI; *m:* Len; *c:* Gregg Bowen, Neal Bowen; *ed:* (BAED) Univ of WI Madison 1962; (MS) Curr/Instruction, Natl Lewis Univ 1991; *cr:* Kndgtn Teacher Poe Sch 1977-78; 1st Grade Teacher Sandburg Sch 1978-81; 5th Grade Teacher Tarkington Sch 1981-; *ai:* Sch Bd Elections Comm 1989-; Soc Stud Comm 1989; Natl Congress of Parents & Teachers 1967-; NEA 1977-; Univ of WI Madison Alumni Life Mem 1965-; *office:* Booth Tarkington Sch 310 Scott St Wheeling IL 60090

SUNSHINE, HELEN ALBAUM, Second Grade Teacher; *b:* New York, NY; *m:* Herbert I.; *c:* Mark, Lisa, Kenneth; *ed:* (BSED) Elem Ed, 1953, (MAED) Elem Ed, 1956 City Coll of NY; Bd of Ed In-Service Courses; Grad Stud; *cr:* 2nd-4th Grade Teacher Public Sch 61 1953-62; K/2nd-3rd Grade Teacher Public Sch 160 1972-; *ai:* United Fed of Teachers 1962, 1972-; NY St Teachers, AFT 1972-; Greenburgh Hebrew Center (Membership VP 1979-81, Recording Secy 1981-83, Ways & Means VP 1983-85; Programming VP 1985-87, Comm Chm 1985-87).

SUNTHIMER, LENNIE CLARK, Chemistry Teacher/Science Dept; *b:* Fort Worth, TX; *m:* Jon C.; *c:* Corlann De Fontes, James De Fontes III; *ed:* (BS) Home Economics, Univ CO 1951; (MED) Secndry Ed, North TX St Univ 1972; Advanced Academic Trng-60 Hrt; *cr:* Childrens Center Kndgtn Teacher 1962-64; Dallas ISD Phy Sci Teacher 1968-72; Richardson ISD Chem Teacher 1972-84; Richland Cmmty Coll 1979-82; Carrollton-Farmers Branch ISD Chm Teacher/Sci Dept Chair 1984-90; *ai:* Odyssey of the Midn Bldg Coord Coach; Adv Placement Chem Review Coach; Uil-Coach-Chemistry; Science Fair Judge Advisor; Amer Chem Society Act St Sec 1978-89; Assn Supervision Curr Dev 1990-; Cfb Ed Assn TSTA/NEA 1984-89; Turner Soci Fair/Research Chm 1984-88; Chamber Partnership Ed Coord 1986-89; Crow Canyon Research/Field Work Archaeology 1989-; Effective Teacher Pilot Prgm 1985-; TX Jr Acad Sci Dist Dir 1988-90; USAF Recruiting Ad 1986-88; VIP Awd 1990; Career Ladder 1987-89; *home:* 10556 Berry Knoll Dallas TX 75230

SUOMI, MARIA ANN, Spanish/English Teacher; *b:* Ionia, MI; *m:* Tom Carr; *ed:* (BA) Span & Eng, Aquinas Coll 1984; *cr:* Teacher Marion HS 1984-; *ai:* Span Club; Class Spon; *home:* 202 1st St Box 118 Buckley MI 49620

SUPER, BRUCE H., Social Studies Teacher; *b:* Kansas City, MO; *m:* Susan Hadley; *c:* Jeff, Craig; *ed:* (BA) Ec, 1965, (MA) Scndry Ed, 1969 Univ of MO Kansas City; Spec Equivalency Ec Ed, Rockhurst Coll 1982; Concept Therapy; *cr:* Teacher 1969-, Psych Chm 1974-, Ec Ed Coord 1980- Hickman Mills Sr HS; *ai:* Natl Prgm Learning of Ec & Psych Club Adv; Self Esteem Seminar Trng Prgm Spon; NEA, MO Ed Assn, UTA of CSD #1 1969-; Greater Kansas City Ec Ed Cncl Exec Steering Comm 1987-; Natl Awds Prgm Learning of Ec Meritorious Achievement Certificates; *office:* Hickman Mills Sr HS 9010 Old Santa Fe Dr Kansas City MO 64138

SUPER, DEBORAH HARVEY, Gifted Program Teacher; *b:* Ronceverte, WV; *m:* Francis Joseph; *c:* Josh; *ed:* (BA) Scndry Ed, 1974, (MA) Scndry Ed, 1981 WV Univ; (MA) Spec Ed, Marshall Univ 1983; Learning Disabilities, George Mason Univ; Rdng, WV Univ; *cr:* Spec Ed/EMH Teacher 1974-76, Gifted Prgm Teacher 1976-84 Elkins Jr HS; Adjunct Instr Davis & Elkins Coll 1982-85; Gifted Prgm Teacher Elkins Hs 1984-85; Eng Teacher Clarke Cty HS 1985-86; Learning Disabilities Teacher Apple Pie Ridge Elem Sch 1986-87; Gifted Prgm Teacher Elkins Jr HS 1987-; *ai:* Yrbk Adv; NHS Co-Adv; Johns Hopkins Talent Search Coord; NCTE 1989-; Delta Kappa Gamma Intl Pres 1990; WV Assn for Gifted & Talented 1983-; Beta Sigma Phi Pres 1988-, Woman of Yr 1989; 1st Baptist Church, Marshall Alumni Assn; Outstanding Young Women of America 1985; Randolph Cty Lang Art Teacher of Yr 1989; *office:* Elkins Jr HS Robert E Lee Ave Elkins WV 26241

SUPERSON, SUSAN J., Religion Teacher; *b:* Springfield, MA; *m:* Edward S. Jr.; *c:* Heather, Jennifer; *ed:* (BA) Religion, Mt Holyoke Coll 1976; Specializing in Learning Disabilities; *cr:* Elem Teacher Mater Dela Rosa 1976-77, St George 1977-79; Jr HS Teacher Holy Cross 1979-84; Teacher Cathedral HS 1988-; *ai:* Pro-Life Club Adv 1989-; Mabel E Merrick Awd for Excl Religious Stud; *office:* Cathedral HS 260 Surrey Rd Springfield MA 01118

SUPPE, GEORGIANA, 5th Grade Teacher; *b:* Cincinnati, OH; *c:* Barbara; *ed:* (BS) Elem Ed, Wittenberg Univ 1966; (MA) Lib/Media, Univ of CO 1974; *cr:* 4th Grade Teacher Mc Kinley Elem Sch 1966-68; 3rd Grade Teacher Cntrl Elem 1968-71; 3rd/4th Grade Teacher 1971-80, 5th Grade Teacher 1980- Northridge Elem; *ai:* NEA, CEA, St Vrain Valley Ed Assn Secy 1968-; NCTM 1989-; Alpha Delta Kappa Pres 1972-; Co Alpha Delta Kappa Treas 1972-; *office:* Northridge Elem Sch 1200 19th Ave Longmont CO 80501

SURFACE, PATRICIA GAIL (MITCHELL), Music Teacher; *b:* Oklahoma City, OK; *m:* William D. Jr.; *c:* William D. III; *ed:* (BME) Music, 1972, Cert Elem, 1973, (MME) Music, 1977 SW OK St Univ; *cr:* 2nd Grade Teacher Mary Allen Elem 1973-74, Earth Elem Sch 1974-75; K-6th Grade Music Teacher Austin Elem 1975-77; Music/Choir Dir Zia Intermediate Sch 1977-81; 5th Grade Classroom/4th-6th Grade Music Teacher Dupree Elem 1981-83; 1st Grade Teacher Santa Rita Elem Sch 1983-84; Music Teacher/Band Dir Zia Intermediate Sch 1984-; *ai:* Phi Delta Kappa; NM Music Educators Assn; Tau Beta Sigma Pres 1970.

SURFACE, WILLIAM DEAN, Band Director; *b:* Oklahoma City, OK; *m:* Patricia C. Mitchell; *c:* William D.III; *ed:* (BME) Music, Southwestern Ok 1971; (MME) Music, State Univ 1977; Administrative Cert, Western NM 1989; *cr:* Asst Band Dir/Choir Dir Stratford HS 1973-74; Band Dir Earth HS 1974-75; Asst Band Dir Pampa HS 1975-77; Band Dir Artesia HS 1977-81, Monterey HS 1981-83, Lee Jr HS 1983-84, Artesia HS 1984-90; *ai:* Kappa Kappa Psi, Pres 1970; Phi Delta Kappa; Phi Beta Mu; NM Music Educator's Assn; Springlake-Earth Sch Teacher of the Yr 1974-75; Artesia Parent's Advisory Cncl Teacher of the Month 1984.

SURRENCY, FRANK C., Agriculture Education Teacher; *b:* Plant City, FL; *ed:* (AS) Ag, Hillsborough Comm Coll 1976; (BS) Ag Extension/Ed, Univ of FL 1979; *cr:* Teacher Columbia HS 1979, La Belle HS 1979-80, Armwood HS 1986-88, Tampa Bay Voc Tech Center 1980-86, 1988-; *ai:* FFA Adv; Wrestling Coach; Hillsborough Cty Voc-Ag Teacher Assn, FL Voc-Ag Teacher Assn, Natl Voc-Ag Teacher Assn 1980-; FNGA 1979-; *office:* Tampa Bay Voc Tech 6410 Orient Rd Tampa FL 33610

SURRENCY, JOANN THOMAS, 4th & 5th Grade Teacher; *b:* Bradenton, FL; *m:* Millard Michael Jr.; *c:* Millard Michael III; *ed:* (BS) Elem Ed, FL Memorial Coll1971; (MS) Early Chldhd, FL Intnl Univ 1976; Barry Univ; *cr:* Teacher 4th Grade 1971-75, Teacher 3rd Grade 1975-80, Teacher 2nd Grade 1980-85, Teacher 4th-5th Grade 1985- SEminole Elem Sch; *ai:* United Teachers of Dade-Building Steward; Grade Level Chairperson-Intermediate 4-6; Faculty Cncl Chairperson Academic Adv-Spelling Bee Sci Fair; United Teachers of Dade (Building Steward 1982- Building Steward of Yr 1982;) FL Educators Assn; ART; Women Involved Now Secy 1988-; Alpha Kappa Alpha; FL Mem Alumni; BetheL Baptist Church; *office:* Seminole Elem Sch 121 Sw 78th Pl Miami FL 33144

SUSHIL, CATHERINE, Social Studies Teacher; *b:* Fort Meyers, FL; *ed:* (BS) Ed, St Bonaventure Univ 1968; (MS) Ed, St Univ NY Cortland 1975; *cr:* Teacher 1956-66, Prin 1967-70 Sacred Heart Sch; Teacher St Paul Sch 1971-80, St Francis Xavier 1981-; *ai:* NCEA 1970-; NCSS 1978-79; *home:* 2045 Heitman St Fort Myers FL 33901

SUSOR, MARIANNE PHILLIPS, Fourth Grade Teacher; *b:* Toledo, OH; *m:* Glen F. Jr.; *c:* Troy, Michael, Jodi; *ed:* (BA) Elem Ed, Bowling Green St Univ 1962; *cr:* 1st Grade Teacher 1962-65, 1976-78, 4th Grade Teacher 1978- Olney Elem; *ai:* OH Ed Assn, NEA, NW OH Ed Assn; Northwood Local Ed Assn Secy 1978-79, 1983-84, 1989-; *home:* 3303 Curtice Rd Northwood OH 43619

SUSSDORFF, JAY D., 12th Grade English Teacher; *b:* Plattsburgh, NY; *m:* Anne Marie Tenaglia; *c:* Christopher, Amy; *ed:* (BA) Eng/Scndry Ed, St Univ of NY New Paltz 1972, 1974; *cr:* 6th Grade Teacher 1972-74, 7th Grade Teacher 1975-79 Valley Cntrl Mid Sch; 9th Grade Teacher 1980-82, 11th Grade Teacher 1983-85, 12th Grade Teacher 1986- Valley Cntrl HS; *ai:* Curr Comm; Var Girls Bsktbl Coach; Coach of Yr Tri-Cty Area 1989-; *office:* Valley Cntrl HS 63-75 Rt 17-K W Montgomery NY 12549

SUTCLIFFE, HARRY FRANKLIN, Social Studies/English Teacher; *b:* Gary, IN; *m:* Clara Mae Moore; *c:* Priscilla, Craig, Harrison, Cindy, Ruth, Candy, Kathleen; *ed:* (BA) His/Poly Sci, Roosevelt Univ 1957; (MS) Ed Admin, Stephen F Austin 1989; Public Admin, Grad Division Univ of AR Fayetteville; *cr:* Soc Stud/Eng Teacher Eureka Springs HS 1959-60, 1969-81; Prin/Instr/Soc Stud Teacher St Paul HS 1965-69; Soc Stud/Eng Teacher/Acting Prin Dawson Ind Sch Dist 1985-; *ai:* Textbook Comm; Soc Stud, Eng, Gifted Talented Selection Comm; Phi Delta Kappa 1989; Disabled Amer Veterans (Commander 1976, St Chm 1983, St Exec Comm); Eureka Springs Teachers Assn Pres; Carroll Cty Quorum Court (Justice, Adm, Chm Finance Comm); Inst for Free Enterprises Ec TX A&M; *office:* Dawson Ind Sch Dist P O Box Dawson TX 76639

SUTER, WILLIAM HENRY, Mathematics Teacher; *b:* Morton, WA; *m:* Kathleen Ann Cosgrave; *c:* Jeffrey W., Jana L.; *ed:* (BA) Ed/Math, Gonzaga Univ 1967; (MS) Ed/Math, Lewis & Clark; *cr:* Teacher Oregon City HS 1971-75, Jesuit HS 1975-79, Sam Barlow HS 1979-; *ai:* NEA 1980-; *office:* Sam Barlow HS 5105 SE 302nd Ave Gresham OR 97080

SUTHERLAND, HELEN ROBINSON, Fourth Grade Teacher; *b:* Raysal, WV; *m:* Franklin P. Jr.; *c:* Franklin IV, John D., Laura J.; *ed:* (BA) Elem Ed, Concord Coll 1958; Courses for Renewal of Cert; *cr:* 4th-5th Grade Teacher Raysal Grade Sch 1952-54, 1958-59; 7th-9th Grade Eng/Rdng Teacher Bradshaw Jr HS 1959-63; 5th Grade Teacher Prince William Cty Schls, 4th Grade Teacher Anne E Moncure 1967-; *ai:* Coord of Young Authors Contest & Young Writers Fnd; Teacher of Gifted Stu; NEA; Outstanding Teacher of Gifted Awd N VA Cncl for Gifted/Talented Ed 1987; *home:* 612 Courthouse Rd Stafford VA 22554

SUTHERLAND, SUZANNE C., Sixth Grade Teacher; *b:* Greenwich, CT; *ed:* (BS) Early Chldhd Ed, 1974, (MS) Intermediate Upper Ed, 1985 Southern CT St Univ; Design for Effective Instruction 1987; *cr:* 5th/6th Grade Lang Arts Teacher 1976-79, 7th/8th Grade Lang Arts Teacher 1979-85 St James Sch; 6th Grade Teacher Second Hill Lane Sch 1985-; *ai:* Writing Task Force.

SUTTER, FRANCES ROWICKI, Retired 4th Grade Teacher; *b:* Villenova, NY; *m:* Clarence James; *c:* Michael, Phillip, Diane Ireland, Lawrence, Sharon, Timothy; *ed:* (BS) Elem Ed/Speech Therapy, Geneseo St Teachers 1950; *cr:* 5th Grade Teacher Willard Sch 1950-51; 3rd-4th Grade Teacher Gowanda Cntrl Sch 1962-73, Gowanda Elem Sch 1973-89; *ai:* Amer Legion Auxiliary, VFW Auxiliary; Women of Moose #651 Lib Chairperson 1989-; *home:* 11679 Main St Perrysburg NY 14129

SUTTER, SALLY ANN CAMPBELL, Fifth Grade Teacher; *b:* Potsdam, NY; *m:* Joseph Gerard; *c:* Susan Misto, David; *ed:* (BS) Elem Ed/His, Potsdam St Univ 1964; Rdng, Potsdam St Univ; *cr:* 4th/5th Grade Teacher Norwood-Norfolk Cntrl Sch 1964-; *ai:* St Raymonds Altar-Rosary Society; Norfolk Elem Stamp Club Adv; St Raymonds Church Cncl; Norwood-Norfolk PTSA 1977-84; *office:* Norwood-Norfolk Cntrl Sch 13 Hepburn St Norfolk NY 13667

SUTTERFIELD, MONA ARMSTRONG, 7th Grade Teacher; *b:* Lake City, AR; *m:* John P.; *c:* Patti E. Mc Daniel; *ed:* (BSE) Elem Ed, AR St Univ Jonesboro 1964; Mt St Marys Coll, CA Luth Coll, Pepperdine Univ 1975-82; *cr:* 4th Grade Teacher Lake City Elem 1956-69; Head Start Teacher Summer Sessions 1966-69; 5th/7th Grade Teacher Edmondson & Dolland Schls 1969-; *ai:* Teachers Assn Norwalk Lamirada, CA Ed Assn, NEA Mem; *office:* Dolland Elem Sch 15021 S Bloomfield Norwalk CA 90650

SUTTLE, WILLIE MAE SHIRLEY, First Grade Teacher; *b:* Tuscaloosa, AL; *m:* Joseph H. Jr.; *ed:* C Certificate Elem Ed, Stillman Coll 1940; (BS) Elem Ed, 1948, (MED) Elem Ed, 1954 AL St; *cr:* 1st Grade Teacher Duncanville Elem Sch 1941-43, Taylorville Elem Sch 1944-50, Matthews Elem Sch 1950-; *ai:* Childrens Church Teacher; NEA, AL Ed Assn; Tuscaloosa Cty Ed Assn Faculty Rep 1982-; Amer Assn Univ Women 1980-; Delta Kappa Gamma 1976-; GSA Leader; Gamma Phi Delta Phi Teen Adv; Hall of Fame Nom for Tuscaloosa Cty Elem Teacher 1976, 1982; *home:* 2831 18th St Tuscaloosa AL 35401

SUTTLES, NANCY HAWKINS, 6th Grade Teacher; *b:* Greer, SC; *m:* John Coy; *ed:* (AA) Elem Ed, Spartanburg Meth Coll 1974; (BA) Elem Ed/Early Chldhd, Limestone Coll 1975; (MA) Rdng, 1977, (MA) Admin, 1981 Furman Univ; *cr:* Teacher Lyman Elem Sch 1976-; *ai:* 6th Grade Fund Raising; Bus Duty; PTA Teacher of Yr 1988; *office:* Lyman Elem Sch 84 Groce Rd Lyman SC 29365

SUTTMOELLER, JOAN M., Business Teacher; *b:* St Louis, MO; *m:* David L.; *c:* Jennifer, Michael, Stephanie, Stacy; *ed:* (BS) Bus Ed, UMSL 1969; (MS) Bus Ed, SIUE 1971; Grad Hours Ed, Bus Ed; *cr:* Part-Time Bus Teacher Meramec Jr Coll 1970-73; Bus Teacher Mehlville HS 1969-; *ai:* North Cntrl Bus Ed Evaluation Comm Chairperson; SLABEA 1970-; GSA (Brownie Leader 1985-88, Jr Scout Leader 1988-); *office:* Mehlville HS 3200 Lemay Ferry Rd Saint Louis MO 63125

SUTTON, ANN PROBERT, Business Teacher; *b:* Jasper, MO; *m:* Dennis; *c:* Matthew, Christopher; *ed:* (BS) Bus Ed, MO Southern St Coll 1985; SW MO St Univ; *cr:* Bus Teacher Carl Junction HS 1986-; *ai:* NBEA, NEA 1986-; *office:* Carl Junction HS P O Box 4 Carl Junction MO 64834

SUTTON, BILL L., Social Studies Teacher; *b:* Oklahoma City, OK; *M:* Terri Lynn Redmon; *c:* Tony; *ed:* (BA) Poly Sci Ed, 1982, (MED) Educl Admin, 1990 Cntrl St Univ; *cr:* Soc Stud Teacher Del Crest Jr HS 1982-; *ai:* Spon Positive Peer Pressure Club; Staff Dev Comm; Sch Improvement Comm; Mid Del Drug Adv Cncl; Awarded Project Challenge Cert 1989; Head Chemical People Townmeeting 1987; Piloted Quest/Lion Club Drug Ed Prgm 1986; *office:* Del Crest Jr H S 4731 Judy Dr Del City OK 73115

SUTTON, CYNTHIA L., Spanish Teacher; *b:* Battle Creek, MI; *m:* Richard; *c:* Richard Jr., Andrew; *ed:* (BS) Span, Cntrl MI Univ 1973; Span, W MI Univ; *cr:* Span Teacher Battle Creek Cntrl HS 1973-; *ai:* Span Club Adv; Foreign Lang Dept Chairperson; Outcomes Accreditation Attendance, Curr Comms Mem; MI Foreign Lang Assn; Amer Assn Teachers of Span & Portuguese; Excl in Ed Day Outstanding Educator Awd 1985; *office:* Battle Creek Cntrl HS 100 W Van Buren Battle Creek MI 49017

SUTTON, DONNA HURST, English & Gifted Teacher; *b:* Knoxville, TN; *m:* Gary Lynn; *c:* Samuel, Jacob; *ed:* (BA) Eng Ed, Maryville Coll 1980; Smoky Mountain Writing Project, Jr Great Books, Future Problem Solving; *cr:* Eng Teacher 1981-82, Summer Sch Teacher 1987-89 Robertsville Jr HS; Eng Teacher 1980, 1982-, Gifted Ed Teacher Jefferson Jr HS 1989-; Summer Sch Dir Oak Ridge HS 1990; *ai:* AIDS Ed Develop & Teach Curr; Chrldrs Coach; NEA, TN Ed Assn, E TN Ed Assn, Oak Ridge Ed Assn; Selected Charter Mem Smoky Mountain Writing Project; Leader of Wkshps E TN to Teach Writing Process to Other Teachers; *office:* Jefferson Jr HS 200 Fairbanks Rd Oak Ridge TN 37830

SUTTON, JAMES R., Eighth Grade Math Teacher; *b:* Rochester, NY; *m:* Ann A.; *c:* Andrew, Heather; *ed:* (BS) Ed, 1961, (MS) Ed, 1965 St Univ of NY; *cr:* Math Teacher Brockport Cntrl Sch 1961-; *ai:* 8th Grade Team Leader; Jeff Bell Awd Comm

Chm; Brockport Teachers Assn VP 1966, Teacher of Yr 1977; NYSUT, AFT 1961-; Brockport Fire Dept Protectives (VP 1971, Pres 1972-73), Service Awd 1988.

SUTTON, JO ANNE HENSON, Sixth Grade Teacher; *b:* Cullowhee, NC; *m:* James Candler; *c:* Krissie Red, Jill; *ed:* (BS) Elem Ed, 1956, (MA) Ed, 1958, Certified Spec Ed, 1965 W Carolina Univ; *cr:* 3rd-6th Grade Spec Ed Teacher Jackson Cty Public Sch System; *ai:* Sch & Cty Senate Bill Comm; Just Say No Club Spon; NC Ed Assn, NEA, Local NC Ed Assn Mem 1956-; Eastern Star Mem 1952-; *home:* Rt 3 Box 412 Sylva NC 28779

SUTTON, KATHLEEN HUMBERD, Retired; *b:* Cleveland, TN; *m:* Raymond; *c:* Stephen, David, Jana Chambers, Melinda; *ed:* (BS) Elem Ed, Univ TN 1949; *cr:* Teacher Cleveland City Sch System 1946-47; Lenior City Sch System 1947-48; Cocke Cty Sch System 1950-51/1964-65; Newport Grammar Sch 1965-84; *ai:* Mem TN Govt Task Force on Ed; TN Ed Assn Life Mem; NEA Life Mem; *home:* R 1 Box 3 Parrottsville TN 37843

SUTTON, LILLIAN ROBINSON, 6th Grade Teacher; *b:* Raymond, MS; *m:* Walter; *c:* Sharon Collins, Sherry, Karron, Delores; *ed:* Assoc General Ed, Utica Jr Coll 1958; (BS) Elem Ed, 1973, (MS) Elem Ed, 1977 Jackson St Univ; Leadership Conference, Jackson St Univ; *cr:* Teaching Asst Reynolds Elem Sch 1970-71, Clausell Elem Sch 1971-73; Substitute Teacher Jackson Public Sch Dist 1973-74; Classroom Teacher Clausell Elem Sch 1974-; *ai:* Safety Patrol, Sch Stu Cncl, Sch Newspaper, Yrbk Spon; Natl Geographic Society Coach; Jackson Assn of Educators, MS Assn of Educators, NEA Active Mem 1970-; PTA Treas 1980-; Fairfield Baptist Church (Sunday Sch Teacher, Bible Teacher) 1959-; Several Good Apple Awds JPS Sch Dist; Several Certificates of Merits for Teaching; Certificate of Appreciation Plaque Sch Supt Jackson Public Schls; *home:* 422 Glen Rose Dr Jackson MS 39209

SUTTON, MICHAEL ROY, Science Department Chairman; *b:* Denver, CO; *m:* Charlotte A. Cloud Sutton; *c:* Brian, Crystal, Casey, Heather; *ed:* (BA) Soc Stud, Bio, General Sci, LA Coll 1978; *cr:* Teacher Leesville HS 1978-79; Teacher/Coach Glenmora HS 1979-; *ai:* Sci Awareness Coord; LA HS Coaches Assn; LA HS Athletic Assn; Bsbl Coach of Yr Dist 98 1986; Elizabeth Dixie Youth Bsbl (VP 1984-85 Pres 1985-89); Quad Parish Dixie Youth Founder/Pres 1987-89; Dev Parish Bio Exit Exam; *office:* Glenmora H S PO Box 697 Glenmora LA 71433

SUTTON, TOM W. B., Social Studies Teacher; *b:* Salt Lake City, UT; *m:* Mary M. R. Staley; *c:* Brent, Michael, David, Steven; *ed:* (BA) His, 1971, (MA) His/Scndry Ed, 1977 Brigham Young Univ; Grad Stud HS Cnslr; Grad Taft Inst of Poly Sci; *cr:* Soc Stud Teacher Jr HS 1972-82, Taylorsville HS 1982-; *ai:* Peer Leadership Team Adv; His Club Adv; Awds Comm; Granite Sch Dist Soc Stud Textbook Adoption Comm Chm 1986-; Taylorsville HS Close-Up Fnd Coord 1989-; NEA, UEA, GEA Mem 1972-; LDS Church Bishop 1977-82; BSA Asst Dist Commissioner 1987-; Republican Party St Delegate 1984; Dept Chm Golden Apple Awd; Dist & St Curr Dev & St Testing Comm Mem; Dist Dossiers; *office:* Taylorsville HS 5225 S Redwood Rd Salt Lake City UT 84123

SUVAK, DOLORES CLOUGHERTY, Advanced English II Teacher; *b:* Pittsburgh, PA; *m:* Ronald Gregory Sr.; *c:* Ronald G. Jr., Russell G.; *ed:* (BS) Comprehensive Eng, Indiana Univ of PA 1970; (MED) Guidance/Counseling, Duquesne Univ 1977; Journalism, OH Univ 1978; Various Wkshps; *cr:* Remedial Rdng Teacher Wilkinsburg Jr HS 1970; 8th Grade Eng Teacher Dickson Jr HS 1970-71; Eng Teacher Swissvale HS 1971-87, Woodland Hills HS 1987-; *ai:* Yrbk Adv; Quill & Scroll; Newspaper Adv; Swissvale & Woodland Hills HS Cheerleading Coach; Faculty Advisory Comm; NEA, PA St Ed, Woodland Hills Ed Assn Mem; St Anselm Parish (Cncl Worship Comm Chairperson, Festival Comm, Summer Sch Bible Teacher, PTG, Liturgy Lector); Swissvale Cmmty HS Historical Comm; Nom Giant Eagle, KDKA, Westinghouse Thanks to Teachers Honors 1990; Ann Devlin Pittsburgh Talking TV Show; *office:* Woodland Hills HS 2550 Greensburg Pike Pittsburgh PA 15221

SVABEK, JOYCE, Math Department Chair; *b:* Chicago, IL; *ed:* (AA) St Petersburg Jr Coll 1959; (BSE) Math, Univ of FL 1961; Suncoast Area Teacher Trng Prgm, Univ of S FL Supvr Int/Beg Teacher Prgm; *cr:* Math Teacher St Petersburg Sr HS 1961-68, Dixie Hollins HS 1968-87, E Lake HS 1987-; *ai:* Stu Cncl Adv; Sch Advsiory, Curr, Budget, Attendance, Graduation, NHS Faculty, Attendance Appeal Comm; #1 Club; Math Dept Head; Delta Kappa Gamma Treas 1973-; NCTM, FL Cncl of Math; Pinellas Cty Cncl of Math, Teacher of Yr 1989; FL HS Act Assn; FL Assn of Stu Cncls Treas 1980-82; Natl Sci Fnd Teacher; Church Exec Secy 1975-79; Finalist Teacher of Yr Pinellas Cty 1981-82; Consultant for Dept of Ed Review Comm Advanced Alg II, Equicor Outstanding Ed Teacher Nominee 1989-; Participant FL Sch Desegregation Consulting Center; Teacher of Yr Nominee Pinellals Cty 1978; Teacher of Month 1975, 1985, 1989-; *office:* East Lake HS 1300 Silver Eagle Dr Tarpon Springs FL 34689

SVATY, MONICA LANE (MILLER), Algebra/Geometry Teacher; *b:* Newton, KS; *m:* Karl J. Jr.; *c:* Sonya L.; *ed:* (BSE) Math, KS St Univ 1968; *cr:* Algebra/Geometry Teacher Manhattan HS 1968-70; Math Teacher South Jr HS 1974-78; Math/Sci Teacher Pleasant Valley Jr HS 1979-80; Math/Algebra Teacher Valley Center Jr HS 1980-89; Algebra/Geometry Teacher Valley Center HS 1989-; *ai:* Staff Relations & Sick Leave Comm; NEA, KS NEA 1974-; Saddle Club Secy 1978-; *office:* Valley Center H S 800 N Meridian Valley Center KS 67147

SVOBODA, BEVERLY R., Science Department Teacher; *b:* Pery, IL; *m:* Howard C.; *c:* Rebecca Greenberg, Stephanie Guziec; *ed:* (BA) Bio Sci, North Cntrl Coll 1957; Natl Coll of Ed; *cr:* Scientific Assn Argonne Natl Lab 1957-63; Bio Teacher Lemont HS 1978-80; Sci Teacher Lemont Cntrl Jr HS 1981-; *ai:* Delta Kappa Gamma Socty Intnl 1988-; Beta Beta Beta Honorary Socty 1955-; Earth Sci Club of Northern IL 1965-; Il Sci Teachers Assn 1985-; Publishes Annuals NY Acad of Sci; Proceedings Amer Assn Cancer Research; Syrgical Forum; *office:* Lemont Central Jr HS 410 Mc Carthy Rd Lemont IL 60439

SVOBODA, PATRICIA NEWBY, English/Cmptr Sci Teacher; *b:* Dallas, TX; *m:* Mark C.; *c:* Elizabeth S.; *ed:* (BA) Eng, Univ of TX Tyler 1983; Grad Work in Eng; *cr:* Cmptr Sci/Eng Teacher Arp HS 1983-; *ai:* Sr Class Spon 1985-; Cmptr Club & Univ Interscholastic League Prose & Poetry Interpretation Spon; Assn of TX Prof Educators; *home:* 14426 CR 247 Arp TX 75750

SVOBODA, RUTH C. GANSKE, 4th/5th Grade Teacher; *b:* Sumner, IA; *c:* Stephen H.; *ed:* (BA) Ed, 1966, (MA) Learning Disabilities, 1982 Univ of IA; Grad Work Beyond Masters Degree; *cr:* 3rd Grade Teacher 1966-83, 4th Grade Teacher 1984-88, 4th/5th Grade Teacher 1988- Wright Elem; *ai:* Wright Elem Rep Cncl Cedar Rapids Cmmty Schls; NEA; Cedar Rapids Ed Assn (Rep 1982-86, Mem) 1966-; IA Rdng Assn 1980-; *home:* 2049 Eastern Blvd SE Cedar Rapids IA 52403

SWAFFORD, CARLETON LEE, Science Teacher; *b:* Chattanooga, TN; *m:* Beverly Dean; *ed:* (BA) Bio/Comm, Southern Coll 1975; (MS) Sci/Environmental Ed, Univ of TN 1978; *cr:* Bio Instr Knoxville Jr Acad 1974-77, Little Creek Acad 1975-77; Jr HS Coord/Life/Phys Sci Teacher A W Spalding Sch 1977-; Bio/Ed Dept Teacher Southern Coll 1977-; *ai:* Cmmty Sci Fair & Project Wild Coord; Sch Camping Club, Amateur Radio, 8th Grade Spon; NSTA; Amer Birding Assn Life Mem 1973-; TN Ornithdogical Society Mem 1965-; Natl Audubon Society (Pres 1989, Ed Chairperson 1987-88); Zapora Awd Teacher of Yr 1990; NASA Teacher in Space Prgm; Kodak Photography Awd; *office:* A W Spalding Sch P O Box 568 Collegedale TN 37315

SWAFFORD, MAXINE SMITH, Social Studies Teacher/Chair; *b:* Villa Rica, GA; *m:* Mack Dale; *c:* Michael, Pamela; *ed:* (BA) His, Coll of Charleston 1977; *cr:* 5th Grade Teacher Men R-IV Elem 1977-78, Marrington Elem 1978-79; 5th/6th Grade Teacher Marrington Mid 1979-; *ai:* Guest Academic Team Spon; Awards Ceremony Coord; Team Leader; SACS Steering Comm; NEA, SCEA, BEA, NCSS; Daughters of King Pres 1983-87; Holy Trinity Episcopal Church Vestryperson; Phi Kappa Phi; *office:* Marrington Mid Sch 00 Gearing St Goose Creek SC 29445

SWAIM, GARY G., 7th-8th Grade Teacher; *b:* Harmony, NC; *c:* Aaron L.; *ed:* (BS) Phys Ed, 1971; (MA) Admin Superv, 1985 Appalachian St; *cr:* Teacher/Coach Forbush Elem 1973-87; 7th-8th Grade Teacher East Bend Elem 1987-88; Jonesville Elem 1988-; *ai:* Prin Adv Cncl; NC Assn of Ed 1973-; Yadkin Cty Assn of Ed 1973-; Teacher of Yr Forbush Elem Sch 1982; *office:* Jonesville Elem Sch 101 Cedarbrook Rd Jonesville NC 28642

SWAIN, SALLY ANN, Physical Ed/Health Teacher; *b:* Akron, OH; *c:* Laura A.; *ed:* (BS) Phys Ed/Health, 1978, (MED) Scndry Sch Admin, 1979 Miami Univ; Grad Stud, Butler Univ; *cr:* 7th-9th Grade Phys Ed/Health Treacher Clay Jr HS 1979-; *ai:* Frosh Girls Tennis Coach 1982; IN St Teachrs Assn; *office:* Carmel Clay Schls 5150 E 126th St Carmel IN 46032

SWALGA, FRANK MICHAEL, Biology Teacher Sci Dept Chm; *b:* New Kensington, PA; *m:* Mary Geary; *c:* Cristina Sittimio, Francis M., Marc D.; *ed:* (BS) Bio 1963; (MS) Bio, 1968 in Univ of OA; (MS) Scndry Admin, Penn ST Univ 1976; *cr:* Sci/Bio Teacher 1963-89; Sci Dept Chm 1970-89 Keith Jr HS; *ai:* 9th Grade Class Adv; Natl Sci Teacher Organization; *home:* 206 Coleridge Ave Altoona PA 16602

SWAN, LINDA PARKER, 5th Grade Teacher; *b:* Omaha, NE; *m:* Lloyd S.; *ed:* (BA) Psych, CA St Univ Long Beach 1972; Private Pilots License 1983; *cr:* 4th-6th Grade Teacher Cordova Villa Elem Sch 1975-82; Teacher of 5th Grade Gifted & Talented Cordova Gardens Elem Sch 1982-88; 5th Grade Teacher Cordova Villa Elem Sch 1988-; *ai:* Peer Coaching Inservice Coord;4th-6th Grade After Sch Rocket Club; Curr Advisory Comm; Just Say No Club Campus & Bicycle Safety Prgm Campus Coord; CA Teachers Assn, NEA, Folsom Cordova Ed Assn 1975-; CA Assn for Aerospace Ed (Mem Bd of Dir 1983-) 1982-, Civil Air Patrol 1980-; Cameron Park Ninety-Nines (Secy, Vice-Chm, Aerospace Ed Chm) 1983-89; 1985-86 NASA Teacher in Space Prgm Participant; Civil Air Patrol Aerospace Ed Wkshp Dir; Earl Sams Aviation Teacher of Yr 1988; *home:* 2820 Catania Way Sacramento CA 95826

SWAN, STEVEN R., Social Studies Chairman; *b:* Columbus, OH; *m:* Cheryl R.; *c:* Amy; *ed:* (BSED) Ed, OH Univ 1970; *cr:* Teacher Unioto HS 1971-; *ai:* Soc Stud Chm; Sr Class Adv; Mock Trial Team-Coach; Union-Scioto Ed Assn Pres 1984-89; Cntrl OH Teachers Assn Area Rep 1987- Meritoreous Service 1988; Civil War Roundtable Pres 1981-83; Ross Cty Historical Society 1980-; Unioto Stu Cncl Teacher of Yr 1979, 1985, 1986, 1987; *home:* 1252 Nelson Dr Chillicothe OH 45601

SWANGEL, PATRICIA ARLENE (ENGELHARD), English Teacher; *b:* Inglewood, CA; *m:* Gordon; *c:* Pamela Swangel Lee, Mark; *ed:* (BA) Eng, Dordt Coll 1967; (MA) Eng, CA Poly Pomona 1974; Inland Area Writing Project Consultant 1982; *cr:* Teacher Taipei Taiwan 1962-64, Ontario Chrstn HS 1967-69, Substitute Teacher 1969-74; Teacher Continuation Buena Vista 1974-80, Don Lugo HS 1980-; *ai:* Natl Eng Teachers; Womens Bible Study Leader 1984-; *office:* Don Lugo HS 13400 Pipeline Ave Chino CA 91710

SWANGER, KATHY LYNN, Soc Stud Teacher/Chairperson; *b:* Columbus, OH; *ed:* (BS) Comprehensive Soc Stud, Bowling Green St Univ 1985; Working on Masters Degree Guidance, Counseling, Univ of Toledo; *cr:* Soc Stud Teacher Stryker HS 1985-; *ai:* Girls JR Var Bsktbl, Sftbl Coach Stu Government, Soph Class, Jr Class Adv; Citizen Bee Coord; OH Mock Trial Coord & Coach; OEA 1986-; Stryker Ed Assn (VP 1987-88, Pres 1988-89); Stryker United Meth Church; *office:* Stryker HS PO Box 624 S Defiance St Stryker OH 43557

SWANGO, BRUCE E., Mathematics Department Chair; *b:* Winchester, KY; *m:* Barbara; *c:* Carolyn; *ed:* (BS) Math/Philosophy, E KY Univ 1969; *cr:* Teacher Hazard HS 1969-70; Cnslr US Army 1970-72; Math Teacher Crescent City HS 1972-74; Math Dept Head Coral Shores HS 1974-; *ai:* Math Club Spon; Union Rep; Math Tutor; *office:* Coral Shores HS P O Drawer 416 Tavernier FL 33070

SWANGO, COLLEEN JILL, Science Teacher; *b:* Izmir, Turkey; *ed:* (BS) Ed, IN Univ 1978; (MS) Ed/Sci, IUPUI 1984; *cr:* Supervising Teacher Brandywine Pre-Sch for Developmentally Disabled Children 1978-85; Sci/Quest Teacher Brownsburg Jr HS 1986-; *ai:* Stu Cncl Adv; Cheerblock Spon; Yrbk & Newspaper Co-Editor; Academic Superbowl Spon for Sci; SAFARI; NEA 1986-; Hoosier Assn of Sci Teachers Inc 1990; *home:* 4 Janean Dr Brownsburg IN 46112

SWANK, ELAINE, Fourth Grade Teacher; *b:* Quemahoning Twnshp, PA; *ed:* (BS) Elem Ed, 1951, (MED) Elem Ed, 1953 Univ of Pittsburgh; Field Study Prgms Univ of Pittsburgh, Univ of AL, St Marys Coll, Coll of Notre Dame, Univ of Santa Clara; *cr:* 3rd/4th Grade Teacher Paint Township 1952-55; 5th Grade Teacher Forbes Sch Dist 1955-62; 4th Grade Teacher Conemaugh Township Area Sch Dist 1962-; *ai:* PA St Ed Assn 1952-; NEA Life Mem; Conemaugh Township Area Ed Assn (Former Secy, Various Comms); Stoystown Lioness Club (Pres 1986-87, Charter Mem); St Pauls United Church of Christ COnsistory Secy.

SWANN, KAREN JONES, Dance/Drill Team Director; *b:* Dallas, TX; *m:* Warren B.; *ed:* (BS) Health/Phys Ed, 1979, (MS) Health/Phys Ed, 1986 E TX St Univ; *cr:* Eng Teacher 1984-85, Eng/Health Teacher 1985-86, Eng Teacher 1986-88 Farmersville HS; Eng/Dance Teacher 1988-89, Dance/Drill Team Teacher 1989- Mc Kinney HS; *ai:* Drill Team Dir; *office:* Mc Kinney HS 1400 Wilson Creek Pkwy Mc Kinney TX 75069

SWANN, MARIE MC KEEL, Physical Science Teacher; *b:* Goldsboro, NC; *m:* Jeffrey S.; *c:* Jeffrey S. Jr., Kevin M.; *ed:* (BA) Home Ec, 1979, (MS) Scndry Sci Ed, E Carolina Univ 1985; Mentor Teacher Trng; *cr:* Home Ec Teacher Mt Olive Jr HS 1980-81; Bio/Chem Teacher Creswell HS 1981-83; Phys Sci Teacher P S Jones Jr HS 1983-; *ai:* Mentor Teacher; Climate Comm Mem; NC Assn of Educators 1979-; First Presbyn Church; Innovative Teachers Awd 2nd Place Grant 1989; Prin Awd Best Ed Project Creswell NC 1982; *office:* P S Jones Jr HS 820 W Bridge St Washington NC 27889

SWANN, MARJEAN DOROTHY, Math Department Teacher; *b:* Obrien County, IA; *c:* Lara, Sonya, Eric; *ed:* (BS) Home Ec/Bio-Sci Ed, IA St Univ 1960; (MA) Ed/Psych, USIU San Diego 1988; *cr:* Home Ec Ed Teacher Oakland Unified Schls 1960-61; Math/Sci Teacher Alameda Cty Spec Schls 1961-64; Sci Teacher 1964-70, Math/Sci Teacher 1978- ABC Unified Schls; *ai:* CA Jr Scholastic Fed, Chinese Club Adv; Jr Var Girls Bsktbl, Mathcounts Team Coach; Sci Curr Comm; CTA 1960-70; Colusa Cty Schlsp Comm Treas 1974-78; Mentor Teacher Natl Sci Fnd Summer Sci Inst Univ of CA Irvine; *office:* Whitney HS 16800 Shoemaker Ave Cerritos CA 90701

SWANN, RANDALL HAROLD, Drafting Teacher; *b:* Birmingham, AL; *m:* Vicki Colafrancesco; *c:* Michael, Andrea, Mark; *ed:* (AS) Engineering Technology, Jefferson St Jr Coll 1979; (BS) Voc Ed, Univ of AL Birmingham 1988; *cr:* Draftsmans Natural Gas Company 1974-77; Estimator/Engineering Technician Dixie Electrical Manufacturing Company 1977-80; Part Time Instr Jefferson St Comm Coll 1979-; Teacher Pinson Valley HS 1980-; *ai:* Jefferson Cty Fed of Teachers (Building Rep, Area Coord, VP); Voc Industrial Clubs of Amer Adv, Dist II Adv of Yr.

SWANN, RUDOLPH, 6th Grade Teacher; *b:* Fayetteville, NC; *m:* Saunda; *c:* Shauna; *ed:* (BS) Elem Ed, Fayetteville St Univ 1970; *ai:* Bsktbl & Bsbl Coach; NCAE, NEA; *office:* Aberdeen Mid Sch 503 Sandhills Blvd Aberdeen NC 28315

SWANNER, DARLA C., English Teacher; *b:* Snyder, TX; *m:* Joseph Brooks; *ed:* (BA) Eng/Speech, Hardin Simmons Univ 1982; Writing Inst; *cr:* Eng Teacher Cooper HS 1982-; *ai:* Literary Magazine; Curr Comm; ATPE; Juvenile Diabetes Assn Bd of Dirs 1988-; *office:* Cooper HS 3639 Sayles Abilene TX 79605

SWANSON, BARBARA JEAN, Fourth Grade Teacher; *b:* Honolulu, HI; *ed:* (BS) Elem Ed, OK St Univ 1970; Grad Stud OK St Univ, Central St Univ & OK Univ; *cr:* 2nd Grade Teacher Glenwood Townsend Elem 1970-74; 1st-3rd Primary Teacher Parkview Elem Schl 1974-80; 2nd Grade Teacher Dexheim Elem Germany 1980-82; 3rd Grade Teacher Highland Park Elem 1982-84; 4th Grade Teacher Parkview Elem Schl 1984-; *ai:* Primary Team Leader 1974-80; Parent Helper Prgm Spon 1978-80; Stu of Month Prgm Spon; Dist Rep Sci Curr & Supt

Advisory Comm; NEA 1970-; OK Ed Assn 1970-; Mid-Del Assn of Classroom Teachers (Site Rep 1983) 1970- 10 Yr Service Awd 1982, 20 Yr Service Awd 1990; PTA 197-84 Educl Achievement Awd 1973; OSU Alumni Assn 1970-; Natl Geographic Society 1970-; Midwest City-Del City Teacher of Yr 1979; Outstanding Young Women of Amer 1979; Article Published in Teachers Magazine; Mid-Del Outstanding Service Awd 1989; *office:* Parkview Elem Sch 5701 Mackelman Oklahoma City OK 73135

SWANSON, BARBARA RANDEAU, English Teacher; *b:* Tulsa, OK; *m:* Charles H.; *c:* Kjalein; *ed:* (BAED) Eng, NE St OK Univ 1963; (MA) Curr/Instruction/Rdng, WV Univ 1980; Gestalt Inst of Cleveland, Natl Trng Laboratories; *cr:* 10th Grade Eng Teacher Sapulpa HS 1963-64, Barstow Union HS 1964-66; Teacher/Dir of Trng N Cntrl OIC 1978-81; 8th Grade Lang Art Teacher Fairview Mid 1983-; *ai:* Spirit Club; Peer Tutoring Spon & Developer; Lang Art Cty Curr, Rdng Cty Learning Outcomes Comms; NCTE 1963-; Intnl Rdng Assn 1979-83; Marion Cty League of Women Voters Treas 1974-80; *office:* Fairview Mid Sch Fairview Rt Fairview WV 26570

SWANSON, CARYN A., English/Journalism Teacher; *b:* Punxsutawney, PA; *m:* Randy A.; *c:* Erin L.; *ed:* (BS) Eng Ed, Indiana Univ of PA 1977; *cr:* Eng Teacher 1982-, Journalism Teacher 1983- Punxsutawney Area HS; *ai:* PA St Ed Assn; *office:* Punxsutawney Area HS N Findley St Punxsutawney PA 15767

SWANSON, CONSTANCE ANN (KAWA), Fifth Grade Teacher; *b:* Omaha, NE; *m:* Larry J.; *c:* Andrea, Erica; *ed:* (BS) Elem Ed, IA St Univ 1967; (MS) Improvement of Instruction, Univ of NE Omaha 1979; *cr:* 5th-6th Grade Teacher Rockbrook Elem 1967-71; 3rd-4th Grade Teacher St Francis of Assiss 1977-78; Kndgtn Teacher Immaculate Conception Sch 1978-79; 6th Grade Teacher 1980-82, 5th Grade Teacher 1982- Pawnee Elem Sch; *ai:* Drug Free NE Team Mem; Stu Asst Prgm; NEA, Omaha Ed Assn, NE St Ed Assn; Metropolitan Rdng Cncl; NE PTA Honorary St Life Membership 1989; Holy Cross Grade Sch (Treas, Bd Mem); Holy Cross Sch Bd; *office:* Pawnee Elem Sch 7310 S 48th St Omaha NE 68157

SWANSON, JANICE KAY, Third Grade Teacher; *b:* Royal, IA; *ed:* (BA) Elem Ed, Buena Vista Coll 1971; Grad Stud; *cr:* 3rd Grade Teacher Webb Consolidated Sch 1957-61, Spencer Cmmty Sch 1961-62; 2nd Grade Teacher Webb/South Clay Cmmty Sch 1962-70; 3rd Grade Teacher Ruthven/Ruthven-Ayrshire 1971-; *ai:* Office Volunteer at Camp Okoboji; PACK Rdng Cncl; Intnl Rdng Assn; Spencer Municipal Hospital Auxiliary Mem 1989; First Eng Luth Church Bd of Ed; *home:* RR 1 Box 270 Ruthven IA 51358

SWANSON, KATHRINE ELMA, Science Department Chairperson; *b:* Erie, PA; *ed:* (BS) Bio - Magna Cum Laude, Gannon Univ 1975; (BA) Music - Summa Cum Laude, Mercyhurst Coll 1985; (MED) Natural Sci, Gannon Univ 1989; *cr:* Laboratory Work BVM Plastics 1976-77; Permanent Substitute Bio Teacher Fairview HS 1977; Substitute Teacher Fairview HS & Girard HS & General Mc Clane HS 1977-81; Sci Teacher 1981-, Sci Dept Chairperson 1982- Mercyhurst Preparatory Sch; *ai:* Diocesan Moderator of Natl Cath Forensic League; Debate Coach Mercyhurst Preparatory Sch; PA Acad of Sci, NSTA, Natl Fed Interscholastic Speech & Debate Assn, Natl Guild of Piano Teachers; PA Jr Acad Sci Exec Bd; Erie Jaycees Outstanding Young Educator 1987-88; Publication of Article 1989; *office:* Mercyhurst Preparatory Sch 538 E Grandview Blvd Erie PA 16504

SWANSON, MARCIA KAY, 2nd Grade Teacher; *b:* Chicago, IL; *ed:* (BA) Ed, Univ of IL 1972; Lang Art Instructional Writing Skills; *cr:* 1st/2nd Grade Teacher Funston Sch 1973-; *ai:* City Teacher Appreciation Day Faculty Rep; *office:* Funston Sch 2010 N Central Park Chicago IL 60647

SWANSON, MARGARET HANNAH, Teacher of Gifted & Talented; *b:* Chestnut Hill, PA; *m:* Steven Timothy; *ed:* (BA) Elem Ed, Trenton St Coll 1977; Working towards Masters; *cr:* 6th Grade Teacher 1977-81, 5th Grade Teacher 1981-88, 4th Grade Teacher of Gifted & Talented 1989- Lower Towns Sch Dist; *ai:* Track & Field Offcl for Cape-Atlantic Cty; Delta Kappa Gamma (VP 1990-, Convention Chairperson 1988); Governors Teacher Recognition Awd 1990; *home:* 1011 Lafayette St Cape May NJ 08204

SWANSON, MELFORD CARL, 5th/6th Grade Science Teacher; *b:* Jamestown, NY; *m:* Mary K. Sharpe; *c:* Nolan, Patrick, Lesley, Ryan; *ed:* (BS) Elem Ed, Fredonia St Coll 1977; Grad Stud Gannon Univ; *cr:* 5th/6th Grade Sci Teacher Sherman Cntrl Sch; *ai:* Bsktbl & Bsbl Coach; NEA Local Pres 1983-89; IATS E266 Local Membership Chm 1988-89; Chautauqua Cty Girls Bsktbl Coaches Pres; Girls Bsktbl Coach of Yr 1983-84, 1986-87; *office:* Sherman Cntrl Sch Park St Sherman NY 14781

SWANSON, PATRICIA M. PARKS, Fourth Grade Teacher; *b:* Mason City, IA; *m:* Steven Charles; *c:* Jason, Amanada; *ed:* (AA) Elem Ed, North IA Area Coll 1965; (BA) Elem Ed, Univ of Northern IA 1967; (MA) Elem Sch Admin, Creighton Univ 1990; Trainers Prgm TESA Trainer, Cooperative Learning Trainer; *cr:* Kndgtn Teacher Newton Cmmty Schls 1967-68, Council Bluffs Cmmty Schls 1968-70; 1st Grade Teacher 1970-80, 4thGrade Teacher 1980- Glenwood Cmmty Sch Dist; *ai:* TESA Instr IA Sch for Deaf; Cooperative Learning Inservice Instr; Assn for Sch Curr Dev 1988-; NCSS 1988-; NEA Life Mem; Glenwood Ed Assn 1970-; IA St Ed Assn 1967-; Midlands OF IA Rdng Assn 1975-; Chairperson 1st in Nation Ed Winning Awd; Excl in Ed Awd; *office:* Northeast Elem 8th & Linn St Glenwood IA 51534

SWARR, LORA HOLMAN, Gifted Education Teacher; *b:* Parkersburg, WV; *m:* J. Timothy; *c:* Christopher, Jason, Steven; *ed:* (BS) Soc Stud/Phys Ed, WV Wesleyan Coll 1968; (MA) Gifted Ed, WV Univ 1985; Post Grad Stud WV & Marshall Univs; *cr:* Health/Phys Ed Teacher 1968-72, Substitute Teacher 1972-79, Health/Phys Ed Teacher 1979-84, Gifted Ed Teacher 1984- Wood Cty WV Schls; *ai:* Co-Spon Parkersburg HS TV Honor Society, WV St Model United Nations; Spon Mat Maids, Sch Literacy Publication; WV Gifted Ed Assn 1984- Article Published Newsletter 1984; Delta Kappa Gamma (Legislative Affairs Chm 1986- 2nd VP 1990); Parkersburg Area Diabetes Assn; Greater Parkersburg Area Chamber of Commerce; Presenter St & Local Wkshps Soc & Emotional Needs of Gifted Children; Greater Parkersburg Area Chamber of Commerce Leadership Services 1990; Article Published in St Gifted Newsletter; *home:* 104 Briarwood Pl Parkersburg WV 26101

SWART, JOANNE M., Second Grade Teacher; *b:* Lake Village, IN; *m:* Warren; *c:* Diana Boersma, Dale; *ed:* (BS) Elem Ed, 1971; (MS) Elem Ed, 1975 in Univ; Gifted Endorsement Purdue Univ 1990; Comp Endorsement Purdue Univ 1990; *cr:* 1st Grade Teacher 1971-81; 2nd Grade Teacher 1981-88; 2nd Grade Gifted/Talented Teacher 1988- Kankakee Vly Sch Corp; *ai:* Presented Wkshps Using Comps to Teach Creative Wrting 2nd Grade; Speaker Intnl Conf Comps in Ed; NEA 1971; in St Teachers Assn 1971; Kankakee Vly Teachers Assn Bldg Rep 1971- Good Apple Awd 1988-89; IN Assn/Gifted 1988; IN Teachers of Writing 1986; IN Comp Ed 1986-; Creative Writing Curr Grades K-5; Co-Authored Scope/Seq for Gifted Prgm; Several Arcitles Published on Comps; Ed Conf; Teacher Quality Grant Creative Writing 1986; Teacher Quality Grant Math, Sci, Soc Stud 1988; Runner Up Comp Writing Teacher 1986; *home:* 16111 N 700 W De Motte IN 46310

SWART, JOHN SCOTT, German Teacher; *b:* Luanshay, N Rhodesia; *m:* Mary A.; *c:* Paula, Jessica; *ed:* (BA) Fr Lit, NY Univ 1959; (MA) Ger Lit, Univ of Cincinnati 1972; *cr:* Latin/French Teacher Germanto N HS 1963-66; Fr/Ger/Span Teacher Town Heights Mid Sch 1966-69; Mithergreen Mid Sch 1966-68; Ger Teacher Watts Mid Sch 1969-; *ai:* AATG 1971-88; *office:* Watts Mid Sch Mc Ewen Rd Dayton OH 45429

SWARTS, CYNDI SIMS, Teacher; *b:* Boulder, CO; *m:* Kem Winthrop; *c:* Heather A., Brett W.; *ed:* (BS) Elem Ed, Univ of NE 168; Grad Work UNL, Wayne St Coll; *cr:* Teacher Bellevue Public Schls 1968, Lincoln Public Schls 1968-71, N Platte Public Schls 1971-72, Wayne City Schls 1972-89; *ai:* Univ of NE Teachers Ambassador; Phi Delta Kappa; Lincoln Public Schls Gifted Advisory Comm; Conceived & Direct Wayne St Coll 5th-8th Grade Creative & Fine Art Camp.

SWARTZ, JANE LEE, Spanish Teacher; *b:* Martins Ferry, OH; *ed:* (BA) Scndry Ed/Span, W Liberty St Coll 1975; WV Univ, Coll Mount St Josephs, Univ of Dayton; *cr:* Lang Art Teacher Pleasants Cty Mid Sch 1975-77; Span Teacher Cadiz HS 1977-; *ai:* Sociedad Honaria Hispanic Adv; Amer Assn Teachers of Span & Portuguese; OH Foreign Lang Assn; NEA, OEA, HHTA; W Liberty St Highest Honors Grad; *home:* Box 402 Dillonvale OH 43917

SWARTZ, JON C., English Teacher; *b:* Goshen, IN; *m:* Jeanie Carolyn Davis; *c:* Mark, Jeremy, Heidi; *ed:* (BA) Eng, TX A&I Univ 1965; *cr:* Teacher Falfurrias HS 1965-78, Benjamin Logan HS 1978-; *ai:* One Act Play, Soph Class, Newspaper Adv; Dir Jr Class Play; *home:* 6558 Rd 18 Bellefontaine OH 43311

SWARTZ, RANDY MARK, Junior High Supervisor; *b:* Muncy, PA; *m:* Kim Ellen Phillips; *c:* Carleton; *ed:* (BS) His Ed, Pensacola Chrstn Coll 1986; *cr:* HS Teacher 1986-89, Jr HS Supvr 1989- Sumter Chrstn Sch; *ai:* Jr Varsity Bsktbl Coach; Honor Society Spon; Field Day Coord; *home:* 1400 Hidden Oak Dr Wedgefield SC 29168

SWEARENGIN, CAROL H., Fifth Grade Teacher; *b:* Fordland, MO; *ed:* (BSED) Elem, SW MO St Univ 1960; (ME) Elem, Drury Coll 1971; Grad Stud S MO St Univ, Drury, NE MO St Coll Kirksville; *cr:* 5th Grade Teacher Fordland Elem 1958-67, Willard Elem N 1967-; *ai:* Math Curr Comm; SNEA Pres 1957-58; MSTA Secy 1958-70; NEA (Pres, VP, Secy, Treas) 1980-; Local & St Intnl Rdng Assn 1988-; PTA 1958-; *office:* Willard R-2 Schls PO Box 98 Willard MO 65781

SWEAT, NORA VAILLANCOURT, Home Economics Teacher; *b:* Glendale, KY; *m:* Michael Francis; *c:* Joseph; *ed:* (BS) Home Ec, 1970, (MA) Home Ec Ed, 1977 W Ky Univ; *cr:* Home Ec Teacher W Hardin HS 1970-; *ai:* FHA Adv; KY Voc Assn Home Ec VP 1988-; KY Assn Home Ec Teachers St Pres 1986; 4-H Cncl Treas 1979-80; KY Home Ec Teacher of Yr 1987; Grant Co-Write Nutritional Sci Curr & Domestic Violence; *home:* 2862 Shepherdsville Rd Elizabethtown KY 42701

SWEATT, LINDA ESPINOLA, Mathematics Teacher/Dept Chair; *b:* Plainfield, CT; *m:* Ronald Burnett; *c:* Tanya, Jason; *ed:* (BA) Math, Nasson Coll 1969; (MA) Scndry Math/Rdng, Univ of CT 1974; Data Processsing & Programming in BASIC Courses; Cooperating Mentor Teacher Trng; *cr:* Math Teacher Ayer Jr/Sr HS 1969-71; Adjunct Cmptrs Teacher Quinebaug Valley Comm Coll 1984-86; Math Teacher 1971-, Math Dept Head 1989- Plainfield HS; *ai:* Frank L. Roediger Chapter NHS Adv; Cooperating Mentor Teacher; Disciplinary Panel; Pomfret Cmmty Sch Parent Organization; NCTM 1971-; CT Assn Teachers of Math 1976-; NEA, CT Ed Assn, Plainfield Ed Assn 1971-; Pomfret Cmmty Sch Booster Club Secy 1989-; GSA Asst Leader 1982-, 5 Yr Service Pin 1987; Bustins Island Cottagers Assn (Secy 1985-88, Treas 1990); Bustins Island Historical Society 1980-; Pomfret Historical Society 1988-; CT Math Teacher Recognition Awd; Helped with Young Scholars Saturday Semester; *office:* Plainfield HS 87 Putnam Rd Central Village CT 06332

SWEATT, MARTHA BULLARD, Third Grade Teacher; *b:* Tupelo, OK; *m:* John Woodlief Jr.; *c:* Kelsey Blackwell, John Woodlief III; *ed:* (BSED) Home Ec, 1951, (MED) Elem Ed, 1961 E Cntrl St Univ; *cr:* Rdng Specialist Valley View Hospital 1964-65; Kndgtn Teacher Jack & Jill Kndgtn 1963-64; Elem Teacher Ada Public Schls 1965-; *ai:* OK Ed Assn 1965-; Ada Ed Assn 1970-; Tanti Study Club Chm 1989-; Southwest Church Of Christ Mem; Teacher of Teachers Awd 1987; Teacher of Excl Awd 1988; *office:* Washington Elem Sch 600 S Oak Ada OK 74820

SWECKER, GARY J., Mathematics Teacher; *b:* Valley Head, WV; *m:* Virginia S. Shoulders; *c:* Sharmon, Aaron; *ed:* (BS) Math Ed, WV Univ 1970; Grad Courses Ed & Math; *cr:* Teacher Suncrest Jr HS; Instr WV Univ; *ai:* Curr Cncl Math Comm; Suncrest Jr HS Math Club; WVEA 1970-; *office:* Suncrest Jr HS 360 Baldwin St Morgantown WV 26505

SWEEM, TERENCE ALLEN, English, Speech Dept Chair; *b:* Lincoln, NE; *ed:* (BA) Speech/Eng/Drama, Univ of NE Lincoln 1980; Numerous Grad Courses Eng, Journalism; *cr:* Speech Chm/Eng Teacher W Point Jr/Sr HS 1980-81; Speech Teacher/Eng Chm Pope John XXIII Cntrl Cath 1981-; *ai:* Dir Fall Dinner Theatre & Spring Musical; Speech Team Coach; Ftbl, Boys Bsktbl Asst Coach; NCTE Mem; Knights of Columbus Mem; *office:* Pope John XXIII Cntrl Cath Sch Po Box 179 Elgin NE 68636

SWEENEY, JAMES MARTIN, Bilingual Teacher/Coordinator; *b:* Oak Park, IL; *m:* Juanita Idalia Valdes; *c:* Veronica, Michael, Victoria; *ed:* Working Towards Masters Math, Univ of IL; *cr:* Teacher/Coord William H King Elem 1967-; *ai:* Park Ridge Jr Girls Bsbl Coach; Sci & Math Improvement Comm Mem; IL Cncl Teachers of Math Mem 1989; Univ of IL Urbana Cmptrs in Elem Ed Summer Fellowship 1987; *office:* William H King Elem Sch 740 S Campbell Ave Chicago IL 60612

SWEENEY, JANE L., 6th Grade Teacher; *b:* St Louis, MO; *m:* William M.; *ed:* (BS) Eng-Latin/Amer His, Bradley Univ; Grad Work; *cr:* Eng Teacher Washington HS 1966-68, Jefferson Mid Sch 1968-73, Franklin Mid Sch 1975-80; 6th Grade Teacher Mc Cleery Elem Sch 1980-; *ai:* Building Rep Aurora Ed Assn; West Mc Cleery Sch Discipline Comm; Aurora Curr Advisory Cncl; Alpha Delta Kappa; *home:* 1730 Kenilworth Pl Aurora IL 60506

SWEENEY, MARY LOU ISAACS, Teacher; *b:* Huntington, IN; *m:* George William; *c:* Barbra A.; *ed:* (BA) Eng, 1972, (MAE) Ed, 1977 Ball St; *cr:* Teacher North Side Mid Sch 1972-88, Highland HS 1988-; *ai:* Lang Art Curr Comm; NCTE 1987-; Anderson Fed of Teachers (Secy 1987-, Mem 1972-); *office:* Highland HS Cross St Anderson IN 46012

SWEENEY, MICHAEL LAWLER, Social Studies Teacher; *b:* Scranton, PA; *m:* Jean M. Gwizdala; *c:* Allison, Quinn; *ed:* (AS) Math/Sci, Jefferson Comm Coll 1973; (BA) His, St Univ of NY Oswego 1975; (MS) Scndry Ed, St Univ of NY Potsdam 1986; *cr:* Substitute Teacher Watertown City Sch Dist 1979-82; Soc Stud Teacher Sackets Harbor Cntrl Sch 1982-; *ai:* Sackets Harbor Sr Class Adv, Yrbk Staff Photographer; Advisory Comm; Adams Youth League Bsbl Coach 1989-; *office:* Sackets Harbor Cntrl Sch Broad St Sackets Harbor NY 13685

SWEENEY, THERESE A. (SOBOCINSKI), 8th Grade Teacher; *b:* Salem, MA; *m:* James N. Jr.; *c:* Deborah, Mathew, Patricia, Susan; *ed:* (BSED) Math, St Coll at Salem 1953; *cr:* 3rd/4th Grade Teacher Gloucester MA 1953-61; 1st-12th Grade Tutor/Substitute Teacher Peabody MA 1961-63; 1st-12th Grade Tutor Medford 1968-70; Kndgtn Teacher Melrose Nursery 1974-76; 7th-8th Grade Teacher St Marys 1978-; *ai:* Raising Funds with Stu to Provide Trip to Washinton DC; Prin Search; *office:* St Marys Sch 162 Washington St Winchester MA 01890

SWEENEY, VIRGINIA MARY, RSM, First Grade Teacher; *b:* Providence, RI; *ed:* (BSED) Primary Ed, Cath Teachers Coll 1956; Working Toward Masters in Grad Prgm Rdng, RI Coll 1967-69; *cr:* 2nd Grade Teacher 1946-56; 1st Grade Teacher 1956-60; 3rd Grade Teacher 1959-60; 1st Grade Teacher Holy Family-Holy Name Sch 1960-; *ai:* NCEA; *office:* Holy Family-Holy Name Sch 91 Summer St New Bedford MA 02740

SWEET, LYNDA LEE, American History Teacher; *b:* Cleveland, OH; *m:* Walter E. Walz Jr.; *ed:* (BA) His, Miami Univ 1969; Working Towards Masters Psych, Nova Univ; *cr:* Soc Stud Teacher Driftwood Mid 1970-; *ai:* Soc Stud Teacher of Yr 1981; *home:* 1540 NE 43rd St Oakland Park FL 33334

SWEETLAND, GRETA WOODS, Second Grade Teacher; *b:* Elkhorn, WI; *m:* David; *c:* Anna Marie; *ed:* (BA) Ed, San Diego St 1954; La Verne Univ; San Diego Univ; UCSB; UCR; Pepperdine; Upland Univ; Cal Poly/Pomona; *cr:* Teacher Baldy View Elem 1954-66; Rep Economy Book Company OK 1966-70; GATE & LDS Teacher Citrus Elem Sch 1972-75, Teacher Citrus Elem 1975-; Mentor Upland Unified Sch Dist 1989-; *ai:* Blue Bird Club Leader & Girl Scout Club Bd Mem; Chaffey HS Band Supporter Club Bd Mem; Alta Loma Riding Club Supporter; Upland Teachers Assn Soc/Salary Curr VP/Primary Rep & Pres 1954-; Baldy View PTA; Auditor/Teacher Rep 1954-66 Honorary Life Membership; Citrus PTA Teacher Rep 1972- Honorary Life Membership; Rdng Assn; Master Teacher to 12 Practice Teachers Univ of San Bernardino/Laverne/Upland Univ/Cal Poly; *home:* 5622 Revere Alta Loma CA 91701

SWEETMAN, CLARENCE JAMES, Fourth Grade Teacher; *b:* Lodi, NJ; *m:* Kathleen Krause; *c:* Neil, Patricia; *ed:* (BS) Bus Management/Admin, Fairleigh Dickinson Univ 1957; (MA) Elem Ed, Paterson St Coll 1967; Cert in Admin & Supervision, Uuniv of South FL; *cr:* Supervisor Acme Supermarkets 1953-67; 4th Grade Teacher Paterson Sch System 1965-66, Haskel Elem Sch 1966-68, Mildred Helms Elem Sch 1968-; *ai:* Acting Prin; Team Leader 4th Grade; FL Ed Assn; FL Rdng Assn; NEA; Pinellas Cty Teachers Assn; *home:* 3748 Orchard Grove Ln Largo FL 34640

SWEGER, GLENDA LEE, English Teacher & Mentor; *b:* Harrisburg, PA; *ed:* (BS) Eng Ed, IN Univ of PA 1968; (MA) Comm, CA St Univ Fullerton 1981; *cr:* Eng Teacher Greensburg-Salem Jr HS 1968-69, Northview HS 1969-; *ai:* Newspaper & Yrbk Staff Adv; Mentor Teacher; Accrediation Comm Chairperson; Curr Dev Advisory Bd; Staff Dev Comm; S CA Sch Pub Bd of Dir Secy 1972-82; NEA, NCTE 1968-; Orange Cty AIDS Fnd 1986-; Statue of Liberty Fnd 1982-; Spring 1988-; SGV Educators Grant; Whos Who of Amer Women; 2000 Notable Amer Women; Whos Who in Ed; Cmmty Leaders of America; *office:* Northview HS 1016 W Cypress Ave Covina CA 91722

SWENBERG, LEILA RUTH, Elem Prin/3rd Grade Teacher; *b:* Dunnell, MN; *ed:* Elem 1947, (BS) Elem/Prin, 1955, (MS) Elem, 1963 Mankato St; *cr:* 1st-8th Grade Teacher Dist 42 Rural 1948-49; 1st-6th Grade Teacher Dist 65 Rural 1949-50; 3rd Grade Teacher 1950-54, 3rd Grade Teacher/Prin Ceylon Public Dist 451; *ai:* NEA, MN St Ed Assn, Natl Prin Assn, MN St Prin Assn; *home:* Dunnell MN 56127

SWENSON, CATHERINE WAGNER, Second Grade Teacher; *b:* Faribault, MN; *m:* Paul M.; *ed:* (BS) Elem Ed, ST Cloud ST Univ 1975; *cr:* Chapter 1 Teaching Wells Elem Sch 1975; 2nd Grade Medford Elem Fall 1975-; *ai:* Medford Ed Cncl Comm Mem 1989-; Sci Curr Comm Mem 1990-; Medford Minnesota Ed Assn Sec 1988-89 1989-.

SWENSON, GLORIA KATHLEEN LAMBERT, English/Spanish Teacher; *b:* Chicago, IL; *d:* Marc W. Swenson; *c:* Dorian M., Tristan L.; *ed:* (AA) Music, Olive-Harvey Jr Coll 1967; (BA) Ed/Eng, Univ of IL Chicago 1970; Span/Ed, Univ of Platteville; *cr:* Pre-K/Kndgtn/1st-3rd Grade Teacher Chicago Public Schls 1970-76; Dir/Head Teacher Gingerbread House Pre-Sch 1978-82; HS Eng/Span Teacher Shullsburg Public Schls 1983-; *ai:* Shullsburg Forensics Team Head Coach; HS Play Dir; Sch Newspaper Adv; NCTE 1984-; Pinto Horse Assn oF Amer 1972-; Natl Audobon Society 1977-; Shullsburg Industrial Dev Corporation Bd of Dir 1988-; Badger Historical Society Pres 1977-82; Shullsburg Historical Pageant Dir 1977, 1990; Composed Original Music, Lyrics; Shullsburg Pageant Comm Chm 1990; *office:* Shullsburg HS 444 N Judgement Shullsburg WI 53586

SWENSON, JOANNE R., Third Grade Teacher; *b:* Charleroi, PA; *m:* Gary Robert; *c:* Gregory, Danielle, Jill; *ed:* Assoc Legal Secy, Robert Morris Jr Coll 1969; (BS) Ed, CA St Coll 1972; *cr:* Teacher Aura Elem Sch; *ai:* Elk Township Ed Assn Treas 1984-88; NJ Ed Assn, NEA; *home:* 264 Ivy Dr Woodbury Heights NJ 08097

SWENSON, RHONNA MARY, Language Art Teacher; *b:* Mondovi, WI; *m:* Keith M.; *c:* Krista, Lindsay; *ed:* (BS) Elem Ed, Univ of WI Eau Claire 1968; Grad Stud Univ of WI River Falls, Univ of WI Superior; *cr:* 6th Grade Teacher E P Rock Sch 1968-70; Jr HS Teacher Franklin Sch 1970-71; Teacher Unity Mid Sch 1972-; *ai:* Curr Coordinating Comm Chairperson; WI Assn of Mid Level Ed; *home:* Rt 1 Box 276 Balsam Lake WI 54810

SWENSON, TERRY DEAN, Soclgy/Psych/Soc Stud Teacher; *b:* Milbank, SD; *c:* Eli, Camille; *ed:* (AA) HPER, Fergus Falls St JC 1972; (BS) HPER, SD St Univ 1975; *cr:* Elem Phys Ed/Jr HS Soc Stud/Driver Ed & Health Teacher Florence Schls 1975-81; Sociology & Psych Teacher Elkton Schls 1981-; *ai:* Head Jr HS Ftbl Coach; Defensive Coord HS Ftbl; Intramural Bsktbl Grades 4-6; Track Team Coach; Bsktbl Coach; Head Ftbl Coach; Little League Bsbl Coach 1987-; Elks Club 1980-; *office:* Elkton Public Sch Box 190 Elkton SD 57026

SWETT, KEITH ELLSWORTH, English Teacher; *b:* Marshfield, WI; *m:* Jean Eichinger; *c:* Matt, Laura; *ed:* (BS) Eng, Univ of WI La Crosse 1973; *cr:* Eng Teacher Seymour HS 1973-; *ai:* HS Head Wrestling, Jr Olympic Wrestling, Ftbl Coach; Class Adv; USA Wrestling (Pres 1982-86, VP 1978-82, Area Rep 1975-), Bronze Awd 1990; WFAA Wrestling Area Rep 1983-87; Lions 1980-82; JC VP 1978-80; Meth Church Admin Bd 1986-89; *home:* 733 Woodside Dr Seymour WI 54165

SWICEGOOD, NANCY PARNELL, Algebra & Geometry Teacher; *b:* Lexington, NC; *m:* Tony Clifton; *c:* Jeffrey C., Michael C.; *ed:* (BA) Math, Catawba Coll 1970; *cr:* Teacher S Rowan HS 1970, N Rowan HS 1970-71, N Davidson Jr HS 1971-; *ai:* 9th Grade Chm; NC Cncl Teachers of Math 1984-; NC Prof Educators 1985-; *office:* N Davidson Jr HS Rt 10 Box 1660 Lexington NC 27292

SWIER, SUSAN A., Business Education Teacher; *b:* Jersey City, NJ; *ed:* (BS) Bus Ed, Montclair St Coll 1983; Insurance Brokers License 1984; *cr:* Bus Teacher Cranford Bd of Ed 1983-85; Bus Teacher/Coach Bogota Bd of Ed 1985-; *ai:* Sr Class Adv; Asst Girls Vlybl & Bsktbl Coach; Bogota Ed Assn Union Rep 1989-; NEA, NJEA, NJBEA 1983-; Piscataway Elk Ladies Mem 1988-; Yrbk Dedication 1989; *office:* Bogota HS 1 Luthin Pl Bogota NJ 07603

SWIERCZEK, CLINTON ANDREW, Health Teacher; *b:* London, England; *m:* Debbie Lynn Hofeldt; *c:* Stephanie A.; *ed:* (BS) Phys Ed/Health, Univ of WY 1981; Amer Red Cross CPR & First Aid Instr; Facilitator & Counseling Trng; *cr:* Teacher/Coach Laramie Jr HS 1981-; *ai:* Coach Vlybl, Boys & Girls Bsktbl, Track; Albany Cty Ed Assn, WY Ed Assn, NEA; Laramie Optimist Club Citizen of Yr 1987; *office:* Laramie Jr HS 1355 N 22nd Laramie WY 82070

SWIES, ANN EDDY, First Grade Teacher; *b:* De Kalb, IL; *m:* John; *c:* Michael; *ed:* (BSED) EMH, N IL Univ 1971; Grad Stud Whole Lang, Gifted Ed, Math; Problem Solving & Critical Thinking Courses Corridor for Excl in Ed & Natl Sci Fnd; *cr:* Intermediate EMH Teacher Delano Sch 1971; 2nd Grade EH Teacher Scott Sch 1971-76; 1st/2nd/4th/6th Grade Teacher Roy Sch 1976-; *ai:* Inservices Dist Staff Problem Solving Techniques; Math Test Comm; Mannheim Teachers Organization 1971-; *office:* Roy Sch 533 N Roy St Northlake IL 60164

SWIFT, ANGELA NELSON, English Teacher; *b:* St Louis, MO; *m:* Jesse B. II; *c:* Jesse B. III, Bryan I.; *ed:* (BA) Sociology, Univ of IL 1969; (MS) Cnslr Ed, IL Univ Edwardsville 1978; Teachers of Gifted & Talented Children Trng; Learning Acad Trng for Teachers of Children At Risk; *cr:* Teacher Clark Jr HS 1975-; *ai:* Stu Cncl Co-Adv; Girls Track Coach; NCTE 1988-; ASCD 1989-; *home:* 1410 St Louis Ave East Saint Louis IL 62201

SWIFT, KATHY HALLOCK, English Teacher; *b:* Wenatchee, WA; *m:* Dean Crandall; *c:* Karin Swift Schwenk; *ed:* (BA) Eng, Ft Wright Coll of Holy Names 1964; Grad Courses St Univ of NY Oswego & St Univ of NY Brockport; *cr:* Eng Teacher Batavia Jr HS 1964-65, Princeton Avenue Sch 1965-67, Gates Chili Mid Sch 1968-; *ai:* Dist Leadership Comm; Mid Sch Excl in Ed Team; Mid Sch Organizational Study Group; NY St Union of Teachers 1968-; Teacher of Excl Awd NY St Eng Cncl 1982, 1989; *office:* Gates Chili Mid Sch 910 Wegman Rd Rochester NY 14624

SWIFT, LINDA A. (LUTZ), 6th Grade Teacher/Counselor; *b:* Oakland, CA; *m:* Rod; *c:* Katrina, Kurt; *ed:* (BA) Sociology, Univ of CA Davis 1967; (MS) Psych, Univ of Laverne 1990; *cr:* Primary Teacher Hayward CA 1968-71; Chapter 1 Rdng Teacher Project City Elem 1971-72; Cnslr Dunsmuir Elem 1972-; *ai:* Stu Adv; Stu Cncl; Stu Study Team Leader; Group Discussion Leader; Mentor Teacher 1987-89; *office:* Dunsmuir Elem Sch 4760 Siskujou Ave Dunsmuir CA 96025

SWIFT, PATRICIA HAYNES, 6th Grade Teacher; *b:* Clarkesville, GA; *m:* Walter D.; *c:* Mary L. E., Anna C. L.; *ed:* (BS) Bus Admin; (MS) Mid Grades, Mercer Univ 1989; *cr:* Math Teacher R E Lee Jr HS 1971; East Thomaston Sch 1976-77; Math/Rdng Teacher Thurston Elem 1980-84; 6th Grade Teacher Upson Mid Sch 1984-; *ai:* Jr Beta Club Spon; POD Ldr 1987-; Math Curr Team; St Spelling Bee Spon-Inter Sch; Sunshine Comm; Upson Mid Sch Technlgy Comm; UCAE Teacher of Yr 1988-89; GAE; NCTM; GA NTCM; Thomaston-Upson (Arts Cncl 1987-; Chamber of Commerce 1987-); Upson Cancer Society (Bosom Buddies 1989-; Cncl Child Abuse 1989); *office:* Upson Mid Sch 300 Adams St Thomaston GA 30286

SWIFT, RUBY WILDER, Sixth Grade Teacher; *b:* Raleigh, NC; *m:* W. Joseph; *c:* Broderick, Tatia; *ed:* (BED) Elem Ed/Early Chldhd, Univ of Miami 1972; Classroom Management FL Memorial Coll 1987; Assertive Discipline Technique 1988, Prof Wkshp 1987, Supervision of Intern Teacher Ed Center 1981; *cr:* Teacher Asst Olinda Elem 1969-71, Primary Sch C 1972; Rdng/Math/Title 1 Teacher St Francis Xavier Cath Sch 1972-79; Teacher Olinda Elem 1979-; *ai:* T-Shirt Making & Sewing Club; Black His & Sunshine Comm; Parent Outreach; Saturday Sch Teacher; United Teachers of Dade, PTA 1972-; Natl Sch Volunteer Prgm 1987-; Dade Sch Volunteers Sch Liaison 1987-; Orinda Elem Teacher of Yr 1990; *office:* Olinda Elem Sch 5536 NW 21st Ave Miami FL 33142

SWIFT, VIOLET ANN (ELDER), Third Grade Teacher; *b:* Mc Alester, OK; *m:* Donnie Ray; *c:* Kevin R., Casey D.; *ed:* Elem Ed, Poteau Jr Coll 1961; (BS) Elem Ed, 1962, Elem Ed, 1965 SE OK St Univ Durant; Elem Ed, E NM Univ; NM St Univ; *cr:* 4th Grade Teacher Pawhuska Elem 1963-64; 3rd Grade Teacher Taylor Elem 1964-70; 4th-5th Grade Teacher Coronado Elem 1971-83; 3rd Grade Teacher College Lane Elem 1983-; *ai:* Church & PTA Comm; NEANM Alternate Delegate; NEA 1963-; NM Natl Ed Assn & Hobbs Educl Assn 1964-; Chrstn Center Church; Delta Kappa Gamma 1985-; *home:* 1134 Zuni Hobbs NM 88240

SWIGART, DEBORAH CALVIN, Music Teacher; *b:* Bryan, TX; *m:* Ray L.; *c:* Douglass, Michael; *ed:* (BS) Music Ed, Clarion Univ 1975; Grad Stud PA St Univ; *cr:* Music Teacher Huntingdon Area Sch Dist 1975-79, Butler Area Sch Dist 1979-; *ai:* Core Team Comm Mem; Music Educators Natl Conference; *office:* Butler Area Sch Dist New Castle Rd Butler PA 16001

SWILLEY, DEBORAH RIVERS, Fifth Grade Teacher; *b:* Ft Lauderdale, FL; *m:* James; *c:* Aimee, Katie; *ed:* (BS) Elem Ed, FL Southern Coll 1975; (MED) Elem Ed/Early Chldhd Ed, Univ of N FL 1985; *cr:* 6th Grade Teacher Okeechobee Elem 1975-76; 3rd Grade Teacher 1979-82, 5th Grade Teacher 1982- Chiefland Elem; *ai:* Dicipline Comm; *office:* Chiefland Elem Sch PO Drawer 40 Chiefland FL 32626

SWILLING, MARJORIE CRAFT, Teacher; *b:* Hartwell, GA; *w:* James Wesley (dec); *ed:* (BS) Poly Sci, NC St Univ 1965; Grad Studies Univ of GA; *cr:* Teacher Hart Cty Comprehensive HS & Boddie HS; *ai:* Soc Stud & Sr Adv; Certified Data Collector; GA Assn of Educators VP 1987; Natl Assn of Educators, NCSS; Optimist Club; Amer Cancer Society Bd of Dir 1987-89; Order of Eastern Star Treas; Natl Assn for Advancement of Colored People; Federal Grant from Taft Inst of Government Univ of GA 1983.

SWINDALL, RONNIE EDWARD, Chemistry Teacher; *b:* Jenkins, NY; *m:* Vickie Sturgill; *c:* Michelle, Nathaniel, Reuben; *ed:* (BS) General Sci, 1965, (MS) Bio, 1974 E TN St Univ; Dreyfuss Inst in Chem, Gilford Coll; Spec Chem Topics, Clinch Valley Coll; *cr:* Sci Teacher Appalachia HS 1965-66, Pound HS 1966-73; Sci Teaching Asst E TN St Univ 1973-74; Sci Teacher J J Kelly HS 1974-; *ai:* Jr Class Spon; Audio-Video Engineering Club Spon; VA Assn Sci Teachers; Lions Club; *home:* Rt 1 Box 484 Big Stone Gap VA 24219

SWINDELL, NELLE FULLER, English Teacher; *b:* Abilene, TX; *c:* Mac; *ed:* (BS) Eng, Hardin-Simmons Univ 1955; (MS) Scndry Ed, OK St Univ Stillwater 1976; Lang Art Ed, Cntrl St Univ 1983-84; *cr:* Elem Teacher Noodle-Horn CSD 1963-65; Scndry Eng Teacher Hawley HS 1965-72; Elem Teacher Harrison Elem 1983-85; Scndry Eng Teacher Cushing HS 1985-; *ai:* Cushing HS Yrbk Adv 1985-; NCTE 1985-; AAUW 1983-; 1st Baptist Church (Singles Dept Dir 1972-, Sanctuary Choir Pres 1988-); *office:* Cushing HS 1700 E Walnut Cushing OK 74023

SWINDEN, LARRY ALLEN, Special Education Teacher; *b:* Chicago, IL; *m:* Laura Francis O Callaghan; *c:* Shawn, Andrew; *ed:* General Liberal Arts Coll of Du Page 1973; (BSED) Spec Ed, 1976, (MSED) Spec Ed, 1981 IL St Univ; Ed Admin, NE IL Univ; *cr:* Cross Catagorical Teacher Wheaton North HS 1979-81; LB/BD Teacher Hersey HS 1982-83; BD Coord Schaumburg HS 1984; BD Teacher Leyden HS 1985-; *ai:* Fellowship Chrstn Athletes Spon; Ftbl, Track & Field, Bowling Coach; IL Track N Field & Cross Cntry Coaching Assn; Kappa Delta Phi Honor Society Mem; IL St Univ Deans Talent Awd of Excl; Outstanding New Coach Leyden HS; *office:* Leyden HS 340 Rose St Franklin Park IL 60131

SWINEY, JAMES MARVIN, Pres/Music/Choir/Guid Cnslr; *b:* Bristol, VA; *m:* Charliece Sublett; *c:* Cynthia Swiney Rodda, Alyssa Swiney Janney; *ed:* (BA) Music, Milligan Coll 1957, (MA) Amer Univ 1962; Univ of VA Ed & Psych Courses; Psych, Liberty Univ; Certified Guidance Cnslr; Music, Univ of FL; *cr:* Music & Sci Teacher Cloudland HS 1957-58; U S Army Arlington Hall Sta 1958-61; Music Teacher/Band Trenton HS 1961-63; Music Teacher/Band & Chorus Herndon HS 1964-68; Dir of Ed/Choir & Sci/Guidance Mountain Mission Sch 1964-83; *ai:* Public Relations Work; Leader Parenting Wkshp & Seminars; FL Bandmasters Assn 1962-64; Natl & St Ed Assn 1964-68; VA Music Ed Assn 1964-; Lions Intl (Pres Local Club 1964-76, St Pres 1973-74); Milligan Coll Trustee 1980-; Free-Lance Writer Religious Publications; Choir & Bands won Numerous Awds; MMS Choir Performed in Europe 1983, Canada 1973; Wolf Trap Gala 1980; Mountain Mission Sch Day Washington DC 1988; Natl Republican Governors Conference Williamsburg Choir Entertained 1978; VA Gubenatorial Gala Richmond 1987; *office:* Mountain Mission Sch 1 Hurley St Grundy VA 24614

SWINGER, DE LOIS YVONNE CARTER, Mathematics Teacher; *b:* Anderson, SC; *c:* Monique Y., Melanie B., Winard C.; *ed:* (BA) Sociology NC Cntrl Univ 1972; Math, 1973, (MED) Ed/Rdng, 1975 Clemson Univ; *cr:* Math Teacher Palmetto HS 1972-85, Southwood Mid Sch 1985-; *ai:* NEA; *home:* Rt 8 114 Leawood Ave Anderson SC 29621

SWINGLER, MICHAEL G., Upper School Science Teacher; *b:* Ft Sill, OK; *m:* Jill Owens; *c:* Tara, Jason; *ed:* (BS) Physics Ed, 1971, (MS) Astrophysics Ed, 1975 E IL Univ; AP Wkshps & Seminar in Physics; NSF Chem Ed; *cr:* Sci/Math Teacher Bradley/Bourbonnais HS 1971-81, Pace Acad 1981-88; Sci Teacher Phoenix Cntry Day 1988-; *ai:* Teams & Tennis Coach; Jr Class Spon; Cum Laude Society Mem Inducted 1990; AAPT, NSTA Mem; NSF Chem Ed Fellowship; Article in Physics Teacher; *office:* Phoenix Cntry Day Sch Stanford & 40th St Paradise Valley AZ 85327

SWINNEY, JO ANN WILSON, Chapter I Reading Teacher; *b:* Russellville, AL; *m:* Curtis Jr.; *c:* Trampas; *ed:* (BS) Home Ec, 1964, (BS) Elem Ed, 1975 Univ of N AL; *cr:* Home Ec Teacher Springville HS 1964-65; 6th Grade Teacher Phil Campbell Elem 1966-; *home:* PO Box 147 Hodges AL 35571

SWINNEY, JOYCE JEANNE, Choral Music Teacher; *b:* Texarkana, AR; *ed:* (BMusED) Choral Music/Piano/Voice 1976, (MMusED) Choral Music, 1987 Henderson St Univ; Certified Dir of Music in United Meth Church Perkins Sch of Theology Southern Meth Univ; *cr:* Choral Music Teacher Mabelvale Jr HS 1984-; *ai:* Yrbk Adv; Delta Omicron 1974-; Music Educators Natl Conference 1988-; AR Choral Dir Assn 1984-; *home:* 20 Connolly Ct Little Rock AR 72209

SWINNEY, SARAH ELIZABETH (JOHNSON), Chapter I Rdng/Math Teacher; *b:* Ranger, TX; *m:* James Clayton; *c:* Ben, Marc; *ed:* (BSED) Elem Ed, 1964, (MA) Rdng Specialist, 1981 N TX St Univ; *cr:* 1st Grade Teacher Murray Elem 1964-66; 2nd Grade Teacher 1974-81; Chapter I Teacher 1981- Cannon Elem; *ai:* ESSA Math Comm; TX St Teachers Assn (VP 1978-79, Pres 1987-88, Faculty Rep 1977-78, 1986-89); PTA VP 1973-74; Set Up Parent Volunteer Prgm at Cannon 1978-79; Teacher of Yr Veterans of Foreign Wars 1978-79 & Teacher of Yr Cannon Elem Faculty Choice 1986-87; *office:* Cannon Elem Sch 1300 W College Grapevine TX 76051

SWINSON, SUE WHITLOW, Latin Teacher; *b:* Rocky Mount, VA; *m:* William Edward Jr.; *c:* Robert A. Burgess, William E. III, Evelyn K., Susan G. Stansbury; *ed:* (AB) Latin, Coll of William & Mary 1961; (MEd) His, 1978, Latin, 1981 GA St Univ; *cr:* Latin Teacher Huguenot HS 1961-62; Eng/His Teacher US Armed Forces Inst 1962-64; Latin Teacher Tucker HS 1965-68, Dekalb Cty Schls 1973-; *ai:* Spon Jr Classical League LatinClub; Natl Latin Honor Society; Coach-Certamen Teams; Cty Comm Textbooks Writing Curr Guides; GA Classical Assn (Co-Editor 1985-86, Mem 1980-) Ga St Latin Teacher of Yr 1986; Amer Classical League 1973-; NEA 1988-; Ga Assn of Educators 1988-; Classical Assn of Midwest & South 1974-88; Organization of Dekalb Educators 1988-; Foreign Lang Assn of GA 1979-; *office:* Lakeside H S 3801 Briar Cliff Rd Atlanta GA 30345

SWINTON, ELLA HUGHES, 6th Grade Language Art Teacher; *b:* Florence, SC; *m:* Roscoe; *c:* Marcus; *ed:* (BA) Soc Stud, Claflin Univ 1971; (MED) Elem, Francis Marion Coll 1975; Prgm for Effective Teaching Trainer; *cr:* Teacher of Learning Disabilities Lake City Mid Sch 1971-73; Lang Art Teacher Hannah-Pamplico Mid Sch 1973-; *ai:* Pro-Team Club Adv; Chm of Eng Book Selection Comm; Florence Cty Ed Assn 1971-; NEA Faculty Rep 1971-; Teacher Incentive Awd 1988-89; *office:* Hannah-Pamplico Mid Sch P O Box 158 Pamplico SC 29583

SWISHER, CHARLES E., JR., School Counselor; *b:* Waynesboro, PA; *m:* Patricia Anita Karle; *c:* Joshua D.; *ed:* (BS) Elem Ed, E KY Univ 1968; (MED) Ed, Shippensburg Univ 1972; Grad Stud; *cr:* 5th Grade Teacher Surrey Elem; 6th Grade Soc Stud Teacher E R Hicks Mid Sch; Cnslr Clear Spring Mid Sch 1987-; *ai:* Washington Cty Crisis Counseling Team 3 Yrs; Mc Donalds Mid Sch Attendance Incentive & Hag Jr Coll Talented & Gifted Summer Prgm Cty Developer Washington Cty; Washington Cty Bd of Ed Equity Cncl; Washington Cty Teachers Assn, MD St Teachers Assn, NEA 1968-; Washington Cty Cnslrs 1987-; Big Brothers of Amer Bd of Dir 1968-78, Special Awd 1979; Washington Cty Childrens Cncl Mem 1979-83; Washington Cty Historical Cmmty Mem 1985-88; Hospice of Washington Cty Mem 1987-; *home:* 12755 Bain Rd Mercersburg PA 17236

SWISHER, PAMELA REESE, Sixth Grade Teacher; *b:* Charleston, WV; *c:* Kenny; *ed:* (BS) Elem Ed, WV St Coll 1976; (MA) Rdng, WV Coll of Grad Stud 1986; Grad Stud Educl Admin; *cr:* Teacher Gay Elem Sch 1977-78, Ripley Mid Sch 1978-; *ai:* Stu Cncl Adv; Class Pres Spon; Asst Track Coach; Sch Improvement Comm; Parent Advisory Cncl; Jackson Cty Rdng Cncl VP 1987; Intnl Rdng Assn 1986-88; Delta Kappa Gamma 1988-; GFWC Jr Womans Club of Ripley (VP, Pres) 1979-80; Teacher of Yr 1989; *office:* Ripley Mid Sch Rt 2 Box 75-A Ripley WV 25271

SWISHER KIEVET, PENNY, Drama Teacher/Director; *b:* Loraine, OH; *m:* Kenneth; *c:* Adam, Emily; *ed:* (BS) Speech/Theatre, MO Valley Coll 1971; (MA) Organizational Comm, Cntrl MO St 1983; *cr:* Speech/Drama Teacher Heidelberg Amer HS 1971-74; Speech/Debate Teacher Truman HS 1974-78; Comm Professor/Debate Coach William Jewell Coll 1978-85; Drama Teacher/Public Relations Dir St Marys HS 1987-; *ai:* Drama Dir; Newspaper & Yrbk Adv; Admin & Diocesan Mrktg Comm; N Cntrl Steering Comm Chairperson; Pi Kappa Delta (Natl Cncl 1981-83, Natl Pres 1983-85, Ed 1985-87) Outstanding Leader 1985, Outstanding Contribution 1987; Speech & Theatre Assn of MO Pres 1979-80, Service Awd 1985; Speech Comm Assn States Advisory 1980-85; Cross Exam Debate Assn Natl VP 1984; Independence Chamber of Commerce Chairs Comm 1990; Co-Author; Articles Published; Presentations at St, Regional, Natl Conventions; Whos Who Among Outstanding Young Women 1981, 1983, 1985; Notable Amer Women; *office:* St Marys HS 622 N Main Independence MO 64050

SWITZER, SANDRA G., 9th-12th Grade Teacher; *b:* Havre de Grace, MD; *m:* Harold; *c:* Lorrie, Scott; *ed:* (BS) Elem, Salisbury St 1969; (MA) Rdng, George Mason 1980; Greater Jr Books; Critical Thinking Skills under Art Costa; Grad Courses Univ of VA; *cr:* K-1st Grade Teacher Anne Green Sch; 1st Grade Teacher Havre de Grace Elem; 3rd-5th Grade Teacher Read-Thomas Manor; 6th-8th Grade Teacher Chpl-St Anthony; 4th-8th Grade Teacher Antilles Sch Syst PR; 9th-12th Grade Teacher Stonewall Jackson HS; *ai:* Kappa Delta Phi 1981-; Greater WA Rdng Cncl 1982-, Nom Agnes Myer Awd Prince William Cty 1990; Grant Greater WA Cncl; *office:* Stonewall Jackson HS 8820 Rixlview Rd Manassas VA 22110

SWOPE, CHARLINE WHITAKER, Retired Fourth Grade Teacher; *b:* Evarts, KY; *m:* George Alfred; *c:* Myra V. Swope Munday; *ed:* (BA) Elem Ed, E KY Univ 1966; Sch Librarian Endorsement; *cr:* Teacher Mercer & Lincoln Cty Schls 1948-51; Currator William Whitley House KY St Parks System 1952-57; Welfare Dir/Secy Lincoln Cty Fiscal Court 1957-67; K-12 Grade Librarian 1967-73, 3rd/4th Grade Teacher 1983-87 Lincoln Cty Schls; *ai:* PTA 1967-, Certificate of Life Membership 1987; Lincoln Cty Ed Assn, KY Ed Assn, NEA 1967-87; KY Lib Sci Assn 1967-73; KY Teachers Retirement Assn 1987-; Democratic Womens Organization Co-Chm 1957-67, Commissioned KY Colonel 1968; Daughters of Amer Revolution 1987-; Eastern Star ADA 1952-72; Calvary Baptist Church (Dir Church Music, Several Comm); Established & Implemented Complete New Lib Facilities Mc Kinney Elem 1967-68 & Highland Elem 1968-69; Title II Grant for Librarians Awd E KY Univ; *home:* Brights Inn 1210 Danville Rd Stanford KY 40484

SWORDS, JAY, Social Studies Teacher; *b:* Moline, IL; *m:* Jeanette Bivens; *c:* Arafel B.; *ed:* (BA) His, Western IL Univ 1982; Educl Counseling Univ of IA; Advanced Trng Madaline Hunter Teaching Prgm; *cr:* Soc Stud Teacher Bettendorf Sch Dist 1983-89; Soc Stud Consultant Quad City Homework Hotline 1985-89; Soc Stud Teacher/Continuing Ed Black Hawk Coll 1988-; *ai:* Bettendorf Var Girls Tennis Coach; Phi Alpha Theta 1981-; Kappa Delta Pi 1982; Phi Kappa Phi 1982; Connie Belin Fellowship for GiFted Ed; MS Athletic Conference Coach of Yr 1987; *home:* 5015 69th Ave Milan IL 61264

SYERS, MARTHA KATHERINE, Mathematics Teacher; *b:* Austin, TX; *ed:* (BS) Elem Ed, SW TX St Univ 1971; (MS) Curr/Instruction Corpus Christi St Univ 1980; Rdng Specialist; *cr:* 4th Grade Elem Teacher Travis Elem 1976-78; 3rd-4th Grade Teacher Fannin Elem 1978-82; 6th Grade Teacher/Media Center Specialist Lozano Spec Emphasis Sch 1982-83; 7th/8th Grade Math Teacher Tom Browne Jr HS 1983-84; Math Teacher Lake Travis Mid Sch 1984-88, Tivy HS 1988-; *ai:* Academic Decathlon, Octathlon, UIL Calculator Coach; Frosh Class Coord; Phi Delta Kappa 1981-; TX Prof Educators Assn; Corpus Christi ATPE (Pres 1980-84, Mem 1978-); ATPE Region 2 (Pres 1982-84, Mem 1978-); Natl Cncl of Teachers of Math 1984-; TX Cncl of Teachers of Math 1989-; First Presbyn Church Youth Coord 1989-; Lake Travis Ind Sch Dist Teacher of Yr Finalist; Corpus Christi St Univ & Corpus Christi Ind Sch Dist Math Grant; *office:* Tivy HS 1607 Sidney Baker Kerrville TX 78028

SYKES, BETTY J. BROWN, Middle Grades Teacher; *b:* Alma, GA; *c:* Deborah D.; *ed:* (BA) Elem Ed, 1977, (MS) Mid Sch Ed, 1983 Ft Valley St Coll; Numerous Seminars; *cr:* Teacher Bacon Cty Mid Sch 1977-; *ai:* 6th Grade Team Chairperson; 7th Grade Graduation; GA Assn for Teachers Building Rep 1987-; 1st AB Sunday Sch Treas 1988-; Lupus Chapter Secy 1987-; Natl Advancement for Colored People Secy 1985-; Deputy Registrar; Recommended for Teacher of Yr; *office:* Bacon Cty Mid Sch E 16th St Alma GA 31510

SYKES, BETTY J. BROWN, 6th & 7th Grade Teacher; *b:* Alma, GA; *c:* Deborah D; *ed:* (BA) Elem Ed, Fort Valleys St Coll 1977, (MS) Mid Grades, 1983 Fort Valley St Coll; *cr:* Teacher Bacon Cty Mid Sch 77-; *ai:* 6th Grade Chairperson; Adv-Spon with 7th Grade Graduation Exercises; GA Assn of Educators Building Rep 1987-; Lupus Chapter Sec 1987-; NAACD Sec 1985-; Bacon Cty Depty Regisra 1989-; 1st AB Church Sunday Sch Treas 1988-; Recommended As Teacher of Yr; *office:* Bacon County Mid Sch 523 E 16th St Alma GA 31510

SYKES, MARCIA MORGAN, English/Speech/Drama Teacher; *b:* Hannibal, MO; *ed:* (BA) Eng, Culver-Stockton Coll 1983; *cr:* Grad Asst Instr Univ of FL 1983-84; Adjunct Instr Culver-Stockton Coll 1984-86; Eng/Speech/Drama Teacher Highland HS 1986-; *ai:* Drama Club Spon; Drama Coach; Schlsp Comm; NCTE, MO St Teachers Assn, Cmmty Teachers Assn 1986-; Amer Assn of Univ Women 1984-; Canton Area Arts Cncl 1988-89; *office:* Highland HS Hwy 6 Ewing MO 63440

SYLVESTER, NANCY WILCHER, Academic Counselor; *b:* Brookhaven, MS; *m:* Herman Lee; *c:* Herman II, Carlton, Larramie; *ed:* (AA) Speech/Theatre, Copiah-Lincoln Jr Coll 1975; (BS) Comm, 1976, (MA) Counseling Psych, 1977 Univ of S MS; Spec Counseling Ed, MS St Univ 1981; Teacher Effectiveness Trng; *cr:* Teacher Prentiss Jr Coll; Cnslr Columbia HS; Teacher/Cnslr Jackson Public Schls; *ai:* Guidance Comm Chairperson; NAVESNP VP 1979-80; MS Counselors Assn Mem, ASCA 1988-; PTA Secy 1990; *home:* 425 Anvil Cir Jackson MS 39212

SYLVESTER, THELMA KINGSTON, English Teacher; *b:* Itta Bena, MS; *m:* Clausell; *ed:* (BS) Eng Lit, Jackson St Univ 1967; (MA) Inner City Stud, Northeastern IL Univ 1973; *cr:* Teacher Muskegon Heights HS 1967-68; Case Worker IL Dept of Public Aid 1968-69; Teacher Chicago Bd of Ed 1969-; *ai:* Lindblom NHS Aetos Chapter Spon; Lindblom Leader Adv; AFT, NCTE; Delta Sigma Theta 1966-; *office:* Lindblom Tech H S 6130 S Wolcott Ave Chicago IL 60636

SYLVESTRO, PHILIP JOSEPH, Social Studies Teacher; *b:* New Britain, CT; *c:* Deborah, Mark; *ed:* (BA) His, Morehead St Coll 1965; (MS) Guidance, Univ of Hartford 1971; Ed, Cntrl CT St Univ 1990; *cr:* Teacher Mark T Sheehan HS 1965-; *ai:* Phi Delta Kappa 1990; Wallingford Ed Assn VP 1981-; CT Ed Assn Bd of Dir 1984-; Wetlands Comm Vice Chm 1972-85; Planning Zonning Comm Secy 1985-; *office:* Mark T Sheehan HS Hope Hill Rd Wallingford CT 06067

SYLVIA, JOHN D., Agriculture Teacher/Dept Chair; *b:* Duquoin, IL; *m:* Joan Van Dorin; *c:* Stacey Logan, John Jr., Mike, Darrin D.; *ed:* (BS) Ag, CA St Univ Fresno 1961; (MS) Ed, CA Poly San Luis 1978; *cr:* Teacher Oroso HS 1961-64; Teacher/Dept Chm Mt Whitney HS 1964-; *ai:* FFA Adv; CATA (Regional Pres 1974) Outstanding Teacher 1985; NUATA; VUTA Pres 1970; St Marys Church; Teacher of Excl 1973; Star St Adv 1974; Honorary Amer Degree 1976.

SYMON, BILL HAROLD, Honors Chemistry Teacher/Coach; *b:* Bluffton, IN; *m:* Carol Hopp; *c:* Bill; *ed:* (BS) Bio, Purdue Univ 1973; (MSE) Bio Ed, TX Womans Univ 1987; *cr:* Bio/Poly Sci/Chem/Physics/Sci Teacher/Coach Aledo HS 1973-83; Poly Sci Teacher/Coach Nichols Jr HS 1983-86; Chem Teacher/Coach Grapevine HS 1986-; *ai:* Var Ftbl & Track; Campers Planning & Employee Benefits Comm; ATPE (Pres 1982) 1978-; NSTA 1973-; Teacher of Yr Aledo 1978 & Grapevine 1990; *office:* Grapevine HS 3223 Mustang Dr Grapevine TX 76051

SYMULESKI, DIANE M. BARYCKI, 5th Grade Elementary Teacher; *b:* Scranton, PA; *c:* Peter; *ed:* (BA) Elem Ed, Mansfield Univ 1972; (MS) Elem Ed, Wilkes Coll & St 1987; *cr:* Elem Teacher Moosic Elem 1973-; *ai:* Marching & Chrldr Co-Adv; Elem Drama Club Co-Dir; Video Pen Pal Co-Adv; Elem Advisory Bd Mem; Elem Discipline Handbook Comm, Art Curr Co-Chairperson; PSEA (Legislative Contact, Rep) 1988-; REA (Rep at Large 1986-, Negotiating Mem) 1985-; NE PA Rdng Assn Exec Bd 1986-87; PTA (PR 1986-87, Legislative Contact) 1987-88; Certified Teacher Drug Abuse; *office:* Moosic Elem Sch Krieg & School St Moosic PA 18507

SYPHER, BEVERLY ANNE, 4th Grade Teacher; *b:* Everett, WA; *m:* James E.; *c:* James, Scott; *ed:* (AA) Grays Harbor Coll 1964; (BA) Ed, Univ of WA 1967; Seattle Pacific Univ, Univ of WA, Cntrl WA Univ; *cr:* Kndgtn Teacher Ashwood Elem; 2nd Grade Teacher Redmond Elem; 2nd-4th Grade Teacher Norman Rockwell Elem; *ai:* Adv Stu Cncl; Staff Comm Soc/Volunteer Tea; Intnl Rdng Assn Recording Secy 1989-; Lake WA Ed Assn Bldg Rep 1986-87, 1989-; Univ of WA Alumni 1967-; Pacific Luth Univ Parent Club 1989-; Faith Lutheran Church 1970-; PTA 1967-; *office:* Norman Rockwell Elem Sch 11125 162nd Ave NE Redmond WA 98052

SYPHER, MARY BETH (BELLANT), French Teacher; *b:* Bay City, MI; *m:* George L. Jr.; *ed:* (BA) Fr/Elem Ed, N MI Univ 1985; (MS) Fr, Wayne St Univ; Numerous Courses; *cr:* Fr Teacher Ladywood HS 1986-; *ai:* Fr Club Adv; Jr Class Moderator Co-Head; Post Prom Comm; Class Trips to France; Discipline Comm; MI Foreign Lang Assn 1987-; *home:* 42430 Parkhurst Dr Plymouth MI 48170

SYRACUSE, ANTHONY VETUS, Science Teacher; *b:* Cleveland, OH; *m:* Eleanor P. Byron; *c:* Anthony T., Patricia A., Diane C., Karen C.; *ed:* (AB) Zoology/Chem, 1963, (MED) Scndry Ed, 1969 OH Univ; Grad Stud Chem, Bio, Physics, Geology, Economics, Cmptrs, Math; *cr:* Sci Teacher Euclid Cntrl Mid Sch 1966-; *ai:* Soc Comm; Prof Growth Comm; OH Ed Assn & NEA Life Mem; Euclid Teachers Assn NEOTA; Outstanding Educator Awd 1984; Euclid Teachers Assn (Sch Rep 1966-72, Exec Bd 1971-72); Jennings Scholar 1984-85; Mem Phi Delta Kappa 1968-; Outstanding Educator Awd 1984; *home:* 10920 Crestwood Dr Kirtland OH 44026

SYRJALA, DEBRA (ORLICH), Second Grade Teacher; *b:* Wakefield, MI; *m:* Paul; *c:* Steven, Scott; *ed:* (AA) Elem Ed, Gogebic Cmmty Coll 1971; (BS) Elem Ed, N MI Univ 1973; Univ of WI Stevens Point, Superior, Oshkosh, Green Bay; Silver Lake Coll, Aurora Univ; *cr:* 2nd Grade Teacher White Lake Elem Sch 1973-; *ai:* Sch Music Prgms Accompianist; White Lake Sch Testing Comm; NEA, WI Ed Assn 1973-; White Lake Ed Assn Treas 1973; Horizon Childrens Center (Bd oF Dir, Historian) 1980-; St Marys Home Sch Assn 1985-; Antigo Music Assn Spon 1983-; Antigo Jr Womens Club 1979-85; St Johns Cath Church Organist 1985-; White Lake 94-142 Sch Dist Teaching Schlsp 1986; Nom Whos Who Among Amer Women; *office:* White Lake Elem Sch PO Box 67 White Lake WI 54491

SZEDELI, BRENDA BLAIR, Eng Teacher of Gifted/Talented; *b:* Lubbock, TX; *m:* Morris W.; *c:* D Lisa, Ryan, Jonathan; *ed:* (BS) Ed, Univ of N TX 1972; (MED) Spec Ed/Gifted, TX Womans Univ 1986; *cr:* Teacher H F Stevens Mid Sch 1976-; *ai:* UIL Drama Spon; 1-Act Play & Talent Show Dir; Detention Hall Supvr; Delta Kappa Gamma Parlimentarian 1989-, Schlsps; ASCD 1989-; Crowley Assn Building Rep 1980-; PTA 1976-; *office:* H F Stevens Mid Sch 1016 FM 1187 Crowley TX 76036

SZELES, FREDERICK JOHN, JR., Science Teacher; *b:* Summit, NJ; *m:* Susan Marie Wasko; *c:* Lori, Cheryl, Julie, Sandra; *ed:* (BA) Scndry Sci Ed, 1970, (MA) Admin/Supervision, 1982 Kean Coll; Electronics Instr US Coast Guard; *cr:* Electronics Teacher US Coast Guard 1970-74; Scndry Sci Teacher Bridgewater Raritan HS East 1974-; *ai:* Var Boys Soccer, Frosh Girls Bsktbl, Asst Var Lacrosse Coach; NJEA, BREA, NEA, Natl Geographic Society; Green Peace; *office:* Bridgewater Raritan H S East PO Box 301 Foothill Rd Martinsville NJ 08836

SZEMAN, EDWARD ROBERT, Music Teacher; *b:* Cleveland, OH; *m:* Penelope Elizabeth Nissen; *c:* Edward M., Robert G., Lisa M.; *ed:* (BS) Music Ed, Univ of Dayton 1961; (MS) Counseling/Psych, Amer Technological Univ 1984; US Army Armor Officers Basic 1961 & Advanced Courses 1966; US Army Command & General Staff Coll 1972; Austrian General Staff Officers Course 1973; *cr:* 8th Grade Music Teacher St Josephs Elem Sch 1982-86; K-6th Grade Music Teacher Willow Springs Elem Sch 1986-; *ai:* Minister of Music 1982-; Killeen Ind Sch Dist Adult Ed Literacy Tutor; TX Music Educators Assn, OR Amer Kodaly Educators 1987-; TX Classroom Teachers Assn 1986-; Retired Officer Assn 1981-; Killeen Elem Music Educators Assn (Treas 1988-89, VP 1989-); Heights Concert Band 1980-; Cntrl TX Mastersingers 1987-; Czech Catholic Union of TX Society #128 VP 1988-; *office:* Willow Springs Elem Schl Old Copperas Cove Rd Killeen TX 76542

SZILAGYI, TAMAS, History Teacher; *b:* Szatmar, Hungary; *m:* Brigitta Risher; *c:* Steven; *ed:* (BA) His, Pedagogic Inst of Budapest 1953; (MA) His, Univ of Pittsburgh 1968; St License Ed Hungary 1954; *cr:* Teacher Gyor HS Hungary 1953-56, Kiski Sch 1963-; *ai:* Soccer & Tennis Coach; Natl Endowment for the Hum Grant 1987; *office:* Kiski Sch 1888 Brett Ln Saltsburg PA 15681

SZUMSKI, CAROLYN ANN, 8th Grade Teacher; *b:* South Bend, IN; *m:* Thomas G.; *c:* Sarah, David; *ed:* (BS) Ed, 1969, (MS) Ed, 1973 IN Univ; *cr:* Teacher St Adalbert Cath Sch 1965-70, Brandywine HS 1975-82, St Baco Cath Sch 1984-; *ai:* Sch Newspaper Spon; Math, Cmptrs, Lang Art, Rdng Diocesan Curr Dev; Pre Cana Counseling 1978-89; Jr Achievement Outstanding Teacher; *office:* St Bavo Cath Sch 513 W 7th St Mishawaka IN 46544

T

TABER, MAXINE FORE, Retired; *b:* Latta, SC; *w:* Albert R. III (dec); *c:* Albert R. IV; *ed:* (BA) Elem Ed, Coker Coll 1958; Univ SC Ext Div Rdng/Audio-Visual Aides; Pembroke St Univ Guidance/Sociology/Phys Ed; Francis Marion Coll European His; *cr:* 4th/5th/6th Grade Teacher Dalcho Sch 1946-50; Principal & 5th/6th/7th Part-Time Teacher Manning Sch 1950-51; 3rd Grade Teacher Floydale Elem 1952-53; 7th Grade Teacher Dillon Elem 1953-54; 5th Grade Teacher Hamer Elem 1957-67; 4th & 2nd Grade Teacher Stewart Heights Elem 1967-83; *ai:* Stewart Heights Elem Sch Stu Teachers Supv 1974/1980; Natl Ed Assn; SC Ed Assn Part-Time Career Mem; Dillon Cty Ed Assn; Dillon Literary Club Pres 1970-72; St Cecilia Music Club Pres 1962-64; Dillon Hs Band Concert Narrator 3 Yrs; St Barnabas Episcopal Church Choir Mem 1949-; St Barnabas Episcopal Church Women Treas; Dillon Cty Diamond Jubilee 1985; Retired Sunday Sch Teacher; Dillon Cty Comm Choir Mem; Mem St Barnabas Episcopal Church Altar Goild; Substitute Teacher; Daughters of Amer Rev Thanksgiving/X-Mas Pgm/Freedom of Our Heritage; Dillon Cty Spelling Bee Pronouncer 1987-; 1st-8th Grade Dillon Sch Dist 2 Teacher of Yr Awd 1973; SC St Teacher of Yr Prgm Nom; *home:* 300 E Wilson St Dillon SC 29536

TABLER, DEBRA GRIFFITH, Math Department Chairperson; *b:* Fukuoka, Japan; *m:* James Stephen Sr.; *c:* James Jr., Jeremy, John P.; *ed:* (BA) Math, Shepherd 1978; (MA) Remedial Rdng, WV Univ 1986; *cr:* Math Teacher 1978-82, 1985-89, Math Chairperson 1989- Clear Spring HS; *ai:* Jr Class Adv; Cmptr Club Adv; Discipline Comm; Soc Comm; Math Sat Adv; MD St Teacher Assn 1978-; MD Cncl of Teachers of Math 1989-; NCTM 1989-; Bedington PTA Pres 1985-; Mt Wesley United Meth 1975-; *office:* Clear Spring H S Rt 2 Box 118 Clear Spring MD 21722

TABOR, DEBBY LYNN, History/Geography Teacher; *b:* Big Spring, TX; *m:* J. W.; *c:* Leslie; *ed:* (BS) Scndry Ed, TX Tech Univ 1984; *cr:* Teacher Lubbock-Cooper HS 1984-; *ai:* Stu Cncl Spon; Phi Sigma Alpha 1984; TX Classroom Teachers Assn 1984-; TX Assn of Stu Cncls 1984-; Dist Adv of Yr 1990; Spec Olympics Volunteer, MDA, MADD; *office:* Lubbock-Cooper Ind Sch Dist Rt 6 Box 400 Lubbock TX 79412

TABOR, JANICE HINSON, 6th Grade Language Art & Sci; *b:* High Point, NC; *m:* Jerome O'Neel Sr.; *c:* Jerome O., Robert L., Paul D., Sentralia D.; *ed:* (BA) Intermediate Ed, Univ of NC Greensboro 1976; *cr:* 5th/6th Combination Teacher Fairview Elem 1977-78; 4th Grade Teacher 1978-81, 3rd Grade Teacher 1981-82 Parkview Elem; 6th Grade Teacher 1983-86, 6th/7th/8th Grade Teacher 1986-87, 6th Grade Teacher 1987- Tabernacle Mid Sch; *ai:* Sci Contact Person; Mem CORE Team; Stu Assistance Prgm; Chairperson Sci Comm; Mentor Teacher; NCAE, OCAE, NEA 1977-; *home:* 114 King St Jacksonville NC 28540

TACKETT, DONALD L., Director of Vocal Music; *b:* San Francisco, CA; *m:* Elaine M. (Proctor); *c:* Laura, Peri, Lon, Jennifer; *ed:* (BA) Music Ed, Cntrl WA Univ 1970; *cr:* Vocal Music Teacher Kilo Jr HS 1970-75, Hoqiuam Sch Dist 1975-; *ai:* Music Groups; Drama & Natural Helpers; NEA, MENC; Elks Club; VFW; Consultant to Other Sch Dist Teaching Self-Esteem; *office:* Hoquiam Sch Dist 501 W Emerson Hoquiam WA 98550

TACKETT, JEAN BLANTON, 7th Grade Math/Eng Teacher; *b:* Ashland, KY; *m:* Ronald G.; *c:* Jason; *ed:* (BA) Elem Ed, 1969, (MA) Elem Ed, 1974 Morehead St Univ; *cr:* 6th Grade Teacher Rockford Lane Elem 1969-71; 5th Grade Teacher Cntrl Elem 1971-74, Mapleton Elem 1974-79; 7th Grade Teacher Mc Nabb Mid 1979-; *ai:* Acadmic Team Ofcl; MCEA, KEA, NEA (Treas 1986-87, Pres 1987-89); *office:* Mc Nabb Mid Sch 3570 Indian Mound Rd Mount Sterling KY 40353

TACKETT, MARION BRADLEY, Mathematics Teacher; *b:* Lake Charles, LA; *m:* Melody Cheryl Westbrooks; *c:* Mary B., Joe P.; *ed:* (BS) Math, Mid TN St Univ 1986; *cr:* Math Teacher Shelbyville Cntrl HS 1986-88, Riverdale HS 1988-; *ai:* Asst Ftbl Coach; Mid TN Teachers of Math 1988-; Edgemont Baptist Church Deacon 1989-; *office:* Riverdale HS 802 Warrior Dr Murfreesboro TN 37129

TACKLESON, JON SCOTT, Guidance Counselor; *b:* Iowa City, IA; *m:* Leslie Jean Hinbaugh; *c:* Jennifer, Rose, Kathryn; *ed:* (BA) Bus Admin, Peru St Coll 1972; (MA) Couseling & Guidance, NE MO St Univ 1983; Univ of N IA; *cr:* Bus Ed/Phys Ed Teacher/Coach Coon Rapids HS 1976-78; Bus Ed Teacher/Cnslr/Dame HS 1978-85; Bus Ed/Admin Teacher/Cnslr/Coach Shellsberg Cmmty Sch Dist 1985-87; Bus Ed Teacher/Cnslr/Coach La Salle HS 1987-; *ai:* Asst Ftbl & Wrestling Coach; IGHSAU Ofcl 1986-; IA Ftbl Coaches Assn 1988-; IA HS Wrestling Coaches Assn 1988-; ICAS 1989-; *office:* La Salle HS 3700 1st Ave NW Cedar Rapids IA 52405

TADLOCK, SUSAN MELADY, Mathematics Teacher; *b:* New Orleans, LA; *m:* Charles Anthony; *c:* Rachael, Joseph; *ed:* (BS) Math, 1976, (MED) Ed Admin, 1985 Univ of New Orleans; *cr:* Teacher Our Lady of Perpetual Help 1973-76, Grace King HS & T H Harris Jr HS & Bonnebel HS 1977-; *ai:* Mu Alpha Theta Spon; Phi Kappa Phi Mem 1976-; Phi Delta Kappa Mem 1985-; Grandlake Estates Civic Organization 1985-; *office:* Bonnabel HS 8800 Bruin Dr Metairie LA 70003

TADROS, NABILA, Mathematics Teacher; *b:* Amman, Jordan; *ed:* (BA) Math, 1977, (MA) Math, 1981 Jersey City St Coll; Supvr of Math 1989; Cmptr & Math CPC TM Certificate Prgm 1985; *cr:* Math Teacher Ferris HS 1977-; *ai:* Math Club Adv; HS Proficiency Test Comm Mem; NJEA, JCEA, NCTM Mem 1977-; Governors Teacher Recognition Awd 1987; *office:* Ferris HS 35 Colgate St Jersey City NJ 07307

TAFFS, JEAN VANCE, English Teacher/Chair; *b:* Alpena, MI; *m:* Anthony; *ed:* (BS) Eng, 1966, (MED) Fnds of Ed, 1968, (PHD) Fnds of Ed, 1974 Kent St Univ; *cr:* Elem Teacher Oak Creek 1962-65; Eng/Soc Stud Teacher Albion HS 1972-74; Elem Teacher Caldwell Sch 1974-84; Eng Teacher/Chairperson Albion HS 1984-; *ai:* Literary Magazine Adv; NCTE 1984-; Conference for Scndry Sch Eng Dept Chairperson 1988-; Albion Choral Society 1980-; Calhoun Child Abuse/Neglect Cncl 1985-; St James Episcopal Church Choir & Jr Choir Dir 1980-.

TAFT, LORA JANE (BAKER), 5th Grade Teacher; *b:* Linton, IN; *m:* Charles W.; *c:* Angeline R., Margie J.; *ed:* (Ba) Ed, 1977; (MS) Mid Grades, 1981 Columbus Coll; *cr:* 5th Grade Elem Teacher Waverly Hall Elem 1978-89; Pine Ridge Elem 1989-; *ai:* Stu Support Team Contact Person; Page 1980-; ROA 1978-; Youth Dir Bapt Church 1985-; US Army Reserve Instr of Yr; Nom Teacher of Yr 1987-89; *office:* Pine Ridge Elem Sch P O Box 129 Ellerslie GA 31807

TAGGART, DIANA L., Math Teacher; *b:* Chicago, IL; *m:* Donald D.; *c:* Ryan, Douglas; *ed:* (BSED) Zoology, E IL Univ 1966; Math, Univ of UT; *cr:* Math Teacher Bingham HS 1985-; *ai:* Academic Decathalon Coach; UT Cncl of Teaching Math, NCTM; Most Influential Teacher Weber St Coll 1987; Participant OH St C2PC Project 1989; *office:* Bingham HS 2160 W 10400 S South Jordan UT 84065

TAHHAN, NANCY BRISBIN, Kindergarten Teacher; *b:* Pittsburg, KS; *c:* Tanya, Sam; *ed:* (BSE) Elem Ed, MO Southern St Coll 1975; (MSE) Adult Ed, Cntrl MO St Univ 1979; Guidance Counseling, Pittsburg St Univ; *cr:* Elem Teacher Golden City R-3 Sch Dist 1975-79, Liberal R-2 Sch Dist 1979-; *ai:* Prof Dev Comm; Kndgtn Advisory Cncl; Beginning Teacher Mentor; MO St Teachers Assn 1975-87; Liberal Cmmty Teachers Assn (Treas 1981-82, Pres 1982-83); *home:* Rt 5 Box 75 Lamar MO 64759

TAKARA, BRIT S., Fourth Grade Teacher; *b:* Hilo, HI; *m:* Jean Kayoko Nishimura; *c:* Tracy Lynn T., Matt S.; *ed:* (BA) Scndry Ed, 1960, (MA) Elem Ed, 1966 Adam St Coll; *cr:* 4th-6th Grade Teacher Sch Dist #60 1960-; *ai:* Team Leader; Cnslr & Staff CO Boys St; NEA; CO Ed Assn Helpmobile, Plaque 1971; Pueblo Ed Assn (Collective Bargaining Negotiation Team 1978-87, Grievance Team 1982-87); BSA Dist Commissioner 1987-89; Natl Eagle Scout Assn Scoutmaster Awd of Merit 1988; Rocky Mountain Cncl Silver Beaver 1987; El Pueblo Dist Awd of Merit 1984; Distinguished Teacher Awd, CO Awd, Ed & Cmmty Achievement 1985; Awd for Volunteer Excl, Volunteer Coord of Pueblo 1988; *home:* 5 Bruce Ln Pueblo CO 81001

TAKES, LARRY L., Mathematics Department Chair; *b:* Manchester, IA; *m:* Linda Markus; *c:* John, Jeanine; *ed:* (BS) Math, Loras Coll 1967; (MAT) Math, Univ of NE 1974; *cr:* Math/Sci Instr Marquette HS 1967-76; Math/Physics Instr Cascade HS 1976-; *ai:* NCTM, IA Cncl Teachers of Math, NEA; Knights of Columbus Grand Knight 1983-84; NSF Grant for Grad Study 1971-74; Discrete Math Wkshp 1986; Physics & Electronics Wkshp 1985; *office:* Cascade HS 505 Johnson St NW Cascade IA 52033

TALAMO, YOLANDA MARIE, Spanish Teacher/Chairperson; *b:* Endicott, NY; *m:* Joseph F.; *c:* Thomas, James, Robert, Richard, Patricia A.; *ed:* (BA) Span, Coll of New Rochelle 1947; (MA) Middlebury Span Sch 1949; Grad Stud, Mexico, Millersville Univ; *cr:* Asst Span Instr Triple Cities Coll of Syracuse Univ 1947-49; 7th/8th Grade Eng Teacher 1951, Latin I Teacher 1951-53 C Fred Johnson Jr HS; Span Teacher Hempfield Sr HS 1966-; *ai:* Dept Chairperson; Honorary Span Society Spon; Hum Day Participation Coord Univ of Pittsburgh; HAEA, PSEA, NEA 1966-; AATSP 1978-; Welcome Wagon Pres 1966-67; Parish Cncl Secy 1968-71; Deanery Cncl Secy 1969-71; Pastoral Cncl VP 1971-73; Seton Hill Coll Certificate of Teaching Excl; Recognition of Spec Service, Achievement, Contribution to Academic & Cultural Act Certificate Awd; Positive Teaching Awd; Awd of Yr Univ of Notre Dame; *home:* 556 Hickory Dr Greensburg PA 15601

TALARIGO, KIM M., Administrative Trainee; *b:* Johnstown, PA; *ed:* (MS) Gifted Ed, Johns Hopkins Univ 1981; (BS) Elem Ed, Towson St Univ 1978; Cert Admin & Supervision, Univ of MD 1987; *cr:* 5th Grade Teacher Hilltop Elem 1978-85; Resource Teacher of Gifted & Talented Anne Arundel Cty Public Sch 1985-88; Ed Struction Specialist IBM 1987-88; Admin Trainee Rippling Woods Elem 1988-; *ai:* Citizens Advisory Cncl Mem; Strategic Planning & Integrated Sch Information System Comm; ASCD, Phi Delta Kappa; NEA, MSTA, TAAAC 1978-; PTO Exec Bd Mem; Whos Who Outstanding Women of America 1984; Natl Sci Fnd Grant Serving Advanced Mid Sch Math Prgms; Nom Phoebe Apperson Hearst Outstanding Educator Awd 1984; Finalist Firene M Steele Most Promising Teacher Awd 1978; *office:* Rippling Woods Elem 530 Nolfield Dr Glen Burnie MD 21061

TALAS, TONI GAIL, Mathematics Teacher; *b:* Newburyport, MA; *ed:* (BA) Math Ed, Framingham St 1975; (MS) Math, Univ of Lowell 1983; Various Math Courses, Univ of NH; Various Math Institutes; *cr:* Summer Sch Teacher Winnacunnet HS; Grad Teaching Asst Coll of Pure & Applied Sci Univ of Lowell 1982; Calculus I Instr Univ of Lowell 1983; Math Teacher Winnacunnet HS 1975-; *ai:* Math Team Adv; Various Comms; Var Bsktbl Coach 1975-79; NCTM 1975-; NH Teacher of Math in New England 1975-; Tri-St Math League Adv (Secy 1979-83, Pres 1989-); Pi Mu Epsilon 1980; NH Vlybl Ofcls Assn (Secy, Treas) 1980-84; Sea Coast Ed Assn Treas 1981-83; NH Ed Assn, NEA 1975-; Nominee Presidential Awd for Excl in Sci & Math Teaching 1987; Calculus Consultant Grant Univ of NH 1989; *office:* Winnacunnet HS Alumni Dr Hampton NH 03842

TALBERT, BENJAMIN MURRAY, 8th Grade English/Lit Teacher; *b:* Emory, GA; *m:* Nancy Morgan Walker; *c:* Rachel, John; *ed:* (MS) Elem Ed, Baylor Univ 1980; (MDIV) Religious Ed, Southeastern Baptist Theological Seminary 1984; *cr:* 4th Grade Teacher Mountainview Elem Sch 1980-81; Extended Day Teacher Wake Cty Public Schls 1982-84; 8th Grade Teacher Swannanoa Mid Sch 1984-; *ai:* Stu Government Spon; Lang Art, Field Day, Sch Improvement Plan Chm; Track Coach; Media & Awds Day Comms; *home:* 78 Forest Hill Dr Asheville NC 28803

TALBERT, LINDA ABSHER, Teacher; *b:* Muncie, IN; *m:* Dick E.; *ed:* (BS) His, 1978, (MA) His, 1981 Ball St Univ; *cr:* Bio Teacher Southside HS 1978-79; Sci/His Teacher 1979-86, Sci Chair/His Teacher 1986-88 Franklin Mid Sch; His Teacher Northside Mid Sch 1988-; *ai:* NCSS; *office:* Northside Mid Sch 2400 W Bethel Ave Muncie IN 47304

TALBOT, FRANK K., Social Studies Dept Chair; *b:* Bellingham, WA; *m:* Cynthia Marie Eakin; *c:* David M., Elizabeth A., Kathleen L.; *ed:* (BA) Child Dev/Ed, W WA Univ 1983; Stan Cert Curr Dev & Instruction Univ of WA; *cr:* Dir Northgate Chrstn Pre-Sch 1984-87; 4th Grade Teacher Chrstn Church Sch 1984-88; 11th-12th Soc Stud Teacher N Seattle Chrstn HS 1988-; *ai:* Dean of Stus & Act Coord; ASB Faculty Adv; Asst Soccer Coach; NCSS; S Sno-Cty Historical Bd of Governors Society 1990-; Teacher of Yr 1989-; *office:* N Seattle Chrstn Sch 12345 8th Ave NE Seattle WA 98125

TALBOT, MARJORIE ANNE BAUMANN, Science Teacher; *b:* Gladwin, MI; *m:* Michael T.; *c:* Anne M., Michelle; *ed:* (MAT) Classroom Management, SVSU 1981; (BS) Health Ed, CMU 1978; *cr:* Teacher St Stephen HS 1978-84, Nouvel Cath Cntrl 1984-85, All Saints HS 1985-; *ai:* Class & NHS Adv; NSTA 1984-; *home:* 3847 Dale Rd Saginaw MI 48603

TALBOT, THOMAS ELBERT, Director of Choral Music; *b:* Earlville, NY; *ed:* (BA) Music Ed, Alfred Univ 1969; Grad Work SUNY Potsdam; *cr:* Choral Music Dir Sauquoit Valley Cntrl 1970-; *ai:* NY St Sch Music Assn, Music Educators Natl Conference 1970-; Natl Assn of Watch/Clock Collectors 1976-; Guest Conductor of 3 All Cty Music Festivals; Performed with The Philadelphia Orch; *office:* Sauquoit Valley Cntrl Sch 2601 Oneida St Sauquoit NY 13456

TALBOTT, LINDA MULLENS, Scndry Soc Stud Teacher; *b:* Dunbar, WV; *m:* William M. II; *c:* Wm. III, Kimberly, Justin; *ed:* (BA) His, Univ of Charleston 1965; Grad Stud St Univ of NY Brockport; *cr:* Teacher Spencerport Cntrl Schls 1965-73, 1985-86, Churchville-Chili Cntrl Schls 1986-; *ai:* SADD Adv; Rochester Area Cncl Soc Stud, NCSS; Spencerport Wesleyan Church Organist 1969-; Dar His Awd; Pi Gamma Mu, Kappa Delta Pi; *home:* 17 Adams Trl Spencerport NY 14559

TALBOTT, SHERRI KATHERINE, Art Teacher; *b:* St Louis, MO; *ed:* (AA) St Marys Coll of O Fallon 1970; (BS) Art Ed, SE MO St 1972; (MS) Educl Processes, Maryville Coll 1989; *cr:* Art Teacher Cedar Hill Mid Sch 1972-; *ai:* Natl Jr Honor Society Faculty Advisory Comm; Northwest Ed Assn (Negotiations Chairperson 1983-87, Pres 1980, Grievance Chairperson 1990, Exec Comm 1987-); Phi Delta Kappa 1987-89; Gateway Ridgers BMW Club 1989-; Northwest R-1 Excl in Ed Apple Awd 1986; MO Ed Assn Jefferson Cty Teacher of Yr 1990; *office:* Cedar Hill Mid Sch Cedar Hill MO 63016

TALBOTT, VIRBLENE FOSTER, Third Grade Teacher; *b:* Olney, TX; *c:* Stephen, Stanley, Stacy D.; *ed:* (BA) Elem Ed, TX Technological Univ 1958; Midwestern Univ Wichita Falls TX; *cr:* 1st Grade Teacher Bowie Elem 1976; 2nd/3rd Grade Teacher Olney Elem 1978-; *ai:* UIL Coord-Ready Writing, StoryTelling, Spelling; Study Teacher Supvr Midwestern Univ; Atheneum Study Club Pres; BSA Leader; Assn of TX Prof Educators; TSTA; West Fnd to Study Geography Wichita Cty & OK Wichita Mountains; *office:* Olney Elem Sch 801 W Hamilton Olney TX 76374

TALIAFERRO, MARY MARGARET, Third Grade Teacher; *b:* Eureka, KS; *w:* Raymond L. (dec); *c:* Marty, Dana, Timothy, Scott; *ed:* Ed, Emporia St Univ 1967; *cr:* 1st-8th Grade Teacher Rural Cty Sch 1945-46; 5th-8th Grade Teacher Rock Grade Sch 1946-47; 1st/2nd Grade Teacher Severy Elem 1947-48; 1st-8th Grade Teacher Union Valley 1948-49; Teacher Severy Elem 1949-; *ai:* Girls Phys Ed Teacher for Several Yrs; Pres of W Elk Ed Assn, Pres PTA & Local Sch Organization; Church Sunday Sch Teacher For Yrs; W Elk Ed Assn Pres; *home:* RR 1 Box 59 Severy KS 67137

TALLENT, SARA BLAIR, Third Grade Teacher; *b:* Kingsport, TN; *m:* Barry N.; *c:* Nicole; *ed:* (BS) Elem Ed, TN Wesleyan Coll 1970; *cr:* Resource Teacher Tellico Elem & Rural Vale 1975; Teacher Tellico Plains Elem; *ai:* NEA/TEA; Delta KAPPA Gamma.

TALLENT, SUSAN ANDERSON, 4th Grade Teacher; *b:* Winchester, TN; *m:* Bobby C.; *c:* Bobby J., Caleb A.; *ed:* (BA) Eng/Ger, Univ of TN 1971; (BED) Elem Ed, TN Tech Univ 1980; Rdng/Spec Ed/TN Tech 1979/1989; *cr:* 7th/8th Eng Teacher

1972-79; 4th Grade Teacher 1979 Dayton City Sch; *ai:* Enrichment Classes Teaching Ger Two Different Age Groups; *home:* Rt 2 Box 439 Gretchen Ln Dayton TN 37321

TALLEY, DELORES MC GRIFF, Kindergarten Teacher; *b:* Detroit, MI; *m:* Rick Kenneth; *c:* Scott, Malaika; *ed:* (BS) Elem Ed, Jackson St Univ 1965; (MA) Ed, Univ of Detroit 1986; *cr:* Primary 1 Teacher Wingert Elem; 3rd Grade Teacher Adams Elem; Primary 1 Teacher Burns; Primary 1/Kndgtn Teacher Crary; *ai:* Co-Chairperson Sch Improvement Comm; Rep Detroit Teachers Credit Union; Delta Sigma Theta 1962-; MI Rdng Cncl 1965-; Detroit Fed of Teachers Union Rep; Greelawn Block Club Pres 1987-; Local Sch Cmmty Organization 1985-88, Cmmty Service Awd 1986, 1988; Booker T Washington Bus Assn Educators Achievement Awd 1989; *office:* Isaac Crary Elem Sch 16164 Asbury Pk Detroit MI 48235

TALLEY, DIANNE BATES, Third Grade Teacher; *b:* Princeton, TX; *m:* Phillipe Benn; *c:* Kim, Casey, Kirk; *ed:* (BA) Home Ec, 1969, (MEd) Elem Ed, 1972 E TX St Univ; *cr:* Home Ec Teacher Royse City HS 1969-70; 5th Grade Teacher 1971-73, 3rd Grade Teacher 1976- Princeton Ind Sch Dist; *ai:* Delta Kappa Gamma (2nd VP 1986-88, 1st VP 1988-, Pres 1990); *office:* Princeton Ind Sch Dist 234 College Princeton TX 75077

TALLEY, GERALDINE ANNE, Language Art/Reading Teacher; *b:* West Chester, PA; *m:* John C.; *c:* Justine, J. Bradford, Kyle; *ed:* (BA) Scndry Eng Ed, Trenton Univ 1972; Educl & Eng Courses, Univ of DE; *cr:* Eng Teacher Vineland Sr HS 1972-73, De La Warr HS 1973-74; Part Time Teacher DE Tech Comm Coll 1989; Eng Teacher Holy Angels Sch 1984-; *ai:* Stu Cncl & Yrbk Adv; NCEA Mem 1985-; Civic Assn Secy 1985-89; *home:* 127 Aspen Dr Newark DE 19702

TALLEY, HARRIETTE WHITWORTH, Mathematics Teacher; *b:* Greenville, SC; *m:* Robert Thad; *c:* Robert, Clay; *ed:* (BA) Math, Furman Univ 1960; (MAT) Math, The Citadel 1980; *cr:* Teacher Wade Hampton HS 1960-62, Central HS 1962-64, Wade Hampton HS 1964-65, Brevard HS 1965-66, Brevard Coll 1966-67, Jonesboro HS 1972, Topeka HS 1973-76, Bishop England HS 1976-78, Summerville 1978-; Adjunct Prof Baptist Coll 1988-; *ai:* Insight Club Spon; NCTM; Alpha Delta Kappa; Dorchester Dist #2 Teacher of Yr 1987; *office:* Summerville HS Gregg Campus 500 Greenwave Blvd Summerville SC 29483

TALLEY, JOE L., Teacher; *b:* Batesville, AR; *m:* Arleene Ichimura; *c:* Frank; *ed:* (BS) Soc Stud/Phys Ed, Cameron Univ 1972; (MED) Guidance/Counseling, Univ of OK 1979; *cr:* Teacher Eisenhower Jr HS 1983-89; *office:* Eisenhower Jr HS 57th & W Gore Blvd Lawton OK 73505

TALLEY, LARRY GENE, 4th Grade Teacher; *b:* Butler, MO; *m:* Karen Lea Harris; *c:* Dennis, Gary, Jeff; *ed:* (BA) His/Elem Ed, S CA Coll 1970; (MA) Sch Admin, W NM Univ 1975; *cr:* Teacher Newport Heights Elem 1970-77, Bureau of Indian Affairs 1971-74, Deming Public Schls 1974-; *ai:* Track, Bsktbl Coach; Budget & Dist Policy Comm, Deming Public Sch; Deming Ed Assn Pres 1987-88; NM Ed Assn (St Bd of Dirs 1988-89, SW Region Chm 1989-); Ayso Soccer (Coach, Bd of Dirs) 1983-87; Little League Coach 1976-80; Church Pastor 1979-86; Zia Educl Research Dir 1987-; *office:* Memorial Elem Sch 1000 S 10th Deming NM 88030

TALLEY, SANDRA KNOWLES, 8th Grade Eng Teacher/Coord; *b:* Fort Lauderdale, FL; *c:* Derrick, Kymberly; *ed:* (BA) Elem Ed, KY St Univ 1973; *cr:* 5th/6th Grade Teacher Randallwood Sch 1973-80; 7th Grade Eng Teacher 1980-82, 7th Grade Geography Teacher 1982-86, 8th Grade Eng Teacher 1986-88, OWA/8th Grade Eng Teacher 1988- Warrensville Jr HS; *ai:* Chrldr Adv Warrensville HS; Washington DC Chaperone; Drug Free & Assembly Comm; Warrensville Ed Assn 1973-; OH Voc Assn, OWA Teachers Assn 1988-; *office:* Warrensville Heights Jr HS 4285 Warrensville Ctr Rd Warrensville Hts OH 44128

TALLMAN, PATRICK H., Guidance Counselor; *b:* Danbury, CT; *ed:* (BS) Elem Ed/Math, 1965, (MS) Guidance, 1970 Cntrl CT St Univ; Grad Work Univ of Hartford; *cr:* Infantry US Army 1965-68; *ai:* Citywide Stu Athlete Mentor Project Coord; CT Sch Counselor Assn, Phi Delta Kappa 1971-; Natl Assn Advancement for Colored People 1970-; CT Black Caucus of AFT 1970; Hartford Fdn of Teachers 1970-, Exec Bd 1990-; Teacher of Yr Hartford Bd of Ed 1981; Disabled Vietnam Veteran Purple Heart 1968; *home:* 432 La Salle St New Britain CT 06051

TALMAGE-BOWERS, KENT LEE, English Department Chairman; *b:* Denver, CO; *m:* Marilyn; *c:* Kaitlyn, Madigan; *ed:* (AB) Eng, Colgate Univ 1970; (MAT) Eng/Ed, Brown Univ 1972; Grad Stud Univ of CO, Univ of Denver, Oxford Univ; *cr:* Eng/Soc Stud Teacher Northglenn Sr HS 1972-; *ai:* Eng Dept Chairperson 1976-; Part Time Prof Artist; NEA; *office:* Northglenn HS 601 W 100th Ave Northglenn CO 80221

TAMBUCCI, SARAH, Art Teacher-Department Chair; *b:* Stowe Township, PA; *m:* Arthur; *ed:* (BS) Art Ed, Edinboro St Coll 1968; (MED) Art Ed, 1972, (PHD) Educl Admin, 1987 Univ of Pittsburgh; *cr:* Art Teacher 1968-, Art Dept Chairperson Chartiers Valley Sch Dist; *ai:* Ed & Curr, In-Service, Prof Dev Comm; NAEA VP Eastern Region 1990; PA Art Ed Assn Pres 1986-87, PA Art Educator of Yr 1987; Chartiers Valley Arts Cncl Pres 1990; PA Fed of Teachers Fnd Awd.

TAMES, SARAH, Head of English Dept; *b:* Hanover, PA; *ed:* Acting/Directing, Howard Univ 1967-69; (BA) Eng, Amherst Coll 1981; (MA) Eng, Rutgers Univ 1983; *cr:* Self-Employed Tames Cleaning Service; Eng Instr Salisbury Summer Sch 1980-83, Rutgers Univ 1981-; Eng Dept Head The Hotchkiss Sch 1988-; *ai:* Educl Policy & Faculty Advisory Comms; NCTE Mem 1988; Natl Womens Stud Assn Mem 1990; Actors Equity Prof Actress 1971; Oblong Valley Players Mem 1977-87; Phi Beta Kappa 1981; Natl Endowment for Hum Summer Fellowship 1986; Commencement Speaker, Yrbk Dedication 1987; *office:* The Hotchkiss Sch Lakeville CT 06039

TAMEZ, RICK, Health Teacher; *b:* Harlingen, TX; *m:* Diana Solis; *ed:* (BS) Health Ed, (BS) Phys Ed, Pan Amer Univ; Safety & First Aid, CPR; *cr:* Phys Ed Teacher Harlingen Ind Sch Dist 1980-81; His/Health/Phys Ed Teacher Los Fresnos Ind Sch Dist 1981-82; Health/Cmptr Literary Teacher 1982-83, Health/Mexican-Amer Stud Teacher 1983-84, His Teacher 1984-85, Health Teacher 1986-87, 1989- San Benito Ind Sch Dist; *ai:* Head Bsbl & Jr Var Ftbl Coach 1988-; Head Jr HS Coach; TX HS Coaches Assn, TX Classroom Teachers Assn, Rio Grande Valley Coaches Assn.

TAMMEN, LINDA BROWN, Kindergarten Teacher; *b:* Galesburg, IL; *m:* Morris; *c:* Alison, Katrina, Evan; *ed:* (BA) Elem Ed, IL Wesleyan Univ 1976; Math Their Way, Whole Lang, Act Integrating Math & Sci; *cr:* Chapter I Teacher 1977, Kndgtn Teacher 1978-83 Ford Cntrl Elem; Dir Thawville Cmmty Nursery Sch Incorporated 1984-85; Kndgtn Teacher Ford Cntrl Elem 1985-; *ai:* Thawville Cmmty Nursing Sch Incorporated Bd of Dir Pres; St of IL Nursery Sch Corporation Registered Agent; Thawville Congregational Church (Religious Ed Comm, Finance Comm); *home:* RR 1 Box 119 Thawville IL 60968

TAMOTO, JANICE CARLSON, Spanish Teacher; *b:* Portland, OR; *m:* Spencer M.; *c:* Bryan Garrison; *cr:* Span Teacher Sinalor Jr HS 1969-71; Span/Eng/Rdng Teacher Mesa Union Sch 1976-77; Span/His Teacher Sequoia Intermed Sch 1978; Span Teacher Simi Valley HS 1978-; *office:* Simi Valley HS 5400 Cochran St Simi Valley CA 93063

TANAKA, KRISTINE URAGAMI, Math Teacher; *b:* Los Angeles, CA; *m:* Arthur Toshio; *ed:* (BA) Math, CSU Los Angeles 1971; *cr:* Math Teacher South Gate Jr HS 1973-76; Carmenita Jr HS 1976-77; Richard Gahr HS 1977-; *ai:* Adv CA Schlstc Fed; Faculty Senate Treas; Math Cncl 1973-; NCTM 1973-; *office:* Gahr HS 11111 Artesia Blvd Cerritos CA 90701

TANEFF, TERESA ANN LEITTEN, Biology Teacher; *b:* Hamburg, NY; *m:* Samuel S.; *c:* John C., Sarah A. Benhatzel; *ed:* (BA) Bio, St Mary of the Woods Coll 1960; (MS) Sncdry Ed, Canisius Coll 1962; *cr:* Gen Sci Teacher-Frontier Cntrl 1960-; Bio Teacher Immaculata Acad 1969-; *ai:* Sci Dept Chairperson; Co-Moderator of the Natl Honor Society; NCEA; NASSP; Recieved Grant for Ap Bio Teachers Course Buffalo St Coll.

TANGEN, JEAN ELIZABETH, 4th Grade Teacher; *b:* La Crosse, WI; *m:* Myron D.; *c:* Julie, Amy; *ed:* (BS) Elem Ed, 1969, (MS) Elem Ed, 1975 Univ of WI La Crosse; Grad Stud; *cr:* 4th Grade Teacher Westside Elem 1969-71, Holmen Area Schls 1971-; *ai:* Midwest Rdng Cncl 1980-; KEA 1969-71; HEA, WWEA 1971-; WEA, NEA 1969-; GSA, Jobs Daughters, Local Nursing Homes; Church Chrstn Ed Comm; *office:* Viking Elem Sch 502 Main St Holmen WI 54636

TANIOKA, ANNE TOKUDA, Star Lab Pilot Teacher; *b:* Lihue, HI; *m:* Dennis M.; *c:* Lara, Daniel; *ed:* (BA) Amer His, Chaminade Coll of Honolulu 1970; *cr:* K-2nd Grade Teacher Kaumakani Sch 1970-80; 5th Grade Math Teacher 1980-84, 5th Grade Sci Teacher 1984-86; 5th Grade Teacher 1986-88; Teacher of Gifted & Talented 1988- Elsie H Wilcox Sch; Star Lab Pilot Teacher Dist of Kauai 1990; *ai:* Delta Kappa Gamma Mem 1986-; *office:* Kauai Sch Dist 3060 Eiwa St Lihue HI 96766

TANIOKA, CHRISTINE NAKAMA, Fourth Grade Teacher; *b:* Ookala, HI; *m:* Harold; *c:* Ian, Meredith; *ed:* (BSED) Elem Ed, Univ of HI 1970; Teachers Certificate Univ of HI 1971; (MA) Elem Ed, Univ of HI Manoa 1973; *cr:* 3rd Grade Teacher Pohakea Elem Sch 1971-73; Kndgtn Teacher Kalanianaole Elem Sch 1974-75; Kndgtn/1st Grade Teacher Naalehu Elem Sch 1975-79; 4th Grade Teacher Pahoa HS & Elem Sch 1979-89, Waiakea Elem Sch 1989-; *ai:* Literacy Through Lit Comm; Intnl Rdng Assn; Lit & Integrating Content Units Wkshp Leader; Literacy Bd Panel Mem; *office:* Waiakea Elem Sch 180 W Puainako Hilo HI 96720

TANNER, BECKY EUBANKS, Third Grade Teacher; *b:* Lucedale, MS; *m:* Steven; *c:* Melanie, Matthew, Brent; *ed:* (BS) Elem Ed, 1980, (MS) Elem Ed, 1984 Univ Southern MS; *cr:* 2nd Grade Teacher Mclain Sch 1980-82; 1st Grade Teacher 1982-84, 7th Grade Teacher 1984-88, 2nd Grade Teacher 1988-89, 3rd Grade Teacher 1989; Rocky Creek Sch; *ai:* Sci Fair Co-Coord; MS Prof Ed 1988-; *office:* Rocky Creek Elem Sch Rt 4 Box 630 Lucedale MS 39452

TANNER, DEAN N., Fourth Grade Teacher; *b:* Auburn, NY; *m:* Judy A. Dunnebacke; *c:* Melanie, Erin, Jeffrey; *ed:* (AA) Liberal Arts, Onondaga Comm Coll 1967; (BS) Elem Ed, SUNY Geneseo 1969; (MS) Ed, Syracuse Univ 1971; Grad Stud Admin, Syracuse Univ & SUNY Cortland; *cr:* 3rd Grade Teacher Union Springs Cntrl Schls 1969-70; 3rd/4th Grade Intern Dr Martin Luther King Elem Sch 1970-71; 4th Grade Teacher Union Springs Cntrl Schls 1971-; *ai:* Dist Computerized Management System Coord; Soc Stud Dist Curr, Sci Curr, Math Curr, Dist Testing Comm; Helped Develop Local His Curr; Kappa Delta Pi Mem 1968-; Union Springs Teachers Assn (Treas, Secy, VP) 1969-; Union Springs Soccer Club (Coach, Co-Dir) 1984-; United Ministry Sunday Sch (Teacher, Dir) 1983-; Village of Union Springs Trustee 1987-89; Fellowship Syracuse Univ Grad Prgm 1970; *home:* 7 Park St Union Springs NY 13160

TANNER, JEANICE BEACHAM, English Teacher; *b:* Senath, MO; *m:* Russell Dale; *c:* Kimberly A.; *ed:* (BSED) Eng/Soc Stud, 1972, (MAED) Eng, 1979 SE MO St Univ; *cr:* Soc Stud/Eng Teacher Bell City HS 1972-74; Eng Teacher Bernie R 13 1975-; *ai:* SE MO Dist Teachers of Eng (Treas 1986-87, Secy 1987-88, VP 1988-89, Pres 1989-); NCTE Dir 1986-; SLATE Rep 1986-; CTA (Pres, Various Offices) 1988-89; MSTA 1972-; Civic Club 1973-76; *office:* Bernie R 13 HS PO Box 470 Bernie MO 63822

TANNER, JOHN WILLIAM, Social Studies Teacher; *b:* Kenora, Canada; *m:* Kathleen Hollandsworth; *c:* Kelly A., Steven; *ed:* (BSED) Soc Stud, Univ of MO Columbia 1966; (MED) Scndry Ed, Univ of MO St Louis 1969; *cr:* Soc Stud Teacher Fort Zumwalt Jr HS 1966-68, Parkway South Jr HS 1969-76, Parkway South HS 1976-; *ai:* Key Club Intnl Faculty Spon 1976-, Planning, Advisory, Challenge & Honors Prgm Dist Comm; Close-Up; MNEA (Public Relations 1971-72, Building Rep 1971-86); NCSS, MO Cncl Soc Stud 1990; Kiwanis Intnl Honary Mem 1976-; Amer Red Cross Blood Mobile Spon; Center for Research & Dev Rep in Law-Related Ed 1987-; Fellowship & Grants to Develop Prgms Law Related Ed Wake Forest Univ Sch of Law; Law Related Lesson Plan Publications; Various Publications; Fellowships Through Amer Bar Assn & Law Ed Prgms; MO Dept of Ed Developed Mastery Testing Prgms; Seminars in Field of Law Ed, Geography Ed; *office:* Parkway South HS 801 Hanna Rd Manchester MO 63021

TANNER, MARTHA MARTIN, Second Grade Teacher; *b:* Cumming, GA; *m:* James Rufus; *c:* Gina L., Chadwick J.; *ed:* (AB) Elem Ed, Brenau Coll 1965; (MECE) Early Chldhd Ed, N GA Coll 1982; *cr:* Teacher Lanier Elem 1965-79, Jones Elem 1979-; *ai:* Jones Elem Curr Comm; HCEA, GAE, NEA 1965-85; Page 1985-; Blackshear Place Baptist (Dir Children Div Sunday Sch, Dir Vacation Bible Sch); Teacher of Yr Lanier Elem 1972-73, Jones Elem 1983; *home:* 5536 Farmhouse Ln Oakwood GA 30566

TANNER, PEGGY P., Sixth Grade Teacher; *b:* Brookhaven, MS; *w:* Luther W. (dec); *c:* Cynthia, Hugh; *ed:* (BS) Elem Ed/Health/Phys Ed, Univ of S MS 1951-53; *cr:* Elem Teacher Moss Point Mid Sch System 1951-55, 2nd/3rd/5th/6th Grade Teacher 1959-; *ai:* 6th Grade Promotion Prgm Coord; Moss Point Educators Treas 1975; MS Assn Educators, NEA; STAR Teacher Awd 1982-83; Chosen by Moss Point STAR Stu Grad with Highest ACT Score; *home:* 5107 Beardslee St Moss Point MS 39563

TANNER, PHYLLIS (SATTER), English/Reading Dept Chair; *b:* Boston, MA; *c:* Lonni, Julie; *ed:* (BA) Eng Lit, Univ MA 1958; (MED) Rdng Northeastern Univ 1969; *cr:* Rdng Spec Holbrook Jr HS 1965; Rdng Eng South Sch Holbrook Jr; Eng & Rdng Chm Holbrook Jr HS; Eng/Rdng Chm 1985 Holbrook Jr/Sr HS; Journalism Teacher 1984; *ai:* The Holbrook Bulldog Spon 1983-; Schl Newspaper 1968-; Faculty Cncl; Kappa Delta Phi Honor Society (ED) 1969; Pres 1986; VP 1985-86; Building Rep 1967 Holbrook Ed Assn; Teacher Service Awd 1986-89; Horace Mann Grant Recipient (College Bd Review Course); Horace Mann Grant Co Recipient (Creating a Journalism Course); *office:* Holbrook Jr Sr H S 245 S Franklin St Holbrook MA 02343

TANNERT, WILLIAM E., Mathematics Teacher; *b:* Houston, TX; *m:* Sara Nellene Lowe; *c:* Michelle Wilder, Cynthia Mc Michen, Patti Tabler; *ed:* (BS) Math, Stephen F Austin St Univ 1957; *cr:* Teacher Nederland HS 1957-62; Sr Analyst EG&G Inc 1962-63; Supvr Programmer/Analyst CDC Data Centers 1963-69; Application Specialist ITT Data Service 1969-70; Teacher Port Neches-Groves HS 1970-82, Jacksonville HS 1982-; *ai:* Math Club Spon; *home:* Rt 1 Box 83-A Reklaw TX 75784

TANNERY, CHARLES N., JR., 7th Grade English Teacher; *b:* Ithaca, NY; *m:* Gail Holmes; *c:* Eve H., Brook E.; *ed:* (BA) Eng, Susquehanna Univ 1971; (MED) Eng Ed, Lehigh Univ 1976; *cr:* Stu Intern Frosh Writing, Susquehanna Univ 1970-71; Scndry Eng Teacher Parkland Sch Dist/Springhouse Jr HS 1971-; *ai:* Newspaper, Stage Crew & Theatre Arts Society Adv; Fun Run Club Adv; Parkland Jaycees Outstanding Young Educator 1980-81; Howard L Klopp Awd for Excl in Teaching from Cedar Crest Coll 1988-89; *home:* 430 Brookside Dr Perkasie PA 18944

TANTON, CAROL LEYH, Eighth Grade CORE Teacher; *b:* Los Angeles, CA; *ed:* (AA) US His, El Camino Coll 1964; (BA) Soc Stud/US His, San Jose St Univ 1966; (MA) Educl Admin, Univ of Santa Clara 1982; Master Teaching, Univ of CA Los Angeles; Peer Coaching; *cr:* Teacher Alum Rock Sch Dist 1967-; *ai:* Stu Act; Sftbl & Track & Field Coach; Coll Readiness Prgm; CA Teachers Assn Exec Cabinet 1967-; NCTE, NCSS 1967-; PTA 1967-, Life Service Awd 1982; San Jose St Spartan Fnd 1975-; CARE for Children 1985-; *office:* Pala Mid Sch 149 N White Rd San Jose CA 95127

TAORMINA, GERALDINE MAUPAI, Science Teacher; *b:* Teaneck, NJ; *m:* James F.; *c:* Andrew, Jeanne M. Monte Marano, Therese Ulanowski, Matthew; *ed:* (BSED) Bio, Fordham Univ Sch of Ed 1956; *cr:* 3rd/6th Grade Teacher St Marys Sch 1967-73; 9th Grade Teacher Morris Knolls HS 1979-80; 9th/10th Grade Teacher Morris Cath HS 1980-; *ai:* Crusaders for Conservation Environmental Sci Club Moderator; NCEA 1980-; Amer Museum Natl HHis Assoc Mem 1985-; *home:* 25 2nd Ave Denville NJ 07834

TAPIA, CARMEN LOBATO, 7th Grade Lang Arts Teacher; *b:* Alamosa, CO; *m:* John O.; *c:* Ronald D., Veronica C.; *ed:* (BA) Elem Ed, NM Highlands Univ 1963; (MA) Elem Ed/Soc Stud, Univ of NM 1967; Univ of Denver, Univ of San Diego; *cr:* 4th Grade Teacher Lowell Elem 1963-68; 6th Grade Teacher Alamosa Elem 1968-72, Governor Bent Elem 1972-76; 6th-7th Grade Teacher Cleveland Mid Sch 1976-82, Eisenhower Mid Sch 1982-83; 7th Grade Teacher Jackson Mid Sch 1983-; *ai:* Sch Newspaper Spon; Childrens Chois Spon 1963-68; Spelling & Geography Bee; Outdoor Ed 1968-77; NEA Life Mem 1963-; Delta Kappa Gamma (Pres, 1st VP); NM Cncl Teacher of Eng; Mothers March of Dimes Volunteer; *office:* Jackson Mid Sch 10600 Indian Schl Rd N E Albuquerque NM 87112

TAPPER, CAROL L., Second Grade Teacher; *b:* Trenton, NJ; *ed:* (BA) Elem Ed, Rider Coll 1972; *cr:* Teacher Roebling Elem Sch 1972-; *ai:* Liason, Curr Comm Mem; Adult Sch GED Prgm Teacher; Florence Township Ed Assn Rep 1980-; PTA Exec Bd Teacher Rep; NJ Governors Teacher Recognition Awd Roebling Sch 1988; *office:* Roebling Elem Sch #5 Hornberger Ave Roebling NJ 08554

TARANGELO, DENISE MARIE, First Grade Teacher; *b:* New York City, NY; *ed:* (BA) His, 1971, (MS) Early Chldhd/Elem Ed, 1973 Lehman Coll City Univ; *cr:* 3rd Grade Teacher Public Sch 153 Bronx 1971-76; 1st/2nd Grade Teacher Public Sch 76 Bronx 1976-; *office:* Public Sch 76 Bronx 900 Adee Ave Bronx NY 10469

TARANTINI, MARY JEAN DELYCURE, World Cultures Teacher; *b:* Wilkes-Barre, PA; *m:* David J.; *c:* David M., Maria E.; *ed:* (BA) Soc Stud, Coll Misericordia 1964; (MS) Soc Stud, Scranton Univ 1972; Grad Stud; *cr:* Teacher Wyoming Valley West 1966-; *ai:* Adv Wy Valley W Delegation & Natl His Day Contests 1980-; Advisory Comm Ed Dept Wilkes Univ; PA St Ed Assn, WY Valley West Ed Assn, NEA 1966-; PA Soc Stud Cncl 1980-; WY Valley Historical Society 1988-; Plymouth Historical Society 1989; Outstanding HS in PA 1988, 1989; Natl His Day Champion 1988; *office:* Wyoming Valley W HS Wadham St Plymouth PA 18651

TAROCHIONE, JAMES MASON, Seventh Grade English Teacher; *b:* Galesburg, IL; *m:* Marjorie Karen Cramer; *c:* Antony Glavanni; *ed:* (BS) Eng, W IL Univ 1960; Techniques & Strategies of Learning, N IL Univ; *cr:* 7th Grade Teacher 1960-61, Eng Teacher 1961- Knoxville Jr HS; *ai:* Free Tutoring Service; Volunteer for Knox Cty Nursing Home; KEA, IEA, NEA; Delta Silma Phi; Knoxville Kiwanis Biography Nom Outstanding Young Men of America; Knoxville Jaycees Outstanding Educator Awd; *office:* Knoxville Jr HS 700 E Mill St Knoxville IL 61448

TARR, JEANIE ANN, Fifth Grade Teacher; *b:* Reno, NV; *c:* Michael, Larry, Randall; *ed:* (BS) Elem Ed, 1971, (ME) Curr/Instruction, 1984 Univ of NV Las Vegas; 32 Credit Hours Beyond Masters; *cr:* 5th Grade Teacher C P Squires/John S Park 1971-72; 4th/5th Grade Teacher O K Adock 1973-89; 5th Grade Teacher Doris Hancock 1989-; *ai:* Rdng Teacher; *office:* Doris Handcock Elem Sch 1661 Lindell Rd Las Vegas NV 89102

TARRANT, NEECIE, English Teacher; *b:* Oak Ridge, TN; *ed:* (BA) Eng, Carson Newman Coll 1980; *cr:* Eng/Jounralism Teacher Clinton Sr HS 1986-87; Eng Teacher Dale Cty HS 1987-; *ai:* Chrldr, Beta Club. & Jr Class Spon; Girls Bkstbl Asst Coach; Dale Cty Ed Assn Mem 1987-; AL HS Athletic Dir & Coaches Assn; TN Governors Teachers Sch 1987; TN Governors Writing Acad 1987; Dale Cty HS Teacher of Yr 1987-; *office:* Dale County H S Drawer J Midland City AL 36350

TARVIN, TERRI LYNN, Music Teacher; *b:* Knoxvile, TN; *ed:* (BS) Music Ed, Univ of TN 1979; *cr:* Teacher Lakeside HS 1980-82, Carter Mid Sch 1982-83, Anderson Cty HS 1983-84, Gibbs Mid & HS 1984-; *ai:* Incentive Comm; Choreographer; ACDA TN Jr HS Rep 1986-90; MENC; TEA/NEA; ETVA Jr HS Chm 1986-; Teacher of Yr Candidate TN 1989; *office:* Gibbs Mid & HS 7628 Tazewell Pike Corryton TN 37721

TASLER, MARGARET GOEKE, Government/Economics Teacher; *b:* San Francisco, CA; *m:* E. J. Jr.; *c:* Troy A., Matthew A.; *ed:* (BA) Eng, Univ of TX Austin 1971; (MED) Curr/instr, Univ of Houston 1974; Amer Economy Inst; Law Related Ed, Summer Inst; *cr:* Teacher Calhoun Cty Ind Sch Dist 1971-78, Texas City HS 1984-; *ai:* Close-Up Coord; TX St Teachers Assn, TX Classroom Teachers Assn 1971-; TX Cncl for Soc Stud 1988; *office:* Texas City HS 1800 9th Ave N Texas City TX 77568

TASSA, LINDA EVELYN, 7th Grade Music Teacher; *b:* Herkimer, NY; *m:* Joseph J. Cerroni; *c:* Marcus; *ed:* (BA) Music Ed/Piano, 1974, (MS) Music His/Piano, 1978 Syracuse Univ; Grad Stud Past Masters; *cr:* K-6th Grade Music Teacher New Hartford Sch Dist 1974-75; K-12th Grade Music Teacher Frankfort Schuyler Sch Dist 1975-80; 1st-7th Grade Music Teacher N Syracuse Sch Dist 1980-; *ai:* Mid Sch Chorus Dir & Accompanist; Private Piano Instruction; NYSSMA; MENC Pres 1973-74; Prof Accompanist Royal Acad Bellet Sch; Accompany Childrens & Prof Exams; *home:* 3117 Dartingbird Ln Baldwinsville NY 13027

TATE, DIANE MITCHELL, English Teacher; *b:* Picayune, MS; *m:* James Thomas; *c:* Belinda Tate Fornea, Cynthia Tate Mills, Cathi Tate Dutton; *ed:* (BA) Eng, Univ of AZ 1973; Spec Needs, Univ of Lincoln; *cr:* Eng Teacher Kubasaki HS Okinawa Japan 1973-76, Papillion La Vista 1976-79, Picayune HS 1982-.

TATE, DONNA MARSH, 6th Grade Soc Stud Teacher; *b:* Chattanooga, TN; *m:* Mark E.; *c:* Emma Bailey; *ed:* (BS) Elem Ed, Univ of TN Chattanooga 1976; *cr:* 4th Grade Teacher Ringgold Intermediate Sch 1976-77; 1st/3rd Grade Teacher 1977-78, 1st Grade Teacher 1978-81, 2nd Grade Teacher 1981-82, 4th Grade Teacher 1982-83, 5th Grade Teacher 1983-84 Harrison Elem; 6th Grade Soc Stud Teacher Ooltewah Mid Sch 1984-; *ai:* Be Kind to Animals Week Spon; Co-Spon 4-H Club; Sch-Wide Talent Show Spon; Cheerleading Judge; Alpha Lamda Delta, Kappa Delta Pi, Alpha Delta Kappa; TN Humane Animal League Mem; Red Cross Service Awd 1981; Chattanooga Humane Society Kindness Awd 1987; Ooltewah Mid Sch Teacher of Yr 1987; Outstanding 6th Grade Teacher 1988; *home:* 8340 Roy Ln Ooltewah TN 37363

TATE, ELIZABETH DEAL, Mathematics Teacher; *b:* Newton, NC; *c:* Ashley, Allison; *ed:* (BSB) Math, Appalachian St Univ 1973; *cr:* Teacher Northeast Jr HS 1973-78; Voc Ed Teacher Cntrl HS 1978-79; Basic Skills Lab Teacher Brentwood Elem 1979-80; Teacher Griffin Jr HS 1980-82, T W Andrews HS 1982-; *ai:* Color Guard TWA Marching Band; Juniorettes Affiliate of Womans Clubs Adv; NCCTM 1982-; AFT 1973-; High Point YMCA Swim Club Secy 1988-; *home:* 3305 Rockingham Rd High Point NC 27265

TATE, JAMES ROGER, Band/Math/Social Stud Teacher; *b:* Knoxville, TN; *m:* June D.; *ed:* (BS) Bus Admin, 1962; Music Ed, 1978 Univ of TN; Elem Ed; Instrumental Music Ed; *cr:* Gen Music Teacher Fairview Elem; Norris Elem; Andersonville Elem; Glen Alpine Elem 1966-68; Band Dir Norwood Elem & Jr HS; Marlow Elem; Clinton Jr HS; Lake City Mid Sch; Dutch Valley Elem 1968-87; Band Dir/Math & Soc Stud Teacher Norwood Mid Sch 1987-; *ai:* Band Dir: Parades/Marching Competition/Band Clinics; Solos & Ensembles Adjudicator; MENC 1968-; East TN Band & Orchestra Assn 1968-; Natl Band Dir Assn 1981-; NEA/Teachers Ed Assn 1968-; Knoxville Jaycees 1960; Kentucky Colonel 1987; "Outstanding Young Educator" Awd Oliver Springs Jaycees; "Teacher of Yr"-Norwood Jr. HS 1973-74; 1st Place Strawberry Festival; Five (5) Superior Ratings - Univ of TN Concert Festival; *office:* Norwood Mid Sch 655 Tri-County Blvd Oliver Springs TN 37840

TATE, JO ANN CHISM, 7th/8th Grade English Teacher; *b:* Talladega, AL; *c:* Jonathan, Samuel, Joseph; *ed:* (BS) Speech, 1977, (MA) Eng, 1980 Univ of Montevallo; *cr:* Teacher Bibb Cty Jr HS 1977-; *ai:* Natl Jr Honor Society Spon; Stu Asst Prgm Core Team Mem; Delta Kappa Gamma Pres 1990; *office:* Bibb Cty Jr HS 335 Walnut St Centreville AL 35042

TATE, JOHN L., Elementary Art Teacher; *b:* Altoona, PA; *m:* Shirley Barnes; *c:* Jennifer L., David J.; *ed:* (BS) Art Ed, IN Univ of PA 1956; (MED) Art Ed, PA St Univ 1960; Grad Stud PA St Univ; *cr:* Art Teacher Cntrl Cove Schls 1956-57, Hollidaysburg Schls 1957-59, Tyrone Schls 1959-; *ai:* Adv Jr Class Prom 1963-75, Yrbk 1976-87; PSEA, NEA; TAEA, VP 1963-64; SPEBSQSA VP 1990; Zion Luth Church (Cncl, Sunday Sch Teacher); Yrbk Dedicatee 1988.

TATE, NORMA FAYE, Media Specialist; *b:* Albany, GA; *m:* Ronnie N.; *c:* Gregory, Gerald; *ed:* (BS) Middle Grades Ed, Albany St Coll 1974; (MSLS) Library Service, Atlanta Univ 1975; *cr:* Librarian Ft. Valley St Coll 1975-77; Librarian/Instr Columbus Coll 1977-80; Instr Central Texas Coll; Teacher Mitchell Baker HS 1986-87; Media Specialist Southside Mid Sch 1987-; *ai:* Media Comm Chm; GAE: GLMA: *office:* Southside Mid Sch 1615 Newton Rd Albany GA 31701

TATMAN, GUINNETTA MIXON, Lang Art/Soc Stud Teacher; *b:* Spalding Cty, GA; *m:* James Cecil; *c:* Rebecca Klase, Cecile Wolf, Lewis, Robert; *ed:* (BS) Soc Work, Valdosta St Coll 1951; (MRE) Religious Ed, Emory Univ 1953; Grad Stud Univ of GA, Auburn Univ, Emory, GA St Univ; *cr:* 5th/6th Grade Teacher Vaughn Elem 1949-50; 2nd/6th Grade Teacher Meadowview Elem 1962-72; 7th/8th Grade Teacher Main Street Mid Sch 1972-79, Conyers Mid Sch 1980-; *ai:* Beta Club Spon 1976-83; RCAE Pres; GAE, NEA (Pres 1989-) 1951-, Membership 1990; GAE Uniserve Pres 1989-, Membership 1990; PTA 1949-; Atlanta Constitution Honor Teacher 1985; 4-H Leader 1967-74; GAE Teacher Hall of Fame Nom; Conyers Mid Sch Teacher of Yr 1983-85; Main Street Sch Teacher of Yr; Rockdale Cty Runner Up Teacher of Yr 1983-85; Outstanding Woman in Ed; Amer Fed of Women 1985; *office:* Conyers Mid Sch 355 Sigman Rd Conyers GA 30207

TATUM, CARLOS DALE, Biology Teacher; *b:* Greenville, KY; *ed:* (BS) Bio, 1981, (MA) Ed, 1988 W KY Univ; *cr:* Bio/Sci Teacher Drakesboro HS 1986-; *ai:* Girls Bsktbl & Sftbl Coach; Champions Against Drugs Spon; Project Graduation Adv; *home:* Rt 1 Box 66 Central City KY 42330

TATUM, NANCY ROBERTS, High School English Teacher; *b:* Owensboro, KY; *m:* Phillip Ray; *c:* Deborah T. Gorley, Heath, Erin; *ed:* (BA) Eng, Brescia Coll 1965; (MA) Scndry Ed, 1982, (Rank I) Scndry Ed, 1985 Western KY Univ; KY Teacher Internship Trng 1987-; *cr:* Eng/Speech/Drama Teacher Washington Cty HS 1965-66; Remedial Rdng Teacher Lebanon Elem/St Augustine Elem 1966-67; Eng/Speech/Drama Teacher Washington Cty HS 1967-; Eng 101-102 Teacher St Catharine Jr Coll 1985-87; *ai:* Stu Cncl Adv 1985-; Drama Class Play 1965-; Jr/Sr Prom Spon 1989; Attended First KY Writing Inst 1985-; CommonWealth Inst for Teachers 1986; Visiting Teachers Inst of Governors Scholars Prgm 1985; Teacher Internship Trng 1987-; WA Cty Ed Assn, KY Ed Assn, NEA, KY Cncl of Teachers of Eng 1965-; St Augustine Young Adult Choir 1975-; *office:* Washington Cty HS Lincoln Park Rd Springfield KY 40069

TATUM, PAMELA HURDLE, Mathematics Teacher; *b:* Oxford, MS; *m:* Arthur; *ed:* (BSE) Math, Delta St Univ 1988; *cr:* Math Teacher Southaven HS 1988-; *ai:* Mu Alpha Theta Co-Spon; *office:* Southaven HS 899 Rasco Rd Southaven MS 38671

TATUM, ROBERT LOWELL, History Department Chair; *b:* Smackover, AR; *m:* Carla Marie Tolar; *c:* John Lowell, Joellen Tatum De Di Donato; *ed:* (BS) Northwestern St 1955; (THM) Theology, Iliff Sch Denver 1959; (MED) Guidance, Northwestern St 1966; (SPED) Guidance, Univ of S MS 1973; Spec Ed Univ of S MS; Hist, Geography SW TX St Univ; *cr:* Meth Chaplain Northwestern St Univ 1958-71; Evaluator Ellisville St Sch 1972-73; Teacher Comal Ind Sch Dist 1973-; *ai:* Outdoor Ed Club; Resource Teacher in His-Academic Decathlon; TX Alliance for Geographic Studs; Camal Educators, TSTA, & NEA Pres 1975-76; *home:* 259 Barcelona New Braunfels TX 78130

TAUBE, JOAN MARIE (LORTSCHER), Third Grade Teacher; *b:* Rochester, NY; *m:* Frederick W.; *c:* Kimberly A. Ward, Kathryn J., Heather M., Heidi D.; *ed:* (BS) Elem Ed, St Univ of NY Brockport 1959; (MED) Elem Ed, Univ of NC 1960; *cr:* 1st Grade Teacher Jacksonville Elem 1967-68; 2nd Grade Teacher Homer Elem 1970-79; 4th Grade Teacher 1979-85, 3rd Grade Teacher 1985- Homer Intermediate; *ai:* Wrestling Cheerleading Coach 1976-84; Building Advisory Comm 1987-; Curr Comm Mem 1970; Homer Teachers Assn (Secy 1981-82, Grievance Chairperson 1985-, Natl & St Delegate Rep 1986-); Homer Music Boosters Club Pres 1974-75; St Univ of NY Cortland Faculty Wives Soc Chairperson 1972-73; Homer Cntrl Sch Prof Staff Dev Action Plan Mem 1988; *office:* Homer Intermediate Sch Clinton St Homer NY 13077

TAUBKEN, CHRISTINE CRAWFORD, 3rd Grade Teacher; *m:* William Oen; *c:* Wm. W., Tamara C., Andrew CrawFord; *ed:* (BA) Elem Ed, 1968, (MS) Elem Ed, 1982 Bowling Green St Univ; *cr:* 3rd/5th Grade Teacher St Joseph Elem 1968-70; Remedial Rdng Teacher 1970-71, Kndgtn/Remedial Rdng Teacher 1971-83, 7th Grade Teacher 1983-88, 3rd Grade Teacher 1988- Wapak City Schls.

TAUCHER, JOHN C., Social Studies Teacher; *b:* Oak Park, IL; *m:* Virginia; *c:* Gretchen, Mark; *ed:* (BA) His/Poly Sci, Univ of WI Eau Claire 1967; (MA) Ed/His, Univ of WI Milwaukee 1978; Univ of Wi; *cr:* Teacher Ripon HS 1967-68; Port Washington HS 1968-; *ai:* Model United Nations Adv; Academic Decathlon Coach; Port Washington Ed Assn Pres 1984-85.

TAULLI, FRANK VINCENT, Elementary Principal; *b:* Pueblo, CO; *w:* Gracie Ellen Elmer (dec); *c:* Terese Wenzel, Patrese J., Frank P.; *ed:* (BS) Elem Ed, Univ of NM 1957; (MA) Admin, W CO Coll 1961; Adams St Coll, W St Coll CO, Wharton Sch of Bus, Univ of CO, CO St Coll; *cr:* 3rd Grade Teacher Fulton Heights Sch 1954-55; 4th Grade Teacher Washington Sch 1957-59; 5th Grade Teacher Sunset Park 1959-62; Prin Highland Park 1962-76, Belmont Sch 1976-; *ai:* Public Employees Retirement Assn (Trustee, Vice Chm) 1976-; CO Ed Assn Pres 1969-70, Service to Ed 1970; Alpha Delta Kappa Outstanding Prin 1978-79; Salvation Army Bd of Dirs 1970-; Governors Awd; Excl in Ed; *office:* Belmont Elem Sch 31 Mac Naughton Rd Pueblo CO 81001

TAVAREZ, JUSTINA C., 2nd Grade Bilingual Teacher; *b:* Rudiosa, TX; *m:* Alcee Manuel; *c:* Alcee M. II, Jennifer M.; *ed:* (BA) Elem Ed, Sul Ross 1982; *cr:* 3rd Grade Teacher 1982-85, Kndgtn Teacher 1985-86, 3rd Grade Teacher 1986-87, 2nd Grade Bi-ling Teacher 1989- Presido Elem; *ai:* Spon HS Chrldr 1982-84, Jr Club 1983-84, 1985-86, Sr Club 1984-85; TSTA Pres 1989-; PTA Pres 1984-86; Lions Club Ladies Auxiliary Pres 1989-; *home:* PO Box 336 Presidio TX 79845

TAVAREZ, RACHEL RAMOS, Mathematics Teacher; *b:* Ft Stockton, TX; *m:* David Gomez; *c:* Nikki, Daven; *ed:* (BA) Phys Ed, Sul Ross St Univ 1983; Grad Level Ed Courses; *cr:* Teachers Aide 1980-81, Math Teacher 1984- Ft Stockton Ind Sch Dist; *ai:* Cheerleading 1985-86; UIL Number Sense Spon 1986-; TX St Teachers Assn, NEA Mem 1986-89; Classroom Teachers Assn Mem 1989-; TX Math & Sci Coaches Assn Sch Membership 1986-; Ft Stockton Golf Assn Mem 1984-; Ft Stockton Ladies Golf Assn Mem 1986-87, 1990; *home:* 1600 W 1st Fort Stockton TX 79735

TAVE, CHARLIE FRANK, Mathematics Team Leader; *b:* Mineola, TX; *m:* C. Anne Hall; *c:* Robert, Cathy; *ed:* (BA) Math, TX Coll 1961; (MS) Math, Prairie View A&M 1970; *cr:* Math Teacher Sulpher Springs HS 1961-64, Greenville Ind Sch Dist 1964-; *ai:* TX St Teachers Assn 1961-; NEA 1970-; Greenville City Cncl Councilman 1979-85; Progressive Voters League Treas 1985-; NAACP Publish Chm 1989-, Outstanding Citizen Awd; TX Coll Alumni Assn Local Chapter Pres 1987-; Natl Sci Fnd Grant; Helping Hand Citizen of Yr 1983; *office:* Greenville Mid Sch 3611 Texas Greenville TX 75401

TAVEL, NORMA LUGO, Spanish Teacher; *b:* Havana, Cuba; *m:* Ramiro C.; *c:* Maria E. Tavel Freyre, Ramiro J., Carmen M., Javier; *ed:* (BA) Elem Ed, Normal Sch for Teachers 1953; (PHD) Ed/Rdng Dissertation, Univ of Havana 1960; (BA) Behavioral Sci - Suma Cum Laude, Mercy Coll 1980; *cr:* 1st-6th Grade Teacher Aguacate Rural Sch 1956-58; Primary Teacher Aguacate Urban Sch 1958-59; Prin Cojimar Sch 1959-61; Religion Teacher Lavernia Bi-ling Sch 1975-77; Kndgtn Teacher St Michaels Cath Sch 1980-84; Span Teacher Epiphany Cath Sch 1984-; *ai:* Epiphany Span Club Adv; Assn of Cuban Educators Mem 1962-; St Timothy Church CCD Adult Instr 1986-; Immaculate Conception CCD Teacher 1970-74; Corpus Christi CCD Teacher 1967-70; Cursillo Movement (Seminars 1975-78, Wkshps 1975-78,

Coord 1972, 1977, Instr 1972, 1977); Aguacate Urban Sch Teacher of Yr; Lavernia Bi-ling Sch Teacher of Yr; *home:* 10730 SW 66th Terr Miami FL 33173

TAVERNARO, GERALD E., Classroom Instructor; *b:* Parsons, KS; *m:* Lois M.; *c:* Michelle, Tina, Gino; *ed:* (AA) Liberal Arts, Phoenix Coll 1964; (BA) His, 1967, (MED) Ed, 1971 Univ of AZ; Maricopa Cty Sheriff Acad, Emergency Medical Technician, Drug Intervention; Various Wkshps; *cr:* Stu Teacher Pueblo HS 1967; Teacher AZ W Coll 1971-76, Rio Salado Comm Coll 1977-88, Gila Bend Jr-Sr HS 1967-; *ai:* Jr HS Stu Cncl & 8th Grade Spon; HS Tennis Coach; Drug Intervention, Drug Curr Comms; N Cntrl Accreditation Sch Philosophy, Services, Soc Stud Comms; NEA, AZ Ed Assn 1967-; Gila Bend Ed Assn Pres 1970-71, 1981-83, 1988-; Natl Historical Society 1968-85; Lions Club (Secy, Treas, Pres, Zone Chm 1985-86) 1981-, Lion of Yr 1986; E European Stud Grant; Energy Stud Grants; Kodak Film Interview Published 1974; *office:* Gila Bend Jr HS 308 N Martin St Gila Bend AZ 85337

TAVIERNE, DEBRA MARIE (DRIVER), Special Education Teacher; *b:* Paulding, OH; *m:* Richard Stephen; *c:* Amy; *ed:* (BS) Spec Ed, Bowling Green St Univ 1985; Hicksville HS 1980; Working Towards Masters in Spec Ed; *cr:* K-6th Grade Tutor Whittier Elem 1985; 7th-12th Grade Teacher of Learning Disabilities Hicksville HS 1986-88, Antwerp HS 1988-; *ai:* Jr HS Vlybl & Bsktbl Coach; Jr Class & Prom Adv; Jr Campus Life Cnslr; *office:* Antwerp HS Archer Dr Antwerp OH 45813

TAYLOR, ANN MONTGOMERY, Fifth Grade English Teacher; *b:* Marshall Cty, AL; *m:* Phillip Howell; *c:* Carol A., Kaye E.; *ed:* (BS) Scndry Ed/Eng, 1957, (BS) Elem Ed, 1978 Jacksonville Univ; Grad Stud Ed, Univ of AL; *cr:* 1st Grade Teacher Mt Hebron Elem 1954-55; 5th Grade Teacher Nixon Chapel Elem 1956-57; 6th Grade Teacher Alabama Avenue Mid Sch 1957-62; 5th Grade Teacher West End Elem 1972-84, Evans Elem 1984-; *ai:* Eng Textbook Selection Comm; Sch Rdng Curr Coord; AEA, NEA, NCTE; Green Lawn Garden Club Pres 1978-79; Thursday Book Club; *home:* 208 Pecan St Albertville AL 35950

TAYLOR, BARBARA NABORS, 8th Grade Reading Teacher; *b:* Nashville, TN; *m:* Norman F.; *c:* Steven A., Karen L.; *ed:* (AS) Ed, Volunteer St Comm Coll 1981; (BS) Ed, TN St Univ 1983; *cr:* 4th Grade Elem Teacher 1984, 6th Grade Sci/Rdng Teacher 1984-85, 6th GRade Sci/Rdng/Advanced Rdng Teacher 1985-87, 8th Grade Rdng/Advanced Rdng Teacher 1987- T W Hunter Mid Sch; *ai:* Just Say No Spon 1985-87; Pom Pon Spon 1985-88; Cheerleading Spon 1988-; 8th Grade Teachers Team Leader; Intnl Rdng Assn Building Rep 1986-; Sumner Cty Teachers Study Cncl Building Rep 1985-; Gamma Beta Phi 1980-83; Hendersonville Elem PTA Pres 1967-68; Lakeside Elem PTA Pres 1968-69; Hawkins Jr HS Pres 1973-74; Lifetime Membership Awd Natl PTA in TN; *home:* 123 Robin Hood Cr Hendersonville TN 37075

TAYLOR, BECKY LAWSON, Government Teacher; *b:* Lubbock, TX; *m:* Kenny; *c:* Kenna, Susan; *cr:* Eng Teacher Coronado Jr HS 1977-81; Government Teacher Plainview HS 1981-; *ai:* ATPE Sch Rep 1988-; Beta Sigma Phi 1988-; Delta Kappa Gamma 1989-; *office:* Plainview HS 1501 Quincy St Plainview TX 79072

TAYLOR, BEVERLY IHLE, 4th Grade Teacher; *b:* Buffalo, NY; *m:* William Aaron Jr.; *c:* Willaim Aaron III; *ed:* (BS) Elem Ed, 1975, (MS) Elem Ed, 1980 SUNY at Fredonia; (MS) Scndry Math; Trained in Third Phase of Effective Teaching; *ai:* Adv Elem Ski Club; TIME Project; Conewango Valley Cntry Club; Firs Presbyn Church; *office:* M J Fletcher Sch 301 Cole Ave Jamestown NY 14701

TAYLOR, BILLIE DALTON, Mathematics Dept Chair/ Teacher; *b:* Hillsville, VA; *m:* Ivan M.; *c:* David, Bonnie Henry, Linda Tawney, Alfred; *ed:* (BA) Elem Ed/Math/Soc Stud, WV St Coll 1971; (MA) Elem Ed, WV Coll of Grad Stud 1974; Grad Stud; *cr:* Elem Teacher Shiloh & Little Valley & Vinson 1 Room Schls 1950-54; 7th Grade Teacher Hillsville Elem 1959-62; Elem Teacher Woodlawn 1962-65; Math Lab Teacher Tiskawal Sch 1971; 1st Grade Teacher Chandler 1971; Elem Teacher Lashmeet 1972-76; 7th-9th Grade Math Teacher Glenwood 1976-; *ai:* Pom Pon Squad Spon; Mathcounts Coach; MCEA, WVEA, NEA Building Rep 1978-86; PTA Treas 1973-74; *office:* Glenwood Jr HS Rt 6 Princeton WV 24740

TAYLOR, BRENDA JOYCE, Health/Physical Ed Teacher; *b:* Grove City, PA; *ed:* (AS) Bus, Robert Morris Coll 1975; (BS) Health/Phys Ed, 1982, (MS) Health Sci, 1987 Slippery Rock Univ; *cr:* Health/Phys Ed Teacher Slippery Rock HS 1982-; *ai:* SADD Adv; Stu Assistance Prgm Coord; Men & Womens Track Coach; PA St Assn Health, Phys Ed & Recreation; *office:* Slippery Rock HS Kiester Rd Slippery Rock PA 16057

TAYLOR, CATHERINE STEELE, Third Grade Teacher; *b:* Eufaula, AL; *m:* Jan Paul; *c:* J.P., Warner; *ed:* (BS) Elem Ed, 1974, (MA) Early Chldhd Ed, 1981 Troy St Univ; *cr:* Classroom Teacher Quitman Cty Elem Sch 1974-; *ai:* Technology Comm; Textbook Comm; GA Assn Educators, Pres 1974-80; Prof Assn GA Educators 1981-; Camerata Music Club 1979-; MADD 1989; Roberts Study Group Charter Mem; Kappa Delta Pi; 1st United Meth Church 1952-; *office:* Quitman Co Elem Sch Rt 2 Kaigler Rd Georgetown GA 31754

TAYLOR, CATHY ROBY, Phys Ed Dept Chairperson; *b:* Kankake, IL; *m:* Kevin Kuster; *c:* Nickolas A., Nicole M.; *ed:* Assoc Phys Ed, San Jacinto Coll 1977; (BED) Phys Ed, Stephen F Austin 1979; *cr:* Phys Ed Teacher/Coach Miller Intermediate 1979-80, S Houston Intermediate 1980-; *ai:* 7th Grade Bsktbl & Vlybl Team Coach; Jump Rope for Heart Coord; Punt Pass Kick; Big Shoot Out; Career Level II; *office:* S Houston Intermediate Sch 900 College South Houston TX 77587

TAYLOR, CEOLA (ENARD), English Teacher; *b:* Arnaudville, LA; *m:* Aubrey; *c:* Aubrey A.; *ed:* (BS) Eng - Cum Laude, Southern Univ 1968; (MED) Eng Ed, TX A&M Southern Univ 1976; Crime Prevention & Drug Ed Wkshp 1978; Preparing Stus For Lang Art Teams Test 1987; TTAS Follow Up 1988; RAP Inst 1988; *cr:* Eng/Speech Teacher Worthing HS 1970-71, Madison HS 1971-78, Eng Teacher Houston Comm Coll 1978-82; Eng/ Speech Teacher Kashmere HS 1978-; *ai:* Commencement Speech Coord & Coach; Schlsp Letter Coord; Sigma Gamma Rho, AFT, TX St Teacher Assn; Pleasant Green Baptist Church (Mission Dept Teacher, Gospel Chorus, Womens Class Sunday Sch Teacher 1986-), Outstanding Teacher Awd 1989; Sterling Green Cmmty Civic Club 1978-; Outstanding Woman Awd James Madison Sr HS 1978; Kashmere YWCA Y-Teens Outstanding Spon Awd 1981-82, 1983-84; *office:* Kashmere Sr HS 6900 Wileyvale Houston TX 77028

TAYLOR, CHARLES EDWARD, Mathematics Department Chair; *b:* Millwood, GA; *ed:* (BA) Scndry Ed, MI St 1975; (MED) Scndry Ed, Auburn 1979; (EDS) Mid Chldhd Valdosta St 1989; Wkshp San Diego St; *cr:* Intern Teacher Sanford Mid Sch 1977-79; Teacher/Coach Willacoochee Elem 1980-83; Teacher/ Math Dept Head Center Jr HS 1983-; *ai:* Math Counts Coach; Effective Schls Leader; GA Assn of Educators 1980-; Teacher of Month; Teacher of Yr; *office:* Center Jr HS 1301 Bailey St Waycross GA 31501

TAYLOR, CHESTER WILLIAM, Social Studies Teacher; *b:* Laona, WI; *m:* Debra A. Burg; *c:* Erin, Matthew, Stephanie; *ed:* (BS) Geography, Univ of WI La Crosse 1973; (MST) Geography, Univ of WI Whitewater; Grad Stud Geography, Coaching; *cr:* Teacher Franklin Jr HS 1974-86, Craig Sr HS 1986-88, Parker Sr HS 1988-; *ai:* Asst Wrestling Coach; WI Cncl for Soc Stud; WI Ger Stud Project Mem; W Germany Study Tour & Developed Curr for St Publication & Use 1989.

TAYLOR, CORA JEAN NORMAN, Eng Teacher/Yrbk Journalism; *b:* Norman Park, GA; *m:* Marion Kenneth; *c:* Alicia Taylor Hiers; *ed:* (BS) Eng Ed, Valdosta St 1957; Trng Updated Classroom & Instructional Procedures; Cmptr Trng; Several Courses Yrbk Journalism; *cr:* Eng/His Teacher 1953-62, Fr Teacher 1964 Colquitt Cty Jr HS; Eng Teacher Norman Park HS 1964-65; Eng/Fr Teacher Colquitt Cty Jr HS 1965-72, Pine Land Ind Sch 1972-83; Eng/Yrbk Journalism Teacher Colquitt Cty HS 1983-; *ai:* Yrbk Adv; Sch Newsletter Comm; NCTE; Delta Kappa Gamma (Secy 1989, Treas 1980-83) 1973-; STAR Teacher; *office:* Colquitt Cty HS 1800 Park Ave Moultrie GA 31768

TAYLOR, DARYL LEE, English Department Chair; *b:* Omaha, NE; *m:* Michael, Stephen;; *ed:* (BS) Ed, 1969; (MS) Scndry Ed, 1975 Omaha Univ; *cr:* Eng Teacher Ralston HS 1969-; *ai:* Eng Dept Chm 1978-; Jr Class, Prom, Homecoming Spon 1971-80; Stu Cncl Spon 1974-78; Debate Speech Coach 1969-74; Head Girls Vlybl Coach 1973-76; Drill Team Spon 1978-82; Concessions Spon 1975-80; Intramural Vlybl Dir 1976-82; Halftime Ceremonies Ftbl Game Annoucer 1978-81; Academic Decathlon Speech & Essay Judge 1987-88; Ralston Ed Assn Pres 1972-73; NEA, NSEA, NASSC, ASCD, NASCD, MRC, NCTE; Lambda Chi Alpha, Phi Mu Alpha Simphonia Mem; Onycron Delta Kappa (Mem, Pres); Christ Cmmty Church Sunday Sch Teacher; Webelos Scout Leader; Whos Who in Amer Colls & Univs 1969; Whos Who in Amer Ed 1988-89, 1989-; Chamber of Commerce Candidate Educator of Yr 1973, 1983; Amer Legion Medal of Merit; Univ of KS Outstanding Teacher & Mentor Recognition 1987; *home:* 3415 S 116th St Omaha NE 68144

TAYLOR, DEBRA LEA, English Teacher; *b:* Oklahoma City, OK; *c:* Joshua; *ed:* (BA) Eng, Midwestern St Univ 1975; Univ of TX Permian Basin, TX Tech Univ, Adams St Coll; *cr:* Social Worker Wichita Falls St Hospital 1974-76; Crosbyton Ind Sch Dist 1977-79; Eng Teacher Crane Ind Sch Dist 1980-; *ai:* Oral Rdng Coach; Public Relations Comm; Classroom Teachers of America (Secy, Pres) 1978-; Delta Kappa Gamma 1984-; NCTE 1986-87; *office:* Crane Mid Sch 511 W 8th St Crane TX 79731

TAYLOR, DIANE DANIEL, Fifth Grade Teacher; *b:* Atlanta, GA; *m:* Samuel Lorie; *ed:* (BS) Elem Ed, Tift Coll 1966; (MED) Rdng, GA St Univ Atlanta 1971; *cr:* Elem Teacher 1966-71, Rdng Specialist Griffin-Spalding Schls 1971-72; Rdng Specialist 1972-75, Asst Prin 1975-76 Lamar Cty Sch System; Rdng Specialist Thomaston City Schls 1976-81; Elem Teacher Griffin-Spalding Schls 1981-; *ai:* Stu Support Team Mem; GAE, NEA 1966-81; PAGE 1981-; Delta Kappa Gamma 1982-; Barnesville Womens League 1982-; Moonflower Garden Club 1989; *home:* 165 Murphy Ave Barnesville GA 30204

TAYLOR, DIANE WALSH, Kindergarten Teacher; *b:* Frankfurt, Germany; *m:* Alvin Lee; *c:* Casey; *ed:* Kndgtn Cert Univ of TN; *cr:* Head Start Teacher Norwood Elem Sch 1973-76; Kndgtn Teacher South Clinton Elem Sch 1976-87, Clinton Elem Sch 1987-; *ai:* Clinton Ed Assn 1987-; PTO Teacher Rep 1987-89; Friends of Lib 1987-88; South Clinton Elem Sch Teacher of Yr 1986; Anderson Cty Schls Teacher of Yr Runner-Up 1986; *home:* 605 Eagle Bend Rd Clinton TN 37716

TAYLOR, DORIS ANN LEMONS, 6th Grade Teacher; *b:* Ronceverte, WV; *m:* Fred Lewis II; *c:* Chad L., Casey L.; *ed:* (BS) Elem Ed/Early Childhd/Soc Stud, Concord Coll 1976; (MA) Learning Disabilities, Radford Univ 1980; *cr:* 4th/6th Grade Soc Stud Teacher 1976-84, 6th Grade Teacher 1984- Union Elem Sch; *ai:* Girls Sftbl Coach; Soc Stud Curr Comm Mem; 6th Grade Homeroom Teacher; NEA, WVEA, Monroe Cty Rdng Cncl 1976-; Sinks Grove Extension Club (Secy, Treas 1983-85,1989-, Session Mem 1983-84); Mt Pleasant Presbyn Church (Organist, Pianist) 1982-; PTA 1987-; Conducted Wkshps; Helped with Teacher In-Service Sci Wkshp; *home:* Rt 1 Box 301-B Sinks Grove WV 24976

TAYLOR, EDITH L., Second Grade Teacher; *b:* Shepherdsville, KY; *ed:* (BA) Elem Ed, 1972, (MS) Elem Ed, 1976 W KY Univ; Rank I Elem Ed, Univ of Louisville; *cr:* 4th Grade Teacher 1972-75, 2nd Grade Teacher 1975- Mt Washington Elem.

TAYLOR, EDWARD E., Assistant Principal; *b:* Oklahoma City, OK; *m:* Lora Carson; *c:* Brooke Anne; *ed:* (BSED) Phys Ed/Bio, E Cntrl Univ 1985; (MS) Admin Secy, Cntrl St Univ 1989; *cr:* Sci Teacher 1985-89, Asst Prin 1989- Eisenhower Mid Sch; *ai:* Dist Grading Policy Task Force, Co-Founder Experiencing Power of Exec; Wrestling, Track Coach; Facilitator & Co-Founder First Outdoor Acad Sch for Metro Area; Detention Prgm, Sci Fair Coord Dist Teacher, Recognition Task Force, Team Leader, Chm Academic Press Comm; OEA 1985-89; Assn for Sup, Curr Dev 1988-89; Quail Springs Baptist Church Chm of Music Comm 1987-89, 1989-; Presentor OK Mid Level Conference, Co-Presentor, Meadows Fnd; Grant Winner OK Public Sch Found Trust; Cmptr Based Inst for At Risk Stu.

TAYLOR, EMMA JEAN DOWNS, Fifth Grade Teacher; *b:* Franklin, NC; *m:* Joe; *c:* Janet T. Gillespie; *ed:* (BS) Primary/ Elem Ed, W Carolina Univ 1959; *cr:* 3rd Grade Teacher 1959-64, 4th Grade Teacher 1964-69, 5th Grade Teacher 1969-, 2nd-8th Grade Summer Sch Teacher Iotla Sch; Adult Ed Teacher Franklin HS; *ai:* Delta Kappa Gamma; Teacher of Yr 1976-77; *home:* 97 Clyde Downs Rd Franklin NC 28734

TAYLOR, ETHEL BURNS, Fourth Grade Teacher; *b:* Thompson Station, TN; *m:* Livingston; *c:* William, Lisa; *ed:* (BS) Bio, TN St Univ 1962; *cr:* Teacher Carver HS, Johnson Elem; *ai:* 4-H Leader; Prof Rights & Responsibilities, Teachers Advisory, Planning Center Comm; TN Ed Assn, NEA; Franklin Spec Schls Assn Prof Rights Chm 1989-; Local Ed Assn; PTO Prgm Chm; *home:* 1906 Carter Creek Pike Franklin TN 37064

TAYLOR, GLENN E., Mathematics Teacher/Coach; *b:* Birmingham, AL; *m:* Teresa Bailey; *c:* Nicholas, Ryan A.; *ed:* Assoc Walker Coll 1977; (BS) Math/Scndry Ed, Univ of N AL 1979; (MA) Admin/Planning, Univ of AL 1986; Numerous Math Wkshps; Coaching Clinics; *cr:* Teacher/Coach Curry HS 1979-81; Teacher Locust Fork HS 1981-82; Teacher/Coach Tuscaloosa Cty HS 1982-; *ai:* Asst Ftbl, Golf, Math Team Coach; AHSCA 1979-; Little League Bsbl 1990; Worked Van Tiffin Ftbl Kicking Camp 1987, Bill Curry Ftbl Camp 1987-89; *office:* Tuscaloosa Cty HS 2200 24th St Northport AL 35476

TAYLOR, GWEN ANN (JUNTUNEN), Mathematics/ Computer Teacher; *b:* Watertown, SD; *m:* James M.; *c:* Amy, Colin; *ed:* (BS) Math, SD St Univ 1981; *cr:* Math/Cmptr Teacher Doland HS 1983-86, Estelline HS 1986-; *ai:* NEA, SD Ed Assn 1983-; SD Cncl Teachers of Math; Estelling Ed Assn Pres 1987-89; Sterling Meth Church Treas 1990; *office:* Estelline HS 1405 Davis Ave Estelline SD 57234

TAYLOR, HELEN VALENTINE, 6th/8th Grade Lang Art Teacher; *b:* San Francisco, CA; *m:* Earl L.; *c:* Laura Eschler, Rodger, Roy, Jennifer Wellard; *ed:* (BA) Eng/Linguistics, San Francisco Univ 1967; *cr:* Substitute Teacher Various San Francisco Elems 1967-68; Math Resource Teacher Bessie Carmichael Elem 1968-69; 6th Grade Self Contained Lincoln Elem 1969-72; 6th/8th Lang Arts Coquille Valley Mid Sch 1972-; *ai:* Benjamin Franklin Stamp Club Adv; Teach Coos Cty Youth Detention Center; Delta Kappa Gamma 1988-; LDS Church (Seminary Teacher 1970-80, 1982-84, Teacher Youth & Adults 1956-); *office:* Coquille Valley Mid Sch 1115 N Baxter St Coquille OR 97423

TAYLOR, IRENE L. JELLON, Vocational Ed Dept Chairperson; *b:* Meriden, CT; *m:* Walter N. F. Taylor; *ed:* (BS) Bus Ed, 1970, (MS) Ed/Psych, 1981 CCSU; *cr:* Bus Teacher Lyman Hall HS 1970-71, Mark T Sheehan HS 1971-; CWE/BOE Coord 1987-, Voc Ed Dept Head 1988- Mark T Sheehan HS; *ai:* SHS & Amer Cyanamid Partnership Ed Coord; FBLA; Phi Delta Kappa 1990; CT Bus Educators Assn 1970-; Wallingford Ed Assn Outstanding St Fundraising 1989-; *office:* Mark T Sheehan HS Hope Hill Rd Wallingford CT 06492

TAYLOR, JACKIE LEE, Sixth Grade Teacher; *b:* Findlay, OH; *m:* James M.; *c:* Jennifer L., Matthew M.; *ed:* (BS) Elem Ed, Findlay Coll 1972; *cr:* 6th Grade Teacher Forest Elem Sch 1972-; *ai:* NEA; OEA; REA; *home:* 308 Wells Rd Forest OH 45843

TAYLOR, JACQUELINE STRINE, Fourth Grade Teacher; *b:* Marion, OH; *m:* Robert; *c:* Megan; *ed:* (BA) Elem Ed, OH St Univ 1972; Grad Stud OH St Univ; *cr:* 4th Grade Teacher Claridon Elem Sch 1973-; *ai:* 4th Grade Outdoor Ed Co-Coord; RVTA Secy 1989-; Claridon PTO Secy; St Pauls Luth Church (Intern Cmm, Vacation Bible Sch); *office:* Claridon Elem Sch 3938 Marion-Mt Gilead Rd Caledonia OH 43314

TAYLOR, JACQUELYN ELAINE, 4th Grade Teacher; *b:* Lake Worth, FL; *ed:* (BA) Sociology, Univ of FL 1975; (BA) Elem Ed, 1978, (MS) Elem Ed, 1986 FL Atlantic Univ; Cert Admin & Supervision/Educl Leadership; *cr:* 2nd Grade Teacher 1978-86, 4th Grade Teacher 1986- Belvedere Elem; *ai:* Safety Patrol Spon; Modern/Jazz Dance Instr; Assertive Discipline Comm & Interim SACS Self Study Chairperson; Palm Beach Cty Rdng Cncl Mem 1989-; Urban League Bd Mem 1984-; Fellowship FL Atlantic Univ; Whos Who Among Coll Stus; *office:* Belvedere Elem Sch 3001 Lake Ave West Palm Beach FL 33405

TAYLOR, JAMES EDGAR, 3rd Grade Teacher; *b:* Houston, TX; *ed:* (BA) Elem Ed, OK Bapt Univ 1967; (MS) Spec Ed, Central St Univ 1976; *cr:* 6th Grade Teacher Del City Elem 1967-70; 4th Grade Teacher Ray Public Sch 1970-71; 5th Grade Teacher Sooner-Rose Elem 1971-72; 6th Grade Teacher 1972-75; 3rd Grade Teacher 1976- Highland Park Elem; *ai:* Math Coord; NEA 1967-; OK Ed Assn 1967-; *office:* Highland Park Elem Sch 4301 S Dimple Oklahoma City OK 73135

TAYLOR, JANE ANN DOLAN, Physics Teacher; *b:* Manchester, IA; *m:* Jerome; *ed:* (BS) Math/Physics/Ed, St Marys Coll 1975; Grad Work Nuclear Sci, Univ of MO Columbia & Energy, Webster Univ & Chem/Cmptr, St Louis Comm Coll & Physics, Univ of MO St Louis; *cr:* Math Teacher Notre Dame Jr HS 1975-77; Math/Physics Teacher Duchesne HS 1977-; *ai:* MO Cncl Teachers of Math, Math Educators of Greater St Louis 1980-; AAPT 1986-; St Mary Magdalen Cath Church Eucharistic Minister 1989-; *office:* Duchesne HS 2550 W Elm Saint Charles MO 63301

TAYLOR, JANET IRENE, 7th Grade Teacher; *b:* Pasadena, CA; *ed:* (BA) Child Dev, CA St Los Angeles 1979; Grad Stud; *cr:* 5th Grade Teacher St Thomas More 1979-81; 7th Grade Teacher Nativity Sch 1982-; *ai:* Stu Cncl & Jr HS Service Moderator; 7th Grade Girls Bsktbl Coach; NCEA; Truck of Love Volunteer Camp Cnslr; Western Assn of Schls & Colls Accreditation Team 1990; *office:* Nativity Sch 1250 Laurel St Menlo Park CA 94025

TAYLOR, JIM CONRAD, Athletic Director; *b:* Williamson, WV; *m:* Connie Stiles; *c:* Tucker, Tammy; *ed:* (BA) Phys Ed, Marshall Univ 1967; (MS) Phys Ed, Univ of N FL 1983; *cr:* Drivers Ed Teacher/Coach Fernandina Beach HS 1967-69; Phys Ed Teacher/Coach Orange Park HS 1969-; *ai:* FL Coaches Assn 1967-; *office:* Orange Park HS 2300 Kingsley Ave Orange Park FL 32073

TAYLOR, JOSHUA, JR., Social Studies Specialist; *b:* Fredericksburg, VA; *m:* Marion Anderson; *c:* Joshua III; *ed:* (BS) Elem Ed, VA St Univ 1963; (MED) Audio/Visual Instruction, Univ of VA, George Mason Univ; Lib Sci, Univ of VA; Art & Educl Tech, Univ of MD; Sch Admin, Univ of VA & George Mason Univ; *cr:* Teacher 1963-86, Sol Stud Specialist 1986- Arlington Public Schls; *ai:* Mem ESOL/HILT Coord Comm; Mem Hum Steering Comm; Dir of Cultural Diversity Project; NCSS 1986-; VA Educl Media Assn 1990; Arlington Historical Society (Bd of Dirs 1987, 1988) 1986-; Arlington Soccer Coach Civitans 1988-89, Mgr of Yr 1987; Nom Teacher of Yr Awd 1982-83; Agnes Meyer Grants in Ed 1983; Kodak, NEA Cameras in the Curr Awds 1983-85; Published Book; Area Captain Amer Cancer Society 1986-89; Co Host Cable TV Prgm; Numerous Photographic Awds; *office:* Arlington Public Schls 1426 N Quincy St Arlington VA 22207

TAYLOR, JUDY JAGGERS, Fourth Grade Teacher; *b:* Mount Vernon, TX; *m:* John T.; *c:* Laurie, Paul; *ed:* (BS) Elem Ed, Univ of TX Tyler 1978; Eng, UT Tyler; *cr:* 4th Grade Teacher Frankston Ind Sch Dist 1978-; *ai:* Coord for Jr HS, Elem UIL Events; Delta Kappa Gamma Society Pres 1985-87; Sci Teachers Assn of TX 1987-; East TX Cncl of Teachers of Math 1988-; Grants from Region VII Ed Service Center in Sci & Soc Stud.

TAYLOR, JUNE STEWART, Chairperson/Kndgtn Teacher; *b:* Chesterfield Cty, VA; *m:* James Flander; *c:* Tracy Yvette; *ed:* (BA) Elem Ed, VA Union Univ 1962; *cr:* 5th Grade Teacher Carter C Woodson Elem 1962-67; 2nd-4th Grades Math Teacher Giles B Cook Elem 1967-70; 5th Grade Teacher Pirmasens Amer Schls 1972-73; 2nd-4th Grades Rdng Teacher 1973-75, Kndgtn Teacher 1975-90 Walnut Hill Elem; *ai:* Chairperson Kndgtn Dept; Mem of Self Study Steering Comm; Black His Spec Prgm Comm; Petersburg Ed Assn 1967-; VA Ed Assn 1967-; NTA 1967-; Merrynettes Civic & Soc Club 1969- 20 Yr Service 1989; Jack & Jill of Amer Inc Treas 1988-89; Girl Scouts of Amer Jr Troup Leader-Ettrick 1980-82; *home:* 4011 Dupuy Rd Ettrick VA 23803

TAYLOR, KAREN WOODWARD, Fifth Grade Teacher; *b:* Conneautville, PA; *m:* Bruce A.; *c:* Craig, Brad; *ed:* (BA) Elem Ed, 1971, (MS) Elem Ed, 1976 Edinboro Univ; *cr:* 3rd Grade Teacher Linesville Elem 1972-75; 5th Grade Teacher Conneaut Valley Elem 1975-; *ai:* Conneaut Ed Assn Pres 1989-; Church of Christ (Choir, Teacher) 1958-; *home:* RD 2 Box 347 Conneautville PA 16406

TAYLOR, LAURIE A., Fourth Grade Teacher; *b:* Anacortes, WA; *c:* Emily K. Frantzen; *ed:* (BA) Soc Sci/Eng Lit, Pacific Luth Univ 1974; Post Grad Stud, Seattle Pacific Univ, Univ of WA; *cr:* 2nd Grade Teacher 1974-80, 2nd/3rd Grade Split Teacher 1980-81, 3rd/4th Grade Split Teacher 1981-82, 3rd Grade Teacher 1982-87 Lakewood Elem Sch; 4th Grade Teacher Lakewood Intermediate Sch 1988-; *ai:* Soc Stud Curr Adoption Comm; Grade Level Sci Rep; NEA, WA Ed Assn, Lakewood Ed Assn 1974-; Cntrl Luth Church; PTA (Local VP 1976) 1974-.

TAYLOR, LYDIA SPENCE, Art Teacher; *b:* New York, NY; *m:* Robert; *c:* Juan D., Lydia J., Lena Scott; *ed:* (BA) Art Ed, Bethune-Cookman Coll 1971; Working Towards MA in Admin & Supervision; *cr:* Teacher Aide Read-Patillo Elem 1971; Art Teacher Westside Elem 1971-76, Colonial HS 1976-, University HS 1990; *ai:* Art Dept Chairperson; Colonial Academic Scholars Prgm; NEA, NAEA 1972-; Cty Art Ed Assn 1976-; Winter Park Sidewalk Art Festival Comm (Sch Exhibit Chairperson 1987-88, Screening Co-Chairperson 1989), Service Awd 1989; Alpha Kappa Alpha Decorations Chairperson for Regional Conference 1990, Service Awd 1990; Painting Donated to City of Orlando by Alpha kappa Alpha; Drawing Selected for Display at Sun Bank Orlando; *office:* Colonial HS 6100 Oleander Dr Orlando FL 32807

TAYLOR, MALCOM GORDON, Science Department Chairman; *b:* Mc Allen, TX; *c:* Darrell J., Britt C.; *ed:* (BA) Bio, Pan Amer Univ 1962; (MED) Admin, Tarleton St Univ 1979; Bio/Wildlife, TX A&M Univ 1975; Mid Management, Tarelton St Univ 1982; *cr:* Gen Sci Teacher Harlingen Ind Sch Dist 1961-62; HS Bio/Chem Teacher 1962-75, Elem/6th Grade Sci Teacher 1975-83, Jr HS Life Sci/Earth Sci Teacher 1983- Copperas Cove Ind Sch Dist; *ai:* Young Astronaut Spon; Dist Inservice Comm; Campus Inservice Comm Co-Chm; TSTA (Life Mem, House of Delegate, Dist 12 Exec Bd 1980-83); Copperas Cove Ed Assn Pres 1978-80; Double C Square & Round Dance Pres 1989-; Heart of TX Square & Round Dance Assn Banner Comm Chm 1990; Natl Sci Fnd Fellowship 1975; VFW Post 8577 Teacher of Yr 1990; *office:* Copperas Cove Jr HS Sunny & Ridge Copperas Cove TX 76522

TAYLOR, MARGARET AUER, Third Grade Teacher; *b:* Fort Wayne, IN; *m:* Richard Aaron Jr.; *c:* Joshua A., Nicholas A.; *ed:* (BS) Elem Ed, 1969, (MS) Elem Ed, 1972 Purdue; Assertive Discipline Trng; *cr:* Kndgtn Teacher 1969-81, 3rd Grade Teacher 1982- Union Township Sch; *ai:* Book Adoption Comms; Writing Curr Guidelines Each Grade Level Rdng; Early Prevention of Sch Failure; IN Rdng Assn; Cub Scouts Den Leader 1988-; First Church of God Life Mem; Teacher of Yr Whitley Cty Schls 1974; *office:* Union Township Sch 2250 S 500 E Columbia City IN 46725

TAYLOR, MARGARET SHOUP, Fourth Grade Teacher; *b:* South Bend, IN; *m:* Russell N.; *c:* Gary A., Michele A. Tucker; *ed:* (BS) Elem Ed, 1971, (MS) Elem Ed, 1976 IN Univ South Bend 1976; *cr:* 3rd Grade Teacher 1971-78, 4th Grade Teacher 1978-83 Lakeville Elem; 4th Grade Teacher La Ville Elem 1983-; *ai:* 5th/6th Grade Girls Vlybl, Bsktbl, Track Coach; NEA, IN St Teachers Assn 1971-; Marshall Cty Rdng Assn 1985-; *home:* 21125 Newton Ave Lakeville IN 46536

TAYLOR, MARTHA ANN, Mathematics Teacher; *b:* Marion, NC; *ed:* (AB) Math, Lenoir Rhyne Coll 1972; (MA) Math, Univ of SC 1978; *cr:* 7th-12th Grade Math Teacher Butler HS 1975-82; 7th/8th Grade Math Teacher Hartsville Jr HS 1982-; *ai:* Chrldr, Mathcounts, Academic Challenge, Knowledge Master Coach; Yrbk Adv; Academic Booster Club Faculty Coord; Sch Improvement Cncl; NEA, SCEA 1975-; Master Teacher Awd 1988; Agnes T Hayes Awd 1989; Hartsville Jr HS Teacher of Yr; *office:* Hartsville Jr HS 437 W Carolina Ave Hartsville SC 29550

TAYLOR, MARY HUDOCK, Mathematics Teacher; *b:* Connellsville, PA; *m:* Allen K.; *c:* Erick B., A. Keith (dec); *ed:* (BS) Math Ed, Trenton St Coll 1958; Cmptr Courses; *cr:* Math Teacher Pennsville HS 1958-59, Sterling HS 1960-63, Eastern HS 1976-; *ai:* Staff Dev Prgm Trainer Eastern HS; Eastern Ed Assn, Camden Cty Ed Assn, NJ Ed Assn; NEA; NCTM, NJ Assn of Math Teachers; Governors Recognition Awd; *office:* Eastern HS Box 2500 Laurel Oak Rd Voorhees NJ 08043

TAYLOR, MARY NEWCOMB, English Teacher; *b:* Clifton Forge, VA; *m:* Fred L.; *c:* Kathryn L.; *ed:* (BA) Eng, Mary Washington Coll 1967; Grad Hrs Ed, Eng, Writing; *cr:* Eng Teacher Kellam HS 1967-68; Eng Teacher 1968-79, Eng Teacher/Dept Chairperson 1971-76 J G Whittier Intermediate Sch; Eng Teacher Oakton HS 1979-82; Eng Teacher 1985-, Eng/Creative Writing Teacher 1988 Thoreau Intermediate Sch; *ai:* Stu Government Spon; VEA, FEA, NEA 1967-82, 1985-; VATE, NCTE 1985-.

TAYLOR, MILDRED NERO, Third Grade Teacher; *b:* Crowley, LA; *c:* Walter E. (dec), Everette P.; *ed:* (BS) Elem Ed, 1958, (ME) Ed, 1970 TX Southern Univ; *cr:* 1st Grade Teacher 1958-80, 2nd Grade Teacher 1980-86, 3rd Grade Teacher 1987- J J Rhoads Elem Sch; *ai:* Shell 2 Sci Teacher; Stu Cncl Adv; Black His Month Chairperson 1990; Faculty Adv Comm Mem; NEA, Assn for Chldhd Ed Inter; Sunnyside Civic Club; HFT; *home:* 8018 Colonial Ln Houston TX 77051

TAYLOR, MONA BRIDGES, Social Studies Chairperson; *b:* Mt Savage, MD; *m:* D. Michael; *ed:* (BA) His/Ed, 1973, (MED) His, 1980 Frostburg St Univ; *cr:* Teacher Bruce HS 1974-78, Mt Savage Sch 1978-; *ai:* Jr Class & Century III Adv; Jr & Sr Prom Spon; MD Cncl Soc Stud 1989-; Allegany Cty Cncl Soc Stud Pres 1990; Phi Eta Sigma Excl Teaching Awd 1987-89; Phi Alpha Theta Moore Awd Excl in His 1973; *home:* Rt 3 Box 108 Cumberland MD 21502

TAYLOR, NANCY JO, English/Phys Ed Teacher; *b:* San Angelo, TX; *m:* Wayne Allen; *c:* David W., Travis W.; *ed:* (BA) Phys Ed, E WA Univ 1972; (MA) Guidance/Counseling, Whitworth Coll 1975; *cr:* Educator Mead Mid Sch 1972-80, Northwood Jr HS 1980-; *ai:* Adv Stu of Month; Coach 8th Grade Vlybl; *home:* E 10918 30th Spokane WA 99206

TAYLOR, NANCY WAKEMAN, 5th Grade Teacher; *b:* Akron, OH; *m:* Robert G.; *c:* Andrea, Stephanie; *ed:* (BSED) Elem Ed, Univ of Akron 1973; Grad Work Akron Univ, Kent St; *cr:* 6th/7th Grade Teacher Southeast Local Schls 1973-75; 5th Grade Teacher Springfield Local Schls 1975-; *ai:* Springfield Local Assn of Classroom Teachers Treas 1981-82; NEA 1973-; Springfield Township Womens Club (Secy 1984-85, Historian 1987-89); Martha Holden Jennings Awd 1981-82; *office:* Milroy Elem Sch 1639 Killian Rd Akron OH 44312

TAYLOR, NORMA LEHMAN, Social Studies Chair; *b:* Wadsworth, OH; *m:* William M.; *ed:* (BS) His/Eng, Kent St Univ 1967; Grad Stud Akron Univ; *cr:* Teacher Brunswick Grade Sch 1962-63, 1964-65, Green HS 1967-; *ai:* Soc Stud Dept Chm; Green Ed Assn (Pres 1983-86) 1990; Martha Holden Jennings Scholar 1951-82; Phi Delta Kappa Mem 1985-; *office:* Green HS 1737 Steese Rd Greensburg OH 44232

TAYLOR, OLLIE MAE, English Teacher; *b:* Wisner, LA; *c:* Allen Johnson, Sherlyn Johnson, Wanda Johnson, Darrell; *ed:* (BS) Phys Ed/Eng, 1971, (MA) Sports Admin, 1983 Grambling St Univ; Grambling Univ; *cr:* Teacher Ouachita HS 1971-; *ai:* River Cities Optimist Bd Mem 1990; Teacher of Yr Ouachita HS 1989-; Outstanding Participation for Chur ch; *home:* 1309 Walton Ln Monroe LA 71202

TAYLOR, ROBBY G., Fifth Grade Teacher; *b:* Sidney, MT; *m:* Anne Marie Zoanni; *c:* Gregory, Lyndsey; *ed:* (BA) Elem Ed, E MT Coll 1979; Phys Ed; *cr:* Jr HS Teacher 1979-82, 5th Grade Teacher 1982- Fairview Consolidated Schls; *ai:* Coach 7th/8th Grade Ftbl 1979-, 5th/6th Grade Bsktbl 1979-; MT Ed Assn, Fairview Ed Assn, NEA 1979-; *office:* Fairview Consolidated Schls 610 W 7th Box 467 Fairview MT 59221

TAYLOR, ROBERTA COOKIE, 8th Grade Teacher; *b:* Galveston, TX; *ed:* (BA) Speech/Drama, Sam Houston St Univ 1979; Working Towards Masters Admin/Supervision, Trinity Coll; *cr:* 6th/7th Grade Lang Art Teacher Stephen F Austine Mid Sch 1979-81; Kndgtn Teacher Holy Comforter & St Cyprian Cath Sch 1983-85; 6th-8th Grade Teacher Nativity Cath Sch 1983-85; 6th-8th Grade Lang Art Teacher St Augustine Cath Sch 1985-; *ai:* Spon Young Achievers Speech Club, Blackademics Team, Dir Christmas Pageants; Coord Archdiocesan Schls for City-Wide Spelling Bee; NCEA 1982-; ASCD 1988-; Delta Sigma Theta VP 1981-82; *office:* St Augustine Cath Sch 1421 V Street NW Washington DC 20009

TAYLOR, ROBIN DARR, Child Care/Guidance Teacher; *b:* Odessa, TX; *m:* Phillip Ross; *ed:* (BS) Home Ec Ed, 1984, (MED) Counseling, 1985 TX Tech Univ; Early Chldhd Ed, Occupational Home Ec; *cr:* Kndgtn Teacher Dunbar Elem Sch 1986; 8th Grade Home Ec Teacher Hood Mid Sch 1986-88; 11th/12th Grade Childcare/Guidance/Management Teacher Berkner HS 1988-; *ai:* Keywanette & FHA Spon; Loving Intervention for Teens Team Mem; Support Group Leader; Assn of TX Prof Educators 1986-; Richardson Ed Assn 1988-; PALS 1990; Future Teacher of America Club Teacher of Month.

TAYLOR, SAMUEL DWIGHT, Social Studies Teacher; *b:* Columbia, KY; *m:* Margaret Loy; *c:* Brian E., Bethany M.; *ed:* (AA) His, Lindsey Wilson Coll 1969; (BA) His, 1971, (MA) His, 1975 W KY Univ; *cr:* US His Teacher John Adair Mid Sch 1971-; *ai:* Adair Cty Ed Assn Pres 1974-76; Mid Cumberland Dist Ed Assn Bd of Dir 1974-76; KY Ed Assn, NEA 1971-; Daughters of Amer Revolution 1988, His Awd; Instrs to Select His Textbooks & Teaching Techniques; *home:* 1769 Weed-Keltner Rd Gradyville KY 42742

TAYLOR, SANDRA D., English Teacher; *b:* Carthage, MS; *ed:* (BS) Eng, Univ of S MS 1972; (MED) Eng, William Carey Coll 1976; *cr:* Teacher Raleigh Elem 1973-75, Raleigh Jr HS 1975-77, Raleigh HS 1977-; Adjunct Instr Hinds Comm Coll 1989-; *ai:* Established & Spon The Lit Club 1983-; Yrbk Staff Spon 1980-; Jr Class Spon 1978-; Sch Play Dir 1980-; Smith Cty Assn Educators, MS Assn Educators, NEA 1978-; Faculty Awd 1978, 1982, 1984, 1990; STAR Teacher 1987, 1989; *office:* Raleigh HS PO Box 188 Raleigh MS 39153

TAYLOR, SHERRA SLAUGHTER, English Teacher; *b:* Wichita, KS; *m:* Daniel M.; *c:* Alyson, Matthew; *ed:* (BA) Ed Eng, Wichita St Univ 1986; *cr:* Teacher Oxford HS 1986-; *ai:* Journalism & Yrbk; NHS; Cheerleading Coach; KS Scholastic Press Assn 1988-; NCTE 1988-; NEA 1986-; Arius Club (Pres 1987-88) 1984-; *office:* Oxford HS 303 E Maple Oxford KS 67119

TAYLOR, SHIRLEY JEAN, Mathematics Teacher; *b:* Atlanta, GA; *ed:* (BS) Math, GA St Univ 1986; *cr:* Math Teacher Mc Intosh HS 1987-; *ai:* Jr Math Team Spon; *office:* Mc Intosh HS 201 E Walt Banks Rd Peachtree GA 30269

TAYLOR, SOL YVONNE (NOBLE), 6th Grade General Sci Teacher; *b:* Quitman, GA; *m:* Willie M.; *c:* Donde, Andrea Greggs, Bryan; *ed:* (BS) Bio Ed, Ft Valley St Coll 1979; Working Towards MS in Mid Grades Ed, GA Coll 1990; *cr:* Phys Sci Teacher T J Elder Jr HS 1979-82; Life Sci Teacher T J Elder Mid Sch 1982-86; Phys Sci Teacher Boddie Jr HS 1986-88; General Sci Teacher Boddie Mid Sch 1988-; *ai:* GA Assn of Educators 1986-; *home:* 174 Forest Hill Rd Milledgeville GA 31061

TAYLOR, STANLEY K., Reading Specialist; *b:* Elkins, WV; *ed:* (AB) Elem Ed, Glenville St Coll 1976; (MA) Ed/Rdng Specialist, WV Univ Morgantown 1984; *cr:* Teacher North Elem Sch 1976-87; Rdng Specialist Valley View Elem 1989-; *ai:* Elkins Area Cmmty Theater & Appollo Civic Theater Acting; Exec Producer

Miss Randolph Cty & Miss Mid Eastern Schlsp Pageant; Phi Delta Kappa Mem 1989-; NEA 1976-; Natl & WV PTA Mem 1976-, (Local Pres, VP, Secy), Honorary Life Membership 1985; US Jaycees Mem 1979-80, Outstanding Young Men of America 1980; Knights of Columbus Mem 1988-; Elkins Area Cmmty Theater Secy 1987-; Mountaineer Millionaire Recognized by WV Secy of St A James Manchin; Ambassador of Cmmty Spirit Recognized by St Treas; Phoebe Hearst Outstanding Educator; Randolph Cty Teacher of Yr 1984; *office:* Valley View Elem Sch Rt 4 Box 269 Martinsburg WV 25401

TAYLOR, SUSAN ANDERSON, Third Grade Teacher; *b:* Cedar City, UT; *m:* Donald Lynn; *c:* J. N., Benjamin; *cr:* 3rd Grade Teacher Grant Elem 1979-; *ai:* Taught Self Esteem Class To Teachers; Grant Sch Started Champions for Life; Wrote & Directed Christmas Play; Murray Cncl PTA Teacher VP 1984-85; *office:* Grant Elem Sch 661 W 6181 So Murray UT 84123

TAYLOR, THOMAS EDWARD, Science Teacher; *b:* Springfield, OH; *m:* Deanne Jean Esterline; *c:* Kylie M.; *ed:* (BS) Sci Ed, OH St Univ 1986; *cr:* Teacher Kenton Ridge HS 1986-; *ai:* Var Boys Bsktbl Announcer; Var Boys Tennis Coach; Vars Girls Tennis Coach; OEA; NEA; Outstanding Young Men of Amer Ica 1988; *office:* Kenton Ridge H S 4444 Middle Urbana Rd Springfield OH 45503

TAYLOR, TIMOTHY FRANCIS, Math Teacher/Computer Coord; *b:* Winchester, VA; *ed:* Teaching Cert Elem Ed, James Madison 1980; *cr:* 4th Grade Teacher Sandy Hook Elem 1980-86; 5th/7th Grade Teacher Strasburg Mid Sch 1986; *ai:* Jr Var Girls & Boys Bsktbl; Var Girls Sftbl; Chamber of Commerce Teacher of Yr 1989; *office:* Strasburg Mid Sch 207 High St Strasburg VA 22657

TAYLOR, TRUDY ELLEN, Third Grade Teacher; *b:* Ellwood City, PA; *ed:* (BS) Elem Ed, Univ of Houston 1972; *cr:* 3rd Grade Teacher Cntrl Elem 1973-77, Gardens Elem 1977-; *ai:* TSTA 1977-82; AFT 1987-; Published Poetry; Whos Who in Amer Ed; *home:* 3402 Preston #213 Pasadena TX 77505

TAYLOR, VIRGINIA GINGER LYNN, 4th Grade Teacher; *b:* Coos Bay, OR; *ed:* (BA) Elem Ed, OR Coll of Ed 1971; 5th Yr Hum, Western WA Univ 1982; *cr:* 5th Grade Teacher Burns Henry L Slater Sch 1972-72; 2nd/4th Grade Teacher Creslane 1972-78; 1st Grade Teacher Stanwood Primary Sch 1978-79; 5th Grade Teacher Arlington Intermediate Sch 1979-86; 6th Grade Teacher Coorparoo St Sch 1984; 4th Grade Teacher Trafton 1986-; *ai:* Odyssey of the Mind Coach; Arlington Ed Assn 1979-; WA Ed Assn 1979-; Arlington Cmmty Educl Project 1982-83; Selected By St Supt of Instruction to Be An Exch Teacher to Brisbane Queensland Australia to Teach in St Sch 1984; *office:* Trafton Schl 12616 Jim Creek Rd Arlington WA 98223

TAYLOR, WILLIAM ANDREW, Science Teacher; *b:* Gladwin, MI; *m:* Dorothy A. Hoffman; *c:* Karen, Linda; *ed:* (BS) Bio, Physics, Walla Walla Coll 1967; Univ of AK; Walla Walla Coll; Home Study Inst; *cr:* Boys Dean/Math Instr Bristol Bay Mission Sch 1967-68; 5th/8th Grade Teacher Sitka AK 1969; Spec Ed Harborview Mem Hospital 1970-75; Sci/Math Instr Valdez HS 1976-; *ai:* Soph Class Spon; Academic Coach; Natl Sci Teacher; Church Sch Bd Mem 1988-;ADFG Advisory Bd; *office:* Valdez H S P O Box 398 Valdez AK 99686

TAYLOR, WILMA (RUGH), English Teacher; *b:* Indianapolis, IN; *m:* Norman T.; *c:* Norma F., Timothy M., Catheen M., Bethany A. Taylor Warren; *ed:* (BA) Eng/Speech Ottawa Univ 1956; (MS) Eng Ed, Butler Univ 1967; *cr:* Missionary Amer Baptist Convention 1956-57; Professional Prgm Secy Young Mens Christian Assn of IN 1957-59; Eng Teacher New Palestine HS 1967-78; Journalism Teacher Warren Cntrl Hs 1978-; Information Office MSD Warren Township 1979-82; Writer/Ed Self Employed 1988-; *ai:* Warren Township PTA 1978, Outstanding Teacher 1986-87; ISTA Publications Local 1978- Outstanding Publication 189; IN Sch Public Relations Assn VP 1981-83 Service Awd 1983; NCTE 1978-; Womens Press Club IN 1985- Writing/Editing Awd 1989; Agwynneville Chrstn Church 1975-; Eng Speaking Union Schlsp for Study Stratford on Avon England; Gold Key Awd/ Columbia Press Assn; Pioneer Awd/Natl Scholastic Press Assn; Dow Jones Outstanding Adv Awd; IN Journalism Teacher of Yr; Outstanding Educator Awd/New Palestine HS; Many Articles Published/Present Editor of In Plant Ford Motor Co Magazine.

TAYLOR, ZENOBIA DAVIS, Music Teacher; *b:* Okmulgee, OK; *m:* Woodley D.; *c:* Diane Taylor Wright, Steven David; *ed:* (BS) Music Ed, TN St Univ 1954; (MA) Music Ed, Montclair St Coll 1975; Kodaly Orff/Music Tech Wkshps: *cr:* 5th Grade Teacher Overture Elem Sch 1954-55; Music Teacher Blanche Ely HS 1955-56; 3rd Grade Teacher Glenfield Sch 1961-73; Montclair Sch System 1973-80; Hillside Gfld/Talented Sch 1980-; *ai:* Montclair/NEA 1961-; NJ Music Educators Assoc 1961-; Music Educators Natl Confernce 1961-; Union Baptist Church Youth Choir Dir 1968-; New Sch for Arts Mem Bd of Dir 1980-84; YWCA Mem/Nominating Comm 1988-; Recipient 1989 Governors Teachers Recognition Grant; Whos Who Among Stu in Amer Coll/Univ 1955; *home:* 15 Stephen St Montclair NJ 07042

TAYSOM, DOUGLAS LEE, Science Teacher; *b:* Salt Lake City, UT; *m:* Janet Maree Fry; *c:* James M.; *ed:* (BA) Bio, S UT St Coll 1985; *cr:* Sci Teacher Tempe HS 1985-; *ai:* Chess Coach, Cycling Club Spon; AZ Sci Teachers Assn 1986-; Outstanding Stu in Scndry Ed; Pestalozzi Awd; St Chess Championship Team 1988-89; Presentation AZ & NV Acad of Sci; *office:* Tempe HS 1730 S Mill Tempe AZ 85281

TEABO, GLENDA PATTERSON, First Grade Teacher; *b:* Otisville, NY; *c:* Geoffrey, Laura A.; *ed:* (BS) Elem Ed, Seton Hall Univ 1970; (MS) Ed, Canisius Coll 1977; *cr:* 5th Grade Teacher 1973-74; 1st Grade Teacher, 1974- Minisink Valley Cntrl Sch; *ai:* Gifted Comm Representing Elem Sch; Effective Schls Rep; NYS Rdng Assn 1973-; ABC Rdng Cncl 1973-; MVTA 1974-; BSA Comm Person 1970; GSA Troop Leader for Brownies 1960; Otisville Church Deacon, Sunday Sch Teacher & Summer Bible Sch Dir; *home:* 162 South St Middletown NY 10940

TEAGNO, MARJORIE, Sixth Grade Teacher; *b:* Jersey City, NJ; *m:* Dante; *c:* Danielle, Rebecca; *ed:* (BA) Elem Ed, Glassboro St Coll 1968; Acad for Advancement of Teaching & Management 1986; Grad Stud Seton Hall Univ & Jersey City St; *cr:* 2nd Grade Teacher 1968-70, 4th Grade Teacher 1970-71, 3rd Grade Teacher 1971-76, 6th Grade Teacher 1979- West Ridge Elem Sch; *ai:* 6th Grade Level Chm 1985-; Safety Patrol Adv 1983-; Dist Sci Comm 1983-; PREA Rep 1969-71; NEA 1968-; Governors Teacher Recognition Awd 1988 & Convocation Princeton Univ 1988; *office:* W Ridge Elem Sch S 1st St Park Ridge NJ 07656

TEAGUE, JOYCE ANN (MATTHEWS), Director; *b:* Memphis, TN; *m:* Thomas Thearon; *c:* Katheryn O.; *ed:* (BS) Bio/ Scndry Ed, Memphis St Univ 1968; (MA) Spec Ed, Univ of AL 1974; *cr:* Life/General Sci Teacher Colonial Jr HS 1969; Spec Ed Teacher Mills River Elem 1970-71, L E Wilson Mid Sch 1971-73, Sheffield HS 1973-74; Spec Ed/Sci Teacher Airways Jr HS 1974-78; Spec Ed Teacher 1983-86, Dir 1987- Concord Acad; *ai:* Learning Disabilities Assn of TN 1987-; CEC 1989-; Concord Acad Teacher of Yr 1985-86; *office:* Concord Acad 4942 Walnut Grove Rd Memphis TN 38117

TEAGUE, REBECCA SLADE, Chem Teacher/Sci Dept Chair; *b:* Oklahoma City, OK; *c:* Lauren Leigh; *ed:* (BS) Natural Sci, Cntrl St Univ 1975; OK St Univ Cmptr Usage IBM; Advanced Chem Manhattan Coll; Grad Studies Equilibrium KS St Univ; Chem Demos Cntrl St U; Adv Chem Univ AL; Inst for Talented Stu Carlton Coll; *cr:* Phys Sci Teacher 1975-79, Chem Teacher 1979-80, Chem Teacher/Dept Chairperson 1980- Edmond Memorial HS; *ai:* Jr Class Spon; Scndry Sci Curr Chairman; Math, Sci Curr Coord; Co Chairperson Scndry Ed Prgm; Chairperson Honors Curr Dev; Testbook Adoption Chairperson; NEA; OK Ed Assn Dist Rep 1975-; Edmond Assn Classroom Teacher 1975-; NSTA 1975-; 1st Presbyn Church 1952-; Kappa Delta Alumnae Assn Membership Adv 1979-; Cntrl St Univ Alum Assn; Cntrl St Uni Fnd; OK Scholar Kerr Fnd; Outstanding Young Woman of America; Dreyfus Fnd Invited Scholar; Outstanding OK Women Educators Charter Mem; Certificates of Merit Westinghouse Corporation, Duracell Corporation, Kerr Mc Gee Corporation; Contributing Author to Duracell Corporation Publications; Dist Teacher of Yr.

TEAL, LINDA SUE (ANDREWS), Principal; *b:* Kinston, NC; *m:* William Robert; *c:* Darren A.; *ed:* (BS) Elem Ed, Atlantic Chrstn Coll 1969; (MA) Early Chldhd Ed, E Carolina Univ 1981; Supervision Cert; *cr:* 2nd Grade Teacher Trenton Elem Sch 1969-82; Prin Comfort Elem Sch 1982-; *ai:* NCASA 1987-; Delta Kappa Gamma (Pres 1988-, VP 1986-88, Secy 1984-86); Jones Cty Prin of Yr 1986, 1987; Region II Alternate Prin of Yr 1987; *office:* Comfort Elem Sch Po Box 188 Comfort NC 28522

TEAT, TERRI ST. CLAIR, English Teacher; *b:* Gadsden, AL; *m:* Terry Owen; *c:* Dustin C., Ansley T.; *ed:* (BS) Office Admin Ed, Jacksonville St 1985; *cr:* Teacher Gaylesville HS 1986-87, Sand Rock HS 1988-89; *ai:* Southern Accreditation Organizations Comm; *home:* Rt 1 Box 210A Leesburg AL 35983

TEATOR, ROBERT H., Industrial Arts Teacher; *b:* New Haven, CT; *m:* Patricia Maddaloni; *c:* Matthew, Mark, John; *ed:* (BS) Industrial Arts, 1969, (MS) Industrial Arts Instruction, 1972 Cntrl CT St Coll; (MS) Industrial Ed, Cntrl CT St Univ 1985; Prof Dev Wkshps, CT Technology Ed Assn & CT St Dept of Ed; *cr:* Teacher Bertram F Dodd Jr HS 1969-; Adjunct Faculty Cntrl CT St Univ 1973-; *ai:* Curr Revision Comm; Practical Life Sci & Technology Dept; Piloting Exploring Technology Ed Curr; CT Cooperating Teacher Mentor Prgm Supervising Stu Teachers; Epsilon Pi Tau 1967-, Life Mem; NEA 1969-, Life Mem; Intnl Technology Assn, New England Assn Technology Teacher, CT Technology Ed Assn 1967-, Life Mem; CT Ed Assn, Cheshire Ed Assn 1969-; Intnl Order of DeMolay Master Cnslr 1962-69, Chevelier Degree 1968; Trumbull Lodge #22 AF&AM Jr Steward 1969-; Cub Scouts of America (Pinewood Derby, Blue, Gold Comm) 1982-89, Volunteerism Awd 1987; BSA Troop #92 (Treas, Merit Badge Cnslr) 1987-, Lord Baden-Powell 1990; *office:* Bertram F Dodd Jr HS 100 Park Pl Cheshire CT 06410

TEBO, MIKE O'DELL, Eng/Creative Writing Teacher; *b:* Magee, MS; *m:* Sheila Breland; *c:* Miranda; *ed:* (BS) Eng, Univ Southern MS 1975; Natl Writing Project Site Trng, Southern MS; Writing Project, Univ of Southern MS 1988, 1990; Working toward Masters Eng, Southern MS; *cr:* Teacher/Coach N Forrest HS 1975-85, Rowan Center 1985-87; Teacher Hattiesburg HS 1987-; *ai:* Bsktbl Coach 1975-89; NCTE, MS Cncl Teachers of Eng, AFT; Maybank Baptist Church; Hattiesburg Public Schls Teacher of Yr 1989; MS Teacher of Yr Finalist 1989-; Coach of Yr Awds; Grants for Publication of Creative Writing Book; *office:* Hattiesburg HS Hutchison Ave Hattiesburg MS 39401

TEDDER, GAIL H., 4th Grade Teacher; *b:* Wilkesboro, NC; *m:* Earl Roland; *c:* Regina Gail; *ed:* (BS) Elem Ed, Appalachian St Univ 1970; *ai:* Chm Beautification Comm; 4th Grade Chm; 5th & 6th Grade Sunday Sch Teacher; Math Teacher of Yr 1978-88.

TEDDER, MOLLIE STEVENS, Fifth Grade Teacher; *b:* Whiteville, NC; *w:* Maxie Drexel (dec); *c:* David, Sylvia T. Elkins, Tyrone; *ed:* (BA) Elem Ed, Flora Mac Donald 1957; (MA) Ed/ Lang Art, Appalachian 1976; *cr:* 4th/6th Teacher Williams Township 1957-59; 6th Grade Teacher Edgewood 1959-60; 5th/ 6th Grade Teacher Chadbourn 1960-70, Edgewood 1970-; *ai:* NCAE (Treas 1975, Pres 1985-86); Alpha Delta Kappa Pres 1980-82, Advanced Study Schlsp 1974-75; 1st Baptist Church Adult Sunday Sch Teacher 1970-; *home:* Rt 1 Box 380-AB Whiteville NC 28472

TEDESCHI, PAMELA ANN (CROWE), 5th Grade Teacher; *b:* E Liverpool, OH; *m:* Brian L.; *c:* Anthony M.; *ed:* (BS) Elem Ed, Kent St 1977; (MS) Child/Youth Guidance, Univ of Dayton 1984; *cr:* 6th-7th Grade Rdng Teacher Harrison Hills City Sch 1976-77; 5th Grade Self-Contained Teacher Irondale Elem 1977-; *ai:* Teach Adult Basic Ed At Edison N; *home:* 1 Summit Dr Salineville OH 43945

TEDESCO, JANET ROUX, Math/Computer Dept Chair; *b:* New Orleans, LA; *m:* Kenneth F.; *c:* Kerri C., Philip E.; *ed:* (BS) Math, Univ New Orleans 1969; Cmptr Literacy; Certified in Eng, General Sci; *cr:* Teacher F W Gregory 1969-70, St Louise De Marillac 1972-74; Teacher/Dept Head Holy Cross 1970-72, 1982-; *ai:* Mu Alpha Theta, Cmptr & Chess Teams Spon; Jets-Teams Coord; NCTM, NCEA 1982-; Greater New Orleans Teachers of Math 1988; *office:* Holy Cross Sch 4950 Danphine St New Orleans LA 70117

TEDFORD, TONI GAIL, Biology Teacher; *b:* Clarksdale, MS; *ed:* (BAE) Bio, Univ of MS 1987; *cr:* Bio Teacher Coahoma Cty HS 1988-; *ai:* Sr Spon; Sci Club; *home:* 509 Colonial Dr Clarksdale MS 38614

TEDFORD, WAYNE JOHN, 7th Grade Teacher; *b:* Manchester, CT; *m:* Tommie Lawkford; *c:* Johnathan, Joanna; *ed:* (BA) Math, St Anselm 1969; (MA) Ed Psych/Guid, Univ TN Martin 1979; *cr:* Teacher Lewis Mills Regional HS 1970-72, Briarwood Sch 1973, Big Sandy HS 1973-83, Huntingdon Jr HS 1983-; *ai:* 7th Guidance; Constitution Comm; NCTM 1990; Teacher Assn (Pres 1978-80/1982-85/1988-89, Spokesperson 1979-83); Lions Club Pres 1989-; Knights of Columbus Grand Knight 1989-; BSA Cub Master, Asst Scout Master, Prgrm Dir, Aquatics Instr 1985-; *home:* 115 Highland Bruceton TN 38317

TEEGARDEN, SHARON MC CLANAHAN, English Teacher; *b:* Cincinnati, OH; *m:* Richard A.; *c:* Troy A., Eric M.; *ed:* (BA) Eng, 1967, (MS) Linguistics, 1970, (Rank I) Ed, 1978 Morehead St Univ; Summer Theater Prgm Internship; Various Writers Conferences; *cr:* Eng/Speech/Drama/Journalism Teacher Montgomery Cty HS 1967-69; Eng/Speech/Drama Teacher Bracken Cty HS 1970-; Eng Instr Maysville Comm Coll 1987-; *ai:* Chrldr Spon; Drama Act; Organized & Led Stu Trips to Europe; Spon & Hosted Foreign Exch Stus; KY Ed Assn, NEA; Poetry Published; *home:* Rt 1 Box 79 Brooksville KY 41004

TEEL, ELIZABETH, English Teacher; *b:* Norfolk, VA; *c:* Erric; *ed:* (BA) Eng, Queens Coll 1973; (MA) Ed, City Coll 1979; *cr:* Eng Teacher Edgar D Shimer Jr HS 1973-75, William Cowper Intermediate Sch 1975-; *ai:* Coach Girls Cheerleading Team; Jewish Stud Grant & Fellowship 1987; Rdng Improvement Prgm Grant 1984; Work Printed in Book 1980; *office:* Wm Cowper Intermediate Sch 70-02 54th Ave Maspeth NY 11378

TEFFETELLER, ELAINE GILLILAND, Second Grade Teacher; *b:* Benton, TN; *m:* Gordon L.; *c:* Sherri Horonjeff, Philip, Steven, Barry; *ed:* (BA) Eng/Elem Ed, Univ of TN 1951; Post Grad Studs Univ of TN & Valdosta St Coll; *cr:* Teacher Porter HS 1951-52, McFarland Park Sch 1952-53, Lutz Sch 1953-54, Lenox Elem 1970-74, S L Mason Sch 1974-; *ai:* NEA, Valdosta Assn of Ed; Valdosta City Schls Teacher of Yr 1984; GA Semi-Finalist Teacher of Yr 1984.

TEGARDEN, JACKSON EAVES, Commercial Drafting Instructor; *b:* Brownsville, TX; *ed:* (BS) Industrial Arts, TX A&I Univ 1974; (MS) Occupational Ed, Corpus Christi St Univ 1985; *cr:* Teacher Austin Ind Sch Dist 1974-76; Ed Specialist US Peace Corps 1976-78; Teacher Brownsville Ind Sch Dist 1978-; *ai:* Spon Regan Outback Expediations 1974-76; Spon Industrial Arts Assn 1978-83; Spon Voc Industrial Clubs of America 1983-; Comm Chm Southern Assn of Schls; VICA 1987-; Top Teachers of TX Univ of TX Ex-Stu Assn 1989-; *office:* Homer Hanna HS 2615 Price Rd Brownsville TX 78520

TEI, CATHARINE MAY (BROWN), Second Grade Teacher; *b:* Pitcher, NY; *m:* William Adrian; *ed:* (BRE) Chrstn Ed, Baptist Bible Seminary 1964; Cortland St Univ, Broome Comm Coll, Oneonta St Univ; *cr:* 2nd Grade Teacher Marathon Cntrl Sch 1965-; *ai:* Marathon Teachers Assn Secy 1971; NY St Teachers Assn, NEA; 1st Baptist Church Youth Leader 1965-73; *home:* Box 402 Marathon NY 13803

TEICHERT, V. DALENE, Teacher of the Gifted; *b:* Idaho Falls, ID; *m:* Fredrick; *c:* Scott, Jeff; *ed:* (BS) Elem Ed, Brigham Young Univ 1975; *cr:* Teacher of Gifted Salt Lake City Sch Dist 1979-; *ai:* Gifted Curr Writing; Debate & Future Problem Solving Coach; VASCD, VAGT, NEA, VEA; Salt Lake City Sch Dist Teacher of Yr 1988-89; *office:* Salt Lake City Sch Dist 1450 W 600 N Salt Lake City UT 84116

TEIGLAND, JOHN B., 6th Grade Teacher; *b:* Buffalo Center, IA; *m:* Mary A. Nesheim; *c:* Peter, Heidi, Jennifer; *ed:* (BS) Elem Ed, Mankato St 1967; (MS) Elem Ed, Univ of WI River Falls 1980; *cr:* 6th Grade Teacher Madelia 1966, Hastings 1967-; *ai:*

NEA, MEA 1966-; HEA Treas 1966-; *office:* Hastings Mid Sch 9th & Vermillion Hastings MN 55033

TEKELL, CHRISTIE DIANNE, Fifth Grade Teacher; *b:* Bryan, TX; *m:* Craig; *ed:* (BA) Elem Ed, Baylor Univ 1980; (MS) Elem Ed, Stephen F Austin 1985; *cr:* 6th Grade Teacher CHolson ISD 1980-81; Maypearl ISD 1981-83; 3rd Grade Teacher 1983-84, 5th Grade Teacher 1984-87, 5th Grade Gifted/Talented Teacher 1987-Corsicana ISD; *ai:* Stat 1988-; *office:* Lincoln Elem Sch 1101 E. 13Th Ave. Corsicana TX 75110

TELIGA, DARLENE ANNETTE, English Teacher; *b:* Martins Ferry, OH; *ed:* (BS) Eng, OH Univ 1978; *cr:* Jr HS Teacher 1978-88, Acting Prin 1987-88 St Mary Cntrl; Instr Belmont Tech Coll 1989-; Eng Teacher Belmont Career Center 1988-; *ai:* Levy Comm; NCTE 1988-; NCEA 1978-88; Belmont Cty Spelling Bee Appreciation; Levy Sch Certificate of Appreciation; *office:* Belmont Career Center 110 Fox-Shannon Pl Saint Clairsville OH 43950

TEMME, JAMES JOSEPH, American History Teacher; *b:* St Louis, MO; *m:* Carol Ann Wright; *c:* James G., Mary K.; *ed:* (BS) Geography, 1961, (MA) Geography, 1963 St Louis Univ; Scndry Admin & Voc Ed; *cr:* Teacher St Marys HS 1963-64; Teacher/Admin St Thomas Aquinas HS 1964-66; Teacher/Dept Chm Crosskeys Jr HS 1968-75; Teacher Westwood Jr HS 1975-; *ai:* Tennis Coach; Phi Delta Kappa 1986-; Whos Who in MO Ed 1974; Most Influential Teacher Awd 1987-89; *office:* Westwood Jr HS 7630 Arapaho Rd Dallas TX 75248

TEMPERILLI, JOHN ROBERT, Biology Instructor; *b:* Ft Sill, OK; *m:* Paula Elaine Smith; *c:* John P., Patrick; *ed:* (MPA) Marine Resource Management, 1981, (BA) Poly Sci, 1976 TX A&M Univ; Grad Stud Bio, TX A&M 1988; Grad Fellow Sci, Baylor Coll of Medicine 1985; *cr:* Research Asst TX A&M 1979-81; Fisheries Observer Natl Marine Fisheries Service 1981-83; Marine Biologist Natl Marine Mammal Lab 1984; Bio Instr Booker T Washington HS 1984-; Chem/Bio Instr Upward Bound Univ of Houston 1987-; *ai:* Faculty Advisory & Greenhouse Curr Comm; Project Access Sci Rep; People to People Delegation Leader USSR Summer Trip 1990; Asst Var Bsbl Coach; Testing Coord Bio Dept; Honors Instr; Sci Tutor; Faculty Advisory Comm; SW Bsbl Umpires Assn 1989-; Natl Wildlife Fed, Nature Conservancy 1990; *office:* Booker T Washington HS 119 E 39th St Houston TX 77018

TEMPLE, MICHAEL EDWARD, Fifth Grade Teacher; *b:* Houston, TX; *m:* Kristine Marie Hassen; *c:* Cody, Cassidy; *ed:* (BS) Ed, E OR Coll 1968; (MS) Ed, Univ of OR 1971; *cr:* 4th/5th Grade Teacher Twin Oaks 1968-83; 5th Grade Teacher Washington Elem 1983-; *ai:* Teacher Advisory Comm; Sch Leadership Team Mem; Eugene Ed 1981-82; Bargaining Team 1987-88.

TEMPLETON, ALLEN, Science Teacher; *b:* Albuquerque, NM; *c:* Sandra A., Dina D. Ward, Evan A., Vanessa J., Amanda N.; *ed:* (BA) Ed, Univ of NM 1969; Grad Work Environmental Stud & Admin; *cr:* Teacher Albuquerque Public Schls 1969-; Consultant BLM 1975-77, US Forest Service 1975; Teacher Albuquerque Tech Voc Inst 1984-; *ai:* Spon of Environmental Stud Field Trips; ACTA 1969-86, NSTA 1969-83; Bosque Del Rio Grande Nature Preserve Society (Pres 1977-79, Bd Mem 1979-83), Teacher of Yr 1976; Volunteers for The Outdoors Chm Bd of Finance 1983-85, Volunteer of Yr 1984; Bernilibo Cty Soil Dist Teacher of Yr 1976; St of NM Volunteer of Yr 1984; *home:* 12713 Hugh Graham NE Albuquerque NM 87111

TEMPLETON, M. ARDIS POSSANZA, Reading/English Teacher; *b:* Scranton, PA; *m:* Thomas; *c:* Milena, Janine; *ed:* (BA) Eng, Marywood Coll 1971; Working on MFA Creative Writing; *cr:* Rdng Specialist Hurley 1978-83; Rdng/Eng/Creative Writing Forest City Regional 1983-; *ai:* HS Newspaper & Sr Class Adv; NEA 1983-; NE PA Writing Project 1989-; Poetry Published; *office:* Forest City Regional Sch 100 Susquehanna St Forest City PA 18412

TEMPLETON, MARJORIE COOPER, Retired; *b:* Smithshire, IL; *m:* Elvin; *c:* Jean Hagmeier, Shirley Bauer, Jim; *ed:* Elem Ed, Western IL Univ 1942; (BA) Elem Ed, IA Wesleyan 1959; (MS) Elem Ed/Remedial Rdng, Western IL UNIV 1969; *cr:* 1st/8th Grade Teacher Stine Sch 1942-43, Belmont 1955-59; 3rd Grade Teacher Keokuk Comm Schls 1959-83; *ai:* Organized Carrie Raich Schlsp; NEA 1955; IA St Ed Assn 1955-87; Keokuk Ed Assn 1955-87; Lee Cty Rdng Cncl 1965-70; Lincoln Sch PTA 1959-87; Delta Kappa Gamma IA; Lifetime PTA Memership; Nom Natl PTA Phoebe Apperson Hearst Outstanding Ed Awd; *home:* R R 2 Box 167 Keokuk IA 52632

TEMPLIN, DON LYNN, Mathematics Department Chair; *b:* Speedwell, TN; *m:* Nancy Fowler; *c:* Daryl, Bryan; *ed:* (BS) Math, Lincoln Memorial Univ 1967; (MS) Health/Ed, Union Coll 1974; Grad Stud Univ of TN; Trained Medic US Natl Guard; *cr:* Teacher Murray Cty HS 1967-69, Lafollette HS 1969-75, Campbell Cty HS 1975-; *ai:* Math Dept Chm; Math Club; AFT 1977-; TN Scndry Math Teacher Assn 1979-; NCTM 1967-79; Campbell Cty Teacher Advisory Comm 1988-; Campbell Cty 4-H Lifestock Advisory Comm 1987-, Chm 1987; Outstanding Young Teachers of America 1972; Math Dept Chm Campbell Cty HS 1979; Campbell Cty HS Outstanding Teacher 1982; TN Career Ladder Level III 1987-88; Campbell Cty Outstanding Teacher Awd, Scndry 1988; *home:* Rt 1 Box 191 La Follette TN 37766

TENCH, LYNN BARNETT, Media Specialist; *b:* Demorest, GA; *m:* Marcus; *c:* Allison T.; *ed:* (BA) Eng, Piedmont Coll 1978; (MED) Eng Ed, N GA Coll 1980; (EDS) Instructional Technology, Univ of GA 1990; *cr:* Eng Teacher 1977-88, Media Specialist 1988- S Habersham Jr HS; *ai:* Stu Cncl Spon; HAE, GAE, NEA Building Rep 1989-; GMLA 1988-; Delta Kappa Gamma (2nd VP 1990, Prgm Chm 1988-); Phi Kappa Phi 1980-; Torch Honor Society (VP 1981-83, Pres 1983-85); Alpha Chi Treas 1977; Teacher of Yr 1983-84; State-Wide Eng Faculty of Yr Mem 1988; Nom for St Eng Teacher of Yr Awd 1988; Outstanding Young Woman of America 1988; Whos Who in Amer Colls & Univs 1976-77; *office:* S Habersham Jr HS Cleveland Rd Cornelia GA 30531

TENGES, JOHN WILLIAM, Math/Computer Science Teacher; *b:* West Allis, WI; *m:* Gwyn L. Nodolf; *c:* Joshua, Ryan; *ed:* (BS) Math, 1971, (BS) Scndry Ed, 1973 Univ WI Platteville; Master Prgm, Cardinal Stritch Univ; *cr:* Math/IA Instr Janesville Public Schls 1973-74; Math/Cmptr Instr Blackhawk Cmmty Schls 1974-83, Sch Dist of Random Lake 1983-; *ai:* Girls Track, Boys & Girls Cross Cntry Head Coach; NCTM (Regional Conference Organizing Comm Mem 1987) 1973-; Milwaukee Educl Computing Assn 1979-; WI Math Cncl 1973-; WI Track Coaches Assn Dist Rep 1975-; WI Cross Cntry Coaches Assn 1983-; *office:* Sch Dist of Random Lake 605 Random Lake Rd Random Lake WI 53075

TEN HOOR, JANICE HEATH, 9th Grade English Teacher; *b:* Montezvma, GA; *c:* Terri L.; *ed:* (BS) Bus Admin, GA Coll 1957; (MS) Management/Supervision, Cntrl MI 1977; Working Beyond Masters Eng 1979-81; *cr:* Bus Ed Teacher Carrollton HS 1957-58, Albany HS 1958-61, Warner Robins Jr HS 1972-75; Eng Teacher Warner Robins Jr HS 1979-; *ai:* Drama Club Spon; SDV Team Mem; Staff Dev; Worked With Writing Current Eng Curr; PAGE 1986-; Pilot Club Intnl 1973-75, Rewarded for Starting Helpine Hand in Warner Robins 1975; Rape Advocate 1982-83; Lang Art Teacher of Yr 1985; Warner Robins Jr Teacher of Yr 1989; *office:* Warner Robins Jr HS Mary Ln Warner Robins GA 31088

TENNER, FRANK HARRISON, 6th Grade Teacher/Science/Math; *b:* Mt Holly, NJ; *m:* Carol D'Alessandro; *c:* Jason, Jaime; *ed:* (BA) Psych, Roger Williams Coll 1974; (MA) Psych, Glassboro St Coll 1980; *cr:* Teacher Clara Barton Sch 1974-; *ai:* Cmptr, Sci Curr Comm; NEA/NJ Ed Assn 1974-; Bordentown Regional Ed Assn VP 1974-; Cncl for Elem Sci Intnl 1989-; Prof Photographers of America 1989-; Jacksonville Cmnty Center Treas 1981-87; Eastampton Soccer Club Coach 1981-89; *office:* Clara Barton Schl 100 Crosswicks St Bordentown NJ 08505

TEPPER, WINNIE BARNES, Third Grade Teacher; *b:* Crestview, FL; *m:* William Louis; *c:* William, Sherrilyn, Nancy; *ed:* (BS) Elem Ed, 1975, (MA) Elem Ed, 1980 Univ of N AL; *cr:* 2nd/3rd Grade Teacher Priceville Sch 1975-; *ai:* Parent Volunteer Prgm; Chairperson of Steering Comm for Accreditation of Sch; Kappa Delta Pi 1974-; Phi Kappa Phi 1980-; Phi Delta Kappa 1986-; Teachers Credit Union (Pres 1983-89, VP 1990); PTO VP 1989-; *home:* Rt 4 Box 363 Hartselle AL 35640

TER HARK, JEAN (MACK), Chorus Teacher; *b:* Spiril Lake, IA; *m:* Ronald; *c:* David, Douglas; *ed:* (BA) Music Ed, Buena Vista Coll 1964; (MA) Music Ed, Univ of ID 1983; *cr:* Eng Teacher Holstein HS 1964-65; K-12th Grade Music Teacher Post Falls Sch Dist 273 1965-67; Jr HS Chorus Teacher Coeur D Alene Jr HS 1968-70; Chorus Teacher Coeur D Alene Sr HS 1973-; *ai:* Sr Class Adv; Wrestling Pep Club; Amer Choral Dir Assn of ID Pres 1987-89; ID Music Educators Dist 271 (Choral Chairperson 1989-) Educator of Month 1986; Dist Music Teachers Assn (Secy, Pres, Treas); 1st Presbyn Church (Deacon 1978-89, Elder 1987-89); *office:* Coeur D Alene Sr HS N 5530 4th Coeur D'Alene ID 83814

TERIBURY, THOMAS MOTT, 5th Grade Teacher; *b:* Elmira, NY; *m:* Katie Shannon; *c:* Thomas; *ed:* (AS) Sci, Mid GA Coll 1973; (BS) Mid Sch Sci/Soc Sci, 1975, (MED) Mid Sch Sci/Soc Sci, 1978 Univ of GA; Addl Stud Environmental Affairs & Archaeology; *cr:* 5th Grade Teacher Peachtree City Elem Sch 1975-80, Huddleston Elem Sch 1980-; *ai:* Gymnastics Coach; Young Astronauts Club Co-Spon; Numerous Curr & Textbook Adoption Comms; GA Assn of Educators Rep 1980-; The Roundtable Excl Elem Sci Teaching 1987; Nom GA Power Company Sci Teacher of Yr 1987; *home:* 280 Palmetto Rd Tyrone GA 30290

TERLIZZI, RICHARD SAMUEL, Observer/Evaluator; *b:* Jacksonville, FL; *m:* Vannah Richardson; *c:* Christy, Anna; *ed:* (BS) Math, Furman Univ 1983; (MAT) Math, Univ of NC Chapel Hill 1984; Admin Cert; Supervision Cert; *cr:* 7-9 Math Teacher/Chm Piedmont Open Mid Sch 1984-88; Observer/Evaluator Charlotte-Mecklenburg Schls 1988-; *ai:* TAC; FAC; Chess Club Spon; NCCTM 1984-; NCTM 1980-; Phi Delta Kappa 1988-; Lyndhurst Fellowship; *home:* 9412 Errington Ln Charlotte NC 28227

TERMAN, KEN L., Chemistry Teacher/Tennis Coach; *b:* Mansfield, OH; *m:* Rosalie Black; *c:* Kecia, Joel; *ed:* (BS) Chem, Ashland Univ 1958; (MS) Chem, Miami of OH; Wkshps Brown Univ, Hope Coll, Miami of OH, Bowling Green Univ; *cr:* Chem/Bio Teacher/Ftbl Asst Smithville HS 1958-60; Chem/Bio Teacher/Bsktbl/Golf/Tennis Coach Shelby HS 1960-; *ai:* NEA, OEA, ACS, SEA; Shelby City Cncl Councilman 1980-84; NSF Grants Miami of OH, Brown Univ, Bowling Green Univ, Hope Coll; *home:* 72 Louise Dr Shelby OH 44875

TERMINI, JOSEPHINE, 5th Grade Teacher; *b:* Brooklyn, NY; *ed:* (BS) Elem Ed, OK St Univ 1973; *cr:* 2nd Grade Teacher 1973-75, 3rd Grade Teacher 1975-78, 4th Grade Teacher 1978-80, 6th Grade Teacher 1980-81, 3rd Grade Teacher 1981-89, 5th Grade Teacher 1989- Madison Park Elem Sch; *ai:* OBEA, MCEA, NJEA, PTA, NEA; *home:* 10 Pensacola St Old Bridge NJ 08857

TERMUHLEN, HELEN FORREST, 4th Grade Teacher; *b:* Jefferson Township, OH; *c:* Richard, David, Douglas; *ed:* (BS) Ed, 1970; (ME) Ed, 1982 Miami Univ; *cr:* 1st Grade Teacher 1968-71, 4th Grade Teacher 1971- Franklin City Sch; *ai:* Franklin Ed Assn 1970-; Miamisburg Bus & Prof Women 1982-89; Literary Club (Pres, VP, Treas) 1989; Excl in Teaching Awd 1989.

TERNES, LINDA (WOODWORTH), Mathematics Teacher; *b:* Santa Clara, Cuba; *m:* Jerry Bruce; *c:* Joshua, Tyler; *ed:* (BA) Math, S CA Coll 1979; Grad Work Math, CA St Univ Fullerton; Cmptr Software Ed; *cr:* Math Teacher Costa Mesa HS 1979, Chrstn Challenge Acad 1979-80, Newport Chrstn HS 1980-; Editorial Asst Chrstn Trng Network 1983-; Span/Math Instr S CA Coll 1983-; *ai:* Asst Ed for Chrstn Trng Network which Publishes Educl Textbrooks, Other Materials & a Quarterly Magazine in Span; *office:* Newport Chrstn HS 3101 Pacific View Dr Corona Del Mar CA 92665

TERPAK, DOROTHY ANN, First Grade Teacher; *b:* New York, NY; *ed:* (BA) His/Rdng, Aquinas Coll 1981; *cr:* Religion Tutor St Mary Magdalen 1973-; 1st-3rd Grade Teacher St Marys Visitation 1981-; *ai:* MI Rdng Assn 1980-; *office:* St Marys Visitation Sch 2459 146th Ave Byron Center MI 49315

TERRANOVA, LOUIS JAMES, Sixth Grade Teacher; *b:* Jersey City, NJ; *m:* Patricia Ann Clark; *c:* Kim M., Ken D.; *ed:* (BA) Elem Ed, 1970, (MA) Rdng, 1975 Jersey City St; Ed Credits, JCSC & Rutgers Univ; Cmptr & In-Service Credits; Rdng Specialist Certificate in Rdng, Jersey City St 1975; *cr:* 5th-8th Grade Teacher Kennedy Sch 1970-; *ai:* Girls Sftbl Team Head Coach; Audio-Visual Coord; Reach Out Action Prgm Comm Mem; North Bergen Fed of Teachers, AFT 1970-; NJ Ed Assn, North Bergen Ed Assn 1986-; Jaycees 1977-84; Hudson Cty Umpires Assn 1972-86; Governors Teacher Recognition Prgm Outstanding Teacher 1989-; Hudson Cty Recognition for Outstanding Prgm Establishing Mini-Cmmty in Classroom; *office:* Kennedy Sch 1210 11th St North Bergen NJ 07047

TERRASI, ROBERT MICHAEL, Counselor; *b:* Monroe, MI; *m:* Rose Fiorini; *c:* Robert, Renee; *ed:* (BS) Soc Sci, 1976, (MA) Guidance/Counseling, 1979 E MI; *cr:* Teacher Christianity Sch 1976-87; Cnslr Monroe & Cantrick Jr HS 1987-; *ai:* Elem Counseling Comm; MI Ed Assn Local Pres 1986-; Monroe Cty Teachers Credit Union Bd Mem; *home:* 448 St Marys Ave Monroe MI 48161

TERRAZAS, BILL, JR., Teacher; *b:* Los Angeles, CA; *m:* Teresa M. Corona; *c:* Stefanie, Noah; *ed:* (AA) Sociology, E Los Angeles Comm Coll 1970-; (BS) Recreation/Sociology, CA St Univ Los Angeles 1971; (MA) Bi-ling/Bilcultural Ed, Univ of S CA 1973; High Intensive Lang Trng; Specification in Teaching Eng to Speakers of Other Lang; St Licensed Contractor Building; Real-Estate Investor, Developer; *cr:* Aquatics Dir/Life Guard Eastside Boys Club 1965-70; Teacher Briggs Sch 1971-73, Channel Islands HS 1973-; *ai:* Started Bi-ling/Migrant Ed Open House; Fought for Legal Rights of Lep Stus; Won Fellowship to USC Sch of Ed 1971; Teacher of Yr 1975; *office:* Channel Islands HS 1400 Raider Way Oxnard CA 93033

TERRELL, CAROLYN WELLS, Science Department Chair; *b:* Murray, KY; *m:* James A.; *ed:* (BS) Bio, Murray St Univ 1970; (MA) Educl Admin, Univ of TX San Antonio 1976; Administrative Mid-Management Cert; *cr:* Sci Teacher Harris Mid Sch 1970-71, Sci Teacher/Coach Horace Mann Mid Sch 1971-76; Math Teacher Wheatley HS 1976-77; Sci Teacher Holmes HS 1977-82, Hobby Mid Sch 1982-; *ai:* Sci Dept Coord; Sci Fair Team Coach; Assn of TX Prof Educators, Sci Teachers Assn of TX 1982-; Coached Regional Sci Fair Championship Teams 1988, 1990; *office:* Hobby Mid Sch 11843 Vance Jackson San Antonio TX 78230

TERRELL, KATHY (QUARY), 2nd Grade Teacher; *b:* Prague, OK; *m:* Audie; *c:* Austin, Shai; *ed:* (BS) Elem Ed, OK Baptist Univ 1980; *cr:* 5th/6th Grade Teacher Bethel Elem Sch 1980-81; 2nd Grade Teacher Prague Elem Sch 1981-; *ai:* Czech Club Mem; Staff Dev Comm Chairperson 1985; 1st Baptist Church 1983-; Teacher of Yr 1985-86; *home:* Rt 2 Prague OK 74864

TERRELL, KATHY ZYCH, Chorus & Music Teacher; *b:* Marianna, FL; *m:* Terry David; *ed:* (BFA) Music, Univ of FL 1968; (MS) Music, Univ of AZ 1974; Cert Courses Varying Exceptionalities, FL St Univ; *cr:* Music Teacher Okeechobee Elem 1968-69, White City Elem 1969-72; Spec Ed Teacher Leon Detention Center 1975-77; Music Teacher Ferry Pass Mid 1977-; *ai:* Cty Comm Paperwork & Forms; Beta Club Spon; Dept Chairperson Fine Arts; Advisory Comm; Curr Cncl; Escambia Cty Music Educators Assn Pres 1987-89; Music Educators Natl Conference 1988-; Escambia Ed Assn VP 1989-91; Democratic Exec Comm 1984-; Escambia Employee of Month; Teacher of Yr Ferry Pass Mid Sch; Chorus Rated Superior at Dist Festival; Fnd for Excl Grant for Music; *office:* Ferry Pass Mid Sch 8355 Yancey Ave Pensacola FL 32514

TERRELL, MARYETTA VAN DEVENDER, 5th Grade Mathematics Teacher; *b:* Mobile, AL; *m:* Robert Allen; *c:* C. Allen, R. Brandon; *ed:* (BS) Home Ec Ed, Auburn Univ 1960; (MA) Elem Ed, Univ of AL 1978; *cr:* Spec Ed Teacher AL Avenue

Mid Sch 1974-75; 4th Grade Teacher West End Elem 1975-83, Evans Elem 1983-85, East Elem 1985-88; 5th Grade Math Teacher Evans Elem 1988-; *ai:* Gamma Belles; Teacher of Yr 1985; Nom Jacksonville Teacher of Yr 1976.

TERRELL, SOPHIA BROWN, English/Gifted Ed Teacher; *b:* Cantonment, FL; *m:* Earl Frank; *c:* Gregory D., Valeria L.; *ed:* (BS) Eng, Southern Univ 1965; (MAT) Eng, Univ of W FL 1984; *cr:* 2nd Grade Teacher Ransom Sch 1965-66; Eng/Soc Stud Teacher Ransom HS 1966-68; Eng/Speech Teacher Wedgewood HS 1968-69; Eng Teacher Carver Mid Sch 1971-72, Woodham HS 1969-70, 1972-; *ai:* 10th Grade Eng Grade Level Chairperson; Faculty Advisory Comm Mem; Escambia Cty Cncl Teachers of Eng Corresponding Secy 1983-84; FL Cncl Teachers of Eng, Escambia Ed Assn, FL Ed Assn, NEA; Debuaires Civic Club Incorporated Pres 1985-86; St Paul AMEZ Church Secy 1968-, Woodham HS Teacher of Yr ; *home:* 1135 Germain St Pensacola FL 32534

TERRELL, TERRY RAY, 5th/6th Grade Teacher; *b:* Durant, OK; *m:* Candy Robinson; *c:* Karale; *ed:* (BA) Elem Ed, SE OK St Univ 1980; Drivers Ed, Phys Ed, Soc Stud; *cr:* 5th-8th Grade Teacher Yuba Sch 1980-; *ai:* 4-H Judging Team Coach; 5th-8th Grade Bsktbl Coach 1981-88; *office:* Yuba Elem Sch R R 1 Hendrix OK 74741

TERRELL JR, GOLDIE JACKSON, 9th Grade English Teacher; *b:* Memphis, TN; *m:* Karen Patterson; *c:* Jonathan P.; *ed:* (BA) Eng, Chrstn Brothers Univ 1970; (MED) Educl Admin/ Supervision, Memphis St Univ 1973; *cr:* 6th Grade Elem Teacher Woodstock Elem Sch 1970-72; Teacher/Asst Bsktbl Coach Germantown HS 1972-; 10th Grade Eng Teacher Millington HS 1980-81; *ai:* Asst Var Bsktbl Coach; Head Coach of Jr Var Bsktbl Team; NEA, TN Ed Assn, Shelby Cty Ed Assn 1970-; *home:* 4121 Sassafras River Dr Memphis TN 38125

TERRY, BETTY DAVIS, 5th/6th Grade Lang Art Teacher; *b:* Cheswold, DE; *m:* Raymond; *c:* Elizabeth, William, Frances, Ellen Reichard, David; *ed:* (BA) Elem Ed, Antioch Coll 1954; (MED) Elem Ed, Wittenberg Univ 1962; Univ of MD, Trinity Coll, Western MD Coll; *cr:* Ed Instr Antioch Coll Lab Sch 1954-61; 3rd Grade Teacher Burns Park Elem 1961-62; Ed Instr Univ of HI 1962-64; 3rd-6th Grade Teacher Prince Georges Cty Public Schls 1983-; *ai:* LDS Church Teacher 1963-; Danforth Grant; Article Published; *home:* 11505 Montgomery Rd Beltsville MD 20705

TERRY, BRUCE DAVID, K-8th Grade Principal; *b:* San Bernardino, CA; *m:* Maureen Thomas; *ed:* (BA) Sociology, Univ CA Riverside 1971, (MS) Ed Admin, CA St Fullerton 1985; Admin Services Credential Univ CA Irvine 1990; *cr:* Teacher Sunnymead Sch & Edgemont Sch 1971-79, Univ Park Sch & Vista Verde Sch 1979-85; Vice Prin 1985-87, Prin 1987- Vista Verde Sch; *ai:* Sch Site Cncl; Cmptr Classes; Assn of CA Sch Admin; Irvine Admin Assn 1987-; PTA; AB803 & Copen Fnd Grant; *office:* Vista Verde Sch 5144 Michelson Dr Irvine CA 92715

TERRY, DIANE DUNN, 4th Grade Teacher; *b:* Toledo, OH; *m:* Ron; *c:* Derek, Dina; *ed:* (BA) Elem Ed, Univ of Toledo 1972; Grad Stud; *cr:* Teacher Benton-Carroll-Salem & Oak Harbor & R C Waters 1972-73, Genoa-Brenner 1973-; *ai:* Head of White Christmas Prgm; Photographs for Brunners His Photo Album; Designer & Care Taker of Brunners Flower Beds; Served on Staffing & Curr Comm; Grandparents Day & Right to Read Week; Educl Excl Comm 1985-88; Vacationland Rdng Mem 1980-; Intnl Rdng Assn; Adults for Brunner to Camper Mem 1983-; Grants for Bird Watching & Learning Value of Money; Wrote Song & Slide Presentation; *office:* Genoa Area Schls West St Genoa OH 43430

TERRY, ILENE SWEETEN, 7th Grade Civics; *b:* Rock Island, OK; *m:* Calvin R.; *c:* Scott, Calene, Ty; *ed:* (BA) Elem Ed, SE OK Univ 1978; Spec Ed; *cr:* 2nd Grade Teacher 1979-87, 7th/8th Grade Rdng/His/Civics Teacher 1987- Shady Point Elem; *ai:* Drug Prgm Coord; 7th Grade Spon; Fund Raising Prgms; Yrbk; Alpha Delta Kappa (Pres 1989-92, St Treas 1988-); NEA, OEA/ Cty Delegate 1986-; OK Rdng Cncl; Kibois Cmmty Action Volunteer, Volunteer for Cty Awd 1989; *office:* Shady Point Elem Sch Box C Shady Point OK 74956

TERRY, JANET E., Fifth Grade Teacher; *b:* Washington, DC; *ed:* (BS) Elem Ed, Radford Univ 1964; (MS) Counseling, VA Tech 1991; *cr:* Classroom Teacher Cameron Elem 1964-67, Graham Road Elem 1967-; *ai:* Safety Patrols Spon; Intergrated Lang Arts Steering Comm; Grade Level Chm; NEA, VA Ed Assn, Fairfax Ed Assn 1964-; Amer Assn for Counseling & Dev, Assn for Multicultural Counseling Dev 1988-; Church Choir Pres 1986-88; PTA Teacher Rep 1980-82; Amer Heart Assn Coord 1987-89; Career Level II Teacher 1989-; Inner City Work with Youth; *office:* Graham Road Elem Sch 3036 Graham Rd Falls Church VA 22042

TERRY, JOYCELYN HARRIS, English II Teacher; *b:* Center, TX; *m:* James David; *c:* Joshua, Jordan; *ed:* (BA) Eng, Lamar Univ 1979; Elem Certificate, Lang Art, Soc Stud; *cr:* World His Teacher 1981-89, Eng II Teacher Lumberton Ind Sch Dist 1988-; *ai:* NHS Spon 1987-89; Future Teachers of America 1980-81; *office:* Lumberton Ind Sch Dist HS P O Box 8123 Lumberton TX 77711

TERRY, KATHEE GERDE, Chemistry Teacher; *b:* Seattle, WA; *m:* Scott A.; *c:* Travis, Mc Kenzie; *ed:* (BA) Chem, Whitman Coll 1971; *cr:* Sci Teacher De Sales Jr/Sr HS 1972-77; Sci/Math Teacher Frazer HS 1977-78; Sci Teacher Marcus Whitman Jr HS 1978-85, Ringdall Mid Sch 1985-86; Chem Teacher Lake Washington HS 1986-; *ai:* NSTA, Amer Chemical Society, WA Sci Teachers Assn; Curr Writing Team 1985-86; WA St Cmptr Ed Guidelines; Currently Reviewing Health Chem Text; Local Sci Teachers& Sci Alliance Pres 1988-89; Ford Fellow Mentor Teacher 1989-; *office:* Lake Washington HS 12033 NE 80th Kirkland WA 98033

TERRY, LORRAINE ANN, Fifth Grade Teacher; *b:* Saint Louis, MO; *m:* Robert E.; *c:* Stephanie L. Bond; *ed:* (BS) Elem Ed, Southeast MO St Univ 1964; *cr:* 5th Grade Teacher Trautwein Elem 1969-; 6th Grade Teacher Franklin Elem 1964-66; *ai:* Stu Cncl Spon; Sci Curr Comm Mehlville Dist; NEA 1969-; MNEA 1980-; Mehlville Sch Dist Teacher of Yr Runner Up 1982; *office:* Trautwein Elem Sch 5011 Ambs Rd Saint Louis MO 63128

TERRY, MICHAEL DARNELL, 7th Grade Physical Ed Teacher; *b:* Henderson, NC; *c:* Shelley, Michael; *ed:* (AS) Phys Ed, Kittrell Jr Coll 1972; (BS) Phys Ed, Fayetteville St Univ 1975; *cr:* Sci/Health Phys Ed 1977-79; Phys Ed 1979- Henderson Jr HS; *ai:* Varsity Bsktbl Head Coach; Varsity Ftbll Asst Coach; Track Head Coach; Intramurals; NCAE; NEA; NC Coaches Assn; Henderson Hr HS Teacher of Yr 1979-86; *office:* Henderson Jr H S 219 Charles St Henderson NC 27536

TERRY, NANCY KEITH, Spanish Teacher; *b:* Columbia, SC; *m:* William David; *c:* Brian, Mandy; *ed:* (BA) Span, Furman Univ 1974; (MAT) Span, Univ of SC 1980; (MARE) Religious Ed, SW Baptist Theological Seminary 1984; *cr:* Span/Eng Teacher Dent Jr HS 1975-79; Span Teacher Spring Valley HS 1979-82; 6th Grade Span Teacher Seminary S Day Sch 1984-85; Span Teacher Parkview HS 1986-; *ai:* Span Club Spon; Foreign Lang Assn of GA, Amer Assn Teachers of Span & Portuguese; Atlanta Baptist Assn BWMU Acteens 1986-89; Briarlake Baptist Church (Dir, Mission Friends, 1st Grade Choir Worker); Lead Wkshps at Foreign Lang Assn of GA; Lead FL Assn Wkshp Span Immersion Camp 1990; *office:* Parkview HS 998 Cole Rd Lilburn GA 30247

TESDAHL, JILL KRISTINE, Phys Ed Teacher/Asst Principal; *b:* Hawarden, IA; *ed:* (BA) Psych/Scndry Ed, Coe Coll 1986; Sch Psych, N AZ Univ; Nutrition, CASA Certificate; *cr:* Customer Service Rep Teleconnect 1986-87; Grad Asst N AZ Univ 1987-88; Substitute Teacher Flagstaff Public Schls 1988-; Sch Cnslr/Admin Asst Ash Fork JUSD #31 1988-; *ai:* NHS & Peer Tutor Adv; Calender Comm; Self Esteem Team; Homeless Project; Academic Hall of Fame; Chi Sigma Iota Mem 1989-, Prof Honor Society Awd 1989; N AZ Gerontology Assn Mem 1988-; Ash Fork Area Ed Assn Mem 1988-89; Wrote Sr Companion Prgm Manual; *office:* Ash Fork JUSD #31 PO Box 247 Ash Fork AZ 86320

TESSITORE, NICK, JR., 1st Grade Teacher; *b:* Walsenburg, CO; *m:* Kathryn Alessie; *c:* Nicholas III, Angelea; *ed:* (BA) Elem Ed/Spec Ed, Adams St Coll 1975; (MA) Rdng/Elem, Univ of N CO 1980; Working Towards Admin Cert; Working Towards Masters Admin; *cr:* EMH/EMR Teacher Eleven Mile Corner Sch 1975-76; TMR Teacher Developmental Trng Services 1976-77; 3rd Grade Teacher 1977-88, 1st Grade Teacher 1988- Longfellow Elem Sch; *ai:* Collegiate Peaks Rdng Cncl Pres; Elem Accountability Comm; NEA 1977-83; Intnl Rdng Assn (Pres, VP) 1983-; ASCD 1989-; Longfellow Teachers Assn Pres 1985-87; High Cntry Fine Arts Assn Bd Mem 1983-87; Univ of N CO Admin Internship; *office:* Longfellow Elem Sch 8th & I Street Salida CO 81201

TETER, JANET T., Fourth Grade Teacher; *b:* Staunton, VA; *m:* Frank E.; *ed:* (BA) Elem/Sci, Madison Coll 1965; Many Ed Courses; *cr:* 5th/6th Grade Teacher Patrick Henry Elem 1965-84; 5th Grade Teacher James K Polk Elem 1984-89; 4th Grade Teacher George Mason Elem 1989-; *ai:* Faculty Cncl Mem; NEA, VEA, EAA, (Local, Sch Rep); PTA; Local Citizens Assn.

TETERS, PEGGY L., Elementary Science Supervisor; *b:* Fort Scott, KS; *w:* Clarence J. (dec); *c:* Larry, Susan Forte, Patti Smith; *ed:* (BSED) 1969, (MSED) 1978, Elem Admin 1979 SW MO St Univ; *cr:* Elem Teacher 1969-85, Elem Sci Resource Teacher 1981-85 Springfield Public Schls; Instr Evangel Coll 1987-89; Curr Supvr Springfield Public Schls 1986-; *ai:* Adopt-A-Sch & Jr League Hands on Sci Prgms; Super Sci Saturday Elem Sci Fair; NSTA (Division Dir 1982-84, Exec Comm Mem 1983-84, Prgm Chairperson 1989-); Elem Sci Nationwide; *office:* Springfield Public Schls 940 N Jefferson Springfield MO 65802

TEUFEL, GEORGE WILLIAM, Social Studies Teacher; *b:* Mount Carmel, PA; *m:* Mary Edwards; *c:* George R., Robert S.; *ed:* (BS) Health/Phys Ed, Lock Haven Univ 1949; (MED) Admin, PA St Univ 1954; Working Towards Ed Penn St Uniiv; *cr:* Health/ Phys Ed Teacher 1950-63, Prin 1963-66 Jersey Shore Sr HS; Scndry Ed Dir Williamsport Sch Dist 1966-74; Soc Stud Teacher Jersey Shore Jr HS 1974-; *ai:* Jr HS Bsktbl Coach 1989-; Stu Cncl Cnslr & Adv; NEA, PSEA 1950-; Phi Delta Kappa 1963-; Masonic Lodge 1954-; Lions Club Mem 1951-; Williamsport Consis Troy W Branch Sports Hall of Fame VP 1980-; Jersey Shore Borough Mayor 1978-; Jersey Shore Kiwanis Club Outstanding Service Awd 1989; Lock Haven Univ Outstanding Distinguished Alumni Awd 1989.

TEVENDALE, RICHARD MICHAEL, Science Department Chair; *b:* Rochester, NY; *m:* Janet Lacy; *c:* Shawn, David; *ed:* (BA) Bio, 1974, (MED) Sci Ed, 1976 Univ of VA; Emphasis on Rdng in Content Areas Cntrl VA Project & Writing to Learn; *cr:* 6th Grade Sci Teacher Walton Mid Sch 1976-77; 7th/8th Grade Teacher Jack Jouett Mid Sch 1977-; *ai:* In-Service Trng of Teachers in Rdng to Learn, Writing to Learn; NSTA 1978-; Charlottesville-Albemarle Volunteer Rescue Squad 1987-; *office:* Jack Jouett Mid Sch 2065 Lambs Rd Charlottesville VA 22901

THACKER, CHARLES ERNEST, Fourth Grade Teacher; *b:* Inglewood, CA; *m:* Jacquelyn Harris; *c:* Nathaniel; *ed:* (BA) His, Long Beach St 1972; Working Towards Masters Bus & Clinical Supervision; *cr:* 6th Grade Teacher Tarpey Elem 1973-77; 5th Grade Teacher Phoenix Elem 1977-79; 4th Grade Teacher Lincoln Elem 1979-86, Bellview Elem 1986-; *ai:* Intramural, Babe Ruth Bsbl, YMCA Bsktbl Coach; Dist Soc Stud & Sch Grant Comm; Ashland Ed Assn Building Rep 1989; OR Ed Assn Mem; Church Sunday Sch Teacher *office:* Bellview Elem Sch 1070 Tolman Creek Ashland OR 97520

THACKER, DELLA KAY, Math Dept Chair/Asst Professor; *b:* Vincennes, IN; *m:* Tim; *c:* Wade; *ed:* (BS) Math, 1982, (MS) Math, 1985 IN St Univ; Gifted & Talented Endorsement 1988-; *cr:* Math Instr IN St Univ Sch 1983-; *ai:* Math Contest Coach; Girls Club Adv; Faculty Affairs Comm; NCTM, IN Cncl of Teachers of Math, Natl Assn of Laboratory Schls 1982-; IN Assn of Gifted 1988-; YWCA Y-Teens Teacher of Yr 1985; First Chrstn Church; Mid Grade Assessment Prgm; Lilly Endowment Mid Sch Prof Dev Sessions; Presented Math/Sci Make-It-Take-It for Natl Assn of Laboratory Sch; Regional & Natl Conventions Shelburn Sch Systems; *home:* RR 16 Box 404 Brazil IN 47834

THACKER, RANDALL, HS Social Studies Teacher; *b:* Youngstown, OH; *m:* Robin Grissom; *c:* Rachelle, Matthew; *ed:* (BS) Soc Stud, SW MO St Univ 1981; Grad Stud Counseling; *cr:* 6th Grade Teacher Univ Christian 1981-82; Soc Stud Teacher Decatur Christian 1982-85; Sr HS Soc Stud Teacher/Admin Decatur Christian 1985-; *ai:* HS Bsktbl Coach 1983-; Sr Class Spon 1986-; *office:* Decatur Christian 3770 N Water Decatur IL 62526

THANNER, JAMES FREDERICK, English Department Chair; *b:* Baltimore, MD; *m:* Julia B., Jesse;; *ed:* (BS) Elem Ed, Salisbury St Coll 1976; (MED) Elem Ed, Towson St Univ 1984; *cr:* 5th Grade Teacher Victory Villa Elem 1976-81; 5th/6th Grade Teacher Edgemere Elem 1981-87; Eng Teacher Sparrows Point Mid Sch 1987-; *ai:* Phi Delta Kappa 1986-; *home:* 2136 Riverview Rd Baltimore MD 21221

THARP, PATRICIA CORDELL, 6th Grade Teacher; *b:* Nacogdoches, TX; *m:* Martin Allen; *c:* Teague, Tana, Trudi; *ed:* (BS) Elem Ed, Stephen F Austin 1970; *cr:* Houston Ind Sch Dist 1970-72; Wells Ind Sch Dist 1973-74; Caldwell Ind Sch Dist 1975-; *ai:* Detention Hall Teacher; TCTA; Burleson Cty Soil & Water Conservation Teacher of Yr Awd; *office:* Caldwell Mid Sch 203 N Gray Caldwell TX 77836

THARPE, DEBORAH C., English Teacher; *b:* Ft Belvoir, VA; *ed:* (BSE) Eng, Cntrl MO St Univ 1979; *cr:* Teacher Tuscumbia HS 1979-; *ai:* Cheerleading Spon; Drama Dir; Newspaper & Yrbk Adv; Schlsp Comm; Sigma Tau Delta.

THAUT, GERALD EDWARD, Junior High Science Teacher; *b:* Custer, MT; *m:* Niki Buechler; *ed:* (BS) Scndry Ed, Eastern MT Coll 1971; *cr:* Sci Teacher Shepherd Jr HS 1972-77 & 1980-; *ai:* Jr HS Bsktbl; MT Sci Teacher Assn; *office:* Shepherd Jr HS P O Box 8 Shepherd MT 59079

THAYER, JANICE ANN, First Grade Teacher; *b:* Bristol, VA; *ed:* (BS) Elem Ed, Carson Newman Coll 1974; (MED) Elem Ed, Univ of VA 1982; Natl Geographic Summer Geography Inst for Teachers at James Madison Univ 1989; Clinch Valley Coll Univ of VA, Radford Univ, Univ of VA; *cr:* Kndgtn Teacher Stonewall Jackson Elem 1974-75, Joseph B Van Pelt Elem 1975-79; 1st Grade Teacher Joseph B Van Pelt Elem 1979-; *ai:* Bristol VA Schls Communication Comm Mem 1989-; NEA, VEA, Bristol VA Ed Assn Building Rep 1978-79; Alpha Delta Kappa (Corresponding Secy 1986-88, VP 1990); SW VA Cncl Teachers of Math Mem 1985-; Van Pelt PTA (Historian, Exec Bd Mem, Cultural Arts Chm) 1987-88, Awd for Distinguished Service VA Congress of PTA 1988; Euclid Avenue Baptist Church (Stewardship Comm, Schlsp Comm, Library Comm); Co-Chairperson of Van Pelt Elems Self Study for Southern Assn of Schls & Colleges 1987-89; Nom Rotary Club Outstanding Teacher Awd 1987, 1989; *office:* Joseph B Van Pelt Elem Sch 200 Springhill Terr Bristol VA 24201

THAYER, MARGARET MAY (ACORD), First Grade Teacher; *b:* Susanville, CA; *m:* Douglas James; *c:* Elizabeth, Mathew, Jeanette; *ed:* (BA) Child Dev, UC Berkeley 1956; Life Teaching Credential Elem Ed, UC Chico; *cr:* 4th Grade Teacher Williams Elem Sch 1956-57; Kndgtn Teacher 1968-84, 1st Grade Teacher 1984- Alturas Elem Sch; *ai:* AAUW (Secy, VP); IRA Secy, Annual Rdng Awd 1988; Alturas Elem Site Cncl Secy; Cmmty Choir 1980-; Published Article CA Rdng Assn Proceedings 1977.

THEDE, AUDREY STEWARD, 7th-8th Grade Soc Stud Teacher; *b:* Shiocton, WI; *m:* Quintin I.; *c:* Debbie D. Thede Croell, Dana D., Diana D. Thede Oberg; *ed:* (BA) Elem Ed, WI St Univ Oshkosh; Miscellaneous Classes; Unit Leadership Trng, Milwaukee; *cr:* 1st-8th Grade Teacher Cedar Grove Elem 1955-58, Springbrook Sch 1958-63; 7th Grade Teacher Shiocton Grade 1963-65; 1st-2nd/7th-8th Grade Teacher Little Chute Elem 1965-67; 6th-8th Grade Teacher Black Creek Grade 1967-; *ai:* Coaching Conservation Speaking Contests; WI Ed Assn, Seymour Ed Assn; *home:* R 1 Box 146 Thede Rd Black Creek WI 54106

THEILER, TULA DRIVAS, 3rd Grade Elementary Teacher; *b:* Wisconsin Rapids, WI; *m:* Charles; *c:* Kristina, Jeremy; *ed:* (BS) Elem, Univ of WI Stevens Point 1975; Grad Stud; *cr:* Kndgtn Teacher Washington Sch 1975-76; 3rd Grade Teacher Bradley Sch 1976-78, Harrison Sch 1978-80, Tomahawk Elem Sch; *ai:* Elem Stu Cncl Adv; Ed Week Comm; Great Booksleader; Project Charlie Leader; *home:* 1415 Theiler Dr Tomahawk WI 54487

THEILLE, ANTHONY, English Teacher; *b:* New York, NY; *ed:* (BA) Eng, Hunter Coll 1968; (MS) Rdng/Learning Disabilities, Univ of S ME 1976; (ED) Eng/Lang Art, Boston Univ 1990; *cr:* 6th Grade Teacher Whitefield Elem Sch 1970-72; Eng Teacher Westbrook Jr HS 1972-74; Spec Ed Teacher Westbrook HS 1974-76; Rdng Consultant Exeter Area Sch Dist 1976-77; Eng Teacher Portsmouth Jr HS 1977-; *ai:* Trng Stus John Hopkins Talent Search; NCTE, Intnl Rdng Assn, Linguistic Society of Amer; *office:* Portsmouth Jr HS Parrott Ave Portsmouth NH 03842

THEISEN, TERESA JUNE, English Teacher; *b:* Osmond, NE; *ed:* (BAE) Eng/His, 1979, (MAE) Eng/Amer Lit, 1984 Wayne St Coll; Eng as 2nd Lang; Prof Leadership Trng; Gifted & Talented Ed; *cr:* Eng Teacher Wayne HS 1979-80; Eng/Journalism Teacher Norfolk Jr HS 1980-85; Eng Teacher San Marcos HS 1985-; *ai:* Key Club Kiwanis; Gifted & Talented Prgm; Mentor Prgm San Marcos Schls; NCTE 1980-; Classroom Teachers Assn 1985-; Sigma Tau Delta 1976-79; Natl Cardinal Key Honorary 1977-79; *office:* San Marcos HS 1901 Hwy 123 San Marcos TX 78666

THEISS, KATHRYN BARKER, 6th Grade Teacher; *b:* Leavenworth, KS; *m:* Thomas V.; *c:* Marianne, John; *ed:* (BS) Elem Ed, Cntrl MO St Univ 1971; (MA) Elem Ed, Univ of MO 1982; Math; *cr:* 4th Grade Teacher Green Ridge Public Schls 1971-72; 6th Grade Teacher Warrensburg Public Schls 1972-74; 7 & 8 Grade Teacher Nativity Sch 1976-77; 6th Grade Teacher Randall Elem 1978-; *ai:* Randall Math Club Spon 1984; Math Comm; Cognitive Goals Chm North Central Accreditation; Provide Dist Inservice Elem Teachers Math; Independence NEA (Bldg Rep) 1989; MNEA; NEA; NCTM 1980-; MO Cncl Teachers Math; KS City Area Teachers Math; PTA; Nom Excl in Teaching Awd; Achievement Awd Univ of MO 1983; *office:* Randall Elem Sch 509 Jennings Independence MO 64056

THELIN, DIANE (PATCH), English Teacher; *b:* Des Moines, IA; *m:* Kirk R.; *c:* Allison, Ryan; *ed:* (BA) Eng/Fr, Simpson Coll 1980; Promoter of IA Writers Project; *cr:* Eng/Drama Teacher Scranton Cmmty Sch 1980-83, Glidden Ralston Cmmty Sch 1983-; *ai:* Yrbk & Newspaper Adv; 1 Act Play Dir; Class Spon; JEA, IRA, NCTE; Dow Jones Schlsp for Stud in Jornalism 1988; *office:* Glidden Ralston Cmmty Sch 602 Idaho St Glidden IA 51443

THEODORE, JO ANNA MC GEE, Lang Arts/Soc Stud Dept Chair; *b:* Chicago, IL; *m:* Wilbert Ruben Sr.; *c:* De Anna Decinta, Wilbert R. Jr.; *ed:* (BS) Elem Ed, Loyola Univ 1978; Math Grad Level Courses; Educably Mentally Handicapped Grad Courses; Gifted Stu Grad Level; Working Towards Masters in Sch Guidance & Counseling, Chicago St Univ; *cr:* Acct/Bookkeeper Trainee Cmmty Service Admin 1974-77; Teacher Edwards Elem Sch 1978-80, Hearst Elem Sch 1980-83, J C Orozco Acad 1983-; *ai:* Comm for Academic Competitions & Prof Problems; Chicago Teachers Union, AFT Mem 1981-; Chosen as Consulting Teacher By Chicago Teachers Union Chicago Public Schls 1989; *office:* J C Orozco Acad 1645 W 18th Pl Chicago IL 60608

THERBER, MARVIN KENT, Department Chair; *b:* Rockport, IN; *m:* Judy Mack; *c:* Jeffrey Kent; *ed:* (BA) Eng/Scndry Ed, 1967, (MA) Eng Lit, 1969 George Peabody Coll; (JD) Law, Nashville Sch of Law 1979; Grad Stud Ed Admin, Supervision, Educl Psych; *cr:* Teacher Wright Jr HS 1967-71; Teacher/Dept Chm Rose Park Jr HS 1972-78; Teacher Watkins Inst 1973-76; Teacher/Dept Chm Glencliff HS 1979-; *ai:* Civitan Club Spon; Golf Coach; Academic Olympics & Advanced Placement Adv; United Way Co-Chm; NCTM 1967-; TN Bar Assn 1979-; Nasville Cncl of Teachers of Eng 1985-89; Amer Bar Assn 1979-80; NEA 1967-; TEA; Metropolitan Nashville Ed Assn; Glencliff Teacher of Yr 1988; Metropolitan Nashville Davidson Cty Teacher of Yr; Mid-Cumberland Dist Teacher of Yr 1988; *home:* 700 Baxter Ln Brentwood TN 37027

THERIOT, JANE HARRINGTON, Teacher of Gifted & Talented; *b:* Mercedes, TX; *m:* Donald J.; *c:* Jeffery, Jennifer; *ed:* (BS) Elem Ed/Art, Pan Amer Univ 1977; Gifted/Talented Trng Sessions; *cr:* Paraprofessional Headstart Smith Elem 1966; 5th Grade Teacher St Martinville Elem 1968-69; Paraprofessional Harlingen Consolidated Ind Sch Dist 1972-76; 2nd/5th Grade Teacher Bonham Elem 1977-; *ai:* UIL Coach Creative Dramatics; Bonham Courtesy Comm; Assn of TX Prof Educators; Delta Kappa Gamma Intnl 1988-; PTA Beautfication Comm 1988-; Teacher of Month 1988; TX Career Ladder; Textbook Comm Rep; Inservice Presenter; Curr Writer Soc Stud, Sci, Gifted/Talented; Sci Fair Chm; Teacher Cmmty Comm; Instructional Advisory Comm; St Gifted/Talented Convention Rep; *office:* Bonham Elem Sch 2400 E Jefferson Harlingen TX 78550

THERIOT, JUDINE, History Teacher; *b:* New Orleans, LA; *ed:* (BA) His, Marillac Coll 1973; (MA) His, Univ of Dayton 1980; *cr:* Teacher Notre Dame HS 1973-79, St Louis HS 1979-83, St Bonaventure Acad 1983-86, Sullivan Cath HS 1986-; *ai:* Attendance Officer; NCEA 1973-; LA Cncl for Soc Stud 1986-; Inter Civic Cncl of Baton Rouge Outstanding Educator 1989; Diocesan Sch Bd 1989-; Named Outstanding Educator Scndry Level Inter Civic Cncl of Baton Rouge; *office:* Bishop Sullivan HS 17521 Monitor Ave Baton Rouge LA 70816

THEROFF, MARV W., Biology Teacher; *b:* Russellville, MO; *m:* Annita Moore; *c:* Eric, Erin; *ed:* (BS) Ed/Bio, Lincoln Univ 1966; (MS) Ed/Admin, Cntrl MO St Univ 1977; Univ of MO Kansas City; Maryville Coll; *cr:* Bio/Gen Sci/Phys Ed Teacher Cole R-1 1966-68; Bio Teacher Blue Springs R-4 1968-; *ai:* Prins Advisory; Discipline & Performance Based Teacher Ed Review Comm; NSTA, Sci Teachers of MO, Greater Kansas City Sci Teachers Assn, MO St Teachers Assn; Timothy Luth Church; *office:* Blue Springs HS 2000 Ashton Dr Blue Springs MO 64015

THESING, TERI A., Mathematics Teacher/Dept Chair; *b:* Charles City, IA; *m:* Jay; *ed:* (BS) Math, IA St Univ 1981; (MA) Scndry Math Ed, E KY Univ 1989; *cr:* Volunteer St Pauls Church 1981-83; Math Teacher Jackson Cty HS 1983-; *ai:* Sftbl Team Coach 1983-; Acad Team Coach 1988-89; Math Club Spon 1983-87; Pep Club Spon 1983-84; KY Ed Assn; KY Commonwealth Inst for Teachers 1988; Power of Positive Stus Multimedia Prgm 1988; *office:* Jackson Cty HS Hwy 421 Mc Kee KY 40447

THEW, FRANCES MARION, HS Computer Teacher; *b:* Milwaukee, WI; *c:* Jerome L. Ashcroft *ed:* (BA) Span/Bio/Scndry Ed, Rollins Coll 1974; (MS) Admin/Supervision, FL Atlantic Univ 1978; (EDS) Cmptr/Sci Ed, Nova Univ 1986; Summer Institutes Bio, Marine Bio, Pascal, A P Pascal, Applications Model Technology Sch; *cr:* Teachers Aid/Resource Teacher Mead Gardens Environmental Center 1974; 7th-8th Grade Sci Teacher Robert E Lee Jr HS 1974-75; 7th-9th Grade Sci/Bio/Chem/Span I-II/Alg I-II Teacher Orlando Chrstn Sch 1975-77; 7th Grade Life Sci Teacher Golfview Jr HS 1977-85; Cmptr Programming/Cmptr Literary/Applications John I Leonard HS 1985-; *ai:* Class of 1989, Human Relations Club & Cmptr Club Spon; Lang Art Academics Games Coach; FAST 1974-86; FACE Local VP 1987-; Audubon Society Educl Comm Chairperson 1977-79; Lakeside Presbyn Church Choir Alto 1968, Bible Sch Teacher 1986 & Deacon 1978-81; 1st Presbyn Church Sunday Sch Teacher 1975-77; Curr Writing Team; Assoc Masters Teacher of Cmptr Ed 1985-87; *home:* 159 Lake Arbor Dr Lake Worth FL 33461

THIBODAUX, CHARLIE JANET, Curriculum Coordinator; *b:* New Iberia, LA; *m:* Al; *c:* Steven, David, Barbara, Kathleen Darnall, James, Patrick; *ed:* (BA) Elem Ed, 1961, (MED) Elem Ed, 1984 Univ of Southwest LA; *cr:* 5th Grade Teacher Mount Carmel Acad 1962-71; 3rd Grade Teacher 1971-89, Curr Coord 1990 Cecilia Primary; *ai:* Amer Fed of Teachers; Republican Womens Assn; PTO Parliamentarian 1987-88; Sch Nom Teacher of Yr 1988-.

THIBODEAU, CAROL H., Biology Teacher; *b:* Caribou, ME; *m:* Richard W.; *c:* Robyn R., Renee J., Cara A.; *ed:* (BA) Life Sci, Univ of ME 1976; (MS) Sci of Ed Instructional Leadership, Univ of Southern MA 1989; *cr:* Bio Teacher Limestone HS 1976-80; Bio & Chem Caribou HS 1980-; Teacher Hands on Sci Univ of MA at Presque Isle 1986-88; Adult Ed Anatomy Caribou HS 1986-; Anatomy & Physiology for Nursing Prgm Northern MA Tech Coll 1989-; *ai:* Class Adv 1984-87; MA Sci Techers Assn 1987-; Natl Bio Teachers Org 1988-; Natl Sci Teachers Org 1986-; Phi Delta Kappa 1987-; NEA & MTA 1980-; Cary Medical Hospital Auxiliary Pres 1970-73; Beta Sigma Phi Pres/Treas/Sec 1969-; Natl Sci Teacher Awd Summer 1986; Life Sci Prgm Simmons Coll Boston MA; Edited Elem Sci Texts Prentice Hall 1989; *office:* Caribou H S 410 Sweden St Caribou ME 04736

THIBODEAUX, BRENDA BERTRAND, Teacher of Gifted Students; *b:* Abbeville, LA; *m:* Michael; *c:* Dedra, Ellen, Seth; *ed:* (BA) Ed, 1971, (MED) Ed, 1984 USL; Grad Stud Elem & Gifted Ed; *cr:* Teacher J W Faulk Elem 1971-76; Teacher 4th-5th Grade Teacher of Gifted Myrtle Place Elem 1977-; *ai:* Grade Level, Soc Stud Fair, Young Authors Contest Chairperson; Carnival Comm; LAE, NEA 1971-; LA Assn of Teachers of Math 1989-; Lafayette Parish Assn of Classroom Teachers; Assn for Gifted & Talented Stus 1983-; PTO Treas; *office:* Myrtle Place Elem Sch 1100 Myrtle Blvd Lafayette LA 70506

THIBODEAUX, MARY LOU BOREL, 5th Grade Teacher; *b:* St Martinville, LA; *m:* Waldo J.; *c:* Glenda S., Thomas, Debora J. Wilkerson, Keith J.; *ed:* (BA) Ed, 1975; (MED) Ed, 1979 USI; Tax Consultant H&R Block; *cr:* Teacher Lafayette Parish Sch Bd 1975; *ai:* Girl Scouts Leader 1958-61; Boy Scouts Den Mother 1964-65; *home:* 1007 Auburn Ave Lafayette LA 70503

THIE, GENEVIEVE ANN, Mathematics Department Chm; *b:* Aledo, IL; *m:* Irvin E.; *c:* Vyona Hetzendorfer, Daryl I.; *ed:* (BA) Jr HS Ed Math/Sci, IA St Teachers Coll 1961; (MA) Math, Univ of N IA 1969; Various Summer Insts & Inservice Trng; *cr:* Math Teacher Cedar Rapids Cmmty Sch Dist 1961-64; Math/Sci/Teacher New Hartford 1965-68; Math Teacher Cedar Falls Cmmty Sch 1968-77; Math Teacher/Dept Chm Hillsborough Sch Bd 1979-; *ai:* Mu Apha Theta Spon; FL Cncl of Teachers of Math; IA Cncl of Teachers of Math (St Journal Ed 1973-77), Certificate of Commendation 1978; NCTM, MAA, NEA; *office:* Armwood HS 12000 US Hwy 92 Seffner FL 33584

THIEBAUD, SHIRLEY WEAVER, Vocal Music Teacher 6-8; *b:* Vivian, LA; *m:* Ronald Bennett; *c:* Ronson Benet; *ed:* (BMED) Vocal Music Ed, Northwestern St Univ 1969; Grad Work LA Tech Univ; LA St Univ; *cr:* K-12th Grade Vocal Music Teacher Marthaville Sch 1969-70; K-6th Grade Elem Music Teacher Cntrl Elem Sch 1971; 7th-12th Grade Vocal Music Teacher Northwood Jr/Sr HS 1973-81; 6th-8th Grade Vocal Music Teacher Byrd Jr HS 1981-; *ai:* Choral Dir Byrd Jr HS; 7th & 8th Grade Choirs & Daniel Intermediate Sch; 6th Grade Choirs; Mem Northside Baptist Church; Choir Accompanists and Church Organist; TX Choral Directors 1981-; TX Music Ed Assn-Solo/Ens Chairperson 1981-; LA Music Ed Assn 1973-81; Northside Baptist Church Accompanist 1988-; First Division Winners Solo/Ensemble Competitions; Sweepstakes Winners Concert/Sight-Reading Competitions TX &LA; Byrd Choirs Won Best in Class Trophy Six-Flags Over TX Music Festival; Dist XX TMEA All-Region Choir; *office:* Byrd Jr H S 1040 W Wheatland Rd Duncanville TX 75116

THIEL, MARION MARQUART, 4th-6th Grade Teacher; *b:* Bismarck, ND; *m:* Dwayne; *c:* Jeffrey; *ed:* (BA) Elem, Univ of Mary 1980; Grad Stud at Univ of ND & ND St Univ; *cr:* Elem Teacher Steele Public Schls 1963-65, Central Elem 1965-67, Custer Elem 1967-; *ai:* NEA 1963-; Natl Math Assn 1988-; ND Ed Assn 1963-; Mandan Ed Assn (Treas 1966) 1965-; S Cntrl Rdng Assn 1985-; *office:* Custer Elem Sch 205 8th Ave N E Mandan ND 58554

THIEMAN, CYNTHIA JEAN (STRODTMAN), Third Grade Teacher; *b:* Kansas City, MO; *m:* Terry Lynn; *c:* Matthew S., Micah K.; *ed:* (BA) Elem Ed, S MO St Univ 1978; (MS) Elem Ed, Pittsburg St Univ 1989; *cr:* 6th Grade Teacher 1978-79, 3rd/4th/6th Grade Teacher 1979 El Dorado Springs; *ai:* Curr Comm; MSTA; Beta Sigma Phi; *home:* 400 W 11th St Lamar MO 64759

THIESSEN, PAUL G., Music Director; *b:* Pittsburgh, PA; *m:* Suzanne Mc Candless Stone; *c:* Paul G. Jr., Gretchen L.; *ed:* (BA) Music Ed/Performance, 1969, (MFA) Music Ed, 1970 Carnegie Mellon Univ; *cr:* Jr HS Band Dir 1969-72, Mid Sch Band Dir 1972-74, Mid Sch Band Dir/Asst HS Band Dir 1974-87, Dir of Music 1987- New Brighton Area Sch Dist; *ai:* Phi Mu Alpha 1966-; Music Ed Natl Conference 1984-; US Power Sq (Ed Officer 1972-76, Admin Officer 1976-78, Exec Officer 1978-80, Commander 1980-82), Outstanding Teaching Awd 1976, 1977; PMEA Citation of Excl Awd MS Band Dir 1985; *office:* New Brighton Area Sch Dist Allegheny & Penn Ave New Brighton PA 15066

THIGPEN, MARY POWERS, Retired Teacher; *b:* Windsor, NC; *m:* Orzo S.; *c:* O. Sloan, Lonnie P., Ada T. Brown; *ed:* (BS) Elem Ed, 1960, (MS) Elem Ed, 1964 E Carolina Univ; *cr:* Teacher Beulaville Elem 1959-85; *ai:* Girls Bsktbl Coach; Jr Beta Club Spon; NEA, NCEA; *home:* Rt 2 Box 24 Beulaville NC 28518

THIMM, JOSEPH O., History Teacher; *b:* Park Falls, WI; *m:* Dawn; *c:* Treva, Ashley; *ed:* (BA) His, IA Wesleyan Coll 1977; (MEPD) His, Univ of WI Platteville 1980; *cr:* Teacher/Coach Glidden Ralston HS 1977-79, Taylors Falls HS 1980-; *ai:* Stu Cncl Adv; Mrktg & Recertification Comm; Cnslr; Boys Bsktbl Head Coach; Taylors Falls Ed Assn 1980-, Teacher of Yr 1987; MN HS Coaches Assn 1980-; Grad Asst Univ of WI Platteville 1979-80; *office:* Taylors Falls Sch 670 West St Taylors Falls MN 55084

THOENEN, ROSE ANN, Science/Amer History Teacher; *b:* Jefferson City, MO; *ed:* (BA) Health/Phys Ed, Lincoln Univ 1980; *cr:* 4th Grade Teacher 1980-82, 7th/8th Grade Teacher 1982- St Peter Sch; *ai:* Coach Track, Vlybl, Bsktbl; Dir Annual Major Musical; Jr HS Coord; Taught Piano Lessons; NCEA 1980-; Church (Organist 1988-, Choir 1985-); *office:* St Peter Sch 314 W High Jefferson City MO 65101

THOMAS, ANNIE SCOTT, Fourth Grade Teacher; *b:* Columbus, GA; *m:* Robert Aaron; *ed:* (BA) Elem Ed, FL Memorial Coll 1970; (MS) Varying Exceptionalities, St Thomas Univ 1980; Grad Stud Various Courses; *cr:* 3rd Grade Teacher 1970-71, 3rd/4th Grade Teacher 1971-72 Palm Springs North Elem; Teacher of Learning Disabilities Stevens Jr HS; 4th Grade Teacher Palm Springs North Elem 1974-; *ai:* Palm Springs North Steering Comms Mem; Supvr Behavioral Modification Prgm; Stu Cncl Spon 1983; Peer Teacher 1988; United Teachers of Dade, AFT 1972-; Order of Eastern Star Assoc Matron 1986-87, Outstanding Service Plaque 1987; FL Masonic Choir Asst Dir 1986-; NAACP 1984-; Democratic Voter Registration (Cnslr, Asst) 1985; Certificate of Awd Implementation of Newspaper in Classroom 1975; Grade Level Chairperson 1988-89; Educl Travel to Kingston Jamaica, Montego Bay & Ochio Rio 1985, San Juan PR, Caribbean Islands of St Thomas, St Maarten, St John 1990; *office:* Palm Springs North Elem Sch 17615 NW 82nd Ave Hialeah FL 33015

THOMAS, AURELIA, Mathematics Teacher; *b:* Mobile, AL; *ed:* (BS) Elem Ed, Jackson St Univ 1972; *cr:* 6th Grade Math Teacher Phillips Prep 1974-; *ai:* Natl Jr Honor Society Adv; Alpha Kappa Alpha Grammateus; Teacher of Yr 1988-89; *office:* Phillips Prep Sch 3255 Old Shell Rd Mobile AL 36607

THOMAS, BARBARA JEAN, Chapter I Coordinator; *b:* Gulfport, MS; *ed:* (BS) Elem 1974, (MS) Elem, 1976 Univ of S MS; Doctoral Prgm Educl Admin & Supervision; *cr:* 2nd Grade Teacher Gaston Point Elem 1974-77, 28th Street Elem 1977-83; 1st Grade Teacher 1983-84, Chapter I Math Teacher 1984-87 28th Street Elem; Chapter I Coord/Teacher Gulfport Schls 1984-; *ai:* Gulfport Sch Dist Staff Dev Team Mem; Chapter I Parent Advisory Cncl Mem; Greater Mount Olive Baptist Church; Phi Delta Kappa Pres 1989-; MS Rdng Assn, Intnl Rdng Assn, MS Cncl of Teachers of Math; GSA Troop Leader 1987-; Phi Delta Kappa Pres 1989-; Outstanding Young Woman of America 1984; Recognition Outstanding Teacher 1981; 28th Street Elem Sch Teacher of Quarter; NIE Teacher of Week; *office:* Gulfport Schls PO Box 220 Gulfport MS 39501

THOMAS, BARBARA OVERTON, Fifth Grade Teacher; *b:* Indianapolis, IN; *m:* Gerald W.; *ed:* (BA) Poly Sci/Ec, Bishop Coll 1976; (MED) Elem Ed, Praire View A&M 1981; Univ of Dallas; *cr:* 8th Grade Classroom Teacher John XXIII Regional Sch 1977-83; 5th/6th Grade Teacher John Neely Bryan Sch 1983-; *ai:* Stu Cncl, Math & His Club Spon; Instruction Support Team, Incentives Prgm Dir; TSTA, NEA, Classroom Teacher of Dallas; Delta Sigma Theta Inc Treas 1974-76; Delta Sigma Theta Arlington Treas 1989-; Teacher of Yr; *office:* John Neely Bryan Sch 2001 Deerpath Dallas TX 75216

THOMAS, BENJAMIN L., English Teacher; *b:* Philadelphia, PA; *m:* Carol Lynn; *c:* Lisa Honey, Sally Tollens; *ed:* (BS) Comprehensive Eng, Chester St Coll 1964; Working Towards Masters; *cr:* 7th/9th/10th Lang Art Teacher Avon Grove Area Sch 1964-71; 5th-8th Grade Lang Art Teacher Mascenic Regional Sch 1971-73; 7th Grade Lang Art Teacher Alexis I Dupont Mid Sch 1973-; *ai:* Newspaper Spon; Var Bsbl, Jr Var Bsbl, Bsktbl Coach; Intramural Hockey, Soccer, Sftbl, Field Hockey; Represent Lang Art Dist Curr Revision; NCTE; Newspaper Use Team Teaching Mini-Grants.

THOMAS, BETTY ALEXANDER, Student Services Chair; *b:* Madison, FL; *m:* Lorenzo Lamar; *c:* Joseph D., Jennifer D.; *ed:* (BS) Poly Sci, FL A&M Univ 1974; (MS) Math Ed, Nova Univ 1983; *cr:* Math Teacher Key West HS 1974-79; Math Teacher 1979-87, Guidance Cnslr W R Thomas Mid Sch 1987-; *ai:* Advisement Coord; Mid Sch Trainer; United Teachers of Dade Building Stewart; Dade Cty Assn for Counseling & Dev Mem 1987-; Advisement Grant; Teacher of Yr; *office:* W R Thomas Mid Sch 13001 SW 26th St Miami FL 33175

THOMAS, BETTY J., English Teacher; *b:* Columbus, GA; *ed:* (MS) Learning Disabilities/Behavior Disorders, GA Southwestern 1984; Advanced Preparation in Rdng, Classroom Management & Eng Grammar; *cr:* Music Specialist Dougherty Cty Sch Dist 1971-81; Sales Asst Gayfers 1978-; Spec Ed Instr Muscogee Cty Sch Dist 1981-; *ai:* Key Club Adv 1984-; Arrive Alive Spon 1989-; Frosh Class Spon 1986-87; Orginator/Coord Faculty Honoring Honor Stus 1985-89; Natl Assn of Bus & Prof Women 1984-; Kiwanis of Columbus Key Club Adv 1989-, Honorary Mem 1989; Natl Assn of Educators 1971-; A J Mc Clung YMCA Secy 1989-; 10th Street Cmmty Center 1985-; Outstanding Young Women of America 1984; Nom Teacher of Yr; *office:* Jordan HS 3200 Howard Ave Columbus GA 31904

THOMAS, BRUCE GORDON, Social Studies Teacher; *b:* Williamsburg, KY; *m:* Deborah Lynne Ryan; *c:* Ryan G., Brittany L.; *ed:* (AS) His, Somerset Comm Coll 1980; (BA) Poly Sci, Univ of KY 1981; Cert Elem Ed, Union Coll 1986; *cr:* Self-Contained Teacher 1983-84, Soc Stud Teacher 1984-86, Math/Eng Teacher 1986-87, Amer His Teacher 1988-89 Whitley City Mid Sch; Soc Stud Teacher Pine Knot Mid Sch 1989-; *ai:* Stu Cncl Adv 1984-; Visiting Teachers Inst; Governors Scholars Prgm 1989-; NEA, KEA 1983-; Commissioned KY Colonel for Work Done Through Governors Scholars Prgm 1989; Appreciation Awd for Service to FHA 1988-89; Distinguished Faculty Mem Awd 1987-88; *home:* HC 82 Box 516A Pine Knot KY 42635

THOMAS, CARITA CHAPMAN, Bio/Anat/Physiology Teacher; *b:* Montgomery, AL; *c:* Tiffany; *ed:* (BS) Bio/Chem/Ed, AL St Univ 1971; Research Trng Southwest Fnd for Research & Ed; Biochem & Molecular Bio, San Antonio Coll; *cr:* Phys Sci Teacher Horace Mann Jr HS 1971-72; Asst Research Scientist Southwest Fnd for Research & Ed; Bio/Anat omy/Physiology/ Chem Teacher Jefferson HS 1978-; *ai:* Class of 1982, 1988 Spon; Physics Olympic Spon; Ford Fnd Fellowship in Molecular Bio; Honorable Mention in Lead Research Project Reprint & Publication 1977.

THOMAS, CARMEN JEANINE, Physical Education Teacher; *b:* Medford, OR; *ed:* (BA) Phys Ed, 1977, (MA) Sec Ed, 1980 Morehead St Univ; Elem Phys Ed Stud; *cr:* 6-8 Sci Teacher/Coach Beth El Elem 1977-81; K-6 Phys Ed Bio Teacher/Jr High Coach Seymour High & Elem Sch 1981-85; 7-12 Phys Ed/Bio Teacher/ HS Coach, 1985- Seymour HS; *ai:* Jr HS Bsktbl Coach; HS Bsktbl Coach; HS Sftbl Coach; Booster Club Mem; PTA Mem; Career Ladder Comm; NEA Local VP 1977-; KKOZ Coach of Yr 1986; *home:* PO Box 478 Seymour MO 65746

THOMAS, CAROL MERCEDES (CLEWS), First Grade Teacher; *b:* Strong, PA; *m:* Bernard J.; *c:* Lora L., Joshua; *ed:* (BS) Elem Ed, St Francis 1976; Ed, Indiana Univ of PA; Cmptr, Univ of Pittsburgh; Elem-Jr HS Physics, Wilson Coll; *cr:* 1st Grade Practice Teaching Pittsburgh-Greensburg Sch; 4th Grade Homeroom Teacher 1969-72, Primary Teacher 1976-78, St Bernard Sch; 2nd Grade Teacher N Cambria Cath 1978-79; 5th Grade-Jr HS Sci Teacher St Bernard Sch 1980-89; 1st Grade Teacher Cambria Heights 1989-; *ai:* PA Jr Acad of Sci 1987-89, St Awd 1988; Natl Rdng Assn 1990; Red Cross/Bloodmobile Chairperson 1987-88; *home:* PO Box 382 Hastings PA 16646

THOMAS, CHARLES MICHAEL, Mathematics Teacher; *b:* Shreveport, LA; *m:* Paula Gladney; *c:* Michael, Stefanie; *ed:* (BA) Soc Stud, Baptist Chrstn Coll 1973; (MS) Math Ed, LA Tech Univ 1978; *cr:* Math Teacher Webster HS 1970-75, Webster Jr HS 1975-85, Haughton HS 1985-; *ai:* Admin Selection Comm 1989; NCTM 1988-; Jamestown-Fryeburg Water System Bd of Dir 1989-; Nom Presidential Awd For Excl in Sci & Math 1989; Teacher of Yr 1989-; *home:* Rt 1 Box 827 Dubberly LA 71024

THOMAS, CHARLES P., 8th Grade Team Leader; *b:* Frederick, MD; *m:* Rosemary A.; *ed:* (BA) His, Western MD 1978; (MA) Poly Sci, Hood Coll 1983; *cr:* Teacher Brunswick Mid Sch; *ai:* Academic Adv; Sch Improvement Team; *office:* Brunswick Mid Sch Cummings Dr Brunswick MD 21716

THOMAS, CHARLIE A., Home Economics Teacher; *b:* Tallahassee, FL; *c:* Kimberly B; *ed:* (BS) Voc Home Ec, FL A & M Univ 1970; *cr:* Headstart Teacher, Charlotte Cnty H S Prgm, 1970-72; Home Ec, Punta Gorda Jr H s1973-; *ai:* Spon-Future Homemkrs Of Amer; Minority Parents Advis Cncl Chm; Cooper St recreation Cntr; Aft Sch Tutor Prgm; Better "U" Girls Clb Co-Spon; *office:* Punta Gorda Jr H S 825 Carmalita St Punta Gorda FL 33950

THOMAS, CINDY FUNKHOUSER, Mathematics Teacher; *b:* Petersburg, WV; *m:* Terry Douglas; *c:* Brian, Brittany; *ed:* (BA) Math, Shepherd Coll 1980; *cr:* Math Teacher Hedgesville HS 1980-; *ai:* Soph Class Coord; Math Dept Chm; *office:* Hedgesville HS Rt 1 Box 89 Hedgesville WV 25427

THOMAS, CLAIR OLIVER, Biology Teacher; *b:* Spokane, WA; *m:* Patricia May Carlson; *c:* Cherish D., Karissa R.; *ed:* (BS) Bio, George Fox Coll 1978; (MS) Sci Ed, OR St Univ 1986; *cr:* Sci Instr Santiam Chrstn HS 1979-87; Phys Sci Teacher 1987-88, Bio Teacher 1988- Lakeview HS; *ai:* Head Wrestling Coach, Soph Class & Honor Society Adv, Drug & Alcohol Advisory Comm; NEA, OR Ed Assn, NSTA 1979-; Stu Elected Teacher of Month; Chamber of Commerce Elected Teacher of Month; *office:* Lakeview HS 906 S 3rd St Lakeview OR 97630

THOMAS, CONSTANCE BETH TOMPKINS, Fourth Grade Teacher; *b:* Lansing, MI; *m:* Jim Phill; *c:* Constance C. (dec), Timothy R.; *ed:* (BA) Music/His, CA St Univ Fresno 1970; Working Towards Masters in His; *cr:* 4th Grade Teacher Oakhurst Elem 1970-; *ai:* Sch Festival of Oral Interpretion & Spelling Bee Contest Coord; His/Soc Sci Summer Inst 1989; Facilitator 1990; Oakhurst Union Sch Teacher Assn (Secy 1976-79, Treas 1986-87); Bass Lake Teachers Assn Communication Laison 1987-; Modera Cty Historical Society 1988-; Mentor Teacher Fine Art 1982-83; Local His Field Stud Grant 1979-80; Master Teacher Prgm Grant CA St Univ Fresno; *office:* Oakhurst Elem Sch 49495 Rd 427 P O Box 395 Oakhurst CA 93644

THOMAS, CONSTANCE TERZOPOLOS, Biology Teacher; *b:* Shamokin, PA; *m:* Richard W.; *c:* Kim, Scott; *ed:* (BS) Ed, Bloomsburg Univ 1961; Grad Stud Univ of DE & George Mason Univ; *cr:* 7th Grade General Sci Teacher Springer Jr HS 1961-64; 10th Grade Bio Teacher George C Marshall HS 1980-; *ai:* Class Adv; BTAP Colleague Teacher Coord; Self Study Steering Comm; Sch-Bus Partnership Rep & Mentor; Sci Fair Registration Chm; Skillful Teacher Part Time Consulting Teacher; VEA, FEA 1980-; NABT 1985-; *office:* George C Marshall HS 7731 Leesburg Pike Falls Church VA 22043

THOMAS, D. R. BOB, Mathematics Teacher; *b:* St Charles, IL; *m:* Cynthia L. Falkenstein; *c:* Dominique; *ed:* (AS) Math/Ec, Univ of WI Rock Cty 1979; (BS) Math/Ec, Univ of WI Whitewater 1982; (MA) Scndry Ed/Admin, N AZ Univ 1988; Scndry Admin; Qualified Supvr of Instructional Delivery; Cmptr Sci; *cr:* Math Assoc Instr AZ Western Coll; Math Teacher Kofa HS; *ai:* ASCD 1989-; Phi Kappa Phi Mem 1979-82; Kappa Delta Pi Mem 1979-84; Tandy Technology Scholars Outstanding Teachers Math Awd 1990; Natl Reference Inst Whos Who in Amer Ed 1989-.

THOMAS, DAN B., Language Arts Teacher; *b:* Spokane, WA; *m:* Linda Marie Avery; *c:* Nicholas A., Kristin N.; *ed:* (BA) Eng Ed, E WA Univ 1980; N ID Writing Project 1983; MT Writing Project 1987; *cr:* Lang Art Instr Priest River Lamanna HS 1980-84, Beaverhead Cty HS 1984-; *ai:* Beaverhead Yrbk Adv; Lang Art Curr Comm; Beaverhead Fed of Teachers Pres 1989-91; NCTE; Amer Legion; MT Boys St Cnslr 1985-; Published MT Eng Journal 1987; Yrbk Best Wkshp Adv 1990; *office:* Beaverhead Cty HS 104 N Pacific Dillon MT 59725

THOMAS, DEBBIE UNTERNAHER, Teacher; *b:* San Rafel, CA; *m:* David W.; *c:* Whitney L., Benjamin; *ed:* (BS) Elem Ed, OH St Univ 1979; Kndgtn Cert OSU 1982; Learning Disabilities Course Work OSU 1983; Teacer Effectiveness Trng Mt St Joseph Coll 1981; Cmptr Prgmg Ashland Coll 1983; *cr:* 4th Grade Teacher 1979-81; 3rd Grade Teacher 1981-82; Kndgtn Teacher 1982-86 Toboso Elem; *ai:* Licking Valley Ed Assn 1979-86.

THOMAS, DONITA BUSH, 7th Grade English Teacher; *b:* Glasgow, KY; *m:* Dennis Cary; *c:* Laura, Rebecca; *ed:* (BA) Elem Ed, 1972, (MA) Elem Ed, 1974, Rdng Specialist 1983, (Rank I) Ed, 1985, 1986 W KY Univ; Eng as 2nd Lang Class; *cr:* Rdng/2nd Grade Teacher Franklin Simpson Schls 1973-74; Rdng/Eng Teacher Charlotte Mecklenburg Schls 1975-78; Remedial Rdng/ Math Teacher Lumberton City Schls 1978-83; Rdng/Eng Teacher Bowling Green City Schls 1983-; *ai:* Help with Stu Cncl, Work with Kids Writing on Cmptrs; NEA, Local Bowling Green Ed Assn Secy; KY Ed Assn Delegate; GSA 1987-; Twelfth Street Church of Christ 1970-; Awarded Jaycees Outstanding Young Elem Educator in 1985; *office:* Bowling Green Jr HS 1141 Center St Bowling Green KY 42101

THOMAS, DORIS DAVENPORT, Fifth Grade Teacher; *b:* Giddings, TX; *m:* Horace Nelson; *c:* Reginald; *ed:* (BS) Elem Ed, TX Southern Univ 1963; Grad Stud & Numerous Prof Growth Courses; *cr:* 5th/6th Grade Teacher Houston Ind Sch Dist 1963-; *ai:* Discipline Comm; Math Club; Stu Cncl; Houston Teachers Assn, TX St Teachers Assn, NEA 1963-85; Houston Fed of Teachers 1986-; GSA Leader 1963-70; Friends of Scouting 1982-; Young Womens Chrstn Assn 1987-; Good Hope Baptist Church Missionary Society VP 1983-87; Houston Jaycees Outstanding Young Educator 1968; *home:* 5030 Ventura Ln Houston TX 77021

THOMAS, DOROTHY ROSANNE, Fifth Grade Teacher; *b:* Albuquerque, NM; *c:* Jason A., Jarred A.; *ed:* (BS) Elem Ed, N AZ Univ 1974; Sch Admin, N AZ Univ; *cr:* Kndgtn Teacher 1974-85, Math Teacher 1985-87, 5th Grade Teacher 1988- Laguna Elem Sch; *ai:* NCA Steering Comm Chairperson 1986-87; Les Support Team & Teacher Assistance Team Mem 1989-; Sch Effectiveness Team Co-Chairperson 1989-; NCTM 1987-; Discovery Learning Math Teacher 1986-87; *home:* PO Box 1466 Laguna NM 87026

THOMAS, ELIZABETH ARCHIBALD, Fourth Grade Teacher; *b:* Elaine, AR; *m:* Albert James; *c:* Thomas G. Hicks, Carolyn D. Hicks Larkin; *ed:* (BS) Elem Ed, Southern IL Univ 1966; (MED) Elem Ed, Univ of MO St Louis 1971; Summer Sessions & Extension Courses, SIU Edwardsville, Webster Univ, CA St Univ Hayward; *cr:* Stu Teacher Geneva Girls Trng Sch 1966; Continuing Ed Instr Florissant Valley Comm Coll 1983-84; Teacher E St Louis Sch Dist 189 1966-; *ai:* Chairperson; Faculty Courtesy Comm; Amer Ed Week Comm Mem; Judge Upward Bound Sci Fair; After Sch Tutoring; Intnl Rdng Assn, Greater St Louis Eng Teachers Assn, Intl Trng in Comm; Phi Delta Kappa Eminent Educator Awd 1987; Delta Sigma Theta Secy 1978-80; St Louis Alumnae Chapt (VP, Pres) 1986-89; New Sunny Mount Baptist Church Chairperson Bd Chrstn Ed 1986-87; United Way Volunteer 1988-89; Rhodia Miller Memorial Awd Mathews-Dickey Boys Club; Teachers Center Project SIUE; *office:* Donald Mc Henry Elem Sch 2700 Summit Ave East Saint Louis IL 62205

THOMAS, EVA M., 6th Grade Teacher; *b:* Robbinsville, NC; *m:* Richard J.; *c:* Kamilla Wright, Richard, Tammy; *ed:* (BA) Elem Ed, 1972; (MED) Aerospace Ed, 1986 Mid TN St Univ; *cr:* 3rd Grade Teacher North Coffee Elem Sch 1973-75; 6th Grade Teacher Hillsboro Elem Sch 1975; *ai:* Organizer Spon 6th Grade Save Trees Club; Chm Annual Hillsboro Homeco Ming Arts Crafts Festival; Knowledge Master Open Club Spon; Textbook Adoption Comm-Rdng; Baptist Womens Union; Vacation Bible Sch Dir/Coord 1985-; *office:* Hillsboro Elem Sch Rt 2 Hillsboro TN 37342

THOMAS, F. KAY (WESTBROOK), Special Ed Teacher; *b:* Holdenville, OK; *m:* Arthur; *c:* Trent, Dominic; *ed:* (BS) Elem Ed, Langston Univ 1971; (MS) Spec Ed, OK St Univ 1973; Working Toward PhD in Spec Ed, N TX St Univ 1976; *cr:* Spec Ed Teacher Ft Worth St Sch 1977-78; Case Mgr Cath Family Services 1978-80; Day Care Provider Quality Day Care 1980-83; Bowling, Bsktbl, Track & Field, Spec Olympics Coach; *ai:* Spec Olympics Coach Bowling, Bsktbl, Track & Field; Dallas Federated Teachers Union 1989-; N Euless Elem PTA 1986-; Delta Sigma Theta 1969-; Curr Writer Spec Ed; Pre-Voc Curr for DISD; Teacher of Yr John B Hood 1990; Perfect Attendance Awd 1988-89; *office:* John B Hood Mid Sch 7625 Hume Dr Dallas TX 75227

THOMAS, FAYE E. JOHNSON, Fifth Grade Teacher; *b:* Summerfield, LA; *w:* Archie (dec); *c:* Dwayne; *ed:* (BA) Eng, Southern Univ 1954; (MS) Early Chldhd Ed, Univ of Cntrl AR 1971; (MSE) Curr Instruction, Cleveland St Univ 1979; *cr:* Eng Teacher Charles Brown HS 1957-69; Eng Teacher Upward Bound Prgm Grambling St Univ 1968; Eng Teaher Springhill HS 1970; Elem Teacher Riveredge Sch 1971-; *ai:* Safety Patrol Dir; Grade Level Chairperson; Math Team Dir; Mem of Intervention Asst Team; NEA, OH Ed Assn,Berea Ed Assn 1971-; NCTE 1990; Assn for Supervision & Curr Dev 1990; Intnl Platform Assn 1990; C H Brown Society Organization Trustee 1984-; Order of Eastern Star; Antioch Baptist Church; NDEA Grantee; Martha Holden Jennings Scholar; Whos Who in the Midwest; *home:* 19353 E Bagley Rd Middleburg Heights OH 44130

THOMAS, FRANCIS J., 2nd Grade Teacher; *m:* John E.; *c:* Ann Bucci, Debra Slaughter, Carolyn Hall, John II, Nathan; *ed:* (BS) Elem Ed, Drake Univ 1970; Grad Stud Cntrl St Univ; *cr:* 4th-5th Grade Teacher Panora IA; 1st-2nd Grade Teacher Guthrie Public Schls; *ai:* NEA, OEA; GACT Treas 1985-86; PTA Pres 1978-79.

THOMAS, GERALD E., American History Teacher; *b:* Detroit, MI; *c:* Matthew; *ed:* (BA) Sociology, Wayne St Univ 1971; Soc Stud Ed; *cr:* Teacher Warren Consolidated Schls 1971-80, Klein Ind Sch Dist 1982-; *ai:* Natl Jr Honor Society Spon; Klein Dist Teacher Who Makes Difference 1988; *office:* Klein Intermediate Sch 4710 W Mount Houston Rd Houston TX 77088

THOMAS, GINNY A., English Teacher; *b:* Jackson, TN; *ed:* (BS) Soc Stud, Bethel Coll 1962; (MED) Curr/Instruction, Memphis St Univ 1978; Sociology, Health; *cr:* Teacher Madison Cty TN 1961-63, Bloomfield HS 1963-67, San Antonio Ind Schls 1967-69, Memphis City Schls 1969-; *ai:* YUrbk Adv; NCTE 1980-; *home:* 3788 Dagmar Memphis TN 38107

THOMAS, JAMES A., 8th Grade Teacher; *b:* Hopkinsville, KY; *m:* Sandi Webster; *c:* Jonathan; *ed:* (BS) Elem Ed, 1974, (MA) Elem Ed, 1975, (Rank I) Admin, 1977 E KY Univ; *cr:* 8th Grade Teacher Conkwright Jr HS 1975-76; Mid Sch Teacher Model Lab Sch 1976-77; Teacher Hearn Elem 1977-80; 8th Grade Teacher Bondurant Mid Sch 1980-; *ai:* Bsktbl & Bsbl Coach; Bsktbl Ofcl; Bsbl Umpire; Franklin Cty Discipline Comm; NEA, KY Ed Assn, KY Mid Sch Assn; Red Cross CPR Instr 1983-; *home:* 965 Stoney Creek Dr Frankfort KY 40601

THOMAS, JAMES LAWRENCE, III, English Teacher/Coach; *b:* Dallas, TX; *m:* Amy Jo De Groot; *cr:* His Teacher Bay City Ind Sch Dist 1975-76; Eng Teacher/Coach Plano Ind Sch Dist 1976-; *ai:* Ftbl Coach; Sch Improvement Plan Comm; Driver Ed Instr; TX Joint Cncl for English Teachers, TX HS Coaches Assn, TX St Teachers Assn; Collin Collin Task Force 1986-88; Plano Palnning & Zoning Revision Comm 1984-86; H Ross Perot Excl in Teaching Awd 1987; Natl Exemplary Sch Awd for Pres Bush 1989; Natl Jr Honor Society Teacher of Yr; *office:* Wilson Mid Sch 1001 Custer Rd Plano TX 75075

THOMAS, JANET (HENDRIX), 4th Grade Teacher; *b:* Coffeyville, KS; *m:* Jerry D.; *ed:* (AA) Coffeyville Comm Coll 1966; (BS) Elem Ed, 1968; (MS) Eng/Speech/Soc Sci, 1979 Pittsburgh St Univ; *cr:* 3rd/4th Grade Teacher Cedar Bluff Elem 1968-78; 4th Grade Teacher Garfield Elem 1978-; *ai:* NEA; PTA;

Alpha Delta Kappa; *office:* Garfield Elem Sch 701 W 4th Coffeyville KS 67337

THOMAS, JEFFREY M., Health Coordinator; *b:* Ossining, NY; *m:* Linda Pheifer; *ed:* (BSED) Health/Phys Ed, Univ of Dayton 1970; Grad Stud Geneseo & Brockport St 1970-73; *cr:* Health/Phys Ed Teacher Warsaw Cntrl Sch 1970-71; K-12th Grade Health Coord Letchworth Cntrl Sch 1971-; *ai:* NHS, SADD, Chemical Free Athletes Adv; WY Cty Youth Bureau Pres 1979, Outstanding Youth Workers 1979; *office:* Letchworth Cntrl Sch School Rd Gainesville NY 14066

THOMAS, JOAN M., Kindergarten Teacher; *b:* Kansas City, MO; *m:* Spencer Ray; *c:* M. Scott, Becky M.; *ed:* Elem Ed, Cntrl MO St Univ 1959; Elem Ed, Univ of WA 1976; Early Chldhd Ed, Seattle Pacific Univ 1990; *cr:* 2nd Grade Teacher Raytown MO 1959-61; 4th Grade Teacher Clearwater FL 1961-63; 1st Grade Teacher Sarasota 1963-65; 2nd Grade Teacher Windwood MO 1968-70; Kndgtn/2nd Grade Teacher Lake Washington 1976-; *ai:* NEA, LWEA, WEA 1976-; Beta Sigma Phi Ways & Means Comm 1970-80, Girl of Yr 1975; Golden Acorn PTSA Awd; *office:* Helen Keller Elem Sch 13820 108th Ave NE Kirkland WA 98034

THOMAS, JOANNE DUKE, Kindergarten Teacher; *b:* Nashville, TN; *m:* Jesse H.; *c:* Jessanne Cole, Kimberly; *ed:* (BS) Elem Ed, Univ of TN 1968; (MA) Elem Ed, Union Coll 1973; *cr:* 1st Grade Teacher 1968-74, Kndgtn Teacher 1974- Clayton Elem Sch; *ai:* Cooperating Stu Teacher Univ of TN; Phi Delta Kappan, Anderson Cty Teachers Assn, TN Teachers Assn, Natl Teachers Assn; *office:* Claxton Elem Sch Rt 8 Powell TN 37849

THOMAS, JOHN DOUGLAS, Science Teacher; *b:* Commerce, TX; *m:* Cynthia Denise; *c:* Courtney, Drew; *ed:* (BS) Health & Phys Ed/His, 1979, (MS) Geology, 1983 E TX St Univ; *cr:* Teacher/Coach Como-Pickton Ind Sch Dist 1980-81, Sulphur Springs Ind Sch Dist 1981-82; Sci Teacher Wolfe City Ind Sch Dist 1983-; *ai:* Sci Club Spon; Literary Coach in Sci; Classroom Teachers Assn 1987-; TX Sci Teachers 1989-; *office:* Wolfe City Ind Sch Dist Drawer L Wolfe City TX 75496

THOMAS, KATHERINE ERIN ROSS, French & English Teacher; *b:* San Francisco, CA; *m:* Eric A.; *c:* Julia; *ed:* His/Fr, Stanford Univ 1973-76; (BA) Hum, Univ CA Berkeley 1981; Credential, CA St Hayward; Sch of Ed Univ CA Berkeley; *cr:* Teacher Calvin Simmons Jr HS 1982-83; Joaquin Moraga Intermediate Sch 1983-; *ai:* Foreign Lang Assn of Northern CA; ACTFL; Amer Assn Teachers of Fr; Rockefeller Fellowship Foreign Lang Teachers 1989; *office:* Joaquin Moraga Sch 1010 Camino Pablo Moraga CA 94556

THOMAS, KEITH A., Computers Chair/Instructor; *b:* Millsboro, PA; *m:* Jolley Nash; *ed:* (BS) Ed/Industrial Art, CA St Coll 1960; General & Tech Ed & Cmptr Related Courses; *cr:* Tech Drawing Teacher Pittsburg Schls 1960-61; Math/Tech Drawing Teacher Berkeley Schls 1961-63; Industrial Art/Cmptrs Teacher Walnut Creek Sch Dist 1963-; *ai:* Cmptr Oriented Admin Duties & Teacher In-Service Trng; Walnut Sch Dist Cmptr Mentor; *office:* Walnut Creek Intermediate Sch 2425 Walnut Blvd Walnut Creek CA 94596

THOMAS, KENNETH, Business Teacher/Dept Chair; *b:* Kingston, PA; *m:* Emily May Smith; *c:* Heather L.; *ed:* (BS) Bus Ed, Bloomsburg Univ 1960; Bus Courses Wilkes Univ, Univ of Scranton, Bloomsburg Univ; *cr:* Bus Teacher Phelps & Clifton Springs Cntrl Schls 1960-61, Clifton Springs Cntrl Sch 1961-62, Lackawanna Trail Jr-Sr HS 1962-; *ai:* Dept Chm; Ski Club, FBLA Adv; NEA Life Mem 1960-; PSEA Life Mem 1962-; Local LTEA (VP, Secy, Treas, Chief Negotiator, Building Rep) 1962-; F&AM 1961-; Order of Eastern Star Worthy Patron 1969-; WY Cty Sch Employees FCU Pres; *home:* RD 2 Box 301 Dalton PA 18414

THOMAS, KERRY DON, U S History Teacher; *b:* Beaumont, TX; *m:* Deborah D. Britain; *c:* Reid; *ed:* (BS) His Ed, Lamar Univ 1980; *cr:* Teacher Beaumont Ind Sch Dist 1981-82; His Teacher Magnolia Ind Sch Dist 1982-85, Dayton Ind Sch Dist 1988-; *ai:* Youth for Christ Spon; TX St Teachers Assn 1988-; NEA 1988-; *home:* 9265 Landis Beaumont TX 77707

THOMAS, LANNY E., Health/Physical Education; *b:* Fort Oglethorpe, GA; *m:* Chrysan Ramsey; *c:* Chaz C., Ramsey E.; *ed:* (BS) Health/Phys Ed, West GA Coll 1985; *cr:* 5th-8th Grade Phys Ed Teacher Pennville Elem 1985-88; Phys Ed Teacher La Fayette HS 1988-; *ai:* FCA Club Spon; Asst Ftbl Coach; Head Bsktbl Coach; *office:* Lafayette H S 301 N Cherokee St La Fayette GA 30728

THOMAS, LAUREL GRACEY, Math/English Teacher; *b:* Mooreland, OK; *m:* Joe Noble; *ed:* (BA) Math, Mc Murry Coll 1962; (ME) Ed, West TX St Univ 1969; Cmptr Cert 1984; *cr:* Teacher Kress Ind Sch Dist 1963-64, Channing Ind Sch Dist 1964-; *ai:* Class Spon; UIL Coach Number Sense, Calcualtor, Ready Writing, Literary Criticism, Spelling; TSTA/NEA Secy 1967-68; United Meth Church (organist 1967-, Secy/Treas 1973-); Order of Eastern Star 1973-75 & 1984-85; Math Grant to West TX St Univ 1965.

THOMAS, LAURIE HENDERSON, First Grade Teacher; *b:* Alliance, OH; *m:* Paul; *c:* Sean, Lindsay; *ed:* (BA) Elem Ed, Mt Union Coll 1974; (MED) Rdng Specialization, Kent St Univ 1988; Cmptr Trng, Youngstown St Univ; *cr:* Elem Phys Ed Teacher 1986-87, 1st Grade Teacher 1974-86, 1987- Sebring Local Sch Dist; *ai:* Girls HS Vlybl Coach; Mahoning Cty Lang Art Curr Comm; Educl Advisory Cncl Mt Union Coll 1988-90; Sebring Local Ed Assn Treas 1974-76; OH Ed Assn, NEA, NE OH Ed Assn 1974-; OH Cncl of Intnl Rdng Assn 1980-; Partners in Ed Secy 1989-; Park & Recreation Bd Mem 1985-; *office:* B L Miller Elem Sch 506 W Virginia Sebring OH 44672

THOMAS, LINDA DENGER, Second Grade Teacher; *b:* Athens, OH; *m:* Doug; *ed:* (BA) Ed, Wright St Univ 1971; (MS) Ed/Rdng, Miami Univ 1986; *cr:* 5th Grade Teacher 1972-75, 4th Grade Teacher 1975-86, 2nd Grade Teacher 1986- Greeneview North; *ai:* Strategic Planning & Sci Curr Comm; NEA, OEA, GEA; Martha Holden Jennings Scholar 1989; *office:* Greeneview North Elem Sch 1795 S Charleston Rd Jamestown OH 45335

THOMAS, LINDA F., Teacher/Coach/Dept Chair; *b:* Beaumont, TX; *ed:* (BS) Health/Phys Ed, 1969, (MS) Health/Phys Ed, 1974 Lamar Univ; Prof Mid-Management Admin; *cr:* Teacher/Coach Vidor Jr HS 1969-; *ai:* Girls Bsktbl & Track Coach; TX Classroom Teachers Assn 1988-; Alpha Delta Kappa 1979-; ADK Alpha Upsilon Chaplain 1989-; 1st Baptist Church Bevil Oaks (Lib Comm Chm 1977-, Policy Comm Mem 1988-, Building Comm Mem 1990); *office:* Vidor Jr HS 945 N Tram Vidor TX 77662

THOMAS, LOLA (SHREVES), Spanish/English Teacher; *b:* Crescent, IA; *m:* Roger L.; *c:* Nicolas; *ed:* (BA) Span, Westmar Coll 1971; Grad Stud Eng, Rdng, Span; *cr:* Span/Eng Teacher Ft Calhoun Cmmty Schls 1971-; *ai:* Dept Chairperson; Span Club Spon; Ft Calhoun Ed Assn Pres 1988-89; NCTE, Metropolitan Rdng Cncl, NSEA, NEA; Grant Sch PTA; Emmanuel Baptist Church; Baptist Womens Missionary Union VP 1988-; *office:* Ft Calhoun Cmmty Sch 1506 Lincoln St Fort Calhoun NE 68023

THOMAS, LOLA MILLS, 4th Grade Teacher; *b:* Tomahawk, KY; *m:* Joe Allen; *c:* Michelle, Greggory; *ed:* (BA) Elem Ed, 1970, Elem Ed, 1976 Moorehead St Univ; *cr:* 1st-2nd Grade Teacher Hitchins Elem 1970-71; 5th Grade Teacher Camargo Elem 1971-78; 4th Grade Teacher Menifee Cty Elem 1978-; *ai:* 4th-5th Grade Academic Coach; Textbooks Selection & Curr Guide Comm; KY Ed Assn, NEA 1970-; Menifee Cty Ed Assn 1982-; PTA Treas 1979-80; Menifee Cty Homemakers Pres 1981-82; Menifee Cty Public Lib Bd Treas 1985-; KY Commonwealth Inst for Teachers; *home:* HCR 71 Box 745 Frenchburg KY 40322

THOMAS, LORELYN GARBINI, 5th Grade Teacher; *b:* Sewickley, PA; *m:* David V.; *c:* Ryann E.; *ed:* (BA) Elem Ed, Univ of AZ 1979; Grad Work Univ of AZ; *cr:* 6th Grade Teacher Marshall Sch 1980-81; 5th Grade Teacher Cragin Sch 1981-82; 4th Grade Teacher 1982-83, 5th Grade Teacher 1983- Sam Hughes Sch; *ai:* Pilot Prgm for Sci Adoption Lab Book & Soc Stud Enrichment Curr Team Mem; Faculty Rep Child Abuse Prevention Through Ed; Asst Comm & Comm Chairperson Artist in Residence Prgm; Cooperating Teacher Stu Teaching Prgm Univ of AZ; Individual Rdng Prgm; Lit Based Rdng Prgm; Enrichment Prgm for Sci; *office:* Sam Hughes Elem Sch 700 N Wilson Ave Tucson AZ 85719

THOMAS, LORRAINE MARY (SAOUR), Sci Dept Head/Teacher; *b:* Jacksonville, FL; *m:* Michael Thomas; *c:* Luanne, Brian; *ed:* (BS) Elem Ed, Barry Coll 1967; Sci, FL St Univ 1968; *cr:* 5th Grade Teacher 1970-72, 1974-75, Sci Dept Head/5th-8th Grade Teacher 1980- St Michael Sch; *ai:* Planned & Coordinated Annual Sci Fair; Madonna Coll Stu Teacher Supvr; Oakland Schls Growing Healthy Teacher Trainer; Assisted Test Revision Oakland Schls; Selected New Sci Book Series; MI MADD 1987-; *office:* St Michael Sch 25175 Code Rd Southfield MI 48034

THOMAS, M. MONICA HILTON, Third Grade Teacher; *b:* Kokomo, IN; *m:* Patrick M.; *c:* Amy, Adam, Christina; *ed:* (BS) Elem Ed, Ball St Univ 1973; (MS) Elem Ed, IN Univ 1977; Many Wkshps on Early Chldhd Ed, Rdng, Lang Art & Elem Sch Subjects; *cr:* 6th Grade Teacher 1973-78, 4th Grade Teacher 1978-82, 4th/5th Split Teacher 1980-81 Ervin Elem; Kndgtn Teacher Ervin & Northwestern Elem 1982-85; 3rd Grade Teacher Northwestern Elem 1986-89; *ai:* Served on Many Textbook Adoption Comm; Chairperson N Cntrl Accredidation Comm; 4th Grade Little Hoosiers Chairperson; Young Authors; Book Fairs; Chi-Omega Alumnus 1973-; Pilot Teacher for Gifted & Talented Prgm; Wrote, Request & Received Money to Extend His Prgm; *office:* Northwestern Elem Sch 4223 W Co Rd 350 N Kokomo IN 46901

THOMAS, MELBA CARTER, Art/English Teacher; *b:* Elk City, OK; *m:* Gordon; *c:* Chelsea, Sam; *ed:* (BA) Art, SW OK St Univ 1973; *cr:* Teacher Dill City Schls 1973-74, Reydon Schls 1974-; *ai:* Soph Class Spon; DEA, NEA.

THOMAS, MICHAEL D., Guidance Counselor; *b:* Litchfield, IL; *m:* Frostine R. Miller; *c:* Matthew, Stephanie; *ed:* (BSED) Math, E IL Univ 1971; (MS) Sch Counseling, IL St Univ 1988; *cr:* Chem/Physics Teacher 1971-84, Math Teacher 1984-89, Guidance Cnslr 1989- Herscher HS; *ai:* NHS Spon; Peer Helpers Adv; *office:* Herscher HS 501 N Main St Herscher IL 60941

THOMAS, NANCY DIXON, Kindergarten Teacher; *b:* Fulton, KY; *m:* Richard S.; *c:* Ashley L.; *ed:* (BS) Home Ec/Child Dev, 1974, (MA) Elem Ed, 1979 Murray St Univ; *cr:* Kndgtn Teacher Hickman Cty Elem 1975-; *ai:* KY Ed Assn, NEA 1975-; KY Assn of Gifted Ed 1989-; *office:* Hickman Cty Elem Sch E Clay St Clinton KY 42031

THOMAS, PAMELA RISNER, Fifth Grade Teacher; *b:* Wichita, KS; *m:* Johnny; *c:* Mary A.; *ed:* (AA) Church Recreation, Southern Baptist Coll 1980; (BSE) Elem Ed, Univ of Cntrl AR 1982; *cr:* 4th Grade Teacher Ft Smith Chrstn Sch 1983-84; 5th Grade Teacher Rural Spec Sch 1984-; *ai:* Gifted & Talented Identification Comm; *office:* Rural Spec Sch Rt 64 S Fox AR 72051

THOMAS, PAT, Mathematics Teacher/Dept Chair; *b:* Altus, OK; *m:* Richard E.; *c:* Rick, Terri, Steve; *ed:* (BS) Bus/Math, OK St Univ 1963; (MED) Scndry Ed/Math, Cntrl St Univ 1984; Grad Stud; *cr:* Math Teacher Hoover Jr HS 1963-66, Edmond Public Schls & Cntrl Mid HS 1981-; Math Dept Chairperson Edmond Cntrl Mid HS 1983-; Adjunct/Lecture Teacher Cntrl St Univ; *ai:* Chairperson N Cntrl Evaluations; Rose St Scholastic Meet Chairperson; Discipline Comm; NEA, OK Ed Assn 1963-66, 1981-; Edmond Ed Assn 1981-; NCTM 1982-; OK Cncl Teachers of Math, Cntrl OK Cncl Teachers of Math 1984; Mathematical Assn of America 1989-; Edmond Panhellenic Pres 1987-88; *office:* Edmond Cntrl Mid HS 500 E 9th Edmond OK 73034

THOMAS, PAT MEHRINGER, 8th Grade Teacher; *b:* Pittsburgh, PA; *m:* Paul E.; *c:* Natalie M.; *ed:* (BS) Elem Ed, Univ of Steubenville 1974; (MS) Rdng/Lang Arts, Du Quesne Univ 1979; *cr:* 2nd/3rd Grade Teacher St Alphonsus Sch 1977-80; 7th/8th Grade Teacher Aquinas Cntrl 1981-; *ai:* 8th Grade Stu Cncl Moderator; OCEA, NCEA 1981-; *home:* 127 S Avalon Dr Wintersville OH 43952

THOMAS, PATRICIA ANN, 3rd Grade Teacher; *b:* Canton, OH; *m:* Dennis J.; *c:* Denny Jr., Christopher M.; *ed:* (BS) Elem Ed, Kent St Univ 1974; Assertive Discipline; *cr:* 2nd Grade Teacher 1974-75, 3rd Grade Teacher 1975-85, 2nd/3rd Split Grade Teacher 1986-87, 3rd Grade Teacher 1988- Pleasant Grove Sch; *ai:* Mid Sch & Art Comm; OEA, NEA; BSA Chm; *home:* 5709 Maplegrove Louisville OH 44641

THOMAS, PATRICIA MONCURE, Teacher; *b:* Chicago, IL; *c:* Kisha, Jamey; *ed:* (BS) Sociology/Soc Work, Western MI Univ 1969; (MA) Elem Ed, Wayne St Univ 1972; *cr:* Teacher Olalla Elem 1974-; *ai:* Art Comm; Prototype Elem Schls Building Comm; South Ritsap Centennial Comm; Principal Interviewing Comm; South Kitsap Assn Rep 1974; Washington Ed Assn 1974-; NEA 1974-; Creative Womens Leadership Awd 1988; Kitsap Cty Black Historical Comm Pres 1984-; Martin Luther King Schlsp Comm VP 1987-; Washington Black Heritage Society 1987-; Comm Svc 1988; Creative Womens Leadership Awd; Comm Svc Awd; *office:* Olalla Elem Sch 6100 SE Olalla-Burley Rd Olalla WA 98359

THOMAS, PAUL LEE, II, English Dept Chair; *b:* Woodruff, SC; *m:* Frances E. Mc Crary; *c:* Jessica F.; *ed:* (AA) Lib Art, Spartanburg Meth Coll 1981; (BA) Eng/Scndry Ed, Univ SC Spartanburg 1983; (MED) Eng/Scndry Ed, Univ SC 1985; Advanced Placement Cert; PET; SC Writing Project; *cr:* Teacher Dawkins Mid Sch 1984, Univ SC Spartanburg 1987, Spartanburg Tech Coll 1988; Teacher/Dept Chm Woodruff HS 1984-; *ai:* Journalism Dept Chm; Southern Assn Chm & Eng Curr Comm; NCTE Promising Young Writers 1989-; SCCTE Ed Stu Publishers 1988-; Various Publishings; *office:* Woodruff HS Cross Anchor Hwy Woodruff SC 29388

THOMAS, PEGGY AMMONS, Eighth Grade Teacher; *b:* Mars Hill, NC; *m:* Paul Woodson; *c:* Kay De Bruhl, Susan Honeycutt; *ed:* (BS) Elem Ed, W Carolina Univ 1959; *cr:* Teacher Mars Hill Elem Sch 1959-; *ai:* Jr Beta Club Spon; Grade Level Chairperson; Consolidated Mid Sch Planning Comm; NC Ed Assn Cty Pres; NEA; Civitan Club Teacher of Yr 1975; Mars Hill Sch Teacher of Yr 1989; Mentor Teacher 1985-86; *home:* Forest St Mars Hills NC 28754

THOMAS, PENELOPE APRIL, Business Admin Educator; *b:* Detroit, MI; *ed:* (BBA) Accounting, Niagara Univ 1963; (MS) Urban Ed Problems, St Univ of NY Buffalo 1970; Grad Stud; *cr:* Educator Buffalo Bd of Ed 1963-; *ai:* Drill Team 1970-72; *office:* Riverside HS 51 Ontario Ave Buffalo NY 14207

THOMAS, RICHARD JOHN, German/Social Studies Teacher; *b:* Aberdeen, SD; *m:* Kathryn F. Hayman; *c:* Aaron Hinton, Michael; *ed:* (BA) His/Poly Sci 1977, (MA) is 1980 Univ of SD; *cr:* Ger/Soc Stud Teacher New Castle HS 1979-; *ai:* Head Spon Jr Class; Closeup Spon; Ger Club; WFLTA Bd Mem 1988; NEA/WEA 1979-; City Cncl Councilman 1989-; Parish Cncl 1980-88; Fulbright Exch West Germany 1986; WY Foreign Lang Teacher of Yr 1989: Semi-Finalist WY Teacher of Yr 1989; Dist Teacher of Yr Masonic Order 1989; *home:* 440 Pine Newcastle WY 82701

THOMAS, RICHARD N., 5th Grade Teacher; *b:* Coraopolis, PA; *m:* Lee Clancy; *c:* Robyn; *ed:* (BS) Elem Ed, Edinboro St 1966; (MEQ) Elem Ed, St of PA 1973; *cr:* 5th Grade Teacher Warren Cty Schls 1966-67, Montour Sch Dist 1967-; *ai:* Ingram Sch Intramurals; Montour Ed Assn Treas 1976-80; NEA, PSEA; Coraopolis VFD Captain 1985-88; OH Valley Firemens Assn Secy 1978-88, Outstanding Service 1988; Coraopolis Centennial Cty Chairperson 1986; *home:* 1216 Ridge Ave Coraopolis PA 15108

THOMAS, ROBERT JOHN, High School Science Teacher; *b:* Pittsburgh, PA; *m:* Janice M.; *c:* Jamie, Jason; *ed:* (BS) Scndry Ed, Clarion Univ of PA 1967; (MED) Ed, 1975, (PHD) Ed Admin, 1984, Univ of Pittsburgh; TESA, ADAPT Prgm; *cr:* Teacher Penn Hills Sch Dist 1967-; *ai:* Swimming & Diving Coach; PSEA, NEA; MASA 1st VP 1980-84; FRSB Pres; BSA Teacher of Yr; Penn Hills Teacher of Month; Penn Hills Kiwanis Coaching Awd; Special Olympics Merit Certificate; *home:* 3306 Windgate Dr Murrysville PA 15668

THOMAS, ROSE ANNETTE, French & Spanish Teacher; *b:* St Louis, MO; *ed:* (BA) Fr, Univ of MO St Louis 1979; (MA) Fr, Univ of CA Santa Barbara 1984; *cr:* Asst Eng Teacher Lycee Robert Shuman 1979-80; Fr/span Teacher Parkway South Jr HS

1980-81, Parkway West Jr HS 1981-; *ai:* Fr Team Spon; Amer Assn Teachers Treas 1980-; AATF, Amer Assn Teacher Span 1986 & 88; Amer Cncl Teachers Foreign Lang 1986-; Foreign Lang Teachers Assn 1980-89; AFS Intnl 1973-; ACTFL Certified Oral Proficiency Testor 1986; Stage DE Formateur Schlsp of Fr Government Recipient 1990; Fr Summer Institute Univ of CA Santa Barbara Distingushed Stu Awd 1984; *office:* Parkway West Jr H S 2312 Baxter Rd Chesterfield MO 63017

THOMAS, RUBYE TROXELL, Science Teacher; *b:* Stevenson, AL; *m:* Walter Russell; *c:* Charles W.; *ed:* (BS) Soc Stud/ Biological Sci, 1974, (MAED) Biological Sci, 1980 AL A&M Univ; AP Bio/Chem Cert, Univ of AL; Physics Cert, AL A&M Huntsville; *cr:* Sci Teacher Stevenson HS 1962-88, N Jackson HS 1989-; *ai:* Sr Class Spon; Teacher Incentive Prgm Dev Comm; NSTA, NEA, AL Ed Assn, Jackson Cty Ed Assn; PTO; Delta Kappa Gamma Treas 1987-88; Jackson Cty Teacher of Yr Awd 1987; Stevenson HS Sci Building Named after Teacher; *home:* PO Box 413 Stevenson AL 35772

THOMAS, SARAH BELL, 8th Grade Reading Teacher; *b:* Mobile, AL; *c:* Leonard Jr., Lester; *ed:* (BS) Ed, Chicago St Univ 1967; (MED) Ed, Natl Coll of Ed 1981; *cr:* 6th Grade Teacher 1967-84, 8th Grade Chm 1984-89, 7th/8th Grade Rdng Teacher 1989- Robert Nathaniel Dett; *ai:* Royalites Mem; Chicago St Univ Alumni Bd (Past VP 1985-86, TAGers Mem); Pilgrim Baptist Church IKA Pres; Soc & Charity Club; Nom Teacher of Yr 1980.

THOMAS, SHIRLEY WESLEY, Mathematics Teacher; *b:* Gilmer, TX; *m:* Archie; *c:* Derrick D. Wesley; *ed:* (BS) Math, TX Coll 1964; (MS) Math Ed, Counseling/Guidance, East TX St Univ 1973; Advanced Math Wkshps, San Diego St Univ & Mc Pherson Coll; *cr:* Teacher Hawkins Ind Sch Dist, Ft Worth Ind Sch Dist, Galena Park Ind Sch Dist, Dallas Ind Sch Dist, Chula Vista Ind Sch Dist; Houston Ind Sch Dist; *ai:* Sr Class Spon; TX St Teachers Assn; Delta Sigma Theta; Phi Delta Psi; Natl Sci Fnd Grant; Whos Who Among Stu in Colls & Univs; *home:* 11523 Ainsworth Dr Houston TX 77099

THOMAS, STEVE D., 6th Grade Teacher/Principal; *b:* Laurel, MS; *m:* Mary Martin; *c:* Matthew N., John M.; *ed:* (BA) Elem Ed, Millsaps Coll 1972; (MS) Sch Admin, Troy St Univ 1980; (MS) Educl Leadership, Univ of S AL; *cr:* 5th Grade Teacher Poindexter Elem 1972-74, Perdido Jr HS 1977-79; 6th Grade Teacher/Prin Stapleton Sch 1979-88; Prin Stapleton Sch & White House Fork Sch 1988-;6th Grade Teacher/Prin Stapleton Sch 1990; *ai:* NAESP 1985-; AL Cncl Sch Admin & Supervision 1985-; AL Ed Assn 1987-; NEA 1988-; AL Assn of Elem Sch Prin 1985-; St Agatha Cath Church (Parish Cncl, Pres 1986-87); *office:* Stapleton Elem Sch PO Box 155 Stapleton AL 36578

THOMAS, TERESA E., HS Business Education Teacher; *b:* Philadelphia, PA; *m:* Merle C.; *c:* John, Christina Bjorgen, Mark, Merle, Joel, Teresa Hickerson, Michele Rink, Monica; *ed:* (BA) Elem Ed, Univ of PR 1976; (BS) Scndry Ed Bus, Bemidji St Univ 1977; Working Towards Masters Voc Ed, Univ of AK Juneau; *cr:* Admin Asst/Bus Instr Bering Strait Sch Dist 1977-83; Bus Instr Mountain Village Voc Center 1983-85, Nome-BeltzJr/Sr HS 1986-; *ai:* Nome Beltz Chrldrs Spon; AK St Voc Assn (Pres, Pres Elect) 1982-85, Outstanding St Voc Educator 1985; Lower Yukon Sch Dist Teacher 1984-85, Outstanding Service 1985; Bering Strait Sch Dist Teacher 1980-83, Outstanding Service 1981, 1982; Bering Sea Lions Club VP 1987-88; Bus Prof of Amer Adv; St Josephs Cath Church Treas 1985-; *home:* PO Box 653 Nome AK 99762

THOMAS, VERITY PETRE, Language Arts Teacher; *b:* Stoke-On-Trent, England; *c:* Jennifer E.; *ed:* (BA) Eng, Univ of OR 1968; Working Towards Certificate Portland St Univ 1985-; OR Writing Project Lewis & CLark 1989; *cr:* Eng Teacher Myrtle Point HS 1969-71, Poynter Jr HS 1988, Hillsboro HS 1988-; *ai:* Newspaper, Literary Magazine, Natural Helpers Adv; Hillsboro Ed Assn, OR Ed Assn, NEA; Hillsboro HS Staff Writing Wkshp Teacher; Started Sch Literary Magazine; *office:* Hillsboro HS 3285 SE Rood Bridge Rd Hillsboro OR 97123

THOMAS, WILLIAM CORBIN, English Teacher; *b:* Denver, CO; *m:* Joanne Mc Lain; *ed:* (BA) Eng/His, Univ of CO Denver 1981; Grad Stud Eng, Univ of CO Denver 1990; Grad Trng Forensics & Speech; *cr:* Eng Dept Chm Frenchman RE-3 Sch Dist 1984-85; Forensics Dir Montbello HS 1985-89; Eng Teacher/ Creative Writing Dir Montbello HS 1989-; *ai:* Montbello HS Literary Magazine Dir & Spon; Montbello HS Building Comm Secy 1987-; Douglas Cty Sch Dist Long Range Planning Comm 1989-; Silverstate Toastmasters Sergeant at Arms 1987-89; Mountain View Ranch HOA Treas 1989-; Del Mar Parkway HOA VP 1987-89; NEH Writing About Lit Summer Inst Grant 1985; Oxford Univ Eng Speaking Union Schlsp 1990; Natl Forensic League Coach of Distinction 1989; *office:* Montbello HS 5000 Crown Blvd Denver CO 80239

THOMAS, WILLIAM HENRY, Military Science Instructor; *b:* Fall River, MA; *m:* Christine Mc Gregor; *c:* Alison, Heather, David; *ed:* (BS) Chem, SE MA Univ 1964; (MS) Management, Naval Postgrad Sch 1976; (MED) Scndry Ed, Univ of Las Vegas 1989; *cr:* Commissioned Naval Officer US Navy 1964-85; Teacher Eldorado HS 1985-; *ai:* Rifle Firing Club; Drill Team Coach; NV St Ed Assn St Delegate 1990; Clark Cty Classroom Teachers Assn Senator 1989-; S NV Sci Teachers Assn; *office:* El Dorado HS 1139 Linn Ln Las Vegas NV 89110

THOMAS, WILLIAM J. A., Biology Teacher; *b:* Waynesburg, PA; *m:* Deborah Kay Smith; *c:* Erin N., Jennifer M., Katy Kerrigan; *ed:* (AB) Zoology, WV Univ 1967; (MS) Bio, CA St Coll 1972; Grad Stud; *cr:* Bio Teacher Fairfax Cty Public Schls 1967-; *ai:* Bio Coord; Lead Sci Cmptr Teacher; Self Study Comm Chm 1988; Local FEA, St VEA, NEA 1967-; N VA Enviromental Ed Assn Past Pres; 5 Articles Published; *office:* Robinson Scndry HS 5035 Sideburn Rd Fairfax VA 22031

THOMASON, DIANE LYNN (CLARK), Business Teacher; *b:* Mt Vernon, IL; *m:* Rahn M.; *c:* Murisa L., Reed C., Ryne M.; *ed:* (AA) Bus Ed, Rend Lake Coll 1968; (BS) Bus Ed, 1970, (MS) Bus Ed, 1973 E IL Univ; *cr:* Bus Teacher Carlyle HS 1970-72, Fairfield Cmmty HS 1972-; *ai:* FBLA Club Adv, Advisory Comm Mem; IL Bus Ed Assn 1972-; Lions Club STAR Teacher 1982; *office:* Fairfield Community HS 300 W King Fairfield IL 62837

THOMASON, JON KEITH, English Teacher; *b:* Valley City, ND; *ed:* (BA) Eng/Math, Luther Coll 1984; (MA) Eng, CO St; *cr:* Librarian Luther Coll 1980-84; Teaching Asst CO St 1984-86; Teacher Davidson Fine Arts 1987-; *ai:* Facing the Wall Schls Literary Magazine Spon; Intramurals & Bsktbl Coach; *home:* 110 Fornum Grovetown GA 30813

THOMASON, WILLIAM DALE, Sixth Grade Teacher & Coach; *b:* Pomona, CA; *m:* Ann Resmick; *c:* Tom S., Robyn J.; *ed:* (BA) Phys Ed/His/Geography/Eng, Univ of La Verne 1964; (MA) Elem Ed, CA St Univ Los Angeles 1970; Driver Trng & Ed Credential; *cr:* Teacher Azusa Unified Sch Dist 1964-65; Acting Prin/Teacher/Coach San Juan Unified Sch Dist 1965-67; Teacher/Coach Claremont Unified Sch Dist 1967-81, Bend-La Pine Schls 1981-; *ai:* Vlybl, Bsktbl, Track Coach; NEA 1964-; OR Ed Assn 1981-; CA Teachers Assn 1964-81; Bend Ed Assn 1981-; YMCA 1957-81; *office:* Cascade Jr HS 19740 SW Century Dr Bend OR 97702

THOMBS, HATTIE CLEMENT, Fifth Grade Teacher; *b:* Fountain Inn, SC; *c:* Gloria E.; *ed:* (BS) Elem Ed, Barber-Scotia Coll 1970; (MA) Rdng, Furman Univ 1979; Grad Stud Ed & Admin, Furman Univ, Univ of SC; *cr:* 5th Grade Teacher Fountain Inn Elem 1971-; *ai:* Phi Delta Kappa, ASCD 1988-; NEA & Affiliates 1971-; Zeta Phi Beta (Secy, Collegiate Adv, SC Collegiate Coord) 1981-, Zeta Schlsp 1987; Order of Eastern Stars 1984-; Natl Cncl of Negro Women 1982-; Lions Club Outstanding Educator Awd 1984; Fountain Inn Elem Teacher of Yr 1983; Outstanding Young Woman in America 1984; *office:* Fountain Inn Elem Sch 311 N Main St Fountain Inn SC 29644

THOMPKINS, EDNA BUTLER, Librarian/Media Specialist; *b:* Jacksonville, FL; *m:* Leo; *c:* Wanda P. Thompkins Harris, Zandra B. Thompkins Faulks, R. Tara Thompkins Wilson, Yolanda S. Thompkins Davis, Schandra K. Thompkins Gerdes; *ed:* (BS) Elem Ed, FL Memorial Coll 1970; (MA) Elem Ed, Nova Univ; Working Toward Ed Specialist Degree Lib Media Specialist, Nova Univ; *cr:* 5th Grade Classroom Teacher Miami Gardens Elem 1970-80; 5th Grade Classroom Teacher 1980-83, Librarian/ Media Specialist 1983- North Glade Elem; *ai:* Sch Patrol, Stu Cncl, Lib Club Adv; Comm for Stu Activity Mem; United Teachers of Dade Building Steward 1987-; Phi Delta Kappa 1990; Off Campus Stu Organization Pres 1968-70, Best all Around Stu 1970; Natl Assn for the Advancement of Colored People Youth Cncl Adv 1980-; Delta Sigma Theta Comm Chairperson 1987-; Top Ladies of Distinction 1st VP 1987-89; New Way Fellowship Baptist Church (Hospitality Comm Chairperson, Childrens Dept for Sunday Sch Dir, Childrens Drams Dept Dir); Teacher of Yr Awd Miami Gardens Elem 1978-79, N Glade Elem 1985-86; *home:* 3230 NW 205th St Miami FL 33056

THOMPSON, ALICE KAY, Mathematics Teacher; *b:* Ashland, KY; *m:* Omer C.; *c:* Sally Dunaway, Amy; *ed:* (BA) Elem Ed, Morehead St Univ 1962; (MA) Math/Scndry Ed, 1988, (Rank I) Admin/Supervision, 1989 Marshall Univ; Rank I & Planned 6th Yr Prgm; *cr:* Teacher Russell Ind Sch System 1962-, Marshall Univ 1987-; *ai:* Prayer Group Leader; Math Advisory Comm; Russell Ed Assn (Building Rep 1989-, Treas 1981-83); KY Ed Pol Act Comm Chm 1988-; Teachers Credit Union (Pres 1988-, Secy 1984-88); Delta Kappa Gamma; Russell Womens Club 1984-85; KY Dept of Ed Math & Sci Incentive Schlsp 1982-85; Math Grad Assistantship at Marshall Univ 1986-; Merrill Publishing Company Honorable Mention & Cash Gratuity;Paticipated Commonwealth Inst of Teachers 1987; Commonwealth Inst of Teachers Faculty Mem 1988 & Steering Comm Mem 1989, Conducted Wkshp; Educal Forum Panel Participant; Tristate Leadership Prgm; Nom Ashland Oil Individual Teacher Achievement Awd 1990; *office:* Russell Mid Sch Red Devil Ln Russell KY 41169

THOMPSON, ANN PHILLIPS, Mathematics Dept Chairperson; *b:* Tyler, TX; *m:* Larry Kalvy; *c:* Amy K., John K.; *ed:* (BS) Math/Eng, Sul Ross St Univ 1966; (MED) Ed, TX Tech Univ 1972; AAT Courses in Classroom Management; *cr:* Teacher Cobre Consolidated Schls 1966-67, Ft Stockton HS 1967-68, R W Matthews Jr HS 1968-69, Columbus HS 1969-70, Hutchinson Jr HS 1970-71, W TX Coll 1971-73, Lubbock HS 1973-; *ai:* Chrldr & Female Astronomy Spon; Trig & Analytic Geometry Textbook & Goal Comm; AFT 1988-; LCTA 1973-88; South Plains Math Organization 1989-; Finalist Outstanding Math Teacher; Summer Work TX Tech Univ in Youth Unlimited Opportunity Prgm for Disadvantaged Stus; *home:* 3005 66th St Lubbock TX 79413

THOMPSON, BARBARA L., 4th Grade Teacher; *b:* Pittsburgh, PA; *m:* James L.; *c:* Teresa Andress, Beverly Sammons, Carrie; *ed:* (BA) Span, Univ of TX Austin 1961; (MS) Elem Ed, Univ of N TX 1987; Elem Cert, Univ of N TX 1980; *cr:* 4th Grade Teacher Butler Elem 1980-; *ai:* Assn of TX Prof Educators 1990; *office:* Butler Elem Sch 2121 Margaret Arlington TX 76012

THOMPSON, BARBARA PRESTON, Lang Arts & Journalism Teacher; *b:* West Library, KY; *m:* Charles W.; *ed:* (AB) Area of Concentration/Eng, 1972, (MA) Ed, 1976, (Rank I) Ed/Eng Emphasis, 1984 Morehead St Univ; Grad Stud St of KY; *cr:* 8th Grade Rdng Teacher Williamson HS 1972-74; 7th-8th Grade Lang Arts Teacher Bath Cty HS & Mid Sch 1974-; *ai:* Spon Dev & Publication of BMS Monitor Mid Sch Newspaper; Textbook Selection & Sch Comm; NEA Mem; KEA; BCEA Secy; NCTE; *office:* Bath Cty Mid Sch 423 Main St PO Box 37 Owingsville KY 40360

THOMPSON, BERTINA SATTERFIELD, Teacher/Business Dept Head; *b:* Muskogee, OK; *c:* Curtis L., Patrick K.; *ed:* (BSED) Bus Ed, 1958, (MS) Bus Ed, 1967 Northeastern St Coll; Univ MO Columbia, Univ N FL Jacksonville, FL Technological Univ; *cr:* Teacher Shidler Public Schls 1961-64, R-7 Sch Dist 1966-71; Teacher/Dept Head Clay HS 1971-76, Orange Park HS 1976-; Adjunct Professor FL Comm Coll Jacksonville 1985-; *ai:* FBLA Adv; S Accreditation Assn Steering & Orange Park HS Curr Comm; FL Bus Ed Assn, FL Voc Assn Mem 1972-; Delta Pi Epsilon Mem 1985-89; Delta Kappa Gamma VP 1973-85; Orange Park United Meth Church Sunday Sch Coord 1988-; Amer Cancer Society Bd of Dirs 1984-86; Excl in Ed Awd 1989; Orange Park HS Techer of Yr Finalist 1990, Teacher of Month 1985; Clay Cty Chm St Textbook Adoption, Statewide Test Dev; Consultant Cmptr Awareness; *office:* Orange Park HS 2300 Kingsley Ave Orange Park FL 32073

THOMPSON, BETTY LAWLESS, 3rd Grade Teacher; *b:* Portland, MI; *m:* James H.; *c:* Karen Mullane, Dennis, Joan, Robert, Judy Zimmerman; *ed:* (BA) Elem Ed, Cntrl MI Univ 1958; Updated Inservices; *cr:* Kndgtn Teacher 1959-60, 1960-61 Pewamo Wostphalia Public; 3rd Grade Teacher Portland Public 1968-; *home:* 215 Barley Ave Portland MI 48875

THOMPSON, BEVERLY CARUTHERS, Fourth Grade Teacher; *b:* Kansas City, KS; *m:* Emmett W. Sr.; *c:* Emmett W. II, Jennifer A.; *ed:* (BA) His, KS Univ 1959; (ME) Elem Ed, Washburn Univ 1971; *cr:* Teacher Quinton Heights Elem Sch 1961-63, Mc Carter Elem Sch 1968-; *ai:* Poetry Club Spon; Proposal Bus/Elem Sch Partnership; Delta Kappa Gamma Intnl Pres 1982-84; Links Inc Pres 1988-; Cmmty Housing Resource Bd VP 1988-; Topeka Performing Arts Center Assoc Pres 1990; Governors Cncl on Arts; St Advisory Comm for Chapter 2, Ed Consolidation & Improvement Act; *home:* 1025 Prairie Rd Topeka KS 66604

THOMPSON, BEVERLY HOOVER, English/Mathematics Teacher; *b:* Aberdeen, MD; *m:* Ted N.; *ed:* (BSE) Ed, Univ of TX El Paso 1973; (MA) Eng Ed, Pembroke St Univ 1986; Cert Admin & Supervision, Winthrop Univ; *cr:* Lang Art Teacher Enfield Acad 1974-75; Rdng Teacher Coll Park Mid Sch 1978-79; Eng/Fr Teacher Bennettsville HS 1979-85, Cheraw HS 1985-; Eng/Math Teacher Evans Correctional Institution 1990; *ai:* Eng Dept Chm Cheraw HS; Tennis Coach Cheraw HS; Quill & Sroll Spon Cheraw HS; Drama Club Spon Bennettsville HS; NEA 1978-; SC Ed Assn 1978-88; Palmetto St Teachers Assn 1988-; NCTE 1985-; Amer Cncl of Teachers of Foreign Lang 1985-; Correctional Ed Assn 1990.

THOMPSON, BYRON KEITH, 6th Grade Teacher; *b:* Denver, CO; *ed:* (BS) Elem Ed, OR St Univ 1982; Cmptr & Outdoor Ed; *cr:* 5th/6th Grade Teacher Juchem Elem Sch 1983-87, Betty Adams Elem Sch 1987-88; 6th Grade Teacher Fairmount Elem Sch 1988-; *ai:* Cmptr Club; Time Magazine Club; Cmptr Building Level Consultant; Math Comm; Rain Forest Protection Fund Drive Spon; PTA; *office:* Fairmount Elem Sch 15975 W 50th Ave Golden CO 80403

THOMPSON, CARMEN (WRIGHT), Jr/Sr English Teacher; *b:* Cairo, IL; *c:* Brandon H.; *ed:* (BS) Eng, S IL Univ Carbondale 1970; *cr:* HS Eng Teacher Century Unit Dist 100 1971-81, Dongola Unit Dist 66 1984-86, Century Unit Dist 100 1987-; *ai:* 7th Grade Class Spon; Co-Adv Schls Literary Magazine; *office:* Century Unit Dist 100 Shawnee College Rd Rt 1 Ullin IL 62992

THOMPSON, CAROL ANN (CARLSON), Health/Physical Ed Instructor; *b:* Red Wing, MN; *m:* Ralph M.; *c:* Kristin, Jennifer, Erik; *ed:* (BS) Phys Ed/Health, Univ of WI River Falls 1971; Facilitator Alcohol & Other Drugs of Abuse, Johnson Inst; *cr:* Phys Ed Teacher Mondovi Cmmty Schls 1971-73; Day Care Teacher Saint Paul Theological Seminary 1973-74; Health/Phys Ed Teacher Boyceville Cmmty Schls 1975-; *ai:* Stus Offering Support Adv; Prin Advisory Comm Mem 1988-; NEA 1971-; Holy Cross Luth Church (Youth Choir Dir 1987-, Handbell Cty Dir 1985-); Mid Sch Teacher of Yr Boyceville Cmmtys Schls 1988, 1989; *office:* Boyceville Comm Schls Box 98 Tiffany St Boyceville WI 54725

THOMPSON, CAROLINE SUE, English Teacher; *b:* Mineola, NY; *m:* Lloyd; *ed:* (BS) Eng Ed, Evangel Coll 1987; Working Toward Masters Eng, Univ of CA Irvine; *cr:* Eng Teacher Fullerton Union HS 1987-; *ai:* Speech & Debate Coach; Sigma Tau Delta 1986-; MO Assn of Teachers of Eng Outstanding Eng Grad 1987, Robert J Greef Awd; NCTE 1986-; *office:* Fullerton HS 201 E Chapman Fullerton CA 92634

THOMPSON, CARROLL RICHARD, Mathematics Teacher; *b:* Limestone, ME; *ed:* (BA) Elem Ed, Farmington St 1956; (MS) Math Instruction, Reed Coll 1967; Natl Sci Fnd Schlshp, Rutgers Univ; *cr:* 6th-8th Grade Teacher Limestone Grammar Sch 1953-55; Prin/7th/8th Grade Teacher Lee Grammar Sch 1956-63; 8th/9th Grade Math Teacher Fanwood Jr HS 1963-65; Eng/7th/ 8th Grade Math Teacher Plainville Jr HS 1965-; *ai:* Math Club Adv; Mathcounts Coach; NEA, CEA, PEA; Mathcounts Team

Coach Won 4 St Championships 1987-, Natl Competition in Washington; *home:* 65 East St Plainville CT 06062

THOMPSON, CLIFF HENRY, Athletic Dir/Religion Teacher; *b:* Rantoul, IL; *m:* Cindy Gerken; *c:* Taya, Ryan, Casey; *ed:* (BA) Ed/Phys Ed, Concordia Univ 1977; (MS) Human Kinetics, Univ of WI Milwaukee 1984; *cr:* K/7th/8th Grade Teacher Holy Ghost Luth Sch 1977-79; 10th-12th Grade Religion Teacher/Athletic Dir Milwaukee Luth HS 1979-; *ai:* Athletic & Co-Curr Act Dir; WI Bsktbl Coaches Assn Private Sch Rep 1981-, 100 Victories 1989; Natl Athletic Dir Assn 1980-; WI Athletic Dir Assn 1980-; Mid-West Athletes Against Childrens Cancer Dir 1977-; Bsktbl Coach of Yr 1984-85; Metro Conference Bsktbl Coach of Yr 1984-85; *office:* Milwaukee Luth HS 9700 W Grantosa Dr Milwaukee WI 53222

THOMPSON, CLIFTON C., Math Dept Chm/Dist Cmptr Coord; *b:* Johnstown, PA; *m:* Janet Steward; *c:* Scott, Gary, Jeffrey, Michael; *ed:* (BA) Math, Gannon Univ 1965; (MS) Math/Ed, St Univ of New York Buffalo 1971; Grad Stud Math & Cmptr Sci; *cr:* Cmptr Instr Jamestown Comm Coll 1983-88; Math Instr Southwestern HS 1965-; *ai:* Cmptr Coord; NEA, SW Teachers Assn, NY St Teachers of Math; Chautauqua Cty Athletic Assn (Secy, Treas 1972-82) Dist Service 1982; Chautauqua Cty Sch Bd Assn for Gifted & Talented Cmptr Summer Enrichment Prgm Instr; *office:* Southwestern Cntrl HS 600 Hunt Rd Jamestown NY 14701

THOMPSON, DEBRUAH ABRUETTE GREEN, French & Latin Teacher; *b:* Baltimore, MD; *m:* Eddy M.; *c:* Sherril Y., Patricia A., Yolanda L., Jacqueline M., Darrel L.; *ed:* (BA) Fr, Morgan St Univ 1966; Current Trends in Ed, Towson St 1980; John Rassias Intensive Foreign Lang Wkshp 1982-83; Span & Fr Natl Endowment of Summer Inst, Univ of MD Baltimore Cty 1984, 1986; Intensive Foreign Lang Summer Inst, Univ of MD College Park 1988; *cr:* Correspondence Dictator Natl Geographic Society 1967-70; Substitute Teacher DC Public Schls 1970-72; Nursery Directress Progressive Day Care Center 1973-74; Foreign Lang Teacher Garrison Jr HS 1975-87, Mt Royal Elem & Mid Sch 1987-; *ai:* Awds Assemblies; Spring & Winter Festivals; MD Foreign Lang Assn Mem 1976-; Interdenominational Alliance of Ministers Wives & Widows Mem 1989-; Progressive 1st Baptist Church (Sr Choir Pres 1958-88, Deaconess Bd Pres), 30 Yrs Service to Church Awd 1988; *home:* 3801 Hendon Rd Randallstown MD 21133

THOMPSON, DENISE GUPTON, 6th Grade Teacher; *b:* Marion, KY; *m:* Michael L.; *c:* Kerry, Kristi; *ed:* (BS) Elem Ed, 1978; Elem Ed, 1984 Murray St; *cr:* Spec Ed Teacher 1980-81; 6th/8th Grade Teacher 1981- Carlisle Cty Mid Sch; *ai:* Ky Ed Assn Legislative Contact Tm; PTSA Treas 1987-; *home:* Rt 2 Box 288C Bardwell KY 42023

THOMPSON, DONALD NEAL, Mathematics Teacher; *b:* Pontiac, MI; *m:* Sara Jo Cray; *c:* Denisse R., Kathryn L. Thompson Jones, Elizabeth S. Thompson Jones; *ed:* (BA) Bus Admin/Accounting, Univ of S FL 1978; Teacher Cert, Scndry Math 1981; *cr:* Math Teacher Hernando HS 1981-; *ai:* NCTM, FCTM, NEA 1981-; *office:* Hernando HS 200 Kelly St Brooksville FL 34601

THOMPSON, DONNA MARSH, 5th/6th Grade/Jr HS Teacher; *b:* Wenatchee, WA; *m:* Charles W. Sr.; *c:* Charles W. Jr., John, Cynthia, Webster, David; *ed:* Bus, Secretarial, Aunswalds Coll 1950; Choral Conducting Music, Univ of Puget Sound 1961; *cr:* Elem Music Teacher Faith Baptist Sch 1968-76; 5th/6th Grade Music/Speech Teacher Calvary Baptist Sch 1977-; *ai:* Prgms Dir; ACSI Speech Meet & Math Olympics Coord; *home:* 2102 Lake Farm Rd Port Angeles WA 98362

THOMPSON, DORIS E. YOUNG, Business Dept Chairperson; *b:* Vaughnsville, OH; *c:* Lori Meyers, Daniel G. Myers, Lee Ann; *ed:* (BS) Bus Ed, Bowling Green St Univ 1953; (MA) Bus Ed, AZ St Univ 1967; Soc Stud, Bus & Related Areas Grad Stud; *cr:* Teacher/Dept Chair Mc Clintock HS 1967-; *ai:* Sr Class Spon; Delta Pi Epsilon, NBEA; Gamma Phi Beta; Mc Clintock HS Teacher of Excl 1989; *office:* Mc Clintock HS 1830 E Del Rio Tempe AZ 85282

THOMPSON, EARLINE KAY (MILLER), Sixth Grade Teacher; *b:* Logansport, IN; *m:* Jerry Dean; *c:* Kyle V., Tisha M.; *ed:* (BS) Elem Ed, Ball St Univ 1969; (MS) Wright St Univ 1988-91; *cr:* 3rd Grade Elem Teacher 1971-74, 2nd Grade Elem Teacher 1974-76 C R Coblentz Elem Sch; 5th Grade Teacher 1979-82, 6th Grade Teacher 1982- C R Coblentz Mid Sch; *ai:* CCTA Mem 1982-; Delta Kappa Gamma 1987-; Society Intnl; OEA Mem 1971-76; NEA Mem 1979-81; United Meth Church Mem 1971-; Right To Read Dist Dir 1974; Quest & Cope Leader 1986; Natl Sci Fnd Grant Chem Miami Univ 1989-; *office:* C R Coblentz Mid Sch 9088 Monroe Central Rd West Manchester OH 45382

THOMPSON, EDNA WAITS, English Teacher; *b:* Earle, AR; *ed:* (BA) Eng/Speech/Drama, Univ of AR Pinebluff 1965; (MA) Eng/Urban Stud, Governors St Univ 1976; Teaching Gifted; Teaching Creative Process; Teaching Writing Process; *cr:* Eng Teacher 1965-72, Dept Chairperson 1970-72 Wendell Phillips HS; Eng Teacher Lindblom Tech HS 1972-; *ai:* Frosh Class Adv; North Cntrl Accreditation Steering Comm; Drama Coach & Spon; NCTE 1975-; UAPB Alumni Assn Secy 1980-82; Chicago Urban League 1986-89; NAACP 1985-89; Lindblom HS Teacher of Yr 1987; *office:* Lindblom Tech HS 6130 S Wolcott Chicago IL 60636

THOMPSON, EVA SUSONG, Sixth Grade Teacher; *b:* Greene Cty, TN; *m:* Daryl Wayne; *c:* Andee T. Lockwood, Ami T.; *ed:* (BS) Home Ec, E Tn St Univ 1952; Elem Ed, E TN St Univ 1952; Grad Work at Univ of VA, Wm & Mary, E Carolina Coll, Lynchburg Coll; *cr:* 6th Grade Teacher 1952-54, 7th Grade Math Teacher 1954-58 Greeneville Public Schls; 6th Grade Teacher Camp Lejeune Schls 1958-60, Fairfax Public Schls 1968-; *ai:* SCA Spon; NEA, VA Ed Assn, Fairfax Ed Assn 1968-.

THOMPSON, FRANK RALPH, English Instructor; *b:* Portsmouth, OH; *m:* Cynthia Johnette Merritt; *c:* Sheri, Wesley, Neal, Jill; *ed:* (BSED) Eng, 1974, (MSED) Scndry Ed, 1983 OH Univ; OH Writing Project Miami Univ, OH Wesleyan Advanced Placement Seminar, Teacher Trng for Jr/Sr HS Gifted Stu Miami Univ; *cr:* Dir West End Tutoring Prgm 1970-72; Teacher Valley Local HS 1974-; *ai:* OH Mock Trial Prgm Team Spon; Drug & Alcohol Abuse Faculty Consultant; Valley Teachers Assn & Valley Alumni Schlsp Comms Mem; Valley Teachers Assn (Pres 1984, VP 1983, Building Rep 1976-82); Portsmouth N Div Minor League Bsbl 1989-; *home:* 2810 Brant Ave Portsmouth OH 45662

THOMPSON, GAYLE HOOD, Mathematics Teacher; *b:* Harrodsburg, KY; *m:* Paul Yates; *c:* Lynn A. Thompson Cole, Jeffrey Yates, Michael K.; *ed:* (BS) Accounting/Ec, Univ of KY 1959; GA St Coll, Univ of NM Ed; *cr:* 5th Grade Teacher R W Lindsey Elem 1959-60; 8th Grade Math Teacher Tabor Jr HS 1960-61; 5th Grade Teacher Rockford Lane Elem 1968-69; 8th Grade Math Teacher Everitt Jr HS 1974-77, Math Teacher Jinks Jr HS 1982-86, Bay HS 1986-; *ai:* Algebra II Math Competition & Swim Coach; Bay Cty Algebra Comm; Bay Dist Math Cncl; *office:* Bay HS 1200 Harrison Ave Panama City FL 32401

THOMPSON, JAMES L., Air Science Teacher; *b:* West Chester, PA; *c:* James M., Richard B., Dina L.; *ed:* (BA) Government, Univ of NH 1960; (MS) Ed/Mid Management, TX A&I Univ 1989; USAF Pilot Trng, Armed Forces Staff Coll, Numerous Military Schls; *cr:* Air Sci Teacher Univ of NH 1956-60; Flight Instr USAF 1960-72; Air Sci Instr O W Holmes HS 1980-; *ai:* Spon AFJROTC Prgm; Commandant AFJROTC Summer Leadership Sch; *office:* Oliver Wendell Holmes HS 6500 Ingram Rd San Antonio TX 78238

THOMPSON, JEANNE A., Mathematics Dept Chair; *b:* Beaumont, Panama; *m:* Jefferson D.; *c:* Jeffrey D., Janene D. Lain; *ed:* (BSED) Math, N TX St Univ 1961; (MAT) Math, Angelo St Univ 1973; *cr:* Math Teacher Dallas Ind Sch Dist 1964-65, Lawton Public Schls 1965-67, Texarkana Ind Sch Dist 1967-68, San Marcos Ind Sch Dist 1968-69, Kerrville Ind Sch Dist 1969-70, Brady Ind Sch Dist 1970-73, Kerrville Ind Sch Dist 1973-; *ai:* NHS Spon; Campus Improvement Team Comm; Math Dept Chm & Curr Coord K-12th Grade; TX St Teachers Assn 1965-; NEA 1979-; NCTM, TX Cncl of Teachers of Math; Schreiner Coll Teacher Ed Advisory Comm 1988-; *office:* Tivy HS 1607 Sidney Baker Kerrville TX 78028

THOMPSON, JENNY MC ALHANY, Sixth Grade Teacher; *b:* Branchville, SC; *m:* David L.; *c:* Lauren E.; *ed:* (BA) Elem Ed, Univ of SC 1975; Grad Stud; *cr:* 5th Grade Teacher Barnwell Sch Dist 1976-83; 6th Grade Teacher Orangeburg Sch Dist 1983-; *ai:* Jr Var Chrldr Spon; Orangeburg Sch Dist Lang Art Comm Chairperson; Reach Co Chairperson; Raylrode Daze Festival Comm Bd of Dirs 1987-88, 1988-89; Received Teacher Incentive Prgm Awds 1987-89; *home:* 605 W Edward St Branchville SC 29432

THOMPSON, JOE EARL, Assistant Principal; *b:* Oak Ridge, TN; *m:* Jeanne Brown; *c:* Melanie; *ed:* (BS) His, 1974, (MED) Admin/Supervision, 1985 Mid TN St; Elem Ed, Trevecca Nazarene Coll; *cr:* Teacher/Coach Lewis Cty Schls 1975-77, Mid TN Chrstn Sch 1978-79; Teacher Bradley Model 1980-87; Asst Prin Bellwood Elem 1987-, Black Fox Elem 1990; *ai:* Tennis, Ftbl, Bsktbl, Cross Cntry Coach; Peer Evaluator 1985; Prin Designee 1982-86; TEA, NEA, MEA 1975-; TASSA 1987-; Belle Aire Baptist Church (Deacon, Adult Sunday Sch Teacher, Head Cnslr); Whos Who in Amer Ed 1987-88; *home:* 5020 Creekside Dr Murfreesboro TN 37129

THOMPSON, JOHN TYRUS, Biology Instructor; *b:* Bozeman, MT; *m:* Evelyn L. Panice; *ed:* (BS) Bio, Bradley Univ 1970; (MST) Bio Ed, Univ of Chicago 1975; *cr:* Biologist S Cook Cty Mosquito Abatement Dist; Curr Consultant/Teacher John G Shedd Aquarium; Consultant/Teacher NE IL St Univ Teacher Center; Teacher Moraine Valley Comm Coll; Sci Chm/Teacher Du Sable Upper Grade Center 1970-74, Oak Lawn Cmmty HS 1974-88; Sci Chm Lyons Township HS 1988-89; Bio Instr IL Math & Sci Acad 1989-; *ai:* NABT, NSTA 1980-; EEAI 1983-, Environmental Educator of Yr 1984; Governors Master Teacher 1984; Univ of Chicago Outstanding HS Teacher Awd 1987, 1989; IL Math/Sci Acad Awd of Excl 1988; Sigma XI Research Society Outstanding Teacher Awd 1990; *office:* IL Math & Sci Acad 1500 W Sullivan Rd Aurora IL 60506

THOMPSON, JON STEVEN, 7th Grade English Teacher; *b:* Zanesville, OH; *m:* Karen L. Johnsen; *c:* Brian, Jeremy, Julie; *ed:* (BS) Ed, OH Univ 1969; (MA) Ed, John Carroll Univ 1976; Ed; *cr:* Eng Teacher Sheffield/Sheffield Lake Mid Sch 1969-70; Lee Burneson Mid Sch 1970-; *ai:* Coach Ftbl, HS Tennis; Mid Sch Yrbk; NEA/OEA 1973-; WTA 1970-; OCTELA 1990-; Westlake Teacher of Yr 1987; Burneson Teacher of Yr 1986-87; Martha Holden Jennings Scholar 1987; Recipient of Westlake Ed Fnd Grant 1989; Presentations OH Mid Sch Conference; OH Cncl of Teachers Eng/Lang Arts Conference; *office:* Lee Burneson Mid Sch 2240 Dover Center Rd Westlake OH 44145

THOMPSON, JUDY JANE CARPENTER, Math Teacher; *b:* Bakersfield, CA; *m:* William Everett; *c:* Cydney E., Patrick E. Lee; *ed:* (AA) Math/Sci, Bakersfield Coll 1961; (BS) Math Sci, CA Poly San Luis Obispo 1963; CA Lutheran; Bakersfield Coll; CA St Coll; Fresno St Univ; Pacific Coll; *cr:* Math Teacher North HS 1966-68, Carden 1968-72, North HS 1975-; *ai:* Textbook & Dist Math Curr; Adv Comm; CA Math Assn, Bakersfld Math Assn; PTA 1975-88 Founders Outstanding Honor 1988; Order of Eastern Star Office; *office:* North H S 300 Galaxy Ave Bakersfield CA 93308

THOMPSON, JULIE LORRAINE, English Teacher; *b:* Salt Lake City, UT; *m:* Jeffrey D.; *c:* Bryan Baumgartner, Thomas Baumgartner; *ed:* (BA) Eng, Univ of CA Santa Barbara 1968; (MA) Ed, CA St Univ San Luis Obispo 1970; (MA) Eng, Univ of Pacific 1986; Bay Area Writing Project, Cap Writing Prgm, Clinical Teaching; *cr:* Eng Teacher Ernest Righetti HS 1969-70, Alhambra HS 1970-73; Yrbk Adv/Eng Teacher Thornwood HS 1974-77; Eng Teacher San Joaquin Delta Jr Coll 1980-87, Lodi HS 1977-; *ai:* Schlsp Comm; Graduation Prgm; Sr Class Adv; San Joaquin Cty Teachers of Rdng 1977-80; Lodi Ed Assn 1977-; Lambda Theta Phi Newsletter 1989-; Faculty Cncl Pres; Mentor Teacher; Lodi HS Teacher of Yr 1985; *office:* Lodi HS 3 S Pacific Ave Lodi CA 95242

THOMPSON, KATHRYN HOLCOMB, 7th Grade English Teacher; *b:* Bristow, OK; *m:* David L.; *c:* Megan L., David C.; *ed:* (BA) Art, 1960, (MED) Ed, 1975 Northeastern St Univ; Grad Stud Eng Elem Ed; *cr:* Elem Lang Art Teacher 1960-61, Elem Art Teacher 1961-70, Scndry Art Teacher 1970-80, 7th Grade Eng Teacher 1980- Bristow Public Schls; *ai:* Co-Teaching Gifted/Talented; Jr HS Newspaper Spon; OEA & NEA; BEA Bldg Rep 1982-84; *home:* Rt 4 Box 122 Bristow OK 74010

THOMPSON, KAY VAN ZANT, Third Grade Teacher; *b:* Winchester, TN; *m:* Carey F.; *c:* Karen Thompson Helton; *ed:* (BS) Elem, Mid TN St Univ 1972; Grad Stud Kndgtn Cert; *cr:* 3rd Grade Teacher Buchanan Elem Sch 1973-; *ai:* Chrldr Spon, Textbook Comm Chairperson; Calander & Attendance Comm; REA Rep; TEA, NEA; MTMC Hospital Volunteer 1985-.

THOMPSON, LEE ANN LEFLER, Mathematics Teacher; *b:* Grinnell, IA; *m:* Bradley Bruce; *c:* Kelsey J.; *ed:* (BS) Math, 1971, (MS) Curr/Instruction, 1974 Univ of OR; *cr:* Math Teacher Roosevelt Mid Sch 1971-84, South Eugene HS 1984-; *ai:* Phi Beta Kappa; *office:* South Eugene HS 400 E 19th Ave Eugene OR 97405

THOMPSON, LINDA BAXTER, Elementary Spanish Teacher; *b:* Pinehurst, NC; *m:* Jerry Moore; *c:* Kelly, Matthew; *ed:* (BA) Span, Meredith Coll 1963; (MS) Intermediate Ed, NCA&T 1980; *cr:* Span/Eng Teacher Sunset Park Jr HS 1963-64, New Hanover HS 1964-66; Span Teacher N Moore HS 1966-68; 7th Grade Lang Art Teacher Mt Gilead Elem & Highland Mid Sch 1972-87; Elem Span Teacher Mt Gilead & Star Biscoe & Candor Elem Sch 1987-; *ai:* Coord Elem Span Prgm for Montgomery Cty Schls; NC Certified Mentor Teacher; NC St Second Lang Ed Evaluation Comm Mem; NEA 1963-68; NCAE 1972-; FLANC 1987-; Delta Kappa Gamma (Membership Chm, Parliametarian); Bd of Trustees Meredith Coll 1979-82; Montgomery Cty Teacher of Yr 1973; Mt Gilead Sch Outstanding Young Educator 1975; Montgomery Cty Terry Sunford Awd 1981; *office:* Mt Gilead Elem Sch PO Box 308 Mount Gilead NC 27306

THOMPSON, LINDA BEAN, English Teacher; *b:* Longview, TX; *m:* Darrell H.; *c:* Melissa, Jennifer, Kristi; *ed:* (BA) Eng, Sam Houston St Univ 1968; (MA) Eng, UTA 1979; Working Toward PhD; *cr:* Eng Teacher Travis Jr HS 1969-71, Mountain View Coll 1978-83, Christ Way Acad 1983-85, Midlothian HS 1985-; *ai:* Dept Head; Coach UIL; Literary Criticism; Ready Writing; TSTA 1985-; Kappa Delta Pi Pres; Alpha Chi; Published Book; *office:* Midlothian HS 925 9th St S Midlothian TX 76065

THOMPSON, LINDA GUARINO, Seventh Grade Science Teacher; *b:* New Orleans, LA; *m:* Lloyd J. Jr.; *c:* Lloyd III, Joshua; *ed:* (BA) Elem Ed, 1975, (MED) Guidance/Counseling, 1979 SE LA Univ; Grad Courses Drug Ed; *cr:* 7th Grade Teacher Mandeville Mid Sch 1975-79; 7th Grade Sci Teacher Mandeville Jr HS 1979-; *ai:* Stu Cncl Spon; Sci Dept Head; Sex Ed Teacher; Phi Kappa Phi Intnl Honor Society 1979-; Writing Sex Ed Curr for St Tammany Parish Comm Mem; *office:* Mandeville Jr HS 639 Carondelet St Mandeville LA 70448

THOMPSON, LOIS DRINKWATER, Mathematics Teacher; *b:* Phoenix, AZ; *m:* Edward M.; *c:* Barbara, Michael; *ed:* (BA) Elem Ed, 1976, (MNS) Phys Sci, 1986 AZ St Univ; *cr:* 8th Grade Math Teacher Laveen Sch Dist 1976; 7th/8th Grade Teacher Hopi Elem 1976-77; 8th Grade Sci Teacher Pueblo Elem 1977-78; 7th Grade Soc Stud/Lang Art Teacher 1978-79, 7th Grade Sci/Math Teacher 1979-85 Cocopah; Math Teacher Chaparral HS 1985-; *ai:* Track Team Clerk; Discipline Comm Mem; United Teachers of Scottsdale 1976-; NCTM 1989-; *office:* Chaparral HS 6935 E Gold Dust Ave Scottsdale AZ 85253

THOMPSON, LOLA BEATRICE (RUSH), Fifth Grade Teacher; *b:* Sapulpa, OK; *m:* Paul Franklin; *c:* Cynthia L. Thompson Roach; *ed:* (BS) Ed, 1970, (MA) Ed, 1973 E Cntrl Univ; *cr:* Elem Teacher Byng Sch 1970-; *ai:* 4th-12th Grade 4-H Club Leader; 4-H Cty Leader of Yr & Nom St Leader; *office:* Byng Sch Rt 3 Ada OK 74820

THOMPSON, MARGARET DUFF, Retired Teacher; *b:* Walla Walla, WA; *c:* Reid A., Rebecca Thompson Schaad; *ed:* (BA) Elem Ed, E OR St Coll 1965; *ai:* OR Retired Teachers

Corresponding Secy 1988-; *home:* 735 SW 29th Pendleton OR 97801

THOMPSON, MARGARET MARY (WELTON), English Teacher; *b:* Waterbury, CT; *c:* Derrick; *ed:* (BA) Scndry Ed/Eng, Coll of Our Lady of The Elms 1968; Media Specialist, Univ of South FL; *cr:* Eng Teacher Watertown HS 1968-74, Sts Peter & Paul 1976-79, Lauderhill Mid Sch 1979-; *ai:* Southern Assn of AccreditationComm on Lang Arts; Media, Newspaper & Yrbk Adv; Lang Arts & Literary Fair Coord; Sch Adv; Prime Steering Comm; Broward Teachers Union Local & Natl Mem 1988-; Lauderhill Mid Sch Teacher of Yr Awd 1990; Lauderhill Womens Club Teacher of Yr Awd 1990; *home:* 1210 SW 4th Ave Pompano Beach FL 33060

THOMPSON, MARIAN LOUISE (WEBER), Learning Disabilities Teacher; *b:* Hamlin, KS; *m:* James Elliot; *c:* Franklin J., David E., Ross S., Clark W.; *ed:* (BS) Elem Ed, Peru St 1963; (MS) Spec Ed/Learning Disabilities KS Univ Lawrence 1971; Ed, Emporia KS, Univ of NE, KS St; *cr:* 1st-8th Grade Teacher NE Rural Schls 1944-49; 4th Grade Teacher Humbolt Elem 1961-68; Teacher of Learning Disabilities Don Cty Cooperative 1969-79; 4th Grade Teacher Highland Grade Sch 1979-89; *ai:* Delta Kappa Gamma (2nd VP 1988-89, VP 1989-); Intnl Rdng Assn Pres 1978-79; KS Math Teachers Assn; Natl Teachers Assn (Secy, Treas) 1986-89; *home:* 501 N Elmira Highland KS 66035

THOMPSON, MARTHA BARRETT, Sixth Grade Teacher; *b:* Abingdon, VA; *m:* Walter David; *c:* Paul D.; *ed:* (BSED) H E Ed, James Madison Univ 1950; (MSED) Rdng, Longwood Coll 1981; Various Univs; *cr:* Classroom Teacher Wilson Memorial HS 1950-53; Home Ec Teacher Halifax Cty HS 1953-69; 6th Grade Teacher Volens Elem Sch 1974-; *ai:* Stamp Club Adv; Textbook Comm Mem; NEA, VA Ed Assn 1950-69, 1974-; Halifax Ed Assn (Treas 1988) 1958-69, 1974-; Delta Kappa Gamma Various Offices 1963-; Phi Delta Kappa 1988-; Halifax Cty Assn of Mental Heath (Bd of Dirs, Various Offices) 1965-73; Young Homemakers of VA Adv 1960-67; VA FFA & FHA Camp Bd 1964-65; *home:* PO Box 371 18 Banister Rd Halifax VA 24558

THOMPSON, MARVIN RUSSELL, Theatre Arts Teacher; *b:* Raymondville, TX; *m:* Lorayne Doom; *c:* John Stephen, Mark Daniel; *ed:* (BA) Speech/Bible, East TX Baptist Coll 1955; (MA) Eng/Drama, Univ of TX A&T 1966; Drama Univ of Houston 1947-49;; Southwestern Bapt Theologigcal Seminary; Doctoral Work Drama East TX St Univ Commerce; *cr:* Eng/Speech Teacher Delhart HS ISD 1956-57; Eng Teacher Valley Baptist Acad 1958-66; Dir of Theatre East TX Baptist Coll 1966-72; Eng Teacher North Battleford 1972-73; Theatre Arts Teacher New Caney Mid Sch ISD 1982-; *ai:* Adv Natl Jr Honor Society; Spon Theatre Arts Acts; Dept Head Speech/Drama; Campus Goals Comm; TX Ed Theatre; TX Non-Profit Theatre; Northwest Baptist Convention Exec Bd 1977-81; Lynwood Extended Care Center (Dir 1980-81/Dev Pastoral Care 1981); Baptist Stud Union Dir 1976-78; Admitted Alpha Psi Omega Univ of Houston 1947-49; Pres Delta Psi Omega East TX Baptist Coll 1953-55; Whos Who Amer Coll/Univ 1955; Writer for South Baptist Convention on Sunday Sch Bd 1976-79; Whos Who in Alberta 1979; Outstanding Frosh Stu Drama Awd; Soph Stu in Drama Awd; VP Sr Class; *home:* 23 Era Ln Porter TX 77365

THOMPSON, MARY K. (JONES), Social Studies Teacher; *b:* Elbert, WV; *m:* Leonard L.; *c:* Tara D., Shannon L.; *ed:* (AAS) Child Dev, Olive Harry Jr Coll 1984; (BS) Ed, Chicago St Univ 1987; *cr:* Librarian/Story Teller/Teacher-Aide St Thaddeus 1980-82; Asst Dir DEMY 1982-84; Part-Time Kndgtn Teacher St Collabanus 1986; 5th Grade Teacher St Joachim 1987-89; Soc Stud Teacher Acad of Our Lady HS 1989-; *ai:* Bowling Club; Frosh Sch Act, Bake Sales, Fund Drives; Sr Luncheon Coord; Soc Comm; Pi Kappa Delta Mem 1987-, Honor Certificate 1987; Chicago St Univ Mem 1985-; Parent Club (VP, Recording Secy), *home:* 7928 S Kimbark Chicago IL 60619

THOMPSON, MARY LEA, Gifted/Talented Teacher; *b:* Fort Worth, TX; *m:* Dwight O.; *c:* Todd, Jana L. Ritchie; *ed:* (BA) Elem Ed, Glassboro St Coll 1975; *cr:* 7th & 8th Grade Sci/Eng Teacher Southampton Twp Sch 1962-64; 7th & 8th Grade Teacher Indian Mills Elem Sch 1966-68; Kndgtn Teacher Anita Metzger ITA Sch 1970-78; Gifted & Talented Teacher Hammonton Elem Sch 1978-; *ai:* NJ Math League Spon; NJ Educators of Gifted & Talented 1985-; Atlantic Cty Educators of Gifted & Talented 1988-; NEA, NJ Ed Assn 1978-; Womens Civic Club 1988-; Cmmty Bible Group Leader 1976-; Seminar to Study Environmental Ed Sponsored by Regional Environmental Ed Prgm; *home:* 339 Central Ave Hammonton NJ 08037

THOMPSON, MARY LOU, Third Grade Teacher; *b:* Ada, OK; *m:* Charles Donald; *c:* Michael O., Jon R.; *ed:* (BS) Elem Ed/Home Ec, 1968, (MED) Elem Ed, 1975 E Cntrl Univ; Inservice Wkshp; *cr:* Teachers Asst Konawa Public Sch; Speech Therapist Valley View Hospital; Jr/Sr HS Lang Teacher Waurika OK; Elem Teacher Ardmore OK; *ai:* Fine Art Curr & Elem Math Review Comm Mem; Arts-in-Ed Comm Chm; Beta Club Spon; HS Stu Cncl; Speech & Drama Club; Ardmore Ed Assn Building Rep 1981-87; OK Ed Assn, NEA 1968-; Baptist Church Bible Teacher 1952-80; *office:* Will Rogers Sch Monroe & Mt Washington Ardmore OK 73401

THOMPSON, MARY PAMELA, 10th Grade English Teacher; *b:* Bradford, PA; *m:* William G.; *c:* Sean R.; *ed:* (BA) Eng, Mercyhurst Coll 1969; (MSED) Rdng, Univ of S ME 1976; S ME Writing Project; *cr:* Eng Teacher Noble HS 1969-; *ai:* Drama Dir 1990; K-12th Grade Curr Review Team; NEA, ME Teachers Assn, NCTE 1969; NCTE, Local Assn Treas; St Matthews Church; Adult Ed Sequential Eng Curr; *office:* Noble HS Cranberry Meadow Rd Berwick ME 03901

THOMPSON, MILTON BLAIR, III, Biology Teacher/Coach; *b:* Odessa, TX; *m:* Mary Ellen Bynum; *c:* Tommy, Tamara, Joe D.; *ed:* (AS) Bio, Odessa Coll 1968; (BS) Bio, TX A&M 1970; *cr:* Teacher/Coach San Saba HS 1971-76, Hood Jr HS 1976-81, Odessa HS 1981-; *ai:* Var Ftbl Wide Receivers & Head Bsbl Coach; Former Athletic Dir & Head Coach San Saba; Tx St Teachers Assn Lifetime Mem 1971-; TX HS Coaches Assn Mem 1971-; Odessa 1st Presbyn Church (Elder, Deacon) 1979-81; San Saba 1st Presbyn Church Deacon 1973-76; *home:* 1106 Douglas Odessa TX 79762

THOMPSON, NANCY WAGNER, Vocational Home Ec Teacher; *b:* Hammond, IN; *c:* Angela B. Christopher; *ed:* (BS) Home Ec Ed, 1970, (MS) Home Ec Ed, Purdue Univ 1971; Wright St Univ; Lake Sumter Comm Coll; *cr:* Cnslr IN St Girls Sch 1971; Teacher Northmont HS 1971-77, South Sumter HS 1983-; *ai:* Var Chrldr Spon; FHA/HERO Dist Adv; FL FHA/HERO Dist Adv 1988-88 Distinguished Service 1988; Natl Campers & Hikers Assn (Natl Corresponding Secy 1982-84) 1972-85; *home:* 318 Central Ave Bushnell FL 33513

THOMPSON, PATRICIA CAMPBELL, English/Journalism Teacher; *b:* Richmond, VA; *m:* Robert Rodney; *c:* Taylor C. Jones, Jocelyn D. Jones; *ed:* (BA) Eng, Coll of William & Mary 1971; (MA) Eng, Univ of DE 1978; Grad Stud; Cooperative Learning Awareness Leader; *cr:* Teacher/Newspaper Adv Caesar Rodney HS 1971-75; Teacher/Prgm Developer DE Tech/Comm Coll 1975-78; Teacher/Yrbk Adv Lake Forest HS 1978-84; Teacher/Newspaper Adv Dover HS 1985-; *ai:* Dover HS Sch Newspaper Adv; Mid Sts Evaluation of Dover HS Steering Comm Vice Chm; Quill & Scroll Intnl Spon; NEA, DE St Ed Assn 1971-75, 1978-; DE Teacher Center Vice-Chairperson 1987-, Service Awd; DE Scholastic Press Assn (Pres 1973-74, VP 1972); Amer Assn of Univ Women (Pres 1977-79, VP 1975-77), AAUW Division All Stars 1980, Named Gift 1979; Teacher of Yr Lake Forest Dist 1981; Outstanding Young Women of America 1980; Publication; *office:* Dover HS 625 Walker Rd Dover DE 19901

THOMPSON, PEGGY S., Home Arts Teacher; *b:* Spartanburg, SC; *m:* Michael H.; *c:* Stacey Cabaniss, Angela, Timothy; *ed:* (BS) Home Ec, Limestone Coll 1964; *cr:* Sci Teacher Fairforest Jr HS 1964-65; 5th Grade Teacher Roebuck Intermediate 1968-69; Home Arts Teacher L E Gable Mid Sch 1976-; *ai:* Decorating Comm; Sch Improvement Cncl; Crestwood Garden Club 1965-; Roebuck Improvement Assn 1975-; PTA, Assn of Bridal Consultants; Co-Owner Carolina Traditions; *office:* L E Gable Mid Sch Box 246 Ott Shoals Rd Roebuck SC 29376

THOMPSON, REBA DENLEY, First Grade Teacher; *b:* Grenada, MS; *m:* Warren Jr.; *c:* Lacy, Tommy; *ed:* (BS) Home Ec, MS Coll 1969; (BA) Elem Ed, 1970, (MA) Rdng, 1975, (MA) Elem Ed, 1980 Delta St; *cr:* Elem Teacher Greenville Public Schls 1975-; *ai:* Cub Scout & Chrstn Womens Club Leader; Cmmty Bible Study Childrens Dir; *home:* 3554 Sherwood Dr Greenville MS 38703

THOMPSON, ROBERT ROSEDON, JR., Biology Teacher; *b:* New York, NY; *m:* Janet P.; *c:* Katherine Fluharty, Robert R. III, S. Kirk; *ed:* (BA) Bio, TX A&I Univ 1955; (MED) Stu Pers Guidance, Trenton St 1973; Hon DD Religion, Universal Life Ch CA 1980; Sci, Physics; Padi Master Instr; *cr:* 7th Grade Teacher Kennedy HS 1955-56; 7th Grade Sci Teacher Scotch Plains Jr HS 1960-62; 7th-9th Grade Teacher Thomas Jefferson HS, 10th-12th Grade Bio Teacher Edison HS, 7th Grade Sci Dept Chm John Adams Jr HS, Bio Teacher 1962- J P Stevens HS; *ai:* Acad of Sci, Photography Club Adv; Natl Chem Soc Pres 1954; Kappa Sigma 1953-; Natl Dramatic Soc 1953-, Outstanding Drama Awd 1955; Lions Club Pres; BSA Scoutmaster 1979-81; Sheriffs Underwater Search & Recovery Team Trng Officer 1975-; HS Paper Delveloped for Curr; Oceanography Grant Awd 1968-72; Teacher in Space Prgm; *office:* John P Stevens HS Grove Ave Edison NJ 08820

THOMPSON, ROBYN WALKER, Fourth Grade Teacher; *b:* Warrenton, VA; *m:* John Robert Jr.; *ed:* (BS) Elem Ed, Adelphi Univ 1974; Univ of VA/VA Commonwealth Univ; James Madison Univ; *cr:* 3rd Grade Teacher 1974-75, Rdng Lab Teacher 1975-77, 3rd Grade Teacher 1977-80, 5th Grade Teacher 1980-87, 4th Grade Teacher 1987- Coleman Elem Sch; *ai:* W G Coleman Leadership Team Mem; Chairperson 4th Grade; Child Study Comm Mem; Fauquier Ed Assn 1974-; VA Ed Assn 1982; Comm for Excl in Ed Fellowship Awd 1986; Mem Lee Hill Elem Self Study & Interim Review Visiting Teams 1983-84 /1988-89; *office:* W G Coleman Elem Sch P O Box 68 Marshall VA 22115

THOMPSON, SANDRA KAY, Kindergarten Teacher; *b:* Kokomo, IN; *ed:* (BS) Elem Ed, 1969, (MS) Elem Ed 1972 IN Univ; *cr:* Kndgtn Teacher Southeastern Sch Corporation 1969-; Teacher Walton Elem Elem & Thompson Elem; *ai:* Campbell Soup Contest Coord; Alpha Delta Kappa Pres 1987-89; Delta Kappa Gamma; SE Teachers Assn; AAUW; PTO Teacher Rep Curr Comm; Home Ec Pres 1985-87; Upper Creek Church of Christ Sunday Sch Supt; Jaycees Outstanding Young Educator 1974; Outstanding Elem Teachers of Amer 1972; *office:* Thompson Elem Sch Box 514 Walton IN 46994

THOMPSON, SANDRA LEE, Mathematics Teacher; *b:* San Francisco, CA; *ed:* (BA) Phys Ed/Driver Ed, CA St Univ Sacramento 1970; Cmptr Courses Cosumnes River Coll; Phys Ed Wkshp CA Poly San Luis Obispo; Advanced Math Classes Shasta Coll; *cr:* Teacher Luther Burbank HS 1971-79, Columbia Sch 1980-86, Sequoia Mid Sch 1986-; *ai:* HS & Jr HS Sftbl, Track, Bsktbl, Vlybl Coach; HS Class, 8th Grade Class, Jr HS Newspaper Adv; CA Teacher Assn; Natl Assn of Health Phys Ed & Recreation; Natl Teachers Assn; CA Assn of Health Phys Ed & Recreation; NCTM; Redding Tennis Club; Shasta Wheelmen; Haven Humane Society; *office:* Sequioa Mid Sch 1805 Sequoia Redding CA 96001

THOMPSON, SHARON ANN, Math Teacher; *b:* Bolivar, MO; *m:* Doyle Michael; *ed:* (BS) Math, 1974, (MS) Scndry Teaching, 1987 Pittsburg St Univ; *cr:* Math Teacher Attica HS 1974-77, West Elk Jr HS 1977-78, Jefferson West HS 1978-84, Cherryvale Mid Sch 1984-; *ai:* Math Club Spon; Academic Team Spon/Coach; Annual Math Competitor Organizer; NEA; Cherryvale Teacher Assn-Pres 1988-89; First Baptist Church; Natl Guard Auxilary-Pres 1986-88; Cherryvale Master Teacher-1989; Phi Kappa Phi.

THOMPSON, SHERRIL, 3rd Grade Mentor Teacher; *b:* Glendale, CA; *m:* George Irvin; *c:* Chris Eberlein, Patrick Eberlein, Samuel; *ed:* (BA) Span, San Diego St Univ 1972; (MSED) Teacher Ed, USC 1982; Admin Services Credential CA St Dominguez Univ 1989; *cr:* Primary Teacher Los Angeles Unified Sch Dist 1979-; Instr Bi-ling Methodology for BCC Candiates 1984-; Mentor Teacher Los Angeles Unified Sch Dist 1990; *ai:* Sch Schlsp Grant Writing Comm; Phi Delta Kappa Mem; Assn Mexican Amer Educators Mem 1984-; CA Assn of Bi-ling Educators Mem 1989-; LAEP Mini-Grants, ECIA Mini-Grants for In-Class Cmptrs & Software: *office:* Wilmington Park Elem Sch 1140 Mahar St Wilmington CA 90744

THOMPSON, STEVE A., Teacher; *b:* Houlton, ME; *ed:* (BS) Ed, Univ of TN 1979; (MED) Supervision/Admin, E TN St Univ 1988; *cr:* Math Teacher Tennessee HS 1979-81, Sullivan South HS 1981-; *ai:* Girls Bsktbl & Boys Bsbl Coach; Upper E TN Teachers of Math, Sullivan Cty Ed Assn, TN Ed Assn, NEA; Governors Spec Task Force Cmptr Curr; Sullivan Cty Supt of Schls Candidate; *office:* Sullivan South HS 1236 Moreland Dr Kingsport TN 37664

THOMPSON, SUSAN BISSETT, 11th/12th Grade Eng Teacher; *b:* Bayonne, NJ; *m:* Charles L.; *ed:* (BA) Eng, Marshall Univ 1970; Drama Trng Circle in the Square NUC NY; Teaching Cert 1980; *cr:* Teacher Ft Gay HS 1981-87, Tolsia HS 1987-; *ai:* Yrbk Spon; Prgm in the Hum Contributor; Advanced Lit Class; *office:* Tolsia HS 1 Rebel Dr Fort Gay WV 25514

THOMPSON, SUSAN KINLAW, Mathematics Teacher; *b:* Elizabethtown, NC; *m:* James W. Jr.; *c:* James W. III, Jacob G.; *ed:* (BA) His, Univ of NC Wilmington 1981; *cr:* Teacher Tar Heel Jr/Sr HS 1988-; *ai:* Sch Improvement & Senate Bill II Comm; SCAT Team Spon; NC Assn of Educators; NC Cncl Teachers of Math; Baptist Church; *home:* PO Box 221 Elizabethtown NC 28337

THOMPSON, TERRI SNAVLEY, 6th Grade Teacher; *b:* Sidney, OH; *m:* Michael Le Roy; *c:* Erica, Rachel; *ed:* (BS) Elem Ed, OH St 1978; (MA) Ed, Wright St 1986; *cr:* Teacher Sidney City Schls 1979-; *ai:* Spelling Bee Chm; Church Youth Group; YMCA Swim Team Boosters Pres; Sidney Ed Assn Soc Comm Chm; Sidney Ed Assn Building Rep 1986-88, 1989-, Doers Awd 1988; W OH Ed Assn, OH Ed Assn, NEA; 1st United Meth Church Athletic Comm Mem 1988-; OH St Alumni Assn; *office:* Northwood Sch 1152 St Marys Sidney OH 45365

THOMPSON, VALERIE HAMILTON, English/History Teacher; *b:* Los Angeles, CA; *m:* M. Eugene; *c:* Diana Thompson Zeigler, Alan, Merrilee Thompson Hauser, Randy; *ed:* (BA) Span, Stanford Univ 1957; *cr:* Eng/His Teacher/GATE Coord Pioneer Jr HS 1974-; *ai:* Dist & Cty Land Art Wkshps Presenter; Academic Scholar Teams Coach; Ecology Club Spon; Dist GATE Comm; Pioneer Literary Magazine & Sch Team Adv; NCTE Mem; AAUW Past Pres Grant Recipient 1976, 1982; NEA, CTA, UTA Secy; PTA (Valencia Sch Pres 1972-73, Pioneer Jr HS Pres 1973-74); Lang Art Mentor Teacher Upland Unified Sch Dist; CA Writing & Lit Project Fellow; CA Outstanding Writing Teacher Awd; St San Bernardino Writing Competition; *office:* Pioneer Jr HS 245 W 18th St Upland CA 91786

THOMPSON, VICTORIA CHIARELLI, Art Teacher; *b:* Philadelphia, PA; *m:* Charles; *c:* Gloria Thompson Schlemmer; *ed:* (BA) Art Ed, 1967, (MS) Art Ed, 1970 IN Univ; Philadelphia Museum Coll of Art; Cmptr Graphics Trng, in Univ; *cr:* Art/Eng Teacher Sharon Hill Acad 1954-55; Industrial Arts Teacher Hobart Jr HS 1967-75; Art/Crafts Teacher 1976-, Cmptr Graphics 1987- Hobart Mid Sch; *ai:* Local Sch Systems Cmptr Graphics Presenter 1989-; Ceramic Wall Mural Mid Sch; St Cmptr Art Proposal Grant 1988; Cmptr Prgm Grant 1989; Several Articles; Teacher of Yr 1986; *office:* Hobart Mid Sch 705 E 4th St Hobart IN 46342

THOMPSON, VIRGINIA R., Gifted/Talented Teacher; *b:* Columbus, OH; *ed:* (BS) Elem Ed, Miami Univ 1969; (MS) Guidance/Counseling, OH St 1974; *cr:* 1st Grade Teacher 1969-82, 2nd Grade Teacher 1982-87, 3rd-5th Grade Gifted/Talented Teacher 1987- J Burroughs; *ai:* Columbus Ed Assn, OH Ed Assn, NEA, PTA; Capital Area Humane Society, Humane Educator Awd 1982; PTA Teacher of Yr 1985; Ashland Oil My Spec Teacher 1989; *office:* John Burroughs Elem Sch 2585 Sullivant Ave Columbus OH 43204

THOMPSON, WANDA CAIRNCROSS ADAMS, 6-8th Grade Soc Stud Teacher; *b:* Misawa Air Base, Japan; *m:* Michael; *ed:* (AA) General, Pasadena City Coll; (BS) Soc Sci, Elem K-9, San Diego St Univ; *cr:* Teacher Mountain View Elem 1979-83,

Grace Yokley Sch 1983-; *ai:* Stu Cncl Adv Dances, Stu Store, Promotions, After Sch Ski Prgm; Coord Adopt a Sch Prgm General Electric; CA Ridge Pres 1989-; Adelphians (VP, Pres) 1971-72 Miss Congeniality; Spartans 1971-72; Omicron Mu Delta 1971-72; Jobs Daughters Honored Queen 1970-71; *office:* Grace Yokley Jr H S 2947 S Turner Ave Ontario CA 91761

THOMPSON, WILLIAM ANTHONY, Sixth Grade Teacher; *b:* Palmersville, TN; *m:* Jerita Essary; *c:* Kristy; *ed:* (BS) Elem Ed, Univ of TN Martin 1973; *cr:* Classroom Teacher Sharon Sch 1974-; *ai:* Jr HS Beta Club Spon; NEA Mem; TN Ed Assn; Weakley Cty Ed Assn (Faculty Rep 1980) 1974-; Adams Chapel Missionary Baptist Church (Deacon 1986-, Sunday Sch Supt 1986-87, Sunday Sch Teacher 1988-; Outstanding Young Men of America 1984; *office:* Sharon Sch North Woodlawn Ave Sharon TN 38255

THOMPSON-DUNN, ROBERT LYNN, English/Journalism Teacher; *b:* Oakland, CA; *m:* James; *c:* Jessica, Ashley; *ed:* (BA) Eng, OH Univ 1973; (MA) Ed Technology/Lib Media Specialist, San Francisco St Univ 1983; *cr:* Eng Teacher Hyde Park Jr HS 1978-86; Eng/Journalism Teacher Rancho HS 1986-; *ai:* Adv for Rampage Ranchos Sch Newspaper; CCCTA; NEA; *office:* Rancho HS 1900 E Owens Ave Las Vegas NV 89030

THOMSEN, TIMOTHY SCOTT, Teacher/Act-Athletic Dir/Coach; *b:* Tacoma, WA; *ed:* (BAE) Soc Sci, Pacific Luth Univ 1980; Educl Admin Prgm, Pacific Luth Univ; *cr:* Asst Bsktbl Coach 1981-86, Teacher 1981-, Traffic Safety Coord/Head Bsbl Coach 1982-, ASB Adv 1986-, Head Bsktbl Coach 1987-, Act/Athletic Dir 1987- Sumner HS; *ai:* Head Bsbl, Bsktbl Coach; ASB Adv; Athletic/Act Dir; *office:* Sumner HS 1707 Main St Sumner WA 98390

THOMSON, JUDITH ANN VAN CAMP, 5th Grade Supervising Teacher; *b:* Des Moines, IA; *m:* Malcolm John; *c:* Kevin Knott, Kepler Knott; *ed:* (BS) His/Psych, Memphis St Univ 1960; Grad Ed Eng, Univ of N IA, Memphis St Univ; Writers Wkshp Eng Dept Memphis St; *cr:* Teacher Westwood Public 1960-62, Knight Road Public 1962-64, Auburndale Private 1978-79; Supervising Teacher Memphis St Univ Laboratory Campus Sch 1981-; *ai:* Started Classics Lit Club; Great Grammarian Club Spon; Contact Teacher; Write & Edit Curr Guides TN Schls Arts in Schls Prgm; Judge, Wordmaster Writing Prgm; City-Wide Comm for Lang Art Called Future Tense; Co-Writing & Coll Eng Class Spon; W TN Ed Assn, TN Rdng Assn 1985-; Natl Cncl of Chrstn & Jews Worked with Disturbed Children Cmmty Service Awd 1974; Memphis Arts Cncl Advisory Bd 1986-; Mayors Cmmty Relations Ed Comm 1988-; Cmmty Career Ladder III Teacher, Rotary Club Grant, Presentor of Collaborative Elem/Coll Writing at Eng Conference; Compiled, Edited, Published 2 Childrens Poetry Books; Memphis Art Cncl Summer Inst; Participated in 2 Videos; *office:* Campus Sch Memphis St Univ 535 Zach Curlin Memphis TN 38152

THOMSON, ZINA, 7th/8th Grade Soc Stud Teacher; *b:* Bivona Sicily, Italy; *m:* Albert D.; *ed:* (BA) Soc Stud, Kent St Univ 1964; His, Ed Courses, John Carroll Univ & Cleveland St; *cr:* Teacher Shaw HS 1964-67, St Gregory the Great 1968-; *ai:* NCEA; *office:* St Gregory the Great Sch 4478 Rushton Rd South Euclid OH 44121

THORBURN, STUART C., Social Studies Teacher; *b:* Lansing, MI; *m:* Kathleen E. Knechtel; *c:* Steven, Jay; *ed:* (BS) Geography, Cntrl MI Univ 1964-68; (MA) Scndry Ed, MI St Univ 1976; ITEP Teacher Effectiveness Trng Seminar; *cr:* His Teacher Leslie HS 1968-72, Fowlerville HS 1972-75; Cooperative Coord Williamston HS 1975-79; Soc Stud Teacher Dansville HS 1982-; *ai:* Bsktbl & Ftbl Coach; Class Spon; Teacher Assn Pres; Close-Up Coord; Bsktbl Coaches Assn of MI Clinic Comm 1982-; Alaiedon Township Bd Treas 1978-; *home:* 3120 Willoughby Rd Mason MI 48854

THORN, JEAN E., Home Careers Teacher; *b:* Newburgh, NY; *c:* Debbie J. Zegel, Peter E. Zegel; *ed:* (BS) Home Ec Ed, St Univ of NY Plattsburgh 1951; (MS) Elem Ed, St Univ of NY New Paltz 1962; Various Classes in Soc Work, Counseling, Crafts, Horticulture; Floral Design, Parsons Sch of Design; *cr:* Home Ec Teacher South Kortright Cntrl Sch 1951-53; Case Worker/Supvr Public Welfare Newburgh 1954-59; Elem Teacher Rondout Valley 1959-; Home & Careers Teacher Rondout Valley 1990; *ai:* Sch Comm Volunteer; Rondout Valley Fed (Corresponding Secy 1985) 1980-; Sierra Club Life Mem; Fire Company; SPCA *office:* Rondout Valley Jr HS Accord NY 12404

THORNBURG, DONOLA PANNELL, Science Teacher; *b:* Ada, OK; *c:* Dani R., David; *ed:* (BA) Sci/Bio 1978, (MS) Ed, SE OK St Univ; *cr:* Sci Teacher Boswell HS 1978-80, Wynona HS 1980-81, Achille HS 1982-; *ai:* Jr Class & Cheerleading Spon; Stu Cncl Adv; AIDS Ed Prgm Dir; Sci Fair Coord; OK Ed Assn, NEA.

THORNBURG, JOANNE CANARY (SHEPHARD), English Instructor; *b:* Indianapolis, IN; *m:* Myron A.; *c:* Cristofer A. Rudyk, Deborah E. Yarnes, Stephen P. Morgan, Philip B., David, Laura T. Ahlgrim; *ed:* (BA) Lang Art, 1951, (MA) Eng, 1964 De Pauw Univ; Journalism, Speech, Lit Wkshps; Amer Stud, De Pauw Univ; *cr:* Eng/Journalism/Speech Instr Elston HS 1951-55; Eng/Speech Instr La Porte HS 1956-; *ai:* Stu Cncl Co-Spon; Spec Events Chairperson; NCTE, IN Cncl Eng Teachers, Folklore Cncl; Delta Kappa Gamma; Teaching Fellowship De Pauw Univ; *home:* 201 Forest Dr La Porte IN 46350

THORNBURY, SANDRA KAY, English & Latin Teacher; *b:* Ashland, KY; *m:* L. Cecel; *c:* Tara, Shawn; *ed:* (BA) Eng, 1968, (MA) Amer Lit, 1974 Morehead St Univ; *cr:* Teacher Boyd Cty HS 1968-74, Summit Jr HS 1982-; *ai:* Beta Club Spon; Amer Assn Univ Women Pres 1980-82; Stu Ally United; *office:* Summit Jr HS 1226 Summit Rd Ashland KY 41101

THORNE, ARNEDA ELLIS, Chapter I Teacher; *b:* Hattiesburg, MS; *m:* Hardy E. Jr.; *c:* Eugene III, Monigue, Monica; *ed:* (BS) Elem Ed, 1970, (MED) Elem Ed, 1976 Wm Carey; *cr:* Teacher Sunrise Elem 1970-72, Runnelstown 1972-74, Cntrl Forrest 1974-82, Earl Travillion 1982-; *ai:* NEA 1974-; MS Assn of Ed Building Rep 1986-87; *home:* 212 Dossett Ave Hattiesburg MS 39401

THORNE, JAMES O., Mathematics Department Chair; *b:* Huntsville, AL; *ed:* (BA) Math, Univ of AL Huntsville 1972; *cr:* Math Teacher S R Butler HS 1971-; *ai:* Competitive Math Teams Spon; N AL Assn Teachers of Math (VP 1988-, Pres Elect 1988-, Pres 1990); Madison Cty Assn for Retarded Citizens Bd of Dir 1980-; TRW Fnd Schls Math Inst Long Island Univ at Southampton 1988; Coll Bd Schlsp AP Calculus Inst Oglethorpe Univ 1988; Woodrow Wilson Fnd Schlsp Math Inst Princeton Univ 1990; *home:* 704 Hal St Huntsville AL 35805

THORNHILL, DENISE BACCHINI, Math/Phys Ed Teacher; *b:* Pittsburg, CA; *m:* Victor J.; *c:* Joseph, Aimee; *ed:* (BS) Phy Ed, San Jose St Univ 1977; *cr:* Phy Ed Teacher Edna Hill Sch 1978-79; 3rd Grade Teacher Brentwood Elem Sch 1979-80; 6th Grade Teacher 1980-81; Math Mentor Teacher 1989 Edna Hill Sch; *ai:* Chrldr Adv; Honor Society Adv; Leadership Team (Prgrm Quality Review); Math Dept Chair; NCATM Mem 1981-; Edna Hill Activity Fnd Mem 1987-; *office:* Edna Hill Schl 140 Birch St Brentwood CA 94513

THORNTON, BARBARA ANN, French & German Teacher; *b:* Alexandria Bay, NY; *ed:* Degre Semestriel Cours de Langue et Civilisation de la Sorbonne, Universite de Paris 1984; (BA) St Univ of NY Oswego 1984; (MS) Fr, Univ of GA Athens 1984-86; (MS) Rdng, 1988; *cr:* Grad Teaching Asst Fr Univ of GA 1984-86; Fr/Ger Teacher S Jefferson Cntrl Sch 1986-; *ai:* Faculty Adv 1990 Class; NY St Assn of Foreign Lang Teachers 1986-; AATG 1990; Little Theatre of Watertown Corresponding Secy 1988-; Beta Sigma Phi 1990; Foreign Lang Dept James E Allen Awd for Excl in Foreign Lang Teaching 1986; *home:* 350 N California Ave Watertown NY 13601

THORNTON, FRANCILLE TAYLOR, Chapter I Teacher; *b:* Caddo, OK; *ed:* (BA) Elem, 1963, (MS) Ed, 1969, Rdng Specialist, 1978 SE OK St Univ; *cr:* 3rd-5th Grade Teacher Harmony OK 1963-64; 2nd-6th Grade Chapter I Rdng/6th-8th Grade Lang Art Teacher Caddo OK 1964-; *ai:* OEA Lifetime Mem 1963-; NEA Life Mem 1980-; Intnl Rdng Assn Mem; SE Rdng Cncl Pres 1977-78; OK Rdng Cncl Mem; Delta Kappa Gamma Pres 1990; Caddo Indian Territory Museum & Lib (Secy, Treas) 1979-; Intnl Rdng Assn World Congress Australia 1988, Annual Convention Delegate 1978, Regional Conferences OK.

THORNTON, JANE LYSBETH, 4th Grade/Admin Asst; *b:* Knoxville, TN; *ed:* (BS) Elem Ed, Winthrop Coll 1970; (MED) Supervision/Admin, East TN St Univ 1988; *cr:* 4th Grade Teacher 1970-74, Orth Hand K-8 Teacher 1974-76 Pate Elem; 7th Grade Jr HS Teacher 1976-77, 2nd & 4th Grade Elem Teacher 1977- Kingsley Elem; *ai:* 4-H Leader; Career Ladder 2 Extended Contract Work; Admin Asst; PTA; Sullivan Cty Ed Assn Mem 1970-; TN Ed Assn Mem 1970-; NEA Mem 1970-; ASCD 1988-; Singles Cncl 1st Baptist Church 1989-; 4-H Club Leader 1978-; Wrote Pamphlet Teachers Communicating W/Parents; Freedom Fnd Awd Pilot Club; Kinglsey Teacher of Yr 1984 & 1989 Pate Elem Teacher of Yr 1972-73; Ruritan of Kingsport Teacher of Yr; *office:* Kingsley Elem Sch 100 Emory Ln Kingsport TN 37660

THORNTON, MARK MC KINNEY, Principal; *b:* Dallas, TX; *ed:* (BS) Ed, 1981, (MS) Ed, 1985 Stephen F Austin St Univ; *cr:* Teacher/Coach Elkhart Ind Sch Dist 1981-84, Palestine Ind Sch Dist 1984-86; Asst Prin Athens HS 1986-; Prin Terrell Mid Sch 1990; *ai:* Natl Society of Sons of Amer Revolution 1989; Phi Delta Kappa Mem 1988-; NASSP 1986-; TX Assn of Scndry Prins 1986-; Honorary Chapter FFA Degree; *office:* Terrell Mid Sch 701 Town North Dr Terrell TX 75160

THORNTON, MARY HARDIN, Jr-Sr Counselor; *b:* Oakland, CA; *m:* Clinton; *c:* Travis; *ed:* (BA) Art, 1976, (BA) Art Ed, 1977, (BS) Elem Ed, 1977 Friends Univ; (MS) Counseling, NSU 1985; Psychometris Certificate; Gessell Testing; *cr:* 1st-6th Grade Art Teacher Andover Elem 1977-80; 1st-5th Grade Teacher of Gifted Jay Elem 1980-89; Jr/Sr Cnslr Jay HS 1989-; *ai:* OAGCT VP 1980-89; JPACT, OK Ed Assn 1980-; Delta Kappa Gamma (Secy, VP) 1985-.

THORNTON, MELANIE ALFORD, Math Dept Chr/Teacher; *b:* Beaumont, TX; *c:* Rita F.; *ed:* (BS) Elem Ed, 1983; (BS) Advertising, 1982 Univ of TX; Math, Southwest TX St Univ; Marilyn Burns - Math Solution Institute; TX Math Teacher Trng Modules; *cr:* G/T Math Teacher/Lang Bulverde Mid Schl 1983-88; Math Dept Head/Math Teacher Smithson Valley Mid Sch 1988-; *ai:* UIL Academic Coord; Calculator Applications Coach; Math Club Spon; TX St Teachers Assn 1983-; ComaL Educators Assn-Secy 1983-; Faculty Rep; Teacher Month May 1988; Nom Presidential Awd for Excl in Math Teaching; *home:* 163 N Sycamore New Braunfels TX 78130

THORNTON, NANCY JEAN, Classroom Teacher/Elem Prin; *b:* Chicago, IL; *m:* Alpheus Marty; *c:* Dennis P O'Neill, Deirdre J. O'Neill; *ed:* (BA) Elem Ed/Scndry Ed/Speech/Drama, Clarke Coll 1969; (MA) Elem Sch Admin, Univ of IA 1981; *cr:* 6th Grade Teacher St Anthonys Elem 1969-70; 5th/6th Grade Teacher 1970-75, Remedial Bi-ling Prgm Teacher 1973-75 Franklin Elem; 4th Grade Teacher Mc Kinley Elem 1975-79; 6th/8th/9th Grade Teacher West Mid Sch 1979-87; Elem Prin Mulberry Elem 1988-; *ai:* Summer Inst Teacher Gifted & TAlented Kollege for Kids 1980-84; Directed Plays Musser Public Lib 1969-72; Wkshps Dir 1969-89; Muscatine Cmmty Elem Schls Talented/Gifted Coord; Muscatine Cty Fine Art Cncl Childrens Musical Dir; Muscatine Chamber of Commerce Leadership; Muscatine Ed Assn, IA St Ed Asn 1970-87; IA Fine Arts Cncl Bd Mem 1982-83; Women in Educl Admin 1982-83; Alpha Delta Kappa VP 1990; Sch Admin of IA, IA Assn of Elem Prins; Miss Muscatine Pageant (Dir, Producer), Cmmty Awd 1979; Muscatine Masquers Theatre Group Bd of Dirs 1974-76; Muscatine Welcome Wagon VP 1976-78; *office:* Mulberry Elem Sch 3211 Mulberry Ave Muscatine IA 52761

THORNTON, NORMA BARBERO, Third Grade Teacher; *b:* Las Vegas, NM; *m:* Thomas F.; *c:* Krystal L., Sandra L., Helene Bianca; *ed:* (BA) Elem Ed 1971, (MA) Bi-Ling Ed, 1974 Highlands Univ; Bi-Ling Classes in Mexico; Cultural Classes in Ghana Africa; *cr:* 1st/2nd/3rd Grade Teacher 1971-78, Part Time Librarian 1971-73 North Public Elem; 1st/3rd Grade Teacher 1978- , 3rd Grade Teacher 1989- Our Lady of Sorrows Elem; *ai:* Alpha Delta Kappa (Mem 1974-82, Chaplain 1976-77); 1 of 3 NM Teachers Selected to Go Western Africa Senegal Ivory Coast & Ghana to Attend Cross Cultural Ed Classes & Visit with People 1977; *home:* PO Box 2062 2500 Dalia Las Vegas NM 87701

THORNTON, SARAH P., English Teacher/Chm Eng Dept; *b:* Carlton, GA; *ed:* (BA) Eng, Paine Coll 1963, (MED) Eng Ed, 1970; (ESP) Eng Ed, 1979 Univ of GA; NDEA; Eng Inst; Eng/Lang Inst; Writing Conference *cr:* Eng Teacher Elbert Cty Mid Sch 1963-; Data Collector Teacher Evaluation Elbert Co Sch Sys 1976-; Staff Dev Coord Pod Leader Elbert Cty Mid Sch 1977-; *ai:* Adv of Tri Hi Y; Facilitator/After Sch Prg ECMS; ECAE/GAE/NEA (Sec Pres Chm Various Comm) Outstanding Service 1986; GCTE/NCTE (Sec Newsletter Editor Dir Presenter); Cystic Fibrosis Chm Fund Drive Service 1982; Coor Debutante Cotillion Alpha Phi Alpha 1968-85 Service & Book Ded; Alpha Forum Pres Cultural Affairs Coord 1983; Fork Creek Baptist Church (Gen Consultant & Prgm Coord Asst Sec Sun Sch Teacher Youth Dir Teacher Dist Sun Sch Congress Oratorical Co Chr); NDEA EPEA Stipends; Undergrad Acad Schlsp; Teacher of Yr; Coauthor High Interest Easy Rdng; Item Writer Ga Crt; Item Writer & Evaluator GA TCT; St Advisory Bd GA Schls; *home:* PO Box 153 Carlton GA 30627

THORNTON, SIDONIE SIMPSON, Chapter I Reading Teacher; *b:* Temple, TX; *m:* Thomas; *c:* Seth, Joshua, Jonathan; *ed:* (BSED) Elem Ed, 1971, (MSED) Elem Ed, 1975 SW TX St Univ; *cr:* 4th Grade Lang Art Teacher 1971-72, 2nd-6th Grade Remedial Rdng Teacher 1972-73 Marion Elem Sch; 3rd Grade Teacher 1973-74, K-2nd Grade Remedial Rdng Teacher 1974-77 Fredericksburg Elem Sch; Kndgtn Teacher 1977-78, 2nd Grade Teacher 1978-84, 1st-5th Grade Chapter I Rdng Teacher 1984- Llano Elem Sch; *ai:* UIL Literary Listening & Oral Rdng Coach; TSTA 1971-81; ATPE 1981-; First Baptist Church (Sunday Sch Dir 1989-, Sunday Sch Teacher 1977-89); Beta Signa Phi VP 1974-77; Mem Kappa Delta Pi, Alpha Phi; *home:* HC 13 Box 32 Valley Spring TX 76885

THORP, CAROL CROSSLEY, Spanish Teacher; *b:* Wilmington, NC; *m:* Frederick Lee; *c:* Christopher Garner, Tamala Garner; *ed:* (BA) Span, Univ of NC Wilmington 1971; *cr:* Span/Eng Teacher Pender Acad 1971-74, Cape Fear Acad 1982-85; Span Teacher East Mecklenburg HS 1985-; *ai:* Span Club Adv; Amer Assn Teachers of Span & Portuguese; Advisory Cncl Stu Teachers Davidson Coll; *office:* East Mecklenburg HS 6800 Monroe Rd Charlotte NC 28212

THORP, DON G., Choir Director; *b:* Artesia, NM; *m:* Maud O. Duncan; *c:* Steven M., Barry W.; *ed:* (BME) Music Ed, 1959, (MME) Music Ed, 1966 E NM Univ; *cr:* Choir Dir Tucumcari HS 1959-60, Morton HS 1961-63, Little Field HS 1963-65, Alamogordo HS 1966-; *ai:* NMMEA Choral VP 1971-73; SWDNMMEA Pres 1975-77; ACDA; *office:* Alamogordo HS 103 Cuba Ave Alamogordo NM 88310

THORPE, EILEEN AABERGE, Business Teacher; *b:* Conrad, MT; *m:* Forrest L. III; *c:* Joshua, Kelly; *ed:* (BA) Ed, Univ of MT 1977; *cr:* Bus Teacher Outlook HS 1977-79, Power HS 1979-82, Huntley Project HS 1983-; *ai:* Elem Vlybl Coach; MT Bus Ed Assn (VP 1987-89, Secy 1986-87, Membership 1985-86), Robert Thompson Awd 1986; *office:* Huntley Project HS 1477 Ash St Worden MT 59088

THORPE, REBECCA JEAN, Fifth Grade Teacher; *b:* Parkersburg, WV; *ed:* (BA) Elem Ed - Magna Cum Laude, Marshall Univ 1978; (MA) Learning Disabilities 1983, (MA) Ed Admin, 1990 WV Univ; *cr:* 6th Grade Music Teacher 1979-86, 5th Grade Sci Teacher 1987- Greenmont Elem; *ai:* Mem of Sch Improvement Team Greenmont Elem; Dir Greenmont Glee Club 1979-86; Adult Basic Ed Instr; Various Curr Selection Comm; Vienna Baptist Church (Youth Fellowship Leader, Jr Choir Dir); Received Benedum Schlsp at Marshall Univ; Teacher of Yr Finalists Wood Cty 1987; *office:* Greenmont Elem Sch 209 58th St Vienna WV 26105

THORSON, PAM AGRIMSON, English Teacher; *b:* Brookings, SD; *m:* Kenneth; *c:* Todd, Kara; *ed:* (BA) Eng, Augustana Coll 1970; Grad Work Univ of SD, Marycrest, Univ of N IA, Sioux Falls Coll; *cr:* Eng Teacher Veblen Cmmty Sch 1970-71, Elk Point Cmmty Sch 1971-76, Hudson Cmmty Sch 1976-77, Boyden-Hull Cmmty Sch 1983-; *ai:* Stu Newspaper Spon; NCTE, IA Cncl Teachers of Eng, NEA; Faith Reformed Church; Faith Reformed Church Women Pres 1982-83.

THORTON, LISA HARPER, Spanish Teacher; *b:* Scottsbluff, NE; *m:* Bradley J.; *c:* Sarah, Geoffrey; *ed:* (BA) Span, Univ of Denver 1982; *cr:* Span Teacher Westminster HS 1984-; *ai:* Spon Intnl Club; Chairperson Dist Curr Review Comm for Lang other than Eng; CO Congress of Foreign Lang Teachers 1984-; Chaperone Stu Travel Group Venezuela; *office:* Westminster HS 4276 W 68th Ave Westminister CO 80030

THRASHER, JAMES STANLEY, Fourth Grade Teacher; *b:* Sullivan, IN; *ed:* (BS) Elem Ed, 1958, (MS) Elem Admin/ Supervision, 1963 IN St Coll; *cr:* 5th Grade Teacher New Lebanon Elem 1958-66; 3rd/4th/5th Grade Teacher Cntrl Elem 1967-; *ai:* 4-H Club Leader 1958-68; Wabash Valley Intnl Rdng Cncl; IN St Teachers Assn; Southwest Sullivan Ed Assn; Life Mem NEA; Scottish Rite Valley of Terre Haute; Graysville Lodge 627 F & AM; *home:* 107 N Wolfenberger Sullivan IN 47882

THRASHER, JOHN P., Chemistry Teacher; *b:* Boston, MA; *m:* Linda Bowen; *c:* Alice Bowen, Rachel E.; *ed:* (BS) Chem, Valdosta St Coll 1974; Grad Courses Scndry Ed; *cr:* Prod Dev Chemist 1966-84, Analytical Chemist 1984-87 Union Camp Corporation; Teacher Lowndes HS 1987-; *ai:* Amer Chemical Society 1974-; *office:* Lowndes HS 1112 N St. Augustine Road Valdosta GA 31601

THRASHER, THOMAS NEWTON, Mathematics Teacher; *b:* Decatur, AL; *m:* Jerretta Lois Barber; *c:* Thomas N. Jr.; *ed:* (BS) Math, Univ of AL 1970; (MED) Sch Admin, AL A&M Univ 1974; Grad Stud Univ of AL; *cr:* Math Teacher Austin HS 1970-82, Decatur HS 1985-; *ai:* Math Team Coach; Chess Club & Mu Alpha Theta Spon; Decatur Ed Assn Pres 1981-82; AL Cncl Teachers of Math Secy 1982-83; Mu Alpha Theta Governor 1978-82; Coach Mu Alpha Theta Natl Math Convention Championship Teams 1978-79; *home:* 1705 Sandra St SW Decatur AL 35601

THREADGILL, OLLIE RIX, JR., Teacher; *b:* Mobile, AL; *m:* Dorothy Riggins; *c:* Mary M., Amy E., Michael Rush, John M., Ollie R. III, Stephen P., Christina M., Robert D., Asha A., Kathryn K., Benjamin R., Sarah G.; *ed:* (BA) His/Poly Sci, Univ of Montevallo 1964; (MA) Intnl Stud, George Washington Univ 1967; (MA) Scndry Ed, 1973, (AA) Scndry Admin, 1979 Univ of S AL; Alliance Francaise Fr Lang, Brussels Belgium 1968-69; *cr:* Teacher Davidson HS 1967-68; Teacher/Admin Presbyn Scndry Sch Bibanga Zaire 1969-70, Presbyn Scndry Sch Lemba Kinshasa Zaire 1970-71; Teacher Fairhope HS 1971-;Part Time Instr Faulkner St Jr Coll 1977-; *ai:* Jr Var Soccer, Fairhope HS Amnesty Intnl Faculty Spon; AL Ed Assn, NEA 1971-; Amnesty Intnl; Amer Civil Liberties Union; People for Amer Way; Christic Inst; Greenpeace; Phi Alpha Theta Univ of Montevallo; Phi Kappa Phi Schlsp Univ of Montevallp Scottish Rite Fellowship George Washington Univ; Outstanding Young Men in America 1970; Honors Annual Awd Coll of Ed Univ of S AL 1980; *home:* 19940 Cty Rd 13 Fairhope AL 36532

THREATT, PEGGY F., 5th Grade Teacher; *b:* Pell City, AL; *m:* Donald; *c:* Shawnda A., Erin S.; *ed:* (BA) Sociology, AL A&M Univ 1973; (MS) Elem Ed, AL St Univ 1986; Elem Ed, Univ of AL Birmingham 1978-79; *cr:* Teacher DPS Daycare 1973-75, Walter M Kennedy Sch 1975-; *ai:* Church Youth Adv; Soc Club Secy; Comprehensive Needs Assessment, Goals, Textbook Selection Comm Mem; Pell City Ed Assn, AL Ed Assn, NEA; *office:* W M Kennedy Sch 813 16th St S Pell City AL 35125

THREET, JOHN THOMAS, English Teacher; *b:* Ft Worth, TX; *m:* Nina Kay Moore; *c:* Emily, Elizabeth; *ed:* (BS) Elem Ed, Univ of TX Austin 1979; (MED) Ed Admin, Houston Baptist Univ 1989; *cr:* 2nd Grade Teacher Brill Elem Sch 1979-80; Eng Teacher Louie Welch Mid Sch 1984-; *ai:* Asst Ftbl Coach; Houston Area Cncl Teachers of Eng 1985-; Congress of Houston Teachers 1985-, Schlsp 1988; Kappa Delta Pi 1988, Pi Eta Awd 1989; Outstanding Grad Stu in Ed Houston Baptist Univ 1988-89; *office:* Louie Welch Mid Sch 11544 S Gessner Houston TX 77071

THRIFT, REBECCA MALLARD, 6th Grade Teacher; *b:* Savannah, GA; *m:* William Glyn; *c:* Kyle; *ed:* (BA) Elem Ed, 1973, (MED) Elem Ed, 1979, (EDS) Elem Ed, 1984 GA Southern; *cr:* Pre-1st Grade Teacher 1973-74, 4th Grade Teacher 1974-76 Metter Primary Sch; Teacher of Gifted 1977-81, 6th Grade Teacher 1981- Metter Mid Sch; *ai:* Mentor; Chorus Dir; GAE Secy; PAGE Building Rep; Pi Kappa Phi; Beta Sigma Phi Pres 1979-80; Teacher of Yr; *office:* Metter Mid Sch Lillian St Metter GA 30439

THUDIN, RANDY CARL, Elementary Principal; *b:* Duluth, MN; *m:* Elaine Van Dorn; *c:* Carrie, Lindsey, Amanda; *ed:* (BS) Elem Ed, Univ MN Duluth 1973; (MS) Educl Admin, 1984, (ES) Educl Admin, 1989 Univ WI Superior; *cr:* Elem Teacher Carlton Elem Sch 1973-88; Elem Prin Cromwell Elem Sch 1988-; *ai:* Head Bsbl Coach; Asst Ftbl Coach; Asst Girls Bsktbl Coach; Asst Track Coach Boys & Girls; Head Track Coach Boys & Girls; Cloq Gospel Tabernacle (Trustee 1978-83 Elder 1985-); *office:* Wright Elem Sch-Cromwell Wright MN 55798

THUMMEL, WANDA DEGES-THYFAULT, Fifth Grade Teacher; *b:* Quinter, KS; *m:* Ralph G.; *c:* John P. Thyfault; *ed:* (BA) Sociology/Elem Ed, Marymount Coll of KS 1971; (MS) Elem Ed, Fort Hays St Univ 1972; *cr:* 3rd Grade Teacher St Joseph Grade Sch 1971-75; 5th Grade Teacher Plainville Elem 1976-; *ai:* USD 270 Cmptr Comm; Summer Sch Instr USD 270; KNEA/NEA 1988-; Sacred Heart Ladies Guild 1975-; Plainville Elem Teacher of Yr 1988-89; Nom KS Teacher of Yr 1988-89; *office:* Plainville Elem Schl 203 SE 3rd Plainville KS 67663

THURBER, ROBERT EVAN, 12th Grade Economics Teacher; *b:* Jamestown, NY; *m:* Julie Anne Pritz; *c:* Melissa A., Andrew E.; *ed:* (BS) Soc Sci, Penn St Univ 1969; (MS); Career Seminars Europe; *cr:* Scndry Ed Teacher Jamestown Public Schls 1970- *ai:* Ec Ed Coord 1987-; US Power Squadron Instr 1986-; *home:* Box 1 Lake St Greenhurst NY 14742

THURE, RHETA V., Mentor Teacher; *b:* South Gate, CA; *c:* Brian, Shelly; *ed:* (AB) His, Univ of CA Berkeley 1966; Univ of MD, Univ of CA Berkeley, Los Angeles; Seminars CA St Univ San Jose; *cr:* Teacher Roger B Taney Jr HS 1968-71, William Neff Sr HS 1972-73, La Mirada HS 1973, Salinas HS 1983-; *ai:* Jr Class & Chrldr Adv; Soc & Employee Recognition Comm; Union Building Rep; Monterey Bay Cncl of Soc Stud Secy 1988-89; CCSS 1987-; AFT Building Rep 1983-; AAUW Treas 1977-79; Women for Women 1977-79; Teacher of Yr 1989; Finalist Harden Fnd Awd 1989; *office:* Salinas HS 726 S Main St Salinas CA 93908

THURMAN, JO ANN TRUAX, Mathematics Department Chair; *b:* Rome, NY; *m:* John Fulton; *c:* Poppy, Zeke; *ed:* (BA) Math, SUNYAB 1969; Cmptr Classes; *cr:* 9th Grade Math Teacher Starpoint Cntrl 1969-70; 8th Grade Math Teacher Highland Jr HS 1970-71; Math Chairperson E Carter R-2 1975-; *ai:* Sr Class Spon; NCTM; SMCTM (Pres, Past Pres 1988-); MCTM VP Scndry 1990; MSTA CTA Pres 1989-; MO St Incentive Grant 1987-88; MO St Continuing Grant 1988-89; *office:* E Carter R-2 Schls P O Box D Ellsinore MO 63937

THURMAN, MARY NANCY MILLER, Fourth Grade Teacher; *b:* Rogersville, TN; *m:* Phillip Wayne; *c:* Karen; *ed:* (BS) Elem Ed, ETSU 1969; *cr:* 4th Grade Teacher Hawkins Cty Elem Sch 1969-70, Hampton City Sch 1970-71, Surgoinsville Elem Sch 1971-; *ai:* Hawkins Cty Ed Assn, TEA, NEA 1969-; 4-H Club Adult Leader 1969-; *office:* Surgoinsville Elem Sch PO Box 239 Surgoinsville TN 37873

THURMAY, BRENDA GORICK, Science/Social Science Teacher; *b:* New York, NY; *c:* William, Tony J.; *ed:* Assoc Liberal Arts, Miami Dade Comm Coll 1965; (BS) Sci/Liberal Arts, FL Atlantic Univ 1967; Working on Masters Nova Univ; *cr:* 2nd Grade Teacher Village Green Elem 1970-72; 1st-3rd/5th Grade Teacher Lillie C Evans Elem 1972-78; 6th Grade Teacher Morningside Elem 1978-83; 5th/6th Grade Teacher Hibiscus Elem 1983-; *ai:* Academic Excl Prgm, Sci Fair, Sci Club Spon; Sci Bowl & Olympiad Teams, Bsbl Coach; Act Dir; Career Ed Chairperson; Delta Kappa Gamma 1988-89; Alpha Upsilon (Chairperson Environemntal Com 1990) 1989-; United Teachers of Dade 1970-; North Miami Beach Optimist Secy 1990; Spec Olympics 1989-; Faculty Cncl 1986-; Academic Excl & Sci Grant; Teacher of Yr 1974, 1986; Career Ed Awd 1987; TV Prgm Ed 2000 The Everglades; Co-Wrote Career Ed Prgm for Dade Cty; *home:* 18380 NE 21st Ave North Miami Beach FL 33179

THURN, JULIE K., Art Teacher; *b:* Pittsburgh, PA; *ed:* (BFA) Art/Ed, Indiana Univ of PA 1984; Grad Stud Kent St Univ; Creative Art Stud Lucca Italy; *cr:* Art Teacher South Fayette Township Jr-Sr HS 1986, Greater Latrobe Hs 1986-; *ai:* Var Girls Bsktbl Coach; NAEA 1986-; Associated Artists of Pittsburgh 1986-, Jurors Awd 1986, 1988; Pittsburgh Society of Artists 1985-; Univ of Pittsburgh Gallery Solo Show 1989; *office:* Greater Latrobe HS Country Club Rd Latrobe PA 15650

THURSTON, MARLENE GILLEN, Second Grade Teacher; *b:* Dover, NH; *m:* David; *ed:* (BA) Elem Ed/Eng, Mount St Mary Coll 1970; Writing Process, Whole Lang, Creative Writing in Lit, Cooperative Teaching Pharmacology for Educators; *cr:* 3rd Grade Teacher 1975-76, 4th Grade Teacher 1977-79, 2nd Grade Teacher 1980- Henry W Moore Sch; *ai:* Granite St Cncl of Intnl Rdng Assn; NH Ed Assn; Supervisory #15 Teacher Incentive Awd 3 Yrs; Amer Legion Citation of Appreciation; Notre Dame Internship Prgm Cooperating Teacher; *home:* 37 Exeter Rd Kingston NH 03848

TIBBETT, ROBERT ANTHONY, English Teacher; *b:* Chicago, IL; *ed:* (BED) Ed, Chicago Teachers Coll 1962; (MED) Ed, Chicago St Univ 1971; Eng & Philosophy, Northwestern Univ & Loyola Univ; *cr:* Teacher Robert Healy Elem 1962-70, J C Orozco Acad 1970-; *ai:* Study Group; Coach Sftbl; Cmptr Camp; Art Camp; Phi Delta Kappa 1962-; NEA & IEA 1962-; Union Leage Boys & Girls Club 1989- Recognition 1990; Midtown Boys Club 1972-; Dedication, Service, Teaching Awds; *office:* J C Orozco Acad 1645 W 18th St Chicago IL 60608

TIBBETTS, LUTITIA BOWEN, 3rd Grade Teacher; *b:* Chicago, IL; *m:* Richard T.; *c:* Karen M. Goggin, Richard B., Lisa Morrison; *ed:* (BM) Piano, 1953; (MM) Piano 1954 Boston Univ; Elem Educ, Univ of Bridgeport 1961; *cr:* 2nd/3rd Grade Teacher Washington Sch 1956-57; 3rd Grade Teacher 1957-58; 6th Grade Tacher 1958-59 Dawes Sch; 2nd Grade Teacher Kings Highway Sch 1959-61; 1st Grade Teacher Great Neck Sch 1962; 1st Grade Teacher 1968-79; 3rd Grade Teacher 1979- Northeast Sch; *ai:* Dist Sci Comm, Mentor, Sch Evaluation Comm, Cooperating Teacher, Team Leader for Grade Level; NEA/CEA/SEA 1968- Finalist for Stamford Teacher of Yr 1989; Amer Assn of Univ Women Publicity/Social Chm 1968-87; Schubert Club 1968-; Article in It Starts in the Classroom; *office:* Northeast Sch 82 Scofieldtown Rd Stamford CT 06903

TIBERT, PRISCILLA CHURCH, Third Grade Teacher; *b:* Boston, MA; *c:* James, Ellen Cordo, Christopher, Susan Susalka; *ed:* (BA) Soc Stud, Emmanuel Coll 1954; *cr:* 3rd Grade Teacher Quincy Sch 1954-57; 6th Grade Teacher St Catherines Sch 1965-66; 3rd Grade Teacher Balch Sch 1967-; *ai:* Soc Stud & Rdng Curr, Report Card Study Comm; Supts Advisory Comm Building Rep; NTA, NEA; PTA Teacher Rep; *office:* Balch Sch Washington St Norwood MA 02062

TICHENOR, GLENDA HILL, French & English Teacher; *b:* Bowling Green, KY; *m:* Bill R.; *c:* Paul K., John M.; *ed:* (BA) Eng, 1960, (MA) Ed, 1979 Western KY Univ; (Rank I) Planned Ed, Murray St Univ 1987; *cr:* Eng Teacher Louisville Public Schls 1959-61, Scottsville HS 1967-77; Fr/Eng Teacher Caldwell Cty HS 1978-; *ai:* Fr Club Spon; Graduation Club; NEA, Amer Assn of Teachers of Foreign Lang; KY Endowment for Hum Grant; KY Inst of European Stud Paris France 1989; *office:* Caldwell Cty HS Rt 1 Box 137 B Princeton KY 42445

TIDBALL, DEE OAKES, Science Teacher; *b:* Evansville, IN; *m:* Curt; *c:* Marcie, Jason; *ed:* (BS) Bio, Greenville Coll 1970; Grad Stud Butler Univ; *cr:* Teacher Pleasant Plains 1970-71, Hillsboro Schls 1971-72, Mooresville Schls 1972-73, Bethesda Chrstn Schls 1981-; *ai:* Sci Fair; Frosh Class, Marine Bio Field Trip, CO Rocky Mountain Ecology Spon; Delta Kappa Gamma Mem 1988-; *office:* Bethesda Chrstn Schls 7950 N 650 E Brownsburg IN 46112

TIDD, BECKIE KAIN, Principal; *b:* Seymour, IN; *m:* Jerry; *c:* Ryan, David; *ed:* (BS) Elem Ed, IN St Univ 1974; (MS) Elem Ed, IN Univ 1984; Sch Admin & Cert Gifted/Talented, 1986; EDS Sch Admin, 1990 IN Univ; *cr:* Teacher Smith Elem 1974-86; Prin North Elem 1986-; *ai:* Admin Bd 1st United Meth Church; Bd of Trustees; Phi Delta Kappa; ASCD; IAEMSP; NAEMSP; Little League Pres 89-; Whos Who Amer Ed 1987- Women Exec 1989-; *home:* 280 Bailliere Dr Martinsville IN 46151

TIDMORE, LINDA JUNE HILL, Counselor; *b:* Ft Worth, TX; *m:* Maynard E.; *c:* Trent M.; *ed:* (BS) Elem Ed, TX Tech Univ 1964; (MA) Elem Ed, AZ St Univ 1970; Rdng Specialization; *cr:* Teacher Maie Bartlett Heard Sch 1964-71, Lincoln Sch 1971-72, Hyde Park Sch 1972-73, Eubank Sch 1974-78, Gallup Mid Sch 1978-80; Teacher/Cnslr Grapevine Mid Sch 1980-; *ai:* Dist Teacher Incentives & Chrldr Task Force; GMS Chrldr & Peer Helper Spon; GMS Stu Advocate Services; Dist Gifted & Talented, New Jr HS Planning Comm; TX Assn for Counseling & Dev 1987-; Alpha Delta Kappa 1978-80; Intnl Rdng Assn Recording Secy 1978-80; Kappa Kappa Gamma Pres 1963-64, Mem of Yr 1964; Beta Sigma Phi (Pres 1976-77, Mortar Bd 1963-64), Mem of Yr 1977; Finalist Meadows Prin Improvement Prgm East TX St Univ; Teacher of Yr for Dist & Sch; *home:* 2822 Wentwood Grapevine TX 76051

TIDMORE, ZAN E., English Teacher; *b:* Port Sulfur, LA; *m:* Charles Bradley; *c:* Tammy, Tori, Blythe A.; *ed:* (BS) Ed/Eng/ His, TX Eastern Univ 1979; (MS) Ed/Curr/Instruction, Univ of TX Tyler 1982; *cr:* Sci Teacher Athens Jr HS 1979-83; Eng Teacher Athens HS 1984-; *ai:* Athens Jr HS Drill Team & Athens HS Stingerette Spon; Jr & Sr Class Spon; TX & Athens Classroom Teachers Assn 1979-; E TX Cncl of Eng Teachers 1985-; *office:* Athens HS 708 E College Athens TX 75751

TIDWELL, HARVEY EUGENE, Physical Education Teacher; *b:* Orange, CA; *ed:* (BA) Phys Ed, Chapman Coll 1981; (MA) Educl Admin, CA Luth Univ 1986; *cr:* Phys Ed/Soc Sci Instr Luth HS 1981-89; Asst Bsktbl Coach Biola Univ 1986-; Athletic Dir/ Head Bsktbl Coach Luth HS 1989-; *ai:* Head Bsktbl Coach La Verne Luth HS; Asst Bsktbl Coach Biola Univ; Summer Bsktbl Coach IN Univ 1986-, GA Tech 1986-, Biola Univ 1986-; Natl Assn of Bsktbl Coaches Mem 1988-; Natl Assn of Sports Ofcls Mem 1978-; Bsktbl Championships 1981, 1985-86; Coach of Yr 1981, Runner Up 1990; Rookie Coach of Yr 1990; Most Improved Bsktbl Team 1990; *home:* 1724 Sunview Dr Orange CA 92665

TIDWELL, MERLENE PRESLEY, English Department Chairperson; *b:* Commerce, TX; *c:* Derek Kyle, Alicia Karen; *ed:* (BA) Eng, East TX Univ 1958; East TX Univ/TX Wesleyan Coll; *cr:* 7th & 8th Grade Teacher Lee Mid Sch 29 Yrs; 7th Grade Teacher Blocker Jr HS 2 Yrs; *ai:* Dept Chm; Prin Adv Comm; UIL Spelling & Ready Writing Coach; Natl Jr Honor Society Spon; Book Adoption Comm; PTA Mem 1958 Pres- Life Membership 1986; PTA Secy 1980; ATPE 1980-; TSTA 1958-80; Tx Joint Cncl of Teachers of Eng; Nom Teacher of Yr 1982 & 1987; *office:* Robert E Lee Mid Sch 401 E Grand Prairie Rd Grand Prairie TX 75051

TIDWELL, TOMMY NOEL, Science Teacher; *b:* Taylor, TX; *m:* Tammy Lorraine Wagner; *c:* Tiffany, Tessa; *ed:* (AA) General, Temple Jr Coll 1973; (BS) Wildlife/Fisheries Sci, TX A&M Univ 1976; Teacher Certification Trng, TX A&M Univ 1977; *cr:* Sci Teacher Round Rock HS 1977-78; 9th Grade Sci Teacher Round Rock Ind Sch Dist 1978-81; Sci Teacher Round Rock HS 1981-; *ai:* Class Spon; Curr Writing Comm; *office:* Round Rock HS 300 Lake Creek Dr Round Rock TX 78681

TIEGGS, RUTH STREEB, Principal; *b:* Windsor, CO; *m:* Leland Ernest; *c:* Chris P., Karri L.; *ed:* (BA) Elem Ed, Univ of N CO 1959; (MS) Elem Ed, E MT Coll 1969; Rdng, Spec Ed, Admin Endorsement; *cr:* Teacher Grand Island 1959-70; Rdng Teacher Specialist 1970-73, Demonstration Grant Teacher 1977-80, Admin Billings MT 1980-; *ai:* Foreign Lang Dept, Hearing Impaired Dept,

Legislative Comm Chairperson; Billings Assn for Elem Sch Prin Pres 1980-; NAESP, MT Assn for Elem Sch Prin 1980-; Phi Delta Kappa Pres 1987-; Rose Park Task Force 1987-; Interpretive Rdng, Foreign Lang in Elem Sch, Learning Center Approach to Individualized Instruction, Robotic Awareness, Thinking Skills Prgm Grants; *office:* Billings Sch Dist 1812 19th St W Billings MT 59102

TIEMANN, PATRICIA (SCHIELE), Sixth Grade GATE Teacher; *b:* Philadelphia, PA; *m:* Roger A.; *c:* Christina, Scott; *ed:* (AA) Liberal Arts, Citrus Jr Coll 1969; (BA) Liberal Stud, Univ of CA 1981; (MA) Soc Sci, Azusa Pacific Univ 1989; *cr:* Teachers Aide Valencia Elem 1976-80; 3rd Grade Teacher Baldy View Sch 1982; 4th/5th Grade Teacher 1982-85; GATE Teacher 1985- Ben Lomond Elem; *ai:* CAG 1986-; Delta Kappa Gamma Mem 1989-; *home:* 11666 Pescana Rd Rancho Cucamonga CA 91730

TIERNEY, MICHAEL PATRICK, Social Studies Teacher; *b:* Beacon, NY; *m:* Sue Houston; *ed:* (BA) Soc Stud, Mount Saint Mary 1986; Scndry Soc Stud, SUNY New Paltz 1988; Univ of London 1985-86; Cultural Studies, Japan; *cr:* Soc Stud Teacher Dover Jr/Sr HS 1988-; *ai:* Coach Varsity Ftbl & Modified Bsktbl; NE Regional Project Team; *home:* 78 Ninham Ave E Wappingers Flls NY 12590

TIERNEY, NOREEN T. (KENNEDY), Eighth Grade Teacher; *b:* Chicago, IL; *m:* Edward; *c:* Kathleen, Edward, Mary, John, Patrick; *ed:* (BA) Eng, Coll of St Francis 1957; *cr:* Eng/Soc Stud Teacher St Lous Acad 1957-59; 8th Grade Teacher St Lous ELem Sch 1959-60; 7th/8th Grade Teacher ST Bernadette Sch 1972-; *ai:* Co-Chairperson Lang Art Curr; Moderator of Stu Safety Patrol; NCEA 1990; *office:* St Bernadette Sch 9311 S Francisco Evergreen Park IL 60642

TILDEN, BYRON DENNIS, Mathematics Teacher; *b:* Valparaiso, IN; *ed:* (BS) Math, 1972, (MS) Math Ed, 1978 Purdue Univ; Working Towards Endorsement Gifted/Talented Ed; *cr:* Math Teacher Krueger Jr HS 1972-74; Part-Time Math Instr Purdue Univ 1978-87; Math Teacher Elston HS 1974-; *ai:* Math Club Co-Spon 1974-80; NCTM 1972-82; IN Cncl of Teachers of Math 1985-88; Mapco Teacher Achievement Awd 1985; Univ of Chicago Outstanding Teacher Awd 1984-86; MI City Area Schls Certificate of Commendation for Teacher Achievement Awd 1985; *office:* Elston HS 317 Detroit St Michigan City IN 46360

TILFORD, BARBARA L., 8th Grade Core/Drama Teacher; *b:* Mc Alester, OK; *m:* Baxter L.; *c:* Patrice, Vonetta, Terri, Baxter Jr.; *ed:* (BA) Soc Sci, Langston Univ 1957; (MA) Ed, St Marys Coll Moraga 1983; Rdng Specialist St Marys Coll Moraga CA 1983; *cr:* Teacher-Aide Bruce Elem 1973; 7th/8th Grade Eng/Drama Teacher Maplewood/Richmond Hgts 1974-77; Longterm Sub Ayers Elem 1978; 6th Grade Rdng/8th Grade Core/Drama Teacher Riverview Mid Sch 1979-80; *ai:* Christmas & Spring Production; Delta Sigma Theta VP 1986-88; Vallejo Alumnae Chapter; St Paul AME Church Drama Teacher 1980, Outstanding Contribution 1988; Black Educators Assn of Mt Diablo; Unified Sch Dist Pres 1987-89; Dist Cmmty on Human Relations 1987-; Teacher of Yr W Pittsburg Cmmty 1982; *home:* 3716 Liscome Way Concord CA 94518

TILL, SUZANNE WEATHERALL, 4th Grade Teacher; *b:* Longview, TX; *m:* Curtis; *c:* Cody; *ed:* (BS) Elem Ed, E TX Baptist Coll 1982; *cr:* 4th Grade Teacher Weldon Intermediate Sch 1982-; *home:* 404 N Central Hallsville TX 75650

TILLERY, CYNTHIA R., Science Teacher; *b:* Rogersville, AL; *m:* Olie B. Jr.; *c:* Gail Richardson, Lois; *ed:* (BA) Bio/Chem, Florence St Univ 1961; (MA) Bio/Scndry Ed, Univ of N AL 1980; *cr:* Lab Technician Southern Research Inst 1961-62; Biochemist Veterans Hospital 1962-66; Sci Teacher Decatur HS 1966-67, Bradshaw HS 1977-; *ai:* Sci Club & AL Jr Acad of Sci Spon; Sci Olympiad Team Coach; Phi Kappa Phi 1969-; Delta Kappa Gamma Treas 1984-; NEA, AEA 1977-; AL Jr Acad of Sci Teacher of Yr; *office:* Bradshaw HS 1201 Bradshaw Dr Florence AL 35630

TILLES, REBECCA WYNN, 9th-12th Grade English Teacher; *b:* Pensacola, FL; *m:* Stephen Andrew; *c:* Katie B.; *ed:* (BA) Eng, Univ of CA Irvine 1982; Working Toward Masters Liberal Arts; *cr:* Eng Teacher Corona Del Mar HS 1986-87, Poway HS 1987-; *ai:* Poway Young Playwrights Adv; Sr Schlsp Comm; NCTE 1986-; Bread for the World 1983-, Spec Service 1986; *office:* Poway HS 15500 Espola Rd Poway CA 92064

TILLETT, HARRIETT JONES, Chemistry Teacher; *b:* Roxboro, NC; *m:* Benjamin Wyche Jr.; *c:* Cera B., Christen S.; *ed:* (BA) Religion/Math, Meredith Coll 1977; Chem Cert, Duke Univ & Univ of NC Chapel Hill; *cr:* Dir of Chrstn Ed Long Memorial United Meth Church 1977-78; Chem Teacher 1978-, Sci Dept Chairperson 1982- Person Sr HS; *ai:* NC Sci Teachers Assn Mem 1987-; Alpha Delta Kappa Pres 1990; Delta Kappa Gamma Mem 1989-; Roxboro Jr Service League (Mem 1978-83, Secy 1981-82); Roxboro Jaycees Outstanding Young Educator 1987; *office:* Person Sr HS 1010 Ridge Rd Roxboro NC 27573

TILLEY, DARRELL GLEN, 4th Grade Teacher; *b:* Burley, ID; *m:* Karen Sue Pratt; *c:* Michelle, Jennifer, Ryan, Landon, Curtis, Kaleena, Amanda, Annette; *ed:* Assoc Elem Ed, Ricks 1971; (BS) Elem Ed, Brigham Young Univ 1973; Grad Courses Elem Ed, ISU 1974-89; *cr:* Migrant Teacher Minidoka Cty Sch Dist 1989; 4th Grade Teacher Heyburn Elem 1973-; *ai:* 4th Grade Chm; Recreational Dir 1975-79; Scouting Commissioner 1988-; Cub Scout (Leader, Comm Mem) 1986-; *office:* Heyburn Elem Sch 18 & O Street Heyburn ID 83336

TILLEY, W. CAROLYN HUGHES, 6th Grade Teacher; *b:* Lancaster, OH; *m:* Jack E.; *c:* Cathryn, Jeffrey P.; *ed:* (BS) Ed, Capital Univ 1959; 5th Yr Ed Los Angeles St, San Bernardino, Valley Coll & Capital Univ; *cr:* 4th Grade Teacher Copley Local 1959-62; 3rd-5th Grade Teacher San Bernardino CA 1962-70; 6th Grade Rdng Teacher Amanda Clearcreek Local 1974-; *ai:* Play Adv; Educl Comms; Amanda Clearcreek Ed Assn Pres 1980-82; OEA, NEA; Fairfield Cty Bd of Mental Retardation & Developmental Disabilities Secy 1989-; Green Mound Cemetery Assn Pres 1986-; Martha Jennings Holden Schlsp 1990; *office:* Amanda Clearcreek Sch Dist Box 188 Amanda OH 43102

TILLIS, GINA R., English Teacher; *b:* Gallipolis, OH; *m:* Don B.; *ed:* (BS) Comm/Eng Scndry Ed, Rio Grande Coll 1986; *cr:* Eng Teacher Meigs HS 1986-87, Eastern HS 1987-; *ai:* Yrbk Adv 1987-, Sr Play 1988; Eastern HS Intervention Remediation & Meigs Cty Course of Study Comms; Academic Quiz Team Moderator 1987-; Alpha Lambda Delta (Secy 1984-85, Charter Mem 1984-); NCTE 1987-89; Meigs Cty Pioneer & Historical Society 1989-; *home:* PO Box 383 Main St Rutland OH 45775

TILLITSON, MARY LOU, 5th Grade Teacher; *b:* Ransom, KS; *ed:* (BS) Elem Ed, St Mary of the Plains Coll 1975; *cr:* Kndgtn Teacher 1975-77, 2nd Grade Teacher 1977-80 St Mary Sch; 5th Grade Teacher Ransom Grade Sch 1980-; *ai:* Curr Cncl; Crisis Intervention Team; *home:* Box 104 Ransom KS 67572

TILLMAN, CAROL SMITH, Teacher; *b:* Vicksburg, MS; *m:* Charles J. D.; *c:* Daphne, Tara, Cassandra, Andrea, Joel; *ed:* (BS) Bio, Alcorn St Univ 1963; (MS) Combined Sci, Univ of MS 1976; (EDS) Combined Sci, Alcorn St Univ 1985; *cr:* Teacher Westside HS 1967-70, Franklin HS 1970-74, Pearisburg HS 1974- 76, Franklin HS 1976-; *ai:* Sci Club Adv; 4-H Club Spon; NSTA, NEA, MS Assn of Educators; Franklin Cty Chamber of Commerce 1990; Amer Cancer Society Local Ed Chm 1990; St Paul United Meth Church (Sunday Sch Teacher, Pianist); Natl Sci Fnd Grant 1980; *home:* Rt 2 Box 209 Roxie MS 39661

TILLMAN, MARION INGRAM, Second Grade Teacher; *b:* Laurel, MS; *m:* Stephen E.; *c:* Stephen L.; *ed:* (BA) Elem Ed, William Carey Coll 1963; *cr:* 3rd Grade Teacher Stainton Elem 1963-65; 3rd/4th Grade Teacher Stonegate Elem 1965-77; 1st/2nd Grade Teacher Soso Elem 1979-; *ai:* Helped Develop Dist Wide Instructional Management Prgm & Dist 5 Yr Long Range Prgm; Team Coord Grade Level in Team Teaching Prgm Jones Cty; NEA 1963-; TX St Teachers Assn 1965-77; MS Assn Educators 1979-; Delta Kappa Gamma (Pres 1976-77, Mem 1976-); *home:* PO Box 311 Soso MS 39480

TILLMANN, MICHAEL L., Staff Development Coordinator; *b:* Prescott, WI; *m:* Mary K. Kuntz; *c:* Patrick, Megan, Sean; *ed:* (BS) Eng/Speech/Theatre, Univ of WI River Falls 1968; (MA) Speech, Univ of ND 1972; Various Colls; *cr:* Teacher Hayward Schls 1966-69, Thief River Falls Schls 1969-71, Marshall Schls 1972-87, Owatonna Schls 1987-; *ai:* Theatre Dir; Speech Assn Exec Bd 1971-, Outstanding Individual 1989; Theatre People Exec Bd 1987-, ASCD 1988-; Owatonna Art Center Bd of Dirs 1988-; MN Ed Assn St Cncls 1970-; Ashland Oil Teacher Achievement Awd 1989; Owatonna Teacher of Yr 1990; *office:* Owatonna Public Schls 500 15th St NE Owatonna MN 55060

TILLOTSON, BILLIE MARIE (FORD), 6th Grade Math Teacher; *b:* Ft Worth, TX; *c:* Mark, Lynette Tillotson Welch; *ed:* (BA) Psych/Bus, TCU 1948; (ME) Ed/Eng, W TX St Univ 1971; *cr:* Teacher Eastridge Elem Sch 1965-88, Sam Houston Mid Sch 1988-; *ai:* Sci Fair; TX St Teachers Assn.

TILLPAUGH, HERBERT ALLAN, Head Teacher; *b:* Kalispell, MT; *m:* Betty Ann Wellman; *c:* Ann Longnecker, Tom, Ralph, Ronald; *ed:* (BA) Soc Stud, Valley City St Univ 1954; ASU Tempe; *cr:* Head Teacher Heron Elem 1954-62; Prin Brockton Elem 1962-65; Supt Eckelson Public Sch 1965-67; Head Teacher Wenden Elem #19 1967-; *ai:* Sch Admin; Coaching; La Paz Cty Sch Admin Assn Pres 1982-85; Wenden Elem Chosen Outstanding Sch in AZ Curr K-3 Grades; Formally Recognized MT, ND & AZ Outstanding Rural Sch Admin; *home:* 101 E Elm Wenden AZ 85357

TILLY, MELODY A., Fourth Grade Teacher; *b:* Kansas City, MO; *c:* Shaun C., M. K.; *ed:* (BS) Elem Ed, 1970, (MSE) Classroom Teaching, 1975 Cntrl St Coll MO; Grad Courses, Univ MO; *cr:* 2nd Grade Teacher Wellington/Napoleon R 9 Sch 1970-73; 3rd Grade Teacher 1973-84, 4th Grade Teacher 1984- Lafayette Cty CI Schls; *ai:* MO Lafayette Teachers Assn Pres 1983-84; MO Ed Assn St IPD Comm 1985-87; NEA; Order Eastern Star Worthy Matron 1986; Rebekah Lodge Noble Grand St Musician 1989-.

TILTON, CRAIG ROBERT, Amer & Modern History Teacher; *b:* Tachikawa, Japan; *m:* Cindy Underhill; *c:* Nathan, Sarah, Hannah; *ed:* (BS) His, Mid TN St Univ 1982; Addl Studies Mid TN St Univ; Bicentennial Comm TN Tech Univ; *cr:* Amer His Teacher 1987; Modern His Teacher 1990 Warren Cty Jr HS; *ai:* Chm Philosophy & Goals Comm; Southern Assn of Coll & Sch Accreditation; Warren Cty Jr HS; Chm Maj Ed Priorities Comm; Soc Stud Textbook Adoption Comm Mem Warren Cty Sch; Soc Stud Comm Mem; Action Team Mem Strategic Planning; Prof Dev Warren Cty Sch Comm; NEA; TN Assn Legislative Rep 1987; Warren Cty Ed Assn Pres 1989; NCSS; TN Cncl for Soc Stud; St Catherines Cath Church Religious Ed Teacher 1989; Action Team Awd-Warren Cty Sch Strategic Plan; Research Comm-Warren Cty Ed Assn Chm; Negotiating Team-Warren Cty Ed Assn Spokesperson; *home:* Rt 8 Box 55 Mc Minnville TN 37110

TIMBERLAKE, CAROLYN P., 10th Grade English Teacher; *b:* Richmond, VA; *m:* Mervyn C. Jr.; *c:* Stephen, Mary P., Paul; *ed:* (BA) Ancient Lang, Coll of Wiliam & Mary 1969; (MA) Eng Ed, VA Tech 1985; *cr:* Eng/Latin Teacher Auburn HS 1981-85; Latin Teacher Blacksburg HS 1985-88; Eng Teacher Atlantic HS 1989-; *ai:* NHS Spon; Intnl Baccalaureate Adv; Tutor; VA Classical League 1981-88; Montgomery Cty Cncl of Teachers of Eng (Treas 1986-88) 1985-88; Palm Beach Cncl Teachers of Eng 1989; Montgomery Cty Christmas Store 1985-88; Newcomers of Boca Raton Chm 1989-; Book Reviews in VA Eng Bulletin; Local Teacher Incentive Grants; SW VA Writing Project; *office:* Atlantic HS 2501 Seacrest Blvd Delray Beach FL 33444

TIMBS, DIANA FORBES, Lang Art & Math Teacher; *b:* Crosstown, TN; *m:* O. P.; *c:* Alicia C., Ashley M., Alex R.; *ed:* (BS) Bus Ed, Lambuth Coll 1969; (MED) Elem Ed, Memphis St Univ 1971; *cr:* Teacher E E Jeter 1969-74, Raleigh Egypt Elem 1974-75, Millington Cntrl Elem 1975-; *ai:* Grade Chm; Cty In-Service Comm; IN Ed Assn, NEA, SCEA, WTRA; Beta Sigma Phi Pres 1977-78; United Meth Women Choir Dir; Cty Grade Level Chm; TN Governors Acad 1988; *home:* 204 Carol Dr Atoka TN 38004

TIMKEN, JUDITH HUFFMAN, Kindergarten Teacher; *b:* Great Bend, KS; *m:* Roger D.; *c:* Chad, Jacey, Jenna; *ed:* (BS) Elem Ed, KS St Univ 1973; *cr:* 4th Grade Teacher Wamego Elem Sch 1973-74; Primary Teacher Lincoln Primary Sch 1974-; *ai:* Substance Abuse Team; Dist Staff Dev Comm Chairperson; NEA; Dighton Housing Authority Chm 1984-; Baptist Church Active Mem; Extension Homemakers Unit (Mem, Past Pres); Cmmty Youth Group Leader; *home:* 335 N 5th Box 911 Dighton KS 67839

TIMM, BETTYE, Curriculum Coordinator; *b:* Yoakum, TX; *m:* Harold G.; *c:* Karen L. Timm Winn, Constance L. Timm Van Zandt; *ed:* (BS) Eng/Ed, SW TX St Univ 1973; (MS) AED Supervision/Ed, Univ of Houston 1989; *cr:* 7th/8th Grade Eng Teacher Hallettsville Jr HS 1973-88; Curr Coord Hallettsville Ind Sch Dist 1988-; *ai:* ASCD 1987-; *office:* Hallettsville Ind Sch Dist 200 N Ridge Hallettsville TX 77964

TIMM-KNUTH, LORA LEE, Home Ec Dept Chair & Teacher; *b:* Springfield, MN; *m:* Dale Henry Knuth; *ed:* (BS) Home Ec Ed, Mankato St Coll 1967; Grad & Undergrad Stud, MN Colls; Spec Impact Stud, Haiti; Visual & Journal Writing, Split Rock Arts; *cr:* Jr/Sr Home Ec Teacher Elkton HS 1968; Enrichment Teacher St Raphaels Parochial Sch 1968; Living Skills to Handicapped Stus EMR Summer Project 1970; Home Ec Teacher Worthington Area Jr HS 1968-; *ai:* Future Leaders of America & FHA Adv; Voc Relicensure Chairperson 1988-89 & Recorder 1989-; Teacher Asst Team Mem; Building & Dist Faculty Advisory Bd; NEA, MN Ed Assn; Worthington Ed Assn (Secy 1986-, Mem 1968-); Amer Home Ec Assn 1968-; MN Home Ec Assn (Dist Pres 1970-72, 1980-81, Treas 1980-88); Worthington Prof Home Ec Club (Pres 1980-, Secy 1986-87, Treas 1985-86); Amer Legion Auxiliary Pres 1990; Cty Extension Club Local Study Group Mem; Judge Numerous 4-H Functions; City Turkey Day Celebration; Field Tested Book for Mc Knight & Company; *home:* 1734 S Shore Dr Worthington MN 56187

TIMMER, DENNIS JOHN, Mathematics Teacher; *b:* Bellingham, WA; *m:* Marilyn Mae Murray; *c:* Craig, Charlene, Renee, Lynnette; *ed:* (BA) Math, W WA Univ 1963; (MA) Ed, Whittier Coll 1969; Grad Stud UCLA, City Univ Seattle; *cr:* Teacher Fremont Jr HS 1963-69, Fountain Valley HS 1969-78, Waputo HS 1978-; *ai:* NHS Adv; Math Team Coach; CA St Math Assn 1963-78; WA St Traffic Safety Assn 1978-; *office:* Waputo HS Box 38 Wapato WA 98951

TIMMERDING, DIANA WILBERS, English Teacher; *b:* Covington, KY; *m:* Thomas F.; *c:* Brandon, Kirsten, Robin, Kevin; *ed:* (BA) Eng/Ed, Thomas More Coll 1967; (MA) Eng/Ed, N KY Univ 1984; Grad Stud Teaching Writing, N KY Univ 1986; *cr:* Eng Teacher Our Lady of Providence 1967-70, Villa Madonna Acad 1983, Boone Cty HS 1984, Notre Dame Acad 1985-; *ai:* Faculty Adv Facilitator; 9th Dist Sch PTA Pres 1980-81, Lifetime Membership; NEA Grants Writing; Various In-Service Presentations; Natl Scholastic Awds Judge 1986.

TIMMONS, SANDRA GROVES, English Teacher; *b:* Shreveport, LA; *m:* Wm Earl; *c:* Kristy, Lori; *ed:* (BA) Eng Ed, LA St Univ ShrevePort 1977; *cr:* HS Eng Teacher/Librarian Calvary Baptist Acad 1977-87; HS/Mid Sch Eng Teacher Trinity Heights Chrstn Acad 1987-; *ai:* Stu Government Assn; Chrldrs; NHS; Homecoming Court; NASSP 1989-; Summer Grove Baptist Church Active Mem 1984-; *office:* Trinity Heights Chrstn Acad 4800 Old Mooringsport Rd Shreveport LA 71107

TIMMONS, TERI DOWNARD, Guidance Counselor; *b:* Charlotte, NC; *c:* Julia, Jon; *ed:* (BS) Bio, Cntrl MI Univ 1970; (MA) Ed, Lindenwood Coll 1982; (MA) Counseling, Univ of MO St Louis 1984; *cr:* Teacher Battle Creek Public Schls 1969-70; Substitute Teacher Portage Sch Dist & Battle Creek Lakeview Sch Dist 1969-72; Teacher/Cnslr Francis Sch Dist 1978-; *ai:* Francis Howell N Chrldr & Intramurals Spon; Hollenbeck Jr HS Summer Sch Earth Sci Teacher; *office:* C F Hollenbeck Jr HS 4555 Central Schl Rd Saint Charles MO 63303

TIMPONE, JOSEPH A., Science Teacher-Dept Chair; *b:* Renton, WA; *m:* Jo Ann Larson; *c:* Jolene; *ed:* (BA) Bio, Cntrl WA St Coll 1971; (MED) Sci Ed, Seattle Pacific Univ 1979; Initial Scndry Prin Certificate Cntrl WA Univ 1984; *cr:* Sci Teacher Pe Ell HS 1971-85, W F West HS 1985-; *ai:* Asst Track Coach; NSTA 1971-; WA Sci Teachers Assn 1984-; Kiwanis Club; *office:* W F West HS 342 SW 16th Chehalis WA 98532

TINAJERO, SARA GARCIA, English Dept Chair; *b:* Laredo, TX; *c:* George, Patricia Rooney, Pamela Rooney; *ed:* (BS) Scndry Ed/Eng/Span, TX A&I Laredo 1973; (MAIS) Eng/Span/Soc Stud, Laredo St Univ 1988; Numerous Courses, Bowling Green Univ, Madrid Spain; *cr:* 9th-12th Grade Eng Teacher Nixon HS 1973-77; Eng Teacher United Intermediate Sch 1979-80; 7th-12th Grade Ace Supvr Laredo Chrstn Acad 1982-83; 7th Grade Eng Dept Chairperson Memorial Mid Sch 1983-; *ai:* Schls Newspaper Ed; Chairperson Schls Discipline Comm; Mem Textbook Comm 1989-; LISD Writing Comm Mem; Bowling Green Univ Teaching Asst for AYA Prgm in Madrid Spain 1987; Several Poems Published in Natl Anthologies; Conducted Var Summer Wkshps for Teachers; Whos Who in TX Ed 1975; *home:* 619 Corpus Christi St Laredo TX 78040

TINGELHOFF, SUZANNE M. (WORTMAN), Fifth Grade Teacher; *b:* West Point, NE; *m:* George R.; *c:* Brian, Brenda, David, Kathy, Steven, Timothy; *ed:* (BS) Elem Ed, Univ of NE Omaha 1979; *cr:* 2nd Grade Teacher St Patricks Elem Sch 1960-61; 4th Grade Teacher Guardian Angels Elem Sch 1963-64; 2nd Grade Teacher St Richards Elem 1967-69; 4th Grade Teacher Holy Ghost Elem 1969-75; 5th Grade Teacher Our Lady of Lourdes Elem 1975-; *ai:* Consultant Weekly Reader 1978-80; Religious Coord Our Lady of Lourdes Sch 1987-; NCEA 1970-; Our Lady of Lourdes Parish Worship Space AD HOC Comm 1982-84; Archdiocese Omaha Soc Stud Curr Comm 1976-77, 1983-84; Our Lady of Lourdes Ed Comm 1982-86; Cooperating Teacher for Univ of NE Omaha 1984 & Creighton Univ 1986; *office:* Our Lady of Lourdes Sch 2124 S 32 Ave Omaha NE 68105

TINGLE, PHYLLIS IRENE, 6th Grade Teacher; *b:* Louisville, KY; *ed:* (BA) Elem Ed, Brescia Coll 1979; (MA) Elem Ed, W KY Unin 1986; *cr:* Elem Teacher 1979-81, Jr HS Teacher 1981-86 St Mary of the Woods Sch; Elem Teacher St Egberts Sch 1986-87; Asst Prin/Jr HS Teacher St Pius X 1987-89; Elem Teacher Bishop Cotton Elem 1989-; *ai:* Consolidated Schls Teacher Advisory Bd; KY Colonels 1983-; Outstanding Young Woman of America 1985; *office:* Bishop Cotton Elem Sch 3418 Hardinsburg Rd Owensboro KY 42301

TINGUE, MARY LOU BURLAGE, Third Grade Teacher; *b:* Cleveland, OH; *c:* David, Patricia Tornow, John; *ed:* (BA) Elem Ed/Music, Fredonia St Teachers Coll 1954; Numerous Courses; *cr:* 2nd Grade Teacher Kenmore Public Schls 1954-55; 3rd Grade Teacher West Seneca Cntrl Schls 1968-; *ai:* Dissemiator AFL-CIO Educl Research; Curr Writing; PTL Bd; Dist Strategic Planning Team; *office:* Allendale Elem Sch 1399 Orchard Park Rd West Seneca NY 14224

TINKLE, JEANETTE STANLEY, Office Education Coordinator; *b:* Center, TX; *m:* Patric L.; *c:* Todd Thompson, Jodi Thompson, Jill Thompson; *ed:* (BS) Bus/Secratarial Sci 1966, (MED) Bus Ed 1972 Stephen F Austin St Univ; Real Estate; Bus; *cr:* Bus Ed Teacher Center HS 1967-70, Joaquin HS 1972-73; Vocational Office Ed Teacher Carthage HS 1974; *ai:* Spon Bus Profs of Amer-Carthage Chapter; TX Classroom Teachers Assn; Vocational Office Ed Teachers of TX; Beta Sigma Phi-Epsilon Tau Chapter; Panola Cty Chapter TX A&M Mothers Club; Service Awds-Bus Profs of Amer; *office:* Carthage H S 1 Bulldog Dr Carthage TX 75633

TINNEY, DONALD LEWIS, English Department Chair; *b:* Burlington, VT; *ed:* (BA) Mass Comm, 1980, Certificate Scndry Ed, 1985 Univ of VT; *cr:* Chm 1988-, Eng Teacher 1986- VT Acad; *ai:* Dormitory Parent; Head Athletic Trainer; Literary Magazine & Sr Class Adv; Coll Counseling Comm; NCTE 1986-; New England Assn of Teachers of Eng 1987-; Article Published; *office:* Vermont Acad Saxtons River VT 05154

TINSELY, JANET MURRAY, Third Grade Teacher; *b:* Moncks Corner, SC; *m:* John Kelvin; *c:* Joshua, Jonathan; *ed:* (BS) Ed, Baptist Coll 1974; *cr:* Teacher Berkeley Elem 1974-75, Penrose Elem 1976-77, Straus Elem 1976-; *ai:* Faculty Cncl & Staff Dev Rep; Discipline Comm; Steering Comm for Senate Bill 2; *home:* PO Box 64 Pisgah Forest NC 28768

TIPPIN, MARK T., Mathematics Teacher; *b:* Oklahoma City, OK; *m:* Robin Finch Ray; *c:* Daniel C.; *ed:* (BS) Math Ed, 1978, (BS) Accounting, 1985 Cntrl St Univ; *cr:* Math Teacher/Coach Putnam City North HS 1978-80; Math Teacher Edmond Cntrl Mid HS 1985-86, Edmond Memorial HS 1986-; Accounting Teacher OK St Univ Tech Branch 1986-; *ai:* Key Club, Sr Class & Jr Class Spon; Asst Golf Coach; Outstanding Young Man of America Mem 1985; *home:* 512 Cherryvale Edmond OK 73034

TIPPING, WILLIAM DAVID, Mathematics Teacher; *b:* Blooming Grove, TX; *m:* Eva La Vonne; *c:* Shonda, Renee; *ed:* (BA) Math/Physics, N TX Univ 1967; *cr:* Programmer General Dynamics 1967-69; Analyst/Consultant Control Data Corporation 1969-87; Teacher Italy Ind Sch Dist 1987-; *ai:* Number Sense Coach; *office:* Italy Ind Sch Dist Drawer 909 Italy TX 76651

TIPPS, SHERRY S., Biology/Botany/Zoology Teacher; *b:* Yakima, WA; *m:* Alan Wayne; *c:* Angela L., Kyle W.; *ed:* Veterinary Medicine, Phillips Univ; (BS) Sci Ed, 1969, (MS) Curr/Instruction, 1988 OK St Univ; Biotechnology, Genetics, Outdoor, Curr Design; *cr:* Teacher/Dept Chairperson Cleveland HS 1969-79, Blackwell HS 1979-86; Teacher Stillwater HS 1986-; *ai:* Environmental Awareness Club; Sci Fair & Jr Acad of Sci Coord; Jr Class Spon; NEA, OK Ed Assn 1969-; Stillwater Ed Assn 1986-; 1st Chrstn Church Disciples of Christ; Stillwater Ed Fnd Grant Recepient; OK Sci Fair Teacher of Best Project; Blackwell Teacher of Yr 1981; Co-Author of Materials on Marine Ed; Co-Author of Laboratories in Biotechnology for HS.

TIPTON, CHARLES LEE, Choral Activities Director; *b:* Big Spring, TX; *m:* Suzanne Leisa Cotton; *c:* Andrew; *ed:* (BA) Choral Ed, E NM Univ 1983; Wkshps; *cr:* Choral Dir Post Ind Sch Dist 1984, Yucca Jr HS 1985-; *ai:* Youth Dir; Phi Mu Alpha Sinfonia 1981-; Magazine Article Published 1987; Outstanding Young Men of America 1984; *home:* 1924 Hull Clovis NM 88101

TIPTON, DEAN D., Business Education Teacher; *b:* Wessington, SD; *m:* Shirleen; *c:* Tricia, Todd, Terry; *ed:* (BS) Bus Ed, 1969, (MS) Bus Ed, 1971 Northern St; Grad Work Bus Ed, Educl Admin, Cmmty Ed, Cmptr Technology; *cr:* Bus Ed Teacher 1969-, Cmmty Ed Teacher 1976- Southland HS; *ai:* Southland Ed Assn Pres; Bus Profs America (Pres, Adv) 1976-89, Distinguished Service Awd 1988; MN Bus Educators SE Treas 1978; NEA, NBEA; Lions Club Secy 1989-; Cedar River Cty Club (Treas, Bookkeeper) 1972-; Little Cedar Luth Church Financial Secy 1989-; St MN Integrated Bus Simulation Manual Co-Author; *home:* 506 Lincoln St NW Adams MN 55909

TIPTON, DEBORAH DIEKMANN, Math/Spanish Teacher; *b:* San Francisco, CA; *m:* Gary Wayne; *c:* Levon J., Randy W.; *ed:* (BA) Hispanic Stud, Monterey Inst of Intnl Stud 1979; Universidad de Salamanca Spain Summer 1981-82; Working Towards Masters Scndry Ed, E Cntrl Univ 1990; *cr:* Span Teacher Marina HS 1980-82, Arroyo HS 1982-83; 7th-12th Grade Math/Span Teacher Stuart HS 1985-; *ai:* Soph Class Spon; Hughes Cty Ed Assn (Treas 1988-, VP 1990-); OEA Delegate 1988-; *office:* Stuart HS P O Box 145 Stuart OK 74570

TIPTON, JUDY ANN, Speech Teacher; *b:* Dallas, TX; *m:* James Dean; *c:* Jaye, Jeramy; *ed:* (BA) Speech/Drama 1971, (MS) Ed, 1975 East Cntrl Univ; *cr:* Speech Teacher East Cntrl Univ 1975-87; Speech/Drama Teacher Byng HS 1978-88; Speech Teacher East Cntrl Univ 1989-; *ai:* ECU Play Asst Dir; Ada Cmmty Theatre Bd of Dir 1989-; Miss Ada Pageant Dir 1972-75; Teacher of Yr 1988; Outstanding Speech Coach 1985; *home:* 311 S 14th Pl Ada OK 74820

TIPTON, VALERY SULLIVAN, Elementary Teacher; *b:* Elkton, KY; *m:* Willard Darrel; *c:* Tana L. Tipton Hightower; *ed:* (BS) Elem Ed, W KY Univ 1961; *cr:* Teacher Highland Elem 1961-69, Sinking Fork Elem 1969-; *ai:* Math Comm; NEA, KEA, CCEA; 2nd Baptist Church (Mem, Nursery Worker, Choir Mem); *home:* 2055 Everetts Ln Hopkinsville KY 42240

TIRADO, CARMEN M., Third Grade Teacher; *b:* Caguas, PR; *m:* Angel L. Viera; *c:* Angel L. Viera, Cynthia Viera; *ed:* (BA) Elem Sch, Univ of PR 1960; Admin, Supervision Sch; *cr:* Teacher Beatriz Sch 1957-59, John D Stubbe Sch 1959-60, Andres Gonzalez Sch 1960-65, John F Kennedy Sch 1965-68, Benita Gonzalez Sch 1968-; *ai:* GSA; Mothers & Fine Art Club; Cmmty Sports; Teachers Assn; NEA Mem; Teacher of Yr; Excl Teacher; Sch & Room Discipline Articles; 6th Grade Graduation Dedication; Red Cross Annual Activity Dedication.

TISDALE, HAZEL ANN, Third Grade Teacher; *b:* Kingstree, SC; *ed:* (BA) Elem Ed, Lander Coll 1973; (MS) Elem Ed, Clemson Univ; CBE Trained-Concensus Based Evalutaion for Teachers; ECRI Trained-Exemplary Center Rdng Improvement; Rdng Prgm to Enhance Learning; *cr:* 3rd Grade Teacher Ware Schoals Primary 1973-; *ai:* Sch Improvement & Teacher Evaluation Comm; Greenwood Cty Ed Assn Recording Secy 1975; NEA, SCEA Delegate 1980-81.

TISON, ROY FREDERICK, History/Geography Teacher; *b:* Chicago, IL; *m:* Marianne Elsa Uebele; *c:* Eric, Mark; *ed:* (BA) His, Elmhurst Coll 1968; (MA) His, NE IL Univ 1972; (MS) Environmental Ed, George Williams Coll 1978; Admin Endorsement Natl Coll of Ed 1976; *cr:* Soc Stud Teacher Peacock Jr HS 1968-; *ai:* Teacher Insurance Comm; Itasca Sch Dist 10 Academically Talented Stu Prgm Building Coord 1978-81; Dist Bd of Ed Mem & Secy; Itasca Teachers Ed Assn (Grievance Comm Chairperson 1974, Negotiation Comm Chairperson 1972-76, Chief Negotiator 1972-76, Pres 1971); Phi Delta Kappa 1976-; Natl Cncl for Geographic Ed (Exec Bd Mem 1980-83, 1985-88, Nominating Comm Chairperson 1981), Distinguished Teaching Awd 1982, Merit Teacher Awd 1977; IL Geographical Society Exec Bd Mem 1981-; NCSS, IL Cncl for Soc Stud, IL Ed Assn, NEA Mem 1968-; Bensenville Boys Athletic Assn (Bsktbl Coach 1974-75, Bsktbl Commissioner 1975-78, Bsbl Coach 1983-89); BSA Educl Resource Person 1975-89; Educl Consultant for Encyclopedia Britannica Films 1982 & Scholastic Incorporated Geography Textbook 1977, 1981; Articles Published 1979, 1982, 1984; Audio Visual Inst of Du Page Bd Mem 1975-80; Natl Geographic Society Natl Coll Summer Geography Inst 1989; *office:* Peacock Jr HS 301 E North St Itasca IL 60143

TITKEMEYER, RAMONA SWANSON, Kindergarten Teacher; *b:* Patriot, IN; *m:* Roy; *c:* Randy, Roger, Rhonda Carnevali; *ed:* (BA) Ed, Miami Univ 1974; OH Writing Proj; Teach; Pride; *cr:* 1st-3rd Grade Teacher, Harbor Springs Public Sch 1958-59; 3rd Grade Teacher Lakewood Public Sch 1964-67; Kngtn Teacher Edgewood Public Sch 1969-; *ai:* Lang Arts Comm; Kndgtn Unit Leader; NEA 1967-;OH Ed Assn 1967-; Eddewood Teacher Assn Treas 1985-87; Disciples Chrstn Chruch Ed Chairperson 85-86; Shiloh Knothole League Bd Mem 68-71 *home:* 3070 Jacksonburg Rd Hamilton OH 45011

TITUS, VALERIE PELLUM, High School Guidance Counselor; *b:* Englewood, CA; *m:* Eugene Sr.; *c:* Eugene III, Chekesha; *ed:* (BA) Sociology, 1973, (MS) Counseling, 1983 CA St Univ Fullerton; Prof Modeling; *cr:* Cnslr Moreno Valley Unified Sch 1984-; *ai:* Black Stu Union & Asst Cheer Adv; Asst Girls Bsktbl Coach; Schlsp Coord; Speechcrafters 1990; CA Stu Opportunity Access Prgm Vice Chairperson 1989-; Loveland Choir 1988-; *office:* Moreno Valley HS 23300 Cottonwood Ave Moreno Valley CA 92388

TOALSON, BOBETTE CURRY, English/Speech Teacher; *b:* Columbia, MO; *m:* Dennis R.; *c:* Dennis A., Martin W., Mary K.; *ed:* (BSE) Eng, Univ of MO Columbia 1973; Mastery Learning; ITEPS; Cooperative Learning; *cr:* Librarian NE Cmmty R-6 Schls 1973-74, Keytesville R III Schls 1974-78, N Callaway Schls 1980-82; Eng/Speech Teacher Lyon-Decatur NE Schls 1984-; *ai:* Supt Advisory Comm; Speech & Drama Coach; 7th Grade Class Spon; NSEA Local Negotiator 1984-; NE Speech Comms Assn 1988-; Womens Club 1982-84, Outstanding Mem 1983; 4-H 1984-90, 5 Yr Leader Awd 1989; ESU Advisory Comm on Prof Dev, Outstanding Teacher in NE Schls 1985-86; *office:* Lyons-Decatur NE Schls 5th & Crystal Lyons NE 68038

TOBIAS, DEANNA WHITE, Fourth Grade Teacher; *b:* Evansville, IN; *m:* Dale Allen; *c:* Erin, Brooke; *ed:* (BS) Elem Ed, 1971, (MS) Elem Ed, IN Univ 1974; Lion Quest Skills for Growing Trainee; *cr:* 6th Grade Teacher 1971-72, 4th Grade Teacher 1972-78 Wakarusa Elem 1972-78; Kndgtn Teacher Union Elem 1978-83, 4th Grade Teacher Central Elem 1983-; *ai:* Broad Based Planning Comm for Gifted & Talented Ed; NEA, IN St Teachers Assn, Wa-Nee Ed Assn 1971-; Psi Iota Xi (Recording Secy 1972-89, Corresponding Secy, Conductoress); *home:* 652 E Van Buren Nappanee IN 46550

TOBIN, PAMELA PATTERSON, Mathematics Teacher; *b:* Yonkers, NY; *m:* William B.; *c:* Megan, Brett, Taylor; *ed:* (BSED) Math Ed, 1977, (MED) Ed/Math, 1980 GA Southern Coll; *cr:* Math Teacher Statesboro HS 1977-79, Lombardi Jr HS 1979-86, St Norbert Coll Amer Indian Summer Math Camp 1989, 1990, Lombardi Mid Sch 1986-; *ai:* Dist Math Comm & Building Leadership Team Mem; Team & Math Content Area Unit Leader; NEA, WI Ed Assn, Green Bay Ed Assn, NE WI Ed Assn 1979-; Hillcrest Parent Organization (Co-Chairperson 1989-, Secy/Treas 1986-89); Parent Advocacy Group for Gifted & Talented Ed, United Way Rep 1984-; *office:* Lombardi Mid Sch 1520 South Point Rd Green Bay WI 54313

TOCZYLOWSKI, CONSTANCE MORRIS, 6th Grade Teacher; *b:* Philadelphia, PA; *ed:* (BS) Ed, Villanova 1965; *cr:* Teacher Parochial Sch System 1954-68, Public Sch System 1968-; *ai:* PTA Pres; Maple Shade Ed Assn Building Rep 1968-; Teacher Recognition Awd NJ 1988; *office:* Steinhauer Sch North Fellowship Rd Maple Shade NJ 08052

TODD, CLEDA LATTA, Third Grade Teacher; *b:* Casa Grande, AZ; *m:* Sam D.; *c:* Holly, Dellise, Brec; *ed:* (BS) Elem Ed/Soc Stud/Eng NE ST Univ 1963; *cr:* 3rd Grade Teacher Ind KS Public Schls 1963-64; K-8th Grade Chester NE Excelsior 1964-65; 5th-6th Grade Teacher/Coach Sunnyside Cushing 165-66; HS Eng Teacher Calvin HS 1966-69; 5th-6th Grade Teacher Moss Elem 1969-71; 3rd Grade Teacher Morris Elem 1973-; *ai:* Staff Dev & Textbook Selection Comm; 4-H Club Leader; Sftbl Coach; Morris Assn of Classroom Teachers 1973-; OK Ed Assn, NEA 1965-; Beta Sigma Phi Pres 1982-83, Woman of Yr 1983; Alpha Chi Natl Honor 1962-63; Morris Assn of Classroom Teachers Rep; *home:* Rt 1 Morris OK 74445

TODD, DARLENE LAWRENCE, Spec Ed Learning Disabilities; *b:* Tulsa, OK; *m:* David Todd; *c:* Dana, Michael; *ed:* (BSED) Elem Ed, 1967, (MED) Elem Ed,1970 Abilene Chrstn Coll ; *cr:* 2nd Grade Teacher Pacedo Elem 1697-68, R A Hall Elem 1970-71; 4th Grade Teacher 1974-75, 3rd Grade Teacher 1975-77 F M C Elem; 4th Grade Title I Resource Teacher 1977-81, 4th Grade Teacher 1981-85 R A Hall Elem 1981-85; Spec Ed Tyler Elem 1986-; *ai:* NEA; TSTA; Beeville Fac Assn; *office:* Tyler Elem 815 N Tyler Beeville TX 78102

TODD, DOLORES ADKINS, Teacher; *b:* Henderson, KY; *m:* Obbie U.; *c:* Steven E., Obbie D., Linda Todd-Ferguson; *ed:* (BS) Elem Ed, 1973, (MA) Elem Ed, 1977 IN St Univ; (Rank I) Elem Ed, Murray St Univ 1980; FL Performance Testing & Beginning Teacher Internship Trng Prgm; *cr:* K/2nd/3rd/6th Grade Teacher E Heights Elem Sch 1973-; *ai:* KEA, NEA Building Rep 1985-86; West Home for Girls Chm Public Relations Comm 1989-; Competency Based Prgm Comm Chm 1976-77; *home:* 7350 Airline Rd Henderson KY 42420

TODD, DONNIE MAE, Substitute Teacher; *b:* Forest Hill, TN; *ed:* (BA) Elem Ed, Lane Coll 1953; (MS) Elem Ed, Memphis St Univ 1972; Adult Basic Ed; *cr:* Teacher Millington East Elem 1986, E A Harrold HS 1953, Millington East Elem 1986; Substitute Teacher Woodstock Elem Sch 1990; *ai:* Activity Sponsorship; 2nd Grade Club Adv; Chm Costumes & Decorations; Natl Teacher (Sch Rep 1980, Homeroom Chm 1986-), 20 Yr Certificate 1985-86, Life Time Membership Pen & Plaque 1986; Shelby Cty Involvement-Mental Improvement 1985-, Certificate 1988; Scientific Grant; *home:* 2582 Moon Beam Millington TN 38053

TODD, JAMES WILLIAM, 7th Grade Soc Stud Teacher; *b:* Independence, LA; *ed:* (BA) Soc Stud Ed, Southeastern LA Univ 1983; *cr:* Amer His Teacher Ponchatoula Jr HS 1984-; *ai:* Stu Cncl Adv/Chief Spon; Soc Stud Fair Coord; Educl Tour Coord; Substance Abuse Prevention Ed Spon; Tangipahoa Fed of Teachers Mem 1984-; *office:* Ponchatowa Jr HS 315 E Oak St Ponchatoula LA 70454

TODD, JOHN PHILIP, G/T Resource Teacher; *b:* Smithville, IN; *m:* Sharon Sierp; *c:* Daniel, David, Kathleen; *ed:* (BA) Ed, Indianapolis Univ 1964; (MA) Ed, Butler Univ 1967; *cr:* Teacher Burkhart Elem 1964-80, Keystone & Meridian Mid Schls 1980-85,

Keyston Mid Schls 1985-; *ai:* G/T Parent Organization Mem; Broad Base Planning Team Mem Further Advancement G/T Prgm; ISTA St Rep 1971; St G/Y Organization; Curr Various Articles Challenge Mag; *office:* Keystone Mid Sch 5715 S Keystone Ave Indianapolis IN 46227

TODD, JUDITH ANN (MURDOCK), 4th Grade Teacher; *b:* Webster, MA; *m:* Richard M.; *c:* Michael M.; *ed:* (BA) Elem Ed, Notre Dame Coll 1979; Univ of NH 1971/1989; *cr:* 1st Grade Teacher Canterbury Elem Sch 1966-67; Act Dir Mc Kerley Nursing Home 1967-72; Folks Recreation Dir NH Recreation & Park Society 1972-74; Prgm Dir Havenwood Retirement Cmmty 1974-75; Elem Teacher Pembroke Hill Sch 1980-; *ai:* Sci Comm; Lang Art Comm; Soc Stud Comm; Career Ed Comm; Staff Dev Comm; Staff Comm Sch Wide Literacy Through Motivational Act; Granite St Rdng Cncl; NHEA/NEA 1980-; Ed Assn of Pembroke (Building Rep 1987-89 Secy 1972-73 Mem 1970-); NH Recreation & Park Society; Natl Recreation & Park Assn 1971-; Notre Dame Coll Alumni 1979-; Amer Legion Aux 1979-; South Congregational Church Choir/Soloist 1967-; Recognition for Contribution to Collection of Math & Sci Act Elem Stu from Acad of Applied Sci; Contributor to Book-Fun is Therapeutic 1972; Contributor to Magazines-Nursing Homes 1973; *home:* P O Box 142 Epsom NH 03234

TODD, LARRIE ANN, Consultant; *b:* Dayton, OH; *m:* Richard; *c:* David Sinck, Eric T.; *ed:* (AB) Eng, Western Coll 1962; Working Towards Masters at Wright St Univ; Numerous Writing Courses; Working Towards CA Certificate; *cr:* Teacher Dayton Public Schls 1962-80; Consultant Placerville Public Schls 1980-; Teacher El Dorado Union HS 1988-; *ai:* Consulting, in Class, Writing & Related Projects Publications; NEA, Journalism Ed Assn, N CA JEA 1988-; Numerous Articles Published in Intnl Publications.

TODD, MARCIA FRIEDRICH, Sixth Grade Teacher; *b:* Parkston, SD; *m:* Jon Larry; *c:* Jeffrey, Rebecca, Jason; *ed:* (BS) Elem Ed, Northern St Coll 1965; (MED) Curr/Instruction, Univ of S MS 1984; *cr:* 4th Grade Teacher Longfellow Sch 1965-66, Aurora Sch 1966-69; 6th Grade Teacher Our Lady of Fatima 1978-; *ai:* Civil Defense Coord; Sch Choir, Recorder Band, Sch Extension Prgm Dir; NEA 1965-69; NCEA 1978-; Mercy Cross HS PTO Pres 1982-; Mercy Cross HS Band Boosters Treas 1983-; Cmmty Concert Assn 1986-; Newspaper in Ed Teacher of Week; *office:* Our Lady of Fatima Sch 2090 Pass Rd Biloxi MS 39531

TODD, SHEILA WOOD, Chapter I Reading Teacher; *b:* Somerset, KY; *m:* Marshall L.; *c:* Sarah E.; *ed:* (AA) Elem Ed, Somerset Comm Coll 1977; (BS) Elem Ed, 1979, (MA) Elem Ed, 1981 E KY Univ; (Rank I) Elem Ed; *cr:* 5th Grade Teacher 1979-86, Chapter I Rdng Teacher 1986- Nancy Elem; *ai:* Cheerleading Spon; Lake Cumberland Intnl Rdng Assn Mem 1986-; KY Educl Assn Mem 1979-; PTA Mem 1979-; *home:* Box 2466 Hwy 80 E Nancy KY 42544

TODD, WILLIAM ERIC, Auto Technology Instructor; *b:* Los Angeles, CA; *c:* Erica, David; *ed:* (BS) Industrial Technology, CA Poly Univ 1968; (MA) Ed, 1973 CA Poly Univ; Factory Trng GM; Ford; Toyota;Chrysler; US Army Electronic; *cr:* Instructor North HS 1969-; *ai:* Auto Club Adv; Auto Technology Advisory Comm; Treas 1978; Chm 1978; ME 1968- CA Ind Tech Ed Assn; CA Teacher Assn/NEA 1968-; CA Auto Teachers 1980-; Alpha Psi Omega; Boy Scouts of Amer Scout Master 1978-80; Automotive Svc Cncl; Plymouth Trouble-Shooting Natl Contest 1971 & 74 8th Place 1974; CA Model Sch Site & Grant 1985; Natl Cert Trng Ctr NIASE 1986; *office:* North H S 300 Galaxy Ave Bakersfield CA 93308

TOEQUE, SANUBO, Curriculum Director; *b:* Monrovia, Liberia; *m:* Mona Nimley; *c:* Veneta J., Sanubo, Koffa-Juah, Mona, Sieh-Nimley; *ed:* (AS) Chem, Bronx Comm Coll 1974; (BSC) Chem, Pepperdine Univ 1977; (MA) Educl Admin, CA St Univ Dominguez Hills 1988; Grad Stud Organic Polymer; *cr:* Asst Coord United Nations Refugee Prgm 1968-71; Asst Chemical Engineer Electro Chemical Company 1971-75; Nursing Chem Tutor Bronx Comm Coll 1971-75; Math/Sci Teacher Various Local Private Schls & Toeque Tech Chrstn Acad 1975-; *ai:* Amer Chemical Society Mem 1974-, Certificate 1974; Natl Organization of Black Chemist & Engineer Mem 1989-, Certificate 1989; Society of Plastic Engineers Mem 1982-, Certificate 1982; ASCD 1990, Certificate 1990; Outstanding Chem Tutor Awd; Project Wild Certificate of Prof Dev; *office:* Toeque Tech Chrstn Acad 5944 S Avalon Blvd Los Angeles CA 90003

TOIFL, KARLYN J., 4th Grade Teacher; *b:* Meriden, CT; *ed:* (BA) Elem Ed, Central CT St Coll 1965; Ferguson-Florissant Writers Project; *cr:* 4th Grade Teacher Hanover 1965-; *ai:* Mem City-Wide Lang Arts Curr Comm; after Sch Folk Dance Group; Mentor Teacher; Cooperating Teacher; Hanover Writing Resource Person; Meriden Ed Assn/NEA 1965-; Delta Kappa Gamma (Lambda Chapter 1978- Prgm Chm 1980-82 Svc Chm 1982-); Girl Scouts (Wider Opportunity Chair 1984-86 Statewide Camp Evaluation Comm 1987-88 Thanks Badge 1969); Prebus Club Ed of Yr 1977; Jaycee Woman of Yr 1981; *office:* Hanover Elem Sch 208 Main St South Meriden CT 06450

TOLAND, DEBRA YZENSKI, German/English Teacher/Chair; *b:* Wheeling, WV; *m:* William F. Jr.; *ed:* (BA) Ger/Ed, W Liberty St Coll 1975; (MA) Speech Comm, WV Univ 1983; *cr:* Instr Cntrl Cath HS 1976-, WV Northern Comm Coll 1986-; *ai:* NHS & Foreign Lang Honorary Moderator; AATG 1976-; NCTE 1989-; Outstanding Young Women of America 1981; *office:* Cntrl Cath HS 14th & Eoff Sts Wheeling WV 26003

TOLES, SUE LATTIMORE, 9th/10th Grade English Teacher; *b:* Brownsville, TN; *c:* Kylan L., Kenya L.; *ed:* (BS) Eng/Bus Ed, Lane Coll 1966; Grad Stud Spec Ed, Memphis St Univ; Working Toward Masters Ed, Trevecca Nazarene Coll; *cr:* Eng Teacher Lauderdale HS 1966-68, W P Ware HS 1969-70; Spec Ed Teacher Ripley Elem & Lauderdale Mid Sch 1971-87; Eng Teacher Ripley HS 1987-; *ai:* Soph Class Spon; Lauderdale Cty Ed Assn (Treas 1985-86, VP 1989-, Pres 1990) Pres Awd 1986; TN Ed Assn, NEA; Lauderdale Cty Drug-Free Alliance Co-Chairperson 1988-; Holly Grove Baptist Church Typist; Spec Art Festival Coord 1985; TN Career Ladder Level II; *office:* Ripley HS 254 Jefferson St Ripley TN 38063

TOLL, LUVERNE FRANZMAN, Fourth Grade Teacher; *b:* Grygla, MN; *m:* Lloyd William; *c:* Nancy Roussin, Lauri, Sharon, David, Michelle; *ed:* (BS) Elem Ed, St Cloud Univ 1971; (MS) Elem Ed, Univ of MN 1984; 2 Yr Elem Ed, St Cloud Univ 1949; *cr:* 4th Grade Teacher Kingston MN Sch 1949-51, Two Harbors MN Sch 1951-52, St Louis Park MN 1952-55; 4th & 5th Grade Teacher St Francis & East Bethel 1968-; *ai:* Math Steering Comm; Soc Stud Steering Comm; MFT 1968-; Church Personnel Comm Chairperson 1982-84 Councilman 1981-84; Nom Ashland Oil Awd for Teachers; *home:* 3007 O Henry Rd Brooklyn Center MN 55429

TOLLEY, BETTY RUBY, Chairperson Foreign Language; *b:* Albany, CA; *m:* Robert Bryan; *c:* Jeannie R.; *ed:* (BA) Ed, Pepperdine 1956; Soc Sciences & Span USC, Pepperdine, S AR Univ; *cr:* 5th Grade Teacher Miller Street 1956-57; Elem Schls Teacher Los Angeles Public Schls 1957-63; Span Teacher Fairview HS 1970-; *ai:* Span Club & Class Spon; Future Teachers of America; Planning & In-Service Trng Comm; AR Ed Assn 1970-; Amer Assn Teachers Span/Portuguese; PTA 1952-, Outstanding Service Awd 1990; Amer Poll-ettes Natl Dir 1989-; AR Poll-ettes (Pres, VP) 1986-87, AR Poll-ette of Yr 1988; Cty 4-H Cncl Bd 1980-84; Teacher of Yr Fairview HS 1987; SW AR Foreign Lang Alliance Mem.

TOLLIVER, JAMES EDWARD, 4th Grade Teacher; *b:* Jenkins, KY; *m:* Julia Hale; *c:* Jennifer, Jessica; *ed:* (BA) Phys Ed, Morehead St Univ 1962; Elem Cert Wright St Univ; *cr:* 6th Grade Teacher Overlook Elem 1962-76, Page Manor Elem 1976-78; Phys Ed Teacher Page Manor Elem 1978-81; 4th Grade Teacher Beverly Gardens Elem 1981-; *ai:* Safety Patrol Supvr; NEA, OEA, WOEA; Norma Jane Zappin Doer Awd; *office:* Beverly Gardens Sch 5555 Enright Ave Dayton OH 45431

TOLLIVER, WILMA COLE, 5th/6th Grade Teacher; *b:* Sharps Chapel, TN; *c:* Jeannie; *ed:* (BS) Elem Ed, Lincoln Memorial Univ 1959; *cr:* Teacher/Prin Oak Grove Elem 1960-65, Sharps Chapel Elem 1976-83; Teacher Sharps Chapel Elem 1965-76, 1983-; *ai:* Bsktbl Coach 1976-89; 4-H Leader; Local Teachers Assn, TN Ed Assn, NEA; *office:* Sharps Chapel Elem Sch RR 1 Sharps Chapel TN 37866

TOLMEN, PATRICIA STEPHENS, Language Arts Teacher; *b:* Muncie, TX; *m:* Harry D.; *c:* Judson, Lorie, Stacie; *ed:* (BS) Soc Service, IN Univ 1961; (BS) Eng, Ball St Univ 1967; *cr:* Lang Arts Teacher Coolspring Sch 1961-62/1964-65/1968, New Prairie 1965-66/1968-71/1973-; *ai:* HS Asst Girls Track Coach; New Prairie Classroom Teachers; ISTA; NEA; Gleaner Society; *office:* New Prairie Jr H S 5331 N 700 E New Carlisle IN 46552

TOLOMAY, LAWRENCE JOSEPH, Mathematics Teacher; *b:* Renovo, PA; *m:* Helen Marie Sobota; *c:* Elizabeth, Daniel; *ed:* (BS) Math, Lock Haven St Coll 1968; (MED) Math, Rutgers Univ 1974; *cr:* Math Teacher Union Springs Cntrl Sch 1968-; *ai:* NY St Math Teachers Assn; Natl Sci Fnd Grant 1971-74; *home:* 6 Yale Ave Auburn NY 13021

TOLSDORF, MARGARET ANN WRIGHT, French/English Teacher; *b:* Jefferson, IA; *m:* Thomas Dale; *c:* Kelley, Scott; *ed:* (BS) Child Dev/Elem Ed, IA St Univ 1967; (MA) Eng, Sangamon St Univ 1990; Numerous Courses Fr; *cr:* Elem Teacher CO Cmmty Sch 1967-69, Sioux City Cmmty Sch 1970-71; Elem Teacher/Tutor Ankeny Cmmty Sch 1974-81; Grad Asst Sangamon St Univ 1984-86; Jr HS Teacher Waverly Cmmty Sch 1986-; *ai:* Fr Club & Soph Class Spon; Foreign Exch Coord; Amer Assn of Univ Women SpringField Branch Treas 1989-; IL Foreign Lang Teachers Assn, NEA, IEA, WEA, Natl IL Waverly Educl Assn; Beta Sigma Phi Pres 1978-79; *home:* 2012 Vista Lake Ct Springfield IL 62704

TOMAN, VINCENT, Social Studies Teacher; *b:* Milwaukee, WI; *m:* Julie Elizabeth Geidel; *c:* Nicholas S., Christopher R.; *ed:* (BS) His/Philosophy, Univ of WI-Stevens Point 1975; Teacher Cert Cardinal Stritch 1980; *cr:* Medical Admin USAF 1972-74; Writer/Photographer Post Newspapers 1975-80; Teacher Muskego-Norway Sch Dist 1980-; *ai:* Stu Cncl Adv; WEA/NEA; Waukesha Little League Coach 1987-; *office:* Bay Lane M S S75 W16399 Hilltop Dr Muskego WI 53150

TOMAS, DORIS DAVIS, Science Dept Chairperson; *b:* Mc Allen, TX; *m:* Eugene Emil; *ed:* (BS) Bio, Pan Amer Univ 1976; (MS) Sci Ed, Univ of Houston 1986; *cr:* Teacher Donna HS 1976-77; Teacher/Dept Chairperson George Jr HS 1977-; *ai:* Task Force Comm Mem; Sci Olympiad Coach; Knowledge Master Bowl & Sci Club Spon; Cncl of Natl Jr Honor Society; Sci Teachers Assn of TX 1980-; Lamar Classroom Teachers Assn 1977-, Schlsp; New Century Garden Club 1989-; Prairie View A&M Energy Conference Schlsp; Baylor Coll of Medicine Summer Inst for Teachers; *office:* George Jr HS 4201 Airport Rd Rosenberg TX 77471

TOMASE, CAROL ALESSANDRI, English/Music Teacher; *b:* Taunton, MA; *m:* Guy R.; *c:* Holly J.; *ed:* (BA) Eng/Music, Emmanuel Coll 1964; *cr:* Vocal Music Teacher Mansfield Public Schls 1964-71; Operation Head Start Teacher Mansfield 1964-65; Substitute Teacher Mansfield & PLainville & Foxoboro 1977-83; 7th/8th Grade Eng/Music Teacher Ursuline Acad 1983-; *ai:* Glee Club Moderator; Liturgy Comm; Sch Bd Rep 1980-83; NCEA 1983-; Cath Womens Club Prgm Chairperson 1977-81; *office:* Ursuline Acad 65 Lowder St Dedham MA 02026

TOMAYKO, MARY ANN, Business Education Teacher; *b:* Monessen, PA; *m:* Charles L. Jr.; *c:* Kelly, Tracy Mosco; *ed:* (BS) Bus Ed, Indiana Univ of PA 1961; *cr:* Teacher Redstone HS 1961-62, Rostraver HS 1962-64, Douglas Sch of Bus 1964-68, Charleroi HS 1968-; *ai:* FBLA; Stu Assistance Team Mem; NEA, PSEA, CAEA; *office:* Charleroi Sr HS Fescen Dr Charleroi PA 15022

TOMBERLIN, CAROL ROWAN, Mathematics Teacher; *b:* Paris Island, SC; *m:* James Ronald; *c:* Amanda, Ryan; *ed:* (BSED) Math, GA Southern 1969; (MED) Math, Valdosta St 1977; *cr:* Math Teacher Tift Cty HS 1969-70, Berrien Jr HS 1970-72, Berrien HS 1972-73, Turner Cty Jr HS 1973-75, Tift Cty HS 1975-78, Berrien HS 1978-; *ai:* Youth Chrstn Fellowship Club Adv; NEA, GA Assn of Educators; STAR Teacher 1978, 1985; *office:* Berrien HS 909 N Davis Nashville GA 31639

TOMKO, MARGARITA OSSANDON-DUNCAN, English Teacher; *b:* Chuquicamata, Chile; *m:* David; *c:* Gary Duncan, Richard Duncan, Diane Duncan Carpenter; *ed:* (BA) Span/Ed, Hunter Coll 1950; Grad Stud Eng & Ed, Hofstra Univ; *cr:* Physically Handicapped Teacher Wm J Gaynor Jr HS 1953-54; Elem Sch Span Teacher Main Street Sch 1959-63; Jr HS Span Teacher W E Howitt Jr HS 1963-81; Mid Sch Eng Teacher W E Howitt Sch 1982-; *ai:* Natl Jr Honor Society Spon; NY St Foreign Lang Teachers Assn, Amer Assn Teachers of Span/Portuguese, NCTE; Farmingdale Fed of Teachers Building Rep; NY St PTA Teacher Rep, Honorary Lifetime Mem 1986; Natl Defense Ed Act Summer Inst Span Hofstra Univ 1963; Recognition by Sch Dist 25 Yrs of Service; *office:* Weldon E Howitt Sch Farmingdale Public Schls Van Cott Ave Farmingdale NY 11735

TOMLIN, CAROL GARRISON, Mathematics Teacher; *b:* Buffalo, NY; *m:* Robert Earl; *c:* Lora T. Hickey, Robin T. Dyer, Stephen, William G., Melissa, Victoria; *ed:* (BA) Math, Winthrop Coll 1954; Grad Courses Ed, Winthrop Coll & Univ of SC; *cr:* Math Teacher Richmond Drive Sch 1954-56; Teacher Orangeburg Jr HS 1956-57; Math/Sci Teacher Fulmer Mid Sch 1978-87; Math Teacher Brookland-Cayce HS 1987-; *ai:* Honor Society Spon; Academic Team Coach; Math Team Co-Spon; Book Selection Comm; Faculty Cncl Mem; NCTM 1979-; SC Cncl Teachers of Math 1979-, Outstanding SC Math Teacher Candidate 1988; Palmetto St Teachers Organization 1984-; Delta Kappa Gamma 1987-; *office:* Brookland-Cayce HS 1300 State St Cayce SC 29033

TOMLIN, LELA BOULDIN, Science/Computer Teacher; *b:* Remo, VA; *m:* Charles E. Jr.; *c:* Charles, Thomas, Evelyn; *ed:* (BA) Eng, Longwood Coll 1948; *cr:* Eng/His Teacher Cople HS 1949-53; 4th Grade Teacher 1969-74, 5th-7th Grade Teacher 1975-81 Fairfields Elem; Coord of Gifted & Talented Northumberland Cty 1983-84; Cmptr/Sci Teacher Northumberland Mid 1982-; *ai:* NSTA; *office:* Northumberland Mid Sch Box 100 Heathsville VA 22473

TOMOSKE, ROGER L., English Teacher; *b:* Benton Harbor, MI; *m:* Christine Lazarek; *ed:* (BA) Ed, W MI Univ 1967; *cr:* 10th-12th Grade Teacher New Buffalo HS 1967-; *ai:* Saturday Detention Prgm Supvr; *office:* New Buffalo HS 222 S Whittaker St New Buffalo MI 49117

TOMPKINS, SANDRA ORR, Elementary Art Teacher; *b:* Kerrville, TX; *m:* John William Jr.; *c:* Becky; *ed:* (BS) Elem Ed, 1971, (MED) Methods & Materials, 1972 SW TX St Univ; *cr:* 3rd/4th Grade Teacher 1973-76, Art Teacher 1976- Kline Whitis Elem; *ai:* TSTA, NEA 1973-88; ATPE, TAEA, NAEA 1988-; Freedoms Fnd Valley Forge Teachers Medal Awd 1976; *office:* Kline Whitis Elem Sch 500 S Willis Lampasas TX 76550

TONEY, PATRICIA NORTHROP, Senior English Teacher; *b:* Boise, ID; *m:* Richard L.; *c:* Bradley D., Katherine S.; *ed:* (BA) Eng, Univ of ID 1970; Post Gradn Stud Advanced Placement Inst Pacific Luth Univ; *cr:* Eng/Soc Stud Teacher Columbia HS 1970-71; 9th Grade Eng Teacher Meridian Mid HS 1972-73; Rdng Teacher Buhl HS 1975-76; 7th/9th Grade Eng Teacher Lake Hazel Jr HS 1981-85; 10th-12th Eng Teacher Meridian HS 1985-87, Centennial HS 1987-; *ai:* Sr Class Adv; Advanced Placement Comm; NCTE, ID Cncl Teachers of Eng 1981-; Kappa Kappa Gamma Alumni Assn Reference Chm 1990; Wkshp Presenter ICTE Conference 1989; Curr Writer for Scndry Eng in Dist; *office:* Centennial HS 4600 Mc Millan Rd Meridian ID 83642

TONEY, PATRICIA REMBERT, 4th-5th Grade Lang Art Teacher; *b:* Bishopville, SC; *m:* Joseph; *c:* Robin Cornell, Jonora Nichelle; *ed:* (BS) Elem Ed, 1973; (MS) Elem Ed, 1980 Francis Marion Coll; *cr:* 1st-6th Grade Teacher 1974-85; Remedial Rdng Teacher 1985-88; Lang Arts Teacher 1988- West Lee Elem; *ai:* Stud Cncl Adv; Pee Dee Rdng Assoc; Alpha Kappa Alpha Soroity; Natl Cncl of Negro Women; Lee Cty Arts Cncl; Teacher of Yr West Lee Elem 1980; West Lee Elem 1989; Distinguished Teacher of Yr Pee Dee IRA 1983.

TONSOR, DIANA THOMAS, Phys Ed-Health Teacher; *b:* Sprucepine, NC; *m:* Tom; *c:* Tracey, Brandi; *ed:* (BS) Phys Ed, Health, High Point Coll 1981; *cr:* 7th Grade Science Teacher; 6th Grade PE Teacher 1984-87 Denton Jr HS; 7th/8th/9th PE Health North Davidson Jr HS 1987-; *ai:* Coach Tennis Bsktbl Sftbl; Alliance Health/Phys Ed/Recreation/Dance 1989-; NC Assn Educators 1987-; Baptist Young Women; Phys Educators Awd High Pint Coll 1981; *office:* N Davidson Jr H S Rt 10 Box 1660 Lexington NC 27292

TONTIMONIA, GUY C., 8th Grade Amer History Teacher; *b:* Ravenna, OH; *ed:* (BS) Ed/Soc Stud, 1975, (MA) Athletic Admin, 1982 Kent St Univ; *cr:* Soc Stud Instr Maplewood JVS 1975-76; His/Ec Instr Ravenna Brown Mid Sch 1976-; *ai:* Brown Mid Sch Bus Mgr; Intramural; Brown Mid Sch Field Trips Dir; Brown Mid Sch Vlybl, Head Boys Bsktbl Coach; Asst HS Sftbl Coach; OH Cncl of Soc Stud 1976-; Ravenna Elks; Jr Achievement Project Bus 1980-82; Ravenna Parks & Recreation Bd Mem; Athletic Journal Article 1980; Kent St Univ Distinguished Teaching Awd 1981; *office:* Ravenna Brown Mid Sch 228 S Scranton Ravenna OH 44266

TOOLE, MARIETTA RESIO, First Grade Teacher; *b:* Pittston, PA; *m:* Michael Patrick; *c:* Erin; *ed:* (BS) Elem Ed, Coll Misericordia 1967; *ai:* PA Ed Assn, NEA, Lake Lehman Ed Assn; Alzheimers Assn of NE PA Asst Treas; Outstanding Teacher of Yr 1984; *home:* 1339 Chase Rd Shavertown PA 18708

TOOMEY, CAROL J. BLOOD, Third Grade Teacher; *b:* Nashua, NH; *c:* Thomas, Scott, Steven, Lynn; *ed:* (BA) Elem Ed, Fitchburg St 1957; *cr:* 2nd Grade Teacher Pepperell Elem Sch 1957-61; 3rd Grade Teacher Peter Fitzpatrick Sch 1967-; *ai:* Report Card, Soc Stud, Communication, Comm; Fund Raisers Chairperson; Bldg Representative P.F.S. 1986-87; Cultural Arts Ed Collaborative 1989-; 4th Grade Chorus Dir 1956-57; 3rd Grade Players Dir 1967; Grange Players 1980; Assn of Elem Teachers Secy 1980-81; PTO Mem; Townsend Recreation Dept Dir 1978-83; Pepperell Recreation Dept Dir 1983-85; Prof Ballroom Dancing Instr at Highgate Dance Acad, Adult Ed Classes NMRHS, YMCA Classes.

TOOMEY, NANCY S., Second Grade Teacher; *b:* Boston, MA; *m:* John J. Jr.; *c:* Karen A., John J., Kathleen B.; *ed:* (BA) Ed, Univ of ME 1958; *cr:* Teacher New Britain CT 1958-59, Monterey CA 1959-60, Canajoharie NY 1961-67, Sharon Springs NY 1967-; *ai:* GSA Leader, Colonial Club Fed of Womens Clubs; Ames Firemens Auxiliary; Sharon Springs Cntrl Sch Dedication of Yrbk 1989; *office:* Sharon Springs Cntrl Sch Rt 20 Sharon Springs NY 13459

TOON, PAM J., 6th Grade Language Art Teacher; *b:* Cincinnati, OH; *ed:* (AAB) Secretarial Sci/Medical, Rio Grande Comm Coll 1982; (BS) Comprehensive Bus Ed, Rio Grande Coll 1984; (MS) Counseling, Univ of Dayton 1990; *cr:* Mid Sch Rdng/Lang Art Teacher Hamden Elem Sch 1984-88; 6th Grade Rdng/Lang Art Teacher Allensville Elem Sch 1988-; *ai:* 6th Grade Safety Patrol Adv; NEA Building Rep 1984-; NEA 1984-; Eastern Star 1979-.

TOPF, VIRGINIA VERONICA, Fifth Grade Teacher; *b:* Bronx, NY; *ed:* (BA) Soc Sci/Elem Ed, Mt St Mary Coll 1974; (MS) Elem Ed, Long Island Univ 1977; *cr:* 3rd Grade Teacher St Patricks Sch 1955-56; 2nd/4th Grade Teacher St Josephs 1957-65; 1st Grade Teacher St Joan of Arc 1965-66; 1st/7th Grade Teacher St Cecelias 1966-68; 6th Grade Teacher Holy Family 1968-72; 5th/6th Grade Teacher Holy Rosary 1972-75; 5th-8th Grade Teacher St Marys 1975-; *ai:* Coord Sch Testing Prgm; *office:* St Marys Sch Jackson St Fishkill NY 12524

TOPOVSKI, SHIRLEY ELSER, First Grade Teacher; *b:* West Salem, OH; *m:* Steve; *c:* Mark, Gregg, Neil, Brian; *ed:* (BS) Elem Ed, Ashland Univ 1964; (MS) Elem Ed, Univ of Akron 1979; Wkshps & Seminars in Whole Lang Field; *cr:* 2nd/3rd Grade Teacher Northwestern Local 1960-64; 5th Grade Teacher Sea Gate Elem 1964-65; 1st Grade Teacher Wooster City Schls 1967-68; Music Therapist 1968-69, K-1st Grade Teacher for Retarded 1969-70 Apple Creek St Inst; 1st Grade Teacher Northwestern Local 1972-; *ai:* Building Rep 1987-89; Negotiating Team 1987, 1988; Northwestern Local Ed Assn, OH Ed Assn, NEA 1972-; Worldwide Church of God (Pianist, Choir Accompanist) 1970-; Annual Ruritan Musical Pianist 1989-; People to People HS Ambassador Prgm Teacher Leader 1987, 1989-; Nom Ashland Oils Outstanding Teacher Awd 1990; Laura B Frick Grant for 1st Grade Rdng 1989-; Poetry Published; *home:* 6212 Lattasburg Rd Wooster OH 44691

TORBETT, C. JOLENE, Teacher; *b:* Ada, OK; *m:* Bruce G.; *c:* Kristy Mc Calister, Lisa Meyer; *ed:* (BA) Ed - Magna Cum Laude, Cntrl St Univ 1972; *cr:* 4th Grade Teacher Indian Meridian 1973-80; Teacher of Gifted 1981-85, 6th Grade Teacher 1986- James Griffith; *ai:* OEA Mem 1972-85; Alpha-Chi Mem 1971-; Deans Honor; Pres Honor Roll; *office:* James Griffith Intermediate 1861 S Indian Meridian Rd Choctaw OK 73020

TORBUSH, LIBBY MARTIN, Gifted Resource Teacher; *b:* Anniston, AL; *m:* John Raymond; *ed:* (BED) Behavioral Disturbances - Magna Cum Laude, Auburn Univ 1975; (MED) Gifted Ed, GA St Univ 1980; Cmptr Literacy Courses; Sci Coursework; Taught Childrens Cmmty Courses Clayton St Coll; *cr:* Behavior Disorders Specialist Spalding Cty 1975-77; Educl Therapist S Metro CDC Blair Village 1977-79; Gifted Resource Teacher Pointe South Elem 1980-; *ai:* Sch Sci Chairperson & Contact; Sch Cmmty Advisory Comm Faculty Rep; Media Comm Mem; Odyssey of Mind & Quiz Bowl Teams Coach; Cncl for Exceptional Children 1974-; Kappa Delta Pi 1980-; GA Sci Teachers Assn 1986-; New Hope Baptist Church (Youth Sunday Sch Teacher, Adult Choir Mem) 1987-; Appaloosa Horse Club Mem 1980-; Auburn Schlsp; GA St Univ Grant; Pointe South Elem Outstanding Young Educator 1986 & Techer of Yr 1990; Outstanding Young Women of America 1987.

TORETTI, MARGARET ANN, First Grade Teacher; *b:* Monongabela, PA; *ed:* (BA) Elem Ed, Bethany Coll 1975; (MED) Rdng Specialist, California Univ of PA 1979; *cr:* 1st Grade Teacher Bethel Park Sch Dist 1975-.

TORGERSEN, TARVAL A., 5th/6th Grade Teacher; *b:* Koosharem, UT; *m:* Louise Sorensen; *c:* Tarval A., Joanne, Charmian Robinson, Chet H., Russell M., Allison, Wesley R., Megan, Kimala; *ed:* (BS) Elem Ed, Coll of S UT 1963; *cr:* Teacher Uintah Sch Dist 1963-65; Teacher/Prin Sevier Sch Dist 1965-; *ai:* BSA Scoutmaster 1985-.

TORGERSON, MARY JO JOE CALLOWAY, English Teacher; *b:* Aztec, NM; *c:* Tod, Greg, Brad; *ed:* (MA) Eng, Univ of NM 1954; *cr:* Eng Teacher Garfield Jr HS 1954-55, Monroe Jr HS 1955-56; Part-Time Bus Teacher Adult Ed 1956-68; Eng/ Typing Teacher Jefferson Jr HS 1968-76; Eng Teacher Highland HS 1976-; *ai:* Volunteer Academic Decathlon Team Lit Coach; Teachers Advisory Comm; Advanced Placement Inst UNM 1987; UNM APS Inst on Short Story 1988; NEH SW Lit Seminar 1989; NEH 5 Week Inst on Emily Dickinson, Gustavus Adolphus Coll 1990; *office:* Highland HS 4700 Coal Ave SE Albuquerque NM 87108

TORNS, ROBERT LOUIS, Music Teacher; *b:* Lindenhurst, NY; *m:* Carol Lee Paul; *c:* Robert Jr., Paul, Scott; *ed:* (BS) Music Ed, Ithaca Coll 1963; (MS) Music Ed, Long Island Univ 1986; *cr:* Music Teacher Penn Yan Cntrl Schls 1968-72, Dundee Cntrl Sch 1972-74, Deerpark Schls 1976-77, Copiague Schls 1977-; *ai:* Long Island Philharmonic Chorus Mem; Suffolk Cty Music Ed Assn (Exec Comm 1978-82), 1977-; NY St Sch Music Assn 1967-; NY St Band Dirs Assn 1988-; BSA Chm Troop 97 1984-89; Free & Accepted Masons Purdue Lodge 123 1970-; S Festival Band Elem Level Chm 1978-81; *office:* Copiague Schls Great Neck Rd Copiague NY 11726

TORRENS, ALEJANDRINA, Mathematics Teacher; *b:* Marianao, Cuba; *ed:* (BA) Math, St Peters Coll 1974; (MA) Bi-ling Ed, Kean Coll 1985; *cr:* Title I/Remedial Math Teacher St Bridgets Sch 1974-77; Math Teacher Dickinson HS 1977-.

TORRES, BERTHA NOYOLA, Art Teacher; *b:* Del Rio, TX; *m:* Israel B.;; *c:* Jason; *ed:* (BS) All Level Art, 1971, (BS) Elem Ed, 1973, (MS) Ed, 1976 Sul Ross Univ; Bi-Ling Ed; Manuscript Writing 1968; *cr:* 6th Grade Teacher Memorial Elem Sch 1971-75, Eastside Elem Sch 1975-81, Buena Vista Elem Sch 1981-82; Eng Teacher 1982-85, Art Teacher 1985- Memorial Mid Sch; *ai:* Yrbk Spon/Textbook Advisory Comm Rep; Univ Interscholastic League Spon; Campus Rep; TX St Teachers Assn Rep; 6th Grade Leader; TX St Teachers Assn 1971-; San Felipe Ex Stu Assn Secy 1989; San Felipe Stu Cncl Secy 1965-66; San Felipe Band Cncl Secy 1965-66; Sul Ross Univ Stu Assn 1969-70; TX Career Ladder Levels II & III Teacher; *home:* 103 Boulder Ridge Del Rio TX 78840

TORRES, ELADIO, Science Teacher IPS; *b:* Yauco, PR; *m:* Evelyn Solivan; *ed:* (BA) Bio/Ed, Rutgers-Newark 1977; (MA) Cmptr Programming/Data Processing/Ed, St Peters Coll 1989; *cr:* Exec Dir Latin Amer Cultural Center 1977-80; Supvr Cath Cmmty Services 1980-84; Case Worker Div of Youth & Family Services 1984-85; Teacher East Side HS 1986-; *office:* East Side HS 238 Van Buren St Newark NJ 07105

TORRES, ELMA DE SANTOS, Gifted/Talented Teacher; *b:* Corpus Christi, TX; *m:* Diego; *c:* Ronnie, Olivia M.; *ed:* (BA) His/ Scndry Ed, TX Womans Univ 1965; Bi-ling Ed, Gifted/Talented Ed; *cr:* Remedial Rdng Teacher Corpus Christi Ind Sch Dist Elem; His Teacher Corpus Christi Ind Sch Dist Jr HS; 3rd Grade Teacher Orange Grove Ind Sch Dist Elem; His Teacher Orange Grove Ind Sch Dist Jr HS 1987-89; Gifted/Talented Lang Arts Teacher Orange Grove Ind Sch Dist Mid Sch 1989-; *ai:* Stu Cncl Spon; UIL Academic Coach; NHS, Career Ladder Comm; TSTA, NEA, Orange Grove Ed Assn; Orange Grove Civic League Secy 1988-; TX Womans Univ Alumnae Assn 1989; *office:* Orange Grove Mid Sch Box 534 Orange Grove TX 78372

TORRES, IRENE CALDERON, Spanish/Portuguese Teacher; *b:* El Paso, TX; *m:* Frank; *c:* Michael A.; *ed:* (BA) His, 1971, (MA) His, 1983 Univ of TX El Paso; TFLA Conferences; Conference on Teaching Portuguese Austin 1989; *cr:* Span Teacher Scotsdale Elem 1971-72; Span/Mexican-Amer Stud Teacher Ysleta HS 1972-75; Amer His Teacher Ysleta Jr HS 1978-79; Span/Portuguese Teacher Bel Air HS 1979-81, Ysleta HS 1981-; *ai:* Span NHS Spon; Sr Class Co-Spon; Ran Teacher of Yr Elections; Amer Assn Teachers of Span & Portuguese (Local Chapter Secy 1979-80, VP 1980-81, Pres 1982-83); TX Foreign Lang Assn, Ysleta Teachers Assn, TX St Teachers Assn, NEA; Presented Paper at AATSP Convention 1984 & TX Foreign Lang Assn 1989; *office:* Ysleta HS 8600 Alameda Ave El Paso TX 79907

TORRES, MARCO, JR., Earth Science Teacher; *b:* Halauka, HI; *ed:* (BS) Tropical Crop Production, Univ of HI 1956; (MS) Fnd of Ed, 1974, Ed Cert Biological Scndry Sci, 1984 Troy St Univ; Army Aviation Trng US Army Aviation Sch 1962; *cr:* US Army Officer Dept of Army 1956-83; Earth Sci Teacher Dauphin Jr HS 1987-; *ai:* Dauphin Jr HS Sci Club Adv; Sch Concession Chairperson; Enterprise Ed Assn Rep 1987-; AL Ed Assn, NEA, AL Sci Teachers Assn 1987-; NSTA 1990; St John Cath Church Religious Ed Staff 1984-; *office:* Dauphin Jr HS Dauphin St Extension Enterprise AL 36330

TORRES, PRISCILLA CHACON, Spanish Teacher; *b:* Taos, NM; *m:* Joseph L.; *c:* Joseph, Fidel, Enrico; *ed:* (BA) Bus Ed/ Span, NM Highlands Univ 1968; Span & Bi-Ling Ed; *cr:* Span/ Typing/Bi-Ling Teacher West Las Vegas Schls 1968-; *ai:* Cultural Dance Club Spon; NEA 1970-; Comprendio De Cuentos De BrujeRia En El Norte De Nuevo Mexico; *home:* 713 Coronado Dr Las Vegas NM 87701

TORRES, RAQUEL LILLY DURAN, Second Grade Teacher; *b:* Penasco, NM; *m:* Leonard N.; *c:* Frank; *ed:* (BS) Elem Ed, Univ of Albuquerque 1970; *cr:* 3rd Grade Teacher Heights Cath 1963-65; 2nd Grade Teacher Holy Rosary 1967-70; Embudo 1971-74; Mark Twain 1974-; *office:* Mark Twain Elem Sch 6316 Constitution Ave N E Albuquerque NM 87110

TORRES, YOLANDA V., 6th Grade Teacher; *b:* San Diego, TX; *c:* Ismael A., Audrey A.; *ed:* (BS) Elem Ed, TX a & I 1979; Sci Cert; *cr:* 3rd Grade Teacher Anna Norman Collins Primary 1979-80; 5th Grade Teacher Archie Parr Elem 1980-82; 1st Grade Teacher Anna Norman Collins Primary 1982-84; 8th Grade Sci Teacher 1984-85; 7th Grade Sci Teacher 1985-89; 6th Grade Teacher 1989- Bernarda Jaime Jr HS; *ai:* Pep Squad Spon; UIL Sci Coach; TCTA Mem 1989-; TSTA Mem 1979-89; *home:* 85 Madison Alice TX 78332

TORREY, VICKI SUSAN, History Teacher/Asst Principal; *b:* Port Huron, MI; *ed:* (BS) Scndry Ed/His, Maranatha 1976; (MS) Educl Admin, Pensacola Chrstn 1983; Working Toward PhD in Counseling; *cr:* His Teacher in Chrstn Acad 1976-81; His Teacher/Asst Prin Cmmty Baptist Chrstn 1981-; *ai:* Vlybl & Sftbl Coach; Citizen Bee Sch Spon; *office:* Cmmty Baptist Chrstn Sch 2340 Gratiot Saginaw MI 48603

TORTORELLO, ANTHONY L., Social Studies Teacher; *b:* Newark, NJ; *m:* Linda Ann; *ed:* (BA) Elem Ed, William Paterson Coll 1973; (MA) Admin/Supervision, Kean Coll 1978; Accounting, Sch Finance; *cr:* Elem Teacher S 17th St Sch 1973-78; Teacher of Gifted & Talented 1978-84, Soc Stud Teacher 1984- University HS; *ai:* Sch Treas; Class Adv; Sch Improvement Team Mem; Newark Museum 1987-; Governor Teachers Grant Prgm; Jaycees Outstanding Young Men of America, Master Teacher Awd 1985; *office:* University HS 55 Clinton Pl Newark NJ 07108

TOTH, LARISSA MUIZNIEKS, English/German Teacher; *b:* Rochester, PA; *m:* Charlie; *c:* Stephanie, Allison, Sarah; *ed:* (BSSED) Ger/Eng, WV Univ 1975; Grad Work Foreign Lang, WV Univ; *cr:* Scndry Ger/Eng Teacher Magnolia HS 1975-79; Adult Lang Teacher WV Northern Comm Coll 1978; Scndry Ger/ Eng Teacher Osterholz Amer HS 1979-83, Bitburg Amer HS 1983-85; Scndry/Mid Level Lang Art Teacher Giessen Mid Sch 1985-; *ai:* Stu Cncl Spon; 8th Grade Adv/Advisee Prgm; Lang Art/Soc Stud Dept, Sch Improvement Plan, Stu Placement Comm; Natl Jr Honor Society Review Bd; Assn of Amer Ger Teachers Mem 1975-79; Kappa Delta Pi Mem 1974-79; NEA Mem 1975-79; Overseas Ed Assn Mem 1979-; Explorer Scouts Adult Leader 1978-79; New Martinsville Emergency Medical Services EMT Aide 1978-79; *office:* Giessen Mid Sch Froebelstrasse 70 Bldg 1717 Giessen APO New York NY 09169

TOTH, MARY ANN A., Second Grade Teacher; *b:* Rapid City, SD; *m:* James Floyd; *c:* Kristen Monet; *ed:* (BA) Elem Ed, Univ of WY 1968; Addl Stud; *cr:* 1st Grade Teacher Shanner Elem 1969-71, Washington Elem 1971-73; 2nd Grade Teacher Shanner Elem 1973-; *ai:* Stu Intervention Comm; Meals on Wheels 1973-; Democrat Delegate to St Convention 1988; Drug Ed Grant; Published Learning Innovations; *home:* Box 373 Holly CO 81047

TOTH, TWILA STONE, English Teacher; *b:* Clarksburg, WV; *m:* Gabriel J.; *c:* Todd, Scott; *cr:* 9th Grade Speech Teacher Wadsworth Jr HS 1961-71; 9th/11th Grade Eng Teacher Wadsworth HS 1972-; *ai:* Dept of Eng Chm; NEA, OEA, NCTE; Teacher of Yr 1989; *office:* Wadsworth HS 625 Broad St Wadsworth OH 44281

TOTHERO, MELISSA LE BEOUF, Physical Science Teacher; *b:* Dallas, TX; *m:* Kenneth Dwight; *ed:* (BA) Psych/Bio, Univ of TX Austin 1984; *cr:* Conversational Eng Teacher Asahigankyo Lang Sch 1984-85; Scndry Tutor America II Syndicate Perth Australia 1985-87; Physics/Phys Sci Teacher Robert E Lee HS 1987-; *ai:* Explorers Post #13 High Adventure Adv; Amer Field Service Spon; AFT, Sci Teachers Assn of TX; Inst of Phys Sci Grant.

TOTTY, THIXE KAY (HENDERSON), Mathematics/Bible Teacher; *b:* Shawnee, OK; *m:* Delbert Ray; *c:* Shannon S., Scott A.; *ed:* OK Sch of Banking & Bus; *cr:* Teller Federal Natl Bank 1969-71; Teacher Liberty Acad 1979-; *ai:* Cheerleading Coach; KOCO-TV OK Best Teachers 1989; *office:* Liberty Acad PO Box 1176 Shawnee OK 74802

TOUCHET, DIANE ROBERTS, Gifted English I & II Teacher; *b:* Denver, CO; *m:* Patrick James; *c:* Andree, Todd; *ed:* (BA) Fr, Eng Ed, 1977; (MA) Gifted Ed, 1987 Univ Southwestern LA; Schlsp to Sorbonne 1981; *cr:* Fr Teacher Cecilia Jr HS 1978-79; Ferncrest Sch 1979-80; Gifted Teacher Pesson Elem 1980-84; Lafayette HS 1984-; *ai:* Quiz Bowl Spon; LEA; APEL; NCTE; Acad Cncl Teachers of Eng; *home:* 203 Laurence Ave Lafayette LA 70503

TOUCHTON, GARY D., Social Studies Teacher; *b:* Philadelphia, PA; *m:* Elaine Stevens; *c:* Michelle, Melissa; *ed:* (BS) Ed/Soc Sci, Shippensburg St Coll 1974; (MS) Ed, West Chester St Coll 1980; *cr:* Soc Stud Teacher Abington Sch Dist 1974-76, Upper Moreland Sch Dist 1976-; *ai:* 8th Grade Girls Sftbl Coach; Stage Mgr for Sch Musical; Key Teacher Soc Stud Dept; King of Prussia Volunteer Fire Company Fire Chief 1974- Fireman of Yr 1986; Merion Township Fire Advisory Bd Secy 1982-; *office:* Upper Moreland Mid Sch Orangemans Rd Hatboro PA 19040

TOUGAS, CAROLINE A., Reading Teacher; *b:* Springfield, MA; *m:* Roger J.; *c:* Kristen, Rebecca, Katherine, Lauren, Jennifer; *ed:* (BA) Eng, St Mary of the Plains Coll 1970; (MED) Rdng, RI Coll 1973; *cr:* Eng Teacher Stafford HS 1970-72; Rdng Teacher Ahern Intermediate Sch 1973-78, Duggan Jr HS 1984-; *ai:* Run At Risk After Sch Prgm 1988-; Newspaper Adv 1988-89; Site Based Management Bd Duggan Jr HS Mem; MA Rdng Assn 1985-; Grad Assistantship Awd RI Coll 1972-73; *office:* Duggan Jr HS 1015 Wilbrham Rd Springfield MA 01109

TOUMBS, MARION MOORE, Science Teacher; *b:* Tampa, FL; *m:* Earnest B.; *c:* Julie, Sandy Cline, Chris; *ed:* (BS) Bio/Chem, 1974, (MS) Broadfield Chem, 1977 E TX St Univ; Courses at E TX Chem, Physics, Bio; Wkshps Chem & Physics; *cr:* Teacher Royse City HS 1974; Grad Asst E TX St Univ 1975; Teacher Farmersville HS 1975-; *ai:* Sci Club; JETS; NSTA; STAT; ATPE; *office:* Farmersville HS Gaddy St Farmersville TX 75031

TOURNEAR, SUSANNAH M., Spanish/English Teacher; *b:* Sparta, IL; *ed:* (BA) Eng/Span, IL Wesleyan Univ 1983; *cr:* Span/Eng Teacher Yorkwood HS 1983-88, Unity HS 1988-; *ai:* Foreign Lang Club Adv; Stu Cncl Adv; Curr Comm; Delta Kappa Gamma Active Mem 1988-; *office:* Unity HS 380 Collins Mendon IL 62351

TOW, GLADYS MAE (DULEY), Kindergarten Teacher; *b:* Corydon, IN; *m:* Ralph; *c:* Mark, Paul; *ed:* (BA) Elem Ed, Olivet Nazarene Univ 1972; (MS) Elem Ed, Purdue Univ 1976; Gesell Institute-Kndgtn Screening Trng 1985; Gesell Institute-Kndgtn Screening Adv Trng 1986; *cr:* Elem Teacher Oak Bank Sch 1948-49; Substitute Teacher Knox Commty Sch 1962-71; 1st Grade Elem 1972-74; 5th Grade Elem Teacher 1974-75; 1st Grade Elem Teacher 1975-79; 2nd Grade Teacher 1979-83; Kndgtn Elem Teacher 1983- Knox Cmmty Sch; *ai:* KCTA Secy & VP 1970; NEA ISTA 1972-; Church of the Naz Secy Church Bd 1962-89 Secy/Treas Sunday Sch 1962-; Chm of Adult Ministries of Church of the Nazarene 1989-90; Sunday Sch Teacher/Youth Jrs Primary; Rensselaer Church of the Nazarene; *home:* R 2 Box 100 Knox IN 46534

TOW, SHELLIE W., 7th/8th Grade Science Teacher; *b:* Winston-Salem, NC; *m:* Larry Gayle; *c:* Joshua S., Loyd C.; *ed:* (BS) Ed/Earth Sci, Guilford Coll 1973; Ag Ed, Wake Forest Univ 1982; *cr:* Teacher Hanes HS 1973-74, Glenn Jr HS 1974-84, Hill Mid Sch 1984-; *ai:* Sci Dept Chm; Senate Bill 2 Comm Vice Chm; Mid Sch Curr Comm; NCAE, NEA, AFT, NSTA 1975-; *office:* Hill Mid Sch 2300 Tryon St Winston-Salem NC 27107

TOWE, LINDA MILLER, Music & Choral Teacher; *b:* Madison, TN; *m:* William Harding; *c:* Christopher M. Henson, Angela R. Henson; *ed:* (BA) Music Ed/Vocal, Belmont Ccll 1962; (MME) Music Ed, Murray St Univ 1967; *cr:* Elem Music Teacher Wintergarden & Forrestdale & Dillard St Elem Schls 1962-63, Reidland & Farley Elem 1964-71; Elem Music Teacher Lakeside Elem 1971-8 Jr/Sr HS Music/Chorus Teacher Hawkins Jr HS & Hendersonville HS 1985-; *ai:* Select Chorus Hawkins Mid Sch & Hendersonville HS; Morning Chorus; Select Soloists for Ballgames; All-St Rehearsals; Honors & Mid St Chorus; Choral Contests; Cmmty Performances by Groups; Mid TN Vocal Assn, Music Ed Natl Conf 1985-; First Baptist Church Choir Solo-Ensemble Coord 1987-; Cmmty Chorus 1984-; ADK Teachers 1985-; *office:* Hawkins Mid Sch Walton Ferry Rd Hendersonville TN 37075

TOWER, ROBERT HOWARD, Physical Ed/Health Teacher; *b:* Glen Ridge, NJ; *m:* Deborah Denker; *c:* Emily, Justin, Liam, Darren; *ed:* (BS) Phys Ed, Univ of Bridgeport 1967; (MA) Sch Admin, Johnson St Coll 1979; Gifted/Talented Degree 1981; *cr:* Const Worker J R Steers Inc 1970-71; 6th Grade Teacher Enosburg Falls Elem Sch 1971-85; Admin Position VT Army Natl Guard 1985-88; Phys Ed/Health Teacher Alburg Elem Sch 1988-; *ai:* Asst Prin; Bsktbl Coach; Comprehensive Health Curr Comm; VT Assn of Health, Phys Ed, Recreation & Dance; NEA, VT Soccer Ofcl Assn; Knights of Columbus, Amer Legion; Town Moderator; *office:* Alburg Elem Sch Alburg VT 05440

TOWLE, DONALD ALAN, Science Teacher; *b:* Beverly, MA; *m:* Charlotte Roberts; *c:* Kimberly, John Wiedenmann, Marc Wiedenmann; *ed:* (BA) Math/Sci, 1963, (MA) Ed, 1969 Salem ST Coll; Meteorology, North Shore Math Sci Collaborative 1988; *cr:* 7th/8th Grade Math/Sci Teacher 1963-64; Sci Teacher 1964-80 Marblehead Jr HS: 8th Grade Sci Teacher Marblehead Mid Sch 1980-; *ai:* Cmptr Weather; Weather Club Elective; Team Leader; Sch Reporting Comm; Report Cards/Reports of Progress Etc; Coord Stu Trips to Wwshington DC; Developed Lead 4 Day Cardigan Mountain Experience 89; Amer Meteorlogical Soc 1986-; Bill Hills Weather Obs 1989-; North Shore Math-Sci Collaborative 1986-; MA Teachers Assn Life Mem; BSA Scoutmaster 1960- Dist Awd of Merit 1988; Asst Scoutmaster Comm Chm #1 Asst; Seaside Firemens Club 1973-; Manchester Club 1976-; Asst Dir of Manchester Summer Playground 32 Yrs at this Summer Job; Marblehead Faculty Forum Elected Mem 1984-89; *office:* Marblehead Mid Sch Village St Marblehead MA 01945

TOWNE, LINDA WINNIE, Jr HS Health Teacher; *b:* Albany, NY; *m:* Kenneth B.; *c:* Kenneth B. II, Michael G.; *ed:* (BS) Health/Phys Ed, W Chester Univ 1978; (MS) Health Ed, Cortland St Univ 1984; *cr:* K-12th Grade Health/Phys Ed Teacher/Health Coord/Var Soccer Coach Lyme Cntrl Sch 1978-86; Jr HS Health Teacher Case Jr HS 1986-; *ai:* Girls Modified Soccer Coach; Sadd Adv; Aids Advisory Comm Mem; Current Aids & Human Sexuality Curr Jr HS Comm Mem; NY St Fed of Prof Health Educators 1984-; World Wildlife Fund, Nature Conservacy 1989-; Drug & Alcohol Cncl of Rochester 1986-; Graduated Cum Laude W Chester Univ; Received Mini-Grant from Jefferson-Lewis Teachers Center for Early Birds Fitness Prgm, Designed to Improve the Cardiovascular Fitness of Elem Sch Children; Turnkey Trainer for St Ed; *office:* Case Jr HS 1237 Washington St Watertown NY 13622

TOWNLEY, STEVEN HENRY, 5th/6th Grade Teacher; *b:* Rush Springs, OK; *m:* Mickie Sue Mason; *c:* Amy, Sara, Jeremy, Scott; *ed:* (BS) Bus Admin, 1977, (BS) Elem Ed, 1982 USAO Chickasha; *cr:* 5th/6th Grade Lang Art Teacher 1982-85, 5th/6th Grade Sci/Math Teacher 1985- Amber-Pocasset Elem; *ai:* Amber-Pocasset Sch Staff Dev Comm Chm; *office:* Amber-Pocasset Sch PO Box 927 Pocasset OK 73079

TOWNS, REX L., Vocal Music Teacher; *b:* Sioux City, IA; *m:* Janelle M. Adkins; *c:* Prudence, Zechary, Noah; *ed:* (BME) Music Ed, Mornignside Coll 1975; (MM) Music/Music Ed, Univ of SD 1983; Orff Cert; *cr:* Elem Music Specialist 1975-77, Mid Sch Vocal Music Teacher 1977-89, HS Choral Dir 1989- Sioux City Schls; *ai:* Musical Production Spon; All Vocal Ensembles; Amer Choral Dirs Assn, ICDA; Holy Family Sch Bd (VP 1987-88, Pres 1988-89, Mem 1987-); Church (Organist 1977-, Cantor 1977-); *office:* North HS 4200 Cheyenne Blvd Sioux City IA 51104

TOWNSEND, ANGELA ALEXANDER, English Teacher; *b:* Bowling Green, KY; *m:* Wendell; *c:* Jacinda, Harvard, Akisha; *ed:* (BA) Eng, Univ of KY 1965; (MA) Eng, W KY Univ 1979; Rdng Specialist, Univ of Louisville & Xavier Univ; *cr:* Teacher Bowling Green HS 1967-70, Lincoln Sch 1970-71, Princeton HS 1971-72, Bowling Green Jr HS 1975-78, Bowling Green Bus Coll 1975-78, Warren Cntrl HS 1979-; *ai:* Miss Bronze Bowling Green/Youth Achievement Prgm & Pageant; Stu United to Excel; Schlsp Prgm; KEA, NEA, WCEA Mem; NAACP 1986-87, Outstanding Youth Awd; DAR 1988-89, Thacker Awd; Amer Legion 1987-88, Outstanding Youth Leader Awd; Highly Motivated Minority Stu Achievement Schlsp Prgm; *office:* Warren Cntrl HS 559 Morgantown Rd Bowling Green KY 42101

TOWNSEND, FRANCES WILDER, US His/Broadcasting Teacher; *b:* Summerville, SC; *m:* Henry Evans III; *c:* Evans, Alicia; *ed:* (BS) Eng/His, Coll of Charleston 1964; Grad Work Clemson Univ, Coll of Charleston, Univ of SC, The Citadel; *cr:* Dept Chairperson/Soc Stud Teacher 1973-88, Teacher 1968- Summerville HS; *ai:* Mock Trial, WAVE-TV, Video Yrbk Spon; Teacher Evaluation Comm; Alpha Delta Kappa; NEA, SC Ed Assn, Summerville Ed Assn Pres 1974-75, 1989-; Dorchester Cty Election Commission Chm 1984-88; *home:* 304 Marion Ave Summerville SC 29483

TOWNSEND, JOYCE C. GORDON, Algebra/Personal Dev Teacher; *b:* Sequoyah Cty, OK; *m:* John G.; *c:* Johnna L. Townsend Flanner; *ed:* (BA) Eng, 1966, (BS) Math, 1966 Northwestern St Univ; *cr:* Teacher Sapulpa Jr HS 1966-70, Foster Jr HS 1970-83, Foster Mid Sch 1983-; *ai:* Teachers Lobbist; Benjamin Benneker Assoc Mem; NHS & Stu Cncl Spon; Tulsa Cncl of Math (Pres Elect, Pres) 1987-, Math Awd 1989, Pres Awd of Excellents Nominee 1990; NC TM Rep 1989-; Democratic (Local, St Delegate 1967-88, Chairperson, Mem 1989-); Carrie Neely Guild (Singer, Mem, 1980-); Church Ed Comm 1980; Writer Mid Sch Guides & Curr Adv Guide; Martin Luther King Non Violence Prgm Delgate; Teacher of Week; Nom St Teacher of Yr; *office:* Foster Mid Sch 12121 E 51st Pl N Tulsa OK 74129

TOWNSEND, KATHLEEN ASHLEY, French Teacher/Dept Chair; *b:* Richmond, VA; *ed:* (BA) Fr/Latin, Winthrop Coll 1967; (MA) Fr, NY Univ 1981; Intensive 2nd Lang Wkshp VA Polytechnic Univ 1987; Fr Summer Wkshp Millersville Univ 1987-88; Dartmouth/Rassias Intensive Lang Method Wkshp Hampton-Sydney Univ 1989; *cr:* Teacher Stonewall Jackson Jr HS 1970-; *ai:* Fr Club Spon; Amer Cncl on Teaching of Foreign Lang Mem, Amer Assn of the Teachers of Fr Mem, Hanover Ed Assn, VA Ed Assn, NEA; Hanover Ctys VA Distinguished Foreign Lang Teacher Awd Nominee 1984, 1989-; Stonewall Jackson Jr HS Teacher of Yr 1988; Flannals Article Collaborator; Conducted Methodoly Wkshps; Statewide Comm to Develop Standards of Learning.

TOWNSEND, MARCIA ELLEN, 6th Grade Co Dept Chairperson; *b:* Princeton, IN; *m:* Paul D.; *c:* David S., Steven C.; *ed:* (BS) Elem Ed, Murray St Univ 1974; (MED) Elem Ed, IN St Univ 84; *cr:* 2nd Grade Teacher South Elem 1974-76; 7th/8th Grade Teacher St Rose 1976-78; 8th Grade Teacher St Edwards 1978-79; 6th Grade Teacher/Co Dept Chairperson Ottercreek Jr HS 1980-; *ai:* Lilly Endowment Comm; Flower Comm Chm; VCTA Jr HS Rep/Secy; Order of Martha Star Point 1990; Eastern Star Mid Sch Assn 1989-; Mentor Teacher St of IN 1986-87; Article in Hoosier Sci Teacher 1983; *home:* 4244 N 19th Terre Haute IN 47805

TOWNSEND, NANCY MAY, Sixth Grade Teacher; *b:* Rochester, NY; *c:* Richard R.; *ed:* (BS) Soc Sci, 1967, (MS) Soc Sci, 1970 Brockport St; Working Toward Masters Degree; *cr:* 6th Grade Teacher Lyndonville Cntrl Sch 1967-; *ai:* Operetta Asst; Sci Mentor; Sci Textbook & Advisory Comm; Action Plan Teams; PTA 1986-; NY St Teachers Assn 1967-; 4-H Asst Leader 1985-; Carlton Ladies Auxiliary Treas 1979-; Energy Mini Grant Prgm 1986-8 7; BOCES Mini Grant Awd 1988-89; *office:* Lyndonville Cntrl Sch Main St Lyndonville NY 14098

TOWNSEND, PAUL KEITH, Lang Arts Acad Gifted Teacher; *b:* Raleigh, NC; *m:* Karen Feimster; *c:* Jill, Allyson; *ed:* (BS) Poly Sci, Western Carolina 1973; (MA) Hist UNC-Greensboro 1976; *cr:* Dir Extended Day Sch 1977-81; Hist Teacher South Iredell HS 1981-83; Lang Arts Ag Teacher West Rowan Mid Sch 1983-; *ai:* Bsktbl Coach 7th Grade Boys; Bsbl Coach 7th-8th Grade; NC Assn Mem 1987-; Gifted & Talented; Teacher of Yr West Rowan Mid Sch 1987; Rowan Cty Academically Gifted Teacher of Yr 1989.

TOWNSON, PATSY J., Spanish Teacher; *b:* Albertville, AL; *m:* Randy Earl; *c:* Heather Mc Kay; Hillary; *ed:* (BS) Lang Arts, Jacksonville St Univ 1982; *cr:* Chapter I Teacher Sylvania Sch 1984-86; Eng/Span Teacher Ider HS 1986-88; Span Plainview/Sylvania Sch 1988-; *ai:* AL Ed Assn 1984-; De Kalb Cty Ed Assn 1984-; NEA 1984-.

TOWRY, LINDA WILLIAMS, First Grade Teacher; *b:* Lebanon, TN; *m:* Wade; *c:* Amy; *ed:* (BA) Elem Ed, TN Tech 1970; (MS) Elem Ed, A&M Univ 1976; *cr:* 1st Grade Teacher New Sharon Jr HS 1970-79, Hazel Green HS 1980-; *ai:* Kndgtn/1st Grade Rdng Rep; *office:* Hazel Green HS Po Box 699 Hazel Green AL 35750

TOY, KAILIM, History Teacher; *b:* Los Angeles, CA; *m:* Laurie Chatham; *c:* Leslie; *ed:* (BA) His, Princeton Univ 1976; His, Ca St Univ Los Angeles; Ec, Univ of Los Angeles; *cr:* His Teacher Madison Jr HS 1978-80, Van Nuys Jr HS 1980-81, King Jr HS 1981-83, Eagle Rock HS 1983-; *ai:* Chinese Club Spon 1986-89; Dungeons & Dragon Club Spon 1981-83; Advanced Placement Amer & European His Teacher 1985-; Los Angeles United Teachers Chapter Chm 1989-; *office:* Eagle Rock HS 1750 Yosemite Dr Los Angeles CA 90041

TOZZIE, JAMES J., Social Studies Teacher; *b:* Los Angeles, CA; *c:* Ryan; *ed:* (BA) His, 1970, CA St Fullerton Univ 1970; (BA Psych, 1973; (MA) His, 1977 CA St Fullerton Univ 1970; *cr:* Soc Stud Teacher Katella HS 1971-81, Western HS 1981-; *ai:* Co-Spon Var Club 1975-; Adv NHS; Decathalon Coach for Academic Team; Academic Decathalon Coach for Kiwanis Bowl Team; Asst Var Bsktbl & Head Jr Var Bsktbl Coach; NEA 1971-; CA Teachers Assn 1971-; Orange Cty Mental Health Asst 1975-; Amer Civil Liberties Union 1970-; Alumni Assn CA St Fullerton 1971-; Amnesty Intnl and Greenpeace Mem; Phi Alpha Theta 1970-; *office:* Western H S 501 S Western Ave Anaheim CA 92804

TRACHSEL, MARGARET COPPING, Vice Principal; *b:* Seattle, WA; *m:* Edward C.; *c:* Edward T., Kevin L., Marlee E. Alexander, Michael; *ed:* (BS) Speech Arts, 1966, (MAT) Lang Art, 1973 Lewis & Clark Coll; Prin/Supt Admin Cert Univ of OR Eugene 1977-89; *cr:* Drama Teacher/Dir Parkrose Sr HS 1967-69, W Linn HS 1970-72; Drama Teacher/Dir/Dept Chairperson Sandy Union HS 1975-78; Prin Scio HS 1978-82; Vice Prin Yamhill-Carlton Union HS 1983-89; *ai:* Volunteer Theatre Dir Yamhill-Carlton; All Act Support Person; COSA, OASSA, NASSP (Chairperson COSA Membership Comm, HS/Coll Relations Comm) 1978-; OR Theatre Arts Assn (Pres, VP, Secy) 1967-77; Scndry Sch Theatre Assn of Amer Region 9 Dir 1969-75; *office:* Yamhill Carlton Union H S 275 N Maple Yamhill OR 97148

TRACY, CHARLES LEE, Math Teacher; *b:* Olney, IL; *m:* Sally I. Stimpson; *c:* Christopher; *ed:* (BSED) Math, Eastern IL Univ 1972; *cr:* Math Teacher Bradley Elem 1972-; *ai:* Bsktbl & Track Coach; NEA, IEA 1972-; PTA 1972-; *office:* Bradley Central Jr H S 235 N Michigan Bradley IL 60915

TRACY, CHRISTINA GOEKLER, Science/Computer Teacher; *b:* Clark Cty, IL; *m:* Darrell Maurice; *c:* Lawrence M., Melissa A., Melanie D., Megan M., Mynda L.; *ed:* (BSED) Math, E IL Univ 1964; Cmptr Sci; *cr:* Math Teacher Arcola HS 1964-65; Math/Physics/Chem/Cmptr Sci Teacher Rossville Alvin HS 1966-; *ai:* Stu Cncl, Yrbk, Sci Fair Spon; Scholastic Bowl Coach; Vermilion Cty Conservation Bd Pres 1980-89; Sigma XI IL Outstanding Sci Teacher 1990; *office:* Rossville Alvin HS N Chicago St Rossville IL 60963

TRACY, JANET WOODYARD, Health Teacher/Dept Head; *b:* Houston, TX; *m:* Henry Clay Jr.; *c:* Henry C. III, Elizabeth C.; *ed:* (BS) Phys Ed/Health, TX A&M Univ 1976; (MS) Counseling, Sam Houston St 1989; Admin, Stephen F Austin Univ; *cr:* Health Teacher Kingwood Mid Sch 1977-81, Creekwood Mid Sch 1981-; *ai:* Stu Taking a Responsible Stand Spon; Teacher/Stu Mentor Bright Lights Prgm; GSA Troop Leader 1988-; Kingwood United Meth Church (Choir, Childrens Aide) 1989-; Volunteer Certificate of Appreciation Amer Red Cross; *office:* Creekwood Mid Sch 3600 Lake Houston Pkwy Kingwood TX 77339

TRADER, RICHARD EUGENE, Office Administration Coord; *b:* Parkersburg, WV; *m:* Marilyn Ann Calloway; *c:* Mike E., Kay L.; *ed:* (BBA) Accounting, 1970 (MBA) Accounting 1976 W TX St Univ; *cr:* Accountant; Teacher Amarillo AISD; *ai:* Office Admin Club; Jr & Sr Proms; Area St & Natl Youth Leadership Conferences; 25 Yr Awd & 10 Yr Awd; *home:* 3611 Eddy St Amarillo TX 79109

TRAFICANTE, MICHAEL FRANCIS, Reading Teacher; *b:* Altoona, PA; *m:* Constance Thompson; *c:* Brandon, Megan; *ed:* (BS) Elem Ed, Clarion Univ 1972; Advanced Coursework, Penn St

Univ; *cr:* Teacher Roosevelt Jr HS 1972-; *home:* 5720 Maryland Ave Altoona PA 16602

TRAHAN, MOTIE GAIL LONGO, English Teacher/Dept Chair; *b:* New Orleans, LA; *m:* Leo Joseph Jr.; *c:* Andrew, Brianna; *ed:* (AA) Phys Ed/Health, Pearl River Jr Coll 1973; (BS) Scndry Ed/Phys Ed/Eng, Univ of S MS 1976; *cr:* Lang Art/5th-8th Grade Phys Ed Teacher/Athletic Dir St Clair Elem Sch 1976-78; Eng/Phys Ed Teacher Magnolia Jr HS 1979-81; Eng/Phys Ed Teacher 1981-, Eng Dept Chm 1985-, Staff Dev Coord 1986- Resurrection Cath Mid/HS; *ai:* NHS & Natl Jr Honor Society Spon 1985-; Discipline Comm 1984-85; Guidance Comm 1989-; Var Vlybl Coach 1979-88; Amer Alliance for Health, Phys Ed, Recreation, Dance 1975-85, 1989-; MS Amer Alliance for Health, Phys Ed, Recreation, Dance 1984-85; NCEA 1981-; NCTE; Amer Red Cross (Water Safety Instr 1971-, Lifeguard Instr 1990); STAR Teacher 1988-89; Annual Dedication 1988-89.

TRAHMS, ALICE SPOONER, Retired Elem 4th Grade Teacher; *b:* Woodville, WI; *m:* Walter; *c:* Scott De Motts, Stanley De Motts, Brian De Motts, Rick De Motts; Ron De Motts; *ed:* (BS) Elem Ed/Lib Sci, River Falls Coll 1972; *cr:* 1st/8th Grade Teacher Apple River Sch 1950-54; 1st Grade Teacher Turtle Lake Sch 1954-55; Leavenworth Sch 1955-60; 4th/5th Grade Teacher Baldwin Woodville Sch 1968-89; *ai:* River Falls Rdng Cncl Building Rep 1987-89; NEA/WEA 1968-89; Woodville Bapt Church Pianist 1968-; *home:* 870 6th Ave Baldwin WI 54002

TRAINA, DIANE CIARLO, English Teacher; *b:* San Francisco, CA; *m:* Roger; *c:* Alyssa; *ed:* (BA) Eng, San Francisco St Univ 1973; (MA) Scndry Ed, Univ of San Francisco 1978; *cr:* Eng Teacher Tracy Joint Union HS 1974-; *ai:* Literary Magazine Co-Ed; NCTE, CA Assn Teachers of Eng; *office:* Tracy Joint Union HS 315 E 11th St Tracy CA 95376

TRAINOR, ELIZABETH GAENSLEN, Middle School Science Teacher; *b:* San Antonio, TX; *m:* J. King; *c:* Trish Kelton, Michael, William, Valerie Skloss; *ed:* (BS) Phys Ed/Bio, SW TX Univ 1957; Environmental/Earth Sci Stud; *cr:* Phys Ed Teacher Leal Mid Sch 1957-58, Garner Mid Sch 1959-60; Sci Teacher Holy Name 1979-; *ai:* Stu Cncl Adv; Natl Sci Fnd Grant; *office:* Holy Name Sch 3814 Nash San Antonio TX 78223

TRAISMAN, ANDREW M., Soc Stud/Lang Art Teacher; *b:* Chicago, IL; *m:* Molly Wilson; *c:* R. Nathaniel Wilson-Traisman; *ed:* (BS) Sociology, N AZ Univ 1978; Teacher Cert Univ of WA 1982; Continuing Techer Cert Univ of WA 1987; *cr:* Teacher Finn Hill Jr HS 1983-; *ai:* Var Bsktbl Coach 1985-; NCSS; *office:* Finn Hill Jr HS 8040 N E 132nd St Kirkland WA 98034

TRAMBLEY, MARLENE KRUG, Science Department Chair; *b:* St Marys, PA; *m:* Gerald Patrick; *c:* Adam, Joel; *ed:* (BS) Chem, Villa Maria Coll 1966; (MS) Phys Chem, IL Inst of Tech 1970; Grad Stud Ed St Cert; *cr:* Sci Instr Cannon Univ 1974-78; Math Adjunct Professor Mercyhurst Coll Career Inst 1982-87; Sci Instr/Math Teacher St Benedicts Acad 1978-88; Chem/Math Instr Villa Maria Acad 1988-; *ai:* Homeroom Adv; PA Jr Acad of Sci Moderator; Forensics Moderator; Sci Club; NSTA, Math Cncl of W PA; St Marys Parochial Sch Bd Pres 1982-; St Marys Parish Liturgy Comm Chairperson 1986-; Mount St Benedict Assoc Mem 1980-; *office:* Villa Maria Acad 2403 W 8th St Erie PA 16505

TRAMMEL, ROBERT WAYNE, Mathematics Department Chair; *b:* Fort Wayne, IN; *m:* Cheryl D. Garringer; *c:* Valerie Priller, Joseph; *ed:* (BS) Math, Purdue Univ 1971; (MS) Math, Notre Dame Univ 1974; *cr:* Math Teacher Northrop HS 1971-; *ai:* Boys Track & Field Head Coach; Cmptr Usage Grant Kent St Univ 1990; *home:* 5012 Desoto Dr Fort Wayne IN 46815

TRANZ, EILEEN MARY NEWTON, Kindergarten Teacher; *b:* Jersey City, NJ; *m:* James A.; *c:* James, Douglas, Jennifer; *ed:* (BA) Kndgtn/Primary, Jersey City St Coll 1965; Jersey City St Coll Grad Sch; Gesell Inst Trng; *cr:* Kndgtn Teacher Cresskill Sch System 1965-67, Lanoka Harbor Sch 1971-; *ai:* Building Coord of Parent/Child Kndgtn Orientation; Chairperson of Schlsp Comm; Mem Kndgtn-Transitional 1st Comm; Prof Day Planning Comm & Curr Comm; NJ Ed Assn, NEA, Lacey Township Ed Assn, Assn of Kndgtn Educators 1971-; PTA 1971-; Lacey Lib Assn 1975-; *office:* Lanoka Harbor Sch PO Box 186 Manchester Ave Lanoka Harbor NJ 08734

TRAPALIS, SYLVIA, World His/Church His Teacher; *b:* Charleston, SC; *ed:* (BA) His/Ed, Univ of AL Huntsville 1977; (MA) His, The Citadel 1983; *cr:* Divine Redeemer Cath Sch 1979-81; 9th Grade World His/11th Grade Church His Teacher Bishop England HS 1981-; *ai:* Bishop England Newspaper, Debate Club, Stu Government Adv; Bishop England Advisory Cncl 1985-89; *office:* Bishop England HS 203 Calhoun St Charleston SC 29401

TRAUN, CARLA JEAN, English Teacher; *b:* Durand, WI; *ed:* (BA) Eng Ed, 1984, (MS) Eng Ed, 1990 Univ of WI Eau Claire; *cr:* Teacher St Croix Cntrl HS 1984-85, Burnsville HS 1985-86, Altoona HS 1986-; *ai:* Burnsville HS Newspaper Adv 1985-86; Altoona HS Drama Dir 1986-88; Altoona HS Forensics Coach 1986-; NCTE 1984-89; WI Cncl Teachers of Eng 1984-; Article Published; Altoona Forensics Teams in Top 5 Percent of Schls St of WI; *office:* Altoona HS 711 7th St W Altoona WI 54720

TRAUTMAN, DIANE DOREEN, Language Art Teacher; *b:* Hampton, IA; *ed:* (BA) Eng, Univ of IA 1984; *cr:* 7th-12th Grade Eng Teacher Kanawha Cmmty Sch 1985-89; 7th/8th Grade Lang Art Teacher W Hancock Jr HS 1989-; *ai:* Newspaper, Drama; NCTE 1985-.

TRAUTMAN, NED R., Music Teacher; *b:* Lebanon, PA; *m:* Lareen N. Zito; *c:* Christopher A., Darren R.; *ed:* (BS) Music Ed, Penn St Univ 1969; (MED) Music Ed, Edinboro Univ of PA 1973; *cr:* Music Teacher Cameron Cty HS 1969-71, James S Wilson Mid Sch 1971-; *ai:* MENC, PMEA, NEA, PA St Ed Assn, Oma Sinfonia; Penn St Club of Erie Cty VP 1988-; Zem Zem Shrine Temple Brass Band Dir 1986-88; *office:* James S Wilson Mid Sch 900 W 54th St Erie PA 16509

TRAUTNER, BRENDA KAY, Second Grade Teacher; *b:* Greeley, CO; *m:* Michael V.; *c:* Nicolas; *ed:* (BA) Elem Ed, 1980, (MA) Elem Ed, 1984 Univ of N CO; *cr:* 4th Grade Teacher 1981-88, 2nd Grade Teacher 1988- Scott Elem; *ai:* Alpha Delta Kappa Treas 1986-; *office:* Scott Elem Sch 13th St 30th Ave Greeley CO 80631

TRAUTVETTER, LESLIE C., 8th Grade Math & Sci Teacher; *b:* Keokuk, IA; *m:* Darla J.; *c:* Shane, Todd, Jeff, Sheri, Brock, Cory; *ed:* (BS) Physics/Math, W IL Univ 1962; (MS) Admin, N IL Univ 1971; Admin, N IL Univ; *cr:* Math/Physics Teacher Orion HS 1962-68; Math/Sci Teacher Huntley Mid ScH 1968-; *ai:* Huntley Mid Sch Building Coord 1987-89; 8th Grade Ftbl & 7th-8th Grade Wrestling Coach; DCTA Welfare Comm 1982-83, 1990; Malta Public Lib VP 1985-; Malta Little League Coach 1990; De Kalb Summer Sftbl Coach 1969-72; *home:* 506 S 5th Malta IL 60150

TRAVERSO, TERESA BOLLELLA, High School English Teacher; *b:* Detroit, MI; *c:* Nicolina; *ed:* (BS) Eng, Wayne St Univ 1974; Remedial Rdng; Counseling Oakland Univ; *cr:* Teacher Hazel Park Sch Dist 1974-77, Hamtramck Sch 1985-; *ai:* Jr/Sr Class Spon; Key Club Adv; Sch Improvement Comm; Pres of Staff Dev Policy Bd; Stu Cncl Adv; SADD Adv; Mem Project Click & Editor for Cncl Newsletter; Staff Dev Pres 1989-; Teacher of 1989; Nom By Stu & Staff Teacher of Yr from Hamtramck HS; *office:* Hamtramck H S 11410 Charest Hamtramck MI 48212

TRAVIS, BILLIE ANN, 7th/8th Grade Math Teacher; *b:* Georgetown, KY; *m:* John Carroll; *c:* Christopher, Logan; *ed:* (BA) Elem Ed, Morehead St Univ 1980; (MS) Elem Ed, Georgetown Coll 1987; (Rank I) Elem Ed, 1989; *cr:* 6th Grade Teacher Great Crossings Elem Sch 1980-81; 6th/7th Grade Teacher Scott Cty Mid Sch 1981-82; 7th/8th Grade Teacher Georgetown Mid Sch 1982-; *ai:* Scott Cty Comm for Educl Excellence; Writing Across the Curr; *office:* Georgetown Mid Sch Clay Ave Georgetown KY 40324

TRAVIS, CLAUDIA J., Mathematics Teacher; *b:* Millville, NJ; *ed:* (AA) Liberal Art/Math/Sci, Cumberland Cty Coll 1971; (BA) Math/Scndry Ed, Glassboro St 1973; (MED) Ed, Rutgers 1989; *cr:* 7th Grade Math Teacher Pleasantville Jr HS 1973-74, W Deptford Mid Sch 1974-75; 8th Grade Math Teacher Willingboro Memorial Jr HS 1975-78; Alg I/Geometry/Alg II Teacher Tasis England Thorpe Surrey UK 1978-81; 8th Grade Math Teacher Pinelands Regional HS 1981-82; Algebra II/Cmptrs/Elem Algebra Teacher A P Schaliek 1983-; *ai:* Asst Cross Cntry Coach; Academic League Co-Adv; Good Ideas Teaching Pre-Calculus Rutgers Participant; NCMT; ABWA Treas 1987, Woman of Yr 1988; *office:* A P Schalick HS RD 1 Box 509A Elmer NJ 08318

TRAVIS, DENNIS, Teacher/Science Coordinator; *b:* Plymouth, MI; *ed:* (BS) Bio, Adrian Coll 1961; (MS) Bio, 1962, (EDD) Sci Ed/Curr, 1988 Univ of MI; *cr:* Teacher East Hills Jr HS 1962-68, Lahser HS 1968-; Dept Head 1983-87, Dist Sci Coord 1980- Lahser HS; *ai:* Environmental Concerns Club Adv; MI Assn of Bio Teachers Pres 1986-88; NABT 1980-; NSTA 1983-; Bloomfield Hills Schls Dist Teacher of Yr 1988; Presidential Awd for Excl in Sci Teaching 1986; Outstanding HS Sci Teacher 1986; MI Outstanding Bio Teacher 1984; *home:* 3325 Franklin Rd Bloomfield Hlls MI 48013

TRAVIS, ELLEN M., Language Arts Teacher; *b:* Portsmouth, OH; *c:* Tori Porginski, Blake, Tracy, Devon; *ed:* (BS) Ed, OH Univ 1978; OH Univ, OH St; *cr:* 2nd Grade Teacher Mc Dermott Elem 1965-67; 5th Grade Teacher 1975-76, 3rd Grade Teacher 1976-81, 6th-8th GradeLang Teacher 1981- Union Elem; *ai:* Lang Art & Curr Dev, Writing Project, CBE Leadership Comm Scido Cty; OH Ed Assn, NEA 1975-; NW Local Ed Assn Secy 1984-; OH Teacher Leader Network 1987-88; Union Booster Club (Pres 1982-83, Secy, Treas, Mem 1975-; *home:* Rt 1 Box 71-A Mc Dermott OH 45652

TRAVIS, JANE ANDERSON, English/Language Arts Teacher; *b:* Dallas, TX; *m:* Edwin Jay; *c:* Melissa Wright, Jessica; *ed:* (BA) Anthropology, 1971, Cert Eng Lang Art, 1975 Univ of TX; TX Hill Cntry Writing Project; *cr:* Eng/Speech/Journalism Teacher Bastrop Ind Sch Dist 1975-80; Eng I/II Teacher Clear Creek Ind Sch Dist 1980-84; Eng I/Drama Teacher Elgin Ind Sch Dist 1984-85; Eng IV/III/Journalism Teacher Bastrop Ind Sch Dist 1985-; *ai:* Bastrop Fed of Teachers Secy 1985-; TX Joint Cncl of Eng Teachers 1986-; Walk Against Hunger Dir 1989; Bus & Prof Women Nike Club Spon; Article Published; *office:* Bastrop Ind Sch Dist 1614 Chambers St Bastrop TX 78602

TRAVIS, MARCIA HELAINE, History-Social Studies Teacher; *b:* Sandwich, IL; *ed:* (BA) His, Aurora Univ 1960; Roosevelt Univ Ed; *cr:* Teacher Leland Schls Unit Dist 1 1960-; *ai:* Sr Class Spon; LEA Schlsp 1960-; IEA 1960-; NEA 1960-; *office:* Leland Schls Unit Dist #1 370 N Main St Leland IL 60531

TRAVIS, MELISSA JANE, Mathematics/Chemistry Teacher; *b:* Middletown, OH; *m:* Harvey Anderson; *c:* Amanda, Megan; *ed:* (BS) Botany, Miami Univ 1981; Middletown Regional Hospital Sch Medical Laboratory Technicians, Attended 1983-84; Received Certificate & Qualified to take ASCP Registry MLT Cert; *cr:* Laboratory Stu/Asst Middletown Hospital 1983-84; Medical Laboratory Technician Conover Clinic 1984-85, Southview Hospital 1985-86; *ai:* American Society of Clinical Pathologists 1984-; Math/Chem Teacher Oneida Baptist Inst 1986-; *office:* Oneida Baptist Inst Box 67 Oneida KY 40972

TRAVIS, PATRICIA ANN (AVINGTON), English Teacher; *b:* Houston, TX; *m:* Edwin Lee; *c:* Eyan T., Keenan G.; *ed:* (BA) Eng/Span, Prairie View A&M Univ 1967; (MA) Eng, TX S Univ 1985; Mid-Management Admin Cert 1989; *cr:* Eng Teacher Fidelity Manor Jr/Sr HS 1967-70; Eng Teacher/Dept Chairperson 1972-87, Eng Teacher 1987- Galena Park HS; *ai:* Hum Society, Univ Interscholastic League, Literary Criticism, Ready Writing, Stu Coping with Stus Spon; Mentor & Supervising Teacher; NCTE 1967-87; NEA, TX St Teachers Assn Exec Secy 1967-; Galena Park Ind Sch Dist Prof Growth Comm 1987-; Miss Lucies Acad Outstanding Parent 1976; Fidelity Manor Alumni Assn; Lambda Iota Tau Literary Honor Society; John Hoke Honor Society Teacher of Yr 1981-82; Galena Park HS Teacher of Yr 1988-; *office:* Galena Park HS 1000 Keene St Galena Park TX 77547

TRAVIS, WANDA LEE MUNTZING, Third Grade Teacher; *b:* Maysville, WV; *c:* Loren; *ed:* (BA) Lang Art/Soc Stud, Shepherd Coll 1964; (MA) Elem Ed, WV Univ 1972; *cr:* 4th Grade Teacher New Creek Sch 1964-68; 2nd-6th Grade Teacher Maysville Elem Sch 1969-; *ai:* WVEA, GCEA.

TRAWEEK, KATHRYN SHAVER, English Teacher; *b:* Monroe, LA; *ed:* (MED) Scndry Eng Ed, NE LA Univ 1973; Grad Work Admin/Supervision, Univ of MS 1976; *cr:* Eng/Rdng/Speech Teacher Logtown Jr HS 1970-73; Eng Teacher Itawamba Jr Coll 1973-74, Nettleton HS 1974-75, Logtown Jr HS 1975-80; Eng/Lang Art/Speech Teacher West Monroe Jr HS 1980-; *ai:* Spon West Monroe Jr HS Drill Team; LA Assn of Educators, NEA, NCTE; Assn of St Teachers of Yr; Jr League of Monroe; Outstanding Young Educator LA 1980; LA Teacher of Yr 1986; Educator of Distinction US 1987; *home:* 811 Good Shepherd Ln Monroe LA 71201

TRAWICK, FLORENCE HALL, Retired; *b:* St Andrews, FL; *M:* Harry L. Sr.; *c:* Julia Braddy, Marcia Tanner, Dorothy Mauriello, Harry I. Jr., Evelyn Hopkins; *cr:* K-5th Grade Teacher/Acad Dir ABC Kndgtn 1967-88; *home:* 1609 Cassidy Rd Thomasville GA 31792

TRAXLER, DAVID EDWARD, Physics Teacher; *b:* Mansfield, OH; *m:* Brenda Louise Bohl; *c:* David Jr., Paul R.; *ed:* (BS) Ind Management, Univ of Cincinnati 1977; (MA) Scndry Ed, Xavier Univ 1989; *cr:* Insurance Claims Adjuster Safeco & Allstate & Republic Franklin 1978-84; Physicis Teacher Moeller HS 1985-; *ai:* Boys Var Tennis Coach; Faculty Band Asst; Sci Club, Physics, Sci Olympics Teams Adv; AAPT, NSTA 1985-; S OH Section Treas 1990; Marianist Ed Consortium Grant to Attend Space Camp 1988; Participated in Tools for Discovery Wkshp; Published Lesson Plans; Developed Sci Discovery Camp from Tools for Discovery Wkshp; *office:* Moeller HS 9001 Montgomery Rd Cincinnati OH 45242

TRAXLER, MARY THERESE, First Grade Teacher; *b:* Le Center, MN; *ed:* (BS) Elem Ed, Mankato St Univ 1963; Mankato St Univ; St Thomas Coll; *cr:* Teacher Deephaven elem 1963-87, Groveland Elem 1987-; *ai:* Parent Teacher Group; Soc Stud Comm; Anchor Awd 1989; *office:* Minnetonka-Groveland Elem Sch 3325 Groveland School Rd Wayzata MN 55391

TRAXSON, TIMOTHY LEE, 8th Grade Science Teacher; *b:* Wichita, KS; *m:* Vikki Diane Barnett; *ed:* (AA) Phys Ed, Coffeyville Comm Coll 1981; (BAED) Phys Ed, Emporia St Univ 1983; (MS) Scndry Admin, Pittsburg St Univ 1990; *cr:* Teacher Coffeyville Mid Sch 1984-; *ai:* 8th Grade Girls Bsktbl & F K HS Var Bsbl Coach; Table Tennis & Archery Clubs Spon; NFICA 1988-89; *office:* Roosevelt Mid Sch 1000 W 8th St Coffeyville KS 67337

TRAYNHAM, CARROLL, Fourth Grade Teacher; *b:* Anderson, SC; *ed:* (BS) Elem Ed, Lander Coll 1969; (MA) Elem Ed, Clemson Univ 1977; *cr:* Teacher A Dorothy Haines Sch 1969-70, Hickory Tavern Elem 1970-; *ai:* NEA, NCTM; Teacher of Yr 1990; *office:* Hickory Tavern Elem Sch Rt 1 Gray Court SC 29645

TRAYNOR, BARRY, Science Department Chairperson; *b:* Brooklyn, NY; *m:* Jane Ellen Zimmerman; *c:* Jessica, Andrew; *ed:* (BA) Elem Ed/Soc Stud, 1970, (MS) Admin/Supv, 1975 Natl Coll of Ed; *cr:* Teacher Indian Grove Sch 1970-72, Carl Sandburg Jr HS 1972-79; Dept Chm Sci Deerfield Beach Mid Sch 1980-; *ai:* Girls Varsity Bsktbl Coach; Sch Publicist; BTU; AOS Secy 1978-80; BCAA VP 1989; *office:* Deerfield Beach Mid Sch 701 SE 6th Ave Deerfield Beach FL 33441

TRBOVICH, HELEN, Third Grade Teacher; *b:* Lorain, OH; *ed:* (BS) Elem Ed, Kent St Univ 1969; Assertive Discipline Trng; Creative Writing; Cmptr Uses in Classroom; Cooperative Ed; Rdng-Using Lit-Basal Readers; Elem Ed, Bowling Green St Univ 1978; *cr:* 3rd-6th Grade Teacher Maplewood Elem 1969-78; 3rd Grade Teacher Franklin Elem 1979-; *ai:* Elyria Ed Assn, OH Ed Assn, NEOTA Mem 1969-; Ruby Ashburn Rdng Cncl Mem 1969-78; Tutoring Adult Rdng Illiteracy Prgm; *office:* Franklin Elem Sch 446 W 11th St Elyria OH 44035

TREADWAY, GEORGE EDWARD, Math Teacher/Dept Chair; *b:* Paragould, AR; *m:* Melba Jean Stepp; *c:* Sheila, Tonya; *ed:* (BA) Math, Harding Coll 1960; (MSE) Math, Univ of AR Fayetteville 1966; *cr:* Teacher Carlisle HS 1960-; *ai:* Jr Class Spon; Policies Comm Carlisle Schls; AR Ed Assn, NEA 1960-; AR Cncl Teachers of Math Pres 1970-; Carlisle Ed Assn (Bd of Dir, Salary Comm); *home:* 1110 E 5th St Carlisle AR 72024

TREANOR, MARILYN J. (PARKER), High School Math Teacher; *b:* Findlay, OH; *c:* Tanya, Scott; *ed:* (BS) Math, OH Univ 1972; (MS) Educl Admin, National Univ 1986; *cr:* Math Teacher San Felipe HS 1969-70, Lehman HS 1972-74; Group Home Admin 1975-76; Math Teacher Chaparral HS 1978-83, Basic HS 1984-; *ai:* Mu Alpha Theta Adv; AP Calculus Teacher; CCTA Mem 1978-; GSA Troop Leader 1982; Recreation Dept (T-Ball, Soccer, Floor Hockey, Sftbl Coach 1979-84); St Andrews Church Youth Group Leader 1985; *office:* Basic H S 400 Palo Verde Dr Henderson NV 89015

TREANOR, RONALD JAMES, Curriculum Resource Teacher; *b:* New York, NY; *m:* Donna Devoto; *c:* Noelle; *ed:* (BA) Elem Ed, Jersey City St Coll 1971; (MA) Learning Disabilities, Fairleigh Dickenson Univ 1979; Peer Leadership, Cmptr Ed, Gifted & Talented Ed, Philosophy for Children; *cr:* 5th Grade Teacher 1969-70, 6th-8th Grade Math/Sci Teacher 1970-71 St Josephs Grammail; Math/Lang/Soc Stud Teacher Hudson Sch 1972-79; Math/Cmptrs/Soc Stud Teacher Jefferson Magnet Sch 1979-89; Curr Resource Teacher 1990; *ai:* Rogate, Symposium for Arts, Forensic Team Adv; Bsktbl Team Coach; NEA, NJEA, HCEA, UCEA 1972-; PTA Faculty Adv 1972-, Outstanding Teacher 1989; NAI; Natl Talent Network Golden Apple Awd 1986; Critical Issue Environmental Selectee 1986; NJ Teacher of Yr Nom 1986-89; Appointed Dist Enrichment Consultant; Appointed Grant Writer for Federal Assistance for Magnet Schls; *office:* Jefferson Magnet Sch 545 35th St Union City NJ 07087

TREAT, THOMAS PAUL, Fourth Grade Teacher; *b:* Dansville, NY; *c:* Ryan, Thomas, Jon; *ed:* (AA) Bus Admin, Corning Comm Coll 1975; (BA) Bi-ling/Bicultural Elem Ed, Univ of N CO 1978; (MA) Elem Ed, Adams St Coll 1989; *cr:* 4th Grade Teacher Red Sandstone Elem 1979-; *ai:* 3rd/4th Grade Co-Ed Bsktbl Coach; 4th Grade Team Leader; NEA 1979-89; USMC 1968-70; VFW 1984-; Eagle Cty Sch Dist Fellowship Awd; *home:* 2000 Chamonix Ln #2 Vail CO 81657

TREECE, JUNE EVANS, Retired; *b:* Goin, TN; *m:* Eugene; *c:* Darrell R., Donnie A., Gary W., Deborah Treece Chumley; *ed:* (BS) Ed, Lincoln Memorial Univ 1966; (MS) Ed, Union Coll 1975; *cr:* Teacher Claiborne Cty Bd of Ed 1945; Prin Highland View Elem 1964-65; Teacher Fergerson Elem, Clairfield Elem, Ellen Meyers Elem, & Powell Valley Elem 1966-86; *ai:* Clairborne Cty Ed Assn Secy 1982; East TN Ed Assn, TN Ed Assn, NEA 1945-86; Delta Kappa Gamma 1983; Claiborne Cty Nursing Home & Hospital Bd of Dirs Mem 1971-86 Appreciation Dinner & Plaque 1986; TN Hospital Assn Mem 1986; Eastern Star Shawanee 436 Mem; *home:* Rt 1 Box 261 Cumberland Gap TN 37724

TREECE, PAMELA KAY, 6th Grade Science Teacher; *b:* Ft Worth, TX; *ed:* (BA) Ed/Zoology, Univ of OK 1978; *cr:* Geological Technician Robinowitz Oil Co 1981-82; 6th/7th/8th Grade Sci Teacher Clinton Mid Sch 1983-; *ai:* Tulsa Classroom Teachers Assn 1983-; OK Ed Assn 1983-; NSTA 1983-85; Jr League of Tulsa 1985-; Summer Institute Biotechnolog Y of Tulsa; *office:* Clinton Mid Sch 2224 W 41 St Tulsa OK 74107

TREGO, MICHAEL ROBERT, Instrumental Music Teacher; *b:* Reading, PA; *m:* Rebecca Gilson; *ed:* (BM) Music Ed, Susquehanna Univ 1981; Vandercook Coll of Music, West Chester Univ, Hartt Sch of Music, Cntrl CT Univ; *cr:* Instrumental Music Teacher/Band Dir Tuscarora Jr HS 1981-; *ai:* Jazz Band Dir; PSEA, NEA 1981-; Intnl Trpt Quild 1979-; *office:* Tuscarora Jr HS Rd 2 PO Box 99 Mifflintown PA 17059

TREIBEL, KAREN ZLOTKOWSKI, Reading Teacher/ Consultant; *b:* Fort Benning, GA; *m:* Wayne A.; *c:* Adam A., Ashley A.; *ed:* (BA) Scndry Ed-Engl 1975; (MA) Scndry Ed-Rdng, 1979 Univ of NM; *cr:* Teacher Albuquerque Public Schs 1975-;Teacher Alburquerque Tech Voc Inst 1977-;Rdng Teacher/ Consultant Albuquerque Pub Sch 1990; *ai:* Sch Improvement Team; TASA; Adopt-A-Sch Prgm; Intnl Rdng Assn/Bernalillo By-Laws Chairperson 1985-87; Cty Cncl Exec Bd Literacy Awds Chairperson 1988-89.

TREIBER, ALICE POWERS, Third Grade Teacher; *b:* Huntington, WV; *m:* Robert G.; *c:* Linda Ferrill, Mona Keeley, Daniel, Laura Kochan, David; *ed:* (BA) Elem Ed, Univ of AZ 1947; *cr:* 2nd Grade Teacher Davidson 1947-49; 1st Grade Teacher Whittier 1949-50; 2nd Grade Teacher 1969-78, Vice Prin 1972-77, 3rd Grade Teacher 1978- S S Peter & Paul; *ai:* Primary Dept Head.

TREIBLE, GRACE ALMOND, Retired Teacher; *b:* Millburn, NJ; *m:* William B.; *c:* Bryan, Kirk; *ed:* (BA) Elem Ed, Paterson St 1963; (MED) Rdng, Lehigh Univ 1967; *cr:* Teacher Plainfield Elem Sch 1937-39, Branchville Elem Sch 1945-76; Adjunct Professor Paterson St 1969; *ai:* Teacher in Charge 1965-76; Title I Coord 1973-76; NJ Ed Assn, NEA (Nominating Comm 1970-77, Exec Comm 1960-63, Instruction & Prof Dev 1972-77); Delta Kappa Gamma Prgm Chairperson 1965-69; Alumni Cncl Sch of Ed Charter Mem Lehigh Univ 1980-82; Intnl Rdng Assn; Kappa Delta Pi; NJ Rdng Teachers; NJ Scndry Rdng Teachers; NJ Schoolwomen; NW NJ Rdng Teachers; Sussex Cty Educl Assn; Sussex Cty Mental Health Bd Chairperson of Bd Mgrs 1965; Convention of Intnl Rdng Assn Respondent 1970; NJ Assn Convention for Demonstration of Rdng Chairperson 1970; Educl Testing Service Natl Teacher Examination Consultant 1970; Natl Cncl for Accreditation of Teacher Ed Evaluating Team Mem; US Office of Ed on Cooperative Accountability Speaker Consultant 1975.

TREIBS, GLEN R., Texas History Teacher; *b:* Fredericksburg, TX; *m:* Peggy Logan; *c:* Jeffrey; *ed:* (BS) SW TX Univ 1967; (MED) Sam Houston St Univ 1975; Grad Work Univ of TX, N TX St Univ, SW TX St Univ; *cr:* Teacher Fredericksburg Ind Sch Dist 1967-; *ai:* Jr Historians Chapter 21 Spon; TX St Teachers Assn Pres 1977, Cert of Appreciation 1974; PTA Pres 1985, (St Life Mem 1984, Natl Life Mem 1989); District PTA VP 1986-; Gillespie Cty Historical Society Pres 1985, Awd of Merit 1984; TX St Historical Commission Gillespie Cty Chm 1989-, Citatian for Distinguished Service 1976; Fredericksburg Heritage Fed, Recognition of Distinguished Service 1985; Certificate for Outstanding Cmmty Achievement of Vietnam Era Vetrans 1979; TX St House of Rep Teacher Career; Outstanding Young Man of Fredericksburg 1980-81; *office:* Fredericksburg Mid Sch 202 W Travis Fredericksburg TX 78624

TRELFA, EUGENIA HENDERSON, Sixth Grade Teacher; *b:* San Francisco, CA; *m:* Timothy Jan; *c:* Natasha A., Danielle M.; *ed:* (BA) Eng, Univ of CA 1967; (MA) Developmental Rdng, Univ N CO 1975; *cr:* 4th/6th Grade Teacher Agnew Elem 1969-72; 5th Grade Teacher Northeast Elem 1972-79; 6th Grade Teacher Willow Creek Elem 1979-; *ai:* Dist AAA Supplemental Pay, Lang Art, Gifted & Talented, 6th Grade Moving to Mid Schls Liason Comms; NEA, NCTE, Intnl Rdng Assn; Artist to Teach 6th Grade Shakespeare Grant; *home:* 10577 Pinewood Dr Parker CO 80134

TRELINSKI, PATRICIA OLSON, Learning Disability Teacher; *b:* Hammond, IN; *c:* Michael; *ed:* (BS) Elem Ed, IN Univ Gary & Bloomington 1969; Cmptr Programming, Spec Ed; *cr:* 3rd/4th Grade/Spec Ed Teacher Wagoner Sch 1970-79; COBOL Programmer J & L Steel Corp 1979-81; 6th/7th Grade Math Teacher Rickover Jr HS 1983-87; Learning Disabilities Resource Teacher Wagoner Sch 1987-; *ai:* Stu Cncl Adv; Math Objectives, Cmptr Curr Comm Mem; Write & Organize Math Contest; NEA; IL Ed Assn; Sauk Village Ed Assn Treas 1975-79, 1987-; PTA 1969-79, 1983-; *office:* Cmmty Consolidated Schls 1831 215th St Sauk Village IL 60411

TREMBLE, JOYCE ADAMS, English Department Head; *b:* Lodge Pole, NE; *m:* Neal; *c:* Michael, Kim Mc Lain, Diane Tremble-Ball, Steve, Scott; *ed:* (BA) Music/Eng, 1947, (MSE) Curr/Instruction, 1976 Drake Univ; *cr:* Teacher Madrid IA 1948, MD 1965; Teacher/Admin Southeast Polk HS 1966-; *ai:* NHS Spon; Phi Delta Kappa 1980-; *office:* Southeast Polk HS 8325 NE University Ave Runnells IA 50237

TREME, LYNNE MITCHELL, Math Teacher; *b:* De Quincy, LA; *m:* Timothy; *c:* Seth; *ed:* (BA) Elem Ed, Mc Neese St Univ 1983; *cr:* 1st Grade Teacher De Quincy Elem Sch 1981; 8th Grade Teacher De Quincy Mid Sch 1984-; *ai:* Natl Jr Society Spon; Past Chrldr Spon; Math Dept Contact Person; Cmptr Comm; Calcasieu Assn of Ed; LA Assn of Ed; NEA; De Quincy Fed Svc Leag (VP 1986-88 Pres 1988-); Sunday Sch Teacher 1983-; De Quincy Mid Sch Teacher of Yr 1989-; *office:* De Quincy Mid Sch 502 Grand Ave De Quincy LA 70633

TREML, MILLIE YURCHIK, 7th Grade Reading Teacher; *b:* Portage, PA; *m:* Raymond F.; *c:* Russell, Allen, Heidi; *ed:* (BS) Elem Ed, St Francis Coll 1962; PA St Univ; In Service Credits Various Insts; *cr:* 1st Grade Teacher Portage Area Schls 1962-63, Bellefonte Area Schls 1963; 3rd-4th Grade Teacher Chief Logan Sch 1964-67; Title I Rdng Teacher Jeannette City Sch 1970-72; 6th-8th Grade Eng Teacher Ridgway Area Mid Sch 1978-79; 7th-8th Grade Rdng Teacher James Buchanan Mid Sch 1981-; *ai:* Newspaper Adv 1981-85; Class Adv 1981-84; Tuscarora Ed Assn Pres 1987-88; James Buchanan Athletic Boosters Secy 1981-87; *home:* 8775 Orchard Dr Mercersburg PA 17236

TRENDLER, GERALD J., 5th Grade Teacher; *b:* Phila, PA; *m:* Sandra; *c:* Jennifer, Laurie; *ed:* (BS) Bus Admin, LaSalle Univ 1967; *cr:* 5th Grade Teacher BB Comegys Elem Sch 1967-; *ai:* Vlybl Coach; Phila Fed Teachers Bldg Rep 1970-73; Llanerch Hills VP Girl 1985; Sftbl Assn Sftbl 1986; *office:* Benjamin B Comegys Elem Sch 51st & Greenway Ave Philadelphia PA 19143

TRENT, JANE WILSON, English/Journalism Teacher; *b:* Paducah, TX; *m:* Kenneth; *c:* Kerry; *ed:* (BS) Eng, Midwestern Univ 1970; *cr:* Teacher Wichita Falls HS 1970-71, Paducah 1972-; *ai:* Coach Literary Univ Interscholastic League; 1964 Study Club 1972-89; Delphian Study Club 1990.

TRENT, JOYCE TOURANGEAU, Language Art Specialist; *b:* Chicago, IL; *m:* Jim; *c:* Sara, Heidi; *ed:* (BED) Elem Ed, Chicago St Univ 1965; (MA) Rdng Instruction, MI St Univ 1971; San Diego St Univ 1975-76; *cr:* 3rd Grade Teacher Ridgeland Dist 122 1965-69; 3rd/4th Grade Teacher San Diego City Schls 1969-70; 3rd/4th Grade Teacher 1971-73, Rdng/Lang Art Specialist 1973- Chula Vista City Sch Dist; *ai:* PTA Auditor 1985-86, 1990; Honorary Service Awd 1989; *home:* 564 Mariposa St Chula Vista CA 92011

TRENT, KENNETH EUGENE, Mathematics Teacher; *b:* Childress, TX; *m:* Jane Wilson; *c:* Kerry; *ed:* (BBA) Bus, W TX St Univ 1964; *cr:* Math Teacher Paducah Schls 1985-; *ai:* UIL Math Coach; *office:* Goodwin Jr HS Drawer P Paducah TX 79248

TRENT, ROBBIE WEST, Kindergarten Teacher; *b:* Lebanon, TN; *m:* George; *c:* Jason, Nicholas; *ed:* (BS) Home Ed/Nutrition, 1977, (MA) Early Chldhd Ed, 1982 TN Tech Univ; *cr:* Kndgtn Teacher Enon Kndgtn 1977-; *ai:* NEA, TEA; MCEA Secy 1988-89; TN Career Ladder Level III; *home:* R 5 Box 117 Lafayette TN 37083

TRESCOTT, EUGENE HYER, JR., Science Department Teacher; *b:* Pensacola, FL; *ed:* (BS) Bio, Old Dominion Univ 1975; Alternative Cert Prgm SC PET Trng; Prgm for Effective Teaching 1986; Environmental Study Citadel; *cr:* Teacher James HS 1984-87, Citrus HS 1987-; *ai:* CHS Bio Club; Sci Fair Judging Comm; League of Env Educators of FL 1989; Society for Study of Reptiles, Amphibians; Natl Geographic Society 1953-; Nature Conservancy; Friends of Flying Eagle VP 1988-89; Tampa Bay Herpetological Society Ed 1990; Gainesville Herpetological Society 1988-; Cntrl FL Herpetological Society 1988-; Gopher, Tortoise Cncl 1988-, Ed Comm 1990; Excl in Ed Awd; FL St Bio Teacher of Yr Citrus Cty Nom 1989; *office:* Citrus HS 600 W Highland Blvd Inverness FL 32650

TRESNER, ROY WAYNE, English/Lang Art Teacher; *b:* Luling, TX; *m:* Sharon Ann Miculka; *ed:* (AA) His, SW TX Jr Coll 1969; (BS) Ed/His, SW TX St Univ 1971; *cr:* Eng Teacher Waelder Ind Sch Dist 1972-73; His Teacher Van Vleck Ind Sch Dist 1973-75; His Teacher 1976-80, Eng Teacher 1987- Waelder Ind Sch Dist; *ai:* UIL Academic & Class Spon; Bsbl Coach; Discipline Management, At-Risk, Textbook, Sch Improvement, Attendance Comms; Phi Theta Kappa 1969; Taft Inst Two-Party Government Grant; *office:* Waelder Jr-Sr HS PO Box 247 Waelder TX 78959

TRESSEL, REBEKAH BEAN, Retired 1st Grade Teacher; *b:* Marlinton, WV; *m:* Paul Samuel; *c:* Julia C., Paul S. Jr., Virginia R., Jane A.; *ed:* (BS) Early Chldhd/Elem, James Madison Univ 1938; *cr:* 1st Grade Teacher Elem 1938-41, Bethany Luth 1956-81; *ai:* Hospital Auxiliary; Womans Club; *home:* 205 Maple Ave Waynesboro VA 22980

TREVEY, MARILYN S., 8th Grade Eng/Rdng Teacher; *b:* Beaumont, TX; *m:* Robert Edward; *c:* Meghan D., *ed:* (BA) Eng, 1965, (MA) His, 1974 Lamar Univ; Grad Stud Rdng, Ed, Spec Ed; *cr:* 7th Grade Eng/Rdng/Soc Stud Teacher Linwood Jr HS 1965-66; 7th-9th Grade His/Eng Teacher Cntrl Mid Sch 1966-; *ai:* Campus Communication Comm; Ready Writing Coach; Campus Improvement Team; TX St Teachers Assn (Local Pres, Treas, Faculty Rep) 1966-; NEA (Local Pres, Treas, Faculty Rep, Delegate to Natl Convention) 1975-; Phi Delta Kappa 1975-82; Delta Kappa Gamma 1974-82; TX Classroom Teacher Assn 1966-82; Amer Assn of Univ Women (VP, Treas) 1976-; Sierra Club 1974-; Nom TEacher of Yr 1976; *home:* 1008 Mimosa Nederland TX 77627

TREVILLION, JANIS PEPPER, English Teacher; *b:* Delhi, LA; *ed:* (BA) Eng, 1964, (MED) Guidance/Psych, 1979 Northeast Univ; *cr:* Eng Teacher Evergreen Jr HS 1967-71; Bus Teacher Ouachita Jr HS 1974-84, Ouachita HS 1984-; *ai:* NEA; *office:* Ouachita Parish HS 681 Hwy 594 Monroe LA 71203

TREVINO, IRMA, Life Science Teacher; *b:* Brownsville, TX; *ed:* (BS) Bio, Pan Amer Univ 1983; Working on Masters Degree Counseling; *cr:* 7th Grade Life Sci Teacher Faulk Intermediate 1983-; *ai:* Sci Club Spon; Sci UIL Coach; Campus Improvement Team; Dept Chairperson; Prin Advisory Cncl Mem; Rio Grande Valley Sci Assn 1989-; Brownsville Nite Lioness (Tail Twister 1987-88, Treas 1988-89, 2nd VP 1989-); *office:* Faulk Intermediate Sch 2200 Roosevelt St Brownsville TX 78520

TREWATHA, ROBERT ALAN HERSHEL, Mathematics Teacher; *b:* Lake Preston, SD; *m:* Mary Elizabeth Schnell; *c:* Jennifer M., Sarah M., Katherine E.; *ed:* (BS) Math, Dakota St Coll 1982; Grad Work Cmptr Lang; *cr:* Math/Cmptrs Teacher Deubrook HS 1982-; *ai:* Head Ftbl & Asst Vlybl Coach; Jr Class Adv; NEA, SD Ed Assn (Chief Negotiator 1986, 1987, 1990) 1982-86, 1988-; NCTM, SD Cncl Teachers of Math 1982-; St Pauls Cath Church Cncl Mem 1990; Jaycees 1990; *office:* Deubrook HS 204 School St White SD 57276

TREXLER, DEBRA CAIN, English Teacher; *b:* Ft Worth, TX; *m:* John Barry; *c:* Lindsay A.; *ed:* (BS) Eng, Longwood Coll 1979; *cr:* Eng Teacher N B Clements Jr HS 1979-; *ai:* Young Authors Contest; Beta Club; 7th Grade Dinner Theatre Chm; NCTE 1989-; VEA, NEA 1979-.

TREXLER, JUDY H., English Dept Chair; *b:* Winston Salem, NC; *m:* Henry L. Jr.; *c:* Rebecca; *ed:* (BS) Eng, Appalachian St Univ 1973; (MA) Ed, Univ of NC Charlotte 1977; *cr:* 8th Grade Lang Art Teacher Lexington Mid Sch 1973-79; 7th-9th Grade Eng/Lang Art/Academically Gifted/Drama Teacher China Grove Jr HS 1979-; *ai:* Newspaper Spon; Academic Awds Assembly; Eng Dept Chairperson; NEA; NC Assn of Educators Unit Treas 1977-78; NC Assn for Gifted & Talented; Rowan Cty Parents Assn for Gifted Ed; Women of Evangelical Luth Church in America Church Circle Leader 1983-84; Rowan Cty Academically Gifted Teacher of Yr; China Grove Jr HS Teacher of Yr; Rowan-Salisbury Sch System Drama Minigrant; *office:* China Grove Jr HS 1013 N Main St China Grove NC 28023

TRIBBLE, PAULA B., Fourth Grade Teacher; *b:* Paragould, AR; *m:* D. Kerry; *c:* Casey, Christopher; *ed:* (BSE) Elem Ed, AR St Univ 1975; *cr:* Kndgtn Teacher 1975-81, 4th Grade Teacher 1981- Walnut Ridge Elem; *ai:* Beta Sigma Phi 1976-86; *office:* Walnut Ridge Elem Sch 510 E Free Walnut Ridge AR 72476

TRICE, AMY RUTH, Fourth Grade Teacher; *b:* Tuscaloosa, AL; *ed:* (BS) Elem Ed, 1977, (MA) Elem Ed, 1979, (AA) Elem Ed/ Rdng 1981 Univ of AL; *cr:* 3rd-6th Grade Teacher Myrtlewood Elem Sch 1977-; *ai:* NEA, AL Ed Assn; Jr League of Tuscaloosa Mem 1980-; March of Dimes & Amer Heart Assn Volunteer; Nom for Teacher Hall of Fame & Teacher of Yr 1980-; *home:* 556 35th St Tuscaloosa AL 35405

TRIEZENBERG, HENRY J., Science Dept Chairperson; *b:* Kent Cty, MI; *m:* La Verne Carol Pruim; *c:* Daniel J., Cynthia R. Nanninga, Steven J., Lawrence D., Heidi J.; *ed:* (BA) Bio Ed, Calvin Coll 1951; (MS) Bio, Univ of IL 1952; (MS) Chem, Purdue Univ 1963; (PHD) Sci Curr/Instr, Univ of WI 1967; *cr:* Sci Teacher/Dean of Boys Timothy Chrstn HS 1955-64; Visiting Asst Prof Cornell Univ 1969; Visiting Assoc Professor FL St Univ 1970-71; Curr Admin Chrstn Schls Intnl 1967-84; Chem/Physics Teacher Timothy Chrstn HS 1984-; *ai:* P-12 Sci Supvr; NSTA; Natl Assn Research in Sci Teaching; NABT; Amer Scientific Affiliation W MI Pres 1974, 1983; MI Sci Teachers Assn Pres 1974-5; W MI Enviromental Action Cncl Chm 1974-76; Calvin Coll Bd of Trustees 1964-70.

TRIM, DAVID T., English/Journalism Teacher; *b:* Forrest City, AR; *m:* Brenda Callender; *c:* Terry, Clair, Charlie; *ed:* (BA) Eng, Memphis St Univ 1974; Working Towards MA Eng Ed, MS Coll 1991; *cr:* Teacher Bishop Byrne HS 1975-76; Teacher/Drama Coach Forrest City HS 1976-81; Teacher/Bsbl Coach Union Acad 1987-89; Teacher/Journalism Adv Crystal Springs HS 1989-; *ai:* Newspaper Adv; Amer Assn of Supervision & Curr 1989-; ITS 1976-; NCTE 1974-; Quill & Scroll; Optimist Intnl 1988-; Jaycees VP 1976-; Forrest Cty HS Teacher of Month 1978; *office:* Crystal Springs HS 213 Newton Crystal Springs MS 39059

TRIMBLE, BARBARA PUTMAN, 8th Grade Earth Sci Teacher; *b:* Cullman, AL; *m:* Wayne Alan; *c:* Alana, Adi; *ed:* (BS) Elem Ed, Univ of AL 1967; (MA) Elem Ed, AL A&M Univ 1980; *cr:* 2nd Grade Teacher Vinemont Sch 1969-71; 6th-8th Grade Teacher Arab Jr HS 1974-; *ai:* AL Ed Assn, NEA 1969-71, 1974-; Arab Classroom Teachers Assn 1974-; Teacher of Yr 1986-87; Arab Jr HS Annual Dedication 1986-87; Nom for Presidential Awd for Excl in Sci & Math Teaching 1987-88, 1989-; Chairperson of 1st Sci Fair 1986; *office:* Arab Jr HS Old Cullman Rd Arab AL 35016

TRIMBLE, MARY MARIE, Social Studies Teacher; *b:* Fayette, MS; *c:* Barte, Justin Rice; *ed:* (BS) Soc Sci, 1972, (MS) Soc Sci Ed, 1976 Alcorn St Univ; Futher Stud Univ of S MS; *cr:* Teacher Jefferson Cty Schls 1972-; *ai:* Jefferson Cty Jr HS Yrbk & Soc Stud Club Co-Spon; MS Assn of Educators, Natl Teachers Assn Mem 1974-; Mt Pleasant United Meth (Usher Bd Asst Secy 1976-89, Church Sch Secy 1975-); *home:* Rt 1 Box 324-A Fayette MS 39067

TRIMBLE, VICTORIA MONKO, Second Grade Teacher; *b:* Coatesville, PA; *m:* James C. III; *ed:* (BS) West Chester Univ 1971; Grad Stud; *cr:* 2nd Grade Teacher Coatesville Area Schls 1971-; *ai:* Leadership Role in Writing Long Range Plan Coatesville Area Schls; Grade Level Chairperson; Coatesville Area Teachers Organization (Teacher 1971-72, Rep 1986-88); Chester Cty Rdng Assn 1985; Outstanding Service Awd 1987-88; Positive Teaching Awd 1985-86, 1987-88.

TRINER, SUSAN LAURIE, Seventh Grade Teacher; *b:* Canton, OH; *ed:* (BA) Ed, Walsh Coll 1976; *cr:* 4th Grade Teacher 1977-81, 6th Grade Teacher 1981-83, 7th Grade Teacher 1983- St Clement Sch; *ai:* Sci Fair Chm; Cantor; Lib Asst; Cath Schls Week & Right-To-Read Week Comm; NCEA 1977-.

TRINNEER, JUDITH WYATT, 1st Grade Teacher; *b:* Caruthersville, MO; *m:* Michael; *c:* Matthew, Connor, Megan; *ed:* (BA) Early Chldhd Ed, Cntrl WA Univ 1977; *cr:* Parent Ed/ Infant/Toddler Instr 1975-77 Columbia Basin Coll 1975-77; 1st Grade Teacher Kalama Elem 1978-; *ai:* WA Centennial Celebration Comm; Leadership Team; Primary Coord; Art Show Chm; Kalama Ed Assn (Negotiating Team, Building Rep) 1978-; WA Ed Assn, NEA 1978-; Cowlitz Rdng Cncl 1989-; Fellowship of Reconciliation 1985-; Kiltie Parent Booster Club 1986-88; Religion Society Friends 1973-; Curr Materials Contributor; USA Today Newspapers Ed Grant; Kalama Sch Bd Recognition Awd; *office:* Kalama Elem Sch 548 China Garden Rd Kalama WA 98625

TRIOLO, JOSEPH JOHN, Counselor; *b:* Wilkinson, WV; *m:* Katherine Elizabeth Despot; *ed:* (BA) His, Lake Forest Coll 1964; (MA) Ed Supervision/Admin, Roosevelt Univ 1969; Instr Trng Sch Norfolk VA/Great Lakes IL; Phy Sci, Univ of WI; Clin Prac Guid/Coun Ed, Roosevelt Univ; Phys Ed Handicapped, Univ of IL; Organ & Admin of Guid Ser, Roosevelt Univ; Negro Hist, Univ of Chicago; *cr:* Teacher Sch Dist 64 1963-89; Cnslr N Chicago HS Dist 187 1989-; *ai:* Lake Cty Cnslrs Assn 1989-; Notaries Assn of IL 1983-; Fleet Reserve Assn 1969-; Pearl Harbor Survivors 1990; Knights of Columbus 1956-; North Chicago Teachers Assn Pres 1963-; *office:* North Chicago HS 1717 17th St North Chicago IL 60064

TRIPLETT, GWENDOLYN BYRD, World History Teacher; *b:* Mound Bayou, MS; *m:* Arnold Anthony; *ed:* (BS) Sociology/His, MS Valley St Univ 1972; His, Delta St Univ; *cr:* Processing Analysis Amer Lib Assn 1974-77; Teacher Gentry HS 1977-; *ai:* Coord Citizen Bee Academic Competition; *office:* Gentry HS 801 B B King Rd Indianola MS 38751

TRIPLETT, KAREN (WILLIAMSON), 6th Grade Gifted Ed, 6th House; *b:* Tacoma, WA; *m:* Darrell; *c:* Laura; *ed:* (BA) Ed/ Bio, Western WA Univ 1968; 5th Yr Cert Univ Puget Sound 1974; Trng in Outcomes Based Ed & Reality Therapy-Control Theory; *cr:* 5th/6th Grade Teacher Crownhill Elem 1969-84; 6th/7th Grade Rdng/Lang Art Teacher Liberty Mid Sch 1984-85; 6th-8th Grade Gifted/Math Teacher Bremerton Mid Sch 1985-; *ai:* Coord all Bremerton Mid Sch Clubs, Act; Adv for Newspaper; Dist Spelling Bee Coord; Phi Delta Kappa 1985-; Alpha Delta Kappa 1988-; *office:* Bremerton Mid Sch 1300 E 30th Bremerton WA 98310

TRIPLETT, STEVEN MARK, Associate Principal; *b:* Storm Lake, IA; *c:* Tricia, Laura; *ed:* (BA) Phys Ed/Health, Univ of Northern IA 1974; (MS) Ed Admin, Western IL Univ 1989; *cr:* Jr HS Phys Ed Teacher/Athl Dir Central Catholic 1975; K-12th Phys Ed Teacher Fonda Cmmnty Sch 1975-77; 5th-12th Phys Ed North Winneshick Cmmnty Sch 1977-78; Jr HS Phys Ed Teacher 1978-; Assoc Prin 1984- Maquoketa Mid Sch; *ai:* Athletic Dir; Head Sftbll Coach; Freshmen Boys Bsktbll & Freshmen Girls Vlybl; NASSP 1987-; Sch Admn of IA 1987-; IA HS Athletic Dir Assn 1984-; Maquoketa Chamber of Commerce 1989-; Maquoketa Athletic Boosters 1979- Booster of Yr 1988; *office:* Maquoketa Mid Sch 200 E Locust Maquoketa IA 52060

TRIPLETT, SUSAN MARIE, Former Teacher; *b:* Fairbanks, AK; *ed:* (BA) Area of Concentration Carroll Coll 1977; Phys Ed/ Health/Recreation/Elem Ed, N MT Coll 1984; Endorsement Math, Eastern OR St Coll 1987; *cr:* Teacher/Coach Chester Public Schls 1977-79, Utterback Mid Sch 1979-86, Mead Jr HS 1986-87; Teacher E OR St Coll 1987; *ai:* 8th-9th-Jr Var Girls Bsktbl & Vlybl; Coed Track; Intramurals; Drug & Alcohol Facilitator Cnslr; Phys Ed & Health Curr Comms; MT Ed Assn 1977-86; WA Ed Assn 1986-87; *home:* Rt 1 Box 15 Haines OR 97833

TRIPP, ELIZABETH HARRIS, Fourth Grade Teacher; *b:* Portsmouth, VA; *m:* John Terry; *ed:* (AA) Ministerial, Emmanuel Coll 1972; (BS) Elem Ed, Univ of GA 1975; (MS) Elem Ed, Campbell Univ 1990; *cr:* 1st Grade Teacher Washington Wilkes Elem Sch 1975-76; 9th/12th Rdng Lab Plymouth HS 1976-77; K/ 1st Grade Teacher Roper Elem Sch 1976-77; Kndgtn Teacher Corinth Holders Sch 1978-81; 4th Grade Teacher Clayton Elem Sch 1981-; *ai:* Kappa Delta Pi, NEA; *office:* Clayton Elem Sch 105 2nd St Clayton NC 27520

TRIPP, PAUL CLARK, 5th Grade Teacher; *b:* Pilot Knob, MO; *c:* Karan Ashlock, Kenneth, Keith; *ed:* (BS) His, Southwest Baptist Univ 1970; (MTH) Theology, 1975, (DD) Honorary, 1978 Intnl Seminary; Southwest MO St Univ/Drury Coll/Governors St Univ; *cr:* Teacher/Prin Long Lane Elem 1970-74; Minister First Baptist Church 1974-78; Teacher Strassburg Elem Sch 1981-; *ai:* Sch Saftey Patrol; Discipline Comm; Cmptr Comm; Textbook Selection Comm; Natl Prin Assn 1972-74; MO St Prin Assn 1972-74; *home:* 951 Sherwood Lk Dr 4A Schererville IN 46375

TRIPP, RICHELLE THADEN, Vocal Music Teacher; *b:* Omaha, NE; *m:* David; *c:* Joshua; *ed:* (BME) Vocal/Instrumental Music, NE Wesleyan Univ 1980; Continuing Ed Cert, Cntrl Wa Univ 1985; Post Grad Credits, WA, CA, OR Univs; Orff-Schulwerk Method of Music Ed, Seattle Pacific Univ 1987; *cr:* Beginning Band Teacher 1980-83; Vocal Music Teacher 1983- Marysville Mid Sch; *ai:* Faculty Natural Helper; Co Chairperson Dist Music Curr Adoption; Faculty Advisory & Project Link Comm; Assisted Sponsorship of Snohomish King Cty Jr HS Solo & Ensemble Festival; Music Educators Natl Conference 1977-; Amer Choral Dir Assn 1985-; Everett Comm Coll Symphonic Band 1981; Trinity Luth Church Choir Dir 1982-84; Peace Luth Church Contempory Choir 1990; Secy of Northwest WA Amer Choral Dir Assn 1987-; Clinician Amer Choral Dir Winter Wkshp 1989; *office:* Marysville M S 4923 67th NE Marysville WA 98270

TRIPPE, CAROL ELIZABETH, Chapter I Reading Teacher; *b:* Adel, GA; *ed:* Assoc Art Ed, Clayton St Coll 1983; (BA) Mid Grades Ed, W GA Coll 1984; *cr:* 6th Grade Rdng Teacher 1984-86, 5th Grade Teacher 1987-88, 4th Grade Teacher 1988-89, Chapter I Rdng Teacher 1989- E Clayton Elem; *ai:* Intnl Rdng Assn, Kappa Delta Pi.

TRIPPE, VICKY LYNN, English Dept Chair/Teacher; *b:* Pratt, KS; *m:* David; *c:* Andrea Leak, Erica Leak; *ed:* (AA) Pratt Comm Coll 1965; (BS) Eng Ed, Phillips Univ 1967; (MAT) Eng Ed, Univ of Chicago 1970; *cr:* Eng Teacher Hinsdale HS 1969-72, Norwood HS 1975-77; Eng/Journalism Teacher Cabool HS 1977-84, Nixa HS 1984-; Eng Instr Drury Coll 1984-; *ai:* Newspaper & Yrbk Adv; Lang Art Dept Rep 1989-; Ozark Publications Advs Rep 1982-85, 1989-.

TRITT, TERRY LEE, Music/Band/History Teacher; *b:* Harvey, IL; *m:* Jill Ann Schenck; *c:* Corey, Noreen, Sarah; *ed:* (BA) Music Ed, Univ of IL Urbana 1971; *cr:* Classroom Music Teacher Sch Dist 152 1/2 1971-78; Band Dir/Music Teacher General George S Patton Sch Dist 133 1978-; *home:* 157 Emelia Chicago Heights IL 60429

TROISI, BARBARA JACOBSEN, First Grade Teacher; *b:* Great Falls, MT; *m:* Guy V.; *c:* Allyn V.; *ed:* (BS) Elem Ed, MT St Univ 1959; Clinical Supervision Inst for Master Teachers, CA St Univ Fresno; Continuing Ed CA St Univ & Pacific Coll Fresno; *cr:* 3rd Grade Teacher Hawthorne Sch 1959-60; 1st Grade Teacher Waterman Primary 1960-61, Washington Sch & Kingsburg Elem 1961-; *ai:* Supvr Stu Teacher; Delta Kappa Gamma 1970-; CA Media Lib Ed Assn 1988-; PTA Pres 1961-75, Honorary Service Awd 1972; CA Rdng Assn 1985-; Mentor Teacher 1987-88; Presenter CA St CMLEA Conference 1989; Teachers Helping Teachers Fresno Cty Small Sch Inst & CA St Univ Future Teachers Assn; *home:* 2350 24th Ave Kingsburg CA 93631

TROLLER, CHRISTINE LOVELAND, Jr HS Social Studies Teacher; *b:* Rockford, IL; *m:* Ronald D.; *ed:* (BS) His, N IL Univ 1976; *cr:* Jr HS Soc Stud Teacher St Edwards Sch 1976-78, Manchester Sch 1978-; *ai:* Yrbk Adv; IL St Bd of Ed Those Who Excel Awd of Merit 1989-; *home:* 651 Cummings Rd Caledonia IL 61011

TROPELLO, DARIA FENNIMORE, Mathematics Teacher; *b:* Montclair, NJ; *m:* David D.; *ed:* (BA) Math, Newark St Coll 1970; *cr:* Math Teacher Roosevelt Jr HS & Mid Sch 1970-; *ai:* NEA 1970-; Assn Math Teachers of NJ 1970-87; *office:* Roosevelt Mid Sch 36 Gilbert Pl West Orange NJ 07052

TROPP, PERLE RYAVE, 4th Grade Teacher; *b:* Pittsburgh, PA; *m:* Harold; *c:* Eden, Richard; *ed:* (BS) Eng, Carnegie Tech 1957; Elem Ed, Univ of Pittsburgh; *cr:* Teacher Sunnydale Sch 1974-83, Piute Intermediate Sch 1983-87, Monte Vista Sch 1987-; *ai:* Faculty Advisory Comm; Delta Kappa Gamma Recording Secy 1987-; CTA Membership Chairperson 1988-; Optimist Club 1988-; Cedar St Theater Bd Mem 1989-; Antelope Valley Symphony Assn 1st VP 1988-; *home:* 43723 Albeck Ave Lancaster CA 93536

TROSPER, RAY LYNN, Soc Stud/Eng Teacher; *b:* Perryton, TX; *m:* Rita Louise Reed; *c:* Renee, Rachel, Robyn, Reed; *ed:* (BAT) His/Government, Sam Houston St Univ 1971; (MED) Ed Admin, Tarleton St Univ 1987; Martin Luther King Sch of Law; *cr:* Teacher/Coach Blanket Ind Sch Dist 1976-; Mgr Wes-Tex Finance Company 1977-85; Asst Mgr Tandy Corporation-Radio Shack 1985; Teacher Sidney Ind Sch Dist 1985-; *ai:* Academic All-Amer Cncl Chm; Adult 4-H Leader; Sci Fair Judge; UIL Spelling Coach; Assn TX Prof Educators, TX St Teachers Assn, Channelview Teachers Assn; TX Panhandle Oil Producers, Royalty Owners Assn; Sidney PTO Pres; Election Judge; Precinct Chm; Delegate to St Political Party Convention; Governors Cncl on Drugs; *home:* Box 158 Sidney TX 76474

TROTIER, AUDREY PRISCILLA, Gifted Education Teacher; *b:* Madison, WI; *m:* Donald L.; *c:* Brian, Jeffrey, Erin P. Shine; *ed:* (BS) Elem Ed, 1969, (MA) Ed, 1979 OH St Univ; Course Work Ec for Elem Stu, Cmptr Ed, Future Problem Solving, Jr Great Books Trng; *cr:* 3rd Grade Teacher Upper Arlington Schls 1969-73; 4th/5th Grade Teacher Centerville City Schls 1973-76; 5th/6th Grade Teacher 1976-86, K-5th Grade Gifted Ed Teacher 1986- Upper Arlington Schls; *ai:* Phi Delta Kappa, NSTA 1980-; OH Assn for Gifted Children 1987-; NEA, OEA, UAEA 1976-; Franklin Cty Sch Employees Federal Credit Union Dir 1982-; Arthritis Fnd Volunteer 1988-; *office:* Wickliffe Elem Sch 2450 Wickliffe Rd Columbus OH 43221

TROTMAN, BEVERLY BARRETT, Principal; *b:* New London, CT; *m:* Will E.; *c:* Wrenn Trotman Turner; *ed:* (BS) Elem Ed, Atlantic Chrstn Coll 1960; *cr:* 6th/7th Grade Teacher Newland Sch 1955-65; 7th Grade Teacher Cntrl Sch 1965-70; 4th-6th Grade Teacher Pasquotank Elem 1970-86; Prin Albermarle Acad 1986-; *ai:* NCAE (Secy, Treas, VP, Pres) 1955-86; NEA 1955-86; CTA; Order of The Eastern Star (Worthy Matron, Dist Deputy Grand Matron, Grand Officer, Grand Rep); Alpha Delta Kappa; Bus & Prof Women Past Pres, Woman of Yr; United Meth Church Layspeaker; Teacher of Yr; Elizabeth City Womens Club Teacher of Month; Radio Station WGAI Teacher for Day.

TROTTA, CARMEN LEYVA, Physical Education Teacher; *b:* Chicago, IL; *m:* Joseph; *c:* Michael J; *office:* Mannheim Jr H S 2600 Hyde Park Ave Melrose Park IL 60164

TROTTA, LAURA, English Teacher; *b:* Mt Vernon, NY; *m:* James V.; *ed:* (BA) Eng, SUNY Cortland 1971; (MA) Ed, Univ of CT 1979; Teaching Certificate Credits SUNY Cortland 1971-75; *cr:* 9th-12th Grade Eng Teacher Maraton Cntrl Sch 1971-75; 11th Grade Eng Teacher Groton Cntrl Sch 1977-78; 9th-12th Grade Eng Teacher Mt Vernon HS 1979-; *ai:* Faculty Awds Comm; Aronson Writing Contest Judge; *office:* Mt Vernon HS 100 California Rd Mount Vernon NY 10552

TROTTER, JEWEL WALLACE, Fifth Grade Teacher; *b:* Mississippi Cty, AR; *m:* Charles Daniel Sr.; *c:* Charles D. Jr., David W.; *ed:* (BSE) Elem Ed, AR St Univ 1952; Grad Stud Univ of N AL 1963-; *cr:* Teacher Mississippi Cty Elem 1945-52, Avalon Ave Sch 1962-; *ai:* Southern Assn Comm Chm Avalon Mid Sch; Grade Level Leader; Rdng Textbook Comm Sch Chm; NEA, AEA, MSEA 1962-; Alpha Delta Kappa (Pres, Corresponding Secy 1976-78); Highland Park Garden Club Pres 1985-87, 1988-89; Sunday Sch (Pres, Secy, Group Captain); Outstanding Elem Teacher of America 1973; *office:* Avalon Mid Sch 1400 Avalon Ave Muscle Shoals AL 35661

TROTTER, JIMMIE FAYE, Language Arts Teacher; *b:* Middlesboro, KY; *c:* Ryan, Vince; *ed:* (BS) Home Ec Ed, Univ of TN 1968; Elem Cert, Ag Extension Trng; *cr:* Home Ec Teacher Sevier Cty HS 1968-69, 1972-73, Seymour HS 1969-72, Sevierville Mid Sch 1975-77; Lang Art Teacher Pigeon Forge Mid Sch 1984-; *ai:* Yrbk & Newspaper Staffs Adv; NEA, TEA, SCEA; NCTE 1990; Natl Mid Sch Assn 1989-; Delta Kappa Gamma (Secy, 2nd VP) 1986-; Teacher of Yr; Governors Sch of Writing Univ of TN; Attended Natl Mid Sch Conference Toronto Canada; *home:* 310 Lonesome Valley Rd Sevierville TN 37862

TROTTER, ROSEMARY HOLDER, Second Grade Teacher; *b:* Columbus, IN; *m:* Ronald E.; *c:* Bryan, Marla Batt, Barry; *ed:* (BS) Pre-Sch, Purdue Univ 1956; (MS) Elem Ed, IN Univ 1972; IUPUI; *cr:* 2nd Grade Teacher Hope Elem 1970-; *ai:* Asst Prin;

Delta Kappa Gamma Society 1984-; DAR; 4-H Leader 1965-80 15 Rr Awd 1980; Moravian Church (Christian Ed Teacher Committees Ladies Soc VP Sunday Sch Supt Choir); *home:* 10100 E 500 N Columbus IN 47203

TROTTER, SHARON CALVERT, Second Grade Teacher; *b:* Oak Ridge, TN; *m:* Les; *ed:* (BS) Art Ed, 1969, (MS) Remedial Rdng, 1977 Univ of TN; *cr:* 4th Grade Teacher Newport Grammar Sch 1971-73; Remedial Rdng 1976-77, 2nd Grade Teacher 1977- Eaton Elem; *ai:* Young Astronaut Spon; Rdng is Fundamental & Art Contest Chm; Spon Artist of Month; Chm PTO Financial Fundraising Comm; Eaton Teacher of Yr, Loudon Cty Teacher of Yr 1978; Career Ladder Level II 1984; TN Governors Writing Acad 1986; *home:* 10520 Shirland Ct Knoxville TN 37922

TROTTY-SELZER, THELMA, Social Science Dept Teacher; *b:* Fargo, ND; *m:* Jon Neal; *c:* Haniya J.; *ed:* (RN) Clinical Nursing, Waterbury CT Hospital Sch 1953; (BS) Soc Sci, 1956, (MA) Soc Sci/His, 1964 Syracuse Univ; Grad Stud, Syracuse Univ; Viskadalens Folkhogskola, Boras Sweden; *cr:* Teacher Levy Jr HS 1963-68, Wm Nottingham HS 1968-; *ai:* Syracuse City Sch Dist Prof Responsibilities Soc Stud Comm Mem; Native Amer Stus Exhibits & Lit Natl Ed Week Adv; Ed Unit, Non Secure Detention Prgm, Cath Charities Curr Adv 1983; Sci Dept Nichols Road Mid Sch Consultant 1982-84; NY St Teacher Assn; Assn Native Amer Affairs; Juvenile Detention Assn of NY 1990; St Ed Dept NY Video Tape Teaching 1987; NOW Leadership in Feminist Ed 1983; Metropolitan Sch for Arts Bd Mem 1985-88; Juvenile Detention Assn Consultant 1986-87; PTA (Adv to Pres 1986-87, Secy 1985-86); John Hay Whitney Fellowship 1957; Amer Indian Assn Schlsp 1957; Master Teacher Le Moyne Coll 1984-88; Panelist Presenter SUNY Cortland 1986-87; Nom NY St Bd of Regents Examination Comm 1987-88; Participant Contributor St Ed Dept 1987; Guest Lecturer Syracuse Univ 1984-87; Participant Contributor St Ed Dept 1987; Guest Lecturer Syracuse Univ 1984-87; *office:* William Nottingham HS 3100 E Genesee St Syracuse NY 13224

TROUP, VERONICA MURPHY, Advanced Geography Teacher; *b:* Jacksonville, FL; *m:* Robert; *c:* Robvonita L., Ravershawn D.; *ed:* (BS) Soc Stud, Edward Waters Coll 1970; Working Towards Masters Degree Nova Univ; Ed FL A&M Univ, Unif of N FL; *cr:* Teacher Smart Pope Livingston Elem 1972-81, Stanton Coll Prep Sch 1981-; *ai:* Natl Jr Honor Society; Spon of Stantonian Club & 2 Chrstn Children Through Chrstn Childrens Fund Incorporated; Eta Phi Beta 1978; Duval Teachers United Mem 1972; Duval Cncl for Soc Stud Mem 1981; NCSS 1985; ASCD Mem; Cmmty Strike Force Mem 1989; Duval Cty Geography Teacher of Yr 1988; Nom by Peers for Duval Cty Teacher of Yr; Natl Jr HS Club of Yr 1989; *home:* 3029 Lagny Dr Jacksonville FL 32208

TROUSIL, JEANNE ALBERS, Mathematics Teacher; *b:* Green Bay, WI; *m:* Clark E.; *c:* Heather, Jeremy; *ed:* (BS) Math, Univ of WI Green Bay 1976; Cmptr Applications Trng; *cr:* Math Teacher Denmark HS 1979-; *ai:* Academic Math Team Coach; *office:* Denmark HS 450 N Wall PO Box 308 Denmark WI 54208

TROUT, DANNY JOE, Sixth Grade Teacher; *b:* Biloxi, MS; *m:* Leesa Daurice Cato; *c:* Emily; *ed:* (BS) Ed, N TX St Univ 1975; Post Grad Work Center for Ec Ed N TX St Univ; *cr:* Teacher Carrollton F B Ind Sch Dist 1975-; *ai:* Campus Rep Partners for Positie Youth Dev; Ec Ed & Thinking Skills Comms 1990; Software Selection Comm; 6TH Grade Pilots Cmptr Literacy & Word Processing; TX Cmptr Ed Assn, TX Cncl Teachers of Math, N TX Cncl Teachers of Rdng; PTA 1976-; Mem Omicron Delta Epsilon Ec Honor Society; Research at TX Cmptr Ed Assn Spring Conference 1987; Outstanding Young Man of Amer Nom 1984; Research & Teaching Fellowship Dept of Ec N TX St Univ; *office:* Blanton Elem 2525 Scott Mills Carrollton TX 75006

TROUT, LORRAINE M. SMITH, Retired 5th Grade Teacher; *b:* Browerville, MN; *m:* Arthur R.; *c:* Kathryn Pitcher, Joyce Brever, Alan; *ed:* (BS) Elem Ed/Soc Stud, Bemifji St Univ 1970; Rdng Prgms Wkshps; Soc Stud & Sci Seminars Implement Prgms; *cr:* 1st-8th Grade Teacher Rural Schls Dist 20 & 45 1949-52; 5th Grade Teacher 1963-86, Asst Prin 1974-86 Sacred Heart Sch; Subsitute Teacher Various Schls 1986-; *ai:* NCEA 1963-86; *home:* R 1 Box 152 Browerville MN 56438

TROUTMAN, BARBARA JANE (ROTHENBERGER), 2nd Grade Teacher; *b:* Buffalo, NY; *m:* Martin; *ed:* (BA) Early Chldhd Ed, Univ of Buffalo 1965; *cr:* 1st Grade Teacher Lincoln Sch 1965-71; 2nd Grade Teacher Cayuga Heights 1971-; *ai:* Teaching 2nd Graders; Sch & Parents Musical Prgm; NY St United Teachers; Depew Teachers Organization & PTO; *office:* Cayuga Heights Elem Sch 1780 Como Park Blvd Depew NY 14043

TROUTMAN, CAROL E., Fourth Grade Teacher; *b:* Wellersburg, PA; *ed:* (BS) Elem Ed, CA St Univ 1957; (MA) Elem Ed, WV Univ 1966; *cr:* 4th Grade Tacher Hyndman Intermediate Sch 1956-59, Lorain City Schls 1959-60, Bedford Intermediate 1960-66, Chestnut Ridge Elem 1966-68, Meyersdale Elem 1968-; *ai:* NEA, PSEA 1956-; MAEA (Pres, Secy, Membership) 1968-; Delta Kappa Gamma 1975-; Volunteer Work Local Nursing Homes; New Tribes Mission 1989; *home:* RD 4 Box 134C Meyersdale PA 15552

TROUTMAN, ELIZABETH LEE, 7th/8th Grade Lang Art Teacher; *b:* Columbia, KY; *ed:* (AA) Elem Ed, Lindsey Wilson Coll 1971; (BS) Elem Ed, 1973, (MA) Elem Ed, 1974 W KY Univ; *cr:* 8th Grade Teacher 1974-75, 5th Grade Teacher 1975-76 Salem Elem; 7th Grade Math 1976-77, 1st/2nd Grade Teacher 1977-78, 7th-8th Grade Lang Art Teacher 1978-88 Russell Elem; 7th-8th Grade Lang Art Teacher Russell Cty Jr HS 1988-; *ai:* Guidance Comm; Academic Team Coach; KEA, NEA 1974-; Columbia Chrstn Church Pianist 1971-.

TROVICH, DONNA SERGI, 3rd/4th/5th Grade Teacher; *b:* Canton, OH; *m:* William P.; *c:* Matthew; *ed:* (BS) Elem Ed, 1966, (MS) Elem Ed Supervision, 1969 Kent St Univ; *cr:* 3rd/4th Grade Teacher Dueber Elem Sch 1966-77; 3rd-5th Grade Teacher Belle Stone Elem Sch 1978-; *ai:* Child Abuse Prevention & Statewide Proficiency Testing Comms; Canton City Schls New Teacher Mentor; Kappa Delta Pi 1964-; *office:* Belle Stone Elem Sch 2100 Rowland Ave NE Canton OH 44714

TROWBRIDGE, CATHY L., 8th Grade Lang Art Teacher; *b:* New Albany, IN; *ed:* (BS) Elem Ed, Univ of Indianapolis 1978; (MS) Elem Ed, IN Univ Southeast 1984; *cr:* Teacher South Newton Jr-Sr HS 1979-; *ai:* Yrbk Adv; South Newton Jr HS Stu Against Drugs Co-Spon; NEA, ISTA, SNCTA (Mem, Treas, Local Pres) 1979-; SNSAP Advisory Comm Chairperson 1989-; IMPACT Core Team Mem 1988-; *office:* South Newton Jr-Sr HS R 1 Kentland IN 47951

TROY, MELODY MC INTYRE, 5th/6th Grade Teacher; *b:* Rutland, VT; *m:* John P.; *c:* Catherine, Lisbeth; *ed:* (AA) Liberal Art, Adirondack Comm Coll 1973; (BS) Sociology/Ed, SUC Geneseo 1976; (MS) Elem Ed, Elmira Coll 1979; *cr:* Elem Teacher Arkport Cntrl Sch 1976-; *ai:* K-6th Grade Sci Coord; Arkport Faculty Assn Pres 1982-; Delta Kappa Gamma, Kanakadea Rdng Cncl; Campfire Org (Bd Mem, Leader) 1987-; Several Wkshps Presentor; *office:* Arkport Cntrl Sch 35 E Avenue Arkport NY 14807

TROY, THOMAS JAMES, Fourth Grade Teacher; *b:* Coudersport, PA; *m:* Frances Marie Caldwell; *c:* Tara, Tracy, Jennifer; *ed:* (BS) Elem Ed, Bloomsburg Univ 1970; Penn St Univ, Mansfield Univ; *cr:* 4th Grade Teacher Coudersport Elem Sch 1970-; *ai:* Coudersport Area Ed Assn Project Comm Chm; PA St Ed Ass, NEA 1970-; Coudersport Area Ed Assn (Treas 1975-76) 1970-; 4-H Leader 1989-; GSA Camp Cnslr 1987; *office:* Coudersport Elem Sch 802 Vine St Coudersport PA 16915

TROYER, GENEVIEVE LEE YODER, K-6 Elementary Principal; *b:* Comins, MI; *m:* Richard W.; *c:* Lee, Tiffany; *ed:* (BA) Hum/Soc Sci, Saginaw Valley St Univ 1977; (MA) General Classroom Teaching, 1981, (SPED) Educl Leadership, 1985 Cntrl MI Univ; Dyslexia Cert MI Dyslexic Inst 1989; Natl Prin Acad San Diego CA 1989; *cr:* Teacher 1978-81, Prin 1981- Fairview Area Schls; *ai:* Chairperson Fairview Area Schls Sch Improvement Project & Oscoda Cty Human Services Coordinating Cncl; MI Elem & Mid Sch Principals (Region 13 Pres 1989-, Rep Assembly Delegate 1989-), Service Recognition FAS Bd 1989-; Recognized by St of MI & Cheboygan-Otsego-Presque Isle Intermediate Sch Dist for Work with Comprehensive Sch Health Ed 1988; *office:* Fairview Area Schls 1800 Miller Rd Fairview MI 48621

TROZZI, JANET G. (KISKI), Gifted Education Instructors; *b:* Bentleyville, PA; *m:* David B.; *c:* Robert J.; *ed:* (BS) Elem Engl, Speech 1966; (MS) Elem Ed, 1971 Univ of PA; Court Steno Grace Martin Bus Sch 1959; *cr:* 4th Grade Teacher Bentworth Sch Dist 1966-67; Kndgtn Teacher 1967-68; 3rd Grade Teacher 1968-78; Gifted Ed Teacher 1978 Canon-Mc Millan Sch Dist; *ai:* Washington Cty Gifted Consortium; Beta Zeta Chapter 1979-; Delta Kappa Gamma Society Intl Treas 1982-84; *office:* Canon-Mc Millan Schl Dist 230 S Central Ave Canonsburg PA 15317

TRUDNICH, SHERI LYNN, Sixth Grade Teacher; *b:* San Pedro, CA; *m:* Laurence Jack; *c:* Alyssa; *ed:* (BA) Liberal Stud, Long Beach St Univ 1980; *cr:* 5th/6th Grade Teacher Denker Avenue Sch 1982-; *ai:* Lang Arts Comm Chairperson; *office:* Denker Avenue Sch 1620 W 162nd St Gardena CA 90247

TRUELOCK, VICKY CRUPPER, 4th Grade Teacher; *b:* Borger, TX; *m:* Harvey Darrel; *c:* Shane, Nikki; *ed:* (BS) Elem Ed, W TX St Univ 1972; Advanced Academic Trng for Career Ladder; *cr:* 3rd Grade Teacher Carencro Elem 1974-77; 8th Grade Lang Art/His Teacher Wilson Jr HS 1979-80; 4th Grade Teacher Goodwin Elem/Paducah Ind Sch Dist 1981-; *ai:* Number Sense Coach 1989; TX Classroom Teachers Assn 1989-; *home:* Rt 1 Box 104 Paducah TX 79248

TRUELOVE, TONY LEE, Mathematics Teacher; *b:* Canyon, TX; *m:* Bobbie Lou Walker; *c:* Jacob A.; *ed:* (BS) Math/Phys Ed, Angelo St Univ 1984; *cr:* 7th Grade Math Teacher/Coach 1984-85, 7th Grade Math Teacher 1985-86 Coahoma Jr HS; Math Teacher Kermit HS 1986-; *ai:* Fellowship of Chrstn Athletes Spon; Var Ftbl Defensive Coord; Boys & Girls Var Golf Coach; Curr & Crisis Comm; Assn of TX Prof Educators 1984-; *office:* Kermit HS 601 S Poplar Kermit TX 79745

TRUEMPER, MARY ANNE COOKE, Spanish/English Teacher; *b:* Gorman, TX; *m:* James; *c:* Justin, Joshua M.; *ed:* (BA) Span, Pan Amer Univ 1971; Univ of AR Grad Sch; *cr:* Span/Eng Teacher Eureka Springs HS 1972-78; *ai:* UIL Spelling Spon; Insurance Comm; Frosh Class Spon; Assn of TX Prof Educators (Local Secy 1988-89, Local Pres 1989-); *office:* Farmersville HS N Hwy 78 PO Box 472 Farmersville TX 75031

TRUEX, PATTY ANKROM, 6th Grade Teacher; *b:* Circleville, OH; *m:* David M.; *c:* Jada, Mitch, Jill; *ed:* (BA) Ed, 1976, (MS) Early Chldhd Ed, 1980 OH St; *cr:* 6th Grade Teacher Teays Valley Schls 1977-; *ai:* OH Ed Assn Building Rep, NEA 1977-; Trinity Luth Church (Cncl Mem 1983-, Sunday Sch Teacher); Grant for Survival Skill Rdng 1979; Recognized Among Whos Who Among Prof Women.

TRUILLO, JAMES NICHOLAS, Math Teacher; *b:* Johnson City, NY; *m:* Marie Barnaba; *c:* Nicole M, Mary R.; *ed:* (AA) Math, Broome Cmmty Coll 1971; (BA) Math, Albany St Univ 1973; Math St Univ of Binghampton 1981; *cr:* 2nd-8th Grade Math Teacher Red Cloud Indian Sch 1975-76; Math Teacher Elmcrest Childrens Ctr 1976-77; 7th-9th Grade Math Teacher Christian Brothers Acad 1977-78; 7th & 8th Grade Math Teacher Jennie F Snapp Mid Sch 1978-; *ai:* Frosh Ftbl Coach 1979-; Jr HS Wrestling Coach 1978-88; Jr HS Track Coach 1980-; Mathcounts Coach; Cath Youth Organization Moderator 1982-83; BSA Explorer Adv 1989-; Alhambra 1983-; *home:* 2921 Twilight Dr Endwell NY 13760

TRUITT, SUSAN MILLER, First Grade Teacher; *b:* Birmingham, AL; *m:* F. Barry; *ed:* (BS) Elem Ed, Univ of Al Birmingham 1974; (MED) Early Chldhd Ed, 1980, (AA) Early Chldhd Ed, 1986 Auburn Univ; Life Saving, Open Water Scuba Diving Cert; *cr:* 2nd/3rd Grade Combination Teacher Appalachian Sch 1974-75; 4th-6th Grade Lang Arts Teacher New Site Sch 1975-77; 1st Grade Teacher Dadeville Elem 1977-; *ai:* Tallapoosa Cty Ed Assn Pres 1980-81, 1987-88, 1989-.

TRUJILLO, LORENA J. BETANCUR, Fifth Grade Teacher; *b:* Lovington, NM; *m:* Benjamin M.; *c:* Benjamin R., Timothy J.; *ed:* (BS) Elem Ed, 1973, (MA) Elem Ed/Rdng, 1978 E NM Univ; *cr:* 2nd Grade Teacher Clovis Municipal Schls 1974-78; 5th Grade Teacher Artesia Public Schls 1982-; *ai:* Delta Kappa Gamma 1985-86; NEA, AEA Building Rep 1983-84; *home:* 615 Hermosa Dr Roswell NM 88201

TRULL, SHARON ROLLINS, Business Education Teacher; *b:* Monroe, NC; *m:* Marty Wayne; *c:* Marshall W.; *ed:* (BS) Bus Admin, Univ of NC Greensboro 1983; *cr:* Mortgage Loan Officer/ Branch Manager Heritage Federal S&L Assn 1983-87; Bus Ed Teacher Monroe City Schls 1987-; *ai:* Spon FTA & Jr Class; Teacher Recruiter.

TRUMAN, NORRIS WESLEY, Director of Counseling; *b:* Long Beach, CA; *m:* Therese Prizmich; *c:* Kristine A., Sara M.; *ed:* (BA) Health Sci/Driver Ed/Geography, CA St Univ Long Beach 1970; (MA) Counseling, CA St Univ Dominguez Hills 1978; (MA) Sch Admin, Azusa Pacific Univ 1985; *cr:* Driver Ed Teacher San Pedro & Banning HS 1971-78; Dir of Counseling Calipatria HS 1978-81; Head Cnslr Bellflower HS 1981-85; Dir of Counseling Strathmore HS 1985-; *ai:* Sr Class, CA Schlsp Fed, Natural Helpers Adv; Friday Night Live Co-Adv; Cnslr; Tulare/Kings Cty Guidance Assn 1988-; CA Sch Cnslr Assn 1980-; Kappa Delta Phi 1971-; Citizens Schlsp Fnd Charter Mem 1988-; PTA 1986-; Yrbk Dedications from 3 Schls; Top Driver Trng Teacher LA Unified Sch Dist 1975; *home:* 1571 Median Cir Porterville CA 93257

TRUMPER, ROGER K., Guidance Director; *b:* Holyoke, CO; *m:* Jo Ann Weiss; *c:* Kerry, Marcy, Lori; *ed:* (BS) Phys Ed, 1961; (MED) Guidance/Counseling, 1965 CO St Univ; *cr:* Classroom Teacher Sidney Public Sch 1961-65; Guidance Cnslr Geneva Public Sch 1965-; *ai:* 9th Grade Boys Bsktbl Coach; NPCA Dist 6 Pres 1986; ESU Cnsler Chm 1986-, Service Awd 1986; Lions Club Bd Mem 1988-89; United Meth Pres; *office:* Geneva Public Sch 1410 L St Geneva NE 68361

TRUNCELLITO, CAROLYN, First Grade Teacher; *b:* Philadelphia, PA; *m:* John; *ed:* (BED) Elem Ed, Univ of Miami 1964; *cr:* 3rd Grade Teacher Warren Snyder Sch 1964-; 3rd Grade Teacher 1966-83, 1st Grade Teacher 1983- Sherman Sch; *ai:* NJ Governors Outstanding Teacher Awd 1989; *office:* Sherman Sch Grant Ave Roselle Park NJ 07204

TRUTNA, TOM CHARLES, 4th Grade Teacher; *b:* Melrose, MN; *m:* Patricia Jungers; *c:* Nicole, Todd; *ed:* (BS) Elem Ed, 1968, (MS) Elem Ed, 1975 St Cloud St; Grad Stud Elem Admin; *cr:* 3rd Grade Teacher Mt Morris 1966-67; 5th Grade Teacher Long Prairie 1968-70; 6th Grade Teacher 1970-82, 4th Grade Teacher 1982- Sauk Centre; *ai:* Boys & Girls Cross Cntry Head; Boys & Girls Track Asst; SCEA, MEA Negotiations Cncl 1970-; Boys Coaches Assn Rep 1980-; Girls Coach Assn Reg 6 Cross Cntry Rep 1988-, Coach of Yr 1989; Jaycees (Pres, VP, Dir) 1969-80, Silver Key 1976-77; Sauk Centre City Cncl VP 1970-74; Sauk Centre Park Bd Pres 1974-85; *home:* RR 1 Box 1 Sauk Centre MN 56378

TSCHANTZ, DWIGHT ALAN, Prescriptive Math Teacher; *b:* Canton, OH; *m:* Diane R. Battista; *c:* Deidra R., Daniel A.; *ed:* (BS) Elem Ed, Malone Coll 1968; (MS) Master Teacher/Elem Ed, Univ of Akron 1976; Univ of Akron; *cr:* 5th Grade Teacher Belden Sch 1967-68; 8th Grade Math Teacher Clarendon Sch 1968-75; Prescriptive Math Teacher Lathrop Sch 1976-77; Clarendon Sch 1978-; *ai:* Sch Safety Patrol Supv; Sch Intraumural Dir; Sch Store Supervisor; NEA 1970-; OH Ed Assn 1970-; Canton Prof Ed Assn 1970-; Early Ford V-8 Club 1984-; 2nd Place 32 Ford 1988-; Natl Street Rod Assn 1978-; 1st Church of Nazarene Asst Head Usher 1955-; Curr Dev Projects-Chapter I; Chapter I Math Grant ES#89 B6E 1980; *office:* Clarendon Elem Sch 412 Clarendon Ave NW Canton OH 44708

TSCHIDA, SHEILA M. JERIKOVSKY, 8th Grade English Teacher; *b:* Minneapolis, MN; *m:* Roger J.; *ed:* (BS) Eng, St Cloud St Univ 1973; Trained in Outcome Based Ed & Mastery Learning; *cr:* 7th/8th Grade Eng Teacher Melrose Jr HS 1973-80; 7th-9th Grade Eng Teacher Oltman Jr HS 1980-82; 10th-12th Grade Eng Teacher Woodbury Sr HS 1982-84; 8th Grade Eng Teacher Oltman Jr HS 1984-; *ai:* Staff Cncl Mem; Homeroom Adv & Advisee Chairperson; Melrose MFT Secy 1978-80; Outstanding Teacher Awd 1979; Sch Effectiveness Team; *office:* Oltman Jr HS 1020 3rd St Saint Paul Park MN 55071

TSHUDY, DEAN JON, 7th Grade Teacher; *b:* Jersey City, NJ; *m:* Marilou Holland; *ed:* (BS) Elem Ed - Cum Laude, Taylor Univ 1978; Grad Stud Farleigh-Dickinson Univ, Kutztown Univ, Montclair St Coll, E Stroudsburg Univ, Jersey City St Coll; *cr:* 6th Grade Teacher Marion Public Schls 1978-79, Allentown Sch 1979-80; 7th Grade Teacher Liberty Township Sch 1980-; *ai:* Soccer, Boys Bsktbl, Boys Sftbl Coach; Ski Club & Cmptr Club Adv; Cmptr & Sci Curr & Resourse Room Comm; Liberty Township Assn (VP 1983-84, Pres 1984-86, Negotiations 1984-); Warren Cty Ed Assn, NJ Ed Assn; Belvidere United Meth Church (Lay Leader 1988-, Sunday Sch Teacher 1987-); Cty Gate Players Cmmty Theater 1982-; Rutgers Merck Elem Sci Inst 1988; Salzburg Austria Comparative Ed 1985; Featured in Math Teacher 1978; *office:* Liberty Township Sch Box 302 Belvidere NJ 07823

TSIROS, ANASTACIA HANZAS, Kindergarten Teacher; *b:* Asheville, NC; *m:* Nicholas George; *c:* Virginia, George, Thomas; *ed:* (BA) Elem Ed, Mars Hill Coll 1980; Diploma Elem Ed/Greek Lang, St Basils Teachers Trng 1964; Working Towards Masters in Early Chldhd; *cr:* Chapter 1 Teacher 1981-82, 4th/5th Grade Teacher 1982-83, 5th Grade Teacher 1983-84, 1st Grade Teacher 1984-85, 1st/2nd Grade Teacher 1985-86, 1st Grade Teacher 1986-88 Claxton Sch; Kndgtn Teacher Vance Sch 1988-; *ai:* Teach Greek Folk Dancers; Tutor Stus Greek Lang; Report Card & Lang Curr Guide Comm; NCAE 1979-87; Prof Educators of NC 1987-; NAEYC 1989-; Philoptochos Ladies Club 1966-; Family Counseling Bd 1975-76; *office:* Vance Sch 98 Sulphur Springs Rd Asheville NC 28806

TUBB, NANCY WILLIAMS, Mathematics Teacher; *b:* Wichita Falls, TX; *m:* Francis Harvey; *c:* Francesca, Forrest; *ed:* (BS) Math/Bus Ed, E TX St Univ 1973; Working Towards Masters in Math, Univ of Houston Clear Lake; *cr:* Math Teacher Carlsbad Mid-HS 1973-74, Lamarque Intermediate Sch 1974-76, Alvin Jr HS 1976-78, Santa Fe HS 1978-; *ai:* Santa Fe HS Math/Sci/Cmptr Sci Club Spon; Number Sense & Calculator Coach; Santa Fe HS Pride Comm; NCTM, TX Cncl Teachers of Math 1985-; TX St Teachers Assn 1974-; AFT, TX Fed Teachers 1987-; Pizza Inn of America Teacher of Yr 1988-89; *office:* Santa Fe HS PO Box 370 Santa Fe TX 77510

TUBB, PAT BRIDGES, Special Education Supervisor; *b:* Brownfield, TX; *m:* Dick; *ed:* (BS) Ed, W TX St Univ 1967; (MA) Ed, Sul Ross Univ 1981; Spec Ed, Supervision; *cr:* 1st Grade Teacher Hereford Ind Sch Dist 1966-72; Early Chldhd Teacher Levelland Ind Sch Dist 1972-73; 1st Grade Teacher Lubbock Ind Sch Dist 1973-74; 1st Grade Teacher/Spec Ed Supvr Levelland Ind Sch Dist 1974-; *ai:* NEA, TSTA, CTA 1966-82.

TUBBS, KATHERINE YATES, Kindergarten Teacher; *b:* Oak Grove, LA; *m:* Zane; *c:* Mike, Steve; *ed:* (BA) Music, LA Coll 1965; *home:* 1504 Summerlin Ln Bastrop LA 71220

TUBBS, KATHLEEN HUCHRO, Physical Education Teacher; *b:* Plattsburgh, NY; *m:* Bruce; *c:* Meagan; *ed:* (BS) Phys Ed, Springfield Coll 1980; (MS) Elem Ed, SUNY Plattsburgh 1985; *cr:* Phys Ed Teacher Ticonderoga Elem Mid Sch 1980-; *ai:* Girls Var Soccer Coach; JOHPERD 1980-; Ticonderoga Youth Commission 1987-; Champlain Valley Athletic Conference Girls Var Bskbl Coach of Yr 1984; CVAC Girls Var Soccer Coach of Yr 1988; *office:* Ticonderoga Elem-Mid Sch Alexandria Ave Ticonderoga NY 12883

TUCCI, MARIA, English Teacher/Journalism Adv; *b:* Greensburg, PA; *ed:* (BA) Eng/Scndry Ed, Seton Hill Coll 1976; (MA) Eng, Duquesne Univ 1978; *cr:* Teaching Asst Duquesne Univ 1976-78; Eng Teacher Greensburg Cntrl Cath HS 1978-; Composition Instr Seton Hill Coll 1984-; *ai:* Stu Newspaper & Literary Magazine Adv; Greensburg Cath Teachers Assn Mem 1981-; Laurel Valley Writers Assn Mem 1989-; *office:* Greensburg Cntl Cath HS 901 Armory Dr Greensburg PA 15601

TUCHAWENA, EDDIE E., Mathematics Teacher; *b:* Tuba City, AZ; *m:* Arlene M. Spencer; *c:* Shelly, Rik, Keri; *ed:* (BS) Elem Ed, 1974, (MA) Ed, 1980 N AZ Univ; Educl Admin; *cr:* Teacher Tuba City Jr HS 1974-80; Prin Second Mesa Day Sch 1982-83; Teacher Tuba City Jr HS 1983-; *ai:* Boys Var & Jr HS Bsktbl Coach; Tuba City HS Girls Jr Var Sftbl Coach; AZ Assn Teacher of Math 1987-; Moencopi Day Sch PTO Pres 1983-84; US Marine Vietnam 1969-70; Moencopi Day Sch Sch Bd Pres 1978-80; *home:* 14 Warrior Dr Box 515 Tuba City AZ 86045

TUCK, DARRELL ALAN, 7th Grade Soc Stud Teacher; *b:* Loudon, TN; *ed:* (BS) Soc Stud, Univ TN 1980, (MS) Elem Ed, Univ TN 1983; Admin & Supervision; *cr:* 6th Grade Math Teacher 1981-83, 7th Grade Math Teacher 1983-87, 7th Grade Soc Stud Teacher 1987- North Mid Sch; *ai:* Spon Fellowship of Christian Athletes; Coach Boys Bsktbl; NEA 1981-; Lions Club 1982-85; *home:* 102 Coulter St Loudon TN 37774

TUCKER, ALAINE L., Dance Teacher; *b:* San Antonio, TX; *m:* G. W.; *c:* Brannon, Brent, Blake; *ed:* (BS) Health/Phys Ed, Univ of Houston 1980; Dance, Stephen F Austin St Univ 1990; *cr:* Fitness Dir Court House Athletic Club 1984-88; Health/Dance Teacher Longview HS 1988-; *ai:* Court House Athletic Club Aerobics Coord 1983-88, Fitness Dir & Wellness Consultant 1985-; IDEA 1986-, Cert 1986-; Jr League of Longview 1988-; *office:* Longview HS 201 W Tomlinson Pkwy Longview TX 75604

TUCKER, ALLAN LEE, Drafting Teacher; *b:* Edmore, MI; *m:* Kathleen A. Laine; *c:* Tracey, Holly; *ed:* (AA) Tech Drafting, 1966; (BA) Trade-Tech Teaching, 1968 Ferris St Univ; (MA) Vocational Ed, Univ of MI 1974; Officer Candidate Sch-Commission 2nd Lt; Educl Specialist; *cr:* Teacher Mt Pleasant HS/Area Center 1968-; Mid-MI Cmmty Coll 1969-81; Instr US Army 1970-71; Central MI Univ 1989-; *ai:* Drafting Team Coach-6 Yrs; Teachers Union Rep Officer-20 Yrs; Mem Chairperson of Union Comm-8 Yrs; Mt Pleasant Ed Assn (Secy Negotiator 1968- Chief Neg 1973); AVA 1968-Inter Tech Assn 1984-; Vietnam Vet Assn 1988- Designed Viet Memorial Bridge for Mt Pleasant 1989; Amer Legion; Cmptr Aided Drafting Grants; Drafting Updates; Trng Ctr Awds; *office:* Mount Pleasant HS 1155 S Elizabeth Mount Pleasant MI 48858

TUCKER, BONITA FRAZIER, Third Grade Teacher; *b:* Columbus, OH; *m:* Sammie Lee; *c:* Avra, Alena; *ed:* (BS) Early Mid Chldhd Ed, 1972, (MA) Early Mid Chldhd Ed, 1979 OH St Univ; *cr:* 1st Grade Teacher Deshler Elem 1972-79; Rdng Teacher Fair Avenue Sch 1979-81; 3rd Grade Teacher Hudson Elem Sch 1981-; *ai:* Stu Cncl & Safety Patrol Adv; Columbus Ed Assn, OH Ed Assn, NEA 1972-; *office:* Hudson Elem Sch 2323 Lexington Columbus OH 43211

TUCKER, BRAD, Head Bsktbl Coach/Bus Teacher; *b:* Terre Haute, IN; *ed:* (BS) Bus Ed, 1984, (MS) Bus Ed, 1987 IN St; *cr:* Teacher Madison HS 1984-89; Teacher/Coach South Knox HS 1989-; *ai:* Boys Head Bsktbl Coach; Delta Pi Epsilon Bus Ed Honor Society, IBCA, HBCA; *home:* 121 Fox Ridge Dr Vincennes IN 47591

TUCKER, COZY H., Chapter I Reading Teacher; *b:* Pleasant Hill, NC; *m:* James Melvin; *c:* Natalie, Anrenee, Melvin, Chelle; *ed:* (BA) Elem Ed, Winston Salem St Univ 1962; (MA) Elem Ed, VA Commonwealth Univ 1979; Rdng VA St Univ 1986; *cr:* 2nd Grade Teacher R B HS 1962-66; 4th Grade Teacher Hicksford Elem Sch 1970-84; Chapter I Rdng Teacher Belfield Elem Sch 1984-; *ai:* Lang Art Comm; Sch Discipline Comm/Supt Comm on Vocational Ed; GEA VEA NEA Building Rep 1975-89 Merit Awd 1980; Intnl Rdng Assn 1985-; Kappa Delta Pi 1985; 4-H Volunteer Secy 1975- St Awd 1980; NAACP Executive Bd 1980-; Antioch Baptist Church Asst Financial Secy 1984; Grant from SCORE to Complete Rdng Cert; *home:* Rt 1 Box 159 Emporia VA 23847

TUCKER, E. CAROLYN, Language Arts Instructor; *b:* Henderson, KY; *m:* Larry Allen; *c:* Tarrolyn A., Tami A.; *ed:* (BS) Poly Sci/Geography/Eng, 1972, (MA) Ed, 1980 Murray St Univ; EMT; Writing Project; Working Towards Ed Writing, Murray St Univ; *cr:* Owner/Operator Flower Shop Carolyns Corner 1981-82; Instr for Gifted/Talented Webster Cty Bd of Ed 1982-83; Lang Art Instr Dixon Elem Sch 1983-; Eng Instr Madisonville Comm Coll 1987-; *ai:* Acad & Speech Coach; Jr Beta & 8th Grade Spon; Church Music Dir; Sunday Sch Teacher; Purchase Area Writing Project; KY Cncl Teachers Eng, NCTE 1987-; DAR 1990; Hospice 1984-85; KY Colonel 1990; Notary Public 1990; Articles Published Religious Magazines; KY St Assessment Comm; Nom Ashland Teacher Awds; Speaker St KY Cncl Teachers Eng; Whos Who Amer Ed 1990; *home:* R 2 Burnt Mill Rd Dixon KY 42409

TUCKER, FRANCES, Fourth Grade Teacher; *m:* A. J.; *c:* Clifton, Janet Tucker White; *ed:* (BA) Eng/Elem Ed, MS Coll 1950; *cr:* 4th Grade Teacher Meadville Sch 1950-51; 3rd Grade Teacher Crystal Springs 1951-57; 4th Grade Teacher Florence Mid Sch 1958-65, 1970-; *ai:* MAE, NEA; *home:* 135 W Tucker Rd Florence MS 39073

TUCKER, GLYNN, Bio Teacher/Sci Dept Chm; *b:* Dallas, TX; *m:* Connie M.; *c:* Justin R.; *ed:* (BS) Bio, Stephen F Austin Univ 1974; Advanced Placement Trng S Meth Univ; *cr:* Teacher 1976-, Teacher/Dept Chm 1984- Woodrow Wilson HS; *ai:* Soph Class Spon; NHS Comm; AFT 1976-; Masonic Lodge 1979-; PTA St Lifetime Mem 1990; Woodrow Wilson HS Teacher of Yr 1990; *office:* Woodrow Wilson HS 100 S Glasgow Dallas TX 75214

TUCKER, JOHN LARRY, High School Math Teacher; *b:* Blanche, AL; *m:* Phyllis Walker; *c:* John, Benjamin; *ed:* (BS) Math, Berry Coll 1972; *cr:* Teacher La Fayette HS 1972-77, 1980-; *ai:* Star Teacher 1988; *home:* HC 65 Box 219 Cloudland GA 30731

TUCKER, LARRY GENE, Guidance Counselor; *b:* Lewis Cty, KY; *m:* Brenda Willocks; *c:* Scott, Ann M., Michael; *ed:* (BA) Eng/Bible, Milligan Coll 1964; (MA) Ed/Guidance, Morehead St Univ 1970; Leadership Trng; *cr:* Jr HS Bsktbl Coach 1986-88, Teacher/Cnslr 1964- Tollesboro HS; *ai:* Project Destination Graduation Bd; Lions Club Eye Conservation Comm; Lewis Cty Teachers Organization Pres 1970; KY Ed Assn, E KY Guidance Assn; Lions Club (Secy, Treas, Pres) 1967-; Tollesboro Volunteer Dept Secy 1965-; STAR Teacher Awd; Buffalo Trace Area Dev Bd; *office:* Tollesboro HS Box 1 Hwy 575 Tollesboro KY 41189

TUCKER, LINDA GAIL, English Teacher; *b:* Silver Point, TN; *m:* Ralph Bud; *c:* Jimmy, Carol Duke, June Betty; *ed:* (BS) Ed/Eng, 1976, (MA) Rdng Specialist, 1982 TN Tech Univ; *cr:* Teacher Chm of Rdng Cookeville Jr HS 1976-88; Teacher Upperman HS 1988-; *ai:* Pep Club, Sr HS 4-H Club, Sr HS Just Say No Spon; PCEA (Pres 1985-86, Faculty rep 1986-87, VP 1980-81, Secy 1978-79); NEA 1985-86; *office:* Upperman HS Rt 2 Box 1 Baxter TN 38544

TUCKER, MARY HELEN (PRICE), English Teacher; *b:* Monroe, LA; *m:* James; *c:* Tarvis, Terrence, Tony; *ed:* (BA) Eng, NE LA Univ 1972; *cr:* Teacher Neville HS 1975-76, 1989-; *ai:* Frosh Class Head Spon; MCAE, LEA, NEA 1976-; NCTE 1968-; Zeta Phi Beta Secy 1978-80; *office:* Neville HS 600 Forsythe Ave Monroe LA 71202

TUCKER, MCKINLEY R., JR., Teacher/Coach; *b:* Radford, VA; *m:* Wilhelmina L. Lamb; *c:* Ashley E.; *ed:* (BS) Health/Phys Ed, Univ of VA 1977; *cr:* Teacher/Coach Prince Edward Cty HS 1977-80, Mills Godwin HS 1980-81, Moody Mid Sch 1981-; *ai:* Ftbl, Bsktbl, Tennis, Wrestling, Bsbl, Soccer Coach; Tennis Club; Mid Sch Athletic Cncl 1989-; Natl Mid Sch Assn; Henrico Coaches Assn 1987-, Mid Sch Coach of Yr 1988-89; Moody PTA; *office:* George H Moody Mid Sch 7800 Woodmar Rd Richmond VA 23228

TUCKER, SHIRLEY THOMPSON, 7th Grade Teacher; *b:* Newark, NJ; *m:* George H. Jr.; *c:* Nicholas, Thelton; *ed:* (BA) Elem Ed, 1973, (MA) Stu Personnel Services, 1985 Kean Coll of NJ; *cr:* Pre-Sch Teacher Friendly Fuld Neighborhood Centers 1971-72; 6th Grade Teacher Hawthorne Avenue Sch 1973-84; 6th-7th Grade Teacher Dr E Alma Flagg Sch 1984-; *ai:* Stu Cncl Adv, NJEA 1973-; St Luke A M E Church Schlsp Club 1973-; *home:* 72 Leslie St East Orange NJ 07017

TUCSNAK, JOSEPH FRANK, 7th Grade Teacher; *b:* Newark, NJ; *m:* Judy; *c:* Leeanne, Heather; *ed:* (AA) S Baptist Coll 1973; (BA) Ed, Union Univ 1976; Memphis St Univ, Univ of TN Martin; *cr:* Teacher Scotts Hill Jr HS 1982-; *ai:* Decatur Cty Ed Assn 1980-; NEA, TN Ed Assn 1976-; Parsons Public Lib Chm 1985-; Phi Gamma Mu Honorary Soc Stud Society 1976-; *home:* Rt 3 Box 124 Parsons TN 38363

TUDRYN, ELAINE MARY, Fifth-Sixth Grade Teacher; *b:* Hadley, MA; *m:* James P.; *c:* Matthew; *ed:* (BA) Eng/Elem Ed, Our Lady of the Elms 1974; *cr:* 6th Grade Teacher 1975, 1st Grade Teacher 1976, 2nd Grade Teacher 1977, 5th/6th Grade Teacher 1977- Hadley Public Schls; *ai:* MA Teachers Assn 1975-; Hadley Ed Assn Secy 1987-89; NEA; Hadley Mothers Club Secy 1985-87; *office:* Russell Sch Russell St Hadley MA 01035

TUFFORD, RAWLINS DALE, Science Teacher; *b:* Hobart, OK; *m:* Peggy Dark; *c:* Kerry D., Amy L.; *ed:* (BS) Zoology, OK St Univ 1964; (MED) Sci, Cntrl St Univ 1971; Grad Work Sci & His; *cr:* Sci Chm Wellston Public Schls 1968-69; Sci Teacher Oklahoma City Public Schls 1969-; *ai:* Sch Store Mgr; AFT, OK Sci Teachers Assn; *home:* 2824 SW 80th St Oklahoma City OK 73159

TUFFY, JEAN M., HS Physical Ed Teacher; *b:* Lyons, NY; *ed:* (AS) Liberal Art, Auburn Comm Coll 1969; (BS) Phys Ed/Psych, SUNY Brockport 1971; (MS) Phys Ed, Ithaca Coll 1978; CPR & First Aid; *cr:* Phys Ed Teacher South Jefferson Sch Dist 1972, Phelps-Clifton Springs Sch Dist 1972-; *ai:* Tennis, Track, Vlybl, Bsktbl, Field Hockey Coach; Section 5 Ofcls Fee Comm; Girls Bsktbl Coach; Midlakes Athletic Assn Asst Adv Friend Awd, Spec Appreciation Awd; *office:* Phelps-Clifton Springs Sch Rt 488 Clifton Springs NY 14432

TUFTS, FRANK EDWARD, American History Teacher; *b:* Mc Veigh, KY; *m:* Betty Jane Zumwalt; *c:* Tamara L. Boyer, Todd E.; *ed:* (BS) Phys Ed, Anderson Univ 1957; Ball St Univ/Western MI Univ; *cr:* Teacher/Coach Akron Ind HS 1958-61; Sturgis PubliC Schls 1961-; *ai:* NEA 1961-; MI Ed Assn 1961-; Sturgis Ed Assn Pres/VP 1976-78; *home:* 508 Mortimer St Sturgis MI 49091

TUGGLE, MYRA WILLIAMS, Sixth Grade Teacher; *b:* Big Spring, TX; *m:* Rusty W.; *c:* Kate J.; *ed:* (MS) Elem Ed - Cum Laude, Cntrl MO St Univ 1985; *cr:* 6th Grade Teacher Cole Camp Sch 1985-; *ai:* Cmmty Teachers Assn 1985-; MO St Teachers Assn 1986-89; *office:* Cole Camp Sch Rt 2 Cole Camp MO 65325

TULEY, HERSCHIEL D., Science Department Chair; *b:* Austin, TX; *m:* Belen Palos; *c:* Alfred; *ed:* (BS) Scndry Composite Sci, Univ of TX Austin 1979; (MS) Scndry Sci, Corpus Christi St 1989; Electronics, Comm, Servicing, Repair, Del Mar Tech; *cr:* Sci Teacher Shannon Jr HS 1980-88, Kaffie Mid Sch 1988-.

TULIUS, PATRICIA PONASIK, First Grade Teacher; *b:* Milwaukee, WI; *m:* James J.; *c:* Jacob, Joseph, Megan, Sarah; *ed:* (BA) Elem Ed, Univ of WI Whitewater 1971; *cr:* 1st Grade Teacher Mukwonago Area Schls 1971-; *ai:* Waukesha Cty Rdng Cncl 1988-; WI St Rdng Assn 1989-; Mukwonago Jaycees Outstanding Young Educator 1988-89; *office:* Prairie View Sch Hwy E Mukwonago WI 53149

TULLEY, KATHLEEN CROSBIE, English Department Chair; *b:* Tulsa, OK; *m:* James Alford; *c:* Jennifer R., Scott A.; *ed:* (BA) Eng, Butler Univ 1968; Grad Hrs in Eng, Ed, Courses, Drug/Alcohol Trng Suicide Prevention; *cr:* 8th Grade Lang Teacher East Ladue Jr HS 1968-74; Eng/Journalism Teacher Sweet Grass Cty HS 1979-; *ai:* Cheerleading Coach; Sch Newspaper Adv; Class Spon; Eng Dept Chairperson; Organized Sch Care Team; Creative Writing Magazine Past Adv; Ladue Sch Dist 8th Grade Curr Writing Team; MT Assn Teachers of Eng/Lang Art 1978-; Sweet Grass Cty Suicide Test Force 1987-; NEA, MT Ed Assn; Sweet Grass Cty Ed Assn (Pres 1985, Secy 1987); MO St Teachers Assn, St Louis Suburban Teachers Assn; St Louis Metropolitan Area Sch Publication (Spon, VP 1973, Pres 1974); Womans Club 1978-; Drug & Alcohol Task Force 1986-89; MO Journalism Teacher of Yr 1974; MT Ed Commission Outstanding Teacher; Coordinated Big Timber Educl Telecommunications System; MT St Univ Inspirational Teacher Awd; *office:* Sweet Grass Cty HS Box 886 Big Timber MT 59011

TULLOCK, VENDEDA H., Chair Sci Dept/Teacher; *b:* Cintwood, VA; *m:* Robert Lee; *c:* Roberta K. Caldwell, Janet L. Small; *ed:* (BA) Fr/Sci, Maryville Coll 1950; (MS) Curr & Instruction, Univ of TN 1976; *cr:* Teacher Townsend HS 1950-56, Porter HS 1957-79, William Blount 1979-; *ai:* Chairperson Sci

Dept; R A Rep BCEA Our Local Organization; Sci Spon; BETA, FTA Club; NEA, TEA, BCEA & ETEA; Alpha Delta Kappa (Pres, VP, Secy, Treas) 1963-; Pi Lambda Theta 1987-; Teacher of Yr Awd Porter.

TULLOCK, VICKI WATSON, Fifth Grade Teacher; *b:* Detroit, MI; *m:* James Kenneth; *c:* Kari E., Jonathan C.; *ed:* (BS) Elem Ed, Carson-Newman 1974; Grad Work Univ of TN; *cr:* Kndgtn Teacher 1974-79, 4th Grade Teacher 1980-83, Kndgtn Teacher 1984-86, 5th Grade Teacher 1986-89 Manley Elem; *ai:* Just Say No Club & Button-Badge Prgm Spon; Scholastic Bowl Coach; Hall Monitor Prgm; Sch Building Comm; HCEA, TEA, NEA Local Rep 1974-88; Lakeway Rdng Cncl; *office:* Manley Elem Sch 3685 W Andrew Johnson Hwy Morristown TN 37814

TULLY, DEBORAH IMRI, Teacher of Lit/Comm/Quest; *b:* Norwalk, CT; *m:* John G; *c:* David G,Katharine J. *ed:* (BA) Psych/Sociology, Boston Coll 1974; (MS) Early Childhood Ed, Wheelock Coll 1975; Quest Training; Numerous Seminars; *cr:* K-2 Teacher 1975-77, K-1 Teacher 1977-78 Pierce Sch; LD Tutor Boone Station Sch, Enon Elem 1978; 2nd Grade Teacher Enon Elem 1978-79; 7th Grade Lit/Comm Teacher Indian Valley Sch 1979-; *ai:* Lang Arts Curr Dev; Levy Passage Comm; Adv Oration Contest; Advisory Cncl Building Level; Drug Intervention Comm; Cty Writing Competency Comm; Mad River Green Local Ed Assn (VP 1983-85, Pres 1986-); OH Fed of Teachers Exec Comm 1990; *office:* Indian Valley Mid Sch 510 Enon-Xenia Rd Enon OH 45323

TUMBERLINSON, ARLENE R., Fourth Grade Teacher; *b:* Magnolia, AR; *m:* Don; *c:* Le Ann; *ed:* (BS) Elem Ed, North TX Univ 1963; *cr:* 4th/6th Grade Teacher Fort Huachuca AZ 1964-66; 4th Grade Teacher Mae Smythe Elem 1966; *office:* Mae Smythe Elem Sch 2202 Pasadena Blvd Pasadena TX 77502

TUMEY, RITA MARIE, English Teacher; *b:* Jackson, MI; *m:* John H; *c:* Patrick J.; *ed:* Assoc Educl Liberal Art, Jackson Comm Coll 1967; (BA) Liberal Arts/Scndry Ed, MI St Univ 1969; Continuing Ed/Elem Ed, E MI Univ 1972; *cr:* 6th-8th Grade Soc Stud TeacherSt Marys Grade Sch 1970-71; 5th/6th Grade Math/Sci Teacher St Philips Grade Sch 1971-73; 7th/8th Grade Eng Teacher Jackson Cath Mid Sch 1976-; 5th-8th Grade Math/His Teacher St Stanislaus Kostka 1973-75; *ai:* Newspaper Adv 1976-; *office:* Jackson Catholic Mid Sch 915 Cooper St Jackson MI 49202

TUNGATE, VICKY MADDOX, Third Grade Teacher; *b:* Covington, KY; *m:* Harry Edward; *c:* Ashley Nicole, Joshua William; *ed:* (BA) Elem Ed, Univ of KY 1980; (MA) Elem Ed, Northern KY Univ 1984; *cr:* 3rd Grade Teacher Burlington Elem Sch 1980-; *ai:* Youth Leader at Walton First Bapt Church; NEA 1980-; KEA 1980-; BCEA 1980-; *home:* 14082 Walton-Verona Rd Verona KY 41092

TURBIDE, JANET CHAMBERLAIN, Fifth Grade Teacher; *b:* Watertown, NY; *c:* Paul, Blake, Richard L.; *ed:* (BA) Liberal Arts, Potsdam St 1974; Grad Stud Potsdam St, Colgate Univ; *cr:* 1st Grade Teacher 1975-80, 2nd Grade Teacher 1980-88, 4th Grade Teacher 1988-89, 5th Grade Teacher 1989- Lisbon Cntrl; *ai:* Gifted & Talented Prgm; N Cntry Rdng Cncl; Teachers Center Mini Grant Chm 1986-; SLVTC Secy 1987-88; Colgate Univ Inst Cmptrs in Elem Ed N Cntry Winner; *home:* 41 Hillcrest Dr Potsdam NY 13676

TUREK, HENRY JOHN, 6th Grade Teacher/Asst Prin; *b:* Chicago, IL; *m:* Janet Rose Lloyd; *c:* Sarah, Laura, Henry; *ed:* (BA) Psych, MSU 1965; (MED) Admin/Supervision, Loyola 1976; IL Acad; *cr:* 6th Grade Teacher 1965-67, 7th Grade Teacher 1967-69 St John of God; 6th Grade Teacher Lied Sch #122 1969-79; 6th Grade Teacher/Asst Prin Harnew Sch #122 1979-; *ai:* Invention Convention; Patrol Boys & Girls; Lang Art Curr; Catechist; Phi Delta Kappa 1976-; Justice Public Lib Bd Mem 1987-89, Service 1989; St Patricia Sch Bd (Pres, Bd Mem) 1985-89; Elected Justice Public Lib Bd; *office:* Harnew Sch 9100 S Austin Ave Oak Lawn IL 60453

TUREK, PATRICIA BEAL, Elementary Teacher; *b:* Shiner, TX; *m:* Billy; *c:* Tamara, Tiffany, Victoria; *ed:* (BS) Elem Ed, 1973, (MS) Elem Ed, 1980 SW TX St; *cr:* Elem Teacher Corpus Christi Ind Sch Dist 1973-74, Spring Branch Ind Sch Dist 1974-75, Shiner Ind Sch Dist 1976-; *ai:* UIL Number Sense.

TURK, MARIA NORMA (SCHEMBRI), Chemistry & Science Teacher; *b:* Cleveland, OH; *m:* Lawrence A.; *c:* John, Mary J., Susan; *ed:* (BA) Sci Comprehensive/Bio/Chem, Ursuline Coll 1962; (MA) Ed/Admin/Supervision, John Carroll Univ 1969; *cr:* Bio/Chem Teacher John Adams HS 1962-69; Sci/Chem Teacher/Dept Chm Jane Addams HS 1969-71; Chem Teacher Shaw H S 1981-; *ai:* Chem Olympics Coach; Delta Kappa Gamma 1989-; Jennings Scholar Awd 1966-67; *office:* Shaw HS 15320 Euclid Ave East Cleveland OH 44112

TURK, PEGGY ANN (BEAGLE), 1st-4th Grade Teacher; *b:* National City, CA; *m:* Mark; *c:* Matthew; *ed:* (BA) Liberal Art, La Sierra/Loma Linda Univ 1982; *cr:* 1st-4th Grade Teacher Riverview Memorial Sch 1982-86, Forestdale Sch 1986-; *ai:* Yrbk & Class Spon & Adv; *office:* Forestdale 7th Day Adv Sch Perkins Valley Rd West Paris ME 04289

TURK, TONY, English Teacher; *b:* Virginia, MN; *ed:* (AA) Eng, Mesabi Jr Coll 1967; (BS) Eng, Univ of MN Duluth 1969; Eng Ed, Univ of MN Duluth; *cr:* Eng Teacher Benilde HS 1969-70; Eng/Speech Teacher Virginia Scndry Schls 1970-; *ai:* Sr Class & Key Club Adv; MEA Comm 1987-88; VEA Comm 1986-88; *office:* Virginia Scndry Schls 4th St & 5th Ave S Virginia MN 55792

TURKAL, THOMAS GEORGE, Physics Teacher; *b:* Massillon, OH; *ed:* (BS) Bio, Mt Union Coll 1979; (MSE) Educl Admin, Univ Of Akron 1986; Candidate for Doctoral Degree Educl Admin, Univ of Akron; *cr:* Bio/Chem/Earth Sci Teacher Strasburg HS 1979-81; Bio/Physics Teacher Louisville HS 1981-85; Physics Teacher Jackson HS 1985-; *ai:* Ski Club Adv; Gifted & Talented, Stu of Month Selection, Grad Gurvey Stud Comms; NEA, OH Ed Assn 1979-; Sci Ed cncl of OH 1983-; Pi Lambda Theta 1984-; Phi Delta Kappa, ASCD, NSTA 1985-; Moose Lodge 1980-; Special Olympics 1989-; *home:* 3414 Amherst Ave NW Massillon OH 44646

TURKASZ, EDWARD STEPHEN, JR., 7th Grade Biology Teacher; *b:* Buffalo, NY; *m:* Janice Klimtzak; *c:* Jennifer, David; *ed:* (BS) Bio, Niagara Univ 1979; (MS) Bio, Buffalo St 1985; Ftbl, Lacrosse NY St Coaching Cert; Ftbl Ofcls NY St Assn Cert; *cr:* Educator Frontier Summer Sch 1981-; Mgr Erie Cty Fair Grandstand 1981-88; Mgr Stadium Services Incorporated 1989-; Educator Hamburg Cntrl Sch Dist 1980-; *ai:* Lake Shore HS Head Frosh Modified Ftbl Coach; Hamburg HS Asst & Head Modified Ftbl Coach; Hamburg HS Var Lacrosse Head Coach; NY St PTA 1989; Natl Fed of Interscholastic Coaches & Ofcls Assn 1980-; *office:* Hamburg Cntrl Sch Dist 4111 Legion Dr Hamburg NY 14075

TURNAGE, SANDRA ANN, Language Arts Teacher; *b:* Brownsville, TN; *ed:* (BA) Eng/Scndry Ed, Union Univ 1969; (MED) Admin/Supervision, Memphis St Univ 1977; *cr:* Lang Art Teacher Mc Nairy Cntrl HS 1970-78, Alamo 1978-84, Crockett Cty Jr HS 1984-; *ai:* Beta Club Spon 1980-; 1st Baptist Church Pianist 1978-; Teacher of Yr Crockett Cty Jr HS 1987; Excl in Teaching Awd Univ of TN 1987; Career Ladder III 1987-; *office:* Crockett Cty Jr HS Rt 2 Conley Rd Alamo TN 38001

TURNBOW, SHELLY DUNHAM, 6th Grade Soc Stud Teacher; *b:* Muleshoe, TX; *m:* James; *c:* Trevor; *ed:* (BS) Mrktg/Distributive Ed, Angelo St Univ 1984; Phys Ed, Soc Stud Advanced Classes; *cr:* Teacher/Coach Muleshoe Jr HS 1985-; *ai:* Jr HS Girls & Boys Tennis Coach 1985; Jr HS Girls Bsktbl & Track Coach 1985-89; Fellowship of Chrstn Athletes Spon 1985-89; *home:* Box 695 Muleshoe TX 79347

TURNBULL, DIANE LUCAS, English Teacher; *b:* Florence, SC; *m:* Esmond; *ed:* (BA) Ed, Brooklyn Coll 1972; (MA) Eng, City Coll 1976; *cr:* Eng Teacher Jefferson HS 1974-75, Prospect Heights HS 1975-76, Adult Educl Trng Center 1976-77, New Utrecht HS 1977-78, Prospect Heights HS 1978-; *ai:* Human Resources Club Adv, Prospect Heights HS Assoc Dean; NY Transit Police Sch Outreach Adv, United Negro Coll Fund Sch Coord; UFT Prospect Heights HS Delegate 1988-; NY Transit Police Sch Adv Certificate 1989; Lehman Coll Fellowship Writing Project 1978; *home:* 92 Madison St Brooklyn NY 11216

TURNBULL, JOANNE TATE, Pre-School Teacher; *b:* New Orleans, LA; *m:* Sammy L. Sr.; *c:* Melissa, Sammy Jr., Jason; *ed:* (BA) Music Ed Tougaloo Coll 1970; Atlantic Union Coll; *cr:* 1st Grade Teacher Westchester Area Sch 1980-83; Pre-Sch Teacher Hackensack Med Center 1984-85; Coord Nursey Sch Lakeside Day Nursery 1985-87; Pre-Sch Teacher Westchester Area Sch 1987-; *ai:* Choir Dir & Church Pianist; Cnslr Pathfinder Club; Original Composition Pulbished; *home:* 5 Valley Dr Spring Valley NY 10977

TURNBULL, KATHLEEN ANN, Science & Reading Teacher; *b:* Lansing, MI; *ed:* (BED) Fr, Univ of Toledo 1978; MI Model Certified; Stu Assistance Prgm, Drug Abuse Facilitator; *cr:* Teacher St Mary Parish Sch 1978-83, Air Force Acad HS 1983-85, St Mary Parish Sch 1986-; *ai:* 7th & 8th Grade Act Co-Spon; Mardi Gras Stu Leader; Earth Day Chairperson; Talent Show Coord; Yrbk; Field Day Act & All-A-Day Coord at Boblo; Halloween Festivities Dir; *office:* St Mary Parish Sch 151 N Monroe St Monroe MI 48161

TURNER, ALAN D., Drafting Instructor; *b:* Salt Lake City, UT; *m:* Linda Jane Smith; *c:* Laura, Lynnette, Le Anne, Alicia, Alana, Ashley; *ed:* (BS) Ind Tech Ed, UT St Univ 1969; *cr:* Shop Teacher Jordan Jr HS 1969; Drafting Instr Bonneville HS 1969-, Ogden-Weber Applied Technology Center 1990; *ai:* Weber Sch Dist Drafting Coord; VICA Adv 1980-; VIEA, NEA, VEA, WEA 1969-; BSA (Dist Comm, Scoutmaster, Var Coach) 1969-, Scouters Key Awd 1975, 20 Yr Service Awd 1990; UT Hunter Safety Instr 1974-, 15 Yr Pin Awd 1989; *office:* Bonneville HS 251 Laker Way 559 E Atelane Ogden UT 84905

TURNER, ALEXANDER L., Art Teacher; *b:* Topeka, KS; *m:* Rosemary Sullivan; *c:* John C., Mary E.; *ed:* (BS) Art Ed, 1962, (MS) Art Ed, 1962 Univ of Bridgeport; 6 Yr Cert Public Sch Admin/Supervision, Cntrl CT St Univ 1985; *cr:* Art Dept Chm George J Penney HS 1974-85; Art Teacher E Hartford HS 1962-; *ai:* Art in Public Places, Fine Arts Annual Arts Exhibit & Art League; E Hartford Ed Assn, CT Ed Assn, NEA; *office:* E Hartford HS 869 Forbes St East Hartford CT 06118

TURNER, ANGELINE NEASE, Science Teacher; *b:* Blairsville, PA; *m:* Robert M.; *c:* Ken, Laura, Dan; *ed:* (BS) Bio, Indiana Univ of PA 1966; Grad Stud Indiana Univ of PA, Univ of PA, Carlow Coll; Grad Work San Jose St; *cr:* Sci Teacher Ligonier Jr HS 1966-68; Bio/Advanced Bio Teacher Ligonier SR HS 1969-71; Chem/Bio/Phys Sci/Earth Sci Teacher Silver Creek HS 1984-; *ai:* Sr Class Adv; NEA, CTA, CA Sci Teachers Assn; *office:* Silver Creek HS 3434 Silver Creek Rd San Jose CA 95121

TURNER, CHERYL YOUNG, Pre-School Teacher; *b:* Columbus, OH; *m:* James C.; *c:* Narcissa M., Camille E.; *ed:* Elem Ed, OH St Univ 1972-75; Spec Ed/Early Chldhd Ed, Cntrl St Univ 1975-87; *cr:* Teacher Eclc Learning Center 1968-71; Rdng Teacher OH St Univ Columbus Public Sch 1971-72; Kndgtn Teacher Little Dudes of Dayton OH 1976-79; Head Teacher Neighborhood House Infant Toddler Day Care 1979-81; Pre-Kndgtn Teacher/Prgm Dir/Asst Dir Edu-Care Guidance Center 1981-88; Pre-Sch Teacher Tendercare Learning Center 1990; *ai:* Franklin Cty Bd of Elections Presiding Judge; Columbus Symphony Orchestra Docent; Action for Children; Parenting Instr; Columbus Urban League Mem; Edu-Care Guidance Center Certificates of Appreciation; Child Abuse Recognition & Prevention Wkshp; *office:* Tendercare Learning Center 625 Scherers Ct Worthington OH 43085

TURNER, DEBORAH L., Soc Stud/Geography Teacher; *b:* Florence, SC; *c:* Jessica, Lindsay; *ed:* (BS) Sociology/Scndry Ed, Francis Marion Coll 1986; *cr:* Soc Stud Teacher South Florence HS 1987-89; *ai:* Dist Geography Textbook Adoption Comm.

TURNER, DIANA LEATHERWOOD, Science Teacher; *b:* Union, MS; *m:* Jerry D.; *c:* Lee; *ed:* (BS) Sci Ed, MS St Univ 1969; Grad Courses, Memphis St Univ 1969-, MS St Univ 1985-87, 1990; *cr:* Bio Teacher Wooddale HS 1969-70, Booker T Washington HS 1970-73; Chem/Physics/Advanced Bio Starkville Acad 1983-; *ai:* NHS Spon; Sci Fair, Math & Sci Team Coord; NSTA 1989-; MS Private Sch Assn 1983-; Delta Kappa Gamma 1984-; Starkville Jr Auxiliary Recording Secy 1977-; Exch Club Teacher of Month 1987; STAR Teacher 1987; *office:* Starkville Acad Academy Rd Starkville MS 39759

TURNER, DIANE MC BRAYER, Mid Sch Band Director; *b:* Gadsden, AL; *m:* James D.; *ed:* (BS) Music Ed, 1977; (MS) Music Ed, 1979; (EDS) Music Ed, 1985 Jacksonville St Univ; *cr:* Band Dir General Forrest Mid Sch 1977-; *ai:* MENC; AEA; Delta Omicron; *home:* Rt 5 Box 157A Gadsden AL 35903

TURNER, DONALD EUGENE, Art Teacher; *b:* Terre Haute, IN; *c:* Jeffery D., Adrian T.; *ed:* (BS) Art Ed, 1973; (MS) Art Ed, 1974 IN St Univ; Art Ed IN St Univ 1975; *cr:* Art Teacher South HS 1974-85; North HS 1985-; *ai:* Spon North HS Art Club 1989-; Turman Gallery of Art Adv Bd in St Univ 1989; ARTS Illiana Cmmty Arts Organization; Amer Fed of Teachers; Kappa Alpha PSI Polemarh 1984; Vigo Cty Lib Bd of Trustee VP 1989; 20 1-Man Art Shows Paintings & Drawings; Hew Grant West Africa 1979; Numerous Group Art Shows; US Press Articles Afro-Amer Art.

TURNER, ELIZA M. TAYLOR, Fourth Grade Teacher; *b:* Jackson, TN; *m:* Walter; *ed:* (BA) Elem Ed, Lane Coll 1970; *ai:* NW Festival Assn Inc Teen Queen Pageant Judge 1989; Milwaukee Public Schls Human Relations Awd 1980-81; Excl in Teaching Awd 1988-89; Whos Who of American Women 1983-84; *home:* 5877 N 78th St Milwaukee WI 53218

TURNER, ELIZABETH TART, 6th Grade Teacher; *b:* Goldsboro, NC; *m:* William Mc Neil Jr.; *ed:* (BS) Elem Ed/Math/Soc Stud, E Carolina Univ 1975; *cr:* 4th Grade Teacher Hobbton Elem 1975-76; 6th/7th Grade Teacher Buies Creek Sch 1976-77; 5th Grade Teacher Erwin Sch 1977-80; 6th Grade Teacher Hargrove Elem 1980-; *ai:* Jr Beta Club Adv 1976-77; Kappa Delta Pi 1973-75; NEA, NCACT 1975-; NCAE (Building Rep 1978-79) 1975-; Mentor Teacher 1990; Hargrove Sch Teacher of Yr 1989; *home:* PO Box 61 Newton Grove NC 28366

TURNER, GAIL WHEELER, Second Grade Teacher; *b:* Dallas, TX; *m:* Ralph A.; *c:* Tony Deon, Ralph A. Jr; *ed:* (AA) Liberal Arts, Mt View Jr Comm Coll 1973; (BS) Elem Ed, Univ of North TX 1975; Elem Ed, East TX St Univ 1990; Summer Schls Enrichment Prgms; Composition Writing/Holistic Grading of Papers; *cr:* 2nd Grade Teacher B C Darrell Elem 1975-; *ai:* 2nd Grade Chairperson; Faculty Advisory Comm Chairperson; Math Chairperson; PTA Exec Bd; United Way Fundraiser; Mem Hospitality Comm; Sch Fundraiser Chairperson; Mem Internal Monitoring Team; Classroom Teacher of Dallas 1986-; Natl Alliance of Black Educators 1988-; Teacher of Yr 1984-85; *office:* B F Darrell Elem Sch 4730 S Lancaster Rd Dallas TX 75216

TURNER, GARLENE RALEIGH, Remedial Reading Teacher; *b:* Ft Thomas, KY; *m:* Mackie; *c:* Nathan, Nicholas; *ed:* (BA) Elem Ed, 1976, Rdng, 1980 Northern KY Univ; *cr:* Remedial Rdng Teacher 1988-, 4th Grade Teacher 1983-88, 5th Grade Teacher 1981-83 Fourth St Elem Sch; 5th Grade Teacher Dora Cumming Elem Sch 1976-81; *ai:* Improvement Team; Bus in Ed & Parent Involvement Comm; NEA 1976-; KY Ed Assn 1976-; Newport Teacher Assn 1976-; PTA Mem 1976-; Published Trilogy Brief Stories with Comprehension Questions & Act-Published by Alleyside Press; *office:* 4th St Elem Sch 4th & Monmouth Sts Newport KY 41071

TURNER, JAI B., Fourth Grade Teacher; *b:* Terre Haute, IN; *ed:* (BS) Elem/Spec Ed, Chicago St Univ 1977; Contemporary Concepts Theology Chicago St Univ; Classroom Management Teacher Effective Trng Natl Teachers Coll Career Ed Leadership SC Univ; PTA Information Course 1989; *cr:* 1st Grade Teacher Fairchild Elem Sch 1978-80; 6th Grade Teacher E Park Mid Sch 1981-86; 4th Grade Teacher Liberty Elem Sch 1986-; *ai:* NEA, Phi Delta Kappa; PTA Certificate Honorary Life Membership 1986; 4-H (Leader 1983-86, Youth Cncl 1984-, Exec Bd Treas 1986-88); People for Educl Concerns; Laura Lee Fellowship House Assn Mem; Volunteer Tutor; Certificate of Recognition Outstanding Educator; *home:* 814 South St Danville IL 61832

TURNER, JAMES WALTER, English Teacher; *b:* Detroit, MI; *m:* Lois Ann; *c:* Lori, Kenneth, Jeanette; *ed:* (BA) Eng, Wayne St Univ 1968; (MA) Ed, Univ of MI 1970; Innovative Techniques for Classroom Instruction, Univ of MI Fellowship Prgm 1969-70; *cr:* Eng Teacher Highland Park HS 1968-69, Parker Elem Sch 1970-74, Ann Arbor Trail Mid Sch 1974-; *ai:* Curr Comm; Chess Club Adv; NCTE 1989-; ASCD 1990; Univ of MI Fellowship 1969-70; *office:* Ann Arbor Trail Mid Sch 7635 Chatham Detroit MI 48235

TURNER, JAYLEN SPERRY, Phys Ed Chair/Intramural Dir; *b:* Huntington, WV; *m:* David William; *c:* Dani L.; *ed:* (AB) Phys Ed, 1975, (MA) Scndry Ed, 1988 Marshall Univ; *cr:* Substitute Teacher Wayne Cty 1975-78; Teacher/Coach Buffalo HS 1978-; *ai:* Track Coach; Intramural Dir; YMCA Nautilus & Aerobics Instr; Special Olympics Time Keeper; Regional Chrldr Judge; Nationally Ranked Roller Skater 1984-86; WV Ed Assn 1985-88; Special Olympics Track Head Timer 1987-; *home:* 4749 Sunset Dr Huntington WV 25704

TURNER, JERRY DONALD, Science Teacher/Coach; *b:* Hope, AR; *m:* Delores Jean Tims; *c:* Jereme, Jason; *ed:* (BSE) Phys Ed, Ouachita Baptist Univ 1972; Sci Cert, Henderson St Univ, Stephen F Austin Univ; *cr:* Head Jr HS Ftbl/Bsktbl/Track Coach/Asst HS Ftbl/Bio/Earth Sci & Life Sci Teacher Union Hill Ind Sch Dist 1986-; *ai:* 8th Grade Spon; Textbook & Curr Guide Comm; Sci Fair, Sci Club, UIL Sci Spon; Sci Teachers Assn of TX, TX HS Coaches Assn 1986-; TX Assn of Bsktbl Coaches; Reserve Officers Assn 1985-; *home:* 3714 Dowell Dr Longview TX 75604

TURNER, JOYCE GREGOR, Librarian; *b:* Bethlehem, PA; *c:* Geoffrey, Stephanie; *ed:* (BED) Ed, Natl Coll of Ed 1964; (MS) Urban Ed, Univ of NE 1981; *cr:* Classroom Teacher Washington Sch 1964-65, Glencairn Sch 1965-67, Neihardt Sch 1977-84, Norris Sch 1984-85, Colony Bend Sch 1985-86, Highlands Sch 1986-89; Librarian Clements HS 1989-; *ai:* TX Lib Assn 1988-; *office:* Clements HS 4200 Elkins Sugar Land TX 77479

TURNER, JUDITH FORSYTH, Assistant Principal; *b:* Adamsville, TN; *m:* James D.; *c:* Donald E., Timothy L., Thomas F.; *ed:* (BS) Scndry Ed, 1966, (MED) Scndry Ed, 1974 Memphis St Univ 1974; Educl Admin, Memphis St 1984; Doctoral Work 1989; *cr:* Sci/Bio Teacher Hillcrest HS 1966-68; Soc Stud/Eng Teacher Bells HS 1969-70; Sci/Geography Teacher Humboldt Jr HS 1970-76; CDC/5th/6th Grade Teacher 1977-84, 7th/8th Grade Teacher/Asst Prin 1984- Selmer Mid Sch; *ai:* Yrbk Spon; Act, Elem Sch & Mid Sch Coord; NEA, TEA, MCEA Pres 1984-86; Delta Kappa Gamma VP 1987-89, Schlsp 1987; Phi Delta Kappa 1987-; Freed-Hardeman Coll Assocs (Local Pres, Natl VP); Democrat Comm 1977-; Democrat Women Pres; Article Published; Career Ladder III Admin; In-Service Wkshps Conductor; *home:* Rt 3 Box 41A Selmer TN 38375

TURNER, KATHRYN BUTLER, Guidance Counselor; *b:* Enid, OK; *ed:* (BS) Elem Ed, OK St Univ 1977; (MA) Guidance/ Counseling, Cntrl St Univ 1983; *cr:* Teacher of Gifted & Talented 1978-82, Cnslr 1982-84; Cnslr 1988-, Dir of Curr 1990 Bridge Creek Schls; *ai:* Eason Awd 1981; Bridge Creek Outstanding Staff Mem 1989; The Wounded Child Heart 1990; *office:* Bridge Creek HS Rt 1 Box 407 Blanchard OK 73010

TURNER, KRISTIN MALIA, Spanish Teacher; *b:* San Francisco, CA; *ed:* (BA) Eng 1987; (MA) Ed Admin, CSU; *cr:* Eng Teacher 1989; Span Teacher1989-; Clovis HS; *ai:* Amer Field Services Club Adv; Asst Aquatics Dir; Varsity Swim Coach; Swim America Prgm Dir; SCU-Fresno Alumni 1987-; Central Valley Recreation Swim Leag (Sec/Treas 1990); *office:* Clovis H S 1055 Fowler Ave Clovis CA 93612

TURNER, LINDA MERRELL, 2nd Grade Teacher; *b:* Madisonville, KY; *m:* Gary; *c:* Scott, Tiffany; *ed:* (BS) Elem Ed, 1975, (MS) Elem Ed, 1984 Murray St Univ; *cr:* 1st Grade Teacher St Charles Elem 1976-77; 1st Grade Teacher Mt Pleasant Sch 1977-78, St Charles Elem 1978-79; 2nd Grade Teacher Hanson Elem 1979-; *home:* 179 Pennyville Dr Madisonville KY 42431

TURNER, MARC MORGAN, Fourth Grade Teacher; *b:* Butte, MT; *m:* Jean Marie; *c:* Dillon; *ed:* (BS) Elem Ed, Eastern OR St Coll 1972; *cr:* 4th Grade Teacher Yankton Elem Sch 1972-87, John Gumm Elem Sch 1987-; *office:* John Gumm Elementary School 251 St Helens St Saint Helens OR 97051

TURNER, MARCIA MILLER, Eng, AP Amer His Teacher; *b:* Sedalia, MO; *m:* David Emmett; *c:* Mollie, David G.; *ed:* (BS) Soc Sci, Univ of MO Columbia 1970; *cr:* His Dept Chairperson LA Monte R-IV Sch 1971-80; Eng/His Teacher Sacred Heart Sch 1980-; *ai:* 7th Grade Moderator; Scndry Review Cncl; NHS Advisory Cncl; Boys Golf Team Coach; NCEA; Sedalia Cmmty Theatre (Lead Roles, Asst Dir) 1978-; Whos Who MO Ed 1974; Area Rep Pettis Cty Law Related Ed; *office:* Sacred Heart Sch 416 W 3rd Sedalia MO 65301

TURNER, NANCY DRAPER, Reading Department Chair; *b:* Levelland, TX; *m:* C. Wayne; *c:* Kelley, Connie; *ed:* (BS) Elem Ed, W TX St 1962; Spec Ed, Univ of TX Austin, IN Univ; Advanced Math Univ of TX Austin; *cr:* Elem Teacher Copperas Cove Ind Sch Dist 1963-; *ai:* Textbook Comm Adv; Amer Assn Univ Woman 1987-; TX Adoption Agency 1975; Exchange Club Teacher of Month & Yr 1985; *office:* Avenue E Elem Sch PO Box 580 Copperas Cove TX 76522

TURNER, NATALIE WELBORN, Soc Stud/Journalism Teacher; *b:* Picayune, MS; *m:* Thomas M.; *c:* Amee R.; *ed:* (BSED) Soc Stud, MS Coll 1984; *cr:* Soc Stud/Eng Teacher 1984-89, Soc Stud/Journalism Teacher 1989- Pascagoula Jr HS; *ai:* Sch Newspaper The Panther Press & Stu Cncl Faculty Adv; Secy for Choral Booster Club; Eastern Star 1989-; Mem Sch Improvement Comm; Teacher of Month 1987-88, 1988-89, 1989-; Teacher of Yr 1988-89; *office:* Pascagoula Jr HS 2234 Pascagoula St Pascagoula MS 39567

TURNER, NORMA FOLEY, Literature Teacher; *b:* Knox Cty, KY; *m:* James Paul; *c:* James P. II; *ed:* (BS) Elem Ed/Eng, 1966, (MA) Eng/Ed, 1968 Union Coll; Eng, Georgetown Univ; Eng/ Curr, Univ of Cincinnati, Miami Univ; *cr:* Eng/Lit Teacher Glen Este Mid Sch 1966-89; *ai:* Yrbk Adv; WCEA Secy 1974-75; OEA, NEA; Martha Holden Jennings Scholar; Eng Awd Union Coll 1966; Helped Write Curr Guide; Dept Chm; *home:* 3109 St Rt 222 Bethel OH 45106

TURNER, PATRICIA CURRY, English & Spanish Teacher; *b:* Rochester, NY; *m:* Robert W. Jr.; *c:* Melita; *ed:* (BA) Span, Univ of MS 1967; Grad Stud Univ of S MS; Span Summer Wkshp FL St Univ 1986; *cr:* Eng/Span Teacher Beaumont HS 1976-77; Eng Teacher Hattiesburg HS 1977-78; Span Teacher Perry Cntrl HS 1984-85, Shanks HS 1985-87; Eng/Span Teacher Sumrall Attendance Center 1987-; *ai:* Annual Staff & Span Club Spon; MS Foreign Lang Assn, Delta Kappa Gamma; Amer Assn Teacher of Span & Portuguese, NEA 1985-89; Alpha Omicron Pi Alumna, Univ of MS Alumni Assn; 1st Presbyn Church; Daughter of Amer Revolution 20th STAR Vice-Regent 1989-; *office:* Sumrall Attendance Center P O Box 187 Sumrall MS 39482

TURNER, PATRICIA SAYLES, High School Counselor; *b:* Chicago, IL; *m:* Lawrence Bruce; *c:* Stephen, Tiffany; *ed:* (BS) Intermediate/Upper Grade, 1971, (MS) Guidance/Counseling, 1986 Chicago St Univ; *cr:* 6th Grade Teacher Willaim Q Gresham 1972; 7th Grade Teacher Van Vlissingen Elem 1972-77; Adjustment Teacher/Clslr Van Vlissingen 1977-86; HS Cnslr Christian Fenger 1986-; *ai:* Practical Nursing Prgm Spon; Prin Scholars Prgm Co-Spon; Fenger Dist Midwest Regional Conference Team Leader; Stu Teacher Bd; Amer Assn of Counseling & Dev 1988-; Scndry Sch Cnslrs Cncl 1986-; Christians Workers Pres 1988-; Fenger HS & 111th Street YMCA Liaison Project DETER; Project IMPACT Liaison Developing Communities; Academic Achievement Banquet Prgm Chairman; Joyce Fnd Retreat Presenter; *office:* Christian Fenger Sch 11220 S Wallace Chicago IL 60628

TURNER, REBECCA COLE, Fourth Grade Teacher; *b:* Villa Rica, GA; *m:* Charles D.; *c:* Jennifer, Ashley, Brandon; *ed:* (BS) Elem Ed, West GA Coll 1976; Student Teacher Supv; TPAI; *cr:* 5th/6th Grade Teacher New GA Elem 1976-78; 5th Grade Teacher Newton Estates Elem 1978-79; 4th Grade Teacher Pathway Chrstn 1979-80; 3rd/4th Grade Teacher New GA Elem 1981-; *ai:* Teacher Advisory Comm; Testing Coord; Stu Support Team Comm; Lib/Media Comm; Grade Level Lead Teacher 1981-89; Textbook Adaption Comm; GA Assn of Educators 1976-79/81-; Douglasville Chrstn Church Teacher 1986-89; Mentor Teacher 1988-; Teacher of Yr 1983; *home:* 9008 Seals Rd Dallas GA 30132

TURNER, RICHARD W., 8th Grade Soc Studies Teacher; *b:* Lawrence, MA; *ed:* (BED) Soc Stud/Scndry, Keene St Coll 1967; *cr:* Teacher 1967-, Past Dept Head 1980-88 Hudson Memorial Sch; *ai:* Sch Sign Comm; Washington Dc Tour Coord; 8th Grade Class Adv; Soc Stud Curr Comm Chm; NEASC Comm; Christman Party Dir; AFT Past Pres 1975-; NCSS 1980-; Clarion Corner Comm 1988-; Good Apple Awd 1989; *office:* Hudson Memorial Sch 1 Memorial Dr Hudson NH 03051

TURNER, RODELL, Biology Teacher; *b:* Melbourne, FL; *m:* Janice Boykin; *c:* Rodell, Jarod, Rojan; *ed:* (BS) Bio, Troy St Univ 1977; Techniques for Teaching Biological Concepts; *cr:* Teacher/ Coach Palm Bay HS 1977-79, Sam Houston HS 1980-; *ai:* Sci Club Founder & Spon; Sr Class Spon; Ftbl, Bsktbl Track Coach; NSTA 1987-; Bio Teachers Assn 1987-89; Teacher Coaches Assn, TX Ed Assn, TX St Teachers Assn 1979-; NEA 1977-; *office:* Sam Houston HS 4635 E Houston San Antonio TX 78220

TURNER, SARAH HILL, 4th Grade Teacher; *b:* Belden, MS; *c:* Gary, Eddie, Tami Lindsey; *ed:* (BA) Elem Ed, MS St Univ 1972; (MA) Elem Ed, Univ of MS 1975; *cr:* Teacher Mantachie HS 1972-; *ai:* NEA 1972-88; MEA 1972-88; Itawamba Educators Assn 1972-88; MS Prof Eduators 1988-; Kappa Delta Pi Ed Honorary 1971-72; Phi Kappa Phi 1971-72; Graduated with Distinction from MS St Univ 1972; *home:* 208 Nanney Tupelo MS 38801

TURNER, SHARON CLARK, First Grade Teacher; *b:* Asheville, NC; *m:* Justin H. Jr.; *c:* Dustin H.; *ed:* (AS) Early Chldhd Ed Walters St Comm Coll 1974; (BS) Elem Ed East TN St Univ 1976; Univ of TN Grad Sch; *cr:* 2nd Grade Teacher Washburn Elem Sch 1976-78; 1st Grade Teacher 1978-84; 2nd Grade Teacher 1984-86; 1st Grade Teacher 1986- Fairview Marguerite Elem Sch; *ai:* TEA 1978-82; NEA 1978-82; Hamblen Cty EA 1978-82; Career Ladder Level I Teacher; *office:* Fairview-Marguerite Elem Sch 2125 Fairview Rd Morristown TN 37814

TURNER, SHIRLEY ANN THOMPSON, 2nd Grade Teacher; *b:* Monroe, LA; *c:* Chautauqua, Tiffany; *ed:* (BS) Elem Ed, Grambling Coll 1971; (MS) Elem Ed, Grambling St Univ 1980; Grad Stud NE LA Univ; *cr:* Teacher Columbia Elem 1971-73, Boley Jr HS 1973-74, Claiborne Elem 1974-; *ai:* Zeta Phi Beta Spon for Amicae Friends of Zetas; NEA, LA Ed Assn, Apple Mem; Zeta Phi Beta Secy 1980-82; Stone Baptist Church Matron; March of Dimes/Amer Cancer Society; Bosom Buddies Cnslr; *home:* 324 Nevada Dr Monroe LA 71202

TURNER, WILLIAM DAVIS, Band Director; *b:* Philadelphia, PA; *c:* William; *ed:* (BME) Flute/Music Ed, Philadelphia Musical Acad 1966; Graduate Stud in Music Ed, Ithaca Coll; Advanced Stud, GA St Univ; *cr:* Elem Band Dir Shenendehowa Cntrl Schls 1966-72; Orch Dir DeKalb Cty Schls 1975-80; Atlanta Public Schls 1980-81; Band Dir Georgetown Day Sch 1984-; *ai:* Coaching Boys JV Soccer and Sftbl; *office:* Georgetown Day Sch 4530 Mac Arthur Blvd N W Washington DC 20007

TURNER, ZELMA TURLEY, Fourth Grade Teacher; *b:* Edmonson, KY; *m:* Donald C.; *c:* Woodford G; *ed:* (BS) Elem Ed, 1972, (MA) Elem Ed, 1979 W KY Univ; *cr:* 3rd Grade Teacher Bonnieville Elem/Jr HS 1972-73; 4th/5th/6th Grade Teacher Park City Elem/Jr HS 1973-; *ai:* NEA, KEA, BCEA; *office:* Park City Elem & Jr HS Box 247 Park City KY 42160

TUROK, LINDA CARLTON, Home Economics Teacher; *b:* Aurora, IL; *m:* Charles; *ed:* (BS) Home Ec Ed, S IL Univ 1976; (MS) Home Ec Ed, E MI Univ 1987; *cr:* Home Ec Teacher Lowpoint-Washburn HS 1976-82, Beach Mid Sch 1984-; *ai:* 7th Grade Vlybl Coach; 6th Grade Camp Comm; Sch Newspaper Adv; Co-Facilitate Concerned Persons Substance Abuse Group; MI Home Ec Educators Nom Outstanding Home Ec Teacher 1989; Brief Article Printed in Forecast; *office:* Beach Mid Sch 445 Mayer Dr Chelsea MI 48118

TUROWSKI, DONALD ALEX, Computer/Mathematics Teacher; *b:* Natrona, PA; *m:* Joann Lewandoski; *c:* Donald S., Kimberly A.; *ed:* (BS) Ed, Clarion St Coll 1969; PA St Univ New Kensington Campus; *cr:* Math/Cmptr Teacher Burrell Sch Dist 1969-; *ai:* Asst Girls Bsktbl Coach; Cmptr Core Comm; Cmptr Prgms Published; *home:* 1236 9th Ave Natrona Heights PA 15065

TURPIN, JIMMIE NELL, Fifth Grade Teacher; *b:* Atwood, OK; *m:* Ralph; *c:* Greg, Paula Turpin Jones; *ed:* (BS) Elem Ed, East Cntrl Univ 1962; Head Start Prgm Cert, OK St Univ; *cr:* 3rd/4th Grade Elem Teacher 1963-65, 3rd-5th Grade Elem Teacher 1965-67 Gerty Grade Sch; 3rd/5th Grade Elem Teacher Allen Elem Sch 1967-; *ai:* 4-H Leader 1967; Cub Scout Den Mother 1969-72; Staff Dev, Sch Policy, Curr Comm; OEA 1963-; NEA 1963-; Allen Ed Assn VP; Chamber of Commerce 1986-89; Allen Teacher of Yr 1983; Pontotoc Cty Teacher of Yr 1983; *home:* Rt 2 Box 248 Allen OK 74825

TURSAK, ROSEMARY K., English Teacher; *b:* Morenci, MI; *m:* Frank E.; *c:* John, Judith Kennedy Pfund; *ed:* (BA) Eng, 1970, (MA) Curr/Instruction, 1973 Siena Heights Coll; *cr:* HS Eng Teacher Morenci HS 1970-; *ai:* Yrbk, Sr Class, Frosh Class Adv; Sch Improvement Team; Gifted & Talented Steering & Faculty Advisory Comm; MI Cncl of Teachers of Eng; NCTE, ASCD; Recognition from Taylor Publishing for being in Top 10 of all Yrbks Taylor Published; Yrbk Awds from MI Interscholastic Publication Assn; *office:* Morenci HS Coomer St Morenci MI 49256

TUTCHER, LARRY CLIFFORD, Mathematics Instructor; *b:* Topeka, KS; *ed:* (BS) Math, GA Southern Coll 1967; *cr:* 7th Grade Teacher Mc Intosh Jr HS 1967-84, Albany Mid Sch 1984-; *ai:* GA Math League Spon; GA Nom for Excl Teaching of Math Presidential Awd 1988; *home:* 1202 Water St Bainbridge GA 31717

TUTT, MARY LOUISE, Mathematics Teacher; *ed:* (BS) Math/ Bus Ed, 1976, (MAT) Math, 1980, (Rank I) Scndry Ed/Math, 1983 Murray St Univ; *cr:* Math Teacher Fort Campbell HS 1976-; *ai:* NCTM, KY Ed Assn, NEA 1976-; Kenlake Cncl Teachers of Math 1987-.

TUTT, SHIRLEY EPPS, Gifted/Talented Teacher; *b:* Lunenburg Cty, VA; *m:* Tyrone; *c:* Anthony, Kimberly, Mark, Jeffrey; *ed:* (BA) Elem Ed, 1974, (MA) Elem Ed, 1988 Kean Coll of NJ; Interior Decorating, Assertiveness Trng, Gifted/Talented Seminars; *cr:* Teacher 1972-87, Gifted/Talented Teacher 1987 Stockton Sch; *ai:* TALC; Textbook Selection Consultant; Career Day, Lang Arts, Cmptr Ed, & Awds Day Comms; East Orange Ed Assn, NJ Ed Assn, NEA 1972-; Alpha Kappa Alpha, South Orange Maplewood Action Comm, Natl Congress of Negro Women; Teacher of Yr 1980; 1st Place Non-Fiction Awd Kean Coll 1985; 3rd Place Art Illustration Awd Kean Coll 1985; *home:* 239 Irving Ave South Orange NJ 07079

TUTTLE, JOHN G., 6th Grade Teacher; *b:* Liberal, KS; *c:* Chris, Kathy; *ed:* (BS) Elem Ed, Panhandle St 1979; Grad Work Univ of OK, OK St Univ, Northwestern St Univ; *cr:* Teacher Guymon Public Schls 1979-; *ai:* 6th Grade Track Coach; 5th/6th Grade Sci Fair Co-Dir; High Plains Rdng Cncl Pres 1982; Phi Delta Kappa Mem 1988-89; OK Ed Assn, NEA 1979-89; BSA Scoutmaster 1985-; Kids Incorporated (Bd Mem 1983-, Ftbl Dir 1987-88); City of Guymon Parks Bd Mem 1988-; *office:* Guymon Public Schls Box 1307 Guymon OK 73942

TUTTLE, MARK F., English Teacher; *b:* Oceanside, CA; *m:* Brenda Bowser; *ed:* (BA) Eng, US Intnl Univ 1972; (MA) Ed, Point Loma Coll 1985; *cr:* Eng Teacher Mt Carmel HS 1975-; *ai:* Master Teacher of Univ Stu Teacher; Eng Dept Chairperson 19852-88; AFT 1975-; *home:* 1811 E Grand Ave #146 Escondido CA 92027

TWADDLE, DONALD D., German/Russian Teacher; *b:* Council Bluffs, IA; *c:* Michael; *ed:* (BA) Russian, Univ of IA 1960; Russian, Ger, Univ of S IL, Univ of N IA, Univ of NE; *cr:* Ger Teacher Edwardsville IL 1964-65, Schuyler NE 1966-68; In Service Dir Glenwood St Hospital Sch 1971-76; Farming 1976-84; Ger/Russian Teacher Henning HS 1985-; *ai:* Knowledge Building Adv; Goethe Inst Munich West Germany Prgm Awd 1986; *home:* RR 2 Staples MN 56479

TWEDELL, LESTER RALPH, JR., Teacher/Mathematics Dept Chair; *b:* Grand Forks, ND; *ed:* (BS) Math, 1966, (MED) Math, 1968 Univ of ND; Numerous Univs; *cr:* Teacher Elgin HS 1968; Teacher/Math Dept Chm Marshall-Univ HS 1968-82, Moreno Valley HS 1982-87, Canyon Springs HS 1987-; *ai:* Prins Advisory Cncl; Minneapolis Math Club (Pres 1974-75, Membership 1968-82); NCTM Membership 1968-; CA Math Cncl Southern Section Membership 1982-; Sons of Norway, Natl Wildlife Fed; Dale Seymour Publication Project Team Mem; *home:* 4695 Maxwell Ct Riverside CA 92501

TWEEDIE, MARY JO (SUTTON), Counselor; *b:* Uniontown, KY; *m:* John Telfer Jr.; *c:* Andrea A., John T. III, James M.; *ed:* (BS) Bus Ed, 1963, (MA) Ed/Counseling, 1969 Murray St Univ; Grad Work Southeast St Univ of MO Columbia, Lincoln Univ, MS Coll; *cr:* 7th/8th Grade Eng Teacher Wingo HS 1963-65; Bus Ed Teacher Middletown HS 1965-68; Cnslr Potosi Elem 1969-77; Cnslr Potosi HS 1977-; *ai:* HS Bstkbl Chrldr, Pom Pon, HELP Club Spon; MO St Teachers Assn 1970-; SE MO Guidance Assn 1975-; Potosi Bus Prof Women (Pres 1981-82, Treas 1985-89), Women of Yr 1982; *office:* Potosi R-III HS 1 Trojan Dr Potosi MO 63664

TWILLEY, JUDY KIRK, Speech/History Teacher; *b:* Orrville, AL; *m:* Henry F. Jr.; *c:* Lisa Twilley Haugen; *ed:* (BA) Speech, Univ of Montevallo 1967; *cr:* Teacher Winnacunnet HS, Robert W Traip Acad, John T Morgan Acad; *ai:* Sr Class Stu Government Assn Adv; Theater Dir; HS Teacher Rep; Drama Coach; *home:* 35 Park Ln Selma AL 36701

TWOMBLY, PATTY DAVID, Third Grade Teacher; *b:* Joplin, MO; *m:* Glenn Allen; *c:* David A., Kari A.; *ed:* (BS) Elem Ed, MO Southern St Coll 1973; (MS) Elem Ed, Pittsburgh St Univ 1978; Taskboard Wkshp 1989; Make It Take It Wkshp 1988; Kids at Risk Outdoor Classroom Inservice 1990; *cr:* 2nd Grade Teacher 1973-88, 3rd Grade Teacher 1988- Carl Junction Schls; *ai:* Cubscout Den Leader; Sick Leave, MO St Teachers Assn Banquet, NCA Design for Learning Comms; NCA Health Comm Chairperson; MO St Teachers Assn (Pres 1984-85, Building Rep 1986-88, 1990); Cub Scouts Cubmaster 1988-; *office:* Carl Junction Schls P O Box 4 Carl Junction MO 64834

TYDE, CHERRY CONRAD, Mathematics Teacher; *b:* Lancaster, OH; *m:* Steve; *c:* Steve Jr., Jennifer; *ed:* (BS) Math Ed, Northeastern St Univ 1987; *cr:* Math Teacher Union HS 1988-; *ai:* Jr Class Spon; Kappa Delta Pi, Kappa Mu Epsilon, Rho Theta Sigma; *office:* Union HS 6636 S Mingo Rd Tulsa OK 74133

TYLAVSKY, GERRY BALTES, English Teacher; *b:* Hampton, VA; *m:* Michael John Jr.; *c:* Michael J. III, Elizabeth A.; *ed:* (BA) Eng, William & Mary 1970; (MS) Ed/Eng, Old Dominion Univ 1986; *cr:* Eng Teacher Bethel HS 1970-72; Eng Teacher/Dept Head C Vernon Spratley Jr HS 1972-80; Eng Teacher Tabb HS 1983-; Continuing Ed Teacher Christopher Newport Coll 1987-; *ai:* NHS Adv; Schlsp Comm; VA Assn of Teachers of Eng 1970-; PTA Prgm Comm 1988-89; College of William & Mary Networkshop Comm 1988-; *office:* Tabb HS 4431 Big Bethel Rd Tabb VA 23602

TYLENDA, DONNA MARIE (RESSLER), Fourth Grade Teacher; *b:* Northampton, PA; *m:* Nicholas F.; *c:* Nicholas; *ed:* (BS) Elem Ed, Kutztown St Coll 1972; Post Grad Stud Penn St & Lehigh Univ; *cr:* Teacher St Anne Sch 1972-; *ai:* Rdng Coord; Crisis Intervention Rep; NCEA; *office:* St Anne Sch Easton Ave & Hickory St Bethlehem PA 18017

TYLER, EDWIN A., Band Director; *b:* New York City, NY; *ed:* (BME) Instrumental Music Ed, Univ of N CO 1978; Grad Work Univ of N CO, Adams St Coll, Western St Coll; *cr:* Band/Choir Dir Fowler Public Schls 1978-81; Band Dir La Junta Jr HS 1981-86, La Junta HS 1986-; *ai:* Curricular 5th Grade, HS Symphonic, Marching, Jazz Band; Color Guard; Music Theory; HS Drama Orch; Cmmty Theater; CO Bandmasters Assn Pres 1981-82; Natl Bandmasters Assn St Pres 1981-82; CO Music Educators Assn, Music Educators Natl Conference, Natl Assn of Jazz Educators; Benevolent & Protective Order of Elks; Performing Groups Selected by Audition to Perform at CMEA Convention 1984, 1988; St Champion Marching Band 1980; Numerous Superior Ratings, Festival Championships; Adjudicator & Clinician in Southern CO; *home:* 1406 Sunrise La Junta CO 81050

TYLER, JUNE PARKER, Third Grade Teacher; *b:* Alton, IL; *m:* Bruce D.; *c:* Pamela S. Iacullo, Terriann Hidaka, Kevin B.; *ed:* (BSED) Ed, Washington Univ 1946; Grad Courses, Math, Rdng, Sci, Soc Stud; *cr:* Kndgtn Teacher Woodrive Sch System 1946-49; 3rd Grade Teacher Urbana Sch System 1949-50, Schaumburg Dist #54 1962-; *ai:* Hillcrest Sch & Churchill Stu Cncl Spon; Hillcrest Talent Show Co-Spon; Soc Comm; Delta Kappa Gamma; PEO 1971-; Chrstn Womens Fellowship (Pres, Sunday Sch Supt); *home:* 660 Michigan Ln Elk Grove Village IL 60007

TYLER, SHIRLEY TUDAS, Third Grade Teacher; *b:* Pittsburgh, PA; *m:* Donald Leroy; *ed:* (BS) Ed, PA St Univ 1967; Numerous Courses, Univ of CA Berkeley, Univ of CA Hayward, Penn St, San Francisco St; Great Books Trng; *cr:* Teacher E Cleveland Schls 1967-70, Lafayette Sch 1970-72; Teacher of Gifted & Talented Highland Elem 1972-85; Teacher Carl B Munck 1985-; *ai:* Bay Area Math Project; Master Teacher Stu Teachers; Dist Lang Art Curr Task Force; Native Amer Model Classroom Teacher OPS; Math & Lang Art Inservice Teacher Trainer; Mentor Teacher; Writer of Units of Study Core Lit; NCTM; Oakland Ed Assn Building Rep 1988-89; Parent Faculty Club Braggin Dragon Awd for Outstanding Contributions to Carl B Munck Sch; Stomp Grant to Enhance Classroom Music Prgm; *office:* Carl B Munck Sch 1190 Campus Dr Oakland CA 94619

TYLER, SUSAN CARTER, 5th Grade Teacher; *b:* Fredericksburg, VA; *m:* Robert C.; *ed:* (BS) Chem, Mary Washington Coll 1964; (MED) Elem Ed, Univ of VA 1968; *cr:* 5th Grade Teacher Fredericksburg City Schls 1966-; *ai:* Alpha Delta Kappa 1988-; *office:* Walker Grant Mid Sch 1 Learning Ln Fredericksburg VA 22401

TYNDALL, WILLIAM ALAN, Mathematics/Computer Teacher; *b:* San Mateo, CA; *m:* Mary-Ellen Knox; *ed:* (BA) Math, Edison St Coll 1983; (MS) Math, Fairleigh Dickinson Univ 1986; *cr:* Math/Cmptr Teacher Chatham Township HS 1985-86, Pompton Lakes HS 1986-; *ai:* Sr Class & Cmptr League Adv; Math Assn of Amer 1986-; NCTM 1986-; MENSA 1985-; Dodge Fellowship Geraldine Dodge Fnd 1986; *office:* Pompton Lakes HS Lakeside Ave Pompton Lakes NJ 07442

TYNER, JOHN CHARLES, Music Coordinator; *b:* Detroit, MI; *m:* Catherine; *c:* Matthew, Sara; *ed:* (BM) Music Ed, Wayne St Univ 1976; (MA) Educl Admin, E MI Univ 1981; *cr:* Vocal Music Teacher Monroe HS 1976-; Music Coord Monroe Pre-Sch 1982-; *ai:* Little League Soccer & Bsbl Coach; MI Sch Voc Assn (Choral Music Adjudicator, Bd Mem 1976-); Amer Choral Dir Assn Bd Mem 1988-; MENC; MI Music Educators Assn; St Pauls United Meth Church Music Dir; Kiwanis Bd Mem 1988-; Fine Arts Cncl Bd Mem 1980-; MI Sch Vocal Assn Music Teacher of Yr 1989; St Honors Choir Dir 1984; *office:* Monroe Public Schls 901 Herr Rd Monroe MI 48161

TYSON, BETH MILNER, Mathematics Department Chair; *b:* Grove City, PA; *m:* John R.; *c:* Loralee; *ed:* (AB) Math, Grove City Coll 1975; (MS) Ed, Alfred Univ 1983; *cr:* Math Teacher Bryant Station HS 1975-77, Randolph HS 1977-78, Madison Jr/Sr HS 1978-79; Math Dept Chairperson Wellsville HS 1979-; *ai:* AMTNYS 1985-; Wellsville Ed Assn (Pres 1984-87, Treas 1988-89); NEA, NY Ed Assn (Alternate Delegate 1987-89) 1977-; Fillmore United Meth Church (Chair Finance Comm 1986-87); *office:* Wellsville HS 126 W State St Wellsville NY 14895

TYSON, LAURA BOGGAN, Reading Teacher Chapter I; *b:* Simpson Cty, MS; *m:* Billy E.; *c:* Ann, Barry; *ed:* (BS) Bio, 1957, (MS) Elem Ed, 1979 Univ of S MS; Charity Hospital Sch of Medical Technology; *cr:* Medical Technologist Franklin Memorial Hospital 1958-61; Classroom Teacher Franklin Elem Sch 1969-88; Chapter I Rdng Teacher Franklin Elem 1988-; *ai:* Delta Kappa Gamma Recording Secy 1978-86; Rdng Cncl (Pres, VP) 1980-88; MS Prof Ed Assn 1988-; Franklin Womans Club (Pres, VP, Secy) 1961-; Franklin Cty Chamber of Commerce 1988-; Bude Public Lib VP 1989-; *office:* Franklin Elem Sch Rt 1 Box 15 Meadville MS 39653

TYSON, RONALD LYNN, Science Instructor; *b:* Lubbock, TX; *m:* Karol King; *c:* Ronna, Tonya, Trent; *ed:* (BS) Ag Ed, 1967; (MED) Ed, 1974 TX Tech Univ; Scndry Bio; Vocational Supvr Cert; *cr:* Ag Sci Teacher 1970-78, Sci Teacher 1978-83 New Deal HS; Ag Sci Teacher Monterey HS 1983-84; Sci Teacher New Deal HS 1984-; *ai:* NHS, Stu Cncl & Sr Class Adv/spon; TX St Teachers Assn 1970-; TX Excl Awds Outstanding HS Teachers; *home:* Box 153 New Deal TX 79350

U

UCHIUMI, GERALD M., Phys Ed Teacher/Athletic Dir; *b:* Oakland, CA; *ed:* (BS) Phys Ed, CA St Univ Hayward 1973; (MA) Phys Ed, CA St Univ San Francisco 1983; *cr:* Ftbl Coach Berkeley HS 1972-76; Phys Ed Teacher Pine Grove Intermediate 1975; Ftbl/Bsbl Coach Albany HS 1976-78; Phys Ed Teacher/Athletic Dir Albany Mid Sch 1976-; Phys Ed Teacher/Ftbl Coach Laney Coll 1978-; *ai:* Noontime Sports Dir; Sch Store Organizer; Bsktbl & Comm Coll Ftbl Coach; *office:* Albany Mid Sch 1000 Jackson St Albany CA 94706

UDELL, JUDITH A., 5th Grade Teacher; *b:* New York, NY; *ed:* (BA) Speech Pathology/Audiology, Brooklyn Coll 1962; (MED) Psych, PA St Univ 1965; Cmptr Sci, CUNY System; *cr:* Teacher New York City Bd of Ed 1963-; *office:* Public Sch 29-Bardwell Sch 1580 Victory Blvd Staten Island NY 10314

UGLOW, MARY F., 4th Grade Teacher; *b:* Waukesha, WI; *ed:* (BS) Primary Ed, 1967, (MS) Elem Ed, 1977 Whitewater St Univ; Grad Stud; *cr:* 2nd/3rd Grade Teacher Kettle Moraine Schls 1967-68; 1st-4th Grade Teacher Muskego Norway Schls 1968-; *ai:* Phi Kappa Phi; WI St Rdng Assn, Intnl Rdng Assn; *office:* Muskego-Norway Schls Lakeview Sch 26335 Fries Ln Wind Lake WI 53150

UHING, RUSS, Business Instructor; *b:* Yankton, SD; *m:* Kim Buhl; *ed:* (BS) Bus Ed, Wayne St Coll 1985; *cr:* Bus Instr West Point Cntrl Cath HS 1985-87, Pius X HS 1987-; *ai:* Frosh Class Spon; Bsktbl Coach, Head Golf Coach; Faculty Rep Admin Cncl; NCA 1985-; *office:* Pius X HS 6000 A St Lincoln NE 68506

UHLHORN, SCOTT DAVID, 7th/8th Grade Science Teacher; *b:* Minneapolis, MN; *m:* Karen Nasser; *c:* Anna; *ed:* (BS) Sci/Art, 1981, (MS) Sci Ed, 1985 IN St; *cr:* Teacher/Coach Owen Valley Mid Sch 1981-; *ai:* Var Ftbl Asst Coach; 7th Grade Boys A Team Bsktbl & 8th Grade Girls Bsktbl Coach; IN St Teacher Assn Sch Rep 1981-; NEA 1981-; Hoosier Assn of Sci Teachers 1984-; IN Bsktbl Coaches Assn, In Ftbl Coaches Assn 1983-; Published Article; *office:* Owen Valley Mid Sch RR 4 Box 12 Spencer IN 47460

ULAKOVIC, LORETTA M., Fourth Grade Teacher; *b:* New Kensington, PA; *w:* John (dec); *ed:* (BA) Elem Ed, 1959, (MS) Elem Ed, 1963 Duquesne Univ; Lib Sci, St Francis Coll; *cr:* Teacher/Prin Holy Trinity 1954-64; Prin Mc Keesport Cntrl Cath 1964-74; Teacher St Angela Merici 1975-; *ai:* Chess Club Adv; Long Range Planning Comm; Angel Club & Missions Moderator; NCEA 1964-; Mc Keesport Coll Club 1978-; Hospital Volunteer 1977-; *office:* St Angela Merici Sch 1640 Fawcett Ave White Oak PA 15131

ULAND, LARRY LEE, Science Teacher; *b:* Dallas, TX; *m:* Charlene Myers; *c:* Daniel B., Andrew J.; *ed:* (BS) Health/Phys Ed/Sci/Psych, Austin Coll 1961; (MED) Counseling/Guidance, Our Lady of the Lake Univ 1967; *cr:* Teacher/Coach Alamo Heights HS 1961-63, John Marshall HS 1964-68, Duncanville HS 1969-72, Waco-Richfield HS 1973-76; Athletic Dir/Coach Cedar Hill HS 1977-84; Teacher/Coach Thomas Jefferson HS 1985-; *ai:* Fellowship of Chrstn Athletes Spon; Ftbl Defensive Coord & Power Lifting Coach; TX HS Coaches Assn 1961-; TX HS Powerlifting Assn, Dallas Coaches Assn 1986-; TX St Teachers Assn 1961-; Lions Club Pres 1984; *office:* Thomas Jefferson HS 4001 Walnut Hill Ln Dallas TX 75229

ULREY, DONALD GLENN, Education Specialist; *b:* Sacramento, CA; *m:* Roxy G. Hardman; *c:* Bradley, Jake, Justin, Julee; *ed:* (BS) Ed, 1970, (MS) Elem Ed, 1984 E OR St; Admin Elem Prin, Univ of OR 1984; Numerous Courses; *cr:* 5th/6th Grade Teacher La Grande Sch Dist 1970-76; 3rd/4th Grade Teacher 1976-84, Rdng/Math/Lang Art Dir 1984-87, Elem Prin 1987-88 Pendleton Sch Dist; Ed Specialist/ESEA OR Dept of Ed 1988-; *ai:* OR St Chapter I Parent Advisory Panel Children Adv & Winter Conference for 1600 Chm; Neglected & Deliquent Prgms Coord St Projects; Intnl Rdng Assn 1984-; ASCD 1980-; Eggs & Equity Breakfasts 1988-; United Way of Umatilla Cty (Pres 1985-88, Campaign Chm 1987, Bd Chm) Saturday Acad Grant Writer for Talented & Gifted Children of Umatilla Cty; Exemplary Compensatory Ed Secy of Ed Awd Effective Chapter I Prgm & Prgm Coord 1987; Textbook Co-author; *office:* OR Dept of Ed 700 Pringle Pkwy SE Salem OR 97310

ULRICH, DAVID RICHARD, High School Generalist; *b:* Euclid, OH; *m:* Phyllis Arlene Pearson; *c:* Matthew; *ed:* (BA) Bio Ed, Univ of MT 1975; Addl Stud, W MT Coll, Univ of AK, Islands Comm Coll; *cr:* Teacher Darby HS 1975-82, Southeast Island Sch Dist 1985-; *ai:* Cross Cntry Coach; Weight Trainer; Photography Club Adv; Natl Sci Assn 1989-; West Inst Preparing for Tommorrows Future; *office:* John Green Sch PO Box 8340 Ketchikan AK 99901

ULRICH, KURT S., English/Gifted Teacher; *b:* Hartford, CT; *m:* Anne Dorrance; *ed:* (BA) Eng/Soc Stud, 1962, (MED) Ed/Eng, 1966 PA St Univ; Natl Endowment for Hum Inst Beaver Coll 1986; *cr:* Eng Teacher 1963-86, Eng/Gifted Teacher 1986- Methacton HS; *ai:* Montgomery Cty Cncl on Hum & Academic Thought; NEA, PSEA 1963-; Methacton Ed Assn VP 1988-; Natl Endowment for Hum Grant Beaver Coll 1986; *office:* Methacton HS Kriebel Mill Rd Fairview Village PA 19403

ULRICH, SHARON ANN, 5th/6th Grade & French Teacher; *b:* Honolulu, HI; *ed:* (BA) Elem Ed, TN Temple Univ Chattanooga 1977; *cr:* 3rd Grade/Fr Teacher Greenville Chrstn Acad 1977-80; Kndgtn/3rd Grade Teacher Norwood Chrstn Sch 1980-82; 1st/5th-6th Combined Class/5th Grade/Fr Teacher Faith Chrstn Sch 1982-; *ai:* Fr Club Spon & Adv; Published Sunday Sch Lit; *office:* Faith Chrstn Sch Russ Rd Greenville OH 45331

ULRIKSEN, JANICE, Chemistry & Physics Instructor; *b:* Oakpark, IL; *m:* John David; *ed:* (BA) Chem, Univ of WA 1966; (MA) Sci Ed, CA St Univ at Fullerton 1989; *cr:* Teacher/Dept Chairperson Bolsa Grande HS 1966-; Mentor Teacher Garden Grove Unified Sch Dist 1984-; Teacher Coast Line Comm Coll 1986-; *ai:* Coord Western Assn of Schls & Colls 1990; WASC Accreditation Report; Sci Dept Chairperson; Sci Mentor Teacher; Sci Olympics Coach; Sci & Math Club Adv; Orange Cty Sci Ed Assn, Amer Chemical Society; Univ of CA Irvine; NSF Mentor Teacher Recipient of Orange Cty Sci Educators Awd for Excl 1989; *office:* Bolsa Grande HS 9401 Westminster Ave Garden Grove CA 92644

ULSH, E. JANE, Social Studies Teacher; *b:* Pottsville, PA; *m:* Roger; *ed:* (BS) Scndry Ed/Soc Stud, Kutztown Univ 1982; *cr:* 5th-8th Grade Soc Stud/8th Grade Teacher St Ambrose Sch 1982-; *ai:* 8th Grade & Dance Club Advs; Talent Show, Natl Geography Week, GeograpHy Bee Coord; Phi Alpha Theta 1980-; Sch Cty Ballet Co 1978-83; Teacher of Yr St Ambrose Sch 1977; Graduated Sunna Cum Laude & Received Eugene Grossman Awd; Received Awd from Local Vietnam Vets Work in Sch with Pow-mia Issue; *office:* St Ambrose Sch 302 Randel St Schuylkill Haven PA 17972

ULVEN, BONNIE, Lang Art/Soc Sci Teacher; *b:* Le Mars, IA; *m:* Marvin E.; *c:* Mark, Matthew, Sara; *ed:* (BS) Soc Sci, Morningside Coll 1951; Hours Towards Masters; *cr:* Home Ec Teacher Soldier Public Sch 1951-53, Meriden Public Sch 1956-57; Home Ec/Soc Sci Teacher Paullina Cmmty Sch 1957-; *ai:* Jr Class Spon; Paullina Educators Assn 1957-; Daughters of Amer Revolution; Daughters of Colonies; Descendants of Mayflower; *home:* 514 E Green PO Box 517 Paullina IA 51046

UMBAUGH, JOYCE ANN, English Teacher; *b:* La Porte, IN; *m:* Dennis Roy; *c:* Dana, Jay; *ed:* (BS) Scndry Ed, Ball St Univ 1967; (MS) Scndry Ed, IN Univ 1975; *cr:* Eng Teacher Washington HS 1968-71; Substitute Teacher South Bend Sch Corporation 1971-72, Union-North Sch Corporation 1974-79; Eng Teacher John Glenn Sch Corporation 1980-; *ai:* Class & Pom Pon Spon; Newspaper Adv; NHS Advisory Comm; NEA, ISTA 1980-; John Glenn Teachers Assn (Building Rep 1980-81) 1989-; St Johns Luth Church Women VP 1975-80; GSA Leader 1976-79; *office:* John Glenn HS John Glenn Dr Walkerton IN 46574

UMBREIT, BONNIE MUIR, 8th Grade Bible Teacher; *b:* Wilkes Barre, PA; *m:* A. Dale; *c:* Gail Umbreit Moore, Timothy; *ed:* Bible/Religion, Philadelphia Coll of Bible; Montessori Spec Trng; *cr:* K-5th/Pre-1st Grade Teacher Castle Heights Acad 1974-80; 7th-8th Grade Bible Teacher Ind Presbyn 1978-79; 8th Grade Bible Teacher Calvary Day Sch 1980-90, Westminister Sch of Savannah 1990; *ai:* Natl Jr Honor Society Adv; Womens Propeller Club Intnl Chaplain; *office:* Westminster Sch of Savannah 6600 Howard Foss Dr Savannah GA 31412

UMSTEAD, TERRY LYNN, Jr HS Mathematics Teacher; *b:* Nebraska City, NE; *m:* Laura Grinder; *c:* Jennifer, Matthew, Seth Wilson; *ed:* (AA) Liberal Arts, Moorpark Jr Coll 1971; (BS) Math, CA Poly San Luiz Obispo 1973; QUEST Trainer; Heres Looking at You Trainee; NLP Practitioner; Scuba Diving Instruction; Yes & Impact Drug Trainer; *cr:* Math Teacher Paso Robles HS 1973-74, Debney Park HS 1974-77; Phys Ed/Math Teacher Pajaro Valley Unified Sch Dist 1977-82; Math Teacher San Lorenzo Valley Jr HS 1982-; *ai:* Surfing, Cross Cntry, Track, Wrestling Coach; ATAP Dir; Sports Adv; Graduation Comm; Cal Poly VP Math Club 1973-74, Camera Club 1972-73; Capher X-Cntry Rep 1973-74; Wrestling Club VP 1979-81; *home:* 322 Plateau Ave Santa Cruz CA 95060

UNDERBERGER, CAROL R., English Teacher; *b:* Bay City, CA; *ed:* (BA) Eng, Univ of CA Berkeley 1973; (MA) Ed, San Francisco St Univ 1974; *cr:* Teacher of Blind/Partially Sighted Rowland Unified Sch Dist 1975-78; Eng Teacher Alvarado Intermediate 1978-85, Rowland HS 1985-; *ai:* Yrbk & Newspaper Adv; CTA (Public Information Officer 1987-, Treas 1985-87); *office:* John A Rowland HS 200 S Otterbein Rowland Heights CA 91748

UNDERDOWN, JOY, Third Grade Teacher; *b:* Boston, MA; *ed:* (AA) Child Stud, 1954, (BA) Elem Ed, 1972 Stephens Coll; (MED) Curr/Instruction, Univ of MO Columbia 1974; Grad Stud; *cr:* Kndgtn/1st Grade Teacher Buckley Sch 1955-57, 1966-70; Nursery/Kndgtn Teacher John Thomas Dye Sch 1959-63; Kndgtn Teacher Palm Valley Sch 1963-66; 3rd Grade Teacher Fairview Elem Sch 1974-; *ai:* Sch & Cmmty Partnership Steering Comm; NSTA; Cncl for Elem Sci Intnl Treas 1982-86; Phi Delta Kappa Treas 1981-82; Delta Kappa Gamma; Pi Lambda Theta Pres 1974-76, Certificate of Merit for Service 1975; Amer Assn of Univ Women; Columbia Cmmty Teachers Assn Teacher of Yr 1978-79; Univ of MO Columbia Citation of Merit for Distinguished Service to Ed 1984; *home:* 2610 Wee Wynd Columbia MO 65203

UNDERKOFFLER, TERRY MARVIN, Teacher/Computer Coordinator; *b:* Allentown, PA; *m:* Theresa Ulrich; *c:* Tommy, Michael, Susan; *ed:* (BA) Ed, Kutztown Univ 1977; Grad Work Kutztown Univ; *cr:* Teacher Methacton Sch Dist 1977-; *ai:* Cmptr Coord; Safety Patrol Spon; HS Soccer Var Coach; NEA 1977-; SPSCAA Coach 1980, Coach of Yr 1988; Cousteau Society 1976-; USYSA Soccer Regional Coach 1979-; EPYSA St Staff Coach 1979-; Methacton Mini Grant for Word Processing Cooperative Learning in Interface; *office:* Methacton Sch Dist 232 Level Rd Collegeville PA 19426

UNDERWOOD, GLENDENE KALERNER, 5th/6th Grade English Teacher; *b:* Fredericksburg, TX; *m:* Tim D.; *c:* Dave; *ed:* (BS) Elem Ed, TX Tech Univ 1970; Cmptr Literacy, TX St Bd of Ed; *cr:* 4th Grade Teacher Mason Elem 1970-71; 5th/6th Grade Teacher Mason Elem & Jr HS 1971-; *ai:* UIL Ready Writing Coach; Career Ladder Comm 1988-; TX Joint Cncl Teachers of Eng, NCTE; Delta Kappa Gamma; Assn of TX Prof Educators; TX Tech Ex-Stus Assn; Alpha Beta Psi; TX Career Ladder Level 3 1988-; *home:* PO Box 752 Mason TX 76856

UNDERWOOD, MARILYN SUE, 6th Grade Teacher; *b:* Plymouth, IN; *m:* David; *c:* Dustin; *ed:* (BS) Elem Ed, IN St Univ 1975; (MS) Elem Ed, IN Univ 1979; Endorsement in Soc Work; *cr:* Teachers Aide Washington Elem 1975; Kndgtn/1st/5th/6th Grade Teacher Oregon-Davis Elem 1975-; *ai:* Lang Spelling Textbook Adoption Comm; Jr Great Books Certified Leader; Inst of Creative Ed Instr; Certified Instr of Lions Quest Skills for Adolescence Prgm; Building Intervention Team Chm; Oregon-Davis Classroom Teachers Assn, IN St Teachers Assn, NEA, Intnl Rdng Assn; Marshall Cty Rdng Cncl (Bd Mem, Building Rep, Coord) 1988-; NIPSCO Sci Grant 1987; *office:* Oregon-Davis Elem Sch RR 2 Box 51 Hamlet IN 46532

UNDERWOOD, PEGGY SUE (CARTER), Advanced English I Teacher; *b:* Shreveport, LA; *m:* Charley B.; *c:* Ellen Sue Underwood Ormes, Carey B.; *ed:* (BA) Eng/Ed, LA Coll 1960; Grad Courses; *cr:* Eng Teacher Hogg Jr HS 1960-61, St Francisville HS 1961-62; His/Rdng/Eng Teacher River Oaks Sch 1972-80; Civics/Lang Art/Eng Teacher Jack Hayes Jr HS 1980-84; Advanced Eng Teacher Ouachita HS 1984-; *ai:* Co-Spon NHS Comm; Textbook; Chrldr, Curr, Stu Cncl, Pep Squad Spon; Kappa Kappa Iota (Secy, VP) 1970-; NCTE; Began Rdng Lab for River Oaks Sch Jr & HS.

UNDERWOOD, ROBERT DEAN, English Teacher; *b:* Abilene, TX; *ed:* (BA) Eng, San Francisco St Coll 1966; Grad Stud Adolescent Lit, Discipline With Dignity, Suicide Prevention; Teacher Credential Eng, San Francisco St Coll 1968; *cr:* Eng Teacher Will C Wood Jr HS 1968-69; Eng/His Teacher Davis HS 1969-73; Rdng/Eng Teacher Saunders Tech & Trade HS 1974-76; Eng/His Teacher Niwot HS 1978-; *ai:* Sch Athletic Mgr; Knowledge Trivia Bowl; Chess Club; Sch Team; Onward to Excl Team; Cco/Ala Curr Writer; Sch Bsktbl, Gymnastics, Wrestling, Ftbl, Track, Vlybl Sports Announcer, Timer, Bookkeeper; Phi Delta Kappa 1968-; *office:* Niwot HS 8989 E Niwot Rd Longmont CO 80501

UNDERWOOD, SUSAN GEBSTADT, Mathematics Department Chair; *b:* Flint, MI; *m:* James M. Jr.; *c:* James M. III; *ed:* (BA) His/Ed, MI St Univ 1966; Grad Stud CA St Long Beach, CSUN; *cr:* 6th Grade Teacher Livonia Public Schls; 4th Grade Teacher Los Angeles Unified Dist; 7th/8th Grade Teacher Lancaster Sch Dist; *ai:* Academic Olympics Knowledge Master Club; Lancer Dance Team; Math Dept Chairperson; Phi Delta Kappa; BSA (Den Mother 1971-81, Weblo Asst), Service Pin 1981; *office:* Park View Intermediate Sch 808 W Avenue J Lancaster CA 93534

UNDSETH, STEVEN PAUL, English Dept Chairman; *b:* Minneapolis, MN; *m:* Lois Blikstad; *c:* Trevor, Joseph; *ed:* (BA) Lang Art/Soc Sci/Ed, W OR St Coll 1981; *cr:* Eng Instr Hillcrest Luth Acad 1982-; *ai:* Jr Class & Yrbk Adv; NCTE 1982-; Phi Kappa Phi 1981-; *office:* Hillcrest Luth Acad 815 W Vernon Ave Fergus Falls MN 56537

UNGER, CYNTHIA JANE (BRANDT), Fourth Grade Teacher; *b:* Frankfort, IN; *m:* Jon R.; *c:* Jill S.; *ed:* (BS) Elem Ed, 1973, (MA) Elem Ed, 1977 Ball St Univ; *cr:* 4th Grade Teacher Daleville Cmmty Schls 1973-; *ai:* Organized Daleville Elem Little Hoosiers; Delaware Cty Rdng Cncl 1988-; Kappa Kappa Sigma Historian 1990-; *home:* 8601 W Tulip Tree Dr Muncie IN 47304

UNGER, LOLITA SEGHETTI, Fourth Grade Teacher; *b:* Oak Park, IL; *m:* Kenneth N.; *c:* Nancy; *ed:* (BA) Sociology, Univ of IL 1948; (MA) Ed, Northwestern Univ 1955; *cr:* 5th/6th/8th Grade Teacher Longfellow Sch 1953-59; 6th-7th Grade Teacher L J Hauser Jr HS 1972-83; 4th Grade Teacher Blythe Park Sch 1984-; *ai:* Chicago Motor Club Patrol Spon; Pi Lambda Theta 1955; W Suburban Rdng Cncl Treas 1974-75; Amer Assn of Univ Women Pres 1984-86; Amer Assn of Univ Women Educl Fnds Prgm Honoree 1987; *home:* 195 Olmsted Rd Riverside IL 60546

UNGER, ROBERTA MARIE (RANDOLPH), Spec Ed Teacher; *b:* Oakland, CA; *m:* William Mitchell Jr.; *c:* Diana M. Holt, William M. III; *ed:* (BA) Ed, San Francisco St Coll 1965; (MA) Ed Admin, WV Univ 1984; Eng & Spec Ed, WV Univ 1971-; Spec Ed, UT St Univ 1966-67, 1973, 1986; Ed, Frostburg St Coll 1973, 1984; *cr:* 2nd Grade Elem Teacher North Park Elem 1965-67; 4th-8th Grade Spec Ed Teacher Centre Street Sch 1967-68; 3rd Grade Teacher Dennett Road Elem Sch 1968-69; 2nd/3rd Grade Teacher Grantsville Elem Sch 1969-70; Undergrad/Grad Spec Ed Supervising Teacher WV Univ 1973-76; K-12th Grade Spec Ed Teacher Short Gap Elem Sch 1970-77; 5th-9th Grade Gifted Ed Summer Satelite Prgm Teacher Frostburg St Coll 1985; 3rd-12th Grade Teacher Mineral Cty Fostering Gifted Ed Summer Prgm 1985-86; Spec Ed Teacher Frankfort HS 1977-; *ai:* Spec Olympics Ski Instr; AFS, OM Ski Club; Classics Club Spon; WV St OM Champion Team World Competition 1987-88; Sch Spon; Amer Field Service; Team Coach for Odyssey of Mind & Jr Engineering Tech Society; Acceleration & Remediation Comm Chairwoman; Mentally Retarded Curr Comm; SEERS Comm; Cty Rdng Comm; Jr Class Play; NEA, WVEA, MCEA Building Rep 1973-75; CEC (Mem, Delegate Natl Convention to Toronto 1990); WV DLD (VP, Membership Chairperson, Pres Elect, Pres 1990); Allegany & Mineral Cty Historical Society, Cmmty Concert Assn, Allied Arts Cncl, St Thomas Womans Study Group, Northern Maidu Tribe of CA Indians; Mooretown Rancheria, Amer Indian Society of Washington DC; Emmanuel Episcopal Church Mem; Awarded WV St Competitive Grant 1990; WV Minigrant Innovative Classroom Instruction 1985, 1987, 1990; Mineral Cty Exemplary Teacher Status 1986-87, 1989; Natl & WV CEC Conference Presenter 1984-89; Past Elected Mem Cty Continuing Ed Comm; *home:* Box 307 Patterson Creek WV 26753

UNGERMAN, ROSANNA WEEKS, Grade Drama Dept Chair; *b:* Provo, UT; *m:* Mark D.; *c:* Alexander, Andrew; *ed:* (BA) Theatre Ed, Brigham Young Univ 1981; *cr:* Eng/Drama/Hum Teacher Mountain View HS 1981-83; Drama/Stu Government/Eng Teacher Provo HS 1983-; *ai:* Drama Club, Stu Government Assemblies Adv; AFT 1981-82; NEA 1983-84; UT Ed Assn 1983-84; Sandgren Sounds Civic Choir Secy 1989; Recording Artist, Best Actress UT Valley Theatre Guild 1986; *office:* Provo HS 1125 N University Ave Provo UT 84604

UNRUH, MARY ANNE, 3rd Grade Teacher; *b:* Winstead, CT; *m:* Arch; *c:* Jim, Jon, Joe, Jannele; *ed:* (BA) Elem Ed, Goshen Coll 1953; Psych & Music Trng; *cr:* Teacher Trailwood Elem 1969-; *ai:* Friends of Art Nelson Gallery Membership; Nom D O Connor Teaching Awd; Nom Excl in Teaching Awd; Environmental Curr Published; *office:* Trailwood Elem Sch 5101 W 95th St Overland Park KS 66207

UNSELD, BARBARA KING, Social Studies Teacher; *b:* Huntsville, AL; *m:* Reginald B.; *c:* Stephanie, Monica; *ed:* (BA) His, E KY Univ 1973; (MED) Spec Ed, Univ of Louisville 1978; *cr:* Teacher T T Knight Mid Sch 1973-76, Jefferson Cty Traditional Mid Sch 1976-; *ai:* Stu Cncl Co-Spon; Management Team; Resource Teacher KY Beginning Teachers Internship Prgm; Oasis Team Leader; NEA, KEA, JCTA; Green Castle Baptist Church; *office:* Jefferson Cty Traditional Sch 1418 Morton Ave Louisville KY 40204

UPCHURCH, RENEE JOYALINE, Mathematics Department Chair; *b:* Denton, TX; *ed:* (BS) Math/Phys Ed, 1980, (MS) Admin/Phys Ed, 1989 TX A&I Univ; Drivers Ed Cert; Grad Stud; *cr:* Math Teacher San Diego Ind Sch Dist 1980-83, San Antonio Ind Sch Dist 1983-84, San Diego Ind Sch Dist 1984-; *ai:* UIL Math Spon; Jr HS Bsktbl, HS Var Vlybl, HS Jr Var Bsktbl Coach; ISTA 1980-; Mini Thesis; *office:* San Diego Ind Sch Dist 609 Labbe Ave San Diego TX 78384

UPTON, BARBARA LYNNE, Jr HS Mathematics Teacher; *b:* Windsor, MO; *ed:* (BSE) Elem Ed/Jr HS Math, Cntrl MO St Univ 1981; Curr/Instruction, Cntrl MO St Univ 1990; *cr:* Jr HS Math Teacher Wellington-Napoleon R-9 1981-; *ai:* HS Vlybl Coach; Class Spon; MSTA; *office:* Wellington-Napoleon R-9 Hwy 131 Wellington MO 64097

UPTON, LORRAINE COHEN, Third Grade Teacher; *b:* Baltimore, MD; *m:* Michael K.; *c:* Matthew C.; *ed:* (BS) Elem Ed, Boston Univ 1969; (MED) Psych of Rdng, Temple Univ 1974; Post Masters Studies Univ of Arts Archaelogy/Drama/Colonial Stud; East Stroudsburg; *cr:* 3rd Grade Teacher Boston Public Sch 1969-70; Neshaminy Sch Dist 1972-; *ai:* Mem Lang Art Comm; Peer Coaching Prgm; Dist Soc Stud Comm Mem; Boston Uvin 1968 Harold C Case Schlsp Awd; Intnl Rdng Assn Mem 1987-; 1989 Whos Who in Amer Ed; Published Work in Instructor Mazagine/The Rdng Teacher & Teacher Magazine; Cultural & Social Outreach Prgms; *home:* 5 Beechwood Ln Yardley PA 19067

URBICK, ROBERT J., 6th Grade Teacher; *b:* Hibbing, MN; *m:* Patricia J. Jonell; *c:* Joseph, Jill, Susan, Jessica, Nicholas; *ed:* (BS) Ed, Univ of MN-Duluth 1965; (MA) Admin, Univ of WI-Superior 1970-; *cr:* 6th Grade Teacher Lakeside Schl 1965-70; 5th & 6th Grades Teacher Park Point Sch 1970-80; Math-Sci Teacher Arrowhead Juvenile Center 1980-82; 6th Grade Teacher Homecroft Sch 1982-; *ai:* Sch Cmptr Coord; Audio Visual Coord; Finance Comm Mem for ISD 709 Budget; Math Curr Comm; Duluth Teacher of Yr 1975; AFT 1965- Union Rep; *home:* 5324 Oakley St Duluth MN 55804

URBIN, CHRISTINE A., Art Teacher; *b:* Schuylkill Haven, PA; *m:* Robert; *c:* Christl Zaccagnino; *ed:* (BSED) Art, 1960, (MSED) Art, 1967 Kutztown Univ; *cr:* Art Teacher Minisink Valley 1960-69; Substitute Art Teacher 1969-70; Art Teacher Ft Plain Cntrl 1970-; *office:* Ft Plain Cntrl Sch West St Fort Plain NY 13339

URCIUOLI, ROBERT JOHN, Science Teacher; *b:* Jersey City, NJ; *m:* Karen Pawelek; *ed:* (BA) Sci Ed, 1967, (MA) Sci Ed, 1973 Jersey City St; Grad Stud; *cr:* Sci Teacher Kawameeh Jr HS 1967-; *ai:* Union Township Fed of Teachers 1967-80; Union Township Educl Assn 1980-; NJ Ed Assn, NEA 1967-; Mini Grant Union Bd of Ed; Testimonial Resolution Bsbl Coach Union Township; Assembly Resolution Coach; *office:* Kawameeh Jr HS Union NJ 07083

URDAHL, KARLYN KESSLER, Home & Family Life Teacher; *b:* Bozeman, MT; *m:* Richard Marlowe; *c:* Richard T., Marlo M.; *ed:* (BA) Home Ec Ed, MT St Univ 1974; Working on Drug Alcohol Counseling Cert; *cr:* Home Ec/Phys Ed/Soc Stud Teacher Cheney Jr HS 1974-; *ai:* FHA & Natural Helpers Adv; Vlybl, Gymnastics, Orchesis Coach; Jr HS Drama Costume Designer; Spokane Home & Family Teachers Organization Chm 1987; Cheney Ed Assn, WA Educators Assn 1974-; WA Voc Assn 1982-; Beta Sigma Phi 1978-79; Campfire Leader 1986; Luth Church Sunday Sch Teacher 1988-89; Curr Design Chairperson Cheney Jr HS Accreditation Process; *office:* Cheney Jr HS 2716 N 6th Cheney WA 99004

U REN, GERI PALZKILL, Kindergarten Teacher; *b:* Belmont, WI; *m:* Ron; *c:* Sean, Tasha, Kirk; *ed:* (BS) Presch/Kngtn, UW Madison 1968; (MA) Elem Ed, UW Platteville 1972; UW Plattville; *cr:* Kngtn Teacher 1968-73; 1st Grade Teacher 1973-82; Kndgtn Teacher 1982-Darlington Sch; *ai:* DEA (Sec/Treas 1971-72/Pres 1978-79); Local/Area/St & NEA 1968-; Music Bstrs (VP 1988-89/Pres 1989-); Coll for Kids (Bd of Dir) 1979-80; Humpty Dumpty Presch (Bd of Dir) 1976-80; *office:* Darlington Cmmty Schls 627 N Main Darlington WI 53530

URIBE-CANO, GRACIE, Fifth Grade Teacher; *b:* Alice, TX; *m:* Noel S. Cano; *ed:* (MS) Elem Ed; (MA) Elem Ed/Rdng, 1982 TX a & I; *cr:* 3rd Grade Teacher Freer Elem 1979-84; 5th Grade Teacher Norman Thomas Elem 1984-; *ai:* Picture Memory UIL

Coach; TSTA VP 1988-; Delta Kappa Gamma Sec 1986-88; PTA Pres 1988-; Catholic Daughter of Amer Pres 1989-; CCD 4th Grade 1984-; *home:* P O Box 853 Freer TX 78357

USELTON, BILL W., European History Teacher; *b:* Oklahoma City, OK; *m:* Catherine Sue Hutchings; *c:* Kelly I.; *ed:* (AA) His Ed, Rose St Coll 1980; (BA) His Ed, Central St Univ 1982; *cr:* OK His/US His/Enrichment Teacher Choctaw Jr HS 1984-85; Ancient/Med European His/US His Teacher Choctaw Sr HS 1986-; *ai:* Chess Club; Philosophy Comm; Inst for Legislative Action, S Youngs Baptist Church Mem 1987-89; Natl Rifle Assn Life Mem 1987-89; Articles Written for Several Papers; *office:* Choctaw Sr HS 14300NE 10th Choctaw OK 73020

USERY, GWEN R., 12th Grade English Teacher; *b:* Camden, AR; *m:* Billy Ray; *c:* Stephen, Gary, Angel Usery Black; *ed:* (BA) Eng, Univ of Ozarks 1977; Eng, AR Tech Univ; Prgm for Effective Teachers; Laubach Literacy Trng; *cr:* 12th Grade Eng Teacher Clarksville HS 1977-78; Soc Stud Teacher Clarksville Mid Sch 1978-79; 12th Grade Eng Teacher Clarksville HS 1979-; *ai:* Chm Sr Class Spons; Stud Cncl Spon; Quiz Bowl Coach; NEA, AEA, CTA, NCTM; First Baptist Church Librarian 1975-82; Grant AR Writing Project 1983; Teacher of Month 1990; Tutor Laubach Literacy Prgm; *office:* Clarksville HS 1701 Clark Rd Clarksville AR 72830

USIFER, PETER JOSEPH, Science Teacher; *b:* Beacon, NY; *m:* Barbara Jean Sitler; *c:* Lori, Kyle, Teri; *ed:* (AA) Liberal Art, Dutchess Comm Coll 1963; (BA) Bio, SUNY Cortland 1966; (MS) Bio/Ed, SUNY New Paltz 1970; *cr:* Sci Teacher Arlington HS 1966-; Anatomy/Physiology Teacher Dutchess Cmmty Coll 1982-; *ai:* Soph Class Adv; Golf Coach; Gifted & Talented Stu Organization Comm; NABT, NYS Conservation 1970-; Hudson Valley Green 1980-; Local Little League Coach 1983-; *office:* Arlington HS Rt 55 Lagrangeville NY 12540

USNIK, PATRICIA ANN, Mathematics Teacher; *b:* Johnstown, PA; *ed:* (BS) Math, Univ of Pittsburgh 1973; (MA) Math Ed, WV Univ 1979; Accounting, Potomac St Coll; Math, Sci, Cmptr, Davis & Elkins Coll; *cr:* Substitute Teacher Forest HillS HS 1973-74; Math Teacher Parsons HS 1974-78, Parsons Elem Mid Sch 1978-82, Tucker Cty HS 1982-; *ai:* Class Spon; Homecoming Co-Chairperson; Ticket Seller Continuing Ed Cncl Mem; JTPA after Sch Tutor; WV Cncl Teachers of Math, NCTM, WV Ed Assn, NEA; Tucker Cty Ed Assn Exec Comm Mem 1986-89; Our Lady of Mercy Cath Church; *office:* Tucker Cty HS Rt 1 Hambleton WV 26269

USRY, JACKIE NEELY, 8th Grade Math & His Teacher; *b:* Jackson, MS; *m:* Thomas Stephen; *c:* Stephen C., Thomas J., Micah Chase; *ed:* (BS) Elem Ed, Belhaven Coll 1980; *cr:* 7th Grade Soc Stud Teacher Mc Laurin Jr HS 1980-81; 8th Grade US His Teacher 1981-85; 8th Grade US His/Math Teacher 1988- Richland Attendance Center; *ai:* Natl Jr Beta Club Spon; *office:* Richland Attendance Center 1202 Hwy 49 So Richland MS 39218

USSERY, EVELYN GUEST, 8th Grade Math Teacher; *b:* Lott, TX; *m:* Glen H.; *c:* David, Stephen, Paul; *ed:* (BA) Elem Ed, 1969; (MA) Elem Ed, 1975 Univ of Houston; *cr:* Math Teacher Bay City Jr HS 1969-; *ai:* Mathcounts - Coach; Gulf Coast Cncl of Teachers of Math Treas 1978-89; *home:* 119 Kingswood Dr Van Vleck TX 77482

USSERY, HELEN OUTON, 5th Grade Teacher; *b:* Clarksville, TX; *m:* Dean; *c:* Randy, Mike, Terry; *ed:* (BS) Elem Ed, Univ of N TX 1955; Gifted Ed, TX Womens Univ; *cr:* 5th Grade Teacher Cedar Hill Elem Sch 1955-56; 4th Grade Teacher Irving Ind Schls; 5th Grade Teacher Shultz, J R Good; 6th Grade Teacher A S Johnston/Lee Britain; *ai:* TX St Teachers Assn; *home:* 1500 Upton Pl Irving TX 75060

USSERY, SALLY DOMINEY, Fifth Grade Teacher; *b:* Vienna, GA; *m:* Joseph Theron Jr.; *ed:* (BS) Elem Ed, 1969, (MED) Elem Ed, 1973 GA Coll; Trained as Data Collector & Supvr of Stu Teachers; *cr:* 2nd Grade Teacher 1969-75, 5th Grade Teacher 1975- Mattie Wells; *ai:* Textbook Selection & Sch Sunshine Comm; 5th Grade Chm 1975-84; PAGE; PTA Legislative Chairperson 1989-; Childrens Hospital-Medical Center (Advokids 1989-, Fairy Godmother 1989); Macon Jr Womans Club (2nd VP, Corresponding Secy, Dept Chairperson) 1975-84; Partner in Nutrition Awd; Trained Stu Teachers; *office:* Mattie Wells Elem Sch Rt 6 Box 272R Macon GA 31211

USZENSKI, WALTER, Special Ed Teacher; *b:* Jersey City, NJ; *m:* Maureen T. Mc Elroy; *c:* Carrianne, Jacqueline, Ryan; *ed:* (BA) Spec Ed, 1974, (MA) Spec Ed, 1981 Jersey City St Coll; Math & Psych; Admins Certificate; Math Credits, Jersey City St Coll & Kean Coll; *cr:* Teacher 1973-81, Vice Prin 1980-81, Prin 1981-89 St James Sch; Teacher Colonial HS 1989-; *ai:* Asst Boys Var Bsktbl Coach; NCTM 1978; Educl Leadership 1975; NEA, NJEA 1989; NAEP 1980; Knights of Columbus Mem 1971-; Woodbridge Elks Mem 1978-; Woodbridge Emergency Squad Mem 1985-88; All Cty Bsktbl, 2nd Team All St Bsktbl; Citizenship of Month Awd; MVP Awd 1970; Honor Carrier for Local Newspaper Voc Grant; Whos Who Outstanding Young Men in America 1982; *office:* Colonia HS East St Colonia NJ 07067

UTHOFF, ANTOINETTE MARIA, English Teacher; *b:* Long Beach, CA; *m:* Stephen; *ed:* (BA) Eng, UCLA 1987; Credential Prgm CA St Univ; *cr:* Eng Teacher Pius X HS 1987-; *ai:* Natl Cath Teachers 1987-; *office:* Pius X H S 7851 Gardendale Downey CA 90242

UTTER, PATRICIA WEIGEL, Business Department Chair; *b:* Akron, OH; *m:* Robert; *c:* Matthew; *ed:* (BA) Bus, 1965, (MA) Bus Ed, 1972, Ed Specialist Bus Ed, 1980 MI St Univ; Cmptr Classes, Counseling Family Difficulties, Drugs, Suicides, Abuse Courses, ITIP Classes; *cr:* Teacher Morrice Area Schls 1965-66, Everett HS 1966-73; Instr Lansing Comm Coll 1974-76; Counseling Coord Lansing Sch Dist 1977-81; Bus Dept Chairperson Everett HS 1982-; *ai:* Chairperson City Wide Steering Comm; OEA Adv; Schlsp Comm; Delta Pi Epsilon (Pres Comm 1981) 1967-; Pi Omega Pi Pres 1964-66, Outstanding MSU Undergrad 1965; NBEA, MEA 1965-, Convention Speaker 1979-82; Bus & Prof Women Guild Bd Mem; YWCA Advisory Bd; BSA Dist Comm; Consultant on Sex Equity to Various Sch Dist & MS Univ; *office:* Everett HS 3900 Stabler St Lansing MI 48910

UYEDA, SHARON, Resource Specialist/Spec Ed; *b:* San Jose, CA; *ed:* (BA) Natural Sci, San Jose St Univ 1968; Ryan Learning Handicapped & Rdng Specialist Credential; *cr:* 1st-4th Grade Classroom Teacher Ruskin & Birchwood & Brooktree Schls 1969-83; Rdng Specialist Summerdale Sch 1983-85; Resource Specialist Vinci Park & Brooktree Schls 1985-; *ai:* Santa Clara Cty Rdng Cncl Recording Secy 1989-; ASCD; Japanese Amer Citizens League Bd Mem 1982-; Classroom Teacher Instructional Improvement Grant; Mentor Teacher; *home:* 3566 Barley Ct San Jose CA 95127

UZZELL, MELBA SMITH, First Grade Teacher Chair; *b:* Goldsboro, NC; *m:* J. P.; *c:* Kenyatta, Kamala; *ed:* (BS) Elem Ed, Fayetteville St Univ 1965; (MA) Early Chldhd, E Carolina Univ 1981; Certificate of Advance Study E Carolina Univ 1983; *cr:* 2nd Grade Teacher Carver HS 1965-68; 3rd Grade Teacher Mount Olive Elem 1968-70; 2nd Grade Teacher Brogden & Meadow Lane 1970-73; 1st Grade Teacher Eastern Wayne Elem 1973-; *ai:* Senate Bill, Southern Assn, Curr Comm; NCAE, NEA; Phi Delta Kappa; Kappa Delta Pi; Alpha Kappa Alpha (Financial Secy 1970-74, Grammateus 1974-76); Eastern Wayne Elem Teacher of Yr.

V

VACCARP, ELAINE BULLOCK, Librarian; *b:* San Marcos, TX; *m:* Andrew Edwin Jr.; *c:* Aaron A., Micah E.; *ed:* (BSE) Elem Ed, Univ of AR Fayetteville 1975; (MSE) Early Chldhd Ed, AR St Univ 1979; Working Towards Masters Lib, Media, Information Technologies; *cr:* Kndgtn Teacher De Witt Public Schls 1975-76; 2nd Grade Teacher Forrest City Public Schls 1976-77; Kndgtn Teacher 1977-80, Librarian 1980-82, 1983- Marianna Public Schls; *ai:* Support Team, Governance, Management, Staff Dev Comm; Delta Kappa Gamma 1988-; PTA (VP, Treas) 1987-; *office:* Whitten Elem Sch 175 Walnut St Marianna AR 72360

VACHA, FAYE REBMAN, 6th Grade Teacher; *b:* Lodi, OH; *c:* James S., John F., Joseph E., Jerald J.; *ed:* Cadet Certificate Elem Ed, 1962, (BS) Elem Ed, 1976 OH Univ; (MED) Gifted Ed, Ashland Coll 1989; Supervision Cert, Ashland Univ; *cr:* 6th Grade Teacher Lodi Elem 1964-65; Title/Rdng Teacher Apple Creek Elem 1976-77; 5th Grade Teacher Dalton Elem 1977-89; 6th Grade Teacher Dalton Intermediate 1989-; *ai:* 7th & 8th Girls Vlybl Coach; Enrichment Acad Teacher of Cmptrs; Various Comm; Sci Olympiad Coach; Elemsch Newspaper; OAGC 1988-; ASCD 1989-; OEA, NEA 1977-; OH Cncl for Soc Stud 1989-; Martha Holden Jennings Fnd Grant 1988; OH Edison Grant 1987; *office:* Dalton Intermediate Sch 151 W Main St Dalton OH 44618

VADALA, JOESEPH D., 5th Grade Teacher; *b:* Troy, NY; *m:* Judith Franke; *c:* Adam Walter; *ed:* (BS) Bus Admin, NY St Univ 1966; (MS) Ed Admin, IL St Univ 1977; Univ of VA/George Mason Univ; *cr:* Teacher Fairfax Cty VA Public Schls 1972-74; Mc Leon Cty Unit 5 Schls 1974-; *ai:* NEA 1972-; ILEA 1974-; Unit 5 EA 1974-.

VAFFIS, CAROL FEICK, Third Grade Teacher; *b:* Toledo, OH; *m:* Peter James; *c:* Christopher, Shannon, Jonathon; *ed:* (BSED) Elem Ed, OH Univ 1969; Grad Ed, Univ of Toledo; *cr:* 2nd Grade Teacher Green Springs Elem 1968-69; 2nd Grade Teacher 1969-71, 5th Grade Teacher 1971-79, 3rd Grade Teacher 1979- Atkinson Elem; *ai:* Surrogate Prin; FEA, OEA, NEA; *office:* Atkinson Elem Sch 1100 Delaware St Fremont OH 43420

VAHEY, REGINA GRANT, Mathematics Department Chair; *b:* New York, NY; *m:* Harry M.; *ed:* (BA) Math, Georgian Court Coll 1968; (MA) Math, OH St Univ 1971; Trenton St Coll, Shenadoah Coll, Music Conservatory; *cr:* 3rd Grade Teacher St James Grammar Sch 1956-59; Math Teacher Red Bank Cath HS 1959-66; Math Teacher/Dept Chairperson Notre Dame HS 1966-72, Holy Cross HS 1972-; *ai:* NHS Adv; Peer Tutor Moderator; Review of Policy Comm Chairperson; NCTM 1963-; NJ Assn of Math Teachers 1960-, 25 Yrs Service Citation; Natl Assn of Stu Activity Advs 1986-; NCEA 1982-; CCD Teacher; Natl Sci Fnd In-Service Grants; Diocesian Citation for Yrs of Service; *office:* Holy Cross HS Rt 130 Delranco NJ 08075

VAHSEN, FAUSTENA FRADD, Science Teacher; *b:* San Diego, CA; *m:* George Martin; *c:* David Martin, Cathleen Faustena, Sharon Vahsen Sicher, Steven S., James J.; *ed:* (BA) Pre-Sch Ed, Hood Coll 1953; (MA) Ed, Loyola Trinity & Western MD 1988; *cr:* K-9th Grade Substitute Teacher Schls IN, HI, CT, VA & MD 1967-84; Permanent Substitue Teacher 1984-85; Sci Teacher 1985- Magothy River; *ai:* Intramural Dir; Faculty Cncl Chairperson; Interdisciplinary Team Chairperson; Anne Arundel Recreation Dept Leader Of Umpiring Clinic 1987-; Spon Midshipmen U S Naval Acad; Navy Wife of Yr 1970; Anne Arundel Cty Teacher of Yr 1988-89; Interviewed on Good Morning America CBS 1989; Interviewed on Evening Magazine & PM Magazine TV 1986; Naval Institute Proceedings Blacks in White Hats; *home:* 313 Halsey Rd Annapolis MD 21401

VAILLANCOURT, HOWARD V., English Teacher; *b:* St Cloud, MN; *ed:* (BS) Lang Art, St Cloud St Univ 1969; Speech/Eng/Ed/Ed Admin, St Cloud St Univ, Coll of St Thomas, Univ of Luverne 1969-; *cr:* Scndry Eng/Drama Instr Princeton Public Schls 1969-; *ai:* Fine Arts Curr Evaluation Comm Mem 1983-84; Var Speech, Asst Jr Var Speech Head Coach; Dir Frosh Drama Prgm 1971-90; Jr HS Speech Chm; Princeton HS Marching Band (Founder, Dir, Auxiliary Unit, Colorguard 1970-77, Advisory Bd Mem 1977-); NHS Adv 1987-; Cntrl MN Speech Coaches Assn Founding Mem 1970-; MN Speech Coaches Assn Mem 1985-; Princeton Schlsp Fnd (Bd of Dir, Mem) 1989-; VFW Voice of Democracy Prgm Adv 1986-; Princeton Cmmty Theatre (Mem, Bd of Dir 1980-84, 1988-, Pres 1983-84) 1975-; *office:* Princeton HS 807 S 8th Ave Princeton MN 55371

VAIRA, MARY REHBEIN, 4-6th Grade Science Teacher; *b:* Sidney, MT; *m:* Collin; *c:* Gillette A.; *ed:* (BA) General Stud, Dawson Coll 1972; (BS) Elem Ed, Coll of Great Falls 1974; Minot St/Northern Eastern/Univ of ND; *cr:* 4th Grade Teacher Poplar Mid Schls 1974-76; 3-4th Grade Sci Teacher Fairview Migrant Prgm 1976 & 77 & 80-81; 3rd-4th Grade Teacher Fairview Consolidated 1976-82; 5th & 6th Grade Teacher Lambert Public 1982-; *ai:* Lambert Ed Assn Secy; Delta Kappa Gamma Music Chairperson 1980-82, 1st & 2nd VP of Theta 184-86/1986-88; Alpha Mu St Legislative Comm 1989-91; 4-H Springlake Steamers Organizational Leader 1977-81; 8th Grade Grad Speaker 1984; Commencement Speaker 1989; Presenter of Wkshp at Inservice Day in Wolf Point; *home:* Star Rt Box 21-F Lambert MT 59243

VAISA, THERESA LOBATO, Home Ec Teacher/Dept Chair; *b:* Santa Fe, NM; *m:* G. Michael; *c:* John M., Christopher, Melissa; *ed:* (BS) Home Ec Ed, NM St Univ 1976; (MED) Voc Home Ec/Voc Guidance/Counseling, CO St Univ 1980; *cr:* Home Ec Instr Socorro HS 1976-78; Facilitator CO St Univ 1979; Home Ec Instr/Asst Track Coach Lincoln Jr HS 1979-80; Career Ed Instr Alternative Learning Center 1979-80; Home Ec Instr Alameda Jr HS 1980-; *ai:* Home Ec Curr Coord & Dist Chairperson; NHS Co-Spon; Alameda Jr HS Mentor; Sch Improvement Prgm Chairperson; Omicron Tau Theta VP 1979, 1980; Stipend Natl Federal Voc Prgm Grad Leadership Dev Grant; *office:* Alameda Jr HS 450 La Madera Santa Fe NM 87501

VALADE, EDMOND JOSEPH, 11th-12th Grade His Teacher; *b:* Manchester, NH; *m:* Doris; *c:* Vincent, John, Judith Ayers; *ed:* (BA) His, St Anselm Coll 1959; (MS) His, Univ of NH 1967; Inst Non-Western His 1966; *cr:* His Teacher Somersworth HS 1959-62, Manchester Memorial HS 1963-; *ai:* Amnesty Intnl Club Adv; NHS Comm; Newcomb Writing Awd 1967; His Teacher Awd 1981; *home:* 35 Plimpton Rd Goffstown NH 03045

VALDEZ, JANNAY PARKINS, Government Teacher; *b:* Dallas, TX; *c:* Kevin, Kelly, Sidney; *ed:* (AS) Phys Ed, Mt View Dallas 1972; (BA) His, Univ of TX Arlington 1969; (MED) Spec Ed, 1981, (MED) Educl Admin, 1984, (MS) Scnry/Higher Ed, 1987 E TX St Univ; *cr:* Teacher Arlington Ind Sch Dist; Dean Hill Coll; Prin Kemp Ind Sch Dist; Dept Head De Soto Ind Sch Dist; Teacher Kaufman Ind Sch Dist; Teacher/Coach Garland Ind Sch Dist; *ai:* Bio Hiking Club; Hoop-D-Do Bsktbl; Phi Delta Kappa, Doctoral Stu Assn 1985-; TX Jr Coll Teachers Assn 1987-; Church 1970-; *home:* PO Box 3043 Desoto TX 75115

VALDEZ, LYDIA CARDENAS, 4th & 5th Grade Teacher; *b:* El Paso, TX; *m:* Raul; *c:* Raul A., Ruben G.; *ed:* (BS) Elem Ed, UTEP 1964; *cr:* Teacher Navarro Elem Sch 1964-65, Lamar Elem Sch 1965-74, Crockett Elem Sch 1974-75, Hillside Elem Sch 1975-; *ai:* Spelling Bee Coord; Stu with Rdng Disorders Teacher; Amer Assn of Univ Women Historian 1968; El Paso Teacher Assn Legislative Chm 1969; ACEI Secy 1970; Delta Kappa Gamma; NEA; Intnl Rdng Assn; St Josephs Altar Society 1988-; Outstanding Young Women of America 1970; *home:* 632 Loretto Rd El Paso TX 79903

VALDEZ, MARY ALICE MURRAY, Reading/Lang Arts Teacher; *b:* Carizzo Springs, TX; *m:* Jesse; *c:* Rachel, Omar; *ed:* (BA) Elem Ed/Eng, SUL Ross 1978; Grad Stud; *cr:* Teacher Carrizo Springs Mid Elem 1971-; *ai:* Lang Arts Dept Head; UIL Spelling Coach; *home:* 112 Old Eagle Pass Carrizo Springs TX 78834

VALDEZ, MAXINE CLEMMER, Spanish Teacher; *b:* Edmonton AB, Canada; *c:* Daniel, David, Victoria; *ed:* Span, Mexico City Coll 1951; (BA) Span, 1966, Credential Scndry Ed, 1968 Univ CA Riverside; Eng 2nd Lang Teaching Certificate, Univ of CA Riverside; Eng 2nd Lang Practice Teaching for Peace Corps, Memphis St Univ; *cr:* Span Teacher Norte Vista HS 1968-69, La Sierra HS 1969-80; Eng Teacher Karoti Girls Scndry Kenya E Africa 1980-81; Span Teacher La Sierra HS 1982-; *ai:* Span Club; Schlsp Comm; CA Teachers Assn, NEA 1982-; CA Foreign Lang Teachers Assn, Inland Empire Foreign Lang Assn

1989-; Sister City Assn of Riverside Coord Youth Exch for Mexico 1973-76; US Peace Corps Volunteer Eng Teacher 1980-81; *office:* La Sierra HS 4145 La Sierra Ave Riverside CA 92505

VALENTI, JOHN MICHAEL, Science Teacher; *b:* Bayshore, NY; *m:* Joyce Johnson; *c:* Serena, Genevieve; *ed:* (BS) Bio, 1972, (MSED) Sci Ed, 1975 St Univ Coll Cortland; Cardio Pulmonary Resuscitation, Advanced First Aid, Winter Emergency Care; *cr:* Sci/Math Teacher Marion Cntrl Sch 1975-77; Earth Sci/Bio Teacher Stamford Cntrl Sch 1977-80; Earth Sci/Chem/Physics Windham, Ashland, Jewett Cntrl Sch 1980-; *ai:* Track & Ski Coach; Class & NHS Adv; Faculty Assn Treas; Sci Teachers Assn of NY St 1977-; Ski Windham Ski Patrol 1984-; Ashland Fire Dept Secy 1979-; *office:* Windham Ashland Jewett Cntrl Main St Windham NY 12496

VALENTINE, ANNIE MARION, Retired Teacher; *b:* Milton, NC; *m:* Leonard R.; *c:* John, Mitchell; *ed:* (BS) Elem Ed, WV St & Bluefield St 1967; *cr:* Teacher Mullens Mid Sch, Marianna; Secy Conley HS; *ai:* Vlybl Coach; Saving Club Treas; Church (Secy, Building Fund Secy, Usher Bd).

VALENTINE, CAROLYN WRIGHT, Gifted & Talented Teacher; *b:* Jersey City, NJ; *m:* Milton P. Jr.; *c:* Milton, Audra; *ed:* (BA) Elem Ed, Jersey City St Coll 1964; Rdng; *cr:* 1st Grade Teacher Public Sch 29 1964-66; 1st Grade Teacher 1966-84, 4th Grade Teacher 1984- Public Sch 41; *ai:* 4th Grade Chairperson; In Sch Child Study Team; Jersey City Ed Assn, NJ Ed Assn, NEA; Governors Teacher Recognition Awd 1989; *office:* Fred W Martin Sch 59 Wilkinson Ave Jersey City NJ 07305

VALENTINE, LEROY, Social Studies Teacher; *b:* Anderson, SC; *ed:* (AA) Anderson Coll 1977; (BA) Drama Ed, Lander Coll 1980; (MA) Ed/His, Furman Univ 1981; Erskine Coll, Clemson Univ, Converse Coll; *cr:* Teacher Pendleton Jr HS 1981-; *ai:* Stu Cncl Adv; Art in Basic Curr Comm; SCEA, NEA; *home:* 201 Chantilly Cir 90 Anderson SC 29624

VALENTINE, PEGGY JOYCE, Mathematics Teacher; *b:* Fort Worth, TX; *ed:* (BS) Ed/Math/Sci, TX Wesleyan Coll 1974; *cr:* Math Teacher/Track Coach Leonard Mid 1977-; *ai:* Math Club & Spirit Force Spon; Track Coach; Fort Worth Classroom Teacher 1988-; Assn of TX Prof Educators 1986-89; NCTM 1986-88; Teacher of Month 1988-89; Spec Recognition for Classroom Accomplishment 1990; *office:* Leonard Mid Sch 8900 Chapin Rd Fort Worth TX 76116

VALENZUELA, VICTOR HUGO, Sr English Teacher/Yrbk Adv; *b:* Eagle Pass, TX; *ed:* (BA) Eng, Univ of Tx San Antonio 1988; Grad Stud Writing Inst Grand Prairie; *cr:* Eng Teacher/ Yrbk Adv S Grand Prairie HS 1988-; *ai:* Yrbk & Sr Class Adv; Classroom Teachers Assn, NCTE 1988-; Natl Geographical Society 1989-; Amnesty Intnl 1989-; Nom Outstanding Teachers TX 1989-; *office:* S Grand Prairie HS 301 Warrior Trl Grand Prairie TX 75051

VALERIUS, LINDA HEITMAN, English Teacher; *b:* Cincinnati, OH; *c:* Suzan, Lisa; *ed:* (BA) Eng Lit, 1974, (BS) Scndry Ed, 1975 Univ of Cincinnati; Grad Stud Adolescent Lit 1976 & Hum 1987; Report Writing, Daytona Beech Comm Coll 1987; *cr:* Eng Teacher Colerain Jr HS 1975-79; Metal Sales Williams & Company 1979-83; Purchasing Agent A R Industries 1983-86; Eng Teacher New Smyrna Beach 1986-; *ai:* Jr Var Ftbl, Bsktbl Chrldng Spon; FL Cncl of Teachers of Eng 1986-; Volusia Cty Cncl of Teachers of Eng 1986-; New Smyrna Beach Mid Sch PTA Pres 1989-; HS Teacher of Yr Runner Up; *home:* PO Box 1891 New Smyrna Beach FL 32170

VALINE, RALPH JAMES, Teacher/English Dept Chair; *b:* Iron River, MI; *m:* Gail Roberts; *c:* Debra, Roger, Jeffrey; *ed:* (BA) Ed/Speech, 1962, (MA) Ed/Eng, 1967 N MI Univ; Univ of WI Eau Claire; *cr:* Teacher Florence HS 1966-, Iron River HS 1962-66, Wausaukee HS 1962; *ai:* Forensics Coach; Drama Dir; NHS, Sch Newspaper, Class Adv; Town Bd Supvr 1980-84; Water & Light Commission Supvr 1990.

VALLAR, MARY ANCILLA, OP, Retired Teacher; *b:* St Louis, MO; *ed:* (BA) Ed, Webster Coll 1951; Numerous Wkshps Harris Teacher Coll 1965-66, St Louis Univ 1966-67, St Louis Archdiocese 1967, 1969-70; *cr:* Primary Grades Teacher NY & St Louis & Outstate MO 1931-48; 5th/6th Grade Teacher Epiphany Sch 1948-66; 6th Grade Teacher St James Sch 1966-70; 5th/6th Grade Teacher St Simon Sch 1970-88; *ai:* St Louis Archdiocese 50 Yrs Teaching Awd 1981; *home:* 11015 Mueller Rd Saint Louis MO 63123

VALLENTINE, ROXANN ELIZABETH, Mathematics Teacher; *b:* El Paso, TX; *ed:* (BA) Elem Ed, 1969, (MED) Counseling/Guidance, 1973 Univ of AZ; Math; *cr:* Coach Santa Cruz Sch 1965-66; Teacher Jewish Cmmty Center 1966-67; Teacher/Coach Canyon Del Oro HS 1969-72, 1973- Cross Mid Sch; *ai:* Alateen Youth Group Spon; Weekly Cmmty Service Work; Amphitheater Math Cues Test Chairperson to Rewrite Test 1982-84; Mathcounts Contest Spon for Stus 1980-82; AlAnon Treas 1987-88; EST Trng Participate & Group Coord 1977-88; Forum Wkshp 1987-88; Nom Cross Mid Sch Teacher of Yr 1974; Nom Cross Mid Sch Teacher of Month 1972, 1977; Nom Cross Mid Sch Favorite Teacher 1983; Nom Cross Mid Sch Yrbl Dedication 1984; *office:* Cross Mid Sch 100 Chapala Tucson AZ 85704

VALLIEU, KENNETH S., Science Teacher; *b:* Dayton, OH; *m:* Barbara E. Hart; *c:* Brian, Kristin; *ed:* (BS) Crop Sci/Ag/Ed/Bio/ Phys Sci, 1967, (MA) Scndry Ed, 1971 MI St Univ; *cr:* Secy/Mid Sch Sci Teacher Camden-Frontier Schls 1968-; *ai:* Asst Var Ftbl & Jr Var Bsktbl Coach; MI Sci Teachers Assn, NSTA; MI Assn for Cmptr Use in Learning; Natl Fed of Coaches; Amer Assn of Bio Teachers; 1st United Meth Church Trustee 1987-89; Hillsdale Golf & Cntry Club Bd Mem 1988-; *office:* Camden-Frontier Schls 4971 Montgomery Rd Camden MI 49232

VALOIS, RICK, Mathematics Department Chair; *b:* Woonsocket, RI; *m:* Karen; *c:* Amber, Andrea, Amy, Allison; *ed:* (BA) Soc Sci, CA St Univ Long Beach 1966; Math Ed, CA St Fullerton, Univ of CA Los Angeles, USC; *cr:* Math Teacher 1967-81, Dept Chm 1981- Artesia HS; *ai:* Math Club Adv; Jr-Sr HS Articulation Comm; AFT Mem 1972-81; CTA Mem 1967-71; From Algebra to Geometry Grant; Coached Natl Jr Track Tem World Univ Games & Natl Record Holder; *office:* Artesia HS 12108 E Del Amo Blvd Lakewood CA 90715

VALONE, KATHERINE G., Sixth Grade Teacher; *b:* Chicago, IL; *ed:* (BA) Liberal Arts, 1953, (BSED) Ed Curr Supervision, 1955, (MA) Admin, 1967 Univ of Chicago; Post Masters Studies PHD Stu Univ of Chgo; *cr:* Elem Teacher William Penn Elem Sch 1955-59; 6th Grade Teacher US Air Force Sch Morocco 1959; 9th Grade Teacher Amer Comm Sch Athens, Greece 1959-60; 8th Grade Teacher Oliver Wendell Holmes 1960-67; 6th Grade Teacher Florence Nightingale Elem Sch 1967-; *ai:* Chairperson Parochial Sch Bd; Dir Religious Ed; Greek Orthodox Religious Ed Comm; Nightingale Sch Essay Contest Spon for Bd of Ed; Local Sch Cncl, Nightingale 1969, Chairperson; Phi Delta Kappa Mem 1980-; IL Cong Par Par & Teachers (PTA) Mem 1955-; Service Distinguished 1972; IL Cncl of Ethnicity Mem 1970-; Hellenic Cncl of ED Co-Founder 1970-; Greek Orthodox Archdiocese Religious Ed Comm, Missions, 1950-; Outstanding St Paul Layman's Awd 1980; Pho Mission, Inc. Founder-Dir 1971-; United Southwest Asson of Greek Amer Founding Dir Pres 1983-; Outstanding Mem 1984; Schlsp Recipient 1950-53, Fellowship PhD Offered 1967, Univ of Chgo; Weekly Journalist Greek Star & Greek Press 1953-; *home:* 10716 S La Crosse Ave Oak Lawn IL 60453

VALVO, FRANCES ANDOLINO, Sixth Grade Teacher; *b:* North Collins, NY; *m:* Joseph R.; *c:* Julie A.; *ed:* (BS) Elem Ed - Cum Laude, Buffalo St Coll 1961; Elem Ed In-Service Courses; BOCES; *cr:* 2nd Grade Teacher Eden Cntrl 1961-62; 5th Grade Teacher Starpoint Cntrl 1962-63; 4th Grade Teacher Eden Cntrl 1963-64; 5th Grade Teacher Hamburg Cntrl 1964-65; Phys Ed Teacher Farnham Sch 1965-66; 4th-6th Grade Teacher Lake Shore Cntrl 1966-; *ai:* Tutoring Private Stu; Various Sch Comms; NY St Teachers Assn 1961-; Lake Shore Teachers Assn 1966-; Kappa Delta Pi 1959-61; Zonta Club; *home:* 3 Bartus Ln Angola NY 14006

VAN ACKEREN, JOHN LEONARD, AP Calculus/Physics/ Dept Chair; *b:* Washington, DC; *m:* Donna Kelly; *c:* John W.; *ed:* (BS) Bio, 1971, (MED) Bio, 1977 Frostburg St Coll; Numerous Courses Various Univs; *cr:* Phys Sci Teacher N Harford JR/Sr HS 1971-72; Chem Teacher Fort Hill HS 1972-81; Chem/Physics Teacher Madeira Sch 1981-84; Sci/Math Teacher Port Townsend HS 1986-; *ai:* Math & Sci Dept Chm; Co-Chm Self Study; Chm Curr Review Math & Sci; NHS; Inservice Comm; Tennis, Cross Country Coach; Amer Chem Society; Amer Assn of Physics Teachers; NEA, NCTM, WA Cncl Teachers of Math, WA Sci Teachers Assn; Article Published 1984; *office:* Port Townsend HS 1610 Blaine St Port Townsend WA 98368

VAN ACKOOY, HOWARD JOHN, 6th Grade Soc Stud Teacher; *b:* Poughkeepsie, NY; *ed:* (BS) Art Ed, 1972, (BS) Elem Ed, 1974, (MS) Ed, 1978 St Univ New Paltz; *cr:* 6th Grade Teacher La Grange Elem Sch 1974, Noxon Road Elem Sch 1974-80; 6th Grade Teacher Soc Stud/Rdng Arlington Mid Sch 1980-; *ai:* Bowling & Sftbl Intramural Prgm; Mid-Hudson Soc Stud Cncl Outstanding Teacher Awd 1987; *office:* Arlington Mid Sch 5 Dutchess Tnpk Poughkeepsie NY 12603

VANALEK, GEORGE JOSEPH, Biology Teacher; *b:* Oak Park, IL; *m:* Andrea N. Salazar; *ed:* (BS) Bio, Culver-Stockton Coll 1964; (MS) Bio/Mammalogy, NM Highlands Univ 1968; *cr:* Sci/ Bio Teacher West Las Vegas Sch Dist 1970-; *ai:* Amer Assn Adv of Sci, NM Acad of Sci Mem 1975-; Sigma Xi Mem 1980-; Kettering Fnd Sci Service Project Grant 1962-63; Scientific Publications; *office:* West Las Vegas HS 179 Bridge St Las Vegas NM 87701

VAN BEEK, RICHARD RAY, Administrator; *b:* Newport Beach, CA; *m:* Charleen Kitabjian; *c:* Jimmy, Katie, Ryan; *ed:* (LS) Liberal Stud, Mendocino Jr Coll 1977; (BA) Bus Admin, Le Tourneau Univ 1980; (MA) Sch Admin, Univ of San Francisco 1987; *cr:* Substitute Teacher Potter Valley Cmmty Unified 1981; Teacher/Coach Pasadena Chrstn Sch 1981-85, Kelseyville HS 1985-87; Admin Pasadena Chrstn Sch 1987-; *ai:* Stu Cncl Adv; Bsktbl & Ftbl Coach; Church of the Open Door; *office:* Pasadena Chrstn Sch 1515 N Los Robles Pasadena CA 91104

VAN BUREN, BARBARA BACHEMIN, 8th Grade Homeroom/Soc Chair; *b:* New Orleans, LA; *m:* William Douglas III; *c:* Charlotte, Leslie, Barbara, Susan, William, Tobias, Theodore, Ivan, Erika, Joachim, Christopher, Tabitha; *ed:* Liberal Art, Xavier Univ; Ed, Southern Univ; Fashion Design, Univ of CA Los Angeles; Span, CA St Dominguez; Basic Nursing Care, Southern Baptist Hospital; *cr:* 3rd Grade Teacher St Philip Sch 1957-59; ESAA Project Teacher Home Learing Center Compton Unified Sch Dist 1977-78; 4th/5th Grade Teacher 1978-80, 5th/ 6th Grade Teacher 1982-83, 7th/8th Grade Sci/Lang Art/Life/ Earth Sci Teacher 1983-89, Sci Dept Chairperson 1984-89 Our Lady of Victory Sch; *ai:* Stu Cncl Moderator 1982-89; Academic Competition Coord 1983-89; Evaluation Team Chairperson 1981, 1985, 1987; Pentathlon Coach 1989; Jr HS & 8th Grade Coord; Faculty Secy; NCEA Membership 1976-; CA Sci Teachers Assn Mem; Assn of Cath Stu Cncls (Mem, Summer Leadership Camp Coord/Speaker 1983-88, S CA Planning Comm Mem); Knights of Peter Claver Ladies Auxiliary Jr Moderator; Natl Cncl Negro Women Charter Membership; Smithsonian Inst Membership; Museum of Sci & Industry Mem; Economic Literacy Grant; Los Angeles Cty Hospitality Awd; Diocese of Los Angeles 10 Yr Teaching Certificate; Outstanding Teacher Certificate; *office:* Our Lady of Victory Sch 601 E Palmer Ave Compton CA 90221

VAN CAMP, PAUL SAMUEL, Science Department Chair; *b:* Danville, IL; *m:* Pamela Ann Brown; *c:* Ronald, Leslie; *ed:* (BA) Zoology, E IL Univ 1968; Working Towards Masters Fisheries Bio, *cr:* Teacher Farmer City Jr HS 1968-70, Mary Miller Jr HS 1970-; *ai:* Conservation Olympics Coach; Head of Sci Dept; Head of Insurance Comm for Union; Georgetown Ridge Farm Ed Assn 1970-; Luth Laymans League 1980-; Outdoor Writer Commercial News; *office:* Mary Miller Jr HS 414 W West St Georgetown IL 61846

VANCE, AMEE M. LEWIS, Kindergarten Teacher; *b:* Colver, PA; *m:* Ronald F.; *c:* Andy Lewis, Marty Lewis; *ed:* (BA) Early Chldhd, Lock Haven Univ 1975; (MS) Elem Ed, Penn St Univ 1980; *cr:* Kndgtn Teacher Forge Road Sch 1975-86, Pine St Sch 1986-; *ai:* Nursery Task Force (Vice Chairperson, Nursery Coord, Cong Life) 1990; Zeta Tau Alpha (Pres 1983, 1985, VP 1987-), Certificate of Merit 1988; PTO Teacher Rep 1978-79; Derry Presbyn Church Elder; PAEA of PSEA (Building Rep, Treas) 1978-79; *office:* Pine St Elem Sch W Pine & College Palmyra PA 17078

VANCE, BARBRA BROWNING, Business Teacher; *b:* Logan, WV; : Danny E.; *c:* Keith, Joseph; *ed:* (AB) Bus Ed Comp, Marshall 1969; *cr:* Bus Ed Teacher Logan Sr HS 1969-; *ai:* Sunday Sch Teacher; Logan Cty Ed Assn; WV Ed Assn; *office:* Logan HS Midelburg Island Logan WV 25601

VANCE, HAROLD, 7th & 8th Math Teacher; *b:* Colson, KY; *m:* Darlene Slone; *c:* Angela Vance Whitaker; *ed:* (BS) Elem Ed, Eastern KY Univ 1966; (MA) Elem Ed, Morehead St Univ 1975; *cr:* Teacher Dry Fork Sch 1961-64; 5th Grade Teacher Hartland Sch 1964-65; 7th & 8th Grade Teacher Fleming Neon Elem Sch 1966-; *ai:* Bsktbl, Sftbl Coach; LCTO, KEA, NEA; *home:* PO Box 116 Neon KY 41840

VANCE, MARGAURITE DE MOSS, English Teacher; *b:* Kirksville, MO; *m:* Dennis; *c:* Russel Phelps, Brendan Phelps, Christopher Phelps; *ed:* (MA) Eng, Univ of N IA 1976; *cr:* Eng Teacher Cedar Falls HS 1972-; *ai:* IA Cncl of Teachers of Eng 1980-; NCTE 1974-; Hemingway Society 1989-; Romance Writers of America; Summer Seminar by Natl Endowment of Hum in Italy; Natl Inst of Hum NC Grant; Readers Digest & NEH Teacher, Scholar for IA; Articles Published Critical Writing; 1 Published Novel; *office:* Cedar Falls HS 10th And Division Cedar Falls IA 50613

VAN DEMAN, BRENDA TETER, 7th/8th Grade Teacher; *b:* Harman, WV; *m:* Thomas Marion; *c:* Thomas D., Timothy S., Rebaka A. Ragland; *ed:* (AA) Ed, Tyler Jr Coll 1980; (BA) Ed, Baptist Chrstn Coll 1984; SW Assemblies of God Coll 1961-62; Univ of TX Tyler 1980-81; *cr:* Teacher Tyler Chrstin Acad 1977-79; Medical Secy/Bookkeeper Doctor J R Bergeron 1982-84; 7th/8th Grade Teacher Westland Chrstn Acad 1984-; *ai:* Westland Baptist Church (5th/6th Grade Sunday Sch Teacher, Choir Mem); Westland Chrstn Acad Teacher of Yr 1988; *office:* Westland Chrstn Acad 430 S Kipling St Denver CO 80226

VAN DEMAN, JAMES EDWARD, History Teacher; *b:* Monticello, IN; *m:* Verna Jean Rogers; *c:* Scott F., Edward W.; *ed:* (BS) Phys Ed, 1959, (MS) Ed Admin, 1964 Purdue Univ; NDEA His Inst Purdue Univ 1968; Grad Admin Prgm Univ of MS 1969-71; Systems Analysis for Ed Duval Cty Sch Bd 1973-74; *cr:* Coach 1960-67, His Teacher 1960-69, Asst Prin 1967-69 East Tipp HS; Instructional Materials Supvr Duval Cty Sch Bd 1971-77; Teacher Paxon Jr HS 1977-81; Curr/Personnel Dir Okeechobee Sch Bd 1981-82; Teacher Okeechobee Jr HS 1982-; *ai:* Phi Delta Kappa, Kappa Delta Pi 1970-; Okeechobee Fed of Teachers (Building Rep, Exec Bd Mem) 1982-; Tippecanoe CTA (Pres 1967-68, VP 1966-67); FL Assn of Instructional Materials Mgrs Pres 1973-74; Cub Scouts Pack Chm 1974-76; Presbyn Church Elder 1978-81; Univ of MS Grad Teaching Asst 1969-71; Nova Univ Admin & Supervision Adjunct Professor 1976-81; NDEA Amer His Fellowship 1968-69; Project Bus Teacher Awd 1978; *office:* Okeechobee Jr HS 925 NW 23rd Ln Okeechobee FL 34974

VANDENBERG, RONALD, Mathematics Teacher; *b:* Appleton, WI; *m:* Bette Ann Smith; *c:* Kevin, Kenneth, Kirk; *ed:* (BS) Math, St Norbert Coll 1962; Grad Work in Math & Ed; *cr:* Math Teacher Abbott Pennings HS 1961-62, Waunakee HS 1965-68; Math/Eng Teacher Brillion HS 1969-70; Math Teacher Kaukauna HS 1970-; *ai:* Asst Math Team Adv; NEA, WI Ed Assn 1965-; *home:* 224 Ryan St Combined Locks WI 54113

VANDENBERGE, DONALD ROBERT, 5th/6th Grade Music Teacher; *b:* Mt Vernon, NY; *m:* Elaine P.; *c:* Brian, Neil, Craig; *ed:* (BA) Music, Trenton St Coll 1974; Working Towards Masters Admin, Supervision, Jersey City; *cr:* Instrumental Music Teacher 1975-; *ai:* Intramural Act 1982-88; *office:* S Toms River & Beachwood Elem 54 Washington St Toms River NJ 08753

VANDENBOSS, ARDIS MARY (ELLIS), Jr HS English Dept Teacher; *b:* Battle Creek, MI; *m:* Donald Peter; *c:* Nicole S., Sean D.; *ed:* (AA) Kellogg Comm Coll 1971; (BS) Eng/Elem, 1972, (MA) Elem Ed, 1974 W MI Univ; Essential Elements of Effective Instruction, Peer Trng, Skills for Adolescence, Power Writing, Healthy Lifestyles, Numerous Drug Prgms & Wkshps; CPR Red Cross; *cr:* 2nd Grade Teacher 1972-74, 1st/2nd Split Grade Teacher 1974-75, Substituting/Pre Sch 8th Grade Teacher 1975-81 Battle Creek Public Sch; Pre Sch/Substitute/8th Grade Teacher Gull Lake Public Schls 1981-85; 7th/8th Grade Eng/Math/Spelling/Rdng/Lit/Earth Sci/Life Sci/Cath Religion/Quest/Phys Ed/Sex Ed/Confirmation/Civics Teacher St Philip Elem/Jr HS 1985-; *ai:* Yrbk, Newspaper Ed/Adv; 8th Grade Graduation Coord; Confirmation Adv & Spon; 7th/8th Grade Homeroom Teacher, Organizer of Dances; Progressive Dinners, Caroling Parties, Money Makers, Field Trips; Elem Gifted & Talented; B C Symphony Orch Violin 1963-88; Brownie Leader Asst 1983-85; Religion Instr 1967-86; PTA Mem 1980-; Band Boosters, Sports Organizations, St Jerome Parish; *office:* St Philip Jr HS 20 Cherry St Battle Creek MI 49017

VANDEN BROOKS, KATHRYN G., Teacher of Gifted/Reading; *b:* Bay City, MI; *ed:* (BA) Eng, Marygrove Coll 1971; (MAED) Rdng, Univ of CA Santa Barbara 1977; Grad Work Ed & Ed of Gifted; *cr:* Scndry/Intermediate Eng Teacher Bay City Public Schls 1971-75, 1978-82; Researcher/Writer Effective Educl Systems 1976; Research/Asst Teacher Univ of CA Santa Barbara 1977; 7th/8th Grade Teacher St Anne Cath Sch 1983-84; Rdng Specialist/Teacher of Gifted Bay City Public Schls 1984-; *ai:* Yrbk Supvr; Needy Stu & Gifted Prgm Curr Writing Comm; St Boniface HS Youth Group Spon 1982-86; Bay City Ed Assn, MI Ed Assn, NEA; Cath Schls Curr Dev Comm 1986-89; St Boniface Parish (Cncl Pres 1987-89, Mem Admin, Finance, Chrstn Service, Ed Comm 1982-88); Bay Arts Fnd Schlsp Comm Mem 1990; Co-Authored Curr Guides K-6th Grade; Developed Rdng Prgms HS & Intermediate Levels; Developed Gifted Intermediate Curr; *home:* 122 Little Killarney Beach Bay City MI 48706

VANDENBULCKE, NORA JANE, First Grade Teacher; *b:* East Orange, NJ; *m:* Charles F.; *ed:* (BA) Elem Ed, Newark St Coll 1971; Certificate Cmptr Ed, Georgian Court Coll 1990; Continuing Ed, Toms River Regional Sch System & Toms River Instructional Theory Into Practice Wkshps 1987-88; *cr:* 4th Grade Teacher 1971-81, 1st Grade Teacher 1981- Toms River Regional Sch Dist; *ai:* Plan & Organize Special Prgms; Organize Annual Sch Fair; Worked on Comm for First Grade Practice Testing Booklet; Governors Teacher Recognition Awd 1987-88; *office:* Cedar Grove Elem Sch Cedar Grove Rd Toms River NJ 08753

VAN DERBEEK, SHARON DONOHUE, Third Grade Teacher; *b:* Newark, NJ; *m:* Richard; *c:* Devon, Dana; *ed:* (BA) Elem Ed, Plattsburgh Univ 1975; Grad Classes; *cr:* 4th Grade Teacher Joyce Kilmer Sch 1977-81; 3rd Grade Teacher George Washington Sch 1981-; *ai:* Rdng & Lang Comms 1989-; NJEA, NEA, AARP 1977-; *office:* George Washington 39 Fardale Ave Mahwah NJ 07430

VANDERBURG, TIMOTHY WARREN, Asst Prin/Athletic Director; *b:* Concord, NC; *m:* Marsha Turner; *c:* Zachary; *ed:* (BA) Poly Sci, Gardner-Webb Coll 1981; Admin Seminar, Pensicola Chrstn Coll; *cr:* His/Phys Ed Teacher 1981-83, His Teacher 1983-89, Asst Prin/Athletic Dir 1989- First Assembly Chrstn Sch; *ai:* Lib Comm; Intnl Relations Organization Adv; Civil Air Patrol Squad Vice Commander 1989; Republican Party (Cty Exec Comm 1987-, Precinct Chm 1985-87); Outstanding Young Men of America 1984; *office:* 1st Assembly Chrstn Sch 154 Hwy 601 Bypass N Concord NC 28025

VANDER DOES, JERRY R., Choral/Musical Theatre Teacher; *b:* Blackfoot, ID; *m:* Shaunna Beesley; *c:* Ryan, Brock, Elise, Nicole; *ed:* (BA) Music Ed/Choral, Univ of UT 1979; *cr:* Choral Music/Musical Theatre Teacher N Davis Jr HS 1980-; Music Dir Clearfield HS 1989-; *ai:* Joint Staff Comm Chm; Musical Theatre; Layton Choral Arts Ensemble Asst Dir 1988-; Earthrise Show Choir Dir 1984-88; Layton Arts Cncl Music Dir; Latter Day Saints Church Production Music Dir; Musical Dir Various Schls; *office:* N Davis Jr HS 835 S State St Clinton UT 84015

VANDERFRIFT, MAVIS JOHNSON, 3rd Grade Teacher; *b:* Alexandria, MN; *m:* Ronald L. Sr.; *c:* Ronald L. Jr., Jane E.; *ed:* Assoc Elem Ed, St Cloud St Univ 1955; (BS) Elem Ed, Univ Northern CO 1959; (MED) Elem Ed, Univ Hartford 1970; Western MD Coll; *cr:* Elem Teacher Columbia Heights Schls 1955-57; 3rd/4th Grade Teacher Robbinsdale Schls 1957-59; 3rd/5th Grade Teacher Denver Sch System 1959-61; 3rd/5th/6th Grade Teacher Hartford Sch System 1961-63 & 1966-70; 3rd/4th/5th/6th Grade Teacher Montgomery Cty Schls 1972-; *ai:* Stu Cncl Adv; Drama Coach; Grade Chm; NEA; Delta Kappa Gamma Intnl 1988-; Cncl of Basic Ed Fellow 1989; Amer Scandinavian Assn; Cty & St Winner Production Animated Films; Intnl Film Winner Production of Animated Film 1988; Montgomery Co Fellow for Ind Study in Hum 1989; *home:* 7902 Quarry Ridge Way Bethesda MD 20817

VAN DER LINDEN, SHERRIE L., 5th Grade Teacher; *b:* Syracuse, NY; *c:* Katie, Kim, Kris; *ed:* (BA) Elem Ed, St Univ Potsdam 1967; (MS) Elem Ed, Nazareth Coll 1987; *cr:* Teacher Clifton Springs Elem 1967-70, Phelps Elem 1978-; *ai:* Organist UMC Clifton Spgs NY; Delta Kappa Gamma Mem; *office:* Phelps-Clifton Spgs Cntrl Sch Phelps Elementary Sch Phelps NY 14532

VANDER MEER, PETER CORNELIUS, 7th/ 8th Grade Teacher; *b:* Aalsmeer, Netherlands; *m:* Patricia Louise De Vries; *c:* Melissa A., Matthew P.; *ed:* (BA) US His, CA St Univ Dominguez Hills 1971; (MA) Ed, Univ of San Francisco; Quest-Dealing with Adolescents; *cr:* Metal Finisher Dyer Plating Incorporated 1963-65; US Army Vietnam 1965-67; Teacher Fred Moiola Elem Sch 1972-; *ai:* Girls Vlybl, Bsktbl, Soccer, Track, Sftbl Coach; Selection & Sch Improvement Comms Mem; NEA 1972-; CA Teachers Assn 1972-; Fountain Valley Ed Assn Rep 1983-87; Nature Conservancy 1983-; Natl Wildlife Fed 1981-88; Greenpeace 1984-; PTA Service to Children Awd; Teacher Exch to ME 1980-81; *home:* 16552 Potter Cir Huntington Bch CA 92647

VANDER MOERE, FRANKLYN J., Social Studies Teacher; *b:* Byron Center, MI; *m:* Barbara Jean Wieten; *ed:* (BS) His/Phys Ed, W MI Univ 1964; *cr:* Teacher Holton HS 1963-68, Byron Center Public Schls 1968-; *ai:* Mid Sch Athletic Dir; Var Bsbl & Ftbl Coach; NEA, MI Ed Assn 1963-; Byron Center Ed Assn 1968-; *office:* Nickels Mid Sch 8548 Byron Center Ave Byron Center MI 49315

VANDERVEEN, ERIC WILLIAM, English Teacher; *b:* Akron, OH; *ed:* (BA) Eng, Thiel Coll 1985; MD Writing Project; Working on Masters Degree Scndry Ed, Sch Admin, Bowie St Univ; *cr:* Eng Teacher North Caroline HS 1985-87; Eng Tutor Portugal 1987-88; Eng Teacher Northern HS 1988-; *ai:* Newspaper Adv; Head Bsktbl Coach; MD St Final 4 1988-; Chairperson Stu Act Comm Mid St Evaluation; MSTA, NEA 1985-; CEA 1988-; Coach of Yr 1989-; *office:* Northern HS 2950 Chaneyville Rd Owings MD 20736

VANDER WAL, VELMA ANN (KILBORN), Third Grade Teacher; *b:* Missoula, MT; *m:* William C.; *c:* Gretchen, Mike Johnsrud, Dan, Sean Johnsrud, Erin Johnsrud; *ed:* (BA) Elem Ed/Elem Sci/Phys Ed, Cntrl WA Univ 1962; Ed, Univ of WA 1975; *cr:* HS Eng/Government Teacher Army Ed Center France 1962-63; 3rd Grade Teacher 1965-66, 2nd Grade Teacher 1967-68 Highline Sch Dist; 1st Grade Teacher 1978-84, 2nd Grade Teacher 1984-87, 3rd Grade Teacher 1987- Moses Lake Schls; *ai:* Chapter I & II Comms 1989-; Curr Cncl 1988-; WEA, NAE; Moses Lake Ed Assn Local VP 1989-; Chapter I Sci Grant 1982-83; WA Ed Assembly Rep 1990; *office:* Garden Heights Elem Sch 707 E Nelson Rd Moses Lake WA 98837

VAN DESSEL, DON, Jr HS Phys Ed/Sci Teacher; *b:* Chester, MT; *m:* Sharon Lamping; *c:* Terri Perry, Karla; *ed:* (BA) Phys Ed, N MT Coll 1962; *cr:* Phys Ed/Sci Teacher Chester HS 1962-: *ai:* Soph Adv; Var Girls Vlybl Coach; NEA 1962-; *office:* Chester HS Box 550 Chester MT 59522

VANDESTEEG, MARIE PANSY, Science Teacher; *b:* Joliet, IL; *m:* Gerrit Jacob; *c:* Xavier; *ed:* (BA) Bio, 1962, (MS) Bio, 1965 Univ of IL Urbana; CA St Univ Long Beach, AZ St Univ, CO St Univ, Univ of CA Irvine & Fullerton; *cr:* Sci Teacher St Francis Acad 1962-63, Marywood Acad 1963-65, Forest View HS 1965-67, Savanna HS 1967-; *ai:* Timer for Swim Meets; NABT; Orange Cty Sci Ed Assn Outstanding Sci Teacher 1989; NEA, CA Teachers Assn, Anaheim Scndry Teachers Assn; Mentor Teacher for Anaheim Union HS Dist; Masonic Lodge Awd Excl in Public Ed; Classroom Teachers Instructinal Improvement Grant; NTL Sci Fnd Schlsps; *office:* Savanna HS 301 N Gilbert Anaheim CA 92801

VAN DEUENTER, WILLIAM ROBERT, Science Teacher; *b:* New Brunswick, NJ; *m:* Bette Jane; *c:* Kristen, Jason; *ed:* (BS) Botany, Univ of AZ 1967; (MS) Bio, Univ of WI 1973; Marine Bio, Suffolk Univ; Physics, St Cloud Coll; Environmental Sci, Univ of WI; Physics, Trenton St Coll; *cr:* Sci Teacher Madison Township HS 1968-69, Keansburg HS 1969-; *ai:* Right-To-Know Dist Coord; Sci Club Adv; Inquiries in Sci Stu Research Project; NJEA 1968-; NSTA 1969-; Atlantic Highlands Historical Society VP 1977-; Atlantic Highlands Recreation Comm 1976-79; Sci Fellowship Univ of WI 1973; JCP&L Grant Energy Conservation 1988; NJ St Mini Grant Environmental Sci 1976; *office:* Keansburg HS 140 Port Monmouth Rd Keansburg NJ 07734

VAN DEUSEN, ROBERT MOON, Technology & Assessment Coord; *b:* Jacksonville, FL; *m:* Jean Donham; *c:* Andrew Donham, Joel Donham; *ed:* (BA) Poly Sci, Coe Coll 1974; (MA) Elem Ed, 1977, (PHD) Elem Math Ed, 1980 Univ of IA; *cr:* 3rd-6th Grade Teacher Nixon Sch 1974-79; 5th-6th Grade Teacheer Squaw Creek Sch 1980-82; Computing Consultant Grant Wood Area Ed Agency 1983-; Technology/Assessment Coord Linn Mar Cmmty Schls 1990; *ai:* Published Cmptr & Higher Order Thinking Skills Mitchell Publishing 1989; Articles Published The Computing; Teacher/Prin/Connect Sch Lib Media Act Monthly; Honorable Mention Electronic Educator of Yr; *office:* Linn-Mar Cmmty Schls 3333 10th St Marion IA 52302

VANDEVENTER, LINDA MARIE, Social Studies Specialist; *b:* Des Moines, IA; *ed:* (BA) Elem Ed, Univ of N IA 1971; *cr:* 5th Grade Teacher Hayes Elem 1971-76; Soc Stud Specialist Harrison Elem 1976-; *ai:* Safety Patrol Supvr Harrison Elem; Antarctica Research Club Spon; IA Cncl for Soc Stud Dir of Exhibits 1985-; NCSS, Delta Kappa Gamma Society 1990; Miss Scott Cty Pageant Assn Public Relations 1982-; *office:* Harrison Elem Sch 1032 W 53rd St Davenport IA 52806

VANDEWALKER, DAVID RICHARD, Band Director; *b:* Stillwater, OK; *m:* Glenda Jane Russell; *c:* Amy D., Leslie J.; *ed:* (BS) Math/Music, 1971, (MED) Ed, 1981 E Cntrl Univ Ada; *cr:* Band/Math Teacher Healdton Public Schls 1971-73; Band Teacher Seminole Public Schls 1973-77; Band/Math Teacher Holdenville Public Schls 1977-80; Band Teacher Konawa Public Schls 1980-82, Ada Public Schls 1982-; *ai:* 6th-8th Grade Band Dir; ECBDA Treas 1981-; OBA 1987-88; Active Guest Clinician & Adjudicator; *office:* Ada Mid Sch 223 W 18th Ada OK 74820

VAN DOREN, TIMOTHY PAUL, Physical Education Specialist; *b:* Indianapolis, IN; *M:* Nancy L. Payne; *c:* Ryan, Kelsey; *ed:* (BA) Phys Ed, Eastern WA Univ 1980; *cr:* K-8th Grade Teacher Mead Sch Dist 1980-82; Elem Phys Ed Specialist Whitworth-Shiloh Hills Elem 1982-83, Whitman Elem 1973-; *ai:* Coaching-Ftbl/Vlybl/Bsktbl/Sftbl Whitman Elem; Trainer-Stallings Effective Use of Time Wkshps-Spokane Sch Dist; WA Ed Assn 1983-; WA Alliance for Hlth Phy Ed Recreation & Dance 1986-88; Summer Camp Coach Skyhawks Sports Acad 1987-89; Northwest Bsbl Acad 1990; Spokane Metro Sftbl Assn 1976-; Spokane Pony Bsbl Coach 1990; Clinician/Presenter 1987 IAHPERD; Conv; 1988 Inland Empire AGPERD; 1990 WASCD St Conf; *office:* Whitman Elem Sch N 5400 Helena Spokane WA 99207

VAN DYKE, MARGARET MARIE KRAFT, 5th Grade Teacher; *b:* Strasburg, ND; *m:* Harry; *c:* Michael, Janet Panian; *ed:* Elem, St Normal & Industrial Coll 1958; Northern St Coll 1963; Maryville Coll 1973; *cr:* Teacher Biegler Sch 1958-60; Henry Sch 1960-61; Sacred Hearth Sch 1961-65; Remedial Rdng Teacher Aberdeen Ind 1965-67; Teacher Holy Infant 1967-; *ai:* Holy Infant Mission Coord; SD Teachers Assn 1958-67; NCEA 1967-; St Louis Archdiocesan Religious Inst Speaker; Wrote Article for Natl Holy Childhood Assn; Holy Infant Faculty Lay Coord; *home:* 265 Churchill Ln Ballwin MO 63011

VAN DYKE, PATRICIA WESTRA, Teacher/Guidance Counselor; *b:* Artesia, CA; *m:* Peter; *c:* Alice, Mary; *ed:* (BA) Home Ec, Central Coll 1969; *cr:* Home Ec Teacher Hudsonville Jr HS 1969-72; Teacher/Cnslr Temple Chrstn HS 1981-; *ai:* Sr Class & Honor Society Adv; Canyon Lake Cmmty Church Womens Ministry Adv 1977-; Educator of Yr Temple Chrstn Schls 1989-; *office:* Temple Chrstn HS 745 N Perris Blvd Perris CA 92370

VAN DYKE, PETER JOHN, Social Studies Teacher; *b:* Glen Cove, NY; *m:* Patricia Cornetta; *c:* Jonathan; *ed:* (BS) Ed, Univ of ME 1977; Alternative Ed & Dropout Prevention; *cr:* Alternative Ed Teacher Largo Alternative Sch 1979-81; Graphic Arts/Soc Stud Teacher Clearwater Comphrehensive Mid Sch 1981-84; Soc Stud Teacher Tarpon Springs Mid Sch 1984-86, Tarpon Springs HS 1986-; *ai:* Tarpon Springs HS Magazine Ed; Schl Public Relations Comm; Stu Assistance Prgm; Case Mgr; Goals Team for Dropout Prevention; NEA 1982-; Bsa Cub Master 1970-71 Medal of Merit 1971; Boys Club Volunteer 1988-; 1st Place Pinellas Cty Economics Fair; Secy Pinellas Cty Soc Stud Cncl 1984; Clearwater Police Dept Sch LaisonPrgm; Curr Dev Comm 1982-84; *home:* 2665 Ullman Ct Palm Harbor FL 34684

VAN DYKE, REBECCA LAYTON, A P English Teacher; *b:* Ogden, UT; *m:* Stephen Allan; *c:* Stephenie M., Eric L., Yvette M., Anne E., Diana R.; *ed:* (BA) Eng Ed, Brigham Young UniV 1977; Elem Endorsement, 1977 S UT St Coll; Enrichment Coursework; *cr:* Teacher Hillcrest HS 1967-68; Librarian S UT St Coll 1977-78; Teacher Lehi HS 1978-81; Adjunct Teacher Weber St Coll 1984; Teacher Clearfield HS 1983-; *ai:* Clearfield HS Sterling Scholars Adv; Write Curr for Cmptr Writing Lab; UT Cncl Teachers of Eng 1988-; NEA, UT & Davis Ed Assns, PTSA 1982-; Published Book Review; Voted by Lehi HS as 1 of 4 Teachers who Taught Them the Most; Most Influential Teacher for Clearfield HS from Weber St Coll; *office:* Clearfield HS 938 S 1000 E Clinton UT 84015

VAN EEDEN, CECILIA FAZZI, Foreign Language Dept Chair; *b:* Lynchburg, VA; *c:* Patricia, Emily; *ed:* (BA) Fr, Mary Washington Coll 1967; (MED) Fr, Bloomsburg Univ 1972; *cr:* Fr Teacher Bethlehem Cath HS 1967-68; Fr/Span Teacher York Cath HS 1968-69; Fr Teacher Muncy HS 1969-73; Fr/Span Teacher/Foreign Lang Chairperson Bishop Hafey HS 1980-; *ai:* Fr Club; Fr Travel & Foreign Exch Prgm; AATF 1980-; Amer Assn Teachers of Span & Portuguese 1985-; *office:* Bishop Hafey HS 1700 W 22nd St Hazleton PA 18201

VAN EVERY, BARBARA E., Jr HS Language Arts Teacher; *b:* Lincoln, NE; *ed:* (BSC) Phys Ed/Biological Sci, Univ of NE Lincoln 1950; (MA) Scndry Ed/Eng, Univ of SD 1967; *cr:* Jr HS Phys Ed/Lang Art/Soc Stud/Sci Teacher East Jr Sioux City Comm Schls 1950-79; Jr HS Lang Art Teacher Interstate 35 Comm Schls 1979-; *ai:* Jr HS Stu Cncl Spon; Interstate 35 Ed Assn Pres 1987-88; IA St Ed Assn; NEA Life Mem; NCTE; IA CTE; Delta Kappa Gamma Society Intnl Honorary for Women Educators Mem 1962-; Mem of Delta Kappa Gamma Society Intnl Honorary for Women Educators 1962-; St Pres of IA Organization 1985-87; Intnl Membership Comm 1988-; *office:* Interstate 35 Comm Schls P O Box 98 New Virginia IA 50210

VAN FLEET, BYRON, Science Teacher; *b:* Upland, CA; *m:* Sheryl Jean Rosvall; *c:* Andrew, Tyler; *ed:* (BS) Zoology, 1968, (MS) Sci Ed, 1971 OR St Univ; *cr:* Sci Teacher Salisbury HS 1972, Spotswood Coll 1973-74; ENg Teacher LABO 1975; Sci Teacher Mazama HS 1976-; *ai:* OR Ed Assn 1976-; Natl Sci Teacher of Yr St Nom; *office:* Mazama HS 3009 Summers Ln Klamath Falls OR 97603

VANGILDER, ALVIN JAY, 7th & 8th Grade Sci Teacher; *b:* Rector, AR; *m:* Regina Kay Travillian; *c:* Joshua; *ed:* (BSE) General Sci, AR St Univ 1977; *cr:* Teacher Piggott Sch Dist 1977-; *ai:* Sci Club & Fire Marshall Spon; Personnel Policies Chairperson; Earthquake Preparedness Comm Chairperson; NSTA 1987-88; ASTA 1989; Hopewell RCI Club Pres 1983; AR Cattlemens Assn 1985-; *office:* Piggott Mid Sch East Court Piggott AR 72454

VAN HAREN, JANE MARIE STODOLA, Middle School Teacher; *b:* Green Bay, WI; *m:* James; *c:* Katherine, Jenna; *ed:* (BS) Elem Ed, Univ of WI-Stevens Point 1978; Lang Arts, Rdng, Univ of WI-Stevens Point; *cr:* 4-5 Grades Teacher All Saints Elem 1978-79; Intermediate Summer Sch Stevens Point WI 1979-82; Jr Authors Univ of WI-Stevens Point 1986; 6-8 Grades Teacher Rosholt Mid Sch 1979-; *ai:* Young Authors Comm; Play Dir; Rdng is Fundamental Comm; Jr Great Books Leader; Writing Comm/ Gifted & Talented Steering Comm; Cntrl WI Rdng Cncl 1979-; Fellowship-Natl Writing Project 1985; *office:* Rosholt Mid Sch 346 W Randolph St Rosholt WI 54473

VAN HAREN, ROGER JAMES, Dir Stu Activities/Eng Instr; *b:* Oconto Falls, WI; *m:* Marilyn Anne Schroeder; *c:* Jill Bornor, Timothy, Michael, Christopher, Mark; *ed.* (BS) Eng, Univ of WI Oshkosh 1961; (MA) Eng, Univ of WI Madison 1969; *cr:* Eng Teacher/Dept Chm Beaver Dam HS 1961-74; Eng Teacher 1974-, Fine Arts Chm 1984-86, Dir of Stu Act 1987- Wayland Acad; *ai:* Stu Act Dir; NCTE, NASSP; Beaver Dam Cmmty Theatre Pres 1971, 1982-83, 1985; Beaver Dam Lions Club Secy 1964-89, Distinguished Service Awd 1989; Natl Defense Ed Act Grant 1968; Outstanding Young Educator Beaver Dam Jaycees 1968; Outstanding Young Men of WI Beaver Dam Jaycees 1969; *office:* Wayland Acad PO Box 398 P O Box 398 Beaver Dam WI 53916

VAN HORN, ELLEN MCGRANE, Second Grade Teacher; *b:* Toledo, OH; *c:* Alison, Michael; *ed:* (BED) Ed, Univ of Toledo 1967; Primary Ed Courses Rdng, Lang Art, Cmptr; *cr:* 3rd Grade Teacher Oregon Public Schls 1967-75; 2nd Grade Teacher St Josephs 1983-; *ai:* Rdng Comm; *office:* St Jospephs Sch 5411 Main St Sylvania OH 43560

VAN HORN, KAREEN L., 2nd Grade Teacher; *b:* Richmond, CA; *ed:* (AA) Liberal Arts, Arapahoe Comm Coll 1978; (BA) Elem Ed, Univ of N CO 1981; *cr:* 1st Grade Teacher Elizabeth Elem 1982-84; Jr Var Vlybl Coach 1982-85, Var Sftbl Coach 1982-88 Elizabeth HS; 2nd Grade Teacher Elizabeth Elem 1984-86; 2nd Grade Developmental Teacher Running Creek Elem 1986-; *ai:* Intramural Vlybl Coach; CO Womens Sftbl Assn Secy 1983-85; *office:* Running Creek Elem Sch Box 550 Elizabeth CO 80107

VAN HORN, PAMELA LEE (LOUDENBECK), Third Grade Teacher; *b:* Belvidere, IL; *m:* Frank; *ed:* (BS) Ed, Univ WI Whitewater 1971; (MEPD) Ed, Univ WI Platteville 1981; Grad Stud Span; *cr:* 3rd Grade Teacher Fontana Sch Dist 1971-77; 4th Grade Teacher 1977-81, 3rd Grade Teacher 1981- Brodhead Sch Dist; *ai:* Sch Effectiveness Team, Assertive Discipline, Power of Positive Stu, Dist Teacher Incentive Comm; Brodhead Ed Assn (Negotiator 1982-87, VP 1985-86, Pres 1986-87); Keynote Inservice Speaker; *home:* N2595 Richland Rd Monroe WI 53566

VAN HORN, PATRICIA LYNN (BAER), First Grade Teacher; *b:* Mechanicsburg, PA; *m:* Mark Steven; *c:* Kyle S., Blair A.; *ed:* (BA) Elem Ed, OH St Univ 1977; Gesell Testing for Kndgtn Screening, Columbus OH 1987; *cr:* 8th Grade Eng Teacher Indian Lake Mid Sch 1977-78; 1st Grade Teacher Lakeview Elem 1978-; *office:* Lakeview Elem Sch 850 W Lake Ave Lakeview OH 43331

VAN HORN, REGINA RENEE, Director of Choral Activities; *b:* Valdese, NC; *ed:* (BM) Vocal Music, Mars Hill Coll 1987; (MS) Music Ed, Univ of IL 1988; *cr:* Faculty Mars Hill Coll Summer Band Clinic 1988-; Choral Dir A C Reynolds HS 1988-; *ai:* Marching Band Flag Corps Instr; Amer Choral Dir Assn 1987-; NC Music Educators Assn, Music Educators Natl Conference 1986-; Choral Music Publication 1988; From This Day Forward Music Dir 1988; *office:* A C Reynolds HS Rt 5 Box 592 Asheville NC 28803

VAN HOUTEN, CONSTANCE LAFOND, English Teacher; *b:* Manchester, NH; *ed:* (BA) Eng Ed, Univ of NH 1971; MED) Learning & Lang Disabilities, Notre Dame Coll 1986; Certificate of Specialization in Ed Gifted & Talented; *cr:* Eng Teacher Memorial HS 1971-; *ai:* Honors Prgm Coord; Spec Ed Evaluation/ Placement Team Secy; Adv to Honors Prgm Steering Comm; Phi Delta Kappa 1985-; NEA 1971-; NH Assn for Gifted Ed 1990; Notre Dame Alumni Assn 1986-; Memorial Booster Club 1980-; *office:* Memorial H S S Porter St Manchester NH 03103

VAN HOUTEN, JACQUELYN LOU (BRUMBAUGH), Fifth-Sixth Grade Teacher; *b:* Canton, OH; *M:* Roger; *c:* Tracy, Christopher; *ed:* (BS) Elem Ed, Bowling Green St Univ 1967; (MA) Educl Ldrshp, Eastern MI Univ 1989; *cr:* 4th Grade Teacher 1967-70, 2nd-6th Grade Teacher 1980- Monroe Public Schls; *ai:* Monroe Ed Assn Treas 1985-87; MI Ed Assn; Phi Delta Kappa; Assn for Supervision & Curr Dev; Tawanka Cncl Campfire Pres 1984-86; Amer Assn of Univ Women; Model a Restorers Cub; Natl Deans List 1988; Whos Who in Amer Ed 1989; *home:* 2467 La Salle Rd Monroe MI 48161

VAN HOY, NAN NICHOLS, Science/Mathematics Teacher; *b:* N Wilkesboro, NC; *m:* J. P.; *ed:* (BS) Bio, 1980, (MA) Bio, 1982 Appalachian St Univ; *cr:* Sci Teacher Davie HS 1982-83; Cmptr Instr Wilkes Comm Coll 1984-86; Sci/Math Teacher Maiden HS 1983-; *ai:* Beta, Sci Club, Cmptr Club Spon; Sr Adv; High-Q Coach; Senate Bill 2 Comm; NABT 1985-; ASCD 1989-; NSTA 1986-; GTE Growth Incentives for Teachers Grant; Catawba Valley Fnd Grant; IBM Teacher of Yr Nominee; St Nominee for Governors Bus Awd for Excl in Teaching Sci; *home:* Rt 1 Box 145AA Olin NC 28660

VANIMAN, RICHARD R., Psychology Teacher; *b:* Culver City, CA; *m:* La Verna Lambrecht; *c:* Timothy; *ed:* (BA) Soc Sci - Cum Laude, 1965, (MA) His Teaching, 1970 La Verne Coll; *cr:* HS Teacher Chino HS 1966-; *ai:* Girls Vlybl Coach; Yrbk Adv; Teacher of Yr 1978; Yrbk Dedication 1975, 1988; *office:* Chino HS 5472 Park Pl Chino CA 91710

VAN LANDINGHAM, WANDA SHOWALTER, 8th Grade Science Teacher; *b:* Falmouth, KY; *m:* Bob G.; *c:* Robert H., Rebecca L., Michael D.; *ed:* (BS) Home Economics, Univ KY 1965; (MA) Educl Admin, Morehead St Univ 1974; Principalship & Supervision, Univ KY 1979; Personal Dynamcics Attitude Prgms; *cr:* Vocational Home Economics Teacher Bellevue Public Schls 1965-1967; Sci Teacher Pendleton Cty Schls 1970-; *ai:* Sci Club Spon; Developing Your Potentials Club Spon; Attendance Comm; NEA PCEA Pres 1980-; KEA Public Relations Comm 1984-88; KMSA; NSTA; Pend Cty Womens Co Dept Chairperson 1970-71; Plum Creek Chrstn Church; Pend Cty Conservation/ Conservation Teacher Yr 1987; *home:* 706 W Shelby Falmouth KY 41040

VAN LENTEN, MARY SHAW, 8th Grade Math Teacher; *b:* Paterson, NJ; *ed:* (BS) Math - Cum Laude, Montclair St Coll 1979; *cr:* 8th Grade Math Teacher Robert R Lazar Mid Sch 1979-; *ai:* Gifted/Talented & BSI Teacher; 8th Grade Adv; NEA, NJ Ed Assn, Assn Math Teachers of NJ 1979-; Amer Power Boat Assn (Referee, Competitor) 1980-; *office:* Robert R Lazar Mid Sch 123 Changebridge Rd Montville NJ 07045

VAN LIEW, JANET CRADDOCK, Social Studies Teacher; *b:* Seymour, IN; *m:* Michael Eugene; *ed:* (BA) Poly Sci, Univ of Louisville 1985; (MA) Guidance/Counseling, IN Univ 1990; *cr:* Teacher Brownstown Cntrl Sch Corp 1986-; *ai:* Coach Vlybl 1986- & Bsktbl 1986-88; Class Spon; Athletic Cncl; Jackson Cty Leadership Awd Nom 1989; *home:* 715 Sweetbriar Ct Seymour IN 47274

VAN LOO, JOAN MEIRE, US History Teacher/Dept Chair; *b:* Paterson, NJ; *m:* Norman Peter; *c:* Joanne Van Loo Slapkowski, Nancy L.; *ed:* (BA) His, William Paterson Coll 1988; *cr:* Teacher Mary Help of Chrstn Acad 1988-; *ai:* Jr Class Adv; Art & Crafts Club; *office:* Mary Help of Chrstn Acad 659 Belmont Ave North Haledon NJ 07508

VAN LUE, MARION I. (MARSHALL), 6th Grade Teacher; *b:* Twin Lake, MI; *m:* Wayne; *c:* Lu Ann; *ed:* St Limited 1956, (BS) Elem Ed, 1968, Permanent Certificate 1974 W MI Univ; *cr:* K-8th Grade Teacher Johnston Sch 1956-58; K-4th Grade Teacher Cooper Sch 1958-60; 3rd Grade Teacher Baker-Reeths Puffer Schls 1960-65; Jr-SR HS Art/Math/Eng/Phys Ed/6th Grade Teacher Holton Public Sch 1965-; *ai:* 6th Grade Outdoor Ed Camp & Money Making Projects Adv; Holton Ed Assn (Pres 1984-87, Chm PN Comm 1987-); Teacher Excl Awd 1984; 4-H Leader 1966-68; *office:* Holton Public Sch Box 159 Holton MI 49425

VAN MEER, DEBRA JOYCE, Sixth Grade Teacher; *b:* St Louis, IA; *ed:* (AA) Pre-Ed, Jackson Comm Coll 1973; (BA) Elem Ed, 1975, (MA) Classroom Ed, 1980 MI St Univ; *cr:* 6th Grade Educator Onsted Cmmty Schls 1975-86; Eng/Bible Instr VISA Japan 1986-87; 6th Grade Educator Onsted Cmmty Schls 1987-; *ai:* 6th Grade Camp Co-Dir; OEA Membership Chairperson; Jackson Tennis Club Pres; Womens Ministries Intnl Pres of Cncl 1989-; *office:* Onsted Mid Sch 1000 Slee Rd Onsted MI 49265

VAN METER, DONALD RAY, Science Teacher/Chair; *b:* Frankfort, KY; *m:* Alice Kay Dean; *c:* Lori A. Roberts, Donald A., Joel D.; *ed:* (BS) Bio, 1968, (MAED) Bio, 1976 E KY Univ; *cr:* Teacher Eminence HS 1968-; *ai:* Bsbl, Asst Boys Bsktbl, Girls Var Bsktbl Coach; Maintenance of Ftbl & Bsbl Fields; Optimist Charter Pres 1978, Life Mem; NSF Summer Inst E KY Univ 1971, UL 1973; STAR Teacher 1971: Outstanding Educator W KY Univ 1980; *home:* Rt 3 Box 694 Eminence KY 40019

VAN METER, MARY JANE (BIRCH), Eng Dept Chairperson/ Teacher; *b:* Waynesburg, PA; *m:* John C.; *c:* Beth Roberts, Lori, Carly; *ed:* (BS) Scndry Eng, 1970, (MS) Rdng Specialist, 1976 CA Univ; WV Writers Project; WV Teachers Acad; Project Horison, Journalsim I & II, Learning Disabilities; *cr:* Rdng Specialist West Greene HS 1971-73; Substitute Teacher Greene Cty Schls 1974-80; Rdng/Eng Teacher Clay Battelle HS 1980-; *ai:* NHS & Jr-Sr Prom Adv; Class & Sch Newspaper Spon; Textbook Selection Comm; Curr Cncl Mem; WVEA 1980-; NCTE 1985-; WV Writers Assn 1989-; Mon Cty Rdng Assn 1981-; WV Mid Sch Assn 1986-; Articles & Poetry Published; Spec Ed Cty Awd; Nom Teacher of Yr Monongalia Cty; *home:* 3240 Sherman Ave Waynesburg PA 15370

VANN, BEVERLEY GAY, 7th Grade English Teacher; *b:* Lufkin, TX; *m:* Larry Wayne; *c:* Lori Gayle, Lance Allen; *ed:* (BS) Elem Ed/Eng, Stephen F Austin St Univ 1971; (MED) Ed; *cr:* 5th/6th Grade Sci/Health Teacher 1971-73, 4th Grade Teacher 1973-80, 7th/8th Grade Lang Art Teacher 1980-, 7th/8th Grade Teacher of Gifted & Talented/Lang Art Teacher 1989- Cntrl Ind Sch Dist; *ai:* Jr HS Stu Cncl Spon; UIL Spelling & Houston Chronicle Spelling Bee Coach; Annual Talent Show Spon; Area Go Texan Comm Mem; Adult 4-H Leader; Cty Project Rescue Educl Summit & Cntrl Ind Sch Dist Strategic Planning Comm Mem; TPEA, TSTA, Phi Delta Kappa Mem; Angelina Cty Teacher of Yr Awd 1988-89; *home:* Rt 1 Box 111E Pollok TX 75969

VANN, MELODY HICKS, Home Economics Instructor; *b:* Hico, TX; *m:* Leslie Lee; *ed:* (BS) Home Ec, Tarleton St Univ 1985; Working Towards Masters Sul Ross St Univ; *cr:* Home Ec Instr Henrietta HS 1985-86, Klondike HS 1986-; *ai:* FHA Spon, Soph Class Spon 1989-; Sr Class Spon 1986-88; Voc Home Ec Teachers Assn of TX 1989; Educl Task Force for Critical Issues Dawson Cty 1990; *home:* Rt 1 Box 284 Lamesa TX 79331

VANN, SYLVIA SCARBOROUGH, Mathematics Teacher; *b:* Manchester, NC; *m:* G. Lawson; *c:* George, Carlton, James; *ed:* (BS) Math Ed, Auburn Univ 1957; (MA) Math Ed, GA Southwestern Coll 1979; Ed Specialist Math Ed, Valdosta St Coll 1989; *cr:* Teacher Albany Mid Sch 1957-65, Stephens Cty Jr HS 1977-78, Peach Cty HS 1978-80, Lee Cty HS 1980-; *ai:* GA Cncl Teachers of Math, Prof Assn of GA Educators; *office:* Lee Cty HS Firetower Rd Leesburg GA 31763

VAN NOORD, RUTH, Phys Ed Teacher/Coach; *b:* Winnie, TX; *ed:* (AA) His, Temple Jr Coll 1970; (BS) His/Health/Phys Ed, Lamar Univ 1972; Phys Ed, Mary Hardin Baylor 1974; Counseling, Sam Houston St; Gifted & Talented, Lamar Univ; *cr:* Teacher/Coach Georgetown Ind Sch Dist 1972-73, Ganado Ind Sch Dist 1973-77, Palacios Ind Sch Dist 1977-78, East Chambers Ind Sch Dist 1978-79, Hardin Jefferson Ind Sch Dist 1986-; *ai:* Vlybl Var, Bsktbl Asst Var, Bsktbl Jr Var, Track, Tennis Coach; TX Girls Coaches Assn, TX Bsktbl Coaches Assn 1986-; TX St Teachers Assn 1986; Regional Runner-Up Girls Vlybl Coach 1986-88; Regional & St Champions Bsktbl Asst Coach 1988; St Runner-Up Track Coach 1989; *home:* Rt 2 Box 51 Winnie TX 77665

VAN NOSTRAND, TERRY LYNNE, Science Teacher/ Chairperson; *b:* Henderson, KY; *m:* Marvin Ray; *c:* Christopher; *ed:* (BS) Bio, Erskine Coll 1972; (MS) Wildlife/Fisheries Sci, TX A&M Univ 1974; *cr:* Sci Teacher 1982-, Sci Dept Chairperson 1986- Buffalo HS; *ai:* Leon Cty Sci Fair Coord 1989; Sci Teachers Assn of TX Mem 1985-; TX Assn Bio Teachers Mem 1986-; *office:* Buffalo HS PO Drawer C Buffalo TX 75831

VAN NOY, BETTY ALDEN, Choral Music Teacher; *b:* San Francisco, CA; *m:* Rex D.; *c:* Amy, Rosalie; *ed:* (BA) Music, San Francisco St Univ 1965, (MAED) Ed, Univ of San Francisco 1978; *cr:* Instrumental/Choral Music Teacher Rincon Valley Jr HS 1965-; *ai:* Dir of Annual Spring Musical; CA Teachers Assn, Music Ed Natl Conference 1965-; Civic Arts Commission Awd City of Santa Rosa 1974; *office:* Rincon Valley Jr HS 950 Middle Rincon Rd Santa Rosa CA 95409

VANNOY, RON L., Health Teacher/Coach; *b:* Lafollette, TN; *m:* Lisa Essary; *c:* Jenna J.; *ed:* (BA) Health/Phys Ed, 1977, (MS) Ed Admin/Supervision, 1989 Lincoln Memorial; *cr:* Phys Ed Teacher Midway Elem 1977-78, Soldiers Memorial Mid 1978-79, Claiborne Cty HS 1979-80; Health Teacher/Coach Powell Valley HS 1980-; *ai:* Head Girls Bsktbl, Boys Bsktbl, Girls Sftbl, Girls/ Boys Cross Cntry Coach; Claiborne Cty Ed Assn, TN Ed Assn, NEA 1977-; *office:* Powell Valley HS Box 275-A Speedwell TN 37870

VAN OVER, GILBERT LEE, JR., A P History Teacher & Instr; *b:* Sawyer, KY; *m:* Ruth Ann King; *c:* Gilbert III, James II, Vaughn, Pamela A., Shiela J.; . *ed:* (BS) Ed, Cumberland Coll; (MA) His/Poly Sci, Union Coll; (PhD) His, Pacific Univ; Certificate Management, Univ MD; Assoc Pikes Peak Comm Coll 1989-; *ai:* Lions Club Whitley Cty KY Past Pres; Empire Lodge 213 Mauldin SC; Amer Legion Post 200 Louisville KY UFW; Phi Delta Kappa Mem 1986-; KY Assn of Gifted Ed 1988-; Organization of Amer Historians Mem 1987-; Order of KY Colonels Mem 1962; Military Career Sports Writer Pacific Stars & Stripes, Sports Ed Korean Dogpatch Truckbuster, Okinawian Kadena News, Dissertation Diest View; *home:* P O Box 25 Stearns KY 42647

VANOVER, JOAN HURST, 1st Grade Teacher; *b:* Savannah, GA; *c:* Jason D., Holly N.; *ed:* (BA) Elem Ed, GA Southern Univ 1962; Working Towards Masters Vanderbilt Univ & Augusta Coll; *cr:* Teacher A Brian Merry Elem, Augusta Cntry Day, S Columbia, Garrett Elem; *ai:* Garrett Sch Fine Art & Extracurricular Coord; Stu Teachers Supervising Teacher at Various Univs; Consulting Services Co-Owner; Minute Made Soc Stud & Math Co-Author; GA Cncl Soc Stud Pres; NEA, Richmond Cty Assn of Educators; Historic Augusta 1987-89; Westlake Cntry Club Tennis 1969-85; Forest Hills Raquet Club 1985-; Augusta Coll Wives Auxiliary; Richmond Cty Teacher & Soc Stud Teacher of Yr; US Geographic Teacher of Yr; Media Oils Art Exhibits Winner; *office:* Garrett Elem Sch 1100 Eisenhower Dr Augusta GA 30904

VAN PAEPEGHEM, A. QUINN, Teacher; *b:* Auburn, WA; *m:* Shirley Lynn Pyle; *c:* Jacob; *ed:* (BM) Music Ed, Boise St Univ 1980; (MME) Music Ed, Univ of OR 1989; *cr:* Choir Dir Meridian HS 1980-84, Bend Sr HS 1984-; *ai:* Concerts & Musicals Cntrl OR; Cmmty Coll Jazz Choir; MENC 1976-; ACDA 1978-; NAJE 1986-; *office:* Bend Sr HS 230 NE 6th St Bend OR 97702

VAN PELT, BARBARA ANN, Social Studies Chair; *b:* El Paso, TX; *ed:* (BA) Scndry Ed 1968, (MA) Educl Admin, 1980, (MBA) Bus Admin, 1988 NM St Univ; *cr:* Teacher/Coach Roosevelt Jr HS 1973-75, Mayfield HS 1975-77, Del Norte HS 1977-79, Lynn Jr HS 1978-82, Las Cruces HS 1982-; *ai:* Head Track Coach; St Vllybl Match Assigner; St Ofcls Bd; Jr Class Spon; Attendance, Improvement Sch Spirit, Dist Grievance Comm; Phi Delta Kappa 1979-; Natl Coaches Assn, Natl Ofcls Assn 1980; NM Act Assn Ofcls Bd 1980-; *office:* Las Cruces HS 1755 El Paseo Las Cruces NM 88001

VAN PETTEN, JACKIE BAKER, Journalism Teacher; *b:* Topeka, KS; *m:* Jeffrey Franklin; *c:* Jolie; *ed:* (BS) Journalism, 1983, (BS) Phys Ed, 1983 KS St Univ; Working Towards Teaching Certificate in Eng; *cr:* Journalism Teacher Shawnee Heights Sr HS 1984-; *ai:* Yrbk & Newspaper Adv; Vlybl Coach; KS Scholastic Press Assn 1984-; Journalism Ed Assn 1988-; HS Teacher Recognition Awd KS Univ 1988; Appointed to Comm to Help Establish a St Wide Publications Contest & Critique Service for KS; *office:* Shawnee Heights Sr HS 4201 SE Shawnee Heights Rd Tecumseh KS 66542

VAN RADEN, HINDERENE, Retired; *b:* Shell Rock, IA; *m:* Leslie T.; *c:* Joyce Keeling, Debra, Rodney; *ed:* Elem Ed, Univ Northern IA; *cr:* K-8th Grade Teacher Jackson Township 1946-49; 2nd Grade Teacher 1972-81; 6th Grade Teacher 1981-87; 2nd Grade Teacher 1987-89 Allison Bristow Comm Sch; *ai:* Substituting K-6th Grade.

VAN RENSSELAER, MICHAEL JEFFREY, Mathematics Dept Chair; *b:* Evanston, IL; *m:* Pamela J. Cooper; *c:* Paul S. Terry, Jana M. Terry, James K.; *ed:* (BA) Religion/Philosophy, 1972, (MAT) Soc Stud, 1976 De Pauw Univ; Cert Scndry Math, De Pauw 1977-79; Cmptr Trng 1985-86; *cr:* Sports Ed Greencastle Banner Graphic Newspaper 1973-75; Math/Cmptr Teacher Greencastle Mid Sch 1976-; *ai:* 8th Grade Boys Bsktbl Coach; Math Dept Chm; North Cntrl Assn Performance Based Accreditation Self-Study Steering Comm Co-Chm; IN St Teachers Organization, NEA 1989-; *office:* Greencastle Mid Sch 400 S 1st St Greencastle IN 46135

VAN RIPER, N. LYNN, 7th/8th Grade Art Teacher; *b:* Lima, OH; *c:* Terry Van Riper Zornow, Robert; *ed:* (BS) Elem Ed, OH St 1973; (MA) Elem Ed, MT St Joseph 1988; *cr:* 3rd/4th Grade Teacher Middletown Public Schls 1955-58; 2nd/3rd Grade Teacher Marion OH 1973-76; Kndgtn-5th Grade Elem Art Teacher Marion City Schls 1976-79; 7th/8th Grade Art Teacher Marion City Schls 1979-; *ai:* Marion City Art Ed Display at Ed Fair; OH Arts Ed Assn Regional Office 1980; MEA, OEA, NEA Teachers Unions 1957-; Phi Delta Kappa 1988-; Jennings Schlsp Awd 1986-87.

VANSANT, ANN M., Fifth Grade Teacher; *b:* Newfoundland, KY; *w:* Charles A. (dec); *c:* William C. (dec), Robert M.; *ed:* (BS) Elem Ed, OH Univ 1970; *cr:* Teacher Elliott Cty Schls 1952-55, Scioto Valley Dist 1960-63, Waverly City Schls 1964-; *ai:* Waverly Classroom Teachers, OH Ed Assn, NEA; Jennings Scholar Awd 1979-80; *home:* 360 Oak Ave Waverly OH 45690

VANSANT, ANNE BURTON, Third Grade Teacher; *b:* Chestertown, MD; *ed:* (BA) Psych, Wilson Coll 1968; (MA) Psych, Washington Coll 1973; *cr:* Teacher Kent Sch Inc 1968; Chm of the Lower Sch 1985; *ai:* Long Range Planning Comm; Natl Assn of Ind Schls, Assn of Ind MD Schls; Friends of Kent Cty Public Lib Past Pres; Historical Society of Kent Cty; Bd of Appeals Chestertown Md; *office:* Kent Sch Inc Wilkins Ln Chestertown MD 21620

VAN SANT, BRENDA B., Science Teacher; *b:* Macon, GA; *m:* C. V. III; *c:* Jami, Levi; *ed:* (BS) Bio, GA Coll 1987; Research Laboratory Technology Cert; *cr:* Sci Teacher Thomson HS 1987-; *ai:* Sci Club, Quiz Bowl, Jr Class Spon; Prom Coord; Prof Assn of GA Educators Building Rep 1988-; Paper Published 1988; Sci Teacher Research Involvement for Vital Ed Prgm 1990; *home:* Rt 3 Box 133 Thomson GA 30824

VAN SCOTER, MARYANN CICERO, Fifth Grade Teacher; *b:* Dansville, NY; *m:* Ronald O.; *c:* Linda Krahe, William, Andrew, Kristopher; *ed:* (AA) Liberal Arts, Genesee Comm Coll 1970; (BS) Elem Ed, SUNY Geneseo 1972; (MS) Ed, Elmira Coll 1976; Grad Work, Univ of KY & Alfred Univ; *cr:* 5th Grade Teacher St Patricks Sch 1972-74, Hornell City Sch System 1974-; *ai:* Effective Schls, Cmptr Comm; Hornell Educators Assn, NEA, NY Ed Assn 1974-; St Anns Contemporary Choir (Guitarist, Dir) 1976-; Hornell Area Wind Ensemble Trumpet Player 1987-; Arkport Exch Club 1989-; *office:* Hornell Intermediate Sch 21 Park St Hornell NY 14843

VAN SICKLE, REECY MASON, Fifth Grade Teacher; *b:* Millstone, KY; *m:* Richard L.; *c:* Scott, Terah; *ed:* (AA) Elem Ed, Lees Jr Coll 1965; (BS) Elem Ed, 1969, (MA) Rdng Specialists, 1975 E KY Univ; *cr:* Kndgtn Teacher Marengo Elem Sch 1965-67; 3rd Grade Teacher Pilot View Elem Sch 1969-70; 6th Grade Teacher 1981-83, 5th Grade Teacher 1983- Shearer Elem Sch; *ai:* Cmmty Sch Relations Chairperson; Sch Patrol & Newspaper Spon; Clark Cty Ed Assn (Shearer Sch Building Rep 1989-) 1981-; KY Ed Assn 1981-; Clark Cty 4-H Cncl Pres 1982-83; *home:* 284 Cabin Creek Rd Winchester KY 40391

VAN SLYKE, LINDA LEE, Spanish/Mathematics Teacher; *b:* Fort Dodge, IA; *c:* Reece Sheeler, Necia Hoffman, Bobbi Marsh, Michael Marsh; *ed:* (AA) Span/Math, Ellsworth Jr Coll 1973; (BS) Span/Math, 1977, (MS) Curr/Instruction/Span/Math, 1987 Mankato St Univ; *cr:* Math Teacher New Ulm 1977-78; Span Teacher Mankato East HS 1978-80; Math/Cmptr Sci Teacher Janesville 1980-83; Math/Span Teacher Mankato East HS 1983-; *ai:* Coach Math League Team & Math Portion of Academic Decathalon; Jr Class Adv; Fall Play Costumes Chairperson; MN Ed Effectiveness Prgm Treas 1988-; AFS (Screening Coord 1983-85, Sch Rep 1978-80); Coach MN All Star Math League Team to Natl Competition 1988; Nom MN Teacher of Yr 1990; *home:* 318 Meadow Woods Dr Mankato MN 56001

VAN STEENBERG, SUZANNE J. RICHARDS, Third Grade Teacher; *b:* Johnson City, NY; *m:* Walter Lee; *c:* Michelle L.; *ed:* (BS) Early Chldhd/Elem Ed, Univ of Akron 1971; Outdoor Ed, Univ of Akron; *cr:* Learning Disabilities Tutor 1973-75, 3rd Grade Teacher 1975-76, 2nd Grade Teacher 1976-78, 3rd Grade Teacher 1978- Wadsworth City Schls; *ai:* Right-to-Read, Adopt a Family, Hall of Fame, Right-to-write, Soc, Young Author, Written Competency, Rdng for Revision Curr Comms; Summer Sch Rdng 1988-89; Wadsworth Ed Assn, NE OH Teachers Assn, NEA 1975-; *office:* Wadsworth City Schls 160 W Good Ave Wadsworth OH 44281

VAN VALKENBURG, EDRIS OWSLEY, Mathematics Teacher; *b:* Paris, KY; *m:* George F.; *c:* Rebecca Reuss, George R., Edris J., Katherine A., Wesley E.; *ed:* (BA) Scndry Ed Math, 1982, (MS) Math Ed, 1989 SUNY Buffalo; CUNA Management Sch 1986-87; Schenectady Cty Comm Coll, Math Tele-Inst 1990; *cr:* 7th/8th Grade Math Teacher Pioneer Mid Sch 1983-; *ai:* Grading Policy Comm; Mentor Prgm; Tutoring; NY Assn of Math Teachers 1985-; Tri-Cty Federal Credit Union Treas 1986-; Free Meth Church (Pianist 1985-, Sunday Sch Teacher 1972-, Genesee Conference Delegate 1987-), 10 Yr Service Awd 1983; Machias Youth Commission Pool Coord 1980-88; *office:* Pioneer Mid Sch Old Yorkshire Rd Yorkshire NY 14173

VAN VELZER, SHARON THILL, Second Grade Teacher; *b:* Glendale, CA; *c:* Traci A., Darren G.; *ed:* (BA) Ed, CA St Univ Northridge 1965; Working Toward Bi-ling Credential in Span, Methodology, Culture, Lang; Getty Art, Cmptr, Violence Prevention Trng; Inservice Classes; *cr:* 2nd Grade Teacher Arminta St Elem 1965-72; 3rd Grade Teacher Shepherd of Valley Luth Sch 1977-85; 2nd Grade Teacher Woodland Hills Elem 1985-; *ai:* CA St Univ Northridge Master Trng Teacher; Shepherd of Valley Luth Sch Bd Mem 1988-; Grade Level, Soc Comm Chm; Gifted Comm; Cmptr Lab Coord; After Sch Tutor; Intern for Kndgtn Intervention Prgm Supvr; United Teachers of Los Angeles Mem 1989-; CSUN CA New Teacher Awd of Gratification; *office:* Woodland Hills Elem Sch 22201 San Miguel Ave Woodland Hills CA 91364

VAN VICKLE, CONNIE SUE, English Teacher; *b:* Dyersburg, TN; *c:* Shelley R.; *ed:* (AS) Bus, Dyersburg St Comm Coll 1972; (BS) Ed/Comm/Speech/Eng/Drama 1975, (MS) Ed/Eng 1980 Univ of TN; *cr:* Eng Teacher Newbern Jr HS 1975-86, Dyer Cty HS 1986-; *ai:* Frosh Chrldr, Jr Class Spon; TN Ed Assn, NEA 1975-; Dyer Cty Ed Assn Secy; Alpha Delta Kappa Corresponding Secy 1988-; Life Blood 1980-; First United Meth Church; Teacher of Yr 1970; *home:* 603 E Main Newbern TN 38059

VAN WAGONER, JANE ELLEN (SCHOBE), Home Economics Teacher; *b:* Kansas City, MO; *ed:* (BS) Home Ec, Pepperdine Coll 1966; (MA) Psych, Pepperdine Univ 1983; Marriage & Family Therapist; *cr:* Home Ec Teacher Fullerton HS 1967-69, Walnut HS 1969-; M F C C Private Practice 1986-; *ai:* Peer Counseling Adv Walnut HS; CA Teacher Assn 1967-; CA Assn of Marriage and Family Therpists 1983; Walnut Valley Unified Sch Dist Teacher of Yr 1985; Walnut HS Teacher of Yr 1985; *office:* Walnut HS 400 N Pierre Rd Walnut CA 91789

VAN WIEL, JOHN EDWARD, Chemistry Teacher; *b:* Moline, IL; *ed:* (BS) Chem, Loyola Univ 1964; (STB) Theology, 1966, (MS) Chem, 1970 Cath Univ; (MED) Educl Admin, Univ of NC Charlotte 1973; *cr:* Sci Teacher St Viator HS 1966-67; Teacher/Dean/Prin Bishop Mc Namara HS 1967-73; Prin Alleman HS 1973-84; Sci Teacher/Dean Griffin HS 1985-87; Chem Teacher St Viator HS 1987-; *ai:* NASSP 1972-84; NCEA 1987-; *office:* St Viator HS 1213 E Oakton St Arlington Heights IL 60004

VAN ZANT, CAROL SALATO, 6th-8th Grade Math Teacher; *b:* Louisville, KY; *m:* Russell Norris; *c:* Susan, Russ; *ed:* (BS) Elem Ed, 1973, (MA) Elem Ed, 1975, (Rank I) Sch Admin, 1987 W KY Univ ; *cr:* 5th/6th Grade Teacher Edmonton Elem 1970-71; 6th Grade Teacher Summer Shade Elem 1973-74; 7th/8th Grade Math Teacher Edmonton Elem 1974-77; 5th/6th Grade Math Teacher Dixon Elem 1977-79; 2nd Grade Teacher Tompkinsville Elem 1979-80; 7th/8th Grade Math Teacher Tompkinsville HS 1980-83; 6th-8th Grade Math Teacher Radcliff Jr HS 1983-87, Hardin Cntrl Mid Sch 1987-; *ai:* Cheerleading Boys, Girls Var Bsktbl Spon Tompkinsville HS 1980-83; Beta Club Spon Hardin Cntrl Mid Grades 1988; KEA, NEA 1970-; *home:* 904 Tyler Cir Elizabethtown KY 42701

VAN ZANT, DONNA JOHNSON, French Teacher; *b:* Minneapolis, MN; *m:* David L.; *c:* Diane Osbourn, David Jr., Stephen; *ed:* (AA) Fr/Ger, Elizabethtown Comm Coll 1973; (BA) Fr/Ger, E KY Univ 1975; (MA) Scndry Counseling, W KY Univ 1984; *cr:* Fr Teacher North Hardin HS 1979-; *ai:* Fr Club Spon; KY Cncl Teachers of Foreign Lang 1979-; AATF; Alpha Gamma Delta; *office:* North Hardin HS 801 S Logsdon Pkwy Radcliff KY 40160

VAN ZUIDEN, JOY ANN, Kindergarten Teacher; *b:* Clinton, IA; *m:* Thomas Edward; *c:* Janet L., Dustin T.; *ed:* (MA) Lang Art, N IL Univ 1990; *cr:* 2nd Grade Teacher 1977-79, Kndgtn Teacher 1980-81, 1985- Fulton Elem Sch; *ai:* NEA, IEA 1977-79, 1985-; Riverbend Ed Assn (Area Rep 1989-) 1977-79, 1985-; 2nd Reformed Church Various Offices 1977-; Fulton Dutch Days Organizer 1981-; *home:* 1114 9th Ave Fulton IL 61252

VARDEMAN, DAVID A., English Teacher; *b:* Waco, TX; *ed:* (BA) Eng/His, 1969, (MS) Sci Ed, 1974 Baylor Univ; *cr:* Eng Teacher Univ Jr HS 1969, Midway Jr HS 1969-; *ai:* Midway Jr HS Communictions Comm; TSTA, NEA 1969-83, 1986-; *home:* PO Box 331 Hewitt TX 76643

VARIS, LINDA TREECE, Spanish/English Teacher; *b:* Herrin, IL; *m:* Barry Kohl; *c:* Cristina, Robby; *ed:* (BA) Span, 1971, (MS) Educl Admin, 1984, Level III Admin Cert, 1988 S IL Univ; Completed Classes PHD in Educl Admin; *cr:* Span Teacher/Librarian Barr-Reve Sch Dist 1971-72; Span/Eng Teacher/Librarian Cntrl Jr HS 1973-; *ai:* Span Club & Lib Club Spon; Scholastic Bowl Coach; Admin Duties in Absence of Prin; Franklin Cty Technology Advisory Cncl Mem; IL Fed of Teachers (Negotiator, Officer 1973-88); Phi Delta Kappa, Phi Kappa Phi 1984-; IL Foreign Lang Teachers Assn 1978-; W Frankfort Civic Center Authority Bd 1988-; W Frankfort Planning Commission 1982-87; Assn of IL Mid-Level Schls St Bd Mem; IL St Bd of Ed Foreign Lang Consultant for S IL; *home:* 509 Franklin Ave West Frankfort IL 62896

VARNADORE, VIDERA KOOGLER, Remedial Math & Rdng Teacher; *b:* Barberton, OH; *m:* Terry R.; *c:* Melissa K.; *ed:* (AA) Elem Ed, Greenville Tech Coll 1974; (BA) Elem Ed, 1975, (MED) Personnel Services/Elem Ed, 1977 Clemson Univ; Certified in Rdng Clemson Univ & Furman Univ 1987; *cr:* 3rd Grade Teacher 1975-84, 4th Grade Teacher 1984-85, 3rd Grade Teacher 1986-87, Remedial Rdng/Math Teacher 1987- Westcliffe Elem; *office:* Westcliffe Elem Sch 105 Eastborne Dr Greenville SC 29611

VARNER, BETTY R., 5th Grade Teacher; *b:* Bucksport, SC; *m:* John K.; *c:* Kirk, Kyle; *ed:* (BA) Elem Ed, Univ of SC 1955; *cr:* 6th Grade Teacher Oak Terrace Elem 1955-57; 7th Grade Teacher Morningside Elem 1957-60; 6th/7th Grade Teacher Dorchester Terrace Elem 1962-66; 5th/6th/7th Grade Teacher Corcoran Elem 1968-; *ai:* NEA; *office:* A C Corcoran Elem Sch 8585 Vistavia Rd North Charleston SC 29418

VASILE, JUDITH GLOVER, Mathematics Teacher; *b:* Englewood, NJ; *m:* Eugene J.; *c:* Jeffrey R. Fagan; *ed:* (BA) Math, Beaver Coll 1964; Kean Coll of NJ; Jersey City St Coll; *cr:* Teacher Bogota Public Sch 1964-66, Parsippany Public Sch 1966-69, Kittatinny Reg Adult Summer Sch 1985-88; *ai:* Ski Club Adv; Cooperative Relations Site Management; NCTM; AMTNJ; Beaver Coll Alumni Admissions Rep; Morris Cty Club-Fund Agent Class 64; Sussex Cty Assn for Retarded Citizens Volunteer.

VASILE, MARY ANN R., Second Grade Teacher; *b:* Wilkes-Barre, PA; *ed:* (BS) Elem/Soc Stud, Coll Misericordia 1968; (MS) Elem Counseling/Early Chldhd, Bloomsburg Univ 1971; Grad Stud Penn St Univ; *cr:* HUD Supvr US Government 1972; Teacher Wilkes-Barre Area Sch Dist 1969-; *ai:* 3rd Grade Pilot Prgm; Wrote K-6th Grade Math Curr; PSEA, NEA, Womens Club; Hospital Volunteer 1975-79; Local Soup Kitchen Donor 1988-89; GSA 1972-75; Heart Fund Comm Chm 1969; Volunteers Service to America Donor 1980-86; *office:* Wilkes-Barre Area Sch Old River Rd Wilkes-Barre PA 18702

VASKE, MARY LOU (SIMMONS), Home Ec Teacher; *b:* Cuba City, WI; *m:* David Victor; *c:* Philip John, Craig David; *ed:* (BS) Scndry Ed, Univ of WI-Platteville 1966; (BS) Commerce & Industry-Accounting, Univ of WY 1989; *cr:* Home Ec Teacher Dubuque Cmmty Sch Dist 1966-71, Albany Cty Sch Dist 1978-; *ai:* Dept Co-Chairperson Home Ec; Albany Cty Ed Assn Treas 1989-; WY Ed Assn; NEA; *office:* Laramie JR HS 1355 N 22nd Laramie WY 82070

VASQUEZ, ANTHONY JUDE, History Teacher; *b:* Upland, CA; *m:* Rita Ambroso; *c:* Michael; *ed:* (BA) His, Univ of La Verne 1980; *cr:* Teacher Imperial Jr HS 1981-84; Head Bsktbl Coach 1984-87, Teacher 1984- Ontario HS; *ai:* Asst Var Bsbl Coach; Selected Head Coach Pomona Valley All-Star Bsktbl Team; *office:* Ontario HS 901 W Francis Ave Ontario CA 91762

VASS, SUSAN J., Reading Teacher; *b:* Philadelphia, PA; *ed:* (BA) Elem Ed, Holy Family Coll 1977; Grad Work in Crisis Intervention; *cr:* 3rd Grade Teacher 1978-86, 7th/8th Grade Teacher 1986- Our Lady of Calvary; *ai:* Jr HS Rdng Coord; NCEA 1978-; *office:* Our Lady of Calvary Sch 110 23 Kipling Ln Philadelphia PA 19154

VASSEY, CONNIE LYNN, 7th/8th Grade Soc Stud Teacher; *b:* Greenville, SC; *ed:* (BA) Scndry Ed/Soc Stud, Clemson Univ 1979; (MA) Scndry Ed/Soc Stud, Furman Univ 1983; *cr:* Sci Teacher 1980-82, Soc Stud Teacher 1982- Bryson Mid Sch; *ai:* Sch Improvement Cncl; Grant Recipient Greenville Alliance 1989-; *office:* Bryson Mid Sch Box 338 Bryson Dr Fountain Inn SC 29644

VASSILAROS, CONSTANTINE GEORGE, Anatomy/Physiology/Bio Teacher; *b:* Piraeus, Greece; *m:* Barbara Gray; *c:* George, John; *ed:* (BS) Bio, California Univ of PA 1957; (MED) Bio, Indiana Univ of PA 1963; Univ of Pittsburgh, Univ of IN, OK St Univ, Seattle Pacific Coll; *cr:* Teacher Gateway HS 1958-; Part Time Teacher Westmoreland Cty Comm Coll 1971-75, Allegheny Cty Comm Coll 1983-; *ai:* Sci Club Adv 1958-; Supt Advisory Comm; W PA Bio Teachers Organization Pres Elect 1990; NABT; PA Jr Acad of Sci (St Treas 1969-70, Asst Dir 1966-71); Articles Published; PA Jr Acad of Sci Awd Outstanding Work With Sci Stu; Calvin Burns Awd of Merit Outstanding Sci Teaching Amer Spectorscopy Society; Teacher Awd for Tomorrows Scientists & Engrs; *office:* Gateway HS Mosside Blvd Monroeville PA 15146

VATHIS, JAMES B., World History Teacher; *b:* Philadelphia, PA; *m:* Erika Varhalmi; *c:* Erika, Christina; *ed:* (BS) Soc Stud/Ed, 1972, (MED) Ed/His, 1974 Shippensburg St; *cr:* Teacher Stephen Decatur HS 1973-; *ai:* Current Events Club; NCSS, NEA, Md St Teachers Assn; Kodak Cameras Classroom Grant 1982; Natl Endowment for Hum Inst Princeton Univ Ottoman Empire 1982, Princeton on Islam 1986, Marshall Univ on Ancient Rome

1989;Natl Endowment for Hum Seminar Univ of MN Morris on Rousseau 1984; *home:* 9017 Ocean Pines Berlin MD 21811

VAUGHAN, NANCY BRYSON, Social Studies Teacher; *b:* Murfreesboro, TN; *c:* Randall, Russell; *ed:* (BA) His/Poly Sci, TN St Univ 1957; (MS) Curr/Instruction Mid TN Univ 1969; TN Career Level Teacher II Mid TN St Univ; *cr:* Teacher US Army, 1963-64; Dir Headstart Prgm Federal Government 1965-67; Teacher Rutherford Cty Sch System 1967-, Mid TN St Univ 1987-; *ai:* Advisory & Sr Planning Comm; Rutherford Ed Assn Rep 1971-81 Teacher of Yr 1976; TN Ed Assn Teacher of Yr 1980; NEA; Amer Bus Womens Assn (Secy, Ways & Means Comm Chairperson) 1988-, Assoc of Yr 1989; *office:* La Vergne HS Wolverine Trl La Vergne TN 37086

VAUGHAN, SHARON R., English Teacher; *b:* Oak Park, IL; *m:* Harry W.; *c:* Holly, Heather, Hilary; *ed:* (BSED) Ed/Eng, 1962, (MAED) Ed/Eng, 1967 Concordia Coll; Gifted Ed, N IL Univ; *cr:* 6th Grade Teacher Cntrl Luth Sch 1962-64; 10th Grade Eng Teacher Luther HS 1964-66; Asst Prof Ed/Speech/Theater Concordia Coll 1967-74; 9th-12th Grade Eng Teacher/6th-12th Grade Art Teacher Ohio HS 1985-; *ai:* Yrbk & Class Spon; IL Assn Teachers of Eng; GSA Leader 1979-89; Centrillio Cncl Family Awd 1986; NEH Fellowship 1989; Articles Published 1964 & 1990; *office:* Ohio HS 103 Memorial St Ohio IL 61349

VAUGHN, ADRIAN J., Speech/Language Therapist; *b:* Staunton, VA; *c:* Derian; *ed:* (BS) Speech Pathology/Audiology, James Madison Univ 1974; Working Towards Masters Ed Admin, VA Tech Univ; Grad Stud Speech Pathology, James Madison Univ; *cr:* Speech Therapist Fauquier Cty Public Sch 1974-79; Summer Youth Employment Coord Fairfax Cty Manpower Services 1974-87; Speech Therapist Prince William Cty Public Schls 1979-; *ai:* Safety Patrol Spon & Coord; Sch Advisory Cncl Mem; Spec Ed Staff Rep; *office:* John F Pattie Elem Sch 16125 Dumfries Rd Dumfries VA 22026

VAUGHN, C. DENNIS, 6th Grade Teacher; *b:* Springfield, OH; *m:* Robin M. Downey; *ed:* Christie, Katy, David, Robbie, Daniel; (BA) Elem Ed, Cntrl St Univ 1972; (MS) Principalship, Univ of Dayton 1978; *cr:* 6th Grade Teacher Cedar-Cliff Elem 1972-; *ai:* Var Bsbl, Ftbl, Golf; Boys Bsktbl Reserve & Jr HS; Girls Var Bsktbl; OEA, NEA, PTO 1972-; Cedar Cliff Ed Assn; Wrote Book 1978; Honored by Mayor for Girls Bsktbl Tm; *office:* Cedar-Cliff Elem Sch Box 45 Cedarville OH 45314

VAUGHN, ELIZABETH CANE, English Teacher; *b:* Marion, MD; *m:* Moses W.; *c:* Rex, Royace; *ed:* (BA) Eng, Howard Univ 1950; (MA) Equivalence 1972; Cath Univ, Howard Univ, Salisbury St Univ, Trinity Coll; *cr:* Eng Teacher Bel Alton HS 1950-61, Wicomico Jr HS 1969-87, Wicomico Mid Sch 1988-; *ai:* Eng Club Spon; Essay Contest Comm Chm; Mem Admin Advisory, Partnership in Ed Comm; Coach Sch Participants Optimist Oratorical Contest; Wicomico Cty Ed Assn Intercom Chairperson 1984-87; MD St Teachers Assn, NEA; Alpha Kappa Alpha; *office:* Wicomico Mid Sch E Main St Salisbury MD 21801

VAUGHN, EVA K., 5th Grade Teacher; *b:* Brodhead, KY; *m:* Paul Jr.; *c:* Thomas; *ed:* (BS) Elem, E KY Univ 1959; *cr:* 6th Grade Teacher 1959-63, 5th Grade Teacher 1964-78 Saffell Street Elem; 5th Grade Teacher Emma B Ward Elem 1978-; *ai:* Leadership & Counseling Comm; NEA, KEA; ACTA (VP, Building Rep); *office:* Emma B Ward Elem Sch West Broadway Lawrenceburg KY 40342

VAUGHN, GEORGIANNE C., 5th/6th Grade Reading Teacher; *b:* Troy, TN; *m:* John E. III; *c:* Amy, Michelle; *ed:* (BS) Ed, Memphis St Univ 1969; *cr:* 1st Grade Teacher 1971-76, 1st/2nd Grade Chapter Teacher 1976-79, 5th/6th Grade Rdng Teacher 1979- Margaret Newton; *ai:* Textbook Adoption Comm 1988-89; Sunshine Fund Comm 1989-; Delta Kappa Gamma Treas 1988-.

VAUGHN, JAMES HAROLD, Mathematics Teacher; *b:* Cardwell, MO; *m:* Carolyn Jeanette Bishop; *c:* James S.; *ed:* (BS) Math, 1962, (MS) Math, 1965 AR St Univ; St Louis Univ, OH St Univ, Marquette Univ, S IL Univ Edwardsville; *cr:* Math Teacher Hayti HS 1962-63, Fox HS 1963-67, Lindbergh HS 1967-; *ai:* Math Club Spon; Dist Math Curr Comm; NEA, AFT, NCTM, MCTM; Intnl Baccalaureate Teacher of Yr 1988-89; *office:* Lindbergh HS 4900 S Lindbergh Saint Louis MO 63126

VAUGHN, JANICE CHILCUTT, Math/Soc Stud Mid Sch Teacher; *b:* Buchanan, TN; *m:* William Dalton; *c:* Michael, Timothy; *ed:* (BS) Elem Ed/Eng, 1971, (MA) Elem Ed, 1976, (Rank I) Elem Ed, 1980 Murray St Univ; Intern Teachers Resource Teacher; *cr:* 6th Grade Teacher Hardin Elem 1971-73; 4th Grade Teacher S Marshall Elem 1973-77; 5th Grade Teacher Sharpe Elem 1977-88; Mid Sch Teacher N Marshall 1988-; *ai:* 6th Grade Team Leader; Cnslr Comm Mem; Marshall Cty Ed Assn Secy 1978; KY Gifted Prgm 1980-86; NEA, KY Ed Assn 1971-; *office:* N Marshall Mid Sch Rt 2 Calvert City KY 42029

VAUGHN, LINDA SUE (SEATON), 6th Grade Teacher; *b:* Valparaiso, IN; *m:* Lanny Steve; *c:* Moneca, Heather; *ed:* (BS) Ed, 1963, (MS) Ed, 1967 Memphis St Univ; Mercer Univ, Olgethorpe Univ, AZ St Univ; *cr:* 6th Grade Classroom Teacher Memphis City Schls 1963-64; Phys Ed Instr William C Jack 1964-65; 5th/7th Grade Teacher Dekalb Cty Schls 1975-78; 6th Grade Classroom Teacher Gwinnett Cty 1978-; *ai:* Spon Stu Cncl, Red Cross; Grade Level Chairperson; Teacher of Yr 1985, 1989; *home:* 4457 Ridgegate Dr Duluth GA 30136

VAUGHN, NELL JONES, Fourth Grade Teacher; *b:* Selma, AL; *m:* Edward C.; *c:* Susan V. Hall; *ed:* (BA) Religious Ed, Samford Univ 1951; (MA) Religious Ed, SW Baptist Theological Seminary 1954; Met Requirements for Bachelors & Masters Cert Livingston Univ; *cr:* Youth Dir Istrouma Baptist Church 1954-56; Secy GA Baptist Convention 1956-60; Campus/Youth Dir Livingston Univ Baptist Church 1962-63; 4th Grade Teacher Sumter Acad 1974-; *ai:* Spelling Bee Spon; Sch Bd Faculty Rep; Delta Kappa Gamma 1st VP 1988-; Primrose Club (2nd VP 1984-86, 1st VP 1986-88); Livingston 1st Baptist Church (Teacher, Comm 1978-); *office:* Sumter Acad Rt 1 Box 389 York AL 36925

VAUGHN, ROBERT LEWIS, Sixth Grade Teacher; *b:* Athens, OH; *m:* Michele Rene Ebert; *c:* Sarah E., Michael R.; *ed:* (BSED) Elem Ed, OH Univ 1977; *cr:* 6th Grade Teacher Mississinawa Valley Mid Sch 1977-78, Huntington Elem 1978-; *ai:* OH Army Natl Guard; Retention NCO & Public Relations NCO; SE OH Adult Basic Ed Instr; *office:* Huntington Elem Sch 188 Huntsmen Rd Chillicothe OH 45601

VAUGHT, AUDEAN THORNTON, Business & Health Teacher; *b:* Russell Springs, KY; *m:* William A.; *c:* Dewayne, Shannon; *ed:* (BS) Bus, Campbellsville Coll 1968; Bus, 1974, Bus, 1980 Eastern KY Univ; *cr:* Teacher Eubank HS 1968, Burnside Elem 1968-77, Burnside Hs 1977-82; SOuthern Elem Sch 1982-87, Southern Jr. HS1987-; *ai:* Academic Coach-8th Grade; Club Adv-Just Say No Club-8th & 9th Grade; Guidance Comm Faculty Mem; NEA; KEA; Pulaski Cty Ed Assn ; *home:* 114 Oak Ave Somerset KY 42501

VAZQUEZ, ELAINE C., 6th Grade Teacher; *b:* Lancaster, PA; *m:* Frank J.; *c:* John; *ed:* (BS) Elem Ed, Indiana Univ of PA 1966; Grad & In-Service Courses; *cr:* Teacher Bergstrasse Elem 1969-; *ai:* Peer Helper Adv; EAEA 1969-; *home:* 601 Ridge View Dr Ephrata PA 17522

VEACH, GLORIA WHITE, Fourth Grade Teacher; *b:* Mt Vernon, IL; *m:* Homer; *c:* Teresa, James, Tamara; *ed:* (BS) Elem, IN St 1973; (MA) Elem, De Pauw Univ 1977; *cr:* 4th Grade Teacher Tangier Elem 1973-74; 5th/6th Grade Teacher Tangier & Bloomingdale 1974-75; 4th Grade Teacher Turkey Run Elem 1975-; *ai:* ISTA/NEA 1973-; Delta Kappa Gamma (Cor Secy 1983-85) 1981-; Delta Theta Tau 1981-84; *home:* R R 1 Box 243 Bloomingdale IN 47832

VEAL, DEANNE DODSON, Gifted Stu Resource Teacher; *b:* Americus, GA; *m:* Donald G.; *ed:* (BA) Bio/Health/Phys Ed, Mercer Univ 1959; (MED) Health/Phys Ed, GA Coll 1962; Post Grad Work, Univ of NC Greensboro, FL St Univ, Valdosta St Coll; *cr:* Health/Phys Ed Teacher A L Miller Sr HS 1959-64; Instr/Asst Professor Wesleyan Coll 1964-70; Asst Professor Mercer Univ 1970-72; Resource Teacher for Gifted Silas Mahone & S L Mason Elem Schls 1973-78, Len Lastinger & Annie Belle Clark Elem Schls 1978-; *ai:* Cty Wide Comm Write Art & Sci Curr; Directed Wkshp Inservice Trng Cty Teachers of Gifted; Cty Wide & Sch Rep Environmental Projects; Intnl Rdng Assn Cty Parents & Rdng Chm 1985-, GA St Rdng Teacher of Yr 1987; GA Cncl Intnl Rdng Assn; Tift Cty Cncl of Intnl Rdng Assn (Pres-Elect, Pres); Cncl for Exceptional Children Tift Cty Pres 1984-85, 1990; Baldwin Womans Club (Treas 1980, Pres 1987); Literacy Volunteers of America (Mem, Bd of Dir) 1988-; Elks Auxiliary Pres 1988-; Cty Wide Comm for Earth Day 1990; Teacher of Yr Annie Belle Clark Elem Sch; Planned, Coordinated & Taught Tift Ctys 1st Family Focus Wkshp; Directed & Taught Summer Prgms for Gifted Stus; *office:* Len Lastinger & A B Clark Elem Lake Dr Tifton GA 31794

VEAL, JANE F. (ZEY), Third Grade Teacher; *b:* Abilene, KS; *m:* Stanley R.; *c:* Blain C., Stacia Veal Nelson, Molly Veal Veach; *ed:* (BS) Elem Ed/Psych-Cum Laude Mary Mount Coll 1972; (MS) Ed-Magna Cum Laude, KS St Univ 1980; Rdng Specialist Cert, KS St Univ Manhattan 1980; Grad Stud Ed; *cr:* 4th Grade Teacher Lincoln Elem Sch 1972-73; Kennedy Elem Sch 1973-76; Kndgtn-12th Grade Substitute Teacher Abilene & Solomon Schls 1976-78; 1st Grade Teacher 1978-80, 3rd Grade Teacher 1980- Solomon Elem Sch; *ai:* Water Safety Instr & Adults & Childrens Swimming Teacher Amer Red Cross Prgm; Antique Bus Jesse Janes Trading Co Auctioneer Prairie Land Auctioneers of Abilene; SEA, KNEA, NEA (Building Rep, Teachers Advisory Cncl) 1972-; KS Assn oF Teachers of Sci & Rdng Mem; Saint Andrews Cath Church (Mem & Pres 1980); Cncl St Andrews Abilene Historical Society Mem; Deans Honor Roll; Published Article Creative Teacher Teachers Magazine Behavior Modification 1972; *home:* RR 4 Abilene KS 67410

VEAL, MARY SUE, English Teacher; *b:* Meridian, MS; *m:* C. David; *c:* Richard Schmidt, Gavin Schmidt; *ed:* (BA) Span/Eng/Poly Sci, Univ of MS 1964; *cr:* Span Teacher Fernwood Jr HS 1964-65; Eng Teacher Fernwood Mid Sch 1984-88, Biloxi HS 1988-; *ai:* NHS Adv; Delta Kappa Gamma; Biloxi Ocean Springs Jr Auxiliary Life Mem; Biloxi Chamber of Commerce Outstanding Mid Sch Teacher 1987; *home:* 2629 Parkview Dr Biloxi MS 39531

VEATCH, SARA O., Science Teacher; *b:* Cedartown, GA; *ed:* (AB) Scndry Ed/Bio, Wesleyan Coll 1975; (MED) Scndry Ed/Bio, N GA Coll 1979; Sci Ed Wkshps; *cr:* Classroom Teacher Johnson HS 1975-; *ai:* Beta Club Spon; Several Local Sch Comm Chm; Music Comm 1982-85; GA Ed Assn, NEA 1975-; Auxiliary of NE GA Medical Center 1980-; 1st Baptist Church Youth Comm 1978-85; Gainesville Chorale Cmmty Chorus 1987-; Daughters of Amer Revolution 1988-; Cmmty Leadership Prgm; Nom Local NSTA Teacher of Yr; *office:* Johnson HS 3305 Poplar Springs Rd Gainesville GA 30505

VEAZEY, JUDITH BEUHRING, 4th Grade Classroom Teacher; *b:* Huntington, WV; *m:* Morris K. Jr.; *c:* Morris T., Kathryn E.; *ed:* (AB) Elem Ed, 1975, (MA) Spec Ed Gifted, 1980 Marshall Univ; *cr:* Classroom Teacher Buffalo Elem Sch 1976-; *ai:* Math Field Day Dir 1983-; Wayne Cty Youth Soccer 1989-; Wayne Cty Ed Assn (Treas 1977-83, VP 1989-); *home:* 2293 Meadow Haven Huntington WV 25704

VECHIOLA, DONALD FRANCIS, Business Teacher; *b:* Chicago, IL; *m:* Anne Morse; *ed:* (BS) Bus, 1959, (MS) Guidance, 1964 E IL Univ; Grad Stud; *cr:* Accountant Continental IL Natl Bank 1959-63; Teacher Bremen HS 1963-; *ai:* Bus Club; Prof Cncl; Cmptr & Bus Olympics Coord; Gifted Comm; Ind Accountants Assn of IL Pres 1962-; Club Accountants Assn 1985-; Hospitality Accountant Assn 1985-89; AFT, IFT Treas 1968-72; Home Owners Assn Pres 1990; IAAI (Bd of Dir 1978-82, Secy 1982, Treas 1984, 2nd VP 1985, 1st VP 1986, Past Pres 1988); *office:* Bremen HS 15203 S Pulaski Rd Midlothian IL 60445

VEEH, ALAN BRUCE, Social Studies Teacher; *b:* Hemet, CA; *m:* Ann Elizabeth Golden; *c:* Adam, Allison; *ed:* (BA) Government, Univ of Redlands 1972; (MA) Phys Ed, N AZ Univ 1974; ASU & Univ of Phoenix; *cr:* Housing Coord Univ of Redlands 1972-73; Activity Center Dir N AZ Univ 1974-76; Teacher Mc Clintock HS 1976-; *ai:* Frosh Boys Tennis Coach; Law Related Ed Mentor Prgm Coord; North Cntrl Dept Evaluation Chairperson 1989; NCSS, AZ Cncl for Ec Ed; Mc Clintock Soc Stud Teacher of Yr 1989-; *office:* Mc Clintock HS 1830 E Del Rio Tempe AZ 85282

VELASCO, EDIDTSA R., Spanish/Mathematics Teacher; *b:* Nogales, AZ; *ed:* (BAED) Span/Bus Ed, Univ of AZ 1982; *cr:* Kndgtn Teacher Elizabeth Borton Elem 1979-80; PTA Span Prgm Teacher Sam Hughes Elem 1980-82; Certified Teacher Tuscon Unified Sch Dist 1 1983-; *ai:* Jr Optimist Club & FBLA Spon; Greater Tucson Sch Partnership; Advisory & Band Issue Comm; Sch Newspaper Photographer; Band Mem; NHS for Bus Leaders of America (Mem, Secy); Optimist Intnl Bd Mem 1987-89; Modern & Classical Lang Teacher of Yr 1989-; Nom Southwestern Sts Teacher of Yr 1987-88; At Risk Youth Conference Presenter; Worked on Bi-ling Curr Guide; Developed Placement Test; Organized After-Sch Tutoring Prgm; *home:* 5249 W Avenida Comba Tucson AZ 85745

VELASQUEZ, ALBERT LEE, 6th Grade Teacher; *b:* Fort Meyer, VA; *m:* Maria Aguirre; *c:* April, Tiffany, Cynthia; *ed:* Credential Elem Ed, Sacremento St Coll 1977; (BS) Bio/Ed, Univ of CA Davis 1976; (AA) Bio, Monterey Penninsula Jr Coll 1974; Admin Inservice, Mentor, Phys Ed Trng; Wkshps; *cr:* 4th Grade Teacher Boronda Sch 1977-81; Summer Sch Teacher Salinas City Sch Dist 1977-84; 6th Grade Teacher Boronda Sch 1982-; Mentor Teacher 1984-, Summer Sch Prin 1985- Salinas City Sch Dist; *ai:* Coach Salinas Parks & Recs Ftbl & Vlybl 1977-, Bsktbl 1980-, Sftbl 1988-, Track 1986-, Continental Little League 1978-87, 1989-; CA Teachers Assn 1977-; Knights of Columbus 1987-; Toastmasters of America 1983-; Natl PTA Sch Treas 1985-88, Achievement Honor Pin 1986; Boronda PTA Honor Plaque 1979, 1983, 1987; KDON Radio Station Cmmty Person of Month 1980; Monterey Cty Jaycee Educator of Yr 1990; Assembly Resolution Commendation #195 1990; *home:* 1114 Fontes Ln Salinas CA 93907

VELASQUEZ, JOSIE MARTINA, English Teacher; *b:* Las Vegas, NM; *m:* Elmer W.; *c:* Jennifer, Kimberly; *ed:* (BA) Journalism/Eng, 1980, (MA) Guidance/Counseling, 1988 NM Highlands Univ; *cr:* Secy NM Highlands Personnel Dept 1978-79, NM Coop Extension Service 1981-82; Reporter Las Vegas Daily Optic Newspaper 1981-82; Eng Teacher Espanola Valley HS 1982-; *home:* Box 62817 Espanola NM 87532

VELAZQUEZ, MARIA TORRES, Guidance Counselor; *b:* Yauco, PR; *m:* Rafael; *c:* Jason R., Eric J.; *ed:* (BS) Scndry Ed/Eng - Cum Laude, Cath Univ of PR 1974; (MA) Elem Ed/Eng as Second Lang, Kean Coll 1981; Stu Personnel Services; *cr:* Eng as Second Lang/Eng Teacher Perth Amboy HS 1974-86; Guidance Cnslr William C Mc Ginnis Sch 1986-88, Perth Amboy HS 1988-; *ai:* City Schls of Excl Comm; Parents & Cmmty Subcomm; Participated in Faculty Shows 1982, 1984-86, 1990; Testing & Stu Review Assessment Comm Mem; Middlesex Cty Personnel & Guidance Assn Mem 1986-; *office:* Perth Amboy HS Eagle & Francis Sts Perth Amboy NJ 08861

VELEZ, ESPERANZA, Honors Chemistry Teacher; *b:* Parral, Mexico; *c:* Maria L. Aguilar-Velez; *ed:* (BS) Microbiology, Univ of TX El Paso 1978; Chem, La Univ de Autonoma De Nuevo Leon 1981; Numerous Courses & Schls; *cr:* Plant Physiology/Inorganic Chem/Analytical Chem Teacher Advanced Ag Stud Inst 1978-80; Project Consultant CONACYT Sci & Technology Center 1981; Chem/Immunology Dept Head Lab of the Amer British Cowdray Hospital 1981-82; Honors Chem Teacher Riverside HS 1987-; *ai:* Univ Interscholastic League Sci Club Co-Spon; RHS Chem Tutor; Stu Sci Fair Project Consultant; NEA, TX St Teachers Assn 1987-; Teacher of Month; Certificates of Superior Achievement from Merck Co of Mexico & Boehringer Mannheim Diagnostics Inc; *office:* Riverside HS 301 Midway Dr El Paso TX 79915

VELEZ, VICKEY, 1st Grade Teacher; *b:* Pampa, TX; *m:* Rudy; *c:* Kevin, Valerie; *ed:* (BA) Elem Ed/Psych, W TX St Univ 1977; *cr:* Kndgtn Teacher B M Baker Elem 1977-78; Kndgtn Teacher 1979-80, 1st Grade Teacher 1981- Stephen F Austin Elem; *ai:* TX Classroom Teachers Assn 1981-; *office:* Stephen F Austin Elem Sch 1900 N Duncan Pampa TX 79065

VELLOFF, MICHAEL M., Fifth Grade Teacher; *b:* Alton, IL; *m:* Terrah J. Daech; *c:* Andrew, Terrah, Jodie; *ed:* (BS) Poly Sci, 1963, (MAT) Poly Sci, 1968 St Louis Univ; *cr:* Teacher Logan & Prather Elem Schls; *ai:* Drug Abuse Coord, Patrol Supvr; Soccer Coach; AFL-CLO Teachers Union Building Rep; Godfrey Khoury League Sftbl Comm; IL Khoury League St Sftbl Comm; Parochial Sports League Pres; Appointed Mem Parish Cncl SS Peter & Paul; Elected Mem Parish Cncl St Ambrose Sch; *home:* 800 Taylor Godfrey IL 62035

VELTRI, PATRICIA ANN (CHRISTY), First Grade Teacher; *b:* Walsenburg, CO; *m:* James Richard; *ed:* (AA) Elem Ed, Trinidad St Jr Coll 1969; (BA) Elem Ed, 1971, (MA) Elem Ed, 1976 Adams St Coll; *cr:* 1st Grade Teacher Kearney Elem Sch 1971-82, Longfellow Elem Sch 1983-; *ai:* K-1 Dept Head; Supts Advisory Cncl Needs Assessment Comm; Delta Kappa Gamma (Mem, 1st VP 1986-) 1983-; NEA Mem 1971-89; Raton Ed Assn (Secy 1976-78, Mem) 1971-89; NM Ed Assn Mem 1971-89; NM St Textbook Adoption Spelling Comm 1980-81; *office:* Longfellow Elem Sch 700 E 4th St Raton NM 87740

VENARD, DORIS FERSON, 4th Grade Teacher; *b:* Des Moines, IA; *w:* Leonard V. (dec); *c:* Lendee Hanson; *ed:* (BA) Ed, KS Univ 1967; (MS) Curr/Instruction, Emporia Univ; Effective Sch & Cmptr Ed Trng; *cr:* 4th Grade Teacher John F Kennedy Sch 1968-; *ai:* Mentor Teacher; Curr & Textbook Comm; Math Coord; NEA 1968-; Intnl Rdng Assn 1987-; Alpha Delta Kappa Pres Elect 1990; WYCA Parents Club Swim Team 1980-88; Nom Excl in Teaching 1987, 1990.

VENCKUS, MEG, Teacher/Coach; *b:* Chicago, IL; *m:* Richard; *c:* Jaime, Kerry, Brian; *ed:* (BA) Phys Ed, NE IL Univ 1974; *cr:* Teacher/Coach Farragut 1975-80, Bogan 1980-; *ai:* Var Vlybl Coach; IHSA Region I Coach of Yr 1988-89; Southtown Economist Coach of Yr 1989; News Herold Coach of Yr 1989; Sun Times All Star Coach 1989; *office:* Bogan HS 3939 W 79th St Chicago IL 60652

VENET, TERESA MIMS, 4th Grade Teacher; *b:* Moultrie, GA; *m:* Ernest Jr.; *c:* Lana M., Ernest III, Michael W.; *ed:* (BS) Elem Ed, GA Southern 1972; (MA) Mid Sch, Valdosta St Coll 198 0; Data Collector; *cr:* 2nd Grade Teacher Funston Elem 1972-73; Sunset Elem 1973-75; 1st Grade Teacher Fred Scott Elem 1975-76; 5th Grade Teacher Sunset Elem 1976-89; 4th Grade Teacher R B Wright Elem 1989-; *ai:* Stu Government Assn Adv; GAE, CCAE, NEA (Building Rep 15-80, PAGE 1980-89); Moultrie Jr Womans Club (IntnlAffairs Chairperson 1973) 1972-75; Moultrie Swim Meet Dir 1984-89; Peer Teacher Instr; Data Collector Beginning Teacher Assessment; Teacher Yr Sunset Elem 2 Yrs; Finalist Teacher Yr Colquitt Cty; *home:* 2319 Marseille Ct Tampa FL 33569

VENGHAUS, PHYLLIS LANGHAMER, Science Teacher; *b:* Weimar, TX; *m:* Dennis G.; *c:* Dennis Jr., Brad E., Adam L.; *ed:* Cert Scndry Sci Composite, Univ of Houston 1987; Cert Medical Technology, SW Memorial Hospital 1980; (BA) Bio, Univ of St Thomas 1980; *cr:* 7th Grade Teacher St Michael 1984; Sci Teacher St Rose Sch & Bishop Forest HS 1984-88, St Rose Sch 1989-; *ai:* St Rose Invent America Coord & Pres 1987; TX Sci Teachers Assn 1985-; Soil & Water Conservation Dist 341 Educator of Yr Nom 1990; Todays Cath Teacher Magazine Outstanding Educator Nom 1988; Article Published 1988; US Patent Model Fnd Grants 1987-89; Region IV Invent America Selected Spec Educator 1987; *office:* St Rose of Lima Sch 400 Black Schulenburg TX 78956

VENICK, JOHN JOSEPH, Social Science Department Chm; *b:* Waynesburg, PA; *c:* Nicole, Seth; *ed:* (BA) Elem Ed, CA Univ of PA 1974; (MS) Soc Sci, OH Univ; *cr:* 5th-8th Grade Soc Sci Teacher St Sylvesters Sch 1974-75, Beallsville Elem Sch 1975-; *ai:* Curr Comm Soc Sci; Mgr Sch Supplies Store; Model United Nations Adv; NEA 1974-; OH Ed Assn 1974-; Southeastern OH Ed Assn 1974-; PTO 1975-; *home:* 322 Wiley Ave Barnesville OH 43713

VENN, ROBERT ALLEN, Physics Teacher; *b:* St Louis, MO; *m:* Laurey Nagel; *c:* Brian; *ed:* (BS) Chem/Math, SE MO St Univ 1963; (MA) Math, NE MO St Univ 1967; *cr:* Math Teacher Ritenour Jr HS 1963-80; Math/Physics Teacher Ritenour HS 1980; *ai:* Asst Bsktbl Coach; Salary Negotiation Comm Mem; NEA 1963-; CTA (VP, Pres) 1967-69; *home:* 13155 Royal Pines #1 Saint Louis MO 63146

VENTURA, JO ANN, Mathematics Teacher; *b:* Staten Island, NY; *m:* Rodney; *c:* Heather; *ed:* (BS) Math, 1964, (MS) Ed, 1966 Wagner Coll; Grad Courses, St Univ of NY Oneonta; *cr:* Math Teacher Port Richmond HS 1964-66, Owen D Young CS 1966-67, Richfield Springs CS 1968-78, S Lewis Jr-Sr HS 1978-; *ai:* NHS Adv; Choreographer-Costume Coord; NY Assn Math Teachers 1968-; *office:* South Lewis Jr-Sr HS East Rd Turin NY 13473

VENTURA, LOUIS A., Science Teacher/Dept Chair; *b:* Brooklyn, NY; *m:* Nancy Counts; *c:* Marie, Diana, John; *ed:* (BS) Bio, Brooklyn Coll 1970; (MS) Botany, Univ of RI 1973; *cr:* Sci Teacher Bishop Hendricken HS 1977-; *ai:* Bowling Coach; Sci Chm; Sci Teachers Natl Assn 1980-; NABT 1980-, Outstanding Bio Teachers RI 1980; RI Sci Teachers Assn 1983-; 443d Civil Affairs Cty Captain 1979-, 94th Arcom Jr Officer of Yr 1986; Presidental Awd Excl Sci Teaching 1983; St Awardee 1985; Natl Awardee 1986; *office:* Bishop Hendricken HS 2615 Warwick Ave Warwick RI 02889

VENZOR, SHERL ANN (DANIELS), Mathematics Teacher; *b:* Kirksville, MO; *c:* Sami, Mike; *ed:* (BSE) Math, NE MO St Univ 1973; *cr:* Math/Sci Teacher Novinger R-I HS 1973-74; Sci Teacher Linn Cty R-I HS 1977; Math/Sci Teacher La Plata R-I HS 1981-86; Math Teacher Putnam Cty R-I HS 1986-; *ai:* HS & Jr HS Campus Bowl Coach; Camera Club Spon; MSTA, CTA.

VERBA, STEVEN JOSEPH, 8th Grade Science Teacher; *b:* Wheeling, WV; *m:* Joanne Azallion; *c:* Carrie J., Laurie A.; *ed:* (BS) Elem Ed, OH Univ 1978; (MS) Educl Admin, Univ of Dayton 1983; Capital Univ Sch of Law 1992; *cr:* 4th Grade Inclusive Teacher St Clairsville Elem Sch 1978-83; 8th Grade Sci/ Advanced Sci Teacher St Clairsville Mid Sch 1983-; *office:* St Clairsville Mid Sch 108 Woodrow Ave Saint Clairsville OH 43950

VERBANIC, THOMAS GLEN, US History Teacher; *b:* Olean, NY; *m:* Martha Jo Leech; *c:* Kendra L.; *ed:* (BS) Soc Stud Ed, Univ of VA 1980; *cr:* His Teacher 1981-83, Fairfax HS 1983-; *ai:* Bsbl & Ftbl Head Coach; Northern VA Coaches Assn Pres 1988-89; Natl Bsbl Coaches Awd 1983-; *home:* 4502 Waverly Crossing Ln Chantilly VA 22021

VERDI, KEVIN JAMES, 8th Grade English Teacher; *b:* Rockville Centre, NY; *m:* Janet Brown; *c:* Brian, Megan; *ed:* (BA) Eng Ed, SUNY Cortland 1974; (MA) Liberal Art, SUNY Stony Brook 1980; *cr:* Accounting Dept Clerk Shell Oil Company 1974-75; Production Control Coord Dynell Electronics 1975-76; Sales Engr IMC Magnetics Corporation 1976-79; Teacher West Hempstead Unified Sch Dist 27 1979-; *ai:* HS Var Bsktbl Coach 1984-, Var Lacrosse Coach 1985-; *office:* West Hempstead Mid Sch 450 Nassau Blvd West Hempstead NY 11552

VERDON, H. JOHN, Science Teacher; *b:* Lansing, IA; *m:* Phyllis Jean; *c:* Todd A., Michael P., Jason J.; *ed:* (BS) General Sci, Univ of WI La Crosse 1962; (MNS) Geology/Earth Sci, Univ of SD Vermillion 1967; Field Geology, 1984 & Outlooks 1983 Univ of N IA Cedar Falls; Wild/IDEAS Environmental Wkshp Drake Univ 1989; *cr:* Sci/Math Teacher La Cross Public Schls 1963-65; Sci Instr Waverly-Shell Rock Sr HS 1967-; *ai:* Spon Waverly-Shell Rock Sr HS Sci Club 1970-; Dir Rocky Mountain Alpine Stud Summer Enrichment 1986-; CARE Team Mem 1987-; NCA Steering Comm Mem 1989-; Waverly-Shell Ed Pres 1972-73; NEA 1963-; IA Earth Sci Teachers Mem 1989-; Shell Rock United Meth Chm 1986-; Izaak Walton Local Chapter Comm Chm 1977; Citizens Spec Task Force Comm Mem 1984-85; IA Pres Excl Sci Teaching Awd 1989; IA Acad of Sci Excl Sci Teaching 1979, 1987; Sci Reports Published 1974, 1976; *office:* Waverly-Shell Rock Sr HS 4th Ave SW Waverly IA 50677

VERES, MARGUERITE, 6th Grade Teacher; *b:* Newark, NJ; *m:* Richard John; *c:* Christy; *ed:* (BA) Elem Ed, 1969, (MS) Educl Admin, 1979 Univ of Dayton; Cmptrs For Educators, Wright St; Data Processing, Univ of Dayton; Stress Management, Wright St; *cr:* 1st Grade Teacher Huber Heights City Schls 1970-71; 6th Grade Teacher Northmont City Schls 1972-; Adjunct Professor Univ of Dayton 1985-; *ai:* Cmptr Facilitator; Multi Media Adv; Dist Cmptr Comm; Northmont Ed Assn Secy 1976-83; OH Cncl Teacher of Eng & Lang Arts 1987-; Greater Miami Valley Educl Technology Assn Secy 1985-; Troy Tennis Assn Secy 1982-; Northmont Educator of Yr 1989-; Northmont Fnd Philosophy Grant 1978; MI Assn of Cmptrs Speaker 1986; SW OH Instructional TV Speaker 1990; *office:* Northmont City Schls 515 N Main St Englewood OH 45322

VERGOTH, MARILYN JOHNSON, 5th Grade Teacher; *b:* Evanston, IL; *m:* John R.; *c:* Karin Vergoth Bowman, Carol J., Michael J. C.; *ed:* (BA) Elem Ed, IL St Univ 1961; (MS) Outdoor Teacher Ed, N IL Univ 1983; *cr:* 2nd-3rd Grade Teacher Salk Sch 1961-66; 4th Grade Teacher Sanborn Sch 1975-76; 6th Grade Teacher Mac Arthur Sch 1977-78; 5th Grade Teacher Hale Sch 1978-; *ai:* Hale Sch 4th-6th Grade Ecology Club Spon; Schaumburg Ed Assn, IL Ed Assn, NEA Mem 1977-; Deacons Presbytn Church Moderator 1989-; *office:* Nathan Hale Sch 1300 W Wise Rd Schaumburg IL 60194

VERHINES, STEVE EDWARD, Elementary Teacher; *b:* Independence, KS; *m:* Sheila Marie Privott; *c:* Michael, Garett, Dustin, Aaron; *ed:* (BS) Spec Ed, SW OK St Univ 1979; (BS) Elem Ed, USAD 1985; *cr:* Spec Ed/His Teacher 1980-87, Sci/Soc Stud Teacher 1987- Friend Sch; *ai:* 8th Grade Spon; Cmptr Labs on Software; Elks 1990; Teacher of Yr Friend Sch 1980-81; Five Alive Top 28 Teachers of OK 1989-; *home:* 3023 Glenwood Chickasha OK 73018

VERLINDEN, ROBERT L., 5th Grade Teacher; *b:* Moline, IL; *ed:* (MS) Admin, W IL Univ 1963; Wkshp in Gifted Ed, St of IL; *cr:* Teacher Hillcrest 1959-; *ai:* Bsktbl, Flag Ftbl, Track Coach; E Moline Ed Assn, Pres 1963; Schoolmasters Pres 1962; NCTM 1970-; PTA VP 1967, Life Membership 1970; Co-Founder Prgm for Gifted Stu.

VER MAAS, JANELLE HUSS, 2nd Grade Teacher; *b:* Mc Cook, NE; *m:* Kenneth Jr.; *c:* Kenneth III., Kimberly; *ed:* (BA) Elem Ed, 1976, Endorsement Early Chldhd Ed, 1976, (MS) Elem Ed, 1990 Kearney St; *cr:* Title I/Chapter I Teacher Pershing & Bryan Elem & St Anns HS 1980-86; 6th Grade Eng Teacher 1981-86, 5th/6th Grade Soc Stud/Eng Teacher 1986-87, Kndgtn Teacher 1987-, 2nd Grade Teacher 1990 Pershing Elem; *ai:* Head Stu Asst Team; 6th Grade Odyssey of Mind Team Coach; Alpha Delta Kappa (Pres, Pres Elect) 1987-; Lexington Ed Assn Soc Comm 1980-; NEA 1980-; Bus & Prof Women 1989-, Lexingtons Young Careerist 1989, 1st Runner-Up Dist Young Careerist 1989; Domestic Engineers Extension Club (Pres, VP, Co-Founder) 1979-; Catechism Teacher 1978-79, 1984-86, 1989-; Lexington Jaycees Outstanding Young Educator 1985; Lexingtons Outstanding Young Woman 1986; NE Outstanding Young Woman 1987; Univ of NE Teachers Coll Alumni Assn Outstanding NE Elem Sch Teacher 1987; *office:* Pershing Elem Sch 1104 N Tyler Lexington NE 68850

VERMEER, CONNIE LEE, English Teacher; *b:* Moorland, OK; *m:* Brad; *c:* Jason Ackleson, Jennifer L. Ackleson; *ed:* (BS) Eng Ed, 1971, (MA) Lit, 1978 NM St Univ; *cr:* Teacher Las Cruces HS 1971-; *ai:* NHS Spon; Phi Kappa Phi 1971-; Phi Delta Kappa; NM Cncl Teachers of Eng Sndry Teacher of Yr 1988-89; Las Cruces Public Sch Dist Teacher of Yr 1988-89; *office:* Las Cruces HS 1755 El Paseo Rd Las Cruces NM 88001

VER MERRIS, DONALD ALAN, 3rd Grade Teacher; *b:* Grand Rapids, MI; *m:* Susan; *c:* Kimberly, Kelly, Kara, David; *ed:* (BA) Group Sci, 1978; (MAT) Sch Admin, 1984 Calvin Coll; *cr:* 1st Grade Teacher 1978-85; 3rd Grade Teacher 1985 Creston Chrstn Sch; *ai:* Girls Sftbl Coach; Church Leader; US Space Camp Ambassador; Chrstn Educators Assn Convention Planning 1985-87; Outstanding Educator By Grand Rapids Fnd May 1989; *office:* Creston Chrstn Sch 1031 Page Ne Grand Rapids MI 49505

VERMEULEN, NANCY IRENE, Project Charlie Teacher; *b:* Newark, NY; *c:* Christine, Deborah; *ed:* (BS) Elem Ed, SUNY Plattsburg 1973; Working Towards Masters; *cr:* 2nd/4th/5th Grade Teacher 1973-85, Project Charlie Teacher 1985- Carthage Elem; *ai:* Drug Free Schls & Family Life Ed Comm; NY St United Teachers 1973-; Carthage Traveling Club VP 1975-; GSA (Leader, Asst Leader) 1973-; Carthage Area Hospital Auxillary 1980-88.

VERMEULEN, VICKY LYNN, Social Science Teacher; *b:* Ft Riley, KS; *ed:* (BS) Soc Sci, Dakota St Univ 1976; *cr:* Librarian/ Soc Sci Instr Herreid Public Sch 1976-78, Doland Public Sch 1978-79, Montrose Public Sch 1979-; *home:* PO Box 19 Salem SD 57058

VERMILLION, GREG J., Second Grade Teacher; *b:* Tucson, AZ; *ed:* (BA) Early Chldhd Ed, 1979, (BA) Elem Ed, 1979, (MED) Elem Ed, 1985; *cr:* 1st Grade Teacher 1979-89, 2nd Grade Teacher 1989- Schumaker Elem; *ai:* Tucson Ed Assn Rep 1979-; AZ Ed Assn, NEA 1979-; Christ Cmmty Church Toddler Teacher; Co-Author Tucson Unified Sch Dist Book 1988; *office:* Schumaker Elem Sch 501 N Maguire Tucson AZ 85710

VERMILLION, LINDA DIANNE, Chemistry Teacher; *b:* Athens, TX; *m:* Michael Loyd; *ed:* (BS) Bio/Eng, 1971, (MS) Bio, 1972 E TX St Univ; Composite Sci Cert, E TX St 1975; Marketing/Distributive Ed Cert, Univ of Houston 1980; *cr:* Bio/ Chem Teacher Trinidad HS 1972-75, Athens HS 1975-78, Bay City HS 1978-79; MDE/Chem Teacher Sweeny HS 1979-; *ai:* Omni Sci Club; Univ Interscholastic League Sci Coord; Spon Bulldogs Against Doing Drugs; NEA, TX St Teachers Assn 1972-; Sweeney Ed Assn (Pres 1982-83, VP 1981-82 Secy, Treas); NSTA, Sci Teachers Assn of TX 1983-; NABT 1985-; TX Assn of Bio Teachers 1986-; Assn of Chem Teachers of TX 1984-85; Amer Chemical Society 1990; Delta Kappa Gamma (Secy 1986-88, VP 1990, Legislative Chm 1988-); Future Teachers of America Athens HS Teacher of Yr 1977, St Adv 1977-79; Univ of TX M D Anderson Cancer Centers Sci Prgm 1987; Presented Various Inservices; Writing Policy on TX Hazard Comm Act 1988; Writing Trng Manual & Stu Lab Guide For Safety 1988; Nom Teaching Excl Awd 1986, 1988; SW Regional Outstanding Teacher of HS Chem Awd 1988; Wallace Awd 1988; *office:* Sweeney HS 1310 Elm St Sweeny TX 77480

VERNON, JANE HARPER, Music Teacher; *b:* Kinston, NC; *m:* Richard T.; *c:* Ryan, Will; *ed:* (BME) Music Ed, E Carolina Univ 1977; Working Towards Masters in Ed 1990; *cr:* Music Teacher Arendell Parrott Acad 1977-79, Southwood Elem Sch 1979-; *ai:* Sch Improvement Accountability Act Steering Comm 1989-; Music Educators Natl Conference Dist Pres Elect 1989-; NCAE Assn Rep 1988-89; Southwood Elem Teacher of Yr 1984-85; Nom Southwood Terry Sanford Awd for Excl 1988-89; *office:* Southwood Elem Sch Rt 5 Box 31 Kinston NC 28501

VERNON, RAE ANNE ANNE (COOK), Mathematics Dept Chair/Teacher; *b:* Maryville, MO; *m:* Joel Lee; *c:* Julie, Jody, Jennifer; *ed:* (BS) Scndry Math, Univ of MO 1971; *cr:* Teacher Iberia HS 1971, Tuscumbia HS 1971-78; Teacher/Cmptr Coord Humansville R-IV HS 1979-; *ai:* Future Teachers Assn Adv; Mu Alpha Theta Math Club, Chrldr Spon; MSTA 1972-; MCTM; CTA Pres 1972-, Teacher of Yr 1986-87; Church (GA Dir 1982-85, Acteen Leader 1979, Mission Friends Leader 1980-82); Teacher of Yr 1988; Tandy Scholars Outstanding Math/Sci/ Cmptr Sci Teacher 1989-; Outstanding Scndry Educators of America 1974; *office:* Humansville R-IV HS 307 N Oak St Humansville MO 65674

VERNON, SHARON ROSEMARY, First Grade Teacher; *b:* Greensburg, IN; *m:* Bernard H.; *c:* Cynthia, Tracy; *ed:* (BS) Elem Ed, 1978; (MS) Elem Ed, 1983 IN Univ; *cr:* 1st Grade Teacher North Decatur Elem 1978-; *ai:* Inservice Staff Dev Trainer for TESA; Decatur Cty Teachers Organization Bldg Rep 1983-; ISTA/NEA 1978-; First Bapt Church Adult Educator 1986-; St of IN Presenter Prime Time Fair Summer 1989; *office:* North Decatur Elem Sch RR 1 Box 95 A Greensburg IN 47240

VERONESI, PETER D., Physical Science Teacher; *b:* Kittanning, PA; *ed:* (BS) General/Earth & Space/Bio Scndry Ed, Clarion Univ 1986; Sci Ed, Clarion Univ; *cr:* Substitute Teacher Armstrong Sch Dist 1987; 9th Grade Phys Sci Teacher Philipsburg Jr HS 1987-; *ai:* Slay The Dragon Anti Drug Prgm for Stu; PA Sci Teachers Assn, PA St Ed Assn; Knights of Columbus; St Francis

Church Nursing Home Visitation; *office:* Philipsburg Jr HS 6th St Philipsburg PA 16866

VERONNEAU, DONALD DENNIS, Guidance Counselor; *b:* Acushnet, MA; *ed:* (BA) Philosophy, St Johns Seminary 1971; (MED) Counseling, Bridgewater St Coll 1988; *cr:* Substitute Teacher New Bedford Public Schls 1971-76; Fr/Soc Stud Teacher 1976-86, Guidance Cnslr 1986-89 Normandin Jr HS; Guidance Cnslr New Bedford HS 1989-; *ai:* Class Adv; MA Assn of Guidance Cnslrs 1986-; Greenpeace 1988-; *office:* New Bedford HS 230 Hathaway Blvd New Bedford MA 02740

VERRASTRO, CARMELLA S., English Teacher; *b:* Waterbury, CT; *m:* Robert S. Sr.; *c:* Kellie, Robert Jr.; *ed:* (BA) Eng/Fr/Latin, Annhurst Coll 1960; Grad Credits Bridgewater St Coll, Southern CT Coll, Fairfield Univ 1973; *cr:* Eng/Latin/Fr Teacher Swift Jr HS 1960-63; Eng/Fr Teacher Croft HS 1965; Eng/Latin Teacher Kennedy HS 1965-69; Eng Teacher Sacred Heart HS 1974-; *ai:* Beta Club Adv; Coalition Comm; NCEA, Sacred Heart Teachers Assn; Fairfield Univ Alumnae Club, Annhurst Coll Alumnae Club, Blessed Sacrament Church Ladies Guild; Eng Dept Chairperson 1987-88; *office:* Sacred Heart H S 142 S Elm St Waterbury CT 06722

VERRATTI, MICHELE GAWEL, Mathematics Teacher; *b:* Wilmington, DE; *m:* Nicholas Francis III; *ed:* (BS) Math, Lebanon Valley Coll 1984; Working Toward MED at West Chester Univ 1990; *cr:* Math Teacher Elkton HS 1984-; *ai:* Aerobics Instr; NCTM, MD Cncl Teachers of Math 1989-; Kappa Delta Pi 1990; *office:* Elkton HS James St Elkton MD 21921

VERSAW, FRANCIS EARL, Math Dept Chair/Teacher; *b:* Ainsworth, NE; *m:* Beatrice Joy Gongwer; *c:* Barry, Blaine; *ed:* (BS) Math, S Nazarene Univ 1965; *cr:* Teacher Hefner Jr HS 1965-66, Watson Jr HS 1966-; *ai:* 9th Grade Girls Bsktbl & Track Coach; Dist Math CAT; NCTM 1977-; Athletic Assn of Black Forest (Soccer Coach 1978-84, Soccer Coord 1978-84, Pres 1980-82); *office:* Watson Jr HS 136 Fontaine Blvd Security CO 80911

VER SCHNEIDER, CONSTANCE W., English Teacher; *b:* Potsdam, NY; *m:* Patrick D.; *c:* Kimberly Ingram, Tripp Ingram, David, Daniel; *ed:* (BA) Eng, SUNY Potsdam 1966; Grad Stud Ed/Eng/Soc; *cr:* Eng Teacher Liverpool HS 1966-67, Lansing HS 1967-69, Norwood-Norfolk HS 1973-; *ai:* Adv Honor Society; Norwood-Norfolk Teachers Assn VP 1988-; Jaycees VP 1969-70; Zion Episcopal Church Vestry 1989-; *office:* Norwood-Norfolk Cntrl Sch Rt 56 Norwood NY 13668

VERTREES, KAYE ROGERS (KELLEY), Third Grade Teacher; *b:* Clarksville, TN; *m:* James A.; *c:* David A. Cooper Jr.; *ed:* (BS) Elem Ed, Austin Peay St Univ 1959; (MS) Agriculture, TN St Univ 1984; Certified by Personal Growth Fnd; *cr:* 1st Grade Teacher Clarksville/TN 1959-60, Las Vegas NV 1960-62, Washoe Cty 1962-64, Ft Campbell KY 1964-70; 3rd Grade Teacher Clarksville TN 1970-; *ai:* Cooperating Teacher With Austin Peay St Univ 1966; Curr Coordinating Comm; Grade Level Chm; Sch Chm Rdng, Math & Soc Stud Textbook Adoption; Music Prgm Chm of Art; Southern Assn Sch Evaluation Comms; NEA 1960-82; NV Ed Assn, KY Ed Assn, TN Ed Assn 1959-82; United Meth Church Sunday Sch Teacher 1965-67, 1977-79; Assn for Research & Enlightenment 1980-; *office:* East Montgomery Elem Sch 230 Mc Adoo Creek Rd Clarksville TN 37043

VESCOVI, JAMES CRAIG, Mechanical Drawing Instructor; *b:* Somerville, NJ; *m:* Anne Mc Dermott; *c:* Jason, Melissa; *ed:* (BA) Industrial Arts, William Penn Coll 1976; *cr:* Mech Drwg Instr Manchester Twp HS 1976-79, Toms River HS 1979-; *ai:* Shore Drafting Contest Chm; Past Coach Ftbl/Wrestling/Track; NEA/NJEA Mem 1976-; Shore Shop Teachers Assn Drafting Contest Chm 1979- Shore Shop Teacher of Yr 1983; South Jersey Shop Teachers Assn 1983- Outstanding Teacher Awd 1985/1987/1989; Whos Who in Coll & Univ; Custom Kitchen & Architectural Millwork Designer; Natl Kitchen & Bath Assn Mem; Outstanding Young Men in America; *office:* Toms River H S East Dunedin St Toms River NJ 08753

VESNESKY, KAREN SUE, Social Studies/Quest Teacher; *b:* Altoona, PA; *m:* Joseph V.; *c:* Krista, Joie; *ed:* (BS) Soc Stud, Slippery Rock Univ 1970; (MED) Elem Guidance Counseling, IN Univ 1977; Quest Skills for Adolescence; *cr:* Soc Stud Teacher Glendale Jr/Sr HS 1970-; *office:* Glendale Jr/Sr HS Flinton PA 16640

VEST, THERESA KAYE (ABBOTT), 8th Grade Teacher; *b:* Ada, OK; *m:* Larry Ray; *c:* Doug, Randy, Scott; *ed:* (BS) Spec Ed/Math/Speech, TX Tech 1977; Cmptr Literacy Cert; *cr:* Deposit Validator Tucson Transit 1974-77; Payroll Clerk Northern Electric 1977-78; Math/Speech Teacher CO City Ind Dist 1978-79; Math Teacher/Math Dept Chairperson Snyder Ind Sch Dist 1979-; *ai:* UIL Number Sense Coach; Campus Improvement Team; Locker Decoration Spon; TSTA, NEA Building Rep 1982-83; TCTA; Sigma Kappa Historian 1970; 1st Baptist Church Dept Leader 1985-87; *office:* Snyder Jr HS El Paso St Snyder TX 79549

VESTAL, BRENDA LLOYD, 7th Grade Lang Art Teacher; *b:* Abingdon, VA; *m:* Robert Glenn; *ed:* (BA) Poly/Soc Sci, Emory & Henry Coll 1974; (MED) Counseling, Univ of VA 1975; Grad Stud 4th-7th Grade Lang Art; *cr:* Rdng Teacher Johnson Cty Schls 1974-76; 4th-7th Grade Lang Art Teacher Cleveland Elem 1976-78; 7th Grade Lang Art Teacher E B Stanley Elem 1978-82; 9th-12th Soc Stud Teacher Abingdon HS 1982-86; 7th Grade Lang Art Teacher E B Stanley Elem 1986-; *ai:* Chrldrs & 4-H Spon; Interact Club Adv; Adv & Founder of His Club; Intnl Rdng Assn, SW VA Teacher of Yr 1982-83; ASCD; *home:* 435 Valley St Abingdon VA 24210

VESTAL, DONALD CHARLIE, Agriculture Teacher; *b:* Elkin, NC; *m:* Mary Lynn Coram; *c:* John, Tammy; *ed:* (BS) Ag, NC St 1970; *cr:* Ag Teacher Surry Cntrl HS 1970-; *ai:* FFA & FFA Club Adv; Building & Grounds, Public Relations Comm; FFA Teams Coach; Natl NC Voc Ag Teachers Assn, NEA, NCAE 1970-; NC Cattlemens Assn 1975-; Boonville Baptist Church Asst Sunday Sch Teacher 1970-; Natl Conservation Teacher of Yr 1982; FFA Honorary Carolina Farmer Degree 1985; *office:* Surry Cntrl HS Box 8 Dobson NC 27017

VICARE, GERALD L., Earth Science Teacher; *b:* La Salle, IL; *m:* Helen L. Fandel; *ed:* (AD) Sci, IL Valley Comm Coll 1968; (BS) Geology/Geography, IL St Univ 1970; Geography Grad Sch, W IL Univ 1986; *cr:* Teacher Scndry Sch Tonga South Pacific Peace Corps Volunteer 1971-73; Instr Coll for Kids Monmouth Coll Summer 1984-86; Scndry Teacher Wkshp Sci Instr Western IL Univ Summer 1986; Earth Sci Teacher IL Cntrl Coll 1987-89; Sci Teacher Monmouth HS 1976-; *ai:* Sci Club Spon; Developed HS Weather Station; Dist Teacher Continiuing Ed & Inservice Comm; Peer Coaching Prgm 1987-88; IL Earth Sci Teachers Assn VP 1986-88; Monmouth Ed Assn VP 1977-78; Symposium Steering Comm 1990; Natl Earth Sci Teachers Assn, Geological Society; Warren Cnty Earth Day Comm 1990; NEA, NSTA, ISTA, IESTA, GSA Mem; Monmouth Coll Sci Fair Judge 1987; Speaker for Weather & Earth Sci Topics Monmouth Groups & Radio; Nom for Presidential Awd Excl in Sci & Math Teaching 1988; Nom for Outstanding Earth Sci Teacher 1987; Speaker at IL Earth Sci Assn Convention 1987.

VICKERY, JOYCE JARVIS, Fifth Grade Teacher; *b:* Etowah, TN; *m:* Elvis L. Jr. (dec); *c:* Elvis L. III; *ed:* (BS) Elem Ed, Berry Coll 1956; Grad Work Univ of TN Knoxville & Chattanooga; *cr:* Girls Bsktbl Coach/Teacher Celanese Sch 1956-61; Teacher Vestal Sch 1961-65; Lang Art Teacher Whitthorne Jr HS 1965-71; 5th Grade Teacher Bess T Shepherd 1972-; *ai:* 5th Grade Teachers Chm; Academic Contest Sponsorship & Coach; NEA 1956-; TN Ed Assn 1962-; Chattanooga Ed Assn Building Rep 1972-; Natl Rdng Assn 1988-; Hamilton Cty Cncl for Soc Stud, Chattanooga Cncl for Soc Stud Outstanding Soc Stud Teacher 1982; Tyner United Meth Church (Ofcl Bd 1987-89, Coll Mem Coord 1987-89); Grant to Study GA Barrier Island Ecology 1986; *office:* Bess T Shepherd Sch 6779 E Brainerd Rd Chattanooga TN 37421

VICKREY, PEGGY CHURCH, English Department Chair; *b:* Albuquerque, NM; *m:* Joe T.; *c:* Preston A.; *ed:* (BA) Span/Eng, Stephen F AustiN St Univ 1977; (MLA) Liberal Art, S Meth Univ 1984; Gifted & Talented, Stu Achievment Trng, Teacher Expectation; *cr:* Eng Teacher 1978-, Dept Chairperson 1981- Lamar Jr HS; *ai:* Stu Cncl Spon 1978-81; Natl Jr Honor Society Spon 1985-87; TX Joint Cncl of Teachers of Eng 1981-; Kathy Burks Child Dev Center Instructional Needs Chairperson 1989-; PTA Bd; Outstanding Young Women of America 1986; *office:* Lamar Jr HS 219 Crandall Irving TX 75060

VIDO, FAY WAGNER, English Teacher; *b:* Tamaqua, PA; *m:* Frank; *c:* Victoria I. D., Frank, Paul; *ed:* (BA) Soc Stud, PA St Univ 1956; Univ of Rochester 1958; OH Writing Project 1986; Miami Univ 1978, 1986; Great Books Leader Trng Course 1987; Univ of Cincinnati 1979; *cr:* Teacher West Irondequoit HS 1956-62, Plymouth-Whitemarsh HS 1962-63, Cath Cntrl Cmmty Sch 1974-76, Stephen T Badin HS 1976-; *ai:* NHS Moderator; Hamilton Cmmty Fnd Grant 1986; OH Writing Project Fellow; *home:* 1720 Sunset Dr Hamilton OH 45013

VIENS, CHARLES HENRY, 5th Grade Teacher; *b:* N Adams, MA; *m:* Carol A. Federchuck; *c:* Robert, Kristin, Daniel; *ed:* (AS) Electrical Technology, Berkshire Comm Coll 1964; (BSED) Elem Ed, N Adams St 1968; Grad Stud Russell Sage Coll, Coll of St Rose, St Univ of NY; *cr:* Asst Teacher Berkshire Country Day Sch 1964-65; Elem Teacher West Sand Lake Elem Sch 1968-; Elem Cmptr Coord Averill Park Cntrl Sch Dist 1987-; *ai:* Yrbk Adv 1971-; Cmptr Users Group; Photography, Stamp, Woodworking Clubs; West Sand Lake PTA Pres 1970-72; Hon Life Mem 1973; Sand Lake Historical Society Hon Life Mem 1975; Troy Sculpins Parents Organization (Pres, Founder 1982-84); Author of Various Books; *office:* West Sand Lake Elem Sch Rt 43 & 150 PO Box 427 West Sand Lake NY 12196

VIERIA, BRIAN M., Instrumental Music Teacher; *b:* Fall River, MA; *m:* Suzanne Paquette; *c:* Allyson B.; *ed:* (BMUS) Music Ed, Boston Univ 1972; (MAT) Music Ed, RI Coll 1976; *cr:* Band/Chorus/Classroom Music Teacher Wilson Jr HS 1972-73; Instrumental/Classroom Music Teacher North Mid Sch 1973-87; 5th-12th Grade Instrumental Music Teacher Somerset Public Schls 1987-; *ai:* 6th-8th Grade Band & Stage Band; Report Card & 5th-8th Grade Scheduling Comm 1983, K-8th Grade Rdng Comm Somerset Public Schls 1985; Music Natl Conference 1972-; Intnl Assn of Jazz Educators 1989-; NEA 1972-; Somerset Arts Cncl 1981-87; *office:* Somerset Public Schls Whetstone Hill Rd Somerset MA 02726

VIGIL, ADELMO, Second Grade Teacher; *b:* Jaroso, CO; *m:* Soledad Gamon; *c:* Adrian, Gabriel; *ed:* (BA) Elem Ed, Western NM Univ 1977; Elem Counseling; *cr:* T-1st Grade Teacher Remedial Math 1977-80; 3rd Grade Teacher 1980-86; 1st Grade Teacher 1986-87; 2nd Grade Teacher 1987- Nizhoni Elem; *ai:* Shiprock HS Wrestling Coach 1982-88; NEA 1977-; Natl Fed of the Blind 2nd VP 1982-; Blind Educators Assn Bd Mem 1984-87; Natl Fed of the Blind NM Pres Awd 1989; NM Sch for Visually Handicapped Bd of Regents Mem 1989-; *home:* PO Box 2514 Shiprock NM 87420

VIGIL, IRENE RICHARDSON, Science Teacher; *b:* Hondo, NM; *m:* John A.; *c:* John C., Evonne, Lloyd; *ed:* (BS) Bio/Span, 1971, (MED) Guidance/Counseling, 1977 Univ of TX El Paso; *cr:* Sci Teacher Father Yerno Elem 1975-77; Sci/Math Teacher 1985-89, Asst Prin 1989- Radford Sch; *ai:* Act Dir; Yrbk Adv; NSTA, ASCD; *office:* Radford Sch 2001 Radford St El Paso TX 79903

VIGIL, LAURA, Business Teacher; *b:* Ocate, NM; *ed:* (BA) Bus Admin/Ed, NM Highlands Univ 1975; Grad & Non-Grad Courses NM Highlands Univ & Univ of NM; *cr:* Typing Teacher Estancia Public HS 1976-80; Bus Instr Rio Grande HS 1980-84; Keyboarding Teacher Mc Kinley Mid Sch 1984-; *ai:* Yrbk Adv; *office:* Mc Kinley Mid Sch 4500 Comanche NE Albuquerque NM 87110

VIGNEVIC, CAROL A., Secondary Mathematics Teacher; *b:* Mckeesport, PA; *m:* Nicholas P.; *c:* Katie, Peter, David; *ed:* (BS) Scndry Ed/Math, PA St Univ 1969; *cr:* Scndry Math Teacher Gateway Jr HS 1969, Pitman HS 1969-70, Central Regional HS 1984-; *ai:* NCTM 1985-; Garden St Skating Club (Test Chm 1985-87, Pres 1988-89, Treas 1989-); *office:* Central Regional HS Forest Hills Parkway Bayville NJ 08721

VIGNOLA, EILEEN YOUNG, 8th Grade Teacher; *b:* Philadelphia, PA; *m:* Joseph C.; *c:* Joseph; *ed:* (BS) Elem Ed, St Josephs Univ 1976; *cr:* 3rd Grade Teacher Epiphany Sch 1973-76; Left Teaching for Private Industry 1976-85; 8th Grade Teacher St Marys Interparochial 1986-89; *ai:* Soc Stud Coord; Safety Patrol & Stu Cncl Adv; Cheerleading Coach; Amer Assn of Rdng Teachers 1986-; NACST Mem 1986-; Friends Rehabilitation Guild Bd of Dirs 1987-; *home:* 235 Fitzwater St Philadelphia PA 19147

VIGUS, DANIEL LEONARD, Band Dir 3rd Grade Teacher; *b:* Butte, MT; *m:* Nancy L. Nelson; *c:* Ryan, Randy; *ed:* (BA) Music Ed, Trinity Coll 1972; (MA) Christian Sch Admin, Grace Seminary 1982; *cr:* Band Dir St Mary's Elem Sch 1972-73; Band Dir & 3rd Grade Teacher Ygnacio Valley Christian Sch 1974-; *ai:* Vice Prin; Christian Instrumental Dir Assn 1985-; CA Music Ed Assn 1989-; Natl Assn of Prof Band Instrument Repair Technicians 1984-; Walnut Creek Cmmty Bank 1986-; *office:* Ygnacio Valley Christian Schl 4977 Concord Blvd Concord CA 94521

VILLA, HECTOR E., Spanish Teacher; *b:* Medellin, Colombia; *m:* Emerita; *c:* Hector A., Carlos A., Elsa Marina S.; *ed:* (BA) His/Poly Sci Tusculum Coll 1964; Univ of TN 1961; Univ of NM 1971; Univ of DE 1975; Univ of WI 1972; *cr:* Span Teacher Greenville City Schls 1964-65, Capital Sch Dist 1966-; Eng as 2nd Lang Teacher Capital & Caesar Rodney Sch Dist 1970-; *ai:* Coach & Referee Indoor Soccer; NEA, DE St Ed Assn; DE Cncl on Teaching of Foreign Lang 1990; Capital Sch Dist Teacher of Yr; *home:* 734 West St Dover DE 19901

VILLA, MARY RUSKA, 5th Grade Teacher; *b:* Erie, PA; *m:* Charles N.; *c:* Craig, Charley; *ed:* (BS) Elem Ed, Villa Maria Coll 1964; Masters Equivalency St of PA 1990; Grad Stud Wayne St, Behrend Coll, Edinboro Univ, Gannon Coll; *cr:* 3rd Grade Teacher Edgewood Sch 1964-65, Max Paun Sch 1966-69; 5th Grade Teacher Perry & Harding Schls 1969-; *ai:* Safety Patrol; Various Sch Events & Comms; Erie Ed Assn, PSEA, NEA 1969-; *office:* Harding Elem Sch 820 Lincoln Ave Erie PA 16505

VILLALOBOS, BERTA DE LOS SANTOS, English Teacher; *b:* Roma, TX; *m:* David F. Jr.; *c:* Amanda V.; *ed:* (BAED) Span/Eng Ed, 1981, (MAED) Eng/Span Ed, 1988 TX Tech Univ; *cr:* Eng Teacher Roosevelt Ind Sch Dist 1981-; *ai:* HS Chrldr Coach; UIL Ready Writing Adv; TX Joint Cncl Teachers of Eng 1984-; NCTE 1985-; League of United Latin Amer Citizens Stu Schlsp Comm Mem 1988-; Nom TX Excl Awd Outstanding HS Teachers 1987-88; Outstanding Young Women of America 1983; *office:* Roosevelt Ind Sch Dist Rt 1 Box 402 Lubbock TX 79401

VILLAMAGNA, GEORGE, US History Teacher; *b:* Elmont, NY; *m:* Leila Anwari; *ed:* (AA) Liberal Art, Broome Comm Coll 1980; (BS) Soc Sci Ed, SUNY Oneonta 1981; (MS) 19th Century US His, Univ of Houston 1990; *cr:* Teacher/Coach Mc Adams Jr HS 1982-83, Dean Jr HS 1983-86, Cook Jr HS 1986-; *ai:* Asst 8th Grade Ftbl & Head Bsktbl Coach; TX HS Coaches Assn 1982-; Assn of TX Prof Educators, Cypress Fairbanks Cncl for the Soc Stud 1983-; TX St Career Ladder Level 3; Teacher that Exemplifies Dist 1989; *home:* 10202 Wayward Wind Houston TX 77064

VILLAREAL, MARIA TERESA, Second Grade Teacher; *b:* Roma, TX; *m:* Guadalupe Gil; *c:* Denise, Danette, Guadalupe Jr.; *ed:* (BS) Elem Ed, Pan Amer Univ 1976; *cr:* 2nd Grade Teacher F J Scott Elem 1976-; *ai:* UIL Spelling Spon; ATPE Club Mem.

VILLAREAL, ROXANNE BEALL, 5th Grade Teacher; *b:* Conroe, TX; *m:* John A.; *c:* Nicole, Danielle; *ed:* (BS) Elem Ed, Stephen F Austin Univ 1977; *cr:* Teacher Tatum Mid Sch 1978-86, Tatum Elem Sch 1986-; *ai:* TSTA; TCTA; *office:* Tatum Elem Sch PO Box 808 Tatum TX 75691

VILLELLA, KATHLEEN LYNN (COPPOLA), 8th Grade Teacher; *b:* Youngstown, OH; *m:* Edward Fiore; *c:* Samantha, Nikki, Brent; *ed:* (BS) Elem Ed, Youngstown St Univ 1974; Masters Certificate Catechists, Comprehensive Thru Newspaper Rdng, Introduction Cmptr Systems, Rdng/Writing Lang Growth; *cr:* 2nd/3rd Grade Teacher Our Lady of Loreto 1974-77; 5th Grade Teacher St Christine 1980-83; 4th-8th Grade Teacher St Joseph 1983-; *ai:* Jr HS Field Trips; Dir Gates Mc Ginities; Day of

Reflection, Spelling Bee Grades 1st-8th, Monthly Guest Speaker 8th Grade, Jr HS Dance Chairperson; Co-Chairperson Cath Sch Week; Eng Festival Monitor; Intnl Rdng Assn 1987-; Volunteer Amer Cancer Society 1985- & March of Dimes 1984-; *office:* St Joseph Sch 4565 New Rd Youngstown OH 44515

VILLEMAIRE, MAUREEN FRAIN, Fifth Grade Teacher; *b:* Waltham, MA; *c:* James, Elizabeth, Susan; *ed:* (BS) Elem Ed, Framingham St Coll 1961; (MA) Cmptr Ed, TX Wesleyan Univ 1985; *cr:* 5th Grade Teacher Maynard Public Schls 1961-63; 5th Grade Teacher Natick Public Schls 1963-65; 5th/6th Grade Teacher Arlington Ind Sch Dist 1979-; *ai:* Lead Teacher.

VILLINES, SANDRA DAWN HALBROOK, Fifth Grade Teacher; *b:* Clinton, MO; *m:* Gary Glenn Jr.; *c:* Elizabeth, Glenn; *ed:* (BS) Elem Ed, SW MO St 1984; Working Towards Masters Counseling, Sch Psych; *cr:* 5th Grade Teacher Tanglewood Elem 1984; *ai:* KS Ed Assn Mem 1984-; Pleasantville Baptist Church; *home:* 1600 Cresthill Derby KS 67037

VINCENT, C. TERRY, History Teacher/Coach; *b:* Huron, SD; *m:* Patty Aalbers; *c:* Angel, Cheryl; *ed:* (BA) His, Dakota St 1969; Working toward Masters; *cr:* His Teacher/Coach Elkton HS 1970-; *ai:* Girls & Boys Cross Cntry, Track Head Coach; Bsktbl & Ftbl Asst Coach; NFICA; Coach of Boys St Champions Cross Cntry 1978, Track 1980; 15 Conference Cross Cntry Championships, 8 Track Championships, 5 Region Cross Cntry Championships, 3 Region Track Championships; *home:* Box 269 Elkton SD 57026

VINCENT, CAROLYN H., Language Arts Teacher; *b:* Wayne Cty, NC; *m:* Charles E.; *c:* Charles Jr., Carmen; *ed:* (BA) Eng, 1976, (MA) Eng, 1980 NC Cntrl Univ; Speech Pathology & Audiology, NCCU; Gifted Ed Class, NCSU; *cr:* Lang Art Teacher Carrington Jr HS 1976-; *ai:* PTSA Faculty & Teacher Cncl Rep; Senate Bill 2 Comm; Team Leader; Cooperating Teacher 1985-86; NCAE, NEA, DCAE; Eno Valley PTA Membership Comm 1985; Carrington PTA Faculty Rep 1989-; GSA; Teacher of Yr 1984-85 Carrington; Outstanding Young Educators Durham Jaycees 1985; *office:* Carrington Jr HS 227 Milton Rd Durham NC 27712

VINCENT, ESTHER DAVIS, Middle School Counselor; *b:* Lake Charles, LA; *m:* Griffin Kary; *ed:* (BS) Vocal Music Ed, Grambling St 1969; (MMED) Music Ed, Mc Neese St 1974; Lamar Univ; *cr:* Vocal Music Teacher 1969-85, Mid Sch Cnslr 1985- Calcasieu Parish Schls; *ai:* Sch Spon Act Faculty Liaison; Partners in Ed & SAPE Prgm Coord; CAE Membership Chairperson 1988-, Honor Chorus; LAE, NEA, VMTO, LMEA, MENC, CCA, LACD; Delta Sigma Theta (Corresponding Secy, Recording Secy, VP, Pres) 1969-, Delta Awd 1982, 1989, Torch Awd 1989, Founders Awd 1990; Amer Legion Auxiliary 1963-; Outstanding Young Women of America 1977; *home:* 2912 General Patton Lake Charles LA 70601

VINCENT, FRANKLIN ANDERSON, Fourth Grade Teacher; *b:* Maquoketa, IA; *M:* Nancy J. Southwick; *c:* Steve E., James F.; *ed:* (BS) Elem Ed, 1963; Cert Elem Ed, 1974 Mankato St Coll; (MS) Elem Ed, Mankato St Univ 1976; Driver Ed; Health Ed; Specialist Degree Prgm; *cr:* Elem Teacher Wells-Easton Public Sch 1963-; *ai:* Soc Stud Curr Comm; High Potential Selection Comm; Planning Evaluating & Reporting Comm; NEA 1963-; MEA Assn 1963-; Wells-Easton Ed Assn 1963-; Past VP of Wells-Waston Ed Assn; Meals on Wheels Volntr; Nom for Wells Jaycees Outstanding Young Educator Awd; *office:* Wells-Easton Public Elem Sch 250 2nd Ave Sw Wells MN 56097

VINCENT, JO ANN DE SALLE, Third Grade Teacher; *b:* Raton, NM; *m:* William A.; *c:* Janet Riley, Judy Culler, Brian Patterson; *ed:* (BA) Elem Ed, Ft Lewis Coll 1972; Facilitator for Parenting Groups; Grad Stud Ft Lewis Coll; *cr:* Substitute Teacher 1964-71, 4th Grade Teacher 1972-75, 3rd Grade Teacher 1976- Farmington Municipal Schls; *ai:* Facilitator for Parenting Group at Cntry Club Elem; Working with At-Risk Children; PTO 1972-; NM Natl Ed Assn; Parents for Drug Free Youth 1988-; Precinct Co-Chairperson; Four Corners Conference for Women; Cmmty Concert Assn; Grant from PTO for Math Manipulatives; *office:* Farmington Municipal Schls 5300 Foothills Dr Farmington NM 87401

VINCENT, JUANITA PARSONS, Choir Teacher/Music Dept Chair; *b:* Atlanta, GA; *m:* Carl; *c:* Victor, Toni N., Vaughn; *ed:* (BA) Music Ed, Clark Coll 1964; (MA) Arts/Liberal Stud, Valparaiso Univ 1976; Teachers Performance Inst, Oberlin Coll; *cr:* Teacher Brookwood Elem 1966-68, Garnett Elem 1968-69, Douglass Elem 1969-74, Tolleston Mid Sch 1974-; *ai:* Gary Sch Employees Bowling League Treas; Curr Writing Team; Vocal Music Project STAY Tolleston Sch; Gary Rdng Cncl; Gary Alumnae Delta Sigma Theta Pres 1978-80; Emerson Sch Visual & Performing Art (PTSA Pres 1982-84, Treas 1988-; Gary Alumnae Delta Sigma Theta Parliamentarian 1989-; Midwest Regional Centers Trng Drug-Free Schls & Communities; Project US Dept of Ed; *office:* Tolleston Mid Sch 2700 W 19th Ave Gary IN 46407

VINCENT, SANDRA LYNN (RAINEY), Music/Choral Director; *b:* Savannah, GA; *m:* Blair; *c:* Kristi L.; *ed:* (AA) Music, Brewton-Parker Coll 1967; (BS) Music Ed, GA Southern Univ 1969; (MCE) Mid Chldhd, Valdosta St Coll 1986; *cr:* Music Teacher Winder-Barrow HS 1971-73, East Augusta Mid Sch 1979-81; Teacher Camden Mid Sch 1981-; *ai:* Chrldr Coach; Yrbk Adv; Dir of Broadway Singers; Stu Cncl Comm; GEA; GMEA 1970-80; PAGE 1986-; Fellowship European Study 1973; *home:* 2876 Hwy 110 Woodbine GA 31569

VINECOMBE, BRENDA, 5th Grade Teacher; *b:* Lowell, MA; *ed:* (BS) Ed, 1961, (MS) Supervision/Admin, 1974 Lowell Univ; *cr:* 4th Grade Teacher Burlington Elem Sch 1961-63, Army Dependent Sch Kitzingen Germany 1964-67; 3rd-5th Grade Teacher Burlington Elem & Mid Schls 1968-; *ai:* Yrbk Comm Teacher Liason; MA Teachers Assn, NEA 1967-; Burlington Ed Assn (Prof Rights, Responsibilities Comm 1973) 1967-; Amnesty Intnl 1975-; Natl Organization for Women 1970-89; New England Historic Genealogical Society 1984-; *office:* Wildwood Sch Francis Wyman Rd Burlington MA 01803

VINELLA, PAUL VICTOR, 6th Grade Teacher; *b:* Oakland, CA; *ed:* (BA) Poly Sci, Univ of San Francisco 1970; K-8 Credential Coll of Holy Names 1972; Gifted & Talented Ed; Substance Abuse Trng Ed; *cr:* 6th Grade Teacher Fallon Sch 1973-76, Cronin Sch 1976-81, Frederiksen Sch 1981-88, Wells Mid Sch 1988-; *ai:* Gifted & Talented Prgm 1981-87; Dublin Substance Abuse Cncl 1987-; Murray Ed Assn (Schl Rep 1975-76/Zone Rep 1977-78/Negotiator 1978-79); Mentor Teacher Murray Sch Dist 1986-87; *office:* Wells Mid Sch 6800 Penn Dr Dublin CA 94568

VINES, GEAN WEATHERLY, Sixth Grade Teacher; *b:* Des Arc, AR; *m:* Gary L.; *c:* Brian L., Joanna M.; *ed:* (BBE) Elem Ed, 1961, (MSE) Elem Admin, 1984 Univ of Cntrl AR; Instr Prgm for Effective Teachers; *cr:* Teacher Little Rock Public Schls 1969-70, Pulaski Cty Spec Sch Dist 1971-; *office:* Bayou Meto Elem Sch Rt 2 Box 200 Jacksonville AR 72076

VINSON, ALAN KARR, 8th Grade Teacher; *b:* Franklin, NC; *m:* Brenda R. Marsengill; *c:* Michael W., Christopher A., Zachary M.; *ed:* (BS) Soc Sci, 1970; (MA) Mid Grades, 1980 Western Carolina Univ; *cr:* HS Math Teacher Franklin HS 1970; 7th Grade Teacher 1970-71; 8th Grade Teacher 1971-77 Franklin Jr HS; 8th Grade Teacher Macon Mid Sch 1977-; *ai:* Bsktbl Coach 1970-; Mem Personnel Policy Comm 1989-; Coaching 7th & 8th Grade Boys Bsktbl 1983-; Math Counts Chm MMS 1988; HS Varsity Girls Bsktbl Coach 1981-83; NEA 1970-; NCAE 1970-; Church League Sftbl (Chm 1976-86, Super Pres 81); United Methodist Men Pres 1986-87; Asbury Meth Supt Sunday Schls 1972-88; Little League Bsbl Coach 1986-; NC Filmstrip Series Advisory Cncl 1982; *home:* 186 Corn Rd Otto NC 28763

VINSON, BETSY, 1st Grade Teacher; *b:* Maysville, KY; *m:* Bob; *c:* Brian, Breck, Brandon; *ed:* (BA) Elem Ed, Morehead St Univ 1973; (MS) Elem Ed, Univ of Evansville 1975; *cr:* 1st Grade Teacher St Meinrad Elem 1975-; *ai:* ISTA 1975-; N Spencer Rdng Cncl 1975-; Local Rdng Cncl Pres 1982: *home:* 45 N Melchior Dr Santa Claus IN 47579

VINSON, CHARLOTTE A., Mathematics Teacher; *b:* Jackson, MS; *m:* David E.; *c:* David B.; *ed:* (BS) Bus Ed, 1965, (BS) Math, 1983 Univ of S MS; *cr:* Math Teacher Jackson Public Schls, Whitten Jr HS 1982-; *office:* Whitten Jr HS 210 Daniel Lake Blvd Jackson MS 39212

VINSON, DAVID LLOYD, English/History Teacher; *b:* Everett, WA; *ed:* (BS) Ed/Eng, Univ of ID 1987; (MS) Creative Arts, Lesley Coll 1990; Drug & Alcohol Counseling; *cr:* Teacher Lochburn Jr HS 1987-; *ai:* Friendly Helper, Chrldr, Care Team Adv; Health Week Chairperson; Honor Society, Odyssey of Mind Co-Chairperson; Kidsday Coord; Teacher of Yr Clover Park Sch Dist 1987-88; GTE Nom Outstanding Teacher Lochburn Jr HS; *home:* 25910 29th Ave S #D-206 Kent WA 98032

VINTRO, RICHARD ALLEN, 6th Grade Soc Stud Teacher; *b:* Taunton, MA; *m:* Barbara Ann Welch; *ed:* (BS) His/Soc Stud, Bridgewater St Coll 1968; Methods Courses Soc Stud, Rdng Introductory Cmptr Courses; Abnormal Psych; *cr:* Sci Teacher Peter Thatcher Jr HS 1968-69; Developmental Rdng Teacher Lee HS 1969-72; Soc Stud Teacher Qualters Mid Sch 1972-; *ai:* Drama Club Adv; Cribbage & Fishing Activity Spon; Mansfield Educators Assn (VP 1976-77, 1980-81, Pres 1981-82); *office:* Qualters Mid Sch East St Mansfield MA 02048

VIPPERMAN, E. JUNE, Retired Teacher; *b:* Chapman, NE; *m:* Fred; *c:* Elizabeth Hodtwalker, John F.; *ed:* (BS) Elem Ed, Univ of NE; Grad Hrs Kearney St Coll; *cr:* K-8th Grade Teacher 1936-37, K-6th Grade Teacher 1939-41 Merrick Cty Rural Sch; Prin Chapman Public Sch 1956-71, Seedling Mile Sch 1971-74; Title I Rdng/Kndgtn Teacher Chapman Public Sch 1974-82; *ai:* Music Prgms; Phys Ed Prgms Dir; Lunch Prgm Mgr; Outstanding Hall Cty Teacher Awd 1973; Grand Island Retired Teachers Schlsp Comm 1986-89; Eastern Star Chapman, Secy 1980-; Meth Church Organist 1972-; Betsey Hager Chapter D A R 1983-; Helped Organize Merrick Arts Cncl; *home:* Rt 1 Box 7 Chapman NE 68827

VIPPERMAN, REBECCA HILL, Chapter I Teacher; *b:* Panama City, FL; *m:* Gary; *c:* Joseph, Laura, Jennifer; *ed:* (BS) Elem Ed, VA Polytechnical Inst & St Univ 1977; *cr:* 4th Grade Teacher Pembroke Elem Sch 1978-79; 4th/5th Grade Teacher Critzer Elem Sch 1979-85; 3rd Grade Teacher Claremont Elem Sch 1985-86; 4th Grade Teacher 1986-, 4th/5th Grade Rdng Teacher 1988- Critzer Elem Sch; *ai:* Just Say No Club Spon; VA Ed Assn, Pulaski Ed Assn, NEA 1979-; Pulaski Jr Womans Club 1980-81; Pulaski Cty CADRE 1987-; *office:* Critzer Elem Sch 100 Critzer Dr Pulaski VA 24301

VIPPERMAN, REGINALD GRAHAM, Seventh Grade Science Teacher; *b:* Seneca, SC; *m:* Carl Jackson; *c:* Carl J. Jr.; *ed:* (BA) Elem Ed, Furman Univ 1954; Clemson Univ, Univ of SC, Univ of VA; *cr:* 4th Grade Teacher Seneca Elem Sch 1954-56; 7th Grade Teacher Dinsmore & Pason Jr HS 1956-59; 4th Grade Teacher Alps Road Elem 1959-61; 7th Grade Teacher Johnson Elem 1961-65, Coll Preparatory Sch 1965-67; 4th Grade Teacher West Broad Street 1967-68; 6th/7th Grade Teacher Athens Acad 1968-; *ai:* Athens Clark Heritage Assn; German Amer Teacher Exch; *home:* 375 W Cloverhurst Ave Athens GA 30606

VIRANDA, KARLA KAY, 7th/8th Grade Teacher/Coach; *b:* Pittsburg, KS; *ed:* (BS) Elem Ed, Pittsburg St Univ 1984; Working on Masters in Ed; *cr:* 7th-8th Grade Soc Sci Teacher/Coach Meadow View USD 506 1984-; *ai:* Coaching Jr HS Vlybl & Bsktbl; Yrbk Adv; Cheerleading Spon; Steering & KS Textbook Comms; Teacher of Yr; *office:* Meadow View USD 506 R R 2 Parsons KS 67357

VIRDELL, DIANA WILDE, Math Teacher; *b:* San Angelo, TX; *m:* Micky; *c:* Kevin K., Keith K.; *ed:* (BS) Math, 1971; (MAT) Phys Ed, 1975 Angelo St Univ; Guidance/Counseling; *cr:* Teacher Cook Ballinger HS 1971-78; Cook Stanton HS 1980-84; Cnslr Marble Falls HS 1984-89; Teacher Needville HS 1989-; *ai:* Coaching Bsktbll-Track-Vllybll; Annual Adv; VIL Calculator Spon; ATPE 1980-89; Delta Kappa Gamma 1987-; *office:* Needville HS 16319 Hwy 36 Needville TX 77461

VISSER, KONRAD JOHN, German Teacher; *b:* Traverse City, MI; *m:* Diana De Liefde; *c:* Franciska; *ed:* (BS) Eng, Cntrl MI 1976; (MA) Ed, Grand Valley St 1988; Grad Stud Klagenfurt Austria Through Univ of IA; Ger, Purdue; *cr:* Teacher Edmore Montabella 1976-78, Jenison 1979-85, Traverse City 1986-; *ai:* Jr Var Ftbl, Asst Var Track Coach; Amer Teachers of Foreign Lang, Amer Teachers of Ger; Natl Endowment for Hum Grant; *office:* Traverse City Public Schls 1150 Milliken Dr Traverse City MI 49684

VISSIA, LARRY DEAN, English Teacher; *b:* Alexandria, SD; *ed:* (BA) His/Eng, Dakota St Univ 1968; His, Span, Eng; *cr:* Eng Teacher Mc Gregor 1968-69; Eng/His Teacher Tri Valley Schls Colton 1969-79; Eng Teacher Alester Schls Alcester 1981-85; Eng/Span Teacher Newell 1985-; *ai:* Jr HS Ftbl Coach Tri-Valley & Alcester Schls; Jr HS Bd Coach Newell Schls; Head Track Coach Alcester Schls; SD Ed Assn, NEA 1969-79, 1987-; Optimist Club VP 1980-81, Outstanding Service 1981; Lyons Cmmty Club 1976-79; Tri-Valley Ed Assn Pres; Outstanding Teacher Awd 1988-89; Teacher of Yr 1978; *home:* RR 1 Box 6A Vale SD 57788

VISSING, PAMELA ANN, Director of Student Activities; *b:* Cincinnati, OH; *ed:* (BA) Eng, Xavier Univ 1978; *cr:* Eng Teacher 1978-84, Dir of Stu Act 1984- Mc Auley HS; *ai:* In Charge of all Non Athletic Extra Curriculars; NASSP 1984-; NCTE 1978-; Leadership Magazine Articles Published; Conduct Leadership Wkshp Girls in Sister of Mercy Schls; *office:* Mc Auley HS 6000 Oakwood Ave Cincinnati OH 45224

VITALE, CAROL COTTONE, Mathematics Teacher; *b:* Montclair, NJ; *m:* John B.; *c:* Lisa, John Jr., Jeffrey; *ed:* (BA) Math, Immaculata Coll 1961; Cmptr Courses, Brookdale Comm Coll; Italian, Brookdale; *cr:* Elem Algebra I & II/Algebra/Basic Geometry Teacher Raritan HS 1983-; *ai:* Field & Track Events Timer; NJ Assn of Math Teachers; NCTM 1983-; NJEA; *office:* Raritan HS 419 Middle Rd Hazlet NJ 07730

VITALE, JANET L., 5th Grade Teacher; *b:* Lorain, OH; *c:* Joseph, Suzanne; *ed:* (BS) Elem Ed, Baldwin-Wallace Coll 1963; Grad Work at Akron Univ, Ashland Univ, Kent St Univ; *cr:* Teacher Warrenton Sch 1962-63, Emerson Sch 1963-66, Bonita Springs Sch 1966-69, Palm Sch 1972-77, Masson Sch 1977-; *ai:* Girls Vlybl & Soccer Coach; Classroom of the Future Membership Comm; IRA, Lorain Ed Assn, OH Ed Assn, AAUW; Traveled to France with Elem Stus as Part Prof Exch Prgm; Supervised Stu Teaches; *office:* Masson Sch W 38th St & Edgewood Dr Lorain OH 44053

VITANZA, BEATRICE SEPULVEDA, Bilingual Teacher; *b:* New York, NY; *m:* Carl David; *c:* Lisa M., Michael D.; *ed:* (BSED) Bi-ling Ed, City Coll of NY 1976; (MSED) Bi-ling Ed, Long Island Univ 1985; Various Integrated Subjects; Sch Within a Sch Teacher; *cr:* Bi-ling Teacher Public Sch 1976-89, Lafayette-Pershing Sch 1990; *ai:* 8th Annual New York Teacher Recognition Day Ceremony Teachers of Dist 17 Rep 1985; *office:* Penns-Grove Carney Point Sch 113 W Harmony St Penns Grove NJ 08069

VITELLO, JOSEPH JOHN, Mathematics Teacher; *b:* Cambridge, NY; *m:* Anne Marie Mc Carthy; *c:* Elise, Carrianne; *ed:* (BA) Math Ed, Oneonta St 1971; *cr:* 5th/9th Grade Math Teacher Our Lady of Victory 1971-72; 7th/12th Grade Math Teacher Cambridge Cntrl 1972-; *ai:* Faculty Assn Negotiator; Cambridge Cntrl HS Summer Sch Dir; Boys Var Bsktbl Coach; Nom Capital Dist Regional Teaching Centers TV Teaching Prgm; Boys Bsktbl Coach of Yr WASAREN League 1984; *home:* 10 Avenue A Cambridge NY 12816

VITTETOE, REBECCA KINMAN, Fourth Grade Teacher; *b:* Owenton, KY; *m:* Henry Thurman III; *c:* Nicole, Carrie; *ed:* (BA) Elem Ed, 1976, (MA) Elem Ed, 1983 N KY Univ 1983; *cr:* Substitute Teacher Kenton Cty 1976-77; 4th Grade Teacher Beechgrove Elem 1977-; *ai:* KEA 1977-79; Ft Mitchell Baptist Church (Dept Dir, Teacher) 1978-; PTA 1977-, Schlsp 1981; *office:* Beechgrove Elem Sch 1029 Bristow Rd Independence KY 41051

VITTOR, NANCY ANN, Lang Art/Soc Stud Teacher; *b:* Madison, WI; *m:* Timothy Mc Kibben; *ed:* (BA) Eng, 1969, (MED) Ed, 1970 Univ of OR; Post Grad Stud, Univ of OR, Univ of WA, Seattle Pacific Univ; *cr:* Eng Teacher Hamlin Jr HS

1970-76, Singapore Amer Sch 1976-80, Amer Sch of Lima Peru 1980-82; Lang Art/Soc Stud Teacher Lake Stevens Mid Sch 1983-; *ai:* Peer Helpers Adv; Mem Dist Lang Art Comm; Mem Dist Teacher Cadre Team; Lake Stevens Ed Assn Mid Sch Dir 1988-89; *home:* 9510 2nd Ave SE Everett WA 98208

VIVIAN, SHIRLEY FRANCES, Language Arts Teacher; *b:* Mendota, IL; *m:* Richard T.; *c:* Christopher, Jeremy; *ed:* (BS) Elem Ed, IL St Univ 1971; (MS) Rdng, N IL Univ 1974; Gifted Trng; Jr Great Books; IL Writing Project; Rdng Specialist; *cr:* 2nd/4th/5th Grade Teacher 1970-74, Kndgtn Teacher 1976-78 Amboy Public Schls; Remedial Rdng Teacher 1978-86, Gifted Lang Arts Teacher 1987- Dixon Public Schls; *ai:* Newspaper, Young Authors, Spelling Bee Spon; Lang Art Dist, Sch Cmmty Relations Dist, Consulting Mentor Teacher Instructional Improvement Comm; Sauk Valley Rdng Cncl (Pres, VP) 1987-89; IL Rdng Cncl, Intnl Rdng Assn, IL Assn Teachers of Eng, IL Ed Assn, NEA; Petunia Festival Bd Mem 1986-89; Received 7 Curr Improvement Grants; Dist & Building Teacher of Yr; Those Who Excel Awd of Recognition St of IL; Asst Ed IL Rdng Cncl Journal; *office:* Madison Jr HS 620 Division Dixon IL 61021

VLAHOS, PETE A., 4th/5th Grade Teacher; *b:* Stenoma-Karpenisi, Greece; *m:* Fotini A. Petmeza; *c:* Paraskevi, Angelike; *ed:* Elem Ed, Maraskleias Acad Greece 1953; (BA) Elem Ed/Classics, Univ of WA 1962-63; Grad Stud Ed; *cr:* Teacher Elem Public Sch Greece 1955-58, Surrey Downs Elem Sch 1955-82, Enatai Elem Sch 1982-; *ai:* Various Comm Bellevue Sch Dist; Natl Soc Stud Mem 1988-; Nom PTA Outstanding Teacher of Yr; Elected Sch Dist Rep Washington DC Wkshp 1988-89.

VLASSIS, SOPHIE PARGAS, Social Science Teacher; *b:* Des Moines, IA; *m:* Thomas; *ed:* (BA) Sociology/Psych, Drake Univ 1963; *cr:* 7th Grade Geography Teacher Harding Jr HS 1963-83; 7th Grade Geography/8th Grade Government/Ec Teacher Hoyt Mid Sch 1983-; *ai:* Cmmty Specialist; Mrktg & Adopt-A-Sch Chm; Sister Cities Club Spon; IA St Ed Assn Mobile Inservice Trng Lab Speaker; IA Sch Public Relations Assn, IA Cncl for Soc Stud Mem; Delta Kappa Gamma, NEA, Des Moines Ed Assn; Auxiliary to Amer Pharmaceutical Assn Pres 1986-88; Auxiliary to IA Pharmacy Assn Pres 1981-82; Des Moines Sister Cities Commission Mem; Readers Digest Fnd Youth/Ed Prgm Awd 1982; YWCA Volunteer Service Awd 1983; Amer Cancer Society Outstanding Service Awd 1967; Alpha Phi Ursa Major Awd 1980; Des Moines Outstanding Service Awd 1981; IA Teacher of Yr Runner-Up 1985-86; Rotary Mid Sch Teacher of Yr 1989; IA Congress of Parents Distinguished Service Awd 1968; *home:* 5001 Lyndale Dr Des Moines IA 50310

VODOLA, CATHERINE M., Fifth Grade Teacher; *b:* New York, NY; *ed:* (BA) Ed, 1970, (MS) Ed, 1975 Queens Coll; Nutrition/Sex Ed, Queensboro Comm 1989; *cr:* Elem Teacher Holy Family Sch 1962-68, Public Sch 1970; *ai:* Teacher Trng Multicultural Prgm; Soc Comm; Tutor Math & Rdng; Kappa Delta Pi Membership 1970; Cath Teachers Assn 1970-; Taught Tennis to Deaf Students Lexington Sch for Deaf 1970.

VOELKER, SHARON BUETENBACH, 6th/7th Grade Math Teacher; *b:* Louisville, KY; *m:* Stanley G.; *c:* Kathleen, Peter; *ed:* (BS) Elem Ed, Univ of Louisville 1981; Mid Sch Math Project, Univ of Louisville; *cr:* 6th Grade Teacher St Polycarp Sch 1981-82; 4th Grade Teacher St Vincent De Paul Sch 1982-83; 4th-6th Grade Math/Sci Teacher St Leonard Sch 1983-89; 6th/7th Grade Math Teacher Southern Mid Sch 1989-; *ai:* Mathcounts Coach 1989; Sci Fair Coord 1983-89; *office:* Southern Mid Sch 4530 Bellevue Ave Louisville KY 40215

VOELTZ, DIANE FIELLO, Assistant to Principal; *b:* Santa Monica, CA; *m:* Larry Wayne; *c:* Theresa L., Larry R.; *ed:* (AA) Psych/Elem Ed, El Camino Jr Coll 1970; (BA) Psych/Elem Ed, Marymouth Coll 1972; (MS) Sch Admin, Pepperdine Univ 1990; *cr:* 5th/6th Grade Teacher Rosedell Elem Sch 1980-87; Mentor Teacher Saugus Union Sch Dist 1987-89; Prin Asst Rosedell Elem Sch 1989-; *ai:* Head Teacher; Stu Cncl Adv; Reviewer CA St Prgm Quality Review Team; Sch Site Cncl; Dist Soc Stud & Staff Dev Comms; Math & Lang Art Textbook Adoption Comms; NCSS 1989-; CA St Dept of Ed Instructional Materials Evaluation Panel 1990; GA Assn of Sch Bds Golden Bell Awd 1986; Masonic Lodge Outstanding Teacher Awd 1985, 1987; Classroom Teacher Instructional Improvement Prgm Grant 1985; *office:* Rosedell Elem Sch 27853 Urbandale Ave Santa Clarita CA 91350

VOELZKE, JOYCE BARTTRAM, German & English Teacher; *b:* Gadsden, AL; *m:* Hans D.; *c:* Sonja, Dan; *ed:* (BS) Health/Phys Ed/Eng, Samford Univ 1972; (MA) Eng, Univ of AL Birmingham 1980; *cr:* Teacher Moody Jr HS 1972-74, Moody HS 1978-; *ai:* German Club Spon 1985-; Univ of AL Birmingham Kappa Delta Pi; AL Assn of Foreign Lang Teachers, AL Assn of German Teachers; *home:* Rt 1 Box 123 Springville AL 35146

VOGEL, CHARLENE SUE, Sixth Grade Teacher; *b:* El Paso, TX; *m:* Edward Charles Sr.; *c:* Edward Jr., Scot A.; *ed:* (BS) Elem Ed, Univ of TX El Paso 1970; Grad Stud Curr Univ of S CA San Diego 1972; Sci 1986, Admin 1979-80 Univ of TX El Paso; *cr:* 5th Grade Teacher 1970-76, 6th Grade Teacher 1976- Eastwood Heights Elem; *ai:* 6th Grade Teacher of Gifted & Talented; OM Judge Regional & St Levels 1989-; NEA, TSTA 1970-; Intl Rdng Assn 1982-90; Delta Kappa Gamma (Recording Secy 1985-, 1st VP 1990); Teacher of Yr 1990; Level III Career Ladder 1987; UIL Coach 1984-87; Primary Tournament Dir 1985-87; St Textbook Adv Comm 1981; *office:* Eastwood Heights Elem Sch 10530 Janway Dr El Paso TX 79925

VOGEL, RUTHANNE GAUGH, Sixth Grade Teacher; *b:* Dayton, OH; *ed:* (BA) Elem Ed, Otterbein 1961; IN Univ, OH Univ, Otterbein Coll, OH St Univ; *cr:* 6th Grade Teacher Bath OH 1961; 3rd/4th Grade Teacher Lorain OH 1961-63; 5th Grade Teacher South Bend IN 1963-66; 5th/6th Grade Teacher Columbus OH 1979-; *ai:* Musical Dir; Staff Dev; 6th Grade Lang Art Head; NEA, OH Ed Assn 1961-; *office:* Starling Mid Sch 120 S Central Ave Columbus OH 43222

VOGT, JEFFREY VON, 6th Grade Teacher; *b:* Mt Vernon, OH; *m:* Belinda Mae Jackson; *c:* Torrey L.; *ed:* (BSED) Elem Ed, OH Univ 1973; Natl Sci Fnd Lead Sci & Math Teacher Project; *cr:* 8th Grade Sci Teacher Federal Hocking Mid Sch 1974-77; 6th Grade Teacher Coolville Elem 1977-; *ai:* Sci Olympiad Coach; Safety Patrol Adv; Math Educl Dev Comm; Federal-Hocking Teachers Assn VP 1980-81; Sci Ed of OH; N A Fishing Club Field Tester 1990; Eisenhower Project Mini-Grant Earth Sci Ed 1989-; *office:* Coolville Elem Sch Main St Coolville OH 45723

VOGT, M. WAYNE, JR., Instrumental Music Director; *b:* St Louis, MO; *m:* Viki L. Stanich; *c:* Jacob; *ed:* (BME) Instrumental Music, Univ of OK 1979; *cr:* Band Dir Fox Public Schls 1979-82; Instrumental Music Dir Wilburton Public Schls 1982-; *ai:* OK Music Educators Assn, OK Bandmasters Assn, OK Ed Assn 1979-; *office:* Wilburton Public Schls 1201 W Blair Wilburton OK 74578

VOGT, MELANIE POLKING, English Teacher; *b:* Ft Dodge, IA; *m:* Thomas R.; *c:* Lindsay, Ryan; *ed:* (BA) Span/Eng, Briar Cliff Coll 1977; *cr:* Eng Teacher St Edmond HS 1977-; *ai:* Yrbk Adv; Schlsp Comm; NHS Faculty Cncl; Long-Range Planning Achievements Comm; NCTE 1977-; NCEA 1987-; Alpha Delta Kappa Pres Elect 1985-; Ft Dodge Tennis Assn 1983-; *office:* St Edmond HS 501 N 22nd Fort Dodge IA 50501

VOGT, SANDRA JOSETTE, English/Reading Teacher; *b:* Bristol, VA; *m:* Robert David; *c:* Amanda, Jared; *ed:* (BA) Eng, 1972, (MS) Ed, 1981 Univ of Dayton; *cr:* Eng/Rdng Teacher Centerville HS 1972-73; Eng Teacher Laurel Sr HS 1973-74; Eng/Rdng Teacher Centerville HS 1974-; *ai:* Competency Intervention Facilitator; Unit Coord Eng Dept Chm; Centerville Classroom Teachers Assn, OH Ed Assn, NEA 1974-; NCTE 1986-; Dayton Area Intnl Rdng Assn 1987-; Twigs Auxiliary of Childrens Medical Center 1986-; Wee Elk Pee Wee FtbL Cheerleading Coach; Outstanding Educator Centerville HS Awd 1979-80, 1986-87; Stu Choice Awd Centerville HS 1986-88; *office:* Centerville HS 500 E Franklin St Centerville OH 45459

VOGT, STEVEN F., Science Teacher; *b:* Wood River, IL; *c:* Amber, Brock; *ed:* (BS) Earth Sci/Geo/His, S IL Univ 1972; *cr:* Sci Teacher Maries Cty R-2 Sch Dist 1974-; *ai:* Sr Class Spon; Belle Lions Club (Secy, Treas) 1978-83, Outstanding Service 1983; Belle Volunteer Fire Dept Asst Chief 1976, Fireman of Yr 1979, 1982; Belle Fair Bd; Belle Chamber of Commerce; Meramec Regional Planning Commission Commissioner; Belle City Cncl Alderman 1982-, Mayor 1989-; *home:* PO Box 542 Belle MO 65013

VOITLEIN, MICHAEL LEE, Biology Teacher; *b:* Portsmouth, VA; *m:* Peggy Richardson; *ed:* (BS) Phys Ed/Health/Bio, 1972, (MA) Ed, 1973 E TN St Univ; *cr:* 2nd Grade Teacher Thomas Jefferson Elem 1972-73; 7th-9th Grade Teacher Holston Valley Jr HS 1973-74; 10th-12th Grade Teacher Science Hill HS 1974-; *ai:* Asst Head Ftbl, Boys Head Tennis Coach; *office:* Science Hill HS John Exum Pkwy Johnson City TN 37604

VOLBRECHT, RICHARD E., JR., Mathematics Teacher; *b:* Milwaukee, WI; *c:* Ashley, Tara; *ed:* (BS) Math, 1970, (BS) Math Ed, 1971 Purdue Calumet; (MS) Industrial Management, Purdue Lafayette-Krannert Sch of Management 1977; (MS) Math Ed, Purdue Calumet 1977; *cr:* Math Teacher/Coach Scott Mid Sch 1971-77, Morton HS 1977-80, Scott Mid Sch 1980-86; Math Teacher/Coach 1986-89, Math Teacher 1989- Morton HS; *ai:* Scott Mid Sch Cross Cntry Coach 1980; 8th Grade Cmmty Chm 1984-86; Scott Mid Sch Track Coach 1971-77; Scott Mid Sch 7th & 8th Grade Bsktbl Coach 1971-76; Morton HS 9th Grade Bsktbl Coach 1976-87; Morton HS Jr Var Bsktbl Coach 1987-89; Morton HS Var Asst Ftbl 1971-80, Frosh Ftbl 1981-83, Var Asst Ftbl Coach 1984; IN Bsktbl Coaches Assn 1971-89; Highland Youth Sftbl Mgr 1985-89, League Champ 1989; *office:* Morton Sr HS 6915 Grand Ave Hammond IN 46323

VOLEK, DAN R., Speech/English Teacher; *b:* Taylor, TX; *m:* Anita; *c:* Leighanne; *ed:* (BS) Ed, Baylor Univ 1977; (MA) Ed, Univ of TX 1990; Several Debate Wkshps; *cr:* Speech Teacher Waco Ind Sch Dist 1977-82; Speech/Eng Teacher Taylor Ind Sch Dist 1982-; *ai:* One Act Play Dir; UIL Coord; UIL Prose, Poetry, Extemporaneous Speaking Coach; C-X & L-D Debate; Drama Club, Sr Class, Young Life Adv; Assn of TX Prof Educators; TX Forensic Assn; TX Speech Comm Assn; *home:* 2207 Carolyn Taylor TX 76574

VOLENTINE, ROGER WILBUR, Mathematics Instructor; *b:* Kearney, NE; *m:* Kristy Marie Oldenburg; *c:* Jason, Angela; *ed:* (BA) Math Ed, 1976, (MS) Math Ed, 1982 Kearney St Coll; *cr:* Math Instr Thedford HS 1976-81, Geneva HS 1981-82, Mullen HS 1982-; *ai:* Athletic Dir; NCTM 1976-; NE Assn of Teachers of Math 1985-; NEA 1976-; *office:* Mullen HS Box 127 Mullen NE 69152

VOLK, DEBORAH J., French Teacher; *b:* Presque Isle, ME; *ed:* (BA) Fr/Eng - Magna Cum Laude, Univ of Akron 1976; (ME) Fr/Ed, Kent St Univ & Univ of Akron; Fr/Ed, KSU & Univ of Akron & Ashland; *cr:* Fr Grad Teaching Asst Kent St Univ 1976-77; Fr Teacher Streetsboro HS 1978-; *ai:* Overseas Stu Travel Cnslr; Intnl Culture Club; Curr Advisory & N Cntrl Comm; Stu of Month Prgm Coord; Cmmty Intervention Group Facilitator; Essential Elements of Ed Meeting Facilitator & Participating Teacher; OH Modern Lang Teachers Assn, NE OH Teachers Assn 1978-; Streetsboro Teachers Assn (Building Rep, Comm Chairperson) 1978-; Akron Cath Commission Bd of Dirs 1982-87; Intnl Inst (Volunteer Teacher, Tutor) 1983-85; Peace & Justice Task Force 1982-; Teacher of Yr 1984-85; Runner-Up Teacher of Yr 1989; NHS Teacher of Yr 1986; *office:* Streetsboro HS 1900 Annalane Dr Streetsboro OH 44241

VOLK, ELIZABETH ANN, Choral Dir; *b:* Kew Gardens, NY; *ed:* (BM) Music, 1973, (MM) Music, 1978 Southern Meth Univ 1978; *cr:* Choral Dir Edward H Cary Jr HS 1973-80, Thomas Jefferson HS 1980-; *ai:* Performing Choral Organizations Spon;; Annual Sch Musical Producer; Pi Kappa Lambda 1989-; TX Music Educators Assn Regional Vice Chairperson; TX & Amer Choral Dir Assn; TX Music Adjudicators Assn; Multi-Yr Teacher of Yr Awds; Choral Groups Won Countless Awds, Interscholastic Sweepstakes Awds 1989; Show Choir Outstanding Performer Awd; 18th Intnl Youth & Music Festival in Vienna 3rd Prize Winner; *office:* Thomas Jefferson HS 4001 Walnut Hill Ln Dallas TX 7229

VOLK, HERBERT JAY, Business Education Teacher; *b:* Johnstown, PA; *m:* Connie; *c:* Michael, Kevin, Steven; *ed:* (BS) Bus Ed, Shippensburg Univ 1965; *cr:* Bus Teacher Conemaugh Township Area HS 1965-; *ai:* Frosh Class Adv; Yrbk Bus Mgr; PA Bus Ed Assn 1965-; Boswell Area Jaycees Pres 1973-74, JCI Senator 1975; St Andrews Luth Church Pres 1980-82; *home:* 704 Morris Ave Boswell PA 15531

VOLK, LOUIS J., Sixth Grade Teacher; *b:* Cincinnati, OH; *m:* Marguerite Nuyrah; *c:* Aaron J., Max L.; *ed:* (BBA) Bus Management, 1969, (MS) Elem Ed, 1974 E KY Univ; Grad Stud Univ of KY 1971 & Univ of TN; *cr:* Teacher Willow Brook Elem 1974-85, Woodland Elem 1985-86, Jefferson Jr HS 1986-; *ai:* AM Homework Help; Young Environmental Stu & Inventors Club; Salary Comm; Sex Ed Task Force; Oak Ridge Ed Assn, TN Ed Assn, NEA, E TN Ed Assn; Oak Ridge Jr Playhouse Comm; Amer Youth Soccer League Coach; Oak Ridge Teacher of Yr 1986; Invent America Regional & Natl Awd 1988; *office:* Jefferson Jr HS 200 Fairbanks Rd Oak Ridge TN 37830

VOLKMER, RONA K., English Teacher; *b:* Deshler, NE; *m:* Ronald; *c:* Ross; *ed:* (BA) Eng, NE Wesleyan 1984; Grad Courses in Ed; *cr:* Eng/Journalism Teacher/Coach Sandy Creek Jr/Sr HS 1985-87; Eng/Speech/Journalism Teacher/Coach Bruning Public Sch 1987-; *ai:* Head Vlybl Coach; Soph Class Spon; Yrbk Adv; NE Coaches Assn 1985-; Bruning Ed Assn 1987-; *home:* RR 1 Box 65 Carleton NE 68326

VOLLENDORF, SHARON ANN, Phys Education/Health Teacher; *b:* Manitowoc, WI; *ed:* (BS) Phys Ed, Univ of La Crosse 1971; (MA) Health Ed, Marion Coll 1989; *cr:* Phys Ed/Health Teacher Campbellsport Public Sch Dist 1971-; *ai:* Kndgtn-12th Grade Dist Health Coord; Stu Asst Prgm Facilitor; NEA, WI Ed Assn 1971-; Campbellsport Ed Assn (Pres, Negotiations Chm) 1985-; GSA Leader 1971-; Amer Legion Aux 1988-; *office:* Campbellsport Public Sch Dist 114 W Sheboygan St Campbellsport WI 53010

VOLLENWEIDER, BETTY H., 6th Grade Teacher/ Chairperson; *b:* Campbellton, FL; *m:* John Charles; *c:* Delene M., William C., Iris G.; *ed:* (BS) Elem Ed, FL St Univ 1959; (MS) Elem Ed, Oglethorpe Univ 1976; *cr:* Teacher McLendon Elem 1956-61, Fair Oaks Elem 1961-62, New Hope Elem 1970-73, Hiram Elem 1976-; *ai:* Americas Pride, Just Say No Club, 4-H Club Adv; Campbells Soup Level Sch Chairperson; Paulding Assn of Educators, GA Assn of Educators, NEA 1970-73, 1976-; PTA 1968-; 4-H Adult Volunteer (Pres, VP, Secy) 1976-80, GA Volunteer Leader Awd 1978; Leader Assn United Meth Women LifeTime Membership 1967; New Hope PTA Pres 1970-72, Honorary Life Membership 1972; Proclamation from Gov Harris 1990; Teacher of Yr Hiram Elem 1982-83, 1987-88.

VOLLMER, FRED L., Drafting Teacher; *b:* Francisville, IN; *m:* Deloris Ann; *c:* Tique A.; *ed:* Executive Automation Technician, Porter Bus Coll 1958; (BS) Industrial Art, 1966, (MA) Industrial Art, 1967 Ball St Univ; Technology/Cmptrs, Ball St UniV; *cr:* IA Teacher Grad Asst Ball St 1966-67, Irvine Jr HS 1967-68, Elston HS 1968-69, Peru HS 1969-; *ai:* Industrial Art Teacher Grad Asst Ball St 1966-67, Irvine Jr HS 1967-68, Elston HS 1968-69, Peru HS 1969-; Peru Comm Ed Assn, IN St Teachers Assn, NEA; Cub Scout Leader 1988-; 1st Baptist Church Mem 1988-, Eternal Life; CADD Grant Jr Drafter 1989-; Summer Youth Employment Prgm Grant 1988-89-; *office:* Peru HS 401 N Broadway Peru IN 46970

VOLPE, DEBORAH LOVE, HS Mathematics Teacher; *b:* Williamsport, PA; *m:* Steven; *c:* Michelle R., Marie E.; *ed:* (BS) Math Ed, IN Univ of PA 1976; (MA) Math, OH St Univ; *cr:* Teacher Westerville S 1977-; *ai:* ACT/SAT Assessment Coach; *office:* Westerville South HS 303 S Otterbein Ave Westerville OH 43081

VOLPE, TECKLA ANNE, English Teacher; *b:* Camp Le Jeune, NC; *ed:* (BA) Eng Lit, Rosemont Coll 1967; Cert Scndry Ed, Glassboro St Coll 1974; *cr:* Eng Teacher Pleasantville HS 1974-86, Hammonton HS 1986-; *ai:* NHS & Rutgers NJ Bowl Team Adv; Womens Civic Club of Hammonton 1988-; *office:* Hammonton HS N Liberty St Hammonton NJ 08037

VOLPE, TINA MARIA, Enrichment Teacher; *b:* Manhattan, NY; *m:* Joseph; *c:* Christopher, Elizabeth; *ed:* (BS) Ed, SUNY New Platz 1964; (MS) Ed, Brooklyn Coll 1969; *cr:* Teacher Glen Head Sch; New York City Public Schls; Teacher/Staff Developer Public Sch 172K; *ai:* Several Sch Based Management Comm; Visiting Nurse Assn Mem 1975-76; Art Partners Public Sch 172K Liaison 1987-88; Several Legislative Grants; Dist Mini Grants; *office:* Public Sch 172K 825 4th Ave Brooklyn NY 11232

VOLTMER, RENEE, Home Economics Teacher; *b:* Maryville, MO; *ed:* (BS) Home Ec Ed - Magna Cum Laude, 1976, (MS) Ed, 1979 NW MO St Univ; Working Towards PHD in Curr & Instruction, Univ of MO Columbia & Univ of MO Kansas City; *cr:* Home Ec Teacher Spring Garden Mid Sch 1977-; *ai:* Spring Garden Youth Advisory Cncl Spon; Educl Technology Software, Faculty Advisory Comm Mem; Metropolitan Instructional Leadership Prgm Mem; Nominating Comm MO St Teachers Assn Dist Level; Dist Level Prof Dev Comm Mem; Phi Delta Kappa, MO St Teachers Assn, Cmmty Teachers Assn, Kappa Omicron Phi; United Way Chm Building Level 1988-; Prof Home Ec Club; Published Article Sch & Cmmty Magazine; *office:* Spring Garden Mid Sch 5802 S 22nd St Saint Joseph MO 64503

VOLZ, PHYLLIS CHANEY, Freshman English Teacher; *b:* Winchester, KY; *m:* Richard J.; *ed:* (BS) Eng/Music, Union Coll 1968; (MA) Ed/Eng, 1973, (Rank I) Scndry Prin/Supervision, E KY Univ; Certified Resource Teacher KY Teacher Intern Prgm; *cr:* 9th-12th Grade Speech/Eng Teacher George Rogers Clark HS 1968-; *ai:* Clark Cty Ed Assn (Secy, Building Rep) 1968-; KEA, NEA 1968-; Alpha Delta Kappa 1968-89; Trinitity United Meth Church (VP United Meth Women, Ofcl Bd, Choir Dir, Bell Choir Dir, Chairperson Susannah Wesley Group); Clark Cty Homemakers; Outstanding Young Women of America 1973; Local, Dist Young Career Woman by BPW 1973; *home:* 318 S Burns Winchester KY 40391

VONA, BEVERLY JEAN, Fifth Grade Teacher; *b:* Sodus, NY; *m:* John L.; *c:* John D., Lynn M., Kathleen A.; *ed:* (BS) Elem Ed, Cortland St 1958; (MS) Elem ED, Elmire Coll 1976; *cr:* 5th Grade Teacher Canandaigua Cntrl 1958-60; 4th Grade Teacher Watkins Glen Cntrl 1960-62; 4th/5th Grade Teacher Odessa-Montour 1969-; *home:* 200 S Decatur St Watkins Glen NY 14891

VON AXELSON, CODYLENE SIMMONS, Guidance Counselor; *b:* Pensacola, FL; *m:* Albert; *c:* Becky Bondurant *ed:* (BA) Elem Ed, Univ of W FL 1976; (MED) Guidance, Livingston Univ 1982; *cr:* 6th Grade Teacher King Mid Sch 1977; Math Teacher Pace Mid Sch 1977-82; Itinerant Guidance Cnslr Allentown/Chumuckla/Munson HS 1982-83; Guidance Cnslr Central HS 1983-; *ai:* Key Club, Project Graduation Spon; Santa Rosa Prof Educators 1982-; *office:* Central HS Rt 6 Box 230 Milton FL 32570

VON BENKEN, WILLIAM DAVID, Chemistry Teacher; *b:* Cleveland, OH; *m:* Laura Shumaker; *c:* Megan; *ed:* (BA) Chem, Hiram Coll 1966; (MS) Chem, Case W Reserve Univ 1969; *cr:* Euclid HS 1969-; *ai:* Ski Club Adv 1969-; Sychronized Swimming Adv 1975-77; Yrbk Adv 1985-; Euclid Teachers Assn Rep 1976-; *office:* Euclid HS 711 E 222nd St Euclid OH 44123

VON DECK, JOSEPH FRANCIS, Social Studies Dept Chair; *b:* Athol, MA; *m:* Evelyn Strachan; *c:* Scott, Philip; *ed:* (BA) His - Summa Cum Laude, Univ of MA 1961; (MED) His, Fitchburg St Coll 1971; NDEA Insts East Asian Stud, Bucknell Univ 1965; Teaching Adult Communism, Russell Sage Coll 1967; Courses Worcester St Coll, Clark Univ, Mt Wachusett Comm Coll; *cr:* Teaccher 1961-67, Teacher/Dept Chm 1967- Oakmont Regional HS; *ai:* Chess & Debate Club; K-12 Curr Comm; Harrisonburg-Rockingham Historical Society; Natl Trust for Historic Preservation; New England Historic Geneological Society; New England His Teachers Assn; Society of Civil War Historians; Sons of Union Veterans Charter Mem; Oakmont Teachers Assn (Treas 1962, Pres 1964, 1967); MA Teachers Assn, NEA; Amer Military Inst; Antietam Battlefield Preservation Society; Assn for Preservation of Civil War Sites; Civil War Necrolithographers; *home:* Russell Hill Rd Ashburnham MA 01430

VON ROSENBERG, GARY MARCUS, JR., Science/Math Teacher; *b:* Baumholder, West Germany; *ed:* (BA) Poly Sci, Cleveland St Univ 1979; *cr:* Lieutenant US Army Field Artillery Ft Hood TX 1980-82; 7th/8th Grade Sci Teacher St Andrews Cath Sch 1982-86; 7th/8th Grade Math Teacher Nolan HS 1986-; *ai:* Jr HS Division, Math Counts & Math Club Moderator; CORE Team Adv; Chess Club Coach; Sci Fair Coord; NCTM 1986-; Math Assn of America 1986-; NSTA 1982-; Knights of Columbus Cncl 2813 1983-; Ft Worth Regional Sci Fair Teacher of Yr 1984, Runner Up 1983; *office:* Nolan Jr H S 4501 Bridge St Fort Worth TX 76103

VON RUDEN, DENISE KAY, Mathematics/Computer Teacher; *b:* Mayville, ND; *ed:* (BSED) Math, Mayville St Univ 1987; *cr:* Math/Cmptr Teacher Walhalla Public Sch 1987-; *ai:* Annual Staff & Frosh Class Adv; ND Cncl Teachers of Math, ND Eeucl Cmptr Assn, Walhalla Ed Assn, ND Ed Assn, NEA; *office:* Walhalla Public Sch Box 558 Walhalla ND 58282

VORBA, JED HAROLD, Science Teacher; *b:* Waterloo, IA; *ed:* (BA) Bio/Phys Ed, Coe Coll 1982; Grad Stud Drake Univ; *cr:* Earth/Life Sci/Phys Ed Teacher West Liberty HS 1982-83; Jr HS Sci/Phys Ed Teacher BCL-UW Schls 1983-; *ai:* Jr HS Ftbl; Head Var Boys BsktBl, Track, Bsbl; IA HS Ftbl Coaches Assn, IA HS Bsktbl Coaches Assn, IA HS Track Coaches Assn, IA HS Bsbl Coaches Assn; United Meth Church; *office:* UW-BCL Schls Box A Union IA 50258

VORTHERMS, DAVID LEE, Business Teacher; *b:* Worthington, MN; *m:* Kari Behnke; *ed:* (BS) Bus Ed, Mankato St Univ 1985; *cr:* Bus Teacher Prescott HS 1985-; *ai:* Stu Assistance Prgm Group Leader; Stu Cncl Adv; Boys Track Head Coach; Finance Comm.

VORTHMANN, MARLENE HAIBECK, Speech & English Teacher; *b:* Bismarck, ND; *m:* Everett A.; *c:* Dawn Patton, Scott A., Layne Lovett; *ed:* (BA) Eng/Speech/Journalism, Wartburg Coll 1959; *cr:* Drama/Foreign Lang Teacher Carl Sandburg Mid Sch 1981-82; Farm Programming Dir WFRL/WXXQ Radio 1982-84; Speech/Eng Teacher Freeport HS 1984-; *ai:* Key Club Adv; Speech Team Coach; *office:* Freeport HS Locust at Moseley Freeport IL 61032

VOSKUHL, DIANNE P., 2nd Grade Teacher; *b:* Minster, OH; *m:* Ralph; *ed:* (BS) Elem Ed, Bowling Green St Univ 1963; *cr:* 2nd Grade Teacher Minster Local 1962-; *ai:* Jr HS Girls Track Coach.

VOSS, DAVID JOHN, Social Studies Chair; *b:* Fond Du Lac, WI; *m:* Lorraine G. Banick; *c:* Kelley M., Kasey M.; *ed:* (BS) Soc Stud, Dr Martin Luther Coll 1977; Working Towards Masters Ed, Admin, N AZ Univ; *cr:* Vice-Prin/Athletic Dir/Soc Stud Chm East Fork Luth HS 1977-; *ai:* Head Ftbl Coach; Sftbl Coach; AZ Ind Athletic Assn Pres 1982-; AIAA Coach of Yr 1989; *office:* East Fork Luth HS Box 489 Whiteriver AZ 85941

VOSS, JEFFREY CHARLES, Third Grade Teacher; *b:* Milwaukee, WI; *c:* Robert; *ed:* (BS) Elem Ed, Univ of WI Stevens Point 1977; Learning Styles Madeleine Hunter Model; Cray Acad Technology in Elem, Sci in Elem; Introduction to Cmptrs; *cr:* 3rd Grade Teacher Abbotsford Elem Sch 1978-; *ai:* 8th Grade Bsktbl Coach 1978-; Sci Curr Comm 1989-; Dorchester Recreation Co-Coord 1982; AEA Union 1978-; *home:* Rt 1 Box 178 Dorchester WI 54425

VOSSLER, JAMES ALAN, Mathematics Teacher; *b:* Williston, ND; *m:* Kristin L.; *c:* Annie M., Maddie J.; *ed:* (BS) Math/Phys Ed, 1977, (MAT) Math, 1990 Minot St Univ; *cr:* Math Instr Minot Bishop Ryan HS 1977-79, Williston Jr HS 1980-82, Williston HS 1983-; *ai:* Drug & Alcohol Awareness Teacher; Prom Adv; NCTM 1982-; NDEA 1980-; WEA 1980-, Teacher of Yr 1990; Lions 1985-; Elks 1980-; Bd of Higher Ed Schlsp; ND Team NCTM Stan Conference Mem; *office:* Williston HS Box 1407 Williston ND 58801

VOTH, MARLA SUE (ROWE), Third Grade Teacher; *b:* Denver, CO; *m:* Dale Michael; *c:* Polly, Daniel; *ed:* (BA) Elem Ed, Southwestern Coll 1975; Grad Courses WSU Wichita, Ft Hays St, Emporia St; *cr:* 3rd-4th Grade Teacher St Cecilia Cath Sch 1975-76; 2nd Grade Teacher 1976-82, 3rd Grade Teacher 1983- Cimarron Elem; *ai:* Sch Coord Jump Rope for Heart & Campbell Soup Labels for Equipment; PTA 1990; KS Rdng Cncl 1986-; United Meth Women Ed Comm 1982-, Spec Membership 1988; United Meth Church Trustee 1988-; *home:* Box 674 Cimarron KS 67835

VOTO, JAMES A., Band Director; *b:* Teaneck, NJ; *m:* Cristina M. Scaglione; *ed:* BMm) Music Ed, Hartt Sch of Music 1984; (ME) Admin, Bridgewater St Coll 1990; *cr:* Music Teacher Boston Publis Schls 1985-86; Band Dir Bridgewater Raynham Reg HS 1986-; *ai:* Producer Muscial Dir Sch Musicals; Quality Circle Mem; MENC 1986-; MMEA S E Dist Exec Bd 1986-; NEA & MTA 1985-; Metropolitan Wind Symphony 1986-88; *office:* Ridgewater Raynham Regnl H S Mt Prospect St Bridgewater MA 02324

VOYLES, DENISE DUKES, Mathematics Teacher; *b:* Jesup, GA; *m:* Bennett Andrew Sr.; *c:* Bennett A. Jr.; *ed:* (AA) Music, Brewton-Parker Coll 1980; (BS) Ed, Tift Coll 1984; (MED) Ed, 1988, (EDS) Ed, 1990 GA Southern Coll; *cr:* Math Teacher Wayne Cty Jr HS 1984-; *ai:* Cluster Leader; Mathcounts & GA Math League Coach; Honors Day Chairperson; Media Comm; Beta Club & Annual Staff Spon; GA Cncl Teachers of Math, Phi Kappa Phi 1988-; Prof Assn of GA Educators 1987-; Jr HS Handbells Dir 1988-; *office:* Wayne Cty Jr HS 1425 W Orange St Jesup GA 31545

VRANISH, JANE, String Teacher; *b:* Mc Keesport, PA; *ed:* (BA) Music Ed, 1968, (MMED) Music Ed, 1970 Duquesne Univ; *cr:* Elem Music Teacher W Mifflin Area Schls 1970-71; String Teacher Mc Keesport Area Sch Dist 1971-; *ai:* Dance Critic Pittsburgh Post Gazette; Directed, Choreographed, Conducted Musicals at Mc Keesport HS; MENC, PMEA, NSOA 1971-; *office:* Mc Keesport Area Schls 1960 Eden Park Blvd Mc Keesport PA 15132

VRBA, GLENN WILLIAM, Health Teacher/Coach; *b:* Waco, TX; *m:* Teri Lyn Story; *c:* Andrew C.; *ed:* (BS) Ed, N TX St Univ 1980; Grad Work; *cr:* Phys Ed Teacher/Coach 1980-83, Eng Teacher/Coach 1983-84 Allen Mid Sch; Health Teacher/Coach Allen HS 1984-; *ai:* Asst Var Ftbl & Head Bsbl Coach; TX HS Coaches Assn 1980-; TX HS Bsbl Coaches Assn 1983-; St Judes Cath Church 1982-; Bsbl Coach of Yr 1983-84; *home:* 1323 Woodland Ct Allen TX 75002

VUKOTICH, DOROTHY, French Teacher; *b:* Burgettstown, PA; *m:* Stanley M.; *ed:* (BA) Eng/Fr, Bethany Coll 1949; Grad Stud Pittsburgh; *cr:* Teacher Burgettstown Area HS 1950-; *ai:* Fr Club; Kolo Club; 7 Stu Trip to France Spon; Burgettstown Ed Assn (Secy, Pres); PA Ed Assn, NEA; Char Valley Singers (Pres, Bd of Dirs); St Agatha Church Choir; Croatian Fraternal Union Jr Nest Secy, 4 Cty Woman of Yr 1990; *office:* Burgettstown Area HS 99 Main St Burgettstown PA 15021

VULCANO, PAT, JR., Teacher/Coordinator; *b:* City of Easton, PA; *m:* Sandra P. Alercia; *c:* Michele; *ed:* (ASB) Accounting/ Finance, Churchman Bus Coll 1968; (BBA) Bus Admin/ Accounting, Ft Lauderdale Coll 1970; (BSED) Mrktg/Bus Ed, IN Univ of PA 1973; (MED) Cooperative/Career Ed, Lehigh Univ 1976; *cr:* Mrktg Rep/Territory Mgr Burrough Corporation 1969-71; Mrtkg Teacher Cntrl Chester Voc Tech Sch 1973-75, Bethlehem Voc Tech Sch 1975-76; Mrktg/Bus Teacher/Coord Northampton Area Voc Tech Sch 1976-; Part-Time Cncl Mem/ City Treas City of Easton PA 1980-; *ai:* 10th, 11th, 12th Grade Class, Stu Cncl, Distributor Ed Clubs of America Adv; NEA, PA St Ed Assn, DECA Prof Mem; PA Jaycees Outstanding Young Educator of Yr 1982; PA Dept of Ed Best Teacher of Yr 1984-85; *office:* Northampton Area Sr HS 1619 Laubach Ave Northampton PA 18067

W

WAARVIK, JANICE L., Science Teacher; *b:* Chicago, IL; *ed:* (BA) Bio/Composite Sci, Luther Coll 1968; (MS) Curr/ Instruction, St Thomas 1988; Grad Stud Various Univs & Wkshps; *cr:* Life Sci Teacher Carl Sandburg Jr HS 1968-69, Minnetonka East Jr HS 1969-70; Phys Sci/Algebra Teacher Ketchikan HS 1970-72; Phys Sci/Life Sci Teacher St Anthony Village HS 1972-73; Chem/Physics/Earth Sci/Home Ec Teacher/Hot Lunch Coord Bethlehem Acad 1978-; *ai:* Sci Olympic Coach; Jr Class, Yrbk Adv; Jr & Sr HS Sci Challenge Teams Coach 1985-; Weekly Presenter Search Bible Study 1984-87; Northfield Arts Gallery Bd Mem & Fine Art Fair Chairwoman 1985-86; Helped With Youth Group & Overnight Act & Retreats 1976-88; Cooperative Teacher/Industry Experience Sheldahl with Chem Engr 1985; Organized & Donated Time Orchesis Group Modern Dance Bethlehem Acad 1979-83; NSTA 1978-; MSTA, MESTA 1985-; AAPT, PTRA 1986; Faribault Amer Assn of Univ Women Schlsp Awd 1988; Finalist Presidential Awd Excl in Sci Teaching 1989; Nom Assn of Commerce & Industry Fnd for Excl in Ed 1986, 1989.

WABLE, RAYMOND A., Fifth Grade Teacher; *b:* Clarksburg, WV; *ed:* (BS) Elem Ed, OH St Univ 1971; (MED) Elem Ed, Miami Univ 1975; Ashland Coll; *cr:* Teacher Lucas Local Schls 1968-; *ai:* Right to Read Comm; OH Ed Assn 1968-; Lucas Teachers Assn (Pres, VP); North Cntrl OH Ed; OH Sci Teachers; Jennings Scholar; Electric Cooperatives Sci Grant 1989-; Apple Cmptr Grant; Article Published 1988; *home:* 444 Wood St Mansfield OH 44907

WACEK, SUSAN (NASS), Mathematics/Computer Teacher; *b:* Owatonna, MN; *m:* Edward James; *c:* Carrie J., Kimberly A.; *ed:* (BA) Math, Coll of St Teresa 1968; Grad Work Winona St Univ, Mankato St Univ; *cr:* Math Teacher Winona Public Schls 1968-70, Marian HS 1970-75, St Marys Sch 1976-85; Math/Computer Teacher St Marys Sch 1985-; *ai:* Mathcounts Team & Mathmasters Coach; Math Curr Comm; Magazine Drive Chairperson; NCTM 1987-; NCEA 1980-; Cath Daughters Treas 1983-86; Sacred Heart Parish 1970-; MN Teacher of Excl Nominee; Organized & Taught Summer Cmptr Sch 1984-; Developed K-8th Grade Cmptr Lab & Curr; *office:* St Marys Sch Marian Dr Owatonna MN 55060

WACH, DOUGLASS R., Mathematics Teacher; *b:* Salt Lake City, UT; *m:* Leslie Gerrard; *c:* Jessica, Ashley; *ed:* Assoc Snow Coll 1978; (MA) Phys Ed/Health, S UT St Coll 1982; Psych Weber St COll 1987; Licensed Cosmetologist Inst of Hair Design 1979; *cr:* Chem Teacher Davis HS 1982-83; World Geography Teacher 1983-84, Math Teacher 1983- Cntrl Davis Jr HS; *home:* 2115 N 1650 E Layton UT 84040

WACKER, JOHN M., Band Director; *b:* Cheyenne, WY; *m:* Laura Fowler; *ed:* (BME) Music Ed, Univ of N CO 1983; Jamey Abersold Jazz Improvisation Seminar; Trng in MIDI & Cmptrs in Music; *cr:* Band Dir Burns Jr/Sr HS 1983-85, Carpenter/Hillsdale Elem 1983-85, Cheyenne Cntrl HS 1985-; *ai:* Direct Marching Band & Pep Band; Jr Class & NHS Spon; Perform in Brass Quintet; Intnl Assn of Jazz Educators 1989-; Music Educators Natl Conference 1983-; NEA 1983-; Mem Cheyenne Symphony Orch; St Champion Marching Band; Clinician & Adjudicator in WY & NE; Exclusively Superior Rating at Dist Festival; Perform Extensively in Cheyenne Area; Selected to Represent St of WY at Re-Dedication of Statue of Liberty; *office:* Cheyenne Cntrl 5500 Education Dr Cheyenne WY 82009

WACKER, RONNIE LOUISE, 4th Grade Teacher; *b:* Hollywood, CA; *ed:* (BAE) Elem Ed, 1963, (MED) Elem Ed, 1971 Univ of AZ; Grad Stud Univ AZ; *cr:* 3rd Grade Teacher 1963-71, 1973-78, Kndgtn-12th Grade Resource Teacher 1971-73, Instr for Gifted 1979-83, 4th/5th Grade Teacher 1983-, Tucson Unified Sch Dist; *ai:* Stu Cncl Spon; Prin Designee; Demonstration Teacher; Tucson Ed Assn (Building Rep 1973-78) 1963-; AZ Ed Assn, NEA 1963-; PTA (Bd Teacher Rep 1967-70) 1963-; Univ of AZ Alumni Study Grant; Sr Honors Univ of AZ; Book Published; Developed Prgm for Gifted; *office:* W A Sewell Elem Sch 425 H Sahuara Ave Tucson AZ 85712

WADAS, FRANK CASMIER, JR., Fine Arts Department Chair; *b:* Nanticoke, PA; *ed:* (BA) Theatre/Theology, Kings Coll 1978; Theatre Stud, Directing & Acting, Amer Univ & The Studio Theatre; *cr:* Adjunct Professor Amer Univ 1979-80; Asst Dir Arena Stage 1980; Fine Arts Dept Chm La Reine HS 1980-; Artistic Dir Sword of Peace Summer Repertory Theatre 1981-; *ai:* Dir, Choreographer, Designer for Musical Productions La Reine HS; Mid Sts & Exemplary Scndry Sch Steering Comm; NCEA 1980-; SE Theatre Conference 1982-; Dir Tantallon Cmmty Theatre 1989-, Best Dir 1989; Trinity Theatre, NRL Showboaters 1987-89; *office:* La Reine HS 5100 Silver Hill Rd Suitland MD 20746

WADDELL, DEBRA HOBBS, Language Art Teacher; *b:* Timmonsville, SC; *m:* Alton Van; *c:* Matthew; *ed:* (BA) Eng, 1973, (MED) Elem Ed, 1977 Francis Marion Coll; *cr:* Eng Teacher Southside Mid Sch 1973-; *ai:* Newspaper Spon; Weathervane Comm; Palmetto St Teachers Assn; Baptist Young Women (Pres 1989, Missions Chm 1990); Teacher of Yr.

WADDELL, GELENE WILLIAMS, Physical Education Teacher; *b:* Colorado City, TX; *m:* Jay Ross; *c:* Leslie J.; *ed:* (BS) Elem Ed, Abilene Chrstn Univ 1977; *cr:* 2nd Grade Teacher 1977-81, 1984-87, Phys Ed Teacher 1982-84, 1987- E Ridge Elem; *ai:* TCTA 1977-; Beta Sigma Phi 1982-89; *office:* E Ridge Elem Sch 1101 Hoyt Sweetwater TX 79556

WADDELL, MARVENE (FRITZEN), English Teacher; *b:* La Porte, IN; *m:* Wayne; *c:* Deborah Haggard, Doria, Eric; *ed:* (BM) Piano, 1956, (BS) Ed, 1957 IN Univ; (MS) Ed, Butler Univ 1967; *cr:* Music/Eng Teacher La Porte Jr HS 1957-58; Music Teacher Connersville Jr HS 1958-59; Eng Teacher Arsenal Tech Day Adult HS 1965-70, Muncie Cntrl HS 1971-; *ai:* Extended Learning Prgm Dir; Advanced Composition Instr; NCTE, IN Teachers of Writing, Intnl Rdng Assn; *office:* Muncie Cntrl HS 801 N Walnut St Muncie IN 47305

WADDELL, ROBERT JOHNSON, Fifth Grade Teacher; *b:* Amigo, WV; *m:* Judith Anne Vosberg; *c:* Christopher R., Marcus A.; *ed:* (BA) Ed, San Diego St Univ 1964; (MA) Ed, US Intnl Univ 1988; Air Force Schls Aerial Gunnery B-29; Air Frame & Engine Mechanics B-52 & Jet; Engine Specialist, Boeing Factory Sch; *cr:* 5th-6th Grade Teacher Riverview Elem Sch 1964-69, 1970-73; 5th Grade Teacher 1969-70, 1973-80; Head Teacher 1969-70, 1976-80 Winter Gardens Elem Sch; 4th-5th Grade Teacher Lakeview Elem Sch 1980-; *ai:* Sch Safety Patrol Spon 1965-; Math Book Selection & Earthquake Safety Comm; Lakeside Teachers Negotiating Comm 1969-72; CA Teachers Assn & NEA 1964-; Kiwanis Jr Olympics Coach 1969-; Little & Pony League Bsbl, Soccer League (Mgr, Coach) 1976-86; Dist Employee of Month 1969; Dist Golden Apple Awd 1989; Greater San Diego Cty Math Cncl Awd Certificate; *office:* Lakeview Elem Sch 12335 Woodside Ave Lakeside CA 92040

WADDLE, JOHN LENORD, HS Mathematics Instructor; *b:* Cedar Rapids, IA; *m:* Lisa Michelle Scheffert; *c:* Jacob D.; *ed:* (BA) Math, Luther Coll 1983; *cr:* HS Math Instr Coon Rapids-Bayard HS 1983-; *ai:* Head Bsbl & Asst Bsktbl Coach; Math Competitions Adv; IA Cncl of Math Teachers Mem 1984-; IA Bsbl Coaches Assn Membership Comm 1988-89; Teacher of Yr Coon Rapids-Bayard HS 1987; 6 Conference Math Team Titles; 3 Creighton Univ Math Team Titles; 4 Conference & Dist Bsbl Championship; Math Dept Co-Chairperson 1988-89; *office:* Coon Rapids-Bayard HS 905 North St Coon Rapids IA 50058

WADDY, SUSANNE WILLIS, Bible/Latin Teacher; *b:* Atlanta, GA; *m:* Charles Gerald; *c:* David P., Jonathan H.; *ed:* (AB) Latin, Randolph-Macon Womans Coll 1951; (MRE) Religious Ed/Youth Emphasis, SW Baptist Theological Seminary 1960; Amer Lit, Ogelthorpe Univ; Advanced Latin Lit, Emory Univ; Numerous Seminars, Conferences Chrstn Ed Trng; *cr:* Latin/Fr Teacher Atlanta Public Schls 1951-58; Mission Worker/Teacher Baptist Home Mission Bd 1960-62; Latin/Fr Teacher Atlanta Public Schls 1962-64, 1965-66; Teacher DeKalb Chrstn Acad 1973-; *ai:* NHS & Latin Club Spon; Sr Class Co-Spon; GA Ed Assn 1951-58; Assn of Chrstn Schls Intnl 1975-; Randolph Macon Womans Coll Alumnae Assn Pres 1955-56; Trinity Baptist Church 1973-; DeKalb Chrstn Acad STAR Teacher 1989; *office:* DeKalb Chrstn Acad 1985 La Vista Rd NE Atlanta GA 30306

WADE, AFRA BROUWER, Mathematics Teacher; *b:* Bradenton, FL; *m:* Theodore James; *c:* Aaron T., Afra H.; *ed:* (AA) Music, Manatee Jr Coll 1977; (BME) Music, FL St Univ 1979; Math, Univ of S FL, MCC, FL St Univ; *cr:* Band Dir 1980-84, 7th Grade Math Teacher 1984-87 Bradenton Mid Sch; Math Teacher Bayshore HS 1987-; *ai:* Awds Co-Coord; FL Cncl Teachers of Math 1987-; *office:* Bayshore HS 5323 34th St W Bradenton FL 34207

WADE, BARBARA HARTUNG, Spanish Teacher; *b:* Plainfield, NY; *m:* Allan M.; *c:* Kimberly; *ed:* (BA) Span/Eng Lit, 1963, (MED) Ed, 1964 Cornell Univ; *cr:* Eng Teacher Dryden HS 1964-65, Ithaca HS 1965-66; Span Teacher Brighton HS 1966-67; Eng/Speech Teacher Cheyenne Mountain HS 1967-69; Span/Sr Eng Teacher Valley Stream Cntrl HS Dist 1969-71, 1981-; *ai:* Sch of Excl Application Comm; LILT, NYSTAFLT, AATSP 1981-; Malverne Park Civic Assn Pres 1974-81, Distinguished Service Awd 1981; PTA (VP, Pres) 1985-88; GSA Brownie Leader 1976-77; Cornell Univ Alumni Assn (VP, Class Correspondent) 1973-83; Ford Fellowship; Krista Mc Auliffe Fellowship Nom; Mentor Teacher; Cornell Assn of Class Officers Bd of Dirs; *office:* Memorial Jr HS 1 Kent Rd Valley Stream NY 11580

WADE, DONNA DOBBS, Jr High English Teacher; *b:* Geraldine, AL; *m:* Charles Lavon; *c:* Victor C., Valerie M. Wade Pittman; *ed:* (BA) Elem Ed, Jacksonville St Univ 1980; Working Towards Masters; *cr:* Teacher of Migrant Geraldine HS 1981-82; 3rd Grade Teacher 1982-83, Kndgtn/Chapter I Teacher 1983-84 Geraldine Sch; Teacher of Migrant 1984-86, Jr HS Eng Teacher 1986- Geraldine HS; *ai:* Beta Club; Chrldr Spon; Sr Class Play Dir; Sch Associational Rep; Girls Bsktbl Coach; Boys Bsktbl Statistician; Spelling Bee & Awds Day Dir; AEA, NEA 1981-; Delta Kappa Gamma VP 1990; Delta Kappa Epislon; PTA Pres 1975-76; Geraldine 1st United Meth Church; *office:* Geraldine HS Hwy 227 PO Box 157 Geraldine AL 35974

WADE, GORDON LEE, Social Studies Dept Chair; *b:* Washington, IN; *m:* Patricia J.; *c:* Jay, Ryan; *ed:* (AA) Liberal Arts, SE Chrstn Coll 1966; (BS) Ed Soc Stud, 1969, (MS) His, 1972 IN St Univ; *cr:* His Teacher 1969-82, Soc Stud Dept Chm 1982- Washington HS; *ai:* Bsbl, Ftbl Asst Coach; NCSS; Cty Government (City Councilman 1980- Pres 1984); Jaycees; Jaycees Distinguished Service Awd; Curr & Gifted & Talented Comm; *home:* 307 N Meridian St Washington IN 47501

WADE, GWEN ELAINE, Principal; *b:* Pensacola, FL; *m:* James; *c:* Gerald, Rolando; *ed:* (BA) Elem Ed, Prairie View Univ 1971; (MA) Admin/Supervision, Univ of TX San Antonio 1975; Admin Trng Prgm Northeast & St Tammany Parish Sch System; *cr:* Teacher 1972-76, Admin Asst 1976-79 El Dorado Elem; Teacher Boyet Jr HS 1979-89; Prin St Tammany Parish & Alton Elem Sch 1989-; *ai:* St Tammany Assn of Educators (Legislative Chairperson 1982-83, Pac Comm 1982-83, VP 1983-84, Pres 1984-85); LA Assn of Educators (Appraisal Comm, Minority Affairs Comm, AD Hoc Code of Ethics, Exec Cncl 1984-86); NEA Womens Caucus; NEA/LAE Congressional Contact Team 1982-87, Black Caucus; Amer Assn of Univ Women; Slidell Bus & Prof Women (Membership, Schlsp, Fashion Show & Home Tour Comm, Amigo Friends Intnl Stu Organization; Slidell Chamber of Commerce (PR, Ed Comm) 1985-; Childrens Endowment Fund Advisory Bd 1990; Leadership Slidell Bd of Trustees 1990; Sch System & Educators Days (Membership 1988, Ed 1989) 1987; Miss Trade Fair 1989; Sister Cities Intnl Panama City Co-Chairperson 1988-89; Annual St Margaret Mary Fund Raiser Baby Contest Judge 1987; Wal Mart Schlsp Judge 1985-89; Teacher of Yr El Dorado Sch 1974; Outstanding Young Woman of America 1976; Nominee Carter G Woodson Natl Human Relations Awd 1978; Slidell Woman of Yr 1986; Slidell Chambers Outstanding Mem of Quarter Awd 1986; Local & St Honoree Women of Accomplishment Womens Health Fnd of LA 1987; Top 50 Most Influential Tri-City Area Slidell 1987; Featured Articles Sentry Day News 1987; LA BPW St Pr Awd 1988; Slidell BPN Nikki Awd 1988; *home:* 115 Kings Way Slidell LA 70458

WADE, JACQUELINE MARIE, Science Teacher; *b:* Orlando, FL; *ed:* (BS) Bio, Troy St Univ 1981; (MS) Bio, Univ of Cntrl FL 1984; *cr:* Sci Teacher Lake Mary HS 1984-; Bio Teacher Seminole Comm Coll 1984-; *ai:* Key Club Kiwanis Educated Youth Spon; Published Article; Golden Apple Awd for Excl in Teaching; *office:* Lake Mary HS 655 Longwood Lake Mary Rd Lake Mary FL 32746

WADE, JENNY SCHAFFER, Biology Teacher; *b:* Enid, OK; *m:* Harold C.; *c:* Leanne, Laurie; *ed:* (BS) Bio, Phillips Univ 1969; (MA) Person Centered Ed, US Intnl Univ 1990; Math, Sci Technology Inst, Lawrence Hall of Sci 1987; *cr:* Sci/Health/Math Teacher Gateway Sch Pregnant Minors 1969-79, Gateway Sch & Golden Valley Continuation 1979-82; Bio/Life Sci Teacher Amos Alonzo Stagg HS 1982-; *ai:* Sci Olympiad Club, Class of 1993 Adv; Sch Site Cncl; Stuart Fnd Curr & Budget Comm; CA Sci Teacher Assn 1988-; Campfire Trainer for Leaders 1982-, Luther Halsey Gulick 1989; Oak Grove Docents Mem 1985-; AIDS Speakers Bureau Mem 1988-; San Joaquin Cty Parks & Recreation Outstanding Cmmty Volunteer; *office:* Amos Alonzo Stagg HS 1621 Brookside Rd Stockton CA 95207

WADE, MARY CLOW, English Teacher; *b:* Centralia, IL; *m:* Jack Franklin; *c:* Mark F., Michael Clark, Donna B. W. Champa; *ed:* (AB) Eng/Soc Stud, Marshall Univ 1950; *cr:* Teacher Huntington Sch of Bus 1951-56, Princeton Jr HS 1964-72, Princeton Sr HS 1972-81, Mercer Chrstn Acad 1981-89; *ai:* Yrbk Adv; Bible Club Spon; Sr Class Adv; Baptist Church (Sunday Sch Teacher 1965-75, Jr Church Teacher 1965-75, Librarian 1983-89); Scndry Lang Art; Textbook Comm; *office:* Mercer Christian Acad 314-A Oakvale Rd Princeton WV 24740

WADE, PEGGY JOYCE (BRADSHAW), Chapter I Reading; *b:* Herrin, IL; *m:* Fred Junior; *c:* Randall D., Rhonda A., Rodney A., Ranetta J.; *ed:* (BA) Elem Ed, 1966, (MS) Elem Ed, 1972 Southern IL Univ Carbondale; Specialist Degree Curr Specialist; *cr:* Elem Ed Teacher W Frankfort IL 1966-; *ai:* PTA Treas 1974-77; Women of the World Fraternal Order Treas 1976-80 Women of Woodcraft 1979; Woodmen of World Fraternal Order (Youth Leader 1962-73 & 1975-81, Camp Cnslr 1962-81); *office:* Denning Elem Sch 701 N Columbia West Frankfort IL 62896

WADE, REED ASHBY, 5th Grade Teacher; *b:* Nephi, UT; *m:* Betty Romney; *c:* Russell, Stephanie Wade Brockbank, Donalynn, Gordon, Richard; *ed:* (BS) Elem Ed, 1964, (MS) Elem Ed Admin, 1977 Brigham Young Univ; Univ of UT, UT St Univ, Brigham Young Univ; *cr:* Intermediate Grade Teacher Morningside Elem 1964-; *ai:* Granite Dist Core Curr Comm Mem; Granite Sch Dist Mill Hollow Sci Instr; Math Olympiad Coord; Granite Dist Prof Improvement Comm Mem; Granite Ed Assn Exec Bd 1986-; UT Ed Assn Voting Delegate 1986-; NEA (Voting Delegate, Natl Convention) 1986-; BSA Scout Master 1976-78; Jr Jazz Bsktbl Coach 1982-85, Championship 1983; Published Sci Prgm; *office:* Morningside Elem Sch 4170 S 3000 E Holladay UT 84124

WADE, STEVE, Mathematics Teacher; *b:* South Bend, IN; *ed:* (AB) Math, Wabash Coll 1982; (MS) Scndry Ed, IN Univ South Bend 1986; MAPS Wkshp Purdue Univ 1987; Advanced Topics in Geometry, Univ of Notre Dame 1988; Woodrow Wilson Fellowship Fnd Inst on Math Modeling Butler Univ 1989; *cr:* Math Teacher Boone Grove Jr/Sr HS 1982-85, New Prairie HS 1985-; *ai:* Girls Vlybl & Bsktbl, Boys Bsktbl Scorekeeper; Cross Cntry & Track Head Timer; *office:* New Prairie HS 5333 N Cougar Rd New Carlisle IN 46552

WADLEY, BARBARA ANNE BROPHY, 8th Grade English Teacher; *b:* Newark, NJ; *m:* John A.; *c:* John III, Eddie; *ed:* (BA) Eng, Univ of St Thomas 1961; (BA) His/Ed, Univ of Houston 1981; Grad Work Eng, His; *cr:* 3rd Grade Teacher St Vincent De Paul 1961-63; 4th Grade Teacher Corpus Christi 1964; Eng Teacher Highlands Jr HS 1980-; *ai:* SADD Spon; Eng Dept Chairperson; NCTE, TX Classroom Teachers Assn, Baytown Classroom Teachers Assn; Sterling Lib Literacy Volunteer; Greater Houston Area Writers Fellowship; Highlands Jr HS H B Awd; Poetry Published; *office:* Highlands Jr HS 1212 E Wallisville Rd Highlands TX 77562

WADLEY, BARBARA FRANKLIN, Language Arts Teacher; *b:* Mt Vernon, GA; *c:* Rico, Kristopher; *ed:* (BS) Eng, 1971, (MS) Elem Ed, Ft Valley St Coll 1979; *cr:* Teacher Toombs Cntrl Sch 1971-76, Montgomery Cty Elem Sch 1976-; *ai:* Chairperson Lang Art Comm; Coord Sch Advisory Comm; GA Assn of Educators Secy 1982-83; Natl Assn of Educators; Concerned Citizens 1990; *home:* 810 Martin Luther King Dr Soperton GA 30457

WADMAN, SHARON RENEE, Biology/Physical Ed Teacher; *b:* Coffeyville, KS; *ed:* (BS) Phys Ed, 1965, (MS) Phys Ed, 1968 Pittsburg St Univ; *cr:* Bio/Health/Phys Ed Teacher Burlington HS 1965-68; Phys Ed Teacher Independence Jr HS 1968-69, Cottey Coll 1969-70; Bio/Health/Phys Ed Teacher Cherryvale HS 1972-; *ai:* Vlybl & Bsktbl Coach; Class Spon; NEA, KS Assn Sci Teacher, KS Assn Phys Ed, Health, Recreation & Dance; Cherryvale Teachers Assn Pres 1985-86, Outstanding Teacher 1980-81, Master Teacher 1985-86; KS Ed Assn Uniserv Southeast Thank You Awd 1985-86; *office:* Cherryvale HS 7th & Carson Cherryvale KS 67335

WAETJE, KATHRYN JOYCE, German Teacher; *b:* Douglas, AZ; *c:* Liam J.; *ed:* (BA) Ger, San Diego St Univ 1973; (MA) Ed/Ger, W WA Univ 1981; Various Wkshps; *cr:* Ger Teacher Vista HS 1973-78, Sehome HS 1979-82, Burlington HS 1982-; *ai:* Ger & Intnl Club Spon; Debate Team Asst; AATG WA Chapter (Pres Elect 1989-, Pres 1990); Fulbright Exchange Teacher 1976-77 to Berlin; WA Assn of Foreign Lang Teachers Awd for Creative Innovation 1989; Teacher Trainer for Pacific NW Ger Teachers; *office:* Burlington-Edison HS 301 N Burlington Blvd Burlington WA 98233

WAFER, CLARETTE S. THOMAS, Vocational Education Chair; *b:* Tyler, TX; *m:* Carl Lee; *c:* Roderick F. Davis; *ed:* (AA) Bus Admin, Tyler Dist Coll 1966; (BS) Bus Integrated, Bishop Coll 1970; (MED) Elem Ed, Prairie View A&M Univ 1975; Grad Stud ETSU Lib Sci 1980; Cert Voc Office Ed, N TX St Univ 1983; Prof Dev Improvement Conferences; *cr:* Office Admin Coord/Bus Ed Teacher Wilmer-Hutchins Ind Sch Dist; *ai:* Class Spon 1989-; Bus Prof of America TX Assn Spon 1989-; Zeta Phi Beta 1979; FBLA Mem 1983; Wilmer-Hutchins Gospel Grammy Choir; Voc Office Careers of TX Mem 1980-89; TX St Teachers Mem; NEA Life Mem; *office:* Wilmer-Hutchins HS 5520 Langdon Rd Hutchins TX 75141

WAFFORD, FRANCIS CATHERINE, First Grade Teacher; *b:* Fletcher, OK; *m:* Francis B.; *c:* Terell, Michael, Pam Holland, Rebecca Smith; *ed:* (BS) Elem Ed, Univ of OK 1974; *cr:* 5th Grade Teacher 1974-75, 2nd Grade Teacher 1975-86, 1st Grade Teacher 1987- Indian Meridian Elem.

WAGAMAN, CRAIG CARPENTER, 5th Grade Teacher; *b:* Lancaster, PA; *ed:* (BS) Elem Ed, 1974, (MED) Elem Ed, 1977 Millersville St; *cr:* 4th Grade Teacher 1975-88, 5th Grade Teacher 1988- Warwick-Lititz Elem; *ai:* Var Girls Bsktbl Coach; Warwick Ed Assn, PA St Ed Assn, NEA; *home:* 335 E 2nd Ave Lititz PA 17543

WAGENER, JOHN ANDREAS, JR., Earth Science Teacher; *b:* Nyack, NY; *m:* Barbara Elaine Sage; *ed:* (BS) Sci Ed, Cornell Univ 1970; (MS) Sci Ed, Elmira Coll 1975; Emergency Medical Technician; Advanced First Aid/CPR; Certified Scuba Diver; *cr:* 7th-12th Grade Sci Teacher Mynderese Acad 1970-; *ai:* Sportsmens & Bowhunter Ed Instr; NEA, NY Ed Assn 1970-; Sci Teachers Assn of NY St 1973-; Pochontas Lodge 211 F&AM Jr Waren 1980-; Seneca Upland Game Pres 1970-; Cornell Hockey Boosters Assn 1975-; Natl Rifle Assn 1970-; NY St Rifle & Pistol Assn 1989-; *office:* Mynderse Acad 105 Troy St Seneca Falls NY 13148

WAGENER, WILLIAM LUDWIG, III, Earth Science Teacher; *b:* Miami Beach, FL; *ed:* (MS) Soc Stud, Nova Univ 1978; *cr:* Soc Stud Teacher Dade Cty Public Schls 1973-81; Earth Sci Teacher Belen Jesuit Prep Sch 1983-; *ai:* Belen Acad Earth and Space Sci Club; Meteorology Club Adv; Asst Jr Varsity Ftbl Coach; Head Swimming-Water Polo Coach; Asst Ftbl Coach; Sons of Amer Revolution 1971-; Union Concerned Scientists 1986-; Fraternal Order of Eagles 1986-; *office:* Belen Jesuit Prep Sch 500 Sw 127 Ave Miami FL 33184

WAGERS, LOIS BROWN, Business Teacher; *b:* London, KY; *m:* Curtis James; *c:* David W.; *ed:* Bus Ed, Sue Bennett Jr Coll 1967-69; (BS) Commerce, Cumberland Coll 1972; (MA) Scndry Ed, Union Coll 1977; *cr:* Library Clerk Sue Bennett Jr Coll 1969; Clerical US Dept of Ag 1969-70; Secretarial Cumberland Coll 1969-72; Cnslr Church of God St Youth Camp 1972; Teacher Bush Jr HS 1972-77; Teacher Laurel Cty Sr HS 1977-; *ai:* Assist FBLA, Regional & St Honor Club, Coord Sr Awds Prgm; KY Ed Assn, NEA 1972-; Church of God (Sunday Sch Supt 1982, Family Trng Hour Dir 1981, Ladies Dir Pres 1981-) Dir of Yr KY 1981; KY Pres of Yr 1981; Childrens Church Dir 1978-81; Sunday Sch Teacher 1973-; Bible Inst Instr; Ministerial Intern Prgm InStr 1984-; Bible Quiz Coach; Natl Bible Quiz Judge, Church of God Natl Teen Talent 1984; Cmmty Efforts for Leukemia Society; Bush Sch PTA Planning Comm 1972-79; Outstanding Young Women of America 1982; *home:* 105 Lyttleton Rd Manchester KY 40962

WAGGONER, LAURA NOEL, Math Teacher; *b:* Kittanning, PA; *m:* Leil J.; *c:* Stephen, Jennifer; *ed:* (BS) Math, Indiana Univ of PA 1974; (MSED) Math, W MD Coll 1981; *cr:* Full-Time Math Teacher West Frederick Jr HS 1974-77, Frederick HS 1977-; Part-Time Math Teacher Frederick Comm Coll 1984-; *ai:* Math Team Adv; Mentorship Prgm for New Teachers; SAT Math Comm; Coord of Math Clinic; MD St Teachers Assn, Frederick Cty Teachers Assn, NEA; *office:* Frederick HS 650 Carroll Pkwy Frederick MD 21701

WAGGY, PAULA JEAN (DICKERSON), 6th & 7th Grade Sci Teacher; *b:* Lima, OH; *m:* Charles Douglas; *c:* Edward, Gretchen; *ed:* (BS) Wildlife Management, WV Univ 1971; Grad Stud; *cr:* 3rd Grade Teacher Marlinton Elem Sch 1972-74; 5th-8th Grade Sci Teacher Franklin Elem Sch 1974-; 7th/8th Grade Sci Teacher Franklin HS 1990-; *ai:* GSA Troop Leader; Potomac Valley Sci Teachers Assn, WV Sci Teachers Assn, NSTA; Franklin Elem Sch PTO; WV Dept Natural Resources Non-Game Wildlife Grant 1985; WV Mini Grant 1989; *home:* Rt 1 Box 61B Franklin WV 26807

WAGNER, BARBARA ELLEN (SIMMONS), 2nd Grade Teacher; *b:* Fairview, OK; *m:* Robert E.; *c:* Robert S., Randall H.; *ed:* (BS) Elem Ed/Bio, NW OK St Univ 1962; Grad Stud Wichita St Univ, Fort Hays St, KS St Univ; *cr:* 3rd Grade Teacher Bridgeport Elem 1962-65; 1st Grade Teacher 1977-87, 2nd Grade Teacher 1988- Oxford Elem; *ai:* Playground Equipment Comm; NEA Building Rep 1987-88; Honor Society 1956-58; EHU (Pres, Secy, VP) 1987-89; *office:* Oxford Elem Sch 500 N Michigan Oxford KS 67119

WAGNER, CLIFFORD, Science Teacher; *b:* Teaneck, NJ; *m:* Barbara; *c:* Jason, Derek, Brett; *ed:* (BS) Bio, St Peters Coll 1972; (MS) Bio, Fordham Univ 1978; *cr:* Sci Teacher Bergen Cath HS 1978-79, Crystal River HS 1979-85; Adjunct Instr Pasco Hernando Comm Coll 1984-; Sci Teacher Springstead HS 1985-; *ai:* Peer & Beginning Teacher Prgm; NSTA 1990-; Hernando Classroom Teachers Assn Assn Rep 1988-; *office:* F W Springstead HS 3300 Mariner Blvd Spring Hill FL 34609

WAGNER, DONALD JOSEPH, Science Teacher; *b:* Baltimore, MD; *ed:* (BA) Biological Sci, Univ of DE 1973; (MS) Zoology, 1978, (DAGS) Zoology, 1978 MI St Univ; Ed Trng Univ of Pittsburg 1984-85; *cr:* Scientist Energy Impact Assocs 1978-82, Self Employed Environmental Consultant/Scientist 1983-85; Sci Teacher Franklin HS 1985-; *ai:* Class Adv; WV Sci Teacher Assn 1986-; Pendleton Cty Lib (VP, Bd Trustees) 1989-; Friends of Pendleton Cty Lib Treas 1987-89; *office:* Franklin HS Franklin WV 26807

WAGNER, EDWARD DEMMY, Sixth Grade Teacher; *b:* Harrisburg, PA; *m:* Mary Jane Higgins; *c:* Joshua, Tracy; *ed:* (BS) Elem Ed, Bloomsburg St 1973; *cr:* 7th/8th Grade Math Teacher Cntrl Darphin East Jr HS 1973-75, Linglestown Jr HS 1976-80; 6th Grade Teacher North Side Elem 1981-; *ai:* Ftbl Coach; Intramural Adv Flag Ftbl/Sftbl/Bsktbl/Soccer Scenery Asst; Cntrl Dauphin Ed Assn 1987-; Service Awd; Whos Who of Amer Teachers.

WAGNER, ELIZABETH ANN, English/Reading Teacher; *b:* Jacksonville, IL; *m:* Karl B.; *c:* David, Susan, Robert; *ed:* (BA) Elem Ed/Eng, Mac Murray Coll 1972; (MS) Rdng, W IL Univ 1977; Grad Stud; *cr:* 1st Grade Teacher Triopia Elem Sch 1971-77; Spec Rdng Teacher Northwestern Elem 1977-79; Eng/Rdng/Skills for Adolescents Teacher Northwestern Jr-Sr HS 1979-; *ai:* Phi Delta Kappa VP 1987-; *office:* Northwestern Jr-Sr HS RR 1 Box 8 Palmyra IL 62674

WAGNER, HENRY VINCENT, JR., Assistant Principal; *b:* Baltimore, MD; *m:* Carol Ann Kornick; *c:* Amy, Carol, Steven, Laura; *ed:* (BA) His/Scndry Ed, Loyola Coll 1974; (MS) Guidance/Counseling, 1980, (MS) Admin/Technology for Educators, 1988 John Hopkins Univ; Computerized Schedule Building Trng; *cr:* Teacher Baltimore City 1974-83; Cnslr 1983-85, Dept Chm 1985-88, Asst Prin 1988- Baltimore Cty Public Schls; *ai:* Admin Rep Parkville HS Stu Assistance Team; Scndry Sch Admin Assn 1988-; Natl Certified Cnslrs 1984-; NEA, MSTA, TABCO 1980-; Knights of Columbus 1976-; Baltimore Cty Cnslrs Assn Treas 1986-88; Baltimore Cty Curr Analysis Mem 1988.

WAGNER, JOAN S., Science Teacher; *b:* Brooklyn, NY; *m:* Norman K.; *c:* Hunter, Dylan; *ed:* (BA) Psych/Bio, Syracuse Univ 1966; (MA) Sci Ed, Teachers Coll Columbia Univ 1967; Hofstra Univ, St Univ of NY Albany; Admin Ed, Coll St Rose; *cr:* Bio Teacher Freeport HS 1967-71; Sci Teacher Burnt Hills Ballston Lake Schls 1973-; *ai:* Sci Club; Coach of HS & Mid Sch Sci Olympiad Teams; Staff Dev Comm; Co-Chairperson Sci & Engineering Fair; STANYS Eastern Section Chairperson 1990; STANYS Bd of Dir 1988; STANYS, NYSUT, NSTA; Excl in Sci Teaching 1986; Capital Dist Sci & Eng Fair Co-Chairperson 1989-; 1986 Excl in Sci Teaching Awd; 1989 Publications Back to Dayton Amer Bio Teacher; Publications 1989; *office:* Burnt Hills-Ballston Lk Cntrl Lake Hill Rd Burnt Hills NY 12027

WAGNER, JOYCE C., 4th Grade Teacher; *b:* Galion, OH; *m:* Erwin J.; *c:* Douglas E., Tony D. Radebaugh; *ed:* (BS) Elem Ed, Ashland Univ 1972; Toledo Univ; Bowling Green St Univ; Mount St Joseph; *cr:* 1st Grade Teacher Lykens Sch 1955-56; 2nd Grade Teacher Bucyrus City Schls 1956-57; 6th Grade Teacher Leesville Sch 1957-58; 5th Grade Teacher Suphur Springs Sch 1958-59; 1st Grade Teacher Wynford Schls 1966-69; 2nd/4th Grade Teacher Colonel Crawford Schls 1969- ; *ai:* Chairperson Philosophy Comm; Supervised Stu at Center of Sci & Industry; Colonel Crawford Teachers Assn 1959-; OH Ed Assn 1959-; Crawford Cty Intl Rdng Assn 1980-; VP Colonel Crawford Teachers Assn; Pres of Colonel Crawford Teachers Assn; *home:* P O Box 122 Sulphur Springs OH 44881

WAGNER, JUANITA THERIOT, 3rd Grade Teacher; *b:* New Orleans, LA; *m:* Jacob G.; *c:* Robyn Hinds, Dawn Mills, Jeffrey N.; *ed:* (RN) Nursing Mather Sch of Nursing 1957; (BA) Nursing, Elem Ed, 1976; (MA) Comm 1986 Webster Univ; *cr:* Head Nurse Deaconess Hosp 1958-59; 5th Grade Teacher 1978-88; 3rd Grade Teacher 1988- Brennan Woods Elem; *ai:* Substance Abuse Comm; Discipline Comm; Hope United Church of Christ Teacher/Wkshp 1963-70; Camp Fire Girls Leader 1967-74; St Lucas United Church of Christ Cncl Mem 1983-86; Camp Fire Girls Dist Chm Training Comm 1972-74; St Lucas UCC Cncl Secy, Mission & Outreach Comm 1984-85; St Lucas UCC Chm Membership Comm 1985-86; *home:* 12826 Tammy Kay Dr St Louis MO 63128

WAGNER, LA WANDA JOYCE, 6th Grade Teacher; *b:* Henderson, TX; *m:* Paul Alan; *c:* Matthew R., Aaron M.; *ed:* (BSE) Elem Ed, N IL Univ 1971; *cr:* 3rd Grade Teacher Crystal Lake Public Schls 1971-72; 3rd Grade Teacher 1979-80, 5th Grade Teacher 1980-82, 6th Grade Teacher 1982- Quincy Public Schls; *ai:* Delta Kappa Gamma 1987-; MS Valley Rdng Cncl 1980-; Quincy Coll Ed Advisory Comm 1988-; *office:* Baldwin Intermediate Sch 30th & Maine Quincy IL 62301

WAGNER, MARY EILEEN, Retired Mathematics Instructor; *b:* Upper Sandusky, OH; *ed:* (BA) Ed, Mary Manse 1947; Grad Work at Bowling Green St Univ, John Carroll Univ, Case Western Reserve; *cr:* Put-in-Bay HS 1947-49; Ottoville HS 1949-52; St Paul HS 1952-60; Math Teacher/Dept Chairperson Bay HS 1960-80; Adv Math Instr/Dept Chairperson St Mary Cntrl Cath HS 1981-89; *ai:* Academic Team & Sr Homeroom Adv; Delta Kappa Gamma VP 1990; Coll Womens Club; Martha Holden Jennings Scholar; *home:* 4612 Venice Hts Blvd #158 Sandusky OH 44870

WAGNER, MARY JON, Principal; *b:* Toledo, OH; *ed:* (BA) Ed, Mary Manse Coll 1965; (MA) Admin Ed, Univ of Detroit 1975; (EDS) Admin Ed, St Thomas Coll 1985; Cmptr; Data Processing; Mrktg & Dev; *cr:* Teacher St Joseph Sch 1963-67, St Raphael Sch 1968-76; Prin/Teacher NE Regional Cath Sch 1977-84; Prin Sts Peter & Paul Sch 1985-; *ai:* Sch Bd; Gifted, Pre-Sch, Extended Day Prgm; Athletic Act & Scouts Coord; NCEA, ASCD; World Futurist Society; Providence Hospital Bd of Trustees Secy 1984-; Bishops Grants Preschool, Extended Day, Telecommunication System for Stus; *office:* Sts Peter & Paul Sch 514 Jackson St Sandusky OH 44870

WAGNER, MAUREEN SCHAEFFER, Fourth Grade Teacher/Principal; *b:* Lewisburg, PA; *m:* Robert; *c:* Nathaniel; *ed:* (BS) Elem, 1970, (MS) Elem, 1977 Bloomsburg Univ; *cr:* 4th Grade Teacher Freeburg Elem 1970-73; 4th/5th Grade Teacher 1973-, Prin 1980, 1983- Chapman-Union Elem; *ai:* Staff Dev Comm; Lay Speaker United Meth Church; Organist; Soc Stud Teacher of Adults; Delta Kappa Gamma (Pres 1990) 1980-, Founders 1989; ASCD 1990; Gideon Auxiliary Chaplain 1989-; Amnesty Intnl, Green Peace 1985-; Governors Acad for Instructional Leadership; Governors Incentive Grant 1989-; *office:* Chapman-Union Elem RD 1 Box 615 Port Trevorton PA 17864

WAGNER, MIRIAM DAVIS, Mathematics Teacher; *b:* Hazleton, PA; *c:* Howard, Valerie; *ed:* (BS) Math Ed, Bloomsburg Univ 1968; (MED) Math, Kutztown Univ 1972; *cr:* Math Teacher Pottsville Area HS 1968-; Part Time Instr Penn St Univ 1980-; *ai:* NCTM, PA Cncl Teachers Math; 1st United Meth Church; *office:* Pottsville Area HS 16th & Elk Ave Pottsville PA 17901

WAGNER, NANCY BROWN, 7th & 8th Grade Teacher; *b:* Greeneville, TN; *m:* David; *c:* Jared; *ed:* (AS) Scndry Ed, Walters St Comm Coll 1975; (BA) Elem/Spec Ed, Tusculum Coll 1977; (MED) Spec Ed, East TN St Univ 1983; *cr:* Resource Teacher 1977-84; 7th/8th Grade Teacher 1984-86 Mc Donald Elem Sch; 6th Grade Teacher 1986-87, 7th/8th Grade Teacher 1987 Chuckey Elem Sch; *ai:* Co-Spon Round Robin Team; TEA/NEA/GCEA 1977-; ETEA; *home:* Rt 2 Box 684 Mosheim TN 37818

WAGNER, ROBERT JAMES, Mathematics Professor; *b:* Philadelphia, PA; *m:* Mary Jane Cameron; *c:* Bob Jr., Scott, Michael, Edwin, Mary K.; *ed:* (BA) Geography/Physics, Temple Univ 1968; Math, West Chester St Univ; Villanova Univ; Temple Univ; Real Estate Institute; Broker License/Educl Requirement; *cr:* Teacher Cardinal O Hara HS 1968-70; Teacher/Coach Archibishop Kennedy HS 1971-73, Bishop Egan HS 1973-75; Ftbl Coach 1977-84, Athletic Dir 1977-79, Roman Catholic HS; Teacher/Coach Bishop Kenrick HS 1977-; *ai:* Head Ftbl Coach; Current Coll & HS Bsktbl Official; Aircraft Owners & Pilots Assn 1978-; Intnl Assn of Approves Bsktbl Officials 1970-; PA Inter Scholastic Athletic Assn Official 1970-; Hereford Township Tax Payers Spokesman 1988-; Berks Cty Bd of Dir 1989-; Taxpayers Assn; Philadelphia Inquirer HS; Ftbl Coach of Yr 1979; Philadelphia Journal HS Coach of Yr 1981; Outstanding Educator of America 1972.

WAGNER, WILLIAM GLENN, Science Teacher; *b:* Sistersville, WV; *m:* Deborah Ann Mc Culley; *c:* William M., Gwendolyn G.; *ed:* (AB) Chem Comp, WV St Coll 1972; OH St Univ, WV Univ, WV Northern Comm Coll; *cr:* Sci Teacher Martins Ferry HS 1970; *ai:* Chy-Phy Adv; Martins Ferry Ed Assn Building Rep 1970-; West Liberty Volunteer Fire Dept (Pres 1982-86) 1976-; West Liberty City Cncl 1980-89; Northern Panhandle Firemens Assn (VP 1986-89, Treas 1990); Natl Sci Fnd Grant 1972; *office:* Martins Ferry HS Hanover St Martins Ferry OH 43935

WAGNER, YVONNE D., English Department Teacher; *b:* Newark, NJ; *m:* Mervin D.; *c:* Megan L.; *ed:* (BS) Bus/Scndry Ed, Youngstown St Univ 1985; *cr:* Sch Secy 1976-85, Eng/Cmptr Sci Teacher 1985- Calvary Chrstn Acad of Higher Learning; *ai:* Speech Team Coach & Coord; *office:* Calvary Chrstn Acad 104 W Evergreen Youngstown OH 44507

WAGNER GEORGI, MARY, Eng/Journalism/Speech Teacher; *b:* Ord, NE; *m:* Todd; *ed:* (BS) Speech/Drama, Univ of NE Lincoln 1969; *cr:* Speech/Debate Teacher Grand Island Sr HS 1969-70, Ogallala Sr HS 1970-76; Eng/Speech Teacher Omaha Tech HS 1976-79; Eng/Speech/Drama/Journalism Teacher Crete Jr Sr HS 1979-; *ai:* Competitive Public Speaking Coach; Yrbk & Drama Club Adv; NCTE 1980-; NE HS Pres Assn 1981-; NE Speech Comm Assn 1980-; *office:* Crete Public Schls 1500 E 15th Crete NE 68333

WAGONER, DAVID LEE, Fourth Grade Teacher; *b:* Paris, KY; *ed:* (BS) Elem Ed, 1971, (MS) Elem Ed, 1976 E KY Univ; *cr:* 4th/6th Grade Teacher Clintonville Elem Sch 1971-89; 4th Grade Teacher Bourbon Cntrl Elem Sch 1989-; *ai:* 4-H Club; Curr Guide Comm; NEA, Ky Ed Assn, Bourbon Cty Ed Assn 1971-; Clintonville Chrstn Church (Historian, Clerk) 1971-76; Clintonville Cemetery Bd Mem 1971-77; Clintonville-Bourbon Cntrl PTA 1971-, Life Membership 19 76; Clintonville Sch Outstanding Teacher Rep 1984; Bourbon Cty Bd of Ed Awd 1982, 1989; *office:* Bourbon Cntrl Elem Sch 367 Bethlehem Rd Paris KY 40361

WAGUESPACK, GERALD EDWARD, Director of Bands; *b:* New Orleans, LA; *m:* Aimee Hebert Waguespack; *ed:* (BME) Instrumental Music, Nicholls St Univ 1971; (MME) Instrumental Music, Univ of Southwestern LA 1977; *cr:* Dir of Bands, Vinton HS 1971-73; Rayne HS 1973-79; Acadiana HS 1979-; *ai:* Coord Acadiana HS Band Prgm: Marching Band; Concert Band, Symphonic Band, Dance Line Color Guard; Music Educatrs Natl Assn; La Music Educators Assn; LA Band Masters Assn; Amer Sch Band Dirs Assn; Southwest LA Band Dir Assn; Phi Beta Mu; Natl Band Assn; First Chair of America; MENC - Active Research; Krewe of Triton Mem; Lafayette Cmmnty Band Assoc Conductor; Lafayette Cmmnty Band Performer; Summer Music Camp Staffs Mem; Special Olympics; LA Takes a Stand Drug Abuse and Prevention Prom Steering Comm; Jerry Lewis Telethon; Viet Nam Veterans of America Acadiana Chapter-Hill 141; Natl Band Assn Citation of Excl 1988; Acadiana HS Teacher of Yr 1987-88; Nom Lba Band Dir of Yr 1988; Certificate of Appreciaton Viet Nam Veterans of Amer 1987;Membership a Band Dir Assn 1985; Recipient Outstanding Young Men of America Awd 1984; Awd Appreciation LA Music Educators Assn 1983; Phi Beta Mu Outstanding Band Dir LA Awd 1981; Certificate Apprecation Acadia Special Olympics Comm 1979; Membership Phi Beta Mu 1977; *office:* Acadiana H S 315 Rue Du Belier Lafayette LA 70506

WAGUESPACK, ROYCE G., Science-Mathematics Teacher; *b:* Vacherie, LA; *m:* Cosmella Recatto; *c:* Karen; *ed:* (BS) Sci/Math Ed, 1953, (MED) Ed/Sci/Math, 1956 LA St Univ; Grad Work Nicholls St Univ 1968; *cr:* Sci/Math Teacher 1953-74, Asst Prin 1964-70, Prin 1970-74 St James HS; Sci/Math Teacher Ascencion Cath HS 1974-; *ai:* Faculty Advisory Comm; Sci Dept Chm; NSTA, NCTM, NCEA 1974-89; Knights of Columbus Financial Secy 1954-, Knight of Yr 1989; Natl Sci Fnd Grants 1956, 1959, 1961, 1964; LA St Univ Nuclear Physics, Radioisotope Technology 1956, 1959, 1964; Univ of SW LA Geology 1961; *home:* 1198 St James St Vacherie LA 70090

WAHLSTEDT, WILMA ANN, 7-8th Grade Teacher; *b:* Pikeville, KY; *ed:* (BA) Eng & Elem Ed, TN Temple Univ 1965; (MA) Elem Ed, Union Coll 1970; *cr:* Teacher Panama City Chrstn Sch 1965-68, Jackson Cty Chrstn Sch 1969-73, Dewitt Elem Sch 1973-; *ai:* Coach-Chrldrs/Academic Team & Mathcounts Team; KEA 1973-; NEA 1973-; Artemus Baptist Church Sunday Sch Teacher 1973-; Emmanuel Bible Camp Athletics Dir 1969-; *home:* HC 66 Box 209 Barbourville KY 40906

WAHRMUND, JANICE EVELYN KLEIN, Fourth Grade Teacher; *b:* Kerrville, TX; *m:* Lyndon G.; *ed:* (BS) Elem Ed, TX Luth Coll 1965; (MED) Elem Ed, West TX St U 1970; *cr:* 4th Grade Teacher Beeville Ind Sch Dist 1965-66; 3rd Grade Teacher Midland Ind Sch Dist 1966-69; Northeast Ind Sch Dist 1970-74; 1st/2nd Grade Teacher Kerrville Ind Sch Dist 1974-78; 4th Grade Teacher Fredericksburg Ind Sch Dist 1978-; *ai:* TX St Teachers Assn; PTA.

WAID, LOUISE RABER, Retired Teacher; *b:* Mt Tabor, VT; *w:* Lee M. (dec); *c:* Kathryn Waid Greenlee, Jean L.; *ed:* (BS) Phys Ed, Syracuse Univ 1939; Masters Equivalency Various CO Colls & Univs 1968-80; *cr:* Classroom Teacher Lincoln Orchard Mesa Sch 1969-83; *ai:* Stu Cncl Spon; Intnl Trng in Comm Mem; Kids on the Block Puppeteer; Local Museum Docent; Outreach Prgm; St of CO Travel Adv; *home:* 1620 N 18th St Grand Junction CO 81501

WAIHMAN, LISA GIRARD, Mathematics Teacher; *b:* Suisun, CA; *m:* Vernon Ross; *c:* Nicole L., Nanci L.; *ed:* (BA) Rhetoric, Univ of IL 1976; Ed, Univ of CO 1981; (MA) Math, Univ of Houston 1987; *cr:* Eng Teacher Hambrick Jr HS 1981-85; Eng Teacher 1985-88, Honors Math Teacher 1988- Crosby Mid Sch; *ai:* Natl Jr Honor Society Adv; 8th Grade Trip Washington DC Spon; Sch News Writer 1985-89; NCTE 1981-; NCTM 1987-; TX Joint Cncl Teachers of Eng, Houston Teachers of Eng 1981-89; PTA Treas 1989-; Epsilon Sigma Alpha (Publicity 1987-88, Yrbk 1989-, Educl Dir 1988-89); Natl Sci Fnd Univ of Houston Master Teachers Math Participant; *home:* 19918 White Dove Tr Crosby TX 77532

WAINSCOTT, SUSAN BROD, Mathematics Teacher; *b:* Boscobel, WI; *m:* Stephen H.; *c:* Jonathan, Kirsten, Stephanie; *ed:* (BS) Bus Analysis, Miami Univ Oxford 1969; (MED) Post Scndry Personnel Services, Clemson Univ 1980; Math Specialist Certificate Clemson Univ 1985; *cr:* Math Teacher Pendleton HS 1977-78; Math Teacher/Cnslr Simpson Spec Prgms 1978-83; Math Teacher Edwards Jr HS 1983-; *ai:* Stu Cncl Adv; Mathcounts Asst Coach; Sch Improvement Cncl; Phi Delta Kappa 1988-; NCTM, SC Cncl Teachers of Math 1986-; Natl Sci Fnd Mid Sch Math Inst Master Teacher 1985, 1986, 1987, 1988; Educl Incentive Act Problem Solving Master Teacher 1988, Teacher Grant 1989-; *home:* 215 Highland Dr Clemson SC 29631

WAISANEN, RICHARD A., Department Chair/Counselor; *b:* Moose Lake, MN; *m:* Sharon L. Ukura; *c:* Kyle, Suzanne, Sara; *ed:* (BS) Elem Ed, Univ of MN Duluth 1967; (MS) Counseling/Guidance, Univ of WI Superior 1974; Stu Assistance; Drug & Alcohol Ed; Marriage Enrichment Trainer; *cr:* 3rd Grade Teacher Fairmont Elem 1967-69; 4th Grade Teacher Juneau AK 1969-70; Prin/Teacher AK St Schls 1970-76; Cnslr/Elem Teacher Kenai Peninsula Sch Dist 1976-85; Cnslr Soldotna HS 1985-; *ai:* Soldotna HS Jr Var Hockey Coach 1989-; Soldotna Elem Sch Yrbk Adv 1977-85, Soccer Coach 1977-83, Cross Cntry Running Coach 1977-85; AK Sch Cncl Assn, NEA; Kenai Peninsula Ed Assn Teacher Rights Chm 1978-82; Soldotna United Meth Church (Trustee 1987-, Parish Relations Pastor 1984-86, 1990); Stu Support Groups AK Merit Awd 1989; *home:* 35985 Pioneer Dr Soldotna AK 99669

WAISNER, BETTY DARLENE (TERSINAR), 4th Grade Teacher; *b:* Arlington, KS; *m:* Robert Thomas; *c:* Bret A., Beth A.; *ed:* (BS) Ed, Pittsburgh St Univ 1955; (MS) Ed, Webster Univ 1980; *cr:* 3rd Grade Teacher Santa Fe Trail Elem Sch 1955-58, Apache 1958-59; 3rd/4th Grade Teacher Santa Fe Trail Elem Sch 1969-; *ai:* NEA 1969-; *home:* 7915 W 77th St Overland Park KS 66204

WAITE, EDWARD R., Social Studies Teacher; *b:* Bennington, VT; *ed:* (BA) His/Liberal Arts, 1979, (MED) Ed, 1983 St Michaels Coll; *cr:* Soc Stud Teacher Christ the King 1981-84; Religion Teacher Stamford Cath HS 1984-88; Soc Stud Teacher Port Chester Sr HS 1988-; *ai:* Peer Leadership Prgm & Frosh Class Adv; ASCD 1989-; Knights of Columbus 1982-; Apartheid & S Africa Educl Wkshp Seminar Schlsp 1990; *office:* Port Chester Sr HS Tamarack Rd Port Chester NY 10573

WAITE, RANDY GLEN, Physics/Chemistry Teacher; *b:* Logan, UT; *m:* Carol Reeve; *c:* Rachelle, Jeanette, Kaylynn, Diana, Julie A., Douglas G., Sharon; *ed:* (BA) Physics, Brigham Young Univ 1974; Sci & Engineering, UT St Univ; Physics, Univ of ID; Sci, ID St Univ; *cr:* Physics/Chem Teacher Bonneville HS 1974-; *ai:* Sci Club Faculty Adv; AAPT, ID Sci Teachers Assn; BSA Dist Comm 1988-; Univ of ID Summer Physics Inst Grant; Intermountain Sci & Hum Symposium Participation Grant; *home:* 3570 Taylorview Ln Idaho Falls ID 83406

WAITS, DONNA BOTTOM, 4th Grade Teacher; *b:* Shelbyville, KY; *m:* Charles Wade; *c:* Kelly R., Zachary; *ed:* (BS) Elem Ed, Eastern KY Univ 1979; (MA) Elem Ed, Georgetown Univ 1985; *cr:* 2nd Grade Teacher Southside Elem 1980-82; 5th Grade Teacher Cropper Elem 1982-85; 4th Grade Teacher Northside Elem 1985-; *ai:* SCEA 1980-; KEA 1980-; *office:* Northside Elem Schl 821 College St Shelbyville KY 40065

WAJDA, MARY J. DEROCHER, 5th Grade Teacher; *b:* Escanaba, MI; *m:* George L.; *c:* David, Katherine; *ed:* (BA) Elem Ed, N MI Univ 1972; Grad Stud; *cr:* 2nd Grade Teacher E Tawas Elem 1973-79; 4th Grade Teacher 1979-83, 5th Grade Teacher 1984- Tawas City Elem; *ai:* 3rd-6th Grade Stu Cncl Co-Adv; *home:* 150 N Rempert Tawas City MI 48763

WAKEFIELD, LOU ANN, Third Grade Teacher; *b:* Ogden, UT; *ed:* (BS) His, Weber St Univ 1964; *cr:* 3rd Grade Teacher Crestview Elem 1964-; *ai:* Field Day Coord; Organize Sports Events; NEA 1964-; UT Ed Assn 1964-; Davis Ed Assn 1964- 25 Yr Pin 1989; Davis Dist PTA Cncl Treas 1967-69; Perfect Attendance 1975-; *home:* 1430 E 275 N Layton UT 84040

WALASINSKI, ALICE JOYCE DZIEWIATKA, Jr High Teacher; *b:* Toledo, OH; *m:* Leo Joseph; *c:* Kevin, Michael, Mary A.; *ed:* (BA) Ed, Mary Manse Coll 1962; Basic Level Catechist Certificate; *cr:* 1st Grade Teacher St Vincent De Paul Sch 1962-65; 4th Grade Teacher St Catherines Sch 1965-66; Substitute Teacher Toledo Cath Schls 1966-81; 7th/8th Grade Teacher Little Flower Sch 1981-; *ai:* Quiz Bowl & Sch Newspaper Adv: Spelling Bee & Speech Contest Coord; Positive Action Week; Jr HS Dances; NCEA 1962-; Quiz Bowl Champs Awd 1989-; *home:* 612 Cloverdale Toledo OH 43612

WALCH, SHIRLEY CASTO, First Grade Teacher; *b:* Akron, OH; *m:* Carl L.; *c:* Phil Casto, Mark Casto; *ed:* (BS) Early Chldhd Ed, Kent St Univ 1956; Rdng, Bowie St Univ; *cr:* Kndgtn Teacher Wildflecken Germany 1956-57; 3rd Grade Teacher Killeen Public Schls 1957-60; Rdng Teacher Rittman Public Schls 1960-61; 1st Grade Teacher Grace Chrstn Sch 1976-; *ai:* Amer Assn of Chrstn Schls 1976-, Teacher of Yr Mid-Eastern Section 1978; *home:* 12229 Foxhill Ln Bowie MD 20715

WALCOTT, JUDY ENGSTROM, Kindergarten Teacher; *b:* Rawlins, WY; *m:* Edward William; *c:* John, Michael; *ed:* (BA) Ed, Univ of WY 1964; *cr:* 2nd Grade Teacher John Muir Sch 1964-69; Pre-Sch Teacher Title VII Fountain Valley Sch Dist 1972-75; Kndgtn Teacher Masuda Sch 1975-83, James Cox Sch 1983-; *ai:* Kndgtn Team Lead Teacher; Various Comms; PTO Rep; Masuda PTO 1975-83, Lifetime Membership 1983; Cox PTO 3rd VP 1983-, Lifetime Membership 1987; PTSA Fountain Valley 1983-89; *office:* James Cox Sch 17615 Los Jardines E Fountain Valley CA 92708

WALDAHL, BALDY JEROME, 7th/8th Grade Math Teacher; *b:* Clarissa, MN; *ed:* (BS) Math/Phys Ed, St Cloud St Univ 1958; Grad Stud Bemidji St & Moorhead St; *cr:* 7th-12th Grade Math Techer Verndale MN 1958-65; 7th-9th Grade Math Teacher Wadena Jr HS 1966-; *ai:* Math Team; Jr HS Ftbl, Bsktbl, Golf; Stu Cncl Adv; Referee; Ftbl & Bsktbl Statistician; MN Math Teachers 1960-; NCTM 1960-; MN Coaches Assn 1958-, MN Golf Coach of Yr 1987-88; MN Golf Assn Dir 1972-; MN St Ftbl Statistician 1983-; MN St Golf Scorepeeker 1970-; *home:* Aldrich MN 56434

WALDECK, EILEEN T., Math Department Chairperson; *b:* Olean, NY; *ed:* (BS) Cmptr Sci, 1969; (MED) Math, 1978 PA St; Staff Dev; TESA; *cr:* Sub Teacher 1970-73; Teacher 1973- Warren Cty Sch Dist; *ai:* PCTM; *office:* Beaty Warren Mid Sch 2 3rd Ave Warren PA 16365

WALDEN, JERRY LEE, Fifth Grade Teacher; *b:* Wrightsville, GA; *m:* Katherine Wiley; *c:* Jerilyn; *ed:* (BS) Soc Sci, Ft Valley St 1975; GA Coll; *cr:* Teacher Tennille Elem 1975-; *ai:* Washington Cty Assn of Educators Pres 1987-88; GA Assn of Educators, NEA; Sandersville Tennille Optimist Club Pres 1989-; *home:* Rt 1 Box 258 Warthen GA 31094

WALDEN, JERRY LEE, Drafting Teacher; *b:* New Castle, IN; *m:* Kathy Jo Huffman; *c:* Taylor G., Kyle A.; *ed:* (BS) Industrial Ed, IN St Univ 1980; (MS) Industrial Ed, Ball St Univ 1987; Currently Working on Degree in Cnslng; *cr:* Teacher/Coach New Castle Chrysler HS 1980-; *ai:* 9th Grade Ftbl; Jr HS Ftbl Coord; Intramural Prgm Coord; NEA 1980-; IN St Teachers Assn 1980-; IN Industrial Technology Ed Assn 1980-; Optimist Intern 1990; *office:* New Castle Chrysler H S 801 Parkview Dr New Castle IN 47362

WALDEN, LINDA L., Teacher; *b:* Moultrie, GA; *m:* Corey J.; *c:* Corey II, Marlon, Christopher, Crystal; *ed:* (AA) Ed, Miami Dade Comm Coll 1979; (BS) Bus Ed, FL Intnl Univ 1980; Grad Stud Cmptr Prgm, Barry Univ; *cr:* Typist/Secy Southeast Bank 1968-69; Admin Asst The Osiris Group 1969-75; Teacher SER Jobs for Progress Inc 1980-82, Miami NW Sr 1982-; *ai:* Jr Fed Class & Co-Chairperson of Teacher Advisory Comm; Alpha Kappa Alpha 1989-; Dade Cty Bus Ed Assn; Future Bus Leaders of America (Secy, Adv) 1984-; Nom Teacher of Yr 1988-89; *office:* Miami NW Sr HS 7007 NW 12th Ave Miami FL 33150

WALDEN, PATRICIA, Special Education Counselor; *b:* Tompkinsville, KY; *ed:* (BA) Health Ed, 1976, (MS) Elem Ed, 1980, (Rank I) Cnslr Ed, 1985 W KY Univ; Endorsement to Administer Individual Intellectual Assessments; *cr:* 5th/6th Grade Teacher Tompkinsville Elem 1978-88; Cnslr Monroe Cty Schls 1988-; *ai:* KY CASE 1988-; *office:* Monroe Cty Schls PO Box 518 Tompkinsville KY 42167

WALDO, JANICE CURTIS, French Teacher; *b:* Topeka, KS; *c:* Jeannette; *ed:* (BSE) Fr, Univ of KS 1975; *cr:* Fr Teacher Unified Sch Dist #501, Highland Park HS 1980-88, Topeka W HS 1988-; *ai:* Chrldr Spon; French Club; KFLA 1980-.

WALDO, NANCY (ALLEN), Biology Teacher; *b:* Washington, DC; *m:* Allen Edward; *c:* Stephen E., Gregory A., Michael C.; *ed:* (BS) Zoology/Entomology, PA St Univ 1963; (MA) Bio, Stanford Univ 1965; Teacher Cert & Chem, TX Womans Univ; *cr:* Asst Professor Univ of ID 1967-72; Bio/Chem Teacher Denton HS 1985-; *ai:* Ecology Club & Jr Class Spon; Discipline Comm; Sci Teachers Assn of TX 1989-; Woodrow Wilson Fellow Honorary Fellow 1963; Natl Sci Fnd Grad Fellowship 1963; NEA 1986-; Phi Kappa Phi 1962-; BSA Asst Scoutmaster 1989-; *home:* 1306 Churchill Cir Denton TX 76201

WALDREN, PATRICIA J., Sixth Grade Teacher; *b:* Fayetteville, AR; *c:* Robert L.; *ed:* (BSE) Elem Ed, 1962, (ME) Elem Ed, 1984 Univ of AR; *cr:* 7th Grade Teacher Springdale Public Schls 1962; 5th Grade Teacher Root Elem 1962-65; 6th Grade Teacher Overland Park Dist 110 1965, Root Elem 1966-; *ai:* Sch Dist Lang Art, Sch Bd Salary & Budget Comm; Stu Act, Stock Market Game Spon; NEA (Delegate 1979) 1962-; AR Ed Assn Delegate 1962-; Fayetteville Ed Assn (Treas, Pres) 1962-; Fayetteville Elem Teacher of Yr 1980; *office:* Root Elem Sch 1529 Mission Blvd Fayetteville AR 72701

WALDREP, MARY LORENE, First/Second Grade Teacher; *b:* Cullman, AL; *m:* Rudolph Waldrep; *c:* Pamela Gable, Lougena Hudson, Debbie Yearwood, Vickie Nichols, Heather; *ed:* (BA) Elem, S Benedictine 1976; (MA) Elem, Univ of AL Birmingham 1979; *cr:* Teachers Aid 1968-71, Teacher 1971-77 Head Start Prgm; 1st/2nd Grade Teacher Dowling Jr HS 1977-; *ai:* Chrldr Spon; Text Book Comm; Key Rdng Teacher; Rainbow Rdng Mem 1987-; AEA, NEA, CCEA Mem; New Mt Zion Baptist (Clerk, Soc Stud Teacher); Liberty Baptist Vacation Bible Sch Dir 1990; *home:* Rt 1 Box 149 Logan AL 35098

WALDRON, DAVID L., Sixth Grade Instructor; *b:* Holly, CO; *m:* Doris E. Ackerman; *c:* Renee, Kent; *ed:* (AA) Elem, Dodge City Comm Coll 1965; (BS) Elem, St Mary of Plains 1967; (MS) Ed, KY St Univ 1980; *cr:* 5th Grade Teacher Spearville Grade Sch 1967-70; 6th-8th Grade Teacher St Andrews Grade Sch 1972, Spearville Grade Sch 1972-73; 6th Grade Teacher Unified Sch Dist 214 1973-; *ai:* Dream Team; Math & Eng Curr Comm; Human Growth & Dev Task Force; NEA, KS Ed Assn, Grant Cty Teachers Assn (Pres, Teas); Phi Delta Kappa (Treas, Membership); Knights of Columbus Secy 1988-, Outstanding Knight 1985, Family of Yr 1981; Grant Cty Schlsp Reporting Secy 1987-; Grant Cty Jaycees Various Offices 1966-75, Outstanding Jaycee 1975; Outstanding Young Educator.

WALDRON, MARK ALLEN, Media Teacher/Music Dir; *b:* Milwaukee, WI; *m:* Cynthia West; *c:* Lucas, Benjamin; *ed:* (BA) Ed/Music, Concordia Coll 1980; (MA) Rdng/Lang Art, Univ of Houston 1986; *cr:* Teacher Immanuel Luth Sch 1980-87; Teacher/Dir of Music St John Evangelical Luth Sch 1987-; *ai:* Soc, Fine Art, N IL Dist Worship Comm; Choristers Guild 1980-; NCTE Assembly on Lit for Adolescents 1986-; *home:* 7651 Monroe Forest Park IL 60130

WALDROP, WINIFRED DALE PREDDY, Fourth Grade Teacher; *b:* Richmond, VA; *m:* Douglas Crawford; *ed:* (BS) Eng/Elem Ed, Longwood Coll 1960; (MED) Teaching of Rdng, Univ of VA 1968; *cr:* 4th/5th Grade Teacher Highland Springs Elem 1960-63; 4th Grade Teacher Crestview Elem 1963-64, Short Pump Elem 1965-71, Pemberton Elem 1971-; *ai:* Henrico Ed Assn (Bd of Dir 1984-85, Elections Comm); VA Ed Assn, NEA; The Elizabeth Kates Fnd Inc Treas 1989-91; *office:* Pemberton Elem Sch 1400 Pemberton Rd Richmond VA 23233

WALDRUM, DOLORES MOORE, Science Chair; *b:* Baytown, TX; *m:* Archie Larimore; *c:* Philip L., Mark L.; *ed:* (BS) Bio, Abilene Chrstn Coll 1948; Working Towards Master; *cr:* Elem Teacher Falls Cty Schls 1946-50; Substitute Teacher Alice Ind Sch Dist 1973-74; Bio/Anatomy/Psych Teacher Alice HS 1974-; *ai:* Delta Kappa Gamma; *office:* Alice HS 1 Coyote Trl Alice TX 78332

WALISH, MYRNA MEAD, Social Studies Teacher; *b:* Cherry Valley, OH; *m:* Richard C.; *c:* Rachel, Rebecca; *ed:* (BED) Soc Stud Ed, Univ of FL 1965; *cr:* Teacher Williston HS 1966-68, Martin Cty Sch System 1968-72, Gulf Breeze Mid Sch 1976-82, Hobbs Mid Sch 1982-; *ai:* Budget Chairperson; Prgm Adv; NCSS; Santa Rosa Cty Mid Sch Soc Stud Teacher of Yr 1988; Hobbs Mid Sch Teacher of Yr 1990; *office:* Hobbs Mid Sch Glover Ln Milton FL 32570

WALKER, ANDREA MARIE, 7th Grade Lang Arts Teacher; *b:* Boise, ID; *m:* Lawrence R.; *c:* Francesca Benoit, Kim Leegard, Judd; *ed:* (BA) Eng, 1969, Ed Degree 1970 WA St Univ; *cr:* Teacher Shelton Mid Sch 1970-; *ai:* Team Leader Inter-Disciplinary Teams; Shelton Ed Assn, WA Ed Assn, NEA; *office:* Shelton Mid Sch 9th & Franklin Shelton WA 98584

WALKER, BEVERLY MC GRAW, 1st-4th Grade Math Teacher; *b:* Tuscaloosa, AL; *m:* Kenneth Wade; *ed:* (BA) Elem Ed, 1975, (MA) Elem Ed, 1978 Univ of AL; *cr:* Title I Rdng Teacher, 3rd Grade Teacher, 2nd Grade Teacher, 4th Grade Teacher, Chapter I Rdng/Math Teacher, Chapter I Math Teacher 1976- Myrtlewood; *ai:* Adopt a Sch Comm; Steering Comm for 10 Yr Self Study Southern Assn Accreditation; Delta Kappa Gamma 1983-86; Aglaia Jr Womans Club (Ed Dept Chm, Soc Chm); Jr League of Tuscaloosa 1987-; *office:* Myrtlewood Elem Sch PO Box 130 Fosters AL 35463

WALKER, BRIAN LUVERN, Fifth Grade Teacher; *b:* Glenwood, MN; *m:* Therese Vilina; *c:* Paige, Justine, Blake; *ed:* (AA) General Ed, Fergus Falls Comm Coll 1981; (BA) Elem Ed, Univ of MN Morris 1983; *cr:* 5th Grade Teacher/Coach Sanborn, Lamberton Public Sch 1983-; *ai:* Ftbl, Girls Bsktbl, Bsbl Asst Coach; Sanborn Ed Assn Pres 1988-89; MN Coaches Assn, MN Ed Assn 1983-; *home:* Rt 2 Box 1 Sanborn MN 56083

WALKER, CAROL U., Mathematics Dept Chairman; *b:* Attalla, AL; *w:* David R. (dec); *c:* Melinda, Theresa Hagan, Susan; *ed:* (BA) Math, Samford Univ 1956; Math Courses; Ed; *cr:* Teacher Jones Valley HS 1956-58, Brookwood HS 1961-67; Teacher/Math Dept Chairperson Summerville HS 1974-; *ai:* Math Team Spon; NCTM 1987-88; SEA; NEA 1974-; Selected by Addison Wesley Publishing Company to Evaluate Geometry Book; *home:* 202 Grouse Rd Summerville SC 29485

WALKER, CHARLENE ELLEDGE, Fifth Grade Teacher; *b:* Chilicothe, OH; *ed:* (BA) Elem Ed, VPI & SU 1977; *cr:* 2nd/4th Grade Teacher Spiller Primary 1977-79; 5th/6th Grade Teacher Rural Retreat Elem 1979-; *ai:* Aerobics Instr for Faculty;

Governors Phys Fitness Awd for Teachers-Gold; *home:* 510 Umberger St Wytheville VA 24382

WALKER, CHERI DUNCAN, 4th Grade Language Art Teacher; *b:* Huntington Park, CA; *m:* Bill; *c:* Bethany, Leslie; *ed:* (AA) Elem Ed, AR St Univ Beebe 1977-78; (BSE) Elem Ed, UCA Conway 1979; *cr:* 1st/2nd Grade Splint Teacher Harris Elem 1979; 4th Grade Teacher Lake Hamilton Intermediate 1980-; *ai:* AEA 1979-88; *office:* Lake Hamilton Intermediate Sch 107 N Wolf Dr Pearcy AR 71964

WALKER, DENNIS DEE, Assistant Principal; *b:* Roxboro, NC; *m:* Belinda Jo Brown; *c:* Amber, Megan; *ed:* (BA) Human Services, Elon Coll 1980; (MA) Sch Counseling, NC Cntrl Univ 1983; (MS) Sch Admin, NC A&T St Univ 1987; NC Assessment Center; Initial Cert Prgm for Admin; *cr:* Sch Cnslr Northern Jr HS 1981-82, Southern Jr HS 1982-83, Turrentine Mid Sch 1983-86; Asst Prin Walter M Williams HS 1986-; *ai:* Boys & Girls Track Team Coach; Prof Educators of NC 1986-; Tarheel Assn of Prins & Asst Prins 1988-; Outstanding Young Men in America; *office:* Walter M Williams HS 1307 S Church St Burlington NC 27215

WALKER, ELIZABETH MOORE, Mathematics Dept Chairperson; *b:* Dunedin, FL; *c:* Laura M., Melissa Coy; *ed:* (BA) Math/Ed, Univ S FL 1968; (MED) Guidance, MS Coll 1973; (ABD) Curr/Instruction Cmptrs, Univ S FL 1989; Writing Dissertation for PhD Degree; *cr:* Teacher Buchanan Jr HS 1968-69, Cadan Jr HS 1969-71, Pearl HS 1971-72, St Pete HS 1972-74; Math Dept Chm Dunedin HS 1974-; *ai:* NHS Spon; Cmptr Club; Awds Comm; Alpha Delta Kappa Past Pres 1979-; Phi Kappa Phi 1987-; Masonic Lodge Teacher of Yr; Articles Published 1986.

WALKER, ELLA HYSLIP, Sixth Grade Teacher; *b:* Wellsville, NY; *m:* Richard E.; *c:* Robert C., Richard M.; *ed:* (AAS) Liberal Arts, Greenbrier Jr Coll 1957; (BDS) Elem Ed, 1973, (MS) Elem Ed, 1977 Alfred Univ; Lions Quest Intnl Prgm; *cr:* Womens Phys Ed Teacher Boces 1965-66; 5th Grade Teacher 1973-75, 6th Grade Teacher 1975-81; 5th Grade Teacher 1981-84; 6th Grade Teacher 1984- Scio Cntrl Sch; *ai:* Chrldr Adv; Class Adv 5th/6th Grades; Scio Teachers Assn Pres 1985-86; Beta Sigma Phi (Pres) 1961-86; Sigma Phi Honorary Mem 1975-; Kanakadea Rdng Cncl 1980-; Allagany Cty Teachers Assn 1973-; Allegany Cty Rdng Cncl 1973-80; Gifted Talented Comm 1976-83; *home:* RD 1 Balcom Beach Rd Rushford NY 14777

WALKER, ELSIE PITTMAN, 6th Grade Teacher; *b:* Itta Bena, MS; *m:* John A.; *c:* Jennifer Momodu; *ed:* (BS) Elem Educ, 1967; (MS) Elem Educ, 1980 MS Valley St Univ; *cr:* Elem Teacher Leflore Cty Elem Sch 1966-; *ai:* Chm Courtesy Club LCES; Staff Dev Comm Mem; Elem Spelling Bee Chairperson LCES; LCAE 1966- Teacher Yr Awd 1988; MAE; NEA; Zeta Phi Beta Inc 1989-; Prgm for Effective Teaching Certificate; *home:* P O Box 344 Itta Bena MS 38941

WALKER, ERIC MICHAEL, English Instructor; *b:* Rantoul, IL; *ed:* (BA) Eng, Univ of N TX 1987; Grad Work Eng, Univ of N TX; *cr:* Eng Instr Sunset HS 1988-; *ai:* NHS Spon; Accompany All Sch Choir, Band Solo, Group Performances; Chm Amer Airlines Mini-Grant Comm; Voted Teacher of Month 1990; *office:* Sunset HS 2120 Jefferson Dallas TX 75208

WALKER, GEORGE RANDY, Biology Teacher/Coach; *b:* Littlefield, TX; *m:* Gaye Ann Cleveland; *c:* Lauren, Jody; *ed:* (BS) Bio/Chem, Abilene Chrstn Univ 1974; (MS) Admin Ed, Univ of N TX 1990; *cr:* Phys Sci Teacher/Coach Duncanville HS 1974-84; Bio Teacher/Coach Bryan Adams HS 1985-86, Cedar Hill HS 1986-87, Skyline HS 1987-; *ai:* Asst Head Coach & Offensive Coord Ftbl; Head Power-Lifting Coach; Classroom Teachers of TX Mem 1989-; NEA Mem 1974-84; *office:* Skyline HS 7777 Forney Rd Dallas TX 75227

WALKER, GLORIA EDWARDS, Teacher/Mathematics Dept Chair; *b:* Eudora, AR; *m:* Walter Ricks; *c:* Adrienne, Eunice, Byron; *ed:* (BS) Math, AM&N Coll 1964; (MA) Ed Admin/Supervision, Chicago St Univ 1989; *cr:* Teacher Cntrl HS 1964-65, Roosevelt Jr HS 1966-71, Bowen HS 1971-; *ai:* Homecoming, Honor Roll, Early Involvement Coord; Math Team Coach; Prof Problems Advisory Comm; Chicago Citywide Math League Bd of Dirs; IL Cncl Teachers of Math, NCTM; Teacher of Yr; Educator of Yr; Service Awd; Math Coach of Yr; Teacher Incentive Awd; *home:* 12316 S La Salle Chicago IL 60628

WALKER, HARRIET NELMS, 7th Grade Science Teacher; *b:* Fort Bragg, NC; *ed:* (BA) Ed, Rider Coll 1975; *cr:* Teacher Newcomb Sch 1975-81, Mac Farland Jr HS 1981-; *ai:* Core Team Mem; Bordentown Teaching Staff Mem; NJ Sch Conservation; Ceramics Club; Governors Teacher Recognition Awd 1987; Nom for Presidential Awd Excl in Math & Sci Teachers 1987; *office:* Macfarland Jr Sch 87 Crosswick St Bordentown NJ 08505

WALKER, HELENE BYRNES, English & Reading Teacher; *b:* Winnfield, LA; *m:* James R.; *c:* Rachel, Drew; *ed:* (BA) Speech Pathology, 1971, (MA) Speech Pathology, 1972 LA Tech Univ; *cr:* Speech Therapist Anne Arundel Cty Bd of Ed 1972-74, Winn Parish Sch Bd 1974-75; Spec Ed Teacher Pasadena Ind Sch Dist 1976-78; Lang Art Teacher Winn Parish Sch Bd 1980-; *ai:* Beta Club & Academic Pentathlon Team Spon; Delta Kappa Gamma; 1st Meth Church; Humana Hospital Winn Parish Bd of Trustees; Beta Sigma Phi; Winn Parish Teacher of Yr 1988-89.

WALKER, IVA LOUISE, Social Studies Teacher; *b:* Oberlin, OH; *ed:* (BA) His/Poly Sci, Hiram Coll 1964; (MED) Guidance/Counseling, Kent St Univ 1976; Ec, Univ of Akron; Theatre Storytelling, Kent St Univ; *cr:* Teacher James A Garfield Mid Sch 1964-; *ai:* Head Teacher; Scorekeeping Vlybl, Wrestling; Cheerleading Coach; Announcing for Marching Band & Track Meets; Drama Mid Sch & HS Musical; Garfield Ed Assn, NE OH Ed Assn, OH Ed Assn, NEA, OH Cncl Soc Stud; 20th Century Club of Garrettsville Secy 1975-76; Martha Holden Jennings Scholar; Article Published; *office:* James A Garfield Mid Sch 8233 Park Ave Garrettsville OH 44231

WALKER, JAMES DANIEL, 8th Grade Lang Arts Teacher; *b:* Jacksonville, IL; *m:* Diana Lynn Murphy; *c:* Ian, Rachel; *ed:* (AA) Eng, Robert Morris Jr Coll 1968; (BSED) Eng, Northeast MO St Univ 1970; Defense Lang Inst Monterey CA;; Successful Completion of Russian Basic Course; Univ of AR Various Russian Lang/Lit Courses; Completed 4th/5th Levels of Russian Lang at Summer Slavic Wkshps; *cr:* Russian Translator/Voice Processing Specialist USAF 1971-74; Lang Arts Teacher Lincoln Mid Sch 1974-86; Deput Y Dir of Russian Translation Worldview Inc 1986-87Lang Arts Teacher Lincoln Mid Sch 1987-; *ai:* Var Tennis Coach; NEA Mem 1974-; IA St Ed Assn Mem 1974-; Albia Cmmty Theater Original Bd of Governors 1976-82; Restoration Days Comm Dir of Variety Show 1984-; St Marys Cath Church Choir Dir 10 Yrs; Selected to Co-Lead a Group of 32 IA HS Students on a 3 Week Tour of the USSR Under the Auspices of Seattle Based Group People to People 1989; *home:* 115 1/2 Benton Ave E Albia IA 52531

WALKER, JEAN GENNARO, Fourth Grade Teacher; *b:* Brooklyn, NY; *d:* Howard; *c:* Lisa Bauer, Glenn; *ed:* (BA) Ed, SUNY Oswego 1961; Grad Stud Lit, Whole Lang, Cmptr Usage; *cr:* 4th Grade Teacher Parish Elem Sch 1961-63; 5th Grade Teacher Main Street Sch 1964-65; Substitute Teacher New Hartford NY 1966-69; 4th Grade Teacher Westmoreland Cntrl Sch 1969-; *ai:* Soc Stud Curr Chairperson & Rep;Center St Teachers Center Bd of Dirs Mem; Evaluation Comm; Rdng Comm Rep; Delta Kappa Gamma (1st VP, 2nd VP, Secy) 1977-; Westmoreland Teacher Assn Negoitiation Comm VP 1980-81; ABC Nursery Sch Chairperson 1988-89; Annunciation Church Renew Chm 1986-88; Published 4th Grade Textbook; *office:* Westmoreland Cntrl Sch Rt 233 Westmoreland NY 13490

WALKER, LINDA MILLER, English Teacher; *b:* Mobile, AL; *c:* Geoffrey, Jessica; *ed:* (BA) Eng, Auburn Univ 1976; (MA) Eng, Univ of AL Birmingham 1986; Working on EDS Degree Univ of AL Birmingham; *cr:* Eng Teacher LaGrange HS 1976-77, Pelham HS 1977-; *ai:* Yrbk & Sr Class Spon; Kappa Delta Epsilon 1989-, Teacher of Yr 1986-87; AEA, NEA 1977-; Univ of AL Birmingham Grad Fellowship 1985; *home:* 2526 Tahiti Terr Alabaster AL 35007

WALKER, LORI LENETTE, 8th Grade Teacher; *b:* Rapid City, SD; *m:* Harlan K.; *c:* Chad, Haley; *ed:* (BS) Elem Ed/Child Dev/Family Relations, SD St Univ 1974; Masters Work Guidance & Counseling, SD St Univ 1991; *cr:* 8th Grade Lang Arts/Soc Sci Teacher Wall Public Sch 1974-; *ai:* Adv 8th Grade Class 1974-, Jr HS Cheerleading 1974-80; Lang Arts Curr Comm 1987-88; Soc Stud Curr Comm 1989-; NEA, SD Ed Assn 1974-; Wall Ed Assn (Secy, Treas 1989-) 1974-; Amer Legion Auxiliary 1987-; United Meth Women, SD Thoroughbred Breeders Assn 1974-; TX Longhorn Breeders Assn 1980-; Outstanding Young Educator Awd 1975-76; *home:* PO Box 301 Wall SD 57790

WALKER, LYNDA BINNS, Fourth Grade Teacher; *b:* Athens, GA; *m:* Robert W.; *ed:* (BS) Elem Ed, Paine Coll 1970; (MED) Elem Ed, GA Univ 1977; *cr:* 2nd Grade Teacher Taliaferro Cty Elem 1970-71; 6th Grade Teacher Beaverdam Elem 1971-83; 4th Grade Teacher Chase St Elem 1983-; *ai:* Clarke Cty Assn of Educators, GA Assn of Educators, NEA; Athens Alumnae Chapter of Delta Sigma Theta Secy 1988-; GSA; Chase Street Teacher of Yr 1988; GSA Troop Leader; *office:* Chase St Elem Sch 757 N Chase St Athens GA 30601

WALKER, MAE CHARLOTTE JONES, Fourth Grade Teacher; *b:* Troy, AL; *c:* Cheryl F., Ronald K., Adrian V., Evelyn G. Mc Lin, Stewart M.; *ed:* (BS) Elem Ed, AL St Coll 1957; (MS) Elem Ed, 1972, (EDS) Elem Ed, 1977 Jackson St Univ; *cr:* Teacher Meridian Public Schls 1957-58, Jackson Public Schls 1960-80; Asst Prin 1980-81, Prin 1981-82, Teacher 1982- Jackson Public Schls; *ai:* 4th Grade Chm; Staff Courtesy Comm Mem; Jackson Assn of Ed, MS Assn of Educators & NEA Life Mem 1960; Phi Delta Kappa Mem 1981; Pentecostal Temple Church Vacation Bible Sch Dir, Youth Sunday Sch & St Church Secy.

WALKER, MARTHA LAWTON, 3rd/4th Grade Teacher; *b:* Kiowa, KS; *m:* William L.; *c:* Barry, Brad; *ed:* (BA) Elem Ed, Univ of KS 1959; Addl Training Elem Econ; Cmptr Ed for Teachers Univ of AR; *cr:* 2nd Grade Teacher Potwin Elem 1958-59; 1st Grade Teacher Minnie Gant Elem 1960; 2nd Grade Teacher T T Minor Elem 1960-61; Hillside Elem 1961-62; 5th Grade Teacher Bel-Aire Elem 1962-63; 2nd/4th Grade Teacher Metro Christian 1979-; *ai:* Conducted Visual Aids Wkshp at OK Christian Coll Lectureship; *office:* Metro Chrstn Sch 900 Waldron Rd Fort Smith AR 72903

WALKER, MARY V., Teacher/English Dept Chair; *b:* Carlsbad, NM; *c:* Mary L. Davis, James B., John W.; *ed:* (BA) Eng, Univ of AZ 1954; *cr:* Teacher Austin HS; Teacher/Dept Chairperson Carlsbad Mid HS; Teacher Carlsbad HS; Instr NM St Univ Carlsbad; *ai:* PEO 1957-; *home:* 908 N Alameda Carlsbad NM 88220

WALKER, MICHAEL J., Assistant Principal; *b:* Owensboro, KY; *c:* Mischelle, Michael Jr., Jennifer, John; *ed:* (BS) Elem Ed, 1976, (MED) Ed Admin, 1979 Auburn Univ; *cr:* Teacher Highland Gardens Elem 1976-78, Brewbaker Elem 1978-84; Asst Prin Wares Ferry Elem 1984-; *ai:* Chm Local Self Study Comm SACS Accreditation Chm; Law Awareness Club, Sch Yrbk Staff, Jr Traffic Police, Sch Supply Store Spon; NEA, AL Ed Assn, Montgomery Cty Ed Assn 1976-; Wares Ferry PTA (1st VP 1984-86, 2nd VP 1987); Montgomery Cty Cncl PTA Rep; *office:* Wares Ferry Elem Sch 6425 Wares Ferry Rd Montgomery AL 36117

WALKER, MICHAEL M., Mathematics Instructor; *b:* Euclid, OH; *m:* Meg Tanaka; *c:* Denise, Deborah; *ed:* (BS) Operations Management, Marquette Univ 1978; Grad Stud Ed, Natl Univ 1986; *cr:* Infantry Officer US Marine Corps 1978-85; Math Instr Twentynine Palms HS 1986-87, Yucca Valley HS 1987-; *ai:* Math Club Adv; Dist Curr/Instruction Comm, Math Task Force, 9th Grade Restucturing Study Group Mem; NCTM 1989-; ASCD 1988-; Marine Corps Assn 1979-; Marine Corps Res Off Assn 1986-; Natl Geographic Society 1988-; *office:* Yucca Valley Sr HS 7600 Sage Ave Yucca Valley CA 92284

WALKER, OPAL COOPERWOOD, 7th & 8th Grade Sci Teacher; *b:* Aberdeen, MS; *m:* Clarence; *c:* Vincent, Reginald; *ed:* (BA) Sci, Rust Coll 1955; *cr:* Teacher Coleman HS 1955-58, Higgason Rosenwald 1958-60, Prairie Jr HS 1960-88, Shivers Jr HS 1988-; *home:* 419 N Franklin Aberdeen MS 39730

WALKER, PATRICIA ANN, English Teacher; *b:* McRae, GA; *m:* Johnny; *ed:* (BS) Eng Ed, Valdosta St Coll 1977; (MED) Mid Grades Ed, 1983; (Ed Specialist) Mid Grades Ed, 1984 GA Southwestern Coll; *cr:* Eng Teacher Irwin Cty HS 1977-81; Eastman Mid Sch 1981-; Eng Instr (Part-Time) Mid GA Coll 1987-88; *ai:* Rdng Cncl 1988-; *home:* Rt 1 Box 292 Rhine GA 31077

WALKER, RAYDENE LEWIS, Counselor; *b:* Booneville, MO; *m:* Harold E.; *c:* Brad; *ed:* (BS) Elem Ed, 1969, (MA) Counseling, 1981 NE OK St Univ; Cmptr Ed; *cr:* 5th-8th Grade Soc Stud Teacher 1969-71, 7th/8th Grade Eng/Lit Teacher 1971-85, 5th/6th Grade Eng Teacher 1985-86, 7th/8th Grade Cmptr Lab Teacher 1986-87, Asst Prin/Cnslr 1987- Allen Bowden; *ai:* 8th Grade, Cheerleading, Stu Cncl Spon; OK Ed Assn; Creek Cty Ed Assn Pres 1987-88; Delta Kappa Gamma 1987-; Allen Bowden Ed Teacher of Yr 1985-86; *office:* Allen Bowden Elem Sch 7049 Frankoma Rd Tulsa OK 74107

WALKER, RICHARD WALTER, 6th Grade Teacher; *b:* Chattanooga, TN; *m:* Schley Dunn; *c:* Matthew, Brandi; *ed:* (BS) Elem Ed/Spec Ed, Lincoln Memorial 1976; (MS) Supervision/Admin, E TN St 1986; TN Math Laser Prgm; *cr:* Resource Teacher Jones Cove/Catons Chapel 1976-79; Teaching Prin Catons Chapel 1979-82; Chapter I Tutor 1985-87, 6th Grade Teacher Sevierville Mid Sch 1982-; *ai:* AYSO Division 4 Soccer Coach; TEA, NEA; BSA Den Leader 1986-88; UMYF Youth Leader 1985; *office:* Sevierville Mid Sch 420 High St Sevierville TN 37862

WALKER, SCOTT M., Music Director/Spanish Teacher; *b:* Whittier, CA; *m:* Virginia Cox; *c:* Marissa; *ed:* (BMU) Music Ed, Brigham Young Univ 1987; (MS) Ed, Azusa Pacific Univ 1989; *cr:* Choral/Span Teacher Juab Mid Sch 1986-87; Elem Music/Band Teacher Baldy Mesa Elem 1987-88; Span/Band/Choral Teacher Serrano HS 1988-; *ai:* Marching Band, Show Choir, Concert Choir, Jazz Band; MENC 1986-; *office:* Serrano HS 9292 Sheep Creek Rd Phelan CA 92371

WALKER, STEPHEN MICHAEL, 1st Grade Teacher; *b:* Spencer, WV; *m:* Janet Marie Tallman; *c:* Melinda, Megan; *ed:* (AB) Elem Ed, Glenville St Coll 1973; (MA) Early Chldhd Ed, WV Univ 1983; Early Chldhd Ed, WV Univ; *cr:* 5th-8th Grade Teacher Smithville Grade Sch 1973-74; 1st Grade Teacher Ellenboro Primary Sch 1974-; *ai:* WV St Teachers Acad 1989-; Ritchie Cty Ed Assn (Faculty Rep 1973-75/Treas 1975-77); Sports Car Club of America 1976-; PTO 1973-; Ritchie Cty Teacher of Yr 1990; *home:* Rt 1 Box 33-A Pennsboro WV 26415

WALKER, SUSAN M., English Teacher; *b:* Seaford, DE; *ed:* (BA) Eng, Shepherd Coll 1984; Trng for Honors Classes; *cr:* Teacher Charlestown Jr HS 1985-86, Jefferson HS 1986-; *ai:* Spon Jefferson HS Stu Government Assn Policy Comm; IAO 1983-; NEA 1985-; Old Opera House 1st VP 1990; *office:* Jefferson HS Rt 1 Box 83 Shenandoah Jct WV 25442

WALKER, TERRY L., United States History Teacher; *b:* Washington, PA; *m:* Valencia A.; *c:* Josh, Matthew; *ed:* (BA) Soc Stud, Univ of S FL 1977; Grad Stud Univ of S FL; *cr:* US His Teacher Seminole Mid Sch 1977-; *ai:* Kiawanis Charter Builders Club Spon; Track & Bsktbl Coach; NEA, PCTA 1977-; FL Real Estate Assn 1982-.

WALKER, TONY ALAN, Physical Education Teacher; *b:* Dallas, TX; *m:* Sherrie M. Benson; *c:* Cameron R.; *ed:* (BS) Phys Ed, TX A&M 1986; His/Bio; *cr:* Teacher/Coach Central HS 1987-; *ai:* Womens Gymnastics/Mens Soccer; TX HS Gymnastics Coaches Assn 1987-90 Coach of Yr 1989; Natl HS Gymnastics Coaches Assn 87, Coach of Yr 1989; TX A&M Assn Former Stu 1986; *office:* Central H S 100 Cottonwood San Angelo TX 76901

WALKER, WANDA BENTON, Guidance Counselor; *b:* Jasper, AL; *m:* Joseph Douglas; *c:* Jerrod, Joseph; *ed:* (BA) Ed, 1978, (MS) Guidance/Counseling, 1986 Univ of AL; *cr:* Teacher Brilliant Elem Sch 1983-86; Cnslr/Math Teacher Brilliant HS

1986-; *ai:* SADD, 4-H, His Bowl, Jr Scholars Bowl & His Bowl Spon; Attendance Clerk Athletic Boosters; Homeroom Mother; Testing Supvr; Working Concessions & Gate Athletic Events; Marion Cty Ed Assn Sch Rep 1983-; AL Ed Assn, NEA 1983-; Delta Kappa Gamma Comm Rep 1986-; AL Cnslrs Assn 1986-; PTO 1983-; *office:* Brilliant HS PO Box 195 Brilliant AL 35548

WALKER, WILLIAM MARTIN, Sixth Grade Teacher; *b:* Scranton, PA; *c:* Dana M., Devin E.; *ed:* (BS) Elem Ed, Mansfield St Coll 1970-74; (MS) Elem Admin, Univ of Scranton 1984; Co-Operative Learning/Peer Coaching, Johns Hopkins Univ; NEIU Advisory Comm Lead Teacher & In-Service Advisory Comm; *cr:* Elem Teacher Mid Valley 1974-; Coll Teacher Lack Jr Coll 1976-80; In-Service Cncl Teacher Northeastern Ed Intermediate Unit 1989-; *ai:* Tee-Ball Coach; Phi Delta Kappa 1976-80; North Cntrl Lead Teacher Center Team 1989-; PA Advisory Bd Lead Teacher Center Team 1989-; *office:* Mid Valley Elem Sch Underwood Rd Throop PA 18512

WALL, ALICIA ANDERSON, 7th/8th Grade English Teacher; *b:* Toledo, OH; *m:* A. David; *c:* Ian; *ed:* (BA) Comm, Azusa Pacific Univ 1979; Ryan Single Subject Credential Eng, CA St Univ Los Angeles 1983; *cr:* Jr HS Eng Teacher Oak Avenue Intermediate 1982-83; Jr HS Teacher Cantua Elem 1983-86; K-5th Grade Lit Specialist John Swett Elem 1986-87; Jr HS Eng Teacher Kings River Union Elem 1987-; *ai:* Stu Cncl Adv; Vlybl, Sftbl, Track Coach; Newspaper & Yrbk Ed; CA Assn Teachers of Eng, Natl Rdng Assn 1988-; CA League of Mid Schls 1987-.

WALL, ANNA MORRIS, English Teacher; *b:* Suffolk, VA; *m:* Michael E.; *c:* Elizabeth Ashley; *ed:* (BA) Eng, Longwood 1974; Grad Stud Eng, Univ of NC Greensboro 1974-75; *cr:* Eng Teacher Suffolk HS 1974-76, Woodrow Wilson HS 1978-; *ai:* Organized & Taught Poetry Wkshp; VA Assn Teachers of Eng, Tidewater Assn Teachers of Eng Mem 1980-; Longwood Coll Alumni Assn; St Christophers Episcopal Church Women; Advanced Placement Courses 1989; Comm to Write Curr for Advanced Plcement Eng Portsmouth 1989; *office:* Woodrow Wilson HS 3701 Willett Dr Portsmouth VA 23707

WALL, DEBORAH WILLIAMS, English Teacher; *b:* Shelby, NC; *m:* Frank Miller Jr.; *c:* Gabriel D., Holly M.; *ed:* (BSED) Scndry Fr, W Carolina Univ 1973; (MA) Scndry Eng, Converse Coll 1988; Advanced Placement Eng Trng; *cr:* Rdng/Lang Art/Soc Stud Teacher Canton Jr HS 1974; Eng Teacher E Rutherford HS 1974-; *ai:* Beta Club Adv; High-Q Team Coach; Kappa Kappa Iota 1989-; Kappa Delta Pi 1972-; NC Assn of Educators, NC Eng Teachers Assn; Lattimore Jr Womens Club (VP 1985-86, Treas 1989-); Sandy Plains Baptist Church Sunday Sch Teacher; Rutherford Cty Career Dev Steering Comm Secy; Outstanding Young Educator 1977; *office:* E Rutherford HS Box 668 Forest City NC 28043

WALL, JOYCE ANN, Physical Education teacher; *b:* Perry, OK; *ed:* (BA) Health/Phys Ed/Recreation, Cntrl St Univ 1971; (MS) Ed, Pittsburg St Univ 1977; *cr:* Teacher Miami Public Schls 1972-; *ai:* Teachers Expectations of Stu Achievements Co-Leader; OEA, NEA 1972-; *home:* 1922 A Street NE Miami OK 74354

WALL, LINDA BETH, Fourth Grade Teacher; *b:* Carnegie, OK; *m:* Gerald Lee; *c:* Kyle; *ed:* (BS) Elem Ed, SE OK St Univ 1975; *cr:* Teacher Gracemont Elem, 1977-79, Fort Cobb 1979-80, Caddo-Kiowa Vo-Tech 1980-81, Fort Cobb Elem 1981-; *ai:* Elem Sci Coord; FCTA Reporter: Elem Scorekeeer; OEA, NEA 1977-; Fort Cobb Teacher of Yr 1988-89; *office:* Fort Cobb Elem Sch Box 130 Fort Cobb OK 73038

WALL, PEGGY LEA (ELLS), Business Education Teacher; *b:* Platte, SD; *m:* Dan C.; *ed:* (BS) Bus Composite, Univ of SD Springfield 1975; Grad Stud for Renewal; *cr:* Bus Teacher Gregory HS 1975-76, Ethan HS 1976-; *ai:* Adv Annual, Newspaper, Frosh Class; All-St Annual 1982, 1983, 1989, All-St Newspaper 1982, 1983, Top of Class Publications 1982, Annual PICA Awd 1988, 1989; Ethan Ed Assn Pres 1985-; SD Ed Assn, NEA 1975-; SD Bus & Office Ed Assn; Jaycee Women 1981-83; Welcome Wagon Chairperson 1982; Amer Ed Week, Natl Teacher Day Act & Events Chairperson 1985-; Ethan Teacher of Yr 1987; *home:* Box 581 Parkston SD 57366

WALL, RONNIE L., Science Teacher; *b:* St Louis, MO; *m:* Kathy Elliott; *c:* Noel, Elliott; *ed:* (BA) Religion, Furman Univ 1976; (MED) Scndry Ed, Univ of SC 1984; *cr:* Soc Stud/Sci Teacher Heath Springs Elem Sch 1978-79; Sci Teacher Flat Creek Mid Sch 1980-84, Andrew Jackson Mid Sch 1984-; *ai:* Yrbk Adv; Sci Fair & Past Sci Dept Chm; NSTA, SC Sci Cncl 1984-; Lancaster Cty Conservation Teacher of Yr 1990; *office:* Andrew Jackson Mid Sch Rt 2 Box 139-B Kershaw SC 29067

WALL, SHARON PAVOGGI, Jr HS Physical Ed Teacher; *b:* Blue Island, IL; *m:* Michael Edwin; *c:* Matthew, Luke; *ed:* (BS) Phys Ed, Univ of Mary Hardin-Baylor 1974; (MS) Phys Ed, Baylor Univ 1975; *cr:* Grad Asst Baylor Univ 1974-75; Phys Ed Teacher Pasodale Elem 1975-79, Normandy HS 1979-80, N Kirkwood Mid Sch 1980, Hollenbeck Jr HS 1980-; *ai:* Francis Howell Frosh Vlybl Team Coach; Spec Projects Comm Chm; Outstanding Stu Comm; MO Ed Assn 1980-; Phi Delta Kappa Ed 1987-; *home:* 4 Kandahar Ct Saint Charles MO 63303

WALL, SUE LINGLE, First Grade Teacher; *b:* Salisbury, NC; *m:* E. Glenn; *c:* John S., Susan M.; *ed:* (BS) Elem Ed, Appalachian St Univ 1970; *cr:* Teacher Oakdale Elem 1970-73, Beverly Hills Elem 1973-77, Rockwell Elem 1977-; *ai:* Grade Team Chairperson; Delta Kappa Gamma Secy 1988-; Kappa Delta Pi; NEA, NCAE Faculty Rep; Rowan Cty Elem Math Teacher Awd 1987; Beverly Hills Teacher of Yr 1975; Rockwell Teacher of Yr 1985; *office:* Rockwell Elem Sch 114 Link St Rockwell NC 28138

WALLACE, ANNA SMACCHI, English Teacher; *b:* Scranton, PA; *m:* James Michael, Ph.D.; *ed:* (AA) Liberal Arts, Keystone Jr Coll 1977; (BA) Eng, Wilkes Univ 1979; (MA) Eng, Lehigh Univ 1983; *cr:* Teaching Fellow Lehigh Univ 1980-82; Eng Teacher Southern Lehigh HS 1983-84; Adjunct Professor Northampton Comm Coll 1982-; Eng Teacher Palmerton HS 1984-; *ai:* Soph Class Adv; 7th Thru 12th Grade Lang Arts Curr Coord; Mentor Teacher; Sigma Tau Delta 1981-; Teaching Fellowship at Lehigh Univ 1980-82; *office:* Palmerton HS Rd #3 Box 3681 Palmerton PA 18071

WALLACE, BONNIE JUNE HAMBLETON, Third Grade Teacher; *b:* Dora, MO; *m:* Richard Estel; *c:* Teresa Ann Poppitz; *ed:* (BS) Elem Ed, Southwest MO Univ 1973; *cr:* 1st-8th Grade Teacher Bakersfield Sch 1956-59; 3rd/4th Grade Teacher Glenwood Sch 1967-68; 3rd Grade Teacher Dora R-III 1968-; *ai:* Beautification Club Spon; Field Day Coord; Ozark Cty Spelling Bee Dora Sch Coord; MSTA 1968-; CTA VP 1988-89; JRA 1987-89; *home:* 2108 Gleghorn West Plains MO 65775

WALLACE, CHARLES ROBERT, American Government Teacher; *b:* Detroit, MI; *m:* Karen V.; *c:* Paige, Jackie, Tara; *ed:* (BA) His/Poly Sci, Muskingum Coll 1966; (MED) Admin, Xavier Univ 1970; Archaeology & Japanese Lang Stud, OH Univ; General Course Stud at OH Univ 1987-; *cr:* Soc Stud Teacher Miami Trace HS 1966-73, Chillicothe HS 1973-; *ai:* AFS Stu Coord; Frosh Ftbl & Track Asst Coach; OEA, NEA 1979-; Miami Trace Teachers Assn Past Pres; Trinity United Meth (Chm 1974-, Trustees 1989-); Wrestling Gold Medal Scholastic Coach Awd; *office:* Chilliocthe HS 381 Yoctangee Pkwy Chillicothe OH 45601

WALLACE, CYNTHIA KAY (JONES), Third Grade Teacher; *b:* Merced, CA; *m:* Alan William; *c:* Shane, Lindsey; *ed:* (AA) General, Merced Jr Coll 1973; (BS) Child Dev - Cum Laude, CA St Univ Fresno 1975; Bay Area Writing Project, Bi-ling Ed Cultural Classes, Drug Awareness; *cr:* 5-7th Grade Teacher Merced Cty Summer Sch 1979-81; K-1st Grade Teacher 1975-81, 4th Grade Teacher 1981-88, 3rd Grade Teacher 1988- Denair Elem; *ai:* Grade Level Lead Teacher; Report Card Revision Comm; Rdng & Lang Art Comm Chairperson; Denair ELem Sch Site Cncl Mem 1984-86; Mentor Selection Comm 1986; Denair United Teachers Assn (Treas, Negotiator) 1986-; CA Teachers Assn, NEA, CA Math Assn; Master Teacher 1980-; *office:* Denair Elem Sch 3773 Madera Ave Denair CA 95316

WALLACE, DONNA M., Fifth Grade Teacher; *b:* New York, NY; *m:* Robert; *c:* Christopher, Nicole, Jonathan; *ed:* (BA) Sociology, Hunter Coll 1980; (MS) Elem Ed, City Coll of NY 1987; *cr:* 3rd Grade Teacher 1981-82, 6th Grade Teacher 1982-87, Health Teacher 1987-89, 5th Grade Teacher 1990 PS 57 M; *ai:* Cities in Sch after Sch Prgms; Homework & Tutorial Adv 1989-; Cub Scouts Den Leader 1989-; *office:* PS 57 M 176 E 115th St New York NY 10029

WALLACE, FRANCES C., Business Education Teacher; *b:* Castine, ME; *m:* Malcolm W.; *c:* Deborah Gilbert, Randall, Timothy, Gregory; *ed:* (BA) Bus Ed, Bliss Bus Coll 1953; *cr:* Bus Ed Teacher Canton HS 1953-54, Weld HS 1954-55, Canton HS 1955-65, Livermore Falls HS 1965-; *ai:* Frosh Class Adv; NHS Selection, Schlsp Selection, Disciplinary Action Comm; MSAD 36 Teachers Assn 1965-; MA Teachers Assn, New England Ed Assn 1953-; *home:* RFD 1 Box 201 Canton ME 04221

WALLACE, GARY DONALD, US History Teacher; *b:* Great Falls, MT; *ed:* (BS) Soc Stud, 1970, (MS) Ed, 1974 W MT Coll; Several Seminars; MT Law Enforcement Acad, Care Team Drug & Alcohol Trng; Grad Courses His, Law, Counseling; Amer His Wkshps 1987-89; 1st Teaching MT Law Conference; *cr:* Soc Stud Teacher Paris Gibson Jr HS 1970-73, West Jr HS 1973-85, C M Russell HS 1985-; His Instr Park Coll, Malmstrom AFB 1989-; *ai:* Adv Honor Society 1986-, Stu Government 1987-; Close-Up Fnd Coord; NEA Life Mem 1970-; MT Ed Assn 1970-; Cascade Cty Historical Society Bd Mem 1983-84; NASSP Division of Sch Act 1988-; Order of De Molay (Organist 1964-66, Adv 1969-72), Chevalier Legion of Honor 1967, 1980; Scottish Rite Organist 1969-, Knight Commander Court of Honor 1981; Uptown Optimist Club Secy 1981-, Life Membership 1987; City of Great Falls Certificate of Appreciation 1987; Du Fresne Fnd Awd; C M Russell HS Outstanding Educator Awd 1989; C M Russell Chapter NHS Doctor of Service Awd 1990; *office:* Charles M Russell HS 228 17th Ave N W Great Falls MT 59404

WALLACE, GEORGE WEST, 5th Grade Teacher; *b:* Buffalo, NY; *m:* Therese Marie O Grady; *ed:* (BS) Ed, 1969, (MS) Ed, 1973 SUNY Coll Buffalo; *cr:* 5th Grade Teacher Orchard Park Cntrl Schls 1969-; *ai:* Ed & Publisher of Creative Writing Magazine; Orchard Park Teachers Assn Mem 1969-, Outstanding Teacher 1984-85; NY St United Teachers, AFT Mem 1969-; Niagara Frontier Bicycle Club Inc Mem 1987-; Orchard Park Jaycees Mem 1977-80; Orchard Park Running Club Mem 1982-86; Founder South Davis Flag Team & Monday Morning Radio Show; Organized & Implemented 1st Cmptr Lab at South Davis Elem Sch; Constructed Castle in Classroom; *office:* Orchard Park Cntrl Schls S Davis Elem Orchard Park NY 14127

WALLACE, JOHN WAYNE, Eighth Grade Teacher; *b:* Davis, OK; *m:* Nancy Lynn Moore; *c:* Leslie J., Scott D.; *ed:* (BA) Soc Sci, Chico St 1961; Quest Instr; Upper Division Unions Toward Several Degrees; *cr:* Teacher Weaverville Elem Sch 1961-64, Loma Vista Elem Sch 1965-66, Weaverville Elem Sch 1966-; *ai:* Class Adv; 8th Grade Sacramento Trip & Upper Grade Elective Coord; Graduation Requirements Sch Comm; Weaverville Elem Head Teacher; CTA, NEA 1961-; TCTA Pres 1963-64; WESTA Pres 1975; Weaverville Lions Club Pres 1970-71; Masonic Lodge #27 Chaplain 1978-80; Ford Fnd Grant Team Soc Sci 1965-66; Team Leader Teaching Team; *home:* PO Box 152 Weaverville CA 96093

WALLACE, KURT ALISON, Math/Computer Prog Teacher; *b:* Greenfield, IA; *m:* Lynne Elaine Prusha; *ed:* (BA) Industrial Arts/Math/Coaching, Westmar Coll 1985; Project Teach; Madeline Hunter; Assertive Discipline Lee Center; *cr:* Math Teacher/Cmptr Prgm BGM 1985-; *ai:* Asst Ftbl & Head Wrestling, Phase III & Wellness Comm, Soph Class Spon; Wrestling Coaches Assn 1988-, Nom for Coach of Yr 1990; MYF Chm 1989-; *home:* 212 High St Box 20 Brooklyn IA 52211

WALLACE, LINDA KAY, 5th Grade Teacher; *b:* Ilion, NY; *m:* Henry C.; *c:* Austin K. Thomas III, John Z. Thomas, Leda M. Thomas; *ed:* (BA) Elem Ed, 1977, (APC) Elem Ed, 1988 Univ of NV Las Vegas; Advanced Prof Certificate; *cr:* 6th Grade Teacher Smithfield Mid Sch; 4th/5th Grade Teacher Urbana Elem; *ai:* Team Leader; Coaching & Cooperative Learning Team; Effective Teacher Leader Prgm; Gifted & Talented Rep; Frederick Cty Teachers Assn Rep 1989-; MD St Teachers Assn Exhibits Comm 1989-; NEA; Francis Scott Key; Amer Legion Auxiliary Pres 1988-; Western MD Amer Legion Auxiliary Cmmty Chm 1989-; PTA Teacher Rep; *office:* Urbana Elem Sch 3554 Urbana Pike Frederick MD 21701

WALLACE, MARY KERSHAW, Social Studies Teacher; *b:* Harrisburg, PA; *m:* George E.; *c:* Eric, Jason, Damon; *ed:* (BA) Span/His, NC Cntrl Univ 1958; (MA) His, Hampton Univ 1968; Coll of William & Mary, Old Dominion Univ; *cr:* Span Teacher Clearwater HS 1959-60, G W Carver & Eaton Jr HS 1960-69; Dept Chairperson/His Teacher Syms Jr HS 1970-86; His Teacher Bethel Sr HS 1986-; *ai:* Coord Gifted Ed; Spon Odyssey of Mind; NEA, VA Ed Assn, Hampton Ed Assn, VA Cncl Soc Stud; Delta Sigma Theta; Hampton Chapter of Links Inc VP 1982-83; Jack & Jill of America Inc Mother of Yr; *home:* 145 Pamela Dr Hampton VA 23666

WALLACE, MURIEL ORITA, Kindergarten Teacher; *b:* St Thomas, VI; *m:* Romel Valentino Sr.; *c:* Elizabeth, Romel Jr., Andrea; *ed:* (BA) Elem Ed/Early Chldhd Ed, Univ of VI 1974; *cr:* Kndgtn Teacher Michael Kirwin Terrace Sch 1975-85, Gladise Gabriel Schls 1985-; *ai:* NAEYC 1988-; Rdng Cncl of VI, Natl Cncl of Negro Women Inc 1987-; Iota Phi Lambda (Mem, Journalist) 1986.

WALLACE, NATHAN, Secondary Teacher/Adminstrator; *b:* San Diego, CA; *w:* Janet L. Henline (dec); *c:* Scott, Laura, Daniel; *ed:* (BA) Soc Sci, 1959, (MA) Curr/Instruction, 1963 San Diego St; Grad Course, San Diego St; *cr:* Teacher Granger Jr HS 1956-64, Castle Park HS 1964-; *ai:* Chrstn Club Adv; 7th-8th Grade Team Bkstbl Coach Hilltop Jr HS; Patrick Henry Medallion Patriotic Achievement 1989.

WALLACE, NEIL D., Science Teacher; *b:* Athens, OH; *m:* Camille Lynn Stanson; *c:* Tyler, Jennifer; *ed:* (BSED) Earth Sci/General Sci, OH Univ 1974; (MED) Scndry Admin, OH Univ 1981; Post Masters Stud in Ed, Ashland Coll, OH Univ, Wright St Univ; OH Energy Ed Conferences; *cr:* Summer Youth Employment Training Prgm Coord Tri-Cty JVS 1983-87; Teacher 1974-, Admin Asst 1982- New Lexington Jr HS; *ai:* SCUBA Elem Stu Introduction & Scndry Stu Experience; Sci Fair Adv; Natl Sci Teachers Assn; Kenney Memorial Wesleyan Church (Bd Mem 1987-, Trustee 1988-, Financial Guidance 1987-); Martha Jennings Fnd Jennings Scholar 1979-80; *home:* 10 Cardiff Ln Athens OH 45701

WALLACE, ROBERT SCOTT, Social Studies Teacher; *b:* San Carlos, CA; *m:* Linda Ann Hawkins; *c:* Trevor Hawkins, Collin W., Jarred L.; *ed:* (BA) His, Univ of N CO 1975; Grad Stud Geography, Eng, Counseling; *cr:* Teacher/Coach N Valley Mid Sch 1977, S Valley Mid Sch 1978-; Coach Valley HS 1987-; *ai:* Dist Affective Ed Action Comm; Mid Sch & HS Transition Team; 7th-8th Grade Ftbl, Frosh Jr Var Bsbl Coach; Stu Cncl Spon 1981-89; Chm Dist Soc Stud Textbook Selection Comm 1982; Dist Soc Stud Curr Comm 1985-86; Developed Dist-Wide 8th Grade Affective Ed Curr 1986; Dist Profession Rights & Responsibilities Comm 1985-86; Valley Ed Assn (Pres 1981-83, Building Rep); *home:* 3813 W 6th St Greeley CO 80634

WALLACE, RONNIE GLENN, Language Arts Teacher; *b:* Durant, OK; *m:* Jane Brantley-Wallace;; *c:* Matthew B.; *ed:* (BA) Lang Art Ed, 1977, (MS) Lang Art Ed, 1983 SE OK St Univ; *cr:* Lang Art Teacher Colbert Public Schls 1978-; *ai:* Frosh Class Spon; OK Ed Assn, NEA 1978-; Kappa Delta Pi 1976-; Durant Jaycees 1984-; Collection of Poems Published; *office:* Colbert Public Sch Box 310 Colbert OK 74733

WALLACE, TERRY WHITE, Mathematics Teacher; *b:* Decatur, AL; *m:* Edison Kim; *ed:* (BS) Math, Athens St Coll 1979; Numerous Cmptr Wkshps, Basic Programming Courses, Jr Coll; Sign Lang; Instruction Teaching Handicapped Children; *cr:* Classroom Teacher Priceville Sch 1979-; *ai:* Beta Club; Math Team Coach; Cmptr Lab Coord; Various Church Act; Outstanding Young Educator Nom 1988-89; *office:* Priceville Jr HS Rt 4 Box 114 Decatur AL 35603

WALLACE, THOMAS CHARLES, English Department Chairman; *b:* Philadelphia, PA; *c:* Stephanie, Christina; *ed:* (BA) Fr - Summa Cum Laude, Marshall Univ 1971; (MA) Fr, 1976, (MA) Eng, 1978 MI St Univ; Studied Under Madeline Hunter AZ St Univ; *cr:* Eng as Foreign Lang Teacher Coll Denseignement General W Africa 1972-75; Eng/Span/Fr Teacher Flint Chrstn

Sch 1978-80, Scottsdale Chrstn Acad 1980-87; Educl Consultant Genesee Intermediate Sch Dist 1987-88; Eng Dept Chm N Branch Wesleyan Acad 1988-; *ai:* MI Dept of Ed Goals & Objectives for Foreign Lang Ed, Global/Intnl Ed Guidelines Project Comm; Sr Class Spon; NCTE, MI Foreign Lang Assn, Alliance Francaise, Phi Kappa Phi Mem; Church Youth Classes (Teacher, Teacher Trainer); Pi Delta Phi Schlsp Grad Stud Fr; Project Dir MI EESA Exemplary & Demonstration Educl Project Grant; *office:* N Branch Wesleyan Acad 3164 N Branch Rd North Branch MI 48461

WALLACE, VALERIA HEDRICK, Third Grade Teacher; *b:* Greensboro, NC; *m:* Felix W.; *c:* Troy J., Kristie F. A.; *ed:* (BA) Primary Ed, Bennett Coll 1964; A&T St Univ; Inservice Wkshp Guilford Cty Schls; Learning Style Inst; *cr:* 2nd Grade Teacher Dunbar Elem 1964-67; 4th Grade Teacher Popular Grove 1967-68; 1st/3rd Grade Teacher Brightwood Elem Sch 1969-; *ai:* Curr Comm; Rdng Lang Art Rep; Grade Level Chm; NC Assn of Educators, NEA 1964-; Cedar Grove Baptist Church (Hospitality Chm, Choir Adv) 1970-; Black Caucas 1989-; *office:* Brightwood Elem Sch 2500 Lees Chapel Rd Greensboro NC 27405

WALLACE, VICKIE KINSLEY, Kindergarten Teacher; *b:* Morgantown, WV; *m:* Conley E. Jr.; *c:* Bruce A., Christopher P.; *ed:* (BS) Elem Ed, WV Univ 1965; (MED) Early Chldhd, Lynchburg Coll 1987; *cr:* 4th-6th Grade Teacher 2nd Ward Elem 1965-67; 3rd Grade Teacher Poquoson Elem 1967-69; 5th Grade Teacher Dare Elem 1971-72; Kndgtn Teacher Bedford Primary 1977-; *ai:* Grade Level Chm; Supt Advisory Comm Rep; NEA, VEA, PAECE, Kappa Delta Pi; *office:* Bedford Primary Sch 807 College St Bedford VA 24523

WALLEMAN, DARYL, Social Studies Teacher; *b:* St Louis, MO; *m:* Teresa Sheldon; *c:* Kimberley Walleman Diamond; *ed:* (BSE) His, 1971, (MA) His, 1976 NE MO St; Grad Stud; *cr:* Soc Stud Teacher Milan Jr HS 1971-72, Mehlville HS 1972-; *ai:* Phi Alpha Theta Mem 1976-; *office:* Mehlville HS 3120 Lemay Ferry Rd Saint Louis MO 63125

WALLENS, THOMAS J., English Teacher/Yearbook Adv; *b:* Aurora, IL; *m:* Gail M. De Dera; *c:* Sarah, Joseph, Diana; *ed:* (AGE) Liberal Art, Mc Henry Cty Coll 1970; (BSED) Speech Comm, 1973, (MA) Eng, 1981 N IL Univ; Post Grad Stud Journalism, Univ of WI Whitewater 1982; *cr:* Eng Teacher/Debate Coach 1973-82, Eng Teacher/Publications Adv 1983-89 Rockford West HS; Eng Teacher/Yrbk Adv Rockford Auburn HS 1990; *ai:* Rockford Fed of Teachers VP 1973-84; Rockford Ed Assn; *office:* Rockford Auburn Hs 5110 Auburn St Rockford IL 61103

WALLER, ANNE BONDS, 5th Grade Teacher; *b:* Kilgore, TX; *m:* Carnell; *c:* Gordon; *ed:* (BS) Elem Ed, 1966; (MED) Elem Ed, 1973 Stephen F Austin Univ; North TX Univ; *cr:* 4th Grade Teacher Overton Elem 1966-71; 6th Grade Teacher Elder Elem 1971-78; 5th Grade Teacher Eastview Elem 1978-; *ai:* Gifted/Talented Comm Mem; TX St Teachers Assn 1971-; Classroom Teachers Assn VP 1971-89; Alpha Delta Kappa (Corresp Secy/Treas/Historian 1973-); *home:* Rt 2 Box 153 Kilgore TX 75662

WALLER, CAROL, Third Grade Teacher; *b:* Nashville, TN; *m:* Robert Curtis Sr.; *c:* Robert C. Waller Jr., Wendell Blake; *ed:* (BA) Elem Ed, Univ of Chattanooga 1965; *cr:* 3rd Grade Teacher Alpine Crest Elem 1965-87, Signal Mtn Elem 1987-; *ai:* Rdng Comm Grade Level Chr 3; Celebration Comm; Finance Comm; TEA 1965-; NEA 1965-; HCEA Soc Comm Chm 1986-88; Distinguished Classroom Teacher 1985; ETEA 1965-; Red Bank Outstanding Educator 1985; Alpha Delta Pi State Day Chr/Record Secy 1965; Outstanding AAum 1978-85/Best Alum 1972-79/Mae Saunders Awd 1984; Alpha Delta Kappa Guard/Corresp Secy 1972-86; Teachers Chatta-Girls Collition 1988-; Dir Alpha Delta Pi Natl Pledge Comm; Career Ladder III Teacher St Ed Dept 1985-.

WALLER, DAVID LEE, Vice Principal; *b:* Kalamazoo, MI; *m:* Amy Ethel Thacker; *ed:* (BA) Theology, Southern Coll 1969; (MED) Admin/Supervision, George Mason Univ 1986; Doctorate Admin/Supervision, George Mason Univ; *cr:* Teacher Highland Lakes Jr Acad 1969-73; Prin Fort Myers Jr Acad 1973-77, Jacksonville Jr Acad 1977-82; Vice Prin John Nevins Andrews Sch 1982-; *ai:* 8th Grade Class & Annual Spon; Sch Bd Mem; Finance Comm Mem; Chm Environmental Concerns Comm for Potomac Conference of 7th Day Adventists; ASCD Mem 1987-; *office:* John Nevins Andrews Sch 117 Elm Ave Takoma Park MD 20912

WALLER, MILDRED WALL, Retired Third Grade Teacher; *b:* Alto, TX; *m:* Carl R.; *c:* Phil R.; *ed:* (BSE) Elem Ed, SFA St Univ 1971; *cr:* 3rd Grade Teacher Joe Wright Elem 1972-88; *ai:* TX St Teachers Assn Life Mem 1971-; *home:* 1514 Quevado St Jacksonville TX 75766

WALLER, PHIL RAY, US History Teacher; *b:* Jacksonville, TX; *ed:* (BA) His/Eng 1972; (MED) His/Ed 1976 Stephen F Austin St Univ; *cr:* US His Teacher Jacksonville HS 1973-; *ai:* TX St Teachers Assn 1973-; Phi Alpha Theta-Natl His Honorary; Sigma Tau Delta-Natl Eng Honorary; Kappa Delta Pi-Nat; Teachers Ed Honorary; Phi Theta Kappa-Natl Jr Coll Honorary; *office:* Jacksonville H S 1602 Mason Dr Jacksonville TX 75766

WALLER, ROBERT BENJAMIN, Algebra II Teacher; *b:* Yazoo City, MS; *m:* Mila Jenkins; *c:* Brandi C., Adam B.; *ed:* (BSE) Phys Ed/Math, 1975, (MED) Guidance/Counseling, 1975 Delta St UniV; (MA) Mc Neese St Univ 1985; *cr:* Grad Asst Guidance Dept Delta St Univ 1974-75; Math Teacher/BB Coach Moss Point HS 1975-76; Math Teacher/Ftbl Coach Jennings HS 1977-79, Westlake HS 1980-; *ai:* Ftbl & Track Coach; Chm for Math Dept Westlake HS; Calcasieau Assn of Educators 1985-; LA Assn of Ed 1980-; Westlake United Meth Church (Pastor-Parish Comm 1986-, Admin Bd 1987-, Bd of Trustees 1985-88); Athletic Schlsp & Grad Assistantship Delta St Univ; *office:* Westlake HS 1000 Garden Dr Westlake LA 70669

WALLER-KEOHO, BARBARA ELAINE, Middle School Teacher; *b:* Thomaston, GA; *c:* Lara R.; *cr:* 5th Grade Teacher Watson Elem 1964-66; Teacher Carrollton Jr HS 1966-73; 7th Grade Teacher Griffin Mid Sch 1973-; *ai:* Spon Carrollton Jr HS Stu Newspaper; Supervising Teacher of Stu Teachers; Speaker What is Teaming Mentoring in Ed, Motivation; Mid Sch Organizational Restructure; Clark Cty & Carrollton City Schls Accredition Comm; Carrollton Assn of Educators Pres 1968; PTA 1964-; Prof Assn of Educators 1989-; Alpha Delta Kappa 1986-89; 1st Meth Church Organist 1967-73; Kingspring Baptist Church Organist 1985-; Stonewall Assn Bd Mem 1988-; GA Senate Music Industry Advisory Comm 1989-; Outstanding Young Women of Amer 1979; Grant His Inst W GA Coll 1966; Smyra Jaycees Outstanding Young Educator Awd 1977; Cobb Cty Teacher of Yr 1987-88, Sci Teacher of Yr 1985; *home:* 3506 Stonewall Pl NW Atlanta GA 30339

WALLESHAUSER, BARBARA MARY, Mathematics Instructor; *b:* Buffalo, NY; *m:* James J.; *c:* Mary B. Porter, James B.; *ed:* (BA) Math, D Youville Coll 1960; (MS) Math Ed, Canisius Coll 1976; Grad Stud Cmptr Courses, St Univ of NY Buffalo; *cr:* Math Instr Clarence Sr HS 1974-; *ai:* Schlsp & Awds Comm; Alpha Delta Kappa VP 1984-; Clarence Teachers Assn Building Rep 1984-88; Nativity Church Soup Kitchen Volunteer 1989-; *office:* Clarence Sr HS 9625 Main St Clarence NY 14031

WALLING, GREGORY ALLEN, Science Teacher/Play Director; *b:* Munday, TX; *ed:* (BS) Composite Sci, W TX St Univ 1984; *cr:* Sci Teacher 1984-, One Act Play Dir 1986- Aspermont Ind Sch Dist; *ai:* 1 Act Play Dir; UIL & Soph Class Spon; 1st Baptist Church; *home:* Rt 1 Box 331 Aspermont TX 79502

WALLIS, ALBERTA J., English Teacher; *b:* New York, NY; *m:* William Lee; *c:* Elizabeth, William, Michael; *ed:* (BA) Eng, Good Counsel Coll 1961; *cr:* Eng Teacher Sacred Heart HS 1961-67; *ai:* NCEA 1977-; *office:* St Mary on the Hill Sch 1220 Monte Sano Ave Augusta GA 30904

WALLIS, BARBARA PRINCE, Second Grade Teacher; *b:* Northampton, MA; *m:* Samuel Gilbert; *c:* David Norcross, Gregory T., Sally Prince Andriot; *ed:* (BS) Ed, Westfield Teachers Coll 1952; (MS) Ed, Lesley Coll 1979; *cr:* 1st Grade Teacher W Springfield Public Schls 1952-53, Oxnard Public Schls 1953-54; 4th Grade Teacher E Aurora Public Schls 1960, Cape Elizabeth Public Schls 1964-67; 2nd-4th Grade Teacher Sudbuury Public Schls 1968-; *ai:* Sudbury Teachers Assn (Bd Mem 1989-, VP 1979-80, Pres 1980-85); Framingham Cmmty Concerts Bd Mem 1971-84; Jr Assoc of Elliot Hospital 1961-64; *home:* 17 Chester Sq Gloucester MA 01930

WALLIS, MICHAELL JAMES, Technical Graphics Instructor; *b:* Doylestown, PA; *m:* Marcia A.; *c:* Lauren A., Robert C.; *ed:* (Ba) Industrial Technology, Millersville Univ 1973; (MS) Counseling Pysch, Trenton St Coll 1976; *cr:* Industrial Technology Instr Cntrl Bucks East HS 1973-; *ai:* HS Athletic Dir; Track & Golf Coach; Leaders Against Drugs; Masonic Lodge #127 1989-; Elected Supvr of Plumstead Township; *office:* Cntrl Bucks E HS Holicong & Anderson Rds Buckingham PA 18912

WALLMANN, BILLIE GOMEZ, Spanish/English/Lit Teacher; *b:* Havana, Cuba; *m:* Achim; *c:* David, Amy; *ed:* (BA) Span, 1972, (MA) Span, 1974 Purdue Univ; *cr:* Teaching Asst Purdue Univ 1972-74; Lecturer Marian Coll 1974-79, IUPUI 1975-81; Eng as Second Lang Teacher ELS Sch 1981-83; Span/Lit/Eng Teacher Frontier Mid Sch 1983-; *ai:* Jr HS Spon; Spelling Bee Chm; *office:* Frontier Mid Sch 8th & Prairie Brookston IN 47923

WALLMANN, EVELYN TSCHETTER, 2nd Grade Teacher; *b:* Bridgewater, SD; *m:* Kenneth L.; *c:* Twila M. Wallmann-Ford, Skyla R.; *ed:* (BA) Elem Ed, Huron Coll 1971; *cr:* Classroom Teacher Rural Hutchison Cty 1957-58, Rural Mc Cook Cty 1958-59, Rural Beadle Cty 1959-60; 2nd Grade Teacher Iroquois Sch Dist 2-3 1972-; *ai:* Adv when Prin is Absent; SD Ed Assn Mem; *home:* Rt 4 Box 299 Huron SD 57350

WALLOCH, HEIDI M. (HAYDUK), Vocal Music Teacher; *b:* Milwaukee, WI; *m:* Thomas M.; *c:* Kathryn, Anne, Allison; *ed:* (BSE) Music Ed, Univ of WI Whitewater 1976; Various Ed Courses & Wkshps; *cr:* Vocal Music Teacher Sch Dist of W Allis-W Milwaukee 1976-85, 1987-; *ai:* Pershing Elem Sch Chorus & Swing Choir Dir; Pershing Sch PTA Exec Bd 1976-85, 1987-; *home:* 2809 S Seymour Pl West Allis WI 53227

WALLOCH, LAWRENCE RAY, Third Grade Teacher; *b:* Los Angeles, CA; *m:* Jennifer Ann; *c:* Elysia; *ed:* (BA) Sociology, CA St Univ Long Beach 1970; Spec Ed, Teacher Cert; *cr:* Teacher of Emotionally Handicapped Paramount Sch Dist 1972-74; Spec Ed Resource Teacher Eagle Point Dist 9 1974-76; 1st/3rd-4th Grade Teacher Elk Trail Dist 9 1976-; *ai:* Supervise Sch Greenhouse; Multi-Disciplinary Team; Union Rep; *home:* 1900 Buck Rock Rd Trail OR 97541

WALLS, FAYE DRUMMOND, AP American History Teacher; *b:* Birmingham, AL; *m:* James Glenn; *c:* Jarrod, Jenny F.; *ed:* (BS) Scndry Ed/Soc Stud/Eng, Samford Univ 1971; *cr:* 11th/12th Grade Eng Teacher St Clair Cty HS 1971-72, Midfield HS 1972-77; 9th/10th Grade Eng Teacher Briarwood Chrstn Sch 1985-86; Advanced Placement Amer His Teacher Pelham HS 1986-; *ai:* Stu Cncl Spon; AL Cncl for Soc Stud Mem 1988-; Pelham HS Teacher of Yr 1989-; *office:* Pelham HS P O Box 38 Pelham AL 35124

WALLS, JILL K., Business Teacher; *b:* Ohio City, OH; *m:* Marvin D.; *c:* Karen Schroeder, Lori, Jason; *ed:* (BA) Comprehensive Bus/IOE, Univ of Findlay 1975; *cr:* Secy Marathon Oil Co 1959-67; Teacher Leipsic HS 1975-; *ai:* Adv Bus Prof of America; OH Ed Assn Treas 1982-; Bus Prof of America 1975-; *office:* Leipsic H S 232 Oak St Leipsic OH 45856

WALLS, JUDITH A., 3rd Grade Teacher; *b:* Lewes, DE; *ed:* (BS) Elem Ed, Salisbury St Coll 1975; (MS) Curr/Instruction, DE St Coll 1990; *cr:* 1st Grade Teacher H O Brittingham Elem 1975-76; Savannah Road Elem 1976-80; 3rd Grade Teacher Savannah Road Elem/Shields Elem 1980-; *ai:* Child Study Team; Savannah Road/Shields PTA Pres; Score 1975-; DSEA 1980-; CHEA 1980-; NEA 1980-; Girl Scouts of America Leader 1975-79; De Janecees Mem 1975-79; Milton Janecees VP 1975-79 Outstanding 1st Year Janecee of Yr 1975; Outstanding Janecee of Yr 1976; De Jayceettes Mem 1980-82; Harrington Jayceettes Pres 1981-82; De Jayceettes St Internal VP 1979-81; Outstanding St Officer of Yr 1983; Region II Internal VP Jayceettes Awd 1983; De Jayceettes Extrordinaire 1984;De Jaycees VP 1982-84; Excl of Exemplary Attendance 1983-; Outstanding Young Women of Amer 1980-82/1985-86; Nom Teacher of Yr 1989; *office:* Shields Elem Sch Sussex Dr Lewes DE 19958

WALLS, KAREN NANCY, 7th/8th Grade Lit Teacher; *b:* Huntsville, AL; *ed:* (BS) Elem Ed, Jacksonville St Univ 1975; (MS) Elem Ed, AL A&M Univ 1979; *cr:* 7th/8th Grade Lit Teacher New Hope HS 1976-; *ai:* Textbook Selection Comm; Key Rdng Teacher; Field Day Chairperson; Lions Quest Prgm; AL Ed Assn Contact Team; New Hope HS Day Spon Awd; Broadway Theater League Field Trips Chairperson; World Book Rdng Prgm Spon; AL Cncl Teachers of Eng, Intnl Rdng Assn, AL Rdng Assn, Patchwork Rdng Cncl; AL Classroom Teachers Assn Contact Person; Alpha Delta Kappa Treas 1990; NEA Delegate 1982; Madison Cty Ed Assn (Building Rep, Bd of Dir) 1981-89; AL Ed Assn Delegate 1981-; PTA Faculty Rep 1990; American Red Cross 1979-; United Way; Big Cove Holiness Church; 4-H Club Spon 1985-86; Huntsville Christmas Charities; Chi-Ho Mansion; Huntsville/Madison Cty Hospitality House; Teacher-Made Exhibits 2nd Place 1981, 3rd Place 1982, Southeast Regional Assn Classroom Teachers; Nom Outstanding Young Educator Huntsville Jaycees 1985; Teacher Volunteer Honoree 1990 New Hope Sch Yrbk; 1st Runner Up Teacher of Yr Madison Cty Schls 1990; *home:* 180 Mohawk Rd Brownsboro AL 35741

WALLS, VIVIAN BURGESS, First Grade Teacher; *b:* Bangor, ME; *m:* Bernard Kelsie; *c:* Anthony, Randal, Karen; *ed:* (BS) Elem Ed, Univ of ME 1962; *cr:* 1st Grade Teacher Valentine Sch 1962-64; 2nd Grade Teacher Hermon Elem Sch 1966; 6th Grade Teacher Rose M Gaffney Sch 1975-76; 1st Grade Teacher Hillgrove Sch 1976-85, Campus Sch 1985-86, Rose M Gaffney Sch 1986-; *ai:* Delta Kappa Gamma 1988; Little League Sftbl VP 1979-84; Holy Name Parish Cncl Pres 1984-86; Recreation Comm Chairperson 1988-; *office:* Rose M Gaffney Sch 99 Court St Machias ME 04654

WALLSCHLAEGER, JOY DOROTHY (REDLIN), 6th-8th Grade History Teacher; *b:* Milwaukee, WI; *m:* David; *c:* Amy, Todd; *ed:* (BS) Bio/Life Sci/His, Univ of WI La Crosse 1971; Drug Courses; Continuing Ed Prgms for Teachers; Space Acad Prgm for Teachers Huntsville; *cr:* Teacher Oak Grove Jr HS 1971; Substitute Teacher Milwaukee Sch Dist 1971-73; Sci Resource Center Brown Deer HS 1973-74; Teacher ST Marys Parish Sch 1976-; *office:* St Marys Parish Sch 9553 W Edgerton Ave Hales Corners WI 53130

WALLSHIELD, ERNEST MATTHEW, JR., Social Studies Dept Chair; *b:* Louisville, KY; *m:* Pat; *c:* John; *ed:* (BA) His, Univ of Louisville 1968; (MA) Ed, Spalding Coll 1972; Rank I Univ of Louisville; *cr:* Airman USAF 1960-64; Foreman Brown & Williamson Tobacco Company 1970; Teacher Thomas Jefferson Jr HS 1968-73; Team Leader/Soc Stud Dept Head Teacher Virginia Carrithers Mid Sch 1973-; *ai:* Chess Club & Chess Tourn Spon; Lasso & Discipline Comm Mem; Supervising Teacher for Stu Teachers; NEA, KY Ed Assn, JCTA Mem 1968-; *office:* Carrithers Mid Sch 4320 Billtown Rd Louisville KY 40299

WALLWORK, ANNE E. SONNENSCHEIN, Kindergarten Teacher; *b:* Newark, NJ; *m:* John; *c:* Richard; *ed:* (BS) Kndgtn/Primary, Newark St Teachers Coll 1955; *cr:* 3rd Grade Teacher Madison Ave Sch 1955-56; Kndgtn Teacher Union Ave Sch 1956-59;Kndgtn Teacher 1967-74; 1st Grade Resource Teacher 1974-80; Kndgtn Teacher 1981- Menlo Park Terrace Sch; *ai:* Prof Membership NAEYC; NJAKE Middlesey Cty Rep 1988-; Governors Teacher Recognition Prgm 1988; *office:* School 19 Menlo Park Terr Maryknoll St Metuchen NJ 08840

WALMER, ELLEN K. (GLAZIER), 3rd Grade Teacher; *b:* Gardiner, ME; *m:* John I.; *c:* Bruce, Keith; *ed:* (BS) Ed, Gorham St Teachers Coll 1957; *cr:* 3rd-6th Grade Elem Teacher Frederick Harris Sch 1957-; *ai:* AFT, MA Fed of Teachers, Springfield Fed of Teachers 1958-80; NEA, MA Ed Assn, Springfield Ed Assn 1985-; *home:* 15 Buick St Springfield MA 01118

WALPOLE, DAVID BUNCH, Mathematics Teacher; *b:* Indianapolis, IN; *m:* Debra Mae Johnson; *c:* Leslie A., David M., Nicholas J.; *ed:* (BA) Math, Wabash Coll 1977; (MAT) Math, Purdue Univ 1984; Schl Admin Courses; *cr:* Math Teacher/Head

Wrestling Coach Decatur Cntrl 1977-; *office:* Decatur Cntrl HS 5251 Kentucky Ave Indianapolis IN 46241

WALRATH, PAT ANN (COLLINS), K-3rd Grade Elementary Teacher; *b:* Wilkes-Barre, PA; *m:* Dan G.; *c:* Jennifer, Ryan, John; *ed:* (BA) Spec Ed 1976, Elem Ed, 1978 Kearney St Coll; *cr:* Kndgtn/Spec Ed Teacher Wolbach Public Sch 1976-77; K-12th Grade Spec Ed Teacher Newman Grove Public Sch 1978-80; K-6th Grade Elem Teacher Midvale 4-M 1980-81; K-8th Grade Elem Teacher 1981-82, 5th-8th Grade Elem Teacher 1984-85; K-2nd Grade Elem Teacher 1985-89, K-3rd Grade Elem Teacher 1989- Primrose PublicSch; *ai:* Music K-6; Art K-6; Boone Cty Ed Assn Pres 1986-; NEA; NE St Ed Assn; Bible Sch (Aide 1968-72, Teacher 1972-76); *home:* Box 96 Primrose NE 68655

WALSH, BONNY TRENT, English as Second Lang Teacher; *b:* Evanston, IL; *m:* James P.; *c:* Brian, Dennis; *ed:* (BA) Eng, Univ of Santa Clara 1966; *cr:* Teacher Memorial Jr HS 1967-73; ESL Specialist Whittier Elem 1977-81; Teacher Lindbergh Jr HS 1981-84, Lakewood HS 1984-; *ai:* Dist LEP Plan, Dist Soc Stud Comm; Teachers Assn of Long Beach; Mentor Teacher 1984-93; *office:* Lakewood H S 4400 Briercrest Ave Lakewood CA 90713

WALSH, IRENE C. PLISKO, Science Dept Chair; *b:* Kingston, PA; *m:* Gerard P.; *c:* Maureen, Brian; *ed:* (BS) Chem, Coll Misericordia 1965; (MED) Scndry Sci Ed, Univ of Pittsburgh 1974; *cr:* Analytical Chemist Bettis Atomic Power Lab 1966-67; Physics Teacher St Wendelin HS 1967-68; Sci Teacher St Bernadette Sch 1974-75; Chem Teacher/Sci Dept Chairperson St Andrews Episcopal Sch 1979-; *ai:* SGA Spon; NSTA, MD Assn Sci Teachers; Woodrow Wilson Inst for HS Chem Teachers 1986; Natl Sci Fnd Sponsored Grant Women in Sci Prgm Amer Univ 1976-77; *office:* St Andrews Episcopal Sch 8935 Bradmoor Dr Bethesda MD 20817

WALSH, JACQUELINE M., Director of Elem Education; *b:* Pawtucket, RI; *ed:* (BS) Elem Ed, 1969, (MED) Elem Ed, 1972, (CAGS) Curr, 1983 RI Coll; (PHD) Curr/Instruction, Univ of CT 1989; *cr:* 6th Grade Teacher Agnes E Little Sch 1969-82; Elem Gifted Prgm Teacher Pawtucket Sch Dept 1982-84; Elem Prin Currin-McCabe Sch 1984-89; Dir of Elem Ed Pawtucket Sch Dept 1989-; *ai:* ASCD; Pi Lambda Theta; RI Assn of Elem Sch Prin & NAESP; Delta Kappa Gamma (St Secy, Chapter Secy & Pres), Intnl Schlrshp, St Schlrshp; Quota Club of Pawtucket 1989; *office:* Pawtucket Sch Dept Park Pl Pawtucket RI 02860

WALSH, JOHN ALLEN, Assistant Principal; *b:* Ft Worth, TX; *c:* Heather; *ed:* (BA) Phys Ed, Univ of TX Arlington 1981; (MS) Public Sch Admin, Univ of N TX 1989; Math, UTA; Cmptr Literacy; *cr:* Math/Cmptr Teacher/Coach Jefferson Mid Sch 1981-88; Admin Intern/Asst Prin Bonham & Milam Elem 1989-; *ai:* TAESP, Phi Delta Kapa 1989-; *office:* Bonham Elem Sch 1309 E Coral Way Grand Prairie TX 75051

WALSH, LUCILLE NILES, Reading Teacher; *b:* Boston, MA; *m:* Michael Stephen; *ed:* (BA) Ed, Boston Coll 1972; (MED) Rdng, Suffolk Univ 1982; In-Service, Cmptr Courses; Various Seminars & Wkshps; *cr:* Elem Teacher 1972-80, Acting Asst Prin 1979-80 Gridley Bryant Sch; 3rd-6th Grade Teacher Adams Sch 1980-82, Lincoln Hancock Cmmty Sch 1982-83; 6th-8th Grade Rdng Specialist Cntrl Mid Sch 1983-; *ai:* Blue Hills Tennis League Treas; Alpha Delta Kappa Mem 1990; *office:* Cntrl Mid Sch 1012 Hancock St Quincy MA 02169

WALSH, MARION WYWORSKI, Science Department Chair; *b:* Avoca, PA; *m:* Thomas M.; *c:* Raoul, Kevin, Kim; *ed:* (BS) Chem, East Stroudsburg St Coll 1951; Chem, Univ of Scranton & Wilkes Univ; *cr:* Sci Teacher Glen Burnie HS 1951-53; Chem Teacher/Sci Dept Chairperson Bishop Hannan HS 1962-; *ai:* PA Jr Acad of Sci Adv; Lackawanna River Corridor Watch Network; Amer Chemical Society 1970-; PTA Pres 1970; Altar & Rosary Society Pres 1972; Fox Hill Cntry Club 1980-; Natl Sci Fnd Grant.

WALSH, MARY RHETA, Fourth & Fifth Grade Teacher; *b:* Valdese, NC; *ed:* (BA) Grammar, Lenoir-Rhyne Coll 1962; *cr:* 4th Thru 6th Grade Teacher Chesterfield Elem 1962-; *ai:* Chairperson Fund Raising Comm; Testing Coord; NCAE, NEA Mem 1962-; NCAE Treas 1975-81, Membership Chairperson 1984-; East Valdese Baptist Church; Old Colony Players Mem 1966-76; Outdoor Drama Actree 1967-75; Teacher of the Yr Chesterfield Elem Sch 1976; *office:* Chesterfield Elem Sch Rt 3 Box 945 Morganton NC 28655

WALSH, MICHAEL PADEN, Mathematics Dept Chair/ Teacher; *b:* Indianapolis, IN; *c:* Darin, Deanna; *ed:* (BS) Math, 1969, (MS) Math, 1972 IN St; *cr:* Teacher Woodview Jr HS 1969-72; Teacher/Dept Chm Stonybrook Jr HS 1972-; *ai:* 8th Grade Head Ftbl; Math Team Contests; Stonybrook Improvement Cncl; NCTM, IN Cncl Teachers of Math, NEA, IN St Teachers Assn; Sigma Chi 1964-; Englewood Lodge 715 F&AM 1971-; *office:* Stonybrook Jr HS 11300 Stonybrook Dr Indianapolis IN 46229

WALSH, RICHARD HAROLD, Librarian; *b:* Bellingham, WA; *m:* Rebecca Jane; *c:* Nathan, Nicholas; *ed:* (BAED) Ed, 1969, (BA) Poly Sci, 1969 W WA St Coll; (MED) Admin, W WA Univ 1982; Willamette Univ Coll of Law, OR Coll of Ed; *cr:* Prin/ Teacher Bureau of Indian Affairs 1972-77; Eng Teacher Coupeville HS 1977-78; Teacher Sunnyside Elem 1978-89; Librarian Marysville Jr HS 1989-; *ai:* Bsktbl Coach; Intramural Dir; Marysville Ed Assn, WA Ed Assn 1978-; W WA Univ Alumni Assn Pres 1979-, Distinguished Service Awd 1984; Adopt-A-Stream Fnd Treas 1986-; Teacher of Yr Marysville Sch Dist 1984; Christa Mc Auliffe Awd St of WA 1989; Golden Acorn Awd PTSA of Marysville 1982; *home:* 1909 W Big Lake Blvd Mount Vernon WA 98273

WALSH, VIANNEY, Spanish/7th Grade Teacher; *b:* Kill, Ireland; *ed:* (BA) Geography, Natl Univ of Ireland 1965; (HDE) Scndry Ed, 1967, Eng, 1976 Univ Coll Cork of Ireland 1976; Grad Stud Mt St Agnes Coll; *cr:* Pre-Sch Teacher N Presentation Ireland 1952-56; 1st/3rd/4th Grade Teacher Parochial 1956-62; 3rd Grade Elem Teacher Farrauree Ireland 1962-64; 7th-12th Grade Geography Teacher N Presentation HS Ireland 1965-72; Prin N Presentation Scndry Ireland 1972-76; 7th Grade/Soc Stud/ Math/7th/8th Grade Span Teacher Sacred Heart 1976-; *office:* Sacred Heart Sch 250 S Davis Dr Warner Robins GA 31088

WALSH, YVONNE KATHERYN, 4th Grade Teacher; *b:* Detroit, MI; *m:* James B. III; *c:* Matthew, Marcus, Katheryn; *ed:* (BA) Eng, Adrian Coll 1975; (MA) Elem Ed/Rdng, Siena Heights Coll 1986; *cr:* 4th Grade Teacher Sand Creek Cmmnty Schls 1977-; *ai:* Sand Creek Ed Assn Treas 1983-; Lenawee Rdng Assn Treas 1978-80; *home:* 2360 Porter Hwy Adrian MI 49221

WALSTON, KATHLEEN BARNHART, 4th Grade Teacher; *b:* Dougherty, IA; *m:* Dean; *c:* Susan Ziegenbusch, Dennis; *ed:* (BA) Elem Ed, Upper IA 1964; Grad Credits, Univ of IA; *cr:* 5th/6th Grade Teacher 1947-48 , 6th Grade Teacher 1948-50 Monticello IA; 4th Grade Teacher West Delaware 1961-88; *ai:* Talented & Gifted Curr Wellness for Staff Comm; ISEA, NEA; IA Rdng Cncl Secy 1980-83; BPW 1948-50; Amer Legion Aux Secy 1960-70; Ed Chm; Article on Teaching Math Facts in Grade Teacher & Teaching Math Facts in Area Keystone Bulletin; *home:* RR 5 Box 21 Manchester IA 52057

WALTER, DOROTHY RALSTEN, Bio Teacher/Staff Dev Trainer; *b:* Clifton Forge, VA; *m:* David L.; *c:* Kimberly L., Christopher L.; *ed:* (BA) Bio, Emory & Henry Coll 1969; (MS) Ed Dev, Wilkes Univ 1990; Cert, Shippensburg Univ; Summer Inst of Biotechnology, Univ of Rochester; Models of Teaching, Bruce Joyce-Washington Univ; Learning Styles of At-Risk Stus, Rita Dunn-St Johns Univ; *cr:* Math Teacher 1969-70, Substitute Teacher 1970-76 James Buchanan HS; Bio Teacher 1979-89, Bio Teacher/Staff Dev Trainer 1989- Waynesboro Area Sr HS; *ai:* Stu Cncl Adv; NEA, Waynesboro Area Ed Assn, PA St Ed Assn, Assn for Supervision & Curr Dev, NABT; March of Dimes Division Bd Chairperson 1988-; Outstanding Teacher & Univ Lecturer Shippensburg Univ 1986-87; Gonzalas Memorial Faculty Recognition Awd 1985; Math-Sci Mini Grant Lincoln Intermediate Unit; *office:* Waynesboro Area Sr H S 550 East 2nd Street Waynesboro PA 17268

WALTER, GEORGIA HILL, Fifth Grade Teacher; *b:* Evanston, IL; *c:* Elizabeth Baranski, Katherine, Laura Crain, Anne; *ed:* (BS) Child Dev, Rockford Coll 1980; (MS) Ed, Loyola Univ 1982; Gifted Ed; Literature; *cr:* 3rd Grade Teacher North Elem Sch 1980; 5th Grade Teacher Canterbury Sch 1980-; *ai:* Gifted Ed Dist Comm Bldg Coord; Rdng Adoption Comm; Soc Stud Adoption Comm; TAT Team; Delta Kappa Gamma; Congregational Church; Girl Scouts of Amer; Mayflower Descendants; Dist Apple Awd Above & Beyond; Master Teacher St Nom.

WALTER, JAMES COYNE, Band Director; *b:* Port Townsend, WA; *m:* Linda Griffin; *c:* Kerry, Melissa Bjorn, Ryan, Devin Bjorn; *ed:* (BA) Music Ed, Cntrl WA Univ 1966; Grad Stud W WA Univ, Cntrl WA Univ, Univ of WA, Seattle Pacific Univ; *cr:* Music Dir Napavine Sch Dist 1966-68; Band Dir Evergreen Mid Sch 1968-84, Cascade HS 1975-84, Evergreen Mid Sch 1984-; *ai:* Music Educators Natl Conference 1966-; Sno-King Music Educators (Secy 1989-) 1968-; NEA 1966-; Choir Dir Prince of Peace Luth Church 1968-69, Trinity Luth Church 1969-71, 1st United Meth Church 1972-84, Trinity Episcopal Church 1984-89; *office:* Evergreen Mid Sch 7621 Beverly Ln Everett WA 98203

WALTER, JUDITH JOHNSON, Science Teacher; *b:* Coleman, GA; *m:* Hawley Drayton; *c:* Susan, Joe; *ed:* (BS) Chem, Univ of GA 1961; (MED) Bio, GA Southwestern 1974; Advanced Placement Bio Wkshp; Univ of FL Cmptr Wkshp for Teachers; *cr:* Sci Teacher Sylvan Hills HS 1961-64, Albany HS 1975-82, Randolph Clay HS 1982-85, Thomas Cty Cntrl HS 1985-; *ai:* Tri-Hi-Y Adv; Sci Olympiad Coach; NEA, GEA 1985-89; Prof Assn of GA Educators 1989-; GA Sci Teachers Assn, Natl Sci Teachers Assn, Assn for Supervision & Curr Dev 1989-; Natl Sci Fellowship Grant 1963; Outstanding Bio Teacher of GA 1976; SECMC Teacher Nominee 1980; Thomas Cty Outstanding Sci Teacher 1989; Nominee for WCTV 6 Excl Awd 1990; *home:* 111 Roundcrest Dr Thomasville GA 31792

WALTER, JUDITH VAN DYCK, Mathematics Teacher; *b:* Portsmouth, VA; *m:* Donald L.; *c:* Jeffrey, James; *ed:* (BA) Math, Duke Univ 1963; (MSED) Ed, N IL Univ 1983; Cmptr Sci, Univ IL Chicago; *cr:* Systems Engineer IBM Corp 1963-67; Programming Instr Mc Donnell-Douglas Aircraft 1967-69; Math Teacher Palatine-Schaumburg HS Dist 211 1978-; *ai:* Math Team Orals Coach; *office:* Schaumburg HS 1100 W Schaumburg Rd Schaumburg IL 60194

WALTER, LINDA LARSON, Chemistry/Physics Teacher; *b:* Payson, UT; *m:* George A.; *c:* Curtis, Lynn, Jared, Michael, Rochelle, Tracy, Melinda, Christopher, Jennifer; *ed:* (BS) Phys Sci/Math Composite, Weber St Coll 1985; *cr:* Chem/Physics Teacher Payson HS 1985-; *ai:* Sci Bowl Team; Teams & Jets; Elem Sci Demonstrations; UEA, NEA Faculty Rep 1987-; PTA Thank-A-Teacher Awd; *office:* Payson HS 1050 S Main St Payson UT 84651

WALTER, VALERIE CECCHERELLI, Earth Science Teacher; *b:* Brooklyn, NY; *m:* Theodor; *c:* Karen, Krista; *ed:* (BS) Bio, SUNY Brockport 1964; (MS) Bio/Earth Sci, SUNY 1975; Grad Work in Earth Sci; *cr:* General Sci/Regents Earth Sci Teacher Connetquot Sch Dist #7 1964-71; Bio Teacher Quakertown 1983-85; Earth Sci/General Sci/Bio Teacher Freedom HS 1985-; *ai:* Freedom HS Acts Dir; Freedom HS Stu Cncl & Class of 1991 Adv; NEA, PSEA Delegate 1985-; Bethlehem Ed Assn (Exec Comm, Public Relations Chairperson) 1989-; NESTA 1990; Bethlehem Musikfest Site Design Volunteer 1985-; Co-Founded with Lehigh Univ Geo-Sci Educators Assn of Lehigh Valley; *office:* Freedom HS 3149 Chester Ave Bethlehem PA 18017

WALTERS, BARBARA J., English Grammar & Literature; *b:* New York City, NY; *ed:* (AAS) Advertising, NYC Comm Coll; BA) Mass Media Comm, Hunter Coll 1976; Masters in Amer Lit; *cr:* Eng Departmental Teacher St Thomas Comm Sch 1976; Career Educator Save-RTP Inc 1980-81; Adjunct Instr Coll of New Rochelle 1984-85; Lang Arts Instr Holy Name Sch 1978-; *ai:* Yrbk Coord; Career Day Coord; Appreciation Awd/Excell in Ed; USAF Articles Pblshd; *office:* Holy Name of Jesus 202 W 97th St New York NY 10025

WALTERS, BILLIE SPENCER, Fifth Grade Teacher; *b:* Douglass, TX; *m:* Billy Mosby; *c:* Kelle D. Foxworth, Mollie A.; *ed:* (BS) Elem Ed, 1961, (MED) Elem Ed, 1965 Stephen F Austin Univ; TX Career Ladder III; *cr:* 7th/8th Grade Teacher Maydelle Ind Sch Dist 1961-64; 4th Grade Teacher Redland Ind Sch Dist 1965-67; Elem Prin 1968-70, 2nd-8th Grade Teacher 1967- Douglass Ind Sch Dist; *ai:* Attendance, Goals, Disciplinary, Homecoming Comm; Cherokee Cty TSTA (Mem, VP 1962-63; Douglass Booster Club 1989-; TCTA Mem 1970-; Douglass PTO Outstanding Achievement Plaque 1983; *office:* Douglass Ind Sch Dist P O Box 38 Douglass TX 75943

WALTERS, GEORGIA CATO, English Teacher; *b:* Bowman, SC; *m:* Timothy; *c:* Timothy V., Alexia, Georgette; *ed:* (BA) Eng, Claflin Coll 1974; (MA) Ed, SC St 1984; Advanced Placement Trng for Teaching Eng; *cr:* Rdng Teacher Harleyville-Ridgeville HS 1974-75; Eng Teacher Williams Memorial Mid Sch 1975-79, Orangeburg-Wilkinson 1979-; *ai:* Advanced Placement Coord; Graduation Comm; NCTE 1988-; New Mt Zion Baptist Church (Sunday Sch Teacher 1978-, Sunday Sch Supt 1990); *home:* Rt 1 Box 2157 Bowman SC 29018

WALTERS, MELVINA JO REFINE, 5th Grade Teacher; *b:* Springfield, IL; *m:* John A.; *c:* Margaret I. Kruckemeyer, Linda L. Maurer, James M.; *ed:* (BED) Scndry His, E IL Univ 1946; Grad Stud S IL Univ Edwardsville, NE MO St Kirksville; Elem Ed, Univ of MO 1970-72; *cr:* Teacher Koch Elem 1972-75, Riverview Gardens HS 1975-80, Koch Elem 1980-; *ai:* Greater St Louis Teachers Assn; MO St Teachers Assn Local Riverview Gardens Pres 1985; Delta Kappa Gamma 2nd VP 1988-; Kappa Delta Pi VP 1943-46; Church Act; *office:* Koch Elem Sch 1910 Exuma Saint Louis MO 63136

WALTERS, PATRICIA HARRIS, English Department Chair; *b:* Lexington, KY; *m:* John Lindsay; *c:* Lisa W. Solise, Matthew Harris; *ed:* (BA) Eng, Univ of KY 1962; (MAEE) 1971, (Rank I) Supervision, 1984 Murray St Univ; *cr:* Eng Teacher Madisonville N Hopkins HS 1964-; *ai:* Leadership Team; Eng Dept Chairperson; Lang & Fine Art Chairperson; Beta Club Spon; NCTE, KCTE 1964-, Outstanding Teacher 1970; HCEA, KEA, NEA 1964-; Delta Kappa Gamma 1968-; Alpha Delta Kappa 1987-; Phi Beta Kappa 1962-; Earlington Chrstn Church 1964-; Outstanding Teacher Awd 1989; *office:* Madisonville N Hopkins HS 4515 Hanson Rd Madisonville KY 42431

WALTERS, WILLIAM MONROE, JR., Mathematics Dept Chair/Teacher; *b:* Bancroft, WV; *m:* Shirley Lee Dolin; *c:* Lora N.; *ed:* (BA) Math/Physics, WV St Coll 1965; (MA) Math/Ed, WV Univ 1971; Grad Stud Industrial Engineering & System Analysis, WV Coll; Grad Stud, Marshall Univ; *cr:* Math Teacher Poca HS 1965-; *ai:* Faculty Advisory Cncl Chm; Athletic & Choir Boosters; Academic & Band Boosters VP; Sftbl Coach; NHS Selection, Textbook, Curr & GHA Comms; WV Fed of Teachers 1989-; WV Ed Assn 1965-; Natl Sci Fnd Fellowship Math Grad Degree Work; Putnam Cty Chamber of Commerce Teacher of Yr Awd; Nom for Ashland Oil Teacher Achievement Awd; *office:* Poca HS Rt 1 Box 5-B Poca WV 25159

WALTHOUSE, FRANCES J. (NOVAK), Math Teacher; *b:* Chicago, IL; *m:* Thomas C.; *c:* Kathy Englund, Thomas P., Robert; *ed:* (BS) Math, IL St Univ 1959; (MS) Scndry Ed, Northern IL Univ 1984; *cr:* Math Teacher Rich Twnshp HS East 1959-60, York HS 1960-62, Lake Park HS 1977-; *ai:* Mathlete Coach; ICTM; NCTM.

WALTON, BOBBIE NOWELL, Business Coordinator; *b:* West Point, MS; *m:* Johnny G.; *c:* John J., Jeffrey P.; *ed:* (BS) Voc Bus Ed, 1970, (MED) Voc Bus Ed, 1976 MS St Univ; *cr:* Bus Ed Teacher Pascagoula HS 1970-74; Bus Technology Teacher 1975-89, Bus Coord 1989- Pascagoula HS Voc Tech Center; *ai:* FBLA Adv; Adult Word Processing Teacher Night Classes; Outstanding Voc Stu Comm 1990; Phi Delta Kappa VP 1982-; Alpha Delta Kappa (Secy, VP) 1979-; SBEA, NBEA 1970-90, Outstanding Scndry Teacher 1988; MBEA Secy 1970-; *office:* Pascagoula HS Voc Tech Center 2602 Market St Pascagoula MS 39567

WALTON, CLAUDIA MAE EDWARDS, Marketing/DECA Teacher; *b:* Hutchins, TX; *m:* Willie; *c:* Dwayne; *ed:* (BAED) Bus Ed, 1959, (MAED) Spec Ed, 1975 AZ St Univ; *cr:* General Office/Sales Clerk Hannys Clothing Store 1959-65; Substitute Teacher Phoenix Elem & Phoenix Union HS Dist 1965-67; Spec

Ed Teacher Maracom 1967-71; Pre-Sch/Nursery Sch Teacher Cath Soc Services 1971-72; Special Ed/EMH/LD Teacher South Mount HS 1972-85; Bus Ed/Mrktg Ed Teacher Carl Hayden HS 1985-; *ai:* Distributive Ed Clubs of America Adv Carl Hayden HS 1987-; CTA, AEA, NEA Cncl of Rep 1965-; AZVA, AVA, AME, MEA 1985-; Antioch Baptist Church Pres Ed Bd 1975-; Tau Gamma Delta West Regional Dir 1984-87, Soror of Yr 1983; Classroom Teachers Assn Cncl of Rep Mem 1990; AZ Dept of Ed Sch Improvement Unit Task Force on Teacher Performance Evaluation 1986; *office:* Carl Hayden HS 3333 W Roosevelt Phoenix AZ 85009

WALTON, ELIZABETH BLANTON, English Teacher; *b:* Mooresville, NC; *m:* Terry Lee; *c:* Christopher, Megan; *ed:* (AB) Eng, Pfeiffer Coll 1970; *cr:* 7th-8th Grade Lang Arts Teacher 1970-86, 9th Grade Eng Teacher 1986- China Grove Jr HS; *ai:* Coord Adopt-A-Sch; Rowan-Salisbury Voc Cooperative Comm Mem; Chm Southern Comm; NEA, NC Assn of Educators; Trading Ford Baptist Church Secy of Sunday Sch Class 1986-; *home:* Rt 4 Box 715 Salisbury NC 28144

WALTON, JANETTA ELIZABETH, Learning Disabilities Teacher; *b:* Antlers, OK; *c:* Monteous; *ed:* (BA) Elem Ed, S OK St Univ Durant 1981; (BA) Learning Disibilities, Cntrl St Univ Edmond 1983; *cr:* Learning Disibilities Teacher Taft Mid Sch 1981-; *ai:* Chldrs 1981-; Pep Club 1985-; Girls Bsktbl Assistance 1986-89; Boys Bsktbl Coach 1989-; AFT 1981-; *office:* Taft Mid Sch 2901 NW 23rd Oklahoma City OK 73107

WALTON, JULIE S., Biology Teacher; *b:* Atlanta, GA; *ed:* (BS) Bio, Berry Coll 1986; Masters Work in Bio, GA S Univ; *cr:* Bio Teacher East Rome HS 1988-; *ai:* Sci Club Spon; Var Cheerleading Coach; Schlsp Comm; NSTA, GA Sci Teachers Assn, Southern Biologists Assn; Earth Day Comm; Nature Conservancy; Natl Wildlife Fed; Mellon Grant Summer Advanced Placement Inst; *office:* East Rome HS 1401 Turner Mc Call Blvd Rome GA 30161

WALTON, KEVIN DEANE, American History Teacher; *b:* Wooster, OH; *ed:* (BA) His, Coll of Wooster 1978; *ai:* OEA; NEA.

WALTON, LORENE KINER, Fifth Grade Teacher; *b:* Ocala, FL; *m:* Mc Arthur; *c:* Keith, James, Antonio; *ed:* (AA) Elem Ed, Hampton Jr Coll 1966; (BS) Elem Ed, FL A&M Univ 1968; *cr:* 4th Grade Teacher 1969-70, 2nd/3rd Grade Teacher 1970-71, 1st Grade Teacher 1971-72, Title I Rdng Teacher 1974-75, 5th Grade Teacher 1989-; *ai:* Textbook Comm; Grade Level Chairperson; Marion Cty Chldhd Dev Cncl; Sports Person; FL Teaching Profession; Marion Ed Assn Cncl Policy Co-Chairperson; NEA; S Marion MA Cmmty Choir Pres 1989-, Outstanding Leader 1989; Anti Recidivist Organization 1989, Outstanding Contribution & Support; Missionary Helpers Cncl Pres 1978-; Young Women Cmmty Club (Treas, Adv); Nom Teacher of Yr 1986; Teacher Appreciation Awd 1973; Cmmty Helpers Awd; *office:* Belleview-Santos Elem Sch 9600 US Hwy 441 Belleview FL 32620

WALTON, MICHAEL IRA, Fifth Grade Teacher; *b:* Brooklyn, NY; *m:* Helen Friedlander; *c:* Leslie Watkins, Sandra; *ed:* (BS) Elem Ed, 1963, (MS) Elem Ed, 1973 New Paltz; Certified Paramedic Nyack Hospital NY 1985; *cr:* Teacher Montgomery Elem Sch 1962-; *ai:* Elem Wrestling & Bsktbl; Valley Cntrl Teachers Assn 1962-; Pine Bush Volunteer Ambulance Corps Dir of Trng 1977-; Orange Cty EMS Cncl Chm 1986-; Town of Wallkill Volunteer Ambulance Corps 1978-; *home:* RD 2 Box 313 Montgomery NY 12549

WALTON, SANDRA CASPER, English Teacher, Dept Chair; *b:* Murray, UT; *m:* Harold H.; *c:* Jeff Colegrove, Craig Colegrove, Jeff, Robb, James; *ed:* (BA) Eng, Univ of UT 1972; (MAT) Eng, Tarleton St Univ 1981 Model for Effective Teaching & Supervision Instructional Leadership Inst; Master Teacher Acad; *cr:* 8th-12th Grade Eng Teacher Gordon HS 1974-79; 9th-12th Grade Eng Teacher 1979-87, 9th Grade Honors Eng Teacher 1987-, Stephenville HS; *ai:* Gordon HS Drill Team & Pep Squad; UIL Speech, Writing, Class & Spelling Spon; Prose Interpretation; Assn of TX Prof Educators Campus Rep; *office:* Stephenville HS 2650 W Overhill Stephenville TX 76401

WALTON, TERRI POLKINGHORN, Fifth Grade Teacher; *b:* Bozeman, MT; *m:* John I; *c:* Brandon, Brian; *ed:* (BA) Soc Work, ID St Univ 1979; *cr:* 5th/6th Grade Teacher Fruitland Elem 1981-; *ai:* Fruitland Ed Assn Secy/Treas 1984-85; *home:* 520 S Whitley PO Box 813 Fruitland ID 83619

WALTON, YVONNE STATON, Fifth Grade Teacher; *b:* Elizabeth City, NC; *m:* Jesse Rudolph; *c:* Trisha, Jevon; *ed:* (BS) Intermediate Ed, Elizabeth City St Univ 1976; (MAED) Elem Ed, E Carolina Univ 1986; Pursuing Educl Specialist Degree; *cr:* Migrant Teacher Pasquotank Elem 1976-80; Summer Sch Teacher Elizabeth City Pasquotank Schls 1990; 5th Grde Teacher Pasquotank Elem 1981-; *ai:* Mentor Teacher, Senate Bill II Steering, System-Wide Calendar, Southern Assn Accreditation, United Way Comm; NEA 1976-; Elizabeth City Pasquotank Treas 1984-86; Intnl Rdng Assn 1989-; NC Assn of Educators (Rep, Treas 1984-86) 1976-; Delta Sigma Theta Alumnae (Secy 1985-89, VP 1989-); PTA Teacher Rep; Outstanding Soc Stud Teacher 1988-89; Jaycee Teacher of Yr; *home:* Rt 6 Box 234 A Elizabeth City NC 27909

WALTZ, CAROLYN JEAN, Spanish Teacher; *b:* Cleveland, OH; *ed:* (BA) Span, Alma Coll 1966; (MED) Instr Design, Wayne St Univ 1980; *cr:* 7th/8th Grade Teacher Our Lady of Sorrows Elem 1967-69; 7th/8th Grade Teacher St Ambrose Acad 1969-85; Span Teacher St Martin De Porres HS 1985-; *ai:* Span Club; Soph Class Moderator; Honors Assembley/Baccalaureate Ceremony Coor; Metro Detroit; Foreign Lang Assn 1988-; MI Fair Housing Assn 1975-; Grosse Pointe Inter-Faith for Racial Justice 1978-80; Detroit Youth Action Comm Bd Mem 1978-80; Cert of Appreciation/Detroit Bd of Ed; Cert of Commendation/MI Dept of Civil Rights; *home:* 1139 Beaconsfield Grosse Pointe Park MI 48230

WALTZ, JAMES ROLAND, Science Teacher; *b:* Newark, NJ; *ed:* (BA) Poly Sci, William Paterson Coll of NJ 1972; (AA) Bio, Essex Cty Coll 1977; Dental Sch NJ Coll Medicine & Denistry 1978; *cr:* Sci Teacher Science HS 1985-; *ai:* NHS Selection Team; NJ St Sci Teachers Assn 1988-; Newark Ed Cncl 1990; Optimist Club of America Lecture 1989; Bethany Baptist Church Lecture Comm; Newark Collaboration Comm 1988-; William Paterson Coll Alumni Assn; Intern for Summer Associateship Prgm for HS Sci & Math Faculty; Dept of the Army Armament Research Dev & Engineering Summer Consortium Pre-Coll Ed; *home:* 241 S Burnet St East Orange NJ 07018

WALZER, MICHAELENE ANN (BAKER), 6th Grade Teacher; *b:* Lewisburg, PA; *m:* David Alan; *c:* Sara; *ed:* (BS) Elem Ed, IN Univ of PA 1973; Curr/Instr, Ashland Univ; *cr:* 6th-7th Grade Teacher S S Cyril & Methodius Cath Sch 1974-76; 6th Grade Teacher Langston Mid Sch 1976-; *ai:* Sch Newspaper Adv; Sch Yrbk Adv; *office:* Langston Mid Sch 150 N Pleasant St Oberlin OH 44074

WAMPLER, CATHERINE PHILLIPS, Second Grade Teacher; *b:* St Joseph, MO; *m:* Darwin Andrew; *c:* Marcy, Mark, Megan; *ed:* (BS) Elem Ed, MO Western St Coll 1971; Lee Canters Assertive Descipline; *cr:* 3rd Grade Teacher 1971-83, 2nd Grade Teacher 1983- Minnie Cline Sch; *ai:* Mentor Comm; TAB Comm; CTA; MSTA; Beta Sigma Phi Valentine Princess Sweetheart 1990; PTA Hospitality Chm 1987-88; *home:* 303 W Swenson Savannah MO 64485

WAMPLER, PORTIA SPITLER, First Grade Teacher; *b:* Argos, IN; *m:* Barry Wayne; *c:* Krista, Kara, Katie, Jed, Chelsea; *ed:* (BS) Elem Ed, Manchester Coll 1970; (MS) Elem Ed, IN Univ 1984; *cr:* 4th Grade Teacher Chelsea Sch 1970-74; 1st Grade Teacher Argos Cmmty Sch 1977-.

WANCHO, AMY ANN (CLARK), Third Grade Teacher; *b:* Kankakee, IL; *m:* Kevin; *c:* Katie, Cassie; *ed:* (BA) Elem Ed, Millikin Univ 1977; Working Towards Masters Rdng, Olivet Univ; *cr:* 4th Grade Teacher 1977, 3rd Grade Teacher 1977-87, Chapter I Rdng Teacher 1987-88, 3rd Grade/Chapter I Teacher 1988- Reddick Grade Sch; *ai:* ASCD; NEA, IEA 1975-89; Lioness 1986-87; PTA (Secy 1987-89) 1977-; Reddick Grade Head Teacher 1984-87; *office:* Reddick Grade Sch Box 67 Main St Reddick IL 60961

WANDRO, KATHLEEN O'ROURKE, Eng/Performing Arts Teacher; *b:* Chicago, IL; *m:* William D.; *c:* Jennifer, Sean; *ed:* (BA) Speech Comm/Eng, Drake Univ 1975; (MA) Admin, Roosevelt Univ 1985; Northwestern Univ Eng, Writing, Performing Arts; *cr:* Teacher Hoffman Estates HS 1977-; *ai:* Performing Arts Spon; Musical Dir; *office:* Hoffman Estates HS 1100 W Higgins Rd Hoffman Estates IL 60195

WANG, JUNE LIANG, Business Education Teacher; *b:* Kiang-si, China; *m:* Joseph C.; *c:* Michael, Mei-Lun, Vincent, Xiao-Wei; *ed:* (BA) Bus Ed, DC Teachers Coll 1960; (MA) Bus Ed, Cath Univ of America 1969; *cr:* Instr Thornton Township HS & Jr Coll 1961-65; Teacher Blacksburg HS 1978-; *ai:* Faculty Spon FBLA 1978-; Chm of Bus Ed Self-Study Comm 1989-; MCEA, VBEA 1978-; Blacksburg HS Parent Teacher Stu Assn Faculty Rep 1986-88; 2nd Place Winner Free Enterprise Project Regional Competition 1989; 1st Place Regional Winner Free Enterprise Project 1981; *office:* Blacksburg HS Patrick Henry Dr Blacksburg VA 24060

WANSOR, COLLIN TERRANCE, English Department Chair; *b:* Sharon, PA; *m:* Nancy Jean Lape; *c:* Lynna, Janeen, Charles, Patrick; *ed:* (BSED) Eng, 1965, (MSED) Eng, 1971, (PHD) Rhetoric/Linguistics, 1990 Indiana Univ of PA; Rdng Specialist; NEH Fellow; *cr:* Classroom Teacher 1965-72, 1973-86, Dept Chm 1982- Hempfield Area HS; *ai:* NEA 1965-; Hempfield Area Ed Assn (Pres, Past Pres) 1965-; NCTE; Teaching Fellow Kent St Univ 1972-73; Natl Endowment for Hum Fellowship Penn St 1982; Amer Family Inst Tribute Distinguished Teaching 1986; Univ of Chicago Commendation 1988; Whos Who Amoung Amer Educators 1989-; Published 1983, 1986, 1989, 1990; *office:* Hempfield Area HS RD 6 Box 77 Greensburg PA 15601

WAPPEL, LOUIS C., Principal/Teacher; *b:* Chicago, IL; *ed:* (BA) Comm, Columbia Coll 1972; (MEPD) Ed, Univ of WI 1982; *cr:* Prin/Teacher Divine Word Seminary 1977-; *ai:* ASCD, NCTE, Phi Kappa Phi; *office:* Divine Word Seminary HS PO Box 107 East Troy WI 53120

WARBIS, MEDA CATCHPOLE, Math/Cmptr Sci Teacher; *b:* Belle Fourche, SD; *m:* Roger D.; *c:* Robert, Joseph; *ed:* (BS) Math, Dickinson St Univ 1987; *ai:* Jr Class Adv; *office:* St Marys HS Box 367 New England ND 58647

WARD, BARBARA B., English Teacher; *b:* Provo, UT; *m:* William S.; *c:* Mary A.; *ed:* (BS) His, 1962, (MS/MA) Eng Ed, 1975 Univ of UT; Grad Stud; *cr:* Eng Teacher Hillcrest HS 1962-74, Jordan HS 1975-78, Alta HS 1978-; *ai:* Sterling Scholar Adv; St Wide Prgm Honor Outstanding HS Scholars; Alpha Delta Kappa; Phi Kappa Phi 1962; Mortar Bd 1975.

WARD, BLENDA RICHARDS, Observer/Evaluator; *b:* Valdese, NC; *m:* Earl Clarence; *c:* Wesley Earl; *ed:* (BA) Grammar Ed, 1967, (MA) Early Chldhd Ed, 1985 Lenoir Rhyne Coll; *cr:* Teacher Chesterfield Elem Sch 1966-69, Glen Alpine Elem Sch 1975-89; Observer/Evaluator Career Dev Office Burke Public Cty Schls 1989-; *ai:* Phi Delta Kappa 1987-; Valdese Fire Dept Ladies Auxiliary Secy 1988-; *home:* Rt 3 Box 401 Valdese NC 28690

WARD, CATHERINE, Substitute Teacher; *b:* Wiconisco, PA; *c:* Beth Brown, John; *ed:* (BS) Elem Ed, Villanova 1957; (MS) Elem Ed/Admin Fordham 1962; Admin, Loyola, Xavier; *cr:* Teacher Corpus Christi Sch 1948-53, All Saints 1953-60; Prin All Saints 1960-62; Teacher St Bridget 1962-65; Prin St Elizabeth 1965-67, Blessed Sacrament 1967-70, Los Angeles 1970-72, Houston 1972-77, Blevins 1977-89; *ai:* NCTM; City Cncl Alderman 1983-; *home:* Rt 1 Box 1 A Mc Caskill AR 71847

WARD, CHARLES RANDOLPH, Guidance Counselor; *b:* Washington, DC; *m:* Mary Louise Speas; *c:* Sarah, Jay, Adam; *ed:* (AA) His, Ferrum Jr Coll 1970; (BS) Health/Phys Ed, 1972, (MS) Guidance/Counseling, 1974 VA Tech; Univ of VA, Radford Univ, James Madison Univ; *cr:* Phys Ed/His Teacher Cave Spring Jr HS 1972-73; His/Driver Ed Teacher Glenvar Jr/Sr HS 1973-82; Guidance/Phys Ed Teacher Page Cty HS 1982-83; His Teacher Andrew Lewis Jr HS 1983-88; Asst Prin/AD Teacher James River HS 1988-89; Guidance Cnslr Salem HS 1989-; *ai:* Var Girls Sftbl; Monogram Club; VA HS Coaches Assn 1972-; *home:* 1855 Tinker Mountain Dr Daleville VA 24083

WARD, CHARLES ROBERT, Sixth Grade Teacher; *b:* Wiesbaden, West Germany; *ed:* (BS) Ed, MO Southern St Coll 1976; *cr:* 6th Grade Instr Neosho Heights Elem Sch 1976; Capt US Army Reserve 1977; Cmptr Instr Labette Comm Coll 1984-; *ai:* Dist Cmptr Coord; KNEA (VP 1978-79/Pres 1979-81); Teacher of Yr 1983-84; 418th CA CO US Army Reserve Officer of Yr 1989; *office:* Neosho Heights Elem Sch N Oregon Oswego KS 67356

WARD, CHRISTOHPER WILLIAM, Medical Magnet Chairman; *b:* Flushing, NY; *m:* Marie T. Ferranto; *c:* Christopher, Dana, William, Rebekah, Jason; *ed:* (BS) Bio, Manhattan Coll 1969; (MS) Medical Bio, C W Post LIU 1974; Educl Research & Dissemination Prgm; Train the Trainer; TESA; Human Relations I & II; NSF Wkshps; Project Outreach; More Effective Schls; *cr:* Teacher St Domonics HS 1969-70, Emerson Jr HS/Mid Sch 1970-81, Lincoln HS 1981-86; Instr/Chm Gorton HS 1986-; *ai:* SADD Intrum Spon; Stu Service League Mem; Medical Club & Red Cross Interschool Cncl Spon; Sr Class Adv; Stu Human Relations Cncl Mem; Medical Magnet Advisory, Burrows Jr HS Medical Magnet Advisory Cncls; Medical Magnet Curr Advisory Cncl Chm; NY St United Teachers 1970-; Yonkers Fed of Teachers (Election Comm 1976-79) 1970-; BSA (Cubmaster, Comm Chm, Cnslr, Dist Comm, Dist Chm Swim Prgm, Dist Trng Chm) 1977-, Wood Badge 1990, Trng Awd 1984, 1987, 1988, 1990, Bronz Pelican Awd 1987, St George Awd 1990; Amer Red Cross (Volunteer, Instr, Trainer) 1987-, Certificate of Merit 1989; Intnl Brotherhood of Magicians 1965-, Society of Merlin 1989; Knights of Columbus 1969-; PTA-Jenkins Memorial Awd; NSF Grants Bio, Chem, Astronomy; *office:* Gorton HS Shonnard Pl Yonkers NY 10703

WARD, DEBRA LEE (WOOD), Computer Teacher; *b:* Parkersburg, WV; *m:* Joe Francis; *c:* Amy, Tony, Daniel, Mary; *ed:* (AB) Phys Ed, 1979; (MA) Phys Ed, 1982; (AB) Math, 1985 Morehead St Univ; Rank I Principalship; Endorsements Elem Phys Ed, Cmptrs; Minors Health & Athletic Trng; *cr:* Elem Phys Ed Teacher Louisa Elem/Blain Elem/Fallsburg Elem 1980-84; Math Teacher Louisa Mid Sch 1984-87; Cmptr Teacher Lawrence Cty HS 1987-; *ai:* Co-Spon Fellowship of Chrstn Athletes; Instr Introduction Cmptr Course for Adults Tolsia HS; NEA; KY Ed Assn; Lawrence City Organ of Teachers Treas 1985-86; Louisa First Baptist Church; *office:* Lawrence Cty HS Hwy 644 Bulldog Ln Louisa KY 41230

WARD, DIANA LYNN (ELMORE), Physical Ed Teacher/ Coach; *b:* Ponca City, OK; *m:* Roger Lynn; *c:* Roger L. II, Rinda L.; *ed:* (BS) Health/Phys Ed/Recreation, Univ of NM 1970; (ME) Cmptrs in Ed, Lesley Coll 1987; Grad Stud; *cr:* Teacher/Coach Hermosa Jr HS 1970-72, 1974-; *ai:* Frosh Girls Vlybl, 7th-9th Grade Boys & Girls Track Coach; AAHPERD 1975-; Alpha Delta Kappa 1976-78; Phys Ed for Overweight Teenagers Grant; St Dept of Ed Phys Ed Sub-Comm of Sch Health Advisory Comm Chairperson; *office:* Hermosa Jr HS 1500 E 25th Farmington NM 87401

WARD, DIXIE KROENCKE, Jr HS Language Arts Teacher; *b:* Adams Cty, IL; *m:* Robert Doyle; *c:* Mark D., Michelle L.; *ed:* (BS) Elem Ed, S IL Univ 1961; Individual Stud Elem Ed, W IL Univ; Microcmptrs for Information Management/Apple Software Enhancement, Natl Coll of Ed; Fundamental Issues in Helping, Sangamon St Univ; *cr:* 2nd Grade Teacher O Fallon Grade Sch 1961-63; 3rd Grade Teacher Springfield Public Schls 1963-64; 1st Grade Teacher Grovetown GA Public Schls 1964-65; 7th-8th Grade Lang Art/Soc Stud Teacher W Pike 1974-; *ai:* 8th Grade Class Spon; NEA 1974-; IL Ed Assn (VP 1990) 1974-; Delta Kappa Gamma 1976-; Hull United Meth Church (Mem 1953-, Admin Bd Secy 1986-); Pike Cty Mental Health Bd Mem 1974-77; Hull His Lives Inc (Founder, Pres) 1985-; *office:* W Pike Jr Sr HS Chaney Ave Kinderhook IL 62345

WARD, DONALD WEBSTER, Biology Teacher; *b:* Monticello, AR; *m:* Janna Hold; *c:* Will Wheeler, Clare Wheeler, Russell; *ed:* (BS) Bio, Univ of AR Monticello 1969; (MED) Bio/Biochem, Sam Houston St Univ 1975; Grad Stud; *cr:* Classroom Teacher Cy-Fair

HS 1969-81; Tech Mkt Rep Durango Assoc 1981-83; Teacher/Dept Chm 1983-88, Teacher 1988- Cy-Fair HS; *ai:* Sci Fair Coord; Class Spon; TX Ed Agency Textbook Adoption Comm; Cy-Fair Ed Assn Pres 1977-78, Teacher of Yr 1985; TX Marine Educators 1987-; TX St Teachers Assn Natl Conv Delegate 1969-; Cy-Fair Lions Club VP 1975-81; Houston Math & Sci Improvement Consortium Fellowship; Harris Cty Comm Coll Grant; Nominee TX Excl Awds For Outstanding HS Teachers; Nominee Outstanding Bio Teacher, Excl Sci Teaching Awd, TX Medical Assn Excl Teaching; *office:* Cy-Fair Sr HS 22602 Hempstead Hwy Houston TX 77040

WARD, GWENDOLYN HANNA, Instructor; *b:* Gastonia, NC; *m:* Jonathan Bishop Jr.; *c:* Catherine, Andrew, Cynthia; *ed:* (AB) Bio, Wesleyan Coll 1968; (MST) Bio Ed, Cornell Univ 1971; *cr:* 6th-12th Grade Sci Teacher; Technician/Research Lab UTMB Galveston TX; *ai:* GSA Leader & Consultant; *home:* 3219 Dominique Galveston TX 77551

WARD, IRIS FRAZIER, 5th Grade Teacher; *b:* Bonifay, FL; *m:* George Addicus Jr.; *c:* Nancy J. Ward Bessinger, George A. III; *ed:* (AB) Bio/Chem, GA Coll 1952; Univ of GA; *cr:* Sci Teacher Elberton HS 1952-56; Bio Teacher 1956-57, 7th/8th Grade Teacher 1957-65 Nancy Hart Elem Sch; 7th Grade/Math Dept Teacher Stillwell Elem Sch 1965-70;7th Grade Journalism Teacher Samuel Elbert Acad 1970-83; 5th Grade Teacher Beaverdam Elem Sch 1983-; *ai:* Math Textbook, Lib, Supts Advisory Comm; Prof Assn of GA Educators 1983-; Beta Sigma Phi Pres 1960, 1967, Girl of Yr 1965; Elbert Cty Homemaker of Yr 1963; Eliam Meth Church (Sunday Sch Teacher, Dir of Youth); Star Teacher 1980; Teacher of Yr 1986; *office:* Beaverdam Elem 739 New Ruckersville Rd Elberton GA 30635

WARD, JANET RYKOSKEY, Basic Skills Remedial Teacher; *b:* Morgantown, WV; *m:* Billy R.; *c:* Aaron F. Moore, Jeremy J. Moses Moore; *ed:* (AB) Elem Ed, 1968, (MA) Counseling/Rehabilitation 1972 Marshall Univ; Religious Theory Class; Authorization K-12th Grade Remedial Rdng, 7th/8th Grade Dev Rdng, Marshall Univ 1988; *cr:* 3rd Grade Teacher St Anthony Elem 1968-70; 1st/2nd/4th Grade Teacher St Joseph Elem 1970-74; 3rd-4th Grade Teacher Sacred Heart Elem 1974-75; 2nd Grade Remedial Rdng Teacher/5th-7th Grade Cnslr St Joseph Elem 1975-83; Remedial Teacher Hamin HS 1983-; *ai:* Teacher Rep Positive Peer Pressure Group; Teacher Advisory Bd; Natl Jr Honor Society; Staff Dev Comm 1988-; *office:* Hamlin HS P O Box 558 Hamlin WV 25523

WARD, JON CLESMER, German/English Teacher; *b:* Brigham City, ID; *m:* Ann Thomas; *c:* Cles, Lydia, Kristin; *ed:* (BA) Ger, ID St Univ 1979; (MA) Eng, UT St Univ 1988; *cr:* Ger/Eng Teacher Malad HS 1979-88, Bonneville HS 1988-89, Rigby HS 1989-; *ai:* Foreign Lang Chm; ID Regional Ger Teacher Inservice Dir; Rigby HS Ger-Amer Exch Dir; ID Assn Teachers of Lang & Cultures Pres 1986; ID Assn Teachers of Ger Pres 1984-85, 1989; ID Ed Assn, NEA 1979-; Malad Valley Cmmty Choir 1980-82; Teton BSA Comm Mem 1989-; Eagle Scout 1968; Whittenberger Writing Fellowship; Ger Democratic Republic Landeskunde Seminar; Poetry Published.

WARD, MARION S., English Teacher; *b:* Pauls Valley, OK; *ed:* (BS) Ed Eng, Univ of OK 1974; (ME) Spec Ed, E TX St Univ 1980; Elem Ed, Univ of OK; *cr:* Eng/Journalism Teacher Jourdanton HS 1974-75; Eng Teacher Big Pasture HS 1975-76; Journlism/Eng Teacher W W Samuell HS 1976-79; Eng Teacher Seagoville Jr HS 1979-80; SPED/SED Teacher Jarmen Jr HS 1980-82; SPED/Eng Teacher West Mid HS 1982-; *ai:* Yrbk Photography Adv; Prof Educators of Norman (Secy 1986-88, Public Relations Chairperspn 1988-; OK Ed Assn; NEA; US Dept of Ed Outstanding Scndry Sch Awd 1988-89 & Drug-Free Schls Awd 1990; *office:* West Mid Sch 1919 W Boyd Norman OK 73069

WARD, NANCY BENSON, English Teacher; *b:* Hampton, AR; *m:* Dennis E.; *c:* Melissa; *ed:* (BSE) Eng Ed, Univ of AR Monticello 1973; (MA) Writing, Univ of AR Little Rock; Facilitator AR Writing Project; *cr:* Eng Teacher Watson Chapel HS 1973-; *ai:* Sr Class Spon; Former Spon Stepperette Drill Team; AR Cncl Teachers of Eng (Secy 1987-88, VP 1989-); AR Ed Assn 1989-; Article Published; St Grant Recognition of Outstanding Classroom Teachers; *home:* 255 Victoria Dr Rt 11 Pine Bluff AR 71603

WARD, NITA ANDRESS, Second Grade Teacher; *b:* Andalusia, AL; *m:* William C; *c:* Ricky, Emily W Newell; *ed:* (BS) Elem Ed, Fl St Univ 1974; *cr:* 1st Grade Teacher St Bede Elem Sch 1975-77, Southlawn Elem Sch 1978-81; 2nd Grade Teacher Dannelly Elem Ech 1982-; *ai:* Organizer & Spon Stud Cncl; Grade Level Chm; Delta Kappa Gamma (SEC) 1987-; Ed Assn 1978-; Montgomery Cty Ed Assn 1978-; Sunday Sch Teacher Childrens Div; Choir Mem Heritage Bapt Church; Dannelly PTA 1988; Teacher of Yr Outstanding Educator Awd.

WARD, RANDALL LEE, 5th Grade Teacher; *b:* Wilmington, DE; *m:* June Rennie; *c:* Bryce R., Sean C., Ryan W.; *ed:* (BS) Elem Ed, 1975, (MSED) Educl Leadership, 1978 Univ of DE; DE Geographic Alliance Geography Inst Trng; Math Geometry Spokesperson Trng; *cr:* 6th Grade Teacher 1975-78, 4th Grade Teacher 1978-86, 2nd Grade Teacher 1986-88, 5th Grade Teacher 1988- Lake Forest North Elem; *ai:* Lake Forest HS Jr Var Bsbl Coach; Lake Forest Sch Dist Coord for Natl Geographic, Dist Spelling Bee Enunciator; Lake Forest North Audio Video Coord; DE Geographic Alliance, DE Cncl for Soc Stud 1989-; S DE Chamber of Commerce 1988-; *home:* 2 Hudson Branch Dr Frederica DE 19946

WARD, RAYBURN WESLEY, Language Arts Teacher; *b:* Frederick, OK; *m:* Lamona Custer; *c:* La Shanna Z., Wesley Mc Crae; *ed:* (BA) Lang Art, 1967, (MS) Ed, 1976, Admin Scndry Prin, 1989 NW OK St Univ; *cr:* Eng/Soc Stud Teacher La Verne Jr HS 1967-68; Lang Art Teacher Vici HS 1968-89; *ai:* Drama Coach; Class Spon; Staff Dev Comm; St Lang Art Curr Comm Mem; NCTE 1968-89; NW Dist Eng Teachers Pres 1972-74; Dewey Cty OK Ed Assn Pres 1974-75, 1980-81, 1986-87, Teacher of Yr 1977; Vici Ambulance Service Emergency Med Tech 1973-77; Cub Scouts Pack 265 Pack Leader 1976-78; BSA Troop 265 Scoutmaster 1978-86; Society of Outstanding Leaders in Scndry Ed; Republican Party Precinct Chm; Delegate to St Convention; *office:* Vici HS PO Box 60 Vici OK 73859

WARD, STEVEN EDWARD, Mathematics Teacher; *b:* Stella, MO; *ed:* (BSED) Math, SW MO St Univ 1987; *cr:* Math Teacher Bolivar HS 1988, Clinton HS 1988-; *ai:* Boys & Girls Tennis & Asst Wrestling Coach; Kappa Delta Pi, MO Cncl Teachers of Math; *office:* Clinton HS 600 E Clinton Clinton MO 64735

WARD, SUANNE STRAND, 3rd Grade Teacher; *b:* Erie, PA; *m:* Thomas Michael; *c:* Gustauve; *ed:* (BA) Elem Ed, 1972, (MA) Elem Ed, 1975 Edinboro St Coll; *cr:* 3rd Grade Teacher Edinboro Elem 1972-; *ai:* General Mc Lane Ed Assn, PA St Ed Assn, NEA, PTA 1972-; *office:* Edinboro Elem Sch 6 N West Edinboro PA 16412

WARD, SUELLEN GLOVER, Home Economics Teacher; *b:* Conway, AR; *m:* Donald Ray; *c:* Jason, Brian; *ed:* (BSE) Home Ec, 1973, (MSE) Home Ec, 1974 Univ of Cntrl AR; Earth Sci, AR Tech Univ; Sci & Cmptr in Home Ec, Univ of AR; Occupational Home Ec New York Fashion Tour, Univ of Cntrl AR; *cr:* Sci Teacher 1974-76, Home Ec Teacher 1976- Guy Perkins Sch; *ai:* FHA Spon & Adv; AVA, AR Voc Assn 1976-; AR Assn of Voc Home Ec Teachers Secy 1976-; Home Ec Ed Assn 1988-; Phi Upsilon Omicron 1976-; FHA Alumni 1987-; Cub Scouts/Weeblos Den Leader 1989-; Grant to Develop Curr Guide for Home Ec; *office:* Guy Perkins Sch P O Box 96 Guy AR 72061

WARD, TERESA J., English Teacher; *b:* Ft Bragg, CA; *m:* Dustin T.; *c:* Dustin G., Teresa N.; *ed:* (BA) Eng, 1970, (MED) Ed, 1973 Univ of OK; (MED) Admin, Cntrl St Univ 1990; *cr:* Intern Teacher Corps 1971-73; Teacher Harding Mid Sch 1973-81; Lease Mgr Plumb Oil Company 1981-83; Teacher Choctaw Jr HS 1983-; *ai:* In-Service Planning Comm; Frosh Class Spon; In-Sch Suspension Supvr; Spelling Bee Coord; Assn of Classroom Teachers; OK Ed Assn; NEA; PTA Pres 1987-89, Outstanding Service 1989; 5 Yr Improvement Plan Mem 1987-; Cub Scouts Asst Leader 1983-85; OK Arts & Hum Cncl Mem 1975-; Outstanding Teacher of Eng 1989; Writing About Eng NEH Summer Inst; *office:* Choctaw Jr HS 14667 NE 3rd Choctaw OK 73020

WARD, THELMA MAE, Third Grade Teacher; *b:* Sallis, MS; *ed:* (BA) Elem Ed, Univ of MO Kansas City 1976; *cr:* Paraprofessional, 1968-77, Teacher 1977- Bd of Ed Kansas City; *office:* Phillips Sch 1619 E 24th Terr Kansas City MO 64108

WARD, VINCENT, Math/Physics/Chem Teacher; *b:* Eglin AFB, FL; *ed:* (BS) Chem Engr, Univ of Fl 1982; (MA) Ed, CA St Doming Hills 1990; Several Chem Wkshps; Teach SAT Prep Course; *cr:* Project Engr Industrial Outfitting Incorporate 1983-84; Sales Engr Trinity Fabrication 1984-85; Teacher Banning HS 1985-; *ai:* Sci Olympiad Team Spon & Coach; Tutoring Coord; Co-Authored Papers; *home:* 126 A Paseo Conclia Redondo Beach CA 90277

WARDELL, MARIAN LISMAN, Sixth Grade Teacher; *b:* Sullivan, IN; *m:* Robert Wendell; *c:* Michael, Cheryl Holladay, Lisa Stepro, David; *ed:* (BS) Elem Ed, 1962, (MS) Elem Ed, 1977 IN St Univ; *cr:* 3rd Grade Teacher Dugger Elem 1962-63, Fairbanks Elem 1963-64; 6th Grade Teacher Hymera Elem 1965-70, MSD of Shakamak 1970-; *ai:* Building Rep; Discussion & Schlsp Comm; NEA, ISTA, CTA; *home:* RR 4 Box 182 Sullivan IN 47882

WARDEN, CECILIA HARLESS, Mathematics Teacher; *b:* Oak Hill, WV; *m:* Abner S.; *c:* Laura; *ed:* (AB) Math, 1968, (MA) Speech Comm, 1981 WV Univ; Grad Stud WV Coll; *cr:* Math Teacher Clay-Battelle HS 1969-70, Stoco HS 1971-72, Mt Hope HS 1972-; *ai:* NHS & Academic Bowl Spon; Mt Hope HS Schlsp Comm; Delta Kappa Gamma 1st VP; WV Cncl Teachers of Math; Oak Hill Jr Womans Club Past Pres 1972-76; Oak Hill Civic League Past Treas 1987-89; Tandy Math Teacher Honoree; *office:* Mt Hope HS 110 High School Dr Mount Hope WV 25880

WARDEN, KENNETH BRUCE, Guidance Counselor; *b:* New York, NY; *c:* Tyrone, Naima; *ed:* (BA) His/Government, St Augustines Coll 1971; (MS) Counseling Ed, Lehman Coll 1975; Prof Diploma Admin Supvr, Brooklyn Coll 1989; *cr:* Music Teacher 1977-89, Guidance Cnslr 1989- JHS 126; *ai:* Band Prgm; Greenpoint Civic Cncl 1984, Educator of Yr 1984.

WARE, CHRISTINE G. SHOWALTER, English Teacher/Dept Chair; *b:* Kansas City, MO; *c:* Gretchen, Jason; *ed:* (BA) Eng/Sncdry Ed, 1973, (MA) Eng/Ed, 1987 Univ of MO Kansas City; Ventures for Excl; Teacher Expectation/Stu Achievement; Instructional Theory Into Practice; *cr:* Instr Lees Summit HS 1979-; *ai:* 9th/10th Grade Eng Dept, Grammar Comm, Division I Courtesy Chairperson; Performance Based Teacher Evaluation, Philosophy, Goals, Building Comms; Building Based Team; Inservice Instr; MATE, NCTE 1979-; NEA 1989-; Phi Kappa Phi 1987-; NCEA 1988-; Stu Cncl Teacher of Month 1989; Nom Kansas City Excl in Teaching Awd; Lee Summit Chamber of Commerce Excl Awd 1987; Ventures for Excl Outstanding Teacher; Kansas City Chamber of Commerce Excl Awd 1988; Nom Outstanding R-7 Teacher Awd 1989; *office:* Lees Summit HS 400 E 8th St Lees Summit MO 64063

WARE, HELEN, 3rd Grade Rdng & Math Teacher; *b:* Newark, NJ; *c:* Jeffrey, Derek; *ed:* (BS) Elem Ed/Early Chldhd, Seton Hall Univ 1974; Montclair St Coll, Kean Coll; *cr:* 5th Grade Teacher 1974-75, 2nd/3rd Grade Teacher 1975-79 Morton Street Sch; 4th Grade Teacher 1979-87, Basic Skills/Remedial Rdng/Math Teacher 1987- George Washington Carver; *ai:* Rdng Comm; Sch Improvement Team; Building Comm Chairperson; NJ Rdng Assn, Intnl Rdng Assn 1987-; Newark Early Chldhd Assn 1989-; Newark Alliance of Black Sch Educators Comm Chairperson 1989-; Newark Teachers Union Rep 1986-; NJ Historical Society 1989; Carol A Graves Civic Assn 1988; *office:* George Washington Carver Sch 333 Clinton Pl Newark NJ 07112

WARE, LEONA YELTON, Fourth Grade Teacher; *b:* Greenville, SC; *m:* R. W. Jr.; *c:* Chris, Jason; *ed:* (BA) Span/Elem Ed, Bridgewater Coll 1966; Univ of VA, JMU; *cr:* Elem Sch Teacher Augusta Cty Schls 1968-89; *ai:* NEA, VEA, ACEA; *office:* Verona Elem Sch Rt 2 Verona VA 24482

WARE, SARAH R., 5th Grade Teacher; *b:* Lexington, MS; *m:* John H.; *c:* Johnny T., Marcus L., Latonya S., Terrance L., Adrian D.; *ed:* (BA) Bus Ed, 1963, (BA) Elem Ed, 1965 MS Valley St; Grad Stud Delta St Univ; *cr:* Teacher Carver Elem & Mid; *ai:* Rdng Dept Chm; Schlsp Fund Mem; Sch & Cmmty Teacher 1990, Good Apple 1990; Church Asst Pastor 1982, Plaque 1982-; PTA Advisory Bd Mem.

WARE, VALETA RUTH, 6th Grade Teacher; *b:* Browning, MO; *m:* Clyde Eldon; *c:* Vicki Elliott, Linda Stecher, Sandra Willsie, James E.; *ed:* Ed, Kansas City Jr Coll 1959-60; (BS) Elem Ed, KS Univ Lawrence 1965; Jr HS Soc Stud Cert; *cr:* 1st-8th Grade Teacher Rural Sch 1948-49; Full-Time Substitute Teacher 1957-58, 6th Grade Teacher 1965-73 Kansas City Public Schls; Mid Sch Teacher Clinton Public Schls 1973-75; 6th Grade Teacher Bucklin R-2 Public Sch 1975-; *ai:* Elem Math Contest & Spelling Bee Coord; MSTA 1973-; CTA (Secy, Treas) 1983-; Eastern Star Secy 1990; Rebekah Lodge Pianist 1985-; *home:* RFD 1 Box 60 New Boston MO 63557

WARKE, HELEN JAROSCH, English Teacher; *b:* Chicago, IL; *m:* Guy D.; *c:* Kathleen Stefans, Amy Gundersen, Christopher; *ed:* (BA) Elem Ed, 1978; (MA) Eng Ed Olivet Nazareen Univ; *cr:* Eng Teacher Bourbonnais Upper Grade Ctr 1978-80; *ai:* Literary Team Adv; Sch Spelling Bee Coord; Rep Cty Bee; Lang Arts Block Comm; Sch Rep Supt/BEA Comm; Negotiations Team Mem; NCTE; IL Assn of Teachers of Eng; Our Savior Luth Church (Sundaysch Teacher) Choir Mem/Dir (Substitute Organist); Valparaiso Univ Guild Pres 1988-; *office:* Bourbonnais Upper Grad Ctr 200 John Casey Rd Bourbonnais IL 60914

WARKENTIN, ROSE MARIE, 4th Grade Teacher; *b:* Huron, SD; *ed:* (BA) Elem Ed, Knox Coll 1962; (MA) Curr Teaching, Teachers Coll/Columbia Univ 1967; Bible Credits, Moody Bible Inst 1978; *cr:* 3rd Grade Teacher Crystal Lake Elem Sch 1962-65; 3rd-4th Grade Teacher Hamilton Elem Sch 1965-67; 3rd Grade Teacher Todd Elem Sch 1967-74; 4th/6th Grade Teacher Delaware Cty Chrstn Sch 1974-; *ai:* Speech Contest Coord; Assn of Chrstn Schls Intnl, Intnl Rdng Assn; Historic 1696 Thomas Massey House Bd of Dir 1985-; *home:* 13 Penn Way Media PA 19063

WARMBROD, DAVID EDWARD, Phys Sci/Phys Ed Teacher; *b:* Winchester, TN; *m:* Deborah Mc Kenzie; *c:* Jeanette, Angela; *ed:* (AA) Phys Ed, Jackson St Comm Coll 1971; (BS) Health/Phys Ed, Univ of TN Martin 1973; (MS) Phys Ed, Memphis St Univ 1983; *cr:* Teacher/Coach Memphis Preparatory HS 1974-82; Grad Stu Memphis St Univ 1982-83; Teacher/Coach Memphis Preparatory HS 1983-86, Crockett Cty HS 1986-; *ai:* Girls Vlybl & Bsktbl, Boys Bsbl Coach; TN Assn of Health, Phys Ed, Recreation (Legislative Comm 1989-) 1971-; Assn of Health, Phys Ed, Recreation & Dance 1974-; Assn of Prof Ball Players of America 1968-; Church Atletic Comm Chm 1985-87, 1988-; *office:* Crockett Cty HS Rt 2 Alamo TN 38001

WARNE, SANDRA PARISH, Language Arts/Reading Teacher; *b:* Keyser, WV; *ed:* (BS) Elem Ed, 1976, (MS) Elem Ed, 1980 Frostburg St Univ; *cr:* Key Punch Operator IBMI 1968; Salesclerk Dept Store 1968-69; Teacher Garrett Cty Bd of Ed 1978-; *ai:* Newspaper Adv; Lang Dept Chm & Arts Coord; Lib Media Evaluation Comm; GCTA, MSTA, NEA 1976-; Intnl Rdng Assn; Amer Legion Auxiliary; Northern Mid Sch & Stu Cncl Awd; Commendation Awd; *office:* Northern Mid Sch Rt 2 Box 5 Accident MD 21520

WARNER, DEBORA PAYNE, Physical Education Teacher; *b:* Utica, NY; *m:* C. David; *c:* Amber L., C. Adam; *ed:* (BS) Health/Phys Ed/Recreation/Cmptr Bus, Findlay Coll 1976; (MS) Sch Guidance/Counseling, Univ of Dayton 1985; Cmptr Usage for Teachers; *cr:* Bus Teacher Wapakoneta Jr HS 1976-89; Phys Ed Teacher Northridge & Centennial Elem Schls 1989-; *ai:* Jr Service League; Var Vlybl & Jr HS Cheerleading Coach; Var Track & Gymnastics Asst Coach; *home:* 118 Phillips Dr Wapakoneta OH 45895

WARNER, DENNIS JAY, Mathematics Department Chair; *b:* Peoria, IL; *m:* Linda Bowlus; *c:* Jason; *ed:* (BS) Math Ed, S IL Univ 1973; Math, IL St Univ; *cr:* HS Math Teacher De Pue HS 1973-76; Jr HS Math Teacher Elmwood Grade Sch 1976-81; HS

Math Teacher Brimfield HS 1985-; *ai:* Var Girls Bsktbl; Var Boys Bsbl; *office:* Brimfield HS 201 E Clinton Brimfield IL 61517

WARNER, DRUSILLA DEITCH, 5th Grade Teacher; *b:* Shreveport, LA; *m:* Rodney A.; *ed:* (BS) Elem Ed, 1966; Span, 1969; (MED) Elem Ed, 1969 Shippensburg St Coll; *cr:* 5th Grade Teacher Eisenhower Elem Sch 1966-67; Keefauver Elem 1967-69; James Gettys Elem Sch 1969-; *ai:* Teacher Spon Rocketry Interest Group; James Gettys Sch Building Rep Gettysburg Area Ed Assn; GAEA Social Comm; Mem Meet and Discuss Comm; Recording Secy Historical Records 1975-; Chm; Delta Kappa Gamma Newspaper; Society Intnl; GAEA 1966-; PA St Ed Assn 1967-; NEA 1967; Adams Cty Chapter Amer Red Cross Red Cross Youth Teacher Spon 1970-83 Yrs of Service Awds Pins 1970-83; Adams Cty SPCA 1984-; Amer Assn of Univ Women (VP, Membership Chm 1966-72); Church of Gettysburg-250th Anniversary Comm 1989-; *office:* James Gettys Elem Sch 900 Biglerville Rd Gettysburg PA 17325

WARNER, JEFFREY MYRON, 8th Grade Science Teacher; *b:* Newton, MA; *m:* Phyllis Ann Hendrix; *c:* Angela A., Shannon R.; *ed:* (AA) Sci, Wingate Coll 1966; (BA) Geography, Univ of NC Chapel Hill 1968; Ed, Catawba Coll 1969; (MED) Earth/Space Sci, Univ of NC Charlotte 1973; *cr:* Sci Instr W Rowan Mid Sch 1968-; *ai:* Sci Fair Cty Comm; Sci Chm W Rowan Mid Sch; Sci Club Adv; W Rowan Mid Sch NC Assn of Educators Rep; Assn of Classroom Teachers Pres 1970; NC Sci Teachers Assn; NC Assn of Educators; Natl Assn of Geology Teachers; NEA; NC Alumni Assn; W Rowan Mid Sch Teacher of Yr 1981; NC Sci Olympiad 2nd Place Coach AWD 1987, 3rd Place Coach Awd 1988; Rowan Cty Sci Teacher of Yr 1988; NC Outstanding Earth Sci Teacher 3rd Place 1989; NC Assn of Educators Terry Sanford Awd Nom 1990; *office:* W Rowan Mid Sch Box 106 Cleveland NC 27013

WARNER, JUDITH KNAPP, German Teacher; *b:* Bloomfield, NJ; *m:* Richard H.; *c:* Eva Cornelia, Richard H.; *ed:* (MA) Ger Linguistics, NY Univ 1968; Russian Lang Stud, Columbia Univ, Inst Fuer Ost und Sudost Kunde, Linz Austria; Fr Stud, Millersville St Coll; E Germany Seminar, Lebanon Valley Coll; *cr:* Ft Lee HS 1961-62; Bergenfield HS 1962-64; Steglitzer Gymnasium W Berllin Germany 1966; Mary Washington Coll 1970-77; N Stafford HS 1977-; Germanna Comm Coll 1989-; *ai:* German Club Spon; VA Organization of Ger Stu 1989; Battle of the Brains Champions N Stafford HS; AATG 1970-; Foreign Lang Assn of VA 1980-; Whos Who in Arabian Horses Certified Judge; Natl & St-Wide Arabian Horse Memberships; Canadian Natl Championships Judge 1990; Hofstra Coll Summer Inst for Ger Stud Natl Defense Bd Act Grant; *office:* N Stafford HS 839 Garrisonville Rd Stafford VA 22554

WARNER, KENNETH EMIL, Mathematics Teacher; *b:* Fulton, MO; *m:* Ramona Marlene; *c:* Melissa, Tracy, Ryan; *ed:* (BSED) Math, 1971, (MSED) Scndry Sch Admin, 1980 Lincoln Univ; Univ of MO Columbia; *cr:* Math Teacher Fatima HS 1971-76, South Callaway R II 1977-; *ai:* Math Relays Spon; MO Cncl Teachers of Math 1980-; NCTM 1986-; *office:* South Callaway R II Box 37 Mokane MO 65059

WARNER, MARYLIN S., English Teacher; *b:* Kansas City, MO; *m:* James H.; *c:* Molly E.; *ed:* (BA) Eng/Speech, Mc Pherson Coll 1971; (MAT) Arts/Hum, CO Coll 1979; *cr:* Eng Teacher Mitchell HS 1971-74; Eng/Speech Teacher Doherty HS 1974-; *ai:* NEA, CEA, CSEA, NCTE; Natl League of Amer Pen Women VP 1989-; Natl Endowment for Hum Grant 1984; Pen Women for Best Fiction 1990; *office:* Doherty HS 4515 Barnes Rd Colorado Springs CO 80917

WARNER, MICHELLE BUTLER, Chairman English Department; *b:* Columbus, OH; *m:* Robert E.; *c:* Megan B., Rob; *ed:* (BA) Scndry Ed, PA St Univ 1969; (ME) Scndry Ed/Eng, Univ of W MD & Penn St Univ; Effective Elements of Instruction; *cr:* Eng Teacher William Penn Sr HS 1969-75, York Coll of PA 1978-83; Eng Teacher/Dept Chm York Cath HS 1983-; *ai:* Spectator Moderator Sch Newspaper; Mock Trial Coord; Stu Assistance & Eng Dept Chm; Steering Comm Mid States Evaluation; NCTE 1983-; Eastminster Presbyn Church Sunday Sch Supt 1987-; *office:* York Catholic HS 601 E Springettsbury Ave York PA 17402

WARNER, PATRICIA ANN, English Teacher; *b:* Wooster, OH; *ed:* (BA) Eng, 1972, (MAT) Eng, 1973 The Coll of Wooster; *cr:* Eng Teacher Orrville HS 1974-; Eng Instr Wayne Coll 1988-; *ai:* NEA, NCTE, OH Cncl Teachers of Eng & Lang Arts; Orrville HS & City Schls Teacher of Yr 1987-88; *office:* Orrville HS 841 N Ella St Orrville OH 44667

WARNER, ROBERT EUGENE, HS Social Studies Teacher; *b:* York, PA; *m:* Michelle Butler; *c:* Megan, Robbie; *ed:* (BA) Soc Stud, Penn St 1967; Masters Equivalency Penn St, W MD, AR St 1972; Stud Beyong Masters Equivalent; *cr:* Soc Stud Teacher York City Sch Dist 1968-; *ai:* Asst Ftbl & Bsbl Coach; *office:* William Penn Sr HS 101 W College Ave York PA 17403

WARNING, GERALD PAUL, 6th-8th Grade Teacher/Prin; *b:* Green Bay, WI; *m:* Kimberly Ann Wallquist; *c:* Katherine; *ed:* (BA) Elem Ed, Dr Martin Luther Coll 1976; *cr:* Teacher/Prin Zion Ev Luth Sch 1976-; *ai:* Head Coach Boys Vlybl, Bsktbl & Track; Child Study Comm Mem 1988-; *home:* 241 River St Sanborn MN 56083

WARNOCK, GLORY DEAN (POWELL), English/Science Teacher; *b:* Dublin, GA; *m:* A. T.; *c:* Keith, Jerry; *ed:* (AA) Bus, Brewton Parker Coll 1964; (BSED) Eng Ed, Univ of GA 1969; Working Towards Masters Degree Ed, Auburn Univ; *cr:* Teacher Monroe HS 1971-72, Prattville Jr HS 1972-73, Autauga Acad 1976-83; Government Employee Gunter AFB 1984-85; Teacher Autauga Acad 1986-; *ai:* Jr Beta Club Spon; Prom Co-Spon; Bible Sch Dir, Sunday Sch Teacher; Scout Den Mother; Eng Dept Coord; Sci Fair Spon; Arts & Crafts Day Class Coord; Kappa Kappa Iota Mem; Spinners Secy 1973-82; Annual Dedication 1981; Sustained Performance Awd 1984; Suggestion Awd 1985; *home:* 308 Poplar St Prattville AL 36067

WARREN, AUDREY ANN, Fifth Grade Teacher; *b:* Hollywood, FL; *m:* Dennis Clay; *c:* Avery A., Cambreia D. Ann; *ed:* (BA) Elem Ed, KY St Univ 1976; *cr:* 2nd Grade Teacher Pembroke Lakes Elem 1977-79; 5th Grade Teacher Pasadena Lakes Elem 1980-93; 4th & 5th Grade Teacher Driftwood Elem 1983-; *ai:* 5th Grade Chairperson; Arbor Day Chm; Former Lan Dept Rep; Former Co-Chm of Soc Services Comm; Broward Teachers Union 1984-; Carver Ranches Homeowners 1985-; Mt Zion AME Church Youth Choir Dir 1989-; Woman of Year 1989; *office:* Driftwood Elem Sch 2700 NW 69th Ave Hollywood FL 33024

WARREN, BETTIE MURPHY, 2nd Grade Teacher; *b:* Richmond, KY; *c:* Mark Murphy, Carolyn J.; *ed:* (BS) Elem Ed, 1976, (MS) Elem Ed, 1978 Eastern KY Univ; *cr:* 1st Grade Teacher 1976-80, 2nd Grade Teacher 1980- Silver Creek Elem; *ai:* Textbook Selection & Lesson Plan Comm; 2nd Grade Chm; Resource Teacher for KY Internship Prgm & Stu Teachers; Sunday Sch Teacher & Youth Worker; NEA, MCEA 1986-; Heard Fund Drive Worker; Mothers March of Dimes; United Way; Brownie Scouts Leader 1968; Certificate of Teaching Excl & Dedicated Service Awd 1979; *office:* Silver Creek Elem Sch 75 Old US 25 S Berea KY 40403

WARREN, BETTY JANE, Third Grade Teacher; *b:* Oswego, NY; *m:* Marvin; *c:* Robin, Robert, Donna; *ed:* (BS) Nursery/Kndgtn/1st-6th Grade, St Univ Coll Oswego 1968; *cr:* 3rd Grade Teacher Pulaski Sch Systems 1968-; *ai:* Public Relations Comm Mem; Alpha Delta Kappa Teachers Secy 1974-75; 4-H Leader 1968-69; Eagles Fan Club Supermodified Racing Group (VP 1979, Pres 1980-83, Treas 1976-77, 1985-87), Appreciation Awd 1978, Past Officers Awd 1984; 7th/8th Grade Religious Ed Teacher 1987-88; Pulaski Band Boosters (VP 1983-84, Pres 1985-88); Pulaski Parent-Teacher Group Treas 1984-; *home:* 8352 Richland Rd Richland NY 13144

WARREN, BETTY WOOD, Kindergarten Teacher; *b:* Castor, LA; *m:* Donnie; *c:* Timothy, Paula Warren Weaver, Crystal Warren Gardner; *ed:* (BA) K-8th Elem Ed, Northwestern St Univ 1977; *cr:* Teacher Castor Sch 1977-; *ai:* LAE, NEA 1977-; Teacher of Yr Castor Elem Sch 1988-89; Teacher of Yr Castor Elem Sch 1988-89; *office:* Castor Sch P O Box 69 Castor LA 71016

WARREN, FRANCES, First Grade Teacher; *b:* Glen Allen, MO; *ed:* (BSE) Ed, SE MO St Univ 1957; (MA) Elem Ed/Rdng, MO Univ Columbia 1964; Continuing Ed, Webster Coll; *cr:* Elem Teacher Trace Creek Sch 1951-52, Snowdenville Sch 1952-53; Primary Teacher Zion Sch 1953-54; 1st Grade Teacher Fox C-6 1954-; *ai:* Natl Teachers Assn, MO St Teachers Assn Life Mem; Amer Assn Univ Women Legislation 1987-; Jefferson Heights Baptist Church (Youth Dir 1956-76, Childrens Teacher 1978-86, Adult Teacher 1989-); PTO; Amer Legion Girls St Beta Club Mem; Amer Fed of Women Schlsp; Deans Honor Roll SE MO St Univ; *home:* 3333 Hwy M #97 Imperial MO 63052

WARREN, GEORGE CLAYTON, Mathematics Dept Chair; *b:* London, KY; *m:* Sally Ann Siler; *c:* Randy, Cynthia; *ed:* (BS) Math, Cumberland Coll 1968; (MED) Admin, Univ TN Chattanooga 1978; *cr:* Teacher Middlesboro HS 1968-69; Signal Corps US Army 1969-71; Teacher 1971-85, Teacher/Math Chair 1985- Bradley Cntrl HS; *ai:* Mu Alpha Theta Math Club & Chrstn Crusader Spon; Math Coach for Academic Contest; BCEA, TEA, NEA, 1971-; Building Level Teacher of Yr 1990; TMTA 1987-89; NCTM 1989-; Hopewell Church of God Adult Teacher 1984-; Faculty Honoree by Class of 1985; Advanced Placements Calculus Summer Inst at Univ of Cntrl FL 1989.

WARREN, KENNETH M., Chemistry Teacher; *b:* Chicago, IL; *m:* Judy Adams; *c:* Jeffery, Jennifer; *ed:* (BA) Chem, NE IL Univ 1968; *cr:* Teacher 1968-, Registrar 1987- Lane Tech HS; *office:* Lane Tech HS 2501 W Addison St Chicago IL 60618

WARREN, LINDA HENDERSON, Social Studies Teacher; *b:* Brookhaven, MS; *m:* Larry Leon; *c:* Tecompsha J., Karmen T.; *ed:* (BS) Soc Sci, Alcorn St Univ 1973; Alcorn St Univ, Jackson St Univ; *cr:* Resident Cnslr Alcorn St Univ 1974-77; Sch Attendance Officer Brookhaven Public Schls 1983; Teacher Brookhaven HS 1983-; *ai:* Chrldr Spon; Lincoln Cty Alcorn St Alumni Assn Secy 1989-; *office:* Brookhaven HS 443 E Monticello St Brookhaven MS 39601

WARREN, MARTHA MELTON, Career Exploration Teacher; *b:* Charlotte, NC; *m:* Thomas F.; *c:* Tracie W. Simma, Tammie M., Teri L.; *ed:* (BS) Home Ec, E Carolina Univ 1964; Cert Sci & Career Exploration Mid Sch Ed; *cr:* Teacher Blue Creek Elem 1964-67, Clyde A Erwin 1967, Northwoods Park Mid Sch 1967-; *ai:* Cmmty Awareness Club Spon; Career Exploration Clubs 1983-; Chairperson Annual Sch Fund Raisers; NEA, NC Assn of Educators 1964-; Onslow Cty Ed Assn 1964-, Cty & Regional Voc Teacher Awds. St Level Career Exploration Teacher Recognition; NC Voc Assn Pres 1989; AVA 1976-; Cncl for Career Exploration Regional Advisory (Region II Past Chairperson, Adv) 1988-; Onslow Cty Voc Assn (Pres 1990) 1976-, Teacher of Yr; Onslow Cty Volunteer 4-H Fund Raising Campaign Co-Chairperson 1989-; Ronald Mc Donald House Fund Raising Chairperson; Brookwood Baptist Church Mem; Outstanding Young Women of America 1978; Jaycees Outstanding Young Women of Jacksonville 1978, Outstanding Young Educator of Jacksonville 1976; Northwood Park Mid Sch Teacher of Yr 1976; NC Center for Advancement of Teaching Voc Dept Chairperson; Curr Comm for Senate Bill II; *office:* Northwoods Park Mid Sch 904 Sioux Dr Jacksonville NC 28540

WARREN, MARTHA MORRIS, Kindergarten Teacher; *b:* Parkersburg, WV; *m:* H. Gerald; *c:* Stephen, Ronald, Elizabeth; *ed:* (BA) Kndgtn/Primary, Oberlin Coll 1956; (MA) Early Chldhd, WV Univ 1983; WV Univ Writing Project 1989; *cr:* 3rd Grade Teacher Athens City Schls 1956-57; Kdngtn Teacher Washington Cty Schls 1957-58, Belpre Township Schls 1960-62, Marion Cty 1968-; *ai:* Marion Cty Schls Curr Comm; Rdng Cncl, NAEYC, Phi Delta Kappa; Jayceettes St Pres 1968-68; Lioness; WV Early Chldhd Eng Lang Art Teacher 1987; *home:* 26 Hollen Cir Fairmont WV 26554

WARREN, MARY COFFMAN, Third Grade Teacher; *b:* Hector, AR; *m:* Michael E.; *c:* Karen Casto; *ed:* (BS) Elem Ed, AR Tech Univ 1963; *cr:* 4th Grade Teacher Hughes Elem Sch 1963-65; Comptroller's Sec Firestone Tire & Rubber Manufacturing 1966-73; 3rd Grade Teacher Atkins Elem Sch 1973-; *ai:* Sci Curr Comm; Soc Comm; Atkins Local Ed Assn 1973-88; AR Ed Assn 1973-88; NEA 1973-88; Cmmty Concert Assn Mem Bd 1968-75; *home:* 807 Avenue 3 SE Atkins AR 72823

WARREN, MARY LOUISE, Third Grade Teacher; *b:* Ft Worth, TX; *ed:* (BA) Elem Ed, TX Southern Univ 1982; *cr:* Substitute Teacher Houston Ind Sch Dist 1979-81, Wilmer Hutchins Ind Sch Dist 1982; 3rd Grade Teacher Lobias Murray Chrstn Acad 1982-; *ai:* Co-Founder Young Sophisticates Club Girls & Esquire Club Boys Lobias Murray Chrstn Acad; Whos Who in Amer Ed 1989-; Full Gospel Holy Temple Church Coord Childrens Wkshp; Several Articles Published Church Souvenir Convention Book/Magazine; *office:* Lobias Murray Chrstn Acad 330 Ann Arbor Dallas TX 75216

WARREN, REBECCA WRIGHT, 8th Grade Language Art Teacher; *b:* Huntington, WV; *m:* Donald Ray; *c:* Anna, Elizabeth; *ed:* (BA) Elem Ed, 1974, (MA) Elem Ed, 1980 Marshall Univ; AFTS Educl Research & Dissemination Prgm; *cr:* Lang Art/Soc Stud Teacher St Joseph Elem 1974-75; 6th Grade Teacher Ft Gay Elem 1975-79; 8th Grade Lang Art Teacher Wayne Mid Sch 1979-; *ai:* AFT 1988-; Johnson Memorial United Meth Church Teacher 1989-.

WARREN, RUSSELL E., JR., Principal; *b:* Astoria, NY; *ed:* (BA) Eng, St Peters Coll 1977; (MA) Urban Admin, Jersey City St Coll 1984; *cr:* Teacher Stuyvesant Private Sch 1979-81, St Columba Sch 1981-86; Principal St Angela Merici Sch 1986-; *ai:* Athletic Dir; HS Cnslr; NCEA, ASCD Mem 1986-; *office:* St Angela Merici Sch 266 E 163rd St Bronx NY 10451

WARREN, S. IMOGENE (REINIER), First Grade Teacher; *b:* Leon, IA; *m:* Chester W.; *c:* Melvin L., Renee Warren O Rourke; *ed:* Simpson Coll 1950; (BA) Ed, Drake Univ 1969; Additional Courses Ed; *cr:* Elem/Intermediate Teacher Pleasant Hill 1945-52; Kndgtn Teacher Garden Grove Consolidated 1952, Van Wert Consolidated 1965-67; 1st Grade Teacher Clarke Cmmty-Weldon Elem 1968-; *ai:* Lang Art & Effective Schls Comm; ISEA 1967-; NEA 1968-; Leon Bible Church; *home:* Rt 2 Box 18 Weldon IA 50264

WARREN, SALLY KENNEDY, Eng/Creative Writing Teacher; *b:* Corinth, MS; *m:* Brady; *ed:* (BS) Eng Ed, MS St Univ 1986; *cr:* Teacher Starkville HS 1986-; *ai:* Creative Writing Club; Frosh Adv; Sr Spon; Faculty Advisory Comm; NCTE; MS Prof Educators Secy 1988-89; Governors Awd for Excl in Art 1990; *office:* Starkville HS Yellowjacket Dr Starkville MS 39759

WARREN, SUE (KENNEDY), Fifth Grade Teacher; *b:* Poteau, OK; *m:* Wayne; *c:* Jeremy, Justin; *ed:* (BA) Elem Ed, 1974, (MS) Scndry Counseling, 1989 Northeastern St Univ; *cr:* 1st Grade Teacher 1974-75, 5th Grade Teacher 1976- Mc Curtain Sch; *ai:* 4-H Leader; Christmas Prgm Choir; Haskell Cty OEA (Mem, Secy 1979-80) 1974-; *home:* Rt 1 Box 166 Mc Curtain OK 74944

WARRICK, ROBERTA BERGMAN, 6th Grade Teacher; *b:* Pittsburgh, PA; *m:* William R.; *c:* Rachel; *ed:* (BS) Elem Ed, Edinboro Univ of PA 1979; (MA) Spec Ed, WV Univ 1984; *cr:* Teacher of Gifted Ed A I Boreman Elem Sch 1979-84; 6th Grade Teacher t Benton Gayle Mid Sch 1984-; *ai:* In-Service Comm; TESA Instr; Phi Delta Kappa; SEA, VEA, NEA; *home:* 5508 Elder St Fredericksburg VA 22401

WARRINGTON, GLORIA BODELL, First Grade Teacher; *b:* Marion, OH; *m:* Phillip Chris; *c:* Molly, Matthew, Adam; *ed:* (BS) Elem Ed, OH St 1966; Bowling Green Univ; *cr:* 3rd/4th Grade Teacher Pleasant Elem 1967-70; Kndgtn/1st/5th/6th Grade Teacher Hopewell Loudon 1970-; *ai:* Jr HS Vlybl Coach; Sr Class Adv; Alpha Delta Kappa 1987-; OEA, NEA Life Mem; Local Ed Assn Pres 1986-87; *office:* Hopewell Loudon Sch Box 400 Cty Rd 7 Bascom OH 44809

WARTER, SHIRLEY ANN (NELSON), Fifth Grade Teacher; *b:* Butternut, WI; *m:* Marvin N.; *ed:* (BS) Elem Ed - Cum Laude, Univ of WI Eau Claire 1959; Univ of WI Parkside, Carthage Coll; *cr:* 5th Grade Teacher Lincoln Elem 1959-60, Wilmot Elem 1961-63; 5th/6th Grade Teacher Forest Park Elem 1963-; *ai:* Math Club & Contest Adv; Faculty Rep Math Sci Comm; NEA, WEA, KEA, WI Math Cncl; PTA Faculty Rep; Elem Teacher of Yr 1981; *office:* Forest Park Elem Sch 6810-45th Ave Kenosha WI 53142

WARUS, JUNE MARIE, Eighth Grade Reading Teacher; *b:* Jersey City, NJ; *ed:* (BA) Elem Ed, 1973, (MA) Rdng Specialist, 1978 Jersey City St Coll; Working Toward PhD NY Univ 1980-81 & Rutgers 1981-82; Sci Cert, JCSC 1987-89; *cr:* Elem Teacher St Paul of the Cross 1969-73, Little Falls Sch #1 1973-74, Elem Teacher 1974-80, Reading Specialist 1980-82, Elem Teacher 1982- Jersey City; *ai:* Jersey City Joint Act, Lincoln Center Performing Arts, Teach Adult HS, Rdng Curriculum Comm; Home Study Prgms; ESL Classes; JCEA Rep 1981-; NJEA, NEA 1973-; City Schls of Excl Grant 1988-89; *home:* 550 Central Ave Harrison NJ 07029

WASHAUSEN, VICTORIA ELAINE (PARKER), Social Studies Teacher; *b:* Hazelwood, MO; *m:* Wilbur C.; *c:* Gary, Adam; *ed:* (BA) Elem Ed, Southern Baptist Jr Coll 1973; (BSE) Elem Ed/Soc Stud, AR St Univ 1975; *cr:* 6th Grade Teacher Winona Public Sch 1975, Bunker R-3 1976-78; Jr HS Teacher Phelps Cty R-3 1978-; *ai:* Stu Cncl Spon; CTA Pres 1989-; *office:* Phelps County R 3 Sch HC 3 Box 175 Edgar Springs MO 65462

WASHBURN, BEVERLY ANN, English/Literature Teacher; *b:* Anderson, IN; *ed:* (BS) Eng, 1969, (MA) Eng, 1974 Ball St Univ; *cr:* Teacher Harrison-Washington Cmmty Sch Corporation 1969-; *ai:* Mid & HS Spell Bowl, Mid Sch Lang Art Super Bowl Team Spon; Accreditation Comm; IN St Teachers Assn, NEA 1987-; IN Academic Coaches Assn 1989-; Psi Iota Xi 1977-82; *office:* Wes-Del Mid Sch Rt 1 Gaston IN 47342

WASHBURN, CINDY KARLIN, Kindergarten Teacher; *b:* Hays, KS; *m:* Mark; *c:* Dusty; *ed:* (BS) Elem Ed, Fort Hays St Univ 1977; *cr:* 2nd Grade Teacher 1978-81, 1st Grade Teacher 1981-89, Kndgtn Teacher 1989- St Joseph Sch; *ai:* NCEA; St Johns Auxiliary; Thomas More Prep Trustee 1983-84; Marian Alumni Assn VP 1984-85; *office:* St Joseph Sch 210 W 13th St Hays KS 67601

WASHBURN, ELIZABETH BROWN, English Teacher/ Counselor; *b:* Helena, AR; *m:* Robert; *c:* Bill, Neil, Donald; *ed:* (BSE) Eng, AR St Univ 1952; *cr:* Eng Teacher Brinkley Jr HS 1952-63, Marvell HS 1964-70; Jr HS Eng Teacher/Cnslr 1970- Marvell acad; *ai:* Sr Class & Yrbk Staff Spon; MPSA Dist Chm Eng 1983.

WASHBURN, FLORENCE KATHRYN, Teacher of Gifted & Talented; *b:* Ironton, OH; *ed:* (BSED) Elem Ed, OH Univ 1972; (MA) Gifted Ed, Marshall Univ 1987; *cr:* 1st Grade Teacher 1972-85, Elem Teacher of Gifted & Talented 1986- Rock Hill; *home:* 1415 Park Dr Ironton OH 45638

WASHBURN, MARGARET ELAINE, Kindergarten Teacher; *b:* Lawrence, MI; *ed:* (BS) Music, 1971; (MA) Counseling, 1973 Western MI Univ; Early Chldhd Ed Endorsement 1990; Reproductive Health Inservice Pgm Teacher; *cr:* Middle Sch Music 1972-73; 3rd Grade Teacher 1973-76; Kndgtn 1976-; Dev Kndgtn 1986-89 Hartford Public Sch; *ai:* Rdng Comm; Math Comm; MI Ed Assn; NEA; Hartford Ed Assn; NAEYC; MI Rdng Assn; United Meth Church Worship Chairperson/Family Coord; Van Buren Youth Camp Leadership Consultant; Folk Dance Specialist; *home:* 40304 Cr 374 Paw Paw MI 49079

WASHBURN, VIOLA J., 4th Grade Teacher; *b:* Atlanta, GA; *m:* James E. (dec); *c:* Valencia M., James E. Jr.; *ed:* (BA) Elem Ed, Morris Brown Coll 1958; (MS) Rdng, Atlanta Univ 1973; Advanced Trng Cmptr Sci; *ai:* NEA, AEA; Public Service Work with Church Feeding Homeless; *home:* 124 Oakcliff Ct NW Atlanta GA 30331

WASHERLESKY, JANET JOHNSON, Lead Teacher; *b:* Bonham, TX; *m:* William E. Jr.; *c:* Jeff, David, Bill; *ed:* (BA) Eng, TX Tech Univ 1965; (MED) Elem Ed, E TX St Univ 1972; Prof & Supervision Cert 1988; Grad Classes Toward Mid Management Cert; *cr:* Jr Eng Teacher Lubbock HS 1965; Eng/Speech/Drama/ Fr Teacher Bonham HS 1967-69; 3rd Grade Teacher Bailey Inglish Elem 1969-75, Princeton Elem 1975-; *ai:* Lead Teacher; Facilitator for Inservice; UIL Coord; Coordination Elem Gifted and Talented; TSTA, NEA 1974-; ATPE 1978-; Delta Kappa Gamma Parliamentarian 1986-; Kappa Delta Pi 1985-; *home:* 406 Willow Ln Princeton TX 75077

WASHINGTON, BRENDA CROCKETT, Fifth Grade Teacher; *b:* New Orleans, LA; *m:* George Jr.; *c:* Dameon; *ed:* (BA) Ed, S Univ 1977; Stenoscript, Jefferson Voc Tech Sch 1981-; MA Early Chldhd, Xavier 1992; *cr:* Teacher Lafayette Elem Sch 1977-89, Murray Henderson Sch 1989-; *ai:* Grade Chairperson; Summer Sch Day Camp Operator; Tutor; Choir Mem; Stu Cncl Adv; Soc Stud Chairperson; Teacher of Yr 1985-86; *home:* 2703 Pritchard Rd Marrero LA 70072

WASHINGTON, CARNELL S., History/Law Teacher; *b:* Fayette, MS; *m:* Zenobia Bridges; *c:* Karnesha, Kartedra; *ed:* (BS) Ed/Scndry Soc Stud, 1972, (MS) Soc Stud, 1974 Southern Univ; Law Cert/Law Ed, LA St Univ 1976; US Constitution, Univ of S MS 1986; Amer Government Teacher, Southern Univ 1985; Grad Stud, Southern Univ 1980; *cr:* Teacher/Coach Pride HS 1972-81, Northeast HS 1981-; *ai:* Coaching Bsktbl, Ftbl, Cross Cntry; Head Track Coach; Mock Trial Team Coach; LA Fed of Teachers VP 1988, Membership Awd 1989; Soc Stud Club 1976; Law Teacher of Yr 1990; *office:* Northeast HS 12828 Jackson Rd Zachary LA 70791

WASHINGTON, DANNY J., Drivers Ed Teacher/Coach; *b:* San Antonio, TX; *ed:* (BA) Safety Ed/Phys Ed, 1980, (MS) Safety Ed/Ind Safety, 1984 Cntrl St Univ; Handicapped Drivers, Driver Improvement; *cr:* Teacher/Coach Lawton Eisenhower HS 1980-; *ai:* Coach Ftbl & Track; Afrs Amer & Booster Club Chm; Alpha Phi Alpha, OK Ed Assn, NEA; Prof Ed Assn of Lawton, OK Coaches Assn; Whos Who of Amer Univ Stu; Phi Beta Chi; *office:* Lawton Eisenhower HS 5202 W Gore Blvd Lawton OK 73505

WASHINGTON, JANNETTE MAXINE, Fifth Grade Teacher; *b:* Boca Grande, FL; *ed:* (BS) Health/Phys Ed, 1958, (MA) Elem Ed, 1980 FL A&M Univ; *cr:* Phys Ed Teacher Carter Paramore Sr HS 1958-59, Pinellas Sr HS 1959-60, Smith-Brown Elem/HS 1960-68; 5th Grade Teacher Little River Elem & Flagami Elem 1968-; *ai:* United Teachers of Dade Cty; *home:* 1150 NW 76th St Miami FL 33150

WASHINGTON, JOE IVA, JR., Physical Education Teacher; *b:* Lynch, KY; *m:* Youlanda Cumings; *c:* Joe I. III, Kevin L.; *ed:* (AA) Recreational Therapy, 1971 (BS) Phys Ed, 1973 E KY Univ; (MS) Counseling, W KY Univ 1976; Teacher Learning Process; Cooperative Learning; Mid Sch Strategies; Mid Sch Concepts Team Approach; *cr:* Teacher/Coach Mac Donald Mid Sch 1973-; *ai:* Sch Dances, Parties, Organizations Disc Jockey; Career Day Prgm Kingsolver Sch With Disco Demonstration Participant; Asst HS Ftbl Coach Fort Knox HS; Mid Sch Gymnastics Coach Mac Donald Mid Sch; Certified Correction Therapist, Veterans Hospital; Jr Var Coach; Fort Knox Teachers Assn 1975-; KY Ed Assn 1973-; KY Assn for Health & Phys Ed & Dance 1973-; KY Trackers Ftbl Team Mem; Amer Ftbl Assn; Sunday Sch Teacher; S Jefferson Chrstn Church Deacon; Wkshps Various Colls; Church Banquets Speaker; Wkshps at Sr Citizens Homes; Presenter Sr Citizens Day; Governors Cncl on Phys Fitness & Sports Clinician; Head Bsktbl Coach; Pres Cncl on Phys Fitness & Sports Clinician; Fitness Mobile for Mayors Summerscene Prgm Dir; Conducted Nutrition & Health Fitness Wkshp in Somerset Sponsored by KY Public Health Assn & KY Heart Assn; Natl Teacher of Yr 1979; KY Teacher of Yr 1980; Recruiting Day Prgm KY St Univ Speaker 1987; Symposium & Luncheon with Martha Collins Guest 1987; Bluegrass St Games, Opening Ceremonies Torch Bearer 1987; Golden Armor Festival 1986; Golden Field Day Act & Heartland Festival Participant 1986; Bluegrass St Games Gymnastics Coach 1986; Gold Medalist & Silver Medalist Bluegrass St Games 1986; Inservice Day Wkshps; Teacher of Yr Conference Omaha NE 1980; *home:* 3030 Garry Ct Radcliff KY 40160

WASHINGTON, LA VONNE CAISE, English/Reading Teacher; *b:* Versailles, KY; *m:* Fred O Neal Sr.; *c:* Fred O. Jr., Montez L.; *ed:* (BA) Eng, KY St Univ 1975; (MA) Rdng Specialist, Univ of KY 1980; Ec Ed Courses, Univ of Cincinnati; *cr:* Eng Teacher Woodford Cty HS 1976-77; Rdng Teacher Scott Cty Mid Sch 1977-80; Eng/Rdng Teacher KY St Univ 1980-83, Cincinnati Bd of Ed CAPE HS 1983-; *ai:* NHS Adv; Sr Class Spon; CAPE After Sch Tutorial & Honor Teacher 1986-; Instructional Assessment Test Writer; Black His Comm; GED Teacher 1988; NCTE 1989-; Cincinnati Fed Teachers 1983-; NAACP; Nom for Ashland Oil Teacher Achievement Awd 1989; *office:* CAPE HS 5425 Winton Ridge Ln Cincinnati OH 45232

WASHINGTON, LUE PEARL ROBINSON, English/Reading Teacher; *b:* Houston, TX; *w:* Willie Sr. (dec); *c:* Jeanice, Willie Jr.; *ed:* (BS) Eng, Southern Univ 1975; Coord Adult Ed *cr:* Adult Ed Teacher 1975-76; Housing Dir 1976-78 Southern Mutual Help Assn; Teacher Jeanerette Mid-Iberia Parish 1978-; *ai:* Chrldr Spon; Drug-Free Sch Coord; Coach Girls Vlybl/Bsktbl/Sftbl; Core Comm for Model Sch;Parish Cncl Mem; Iberia Assn of Ed Assoc Rep 1980- Most Increase Mem 1985-87; M Polk Schlsp Org Pres 1984-87; Southern Alumni Pres 1985-; Religion Ed Dir 1977-86 Cert 1985; Knights of Peter Clauer Ladies Aux Grand Lady 1990 Svc Awd 1990; Gamma Sigma Gamma Svc Pres 1975-75 Svc Awd 1974; Pips; Assoc Rep LA Assn of Educator; *office:* Jeanerette Mid Sch 609 S Pellerin Jeanerette LA 70544

WASHINGTON, MICHAEL JAMES, Biology I Teacher; *b:* Houston, TX; *m:* Linda Lillie Wilson; *c:* Jordon R.; *ed:* (BA) His, Lamar Univ 1982; *cr:* Teacher/Coach Lincoln HS Port Arthur 1985-; *ai:* Var Ftbl & Track Coach; TX St Teacher Assn 1985-; Kappa Alpha Psi VP 1989-; *office:* Port Arthur Lincoln Sch 1023 Abe Lincoln Port Arthur TX 77640

WASHINGTON, MILDRED CHISHOLM, French Teacher; *b:* Charlotte, NC; *m:* Emanuel Ezra; *c:* Emanuel Jr., Ronald P., Granville C.; *ed:* (BA) Fr/Eng, Johnson C Smith Univ 1950; Fr/ Eng, Univ TX Arlington; Fr, Univ NC Greensboro; *cr:* Teacher Como Jr-Sr HS 1962-69, Western Hills HS 1970-73, W Charlotte HS 1973-80, John T Williams Jr HS 1980-; *ai:* Fr Club Spon; Foreign Dept Chairperson; NEA, NC Assn of Educators, Charlotte-Mecklenburg Assn of Educators 1980-; *home:* 5707 Snow White Ln Charlotte NC 28213

WASHINGTON, PRINCE HALL, Principal; *b:* Slidell, LA; *m:* Marhsa Kimbrough; *c:* Arnel T.; *ed:* (BA) Teacher Elem Grades, Dillard Univ 1957; (MA) Admin/Supervision, Loyola Univ 1981; Numerous Educl Prgms, Wkshps, Act; Prof Improvement Prgm; Post Masters Stud Guidance, Counseling, Principalship, Loyola, Tulane 1981; Child Welfare, Attendance,Curr, Southeastern Univ, Univ of New Orleans; *cr:* Teacher 1957-77, PEA Coach 1977-78 Frederick Douglass Elem; Soc Stud Teacher Gretna Park Elem 1979; Admin Asst Frederick Douglass Elem 1979-80; Prin Elm Grove Elem 1980-; *ai:* Phi Delta Kappa, LA St Educl Organization, LA St Prin Assn, Jefferson Parish Prin Assn, NAESP, St Paul AME Church; Echelon of 59 Pres; Kappa Alpha Psi Polemarch; Urban League, NAACP Mem.

WASIK, CAMILLE S., Jr HS Teacher; *b:* Detroit, MI; *ed:* (BS) Elem Ed/Soc Stud/Eng, 1974, (MED) Elem Ed/Math, 1981 Wayne St Univ; *cr:* Teacher Our Lady of Mt Carmel Sch 1974-77; Part Time Math Therapist Marygrove Coll 1981-83; Teacher Sts Peter & Paul Sch 1977-; *ai:* Math Dept Head; Cmptr Lab Coord; Sch Safety Patrol Moderator; NCEA, NCTM, DACTM, MCTM, MACUL; Wayne St Univ Alumni Assn.

WASINGER, JOHN ROBERT, Reading Teacher/Dept Chair; *b:* Hays, KS; *ed:* (BA) Eng, 1959; (MS) Scndry Ed, 1968 Ft Hays St Univ; *cr:* Eng Teacher Bazine HS 1964; Lang Art Teacher Hickock Jr HS 1964-67, Orr & Hyde Park Jr HS 1967-81; Rdng Teacher Woodbury Jr HS 1981-; *ai:* Publications Adv; CO St Univ NDEA Rdng Inst 1966; *office:* Woodbury Jr HS 3875 E Harmon Ave Las Vegas NV 89121

WASON, JUDITH NASERS, Mathematics Teacher; *b:* Watseka, IL; *ed:* (BS) Math Ed, Univ of IL 1962; (MS) Math Ed, NE IL Univ 1973; Lake Forest Coll; Univ of IL Chicago; *cr:* Math Teacher W Aurora Sr HS 1962-66, Glenbard East HS 1966-68, Deerfield HS 1968-; *ai:* Test Dir for ACT & SAT Tests; NCTM, IL Cncl of Teachers of Math, N IL Math Educators, Metropolitan Math Club of Chicago; Deer Park Federal Credit Union Loan Officer 1980-; *office:* Deerfield HS 1959 N Waukegan Rd Deerfield IL 60015

WASSERMAN, HONI, Media Specialist; *b:* Newark, NJ; *m:* Bennett N.; *c:* Adam, Rebecca; *ed:* (BS) Elem Ed/Lib Sci, Trenton St Coll 1972; Educl Policy Sci, Kean Coll; *cr:* 6th Grade Teacher Grove Street Sch 1972-78, Madison Avenue Sch 1983-88; Media Specialist Grove Street Sch 1988-89, Collins Sch 1989-; *ai:* Gifted & Talented Steering, Geography, Writing Handbook 3rd-5th Grade Comm; NJ Ed Assn Mem 1972-78; NEA Mem 1982-; PTA Mem 1972-78, 1982-; *office:* Collins Sch 67 Martin Rd Livingston NJ 07039

WASSON, DANNY ALAN, United States History Teacher; *b:* Georgetown, KY; *m:* Reba Faye Mc Gehee; *c:* Jeremy, Todd, Christopher; *ed:* (BS) His, Cumberland Coll 1978; *cr:* His Teacher Williamsburg HS 1978-79; Life Sci Teacher 1981-83, His Teacher 1983-88 N Shore Mid Sch; His Teacher N Shore HS 1988-; *ai:* Head Frosh Ftbl, Asst Var Bsbl Coach; Headmaster Cmptr Comm; NEA 1979-; TX St Teachers Assn 1981-; TX HS Coaches Assn 1986-; NE Umpire Assn Secy 1988; NCES 1990; TX PTA Lifetime Membership; *office:* N Shore HS 13501 Holly Park Houston TX 77015

WATCHMAN, PAULINA YELLOWHAIR, Language Arts Teacher; *b:* Luepp, AZ; *m:* Leo C.; *c:* Derrick, Derrith Moore, Debra Watchman-Dole, Leo Jr.; *ed:* (BA) Ed, 1965, (MS) Eng, 1971 N AZ Univ; Grad Stud Admin; *cr:* Kndgtn-9th Grade Teacher Navajo Elem Sch 1965-79; 7th/8th Grade Lang Art Teacher/7th-12th Grade Dept Head Navajo Pine HS 1980-; *ai:* 7th-12th Grade Speech Spon; Screening Co-Chairperson; Intnl Rdng Assn, NM Teachers of Eng; *office:* Navajo Pine HS Box 1276 Navajo NM 87328

WATERS, GINGER KAY, Science Teacher; *b:* Rigby, ID; *ed:* (BS) Phys Ed/Sci, Boise St Univ 1974; *cr:* His/Phys Ed Teacher/ Coach Adelaide HS 1974-77; His/Health/Phys Ed Teacher/ Coach Bonneville HS 1977-80; 7th Grade Teacher/Coach Meridian Mid Sch 1982-; *ai:* Girls Athletic Dir; 8th Grade Girls Bsktbl Coach; Core Subject Team Leader; Nature Conservancy Natl Wildlife Fed; Sierra Club; Natl Aubudon Society; Teacher of Yr 1988; *office:* Meridian Mid Sch 1507 W 8th Meridian ID 83642

WATERS, MARY BURWELL, Mathematics Teacher; *b:* Yazoo City, MS; *m:* G. Keith; *c:* Hal, Brent; *ed:* (BA) Elem Ed, Univ of S MS 1974; (MS) Ed, William Carey Coll 1982; *cr:* Teacher Lamar Cty Schls 1974-; *ai:* HS Chrldr Spon; Natural Helper Adv; DAR 1989; Delta Kappa Gamma 1985-87; Meth Church Youth Dir 1989; *home:* Rt 1 Box 552 Sumrall MS 39482

WATERS, PATRICIA JEANNE (YOST), 1st Grade Primary Teacher; *b:* Miller, SD; *m:* Dale Francis; *c:* Victor F.; *ed:* (BA) Elem Ed, Huron Coll 1948; (MS) Elem/Rdng, Northern St Univ 1982; Nutrition; Growing Healthy; Effective Sch Dev; *cr:* 1st-8th Grade Rural Elem Teacher Hurd Cty Schls 1946-55; Urban Elem Teacher Miller Public 1955-; *ai:* Negotiations, Local Level Legislative Comm; Miller Ed Pres 1968-70; Bus Prof Woman (Local Pres 1981-83, St By-Laws 1978-83); SD Ed Assn Plains Uni-Serv Exec Comm; VFW Pres 1978-80.

WATERS, SANDRA CAROL, English Teacher; *b:* Steubenville, OH; *ed:* (BA) Scndry Ed, West Liberty St Coll 1973; (MA) Scndry Ed, WV Univ; Grad Stud; *cr:* Teacher Brooke HS 1974-; *ai:* WVLAC Brooke Cty Teacher of Yr 1990; *home:* 131 Hawthorne Acres Wellsburg WV 26070

WATERS, TED A., Mathematics Teacher/Dept Chair; *b:* Bluffton, IN; *m:* Marilyn L. Jones; *c:* Sheri, Scott; *ed:* (BA) Math/ Bus, Huntington Coll 1968; (MS) Math/Ed, St Francis Coll 1970; Grad Stud Ball St Univ Bowling Green St; *cr:* Teacher 1968-86, Dept Chm/Teacher 1987- Norwell HS; *ai:* Curr & Code Book Rewrite Comm Chm; NCTM 1970-; ISTA 1968-; Park United Brethren Church Treas 1975-; Natl Sci Fnd Summer Inst Grant; *office:* Norwell HS 1100 E U S 224 Ossian IN 46777

WATERS, VERNON EDWARD, Social Studies Teacher; *b:* Jacksonville, FL; *m:* Anne Rogers; *c:* Daniel L., Michael J.; *ed:* (BA) Sociology, Stetson Univ 1964; *cr:* Soc Stud Teacher John M Tutt Jr HS 1970-87, Westside HS 1987-; *ai:* Chm Textbook Comm; NEA 1972-89; Augusta Audubon Society Pres 1987-88,

1990; Crestview Baptist Church (Vice Chm, Deacon Bd) 1986-88; *office:* Westside HS 1002 Stelling Rd Augusta GA 30907

WATERS, VICKY RHODES, Science Teacher; *b:* Alexander City, AL; *m:* Joseph Edward; *c:* Kristi; *ed:* (BS) Chem/Bio, Auburn Univ 1978; *cr:* Teacher Beulah HS 1978-79, Goodwater HS 1979-80, Dadeville HS 1980-; *ai:* Attendance Clerk; Jr HS Chldr Spon; STRIPE & Core Team Mem; SADD Asst & Sr Sci Adv; AEA, NEA, NSTA, AL Sci Teachers Assn; GSA Asst Leader 1989-; New Concord Baptist Church Mem; Nom AL Teacher of Yr; Nom Natl Sci Teacher of Yr; Tallapoosa Cty Chem Teachers Curr Guide; *office:* Dadeville HS 611 E South St Dadeville AL 36853

WATHEN, HARRIET SEABROOK, Fourth Grade Teacher; *b:* Florence, SC; *w:* William Thales Jr. (dec); *c:* Maribeth Wathen Niager, Rebecca, Thales T., Kenneth Seabrook; *ed:* (AB) His, Coll of Charleston 1948; FL St Univ 1950; Univ of Houston 1966; *cr:* 7th/8th Grade Eng Teacher Beaufort HS 1948-49; 5th Grade Carrabelle Sch 1949-51; 4th Grade Teacher Brazoria Elem Sch 1951-52, 1965-; *ai:* Columbia Brazoria Ind Sch Dist Lang Art, Dist Career Ed, Numerous Textbook Comms; TX St Teachers (VP, Pres, Life Mem) 1968-; Alpha Delta Kappa Pres 1986-88; TAIR; 1st Presbyn Church (Deacon 1969-, Elder 1988); *office:* Brazoria Elem Sch PO Box O Brazoria TX 77422

WATIN, GEMMA B., Mathematics Dept Chairperson; *b:* Mahayag, Philippines; *m:* Rosli Habibullah; *c:* Monah Merced; *ed:* (BSE) Math/Physics, Immaculate Conception Coll Philippines 1972; (MAT) Math, SE MO St Univ 1986; *cr:* Math Teacher Immaculate Conception Coll 1973-75, Sacred Heart Sch for Girls 1975-77, San Jose Recoletos 1977-78, Cebu Intnl Sch 1978-81; Math Dept Grad Asst SE MO St Univ 1984-86; Math Dept Chairperson St Piux X HS 1986-; *ai:* Math Club; Gifted Math Prgm; 1-8-1-8 Prgm St Louis Univ; NCTM; *office:* St Pius X HS Rt 5 Box 83 Festus MO 63028

WATKINS, ANTHONY KEITH, Teacher/Lang Art Dept Chair; *b:* Henderson, KY; *m:* Patricia Lynn Crowder; *c:* John C.; *ed:* (BA) Eng/Scndry Ed, Univ of S IN 1975; (MA) Scndry Ed, 1981, (Rank I) Sch Admin, 1987 W KY Univ; *cr:* Teacher Henderson Cty Mid Sch 1976-77, 1977-88, Teacher/Dept Chm 1988- Henderson Cty North Jr HS; *ai:* 7th Grade Boys Bsktbl Coach; Henderson Cty In-Service Calendar Comm Mem; NEA, KEA 1976-; NCTE 1981-86; Henderson Cty Potential Admin Prgm 1989; Selected to Attend NASSP Prin Assessment Center; *office:* North Jr HS 1707 2nd St Henderson KY 42420

WATKINS, BRENDA KILPATRICK, Spanish Teacher; *b:* Athens, GA; *m:* Jerry W.; *c:* Cameron, Joey, Robbie; *ed:* (BA) Span, Lee Coll 1969; *cr:* Sci Teacher Belwood Sch 1970-71; Span Teacher Calhoun HS 1971-73, Northwest Whitfield HS 1981-83, Southeast Whitfield HS 1983-; *ai:* Span Club & Honor Society; Foreign Lang Assn of GA; Amer Assn of Teachers of Span & Portuguese; GA Assn of Educators; *office:* Southeast Whitfield HS 1954 Riverbend Rd Dalton GA 30720

WATKINS, E. MAUREEN SHEPHERD, Eng/Lang Art/ Comm Teacher; *b:* Lancaster, MO; *m:* Robert K.; *c:* Daniel E., Donna L. Norman, Dianna S. Kinney; *ed:* (BSE) Music, 1949, (MA) Eng Ed, 1967- NW MI St Univ; *cr:* Music Teacher Lancaster Public Schls 1949-50, Livonia Public Schls 1950-51, Lancaster Public Schls 1952-53, Livonia & Downing Public Schls 1956-57; Eng Teacher Schuyler R-I Schls 1960-; *ai:* Amer Field Service Club, Quiz Bowl Teams, Jr Class of 1990 Spon; Yrbk Class Adv; MSTA 1949-; Local CTA (Pres, Membership Chairperson) 1988-; NCTE, MO Assn Teachers of Eng 1960-; OES 1946-; PEO 1966-; Delta Kappa Gamma 1978-; Lancaster Chrstn Church Organist 1940-; NE MO Dist Eng Teachers Past Pres; Articles Published; *home:* Rt 3 Box 3 Lancaster MO 63548

WATKINS, JACQUELINE C. (KLEIN), 5th Grade Elementary Teacher; *b:* Dayton, OH; *m:* Larry L.; *c:* David, L. Douglas; *ed:* (BSED) Elem Ed, Youngstown St Univ 1971; Gifted Ed; *cr:* 3rd Grade Teacher Howland 1968-69; Kndgtn Teacher 1970-74, 3rd Grade Teacher 1974-83, 5th Grade Teacher 1983- Niles City Schls; *ai:* HS Girls Tennis Team Coach 1974-77; Sci Fair Chairperson; Gifted Comm; Natl Forensic League Judge; Amer Field Service Area Rep; OH Cncl/Gifted, OEA, NEA, NCTA; AFS (Area Rep 1983-87) 1976-88; Welcome Wagon; *office:* Niles City Schls-Lincoln 960 Frederick Ave Niles OH 44446

WATKINS, JOAN MOORE, HS Mathematics Teacher; *b:* Palestine, TX; *m:* Roy Paxton Sr.; *c:* Roy Jr., Kathy A., Mary J. Henderson; *ed:* (BS) Ed/Math, 1980, (MS) Ed, 1982 Stephen F Austin St Univ; Cmptr Programming; Cmptr Literacy; *cr:* Teacher Slocum Ind Sch Dist 1980-; *ai:* One-Act Play Dir; 8th Grade Spon; Kappa Delta Pi, Pi Mu Epsilon 1979; Alpha Chi 1981; CREST; *office:* Slocum Ind Sch Dist Rt 2 Elkhart TX 75839

WATKINS, LOUIS RALPH, Science Teacher; *b:* Manchester, NH; *m:* Rachel N. Roy; *c:* Shane, Mandi; *ed:* (BED) General Sci, Keene St Coll 1971; *cr:* 8th Grade Sci Teacher 1973-86, 6th Grade Sci Teacher 1986- Mastricola Mid Sch; *ai:* Sci Curr Steering & Curr Evaluation Comm Chairperson; Olm Religious Ed (Baptismal Co-Coord 1985-, Coord/Promoter of Charity Fund Concert 1990); Excl In Ed Awd Merrimack Teachers Assn; *office:* James Mastricola Mid Sch Baboosic Lake Rd Merrimack NH 03054

WATKINS, MARK N., English Teacher; *b:* Orange, CA; *m:* Kathryn A. Barton; *ed:* (BA) Comm, CA St Univ Fullerton 1980; Certificate Cmptr Instruction, CA St Univ San Bernardino; *cr:* Eng Teacher Yucaipa HS 1981-; *ai:* Cross Cntry Coach 1983-; Nominee Teacher of Yr 1988-89; Mt Sac Coach of Yr 1986, 1988-89; Article Published; *office:* Yucaipa HS 33000 Yucaipa Blvd Yucaipa CA 92399

WATKINS, RONALD, 5th Grade Teacher; *b:* Aliquippa, PA; *m:* Thelma Gist; *c:* Garrett, Stewart; *ed:* (BS) Elem Ed, CA ST Coll 1968; (MED) Elem Ed, Univ of Pittsburgh 1971; *cr:* Classroom Teacher Hopewell Area Sch 1968-; *ai:* NEA 1968-; PA ST Ed Assn 1968-; Hopewell Ed Assn Bldg Rep 1968-; *office:* Hopewell Area Schls 2121 Brodhead Rd Aliquippa PA 15001

WATKINS, RUTH COCKE, Retired; *b:* Birmingham, AL; *m:* Nathan G.; *c:* Nathan Jr., Grace E., Pat, Sandra; *ed:* (BS) Soc Sci, Livingston Univ 1977; *cr:* 7th-12th Grade Teacher Sumiter Acad 1978-89; *ai:* Drama Club Spon; Jr Beta Club Spon; Yrbk Adv; Faculty Rep; Authored Curr Guide for Teachers of Stud in HS; Delta Kappa Gamma 1987-89; AL Writers Conclave (Mem 1980- Historian 1984-86 Corresponding Sec 1986-88) Short Story/ Poetry Awds 1980-82; AL St Poetry Socty (Mem 1980- 1st VP 1987-89); Sumter Acad Yrbk Won Awds in 1987-89; Yrbk Dedicated to Me 1985; *office:* Sumter Acad Sch Rt 1 Box 389 York AL 36925

WATKINS, TONY IRVIN, 7th/8th Grade Math Teacher; *b:* Starkville, Miss; *c:* Anna Caroline; *ed:* (BS) Math, 1975, (BS) Math Sec Ed, 1976, (MA) Ed Sec Math, 1978 Univ of North AL; Univ of AL Birmingham 1986; *cr:* Teacher-Adult Basic Ed Muscle Shoals Tech Inst 1977-; 6th/7th/8th Grade Math Teacher Jackson Cty Bd of Ed Hollywood Jr HS 1977-78; Walker Cty Bd of Ed 1978-; 7th & 8th Grade Math Teacher Bankhead Mid Sch; *ai:* 7th Grade Bsktbl Coach Boys/Park Dir Cordova Park & Rec; 8th Grade Bsktbl Coach Boys/Chm Walker Co Girls Sftbl League; 7-8 Grade Girls Sftbl Coach; Lions Club Citizen of Yr 1988; Awd Dizzy Dean Bsbl Walker Cty; Coached Cty Champions in 7th Grade Bsktbl 1980; *office:* Bankhead Mid Sch 500 School Rd Cordova AL 35550

WATKINS SCHORR, CHRISTINE SMITH, English & History Teacher; *b:* Denver, CO; *m:* Peter A.; *ed:* (BA) His, Lake Forest Coll 1970; (MLITT) Interdisciplinary, Drew Univ 1981; 19th Century Stud, Drew Univ; *cr:* Teacher Libertyville Elem Sch 1970-72, Southern Boulevard Elem Sch 1972-75, Lafayette Mid Sch 1975-80; Eng Dept Chairperson 1987-88, Eng/His Teacher 1978- Chatham HS; *ai:* Design & Dev Interdisciplinary Courses His & Eng Chatham HS; Chatham Township Teachers Assn (Pres 1980-82, Chief Negotiator 1978, 1983-84); NJ Cncl of Teachers of Eng 1982-; Legislative Aide to Rep James Barry 1979-81; Harding Township Recycling Comm Co-Chairperson 1974-79; NJ Governors Outstanding Teacher Awd 1989; Geraldine R Dodge Fnd Grant 1988; Alternate NEH Summer Inst 1987; NJ Fellowship Summer Study Princeton 1985; Chatham Township Bd of Ed Spec Recognition Awd 1981; Drew Univ Commencement Address 1979; *home:* 31 Shadylawn Dr Madison NJ 07940

WATSON, ANNIE LITES, Second Grade Teacher; *b:* Greenwood, SC; *w:* Henry M. (dec); *c:* Elaine W. Hunter, Bettye W. Booker, Harry M., Henry M., Gregory I., Vivian W. Morris, J. Leanne; *ed:* (BS) Elem Ed, Allen Univ Columbia 1955; Certified Rdng Teacher Ed, Clemson Univ 1973; Courses for Pay Increases as Well as Recert Purposes; *cr:* 6th Grade Teacher Mims Elem Sch 1965-68; 2nd Grade Teacher Promisedland Elem Sch 1968-70, Mathews Primary Sch 1970-; *ai:* Palmetto Teachers Assn 1987-; Piedmont Rdng Cncl 1970; Harmony Lodge Order of Eastern Star #282 Assn Matron, Daughters of Isis Shriners 1980-.

WATSON, CAROLYN CAUFFMAN, Sixth Grade Teacher; *b:* Allentown, PA; *m:* Lynn Allen; *c:* John D., Barbara E.; *ed:* (BSED) Scndry Eng/Elem Ed, Shippensburg Univ 1958; Penn St Univ, Bloomsburg Univ, Clarion Univ; *cr:* 5th Grade Teacher Hamilton Sch 1958-61; 9th Grade Eng Teacher Carlisle Jr HS 1961-63; 6th Grade Teacher L R Appleman Elem Sch 1968-; *ai:* Lang Art Curr Comm; PSEA, NEA; PA Quilters 1985-; Benton United Meth Church 1968-; *office:* L R Appleman Elem Sch Park St Benton PA 17814

WATSON, CRAIG, English Teacher; *b:* Princeton, IL; *m:* Melody; *c:* Brooke, Ryan; *ed:* (BS) Phys Ed/Eng, IL St Univ 1976; Educl Admin, IL St Univ; *cr:* Eng Teacher Oswego Traughber Jr HS 1976-79; General Mgr Watson Pontiac Buick 1979-86; Eng Teacher Oswego Traughber Jr HS 1986-87, Minooka HS 1987-; *ai:* Var Boys Bsktbl & Var Boys & Girls Cross Cntry Head Coach; Asst Boys & Girls Track; IL Bsktbl Coaches Assn, NEA, IL Ed Assn; Minooka Ed Assn (Spokesperson, Negotiation Comm); Princeton Chamber of Commerce Pres 1984-85; Meth Youth Fellowship Dir 1982-86; *home:* 246 Forest St Oswego IL 60543

WATSON, DARLENE LAW, Resource Teacher for Gifted; *b:* Martinsville, VA; *m:* Ronald L. Sr.; *c:* Jennifer, Ronald II, Nicholas; *ed:* (BS) His, Radford Coll 1970; (MS) Curr & Instruction, Radford Univ 1989; *cr:* Elem Teacher 1970-88, Resource Teacher for The Gifted 1988- Pittsylvania Cty Sch System; *ai:* Young Authors Steering Comm; Enrichment Team Mem for Stony Mill/Whitmill/Mt Hermon Schls; Spon of Brain Waves Academic Competition; Spon of Stony Mill Yrbk; VA Assn for The Ed of the Gifted 1987-; Brosville Womans Club Pres 1976-77; Presenter VAEG Conference Regional Gifted Conference and Northern VA Gifted Conference 1987; Presenter Roaoke Regional Gifted Conference 1988; Pittsylvania Cty Elem Teacher of Yr 1988; *home:* Rt 1 Box 687 Cascade VA 24069

WATSON, GLADYS JUANITA, 5th Grade Teacher; *b:* Port Gibson, MS; *w:* A. W. Jr. (dec); *c:* Terrance, Dexter; *ed:* (BA) Elementary Ed, 1964; (MS) Elem Ed, 1979 Alcorn St Univ ; *cr:* Elem Teacher a W Watson Jr HS; Richardson Primary Sch; *ai:* Prgm Coord Elem Grades; NEA; PTA; NWACP; *home:* 907 Vine St Port Gibson MS 39150

WATSON, JEAN (BALBONI), Mathematics Teacher; *b:* Springfield, MA; *m:* Ronald R.; *c:* Lisa K.; *ed:* (BSED) Ed/Math, Westfield St 1963; PIMS Scholar, Hampshire Coll 1987-89; Trained for Giving Self Esteem Wrkshp 1988-89; Cmptr Courses, UMAS; *cr:* Teacher Classical Jr HS 1963-65, Forest Park Jr HS 1968-72, HS of Commerce 1972-; *ai:* Class Adv; Schlsp, Prin Faculty Advisory Comm; Mentor Teacher 1987-88; Springfield Ed Assn, MA Teacher Assn, NEA 1963-; Phi Delta Kappa 1987-; Delta Kappa Gamma 1984-; Chicopee Sch Comm (Chairperson 1981, 1986, Vice Chairperson 1980) 1978-; GE PIMS Fellowship Grant 1987-89; *home:* 148 La Belle Dr Chicopee MA 01020

WATSON, JEAN WOODS, Science Teacher; *b:* Selma, AL; *m:* Byron Wells Sr.; *c:* Byron W. Jr., David Q.; *ed:* (BS) Elem Ed, 1969, (BS) Bio, 1988 Judson Coll; Grad Study Univ of AL; *cr:* Sci Teacher Macon Acad 1969-70; Sci/Math Teacher 1970-73, Elem Sci Teacher 1974-75, Sci Teacher 1975-80, 1981- Southern Acad; *ai:* Yrbk Spon; 8th Homeroom; Sci Fair Coord; AL Private Sch Teachers Assn 1969-; *home:* PO Box 327 Newbern AL 36765

WATSON, JOHNNIE JEAN (SMALL), Teacher-Medical; *b:* Fort Worth, TX; *m:* Rice Eugene (Gene); *c:* John G.; *ed:* (BS) TX Wesleyan Coll Univ 1954; Several Wkshps; *cr:* Teacher Morningside Elem 1954-61, Bruce Shulkey 1961-87; *ai:* Life Mem PTA 1987; NRTA 1987; AARP 1987; Classroom Teacher Rep; *home:* 6433 Whitman Fort Worth TX 76133

WATSON, JOSEPH LELAND, Drama Teacher; *b:* Charleston, WV; *ed:* (BA) Theatre/Ed, St Andrews Presbyn Coll 1980; Working Towards MED UNCC; *cr:* Drama Teacher Independence HS 1982-83, Eastway Jr HS 1985-; *ai:* NC Theatre Conference Competitions Adv & Dir; Optimist Oratorical Contest Adv; NC Theatre Conference Mem 1985-, Best Play 1985, Honorable Mention 1986-87, Dir Awd 1986-88; Eastway Jr HS Teacher of Yr 1989-; *office:* Eastway Jr HS 3333 Biscayne Dr Charlotte NC 28205

WATSON, JOYCE O'QUINN, Mathematics/German Teacher; *b:* Lackey, KY; *m:* Neil Stanton; *c:* Heather, Matthew; *ed:* (BA) Math/Ger, Morehead St Univ 1973; (MA) Math Ed, E KY Univ 1974; (Rank I) Math/Scndry Ed, Morehead St Univ 1981; Resource Teacher Trng 1986-; Math Conference 1989-; *cr:* Dual Credit Project Alice Lloyd Coll 1976-80; Upward Bound Teacher Prestonsburg Comm Coll 1987-88; Teacher Allen Cntrl HS 1975-; Resource Teacher Floyd Cty 1986-; *ai:* Math & Ger Club Adv; Academic Team Coach; Governors Scholars Selection Comm, Curr Comm Chairperson, Cty Math Curr Comm; Delta Kappa Gamma VP 1982-; E KY Cncl Teachers of Math VP 1988-; KY Cncl Teachers of Math, Foreign Lang; NCTM 1988, Nominee Presidential Awd Excl Math Teaching; KY Ed Assn Delegate 1984-86; Hueysville Church of Christ Pres Womens Chrstn Fellowship 1987-88; Alice Lloyd Coll Alumni Dir 1974-75; Math Challenge Founder 1985-; Articles Published Floyd Cty Times; Grants Sch Partnership Comm 1988-; Awarded Math is Radical Prgm 7th Congressional Dist 1990; *office:* Allen Cntrl HS Eastern Eastern KY 41622

WATSON, MARGARET LEE, Guidance Counselor; *b:* Dothan, AL; *m:* Benjamin Michael; *c:* Ben, Elizabeth; *ed:* (BA) His, 1972, (MA) Counseling/Guidance, 1973 Univ of AL; *cr:* His/Eng Teacher De Kalb Cty 1973-74; Adult Basic Ed Teacher Metropolitan Nashville 1974-75; Eng Teacher Northview HS 1986-87; Teacher of Gifted & Talented/Guidance Cnslr Dothan HS 1987-; *ai:* Schoolwide Enrichment Resource Teacher; Talent Pool & Adopt-A-Sch Coord; NHS Comm & Inducting Teacher; Publicity, Scrapbook, Houston Cty Jr Miss Scholastic Judge Chairperson; Japanese Prgm Liaison; Delta Kappa Gamma 1990; Kappa Delta Epsilon Pres 1971-, Outstanding Mem 1972; Kappa Delta Pi 1973-; AL Assn for Counseling & Dev, AL Sch Cnslr Assn, Dothan Ed Assn, AL Ed Assn, NEA; AL-West FL Conference Pres; United Meth Ministers Wives (VP, Secy) 1975-; Dothan Service League VP 1979-83; Dothan Kappa Delta Alumnae Assn (Pres, Treas, Rush Chairperson) 1979-; Univ of AL Natl Alumni Assn VP; Daugters of Amer Revolution; Amer Assn of Univ Women; Pensacola FL & Columbus GA Assn of Jr Leagues; Wallace Comm Coll Stu Dev & Advisory Comm; *office:* Dothan HS 1000 S Oates St Dothan AL 36301

WATSON, NEZ, Social Studies Teacher; *b:* Scobey, MS; *m:* Dorothy Young; *c:* Julius, Shawn, Coriss; *ed:* (BA) Soc Sci Ed, Jackson St Univ 1972; Course of Study MS Annual Sch Alcohol/ Drug Stud; Trng MS Teacher Assessment Instruments; *cr:* Teacher Drew Public Schls 1972-74, Grenada Public Schls 1975-; *ai:* Stu Cncl Adv; Soc Stud Dept Chm; PTA Mem 1974-; MEA Building Rep 1984-86; Fine Arts Cncl Bd Mem 1978-80; Nom Teacher of Yr 1987-88; *home:* Rt 5 Box 945 Grenada MS 38901

WATSON, PATRICIA MORGAN, English Teacher; *b:* Lubbock, TX; *m:* W.t.; *c:* David, Edwin, Clifford; *ed:* (BMED) Elem Ed/Music, E NM Univ 1973; Cert all Areas Lang Art & all Areas Music, TX Tech Univ; *cr:* 3rd Grade Teacher Deshazo Elem Sch 1974; 6th Grade Rdng Teacher Watson Jr HS 1975-84; 11th Grade Eng Teacher Muleshoe HS 1985-; *ai:* Sch Yrbk Co-Spon; Faculty Advisory Comm; TX St Teachers Assn Pres 1977-78; Classroom Teachers Assn Building Rep 1984-85; PTA Pres 1970-71, Lifetime Mem 1970; Kappa Kappa Iota, Amer Assn of Univ Women; 1st Assembly of God Church Organist; Outstanding Young Women of America 1970; Intnl Whos Who in Music 1975; Author Book 1989; *home:* Rt 2 Box 750 Muleshoe TX 79347

WATSON, RANDALL GREGG, 5th Grade Teacher; *b:* Philipsburg, PA; *m:* Linda; *c:* Ryan, Amanda; *ed:* (BS) Elem Ed, 1971, (MS) Ed Admin, 1977 Penn St; Elem Prin Certificate 1978; *cr:* Elem Teacher Goshen Elem Sch 1973-; *ai:* Head Teacher

Goshen/Girard Elem Bldgs; Ben Franklin Stamp Club Adv; Clearfield Ed Assn; Goshen PTA; *home:* Box 51 Lanse PA 16849

WATSON, REBECCA HOOPER, First Grade Teacher; *b:* Waverly, TN; *m:* Carl; *c:* Susanne, Margaret; *ed:* (MS) Elem Ed, Memphis St 1976; *cr:* 5th Grade Teacher 1975, 1st Grade Teacher 1975- Bolivar Elem Sch; *ai:* Lead Teacher for 1st Grade 1988-; NEA, TN Ed Assn, Hardeman Cty Ed Assn 1975-; Outstanding Young Women of America; Career Level II of TN Career Ladder; *office:* Bolivar Elem Sch Nuckolls Rd Bolivar TN 38008

WATSON, ROGER EVERETT, Math/Physics/Computer Teacher; *b:* Milwaukie, OR; *m:* Mary L. Nally; *c:* Corinne L. Nieman, Roma R. Clewell, Brian E.; *ed:* (BS) Bio/Math, Portland St Univ 1959; (MED) Ed, Univ of OR 1968; Working Towards Masters Cmptr Sci, OR St Univ, S OR St Coll, Walla Walla Coll; Microcmptr Electronics, Natl Radio Inst; *cr:* Bio/Algebra I & II/Chem General Sci Teacher Ophir HS 1959-60; Algebra I & II/Geometry Teacher Molalia HS 1960-69; Algebra I & II/Advanced Math/Geometry/Physics/Cmptrs Teacher Laurelwood Adv Acad 1969-85; Physics/Geometry/Cmptrs Teacher Milo Adv Acad 1985-; *ai:* Jr Class Spon; OR Teachers of Math, NCTM 1960-; Natl Physics Teacher 1970-; Assisted Dr Q Clarkson Portland St Univ Researching Iris & Trilleum on S OR Coast; Taught Cmptrs for Teachers Laurelwood Adv Acad & Portland St Univ; *office:* Milo Adventist Acad P O Box 278 Days Creek OR 97429

WATSON, SHARON DENISE, 8th Grade Lang Arts Teacher; *b:* Detroit, MI; *c:* Dewayne, Frederick, Gregory, Darryl; *ed:* (AA) Lib Arts, WCCC 1972; (BA) Ed/Lang Arts, MSU 1974; Natl Writing Project; *cr:* Intern Teacher MSU Detroit Public Sch 1973-74; Lang Arts Teacher Hamilton Mid Sch 1977-; *ai:* Creative Writing Teacher; 8th Grade Act Comm Gifted & Talented, Future Teachers Club Comm; *office:* Hamilton Mid Sch 14223 Southampton Detroit MI 48213

WATSON, VERA DOLORES (BANKS), Social Studies Teacher; *b:* Raymond, MS; *m:* Lawrence; *c:* Jocylynn L. *ed:* (BS) Soc Sci, 1972, (MAT) Soc Sci, 1976 Jackson St Univ; Working Towards Specialist Jackson St Univ; MS Coll 1983 & MS St Univ 1984; *cr:* Teacher Hinds Cty Schls 1976-79, Clinton Public Schls 1980-; *ai:* Spon Soc Stud Club 1984-, Chrldr 1988-89; Prin Advisory Comm 1988-89; MS Assn of Educators 1982-; Clinton Assn of Educators Building Rep 1987-88; Jackson Dist Jr Matrons Auxiliary (Pres 1987-89, Leadership 1989); Clinton Cmmty Chrstn Corporation Bd of Dirs 1987-; Natl Assn Advancement of Colored People Secy 1986-; Clinton Jr HS Teacher of Yr 1988-89; Educl TV MS His Series Public Advisory Comm; *office:* Clinton Jr HS 400 E College St Clinton MS 39056

WATT, BETTY J., 8th Grade Earth Sci Teacher; *b:* Des Moines, IA; *m:* Charles C.; *c:* Katy Anderson, Kylee Anderson; *ed:* (BS) Bio, Mc Pherson Coll 1969; (MD) Scndry Ed, Univ of NE 1974; Grad Stud Ed, Sci Ed; *cr:* 7th/9th Grade Bio Teacher Beveridge Jr HS 1969-72; 8th Grade Earth Sci Teacher Plattsmouth Mid Sch 1972-; *ai:* Plattsmouth Ed Assn Secy 1974; NSTA; NE Assn of Mid Level Educators; *office:* Plattsmouth Mid Sch 8th & Main Plattsmouth NE 68048

WATTERS, LINDA BROOKS, Fourth Grade Teacher; *b:* Columbus, MS; *m:* Charles Edward; *c:* Derrick; *ed:* (BS) Elem Ed, Rust Coll 1972; *cr:* Teacher New Hope Elem Sch 1972, Grady A Brown Elem Sch 1973-; *ai:* Cultural Arts Comm; NC Assn of Educators; Delta Sigma Theta; Grady A Brown Sch Teacher of Yr; Teacher Awd of Excl; *office:* Grady A Brown Elem Sch Rt 6 Box 1005 Hillsborough NC 27278

WATTERSON, DAWN ZELLEFROW, 6th Grade Teacher; *b:* Kittanning, PA; *m:* Robert E.; *c:* Bria D.; *ed:* (BS) Elem Ed, Indiana Univ of PA 1977; *cr:* 5th/6th Grade Teacher St Josephs Sch 1977-78; 5th Grade Teacher 1978-79, 6th Grade Teacher 1979- Dayton Elem; *ai:* Ecology Meet Coach; Sign Lang Club; Sci & Rdng Curr Integration Comm; Elem Intramural Coach 1978-80; NEA, AEA, PSTA, NSTA; Dayton PTA Treas 1986-87; Mini Grant Prgm 1986-87; *home:* RD 2 Box 236A Ford City PA 16226

WATTS, AUGUSTINE SMITH, Business Education Teacher; *b:* Magee, MS; *m:* Willie E.; *c:* Erica; *ed:* (BS) Bus Ed, Alcorn St Univ 1966; (MS) Bus Ed, Governors St Univ 1979; Cmptr Ed, Purdue Univ; *cr:* Teacher Chicago Bd of Ed 1966-73, Gary Cmmty Sch Corporation 1974-; *ai:* FBLA Spon; Bus & Prof Womens Inc 1989-; Gary Rdng Cncl 1987-; *office:* West Side H S 9th Ave & Gerry St Gary IN 46406

WATTS, BRENDA TURNER, 4th-6th Grade Reading Teacher; *b:* Bowen, KY; *m:* Paul; *ed:* (BS) Elem Ed, 1969, (MA) Ed/Rdng, 1972, (Rank I) Ed/Rdng, 1975 E KY Univ; Gifted Ed; Beginning Teacher Internship; Comp Ed; *cr:* Teacher Jackson City Sch 1969-; *ai:* Academic Mid Sch, Elem Academic Future Problem Solving Team & Girls Bsktbl Team Coach; 4-H Club Leader; Cheerleading Spon; PTA Pres; Jackson Ed Assn Pres Outstanding Teacher; Breathitt Cty Honey Festival Educator of Yr 1988; 4-H Outstanding Leader 1989; *home:* 338 Panbowl Rd Jackson KY 41339

WATTS, DENNIS W., English Teacher; *b:* Lumberton, NC; *m:* Janice Ann Fields; *ed:* (BA) Eng, Pembroke St Univ 1983; MBA, Univ of NC Wilmington; MA Prgm Eng, Pembroke St Univ; *cr:* Eng Teacher S Robeson HS 1986-87, W Robeson HS 1987-89, Purnell Swelt HS 1989; *ai:* NHS Adv; NEA, NC Assn of Educators, Robeson Assn of Educators Mem 1987-; *office:* Purnell Swett HS PO Box 1210 Pembroke NC 28372

WATTS, JAQUELINE MC NEIL, French Teacher; *b:* Charlotte, NC; *m:* Nathaniel Ronald; *ed:* (BS) Fr/Span, Knoxville Coll 1968; (MA) Foreign Lang Ed, OH St Univ 1973; Cert in Rdng Ed, OH St Univ 1988; Post-Grad Courses in Fr, Purdue Univ 1984; *cr:* Fr/Span Teacher Northland HS 1968-74; Eng Teacher Lycee De Luang Prabang 1974-75; Fr/Span Teacher Barrett Jr HS 1975-78; Fr Teacher Columbus Alternative HS 1978-; *ai:* Adv Fr Club; Adv Fr Honor Society; OH Foreign Lang Assn 1968- Outstanding F L Prgm Awd 1989; AATF 1980-Certificate D Honneur 1984-85/1987-88; NEA, OEA, CEA, & COTA 1968-; Alpha Kappa Alpha Basileus Chapter Pres 1967 Silver Awd 1990; Fulbright-Hays Grant to Teach in Laos 1974-75; Foreign Lang Prgm Facilitator NHF Grant Sponsored Position; Natl Endowment Hum Grant Fr Inst 1984; Educator of Yr Columbus Alternative HS 1990; *home:* 1299 Louis Dr Columbus OH 43207

WATTS, JERRY L., 5th Grade Teacher; *b:* Willows, CA; *m:* Ethel Goltz; *c:* Warren, Wendi; *ed:* (BA) Ed/Comm, 1965, (MA) Curr Dev, 1968 Pacific Union Coll; Grad Stud Univ of CA Berkeley, CA St Univ Sacramento, CA St Univ Chico 1969-89; *cr:* Mid Sch Teacher Orangevale SDA Sch 1965-69, Paradise Elem Sch 1969-; *ai:* 4th-6th Grade Fund Raising Chm; Paradise Unified Sch Dist Math & Cmptr Comm Mem; Paradise Elem Cmptr Task Force Mem; CA St Univ Chico Master Teacher; Paradise SDA Church Tape Ministries Dir 1976-; Sch & Dist Cmptr Mentor 1982-83; Wrote 8th Grade His Curr Guide Pacific Union Conference SDA 1968-69; *office:* Paradise Elem Sch 588 Pearson Rd Paradise CA 95969

WATTS, JOYCE ANN (MORGAN), Computer Department Chairman; *b:* Lucedale, MS; *m:* Benjamin Patrick Sr.; *c:* Benny, Jennifer, Morgan; *ed:* (BS) Math/Psych, Univ of S MS 1967; (MED) Math Ed, William Carey Coll 1986; *cr:* Math Teacher Moss Point HS 1969-72, Magnolia Jr HS 1974-78; Math Teacher 1981-85, Cmptr Teacher 1985- Pascagoula HS Annex; *ai:* Soph Class Spon; Phi Delta Kappa Secy 1988-; Chamber of Commerce 1988-; *office:* Pascagoula HS Annex 1520 Tucker St Pascagoula MS 39567

WATTS, NORMA HUGHES, Theatre Arts Teacher; *b:* Anchorage, KY; *m:* Billie Dean; *c:* Jennifer C., Juliet N.; *ed:* (BA) Theatre/Eng, OR St Univ 1968; Elem Ed, Angelo St Univ TX 1978; Advance Academic Trng Educal Theatre, Curr Dev & Wkshp Presentations; *cr:* 2nd Grade Teacher Crockett Elem 1978-84; Theatre Arts Teacher San Angelo Cntrl HS 1984-; *ai:* Intnl Thespian Troupe 3440 Spon; San Angelo Cntrl HS Theatre Productions Dir 1989; TX Ed Theatre Assn Secy Scndry Section 1988-; Theatre Ed Assn 1987-; San Angelo River Stage Advisory Comm 1988-89; Intnl Thespian Festival; *office:* San Angelo Cntrl HS 100 Cottonwood San Angelo TX 76901

WATTS, PATRICIA ANN, English Teacher; *b:* Alexandria, LA; *m:* O'Neil Jr.; *c:* Alexandra, Tammie, Demiatris; *ed:* (BA) Scndry Ed, 1974, (MA) Ed Admin, 1978 Univ of NM; *cr:* Teacher Madison Mid Sch 1974-77, Sandia HS 1977-; *ai:* Sandia HS Natl Jr Honor Society Spon 1986-88; East Area Teacher Advisory Cncl Rep 1984-86; Sandia HS Improvement Team Chairperson 1987-89; N Cntrl Evaluation Co-Chairperson 1989-; NEA Pres 1984-86; Phi Delta Kappa 1987-89; Delta Sigma Theta Pres 1980-81; Natl Assn Advancement of Colored People St Secy 1981-83, Appreciation Awd 1983; Garden City HS of Fame Inductee 1988; Natl Jaycee Outstanding Young Women 1979; Natl Cncl of Negro Women Black Women in Management Awd 1985; Chamber of Commerce Leadership Prgm 1988; *office:* Sandia HS 7801 Candelaria Rd N E Albuquerque NM 87110

WATTS, SANDRA KAY (BROOME), Sci Teacher Dept Chairperson; *b:* Lancaster, SC; *m:* Stephen Paul; *c:* Stephen; *ed:* (BA) Sec Sci Ed, Clemson Univ 1978; (MED) Sec Sci Ed, Univ of SC 1982; *cr:* 8th Grade Sci Southside Jr HS 1978-79; 8th/9th Grade Sci Fairfield Jr HS 1979-82; 8th Grade Sci Kingstree Jr HS 1982-87, Carver Edisto Mid Sch 1987-; *ai:* Sci Dept Chairperson; Stu Cncl, Sci & His Club Spon; Curr Planning Comm; Sci Fair Chairperson; Teacher of Yr 1982-83, 1985; Palmetto St Teachers Assn; SC Sci Cncl; Amer Chem Teachers Assn; Teacher of Yr 1982-83, 1985; Pres Excl in Sci Teaching Awd Nom; *office:* Carver Edisto Mid Sch P O Box 65 Cordova SC 29039

WATTS, WILLIAM HENRY, Amer His Teacher/Soc Stud Chm; *b:* Ft Bragg, NC; *m:* Marilyn Annette Rayner; *c:* Ashley A., Michael W.; *ed:* (BA) Soc Stud, Univ of S MS 1979; Working Towards Masters; *cr:* Amer His Teacher Tylertown HS 1980-; *ai:* MS STAR Teacher 1987-88; *home:* 507 Enochs St Tylertown MS 39667

WAUGH, SUZANNE MARY, Tutor; *b:* Peoria, IL; *m:* George Masurat; *ed:* (BA) Psych/Spec Ed, St Louis Univ 1974; Spirituality, St Catherines Coll; Success in Rdng, Logo Cmptr, Creative Writing, The Learning Center; *cr:* Learning Disabilities Teacher Loretto Center 1974-77; Teacher Neighborhood Sch 1977-79; Teacher 1980-86, Tutor 1986- Childgrove Sch; Logo Classes The Learning Center 1986-88; *ai:* Childgrove Bd of Trustees (Pres 1988-) 1981-; Make Today Count Facilitator 1981-; Success in Rdng Wkshp Presenter 1984; Seattle Pacific Adjunct Faculty Mem; *home:* 1574 Foxham Dr Chesterfield MO 63017

WAVE, KIM FISHER, Sixth Grade Teacher; *b:* Columbus, OH; *m:* John Steven; *ed:* (AA) Elem Ed, Okaloosa Walton Jr Coll 1978; (BA) Elem Ed, Univ of W FL 1980; Working on Masters Public Sch Admin, W Carolina Univ; *cr:* 6th Grade Teacher Jenkins Mid Sch 1980-81; 6th-8th Grade Eng Teacher Lincoln Mid Sch 1981-82; 6th Grade Teacher Pisgah Elem 1984-86, Enka Mid Sch 1986-; *ai:* Eng & Rdng Textbook Adoption Comm; NC Assn of Educators Mem 1987-; ASCD Mem 1990; *office:* Enka Mid Sch 390 Asbury Rd Candler NC 28715

WAX, MARILYN, Phys Ed/Health Teacher/Coach; *b:* Chicago, IL; *ed:* (BS) Ed, N IL Univ 1968; (MA) Comm Sci, Governors St Univ 1977; Additional Course Work Phys Ed, Health & Ed; *cr:* Phys Ed/Health Instr/Coach Evergreen Park HS 1968-; *ai:* Bowling, Golf, Sftbl Coach; Started Girls Bowling Team 1976 & Sftbl Team 1970; Sch Bd Caucus; Lifeguard/Swim Instr Evergreen Aqua Park; Mgr & Coach Khoury League Sftbl Prgm Evergreen Park; Bowling Advisory Bd; Chairperson N Cntrl Media Comm 1983-84; IL HS Assn Sftbl Ofcl 1971-; IL Assn Health, Phys Ed, Recreation Mem; IL Coaches Assn, IL Bsbl Coaches Assn Mem; Chicago Sun-Times All-Area Sftbl Coaches Bd Mem; N IL Univ & Governors St Univ Alumni Assn Mem; Amer Red Cross 1967-, Awds 1972, 1977, 1982, 1987, 1989; Winningest Sftbl Coach; Female Teacher of Yr 1983; Sftbl Coach of Yr Chicago Sun Times 1986; *office:* Evergreen Park HS 9901 S Kedzie Ave Evergreen Park IL 60642

WAY, WANDA STRICKLAND, English Teacher; *b:* Portsmouth, OH; *m:* David E.; *c:* Chad R., William D., Michael J., Rebecca M. Rudd; *ed:* (BA) Elem Ed, Miami Univ 1970; (MA) Supervision/Admin, Univ of Dayton 1985; *cr:* Kndgtn Teacher Scioto Valley Schls 1966-67; Spec Ed Dh, 1970-71; 4th Grade Teacher 1971-76; 8th Grade Teacher OH Hist/Guid 1976-81; Gifted/Talented 1981-82; 8th Grade Teacher Eng/Writing 1982- Middletown City Schls; *ai:* Chm Right to Read Prgm; Chm Black His Month; Chm Dist Spelling Bee; Chmn Language Arts Olympiad; Mem Eng Curr Comm; Educl Honor Society Kappa Delta Pi Mem 1970-; Scholastic Honor Society Phi Kappa Phi 1970-; Middletown Teachers Assn 1970-; OH Ed Assn 1970-; NEA 1970-; Doty House for Handicapped Bd of Trustees 1982-; *home:* 640 Da Vinci Dr Middletown OH 45042

WAYLAND, JOANN LAFLIN, Business Teacher/Dept Chairman; *b:* Aurora, IL; *m:* Frank R.; *c:* Mark, Robert; *ed:* (BS) Bus, W IL Univ 1954; W IL; CA St Univ Northridge; *cr:* Teacher Dunlap HS 1954-55, Macomb HS 1955-57, Madera HS 1958-59, Antelope Valley HS 1961-; *ai:* Substance Abuse Coord; Mentor Teacher; Peer Helper Trainer; Teacher of Yr Comm; Employees Assistance Prgm; Staff Dev Comm; CA Teachers Assn, NEA 1961-; Delta Kappa Gamma (VP 1976-78) 1971-; Antelope Valley HS Teachers Assn 1961-; Toastmistress Club Pres 1965; Antelope Valley HS Booster Club 1971-79; Chm WASC Accreditation Voc Comm; *office:* Antelope Valley HS 44900 N Division Lancaster CA 93535

WAYNE, MARTHA (MORRISON), English Teacher/Dept Chair; *b:* Tulsa, OK; *m:* James L.; *c:* Jeremy, Cassandra; *ed:* (BS) Eng, SE MO St Univ 1970; Grad Stud S OR Coll Ashland, SE MO St Univ Cape Girardeau; *cr:* Teacher/Librarian S Iron Cty Schls 1970-71; Teacher Lesterville R-IV 1971-76, Arcadia Valley Schls 1976-80; Teacher/Dept Chair Lesterville R-IV 1980-; *ai:* Academic Team Coord; Stu Cncl Spon; Drama Club & Debate Coach; *office:* Lesterville R-IV Schls PO Box 120 Lesterville MO 63654

WEAKLEY, SYBIL LEE, 7/8th Grade Lang Arts Teacher; *b:* Dyersburg, TN; *ed:* (BS) Elem Ed, Univ of TN 1971; Grad Work Memphis St Univ 1979; *cr:* Teacher Holice Powell Sch 1972-; *ai:* Events Coord; Cmptr Coord; Play-By-Play Ftbl Announcer; NEA/TEA/DCEA 1972-; Dyer Cty Ed Assn Past Pres; Alpha Delta Phi Alumnae Assn Pres 1988-; Holice Powell Teacher of Yr 1978/1983/1985/1987/1990; Chm Curr Dev Comm Summer Sch Pgm; *home:* Rt 1 Box 387 Dyersburg TN 38024

WEALTHALL, BILL, Music Teacher/Asst Principal; *b:* Ulysses, KS; *m:* Sherry Artherton; *c:* Kimberly, Amber, Dustin; *ed:* (BME) Music Ed, 1978, (MS) Sch Admin 1987 Univ of KS; *cr:* Music Ed West Colomon Valley USD 213 1978-80; Teacher/Asst Prin Perry-Lecompton USD 343 1980-; *ai:* Asst Prin; Band Dir; Flag Team Spon; Stu Cncl Adv; KS Music Ed Assn 1978- St Participant 1987; ASCD 1986-; United Meth Church (Chapel Choir Dir 1976-78, 1980-, Worship Comm 1980-); KS Staff Dev Leadership Conference Presenter 1988; Kaw Valley Regional Inservice Facilitator 1986; USD 343 Curr Coordinating Cncl Chair 1987-88; *office:* Perry-Lecompton HS PO Box 18 Perry KS 66073

WEATHERFORD, KEITHA DAVIS, Mathematics Teacher; *b:* Toccoa, GA; *m:* Charlie J.; *c:* Tonya E., Judy C.; *ed:* (BS) Elem Ed, Berry Coll 1958; *cr:* Teacher W Rome Jr HS 1958-64, Glenwood Elem Sch 1967-82, Armuchee Mid Sch 1982-; *ai:* FCAE, GAE, NEA; *home:* 277 Old Summerville Rd Rome GA 30161

WEATHERFORD, LISA MARLENE, Anatomy and Biology Teacher; *b:* Houston, TX; *m:* David B.; *c:* Angela, Jeff; *ed:* (BS) Scndry Ed, Bio/Psych-Summa Cum Laude, TX Chrstn Univ 1978; *cr:* Teacher Athens HS 1979-; *ai:* Natl Honor Society Co-Spon;textbook Comm; Athens Classroom Teachers Assn 1979-; TX St Textbook Comm Mem 1984; *office:* Athens H S 708 E College Athens TX 75751

WEATHERLY, ELMINA DONETTE, Elementary Principal; *b:* Friona, TX; *m:* Jimmy Stanton; *ed:* (BA) His, Wayland Baptist Univ 1979; (MED) Admin, Sam Houston St Univ 1984; *cr:* Teacher 1980-84, Cnslr 1984-85, Asst Prin 1985-87, Prin 1987- Splendora Ind Sch Dist; *ai:* Phi Delta Kappa, ASCD Mem 1988-; Center for Slow Learners Mem 1989-; Whos Who Among Coll Stus in America 1979.

WEATHERS, GERALD LEE, Mathematics Teacher; *b:* Shelby, NC; *ed:* (BS) Math, Appalachian St Univ 1969; (MA) Math, 1976, (MED) Curr/Instruction, 1976 Univ of NC Charlotte; Mentor Trng; *cr:* Math Teacher Burns Sr HS 1969-76, Burns Jr HS 1976-78, Crest Sr HS 1978-; *ai:* Math Club & Sr Class Spon; Math Team Coach; Mentor Cert 1989; NC Assn of Educators, NEA, NCTM, NC Cncl Teachers of Math; Aldersgate United Meth Church Mem; Meth Men Evangelism Comm Mem; *office:* Crest Sr HS 800 Old Boiling Springs Rd Shelby NC 28150

WEAVER, CHERYL EVERIDGE, Fourth Grade Teacher; *b:* Macon, GA; *m:* Edward Neal; *c:* Lynette, Jaime, Thomas N.; *ed:* (BS) Health/Phys Ed, 1968, (MS) Elem/Mid Grades Ed, 1975 GA Coll; *cr:* Phys Ed Teacher Wilkinson Cty HS 1968-69; Coord Oconee Neighborhood Youth Corporation 1969-71; Sci Teacher Boddie Jr HS 1971-72; 4th Grade Teacher East Laurens Elem 1972-73; Span/Phys Ed Teacher Treutlen Cty HS 1973-75; Sci Teacher Boddie Mid Sch 1976-89; 4th Grade Teacher Southside Elem 1989-; *home:* 137 Admiralty Way NW Milledgeville GA 31061

WEAVER, DEBORAH PARRIS, Kindergarten Teacher; *b:* Wilson, NC; *m:* Danny Lee; *c:* Christopher A., Ashley E.; *ed:* (BS) Early Chldhd, Atlantic Chrstn Coll 1975; *cr:* Teacher of Educable Mentally Handicapped/K-3rd Grade Teacher 1975-76, Kndrgtn Teacher 1976- Nashville Elem Sch; *ai:* Soc Comm Chairperson 1989-; Stu Assistance Team; Teacher Effectivness Trng; Guidance Comm; Dial-R Trng; Parent Activity Comm; Kndgtn Chairperson 1989-; Faculty Advisory Comm 1989-; Kndgtn Report Card Comm Chairperson Nash Cty 1989-; NC Assn of Educators 1975-79, 1989-; NC Assn for Ed of Young Child 1976-; Nash-Rocky Mount Assn for Ed of Young Children (secy, Treas 1988-89, Pres 1989-); Tuition & Fees Awd Division of Exceptional NC Dept of Public Instruction 1975-76; Nash Cty Teacher of Yr Nominee 1989-; *office:* Nashville Elem Sch 209 Virginia Ave Nashville NC 27856

WEAVER, FAY BENSON, French Teacher; *b:* Madison, TN; *m:* John Lawson III; *c:* Edwin W. Benson III; *ed:* (BA) Span/Fr, Peabody of Vanderbilt 1968; (MS) Ed, 1985, (EDS) Ed, 1986 Univ of TN; Lozonov & TOTAL Phys Response Method of Foreign Lang Teaching; *cr:* Span/Fr Teacher N Nashville HS 1968-71; Fr Teacher/Team Leader Mc Gavock HS 1971-; *ai:* Fr Club Spon; Honor Society Adv; Faculty Advisory Comm Secy; Core Team Cnslr Chemical Abuse; Metro Nashville Ed Assn Faculty Rep 1968-; TN Assn Teachers of Foreign Lang 1975-; Pi Lambda Theta Educators Honor Society 1985-; Univ of TN Alumni Assn 1985-; Peabody Vanderbilt Alumni Assn 1968-; Order of Eastern Star Officer 1980-; Shrine Ladies Auxiliary Pres 1986-; Cntry Music Assn 1980-; Nashville Bd of Realtors 1980-; Nom Teacher of Yr 1990; *office:* Mc Gavock HS 3150 Mc Gavock Pike Nashville TN 37216

WEAVER, JO NELL (BRYANT), 4th Grade Teacher; *b:* Dallas, TX; *c:* Carolyn E. Luther B.; *ed:* (BA) Elem Ed, Southern Meth Univ 1968; (MED) Elem Supervision, North TX Univ 1974; *cr:* Classroom Teacher, Mark Twain Elem 1968-79; Hamilton Park Pacesetter 1979-; *ai:* ASCD 1983-88; TX ST Teachers Assn. 1968-79; Alpha Delta Kappa 1981-; Richardson Ed Assn 1968-; North TX Rdng Assn 1988-; Assn of TX Prof Educators 1980-; TX Congress Parents & Teachers Schlsp Grant; Outstanding Elem Teachers of Amer; Ross Perot Awd Teaching Excellance; Critic Reader Silver Burdett Publishing Co; *home:* 4505 Hanover Garland TX 75042

WEAVER, LA DONNA LEWIS, Biology/AP Teacher; *b:* Odessa, TX; *m:* Paul David; *c:* Justin J. Lewis, Whitney R.; *ed:* (AS) Bio, Odessa Coll 1973; (BS) Bio, Univ of Tx 1977; Sci Courses, Univ of TX Austin & Univ of TX Permian Basin; *cr:* Phys Sci Teacher Nimitz Jr HS 1977-79; Bio I Teacher 1979-81, Bio II/advanced Placement Teacher 1983- Odessa HS; *ai:* Lecture Wkshps for Coll Bd; Tutoring to Academic Decathlon Team; Bio Textbook Comm 1986; Bio Teacher of TX 1985-; NSTA 1985-; TX St Teachers Assn Bldg Rep 1979-80; TX Classroom Teachers Assn 1977-; Odessa Classroom Teachers Bldg Rep 1977-; Consultant for Coll Bd 1987-; Nom Outstanding Sci Teacher of TX 1988; *home:* 1720 W 26th Odessa TX 79763

WEAVER, MADGE YVONNE, 4th Grade Teacher; *b:* Munday, TX; *m:* Gary; *c:* Lynette, Eddie; *ed:* (BA) Elem Ed, Coll of the Southwest 1969; Caprock Writing & Ready Rdng; *cr:* Head Teacher Crosbyton Elem 1986-; *ai:* 4th Grade Spon; TCTA Building Rep 1986-87; Step Two Career Ladder; *office:* Crosbyton Elem Sch 202 S Harrison Crosbyton TX 79322

WEAVER, PAMELA ANN, Chapter I Reading Teacher; *b:* South Bend, IN; *m:* William E.; *ed:* (BS) Dramatic Arts for Children/Childrens Lit/Content & Methods, E MI Univ 1978; (MS) Elem Classroom Teaching, MI St Univ 1987; *cr:* Elem Teacher Brandywine Elem Schls 1979-80, Dowagiac Union Schls 1981-84, Brandywine Elem Schls 1984-; *ai:* Human Growth Curr Dev Comm; MI Rdng Assn 1984-85, 1990; *office:* Brandywine Public Schls 2428 S 13th St Niles MI 49120

WEAVER, RUSSELL ANTHONY, English Teacher; *b:* Calhoun, GA; *m:* Jennifer G. Scott; *ed:* (AB) Eng, Univ of GA 1981; *cr:* Eng Teacher N Hall HS 1984-; *ai:* Boys & Girls Cross Cntry Coach; Renaissance & N Hall Media Comm Mem; GA Lib Media Assn 1988-; Yrbk Dedication 1988; *office:* North Hall HS 4885 Mt Vernon Rd Gainesville GA 30505

WEAVER, VELMA MOSELEY, Science Teacher; *b:* Blackstone, VA; *m:* Jerry Lynn; *c:* Shaun M.; *ed:* (BS) Sci Ed, St Pauls Coll 1977; Gifted Ed, VA Commonwealth Univ 1988-89; *cr:* Sci Teacher St Mary CA 1978-80, King William HS 1980-82, Lee Davis HS 1985-; *ai:* Sci Club Spon; Greater Richmond Recording Secy 1988-; Cncl of Sci Educators; VA Assn of Co-Leader for Sci Teacher Bio Section 1989-; NABT 1986-; *office:* Lee Davis HS 6540 Mechanicsville Pike Mechanicsville VA 23111

WEAVER, WALTER ROBERT, 8th Grade Teacher; *b:* Fountain Hill, PA; *m:* Linda Ebeling; *c:* Jason, Meg; *ed:* (BA) His, Muhlenberg Coll 1968; (MED) Elem Ed, Lehigh Univ 1970; Admin Cert Elem 1976, Scndry 1989, Lehigh Univ; *cr:* 6th Grade Teacher 1968-85, 8th Grade Teacher 1985- S Lehigh Mid Sch; *ai:* His Day & Stock Market Game Adv; Lehigh Valley Cncl for Soc Stud, NEA, PSEA, SLEA; Saucon Valley Jaycees Pres 1976-77; Selected as One of Top 10 Teachers of Ecomomics in PA 1989 by PA Cncl of Bus & Industry; Saucon Valley Sch Bd 1989- Dist Treas; *home:* RR 7 Box 7352 Bethlehem PA 18015

WEBB, ANDREA IVIE, Honors English Teacher; *b:* Corsicana, TX; *m:* Ivan Braxton Jr.; *c:* Michael B.; *ed:* (AA) Psych, Navarro Coll 1967; (BA) Eng/His, Stephen F Austin St Univ 1969; (MED) Curr/Supervision/His, E TX St Univ 1981; Amer Stud, Baylor Univ; Intnl Travel, Univ of CA Santa Barbara; *cr:* Teacher Corsicana HS 1970-71, St John HS 1971-79; Evening Division Instr Navarro Coll 1974-86; Curr Dir 1978-79, Asst Prin 1979-81 St John HS; Teacher Ennis HS 1981-; *ai:* Assn of TX Prof Educators 1981-; NCTE 1985-; Delta Kappa Gamma 1988-; EF Inst Outstanding Work Overseas Travel Stu Assoc Status 1986-89; Featured in Books; Prologue Co-Author; *office:* Ennis HS 1405 Lake Bardwell Dr Ennis TX 75119

WEBB, ANNA MANCO, Fifth Grade Teacher; *b:* Bowling Green, KY; *m:* Jimmy Willis; *c:* Alecia; *ed:* (MS) Elem Ed, 1989, (BA) Elem Ed, 1964 W KY Univ; Working on Rank I Natl Writing Inst; *cr:* 6th Grade Teacher Adairville HS 1964-65; 5th Grade Teacher Alvaton HS 1965-68; 4th Grade Teacher Bristow 1968-69, Cumberland Trace Elem 1969-70, Bristow Elem 1970-79; 5th Grade Teacher Brownsville Elem 1979-; *ai:* Chrldr Spon; 4-H Leader; Sftbl Coach; KEA Dist Bd; WCEA, ECEA Pres; Republican Womens Club Pres 1986-88; Grant Brownsville Elem Sch to Teach The Writing Process; *office:* Brownsville Elem Sch Brownsville KY 42210

WEBB, BONITA DABBS, Elementary Principal; *b:* Quincy, MS; *m:* Wilford Robert; *c:* Luther II, Robert, Tully; *ed:* (BS) Elem Ed, MUW 1962; (ME) Admin, DSU 1974; *cr:* 3rd Grade Teacher 1962-65, 1st Grade Teacher 1965-69 Bankston-Greenwood Mid Sch; 1st Grade Teacher Pillow Acad 1969-80; K-1st Grade Teacher First Presbyn Church 1980-81; Elem Prin Pillow Acad 1981-; *ai:* MPSEA (Dist Chairperson 1981-82, 1988-89, Elem Prin 1981-82, 1988-89, St Chairperson 1987-88); Spring Lake Home Owners Assn (Secy, Treas 1988-89); Enon United Meth Church (Pianist, Sunday Sch Music Dir); *office:* Pillow Acad Po Box 1880 Hwy 82 W Greenwood MS 38930

WEBB, CAROL WOODWORTH, Ag Ed Teacher/Dept Chairman; *b:* Cumberland, MD; *m:* Kenneth Edwin; *c:* Megan J.; *ed:* (AA) Ag, Potomac St Coll 1982; (BA) Ag Ed, WV Univ 1984; Grad Work Ag Sci; *cr:* Ag Ed Instr Frederick Cty Mid Sch 1984-; *ai:* FFA Adv; Frederick Cty FFA Alumni, NEA, VEA; Articles Published; VA Outstanding Young Ag Teacher Nom; *office:* Frederick Cty Mid Sch 441 Linden Dr Winchester VA 22601

WEBB, COLLEEN JOHNSON, Business Education Teacher; *b:* Ishpeming, MI; *m:* Lawrence J.; *c:* Nicole, Joseph; *ed:* (BS) Bus Ed, N MI Univ 1973; (MS) Scndry Bus Ed, E MI Univ 1979; St Voc Bus Ed Wkshps; Cmptr Seminars; Gregg Publishing Company & Cntrl MI Univ Summer Methods Conferences; *cr:* Office Ed Algonac HS 1974-75, St Clair HS 1975-79; Bus Teacher St Clair Cty Comm Coll Adult Ed Prgm 1975-81; Accounting/Shorthand/Typing/Law Teacher Marine City HS 1979-; *ai:* N Cntrl Steering Comm Mem; Bus Profs of Amer Local & Regional Adv; Delta Pi Epsilon 1975-; Bus Profs of America 1979-; MI Bus Ed Assn, NBEA 1969-; Marine City Civic Womens Club Treas 1985-88; Appointed by St Voc Ed Dept to Classroom Educators Advisory Comm Bus Prof of America to Represent MI 1987-; Conducted Various Teacher/Adv Wkshps in Bus Profs; St Competitive Events Chairperson 1987-; *office:* Marine City HS 1085 Ward St Marine City MI 48039

WEBB, CYNTHIA WOMACK, 7th/8th Grade English Teacher; *b:* Nashville, TN; *m:* James R.; *c:* Mary Margaret, James Richard II; *ed:* (BS/EE) Elem Ed, Austin Peay St Univ 1970; (MS) Guidance & Counseling, Trevecca 1990; *cr:* 3rd Grade Teacher Ft Campbell Dependent Sch 1970-72; Kndgtn Teacher Walton Ferry 1972-74; K-8th Grade Teacher Coopertown Sch 1974-; *ai:* Jr Beta Club Spon; NEA 1970-; KEA 1970-72; TEA 1972-; *office:* Coopertown Elem Sch 3746 Hwy 49 W Springfield TN 37172

WEBB, DEANA HODGIN, Fourth Grade Teacher; *b:* Moberly, MO; *m:* Robert William; *c:* Laura M., Robert J., Matthew W.; *ed:* (BSED) Elem Ed, AR St Univ 1965; (MSED) Rdng, NW MO St Univ 1987; *cr:* 2nd Grade Teacher Platte City Elem Sch 1965-66; Chapter I Math Teacher 1978-79, 4th Grade Teacher 1979- Eugene Field Elem Sch; *ai:* Delta Kappa Gamma 1984-; *home:* 316 E 14th Maryville MO 64468

WEBB, GERALD EDWIN, Military Science Teacher; *b:* San Diego, CA; *m:* Bonnie La Fleur; *c:* J. D. Jones, Kathy J. Boudreaux, Robert; *ed:* (BA) Bus Admin, Rutgers Univ 1960; (MPA) Public Admin, George Washington Univ 1974; USA Command & General Staff Coll, Industrial Coll of the Armed Forces, Natl Defense Univ; *cr:* Career Army Officer US Army 1960-85; Sr Army Instr Morse HS 1985-; *ai:* ROTC Act Color Guards; Drill Team; Drum Corps; Rifle Team Coach; Military Order of the World Wars 1985-; Assn of the US Army 1964-; Retired Officers Assn 1985-; NEA, Amer Legion, San Diego Teachers Assn 1985-; *office:* Morse HS 6905 Skyline Dr San Diego CA 92114

WEBB, JEAN HEFNER, 3rd Grade Teacher; *b:* Port Arthur, TX; *m:* Billy G.; *c:* Simone Thomas, Victoria; *ed:* (BS) Elem Ed, 1955; (MED) Elem Admin/Supervision, 1964 Univ of North TX; *cr:* 3rd Grade Teacher Fort Worth Ctry Day Sch 1966-; 1st Grade Teacher Greenhill Sch 1962-64; 4th Grade Teacher Santa Ana CA 1959-61; 3rd/4th Grade Teacher Fort Worth TX 1955-58; *ai:* Spon Lower Sch Talent Show; Lower Sch Rep Eng Dept; Delta Kappa Gamma Society (St Archives Chm 1989- St Area Coord 1985-87 Chapter Achievement Awd 1986 Chapter Pres 1982-84); First United Meth Church Admin 1980-; Reviewer Delta Kappa Gamma Educator Awd Books; Wkshp Presenter for Delta Kappa Gamma & Ind Schls Assn of Southwest; Sch Evaluator Ind Sch Assn of Southwest; Interum Prin Lower Sch Fort Worth Ctry 1988; *home:* 2136 Pembroke Fort Worth TX 76110

WEBB, JOHN BADGLEY, French Teacher & Dept Chair; *b:* Cooperstown, NY; *ed:* (BA) Fr, SUNY Albany 1968; (MA) Fr, Middlebury Coll 1972; (EDD) Bi-ling Ed/ESL, NY Univ 1986; *cr:* Fr Teacher/Dept Chair E Ramapo Cntrl Schls 1968-86, Hunter Coll HS 1986-; Adjunct Assoc Professor Hunter Coll 1986-; *ai:* Faculty Cncl; Long Range Planning Comm; Task Force Teacher Qualifications; Telecomm Projects Soviet Union Co-Dir; Exchange Prgm with France Dir; NY St Assn of Foreign Lang Teachers (Pres 1990), Remunda Cadoux Leaderership Awd 1989: AATF; Amer Cncl on Teaching Foreign Lang; Doctoral Fellowship NY Univ; Dodge Fnd Grant; Numerous Conferences, St & Nationwide; Author of Articles in St & Natl Publications; *home:* 175 W 12th St #3k New York NY 10011

WEBB, JOHN CLARK, Band Director; *b:* Little Rock, AR; *m:* Betty Virginia Vandegrift; *c:* Jason, Mollie; *ed:* (BME) Music Ed, 1974, (MME) Music Ed, 1980 Henderson St Univ; *cr:* Band Dir Malvern Jr HS 1974-77, Fairview HS 1977-; Adjunct Instr Henderson St Univ 1990; *ai:* Marching Band, Concert Band, Pageant Band, Musical Orch, FFA St Convention Band Spon; HSU Band Camp Instr; Miss AR Orch; ASBOA Region Clinic Band Dir; AR Sch Band & Orchestra Assn Parliamentarian 1974-; AR Bandmaster Assn (Secy, Treas) 1978-; Amer Sch Band Dir Assn 1986-; FFA 1981-, Honorary St Farmer 1986; ASBOA Region IV (Secy, Chm); Fairview Teacher of Yr 1984-85; ASBOA Marching, Sight Reading & Concert Contest Judge; AR Governors Sch Judge; Trumpet Performances; *home:* 2740 Mimosa Camden AR 71701

WEBB, LARRY LEE, Band Director; *b:* Roanoke Rapids, NC; *ed:* (BM) Music Ed, East Carolina Univ 1988; *cr:* Band Dir Dillon HS 1989-; *ai:* Fellowship Chrstn Athletes Spon; SC Band Dirs Assn Awds Comm; Music Educators Natl ConferencE, SC Band Dirs Assn 1989-; Phi Mu Alpha Sirfonia (Secy, Alumni Secy) 1984-88; Appointment SC Governors Sch for Arts Internship; *office:* Dillon HS Hwy 301 N Dillon SC 29536

WEBB, LINDA SINGLETARY, Fourth Grade Teacher; *b:* Atlanta, GA; *m:* Arley Lee; *c:* Julie, Heidi, Mark; *ed:* (BS) Elem Ed, OH St Univ 1966; (MA) Elem Ed Prin/Elem Ed Curr/Supervision Wright St Univ 1976; Working Towards PhD; *cr:* Teacher Shepard Elem 1966-68; Rdng Specialist Windsor Terrace Elem 1968-69; Teacher Driscoll Elem 1969-; *ai:* Odyssey of Mind Coaching & Judging 1987-; Oration & Speech Contests Chairperson 1974-; Essay Writing Contests Chairperson 1985-; Centerville HS Ice Hockey Chrldr Adv 1988-89; 7th/8th Grade Chrldrs Adv 1987-89; CCTA Local (Building Rep 1975-78; Negotiations 1976, Schlsp Comm Selector 1987-); OH Ed Assn, NEA Mem 1966-; Centerville Washington Township Ed Fnd Grant; *office:* Driscoll Elem Sch 5767 Marshall Rd Dayton OH 45429

WEBB, PATRICIA L., 7th/8th Grade Teacher; *b:* Martin, KY; *ed:* (BS) Bus Ed, E KY Univ 1977; Bus Ed, Morehead St Univ 1986; *cr:* Teacher Maytown Elem Sch 1977-; *ai:* 8th Grade Spon; Comm to Improve Stu Attendance; KY Ed Assn, NEA 1977-; *office:* Maytown Elem Sch PO Box 220 Langley KY 41645

WEBB, PAULA SUE JONES, 7th/8th Grade Lang Art Teacher; *b:* Union City, TN; *m:* Ronald Owen; *c:* Dana R., Robert W.; *ed:* (BS) Scndry Ed/Bio/His, Univ of TN Martin 1971; Elem Endorsement 1973; *cr:* 7th/8th Grade Teacher Rives Elem Sch 1971-; *ai:* Beta Club Spon; Academic Bowl Adv; Obion Cty Ed Assn (Negotiating Team Mem 1988-89) 1971-; TN Ed Assn 1971-; NEA 1975-; Jaycees Distinguished Service Awd; Outstanding Young Educator Nominee 1988; Univ of TN Martin Outstanding Teacher Awd 1989; *home:* 5250 Rives-Mt Pelia Rd Rives TN 38253

WEBB, ROBERT OKEY, English Teacher; *b:* Wallace, WV; *m:* Betty Jo Griffin; *c:* Robert M., Pamela A. Potter; *ed:* (AB) Speech/Dramatics, Fairmont St Coll 1956; (MS) Admin, Youngstown St Univ 1971; Grad Stud Univ of WV & OH St Univ; *cr:* Speech Instr Marion Harding HS 1956-73; Eng Teacher Baker Mid Sch 1973-; Comm Teacher Marion Tech Coll 1978-81; Lang Art Teacher Marion Correctional Inst 1975-; *ai:* Olympics of Mind Coach; Lang Art Curr Dev Comm; St Cncl of Prof Educators, NEA 1985-; OH Ed Assn 1956-; *home:* 423 Normandy Dr Marion OH 43302

WEBB, SUSAN KAY, French/English Teacher; *b:* Vancouver, WA; *m:* Richard C.; *c:* Ashley; *ed:* (BA) Fr, Univ of KY 1965; (MA) Fr Lit, IN Univ 1967; Cert in Art His, Thiel Coll; Cert in Eng, Youngstown St Univ; *cr:* Asst Fr Professor Westminster Coll 1967-71; Fr Teacher Mathews HS 1973-; *ai:* Fr Club Adv; France Trip Coord; OH Modern Lang Assn 1989-; Ideal Literary Club Corresponding Secy 1990; Presbyn Womens Assn Prgm

Chairperson 1985-86; Youth Club 1989-; Church (Sunday Sch Supt, Elder, Fellowship Comm, Chrstn Ed Comm, Sunday Sch Teacher); Trumball Cty Cmmty & Schls Career Information Grants 1987-89; *home:* 8426 State St Kinsman OH 44428

WEBB, WILLIAM DAVID, Science Teacher; *b:* Columbia, SC; *m:* Virginia B.; *c:* Nicholas D.; *ed:* (BS) Physics/Sci Ed, Clemson Univ 1970; (MS) Sci Ed, Radford Univ 1984; Chem, Phys Sci, Geology, Radford Univ; *cr:* Teacher Hargrave Military Acad 1971-73, Jackson HS 1973-74, Chatham HS 1975-; *ai:* Trip Bus Driver; Band Act Asst; Sr Class Spon; Radford Univ Teacher Organization Mem 1989-; Franklin Brass Tuba Player 1987-; Contributing Text Author; *office:* Chatham HS RR 2 Box 122-A Chatham VA 24531

WEBB, WONDA GALE JOHNSON, Math Teacher; *b:* Sugarland, TX; *m:* Fred Jr.; *c:* Karen N., Cristal C.; *ed:* (BS) Math, 1974; (MA) Elem Ed, 1980 Prairie View A&M Univ; *cr:* Math Teacher Fred F Florence Mid Sch 1974-; *ai:* Asst Ldr Girl Scout Troop 1774; Youth Spon Morning Star Bapt Church Mission II; Operation Involvement Rep.

WEBBER, DAVID ERIC, Band Director; *b:* Miami, FL; *m:* Betty Miller; *ed:* (BME) Music Ed, E KY Univ 1981; Psychological Ed, N KY Univ; *cr:* Band Dir Bellevue HS 1982-; *ai:* Tri-M Music Honor Society Spon; Boys & Girls Tennis Head Coach; KY Music Educators Assn Dist Pres-Elect 1990; KY Bandmasters Assn 1990; KY Coaches Assn 1987-; PTSA Dist Teacher of Yr 1987; Golden Apple Teacher of Yr Nom 1990; *office:* Bellevue HS Center & Lafayette Bellevue KY 41073

WEBBER, KELLY ROBINETTE, English Teacher; *b:* Conway, AR; *m:* Ron; *c:* Seth A.; *ed:* (BSE) Speech/Theatre/Eng, Univ of Cntrl AR 1987; *cr:* Teacher Southwest Jr HS 1987-; *ai:* Drama Club Spon; Southwest Assessment Team Mem; NEA, AR Ed Assn, Little Rock Classroom Teachers Assn 1987-; *office:* Southwest Jr HS 3301 S Bryant Little Rock AR 72204

WEBER, BONNIE LEE, Science/Health/English Teacher; *b:* Marietta, OH; *ed:* (AA) General, OH Valley Coll 1967; (BA) Phys Ed/Health/Soc Stud, Harding Univ 1970; Certificate Elem Ed; Wkshps Outdoor Ed, Nutrition, Stress Management; Child Psych Working with Stu, Teachers & Parents; *cr:* Pennsville Elem 1970-74; 6th Grade Sci Teacher 1974-85, 5th/6th Grade Sci/Health Teacher 1985-, Head Teacher 1989- Warren Elem; *ai:* Textbook & Spelling Bee Comms; Warren Local Teacher Assn Pres 1971-72; Amer Assn of Univ Women 1978-83; Amer Heritage 1979-83; 4-H (Mem, Adv) 1965-85, 20 Yr Pen; *office:* Warren Elem Sch Rt 4 Marietta OH 45750

WEBER, DAMON FRANKLIN, Fine/Performing Art Coord; *b:* Caldwell, KS; *m:* Patricia Zoe Frazier; *c:* Stephen, Kurt, Gretchen, Becky Kretchmar, Erika; *ed:* (BM) Music/Voice, Univ of TX Austin 1953; (MS) Curr/Admin, Euporia St Univ 1968; Spec Stu Paris Conservatory of Music, Julliard, Univ of KS, Wichita St Univ; *cr:* Voice Teacher Univ of TX 1952-53; 6th Grade Teacher 1963-66, Coord/Elem Ed Teacher 1966-68 Unified Sch Dist 261; Staff Natl Ed Assn Washington DC 1968-73; Elem/Jr HS Music Teacher Unified Sch Dist 261 1986-87; Facilitator of Gifted Campus HS 1987-; *ai:* Coach Chess Team & High Q/Scholars Bowl; Dist Curr Comm; Phi Mu Alpha Sinfonia Pres 1947-; Phi Delta Kappa Secy 1964-; Sigma DeLta Chi 1984-; Kiwanis Pres 1967; Lions Club Prgm Chm 1982; Actors Equity Assn Deputy 1962-63; Division of Vehicles Dir St of KS; Regional Dir Alliance for Art, Ed Kennedy Center; Dir 1st Natl Salute to Ed Washington DC 1972; Author of Book; *office:* Campus HS 2100 W 55th St S Wichita KS 67217

WEBER, EUGENE JOHN, Retired Teacher; *b:* Landeck, OH; *m:* Eileen M. Freund; *c:* Michael, Maria L., Karen Meyer, Patrick; *ed:* (BS) Math/His, Bluffton Coll 1960; (MED) Math Ed, OH St Univ 1964; Numerous Univs; *cr:* Teacher Lincolnview HS 1960-63, Coldwater HS 1964-89; *ai:* Coldwater Leo Club Adv; Cross Cntry, Track, Golf Coach; Sch Athletic & Adult Ed Dir; Coldwater Teachers Organization, OEA, NEA Pres 1967-68, 1974-75; NCTM, Sch Sci/Math Assn; Coldwater Lions Club Secy, Treas 1972-, Lion of Yr 1975; Knights of Columbus Grand Knight 1974-75, Knight of Yr 1987, 89; Veterans of Foreign Wars Commander 1989-; Village of Coldwater Cncl 1973-89; Citizen of Yr 1988; Chamber of Commerce; Coldwater Schls Excl in Ed 1988; CO-Author 1988; Coll Cmmty Arts Cncl Pres 1988-; *home:* 301 N 2nd St Coldwater OH 45828

WEBER, GRACE PICKENS, Retired Teacher/Admin; *b:* Reedsville, OH; *m:* Denver; *c:* David, Mark; *ed:* (BS) Elem Ed, OH Univ 1952; *cr:* Teacher Tuppers Plains Elem 1952-53, Luckey Elem 1953-54, Unioto Elem 1954-55, Washington Elem 1955, Warren Local 1957-59, Chester Elem 1959-60; Teacher/Admin Riverview 1962-87; *ai:* Substitute Teaching at Riverview; Involved in Cmmty & Church Groups; *home:* Box 116 Reedsville OH 45772

WEBER, JACK CARL, Fifth Grade Teacher; *b:* Los Angeles, CA; *m:* Georgia Ann Hatch; *c:* Sue-Ellen Ploeger, Shari-Lyn; *ed:* (BS) Bus Management, 1960, Elem Teaching Cert Elem Ed, 1962 Brigham Young Univ; Equal Opportunity Management Inst Dept of Defense 1979-80; *cr:* 6th Grade Teacher John Enders Sch 1962-63; 5th/6th Grade Teacher Davis Cty Sch Dist 1963-; *ai:* Joint Staff Study Comm Chairperson; Davis Cty Sch Dist Gender/Ethnic Expectations & Stu Achievement Prgm Facilitator; Local Assn Bldg Rep; Davis Ed Assn Building Action Team Mem, UT Ed Assn 1963-; NEA Mem 1962-; Centerville Jaycees Pres 1964; Natl Guard UT Enlisted Assn 1989-; UT Army Natl Guard (Mem, Equal Opportunity Specialist) 1973-, Soldier of Yr Candidate 1975; Salt Lake City Teacher of Week 1967; *home:* 1564 N 300 W Bountiful UT 84010

WEBER, JOAN M., Choral Director; *b:* Manila, Philippines; *m:* Benjamin; *ed:* (BME) Music Ed, Wichita St Univ 1972; *cr:* Choral Dir Dumas Jr HS 1972-76, Canyon Jr HS 1976-; *ai:* Madrigal Chamber of Amarillo Coll; TX Music Educators Assn; Amarillo Opera Choral Dir; *home:* 4101 W 45th #1904 Amarillo TX 79109

WEBER, LINDA BESCH, Spanish Teacher; *b:* Appleton, WI; *ed:* (BA) Scndry Ed Span, Univ of WI Eau Claire 1969; (BS) Curr/Instruction, Univ of WI Milwaukee 1990; *cr:* Span Teacher Einstein Jr HS 1969-; *ai:* Exercise Instr Adult Women; Mem of Steering Comm IQ of Life Sch Dist Wellness Project; WI Assn of Foreign Lang Teachers Mem; Amer Cncl on Teaching of Foreign Lang Mem; Leadership in Lang Awd & Ambassador Awd Concordia Lang Villages; *office:* Einstein Jr HS 324 E Florida Ave Appleton WI 54911

WEBSTER, BRADLEY NEWMAN, English Teacher; *b:* Ellendale, ND; *m:* Faith Ellen Harding; *c:* Nicolas Roy; *ed:* (BS) His, Valley City St Coll 1983; Driver Ed & Lib Sci; *cr:* Eng Teacher Tolna Public Sch 1983-86; Eng Teacher/Libn North Sargent HS 1986-87; Eng & His Teacher/Libn Bowdon Public Sch 1987-89; Eng Teacher/De Steele HS 1989-; *ai:* Annual Staff; Drama Club; Speech Prgm; Track Coach; NDEA Commissioner 1983-85 & 1989-; Masonic Lodge; Mem ND Ed Assn Memsp & Trng Comm; Past Mem NDEA Nogotiations Comm; *home:* Box 503 Steele ND 58482

WEBSTER, CANDACE LYNN, Pre-Kindergarten Teacher; *b:* Conroe, TX; *ed:* (BS) Elem Ed, Sam Houston St Univ 1977; *cr:* Kndgtn Teacher New Caney Elem 1977-78, Ben Milam Elem 1978-88; Pre-Kndgtn Teacher Montgomery Elem 1988-; *ai:* Assn TX Prof Ed 1978-88; TX St Teachers Assn/NEA 1988-89; *office:* Montgomery Elem Sch P O Box 1475 Montgomery TX 77356

WEBSTER, DORIS PERRY, 7th-9th Grades Counselor; *b:* Guin, AL; *m:* Ward; *c:* Allison; *ed:* (AS) Ed/Hist/Phys Ed, Northwest AL Jr Coll 1970; (BS) Ed/Hist/Phys Ed, Athens Coll 1972; (MA) Guidance/Counseling, Univ of North AL 1984; *cr:* Phys Ed Teacher Decatur HS 1972-81; Cnslr East Lawrence HS 1985-; *ai:* AL Counseling Assn 1984-; Hospice of Morgan Cty 1986-; *office:* East Lawrence H S 55 Cnty Rd 370 Trinity AL 35673

WEBSTER, GARY SCOTT, Fifth Grade Teacher; *b:* Gary, IN; *ed:* (BSED) Elem Ed, IN Univ 1974; (MA) Elem Ed, Valparaiso Univ 1978; *cr:* 6th Grade Teacher 1974-86, 5th Grade Teacher 1986- Hayes-Leonard; *ai:* Hayes-Leonard Athletic Dir/Elem Ed; ISTA 1974-; Boys Club Bsktbl Coach 1979-80, Certificate of Appreciation 1980; Parks Bsbl Coach 1978-80; *office:* Hayes-Leonard Elem Sch 653 Hayes Leonard Rd Valparaiso IN 46383

WEBSTER, JENNIFER BRYSON, Home Economics Teacher; *b:* Topeka, KS; *m:* James H. Jr.; *ed:* (BSE) Home Ec Ed, Emporia St 1984; *cr:* Home Ec Teacher Mulvane HS 1984-; *ai:* FHA Adv; Yrbk Spon; NEA, Local MTA Mem 1984-; HEA Mem 1990; *office:* Mulvane HS 915 Westview Mulvane KS 67110

WEBSTER, LINDA SCOTT, 7th Grade Life Science Teacher; *b:* Florence, AL; *m:* Roy M.; *c:* Scott, Rachel; *ed:* (BS) Bio, George Peabody Coll 1963; (ME) Adult Ed, TN St Univ 1976; *cr:* 6th/7th Grade Sci Teacher Nannie Berry Elem 1963-69; Adults Teacher Sumner Cty Adult Ed Classes 1970-76; 7th Grade Sci Teacher Gallatin Jr HS 1976-; *ai:* Mini Sch Team Leader; Help With Sci Club & Sci Olympiad; Drama Club Spon; Carried Stud to NY Theatre Tour; NSTA; Delta Kappa Gamma 2nd VP 1986-; Intnl Rdng Assn; Gallatin Church of Christ Teacher; Adult Spon Teen Group Magazine Work Camp Gallatin Church of Christ.

WECKERLY, RONALD ROY, 4th Grade Instructor; *b:* Freeport, IL; *c:* Heidi, Ginni; *ed:* (BA) Sociology/Anthropology, 1974, (MS) Ed, 1977 IL St Univ; *cr:* Bd Teacher Oak Creek HS 1976-77; Bd Elem Teacher 1977-78, Regular Elem Teacher 1978- Rockford Bd of Ed; *ai:* West HS Track Coach; Helped Local Soup Kitchen; NEA, IL Ed Assn 1976-; *home:* 2315 Eastmoreland Ave Apt 2 A Rockford IL 61108

WEDDELL, ALAN, Athletic Director/Head Coach; *b:* Freeport, TX; *c:* Mark; *ed:* (ME) Admin, Univ of Houston Victoria 1988; *cr:* Math Teacher/Asst Coach Angleton HS 1973-78; Math Teacher/Asst Coach Victoria HS 1978-82; Head Ftbl Coach/Athletic Dir Victoria HS, La Marque HS 1990; *ai:* Athletic Dir La Marque Ind Sch Dist; La Marque City Parks & Recreation Band Mem; TX HS Coaches Assn 1973-; TX HS Athletic Dir Assn 1985-; Dist 26-5A Coach of Yr 1986, 1989; *office:* La Marque HS 300 Vauthier La Marque TX 77568

WEDDING, DAVID JOHN, Health & Phys Ed Teacher; *b:* Toms River, NJ; *m:* Diane Digialinto; *c:* Chrisopher D.; *ed:* (AS) Criminal Justice, Ocean Cty Coll 1976; (BA) Health/Phys Ed, E Stroudsburg St 1978; *cr:* Teacher Lacey Township HS 1985-; *ai:* Weight Trng, Asst Bsktbl & Head Tennis Coach; Phi Espilion Kappa 1978-; Toms River Elks; *office:* Lacey Township HS Haines St Lanoka Harbor NJ 08734

WEDDINGTON, CHERYL DEBRA, Second Grade Teacher; *b:* Queens, NY; *ed:* (MS) Curr & Instruction, VA Tech 1988; (BA) Early Chldhd Ed, Hampton Inst 1977; *cr:* 2nd Grade Teacher Burnt Chimney Elem 1977-; *ai:* NEA, VA Ed Assn, Franklin Cty Ed Assn Mem 1977-; W Rocky Mount Jaycee Women Pres 1983-84; *office:* Burnt Chimney Elem Sch Rt 1 Box 447 Wirtz VA 24184

WEDDLE, HARRY, 7th Grade Soc Studies Teacher; *b:* Lebanon, PA; *m:* Loretta Light Weddle; *c:* Steven M., Kathie A.; *ed:* (BS) Hlth/Phys Ed, West Chester St 1960; *cr:* Soc Stud Teacher Harding Jr HS 1960-69, Lebanon Jr HS 1969-; *ai:* Coach Ftbl/Track Field/Girls Sftbl; PSEA 1960-; Cumberland Club VP 1980-89 Life Mem Awd 1984; 1st Scndry Mem Elected to Lebanon Cty Ed Honor Society 1983; *home:* 751 Locust St Lebanon PA 17042

WEDEL, DEBORAH LYNN (SMITH), Science Teacher; *b:* Duncan, OK; *m:* K. Bruce; *c:* Derek, Heather; *ed:* (BAED) Sci/Voc, 1977, (MS) Scndry Ed, 1985 Cntrl St Univ; Various Courses; *cr:* Home Ec Teacher Dunbar Center 1979-81; CVET/General Sci Teacher Capitol Hill 1981-84; Bio/General Sci Teacher Southeast HS 1984-85; Chem/Phys Sci/Physics/Gifted Teacher Newcastle HS 1985-; *ai:* Stu Cncl, Gifted & Talented, Challenge Bowl, Mock Trial, Art Contest, Model UN, Sci Club, OK-OM, Sci Saturday Spon; Dist/St His Day & Sci Fair Spon & Judge; OEA, NEA, NACT (Local Pres, Secy, Rep 1989-), 1987-; AVA, OVA, NAVESNAP, CVET St Secy 1982-83; CSU Alumni (PreS, VP) 1980-84; OK City Home Ec Teacher Assn (Pres, Vp, Historian) 1981-85; Kappa Delta Pi; Kiwanis Club Outstanding Teacher 1983-84; Music Boosters Secy 1989-; Outstanding Young Women of America 1983; Good Housekeepings 100 Young Women of Promise 1985; KOCO OK Honor RolL of Teachers 1989; Outstanding Teenager OK 1969; Tandys Scholar Outstanding Sci Teacher Natl Semi Finalist 1989; Teacher of Yr Newcastle 1989; Who Whos in Amer Coll & Univ 1973; *office:* Newcastle HS 101 N Main Newcastle OK 73065

WEDEL, GERALD BRADLEY, Business Education Teacher; *b:* Niles, MI; *m:* Marilyn Jeannette Morea; *c:* James D., Robert S., Kim C., Nicole R., Kayla M.; *ed:* (BS) Ed, 1968, (MA) Ed Admin, 1974 Cntrl MI Univ; *cr:* Bus Ed Teacher Vassar Public Schls 1968-70, Fenton Area Public Schls 1970-; *ai:* Sftbl Dir Fenton Cmmty Ed; Hockey Coach Fenton HS 1978-80; NEA, MEA 1968-; Fenton Ed Assn Rep 1970-.

WEDIN, GEORGIA MORGAN, Science Teacher/Coordinator; *b:* Alpine, TX; *c:* J. Michael, Morgan F., Pat Wedin Sierra, Karl E.; *ed:* (BS) HPE/Bio, 1961; (MED) Elem Ed/Sci, 1981 Sul Ross St Univ; Earth Sci, Univ of TX San Antonio; Advanced Acad Trng, UT Marine Sci Center; *cr:* 5th-8th Grade Sci Teacher Notre Dame Cath Sch 1978-79; Sci Teacher Brentwood MS 1980-82; Sci Dept Coord/Teacher Pease Mid Sch 1982-; *ai:* Pease Sci Fair; Sci Textbook, Sci Curr Comm; Assn TX Prof Educators Building Rep 1987-; Sci Teachers of TX 1980-; Earth Sci Teachers of TX 1985-; St Andrews Episcopal Lay Reader 1984-; PTA; Target 90 Grant; Natl Earth Sci Grant Summer Earth Sci Inst Univ TX San Antonio; *office:* Pease Mid Sch 201 Hunt Ln San Antonio TX 78245

WEE, WESLEY Y. H., School Counselor; *b:* Honolulu, HI; *m:* Deborah Shimojo; *ed:* (BED) Psych/Soc Stud, 1973, Prof Diploma Ed, 1975, (MED) Educl Admin, 1983 Univ of HI; *cr:* Scndry Teacher Kailua HS 1972-73, Kalaheo HS 1974-82; Sch Cnslr Pearl Harbor Kai Elem Sch 1982-; *ai:* Partners in Ed Coord; Career Cadre for HI Career Dev Prgm; Drug Cadre, Prgm Comm Mem; Onwards Toward Excl Consultant; HI Sch Cnslrs Assn 1987-; HI St Public Sch Cnslrs Assn 1988-; HI St Teachers Assn, NEA 1974-; Dale Carnegie Prgm Instr 1981; Nom HI St Dept of Ed Teacher of Yr 1976-78, Certificate of Achievement 1987-88; HI St Sch Cnslrs Assn Elem Sch Cnslr of Yr Awd 1987-88.

WEECES, TERRI (VANDER STOEP), Science Teacher; *b:* Hanford, CA; *m:* Tim; *c:* Nolan, Keithen; *ed:* (BS) Natural Sci/Scndry Ed, Midland Luth Coll 1981; (MS) Sci/Scndry Ed, Univ of NE Omaha 1989; *cr:* Sci Teacher Blair Jr-Sr Cmmty Schls 1983-; *ai:* Teacher Advisory, Sci Curr, Schlsp Selection Comms; Blair Ed Assn, NE Ed Assn, NSTA; *office:* Blair Cmmty Schls 9th & Jackson Blair NE 68008

WEED, PATRICIA ANN WHITE, French Teacher; *b:* Denver, CO; *m:* Paul R. Hansen; *c:* Matthew A.; *ed:* (BA) His, CO Coll 1969; (MPA) Public Admin/Criminal Justice, Univ of CO Colorado Springs 1979; Arts & Hum Master of Teaching; *cr:* His Teacher CO Springs Sch 1969-70; Core Subjects Teacher Area Confinement Facility 1972-77; His/Fr Teacher West Jr HS 1977-83; Fr/His/Gifted & Talented His/Stu Govt Teacher Coronado HS 1983-; *ai:* Stu Act; Intervention Team; Child Abuse Team; Gifted & Talented; Ski Club; Santa Fe Trip; Symposium Comm; Phi Delta Kappa 1988-; Danforth Fellowship, Coronado Teacher of Yr; *office:* Coronado HS 1590 W Fillmore Ave Colorado Springs CO 80904

WEED, RUTH KOHLMORGAN, 6th Grade Teacher; *b:* Warren, OH; *m:* Nathan B.; *c:* Susan, Nathan, Wendelin; *ed:* (BA) Soc Sci, Miami Univ of OH 1947; (MA) Counseling, Eastern MI Univ ; Teaching Cert Wayne St Univ 1958; *cr:* Y-Teen Prgm Dir YWCA 1947-49; 5th Grade Teacher Volney-Smith 1958-64; Math/Sci Teacher Hilbert Jr HS 1964-69; 6th Grade Teacher Volney Smith 1969-81; B Beck Elem 1981-; *ai:* Spon Safety Patrol; *home:* 27390 W Ten Mile Rd Southfield MI 48034

WEEKLY, JENAY ATKINSON, Gifted Education Teacher; *b:* Topeka, KS; *m:* Gary W.; *c:* Chelsey, Ashley; *ed:* (BA) Eng, Washburn Univ 1972; (MS) Gifted Ed, KS St Univ 1987; *cr:* Facilitator/Gifted Ed Teacher Unified Sch Dist #501 Topeka Public Schls 1980-; *ai:* Bi-Annual European Study Trips & Sch Spon; Model United Nation, Optimist Oratorical Contest, KS His Day Contest, Spelling Bee Spon; Robinson Sch Play Dir; Various Sch Comm Mem & Dist Task Forces on Gifted Ed; Delta Kappa Gamma 1989-; Topeka Assn for Gifted 1980-; KS Gifted Talented Creative 1980-; Jr League at Topeka Various Chairmanships 1980-; Tau Alpha House Corporation 1968-, Honor Initiate 1969;

Nonoso Corresponding Secy 1971-; Topeka Panhellenic Cncl; AAUW Corresponding Secy; Bishop Elem PTO Pres; Received Dist Grant; Magazine Article Published; *office:* Robinson Mid Sch 1125 W 14th Topeka KS 66604

WEEKS, JAMES DOUGLAS, Third Grade Teacher; *b:* Freer, TX; *m:* Bobbie Jean; *c:* Barbara Jan Dubec; *ed:* (BS) Sociology/His, Univ Corp Us Christi 1963; *cr:* Coach Bartlett HS 1967-73; Elem Prin 1973-87, 3rd Grade Head Teacher 1987- Bartlett Elem; *ai:* TX St Teachers Assn 1967-; NEA 1980-; *office:* Bartlett Elem Sch 404 N Robinson Bartlett TX 76511

WEEKS, NANCY HECK, English & Writing Teacher; *b:* Binghamton, NY; *M:* Francis L.; *c:* Gabrielle S., Alexandra, Curtis; *ed:* (BS) Ed 1965, (MS) 1974 St Univ Coll Oneonta; Clinical Ed Supervision 1976; *cr:* 2nd & 6th Grade Teacher Charlotte Calley Central 1965-70; 8th & 9th Grade Math & Soc Stud Teacher St Marys Sch 1979-84; 7th & 8th Grade Eng & Soc Stud Teacher 1984-87, 7th & 10th Grade Eng/Writing Teacher 1987-, 8th & 9th Grade Math Teacher Stamford Cntl Sch; *ai:* Stu Cncl Adv; Academic Challenge Coach; Pupil Personnel Services Comm Mem; Leadership Cncl Adv; NEA 1984-; Supv Stu Teachers State Univ Coll Oneonta & Hartwick Coll; Church Lector & Eucharistic Minister; Announcer Swim Meets & JV Ftbl Oneonta HS; *office:* Stamford Central Sch 1 River St Stamford NY 12167

WEEKS, PAT HAVENS, Guidance Counselor; *b:* Millington, TN; *m:* Randy; *c:* Jeff, Joel, Jeremy; *ed:* (BSE) Elem Ed, 1973, (MS) Counseling, 1987 Univ of Cntrl AR; *cr:* 3rd Grade Teacher 1973-85, Guidance Cnslr 1985- Ida Burns Elem Sch; *ai:* Prin Advisory Comm; AR Sch Cnslr Assn 1985-; AR Assn Counseling Guidance & Dev 1985-; Delta Kappa Gamma 1986-; Boys & Girls Club of Wonway Bd of Dir Secy 1989-; *office:* Ida Burns Elem Sch 1201 Donaghey St Conway AR 72032

WEEKS, PHYLLIS ERLENE, Second Grade Teacher; *b:* Gray, OK; *c:* Charles; *ed:* (BS) Home Ec, 1958, (BS) Elem Ed, 1967 OK Panhandle St Univ; Draughons Bus Coll 1954; *cr:* Home Ec/8th Grade Sci Teacher Adams OK 1960-61; Kndgtn/Rdng Teacher Balko OK 1967-72; Summer Sch Teacher Beaver OK 1973-76; 2nd Grade Teacher 1973-; Summer Sch Teacher 1983- Balko OK; *ai:* TX Cty OEA 1960-61; OK Ed Assn 1960-; Beaver Cty OEA Public Relations 1967-, Cty Techer 1984; NEA 1978-; High Plains Rdng Cncl Secy, OK Rdng Cncl 1970-84; Delta Kappa Gamma 1989-; Staff Dev Comm 1987-; *home:* Rt 1 Box 54 Balko OK 73931

WEEKS, STEVE WESLEY, Fifth Grade Teacher; *b:* Grangeville, ID; *ed:* (BA) Elem Ed, Lewis-Clark St Coll 1976; *cr:* Chapter I Teachers Aide 1976-80, 4th-6th Grade Phys Ed/5th Grade Teacher Clearwater Valley Elem Sch 1980-; *ai:* Jr HS Boys Bsktbl & Track Coach; HS Asst Ftbl Coach; Prof Dev & Inservice Credit Comm; ID Ed Assn, NEA; Kooskia City Cncl Councilman 1990; *office:* Clearwater Valley Elem Sch 306 Pine Box 100 Kooskia ID 83539

WEEKS, TERRY M., Asst Professor of Education; *b:* Murfreesboro, TN; *m:* Mary S.; *ed:* (BS) Soc Sci, 1972, (MED) Curr/Instruction, 1975 Mid TN St Univ; *cr:* 7th Grade Teacher Rutherford Cty Schls 1973-88; Asst Professor Mid TN St Univ 1989; *ai:* TN Ed Assn St Membership Chm 1987-88; TN Teacher of Yr 1987; Distinguished TN Teacher of Yr 1988; Natl Teacher of Yr 1988; Presidential Scholars Commissioner 1988; Educators Advisory Comm Inaugural Celebration Mem 1989; *home:* Rt 8 Box 367 Murfreesboro TN 37130

WEEMS, MARY ANNE PAULK, Mathematics Teacher; *b:* Pulaski, TN; *m:* Ralph Hicks Jr.; *c:* Ralph III, Belk, Luann Weems Little; *ed:* (BS) Math, 1954, (MED) Math, 1968 MS St Univ; *cr:* Stu Instr MS St Univ 1953-54; Jr HS Instr West Point City Schls 1966-71; HS Instr Oak Hill Acad 1971-86; Instr Joe Cook Jr HS 1986-; *ai:* Mathcounts Coach; Scholastic Honor Club; NCTM, MS Cncl of Math Teachers, Math Assn of America, MS Prof Educators; 1st United Meth Church; Columbus Classroom Teachers; MS Ec Cncl STAR Teacher Awd 1975, 1976, 1982, 1983; Nom Presidential Awd for Excl in Sci & Math Teaching 1988; Oak Hill Acad Master Teacher Awd; *office:* Joe Cook Jr HS 2217 7th St N Columbus MS 39701

WEGHORN, MICHAEL STEVEN, English Teacher; *b:* Spring Valley, WI; *m:* Kathleen Ellen Tollefson; *c:* Wendy, Bryan; *ed:* (BA) Eng, 1968, (MST) Eng, 1975 Univ of WI Eau Claire; *cr:* Eng Teacher Hartford Union HS 1968-73, Barron Sr HS 1974-; *ai:* First Luth Church of Barron Pres 1990; Yrbk Dedications; *home:* 640 Edgewood St Barron WI 54812

WEGMANN, CLARE M., First Grade Teacher; *b:* Bloomington, WI; *ed:* (BA) His, Holy Family Coll 1959; Religious Stud Prgm, St Thereses; *cr:* 1st Grade Teacher St Philips 1987-89, Guardian Angels 1990; *ai:* NCEA Mem 1950-; *home:* 2409 S Alverno Rd Manitowoc WI 54220

WEGMANN, LINDA KAYE, Band Director; *b:* Steelville, MO; *m:* Larry Lynn; *c:* Dana L., Jill L.; *ed:* (BME) Music Ed, SE MO St Univ 1964; (MME) Music Ed, SIU at Edwardsville 1990; *cr:* Music Educator Festus R-6 Public Schls 1968-89; Band Dir Windsor C-1 Schls 1990; *ai:* Marching Band Act; Color Winter Guard Spon; MO Band Masters; MO Music Educators; Pi Kappa Lamda 1987; Delta Kappa Gamma Music Chm 1986-88; Phi Kappa Phi 1987; MO St Teachers Assn 1968-89; Jefferson Cty Music Educators VP, Secy & Treas 1983-; *office:* Windsor HS 6208 Hwy 61-67 Imperial MO 63052

WEGSCHEID, NELLIE HENDRICK, 5th Grade Teacher; *b:* Butler, MN; *m:* Jerome; *c:* Greg, Tim, Vicki, Sally, Scott; *ed:* (BS) Elem Ed, Bemidji St Univ 1980; Kids Teaching Kids; *cr:* Dist 132 1954-56, Dist 32 1956-58, St John The Baptist Sch 1966-67, St Anns Sch 1969-; *ai:* VP Sch Safety Patrol Supvr; KTK Moderator; CAAP Facilitator; BPO Does Pres 1990; VFW Aux Flag Bearer, Voice of Democracy Chairperson; Historical Society Secy; Ed Womens Hall of Fame Awd; BPO Does Inner Guard; 1st Cnslr; *home:* 11 Howard Ave SE Wadena MN 56482

WEHLING, THOMAS MATTHEW, English Department Co-Chair; *b:* E St Louis, IL; *m:* Susan Morice; *ed:* (BA) Eng/Lang/Lit, 1973, (MAT) Eng Ed, 1974 Univ of Chicago; *cr:* Teacher Fox Lane Mid Sch 1974-75, Parkway North HS 1975-; *ai:* Peer Teachers, Seven & Seven Club Spon; Faculty Adv; NHS; Greater St Louis Eng Teachers Assn 1984-; NCTE, Parkway Natl Ed Assn 1976-; Cntrl, Westend, North Inc Pres 1986-88; Parkway North Teacher of Yr 1985, 1986, 1987; *office:* Parkway North HS 12860 Fee Fee Rd Creve Coeur MO 63146

WEHMAN, KAREN KIRKEGARD, English Teacher; *b:* Winston-Salem, NC; *m:* Peter Clement; *c:* Prentiss, Jacob; *ed:* (BA) Eng/Psych, 1969, (MA) Eng/Writing, 1984 Columbia Coll; Various Courses; *cr:* Eng Teacher Gordon Lee HS 1970-71, Berkley Charleston Dorchester Tech 1972-73; Psych Teacher Forsyth Cty Tech 1978-80; Eng Teacher Irmo HS 1984-; *ai:* Sch Improvement & Curr Cncl; Tardy Policy Comm; SAT Verbal Coord; Various Church Comm; NEA, SCEA, ICEA 1984-89; Natl Republican Party, SC Republican Party; *office:* Irmo HS 6671 St Andrews Rd Columbia SC 29212

WEHNER, DAVID JOEL, Bio/Microbiology/Dept Chair; *b:* Wyandotte, MI; *m:* Connie Haller; *c:* Matthew, Stephanie, Jennifer; *ed:* (BA) Bio, W MI Univ 1969; (MS) Bio, E MI Univ 1976; *cr:* 8th Grade Sci Teacher Wilson Jr HS 1970-76; Bio/Microbio Teacher Roos evelt HS 1976-; *ai:* Curr, Educl Fnd, North Cntrl Visitation Comm; NABT 1984-, Bio Teacher of Yr 1988; MABT 1984-, Bio Teacher of Yr 1989; MSTA 1986-; NSTA 1984-; Tandy Corporation Tandy Scholar Finalist 1990; Mini Grant 1986; Lab on DNA Extraction Pub in NABT Monograph 1989; Research Fellowship Ford Motor Company Laboratories Teacher 1990; *home:* 2394 21st Wyandotte MI 48192

WEHR, DONALD LEE, Teacher; *b:* Middletown, OH; *m:* Marilyn Brown; *ed:* (BS) Soc Sci/Scndry Ed, FL Southern Coll 1963; (MAT) Soc Sci/Admin Supvr, Rollins Coll 1965; *cr:* Teacher Edgewater HS 1963-72; Teacher/Pres Asst Lake Highland Preparatory Sch 1972-79; Teacher Apopka HS 1979-; *ai:* Sch Textbook Mgr; Stu Assistance Team; Phi Delta Kappa; Organization of Amer Historians; FL Prof Educators; Society for His Ed; Masonic Order Chaplain/Tyler 1982-83; Military Order Stars & Bars Com FL Soc 1984-86, Jackson Awd 1984; Order of Southern Cross Adj-in-Chief 1986-; Hon Order of Ken Cols; Outstanding Scndry Educator of America 1974; Distinguished Service Awd FL Southern Coll 1974; *office:* Apopka HS 555 W Martin St Apopka FL 32712

WEHRLE, JOHN GEORGE, Teacher-US History; *b:* Altoona, PA; *m:* Nancy Jean Milne; *c:* John G. (dec), Matthew M.; *ed:* (BA) His, St Vincent Coll 1968; (MA) His, Georgetown Univ 1972; Grad Stud His Univ MD; Eastern European Educ Stud; *cr:* Teacher Cabin John Jr HS 1968-84, Thomas S Wootton HS 1984-; *ai:* Class Spon-Sr Class Adv 1989; Amer Historical Assn; MD Cncl for Soc Stud; Greater Laytonsville Pres 1979-81; Civic Assn; Solid Waste Advisory Mem 1981-82; Montgomery Cty Govt Comm; Corma Higgins Schlsp Georgetown Univ 1972; Natl Fellow, Natl Endowment for Hum Cncl for Basic Ed 1989; *home:* 8200 Rocky Rd Laytonsville MD 20879

WEICHINGER, DAVID C., Fifth Grade Science Teacher; *b:* Cameron, MO; *m:* Terrilyn Keever; *c:* Colby; *ed:* (BSED) Elem Ed, 1975, (MSED) Elem Admin, 1978 Northwest MO State Univ; Post Grad Work Ed/Admin/Counseling NWMSU; *cr:* 4th Grade Class Teacher Maysville R-I Schls 1975-76; 5th Grade Class Teacher 1976-88, 5th Grade Sci Teacher 1988- Maryville R-II Sch Dist; *ai:* MO St Teachers Assn 1975-; Sci Teachers of MO 1989-; Nominee Presidential Awd for Excl in Sci Teaching 1990; *home:* Rt 2 Box 46 Maryville MO 64468

WEICK, DAVE LEE, Computer/Math Jr High Teacher; *b:* Grand Haven, MI; *m:* Susan Jane Tiles; *c:* Brianne, Tyler, Grant; *ed:* (BS) Math, Univ of MI 1975; *cr:* Swim Coach/Math/Cmptr Teacher Grandville Public Schls 1975-; *ai:* Boys Varsity Swim & Boys Water Polo Coach; Interscolastic MI Swim Coaches Assn; Grandville Athletic Booster Club; *office:* Grandville Public Sch 3100 Ottawa Grandville MI 49418

WEICK, SUE, Fifth Grade Teacher; *b:* Deridder, LA; *m:* Robert Raleigh; *ed:* (BS) Ed, TX Womans Univ 1969; *cr:* 5th Grade Teacher Ysleta Ind Sch Dist 1974-; *office:* Edgemere Elem Sch 10300 Edgemere El Paso TX 79925

WEIGAND, CAROLYN STOUT, Fifth Grade Teacher; *b:* Franklin Cty, OH; *m:* Louis G. III; *c:* Richard S., Robert M.; *ed:* (BSED) Elem Ed/Eng, Capital Univ 1961; Post Grad Stud; Numerous Wkshps; *cr:* 6th Grade Teacher Sandusky City Schls 1961-63; 5th Grade Teacher Circleville City Schls 1973-; *ai:* Circleville Ed Assn, OH Ed Assn, NEA; *office:* Nicholas Drive Elem Sch 410 Nicholas Dr Circleville OH 43113

WEIGAND, JAMES PAUL, 8th Grade Teacher; *b:* Buffalo, NY; *m:* Alta Gale Bruce; *c:* Cassandra, Erika, Nathan; *ed:* (BA) Phys Ed, 1984, (MA) Phys Ed, 1984 NE MO St; Univ of UT, Fresno Pacific, Univ of CA Berkeley, Fresno St; *cr:* Teacher Stratford Elem Sch 1964-; *ai:* Coaching Ftbl, Bsktbl, Track, Cross Cty, Free Shots; Dir Sch Play; Math Coach; Phi Delta Kappa 1963-; CTA, NEA 1964-; ASCD 1988-; Kiwanis Club (Pres 1969-, Dist Pres 1983-84); Kings Ct Peace Officers 1968-; ASA Youth Sftbl Equipment First Aid Dir 1985-87; Outstanding Math Coach 1990; Outstanding Track Ofcl 1981, 1982, 1989; Pres Sch Bd 1st Luth Pre Sch 1985-; *office:* Stratford Elem Sch 19348 Empire St Stratford CA 93266

WEIGAND, MARIE CATHERINE TRETTIN, 7th/8th Classroom Teacher; *b:* Grafton, IA; *m:* William L.; *c:* C. W., Thomas R., Jan M., Joel R.; *ed:* (BA) Elem Ed/Soc Stud, Univ of CA Sacramento 1971; Grad Stud IA St Univ, Drake, UNI, Concordia; *cr:* Jr HS Soc Stud Teacher LA Porte City IA Sch 1947-49; Jr HS Soc Stud/Math Teacher Rockford IA Sch 1949-53; Substitute K-6th Grade Teacher Folsom CA Consolidated Schls 1970-73; Jr HS Lang Art Teacher Rudd/Rockford/MarbLe Rock Cmmty Schls 1973-; *ai:* Stu Cncl Adv; Spelling Bee Spon & Coach; Advisee Adv; Stu At Risk, Lib Bd Comm; ISEA (Pres, Chm, Delegate, Unit Bd 1984-86) 1973-; NEA Cluster Delegate; IA Cncl Eng Teachers Assn 1973-; Grace Luth Church All Exec Offices CA 1958-70, Mother of Yr 1966; Zion Luth Church (Civic, Sch, Scout, Sunday Sch, Bible Sch) 1971-; Spelling Champions.

WEIGAND, MARY CATHERINE (SULLIVAN), Fifth Grade Teacher; *b:* Madison, WI; *m:* Raymond John; *c:* Heidi M., Heather C., Joshua J.; *ed:* (BS) Elem Ed, Univ of Platteville 1968; (MEPD) Elem Ed, Univ of WI Whitewater 1989; *cr:* 4th-6th Grade Elem Ed Teacher Seymour Sch Dist 1968-71, Oregon Sch Dist 1972-74, 1975-; *ai:* Rdng & Lang Art Comm; Prof Dev & In Service & I Dare Comm; AODA Support Group Facilitator; WI Ed Assn, NEA, OR Ed Assn, S WI Ed Assn; WI FFA Alumni St Treas 1976-78, Plaque 1978; Rock Cty 4-H Leader Awd & Plaque 1987; Outstanding 4-H Youth Leader 1987; *home:* 1346 Tupper Rd Evansville WI 53536

WEIGANDT, DOROTHY MAE, Kindergarten Teacher; *b:* Scotland, SD; *m:* Larry; *c:* Jamie, Bradley, Melanie; *ed:* (BS) Elem Ed, Univ of SD 1972; *cr:* Kndgtn Teacher Ethan Public Sch 1973-; *home:* 500 E 13th Mitchell SD 57301

WEIGANDT, LARRY EDWARD, Math & Sci Dept Chair; *b:* Murdo, SD; *m:* Dorothy Mae Mehlhaf; *c:* Jamie, Bradley, Melanie; *ed:* (BS) Composite Sci, Univ of SD Springfield 1972; (MS) Scndry Admin, SD St Univ 1978; *cr:* Teacher/Guidance Cnslr/Admin Asst Ethan HS 1972-; *ai:* Phi Delta Kappa 1978-81; Zion Luth Church (Bd of Ed Chm 1984-87, Bd of Trustees Chm 1989-); Local Teacher of Yr; Local Jaycees Outstanding Young Educator; *office:* Ethan HS Box 169 Ethan SD 57334

WEIKLE, MICKEY GILLEY, Home Economics Teacher; *b:* Fries, VA; *m:* Lionel Dale; *c:* Sandra D., Jennifer M.; *ed:* (BS) Home Ec Ed, 1967, (MS) Home Ec Ed, 1971 Radford Univ; *cr:* Teacher Tunstall HS 1967-68; Christiansburg HS 1968-79; Pulaski Cty HS 1979-; *ai:* Spon Home Ec Related Occupations 1977-; Spon FHA 1967-77; Spon Young Homemakers of VA 1968-75; Spon GSA Leader; VA Home Ec Teachers (Treas 1967-89, Secy 1967-79); FHA Lifetime Mem; VA/NEA 1967-; Dublin United Meth Church Class Pres 1988-; Grant for Research on Durable Press & Soil Release Fabrics from the Amer Assn of Textile Colorist & Chemist, Amer Home Ec Assn; Bulletin Bds Published in Forecast in Home Ec.

WEIL, GAYLE GREENBURG, Fourth Grade Teacher; *b:* Chicago, IL; *m:* Norman; *c:* Brian, David; *ed:* (BS) Elem Ed, N IL Univ 1969; Various Grad Work Ed; *cr:* 1st Grade Teacher 1969-76, 3rd Grade Teacher 1976-84, 4th Grade Teacher 1984- Memorial Sch; *ai:* Dist Math Comm; Mem Consulative-Collaborative Pilot Prgm; IL Fed of Teachers Local Pres 1978-80; Developmental Inst Bd of Dir 1982-; Congregation Beth Sholom Religious VP 1990; *office:* Memorial Sch 6701 W 179th St Tinley Park IL 60477

WEILER, FRANCES BAIRD, English Teacher; *b:* Tuscaloosa, AL; *ed:* (BSE) Eng, Delta St Univ 1969; (MS) Eng Ed, Univ of S MS 1990; Public Admin Internship NY St 1977-78; *cr:* Eng Teacher Harrison Cty HS 1969-70; Admin Asst NY St Government 1970-79; Spec Ed Teacher Gulfview Elem Sch 1982-83; Eng Teacher Harrison Cty 9th Grade Sch 1983-84, Gulfview Elem Sch 1984-; *ai:* Gulfview Jr Beta Club Spon; Hancock Cty Staff Dev & Personnel Insurance Comm; NCTE; *office:* Gulfview Elem Sch PO Box 8 Lakeshore MS 39558

WEIMER, CAROL LOGAN, Home Economics Teacher; *b:* Rural Valley, PA; *m:* John S.; *c:* Scott; *ed:* (BS) Home Ec Ed, Indiana Univ of PA 1962; Grad Stud Indiana Univ of PA; *cr:* Teacher Saltsburg Jr/Sr HS 1962-66, 1978-; *ai:* Cheering & Jr HS NHS Adv; Soph Class Spon; Stu Assistance Prgm Team Mem; PA St Ed Assn, NEA 1979-; Home Ec Alumni Assn Indiana Univ of PA (Newsletter Adv) 1962-; Blairsville-Saltsburg Ed Assn 1979-; Amer Legion Auxiliary Secy 198-85; Arin Intermediate Unit Mini Grants; *office:* Saltsburg Jr/Sr HS 84 Trojan Ln Saltsburg PA 15681

WEINER, BERTA MELTZER, Mathematics Teacher; *b:* Brooklyn, NY; *m:* Jack Warren; *c:* Sherri Silver, Elizabeth M.; *ed:* (BS) Math, Brooklyn Coll 1957; (MA) Math Ed, Queens Coll 1961; *cr:* Math Teacher Paul D Schreiber HS 1957-; *ai:* Staff Resource Center Policy Bd Mem 1988-; *office:* New Rochelle HS 265 Clove Rd New Rochelle NY 10801

WEINER, KATHY CROSS, English/Russian Teacher; *b:* Ardmore, OK; *m:* Charles S.; *ed:* (BS) Ed/Lang Art, OK St Univ 1974; (MED) Eng, Cntrl St Univ 1976; *cr:* Eng Teacher Putnam City West HS 1975-81, Cntrl Jr HS 1981-83, Putnam City HS 1983-; *ai:* Spon Ink Inc & Russian Club; NCTE, NEA, OK Ed Assn; Assn of Classroom Teachers Building Rep 1986-88, 1990; Teacher of Yr Putnam City HS 1987; Putnam City Schls Awd for Excl in Ed 1990; *office:* Putnam City HS 5300 NW 50th Oklahoma City OK 73122

WEINERT, SHELDON KEITH, Mathematics/Science Teacher; *b:* Humboldt, NE; *m:* Karla Ann Cook; *c:* Shanna, Andrea; *ed:* (BA) Math, Westmar Coll 1968; (MA) Scndry Admin, Univ of N IA 1971; *cr:* Teacher Dumont Cmmty Sch 1968-72; Jr HS Prin Rockwell-Swaledale Schls 1972-75; Prin Sioux Valley HS 1975-81; Teacher Alta HS 1981-; *home:* 805 W 2nd Alta IA 51002

WEINLEIN, GREGG THOMAS, Alternative Ed Supervisor; *b:* Albany, NY; *c:* Christine, Jesse Colm; *ed:* (BS) Eng Ed, SUNY Albany 1974; (MS) Public Admin, Russell Sage Coll 1990; Masters Equivalent Eng Ed at SUNY Albany, St Rose Coll, NY Univ, Russell Sage; *cr:* Eng/Rdng Teacher Berkshire Farm 1974-80; In-Sch Suspension Coord/Teacher 1980-; *ai:* Free Lance Writer 1973-; Class Adv 1987-; Yrbk Adv 1983, 1984; NYSUT 1974-; The Authors Guild, Poets & Writers 1980-; Capital Dist Vietnam Vets 1988-; Poetry Published 1976, 1987; Essays & Articles Published; *home:* PO Box 6117 Albany NY 12061

WEINMANN, DONALD JOHN, 7th Grade Soc Stud Teacher; *b:* Winona, MN; *m:* Rita E. Shaw; *c:* Christine, James, Catherine Johnson; *ed:* (BS) Soc Sci, Winona St Univ 1963; (MS) His, Oshkosh St Univ 1972; *cr:* Teacher Horace Mann Jr HS 1963-64, Conant Jr HS 1965-79, Shattuck Jr HS 1980-; *ai:* Debate, Track, Wrestling Coach; Archery Club Adv; Soc Stud Curr, Gifted & Talented Comm Mem; WI Ed Assn, NEA Mem 1970-; Neenah Ed Assn Mem 1963-; Teacher of Yr Twice; *office:* Shattuck Jr HS 600 Elm St Neenah WI 54956

WEINMEISTER, MARILYN SCHAEFER, 6th Grade Math Teacher; *b:* Sacramento, CA; *m:* Richard L.; *c:* Kristin, Michelle Podtburg; *ed:* (BA) Elem Ed, Univ of Northern CO 1965; *cr:* 4th Grade Teacher Kullerstrand Elem 1965-67, Park Sch 1969-74; 6th Grade Math Teacher Windsor Mid Sch 1975-; *ai:* NEA; Co Ed Assn; Windsor Ed Assn; *home:* 31703 WCR 23 Greeley CO 80631

WEIR, GAY BREWINGTON, Kindergarten Teacher; *b:* Herington, KS; *w:* John (dec); *c:* Leo D., Sean C. Brewington Weir; *ed:* (BMUSED) Music, Univ of CO 1958; Eng, Sonoma St Univ; *cr:* Music Teacher Bear Creek Jr-Sr HS 1958-59; Kndgtn Teacher Wyckoff Elem 1960-61; Music Teacher Wheatridge Jr HS 1961-62; Kndgtn Teacher Prestwood Sch 1968-; *ai:* Valley of the Moon Teachers Assn (Secy 1974-76, Site Rep 1976-78, 1988-); Teacher of Yr Sonoma 1986; One of Three Teachers to Start Developmental Phase I-II Kndgtn Prgm in Dist 1980; *home:* 719 Madison Dr Sonoma CA 95476

WEIRICH, PHILLIP O., 7th Grade Science Teacher; *b:* Port Clinton, OH; *m:* Brenda Kay Wilkins; *c:* Tiffany, Travis; *ed:* (BA) Elem Ed, Bowling Green St Univ 1984; Skills for Adolescence Cert; Guidance, Counseling; *cr:* 5th Grade Long Term Substitute Teacher Danbury-Lakeside Elem 1985; 7th Grade Sci Teacher Rossford Jr HS 1985-; *ai:* Frosh Ftbl, Var Wrestling, Jr HS Track Coach; Wrestling Club Coach-Prgm & Youth Recreation Dept Coord; Sci Dept Chairperson; Summer Sch Teacher; Cty Teacher of Yr NW OH 1989; *office:* Rossford Jr HS 651 Superior St Rossford OH 43460

WEIRICK, MARIA CIANFLONA, Eighth Grade Teacher; *b:* Columbus, OH; *c:* John Schafer, Debra Trott, Suzanne Marsh; *ed:* (BS) Elem Ed, OH Dominican Coll 1972; Gifted Ed, Ashland Coll; *cr:* Elem Teacher Christ The King Sch 1967-; *ai:* NCEA, OCEA, CDEA; *home:* 2595 Caroline Ave Columbus OH 43209

WEISER, SHARON DESETH, Teacher; *b:* Devils Lake, ND; *m:* Thomas; *c:* Ryan, Jonell, Heather; *ed:* (BS) Phys Ed, Mayville St 1969; Grad Stud Univ of ND; *cr:* Phys Ed Teacher Walhalla Public Sch 1969-71; Teacher Hazelton Moffit HS 1981-; *ai:* Newspaper & 8th Grade Adv; NEA; Luth Ladies Aid (Treas, Secy, Pres) 1989-.

WEISKOPF, SHERRY ROSE, English Teacher; *b:* Cleveland, OH; *m:* Mark A.; *c:* Joseph, Stacy, Jason, Scott; *ed:* (EDB) Scndry Ed/Lang Arts, Univ of HI Manoa 1970; Grad Work HI Pacific Coll, Chaminade Univ, Univ of HI; Masters Prgm Curr & Instruction, Univ of HI; *cr:* Lang Art/Soc Stud/Chapter I Teacher Sanford Ballard Dole Intermediate Sch 1970-89; Lang Art/Eng Teacher Wallace Rider Farrington HS 1989-; *ai:* Soph Class Week Act Adv; *office:* W R Farrington HS 1564 N King St Honolulu HI 96817

WEISLOGEL, ORVILLE WALLACE, Science Teacher; *b:* Erie, PA; *m:* Mary Jane Wilson; *c:* Gregory E., Randy A., Bradley D.; *ed:* (BS) Elem Ed, Edinboro Univ 1962; Ithica Coll, Penn St Herhand Campus, Univ of Pittsburg Erie; *cr:* Asst Bsbl Coach Tri Borough 1949-56; Sch Bd Fairview Sch Dist 1956-59; Asst Wrestling Coach 1970-84, Asst Ftbl Coach 1972-86, Bsktbl Coach 1977- Fairview; *ai:* Stu at Risk Prgm; Intramural Bsktbl; Fairview Amer Legion 1947-; NEA, PSEA, FEA Pres 1965-67; Blood Donor 1950-; Received Dedication of Yrbk 1983-84.

WEISS, BARBARA M., Social Studies Teacher; *b:* Knoxville, TN; *m:* Barry Ronald; *c:* Angela Stacey, Shauna Stacey; *ed:* (BS) Scndry Ed/Soc Stud, Bob Jones Univ 1977; (MS) Scndry Ed/Soc Stud, SUNY New Paltz 1988; Ed Admin, SUNY New Paltz; *cr:* Speech/Debate Teacher Hampton Park Sch 1982-84; Soc Stud Debate Teacher Mauldin HS 1984-87, Newburgh Free Acad 1987-; *ai:* Coord Debate, Speech Prgm; Natl Forensic League 1969-; NCSS, Newburgh Teachers Assn, NY St Teachers Union 1987-; SC Debate Coach of Yr 1984; Faulkner Fellow Univ of MS 1984; Natl Endowment for Hum Fellow Univ PA 1986; Merit Pay Awd Greenville Sch Dist 1986; *office:* Newburgh Free Acad 201 Fullerton Ave Newburgh NY 12550

WEISS, BRETT HIRTH-VINIK, English Teacher/AVID Coord; *b:* San Francisco, CA; *ed:* (BA) Amer Stud, Univ of CA 1978; *cr:* ESL Teacher Sweetwater Adult Sch 1980; Teacher Eng/ASB/Jrnlsm Adv Bell Jr HS 1980-86; Teacher Adv Amer Lit/Avid Univ City HS 1986-; *ai:* Spon Organization for Natural Conservation; Co-Spon Photo Club; PTA Honorary Schl Serv Awd 1985; Initiated/Coord Bus Partnership San Diego Chargers & Bell Jr HS; Featured on TV 8 Looks at Learning; Panel Spkr CA St Dept of Ed; Sch Dist Adv March of Dimes; Edited SD Zoo Endangered Species Qtrly; *office:* University City H S 6949 Genesee Ave San Diego CA 92122

WEISS, DEBRA (STERANKO), Mathematics Teacher; *b:* Anchorage, AK; *c:* John, Catherine; *ed:* (BS) Math, Marywood Coll 1977; *cr:* 7th/8th Grade Math Teacher Shenandoah Valley Sch Dist 1977-84; 7th-9th Grade Math Teacher Chattanooga Public Schls 1984-; *ai:* Math Team Coach; Class Adv; PA Newspaper Publishers Assn; Chattanooga Assn of Math Teachers VP 1988-; TN Math Teachers Assn, NCTM; Title II Grant Recipient 1989-; Participant Preparing Parents & Press Guidelines; *office:* Orchard Knob Mid Sch 500 N Highland Park Ave Chattanooga TN 37404

WEISS, DOLORES HAMITER, Fifth Grade Teacher; *b:* Waskom, TX; *m:* Stanley P.; *c:* Amanda K. Martin, Pamela S.; *ed:* (BS) Elem Ed, Stephen F Austin Univ 1961; (ME) Curr/Instruction, Univ of Houston 1982; *cr:* Music Teacher Green Valley Elem 1961-64; Classroom Teacher/Phys Ed Coach 1967-74, 5th Grade Classroom Teacher 1974- Cimarron Elem; *ai:* TX PTA Life Mem 1981; Outstanding Elem Teachers of America 1973; *home:* 215 Ballantrae Ln Houston TX 77015

WEISS, DOROTHY MARIE, Sixth Grade Teacher; *b:* Aurora, IL; *ed:* (BA) Eng, Coll of St Benedict 1950; FLES Cert, Coll of St Benedict 1970; Numerous Courses; *cr:* 6th Grade Teacher Holy Angels Sch 1961-; *ai:* Teachers Retreat & Recommended Rdng Lists Comms; Jr Chrstn Service Club; NCEA Assoc Teacher 1979-; Holy Angels Parish Cncl (Ed Comm 1969-71, Parish Life Comm 1976-78, Renew Group Leader 1984-85); Widowed Persons Service Leader 1982-84; Nom Rockford Diocese Cath Teacher Magazine 1988; *office:* Holy Angels Sch 720 Kensington Aurora IL 60506

WEISS, IRIS GERSHON, English Teacher; *b:* Chicago, IL; *m:* Mark P.; *c:* Audra, Kerri; *ed:* (BAED) Eng, 1970, (MAED) Rdng, 1974 AZ St Univ; *cr:* Eng/Rdng Teacher East HS 1971-74; Part-Time Rdng Teacher Mesa Comm Coll 1975-76; Eng Teacher Chandler HS 1980-; *ai:* Wolfs Paw Adv; NEA Mem 1980-; Temple Emanuel Religious Sch Chairperson 1985-88; Flinn Fnd Recognition of Distinction in Ed Awd 1988; *office:* Chandler HS 350 N Arizona Ave Chandler AZ 85224

WEISS, JARED L., Eighth Grade Teacher; *b:* Bay City, MI; *m:* Marlyn L. Hartrick; *c:* Theodore, Brandi; *ed:* (AA) Teacher Ed, St Pauls Coll 1975; (BS) Soc Stud Ed, Concordia Teachers Coll 1977; (MED) Soc Stud Ed, Wayne St Univ 1984; *cr:* 7th Grade Teacher/Athl Dir Mt Calvary Luth Sch 1977-85; 8th Grade Teacher/Athl Dir St Luke Luth Sch 1985-; *ai:* Athl Dir; Bsktbl Coach; Track Coach; Sftbl Coach; Spon 8th Grade Class Trip; Fellowship Coord; Sunday Sch Teacher; Luth Ed Assn 1989-; Southeast MI Ofcls Assn 1983-; Luth Fraternities of Amer 1980-; Register Southeast MI Luth Teachers Conf 1984-86; Features Editor MI Luth Sports & Phys Ed Comm 1989; Chm Eastside Luth Schls/Detroit Athl Conf 1980-85; Chm North Suburban Luth Schls/Macomb Cty Athl Conf 1989-; *home:* 20866 Fleetwood Mt Clemens MI 48043

WEISS, MARILYN PETERSON, Home Economics Dept Chair; *b:* River Falls, WI; *m:* Duane E.; *c:* Scott; *ed:* (BS) Home Ec Ed, Univ of WI Stout 1960; Grad Studs Ed, St Thomas Coll, Univ of MN, Univ of WI River Falls; *cr:* Teacher Spooner HS 1960-61, Roseville Schls 1961-; *ai:* Chairperson Curr Writing & Parent Teacher Conference Comms; Faculty Senate Mem; AFT 1961-; *office:* Roseville Schls 1261 Hwy 36 Saint Paul MN 55113

WEISS, MARY ANN, Seventh Grade Teacher; *b:* Jersey City, NJ; *m:* John; *c:* John, Eric; *ed:* (BS) Math/Sci Ed, Jersey City St Coll 1957; *cr:* Kndgtn Teacher Immaculate Heart Sch 1963-78; Math Teacher Sacred Heart Sch 1978-84; 7th/8th Grade Teacher Our Lady of Libera 1984-; *ai:* Sch Newspaper, Bowling Club Adv; NCEA 1978-; GSA 1976-; Public Lib Bd 1983-; *office:* Our Lady of Libera Sch 5700 Kennedy Blvd West New York NJ 07093

WEISS, MICHAEL HOWARD, Physics Teacher; *b:* Miami Beach, FL; *ed:* (BA) Psych, 1983, (BS) Chem, 1983 Univ of Miami; (MS) Sci Ed, FL Intnl Univ 1988; *cr:* Physics/Chem Teacher Hialeah HS 1985-; Adjunct Professor FL Intnl Univ 1987-; *ai:* Club Spon-Sci Honor Society; Feeder Sch Sci Coord; Sci Olympiad Dir; Sci Bowl Coach; Phi Delta Kappa Treas 1986-88; Amer Assn of Physics Teachers; United Teachers of Dade; Phi Beta Kappa; Phi Kappa Phi; Friends of Physics; Scndry Ed Improvement Grants; Labnet Prgm 1989; Leadership Inst for Teachers of Physics 1988; *office:* Hialeah HS 251 E 47th St Hialeah FL 33013

WEISS, NANCY L., Fourth Grade Teacher; *b:* Chicago, IL; *ed:* (BA) Kindergarten Northeastern Univ 1970; *cr:* 3rd Grade 1971-81; 4th Grade Westdale Sch 1981-; *ai:* Westdale's Fun Fair Clown; Textbook Comm Soc Stud, Eng, Spelling & Penmanship; Field Trip Comm; 3rd VP PTA; Asst to Westdale Sch Musical Productions; Co-Spon to Safety Patrol; Mannheim Teacher's Assn 1971-; Mannheim Dist 83 for 15 Yrs of Service; Service Awd Pin 1985; *office:* Westdale Elem Sch 99 W Diversity Ave Northlake IL 60164

WEISS, SHARON MARTIN, French Teacher; *b:* Pontiac, IL; *c:* David J.; *ed:* (BA) Fr, IL St Univ 1976; Human Growth & Dev, Guidance Counseling; *cr:* Fr Teacher Peoria Notre Dame HS 1977-; *ai:* Co-Moderator & Stu Government Cncl; IL Foreign Lang Teachers Assn 1987-90; IL Cncl Teaching of Foreign Lang 1988-; AATF 1986-; Pilot Club 1989-; Teacher/Cnslr Summer Study Abroad 1989; Faculty Rep Leadership Wkshp 1989; *office:* Peoria Notre Dame HS 5105 N Sheridan Rd Peoria IL 61614

WEISSMAN, ADRIENNE Y., English Teacher; *b:* Brooklyn, NY; *m:* Lewis; *c:* Shari, Jaime; *ed:* (BA) Span, Harpur Coll 1964; (MS) Scndry Ed, Hofstra Univ 1965; (MA) Lit, Coll of Staten Island 1990; Courses Queens Coll, NYU, Nassau Comm Coll; *cr:* Eng Teacher Plainedge Jr HS 1965-67, Jr HS 57 1967-71, Ind Sch Dist 220 1982-; *ai:* UFT; Kingswalk Homeowners Assn VP 1986-88; Brunswick Acres Homeowners Assn VP 1976-78; Ed Brunswick Acres Newsletter 1974-78; *home:* 48 Hammock Ln Staten Island NY 10312

WEIST, LAMONT EUGENE, Vice Prin/5th Grade Teacher; *b:* Findlay, OH; *m:* Kathryn Myers Leishman; *c:* Amy L., Jennifer, Matthew, Steven, Katie; *ed:* (BS) Wildlife Management, 1973, (BS) Elem Ed, 1975, (MED) Elem Ed, 1985 UT St Univ; Trng Elem Admin, ID St Univ; *cr:* Elem Teacher Hazel Stuart Elem1975-; Asst Prin Goodsell Elem 1989-; *ai:* ID Centennial Comm; PTSO Faculty Rep, Intramural Comm; Chapter 1 Migrant Dir; SEA Building Rep 1977-78; NEA, IEA; Little League Coach 1975-77/1985-; Shelley Sch Dist Cmmty Ed Dir 1981-87; Scout Master 1976-79 Extra Miler 1978; Church of Jesus Christ of Latter Day Saints (Stake High Cncl Mem 1987-, Bishopric Mem 1979-84); *home:* 577 Holley St Shelley ID 83274

WEISZ, DEL, His Dept Chair/US His Teacher; *b:* Eureka, SD; *m:* Darleen Kenny; *c:* Karen, Barry; *ed:* (BS) His, 1957, (MS) Scndry Admin, 1963 Northern St Univ SD; Graduate Stud, Hofstra Univ, Chapman Coll, Pepperdine Univ; *cr:* Teacher Geddes & Chamberlain 1959-63; HS Prin Canistota 1963-65; Teacher Tustin CA 1965-; *ai:* NEA 1970-; CTA 1965-; TEA 1965-; US Government Institute Hofstra Univ 1965.

WEITH, FRAN GOOD, English Teacher; *b:* Findlay, OH; *m:* Edward L.; *c:* Tammy Weith Miller; *ed:* (BA) Eng, Findlay Coll 1959; (MA) Theatre, Bowling Green St Univ 1965; Grad Work Beyond Masters; *cr:* Eng Teacher Findlay HS 1959-61, Fostoria HS 1965-66, N Baltimore 1966-; *ai:* Drama Club Adv; Play Dir; Eng Curr Revision Comm; NEA 1959-; Alpha Psi Omega 1959; Heidelberg Coll Euglossian Lierary Society 1942-52; Eastern Star Assoc Conductress 1989-; St James Meth Church Organist 1987-; Grad Asst Bowling Green St Univ 1964-65; NEH Fellowship OH Wesleyan 1986; *office:* N Baltimore Mid Sch 124 S 2nd St North Baltimore OH 45872

WEITHERS, MERILLE G., English Department Chairman; *b:* Georgetown, Guyana; *m:* Claudia M. Alford; *c:* Deborah Poole, Theodore, David, Merillee; *ed:* (BED) Scndry Ed, West Indies Coll 1963; (MAT) Eng, 1976, (MA) Eng, 1978 Andrews Univ; *cr:* Vice-Prin Georgetown Acad 1963-65; Acting Prin St Lucia Acad 1965-67; Prin Sharon Elem Sch 1967-72; Eng Dept Chm Peterson Acad 1972-80; *ai:* ASCD Mem 1989; *office:* Northeastern Acad 532 W 215th St New York NY 10034

WELBAUM, MARGARAT ANN, Spanish Teacher; *b:* Lakewood, OH; *m:* Jeffrey M.; *c:* Andrew, Alexander; *ed:* (BA)Fr/Ed, Miami Univ 1977; (MED) Ed, Wright St Univ 1988; *cr:* Fr/Span Teacher Troy HS 1977-80, Bethel HS 1984-; *ai:* NEA, OH Ed Assn, Bethel Ed Assn 1984-; Paralegal 1980-84; Beta Sigma Phi (Recording Secy 1983-84, Treas 1990); *office:* Bethel HS 7490 S SR 201 Tipp City OH 45371

WELBERG, DOROTHY HOLVERSON, Arts Teacher; *b:* Scranton, PA; *m:* George L.; *c:* Holly F. Holverson, Jeffrey S. Holverson; *ed:* (BS) Home Ec, Hood Coll 1944; (MS) Home Ec, Drexel Univ 1948; Scndry Art Ed, Boise St Univ; Correspondence Courses, Inst of Childrens Lit; *cr:* Textiles Instr Intnl Corresponce Sch 1945-46; 1st Grade Teacher Audubon Sch 1946-47; Home Ec Teacher Technical HS 1947-49; Home Ec Instr Drexel Univ 1949-53; Art Teacher Emmett HS 1974-; *ai:* St Bd Evaluation Comm; Dist Art Projects; Pep Club, Sr Class, Future Nurses Adv; Floor-Show Presentation for Elected Personalities; Beta Sigma Phi (Adv & Pres) 1954-74; Delta Kappa Gamma Honary Teachers Org 1977-81; Alpha Delta Kappa Honarary Teachers Org Secy 1978-82; Cty Sch Bd Elected Office 1970-74; Gem Cty Woman of Yr, Teacher of Yr; HS Annual Dedication; Key to City; Homecoming Parade Marshall; Weekly Newspaper Column; *office:* Emmett H S 721 W 12th Emmett ID 83617

WELBORN, LAURA LANCASTER, Middle School Teacher; *b:* Alexandria, LA; *m:* Earnest Paul; *c:* Tim, Samantha; *ed:* (BA) Elem Ed/Speech Therapy, SE LA Univ 1976; *cr:* Teacher Millerville Acad 1983-; *ai:* Yrbk & Cheerleading Spon; Stu Cncl; *home:* 16338 London Ave Baton Rouge LA 70819

WELBORN, LISA, English/French Teacher; *b:* Greenville, SC; *ed:* (BA) Scndry Ed/Eng, 1979, (MS) Scndry Ed/Eng, 1988 Clemson Univ; *cr:* Teacher Easley HS 1980-; *ai:* Chrldr Coach; Chorus Pianist; Pickens Cncl Teachers of Eng Pres 1987-; ADK Secy 1989-; Wolfe Society 1988-; Clemson Centennial Outstanding Grad 1989; NEH Grant Study Hawthorne SUNY Buffalo 1990; Prgm Participant Natl NCTE Convention 1989; SC Bar Assn Grant 1988; *office:* Easley HS Pendleton St Easley SC 29640

WELCH, ARTHUR GLEN, English & History Teacher; *m:* Sandra Kaye Shaffer; *ed:* (BA) Eng/Ed, 1969, (MA) Teaching, 1972 W MI Univ; Univ of IL, Oberlin Coll, W MI Univ; *cr:* Eng Teacher Lumen Christi HS 1969; Eng Instr Jackson Comm Coll 1973-77; Eng/His Teacher Homer Cmmty Schls 1969-; *ai:* Prof Negotiations; Stu Leadership Adv; Stu & Curr Cncl; Advanced Placement; Inservice Comm; Eng & His Dept Chm; Homer Ed Assn Pres 1980-86; MI Ed Assn, NEA; Amnesty Intnl, Sierra Club, Greenpeace, Spectical Lake Conservation Club; Natl Endowment for Hum Univ of IL; Schlsp from Oberlin Coll; MLA Journal Published Article; *office:* Homer Cmmty Schls 412 S Hillsdale St Homer MI 49245

WELCH, DANIEL R., Sci & Human Sexuality Teacher; *b:* Ann Arbor, MI; *m:* Susan V. Harder; *c:* Gail, Jennifer, Erin; *ed:* (BA) Bio, Olivet Coll 1965; (MS) Sci, Eastern MI Univ 1970; Prgm Trng, Admin Management Acad 1988; *cr:* Sci Teacher/Coach Pewamo-Westphalia HS 1965-66; Sci/Sexuality Teacher/Coach Clintondale Mid Sch 1967-; Ed Consultant Lee Canter & Assocs 1988-; *ai:* Improvement Prgm Chairperson; Sci Olympiad Team Dir; HS Cross Cntry, Jr HS Boys Bsktbl Coach; NSTA Mem 1979-; Wrote Human Sexuality Prgm; Detroit-Metro Teacher of Yr 1987; Tri-Cty Outstanding Teacher of Yr; *office:* Clintondale Mid Sch 35300 Little Mack Ave Mount Clemens MI 48043

WELCH, ELI, JR., Physical Education Dept Chair; *b:* New Orleans, LA; *m:* Anita Louise; *c:* Joanna K., Eli III, Michael H.; *ed:* (BS) Health/Phys Ed, Grambling St Univ 1970; *cr:* Phys Ed Teacher Edward H Phillips Jr HS 1970-; *ai:* Started Manhood Club For Problem Boys; Ftbl & Girls Track Head Coach; Awards Comm Chairperson; Head of Dept & Prin Cabinet Mem; United Teachers of New Orleans Coaches 1977-; Natl Fed Interscholastic Coaches Assn 1986-; LA Phys Ed, Health Recreation 1987-89; Concordia Luth Church VP 1976-88, Man of Yr 1980; New Day Lady Stars AAU Summer Track Team Coach 1989; Coached Willie Hall 16 Yr Old Team to Dist Title & Received Appreciation Awd; Received John Mc Donogh HS Awds for Coaching Distance Runners 1987-89; *office:* Edward H Phillips Jr HS 1200 Senate St New Orleans LA 70122

WELCH, ELIZABETH BROWN, 4th Grade Teacher; *b:* Port Arthur, TX; *m:* Stevan E.; *c:* Virginia; *ed:* (BA) Elem Ed, Univ of Houston 1974; Addl Studies Elem Ed Stephen F Austin St Univ; *cr:* 5th/6th Grade Teacher Houston ISD 1974-78; 4th-6th Grade Teacher West Sabine ISD 1978-; *ai:* UIL Spon; Distinguished Svc Awd Houston Teachers Assn 1978; TX Teacher of Yr Prgm Local Awd 81; *office:* West Sabine ISD P O Box 8 Pineland TX 75968

WELCH, HERBERT TIMOTHY, English Teacher/Dept Chairman; *b:* Florence, SC; *m:* Mary Suzanne Stegmier; *c:* Michael, Sarah Holtrop, Jane Saladino, Tim (Dec); *ed:* (Ba) Eng/Speech, Furman Univ 1951; (MA) Admin/Ed Svs, MI St Univ 1959; *cr:* Teacher Cedar Springs HS 1956-; *ai:* Forensics Coach; Yrbk Adv; Co-Chm North Cntrl Accreditation Comm; Publications Adv; Play Dir; CSEA Pres 1975-76; MEA/NEA Teacher of Yr 1988; City Commission Commissioner; *home:* 272 Jeffrey Cedar Springs MI 49319

WELCH, JAMES MONROE, Soc Stud Teacher/Dept Chair; *b:* Kingsport, TN; *m:* Victoria Fox; *c:* James III, Brynn; *ed:* (BS) Sociology/His, E TN St Univ 1975; Grad Stud E TN St Univ 1985-; Phi Delta Kappa Textbook Adoption Services Trng Seminars; *cr:* Teacher Robinson Mid Sch 1976-; *ai:* Soccer Coach; Golf Club Adv; Site Base Management Comm; Kingsport City Schls Soc Stud Dept Chm; St of TN Career Ladder Test Review Panel; Kingsport Ed Assn Pres 1983-84, Nom Outstanding Educator of TN 1988-89; TN Ed Assn (Legislative Liaison 1987-88, St Bd of Ed Liaison 1985-); NEA; 1st Broad Street United Meth Church Lay Leader 1989-; Holston Mental Health Bd Mem 1988-; Rascals Teen Center Bd Mem 1986-89; Rotary 1989-; *office:* Robinson Mid Sch 1517 Jessee St Kingsport TN 37664

WELCH, JEAN CATHERINE, Fifth Grade Teacher; *b:* Rochester, NY; *ed:* (BSED) Ed, Nazareth Coll 1956; *cr:* 1st/2nd Grade Teacher Most Precious Blood Sch 1955-60; 1st-4th Grade Teacher St Thomas More 1960-70; 5th Grade Teacher St Pius Tenth 1970-; *ai:* Rochester Hospital Psychiatric Volunteer 1988-; St Peters Soup Kitchen Volunteer 1989-; Ethic Comm Bd Mem 1987-; *home:* 55 Chestnut Ridge Rd Rochester NY 14624

WELCH, KATHRYN LATIMER, First Grade Teacher; *b:* Hartsville, SC; *m:* Benny E. Jr.; *c:* Benny III, Stephen L.; *ed:* (BA) Elem Ed, Coker Coll 1971; Francis Marion Coll; *cr:* 1st Grade Teacher Bishopville Primary Sch 1971-; *ai:* Grade Chairperson; Supervising Teacher for Stu Teachers; APT Observer; Editor Annual Newspaper Tabloid; Coord Lee Cty Spelling Bee; Delta Kappa Gamma 1985-; Jr Welfare League Treas 1973-86; Dixie Youth Advisory Bd Secy-Treas 1987-; Awarded 5 Mini Grants from Pee Dee Ed Fnd 1988; Awarded 7 Mini Grants from Pee Dee Ed Fnd 1989; Lee Cty Distinguished Teacher 1990; Teacher Incentive Awd 1986/1987/1988.

WELCH, LARRY DEAN, Mathematics Teacher; *b:* Dennison, OH; *m:* Rebecca Ann Cantor; *c:* Jennifer L., Steven A.; *ed:* (BS) Bio, Kent St Univ 1979; (MS) Math, OH Univ 1989; *cr:* Math Teacher Tri-Valley HS 1979-; *ai:* Golf Coach; NCTM; *home:* 2545 Tarkman Dr Nashport OH 43830

WELCH, LYNN BYRD, Language Arts Teacher; *b:* Lancaster, SC; *m:* Charles Jr.; *c:* Lee, Charoline; *ed:* (BA) Scndry Ed, Univ of SC 1975; (MED) Rdng, Winthrop Coll 1980; *cr:* Chapter I Teacher North Jr HS 1975-77; Lang Art Teacher Flat Creek Mid Sch 1977-84, Andrew Jackson Mid Sch 1984-; *ai:* Lancaster Cty Mid & Jr Schls Lang Art dept Liaison; Lancaster Cty Young Writers Conference Coord; Teacher Incentive Prgm Comm Mem; IRA, SCIRA, NEA, SC Ed Assn 1988-; Honorable Mention Distinguished Rdng Teacher 1989-; Andrew Jackson Mid Sch Teacher of Yr 1987-88; SC St Dept of Ed Teacher Incentive Grant 1989-; Lancaster Cty Sch Dist Critical Thinking Grant 1989-; Teacher Incentive Prgm Awd 1988-89; *office:* Andrew Jackson Mid Sch Rt 2 Box 139B Kershaw SC 29067

WELCH, MARY PASSAMANO, Teacher; *b:* New Britain, CT; *w:* Harold B. Jr. (dec); *c:* Mary Welch Mc Gill, Harold B. III, Frank L.; *ed:* (BSED) Elem Ed, 1973, (MS) Rdng, 1980 Cntrl CT St Univ; Rdng Consultant; *cr:* Teacher Dr James Naylor Sch 1974; *ai:* Quality Ed Hartford Sch Ad Hock Comm; Intnl Rdng Assn, CT Rdng Assn.

WELCH, MICHAEL G., 6th Grade Teacher; *b:* Anderson, IN; *m:* Joyce Pitts; *c:* Julie, Lori, Jennifer; *ed:* (BA) Elem Ed, Anderson Univ 1969; (MA) Elem Ed, Ball St Univ 1972; *cr:* 4th/6th Grade Teacher Shadeland Elem/Washington Elem/Killbuck Elem & Coll Corner Elem 1969-; *ai:* Teach GED Madison Cty Jail; Teach Defensive Driving BMV; Anderson Park Dept Sch Dir; Anderson Fed Teachers Bldg Rep 1985-; IN Assn Adult Ed Mem 1979-; Police Merit Comm VP 1987-; *home:* 108 S Mustin Dr Anderson IN 46012

WELCH, MILDRED BAILEY, Third Grade Teacher; *b:* Bryson City, NC; *m:* Robert L.; *c:* Derek, Mark; *ed:* (BS) Elem Ed/Eng, Bethel Coll 1968; (MED) Rdng, E TN St Univ 1983; Post Grad Stud Admin & Supervision, E TN St Univ 1989; *cr:* 2nd Grade Teacher S Pittsburg Elem; 6th Grade Teacher Jasper Elem; 3rd Grade Teacher Hawkins Elem; *ai:* Delta Kappa Gamma (Pres 1983-85, St Achievement Awd Comm), Lottie Mc Cll Schlsp 1988; Hawkins Cty Ed Assn (Pres 1989-, Secy 1976-77, Treas 1976-77); Exch Club Child Abuse Center Bd of Dir 1987-89; ABWA Membership Chairperson 1981; Natl Deans List 1983-84; Sch Annual Dedication 1980-81; *home:* Rt 4 Box 3510 Rogersville TN 37857

WELCH, RENEA GINN, Counselor; *b:* Goldsboro, NC; *m:* Kimsey R.; *ed:* (BS) Elem Ed, W Carolina Univ 1976; (MS) Elem Ed, 1983, (MS) Counseling, 1987 E Carolina Univ; *cr:* Soc Worker Neuse Mental Health 1977-79; Teacher Wilson Cty Schls 1979-81; Teacher 1981-88, Cnslr 1988- Greene Cty Schls; *ai:* Sch Base & Intervention Chm; Leadership Cncl; NCAE 1982-; ABWA Pres 1981-, Woman of Yr Awd 1983; *office:* W Greene Sch 303 Kingold Blvd Snow Hill NC 28580

WELCH, SCOTT WARREN, Social Studies Teacher; *b:* Ashland, KY; *m:* Laura Palmer; *ed:* (BA) His, 1982, (MS) Ed, 1986 Univ of KY; *cr:* Substitute Teacher Fayette Cty Schls 1987; Soc Stud Teacher Lexington Cath HS 1987-; *ai:* Girls Bsktbl, Boys & Girls Track & Intramural Bsktbl Head Coach; Haunted House Fund Raising Comm; Dept Chairperson 1990; Cross Cntry Meet Dir Lexington Cath HS; Phi Alpha Theta 1987-; *office:* Lexington Cath HS 2250 Clays Mill Rd Lexington KY 40503

WELCH, SHARON R., Math Teacher; *b:* Rochester, NY; *m:* Edward; *c:* Nathaniel, Adam; *ed:* (BS) Math/Scndry Ed, 1970, (MS) Scndry Ed, 1973 SUNY Brockport; *cr:* Math Teacher Gates-Chili Jr HS 1970-; *ai:* Organization, Parent Conferencing, Assembly, Final Exam & Substance Abuse Comms; Math Dept Chairperson 1988-; CORE Team Co-Chairperson 1987-; Assn of Math Teachers of NYS Mem 1986-89; Cmmty Organizations Mem 1987-; *office:* Gates-Chili Mid Sch 910 Wegman Rd Rochester NY 14624

WELCH, SHEILA GREENE, Science Teacher; *b:* Americus, GA; *m:* Clarence Roscoe; *c:* M. Keith, Jami I.; *ed:* (BS) Bio, GA Southwestern Coll 1969; *cr:* Bio Teacher Marion Cty 1969-71; Bio Teacher 1973-77, Phys Sci/Earth Sci Teacher 1981- Southland Acad; *ai:* Civinette Club Adv; *office:* Southland Acad PO Box 1127 Americus GA 31709

WELCH, SUSAN DUCOTE, Mathematics/Science Teacher; *b:* Cottonport, LA; *m:* Luke Louis; *c:* Aimee E., Lucas J., Perry L.; *ed:* (BS) Math/Sci Ed, LA Coll 1981; (MED) Admin, LA St Univ 1988; *cr:* Math/Sci Teacher Cottonport HS 1981-88; Math/Sci Teacher/Math Chairperson Bunkie HS 1988-; *ai:* Math Dept Chairperson; LA Assn of Teachers of Math, NCTM; Alpha Delta Kappa Pres-Elect; *office:* Bunkie HS Evergreen Hwy Bunkie LA 71322

WELCH, SUSAN PARKER, History Teacher; *b:* Americus, GA; *m:* Marshall Clinton; *c:* Willaim R. Folsom Jr., Lynsey A.; *ed:* (BS) His 1973; (MED) Soc Sci, 1974 GA Southwestern Coll; EMT; *cr:* Math Teacher Americus HS 1973-74; His Teacher Southland Acad 1974-; *ai:* Var Cheerleading, Soc Sci Coach;Jr Class Spon;7Th Grade WA DC Trip Dir; GA Endowment For Hum Grant 1983; GA His Teachers Handbook; *home:* PO Box 160 Americus GA 31709

WELCH, THELMA FAVORS, First Grade Teacher; *b:* Atlanta, GA; *m:* James Emanuel; *ed:* (BA) Elem Ed, Clark Coll 1963; (MA) Elem Ed, Atlanta Univ 1973; Headstart Trng, Tuskeegee Inst 1966; *cr:* 1st Grade Teacher Newnan City Schls 1963-64; 2nd Grade Teacher Newton Cty Schls 1964-67; 1st Grade Teacher De Kalb Cty Schls 1967-; *ai:* Strategic Planning & Ed Leadership Comm; GAE 1969-72; Sagamore Teacher of Yr 1975, 1976, 1988; *home:* 3820 Morning Creek Dr College Park GA 30349

WELCH, THOMAS R., Reading/Social Studies Teacher; *b:* Elkhorn, WI; *m:* Patricia C; *c:* Laura Moran, Lisa Burch, Mark, David, Patrick; *ed:* Elem Ed, Racine-Kenosha TeodieUS Coll 1957; (BE) Elem Ed, Univ of WI 1968; Univ of WI-Whitewater; CardinaL Stritch Coll Milwaukee; *cr:* 5th/6th Grade Teacher S&L Star Ctr Sch 1957-58; 5th Grade Teacher 1958-59; 6th Grade Teacher 1959-64 Fontana Grade Sch; Bristol Grade Sch 1964-65; 8th Grade Teacher Reele Sch 1965-; *ai:* Outdoor Ed Founder and Dir Reek Sch 12 Years; NEA Mem 1957-; WI Ed Assn Cncl Mem 1957-; Big Foot Ed Assn Bd of Dir Chm 1988-; Reek Sch Dist Teacher of Yr 1977-78; *home:* Rt 3 Box 652 Fontana WI 53125

WELCH, WILLIAM DENNIS, 8th Grade Amer History Teacher; *b:* Somerset, OH; *ed:* (BA) Soc Stud Comprehsensive, OH Univ 1969; *cr:* 7th-9th Grade Soc Stud Teacher New Lexington Jr HS 1969-74; Soc Stud/Eng Teacher St Rose 1974-; *ai:* Asst Var Coach Bsbl 1982-, Bsktbl 1988-; Diocese of Columbus Teacher 1974-84 10 Yr 1984; Somerset Fire Dept 1978-84 5 Yr 1983; Babe Ruth Championship Team St of OH Mgr 1978; *home:* W Main St Somerset OH 43783

WELCOME, ALLEN J., Biology Teacher; *b:* Saugerties, NY; *m:* Angela Anzalone; *c:* Kristen, Brian; *ed:* (BS) Bio, SUNY Albany 1965; (MS) Psych, Coll of St Rose 1971; *cr:* Bio Teacher Scotia Glenville HS 1965-71, Newfield HS 1971-; *ai:* Mid States Cert Steering, Dist Grading Policy, Discipline Policy Comms; More Effective Schls Building Team; Detention Supvr; *office:* Newfield HS 145 Marshall Dr Selden NY 11784

WELCOME, PRESTON M., JR., Principal; *b:* New Iberia, LA; *m:* Janis Scranton; *c:* Tiffany; *ed:* (BA) Soc Stud, Grambling St Univ 1953; (MA) Elem Admin, Univ of OK; (EDS) Elem Admin, Mc Neese St Univ; *cr:* Teacher Teche Elem 1960-65, Paul Breaux HS 1965-68; Asst Prin Paul Breaux Elem 1968-71, N P Moss Mid Sch 1971-72; Prin W a Lerosen Elem 1972-78, N P Moss Mid Sch 1978-; *ai:* Pres of Lafayette Prin Assn 1972; Outstanding Educators Awd Southern Consumers 1971; Citizens for Public Ed Awd; Alpha Kappa Alpha 1982 Svc to Mankind 1982; Phi Delta Kappa Mem 1970-80; North Lafayette Rotary Mem 1989-; Optimist Club North Bd of Dir 1989-; Lafayette Flood Control Mem 1987-; 12 Yrs Service N P Moss Mid Sch; 25 Yrs Service Lafayette Parish Schls 32 Yrs Service to Ed in LA; *home:* 191 Holly St PO Box 92461 Lafayette LA 70502

WELDER, POLLY ANNE WHITTEN, 8th Grade Humanities Teacher; *b:* Jackson, TN; *m:* George E.; *c:* Carl D., Adrienne A.; *ed:* (BA) Eng, N TX Univ 1956; Eng, Cmptr, Psych; *cr:* Teacher Baker Jr HS 1956-60, Robert E Lee 1960-61, Cheyenne WY 1962-63, John Adams & Cleveland & Mc Kinley 1982-; *ai:* Natl Jr Honor Society Spon; NCTE; NMCTE Excl in Eng Ed 1988; GSA Dist Chairperson 1973-74; Scarborough Outstanding Jr HS Teacher Awd 1960; *home:* 8300 Harwood Ave NE Albuquerque NM 87110

WELDON, CHERRI ISON, 2nd Grade Teacher; *b:* Griffin, GA; *m:* Ronald Daniel; *c:* Allison, Claris, Weldon; *ed:* (AA) Sociology, Clayton Jr Coll 1978; (BA) Early Chldhd Ed, Tift Coll 1982; *cr:* 2nd Grade Teacher 1982-83, 4th Grade Teacher 1983-87, 3rd Grade Teacher 1987-88, 2nd Grade Teacher 1988- Beaverbrook; *ai:* Building Reporter; Brownie Asst Leader; Sunday Sch Teacher; PAGE 1982-; PTA Prgm Chm; *office:* Beaverbrook Elem Sch 251 Birdie Rd Griffin GA 30223

WELK, SONIA SUE, Home Economics Teacher; *b:* Grand Forks, ND; *m:* Ronald R.; *c:* Shawn, Rachel, Rebecca; *ed:* (BS) Home Ec Ed, Univ of ND 1973; *cr:* Teacher Big Lake MN 1973-74; Remer MN 1974-; *ai:* Asst Coach Girls Bsktbl/Tracl; Prom Dir; FHA Adv.

WELLER, DIANNA FRIEMEL, Mathematics Teacher; *b:* Groom, TX; *m:* Thomas W.; *c:* Ron, Devian, Paul; *ed:* (BS) Scndry Ed/Math/Chem, W TX St Univ 1971; *cr:* HS Math Teacher Clarendon Ind Sch Dist 1972-75, Claude Ind Sch Dist 1986-; *ai:* Frosh Class Spon; UIL Number Sense Coach; TX St Teachers Assn 1973-; *office:* Claude Ind Sch Dist 500 W 5th St Claude TX 79019

WELLER, LEONE HEIN, 3rd Grade Teacher; *b:* Stevens Point, WI; *m:* Willett P.; *c:* Patrick, Karen Jones, Mark, Thomas, Anne; *ed:* (BS) Ed, WI St Univ Stevens Point 1949; Univ of San Diego/San Diego ST Univ/Univ of MI/Mount Mary Coll/Univ of WI Stevens Point; *cr:* 1st Grade Teacher Waukesha Elem Schl 1949-50, St Stephen Sch 1952-5 3; Kndgtn Teacher San Diego Sch System 1962-66; 1st/3rd Grade Teacher St Stephen 1975-; *ai:* United Way Coor; Educl Curr Comm; NCEA Pres 1975-; Amer Leg Aux 1976-; 40 & 8 Aux 1977-; Knights of Columbus Aux 1978-; 1st Kndgtn Prgm North Stonington CT Public Sch System 1966; *office:* St Stephens Sch 1335 Clark St Stevens Point WI 54481

WELLER, ROBIN FORD, 7th/8th Grade Lang Art Teacher; *b:* Jacksonville, IL; *m:* Michael Lewis; *c:* Christopher, Robert, Morgan L.; *ed:* (BA) Elem Ed/Children & Family Counseling, Sangamon St Univ 1985; *cr:* 7th/8th Grade Lang Art Teacher 1985-86, 6th-8th Grade Lang Art Teacher 1986-88, 7th/8th Grade Lang Art Teacher 1989- Greenfield Jr HS; *ai:* Stu Cncl; Var Cheerleading Spon; Literary Contest Coach; *office:* Greenfield Jr HS 115 N Prairie Greenfield IL 62044

WELLMAN, DEBRA BAKER, Social Stud/Lang Art Teacher; *b:* Springfield, IL; *m:* Ray Wellman; *c:* Loni, Jodi; *ed:* (BA) Phys Ed, IL Coll 1978; (MS) Ed Admin, E IL Univ 1985; Gifted Wkshps; *cr:* Teacher Frazier 1981-82, Mary Miller Jr HS 1982-; *ai:* Stu Cncl; Track & Girls Bsktbl Coach; IL Ed Assn 1983-89; Assn of Women Admin 1985-87; IL Coll Investment Club Treas 1987-89; Toastmasters Intnl Pres 1988-89, Able Toastmaster 1988; Won Dist Speech Contest 1989; Chapter I Prgm Coord 1985; *home:* 202 Delmar Dr Catlin IL 61817

WELLMAN, JOHN B., 6th Grade Sci/Health Teacher; *b:* Portsmouth, OH; *m:* Sandra L. Blakeman; *c:* John Jr., Betsy Wolf; *ed:* (BS) Health/Phys Ed/Bio Sci, E KY Univ 1965; *cr:* Teacher/Coach Miami Trace HS 1965-66, Wilmington HS 1966-76, Clinton Massie Mid Sch 1982-; *ai:* Asst Ftbl Coach; *office:* Clinton Massie Mid Sch 2556 Lebanon Rd Clarksville OH 45113

WELLMAN, JOYCE RIDDLE, German/English Teacher; *b:* Logan, WV; *m:* Bert F. III; *c:* Misti, Cheree, Triplett; *ed:* (BS) Ger, Berea Coll 1972; (MA) Eng, Marshall Univ 1984; (Rank I) Ger/Eng, Univ of KY/Marshall Univ 1986; *cr:* Ger/Eng Teacher Chapmanville HS 1973-74, 1977-78, Hamlin HS 1978-79, Boyd Cty HS 1979-; *ai:* Ger Club Spon; Foreign Lang Dept Chairperson; KCTFL; Goethe Inst Fellowship to Salzburg Sommerschule 1972; *office:* Boys Cty HS 12307 Midland Trail Rd Ashland KY 41101

WELLS, ANGELUS BRACEY, Third Grade Teacher; *b:* Roanoke Rapids, NC; *m:* Michael; *c:* Marcla; *ed:* (BS) Elem Ed, Fayetteville St Univ 1971; (MED) Early Chldhd Ed, NC Cntrl Univ 1980; *cr:* 3rd Grade Teacher Aurelian Springs Elem 1971-; *ai:* Mentor Teacher; Safety Patrol Adv; Sch Improvement Team Testing Coord; A-Team Senate Bill 2 Comm Mem; NEA; Alpha Kappa Alpha Epictoleus 1988-; *home:* Rt 1 Box 147A Skippers VA 23879

WELLS, B. R., Calculus Instr/Gifted Ed Coord; *b:* Pratt, KS; *m:* Judy C. Countryman; *ed:* (AB) Math, Soc Sci, Fort Hays St Univ 1958; (MS) Math, Emporia St Univ 1963; Gifted Ed/Math KS St Univ; *cr:* Teacher Graden City HS 1958-63; Junction City HS 1963-; *ai:* Scholars Bowl Spon; Faculty/StU Advisory Comm; NEA Life Mem; KNEA 1969-83; JCEA Treas 1969-83;Kappa Mu Epsilon; Phi Delta Kappa; NCTM; NATM; 1988 Teacher of Yr Awd JCHS; Governors' Scholars Rep 1984 & 1986-88; HS Teacher Recogniton Awd KU 1986-88; Incentive Pay Awd 7 Yrs; NSF Grants 1961-63; Math Dept Chrm 12 Yrs; Articles in KATM Bulletin; *home:* 702 S Eisenhower St Junction City KS 66441

WELLS, CAROLYN LOUISE, English Teacher/Dept Chair; *b:* Elkton, KY; *ed:* (BS) Eng, 1972, (MAED) Supervision, 1977, (EDS) Supervision, 1981 Austin Peay St Univ; *cr:* Eng Teacher 1972-, Eng Dept Chairperson 1981- Todd Cty Cntrl HS; *ai:* Natl Beta Club Spon; Todd Cty Cntrl HS Faculty Advisory & Public Relations Comms; Todd Cty Master In-Service Comm; Todd Cty Ed Assn, KY Ed Assn, NEA 1972-; Citizens for Academic Excl in Todd Cty (Bd of Dirs 1986-89, Vice-Chm 1989-); Todd Cty Jaycees Outstanding Young Educator 1986; Univ of KY Outstanding Achievement in Teaching 1988; *office:* Todd Cty Cntrl HS S Main St Elkton KY 42220

WELLS, DARLENE ADELLE, Physical Education Teacher; *b:* Cuba, NY; *ed:* (BS) Phys Ed, Houghton Coll 1975; (MS) Ed in Coaching, Alfred Univ 1979; Post Master Studies USA Coaching Accredition Prgm Level I Vlybl Coach; Amer Coaching Effectiveness Prgm Level I Certified Coach; *cr:* Elem Phys Ed 1975-88; Jr Sr High Phys Ed 1988- North FL Christian; *ai:* Varsity Sftbl Coach; Varsity Vlybl Coach; Fellowship of Christian Athletes; Gym Supervisor Tallahassee Pks & Recreation Depts Bsktbl Prgm; Sports Camps; FL Athletic Coaches Assn 1990-; US Vlybl Assn 1990-; Amer Vlybl Coaches Assn 1990-; Fellowship of Christian Athletes 1990-; North FL Christian Teacher of Yr 1986; Vlybl Coach of Yr 1987 (Tallahassee Democrat); NFC Yr Book Dedication 1989; Tachifara Victory Club Awd 1990; *office:* North Florida Chrstn Sch 3000 N Merdian Rd Tallahassee FL 32312

WELLS, IRMA CARTER, Fifth Grade Teacher; *b:* Brandon, MS; *m:* Bennie; *c:* Benji L.; *ed:* (BS) Elem Ed, Jackson St Univ 1969; Addl Studies MS Coll; MS St Univ; *cr:* Elem Teacher Smith Cty Sch 1969-72; 5th Grade Teacher Pearl Public Sch 1972-; *ai:* Girls Circle K Club; Teen Sftbl Adv; City Wide Youth Adv; MS Assn of Ed; Pearl Assn of Ed; PTA; Coord for Summer Youth Prgm; Youth Cnslr for Dist; Outstanding Cmmty Leader; Nom for Teacher of the Year; Woman of the Year-Church; *home:* 140 Huckleberry Lane Brandon MS 39042

WELLS, JOE, 7th English/Soc Stud Teacher; *b:* Grand Island, NE; *m:* Cynthia A. Walters; *c:* Brooks Bradley; *ed:* (BA) Soc Sci, Kearney St Coll 1980; *cr:* Eng/Soc Sci Teacher Walnut Jr HS 1983-; *ai:* Varsity Ftbl Asst Coach; Jr HS Frosh Track Asst Coach; Grand Island Ed Assn; *office:* Walnut Jr H S 1600 N Custer Ave Grand Island NE 68803

WELLS, KAREN KEATING, Third Grade Teacher; *b:* Pittsburgh, PA; *m:* Cary S.; *ed:* (BS) Elem, Edinboro Univ 1973; Univ of Pittsburgh; *cr:* Elem Teacher East Allegheny Sch Dist 1976-; *ai:* EAEA Rep; Mon Valley Consortium Grant in Math; *office:* Westinghouse Elem/E Allegheny Marguerit Ave Wilmerding PA 15148

WELLS, KELLIE WESSELS, English Teacher; *b:* Ft Dodge, IA; *m:* Michael Wells; *c:* Katie L., Kevin M.; *ed:* (BA) Eng Ed, Univ of N IA 1983; *cr:* Mid Sch Lang Art Teacher Fonda Cmmty Sch 1983-; *office:* Fonda Cmmty Sch 3rd And Howard Fonda IA 50540

WELLS, LAWRENCE ARTHUR, Fifth Grade Teacher; *b:* Shelburne Falls, MA; *m:* Gina Marie Baronas; *c:* Christopher J., Matthew C., Timothy J., Stephen M., Lawrence A. Jr.; *ed:* (BSE) Elem Ed, Fitchburg St Coll 1971; (MS) Elem Admin, Westfield St Coll 1987; *cr:* 4th-6th Grade/Head Teacher Colrain Cntrl Sch 1972-88; 5th Grade Teacher Buckland-Shelburne Regional 1988-; *ai:* Chairperson Teacher Center Advisory Bd; BCS Negotiations; Little League Coach; Bsktbl Prgm Coach & Ofcl; BCS Teachers Assn Pres 1976-80; *office:* Buckland-Shelburne Sch Mechanic St Shelburne Falls MA 01370

WELLS, MARY H., Elementary Principal; *b:* Phenix City, AL; *m:* Glenn A.; *c:* Pam, Lisa, Laurie Wells Maskowitz, Mark, Kristy Wells Meyers, David; *ed:* (BA) Scndry Ed, Marycrest Coll 1957; (MS) Rdng, W IL Univ 1981; (PHD) Elem Ed, Univ of IA 1986; Admin, W IL Univ, Univ of IA; Learning Disabilities, N IL Univ; *cr:* HS Teacher Geneseo HS 1957-58; Elem Teacher 1958-61, 1972-87, Chapter I Teacher 1987-89 Rock Island Public Sch; Adjunct Faculty Rdng 1987-88; Prin Alwood Elem 1989-; *ai:* Rdng Wkshp & Presentations; Chapter I Dir; Learning Assessment Coord; Black Hawk Rdng Cncl Pres 1988-89; IL Rdng Cncl Zone Coord 1989-; Phi Delta Kappa 1986-; Intnl Rdng Assn 1984-; IL Cncl for Affective Rdng Ed Pres 1987-88; Jordah Cath Sch Bd VP 1980-81; St Pius X Parish Cncl 1977-80; Delta Kappa Gamma Schlsp for Post Grad Study; *office:* Alwood Elem Sch PO Box 67 Alpha IL 61413

WELLS, ROBERT B., Jr HS Band/Sr HS Bible Teacher; *b:* Ft Smith, AR; *m:* Phyllis Mitchael; *c:* Anne, Sarah, Paul, Philip; *ed:* (BME) Music, John Brown Univ 1976; (MDIV) Theology, Mid-America Baptist Theological Seminary 1987; *cr:* Band/Choir Teacher Siloam Springs Jr HS 1976-77; Band/General Music Teacher Kimmons Jr HS 1977-83; Band/Choir/Bible Teacher Ft Smith Chrstn 1989-; *ai:* Band, Choir Dir; AR Bandmasters Assn Mem 1976- 83; *office:* Ft Smith Chrstn Sch 4201 Windsor Dr Fort Smith AR 72904

WELLS, ROSALIND LENETTE, Language Arts Teacher; *b:* St Louis, MO; *ed:* (BS) Speech Comm/Bus Admin, Southern IL Univ 1977; (MA) Master of Arts in Ed, Maryville Coll 1990; *cr:* Early Chldhd Teacher Aide 1977-79; Speech Teacher 1980-83; Lang Arts Teacher 1983- East St Louis Sch Dist 189; *ai:* Rep to IL Gifted Assn; Jr Beta Club Adv; Head of Eng Dept; Girl Scouts Leader; Ed Week Comm Mem; Jr Varsity Girls Bsktbl Asst Coach; Dist Wide Lang Arts Curr Comm Mem; AFT/IL Federation of Teachers 1980; NEA 1980; Natl Assn Teacher of Eng 1980; Natl Assn for Advancement of Colored People 1981; Delta Sigma Theta 1988; Natl Cncl of Negro Women 1987; Project Speak Awd; Mt Zion M B Church Tape Ministry; Writers Digest Awd; *home:* 1814 Gaty Ave East St Louis IL 62205

WELLS, SUSAN T., Social Studies Teacher; *b:* Vicksburg, MS; *ed:* (BA) Soc Stud Ed, MS Univ for Women 1965; Elem Ed Cert Courses; *cr:* Soc Stud Teacher Warren Cntrl HS 1966-67; 5th Grade Teacher Alpine Crest 1967-68; 3rd Grade Teacher Justiva Rd Sch 1968-69; 6th Grade Teacher Des Peres Elem 1969-74, 7th Grade Math Teacher Vicksburg Mid Sch 1980-85; Soc Stud Teacher Vicksburg HS 1985-; *ai:* Var Chrldr Coach/Spon Vicksburg HS 1985-; Drill Team 1988-89, Sr & Jr Class Spon; Vicksburg Art Assn; Vicksburg Historical Society for Preservation; *home:* 3425 Wisconsin #55 Vicksburg MS 39180

WELSH, JEANNETTE MC WILLIAMS, Mathematics Teacher; *b:* Newport News, VA; *m:* John D.; *c:* Murray G.; *ed:* (BA) Math, Westhampton Coll Univ of Richmond 1960; (AM) Math, Bowdoin Coll 1974; *cr:* Math Teacher Metairie Park Cntry Day 1961-63, Kinkaid Sch 1963-64, Collegiate 1964-; *ai:* TV Quiz Bowl Coach; *office:* Collegiate Schls N Moreland Rd Richmond VA 23229

WELSH, TERRY RANDALL, English Teacher; *b:* Travis AFB, CA; *m:* Joyce Marie; *ed:* (AA) General, Merced Jr Coll 1983; (BA) His, Stanislaus St 1986; *cr:* Ind Study Teacher Merced HS 1985-88; Eng Teacher Le Grand HS 1988-; *ai:* Jr Class Adv; Var Girls Sftbl & Boys Bsktbl Coach; Faculty Staff Salary Comm; Le Grand Cmmty Water Dist Mem 1990; Le Grand Cmmty Park & Recreation Dist Mem 1988-; *office:* Le Grand HS PO Box 67 Le Grand CA 95333

WENCK, ROMONA NELLIS, K-12th Grade Phys Ed Teacher; *b:* Cortland, NY; *m:* Gerald William; *c:* Jonathan W.; *ed:* (BA) Phys Ed, 1977, (MS) Phys Ed, 1981 Cortland St Univ; *cr:* Teacher Laurens Cntrl Sch 1977-; *ai:* Instr Laurens Jaguars Drill Colorguard Adv; Laurens Cntrl Sch Soccer, Bsktbl, Vlybl, Sftbl Coach; *home:* RD 1 Box 192 Laurens NY 13796

WENDELGASS, MARK L., Social Studies Teacher; *b:* Ft Knox, KY; *m:* Patricia; *c:* Jessica, Michael, Thomas; *ed:* (BA) His/Poly Sci, SD St Univ 1973; Grad Work His & Geography; *cr:* Teacher/Coach Huron Public Schls 1973-; *ai:* NHS & Lettermans Club Adv; Boys & Girls Track Head Coach; Boys & Girls Cross Cntry Asst Coach; NEA, SDEA, HEA, Natl & St Coaches Assn; Teachers Credit Union Pres 1986-; St Martins Sch Bd Secy 1988-; St Martins Parish Cncl Pres 1986-; Little League Bsbl Coach 1990; Guest Clinician SD Track Clinic; 2 Time Nominee Track Coach of Yr SD; Boys & Girls Track & Cross Cntry Teams Amassed 5 St Championships & 10 ConferencE Titles; *office:* Huron Sr HS 18th & Arizona S W Huron SD 57350

WENDELKEN, ROBERT JOSEPH, American History Teacher; *b:* Hoboken, NJ; *m:* Margaret Maroney; *c:* Keri, Lori; *ed:* (BS) Amer His/Ed, 1969, (MA) Admin/Supervision, 1980 St Peters Coll; Certified Sch Bus Admin; *cr:* Eng Teacher Bricktownship HS 1969-70, Union City Emerson HS 1970-76; Amer His Teacher Emerson HS 1976-; *ai:* Head Var Bsktbl Coach; His Club & Asst Class Adv; Faculty Cncl Mem; Hudson Cty Umpires Assn 1980-; Hoboken Bd of Ed (Pres 1975-80) 1974-81; *home:* 845 Garden St Hoboken NJ 07030

WENDHAUSEN, DANA RENEE, Science Teacher; *b:* Davenport, IA; *ed:* (BSE) Bio, NE MO St UNiv 1987; HS Guidance & Counseling, Univ of S MS; Summer Grad Prgm; *cr:* Sci Teacher R-3 HS 1987-; *ai:* Cheerleading Spon 1987-; Dist Wide Sci Curr Revision Comm; Sci Teachers of MO 1989-; Alpha Phi Sigma, MO HS Chearleading Assn; *office:* Savannah R-3 HS 701 E William Savannah MO 64485

WENERSKI, LOU ANNE, Business & Marketing Teacher; *b:* Buffalo, NY; *ed:* (BS) Bus/Mrktg, 1980, (MA) Organizational Comm, 1985 St Univ of NY Buffalo; Working Towards MBA St Univ of NY Buffalo; Working Towards Elem Ed Certificate; *cr:* Adult Ed Teacher Cheektowaga-Maryvale Schls 1981-82; Asst Professor Erie Comm Coll 1982-84; Teacher West Seneca West Sr HS 1980-; *ai:* Distributive Ed Clubs of America & FBLA Club Adv; Ski Club Chaperone; *office:* West Seneca West SR HS 3330 Seneca St West Seneca NY 14224

WENGER, JO ANN CRAUN, Mathematics Dept Chairperson; *b:* Harrisonburg, VA; *m:* C. Winston; *c:* C. David, Brian D.; *ed:* (BS) Elem Ed, 1965, (MS) Elem Ed, 1972 James Madison Univ; *cr:* Teacher Linville-Edom Elem 1965-72; Teacher/Prin Bergton Elem 1972-74; Part Time Teacher E Mennonite Coll 1984-86; Teacher John C Myers Mid 1974-; *ai:* Planned Fall Faculty Retreat; NCTM 1983-; VA Cncl Teachers of Math 1974; Valley of VA Cncl Teachers of Math Dir 1972-; Broadway HS Athletic Booster Club Pres 1977-, Outstanding Service 1981; Sunset Drive United Meth Church (Treasof Women 1980, Sunday Sch Teacher); Ec Awd for Unit Taught; Clinical Faculty Mem Mid Valley Consortium for Teacher Ed; *home:* 132 Skymont Broadway VA 22815

WENNER, DOUGLAS KEITH, English Teacher; *b:* Oil City, PA; *m:* Jacqqueline S. Mook; *c:* Brett, Romain, Autumn, Lee; *ed:* (BA) Eng, Asbury Coll 1971; (MED) Eng Ed, Westminster Coll 1977; *cr:* Eng Teacher SR HS 1972-81; Oil City Mid Sch 1981-; *ai:* Young Astronaut Club Adv; Yrbk Adv; PA Comprehensive Rdng Prgm Coord; *office:* Oil City Mid Sch 69 Spring St Oil City PA 16301

WENNERBERG, CARL LAWRENCE, 7th Grade Math Teacher; *b:* Fitchburg, MA; *ed:* (BS) Math, Fitchburg St Coll 1971; *cr:* Math Teacher May a Gallagher Jr HS 1971-; *ai:* Stu Store Adv; Girls Bsktbl Coach; *office:* May A Gallagher Jr H S 24 Church St Leominster MA 01453

WENNING, KAROLANNE PIERCE, Sixth Grade Teacher; *b:* Fort Myers, FL; *m:* Todd G.; *ed:* (AB) Elem Ed, 1967 St Univ of NY Coll; (MED) Elem Ed/Rdng Specialist, 1974; (EDS) Elem Ed/Rdng Specialist/Instructional Supervisor, 1976 Southern Coll; 250 Hr Trng As Right to Read Dir; *cr:* Teacher Kenmore-Town of Tonawanda Sch Syst 1967-69; Teacher Chatham C Ty Bd of Ed 1969-71; Rdng Specialist Brooklet Elem Sch 1971-73; Compensatory Ed Dir 1973-81; Elem Curr Dir 1979-81 Bulloch Cty Bd of Ed; Instr GA Southern Coll 1979; Teacher Tyrone Elem Sch 1981-; *ai:* 4-H Club Adv; 6th Grade Chm; Comm Chm Interim Review Southern Assn of Colleges and Schls; Adv Schl Lib Comm; Curr and Textbook Review Evaluator; Intnl Rdng Assn 1976-81; GA Cncl of Intnl Rdng Assn 1978-81; Core Cncl of GA I R a GA Southern Coll 1979-; ASCD 1978-81; GA Assn for Curr & Instructional Supervisors 1978-81; Statesboro Jr Womans Club (VP 1973-81, Chm 1974-78); Phi Kappa Phi Honor Society; Phi Delta Kappa; Kappa Delta Pi; Alpha Delta Kappa; *home:* 123 Morallion Hills Peachtree City GA 30269

WENTWORTH, CAROLINE SMITH, Eighth Grade Science Teacher; *b:* Jersey City, NJ; *m:* Ross; *ed:* (BA) Elem Ed, Jersey City St Coll 1971; Grad Work Health Sci, Cmptr Ed; *cr:* 3rd Grade Teacher 1971-72, 4th Grade Teacher 1972-74, 6th Grade Teacher 1974-82, 8th Grade Sci Teacher 1982- Thomas A Edison Sch; *ai:* Emerson HS Chrldrs Coach 1975-82; Emerson HS Drill Team Adv/Coach 1982-; Edison Sch Faculty Adv; Honors Awds Club; Curr Comm; K-8th Substance Abuse Ed; Edison Sch Faculty Cncl Mem; Cmmty Church of God Sunday Sch Teacher 1975-82; Outstanding Young Women of America 1973; NJ Governors Teacher Recognition Awd 1987; NJ Commissioners Symposium Ed 1987; Edison Sch Teacher of Yr 1986-87; *office:* Thomas A Edison Sch 507 West St Union City NJ 07087

WENTZEL, HOWARD SCOTT, Social Studies Teacher; *b:* Greensburg, PA; *m:* Elain J. Pudelsky; *c:* Lee A., David S.; *ed:* (BS) Soc Stud Ed, Clarion 1964; Grad Stud, Slippery Rock Univ; Drug & Alcohol Trng; *cr:* Teacher N Hills Sch Dist 1964-; *ai:* Head Track Coach; HS Drug & Alcohol Team; PA Ed Assn, NEA, N Hills Ed Assn 1964-; Natl Soc Stud Cncl 1962-75; Braun-Jeffrey Athletic Assn Secy 1977-81; *office:* North Hills Sch Dist 53 Rochester Rd Pittsburgh PA 15229

WENTZELL, JANET MARIE (FREEL), 6th Grade Language Art Teacher; *b:* Clinton, MA; *m:* Roger D.; *c:* Carolyn; *ed:* (BS) Elem Ed, 1962, (ME) Elem Ed, 1981 Worcester St Coll; *cr:* 3rd Grade Teacher 1962-69, 2nd/3rd Grade Teacher 1969-77, 4th Grade Teacher 1977-82, 6th Grade Lang Art Teacher 1982-, Admin Asst 1986- Boylston Elem; *ai:* Tahanto Schlsp Fundraiser; Spelling & Tradebook Comm; Boylston Teachers Assn Pres 1987-88; MA Teachers Assn, NEA; Boylston Firefighters Auxiliary Pres 1970-75; Boylston Memorial Day Comm 1990; Boylston Lioness Organization 1985-; Alliance for Ed Grant; *office:* Boylston Elem Sch Sewall St Boylston MA 01505

WENZ, MICHAEL F., Business Department Chair; *b:* Jersey City, NJ; *c:* Derek J.; *ed:* (AS) Bus Admin, Champlain Coll 1973; (BS) Bus Ed, 1975, (MA) Curr/Instruction, 1983 Castleton St; *cr:* Industry Management Positions NY & WA St 1961-75; Bus Teacher Oxbow HS & Voc Center 1975-79; D E Instr Mineville BOCES 1979-80; Bus Dept Chm Rome Catholic HS 1980-; *ai:* VT Bus Teachers Assn Pres 1978-79; NY St Bus Teachers Assn Mem 1979-; Jaycess Local Pres 1970, Outstanding Young Men of Amer 1973; Published Articles 1977, 1979, 1983; *office:* Rome Catholic HS 800 Cypress St Rome NY 13440

WENZEL, MARILYN COLE, English/AP English Teacher; *b:* St Louis, MO; *m:* Fred H.; *c:* Keith, Brian, Carolyn S.; *ed:* (BA) Eng/Span, Lake Forest Coll 1961; (MED) Scndry Ed, UT St Univ 1980; UT Writing Project; Natl Hum Inst; MO Univ St Louis; *cr:* Eng Teacher North Kirkwood Jr HS 1961-63, Dixie Jr HS 1973-77, Dixie HS 1977-; *ai:* Sterling Scholar & Advanced Placement Coord; NHS Adv; NEA, UEA, WCEA; NCTE UT Eng Teacher 1986-87; *office:* Dixie HS 350 E 700 S Saint George UT 84770

WENZEL, PATRICIA RUGGLES, 6th Grade Lang Art Teacher; *b:* Norwalk, OH; *m:* Richard A.; *ed:* (BA) Eng, Miami Univ 1970; (MED) Rdng Specialist, Xavier Univ 1982; *cr:* 7th/8th Grade Eng Teacher 1970-78, 7th/8th Grade Rdng Teacher 1978-85, Lang Art Teacher of Gifted 1985-86, 7th Grade Rdng Teacher 1986- Bethel Tate Schls; *ai:* Stu Cncl Adv; Tiger Paw & Staff Recognition Comm; TAWL Clermont Cty Exec Comm 1988-; Little Miami Rdng Cncl Pres 1987-88; Intnl Rdng Assn 1982-; Martha Holden Jennings Scholar; OH Lang Art Teacher Leader Network; *home:* 3234 Pitzer Rd Bethel OH 45106

WERNE, MAUREEN ROSE (SEGER), Second Grade Teacher; *b:* Jasper, IN; *m:* Kevin Lee; *c:* Brock, Asha R., Cameron; *ed:* (BS) Ed, 1977, (MS) Ed, 1981 IN Univ; *cr:* 2nd Grade Teacher David Turnham 1977-78; 1st/3rd Grade Teacher Haysville Grade Sch 1978-79; 2nd Grade Teacher Dubois Elem 1979-; *ai:* Girls Jr Vars Vlybl Coach 1979-83; Textbook Adoption & Social Comm; Teacher Supvr Critic Teacher; IN St Teachers Assn (Natl, St, Local Mem); Jasper Bus & Prof Women Mem 1986-; St Josephs Church; Mini Economic Grant 1989-; *home:* 435 W 33rd St Jasper IN 47546

WERNER, DAVID GARY, Science Supervisor; *b:* Philadelphia, PA; *m:* Joan St Clair Hutchison; *c:* David, Daniel, Andrea; *ed:* (BS) Scndry Ed, Millersville Univ 1969; (MA) Phys Sci, West Chester Univ 1975; Natl Sci Fnd Summer Inst Beaver Coll 1970; *cr:* Teacher/Coach Upper Moreland Jr HS 1969-80, Upper Moreland HS 1980-82; Acting Asst Prin Upper Moreland Mid Sch 1984-85; Scndry Sci Supvr Upper Moreland HS 1982-84, 1985-; *ai:* Upper Moreland New Teacher Induction Comm; ASCD 1989-; Montgomery Cty Sci Teachers Assn, NEA, PA St Ed Assn 1969-; Upper Moreland Ed Admin Assn 1982-; *office:* Upper Moreland HS 150 Terwood Rd Willow Grove PA 19090

WERNER, IVAN E., Mathematics & Computer Teacher; *b:* Goodland, KS; *m:* Verda L. Goetz; *c:* Rhonda K. Fionda, Patti A., Michael E.; *ed:* (BS) Bus Admin, 1958, (MS) Bus Admin, 1972 Ft Hays St Univ; Summer Inst Jr Coll Instruction 1973, Mid Sch Math 1986-87; *cr:* Bus Ed/Ec Teacher Brewster Unified Sch Dist 314 1958-67; Ec Instr KS St Univ 1967-69; Accounting Instr Ft Hays Univ 1972-76; Math/Sci/Cmptr/Soc Stud/Rdng Teacher Victoria Elem Sch 1971-; *ai:* Math Curr Comm Chm; Cmptr Curr Comm Mem; Phi Delta Kappa 1967-; NCTM, KS Assn Teachers of Math 1980-; Brewster Lions Club Pres 1958-67, Perfect Attendance; Victoria City Cncl 1981-87; Victoira Planning Commission 1990; NDEA Inst in Ec KS St Univ 1966; Natl Sci Fnd Inst for Jr Coll Instruction 1973; Summer Inst for Mid Sch Math 1986-87; *home:* 620 Iron St Victoria KS 67671

WERNER, JULIA STEWART, Humanities Teacher; *b:* Washington, IA; *m:* Steven; *ed:* (AB) His, Grinnell Coll 1958; (MA) His, 1969, (PHD) His, 1982 Univ of WI; Inst of Historical Research Univ of London England; *cr:* Teacher Kemper Hall 1962-68; Teaching Asst Univ of WI Madison 1969-71; Teacher Nicolet HS 1972-; *ai:* Amer Historical Assn Teaching division 1987-; Organization of His Teachers Exec Bd 1988-; NEH Teacher-Scholar 1990-91; NEH Summer Seminars 1987, 1990; Basic Ed Ind Study Fellowship Cncl 1985; Book Published 1984; *office:* Nicolet HS 6701 N Jean Nicolet Rd Glendale WI 53217

WERNER, LYNN BOYD, Soc Stud/Teacher of Gifted; *b:* Paducah, KY; *c:* Tracy L.; *ed:* (BS) Elem Ed, David Lipscomb Coll 1967; (MA) Elem Ed, Murray St Univ 1971; *cr:* Teacher R C Longan Elem Sch 1967-68, Lone Oak Mid Sch 1968-; *ai:* Academic Team Coach; Curr Advisory Steering, Spec Ed Placement Comm; NEA, KY Ed Assn; Mc Cracken Cty Ed Assn Secy 1971-75; Delta Kappa Gamma (St Secy 1983-87, Local Pres 1976-80, 1986-); KY Assn Gifted Ed; Lone Oak Womans Club Pres 1980-82; Area Chamber of Commerce Extra Mile Awd; *home:* 167 Atlanta Ave Paducah KY 42003

WERNER, PATRICIA ANN, 6th Grade Teacher/Asst Prin; *b:* Evergreen Park, IL; *m:* Bob; *c:* Michael, Brian, Jim; *ed:* (BS) Ed, 1969, (MS) Ed, 1972 Loyola; Admin & Supervision; *cr:* 2nd-4th/6th Grade Teacher 1969-, Asst Prin 1982- Mc Cord; *ai:* Organizing Act & Spec Events; Chairperson Spelling Bee & RIF Projects; AFT 1969-; Asst Prin Assn 1982-; PTA Public Relations VP 1976-, Life Membership 1979; Nom for Teacher of Yr & Golden Apple Awd; *home:* 4705 W 106th St Oak Lawn IL 60453

WERNER, RICHARD, Fourth Grade Teacher; *b:* New York, NY; *c:* Matthew, Meredith; *ed:* (BA) Ed, Adelphi Univ 1969; (MALS) Liberal Sci, Stony Brook Univ 1973; *cr:* Teacher Intermediate Sch 292 1970-73, Longwood Schls 1975-; *ai:* Co-Authored Play; *office:* W Middle Island Sch Swezey Ln Middle Island NY 11953

WERNER, THOMAS DAVID, Fifth Grade Teacher; *b:* Odebolt, IA; *m:* Renee Jean Van Adestine; *c:* Michael, John, Zachary; *ed:* Assoc Elem Ed, Door-Kewaunee Teachers Coll 1969; (BA) Elem Ed, Univ of WI Oshkosh 1974; *cr:* 3rd Grade Teacher 1969-76, 6th Grade Teacher 1977-84, 5th Grade Teacher 1985- Luxemburg-Casco Schls; *ai:* Elem Bsktbl Coach; Rdng Dev & Rdng Curr Comm; Asst HS Ftbl Coach; LCEA Pres 1972-73; WEA, NEA; Volunteer Fire Dept 1983-; St Johns Church Secy 1980-; YMCA Youth Dir 1972-81; Luxemburg Village Recreation Dept Dir 1972-77; Jaycees Outstanding Young Educator 1974; WI Congress Outstanding Young Men Mem; *home:* R 1 Box 293 Luxemburg WI 54217

WERNTZ, HELEN SHARKEY, Fourth Grade Teacher; *b:* Philadelphia, PA; *m:* Ronald C.; *c:* Elizabeth, Meredith, Adrienne; *ed:* (BS) Elem Ed, West Chester Univ 1971; (MED) Elem Ed, Clemson Univ 1976; *cr:* 4th Grade Teacher Forest Acres Elem 1971-; *ai:* Lang Art Coord; NEA 1978-; SCEA 1978-; PCEA 1978-; Fourth Presby Church- Sunday Sch Teacher 1987-; *home:* 32 Windsor Dr Greenville SC 29609

WERT, DOROTHY GOLDEN, Mathematics Teacher; *b:* Waterbury, CT; *m:* Arthur; *c:* Todd; *ed:* (BS) Math, Millersville St Coll 1953; Univ of WY, Penn St Univ, Millersville Univ; *cr:* Teacher Gordon Swift Jr HS 1953-60, York Suburban Sch Dist 1960-69, 1981-; *ai:* Mathcounts; NEA, PSEA; Delta Kappa Gamma Treas 1974-84; OES PM 1976-; NSF 1963-64; *office:* York Suburban Mid Sch Sundale Dr York PA 17402

WERTH, EDNA REETZ, 2nd Grade Teacher; *b:* Neshkoro, WI; *m:* Karl Wilton; *c:* Martin P., Amy J., Peter K., Karl K.; *ed:* Cert Elem Ed, Greenlake Cty Normal 1948; Cert Elem Ed, Waushara Cty Normal 1949; (BA) Elem Ed, ID St Univ 1975; Univ of WI Oshkosh; *cr:* 1st-8th Grade Teacher North Mackford & Maple Lawn & Mack for Prairie 1949-70; Child Dev Center Teacher St of ID 1970-75; 6th Grade/Chapter I Teacher 1975-78, 2nd Grade Teacher 1978- Elem Sch; *ai:* Local Spec Comms; DAR Mem 1948; *home:* 904 Pine St Buhl ID 83316

WERTHEIM, SANDRA LYDIA, Lang Art & Spanish Teacher; *b:* Mc Allen, TX; *m:* William D.; *c:* Arianna, Derek; *ed:* (BA) Span, E NM Univ 1976; *cr:* Span/Civics Teacher Ft Sumner HS 1977-80; Lang Art/Span Teacher Ft Sumner Mid HS 1986-; *ai:* Class Spon; Spelling Bee Coord; NEA 1986-89; Ft Sumner Ed Assn VP 1979; Beta Sigma Phi (Pres, VP, Secy) 1974-81; Eastern Star 1982; Amer Cancer Society (Secy, Treas) 1981; *office:* Ft Sumner Municipal Schs P O Box 387 Fort Sumner NM 88119

WERTZ, DAVID E., 4th Grade Teacher; *b:* Bedford, PA; *m:* Sharon K. Sciranko; *ed:* (BA) Elem Ed, Clarion Univ 1976; *cr:* 4th Grade Teacher Cumberland Valley Elem Sch 1977-; *ai:* Intramural Athletic Coord; Bedford Area Ed Assn, PA St Ed Assn 1977-; Elks Lodge #1707 Pres Mens Golf Assn 1984-; Moose Lodge #480 1980-; *office:* Cumberland Valley Elem Sch Rd 3 Box 138 Bedford PA 15522

WERTZ, JOAN P., Third Grade Teacher; *b:* Pittsburgh, PA; *m:* Harry O. Jr.; *c:* David; *ed:* (BS) Elem Ed, Edinboro Univ 1960; (MA) Elem Ed, Pitt & Penn St 1983; *cr:* 4th Grade Teacher Bethel Park 1960-63; 6th 1st 3rd Grade Teacher Nesh Twp 1963-65/1973-; *ai:* Mentor Teacher Eng Comm; Soc Stud Comm Twp Rep Tells Wkshp; NTEA Secy/Grievance Chm 1973-;PSEA 1973-; Jr Womans Club Secy 1970; Law Co Fed League Pres 1982; Elder Northminster Presbyn Church 1988; *office:* Neshannock Elem Sch 299 Mitchell Rd New Castle PA 16105

WERYAVAH, DANA ANDREW, High School Counselor; *b:* Lawton, OK; *m:* Janet Lea Cofer; *c:* Brian, Kellen, Jordan; *ed:* (BS) His/Phys Ed, Cameron Univ 1974; (MED) Counseling, Southwestern St Univ 1983; Scndry Admin, Southwestern St Univ; *cr:* Coord Title IV Indian Ed/Lawton Public 1974-80; Teacher/Coach Eisenhower Jr HS 1980-88; Cnslr Lawton HS 1988, Eisenhower Sr HS 1988-; *ai:* Schlsp; Stu Assistance Prgm Mem; NEA, OEA, PEAL; Comanche Tribe Higher Ed Comm 1987-88; Distinguished Achievement Awd Outstanding Certified Prof Lawton Public Schls 1989-90; *office:* Eisenhower Sr HS 5202 W Gore Blvd Lawton OK 73505

WESCHKE, BERT E., Drafting Teacher; *b:* Tuxedo, NY; *m:* Kay; *c:* Erica, Kira; *ed:* Cert Welding, Pikes Peak Comm Coll 1978; (BS) Technology Ed, VA Tech 1984; *cr:* Welding Teacher New River Comm Coll 1978-80; Drafting Teacher Pulaski Cty HS 1985-; *ai:* Yrbk, VICA Spon; NEA, VA Ed Assn, Pulaski Cty Ed Assn 1987-; Va Tech Coll of Ed Sr of Yr & Industrial Art Sr of Yr 1984; *office:* Pulaski Cty HS P O Box 518 Dublin VA 24084

WESCOTT, DIANE BLAKE, Mathematics Teacher; *b:* Glens Falls, NY; *m:* Daniel Joseph; *c:* Lisa, Kyle; *ed:* (AAS) Math, Adirondack Comm Coll 1973; (BS) Ed/Scndry Math, Castleton St Coll 1975; Grad Stud; *cr:* 7th-10th Grade Math Teacher Granville Jr/Sr HS 1977-; *ai:* 8th Grade Class, Natl Jr Honor Society Adv; Mid Sch & Prin Advisory Comm; GSA (Leader 1982-, Area Chm 1989-); *office:* Granville Jr/Sr HS Quaker St Granville NY 12832

WESCOTT, GWENDOLYN STANLEY, English Dept Chairman; *b:* Goldsboro, NC; *m:* William James; *c:* Celeste G., William G.; *ed:* (BA) Eng/Religious Ed, Atlantic Chrstn Coll 1959; (MSED) Eng/Supervision, E Carolina Univ 1979; Various Courses; *cr:* Scndry Eng Teacher Rock Ridge 1959-61, Tar Heel 1962-63; Eng/Soc Stud Elizabeth City HS 1963-67; Mid Grades Lang Teacher Camden Cty 1967-69; *ai:* Jr, Sr, Beta Club Spon; Climate, SAT, Southern Accredition Comm; Phi Delta Kappa Newsletter Editor 1983-84; Alpha Delta Kappa Several Comms 1980-; NC Assn of Educators (Local Pres 1976-77, Local Secy 1990); Baptist Women Pres; Belcross Homemakers Secy 1988; Museum of Albemarle Bd of Trustees 1990; NC St Volunteer Awd 1984; Textbook Comm Albemarle Area; Teacher of Yr Camden HS 1977; NC Eng Teachers Convention Camden HS Rep 1989; NC Mentor Teachers Conference Camden Cty Rep 1989; *office:* Camden HS PO Box 220 Camden NC 27921

WESELOH, VIVIAN UNSETH, 3rd Grade Teacher; *b:* Suttons Bay, MI; *m:* Lawrence G. Jr.; *c:* Matthew, Kirsten Schnackenberg, Christian; *ed:* (BS) Elem Ed, Mankato St 1962; *cr:* 1st/2nd Grade Teacher Trinity Luth Sch 1962-65; 1st Grade Teacher Monee Elem 1966-67, 5th/6th Grade Teacher 1972-75, 4th Grade Teacher 1975-76; 5th/6th Grade Teacher 1976-83; 3rd Grade Teacher 1983 Oakes Elem; *ai:* Sing-N-Aires Pianist/Dir 1977-; Guelph Band Dir 1983-; *home:* PO Box 266 Guelph ND 58447

WESLEY, BETTY JANE SLAUGHTER, 1st & 2nd Grade Comb Teacher; *b:* Kansas City, MO; *m:* Leonard H. Jr.; *c:* Leonard III, Alan E.; *ed:* (BA) Elem Ed, KS St Coll 1959; Addl Studies Wichita St Univ; Brigham Young Univ; *cr:* Teacher Yeager Sch 1959-61; Isely Elem Sch 1961-67; Mc Lean Elem Sch 1968-; *ai:* Staff Dev Laison; Multi-Cultural Ed Task Force; Sch Building Comm; NEA 1961-; KS Natl Ed Assn 1961-; Wichita NEA 1961-; Delta Sigma Theta Sororoty Chaplain 1986-88; Wichita Chapter Links Inc Recording Sec 1986-88; St Matthew CME Church Bd Chrstn Ed 1980-; *home:* 2401 N Bluff Wichita KS 67220

WESLEY, LULA BRADFORD, Supervising Teacher; *b:* Newellton, LA; *m:* Kenneth R.; *c:* Sheddrick Bradford; *ed:* (BS) Elem Ed, 1971, (MED) Elem Ed, 1976 Southern Univ; Rdng Specilist, Post Doctorate, Grambling St Univ; *cr:* Teacher Wright Elem 1971-74, Clark Elem 1975-76; Supervising Teacher Grambling St Univ & Alma J Brown Lab 1976-; *ai:* Brownie Scout Leader; Bsktbl Clock Operator & Scorekeeper; Summer Sch Enrichment Teacher; Courtesy Fund; Calendar; Prgms Chairperson; Honors Assembly; Schlsp Chairperson; Curr; Faculty Handbook; Bsktbl Coach; Youth Dir; Extended Day Teacher; Supt Advisory Cncl; Phi Delta Kappa; LA Educators Assn, NEA 1976-; LA Rdng Assn 1980-; Easter Seal of LA; PTA (Membership Chairperson 1982-84) 1988-; Math-A-Thon Chairperson 1987-88) 1988-; Delta Sigma Theta (Spelling Bee Chairperson 1986-87) 1988-; Faculty Senate Rep 1978-79; Alpha Kappa Alpha; GSA Leader; Teacher of Yr 1987-89; Safety Patrol Winner 1986-87; Marching Unit Chaperone; *office:* Alam J Brown Lab Grambling St Univ Ralph Jones Dr Grambling LA 71245

WESLEY, THOMAS GREGORY, Guidance Counselor; *b:* Elkton, MD; *ed:* (BS) Elem Ed, Salisbury St Coll 1979; (MED) Counseling/Personal Services, Univ of S MS 1984; Working Towards Masters Admin, Univ of DE; *cr:* Teacher/Cnslr Cecil Cty Bd of Ed 1980-; *ai:* Stu Cncl Adv; Odyssey of Mind Competitions Cty Coach; NEA, MSTA 1980-; Wrights AME Church Supt 1982-; *home:* PO Box 54 Elkton MD 21921

WESOLOWSKI, GERMAINE VELICER, Kindergarten Teacher; *b:* Kewaunee, WI; *c:* Katherine Wesolowski Brumm, James; *ed:* (BS) Elem Ed, Oshkosh St Coll 1963; (MS) Curr/Instruction, Univ of WI Milwaukee 1985; *cr:* 3rd Grade Teacher Beaumont Sch 1963-66; Kndgtn Teacher Fairview Sch 1967-69, 1970-81, Sunnyside Sch 1981-; *ai:* Dist Math & Rdng Comm; Early Chldhd Outreach Team; Dist Lead Kndgtn Teacher; WI Ed Assn, NEA 1963-; Sunnyside PTA (Teacher Rep 1987-88) 1981-; Chrstn Mothers (Secy 1967-68) 1966-; Music Boosters (Secy 1983-84) 1981-85; GSA 1966-76; Beginning Experience 1981-; Pulaski Elem Teacher of Yr 1981; *home:* 192 E Cedar St Pulaski WI 54162

WESSLING, SHARON WALSTROM, Math & Physics Teacher; *b:* Spencer, IA; *m:* Alfred J.; *c:* Alfred V., Teresa L., Angela G., Mark W.; *ed:* (BS) Math, IA St Univ 1973; IA St Univ, Drake Univ, Univ of N IA; *cr:* HS Math/Physics Teacher Guthrie Center HS 1973-; *ai:* Physics Olympics; NEA, ISEA, GCEA; CCD Teacher; K-6 Cath Choir Dir; *home:* 203 Allen Bayard IA 50029

WESSON, JANET HUNT, Counselor; *b:* Garwood, TX; *m:* James W.; *c:* Jana Martin, Jay, Jeff; *ed:* (BS) Psych, Abilene Chrstn Univ 1957; (MA) Counseling/Guidance, Univ of AL 1968; Univ of TX, TX Tech Univ; *cr:* Elem Teacher West Elem 1957-61; HS Teacher 1964-66, HS Cnslr 1967- Snyder HS; *ai:* TX Classroom Teachers, Snyder Classroom Teachers, TX Sch Cnslrs Assn; Ko Jo Kai Pres 1956; Campus Service Organization VP 1957; In Psysiders Pres 1956; Univ of AL Fellowship 1966-67; *home:* 2201 45th St Snyder TX 79549

WEST, BARBARA BRUCE, Mathematics Teacher; *b:* Kosciusko, MS; *m:* Bobby Arnold; *c:* Ryan, Brooks; *ed:* (MS) Math, MUW 1971; *cr:* Teacher Ackerman HS 1971-79, Brookhaven HS 1979-82, Brandon Acad 1982-84, Jackson Public Schls 1984-; *ai:* Spon APAC Mu Alpha Theta; MCTM 1975-; *home:* 3830 Greentree Pl Jackson MS 39211

WEST, CAROLYN CAMPBELL, 3rd Grade Teacher; *b:* Mapleton, KS; *m:* Dean A.; *c:* Michael D., Melanie L., Marilee; *ed:* (BSED) Elem, Emporia St Univ 1966; Grad Stud Pittsburg St Univ; *cr:* Teacher Winfield Scott Elem 1966-70, Eugene Ware Elem 1972-; *ai:* KS Ed Assn 1966-; United Meth Church Parish Relations 1987-; Bourbon Cty Jaycees Outstanding Young Educator 1970; *home:* 310 W 23rd Fort Scott KS 66701

WEST, DARRELL A., Mathematics Teacher; *b:* Williamston, MI; *m:* Donna Jean York; *c:* Kelly, Karmi, Dustin; *ed:* (BA) His, MI St Univ 1964; *cr:* Teacher Webberville HS 1964-; *office:* Webberville HS 309 E Grand River Webberville MI 48892

WEST, DONNA PATE, English Teacher; *b:* Asheville, NC; *ed:* (BS) Eng Ed, Univ of NC Chapel Hill/Minot St Univ 1980; *cr:* Eng Teacher Max Public Schls Dist 50 1980-82; Charles D Owen HS 1984-; *ai:* Stu Government & European Trip Spon; Asst Sftbl Coach; Prom, NCAE Prof Rights, SAT Improvement, Homecoming Comm; Issues & Concerns Comm Chairperson; March of Dimes Walk America Capt; Sch Improvement Team; NC Assn of Educators 1984-; Black Mountain Pairing Project Bd Mem 1990-93; Optimist Club 1990; VFW Ladies Auxiliary Voice of Democracy Awd; *home:* 24 Rhododendron Dr Arden NC 28704

WEST, DOROTHY H., Social Studies Teacher; *b:* New Castle, PA; *m:* John C.; *c:* Barbara L., John C. Jr.; *ed:* (BSED) Bus Ed, Youngstown St Univ 1962; Cert Soc Stud, Slippery Rock Univ 1985; Working Towards Masters Bus Ed, Univ of Pittsburgh; *cr:* Bus Ed Teacher South HS 1962-65, Carlynton Sch 1965-67; Bus Ed/Soc Stud Teacher Butler Area Schls 1971-; *ai:* Adv Chrldrs, Golden Kickers Drill Team, FBLA; NEA, PSEA, BEA; Amer Assn Univ Women; League of Women Voters; *office:* Butler Sr HS 167 New Castle Rd Butler PA 16001

WEST, FAITH CRAIG, English Teacher; *b:* Prairie, MS; *m:* James Hilton; *c:* Loren, Holly, C. I., Denny; *ed:* (BA) Eng, Millsaps Coll 1961; Grad Stud MS St Univ, MS Univ for Women; *cr:* Eng Teacher Amory HS 1961-64, 1978-80, Hattiesburg Jr HS 1964-66, West Point 1980-; *ai:* Staff Dev Comm; Chrldr Spon; MS Sch Bd Assn Dist I (Pres 1980-82, Secy 1978-80); NCTE; Aberdeen Sch Bd Pres 1984-; United Meth Women Dist Pres 1974-80, Whos Who 1976; Jr Auxiliary Secy 1976; Compassionate Friends Leader 1985-; Outstanding Young Woman in America 1976; *office:* 5th Street Jr HS PO Box 617 West Point MS 39730

WEST, GAIL MC CARTER, Keyboard Teacher; *b:* York, SC; *m:* Roger Nelson; *c:* Blake, Cayce, Clay; *ed:* (BS) Bus Ed, Winthrop Coll 1979; *cr:* Teacher Sullivan Jr HS 1979-81, Clover Jr HS 1981-; *ai:* Owner Day Care Center; Intnl Society for Technology in Ed; Intnl Cncl Cmptrs in Ed; *home:* 2748 Kingsburry Rd Clover SC 29710

WEST, KENT, Computer Science Teacher; *b:* Hurst, TX; *ed:* (AA) General Bus, Tarrant Cty Jr Coll 1983; (BSED) Cmptr Sci/His, Abilene Chrstn Univ 1987; Microcomputers, Microprocessor Technology, Natl Radio Inst; *cr:* Substitute Teacher Birdville Ind Sch Dist 1987-88; MS DOS Class Teacher Howard Cty Jr Coll 1989; Coahoma HS 1988-; *ai:* Sr Spon; Informal Cmptr Club Master; Technological Comm.

WEST, LYNNE J., English/Speech Teacher; *b:* Canton, IL; *m:* Greg; *c:* Emily J.; *ed:* (BA) Eng/Speech, Univ of IL 1978; *cr:* Eng/Speech Teacher Galva HS 1978-86, Knoxville HS 1986-; *ai:* Class Spon; Drama Coach; Holistic Scoring & K-12 Curr Comm Chairperson; NCTE 1986-; St Bd of Ed Awd of Recognition 1989; United Meth Church; *office:* Knoxville HS Main & Ontario Knoxville IL 61448

WEST, MARY J., Remedial Reading Teacher; *b:* Prentiss, MS; *m:* Frank Jr.; *c:* Tyeed; *ed:* (BA) Poly Sci, Alcorn St Univ 1975; (MS) Ed, CA St Univ 1978; *cr:* Intern Teacher Burbank Elem 1977-78; 6th Grade Core Teacher Matt Kelly Sch 1978-84; HS Rdng Teacher Bassfield HS 1987-; *ai:* Annual Staff Spon 1988-89; Substance Abuse Chm 1989-; *office:* Bassfield HS P O Box 128 Bassfield MS 39421

WEST, MICHEAL, Counselor; *b:* Chicago, IL; *m:* Cynthia J. Mc Calla; *c:* Rachel, Michelle; *ed:* (BA) Psych, 1971, (MS) Counseling, 1974 Chicago St Univ; Loyola Univ, Governor St Univ, Chicago St Univ; *cr:* Cnslr Corliss HS 1972-, De Paul Univ 1987-; Chm Bd Co Mo Lube Incorporated 1989-; *ai:* Scndry Sch Cnslrs Cncl 1980-; Village of Glenwood Bd Mem Zoning Appeals 1988-; Teacher of Yr Awd 1975, 1977-78; US Office of Ed Awd; *office:* Corliss HS 821 E 103rd St Chicago IL 60628

WEST, NANCY RAE PALMER, 1st Grade Teacher; *b:* Hillsboro, OH; *m:* Roger Wayne; *c:* Lora, April, Andrea; *ed:* (BS) Elem Ed, OH Univ 1976; *cr:* Kndgtn Teacher 1977-79, 1st Grade Teacher 1980-81 Belfast Elem Sch; 1st Grade Teacher Concord Elem Sch 1981-; *ai:* Mathathon Dir; O M Coach; NEA, OEA Building Rep 1977-; OH Cncl of Rdng 1986-; Delta Kappa Gamma 1984-; *office:* Concord Sch 2281 State Rt 136 Hillsboro OH 45133

WEST, ROBIN ROBERT, History Teacher; *b:* Crawfordsville, IN; *m:* Deidra Campbell; *c:* Sarah B., Levi H.; *ed:* (AS) Soc Sci, Vincennes Univ 1978; (BA) His, IN Univ 1980; (MA) Ed, IN St Univ 1986; *cr:* General Sci Teacher Cloverdale Jr/Sr HS 1980-81; Soc Stud Teacher WillO Hill Chrstn Sch 1981-82, Mill Road Chrstn HS 1982-85, Faith Heritage Chrstn Sch 1985-; *ai:* Athletic Dir; Boys Bsktbl Coach; Evansville Bsbl Umpire Assn Umpire 1984-; IN HS Athletic Assn Bsbl Umpire 1987-; Articles Published; *office:* Faith Heritage Chrstn Sch 1613 Pollack Ave Evansville IN 47714

WEST, RUTH GRAHAM, 7th Grade Soc Stud Teacher; *b:* Louisa, KY; *m:* Freddie N.; *c:* Janet, Mark, Dwayne; *ed:* (BA) Geography/His, 1972, (MA) Ed, 1973, (Rank I) Ed, 1975 Morehead St Univ; *cr:* 7th Grade Soc Stud Teacher Louisa HS 1972-79, Louisa Mid Sch 1979-; *ai:* Bsktbl, Sftbl & Track Coach; Sponsored Stu Cncl & Yrbk Adv; Louisa Mid Sch Teacher of Yr 1988; Lawrence Cty Organization of Teachers Building Rep 1986-; Lawrence Cty Concerned Citizens Chairperson 1989-; Kentuckians for the Commonwealth (Steering Comm 1983-85, Finance Comm 1988-); KY Colonel 1990; Selected by KY Historical Society to Attend KY His Seminar at UK 1983; *office:* Louisa Mid Sch PO Box 567 Louisa KY 41230

WEST, SHELIA ANDERSON, Fifth Grade Teacher; *b:* Highlands, TX; *m:* Lawrence Nolan; *c:* Scott, Keith, Laurie; *ed:* (MA) Admin, 1984, (BS) Home Ec Ed, 1971 Mc Neese St Univ; Cert Elem Ed, LA Prof Improvement Prgm; FL Math Sci Enhancement Trng; *cr:* 7th Grade Lang Art Teacher Kinder Elem & Jr HS 1979-88; 5th Grade Teacher W Zephyrhills Elem 1988-; *ai:* 4-H Adv; Parent Advisory Comm; Cheerleader Adv; Grade Chm; Delta Kappa Gamma Pres 1986-88; Alpha Delta Kappa Treas 1990-92; Pasco Rdng & Math Cncls; Teacher of Yr Allen Parish 1986-88; *home:* 6998 Ft King Rd Zephyrhills FL 33541

WEST, SUSAN KAPCZYNSKI, Math Dept Chair/Admissions Dir; *b:* El Paso, TX; *m:* Gary T.; *c:* Brenna Bollom; *ed:* (BA) Linguistics/Anthropology/Fr, Rice Univ 1973; (MA) Linguistic Anthropology, WA Univ 1974; Cert Math/Fr, Univ of Houston 1988; Advanced Work Math & Ed; *cr:* Teacher Aide Aldine Contemporary Ed AISD 1979; Fr Teacher Aldine Jr HS 1980; Dept Chairperson/Math Teacher 1981-, Dir of Admissions 1989- St Pius X HS; *ai:* Spon NHS Society, Speech Team, Literary Guild, Math Club, Academic Challenge Team; Academic Competition Coord; Seton Jr HS Asst Sftbl Coach; CAMT, CEATH 1988-; NCTM, NCEA 1981-; NASC, MAA, NASSP, Amer Sftbl Assn 1985-; TCTM 1987-; Seton Jr HS Parents Assn 1988-; Engineers Cncl of Houston Grant; Nom Tandy Outstanding Teacher Awd; Nominee TX Outstanding Teacher of Math; Diocesan Sch Accreditation Team Mem; *office:* St Pius X HS 811 Donovan Houston TX 77091

WEST, TERESA ANNE (WHITAKER), 5th Grade Mathematics Teacher; *b:* Indianapolis, IN; *m:* Kyle K.; *ed:* (BS) Elem Ed, Ball St Univ 1978; (MS) Elem Ed, Univ of Indianapolis 1987; *cr:* 3rd Grade Teacher Center Grove Elem 1978-79; 6th Grade Lang Art Teacher Center Grove Mid Sch 1979; Substitute Teacher 1979-80, 7th/8th Grade Rdng Teacher 1980-82 New Carlisle-Bethel Schls; 5th Grade Math Teacher 1982-83, 4th Grade Teacher 1983-84, 5th Grade Math Teacher 1984- West Grove Elem; *ai:* Center Grove Girls Var Vlybl Asst Coach; West Grove Teacher of Yr 1988-89; *home:* 1075 S State Rd 135 Greenwood IN 46143

WEST-HODGE, ROSEMARIE, Teacher; *b:* Salt Lake City, UT; *m:* J. Whitney Hodge; *c:* David West, Jason West; *ed:* (BA) Elem Ed, UT St Univ 1968; CA St Univ Hayward 1970; Univ of CA 1973; *cr:* Elem Teacher Mt Diablo Unified Sch Dist 1968-80; 6th Grade Core/Study Skills Teacher Valley View Mid Sch 198 7th Grade Core/Math Teacher Glenbrook Mid Sch 1988-; *ai:* Mt Diablo Ed Assn 1980-; PTA 1981-; *home:* 110 Clipper Ln Martinez CA 94553

WEST-LENTZ, TERESA LYNN, English Teacher; *b:* Iowa City, IA; *m:* Kevin Lentz; *c:* Brennan; *ed:* (BSE) Eng, 1980, (MA) Eng, 1983 Drake Univ; Grad Stud Cert in Journalism; *cr:* Lang Art Teacher Schuler Jr HS 1980-82; Eng Teacher Grundy Center HS 1984-86; Intermediate Comp Instr Wartburg Coll 1983-; Eng Teacher Waverly-Shell Rock Jr & Sr HS 1986-; *ai:* Adv Sch Newspaper; Wartbug Coll Teacher Ed Advisory Comm; AEA 7 Lang Art Curr Dev Project; NCTE 1980-; ICTE 1985-; Kappa Delta Pi Pres 1977-80; AAUW 1989-; Bus & Prof Women 1980-82; Beta Sigma Phi Pres 1981-; Teaching Fellowship Drake Univ; *office:* Waverly-Shell Rock HS 4th Ave SW Waverly IA 50677

WESTCOTT, SHIRLEY DALGLISH, French & English Teacher; *b:* Erie, PA; *c:* Nora Westcott Pietrasiewicz, Molly Westcott Cipriani, David, Janet Westcott Laboda, James, Michael; *ed:* (BA) Fr, Grove City Coll 1948; Grad Stud Fr, OH St Univ & Mercyhurst Coll; Eng, Indiana Univ of PA; *cr:* Teacher Lawrence Park HS 1962-65, Iroquois HS 1966-; *ai:* NHS Adv; Academic Challenge Team & Debate Coach; Sr Commencement Speech Dir; NCTE, W PA Teachers of Eng, NW PA Cncl Teachers of Eng; Teaching Fellow Allegheny Coll Natl Endowment Hum 1985; Fellowship NEH Shakespeare Inst Indiana Univ of PA 1987; *office:* Iroquois HS 4301 Main St Erie PA 16511

WESTERBERG, SONJA ELIZABETH, Kindergarten Teacher; *b:* Stillwater, MN; *m:* Michael W.; *ed:* (BS) Elem Ed, WI St Univ-EAU Claire 1968; WI St Univ-Eau Claire/River Falls & Stout; *cr:* 1st Grade Teacher Lake Holcombe Public Schs 1968; Kndgtn Teacher Cornell Elem 1968-; *ai:* Chm of Curr & Instruction Comm Cornell Ed Assn; Cornell Ed Assn; Cornell PTA Chm of Fund Raising 1985-; Sch Annual Dedicated to Me in 1983; *home:* PO Box 247 Cornell WI 54732

WESTERFIELD, BARBARA GREGORY, Economics/Government Teacher; *b:* Jackson, MS; *m:* Ray; *c:* Megan, Andrew, Whitney; *ed:* (BS) Soc Stud, 1973, (MED) Soc Stud, 1980, (EDS) Soc Stud, 1985 MS Coll; *cr:* Teacher Brinkley Jr HS 1973-80; Coord Jackson Public Schls ESSA 1980-81; Teacher Powell Jr HS 1981-82, Peeples Jr HS 1982-85, Forest Hill HS 1985-; *ai:* Spon Mayors Youth Cncl, Co-Spon NHS & Jr Historial Society; Alpha Delta Kappa Pres 1982-, Schlsp 1984; MS Cncl for Soc Stud 1980-; MS Assn for Gifted & Talented 1986-; Neighborhood Watch Block Captain 9-; Outstanding Teacher Brinkley Jr HS 1974; Red Apple Awd Forest Hill 1988; Outstanding Young Women of America; *office:* Forest Hill HS 2607 Raymond Rd Jackson MS 39212

WESTERHOLD, PATRICIA (RUPP), Science Department Chair; *b:* Norwalk, OH; *m:* James R.; *c:* Marie, Andy, John; *ed:* (AB) Elem Ed, Mary Manse; (MS) Bio Sci, Univ of Notre Dame 1971; *cr:* Elem Teacher 1950-63; Jr HS Teacher St Wendelin Fostoria 1963-64; Sr HS Bio Teacher Notre Dame Acad 1964-67; St Mary HS 1967-71; Bio Instr Bellevue Sr HS 1971-; *ai:* Future Nurses of America Club; NSTA, NABT, SECO; Teacher Local Assn (VP, Pres, Past Pres) 1976-79; Red Cross Heart Assn 1964-67, 1980-; Red Cross Secy 1976-78; *office:* Bellevue Sr HS 200 Oakland Ave Bellevue OH 44811

WESTERMAN, GENE L., Math/Chemistry/Physics Teacher; *b:* Batesville, IN; *m:* Ruth Ann Adams; *c:* Jennifer J.; *ed:* (BS) Math, IN St Univ 1965; (MS) Math, Coll of Mt St Joseph 1989; *cr:* Teacher Jac-Cen-Del Sch Corporation 1965-73, 1982-; Instructor Purdue Univ 1990; *ai:* NHS Spon; Several Chem & Physics Demonstrations Published; *office:* Jac-Cen-Del HS R 3 Box 28 Osgood IN 47037

WESTERN, KIM STACY, English Teacher; *b:* Newport, AR; *m:* Wess Gene; *c:* Catherine D.; *ed:* (BA) Speech, Harding Coll 1978; Eng/Eng Cert/Masters Prgm, AR St Univ; *cr:* Eng Teacher 1979, Speech Teacher 1979-80 Newport HS; Eng/Speech Teacher Grubbs HS 1985-86; Newport HS 1985-; *ai:* NHS Newport Chapter Spon; NEA, AR Ed Assn, NCTE; Amer Legion Speech Contest Work Awd; *home:* 1100 Josphine Newport AR 72112

WESTFALL, ADRIENNE E., 4th/5th Grade Teacher; *b:* Schenectady, NY; *ed:* (BS) Elem Ed, 1964, (MS) Ed/Soc Sci, 1967 SUNY Oneonta; *cr:* 2nd Grade Teacher 1964-67, 3rd Grade Teacher 1967-69, 4th Grade Teacher 1969-70, 2nd Grade Teacher 1970-82, 3rd Grade Teacher 1982-88, 4th/5th Grade Lang Art Teacher 1988- Lincoln Elem & Scotia-GLenville Cntrl Schls; *ai:* Stu Government Co-Organizer; PTA Schlsp Comm; Books & Beyond Trng Group; Teachers Assn Liason With Admin; Supervision of Stu Teacher; PTA Rep to Dist Cncl; Stu Loan Comm 1980-; Delta Kappa Gamma Society (Corresponding Secy 1982-84, Mem) 1980-; Scotia-Glenville Teachers Assn (Corresponding Secy, 2nd VP, Building Rep) 1970-; Schenectady Cty Assn for Retarded Children (Dir 1986-, Corresponding Secy 1990); Lincoln Sch PTA (VP, Treas, Various Comm Chairs) 1976-; Beta Sigma Phi (Pres, VP, Secy, Treas, Corresponding Secy) 1970-80; Trinity Reformed Church Choir 1974-84; Life Membership Awd NY St Congress of Parents & Teachers 1981; *office:* Lincoln Elem Sch Albion St Schenectady NY 12302

WESTFALL, DAVID LEE, 4th Grade Teacher; *b:* Greenville, OH; *m:* Joan Himes; *c:* Rachelle, Brian; *ed:* (BA) Elem, Bluffton Coll 1980; Working Towards Masters Gifted Ed; *cr:* 5th/6th Grade Teacher South Gettysburg 1980-83; 4th Grade Teacher East Elem 1983-; *ai:* Jr HS Cross Cntry, 8th Grade Girls Bsktbl, Jr HS Girls Track League Champions; In Charge of East Sci Fair; GEA Mem 1980-89, Teacher of Yr; *office:* East Elem E 5th St Greenville OH 45331

WESTHED, MARK NILS OSCAR, Science Teacher; *b:* Roseau, MN; *m:* Elisabeth Ihlar; *c:* Rachel, David, Sarah; *ed:* (BS) Sci Ed, 1970, (MA) Environmental Stud, 1978 Bemidji St Univ; Grad Research Inst of Physiological Botany of Univ of Uppsala Sweden; Natl Sci Fnd Inst; *cr:* Earth/Phys Sci Teacher East Grand Forks Jr HS 1970-71; 7th-12th Grade Sci Teacher Gary HS 1972-; *ai:* Driver Ed Teacher; Chemical Awareness Coord; Gary Ed Assn Pres 1988-; MN Ed Assn, NEA 1970-; Gary Rescue Squad Pres 1983-89; Gary Fire Dept Fireman 1980-; Cty EMS Paramedics EMT D 1984-; Natl Sci Fnd Stipendums Grants; *office:* Gary HS PO Box 100 Gary MN 56545

WESTLUND, MARGARET WEBB, Elementary Music Teacher; *b:* Topeka, KS; *m:* John Otto; *c:* Allison A., Todd A.; *ed:* (BA) Music Ed, Washburn Univ 1958; (MME) Music Ed, Univ of MI 1960; Carl Orff Wkshps 1982-; *cr:* Kndgtn Teacher Kansas City Bd of Ed 1959-63; Summer Instr William Penn Coll 1968-72; Elem Music Teacher Oskaloosa Cmmty Schls 1971-76; Instr N KY Univ 1978; 7th-12th Grade Eng/Music Teacher Our Lady of the Highlands Cath Girls Sch 1979-82; Elem Music Teacher Norwood View Elem 1982-; *ai:* Norwood View 4th-5th Grade Chorus Dir; Amer Orff-Schulwerk Assn 1982-; OH Music Educators 1987; PEO Sisterhood Recording Secy 1978-79; *office:* Norwood View Elem Sch Carthage & Hannaford Aves Norwood OH 45212

WESTMAN, LINDA NELSON, 3rd Grade Teacher; *b:* Iron Mountain, MI; *m:* Alton K.; *c:* Kenneth, Kristin; *ed:* (BME) Music, 1969; (MA) Elem Ed, 1983 Northern MI Univ; *cr:* 5th Grade Teacher James T Jones 1969-70; 6th Grade Teacher 1971-82; 3rd Grade Teacher 1982-89 Quinnesec Elem; 3rd Grade Teacher Woodland Elem 1989-; *ai:* Coord for Gifted/Talented Prgm; Cmptr Comm; NEA; MEA; BTEA; Church Choir Accompanist; WELCA; *office:* Woodland Elem Sch 2000 Pyle Dr Kingsford Quinnesec MI 49801

WESTMORELAND, ALLYSON B., Marketing Education Teacher; *b:* Atlanta, GA; *m:* Kurt Edward; *ed:* (BSED) Marketing Ed, Univ of GA 1987; New Teachers Inst; *cr:* Teacher E Hall HS 1988-; *ai:* Distributive Ed Clubs of America Spon; Prom & Employer/Employee Banquet Comm; PAGE 1988-; GMA 1989-; GA Assessment Project; *office:* East Hall HS 3534 E Hall Rd Gainesville GA 30501

WESTON, CAROL SCHMIEL, Fourth Grade Teacher; *b:* Abington, PA; *m:* Edward; *ed:* (BA) Bio, Slipper Rock Univ 1969; (MS) Zoology/Physiology, Miami Univ 1972; UCI Summer Sci Inst; Project Wild & AIMS; Family Math; Sci Curr ImplemEntation; Equals; CA Poly Womens Sports Clinic; Freedoms Fnd; *cr:* 1st & 2nd Grade Teacher Tri-Cty Sch 1969-71;

Pharmacologist William H Rorer 1971-74; Bio Teacher Mojave HS 1974-80; Cerro Cosa Coll 1978-81; Aerobics/Vlybl Teacher Bakersfield Coll 1978-81; 4th Grade Teacher Robert P Ulrich Sch 1980-; *ai:* Mentor Teacher Sci; Sch Improvement Prgm; Family Life Curr; Curr Comm; CA Teachers Assn 1974-; NEA 1974-; Univ CA Irvine Summer Sci Grant; Articles Published PA Acad of Sci/Amer Midland Naturalist; *home:* 19711 Kid Place Tehachapi CA 93561

WESTPHALL, M. DIANE, Jr HS Math/English Supervisor; *b:* Grand Rapids, MI; *ed:* (MA) Ed Admin, 1982, (BA) Chrstn Ed, 1968 Bob Jones Univ; *cr:* Teacher Santa Rosa Chrstn 1968-69; Maranatha Baptist Bible Coll 1969-71; Teacher/Supvr Calvary Baptist Chrstn 1971-; *ai:* Sch Newspaper, Yrbk, Speech, Girls Sports Coach; Articles in Newsletter; *office:* Calvary Baptist Chrstn Sch 792 Milford St Watertown WI 53094

WESTRA, ROGER DEAN, Business Teacher; *b:* Hull, IA; *m:* Jacqulyn D.; *c:* Eric, Justin, Jamie; *ed:* (BA) Bus, Westman Coll 1968; (MS) Bus Ed, 1972, (MS) Sch Admin, 1975 Univ of SD; Scndry Learning Disabilities, IA St; *cr:* Bus Teacher Western Chrstn 1968-72, Pomeroy Cmmty Sch 1972-88, Cntrl Valley Chrstn HS 1988-; *ai:* Class Spon; Phi Delta Kappa Pres 1968-88, Research 1972; Stock Investors Pres 1980-88, Investor of Yr 1987; Republican Party Cty Chm 1976-88, Natl Republican Task Force 1978; Kiwanis 1968-72; Liberty Fnd Pres 1986-88; St of IA Bus Curr Grant; Senator Grassley Cty Chm; Lightfoot Election Campaign Rep; *home:* 1102 W Princeton Visalia CA 93277

WESTRAY, SHARON SMITH, Fifth Grade Teacher; *b:* Baltimore, MD; *c:* Jose; *ed:* (BS) Elem Ed, 1971, (MS) Elem Ed, 1989 Coppin St Coll; *cr:* Teacher Baltimore City Publis Schls 1978-; *ai:* Just Say No Club Adv; All Sch Salute Comm; Faculty Gospel Choir Asst Dir; MD St Teachers Assn, Coppin St Alumni Assn; Youth Dept Instr, Inspirational Choir Mem; Educl Excl Grant; Just Say No Grant; *office:* Mt Royal Elem Mid Sch 121 Mc Mechen St Baltimore MD 21217

WESTVANG, SAUNDRA LEE IRWIN, 5th Grade Teacher; *b:* Chicago, IL; *m:* Robert W.; *ed:* (BA) Art/Elem Ed, Cntrl WA Univ 1972-78; (BA) Arts in Ed, Seattle Pacific Univ 1988; *cr:* Substitute Teacher Everett Sch Dist 1974-75; Teacher Aid Everett HS 1975; 4th/5th Grade Teacher Silver Lake Elem 1976-88; 5th Grade Teacher Mill Creek Elem 1988-; *ai:* Teacher Leader Mill Creek; Elem Art Coord; Arts Presentor/Inservice Person for Stu/ Teachers Staff Dev Participant; Beta Alpha-Delta Kappa Gamma 1983-; Lambda Rho Mem 1989-; WA Art Educators Assn Secy, Co-Chm 1983- Educator of Yr 1987; PTA 1st VP 1985-87; Golden Acorn 1983; ESD 189 Art Co-Op Exec Bd Mem 1985-; TIP Grant 1984-88; Book Integration of the Arts; *office:* Mill Creek Elem 3400 148th St SE Bothell WA 98012

WETTA, JANET INGRID, Third Grade Teacher; *b:* Seattle, WA; *ed:* (BA) Speech/Elem Ed, Univ of WA 1976; Grad Stud Univ of WA 1985; Seattle Pacific Univ, W WA Univ; *cr:* 3rd Grade Teacher Kenmore Elem 1977, Canyon Creek Elem 1977-; *ai:* Mentor Teacher; Master Teacher for Teachers in Trng; Phi Beta Kappa 1976; NEA, WA Ed Assn, Northshore Ed Assn; Ballard 1st Luth Church Mem 1968-; Matrix Table Speech Comm 1976; *home:* 10015 Marine View Dr Everett WA 98204

WETTER, JANINE TERESA, English Teacher; *b:* Scranton, PA; *m:* James Michael; *ed:* (BA) Eng/Ed, 1984, (MS) Eng/Thesis Prgm, 1989 Univ of Scranton; *cr:* Eng Teacher Bishop Hannan HS 1984, Bishop O'Hara HS 1984-; *ai:* Bishop O'Hara HS Newspaper Adv; NCTE, NCEA 1984-; Natl Arbor Day Fnd, Care 1990; *home:* 625 E Warren St Dunmore PA 18512

WETZBARGER, NORA AMY (DI FULCO), Fourth Grade Teacher; *b:* Denver, CO; *m:* Larry D.; *ed:* (BA) Elem Ed, Univ of N CO 1975; Classes, Panhandle St Univ Goodwell; *cr:* 3rd Grade Teacher Hugo Public Sch 1975-77; 4th Grade Teacher Tyrone Public Sch 1977-; *ai:* 4 Yr Improvement Plan Comm; Chairperson Staff Dev Comm; TX Cty Ed Assn (Secy/Treas 1984-85, VP 1985-87); Tyrone Teacher of Yr 1986-87; *home:* PO Box 322 Tyrone OK 73951

WETZEL, CORALIE ANN, English Teacher; *b:* Yakima, WA; *m:* Richard; *c:* Patricia; *ed:* (BM) Music, Univ of TX 1961; (MMED) Music, Angelo St Univ 1987; Advanced Trng in Eng for Cert, Angelo St Univ 1985; *cr:* Teacher Lee Jr HS & San Jacinto Elem & Central HS & Bowie Elem & Fannin Elem; *ai:* Eng Dept Head 1988-; TCTA 3rd VP 1988-; Mini Grant Comm Mem Local Sch Dist 1989-; Music Curr Dev Mem San Angelo Ind Sch Dist 1973.

WETZEL, JOAN ANN, Third Grade Teacher; *b:* Buffalo, NY; *ed:* (BS) Elem Ed, Medaille Coll 1981; *cr:* 3rd Grade Teacher Most Holy Redeemer 1981-85, St Barnabas Sch 1986-; *office:* St Barnabas Sch 2099 George Urban Blvd Depew NY 14043

WETZEL, NANCY HOWELL, English Teacher; *b:* East Liverpool, OH; *m:* William D.; *ed:* (BA) His, Mount Union Coll 1951; (MED) Admin, Univ of Dayton 1979; *cr:* His/Eng Teacher Sixth St Sch 1951-56; Eng Teacher E L Mid Sch 1956-; *ai:* Merit Awd Comm; Poetry Booklet Spon; Class Co-Chairperson; E Liverpool Educl Assn Bd of Dir 1980-; OH Educl Assn; NEA; E Liverpool Historical Society; OH Historical Society; DAR Historian; Jennings Scholar 1975-76; Teacher of Month; *office:* East Liverpool Mid Sch 810 W 8th St East Liverpool OH 43920

WETZEL, PAT RYAN, Home Economics Teacher; *b:* Fairmont, WV; *c:* Ryan L., Tera R.; *ed:* (BA) Home Ec Comp, Fairmont St 1971; Working Towards Masters Voc Ed; Supvrs Certificate Kent St Univ; *cr:* Teacher James A Garfield HS 1978-; *ai:* FHA Club Adv; Chemical Awareness Core Mem; OH Ed Assn 1978-; OH Voc Assn 1989-; Jr Womens League 1988-; *office:* James A Garfield HS 10233 St Rt 88 Garrettsville OH 44231

WETZEL, SALLY ANN, Spanish Teacher; *b:* Sewickley, PA; *ed:* (BS) Span, Clarion Univ 1969; (MA) Span, Millersville Univ 1976; Eng Cert, Clarion Univ 1980; Total Phys Response Wkshps Calvin Coll in Methodology; *cr:* Span/Eng Teacher Curwensville HS 1969-; *ai:* Span Club; Act 178 & Long Range Planning Comm; Mid St Evaluator; Curwensville Area Ed Assn Pres; Bus & Prof Womens Club Mem 1985-; Prof Standards & Practices Commission for PA Teachers; *office:* Curwensville HS Beech St Curwensville PA 16833

WEYAND, BRADFORD, 6th Grade Teacher; *b:* Queens, NY; *m:* Marguerite Kay; *c:* Ted, Ernest, Susan, Bradford K.; *ed:* (BA) Elem Ed, Pepperdine Coll 1963; Coll & Univ Work; *cr:* 3rd-6th Grade Elem Teacher 112th St Sch 1963-67, Crestwood St Sch 1967-78; 6th-8th Grade Teacher Fleming Mid Sch 1979-; *ai:* Confederation of OR Sch Admin Act Adv 1987-88; St Mid Level Act Adv of Yr Awd 1988; OR Ed Assn, Josephine Cty Ed Assn 1979-; *office:* Fleming Mid Sch 6001 Monument Dr Grants Pass OR 97526

WHALEN, JAN SHELNUTT, Choral Dir/Gen Music Teacher; *b:* Fairmount, GA; *m:* Andrew J. III; *c:* Andrea D., George L.; *ed:* (BA) Music Ed, Wesleyan Coll 1971; (MM) Music Ed, GA St Univ 1974; *cr:* Chorus/General Music Summerour Mid Sch 1971-73; K-7th Grade General Music Teacher Kingsley Elem 1973-76; Chorus/General Music Teacher Spalding Cty Sch System 1977-; *ai:* Liaison for String Prgm; Accompanist for String Rehearsals & Performances; GMEA, MENC 1971-; Griffin Music Club 1977-; 1st Meth Church Choir Mem; *office:* Flynt Street Mid Sch 1551 Flynt St Griffin GA 30223

WHALEN, NANCY B., HS Mathematics Teacher; *b:* Boonville, MO; *m:* George P.; *c:* Jennifer; *ed:* (BA) Natural Sci/Math, Cntrl Meth Coll 1972; Curr & Instructional Univ MO Columbia; *cr:* Teacher New Franklin HS 1975-; Keytesville HS 1973-75; Iberia HS 1972-73; *ai:* Natl Honor Society Adv NUN FE Chapter; NCTM 1985-; MO Cncl Teachers of Math 1985-; MO St Teachers Assn 1972-; Comm Teachers Assn 1975-; Delta Kappa Gamma VP 1982-; PEO Rec Sec 1988-; BETA Sigma Phi Treas 1989-; Girl of Yr 1989; Xi Kappa Eta Chapter 4-H Proj Ldr 1987-; *office:* New Franklin H S 412 W Roadway New Franklin MO 65274

WHALEN, PRISCILLA KIRTLAND, Jr HS Reading Teacher; *b:* Galion, OH; *m:* Kenneth E.; *c:* Kenneth Jr., David, Christopher, Michael, Andrew, Ted; *ed:* (BA) Elem Ed, Akron Univ Defiance Coll 1981; Quest Prgm Trng; *cr:* Rdng/Eng Teacher Kunkle Mid Sch 1981-; *ai:* NWOEA; NW Region Teacher Leader Network OH Dept of Ed; Consumer Ec Ed Grants; Thematic Units Published; *office:* Kunkle Mid Sch Box 92 Kunkle OH 43531

WHALEN, STEVE P., Physical Education Teacher; *b:* Roswell, NM; *m:* Karen Janice Beason; *c:* Shanna F., Ashley F.; *ed:* (BS) Phys Ed 1977, (MS) Scndry Ed, 1983 E NM Univ Portales; *cr:* Teacher/Coach Goddard HS 1977-81, Artesia HS 1981-85, Berrendo Mid Sch 1985-; *ai:* Head Ftbl & Track Coach; Intramurals Spon; Phys Ed Chm; *office:* Berrendo Mid Sch 800 Marion Richards Roswell NM 88201

WHALEY, ANNE BACKUS, Science Dept Chairperson; *b:* Bluefield, WV; *c:* Hope E.; *ed:* (BS) Bio, Radford Coll 1965; (MED) Sci Supervision, Univ of VA 1974; *cr:* Bio Teacher Laurel HS 1965-68; Life Sci/Phys Sci Teacher Graham Jr HS Mid Sch 1969-87; Bio Teacher/Sci Dept Chairperson Graham HS 1987-; *ai:* Graham HS Pep & Sci Club Spon; Tazewell Ed Assn 1969-; VA Ed Assn 1969-76, 1980-; NEA 1980-; Laurel Ed Assn (VP 1968) 1965-68; Graham Chrstn Church 1970-; Univ of VA NSF Fellowship 1973-74; *office:* Graham HS Double Gates Bluefield VA 24605

WHATLEY, CALVIN ARTHUR, Retired Teacher/Principal; *b:* Dallas, TX; *m:* Julia Katherine Byron; *ed:* (BA) His, 1950, (MS) Ed 1951 E TX St; *cr:* Teacher Reagan Cty Schl 1950-52; 6th Grade Teacher Temple Ind Sch Dist 1952-56; Prin DEG Sch France & Germany 1956-61; His Teacher 1961-63, Prin 1963-71 Temple HS; Prin Scott Elem Sch 1971-86; *ai:* NAEP Rdng Prgm Presenter 1976, 1979; St Admin 1963.

WHATLEY, THERESA PAIGE, Fourth Grade Teacher; *b:* Butte, MT; *m:* Owen N.; *c:* Curtis Rhodes, Shawn, Troy, Brent; *ed:* (BA) Elem Ed, 1979, (MS) Elem Ed, 1981, Certificate Rdng, 1981 OK Univ; *cr:* 4th Grade Teacher Cntrl Elem 1980-; *ai:* Guidance Comm; Kappa Kappa Iota (VP 1987-88, Pres 1988-); Cntrl OK Rdng Cncl 1987-; *office:* Upper Cntrl Elem Sch 400 N Broadway Moore OK 73160

WHEAT, NURLINE JOHNSON, Rdng/Eng Teacher; *b:* Forrest City, AR; *c:* Jonette, Gerald Jr., Patrick; *ed:* (BS) Scndry Eng Ed, Univ of AR Pine Bluff 1969; (MS) Rdng, AR St Univ Jonesboro 1988; *cr:* Secy Stewart Elem 1962-67; Instr/Secy Univ of AR Pine Bluff Eng Dept 1968-71; Eng Teacher 1971-89, Cmptr/Rdng Teacher 1989- Forrest City HS; *ai:* Rdng Club; Dept of Eng & Related Arts Co-Chm; Sr Class Spon; Textbook Selection Comm; NEA, AR Ed Assn Mem 1970-; FCEA Building Rep 1986-87; AR Cncl of Rdng Teachers 1988-; Alpha Kappa Alpha Financial Secy 1989-; Semper Fidelis Charmettes Corresponding Secy 1989-, Pres Awd 1981-82; St Grants 1986; Class of 1974 Outstanding Teacher; *office:* Forrest City HS 467 Victoria St Forrest City AR 72335

WHEATLEY, CAROL NICHOLS, 3rd Grade Teacher; *b:* Wytheville, VA; *m:* Jimmy Lynn; *ed:* (AS) Ed, Ferrum Coll 1970; (BS) Elem Ed, 1972; (MS) Elem Ed/Admin 1976 Radford Univ; *cr:* Teacher Providence Sch 1972-; *ai:* NEA, VA Ed Assn, Grayson Cty Ed Assn 1972-; *office:* Providence Elem Sch Rt 2 Box 185 Fries VA 24330

WHEATLEY, MARGERY MC CRIGHT, 5th Grade Teacher; *b:* Fairfield, IL; *m:* Ben W.; *c:* Carolyn Sturtz, Robert Mc Cright, Wendy Kaufmann; *ed:* (BA) Elem Ed, Univ of N IA 1970; *cr:* Retired 5th Grade Teacher Independence Cmmty Sch 1987; *home:* 302 Park Ave Rowley IA 52329

WHEATLEY, PATRICIA SPAGEL, 4th Grade Teacher; *b:* Seattle, WA; *m:* William L.; *c:* Jamie L., Blake P., Paige L.; *ed:* (BA) Sociology, CA St Univ Humboldt 1973; (MA) Ed, Fresno Pacific Coll 1983; *cr:* 3rd-6th Grade Teacher Crestwood Elem; *ai:* St Aolysius Church Co-Youth Minister 1988-; Tulare Jaycees Cystic Fibrosis Golf Town Cmnty Service Awd 1985; Amer Heart Assn Jump for Heart Chm 1987-88; *home:* 1573 Baywood Tulare CA 93274

WHEATLEY-DYSON, ELIZABETH, French/German Sp Teacher; *b:* New Bedford, MA; *m:* David Taylor; *c:* Erin, Nicole, Barrett; *ed:* (BA) Fr, Univ of MA Amherst 1978; MED Prgm for Scndry Admin, Bridgewater St Coll; Analyzing Observing Teacher Course; *cr:* Foreign Lang Teacher Norwood Jr HS S 1978-83, Norwood Sr HS 1983-; *ai:* Academic Decathlon Coach; Faculty Soc Discipline Comm Co-Chairperson; Involved in Interactive Video Link with Westwood Organized Fund Raiser for Faculty Lounge;Search Comm For Prin; Outstanding Teacher Awd Comm; MFLA, Delta Kappa Gamma; Volunteer Tutor 1989-; Food Drive for Homeless Contest 1990; Golden Apple Awd 1988; Sony Seminar Presenter on Lang Labs; Philosophy & Sch Atmosphere Comms; Foreign Lang Area Comm Chairperson; *office:* Norwood HS Nichols St Norwood MA 02062

WHEATON, MARK G., Instrumental Music Teacher; *b:* Bronxville, NY; *m:* Darla J. Dick; *ed:* (BM) Music Ed, Ithaca Coll 1972; (MM) Music Ed, Eastman Sch of Music 1977; Phd Prgm at Eastman Sch of Music; *cr:* Instrumental Music Teacher Churchville-Chili Jr HS & Mid Sch 1972-, Churchville-Chili Sr HS 1988-; *ai:* Churchville-Chili Sr HS Symphonic Band Conductor; NYSSMA, MENC 1972-; Monroe Cty Sch Music Assn Pres 1979-81; NY St Music Assn Certified Adjudicator 1977-; NY St Band Dir Assn (Conference Clinician, Conductor) 1985; Eastman Sch Grad Asst Awd 1978-79; *office:* Churchville-Chili Sch Dist 139 Fairbanks Rd Churchville NY 14428

WHEELER, CAROLE M., Chairperson/Kndgtn Teacher; *b:* Macon, GA; *m:* Bobby R. Sr.; *c:* Bobby Jr., Christy, Cathy; *ed:* (BS) Home Ec/Nursery Sch Kndgtn, Univ of GA 1967; (MED) Early Chldhd Ed, GA Coll 1980; *cr:* 2nd Grade Teacher 1967-70, 1st Grade Teacher 1970-71, 6th & 7th Grade Teacher 1976-78; 3rd-5th Grade Teacher 1980- Bibb Cty Bd of Ed; Asst/Dir Kindercare Learning Center 1972-74; 1st Grade Teacher Cochran Field Chrstn Acad 1975-76; File Clerk Coliseum Park Hospital 1989-; *ai:* Girl Scout Brownie Troop Leader; Fire Marshall Adv; Speling Bee Adv; Prof Assn of GA Ed Building Rep 1985-; GA Jr Miss Backstage Moms Chairperson 1986-; *home:* Rt 4 Box 1400 Gray GA 31032

WHEELER, CYNTHIA CONNOR, Fifth Grade Teacher; *b:* Morris, IL; *m:* Gary G.; *c:* Amy, Garret; *ed:* (BS) Elem Ed, N IL Univ 1967; *cr:* 5th Grade Teacher Immaculate Conception 1967-68; 3rd Grade Teacher Kishwaukee Sch 1968-69; 6th Grade Teacher Washington Sch 1980-81; 5th Grade Teacher Caledonia Sch 1981-; *ai:* Alpha Delta Kappa 1983-; PTA Secy 1980-; Belvidere Buc Boosters 1985-.

WHEELER, JAMES WILLIAM, American History Teacher; *b:* Louisville, KY; *m:* Sandra Leigh Reiber; *c:* Brooks, Meredith, Lucas; *ed:* (BA) Scndry Ed/US His, 1978, (MS) Scndry Ed/ Rdng, 1983 IN Univ; *cr:* 7th Grade Geography Teacher Westlane Jr HS 1978-81; 8th Grade US His Teacher North Mid Sch 1981-82, Willowcreek Mid Sch 1982-; *ai:* Coach Boys/Girls Bsktbl; IN Bsktbl Coaches Assn 1988-; *office:* Willowcreek Mid Sch 5962 Central Ave Portage IN 46368

WHEELER, JUDY DELORES, AP English/Journalism Teacher; *b:* Detroit, MI; *ed:* (BA) Eng, 1971, (MS) Educl Psych, 1981, Ed Spec Admin, 1990 Wayne St Univ; *cr:* Eng Teacher Detroit Bd of Ed 1971-; *ai:* Adv Publication of Sch Newspaper; Pi Lambda Theta 1985-; NCTE 1984-; ASCD 1985-; Exchequer Unlimited Pres 1985-; Outstanding Commitment in Classroom Awd 1986-; Best Female Teacher Cass Tech Awd 1989; *office:* Cass Tech HS 2421 2nd Ave Detroit MI 48201

WHEELER, JUDY G., Sixth Grade Teacher; *b:* Lexington, KY; *m:* Raymond B.; *c:* John R.; *ed:* (BS) Elem Ed, 1976, (MS) Elem Ed, 1982 IN Univ; *cr:* Music Teacher St Anthony Sch 1978-80; 6th Grade Teacher Parkview Mid Sch 1982-85, River Valley Mid Sch 1985-; *ai:* Alpha Delta Kappa Sergeant-At-Arms 1987-; IN St Teachers Assn, NEA 1982-; *home:* 513 Weaver Rd Memphis IN 47143

WHEELER, MILDRED ZADY, Retired 1st Grade Teacher; *b:* Calhan, CO; *m:* Andrew W.; *c:* Judy Hill, Sherry Groves; *ed:* (BS) Elem Ed, Phillips Univ 1965; *cr:* Classroom Teacher Enid OK

1965-75, Drummond OK 1975-88; *ai:* Delta Kappa Gamma Mem; *home:* Box 143K Lahoma OK 73754

WHEELER, PATRICIA ANN ROSE, Kindergarten Teacher; *b:* Knoxville, TN; *m:* David Little; *c:* Fred S., Lisa R.; *ed:* (BS) Child Dev, Univ of TN Knoxville 1962; Early Chldhd & Elem Ed, Univ of TN Knoxville, Univ of TN Chattanooga, TN Tech Univ; *cr:* Teacher Bledsoe Cty Head Start 1965; Kndgtn Teacher Pikeville Elem Sch 1969-; *ai:* Discipline Comm Mem; Sequatchie Akoliyeti Rdng Assn Pres 1987-88; Alpha Delta Kappa (VP 1983, Treas 1985); Intnl Rdng Assn, TEA, NEA, TN Assn of Young Children; Pikeville Garden Club Treas 1980-; Pikeville United Meth Church Chairperson of Various Comms; Univ of TN Volunteer Alumni Network; Bledsoe-Sequatchie Univ of TN Alumni Assn Pres 1986; *office:* Pikeville Elem Sch College St Pikeville TN 37367

WHEELER, THOMAS LEE, Economics/Amer History Teacher; *b:* Tulsa, OK; *m:* Kim Girl; *c:* Ashley L.; *ed:* (BA) Soc Stud, Southeastern St Univ 1980; Advanced Placement Ec Trng; Intnl Investment; Securities Market; Instructional Skills; *cr:* OK His/Civics Teacher Cntrl Jr HS 1981-82; World Geography/Amer His/Civics Teacher Madison Jr HS 1982-84; Amer His/Government Ec/Advanced Placement Ec Teacher/Building Chm Bartlesville HS 1984-; *ai:* Ftbl, Var Bsktbl, Track Coach; Soc Stud Building Chm; OK Coaches Assn 1981-; Redeemer Luth Church; Bartlesville Public Sch Fnd Grant to Teacher Awd; *office:* Bartlesville HS 1700 Hillcrest Dr Bartlesville OK 74003

WHEELER, VIRGINIA ANN, Choral Director; *b:* Atlanta, GA; *ed:* (BME) Piano, Shorter Coll 1976; (MME) Music Ed, GA St Univ 1981; *cr:* Music Teacher/Choral Dir Floyd Mid Sch & S Cobb HS 1976-; *ai:* Show Choir & Swing Ensemble Choral Act; GA Music Educators Assn, Natl Music Educators Assn 1976-; Powder Springs 1st Meth Church Pianist; *office:* South Cobb HS 1920 Clay Rd Austell GA 30001

WHEELES, JUANITA RUSSELL, Eighth Grade Math Teacher; *b:* Boaz, AL; *m:* William Sidney; *c:* Shellie, Rusty, Tana; *ed:* (BS) Scndry Ed/Math/Eng, 1981, (MS) Scndry Ed/Math, 1986 Univ North AL; *cr:* Math Teacher Waterloo HS 1982-84, Muscle Shoals HS 1984-87, Avalon Mid Sch 1987-; *ai:* Knowledge Master Open Coach; Muscle Shoals City Park & Recreation Bd 1989-; *home:* 2110 Jennifer Ave Muscle Shoals AL 35661

WHEELESS, LINDA COPPIC, Elementary Music Teacher; *b:* Brownwood, TX; *m:* B. Edmond; *c:* Da Lin Wheeless Morrow, Dana; *ed:* (BME) Music Ed, Howard Payne Univ 1969; *cr:* General Music Teacher South Elem 1974-79, Coggin Elem 1977-79, Woodland Heights Elem 1979-; *ai:* TMEA Region Chm 1977-78; TCTA, TSTA; *home:* 3209 Austin Ave Brownwood TX 76801

WHEELEY, BOBBY E., Middle/Upper School Admin; *b:* Midland, TX; *m:* Debra Kay Mc Guire; *ed:* (BA) Hum, 1981, (MED) Scndry Ed, 1984 Stephen F Austin St Univ; Advanced Economic Seminar TX A&M Univ 1986; *cr:* Teacher Pine Tree HS 1981-88; Admin Trinity Sch of TX 1988-; *ai:* AD HOC Mem; NHS Faculty Comm; Mid Sch Boys Bsktbl Coach; E TX Cncl Soc Snoigs Bd Mem 1986; ASCD 1988-; Developed Presentation in Soc Stud Classroom; *office:* Trinity Sch of TX 906 Padon Longview TX 75601

WHEELING, DANIEL FRANCIS, Physical Education Teacher; *b:* Roanoke, VA; *m:* Jean Osborne; *c:* Lauren; *ed:* (BA) Phys Ed, Guilford Coll 1970; Grad Work U of VA, VA Tech, Radford Univ; *cr:* Phys Ed Instr Salem Intermediate Sch 1970-77, West Salem Elem Sch 1977-; *ai:* Salem HS Asst Ftbl, Outdoor/Indoor Track Coach; VA Assn for Health, Phys Ed, Recreation; VA HS League Coaches Assn 1970-; Natl HS Coaches Assn 1980-; 1st United Meth Curch Sunday Sch Teacher; Salem City Cncl Public Service Citation, Outstanding Leadership Salem HS Ftbl Team 1986, 1989; *home:* 987 Stonegate Dr Salem VA 24153

WHEELIS, RUTH LASATER, Mathematics Teacher; *b:* Winters, TX; *m:* Dale Edward; *c:* Matthew E., Lee A.; *ed:* (BA) Math/His, Univ of TX 1967; *cr:* Math Teacher Spring Branch Ind Sch Dist 1967-70, Brownwood Ind Sch Dist 1987-; *ai:* NHS Spon; Brownwood HS Improvement Team; NCTM, Assn of TX Prof Educators Mem; Amer Assn of Univ Women (Pres 1975-76); Womans Club of Brownwood (VP, Charter Mem); Local Rdng is Fundamental (Founder, Coord) 1979-82; Cmmty Cultural Affairs Commission Mem 1980-82; Service Awd by Brownwood Jaycees, Outstanding Woman Under 25 Awd 1974-75.

WHELAN, JOHN JOSEPH, Principal; *b:* Cleveland, OH; *ed:* (BA) Ed, John Carroll Univ 1965; (MS) Educl Admin, Case Western Reserve Univ 1970; Dale Carnegie Course 1988; Dale Carnegie Management Seminar 1989; *cr:* 7th/8th/12th Grade Teacher St Francis 1965-67; 6th Grade Teacher Prospect Elem Sch 1967-69; Prin Chambers Elem Sch 1969-; *ai:* John Carroll Univ Advisory Comm; Bd of Trustees Past Pres of John Carroll Univ Alumni Assn; Ed Monitorys Editorial Advisory Bd; John Carroll Univ Bd of Trustees 1989; Phi Delta Kappa VP 1986-87; NAESP Lifetime Mem; John Carroll Univ Pres 1985-87; Alumni Assn; Whos Who in Amer Ed by Natl Reference Inst 1988-89; Named Natl Distinguished Prin for OH by US Dept of Ed; United Black Fund Educators Awd 1987; Urban League of Greater Cleveland Awd for Educl Excl 1987; Rotary Club of Cleveland Recognition Awd 1986- JCU Alumni Medal; *home:* 344 E 276th St Euclid OH 44117

WHELAN, THOMAS MICHAEL, JR., Social Studies Teacher; *b:* St Louis, MO; *m:* Katherine Anne; *ed:* (BA) Scndry Ed, Univ of MO Columbia 1983; Working on Masters Educl Technology, Webster Univ; *cr:* Soc Stud Teacher Francis Howell; *ai:* Pep Club; Jr Var Cheerleading; Soph Class; Technology Comm; *office:* Francis Howell Sch Dist 7001 S Hwy 94 Saint Charles MO 63303

WHELCHEL, GARY L., Phys Ed Teacher, Dean Students; *b:* Monterey Park, CA; *m:* Susan G.; *c:* Bryan, Penny, Danielle; *ed:* (BA) Elem Ed/Phys Ed, Grand Canyon Coll 1972; (MA) Scndry Ed, AZ St Univ 1977; *cr:* 8th Grade Teacher Toltec Elem Sch 1972-82; Phys Ed Teacher Stanfield Elem Sch 1982-; *ai:* Coaching Vlybl, Bsktbl, Sftbl & Track; Dean of Stu 6th-8th Grade; Natl Assn of Sports Ofcls; *home:* PO Box 891 Stanfield AZ 85272

WHETSTONE, EMILEE ANNE, French/Spanish Teacher; *b:* Middletown, OH; *m:* David E.; *c:* Charlotte M., Stephanie J.; *ed:* (BA) Fr/Span, 1974, (MAE) Eng, 1975 N AZ Univ; Grad Stud Admin; *cr:* Fr/Span Teacher Riverdale HS 1979-; *ai:* Lang Club Spon; HS Newspaper & Jr/Sr Class Adv; Riverdale Ed Assn, OH Ed Assn, NEA, OH Foreign Lang Assn 1979-; Church Choir 1980-; Farm Bureau Cncl 1981-; Martha Holden Jennings Scholar; Attended 2 Jennings Wrkshps Schlsp; *office:* Riverdale HS 20613 SR 37 Mount Blanchard OH 45867

WHETSTONE, PAULA GLIGOR, Retired Elementary Teacher; *b:* Honolulu, HI; *m:* Scott Frederick; *c:* David; *ed:* (BA) Elem Ed/Span, Mt Union Coll 1977; Spec Ed, Univ of Akron 1974-75; Cmptrs, Ashland Univ 1990; *cr:* 6th Grade Teacher 1977-80, 4th/5th Grade Split Class Teacher 1980-81, 5th/6th Grade Split Class Teacher 1981-83, 3rd Grade Teacher 1983-84 Knox Elem Sch; *ai:* Sunday & Bible Sch Teacher; Family Life Comm Chm; Knox PTO 1977-84; NEA; OH Fed of Womens Clubs 1984-; Delta Delta Delta (Pres, Treas, Ways & Means) 1980-89; Mt Union Women 1980-; North Canton Jr Women (Treas, Membership Chm, Home Life Chm) 1984-, Outstanding Club Woman Finalist 1988; Outstanding Young Women of America 1978; *home:* 44601 1665 Ashford Cir NE North Canton OH 44720

WHETZEL, ELAINE, Science Teacher; *b:* Uniontown, PA; *ed:* (BS) Bio, CA St Coll 1963; Grad Courses Sci, Akron Univ & CA St Coll; *cr:* Sci Teacher Brimfield Sch 1963-65, Benjamin Franklin Sch 1965-; *ai:* Ecology Club; NSTA 1965-70; Coll Club 1965-80; Sponsoring Teacher Awd Buhl Planetarium; Ecology Project Governors Awd; *home:* RD 1 East Millsboro PA 15433

WHILLOCK, ARTHUR DWYANE, 6th/7th Grade Sci/Math Teacher; *b:* Wichita, KS; *m:* Doris Shelly; *c:* William; *ed:* (BA) Elem Ed, 1979, (ME) Ed Admin/Supervision, 1989 Wichita St Univ; *cr:* 6th Grade Self-Contained Teacher 1979-87, 6th Grade Math/Sci Teacher 1987-89, 7th Grade Math/Sci Teacher 1989-Santa Fe Mid Sch; *ai:* Mid Sch Vlybl Coach; KS Assn of Mid Level Educators 1982-86; NEA 1984-88; KS Assn Teachers of Sci 1986-89; Natl Mid Sch Assn 1990; 6th Grade Dept Chairperson 1986-87; *office:* Santa Fe Mid Sch 130 W Broadway Newton KS 67114

WHILLOCK, TOM L., English Teacher; *b:* Vinita, OK; *m:* Anita Gaye Palmer; *c:* Lesli A.; *ed:* (BS) Elem Ed/Music Ed, Northeastern St Univ 1981; Health Admin, OK Univ 1983; *cr:* Company Supvr NE Health Care 1981-83; Teacher Sapulpa Mid Sch 1983-; *ai:* Frosh & HS Boys Bsktbl Coach; Impact Crisis Cnslr; Talent Show & Summer Recreation Coord; Staffing, Textbook, Crisis Intervention Public Relations Comm; Adult Basic Ed Teacher; KS Univ Bsktbl Camp Coach; NEA 1983-; OEA 1983-, Teacher of Yr 1986, Humanitarian of Yr 1988; OK Coaches Assn 1984-; FCA Coord 1983-84; Music Educators Natl Conference Pres 1981; Outstanding Young Men of America 1987; Coaching Most Wins in Season 1989-; *home:* 2779 W 115th Pl S Jenks OK 74037

WHIMPENNY, WALTER GEORGE, Mathematics Teacher; *b:* Newark, NJ; *m:* Marie Horwath; *c:* Walter, Kristina; *ed:* (BA) Math, 1966, (MA) Math, 1972 Montclair St; Sabbatica Leave 1976; Cmptr Stud; Continuing Ed Cmptrs; Consortium for Study of Math & Art; *cr:* Teacher Kearny HS 1966-; Math Consultant NJ Commission for Blind 1969-73; *ai:* NJ Math League Team Adv; NCTM 1964-78; NJMA 1964-82; NEA, NJEA, KEA 1966-; Holy Comforter Church Sr Warden 1984-; Cub Scouts Cubmaster 1978-81; Merrill Park Little League (Coach, Mgr) 1976-82; Colonia Soccer League Coach 1978-84; Developed Basic Skills Prgm; Kearny Bd of Ed; Developed Prgm to Improve HS Proficiency Test Scores for Kearny HS; *office:* Kearny HS 336 Devon St Kearny NJ 07032

WHIPKEY, EDITH MARIE (YOST), Retired Elementary Teacher; *b:* Cameron, WV; *w:* Phillip Dinsmore (dec); *c:* Marcia A. Menefee, Marilyn V. Clark; *ed:* (BA) Eng/Soc Stud Elem, West Liberty Teachers Coll 1967; Elem Ed, WV Univ; *cr:* 5th-8th Grade Elem Teacher Mt Hope Sch 1967-69; 3rd-4th Grade Elem Teacher Pleasant Valley 1969-72; 6th Grade Elem Teacher 1972-73, 4th-5th Grade Elem Teacher 1973-85 Cameron Grade; *ai:* Retired from Public Sch; Private Piano Teacher 40 Stu Weekly; Accompanist for Solo-Ensemble Band & Violin; Marshall Cty Retired Sch Employees 1990; GFWC Cameron Womans Club VP 1988-; Literary Short Story-2 Articles 1st 2nd Place 1990; Poetry 1 Entry 3rd Place 1990; Readers Digest April 1989 Life in U S; World Poetry 1989 Anthology; *home:* 54 North Ave Cameron WV 26033

WHIPPLE, MYRON CHARLES, Fifth Grade Teacher; *b:* Detroit, MI; *m:* Lois Ann; *c:* Cindy Foreman, Brian, Susan Hicks; *ed:* (BA) Ed, MI St Univ 1968; *cr:* 5th Grade Teacher Immaculate Heart of Mary 1964-66, Vandercook Lake Sch 1966-67, Dansville Ag Sch 1967-; *ai:* Jr HS Bsktbl Coach; Dansville Ed Assn 1967-; Meth Church Sunday Sch Teacher 1956-86; *home:* 731 Mc Roberts St Mason MI 48854

WHISENANT, SANDRA WALKER, Sixth Grade Teacher; *b:* Arab, AL; *m:* Dwight; *c:* Kerrick; *ed:* (BS) Elem Ed, Jacksonville St Univ 1971; (MA) Elem Ed, Al A&M Univ 1977; *cr:* 5th Grade Teacher Fort Mc Clellan Ind Sch 1971-72; 2nd Grade Teacher Hillcrest Elem Sch 1972-73; 6th Grade Teacher Laceys Spring Sch 1973-; *ai:* Supts, Elem Curr, Morgan Cty Promotions/Retention Comm; Sch Spelling Bee Coord; NEA, AL Ed Assn 1976-; Morgan Cty Teachers Assn 1976-; *home:* Rt 1 Box 614 Laceys Spring AL 35754

WHISENHUNT, AUDREY ELAINE, Span Teacher/Foreign Lang Head; *b:* Wills Point, TX; *m:* David; *ed:* (BS) Psych/Eng, 1978, Span Cert 1985 E TX St Univ; *cr:* Eng/Span Teacher Leonard Ind Sch Dist 1978-82; Span Teacher Bonham Ind Sch Dist 1984-; *ai:* Jr Class Spon, UIL Spelling Dir; TSTA 1978-82, 1984-; *office:* Bonham HS Warpath Dr Bonham TX 75418

WHISENHUNT, BETSY ANN, English Teacher; *b:* Mineral Wells, TX; *m:* Donald Wayne Sr.; *c:* Donald Wayne Jr., William Benton; *ed:* (BS) Speech/Eng, 1963, (MA) Comm, 1976 E NM Univ; (MA) Interdisciplinary Stud/Eng, Univ of TX Tyler 1982; *cr:* Eng Teacher Mac Kenzie Jr Hs 1963-66; Speech/Eng Instr Tx Coll 1978-82; Eng Teacher John Tyler 1982-83; Eng/Speech Teacher Walthill Public Sch 1985-, Wayne St Coll 1990; *ai:* Speech, One Act, Mock Trial Coach; Amer Assn of Univ Women Pres 1967-87; Phi Kappa Phi 1976-; Cooper Fnd Teaching NE Excl Awd 1990; *home:* PO Box 224 Wayne NE 68787

WHISNANT, EVELYN, Math/Science/Health Teacher; *b:* Kings Mountain, NC; *ed:* (BS) Elem Ed, Barber-Scotia Coll 1966; (MS) Elem Ed, NC Cntrl Univ 1978; Univ of VA; *cr:* Teacher Westmoreland Sch 1966-70, Bellevue Elem Sch 1970-81, Edwin A Gibson Mid Sch 1981-; *ai:* Math, Textbook Adoption, Personnel Policy, Sci Comm; Danville Ed Assn, VA Ed Assn, NEA Mem 1966-; *office:* Edwin A Gibson Mid Sch 1215 Industrial Ave Danville VA 24541

WHISONANT, MARY DAWKINS, Third Grade Teacher; *b:* Gaffney, SC; *m:* Jerry W.; *c:* Jerry Jr., Corey, Katrina; *ed:* (BA) Early Chldhd Ed, Livingstone Coll 1975; *cr:* Kndgtn Teacher Hurley Elem Sch 1975-76; 3rd Grade Teacher Mt Ulla Elem Sch 1976-; *ai:* Sch Base Comm for Pupil Services; Math Comm Chairperson; *home:* 1008 Hawkinstown Rd Salisbury NC 28144

WHITAKER, AMELIA BATTS, 3rd Grade Teacher; *b:* Somerville, TN; *m:* Johnnie S.; *c:* Natalie Scates, Cedric, Arlene London, Algerine; *ed:* (BS) Soc Admin, Tn St Univ Nashville 1953; Peabody Coll, Univ TN Knoxville; *cr:* Teacher Miller Elem & Fayette Ware HS 1955-59; Prin/Teacher Morrows Grove Elem 1960-68; Teacher Cntrl Elem 1968-73, Oakland Elem 1974-; *ai:* Career Days Comm; Chm Easter Seal Drive; TN Ed Assn, NEA; Fayette Cty Ed Assn Faculty Rep 1982-89; Natl Assn for Advancement of Colored People; Alexander M B Church; *home:* Rt 5 Box 219 Somerville TN 38068

WHITAKER, BARBARA LINDSAY, Health & Physical Ed Teacher; *b:* Memphis, TN; *ed:* (BS) Phys Ed, 1981, (MED) Phys Ed, 1982 Memphis St Univ; US Vlybl Assn Level II, III Cert in Coaching; *cr:* Teacher Auburndale Sch 1982-84, Germantown Hs 1984-; *ai:* Var Vlybl, Bsktbl, Sftbl, Tennis Coach; Jr Var Bsktbl; NEA, TN Athletic Coaches Assn 1984-, Vlybl Coach of Yr 1985, 1988; *office:* Germantown HS 7653 Poplar Pike Memphis TN 38138

WHITAKER, CAROL DUNAGIN, 3rd Grade Teacher; *b:* Abilene, TX, *m:* Claude D.; *c:* Stephen D., Scott B., Susan C. Henderson; *ed:* (BS) Elem Ed/Eng, 1954, (MED) Elem Ed/Art/Bible, 1956 Hardin-Simmons Univ; *cr:* 3rd Grade Teacher Odessa-Ector Cty Public Schls 1954-56, Snyder Public Schls 1956-58; 5th Grade Teacher Garland Ind Sch Dist 1958-60; 3rd Grade Teacher Allen Ind Sch Dist 1965-; *ai:* Delta Kappa Gamma; ATPE; PTA; Outstanding Elem Teachers of America 1974.

WHITAKER, CYNTHIA LIZABETH (JONES), Third Grade Teacher; *b:* Denver, CO; *m:* Lewis T.; *c:* Lewis L., Lanny R.; *ed:* (BS) Elem Ed/Art, 1972, (MED) Learning Disabilities/Psych, 1975 W TX St Univ; *cr:* 4th Grade Teacher Bushland Ind Sch Dist 1972-73, 1978-79; 3rd Grade Teacher Claude Ind Sch Dist 1979-; *ai:* Spelling & Story Telling Univ Interscholastic League; TX St Teachers Assn Pres 1986-87; Delta Kappa Gamma; Panhandle Rdng Assn Treas 1989-; *office:* Claude Elem Sch Box 209 Claude TX 79019

WHITAKER, DONIS ILENE, Fourth Grade Teacher; *b:* Eaton County, MI; *m:* George W.; *c:* Julie Wilson, Tamara, Eric; *ed:* (BA) Elem Ed, 1961, (MA) Elem Ed, 1965 MI St Univ; *cr:* 4th/5th Grade Teacher Charlotte Public Schls 1961-; *ai:* Mem Charlotte Ed Assn Awds & Retirement Comm; NEA, MI Ed Assn, Charlotte Ed Assn 1961-; Delta Kappa Gamma Intnl Society (1st VP 1974-76, Mem 1970-, Treas 1979-81); Avenue United Meth Church Mem 1955-; *office:* Parkview Elem 301 E Kalamo Hwy Charlotte MI 48813

WHITAKER, HENRY WASHINGTON, English Teacher; *b:* Muskogee, OK; *m:* Janet La Voyce Mc Vay; *c:* Jahan, Michelle, Kwala, Brianna, Brian; *ed:* (BA) Eng, Langston Univ 1976; *cr:* Eng Teacher Boley St Sch for Boys 1976-79, Sadler & West Jr HS 1979-81, Alice Robertson Jr HS 1981-; *ai:* Var Boys Bsktbl & Asst Ftbl Coach; Alice Robertson Jr HS Testing Comm; OK Ed Assn Mem 1976-; NEA, Muskogee Ed Assn Mem 1979-; NCTE Mem

1981; Alpha Phi Alpha Mem 1972-; Jerusalem Missionary Baptist Church (Treas, Deacon); Muskogee HS Educator of Yr Spec Merit Awds 1987-89; *home:* 1209 Georgetown Muskogee OK 74401

WHITAKER, LINDA R., Life Science Teacher; *b:* Kansas City, MO; *ed:* (BSE) Bio, 1966, (MS) Bio, 1968 Cntrl MO St Univ; *cr:* Instr Morristown Jr Coll 1968-69, Blue Mountain Coll 1969-70; Teacher Palmer Jr HS 1972-; *ai:* Coach Sci Olympiad Team; Sci Teachers of MO; NEA; Grad Asst-Cntrl MO St Coll 1966-68; NSF Summer Institute Rocky Mountain Ecology CO St Univ 1969; AEC Summer Institute Radion Bio TX Womens Univ 1970; *office:* Palmer Jr H S 218 N Pleasant St Independence MO 64050

WHITCOMBE, ROXANN ROBIN, Reading Department Chair; *b:* East Chicago, IN; *ed:* Elem Ed, Ball St Univ 1980; Elem Ed, IN Univ 1989; *cr:* K-5th Grade Elem Teacher Hobart Township Schls 1980-83; 6th Grade Rdng/Eng/Soc Stud Teacher 1983-, Rdng Dept Chairperson 1989- Kahler Mid Sch; *ai:* Babysitter Club Spon 1989-; Cheerleading Spon 1985-88; Theater Spon 1983; PEO VP 1990; Hammond Area Rdng Cncl Mem 1980-88; Intnl Rdng Assn; Sch Outcome Driven Developmental Model Core Group Mem; St Mary IN Natl Geography Wkshp Grant; *office:* Kahler Mid Sch 452 Elm St Dyer IN 46311

WHITE, ANITA ANN (BURRELL), Science Teacher; *b:* Birmingham, AL; *m:* Donald Everette; *c:* Mark E., Todd E.; *ed:* (BS) Chem, Parsons Coll 1961; (MS) Chem, IL Inst of Technology 1964; Ed, St Univ Buffalo 1977-78; Essential Elements of Ed; *cr:* Research Asst Northop Space Laboratories 1964-65; Part-Time Instr Univ of AL Huntsville 1966-67; Chemist Starks Assocs Inc 1968-74; Sci Teacher Buffalo Bd of Ed 1974-, Academic Challenge Center 1982-; *ai:* Magnet Sch Resource Unit, Earth Sci Curr, Phys Sci Examination Comm Mem; Stu Cncl Adv; Buffalo Teachers Fed Inc, NEA 1974-; Natl Tech Assn Treas 1987-; Amer Chemical Society 1969-74; PTA 1970-; Alpha Kappa Alpha (Membership Chm, Corresponding Secy, Public Relation Chm) 1982-; Amer Assn Univ Women 1969-75; Article Published in Canadian Journal of Chem 1967; *office:* Academic Challenge Center S Division & Hickory St Buffalo NY 14204

WHITE, BETTY CANTY, Sixth Grade Teacher; *b:* Columbus, OH; *m:* Mc Neil; *c:* Dawn; *ed:* (BSED) Elem Ed, Cntrl St Univ 1965; *cr:* 1st Grade Teacher Kinsman Elem 1966; 2nd Grade Teacher Highlands Elem 1966-69, Arrowood Elem 1969-75; 5th Grade Teacher Shawnee Elem 1975-76; 5th/6th Grade Teacher Simon Kenton Elem 1976-; *ai:* Food for Friends & Talent Show Co-Chairperson; Handwriting Comm; Xenia Ed Assn, OH Ed Assn, NEA; Cooperating Teacher for Stu Teachers & Field Base Stus; *home:* 1193 Brush Row Rd Wilberforce OH 45384

WHITE, BETTY JEAN, Music & Chorus Teacher; *b:* Oak Ridge, TN; *ed:* (BS) Music Ed, Knoxville Coll 1970; Philosophy of Ed, Educl Psych, Vocal & Piano Music for Advanced Learner, Teacher Private Voice & Piano Improvisation; *cr:* Teacher Cuyahoga Boys Sch 1966; 6th-8th Grade Teacher Cleveland Public Schls; 6th-9th Grade Teacher Oak Ridge Schls; *ai:* Co-Spon Southeast Consortium for Minority Engrs; Spon RJHS Show Choir; Mem Oak Ridge Schls Minority Concerns Comm; Mem NAACR; Oak Ridge Recruiting Team 1989-; Music Educators Natl Assn; Recognition Lion Club & Big Brothers Big Sisters; Natl Assn for Advancement of Colored People; Zeta Phi Beta Mem; Mt Calvary Baptist Church (Mem, Minister of Music); Music Dept Chm Robertsville Jr HS; Music Chm Knox Penal Farm & Health Care Center; Guest Soloist Ellis Marsalis Concert; *office:* Oak Ridge Schls 245 Robertsville Rd Oak Ridge TN 37830

WHITE, BETTY RUTH, 8th Grade English Teacher; *b:* Lamar, CO; *c:* Hohn Merriman, James Merriman, Sarah Merriman; *ed:* (BA) Eng, Lincoln Univ 1984; *cr:* 8th Grade Teacher Eldon Mid S H 1985-; *ai:* Spon Jr HS Level Future Teachers of America; Jr HS Girls Track Coach; MSTA 1985-; Published Poetry in Quoin; 15th Place Writers Digest Short Story Competitions; *office:* Eldon Mid Sch Rt C C Eldon MO 65026

WHITE, BRENDA COOKSON, Language Arts Teacher; *b:* Muskogee, OK; *m:* David Charles; *c:* Gregory J.; *ed:* (BAED) Eng, Northeastern St Coll 1972; Grad Work, N TX St Univ; *cr:* Eng/Journalism Teacher North Side HS 1972-74; 7th Grade Self-Contained Teacher Roanoke Valley Chrstn 1974-76; 7th/8th Grade Lang Arts Teacher St John Apostle Day Sch 1976-86, Harleton Jr HS 1984-; *ai:* At-Risk, Gifted/Talented Coord Harleton Ind Sch Dist; TX Classroom Teachers Assn; Harleton Classroom Teachers Assn VP 1988-; E TX Baptist Univ Womens Club Recording Secy 1988-; *home:* 46 Pine Burr Cir Marshall TX 75670

WHITE, BRIAN JOSEPH, Biology Teacher; *b:* Poughkeepsie, NY; *ed:* (BA) Bio, Marist Coll 1979; Suny/Univ of HI/Salem St Coll; *cr:* Phys Sci Teacher Arlington HS 1979-80; Math Teacher Millbrook HS 1980-85; Bio Teacher Danvers HS 1985-; *ai:* Intramural Soccer; Tennis & Bsktbl Coach; Bsktbl Intramural Traveling Team; Sci Team Adv; Stu Teacher Mentor; Exec Bd Comm; MA Marine Educ 1987-; Recipient Natl Sci Fnd Grant; Recipient Proj Oceanology Grant; *office:* Danvers HS 60 Cabot Rd Danvers MA 01923

WHITE, CAROL BENZ, Science Teacher; *b:* Long Branch, NJ; *m:* Allen W.; *ed:* (AA) Liberal Arts, 1966, (BS) Sci, 1968, (MAT) Sci Ed, 1970 Monmouth Coll; *cr:* 7th/8th Grade Sci Teacher Frank Antonides Sch 1968-; *ai:* Yrbk, Class, Graduation, Sci Fair Adv; NEA, NJEA, MCEA, WLBEA 1968-; NJSTA 1970-; EMD of Womens Club of NJ St Chm 1980-82, Honor Roll Recipient 1980; BISECT Mini Grant NJ Winner; *office:* Frank Antonides Sch Locust Ave West Long Branch NJ 07757

WHITE, CARRIE LEE, Mathematics Teacher; *b:* Monroe, LA; *m:* Joseph; *c:* Joey, Erin; *ed:* (BS) Math, 1968, (MED) Math Ed, 1973 TX Southern Univ; *cr:* Math Teacher Westbury HS 1969-85, Waxahachie Jr HS 1985-; *ai:* Univ Interscholastic League UIL Dir; NEA, TX Ed Assn 1969-88; NCTM 1969-85; *office:* Waxahachie Jr HS 2401 E Brown Waxahachie TX 75165

WHITE, CATHRINE GRIFFIN, 5th Grade Teacher; *b:* Douglas, GA; *m:* Bruce; *c:* Sarah C. Atkinson, Joseph G.; *ed:* (BSED) Elem Ed, Univ of GA 1973; (MED) Elem Ed, 1977, (SED) Mid Sch, 1984 Valdosta St Coll; Cert in Data Collecting & Supervision of Stu Teachers; Aerospace Ed Courses; *cr:* Math Teacher Ambrose Elem Sch 1973-81; 5th Grade Teacher Westside Elem Sch 1981-; *ai:* 4-H Club Spon; Coffee Assn of Educators (Pres Elect 1989) 1973-; GA Assn of Educators, NEA 1973-; Civil Air Patrol 1989-; Lobbyed for Educl Issues; 23rd Annual Natl Congress on Aviation & Space Ed; *office:* Westside Elem Sch 311 Westside Dr Douglas GA 31533

WHITE, CLEON EUGENE, Mathematics/Chemistry Teacher; *b:* Spokane, WA; *m:* Sandra Maxine Clough; *c:* Eric J., Suzanne R.; *ed:* (BA) Math, Walla Walla Coll 1963; (MA) Math, Univ of N CO 1969; OR St Univ, Andrews Univ; *cr:* Math/Sci Instr Mansfield HS 1963-65, Campion Acad 1965-76; Math/Sci Instr/VP Andrews Acad 1976-81; Prin/9th Grade Teacher Hermiston Jr Acad 1981-89; Math/Sci Instr Andrews Acad 1984-; *ai:* Primary Stu Assn Adv; Mem of Health/Safety Comm; Stu Affairs Chm Curr Comm; Accreditation; CO SDA Teachers Assn Treas 1975-76; SDA Cmptr Assn 1988; Pioneer Memorial Church Sabbath Sch Early Teen Dir 1984-87; Pioneer Memorial Church Sabbath Sch Yth Dir 1989-; Lake Union Conference of SDA Zappara Awd 1990; NSF Grants Univ of N CO 1972; *office:* Andrews Acad Andrews University Berrien Springs MI 49104

WHITE, CONNIE COOK, Science Teacher; *b:* Chicago, IL; *m:* Robert David; *c:* Zachary; *ed:* (BS) Chem, Gardner-Webb Coll 1984; Math Cert, Physics Endorsement 1990; *cr:* Teacher Burns Sr HS 1986-; *ai:* Cheerleading Spon; Teaching Fellows Schlsp, Bus/Ed, Prom Comms; Class Spon; NC Sci Teachers Assn; NC Alliance Chem Teachers; Dover Baptist Church Mem 1985-.

WHITE, DANIEL W., Physical Education Teacher; *b:* Moline, IL; *ed:* (BA) His, Cameron Univ 1975; *cr:* Phys Ed Teacher Carriage Hills Elem 1975-; *ai:* OK Ed Assn 1975-; OK Assn for Health/Phys Ed/Recreation & Dance S W Coord 1986-88; Dept of the Army Certificate of Appreciation for Patriotic Civilian Service; St Champion Merit Awd Carriage Hills Sch 1977; St Champions Phys Fitness Awd 1983-86; *office:* Carriage Hills Elem Sch 215 SE Warwick Way Lawton OK 73501

WHITE, DAVID MICHAEL, 5th Grade Teacher; *b:* Denver, CO; *m:* Ellen Kay Luke; *c:* Travis; *ed:* (AA) Ed, Phoenix Coll 1971; (MS) Scndry Ed, 1973, (MS) Elem/Spec Ed Learning Disabilities, 1981 N AZ Univ; *cr:* Jr HS Soc Stud Teacher Puerco Elem Sch 1974-76; K-8th Grade Head Teacher Blue Sch 1976-78; Spec Ed Teacher Camp Verde Jr HS 1978-81; 5th Grade Teacher Camp Verde Elem Sch 1981-; *ai:* 5th/6th Grade Bsktbl & Little League Bsbl Coach; *home:* PO Box 1448 Camp Verde AZ 86322

WHITE, DAVID PHILLIPS, JR., Assistant Principal; *b:* Shelby, NC; *m:* Marsha Reid; *c:* David III; *ed:* (BS) Ed, Tusculum Coll 1967; (MED) Admin, Univ of NC Charlotte 1978; (EDS) Admin, Winthrop Coll 1986; Mentor, Performance Appraisal, Effective Teachers Trng; *cr:* Teacher Gaston Cty Schls 1968-70; Salsman Glen Brook Laboratories/Burlington Industries 1970-75; Teacher 1975-81, Asst Prin 1981- Gaston Cty Schls; *ai:* Natl Coalition for Parent Involvement in Ed; Track Coach; N CA Assn of Ed 1980-85; N CA Prin Asst Prin Assn 1985-88; Tar Heel Prin Asst Prin Assn 1988-90; Lions Club (Secy 1988-89, Treas 1988-89, Pres 1990); Dist Asst Prin of Yr 1984; Effective Prin Trng Prgm; *office:* South Gastonia Elem Sch 3005 S York Rd Gastonia NC 28052

WHITE, DEBBIE DODSON, US His/Government Econ Teacher; *b:* Mineala, TX; *m:* Michael Joseph; *c:* Misti S., Haley A., Blake C.; *ed:* (BSE) Soc Stud, S AR Univ 1977; Major in Gen Sci; *cr:* 7th Grade Sci Teacher 1978-80, 8th Grade US His Teacher 1980-82 Blytheville W Jr HS; 7th-8th Grade Sci Teacher Liberty-Eylau Jr HS 1982-84; 9th-12th Grade US His/Psych/Amer Government/Ec Teacher Atlanta HS 1984-; *ai:* Girls Jr Class Spon; Fellowship of Chrstn Athletes; Phi Alpha Theta VP 1976-77; Outstanding Young Woman of America 1977; *office:* Atlanta HS 705 Rabbit Blvd Atlanta TX 75551

WHITE, DELORIS ELIZABETH, 7th Grade English Teacher; *b:* Jacksonville, NC; *ed:* (BA) Intermediate Ed, Winston-Salem St Univ 1977; *cr:* Eng Teacher Jacksonville Mid Sch 1978-; *ai:* Dir Dinner Theater; Mid Sch Coord; Delta Sigma Theta Sorority; Outstanding Educator 1987; Teacher of Yr 1988; Mentor; *office:* Jacksonville Mid Sch 401 New Bridge St Jacksonville NC 28540

WHITE, DOUGLAS DALE, JR., Social Studies Teacher; *b:* Lexington, KY; *m:* Sue Hobbs; *c:* Thomas D.; *ed:* (BA) Soc Stud, 1971, (MA) Scndry Ed, 1976 E KY Univ; *cr:* Substitute Teacher Clark Cty Bd of Ed 1971-73; Teacher George Rogers Clark HS 1973-; *ai:* Stu for a Cause; NEA, KY Ed Assn 1973-; *office:* George Rogers Clark HS 620 Boone Ave Winchester KY 40391

WHITE, EDNA DOTSON, Fifth Grade Teacher; *b:* Richmond, IN; *m:* Robert L.; *c:* Constance White Jones, Christine White Townsend, Catherine White Showalter, Robert J., Ronald L.; *ed:* (BS) Elem Ed, 1973, (MS) Elem Ed, 1976 Ball St Univ; Classes, IN Univ E & Miami Univ OH; *cr:* 5th Grade Teacher Richmond Cmmty Schls 1973-; *ai:* Highland Heights Sch Rdng & Writing Resource Person; Alpha Delta Kappa Chaplain 1990; Richmond Area Rdng Cncl Secy 1977-78; Outdoor Lab Area Grant for Highland Heights Sch.

WHITE, EDNA MEISEKOTHEN, Computer/English Teacher; *b:* Madison, WI; *m:* John F.; *ed:* (BBA) Ec, Univ of WI 1953; (MA) Spec Ed, San Francisco St Coll 1968; Cmptr Literacy Applications; *cr:* Economic Analyst Crown Zellerbach Corp 1954-66; Spec Ed Teacher 1966-70, 1st-8th Grade Teacher 1970-82, Cmptr Coord & Teacher 1983- Jefferson Sch Dist; *ai:* Mentor Teacher 1986-89, Cmptr Skills; CAP Essays 1988-, Reader & Scorer for ETS; CTA Finance Chm 1966-73, Sp Achievement 1970; AFT Building Rep 1973-; CVE Dist Rep 1966-; Sr Net 1990-; Helpers of Mentally Retarded 1960-; AB 803 Grant; *home:* 800 Swindon Ct Vacaville CA 95688

WHITE, ELDRED C., Principal-Owner; *b:* Morgantown, KY; *m:* Lancine E. Zittrover; *c:* Veralynn Malone, Clifton, Chris, Vicki Hubbard; *ed:* (BA) His/Psych, Georgetown Baptist Coll 1957; (MA) Scndry Educl Admin, Rollins Coll 1970; *cr:* Teacher Howard Jr HS 1957-59; Baptist Pastor KY & FL Churches 1957-85; Prin Platts Acad 1960-75; Prin/Owner Cntrl FL Acad Inc 1975-.

WHITE, FAYE PORTER, First Grade Teacher; *b:* Utopia, TX; *m:* Tommy; *c:* Tana White Kehoe, David; *ed:* (BS) Elem Ed, Sul Ross St Coll 1957; *cr:* 5th Grade Teacher Commance Elem 1957-59; 7th/8th Grade Health/Phys Ed Teacher Pearsall Jr HS 1965-68; 1st Grade Teacher Fabra Elem 1968-; *ai:* 1st Grade Tutoring Instr; AFT; *home:* Rt 2 Box 2106 Boerne TX 78006

WHITE, GAYNELL REEVES, Fifth Grade Teacher; *b:* Rossville, TN; *m:* Robert S.; *c:* Tangela G., Robert S. II; *ed:* (BA) Elem Ed, Le Moyne Coll 1965; (MS) Elem Admin/Supervision, Memphis St Univ 1970; Grad Stud; *cr:* 5th Grade Teacher Riverview Elem 1965-71; 5th/6th Grade Teacher Balmoral Elem 1972-77; 5th Grade Teacher Double Tree Elem 1977-; *ai:* Staff Dev Comm Chairperson; Honors Club Spon; Good Behavior Club Co-Spon; IIPEL Liaison Teacher; Memphis Ed Assn Faculty Rep 1975-77; TN Ed Assn, W TN Ed Assn, NEA; NAACP 1966-; YWCC Pres 1976-81; Sci Grant 1985; *home:* 2121 Carmi Cove Memphis TN 38116

WHITE, HELEN CAMBEROS, English Teacher; *b:* Whitesville, WV; *m:* James C.; *c:* James, Marlana, Bert; *ed:* (BS) Eng/Span, Concord Coll 1968; (MA) Rdng Specialist, WVCOGS 1977; *cr:* Eng/Span Teacher Central Jr HS 1968-71, Princeton Jr HS 1971-88; Eng/Writing Teacher Princeton Sr HS 1988-; *ai:* Comm of Sch Excl; NEA, WY Ed Assn, Mercer Cty Ed Assn Faculty Rep 1968-; Mercer Cty Rdng Assn 1986-; WV Ed Mini-Grant 1986; *office:* Princeton Sr HS Princeton Sr H S Princeton WV 24740

WHITE, ILA FAYE, 2nd Grade Teacher; *b:* Dolberg, OK; *m:* Vaskon; *c:* Karen L. White Burris; *ed:* (BS) Elem Ed, 1970, (MS) Rdng Specialist, 1976 East Cntrl Univ; Whole Lang, Math Their Way, Gifted & Talented, Rdng; Various Seminars & Wkshps; *cr:* Elem Teacher Byng Sch 1971-87, Byng-Homer Sch 1988-; *ai:* NEA, OEA, IRA; Pontotoc Cty Rdng Cncl VP 1981; *home:* 102 S Monta Vista Ada OK 74820

WHITE, JACK KENNETH, Fourth & Fifth Grade Teacher; *b:* Charleston, SC; *m:* Sharon Peterson; *c:* Layla, Nathan, Jonathan; *ed:* (BS) Elem Ed, Coll of Charleston 1979; (MA) Bible Exposition, Pensacola Chrstn Coll 1990; *cr:* Elem Teacher Chester Chrstn Sch 1979-85, Charleston Chrstn Sch 1985-; *ai:* Charleston Harbor Bible Church Sunday Sch Teacher; *office:* Charleston Chrstn Sch 2234 Plainview Rd Charleston SC 29414

WHITE, JAMES CLAY, Science Department Chairman; *b:* Piedmont, MO; *m:* Mary Anna Sherrod; *c:* David, Mike; *ed:* (BS) Bio, SE MO St Univ 1965; (MA) Bio, Webster Univ 1975; Grad Stud Sci, Waste Management, Energy Ed; *cr:* Teacher N Jefferson Jr HS 1965-77; Teacher 1978-87, Sci Dept Chm 1988- Northwest HS; *ai:* NSTA, Sci Teachers MO, MO Waste Coalition; IL-MO Gas Engine Club, Model T Club of MO, Public Water Dist #8 Pres.

WHITE, JANE YOUNT, Mathematics Teacher; *b:* Lenoir, NC; *m:* Stephen Elliott; *c:* Sean, Cory, Stephanie; *ed:* (BS) Elem Ed, Appalachian St Univ 1969; (MAT) Math, Winthrop Coll 1977; Spec Ed, Univ of TN 1980; *cr:* 3rd Grade Teacher Harmony Elem Sch 1968-69; 4th Grade Teacher Northview Elem Sch 1969-70; 6th Grade Teacher Catawba Elem Sch 1970-72; 7th Grade Math/Sci Teacher Rawlinson Road Jr HS 1972-77; Resource Teacher 1978-86, Math Teacher E Ridge Mid Sch 1986-; *ai:* Beta Club Spon; Homework Hotline; After Sch Tutoring Prgm; TEA, NEA 1978-89; HCEA (Membership Chm 1982) 1978-89; Career Ladder Level III; *office:* E Ridge Mid Sch 5273 E Andrew Johnson Highway Russellville TN 37860

WHITE, JANIS B., Spanish Teacher; *b:* Brooklyn, NY; *m:* Preston B.; *c:* Kemba, Kamal; *ed:* (BA) Span, Morgan St Univ 1969; (MA) Urban Ed, Univ of PA 1970; (MS) Guidance/Counseling, CCNY 1977; *cr:* Span Teacher Dwight Morrow HS & J E Dismus Mid Sch 1970-; *ai:* Dir Project Elite Farleigh Dickinson Univ; *home:* 126 Mercer Pl South Orange NJ 07079

WHITE, JOHN MARK, Social Studies Teacher; *b:* Mc Kinney, TX; *m:* Donna; *c:* Stacey, Matthew; *ed:* (BA) His, Univ of Houston 1976; Petroleum Stud; Advanced EconoMics Stud; *cr:* World His Teacher 1977-, Sociology Teacher 1977-, Conversational Span Teacher 1980-83, Ec Teacher 1987-89 South Houston HS; *ai:* Life Stu; ATPE.

WHITE, JUDITH DOUGHERTY, English Teacher; *b:* Wheeling, WV; *m:* Willard C.; *c:* Amy L., Philip A.; *ed:* (BS) Scndry Ed/Eng/Home Ec, Concord Coll 1966; (MSED) Rdng Specialist, California Univ of PA 1984; *cr:* Eng/Home Ec Teacher Minford HS 1966, Southeast Jr HS 1967-69; Eng Teacher Trinity HS 1981-; *ai:* NCTE, PSEA; Faith United Presbyn Church Deacon 1986-; *office:* Trinity HS Park Ave Washington PA 15301

WHITE, JUDITH MAES, Third-Fourth Grade Teacher; *b:* Flint, MI; *m:* William H; *c:* Ryan; *ed:* (BS) Elem Ed, 1972; (MS) Elem Guidance, 1974 Southern IL Univ; *cr:* 4th Grade Teacher St Andrew's Grade Sch 1972-73; 2nd, 3rd, 4th Grade Teacher Gorham Grade Sch 1973-; *ai:* Gifted Coord, Benjamin Franklin Stamp Club Adv, Spelling Bee Coord, Curr Comm; Jackson-Perry Co Gifted Coop Dist #166 Coord 1973; IL Cncl of Teacher of Math; PTA Sec 1974-76; Cub Scouts Asst Cubmaster, Quality Unit Pope Paul VI 87-89; World Apostolate of Fatima, Little Egypt Apple Users Group; Challenge to Excl, Aids Ed Grant; *home:* Rt 5 Murphysboro IL 62966

WHITE, KATHY APLIN, Second Grade Elem Sch Teacher; *b:* Medford, OR; *m:* George Harvard Jr.; *ed:* (BA) Child Dev/Ed, E WA St Univ Cheney 1975; (MA) Admin/Curr, Gonzaga Univ 1990; *cr:* 3rd Grade Teacher 1977-84, 2nd Grade Teacher 1984-Trent Elem; *office:* Trent Elem Sch N 3303 Pines Rd Spokane WA 99206

WHITE, KERRY ALLEN, American History Teacher; *b:* Hellam, PA; *m:* Krista Weir; *ed:* (BA) Amer His, York Coll of PA 1972; (MA) Amer His, Millersville PA 1990; *cr:* Classroom Teacher Eastern York HS 1974-; *ai:* NEA/PSEA/EYEA 1974-; Co-Edited York Dispatch Index Catalog of Newspaper Articles Helpful Guide for Writing MA or PHD Theses; *home:* RD 11 Box 314 York PA 17406

WHITE, LARRY DWAYNE, Math/Computer Teacher; *b:* Bakersfield, CA; *m:* Elmona Grounds; *c:* Larry Jr., Eric; *ed:* (BS) Math, 1972, (MAT) Math, 1979 Angelo St Univ; *cr:* 7th/8th Grade Math Teacher Winters HS 1972-77; 7th-12th Grade Math/Cmptrs Teacher/Coach Eden HS 1977-83; 8th-12th Grade Math/Cmptrs Teacher/Coach 1983-85, 8th-12th Grade Math/Cmptrs Teacher 1985- Sterling City HS; *ai:* Math Team Coach; Math Club Spon; Textbook Comm; Cmptr Coord 1990-95; TX Stu Assessment Planning Comm; Leading Math into the 21st Century Natl Comm TX Rep; NCTM, TX Cncl Teachers of Math, TX Cmptr Ed Assn, TX Math/Sci Coaches Assn, TX St Teachers Assn; Math Assn of America; Masonic Lodge 728 1982-; Sterling Cty Hospital Bd 1990; Presidential Awd for Excl Math Teaching 1987; TX Excl Awd Outstanding HS Teachers 1990; Speaker on Math Motivation 1987-; *home:* Box 395 13th St Sterling City TX 76951

WHITE, LAURIE ANN, Spanish/Photo/Yearbook Teacher; *b:* Memphis, TN; *c:* Christy C. Crosson, John S. White; *ed:* (BA) Eng/Photo, E TX St Univ 1981; *cr:* Teacher Greenville Mid Sch 1982-; *ai:* Greenville Mid Sch Yrbk Adv; Greenville Mid Sch Staff Photographer; Photographic Works Published & Displayed 1988; *home:* 1306 Arp Commerce TX 75428

WHITE, LEAH ESKOLA, 2nd Grade Elementary Teacher; *b:* Virginia, MN; *m:* Raymond M.; *c:* Danie, Jayson (dec); *ed:* (BA) Elem Ed, Univ of Duluth 1965; (MS) Elem Ed, Bemidji St Univ 1978; Numerous Courses; *cr:* Kndgtn Teacher Chisholm MN 1953-54, N St Paul MN 1956-58, Hibbing MN 1966-77; 2nd Grade Teacher Hibbin MN 1970-; *ai:* MN Sch Effectiveness Team; Amer Assn Univ Women Mem 1960-77; Bus Prof Women (Pres, Treas); MN Ed Assn 1953-, Teacher of Yr 1984; First Luth 1970-; Range Creative Art (Pres, Treas) 1958-; MN St Fair Outstanding Teacher 1980.

WHITE, LEX, Spanish Teacher; *b:* Springfield, TN; *ed:* (BA) Eng & Span, Belmont Coll 1972; (MS) Rural Dev, TN St Univ 1982; Admin & Supervision, Austin Peay St Univ 1988; *cr:* Sales Person Greenbrier HS 1976-; Teacher Breenbrier HS 1972-; *ai:* Span Club Adv; Freshman Class Spon; Robertson Cty Ed Assn 1972-; TN Ed Assn 1972-; NEA 1972-; TN Foreign Lang Teaching Assn 1985-; Robertson Cty Merit Teacher 1986; Natl Cncl of Teachers of Eng 1980-85; Mid TN Ed Assn 1972-; *home:* 2120 A Mockingbird Lane Springfield TN 37172

WHITE, LUCILLE WATKINS, Principal; *b:* Mer Rouge, LA; *m:* Harry Jr.; *c:* Nedra, Fanette; *ed:* (BA) Poly Sci, Grambling St Univ 1964; (MSED) Urban Ed, Chicago St Univ 1974; Grad Stud Governors St Univ, Sangamon St Univ, Natl Coll of Ed; *cr:* Upper Grade Teacher 1969-86, Teaching Asst/Prin 1986-89 Caldwell Sch; Prin Mary E Mc Dowell Elem 1989-; *ai:* Chicago Chairperson Sch America; Intnl Rdng Assn, Phi Delta Kappa, AFSA; Chatham Presbyn Church, Delta Sigma Theta, Mc Dowell Local Sch Cncl; S Cntrl Cmmty Services Inc Educator of Yr Awd 1984; Kate Moremont Fnd Dedicated Teacher Awd 1985; Those Who Excel Awds Recognition; IL St Bd of Ed 1989; *home:* 8907 S Constance Chicago IL 60617

WHITE, MARGARET WOODS, Extended Day Kndgtn Teacher; *b:* Battle Creek, MI; *m:* Raymond Calvin Sr.; *c:* Robin R., Raymond Jr.; *ed:* (BS) Scndry Ed, Miner Teachers Coll 1955; (MS) Learning Disabilities, Univ of Detroit 1979; *cr:* Stu Miner Teacher Washington DC 1949-55; Teacher/Stu Harris Teachers 157-58, Univ of MI 1967, Univ of Detroit 1973-79; *ai:* Sch Service Squad; Heroines of Templar Crusades Princess Captain 1989-; Eastern Star Worthy Matron 1979; Detroit Teachers Building Rep 1968; Zeta Phi Beta; Breitmeyer Teacher of Yr 1977; *office:* Sherrard Sch 8300 Cameron Detroit MI 48211

WHITE, MARIE V., Head of Middle School; *b:* Medfield, MA; *m:* James; *c:* Ann White Cole, Mary, Barbara White Gorham, James, Peter; *ed:* (BA) Eng, Regis Coll 1956; Grad Stud Univ of MA, Univ of CO; *cr:* Kndgtn Teacher Cristo Rey Sch 1966-70; 5th/6th/8th Grade Eng Teacher 1970-73, 7th/8th Grade Eng Teacher 1973-, Head Mid Sch 1981- Santa Fe Prep Sch; *ai:* Curr Comm Santa Prep Sch; *office:* Santa Fe Prep Sch 1101 Camino Cruz Blanca Santa Fe NM 87501

WHITE, MARILYN KENNEDY, Fourth Grade Teacher; *b:* Cushing, OK; *m:* Bill D.; *c:* Wesley, Alisha; *ed:* (BS) Elem Ed, OK St Univ Stillwater 1976; *cr:* 5th/6th Grade Teacher Olive Public Sch 1976-77; 2nd Grade Teacher 1977-78, 4th Grade Teacher 1978- Garber Public Sch; *ai:* Garber Ed Assn 1977-; OK Rdng Cncl 1989-; OEA, NEA 1976-; Garber Teacher of Yr 1985; Outstanding Young Women of America 1982; Yrbk Dedication 1988; *home:* 224 Versailles Box 282 Garber OK 73738

WHITE, MARILYN MEYER, Business Teacher; *b:* Lincoln, IL; *m:* Sammy B.; *c:* Stephen L.; *ed:* (BS) Bus Ed, 1961, (MS) Bus Ed, 1966 Southern IL Univ; Cmptr Sci & Bus Management; *cr:* Bus Teacher Wesclin Cmmty Schls 1961-75, Gem City Bus Coll 1981-87, West Pike Cmmty Schls 1987-; *ai:* Chrldng, Yrbk, Newspaper, Pep Club, Bus Club, Class Spon; Publicity Dir Sch Dist; Asst Dir of Voc Ed; *home:* Box 75 Hull IL 62343

WHITE, MARJORIE ANN, 5th Grade Teacher/Team Leader; *b:* Portland, ME; *m:* Robert L.; *c:* Cynthia, Allison, Brett; *ed:* (BA) Elem Ed, Elmira Coll 1975; Post Grad Courses UCF; *cr:* Classroom Teacher Goldsboro Elem 1977-79, Lake Mary Elem 1979-; Team Leader Lake Mary Elem 1989-; *ai:* Team Leader; Rdng Comm Mem; Ed 5th Grade Newspaper; Seminole Cty Rdng Cncl 1987-; *office:* Lake Mary Elem Sch 132 S Country Club Rd Lake Mary FL 32746

WHITE, MARK EDWARD, Fifth Grade Teacher; *b:* Greensburg, PA; *m:* Joan Wiley; *c:* Megan, Erin; *ed:* (BSED) Elem Ed, Edinboro Univ of PA 1978; Working Towards Masters Educl Admin, Univ of SC 1990; *cr:* 5th Grade Teacher S Conway Elem 1978-; *ai:* Grade Level Chairperson; Sci Coord S Conway Elem; SC Educl Assn, NEA 1978-; Horry Cty Educl Assn Building Rep 1978-; *office:* S Conway Elem Sch 3001 4th Ave Conway SC 29526

WHITE, MARY ALICE ROBINSON, Mathematics Teacher; *b:* Pulaski, TN; *m:* Cecil Leon; *c:* Andrew, John, Mary L.; *ed:* (BA) Math/Soc Stud/Elem, George Peabody Coll 1954; *cr:* Teacher Minor Hill HS 1954-59, Antioch HS 1959-60, Donelson Chrstn Sch 1971-73; Teacher 1973-78, Prin 1977-78 New Prospect Sch; Teacher Lawrenceburg Public 1978-; *ai:* NEA, TEA, LCEA.

WHITE, MARY CATHERINE, Humanities/World His Teacher; *b:* Chicago, IL; *ed:* (BA) Eng Ed, Mundelein Coll 1964; (MA) Eng, Seattle Univ 1970; Asian Stud, Univ WA; Ed Stud, Seattle Pacific; *cr:* Eng Teacher/Adv Placement/Basic Skills Chicago Public Sch 1964-67; His/Eng Teacher Seattle Cath Sch 1967-70; Drama/Eng Teacher Rainier Beach HS 1970-72; Eng Instr/Dept Head South Shore Mid Sch 1972-76, Eckstein Mid Sch 1976-82; Hum Dept Cleveland HS 1982-; *ai:* Sr Adv 1991; Vietnamese Club & Environmental Club Spon; Partners in Public Ed; Seattle LA Adoption Comm; Faculty Rep Cncl; NCTE; Natl Endowment HumanitieS 1988 Fellow 3 Yrs; WA St Soc Stud Teachers; Womens Univ Club; Kiwanis 1990; St James Parish Homeless Cncl 1976-, Now VA St 1975-; YWCA Alternative Housing Bd 1989; Denney Regrade Cmmty Cncl; Denney Regrade Cmmty Cncl; Seattle Art Museum-Teacher Prgm Liason Coord; Asian Inst Univ WA; Insite Teacher Bus U S West Comm 1986; Nom Excl Ed Awd 1987, Close-Up Teacher Dir U S Hist Prgm; Puget Sound Teachers Writing; Crossroads Seattle; *office:* Cleveland H S 5511 15th Ave S Seattle WA 98108

WHITE, MICHAEL JOSEPH, Mathematics Teacher/Coach; *b:* Brooklyn, NY; *m:* Debbie Diane Dodson; *c:* Misti, Haley, Blake; *ed:* (BSE) Math, S AR Univ 1978; Med Ed Admin, E TX St Univ; *cr:* Math Teacher Bytheville East Jr HS 1978-82, Atlanta HS 1982-; *ai:* Ftbl Coach, Defensive Coord; Tennis Coach; FCA Spon; TX Classroom Teachers Assn 1988-; TX HS Coaches Assn 1982-; *home:* 903 Mockingbird Atlanta TX 75551

WHITE, MIRIAM RECKER, Chemistry Teacher; *b:* Wood Ct, OH; *m:* Andrew J.; *c:* Mary S. Burns, Daniel A, John A, James D,; *ed:* (BA) (BS) Chem, Wittenberg Univ 1953; (MS) Sci Ed, Temple Univ 1971; Beaver Coll Inst 1972; Phys Chem, Univ of MD NSF Inst 1985; Instrumentation, Univ of WI Madison 1987; Cmptrs Indiana Univ of PA 1988; *cr:* Bio Teacher Springfield HS 1953-55; Substitute Teacher Shaw HS 1966-67; Bio/Sci Teacher Hebrew Acad 1967-68; Sci Teacher Chestnut Hill Acad 1968-; *ai:* Assembly Adv ; NSTA 1976-; ACS (Bd of Dirs 1983-89, Cnslr 1987-; Comm Chairperson); NSTA ACS Examination Comm; E Mt Airy Group Homes Treas 1979-85; Reformation Luth Church Cncl 1982-88; Chemist Manufacturers Catalyst Awd 1989; *office:* Chestnut Hill Acad 500 W Willow Grove Ave Philadelphia PA 19118

WHITE, N. GALE, English Teacher; *b:* Nashville, TN; *ed:* (BS) Eng, Mid TN St Univ 1972; Grad Work at Mid TN St Univ, TN St Univ; *cr:* Classroom Teacher Overton HS 1972, Litton Jr HS 1973-76, 1977-; *ai:* Homecoming Chairperson; Cheerleading Spon; NCTE, Mid TN Ed Assn, MNEA, NEA; Amer Heart Assn; TN Career Ladder; *home:* 502 W Angela Cr Goodlettsville TN 37072

WHITE, NOEMI LOPEZ, Mathematics Teacher; *b:* Robstown, TX; *m:* John Micheal; *c:* Joshua, John; *ed:* (BS) Scndry Ed/Math/Chem, TX A&I Univ 1970; (MA) Math Ed, Univ of Houston Clear Lake City 1980; *cr:* Math Teacher Galveston Jr Coll 1982, Ball HS 1970-; *ai:* Stu Cncl 1974-76; Jets 1982-84; Mu Alpha Theta 1985-; TX Cncl Teachers of Math 1988-; NCTM (Newmast Participant 1985) 1974-; Sierra Membership Chairperson 1984-; Delta Kappa Gamma Membership Chairperson 1982-; *office:* Ball HS 4115 Ave O Galveston TX 77550

WHITE, PAMELA J., English Teacher; *ed:* (BA) Eng, Colgate Univ 1979; (MA) Eng, Vanderbilt Univ 1983; *cr:* Eng Instr Harpeth Hall 1986-88, Univ Sch of Nashville 1988-; *office:* Univ Sch of Nashville 2000 Edgehill Ave Nashville TN 37212

WHITE, RHONDA CHAPIN, Reading Teacher; *b:* OKeene, OK; *m:* Jesse Edward; *c:* Derrel, David, Dewayne; *ed:* (BA) Eng, 1969, (MAT) Eng Ed, 1974 OK City Univ; (MED) Spec Ed/Learning Disabilities, Cntrl St Univ Edmond 1977; Doctoral Candidate, OK St Univ Stillwater; *cr:* Eng/Sp/Drama Teacher Minco Public Schls 1969-70; Adjunct Faculty OK City Univ, SW OK St Univ 1973-74, 1981-82; K-12th Grade Learning Disabilities Teacher Minco Public Schls 1976-84; GED Instr Canadian Valley Voc Tech, OK City Comm Coll 1981-85, 1987-88; Rdng Teacher Mustang Public Schls 1987-; Adjunct Faculty OK City Comm Coll 1987-; *ai:* OK St Validation Comm; Eng As Second Lang Stu Coord; OK Ed Assn, NEA 1976-; Mustang Area Rdng Cncl (VP, Pres) 1988-89, 1990; Minco Ed Assn Pres 1982-84; Minco Schls Teacher of Yr 1983; *office:* Mustang HS 906 S Heights Dr Mustang OK 73064

WHITE, RICHARD CARLTON, Mathematics Department Teacher; *b:* Hanover, NH; *m:* Beverly A. Morrow; *c:* Sheri, Kelly, Kimberly, John, Scott; *ed:* (BED) Math, Plymouth St 1964; (MS) Math, Boston Coll 1969; Wesleyan Summer Sch Wesleyan Univ 1966; *cr:* Math Dept Teacher Morgan HS 1965, New Hampton Prep 1965-66; Math Dept Teacher/Coach Williston Acad 1967-69, Loomis Chaffee 1970-79, Cheverus HS 1980-; *ai:* Head Coach Bsktbl, Ftbl; *home:* Box 2141 Beach Rd Raymond ME 04071

WHITE, RICHARD W., English/Journalism Teacher; *b:* New London, CT; *c:* Alison Byrnes; *ed:* (BS) Eng, Cntrl CT St 1957; (MA) Eng, Trinity Coll 1959; *cr:* Cntrl Jr HS 1957-59; Fitch Jr HS 1959-60; E Lyme HS 1973-83; Bishop Guertin HS 1986-; *ai:* Sch Newspaper Adv; Historical Novel Pegma Books 1983; Grand Prize, Writers Digest Competition 1979; CA St Poetry Prize 1979; Miscellaneous Magazine Pieces; Columnist Todays Cath Teacher Magazine; *office:* Bishop Guertin HS Lund Rd Nashua NH 03060

WHITE, RONALD I., Guidance Counselor; *b:* Corinthy, NY; *m:* Roxanne Gardner; *c:* Katherine, Erin, Andrew; *ed:* (BA) His, St Lawrence Univ 1973; (MS) Counseling, 1984, (CAS) Counseling, 1986 SUNY Plattsburgh; *cr:* 7th-12th Grade Eng Teacher Hague Cntrl Sch 1974-76; 7th-8th Grade Eng Teacher 1976-84, 7th-12th Grade Guidance Teacher 1984- Corinth Cntrl Sch; *ai:* Girls Bsktbl Coach; Adir Assn Counseling & Dev 1984-; Amer Assn Womens Bsktbl Coaches 1985-; Corinth Little League Coach 1986-; Corinth Teachers Assn VP 1979-83; *office:* Corinth Cntrl Sch 105 Oak St Corinth NY 12822

WHITE, SANDRA KAY (AUSTIN), Bio Teacher-Staff Developer; *b:* Lansing, MI; *m:* Richard Keith; *c:* Pamela, Richard II, Meredith; *ed:* (BS) Bio, MI St 1967; Instructional Theory Into Practice Trng; Dist Staff Developer; *cr:* 3rd/4th Grade Teacher Corcoran Elem 1963-65; HS Chem/Physics Teacher 1965-67, Bio Teacher 1967- Perry HS; *ai:* Union Rep; Sch Improvement Core Team; Wrkshp Instr; MEA, NEA, ASCD; Meth Church (Lay Leader, Sunday Sch Teacher, Choir Mem); Christa Mac Cauliff Teacher of Yr Nominee; Teacher of Month; *office:* Perry HS 2775 Britton Rd Perry MI 48872

WHITE, SANDRA PARRISH, Choral Director/Fine Art Chm; *b:* Roanoke, AL; *m:* Winfred; *c:* Richard, Allison; *ed:* (BS) Music Ed, Jacksonville St Univ 1963; Elem Ed, Univ of S FL 1978; Master Courses Music, Univ of NC Cntrl & FL St Univ; *cr:* Elem/Music Teacher Etowah Cty 1965-69; Music Teacher Fred Wild Elem 1975-80; Choral Dir Sebring Mid 1981-85, Sebring HS 1985-; *ai:* Sebring HS Fine Art Chairperson; Choral Club Spon; FL Vocal Assn (Exec Bd, Dist 8 Dir, Dist Chm); Delta Omicron Pres 1962-63; 1st Baptist Church Organish 1975-; Alpha Delta Kappa 1978-84; Teacher of Yr Fred Wild Elem 1980, Highlands Cty 1980, Sebring Mid Sch 1983-84, Sebring HS 1986-87; Article Published; *office:* Sebring HS 3514 Kenilworth Ave Sebring FL 33870

WHITE, SCOTT E., History/Ind Arts Teacher; *b:* Des Moines, IA; *m:* Sherry Takes; *c:* Matthew, Sara; *ed:* (BA) His/Poly Sci, Univ of N IA 1973; Industrial Arts, IA St Un iv 1977; Coaching & Mid Level Ed; *cr:* Teacher/Coach Steamboat Rock Cmmty Schls 1978-80, Monticello Cmmty Schls 1980-; *ai:* Jr Class Spon; Var Wrestling Coach; IA St Ed Assn, NEA, Monticello Ed Assn 1980-; Natl Arbor Society; Mid Level Ed Movement Conferences; *office:* Monticello Mid Sch 214 S Maple Monticello IA 52310

WHITE, SHARON ANGLIN, Principal; *b:* Fullerton, CA; *m:* David Paul; *c:* Julie, Adrian, Matthew; *ed:* (BA) Soc Sci/Psych, Univ of CA Irvine 1973; Intl Center for Elem Montessori Ed, Bergamo Italy 1976-77; Primary Montessori Early Chldhd 1974-76; *cr:* Elem Teacher Edwards Montessori Sch 1977-81, Montessori of Orange 1981-83; Prin/Teacher Tustin Hills Montessori Acad 1983-; *ai:* Field Trip Travel with Stu to Albuquerque, ID & HI UAAW 1986-; AMI, EAA 1980-; AMI 1976-; CHOC Childrens Hospital Handicapped Children Fishing Tournaments; Opened & Operated Sch.

WHITE, SHARON JANET, 4th Grade Mathematics Teacher; *b:* Slaton, TX; *ed:* (BS) Elem Ed, NM St Univ 1971; (MED) Curr/Instruction, Univ of El Paso 1978; *cr:* 3rd Grade Teacher Loving Elem 1971-73; 4th/5th Grade Teacher Coll Heights 1973-; *ai:* AFT, Intnl Rdng Assn; Delta Kappa Gamma; *office:* College Heights Elem Sch 1450 N 17th Abilene TX 79601

WHITE, SHERI DE LUE, 4th Grade Teacher; *b:* Denver, CO; *m:* Perry A.; *c:* Ryan, Heather; *ed:* (BA) Elem Ed, Univ of Northern CO 1980; Creative Arts, Lesley Coll; *cr:* 5th Grade Teacher Lincoln Park Elem 1980-81; 4th Grade Teacher Pine Lane Intermediate Sch 1981-89; *ai:* Gifted/Talented Seminar Team Coord; *office:* Pine Lane Intermediate Sch 6450 E Pine Ln Parker CO 80134

WHITE, STEVEN LOY, 9th Grade Algebra Teacher; *b:* Tulsa, OK; *m:* Patresa Sue Branham; *c:* Courtney; *ed:* (BS) Math Ed, AR Tech Univ 1985; *cr:* 9th Grade Teacher Owasso Jr HS 1985-89; *ai:* 7th Grade Ftbl Head Coach; OK Math Teacher Assn 1980-; *home:* 202 W 11th Owasso OK 74055

WHITE, SUE EVELYN (MC DONALD), Second Grade Teacher; *b:* Douglas, GA; *m:* Claude Jr.; *c:* Evelyn M.; *ed:* (AS) Bus Ed, S GA Coll 1971; (BBA) Bus Ed, 1973, Certified Elem Ed, 1974-75; (ME) Elem Ed, 1978 Valdosta St Coll; *cr:* 4th Grade Teacher 1973-77, 2nd Grade Teacher 1976- Pearson Elem Sch; *ai:* Pearson Elem Jump Rope for Heart Co-Coord 1990; Delta Kappa Gamma Intnl 1989-; Amer Heart Assn Chairperson Health Ed of Young 1987-; St Jude Bike-A-Thon Coord 1989, 1990; Holy Family Cath Church (Mem, HS Religious Ed Class Teacher); *office:* Pearson Elem Sch PO Box 578 Pearson GA 31642

WHITE, SUE HOBBS, Secondary English Teacher; *b:* Barbourville, KY; *m:* Douglas Dale Jr.; *c:* M. Thomas Dillon Jr. *ed:* (AA) Eng/Art, Midway Coll 1966; (BA) Eng/Art, 1969, (MA) Eng Ed, 1979 Univ of KY; *cr:* Scndry Eng Teacher George Rogers Clark HS 1970-; *ai:* KY Ed Assn, Clark Cty Ed Assn, NEA 1970-.

WHITE, SUSAN MARIE, Band Director/Computer Teacher; *b:* Grand Rapids, MI; *m:* Daniel; *ed:* (BM) Public Sch Music, W MI Univ 1970; (MA) Cmptr Ed, N MI Univ 1987; *cr:* Elem Band Teacher Muskegon Public Schls 1972-74; Vocal Music Teacher Manistique Area Schls 1975-78; Band Dir/Cmptr/Elem Music Teacher Big Bay De Noc Sch Dist 1978-; *ai:* Cmptr Coord; Band Festivals, Elem, Scndry Music Prgms; MI Sch Band & Orch Assn, MI Assn for Cmptr Users in Learning; Phi Kappa Phi; *office:* Big Bay De Noc Sch Dist M 183 Cooks MI 49817

WHITE, SUSAN WALKER, 5th Grade Teacher; *b:* Orlando, FL; *m:* James Walter Sr.; *ed:* (BS) Elem Ed, Auburn Univ 1976; (MED) Elem Ed, Univ of S AL 1982; Admin Cert Leadership Dept Univ S AL; *cr:* Title I Rdng Teacher Orange Cty Schls 1976-79; Elem Classroom Teacher Mobile Cty Schls 1979-; Eng Instr Phillips Coll 1990; *ai:* Art Appreciation Instr; SACS Accreditation & Steering Comms; Sch Ukulele Band Dir; Delta Kappa Gamma Intnl (2nd VP 1983-84, Mem 1981-); Mobile Cty Teacher of Yr 1982, Hall of Fame Teacher 1987; AL Hall of Fame Nom 1989; Published Article 1982; *home:* 4101 Libby Dr Mobile AL 36693

WHITE, SYLVIA YARBROUGH, Second Grade Teacher; *b:* Tupelo, MS; *m:* Joe T.; *c:* Teresa White Irwin, Paula White Shackelford; *ed:* (BS) Elem Ed, Blue Mountain Coll 1963; *cr:* 3rd Grade Teacher Clarksdale City Sch System 1963-64; 1st Grade Teacher 1968-69, Elem Teacher 1969-75 Pontotoc City Sch System; 1st Grade Teacher North Tippah Sch System 1975-76; Elem Teacher South Tippah Sch System 1976-; *ai:* Lib Comm; Taught Adult Ed Class; MS Assn of Public Continuing & Adult Ed; Outstanding Young Women of America 1970; Pontotoc Cty Outstanding Young Educator 1970; Outstanding Elem Teacher of America 1975; Nom Thanks To Teachers Excl Awd Spon by WMC Television & Apple Cmptr 1990; *office:* Ripley Elem Sch 702 W Terry Ripley MS 38663

WHITE, TOM, Hi-Technology Teacher/Spec; *b:* Louisville, KY; *m:* Sharon Charmoli; *c:* Jamey, Kacy; *ed:* (BS) Biophysics/Bio, 1977, (MA) Ed/Psych, 1980 Western KY Univ; Digital Electronics, Creative Problem-Solving Sci, Univ of Louisville; Digital Interface Services MT St Univ 1989; Honorary Schlsp 1982; Research Dir Briefings & Corp VP Briefings in Hi-Tech Areas Boeing/NASA/GE/Celanese/Rohm & Haas; Intnl Think Tank Dir, Updates with White House/Senate/Research Fnd/ Canadian Prime Minister Mulroney/Soviet Teachers; *cr:* Coach & Sr Physics/Phys & Earth Sci Teacher Eastern HS 1977-78; Coach, Bio & Phys Sci Teachers Waggener HS 1978-80; Space & Earth Sci Teacher Meyzeek Mid Sch 1980-84; Regional Implementation Consultant 1984-85, Assessment Unit for Educl Excl 1985-86 Jefferson Cty Public Schls; Hi-Technology Dir Meyzeek Magnet Mid Sch 1986-; *ai:* ELITE Think Tank Dir for Gifted; Global Outreach of Human Life thru Application of Hi-Technology KY Ed Assn 1977-; NEA 1977-; Acad of Sci 1977-; NSTA 1977-; Red Cross 1977-; YMCA 1977-; Church Civic Outreach 1977-; Intnl Kohl Ed Fnd Commendation; John Darrell Memorial Schlsp Awd 1989; Gustov Ohaus Awd for Sci Innovation 1989; Sci Scope Magazine Profile of Intnl Think Tank 1989; Outstanding Young Man of America for Public Service 1987; Pres Awd Excl Sci Teaching (State Finalist) 1988; Ashland Oil Golden Apple Achiever Awd 1989; First Natl Bank Teachers & Advocates for Pupil Excl Awd 1989; South Cntrl Bell Awd of Excl in Teaching 1988; Governor's Certs of Recognition for Sci Innovations, Top US Inventions 1989, Excl in Teaching 1988; Hurstbourne Rotary Club Speaker Awd 1989; Citizens St Bank Teacher Awd; Southeastern Dairies Teacher of Yr Awd; Commendations from NASA, Dupont, General Learning Corp, White House, Senate, House of Reps, Louisville Police & Fire Depts; *office:* Meyzeek Middle Sch 828 S Jackson St Louisville KY 40203

WHITE, TROY WADE, SR., Social Studies Chm/Teacher; *b:* Brookhaven, MS; *m:* Kathy Morris; *c:* Heather, Wade; *ed:* (BS) Soc Stud, MS St Univ 1972; (MS) Soc Stud, FL St Univ 1975; His Dept Adjunct Professor S FL Comm Coll; *cr:* Teacher Lake Placid HS 1972-; *ai:* Dept Chm; Soc Stud, Citizen Bee, FL Close-up Prgm Sch Coord 1990; Phi Alpha Theta 1972; FL Cncl for Soc Stud 1979, HS Soc Stud Teacher of Yr 1979; Homeless & Orphan Outreach Incorporated Chm 1987-; Memorial United Meth Church Mission Chm 1985-, Meth Womens Awd 1989; Sertoma Man of Yr 1989; *office:* Lake Placid HS 202 Green Dragon Dr Lake Placid FL 33852

WHITE, VELMA LOU LEWIS, Science Teacher; *b:* Dixon, MS; *m:* Troy Dale Sr.; *c:* Troy D. II, Joseph Henderson, Stephanie L. Anne; *ed:* (BS) Biological Sci, Univ of S MS 1950; (MPH) Public Health Ed, Univ of NC 1952; Phys Sci/Remedial Rdng, Univ of S MS, Univ of MS, MS St Univ; *cr:* Sci Teacher Clinton Schls 1972-81, Newton HS 1981-87, Decatur HS 1987-; *ai:* Sci Fairs; MS St Univ Physics Competition; Natl Sci & Math Tournaments Energy Expo; MSTA, NSTA; MS STAR Teacher 1985, 1986; Lunar Sci NASA 1976; Man in Gulf Project Teacher Writer 1982; MS Educl Television Teacher of Yr 1986; Dow Chemical Sci Teacher Wkshp Awd 1987; New Mast Teacher 1986; *home:* 202 N Decatur St Union MS 39365

WHITE, WANDA M., First Grade Teacher; *b:* Mount Vernon, NY; *c:* Nicole, Tremaine; *ed:* (BA) Elem Ed, VA Union Univ 1974; (MS) Counseling, Long Island Univ 1980; *cr:* Child Care Worker Jennie Clarkson Home 1976-79; 2nd Grade Teacher 1980-81, 6th Grade Teacher 1981-86, 1st Grade Teacher 1986- Lincoln Sch; *ai:* Jr Girl Scout Leader; Supvr of Young People & Jr Choir of Macedonia Baptist Church; Team Mother for Jr Minor League Burr Davis Shape; NAACP 1987-; *home:* 145 N High St Mount Vernon NY 10550

WHITE, WILSON HENRY STOUT, III, Mathematics/Cmptr Science Chm; *b:* Parkersburg, WV; *ed:* (AB) Scndry Ed/Math, Shepherd Coll 1968; (MA) Ed Admin, 1972, (MA) Supervision, 1974 WV Univ; Math Ed, James Madison Univ 1976; Math Ed, WV Univ 1979; *cr:* 7th-9th Grade Math Teacher Musselman HS 1968-69; 10th-12th Grade Math Teacher Martinsburg HS 1969-70; 7th-9th Grade Math/Cmptr Teacher Charles Town Jr HS 1971-; *ai:* Cmptr & Math Clubs; WV Cncl Teachers of Math 1971-, Teacher of Yr 1990; Potomac Valley Cncl Teachers of Math Secy 1971-; NCTM 1971-; Mount Nebo 91 Masonic Lodge AF&AM 1980-; 4 Natl Cmptr Winners-Amer Cmptr Sci League Coach; *home:* Rt 3 Box 329 Kearneysville WV 25430

WHITEHEAD, BARBARA ANN, Soc Stud/Amer His Dept Head; *b:* Shreveport, LA; *ed:* (BA) Soc Sci, 1963, (MED) Admin/ Supervision 1967 Mc Neese St Univ; Grad Stud Centenary Coll, LA Tech Univ 1982-83; *cr:* Soc Sci Teacher Calcasieu Parish Sch System 1963-68, Caddo Parish Byrd HS 1968-; Soc Stud Dept Head C E Byrd Math/Sci Magnet HS 1987-; *ai:* Academic Decathlon Team Co-Coach Byrd HS; Ring Comm Supplementary Spon Byrd HS; NEA, LA Assn of Educators, Caddo Assn of Educators; Sigma Tau Delta 1966-; Teacher of Month, Nominee Teacher of Yr LA Grange Sr HS 1967; Lucille B Mc Clendon Awd Excl Amer His; LA St Society of Daughters of Amer Revolution 1979; Pilot Teacher Project Justice 1979-80; Certificate of Recognition Conducting Inservice Ed, Sch Competency Based Ed Seminars, Wkshps 1982; Publication of Book on Methods of Instruction Soc Sci 1982; Teacher of Yr Caddo Parish 1983; *office:* C E Byrd Math/Sci Magnet HS 3201 Line Ave Shreveport LA 71104

WHITEHEAD, BRENDA JUDY, 8th Grade Science Teacher; *b:* Dyer, TN; *m:* James Autry; *c:* Judy L., Christy L.; *ed:* (BS) Biological Sci, Univ of TN 1967; Curr & Instruction, Univ of TN; *cr:* Teacher Weakley Cty Schls 1967-68, Knox Cty Schls 1971-; *ai:* 7th-8th Grade Mid & HS Honor Club Spon; Knox Cty Ed Assn; TN Ed Assn, NEA; Order of Eastern Star 1974-84; *office:* Gibbs Mid & HS 7628 Tazewell Pike Corryton TN 37721

WHITEHEAD, CAROLYN TAFT, High School English Teacher; *b:* Jamestown, NY; *ed:* (BA) Eng, Fredonia Coll 1964; *cr:* Eng Teacher Jamestown HS 1964-; *ai:* Stu Organization & Class Adv; NEA; Chautauqua Chamber Singers 1979-; Judson Fellowship 1983-; *office:* Jamestown HS 350 E 2nd St Jamestown NY 14701

WHITEHEAD, DEBBIE KILLEN, English Teacher; *b:* Florence, AL; *m:* Paul Douglas; *c:* Jacob Killen; *ed:* (BS) Eng, Univ of N AL 1973-; (BS) Lib Sci, Univ of MS 1983; *cr:* Teacher Brooks HS 1978-80, Fairview Jr HS 1981-; *ai:* Beta Club Spon; Tremont Womans Club; *home:* Box 145 Tremont MS 38876

WHITEHEAD, NORMA LEA LUPER, Fourth Grade Teacher; *b:* Owasso, OK; *m:* William Ridgway; *c:* Douglas, Darren; *ed:* (BS) Elem Ed, 1971, (MS) Early Chldhd, 1974 E TX St Univ; *cr:* 4th Grade Teacher Pottsboro Ind Sch Dist 1971-; *ai:* At Risk; Textbook; TX St Teachers Assn Treas 1971-76; Assn of TX Prof Educators 1990; Delta Kappa Gamma Various Comm 1976-; TX St Rdng Assn 1987-; *office:* Pottsboro Ind Sch Dist PO Box 555 Pottsboro TX 75076

WHITEHEAD, SHARON S. (YOUNG), Secondary Mathematics Teacher; *b:* Jamestown, NY; *m:* Michael J.; *c:* Shayne, Jill; *ed:* (AS) Math, Jamestown Comm Coll 1970; (BS) Math, SUNY at Fredonia 1972; (MED) Math Ed, AZ St 1989; *cr:* Math Teacher Marcos De Niza HS 1986-; *ai:* Care Group Facilitator & Mem of Core Team Substance Abuse Prgm; Teachers Teams AZ St Rep 1988-; Parish Cncl Youth Ed Ministry 1988-; Religious Ed Teacher 1965-89; Civil Service Employees Assn Secy 1973-77; Conservatory Dance Bd of Dir 1985-88; Volunteer Work Amer Cancer Society, United Fund, My Sisters Place Shelter for Battered Women; Manpower Advisory Comm; Zonta Club Schlsp; *office:* Marcos De Niza Sch 6000 S Lakeshore Dr Tempe AZ 85283

WHITEHORN, SUE WEBSTER, 4th-6th Grade Math Teacher; *b:* Helena, AR; *m:* Robert B.; *c:* Brian; *ed:* (BSE) Elem Ed, Univ of Cntrl AR 1970; *cr:* 3rd Grade Teacher Lee Elem 1970-1972; 5th Grade Teacher 1972-1976; Migrant Ed Teacher 1976-1977; 3rd Grade Teacher Garland Elem 1977-1988; 4th-6th Grade Math Teacher Clrendon Elem 1988; *ai:* JTPA Rdng Teacher/Tutor Spvr 1988-; Personnel Policy Comm; Math Comm Chairperson; Delta Kappa Gamma 1978-; Clarendon Ed Assn 1976-; AR Ed Assn 1970-; NEA 1970-; *office:* Clarendon Elem Sch 320 N 7th St Clarendon AR 72029

WHITEHOUSE, RAYMOND CHARLES, Biology Teacher; *b:* Boston, MA; *m:* Gail Conti; *c:* John, Kataryn; *ed:* (BS) Bio, 1967, (MS) Sci Ed, 1973 Univ of MA; Doctoral Work Sci Ed, Boston Univ; Curr Writing, Tech Writing, Publications; *cr:* Teacher Cntrl Mid Sch 1967-88, Quincy HS 1988-; *ai:* Quincy HS Vlybl Coach; Yrbk Adv; Prof Assessment Comm; Natl Geographic Society Mem 1960-; NSTA Mem 1967-; Chrstn Ed Comm Chm 1989-; MA Patriots Vlybl Head Coach; Author 1970; Articles Published Vlybl Journals; Involved in Gifted/Talented Curr; *office:* Quincy HS 52 Coddington St Quincy MA 02169

WHITEHURST, BARBARA WOODHOUSE, Sixth Grade Teacher/Dept Chm; *b:* Virginia Beach, VA; *c:* Amon J.; *ed:* (BA) Elem Ed, St Augustines Coll 1963; *cr:* 6th Grade Teacher Princess Anne Elem 1963-68, Malibu Elem 1968-76, Point O View Elem 1976-; *ai:* 6th Grade Dept Chm; VA Ed Assn, NEA, Virginia Beach Ed Assn 1963-; *office:* Point O View Elem Sch 5400 Parliament Dr Virginia Beach VA 23462

WHITELEATHER, DENISE MARIE, Second Grade Teacher; *b:* Findlay, OH; *m:* Larry; *c:* Erin, Allison; *ed:* (BA) Elem Ed, Bowling Green St Univ 1975; *cr:* Elem Supvr/Sec Wood Cty Office of Ed 1975-77; 2nd Grade Teacher E A Powell 1977-; *ai:* Prin Selection & Right to Read Comms; Spring Carnival Co-Chairperson; N Baltimore Ed Assn Building Rep 1977-; Trinity Luth Church Teacher 1987-; Parent Cncl Co-Pres 1988-89; *office:* E A Powell Elem Sch 500 N Main St North Baltimore OH 45872

WHITENER, R. EDGAR, Director of Bands; *b:* High Point, NC; *m:* Karen Pennington; *c:* Shawn Edgar, Rebecca Katherine; *ed:* (BME) Instrumental Music, Appalachian St 1971; Mentor Cert, St of NC; *cr:* Dir of Bands Surry Cty Schls 1971-76; Dean of Stu the Patterson Sch 1977-79; Dir of Bands William Lenoir Mid 1979; *ai:* Bsktbl Time Keeper; Mentor for Beginning Teacher; Co-Chm for Cist Band Sr HS Contest/Festival; Chaperone for Sch Dances; Chm of Sch Music Dept; NEA-NCAE; MENC-NCMEA Pres Dist 3 1973-75; Caldwell Bandmasters Secy-Treas 1982; Zion United Church of Christ (Elder 1986-; Cncl Pres 1987); Comm Mem BSA Troop 254 1976-; Accomplished Teacher Prgm 1988-89; Cmmty Based Alternatives Comm Mem 1989; Church Choir Dir 1988-; *office:* William Lenoir Mid Sch 332 Greenhaven Lenoir NC 28645

WHITESELL, JOAN SNIDER, Computer Teacher; *b:* Lexington, VA; *m:* John Miley; *c:* Terry M., Jon K., Gregory S.; *ed:* (BS) Bus Ed, 1969, (MS) Bus Ed, 1971 Madison Coll; Numerous Cmptr Courses; *cr:* Bus Teacher Parry Mc Cluer HS 1969-71, Lexington HS 1971-89; Cmptr Teacher Parry Mc Cluer HS 1989-; *ai:* FBLA & 9th Grade Class Spon; Dabney S Lancaster Comm Coll Bus Advisory Bd 1986-; VA Ed Information System Assn (Secy, Bd Mem) 1987-; NEA, VA Bus Ed Assn 1969-; *office:* Parry Mc Cluer HS 2329 Chestnut Ave Buena Vista VA 24416

WHITESELL, MARY CLARICE CRISPIN, 7th/8th Grade Math Teacher; *b:* Kansas City, KS; *m:* James; *c:* Joshua, Jessica; *ed:* (BS) Elem, KS St Univ 1971; (MS) Curr/Instuction KS St Univ 1986; Teacher Evaluation Stu Achievement KS Sch Team Trng; *cr:* Kndgtn Teacher Shawnee Mission-Prairie Elem 1970-71; 7th/8th Grade Teacher Green Elem 1972-79, Riley Cty Sch 1979-; *ai:* 8th Grade Spon; Teacher Evaluation; KS Assn Teachers of Math; Riley Cty Educator Assn Pres 1989-; Action Team Chm 1987-; *office:* Riley Cty Grade Sch PO Box 248 Riley KS 66531

WHITEWOOD, LOIS BURNS, English Department Chairperson; *b:* Cleveland, OH; *m:* Fred J. Jr.; *c:* Fred III, Patricia S Knaupp, Vicki A. Ledford, Tammy L.; *ed:* (BM) Music, Sul Ross St Univ 1951; Summer Sch Southwest TX St Univ; TX A&I Univ; *cr:* Teacher Pettus Ind Sch Dist 1958-67; Eng Teacher Fredericksburg Ind Sch Dist 1967-; *ai:* UIL Ready Wrtng Coach; ATPE; NCTE; VFW Voice of Democracy Awd Citation 1982-83; DAV Cert of Appreciation 1980; *home:* Rt 1 Box 97A5A Fredericksburg TX 78624

WHITFORD, JEANNIE ELLEN, Sixth Grade Teacher; *b:* Meyersdale, PA; *ed:* (BS) Elem Ed, Frostburg St Univ 1971; Advanced Trng Credits, Madeline Hunter Inst Williamsburg; *cr:* 5th Grade Teacher 1971-82, 4th Grade Teacher 1982-83, 2nd Grade Teacher 1983-84, 6th Grade Teacher 1984- Meyersdale Area Elem; *ai:* Amer Ed Week Comm 1989-; Open House Comm Chairperson 1988-89; Cheerleading Adv; NEA, PA St Ed Assn, Meyersdale Area Ed Assn 1971-; Local, St, Natl PTA; Meyersdale Church of Brethren 1st Grade Sunday Sch Teacher; Supporter Chrstn Childrens Fund Inc; PRIDE Awd for Excl Teaching 1986-87; *office:* Meyersdale Area Elem Sch RD 3 Meyersdale PA 15552

WHITFORD, LINDA TREANTAFELLOW, English Department Chair; *b:* Sewickley, PA; *m:* Gary A.; *c:* Jeffrey B.; *ed:* (BS) Scndry Ed/Eng, Slippery Rock Univ 1969; (MS) Scndry Ed/Eng, Duquesne Univ 1976; Post BS PA St Univ; Lead Teacher Trng Shippensburg Univ, Schenley Teacher Center; *cr:* Eng Teacher/Teacher of Gifted/Eng Dept Chairperson Ambridge Area HS; *ai:* Ed Sch Dist Brochure; Liaison Comm to Supt; Ed of Cmmty Newsletter; Public Relations Person for Sch Dist; Jr Var Chrldrs, Spon Pep Club, Ftbl Prgm Spon; NEA, PA St Ed Assn 1969-; PA Assn for Gifted & Talented 1980-; PA St Consortium for Comm Skills 1983-; Beaver Cty Teachers of Gifted 1985-; Employee Involvement Team 1989-; Tri St Area Sch Study Cncl 1985-; Amer Cancer Society Volunteer 1985-; Participant SW PA Lead Teachers Governing Bd; Outstanding Young Educators Awd Ambridge Area Jaycees 1971; Mid St Evaluation Teams Rep; Univ Audit Team PA Dept of Ed Mem; *office:* Ambridge Area HS 909 Duss Ave Ambridge PA 15003

WHITFORD, PATRICIA ANNE, Spanish Teacher; *b:* Wakefield, RI; *m:* Gilbert R.; *c:* John, Robert, Melissa; *ed:* (BA) Span Teacher Ed, Univ of RI; (MS) Ed/Human Relations/Span/Italian, E CT St Univ 1983; Ed, Human Relations, Foreign Lang CEU; *cr:* Span/Italian Teacher Warwick Veterans Memorial HS; Span I/II/III Teacher St Bernards HS 1972-84; Span I-IV Teacher Griswold HS 1984-; *ai:* Sr Moderator; Span Act Coord; Philosophy Comm; NEA, CEA, GEA 1984-; Colt 1978-84; BSA Cub & Den Mother & Webelos; Little League Secy; Sr League Secy 1989-; *home:* RFD 1 Box 690 Hyde Park Rd North Franklin CT 06254

WHITLEY, HARRIET COKER, Mathematics Teacher; *b:* Pilot Point, TX; *m:* Tommy J.; *c:* Jade, Evan, Kyle; *ed:* (BS) Ed/Eng, TX Womans Univ 1967; Working Towards Addiction Counseling St Certificate; *cr:* Self-Contained 5th Grade/Chapter I Rdng Teacher Aubrey Mid Sch; 6th/7th Grade Math Teacher Pilot Point Jr HS; *ai:* Concerned Outlook on Life & Graduation Ceremony Coord; Peer Tutoring Prgm; Past Beta Club Spon; TEA, TSTA, CTA; Bus & Prof Womens Club 1980-84; San Antonio TX Sch Bd Convention Speaker 1988; Presented Booklet to Pilot Point Jr HS; *home:* 217 E Mc Kinney St Pilot Point TX 76258

WHITLEY, JAMES, Social Studies Teacher; *b:* Hot Springs, SD; *ed:* (BS) His, Northern St Coll 1973; Grad Stud Ed; *cr:* Soc Stud Teacher Holgate Jr HS 1973-; *ai:* Jr HS Boys Bsktbl; Soc Stud Curr Dev; NEA, AEA 1973-82; BPOE Elks 1976-86; *office:* Holgate Jr HS 2200 N Dakota St Aberdeen SD 57401

WHITLEY, PAMELA KAYE, English Teacher; *b:* Lawton, OK; *ed:* (BA) Psych, 1983, (BA) Eng, 1984 St Marys Univ; (MA) Literature, Univ of Essex 1985; *cr:* Eng Teacher Antonian Coll Preparatory 1986-88, Tom C Clark HS 1988-; *ai:* Great Outdoors Spon; NCTE 1989-; Natl Organization of Women 1988-; *office:* Clark HS 5151 De Zavala Rd San Antonio TX 78249

WHITLOW, FAY RIGHTER, 3rd Grade Teacher; *b:* Norristown, PA; *m:* Clarence M.; *c:* Wendy Murphy, Beth, Scott, Todd; *ed:* (BS) Elem Ed, Univ of PA 1954; (MS) Elem Ed, IN Univ 1972; Rdng Specialist, Rdng Supvr Cert; *cr:* Kndgtn Teacher Oreland 1954-55, Crown Point 1969-72; Rdng Specialist Lebanon 1973-76; 3rd Grade Teacher Fredericksburg 1976-; *ai:* Intl Rdng Assn, Keystone St Rdng Assn, Lancaster Lebanon Rdng Assn 1973-; Cty Honorary Organization 1989-; Fulbright Teacher Exchange England 1990; *office:* Fredericksburg Elem Sch N Pine Grove St Fredericksburg PA 17026

WHITLOW, WANDA CHAMBERS, Mathematics Teacher; *b:* Durham, NC; *m:* Clifton D.; *c:* Scott Morgan, Justin Morgan; *ed:* (BS) Math, Univ of NC Greensboro 1972; Working Toward Masters Degree & Numerous Math & Ed Wkshps; *cr:* Teacher Reidsville Jr HS 1972-75, 1979- Reidsville Sr HS; *ai:* Staff Dev Comm Chairperson; Soc/Courtesy Comm; NCCTM 1984-; NCAE, NEA 1984-86; *home:* 2309 Lemar Dr Reidsville NC 27320

WHITMAN, HARLEY WAYNE, Principal/Eng Teacher/Coach; *b:* Muskogee, OK; *m:* Robin Anne; *c:* Seth Sterling, Micah C., Joel B.; *ed:* Assoc Phys Ed/Health/Safety, Connors St Coll 1980; (BS) Phys Ed/Health/Safety, 1982, (MSED) Phys Ed/Health/Safety 1987 NE St Univ; Supt Certificate Hrs; Federal & St Funding Wkshps; St Teacher Evaluation Wkshps; *cr:* Teacher/Coach Hilldale HS & Mid Sch 1982-86; Teacher/Coach/Prin Midway HS 1986-; *ai:* HS Boys & Girls Bsktbl, HS Girls Vlybl Coach; Athletic Dir; N Canadian Conference Secy 1986-87, Girls Coach of Yr 1989-; OK Bsktbl Coaches Assn 1986-; OK Ed Assn, NEA Local Rep 1982, 1990; OK Girls Bsktbl Assn, OK Scndry Schls Act Assn; Masonic Lodge Worshipful Master 1988, Awd of Excl 1988; Bedovin Shrine Temple Trailblazer Secy 1983-84; Checotah Trailblazers (Secy, Treas) 1983-87; Fred Bear Sports Club; Checotah 1st Baptist Church (Chm of Deacons 1989-, Vice Chm 1988-89); Outstanding Young Men of America 1988; 2 Regional Championships Vlybl; Midway Honorary Chapter Farmer 1988-89; Girls Bsktbl Dist Champions 1988; Outstanding Stu Cncl Spon Hilldale Mid Sch 1984-86; *home:* 506 N Broadway Checotah OK 74426

WHITMAN, JILL TRIPLETT, Kindergarten Teacher; *b:* Lenoir, NC; *m:* Roger W.; *ed:* (AA) Early Chldhd Ed, Wilkes Comm Coll 1976; (BS) Early Chldhd Ed, Appalachian St Univ 1978; *cr:* K-1st Grade Teacher Gamewell Elem Sch 1978-; *ai:* NC Assn of Educators, NEA; Nom Educator of Yr Gamewell Elem 1988-89; *office:* Gamewell Elem Sch Rt 6 Box 274 Lenoir NC 28645

WHITMAN, ROBIN ANNE, English Teacher; *b:* Muskogee, OK; *m:* Harley Wayne; *c:* Seth, Micah, Barrett; *ed:* (AA) Eng, Connors St Coll 1980; (BA) Eng, 1982, (ME) Ed, 1987 Northeastern St Univ; *cr:* Eng Teacher Midway HS 1982-; *ai:* Yrbk, Newspaper, Homecoming & Jr Class Spon; Midway Ed Assn Pres 1987-89; OK Ed Assn Delegate 1987-89; Epsilon Sigma Alpha Public Relations 1984-86; Eastern Star Chaplain 1987-89; *home:* 506 N Broadway Checotah OK 74426

WHITMORE, CRAIG STEVEN, 8th Grade English Teacher; *b:* Ashland, OH; *m:* Dianna Vale; *c:* Heather, Heidi, Jeremy, Hallie; *ed:* (BS) Speech Ed, 1970, (MA) Curr & Instruction, 1986 Ashland Univ; *cr:* 7th Grade Lang Arts Teacher West Holmes Jr HS 1971; Adjunct Instr Radio/TV Ashland Univ 1980-86; Eng/Speech Teacher Ashland Jr HS 1972-; *ai:* Dir Jr HS Drama, Sr HS Thespian Play, Musical; Past Dir Audio-Visual Aids; Coach 8th Grade Power of Pen Interscholastic Writing Team; Instr Creative Comm Gifted Challenge Institute; NEA, OH Ed Assn, NCTE Mem; United Meth Church Certified Lay Speaker 1978-; Martha Holden Jennnings Scholar 1978-79; Published Theatre Ed Assn Magazine 1989; Published Amer & Midwestern Poetry Anthology 1988; *home:* 1558 Southwood Dr Ashland OH 44805

WHITNEY, DEBORAH L., English Teacher; *b:* Farmington, NM; *m:* Chris; *c:* Aaron; *ed:* (BS) Eng, 1971,(MA) Admin, 1978 NM St Univ; *cr:* Eng Teacher Cuba HS 1971-73, Gadsden HS 1973-82, Hermosa Jr HS 1983-86, Farmington HS 1986-; *ai:* Honor Society; NCTE 1971-; Emmanuel Baptist Church; *office:* Farmington H S 2200 Sunset Ave Farmington NM 87401

WHITNEY, JOAN BETTY (LE ROY), Fourth Grade Teacher; *b:* Chicago, IL; *m:* Frank Becht Jr.; *c:* Frank III, Michael K., Jennie E.; *ed:* (BS) His/Elem Ed/Group Sci, 1972, (MA) Jr Coll Teaching/His, 1975 W MI Univ; Assoc Geneaology, Brigham Young Univ 1985; Grad Stud Sci, Provo UT; AIMS; Outdoor Sci Ed; Higgins Lake Outdoor Ed Course; Water Safety Instr & Instr Trainer; *cr:* Secy St Tech Inst 1961-62, Valley Metal Products Company 1962-64, Ford Dealerships 1964-69; 8th Grade Teacher Martin Public Schls 1972-73; 1st/3rd/4th Grade Teacher Gilkey Elem Sch 1973-; *ai:* Coturnix Classroom Project; Class Plays; 4-H Club Leader; Classroom Family Tree Books; Ismond Environmental Laboratory Charter Mem 1973-; Sci Curr Comm 1973-; Soc Stud Curr Comm 1988-; Adv & Chaperone Traverse City & Lansing Sesquicentennial Family Weekend 1987 & Centennial Family Weekend 1976; Bicentennial Comm 1975-76; 2020 Plainwell Advisory Cncl 1989-; Plainwell Ed Assn (Pres, VP, Secy) 1974-88; St of MI Intnl Coturnix Olympics MI St Univ K-4th Grade Supt 1980-; Hillsdale Press Incorporated MI Classroom Materials Advisory Comm 1985; Republican Womens Club Secy 1984-85; MI Jaycette VP 1969-75; MI Jaycee Belize Steel Band Host 1973; Boy Scout Den Leader 1968-70; Amer Red Cross Volunteer; GSA Modeling Wkshp Leader 1980-; Teacher Exch Dominican Republic 1978; Deans Honor List 1970; Dept of Ed Awd of Merit 1980; St of MI Teacher Mini Grant 1989; Gilkey Sch Rdng Grant 1988; Allegan Cty De Lano Fnd & Plainwell Fnd 1989; Wrote, Edited, Published Book 1977-78; Foreign Exch Stu Host Japan 1989; *office:* Gilkey Elem Sch 707 S Woodhams St Plainwell MI 49080

WHITNEY, LINDA HANSEN, Guidance Counselor/Band Dir; *b:* Deadwood, SD; *m:* Steven L.; *c:* Jennifer; *ed:* (BS) Instrumental/Vocal Music, Northern St Coll 1972; (MED) Counseling/Guidance/Personnel Services, SD St Univ 1988; *cr:* K-12th Grade Band/Vocal Music Teacher Timber Lake Sch 1973-75, Pollock Sch 1975-78, New Underwood Sch 1978-80; K-12th Grade Vocal Music Teacher Stanley Cty Sch 1980-83; K-12th Grade Vocal/Band Music Teacher 1984-87, 5th-12th Grade Band Teacher/Guidance Cnslr 1987- Artesian Sch; *ai:* Cheerleading Adv; SDSCA, SDACD (Chapter Secy, Treas) 1989-; SDBA 1984-; City Cncl Trustee 1986-88; *office:* Artesian Sch Dist #55-1 RR 2 Box 88A Artesian SD 57314

WHITNEY, MICHAEL STEPHEN, English Teacher; *b:* Atlanta, GA; *m:* Jane Dempsey; *ed:* (BA) Eng, Univ of S AL 1972; *cr:* Eng Teacher Ernest Ward HS 1982-83, Carver Mid Sch 1983-85, Brownsville Mid Sch 1985-86, Workman Mid Sch 1986-; *ai:* Honors & Awds Comm Membership Workman Mid Sch; Workman Mid Sch Teacher of Yr 1990; *office:* Workman Mid Sch 6299 Lanier Dr Pensacola FL 32504

WHITNEY, PHYLLIS LOUISE (HECKMAN), Choir/General Music Teacher; *b:* Council Bluffs, IA; *m:* William Thomas; *c:* Jason, Heather, Courtney; *ed:* (BM) Voice, Univ of IA 1969; *cr:* Choir Dir Glenwood Jr & Sr HS 1969-70; General Music Teacher/Choir Dir Lewis Cntrl Jr HS & Mid Sch 1970-; *ai:* Swing Choir Dir; Music Curr Comm; IA Music Educators Assn 1970-78; Music Educators Natl Conference 1970-78; Natl Assn of Jazz Educators 1970-74; Service League 1988-89; *office:* Lewis Cntrl Mid Sch 2000 Hwy 275 Council Bluffs IA 51503

WHITSON, ELLISA FRANK, Teacher of Gifted; *b:* Erie, PA; *m:* Ray; *c:* Travis, Jeffrey, Ashlyn; *ed:* (BS) Criminology/Soc Welfare, FL St 1971; Eng, Emotionally Handicapped; *cr:* Itinerant Teacher of Emotionally Handicapped Brevard Sch Bd 1971-72; Teacher of Emotionally Handicapped Mims Elem Sch Bd 1972-77, Apollo Elem Sch Bd 1977-78; Teacher of Emotionally Handicapped 1978-83, Teacher of Gifted Eng/Soc Stud 1983- Jackson Mid Sch; *ai:* Ex Ed Dept Chm; Guidance Comm Chm; LEA Rep; *office:* Jackson Mid Sch 1515 Knox Mc Rae Dr Titusville FL 32780

WHITSON, MARILYN MURPHREE, Second Grade Teacher; *b:* Birmingham, AL; *m:* Hershel Daniel; *c:* Dana, Matthew; *ed:* (BS) Elem Ed, Univ of Montevallo 1968; (MA) Elem Ed, Univ of AL Birmingham 1983; *cr:* 3rd Grade Teacher W Decatur Elem 1968-72; 2nd Grade Teacher Tri-Cty Bible Sch 1979-; *ai:* Geography Bee/Spelling Bee/Sci Fair Spon; Kappa Kappa Iota (VP, Treas, Secy 1971-84), Schlshp Further Ed 1981; *office:* Tri-City Bible Sch 2159 Beltline Rd SW Decatur AL 35601

WHITSON, MARY M., Fifth Grade Teacher; *b:* Santa Monica, CA; *ed:* (BS) Eng, 1968; (MED) Ed, 1970 CA Polytechnic St Univ; *cr:* Elem Teacher Shelyn Elem Schl 1969-; *ai:* PTA Bd - Teacher Rep; Young Achievers Math Club Adv; Phi Kappa Phi; Assn of Rowland Elem Segment Educators Dir 1989-; Natl Wildlife Fed; Leag of Women Voters; Common Cause; Mentor Teacher - Project Wild - 3 Years; *office:* Shelyn Elem Sch 19500 Nacora St Rowland Heights CA 91748

WHITT, ARVILLE PHILIP, Biology & Phys Science Teacher; *b:* Cedar Bluff, VA; *m:* Claudia Mae; *c:* Philip R., Jefrey J., Daniel L., Elizabeth K. Bruan; *ed:* (BAED) Soc Stud, 1959, (MA) Bio, 1971 Pacific Luth Univ; Philosophy of Chrstin Ed; Entomology; ITIP; Geography Seminar; Management; *cr:* Teacher Gault Jr HS 1959-67; Part Time Teacher 1968-88, Teacher 1988- Tacoma Baptist Schls; *ai:* 9th Grade & Juggling Club Adv; Sci Fair Coord; Asst Summer Admin; WEA, NEA 1967-59; USAF Reserve (Adv Cncl 1963-66, Career Cnslr 1973-), NCO of Yr 1965; H P Baptist Church (Deacon, Trustee) 1986-; NSF Grant 1962-63; Article in Whos Who in the Zoo; *office:* Tacoma Baptist Schls 2052 S 64th St Tacoma WA 98407

WHITT, SHIRLEY ANN ROBINSON, Reading Teacher; *b:* Ashland, KY; *m:* Clyde Jr.; *ed:* (BS) Voc Home Ec, 1967, Elem Ed, 1974, (Rank I) Elem Ed, 1990 Morehead St Univ; *cr:* Sci Teacher Breathitt Cty HS 1968-69; Home Ec Teacher Hazard HS 1969-71; Elem Teacher Garner Elem 1975-; *ai:* Garner Elem Spelling Bee Coach; E KY Ed Assn Instructional Conference Coord; Boyd Co Prof Evaluation Review Comm Mem; NEA, KY Ed Assn Mem 1975-; E KY Ed Assn (Pres 1988-89, Mem 1975-); Delta Kappa Gamma 1988-; Garner Elem PTA Pres 1986-87; Pres of Boyd Cty Ed Assn 1982-86; KY Commonwealth Inst for Teachers Participant 1986; KY Educl Fnd Grant 1987; Chm Boyd Cty Report Card Revision Comm 1985; Boyd Cty Transportation Study Comm Mem 1985; Sch Facilities Study Comm 1987-88; *office:* Garner Elem School 19231 St Rt 3 Rush KY 41168

WHITTAKER, SUSAN ROYALL, English/Speech/Drama Teacher; *b:* Richlands, VA; *m:* Randall Bert; *c:* Mary B., Matthew B.; *ed:* (BS) Lang Art, Bluefield St Coll 1973; *cr:* Eng Teacher Honaker HS 1973-74, Richlands Mid Sch 1974-77, Tazewell Mid Sch 1977-85; Eng/Speech/Drama Teacher Tazewell HS 1985-; *ai:* Forensic & Drama Coach; 9th Grade Spon; NEA, VA Ed Assn, Tazewell Ed Assn, VA Assn of Eng Teachers; Delta Kappa Gamma, Tazewell Cty Youth Bd; Teacher of Yr Tazewell HS 1989; Tazewell Rotary Clubs Voc Service Awd 1989; *office:* Tazewell HS 1986 Bulldog Ln Tazewell VA 24651

WHITTEMORE, GEORGE CHARLES, Physics Teacher; *b:* Laconia, NH; *m:* Sandra C.; *c:* Sarah; *ed:* (BS) Math/Physics, KSC & Univ of NH 1977; (MED) Univ of MA Amherst; Grad Stud Physics, WPI & Clark Univ; *cr:* Physics Instr Worcester Acad 1978-87, Leominster HS 1987-; *ai:* Var Ftbl & Bsktbl Coach; Stu Faculty Senate Adv; Academic Decathlon Team Coach; AAPT 1978-; Nom Presidential Awd Excl in Sci & Math Teaching; Most Outstanding Sci Teacher Awd 1988; Worcester Acad Yrbk Dedication 1987; *office:* Leominster HS 122 Granite St Leominster MA 01453

WHITTEN, EFFIE, Creative Writing Teacher; *b:* Acworth, GA; *ed:* (BA) Ed, Villa Madonna Coll 1949; (MED) Ed, Xavier Univ 1954; Lib Certificate, Villa Madonna Coll 1964; Speech, CA St Coll Fullerton 1968; *cr:* Jr HS Teacher Cath Schls in KY 1936-60, Cath Schls in CO & IL 1960-63, 1969-72; Prin Schls in KY 1950-1965; Teacher Villa Madonna Acad 1989-; *ai:* Speech Tournaments & Creative Writing Judge; 4-H Club Leader; Cath Knights of OH 1972-89, Plaques to Schls; CA St Coll Fullerton Grant 1968; *home:* 2500 Amsterdam Rd Villa Hills KY 41017

WHITTEN, GAIL MC GEOCH, 5th Grade Teacher; *b:* Cambridge, NY; *m:* Joseph Lee; *c:* Miriam E.; *ed:* (BS) Chrstn Ed, Bob Jones Univ 1961; (MED) Elem Ed, Univ of Montevallo 1978; Adult Ed, Univ of AL; *cr:* 3rd-5th Grade Teacher Pensacola Chrstn Sch 1964-71; 4th Grade Teacher Panama City Chrstn Sch 1971-73; 5th Grade Teacher Alliance Chrstn Sch 1973-74; 3rd Grade Teacher Ragland HS 1977-80; 5th/6th Grade Teacher Saint Clair Cty HS 1980-; *ai:* SAE Spon; 4-H Leader; Elem Wkshp Comm; Adult Basic Ed Teacher 1977-84; Saint Clair Cty Ed Assn, AL Ed Assn 1977-; PTO Prgm Chm 1986-; Delta Kappa Gamma Treas 1987-; Bethel Baptist Church (Pianist, Sunday Sch Teacher) 1980-; 4-H Club Leader 1984-, Cty Leader of Yr 1986-87; Wm J Calvert Writers Club 1988-; Saint Clair Cty HS Teacher of Yr 1983-85; 4-H Club of Yr 1986-87, 1988-89; *home:* 104 3rd Ave Bartlett Odenville AL 35120

WHITTEN, JOSEPH LEE, Media Specialist; *b:* Bryant, AL; *m:* Gail Mc Geoch; *c:* Miriam E.; *ed:* (BA) Speech Interpretation, Bob Jones Univ 1960; (MED) Counseling, Univ of Montevallo 1977; *cr:* Teacher/Librarian St Clair Cty HS 1961-70, Private Schls 1970-74; Teacher/Cnslr St Clair Cty HS 1974-86; Media Specialist St Clair Cty Elem Sch 1986-; *ai:* NEA, AL Ed Assn, SEA 1961-; William J Calverty Writers Club Vice Chm 1989-; Bethel Baptist Church Mem; Poems & Book Published; Whos Who in AL 1971; *home:* PO Box 125 Odenville AL 35120

WHITTEN, MICHAEL VERN, Mathematics Teacher; *b:* Evansville, IN; *m:* Karen E. Dillon; *c:* Brittney R.; *ed:* (BS) Phys Ed, Oakland City Coll 1986; *cr:* Teacher Pike Cntrl HS 1986-; *ai:* Var Cross Cntry, Asst Var Bsbl, Frosh Bsktbl Coach; Organizer Pike 4-H 5K Road Race 1988-; Consultant Petersburg Harvest

Days 5K Road Race; IN Assn of Track & Cross Cntry Coaches 1989-; IN Bsktbl Coaches Assn 1986-; Hoosier Bsktbl Coaches Assn 1987-; Optimists Intnl 1988-89; *home:* 122 S 2nd Ave Oakland City IN 47660

WHITTEN, SANDRA ELAINE, English Teacher; *b:* Newcastle, IN; *m:* William B. II; *c:* Jennifer, Amanda, Emily; *ed:* (BA) Eng/Soc Sci, Centre Coll 1969; Eng/Soc Sci Rdng, Univ SUNY; *cr:* Eng/Soc Stud Teacher Lincoln Jr HS 1970-71, East Mid Sch 1971-75; Eng Teacher Guilderland Cntrl HS 1975-76; Farnsworth Mid Sch 1976-78; *ai:* Lang Arts Curr Comm; NCTE; NJCTE; NJCTSS; AAUW; Girl Scout Leader 1987-89; Phi Alpha Theta His Honorary; Comm Service United Methodist Church; *home:* 31 Rambling Brook Dr Holmdel NJ 07733

WHITTENBARGER, BIANCA M., Math Department Chairperson; *b:* Copperhill, TN; *ed:* (AA) Music Ed, Truett Mc Connell Coll 1978; (BS) Mid Grades Ed, Brenau Coll 1981; (MED) Mid Grades Ed, W GA Coll 1988; Cert Interrelated Spec Ed; Teacher Evaluation Trng; GA Teacher Evaluation Instrument Trng; *cr:* Teacher Ellijay Elem 1981-83, Fannin Cty HS 1983-84, Remount Road Elem 1984-85, Eastbrook Mid Sch 1985-; *ai:* Mathcounts Coach; PTA, NCTM 1980-; Phi Delta Kappa 1985-; *office:* Eastbrook Mid Sch 700 Hill Rd Dalton GA 30721

WHITTENBURGER, NANCY GULLEY, Music Consultant/Instructor; *b:* Atlanta, GA; *m:* William L.; *c:* Ashley, Valerie; *ed:* (BMUSED) Ed/Voice Concentration, 1971, (MMUSED) Ed/Voice Concentration, 1972 GA St Univ; Cert Independent Study Music & Spec Ed; *cr:* Elem Music Teacher Flat Shoals Elem & Wadsworth Elem 1972-74; K-5th Grade Music Teacher Woodward Acad 1974-77; Music Dir Chapel Heights Baptist Church 1975-81; Music Instr Tarrant Cty Jr Coll 1981-84; Choral Dir/Drama Teacher Alexander HS 1987-89; *ai:* Teach Private Voice & Piano Lessons; Direct Rock Baptist Church Youth & Adult Choirs; Former Choral & Drama Instr; GMEA 1987-; ACDA 1987-, 2 Stus Chosen Natl Jr HS Honors Choir; Mu Phi Epsilon-Alumnae 1969-; PTA; Douglas Cty System Revise HS Music Curr Consultant; Teacher of Month 1987; Alexander HS Teacher of Semester 1988; *home:* 5645 Milam Rd Fairburn GA 30213

WHITTIER, JENNIFER JACKSON, English/Spanish Teacher; *b:* Brookhaven, MS; *m:* Gregory M.; *c:* Lindsey, Carly; *ed:* (BS) Span, MS St Univ 1972; *cr:* Teacher Shivers Jr HS 1972-74, Alexander Jr HS 1974-78, Brookhaven HS 1978-80, Loyd Star HS 1980-; *ai:* Lincoln Cty Schls Staff Dev Comm; MS Prof Educators; STAR Teacher 1984, 1985, 1989; Lincoln Cty Teacher of Yr 1988; MTAI Certified; *office:* Loyd Star HS Rt 3 Box 486 Brookhaven MS 39601

WHITTINGTON, LONA TERESA, English/Drama Teacher; *b:* Cincinnati, OH; *m:* Leslie Max; *c:* Brandy, Cody; *ed:* (BA) Eng 1968, (MA) His Magna Cum Laude, 1976 Sul Ross St Univ; Spec Ed, GA Sourthern; Drama, Univ of TX El Paso; *cr:* Special Ed Teacher Presidio ISD 1970-71; Therapist Ed Service Center 1978-79; Behavior Disorders Teacher Mcintosh ISD 1979-81; Eng/Drama/His Teacher Fort Hancock ISD 1981-; *ai:* UIL Coord Drama Club Spon Jr/Sr Class Spon; Comm Chair Person Gifted & Talented Selection Comm; Mem Lib Comm; Drug Free Sch Comm; 4-H Leader; Eastern Star; Whos Who in Bicentennial Yr 1976; Whos Who in the South 1976; the Road of Sorrow Published 1976; *office:* Ft Hancock H S P O Box 98 Fort Hancock TX 79839

WHITTINGTON, LORIN DALE, Choral Dir/Cultural Arts Chair; *b:* Baltimore, MD; *ed:* (BM) Choral Music Ed, Appalachian St Univ 1979; NC Summer Inst of Choral Art; *cr:* Music Teacher Hall Fletcher Mid Sch 1979-81; Chorus Master Mid-Atlantic Opera Company 1985-86; Choral Dir Owen HS 1981-; Music Dir 1st Chrstn Church 1989-; *ai:* Cultural Arts Chm 1984-90; Sch Improvement & Writing Across Curr Comm; NEA, NCAE, MENC 1979-; Lions Club 1990; 1st Chrstn Church 1989-; Owen HS Teacher of Yr 1989-; Adjudicator E TN Vocal Music Assn Festival 1989; *office:* Owen HS 730 Old US 70 Swannanoa NC 28778

WHITTINGTON, SHIRLEY MORRIS, Chemistry Teacher; *b:* Estill County, KY; *m:* C. Robin; *c:* James R.; *ed:* (BS) Sci Ed, 1967, (MS) Sci Ed, 1970 Radford 1niv; VA Dept of Ed Dev Applied Phys Sci 1987-88, Standards of Learning 1980-86; *cr:* General Sci St Paul Intermediate Sch 1967-68, Hillsville HS 1968-69, Hillsville Intermediate Schl 1969-70; Physics/Chem Teacher 1970-88, Chem Teacher 1988- Carroll Cty HS; *ai:* Teams Co-Coach 1990; Sci Fair Chairperson 1989-; VA Ed Assn (Delegate 1969-79) 1967-; Carroll Ed Assn (Comm Chm 1969-79) 1967-; Delta Kappa Gamma Society Intnl Comms Chairperson 1872-; NEA (Delegate 1975, Mem) 1967-; Honored Amer Optical Society Inclusion Statewide Seminar 1982; *office:* Carroll Cty HS P O Box 1268 Hillsville VA 24343

WHITTLE, DOROTHY DOUGLAS, 8th Grade English Teacher; *b:* Cagayan Misamis, The Philippines; *w:* Jay F. (dec); *c:* Jeff, Doug, Beth W. Ipchurch, Wendy W. Kieutz; *ed:* (BS) Home Ec Ed, FL St Univ 1953; (MS) Supervision/Admin, Nova Univ 1977; Univ of West FL; Pensacola Jr Coll; Univ of FL; FL St Univ; FL Writing Project; *cr:* Voc Home Ec Ed Blount Jr HS 1953-55; Asst Home Demonstration Agent Santa Rosa Cty FL 1955; 6th Grade Teacher Oakhurst Elem 1966; 4th Grade Teacher Berryhill Elem 1966-68; JJ Elem 1968-73; Ft Clarke Mid Sch 1973-84; 8th Grade Teacher Mebane Mid Sch 1984-; *ai:* Clowning Club; Dept Chm Lang Arts; FL Cncl of Teachers of Eng; Alachua Cty Teachers of Eng (Sec Laison Officer) NCTE; Natl Writing Project; FL Writing Project; Alachua Cncl of Mid Sch Teachers; Univ Luth Church Mem; Consultant FL Writing Project; Article Published Idea Factory; Presentations at St Meetings; *home:* 2110 NW 51st Terr Gainesville FL 32605

WHITTLESEY, HOWARD L., Music Dept Head/Choral Instr; *b:* Muskogee, OK; *m:* Colleen J. Guyer; *c:* Leah, Edwin, Nathan, Myron; *ed:* (BED) Music, Northwest MO St Univ 1968; (MME) Music Ed, Univ MO Kansas City 1974; General Music & Cmptr Wkshps, IN St Univ; *cr:* 7th-12th Grade Choral Teacher South Page Comm Sch/Coll 1968-71; 9th-12th Grade Choral Teacher Charleston HS 1971-72; 7th-12th Grade Choral Teacher Oak Grove Comm Sch 1972-75, N Miami Comm Sch 1975-; *ai:* Tri M Spon; Drama Dir; Thespian Spon; Jr HS Track Coach; Amer Chroal Dir Assn Life Mem; NEA Life Mem; IN St Teachers Assn; *office:* North Miami Jr-Sr HS R R 1 Denver IN 46926

WHITWELL, MARTHA VEAZEY, Chemistry/Physics Teacher; *b:* Memphis, TN; *m:* Robert Q. Sr.; *c:* Quentin, Fletcher; *ed:* (BSE) Bio/Chem, Delta St Univ 1968; (MSC) Bio/Chem, Univ of MS 1971; *cr:* Sci/Physics Teacher Coahoma Cty HS 1968-69; Chem/Physics Teacher Oxford HS 1969-71; Sci Teacher North Delta Acad 1971-72; Chem/Physics Teacher SBEC 1978-85, Oxford HS 1986-; *ai:* JETS Teams, MS Math, Sci Competition Team Coach; Chem Olympiad Spon; Delta Kappa Gamma 1987-; Tri Delta Alumnae Schlsp Chairperson; URF; MS Jr Tennis Cncl Ranking Chairperson; Outstanding Young Educator; OH St STAR Teacher; St STAR Teacher; *office:* Oxford HS Bramlett Blvd Oxford MS 38655

WHITWORTH, BETTY ALLEN, 6th Grade Teacher; *b:* Mc Daniels, KY; *m:* David; *c:* Karen S. Williams; *ed:* (BA) Elem Ed, KY Wesleyan Coll 1980; Elem Ed, W KY Univ 1984; Creative Writing, Famous Writers Sch 1969; *cr:* 6th Grade Teacher Ben Johnson Elem 1980-; *ai:* Natl Jr Beta Club Spon; Sch Newspaper Faculty Adv; KY Colonel Lifetime Mem 1976; St Comm Help Write Book of Spelling Act Used by All Public Schls in KY.

WHITWORTH, BRECK HOWARD, Science Teacher/Football Coach; *b:* Folley, AL; *m:* Frances Kay Kelly; *c:* Danielle, Garrett; *ed:* (BS) Athletic Admin/Coaching, 1977, (MS) Health/Phys Ed, 1980 Univ of S MS; AA Certificate in General Sci; *cr:* Head Ftbl Coach/General Sci Teacher Enterprise HS 1977-80, Beat Four HS 1980-83; Asst Ftbl Coach/General Sci Teacher Forrest Cty Ag HS 1983-; *ai:* Offensive/Defensive Linemen & Strength Ftbl Coach; *office:* Forrest Cty Ag HS P O Box 9 Brooklyn MS 39425

WHITWORTH, BRYAN TRUMAN, Teacher/Science Dept Chairman; *b:* Dexter, NM; *m:* Constance J. Denaro; *ed:* (AA) Bio, Hartnell; Teaching Credential Sci, Fresno Pacific Col; *cr:* 7th-78th Grade Sci Teacher Parlier HS; *ai:* Jr & Sci Club Adv; Amer Entomological Society 1972-; Assn of Vector Ecologists 1971-; USPHS Medal of Merit 1970; Wrote Sci Vocabulary Exercises; *home:* 516 S Spruce Tulare CA 93274

WHITWORTH, CATHY MASON, Jr/Sr HS Vocal Director; *b:* Sullivan, MO; *m:* Robert; *c:* Thomas; *ed:* (BS) Music Ed, Univ of MO Columbia 1970; Grad Study, Univ of MO Kansas City; *cr:* Vocal Dir Lincoln Co R-III Sch 1970-76, Crawford Co R-I Sch 1976-77; Elem Music Teacher Bourbon Elem Sch 1977-79; Vocal Dir Lincoln Co R-III Sch 1979-; *ai:* Sch Musical & HS Show Choir Dir; Amer Choral Dir Assn 1975-; Music Educators Natl Conference, MO Music Educators Assn 1970-; Carillon Music Club Dir 1970-; Show Choir Selected to Perform at Intnl Kiwanis Convention; Concert Choir Selected to Perform at Disneyworld; *office:* Lincoln Co R-III Sch 711 W College Troy MO 63379

WIATREK, DEBORAH KOTARA, Speech/English Teacher; *b:* Karnes City, TX; *m:* Archie Paul; *c:* Dawn E., Christopher P.; *ed:* (BS) Speech Comm 1980, (MA) Speech Comm 1983 Southwest TX St Univ; *cr:* Instr Southwest TX St Univ 1980-82, Palo Alto Coll 1986-87, Bee Cty Coll 1989; Teacher Falls City HS 1980-; *ai:* Team & Lincoln Douglas Debate, Informative & Persuasive Speaking, Oral Interpretation Coach; One Act Play Dir Sr HS; Drama Club & Speech Team Spon; Jr HS Speaking Events Ready Writing; TX Educl Theatre Assn 1981-; NCTE 1980-; TX Speech Comm Assn 1986-: Blessed Sacrament Church (Dir Religious Ed 1986-, Youth Ministry Leader 1987-); 4-H Adult Leader 1983-; 4-H Gun Club Adult Leader 1985-; Catholic Daughters Trustee 1986-88; Thesis; Optometry Journal Article; ERIC System Entry Paper Presented Intnl Speech Comm Convention; Journal of Thought Article; Notable Women TX 1984; *office:* Falls City Sch P O Box 399 Falls City TX 78113

WIATROWSKI, JO ANN GAUTHIER, French/English Teacher; *b:* Buffalo, NY; *m:* Christopher R.; *c:* Rachel A., Kyle E.; 0 *ed:* (BS) Scndry Ed/Fr/Eng, Buffalo St Coll 1978; (MED) Scndry Ed, St Univ of NY Buffalo 1982; *cr:* Grad Asst St Univ of NY Buffalo 1980-82; Substitute Teacher Iroquois Cntrl 1982-85; Fr Teacher West Seneca West HS 1984; Eng/Fr Teacher Immaculata Acad 1985-; *ai:* Immaculata Acad Drama Dir & Literary Magazine Moderator; Immaculata Acad Class of 88 Yrbk Dedication; *home:* 23 Rollingwood Dr Lancaster NY 14086

WICH, JOHN JOSEPH, Computer Science/Math Teacher; *b:* St Louis, MO; *c:* David, Michele, Laura; *ed:* (BS) Ec, 1966, (MA) Ed, 1974, (MBA) Bus, 1979 St Louis Univ; Cmptr Sci, Meramec Comm Coll; *cr:* Math Teacher Bishop Du Bourg HS 1966-67; Transportation Officer US Army 1967-70; Math/Cmptr Sci Teacher Oakville Jr HS 1970-; *ai:* Cmptr Club & Math Contest Spon; Track & Field Coach; NEA, MO Ed Assn 1974-; Mehlville Cmmty Teachers Assn (Pres 1985-86, Mem 1970-, Chief Negotiator 1988-89); Mehlville Teacher Advocate 1986; Delegate to St & Natl Conventions 1985-; *office:* Oakville Jr HS 5950 Telegraph Rd Saint Louis MO 63129

WICHMANN, JOAN VESPER, 5th Grade Teacher-Math Dept; *b:* Ft Thomas, KY; *m:* Charles J. Jr.;; *c:* Karen, Charles J. III; *ed:* (BA) Elem Ed, Coll of Mt St Joseph 1968; Grad Work Coll of Mt St Joseph & Xavier Univ; *cr:* 5th Grade Lang Art Teacher Washington Park Cincinnati Pub 1968-70; 3rd Grade Teacher, 5th Grade Teacher St Dominic; *ai:* Math Coord; 5th/6th Grade Knowledge Master Open Coach; Coord Parish CCD Prgm; Greater Cincinnati of Teachers of Math 1989-; OH Cath Ed Assn 1985-; Greater Cincinnati Fnd Grant for Art; *office:* St Dominic Sch 371 Pedretti Cincinnati OH 45238

WICKERSHAM, HUBERT ELTON, JR., Social Studies Teacher; *b:* Charleston, TX; *m:* Nelia C. Humphries; *c:* James B., Teresa L. Wickersham Mc Donaldson, Shelly D., Kyle E.; *ed:* (BS) Soc Sci, 1967, (ME) Elem Ed, 1970 East TX St Univ; Real Estate Broker Commercial Coll; Sch of Theology Southwestern Seminary; *cr:* US Army 1953-55; Dept Mgr A&P Grocery 1955-56; Clerk Corp Court City of Dallas 1956-65; Soc Stud Teacher Garland Ind Schls 1967-; *ai:* Intramural Sports Dir; His Textbook Comm; Dept Head Soc Stud Dept; Comm for Writing Amer His Curr Guide; Garland Ed Assn Treas 1967-; TX St Teachers Assn 1967-; NEA 1967-; Lions Club 1970-80; Eastern Hills Baptist Deacon 1975-; *office:* Bussey Mid Sch 1204 Travis Garland TX 75042

WICKHAM, BRIAN L., Mathematics Teacher; *b:* Roseburg, OR; *ed:* (BS) Math/Speech/Drama/Ed, Southern OR 1970; Univ of OR, Univ of NM, Portland St Univ; *cr:* Math Teacher Coffenberry Jr HS 1970-82, Molalla HS 1982-83, Fremont Jr HS 1983-; *ai:* Math Chm; TALC Mem; Wrestling & Ftbl Coach; Planning Commissioner 1980-82; *office:* Fremont Jr HS 850 W Keady Ct Roseburg OR 97470

WICKKISER, JOHN D., English/Phys Ed Teacher; *b:* Detroit, MI; *m:* Rosanna; *c:* Vanessa, Nicholas; *ed:* (BS) Eng, Univ of ND 1966; (MS) Phys Ed/Physiology, St Cloud St Univ 1974; *cr:* Eng/Phys Ed Teacher & Track/Gym Coach Great Falls HS 1966-68; Eng/Phys Ed Teacher & Track Coach Schweinfurt Jr HS 1968-71; Eng/Phys Ed Teacher & Track/Cross Cntry Voach Vicenza HS 1971-73, Aviano HS 1974-; *ai:* Head Track, Cross Cntry Coach; Articles Published on Masters Thesis; *office:* Aviano HS Box 649 APO New York NY 09293

WICKS, LEANN GEHRKE, Librarian; *b:* Cottonwood, ID; *m:* Dwight Earl; *ed:* (BA) Elem Ed, Lewis-Clark St Coll 1974; Media Endorsement; *cr:* CH I Aide 1974-76, 1st Grade Teacher 1976-84 Clearwater Valley Elem; Media Specialist Clearwater Valley Elem & Jr HS 1984-; *ai:* Jr HS Girls Track Coach; Big Cedar Cmmty Secy 1982-84; Big Cedar Extention Secy 1986-87; *office:* Clearwater Valley Elem Sch Box 100 Kooskia ID 83539

WICKS, NANCY INGRAM, 4th Grade Teacher; *b:* Louisville, MS; *m:* Felix; *c:* Maurice, Monique; *ed:* (BA) Elem Ed, MVSU 1969-73; *cr:* 4th Grade Teacher Hughes Elem Sch 1974-; *ai:* Sunday Sch Teacher; MS Assn of Educators 1974-; Columbus Assn of Ed Teacher of Yr 1987-88, Certificate 1988; GSA Leader; *home:* Rt 1 Box 330-A Columbus MS 39701

WICZEN, LINDA WHITING, Third Grade Teacher; *b:* Youngstown, OH; *m:* Steven C.; *c:* Scott, Brandon; *ed:* (BS) Elem Ed, Youngstown St Univ 1972; (MA) Elem Ed, OH Univ 1983; *cr:* 1st/2nd Grade Teacher 1972-73, 2nd Grade Teacher 1974-77 Noble Local Schls; 3rd Grade Teacher Tri-Valley Schls 1977-; *ai:* Bargaining Team Tri-Valley Ed Assn; Mentor Teacher Comm; Inservice Planning Comm; Tri-Valley Ed Assn Pres 1988-; *office:* Tri-Valley Schls 1318 Main St Dresden OH 43821

WIDENER, LARRY DEAN, Band Director; *b:* Seattle, WA; *m:* Glenna R. Eymann; *ed:* (AA) Music, Los Medanos Coll 1982; (BA) Music Ed, CA St Univ Fresno 1985; *cr:* Band Dir Tulare Western HS 1988-89, Antioch HS 1989-; *ai:* Band Club Adv; Amer Fed of Musicians 1984-; Intnl Assn of Jazz Educators 1988-; CMEA, MENC, CBDA 1988-; Prof Musician Mem Sharp 9 Vocal Jazz Ensemble; *office:* Antioch HS 700 W 18th St Antioch CA 94509

WIDMAN, CONNIE MARIE, First Grade Teacher; *b:* Bucyrus, OH; *ed:* (BA) Soc Stud, Mary Manse Coll 1973; *cr:* 1st Grade Teacher Holy Trinity Sch 1973-; *ai:* NCEA 1973-; NCEA 1973-; Church (Liturgy Comm Chairperson, Parish Cncl Rep, Choir Mem).

WIDSTRAND, CHRISTINE (BOARDMAN), Nursery School Teacher; *b:* Chicago, IL; *m:* Randall Edward; *c:* Katie L., Eric J., Bryan J., Lauren K.; *ed:* (BA) Ed/Music, Concordia Coll 1978; *cr:* 1st-2nd Grade Teacher Salem Luth Sch 1978-80; Nursery Class Teacher St John Luth Sch 1989-; *ai:* Church Choir Dir & Youth Cnslr; Piano & Flute Instr; *home:* 2025 178th St Lansing IL 60438

WIECK, ELAINE HODGES, Rdng/Latin/Japanese Teacher; *b:* Victoria, TX; *m:* Richard Barry; *c:* Valerie A., Elizabeth F.; *ed:* (BSED) Elem Ed, 1965, (MED) Elem Ed, 1968 Univ of Houston; (EDD) Rdng/Ed, Univ of N CO 1972; *cr:* 1st Grade Teacher 1965-68, Title I Teacher 1968-76 Alvin Public Schls; Title I Teacher Greeley Public Schls 1970-72; Asst Professor Univ of NE Lincoln 1972-76; Rdng/Latin/Japanese Teacher Cntrl Cath Jr-Sr HS 1977-; *ai:* Asst Vlybl, Bsktbl Coach; 7th Grade Girls NHS, Gifted & Talented Group, Jr Classical League, Jr HS Newspaper Citizen Bee, Geography Bee, Knowledge Bowl Spon; Intnl Rdng Assn, Cntrl NE Rdng Assn, NE Rdng Assn; Volunteer Line-Help-Line 1990; Handbell Choir 1989-; Continental Gardens Home Owners Assn Bd Rep 1990; Blessed Sacrament Cath Church Parish Cncl; CO St Cncl of Intnl Rdng Assn Outstanding Research Awd 1972; Outstanding Educator 1987; Grand Island Amer Assn of Univ Women; NCEA Scndry Sch Dept; Amer Cath Scndry Ed

Awd 1988; Univ of NE Teachers Coll Freda Battey Distinguished Educator Awd 1990; *office:* Cntrl Cath Jr-Sr HS 1200 N Ruby Grand Island NE 68803

WIEGAND, JUDITH LAPEN, Mathematics Department Chair; *b:* New York, NY; *m:* Steven; *c:* Adam, Jon, Mark; *ed:* (BA) Math, Gettysburg Coll 1963; (MS) Math, NY Polytechnic Inst 1969; *cr:* Math Teacher Patchogue Medford Sch Dist 1964-69; Math Asst Professor Suffolk Comm Coll 1981-; Math Chairperson/Teacher Suffolk Luth Sch 1985-; *ai:* Sr Class Adv; Graduation & Honors Comms; Sigma XI 1969-; NY St Math Teachers Assn, Assn Math Teachers; Colloquoy Luth Teacher Concordia Coll 1988; *office:* Suffolk Luth Sch Moriches Rd & Woodlawn Ave Saint James NY 11780

WIEGEL, A. JEANNE CRINES, Language Art Teacher; *b:* Orange, NJ; *m:* Richard Andrew; *c:* Richard A., Seton O'Neil, John J.; *ed:* Ed, Seton Hall Univ 1955-57; (BA) Soc Stud, Montclair St 1977; (BA) Elem Ed, Kean Coll 1979; *cr:* 5th-8th Grade Teacher Our Lady of Lourdes 1955-64, 1973-74; 6th-8th Grade Soc Stud Teacher Holy Name Sch 1974-77; K-6th Grade Title I Teacher Washington Sch & Our Lady of Lourdes 1977-81; Lang Art Teacher/5th-8th Grade Coord St Cassian Sch 1981-; *ai:* Yrbk Moderator; Transition Adv; 8th Grade Graduation Entertainment; Bicentennial Comm; NCEA 1981-; Developed Soc Stud Curr For Holy Name Sch; Wrote Lang Art Curr for Archdiocese of Newark Evaluation Team Mem; Cath Schls Week Chairperson; *home:* 58 Ridgeway Ave West Orange NJ 07052

WIEGREFFE, TYBA GILLILAND, Fifth Grade Teacher; *b:* Livingston, TX; *m:* Roger Watson; *c:* Emmitt W., Ronnie W.; *ed:* (BS) Elem Ed, 1968, (MED) Admin/Supervision, 1983 Sam Houston St Univ; *cr:* 5th Grade Teacher Huntsville Ind Sch Dist 1968-69; 2nd Grade Teacher 1969-78, 5th Grade Teacher 1978- Livingston Ind Sch Dist; *ai:* Grade Level Chairperson; *office:* Livingston Elem Sch 701 N Willis Livingston TX 77351

WIEHE, JAMES MICHAEL, History Teacher; *b:* Harrisburg, PA; *m:* Deborah Lynn; *c:* Kerry M., Kristin M.; *ed:* (BS) His/Health Ed, IN St Univ 1969; (MS) His, Penn St 1990; Educl Classes; *cr:* Teacher David Brearley HS 1969-70, Harrisburg Schls 1970-71, Susquenita HS 1978-; *ai:* HS Var Bsbl Coach; PA St Educl Assn, NEA 1979-; *office:* Susquenita HS 1765 Schoolhouse Rd Duncannon PA 17020

WIEHE, KARL STEPHEN, Teacher; *b:* Hastings On Hudson, NY; *m:* Kathleen Tunney; *c:* Scott, David, Caroline; *ed:* (BA) Ec, Manhattan Coll 1963; (MA) Math, Columbia Univ Teachers Coll 1969; *cr:* Math Teacher Edgemont HS 1966-71, Haviland Jr HS 1971-; *ai:* Var Bsbl Coach Edgemont HS 1966-71, FDR HS 1973-74; West Chester Cty Bsbl Coaches Assn Pres 1970-71; *office:* Haviland Jr HS Haviland Rd Hyde Park NY 12538

WIELEBA, FRANCES ARLENE, 5th Grade Teacher; *b:* Detroit, MI; *ed:* (BSED) Eng, Univ of Detroit 1952; *cr:* Teacher St Francis Xavier 1952-54, Roosevelt Elem 1954-64, Halfman Elem 1964-; *ai:* Spon Sch Service Squad.

WIELECHOWSKI, ANITA H., Latin Teacher; *b:* Staten Island, NY; *m:* William; *c:* Jeanne M., William, Aimee; *ed:* (BS) Ed/Latin, Seton Hall Univ; (MA) Human Dev, Fairleigh Dickinson; Ed, NJ Acad for Advancement of Teaching & Management; *cr:* Latin/Eng Teacher Sparta HS 1963-64; Latin Teacher High Point Regional 1966-67, Newton HS 1979-; *ai:* Latin Club & Latin Honor Society Adv; Core Team Mem; NJ Classical League 1979-; Recipient Governors Teacher Recognition Prgm 1986; *home:* 18 Jenkins Rd Franklin NJ 07416

WIEMERS, DONNA FRANK, First Grade Teacher; *b:* Pioneer, IA; *m:* Denzil; *c:* Diane Morrison, David, Duane; *ed:* Elem Ed, Univ of N IA Cedar Falls 1954; *cr:* 3rd Grade Teacher 1954-58, Kndgtn Teacher 1965-81, 1st Grade Teacher 1981- Gilmore City Bradgate Sch; *ai:* Early Ed Comm Chairperson; Needs Assessment Comm Secy; Advisory Comm Secy; Drug Prevention Comm; IA Rdng Assn; 1st Luth Church (Sunday Sch Teacher, Dorcas Circle); Luth Brotherhood Branch Officer; *home:* RR 2 Box 125 Gilmore City IA 50541

WIENERS, CHARLES J., Social Stud Department Chair; *b:* Philadelphia, PA; *m:* Mary D. Light; *c:* John, Kathy, Tracey; *ed:* (BA) His, St Josephs Univ 1966; (MA) His, Miami Univ 1968; *cr:* Teacher Cardinal Dougherty HS 1968-85; Teacher/Dept Head Archbishop Prendergast HS 1985-; *ai:* Athletic Dir; Var Sftbl Coach; Operation Santa Claus & Sr Prom Moderator; Soc Stud Curr Comm; Joint Systems Soc Stud Prgm Coord; NCSS, Mid Atlantic Cncl for Soc Stud, PA Soc Stud Cncl; St Bernadettes CYO HS Girls Bsktbl Coach; Llanerch Hills Athletic Assn Sftbl Coach; Philadelphia Inquirer Newspaper in Ed Series Consultant; *office:* Archbishop Prendergast HS 401 N Lansdowne Ave Drexel Hill PA 19026

WIENS, WALDO K., 4th Grade Teacher; *b:* Meade, KS; *m:* Alvina Isaac; *ed:* (BS) Music, (MS) Music 1959, Emporia St Univ; Specialist in Ed Counseling & Admin Degree Eds Institution & Emporia St Univ 1969; *cr:* Scndry Elem & Vocal Music Teacher 1971, 4th Grade Teacher Meade Public Sch; *ai:* Educational Comms; Preparation of Master Playground Schedule Grades 3-6; Phi Mu Alpha Sinfonia of America Life Mem 1958-; KS Bankers Assn Soil Conservation Awd 1982; Meade Jr Chamber of Commerce Rep 1963; Univ of KS Sch of Ed 25 Yrs Service Certificate of Appreciation; *home:* HCR 3 Box 16 Meade KS 67864

WIERENGO, SARAH JANE, Art Teacher; *b:* W Palm Beach, FL; *ed:* (AA) Art, Young Harris Coll 1968; (BFA) Art Ed, Univ of GA 1970; (MVA) Art Ed, GA St Univ 1976; *cr:* Art Teacher Wheeler HS 1970-74, Pebblebrook HS 1975-80, S Cobb HS 1980-; *ai:* Stu Cncl & Art Club Spon; Teacher of Yr Twice; *office:* S Cobb HS 1920 Clay Rd Austell GA 30001

WIERWILLE, NANCY CHAPMAN, Fifth Grade Teacher; *b:* Jersey City, NJ; *m:* Tim; *c:* Chloe Brooke, Nathan C.; *ed:* (BS) Early Chldhd Ed, Geo Peabody Coll at Vanderbilt Univ 1971; Grad Work Univ NM; *cr:* 1st Grade Teacher Los Alamos Schls 1971-72; Dir Presbyterian Pre Sch of Santa Fe 1972-75; Elem Levels Teacher Ruidoso Municipal Schls 1975-; *ai:* Curr Comm RMS; Parent-Teacher Group & Parent Activity Cncl; NEA Pres of Ruidoso 1977-78.

WIES, BONNIE BRAUN, First/Second Grade Teacher; *b:* Norfolk, NE; *m:* Ronald; *c:* Adam; *ed:* (BA) Elem Ed, Kearney St 1973; *cr:* 1st-6th Grade Teacher Petersburg Public Sch 1973-76; 2nd Grade Teacher Fullerton City Sch 1976-77; K-4th Grade Teacher Dist 57 1978-81; 5th-6th Grade Teacher 1981-86; 1st-2nd Grade Teacher 1986- St John Bapt; *ai:* Asst Prin; Pep Club Spon; Petersburg Young Women Pres 1977-82; Petersburg Survey Team 1984-85; *office:* St John The Baptist Sch Box 208 Petersburg NE 68652

WIESEL, MARY HELEN, English Teacher; *b:* Baltimore, MD; *ed:* (BA) Eng, Chestnut Hill Coll 1968; *cr:* Eng Teacher DE Public Sch Dist 1969-70, Holy Spirit Sch 1970-74, Padua Acad 1974-; *ai:* Act Include Youth Leadership Contest; Moderator of Sch Club Related Working with Young People who visit & work with Nursing Home Residents; NCEA 1970-; *office:* Padua Acad 905 N Broom St Wilmington DE 19806

WIESENDANGER, BETTY GRIFFIN, English/Language Arts Teacher; *b:* Union Cty, NC; *m:* Fritz; *c:* Marylou, Jimmy; *ed:* (BA) Soc Stud/Eng, Meredith 1954; *cr:* 7th Grade Teacher Chestnut Mid Sch 1954-56; Soc Stud Teacher Zephyrville Hills Sch 1956-58; 8th Grade Teacher La Drayo Sch 1958-60; 6th Grade Teacher Intnl Sch Tokyo Japan 1960-62; Lang Art Teacher E Union Mid Sch 1980-; *ai:* NCEA, NCA 1980-; *office:* E Union Mid Sch P O Box 666 Marshville NC 28103

WIEST, KAREN MACHTLEY, Gifted Ed/English Teacher; *b:* Johnstown, PA; *m:* William Harvey; *c:* Joel, Rachel, David, Tobias, Elisabeth, Chad; *ed:* (BS) Eng, Clarion Univ 1968; Counseling, Bucknell Univ; Grad Work Kent St Univ, Shippensburg Univ, La Verne Coll; *cr:* Teacher W Perry Sch Dist 1968-69, Shaker Heights Sch Dist 1970-71; Teacher Line Mountain Sch Dist 1971-73, 1986-; *ai:* Odyssey of Mind Coach; Prom Adv; Stu Assistance Team; Faculty Senate; Lead Teacher; PA Assn Gifted Ed 1975-; Northumberland Cty Historical Society 1971-; PA Ger Society 1971-; Dalmatia PTA (Pres 1979-80) 1978-; *home:* Box 206 Dalmatia PA 17017

WIGDAHL, MATTHEW JOHN, English Teacher; *b:* Minneapolis, MN; *m:* Pamela Jeanne Girard; *ed:* (BA) His 1974, (BA) Eng, 1982 CO St Univ; *cr:* Eng Teacher Castle Rock Jr HS 1982-85, Douglas Cty HS 1985-; *ai:* Yrbk Spon; Douglas Cty Fed of Teachers 1982-; Filmed Educl TV Series 1985; *office:* Douglas Cty HS 2842 Front St Castle Rock CO 80104

WIGG, BRUCE JAY, Soc Sci Department Chair; *b:* Harlan, IA; *m:* Karen Bortscheller; *c:* Aaron, Brian; *ed:* (BA) Soc Sci, Buena Vista Coll 1977; Grad Work Drake Univ, Univ of IA, Univ of N IA; *cr:* Soc Stud Teacher La Porte City Schls 1977-; *ai:* Stu Cncl Adv; Tennis Coach; NEA, ISEA; NEIEU, LPCEA (Government Affairs, Negotiations) 1977-; NCSS 1977-; Sacred Heart Church Pres Bd of Ed 1989-; Republican Educators of IA; Taft Fellow Univ of IA; Teacher of Yr Union HS 1986, 1989; *home:* 218 Valley Dr La Porte City IA 50651

WIGGIN, BARBARA JONES, Language Arts Teacher; *b:* Abington, PA; *m:* Tim; *c:* Deborah, Lisa; *ed:* (BS) Eng/Scndry Ed, PA St Univ 1967; Working Towards MA Hum, William Paterson Coll 1991; *cr:* Eng Teacher Westerly Parkway Jr St Coll 1967-68, North Penn HS 1969-70, Hanover Park HS 1983-; Educl Consultant Lawrence-Wiggin Assn Incorporated 1989-; *ai:* Newspaper Adv; NEA 1983-; NCTE 1985-; Journalism Ed Assn 1990-; Ecumenical Cncl for Homeless 1989-; Church Sch Supt 1983-89; NJ Governors Teacher of Yr Awd 1987; *office:* Hanover Park HS 63 Mt Pleasant Ave East Hanover NJ 07936

WIGGIN, ROBERT T., Scndry Curriculum Coordinator; *b:* Rockville Centre, NY; *m:* Caroline Evans; *c:* Christopher; *ed:* (BS) Math, 1959, (MS) Math, 1960 NY St Coll for Teachers; NSF Fellow MIT 1960-61; Grad Stud Lesley Coll, Boston Univ; *cr:* Math Teacher 1961-67, Coord 1967- Brookline HS; *ai:* NCTM Reviewer: New England Math Teachers Assn, Math Assn of America; New England Aquarium, Sierra Club, Trout Unlimited; Amer Scndry Ed Leader 1971; Outstanding Scndry Educator America 1973; *office:* Brookline HS 115 Greenough St Brookline MA 02146

WIGGINS, JAN STAMEY, Health/Physical Ed Teacher; *b:* Waynesville, NC; *m:* Robert Wayne; *c:* Katie E.; *ed:* (BA) Health/Phys Ed, Cntrl Wesleyan 1977; *cr:* Human Resource Dev Teacher Cleveland Tech Inst 1977-78; Phys Ed/Health Teacher Southwest Jr HS 1978-89, Hunter Huss HS 1989-; *ai:* Coach Girls Var Bsktbl Coach Hunter Huss 1989-; 4-H Club Spon; Athletic Dir 1987-89; Girls Jr HS Coach 1978-89; NC Amer Alliance for Health, Phys Ed, Recreation, Dance 1978-; NC & Gaston Cty Coaches Assn 1978-; Coach of Yr 1989-; *office:* Hunter Huss HS 1518 Edgefield Dr Gastonia NC 28052

WIGGINS, MARY JEAN (ALGAR), Fourth Grade Teacher; *b:* Pittston, PA; *m:* David; *c:* Eric, Amy, David J.; *ed:* (BS) Elem Ed, Mansfield St 1971; Grad Courses, St Univ of NY Binghamton, St Univ of NY Cortland; *cr:* 6th Grade Teacher 1971-79, 4th Grade Teacher 1979- Tioga Hills Elem Sch; *ai:* NEA, Vestal Teachers Assn 1971-; Vestal Little League Ladies Auxiliary 1987-; GSA 1955-66, 1985-; *office:* Tioga Hills Elem Glann Rd Apalachin NY 13732

WIGGINS, PATRICA EDISON, Math & English Teacher; *b:* Bay City, TX; *c:* Michael K. Edison, Tiffany D.; *ed:* (BS) Math, Prairie View A&M 1970; Several Wkshps in Eng & Math; *cr:* Teacher Van Vleck HS 1970-86, Palacious Job Trng Prgm 1988, Van Vleck Jr HS 1986-; *ai:* Daughters in Progress Recording Secy 1984-; *office:* Van Ueck Jr H S PO Box Q Van Vleck TX 77482

WIGGINS, ROBERT WAYNE, Physical Education Teacher; *b:* Shelby, NC; *m:* Jan Stamey; *c:* Katie E.; *ed:* (BA) Phys Ed/Health, Cntrl Wesleyan Coll 1975; (MS) Safety/Driver Ed, NC A&T Univ 1987; *cr:* Teacher/Coach/Athletic Dir Ashley Jr HS 1975-82; Teacher/Coach Hunter Huss HS 1982-; *ai:* 4-H Club Spon; Asst Ftbl, Head Golf Coach; Prof Educators of NC 1986-; NC Driver & Traffic Safety Ed Assn, Amer Driver & Traffic Safety Ed Assn 1985-; NC Coaches Assn 1975-; Gaston Cty Coaches Assn 1985-; *office:* Hunter Huss HS 1518 Edgefield Ave Gastonia NC 28052

WIGGS, BRENDA ATKINSON, Jr. HS Math & Science Teacher; *b:* Lambert, MS; *m:* Harold Dean; *c:* Doug, Rhonda, Melody, Barbie; *ed:* (BA) Elem, Univ of MS 1968; *cr:* Jr HS Math/Sci Teacher Delta Acad 1968-87; *ai:* Soil & Water Conservation Auxiliary St VP 1988-, Outstanding 1989; Amer Heart Assn Cmmty Fund Raiser; Quitman Cty Industrial Fnd 1990; Whos Who in MS; MACD Auxiliary St Level Pres; Quitman Cty Circuit Clerk.

WIGGS, CHRISTIE EARLY, Ag-Lang Arts/English Teacher; *b:* Rocky Mount, NC; *m:* James Edward Jr.; *c:* Jonathan A.; *ed:* (BS) Scndry Ed/Eng, 1981, (BA) Eng, 1981 NC Weselyan; Gifted Ed; *cr:* Eng Teacher Northern Nash Sr HS 1982; Ag Lang Arts/Eng Teacher Nash Cntrl Jr HS 1982-83; Eng Teacher Rocky Mount Sr HS 1983-84; Lang Arts/Soc Teacher 1985-87, Ag Teacher 1987- Southern Nash Jr HS; *ai:* Coach Academic Quiz Bowl Team; Adv Coord Spec Pals Prgm; NC Assn Gifted/Talented; Teacher Yr Gifted Ed Nash Cty 1989; *office:* Southern Nah Jr H S Rt 3 Box 54 Spring Hope NC 27882

WIGHT, LINDA ELAINE (RUSH), ESL Teacher; *b:* Medford, OR; *m:* Thomas Earl; *c:* Gregory R., Gary C., Cynthia M.; *ed:* (AA) Fr/Eng, W Valley Coll 1969; (BA) Fr/Eng, 1971, (MA) Eng 2nd Lang, 1986 San Jose St Univ; Teaching Credential, San Jose St Univ 1972; ESL Certificate, Santa Clara Univ 1981, San Jose St Univ 1982; *cr:* Field Teacher Redwood Glen Outdoor Ed Sch 1972-73; ESL Teacher Interstudy Intnl Study Tours 1979; Private Tutor ESL for Business Exch Families 1977-; ESL Teacher Oak Grove Sch Dist 1978-; *ai:* Prof Educators Group Mem 1988-; Cub Scouts Treas 1984-85; Certificate of Recognition, Comm for Outstanding Teachers Awd, Eng Lang Consortium Santa Clara Cty Office of Ed 1984, Schlsp 1967, 1969.

WIGINTON, VICKIE (MC GEE), Drama/Debate Teacher; *b:* Corinth, MS; *m:* B. J. Mc Gee; *c:* Bonnie Mc Gee; *ed:* (BFA) Drama/Speech Ed, OK Univ 1977; Debate Contest Material, Cameron Univ; Creative Drama, Univ of HI; *cr:* Drama/Debate Coach Lawton HS 1978-; *ai:* Debate & Individual Events Speech Team Coach;NFL Spon; Sch Plays Dir; MUN Adv; Arts Planning Team; OK Ed Assn, NEA, Prof Ed Assn of Lawton, ASCD; SW Theatre Assn 1988-; Nom Natl Teacher of Yr 1987; *office:* Lawton HS 601 NW Ft Sill Blvd Lawton OK 73507

WIGTON, TERRY LEE, Mathematics Teacher; *b:* Mount Gilead, OH; *ed:* (BS) Math, E KY Univ 1970; (MS) Educl Psych, W KY Univ 1975; Post Grad Toward Ed S; *cr:* Teacher/Coach Owensboro HS 1970-; *ai:* Asst Ftbl Coach; Sr Class Spon; OEA, KEA, NEA 1970-; Jaycee 1971-73; St Champions 1974; Head Track Coach; St Champions 1974 & 1986; Asst Ftbl Coach; *office:* Owensboro HS 1800 Frederica Owensboro KY 42301

WIIK, SUSAN MERRICK, English Teacher; *b:* Minneapolis, MN; *m:* John Edward; *c:* Katherine, Kristen; *ed:* (BA) Eng Lit - Magna Cum Laude, 1969, (BS) Eng Ed - Magna Cum Laude, 1969 Univ of MN; Grad Work Curr Dev, Rdng, Ed of Gifted Stu, Univ of MN & Coll of St Thomas; *cr:* Teacher/Dept Chairperson Cntrl Jr HS 1969-81; Teacher White Bear Sr HS 1981-; Debate Coach; Odyssey of Mind Coach; Coord of HS Potential Prgms; *ai:* NCTE 1969-; NEA, MEA 1969-; MN Educators of Gifted & Talented 1985-; Published Article 1973; *office:* White Bear Lake Area HS 5040 Bald Eagle Ave White Bear Lake MN 55110

WIKEL, CAROL IRIS, Fifth Grade Teacher; *b:* Boston, MA; *m:* Ronald; *c:* Todd, Brian, Cory; *ed:* (BS) Elem Ed, 1977, (MS) Elem Ed, 1984 Troy St Univ; Space Orientation for Prof Educators; *cr:* 5th Grade Teacher Samson Elem Sch 1977-; *ai:* 4-H Club Teacher-Leader; NEA, AL Ed Assn 1977-; Geneva Cty Ed Assn Secy 1977-; Samson Garden Club 1973-77; Geneva Cty Cowbelles 1978-83; PTO 1st VP 1979-; Samson Elem Teacher of Yr; Geneva Cty Teacher of Yr; Geneva Cty Extension Service Leadership Awd; *office:* Samson Elem Sch 505 N Johnson St Samson AL 36477

WILBANKS, RANDALL THOMAS, Industrial Technology Teacher; *b:* Beaumont, TX; *ed:* (BA) Industrial Ed, 1984, (MED) Scndry Ed, 1985 Sam Houston St Univ; *cr:* Teacher Tom C Clark HS 1985-; Adjunct Professor Webster Univ San Antonio 1987-89;

ai: Industrial Technology Club Spon; Assn of TX Technology Ed Mem 1985-, Regional Outstanding Teacher 1986-87, 1987-88; Alamo Industrial Technology Assn (Bd Mem 1989-, Pres 1988-89, 1986-88); Industrial Technology Ed Assn Mem 1987-; Project 2061 Sci; Curr Writer Extension Intructional Materials Center; Univ of TX Austin; Assn for Advancement of Sci; *office:* Tom C Clark HS 5150 De Zavala Rd San Antonio TX 78249

WILBOURN, MARTHA JEAN, 5th/6th Math/Sci/Rdng Teacher; *b:* Ada, OK; *m:* Donald Ray; *c:* Lorie, Dianne, George; *ed:* (BS) Elem Ed/Health/Phys Ed, 1966, (ME) Ed, 1974 E Cntrl Univ; *cr:* Phys Ed Teacher Pauls Valley 1966-67; Elem/Phys Ed Teacher Tupelo 1968-69; 5th/6th Grade Elem Sci/Math/Phys Ed 3rd/4th Phys Ed Teacher Bearden 1969-; *ai:* 3rd & 4th Grade Bsktbl Coach; Class Selected St Champions Phys Fitness 1988-89; OK Ed Assn, NEA; 1st Baptist Church Okemah.

WILBURN, AVONELL UTTERBACK, Second Grade Teacher; *b:* Dublin, TX; *c:* Kimberly Hansley; *ed:* (BS) Primary/Kndgtn Ed, TX Womans Univ 1957; *cr:* 2nd Grade Teacher Odessa TX 1957-59; 3rd Grade Teacher Midland TX 1959-1961; 3rd Grade Teacher Sherman TX 1961-64; 2nd Grade Teacher Denison TX 1964-; *ai:* Classroom Teachers 1957-; TX St Teachers Assn 1957; Delta Kappa Gamma Society Intnl 1987-; Denison Service League 1986-; Jr Delphians 1965; Beta Sigma Phi 1964; Teacher of Yr-1987-88.

WILBURN, JEAN ANN, Elementary Librarian; *b:* Pittsburgh, PA; *ed:* (BA) Eng, 1950, (ME) Admin/Supervision, 1960 Duquesne Univ; Rdng Specialist Duquesne Univ 1978; *cr:* Elem Teacher Tucson, Phoenix, Pittsburgh Cath Schls 1937-57; Elem Prin Pittsburgh & Phoenix Cath Schls 1957-67; Diocesan Consultant Tucson Cath Schls 1967-70; Supt of Schls 1970-74, Elem Prin 1974-76 Diocese of Phoenix; Elem Teacher Diocese of Baltimore & Pittsburgh 1976-87; Elem Teacher/Librarian Cathedral Sch 1987-; *ai:* Who Whos in Religion; *office:* Cathedral Sch 330 N Main Greensburg PA 15601

WILBURN, MARVA J. (PROTHO), 8th Grade English Teacher; *b:* East Chicago, IN; *c:* Damarr Smith, Marjanii, Adhjamon; *ed:* (BA) Eng, W MI Univ 1972; Grad Stud W MI Univ; *cr:* Day Care Dir Kalamazoo Public Sch; Teacher W K Kellogg Jr HS; *ai:* Chrldr Coach; Yrbk & Newspaper Adv; Textbook & Writing Assessor Comm; BCEA Building Rep; NEA; Kellogg Sch Awd for Influencing Stu; *home:* 405 Boyes Dr Battle Creek MI 49017

WILBURN, WILLIAM JOE, Bus Dept Head/Soc Stud Teacher; *b:* Amherstdale, WV; *m:* Donna Kay Moore; *ed:* (AB) Soc Stud/Bus, Marshall Univ 1966; (MA) Scndry Ed/Soc Stud, WV Univ 1972; Post Grad Stud Cmptr, Nonverbal Comm, Phys Fitness; *cr:* Bus Math/Soc Stud/General Bus Teacher Man HS 1966-68; Typing Teacher 1980, General Bus Teacher 1980-89, His/Government Teacher 1984- Mounds Jr HS; *ai:* Ftbl Side Line Chain Crew; WV His Golden Horseshoe Adv; Marshall Cty Ed Assn Building Rep 1968-, Super Rep 1989-; WV Ed Assn Chm Prof Services 1980; NEA; Benevolent & Protective Order of Elks 1970-; Scottish Rite of Freemasonry 1985-; Ancient Free & Accepted Masons Marsh Union 1984-; Marshall Cty Democrate Exec Comm; Marshall Cty Ed Assn Poly Action Comm Vice Chm; WV Ed Instruction & Prof Dev Comm; Marshall Cty Soc Stud Textbook Comm; *office:* Moundsville Jr HS 401 Tomlinson Ave Moundsville WV 26041

WILCOX, BRENDA RATLIFF, First Grade Teacher; *b:* Brownwood, TX; *m:* James Edward; *c:* Tracy Bowman, Keith; *ed:* (BS) Elem Ed, Howard Payne Univ 1973; (MS) Elem Ed, Tarleton St Univ 1988; *cr:* 1st Grade Teacher Woodland Heights Elem 1973-; *ai:* TX Classroom Teachers Assn 1973-; *office:* Woodland Heights Elem Sch 3900 4th Brownwood TX 76801

WILCOX, MARJORIE SHERRILL JOHNSON, Math Dept Chm/7th Gr Teacher; *b:* Syracuse, NY; *M:* Lonnie E.; *c:* Barbara, Derrick, Robin; *ed:* (AA) Medical Technology, Coll of Medical Technology 1957; (BA) Psych Ed, 1972; (MAT) Ed, Psych, 1976 Manhattanville; *cr:* Pre-K Teacher Longfellow Sch 1974-75; Spec Ed Teacher Greenburgh-Graham 1975-79; Elem Teacher Cleveland Elem 1980-82; Mid Teacher Wilson Jr HS 1982-86; Washington Mid 1986; *ai:* Dept Chm-Math; Coord-Tutoring and Asst Prgm; Spon-Math Fair; Team Mem for Counseling-Drug Related-Impact Prgm; CMC 1986-; NCTM 1986-; Organized Curr Guide for Math 6-7-8th for Dist 1987; Dist Textbook Selection Comm for Math; Inservice Trng for Teachers How to Write Ieps NY 1975-79; *office:* Washington Mid Sch 1505 N Marengo Ave Pasadena CA 91103

WILCOX, NANCY KAREN, Adm/Prin/5th,6th,7th Teacher; *b:* Yakima, WA; *ed:* (BS) Nursing, 1970, (MS) Nursing, 1980 Univ of WA; (BA) Ed, Cntrl WA Univ 1980; Cntrl WA Univ; *cr:* Public Health Nurse Yakima Cty Hlth Dist 1970-73; Nurse Coord Childrens Orthopedic Hosp 1975-79; Elem Teacher 1982-, Prin/Admin 1989-Harrah Cmmty Chrstn Sch; *office:* Harrah Community Chrstn Sch P O Box 68 Harrah WA 98933

WILCOX, PHILLIP DANIEL, Science Department Chair; *b:* Greenville, MS; *m:* Pamela Rene Harrington; *c:* Meghan; *ed:* (BSED) Bio, Delta St Univ 1985; MTAI Certified; MS Teacher Assessment Instrument Evaluation Trng; *cr:* Lab Asst/Teacher Delta St Univ 1985; Earth Sci Teacher 1986, Life Sci Teacher 1986-87 Coleman Jr HS; Bio Teacher/Dept Head T L Weston HS 1987-; *ai:* Sci Dept Head; Academic Teams Coach; Southeastern Consortium Minority Stu Engineering Spon; Prin Academic Advisory Comm Mem; Bio Club Adv; NSTA, MS Sci Teachers Assn, Delta Sci Teachers Assn 1988-; Kappa Sigma (Athletic Coord, Pledge Cncl Adv, Academic Adv) 1982-85; St MS Dept of Ed Night Class Teacher for GED Testing; *office:* T L Weston HS 901 Archer Greenville MS 38701

WILCOX, ROSEMARY, Third Grade Teacher; *b:* Greenbrier, AR; *m:* Freddie F.; *c:* Mary Jane Fulmer, Freddie M; *ed:* (BSE) Elem Ed, Univ of Cntrl AR 1971-; Wkshps; *cr:* 4th Grade Teacher Vilonia Elem 1971-77; 3rd Grade Teacher Greenbrier Elem 1977-; *ai:* AEA Delegate 1971-78; GEA Mem 1978-; North Cntrl Rdng Cncl Mem 1978-; Springhill Baptist Church Sunday Sch Teacher 1968-80; Cattlemans Assn Mem 1980-; Young Democrats Mem 1971-80; PTA; Dept of Labor CPR Awd 1980; Teacher Appreciation Greenbriar PTA 1989-; *office:* Greenbrier Elem Sch Box 68 Greenbrier AR 72058

WILCOX, VERLA SHAFFER, Reading Teacher; *b:* Grayson, KY; *m:* Frank Leland; *c:* Beth, Leslie; *ed:* (BS) Elem Ed, Trevecca Nazarene Coll 1970; (MA) Elem Ed, Morehead Univ 1973; *cr:* 3rd Grade Teacher 1970-72, 2nd Grade Teacher 1972-88, 1st/2nd Grade Rdng Teacher 1988-89, Chapter I Rdng Teacher 1989- Prichard Elem; *ai:* Academic Team Coach 1988-; Hiring in Sch Comm; KEA; Academic Boosters; *home:* PO Box 324 Grayson KY 41143

WILD, JANICE L., 6th Grade Teacher; *b:* Menlo Park, CA; *c:* Elizabeth; *ed:* (BA) General Ed, San Francisco St 1960; Post Grad Work Sci; *cr:* Teacher Lake Tahoe Unified Sch Dist 1960-61; 1st-6th Grade Teacher Cupertino Sch Dist 1961-; *ai:* Lead Sci Camp Teacher; Teach Cmptrs to Other Teachers; CTA; Developing Natural Ecology Area through Grants & Donations; *office:* Garden Elem Gate Sch 10500 Ann Arbor Dr Cupertino CA 95014

WILD, THOMAS RICHARD, Psychology/History Teacher; *b:* Milwaukee, WI; *ed:* (BA) Psych, Univ of WI-La Crosse 1983; Cert His/Ed, Cardinal Stritch Coll 1988; Completing Masters in Prof Dev in Teaching, Cardinal Stritch Coll; Grad Work in Psych; *cr:* Psych Instr Salzburg Intnl Preparatory Sch 1983-85; Substitute Teacher 1985-87, Psych/His Teacher 1988- Milwaukee Public Schls; *ai:* Co-Coord Adopt-A-Stu Prgm; Co-Coach Special Olympic Track Team; Hispanic Task Force; Comm Mem Helped Select New Psych Text for Milwaukee Public Sch System; Nom by WI Improvement Prgm Mem to Participate in Teachers Teaching Teachers Conference; *office:* Riverside Univ HS 1615 E Locust St Milwaukee WI 53211

WILDE, MARY KAYTHREN, Science Teacher/Dept Chairman; *b:* Marengo, IA; *m:* Charles; *c:* Scott, Tamera; *ed:* (BS) Ed/Sci & Math, Concordia Teachers Coll 1969; (MS) Univ Rdng Specialist/Ed, Univ of MO-St Louis 1973; Specialist Mid Sch/Sci, West GA Coll 1987; Teacher Evaluation Data Collector; *cr:* 1st Grade Teacher Rockwood Sch Dist; Primary Teacher Griffin Spalding Dist; 1st Grade/Rdng Teacher Peachtree Elem; 8th Grade Sci Teacher/Dept Chm Booth Mid Sch; *ai:* 8th Grade Sci Club Spon; Sci Olympiad Coach; Track Coach; Long Distance Girls & Boys; GTSA Mid Sch 1989- Sci Teacher of Yr 1987; NSTA Comm Chm for Natl Conference 1990; Christ Out Shepherd Luth Church Secy Church Cncl 1985-87; Fayette Cty Teacher of Yr 1987; NEWMAST 1988; Fayette Cty Teacher Grant 1989; *office:* Booth Mid Sch 250 Peachtree Pkwy Peachtree City GA 30269

WILDER, BARBAR GASKIN, Third Grade Teacher; *b:* Richmond, VA; *m:* James E.; *c:* Laura L., James S.; *ed:* (BS) Elem Ed, Armstrong St Univ 1972; (MA) Early Chldhd Ed, East Carolina Univ 1978; *cr:* 3rd Grade Teacher Summersill Elem 1968; 1st Grade Teacher Shell Point Elem 1971-72; 3rd Grade Teacher Northwest Laurens Elem 1974-76; a W Edwards Elem 1977-; *ai:* Guidance Comm; Media Comm; Chairperson Writing Comm; Team Leader; NCAE; ADK Corresponding Secy 1986-88; Twins Rivers IRA; Cherry Pt Baptist Church (Sunday Sch Teacher 1987-/Tape Ministry Dir 1986-/G a Dir 1986-/Lib Comm 1985-); *office:* A W Edwards Elem Sch PO Box 189 Havelock NC 28532

WILDER, BETTY ANN, Fourth Grade Teacher; *b:* Mt Carmel, TN; *m:* Vernon D.; *ed:* (BS) Elem Ed, 1964, (MA) Ed, 1976, E TN St Univ; *cr:* 2nd Grade Teacher Morristown City Sch System 1964-65; 9th Grade Teacher Hawkins Cty Sch System 1966-67; 2nd/5th Grade Teacher Grainger Cty Sch System 1969-72; 4th/5th Grade Teacher Hamblen Cty Sch System 1972-; *ai:* Hamblen Cty Ed Assn 1972-; TN Ed Assn, NEA 1964-; Lakeway Rdng Assn 1989-; *office:* Fairview-Marquerite Sch 2125 Fairview Rd Morristown TN 37814

WILDER, DONNA BOCOCK, Mathematics Teacher/Dept Chair; *b:* Staunton, VA; *m:* Ernest William; *c:* Ryan, Regan; *ed:* (BA) Ed, 1976, (MA) Ed, 1980 VA Polytechnic Inst & St Univ; *cr:* Kndgtn/2nd Grade Teacher Fallon Park Elem 1976-82; Teacher of Gifted & Talented Raleigh Court Elem 1982-84; Math Teacher Breckinridge Jr HS & Mid Sch 1984-; *ai:* Sch Team Leader; Instructional Cncl; Guidance Support Team, Prin Advisory Team Mem; Math Conference Wkshps & Sessions Presenter; Blue Ridge Cncl of Teachers of Math 1984-; VA Cncl of Teachers of Math 1986-; NCTM 1987-; Cub Scout Pack 584 Treas 1989-; St Johns Episcopal Church Sunday Sch Teacher 1986-89; Currently Writing Book; *home:* 35 Mac Gregor Dr Blue Ridge VA 24064

WILDER, DOROTHY BUNCHE, Eng/Soc Stud/Rdng Teacher; *b:* Windsor, NC; *m:* Hubert; *c:* Tineya A.; *ed:* (BA) Soc Stud/Fr/Eng, St Augustine Coll 1951; (MA) Philosophy/Soc Sci/His/Ed, Columbia Univ 1988; Various Univs; *ai:* Cedar Landing Baptist Church Building Comm Pres; NC Assn of Educators, NEA, Hertford Cty NEA; Delta Sigma Theta; Hollin Coll Fr Inst 1965; *home:* Rt 1 Box 274 Ahoskie NC 27910

WILDER, GERTRUDE, Mathematics Teacher; *b:* Portsmouth, NH; *ed:* (BA) Math, 1957, (MA) Math, 1958 NY St Coll for Teachers Albany; *cr:* Math Teacher Webster HS 1958-; *ai:* AMNYST, AMTRA; Monroe Cty Math League Treas; Univ of Rochester Grad Sch of Ed & Hum Dev Awd for Excl in Scndry Sch Teaching.

WILDER, PEGGY LEE, Fourth Grade Teacher; *b:* Zebulon, NC; *m:* Barna O.; *c:* Barnanne L., Barna O. Jr.; *ed:* (AA) Bus, Louisburg Jr Coll 1960; (BA) Elem Ed, Atlantic Chrstn Coll 1963; (MA) Early Chldhd, East Carolina Univ 1970; Post Masters Studies Univ of NC at Chapel Hill; NC ST Univ; *cr:* 1st Grade Teacher Richlands Sch 1963-65; Zebulon Elem 1965-67; Rolesville Elem 1968-69; Zebulon Elem 1969-79; 4th Grade Teacher Zebulon Elem 1980-; *ai:* Sci Coord Zebulon Elem Sch 1984-; Workshops at NC Cncl of Teachers of Math Regional Conferences Meredith Coll 1988; East Carolina Univ 1990; NC Assn of Educators 1963-; NEA 1963-; NC Cncl of Teachers of Math 1983-; Zebulon Elem Math Teacher of Yr 1989; NC Jr Woman's Club VP Ways & Means Chm 1968-80, Club Woman of Yr 1973, Dist Club Woman 1973; Zebulon Baptist Church 1965-; Zebulon Baptist Church Deaconess 1987-; Zebulon Baptist Church Chm Worship Comm 1988-89; NC Natl Congress of Parents & Teachers 1963-; *home:* Rt 1 Box 212A Zebulon NC 27597

WILDERMUTH, LARRY GUY, World Cultures Teacher; *b:* Reading, PA; *m:* Margaret Kolsecek; *c:* Jenel, Erika; *ed:* (BA) His, Albright 1969; Grad Stud Lehigh Univ; *cr:* Teacher Oley Valley HS 1969-; *ai:* Wrestling & Head Wrestling Coach 1969-; Berks Cty Historical Society Article; Wrestling Clinician; *office:* Oley Valley HS Main St Oley PA 19547

WILDMAN, MARY A. (RATHERT), Second Grade Teacher; *b:* Cresco, Iowa; *m:* John A.;; *c:* Amy, Ann Wildman Parvin; *ed:* (BS) Elem Ed, Upper IA Coll 1968; Drake Univ; Marycrest Coll; Univ of Northern IA; *cr:* 1st Grade Teacher Marengo Sch 1954-55; Fort Dodge Schls 1955-58; 2nd Grade Teacher Cntrl Cmmty Sch 1959-; *ai:* NEA; IA St Ed Assn; Cntrl Ed Assn Mem Northeast IA Rdng Cncl; PEO 1965-; Cntrl Cmmty Hospital Aux Mem; Elkader Historical Society Bd Mem 1989-; 1st Congregational Church Church Cncl Mem; Edition Outstanding Young Women Amer 1965; *home:* 806 1st St NW Elkader IA 52043

WILDNAUER, MARCIA MASCIONI, 2nd Grade Teacher; *b:* Ridgway, PA; *m:* Donald; *ed:* (BS) Elem Ed, Villa Maria Coll 1970; Penn St & Gannon; *cr:* 2nd Grade Teacher Red Bird Elem 1970-71, Ridgway Cntrl 1971-; *ai:* Track Coach 1981-83; PSEA; NEA; RATA; *home:* 416 Willard St Ridgway PA 15853

WILES, GARY CAVEN, Business Teacher; *b:* Troy, OH; *m:* Brenda Sue Davis; *ed:* (BS) Bus Ed, Bowling Green St Univ 1985; *cr:* Teacher Bryan HS 1985-; *ai:* Girls Bsktbl Team Scorekeeper; Asst Track Coach; *office:* Bryan HS 150 S Portland Bryan OH 43506

WILEY, BENNIE K., Elementary Counselor; *b:* Dodge City, KS; *c:* Chasni Briggans; *ed:* (BS) Ed, 1973, (MS) Elem Counseling, 1978 Emporia St Univ; *cr:* Elem Cnslr Miller-Cntrl-Wright Elem; 6th Grade Teacher Miller Elem; *ai:* Miller Sch Just Say No Club Spon; Support Groups for Elem COAS; Sch Team Trng for Drug & Alcohol Prevention; Phi Delta Kappa; *office:* Miller-Cntrl-Wright Elem Sch 1000 2nd Ave Dodge City KS 67801

WILEY, CAROLYN, English Department Head; *b:* Philadelphia, PA; *c:* Amaela; *ed:* (BA) Eng, 1970, (MED) Eng, 1979 Cheyney St; *cr:* 10th-12th Grade Teacher Vineland HS 1970-72; 7th Grade Teacher Douglass Mid 1972-82; 8th Grade Eng Dept Head Showalter Mid 1981-; *ai:* Newspaper & Yrbk Adv; Grade Advisory Chairperson; Competency Based Curr Chairperson; Act 178 Co-Chairperson; NATE 1986-87; Alpha Kappa Alpha 1968-; Newspaper Articles Published.

WILEY, DOROTHY STEWART, Fourth Grade Teacher; *b:* Macon, GA; *m:* James Willie Jr.; *c:* Pamela, Rosalyn; *ed:* (BS) Elem Ed, Ft Valley St Coll 1973; (MS) Elem Ed, GA Coll 1976; *cr:* Teacher Mt Olive Elem Sch 1973-75; Danville Elem Sch 1975-; *ai:* Beta Club Spon; Stu Support Team Chairperson; Participant Writing Test Items for GA Criterion Reference Test; GA Assn of Educators 1973-; Twiggs Assn of Educators Secy 1987-; NEA 1973-.

WILEY, LINDA GAIL, Biology Teacher/Dept Chm; *b:* Topeka, KS; *m:* John H.; *c:* Michele, Todd, Ann, Erin; *ed:* (BS) Bio/Scndry Ed, KS St Univ 1972; (MED) Rdng Specialist, Washburn Univ 1980; Doctoral Candidate Univ KS; *cr:* Research Asst Univ of Ks 1977-80; Bio Teacher Topeka West HS USD 501 1980-; *ai:* Chrldr & Acad Bowl Spon; Stu Environmental Club Spon; Faculty & Staff Mem; Past Rep to Supt Comm Session; NTSA 1984-; KS Assn Teachers of Sci 1984-; Intnl Rdng Assn 1980-85; Phi Delta Kappa 1990; ASCD 1990; Chrstn Church Dev Task Force 1990; Minigrant 1984; Innovative GraNt 1988-89; Nom Presidential Awd Excl In Sci & Math 1986, 1988, & 1990; Distinguished Young Amer Women 1988; Honors KS Univ Coll Arts & Sci Distinguished HS Teachers; *office:* Topeka West HS 2001 Fairlawn Topeka KS 66604

WILFONG, DEBORAH JUNE, Language Arts Teacher; *b:* Charleston, WV; *ed:* (BA) Ed/Eng, Salisbury St Univ 1979; Grad Stud; *cr:* Eng/Speech Teacher Cumberland HS 1980-84; Eng Teacher Marley Jr HS 1986-87, Northeast Sr HS 1987-89; Lang Art Teacher George Fox Mid Sch 1989-; *ai:* Cheerleading Coach; Finance, MD Mid Sts Evaluation Curr, MD Mid Sts Eng Comms; Mentoring At-Risk Stus; Future Teachers of America Spon; Play

Dir; Natl Eng Assn, Anne Arundel Teachers Assn, MD St Teachers Assn, NEA Mem; Salisbury St Univ Grad Assistantship; Remedial Freshment Eng Teacher; Salisbury St Univ Writing Center Tutor; *office:* George Fox Mid Sch 7922 Outing Ave Pasadena MD 21122

WILGUS, JOHN PETER, Math Teacher; *b:* Canton, OH; *m:* Susan Marie DeChant; *c:* Michael, Christopher, Elizabeth, David, Joseph, Stephen, Brian; *ed:* (BSE) Music Ed, 1970, (MED) Educl Admin Elem, 1977 Kent St Univ; *cr:* 5th Grade Teacher Lincoln Elem Sch 1973-74; Math Teacher Emerson Mid Sch 1974-; *ai:* Cedar Point Comm Chm; Soc Comm Chm; Kent St U Alumni Assn 1977-; OH Cncl of Teachers of Math 1985-; Natl Mid Sch Assn 1988-; The Greater Cleveland Cncl of Teachers of Math 1985-; NCTM 1989-; Natl Eagle Scout Assn 1987-; Outstanding Coll Stu of America 1989-; Martha Holden Jennings Fnd Schoolar 1984-85; Martha Holden Jennings Interface Prgm Awd 1989; Jr Achievement Project Bus Prgm Plaque 1979-81; *office:* Emerson Mid Schl 13439 Clifton Blvd Lakewood OH 44107

WILGUS, PATRICIA SNIPES, Social Studies Dept Chairman; *b:* Spruce Pine, NC; *m:* Winton L.; *c:* Suzanne Wilgus Campana, Sharon K.; *ed:* (BS) His, 1972, (MA) His 1977, Old Dominion Univ; Intnl Travel Study Admin Trng; *cr:* Teacher Arrowood Acad 1965-70; Soc Stud Dept Chairperson Brewbaker Ac Ad 1971-81; GED Teacher Norview HS 1978-80-; Soc Stud Dept Chairperson Norfolk Cath HS 1981-; *ai:* Intnl Travel Study Inc Admin; Responsible Planning & Executing Academically Oriented Stu Trips to Europe & Asia During Summer 1983; Natl Honor Society Moderator; Tidewater Challenge Team Moderator; Jr Class Moderator; Cath Ed Assn 1981-; Tidewater Ind Schls Ed Assn 1970-80; Tidewater Ind Schls Most Outstanding Teacher Awd 1975; Listed Outstanding Scndry Educators of America Washington DC 1974; St Johns United Meth Church Worship Chairperson/Admin Bd 1990; Childrens Hospital Kings Daughters Hermitage Circle Founder 1965; Bel-Aire Civic League Officer 1983-84; Old Dominion Univ Schlsp to Scndry Sch; Teachers Soc Stud Motivation 1977; Teachers Economics 1978; Whos Who Amer Scndry Schls 1975; *office:* Norfolk Cath H S 6401 Granby St Norfolk VA 23505

WILHELMSEN, W. GROVER, Music Teacher; *b:* Ogden, UT; *m:* Diana M. Bentley; *c:* Brian, Rebekah, Jared, Kevin, Aaron, Drew, Jaime; *ed:* (BS) Music/Ed, 1974, (MS) Ed, 1984 Weber St Coll; *cr:* Educator/Teacher Ogden City Sch Dist 1973-78; Teacher Box Elder Sch Dist 1978-; *ai:* Orch Adv; Career Ladder Comm; UT Educators Assn (Building Rep 1984-85, Minorities Comm 1984-87); UT Music Educator Assn Mem 1975-78, 1986-87, 1990; BSA (Scout Master, Asst Dist Comm 1983-, Wood Badge Staff 1986, 1988, 1990), Merit Awd 1990; Box Elder Jr HS Teacher of Yr; String Orch Teacher Newspaper Article; Strings Unlimited Private Bus; *office:* Box Elder Jr HS 18 South 500 East Brigham City UT 84302

WILHITE, DOROTHY WIELBON, Sixth Grade Teacher; *b:* Elberton, GA; *c:* Tiffany; *ed:* (BS) Elem Ed, 1974, (MS) Elem Ed, 1985 Buffalo St Coll; *cr:* 6th Grade Teacher Public Sch 57 1979-81, Public Sch 4 1981-82, Triangle Acad 1982-; *ai:* Integration Concerns, Sch Building Concerns, Trauma Comms; *office:* Triangle Acad 1515 S Park Ave Buffalo NY 14220

WILKE, RUSSELL A., 6-8th Grade Principal; *b:* Clintonville, WI; *m:* Diane G. Lortscher; *c:* Russell III, Koreen, Nathan, James, Seth; *ed:* (BS) Elem Ed, Doctor Martin Luther Coll 1974; (MS) Ed, UW Whitewater 1984; *cr:* 6th/8th Grade Prin St Peters 1974-; *ai:* Athletic Dir; Coach All Boys Sports; YPS Dir; WI Synod Sch Vistor; Chm of St Teachers Prgm Cty; VP St Teachers Conf; Teacher Northwestern Publishing House; *office:* St Peters Lutheran Sch Box 117 Hwy 18 Helenville WI 53137

WILKENING, LORRAINE, Fourth Grade Teacher; *b:* Flushing, NY; *m:* George M.; *c:* Karen Orfe, George, Robert, Heidi Holdridge, Holly; *ed:* (BA) Ed, Queens Coll 1951; *cr:* 5th Grade Teacher Richmond Public Schls 1951; 4th Grade Teacher Brooklyn Public Schls 1951-52; 3rd/5th Grade Teacher Springfield Public Schls 1952-54; Dir Warren Pre-Sch 1970-73; K-4th Grade Teacher Warren Public Schls 1973-; *ai:* Rdng, Spelling, Gifted & Talented Curr Comms; Warren Township Ed Assn, NJEA, NEA 1973-; GSA Leader 1964-72; Most Gifted Future Teacher Ed Medal 1951; *office:* Mt Horeb Sch Mt Horeb Rd Warren NJ 07060

WILKERSON, BETTY ETHERIDGE, Second Grade Teacher; *b:* Selmer, TN; *m:* Ronnie David; *c:* Chuck; *ed:* (BS) Elem Ed, Memphis St 1972; Enrichment Courses & Wkshps Memphis St Univ, MS St Univ, Freed-Hardeman Coll; *cr:* 4th Grade Teacher 1972-81, 2nd Grade Teacher 1981- Selmer Elem Sch; Adult Basic Ed Teacher Mc Nairy Cntrl HS 1987-; *ai:* Stu Assistance Prgm Core Team Coord; Southern Assn for Accredited Schls & Colls (Soc Stud Goals & Objectives Comm, Faculty Qualifications Comms); Mc Nairy Cty Band Boosters; Mc Nairy Cty Ed Assn, TN Ed Assn, NEA 1972-; PTO Pres 1987-88; Selmer Elem Teacher of Yr 1988-89; *office:* Selmer Elem Sch 533 E Poplar Ave Selmer TN 38375

WILKERSON, DONNA WATKINS, 2nd Grade Teacher; *b:* Hendersonville, NC; *m:* Carl Franklin; *c:* Greg, Glenn, Carol; *ed:* (BS) Elem Ed, Winthrop Coll 1969; Grad Work; *cr:* 2nd Grade Teacher B C Haynie Elem Sch 1969-71, North Charleston Elem Sch 1973-; *ai:* Palmetto St Teachers Assn 1984-; SC PTA Lifetime Membership Awd 1986; *office:* North Chas. Elem Sch 4921 Durant Ave North Charleston SC 29406

WILKERSON, GARY DWAINE, Kindergarten Teacher; *b:* Manter, KS; *ed:* (BS) Elem Ed, Fort Hays St 1973; (MS) Elem Ed, Wichita St 1980; Specialist in Educl Admin, Wichita St Univ 1990; *cr:* 1st Grade Teacher Oberlin Elem Sch 1973-75; 2nd Grade Teacher 1975-76, 1st Grade Teacher 1976-82, El Paso Elem; Kndgtn Teacher Tanglewood Elem 1982-; *ai:* Stu Cncl Spon; Prof Dev Cncl; Outdoor Landscaping & Read Week Comms; Chief Negotiator; Derby Ed Assn Pres 1980-81; KS Ed Assn Congressional Contact 1983-; KS Assn Ed Young Children 1988-; St Joseph Assoc Prgm 1988-; Cmmty Schlsp Follies 1986-89; Big Brothers 1977-78; Decatur Area Theater Assn Bd of Dir 1974-75; Derby Teacher of Yr 1984; Derby & KS Master Teacher 1989; *office:* Tanglewood Elem Sch 830 Ridgecrest Derby KS 67037

WILKERSON, IDA OGLESBY, Math Teacher & Dept Chair; *b:* Swainsboro, GA; *m:* Richard; *c:* Roderica C.; *ed:* (BS) Math, Paine Coll 1965; Augusta Coll; Univ of GA; *cr:* Teacher John M Tutt 1965-; *ai:* Math Counts Coach; Team Leader 8th Grade; GA Math Leag Coach; Richmond Cty Math Cont Coach for Tutts Team; RCA 1965-; GAE 1965-; NEA 1965-; Greater Young Zion Bapt Church Church Directoress; Mission Society VP 1990; Teacher Ed Ministry Dir 1990; Bible Study Prgm Teacher 1990 Pin & Certificate; Teacher of Yr 1983-84; St Jude Mathathon 1985; Pin & Certificate for Outstanding Service.

WILKERSON, LINDA TARVER, Guidance Counselor; *b:* Natchitoches, LA; *m:* Kenneth; *c:* Kyle K., Brannon K.; *ed:* (BA) Elem, Northwestern St Univ 1968; (MED) Guidance/Counseling, W GA Coll 1971; (MED) Principalship/Supervision, Univ of Southwestern 1984; *cr:* 7th Grade Teacher/Coach Fairview Alpha HS 1968-69; Jr HS Teacher/Cnslr Temple HS 1971-75; Cnslr Church Point Jr HS 1975-79, Crowley Jr HS 1980-; *ai:* Stu Cncl Spon; Acadia Parish Cnslr Assn 1975-; A-Pel Teachers Organization 1988-; Crowley HS Boosters Club 1989-; Crowley Jr HS Parent Organization 1970-; STAR Teacher Temple HS 1973; *office:* Crowley Jr HS 401 W Northern Crowley LA 70526

WILKERSON, MILDRED THOMAS, Science Teacher; *b:* Laurel Hill, FL; *m:* Henry Thomas; *c:* Jerrund T., Shelia W. Edmondson, Sherrell R.; *ed:* (BS) Elem Ed, 1962, Mid Sch/Jr HS Sci, 1965 FL A&M Univ; Earth & Phys Sci; *cr:* Teacher Chapel Hill Jr HS 1962-65, Carver Jr HS 1965-67, Maude Saunders Elem 1967-68, Walton Mid Sch 1968-; *ai:* Sci Dept Chm; Steering & Sch Improvement Comm Mem; FL Sci Teachers; Ladies Bible Class Teacher; *home:* Rt 1 Box 54 Ponce De Leon FL 32455

WILKES, PAUL MICHAEL, Science/Soc Stud/Rdng Teacher; *b:* Dublin, GA; *ed:* Assoc Sci, Mid MA Coll 1977; (BSED) Soc Sci Ed, Univ of GA Athens 1980; Air Univ of USAF, NCO Leadership Sch; *cr:* Military USAF 1973-78, GA Natl Guard 1978-83; Teacher/Coach Boddie Jr HS & Boddie Mid Sch 1981-; *ai:* Jr HS & Mid Sch Ftbl, Bsktbl, Bsbl Coach; NEA, GAE, BAE Mem; Springdale Baptist Church Mem; Yrbk Dedication Boddie Jr HS 1987; *office:* Boddie Mid Sch Orchard Hill Rd Milledgeville GA 31061

WILKES, PEGGY PASSMORE, Mathematics Teacher; *b:* Hahira, GA; *m:* Terry Thompson; *c:* Richard, Barrett; *ed:* (BS) Math Ed, 1975, (MED) Math, 1978, (MED) Guidance/Counseling, 1989 Valdosta St Coll; Working Toward Educl Specialist in Math; *cr:* Math Teacher Valdosta HS 1975-83; Part-Time Math Instr Valdosta St Coll 1983-85; Math/Cmptr Sci Teacher Lowndes HS 1985-; *ai:* Stu Cncl Spon; Homecoming Coord; Miss Lowndes HS Beauty Pageant Dir; NCTM, GA Cncl Teachers of Math 1985-; NEA, GA Assn of Educators 1987-; Valdosta Jr Womans Club (Ed Dept Chairperson 1988, Publicity Chm 1989, Treas 1990), Best New Mem 1987, Outstanding Citizen 1989, 8th Dist Outstanding Citizen 1989; ZTA (Pres, VP, Membership Adv) 1977-; Park Avenue Meth Church 1984-; *office:* Lowndes HS 1112 N St Augustine Rd Valdosta GA 31601

WILKES, SARAJO OWENS, Reading Teacher; *b:* Carnesville, GA; *m:* Joseph T.; *c:* Kara F.; *ed:* (BS) Elem Ed, Paine Coll 1961; (MS) Ed, Wichita St Univ 1970; Grad Work Univ of NM, Univ of HI; *cr:* Classroom Teacher Scott Elem 1961-62, Fairmount Elem 1962-69, Alvah Scott Elem 1969-72, Alamogordo Jr HS 1972-74, Washington DC Jr HS 1974-75; Classroom Teacher Colorado Springs Jr HS South 1975-79, Dept of Defense Sch System England 1979-80, Franklin Cty Jr HS 1981-; *ai:* Jr/Sr Usher Bd Friendship Baptist Church; Sunday Sch Teacher Jr HS; World of Poetry Awd Golden Poet 1989; Outstanding Local Poet Awd; *home:* PO Box 252 Toccoa GA 30577

WILKIE, EILEEN KELLEY, 4th-6th Grade Teacher; *b:* Schnectady, NY; *m:* Craig L.; *c:* Mac Gregor J.; *ed:* (BS) Elem Ed, SUNY Plattsburg 1973; (MS) Elem Curr, SUNY Cortland 1978; *cr:* 1st Grade Teacher 1973-76, 2nd Grade Teacher 1976-79, 3rd Grade Teacher 1979-81, 5th Grade Teacher 1981-87, 4th-6th Grade Enrichment Teacher 1987- Minoa Elem; *ai:* Math & Ski Club Adv; OCMTA 1987-; Cntrl NY Teacher Center Creator Grant 1989; *office:* Minoa ELem Sch N Main St Minoa NY 13116

WILKIE, MARGARET ANNE, English Teacher; *b:* Dodge City, KS; *m:* Dallas A.; *c:* Dustin, Megan, Brandon; *ed:* (BA) Eng, St Mary of The Plains Coll 1975; *cr:* Eng Teacher Hanover HS 1975-79; Elem Teacher Dist 9 Tryon NE 1981-82, Dist 4 Tryon NE 1982-83; Eng Teacher Mc Pherson Cty HS 1983-; *ai:* Annual Spon; Newspaper Adv; Dir Jr & Sr Plays; NCTE; NSEA Local Pres 1989-; *office:* Mc Pherson Cty HS Box 38 Tryon NE 69167

WILKINS, ANN BOSTON, Eng/Rdng/Amer His Teacher; *b:* Twin Falls, ID; *c:* David B. (dec), Daniel G., Michelle A., Ciara N.; *ed:* (BA) Amer Stud, 1965, (MA) Eng, 1970 UT St Univ; *cr:* Eng Instr Dixie Coll 1965-66, Univ of NE Las Vegas 1968-69; Lang Art/Rdng Teacher S Cache Jr HS 1979-86; 7th-8th Grade Lang Art/Eng/Rdng/Cmptr Writing Lab/Amer His Teacher Spring Creek Mid Sch 1986-; *ai:* Stu Schlsp & Recognition Comm Coord; Mr Kenneth Thomasma 8th Grade Writers Wkshp; Lang Art Dept Head; UT Cncl Intnl Rdng Assn 1982-; UT Mid Sch Assn 1987-; Cache Ed Assn, UT Ed Assn, NEA; BSA (Merit Badge Cnslr, Schlsp, Rdng) 1980-; Outstanding Young Women of America 1965; Rdng Rekindling Curiosity; Jack London Champion of Individual; Creative Writing Experience Author Kenneth Thomasma & Spring Creek Stu; *home:* 30 N Satsuma Providence UT 84332

WILKINS, HELEN JENNINGS, First Grade Teacher; *b:* Drew, MS; *m:* William L.; *ed:* (BSE) Eng/Ed, AR St Univ 1952; ID/Nat/NDS Gifted; Edu Proc/MAT Gifted; Fundmentals Cmptr, Phillips Cty Comm Coll; Ed #53730 GW/Great/ELEA Ouachita Baptist Univ; *cr:* 1st Grade Teacher Wynne Public Schls 1949-50, 1952-53, 1955-56, Memphis Public Schls 1953-55; 1st-3rd Grade Classroom Teacher for Exceptional Marianna Public Schls 1956-71; 1st/5th Grade Teacher Lee Acad 1971-87; 1st Grade Teacher Brinkley Public Schls 1987-; *ai:* Spec Stud Comm; NEA, AEA, Brinkley Ed Organization; GSA Local Troop Leader; Meth Missions Dir 1977-80; Lee Cty Marianna Museum Assisted Dir; Cook Book Written 1983; Child Abuse Prgms Educate Teachers; *home:* 527 Knight St Forrest City AR 72335

WILKINS, JOAN SAUCER, Third Grade Teacher; *b:* Monroeville, AL; *m:* Micky B.; *c:* Jeffrey, Amy; *ed:* Assoc of Arts Elem Ed, Patrick Henry Jr Coll 1980; (BS) Elem Ed, Troy St Univ 1981, (MED) Elem Ed, Livingston Univ 1983; *cr:* 4th Grade Teacher 1981-82, 2nd Grade Teacher 1982-83, 1st Grade Teacher 1983-88, 3rd Grade Teacher 1988- Frisco City Elem; *ai:* Stu Cncl & Yrbk Adv; Chairperson St Judes Childrens Hospital Mathathon; Jacksonville St Teacher of Yr; Nom for Frisco Cty Elem Sch 1989-; *office:* Frisco Elem Sch PO Drawer 160 Frisco City AL 36445

WILKINS, KAYE WARREN, 5th Grade Dev Reading Teacher; *b:* Hopkinsville, KY; *m:* Charles R.; *c:* Kayela; *ed:* (BS) Elem Ed, 1975; (MA) Rdng Elem Ed, 1976 Western KY Univ; Western KY Univ 1979; Endorsements Rdng Specialist; Prin Elem Sch; Supv of Instr; Peabody/Vanderbilt Classes Curr & Staff Dev 1982; *cr:* Graduate Asst Elem Ed Western KY Univ 1974; Remedial Rdng Teacher 1974; Developmental Rdng Teacher 1975 Logan Elem; Developemental Rdng Teacher Russellville Mid Sch 1975-; *ai:* Chairperson Rdng Skills; Omicron Delta Kappa 1972-; 1st Woman in KY/TN to Be Initiated; Phi Delta Kappa 1974; Kappa Delta Pi Pres 1975-88; Womans Club 1988-; PTA 1975-; Scholar of Univ Western KY Univ 1974; Ogden Scholar Western KY Univ 1975; Achievement Awd Elem Ed 1974-75; *office:* Russellville Mid Sch 210 E 7th St Russellville KY 42276

WILKINS, LARRY DEAN, Mathematics Teacher; *b:* Portland, OR; *m:* Sandra; *c:* Lori Heydel, Martin; *ed:* (BS) Bus Ed, Lewis & Clark Coll 1959-61; (MS) Ed, Portland St Univ 1965; *cr:* Teacher Milwaukie HS 1961-; *ai:* Bsbl Coach; Var Asst Ftbl Coach; OCTM; OHSCA 1961-; Natl Ftbl Fnd Pres; Pont Chapter 1984-; *office:* Milwaukie HS 11300 SE 23rd Milwaukie OR 97222

WILKINS, PAMELLA TURNER, English Teacher; *b:* Washington, DC; *m:* Furman Clement III; *c:* Danielle T., Raven A.; *ed:* (BA) Eng, 1970, (MA) Guidance/Counseling, 1975 Howard Univ; *cr:* Eng Teacher Backus Jr HS 1970-71, R H Terrell Jr HS 1971-; *ai:* Pep Club Spon; Asst Cheerleading Coach; Sch Chapter Advisory Comm Mem; DC Cncl Teachers of Eng 1990; Alpha Kappa Alpha Epistoleus 1987-88; Iota Gamma Omega; Ward II Teacher of Yr 1983, 1984; *office:* R H Terrell Jr HS 1st & Pierce Sts NW Washington DC 20001

WILKINSON, CAROL E., Art/Mathematics Teacher; *b:* Carbondale, IL; *ed:* (BFA) Art Ed, 1971, (MS) Ed Art, 1977 S IL Univ Carbondale; Math Cert, Rend Lake Coll; *cr:* Art Teacher Mt Vernon Township HS 1971-84, Rend Lake Coll 1982-85; Art/Math Teacher Mt Vernon Township HS 1985-; *ai:* Co-Spon Art & Literary Magazine; Downstate Art Ed (Pres 1988-89, Ed Lesson Books 1990); IL Art Ed Assn 1990; Mt Vernon Art Guild Pres 1989-; Southern IL Arts Grant Time-Line Mural 1988, Historical Mural 1990; *office:* Mt Vernon Township HS 320 S 7th St Mount Vernon IL 62864

WILKINSON, CATHERINE JELENSKY, 8th Grade Teacher/Math Chair; *b:* Pittsburgh, PA; *m:* John A.; *c:* Dennis, Denise Wilkinson Somma; *ed:* (BS) Elem Ed, Univ of Steubenville; Admin, Carlow Coll & Duquesne; *cr:* Teacher St Columbkille 1967, Holy Trinity 1967-70, St Phillip 1971-84, Holy Trinity 1984-; *ai:* Stu Cncl Moderator; Yrbk Adv; CCD Coord; NCEA; Marriott Inn Shared Time Awd; *office:* Holy Trinity Sch 5718 Steubenville Pike Pittsburgh PA 15244

WILKINSON, HARRY L., History Teacher; *b:* North Andover, MA; *m:* Julie O'Hara; *ed:* (BA) His, 1969, (MED) Ed, 1974 Tafts Univ; *cr:* His Teacher Woburn HS 1969-70, Kennedy Jr HS 1970-88, Kennedy Mid Sch 1988-; *ai:* Woburn HS Jr Var Bsktbl; Woburn Teachers Assn (Pres 1981-85) 1965-; MTA, NEA 1969-; BPO Elks 908 1983-; Towanda Club Bd of Dir 1970-; *office:* Kennedy Mid Sch Middle St Woburn MA 01801

WILKINSON, JUANITA S., Home Economics Teacher; *b:* Westlake, LA; *m:* George A.; *c:* Debbie Douglas, Betsy Douglas, Sally Patin, Nancy; *ed:* (BS) Voc Home Ec, McNeese St 1971; Cert Elem Grades; Parenting Skills; *cr:* Substitute Teacher Calcasieu Parish Sch Bd; Church Consultant United Church Directories; Teacher Calcasieu Parish Sch Bd 1983-; *ai:* FHA Adv; Teaching Parenting Skills to Parents; AVA 1988-; LA Voc Assn 1985-; Calcasieu Parish Home Ec Teachers Assn (Secy 1988-, Mem) 1983-, Spotlight Awd 1989; Moss Bluff Order of Eastern Star Secy

1987-; *office:* Sam Houston HS Rt 5 Box 300 Lake Charles LA 70611

WILKINSON, JUDY A. (BLANTON), 3rd-4th/7th-8th Grade Teacher; *b:* St Louis, MO; *m:* George M.; *c:* Donna J. Mc Mahan, Carl L.; *ed:* (AA) Elem Ed, East Cntrl Coll 1987; Working Towards Degree & Cert, Harris St Coll; *cr:* Teacher St Anthony Sch 1981-; *ai:* Nom Natl Deans List; *home:* 440 Scottsdale Sullivan MO 63080

WILKINSON, MARK JAMES, English Teacher; *b:* Anderson, IN; *m:* Cathy Rose Dierdorf; *c:* Zachary C., Emily J.; *ed:* (BA) Ed, IN Univ 1979; (MA) US His, Ball St Univ 1986; *cr:* Eng Teacher Greenfield Cntrl HS 1980-; *ai:* Chrldr Spon; Asst Frosh Ftbl, Head Frosh Ftbl, Head Reserve Ftbl, Head Reserve Bsbl, Academic Teams Coach; HS Ftbl Ofcl; NCTE 1979-; IN Bsbl Coaches Assn; IN Ftbl Coaches Assn; Nom Channel 6 Teacher of Week; *office:* Greenfield-Cntrl HS 810 N Broadway Greenfield IN 46140

WILKINSON, MARY ALICE COURTS, Fifth Grade Teacher; *b:* Logan, WV; *m:* Earl N.; *c:* Steven, Rodney; *ed:* (AB) Eng, Univ of Charleston 1967; *cr:* 1st-6th Grade Teacher Rhode Fork Sch 1962-63, Dial Sch 1963-64; 1st-4th Grade Teacher Hubball Sch 1964-67; 6th Grade Teacher Branchland Elem 1967-73; 5th/6th Grade Teacher West Hamlin Elem 1973-; *home:* Rt 1 Box 224 West Hamlin WV 25571

WILKINSON, MARY ANN (HEAVNER), Third Grade Teacher; *b:* Rock Cave, WV; *m:* John C.; *c:* John C. Jr., Kathy A. Anderson; *ed:* (AA) Elem Ed, Lorain Cty Comm Coll 1972; (BS) Elem Ed, Kent St Univ 1974; *cr:* 3rd Grade Teacher 1975-87, Elem Coord 1982-83 Elyria Chrstn Acad; 3rd Grade Teacher First Baptist Chrstn Sch 1988-; *ai:* Soc Comm; Abbe Road Baptist Church; *office:* First Baptist Chrstn Sch 11400 La Grange Rd P O Box 929 Elyria OH 44036

WILKINSON, SARA DILL, Fourth Grade Teacher; *b:* Milford, DE; *m:* Alfrey Ray; *c:* Teresa Croll, Jeffrey R.; *ed:* (BS) Elem Ed, DE St 1971; (MED) Elem Ed, Univ of Salisbury 1976; *cr:* 4th Grade Teacher Rehoboth Elem 1971-80; Prin 1980-81, 4th Grade Teacher 1981- H O Brittingham; *ai:* Cheerleading Milton Jr HS; Delta Kappa Gamma; Phi Delta Kappa 1983; Milton Historical Society Pres 1990; Teacher of Yr H O Brittingham 1988; *home:* RD 1 Box 122 D Milton DE 19968

WILKS, JANE ANN, Fourth Grade Teacher; *b:* Joplin, MO; *m:* Gregory Blaine; *c:* Stephanie Houk, Jon, Jason, Ashlee Thompson; *ed:* (BS) Elem Ed, 1969, (MS) Elem Ed, 1976 Pittsburg St Univ; Various Grad Stud Gifted Ed; *cr:* 2nd Grade Teacher 1969-72, 4th Grade Teacher 1972- Carl Jct Interm; *ai:* Future Problem Solvers Coord; N Cntrl Accreditation Comm Chm; Prof Dev Comm Mem; MO St Teachers Assn (Sec, Treas, VP, Pres) 1975-80; Intnl Rdng Assn 1989-; Jaycees Secy 1978-79; 1965 Class Reunion Co-Chm 1975-; *office:* Carl Junction Intermediate P O Box 4 Carl Junction MO 64834

WILKS, NADINE O., Retired Elementary Teacher; *b:* Monett, MO; *ed:* Monett Jr Coll 1939; (BS) Ed, Southwest St Coll 1952; Grad Stud UMKC *cr:* 4th Grade Teacher Lawrence Cty, Marionville Jr HS, Grandview Elem 1959-89; *ai:* MSTA, NEA, PTA; *home:* 10804 Cambridge Kansas City MO 64134

WILL, ANGELA M., French/Spanish Teacher; *b:* North Wilkesboro, NC; *m:* Joseph Bryan; *c:* Hunter E., Charles B.; *ed:* (BA) Fr/Span, VA Poly Inst & St Univ 1971; Grad Classes Univ of VA, Richmond & Nancy; *cr:* Teacher Woodrow Wilson Jr HS 1971-75, Brookland Mid 1975-77, Patrick Henry HS 1984-; *ai:* Fr Club Spon; Hanover Ed Assn 1986-; Roanoke City Sch Teacher of Yr 1973; Grant-Schlrshp Fr Govt Study at CRAPEL & Univ of Navy 1986; Fr Cultural Services Schlsp 1986; *office:* Patrick Henry HS Rt 54 Ashland VA 23005

WILLAN, JANYTH SUE (WALTERS), English/Science Teacher; *b:* Jonesboro, AR; *m:* Roy James; *c:* Janyth M., Angela K., Beth, Stephanie, Steven; *ed:* (BS) Eng, IL St Univ 1965; *cr:* 9th Grade Eng/Sci Teacher Chiddix Jr HS 1965-66; Substitute Unit 5 Dist Schls 1966-68; GED Teacher Unit 87 & 5 Dist Schls 1968-73; Eng/Sci Teacher Calvary Baptist Acad 1973-78, 1984-; *ai:* Class of 1991 Spon; *office:* Calvary Baptist Acad 1017 N School P O Box 587 Normal IL 61761

WILLARD, FRANCES TOTTY, Math Teacher; *b:* Mobeetie, TX; *m:* Vernon C.; *c:* Terri Mc Cormick, Dennis, Karl; *ed:* (BS) Ed/Math, 1970, (MED) Ed/Math, 1981 West TX St Univ; *cr:* Jr HS Math Teacher Bovina ISD 1970-; *ai:* Chrldr Spon; Ath & Calculator Coach; TSTA Local Offices 1970-; Bovina Classroom Teacher Pres 1985 & 1989; NCTM 1975-; Bovina UMC; *office:* Bovina ISD 500 Halsell St Bovina TX 79009

WILLCOX, JOANNE SASSI, AP US History Teacher; *b:* Syracuse, NY; *m:* Philip; *ed:* (BA) Amer His, 1970, (MA) Amer His, 1972 SUNY Albany; *cr:* Teacher East Syracuse-Minoa Cntrl HS 1973-; *ai:* Mock Trial Adv; Orginization of Amer Historians; Amer Historical Assn; Positive Influence Outstanding Teacher 1986-87; *office:* East Syracuse-Minoa Cntrl HS Fremont Rd East Syracuse NY 13057

WILLE, SHELLEY VAUGHN, HS English/German Teacher; *b:* Fredericksburg, TX; *m:* Ryan K.; *c:* Christen, Lauren; *ed:* (BA) Eng, TX A&M 1972; Grad Work Ger, TX A&M; TX Ed Agency Center for Developing Proficiency in Ger; *cr:* 1st-8th Grade Ger Teacher St Marys Sch 1976-82; 7th Grade Eng Teacher 1982-83, 10th Grade Ger I & II/Eng Teacher 1983- Fredericksburg Ind Sch Dist; *ai:* Spon Ger Club, Jr Class 1988-89, Sr Class 1989-, UIL Spelling 1988-; Assn of TX Prof Educators; Beta Sigma Phi (Pres 1977-79, VP 1976-77), Woman of Yr 1980; TX Ed Agency Grant; *home:* 112 W Morse Fredericksburg TX 78624

WILLEMS, SHIRLEY J., Learning Director; *b:* Wolf Point, MT; *m:* Johnnie K.; *c:* Jon M., Sheila, Matthew; *ed:* (BA) Liberal Stud - Summa Cum Laude, 1976, (MA) Educl Admin, 1979 CA St Univ Fresno; *cr:* 5th-6th Grade Teacher 1977-89, 7th Grade Teacher of Learning Disabilities 1989- Kingsburg Elem Sch Dist; *ai:* Summer Sch Coord; Mentor & Master Teacher; Prgm Quality Review Team; Cnslr; Spelling Bee Coach & Coord; Drug Awareness & Stu Body Act Adv; Dist Clinical Supervision & Evaluation, SB813 Advisory, Dist Curr, SIP Comm; Kappa Delta Pi Life Membership Schlsp 1975; Alpha Gamma Sigma Life Membership; Teachers & Parents Organization Treas 1988-89; Mentor Teacher CAP Improvement Project; Outstanding Soc Sci Awd 1975.

WILLET, ROMONA COGGINS, Mathematics Teacher; *b:* Sanford, NC; *m:* Gary Louis; *c:* Jeremy, Timothy, Stephen; *ed:* (BS) Math Ed, Liberty Baptist Coll 1982; *cr:* Math Teacher East Lee Jr HS 1982-, Lee Cty Sr HS 1987-; *ai:* Keywanettes Asst Spon; Choir Choir; Agape Singers; *office:* Lee Cty Sr HS 1708 Nash St Sanford NC 27330

WILLEY, DEBRA JANE, 3rd Grade Teacher; *b:* St Louis, MO; *ed:* (BS) Elem Ed, SE MO St Univ 1973; (MED) Elem Ed, Univ of MO St Louis 1980; *cr:* 6th Grade Teacher Nevada Mid Sch 1974-75; 2nd Grade Teacher South Point Elem 1975-78; 2nd Grade Teacher 1979-81, 3rd Grade Teacher 1981- Fairmount Elem; *ai:* MO Ed Assn; *office:* Fairmount Sch 1725 Thoele Rd Saint Peters MO 63376

WILLHELM, BONNIE BELLE, Mathematics/Science Teacher; *b:* Lander, WY; *m:* Dick Ray; *c:* Lisa A. Kisling, C. Dawn; *ed:* (BA) Bio, Univ of WY 1966; *cr:* Math/Sci Teacher Fort Washakie Jr HS 1966-80; Sci Teacher 1980-88, Math/Sci Teacher 1988- Starrett Jr HS; *ai:* Sci Club, Knowledge Bowl Spon; Prin Advisory, N Cntrl Accreditation Steering Comm; Chairperson Sci Curr Comm; NEA, WY Ed Assn 1966-; Lander Ed Assn Secy 1988-; Fremont Cty 4-H Cncl Secy 1982; Outstanding Young Educator 1968; *office:* Starrett Jr HS 863 Sweetwater Lander WY 82520

WILLHITE, GARY L., English Teacher/Dir of Curr; *b:* Denver, CO; *m:* K. T. Thomas; *ed:* (BS) Spec Ed/Theatre Arts, Bob Jones Univ 1980; (MA) Eng, Wichita St Univ 1988; KS Writing Project; ASCD Evaluation Seminar; *cr:* Eng Teacher High Point Baptist Acad 1980-81, Rose Hill Unified Sch Dist #394 1982-85; Eng Teacher/Dir of Curr Marion Unified Sch Dist 408 1986-; *ai:* NHS & Future Educators of America Adv; Literary Magazine Spon; Forensics Coach; Theatre Dir; ASCD 1986-; Pi Kappa Delta, Gamma Rho 1987-; NASSP 1986-; KASCD 1981-; KS SP Assn 1988-; *home:* 909 Maple Marion KS 66861

WILLIAMS, ALICE BRAMLETT, 6th-8th Grade Phys Ed Teacher; *b:* Clinton, AR; *m:* R. Kent; *c:* Hayden W.; *ed:* (BSE) Phys Ed, Univ of Cntrl AR 1977-81; (MS) Phys Ed/Gen Sci, Ball St Univ 1984-88; *cr:* 8th Grade Sci Teacher/7th Grade Coach Conway Jr HS 1981-82; 9th-10th Grade Phys Ed Teacher Frankton HS 1982-83, 1986-87; 6th-8th Grade Phys Ed/8th Grade Sci Teacher Beech Grove Mid Sch 1987-; *ai:* Mid Sch Sci Dept Chm; 8th Grade Girls Bsktbl; Sftbl Sectional Champions 1987; Madison Cty HS All-Star Sertoma Girls Bsktbl Coach 1989-; *home:* PO Box 724 Lapel IN 46051

WILLIAMS, ALMETA, 6th/7th Grade Math Teacher; *b:* Detroit, MI; *m:* Dave; *c:* Derrick, Aaron; *ed:* (BA) Soc Stud, 1974, (MS) Soc Stud, 1979 Wayne St Univ; Essential Elements of Instruction; Sch Admin; *cr:* Teacher Grayling Elem 1974-76, Pulaski 1976-; *ai:* Journalism Spon; Co-Chairperson Spelling Bee & Oratorical Contest; Church Usher & Sunday Sch Teacher; Solicitor for United Way, Black United Fund, UNCF, Rosa Parks Schlsp Fund; Pulaski Sch Cmmty Relation 1988-; *home:* 20030 Picadilly Detroit MI 48221

WILLIAMS, ANNA KATHLEEN, 9th/11th/12th English Teacher; *b:* Phoenix, AZ; *m:* John T.; *c:* Stephen; *ed:* (BA) Ed, Baylor Univ 1952; (MA) Amer His, OH St Univ 1967; Developmental Rdng, Eng/His E TX St Univ; *cr:* 3rd Grade Teacher Cntrl Elem 1952-53; 7th Grade Eng/His Teacher University Jr HS 1955-58; 8th Grade Eng/His Teacher Junior HS 1958-60; 7th-9th Grade Eng/His Teacher Reynoldsburg Jr HS 1964-68; 11th Grade Eng Teacher Maconaqoah HS 1968-70; 11th/12th Grade Eng Teacher Greenville HS 1970-71; 9th/11th/12th Grade Eng Teacher Caddo Mills HS 1978-; *ai:* Stu Cncl Adv; Faculty Advisory Comm; Soc Stud Dept Chm; Delta Kappa Gamma Second VP 1967-; COE Fnd Fellow Abilene Chrstn Univ; Robert Taft Symposion on Government Trinity Univ; Educl Advisory Comm Honorable William Thomas TX House of Rep.

WILLIAMS, ARLENE VAN GALDER, Facilitator of Gifted; *b:* Stafford, KS; *c:* Carlen L., Victoria L.; *ed:* (BS) Elem Ed, 1967, (MS) Elem Ed, 1971 Ft Hays St Univ; Cert Gifted Ed 1986; *cr:* Kndgtn/Elem Music Teacher Anthony Harper Unified Sch Dist 361 1967-68; Kndgtn Teacher Washington Elem 1968-83; Substitute Teacher 5 Cty Area 1983-84; Teacher of Gifted Unified Sch Dist 331 1984-85; Facilitator of Gifted Stafford Cty Spec Ed Coop 1985-; Teacher of Gifted Ed Ft Hays St Univ 1987-; *ai:* Jr/Sr Play Dir; St John HS Knowledge Master Open, Stafford Elem & HS Scholars Bowl Coach; Phi Delta Kappa 1986-; Delta Kappa Gamma 1988-; CEC Talented & Gifted Division 1986-; Order of Eastern Star 1963-; Bus & Prof Women Pres 1988-89; Drama Guild 1984-; Ye Olde Tyme Club 1983-; Coord of Gifted Ed Practicums Ft Hays St Univ; Outstanding Young Educator Anthony Jaycees 1971; Whos Who Among Young Career Women 1971; Admin Coord for R D & Joan Hubbard Grant 1989; *office:* Stafford Cty Spec Ed Coop 505 N Broadway Saint John KS 67576

WILLIAMS, AUDREY ENGLISH, Fourth Grade Teacher; *b:* Amherstdale, WV; *m:* Jarrad; *c:* Jason; *ed:* (BA) Elem Ed, Bluefield St Coll 1971; (MS) Elem Admin, Radford Univ 1979; *cr:* 2nd Grade Teacher Anawalt Elem 1971-72; 5th Grade Teacher 1972-85, 4th Grade Teacher 1985- Switchback Elem; *ai:* Chrldr & Dance Routine Spon; Coach Math Field Day; Faculty Rep; NEA, WV Ed Assn, Mc Dowell Cty Ed Assn; Alpha Kappa Alpha, Maybeury Extension Homemakers; *home:* Rt 52 Box 58 Maybeury WV 24861

WILLIAMS, AVIS FEIRING, 5th Grade Teacher; *b:* Longwood, WI; *ed:* (BS) Scndry Ed/Eng/His/Soc Sci, 1941, (BS) Upper Elem, 1943 Univ of WI Platteville; Numerous Univs; *cr:* 7th-8th Grade Teacher Bellville WI 1941-43; Jr/Sr HS Eng/Math Teacher Beaver Dam WI 1943-46; 6th-8th Grade Teacher 1946-80, 5th Grade Teacher 1980-88 Mc Curdy Sch; *ai:* NEA NM Life Mem; Natl Assn of Deaconess & Home Missionaries; Diakonia Intnl Organization; *home:* 509 4th St NE Waseca MN 56093

WILLIAMS, BARBARA HOLMES, Fourth Grade Teacher; *b:* Grand Ridge, FL; *m:* Melvin; *c:* Marcus, Byron, MarQuita; *ed:* (BA) Elem Ed, Univ of W FL 1974; Early Chldhd, Univ of FL; *cr:* Teacher Grand Ridge Elem 1975-78, Riverside Elem 1978-; *ai:* Sch Policy Comm & Instructional Cncl Mem; JCA 1975-; FTP; J C Health Club Treas 1989-; Riverside Elem Sch Teacher of Yr Awd 1989; Cty Teacher of Yr Runner-Up; *home:* Rt 1 Box 132 Greenwood FL 32443

WILLIAMS, BILLY CRAIG, Health/Phys Ed Teacher; *b:* Pinehurst, NC; *ed:* (BA) Health/Phys Ed/Soc Stud, Cntrl Wesleyan Coll 1984; Effective Teaching Trng Prgm, Choosing For Yourself Comprehensive Drug Ed, Stu Asst Prgm; *cr:* ISS Dir Richmond Sr HS 1985; Teacher Highland Mid Sch 1985-; *ai:* Ftbl, Bsktbl, Bsbl Coach; OSHA & Stu Asst Prgm Comm; Athletic & Intramural Dir; NC Assn of Ed, NEA, NC Coaches Assn, PTA 1985-; Richmond Sr HS Bsbl Asst Head Coach Mid South AAAA Champions 1984-85; Highland Boys Bsktbl Cty Champions 1985-86; Boys Bsktbl Co-Cty Champions 1988-; Won Boys Bsktbl Team Camp High Point Coll 1989; Cty Ftbl Champions 1988-; Teacher of Yr 1986-87.

WILLIAMS, BOBBYE CHANEY, Retired/Substitute Teacher; *b:* Fort Myers, FL; *m:* Macon L.; *c:* Terri K. Chaney; *ed:* (BS) Elem Ed, FL A&M Univ 1954; Attended FL St & Nova Univ; *cr:* 1st-8th Grade Teacher Daniels Elem 1954-56; 2nd Grade Teacher Dunbar Elem 1956-58; 2nd/4th/5th Grade Teacher Franklin Park Elem 1958-; 4th/5th Grade Teacher Bayshore Elem; *ai:* Lee Cty Teachers Assn (Secy, VP); FTP, NEA Mem 1954-89; NAACP, Dunbar Festival Cmmty Pres 1988.

WILLIAMS, BRADLEY C., Business Teacher; *b:* Wayne, NE; *m:* Connie Rae De Jager; *c:* Christopher F., Rachel E.; *ed:* (BA) Phys Ed/Bus, Yankton Coll 1982; *cr:* Bus/Cmptr Teacher Greeley Public Schls 1982-; *ai:* Asst Ftbl & Head Girls Bsktbl Coach; Greeley Ed Assn Pres 1988-; NE Ed Assn, NE Coaches Assn 1982-; Girls Bsktbl St Championship 1990; *home:* Box 165 Greeley NE 68842

WILLIAMS, CARL GLENN, Industrial Technology Teacher; *b:* Houston, TX; *m:* Anna Irene Corbin; *c:* Margie, Terri, Daniel; *ed:* (BS) Industrial Arts, SW TX St Univ 1965; (MS) Industrial Technology, Univ of TX Tyler 1986; Working Toward PhD Technology, Univ TX Tyler; Numerous Wkshps; *cr:* Industrial Arts Teacher Barstow Ind Sch Dist 1965-66; Occupational Trng 1966-67, Industrial Arts Teacher 1967-72 El Paso Ind Sch Dist; Industrial Arts/Technology Teacher Comal Ind Sch Dist 1972-; *ai:* NEA, TX St Teacher Assn 1965-, Life Mem; Comal Educators Assn 1972- (St Conference Delegate 1977, 1983-85, Pres 1984-85) 1972-; Intnl Technology Ed Assn 1965-; El Paso Industrial Art Assn (Pres 1971-72, Bd Mem TIAA), Outstanding Teacher 1972; Technology Stu Assn Bd Mem 1987-89; Hill Cntry Industrial Art Assn Pres 1983-84; Amer Industrial Assn Outstanding Adv 1987; Co-Author & Coord Voc Academic Ed El Paso Ind Sch Dist 1967-68; TX Industrial Art Teacher to Review Curr 1982-85; Develop Rationale for Industrial Technology in TX 1983-84; St Curr Dev for HS in Technology Ed 1985-; *home:* Rt 8 Box 170 New Braunfels TX 78130

WILLIAMS, CAROLYN GAYLE, Pre-Algebra/Algebra I Teacher; *b:* Oklahoma City, OK; *ed:* (BS) Math, S Nazarene Univ 1973; (MED) Scndry Ed, Cntrl St Univ 1978; *cr:* Math Teacher Yukon Jr HS 1973-76, Independence Mid Sch 1976-; *ai:* Mathcounts Coach; North Cntrl Accreditation Assn Self Evaluation Comm; Yukon Prof Ed Assn, OK Ed Assn, NEA; Delta Kappa Gamma Society Treas 1988-; *office:* Indepenence Mid Sch 500 E Vandament Ave Yukon OK 73099

WILLIAMS, CLARA JANE, Teacher; *b:* Ashland, AL; *ed:* (BS) Elem Ed/Spec Ed, 1980, (MS) Elem Ed, 1986 Jacksonville St Univ; *cr:* Teacher Ashland Elem Sch 1980-; *ai:* NEA, AL Ed Assn Mem 1980-; *home:* Rt 3 Box Ashland AL 36251

WILLIAMS, CURTIS, Health & Phys Ed Teacher; *b:* Columbus, GA; *m:* Joyce; *c:* Corey, Natalie; *ed:* (BS) Health/Phys Ed, Albany St Coll 1974; (MED) Phys Ed, Valdosta St Coll 1980; Data Collector; *cr:* Phys Ed Teacher Adel Elem 1976-77; Phys Ed Teacher/Coach Valdosta Jr HS 1977-81; Health/Phys Ed Instr Washington-Wilkes Comprehensive HS 1981-; *ai:* Adv Fellowship of Chrstn Athletes; Defensive Coord Ftbl Team; Jr Var Boys

Bsktbl & Asst Head Ftbl Coach; GA Assn of Educators, NEA, Natl Fed Interscholastic Assn, GA HS Coaches Assn; Recreation Bd of Dirs 1988-; GSA Activity Leader 1986-88.

WILLIAMS, DALT B., Band Director; *b:* Vallejo, CA; *m:* Patricia J. Mecredy; *c:* David B., Jeffrey L.; *ed:* (AA) Music, Vallejo Coll 1957; (BA) Music, San Francisco St Univ 1959; Addtl Courses, Clinics, Wkshps, Seminars Solano Coll, Hayward St Univ, Sonoma St Univ, San Francisco St Univ; *cr:* Band Dir Center Sch 1960-64; Band/Choir Dir Vanden HS 1964-68, Benicia HS 1968-; *ai:* Adv & Dir Music Fed, Concert & Marching Band, Choir, Jazz Band, Combos & Small Ensembles; Solano Cty Band Dirs Pres 1962-64; CA Band Dirs Assn 1966-; CA Music Educators Assn, Music Educators Natl Conference 1960-; Amer Fed of Musicians 1956-; Intnl Assn of Jazz Educators 1960-; Numerous Awds Benicia HS Bands; *home:* 306 Cottonwood Dr Vallejo CA 94591

WILLIAMS, DAVID P, English/Journalism Teacher; *b:* Arkadelphia, AR; *m:* Dana Kaye; *c:* Heather; *ed:* (BA) Eng/Journalism, Henderson St 1978; (MED) Scndry Sch Admin, Univ of AR 1985; *cr:* Teacher Hot Springs Cntrl Jr HS 1978-83, Jessieville Schls 1983-; *ai:* Yrbk & Newspaper Spon; *home:* Rt 2 Box 89 Mountain Pine AR 71956

WILLIAMS, DEBORAH ANDERSON, First Grade Teacher; *b:* Washington, GA; *m:* Roy J. E.; *c:* Audrey, Bernadette; *ed:* (BA) Elem Ed, Johnson C Smith Univ 1961; Univ of CA Los Angeles, CA St Univ Dominguez Hills, Univ of NC Charlotte; *cr:* 3rd Grade Teacher Castle Height Elem 1961-62; Kndgtn Teacher Abraham Lincoln Sch 1967-68, Robert F Kennedy Sch 1968-71; K-2nd Grade Teacher Matthews Elem Sch 1972-; *ai:* Sch Plan Comm Co-Chm; Minority Achievement Comm Mem; NCAE, NEA 1972-; NC Assn for Chldhd Ed Secy 1972-79; Alpha Kappa Alpha 1961-; Teacher of Yr 1983; *home:* 1706 Jennings St Charlotte NC 28216

WILLIAMS, DEBRA PETERS, Eng/Speech/Drama Teacher; *b:* Washington, DC; *ed:* (BS) Eng, SW MO St Univ 1983; Working Towards Masters Scndry Ed; *cr:* Eng Teacher/Coach Parker HS 1984-86; Eng/Speech/Drama Teacher Pierce City HS 1987-; Poetry Teacher Crowder Coll 1990; *ai:* Soph Class Spon; Speech & drama Coach; Mentor Teacher; Sigma Tau Delta 1982-; NCTE 1986-; MO St Teachers Assn 1987-89; Poetry Published; *home:* 432 W County Monett MO 65708

WILLIAMS, DELORES, English Teacher; *b:* Gary, IN; *c:* Janelle E.; *ed:* (BS) Ed, 1975, (MS) Ed, 1988 IN Univ; *cr:* Youth Supvr Gary Manpower Admin Summer Prgm 1977-81; Teacher Gary Sch Cmmty Corporation 1977-; *ai:* Frosh Class Spon 1978-83; Parent Teacher Involvement Prgm; Gary Rdng Cncl Mem 1978-; Gary Eng Cncl Mem 1978-87; Delta Sigma Theta 1974-; Old Path Ministry Ec Dev Secy 1989; AFT 1977-; Evangelistic Outreach Secy 1987-; NAACP Secy 1990; Honorary Gary City Cncl Person; I U Dons Incorporated Distinguished Citizens 25 Yrs Service Awd; IN Univ Deans List.

WILLIAMS, DENNIS RALPH, Counselor/Cmmty Service Coord; *b:* Jefferson City, MO; *ed:* (BSED) Eng, 1971, (MED) Curr Dev/Peace Corps, 1975, (MED) Guidance/Counseling, 1978 Lincoln Univ; Scndry Sch Admin, Drake Univ; *cr:* Eng Instr Lincoln Univ 1971-73; Math/Sci Teacher Trainer/Adult Ed Specialist Peace Corps 1973-75; Eng Instr Ft Dodge Sr HS 1975-78; Dir Desegregation Prgm 1978-80, Cnslr/Cmmty Services Coord 1980- Ft Dodge Cmmty Sch Dist; *ai:* Small Bus Review Comm; Project Try Teacher; Race & Sex Equity Consultant; NCTE, ICTE Mem; Calvary Mem COGIC Deacon 1980-, Outstanding Mem 1980; Nom IA Teacher of Yr; Outstanding Educator of America; Whos Who Among Coll Stus; *office:* Ft Dodge Sr HS 819 N 25th St Fort Dodge IA 50501

WILLIAMS, DIANNE THERESA B., Psychology Teacher; *b:* Washington, DC; *ed:* (AS) Fashion Design, 1966, (AA) Liberal Arts, 1967 Miami Dade Comm Coll; (BS) Bio - Magna Cum Laude, Barry Univ 1969; (MS) Microbiology/Immunology, Univ of Miami 1974; (MA) Counseling/Guidance, WV Sch of Grad Stud 1981; Oak Ridge Natl Laboratories; Summer Stu Honors Prgm; Natl Inst of Dental Health; *cr:* Bio/Phys Sci Teacher Our Lady of the Lourdes 1969-70; Psych/Anatomy/Developmental Teacher Shady Spring Sr HS 1977-84; Part Time Microbiology Instr Beckley Coll 1982-84; Psych/Anatomy/Bio Teacher Miami Coral Park Sr HS 1984-; *ai:* Faculty Cncl 1988-; QUIIP Comm for SAT Scores 1989-; Fire Safety Comm 1984-85; Vlybl Coach Shady Spring HS 1977-78, Tennis Coach 1977-78; Sr Class Spon 1983-84; Assn of Humanistic Psych 1981-; Assn of Transpersonal Psych, Carl Jung Fnd, NEA, Natl Sci Teacher; Miami Parrot Club & Parrot Crime Watch Ed Comms; Natl Appaloosa Horse Club 1970-84; Weimaraner Club of America; Greenpeace; Amnesty Intnl; People for the Amer Way; Animal Defense Fund; Environmental Defense Fund 1988-89; Earth Island Inst; Miami Coral Park Sr HS Sci Teacher of Yr 1986-87; Sci Honor Spec Recognition Awd; Teacher of Yr Coral Park Sr 1986-87, Shady Springs Sr HS 1980-81; Authored & Co-authored Immunolgy Research Articles.

WILLIAMS, DON E., SR., Teacher & Coach; *b:* Richwood, WV; *m:* Patricia E. Hicks; *c:* Don Jr., Paul M., John C., Danielle E., Caroline A., James E.; *ed:* (BS) Math Ed, WV Inst of Technology 1975; Scndry Admin, WVU-COGS; *cr:* Teacher/Coach Gauley Bridge HS 1975-77, Charleston Cath HS 1977-79; Teacher/Coach/Asst Prin Parkersburg Cath HS 1979-82; Teacher/Coach Walton HS 1982-; *ai:* Class Spon 1992; SADD Spon; Var Ftbl, Bsktbl Coach; WV Ed Assn 1983-; Roane Ed Assn VP 1989-; Metro-Index Outstanding Coach 1988; Cub Scouts Cub Master 1985-86; Parish Cncl Pres 1985, 1988-89; OH/WV Scout; *home:* 511 W Main St Spencer WV 25276

WILLIAMS, DONALD WOODROW, Art Teacher; *b:* Saginaw, MI; *m:* Kathy M. Brown; *c:* Sara; *ed:* (BA) Art, W MI 1970; Ed, MI St Univ; *cr:* Painting/Drawing Teacher Delta Coll 1976-77; Jewelry Teacher Northwood Inst 1978-81; Teacher of Gifted Art Delta Coll 1982-86; Art Teacher Saginaw Township Cmmty Schls 1970-; *ai:* 8th Grade Girls Bsktbl; Build Sets for Sch Plays; Saginaw Township Cmmty Sch Teacher of Yr 1982-83 & Grant 1979; 4 Week Artist Exch Japan; Published Visual Art in Gifted Prgm, Natl Directorty K-12th Grade Artistically Talented; *office:* White Pine Mid Sch 505 N Center Rd Saginaw MI 48603

WILLIAMS, DONNY LEE, 7th & 8th Grade Sci Teacher; *b:* Louisville, KY; *m:* Debby Lou Welcher; *ed:* (BS) Elem Ed, Toccoa Falls ColL 1979; (MED) Mid Grades Ed, North GA Coll 1984; *cr:* 7th/8th Grade Sci Teacher Stephens Cty Mid Sch 1979-; *ai:* Stephens Cty HS Bsktbl Coach 179-86; SCMS Tennis Coach 1986-87; Prof Assn of GA Educators 1980-89; Toccoa Falls Coll Alumni Bsktbl Hall of Fame 1986; *home:* 128 Fern Valley Dr Toccoa GA 30577

WILLIAMS, EARL LOUIS, Graphic Arts Teacher; *b:* Lynwood, CA; *ed:* (BVE) Vocational Ed, Ca St Univ 1990; *cr:* Instructional Aide/Vocational 1982-86; Graphic Arts Teacher 1986- Lynwood HS; *ai:* Lynwood Lithographers Club-Spon; Graphic Arts Tech Fnd Mem 1988-; Graphic Arts Assn of Comm Coll Instrs Mem 1988-; Outstanding Teacher, Lynwood Reg Occupation Prgm 1990; *office:* Lynwood H S 12124 Bullis Rd Lynwood CA 90262

WILLIAMS, EDNA RENE MIDDLETON, Second Grade Teacher; *b:* Little Rock, AR; *m:* Keith David; *c:* Kelli, Tacuma Sekou; *ed:* (BA) Speech, S F St Univ 1971; (MA) Ed, Univ of CO Boulder 1987; Lifetime Credential, CA St Univ; *cr:* Kndgtn/2nd Grade Teacher Milpitas Unified Sch Dist 1972-78; 2nd/4th Grade Teacher Harrison Sch Dist 1980-; *ai:* Sch Accountability Comm; Mem of Chancellors Advisory Comm on Minority Recruitment & Retention, Univ of CO Colorado Springs; Mem Pres E Gordon Gees Minority Advisory Comm for CO Coll System; Total Rdng Assn Rdng Consultant; Delta Sigma Theta 1972-; Oak Creek Elem Sch Teacher of Yr 1987; Harrison Sch Dist Teacher of Yr Finalist 1987; Fullbright Fellowship to Kenya E Africa Soc Stud Curr Writing Project 1985; *home:* 2005 Flintlock Terr E Colorado Spgs CO 80920

WILLIAMS, ELAINE R., 5th Grade Teacher; *b:* Kansas City, MO; *m:* Wellington J.; *c:* Wellington Jr., Brian; *ed:* (BS) Elem Ed, Univ of CO 1972; (MA) Cmptr Ed, Lesley Coll 1990; *cr:* Kndgtn Teacher Anderson AFB Guam 1967-69; Math Tutor Denver Public Schls 1969-72; 3rd Grade Teacher 1972-77, 5Th Grade Teacher 1977- Aurora Public Schls; *ai:* Faculty Rep; Safety Patrol Leader; Phi Delta Kappa 1988-; Park Hill United Meth Church; *office:* Virginia Court Elem Sch 395 S Troy St Aurora CO 80012

WILLIAMS, ELIZABETH ANN, Sixth Grade Teacher; *b:* Chicago, IL; *c:* Emily Chaffin, Thomas Chaffin; *ed:* (BS) Elem Ed, Bowling Green St Univ 1973; Elem Ed, Univ of Toledo; *cr:* 2nd Grade Teacher Highland W Elem Sch 1973-75; 4th/5th Split Grade Teacher Northside Chrstn Sch 1975-76; 1st-4th Grade Tutor of Learning Disabilities Delaware City Schls 1977; 5th-8th Grade Teacher Genoa Jr HS & Brunner Elem 1980-; *ai:* Math Curr Comm; NEA 1973-75, 1980-; OEA, GAEA, HEA Building Rep 1974-75; Amer Red Cross Reaching Adolescents & Parents Inst 1989-; Martha Holden Jennings Scholar 1982-83; *office:* Brunner Elem Sch 1224 West St Genoa OH 43430

WILLIAMS, ELIZABETH C., Spanish Teacher; *b:* Memphis, TN; *m:* Bryan E.; *ed:* (BA) Eng/Span, Bible Blue Mountain Coll 1961; Univ of TN, Emory Univ, Univ of NE, Memphis St Univ; *cr:* Teacher Valmeyer HS 1961-63, White Station HS 1963-69, Tech HS 1969-71, Cntrl HS 1971-; *ai:* Span Club Spon; Sch Frosh Comm Mem; Amer Assn Teachers of Span & Portuguese, Memphis Ed Assn, W TN Ed Assn, NEA; Scenic Hills Womens Assn; Natl Defense Ed Act Inst for Foreign Lang Univ of NE 1963; Natl Defence Ed Act Inst for Eng Teachers Emory Univ 1965; *office:* Central HS 306 S Bellevue Memphis TN 38104

WILLIAMS, EVAN PRICE, English Department Chairman; *b:* Easton, PA; *m:* Susan Lee Wamsgans; *c:* Charles; *ed:* (AB) His/Eng, La Fayette Coll 1977; (MED) Eng Ed, E Stroudsburg Univ 1989; PhD Prgm PA St Univ; *cr:* Quality Control Mgr Shaw Plastics Corporation 1982-86; Substitute Teacher N Hunterdon Regional HS 1986; Teacher 1986-88, Eng Dept Chm 1988- Upper Dauphin Area HS; *ai:* Film Club Spon; Var Ftbl Statistician; Boys Track Asst Coach; Advanced Placement Coord; PSEA 1986-; UDAEA Comm Chm 1988-; MLA 1989-; Various Schlsps; *office:* Upper Dauphin Area HS RD 1 PO Box 24 Elizabethville PA 17023

WILLIAMS, FANNIE RANDOLPH, First Grade Teacher; *b:* Brandon, MS; *m:* Moress Sr.; *c:* Yulanda S., Moress Jr., John M., Kewanza Q.; *ed:* Assoc Elem Ed, Piney Woods Jr Coll 1967; (BS) Elem Ed, Jackson St 1969; Rdng, Jackson St, Leadership Inst, Tougaloo Coll; Law Related Ed, Univ of MS; *cr:* 4th Grade Teacher Kilmichael Elem 1970-71; 2nd Grade Teacher Pass Chrstn Elem 1971-73; 1st Grade Teacher Pelahatchie Elem 1973-; *ai:* Girl Scout Leader; Cmmty Club Treas; Rankin Assn of Educators (Secy, Treas 1987-88) Certificate 1988; Piney Woods Alumni Assn Secy; Zeta Phi Beta 1968-69; Outstanding Teacher in Area 1988-89; Teacher of Yr Pelahatchie Elem 1988-89; *home:* 129 Mandy Dr Brandon MS 39042

WILLIAMS, FLOSSIE K., First Grade Teacher; *b:* Ft Myers, FL; *c:* Michelle, Darrell, Robert; *ed:* (BA) Elem Ed, Barry Coll 1968; Grad Stud Early Chldhd Ed, Nova Univ; *ai:* Sunday Sch Teacher; Usher Bd Pres; *home:* 1120 NW 66th St Miami FL 33150

WILLIAMS, FRANCES ELIZABETH, Soc Stud Teacher/Dept Chair; *b:* Eccles, WV; *ed:* (BA) Poly Sci/His, Univ of DC 1973; (MAT) His, Trinity Coll 1975; Post Grad Stud Trinity Coll; *cr:* Cmptr Tape Librarian GSA Federal Government 1966-72; Cmptr Operator HHS Federal Government 1972; Soc Stud Teacher H D Woodson Sr HS 1973-; *ai:* NCSS, US Capitol Historical Society; Jr Achievement DC Area Bd Supt Awd; *office:* H D Woodson Sr HS 55th & Eads Sts NE Washington DC 20019

WILLIAMS, FRANCIS RICHARD, JR., History Teacher/Coach; *b:* Abbeville, SC; *m:* Jamie O Neal; *c:* Anna L., Katelyn P.; *ed:* (BA) His, Presbyn Coll 1984; *cr:* Teacher/Coach Woodruff HS 1984-; *ai:* Fellowship of Chrstn Athletes Spon; Asst Athletic Dir; Asst Ftbl & Boys Tennis Coach; Dist Team Faculty Rep; Sch & Cmmty Comm; SC Athletic Coaches Assn 1984-, Region II-AA Tennis Coach of Yr 1986, Teacher of Month 1989; Region II-AA Secy, Treas 1988-89; *home:* 1 Fowler Dr Woodruff SC 29388

WILLIAMS, GAIL SUZANNE, Language Arts Teacher; *b:* Tiffin, OH; *m:* Thomas M.; *c:* Jill Nicole, Erin Elizabeth; *ed:* (BA) Soc Stud/Eng, MI St Univ 1969; Univ of AR Little Rock; *cr:* Eng & Soc Stud Teacher Mc Grath Jr HS 1969-71, Pulaski Acad 1977-79; Eng Teacher Madison HS 1980-81; Lang Arts Teacher Alief Mid Sch 1981-; *ai:* Team Leader; Sch Newsletter Faculty Spon; West Houston Area Cncl of Teachers of Eng Mem 1986-; Mission Bend United Meth Church 1988-; *office:* Alief Mid Sch 4415 Cook Rd Houston TX 77072

WILLIAMS, GARY, Business Teacher; *b:* Newport, TN; *m:* Debbie Moore; *c:* Franklin; *ed:* (BS) Bus Ed, 1973, (MED) Admin/Supervision, 1989 E TN St Univ; Various Courses Univ of TN Knoxville; *cr:* 8th Grade Teacher Edgemont Elem 1973-87; Bus Teacher Cocke Cty HS 1988-; *ai:* Academic Decathlon Spon; CCEA, TEA, NEA; *office:* Cocke Cty HS Hedrick Dr Newport TN 37821

WILLIAMS, GARY BENNETT, Chemistry Teacher; *b:* Williamsport, PA; *m:* Kathy L. Heckman; *c:* Shawn, Desiree, Tiffany; *ed:* (BA) Chem, Lycoming Coll 1965; (MED) Ed, Temple Univ 1968; Central PA Assn of Chem Teachers; *cr:* General Sci Teacher Brookhaven Jr HS 1965-1967; Chem Teacher Montoursville HS 1967-; *ai:* Bd Mem for Montoursville HS Natl Honor Society; Montoursville Ed Assn Negotiations Team 1967-85; Organization Montoursville Ed 1985-; United Meth Church Bd Mem 1988-89; Office Nom Comm 1990-92; *office:* Montoursville H S 100 N Arch St Montoursville PA 17754

WILLIAMS, GERALD LEE, Electronics Teacher; *b:* Elko, NV; *m:* M. L. Schwartz; *c:* Terral Lee, Trent Lee, Travis Lee; *ed:* (AS) General Ed, Snow Coll 1965; (BFA) Printmaking/Illustration Design, UT St Univ 1967; (MED) Ed, Univ of UT 1971; Electonics, RCA, Heath, Zenith; Ed Admin, Univ of NV Reno; *cr:* Art Teacher Wells HS 1967-70, Elko Jr HS 1971-81; Electronics Teacher Elko HS/Northern NV Comm Coll 1981-; *ai:* Stu Cncl & Frosh Class Adv Elko Jr HS; Sch Plays; Yrbk; Art Club; Stu Cncl Wells HS; Elko Cty Teacher Assn Building Rep 1968-69; JC Secy 1972-73; *home:* PO Box 1344 Elko NV 89801

WILLIAMS, GRACE TWINING, First Grade Teacher; *b:* Denver, MO; *m:* James W.; *c:* Stephanie K.; *ed:* (Bs) Ed, Bethany Nazarene Coll 1959; Grad Hrs Ouachita Univ; Univ Central AR; Prof Grouth Hrs Pulaski Cty Sch Dist; *cr:* 1st Grade Teacher Abbott Elem 1959-60; Riverside Elem 1960-63; 2nd Grade Teacher Badgett Elem 1963-67; 1st Grade Teacher Landmark Elem 1967-; *ai:* Staff Rep Music Dept; Staff Rep Pals; 1st Grade Level Leader, North Central Steering Comm; Primary Team Leader; Adivsory Cncl; Pulaski Assn of Classroom Teachers Mem 1962-89; AR Ed Assn Mem 1959-89; NEA Mem 1959-89; Girl Scout/Brownie Leader 1978-79; Springlake Church of Nazarene Pianist 1964-; Childrens Choir Dir 1970-; Mission Dept Study Chm/Study Recorder 19 70-; PTD (Historian/Teacher Rep); Lifetime Awd 1976; Pulaski Cty Special Member Awd 1986; Sch Dist Teacher of Yr; *home:* 22019 N Springlake Rd Hensley AR 72065

WILLIAMS, HELEN HAYES, Second Grade Teacher; *b:* Rome, GA; *m:* Jimmie L.; *c:* Marcus; *ed:* (BS) Elem Ed, Albany St Coll 1971; (MED) Early Chldhd Ed, West GA Coll 1979; Early Chldhd Ed West GA Coll; *cr:* 3rd Grade Teacher Tallapoosa Elem Sch 1971-73; 2nd Grade Teacher Coll St Schl 1974-82; Cherokee Elem Sch 1982-; *ai:* Gifted Pgm Support Team Monitor 1987-89; 2nd Grade Lead Teacher Cherokee Elem Sch; PAE/GAE; Delta Sigma Theta Sorority Pres 1985-88; South Rome Comm Assn VP 1989-; Nom Romes Woman of Yr -1988; *office:* Cherokee Elem Sch Cedartown GA 30125

WILLIAMS, HENRY WOODSON, III, 6th Grade Teacher; *b:* Greensburg, KY; *m:* Carolyn Scott; *c:* Eric, Matthew; *ed:* (BS) Phys Ed/Bio, 1965, (MA) Elem Ed, 1971, (Rank I) Ed, 1974 Western KY Univ; *cr:* 6th Grade Teacher Daviess Cty Sch System 1965-; *ai:* Mid Sch Ftbl Coach; Teach Adult Ed Class; *home:* 2823 Asbury Pl Owensbow KY 42303

WILLIAMS, INGRID HARVEY, English/Journalism Teacher; *b:* Fort Worth, TX; *m:* Paul E.; *ed:* (BA) Broadcast Journalism, Univ of OK 1985; *cr:* Scndry Eng/Journalism Teacher Trimble Tech 1988-; *ai:* Class of 1992 Spon; Journalism/Sch Newspaper

Adv; *office:* Trimble Tech HS 1003 W Cannon Ave Fort Worth TX 76104

WILLIAMS, JAMES C., 11th Grade Guidance Counselor; *b:* Warren Cty, TN; *m:* Sue Harrell; *ed:* (BS) Psych, M1971, (MA) Counseling/Psych, 1976 Mid TN St Univ; Trng Individual Instruction; *cr:* Building Prin/Teacher Gribble Spec Ed Sch 1971-77; Psych/His Teacher 1978-88, Jr Cnslr 1989- Warren Cty Sr HS; *ai:* NHS Spon; Beta Club & Jr Class Adv; Warren Cty At Risk Stu Comm Mem; NEA, TEA, WCEA 1971-84; TN Assn of Cnslrs 1989-; Veterans of Foreign Wars; Natl Sci Fnd Citizenship Grant; Free Enterprise & Ed Univ of TN Chatanooga; *office:* Warren Cty Sr HS 200 Caldwell St Mc Minnville TN 37110

WILLIAMS, JANET STEENSMA, Reading Teacher; *b:* Sioux Falls, SD; *m:* John F.; *ed:* (BA) Eng, Sioux Falls Coll 1968; (MES) Effective Teaching/Rdng, Drake Univ 1990; *cr:* Teacher Kasson-Mantorville HS 1968-70, Rock Valley 1970-74; Mc Combs Mid Sch 1978-; *ai:* Drug/Alcohol Intervention Cadre; Gifted & Talented Comm; Building Activities Comm; Crafts Club Adv; Odyssey of Mind Judge; DMEA, ISEA, NEA 1968-; IRA 1978.

WILLIAMS, JOAN L., English Teacher; *b:* Eureka, CA; *m:* Michael; *c:* Ryan, Michele; *ed:* (BA) Eng, CA Luth Univ 1971; (MA) Eng, Univ of ME 1973; *cr:* Eng Teacher Univ of ME 1973-75, Coll of the Redwoods 1976-, Arcata HS 1976-; *ai:* Sr Class, Tiger Tales Literary Magazine Adv; CA Teachers Assn 1976-; CA Assn Teachers Eng Redwood Region VP 1989-; Ind Study Fellowship; Natl Endowment for Hum Redwood Writing Project Fellow; *office:* Arcata HS 1720 M Street Arcata CA 95521

WILLIAMS, JOAN MONSER, 4th/5th Grade Lang Art Teacher; *b:* Oneonta, NY; *c:* Amy; *ed:* (BA) Elem Ed, SUNY Oneonta 1969; Grad Work Loyola Coll; *cr:* 7th Grade Lang Art Teacher Shenendehow Cntrl Sch 1969-72; *ai:* St Vincent de Paul Fair Coord; Knights of Columbus Spelling Bee Enunciator; Lang Art Comm Head; NCEA 1975-; Glen Burnie HS PTA Pres 1989; *office:* St Jane Frances Sch 8499 Virginia Ave Riviera Beach MD 21122

WILLIAMS, JOCELYN JONES, Reading Teacher; *b:* Greenville, NC; *ed:* (BS) Home Ec/Clothing & Textiles, Bennett Coll 1970; (MS) Early Chldhd Ed, NC Cntrl Univ Durham 1988; Early Chldh Ed NC Cert; NC Ag & Tech St Univ 1972; Rdng Cert; *cr:* Teacher Greenville Cty Schls 1970-74, Orange Cty Schls 1974-; *ai:* PTO Advisory Bd Mem 1989-; Orange Cty Assn of Educators 1974-; NC Assn of Educators 1970-; Phi Delta Kappa Intnl 1987-; ASCD 1985-; Alpha Kappa Alpha 1977-; Progressive Sertoma Club 1989-; Eugenia Mc Manus Younge Awd for Excl in Rdng Grad Elem Ed Prgm NC Cntrl Univ Durham 1986-87; Teacher Excl Awd Orange Cty Schls 1988; *office:* Grady A Brown Elem Sch Orange Grove Rd Rt 6 Box 1005 Hillsborough NC 27278

WILLIAMS, JOHN E., Fifth Grade Teacher; *b:* Panama City, FL; *ed:* (AA) General Ed, Palm Beach Jr Coll 1968; (BA) Elem Ed, Univ of West FL 1970; *cr:* 5th Grade Teacher Clewiston Elem 1970-81, Gove Elem 1981-; *ai:* Spon Safety Patrol; 5th Grade Chairperson; Sci/Soc Stud Peer Teacher; NEA 1989-; Jaycees Outstanding Youth Educator Awd 1975-76; Goves Teacher of Yr 1989-; *office:* Gove Elem Sch 900 SE Avenue G Belle Glade FL 33430

WILLIAMS, JOMARGARET, Orchestra/Music Teacher; *b:* San Angelo, TX; *m:* Robert S. Fisher Sr.; *ed:* (BM) Music Ed, Univ of Houston 1969; (MS) Music Ed, East TX St Univ 1976; *cr:* Orch Teacher Dallas Ind Sch Dist 1969-; Cello Instr Mountain View Cmmty Coll 1971-73; Curr Writer-Success Through Strings Project-DISD 1974-76; Jr Division Coord Southern Meth Univ 1978-; Teacher Trainer in Montes Sori Music-DISD 1980-; *ai:* Mid Sch Orch Coaching-Before and after Sch; Founder and Exec Dir Youth Concert: Fnd Promotion Creative Arts in Schlsp Assistance; TMEA Mem 1979-89; Kappa Delta Pi Mem 1969: Music Dept Awd 1969; Dallas Music Educators Assn Mem 1969-; Montessori Music Manual for Classroom Teachers-1980; Private Grant Study in Europe-1972; Curr Writer Success Through Strings Project-DISD-Recognized at MENC-1975; Presenter Outstanding Groups TMEA 1972-73; Teacher L L Hotchkiss DISD 1981-83-87-88; *home:* 2310 Freeland Way Dallas TX 75228

WILLIAMS, JOYCE SMITH, Fourth Grade Teacher; *b:* Raleigh, NC; *m:* Paul J.; *c:* Teresa Faison, Paul T., Saul J., Rhonda Alexander; *ed:* (BA) Elem Ed, St Augustine 1955; *cr:* Elem Ed Teacher Clinton City Sch System 1960-; *ai:* NCAE; Sampson HS Alumni Assn Corresponding Secy; *home:* 302 W Carter St Clinton NC 28328

WILLIAMS, JUDY, Chapter I Math Teacher; *b:* Salyersville, KY; *m:* Ralph; *ed:* (BA) Elem Ed, 1973, (MA) Ed/Lib Sci, 1975, (Rank I) Ed, 1978 Morehead St Univ; *cr:* 3rd/6th Grade Teacher Salyersville Grade Sch 1975-84; Librarian/Chapter I Teacher Salyer Elem 1984-; Resource Teacher for Intern Teacher 1987-; *ai:* Magoffin Cty Chapter I Improvement Plan Math-A-Thon Coord; Intnl Rdng Assn 1987-; Society of Sch Librarians Intnl 1989-; Magoffin Cty Ed Assn 1975-; NEA 1980-88; Big Sandy Health Clinic Bd Mem 1985-87; *office:* Salyer Elem Sch 5781 Royalton Rd Salyersville KY 41465

WILLIAMS, JULIE FISHER, Third Grade Teacher; *b:* Evansville, IN; *c:* Amanda J.; *ed:* (BA) Elem Ed, Univ of S IN 1975; (MS) Elem Ed, IN St Univ 1985; *cr:* 3rd Grade Teacher Sts Peter & Paul Cath Sch 1976-81, 1982-; *ai:* Sch PTO Faculty Rep; Stu Achievement Club; Childrens Choir Dir; Kappa Kappa Iota; *office:* Sts Peter & Paul Cath Sch PO Box 368 Haubstadt IN 47639

WILLIAMS, JULIE FOUSHEE, First Grade Teacher; *b:* Ekron, KY; *m:* Ronnie Michael Sr.; *c:* Jennifer L., Ronnie M. Jr.; *ed:* (BS) Elem Ed, Catherine Spalding Univ 1968; (MS) Elem Ed, W KY Univ 1978; *cr:* 3rd Grade Teacher Sara Belle Wellington Elem 1968-71, Radcliff Elem 1971-74; 6th Grade Teacher Radcliff Mid Sch 1976-77; 2nd/3rd Grade Teacher Lincoln Trail Elem 1977-83; 1st Grade Teacher St James Elem 1986-; *ai:* NCEA 1986-; *home:* 567 Fowler Ln Elizabethtown KY 42701

WILLIAMS, KAREN RAUB, 1st Grade Teacher; *b:* Cincinnati, OH; *m:* Michael Howard; *ed:* (AA) Elem Ed, Elizabethtown Comm Coll 1970; (BA) Elem Ed, Univ of KY 1972; (MA) Elem Ed, W KY Univ 1978; *cr:* Elem Teacher Howevalley Elem Sch 1972-; *ai:* NEA, KY Ed Assn, Hardin Cty Ed Assn; Outstanding Young Women of America 1981; Bd of Ed Certificate of Outstanding Performance 1983; *office:* Howevalley Elem Sch 8450 Hardinsburg Rd Cecilia KY 42724

WILLIAMS, KAREY LYNN, English Teacher; *b:* Marion, IN; *ed:* (BPE) Phys Ed, 1984, (MS) Eng Ed, 1988 Purdue Univ; *cr:* Eng Teacher Monroe Cntrl Jr/Sr HS 1984-86, Southmont Jr/Sr HS 1986-; *ai:* Var Vlybl & Asst Girls Bsktbl Coach; Sch Climate & Honor Society Selection Comms; NEA, ISTA 1984-; ICGSA 1989-; *home:* 3069-811 Pheasant Run Dr Lafayette IN 47905

WILLIAMS, KARMEN PETERSEN, English Teacher; *b:* Kansas City, MO; *m:* James E.; *c:* Jan E., James J.; *ed:* (BA) Eng, OK Baptist Univ 1964; (MSE) Rdng, Ouachita Baptist Univ 1983; *cr:* Staff Dev Specialist Division of Family & Children Services; Teacher White Hall HS; *ai:* Drama Club Spon; Debate Coach; Eng Dept Chairperson; NCTE, AR Speech Assn, Natl Fed of Interscholastic Speech & Debate Assn; Wrote Grant Proposal to Place 1st AR Building on Natl Register of Historical Buildings; *office:* White Hall HS 901 Bulldog Dr White Hall AR 71602

WILLIAMS, KATHLEEN S. BROUSE, Fifth Grade Teacher/ Mentor; *b:* Elkhart, IN; *m:* Richard D.; *c:* Mason D.; *ed:* (BA) Liberal Art/Mexican Amer - Summa Cum Laude, Fresno Pacific Coll 1980; (MA) Ed, Fresno Pacific Coll; *cr:* Rural Comm Dev Peace Corps 1968; Teacher Grand View Sch 1980-83, Lincoln Sch 1983-; *ai:* Mentor Teacher Dinuba Public Schls; Lead Teacher Lincoln Sch; Migrant Ed Extended Day Teacher Lincoln Sch; Master Teacher Fresno Pacific Coll & CA St Univ Fresno; CA Rdng Assn, CA Assn of Teachers of Eng, NEA, CA Teachers Assn 1980-; Delta Kappa Gamma (Secy 1988-, 1st VP 1990); Fresno Pacific Coll Church Advisory Cncl 1980-86, 1988-; San Joaquin Valley Writing Project Advisory Bd 1989-; Fellow San Joaquin Valley Writing Project 1989; Recipient of CA TIIP Grant 1987; SBCP Quality Review Team Mem Tulare Cty 1990; *home:* 20736 E Huntsman Reedley CA 93654

WILLIAMS, KATHRYN THELMA, Retired; *b:* Elizabethton, TN; *m:* Carl V. Sr.; *c:* Carl V. Jr.; *ed:* Elem Ed, ETSU 1940; (BS) Milligan Coll 1967; *cr:* Lane Hill Sch 1940-41; Buladeen Sch 1942-45; Midway Sch 1945-51; Unaka Sch 1951-82; *ai:* TN Ed Assn, NEA, Carter Cty Teacher Assn; PTA Life Membership.

WILLIAMS, LANA M., Business Technology Teacher; *b:* Memphis, TN; *m:* David Jr.; *c:* Nina Cobb, Steven, Kathy; *ed:* (BS) Bus Ed, Rust Coll 1965; (MS) Bus Ed, Delta St Univ 1973; (BSC) Bus Technology, Univ of S MS 1987; *cr:* Teacher Rosa Fort HS 1965-87; Bus Technology Teacher Tunica Cty Voc Tech Center 1987-; *ai:* FBLA; MS Assn of Educators, MS Bus Educators Assn 1965-; MS Assn of Voc Educators 1987-; STAR Teacher Awd; *office:* Tunica Cty Voc Tech Center P O Box 1920 Tunica MS 38676

WILLIAMS, LAVARNE, 5th/6th Grade Science Teacher; *b:* Rosedale, MS; *ed:* (BSE) Elem Ed, 1980, (MED) Elem Ed, 1990 Delta St Univ; *cr:* 2nd Grade Teacher 1980-81, 5th/6th Grade Teacher 1981- West Bolivar Elem Sch; *ai:* Youth With Opportunity Girls & Boys Club Secy, Treas 1982-; MAE; *home:* 609 4th Box 594 Rosedale MS 38769

WILLIAMS, LEAH ANN RIEG, Science Teacher; *b:* Pittsburgh, PA; *m:* Michael P.; *ed:* (BS) Pre-Med/Bio, Grove City Coll 1985; Cert Teaching Cert, Slippery Rock Univ 1986; Core Team/Stu Assistance Prgm 1990; *cr:* 10th Grade Bio Teacher Moniteau HS 1986; Sci Teacher Butler Intermediate HS 1987-; *ai:* Asst Cross Cntry & Track Coach; Sci Club & SADD Spon; Cmptr Supvr; Omicron Delta Kappa 1985-; *home:* 324 W Main St Grove City PA 16127

WILLIAMS, LILLIAN POPE, English Chairperson/Teacher; *b:* Newark, NJ; *m:* Franklin L.; *c:* Valerie Williams Mundy, Franklin Jr.; *ed:* (BS) Sociology, Columbia Univ 1958; (MA) Ed, Jersey City St Coll 1978; *cr:* Teacher Head Start 1965-69; Eng Teacher Henry Snyder HS 1970-80; Eng Teacher/Eng Instr NJ Inst of Tech 1978, 1985; Chairperson Henry Snyder HS 1980, 1990; *ai:* Newspaper & Literary Magazine; Prgm, Curr Honor Society Comms; NJ Ed Assn; NAACP Youth Adv 1979; Teacher of Yr City Wide Parents Cncl; Yrbk Dedication; Outstanding Teach Selected by Sch Received Grant; *home:* 52 Culver Ave Jersey City NJ 07305

WILLIAMS, LINDA ANN (DAVIS), Sixth Grade Teacher; *b:* Villa Rica, GA; *c:* Jeffrey, Nicholas; *ed:* (BAE) Kndgtn/Elem, Univ of Fl 1962; *cr:* 1st/2nd Grade Teacher Jacksonville Beach Elem 1962-64; 6th/7th Grade Teacher Main Street & J H House Elem 1966-68; Adult Ed Teacher Div of Continuing Ed 1970-71; 5th/6th/8th Grade Teacher Flat Shoals Elem 1972-78; 6th/8th Grade Teacher Edwards Mid Sch 1978-; *ai:* Sunshine Comm; Adopted Grandparents Nursing Home Spon; GAE/NEA 1980-; Alpha Delta Kappa 1983-; *office:* Edwards Mid Sch 2400 Stanton Rd Conyers GA 30208

WILLIAMS, LINDA DARBY, First Grade Teacher; *b:* St Stephen, SC; *w:* Willie Jr. (dec); *c:* Brian L., Kimberly C.; *ed:* (BA) Elem Ed, Benedict Coll 1970; (MA) Ed, SC St Coll 1978; *cr:* 1st Grade Teacher Goose Creek Elem Sch 1972-76; 1st Grade Teacher 1976-77; 4th Grade Teacher 1977-88; 1st Grade Teacher 1988- St Stephen Elem Sch; *ai:* NEA 1972-; Ed Assn 1972-; Membership/Chairperson 1987-; Treas 1985-86 Berkeley Cty Ed Assn; Berkeley Cty Mental Health Ctr Bd Mem 1987-; Kappa Alpha Zeta Chapter of Zeta Phi Beta Sorority Inc; St Stephen Elem Teacher of Yr 1980-81; *office:* St Stephen Elem Sch P O Box 338 Saint Stephen SC 29479

WILLIAMS, LINDA FAYE, Vocational Office Ed Teacher; *b:* Fayetteville, TN; *ed:* (BS) Bus Ed, 1969, (MED) Scndry Ed, 1973 Mid TN St Univ; Grad Stud Office Ed; *cr:* Phys Ed Teacher Highland Rim Elem 1969-70; Voc Office Ed & Bus Teacher Cntrl HS 1970-79, Lincoln Cty HS 1976-; *ai:* Bus Prof of America Club Adv; NEA, TEA; Lincoln Cty Ed Assn Pres 1977-78; Amer Legion Aux; VFW Aux; Bus Prof of America Teacher Assn; Lincoln Cty Democratic Party; *home:* Rt 1 Box 29 Fayetteville TN 37334

WILLIAMS, LIZZIE MITCHELL, English Teacher; *b:* Marion, AL; *m:* Clarence B. Allen; *c:* Clarence B. II; *ed:* (BA) Eng Ed, FL A&M Univ 1966; (MS) Eng Ed, FL Intnl Univ 1975; Specialist Ed, Nova Univ 1989; Computer Tech; Rdng; *cr:* Eng Teacher Dunbar Sr HS 1966-69, Citrus Grove Jr HS 1970-; *ai:* Stu at Risk Prgm Specializing in Dropout Prevention; NCTE, AFT 1970-; *office:* Citrus Grove Middle School 2153 N W 3rd St Miami FL 33125

WILLIAMS, LLOYD DAVID, Social Studies Teacher; *b:* Winter, WI; *m:* Eunice A. Larson; *c:* Jeffrey, Pamela Putney,kathleen Bolot, Patrick; *ed:* (BS) Scndry Ed, Univ of WI Superior 1958; Counseling, Univ of WI Superi or; *cr:* Teacher Bloomer HS 1958-66, Winter HS 1966-; *ai:* Class Adv; *office:* Winter HS PO Box 7 Winter WI 54896

WILLIAMS, LOIS GERALDINE PHIPPS, 6th Grade Teacher; *b:* Red Rock, OK; *m:* Larry Dean; *c:* Dale Matlock, Gary Matlock; *ed:* (BS) Lang Arts, Phillips Univ 1964; Addl Training Phillips Univ; OK St Univ; *cr:* 4th Grade Teacher 1963-68; 5th Grade Teacher 1968-79; 6th Grade Teacher 1979-89; Enid Public Sch; *ai:* Bd Mem of Enid Political Action (EPAC); Jr Patrol; Stu Cncl; Chm of Steering Comm for North Cntrl Accrediation; Staff Dev Comm; Mem of Cherokee Strip Rdng Cncl; 1989 Teacher Feature in News & Eagle; Dec 1989 Front Page Article in Advocate (Enid Ed Assn Newsletter); *office:* Lincoln Elem Sch 600 W Elm Enid OK 73701

WILLIAMS, LOJEAN MORRIS, 8th Grade Eng/His Teacher; *b:* Pikeville, KY; *m:* Roger Lee; *c:* Roger T., Chadwick L.; *ed:* (BS) His/Poly Sci, Pikeville Coll 1969; (MA) Scndry Ed, 1979, (Rank I) Scndry Ed, 1980 Morehead St Univ; *cr:* Classroom Teacher Millard HS 1969-70, Greasy Creek Elem 1970-; *home:* PO Box 12 Lookout KY 41542

WILLIAMS, LONI R., Counselor; *b:* Pine Bluff, AR; *m:* Robert Jr.; *c:* Susan; *ed:* (BA) Music, 1970, (MA) Music, 1975 CA St Univ Hayward; (MS) Counseling, Univ of Laverne 1982; Admin Course, Univ of Laverne 1983; *cr:* Vocal & Instrumental Music Teacher Richmond Unified Sch Dist 1970-79; Piano/Beginning Instruments/Chorus Teacher Portola Jr HS 1979-82; Counseling Field Work Contra Costa Comm Coll 1981-82; Cnslr De Anza HS 1982-83, Portola Jr HS 1983-87, Contra Costa Comm Coll 1985-88, El Cerrito HS 1988-; *ai:* El Cerrito HS Schlsp Chairperson 1989- & Testing 1988-89; Portola Jr HS Stu Cncl Adv 1985, Coll Readiness Prgm Campus Coord 1987-88; CMEA Wkshp Teachers; Resource Person Supplementary Teaching Materials Afro-Amer Music; CA Curr Dev, Supplemental Materials Commission Advisory Bd; Consult CA Music Educators Assn; Mu Phi Epsilon Mem 1970-; Delta Sigma Theta (Pres 1981-83, Music Coord 1983-84, Membership Intake Trng Team 1985-, Chairperson 1984-85), Salute to 75 Delta Diamonds 1988; Phi Delta Kappa Mem 1983-88; CA Assn Counseling, Development Legislative Relations Comm 1988-; Numerous Public Service Awds Civic, Cmmty.

WILLIAMS, LORETTA FOUST, Sixth Grade Teacher; *b:* Knoxville, TN; *m:* Steve; *ed:* (BS) Eng Ed/Scndry, 1982, (MS) Curr/Instruction, 1988 Univ of TN Knoxville; Governors Acad for Teachers of Writing; Post Grad Stud Elem Ed; *cr:* Teacher Maynardville Elem 1982-; *ai:* MES Stu Volunteer Corps Spon; 4-H Adult Teacher Leader; Faculty Team Leader; Spelling Bee Spon & Organizer; Prof Dev Comm; NEA, TEA, UCEA Mem 1982-; NCTE Stu 1982; TN Geographical Society Mem 1988-; *office:* Maynardville Elem Sch Box 339 Hwy 33 Maynardville TN 37807

WILLIAMS, LORETTA NIESCHWITZ, Mathematics Department Chair; *b:* Floresville, TX; *c:* Jason, Bradley, Holly; *ed:* (BS) Math, SW TX St Univ 1962; (MS) Ed, Lady of the Lake Univ 1965; *cr:* Teacher Alpine HS 1962-64; San Antonio Ind Sch Dist 1964-70; Teacher/Math Dept Chairperson East Cntrl HS 1972-; *ai:* TX St Teachers Assn; Mu Alpha Theta Spon; *office:* East Cntrl HS 7173 Fm 1628 San Antonio TX 78263

WILLIAMS, LUDDIA CHATMAN, Second Grade Teacher; *b:* Picayune, MS; *m:* Arthur; *c:* Alisa; *ed:* (BA) Elem Ed, Alcorn St Univ 1978; (MS) Elem Ed, William Carey 1974; *cr:* Soc Stud Teacher Picayune Jr HS 1976-77; Chapter Teacher 1977-81, 2nd

Grade Teacher 1981-87 East Side Main; 2nd Grade East Side Annex 1987-88, Roseland Park Elem 1988-; *ai:* Sci, Health, Safety & Stu Welfare Comm Mem; NEA, Picayune Assn of Educators Mem 1987-88; Prof Growth Act Awds 1984-; *office:* Roseland Park Elem Sch 1610 Gilcrease Ave Picayune MS 39466

WILLIAMS, LUVENIA REED, English Coordinator; *b:* Chicago, IL; *m:* Peyton La Roy; *c:* Dana; *ed:* (BA) Eng, Roosevelt Univ 1970; (MA) Admin/Supervision, Chicago St Univ 1980; *cr:* Instr/Mgr IL Bell Telephone Co; Teacher/Coord Chicago Bd of Ed; *ai:* Drama Club Spon; ASCD, NTCE; Natl Jack & Jills.

WILLIAMS, LYNDIA MOSES, Vocal Music Teacher; *b:* Summit, MS; *m:* James B. Jr.; *c:* Raymond; *ed:* (BS) Piano/Voice, Southern Univ 1963; (MMED) Music Ed, 1970, Specialist Admin, 1975 LA St Univ; *cr:* Music Teacher St Tammany HS 1963-65, Southern Univ Lab Sch 1965-; *ai:* Sr Class & Music Leaders of Amer Spon; Choral Directress Acapella Choir, Female Honor Chorus, Male Chorus, Choarlettes; Tenure & Promotion, Self Study Comms; Music Educators Natl Conference, LA Music Educators Assn 1975-; Amer Choral Dirs Assn 1986-; Phi Delta Kappa 1975-; Alpha Kappa Alpha 1961-; The Links Inc Recording Secy 1988-; Asst Conductor of All Amer Youth Honor Choir That Toured Rome, London, Paris, Moscow, Leningrad, Malaga Costa Del Sol & Mexico City 1978-; *home:* 1245 Elysian Dr Baton Rouge LA 70810

WILLIAMS, MARIA A. LARA, Spanish Teacher; *b:* Mc Allen, TX; *c:* Lara C., Mark A., Christopher W.; *ed:* (BA) Span, San Diego St 1965; (MSE) Ed, Cntrl MO St Univ 1979; Trng In Bi-ling Spec Ed; Eng as Second Lang; *cr:* Teacher Nashville Davidson Sch Dist 1967-69, Cntrl MO St Univ 1976-81, Kansas City MO Public Schls 1981-87, Warrensburg RVI Dist 1987-; *ai:* Organizes & Spons Span Club; Foreign Lang Assn of MO 1987-; AATSP 1988-; Cntrl Dist Foreign Lang Teachers Assn Pres 1988-; Johnson Cty Food Pantry Volunteer 1989, Service Awd 1986-89; Dist Publication on Early Chldhd for Kansas City MO Public Schls Translated into Span for Distribution; Warrensburg HS Distinction Awd 1988; *office:* Warrensburg HS 1411 S Ridgeview Dr Warrensburg MO 64093

WILLIAMS, MARIA-CRISTINA HALLEY, Spanish Teacher; *b:* Havana, Cuba; *m:* Thomas H.; *c:* Crist, Buckley, Hal; *ed:* (BA) Span/Fr, Univ of Miami 1966; (MAT) Elem/Bi-ling Ed, Jacksonville Univ 1980; *cr:* 5th/6th Grade Elem Teacher Arlington Heights & South Pope Livingston 1970-72; Span/Fr Teacher Ribault Sr HS 1972-78, Jacksonville Cty Day 1978-81, Stanton Preparatory Sch 1983-85; Span Teacher Sandalwood Sr HS 1985-; Adjunct Ed Dept Jacksonville Univ 1986-; *ai:* Span Honor Society Spon; Amer Assn Teachers of Span & Portuguese 1985-; Resurrection Sch Bd Mem 1980-86; *office:* Sandalwood Sr HS 2750 John Prom Blvd Jacksonville FL 32216

WILLIAMS, MARK C., History Teacher; *b:* Albany, NY; *m:* Anne F. Mc Cormick; *c:* Adam, Amy, Benjamin; *ed:* (BA) His, Yale Coll 1970; (MA) His/Ed, Univ of CT 1975; *cr:* His Teacher L P Wilson Jr HS 1971-75, Dept Head 1979-85; His Teacher Loomis Chaffee Sch 1975-; *ai:* Sch Magazine Adv; CT Coordinating Promotions of His Comm 1989-; W Granby Historic Study Comm Chm 1988-; Granby Rovers Soccer Club Coach 1980-; CT Cncl for Soc Stud 1979-; Salmon Brook Historical Society Dir 1975-; Published Series on CT His; Daughters of Amer Revolution St Teacher of Yr 1988; Articles in Teachers Magazines & Historical Periodicals; Published Text on Early Amer His; Edited Granby Town Meeting Records; *office:* Loomis Chaffee Sch Windsor CT 06095

WILLIAMS, MARLENE GRAVES, 4th Grade Teacher; *b:* Siolam Springs, AR; *m:* Thomas R.; *c:* Thomas R., Theodore J.; *ed:* (BME) Music, Ed, John Brown Univ 1954; *cr:* 3rd Grade/Music Teacher Little Kansas Elem 1954-55; Music Teacher Bardolph Elem 1955-56; 3rd Grade Teacher Southern CA Military Acad 1961-63; K-4th Grade Teacher Oak Grove Elem 1964-; *ai:* Just Say No Spon; Bldg Adv Comm; NEA 1964-; KNEA 1964-; KNEAT 1964-; Grandview Park Presbyn Church Deacon 1986; Maple Hill Presbyn Church Elder 1976; Nom Recognition 7th Annual Excl Teaching Awd Prgm Spon By Kansas City Star Co Learning Exchange Chamber of Commerce of Greater Kansas City; *home:* 6518 Lowell Dr Merriam KS 66202

WILLIAMS, MARTHA SWEITZER, Social Studies Teacher; *b:* Richmond, VA; *m:* Ernest N.; *c:* Katherine W. Ponder, Roger L. Severn, John E.; *ed:* (BS) Ed, 1954, (BA) Ed/Supervision/Admin, 1964 James Madison Univ; Doctorate Prgm VA Tech Blacksburg; Univ of VA & Radford Univ; *cr:* 3rd Grade Teacher Ridgeway Elem 1954-55; Eng/Soc Stud Teacher Drewry Mason HS 1955-61; 6th-7th Grade Teacher Ridgeway Elem 1961-63; Prin Fieldale Primary 1963-65; Supervision Henry Cty Schls 1965-70; Prin Rich Acres HS 1970-73, Bassett Mid Sch 1973-77; Soc Stud Teacher Drewry Mason HS 1977-87; Soc Stud Teacher/Dept Head Magna Vista HS 1988-; *ai:* Soc Stud Dept Head; Academic Team Coord & Soc Stud Coach; VA Ed Assn; *office:* Magna Vista HS Magna Vista Rd Ridgeway VA 24148

WILLIAMS, MARY CARR, First Grade Teacher; *b:* Jacksonville, TX; *m:* Azell Lamar; *c:* Darrell, Amelia; *ed:* (BS) Elem Ed, Jarvis C Coll 1967; (MA) Elem Ed, Webster Univ 1987; Mentor Teacher Trng, Assertive Discipline, Teachers Expectation Stu Achievement; *cr:* 1st Grade Teacher Hawthorne Elem 1967-69, Prescott Elem 1969-73, Marlborough Elem 1973-77, Pershing Elem 1977-; *ai:* Site Planning Comm; Stu Cncl Spon; Cadre Rdng Teacher; Grade Level Chairperson; Mentor Teacher; Cooperative Teacher; Youth Trng Dir; AFT Building Rep 1985-; Sigma Gamma Rho Secy 1977; St Stephen Baptist Church Sunday Sch Teacher; Nom Excl Teaching Awd 1985; *office:* John J Pershing Sch 5915 Park Kansas City MO 64130

WILLIAMS, MARY JO, Reading Teacher/Librarian; *b:* Alexandria, LA; *m:* Edward Dean; *c:* Joseph E., Elizabeth L.; *ed:* (BS) Lib Sci, 1970, (MED) Supervision/Admin, 1970 Univ of S MS; Grad Stud; LA Personal Improvement Plan; Supvr of Stu Teachers for NE LA Univ; *cr:* Librarian Jonesville Jr HS 1970-86, Jonesville Consolidated HS 1969-; 7th Grade Rdng Teacher/Librarian Jonesville Jr HS 1987-; *ai:* Honor Society & 4-H Club Spon; Sch Improvement Plan Chairperson; Catahoula Assn of Educators, LA Assn of Educators, NEA 1969-; Girls St of LA 5th Dist Procurement Chairperson 1986-; Jubliee Club Pres 1984-85, Young Woman of Yr 1985; Utility Baptist Church 1960-; 4-H Fnd Bd of LA St Univ 1980-; Sch, Parish, Regional Jr HS Teacher of Yr 1988-89; *office:* Jonesville Jr HS 802 State St Jonesville LA 71343

WILLIAMS, MARY YOUNG, English Teacher Mentor; *b:* St Marys, PA; *c:* Ryan D., Nicole M.; *ed:* (MA) Educl Admin, San Jose St Univ 1986; (BS) Eng/Speech, 1971; (MED) Ed/Rdng, 1974 Edinboro St Univ; *cr:* Lang Arts Teacher 1976-; Mentor Teacher 1985- Fair Middle Sch; Assoc Dir San Jose St Univ 1980-84; Eng Teacher Warren Area HS 1971-76; Adjunct Prof Ottawa Univ 1990; Seminar Presenter Santa Clara Cty Office 1988-; *ai:* Newspaper Club; Desktop Publishing Club; Campus Pride Club; Storybook Theater; Chairperson Eng/Lang Arts Scope Sequence; Core Literature List Comm; Mid Sch Prgm Dev Comm; South Bay Writing Project Assoc Dir 1980-84; Santa Clara Rdng Cncl/Ca Rdng Assn Presenter 1988-; Cntrl CA Cncl of Teachers of Eng Exec Brd 1983; CA Curr Commission Mem 1984; Burnett Elem Sch Parent Faculty Assn 1988- Outstanding Cmmty Support 1989; Cmmty Bd Advisory Burnett Rep 1988; Whos Who in West 1981; Outstanding Young Women in America 1979; Published Author Teaching Writing in K-8 Classrooms 1985; Let Em Talk 1988; Enjoying Written Word 1987; Rdng/Thinking/Writing 1989; Resources for Advisory Prgm 1990; Santa Clara Cty Sch Bd Assn Glen Hoffman Awd; Teacher of Yr Fair Mid Sch 1978; *home:* 483 Cestaric Ave Milpitas CA 95035

WILLIAMS, MICHAEL C., 7th Grade Teacher/Principal; *b:* Washington, DC; *m:* Michele D.; *c:* Jason; *ed:* (BS) Elem Ed, Valparaiso Univ 1974; Natl Luth Schls Prin Acad; *cr:* 4th Grade Teacher 1974-83, 6th Grade Teacher 1983-84, 7th Grade Teacher/Co-Prin 1984- St Matthew; *ai:* Boys Bsktbl Coach; Coord Fund Raising Comm, Various Athletic Extra-Curr Act; NAESP Mem 1984-; Parent-Teacher League Mem 1983-; Various Sch & Church Bds (Coord, Mem) 1980-; *office:* St Matthew Luth Sch 200 Sherman Ave New York NY 10034

WILLIAMS, MICHAEL KEVIN, Honors English Teacher; *b:* Monterey, CA; *ed:* (BA) Phys Ed, 1976, (MEd) Phys Ed, 1977 TX Tech Univ; *cr:* 6th-8th Grade Eng Teacher Eunice Schls 1977-78; 11th Grade Eng Teacher Hanks HS 1978-; *ai:* Head Bsbl & Asst Ftbl Coach; TX HS Bsbl Coaches Assn 1988-89; NEA, TX St Teachers Assn 1978-; El Paso Bsbl Coach of Yr 1982, 1984, 1988; *office:* Hanks HS 2001 Lee Trevino El Paso TX 79936

WILLIAMS, MICHAEL THOMAS, 7th Grade Life Science Teacher; *b:* Pottsville, PA; *ed:* (BS) Sec Ed Bio, Bloomsburg St Coll 1976; (MED) Sec Admin, East Stroudsburg Univ 1985; *cr:* 7th Grade Sci Teacher Holaird Jr HS 1976-78; 7th Grade Life Sci Teacher Philip Laver M S 1980-; *ai:* NSTA; NEA; PSEA; West Park Civic Assn; Nature Conservancy; *office:* Philip F Laver Mid Sch Firmstone & Balata St Easton PA 18042

WILLIAMS, MILDRED WEAVER, Science Teacher; *b:* Blountsville, AL; *m:* James Edward; *c:* Twila Harmon; *ed:* (BS) Scndry Ed, Univ of AL 1964; (MA) Scndry & Sci, 1966; Post Master Studies Double a Awd Sci & Scndry Ed 1970; Several Subjects at UAB; *cr:* Teacher JB Pennington Sch 1963-66; Oneonta HS 1966-; *ai:* Sr Spon; Sci Club Adv; PTSA; OEA; AEA 1966-; NEA 1966-; Phi Epsilon Omicron 1964-70; Univ of South MS Sea Grants; Studied in England Summer of 1977; *office:* Oneonta City Sch Rt 1 Box 14 Oneonta AL 35121

WILLIAMS, NANCY BEATRICE, Second Grade Teacher; *b:* Tulsa, OK; *ed:* (Ba) Elem Ed, 1954; (MED) Elem Ed, 1960 Univ of OK; Gesell Institute Trng; Auditory Discrimation in Depth Trng: ECRI Mastery Teaching Trng; *cr:* 4th Grade Teacher Irving Sch 1954-60; 5th Grade Teacher Pleasant Valley 1960-62; 3rd/4th Grade Teacher Eosemond 1963-64; K-2nd Grade Teacher Soledad Union 1964-; *ai:* Grade Level Chairperson; Adv Comm to Princ; Soledad Teachers Rdng Assn Pres 1973-75; Owl Awd 1983; Girl Scout Leader Cncl 1954-60; Bus Prof Women Sec 1965-70; PTA Comm 1954-1980; Membership on Sch Adv Cncl; Awd Boy Scouts for Civic Svc; Awd VFW Civic Svc; *office:* San Vicente Sch 1300 Metz Rd Soledad CA 93960

WILLIAMS, NANETTE SMITH, 5th Grade Teacher; *b:* Rockford, IL; *m:* Robert O.; *c:* David Ray, Diane Carol Dunn, Melinda Kay; *ed:* (BA) Ed, Millikin Univ 1951; *cr:* 6th Grade Teacher Mansfield Grade 1960; Sub/Bedside Teacher Rock Island IL 1961-65; 3rd-6th Grade Teacher Cayne Center Sch 1966-; *ai:* At Risk Comm; Blackhawk Rdng Cncl 1987-; *home:* 1700 25th St Rock Island IL 61201

WILLIAMS, NICHOLAS M., Vocal Music Teacher; *b:* Batavia, NY; *ed:* (BM) Music Ed, Suc Potsdam 1977; (MM) Music Ed, Eastman Sch of Music 1981; *cr:* Elem Vocal Music Teacher West Ave Sch 1977-88; Vocal Music Teacher Hilton HS 1988-; *ai:* Musicals, Show Choir, Cmmty Choruses Dir; Gala Choruses VP 1989-; *office:* Hilton HS 400 East Ave Hilton NY 14468

WILLIAMS, PAMELA EILEEN, Fourth Grade Teacher; *b:* Washington, DC; *c:* Jennifer, Joyce; *ed:* (BA) Elem Ed, Towson Univ 1966; Grad Work Univ of MD & Shippensburg Coll; *cr:* 2nd Grade Teacher 1966-68, Ungraded Teacher 1968-70 New Carrollton Elem; 2nd Grade Teacher New Springfield Elem 1970-85; 2nd Grade Teacher 1985-87, 4th Grade Teacher 1987- New Middletown Elem; *ai:* Jr Church Leader; Vacation Bible Sch Teacher; Foreign Exch Stu Family Host; Sci Curr Comm; OH Ed Assn 1970-; NEA 1966-; Mahoning Cty Uniserve Chairperson 1987-; Springfield Local Classroom Teachers Assn VP 1987-; Dial-A-Teacher Steering Comm Mem 1989-; Springfield Ruitan Teacher of Yr Awd 1986; *office:* New Middleton Elem Sch 10580 Main St New Middletown OH 44442

WILLIAMS, PATRECIA ANNETTE MURPHY, English Teacher; *b:* Duncan, OK; *c:* Joel O., Patrecia K.; *ed:* (MED) Eng Ed, 1975, (BS) Bus Ed, 1969, (BS) Office Ed, 1969 TX Southern Univ; *cr:* Eng Teacher Sharpstown Jr HS 1970-75, Worthing Sr HS 1975; *ai:* Vlybl Coach; NCTE 1970-; Houston Area Cncl of Eng Teachers 1970-; Southeast Pizza Inn Teacher of Yr 1989; Southeast Teacher of Yr 1988-89; *office:* Worthing Sr HS 9215 Scott St Houston TX 77051

WILLIAMS, PATTY L., Mathematics Teacher/Coach; *b:* Eldorado, IL; *m:* Joseph W.; *c:* Cassandra; *ed:* (BS) Math, S IL Univ Carbondale 1979; *cr:* Math Teacher Easton Cmmty HS 1979-85; Math Teacher/Coach Sparta Cmmty HS 1985-; *ai:* Math Team Coach; IL Cncl Teacher of Math 1980-; IEA, NEA 1979-; *home:* 1009 Belle Valley #3 Belleville IL 62221

WILLIAMS, PEGGY ALFORD, Mathematics Department Chair; *b:* Mullins, SC; *m:* Johnny Larue; *c:* Anita J., Alicia; *ed:* (BS) Elem Ed, Winthrop Coll 1971; (MED) Elem Ed, Univ of SC 1976; Completing Educl Specialist Cert in Admin; *cr:* Math/Sci Teacher Finklea Mid Sch 1971-74, Green Sea HS 1974-76; Math Teacher Green Sea Floyds Mid Sch 1976-; *ai:* Mathcounts Coach 1985-; SACS Steering Comm Chairperson; Math Chairperson 1981-; Big MAC 1980-; Palmetto St Teachers Organization 1987-; NEA, SCEA, HCEA 1971-87; Waccamaw Baptist Assn Mission Action Dir 1987-; TIP Recipient 1988-89; 1st Runner-Up for Horry Cty Teacher of Yr 1985; NEWMAST Awd Recipient 1989; *home:* Rt 1 Loris SC 29569

WILLIAMS, RAINELLE TILLEY, 8th Grade Science Teacher; *b:* Trenton, NJ; *m:* Gregory James Sr.; *c:* Gregory Jr.; *ed:* (BS) Intermediate Ed, E Carolina Univ 1975; NC Cntrl Univ, Lenoir Comm Coll; *cr:* 3rd Grade Teacher Northwest Elem Sch 1975-77; 8th Grade Sci Teacher Kinston Jr HS & Rochelle Mid Sch 1977-; *ai:* Differentiated Pay Voting & Senate Bill 2 Sch Based Comms; NCAE Assn Rep 1975-; NEA 1975-; Natl Teachers Convention Dupont Grant; *office:* Rochelle Mid Sch 301 N Rochelle Blvd Kinston NC 28501

WILLIAMS, REBA KING, Kindergarten Teacher Assistant; *b:* Turkey, NC; *m:* Paul Miles; *c:* Wendy Barrett, Kellie Langston; *cr:* Clerk Typist 1956-58, Proof Reader 1958-61 Justice Dept Washington DC; Teacher Asst Brogden Primary 1972-; *ai:* Sch Safety Cncl; Sunday Sch Teacher; Wayne Cty Assn Teacher Asst 1st VP 1988-89; NC Assn Teacher Asst; Amer A R Persons; Natl Assn for Retired Credit Union People; *home:* 612 Ridge Dr Goldsboro NC 27530

WILLIAMS, RITA MAJETTE, 8th Grade Teacher; *b:* Norfolk, VA; *m:* Alfonso; *c:* Gregory, Alfonso II; *ed:* (BA) Poly Sci, Bennett Coll 1970; (MA) Scndry Ed, Montclair St Coll 1972; Kean Coll Elem Ed Certificate 1972-73, Admin & Supervision Certificate 1988-89; Syracuse Univ Admin & Adult Stud Summer 1988; *cr:* Teacher Dr William H Horton Sch 1970-; *ai:* Natl Jr Honor Society Adv; Dr Horton Sch Building Comm; Phi Delta Kappa (Pres St Coll Chapter 1989-, Pres Elect 1988-89, VP, Membership 1986-88, Fnd Rep 1985-86, His 1984-85); Service Key 1990; Intnl Rdng Assn 1983-;ASCD 1989-; AFT Newark Teachers Union VP 1989-; Natl Cncl of Negro Women 1988-; Natl Assn Advancement of Colored People 1988-; BSA (Cub Scout Leader 1986-, Scout Master 1990-); Carol A Graves Civic Organization 1985-; Awarded Grant Geometry Newark Teachers Center 1977; Natl Teachers Examination Enabling Skills Advisory Comm 1989; Dr Horton Sch Recognition Awd Working with Limited Eng Proficiency Stus 1989; *home:* PO Box 7345 Elmhurst NY 11352

WILLIAMS, RITA PEER, French/English Teacher; *b:* New York, NY; *m:* Phillip Norman; *c:* Marc, Ian; *ed:* (BA) Eng, CT Coll 1966; (MAT) Ed, Johns Hopkins Univ 1968; Grad Stud in Fr & Eng, OH Univ, Univ of N IA; Grad Stud in France; *cr:* Teacher Bedford Jr HS 1967-68, Univ City HS 1968-70, Eastern HS 1977-; *ai:* Jr Class Adv; Grading Comm; ALSG Stu Travel Cnslr for Trips to Europe; NEA, Eastern Local Ed Assn 1977-; *home:* Shadegarden Stables 18521 Bucks Lks Rd Guysville OH 45735

WILLIAMS, ROBERT B. R., English/Social Studies Teacher; *b:* Sandusky, OH; *m:* Sandra Hall; *c:* Robyn Moore, Holly, Megan, Alex; *ed:* (BA) Soc Stud, OH Wesleyan Univ 1961; His Tulane Univ; (MED) Scndry Ed/Soc Stud, OH Univ 1968; Advanced Work Ed Univ of Cincinnati; *cr:* 7th Grade Teacher 1964-67, Eng/Soc Stud Teacher 1968- Forest Hills Sch Dist; *ai:* 7th/8th Grade Athletic Dir & Activity Coord Anderson HS; OH HS Athletic Assn (Swimming, Diving Ofcl 1970-); Mount Lookout Civic Club (Bd Mem 1977-79, Pres 1972); PTA Teaher of Yr 1983; JCS Teacher of Yr 1973; *office:* Anderson HS 7560 Forest Rd Cincinnati OH 45255

WILLIAMS, ROBERT EARL, Social Studies Teacher; *b:* Natchez, MS; *m:* Elize Nevonne Morales; *c:* Cassandra Squalls, Tasiskia, Cedric Morales; *ed:* (BS) Soc Stud, MS Valley St 1966; NE LA Univ, Grambling St Univ,Alcorn St Univ, Northwestern St

Univ; *cr:* Teacher Routhwood Elem Sch 1966-77, Newellton HS 1977-83, Routhwood Elem Sch 1983-; *ai:* Wildlife Club Spon; Chm Stu of Yr, Building Level Comm, Soc Stud Fair, Honors Day Prgm, Sch Handbook Comm; Pres Academic Fitness Awd Coord; TX Ed Assn, LA Assn of Educators 1966-; Kappa Alpha Psi 1978-; Trail Blazers of TX Parish 1989-; KS Parish Mid ScH Teacher of Yr; Task Force Mem; Developed Curr Gui de for Teaching About Drugs; Newellton HS Teacher of Yr; Appointed Comm to Develop Soc Stud Curr Guide TX Parish; Attended Northwestern Univ Wkshp; *home:* 705 Holly St Saint Joseph LA 71366

WILLIAMS, ROBERT ELLIS, Biology Teacher; *b:* Grenada, MS; *c:* Michael L., Bobbie D. Dolan, Mark Sequoiah; *ed:* (BA) Bio/Psych, Memphis St Univ 1956; (MA) Ec Entomology, 1958, (PHD) Medical Entomology/Ecology, 1961 OH St Univ; Post Grad Stud Virology, Yale Univ; *cr:* Branch Chief Army Biological Welfare Laboratories 1961-64, Office of Naval Research 1964-67; Division Chief USN Medical Research Unit Cairo Egypt 1967-73; Bio Teacher Trimble HS 1973-76, Glaydin Sch 1979-85, Ft Chiswell HS; *ai:* Former Track & Field Head Coach; Psy Chi Pres 1954; Amer Society of Tropical Medicine & Hygiene 1969-73; VA Assn of Environmental Educators 1986-; Cub Scouts Cubmaster 1958-61; Little League Sports Umpire 1961-62; BSA Scoutmaster 1961-64; Natl Insts of Health Research Grant; OH St Univ Research Fnd Assoc; Articles & Book Published; *office:* Ft Chiswell HS Rt 3 Box 255 Max Meadows VA 24360

WILLIAMS, ROBERT LEE, HS Mathematics/Science Teacher; *b:* Pittsburg, KS; *m:* Catherine Jo Covert; *c:* Tabitha J., Hannah E., Esther L.; *ed:* (BS) Math Ed, MO Southern St Coll 1980; *cr:* Teacher Lamar HS 1980-; *ai:* Asst Girls Track Coach; Math League, Math Club, Sci Club, Jr Class Spon; MO St Teachers Assn 1980-; Verdella Freewill Baptist Church Sunday Sch Teacher 1987-; *home:* RR 3 Box 28 Liberal MO 64762

WILLIAMS, RONELLA LAZENBY, Fifth Grade Teacher; *b:* Kansas City, KS; *m:* Michael; *c:* Michael II; *ed:* (BS) Elem Ed, 1977, (MED) Elem Ed, 1979, (EDS) Elem Ed, 1983 AL St Univ; *cr:* Teacher Smiths-Station Elem 1977-; *ai:* Smiths-Station Faculty Bsktbl Team Mem; Smiths-Station Elem Sch Choir Directress; Tae Kwan Do Karate Club Secy; Lee Cty Ed Assn Faculty Rep 1979-80; AL Ed Assn, NEA 1977-; Hutchinson Missionary Baptist (Tutoring Sch Prin 1987-, Minister of Music 1983-), Service Plaque 1988, Educl Tutor Certificate 1982; Delta Sigma Theta Sergeant-At-Arms 1981-82; Tau Beta Sigma Co-Adv 1980-81; AL St Univ Alumni Band Assn Corresponding Secy 1983-84; Order of Eastern Star Ruth 1983-85; Kappa Delta Pi 1983-; Smiths-Station Elem Sch Outstanding Choir Dirs Awd 1981; Gospel Music Wkshp Certificate 1981; Outstanding Young Women of America 1983; *home:* 430 Spring Valley Rd Montgomery AL 36116

WILLIAMS, RUBY ANNA TEPE, Math Teacher/6-8 Dept Chm; *b:* Lott, TX; *m:* John Calvin; *c:* John C. Jr., Joe B., James N.; *ed:* (BS) Elem Ed, TX Weslyn Coll 1958; Math, Soc Stud, Educl Courses; *cr:* 5th Grade Teacher Oakridge Elem 1967-70; 6th/7th/8th Grade Math Teacher Webster Mid Sch 1970-; *ai:* Math Chairperson; Started Math Prgms; 6th/7th/8th Grade Advanced Math; Central OK Assn Teachers of Math 1985-; Work in Church with Teenagers; Counsel Children & Adults in Church; Textbook Comm Chairperson; Math Wkshp; Comm Basic Skill 6th Grade Advanced Math; Test for Basic Skills; Present Wkshp Tulsa OK; *home:* 105 SW 57th Oklahoma City OK 73109

WILLIAMS, RUTH ANN (REEVES), Third Grade Teacher; *b:* Saint Louis, MO; *m:* Shirley D.; *c:* Jerry, James, John (dec); *ed:* (AA) Ed, Florissant Valley Comm Coll 1972; (BS) Elem Ed/early Chldhd, Univ of MO St Louis 1975; Certified Catechist, Archdiocese of St Louis 1985; *cr:* K-6th Grade Teacher Asst Jury Sch 1975-77; 6th Grade Teacher St Anthony 1977-78; 2nd Grade Teacher 1978-83, 3rd Grade Teacher 1983- St Simon the Apostle; *ai:* Rdng Tutor Adult Literacy Prgm; Bd Mem Representing Faculty Home & sch assn St Simon the Apostle; Intnl Rdng Assn 1985-; *home:* 4 Eastview Dr Fenton MO 63026

WILLIAMS, RUTHA C., Mathematics Teacher; *b:* Mc Kenzie, TN; *m:* James D.; *c:* Scarlet Taylor, Stacie Arnold; *ed:* (BA) Math, Union Univ 1967; (MA) Guidance, UTM 1977; *cr:* Teacher Grand Junction HS 1967-68, Burnsville HS 1968-69, Savannah Mid Sch 1969-70, W Carroll HS 1971-; *ai:* TEA, NEA, NCTM, TMTA, MT2NW; *home:* 2010 Virdell St Milan TN 38358

WILLIAMS, S. JEROME, Math Teacher/Dept Leader; *b:* Philipsburg, PA; *m:* Norma Jedinak; *c:* Erin Carlson, Stephen, Kristin; *ed:* (BS) Physics/Chem, Juniata Col 1961; (MED) Math Ed, Temple Univ 1964; West Chester Univ; Baldwin-Wallace Coll; Villanova Univ; Southward Polytech Institute-London England; Philadelphia Coll of Textiles & Sci; Penn St Univ; IN Univ of PA; *cr:* Math Institute Delaware Cty Comm Coll 1977-87; Math/Sci Teacher Paxno Hallow Mid Sch 1961-; *ai:* Math Counts Adv; Dist Technology Comm; Mid Sch Advisory Comm; Math Curr Co-Chm; Girls Track Coach and Wrestling Coach Marple-Newtown Sr HS; Ftbl Coach & Math Dept Leader Paxon Hollow Mid Sch; Marple-Newtown Ed Assn St House of Delegates Negotiation Comm 1986-; PSEA 1961-; NEA 1961-; NCTM/MAA/ASCD/PCTM 1961-; Atmopav Natl Midd Sch Assn 1961-; St Agnes Parish Cncl Chm Liturgical Comm 1976-81; Democrat Party of West Chester Zone Leader 1978-82; Jesse Owens Track Meets Dir 1980-86; MSF Grants (1963 1968 1970); Marple-Newtown Teacher Yr (1989); Marple-Newtown Profiles of Excl; Cntrl League Wrestling Coach Yr; Lou Bonder Awd for Contributions to Scholastic Sports; Presenter NCTM Regional Conventions; *office:* Paxon Hollow Mid Sch 815 Paxon Hollow Rd Broomall PA 19008

WILLIAMS, SALENA MAE, Business Teacher; *b:* Richmond, VA; *c:* Tytwan J.; *ed:* (BS) Bus Ed, VA St UNIV 1982; WV Teachers Acad 1989; Jefferson Cty Sch Bd Wkshp Cmptr Literacy; VA St Univ Grad Prgm Supervision; *cr:* Bus Teacher Jefferson HS 1982-; *ai:* Curr & Stus Act Comm 1989-; Stu Act Cashier 1987-; Supvr of Stu Field Experiences Shepard Coll 1987-; NEA, WVEA 1982-; Teach Adult Ed Classes; Certificate Sheperds Coll for Servicing Stu Teachers; Certificate The Teachers Acad WV; *home:* 141 Clayton St Petersburg VA 23804

WILLIAMS, SALLY BURDEN, 4th Grade Teacher; *b:* Rockford, IL; *m:* William R. III; *c:* William IV, Phillip; *ed:* (BA) Elem Ed, Rockford Coll 1977; *cr:* 4th Grade Teacher Kinnikinnick Sch 1977-79, Ledgewood Sch 1979-89, Stone Creek Sch 1990; *ai:* Kinnikinnick Ed Assn, IL Ed Assn, NEA; Red Cross (Volunteer, KISS Instr) 1988-; Family Advocate Auxiliary; *office:* Stone Creek Sch 11633 Southgate Rd Roscoe IL 61073

WILLIAMS, SANDRA ANKROM, Third Grade Teacher; *b:* Circleville, OH; *m:* Greg; *c:* Stacey, Brett; *ed:* (BSED) Elem Ed, OH Univ 1975; Grad Stud Coll of Mount Saint Joseph; *cr:* 3rd Grade Teacher Clearcreek Elem 1976-; *ai:* Curr Cncl, Prin Advisory, PTO Rep Comm; Amanda Clearcreek Ed Assn Building Rep 1989-; OH Ed Assn, NEA; Faithful Friends (Secy, Historian) 1987-89; Jennings Scholar Capital Univ; *home:* 515 Northfield Dr Circleville OH 43113

WILLIAMS, SANDRA JACKSON, Counselor; *b:* Raleigh, NC; *c:* Barry L.; *ed:* (Aa) Sociology, Catawba Coll 1974; (MS) Guidance, NC Ag/Tech St Univ 1980; *cr:* Teacher Asst Hampton Elem Sch 1975-79; Irving Park Elem Sch 1979-80; Guidance Cnslr Hunter Elem Sch 1980-82; Mciver Sch 1982-83; Archer Elem Sch 1983-; *ai:* Stu Cncl; Youth Advisory Cncl; Amer Assn Counseling/Dev; Assn Supv/Curr Dev; Intl Alliance Invitational Ed; Natl Ed Assn; NC Assn of Ed; NC Assn Counseling Membership Tri-Chair 1989-91; NC Assn Multicultural Counseling/Dev; NC Peer Helper Assn; NC Sch Cnslr Assn; Piedmont Chapter NC Assn Counseling Dev Secy 1988-90; Alpha Kappa Alpha; Notary Public; *office:* Archer Elem Schl 2610 4 Seasons Blvd Greensboro NC 27407

WILLIAMS, SANDRA JANE BROWN, Social Studies Dept Head; *b:* Lubbock, TX; *m:* Don R.; *c:* Vicki Hall, Mica Melby; *ed:* (BS) His/Eng Ed, TX Tech 1966; Grad Stud Tech, TX A&M & Wayland Univ; *cr:* Eng Teacher Abernathy HS 1966-69, John Tyler HS 1969-71; US His Teacher Plainview HS 1971-; *ai:* Supt Cabinet 1988-; FTA; Stu Cncl; Gifted & Talented Coord; TCTA; NCSS 1979-; Delta Kappa Gamma 1970-; 1st Baptist Church Teacher; Grad Stipend TX A&M Univ; *office:* Plainview HS 1501 Quincey St Plainview TX 79072

WILLIAMS, SANDRA S. HANNA, 4th Grade Teacher; *b:* Valparaiso, IN; *m:* Glenn A.; *c:* Joanna Gourley, Ronald Bedwell, Rob Bedwell; *ed:* (BS) Elem Ed, 1979, (MS) Elem Ed, 1986 Purdue Univ; *cr:* Elem Teacher Hebron Elem Sch 1979-; *ai:* Porter Cty Teachers Assn Building Rep 1980-81; IN St Teachers Assn St Delegate 1980-81; Beta Sigma Phi (Treas, Secy, Comm Chm) 1966-69; Purdue Univ Distinguished Deans List 1977-79, Certificate 1978-79, Stu Senate Awd 1978; Helping Hands Block Parent Prgm Coord; IN St Schlsp; Purdue Stu Senate Schlsp; Bob Jones Univ Debate Team; Univ Choir Touring NM; Stu Ed Assn; Purdue AIL Poly Day Chairperson 1977; Planning & Stu Advisory Comms; *office:* Hebron Elem Sch 307 S Main St Hebron IN 46341

WILLIAMS, SARA SALLY COBURN, Lang Art Teacher/Dept Chairman; *b:* Fresno, CA; *m:* Russell L.; *c:* Kelly, Kim; *ed:* (BA) Eng, 1966, Eng/Life Sci, 1967 CA St Univ Fresno; *cr:* Teacher Ahwahnee Jr HS 1967-68, Fresno HS 1970-71; Teacher/SIP Admin Lone Hill Intermediate 1976-82; Teacher/Dept Chairperson/Mentor Teacher Divisadero Mid Sch 1982-; *ai:* Mentor Teacher Visalia Unified 1990; CA Jr Schlsp Fed Adv; Lang Art Dept Chairperson 1987-; Dist Lang Art Curr Comm 1989-; Visalia Unified Mid Sch Curr Comm 1989-; Visalia Unified Teachers Assn 1987-; Lone Hill PTA Mem 1976-82; St Pauls Episcopal Church Vestry 1984-87; St Pauls Sch Bd Mem 1984-87; Kappa Kappa Gamma Alumnae Club (Pres, Panhellenic Chm) 1986-87; *office:* Divisadero Mid Sch 1200 S Divisadero Visalia CA 93291

WILLIAMS, SARAH LORING, 7th Grade Reading Teacher; *b:* Scottsbluff, NE; *ed:* (BA) Elem Ed/Early Chldhd, Univ of WY 1979; *cr:* Rdng Teacher Torrington Mid Sch 1979-; *ai:* Yrbk Spon; Quiz Bowl Coach 7th Grade; Intnl Rdng Assn; *office:* Torrington Mid Sch 25th & West E Torrington WY 82240

WILLIAMS, SHARON CHILD, 7th Grade Life Science Teacher; *b:* Ogden, UT; *m:* Douglas R.; *c:* Jeffrey, Jason, Nicole; *ed:* (BA) Sci/Home Ec, NM St Univ 1965; Working Towards Masters Sci; *cr:* Teacher White Sands NM 1966-68, Baton Rouge LA 1969-71, Fresno CA 1984-; *ai:* Stu Cncl Spon; Fresno Public Ed Mini-Grant 1988-; *office:* Ahwahnee Mid Sch 1127 E Escalon Ave Fresno CA 93710

WILLIAMS, SHEILA KELLY, Second Grade Teacher; *b:* Key West, FL; *m:* Thomas F.; *c:* Thomas K., Brian O.; *ed:* (BA) Comm Art/Elem Ed, Mercy Coll 1968; Speech, Drama, TX A&I Univ; *cr:* 4th Grade Teacher St Gertrudes Sch 1968-69; 2nd/4th-8th Grade Teacher St Columba Sch 1970-; *ai:* Stu Cncl; Sch Moderator & Adv; Prepare Stu for Penance & Eucharist; NCEA; *office:* St Columba Sch Rt 82 Box 368 Hopewell Junction NY 12533

WILLIAMS, SHERRY WEBB, Literature Teacher; *b:* Glasgow, KY; *m:* Edd; *c:* Jonathan, Jessica; *ed:* (BS) Phys Ed, Campbellsville Coll 1979; Ed, W KY Univ; *cr:* Phys Ed Teacher Edmonson Cty HS 1979-81; Eng Teacher Edmonson Cty Mid Sch 1984-88; Classroom Teacher Maplewood Sch 1988-89; Lit Teacher Edmonson Cty Mid Sch 1989-; *ai:* Girls Bsktbl Asst Coach 1979-81; Girls Track Coach 1979-81; Girls Sftbl Coach 1985; *office:* Edmonson Cty Mid Sch HC 60 Brownsville KY 42210

WILLIAMS, SHIRLEY ANN (TANQUARY), Elementary Science Teacher; *b:* Bellmont, IL; *m:* Bill J.; *c:* Dan, Brad, Edwin; *ed:* (AS) N OK Coll 1970; (BS) Elem Ed, OK St Univ 1972; Sci Wkshps; Natl Sci Teachers Natl Meeting; *cr:* Elem Sci Teacher Roosevelt Elem Sch 1973-; *ai:* Chaperone Stus to Washington DC; OK Ed Assn, OK Sci Teachers Assn, NSTA; Kappa Kappa Iota Pres; PEO; Marland Mansion Commission; Church Choir; Staff Dev Comm; PTA Outstanding Service Awd 1979, 1988; *home:* 1609 Blake Dr Ponca City OK 74604

WILLIAMS, SHIRLEY CHURCH, Business Education Teacher; *b:* Bud, WV; *m:* Bruce O.; *c:* Kerri D. (Dec), Gary B., Bouie O.; *ed:* (AB) Bus Ed, Marshall Univ 1961; Stetson Univ; WV Univ; *cr:* Bus Math Teacher Du Pont HS 1961-62; Engl Teacher Titusville Jr HS 1962-63; Shorthand Teacher Coca HS 1963-65; Teacher Pineville HS 1965-90; *ai:* Spon Chrldrs; Chaired Grads & Proms; Spon Tri-Hi-Y & FBLA; 4 Yr Yrbk Spon; WV Ed Assn 1965-; NEA 1965-; Gen Fed of Womens Clubs Mem 1976-; Pineville Womans Club Pres 1980-84; GFWC-WVFWC Safety Chm 1984-86; Celebrate Women/Todays Woman 1986-88; HOBY Ldrshp 1988-; Ctzn of Y Awd GFWC-Pineville Womans Club 1982; *office:* Pineville H S Box 219 Pineville WV 24874

WILLIAMS, STEPHEN RAY, Social Studies Teacher; *b:* Metter, GA; *ed:* (BS) Soc Stud, GA S Coll 1980; Working Toward Masters Ed, GA Southern; *cr:* Teacher Metter HS; *ai:* Soc Stud Comm Chairperson; Monitoring Halls During Lunch; Before Sch Tutoring Nonachieving Stus; PAGE, Phi Alpha Theta; Cool Springs Church Mem; *home:* Rt 3 Box 506-A Metter GA 30439

WILLIAMS, SUSAN LYNETTE NINE, First Grade Teacher; *b:* Oakland, MD; *m:* Wayne R.; *c:* Courtney; *ed:* (AB) Elem Ed, Fairmont St Coll 1972; (MA) Rdng, WV Univ 1979; *cr:* 1st Grade Teacher Terra Alta Elem Sch 1973-; *ai:* Lang Art Comm; NEA, WVEA 1973-; Preston Cty Ed Assn Pres 1985-87; Delta Kappa Gamma; Terra Alta Civic Club; *office:* Terra Alta Elem Sch State St Terra Alta WV 26764

WILLIAMS, SUSAN MARY, English Teacher; *b:* Cheyenne, WY; *ed:* (BA) Eng/Soc/Anthropology, 1986, (BA) Ed, 1987 Rollins Coll; Working Towards Masters Liberal Stud, Rollins Coll; *cr:* Eng Teacher Oviedo HS 1987-; *ai:* Asst Tennis Coach; Oviedo HS Counseling Dept Stu Assistance Prgm Aide; PTA 1987-; *office:* Oviedo HS 601 King St Oviedo FL 32765

WILLIAMS, TAMMIE ROUSE, Secondary Mathematics Teacher; *b:* Uniontown, PA; *m:* Larry P.; *c:* Lenny, Diane; *ed:* (BS) Math/Scndry Ed, CA St Coll 1983; Working Towards Master of Ed/Math/Cmptr Sci, California Univ of PA; *cr:* Math Teacher S Laurel Jr HS 1983-84, Redstone Mid Sch 1984-85, Brownsville Area HS 1985-; *ai:* Math Club & Future Mathematicians of America Spon; NCTM, NEA 1983-; *office:* Brownsville Area HS RD 1 Rt 40 Grindstone PA 15442

WILLIAMS, TERRI AVANT, Interrelated Spec Ed Teacher; *b:* Sandersville, GA; *m:* James S. Jr.; *c:* Jess S., Amber L.; *ed:* (BS) Elem Ed, 1976, (MED) Spec Ed/Learning Disabilities, 1986 GA Coll; Interrelated Spec Ed, GA Coll 1986-87; *cr:* 1st Grade Teacher 1976-85, Interrelated Teacher 1985- Elder Primary Sch; *ai:* Elder Primary Sch PRIDE Comm Chm; Oconee Area Learning Disabilities Consortium Chm; Gamma Beta Phi 1983-84; *office:* Elder Primary Sch 316 Hall St Sandersville GA 31082

WILLIAMS, TIMOTHY HARMON, Sr Data Processing Instructor; *b:* Troy, OH; *m:* Sandra Kaye Barbee; *c:* Chad, Michael; *ed:* (BS) Bus Ed, Wright St Univ 1989; Data Processing Certificate Amer Automation Trng Center; *cr:* Programmer/Analyst French Oil Mill Machinery Company 1969-82, Bank One Mortgage 1982-83; Instr Upper Valley Joint Voc Sch 1983-; *ai:* Chapter Adv Bus Prof of America; OVA, AVA 1988-; Bus Prof of America 1983-; 4-H West Cntrl Wrestling (Pres, Adv) 1982-84; Ofcls Assn Pres 1980-81; Masonic Lodge Master 1979; Stu Elected Natl Scndry Pres Bus Prof of America; *home:* 8400 E Miami-Shelby Rd Conover OH 45317

WILLIAMS, TRINA CORNWELL, Scndry Bus Ed Teacher; *b:* Hendersonville, NC; *m:* Louis Alexander; *c:* Alex, Katherine; *ed:* (BS) Bus Ed, 1981, (MA) Bus Ed, 1982 W Carolina Univ; *cr:* Bus Teacher Hickory HS 1982-; *ai:* FBLA Adv 1984-; Enrichment & Teacher-Adv Comm; Stu Cncl Adv 1983-84; Zion Luth Church; *office:* Hickory HS 1234 3rd St NE Hickory NC 28601

WILLIAMS, VAN OLIVER, Special Education Teacher; *b:* Akron, OH; *m:* Regina Renee Gresham; *c:* Brandon; *ed:* (BA) Elem/Spec Ed/Learning Disabilities/BD, Hiram Coll 1976; Rdng, Curr, Instruction; *cr:* 6th Grade Teacher Chambers Elem Sch 1976-78; Remediation Spec Ed Teacher Shaw HS 1978-79; Health Instr Kirk Mid Sch 1979-82; Phys Ed Instr Prospect Elem Sch 1982-87; Sci Teacher 1987-88, Athletic Dir 1986-89 Kirk Mid Sch; *ai:* Head Swim Coach; Labor Management Comm; Natl Interscholastic Swim Coaches Assn; OH Swim Coaches & Office Assn 1980-89, NE OH Coach of Yr 1984-85; NEA, OEA 1976-; East Cleveland Ed Assn (Asst Membership Chm, Exec Bd 1979-83), Building Teacher of Yr 1985-86; Diabetes Assn

Volunteer 1987-89, Appreciation Awd 1987, 1988, 1989; East Cleveland Sch Spec Ed Recognition 1988-89.

WILLIAMS, VERN S., Mathematics Teacher; *b:* Washington, DC; *ed:* (BA) Math Ed, Univ of MD 1972; *cr:* Math Teacher Hayfield Scndry Sch 1972-74, Ellen Glasgow Intermediate Sch 1974-81, H W Longfellow Intermediate Sch 1981-; *ai:* St Champion Longfellow Coach; Mathcounts Team; Fairfax Cty Fed of Teachers 1984-; Fairfax Cty Assn of Teachers of Math 1979-; Fairfax Cty Teacher of Yr 1990; Outstanding Teacher of the Gifted Awd 1990; Human Relation Awd 1988; Natl Society of Prof Engrs Service Awd 1988; *office:* H W Longfellow Sch 2000 Westmoreland St Falls Church VA 22043

WILLIAMS, VICTORIA HOWELL, Jr HS Dev Handicapped Teacher; *b:* Oak Hill, OH; *m:* Roy Jr.; *c:* Lindsay; *ed:* (BS) Elem Ed/Spec Ed, OH Univ 1972; Guidance & Counseling, Univ of Dayton; *cr:* Teacher Hope Haven Sch 1972-86; Teacher of Developmentally Handicapped Jackson HS 1986-; *ai:* Jackson HS Girls Tennis Coach; OEA, NEA 1986-; Cncl for Retarded Citizens 1972-; Gallia-Jackson Meigs Mental Health Bd, Bd Mem; Lib Trustee Secy 1978-; Pals Support Group Pres 1989-; Jackson Cty BPW Young Careerist 1977.

WILLIAMS, WENDY PARKER, English Teacher; *b:* Johnson, VT; *m:* Frederick Allen; *c:* Megan; *ed:* (BA) Eng, WV Wesleyan Coll 1971; (BA) Scndry Ed, Glenville St Coll 1980; (MA) Comm Stud, WV Univ 1988; *cr:* Secy to Asst Supts Wood Cty Bd of Ed 1972-79; Bus/Eng Teacher Mountain St Coll 1980; 7th/8th Grade Eng Teacher Van Devender Jr HS 1981-86; 10th Grade Eng Teacher Parkersburg HS 1986-; *ai:* Writers Wkshp Co-Spon; Future 2000 Promotional, Scndry Eng, Lang Art Textbook Adoption Comm; AAUW 1968-85; Sigma Tau Delta Secy 1970-71; WVELAC Mem 1985-88, Nom Teacher of Yr 1984; Jaycees 1984, Nom Teacher of Yr 1984; N Parkersburg Baptist Church Mem; WV St Dept of Ed, St Writing Assessment Comm 1989-; Ashland Oil Teacher Achievement Awd Nom 1989-; WV St Dept of Ed 1989-; *home:* 3213 Hemlock St Parkersburg WV 26101

WILLIAMS, WILLENA SMITH, K-5th Grade Teacher; *b:* Macon, GA; : Herbert Smart; *c:* Julie E, Jeffrey F, William F; *ed:* Bible, Child Evangelism Fellowship 1970; Ed, Macon Coll 1982; Bible, Moody Bible Institute 1983; Elem Edu, Liberty Univ Sch of Lifelong Learing 1987-89; *cr:* Elem Teacher Central Fellowship Chrstn Acad 1970-; *ai:* GA Assn of Chrstn Schls; *home:* 4302 Elberta Dr Macon GA 31206

WILLIAMS-MONSON, PEGGY JOYCE ELLIS, 8th Grade Teacher; *b:* Campbellsville, KY; *m:* Rodger A Monson; *c:* Laura Williams Bryant, Milton E. Williams, Myra Williams Oliver; *ed:* (BS) Elem Ed, Campbellsville Coll 1964; (MA) Ed, 1987, (Rank I) Sch Admin, 1988 W KY Univ; *cr:* Teacher Campbellsville City Sch 1964-77, Taylor Cty Sch 1977-82, Green Cty Sch 1985-; *ai:* Mid Sch Drama Club; NEA, KY Ed Assn Mem 1964-; Green Cty Ed Assn Mem 1985-; Outstanding Teacher Awd Green Cty Mid Sch 1986; *office:* Green Cty Mid Sch PO Box 369 Greensburg KY 42743

WILLIAMSON, ARTHUR WAYNE, Sports Medicine Teacher; *b:* Florence, SC; *c:* Benjamin, Stephen; *ed:* (BA) Religion/Soc Stud, Gardner-Webb Coll 1976; Sports Med, Wake Forest/Bowman Gray Sch of Med; *cr:* Teacher/Trainer Dixon HS 1979-83; Independence HS 1983-; *ai:* Athletic Trainer Intnl Stud Comm/Stu Asst Prgm/Crisis Asst Team; NC Trainers Assn Dist Dir 1980-; Natl Athletic Trainers Assn 1983-; Trainer for Shrine Bowl 1986, 1988; St Wrestling Championship Trainer 1984-89; *office:* Independence HS 1967 Patriot Dr Charlotte NC 28227

WILLIAMSON, CARMEN OLIVER, English Teacher; *b:* Daytona Beach, FL; *m:* Percy L. Sr.; *c:* D'Artan, Percy II; *ed:* (BA) Eng, Bethune-Cookman Coll 1978; *cr:* Teacher John F Kennedy Sr HS 1978-81, Church Point Sr HS 1981-83, Robert E Lee Sr HS 1983-; *ai:* Jr Class Adv; Forensics Coach; Prom Spon; Duval/Nassau Alumni Assn of Bethune-Cookman Coll Secy 1986-89, Service Awd 1985; Young Matrons of Dayspring Baptist Church Sunday Sch Teacher; Beachwood Civic Assn; Teacher of Yr Awd 1987-88; Key to City of Jacksonville for Public Service; *office:* Robert E Lee Sr HS 1200 S Mc Duff Jacksonville FL 32205

WILLIAMSON, CAROL HONER, 1st Grade Teacher; *b:* Belleville, IL; *m:* Robert E.; *c:* Amy J., Kelly J.; *ed:* (BS) Bus Admin, Washington Univ St Louis MO 1957; (MED) Elem Ed, Univ of AZ 1963; S IL Univ-Edwardsville; *cr:* 4th Grade Teacher 1960-63, 5th Grade Teacher 1963-67, K-6th Grade Substitute Teacher 1967-78 Cahokia Public Schls; 1st Grade Teacher Holy Rosary Sch 1978-; *ai:* Comm Work; NCEA 1978-; Jobs Daughters Bethel Guardian 1979-85; IL Cncl Jobs Daughters-Grand 4th Messenger 1983; Delta Delta Delta 1953-; Advanced Catechist Cert; *home:* 2006 E Main St Belleville IL 62221

WILLIAMSON, CAROLYN BEDSOLE, Kindergarten Teacher; *b:* Butler, AL; *m:* Walter W.; *c:* Barbara A. Williamson Jennings, Michael W.; *ed:* (BS) Mobile Coll 1974; Early Ed Cert Univ of S AL; *cr:* 1st Grade Teacher Semmes Elem 1974-76; Kndgtn Teacher Wilmer Elem 1976-; *ai:* Dropout Prevention Steering Comm; Peer-Tutoring Comm Chairperson; Mobile Ed Assn, AL Ed Assn, NEA; *home:* Rt 4 Box 217 Wilmer AL 36587

WILLIAMSON, DONNA LIZET, Secondary English Teacher; *b:* Waynesboro, MS; *m:* Edward Charles; *c:* Edward O'Brian; *ed:* (BA) Eng/Scndry Ed, Univ of S MS 1981; *cr:* Eng Teacher Baumholder HS W Germany; Eng/Written Comm Teacher Wayne Cty Sch System; *ai:* Sr Spon; Natl Cncl of Teachers; ASCD; Sweet Pilgrim MB Church Bible Study Instr; *office:* Wayne Cty HS Gen Del Hwy 84 E Waynesboro MS 39367

WILLIAMSON, ELLEN MC KERNAN, Guidance Counselor; *b:* Brooklyn, NY; *w:* John Schenck (dec); *c:* Ellen W. Skavla, John S. III, Gretchen Williamson Crowley; *ed:* (BS) Chem, Chestnut Hill Coll 1948; Sci, Adelph Univ; Guidance Prof Cert, C W Post Univ; Advanced Counseling, Univ of RI; Supervision, Hofstra Univ; *cr:* Research Chemist Natl Dairy Research Corp 1948-52; Patent Chemist Natl Starch Products Inc 1952-55; Chem/Physics Teacher Bayport-Blue Point HS 1960-; Guidance Cnslr Sachem HS 1960-; *ai:* Amer Chemical Society 1948-56; Western Suffolk Cnslr Assn 1960-; Concerned Citizens Montauk 1980-; South Sayville Civic Assn 1970-; NDEA Fellowship Univ of RI Advanced Counseling Inst 1963; NDEA Fellowship Hofstra Univ Advanced Physics 1958-59; *office:* Sachem H S North Campus 212 Smith Rd Lake Ronkonkoma NY 11779

WILLIAMSON, JOAN BREWER, English Teacher; *b:* West Blocton, AL; *c:* Amber, Ashley; *ed:* (BS) Eng 1973, (MA) Eng 1981 Univ of AL; *cr:* Eng Teacher West Blocton HS 1973-; *ai:* Sr Class Spon; Anchor Club Adv; Delta Kappa Gamma Secy 1980-82; *home:* Rt 1 Box 254 West Blocton AL 35184

WILLIAMSON, LYNETTE COGGINS, Fifth Grade Teacher; *b:* Cleveland, OH; *m:* Jody; *ed:* (BA) Elem Ed, TN Tech Univ 1980; (MED) Supervision/Admin, E TN St 199 0; *cr:* 5th Grade Teacher Newport Grammar Sch 1980-; *ai:* 5th Grade Honors Clb & Sci Fair; E TN Ed Assn 1980-; *home:* Rt 4 Box 745 Newport TN 37821

WILLIAMSON, MARILYN JOYCE (BURRUS), General Music/Band/Chorus Dir; *b:* Springfield, IL; *m:* Ronnie Frank; *c:* Ryan F., Linda M.; *ed:* (BA) Spec Teaching/Supervising Music, IL St Univ 1966; *cr:* Band Dir Bonfield & Limestone Grade Schls 1966-72, Limestone Grade Sch 1972-75; General Music/Band/Chorus Dir Reddick & Essex Grade Sch & Reddick HS 1984-88, Reddick & Bonfield Grad Schls 1988-; *ai:* Piano Teacher, Entertainer, Performer; Delta Omicron Dir of Music 1965-66, Lifetime Mem; Music Educators Natl Conference (Pres 1966) 1965-66; AFT Exec Bd; Herscher United Meth Church Choir (Accompanist 1966-88, Accompanist & Dir 1988-); *home:* 296 E Kay St Box 434 Herscher IL 60941

WILLIAMSON, MARK ANTHONY, Marketing Teacher; *b:* Knox, TN; *m:* Susan Marie Flynn; *c:* Chelsea; *ed:* (AS) Soc Sci, Rogane St 1982; (BS) Mrktng Ed, Univ of TN 1984; (MS) Ed & Admin, Lincoln Memorial 1989; *cr:* Teacher Oliver Springs 1984-85; William Blount 1985-; *ai:* DECA Club; DECA; TGA/WTA; Masons; *office:* William Blount Sch County Farm Rd Maryville TN 37801

WILLIAMSON, MILDRED ELLISON, First Grade Teacher; *b:* Gouverneur, NY; *c:* Kristi Cusa, Jeff, Lori Hope, Mark; *ed:* (BS) Elem Ed, Oswego St 1975; *cr:* 1st Grade Teacher 1975-77, 4th Grade Teacher 1977-89, 1st Grade Teacher 1989- M W Cuyler Elem Sch; *ai:* M W Cuyler Sch CORE Team; Building & Field Days Comm; Chamber of Commerce 1988-; We Care About Kids 1986-; *office:* M W Cuyler Elem Sch South St Red Creek NY 13143

WILLIAMSON, SCARLET DOIRK, Third Grade Teacher; *b:* Pinehurst, NC; *m:* Robert Lawrence Jr.; *c:* Robert, Jarrod; *ed:* (BS) Primary Ed, East Carolina Univ 1969; *cr:* 1st Grade Teacher 1969-74, 2nd Grade Teacher 1976-81, 3rd Grade Teacher 1982-89 Jones Elem; *ai:* NEA; NCAE; Jones Elem Teacher of Yr.

WILLIAMSON, SUSAN AHRENS, Third Grade Teacher; *b:* Omaha, NE; *m:* Guy C.; *c:* Laura, CHristine; *ed:* (BA) Elem Ed, Wayne St Coll 1969; Midland Luth Coll, Creighton Univ, Kearney St Coll; *cr:* 3rd Grade Teacher Washington Elem Sch 1969-74; 4th Grade Teacher Iekamah Elem 1974-75; 3rd/6th Grade Teacher Twin Ridge Elem 1976-; *ai:* BEA, NSEA, NEA 1969-; MRC 1985-.

WILLIAMSON, THEDA G., Fifth Grade Teacher; *b:* Brownstown, IN; *m:* Jerome C.; *c:* Jay; *ed:* (BS) Elem Ed, 1966, (MS) Elem Ed, 1972 IN ST Univ; Learning Disability Ed; Gifted/Talented Ed; *cr:* 2nd Grade Teacher Brownstown Elem Sch 1966-68; 4th Grade Teacher Banta Sch 1968-70; 5th Grade Teacher Brownstown Elem Sch 1975-; *ai:* Team Leader 5th Grade Teachers; REAP Grant Comm; Mem Book Adoption Team; Revision Comm Lang Arts 1988-; Amer Assn of Univ Women VP 1988-; Beta Sigma Phi Pres 1988-89; *office:* Brownstown Elem Sch R 2 W Jackson Brownstown IN 47220

WILLIG, LOIS (HILCKER), Third Grade Teacher; *b:* Philadelphia, PA; *m:* Wallace P.; *c:* Karen Bateman, Kim Gibson, Kyra; *ed:* (BA) Elem Ed, 1973, (MS) Elem Ed, 1974 Millersville Univ; Foreign Lang in Elem Sch; Process Writing & Rdng; *cr:* Open Ed Teacher Schoeneck Elem 1973-75; Kndgtn Teacher Schoeneck & Reinholds Elem Schls 1975-84; 3rd Grade Teacher Denver Elem 1984-; *ai:* PTA Teacher Liaison; Stu Cncl Adv; Open Process Classroom for Visitors; *office:* Denver Elem South 4th St Denver PA 17517

WILLINGHAM, ANNE SIMPSON, Chapter I Reading Teacher; *b:* Greenville, SC; *m:* Martin B.; *c:* Amy G., Ashley B.; *ed:* (BS) Home Econ, Lander Coll 1971; (MS) Home Econ, Winthrop Coll 1979; PET Evaluator; APT Observer; *cr:* 6th Grade Teacher 1971; 8th Grade Teacher 1971-74; 7th/8th Grade Home Ec Teacher 1974-80 Ninety Six Mid Sch; Continuing Ed Inst Piedmont Tech Coll 1980-81; Asst Professor of H E Erskine Coll 1981-82; 6th Grade Teacher 1982-83 7th Grade Teacher 1983-84; 8th Grade Teacher 1984-85 Ninety Six Mid Sch; Chapter I Rdng Teacher Edgewood Mid Sch 1985-; *ai:* PTO Treas; Rdng Dept Chairperson; Piedmont Rdng Cncl 1985-; SC Intnl Rdng Assn 1985-; Intnl Rdng Assn 1985-; Needlers Quilting Club Pres 1990; Girl Scouts of Amer Ldr 1983-89; Sch Teacher of Yr 1989; Dist Teacher of Yr 1989; SC Teacher Forum Mem 1990; *office:* Edgewood Mid Sch Kinard Ave Ninety Six SC 29666

WILLINGHAM, JANICE DARRAH, Chem Teacher/Sci Dept Head; *b:* Frankfurt, Germany; *c:* Leslie, Kristi; *ed:* (BA) Bio, Cntrl St Univ 1972; (MS) Sci Ed, Cntrl St 1988; Med Technology; *cr:* Med Technologist Childrens Memorial Hospital 1972-79; Sci Teacher Cntrl Mid HS 1979-88, Westmoore HS 1988-; *ai:* Sci Dept Head; Academic Bowl Coach; Scholastic Team Spon; NSTA 1987-; Teacher of Yr 1980-84; *office:* Westmoore HS 12613 S Western Oklahoma City OK 73160

WILLINGHAM, MELISSA WOLFE, 5th Grade Teacher; *b:* Piedmont, AL; *M:* Terry A.; *c:* Molly E.; *ed:* (BA) Elem Educ, 1976; (MED) Elem Ed, 1981 Jacksonville Univ; *cr:* 5th/6th Grade Sci Teacher Alexanderia Elem Sch 1976-77; 6th Grade Eng Teacher Weaver Elem Sch 1977-78; 5th Grade Rdng Teacher 1978-81; 5th Grade Self-Contained Teacher 1981- Wellborn Elem Sch; *ai:* Chairperson Self-Study Southern Accredition Assn; Calhoun Cty Ed Assn 1976-; AL Ed Assn 1976-; NEA 1976-; AL Teacher of Yr 1989- Walter Wellborn Elem Sch; *home:* 81 New Haven Rd Anniston AL 36201

WILLINGHAM, REYNA A., Business Education Teacher; *b:* Reynosa, Mexico; *m:* Arthur L.; *c:* Travis L.; *ed:* (BBA) Bus Ed, Pan Amer Univ 1984; *cr:* Bus Teacher Progreso HS 1984-; *ai:* Stu Cncl & Sr Class Spon; UIL Shorthand Coach; Textbook & Graduation Comm; NHS Faculty Adv; TSTA, NEA Pres 1988-; *office:* Progreso HS P O Box 613 Progreso TX 78579

WILLIS, ANNIECE DURHAM, 4th Grade Teacher; *b:* Wolfforth, TX; *m:* Bill D.; *c:* Billy, Douglas; *ed:* (BBA) Bus Ed, TX Tech 1968/1971; TX Tech Advncd Acad Trng; *cr:* 5th Grade Teacher 1968-75; Jr HS Prin 1975-89; 4th Grade Teacher 1989 Ropes ISD; *ai:* ATPE; *home:* PO Box 68 Ropesville TX 79358

WILLIS, BARBARA CUMMINGS, Business Education Director; *b:* Atlanta, GA; *m:* John Richard; *c:* Joel R.; *ed:* (BS) Bus Ed, GA St Univ 1990; *cr:* Cmptr System Mgr Alston Miller & Gaines 1970-81, Hurt Richardson Garner Etal 1981-84; Admin Asst GA Cumberland Conference 1984-86; Bus Ed Dir GA Cumberland Acad 1986-; *ai:* GA Cumberland Conference Womens Ministries Exec Comm Secy; Sr Class & Maranatha Volunteers Mission Trip Spon; Bus Teachers Wkshp Chm 1990; Delta Kappa Pi 1987; NBEA 1988; ASCD 1989; Voluntary Action Center & Food Bank 1986-; Womens Ministries Secy 1988-; Jr Achievement Volunteer Educator 1988; Golden Key; Mortar Bd; Whos Who Among Young Amer Prof; Natl Collegiate Bus Merit Awd; Nom Volunteer of Yr 1989; *office:* Georgia Cumberland Acad 397 Academy Dr SW Calhoun GA 30701

WILLIS, BECKY JANE (ESTES), Mathematics Teacher; *b:* Tishomingo, OK; *m:* G. C.; *c:* Greg, Reggie; *ed:* (BS) Math, S OK St Univ 1970; *cr:* Math Teacher Marietta Public Schls 1971-73, Ardmore Public Schls 1975-85, Durant Public Schls 1986-88, Graham Public Schls 1988-89, Plainview Public Schls 1989-; *ai:* NEA, OEA; *home:* Box 335 A Murray Rt Ardmore OK 73401

WILLIS, EDWARD WILLIAM, Science Department Chairman; *b:* San Antonio, TX; *m:* Marsha Jane Morgan; *c:* Matthew A. Lukaszewski, Anne M. Morgan; *ed:* (BSED) Bio/Chem, 1980, (MED) Bio/Physics/Ed Admin, 1983 SW TX St Univ; Various Wkshps & Inservices Presented & Attended; *cr:* Lab Instr Botony Prep 1977-81; Sci Teacher Webster Intermediate Sch 1980-82; Instr/Cnslr Space Earth Ocean Center 1987; Public Sch Supervising Teacher for Stu Teachers 1987; 5th Grade Sci Laboratory Teacher Silver-Burdett & Ginn 1989; Instr Summer Sci Camp Teacher Univ of Houston-Clear Lake 1989; 7th Grade Life Sci/8th Grade Earth Sci/Phys SciCVAE Sci Teacher 1982-, Sci Dept Chm 1984 League City Intermediate Sch; Sci/Health Teacher Univ of Houston-Clear Lake Adjunct Elem 5135 1988-; *ai:* Stu at Risk; Clear Lake Ind Sch Dist (Technology Comm, Coord Elem Sci Fair 1990); Phys Sci Textbook Comm; League City Intermediate Sch (Goals Comm, Chm Discipline & Building Management, Coord Sci Fair, Coord/Spon 8th Grade Geology Field Trips); Prin Comm for Academic Excl; Beta Beta Beta 1978; Sci Teachers Assn of TX 1980-; TX PTSA 1980-, TX Honorary Life Mem 1989; Clear Creek Ind Sch Dist Curr Guide Publications 1984, 1987; *office:* League City Intermediate Sch 2451 E Main League City TX 77573

WILLIS, LARRY LEE, Social Studies/Health Teacher; *b:* Lafe, AR; *m:* Judy Louise; *c:* Flynn L., Crystal M.; *ed:* (BA) Phys Ed, AR St Univ 1978; Drivers Ed, Health Ed, Soc Stud; Grad Work Phys Ed; *cr:* Teacher/Coach/AD Lafe HS 1978-84; Teacher/Coach Marmaduke HS 1984-; *ai:* Head Bsbl Coach; Dist 3-A Bsbl Coach of Yr 1989, 1990; *home:* PO Box 204 Lafe AR 72436

WILLIS, NANCY JOE, Third Grade Teacher; *b:* Smithville, MO; *ed:* (BSEd) Elem Ed, Univ of MO Columbia 1971; (MA) Elem Ed, Univ of MO Kansas City 1975; *cr:* 6th Grade Teacher 1971-72, 5th Grade Teacher 1972-77 Mc Coy Elem Sch; 3rd Grade Teacher Alton Elem Sch 1977-82, Santa Fe Trail Elem Sch 1982-; *ai:* Independence Career Ladder & Santa Fe Trail Advisory Comms; Independence Natl Ed Assn (Historian 1982-84, Secy 1984-86, VP 1986-88, Pres 1988-89); MO Natl Ed Assn Womens Concerns Comm 1986-89; *office:* Santa Fe Trail Elem Sch 1301 S Windsor Independence MO 64055

WILLIS, PAULA DEE, Math Teacher; *b:* Houston, TX; *m:* Mark David; *c:* Corey P.; *ed:* (BSE) Elem Ed, Univ of AR 1978; (MED) Math, St Thomas Univ 1985; *cr:* 2nd Grade Teacher Elmdale Elem 1978-79, The Awty Sch 1979-81, W Briar Sch 1981-83, Horne Elem 1983-84; 6th/8th Grade Math Teacher Watkins Jr HS 1985-87; Jr High Math Teacher Duchesne Acad 1987-89; *home:* 3334 Chimney Place Dr Waco TX 76708

WILLIS, PURDY, 8th Grade Science Teacher; *b:* Weona, AR; *m:* Willie J.; *c:* Willie Jr., Timothy W., Gregory A., Sherita D., Frederick A.; *ed:* (BA) Bio, Rust Coll 1964; Sci Stud, Wayne St; Elem Courses, AR St Univ; *cr:* 5th/6th Grade Teacher Rosenwald Elem 1964-65; 6th Grade Sci Teacher West Elem 1965-73; Sci Teacher Feltwell Jr HS 1977-78, Osceola Jr HS 1982-; *ai:* Sci Club & Sci Fair Spon; *office:* Osceola Jr HS 711 W Lee Osceola AR 72370

WILLIS, SAMUEL E., JR., Elementary Administrator; *b:* Haleyville, AL; *m:* Judy Pruitt; *c:* Christopher E., Rebecca Hathcock, Walter P.; *ed:* (BS) His/Phys Ed, Florence St Univ 1960; (MS) Sch Adm/Guidance, 1965, (MS) Elem Ed, 1966 MS St Univ; Post Grad Stud Sch Admin, Supervision, MS St Univ 1968; *cr:* Teacher/Coach Lake Lucinia Sch 1959-60; Elem Prin/Coach Wren Sch 1960-65; Guidance Cnslr Amony Mid Sch 1965-68; Mid Sch Prin Aberdeen Mid Sch 1968-73; Elem Prin Monroe Cty Sch 1973-; *ai:* Monroe Cty Staff Dev Cmmty Chm; Admin Head of 2 Elem Schls; Natl Assn of Sch Admin 1980-; MS Prof Ed Assn 1985-; Lions Club 1960-; Educl Research Grant Rdng, Math; *office:* Becker Elem/Monroe Cty PO Box 6 Becker MS 38825

WILLIS, STEVEN CABOT, Studio Instructor; *b:* Daytona Beach, FL; *m:* Terri; *ed:* (BFA) Fine Art, 1974, (MAT) Art Ed, 1987 FL Atlantic Univ; Several Wkshps & Seminars; *cr:* Adult & Cmmty Ed Administrative Asst, Art Dept Chm 1982-87, Art Instr 1976-, Gallery 900 Dir 1980-, Art Schlsp Coord 1985- Atlantic Cmmty HS; *ai:* FBLA, SADD; Stu Tour of Spain 1982-85; W Palm Beach Curr Dev Writing Team Mem; Co-Chm Northwood Inst Annual Art Stu Exhibition Comm 1988, REAP Comm 1988; St Academic Games Question Writing Team Mem; Art Textbook Adoption Comm Mem 1988; Armory Sch Ed Comm Bd of Dirs Mem 1987-88; FL Art Ed Assn, NAEA, FL Teaching Profession, NEA, Palm Beach Cty Classroom Teachers Assn, Phi Kappa Phi Honor Society Mem; Omega Psi Phi; Greater Delray Beach & Boynton Beach Chambers of Commerce; Sunshine Square Merchants Assn; Palm Beach Cty Cncl of Art; Congressional Art Caucus; Young Audiences of Palm Beach Cty Incorporated Annual Art Festival (Consultant, Participant) 1988; City of W Palm Beach Spring Youth Arts Festival; City of Boynton Beach Annual Festival of Art; Royal Palm Audubon Society Ed Chm 1985; Southern Assn of Colls & Scndry Schls (Steering Comm 1986, Art Comm 1981);Various Publications; Ofcl US Natl Leadership Merit Awd; US Achievement Acad; Academic All-Amer; WPBR Top Teacher Awd; Atlantic Cmmty HS Top Teacher Awd, Top Faculty Awd, Teacher of Yr, Golden Brush Awd, Faculty Awd 1988; Univ of Miami Outstanding HS Teacher Awd Nominee 1988-89; William T Dwyer Excl in Ed Awd Nominee 1988; Whos Who in Amer Ed; Various Radio & TV Interviews; *office:* Atlantic Cmmty HS 2501 Seacrest Blvd Delray Beach FL 33444

WILLIS, VALERIE B., 10th/12th Grade Eng Teacher; *b:* Chicago, IL; *m:* Don; *c:* Steven, Kathleen; *ed:* (BA) Eng, FL Atlantic Univ 1970; (MS) Eng Ed, FL Intnl Univ 1980; Philosophy; *cr:* 9th Grade Eng/Sci Teacher Loyola Cath Sch; 7th-9th Grade Eng Teacher Mays Jr HS; 8th/9th Grade Eng Teacher Ponce de Leon Jr HS; 10th-12th Grade Eng Teacher Southern Door HS; K-8th Grade Teacher Chicago City Schls; 10th-12th Grade Eng Teacher Coral Gables HS; *ai:* Natl Jr Honor Society Spon; Quiip Prgm Eng Leader; Eng Journal; Luth Church Sunday Sch Teacher 1970-72; *office:* Coral Gables HS 450 Bird Rd Coral Gables FL 33146

WILLMAN, JAY, Computer Lit Teacher/Coach; *b:* Odessa, TX; *m:* Beth; *c:* Aaron; *ed:* (BA) Phys Ed, Angelo St Univ 1985; Drivers Ed Endorsement; Working Towards Mid-Management Degree Ed; *cr:* Teacher/Coach Wall Ind Sch Dist 1985-; *ai:* HS Ftbl & Bsktbl Coach 1985-8;; Mid Sch Ftbl, Bsktbl & Track Coach 1988-; Tennis Coach 1989; *office:* Wall Ind Sch Dist P O Box 259 Wall TX 76957

WILLMORE, LEANNA READ, Choir Teacher; *b:* Ogden, UT; *m:* Kenneth P.; *c:* Trent, Florence, West; *ed:* (BS) Music Ed, Weber St Coll 1971; (MM) Music Ed, Univ of UT 1984; *cr:* Band/Choir Teacher Valley Jr HS 1971-73; Choral Teacher Bonneville HS 1973-; Teacher/Leader Weber Sch Dist 1988-; *ai:* Ladies Cross Cntry Coach; Weber Dist Evaluation Comm 1984-86; UT Music Textbook Comm 1986-89; Amer Choral Dir Assn St Pres 1979-81; UT Music Educators Assn (Pres Elect 1989-, Region Rep 1973-75, Secy 1977-79, 1984-87, Awds Comm Chm 1979-82), Superior Accomplishment 1984; UT Ed Assn 1971-; Delta Kappa Gamma St Pres 1989-91; Delta Kappa Gamma Schlsp 1982-83; *office:* Bonneville HS 251 E Laker Way Ogden UT 84405

WILLRETT, MICHELE J., 11/12th Grade English Teacher; *b:* Moberly, MO; *c:* Jennifer; *ed:* Assoc General Ed, Moberly Jr Coll; (BSED) His/Poly Sci, SW MO St Univ; Eng, Cntrl MO St Univ & NE MO St Univ; *cr:* Migrant Teacher Southland Sch Dist 1975-77; Eng/His Teacher Liberty HS 1977-80; Eng Teacher Dora Sch Dist 1982-86, St Genevieve RII 1986-; *ai:* St Genevieve HS LA Incentive Grant Comm; Yrbk Adv; Cheerleading & Class Spon; St Genevieve HS Music Booster; MO St Teachers Assn VP 1985-86; MO Assn Teachers of Eng 1990; AFT (Constitution Revision Comm, Nominating Comm) 1986-; St Genevieve Cncl of Performing Art 1989-; St Genevieve Wind Ensemble 1989-; *home:* 195 N 6th St Ste Genevieve MO 63670

WILLS, BILLIE S., ESOL Department Chair; *b:* Washington, DC; *ed:* (BA) Span/Eng, Univ of Miami 1952; (MA) Span, Middlebury Coll 1964; San Carlos Univ Lima Peru; Univ of the Americas Mexico; *cr:* Span Teacher 1957-61, Stu Act Dir 1962-67 Miami Sr HS; Eng Teacher Univ of Miami 1967-72; Eng/Span/TV Production Teacher Miami Sr HS 1973-; *ai:* Awds, TAP, Lib, Awds in Lang Comm; Stu Government Cnslr; TV Production; NEA, FL Ed Assn, United Teaches of Dade 1957-; NCTE, Natl Assn Foreign Lang Teachers 1985-; Papanicolaoo Cancer Society Secy 1975-80; Candidate FL Teacher of Yr, Univ of Miami Teacher Awd, Pan Amer Awd Best Span Stu; *office:* Miami Sr HS 2450 SW 1st St Miami FL 33135

WILLS, GAIL DOUGLAS, 6th Grade Teacher; *b:* Fresno, CA; *m:* Barbara Crandall; *c:* Katherine, Kelly, Kevin; *ed:* (BE) Ed, Fresno St 1962; Individual Classes for Growth; *cr:* 6th Grade Teacher Le Grand Elem 1960-62; Spec Ed Teacher Merced Cty Schls 1962-76; 6th Grade Teacher Le Grand Elem 1976-; *ai:* Sftbl Coach; Outdoor Ed Adv; CEC Pres; Lions Pres 1968, Monark 1985; Masons Master 1974, 1988; Environmental Ed Outdoor Camp; Jack L Boyd Outdoor Ed Sch Pres; *office:* Le Grand Elem Sch PO Box 27 Le Grand CA 95333

WILLS, GWENDOLYN WILLIAMS, Secondary Counselor; *b:* Calvert, TX; *m:* Timothy W. Jr.; *ed:* (BS) Dietetics, 1960, (ME) Ed, 1965 Prairie View A&M Univ; *cr:* Elem Teacher Hawthorne Elem Sch 1960-66; Elem Cnslr Cntrl Grade Sch 1966-73; Cnslr Argentine Mid Sch 1973-75; Scndry Cnslr Wyandotte HS 1975-; *ai:* Peer Spon; Upward Bound Pgm & United Way Coord; Mem Close-Up, NHS, Drug & Alcohol Subanstance Abuse Committees; Amer Assn Cnslrs Dev, ASCA 1967-; KACD, NEKACD 1975-; NEA 1960-; Parkway Home Owners Assn 1988-; Volunteer of Yr 1985; Female Teacher of Yr 1981-82; A Woman of Distinction 1985; *office:* Wyandotte HS 25th & Minnesota Ave Kansas City KS 66102

WILLSON, JOHN PAUL, Health Teacher; *b:* St Charles, IL; *m:* Nancy Strunk; *c:* Andrew, Eric, Brent, Laura; *ed:* (BS) Health/Safety Ed, IN Univ 1972; (MS) Sch Health Ed, S IL Univ 1976; *cr:* Health Teacher Evanston Township HS 1972-; *ai:* Ftbl, Wrestling, Golf Coach; Drug Awareness, Sexuality, Sexual Abuse Comm; Amer Alliance of Health Phys Ed & Recreation Mem; NEA 1972-; IL Ed Assn; Tree of Rest VP 1989-; Awana Leader 1989-; Young Life Comm Mem 1978-; Article Published Magazine 1977; *office:* Evanston Township HS 1600 Dodge Ave Evanston IL 60204

WILLSON, MARGARET SUE, Vocal Music Teacher; *b:* Sherman, TX; *m:* Charles Emery; *c:* Nanci S., Wade H., Amy L.; *ed:* (BME) Music Ed, 1962, (MS) Sch Admin, 1989 Ft Hays St Univ; *cr:* 6th-12th Grade Vocal Music Teacher Wa Keeney KS 1962-64; 7th-9th Grade Vocal Music Teacher Jefferson Cty CO 1964-69; K-12th Grade Vocal Music Teacher Russell KS 1975-; *ai:* Sch Musical; 6th-12th Grade Performance Groups; Class Spon; Phi Delta Kappa 1989-; Phi Kappa Phi 1962-; KS Music Educators Assn 1975-; Amer Choral Dir Assn 1987-; NEA, KS Ed Assn 1975-; Russell Cty Ed Assn (VP 1985-89) 1975-; Russell Arts Cncl 1976-; Russell Cmmty Theater 1986-; PEO 1980-; *home:* 633 Oakdale Russell KS 67665

WILMARTH, SHELLI ZIMMER, Fifth Grade Teacher; *b:* Lincoln, IL; *m:* Gary J.; *c:* Brian, Neil; *ed:* (BA) Elem Ed, E IL Univ 1982; *cr:* Teacher/Coach Divernon Elem HS 1982-; *ai:* Coaching HS Vlybl 1982-; 8th Grade Spon; Spelling Bee Coord; Read to Succeed Coord; Amer Vlybl Coaches Assn; *office:* Divernon Elem Sch 303 E Kenney Divernon IL 62530

WILMORE, WINIMERIL VONDERSLICE, 5th Grade Teacher; *b:* Wynnewood, OK; *c:* Kevin L.; *ed:* (BA) Elem Ed, 1971, (MA) Elem Ed, 1978 E NM Univ; *cr:* 3rd Grade Teacher Floyd Municipal Schls 1971-72; Mid Sch Eng/3rd/5th/6th Grade/HS Bus Teacher/Athletic Dir Carrizozo Municipal Schls 1972-; *ai:* Vlybl & Bsktbl Bookkeeper; MMEA Secy; *home:* Box 34 Carrizoz NM 88301

WILMOT, BARBARA KLEIN, Social Studies Teacher; *b:* Framingham, MA; *m:* David John; *ed:* (BA) Sociology, Brandeis Univ 1986; *cr:* 8th Grade Soc Stud Teacher Varnum Brook Mid Sch 1986-; *ai:* Odyssey of Mind Coach; Stu Cncl Adv; Mem Soc Stud Curr Comm; Study Group Supvr; Excl in Ed Awd Brandeis Univ; *office:* Varnum Brook Mid Sch Hollis St Pepperell MA 01463

WILSKI, CHRISTOPHER JOSEPH, Orchestra Director; *b:* Wilkes-Barre, PA; *m:* Judith Allen; *c:* Megan A.; *ed:* (BS) Music Ed, Mansfield Univ 1976; Marywood Coll, Wilkes Univ, Univ of Scranton, Penn St Univ; *cr:* Mid Sch Orch Dir 1976-83, HS Orch Dir 1983- Wyoming Valley W; *ai:* Ski Club & Class Adv; Golf & Vlybl Coach; HS Musical Tech Dir; Open-House Comm; NEA, PSEA 1976-; MENC, PMEA 1983-; A F of M Local 140 1969-; Knights of Columbus 1986-; Staff of Wilkes Univ Encore Music Camp 1988-; Euphonium Soloist Local Music Organizations; Orch Mgr Synfonia Da Camera Chamber Orch; *office:* Wyoming Valley W HS Wadham St Plymouth PA 18651

WILSON, AGNES JACKSON, Science Teacher; *b:* Philadelphia, PA; *m:* John H.; *c:* Sally Ashton, Cynthia Marks, Janet, John H.; *ed:* (BA) Psych, Westminster Coll 1945; Natl Sci Fnd Inservice Inst Environmental Sci for Scndry Sch Teachers Gannon Univ; Masters Degree Prgm Gannon Univ 1978; *cr:* Teacher Roosevelt Mid Sch 1963-; *ai:* Roosevelt Sci Fairs; 8th Grade Graduation Dinner Dance; Awds Day; Essay Contests; Mentor Teacher; NEA, PA St Ed Assn 1963-; Pi Delta Epsilon 1942-; Adolescent Task Force 1980-; PTA Honorary Life Membership 1977, Outstanding Ed Achievement Merit Awd 1980, Teacher Service Awd 1981-82; Environmental Sci Natl Sci Fnd Gannon Univ 1978; Presenter Natl Mid Sch Conference 1979; Mem Project 81 Life Skills Competencies Team 1981-; Original & Revised Editions of Basic Skills Curr Guide 1981-85; Certificate of Achievement Aerospace Ed Millersville St Coll 1979; *office:* Roosevelt Mid Sch 2300 Cranberry St Erie PA 16502

WILSON, ANITA FREEZE, 4th Grade Teacher; *b:* Salisbury, NC; *m:* Boyd C. Jr.; *ed:* (BA) Soc Stud, 1977; (MS) Sci, 1981 Appalachian St Univ; *cr:* 6th Grade Teacher 1977-78; 4th Grade Teacher 1978 Hudson Elem Sch; *ai:* Grade Level Chm; Fitness Comm; NCEA 1977; IRA VP 1989-; Hudson Womans Club (Pres/VP/Secy) 1980- Woman of Yr 1985 & 1988; Xi Gamma Rho (Pres/Sec) 1979-; Delta Kappa Gamma 1989-; *home:* PO Box 522 Hudson NC 28638

WILSON, ARDIS KRUEGER, Mathematics Teacher; *b:* Independence, MO; *m:* Gary A.; *c:* Nicholas A., Ryan C.; *ed:* (BA) Math, Cntrl MO St 1972; (MS) Cmptrs in Ed, Lesley Coll 1988; *cr:* Math Teacher William Chrisman Jr HS 1973-77, Fort Osage Jr HS 1979-80, Bridger Jr HS 1983-; *ai:* Cmptr Club & At Risk Math Stus Tutorial Sessions Spon; NCTM 1986-; NEA 1973-77, 1983-.

WILSON, B. BETH, Second Grade Teacher; *ed:* (BS) Elem Ed, St Francis Coll 1968; (MA) Liberal Stud, St Univ NY Stonybrook 1971; Grad Stud; *cr:* Primary Grade Teacher Tackan Elem Sch 1968-; *ai:* Various Local, St & Natl Teachers Groups; *office:* Tackan Elem Schl Midwood Ave Nesconset NY 11767

WILSON, BARRY ROBERT, Industrial Tech Teacher; *b:* Watsonville, CA; *m:* Kathleen Mary Juba; *c:* Patrick, Eric, Danielle; *ed:* (BA) Industrial Ed, IA St Univ 1968; Grad Stud IA St 1975-76; *cr:* Draftsman MS Valley Steel 1969-72; Pres 300 Research 1984-87; Teacher Kennedy HS 1972-, Kirkwood Comm Coll 1973-; *ai:* Industrial Tech Adv Cedar Rapids Schls, Grant Wood Area Ed Agency, Kirkwood Comm Coll; *office:* Kennedy HS 4545 Wenig Rd NE Cedar Rapids IA 52402

WILSON, BESSIE BALL, Language Arts Department Head; *b:* San Augustine, TX; *m:* James Arthur Sr.; *c:* James A. Jr., Letisha A.; *ed:* (BS) Home Ec, TX A&M Prairie View 1957; (MLA) Liberal Art, S Meth Univ 1978; Lang Art Wkshps; *cr:* Homemaking Teacher Blackshear HS 1958-60; 7th/8th Grade Lang Art Teacher Dunbar HS 1963-69, Sarah Zumalt Mid Sch 1969-71, W E Greiner Mid Sch 1971-; *ai:* Lang Art Dept Head; W E Greiner New Sch Steering Comm; TX PTA Honorary Life Membership 1984; NCTE, TX Schls Teachers Assn, Classroom Teachers of Dallas, NEA; Alpha Kappa Alpha 1986; Lib Sci Study Abroad Prgm 1984; W E Greiner Mid Sch Teacher of Yr 1984-85, Finalist 1985; Cabells Golden Apple Teacher of Yr; Dallas Ind Sch Dist Career Ladder Levels II & III; Cliff Chamber of Commerce Nominee Golden Oak Awd 1985; *office:* W E Greiner Mid Sch 625 S Edgefield Ave Dallas TX 75208

WILSON, BETTY KING, 1st Grade Teacher; *b:* San Antonio, TX; *c:* Stephanie R.; *ed:* (BA) Elem Ed, Our Lady of the Lake 1963; *cr:* 1st Grade Teacher, Smith Elem 1963-65; Edgewood Sch 1965-67; San Antonio ISD 1967-; *ai:* Act 1st Grade; NEA; San Antonio Cncl; Zeta Phi Beta Sorority Zeta OfYr 1973; Church Mother of Yr 1989; Cert 25 Yrs Tchg 89; *home:* 622 Canton St San Antonio TX 78202

WILSON, BRIDGETT HAMILTON, Chemistry Teacher; *b:* Lebanon, KY; *m:* Frank Brown; *c:* Ka; *ed:* (BA) Bio/Chem, Bellarmine Coll 1985; Working on Masters in Natural Sci, Univ of Louisville; *cr:* Chem Teacher Nelson Cty HS 1985-; *ai:* Stu Cncl Spon; Tropical Marine Bio Trip FL Keys; KEA, NEA, KAPS; *office:* Nelson Cty HS 1070 Bloomfield Rd Bardstown KY 40004

WILSON, CAROL JANEBA, Sixth Grade Teacher; *b:* Cedar Rapids, IA; *m:* Royce Gill; *c:* Gayle Wilson Ray, John K.; *ed:* (AA) Bus, Lon Morris; (BA) Teaching, Sam Houston; CED; *cr:* Remedial Math Teacher 1975-76, 4th-6th Grade Teacher 1976-82, Advanced Basic Skill Teacher 1982-85, 6th Grade Teacher 1985- Leon Elem; *ai:* UIL Spon; *office:* Leon Elem Sch P O Box 157 Jewett TX 75846

WILSON, CAROLYN NEELY, Sixth Grade Teacher; *b:* Sistersville, WV; *m:* Allen R.; *c:* Jeremy A., Mark D.; *ed:* (AB) Elem Ed, Fairmont St Coll 1974; Grad Stud WV Univ, Salem Coll; Mid Sch Cert Trng; *cr:* Classroom Teacher Sistersville Mid Sch 1975-88, Sistersville Elem 1988-; *ai:* Stu Cncl Adv; Sch Improvement Team; Academics Task Force; WV Ed Assn, Tyler Cty Ed Assn 1975-; WV Effective Schls Prgm Network 1988-; NEA 1975-; BSA (Asst Leader, Aide Volunteer) 1989-; PTA; *office:* Sistersville Elem 651 Terrace Cir Sistersville WV 26175

WILSON, CAROLYN S., Spanish/English Teacher; *b:* Corbin, KY; *ed:* (BA) Eng, Cumberland Coll 1973; (MA) Eng Ed, 1979, (Rank I) Supervision, 1985 E KY Univ; Principalship HS, Elem; KY Internship Prgm; *cr:* Eng/Speech/Theatre/Fr/Span Teacher Williamsburg HS 1974-; Part Time Eng Instr Carson Newman Coll 1988-; *ai:* Sch Play Dir; Spon Span Club; KY Cncl of Teachers of Foreign Lang, NCTE, NEA, KY Ed Assn; Williamsburg Ed Assn (VP, Pres); PTA Exec Bd 1984-; KY Foreign Ambassador; Beta Club Teacher of Yr 1980, 1985; *office:* Williamsburg HS 1000 Main St Williamsburg KY 40769

WILSON, CATHERINE DIANE, 7th Grade Teacher; *b:* Vancouver BC, Canada; *m:* Charles Kyle; *c:* Kyle V., Kathryn L.; *ed:* (BED) Phys Ed/Fr, Univ of BC 1975; (MA) Admin/Curr, Gonzaga Univ 19 89; *cr:* Phys Ed Teacher J Crowe Scndry 1975-81; Substitute Teacher 1981-84; 7th Grade Teacher Northport Elem Schls 1984-; *ai:* Mid Sch Vancouver BC Field Trip; Youth Soccer; Sex Ed Curr Comm; *office:* Northport Elem Sch P O Box 180 Northport WA 99157

WILSON, CHERYL DIANE, Mathematics Teacher; *b:* Providence, RI; *ed:* (MAT) Math, 1980, (BA) Math, 1974 RI Coll; *cr:* Engr Englehard Industries 1974; Math Teacher Seekonk HS 1974-82, Venice HS 1982-; *ai:* Var Cheerleading Coach; Math Tutoring Prgm Supvr; Chaperone Stu to USSR 1990; Sarasota Cty Teachers of Math 1990; Venice HS Teacher of Yr 1988; Chosen for Comp II Comm Sarasota Cty; Dual Enrollment Instr & Adjunct Professor Manatee Jr Coll & Nova Univ; *home:* 748 White Pine Tree Rd #202 Venice FL 34292

WILSON, CLEVELAND THADDEUS, Sixth Grade Teacher; *b:* New Haven, CT; *m:* Antoinette Snodgrass; *c:* Gina, Danita; *ed:* (BS) Elem Ed, AL A&M 1976; Grad Work Toward Admin Certificate; Charter Grad Exec Dev Prgm; ESEA Chapter 2 Cnslr Trng Prgm; *cr:* Teacher Montview Elem 1976-81, Univ Place Elem 1981-84, Acad for Academics & Arts 1984-; *ai:* Sound Engineer Auditorium Performances; Traveling Performing Sch Groups; Adventist Towers Elderly Housing Bd Mem 1985-; *office:* Acad for Academics & Arts 2800 Popular Ave Huntsville AL 35816

WILSON, CLIFFORD DON, Assistant Principal/Teacher; *b:* Indianola, MS; *m:* Cathy Harris; *c:* Clifford II, Crystal; *ed:* (BS) Math, MS Valley St Univ 1973; (MS) Admin, Delta St Univ 1988; *cr:* Math Teacher Carver Mid Sch 1973-88; Asst Prin/Teacher Indianola Jr HS 1988-; *ai:* Stu Government Assn Adv; Prom Comm & Dist-Wide Math Dept Chm; Indianola Ed Assn (Treas 1985-88, Comm Chm 1984-88), Volunteer Service 1986; *home:* PO Box 83 Indianola MS 38751

WILSON, CONSTANTINE LOWERY, Fourth Grade Teacher; *b:* Norfolk, VA; *m:* Anthony Dewitt; *c:* Leigh M., Ericka A.; *ed:* (BS) Elem Ed, Norfolk St Univ 1969; *cr:* 4th Grade Teacher Smithfield Elem Sch 1969-71, Larchmont Elem Sch 1973, Stuart Elem Sch 1973-86, Granby Elem Sch 1986-; *ai:* After Sch Math & Rdng Tutoring; Ed Assn of Norfolk Chm of Instruction Commission 1988-89; Saint Thomas AME Zion Church Class Leader 1988-; Stuart Elem Teacher of Yr 1983; Natl PTA Phoebe Apperson Hearst Outstmding Educator Awd Nom 1984; Teacher of Yr Nom 1990; *office:* Granby Elem Sch 7101 Newport Ave Norfolk VA 23505

WILSON, CYNTHIA OLIVER-BAUMANN, High School English Teacher; *b:* Grosse Pointe, MI; *m:* Perry Wayne; *c:* Darren W., Christy L.; *ed:* (AA) General Ed, Palm Beach Jr Coll 1968; (BA) Eng, 1970, (MED) Curr/Istr Adult Ed, 1978 FL Atl Univ; FL Advanced Placement 1980-88; FL Performance Measurement System 1985; FL Atl Univ Admin Supervision Cert Courses 1987; *cr:* Eng Teacher Glades Cntrl HS 1970-71, Boca Raton Cmmty HS 1971-80, Forest Hill HS 1980-; *ai:* NHS Advisory Cncl 1985-; Budget Comm 1986-88; Stu Advisory Prgm Cnslr, Prof Renewal Cncl 1985-86; Staff Dev Comm 1984-85; Sr Class Spon 1982-83; Yrbk Spon 1972/74; Phi Delta Kappa Mem 1986-; Alpha Delta Kappa Mem 1975-78; EF Inst for Cultural Exch (EF Tour Cnslr Europe 1984-85, Ussr, East & West Berlin 1988-89, Assoc of EF Inst 1989); US Army Educator Tour 1990 Honorary Army Recruiter 1990; S Assn for Coll & Sch Visiting Comm; Trng Module for Testing Test Construction, Stu Preparation, Admin, Feedback, St Curr Team Writer 1986; *office:* Forest Hill H S 6901 Parker Ave West Palm Beach FL 33405

WILSON, CYTHNIA GEORGE, English Teacher; *b:* Bishopville, SC; *ed:* (BA) Eng, Bennett Coll 1973; Grad Stud Ed Courses, Francis Marion 1980; *cr:* Eng Teacher Berea HS 1974-75; Tax Assessor Lee Cty Cncl 1975-78; Eng Teacher Ashwood Cntrl HS 1978-80, Bishopville HS 1980-; *ai:* Yrbk Adv & Spon; Stu Cncl Co-Adv; Head Teacher Lee Cty Adult Ed; NEA, SCEA, LCEA 1978-; SCIRA, NCTE 1989-; Pee Dee Teachers Incentive Awd 1989.

WILSON, DANIEL THOMAS, Director of Bands; *b:* Atlanta, GA; *m:* Kathy Beene; *c:* Brittany, Sarah; *ed:* (BME) Music Ed - Cum Laude, 1978, (MME) Music Ed, 1981 GA St Univ; *cr:* Asst Band Dir Griffin HS 1978-79, Morrow HS 1979-82; Band Dir G P Babb Jr HS 1982-88, Mundys Mill Mid Sch 1988-; *ai:* Music Educators Natl Conference Mem 1979-; GA Music Educators Assn (Band Division Chm 1991-93, Mem) 1979-; Phi Beta Mu Mem 1987-; Natl Band Assn (GA Chm 1987-, Mem 1979-), Citation of Excl 1986; Jr HS & Mid Sch Bands Festival Evaluation/Competitions Highest Ratings; Lecturer, Clinician, Adjudicator & Guest Conductor; *office:* Mundys Mill Mid Sch 1251 Mundys Mill Rd Jonesboro GA 30236

WILSON, DAVID WILLIAM, Mathematics Teacher; *b:* Denver, CO; *m:* Cheryl L. Burrows; *c:* Sarah, Ellen; *ed:* (BA) Math, Univ of N CO 1973; *cr:* Math Teacher Jefferson Cty Schls 1973-84, Target Range Sch 1984-; *ai:* Mathcounts Team Coach & Spon; *home:* 11900 Merwin Ct Missoula MT 59802

WILSON, DOLORES M., English Teacher; *b:* New York, NY; *c:* Claire, Jennifer; *ed:* (BA) Amer Lit, Marymount Manhattan 1960; (MA) Eng Lit, St Johns Univ 1966; 4 Yrs Certified Graphologist; *cr:* Eng Teacher New Hyde Park Memorial HS 1960-64; Substitute Teacher Sewanhaka Dist 1970-75; Eng Teacher New Hyde Park Memorial HS 1976-; *ai:* Talented & Gifted Mentor; Mid States Rep; Coord Writing Contests; NHS 1988; Poetry Published; 3 Plays Produced in New York Art Galleries; Play in Progress 1990; Adirondacks Dist Awd Spon Winner NCTE Writers Contest; *office:* New Hyde Park Memorial HS 500 Leonard Blvd New Hyde Park NY 11040

WILSON, DORA CLINKSCALES, English/Reading Teacher; *b:* Abbeville, SC; *m:* Woodrow Z. Jr.; *c:* Woodrow III, Gwendolyn Summerour, Walter; *ed:* (BS) Bus Ed/Eng, Benedict Coll 1968; Grad Studs Guidance, Univ of TN Grad Sch; *cr:* Teacher Beardsley Mid Sch 1969-; *ai:* Teacher Center Rep; 4-H Club Spon; Mt Olive Baptist Church Media Asst Dir & Newsletter Ed; NCTE 1987-89; Knox Cty Ed Assn 1969-; TN Assn of Mid Sch 1980-; Knoxville Urban League & Guild Treas 1989-; Beck Cultural Exch 1987-; Delta Sigma Theta 1972-; DEJ Travel Club for Youth (Pres, Founder) 1986; Smokey Mountain Writing Project Grant; Knox Cty Sherriffs Dept Juvenile Assistance Awd; VITA Volunteer 1980, *home:* 3517 Riverview Rd Knoxville TN 37921

WILSON, DOROTHY BATTS, Third Grade Teacher; *b:* New Haven, CT; *m:* Donald J.; *c:* Karen, Gail, Donna; *ed:* (AS) Early Chldhd Ed, S Cntrl Comm Coll 1975; (BS) Early Chldhd, 1984, (MS) Early Chldhd, 1987 S CT St Univ; *cr:* Instructional Aide West Hills Sch 1969-84; Kndgtn Teacher Hill Cntrl 1984-85; 3rd Grade Teacher Martin Luther King Sch 1985-; *ai:* After Sch Math Tutoring; *home:* 24 Rock Creek Rd New Haven CT 06515

WILSON, DOUGLAS KENT, English Teacher; *b:* Salem, OR; *m:* Linda Jane; *c:* Cameron, Caitlin, Collin; *ed:* (BS) Lang Arts/Speech, OR Coll of Ed 1976; (MAT) Ed/Eng, W OR St Coll 1980; *cr:* Eng Teacher/Coach Coquille HS 1976-79; Eng Teacher Chemeketa Comm Coll 1987, Douglas Mc Kay HS 1980-; *ai:* Mc Kay HS Mens Asst Bsktbl Coach 1980-85; Willamette Univ Mens Asst Bsktbl Coach 1986-88; Mc Kay HS Girls Bsktbl Head Coach 1988-; OR HS Coaches Assn 1980-85, 1988-; NEA 1980-; OR Ed Assn 1977-; 1st Chrstn Church Deacon 1984-89; Make Wish Fnd Fund Raising Coord 1985-89, Spec Recognition 1989; *office:* Douglas Mc Kay HS 2440 Lancaster Dr NE Salem OR 97305

WILSON, EILEEN LILLEOIEN, 4th Grade Teacher; *b:* Mc Ville, ND; *m:* Richard B.; *c:* Joel R., Debra Westerman, Robert B., Beth Spanton; *ed:* Assoc Elem Ed, Mayville St 1947; (BS) Elem Ed, Valley City St 1978; Grad Stud Various Univs; *cr:* 3rd/4th Grade Teacher Hoople ND; Basic Skills/4th Grade Teacher Roosevelt Sch; *ai:* Sci Comm; JEA, NDEA 1980-; Amer Assn of Univ Women Various Comms 1979-; Delta Kappa Gamma Various Comms 1983-; PTA 1969-; *home:* 301 14th Ave NE Jamestown ND 58401

WILSON, EUGENA ELIZABETH (PERRY), English Teacher; *b:* Gary, IN; *m:* Kenneth H.; *c:* Nathaniel, Kendred, Robert, Julia, Kenneth E.; *ed:* (BS) Ed, IL St Univ 1967; (MS) Ed, IN Univ 1978; *cr:* 9th Grade Teacher IL Sch Dist 218 1967-69; Caseworker I Lake Cty Dept of Public Welfare 1969-71; 9th-12th Grade Teacher Gary Cmmty Sch Corp 1971-; *ai:* Gary Engl Cncl 1972-88; Gary Rdng Cncl 1975-89; NCTE 1975-88; *office:* W Side Sr HS 9th Ave & Gerry St Gary IN 46402

WILSON, EUNICE NAVENE, Social Studies Teacher; *b:* Caruthersville, MO; *m:* George W.; *c:* Kevin, Veronica, Angelique, Mark; *ed:* (BS) Soc Sci, Columbus Coll 1976; Masters Degree Candidate, Columbus Coll; Skillful Teacher & Metorship Course, Fairfax Cty; *cr:* Soc Studies Teacher Shaw HS 1978-84, Luther Jackson Intermediate Sch 1984-86, Fairfax HS 1986-89, Luther Jackson Intermediate Sch 1989-; *ai:* Faculty Advisory, Minority Achievement, Stu Government Task Force Comm; Luther Jackson Mentorship Prgm; AFT 1989-; NEA 1986-89; Grant for Dev of Fairfax HS Mentorship Prgm Literary Awd; Fairfax HS Mentorship Proposal; Published Ideas for Teaching, Mentor Handbook Fairfax HS; *office:* Luther Jackson Intermediate 3020 Gallows Rd Falls Church VA 22042

WILSON, EVELYN FUNDERHURK, Honors English Teacher; *b:* Minco, OK; *M:* Elzie J.; *c:* Gregory J., Michael D., Terri L.; *ed:* (AA) Tarrant Cty Jr Coll 1969; (BA) Eng, TX Wesleyan Coll 1971; (MA) Eng, TX Chrstn Univ 1982; Elem Cert 1977, Scndry Cert 1983 TX Wesleyan Coll; ESOL Cert Ft Worth Ind Sch Dist 1979; Writing Specialist Cert E TX St Univ & Keystone Writing Inst 1986; Honors Eng Course, TX Chrstn Univ 1986; Various Seminars & Wkshps; *cr:* Bookkeeper Amer Life & Accident Insurance Company 1957-59, Almond Orchards 1959-60; Secy TX Wesleyan Coll 1969-70; Sftbl Dir/Coach Univ Athletic Assn 1969-78; Ed/Typist Hageman Assocs 1972-73; Elem Teacher Rabyor Schls 1973-75; Tutor Hill Sch 1973-76; LLD Teacher Hill Elem Sch 1975-78; Part-Time Eng Instr Tarrant Cty Jr Coll 1983-84; Rdng Teacher 1978-80, Eng Teacher 1980-83 Morningside Mid Sch; Eng Teacher Leonard Mid Sch 1983-84, Southwest HS 1984-; Writing Consultant Mc Dougal Littell Publishing Company 1988-89; VP/Co-Bus Partner Gallman-Wilson Electric Company 1985-; Keystone Writing Consultant Ft Worth Ind Sch Dist 1986-; *ai:* Eng Textbook, Multiple List Textbook, TSTA Tally Comm; Campus Coordinating Comm Secy; Wkshps & Seminars Instr; Faculty Rep & Delegate; Whiz Quiz, Acad Decathlon, SHS Ink Spots Writing Club, Natural Helpers Spon; UIL Lang Art Coach; IOTA PI Chapter Pres & VP; Keystone Writing Assessment Team 1979-89; Delta Kappa Gamma, NEA, TX St Teachers Assn, Ft Worth Classroom Teachers Assn, NCTE, TX St Cncl Teachers of Eng, Ft Worth Cncl Teachers of Eng, PTA, Ft Worth Arts Cncl, TX Assn for Gifted & Talented, Ft Worth Gifted Stus Inst, Assn for Supervision & Curr; Notable Women of TX; Whos Who in Amer Ed; Outstanding Sftbl Dirs & Coaches Awds; Volunteer Work Awd; *office:* Southwest HS 4100 Alta Mesa Blvd Fort Worth TX 76133

WILSON, FREDA ANN (SCHREFFLER), English/Speech/Drama Teacher; *b:* Des Moines, IA; *c:* Nicholas, Joseph; *ed:* Certificate Clerical Sci, 1975, (AA) General Stud, 1976 Trenton Juco; (BSE) Comm/Speech/Drama, NE MO St Univ 1978; Life Cert Comm, Speech, Drama, Eng & Bus; Correspondence Courses with Univ of MO, Columbia & SMSU; *cr:* Radio DJ/Copywriter KTTN, KIRX, KRXL Stations 1974-77; Office Mgr Mc Carty Trucking Company 1978-79; Teacher Knox Cty HS 1979-80, Mercer HS 1983-88, Strafford HS 1988-; *ai:* Drama Club, Natl Forensic League & Stu Writers Spon; Play Dir; Speech/Debate Coach; Care Team Mem; Schlsp Selection, Stu Course Requests Comm; CTA, MSTA (Secy, Treas 1990-) 1978-; SW MO Speech Assn, Natl Fed Speech Teachers, Speech/Theatre Assn of MO 1988-; PTA 1986-; Mothers Psych Club 1986-88, Mother of Yr 1987; Beta Sigma Phi (VP, Pres Elect) 1987-88; Church (Teacher, Choir, Dir, Singer) 1970-; Jaycees Wives Chairperson Miss Trenton Pageant 1978-80; Tech in Ed Speaker; VFW Certificate of Merit 1988-89; Certificate of Achievement & Recognition Strafford Elem 1988-89; Poetry, Articles, & Work Published; Stu Speech Recognition in Natl Forensic League; *home:* 2934 S Galahad Ct Springfield MO 65807

WILSON, GAIL PURVIS, English Department Chairman; *b:* Williamston, NC; *m:* Zachariah; *c:* Natasha R., Christy L., Jelisa R.; *ed:* Working Towards Masters Eng 1986-; *cr:* St Remedial Rdng Teacher Bertie Sr HS 1983; Eng Teacher/Chm Jamesville HS 1983-; *ai:* Sr Spon; Southern Assn Co-Chm; Essay Oratory Contest Coord; Discipline Comm; NCAE Rep 1989-; Nom Jamesville HS Teacher of Yr 1989-; *home:* Rt 4 Box 414 Windsor NC 27983

WILSON, HARRIETTA MONTGOMERY, Third Grade Teacher; *b:* Flat Rock, IL; *m:* James L.; *c:* Rebecca Peno, Mark, Eddie; *ed:* (BS) Elem Ed, Eastern IL Univ 1962; *cr:* 3rd Grade Teacher Greenup Grade Sch 1962-66; Cumberland Elem 1967-89; *ai:* Gifted Prgm Grades 3 & 4; CEA; IEA; NEA; Casey White Oak Church of God Asst Pianist 1989-; Greenup Womans Club Pres; *office:* Cumberland Elem Sch Rt 1 Box 182 Toledo IL 62468

WILSON, HAZEL GERALDINE, Sixth Grade Teacher; *b:* Ann Arbor, MI; *m:* William; *c:* Joseph, Douglas; *ed:* (BS) Elem Ed, E MI Univ 1963; Grad Stud E MI; *cr:* Teacher Romeo Cmmty Schls 1963-69, Escanaba Area Schls 1970-; *ai:* Escanaba Ed Assn Building Rep 1972-; MI Ed Assn, NEA.

WILSON, JAMES AUSTIN, Fifth Grade Teacher; *b:* Tyler, TX; *m:* Molly F. Terry; *c:* Kevin, Cheryl; *ed:* (BS) His, East TX Univ 1975; (MEd) Elem Ed, Stephen F Austin St Univ 1980; Ed; *cr:* Loan Mgr Liberty Loan Corp 1966-69; Research Tech Johnson & Johnson 1969-75; Teacher Hawkins ISD 1975-81; Chapel ISD 1981-; *ai:* Ben Franklin Stamp Club; NEA/TSTA 1975-; NSTA 1987-; TX Sci Teachers 1989-; NCSS 1987-89; Sherman Jaycees Project Chm 1967-69 Chm of Yr 1968; Bapt Church Ordained Deacon; Tyler Stamp Club Pres 1988; Winner Lycan Awd Johnson & Johnson; President Hawkins Classroom Teachers 1979-81; *office:* Chapel Hill Mid Sch Rt 7 Box 34 Tyler TX 75707

WILSON, JAMES COPELAND, English Teacher/Yearbook Adv; *b:* Cumberland, MD; *ed:* (BA) Scndry Eng/Journalism Ed, Univ of South FL 1969; (MSLS) Lib Sci, FL St Univ 1973; *cr:* Eng Teacher Walker Jr HS 1969-70; Reference Librarian College of Orlando 1970-71; Yrbk Adv/Eng Teacher/Chm of Eng Dept/Newspaper Adv Conway Jr HS 1971-86; Eng Teacher/Yrbk Adv Dr Phillips HS 1986-; Adjunct Instr Univ of Cntrl FL 1982-87; Adjunct Instr of Eng Boone Cmmty Sch 1984-; *ai:* Yrbk Adv; Orange Cty Cncl of Teachers of Eng Pres 1969-; FL Assn of Teachers of Eng 1969-; Orange Cty Assn of Ed In Media 1989-; FL Assn for Media in Ed 1989-; Teacher of Yr Conway Jr HS; Fellowship Awd Lib Sci; Fl Cncl of Teachers of Eng Comm & Convention Chairperson; Seminar Speaker; Mem of St 9th Grade Exam Writing Comm for Eng; Evaluator of St Teachers Subject Area Tests; *office:* Dr Phillips HS 6500 Turkey Lk Rd Orlando FL 32819

WILSON, JAMES LARRY, Mathematics Teacher; *b:* Hayesville, NC; *m:* Darla Arlene Jackson; *c:* Kristine, Kathryn, Jeanne; *ed:* (MA) Ed/Lib Sci, AZ St Univ 1971; (BS) Math, Univ of UT 1968; Spec Weapons Colibrations US Army; *cr:* Math Teacher Kino Jr HS 1968-72, Samuel Elbert Acad 1972-76, Elbert Cty Comphrehensive HS 1976-; *ai:* Responsible for Office Scheduling for Sch; Handle Cmptr Coord of Scheduling Grading; Stu His & Attendance; Math Dept Chm; Apple Cmptr Room Coord; NEA, GA Assn Ed Local Unit Pres 1988-89, Most Outstanding Membership 1989; Former Optimist Club (Mem, VP) 1981-82; Wrote Sch Drop Out Proposal Operation; *home:* 1216 Robinwood Ln Elberton GA 30635

WILSON, JAMES ROBERT, Earth Science Teacher; *b:* Frankfort, MI; *m:* Dianne Carol Britten; *c:* James T.; *ed:* (BA) Phys Ed, Cntrl MI Univ 1971; *cr:* Phys Ed Teacher 1971-86, Soc Stud Teacher 1986-89, Earth Sci Teacher 1989- Hemlock Mid; *ai:* Hemlock Fed of Teachers; *home:* 9881 Cannonsville Rd Vestaburg MI 48891

WILSON, JAMES WILLIAM, Social Studies Teacher; *b:* Lancaster, SC; *ed:* (BA) His, Johnson C Smith Univ 1964; VA Polytechnic Inst & St Univ, Univ of VA; Photography Courses, Northern VA Comm Coll Manassas; *cr:* Soc Stud Teacher William C Taylor HS 1964-66; Soc Stud/Amer His/AP Amer His Teacher Fauquier HS 1966-; *ai:* African Amer His Month Act Comm; Fauquier Ed Assn, VA Ed Assn, NEA Mem 1964-; NDEA Geography Inst Southern IL Univ Carbondale 1967; NDEA Afro-Asian Inst Bethany Coll 1968; NDEA Afro-Amer Inst Appalachian St Univ 1969; Photographs for Publication; *home:* Rt 2 Box 570-H Amissville VA 22002

WILSON, JANET MC CORD, First Grade Teacher; *b:* Saint Louis, MO; *m:* Paul R. Jr.; *c:* Melanie, Heather; *ed:* (BA) Ed, Drake Univ 1970; (MS) Ed, Univ of IL 1975; Working Toward Cert Sci & Bus Ed; *cr:* Teacher Johnston Elem 1970-71, Northview Sch 1971-75, Dept of Defense overseas Schls 1975-77, Pleasant Acres Sch 1977-; *ai:* Report Card Revision Comm; Heres Looking at You 2000 Trng of Trainers Wkshp; Soc Stud Book Selection Comm; Vlybl Coach 1977-80; Rdng Series Selection comm; NEA, IEA, RCSEA 1977-; 1st United Childcare Bd (Pres 1986) 1984-86; PTO Bd Teacher Rep 1978-80/1988; Champaign Cty Home Extension 1988-; *home:* 591 Hazelcrest Pl Rantoul IL 61866

WILSON, JANET SUE, 5th Grade Teacher; *b:* Hazel Green, KY; *m:* Gerald L.; *c:* Tamara Henson, Rebecca, Jessica; *ed:* (BA) Elem Ed, 1979, (MS) Elem Ed, 1976 Morehead St Univ; *cr:* 3rd Grade Teacher West Liberty Elem 1972-73; 3rd Grade Teacher 1973-76, Remedial Math Teacher 1976-79, 4th Grade Teacher 1979-87, 5th Grade Teacher 1987-Ezel Elem; *ai:* Rdng Club; 4-H Club; *office:* Ezel Elem Sch Rt 460 Ezel KY 41425

WILSON, JANICE (BEAL), Math Teacher; *b:* Bryan, TX; *m:* Frank M. Jr.; *c:* Scott, Susan Wilson Young, Bart; *ed:* (BA) Math, Baylor Univ 1961; (MS) Math, TX Womens Univ 1967; Instr Trng for Kaplan Wkshps; *cr:* Math Teacher Racier Jr HS 1961-62, Crockett Jr HS 1963-65, Bowie Jr HS 1966-67, Mac Arthur HS 1967-79, Irving HS 1979-; *ai:* Academic Decathalon Coach; Sr Class Spon; TX St Tachers Assn 1961-77; Assn of TX Prof Educators 1986-88; NCTM 1984-85; Alpha Delta Kapa 1968-73; Plymouth Park Baptist Church Bible Teacher 1963-; Irving Tennis Assn Secy 1965-78; Baylor Univ Alumni Assn Dir 1984-87; Kappa Kappa Gamma 1976-; Natl Sci Fnd Grants; US Congressman Jim Collins Awd Teacher of Yr 1985-86; Instr Kaplan SAT Preparation Courses; Delegate to TX Energy Symposium Univ of TX; Navy Educator Orientation Tour; Marine Educator Orientation Dist Textbook Comm; *office:* Irving H S 900 O Connor Rd Irving TX 75061

WILSON, JANINE MARKS, K-8th Grade Principal; *b:* Fayetteville, TN; *m:* Robert E. Jr.; *c:* Courtney, Rebecca; *ed:* (BS) Ed, Univ of TN Knoxville 1975; (MA) Ed Admin/Supervision, TN St Univ 1982; *cr:* Speech Therapist Lincoln Cty Schls 1977-81; 8th Grade Math Teacher Cntrl Jr HS 1981-87; Prin Petersburg Sch 1987-; *ai:* 7th/8th Grade Bsktbl Coach; Comm & Act Supervision; NEA Delegate Rep Assembly 1989-; TN Ed Assn (Delegate Rep Assembly 1985-, Admin Task Force 1989-); Chamber of Commerce Ed Comm 1988-; Assn Reformed Presbyn Church Supt 1986-87; CLEAN Ed Comm 1988-; Outstanding Young Women of America 1987; Prin Northwest Sch 1991; *home:* Rt 3 Box 144 Fayetteville TN 37334

WILSON, JEANETTE WEST, Fifth Grade Teacher; *b:* Andrews, NC; *m:* James Terry; *ed:* (BSED) Mid Grades Math/Sci, 1972, (MAED) Mid Grades Math/Sci, 1973 W Carolina Univ; *cr:* 7th Grade Teacher Waynesville Jr HS 1971-72, Canton Jr HS 1972-74; ESEA Math Teacher 1974-75, 5th Grade Teacher 1975- Andrews Elem; *ai:* Andrews Elem Southern Assn Accreditation Math Chairperson, NC Senate Bill 2 Cty Comm & Differentiated Chairperson, Sci Textbook Comm, Mentor; NC Assn of Ed, NEA (Pres 1975-76, Treas 1974-75, Building Rep 1986-); *home:* PO Box 855 Andrews NC 28901

WILSON, JEANNETTE, Third Grade Teacher; *b:* Cushing, OK; *ed:* (BS) Elem Ed, OK Coll of Women 1963; Bethany Nazarene Coll 1967-68; Re-Cert Refresher Courses NM Univ; *cr:* 2nd Grade Teacher Lamar Sch Dist RE-2 1963-67; Supvr Little Tumbleweed Day Care Center 1969; 2nd/3rd Grade Teacher Gallup-Mc Kinley Cty Public Schls 1970-; *ai:* Sch Cooperative Comm; NEA 1963-67; AFT 1977-83; Whos Who in Amer Ed 1989-; Nom Distinguished Teacher Awd 1989.

WILSON, JOAN NELSON, 10th Grade English Teacher; *b:* Tallahassee, FL; *c:* Michael; *ed:* (BS) Lib/Media Service, FL A&M Univ 1973; (MA) Eng, Atlanta Univ 1985; *cr:* 7th-12th Grade Eng Teacher Williston HS 1974-77; 9th/10th Grade Eng Teacher Columbia HS 1977-80; Head of Circulation Ida Williams Branch Lib 1980-81; 8th/9th Grade Eng Teacher Redan HS 1981-83; 7th/8th Grade Eng Teacher Adamson Mid Sch 1983-86; 10th Grade Eng Teacher N Clayton HS 1986; *ai:* Stu Alliance Co-Spon; Eng Textbook & Eng Curr Comm; N Clayton HS Concerned Parent Comm; PTSA; Eng Tutor; GA Assn of Educators 1981-; Clayton Cty Ed Assn Building Rep 1988-; Delta Sigma Theta Incorporated 1972-; Natl Cncl of Negro Women Incorporated 1989; FL A&M Univ Alumni Assn; *home:* 1953 Valleywoods Dr Riverdale GA 30296

WILSON, JOHN ALAN, 4th Grade Teacher; *b:* Williamsport, PA; *m:* Elaine Oleksik; *c:* John, Stephen, Justin; *ed:* (BA) Elem Math, CA St Univ 1972; (MS) Elem Admin, WV Univ 1980; *cr:* Teacher Menallen Sch 1972-; *ai:* PSEA Rep; EDR Comm; Mens Honor Society Secy 1989-; HARC Bsbl VP 1984-; *office:* Menallen Sch RD 6 Box 272 Uniontown PA 15401

WILSON, JOHN DOUGLAS, Math & Social Studies Teacher; *b:* Hendersonville, NC; *ed:* (BS) Scndry Ed/Soc Sci/Geography/ Concentration, Appalachian St Univ 1974; Univ of NC Asheville, Western Carolina Univ; *cr:* 7th Grade Teacher West Buncombe Elem Sch 1975-76; 6th Grade Teacher Clyde A Erwin Mid Sch 1976-; *ai:* NEA/NCAE 1975-; Knights of Columbus 1985-; Secular Franciscan Order (Vice Minister 1985-) 1986-87; *home:* PO Box 452 Mountain Home NC 28758

WILSON, JOHN EVERETT, Science Teacher; *b:* West Memphis, AR; *m:* Amy Jo Huston; *ed:* (AA) Chem, FL Coll 1978; (BS) Chem, 1980, (MS) Chem, 1985 AR St Univ; *cr:* Sci Teacher Monette HS 1982, Ridgecrest HS 1983-; *ai:* Sci Club, Soph Class, Wiffacons Spon; NEA, AEA; CTA Pres 1989-; Natl Rifle Assn; *office:* Ridgecrest HS 1701 W Court St Paragould AR 72450

WILSON, JOHN J., JR., Mathematics Dept Teacher; *b:* Texarkana, AR; *m:* Ruth O.; *c:* David, Robert; *ed:* (BS/BA) Industrial Management, Univ of AR 1969; (MSE) Scndry Sch Leadership, Univ of Cntrl AR 1988; *cr:* Math Teacher/Bsbl Coach 1970-85, Math Teacher 1985- Nashville Public Schls; *ai:* Mathcounts Spon; Phi Delta Kappa 1988-; AR Cncl Teachers of Math 1985-; *office:* Nashville Jr HS 1000 N 8th Nashville AR 71852

WILSON, JONNIE LEWIS, Second Grade Teacher; *b:* Elizabethton, TN; *m:* James M.; *ed:* (BS) Elem Ed/Scndry Eng/ Health, E TN St Univ 1973; Licensed Practical Nurse 1964; Sch Health Curr Amer Lung Assn of TN 1986; Basic Cmptrs, St Area Voc Tech Sch 1988; *cr:* Secy/Clerk Carter Cty Supts Office 1967-69; 3rd Grade Teacher Cntrl Elem 1969-71; 2nd Grade Teacher Hunter Elem 1971-; *ai:* Amer Red Cross Sch Health Prgm; AFT 1971-; GFWC-TFWC Elizabethton Jr Womens Club (Pres 1982-84, VP, Corresponding Secy, Fed Secy, Parlimentarian) 1970-, Outstanding Club Mem 1982; *home:* Rt 7 Box 2735 Hyder St Elizabethton TN 37643

WILSON, JOYCE GARRETT, English Teacher/Dept Chair; *b:* Laurens, SC; *m:* Ronald W.; *c:* Cory, Jonathan, Patrick; *ed:* (BA) Eng, Lander Coll 1978; *cr:* Eng/Span Teacher 1985-88, Eng Teacher 1989- Cmmty Chrstn Acad; *ai:* Span Club Spon; Responsible for Jr & Sr HS Lib; Pro Family Forum Treas 1986-88.

WILSON, JUDITH ANN, Journalism Teacher/Advisor; *b:* Cassville, MO; *m:* David M.; *c:* Melissa; *ed:* (BS) Eng, 1972, (MS) Eng, 1976 SE MO St Univ; *cr:* Journalism Teacher Butler HS 1972-73; Eng Instr SW MO St Univ 1973-74; Journalism Teacher Strafford HS 1974-75; Eng Instr SW MO St Univ 1978-81; Journalism Teacher Parkview HS 1981-; *ai:* Yrbk, Newspaper Adv; NEA, MO Interscholastic Press Assn, Journalism Ed Assn 1981-; Ozarks Publications (Adv 1982-; Pres 1984-86); *office:* Parkview HS 516 W Meadowmere Springfield MO 65807

WILSON, KAREN GARRETT, Math Teacher; *b:* Richmond, VA; *m:* Merwyn Todd; *ed:* (BS) Math, Longwood Coll 1986; *cr:* Math Teacher Henrico Cty Public Schls 1987-89; Math Teacher/ Coach Trionity Episcopal Sch 1989-; *ai:* Womens Field Hockey, Mens & Womens Track Team Coach; Co-Spon SADD; CRCTM 1987-; *office:* Trinity Episcopal Sch 3850 Pittaway Rd Richmond VA 23235

WILSON, KAREN GERDES, English Teacher; *b:* Victoria, TX; *m:* George W.; *c:* Shannon, Kevin; *ed:* (BA) Eng, Trinity Univ 1961; (MS) Early Chldhd, E TX St Univ 1972; Talented & Gifted Ed Trng; *cr:* Eng Teacher Edison HS 1961-62; Kndgtn Teacher Wilson Pre-Sch 1968-72; Elem Teacher 1972-88, Mid Sch Teacher 1988- Denison Public Schls; *ai:* PTA Cultural Arts Chairperson; Natl Jr Honor Society Spon; B Mc Daniel Buzz Ed; TSTA, Delta Kappa Gamma, Phi Delta Kappa, TCTA, Denison Ed Assn; Denison Classroom Teachers Assn; Epsilon Sigma Alpha (VP, Secy, Educl Dir); Delta Kapp Gamma Schlsp; Article Published.

WILSON, KENT, English/Social Studies Teacher; *b:* Johnson City, TN; *ed:* (BSL) Bible, Johnson Bible Coll 1967; (BS) His, East TN St Univ 1971; Elem Cert, East TN St Univ 1974-75; *cr:* 7th-8th Grade Teacher Range Elem 1972-74; 5th Grade Teacher 1974-78, 5th/6th/8th Grade Teacher 1978- Happy Valley Mid Sch; *ai:* Happy Valley Mid Sch Stu Cncl Faculty Spon; NEA, TN Ed Assn, Carter Cty Ed Assn 1972-; Publicity Comm 1986-87; *home:* Rt 6 Dave Buck Rd Johnson City TN 37601

WILSON, L. ALVINE, English & Literature Teacher; *b:* Neath, South Wales; *ed:* (BSE) Eng Comprehensive, OH Univ Athens 1967; (MS) Teaching, Univ of Dayton 1979; Grad Stud Wright St, Bowling Green, Miami Univ, Sinclair Coll; OH Writing Project, Miami Univ 1986; *cr:* Eng Teacher Theodore Roosevelt Jr HS 1967-68; Eng/Lit Teacher 1968-70, Dean of 7th Grade Stus 1970-72, Eng/Lit Teacher 1972- W Carrollton Jr HS; *ai:* Power of Pen Writing Team Coach, Univ of Dayton Regional Writing Tournament Judges Coord, Univ of Denison St Tournament Planning Comm; W Carrollton Ed Assn Building Rep 1968-; OH Ed Assn, W OH Ed Assn 1968-; NEA 1967-; Phi Delta Kappa 1987-; W Carrollton Ed Fnd (Trustee, Grants Chairperson) 1990-93; OH Writing Project Miami Univ Fellowship Awd 1986; W Carrollton Ed Recognition Assn Significant Teacher Awd 1987-89; *office:* W Carrollton Jr HS 424 E Main St West Carrollton OH 45449

WILSON, LAURA KESSLER, German Teacher; *b:* E Chicago, IN; *m:* Robert A.; *c:* Carrie, Ryan; *ed:* (BA) Ger, 1968, (MS) Ed, 1974 IN Univ; *cr:* Ger Teacher Gavit Jr-Sr HS 1968-77; Media Specialist Lincoln Elem 1977-78; Ger Teacher Gavit Jr-Sr HS 1984-; *ai:* HS Chrldrs Co-Spon; Summer & Saturday Expanded Stud Gifted & Talented Prgms 1989-; *office:* Donald E Gavit Jr-Sr HS 1670 175th Hammond IN 46324

WILSON, LEANNA ZAY, Mathematics Teacher; *b:* Brownwood, TX; *m:* Charles Milton; *c:* Perry E., Spencer C.; *ed:* (BS) Math/Phys Ed, 1972, (MS) Phys Ed, 1980 Tarleton St; *cr:* Teacher Gustine Ind Sch Dist 1980-81, Yorktown Ind Sch Dist 1982-83, George West Ind Sch Dist 1983-88, Corsicana Ind Sch Dist 1988-; *ai:* TX Cncl Teachers of Math 1989-.

WILSON, LINDA MARTIN, Assistant Principal; *b:* Nashville, TN; *c:* Jay; *ed:* (BS) Scndry Ed/Eng, Univ of TN Martin 1964; (MED) Scndry Curr, Memphis St Univ 1977; Grad Stud Admin/ Supervision; *cr:* Teacher Mc Kenzie Jr HS 1964-65, Ritta Elem 1965-66, Scenic Hills Elem 1968-72, Millington Mid 1976-83, Millington HS 1983-89; Asst Prin Millington HS 1989-; *ai:* Spon Scholar Athlete Team; Contact TN Teen Inst; Shelby Cty Ed Assn (Secy 1986-87, Pres 1987-88, 1988-89); Phi Delta Kappa 1982-; Tn Ed Assn Bus & Ed Comm; Millington Bd of Aldermen 1988; *office:* Millington Cntrl HS 8057 Wilkinsville Millington TN 38053

WILSON, LINDY B., Mathematics Teacher; *b:* Casper, WY; *ed:* (BS) Math/Scndry Ed, Univ of WY 1987; *cr:* Math Teacher Campbell Cty HS 1987-; *ai:* Chrldr, Jr Class, NHS Spon; BEST Building Comm; Gillette Jaycees; *office:* Campbell Cty HS 1000 Camel Dr Gillette WY 82716

WILSON, MARGARET WEST, English Department Chair; *b:* Rigby, ID; *m:* L. Keith; *c:* James K., Elizabeth A. Watson, Margaret, Steven W.; *ed:* (BA) Speech, 1948, (MA) Speech, 1968, Teaching Certificate Eng, 1969 Univ of UT; *cr:* Teaching Asst Univ of UT 1962-68; Teacher Churchill Jr HS 1969-; *ai:* Journalism Adv Newspaper, Yrbk, Literary Magazine; Awds & Promotion Prgm Comm; Granite Ed Assn Faculty Rep 1980-81; UT Ed Assn 1969-.

WILSON, MARLENE E., 5th Grade Teacher; *b:* Wichita Falls, TX; *m:* Jerrel W.; *c:* Gregory Cook, Alan Cook, Susan Cook, Diane C. Martin; *ed:* (BS) Speech/Hearing, TX Womans 1974; Grad Stud; *cr:* Speech Pathology Teacher 1974-80, Classroom Teacher 1980- Gainesville Ind Sch Dist; *ai:* TX Classroom Teachers 1988-; Retarded Citizens Assn Pres 1973-74; *office:* Edison Elem Sch 1 Edison Dr Gainesville TX 76240

WILSON, MARTHA BOYD, Science Teacher; *b:* Jackson, TN; *w:* Ralph J. (dec); *c:* Laurie L. Anglin, Kimba L. Hopkins, Steven B.; *ed:* (BA) Sociology/Eng, Lambuth Coll 1961; *cr:* East Elem 1977-84; Teacher Northside Jr HS 1984-; *ai:* Delta Kappa Gamma; *office:* North Side Jr HS 3020 Humboldt Hwy Jackson TN 38305

WILSON, MARVIN RICK, US & World History Teacher; *b:* Big Spring, TX; *m:* Karen Mae Pinkerton; *c:* Marvin R. II, Laresa M.; *ed:* (BS) Phys Ed, Howard Payne Univ 1977; *cr:* Coach/US His Teacher Brownwood Jr HS 1977-79; Coach/US & World His Teacher Brownwood HS 1980-; *ai:* Defensive Coord & Ends Ftbl Coach; Track Distance Runners; TX Classroom Teachers Assn 1989-; TX HS Coaches Assn 1977-; Amer Ftbl Coaches Assn 1985-; Teacher of Month; *office:* Brownwood Sr H S 2100 Slayden Brownwood TX 76801

WILSON, MARY L., Guidance Counselor; *b:* Trimble, KY; *m:* George S. Jr.; *c:* Mary E. Capuccio, Stan, Paul; *ed:* (BA) Elem Ed, OK Coll for Women 1964; (MS) Counseling, Univ of OK 1976; Grad Work Univ of KY; Post Grad Stud S OK St Univ; *cr:* Elem Teacher Edison Sch 1964-67, Laurel Hill Sch 1967-68, Taft 1968-69, Van Voorhis 1970-71; Cnslr Ed Center 1971-72; Elem Teacher Meredith Sch 1972-73; Cnslr 1973-74, Eng Teacher 1976-77 Ed Center; Elem Teacher Hoover 1977-85; Eng Teacher 1985-86, Cnslr 1986- Eisenhower Jr HS; *ai:* Stu Cncl Spon; SAP Mem; NEA, OEA, PEAL; *office:* Eisenhower Jr HS 57th & Gore Lawton OH 73505

WILSON, MARY LOU LOU (FELTNER), Home Economics Teacher; *b:* Crawfordsville, IN; *m:* Charles David; *c:* Travis, Kelly, Amy; *ed:* (BS) Voc Home Ec, 1972, (MS) Ed/Child Dev, 1976 Purdue Univ; Trng for Quest Intnl Prgm 1989; *cr:* Home Ec Teacher Edgewood HS 1972-73, Lizton Jr HS 1973-74, Southmont HS 1983-85, Tri West HS 1985-; *ai:* Sr Class Spon; Help in Planning Graduation; AIDS Curr Comm; New Hope Chrstn Church Mem; *office:* Tri West HS RR 1 Box 10 Lizton IN 46149

WILSON, MICHELLE BONITA (AIKEN), Fourth Grade Teacher; *b:* Moncks Corner, SC; *m:* Horace; *c:* Isaac, Nicole; *ed:* (BS) Elem Ed, Baptist Coll Charleston 1982; Working Towards Masters in Elem Admin; *cr:* Teacher Cross Elem 1983-; *ai:* Grade Level Chairperson; Intnl Rdng Assn, Berkeley Cty Rdng Cncl; Teacher of Yr Cross Elem 1983-84; *office:* Cross Elem Sch Rt 1 Box 2 Cross SC 29436

WILSON, MIKE V., Social Studies Teacher/Coach; *b:* Pawnee, OK; *c:* Kena, Shane; *ed:* (BA) Soc Stud/Health/Phys Ed, Cntrl St Univ 1972; Grad Stud Counseling 1988; *cr:* Soc Stud Teacher/ Coach MariettA Public Sch 1972-74, Ralston Public Sch 1974-76; VP Pawnee Natl Bank 1977-87; Soc Stud Teacher/Coach Yale Public Sch 1989-; *ai:* Asst HS Ftbl Coach; Head HS Boys & Girls Bsktbl Coach; Head HS Girls Track Coach; Sr Spon; OK Coaches Assn 1972-76, 1988-; OEA & NEA 1972-76, 1988-; Masonic Lodge; *office:* Yale Public Sch 315 E Chicago Yale OK 74085

WILSON, NANCY MORRIS, Senior English Teacher; *b:* San Angelo, TX; *m:* Troy Michael; *ed:* (BA) Eng, Angelo St 1967; (MA) Eng, Univ of TX Austin 1968; *cr:* Eng Teacher Wall HS 1968-69, Grapevine HS 1970-; *ai:* NCTE, TX Joint Cncl Teachers of Eng, Assn of TX Prof Educators; Sigma Tau Delta, Dallas Museum of Art, Dallas Inst of Hum, The 500 Inc, Univ of TX Exes, Westminster Presbyn Church; TX Excl Awd for Outstanding HS Teachers 1987; *office:* Grapevine HS 3223 Mustang Dr Grapevine TX 76051

WILSON, PATRICE BERHOW, Fourth Grade Teacher; *b:* Crookston, MN; *m:* James A.; *c:* Michael, Katherine; *ed:* (BS) Elem Ed, Moorhead St Univ 1971; ND St Univ; St Johns Univ, Gesell Inst of Human Dev; Univ of HI; *cr:* 3rd Grade Teacher St Wendelin Sch 1972-75; 2nd Grade Teacher Paynesville Public Schls 1975-76; K-4th Grade Teacher Wahpeton Public Schls 1977-; *ai:* Young Astronauts Club Adv; Kndgtn Curr Comm; Gesell Kndgtn Screening Team; Rdng Cncl 1988-; Bethel Church; *home:* 625 N 2nd St Wahpeton ND 58075

WILSON, PATRICIA ANN, Social Stud Prgm Facilitator; *b:* Sumner, IA; *ed:* (BS) Elem Ed, Soc Sci, Mount Mercy Coll 1970; (Ma) Curr & Instr, 1980, (MA) Elem Admin, 1983 Univ of IA; Gifted Ed; Cmptr Tech; Mastery Teaching; *cr:* 5th Grade Teacher 1970-84, Resource Teacher for The G/T 1984-89, Prgm Facilitator 1989- Cedar Rapids Comm; *ai:* Dist Presentor Trained in Madeline Hunter/Coop Learning/Thinking Skills/Mastery Learning; Natl Trainer for Talents Unlimited; Dev Compacting Inservice for IA Talented/Gifted NCSS; Natl Assn Gifted/Talented; IA Gifted/Talented; Phi Delta Kappa; ASCD.

WILSON, PATRICIA ANN, Human Resource Specialist; *b:* Indianapolis, IN; *c:* Paula N.; *ed:* (BS) Elem Ed, W VA St Coll 1964; (MS) Psych/Guidance/Counseling, TN St Univ 1969; Butler Univ, IN Univ NW, Purdue Univ; *cr:* 2nd-5th Grade Teacher Gary Cmmty Sch Corp 1964-78; Parent Specialist Basic Educl Skills 1978-80; 5th/6th Grade Teacher 1980-88, Human Resource Specialist 1988- Gary Cmmty Schls; *ai:* Amer Fed of Teachers 1964-; Gary Rdng Cncl 1964-89; Assn of Chldhd Ed 1964-69; NW IN Alliance of Black Sch Educators; Alpha Kappa Alpha 1983-; Amer Red Cross Service to Military Families 1988-; Tots & Teens (Pres, Sec) 1981-83, 1983-85; Tots & Teens Natl Bound 1985-89; Eli Lilly Grant Math & Sci; *home:* 1962 Cleveland St Gary IN 46404

WILSON, PATRICIA R., Mathematics/Algebra Teacher; *b:* Nashville, TN; *ed:* (BS) Math, 1973, (MED) Admin, 1976 Mid TN St Univ; Working Toward EDS Degree Mid TN St Univ; *cr:* Teacher North Jr HS 1973-86, Cntrl Mid Sch 1986-; Developmental Stud Dept Teacher Mid TN St Univ 1987-; *ai:* Cheerleading & Yrbk Co-Spon; Fellowship of Chrstn Athletes Adv; TN Ed Assn, NEA 1973-; NCTM 1986-; GSA Leader 1973-86; S Assn of Coll & Schls Evaluating Teams Mem 1980-; *office:* Cntrl Mid Sch 701 E Main St Murfreesboro TN 37130

WILSON, PATSY DENSON, Social Studies Teacher; *b:* Birmingham, AL; *m:* Wendell; *c:* Wendy, Jimmy; *ed:* (BA) Phys Ed/Soc Stud, St Bernard Coll 1968; (MA) Phys Ed/Soc Stud, 1972, (AA) Phys Ed 1980, (AA) Soc Stud, 1988 Univ of AL Birmingham; *cr:* Coach 1975-87, Teacher 1968- Addison HS; *ai:* Sr Class Spon; Homecoming Coord; Winston Cty Coaches Assn Secy, Coach of Yr; Cancer Crusade; *home:* Rt 1 Box 122A Addison AL 35540

WILSON, PAUL WADE, Social Science Teacher; *b:* Shoshoni, WY; *m:* Donna Loy; *c:* Laura M., John M.; *ed:* (BA) Poly Sci, Loyola Univ 1977; (MA) Poly Sci, Univ of AZ 1979; *cr:* Instr Univ of AZ 1977-79; Captain US Army Quartermaster Corps 1979-83; Part-Time Professor San Antonio Coll 1984-; Teacher Jourdanton HS 1984-; *ai:* Debate Coach; City Cncl Councilman 1988-; *office:* Jourdanton HS 200 Zanderson Jourdanton TX 78026

WILSON, REBECCA LOVELL, High School English Teacher; *b:* Fort Smith, AR; *c:* Beth E., Benjamin C. III, Brett D.; *ed:* (BS) Eng, Mid TN St Univ 1966; Grad Work at Numerous Univs; *cr:* His/Eng Teacher Central HS 1966-67; Dir of Admissions Edmondon Bus Coll 1968-69; Sci/Math Teacher Ooltewah HS 1969-72; Teacher of Educably Mentally Retarded Lacey Elem Sch 1972-80, 12th Grade Eng Teacher Ooltewah HS 1980-; *ai:* Schl Newspaper & JROTC Spon; Sr Class Adv; Faculty Hospitality Comm Chairperson; Amer Bus Womens Assn VP 1989-; NEA, TN Ed Assn; Hamilton Cty Ed Assn (Human Relations Comm Chairperson) 1988-, Runner-Up Outstanding HS Teacher 1988-89; Intnl Rdng Assn Budget Comm 1989-; United Daughters of Confederacy 1984-; BSA (Asst Scoutmaster 1982-83, Denmother 1980-84); 4-H Club Adult Spon 1974-87; Parent Teacher Stu Assn Lifetime Membership 1989-; 1st Place Laura Handley Brock Awd Excl in Teaching 1987-88; 1st Place Evans Fnd Awd Excl in Teaching 1984-85; Runner-Up Hamilton Cty Outstanding Teacher of Yr 1987-88; Dow Jones Schlsp Winner 1985-86; *office:* Ooltewah HS 6112 Snow Hill Rd Ooltewah TN 37363

WILSON, ROBERT CLEMENTS, Science Teacher; *b:* Lufkin, TX; *m:* Patsy Jones; *c:* Robin L., Robert A.; *ed:* (BS) Bio, Stephen F Austin Univ 1967; Geology, TX A&M Univ; Phys Ed, TX E Univ; Phys Sci, Stephen F Austin Univ; *cr:* Teacher/Coach Tyler Public Schls 1967-80, Winona Public Schls 1980-81, Beckville Public Schls 1982-; *ai:* Girls Ftbl, Bsktbl, Track, Special Olympics Coach; TX Classroom Teachers Assn 1989-.

WILSON, ROBERT EARL, 8th Grade Math Teacher; *b:* Shattuck, OK; *m:* Susan D. Labbe Wilson; *c:* Jamie, Jason; *ed:* (BA) Soc Sci, Northwestern St Coll OK 1971; (MS) Ed, Wichita St 1983; *cr:* 7th/8th Math Teacher Mulvane Jr HS 1971-76; 8th Math Teacher Andover Mid Schl 1976-; *ai:* Head Coach Mid Sch Ftbl & Track; NEA (Mem Negotiation Team 1986-87 Chief Negotiator 1987-90).

WILSON, ROBERT JOHN, English Teacher; *b:* Montpelier, OH; *m:* Cynthia S. G.; *c:* Erica, Margaret M.; *ed:* (BS) Eng, Wittenberg Univ 1979; (MAT) Eng, IN Univ 1986; *cr:* Eng Teacher Edison HS 1980-85, E Noble HS 1985-86, Montpelier HS 1986-; *ai:* Poems Published in Different Periodicals; Assoc Faculty Composition in Univ; *office:* Montpelier HS 309 E Main Montpelier OH 43543

WILSON, RONALD PRESTON, English Teacher; *b:* Evarets, KY; *m:* Linda Jo Foley; *ed:* (BA) His/Poly Sci, 1971, (BA) Eng, 1971 Cumberland Coll; (MA) Ed, Union Coll 1975; *cr:* Teacher Oak Grove Elem 1973-74. Whitley Cty Mid Sch 1974-88, Whitley Cty HS 1988-; *ai:* Whitley Cty HS Teen Leadership Cncl Co-Spon; NEA, KEA 1971-; *office:* Whitley Cty HS Rt 1 Box 357 Williamsburg KY 40769

WILSON, RUTH WALDROP, Retired; *b:* Etowah, TN; *m:* James Benjamin; *c:* Roger, Sarah Ray, Morgan, Benjamin; *ed:* (BS) Soc Sci, Univ of TN 1945; (Ms) Elem Ed, IN Univ 1970; *cr:* Teacher Fair Garden 1945-48, Athens HS 1948-49, Tefft HS 1961-62, South Ripley Elem 1966-85; *ai:* Delta Kappa Gamma-Mu Chapter; *home:* PO Box 237 Versailles IN 47042

WILSON, SHARON CROSSAN, Second-Third Grade Teacher; *b:* Glendale, CA; *m:* Wayne J.; *c:* Terrance, William; *ed:* (AA) General Ed, Pierce Coll 1960; (BA) Elem Ed, CA St Northridge 1962; Grad Stud Elem Curr; *cr:* 3rd Grade Teacher Henry Mingay 1962-64; 4th Grade Teacher Yorba Linda CA 1964-65; 6th Grade Teacher Grazide Hacienda 1964-65; 2nd Grade Teacher Washington 1966-67; 1st Grade Teacher Grazide Hacienda 1968-70; 2nd/3rd Grade Teacher Reeds Creek 1980-; *ai:* Cty Soc Sci Comm; Stu Cncl Adv; AAUW Pres 1980-82, Grant 1984; N CA Writing Project 1986; Elected Sch Bd Mercy HS 1986-88; *office:* Reed Creek Elem Sch 18335 Johnson Rd Red Bluff CA 96080

WILSON, SUSAN RUTH, Social Studies Teacher; *b:* Johnson City, NY; *m:* Cary; *c:* Shannon, Tammy, Jason, Gary; *ed:* (BAE) His, AZ St Univ 1973; Military Trng, Continuing Teacher Ed; *cr:* Teacher Westwood HS 1973-74, Corral Private Sch 1974-75; Material Management Supvr/Staff Sergeant Nyang 174th TFW 1980-84; Teacher Thomas Stone HS 1989; *ai:* Band Front Coord 1985-88; Future Teachers of MD 1988-; Effective Schls Comm 1989-; MSTA, NEA 1985-; NYANG 1980-84, NY Accomendation Medal 1981; Amer Legion Auxiliary 1985-; Natl Historical Society 1986-89; *office:* Thomas Stone HS Box 32 R R 5 Waldorf MD 20601

WILSON, TERRY, History Teacher; *b:* Keokuk, IA; *m:* Roxanne Ranck; *c:* Tania A., Brian T.; *ed:* (BS) Phys Ed/His, Culver-Stockton Coll 1965; Grad Stud W IL Univ; *cr:* Phys Ed/Coach Ewing HS 1965-68; His/Government/Drivers Ed Teacher/Coach Meredosia-Chambersburg HS 1968-; *ai:* Ftbl Asst Coach; Teacher Negotiating & Discipline Bd Comm; Sr Class Spon; Meredosia-Chambersburg Ed Assn Pres; IL Ed Assn 1968-; NEA Life Mem; Meredosia Historical Society; Fed of Fly Fishers; Historic Preservation Advisory Comm; Published Articles; *office:* Meredosia-Chambersburg HS Main St Meredosia IL 62665

WILSON, THOMAS JOSEPH, Social Studies Teacher/Chair; *b:* Ste Genevieve, MO; *m:* Suzanne Kay Steinman; *ed:* (AA) His, Mineral Area Coll 1981; (BA) His, Univ of MO Columbia 1983; (MA) His, Lincoln Univ 1989; *cr:* Soc Stud Teacher/Coach Jamestown HS 1984-87, Blair Oaks HS 1987-; *ai:* Class Spon; Asst Head Ftbl & Head Boys Bsktbl Coach; MO Ftbl & Bsktbl Coaches Assn 1987-; Knights of Columbus 1988-; *office:* Blair Oaks HS Rt 6 Falcon Ln Jefferson City MO 65101

WILSON, THOMAS LINN, 7th Grade Teacher/Chairperson; *b:* Urbana, OH; *m:* Dana Lynne Switzer; *c:* Adrienne; *ed:* (BSED) Bio/General Sci, Cntrl St Univ 1976; Working Towards Masters Sci Ed, Wright St Univ; *cr:* 7th Grade Teacher Northwestern Mid Sch 1976-; *ai:* 7th Grade Chairperson; Bsktbl Coach; Northwestern Teachers Assn (Building Rep, Grievance Rep) 1976-; OH Ed Assn, NEA; OH Assn of Sci 1985; Dist Advisory Cncl Chairperson 1985-87; *office:* Northwestern Mid Sch 5610 Troy Rd Springfield OH 45502

WILSON, THOMAS M., Head of Humanities; *b:* Brooklyn, NY; *ed:* (PHD) Anthropology, CUNY 1985; (MA) Cinema Stud, NY Univ 1985; *cr:* Adjunct Asst Professor of Irish Stud Queens Coll CUNY 1985; *ai:* Columbia UniV Seminar on Irish Stud Chm 1988-; *office:* United Nations Intnl Sch 24-50 Franklin D Roosevelt Dr New York NY 10010

WILSON, VERONICA MARY, Kindergarten Teacher; *b:* New York, NY; *ed:* (BS) Elem Ed, Coll of St Elizabeth; *cr:* 7th/8th Grade Teacher St Joseph 1945-59; 1st Grade Teacher St George 1959-69; Kndgtn/1st Grade Teacher Sts Joseph & Michael 1969-; *office:* Sts Joseph & Michael Of Union 1500 New York Ave Union City NJ 07087

WILSON, VINIE ANN, Science Teacher; *b:* Daleville, MS; *ed:* (BS) Soc Sci/Elem Ed, MS Valley St Univ 1971; (MED) Elem Ed, Jackson St Univ 1977; Further Grad Study Univ Southern MS; *cr:* Teacher SE Lauderdale HS 1971-; *ai:* Sci Comm; Grade Chairperson; LCAE Building Rep 1989-; MS Assn Educator Mem, NEA Mem 1973-; Zeta Phi Beta VP 1982-; Heroines of Jericho Treas 1980-; Order of Eastern Star Mem 1986-; Great Books Leader Trng Course; MS Inst on Law Related Ed Merit Awd; *office:* SE Lauderdale HS Rt 7 Box 477 Meridian MS 39301

WILSON, WILFORD DREW, Science Teacher; *b:* Ogden, UT; *m:* Ann Kogianes; *c:* Stacy, Dean; *ed:* (BS) Biological Sci, 1978, (MS) Scndry Ed, 1983 Weber St Coll; ADM/END Admin Endorsement, UT St Univ 1987; *cr:* Sci Teacher T H Bell Jr HS 1978-84, Bonneville HS 1984-; *ai:* Stu Government Adv; Asst Bsbl Coach; Dist Sci Lib Coord; UT Sci Teachers Mem; Sigma Xi Outstanding Teacher of Yr 1988; Weber Sch Dist I Love Teaching Awd 1989; *office:* Bonneville HS 251 E Laker Way Washington Terrace UT 84405

WILSON III, SAMUEL EARL, Science Teacher; *b:* Hattiesburg, MS; *m:* Ruby Burkett; *ed:* (BS) Phys Ed, Morehouse Coll 1955; (MS) Earth Sci, Univ of S MS 1969; Numerous Univs; *cr:* Teacher Jones HS 1955-56; Army Soldier Army 1956-58; Teacher Jones HS 1958-69, Clarkstown HS South 1970-; *ai:* Sftbl, Vlybl, Bsktbl Coach; NYSTA Mem; CTA, NSTA; NAACP, KAY Mem; Perry Cty Teachers Assn Pres; Coach of Yr in Bsktbl 1967-68; Numerous Sports Championships; *office:* Clarkstown HS South Demarest Mill Rd East West Nyack NY 10994

WILTSHIRE, SHERRY BROWN, Jr HS Mathematics Teacher; *b:* New York, NY; *m:* Henry Loyd; *c:* Matthew, Joshua; *ed:* (MS) Elem Ed, Univ of S MS 1985; *cr:* Teacher Taylorsville HS 1981-; *ai:* 1st Baptist Church Youth Dir 1986 89; Outstanding Young Women of America 1982; Jr HS Math Lib Grant; Elem Math Laboratory Grant; Jr HS Rdng Laboratory Grant; *office:* Taylorsville HS Hester St Taylorsville MS 39168

WILZ, GARY ALLAN, Science Teacher; *b:* Richardton, ND; *m:* Pamela Ann Kuntz; *ed:* (BS) Bio/Ed, Dickinson St Univ 1985; US Army Engr Officer Basic Course, Ft Belvoir VA 1985; US Army Engr Advanced Course, Ft Leonard Wood MO; *cr:* Scndry Sci Teacher Hettinger Public Sch 1985-; *ai:* Jr HS Ftbl Coach Hettinger Public Sch; Jr Class Adv; SW ND Regional Sci Fair Dir 1990; NEA, NDEA, HEA Local Pres 1987-88; *office:* Hettinger Public Sch Box 1188 Hettinger ND 58639

WIMAN, DAVID W., Director of Guidance; *b:* Memphis, TN; *m:* Deborah K. Veach; *c:* Bobby, Billie D., Jeff; *ed:* (BS) Bus/Health/Phy Ed, 1966, (MA) Guidance/Counseling, Murray St Univ 1970; Admin Cert S IL Univ Carbondale 1985; *cr:* Teacher/Coach Potosi Jr HS 1966-67, Shawneetown HS 1967-72; Guidance Dir SE IL Coll 1972-78; Insurance Broker Wiman Insurance Agency 1978-84; 12th Grade Teacher/Guidance Dir Shawnee HS 1984-85, Hardin Cty K-12 Sch 1985-; *ai:* IEA, NEA, Hardin Cty Ed Assn; *home:* RR 1 Box 124 Herod IL 62947

WIMBERLY, ROBERT JAMES, AP US History/US Hist Teacher; *b:* Portland, OR; *m:* Shirley Ann Urych; *c:* David J., Andrea M.; *ed:* (AA) College Transfer, Lane Comm Coll 1967; (BS) Ed, 1966, (MAT) Geography, 1973 OR Coll of Ed; Admin Courses toward Standard Admin Cert; *cr:* 9th-12th Grade Teacher Silverton Union HS 1969-70; 8th/9th Grade Teacher Helen Mc Cune Jr HS 1971-78; 11th Grade Teacher Pendleton HS 1978-; *ai:* Rifle Team, Boys & Girls Bsktbl Team Coach; Stu Government; Jr Class Adv; Teacher Union Pres; Dept Head; Dist Curr & Soc Stud Area Cncl; OR St Textbook Commissioner Eastern OR; Pendleton Assn of Teachers Pres 1988-; OR Ed Assn; NEA; BSA Cnslr 1985-; Pendleton HS Teacher of Yr 1987; Phi Delta Kappa North Eastern OR Region Scndry Teacher of Yr 1987; *office:* Pendleton H S 1800 N W Carden Ave Pendleton OR 97801

WIMER, SHARON CHILDERS, 5th Grade Teacher; *b:* Havre De Grace, MD; *m:* Kirk Douglas; *c:* Kristen, Kimberly, Alison; *ed:* (AA) General Stud, Harford Comm Coll 1976; (BS) Elem Ed, Towson St Univ 1978; Graduate Work Loyola Coll; *cr:* 5th Grade Teacher Halls Cross Roads Elem 1978-80; 4th Grade Teacher Deerfield Elem 1980-81; 5th Grade Teacher Norrisville Elem 1981-; *ai:* Gifted/Talented Comm; Literary Magazine Comm; Cmptr Comm; Amer Heart Assn 1964-74 Bronz E Medallion 1972; Darlington Halloween Planning Comm 1989; Cub Scouts Asst Den Mother 1975-76; Nom for Harford Cty Teacher of Yr 1989; Featured in Aegis Newspaper Creative Teacher Series 1989; *office:* Norrisville Elem Sch 5302 Norrisville Rd White Hall MD 21161

WINBURY, JOHN, English/History Teacher; *b:* La Mesa, CA; *ed:* (BA) Psych/Urban Stud, Occidental Coll 1970; (MA) Ed, US Intnl Univ 1980; *ai:* Mentor Teacher Writing 1988-; Pilot Project Portfolio Writing Assessment 1989-; Greater San Diego Area Cncl Teachers of Eng Bd Mem 1988-; San Diego Area Writing Project (Teacher, Trainer) 1983-; Table Leader CAP Direct Writing Assessment Scoring 1987-89; *office:* Black Mountain Mid Sch 9353 Oviedo St San Diego CA 92129

WINCHELL, JO-ANN PATTERSON, 1st Grade Teacher; *b:* Troy, NY; *m:* Robert; *c:* Kori L., Kasey L., Eric S.; *ed:* (BS) Ed, Norwich Univ 1977; (MS) Elem Ed, Russell Sage Coll 1987; *cr:* 6th Grade Teacher 1978-79, 5th Grade Teacher 1979-84, 1st Grade Teacher 1984- Stillwater Cntrl; *ai:* St Peters Parish Centennial Comm; Stillwater Planning Bd; Stillwater Zoning Bd of Appeals; Stillwater Democratic Club Secy; Stillwater Elem Gifted & Talented Comm; Stillwater PTSA VP 1984-; GSA Parent Leader; *home:* Box 29 RD 2 Munger Hill Rd Stillwater NY 12170

WINDEMUTH, MILLIE K. BARAN, Business Ed & English Teacher; *b:* Preeceville SK, Canada; *m:* Roger; *c:* Todd, Ryan; *ed:* (BA) Behavioral Sci, Andrews Univ 1967; (MPH) Public Health, Loma Linda Univ 1985; Ed, Eng, Bus Ed, Cmptrs; *cr:* Lang Art/Bus Ed Teacher San Francisco Jr Acad 1968-70, Rogue River Jr Acad 1981-83, Grants Pass Jr Acad 1983-87; Bus Ed/Eng Teacher Columbia Adv Acad 1989-; *ai:* Frosh Class Spon; Curr Comm; OR Cncl Teachers of Eng; Church Work (Adult Teacher 1975-, Childrens Teacher 1965-75); *office:* Columbia Adv Acad 11100 NE 189th St Battle Ground WA 98604

WINDHAM, DIANA DORIS, Science Dept Chairperson; *b:* Collins, MS; *ed:* (BS) Sci Ed, 1978, (MED) Scndry Ed, 1983 Univ of S MS; Various Wkshps; *cr:* Sci Teacher Richton Separate Sch Dist 1978-79; Teacher Purvis Jr HS 1979-82, Crowley Jr HS 1982-83; Sci Dept Chm NE Jones HS 1983-; *ai:* Math & Sci

Tournament Spon; Amer Chem Society Ed Division; S MS Regional Assn of Chem Teachers; MS Economic Cncl Stu Teacher Achievement Recognition Awd 1989, 1990; *office:* NE Jones HS Rt 13 Box 15 Hwy 84 E Laurel MS 39440

WINDHORST, JULIE ANN (COVER), Fifth Grade Teacher; *b:* Minden, NE; *m:* Bill L.; *c:* Megan; *ed:* (BA) Elem Ed, Kearney St Coll 1979; *cr:* 2nd Grade Teacher 1979-87, 5th Grade Teacher 1987- Elkhorn Public Schls; *ai:* Teachers Assistance Team; Self-Study Comm; NE St Ed Assn 1979-; Just Say No Coord 1989-; Nom NE Teacher of Yr Awd 1981; *home:* 1210 Cheyenne Elkhorn NE 68022

WINDSOR, JEANETTE LAURA, Physical Education Teacher; *b:* Rochester, NY; *m:* Guy Behenna; *ed:* (BA) Phys Ed, Springfield Coll 1986; *cr:* Teacher Satellite HS 1986-; *ai:* Var Girls Vlybl & Soccer Coach; Fellowship Chrstn Athletes Co-Spon; *office:* Satellite HS 300 Scorpion Ct Satellite Beach FL 32937

WINDSOR, LYN MENZIE, AP English Teacher; *b:* Warsaw, IN; *m:* Arthur David; *c:* Beth W. Kropf, Carrie Najera-Ortega, Conde W. Devine; *ed:* (AA) Stephens Coll 1957; (AB) Eng Lit, 1959, (MAT) Eng/Scndry Ed, 1961 IN Univ; Coll of St Mark & St John, Univ of AL; *cr:* 10th Grade Eng Teacher Broad Ripple HS 1960-61; 7th/8th/11th Grade Soc Stud Teacher Chaffee HS 1973-75; 8th/9th Grade Eng Teacher J Browne Jr HS 197 6-79; 11th/12th Grade Eng Teacher/Dept Chairperson Germantown HS 1979-; *ai:* Delta Kappa Gamma 1982-; NCTE 1980-; TN Cncl Teachers of Eng 1979-; Shelby-Memphis Cncl Teachers of Eng 1979-; *office:* Germantown HS 7653 Old Poplar Pike Germantown TN 38138

WINE, PATRICIA SHIRLEY, English Teacher; *b:* Winchester, VA; *m:* J. Michael; *ed:* (BS) Ed/Lang Art Shepherd Coll; (MED) Sch Admin; Courses Gifted Ed, James Madison Univ, George Mason Univ; *cr:* Teacher Warrenton Jr HS 1970-71, Faquier HS 1971-; *ai:* Sch Newspaper Spon 1977-84; Eng Dept Chairperson 1976-85; Octagon Club 1988-89; Cnty Wide Curr Comm; Warrenton-Faquier Optimists Service Awd; *office:* Faiqioer HS 705 Waterloo Rd Warrenton VA 22186

WINEBARGER, MARY TESTER, Language Arts Teacher; *b:* Johnson City, TN; *m:* Charles S.; *c:* Charles P., Kristel W.; *ed:* (BS) Secretarial Sci/Eng, East TN St Univ 1959; Eng ETSU; Psych ETSU; *cr:* Church Hill HS 1959-60; 2nd Grade Teacher Boones Creek Elem 1978; 3rd Grade Teacher Sulphur Springs Elem 1978-84; 7th/8th Grade Eng Teacher Gray Elem 1985-; *ai:* 7th/8th Grade Scholars Bowl Spon; 7th/8th Grade Sch Magazine Spon; WA Cty Ed Assn Sch Rep 1982-83; TN Ed Assn 1978-; NEA 1978-; WA Cty Republican Comm Delegate 1976-80; Liaison Rep to Supts Ofc 1987-88; *home:* Rt 16 Box 373 Gray TN 37615

WINEMILLER, JEAN CORN, 2nd Grade Teacher; *b:* Mc Leansboro, IL; *m:* Lewis; *c:* Ron, Brooke; *ed:* (BA) Elem Ed, Greenville Coll 1975; *cr:* 2nd Grade Teacher Hamilton Cty Unit 10 1975-; *ai:* Hamilton Cty Fed of Teachers (VP) 1988-89, Pres 1989-); PTO 1975-; *home:* Rt 1 Box 221 Mc Leansboro IL 62859

WINFREY, ELSIE BALMER, Mathematics-Science Teacher; *b:* Seaboard, NC; *m:* Joseph; *c:* Rhonda Winfrey Moses; *ed:* (BS) Ed, Elizabeth City St Univ 1955; Numerous Univs; *cr:* Teacher W S Creecy HS 1957-60, Eastside Sch 1960-64, Willis Hare HS 1964-67, Conway Mid Sch 1967-; *ai:* Conway Mid Sch Stu Cncl & Letters Unlimited Adv; Conway Mid Sch Gator Team Leader; Elizabeth City Alumni Secy 1970-; NC Ed Assn, NEA, NC Sci Assn, Intnl Rdng Assn; Silverlife Stu Asst Society Secy 1969-; Natl Sci Fnd Grant; NC Math Grant 1983-84; *home:* PO Box 367 Rich Square NC 27867

WINGFIELD, JOLENE K., 4th Grade Teacher; *b:* Denver, CO; *ed:* (BA) Elem Ed, CWC 1973; Grad Stud; *cr:* Substitute Teacher Liberty & Idalia 1974-75; 6th Grade/HS Teacher Yuma Schls 1976; 4th Grade Teacher Yuma Mid Schls 1977-; *office:* Yuma Mid Sch 500 S Elm Yuma CO 80759

WINGO, BRENDA NIXON, Chapter I Reading Teacher; *b:* Raton, NM; *m:* Franklin James; *c:* James B., Deborah J.; *ed:* (BA) Elem Ed, Univ of AZ 1960; (MA) Elem Ed, Adams St Coll 1985; *cr:* 5th Grade Teacher P E Howell Elem Sch 1960-62; 2nd Grade Teacher Dept of Defense Elem Sch 1963-64; 1st Grade Teacher Zweibrucken Elem Sch 1978-79; 2nd Grade Teacher 1980-88, Chapter I Rdng Teacher 1988- Raton Public Schls; *ai:* Dept Head; NM Rdng Assessment Comm 1st & 2nd Grade; NM Law Related Ed Elem Sch Rep; Delta Kappa Gamma Pres 1986-; NEA 1980-85; Raton Literacy Prgm (Bd Mem, Tutor) 1989-; Raton Cmmty Concert Assn Bd Mem 1981-; *office:* Columbian Elem Sch 700 N 2nd St Raton NM 87740

WINGROVE, M. LYNN (GROSSCUP), English Teacher; *b:* Yankton, SD; *m:* C H Jr.; *c:* Jill; *ed:* (BA) Eng, Univ of NE Lincoln 1968; Grad Courses Univ of NE Lincoln & Lincoln Public Schls; *cr:* HS Eng Teacher Fullerton Public Schls 1968-69, St Paul Public Schls 1969-70; Jr HS Eng Teacher Lincoln Public Schls 1970-; *ai:* Gifted Facilitator; Eng Dept Liaison; 8th Grade Team Leader; LEA, NSEA, NEA 1970-; Phi Delta Kappa 1987-; Mortar Bd 1968-; MCTE 1987-88; Capitol Humane Society Friend 1987-; Friends of Museum 1987-; Neighborhood Watch Block Captain 1986-; Scottish Rite Distinguished Teacher of Yr 1987; Cooper Fnd Teaching Excl Awd 1987; NASSP Exemplary Prgms Gifted & Academically Talented; Building Class Size Comm Chm; *office:* Pound Jr HS 4740 S 45th Lincoln NE 68516

WINKLE, ALICE MARIE, Jr HS Reading Teacher; *b:* Columbus, OH; *ed:* (BA) Eng/Elem Ed, Wilimington Coll 1971; Rdng Ed, Miami Univ 1990; *cr:* Lang Arts Teacher Blanchester Jr HS 1970-71; 5th & 6th Grade Lang Arts Teacher Main Street Mid Sch 1971-75, Lang Arts Teacher Blanchester Jr HS 1975-; *ai:* Right to Read Comm Chm; Natl Jr Honor Society Comm; NEA/OEA/BEA; Intnl Rdng Assn 1988-; Natl Realtors Assn 1980-; Article Published OH Rdng Teacher Magazine 1988; *office:* Blanchester Jr H S St Rte 28 Blanchester OH 45107

WINKLER, BRADLEY MASON, 8th Grade Amer History Teacher; *b:* Richmond, KY; *m:* Pamela Gail Cox; *c:* Dustin M.; *ed:* (BS) Phys Ed, MS St Univ 1983; *cr:* Minor League Bsbl Player NY Yankees Inc 1983-86; 7th-10th Grade His/Coach Magnolia Acad 1986-87; 8th Grade Amer His Teacher/Coach Hillcrest Chrstn Sch 1987-; *ai:* Asst Ftbl Coach; Head Bsbl; Assn Prof Ball Players of America 1983-; Pres Scholar 1982; Academic All-Southeastern Conference 1983, All Southeastern Conference Bsbl 1983; Coll Bsbl All-Amer 1983; Outstanding Young Man of America 1983/90; Bsbl Coach of Yr South Cntrl AA 1987, South AAA 1989; *office:* Hillcrest Chrstn Sch 4060 S Siwell Rd Jackson MS 39212

WINKLER, CATHERINE ANNA (LOBOCKI), Kindergarten-1st Grade Teacher; *b:* Detroit, MI; *m:* James A.; *c:* Eric A., Jacquelyn C.; *ed:* (BA) Elem Ed/Math/Sci/Soc Stud, MI St Univ 1973; (MA) Rdng, Oakland Univ 1981; *cr:* 2nd Grade Teacher Memphis Cmmty Sch 1973-76; 4th/5th Chapter I Teacher Beaerton Rural Sch 1976-77; 5th Grade Teacher 1977-82; 6th/7th Grade Teacher 1982-84 Pinconning Area Sch; K-1st Grade Teacher 1984-; Rdng Instr Ctr Innovation in Ed 1988-; *ai:* Intnl Rdng Assn 1989-; MI Assn Cmptr Users in Learning 1989-; Quiz Kids Faith Luth Church Coach 1989-; Bd of Evangelism Chairwoman 1987-; See-Saw Co-Op Pre-Sch VP 1982-84; *office:* Mt Forest Elem Sch 4197 11 Mile Rd Pinconning MI 48650

WINN, DAVID ERVIN, Latin Teacher/Foreign Lang; *b:* Fredericksburg, VA; *c:* Jason A.; *ed:* (AB) Ancient Lang, 1966-70, (MA) Latin/Scndry Ed, 1971-74 Coll of William & Mary; *cr:* Visiting Instr Coll of William & Mary 1979; Part Time Instr Mary Washington Coll 1977-83; Latin/Eng Teacher Spotsylvania HS 1970-; *ai:* Latin Club & Sr Class Spon; NEA, VA Ed Assn; Classical Assn of VA Treas 1977-83; Foreign Lang Assn of VA 1978-; Virgilian Society, Classical Assn of Mid West & South 1970; Amer Classical League 1973-; Article Published in Classical Outlook; Teacher of Yr 1976 Spotsylvania Cty; *office:* Spotsylvania HS 8801 Courthouse Rd Spotsylvania VA 22553

WINN, SHIRLEY GRIFFY, Fourth Grade Teacher; *b:* Clarksville, TN; *m:* Michael H.; *c:* Tim, Chris, Steven, Jessica; *ed:* (BS/EE) Elem Ed, Austin Peay Univ 1972; (MA) Elem Ed, APSU 1976; Post Masters Stud Rdng Specialist APSU; *cr:* 2nd-3rd Grade Teacher 1972-73, 4th Grade Teacher 1973- Millbrooke Elem; *ai:* Yrbk; Gifted, Elem Cmptr Comm & Special Comm Improving Skills; Chrstn Cty Ed Assn, KY Ed Assn; Class Won 3rd Place in Math Contest 1st Congressional Dist 1989; *office:* Millbrooke Elem Sch 415 Millbrooke Dr Hopkinsville KY 42240

WINN, SUSAN LEWIS, Fifth Grade Teacher; *b:* Waxahachie, TX; *m:* Tommy; *c:* Misti, Wess, Emilie; *ed:* (BS) Elem Ed, Lamar Univ 1967; *cr:* Elem Teacher Waxahachie Ind ScH Dist 1968-72, 1980-; *ai:* TSTA.

WINNER, KATHLEEN BERNARD, Fifth Grade Teacher; *b:* Lonaconing, MD; *ed:* Eng, Mt St Joseph Coll 1969; (MA) Religion/Theology, Villanova Univ 1979; *cr:* 3rd Grade Teacher St Callistus Sch 1953-54, Holy Comforter Sch 1954-65; 5th Grade Teacher Pius X Sch 1965-66, Our Lady of Mercy Sch 1966-68; 8th Grade Teacher St Timothy Sch 1968-71; 6th Grade Teacher Holy Trinity Sch 1976-78; 5th Grade Teacher St Vincent Sch 1976-78; 5th/6th Grade Teacher St Peter Sch 1978-86; 5th Grade Teacher St Philip Sch 1986-; *ai:* Religion Coord; Sisters of St Joseph Mem 1951; *office:* St Philip Sch 7506 St Philip Ct Falls Church VA 22042

WINNETT, CHERYL ONSTOTT, Kindergarten-5th Grade Teacher; *b:* Bonham, TX; *m:* Jerry D.; *c:* Jeremy, Holly; *ed:* (BS) Elem Ed, 1979, (MS) Early Chldhd, Southeastern St Univ; *cr:* K-5th Grade Teacher Achille Public Schs 1979-.

WINNICKI, MARYANN KEIDA, First Grade Teacher; *b:* Utica, NY; *m:* Lance Stuart; *ed:* (BS) Elem Ed, Keuka Coll 1971; (MS) Elem Ed, Syracuse Univ 1975; *cr:* 3rd Grade Teacher Sauquoit Valley Cntrl Sch 1971-73; Master Teacher Sauquoit Cntrl 1975-76; Stu Teacher Hamilton Coll 1976-77; 1st Grade Teacher Sauquoit Valley Cntrl Sch 1973-; *ai:* Health Curr Comm; Chairperson Report Card Revision Comm 1985 & Rdng Textbook Evaluation Comm 1980; NY St United Teachers, Sauquoit Valley Teachers Assn; NY St Mini Grant Awd 1974-75, 1976-77; *home:* 28 Stonebridge Rd New Hartford NY 13413

WINSETT, RON, Fourth Grade Teacher; *b:* Philadelphia, PA; *m:* Patricia T.; *c:* Michael, Alisa M.; *ed:* (AA) Liberal Arts, Mercer Cty Coll 1968; (BA) Elem Ed, 1970; (MEd) Ed, 1975 Trenton St Coll; Cert for Ed Admin Rider Coll; TABA Teaching Strategies Trenton St; Natl Sci Fnd Grant; *cr:* 4th-7th Grade Teacher 1970-; Coord 1987- Willingboro Public Schls; *ai:* Coaching Bsbl/Bsktbl/Soccer; ASCD; NJ Ed Assn; Burlington Cty Ed Assn; NEA; Knights of Columbus 1975-79; Natl Sci Fnd-Grant; *home:* 9 Tenby Ct Westampton Twp NJ 08060

WINSLETT, FRED N., Math Teacher; *b:* Bessemer, AL; *m:* Judy Draper; *ed:* (AA) Bible, AL Chrstn 1953; (BS) His 1964, (MA) Scndry Ed, 1965, (EDD) Scndry Ed, 1969 Univ of North AL; *cr:* Dd Dept Teachr Univ of Montevallo 1975-77; His, Teacher Morgan Acad 1980-82; Prin Coosa Valley Acad 1982-85; Math Teacher Pell City 1985-; *ai:* Key Club Spon; *home:* Rt 4 Box 67 Montevallo AL 35115

WINSTON, MABLE WILLIAMS, 8th Grade Reading Teacher; *b:* Mer Rouge, LA; *m:* L. J.; *c:* Deidra, Aundrea, Cherlyn W., Lione L.; *ed:* (BS) Bus Ed, 1972, (MA) Elem Ed, 1983 Grambling St Univ; Rdng Specialist, Grambling St Univ 1988; Bus Ed, LA Tech Univ; *cr:* Classroom Teacher Mer Rouge Ellem; Bookkeeper/Accountant W Auto Assoc Store 1972-; Classroom Teacher Bastrop Jr HS 1990; *office:* Bastrop Jr HS W 1001 W Madison Ave Bastrop LA 71220

WINTER, ESTHER JOANNE, Sixth Grade Teacher; *b:* Fairfield, IA; *ed:* (BS) Elem Ed, Bob Jones Univ 1960; *cr:* 3rd Grade Teacher Tryon St Elem Sch 1960-63; Remedial Rdng Teacher Lynnville-Sully Comm Sch 1963-64; 6th Grade Lang Art Teacher Keota Elem Sch 1964-; *ai:* NEA, ISEA; KEA Pres 1988-; *office:* Keota Elem Sch N Ellis St Keota IA 52248

WINTER, SUZANNE, 5th Grade Teacher; *b:* Boston, MA; *ed:* (BS) Elem Ed, 1970, (MED) Counseling, 1990 Univ of MO St Louis; *cr:* 4th-6th Grade Sci Teacher Elmwood 1970-72; 6th Grade Teacher DeHart 1972-76; 5th Grade Teacher Kratz Elem Sch 1976-; *ai:* St Louis Ladies Retreat Chairperson; Chrstn Educators Assn Intnl St Rep 1986-; NEA Negotiations Team 1982-84; *home:* 746 Harvard Saint Louis MO 63130

WINTERBERG, CAROL MC KAY, 4th Grade Teacher; *b:* Galesburg, IL; *m:* Gary Hal; *c:* Garett, Nicholas; *ed:* (BA) Elem Ed, Drake Univ 1965; Whole Lang Approach to Teaching Rdng; Grad Stud Elem Ed, Drake Univ 1975; *cr:* 4th Grade Teacher Willard Elem 1965-70; 5th Grade Teacher Hanawalt Elem 1970-78; 4th Grade Teacher Brooks Elem 1978-; *ai:* Stu Cncl; NEA, Des Moines Ed Assn, IA St Ed Assn 1965; NCTM Mem 1975; NCTM Runner Up Awd 1987; Teach Staff Dev Rdng/Writing Classroom; Spoke 2 Yrs NCTM Insts & Des Moines Teacher In-Service Days; *office:* Brooks Elem Sch 2124 E Des Moines Des Moines IA 50317

WINTERBERG, JAMES JOSEPH, 6th Grade Teacher; *b:* Cumberland, MD; *m:* Sandra K. Snyder; *c:* Shawn, Guy; *ed:* (BS) Elem Ed, 1967; (MS) Admin & Supervision, 1972 Frostburg St Coll; *cr:* 6th Grade Teacher Thurmont Elem Sch 1967-68; Columbia St Sch 1968-84; Braddock Sch 1984-; *ai:* Instr Hunter Safety Ed St of MD; Adv Gifted & Talented Prgm Braddock Mid Sch; Co-Author Outdoor Ed; Math Prgm; Project Basic Curr Guides; ACTA 1967-; MSTA 1967-; NEA 1967-; Knights of Columbus 1964-; Upper Potomac Garden Club Bd of Dir 1989-; *office:* Braddock Mid Sch 909 Holland St Cumberland MD 21502

WINTERS, BETTY A., 3rd/4th Grade Teacher; *b:* Linden, NJ; *m:* Reginald; *c:* Salli Dyer, Joan Hoppes, Kathleen, Cindy Buckner, Bruce, Douglas; *ed:* (BA) Health/Phys Ed/Elem Ed, Univ of NY Brockport 1950; Working Towards Recertification & Elem Certificate Univ of Cntrl FL, Rollins Coll, Brevard Cmmty Coll; *cr:* 4th Grade Teacher 1986-89, 3rd/4th Grade Teacher 1989- St Marys Cath Sch; *ai:* Wuesthoff Hospital Auxiliary Volunteer; *office:* St Marys Cath Sch 1152 S Seminole Dr Rockledge FL 32955

WINTERS, CHARLES STUART, 7th/8th Grade Math Instructor; *b:* Port Huron, MI; *c:* Melody, Dana; *ed:* (AA) His/Sci, Port Huron Jr Coll 1966; (BA) Elem Ed, 1968, (MA) Elem Ed, 1972 MI St Univ; *cr:* 6th Grade Teacher Kimball Intermediate & Garfield Intermediate 1968-76; 7th/8th Grade Teacher Holland Woods Intermediate 1976-80, Cntrl Intermediate 1980-; *ai:* Coin Club Adv; Bsktbl Coach; Textbook Selection Comm; Jaycees Outstanding Educator 1980; Pres Cncl for Outstanding Math & Sci Teachers 1988; Dist 8 Outstanding Math Instr 1989; Nom MI Teacher of Yr 1989; *home:* 712 Ontario St Port Huron MI 48060

WINTERS, LISA SCHUERHOLZ, Soc Stud Teacher/Team Leader; *b:* Middletown, NY; *m:* John R.; *ed:* (BA) Ed & His, Univ of RI 1984; Glsp Prgm Wesleyan Univ; *cr:* Soc Stud Teacher North Kingstown HS; East Hampton HS; *ai:* Model United Nations Adv; Thinking Skills Task Force Chairperson; Ame R Hist Curr Revision Comm; NCSS; ESR; ASCD; CT Sane/Freeze; Pledge of Resistance; CT Planned Parenthood; Natl Orgztn of Women; Abortion Rights Action League; NEA; CEA; Nom East Hamptons Teacher of Yr 1989; *office:* East Hampton HS N Maple St East Hampton CT 06424

WINTERS, PHILLIP B., Vocational Agriculture Teacher; *b:* Clarksburg, WV; *m:* Betty Lou Hayes; *c:* Janet D. Spaur, Anita K. Crouser, Lisa G. Fulmer; *ed:* (BS) Ag Ed, 1962, (MS) Ag Ed, 1969 WV Univ; Grad Work in Ag Ed, Ag Mechanics; *cr:* Voc Ag Teacher 1961-, Part Time Voc Dir 1980-82 Wirt Cty HS; *ai:* Adv Wirt Cty Chapter FFA; WV Voc Ag Teachers Assn, WV Ed Assn 1961-; Wirt Cty Ed Assn Pres 1965; Wirt Cty Fair Assn VP 1964, Lifetime Mem 1970; Elizabeth Meth Church (Chm, Admin Bd) 1989-; Wirt Cty Farm BureAu Dir 1986-; *home:* PO Box 161 Palestine Rd Elizabeth WV 26143

WINTERTON, VICTORIA THOMPSON, Chemistry Teacher; *b:* Placerville, CA; *m:* John Arthur; *c:* Alysa B., Rhett T.; *ed:* (BA) Chem, Anderson Univ 1976; (MA) Educl Admin, CA St Univ Long Beach 1981; *cr:* Math Teacher Hosler Jr HS 1977-81; Chem Teacher Mt Whitney HS 1981-; *ai:* Sci In-Depth Study, Accreditation Comm; Outstanding Sr in Scndry Ed Anderson Univ

1976; Outstanding New Teacher Hosler Jr HS 1978; Visalia Teacher of Yr 1986; *home:* 36940 Millwood Dr Woodlake CA 93286

WINTHROP, JERAULD SAMUEL, English Teacher; *b:* Camden, NJ; *m:* Anita Louise Sterling; *c:* Heather, Jessica; *ed:* (BA) Eng, CA St Univ Chico 1986; Prof Clear Credential 1988; *cr:* Eng Teacher Fairfield HS 1987-; *ai:* Jr Class Co-Adv; Shakespearian Society Adv; *office:* Fairfield HS 205 E Atlantic Ave Fairfield CA 94533

WINTLE, JESSIE OSBUN, Mathematics/English Teacher; *b:* Passaic, NJ; *m:* Marke E.; *ed:* (BA) Eng/Math/Poly Sci, Rutgers Coll 1987; *cr:* Math/Eng Teacher Neumann Prep 1987-; *ai:* Yrbk Moderator; Play Dir; Literary Magazine, Creative Writing Group, Math League, HS Bowl Moderator; *office:* Neumann Prep Sch 970 Black Oak Ridge Rd Wayne NJ 07470

WIPERT, JIMMY DALTON, Principal; *b:* Bainbridge, OH; *m:* Mary Weber; *c:* Angela, Erin; *ed:* (BS) Ed, IA St Univ 1966; (MS) Scndry Ed, Morehead St Univ 1973; (PHD) Scndry Admin, Walden Univ 1978; *cr:* Teacher Ironton HS 1967-73; Prin Rock Hill Mid Sch 1973-; *ai:* OH Assn of Elem Administrators 1973-; Benevolent & Protective Order of Elks Trustee 1965-; *office:* Rock Hill Mid Sch Rt 3 Ironton OH 45638

WIRSIG, GREGORY V., English Teacher; *b:* Keokuk, IA; *m:* Ella Marie Kennedy; *c:* Kasey M.; *ed:* (BA) Eng Ed, Cntrl Univ of IA 1975; (MA) Eng Ed, NE MO St Univ 1984; Grad Stud; *cr:* Substitute Teacher Keokuk Sch Dist 1976-77; CETA Youth Prgm Dir SE IA Regional Planning Inst 1977-78; Eng Teacher CCR1 Jr/Sr HS 1977-; Part Time Eng Teacher Southeastern Comm Coll 1987-; *ai:* Jr/Sr HS Newspaper Spon 1978-84; MSTA Treas 1978-79; *home:* 5 Timberline RR 3 Kahoka MO 63445

WISCOMBE, REM C., Fourth Grade Teacher; *b:* Provo, UT; *ed:* (BA) Elem Ed, Brigham Young Univ 1977; Art Ed; Lib Sci; Cmptr Assisted Instruction; *cr:* 4th Grade Teacher Grandview Elem 1979-; *ai:* Career Ladder Teacher Cmptr Specialist; ; Dist Evaluation Comm; Provo Sch Dist Credit Union Rep; Provo Ed Assn Building Rep 1984-86; UT Ed Assn, NEA Mem; *office:* Grandview Elem Sch 1591 N Jordan Ave Provo UT 84604

WISE, BRENDA OGLETREE, Third Grade Teacher; *b:* Dayton, OH; *m:* Harry H. Jr.; *c:* Robin L., Todd B., Lori R.; *ed:* (BS) Elem Ed, Cntrl St Univ 1966; Curr & Supervision, Wright St Univ 1971-73; *cr:* Teacher Meinecke Ave Sch 1966-67, Carlson Elem Sch 1967-68, Blairwood Elem Sch 1968-; *ai:* HS Bands Drill & Flag Adv; NEA, OH Ed Assn, Jefferson Twp Teachers Assn 1970-; GSA (Leader 1979-88), Youth Service 1986; On Developmental Comm for Compentency Based Math Test, Served on Various Dist Comm for Math, Rdng & Writing Curr Dev; *office:* Blairwood Elem Sch 1241 Blairwood Ave Dayton OH 45418

WISE, ELAINE VANN, English Teacher; *b:* Valdosta, GA; *m:* John F.; *ed:* (BS) Eng Ed, Valdosta St Coll 1967; (MED) Scndry Eng, GA St Univ 1974; Ed Specialist/Scndry Eng, Columbus Coll 1984; *cr:* Eng Teacher Valdosta HS 1967-68, Jordan HS 1970-; *ai:* Chrldr Spon; Sftbl & Flag Corps Coach; Jr Class, Sr Class, Newspaper, NHS Adv; Kappa Delta Pi STAR Teacher 1987, 1988; Prof Assn of GA Educators; Delta Kappa Gamma; Philonian Club (Secy & Pres) 1986-; Page 1 Teacher of Yr Jordan HS; *office:* Jordan HS 3200 Howard Ave Columbus GA 31995

WISE, ELIZABETH LEONARD, 7th Grade Mathematics Teacher; *b:* Lincolnton, NC; *m:* Donald E.; *c:* Evan; *ed:* (AB) Intermediate Ed/Eng/Math, Lenoir Rhyne Coll 1978; *cr:* Teachers Aide Park Elem Sch 1974; 5th Grade Teacher Love Memorial Elem Sch 1978; 8th/9th Grade Eng/7th Grade Math/Psych Teacher Lincolnton Jr HS 1978-; *ai:* Lincolnton Jr HS Builders Club Co-Adv; Alpha Delta Kappa; NC Assn of Educators Sch Rep 1987-; Lincoln Cty Democrat Party Precinct Secy 1986-; NC Skeet Assn (Secy, Treas) 1989-; *office:* Lincolnton Jr HS 511 S Aspen St Lincolnton NC 28092

WISE, JAMES LEWIS, Science/Mathematics Teacher; *b:* Erie, PA; *m:* Sandra Legenzoff; *c:* Geoffrey; *ed:* (BS) Ed, 1964, (MS) Bio, 1975 Edinboro St; (PHD) Bio/Ecology, WV Univ 1978; *cr:* Bio Teacher Northwestern HS 1979-80; Cmptr Teacher Colegio Karl Parrish 1982-83; Sci/Math Teacher General Mc Lane HS 1980-; *ai:* Chess, Photo, Peace Club; BEA, NEA 1979-; *office:* General Mc Lane HS 11761 Edinboro Rd Edinboro PA 16412

WISE, JAMES R., Fifth Grade Teacher; *b:* Fairmont, WV; *m:* Esta Wageley; *c:* James W.; *ed:* (AB) Ed, Fairmont St. Coll 1964; Addl Studies Akron Univ; *cr:* 4th/5th/6th Grade Teacher North Elem 1964-66; 6th Grade Teacher Moffitt Hghts 1966-70; Tuslaw Inter 1970-80; Moffitt Hghts 1980-81; 7th Grade Teacher Tuslaw Inter 1981-85; 5th Grade Teacher Moffitt Hghts 1985-; *ai:* CORE Team (Drugs); Tuslaw Teachers Treasureer 1968-; OH Ed Assn 1964-; NEA 1964-; BPO Elks 1961-; Knights of Columbus Public Relations 1978-; Bishop Massillon Assembly 4th Degree 1987-; Moose Lodge 1981-; Knight of Month Sept 1989; St. Mary Catholic Church Parish Cncl 1989-; *home:* 7311 Knight St. NW Massillon OH 44646

WISE, JUDD A., Life Management Skills Teacher; *b:* Akron, OH; *m:* Penni A. Davis; *c:* Katelyn L., Patrica A.; *ed:* (BS) Phys Ed, 1981, (MAT) Phys Ed, 1983 Jacksonville Univ; Gifted Ed; *cr:* Adjunct Professor Jacksonville Univ 1981-83; Athletic Dir Mary Immaculate HS 1983-86; Life Management Skills Teacher Key West HS 1986-; *ai:* Var Boys Bsktbl & Jr Var Bsbl Head Coach; FACA, FAHPERD; *office:* Key West HS 2100 Flagler Ave Key West FL 33040

WISE, LINDA L. (HORRISBERGER), English Teacher Dept Chair; *b:* St Paul, MN; *c:* Abigail; *ed:* (MST) Eng, 1975, (BS) Eng Ed, 1973 Univ of WI; Coursework Writing, Univ of MN & Hamline; Rdng, Univ of WI; Dale Carnegie Inst; *cr:* Dept Head/Eng Teacher Maple Lake HS 1975-81; Asst Account Exec Carmichael Lynch Advertising Agency 1981-84; Sales Rep Val Pak Advertising 1984-85; Eng Teacher/Dept Head Washington Jr HS 1985-; *ai:* Spelling Bee & Literary Magazine Head; Speech Coach; Organized & Administered Annual Rdng Test; AFT 1975-81; Maple Lake Fed of Teacher (Secy 1981) 1985-; Organized Tutoring Prgms; Nom Excl in Ed Awd; *office:* Washington Jr HS 1041 Marion St Saint Paul MN 55117

WISE, MARSHA SHOBER, 8th Grade Lang Arts Teacher; *b:* Roanoke, VA; *m:* David Kenneth; *c:* Lara N., Emily D.; *ed:* (BS) Eng Ed, Towson St 1972; APC Ed, Hood Coll; *cr:* Eng Teacher Gov Thomas Johnson Jr HS 1972-81; Lang Arts Teacher Monocacy Mid Sch 1981-87, Middletown Mid Sch 1987-; *ai:* 8th Grade Team Leader; Literary Magazine Adv; Dept Writing Liason; Author of Schs Parent Handbook; NEA, MSTA, FCTA; Teacher Plus; Innovative Teaching Awd; Presenter MD Mid Sch Conference; *home:* 2404 Tabor Dr Middletown MD 21769

WISE, ROGER DAVID, Mathematics Teacher; *b:* Andalusia, AL; *ed:* (BS) Math, 1971, (MS) Fnds of Ed, 1973 Troy St Univ; *cr:* Math Teacher Samson HS 1971-72, Enterprise St Jr Coll 1976-81, 1985-, Crenshaw Chrstn Acad 1973-; *ai:* Scholars Bowl & Math Team Spon; *office:* Crenshaw Chrstn Acad Rt 3 Box 8S Luverne AL 36049

WISE, TERESA ANDREWS, 5th Grade Teacher; *b:* Jamestown, NY; *m:* Stephen L.; *c:* Christy L.; *ed:* (BA) Elem Ed, 1973, (MS) Elem Ed, 1977, (CAS/SAS/SDA) Admin, 1990 St Univ Coll Fredonia; Numerous Classes; *cr:* 4th Grade Teacher 1973, Title I Summer Sch Prgm Coord Intermediate Levels 1974-75, Admin Intern 1988-89, 5th Grade Teacher 1974- SW Cntrl Sch Dist; *ai:* Grade Level Chairperson; Sci Mentor; Thinking Skills Club Dir; Curr, Prof Advancement, Public Relations, Inservice, Schlsp, STA Exec Bd, Prof Performance Reviews Comms; SW Teachers Assn Pres 1984-86; NEA Delegate 1984-; Delta Kappa Gamma 1975-; Intnl Rdng Assn ; PTO Treas 1974-76; Little Theater 1988-; Legislative Delegate; US Achievement Acad Awd 1989; SW Exemplary Commitment & Service Awd 1988; Presentations Peer Coaching; Thinking Skills & Author of Dist Sci Curr; Newspapers in Ed Coord; *home:* 77 Dearborn St Jamestown NY 14701

WISEMAN, MARY JANE, Chapter I Teacher; *b:* Houston, TX; *ed:* (BS) Elem Ed, TX Southern Univ 1965; (MA) Counseling/Guidance, Prairie View A&M Univ 1975; Eng as 2nd Lang; Early Chldhd Dev; *cr:* 1st Grade Teacher Robert C Chatham 1965-69, David Crockett 1969-72, Dept of Defense Overseas Sch 1972-73; 2nd Grade Teacher David Burnett 1973-84, John F Kennedy 1984-; *home:* 2704 Cliffdale Houston TX 77091

WISEMAN, RANDY L., Sixth Grade Teacher; *b:* Trenton, MI; *ed:* (BS) Elem Ed, W MI Univ 1968; (MA) Educl Leadership, 1973, (EDS) Educl Leadership, 1978 E MI Univ; *cr:* 3rd-6th Grade Teacher Trenton Public Schls 1968-; *ai:* Conduct Wkshps & Seminars on Critical Thinking; Trenton Jaycees 1975-83; Authored 12 Books & 1 Journal Article 1972-; City of Trenton Outstanding Educator Awd 1974; *home:* 1870 Fort St #3 Trenton MI 48183

WISER, SUSAN VIRGINIA, Span/Eng 2nd Language Teacher; *b:* Philadelphia, PA; *m:* Conrad A.; *c:* Eric M., Kathryn M.; *ed:* (BS) Span, Shippensburg 1971; (MA) Eng, West Chester 1987; Universidad De Las Americas Pucbla Pae Mexico; Penn St Univ; *cr:* Span Teacher Big Spring HS 1971; Span/ESL Teacher Perkiomen Valley HS 1971-; *ai:* Spon-Foreign Trips; Spon-Amnesty Intnl; Kappa Delta Pi 1971-74; Laubach Literacy Assn Tutor Trainer 1986-89; Montgomery Cty FL Assn 1971-; Amnesty Intnl 1988-; Laubach Literacy Assn Tutor-Trainer 1986-89; *office:* Perkiomen Valley H S Rt 29 & Trappe Rd Graterford PA 19426

WISHAM, JANICE WIGGINS, Social Science Teacher; *b:* Americus, GA; *m:* Richard Oscar; *c:* Richard J., Bette A.; *ed:* (BS) Soc Sci, GA Southwestern Coll 1969; (BS) Mid Sch Ed, Columbus Coll 1972; (MS) Soc Sci, 1977, (MS) Mid Sch 1979 GA Southwestern Coll; Career Ed Cert Univ of GA 1982; Certified Data Collector; *cr:* Soc Sci Teacher Marion Cty HS 1969-71; 5th/6th Grade His Teacher Upson Cty Public Schls 1971-72; 6th Grade His Teacher Muscogee Cty Public Sch 1972-74; Soc Sci Teacher Sumter Cty Public Schls 1974-; *ai:* GA His Day Competition & Jr Class Spon; Courtesy Comm Secy-Treas; Enrichment Action Comm Co-Chm; Blue Tide Swim Team Past VP; Jr HS Chrldr Spon 1984-86; GAE 1969-; GA Cncl for Soc Stud 1988-; BSA Cnslr 1989-; GSA Cnslr 1972-74; 4-H Cnslr 1969-71; Liberty Primitive Baptist Church Mem; Cystic Fibrosis Fnd Plaque of Appreciation; GA PECE Prgm 5 Yr Service Awd; *office:* Sumter Cty HS 101 Industrial Blvd Americus GA 31709

WISHNOW, ELAINE, 6th Grade G/T Teacher; *b:* New York, NY; *ed:* (BA) Ed, 1967, (MS) Ed, 1971 Brooklyn Coll; *cr:* Teacher Public Sch 46K 1967-; *ai:* Life Lab Sci Prgm Lead Teacher; Spelling Team Coach; Elem Sch Sci Assn 1986-; Shetland Sheepdog Club of Northern NJ Pres 1987-; Owner Handlers Assn 1986-; Teacher of Yr Dist 13 1986; Article Published; *office:* Public Sch 46K 100 Clermont Ave Brooklyn NY 11205

WISNIEWSKI, LISA KLARES, English/Work Study Teacher; *b:* Cleveland, OH; *m:* Melvin Trenton; *c:* Lindsay M.; *ed:* (BS) Psych, Frostburg St Coll 1980; (MAED) Spec Ed/Adjudicated Youth, George Washington Univ 1984; Ed of Emotionally Disturbed; *cr:* Mental Health Assoc 1980-82, Mental Health Cnslr/Unit Coord 1982-83 Regional Inst Children & Adolescents; Residential Coord Walden/Sierra House 1984-85; Spec Ed Teacher/Dept Chairperson Lackey HS 1985-; *ai:* Sr Adv; Task Force; Alternative Strategies, 8th Grade Writing Assessment Comm; Presenter Writing Wkshps; Juvenile Offenders in Need of Treatment Comm; Charles Cty Ed Assn, Md St Teachers Assn, NEA 1986-; *office:* Lackey HS Rt 224 Indian Head MD 20640

WISNIEWSKI, SHARON ANN (SULLIVAN), 2nd Grade Teacher; *b:* Bryan, OH; *m:* Dennis P.; *c:* Jason, Justin; *ed:* (BS) Elem Ed, Bowling Green StUniv 1965; Addl Studes Theory in Primary Sch; Econ for Elem Ed; Adventures in Econ; Instr Stategy; Classroom Mgmt Stategy; Proj Teach; Proj Pride; Becoming Whole Lang Teacher; *cr:* 4th Grade Teacher Defiance City Schls 1965-69; 3rd Grade Teacher 1969; 2nd Grade Teacher 1970-74; 2nd Grade Teacher 1979- Bryan City Schls; *ai:* Lang Arts Curr Dev Comm; Defiance Ed Assn; Bryan Ed Assn; OEA; NEA; *home:* RD 2 Stryker OH 43557

WISSINGER, CAROLYN CRAWFORD, Teacher; *b:* Wilmington, DE; *m:* Melvin G.; *c:* William, Cynthia Thompson; Melanie; *ed:* (BS) Elem Ed, Towson Univ 1977; *cr:* Art Teacher Elkton Chrstn Sch 1974-75; Teacher Fairwinds Chrstn Sch 1977-82; 5th/6th Grade Teacher Red Lion Chrstn Acad 1982-; *ai:* Missions Comm, Curr & Open House; *office:* Red Lion Chrstn Acad 1400 Red Lion Rd Bear DE 19701

WITBECK, RANDALL S., Guidance Cnslr/Bible Dept Head; *b:* Detroit, MI; *m:* Lynn Sweet; *c:* Brandon, Matthew; *ed:* (BA) Religion, Trevecca Nazarene Coll 1980; (MAR) Chrstn Ed, Wesley Biblical Seminary 1985; *cr:* Cnslr Baptist Childrens Village 1983-84; Pastor Houlka Church of the Nazarene 1984-86; Minister of Youth Princeton Church of the Nazarene 1986-; Bible Teacher Princeton Chrstn Sch 1986-; *ai:* Dean of Discipline; Var Bsbl Coach; Church of the Nazarene Ordained Minister 1985; Outstanding Young Men in America 1986; TNC Minister Assn VP 1979; *office:* Princeton Chrstn Sch PO Box 4299 Princeton FL 33039

WITCHER, CHERYLE TURNER, Earth Science Teacher; *b:* Bentonville, AR; *m:* Loren Ray Sr.; *c:* Elisabeth Clark, Betty ThompsoN, Loren Jr., Jeff; *ed:* (BS) Geology, 1974, (BSE) Scndry Ed, 1974 Univ of AR; Conservation Field Study 1976; Energy Univ Cntrl AR 1976; AR Geology, Field Consortium Univ of AR 1985; AR Field Geology for Earth Sci Teacher Univ of AR 1989; *cr:* Volunteer Jefferson HS 1968; 8th Grade Chem/General Sci/Earth Sci Teacher Walton Jr HS 1980-; *ai:* Discipline Comm; *office:* Walton Jr HS 1501 Cub Blvd Bentonville AR 72712

WITCHER, JAMES DOUGLAS, Science Teacher; *b:* Bryan, TX; *m:* Mary Ann Mc Carty; *c:* John, David; *ed:* (BS) Bio, 1969, (MST) Sci, 1974 Tarleton St Univ; Cmptr Literacy Trng; Mid-Management Cert 1989; *cr:* 1st Lt Medical Corp US Army 1970-72; Sci Teacher Mc Camey Mid Sch 1972-; *ai:* Adult Team Cncl Mem; Mid Sch Newspaper Adv; Sci Teachers Assn 1974-; TX Teachers Assn Past Pres 1973-; Assn TX Prof Educators Past Pres 1982-; MC Camey Emergency Service Instr 1976-82, Mc Camey Volunteer Fire Dept Secy 1977-80; Drug & Alcohol Prevention Bd 1975-77; *office:* Mc Camey Mid Sch 400 E 11th Mc Camey TX 79752

WITHEROW, CATHERINE SASLAWSKY, English Teacher; *b:* West Islip, NY; *m:* Stephen M.; *c:* Jennifer, Eric, Alan, Scott; *ed:* (BA) Eng/Speech, SUNY Geneseo 1971; (MS) Eng, Elmira Coll 1978; *cr:* 10th - 12th Grade Eng Teacher R L Thomas HS 1971-72; Substitute Teacher 1972-77; 9th - 12th Grade Eng Teacher Eng Canaseraga Cntrl Sch 1977-79; 7th - 12th Grade Eng Teacher Andover Cntrl Sch 1981-; *ai:* NCTE, NY St Eng Cncl; *office:* Andover Central School 31 Elm St Andover NY 14806

WITHERS, KIMBERLY DENAE, Biology/Physical Sci Teacher; *b:* Marion, OH; *ed:* (BS) Bio/Zoology, Marshall Univ 1983; (BS) Sci Ed, WV St Coll 1984; VA Polytechnic Inst; Physics Prgm Scndry Teachers 1989-; Working Towards Masters Scndry Sci with Physics Specialization Sponcered by Natl Sci Fnd; *cr:* General/Phys Scci Teacher Wahama HS 1984-88; Bio Teacher Pt Pleasant HS 1988-; Phys Sci Teacher Pt Pleasant Jr HS 1988-; *ai:* Sr Class & Skateboard Club Adv; *home:* PO Box 85 Ashton WV 25503

WITT, CATHY BROWN, Third Grade Teacher; *b:* Meyersdale, PA; *w:* Walter De Sales (dec); *c:* Victoria Witt Hensel, Daniel N., Mark A., Lisa R. Keen; *ed:* (BS) Elem Ed - Cum Laude, 1975 (MED) Elem Ed, 1980 Frostburg Univ; *cr:* 1st Grade Teacher Meyersdale Elem 1975-80; 3rd Grade Teacher & Chair Lynchburg Chrstn Acad 1980-; Textbook Selection & Evaluation Comm, Curr Comm & Soc Comm; *ai:* ACSI; NEA Mem, PHEAA Mem; Deans List; *home:* Rt 7 Box 247 Forest VA 24551

WITT, ELAINE M., 4/5th Grade Lang Arts Teacher; *b:* Trenton, NE; *m:* Bill C.; *c:* Richard C., William Thomas, Harry Ray; *ed:* (BA) Elem Ed, Kearney St Coll 1973; Addl Training Kearney State; *cr:* K-3 Teacher R-4 Phelps Cty 1957-59; Chase Cty Dist 66 1961-63; 6th Grade Teacher Wilsonville Public Sch 1965-67; 5th Grade Teacher Red Willow Sch 1967-68; 4th Grade Teacher MVPS 1968-; *ai:* NEA 1968-; NE Ed Assn 1959-; CEA Bldg Rep 1987-; Curtis Ed Assn 1968-; Royal Neighbors 1950-; Extension Club 1960-64; Den Mother Cub Scouts 1962-64; Bible Study Teacher 1950-82; Helping Hands Club for York Christian Coll; *office:* Medicine Valley Elem Sch 605 Ord Ave Curtis NE 69025

WITTE, EULA ANN, Kindergarten Teacher; *b:* Beeville, TX; *m:* Joddie; *c:* Jeff, Tamra Spain, Donna Elmore; *ed:* (BS) Elem Ed, 1973, (MS) Elem Ed, 1980 SWT; *cr:* Kndgtn Teacher Kyle Elem; *ai:* Phi Delta Kappa; Beta Sigma Phi; Delta Kappa Gama.

WITTEN, SUSAN CAROL, Pre-First Grade Teacher; *b:* Akron, OH; *ed:* (BS) Elem Ed, Kent St 1972; Montessori Pre-Sch Certificate; *cr:* 4th Grade Teacher Sharon Elem 1972-74; 1st-3rd Grade Teacher Hinckley Elem 1974-87; Pre-1st Grade Teacher Black River Primary 1987-; *ai:* Teach Saturday Enrichment Sci Classes Local Joint Voc Sch; Working to Correlate Dist Parenting Prgm; OEA, NEA; Jennings Scholar Awd 1976; *home:* 7153 Northview Dr Wadsworth OH 44281

WITTEN-UPCHURCH, GWENDOLYN, Choral Director; *b:* Elizabethton, KY; *m:* Kenneth W.; *ed:* (BM) Vocal Performance, 1982, (BME) Music Ed, 1982 Univ of Louisville; (MA) Vocal Performance, IN Univ 1985; *cr:* Choral Dir MCCSC 1985-; *ai:* IMEA Reperataire 1989-; ACDA; Delta Kappa Gamma Music Chm 1988-; *office:* Bloomington HS South 3701 Bluebird Ln Bloomington IN 47401

WITTER, JOHN H., Mathematics Teacher; *b:* West Reading, PA; *m:* Linda M. Brubaker; *c:* Ben, Jean, James; *ed:* (BS) Elem Ed, Lebanon Valley Coll 1964; *cr:* 6th Grade Teacher Newmanstown Elem Sch 1964-72; 6th Grade Math/Lang Art Teacher ELCO Mid Sch 1972-; *ai:* ELCO Mid Sch Math Club, Mathcounts, Chess Club; ELCO HS Golf Coach; ELCO Dist Math Task Force; Eastern Lebanon Cty Educators Assn, PA St Educators Assn, NEA; *office:* ELCO Mid Sch 180 ELCO Dr Myerstown PA 17067

WITTMAN, JONATHAN R., HS Band Director; *b:* Milford, DE; *m:* Jacqueline Sue; *c:* Kaitlyn M., Jonathan K.; *ed:* (BA) Bio, 1975, (BM) Music Ed, 1978 Univ of DE; *cr:* Band Dir George Read Jr HS 1979-80; Instrumental Music Teacher Instrumental Music Prgms 1980-81; Band Dir Middletown HS 1981-86, Wilmington HS 1986-; *ai:* Head Bsbl Coach; Intnl Trumpet Guild Mem 1976-; Music Educators Natl Conference Mem 1978-; NEA Mem 1981-; 1st St Symphonic Band Prin Trumpet 1978-.

WITTMAN, LOUANN (BLANDINO), Junior High English Teacher; *b:* Bridgeton, NJ; *m:* Daniel J. Sr.; *c:* Daniel Jr., Gina M., John F.; *ed:* (BA) Eng, S IL Univ Edwardsville 1970; *cr:* 6th-8th Grade Eng Teacher 1970-72, Substitute Teacher 1973 St Marys Sch; Substitute Teacher/Volunteer Immaculate Conception 1979-84; 7th/8th Grade Eng Teacher Sacred Heart Grammar Sch 1985-; *ai:* Literary Magazine Adv; Rdng Coord; NCEA 1985-; Immaculate Conception Chair (Choir Dir 1987-) 1979-; *office:* Sacred Heart Grammar Sch 922 Landis Ave Vineland NJ 08360

WITTMANN, CHARLES MICHAEL, Mathematics Teacher; *b:* Mobile, AL; *m:* Mary E.; *c:* Charles, Heather; *ed:* (BS) Sci/Math, Univ of AL 1963; *cr:* Teacher Hunter HS 1964-66, Northwest Cuberrus 1966-67, Albemarle Road Jr HS 1967-74, West Charlotte Sr HS 1974-; *ai:* NC Cncl Teachers of Math, NCTM 1979-; *office:* West Charlotte Sr HS 2219 Senior Dr Charlotte NC 28216

WITTMANN, MARY EVELYN, Sixth Grade Teacher; *b:* Charlotte, NC; *m:* Charles M.; *c:* Charles H., Heather S.; *ed:* (BA) Elem Ed, 1963, (MS) Elem Ed, 1965 ASU; *cr:* 5th Grade Teacher 1964-68, 7th Grade Math Teacher 1968-71 Charlotte Mec; Spec Ed Teacher 1972-73, 6th Grade Teacher 1973- Cabarrus CO; *ai:* Grade Chm; NCAE Sch Rep 1988-89; ADK Treas 1990; Cabarrus Hospital Bd Mem 1987-; *home:* 402 Dogwood Ln Harrisburg NC 28075

WITWER, WILLIAM FREDERICK, Director of Choral Activities; *b:* Akron, OH; *m:* Lisa Carmen Troullier; *ed:* (BM) Music Ed/Music His/Lit, Univ of Akron 1982; (MM) Choral Music Performance, SW TX St 1986; *cr:* Scndry Vocal Music Dir Jasper Ind Sch Dist 1982-83, Revere Local Schls 1983-84; Grad Asst SW TX St Univ 1984-86; Choir Dir Victoria HS 1986-; *ai:* All HS Choral Act & Contests; TX MEA Region Vocal Chm 1988-; TX ACDA 1983-; ACDA 1979-; Akron Jaycees 1983; Jasper Cultural Art Cncl 1982; Victoria Summer Music Rep 1986-88; Outstanding Young Man of America 1983; ACDA Choral Composition Contest Winner 1986; *office:* Victoria HS 1110 Sam Houston Dr Victoria TX 77901

WIX, JANICE HOPE (PERRY), Coord/Teacher of Gifted Prgms; *b:* La Grange, KY; *m:* Fred Michael; *c:* Jane M.; *ed:* (BME) Music Ed, Georgetown Coll 1978; (MAT) Elem Teaching, 1979, (MA) Rdng Specialist, 1985 Spalding Univ; Grad Stud Gifted Ed; *cr:* 1st/4th Grade Teacher Flaherty Elem 1979-83; Gifted Ed Instr 1986, Music Ed Instr 1979-87 Spalding Univ; Teacher of Gifted Ed 1983-, Coord of Gifted Ed 1988- Meade Cty Bd of Ed; *ai:* Odyssey of Mind Teams Coach; Meade Cty Mid Sch Annual & Advisory Bd Chm for Gifted Ed; Private Piano Teacher; KY Assn for Gifted Ed 1983-; ASCD 1985-; Baptist Young Women 1986-; Meade Assn for Retarded Citizens Annual Auction Co-Chm 1987-; St Advisory Bd Mem Odyssey of Mind; Odyssey of Mind Teams St Winners 1986, 1990; PICA Awd for Annual 1987-; *home:* 412 Trailridge Rd Brandenburg KY 40108

WODOCK, REBECCA BARNETT, Math Teacher; *b:* Frankfort, IN; *m:* Joseph A.; *ed:* (BS) Math Ed 1966, (MS) Guidance, 1969 Purdue; *cr:* Teacher Carmel Jr HS 1966-74, Ft Wayne Cmmty Schls 1974-; *ai:* Project SET Adv; Intramural Staff; 7th Grade Team Leader; FWEA, ISTA, NEA; Joint Cncl of Ec Awd; *office:* Lane Mid Sch 4901 Vance Ave Fort Wayne IN 46815

WOEHLER, CAROL ANNE (NACHTRAB), Fourth Grade Teacher; *b:* Toledo, OH; *m:* David G.; *ed:* (BA) Ed, Wittenburg Univ 1975; (MA) Curr & Instruction, TX A & M Univ 1984; Working on EDD Ed & Rdng; *cr:* Elem Teacher Dominicum Sisters of Adrian 1963-69, St Teresas 1969-70, St Joseph Schls 1975-77, Pulaski Cty Sch 1977-79, Navasota Ind Sch Dist 1980-; *ai:* PTA Parliamentarian; Intnl Rdng Assn 1988-; ASCD 1989-; Navasota Lioness (Secy/Treas 1982-83, Pres 1986-87) Lioness of Yr 1986; *office:* John C Webb Mid Sch P O Box 511 Navasota TX 77868

WOESTMAN, NANCY KAY, 5th Grade Teacher; *b:* Cincinnati, OH; *ed:* (BA) Soc Wk, 1972; Cert Elem Ed, 1976 Coll of Mount St Joseph; (MED) Rdng Specialist, Xavier Univ 1989; *cr:* 2nd Grade Teacher St Pius Sch 1976-77; 5th/6th Grade Teacher 1977-80; 5th Grade Teacher 1980- St Therese Little Flower Sch; *ai:* Intnl Rdng Assn 1988-; *office:* St Therese Little Flower Sch 5555 Little Flower Ave Cincinnati OH 45239

WOFFINDEN, BRENT E., Teacher; *b:* Payson, UT; *m:* Eileen Kunz; *c:* Kori, Jeimi, Vaughn; *ed:* (AS) Math, Snow Coll 1971; (BA) Elem Ed, 1973, (MED) Elem Ed, 1985 UT St Univ; *cr:* Teacher Carl Sandburg Elem Sch 1973-79, Calvin Smith Elem Sch 1979-87, Beehive Elem Sch 1987-; *ai:* Operation of Cmptr Lab; Chm Gifted & Talented Comm; Mem Yr Round Sch Comm; UEA, GEA, NEA 1973-; Latter Day Saints Church; Cmmty Crime Watch Chm; UT Parent Assn of Gifted & Talented St Treas; Co-Authored Granite Sch Dist Sci Dossier; Authored Math Word Problem Solving Workbook.

WOHL, JUDITH R., Middle School English Teacher; *b:* Baltimore, MD; *m:* Anthony; *c:* Victoria, Gillian; *ed:* (BA) Latin/Classics, Brown Univ 1962; (MA) Eng, St Univ NY New Paltz 1972; Certificate Drama Ed, London Univ 1982-83; *cr:* 9th Grade Teacher 1964-65, 8th Grade Teacher 1970-79, 7th Grade Teacher 1964-68, 1980-89 Arlington Mid Sch; *ai:* Drama Club Adv; Play Dir; NYSUT; CERT Secy 1986-87; CCT Bd Mem 1988; Travel Articles; Teacher Trng Consultant; *home:* History Dept Vassar Coll Poughkeepsie NY 12601

WOJCIECHOWSKI, DONALD RAY, Mathematics Teacher; *b:* Little Falls, MN; *m:* Karen Sue LaFond; *c:* Michele R. Sjolander, Kevin D.; *ed:* (BS) Math, St Cloud St Univ 1963; (MS) Math, Univ of Dayton 1972; *cr:* Teacher Ind Sch Dist #16 1963-; *ai:* Math Team, Head Boys Tennis Coach; Boys Tennis Coaches Assn Pres 1989-; MN Math Teachers; MN Fed of Teachers; Knights of Columbus; Natl Sci Fnd Grant 1968-72; *office:* Spring Lake Park HS 8001 Able St N E Spring Lake Park MN 55432

WOJCIECHOWSKI, MICHEAL JOSEPH, U S History 8th Grade Teacher; *b:* Manistee, MI; *m:* Janet Vlajkov; *c:* Joseph, Michael; *ed:* (BA) US His, 1972, (MA) US His, 1977 Western MI Univ; *cr:* 6th Grade Teacher 1972-75, 8th Grade MI His Teacher 1975-80, 6th Grade Teacher 1980-85, 8th Grade US His Teacher 1985- Delton Mid Sch; *office:* Delton Kellogg School 327 N Grove St Delton MI 49046

WOJCIK, NORMAN THOMAS, Guidance Counselor; *b:* Chicago, IL; *m:* L. Judith Chandler; *ed:* (BS) Scndry Ed/Sociology, Lee Coll 1973; (MED) Scndry Guidance Counseling, Univ TN Chattanooga 1976; Ed/Elem Ed Univ TN Knoxville; *cr:* 4th-8th Grade Hlth Teacher North Lee Sch 1973-74; 4th-8th Grade Teacher Taylors Sch 1974-86; Guidance Counseling Bradley Jr HS 1986-; *ai:* Spon of Project 714 Stu Staying Straight; *office:* Bradley Jr H Sch North Ocoee St Cleveland TN 37311

WOJCIK, RICHARD JOHN, Sr HS Language Arts Teacher; *b:* Weirton, WV; *ed:* (BA) Lang Art, Alliance Coll 1952; Univ of Steubenville, Univ of Pittsburgh, WV Univ; *cr:* Faculty Follansbee HS 1955-60; Asst Dir of Admissions Case Inst 1960-65; Faculty Follansbee HS 1965-71, Weir HS 1971-73, Brooke HS 1973-; *ai:* Public Relations; Prins Newsletter; AFT Public Relations 1987-89; Staff Announcer WSTV/WRKY; *home:* 237 May Rd Follansbee WV 26037

WOJCIKEWYCH, JOAN HARRIS, Admin/Language Art Teacher; *b:* Roanoke Rapids, NC; *m:* Raymond; *c:* Andrea, Raymond, Gregory, Kevin, Matthew; *ed:* (AA) Liberal Art, Richard Bland Coll 1968; (BA) Eng, James Madison Univ 1970; Working toward Masters Admin, Bradley Univ; Courses taken Univ of VA, IL St Univ, Bradley Univ, IL Comm Coll; *cr:* Teacher Chesapeake Public Schls 1970-73, Centre Bus Coll 1974-75, St Mark Sch 1980-87; Admin/Teacher Father Sweeney Sch 1988-; *ai:* Yrbk Spon; Oratorical & Declamations Coach; Phi Delta Kappa Newsletter Comm 1989-; St Mark Sch PTO Chairperson 1989-; Bradley Womens Club 1977-; AAUW 1971-73; *office:* Father Sweeney Sch 403 NE Madison Peoria IL 61603

WOJNOWSKI, SUZANNE DICK, English/Phys Ed Teacher; *b:* Carbondale, IL; *c:* Adam; *ed:* (BS) Jr HS Ed, 1976, (MS) Elem Ed, 1987 E IL Univ; *cr:* Jr HS Eng/Phys Ed Teacher St Anne Grade Sch 1976-; *ai:* Yrbk Spon; Lang Art Comm; Vlybl Referee; IL Ed Assn; *office:* Saint Anne Grade School 333 St Louis Saint Anne IL 60964

WOLBERT, ELIN VIRGINIA EAGLESTON, Social Studies Teacher; *b:* Brooklyn, NY; *m:* George A.; *c:* Christine L. Jacobsen, John A.; *ed:* (BS) Elem Ed, ST Univ of NY at Plattsburg 1958; (MA) Soc Sci/Sociology, William Paterson Coll 1978; *cr:* 6th Grade Teacher Unqua Road Elem Sch 1958-60; 5th & 6th Grade Soc Stud Teacher Greenwood Lake Elem & Mid Sch 1968-82; 9th Thru 12th Grade Soc Stud Hudson Sr HS 1984-; *ai:* Steering Comm and Grade Level Chairperson Teachers Adv Prgrm; FL Cncl of Soc Stud 1984-; NCSS 1984-; Pasco Cncl for Soc Stud 1988-; Teacher of Yr 1989; *office:* Hudson Senior High School 14410 Cobra Way Hudson FL 33568

WOLCOTT, JANE AUSTIN, Second Grade Teacher; *b:* Warsaw, NY; *m:* Jeffrey M.; *c:* Katherine, Joseph, Sarah; *ed:* (BS) Ed, SUNY Geneseo 1976; Grad Stud St Bonaventure Univ 1981; *cr:* 4th Grade Teacher 1976-77, 1st Grade Teacher 1977-78, 2nd Grade Teacher 1978- Bolivar Cntrl Sch; *ai:* Liason Comm Mem; NEA; *office:* Bolivar Cntrl Sch 100 School St Bolivar NY 14715

WOLD, JERRI BOWMAN, Advanced Spanish Teacher; *b:* Glasgow, KY; *m:* Vernon E. Jr.; *c:* Michael S., Stephanie B.; *ed:* (BA) Span, 1967, (MA) Speech, 1977 Western KY Univ; *cr:* Span/Fr/Eng Teacher Shawnee Jr HS 1968-69; 3rd/4th Grade on Camera Span Teacher WKPC-TV Channel 15 Instructional TV 1969-75; Span Consultant Jefferson Cty Bd of Ed 1975-76; Advanced Span Teacher Dupont Manual HS 1976-; *ai:* Span Club Spon; Manual Schlsp Comm Mem; Jefferson Cty Ed Assn, Local & St Natl Ed Assn 1968-; KY Cncl for Teaching Foreign Lang 1980-; America Assn for Teacher of Span & Portuguese 1988-; Amer Women in Radio & TV (VP, Pres) 1970-71; Jefferson Cty Foreign Lang Festival Dir 1978-84; *office:* Dupont Manual HS 120 E Lee St Louisville KY 40208

WOLF, CATHERINE ROSE, Sixth Grade Teacher; *b:* Delaware, OH; *ed:* (BS) Elem Ed, Duquesne Univ 1975; *cr:* Adult Basic Ed Teacher Mid-East OH Voc Sch 1984-86; 6th Grade Teacher Holy Trinity Sch 1978-; Critic Reader Silver Burdett & Ginn Incorporated 1988-; *ai:* Art Curr Comm; Sch Art Show Organizer; Advisory Comm Teacher Rep; Asst Prin; Spelling Bee Competition Coach; Diocese of Columbus Art Paddlewheel Participant; NCEA 1975-; Follow the Footsteps Historical Field Trip Prgm Contributor; OH St Univ & Dept of Mental Health Project Conflict & Nuclear War Participant; *home:* 3278 St Rt 22 NW Somerset OH 43783

WOLF, EARL DUDLEY, History/Physical Ed Teacher; *b:* Paso, WA; *ed:* (BA) Soc Ed/Phys Ed/Elem Ed/Traffic Safety Ed, Cntrl WA Univ 1971; *ai:* Head Bsbl Coach; Jr Class Adv; TSE Quincy HS Dept Chm; Quincy Ed Assn, Natl Bsbl Coaches Assn; WA St Bsbl Coaches Assn Dist Rep 1989-, Coach of Yr 1990; Quincy Lions 1988-89; United States Army Reserve (Secy, Instr).

WOLF, JOANN E. (LILLEY), Second Grade Teacher; *b:* Topeka, KS; *m:* Randy J.; *c:* Adam, Justin; *ed:* (BED) Elem Ed, Washburn Univ 1977; (MS) Curr/Instruction, Emporia St Univ 1988; *cr:* Kndgtn Teacher 1977-80, 5th Grade Teacher 1980-84, 2nd Grade Teacher 1984- Silver Lake Elem; *ai:* NEA (Treas 1989-) 1977-; PTA Treas 1989-; *home:* 5348 NW Valencia Rd Silver Lake KS 66539

WOLF, JOANNE SHOSTACK, Alternative Education Teacher; *b:* Miami, FL; *ed:* (BED) Elem Ed, Univ of Miami 1968; *cr:* 6th Grade Teacher Citrus Grove Elem & Phyllis Wheatley Elem 1968-70; 4Th/5th Grade Combined Teacher Doctors Inlet Elem 1971-73; 5th/6th Grade Teacher Rockway Elem 1973-86; 5th Grade Alternative Ed Teacher Joe Hall Elem 1986-; *ai:* Dade Partners Liaison; *office:* Joe Hall Elem Sch 1901 S W 134th Ave Miami FL 33175

WOLF, KATHY SANTORO, 5th Grade Teacher; *b:* Alliance, OH; *m:* Terry A.; *ed:* (BS) Elem Ed, 1974, (MS) Rdng Specialization, 1982 Kent St Univ; *cr:* 7th Grade Soc Stud Teacher Marlington Local Schls 1975-76; Substitute Teacher Stark Cty Schls 1976-78, 4th/5th Grade Teacher Lake Local Schls 1978-; *office:* Lake Local Schls 225 W Lincoln Hartville OH 44632

WOLF, MARTHA E.(VAN LANTSCHOOT), Asst Prin/2nd Grade Teacher; *b:* Fairfield, IA; *m:* Donald Gary; *c:* Susan, John; *ed:* (BA) Elem Ed, Parsons Coll 1963; MA Elem Ed, AL Ag/Mechanical Univ 1983; *cr:* 2nd Grade Teacher Keokuk Sch System 1962-67; Asst Prin 1985, 2nd Grade Teacher, 1970 Lincoln Cty Sch System; *ai:* Chairperson/K-2nd Grade Team; Delegate TN Ed Assembly 1985; K-12th Grade Religious Ed Coord St Anthonys Cath Church 1985; Delta Kappa Gamma Pres 1988-; Phi Kappa Phi Mem; TN Ed Assn (Secy 1980-89, Treas 1982); Distinguished Classroom Teacher Highland Rim 1989; Career Ladder III Educator; Lincoln Cty Extended Contract Supvr 1985-88; *home:* Rt 4 Box 12 Fayetteville TN 37334

WOLF, WENDY, Career Education Director; *b:* Portland, OR; *ed:* (BA) Eng, Willamette Univ 1969; (MA) Eng/Ed, Univ of OR 1970; Grad Work Portland St Univ & W OR St Coll; *cr:* Eng Teacher Stayton Union HS 1970-73; Eng Teacher/Curr Dir Open Meadow Learning Center 1973-77; Eng Teacher 1977-88, Career Ed Dir 1988- Tigard HS; *ai:* Effective Schls Team Leader; OCTE 1978-89; NEBCEA 1989-; Faculty Commencement Speaker 1982, 1984, 1987; Whos Who in Amer Ed; *office:* Tigard HS 9000 SW Durham Rd Tigard OR 97223

WOLFE, ELAINE CLAIRE (DAUGHETEE), Science Teacher; *b:* Indianapolis, IN; *c:* Leah D., Scott A.; *ed:* (BS) Bio Sci, Purdue Univ 1962; (MA) Vertebrate Zoology, UCLA 1964; Organic Chem/His Purdue Univ 1964-65; Audio Visua Medie Testing Except Child TX Chrstn Univ 1965-66; Sch Admin/Spec Sci Stud Penn St Univ 1970-71; Human Genetics Univ of Indianapolis 1985; Cmptrs Butler Univ 1986; Cascades Volcanology & Spec Sci Probs Portland St Univ 1988; Plate Tectonics Geology/Planet Earth Purdue Univ 1989; *cr:* Bio Teacher Canoga Park HS 1963-64; Instr Bio Labs Purdue Univ 1964-65; Teaching Asst-Dept of Ed TX Chrstn Univ 1965-66; Long Term Sub Teacher Ft Worth Public Schls 1966-67; Bio Teacher Upper Merion Sr HS 1967-71; Mother & Artist Prof Home Art Studio 1971-81; Long Term Sub Teacher Fulton Jr HS 1982; Sci Teacher Guion Creek Mid Sch

1982-; *ai:* Faculty Adv-Stu Cncl; Building Rep MSD Pike Twp Outdoor Classroom Adv Bd; Steering Comm Mem-Lilly Endownment Mid Grades Improv Comm; Mentor Sub Comm Mem for at Risk Stu GCMS; Landscape Comm Chairperson; Natl Parks Assn; Hoosier Assn of Sci Teachers; NSTA; Natl Wildlife Fed; Smithsonian Museum; Phi Delta Kappa; Pi Lambda Theta; Purdue Alumni Assn; Purdue Club of Indpls; Lyndhurst Baptist Church Teach Adult Sunday Schl Class; Publ Masters Research in the Amer Bio Teacher 1975; APK & KATT Honoraries Undergrad Sch/Schlsps Undergrad & Masters Prgms; Nom Best Sci Teacher PA 1970; Nom Best Sci Teacher in PA in 1970; Nom Presdntl Awd for Excl in Sci & Math 1987 & 1990; Selected 1 of 10 Runner-Ups for Best Teacher Indianapolis 1988; Selected for Educational Honoraries-Phi Delta Kappa & Pi Lambda Theta 1988; 1988-Received NSF Grant-Cascades Volcanoes Wkshp; NCA Evaluations Teams 1986 & 1990; *office:* Guion Creek Mid Sch 4401 W 52nd St Indianapolis IN 46254

WOLFE, ELLEN M., Third Grade Teacher; *b:* Mt Erie, IL; *w:* William (dec); *c:* Marcia Runyon; *ed:* (BS) Elem Ed, S IL Univ 1967; *cr:* 1st-8th Grade Teacher Wayne Cty 1945-53; 1st-2nd Grade Teacher 1953-54, 8th Grade Prin/Teacher Mt Erie Elem 1954-55; 5th-8th Grade Teacher/Prin Zif Consolidated 1963-64; 5th/6th Grade Teacher Mt Erie 1964-75; 3rd Grade Teacher Mt Erie 1975-; *home:* RR 1 Box 106 Mount Erie IL 62446

WOLFE, HELEN H., Fourth Grade Teacher; *b:* St Marys, PA; *m:* Arthur L.; *c:* Douglas, Ann Haverfield, Robert, Lorraine, Philip; *ed:* (BA) Soc Sci, St Marys Coll 1956; *cr:* 6th/7th Grade Teacher St Leos Sch 1956-57; 4th Grade Teacher Mother of Sorrows 1976-; *ai:* Sch Cmptr Coord; NCEA.

WOLFE, HOLLY G., Second Grade Teacher; *b:* Gastonia, NC; *m:* Robert; *c:* Stephanie, Christopher; *ed:* (BA) Elem Ed, Carthage Coll 1964; *cr:* Teacher Shady Lane 1964-67, Bethesda 1978-79, Rose Glen 1979-; *home:* 3048 Minot Ln Waukesha WI 53188

WOLFE, JOSEPHINE, Retired Third Grade Teacher; *b:* Sneedvile, TN; *ed:* (BS) Elem Ed, Carson-Newman Coll 1958; (MS) Ed, Univ of TN 1972; *cr:* 4th Grade Teacher Fairview Elem Sch 1956-69; 3rd Grade Teacher Manley Elem Sch 1970-86; *ai:* NEA 1956-86; East TN Ed Assn 1956-86; TN Ed Assn 1956-86; Hamblen Cty Ed Assn Treas 1956-86; Fairview Elem PTA Sec 1956-69; Manley Elem Sch PTO 1970-86; TN Retired Teachers Assn 1986-; Morristown-Hamblen Cty Retired Teachers Assn 1986-; 1986 TN NU Chapter Alpha Delta Kappa; Hamblen Chapter 31 Order of Eastern Star 1976-; Calvary Bapt Church Mem; Selected "outstanding Elem Teacher of Amer 1974" By Bd of Adv; *home:* 3427 Vicki St Morristown TN 37814

WOLFE, PAMELA KLINE, Social Studies Chairperson; *b:* Richmond, VA; *m:* Robert Edward; *c:* Fr, Univ of Strasbourg France 1978; (BA) Fr, Bridgewater Coll 1979; (MA) European His, Univ of MD 1983; *cr:* Fr Teaching Asst 1979-80, His Teaching Asst 1980-84 Univ of MD; Fr Teacher 1980-86, Soc Stud Chairperson 1986- Yeshiva of Greater Washington; *ai:* Greenpeace 1983-; Amnesty Intnl 1989-; George C Marshall Research Fellow; *office:* Yeshiva of Greater Washington 1216 Arcola Ave Silver Spring MD 20902

WOLFE, ROBERT, JR., Third Grade Teacher; *b:* Grafton, WV; *ed:* (BA) Elem Ed, Fairmont St Coll 1974; *cr:* 5th Grade Teacher Rowlesburg Elem Sch 1975-86; 3rd Grade Teacher Fellowsville Elem Sch 1986-; *ai:* Elem Bsktbl, Jr HS Boys & Girls Bsktbl Coach; WVEA, PCEA; N Amer Limousin Cattle Fnd Lifetime Mem, Natl Rifle Assn of America; *office:* Fellowship Elem Sch PO Box 265 Tunnelton WV 26444

WOLFE, SHEILA ANNE, Art Teacher; *b:* Beverly, MA; *m:* Robert Franklin Jr.; *c:* Morgan M.; *ed:* (BA) Art Ed, S CT St Univ 1985; *cr:* Art Teacher St Cecilias & St Gabriels 1986-87, Cntrl Cath HS 1987-; 8th Grade Teacher St Gabriels Elem Sch 1990; *ai:* Cheerleading, Var, Jr Var Coach; Var Shop & Art Club Adv; NCA Cheerleading Camp Spirit Stick 1987-89.

WOLFE, SUSAN SLOAN, Second Grade Teacher; *b:* Pittsburgh, PA; *m:* Dennis R.; *c:* Daniel; *ed:* (BA) Elem Ed, 1972; (MED) Elem Ed, 1976 Northern KY St Univ; *cr:* 1st/4th/3rd/5th/2nd/5th/4th & 3rd/4th Split Grade Teacher Crescent Springs Elem 1972-; *ai:* Stu Cncl, Cheerleading, Book-Fair Spon; KEA; Nom for Golden Apple Awd Local Newspaper; Citizen of Day by Local Radio Station; *office:* Crescent Springs Elem Sch 541 Buttermilk Pk Fort Mitchell KY 41017

WOLFE, VENITA (BATES), Second Grade Teacher; *b:* Ladonia, TX; *m:* Neil F.; *c:* Kyle N., Kenneth R.; *ed:* (BA) Elem Ed, Wichita St Univ 1969; (MED) Elem Ed, Washburn Univ 1971; *cr:* 2nd Grade Teacher Polk Elem 1971-73; 2nd/3rd Grade Teacher Cabot Public Schls 1973-75, Clinton Public Schls 1975-; *ai:* AR Ed Assn Spec Serv Comm 1979-80; CEA (Pres 1986-87, Membership Chm 1988-); *office:* Clinton Public Sch Rt 6 Box 103-1 Clinton AR 72031

WOLFE, VIOLET KIRKPATRICK, First Grade Teacher; *b:* Madisonville, TN; *m:* Robert Estel; *c:* Sheila Wolfe Carpenter, Robert N.; *ed:* (AA) Ed, Hiwassee Coll 1965; (BS) Ed, Univ of TN 1967; Ed; *cr:* 1st Grade Teacher Greenback Public Sch 1967-; *ai:* Loudon Cty Ed Assn 1967-; East TN Ed Assn 1967-; TN Ed Assn 1967-; NEA 1970-; Oakland United Meth Church 1951-; Daughters of Amer Revolution Vice Regent 1989-; His of Vonore Group Secy 1990; Delta Kappa Gamma 1984-; Teacher of Yr Loudon Cty TN 1988; *home:* Rt 2 Box 153 Greenback TN 37742

WOLFF, DOROTHY WEYNAND, Home Economics Teacher; *b:* Hondo, TX; *m:* Ray; *c:* Greg, Amy, Brad, Mandy; *ed:* (BS) Consumer/Home Ec, SW TX St Univ 1969; Voc Home Ec Teachers St Prof Improvement Conference 1974-; *cr:* Teacher Hondo Ind Sch Dist 1974-; *ai:* FHA Adv; VHETAT 1984-; DHanis Alters Society 1985-; Holy Cross Church Choir 1989-; DHanis Booster Club 1983-l DHanis Athletic Club 1979-; Honorary Mem Hondo FFA & DHanis FFA; *office:* Hondo HS 2603 Ave H Hondo TX 78861

WOLFF, JUDITH CASSIDY, 8th Grade Lang Arts Teacher; *b:* Philadelphia, PA; *m:* Norman D.; *c:* Karen, Keith; *ed:* (BS) Eng/Soc Stud, West Chester Univ 1957; Grad Stud Guidance & Counseling; *cr:* Teacher Ocean City HS 1957-60, Toms River HS 1960-62, Toms River HS N 1982-83, Toms River Intermediate E 1983-; *ai:* Yrbk Adv; Conflict Mgr, Adv & Trainer; Schl Resource Comm; NEA, NJEA, TREA, NCTE; Contact of Ocean Cty (Telephone Worker 1980-, Bd of Dirs 1982-85, Trainer 1987-); Governors Teacher Recognition Awd 1989-; *office:* Toms River Intermediate E Hooper Ave Toms River NJ 08753

WOLFF, MARSHA BERG, English Teacher; *b:* Madison, MN; *m:* Gary A.; *c:* Jason, Eric, Sarah; *cr:* Prgm Dir Hubbard Cty DAC 1980-81; Eng Teacher Menahga Public Sch 1981-; *ai:* Knowledge Bowl Teams Coach; Spelling Bee Coord; Menahga Ed Assn (Past Pres, Negotiator); *office:* Menahga Public Sch PO Box 160 Menaliga MN 56464

WOLFF, ROGER DENNIS, Fifth Grade Teacher; *b:* Faith, SD; *m:* Patricia Plautz; *c:* Benjamin, Jesse; *ed:* (BS) Ed, Dr Martin Luther Coll 1975; (MEPD) Ed, Univ WI La Crosse 1987; Religion, DMLC 1983; Certified in Reality Therapy, UWL 1987; *cr:* 5th-8th Grade Teacher Mount Clavary Ev Luth Sch 1975-85; Teacher/Prin St Johns Ev Luth Sch 1985-87; 5th Grade Teacher Valley View Elem Sch 1987-; Part Time Instr Oglala Lakota Coll 1988-89; Consultant SD Sch of Mines & Tech 1990; *ai:* SD Dropout Coalition; Faculty Adapt Instr; Phi Sigma Kappa 1971-; St Pauls Church Cncl Mem 1989-; Natl Ski Patrol CPR Trnr 1974-87; Originated MI Luth Sch Sci & Arts Fair; Granted Sabbatical-Graduate Asst at UW-L; *home:* 943 Sitka St Rapid City SD 57701

WOLFORD, MILDRED LOZIER, Seventh Grade Teacher; *b:* Girard, OH; *m:* Donald W.; *c:* Robert, James, David, Elizabeth Myers, Donald Jr.; *ed:* (ABA) Accounting, 1948, (BS) Ed, 1968 Youngstown St Univ; *cr:* Exec Secy Carlson Electric Co 1945-49; Accountant Mc Cune & Co 1949-51; Teacher St Matthias Sch 1965-; *ai:* Sci Fair Spon; Developed Sign Lang Prgm which Resulted in Formation of Singing & Signing Choir; NCEA; *home:* 29 Gertrude Ave Youngstown OH 44512

WOLFSON, ELOISE SYMONS, Retired Teacher; *b:* Edwardsville, PA; *c:* William Symons; *ed:* (BS) Elem Ed, Bloomsburg St Univ 1951; (MA) Curr/Instruction, WV Univ 1977; *cr:* 5th Grade Vocal Music Teacher 1952-74, 5th Grade Sci Teacher 1952-88, 5th Grade Rdng Teacher 1984-88 St Clairsville Mid Sch; *ai:* 5th Grade Annual Pittsburgh Excursion 1959-85; 5th Grade Excursion OH Amish Cntry 1963-66; 5th Grade Opera 1970; Bicentennial Pageant 1976; 6th Grade Outdoor Ed Sci Instr 1982-84; St Clairsville Ed Assn (Mem 1951-88, Secy 1969, Pres 1972-74, Exec Comm 1974-82); OH Ed Assn 1951-; NEA 1970-; St Clairsville-Richland Memorial Park Incorporated (Negotiator, Commissioner 1990, VP 1987-, Trustee 1985-87); Order of Eastern Star 1952-; Belmont Cty Republican Women Pres 1971-75; Support Dogs for the Handicapped Outstanding Service Awd 1982; Collie Club of America, Panhandle of WV Collie Club; St Clairsville OH Kennel Club (Charter Mem 1978, Pres 1985-); Allen Pool Mgr 1968-82, 1988; Entrepreneuship St Clairsville Collies, Breeder & Exhibitor; *home:* 219 Efaw Ave Saint Clairsville OH 43950

WOLKING, PAULA KELLY, Social Studies Teacher; *b:* Odessa, TX; *m:* Dennis Theodore; *c:* Anne E.; *ed:* (BS) Phys Ed, Sul Ross St Univ 1971; (MED) Phys Ed/Scndry Ed, SW TX St Univ 1981; *cr:* Teacher/Coach S San Antonio Ind Sch Dist 1971-79; Grad Asst SW TX St Univ 1979-81; Teacher/Coach San Marcos CISD 1981-; *ai:* Soph Class Spon; Adopt-A-Sch Comm; TX HS Girls Coaching Assn 1973-86; NCSS 1989-; GSA 1989-.

WOLLE, SELAMTAW, IB Economics Teacher; *b:* Debre Tabor, Ethiopia; *ed:* (BA) Economics/Math, Haile Selassie Univ Ethiopia 1971; (MA) Ec, OH Univ 1974; (MAABD) Ec, Cornell Univ 1977; Trng in Teaching Modern Math, Ec Dev, Management; *cr:* Adjunct Asst Professor St Johns UNiv 1981-84; Adjunct Instr Lehman Coll CUNY 1982-; Adjunct Asst Professor Pace Univ 1986-88; Teacher United Nations Intnl Sch 1987-; *ai:* Mentor; Adv Stu Act & Stu Government; Chm of Teachers Cncl; African Scholars Awd & Amer Inst Fellowship; *office:* United Nations Intnl Sch 24-50 Franklin D Roosevelt Dr New York NY 10010

WOLLENBURG, NANCY A., Reading/Language Teacher; *b:* Oak Park, IL; *ed:* (BS) Ed, 1966, (BA) Eng, 1966 Edgewood Coll; *cr:* Team Leader 1972-80, Teacher 1969-87, Teacher 1988- Herrick Jr HS; *ai:* Stu Cncl Adv; Operettas Asst Dir; Girls Bsktbl Coach; Sch Newspaper Spon; *office:* Herrick Jr HS 4435 Middaugh Downers Grove IL 60515

WOLLENHAUPT, JAN K., Business Teacher; *b:* Eagle Grove, IA; *m:* Ralph; *c:* Kurt; *ed:* (BSC) Bus/Ed, Univ of IA 1951; (MS) Bus, Drake Univ 1962; Rotary Fellow Univ of Melbourne; Univ of N IA, Drakke Univ; Summer Wkshps; Intnl Society of Bus Educators Seminars; *cr:* Bus Teacher Ruthven Consolidated Sch 1951-53, Lehigh HS 1953, Bridgewater-Fontanelle HS 1954-; *ai:* Bsktbl & Class Spon; NHS Adv; Curr & Phase III Comm; Delta Kappa Gamma Secy 1990; Delta Pi Epsilon, Pi Omega Pi, Beta Gamma Sigma; NBEA N-CBEA IA Rep; NCBEA (Secy, Convention Liaison); IBEA (Treas, Pres); IA Bus Educator 1982; Amer Legion Auxiliary Teacher of Yr Awd 1989; Published Articles; *home:* 116 Benton Box 367 Fontanelle IA 50846

WOLLENMAN, MAXINE MICHELLE (VEYNA), 7th/8th Grade English Teacher; *b:* Santa Ana, CA; *m:* Joseph M.; *c:* Alexandra; *ed:* (BA) Liberal Stud, CA Poly San Luis Obispo 1982; Pupil Personnel Credential Fresno Pacific Coll; *cr:* 5th Grade Teacher Fairview Elem 1982-85; 7th/8th Grade Math Teacher 1985-86, 7th/8th Grade Eng Teacher 1987-89 Green Acres Mid Sch.

WOLLIARD, LORRAINE J., First Grade Teacher; *b:* Trenton, NJ; *ed:* (BS) Elem Ed, Georgian Court Coll 1970; (MS) Rdng, Glassboro St Coll 1977; Wkshps Learning Disabilities, Diocese of Metuchen; *cr:* 1st-2nd Grade Teacher St Mary 1964-71; 1st Grade Teacher St Paul 1971-73, St Joseph 1973-; *ai:* Dept Head; Sch Supplies; Rdng Coord; NCEA; *home:* 99 Westervelt Ave North Plainfield NJ 07060

WOLLMAN, BARBARA LEWIS, Librarian; *b:* Chicago, IL; *c:* Jamin B., Alicia A.; *ed:* (BA) Eng Lit, Univ of MI 1957; (MAL) Lib Sci, Rosary Coll 1970; (EDD) Curr & Instruction Northern IL Univ 1989; *cr:* K-8th Grade Librarian Bannockburn Sch 1970-71; 4th-5th Grade Librarian Half Day Sch 1971-83; 5th-8th Grade Librarian Daniel Wright Mid Sch 1983-; *ai:* Beta Phi Mu 1970-; Kappa Delta Pi 1980-; *office:* Daniel Wright Mid Sch 1370 Riverwoods Rd Lake Forest IL 60045

WOLPA, BRENDA ANN, Chemistry Teacher; *b:* Tracy, MN; *m:* Bruce A.; *c:* Katherine; *ed:* (BA) Chem/Bio, Univ of MN Morris 1976; Scndry Ed, Univ of AZ 1980; Natl Sci Fnd Inst of Chemical Ed; Wkshps on Demonstrations & Instrumentation; *cr:* Chem Teacher Canyon del Oro HS 1980-; *ai:* Intnl Classroom Cmptr Link-Up with Other Countries; AFS Club Adv; Sch Improvement Comm; Amer Chemical Society 1986-; NSTA 1987-86; Amer Assn Advancement Sci 1988-89; S AZ Section of ACS Outstanding Stus 1987-88, 1990; Intnl Sci & Engineering Fair Teacher Commendation 1988-89; AZ Cncl of Engineering & Scientific Assn; Teacher of Yr 1988; Canyon del Oro/Amphitheater Sch Dist Teacher of Yr 1989-; *office:* Canyon del Oro HS 25 W Calle Concordia Tucson AZ 85737

WOLPER, TIMOTHY M., Social Studies Dept Chairman; *b:* Norristown, PA; *m:* Lisa Gregory; *ed:* (BA) Scndry Ed, La Salle Coll 1975; (MA) His, Villanova Univ 1985; *cr:* Soc Stud Teacher Hallahan Cath Girls HS 1976, Bishop Mc Devitt HS 1977, Roman Cath HS 1977-78; Soc Stud Teacher/Dept Head Lansdale Cath HS 1978-; *ai:* Sch Newspaper Moderator; NCSS 1982-; Phi Alpha Theta His Honor Society Mem; *office:* Lansdale Cath HS 7th & Lansdale Avenues Lansdale PA 19446

WOLPERT, DEBRA ANN (BETZ), Mathematics Teacher; *b:* Canton, OH; *m:* David Scott; *c:* Andrew, Melissa; *ed:* (BS) Math, Mt Union Coll 1973; Grad Work at Various Colls 1984-85; *cr:* Math/Phys Ed Teacher Jackson Memorial HS 1973-74; Math Teacher Louisville Jr HS 1974-; *ai:* Math Dept Chairperson; Dist Math, Dist Testing, N Cntrl Evaluation Steering, Various Building Comms; Mt Union Coll Dept Ed Advisory Cncl; Louisville Ed Assn, OEA, NEA 1974-; Oh Cncl Teachers Math 1977-; Washington Sch PTO 1981-; Finalist Stark Cty Teacher of Yr 1988; *office:* Louisville Jr HS 300 E Gorgas Louisville OH 44641

WOLSELEY, CARRIE HOFHERR, Substitute Teacher; *b:* Ft Wayne, IN; *m:* Paul Vincent; *c:* Ryan M., Kyle N.; *ed:* (BS) Phys Ed/Bio, Ball St Univ; (MS) Scndry Ed, IN Univ; IU-PU Extension Ft Wayne IN 1978-79; *cr:* Bio Teacher Caston Ed Center 1985-87; 8th Grade Earth Sci/Health/Substitute Teacher Crown Point Cmmty Schls 1988-89; Substitute Teacher Porter Cty Township Schls 1988-89; *ai:* Jr HS Vlybl, Asst Boys Var Track Coach; Sci Club; NSTA 1985-87; Four Seasons Homemakers Club 1988-89; Babysitting Coop VP 1987-; Salem United Meth Church (Choir Mem, Teacher) 1987-; *home:* 1557 Happy Valley Rd Crown Point IN 46307

WOLTJER, JOHN GERARD, History Teacher/Dept Chair; *b:* Fort Dix, NJ; *m:* Sonja Godeken-Woltjer; *ed:* (BA) Poly Sci/His, Gonzaga Univ 1983; Univ of WA, Stanford Univ, Princeton Univ; *cr:* Amer Government Teacher 1984-85, Advanced Placement Amer His Teacher 1984-, Dept Head 1986- Bellarmine Preparatory; *ai:* Political Sci Club Adv; Set Design & Construction for Drama; Encounter Crew Chief, Bus Driver; Impact Intervention Team; Wm Robertson Coe Fellowship Stanford Univ, Dewitt Wallace Woodrow Wilson Inst Princeton; OAH Convention Washington DC Presenter 1990; Monticello Stratford Hall Univ of VA Summer Teachers Inst; *office:* Bellarmine Preparatory Sch S 2300 Washington Tacoma WA 98405

WOLVERTON, CAROLYN CESTRA, English/Speech/Drama Teacher; *b:* Pittsburgh, PA; *m:* Raymond B.; *c:* Jennifer, Joanna; *ed:* (BEDd) Soc Stud, 1965, Eng, 1968 Indiana Univ of PA; Soc Stud Ed, Indiana Univ of PA; *cr:* Eng/Soc Stud Teacher Freeport Area Jr HS 1966-68; Soc Stud Teacher Bristol Township Sch Dist 1968-70; 5th Grade Teacher St Michaels 1985; Eng/Speech/Drama/Music Appreciation Teacher Villa Joseph Marie HS 1985-; *ai:* Drama Club; NCTE; Levittown Jaycettes (Pres 1975, Secy 1974), St Speak-Up Awd 1974; Cath Youth Organization (Cultural Adv 1984-, Dir 1 Act Play), 5 Yr Awd 1985; GSA Troop Leader 1982-86; *home:* 17 Border Rock Rd Levittown PA 19057

WOLVERTON, DEBORAH LEANN (COUCH), Art Instructor; *b:* Parsons, KS; *m:* Ronnie Gene; *ed:* (BFA) Art, Pittsburg St Univ 1980; *cr:* Eng Instr Parsons Mid Sch 1981-84;

Art Instr Parsons HS 1984-; *ai:* Fine Arts Dept Chairperson; KNEA 1981-; *office:* Parsons HS 3030 Morton Parsons KS 67357

WOMACK, GAIL WERNER, Choir Director; *b:* Corpus Christi, TX; *m:* Jerald Clay; *c:* Justin Lane; *ed:* (BMED) Vocal Music, Univ of N TX 1979; Show Choir Trng TX Womans Univ; *cr:* Math Teacher S Garland HS 1979-84; Math/Music Teacher Rockwall Ind Sch Dist 1984-; *ai:* Rock City Players Musical Theatre Troupe Grades 7th & 8th; Crescendo & Encore HS Show Choirs; Youth Against Cancer; TX Music Ed Assn; Amer Cancer Soc 1985-89; N TX Meth Ministers Spouses VP 1989-; Service Awd Chamber of Commerce Royse City Tx; *office:* Rockwall HS/Williams Mid Sch 1201 High School Dr Rockwall TX 75087

WOMACK, MONTE CHARLES, Agriculture Education Teacher; *b:* Sherman, TX; *m:* Reina Haworth; *c:* Brian, Brandon, Brent; *ed:* (BA) Ag Ed, E OK St Coll 1981; (BS) Ag Ed, 1983, (MC) Ag Ed, 1985 OK St Univ; *cr:* Ag Ed Teacher Weleetka Public Schls 1983-; *ai:* Co-Fellowship of Chrstn Athletes; OK Voc Ag Teachers Assn St VP 1988, Outstanding Young Teacher 1988; Weleetka Classroom Teachers Assn, NEA, OK Ed Assn Cty Teacher of Yr 1987; Mens Chrstn Fellowship (Pres, VP) 1989-; Weleetka Chamber of Commerce Outstanding Service Awd 1986; Cmmty Pride Day Celebration Chm 1985-; FFA (Alumni Adv, Young Farmer Adv, St VP 1986-); Weleetka Sch Yrbk Dedication 1987.

WOMBLE, EVELYN CROUCH, Gifted Education Facilitator; *b:* Brady, TX; *m:* Harold L.; *c:* David, Ross, Glen, Todd; *ed:* (BA) Speech/Drama, N TX St Univ 1954; (MED) Supervision/Gifted, TX Womans Univ 1979; *cr:* Speech Therapist Teacher Gladewater Ind Sch Dist 1954-56; Elem Classroom Teacher Lubbock Ind Sch Dist 1956-58; Elem Classroom Teacher 1979-80, Teacher of Gifted Ed 1980- Carrollton-Farmers Branch Ind Sch Dist; *ai:* Odyssey of Mind Dist & Regional Dir; Future Problem Solving Trng; TX Assn for Gifted & Talented 1980-; Carrollton-Farmers Branch Talented & Gifted Assn Faculty Rep 1984, 1989, 1990; *home:* 2709 Bay Meadows Cir Dallas TX 75234

WOMMACK, VICTORIA ANNE, Vocational Agriculture Teacher; *b:* Inglewood, CA; *ed:* (BS) Animal Sci, CA Poly Pomona 1980; *cr:* Ag Teacher Calipatria HS 1982-89, Holtville HS 1989-; *ai:* FFA Adv; CA Ag Teachers Assn Section Secy 1984; CATA Section (Pres, Mem) 1985; Natl Voc Ag Teachers Assn; Imperial Valley Barbara Worth Brigidettes; *home:* PO Box 517 Imperial CA 92251

WONDERLING, KATHLEEN MC KILLIP, Computer/ Mathematics Teacher; *b:* Detroit, MI; *m:* Lawrence; *c:* Sarah, Legend, Leah; *ed:* (BS) Math, Siena Heights Coll 1981; (MA) Ed, N KY Univ 1990; *cr:* Math Teacher St Gertrude Acad 1983-84; Cmptr Sci/Math Teacher Dixie Heights HS 1984-; *ai:* Cmptr Club Adv; NCTM, NEA, KY Ed Assn 1989-; *home:* 371 Merravay Florence KY 41042

WONG, ANTHONY MARTIN, Science Instructor; *b:* Sacramento, CA; *m:* April Esther; *ed:* (BA) Genetics, Univ of CA Berkeley 1969; *cr:* Sci Instr Vacaville HS 1971-74, Will C Wood Jr HS 1974-89, Will C Wood HS 1989-; *ai:* Bsktbl Coach-Frosh Boys & Jr Var Girls; Team Adv-Sci Issues & Bioethics Symposium; Intramural Bsktl coord; Sci Fair Judge; Instr for Gifted & Talented Prgm; Greenpeace 1987-; Nature Conservancy 1989-; *office:* Will C Wood H S 998 Marshall Rd Vacaville CA 95687

WONG, FRANCES J. C., English Teacher Jr HS Coord; *b:* Honolulu, HI; *m:* Jack; *c:* Anne, Aaron; *ed:* (BA) Eng, 1973, (BED) Scndry Eng, 1973, (MA) Eng Lit, 1975 Univ of HI; HI Writing Proj Fellow 1984; Teacher Consultant; *cr:* Jr HS Teacher St Theresa Sch 1974-81; Maryknoll Schls 1981-; Jr HS Coord Maryknoll Schls 1989-; *ai:* Maryknoll Ink Bottle-Editor; Quiz Bowl Coach; Stu Cncl Adv 1986-89; Phi Beta Kappa 1973-; Phi Kappa Phi 1973-; *office:* Maryknoll Grade Sch 1722 Dole St Honolulu HI 96822

WONG, JANICE SASAKI, Mathematics Teacher; *b:* Sacramento, CA; *m:* Gary Gene; *c:* Darren, Brian; *ed:* (AA) Math, Sacramento City Coll 1974; (AB) Math, 1976, Teaching Cred Single Subject, 1977 Univ CA Berkeley; (MA) Ed/Curr/ Instruction CSUS 1988; *cr:* Stu Teacher Oakland Tech HS 1976-77, Mc Chesney Jr HS 1976-77; Math Teacher El Dorado HS 1977-79, El Camino HS 1979-; *ai:* CA Schlsp Fed & NHS Adv; Academic Decathlon Team Math Coach; Textbook Selection Comm Mem; CTA, NEA 1979-; *office:* El Camino Fundamental HS 4300 El Camino Ave Sacramento CA 95821

WONG, SANDRA, Math Department Chairperson; *b:* The Dalles, OR; *ed:* (BS) Sci Ed, OR St Univ 1977; (MST) Math, Portland St Univ 1984; *cr:* Math Teacher/Dept Head Wasco Cty Union HS 1977-; *ai:* Stu League & Academic Awds Adv; Task Force Comm; Kappa Delta Pi 1976-; NCTM 1977-; OR Cncl Teachers of Math 1980-; NEA, OR Ed Assn 1977-; Wasco Cty Union HS Ed Assn (Treas 1986-87, Secy/Treas 1987-) 1977-; *office:* Wasco Cty Union HS P O Box 347 Maupin OR 97037

WONG, STANLEY, Mathematics Teacher; *b:* Los Angeles, CA; *m:* Lina Ada Leeman; *c:* Bunny, Rebecca, Maryann, Cosette, Luther; *ed:* (BA) Math, Univ of S CA 1965; (AA) General Bus, Coll of The Desert 1980; (BA) Theology, The Way Coll of Biblical Research 1987; *cr:* Math Teacher 1966-68, Math Teacher/ Athletic Dir 1970-78 Huntington Park HS; Math Teacher Wilson Mid Sch 1978-79, Del Norte HS 1986-; *office:* Del Norte HS 5323 Montgomery NE Albuquerque NM 87109

WONG, VICTOR ALEXANDER, Vocal Music Teacher; *b:* Denver, CO; *c:* Joshua, Gregory; *ed:* (BA) Music, Dartmouth Coll 1967; (MMUS) Choral Conducting, Univ of CO 1970; (MED) Scndry Ed, Univ of Cntrl OK 1978; Choral Conducting & Voice, Univ of OK; *cr:* Vocal Music Teacher Harrah Mid Sch & HS 1978-80; Grad Asst Univ of OK 1980-81; Vocal Music Teacher Putnam City Schls 1981-; *ai:* Stu Cncl Spon; ACDA Jr HS Rep; OCDA (Jr HS Rep, Honor Choir 1987); OMAA, OMEA; OSSAA Achievement Awd 1979; Oklahoma City Bahais Mem; LSA; Outstanding Choir Tri St Festival 1986-89; *office:* Putnam City Cntrl Jr HS 4020 N Grove St Oklahoma City OK 73122

WOOD, ALICE NICHOLS, Kindergarten Teacher; *b:* Pawhuska, OK; *m:* Bob; *c:* Tony; *ed:* (BS) Elem Ed, OK St Univ 1978; *cr:* 5th/6th Grade Teacher Kendrick Sch 1982; 5th Grade Teacher 1982-86, Kndgtn Teacher 1986- Stroud Elem Sch; *ai:* Amer Assn of Univ Women (Cmmty Rep 1987-, Membership VP 1989-); *home:* 523 N 2nd Ave Stroud OK 74079

WOOD, BETTE HIATT, Guidance Counselor; *b:* Ullin, IL; *c:* Jeffrey A., Julie A.; *ed:* (BA) Art, 1970, (MSED) Guidance/ Counseling, 1975 Eastern IL Univ; Cmptr Sci; Sign Lang; *cr:* Art Teacher Tolono HS 1970-75; Dean of Women Liberty Baptist Univ 1977-80; Guidance Cnslr Momence Jr HS 1980-; *home:* 495 Briarcliff Ln #5 Bourbonnais IL 60914

WOOD, BONNIE LOU (TULLAR), Phys Ed/Health Ed Teacher; *b:* Durand, MI; *m:* Richard Dean; *c:* Chad W., Jason E.; *ed:* (BSED) Health/Phys Ed/Recreation, Cntrl MI Univ 1970-71; Human Sexuality Ed; Quest Skills for Adolescence; MI Health Model 7th-8th; *cr:* K-6th Grade Phys/Health Ed Teacher Monroe Public Schls 1970-71, New Lothrop Public Schls 1971-75; Home Ec/Home Family Living Ed/Health Ed Teacher 1980-84, 7th-12th Grade Phys Ed/Health Teacher New Lothrop Public Schls 1975-; *ai:* Jr HS Stus Against Drugs & Drinking Adv; Health Curr Dir; Clinical Peer Coaching Supv; Cty Wide Project Grad Projects; New Lothrop Ed Assn (Pres, Building Rep); Developed Girls Athletics & Health Ed Prgms for New Lothrop & Recognition Honors; *office:* New Lothrop Public Sch 9285 Easton Rd New Lothrop MI 48460

WOOD, CASSIE COGGINS, History-Government Teacher; *b:* Casa Grande, AZ; *m:* Donald G.; *c:* Daryl R., Carri Wood Moore; *ed:* (BA) His, OK Coll of Liberal Arts 1967; (MS) Ed, Du Quesne Univ 1973; Scndry Prin Cert, Du Quesne Univ 1973; *cr:* S S Teacher Blanchard Schls 1967-88, St Ignatius 1968-69, Sharpsburg Mid Sch 1969-79, O Hara Jr HS 1970-76, Blanchard Sch 1976-; *ai:* Spon Gifted/Talented Prgm, Beta Club, Jr HS Academic Team, HS Academic Team, Citizens Bee; Secy, Treas, Alumni Secy Assn of Classroom Teachers; Assn of Classroom Teachers 1976 Teacher of Yr 1983; ACT (Secy, Treas) 1989-; Blanchard Alumni Secy 1983-89; *office:* Blanchard H S Box 2620 400 N Harrison St Blanchard OK 73010

WOOD, CLAUDIA JANE, HS Social Studies Teacher; *b:* Scotia, CA; *ed:* (BA) Soc Stud, Humboldt St Univ 1956; (MA) US His, Sonoma St Univ 1974; *cr:* Eng Teacher Washington HS 1957-59; Eng/Soc Stud Teacher Franklin Jr HS 1959-64; Jr HS Eng Teacher Munich Amer Sch #2 1964-65; Soc Stud Teacher Franklin Jr HS 1965-69, Pt Wheel Jr HS 1969-71, Kubaski HS 1971-75, Bad Krezuznach HS 1975-; *ai:* Sch Advisory Cncl; Sr Class Adv; Extra Curricular Eligibility Comm; CA Teachers Assn 1956-69; Overseas Teachers Assn 1969-; NEA Life Mem 1956-; Phi Delta Kappa 1980-; NCSS 1973-; BSA Merit Badge Adv 1990.

WOOD, CYNTHIA MUTZ, 1st Grade Teacher; *b:* San Antonio, TX; *m:* Theo Noel Jr.; *c:* T. Noel III, Tamarah C.; *ed:* (BA) Elem Ed, St Marys Univ 1976; (MS) Ed, Tarleton St Univ 1986; Early Chldhd Cert, Howard Payne Univ 1984; Mid-Management Cert Ed, Tarleton Univ 1987; *cr:* K-6th Grade Math Teacher Southside Ind Sch Dist 1976-77; K-2nd Grade Elem Teacher 1977-81, K-12th Grade Migrant Math Teacher 1981-83, K-1st Grade Elem Teacher 1983- Richland Springs Ind Sch Dist; *ai:* Effective Schls, Gifted/Talented, Track Awds & Accounting Comm; Bsbl & Bsktbl Coach for Youth; Jr HS Chrldr Spon; Track, Bsktbl Jr HS & HS Bookkeeper; Richland Springs Parent-Teacher Club Pres 1989-; St Teacher Assn 1976-83; Migrant Teachers of TX 1981-83; Kndgtn Teachers of TX Area Dir 1985-86; Assn of Cmmty Small Schls 1977-81; PTA Carnival Coronation Chairperson; Cty Water Cncl Ed Spokeperson 1985-; TX Rural Womens Electric Assn (Chairperson 1988-) 1982-; Cty 4-H Leadership Club, Cty Water Cooperative 1987-; Cty Property Owners Assn 1976-; Parent & Teacher Club (Carnival Fundraiser Chairperson, Treas, Secy); Vacation Baptist Bible Sch Teacher; Sch-Cmmty Relationships Dev Article; Research Proposal in Educl Leadership Tarleton St Univ Ed Dept; *home:* PO Box I Richland Springs TX 76871

WOOD, DENISE, 9th/10th Grade Teacher; *b:* Abington, PA; *m:* Keith; *c:* Justin, Jason, Lauren; *ed:* (BS) Ed, Millersville 1974; (MAEQ) Ed, Temple & Penn St; *cr:* Teacher Sandy Run Elem Sch 1974-76, Sandy Run Mid Sch 1976-86, Upper Dublin HS 1987-; *office:* Upper Dublin HS Ft Washington & Loch Alsh Ave Fort Washington PA 19034

WOOD, DENNIS R., Sixth Grade Teacher; *b:* Jonestown, PA; *m:* Linda G. Gilbert; *c:* Emily S.; *ed:* (BS) Elem Ed, 1974, (MED) Elem Ed, 1977 Millersville Univ; *cr:* Fiscal/Account Clerk Federal Government 1964-69; Personnel Rep Vesely Company 1970-71; Elem Teacher Northern Lebanon Sch Dist 1974-; *ai:* Sch Intramurals; PSEA, NEA Building Rep 1984-; Teacher Honor Society; Jonestown Amer Legion Commander 1967-68, 1990; St Johns UCC of Jonestown Consistory 1986-; Jonestown Memorial Home Assn (Secy 1984-, Pres 1983-84); *home:* 10 Eve Ave Lebanon PA 17042

WOOD, DIANE ALLEN, 8th Grade Lang Art Teacher; *b:* Utica, NY; *m:* Frank Parker; *c:* James, Jeffrey, Alison; *ed:* (BS) Eng Ed, Hartwick Coll 1970; (MA) Ed, Canisus Coll 1983; *cr:* 10th-12th Eng Grade Teacher 1970-73, 7th-12th Grade Substitute Teacher 1974-80, 7th Grade Eng Teacher 1980-81, 8th Grade Eng/Lang Art Teacher 1982- Pioneer Cntrl Sch; *ai:* Odyssey of the Mind Coach; Jr Natl Honor Society & Literary Magazine Adv; Wkshp Coord Facilitator for Scndry Teachers 1990; Arcade Free Lib (Pres, Secy, Trustee of Bd Pres) 1976-; Arcade Youth Ftbl Assn (Secy Bd of Dir) 1989-; UCC Church (Sunday Sch Teacher, Supt of Sch, Diaconate Mem 1988-) 1976-78; *office:* Pioneer Mid Sch Old Olean Rd Yorkshire NY 14173

WOOD, DOLORES ANN, 8th Grade Teacher; *b:* Bath, NY; *c:* Jeffrey; *ed:* (AS) Liberal Arts, Corning Comm Coll 1976; (BS) Elem Ed, Suffolk Univ 1979; Psych of Gifted, Elmira Coll 1979-80; Human Resources, Wilmington Coll; *cr:* Teacher of Gifted & Talented Addison Cntrl Sch 1979-80; Rdng/Eng Teacher Bayou Le Batre-Alba HS 1982; 6th-7th Grade Teacher 1983-85, 8th Grade Teacher 1985- St Mary Regional Sch; *ai:* Co-Supvr After Sch Latchkey Prgm; Co-Dir Summer Sch; Peer Adv Camden Diocese; Assn of Univ Women 1979-82; Cath Assn of Educators (Teacher, Assoc) 1984-; Diocese of Camden Peer Evaluator 1987-88, Cert of Outstanding Service 1987-88; Historical Society Co-Founder 1975-79; Village Planning Bd 1975-79; Addison Assn for Gifted/Talented Facilitator 1978-80; Religious Stud Grant; NY St Merit Awd; Publications Prgm Gifted & Talented Cmptr Sci; Bring Art to Schls Grant 1979; *office:* St Mary Regional Sch 31 Oak St Salem NJ 08079

WOOD, ELIZABETH GUNHUS, 3rd Grade Teacher; *b:* Faribault, MN; *m:* Robert W.; *c:* William; *ed:* (BA) El Ed/Music Ed, Winona St Univ 1966; (MM) Applied Voice, Univ of SD 1971; Univ of SD; *cr:* 2nd Grade Teacher Missoula MT Schls 1966-68; Music Teacher Vermillion SD Schls 1968-71; Vocal Music Teacher Univ of SD 1971-73; Kndgrtn Teacher St Agnes Sch 1974-76; Kndgrtn Teacher 1976-77; Vocal Music Teacher 1977-79; 3rd Grade Teacher 1979 Vermillion Schls; *ai:* ETA Chapter Service; Chairperson of Research Comm; Co-Chairperson of Music Comm for St Conv in Vermillion; Presentations to Chapter; Mem of Publications & Publicity Comm Delta Kappa Gamma; Natl Cncl Soc Stud SD Bd of Dir 8 Yrs; NEA; SD Assn Delta Kappa Gamma Society; ETA Chapter; Modernization Process in India Co-Editor Book Publ By Univ of Poona India 1975; You Are a Model Every Minute of Every Day Instr 1976; a Group Projects Abroad Pgrm in India for Amer Educators the Delta Kappa Gamma Bulletin 1977; Perceptions of India Held By Elem Sch Chldrn India 1980; Reflections of India from Amer Educators 1981; *home:* RR 1 Box 166 Vermillion SD 57069

WOOD, FRANCES M., Language Department Chair; *b:* New York, NY; *c:* Craig, Cori; *ed:* (BA) His, Univ of MA Amherst 1954; (MA) Eng, Wesleyan Univ 1959; (MED) Admin, Univ of ME 1976; *cr:* Teacher Amherst Jr HS 1954-59, Madera HS 1959-60, Bellmore HS 1960-61, Middletown Jr HS 1961-62, Saco Mid Sch 1976-; *ai:* Lang Art Dept Chairperson; Saco Teachers Assn, MTA, NEA, NCTE, Natl Assn for Curr Dev; *office:* Saco Mid Sch Buxton Rd Saco ME 04072

WOOD, HENRY ALBERT, JR., Chemistry/Physics Teacher; *b:* Tylertown, MS; *m:* Alice Dillon; *c:* Henry A. III, Jill Duffee; *ed:* (BS) Sci Ed, 1958, (ME) Sch Admin, 1962 Univ of S MS; Grad Work; *cr:* Sci Teacher St Gabriel HS 1958-74; Asst Prin St Gabriel Elem 1974-77; Chem/Physics Teacher Tylertown HS 1978-; *ai:* BSA Spon; Bsktbl Coach; NEA, Sci Teachers of MS; STAR Teacher; NSF Grants; *office:* Tylertown HS Rt 4 Box 257 Tylertown MS 39667

WOOD, JAMES WALKER, Social Studies Teacher; *b:* Choctaw, MS; *m:* Janis Elizabeth Worsham; *c:* James B., Sara E.; *ed:* (BS) Phys Ed & Soc Stud, MS St Univ 1964; *cr:* Teacher/ Coach Tupelo City Sch 1964-69; Corinth City Sch 1969-70; Partner Worsha Bros Cont Coll 1970-88; Teacher/Coach Burnsville HS 1988-; *ai:* Spon Sr Class; Spon Stu Cncl; Spon Fellowship of Christian Athletes; MS Assn of Coaches 1064-70/ 1988-89; Masonic Lodge Master 1980-81/1986-87; Boy Scouts of Amer Scout Master 1984-85; Explorer Leader 1965-66/1969-70; *home:* 1407 Pine Road Corinth MS 38834

WOOD, JAQUELYN E., Mathematics Teacher; *b:* Denver, CO; *m:* Howard E.; *c:* Michelle; *ed:* (BA) Math, Drake Univ 1966; (MS) Spec Ed of Gifted, Southern IL Univ 1981; Grad Courses in Ed; *cr:* Math Teacher Franklin Jr HS 1966; Math Teacher/Gifted Prgm Coord Fairfield Cmmty HS 1966-; *ai:* Math Club Spon; ICTM Math Team Coach; Frosh Class Spon; NCTM; IL Cncl Teachers of Math; South Cntrl IL Teachers of Math Pres 1988-89; Delta Kappa Gamma VP 1976- Schlsp 1980; Phi Kapp Phi; Lions Club Star Teacher of Yr 1968/1974/1984/1987-; IL Governors Master Teacher 1984; IL Cncl Teachers of Math Delegate to China 1987; Comm Chm Project Cosmic; *office:* Fairfield Community H S 300 W King St Fairfield IL 62837

WOOD, JEAN PETROSUS, English Teacher; *b:* Gary, IN; *m:* Richard Paul Sr.; *c:* Richard P. Jr.; *ed:* (BS) Eng/Ed, IN Univ 1970; (MA) Eng, Purdue Univ 1974; Grad Stud, Sam Houston St Univ; *cr:* Eng Teacher Lew Wallace HS 1970-78; Frosh Composition Instr Valparaiso Univ 1984-85; Eng Teacher Willis HS 1985-; *ai:* Academic Schlsp & Instructional Focus Comm; NHS Cncl; Academic Decathlon Coach; NCTE; *office:* Willis HS 204 W Rogers St Willis TX 77378

WOOD, JOSEPH ALLEN, English Teacher/Dept Head; *b:* Harrison, MI; *m:* Susan Jean Nee De Ryke; *c:* Jonas, Kara; *ed:* (BA) Eng, 1969, (MA) Scndry Eng, 1974 MI St Univ; TAC Level I Track Field Cert; *cr:* Instr MI St Univ 1974; Teacher Potterville Public Schls 1969-; *ai:* Cross Cntry Coach; Jr Var Bsktbl Coach; Teacher to Parent News Ed; MI Cncl Teachers of Eng 1974-; MI Interscholastic Track Coaches Assn VP 1980, Class D Boys Track Coach of Yr 1984; MI Ed Assn 1969-, E Dale Kennedy Public Relations 1972; NEA, MI Ed Assn; Teacher of Yr; Lansing Chamber of Commerce Teaching Excl Awd 1990; *office:* Potterville HS 420 N High St Potterville MI 48876

WOOD, JUDITH CROFT, Business Teacher; *b:* Eccles, WV; *m:* Albert Thurman Jr.; *c:* Teresa A., Albert T. III; *ed:* (BS) Ed/Bus, Concord Coll 1965; *cr:* Bus Teacher Harrington HS 1965-69, Lake Forest HS 1970-; *ai:* Bookstore Adv; Bus Prof of Amer 1980-; DE Bus Educators Assn 1985-; *office:* Lake Forest HS R D 1 Box 847 Felton DE 19943

WOOD, JULIA WOODS, Gifted English Teacher; *b:* Kuling, China; *c:* Elizabeth L. Clore, Catherine E. Clore, Julia Woods Clore; *ed:* (BA) Eng, 1981, (MA) Eng, 1989 Univ of NC Charlotte; Grad Work Academically Gifted; *cr:* ISS Coord King Mountain HS 1983; Academically Gifted Eng/Soc Stud Teacher King Mountain Jr HS 1983-; *ai:* Drama & Pep Club; Liason Rep; Eng Dept Chm; NCAE VP 1987-88; ADK 1990; NCETA 1984-; Kings Mountain Little Theatre VP 1989-; Teacher of Yr 1988-89; *office:* Kings Mountain Jr HS 500 Phifer Rd Kings Mountain NC 28086

WOOD, KATHERINE A., Math Dept Chairman; *b:* Lansing, MI; *ed:* (BS) Math, MSU 1976; (MAT) Math, CMU 1988; *cr:* Dept Chm Dansville HS 1976-; Instr Lansing Comm Coll 1984-; *office:* Dansville H S 1264 Adams St Dansville MI 48819

WOOD, KATHERYN JANE, Fourth Grade Teacher; *b:* Madill, OK; *m:* Danny R.; *c:* Ann Wood Miller, Gary W.; *ed:* (BS) Elem Ed, Cameron Univ 1980; (MED) Elem Admin, Univ of OK 1988; *cr:* Teacher Marlow Elem Sch 1980-; *ai:* NEA, OK Ed Assn Delegate 1979-; Marlow Assn of Classroom Teachers (Building Rep 1980-, PMP Rep 1986-), Nom Teacher of Yr 1990; Young Homemakers Organization Pres 1973; Marlow Youth Cncl VP 1985-89; Marlow Booster Club (Secy, Treas 1986-87, Pres 1987-88); Univ of OK Alumni Assn 1988-; *home:* 912 Scott Marlow OK 73055

WOOD, LEO MILTON, Chemistry Instructor; *b:* Westwood, CA; *m:* Teverly Jan Hermann; *c:* Tonya D., Cory A., Tarina J., Tiffany L., Daniel K. (dec); *ed:* (BA) Music/Bio, 1962, (MA) Music/Sci, 1968 AZ St Univ; NSF Sci Teacher Trng, Mid TN St Univ 1970-71; Chem Teacher Trng NSF, AZ Bd of Regents Northern AZ Univ 1989-; *cr:* Music/Bio/Chem/Math Salome HS 1963-64; Music Teacher 1964-70, Bio/Chem Teacher 1970-75, Honors & Regular Chem Teacher 1975- Tempe HS; *ai:* Sci Club Spon; Curr Comm; Outcome Based Ed Mastery Learning Comm; Optimalearning Trainer & Presenter; NSTA; AZ Sci Teachers Assn; AZ Chem Teachers Assn Secy/Treas 1989-; AZ Ed Assn; NEA; Church of Jesus Christ of LattErday Saints-Morman Elder, Choir, & Sunday Sch Teacher; BSA Scout Leader; Tempe HS Dist Teacher of Excl Awd 1984-85; Diablos Awd of Excl 1984-85; Chem Course Guidelines & Outcomes; Chem Laboratory & Study Guide; Chem Songs Booklet & Tape; *office:* Tempe H S 1730 S Mill Ave Tempe AZ 85281

WOOD, LOUISE, 4th Grade Teacher; *b:* Lafollette, TN; *m:* John; *ed:* (BA) Elem Ed, Lincoln Memorial Univ 1968; Univ of TN; *cr:* Classroom Teacher Pinecrest Elem 1958-74; 4th Grade Teacher Jacksboro Elem 1975-; *ai:* Active 4-H Leader; Asst Youth Dir, Pianist Cumberland View Bapt Church; Campbell Cty Ed Assn; East TN Educl Assn; TN Educl Assn; TN Educl Assn; NEA; Awarded Outstanding Leader 4-H 1987; *home:* Rt 2 Jacksboro TN 37757

WOOD, LU ANN, Religion Teacher; *b:* Minneapolis, MN; *m:* David C.; *c:* Rachel A.; *ed:* (BA) Theology/Ed, Coll of St Benedict 1981; Death Ed, Grief Facilitator Trng; Cooperative & Mastery Learning, Outcome Based Ed, Gifted Stu Wkshps; *cr:* Religion Teacher Hill-Murray HS 1981-; *ai:* Calendar Planning Comm; Coalition for Terminal Care 1986-; Adopted Families of Amer 1987-; Pregnancy & Infant Loss Center 1986-; Grief Group Facilitator; Chm Spring Conference for Coalition for Terminal Care 1988; Speaking Engagements on Death/Grief Ed; *office:* Hill-Murray HS 2625 E Larpenteur Ave Saint Paul MN 55109

WOOD, LYNDA SUSAN, 9th Grade Algebra Teacher; *b:* Wichita Falls, TX; *m:* Edwin J. II;; *c:* Edwin III; *ed:* (BA) Math, Univ of TX Arlington 1984; Marilyn Burns Math Institute 1989; *cr:* Teacher Workman Jr HS 1984-; *ai:* Stu Cncl Spon 1988-; Textbook Comm 1989-; Project Success Co-Founder 1988-; Assn TX Prof Educators 1984-; *office:* Workman Jr H S 701 Arbrook Arlington TX 76014

WOOD, MARYLOU DONOVAN, English Teacher; *b:* Cincinnati, OH; *m:* Paul W.; *c:* Paul Jr., Suzanne M. Bruckner, Douglas L., Rebecca C.; *ed:* (BA) Eng, Coll of Mt St Joseph 1959; Xavier Univ, St Bonaventure Univ; *cr:* Eng/Journalism Teacher Seton HS 1959-62; Substitute Teacher Portville Cntrl Jr Sr HS 1972-; *ai:* Jr Class Adv; United Nations Scholastic Challenge Team; Eng Dept Coord; Faculty Advisory Bd Mem; PCS NHS Bd; WHDL Originator & Moderater; NCTE 1987-; Phi Delta Kappa 1983; St Bonaventure Univ Campus Parish 1973-; Exch Teacher Strassbourg France 1991; *office:* Portville Cntrl Sch Elm St Portville NY 14770

WOOD, PEARL BOTTOMS, Teacher; *b:* Oakland City, IN; *m:* James R.; *c:* James Jr., Gwendolyn Edwards, Mark; *ed:* (BS) Elem Ed, 1965, (MED) Ed, 1975; Admin, 1980 Murray St Univ; *cr:* Teacher Reidland Mid Sch 1965-; *ai:* Coach Mathcounts, Alegebra Team; Resource Teacher; KLCTM Pres 1990; NCTM 1972-; MCEA (Secy, Treas) 1965-; KEA, NEA 1965-; Grant from Paducah Chamber of Commerce Project Designed Remedial Math Stu; *office:* Reidland Mid Sch 5349 Reidland Rd Paducah KY 42003

WOOD, PHYLLIS PARK, 7th-8th Grade English Teacher; *b:* Mayfield, KY; *m:* Randy D.; *c:* Jenny, Amy; *ed:* (BS) His/Eng, 1971, (MA) Scndry Ed, 1974, Scndry Ed, 1984 Murray St Univ; *cr:* Eng Teacher Benton Schls 1972-; *ai:* Academic Team; KEA, NEA; MCEA Rep; *home:* Rt 10 Box 52 Benton KY 42025

WOOD, REBECCA ADELLE, Mathematics Dept Chair; *b:* Navasota, TX; *ed:* (AA) Math, Temple Jr Coll 1970; (AB) Math, Asbury Coll 1972; (MS) Math Ed, Univ of KY 1976; *cr:* Math Teacher 1975-, Math Dept Chairperson 1986- Tates Creek Sr HS; *ai:* NHS; Faculty, Sr Awds Faculty, Fayette Cty Staffing Transfer, Tates Creek Sr Magnet Sch Proposal Comm; Sch Improvement Sub Comm; NCTM, KY Cncl Teachers of Math, Lexington Cncl Teachers of Math; Fellowship of Chrstn Athletes St Bd 1983-; Wilmore United Meth Church (Admin Bd 1985-, Staff Relations Comm 1989-); Miami of OH Outstanding HS Teacher 1989-; Fayette Cty Public Schls Outstanding Teacher 1989-; MA Inst of Technology Recognition Being Influential in Stu Dev 1988; Univ of KY Recognition Outstanding Achievement in Teaching 1988; KY Cncl Teachers Recognition for Excl Teaching Math 1988; *office:* Tates Creek Sr HS Centre Pkwy Lexington KY 40517

WOOD, REBECCA JOLLY, Food Service Teacher; *b:* Houston, TX; *m:* Dennis Dale; *ed:* (AA) Home Ec, E Cntrl Jr Coll 1974; (BS) Home Ec, 1976, (MSE Home Ec, 1977 MS Univ for Women; Post Grad Work & Occupational Ed License in Food Service & Child Care, Univ of S MS; *cr:* Teacher Moss Point HS 1978-; *ai:* Home Ec Related Occupations Club & Jr Class Spon; Phi Delta Kappa Research Chm 1987-; MS Univ for Women Alumni Assn Schslp 1979-; AVA 1979-; MS Voc Assn, Amer Home Ec Assn, NEA, MS Assn of Educators; Moss Point Assn of Educators (Secy 1979, VP 1970, 1988, Pres 1981) Outstanding Service Awd 1987; ASCD; Jr Womens Club (Schslsp Chm 1979-88, VP 1983); Mobile Symphonic Pops Band & Ballet Patron; MS Ec Cncl Schlsp & Published Material; Home Ec Dept Head 1980-86; Elected St VP Stu Cncl Adv; Moss Point Teaccher of Yr 1986; St Comm Mem Wrote MS Curr Guide for Enrichment Food Class 1987; Food Asst S Living Cooking Sch 1990; Whos Who in Ed 1983-84; *office:* Moss Point HS 4924 Church St Moss Point MS 39563

WOOD, ROD A., Social Studies Teacher; *b:* Alma, CO; *c:* Robin, Christy, Shannon; *ed:* (BA) Bio/HPER, 1964, (MA) HPER, 1971 Adams St; Admin, Western St 1987; Human Ecology, Environmental Bio, Emporia St 1970; Earth Sci, KS St Univ 1967; *cr:* Teacher/Coach Loveland HS 1967-72; Private Bus Canon City & Cortez Cty 1972-80; Scndry Teacher Walsenburg HS 1980-81, Gunnison HS 1981-; *ai:* NHS Spon; Knowledge Bowl; Ftbl, Cross Cntry, Girls Bsktbl Coach; Bsbl & Summer Recreation Prgm; Supt & Teacher Advisory Comm; Dept Chairperson; GCEA, CEA, NEA 1980-; BPOE 1963-; Natl Defense Grants Summer 1967, 1970; Grad Asst.

WOOD, SANDRA LEE, Third Grade Teacher; *b:* Pontiac, MI; *ed:* (AAS) Liberal Arts, Monticello Coll 1970; (BS) Elem Ed, 1972; (MS) Ed, 1978 St Bonaventure Univ; *cr:* 3rd Grade Teacher 1972-76; 5th Grade Teacher 1976-78; 3rd Grade Teacher 1978- Scio Central Sch; *ai:* Scio Teachers Assn (Sec) 1980-82; Allegany Cty Teachers Assn Golden Apple Awd 1985; (VP 1985-86; Pres 1986-); Kanakadea Rdng Cncl 1972-; *home:* 21 Coats St Wellsville NY 14895

WOOD, VIRGINIA REED, Chemistry/Physics Teacher; *b:* Petoskey, MI; *w:* Frederick (dec); *c:* Frederick; *ed:* (BS) Chem, Ferris St Univ 1957; Chem, Northern MI Univ; Physics, Univ WI; Oceanography, Univ of HI; *cr:* Sci/Math Teacher Reese HS 1957-59; Chem/Phys Teacher Richmond 1959-63; Sci Teacher Shelby Jr HS 1963-64; Chem/Physics Teacher Richmond HS 1964-; *ai:* Sr Class Adv; Sci Olympiad Coach; NSTA; MI Sci Teachers Assn SecY 1961-70; NEA; MEA; Richmond Ed Assn Secy 1984-; Alpha Delta Kappa Pres 1968-70; NSF Grant Chem 1961; NSF Grant Project Physics 1968; Outstanding Teacher Awd 1987; *home:* 70109 Karen Richmond MI 48062

WOOD, WENDY L., English Teacher; *b:* N Tonawanda, NY; *c:* Christopher L.; *ed:* (BS) Ed Summa Cum Laude, 1972, (MS) Ed/Eng, 1974 SUCNY Buffalo; MS Counseling, St Bonaventure Univ 1991; *cr:* Eng Teacher Pioneer Cntrl HS 1978-; *ai:* NHS, Class, Newspaper, Literary Club Adv; Peer Coaching Comm; Amer Assn for Counseling & Dev, Kappa Delta Pi, Prof Ski Instrs of America; Teacher of Yr Awd 1988; Teacher of Month Awd 1989.

WOOD, WILFORD ROBERT, Science Teacher; *b:* Rio Hondo, TX; *m:* Marie Mercedes Gutierrez; *c:* Jennifer L., Lesley A.; *ed:* (BS) Bio, 1969, (MS) Elem Ed, 1971 TX A&I Univ; (MS) Counseling, Pan Amer Univ 1978; *cr:* Sci Teacher Pharr-San Juan-Alamo Ind Sch Dist 1971-; *ai:* Sr Class Spon; Rio Grande Valley Sci Assn 1989-; TSTA Faculty Rep 1976; *office:* Pharr-San Juan-Alamo HS 1229 South I Rd Pharr TX 78577

WOOD, WILLIAM BOYD, Social Studies Teacher; *b:* Ackerman, MS; *m:* Peggy Wade; *c:* Valarie, Mary A.; *ed:* (BS) Scndry Ed, 1971, (MED) Scndry Ed, 1974, Ed Specialist Scndry Ed, 1985 MS St Univ; Courses in Cnslr Ed & Sch Admin; *cr:* Teacher/Coach Lizana Sch 1971-73, Orange Grove Sch 1973-76; Asst Prin 1976-78, Teacher/Coach 1978-79 Orange Grove Sch; Teacher Ackerman HS 1979-; *ai:* Stu Government Assn & Our Amer Heritage Competition Spon; MS Prof Educators 1985-l MS Cncl for Soc Stud 1984-; Admin Dev Task Force 1987-; Sch Cmmty Guidance Comm 1989-; *home:* Rt 1 Box 99-A Ackerman MS 39735

WOODALL, AUBRIETTA NEWTON, 7th/8th Grade Lang Art Teacher; *b:* Evansville, IN; *m:* Gary Howard; *c:* David, Alissa; *ed:* (BA) Fr, 1970, (MS) Ed, 1980 W KY Univ; *cr:* Teacher Auburn Mid Sch 1973-; *ai:* Academic Coach; Beta Spon; Guidance, In-Service, Gifted Comm; KEA, NEA 1973-; *home:* 619 Mc Reynolds Rd Quality KY 42268

WOODALL, DREW DAVID, Counselor; *b:* Spokane, WA; *m:* Monica Claire Hellar; *c:* Emily N., Asha E.; *ed:* (BA) Tutorial Writing, Univ of CA Santa Barbara 1977; *cr:* Teacher 1980-88, Cnslr 1988- Northside Sch; *ai:* 8th Grade Girls Bsktbl Coach; Amer Assn of Counseling & Dev 1988-; Amer Sch Cnslrs Assn 1989-; *office:* Northside Sch P O Box 217 Cool CA 95614

WOODALL, GARY H., Biology Teacher; *b:* Logan, KY; *m:* Aubrietta Newton; *c:* David, Alissa; *ed:* (BA) Ag/Bio, 1969, (MS) Cnslr Ed, 1977 W KY Univ; *cr:* Teacher Auburn HS 1969-76, W KY Univ 1977; Bank Rep Citizens Natl Bank 1977-78; Teacher Logan Cty HS 1984-.

WOODALL, JO ANN (GIBBS), Third Grade Teacher; *b:* Hannibal, MO; *m:* James Bryan; *c:* Jaime A.; *ed:* (BS) Ed, Univ of MO Columbia 1979; *cr:* 5th Grade Teacher Paris R-II Elem 1979-81; 4th Grade Teacher 1981-82, Transition Room Teacher 1982-83, 2nd Grade Teacher 1983-84, 3rd Grade Teacher 1984- Monroe City R-1 Elem; *ai:* Prof Dev Comm 1989-; Monroe City CTA Mem 1981-; MO St Teachers Assn Mem 1989-; Beta Sigma Phi (Secy 1983-84, Pres 1984-85) 1981-87, Chapter Woman of Yr 1985; Monroe City Womens Club Mem 1987-; United Meth Church Mem; *office:* Monroe City R-1 Elem Sch 420 N Washington Monroe City MO 63456

WOODARD, JUDY FALLIN, Jr HS Language Arts Teacher; *b:* Anniston, AL; *m:* Paul; *ed:* (BA) Speech Hearing Therapy, 1966; (MA) Elem Ed, 1970 LA Tech; *cr:* Speech Therapist Webster Parish 1966-70; Jr HS Teacher Simsboro HS 1970-; *ai:* 4-H Spon; Prof Educator of LA 1986-; Antioch Meth Church Sunday Sch Supt 1988-; Teacher of Yr Schl 1987; Teacher of Yr Parish & North LA 1987; Teacher of Yr Sch & Parish 1989-; *home:* Rt 2 Simsboro LA 71275

WOODARD, LLOYD ERVIN, Art Instructor; *b:* Chicago, IL; *m:* Marcia Rae Whittum; *c:* Nathan P., Joshua M., Anna E.; *ed:* (BA) Arts/Crafts, IN Wesleyan Univ 1976; (MA) Art, Ball St Univ 1982; *cr:* Art Instr Hamilton Hts Jr HS 1976-78; Industrial Art Instr Jones Jr HS 1978-79; Art/Photo Instr Mississinewa HS 1979-83; Instr of Gifted & Talented/Art Instr Shenandoah Mid Sch 1983-; *ai:* N Cntrl & Catalyst Gifted & Talented Broad Based Planning Comm; Cadre for Gifted & Talented ; Chrstns in Visual Arts 1978-; Grant Cty Art Assn 1975-89; Wesleyan Men Bd Mem 1989-; Numerous Art Awds, Exhibitions, Commissioned Paintings; *home:* PO Box 206 Gas City IN 46933

WOODARD, PHYLLIS SUE, English Teacher; *b:* Clinton, IN; *ed:* (BS) Eng, 1974, (MS) Eng/US His, 1979 IN St Univ; *cr:* Eng Teacher Bridgeton Jr HS 1974-86, Rosedale Jr HS 1986-; *ai:* Natl Jr Honor Society, Chrldr Spon; Academic Bowl, Spell Bowl Coach; Power Mem, Lead Comm; Sigma Delta Pi, Delta Kappa Gamma, ISTA, NEA; *office:* Rosedale Jr HS 707 E Central St Rosedale IN 47874

WOODCOCK, LINDA BIRGE, Math Teacher; *b:* Glasgow, KY; *m:* Milton B; *c:* James E.; *ed:* (BS) Math, Eastern KY Univ 1973; (Rank I/Rank II) Scndry Educ, Western KY Univ 1980; *cr:* Math Teacher 9th-12th Hiseville HS 1973-74; 8th-9th Temple Hill Sch 1974-77; 7th-8th Austin Tracy Sch 1977-; *ai:* Beta Club Spon; Austin Tracy Sch Yrbk Adv; Mathcounts Team Coach; Coord St Jude's Childrens Research Hospital Math-A-Thon Coord; NEA 1973-; BCEA 1973-; PTA 1973-; Austin Tracy Vol Fire Dept Women's Aux 1985-; *home:* 225 Birge Road Austin KY 42123

WOODCOCK, THOMAS C., Fourth Grade Teacher; *b:* Philadelphia, PA; *m:* Peg; *c:* Corinne, Megan; *ed:* (BA) Elem, Millersville Univ 1966; *cr:* Elem Teacher Sch Dist of Lancaster 1966-; *ai:* NEA, PSEA, Lancaster Ed Assn 1966-; *home:* 131 Milton Cir Lititz PA 17543

WOODDELL, P. GLENN, Fine Arts Department Chair; *b:* Hutchinson, KS; *ed:* (BMUS) Music Ed, Southwestern Coll 1963; (MM) Choral Stud, Crane Sch of Music 1982; (MA) Performance/Ed Theatre, NY Univ 1988; N TX St Univ Sch of Music; Gifted & Talented, Coll of New Rochelle; *cr:* Dir Head Start 1968-70; Fine Arts Teacher Jeffersonville-Youngsville Central Sch 1965-; *ai:* Co-Adv Stu Cncl Jeffersonville-Youngsville; 8th Grade Class Adv; Music Educators Natl Conference 1965-; Phi Mu Alpha 1964-; Amer Film Institute Charter Mem 1965-; Lions Club 1984-85; WJFF-FM (Advisory Bd 1986-, On-Air Announcer 1990); Saratoga Performing Arts Philadelphia Orch Chorus Mem 1979-83; Amer Guild of Variety Artists Awd; Danforth Fellowship; Articles Published Music Educators Journal; *office:* Jeffersonville-Youngsville Sch School House Rd Jeffersonville NY 12748

WOODELL, PEGGY ANDERSON, Special Education Teacher; *b:* South Boston, VA; *m:* John Norris; *c:* Trudy W Shutt, Joni W. Homlett; *ed:* (BA) Sociology, Univ of NC 1952; *cr:* 3rd Grade Teacher Rustburg Elem 1965-66; 2nd/3rd Grade Teacher

Peter Sarpy Elem 1966-67; 4th Grade Teacher Amer Sch/England 1968-70 & 1971-72; 5th/6th/7th Grade Math/Sci Teacher Patrick Henry Acad 1975-78; Library Gladys Elem 1978-79; 7th/8th Grade Math Teacher William Campbell Mid Sch 1979-81; 7th-12th Grade Special Ed/EMR/LD Teacher William Campbell HS & Mid Sch 1981-; *ai:* SADD; Amer Univ Women Assn Co-Pres 1987-88 & VP 1988-; Campbell Cty Ed Assn Rep 1985-; League of Women Voters; *office:* William Campbell H S P O Box 7 Naruna VA 24576

WOODEN, JACQUELYN LUMPKIN, English Teacher; *b:* Miami, FL; *m:* Johnnie III; *c:* Millanee; *ed:* (BA) Eng, Univ of FL 1984; Writing Inst, Univ of Miami; *cr:* Eng Teacher Miami Northwestern Sr HS 1984-; *ai:* Ladies Cnslrs Club & Stu Newspaper Adv; Zeta Phi Beta Basileus 1983-84; Dade-Monroe Teacher Ed Center Hum Project; Nom Teacher of Yr 1989- ; *office:* Miami Northwestern Sr HS 7007 NW 12th Ave Miami FL 33150

WOODFIELD, DARRILL R., Industrial Art Teacher; *b:* Oklahoma City, OK; *m:* Rita Grabbe; *c:* Dari L., Darrill R. Jr.; *ed:* (BS) Industrial Art, W TX St Univ 1962; (MA) Industrial Art, Univ of Northern CO 1965; Grad Course Work Numerous Univs; *cr:* Industrial Art Teacher Carlsbad Mid HS 1962-80, Carlsbad Jr HS 1980-89, Leyva Jr HS 1989-; Technical Drawing Instr NM St Univ Carlsbad 1985-; *ai:* Accrediting Comm Carlsbad Municipal Schls; NEA, Carlsbad Ed Assn 1962-; NM Ind Art Assn Treas 1982-84; Amer Industrial Arts Assn 1962-; Elks Lodge 1972-; Industrial Art Teacher of Yr NM 1980; *home:* 301 Moore Dr Carlsbad NM 88220

WOODFIN, SUSAN RAINS, Department Chair; *b:* Bedford, England; *m:* Steven Ray; *c:* Marci J., Mica R.; *ed:* (BS) Scndry Ed/General Sci, 1975, (MS) Curr/Instruction, 1990 S IL UniV; *ai:* Christa Mc Auliffe Fellowship Sci Ed for Visually Impaired Stus 1989; *office:* Benton Consolidated HS 511 E Main St Benton IL 62812

WOODIE, CORETHA BOYKIN, 6th Grade Teacher; *b:* Bradenton, FL; *m:* Eddie L.; *c:* Al; *ed:* (AA) Gibbs Jr Coll 1958; (BS) Elem Ed, FL a & M Univ 1962; (MA) Ed/Admin, United States Int Univ 1986; *cr:* Teacher Rosenwald Jr HS 1962-66; Spangdalem Dependent Sch 1966-70; Fairfield Unified Sch Dist 1970-; *ai:* Prgm Mgr/6th Grade Teacher; Co-Chm of Awds Assembly & Comm; Mem Cmptr Comm; Mem Calendar Comm; Chm Spelling Bee Comm; FSUTA; NEA; CTA; XAACP; Mem Martin Luther Kings Birthday Celebration Comm; *office:* Amy Blanc Elem Sch 230 Atlantic Ave Fairfield CA 94533

WOODIS, DORTHY MUECKE, Teacher; *b:* Galveston, TX; *m:* Kenneth W.; *c:* John Hayes, Russell Hayes, Martha Hayes; *ed:* (BS) Elem Ed, N TX St Univ 1957; (MED) Elem Ed, AL A&M 1978; *cr:* Teacher Peaslee Elem 1958-63, Roselawn Elem 1961-63, Coward Elem 1967-; *ai:* Athens Public Schls Textbook Selection Comm; Alpha Delta Kappa; Quest Study Club Pres 1974-78; Friends of the Lib; Friends of Symphony; Federal St Schlsp AL A&M; *office:* James L Cowart Elem Sch 1701 W Hobbs St Athens AL 35611

WOODLE, H. LORAINE, 7th-8th Grade Math Teacher; *b:* Statesville, NC; *ed:* (BS) Elem Ed, Bob Jones Univ 1972; *cr:* 6th Grade Teacher Marietta Chrstn Sch 1972-76; 7th-8th Grade Math Teacher Grace Baptist Acad 1976-84; 6th-8th Grade Math Teacher Cedar Forest Chrstn Sch 1984-87; 7th-8th Grade Math Teacher Calvary Baptist Day Sch 1987-; *ai:* Yrbk Staff Adv; Vlybl Coach; *office:* Calvary Baptist Day Sch 5000 Country Club Rd Winston-Salem NC 27104

WOODRING, MARK EDWIN, Social Studies Teacher; *b:* Tyrone, PA; *m:* Vicki Ann; *c:* Courtney; *ed:* (BA) His, Lycoming Coll 1985; Grad Stud; *cr:* Teacher Claysburg-Kimmel HS 1986-; *ai:* Former Head Ftbl & Jr HS Wrestling Coach; PSEA 1986-; *office:* Claysburg-Kimmel HS Bedford St Claysburg PA 16625

WOODROFFE, MARCIA FREDERICO, Biology/Phys Science Teacher; *b:* Ridgeway, PA; *m:* William; *c:* Michele, Brian, Brad, Cheryl; *ed:* (BS) Scndry Ed/Sci, Penn St Univ 1960; (MS) Curr/Instruction, Univ of TN 1986; Temple Univ & Walters St; *cr:* Sci Teacher York Cty Jr HS 1961-62; Substitute Teacher Haverford Township Schls 1976-78, Morristown East/West HS 1979-83; Teacher Morristown Hamblen HS West 1983-89; *ai:* Keep America Beautiful, Stus Taking a Right Stand, Just Say No Clowns Coord; Hamblen Cty Ed Assn, NEA, TN Ed Assn 1983-; Drug Alliance 1989-; Pilot Intnl Bd of Dir 1990; St Patrick Parish Cncl (Chairperson 1989-) 1988-; Chestnut Hill Coll Natl Sci Fnd; Berea Coll Mellon Scholar; Oak Ridge Associated Univs Sci Teachers Research Involement for Vital Ed; *office:* Morristown Hamblen HS West 1025 Sulphur Springs Rd Morristown TN 37814

WOODRUFF, ARTHUR DEVLIN, Physics/Journalism Teacher; *b:* Sanford, FL; *ed:* (BA) Journalism/Chem, Univ of NC Chapel Hill 1984; *cr:* Teacher Seminole HS 1985-; *ai:* Yrbk Adv; AAPT 1989-; *office:* Seminole HS 2701 Ridgewood Ave Sanford FL 32773

WOODRUFF, HYLA, Educational Director; *b:* Bronx, NY; *ed:* (BA) Eng, 1973; (MS) Elem Ed, 1977 Herbert H Lehman Coll; *cr:* Teacher 1974-86; Ed Dir 1986- Parkway Sch; *home:* 3508 Kings College Pl Bronx NY 10467

WOODRUFF, LINDA DEE, Third Grade Teacher; *b:* Vincennes, IN; *m:* Arthur; *c:* David, Sandra; *ed:* (AS) Bus, Vincennes Univ 1965; (BS) Elem Ed, 1969, (MS) Elem Ed, 1973 IN St Univ; Talented/Gifted IN Univ; *cr:* Librarian L&M Consolidated Schls 1969-70; 3rd Grade Teacher Linton Stockton Elem Sch 1971-; *ai:* Linton Swim Team Coach; Miner Kadet Drill Team Spon 1984-86; N Cntrl Cty Chairperson 1989- Linton Elem Sch; Linton Classroom Teachers Assn Pres 1984-85; IN St Teachers Assn 1971-; United Meth Church (Finance Comm, Mem 1989-, 5th/6th Grade Sunday Schl Teacher 1974-); Psi Iota Xi (Pres, Recording Secy 1970-); *home:* 459 A Street NE Linton IN 47441

WOODS, BONNIE HURLEY, English Teacher; *b:* Cairo, IL; *m:* William E.; *c:* Jason, Ryan, Amy; *ed:* (BS) Eng, SEMO Univ 1967; Working Towards Masters; Numerous Inservice Wkshps; *cr:* Speech Teacher North Kirkwood Jr HS 1967-68; Eng Teacher Charleston HS 1971-76, Cntrl HS 1981-; *ai:* NHS Adv; Lang Art Curr Review Comm & Dept Chm; SMETA, MSTA, CTA; Meth Church; *home:* 1633 Parkmore Cape Girardeau MO 63701

WOODS, CHERYL DENISE, Jr HS English-Science Teacher; *b:* Chicago, IL; *ed:* (BS) Jr HS Ed, IL St Univ 1980; (MA) Sch Admin, Concordia Coll 1985; *cr:* Mid Sch Teacher 1980-83, Jr HS Lang Art Teacher 1983-88 Irving Elem Sch; Jr HS Lang Art/Sci Teacher Glen Haven Elem Sch 1988-; *ai:* Spon Beta Club; Black His Curr Guide Comm; Coached Boys & Girls Vlybl, Track & Field & Girls Sftbl; NEA 1980-88; AFT 1980-88; De Kalb Assn of Educators 1988-89; Alpha Kappa Alpha 1981-; NAACP 1981-86; Chicago Urban League 1981-83; Outstanding Young Women of Amer 1983; *home:* 1007 Tree Hills Pkwy Stone Mountain GA 30088

WOODS, CHRISTOPHER WILDRICK, Anatomy & Physiology Teacher; *b:* Atlanta, GA; *ed:* (BA) His, Yale Univ 1989; Attending Duke Univ Medical Sch 1990; *cr:* Anatomy & Physiology Teacher Yeshiva of Greater Washington 1989-; *office:* Yeshiva of Greater Washington 1216 Arcola Ave Silver Spring MD 20902

WOODS, CINDY LEE, 4th Grade Teacher; *b:* Columbus, OH; *m:* Donald; *c:* Casey; *ed:* (BA) Elem, OH St Univ 1978; Various Elem Courses, OH St Univ; *cr:* 4th/5th/7th/8th Grade Teacher St Anthony Sch 1979-; *ai:* Prin Advisory; Columbus Diocesan Ed Assn 1983-; Cntrl OH Down Syndrome Assn 1988-; *office:* St Anthony Sch 1300 Urban Dr Columbus OH 43229

WOODS, DEBORAH POWELL, Biology Teacher; *b:* Rocky Mount, VA; *m:* Steven Curtis; *c:* Matthew C.; *ed:* (BS) Bio, St Pauls Coll 1985; *cr:* Bio Teacher Franklin Cty HS 1987-; *ai:* Cheer Spon; Black His Month; NEA, VEA, FCEA 1987-; *office:* Franklin Cty HS 506 Pell Ave Rocky Mount VA 24151

WOODS, DOUGLAS ELLIOT, English/Writing Teacher; *b:* New Kensington, PA; *m:* Aimee Rae Haser; *c:* Alexis, Alison; *ed:* (BS) Ed, 1972, (MA) Lit, 1976 IN Univ of PA; *cr:* Eng Teacher Butler Intermediate HS 1972-; Writing Instr Westmoreland Cty Comm Coll 1975-; Eng Dept Chm Butler Intermediate HS 1976-86; Fiction Instr PA Governors Sch for Arts 1985-; *ai:* Butler Area Sch Dist; Core Team; *home:* 519 Oaklake Rd New Kensington PA 15068

WOODS, GRETA GARY, Kindergarten Head Teacher; *b:* Port Arthur, TX; *m:* Albert B.; *ed:* (BSED) Elem Ed/Kndgtn, 1975, (MED) Rdng Specialist, 1980 Stephen F Austin Univ; Cmptr Classes, Stephen F Austin St Univ, Angeline Coll; Writing to Read Cmptr IBM Wkshp; *cr:* Head Kndgtn Teacher Hemphill Elem Sch 1976-; *ai:* Hemphill Ind Sch Dist Textbook Comm; HS & Jr HS Chrldr & Pep Squad Spon 1979-81; Assn of TX Prof Educators 1980-; TX St Teachers Assn 1985-86; Hemphill Sch Service League (Treas 1987-88, Membership Chairperson 1985-87); *home:* Rt 1 Box 560 Pineland TX 75968

WOODS, JOYCE HEWITT, Fifth Grade Teacher; *b:* Rayville, LA; *m:* Terry L.; *c:* Nicole; *ed:* (BA) Elem Ed, Northeast LA Univ 1968; (MED) Elem Ed, Mc Neese St Univ 1979; *cr:* 5th Grade Teacher D S Perkins Elem 1968-69, E K Key Elem 1969-82; 3rd Grade Teacher 1982-83, 5th Grade Teacher 1983- Frasch Elem; *ai:* NEA 1968-87; LA Assn of Educators 1968-87; Calcasien Assn of Educators 1968-87; AFT/LFT 1987-; *office:* Frasch Elem Sch 540 S Huntington Sulphur LA 70663

WOODS, MARIEL GANDER, Third Grade Teacher; *b:* Hutchinson, MN; *m:* Keith; *ed:* (BA) Ed, Bethel Coll 1980; *cr:* Elem Teacher Silver Lake Public Sch 1980-; *ai:* MN Ed Assn (Local Secy 1980-81) 1980-; Bethany Baptist Church (Chrstn Ed Bd 1988, Dir of Music 1987-); Staff Dev Prgm Chairperson; *office:* Silver Lake Public Sch 229 Lake St Silver Lake MN 55381

WOODS, MARTHA CATE, Fifth Grade Teacher; *b:* Athens, TN; *m:* M. Dale; *ed:* (BS) Bus Ed, TN Wesleyan Coll 1974; (MS) Curr/Instruction, Univ of TN Chattanooga 1979; *cr:* 4th Grade Teacher 1974-77, 5th Grade Teacher 1977- Riceville Elem; *ai:* Coach Academic Olympics Contest; 4-H Club Adv; NEA, TEA, ETEA; Alpha Delta Kappa, TN Rdng Assn, Mc Minn Cty Ed Assn; *home:* Rt 1 Box 239 Riceville TN 37370

WOODS, MARTHA STONE, First Grade Teacher; *b:* Charlotte, NC; *m:* John Miller; *c:* John M. Jr., Bonnie Bouche Woods Lawry; *ed:* (BS) Ed, Queens Coll 1957; Early Chldhd, UNCC; Numerous Wkshps; *cr:* 1st Grade Teacher Cotswold Elem 1957-61; K-3rd Grade Teacher Charlotte Cntry Day Sch 1968-; *ai:* Lower Sch Drama, Sci, Soc Stud Rep; Delta Kappa Gamma (Soc Chm, Alpha Sigma Prof Growth & Service, 1st VP 1989-); Outstanding Teacher of Yr 1980; Presented Soc Stud Wkshps; *office:* Charlotte Cntry Day Sch 1440 Carmel Rd Charlotte NC 28226

WOODS, MATTIE SMITH, Third Grade Teacher; *b:* Houston, TX; *m:* Willie H. Jr.; *c:* Theron, Renna; *ed:* (BA) Elem Ed, Prairie View A&M Coll 1967; *cr:* 3rd Grade Teacher Noche Buena Elem 1967-69, Garfield Elem 1969-76, Martin Luther King Elem 1976-; *ai:* Budget Comm; At Risk & Sch Site Cncls; Black His Prgm; King Faculty Club Treas; Soc Stud & Math Rep; FTA, CTA, NEA 1975-; St Rest Baptist Church Clerk 1988-; St John Dist Assn Treas 1985-; Outstanding Teacher of Yr; *home:* 2359 S Banneker Fresno CA 93706

WOODS, RUTH ANNE GUERRY, Mathematics/Science Teacher; *b:* Charleston, SC; *m:* Charles Rudolph; *c:* Charles R. Jr., Pamela Medeiros; *ed:* (BS) Elem Ed, 1973, (MA) Ed, 1975 Univ of SC; *cr:* Math/Sci Teacher Hampton Elem 1973-; *ai:* Awds Prgm, St Jude Math-A-Thon, 3rd/4th Grade Math Curr Chm; Stu Teachers Supvr Univ of SC; NEA, SC Ed Assn, Hampton Cty Ed Assn 1977-; Hampton Cty Historical Society Pres 1978-; Magnolia Garden Club Pres; Gamma Beta Phi, NHS; *home:* 700 Willard Hampton SC 29924

WOODS, SUSAN E., 4th Grade Teacher; *b:* Grand Rapids, MI; *c:* Laura, Steven; *ed:* (BA) Elem Ed, 1964, (MA) Elem Ed, 1967 MI St Univ; *cr:* 1st/2nd Grade Teacher Wainwright Elem 1964-69; Coord Stu Teachers CMU Grand Rapids 1969-70; 3rd/4th Grade Teacher Whitehall Elem 1970-; *ai:* Young Author Coord; Continuous Comm Mem; Grant Writer; Math, SOC, MOORA Grants; *office:* Whitehall Elem Sch Sophia St Whitehall MI 49461

WOODS, SYLVIA MAUFIELD, Fourth Grade Teacher; *b:* Waynesboro, MS; *c:* Katonya W. Smith, Ray; *ed:* (BS) Elem Ed, Alcorn St Univ 1972; (MS) Elem Ed, William Carey Coll 1978; *home:* Rt 2 Box 55E Waynesboro MS 39367

WOODS, VERA GAIL, English Teacher; *b:* Charles Town, WV; *m:* Donald A.; *c:* Teresa Propps Owens, Jeffrey L. Propps; *ed:* (BA) Eng, Hood Coll 1952; Grad Stud Ed, W MD Coll, Shippensburg Univ; *cr:* Teacher Charles Town HS 1958-72, Cumberland Valley HS 1972-78, Jefferson HS 1978-; *ai:* Publicity; Newspaper, Yrbk, Magazine Adv; N Cntrl Evaluation Steering Comm Chairperson; NEA, WVEA, JCEA; *office:* Jefferson HS Rt 1 Box 83 Shenandoah Jct WV 25442

WOODSIDE, SHARON A., Business/Computer Teacher; *b:* Belleville, KS; *m:* Keith A.; *c:* Alan K.; *ed:* (BS) Bus Ed, KS St Univ 1961; (MS) Bus Ed, Univ of MO Kansas City 1970; Additional Trng Cmptrs, Careers, Current Trends in Bus; *cr:* Bus Teacher Excelsior Springs Public Schls 1961-62, Lawson Public Schls 1963-69; Bus/Cmptr Teacher Unified Sch Dist 455 Hillcrest 1969-; *ai:* Yrbk & Sch Paper. Soph Class Spon; Prepare & Spon Schs Annual Team Bus Decathlon Competition; Local Sch Dist Planning Bd for Goals & Objectives Chairperson; Delta Kappa Gamma Local Pres 1990; NBEA 1982-; KS Bus Ed Assn 1975-; NEA, KS Ed Assn (Commission Chairperson 1984, Dist Level VP, Local Pres); Narka Presbyn Church (Elder 1978-80, Clerk of Session 1986-88); Order of the Eastern Star Dist Aide 1987-88; Ladies Auxiliary 1989-; Finalist KS Teacher of Yr 1990; Interview Team for Selecting the KS NEA Comm Dir 1984; Voted Master Teacher of Local Dist; *home:* RR 1 Box 17 Narka KS 66960

WOODSON, LELIA MYATT, Third Grade Teacher; *b:* Mayfield, KY; *m:* Steve; *c:* Matt; *ed:* (BA) Elem Ed, 1973, (MA) Elem Ed, 1974 Murray St Univ; *cr:* 3rd Grade Teacher Wingo Elem Sch 1973-; *office:* Wingo Elem Sch Lebanon St Wingo KY 42088

WOODWARD, ANN JOHNSON, Fourth Grade Teacher; *b:* Atlanta, GA; *m:* Harold D.; *c:* Lorie, Cindi; *ed:* (BA) Sociology, Huntingdon Coll 1961; Elem Ed Cert; GA St Univ; Oglethorpe Univ; *cr:* Teacher De Kalb Cty Sch Sys 1962-65; Atlanta Public Sch Sys 1965-68; Troup Cty Sch Sys 1981-; *ai:* Page 1985-; Jr Svc Leag 1972-; West GA Med Ctr Aux Pres 1973-81; 1st United Meth Church; Mountville Sch Teacher of Yr 1987-88; *home:* 1004 Broad St La Grange GA 30240

WOODWARD, DIANNE GIBSON, Social Studies Teacher; *b:* Whiteville, NC; *m:* Kent T.; *c:* Holt; *ed:* (BS) Elem Ed, Campbell Univ 1973; (MA) Ed & Supvsn, 1976; (EDS) Admin, 1978 East Carolina Univ; *cr:* Classroom Teacher Virginia Beach City Schls 1963-68; Elem Suprv 1974-76; Elem Asst Prin 1977-79 Whitevillle City Schls; Soc Stud Teacher Myrtle Beach Mid Sch 1980-; *ai:* Staff Dev Chairperson; Stu Adv; Chrldr Spon; Youth Group Chruch Adv; NC Prin Assn 1978; NEA; SCTA; Assn of Curr Dev 1974-78; Alpha Delta Kappa Sec 1979; Natl Republican Comm 1985-89; Bus Prof Womens Club VP 1969-70; Garden Club Pres 1971-73; Amer Cancer Soc 1988-89; BPW Outstanding Carreer Woman 1968; *office:* Myrtle Beach Mid Sch 3400 Oak St N Myrtle Beach SC 29577

WOODWARD, JILL RENEE JENKINS, Fourth Grade Teacher; *b:* Madison, IN; *m:* Douglas Lee; *c:* Trent, Trevor, Whitney; *ed:* (BA) Elem Ed, Ball St Univ 1977; (MS) Elem Ed, IN Univ Southeast 1980; *cr:* 4th Grade Teacher Trimble Cty Schls Milton Elem 1978-; *ai:* NEA 1978-; KY Ed Assn 1978-; Phi Beta Psi Reporter 1980-; Cub Scouts Den Leader 1989-; North United Meth Church 1967-; *office:* Milton Elem Sch US Hwy 421 Box 75 Milton KY 40045

WOODWARD, RITA LAMIRAND, Sixth Grade Teacher; *b:* Oklahoma City, OK; *m:* Terry Lee; *c:* Jonathan, Chadd; *ed:* (BS) Elem Ed, Cntrl St Univ 1976; Span; *cr:* 7th Grade Teacher Sequoyah Mid Sch 1976; 1st Grade Teacher Sperry Sch 1977; Kndgtn Teacher 1977-79, 5th Grade Teacher 1979-82, 6th Grade Teacher 1982- Mc Alester Schls; *ai:* Stu Cncl, Safety Patrol, Spelling Bee Spon; Sci Curr Comm Mem; OK Ed Assn 1977-; PTA (Treas 1982-86) 1977-; Beta Iota Treas 1980-81, Pearl Awd 1979; *home:* PO Box 1649 Mc Alester OK 74502

WOODWARD, RONALD LEE, Social Studies Teacher; *b:* New Albany, IN; *m:* Diana Lynn Haley; *c:* Wendy J. Leeka, Heather L., Russell L., Brandy L.; *ed:* (BS) Soc Stud, IN Univ 1971; (MAE) US His, Ball St Univ 1974; *cr:* Military Instr US Navy 1969-71; Teacher Wabash Mid Sch 1974-; Upper Wabash Voc Center 1975-77; *ai:* Spon Wabash Mid Sch His Club, WMS Stamp Club, Beta Club; Washington DC Trip; IN Cncl of Soc Stud 1978-; Wabash Co Historical Soc Pres 1982-84; IN Jr Historical Soc Spon 1977- 10 Yr Recognition 1987; IN Historical Soc Cty Historian 1975-; Creative Teachers Grant Ball St Univ 1982; Jaycees Distinguished Service Awd 1980; Semifinalist Teacher of Yr IN 1984; Teacher in Space Candidate; Asst Curator Wabash Cty Museum 1980; Books Published Brief His of Wabash Cty; *home:* 574 Ferry Wabash IN 46992

WOODWARD, SHIRLEY ANN MC CARROLL, 6th Grade Science Teacher; *b:* Springfield, TN; *m:* Everette R.; *c:* Robin Raymond, Judith A., Shana R.; *ed:* (BS) Home Ec, W KY St Coll 1964; (MA) Ed/Home Ec, W KY Univ 1973; Doctorial Work Early, Mid Chldhd Ed, Nova Univ 1987-89; *cr:* 9th-12th Grade Home Ec/Sci Teacher Auburn HS 1964-65; 7th Grade Sci Teacher Lebanon Jr HS 1965-66; 7th Grade Math/Sci Teacher Hendersonville Jr HS 1966-67; 7th Grade Sci Teacher Portland Jr HS 1967-70; 6th Grade Teacher Clyde Riggs Elem 1970-87; 6th Grade Sci Teacher Portland Mid Sch 1987-; *ai:* Boys & Girls Bsktbl Teams Bookkeeper; Mid Sch Cty Sci Festival Comm; Just Say No Leader; Porland Mid Sch Advisee Prgm Adv; 4-H Classroom Leader; Cty In-Service Work; NEA, SCEA Mem 1966-; ASCD, Amer Educl Reach Assn Mem 1988-89; TEA Rep; Portland Drug Cncl 1987-89; Sulpher Springs Baptist Church; BSA Sign Rocketry Badges Leader 1989-; Mid TN Aerospace Wkshp Schlsp; Sumner Cty Mid Sch Teacher of Yr 1991; Travel Awds; Rocketry Software Grant; *office:* Portland Mid Sch 922 S Broadway Portland TN 37148

WOODWARD, WILLIAM PERRY, Science Teacher; *b:* Bowling Green, KY; *m:* Sharon Huff Woodward; *c:* William B., Brian G.; *ed:* (BS) Bio, Phys Ed, 1966; (MA) Ed, 1968; Ed, 1980 Western KY Univ; *cr:* 8th Grade Sci Teacher Allen Cty Mid Sch 1966-; *ai:* Jr Beta Spon; KY Ed Assn; NEA; *home:* 176 Ormond Dr Scottsville KY 42164

WOODWORTH, LAURA GRAH, 6th Grade Language Art Teacher; *b:* Chester, IL; *m:* Ronald A.; *c:* Lindsey; *ed:* (BS) Elem Ed/Scndry Ed, Murray St Univ 1977; Working Towards Masters S IL Univ Carbondale; *cr:* Teacher SETA Government; Eng Teacher Sparta HS; 7th Grade Rdng Teacher, 6th Grade Lang Art Teacher Sparta Lincoln Attendance Ctr; *ai:* Sparta Lincoln Pom Pom Squad & Pep Club; NEA, IL Ed Assn; Delta Theta Tau Historian 1990; Bus & Prof Womens Club 1989-; Eastern Star 1986-; Sparta Core Group Mem; Pioneer of Sparta Mastery Learning Prgm; Speaker on Mastery Learning; *office:* Sparta Lincoln Attendance Ctr 200 N St Louis St Sparta IL 62286

WOODY, ROSLYN DE CORDOVA, Second Grade Teacher; *b:* Richmond, VA; *c:* James R. Jr.; *ed:* (BA) Elem Ed, VA Union Univ 1969; *cr:* 2nd Grade Teacher Bethany Elem Sch 1969; 3rd Grade Teacher Redd Elem Sch 1970-71; 2nd-5th Grade Teacher ESH Green Elem 1971-; *ai:* Phys Ed Comm; Rich Ed Assn; VA Ed Assn; NEA; Twigs Inc Treas 1980-.

WOOFTER, BETTY LANGFORD, Business Education Teacher; *b:* Glenville, WV; *m:* William Joseph; *c:* Sherry Woofter Jones, Kent J.; *ed:* (AB) Bus Ed, Glenville St 1952; Career Ed, Marshall Univ; *cr:* Bus Teacher Spencer HS 1952-54; Sand Fork HS 1954-55; Substitute Teacher Gilmer Cty Schls 1967-76; Bus Teacher Gilmer Cty HS 1976-; *ai:* Head Spon Frosh Class; Voc Comm Mem; WV Ed Assn 1977-; Gilmer Cty Ed Assn 1977-; Amer Assn Retired Persons 1980-; Pledge to Alpha Delta Kappa; Womens Club 1968-72; Womens Chrstn Service Org 1965-70; FBLA Spon 1980-82; Secy Oak Grove United Meth Church Admin Cncl 1979-; *office:* Gilmer County H S 300 Pine St Glenville WV 26351

WOOL, DEBRA LYNN, Fourth Grade Teacher; *b:* Gary, IN; *m:* Thomas; *c:* Kristopher, Kevin; *ed:* (BS) Elem Ed, 1973, (MS) Elem Ed, 1981 IN Univ; *cr:* Teacher Winfield Elem Sch 1973-; *ai:* IN St Teachers Assn, Crown Point Cmmty Teachers Assn 1973-; Kankakee Valley Rdng Cncl; Lakes of the Four Seasons Ladies Golf; *office:* Winfield Elem Sch 13128 Montgomery Crown Point IN 46307

WOOLARD, DAVID EUGENE, Mathematics Teacher; *b:* Richmond, VA; *ed:* (BA) Math/Music, Univ of Richmond 1977; Musicology, Univ of Chicago 1977; Cmptrs/Math/Ed, VA Commonwealth Univ 1979-89; *cr:* Math Teacher Thomas Dale HS 1978-; *ai:* NCTM, Mathematical Assn of America 1988-; VA Cncl Teachers of Math 1978-; Chesterfield Cty Math Curr & Essential Learnings Comms; *office:* Thomas Dale HS 3626 W Hundred Rd Chester VA 23831

WOOLARD, LINDA ANN, Fifth Grade Teacher; *b:* Newark, OH; *ed:* (BS) Ed, OH St Univ 1970; Grad Work OH St Univ; *cr:* 5th Grade Teacher Hartler Elem 1970-71, Kettering Elem 1971-72; 5th/6th Grade Teacher Wm E Miller Elem 1972-; *ai:* Newark City Schls Lang Art Curr Comm; Literacy Connection, NOTE, NCTE, NEA, PTA, Delta Kappa Gamma; Natl Audubon; Newark Rotary Teacher Awd 1989; *office:* Wm E Miller Elem Sch Granvill Rd & Country Club Dr Newark OH 43055

WOOLDRIDGE, WILLIAM HENRY, Science Teacher/ Athletic Dir; *b:* Hartford, CT; *m:* Lois Kidney; *c:* Kelly, Lindsay; *ed:* (BS) Bio, 1972; (MS) Bio, 1983 Cntrl Ct St Univ; Cmptr Assisted Trng Quinnipiac Coll 1989-; *cr:* Teacher 1973-, Coach 1974- Bennet JR HS; *ai:* Bennet Jr HS Stu Cncl Adv 1980-; Athleic Dir 1989-; Frosh Girls Bsktbl Coach; Stu Act Bookkeeper 1984; Faculty Cncl & 75th Anniversary Comms; MEA, CEA, NEA 1973-; Ct Assn of Athletic Dirs 1989-; CT Coaches Assn 1975-78; Big Brother 1973-76; Manchester Soccer Club Boosters 1988; Bennet Above and Beyond Coll of Duty Awd 1987, 1989; I'll Take Care of It Awd 1987; Mem Faculty Comm Recognise Bennet as Natl Sch Excl; *office:* Bennet Jr HS 1151 Main St Manchester CT 06040

WOOLERY, MARTHA WALLING, English Department Head; *b:* Toms River, NJ; *m:* Mark Crismon; *c:* Jeffrey; *ed:* (AB) Eng, Lafayette Coll 1975; (MED) Rdng, Univ of VA 1976; Tidewater Writing Project 1982; *cr:* Eng/Rdng Teacher Great Bridge HS 1976-; *ai:* Eng Dept Head; Effective Schls Comm Chm; Soph Class Spon; Forensics Coach; Beginning Teacher Colleague; VA Assn of Teachers of Eng 1976-, Service Awd 1985; VA St Rdng Assn 1976-; Alpha Delta Kappa (Pres 1988-, Pres-elect 1986-88, Corresponding Secy 1984-86); Governors Sch For Hum, Univ of Richmond; Presidential Citation for Excl in Ed; Teacher of Yr Great Bridge HS 1984; *office:* Great Bridge HS 301 Hanbury Rd Chesapeake VA 23320

WOOLEVER, GAIL WALUK, Elementary Art Teacher; *b:* Auburn, IN; *m:* Stephen J.; *c:* Zachary; *ed:* (BA) Art Ed, Valparaiso Univ 1974; (MS) Art Ed, IN Univ 1979; *cr:* Art Teacher Wheatfield Elem 1974-; *ai:* Yrbk Spon; Kankakee Valley Teachers Assn (Secy 1978-79), Good Apple 1988-89; NAEA; Delta Kappa Gamma; Zionsville Art Show 1988; *home:* RR 1 Box 379 Wheatfield IN 46392

WOOLF, STEPHEN D., Civics/English Teacher; *b:* Kansas City, MO; *m:* Kellie Kae Mac Farlane; *c:* Stephen D. Jr.; *ed:* (BS) Scndry Ed, 1985; (MS) Ed Admin, KS St Univ 1987; TESA Coord Cert; *cr:* Speech/Drama/Eng Teacher Highland Park HS 1987-88; Civics/Eng Teacher Logan Jr HS 1988-; *ai:* Head Ftbl, Head Track, 8th Grade Bsktbl Coach; Curr Comm; Intramurals; Saturday Study Prgm; Phi Delta Kappa 1985-87; Flinthills Breadbasket Bd of Dirs 1984-87; Northland Chrstn Church Youth Group Dir 1988-; TESA Coord; *office:* Logan Jr HS 1124 NW Lyman Rd Topeka KS 66608

WOOLLEY, JUDITH ROXEY, Fifth Grade Teacher; *b:* Detroit, MI; *m:* Carl T.; *c:* Thomas; *ed:* (BA) Poly Sci 1958, (MA) Elem Ed, 1965 Univ of MI; *cr:* 5th/6th Grade Teacher Henry Ford Elem & Willow Run Schls 1958-; *office:* Henry Ford Elem Sch 2440 Clark Rd Ypsilanti MI 48198

WOOLLEY, VIKI (WALKER), Teacher; *b:* Chevelry, MD; *m:* Gregory Edward; *c:* Jonathan, David, Nathan; *ed:* (BS) Chrstn Ed, Calvary Bible Coll 1979; *cr:* 4th Grade Teacher 1980-81, 5th Grade Teacher 1981-82 Tri-City Chrstn Sch; *office:* Tri-City Chrstn Sch 4500 Selsa Rd Blue Springs MO 64015

WOOLSEY, ROBIN ALICIA, 2nd Grade Teacher; *b:* Camp Lejeune, NC; *ed:* (BS) His/Fr, Auburn Univ 1974; Grad Stud LA St Univ & Jacksonville St Univ; *cr:* Teacher Sacred Heart Sch 1978-; *ai:* After Sch Fr Prgm; Lib Coord; PTO (Exec Bd, Teacher Rep); *home:* 1801 Mimosa Dr Oxford AL 36203

WOOLWORTH, JUDY A. (GOETTEL), 5th Grade Teacher; *b:* Lewistown, MT; *m:* Harlan K.; *ed:* (BS) Elem Ed, Eastern Mt Coll 1968; Cert Renewals; Cooperative Learning; *cr:* 3rd Grade Teacher Stratmoor Hills Elem Sch 1968-69, Nodland Elem 1970-81; 5th Grade Teacher Nodland Elem 1981-; *ai:* Leadership Comm; Safety Patrol Adv; Music Accompanist; *office:* Nodland Elem Sch 5000 Mayhew Ave Sioux City IA 51106

WOOTEN, KATHRYN WILKERSON, Speech-Language Pathologist; *b:* Sylvester, GA; *m:* Steven Dulaney; *c:* Kate L.; *ed:* (BSED) Speech/Lang Pathology, 1981, (MSED) Speech/Lang Pathology, 1982 Univ of GA; *cr:* Speech/Lang Pathologist Worth Cty Sch System 1982-; *ai:* Amer Speech Lang Hearing Assn 1982-; GA Speech Lang Hearing Assn 1980-; Prof Assn of GA Educators 1982-; Sylvester Jr Womens Club (Pres 1986-87) 1983-, Clubwoman of Yr 1987, Good Citizen Awd 1987, Family of Yr 1989; *office:* Worth Cnty Sch System 204a E Frnklin St Sylvester GA 31791

WOOTEN, MONTA FAYE, Team Leader Soc Stud Dept Chm; *b:* Hillsboro, AL; *m:* William Vernon; *c:* Brigette Wooten Tidwell, Pamela Wooten Enzer, Shawn M., Gina Wooten Scott; *ed:* (BA) His/Scndry Ed/Elem Ed/Ec, Judson Coll 1957; Ed Leadership, Univ of West FL; Curr, Pensacola FL; Leadership, FL St Univ; *cr:* Indialantic 1957-58; Melbourne Elem 1958; Oakland Heights 1959-60; Eglin AFB 1960-64; Wright Elem 1965-67; Niagara Whitfield 1967-70; Headstart Consultant Okaloosa Cty Test Team 1970-71, Bruner Jr HS 1971-; *ai:* Yrbk Adv; Visiting Comm Mem; Southern Assn Evaluation Comm; 8th Grade Team Leader; Soc Stud Dept Chairperson & Cncl; Mid Sch Team Leaders Group; Alpha Delta Kappa Chaplain; NCSS; Honorary Educl Society; Okaloosa Cty Soc Stud Chm; Pilot Club (Secy, Schlsp Comm); Amer Assn of Univ Women Schlsp Comm; Okloosa Cty Journalist; Amer Scholastic Press Awd Outstanding Yrbk/Journalism; FL Cncl for Soc Stud & Bruner Jr HS Teacher of Yr Awds; Jr HS Instr Taylor Publishing Company Yrbk Seminar.

WOOTEN, PAMELA JOHNSON, Science, Math, Health Teacher; *b:* Smithfield, NC; *m:* William Carroll; *c:* David; *ed:* (BS) Health/Phys Ed, Atlantic Chrstn Coll 1977; *cr:* Teacher Harrison Jr HS 1978-87, North Johnson Mid Sch 1987-; *ai:* Lead Teacher; Natl Jr Honor Society Comm Mem; NC Comm Teachers of Math 1987-; Nom Pres Math/Sci Teacher of Yr 1989; Teacher of Yr Harrison Jr HS 1985 & North Johnston Mid Sch 1990; *office:* North Johnston Mid Sch Box 69 Micro NC 27555

WORACEK, CLARA ANN (WINDELS), Second Grade Teacher; *b:* Omaha, NE; *m:* Raymond James; *c:* Richard, Gerald, Sandra Woracek Walker; *ed:* Elem Ed, Coll of St Mary 1955; (BA) Elem Ed, 1971, Elem Ed, 1982 Kearney St Coll; *cr:* Lower Elem Teacher Holy Ghost Cath Sch 1955-65; 1st Grade Teacher St Columbkille Cath Sch 1965-66, Sargent Public Sch 1966-68; 2nd Grade Teacher Arnold Public Sch 1968-73, Sargent Public Sch 1973-; *ai:* Sargent Teachers Assn (Pres 1983-84, Chief Negotiator 1984-85); NE St Ed Assn, NEA; Amer Cancer Society Area Crusader 1983-; US Office of Consumer Ed Fellowship SD Cncl E Regional Summer Inst Univ of SD 1977; *home:* HCR 72 Box 41 Sargent NE 68874

WORK, BETTY ANLI, Elementary Teacher; *b:* Talahina, OK; *c:* Darlene; *ed:* (BS) Elem Ed, 1972, (MS) Behavior Stud 1975 SE OK St Univ; (EED) Post Grad, OK Univ 1978; *cr:* Teacher Rattan Public Sch, OK City Univ 1972-75; Teacher/Consultant SE OK ST Univ; *ai:* John O Mally & Title IV Teacher Rep; NEA, Classroom Teachers 1974-; Rattan Assn of Classroom Teachers Pres 1987-89; GSA Leader; 4-H Club Leader; Bicentennial Ed Grant 1987; Choctaw of Yr 1984; St Dept of Ed Rattan Teacher of Yr 1989-; *home:* Rt 1 Box 159 Farris OK 74542

WORK, JAMES JAY, Music Teacher; *b:* Fairmont, WV; *m:* Nancy; *c:* James A., Heather E., Justin A.; *ed:* (AS) Liberal Art, Montreat Anderson Jr Coll 1964; (BM) Music, Westminster Choir Coll 1967; (MME) Music Ed, WV Univ 1971; *cr:* Minister of Music/Youth Emmanuel Baptist Church 1967-69; Minister of Music First United Meth Church 1969-70; Dir of Music Church of The Good Shepherd United Meth 1973-78; Teacher Taylor Cty Bd of Ed 1973-; *ai:* Volunteer Track Coach.

WORKMAN, JULIA GEWEKE, Orchestra Director; *b:* Washington, DC; *m:* Ellis; *c:* John, Paul; *ed:* (BME) Music Ed, IN Univ 1973; Working Towards Masters String Dev Univ WI Madison; *cr:* Elem Orch Dir 1974-82, Jr HS Orch Dir 1977-83, HS Orch Dir 1982- Rochester Public Schls; *ai:* John Marshall String Quartet; Amer String Teachers Assn; Rochester Symphony Orch (Prin 2nd Violin 1975-79, Section 1st Violin 1979-); Rochester Youth Orch Dir 1982-85; All City Elem Orch Dir 1975-79; Article Published 1983; *office:* John Marshall HS 1510 NW 14th St Rochester MN 55901

WORKMAN, TERRY RADTKE, English/History Teacher; *b:* Twin Falls, ID; *m:* Raymond; *c:* C. J. Montgomery, Terry J. Montgomery; *ed:* (BS) Eng/His, Univ of ID 1971; Various Classes & Wkshps ID St Univ; *cr:* Eng/His Teacher Amer Falls Sr HS 1982-; *ai:* Frosh Class Adv; NEA, ID Ed Assn, Amer Falls Ed Assn 1982-87, 1989-; *office:* Amer Falls HS 254 Taylor American Falls ID 83211

WORLEY, BETTY QUINN, 2nd Grade Teacher; *b:* New York, VA; *m:* Harvey L. Jr.; *c:* Lee, Jeffrey; *ed:* (BA) Span, Radford Univ 1961; *cr:* Spanish/French Teacher Deep Creek HS 1961-62; 2nd Grade Teacher Lanahan 1962-63; 3rd Grade Teacher Portsmouth City 1962-63; Elem Teacher VA Beach Sch 1963-69; Henry Elem 1973-; *ai:* VA Ed Assn; NEA; Franklin Cty Ed Assn; Delta Kappa Gamma Ed Society; Ruritan Ladies Aux (Pres; Sec 1988-); *office:* Henry Elem Sch Rt 1 Henry VA 24102

WORLEY, DANIEL OSBORN, Sixth Grade Teacher; *b:* San Diego, CA; *m:* Geriann E. Cox; *c:* Benjamin; *ed:* (BS) Sociology, GA Coll 1973; (MED) Elem Ed, North GA Coll 1978; *cr:* 5th Grade Teacher Ellijay Elem Sch 1973-88; 6th Grade Teacher Ellijay Mid Sch 1988-; *ai:* GAE 1973-; Ellijay Lions Club (Secy 1978) 1973-79; Cartecay Optimist Club (VP 1987) 1982-89; United Meth Men (VP 1978) 1973-79; *home:* PO Box 704 Ellijay GA 30540

WORLEY, DAVID H., Unified Studies Teacher; *b:* Topeka, KS; *c:* Heather, Lauren; *ed:* (BA) Eng, WA Univ 1979; (MA) Spec Ed, Univ of MO 1987; *cr:* Teacher/Asst Prin The Metropolitan Sch 1980-85; Teacher Parkway South Jr HS 1985-; *ai:* Soccer Coach; Care Team Chm; City/Cty Partnership Spon; NEA, Parkway Ed Assn; Natl Soccer Coaches Assn of America 1985-; *office:* Parkway South Jr HS 760 Woods Mill Rd Manchester MO 63011

WORLEY, DAVID WAYNE, Principal; *b:* Herrin, IL; *m:* Bonita J. Mc Graw; *c:* (BRED) Religious Ed, Trinity Coll of Bible; (THB) Theology, (MDIV) Theology/Bible, Trinity Theological Seminary; *ed:* Assemblies of God Theological Seminary; *cr:* Pastor Pentecostal Assembly 1971-73, First Pentecostal Church 1973-; Prin Murphysboro Chrstn Acad 1976-; *ai:* ACSI Spelling Bee Chm 1989; South & Jr HS Speech Meet; Bethel Ministerial Assn, Dir Bethel Ministerial Acad 1990; *home:* 2101 Dewey St Murphysboro IL 62966

WORLEY, RUTH, Social Studies Dept Chairman; *b:* Boston, MA; *m:* Ben F.; *ed:* (BA) Poly Sci, Taylor Univ 1972; Ball St Univ, N TX St Univ; *cr:* Teacher Kennedale HS 1984-; *ai:* NHS & Debate Team Spon; Chamber of Commerce 1972; Internship Philip Hart Washington DC; Teacher of Month; VOCT Honorary

Certificate; *office:* Kennedale HS PO Box 1208 Kennedale TX 76060

WORREL, MARY JO WHITE, Third Grade Teacher; *b:* Elizabeth City, NC; *m:* Livius Fenton Jr.; *c:* Craig F., Kirk J.; *ed:* (BA) Early Chldhd, Meth Coll 1973; *cr:* 3rd Grade Teacher Ferguson Easley Elem 1973-77, Lucile Souders Elem 1977-85, Ferguson Easley Elem 1985-86, Lucile Souders Elem 1986-; *ai:* Mentor Teacher; PACE, NC Assn of Educators, Assn of Classroom Teachers, Cumberland Fayetteville Assn of Educators 1973-; Cub Scouts Awds Chairperson 1989-; *office:* Lucile Souders Sch 128 Hillview Ave Fayetteville NC 28301

WORTH, HELEN R., Student Teacher Supervisor; *b:* Portville, NY; *m:* James William; *c:* Mary K. Kewley, Karen Foster, Bradley; *ed:* (BA) Eng, 1971, (MA) Ed, 1976 St Bonaventure; Grad Stud Rdng; *cr:* Eng Teacher Portville Cntrl Sch 1971-89; Part-Time Eng Instr Jamestown Comm Coll 1988-89; Supvr Stu Teachers St Bonaventure Univ 1989-; *ai:* Gifted/Talented Coord; Yrbk 1976-89, Ski Club 1972-89, IBM Cmptr, Stu Paper 1985-89, Model United Nations, Its Academic Adv; St Bonaventure Coord Teacher; Drama Dir; Phi Delta Kappa 1983-; PTA 1971-; NYSUT (Pres, Secy) 1971-88; St Bonaventure Univ Ed Dept Secy; Faculty Assn Pres; Portville United Meth Church Lay Leader; Bicentennial Pageant Dir; Portville Historical Society Trustee; Organized & Presented Inservice Wkshp; Randolph Cntrl Sch Inservice Wkshp Presenter; Expanded Sr Debate Team to Cattaraugus Cty Level; Implemented Comm Courses I & II; Helped Organize Olympics of Mind; *home:* 84 Brooklyn St Portville NY 14770

WORTHAM, DAVID, Social Studies Chairman; *b:* Fulton, KY; *ed:* (BS) His/Geography, 1969, (MA) Geography, 1972 Murray St Univ; *cr:* 7th Grade Soc Stud Teacher T K Stone Jr HS 1969-; *ai:* Pep Club Spon 1983-86; Yrbk Spon 1984-86; Local Educl Curr Comm; Local Bicentennial Comm 1976; KY Bicentennial Comm 1992; Elizabethtown Ed Assn, KY Ed Assn, NEA; Memorial United Meth Church Mem; Daughters of Amer Revolution Patriotism Awd, Bicentennial Youth Exhibit Awd 1976; Severns Valley Bicentennial Exhibit Awd 1979; Teacher of Yr T K Stone Jr HS, Elizabethtown Ind Schls 1982-83; *office:* T K Stone Jr HS Morningside Dr Elizabethtown KY 42701

WORTHY, CHRISTINE DARE (SWORDS), K-5th Grade Teacher; *b:* Tonkawa, OK; *m:* Lawrence Dee; *c:* Elizabeth A., Margaret D. Peredo, Judy L. Carter; *ed:* (AA) Music, N OK Coll 1961; (BA) Music, Univ of MD 1978; (MA) Learning Disabilities, Ball St Univ 1981; Emotionally Disturbed Cert, OK St Univ; *cr:* 5th-12th Grade Instrumental Music/Soc Stud Teacher 1983-84, 7th-12th Grade Soc Stud Teacher 1984-86, 7-12th Grade Learning Disabilities/Soc Stud Teacher 1986-87 Hominy Public Schls; K-5th Grade Learning Disibilities Teacher Horace Mann Elem 1987-; *ai:* NEA, OEA, 1983-; HEA (Secy, Bargaining Team, Staff Dev, Chairperson) 1983-; OACLD 1986-; ESA 1989-; *office:* Horace Mann Elem PO Box 400 Hominy OK 74035

WORTZMAN, MARILYN B., 5th Grade Teacher; *b:* Boston, MA; *m:* Sidney; *c:* Norman, Jerry; *ed:* (BSED) Elem, Boston St 1948; *cr:* 1st Grade Teacher Roxbury-Garrison Sch 1948-49, Charlestown 1949-; 5th Grade Teacher Donovan 1969-; *ai:* PTO Teacher Rep; *office:* M L Donovan Sch Reed St Randolph MA 02368

WOS, EVELYN MUZIKA, Jr High/Language Arts Teacher; *b:* Chicago, IL; *w:* Michael Vincent (dec); *c:* Vincent, Anthony, Karen; *ed:* (BA) Eng, Mundelein Coll 1960; Exceptional Children, Delourdes Coll; *cr:* Drama/Honors Eng Teacher Harrison HS 1960-62; Honor Eng Teacher Gage Park HS 1962-63; Substitute Teacher 1969; Jr HS Eng Teacher St Charles Borromeo 1985-; *ai:* Drug Abuse Coord 7th-8th Grades; 5th-8th Grade Coord; *home:* 563 N Mt Prospect Rd Des Plaines IL 60016

WOUDENBERG, THOMAS JOHN, Biology Teacher; *b:* Paterson, NJ; *m:* June T.; *c:* Terry Lussos, Deborah Upham; *ed:* (AB) Bio, Rutgers Univ 1956-60; Biophysics, Medical Coll of VA 1960-61; Teaching Cert Montclair St 1962-63; (MA) Bio/Ed, Lehigh Univ 1970-72; Research, Univ of WI 1966, 1967; Sci & Curr Dev, Wesleyan Univ 1983-; *cr:* Bio Teacher Columbia HS 1961-67; Bio Instr Fairleigh Dickinson Univ 1965-67; Sci Dept Head Nkumbi Intnl Coll Zambia Africa 1967-69; Sci Dept Chm Moravian Acad 1970-72; Ed Supvr Compagnie Des Bauxities De Guinee Guinea West Africa 1972-75; Bio Teacher East Lyme HS 1975-; *ai:* East Lyme Adult Ed Diploma Prgm Dir 1977-80; PIMMS Bio Writing Team Mem & Elem Sci Staff Bio Instr 1984-; CCL & Natl Sci Fnd Project St Sci Advisory Comm 1989-; Articles Published; *office:* East Lyme HS 30 Chesterfield Rd East Lyme CT 06333

WOWK, PATRICIA DIANE, English Teacher; *b:* Richmond, KY; *m:* Vitaly; *ed:* (BA) Eng, 1980, (Rank II) Ed/Eng Emphasis, 1982 Eastern KY Univ; *cr:* Eng Teacher Foley Mid Sch 1982-; *ai:* Spon Sch Newspaper; *office:* Foley Mid Sch 211 Glades Rd Berea KY 40403

WOZNIAK, KATHLEEN LOUISE, Fifth Grade Teacher; *b:* Blue Island, IL; *ed:* (BA) Eng, Coll of St Francis 1972; (MS) Ed, Valparaiso Univ 1978; Learning Disabilities Endorsement, IN Univ 1989; *cr:* 3rd Grade Teacher Queen of All Saints Sch 1972-73; 3rd/5th Grade Teacher St Patrick Sch 1973-88; Learning Disabilities Teacher Knapp Elem Sch 1988-89; 5th Grade Teacher Our Lady of Grace Sch 1989-; *ai:* Intnl Rdng Assn Treas 1979-80; Assn of Children & Adults with Learning Disabilities; *home:* 10952 Avenue O Chicago IL 60617

WOZNIAK, STANLEY JOHN, JR., Fourth Grade Teacher; *b:* Chicago, IL; *m:* Julie Ann Rohloff; *c:* Jennifer L.; *ed:* (BA) Elem Ed, Univ of IL Chicago 1978; *cr:* 4th Grade Teacher Jonathan Scammon Sch 1982-; *ai:* Stu Cncl; Prof Personnel Advisory; Scammon Band Dir; Adopt-A-Sch Rep; IL PTA Local; Teacher of Yr; *office:* Jonathan Young Scammon Sch 4201 W Henderson Chicago IL 60641

WRAY, BESSIE HOLLAND, Grade School Teacher; *b:* Rocky Mount, VA; *m:* Robert Elmore Sr.; *c:* Deborah Wray Wilson, Robert E. Jr., Traketa K.; *ed:* (BS) Soc Stud/His/Music Ed, Bluefield St Teachers Coll 1945-65; Cert Elem, Univ of VA; *cr:* Librarian Truvine Elem Sch 1962-69; Teacher Callaway Elem Sch 1969-; *ai:* Outstanding Elem Teachers of America 1972; VA Ed Assn 1962-; NEA 1962-; Title I Fed Prgm Rep Nominee; Personalities of South Nominee 1972; Mary Bethune Civic Organization Secy 1978-; Bd Mem Cmmty Action 1969; Organist-Pianist Church Choir.

WRAY, FARRELL D., 8th Grade English Teacher; *b:* Blackfoot, ID; *m:* Claudia Wheeler; *c:* Kerri, Korden, Kimberly, Kendell, Kelly, Dean, Tyrel, Amy, Karson; *ed:* (BA) Scndry Ed/Foreign Lang/Ger/Eng/Soc Stud, ID St Univ 1971; Grad Stud; *cr:* 8th Grade Eng Teacher Snake River Jr HS 1971-74; 9th Grade Soc Stud Teacher Blackfoot HS 1985-86; 8th Grade Eng/Rdng Teacher Mountain View Mid Sch 1986-; *ai:* Score 8th Grade St of ID Writing Tests; ID Cncl of Eng Teachers; *office:* Mountain View Mid Sch 1340 Mitchell Ln Blackfoot ID 83221

WREN, LOIS JEAN (LEININGER), 4th Grade Teacher; *b:* Gladwin, MI; *M:* Kenneth; *c:* Deborah J. Stewart, Pamela M. Hecht, Paul W.; *ed:* (BA) Delta Comm Coll 1971; (BA) Elem Ed, 1973; (MA) Elem Ed, 1976 Saginaw Valley St Univ; *cr:* 4th Grade Teacher Freeland Elem 1973-; *ai:* Girl Scouts; Sch Carnival; Playground Comm; Prin Selection Comm; Textbook Selection Comm; Freeland Ed Assn 1973-; NEA 1973-; Py Sec 1963-65; St Anne Society Pres 1966; *office:* Freeland Elem Sch 710 Powley Dr Freeland MI 48623

WRIGHT, ANN PROSSER, Sixth Grade Teacher; *b:* Nashville, TN; *m:* Billy W.; *c:* Christi L. Carter, Sara E. Smith; *ed:* (BA) Ed, Mid TN St Univ 1972; *cr:* 5th Grade Teacher Guild Elem 1972-76; 5th/6th Grade Teacher Rucker-Stewart 1976-; *ai:* Delta Kappa Gamma 1980-; *office:* Rucker Steward Elem Sch 600 Small St Gallatin TN 37066

WRIGHT, ANNA BELLE, 2nd Grade Teacher; *b:* Roxana, KY; *ed:* (BS) Elem, Cumberland Coll 1973; (MA) Elem, Union Coll; *cr:* Teacher Eolia 1974-77, Letcher 1978-; *ai:* LCTO, KEA, NEA; *home:* HC 71 Box 995 Roxana KY 41848

WRIGHT, BARBARA LOUISE, 6th Grade Teacher; *b:* St Petersburg, FL; *m:* Willie J.; *c:* Wanda K. Green; *ed:* (AA) Elem Ed, Gibbs Jr Coll 1961; (BS) FL A&M Univ 1966; Cert Math, Mid Sch; *cr:* Teacher Trinity Headstart 1965-66, Royal Elem 1967-68, Eustis Elem/Eustis Mid Sch; *ai:* NEA, Lake Cty Ed Assn, FL A&M Univ Alumni; Church of God (Young Ladies Ministry, Tutor); *home:* 822 Douglas St Leesburg FL 34748

WRIGHT, BARBARA ROBERSON, Math Dept Chair/Math Teacher; *b:* Mobile, AL; *c:* Robert K., Lisa R.; *ed:* (BS) Math, AL St Univ 1967; Ed for Gifted & Talented Math, Advanced Placement Math Conference; Instructional Effectiveness Trng, Kelwyn Incorporated; *cr:* Math/Sci Teacher Paret Hart Jr HS 1968-69; Math Teacher Vista Nueva HS 1969-70, Wagner Mid Sch 1970-71, Vigor HS 1972-74, Centennial Jr HS 1975-76, Star Spencer HS 1978-; *ai:* Academic Coach; Math Club & St Jude Math-A-Thon Spon; OK Academic Coaches Assn 1990; Eta Phi Beta 1986-; Teacher of Yr Star Spencer HS 1988-89; *home:* 963 Kooiman St Mobile AL 36617

WRIGHT, BERNADINE TYLER, Teacher/Math Department Chair; *b:* Greenville, MS; *m:* Sylvester Rogers Jr.; *c:* Sylvester R. Jr., Cedric D.; *ed:* (BS) Math, MS Valley St Univ 1977; Memphis St Univ; Ed, Lemoyne Owens Coll; Math Text, St Tech Inst; *cr:* Teaching Aid Warrensburg Jr HS 1977-78; Teacher Frayser HS 1978-80, Graceland Jr HS 1980-; *ai:* Graceland Jr HS Math Club Spon; Graceland Jr HS AIDS Awareness Comm Mem; Graceland Jr HS Math Dept Chairperson; Memphis Urban Mem 1987-; Math Collabrative; Memphis City Schls Title I Math Grant; Pat Carter Pontiac Incorporated Teacher of Month 1986.

WRIGHT, BETTY JEAN CROOM, Teacher of the Gifted Gr 1-5; *b:* Apalachicola, FL; *m:* Robert Lee, Jr; *c:* Michelle A. Towers, Robert Lee III; *ed:* (BS) Elem Ed, FL A & M Univ 1963; (MA) Spec Ed, OK Univ 1985; Gifted Ed, OK CityUniv 1989-Present 180 Hrs in Staff Dev; *cr:* Teacher Mainz, Germany Public Schls 1964-66; Primary Teacher Lawton Public Schls 1966-78, Tulsa Public Schools 1978-80; Intermediate/Primary/Gifted OK City Public Schls 1980-; *ai:* Trainer for Teachers 1986-; Present Educl Wkshps for Educators; Mem of Task for Federal Grants; Mem of Stu Schlsp Comm at CSU: Invention Dev Soc, Chm Children's Prgms 1985-; First Southern Baptist Church Outreach Ldr 1985-; Cox Cable Multimedia TV, TV Math Teacher 1989-; Public School Fnd Grant Recipient 1986-; George Washington Medal of Honor Winner, Freedom Fnd 1988; 1st Place St Winner, Excl in Ec Ed 1980; Teacher of Yr OK Public Schls 1989; Finer Womenhood Awd 1990; Excl in Architecture Awd 1990; St Public Relations Teacher of Yr 1990; 2 Time Winner State Ed Awd Natl Invent America; Published Articles in Nanaikana Newsletter 1987-88, DAGCT Newsletter 1987 & 89.

WRIGHT, CAROL S., Social Studies Teacher; *b:* Wilmington, DE; *c:* Angela; *ed:* (BA) Elem Ed, 1970, (MA) Curr/Instruction, DE St Coll; Grad Stud Ed, Univ of DE; *cr:* Follow Through Teacher Northeast Elem Sch 1970-75; 6th Grade Teacher Bayard Mid Sch 1975-77; 3rd/5th Grade Teacher William C Lewis Elem Sch 1978-79, Marbrook Elem Sch 1979-; *ai:* DSEA Building Rep; Soc Stud Dept Chairperson; Cadette Girl Scout Leader Troop 1087; Minority Action Comm DE Ed Assn; Phi Delta Kappa 1973-; New Castle Cty Twigs Chaplain 1987-88; *office:* Marbrook Elem Sch 2101 Centerville Rd Wilmington DE 19808

WRIGHT, CORA B. JUDY, 5th & 6th Combination Teacher; *b:* Athens, GA; *w:* Robert C. (dec); *c:* Forrest Cummings, Stephanie Wright-Watson, Tamera, Tonya Logue, Patricia Anderson; *ed:* (AA) Child Dev, Chaffey Coll 1976; (BA) Liberal Arts, 1978; (MA) Ed, 1985 CA ST Univ at San Bernardino; *cr:* Child Dev Specialist II Chaffey Comm Coll 1976-80; Teacher Central Sch Dist 1980-; *ai:* Central Sch Square Dance Instr; Curr Cncl Central Dist; Girl Scouts of Amer Certificate of Appreciation 1959-74; Spanish Trails, Brownie Girl Scout Leader, Jr Girl Scout Leader, Cadette Girl Scout Leader, Girl Scout Troop Organizer, Consultant; Coach Golden Girl Sftbl; Pomona 1st Baptist Church Teacher 1959-; Exemplary Schlsp 1974, Dean's Honor List 1975, Permanent Mem Alph Gamma Sigma Chaffey Coll; Honorary Services Awd Cert CA Congress of Parents & Teachers Inc El Camino Sch , Ontario-Montclair Sch Dist; Cert of Appreciation, Spanish Trails Girl Scout Cncl; *office:* Central Elem Sch 7955 Archibald Rancho Cucamonga CA 91730

WRIGHT, DAMON H., Religion Teacher; *b:* Salem, OR; *m:* Karen C. Seitz; *c:* Rebecca, Joshua; *ed:* (BS) Math/Scndry Ed, OR Coll of Ed 1972; (AA) Biblical Stud, Nazarene Bible Coll 1983; *cr:* Data Processing Dir Clatsop Comm Coll 1976-81; Cmptr Programmer CO Coll 1981-83; Pastor Church of the Nazarene NY, AZ, OK, TX 1983-; Bible Teacher Presbyn Pan Amer Sch 1989-; *ai:* Wesleyan Theological Society 1982-; *home:* 1809 E Caesar Kingsville TX 78363

WRIGHT, DAN L., Secondary Math Teacher; *b:* Tucumcari, NM; *ed:* (BS) Math, Eastern NM Univ 1972; Bus; Ed & Math; Cmptr; Marketing & Accounting; *cr:* Teacher Clovis Public Schls 1972-76; Chama Valley Schls 1976-77, Albuquerque Public Schls 1977-; *ai:* Activity Period Teach Beginning Guitar; Coord/Producer 3 Sch Wide Talent Shows; Self-Employed in a Computerized Accounting Service; *office:* Hayes Mid Sch 1100 Texas NE Albuquerque NM 87110

WRIGHT, DARRELL LEWIS, Health, Phys Ed Teacher; *b:* Columbia, SC; *m:* Cathy Eastmond; *c:* Danielle, Cameron; *ed:* (BS) Health/Phys Ed, NC A&T St 1985; Phys Ed, Gardner Webb Coll; *cr:* Health/Phys Ed Instr/Head Ftbl/Bsktbl Coach Rohanen Jr HS 1985-; *ai:* Act Park Dir Palisade 1988-89; NEA (Sch Rep 1989-) 1985-; NC Coaches Assn 1985-; NC Assn of Educators (Sch Rep 1989-) 1985-; Phi Beta Sigma 1980-; Ind Order of Foresters 1989-; US Jaycees Richmond Cty 1988-; Natl Assn Advancement of Colored People 1989-; Rohanen Jr HS Coach of Yr 1988-89; *home:* 920 Montclair Ave Rockingham NC 28379

WRIGHT, DAVID BRIAN, Physics Teacher; *b:* Denville, NJ; *ed:* (BA) Phys Sci, Glassboro St Coll 1985; *cr:* Physics/Chem Teacher Washington Township HS 1985-; *ai:* Interact Co-Adv; Asst Var Girls Soccer & Track Coach; Ftbl & Bsktbl Games Announcer; Contract Negotiations Team Mem; Amer Chem Society Teachers (Affiliate, Chm) 1987-; NSTA 1985-; Washington Township Ed Assn Building Rep; *office:* Washington Township HS Hurtville-Cross Keys Rd Sewell NJ 08080

WRIGHT, DAVID WALTER, American History Teacher; *b:* Fairmont, WV; *m:* Kelly M.; *c:* Jordan L., Collyn E.; *ed:* (AB) Elem Ed, West Liberty St Coll 1977; (MS) Admin, Univ of Dayton 1980; *cr:* Teacher Cameron Elem 1977-78; Teacher Sardis Elem 1978-; *ai:* Bsktbl/Ftbll Coaching 1977-; Residential Outdoor Ed Teacher/Cnslr 1977-; Various Dist Comm; NEA; OEA; SOEA; Free Masonry; Vol Fire Dept/E Squad; United Meth Church; *office:* Sardis Elem Sch St Rt 7 Sardis OH 43946

WRIGHT, DONNA LOU, Science Dept/Russian Teacher; *b:* Greenville, KY; *ed:* (BS) Bio, 1971, (MAE) Botany, 1979 W KY Univ; *cr:* Sci/Russian Teacher Graham HS 1972-; *ai:* Russian Club; MCEA, KEA, NEA 1972-; *office:* Graham HS Hwy 175 Graham KY 42344

WRIGHT, DOROTHEA HELEN, Science Teacher; *b:* San Angelo, TX; *ed:* (BS) Bio, 1968, (MED) Guidance/Counseling, 1988 Angelo St Univ; Chem Cert 1981; Emergency Medical Technician Spec Skills TX Dept of Health; *cr:* Sci Teacher Rankin Jr HS 1968-69; Bio Teacher Thomas Jefferson HS 1969-75; Recreation Therapist San Angelo St Sch 1975-76; Sci Teacher Robert Lee HS 1976-; *ai:* UIL Sci Team; Order of Eastern Star Past Matron 1984-85; Fellow Amer Petroleum Inst; Soil & Water Conservation Service Wkshp; *office:* Robert Lee HS HC 61 Box 303 Robert Lee TX 76945

WRIGHT, DOROTHYE HARRIS, 4th Grade Teacher; *b:* Thomasville, GA; *c:* Kenneth, Sheila, Jeffrey; *ed:* (BS) Elem Ed, Albany St Coll 1958; Cert Remedial Rdng FL A&M Univ 1965; Cert Renewal Ed FL Atlantic Univ 1966; Cert Data Colledctin Univ of GA 1980; *ai:* Simmon Hill Flora Comm; Attendance & Honor Roll; Way & Means; GAE 1958-; NEA 1958-; Piney Grove Baptist Church (MEm 1947- Choir 1947- Sunday Sch Intermed Teacher 1966-68); New Corinth Bapt Church Woman Day Speaker 19967-68; BYPU Pres 1968-69; 2nd Presbyn Day Care Sch PTO 1969-71; Sr Choir Secy 1977-80; Womans Day Chairperson 1982; Brown Bethal Bapt Family/Friends Day Spkr 1980; Honors Day Speaker Gracie Jeffersons Retirement Prgm

1985; Sr Choir Pres 1988; Whighams Elem Coord Ava Elem Sch Prgm 1956-61; Phys Ed Prgm 1959-62; Buckholt Elem Adult Ed 1966-68; Sch Dramatroupe 1968-69; Quitman Primary Instr for Stu Teacher 1974-76; Wrote Language Art Curr 4th Graders in Brooks Cty 1980; Plaques Outstanding Service Awd 1981; Cert of Excellence for Classroom Appearance & Organization 1977-84; Cert of Service & Contributions to Simmon Hill Elem Sch 1977-79; *office:* Simmon Hill Elem Sch Rt 1 Box 216 Dixie GA 31629

WRIGHT, EARL RAY, Middle School Science Teacher; *b:* Russellville, KY; *m:* Marilyn June Kees; *c:* Shannon; *ed:* (BA) Bio/Phys Ed, 1970, (MA) Ed, 1973 W KY Univ; *cr:* Sci Teacher Auburn Mid Sch 1970-; *ai:* Textbook Adoption Comm for Mid Sch Sci; Code of Conduct/Stu Handbook Comm Chm; Logan Cty Ed Assn Sch Rep 1970-73; *office:* Auburn Mid Sch College St Auburn KY 42206

WRIGHT, ELLEN E., VOE Teacher/Coordinator; *b:* Buffalo, NY; *m:* William T.; *c:* Stephanie D., Alexander; *ed:* (BS) Bus, N TX St Univ 1964; Grad Stud; *cr:* Bus Teacher Forreston HS 1964-65, Yorktown HS 1965-66, Sinton HS 1966-68; Eng Teacher Tatum HS 1969; Voc Ed Teacher Bastrop HS 1981-; *ai:* Bus Prof of America & Office Admin Chapter Adv; Univ of N TX Alumni Assn; Outstanding Service Awd for Conference Co-Chm 1987; Nom Outstanding Teacher 1990; *office:* Bastrop HS 1602 Hill St Bastrop TX 78602

WRIGHT, GARY KEITH, 5th Grade Teacher; *b:* Denison, IA; *m:* Vicki Lee Bromander; *ed:* (BA) Elem Ed, Midwestern Coll 1969; (MS) Elem Admin, Bemidji St Univ 1973; Hospital Corps Sch US Navy; *cr:* 5th Grade Teacher West Monona West 1969-75; 5th Grade Teacher/Asst Prin West Monona Blencoe 1975-82; 5th Grade Teacher West Monona Cntrl 1982-; *ai:* 7th Grade Ftbl Coach; NEA, IA St Ed Assn 1969-; West Monona Ed Assn Pres 1986-; *home:* Box 296 Blue Lake Onawa IA 51040

WRIGHT, GINGER CONNELLEY, Physical Education Teacher; *b:* Houston, TX; *c:* Toby, Mary Quinn; *ed:* (BS) Phys Ed, TX Tech Univ 1965; USPTR Certificate, Dennis Van De Meer Tennis Univ; Grad Courses, Bryn Mawr VA; *cr:* Phys Ed Teacher St Anns Sch 1965-71, Duchesne Acad 1972-74, E Terrell Hills 1975-79, Kingwood HS 1982-83, Wilson Jr HS 1983-; *ai:* Tennis & Girls Sftbl Coach; Chm Ladies Doubles League Kingwood Cntry Club; NEA 1975-; TSTA, LEA 1983-; TAPEHRD, AAPEHRD 1965-; Major/Minor Club Pres 1964-65; Jaycettes 1967-71; Outstanding Coach of Yr St Matthews Church 1977; *office:* Smylie Wilson Jr HS 4402 31st St Lubbock TX 79410

WRIGHT, GLADYS SMITH, Second Grade Teacher; *b:* Sharpsburg, GA; *m:* Charles H.; *c:* Stephen, Jonathan, Joseph; *ed:* (BS) Elem Ed, Berry Coll 1959; *cr:* 3rd Grade Teacher West Griffin Sch 1959-62, Rankin Sch 1962-67; 2nd Grade Teacher Atkinson Sch 1967-70; 2nd & 3rd Grade Teacher Northside Sch 1972-; *ai:* Page; PTO; Bapt Church Sunday Sch Teacher 1960-; *home:* 65 Redwine Dr Newman GA 30263

WRIGHT, GLENN A., Language Art Dept Chairperson; *b:* San Francisco, CA; *m:* Dorothy Ann Lindemann; *c:* Matthew, Peter, Ann; *ed:* (BA) Eng, Univ of San Francisco 1973; (MED) Scndry Ed, Univ of AK 1983; *cr:* Teacher Robert Service HS 1975-; *ai:* Scndry Lang Art Curr Comm Rep; Phi Delta Kappa Mem 1983-; NEA Mem 1975-; Kappa Delta Pi Mem 1988-; PTSA Service HS VP; Outstanding Stu Teacher, Univ of San Francisco 1973; Cncl for Basic Ed Natl Endowment for Hum Fellow 1987; *office:* Robert Service HS 5577 Abbott Rd Anchorage AK 99507

WRIGHT, HAROLD C., Fourth Grade Teacher; *b:* Mc Lean Cty, KY; *m:* Araceli Noblejas; *c:* Dan, Pam Inguaggiato; *ed:* (AA) Ed, Merced Jr Coll 1973; (BA) Liberal Stud, CA St Univ Stanislaus 1976; (MA) Ed, Chapman Coll 1985; *cr:* Sergeant USAF 1951-72; Teacher Atwater Elem Sch Dist 1979-; *office:* Thomas Olaeta Sch 2266 High St Atwater CA 95301

WRIGHT, IVAN C., Art Teacher; *b:* Heidelberg, Germany; *m:* Marianne Knott; *c:* Meredith; *ed:* (BA) Art Ed, 1970, (MA) Art Ed, 1971 Univ of NM; Grad Stud Center for Understanding Media; Brook Inst of Photography Santa Barbara; *cr:* Art Teacher Univ of NM 1970-71, Rio Grande HS 1972-84, Manzano HS 1984-, UNM Comm Coll; *ai:* NMAEA Secy 1981-82; Fellowship to Study Filmaking NY City; *office:* Manzano HS 12200 Lomas Blvd NE Albuquerque NM 87112

WRIGHT, JAMA COVINGTON, 1st Grade Teacher; *b:* Gallatin, TN; *m:* W. Nelson; *c:* James N.; *ed:* (AS) Elem Ed, Volunteer St Comm Coll 1975; (BS) Elem Ed, Austin Peay St Univ 1977; Grad Stud Austin Peay St Univ; *cr:* 1st Grade Teacher 1977-78, 1st/2nd Grade Teacher 1978-79, 1st Grade Teacher 1979- E Robertson; *ai:* NEA, TN Ed Assn, Robertson Cty Ed Assn 1977-; *office:* E Robertson Sch 5571 E Robertson Rd Cross Plains TN 37049

WRIGHT, JAMES EDWIN, Biology Teacher; *b:* Sewickley, PA; *m:* Darla Kay Copeland; *c:* Jason, Justin; *ed:* (BA) Zoology, TX Tech Univ 1973; Grad Work Midwestern St Univ; *cr:* Bio Teacher Burkburnett HS 1973-; *ai:* NEA 1973-; TX St Teachers Assn (Local VP 1975-76, Local Pres 1976-77) 1973-; Nom Teacher of Yr 1982-83, 1986-87; *office:* Burkburnett HS 109 W Kramer Rd Burkburnett TX 76354

WRIGHT, JANET CAROL, School Counselor; *b:* La Grande, OR; *m:* Bert Leroy; *c:* Kelley S. Borresen, Heather L.; *ed:* (BS) Math, Univ of OR 1965; (MS) Counseling, OR Coll Of Ed 1973; Child Abuse & Human Sexuality Wkshps; Impact Trng; *cr:* Sci Teacher 1970, Dean of Girls 1970-72 La Grande Jr HS; Cnslr Lebanon HS 1973-74, Sweet Home Jr HS 1974-; *ai:* Achievement Awd Adv; Sexual Abuse Group & Children of Alcoholics & Addicts Group Facilitators; Mid Sch Master Schedule, Site, Dist Teacher Recognition Comms; Dist & Local Core Team; OR Ed Assn 1970-; Sweet Home Ed Assn 1974-; NEA 1970-; Teacher of Yr 1987-88; *office:* Sweet Home Jr HS 880 22nd Ave Sweet Home OR 97386

WRIGHT, JANET JACKSON, Third Grade Teacher; *b:* Radford, VA; *ed:* (BS) Elem Ed, Longwood Coll 1971; Grad Courses, Univ of Richmond; *cr:* 3rd Grade Teacher Varina Elem 1971-72, Jackson Davis Elem 1972-73; 1st Grade Teacher 1973-79, 3rd Grade Teacher 1979- Jackson Davis Elem; *ai:* Safety & Lib Media Services Comm Self Study; Westhampton Jr Womans Club Secy 1984-85; *office:* Jackson Davis Elem Sch 8801 Nesslewood Dr Richmond VA 23229

WRIGHT, JEAN NORMAN, Sixth Grade Teacher; *b:* Norristown, PA; *w:* John A. (dec); *c:* Lori Lutter, Larry; *ed:* (BA) Eng, Cedar Crest Coll 1953; Western Reserve; Penn St Extension; *cr:* 1st Grade Teacher Upson Sch 1953-55; Art/Music Teacher 1965-70, 3rd Grade Teacher 1970-81, 6th Grade Teacher 1981- Schuylkill Elem; *ai:* PSEA 1970-; Delta Kappa Gamma (VP 1986-, Pres 1990); Cedar Crest Coll Alumnae Bd 1980-84; Cedar Crest Coll Alumnae Pres 1962-64; Presbyn Church Deacon 1988-; Cmmty Concerts Assn Bd 1986-; Valley Forge Sweet Adelines 1987-; Conducted Wkshp on Creative Teaching; *office:* Schuylkill Elem Sch White Horse Rd Phoenixville PA 19460

WRIGHT, JUNE ALDERSON, Kindergarten Teacher; *b:* Mc Alester, OK; *m:* Donald Brown; *c:* Susan D. *ed:* (BS) Voc Home Ec, OK St Univ 1955; (MED) Elem Ed - Cum Laude, Cntrl St Univ 1970; Additional Trng OK City Univ & Cntrl St Univ; *cr:* Home Service Consultant OK Gas & Electric Company 1955-58; Kndgtn Teacher Oklahoma City Public Schls 1958-; *ai:* Sch Organization Comms; Kappa Kappa Iota (Historian, VP, Pres) 1967-; Delta Kappa Gamma Treas 1980-; Phi Kappa Phi 1955-56; Kappa Delta Pi Membership 1955-56; N Cntrl Assn Chairperson; OK City Rdng Cncl Treas 1970-; OK Educl Assn, NEA, OK City Classroom Teachers Assn 1958-87; Received Federal Grant 1984-85; Grants from OK City Public Sch Fnd 1987-88, 1990.

WRIGHT, KATHRYN ANN JONES, Teacher of Gifted/Eng; *b:* Great Falls, MT; *c:* Christopher; *ed:* (BA) Elem Ed/Eng, Coll of Great Falls 1971; (MAT) Ed, Rollins Coll 1978; Grad Stud; *cr:* Math Teacher Mt Dora Mid Sch 1971; 6th Grade Teacher 1972-81, 6th Grade Eng Teacher 1981-86 Dabney 5 & 6 Sch; 7th/8th Grade Eng Teacher 1987-88, Eng Teacher of Gifted 1988- Oak Park Mid Sch; *ai:* Newspaper Adv; Jazzercize Coach; Underprivileged Stu Tutoring; Lake Cty Ed Assn 1972-; Zeta Phi Beta 1975-; Kappa Delta Pi 1978-; Cty-St Textbook Cncl 1989-; Iris Proie Educl Grant 1989-; Mote-Morris House Archealogical Grant 1990; Poem, Short Stories Published 1980, 1986; *office:* Oak Park Mid Sch 2101 W South St Leesburg FL 34748

WRIGHT, LAWRENCE ALFRED, Principal; *b:* Minatare, NE; *m:* Sharon G.; *c:* Jenifer, Toni Mc Garvey, Kim W.; *ed:* (BS) Biological Sci, 1960, (MED) Guidance/Counseling, 1969 OR St Univ; Admin Cert 1979; *cr:* Bio Teacher 1961-69, Cnslr 1967-69 Canby HS; Job Placement Officer Clackamas Comm Coll 1969-75; Asst Prin 1975-85, Prin 1985- Canby HS; *ai:* Head Wrestling Canby 1967-69, Asst Ftbl Canby 1961-66, Wrestling Coach Clackamas Comm Coll 1969-75; Service Club Adv 1977-85; Class Adv 1985-; COSA 1975-; NASSP 1985-; Clackamas Comm Coll (Sch Bd Mem 1976-, Bd Chm 1983); Canby Kiwanis 1st VP 1989-; Wrestling Coaches Assn Pres 1966-; Kiwanian of Month 1989; *office:* Canby Union HS 721 SW 4th Canby OR 97013

WRIGHT, NANCY BARKLEY, 7th/8th Language Arts Teacher; *b:* Ft Eustis, VA; *m:* Greg; *c:* Benjamin; *ed:* (BS) Elem Ed, 1977, (MA) Supervision, 1981 E TN St Univ; Cmptr Wkshps; *cr:* 6th Grade Teacher 1977-81, 7th-8th Grade Teacher 1981- South Cntrl Elem; *ai:* Sch Newspaper, Sch Annual, Scholar Bowl Co-Spon; Developer of Sch Nature Trail; Gifted & Talented Prgm Coord; NEA, TN Ed Assn, WA Cty Ed Assn, PTA; Teacher of Yr 1988; Excel Teacher 1988; Washington Cty Soil Conservation Educator 1989; *home:* Rt 2 Box 91A Telford TN 37690

WRIGHT, NANCY BROWN, Math Teacher; *b:* Glasgow, KY; *m:* Jimmy H.; *c:* Jay, Jalee; *ed:* (BS) Bio/Math, 1965, (MA) Math/Sci Concentration, 1970 W KY Univ; *cr:* Math/Sci Teacher Franklin-Simpson HS 1965-66; Math Teacher Auburn HS 1966-82, Logan Cty HS 1982-; *ai:* LCEA 1966-; KEA, NEA 1965-; *office:* Logan Cty HS 2200 Bowling Green Rd Russellville KY 42276

WRIGHT, PHILORON A., Assistant Principal; *b:* St Augustine, FL; *m:* Cottie Bolling; *c:* Philoron II, Patrick; *ed:* (BS) Sociology, TN St Univ 1970; (MA) Soc Stud, Univ of FL 1976; East India Culture, Univ of Baroda 1976; Cert Admin Univ of FL 1980; *cr:* Teacher Mountain Top Sch 1970-71, Voc Ed Center 1971-72, Mebane Mid Sch 1972-82; Admin Howard Bishop Mid Sch 1982-; *ai:* Sch Prgm Coord; Big Brother to Disadvantaged Boys; FL Assn Sch Admin 1983-; Alpha Phi Alpha 1975-; Developed Prgm Encourage Parents work Closer with Schls; *home:* 9606 NW 62nd Ln Gainesville FL 32606

WRIGHT, RALEIGN K., Math Teacher/Dept Chm; *b:* Warren, OH; *m:* Sandy; *c:* Shannon; *ed:* (BS) Math, Heidelberg Coll 1963; (MED) Scndry Admin, Westminster Coll 1966; Grad Stud Ed; *cr:* Math Teacher Levitsburg OH 1963-67, Youngstown Woodrow HS 1966-67, Antelope Valley HS 1967-; *ai:* Mathlete Spon; Math Dept Chm; Various Comm; NEA, CTA, AVUHS; Elks; *office:* Antelope Valley HS 44900 Division St Lancaster CA 93535

WRIGHT, ROSAYLN C., Kindergarten Teacher; *b:* Andalusia, AL; *m:* Charles Farrell; *c:* Robert, Kim; *ed:* (BS) Elem/Early Chldhd Ed, 1976, (MED) Early Chldhd Ed, 1978 Auburn Univ; *cr:* 2nd Grade Teacher 1976-77, Kndgtn Teacher 1977-78 Lyeffion Elem; Kndgtn Teacher Red Level Sch 1978-; *ai:* Red Level Sch Handbook & Advisory Comm; Covington Ed Assn, NEA, Delta Kappa Gamma, AL Assn of Young Children; Covington Cty Human Resources Dept Bd Mem 1986-; *home:* Rt 2 Box 75 Red Level AL 36474

WRIGHT, RUTH E., Retired Teacher; *b:* Elkmont, AL; *m:* Luther E.; *c:* Beverly Wright Nemanic, Donald E.; *ed:* (BS) His/Eng, 1941, (MA) Psych, 1961 Vanderbilt; Amer Airline Sch Earned Wings; *cr:* Teacher Limestone Cty Schls 1941-42; Airline Stewardess Amer Airlines 1943-44; Teacher Lovett Sch 1950-64, Randolph Sch 1964-84; *ai:* Church Comm, Church Vestry, Local Civic Groups; Vanderbilt Alumni Bd 1960-64; Started Private Sch St Andrews 1945-46; *office:* Randolph Sch 1005 Drake Ave Huntsville AL 35802

WRIGHT, RUTH NELSON, Teacher; *b:* Memphis, TN; *m:* Michael T.; *c:* Jimmy N., Ruth W., Michael T. Jr.; *ed:* (BS) Elem Ed, Le Moyne-Owen 1973; Continuing Ed Eng, Rdng, Lang Art; Supt of Public Instruction 1988; *cr:* Teacher Memphis City Schls 1974-81, Tacoma Public Schls 1982-; *ai:* Spelling Bee Spon 1983-85; Mid Sch Coord 1988-; Advisory Task Force 1988-; GSA Team Leader 1990; Yrbk & Journalism Adv 1988-; WEA, TEA; PTA; Self Study Comm 1989-; Progressive Black Educators Secy 1983-85; *office:* Mc Ilvaigh Mid Sch 1801 E. 56th St. Tacoma WA 98404

WRIGHT, SANDRA LEE, 5th/6th Grade Teacher; *b:* Kellogg, ID; *ed:* (BS) Elem Ed, 1971, (MED) Elem Ed, 1977 Univ of ID; *cr:* 2nd Grade Teacher Pinehurst Elem 1971-72; 5th Grade Teacher 1973-76, 4th Grade Teacher 1976-78, 6th Grade Teacher 1978-85 Hayden Lake Elem; 4th Grade Teacher 1985-86, 4th-5th Combination Teacher 1986-87, 3rd Grade 1987-89 Borah Elem; 5th-6th Combination Grade Teacher Clover Creek Elem 1989-; *ai:* Co-Sci Fair Coord; Inservice Comm; Phi Delta Kappa Pres 1987-89; Coeur d Alene Ed Assn (Pres 1984-85, Secy 1974, VP 1983-84); Alpha Delta Kappa; ID Ed Assn (Delegate 1974-89, Region I VP 1988-89, Region I Pres 1989-); Los Angeles Rep Assembly Delegate 1987; Master Teacher 1976, 1986; Teacher of Month 1987-88; Whos Who in Amer Ed 1989-; *home:* 19111 5th Ave E Spanaway WA 98387

WRIGHT, SANDRA LEE, Fourth Grade Teacher; *b:* Hazleton, PA; *ed:* (BS) Elem Ed, Bloomsburg Univ 1968; Grad Work Bloomsburg Univ; *cr:* 4th Grade Teacher Williams Valley Elem 1969-; *ai:* Williams Valley Educators Assn (VP 1970-71, Pres 1971-72, 1978-79); PA St Educators Assn, NEA.

WRIGHT, SHERRY, English & Theatre Teacher; *b:* San Diego, CA; *m:* Douglas Grant Davidson; *ed:* (BA) Eng, Cal Poly San Luis Obispo 1982; Grad Stud Theatre & Ed, Cal Poly San Luis Obispo 1985; *cr:* Eng/Drama/Journalism Teacher Atascadero Jr HS 1982-85; Eng/Drama/Dance Teacher Morro Bay HS 1985-; *ai:* Drama Club Adv & Dir; San Luis Jazz Dancers (Dancer, Choreographer 1982-); Phi Kappa Phi Honor Society; *office:* Morro Bay HS 235 Altascadero Rd Morro Bay CA 93442

WRIGHT, THERESE LOUISE, 2nd Grade Teacher; *b:* Archbald, PA; *ed:* (BA) Economics, Marywood Coll; (MED) Elem Ed, Univ of DE; *cr:* 6th Grade Teacher Baltz Elem; 2nd Grade Teacher Heritage Elem; *ai:* DSEA; NEA; *office:* Heritage Elem Sch Highlands Ave Wilmington DE 19808

WRIGHT, TONY GENE, Chemistry Teacher; *b:* San Leandro, CA; *m:* Sue Ellen Tatum; *c:* Julie A. Hirons, Trudy L.; *ed:* (BS) Area Sci, IN Univ 1967; (MS) Area Sci, St Francis Coll 1971; *cr:* Sci Teacher Angola HS 1968-; *ai:* Boys & Girls Tennis Coach; Hi-Y/Y Teen Spon; IN St Tennis Coaches Bd of Dir 1990; *office:* Angola HS US Hwy 20 E Angola IN 46703

WRIGHT, WILLIAM MC KINLEY, Social Studies Teacher; *b:* Hagerstown, MD; *m:* Nancy Cook; *c:* Nancy A. Phillips, Mary E., Susan J.; *ed:* (BS) Psych, Juniata Coll 1950; (MAED) Guidance, Columbia Univ 1951-55; Cert PA Schls, Westminster Coll 1964; Orginational Dev, OH St 1976; Assertiveness Trng Specialist, Denison Univ 1975; Group Dynamics Expert, OK St Univ 1970-75; Taught Group Dynamics & Procedures, IN Univ 1972; *cr:* Dean of Stus De Pauw Univ; Dean of Stus Westminster Coll; Guidance Cnslr/Soc Stud Teacher Kennedy Chrstn HS; *ai:* HS Bowl Adv; PA Cnslrs 1986-88; Natl Assn Per Admin, Assn Cnslr of Personnel 1955-82; Kiwanis Int 1956-78; Masons 1956-78; Rotary Int 1978-83; Published Bantas Greek Exch; *home:* 312 S Market St New Wilmington PA 16142

WRISINGER, RICK S., Business Department Teacher; *b:* Camden, MO; *m:* Laura Rosewaren; *c:* Justin, Heather; *ed:* (BA) Bus Ed, William Penn Coll 1977; Grad Stud Cntrl MO St Univ Warrensburg; *cr:* Bus/Soc Stud Teacher Melcher/Dallas 1977-80; Soc Stud Teacher Orrick Jr/Sr HS 1981-88; Bus Ed Teacher Orrick HS 1988-89; *ai:* Stu Cncl; FBLA; Golf, Girls Bsktbl, Ftbl Coach 1977-80; Jr HS Ftbl & Bstkbl Coach 1981-84; ISEA Negotiator 1978-79; NEA 1977-80; OTA 1981-; *office:* Orrick HS Box 37 Orrick MO 64077

WROTEN, MELVIN FRANKLYN, Technology Ed Dept Chm; *b:* Baltimore, MD; *m:* Susan Reckord; *c:* Michael, Daniel; *ed:* (BS) Industrial Art, Univ of MD 1969; Industrial Art, Admin, Cmptr; *cr:* Industrial Art Teacher 1969-71, Tech Ed/Dept Chm 1971- Randallstown Sr HS; *ai:* Dept Chm Advisory Comm Baltimore Cty; Curr Advisory Comm Baltimore Cty; Teachers Assn of

Baltimore Cty 1969-; MD St Teachers Assn 1969-; Tech Ed Assn of MD 1969-; Winfield Rec Cncl Bsktbl Commissioner 1981-, Volunteer of Yr 1985; *office:* Randallstown Sr HS 4000 Offatt Rd Randallstown MD 21133

WUDY, JIM ROBERT, 3rd-8th Grade Phys Ed Instr; *b:* Cherokee, IA; *m:* JoAnn Carol Vetter; *c:* Jeremy, Jonathon; *ed:* (BS) Elem Ed, Concordia St Paul 1971; (MS) Elem Ed, IN Univ 1988; *cr:* 3rd-8th Grade Teacher St Johns Elem 1971-79, Emmanuel-St Michael Elem 1979-; *ai:* Ftbl, Bsktbl, Wrestling, Track Coach; LTA Rep; Athletic Dir; Luth Schls Athletic Assn 1988-; *office:* Emmanuel-St Michael Elem Sch 1123 Union Fort Wayne IN 46802

WUENSTEL, KAREN FOX, 6th-8th Grade Math Teacher; *b:* Wamego, KS; *m:* Francis William; *c:* Christopher, Andrea, Mark; *ed:* (BA) Math, St Mary Coll 1971; Math, Sci Conventions, Wkshps; *cr:* Assumption Grade Sch 1971-74; General Ed Diploma Adult Ed Unified Sch Dist 501 1976-83; 6th Grade Homeroom/6th/7th Grade Math/8th Grade Algebra Teacher Most Pure Heart of Mary Grade Sch 1983-; *ai:* Math Dept Acting Head; NEA Comm Mem Cert; KATM Mem, Nom Outstanding Teacher of Math 1989, 1990; NCEA, NEA Mem; Outstanding Elem Teachers of America 1974; Whos Who Among Colls & Univs 1971; *home:* 101 SW Kendall Topeka KS 66606

WUERTZ, CAROL KRUEGER, English Teacher; *b:* Huron, SD; *m:* Robert; *c:* Katherine K. Wuertz Paggett; *ed:* (BS) Lang Art, Northern St Univ 1963; *cr:* Eng Teacher Bath HS 1963-65, Cntrl HS 1965-; *ai:* Delta Kappa Gamma Pres 1987-; SD Cncl of Teachers of Eng Secy 1989-; Meth Church Coord of Childrens Ed 1963-; Selectd NHC Chaucer Inst 1989; *home:* 814 N Penn Aberdeen SD 57401

WUNDERLIN, KITTY THOMAS, First Grade Teacher; *b:* South Bend, IN; *m:* Richard A.; *c:* Shawn, Jon; *ed:* (BA) Eng, 1961, (MA) Elem Ed, 1985 Western Mi Univ; *ai:* Sci Coord; Kalamazoo Public Schls Curr Comm; Black His Comm; *office:* Winchell Elem Sch 2316 Winchell Ave Kalamazoo MI 49008

WUNNER, JANET HILL, Instructional Lead Teacher; *b:* Newnan, GA; *m:* Richard G.; *c:* Kristin; *ed:* (BSED) Elem Ed, Georgia Southern 1979; (MED) Mid Grades, West Georgia Coll 1983; *cr:* Teacher Madras Sch 1980-88; Instructional Lead Teacher White Oak Elem 1988-; *ai:* Page 1989-; *office:* White Oak Elem Sch 770 Lora Smith Rd Newnan GA 30265

WUNSCH, JOAN MARTIN, 6th Grade Teacher; *b:* Huntington, WV; *c:* Jason, Mark; *ed:* (BS) Elem Ed, Univ of CO 1971; *cr:* Teachers Aide Mead Elem Sch 1971-72; Substitute Teacher Boulder & St Urain Sch Dists 1972-73; 5th/6th Grade Teacher Niwot Elem Sch 1973-77, 1979-; *ai:* Dist Sci & Soc Stud Comms; Adv/Advisee Mid Sch Comm; Ecology Study Team Leader; Delta Kappa Gamma Secy 1988-; Niwot Elem Mini-Grants; Nom Teachers Who Make a Difference; *office:* Niwot Elem Sch 8778 Morton Rd Longmont CO 80503

WURSTER, DOROTHY FOX, Kindergarten Teacher; *b:* Oskaloosa, IA; *m:* Howard E.; *c:* Kathy Russi, Rosann Schutte, Gary; *ed:* (BS) Elem Ed, Graceland Coll 1970; (MSE) Teacher Effectiveness, Drake Univ 1988; Numerous Wkshps; *cr:* K-8th Grade Teacher Center Sch 1949-50; Teachers Aide Mt Ayr Cmmty Sch 1965-68; Kndgtn Teacher East Union Cmmty Sch 1970-; *ai:* Elem & Scndry Sch Curr Comm Chm; Wellness Comm Mem; Needs Assessment Comm; ISEA, NEA (Local Treas 1974-89, Mem 1970-); United Meth Church St Conference Level Bd 1987-; Ringgold Cty Democratic Party St Comm Affirmativ Action Rep 1987-; 4-H Club of America Local Leader 1965-71; Tingley Meth Church (Bd Chm 1984-88, Sunday Sch Teacher 1954-); *home:* RR 1 Box 56 Tingley IA 50863

WUSSOW, REBECA ROUSSO, Biology Teacher/Dept Chair; *b:* Havana, Cuba; *m:* James R.; *c:* Shereen, Joel; *ed:* (BS) Ed/Bio/Span, Univ of TX 1976; (MS) Scndry Ed, Univ of N TX 1988; Scientific Conferences at TX & Natl Level; Completion Team Leader Course; *cr:* Teacher Capitol HS 1976-81; Asst Team Leader/Teacher Clark HS 1981-84; Dept Head/Teacher Shepton HS 1984-; *ai:* Laser Spon; Sci Fair Building Coord; Textbook Comm; Dist Curr, Aids Curr, Dist Test Item Dev; Dist Inservice; Supervision of Stu Teachers; Spon Stus to Natl Sci Symposium West Point NY; NSTA, Assn of TX Prof Educators, Sci Teachers Assn; Delta Kappa Gamma 1987-; Sch & Dist Nom Teacher of Yr 1990; Dallas Morning News Regional Sci Fair Excl in Sci Teaching 1987; US Army Research Office Excl in Sci Teaching Awd 1989; *office:* Stepton HS 5505 Plano Pkwy Plano TX 75093

WUTZLER, LINDA KAY (SMITH), Sixth Grade Teacher; *b:* Centralia, IL; *m:* Robert Dale; *c:* Robert M.; *ed:* (BS) Elem Ed, St Univ of IL EdWardsville 1979; *cr:* 6th Grade Teacher/Band Instr Breese-Beckemeyer; *ai:* ESC Project; Sci Literacy, St Goals & Objectives, Sci Comms; New Life Chrstn Center Music Dir 1985-; Odin First Baptist Church Music Dir 1977-85; *home:* 301 N Tyler Trenton IL 62293

WYANT, RICHARD LEE, Teacher/Mathematics Chairman; *b:* Monroe City, IN; *m:* Betty Kline; *c:* Melinda, Denise Knoy, Andrew R., Richard; *ed:* (AS) Elem Ed, Vincennes Univ 1955; (BS) Oakland City Coll 1958; (MS) IN St Terre Haute 1965; Natl Sci Fnd Summer Grant Valparasio Univ & Ball St Univ; *cr:* Teacher Wabash Cmmty Sch 1955-59, Vincennes Cmmty Sch Corporation 1959-64; Spec Ed Teacher of Mentally Handicapped/Math Dept Chm Clark Mid Sch 1964-; *ai:* Youth for Christ & Educl Game Club Spon; Vincennes Ed Assn Pres 1963-64; NEA Mem 1959-; ISTA Mem 1990; Monroe City Alumni Assn Pres 1973, Distinguished Alumnus Awd 1988; Missionary to Jamaica 1982, 1988.

WYATT, DANNY S., Health Teacher; *b:* Glasgow, KY; *m:* Carolyn Velaszquez; *c:* Justin, Rachel, Anndora; *ed:* (BS) Health-Phys Ed, 1970; (MA) Scndry Ed, 1979 Western KY Univ; Drug Use and Abuse-Prevention; Safety and First Aid Trng; *cr:* Phy Ed/Coach Red Cross Sch 1970-74; Eastern Elem Sch 1974-78; Psych/Health/Coach 1978-86; Health Teacher 1986 Temple Hill Schl; *ai:* Beta Club Spon 7th-8th Grades; NEA; KY Ed Assn; Barren Cty Ed Assn Pres 1976-77; *home:* 501 Old Mayfield Mill Rd Glasgow KY 42141

WYATT, GARY RUSSELL, 7th Grade Science Teacher; *b:* Asheville, NC; *m:* Barbara Riddle; *ed:* (BA) Elem Ed/Soc Stud/Lang Art/Sci, Mars Hill Coll 1974; Mid Sch Sci; *cr:* 6th-8th Grade Teacher Flat Creek Elem 1974-87; 7th Grade Sci Teacher North Bancombe Mid Sch 1987-; *ai:* Bsbl; Bus Driver; Outdoor Club; NEA; BSA Asst Leader 1986-89; *home:* 8 Oakland St Weaverville NC 28787

WYATT, JUDY GAY, Second Grade Teacher; *b:* Paris, KY; *ed:* (BA) Elem Ed, Morehead St Univ 1967; (MS) Rdng Specialist Elem Ed, Eastern St Univ 1972; *cr:* 2nd Grade Teacher Little Rock Elem 1967-74, North Middletown Elem 1974-; *ai:* Curr Revision Comm; NEA, KY Ed Assn 1967-; Bourbon Cty Ed Assn Building Rep 1967-; Lioness Club (Dir 1987-, 2nd VP 1983-84), Lioness of Yr 1985; *home:* 149 Tahoma Dr Paris KY 40361

WYATT, LORENA MOSELEY, First Grade Teacher; *b:* Ayden, NC; *m:* William Wayne; *c:* Megan; *ed:* (AA) Mt Olive Coll 1966; (BS) Ed, 1968, (MAED) Learning Disabilities, 1984 E Carolina Univ; *cr:* 1st Grade Teacher Snow Hill Primary Sch 1968-; *ai:* Snow Hill Primary Media, Leadership, Budget Comm; Sch & St Accreditation, Child-Centered Curr Comm Chairperson; Mentor Teacher Liaison to Standard Laconic; NEA, NCAE 1968-; Gamma Mu, Delta Kappa Gamma Secy 1984-88; ABWA Secy 1988-89; Southern Assn of Colls Comm Chairperson; Whos Who Amoung Outstanding Young Women in Amer 1971; Greene Cty NCAE Pres 1969-70; Greene Cty Terry Sanford Awd Winner 1984-85; Finalist NCAE Terry Sanford Awd 1985; Innovation & Creativity Teaching; *office:* Snow Hill Primary Sch 502 Se 2nd St Snow Hill NC 28580

WYATT, NANCY L., 5th Grade Teacher; *b:* Fullerton, CA; *ed:* (BA) Elem Phys Ed/Elem Subjects, 1972, Elem Curr, 1977 Cntrl WA Univ; WA, OR Colls & Univs; *cr:* 4th Grade/Phys Ed Teacher 1972-79, 2nd Grade Teacher 1979-82, 6th Grade Teacher 1982-85, 5th/6th Grade Teacher 1985-88, 5th Grade Teacher 1988- Quilcene Elem Sch 1988-; *ai:* Public Relations Parent Night; Young Writers Conference; Textbook Selection Comm; Grant Writer; QEA Schlsp Fund Raiser; Quilcene Ed Assn (Pres 1981-82, 1989-, Bargaining Team 1977-78, 1988-); WA Ed Assn, NEA 1972-; Jefferson Cty Fire Dept #2 Volunteer Fire Fighter 1988-; PTK Organizer 1989-; Cooperative Learning Network Facilitator 1989-; ESD Grants for In-services Critical Thinking Skills & Learning Styles; *home:* PO Box 101 Quilcene WA 98376

WYATT, WILMA HOLMES, Music Teacher; *b:* Surry, VA; *m:* Norman Sr.; *c:* Guan O., Norman Jr., Shenon T.; *ed:* (BA) His, Norfolk St Univ 1970; (MA) Elem Ed, VA Commonwealth Univ 1979; Music, VA St Univ; *cr:* Teacher Surry Public Schls 1970-; *ai:* NEA, VA Ed Assn 1970-; Surry Cty Ed Assn (Pres 1988-) 1970-; Citizens Forum Fund Raising Comm; Surrey Elem PTA Pres; Surry Cty Ed Assn Pres 1988-; Trng of Teachers Awd 1981; *home:* Rt 1 Box 29-A Disputanta VA 23842

WYCKOFF, SANDRA SWEARINGEN, Bus Department Chair/Bus Instr; *b:* Texas City, TX; *m:* Leigh Stephen; *c:* Cheri L. Agnew-Munk, Aaron S. Agnew; *ed:* (BS) Bus Ed, CA St Univ Sacramento 1972; (MA) Ed Admin, Univ of San Francisco 1988; Various Wkshps & Seminars; *cr:* Clerk Cashier Fireside Thrift Company 1964-70; Substitute/Long Term Teacher Napa Valley Unified Sch Dist 1972-76; Teacher Napa Cty Supt of Schls 1975-77; Cnslr Juvenille Hall Napa CA 1977; Tour Guide Inglenook Winery 1977-78; Office Mgr Barrel Builders Incorporated 1978-79; Weightroom Instr La Cancha Racquetball Health Center 1979-80; Coach Napa Valley Sch Dist 1980-84; Teacher ROP Duplicating 1979-83; Aerobics Dir La Cancha Racquetball & Health Club 1983-84; Supvr/Aerobics Instr Hyatt Regency Health Club 1984-85; Coord/Intr Golds Gym 1985-87; Bus Teacher Napa HS 1985-; *ai:* Cheer Adv 1986-; Badminton Coach 1986-; Phi Delta Kappa (Secy, Treas) 1988, Perfect Attendance 1988-89; CA Bus Ed Assn Cty Coord 1989-; Soroptimist 1988-; Mental Health Assn (Treas 1973-75, Pres 1976-77); Aldea Incorporated Group Home Treas 1974; *office:* Napa HS 2475 Jefferson Napa CA 94558

WYGANT, PAM MC COY, Second Grade Teacher; *b:* Batesville, IN; *m:* Dean L.; *c:* Allison; *ed:* (BS) Elem Ed, Huntington Coll 1970; (MS) Elem Ed, St Francis Coll 1973; Purdue Univ; Ball St Univ; IN Univ; *cr:* 2nd Grade Teacher South Ripley Sch Corp 1970-; *ai:* Mem Fine Arts Comm; Mem Fund for Riley Hosp; Delta Kappa Gamma (Mem 1983-87 VP 1990-92); St Paul Luth Church Tri Kappa (Sec) 1979.

WYLIE, CHARLOTTE LEE, 5th Grade Teacher; *b:* Mc Keesport, PA; *ed:* (BS) Elem Ed, CA St Coll of PA 1974; *cr:* 5th/6th Grade Eng Teacher 1974-75, 6th Grade Teacher 1975-79, 5th Grade Teacher 1979-80 Jennerstown Elem; 7th Grade Math Teacher 1980-82; 7th Grade Math/Sci Teacher 1982-84 Jennerstown Mid Schl; 5th Grade North Star West 1984-; *ai:* Spec Interest Adv Cermaics/Kickball/Paper Airplanes; Talen Show Adv; Gong Show Adv; Elem Field Day Helper; Al Ost Anything Goes Day Helper; MS PSEA 1974-; *home:* Box 90 Jennerstown PA 15547

WYLIE, M. ELIZABETH CONNERS, Sixth Grade Elementary Teacher; *b:* Junction City, KS; *w:* Walter W. (dec); *c:* Michael, Linda; *ed:* (BA) Ed, Fresno St Univ 1964; Fresno St, Pacific Coll; *cr:* Teacher Geary Cty Schls 1945-49, Topeka SDA 1949-51, Kaw Valley 1953-56, Highland Park 1957-59, Clovis Unified 1964-; *ai:* Gifted Coord; Soc Sci Comm; Lead Teacher; Prin Adv Comm; Dist Golden Key Awd Rdng 1983-84, Math 1974, 1982-87, Lang 1984, 1986-87; Dist Ach Grade Level Teams 1988; *home:* 5548 E Crescent Fresno CA 93727

WYLIE, M.SUE HAGGARD, Ath Director/ICAN Teacher; *b:* Shawnee, OK; *m:* William L.; *c:* Aaron, Sarah; *ed:* (BS) Soc Stud, OSU 1972; ICAN Specialty Trng, QUEST Skills for Adolescence; *cr:* Soc Stud Teacher Hefner 1973-77; Am His Teacher Putnam City Schls 1977-83; ICAN-QUEST Teacher Hefner 1984-; *ai:* Pep Club Head, Stu Cncl Head, Bsbl Club Spon; Athletic Dir; Core Team; Staff Dev Comm; Hefner Advisroy; Kappa Delta Phi 1972; Delta Kappa Gamma (Pres, VP, Treas) 1980-; NEA, OEA, ACT (Negot Team, Secy) 1975-; Teacher of Yr Putnam City Schls 1984; Best in OK Awd 1990; *home:* 5817 Caddo Ct Oklahoma City OK 73132

WYLIE, PAULA COX, Kindergarten Teacher; *b:* Frankfort, KY; *m:* Timothy Robert; *c:* Brian, Katie; *ed:* (BS) Elem Ed, E KY Univ 1976; Elem Ed, Georgetown Coll; Kndgtn Cert; *cr:* Kndgtn Teacher Thorn Hill Elem 1976-80, Collins Lane Elem 1980-; *ai:* FCEA, KEA 1976-; *office:* Collins Lane Elem Sch 1 Cougar Ln Frankfort KY 40601

WYLLY, EMILY RYALS, First Grade Teacher; *b:* Townsend, GA; *m:* Jonathan; *c:* Gregory, Valarie; *ed:* (BS) Elem Ed, Ft Valley St 1954; NC Cntrl Univ, Fayetteville St Univ, Fayetteville Technical Inst; *cr:* Prin Sapelo Island 1948-50; Teacher Eulonia Elem 1950-57,1961-63, Risley Elem 1967-68, Goodyear Elem 1970-71, Murray Elem 1974-; *ai:* Design for Learning Co Chm; NEA; NCAE Secy; Rdng Cncl; NAACP; *home:* 1712 Valley Ridge Dr Fayetteville NC 28303

WYMAN, PATRICIA KATHLEEN, Language Art Teacher; *b:* Lorain, OH; *c:* Lyndie, G. J.; *ed:* (BSED) Elem Ed, OH St Univ 1973; (MED) Curr/Instr, Cleveland St Univ 1985; *cr:* 4th/5th Grade Teacher Charles Dickens Elem 1974-76; 7th Grade Math Teacher Nathan Hale Jr HS 1978-81; 8th Grade Lang Art Teacher Fundamental Ed Center 1981-; *ai:* Stu-At-Risk Support Group Spon; Staff LED Team; Right-To-Read Comm; Cleveland Teachers Union Building Rep 1986-87; Greater Cleveland Cncl of Eng Teachers 1990; Women Speak Out for Peace & Justice 1985-; Cleveland St Univ Grad Asst 1989-, Volunteer Co-Facilitator; Conduct Human Relations Prof Wkshps; Eng Teacher in Poland 1989; *home:* 6100 Laurent Dr #530B Parma OH 44129

WYNNE, BARBARA MINOR, Fifth Grade Teacher; *b:* Oakman, AL; *m:* William Thomas; *c:* Marla J., William M.; *ed:* (BS) Elem Ed, 1959, (MA) Elem Ed, 1976 Univ of N AL; Ed Research & Inservice Center Univ of N AL; Post Grad Stud Amer His, Penn St; *cr:* Teacher Tuscumbia Sch System 1959-63, Florence Sch System 1963-64, Mars Hill Bible Sch 1972-; *ai:* Elem Soc Stud Comm Chm; AL-LA-MS Math Contest & Natl Geographic Geography Bee Spon; Sch Spelling Bee Judge; ASCD 1988-89; Alpha Delta Kappa (Nominating Comm Chm, Chaplain) 1976-; Muscle Shoals Concert Assn 1990; Southern Assn of Accreditation Sch Self-Study Steering Comm; Natl Excl in Ed AWd Application Writing Comm; WA Awds Ceremony Faculty Rep; *office:* Mars Hills Bible Sch 698 Cox Creek Pkwy Florence AL 35630

WYNSMA, BECKY KRYGSHELD, Home Economics Teacher; *b:* Chicago, IL; *m:* Gerard; *c:* Michelle Wynsma Kelly, Deb Wynsma Van Deursen, Keith, Kevin, Kathy, Randolph, Mark, Jonathan, Jessica, Allison; *ed:* (BA) Ed, Trinity Chrstn Coll 1973; (BS) Home Ec, 1975, (MS) Home Ec, 1976 IL St Univ; Numerous Grad Courses; *cr:* Home Ec Teacher Illiana Chrstn HS 1976-; *ai:* Amer Home Ec Assn 1976-; *office:* Illiana Chrstn HS 2261 Indiana Ave Lansing IL 60438

WYRICK, CONSTANCE HELEN, Biology/Chemistry Instructor; *b:* Kirksville, MO; *m:* Kenneth Lynn; *c:* Joshua, Jacob; *ed:* (BSE) Bio Ed, NE MO St Univ 1976; Summer Sci Inst Univ of MO Columbia 1986; *cr:* 7th-12th Grade Teacher Tuscumbia HS 1976-81; Bio/Chem Teacher Eugene HS 1981-88, Eldon HS 1988-; *ai:* FTA Spon; MO Acad of Sci Jr Division Dist Dir 1987-; MO St Teachers Assn Mem; Tuscumbia Alumni Assn Pres 1983; Cntrl MO St Univ Outstanding Sci Teacher; *office:* Eldon HS North & Pine Eldon MO 65026

WYSE, TOBY DEAN, Music Department Teacher; *b:* Wauseon, OH; *m:* Patti G. Loomis; *c:* Matthew, Joshua, Timothy; *ed:* (BA) Sacred Music, Baptist Bible Coll 1976; *cr:* Phys Therapy Aide Arnot Ogden Hospital 1977-78; Minister of Music 1st Baptist Church 1976-; Teacher Twin Tiers Baptist HS 1979-; *ai:* Sr Class Adv; Drama Dir; Jr & Sr HS Choir; *office:* Twin Tiers Baptist HS P O Drawer K Breesport NY 14816

WYSS, ARDIS HARVEY, Family & Consumer Ed Teacher; *b:* Menomonie, WI; *m:* Jerome; *c:* Scott, Jason; *ed:* (BS) Home Ec, 1971, Spec Cert Spec Ed, 1984 Univ of WI 1984; Trng Human Growth Dev Area; *cr:* FACE Home Ec Teacher 1971-, Daily Life Skills Spec Ed Teacher 1984-, HGD/Health Coord 1988-Glenwood City HS; *ai:* Pupil Services Comm; Positive Support Comm Staff; Advisory Comm Chairperson; WHEESE; AODA

Grants; Curr for Sexual Abuse Prevention; *office:* Glenwood City Jr/Sr HS Glenwood City WI 54013

Y

YAEGER, CURTIS LEROY, HS Mathematics Teacher; *b:* Jefferson City, MO; *ed:* (BS) Math, Cntrl MO St 1987; *ai:* Coach Jr Var Vlybl, 7th Grade Bsktbl, Jr Var Bsbl; Math Club Spon; MO St Teachers Assn 1988-; MO Vlybl Assn 1987-; *home:* Rt 1 Oakview Apt 1 Camdenton MO 65020

YAFFIE, DAVID SCOTT, Science/History Teacher; *b:* Sarasota, FL; *ed:* (BA) Bio, Univ of Tx Austin 1985; Ed, Univ TX; *cr:* 7th Grade TX His Teacher 1985-86, 8th Grade US His Teacher 1986-89, 7th Grade Life Sci Teacher 1987- Quail Valley Mid Sch; *ai:* Quail Valley Mid Sch Campus Action Team Mem; Soc Stud Tutorial Teacher; Track Coach; QVMS TX & Ft Bend Ind Sch Dist Acad Pentathlon Coord; TX Assn of Scndry Sch Prins, NAASP; Teacher of Yr Finalist 1988-; Perfect Attendance Awd 1986-89; *office:* Quail Valley Mid Sch 3019 FM 1092 Missouri City TX 77459

YAGER, BRYAN C., American History Teacher; *b:* San Mateo, CA; *m:* Linda Johns Mateo; *c:* Michael, Lisa; *ed:* (BA) Anthropology/His/Industrial Art, Univ of CA Berkeley 1970; Continuing Ed Voc Ed, Industrial Technology, Methods, Self-Esteem Cooperating Learning; *cr:* Instr Taft Sch 1972, Belmont Sch & Ralston Mid Sch 1972-; *ai:* Graduation Requirement & Self Study Comm; CITEC Contractors License; Phi Beta Kappa 1970; Elks Club Mem 1985-; *home:* 1114 S Grant St San Mateo CA 94402

YAGER, JULIE K., Intermediate Lang Arts Teacher; *b:* Superior, NE; *m:* James; *c:* Jessica, Jordan; *ed:* (BA) Elem Ed, Univ of WY 1977; *cr:* 6th Grade Teacher Wagon Wheel Elem Sch 1977-79; 4th/5th Grade Lang Art Teacher Ashgrove Elem 1979-; *ai:* Writers Guild; Various Sch & Dist Comm; NEA, WY Ed Assn, Riverton Ed Assn, Kappa Delta Pi 1977-; Fremont Cty Assn for Retarded Citizens, Presbyn Church, Chi Omega; *office:* Ashgrove Elem Sch 121 N 5th W Riverton WY 82501

YAGGI, CONNIE HOFFMAN, Fourth Grade Teacher; *b:* Washington, IN; *m:* Jack L.; *c:* Terri L.; *ed:* (BA) Elem Ed, St Benedict Coll 1968; (MA) Elem Ed, W KY Univ 1973; *cr:* 6th Grade Teacher 10th Street Elem Sch 1968-70; 3rd Grade Teacher 1970-85, 5th Grade Teacher 1985-87, 4th GradE Teacher 1987 Ireland Elem Sch; *ai:* Jasper HS Bsbl Batgirl Spon; NEA, IN St Teachers Assn 1968-; Jasper Classroom Teachers Assn Treas 1980; Du Bois Cty Rdng Assn 1970-; Jasper Bus & Prof Womens Club Corresponding Secy 1976-82; Jasper Cmmty Art Commission 1981-83; Jasper Park & Recreation Bd of Dir (Secy 1982, 1986, 1989, VP 1983, 1987, 1990, Pres 1984, 1988); IN St Finalist Amateur Bsbl Woman of Yr 1988; Jasper Jaycees Teacher of Yr 1990; *office:* Ireland Elem Sch PO Box 95 Ireland IN 47545

YAGOOBIAN, JERILYNN HEWEY, Kindergarten Teacher; *b:* Long Beach, CA; *m:* Larry John; *c:* Ruth; *ed:* (BME) Music Ed, John Brown Univ 1968; CSUN, CA Lutheran Coll, Biola Coll, Pepperdine Coll; *cr:* 1st Grade Teacher Sulfur Springs Union Sch Dist 1968-71; Pre-sch Teacher First Baptist Church 1971-73; Kndgtn Teacher/Prin Lindley Ave Baptist Sch 1973-88; Kndgtn Teacher N Hollywood Chrstn Sch 1988-89, Hillcrest Chrstn Sch 1989-; *ai:* Choir Dir, Pianist for Chapel; Judge for CDSA Speech Contest; BDSA 1973-, 15 Yr Pin 1988; *home:* 10826 Blucher Ave Granada Hills CA 91344

YAHNE, DAN L., Media Specialist; *b:* Harrisburg, IL; *m:* Lavada Louise Swafford; *c:* Tonya M. Yahne Shea; *ed:* (BS) Eng, 1969, (MS) Scndry Ed/Eng Emphasis, 1974 S IL Univ; Trng Media Production, Curr Integration of Media, Sangamon St Univ; Admin, Utilization of Educl Media Prgms, S IL Univ; *cr:* Eng Instr Rochester Unit Dist #3A 1969-75; Media Specialist Harrisburg Unit Schls 1975-; *ai:* Unit 3 Media, Cmptr, Disaster Preparedness Comm; Media Asst & IL St Media Fair Participant Spon; IL Sch Lib Media Assn; IL Assn for Media in Ed Comm; Harrisburg Ed Assn Comm; Valley of S IL Scottish Rite Bodies; Ainad Temple AAONMS of E St Louis; *office:* Malan Jr HS 124 S Webster St Harrisburg IL 62946

YAMADA, FRANCES S., 2nd Grade Teacher; *b:* Eleele, HI; *m:* Jiro; *c:* Steven, Laurie A.; *ed:* (BA) Elem Ed, ID St Univ 1953; Brigham Young Univ, ID St Univ; *cr:* Teacher Alameda Jr HS 1953-55, Moreland Elem 1955-57, Riverside Elem 195-60, Moreland Elem 1960-; *ai:* Head Teacher; Team Leader; NEA, IEA Secy; JACL, Sigma Kappa, Alpha Delta Kappa; Snake River Sch Dist 52 Teacher of Yr; *office:* Morland Elem Sch Box B Moreland ID 83256

YAMAMOTO, PAUL AKIRA, Science Teacher/Dept Chair; *b:* Milwaukee, WI; *m:* Claudia Koenig; *c:* Matthew; *ed:* (BA) Biological Sci, Univ of La Verne 1968; Stan Biological Sci; *cr:* Laboratory Instr Univ of La Verne 1968-70; Sci Team Rowland HS 1969-70; Sci Teacher Pioneer Jr HS 1971-; *ai:* Regional Dir Blizzard Ski Club; Tennis Team, Ftbl Coach; Regional Sci Fair Jr HS Coord; Sci Act Inland Sci Fair; Dist Sci Mentor; Upland Teachers Assn Jr HS Rep 1977-80; CTA, NEA, 1970-; NSTA; PTSA Honorary Service Awd 1977, Continuing Service Awd 1978; San Digg West End Sci Consortium Presenter Chm; Claremont Grad Sch Math, Sci Coalition Mem; Instr Summer Sci Wrkshp Elem Teachers Cal Poly Pomona; Textbook Review Hought & Mifflen Company; *office:* Pioneer Jr HS 245 W 18th St Upland CA 91786

YANA, PATRICIA (HUEVLER), Kindergarten Teacher; *b:* Milwaukee, WI; *m:* Joseph V.; *ed:* (BS) Early Chldhd, Univ of WI Oshkosh 1976; Working on Master of Arts Degree in Ed, Viterbo Coll La Crosse WI; *cr:* Nursery Sch Teacher Bluemound Nursery Sch 1976-79; Kndgtn Teacher St Casimir 1977-79; Primary Teacher St Peter 1979-80; Kndgtn Teahcer St Mary 1980-85, Oshkosh Area Schls 1985-; *ai:* Joint Task Force Jump Rope for Heart of WI; Kndgtn Roundtable-Chairperson/Rdng Curr Comm; Sch Improvement & Effectiveness Comm; Kndgtn Screening Comm Secy; Kndgtn Specialists Comm; Oshkosh Ed Assn Mem, WI Ed Assn Cncl Mem, NEA 1985-; Numerous Comm in Early Chldhd Field; *office:* Smith Elem Sch 1745 Oregon St Oshkosh WI 54901

YANCEY, ANITA ARCHEY, Fifth Grade Teacher; *b:* Ashland, KY; *m:* Mark Edmund; *ed:* (BA) Elem Ed, 1982, (MS) Elem Ed, 1987 Morehead St Univ; *cr:* Rdng Teacher Warnock Elem 1982-83; 6th Grade Teacher 1983-84, 1st Grade Teacher 1984-86, 2nd Grade Teacher 1986-87, 5th Grade Teacher 1987- Wurtland Elem; *ai:* Safety Patrol & 4-H Club Spon; Asst Sftbl & Hi-Q Coach; NEA, KY Ed Assn, Greenup Cty Ed Assn 1982-; *home:* 520 Collins Ln E K Road Greenup KY 41144

YANCEY, GLORIA S., Third Grade Teacher; *b:* Locust Grove, GA; *m:* Harrison Sr.; *c:* Harrison Jr., Corliss D., Marcus K.; *ed:* (AB) Eng/Elem Ed, Spelman Coll 1956; (MA) Elem Ed, Atlanta Univ 1971; Cert GA St Univ 1979; *cr:* 4th Grade Teacher Bruce Street Elem & HS 1956-59; 4th-5th Grade Teacheer C M Pitts Elem Sch 1963-70; 4th Grade Teacher R L Hope Elem Sch 1970-72; 3rd-6th Grade Teacher G A Towns Elem Sch 1973-; *ai:* Leadership Team; Grade Level Chairperson; Test & Staff Dev Contact; Mentor Teacher; NEA, St & Local Ed Assns 1956-; Intnl Rdng Assn 1978; Parent Teacher & Stu Assn; Friendship Baptist Church; Neighborhood Club; *home:* 3948 Adamsville Dr SW Atlanta GA 30331

YANCY, REGINA MOORE, 3rd & 4th Grade Teacher; *b:* Chicago, IL; *c:* Alan Knight, April K. Brown; *ed:* (BED) Intermediate Upper Elem Ed, Chicago Teachers Coll 1955; (MA) Elem Ed, Governors St 1976; *cr:* 5th Grade Teacher Thomas Jefferson Elem 1955-61; 3rd-8th Grade Teacher Victor Herbert Elem Sch 1961-; *ai:* After Sch Rdng; Government Funded Prgms Coord; NEA, IEA, Chicago Teachers Union; *office:* Victor Herbert Elem Sch 2131 W Monroe Chicago IL 60612

YANCY, RUTH ROBERTSON, Fifth Grade Teacher; *b:* Refugio, TX; *m:* Jerry Warren; *c:* Jeriann; *ed:* (BS) Elem Ed, Sam Houston St Univ 1956; Grad Work Sam Houston St Univ & Univ of TX Tyler; *cr:* 4th Grade Teacher Ramey Elem 1956-60; 3rd Grade Teacher Clarkston Elem 1961-62; 6th Grade Teacher Ramey Elem 1975-78; 5th Grade Teacher Dixie Elem 1978-; *ai:* Classroom Teachers Assn 1978-; Alpha Delta Kappa Treas 1985-87; TX Finance Assn (Recording Secy 1989-, Exec Dir 1990); Nom Dixie Elem Sch Teacher of Yr 1988.

YANDO, RAYMOND A., Mathematics Teacher; *b:* Ludlow, MA; *m:* Judith Brouillette; *c:* Jill, Lee-Ann; *ed:* (BA) Math, Univ of MA 1966; (MA) Math, Worcester Polytechnic Inst 1980; Boston Coll, Univ of CT, Amer Intnl Coll, Westfield St Coll; *cr:* Math Instr Univ of MA 1984-88; Math Teacher Ludlow HS 1966-; *ai:* Ludlow Ed Assn Pres 1983; MA Ed Assn, NEA; *office:* Ludlow HS 500 Chapin St Ludlow MA 01056

YANIGER, MARILYN TRINKLE, Guidance Counselor; *b:* Allentown, PA; *m:* Christopher J.; *ed:* (BS) Eng, Kutztown St Univ 1968; (MS) Guidance/Counseling, Loyola Coll 1983; Towson St Univ; *cr:* Eng Teacher General John Stricker Jr HS 1968-71; Eng/Drama/Speech Teacher Hereford HS 1971-76; Eng/Speech Teacher Loch Raven HS 1976-83; Human Relations Specialist Dundalk HS 1983-85; Guidance Cnslr Chesapeake HS 1985-; *ai:* Baltimore Cty Drug Ed Facilitator; Teachers Assn of Baltimore Cty, MD St Teachers Assn, NEA 1968-; Assn of Counseling & Dev 1983-; Excl in Ed Awd Nom Baltimore Cty 1988; *office:* Chesapeake HS 1801 Turkey Point Rd Baltimore MD 21221

YANITY, LYNNE (PATTERSON), 7th Grade Teacher; *b:* Indiana, PA; *m:* Frederick Allan; *c:* Melissa L.; *ed:* (BS) Elem Ed, 1968, (MED) Elem Ed, 1969 Indiana Univ of PA; Educl Support Team Trng, St Vincents Coll 1990; *cr:* 2nd/3rd/5th/Grade Teacher/5th Grade Teacher of Gifted 1968-73, Teacher of Gifted 1977-79 Southmont Sch; 4th-8th Grade Teacher Westmont Hilltop Mid Sch 1980-; *ai:* Stu Assistance Team Mem; NEA, PA St Ed Assn, Westmont Hilltop Ed Assn Mem 1968-; Oakland United Meth Church (Trustee 1987-, Pastoral Relations Comm 1984-87, Ed Comm 1981-84); Teacher in Space Candidate; *office:* Westmont Hilltop Mid Sch 827 Diamond Blvd Johnstown PA 15905

YANKOWITZ, COLETTE GABORIT, French Teacher; *b:* Le Mayet de Montag, France; *m:* David E.; *c:* Eric; *ed:* (CELG) Fr Lit, Univ of Bordeaux France 1963; (CAP) Ed, Cours Pedagogiques France 1967; (MA) Fr, Seton Hall Univ 1973; *cr:* Eng Teacher Lycee de Jeunes Filles Saintes France 1963-65; Fr/Eng Teacher Coll De Seiqnement General Montlieu France 1965-68; Fr Teacher Millburn HS 1969-71, Cntrl Sch 1976-; *ai:* Spon Fr Festivals & Quebec Trip; Adv in Charge Developing FLES Prgm 5th-6th Grade Fr & Span; AATF; Chrstn & Missionary Alliance; *office:* Cntrl Mid Sch 90 Central Ave Stirling NJ 07980

YARBERRY, TERRY LYLE, Fourth Grade Teacher; *b:* Pueblo, CO; *m:* Deborah Jo; *c:* Amber, Nathan, Jake; *ed:* (AA) Liberal Arts, Canada JC 1972; (BA) Liberal Arts, San Diego St 1976 (MA) Educl Admin, Univ NV Las Vegas 1985; Navy Electronic, Radio Sch; *cr:* 4th/5th Grade Teacher 1976-77, 4th Grade Teacher 1977- Elbert B Edwards; 2nd Grade Teacher Charlotte Hill 1990; *ai:* Teacher Duty Schedule; Math Contest Coord; Safety Patrol; Grade Level Chairperson; Phi Delta Kappa; *office:* Elbert B Edwards Elem Sch 4551 Diamond Head Dr Las Vegas NV 89110

YARBOROUGH, PAULA HAMILTON, First Grade Teacher; *b:* Dublin, TX; *m:* Martin L.; *c:* Taylor; *ed:* (ME) Ed, 1972; (BS) Elem Ed, 1986; All Level Rdng Cert; *cr:* 1st Grade Teacher Granbury Elem 1976-78, Acton Elem 1978-86; Glen Rose Ind Sch Dist 1986-87, Acton Elem 1987-; *ai:* ATPE 1979-; *home:* 21 Oaks Dr Granbury TX 76048

YARBROUGH, DOUGLAS B., AP English/Philosophy Teacher; *b:* Littlefield, TX; *ed:* (BA) Philosophy, Univ TX Austin 1969; (MA) Hum, Univ Louisville 1979; *cr:* Advanced Placement Eng/Philosophy Teacher Countryside HS 1982-; *office:* Countryside HS 3000 SR 580 Clearwater FL 34621

YARBROUGH, HAZEL HILL, Lang Art/Soc Stud Coordinator; *b:* Kinston, NC; *m:* Charles G. Sr.; *c:* Charles Jr., Brian; *ed:* (BA) His/Ed, Wake Forest Univ 1963; (MED) Soc Stud Ed, Campbell Univ 1979; Univ of NC Chapel Hill, Univ of NC Charlotte, E Carolina Univ, Univ of Madras India; Working Towards EdS in Admin/Supervision, Winthrop Coll 1991; *cr:* Teacher Belleville 1963-64, Gainesville HS 1964-65, 1967-70, Harnett Cty Schls 1966-67, 1970-80; Teacher 1980-88, Lang Art/Soc Stud Coord 1988- Union Cty Schls; *ai:* NCSS, NC Cncl for Soc Stud 1981-; NC Cncl of Eng Teachers 1989-; Intnl Cncl of Rdng Teachers 1989-; ASCD 1986-; Phi Kappa Phi 1979-; Alpha Delta Kappa 1989-; Fulbright Faculty Dev Seminar in India 1988; Outstanding Soc Stud Teacher 1987; Whos Who in Amer Ed 1989; *home:* PO Box 3091 Wingate NC 28174

YARBROUGH, MARK ANTHONY, Bio Teacher/Head Ftbl Coach; *b:* Water Valley, MS; *c:* Jeremy S.; *ed:* (BA) Phys Ed, Univ of MS 1980; Sci; *cr:* Earth Sci Teacher/Head Jr HS Coach 1980-85, Phys Sci Teacher/Asst HS Coach 1986-88, Bio Teacher/Head HS Coach/Athletic Dir 1988- Bruce HS; *ai:* Head HS Ftbl, Head Jr HS Ftbl, Golf Coach; MS HS Coaching Assn 1980-.

YARBROUGH, RUTH E., French/Spanish/English Teacher; *b:* Hattiesburg, MS; *w:* Thomas H. (dec); *c:* Camille, Tom, Jim, Ann, John; *ed:* (BA) Fr, USM 1949; *cr:* Classroom Teacher Oakdale HS.

YARDLEY, JANET ELLEN (HARVEY), 6th-7th Grade Math Teacher; *b:* Bellaire, OH; *m:* William C.; *c:* John M., William H.; *ed:* (AB) Elem Ed, W Liberty St Coll 1959; Grad Work OH St Univ 1961; Advanced Trng OH Univ 1989; *cr:* 4th Grade Teacher Linden Elem 1959-65; 7th Grade Teacher Gravel Hill Sch 1967-68; 6th Grade Teacher North 1969-; *ai:* Math Tutor; OH Ed Assn, Martins Ferry Ed Assn 1969-; NEA 1969; Antique Car Assn 1987-; Math Guide Chm 1986; Sci Guide Chm 1987; *home:* 54919 Lawver Dr Bridgeport OH 43912

YARNELL, JIM, Government Teacher/Coach; *b:* Ballinger, TX; *m:* Mary Ann Miller; *c:* Doug, Kali; *ed:* (BS) Health/Phys Ed, Angelo St Univ 1978; Poly Sci, Teaching Constitution; Methods of Effective Teaching Strategies; *cr:* Teacher/Coach Wellington HS 1978-79, Throckmorton HS 1979-80, Nocona HS 1980-84, Weatherford HS 1984-; *ai:* Offensive Ftbl Coord; Asst Head & Head Boys Track Coach; TX HS Coaches Assn 1978-; *office:* Weatherford HS 1007 S Main Weatherford TX 76086

YARRICK, JAMES A., Director of Bands; *b:* South Bend, IN; *m:* Nancy J. Bolhuis; *c:* Patricia; *ed:* (BM) Music, W MI Univ 1967; (MM) Cntrl MI Univ; *cr:* Dir of Bands Chippewa Hills HS 1967-; *ai:* Marching & Pep Band, All Band Tours; Phi Mu Alpha 1965-; Natl Band Dir Assn 1975-; 1st Division Ratings at Dist & St Levels; Chippewa Hills HS Teacher of Yr 1984; *office:* Chippewa Hills HS 3226 E Wheatland Ave Remus MI 49340

YARRICK, NANCY J., History Teacher; *b:* Holland, MI; *m:* James A.; *c:* Patricia *ed:* (BS) Psych, 1968, (MA) Ed, 1974 Cntrl MI Univ; *cr:* Psych/Sociology/Physiology Chippewa Hills HS 1968-71; Amer His/Practical Law Teacher Chippewa Hills Jr HS 1974-; *ai:* Chippewa Hills Ed Assn, MEA, NEA 1968-; Chippewa Hills Jr HS Teacher of Yr; *office:* Chippewa Jr HS 350 W Wheatland Ave Remus MI 49340

YATES, ANGELIA GWEN, Spanish Teacher; *b:* Kingsport, TN; *m:* Don Allen; *ed:* (BA) Span, 1984, (MAT) Scndry Ed, 1987 E TN St Univ; Attended Prgm Univ of Madrid Spain Through E TN ST Univ 1984; *cr:* Span/Eng Teacher Johnson Cty HS 1986-87; Span/Bus Teacher Washington Coll Acad 1987-88, Cloudland HS 1988-89, Span Teacher J Mc Eachern HS 1989-; *ai:* Span Club Spon; Teacher Wellness Comm; Kappa Delta Pi 1987-; Chosen to Attend Univ of TN Governors Acad for Teachers of Foreign Lang 1987; *office:* Mc Eachern HS 2400 New Mac Land Rd Powder Springs GA 30073

YATES, BOBBI JO, Third Grade Teacher; *b:* Harrodsburg, KY; *c:* Amanda J., Michael L.; *ed:* (BA) Elem Ed, Univ of KY 1977; (MA) Early Chldhd Ed, E KY Univ 1980; *cr:* Elem Teacher Burgin Ind Sch 1978-; *ai:* Asst Girls Sftbl Coach; Burgin Ed Assn (Pres 1984-85, Treas 1986-); KY Ed Assn 1978-; Harrodsburg Womans Club (Pres 1983-84, Treas 1989-); Anna Elliott Bohon Dept UK Alumni Assn; Mercer Cty UK Alumni Assn Pres 1986-87.

YATES, BRENDA CARROLL, Language Arts Department Chair; *b:* Carrollton, GA; *m:* G. Ray; *c:* Kasey, Sam Carroll, Tonya; *ed:* (AB) Scndry Ed/Soc Stud, 1970, (MED) Scndry Ed/Eng, 1975, (EDS) Scndry Ed/Eng, 1986 W GA Coll; *cr:* Geography Teacher 1970-71, Eng Teacher 1972-76 Rockmart HS; Eng Teacher Douglas Cty Comprehensive HS 1976-; *ai:* Responsibility for Literary Team Dept Chm; Mem Leadership Team; Douglas Cty Assn of Educators Publicity Comm 1976-; GA Assn of Educators, NCTE 1972-; STAR Teacher; Teacher of Quarter Douglas Comprehensive HS; *office:* Douglas Cty Comprehensive HS 8705 Campbellton St Douglasville GA 30134

YATES, GWEN EDWARDS, Supervisor of Elem Teachers; *b:* Memphis, TN; *c:* Steven, Stephanie; *ed:* (BA) Elem Ed, IN Univ 1975; (MS) Ed Fnds, Univ of Cincinnati 1981; Doctoral Stu Educl Admin, Univ of Cincinnati; *cr:* Classroom Teacher 1975-88, Assoc Elem Supvr 1988- Cincinnati Public Schls; *office:* Cincinnati Public Schls 230 E 9th St Cincinnati OH 45202

YATES, GWENDOLYN DRAPER, Mathematics Teacher; *b:* New Orleans, LA; *c:* Jeanetta; *ed:* (BS) Math, Alcorn St Univ 1970; (MED) Math, 1976, (EDS) Math, 1981 MS Coll; Cmptr Sci, Alcorn St Univ; *cr:* 7th/8th Grade Math Teacher Forest Mid Sch 1970-71; Substitute Teacher 1971, Math Teacher 1972-73 S Vicksburg HS; Math Teacher Vicksburg HS Complex B 1973-75; Coll Algebra Instr Alcorn St Univ 1979; Math Teacher Vicksburg HS Complex A 1975-80, Vicksburg Jr HS 1980-89; Mathematician Water Ways Experiment Station 1985-89; Elem Math for Teachers Instr MS Coll 1989; Math Teacher Vicksburg HS 1989-; *ai:* Math Dept Chm Vicksburg Jr HS; 9th Grade Spon Vicksburg HS & Jr HS; Teacher Advisory & Bulletin Bd Comm Vicksburg HS; MS Cncl Teachers of Math, NCTM, MS Assn of Educators, NEA; Alpha Kappa Alpha (Treas 1980-82, VP 1982-83, 2nd VP 1983-84); Mt Calvary Baptist Church & Inspirational Choir Mem; Honorable Mention Gift Merrill Publishing Company; Teacher of Month; Magna Cum Laude; Valedictorian Summer Associateship Prgm for HS Sci & Math Faculty; Nom Teacher of Yr; Level I Awd for Staff Dev; Whos Who Among Coll Stu; *home:* 104 Skyway Ln Vicksburg MS 39180

YATES, JOY O'DELL, Elementary Guidance Counselor; *b:* Johnson City, TN; *m:* Dale; *ed:* (BS) Elem Ed, 1970; (MA) Spec Ed, 1978 East TN St Univ; Addl Studies, Elem Guidance/Counseling, Admin Supervision Univ of TN; *cr:* Teacher of Emotionally Disturbed, Educational Youth Center 1970-73; Kndgtn Teacher Central Sch 1973-74; Resource Teacher 1974-78; 5th Grade Teacher 1978-85 Charleston Sch;Elem Guidance Cnslr Seminars Schls 1985-; *ai:* Bradley Cty Ed Assn Negotiating Team Mem 1988-;TN Ed Assn Rep Assembly Delegate; Bradley Cty Ed Assn Treas 1987-; TN Ed Assn 1970-; NEA 1970-; Amer Assn Counseling/Dev 1985-; TN Assn Counseling/Dev 1985-; Lookout Assn Counseling/Dev 1985-; TN Sch Cnslr Assn 1985-; Delta Kappa Gamma 1989-; Bradley-Cleveland Health/Ed Comm Chairperson 1988-; Bradley-Cleveland Interagency Cncl 1985-; Nominated for Outstanding Young Women of America 1985; *office:* Bradley County Schs 155 Broad St Cleveland TN 37364

YATES, MARIKO LYNN, Mathematics Teacher; *b:* Okinawa, Japan; *m:* John R.; *ed:* (BA) Math, San Diego St Univ 1987; *cr:* Math Teacher Asst El Capitan HS 1985-88; Math/Bio Teacher Corona Sr HS 1988-89; Math Teacher Centennial HS 1989-; *ai:* Academic Decathlon Asst Coach; Frosh Class Adv, Girls Bsktbl Coach; NCTM; CA Math Cncl; *office:* Centennial H S 1820 Rimpau Ave Corona CA 91719

YEAGER, JAMES WENDELL, 5th Grade Teacher; *b:* Mishawaka, IN; *ed:* (BS) Elem Ed, Manchester Coll 1980; (MS) Elem Ed, Ball St Univ; Lions Quest 1989; *cr:* 2nd Grade Teacher 1980-81, 5th Grade Teacher 1981- Cntrl Elem; *ai:* NEA 1980-; *home:* 624 E South St Bremen IN 46506

YEAGER, ROBERT JAY, Assistant Principal; *b:* New Martinsville, WV; *m:* Barbara L. Smith; *c:* Corey J.; *ed:* (BS) Scndry Ed, 1979, (MA) Ed Admin, 1984 WV Univ; WV Principals Acad 1988; Stud Completed 1989; *cr:* Teacher 1979-87; Asst Prin 1987- Short Line Sch; *ai:* Frosh Boys Bsktbl Coach; Adv 8th Grade Field Trip- Washington DC; NASSP; WVSSPA; Short Line PTA; New Martinsville Jaycees; Loyal Order of Moose; Jaycees Ed of Yr 1982; Grad of WV Prin Acad 1988-89; *office:* Shortline Middle School P O Box 328 Reader WV 26167

YEAMAN, DELORIS BURKS, Fifth Grade Teacher; *b:* Lynchburg, VA; *w:* Gary L. (dec); *c:* Cheryl Y. Yeaman Capron, Kellie Yeaman Grey (dec); *ed:* (BA) Bus/Ed, 1952, (MED) Elem Ed, 1969 Lynchburg Coll; *cr:* Bus Teacher Kempsville HS 1952; 4th/6th Grade Classroom Teacher Linkhorne Elem Sch 1966-; *ai:* Math Resource, Rdng Incentive, Steering Comm; Southern Assn Colls & Schls; Kappa Delta Pi 1968-; Delta Kappa Gamma (Pres 1976-78) 1971-.

YEARA, JAMES CARROLL, English/Drama Teacher; *b:* Rochester, NY; *m:* Claudia Lynn; *c:* Matt, Amanda, Jinny, Alice; *ed:* (BA) Eng/Creative Writing, Nazareth Coll 1981; (MA) Eng Lit, St Univ of NY Albany 1986; Shakesperean Drama, Univ of Birmingham England 1983; Romantic Poetry, Rice Univ 1984; Shakesearean Drama Brown Univ 1989; *cr:* Eng Teacher Marshall HS 1981, Interim Jr HS 1981-82, Migrant Rotorial Outreach Project SUNY 1982-83; Eng/Drama Teacher Averill Park HS 1983-85, Bethlehem HS 1985-; *ai:* Drama Dir; Shakeseare Recitation Competition; Natl Endowment for Hum Grants Rice Univ 1984 & Brown Univ 1989; Golub Scholars Teacher of Yr Awd 1989; Article Published Sunstone Magazine & Sunday Albany Times Union; *home:* 433 Kenwood Ave Delmar NY 12054

YEARSLEY, GARY STANTON, Vice-Prinicpal; *b:* Pocatello, ID; *m:* Wanda Jean Finnell; *c:* Kori, Jeff, Scott, Melissa, Shelley; *ed:* (BS) Phys Ed, Brigham Young Univ 1975; (MED) Admin, ID St Univ 1988; ID Natl Guard 1970-79; 1st Lieutenant Exec Officer Trng; Officer Basic Course, Refresher Course, Ft Sill OK; Maintenance Mangement Course, Ft Lewis WA; *cr:* Phys Ed/Health Teacher Marsh Valley Jr HS 1975-83; Driver Ed Supvr Marsh Valley Sch Dist 21 1976-; Phys Ed/Health Teacher 1983-, Vice Prin 1988- Marsh Valley HS; *ai:* Asst Bsktbl Coach; Stu Cncl Adv; Bannock Cty Child Abuse Task Force; Marsh Valley Jr Hs Teacher of Yr Awd 1978-79; *home:* 50 N High St Arimo ID 83214

YEATTS, MARIAN SUNNY SMITH, Teacher; *b:* Arlington, TX; *m:* Fred H.; *c:* Denise J.; *ed:* (BS) Speech/Drama, 1968, (MA) Theatre, 1976 TX Womans Univ; Grad Stud Eng, Univ of N TX; *cr:* Theatre Teacher R L Turner HS 1974-76; Eng Teacher Dewitt Perry Jr HS 1976-77, Newman Smith HS 1977-78; Eng/Debate/Speech/Theatre Teacher Sanger HS 1978-; *ai:* Natl Forensic League & ITS Spon; Debate & Drama Competition Coach; Univ Interscholastic League Dir; TX Educl Theatre Assn 1987-; TX Speech Comm Assn 1979-; Zeta Phi Eta Adv 1974-76; Denton Cmmty Theatre (Production Bd 1989-, Dir 1977-78, 1989-) Scene Design for Santa Fe Sunshine 1989; Sanger HS Teacher of Yr; Coached Winning Debate Teams & Speakers; Directed Awd Winning 1 Act Plays; *office:* Sanger HS P O Box 188 Sanger TX 76266

YEE, ELIZABETH ANN, English Teacher; *b:* San Francisco, CA; *m:* Eugene; *ed:* (BA) Eng, San Francisco St Univ 1974; Standard Scndry Credential, San Francisco St Univ 1975; *cr:* Eng Dept Chairperson 1983-89, Teacher 1975- N Salinas HS; *ai:* Fine Art & Advanced Placement Club Adv; Championship Gymanstics Team Coach; Cheerleading Squads, Frosh, Soph, Jr, Sr Class Spon; Winter Ball & Prom Chaperone; Delta Kappa Gamma (Historian 1982-85, Recording Secy 1988-, Treas 1990), 1980-; NCTE, CA Assn Teachers of Eng, AFT 1975-; Chinese Amer Teachers Assn 1983-85; Valley Guild Steinbeck House 1986-; KQED Educl Television 1979-; Univ of Santa Cruz Fellowship; Cntrl CA Writing Project 1983; N Salinas HS & Salinas Union HS Dist Teacher of Month 1989; *office:* N Salinas HS 55 Kip Dr Salinas CA 93906

YEE, JAMES C., Math Teacher; *b:* Barstow, CA; *ed:* (BA) Math, CA St Univ Long Beach 1972; (MA) Teaching, Azusa Pacific Univ 1981; *cr:* Teacher Long Beach Unified Sch Dist 1973-74; Victor Valley HS 1974-78; Victor Valley Jr HS 1978-84; Instr Part Time Victor Valley Coll 1981-84; Teacher Hesperia HS 1984-; *ai:* Asst Math Dept Head; NTCM.

YELKOVAC, PENNY, Third Grade Teacher; *b:* Gary, IN; *m:* Peter; *c:* Peter G., Susan; *ed:* (BS) Elem Ed, 1964, (MS) Elem Ed, 1967 IN Univ; Ingalls Substance Abuse Ed/Cert; Brass Fnd Substance Abuse Ed/Cert; *cr:* Teacher Gary Sch Corporation 1964-69; Teacher/Dir Montessori 1969-70; Teacher Trinity Luth Nursery Sch 1973-76, Valpariso Cmmty Schls 1975-; *ai:* Valparaiso Drug & Alcohol Cncl; Ben Franklin Stamp Club; Red Ribbon Spon; Just Say No Club Adv & Spon; Smart Kids-Mc Gruffs Spon; Valparaiso Teachers Assn Teacher Rep 1986; IN St Teachers Assn, NEA, NCTE; Valparaiso Drug & Alcohol Cncl Elem Rep 1987-; Alpha Delta Kappa Courtesy Chairperson 1985-; Join Our Youth Consultant-Coord 1987-; Lilly Fellow for Creativity in Teaching 1989; Published Journals & Newsletters; *home:* 2302 Campbell Valparaiso IN 46383

YELLEN, FRED LEE, 7-9th Grade Math Teacher; *b:* Brooklyn, NY; *m:* Linda Boss; *c:* Mark, Carrie, Sara; *ed:* (BS) Psych, UB SUNYAB 1968; (EDM) Math Ed, SUNYAB 1971; *cr:* 7th-8th Grade Math Teacher Woodlawn Jr HS 1968; 7th/8th/9th Math Teacher North Park Acad 1968-; *ai:* BA Teachers Fed Executive Comm 1973-; NEA/NY Dir 1989-; BA Schoolmasters Dir 1988-; Honored 1978; Author Several Math Tapes; *office:* North Park Acad Parkside & Tacoma St Buffalo NY 14216

YELLOTT, JODY HYATT, Social Studies Teacher; *b:* De Quincy, LA; *m:* Kirk A.; *c:* Dallas, Peyton; *ed:* (BA) Comm Ed, 1973, (MED) Comm Ed, 1979, (BA) Elem Ed, 1981 Mc Ness St Univ; Assertice Discipline Seminar; Cmptr Assisted Ed; *cr:* Teacher De Quincy HS 1974-75, De Quincy Mid Sch 1975-; *ai:* Soc Stud Club Spon; LA Assn of Educators, NEA, Calcasieu Assn of Educators 1974-; Service League (Pres 1976-78, Treas 1978-80); Civic Club; *home:* 301 S Perkins St De Quincy LA 70633

YENCHIK, JOHN A., Spanish Teacher/Dept Chair; *b:* Wilkes-Barre, PA; *m:* Deborah C. Fox; *c:* Rebecca, Althea, Allison, John, Alex; *ed:* (BA) Span/Scndry, Kings Coll 1967; (MA) Span, Villanova Univ 1970; PA St Univ; *cr:* Span Teacher Romulus Cntrl NY 1967-68; Cntrl Cath Kingston PA 1969-70; Coll Misericordia Dallas PA 1970-73; Hanover Area Wilkes-Barre PA 1975-; *ai:* Adjunct & Lecturer in Span PA St Campus 1984-; Amer Assn of Teacher of Span & Portuguese; Part Time ESL Teacher PA Dept of Ed St Correctional Inst Dallas 1985-; Teaching Grad Asst Villanova Univ; *home:* 37 Pearson St Truesdale Terr Wilkes-Barre PA 18706

YERBY, JAMES NATHAN, 7th Grade Mathematics Teacher; *b:* Richmond, VA; *m:* Vernice Charlene Stowers; *c:* Tiffany E., Patrick A.; *ed:* (AS) Elem Ed, Rappahannock Comm Coll 1973; (BS) Elem Ed, VA Commonwealth 1975; Teacher Effective Trng; Cmptr Sci; *cr:* 7th Grade Math/Sci/His Teacher Madison Public Sch 1975-76, Caroline Public Sch 1976-; *ai:* Homebase Activity, Dance for Fun, Math for Real Adv; Stu Behavior Comms; Macedonia Baptist Church Deacon 1975-; New Light Baptist Church Sunday Sch Teacher 1981-; *home:* 3511 Carolina Ave Richmond VA 23222

YETTO-REICHARD, LYNETTE, Teacher of Gifted/Talented; *b:* Kane, PA; *m:* Samuel W.; *ed:* (BA) Theatre Arts, PA St Univ 1977; (BS) Speech/Comm/Theatre, Clarion Univ 1978; *cr:* Eng Teacher Morrisville HS 1978-86; Teacher of Gifted/Talented Morrisville Mid/Sr HS 1986-; *ai:* Drama, Musical, Cheerleading, Gym Show, Assembly Comm; NEA, PA St Ed Assn; Morrisville Ed Assn Pres Elect 1990-; Kane Players Managing Dir 1974-78; Morrisville Cmmty Theatre; Outstanding Young Woman of America 1983; Nom Outstanding Teacher of Yr Morrisville Sch Dist 1986-88; *office:* Morrisville Mid/Sr HS W Palmer St Morrisville PA 19067

YGLESIAS, AUDRY HILL, Rdng Spec/Art Teacher/Prin; *b:* Hammond, LA; *m:* Bernard D.; *c:* Craig B., Maria C.; *ed:* (BFA) Design, MS St Univ for Women 1969; Reg Teacher Cert, 1978, (MA) Ed/Rdng/Admin, 1982 LSU; Completed Coursework & Teaching in Cntrl America; Curr Adv, Diagnostician; *cr:* Teacher MS Public Schls 1973-74; Teacher/Curr Adv Costa Rica Acad 1974-75; Rdng Specialist/Prin/Teacher Millerville Acad 1976-; *ai:* Diagnostic Testing Rdng Clinic Counseling; Fund Raising Motivational Assemblies; Natl Assn for Curr Adv, Natl Prin Assn 1983-; Natl Mid Sch Assn 1989-; Sch Volunteer Org 1973-, Outstanding Service 1973-; Travel Club Cntrl, S America & Europe 1981-86; Comite Baptist Church Charity Volunteer; Group Therapy Facilitator Cmmty Service; MSCW Philosophy Fellowship; Self Help & Childrens Bibliotherapy Series, Stu Handbooks, Brochures, Various Admin & Curr Evaluation Forms; *office:* Millerville Acad 1615 Millerville Rd Baton Rouge LA 70816

YOAKAM, MARK WILLIAM, English Teacher; *b:* Mc Minville, OR; *m:* Joy Colleen Schroeber; *c:* Alyce, Paul; *ed:* (BS) Eng, Dickinson St Coll 1973; (MS) Counseling, E MT Coll 1981; *cr:* Teacher/Coach Garrison HS 1973-74, Glascow Mid Sch 1974-; *ai:* Girls & Boys HS Cross Cntry Head Coach & Track Asst Coach; NEA, MEA, MT Coaches Assn; Glasgow Youth Soccer Pres 1984-85; Glasgow Girls Sftbl Pres 1988-; Coach of Yr 1978, 1980; Articles Published Cross Cntry Journal; *home:* 104 Aberdeen Glasgow MT 59230

YOCOM, ELLEN STAHR, 7th-12th Grade English Teacher; *b:* Chicago, IL; *m:* Thomas A.; *c:* Audrey, Morphett; *ed:* (AB) Eng, Mac Murray Coll 1968; (MA) Lit , Sangamon St Univ 1979; Writing, IL St Univ; *cr:* Eng Teacher Waverly Dist #6 1968-; Composition Instr Lincoln Land Comm Coll 1981-; *ai:* Drama Club Spon Dir for HS Plays; NEA 1970-; IL Ed Assn 1970-; Waverly Ed Assn Pres & Chief Negotiator 1973/1986/1988; Outstanding Teacher of Yr 1975 for Publication; *office:* Waverly District #6 201 N Miller Waverly IL 62692

YOCUM, TIMOTHY ALLEN, Phys Ed Teacher/Athletic Dir; *b:* Mishawaka, IN; *m:* Cynthia Joy Martin; *c:* Daniel; *ed:* (BS) Phys Ed, 1984, Speech Teaching, 1984 Grace Coll; *cr:* Athletic Dir/Phys Ed/Health Teacher Cntrl Baptist Chrstn Acad 1985-; *ai:* Boys Var Soccer Coach; Faculty Adv of Acad of Arts Drama Productions; Var Soccer & Bsktbl Tournament Dir; Triple Cities Soccer Ofcls Assn Ofcl 1985-; *office:* Cntrl Baptist Chrstn Acad 1606 Upper Front St Binghamton NY 13901

YODER, TERRY ROBERT, Social Studies Teacher; *b:* Flint, MI; *m:* Judith Ann Fickies; *c:* Laura J. Jones, Gregory S., Bethany K. Swart; *ed:* (BA) His, MI St Univ 1960; *cr:* Geography/Eng/Phys Ed Teacher Davison Jr HS 1960-61; Soc Stud Teacher Bryant Jr HS 1961-64, Davison HS 1964-81; Eng Teacher Davison Jr HS 1981-84; Soc Stud Teacher Davison HS 1984-; *ai:* Var Vlybl Coach; Driver Ed Instr; MI HS Vlybl Coaches Assn 1981-; First Baptist Church Lapeer Youth Leader 1986-; *home:* 8242 Potter Rd Davison MI 48423

YOELL, MARTHA BONFIGLIO, 5th/6th Grade Teacher; *b:* Hillsdale, MI; *m:* David S.; *c:* Chris Johnstone, Mary J. Blair, Nancy Johnstone, David E. Johnstone; *ed:* (BPH) Music Ed/Fr & Eng, Siena Heights Coll 1960; Spring Arbor Coll 1974-77; *cr:* 4th Grade Teacher St Thomas Aquinas 1960-62; 6th Grade Teacher Our Lady of Fatima 1977-; *ai:* Piano Teacher; Church Choir Mem; Sch Organist/Sch Masses; Tutor; NCEA 1977-; Jackson Symphony 1967-75; NAACP 1968-70; Jackson Musical Theater 1970-73; Clark Lake Players 1970-73; *office:* Our Lady Of Fatima 911 Napoleon Rd Michigan Center MI 49254

YOGI, KAY KEIKO (OYAMA), Computer Literacy Teacher; *b:* Honolulu, HI; *m:* Richard S.; *c:* Kelsey, Reidly; *ed:* (BED) Elem, 1960, Teaching Certificate Elem, 1961 Univ of HI; Grad Courses Ed of Exceptional Children; Lang Arts Wkshps, Inst for Academically Talented Stu; Cmptr Ed Courses/Wkshps; *cr:* 5th Grade Teacher Waianae Elem Sch 1961-65; 3rd-5th Grade Teacher Ala Wai Elem Sch 1965-71; 6th Grade Teacher Princess Kaiulani Elem Sch 1972; 4th Grade Teacher 1973-81, Gifted/Talented Teacher 1981-86, Cmptr Literacy Teacher 1986- Ala Wai Elem Sch; *ai:* Stu Cncl Adv; HI Ed Assn, NEA, HI St Teachers Assn; Alpha Delta Kappa (Secy, Chaplain, Sargeant-At-Arms, Pres) 1986-88; *office:* Ala Wai Elem Sch 503 Kamoku St Honolulu HI 96826

YOKLEY, W. KEITH, English Dept Chair; *b:* High Point, NC; *ed:* (BS) Eng, Appalachian St Univ 1967; (MA) Eng, Univ of NC Chapel Hill 1972; Coursework, Yale, Duke, Univ of NC Greensboro; *cr:* Eng Teacher 1967-71,1972-, Eng Dept Chm 1980- High Point Cntrl HS; *ai:* NHS Selection Comm Chm; Tutoring; Schlshp Comm Mem; Journalism Teacher & Sch Newspaper Spon; AFT, NCTE; Teachers Panel for Task Force Excl in Scndry Ed Mem 1989-; NC Lang Art Teacher of Yr 1986; High Point Teacher of Yr 1985; Whos Who in Amer Ed 1990; *office:* High Point Central HS 801 Ferndale Blvd High Point NC 27265

YOKOZAWA, TAKESHI, Japanese Teacher/Lecturer; *b:* Otaku Tokyo, Japan; *m:* Yukiko Yamamoto; *c:* Fumiko I.; *ed:* (BA) Bus Adm, Tokyo Coll of Ec 1968; (MA) Bi-ling/Bicultural Ed, Seton Hall Univ 1978; *cr:* Ed Assoc Univ of HI Manoa 1968-73; Lecturer Chaminade Univ of Honolulu 1970-71; Teacher Damien Memorial HS 1981-89, Punahou Sch 1989-, Damien Memorial HS 1990-; *ai:* Stu Exchange Prgm Coord; Japanese Club Adv; Cath Sch Dept Certificate of Recognition 1989; Diocese of Honolulu; Society for Teaching Japanese as Foreign Lang 1980-; Japanese Educl Fund of HI Bd of Dir 1978-; Bi-ling Fellowship Prgm Federal Government 1977-78; Japanese Lang Textbooks for Children Vol 1-9 With Teachers Manuals; HS Japanese Lang Text Workbooks Vol I-III; Set of Transparencies for Lang Teaching; *office:* Damien HS 1401 Houghtailing St Honolulu HI 96817

YOKUM, NORA G. (HARDER), Retired Teacher; *b:* Harman, WV; *m:* Troy C.; *c:* Robert D., Theadore M., T. Michael, John W.; *ed:* (BA) Ed, Davis & Elkins 1961; Grad Stud Ed; *cr:* 1st/2nd Grade Teacher Whitmer Elem 1958-71; 6th Grade Teacher Harman 12 Yr Sch 1971-88; *ai:* NEA, WV Ed Assn, Classroom Teachers Assn, Randolph Cty Retired Teacher Assn, PTA.

YOLISH, KATHLEEN T., Second Grade Teacher; *b:* Derby, CT; *m:* Norman L.; *c:* P. Jane; *ed:* (BA) Ed/Eng, Sacred Heart Univ 1971; (MA) Rdng, S CT St Coll 1979; Pursuing 6th Yr Fairfield Univ; *cr:* 3rd Grade Teacher 1971-78, 5th Grade Teacher 1978-80 Ferry Sch; 2nd Grade Teacher Sunnyside Sch 1981-83, La Fayette Sch 1983-; *ai:* Shelton Staff Dev Comm 1989-; Shelton Ed Assn (VP 1973-74, Treas 1977); CT Teachers Applying Whole Lang Charter Mem; Whole Lang Teachers Assn; Lafayette Sch PTA VP 1987-89; Co-Operating Teacher Mentor Prgm St of CT & Shelton Sch System 1987-; *home:* 6 Meadowlake Dr PO Box 663 Shelton CT 06484

YONCHUK, LINDA JEAN, Soc Stud Teacher/Dept Coord; *b:* Binghamton, NY; *ed:* (BA) Soc Stud, 1971, (MA) Ed, 1972 St Univ of NY Albany; Robert A Taft Inst for 2-Party Government; US Constitution Bicentennial Natl Endowment for Hum Grant; Dev Local Law Ed Prgm Project PATCH Grant; *cr:* Soc Stud Teacher Averill Park Cntrl Sch 1971-72; Soc Stud Teacher 1972-, Soc Stud Dept Coord 1982- Windsor Cntrl Sch; *ai:* Jr HS Stu Cncl Adv; HS Challenge Coach & Adv; Jr Var Vlybl & Boys Club Vlybl Coach; Developing Activity Period Faculty Comms; NHS Honorary Mem 1989; Delta Kappa Gamma (Secy 1982-86, Chapter Pres 1986-88, Coordinating Cncl 1988-); Windsor Town Youth Prgm Bsbl Coach 1980-82; Kirkwood Youth Commission Sftbl Coach 1982-83; Cath Youth Organization Vlybl Coach 1989; NE Regional Soc Stud Conference Rep 1987, 1989-; *office:* Windsor Jr/Sr HS Rt 79 S Windsor NY 13865

YONKE, LINDA CARMITCHEL, Dean of Students; *b:* Kankakee, IL; *m:* Gary; *c:* Courtney, Zachary; *ed:* (BA) His, Albion Coll 1975; (MA) Lang/Lit, Governors St 1983; Certificate Educl Admin, Univ of IL 1989; *cr:* Eng Teacher King Upper Grade Center 1976-79, Eastridge HS 1979-88; Eng Dept Chairperson 1988-89, Dean of Stus 1989- Kankakee HS; *ai:* NCTE 1985-; ASCD 1989-; Jr League Treas 1990; Cmmty Art Cncl 1989-; *office:* Kankakee HS 1200 W Jeffery Kankakee IL 60901

YORK, SARA ELLEN, Mathematics Teacher; *b:* Newton, AL; *c:* Craig, Katie; *ed:* (BS) Math, Troy St Univ 1978; *cr:* Math Teacher Ozark City Sch System 1977-81, Dale Cty HS 1983-; Part Time Math Teacher Wallace Comm Coll 1988-; *ai:* Annual Spon; NEA, AEA; *office:* Dale Cty HS PO Drawer J Midland City AL 36350

YORTY, ROLLIN DALE, Retired Teacher; *b:* Lebanon, PA; *m:* Ethel Belle; *c:* Bonnie Brandt, Heather Nelson, Tami Laizure, Melodie; *ed:* (BS) Soc Sci, 1951, (MA) Elem Admin, 1962 Cntrl MI Univ; *cr:* Instr Gerrish-Higgins Schls 1951-59, Saginaw Township Schls 1959-60, Merritt Public Schls 1960-62, Grayling Public Schls 1962-66, Gerrish-Higgins Schls 1966-83; *ai:* MEA, NEA; Whos Who in Midwest; Whos Who in America; *home:* 103 Yorty Dr Roscommon MI 48653

YOSHIOKA, VERNON KOSUKE, 6th Grade Head Teacher; *b:* Wailuku, HI; *m:* Diana Hope Connolly; *c:* Holly Hutchison, Michelle, Matthew, Andrew, Adan, Joshua, Jacob; *ed:* (BS) Elem Ed, 1969, (MS) Ed/Rdng, 1978 E OR St; Prin Certificate Portland St Univ 1988; *cr:* Teacher Island City Sch 1969-87; Head Teacher Riveria Sch 1987-; *ai:* Ftbl, Bsktbl, Track, Wrestling; Sch Newspaper, Onward to Excl, Dist Strategic Planning Comm, Drug & Alcohol Leadership Team; Lions Club 1987-; Whos Who Elem Teachers of America 1974; Outstanding OR Geographer 1975; Ed Radio-TV Governors Comm 1976-78; Natl Career Ed Conference Presenter 1977; Teacher Incentive Grant 1978; *office:* Riveria Elem Sch 2609 N 2nd St La Grande OR 97850

YOST, BILL, Mathematics Teacher; *b:* Omaha, NE; *c:* Christopher; *ed:* (BA) Math, Emporia St Univ 1970; Univ of IA, Marycrest, Peru St Coll; *ai:* Head Boys Bsktbl Coach; NCMT, NEA, ISEA, IBCA; *office:* Louisa-Muscatine Cmmty HS Box 234-A Letts IA 52754

YOST, DEBRA ANN, Home Economics Instructor; *b:* Sunbury, PA; *ed:* (BS) Home Ec Ed, Mansfield St Univ 1973; (MS) Early Chldhd Ed, 1978, 6th Year Early Chldhd Ed, 1983 S CT St Univ; *cr:* Home Ec Instr Warren Harding HS 1973-77, Tomlinson Jr HS 1977-78, Fairfield HS 1978-; *ai:* Peace Corps Partnership Prgm Club Adv; Amer Home Ec Assn; Natl Assn of Family Daycare; *office:* Fairfield HS Melville Ave Fairfield CT 06430

YOST, JOAN FOSTER, English Teacher; *b:* Grenada, MS; *m:* Dennis Robert; *ed:* (BA) Eng, Mary Hardin Baylor Univ 1963; (MA) Scndry Curr/Instruction, San Diego St Univ 1978; Trng for Lang Dev Specialist; Dist Cert for Gifted & Talented Ed; *cr:* Eng Teacher Dickinson Jr HS 1963-65, Mc Clintock HS 1965-67, Pacific Beach Jr HS 1967-84, Mission Bay HS 1984-; *ai:* Restructuring Comm; Gifted & Talented Stu Team Mem; CA Assn Teachers of Eng; Greater San Diego Cncl Teachers of Eng Publicity Chairperson 1977-79; San Diego Teachers Assn, CA Teachers Assn, NEA; CA Teachers Assn Innovative Dev Merit Awd; NDEA Summer Inst Participant AZ St Univ; *office:* Mission Bay HS 2475 Grand Ave San Diego CA 92109

YOST, SANDRA L., First Grade Teacher; *b:* Gloversville, NY; *c:* Jenifer, Emily; *ed:* (BA) Elem Ed, 1971, (MS) Elem Ed, 1975 St Univ Coll Oneonta; Talents Unlimited; Quest Intnl Skills for Growing; Educl Admin; Licensed Real Estate Salesperson; *cr:* 1st Grade Teacher New Lebanon Cntrl Sch 1971-72; 5th Grade Teacher Franklin Cntrl Sch 1972-74; Kndgtn/1st/3rd Grade Teacher South Kortright Cntrl Sch 1976-; *ai:* Gifted & Talented Prgm; South Kortright Teachers Assn, NY Ed Assn; AEI, ARDA Real Estate 1989-, 100 Club 1989; First Presbyn Church; *office:* South Kortright Cntrl Sch Rt 10 South Kortright NY 13842

YOUMANS, MERCEDES NORRIS, 8th Grade Lang Art Teacher; *b:* Savannah, GA; *m:* Donald Ray; *c:* Donald K., Jonathan M., Jason A., Brian M.; *ed:* (BM) Music Ed, Wesleyan Coll 1968; (MED) Mid Grades, GA Coll 1983; *cr:* Choral Music Teacher Southwest HS & Arkwright Elem 1968-70; Lang Art Teacher/Librarian Alapaha Elem 1981-82; Lang Art Teacher T J Elder Mid 1983-; *ai:* Textbook Adoption Comm, Philosophy & Goals Comm, 8th Grade Chm; Choral Dir; Drama Club, Academic Bowl, Stu Cncl Spon; Alpha Delta Kappa 1988-; United Meth Women (Dist VP, Local Offices 1970-); Sandersville Music Club 1986-; Most Cooperative Teacher Awd 1985-87; *office:* T J Elder Mid Sch PO Box 816 Hines St Sandersville GA 31082

YOUNG, ANN MILLER, Third Grade Teacher; *b:* Tuscaloosa, AL; *m:* Terence O.; *c:* Amy Young Mc Daniel, Ellen E.; *ed:* (BS) Elem Ed, Bethel Coll 1957; (MS) Rdng/Elem Ed, Univ of MS 1983; *cr:* 2nd Grade Teacher Memphis City Schls 1957-58, Tyler City Schls 1959-60; 1st Grade Teacher Memphis City Schls 1960-61; 3rd Grade Teacher Greenville City Schls 1966-70; Kndgtn Teacher Greenville Presbyn Sch 1970-72; 3rd Grade Teacher Senatobia City Schls 1975-; *ai:* Sch Newspaper Spon; Childrens Theater Spon & Coach; NEA, MS Ed Assn 1975-85; Senatobia Ed Assn (VP 1980) 1975-85; GSA Leader 1973-78; Sycamore Art Cncl (Pres 1986-87, Bd of Dir 1990); Senatobia Lib Trustee 1979-84; Senatobia Home & Garden Club (Secy, Women of Church Pres, Culture Club VP & Secy); *home:* 69 Country Club Dr Rt 3 Senatobia MS 38668

YOUNG, AUDREY KING, Fourth Grade Teacher; *b:* Bonifay, FL; *m:* Lawrence Sr.; *c:* Debbie Y. Snead, Lawrence Jr., Kyle; *ed:* (BS) Elem Ed, FL Memorial Coll 1956; (MS) S CT St Coll; Various Wkshps; *cr:* Teacher Truman 1965-70, Helene Grant 1972-; *ai:* Cmptr Club; Nuts & Bolts Club; Natl Cncl of Negro Women 1989-; Order of Eastern Star 1980-; Bethel AME Church (Edith B Powers Pres 1967-70, Stewardess Bd 1 Pres 1989-, Gospel Choir Pres 1981-83); BSA Den Mother 1967-71; Little League Team Mother 1983-83, 3 Trophies; *office:* Helen W Grant Sch 185 Goffe St New Haven CT 06511

YOUNG, BARBARA HENSON, 7th-8th Grade English Teacher; *b:* Mc Allen, TX; *m:* David Allen; *c:* Aimee M., Travis H.; *ed:* (BA) Speech/Eng, Univ of TX Austin 1967; *cr:* 7th/8th Grade Eng Teacher Houston Ind Sch Dist 1967-68; 4th Grade Teacher St Francis Episcopal Day Sch 1971-72; 3rd Grade Eng Teacher Weslaco Ind Sch Dist 1968-69; 7th/8th Grade Eng Teacher Mason Ind Sch Dist 1989-; *ai:* 8th Grade Class & Chrldr/Pep Squad Spon; UIL Spelling/Ready Writing; Riata Literary Club; *office:* Mason Jr HS HC 60 Box 31C Mason TX 76856

YOUNG, BETSY WRIGHT, Fourth Grade Teacher; *b:* Huntingdon, PA; *w:* Eugene Richard (dec); *c:* E. Richard Jr., Mark T., Michael W., Matthew A.; *ed:* (BS) Elem Ed, Juniata 1950; Grad Work PA St Univ, & Millersville Univ; *cr:* 1st Grade Teacher 1948-49, Mt Union Elem Sch 1950-54; 3rd/4th Grade Teacher Lincoln Elem 1964-; *ai:* NEA, PA St Ed Assn, Ephrata Area Ed Assn; *home:* 809 Pleasant View Dr Ephrata PA 17522

YOUNG, BEVERLY JEAN, Elementary Reading Specialist; *b:* St Louis, MO; *m:* Kenneth; *c:* Sarah; *ed:* (BA) Psych, St Louis Univ 1973; (MA) Rdng, Univ of MO St Louis 1981; *cr:* 3rd Grade Teacher Sappington Sch 1973-76; 2nd Grade Teacher Watson Sch 1976-81; Elem Rdng Specialist Crestwood Sch 1981-; *ai:* Dist Staff Dev Comm; Intnl Rdng Assn; NEA Comm Chairperson 1987-.

YOUNG, BLANCHE, Second Grade Teacher; *b:* Camden, NJ; *m:* Albert; *c:* Tracy, Alan; *ed:* (BA) Elem Ed, Glassboro St 1983; *cr:* 2nd Grade Teacher Highland Park Sch 1983-; *ai:* Sci Comm 1988-89; Rdng Comm 1989-; NJEA; GCPTA; GCEA; *office:* Highland Park Sch Broadway below Mercer Gloucester City NJ 08030

YOUNG, BONNIE EVANS, Third Grade Teacher; *b:* Valley View, PA; *c:* Walter T.; *ed:* (BS) Elem Ed, West Chester Univ 1960; *cr:* 2nd Grade Teacher 1960-70, Remedial Rdng Teacher 1970-73, 4th Grade Teacher 1973-76, 3rd Grade Teacher 1976- Pennsboro Elem Schls; *ai:* PTO Treas 1967-70; Red Cross Sch Youth Adv 1975-85; *office:* East Pennsboro Area Schls 529 N Enola Dr Enola PA 17025

YOUNG, BRENDA LONG, English Teacher; *b:* Harrodsburg, KY; *m:* Edward Thomas; *c:* Stacy Y. Logue, Mark E., Kristie L.; *ed:* (BA) Eng/His, 1968, (MA) Ed/Eng, 1978 Univ of KY; *cr:* Teacher Mercer Cty Schls 1970-; *ai:* Internship Prgm; Dept Chairperson; Chrldrs, Stu Cncl, Pep Club, Drug Club, Yrbk Spon; MCEA Secy; KY Ed Assn, NEA; Univ KS Alumni (Secy, Treas); Harrodsburg Baptist (Finance Comm 1985-89, Recreation Comm 1989-); Corning Glass Schlsp; *office:* Mercer Cty Jr & Sr HS 937 Moberly Rd Harrodsburg KY 40330

YOUNG, CLAYTON DATHOONG, Science Teacher; *b:* Honolulu, HI; *m:* Lisa Emiko Hiramoto; *ed:* (BED) Scndry Ed/Bio, Univ HI 1983; *cr:* Sci Teacher Hana HS/Elem Sch 1983-85, Pres William Mc Kinley HS 1985-; *ai:* Environmental Ed Chm; Friends of Animals Club Adv; Campus Beautification Comm Co-chm; HI St Teachers Assn 1983-; Duetz-Allis St Awd for Conservation Ed 1986; *office:* Mc Kinley HS 1039 S King St Honolulu HI 96814

YOUNG, CLIFFORD CRAIG, English Teacher; *b:* Topeka, KS; *m:* Sharon Ann Sanders; *c:* Elizabeth, Abigail; *ed:* (BLS) Tech Theatre, 1979, (BS) Scndry Ed, 1982 NM St Univ; *cr:* 7th-8th Grade Eng Teacher/8th Grade Honors Eng Teacher Chaparral Jr HS 1984-; *ai:* Stu Government Spon; NEA (Treas 1989-, VP 1988-89); Alamogordo Ed Assn Treas 1987-88; *office:* Chaparral Jr HS 1400 College Ave Alamogordo NM 88310

YOUNG, CYNTHIA BOYLE, Fifth Grade Teacher; *b:* Pittsburgh, PA; *m:* Patrick L.; *c:* Julie; *ed:* (BS) Elem Ed, Lamar Univ 1966; Grad Work Cntrl St Univ, St Josephs Univ; *cr:* 5th Grade Teacher St Theresa 1966-68; 1st Grade Teacher Bridge City Elem 1968-69; 2nd/4th/5th Grade Teacher Orvis Risner Elem 1976-; *ai:* Spelling Bee Co-ord Orvis Risner; Staff Dev Comm & Public Relations Comm Edmond Schls; EACT, NEA, OKEA 1976-; Edmond Rdng Cncl 1987-; Freedoms Fnd of Valley Forge VP of Youth 1985-, Teacher of Yr 1985; Daughters of Colonial Wars Teacher Awd 1986; Edmond Public Schls Teacher of Yr Finalist 1990; Freedoms Fnd of Valley Forge Teacher Conference, George Washington Medal of Honor; Edmond Historical Society Arts Awd; *office:* Orvis Risner Elem Sch 29th & Rankin Edmond OK 73013

YOUNG, DANA DEAN, 7th & 8th Grade Teacher; *b:* Banner Elk, NC; *m:* Jo Nell Mc Collum; *c:* Karen D. Buchanan, Sandra J. Guinn, Dana Clark; *ed:* (BS) Phys Ed/Sci, Milligan Coll 1962; Math, Lit, ETSU; Math/Sci, Appalachian St Univ; *cr:* Teacher Fall Branch HS 1962-63, Beech Mountain Elem 1963-; *ai:* Elem Bsktbl Coach; NCAE 1964-84; First Baptist Church Sunday Sch Supt 1966-69; *home:* Rt 2 Box 1170 Roan Mountain TN 37687

YOUNG, DARYLE ANN WILLIAMS, Staff Developer; *b:* New York, NY; *m:* Donald Lance; *c:* Zenaya A., Sidiq N., Aneesah F.; *ed:* (BA) Span/Theatre Dance, Queens Coll 1975; (MS) Rdng, 1987, (MS) Admin/Supervision, 1990 Coll of New Rochelle; Adult Ed; Cmmty Mapping Humanizing in Ed; Bi-ling Teacher Internship, City Coll NY; Teaching Strategies & Classroom Organization; Instructional Design; *cr:* Teacher of Eng Lang PS 40X 1975-76; Educl Asst Rdng PS 91X 1976-77; Bi-ling Cluster Teacher PS 115 1977-78; Rdng/Lang Arts Teacher CIS 229X 1978-80; Career Educator NYC Recruitment & Trng Prgm Project SAVE 1981; Promotional GATES Pgrm Eng Teacher 1981-83, Lang Arts Teacher 1981-88, Resident Staff Developer 1988- JHS 142; *ai:* Club Adv; African Amer Cultural Society; Dance Club Instr; ASCD 1988-; Intnl Rdng Assn 1987-; Bronx Rdng Cncl 1986; Prof Islamic Organization of United Sisters 1984-; Proposals Accepted & Presentations to NYSRA NY St Rdng Assn 1988-89; Realistic Lit in Classroom; Multicultural Lit that Enhances Self-Esteem Lecturer; Lehman Coll Teacher Trng Corp 1990; *office:* John Philip Sousa Jr HS 142 3750 Baychester Ave Bronx NY 10466

YOUNG, DAVID ALLEN, 5th/6th Grade Math Teacher; *b:* Williamsport, PA; *m:* Linda Roho; *c:* Matthew, Craig; *ed:* (BA) Elem Ed, Lycoming Coll 1969; Masters Equivalent; *cr:* Elem Teacher Loyalsock Valley Elem Sch 1969-71; Math Teacher Mc Call Mid Sch 1971-; *ai:* Township Auditor Mill Creek 3rd Term; Church Bd of Trustees Pennsdale United Meth; NEA, PSEA 1969-; MAEA Treas 1981-.

YOUNG, DOMINIC G., Religion Teacher; *b:* Frankfort, IN; *ed:* (BA) His, St Meinrad Coll 1972; (MA) Theology, Aquinas Inst 1976; Curr Dev/Classroom Management, GA St Univ; *cr:* Teacher Fenwick HS 1972-74, Clarke Coll 1974-76, St Pius HS 1977-89, Bennett HS 1989-; *ai:* Dir of Religious Ed; Drama Club; Admission Comm; NCEA 1977, Certificate 1989; *office:* Bennett HS 1009 Kem Rd Marion IN 46952

YOUNG, DONNA MAE (MARCELLUS), Second Grade Teacher; *b:* Atkinson, NE; *m:* Geoffrey William; *c:* Casey, Bradley, Melissa; *ed:* (BA) Elem Ed/Early Chldhd, Kearney St Coll 1977; Grad Stud Kearney St Coll; *cr:* 1st Grade Teacher 1977-78, 2nd Grade Teacher 1978- Centura Public Schls; *ai:* Report Card Comm; Centura Ed Assn; *home:* 409 S Nubia Box 2 Cairo NE 68824

YOUNG, DONNA PAULETTE, French Teacher; *b:* Pasadena, CA; *ed:* (BA) Fr, Brigham Young Univ 1979; *cr:* Newspaper Adv 1983-87, Art Teacher 1988-89, Yrbk Adv 1983-, Fr/Journalism Teacher Valley Jr HS 1983-; *ai:* Yrbk Adv; VEA, GEA, NEA Assn Rep; *office:* Valley Jr HS 4195 S 3200 W West Valley City UT 84119

YOUNG, DORIS MUSSEY, Third Grade Teacher; *b:* Sedgwick, CO; *m:* Vincent; *c:* Elaine Gomez, Reva Hewgley, David; *ed:* (BA) Elem, Univ of Northern CO 1958; Grad Stud Elem Ed; *cr:* Teachers Aide Monterey Elem 1967-68; 4th Grade Teacher 1968-76, 3rd Grade Teacher 1976-81, 4th Grade Teacher 1981-84, 3rd Grade Teacher 1984 Westview Elem; *ai:* Alpha Delta Kappa (Chapter Pres 1984-86, St Courtesy Chm 1986-88); *office:* Westview Elem 1300 Roseanna Dr Northglenn CO 80234

YOUNG, EDDIE, Health/Phys Ed Teacher; *b:* Itta Bena, MS; *m:* Terry Byrd; *c:* Michelle, Heather; *ed:* (BS) Health/Phys Ed, 1976, (MS) Athletic Admin, 1978 Alcorn St Univ; Ind Stud Univ of WI Madison, Univ of CA Los Angeles, Univ of S MS Hattiesburg; Woodward & Karolyis Gymnastics; *cr:* Teacher/Coach Alcorn St Univ 1976-78, Madison Public Schls 1978-79, Picayune Jr HS 1979-; *ai:* Gym Owner Eddie Youngs Gymnastics; Head Coach Turners Gymnastics Team; US Gymnastics Fed Mem 1982-; Track Athletic Congress Mem 1984-; Jaycees 1988-; Project Self-Help VP 1975-77; *office:* Picayune Jr HS 702 Goodyear Blvd Picayune MS 39466

YOUNG, ELLEN WIESINGER, Sixth Grade Teacher; *b:* Jamaica, NY; *m:* Russell A.; *ed:* (BA) Poly Sci/Elem Ed, Cedar Crest Coll 1971; (MA) Poly Sci, Long Island Univ 1974; Grad Stud Inservice Courses; *cr:* 3rd/5th/6th Grade Teacher Setauket Sch 1971-; *ai:* Declamation Contest Coord; Setauket Sch Teacher of Yr 1982; Prof Recognition 1989; *office:* Setauket Sch Main St Setauket NY 11733

YOUNG, FELECIA DIAN, Consumer & Home Ec Teacher; *b:* Sulphur Springs, TX; *ed:* (BS) Voc Home Ed, E TX St Univ 1987; *cr:* Home Ec Teacher Sulphur Springs Ind Sch Dist 1988, David W Carter HS 1988-; *ai:* FHA Adv; *office:* David W Carter HS 1819 W Wheatland Rd Dallas TX 75232

YOUNG, FRANCES JEANE TATUM, Business Department Chairman; *b:* Dallas, TX; *m:* Malcolm E. Jr.; *c:* Robert, Kerri, Scott; *ed:* (BS) Bus, Howard Payne Univ 1967; (MBE) Bus Ed, Univ of North TX 1978; Scndry Team Leader Trng; Scndry Curr, Cmptr Literacy, Cmptr Programming in BASIC, SMART Word Processing Trng; Dist Team Leader Trng; *cr:* Teacher Nimitz HS 1970-81; Teacher/Bus Dept Chm Plano East Sr HS 1981-; *ai:* FBLA; Univ Interscholastic League Typing Competition; Assn TX Prof Educators (Pres 1984-85, 3rd VP 1988-); TX Bus Ed Assn Dist Teacher of Yr 1988-89; Delta Pi Epsilon; Natl Bus Ed Awd of Merit 1978; Nom St Textbook Comm 1986; Dist Bus Ed Teacher of Yr 1988-89; Nom Plano East Sr Teacher of Yr 1988-89; *office:* Plano East Sr HS 3000 Los Rios Blvd Plano TX 75074

YOUNG, GARY J., Civics Teacher; *b:* Lexington, MI; *m:* Maureen Burch; *c:* Bradley, Dana Cutler; *ed:* (BS) His/Government, Cntrl MI 1961; (MA) Psych, Wayne St Univ 1969; *cr:* Teacher E China Schls 1961-63, Port Huron Area Schls 1964-; *ai:* MI Ed Assn, NEA Life Mem; NDEA Grant; Eastern Star Schlsp; Honor Grad Cntrl & Wayne St; *home:* 323 Jackson Croswell MI 48422

YOUNG, GEORGANNE MC KENZIE, Social Studies Dept Chair; *b:* Mobile, AL; *c:* John W. III, Elizabeth; *ed:* (BA) Psych, 1974, (MA) Learning Disabilities, 1975 Univ of AL; Soc Stud, W GA Coll; *cr:* Learning Disabilities Teacher Birmingham City Schls 1974-77, Thompson Elem 1977-81, Walton HS 1982-86; Soc Stud Teacher 1986-, Soc Stud Dept Chairperson 1988- Walton HS; *office:* George Walton HS 1590 Bill Murdock Rd Marietta GA 30062

YOUNG, GEORGE E., Science Teacher; *b:* Newark, NJ; *m:* Nadine B.; *ed:* (BA) Sci/His, 1979, (MA) Env Sci/Conservation, 1989 Glassboro St; *cr:* Asst Dir Conservation & Environment Stud Center 1971-80; Teacher Haddonfield Mid Sch 1980-81, Pinelands Regional HS 1981-; *ai:* Cross Cntry, Winter Track, Spring Track Coach; Attendance Appeals; Pinelands Experience Dir; NJEA 1980-; VFW VP 1973; Environmental Chairperson 1984-87; Comission Pemberton Township; Co-Wrote Curr NJ Pinelands; Teacher of Yr 1988; Governors Grant Teacher of Yr 1989; Best Environment Prgm Ocean Cty 1990; Chairperson Pemberton Twp Environment Commission; *office:* Pinelands Regional HS Nugentown Rd Tuckerton NJ 08087

YOUNG, GINGER EILENE, Mid Sch English Teacher; *b:* Hammond, LA; *m:* Ross; *c:* Stephen S.; *ed:* (BA) Elem Ed, 1974; (MED) Early Chldhd Ed, 1979 McNeese St Univ; *cr:* Classroom Teacher Hyatt HS 1975-83; Starks HS 1983-; *ai:* Spon-Starks Jr Beta Club; Spon-SAPE Team; Associated Prof Educators of LA; De Quincy Study Club.

YOUNG, GINNY (KELLER), Social Studies Teacher; *b:* Pottstown, PA; *m:* Lewis E.; *c:* Debra Stickles, Catherine, Holly; *ed:* (BA) His, Ursinus Coll 1960; (MED) Ed/Admin, Univ of Reno 1989; N WV Writing Project Invitational; *cr:* His Teacher N Hunterdon Regional HS 1960-61, WestChester Jr HS 1961; Home/Hospital Teacher 1962-82, His/Government Teacher 1982- Washoe Cty Schls; *ai:* Academic Olympics & Reed HS Bowling Club Adv; Faculty Play Participant; Study Skills Comm; NEA 1960-; NSEA 1962-; Washoe Cty Teachers Assn 1962-, Distinguished Service 1987; WIBC 1964-; RSYABA (Pres 1976-79, 1st VP 1990); RSH600 Club; *office:* Edward C Reed HS 1350 Baring Blvd Sparks NV 89434

YOUNG, GLENNA BLEVINS, English Teacher; *b:* Louisa, KY; *m:* W Maxwell; *c:* Vikki Young Franklin; *ed:* (AB) Eng/His, 1964, (MA) 1977 Morehead St Univ; *cr:* Eng Teacher Louisa HS 1964-77, Lawrence Cty HS 1977-; *ai:* Lawremce Cty Ed Assn 1964-84; Lawrence Cty Organization of Teachers 1985-; KY Ed Assn , NEA 1964-; *home:* PO Box 403 Louisa KY 41230

YOUNG, GLORIA BYRD, Fourth Grade Teacher; *b:* Enoree, SC; *m:* Donald Edward; *c:* Andre L., Brittany D.; *ed:* (BS) Spec Ed, Winthrop Coll 1976; (MA) Spec Ed, Converse Coll 1980; Grad Stud Univ of SC Spartanburg & Converse Coll; *cr:* Resource Teacher 1977-87, 4th Grade Teacher 1988- Woodruff Elem; *ai:* Redskin Cheerleading Squad Spon; NEA, SCEA 1977-80, 1989-; CEC 1977-80; *office:* Woodruff Elem Sch Cross Anchor Rd Box 639 Woodruff SC 29388

YOUNG, INELL BROWN, 6th Grade Elementary Teacher; *b:* Greensboro, AL; *w:* Willie C. (dec); *c:* Darlene, David C.; *ed:* (BA) Elem, Stillman Coll 1955; *cr:* Elem Ed Teacher Tuscaloosa Cty 1966; Rdng Teacher Sumter Cty 1966-67; Elem Phys Ed Teacher 1967-80, 6th Grade Teacher 1980- Hale Cty; *ai:* Courtesy Comm; AL Ed Assn, NEA; PTA Secy 1976-77; Received Flag from Pres Cncl on Phys Fitness & Sports 1979; *home:* 2028 4th Pl E Tuscaloosa AL 35404

YOUNG, JAN ELAINE (MEREDITH), Consultant of Gifted/Talented; *b:* Caro, MI; *m:* James Harvey; *c:* Jerry D. Shackelford, Teri L. Janis, Karen M. Shackelford; *ed:* (BA) Elem Ed, MI St Univ 1959; (MA) Lang Art, Cntrl MI Univ 1978; Gifted & Talented Trng Univ of CT; *cr:* Teacher Lansing Schls 1959-60, Fayette Cty Schls 1960-64, Bullock Creek Schls 1972-89; Consultant Midland Cty Intermediate 1989-; *ai:* Odyssey of Mind & Pentathlon Coach; Delta Kappa 1985, Woman of Distinction 1989; Natl Assn Gifted Ed 1989; Bullock Creek Ed Assn VP 1974-89; Britton Hum Awd; COOR Intermediate Sch Dist Awd Creative Educl Idea; Co-Editor Natl Publication for Teachers; Speaker MI St Gifted & Talented Conference; Speaker MI Rdng Assn Conference; Article Published; Presentor for Numerous Wkshps; Organized & Taught Academically Gifted Prgm & Wrote Federal Grant to Fund Prgm; *home:* 4622 Keen Ct Midland MI 48640

YOUNG, JEAN BAKER, 5th Grade Teacher/ESL; *b:* Houston, TX; *m:* David E.; *c:* Derrick, Dwight; *ed:* (BA) Elem Ed, TX Southern Univ 1971; *cr:* 2nd Grade Teacher Alcott Elem 1972-73; Teacher Briargrove Elem 1973-77, Oak Forest Elem 1977-; *ai:* Grade Level Chairperson; Faculty Advisory Comm; Safety Patrol Spon; Black His Month Coord; Project Access Rep; Natl Women Achievement Inc Youth Spon 1988-; Masonic Grand Chapter OES Secy 1975-; M B Smiley HS PTA 1989-; Pine Crest Church Youth Dir 1989-; Impact II Dev Grant; Oak Forests PTA Yrbk Dedication Awd; Oak Forests Teacher of Yr; *office:* Oak Forest Elem Sch 1401 W 43rd Houston TX 77018

YOUNG, JEFF A., 8th Grade Science Teacher; *b:* Chillicothe, OH; *m:* Karen D. Miller; *ed:* (BA) Elem Ed, Rio Grande Coll 1982; (MS) Admin, Univ of Dayton 1987; *cr:* 5th-8th Grade Sci Teacher Zaleski Elem 1982-83; Jr HS Sci Teacher Jackson HS 1983-.

YOUNG, JIM E., Fifth Grade Teacher; *b:* Anniston, AL; *m:* Carolyn Ann Phillips; *c:* Stacie A., Shannon E.; *ed:* (BS) Elem Ed, 1974, (MS) Elem Ed, 1977, (MS) Sch Admin, 1984 Jacksonville St Univ; *cr:* Classroom Teacher 1973-, Cmptr Coord 1984- Lineville Elem Sch; *ai:* Elem Scholars Prgm; Cmptr Prgm Coord; Lineville HS Var Chrldr Co-Spon; Truancy Task Force Comm; Clay Cty Ed Assn Pres 1986-87; AL Ed Assn Delegate Assembly Mem 1986-89; PTO VP 1978; Lineville Baptist Church (Sunday Sch Dir 1987-, Deacon 1986-); Beeson Fellow Samford Univ 1989; Clay Cty Emergency Coord EOC 1980; Amer Radio Relay League Public Service Awd 1977; Book Published; *home:* Rt 1 Box 18 Delta AL 36258

YOUNG, JO ANN R., 6th Gr Teacher/Multidis Team; *b:* Dubuque, IA; *m:* James; *c:* Andrea Stibal, Kevin Stibal, Nick, Ryan; *ed:* (BA) His, Mount Mercy Coll 1968; Univ of IA; *cr:* 5th Grade Teacher Harrison Elem 1969-76; 6th Grade Teacher Nixon Elem 1977-82; Harrison Elem 1982-85; Rooselvelt Mid Sch 1987-; *ai:* Dist Soc Stud Curr, Building Improvement, Encourage Recreational Rdng Comm; Team Leader; CREA, ISEA, NEA; *office:* Roosevelt Mid Sch 300 13th St Nw Cedar Rapids IA 52405

YOUNG, JOAN (GEIGER), First Grade Teacher; *b:* Wolf Lake, IN; *m:* Hanson; *c:* Carey, Lamar; *ed:* (BS) Voc Home Ec, Ball St Muncie 1964; (MS) Scndry Ed, 1970, Elem Endorsement, 1978, 6th Yr Guidance K-12th, 1979 St Francis; *cr:* Home Ec Teacher W Noble Sch Corp 1964-65, Whitley Cty Schls 1973-78; 1st Grade Teacher Jefferson Center 1978-; *ai:* NEA, ISTA 1964-65, 1973-; IRA Little Turtle Exec Bd Mem 1973-; Delta Kappa Gamma Alpha Zeta Corresponding Secy 1988-; First Brethren Church (Chrstn Ed 1980-, Chrstn Ed Dir 1990, Deaconess, Sunday Sch Teacher); Recipient Creative Teaching Grant Ball St 1986-87; IN St Prime-Time Video 1986-89; *office:* Jefferson Center Schl R 5 Columbia City IN 46725

YOUNG, JOANNE ADAMS, Sixth Grade English Teacher; *b:* Charleston, MS; *m:* M. Joe Sr.; *c:* Donna J., Marvin J. Jr., Joel T.; *ed:* (AA) Elem Ed, Northwest Coll 1969; (BSE) Elem Ed, 1971, (MSE) Elem Ed, 1971 Delta St Univ; *cr:* Elem Teacher Charleston Upper Elem 1971-; *ai:* Faculty Secy; NEA 1971-88; MPE 1988-; Bus & Prof Women 1973-81, Young Career Woman 1974; NW Alumni Assn Secy 1971-74; GSA Troop Leader 1987-89; *home:* 105 Marshall Charleston MS 38921

YOUNG, JUANITA BACHLE, Mathematics Teacher; *b:* Oklahoma City, OK; *m:* William A.; *c:* Christopher Pruett, Kara Pruett, Kevin Pruett, Greg; *ed:* (BA) Math/Piano Music, 1971, (MAT) Ed, 1974 OK City Univ; *cr:* 7th/8th Grade Math Teacher Heritage Hall Mid Sch 1971-72, Pleasant Hill Jr HS 1972-74; HS Math Teacher Del City HS 1974-75, Yukon Mid HS 1975-79; Math Teacher Putnam City HS 1979-80, Western Heights HS 1985-; *ai:* Tutoring Math; Band Parent Group at Deer Creek HS; NCTM 1971-; COCTM 1988-; Alert Neighborhood Watch (Secy, Treas) 1986-89; Textbook Selection Comm Western Heights received CAPR Awd.

YOUNG, KIM B., Kindergarten Teacher; *b:* Winchester, TN; *m:* Steve W.; *c:* Stacy, Ryan; *ed:* (AS) Ed, Motlow St Comm Coll 1976; (BS) Elem Ed, 1977; (MS) Early Chldhd Ed, 1979 Mid Tn St Univ; *cr:* 4th Grade Teacher Rock Creek Elem 1977-80; Kndgtn Teacher Cowan Elem 1980-; *ai:* NEA 1978-; TEA 1978-; FCEA 1978-; Cowan Cumberland Presbyn Church Childrens Dir 1988-; *home:* 537 Davis St Cowan TN 37318

YOUNG, LE MYRA TYLER, Eng I/SC His/Home Arts Teacher; *b:* Wagener, SC; *m:* Garry Jack; *c:* Tyler Alan; *ed:* (BA) Sociology/Eng, Lander Coll 1969; (MED) His, Univ of SC 1981; *cr:* Classroom Teacher Goose Creek HS 1969-71, Ridge Spring/Monetta Mid 1971-75, a L Corbett Mid Sch 1975-; *ai:* 8th Grade Team Leader; Stu Cncl Spon; Drug Week Coord; PTO Prgm Black His Awareness Coord; Acken Cty Assn Rep 1971-; SC Ed Assn 1971-; NEA 1971-; Wagener Garden Club Pres 1984-86; Lifetime Mem of US Garden Club 1989; West Low Cty of Garden Club of SC Chm SC Gardens 1989-91; Wagener Museum (Secy 1989- /Bd of Dir 1989-; A L Corbett Teacher of Yr 1986; Teacher Incentive Prgm Recipient 1987; *office:* A L Corbett Mid Sch PO Box 188 Wagener SC 29164

YOUNG, LINDA AUZOUT, Fifth Grade Teacher; *b:* New Orleans, LA; *m:* Charles Bernard; *c:* Jabari; *ed:* (BA) Elem Ed, Univ of New Orleans 1972; Counseling, Guidance, Spec Ed, Curr & Instruction, Univ of New Orleans; *cr:* 1st Grade Teacher Valena C Jones 1970-71; 5th Grade Teacher Johnson Lockett Sch 1971-72; Lib Aide New Orleans Public Lib 1978; 4th-6th Grade Teacher Henry C Schaumburg Elem 1980; 5th/6th Grade Teacher Mc Donogh 31 Elem Sch 1973-; *ai:* GSA, Stud Cncl, Speech Choir, Awds Day Prgm, Black His Prgm Spon; Summer Sch Enrichment Prgm Team Mem 1989; Testing & Math/Sci Coord; SAFE Teacher Assoc; LEAP/CRT Teacher; Upper Grade Chairperson; Ranking Teacher; Mc Donogh 31 Elem Sch Serivce Citation 1984-85; Mc Donogh 31 Elem Sch Teacher of Yr 1988-89; *office:* Mc Donogh #31 Sch 800 N Rendon New Orleans LA 70119

YOUNG, LYNDA B., Reading Teacher; *b:* Baltimore, MD; *c:* Michael, Kirsten, Casey; *ed:* (BA) Eng, Auburn Univ 1967; Prof Ed/Eng, Mid TN St Univ 1984; TN Instructional Model; *cr:* Rdng Teacher Smyrna Mid Sch 1986-; *ai:* Organized Parent Volunteer Prgm 1989-; Taught Amnesty Prgm; 4th-12th Grade Rdng/Eng Private Tutoring; TEA, REA, NEA 1986-; IRA, TRA, Mary Tom Berry Rdng Cncl 1989-; *home:* 211 E Northfield Blvd Murfreesboro TN 37130

YOUNG, MARGIE F., Head Teacher; *b:* Corinth, MS; *m:* Jeff C.; *c:* Phil, Tim; *ed:* (CDA) Kndgtn Children, Kendrick Head Start 1979; *cr:* Head Teacher Kendrick Head Start; *ai:* Outstanding Employee Awd 1980-81.

YOUNG, MARILYN S., Science Teacher; *b:* New York, NY; *m:* Everett C.; *c:* Joshua; *ed:* (BA) His, 1967, Masters Equivalency Ed, 1972 Temple Univ; Graduate Work Sci, Temple Univ/Beaver Coll/St Josephs Univ; *cr:* 2nd Grade Teacher Dewey Mann Sch 1967-68; 4th/5th Grade Teacher Reynolds Elem 1968-73; Sci/Eng Teacher 1974-82, Sci Teacher 1982 John Story Jenks; *ai:* Sci Fair Spon PA Jr Acad of Sci Carver SF DE Valley Sci Fair; Environmental Ed Camping Prgm Spon; NSTA 1982; Phila Area Elem Sci Teachers Assn Executive Secy 1984-; Phila Scndry Sci Teachers Assn Executive Bd 1986-; Phila Fed Teachers Building Comm 1975-1987/1989-; Awarded 2 Prism Grants Phila Renaissance in Sci & Math 1986-87; Lead Teacher Univ of PA Field Ecology Prgm 1988-89; Articles Published Cmptr Learning Monthly 1988-89; Nom Excl in Ed Awd 1989; *office:* John Story Jenks School Southampton & Germantown Aves Philadelphia PA 19118

YOUNG, MARION, 4th/5th Grade Teacher; *b:* Tuskegee, AL; *ed:* (BS) Elem Ed, 1968, (MS) Guidance Counseling, 1974 AL St Univ; Stu Motivation, Teacher Awareness of Communicable Diseases, Meeting the Needs of Stu With Different Learning Abilities wkshps; *cr:* Teacher Main Avenue Elem 1968-69, Bellingrath Elem 1969-70, Flowers Elem 1970-; *ai:* Youth Adv Cncl; Law Awareness Club Adv; Teens Need Teens; Curr & Inservice Cncl; Montgomery Cty Ed Assn, NEA, PTA; Alpha Kappa Alpha; *office:* Flowers Elem Sch 3510 Harrison Rd Montgomery AL 36109

YOUNG, MARY CEBASEK, Fourth Grade Teacher; *b:* Conneaut, OH; *m:* Rodney L.; *c:* Gary, Michelle, Molly; *ed:* (BA) Elem Ed, Edinboro Univ 1970; Grad Stud Edinboro Impact Trng; Numerous Inservices & Wkshps; *cr:* 3rd Grade Teacher Southeast Sch 1970-75; 4th Grade Teacher Lakeview Sch 1976-; *ai:* CORE Team Lakeview; Prgm Chairperson Various Educl Events; Math Comm; Conneaut Ed Assn, OH Ed Assn, NE OH Ed Assn; *office:* Lakeview Elem Sch Liberty St Conneaut OH 44030

YOUNG, MARY OSBORNE, Mathematics Teacher; b: Roanoke, VA; m: Melvin Jerry; c: Micki M., Darin C.; ed: (BS) Math Ed, VPISU 1972; cr: Math Teacher Oak Hill Acad 1972-79, Fries HS 1978-81, Grayson Cty HS 1981-; ai: Jr Class Spon; office: Grayson Cty HS Independence VA 24348

YOUNG, NAOMI SHEARES, 4th/5th Grade Science Teacher; b: Charleston, SC; m: Richard Jr.; c: Bernard J.; ed: (BS) Elem Ed, SC St Coll 1953; (MA) Elem Ed, NC Coll Durham 1958; Music, Cmptr Sci; cr: 6th Grade Soc Stud/Music Teacher Jennie Moore 1953-59; 5th Grade Teacher Alston Elem 1960-64; 5th/6th Grade Music/Fr/Sci Teacher Wallace Elem 1964-70; 5th Grade Sci Teacher Orange Grove Elem 1970-85; 5th Grade Teacher Buist Acad 1985-87; 4th/5th Grade Sci Teacher Wilmot J Fraser Elem 1989-; ai: Sci Chairperson; Stu Responsibility Comm; Palmetto Teacher Assn 1953-70; SC Ed Assn 1970-84; Natl Teacher Assn 1970-84; Natl Parent Teacher Assn Lifetime Mem 1978; NSTA 1986; Alpha Kappa Alpha Parlimentary 1957-58, 25 Yrs Service Awd 1981; Natl Phi Delta Kappa 1984, Charter Mem; Phi Delta Kappan 1984-; SC Sea Museum (Mem, Volunteer) Chas Cty Plaque; Household of Ruth Secy 1983-85; Fellow of Charleston Area Writing Project; First Minority Instr OASIS; Charleston Cty Ardent Worker Sci Hands on Act Charleston Cty; 1st Teacher of Yr 1985; Buist Acad Sci Fair Elem in Schls 1953-; Schlsp Fund Buist Acad; home: 52 Parkwood Ave Charleston SC 29403

YOUNG, RAYMON DWAINE, Language Arts Teacher; b: Lincoln, IL; m: Marsha K. Wagoner; c: Catlin, Caleb; ed: (BA) English, 1969; (MA) Eng Ed, 1973 Western IL Univ; cr: Jr High Lang Arts Riverton Jr HS 1969-74; English Nokomis HS 1975-76; Freshman Comp Instr Lincoln Lamd Comm Coll 1983-; Jr High/Sr High Lang Arts Auburn Jr/Sr HS 1985-; ai: Jr High Bsbl Coach; Jr High Spelling Bee Coach/Adv; NEA 1989-; Auburn Ed Assn 1989-; AF/AM Masonic Lodge Worshipful Master 1972-74; Natl Assn of Eng Teachers 1986-87; Outstanding Elem Teachers of Amer 1974; Outstanding Scndry Educators of Amer 1974; office: Auburn Jr H S N 7th St Auburn IL 62615

YOUNG, RAYMOND L., Math Teacher; b: Rockland, ME; m: Julianne Boothby; c: Shayne; ed: (BS) Scndry Ed, Univ of ME Gorham 1970; Bowie St Coll; cr: Math Teacher/Dept Chm William Wirt Mid Sch 1972-83; Math Teacher High Point HS 1983-; ai: NEA, MD St Teachers Assn, Prince George Cty Educators Assn 1975-; Provinces Civic Assn 1981-85 1st Good Neighbor Awd 1985; Ridgewood Cmmty Assn 1985-; office: High Point H S 3601 Powder Mill Rd Beltsville MD 20705

YOUNG, REBECCA, Drama Teacher; b: Lawton, OK; m: Jerry W.; c: Brandon M., Clayton M.; ed: (BA) Speech/Drama, Cameron Univ 1974; Eng Ed, Univ of S FL 1974-75; Theater Ed, 1990; cr: Eng Teacher Gulf Jr HS 1976-85; Eng Teacher 1985-86, Drama Teacher 1987- Gulf HS; ai: ITS Troupe #3840 Spon; Class Act Drama Club Adv; Play Dir; Fine Arts Comm Mem; Teacher of Yr 1989-; office: Gulf H S 401 School Rd New Port Richey FL 34652

YOUNG, ROBERT WENDELL, Athletic Trainer; b: Camden, NJ; m: Deborah Nelson; ed: (BS) Phys Ed, Temple Univ 1983; (MS) Athletic Trng, Univ of AZ 1984; cr: Prgm Dir Sports Trng Inst 1984-85; Athletic Trainer South River HS 1985-86, Rancocas Valley Regional HS 1986-88, Edgewood Regional Sr HS 1988-; ai: Supvr Stu Athletic Trainer Prgm; Mentor Gifted & Talented Stu Mentorship Prgm; Sports Medicine Academic Schlsp Temple Univ 1981-83; office: Edgewood Regional Sr HS 250 Coopers Folly Rd Atco NJ 08004

YOUNG, SUSAN ALICE, Biology/Chemistry Teacher; b: Detroit, MI; ed: (BA) Ed/Span/Sci, Mercy Coll 1971; (MA) Ed, Oakland Univ 1981; (MA) Educl Admin, Saginaw Valley Coll 1985; Bio, Chem, Physics, Anatomy Univ of MI 1976-78; cr: 4th Grade Teacher St Matthew Sch 1971-76; 7th/8th Grade Teacher Wyandot Mid Sch 1979-83; 4th Grade Teacher Fox Elem 1983-84; Bio/Chem Teacher Chippewa Valley HS 1984-; ai: Chippewa Valley Scndry Curr Evaulation Comm Mem; MEA, NEA 1979-; home: 42970 Mirabile Tr Mount Clemens MI 48044

YOUNG, SUSAN WENTWORTH, English Teacher; b: Lynwood, CA; m: Douglas R.; c: Benjamin, Kathryn; ed: (BA) Interpretive Speech, Bob Jones Univ 1978; cr: 1st-3rd Grade Teacher Cedar Forest Chrstn Sch 1978-79; Eng Teacher Faith Chrstn Sch 1981-.

YOUNG, THOMAS WILFRED, Teacher/Athletic Director; b: Oklahoma City, OK; m: Gladys Marie Pitts; c: Kendell, Shannon, Sharon; ed: (BA) Soc Stud/Safety Ed, Cntrl St Univ 1976; cr: Soc Stud Teacher 1976-85, Athletic Dir 1986- Guthrie Jr HS; ai: Jr HS Girls Sftbl & Boys Bsktbl Coach; Asst HS Bsbl Coach; Soc Stud Dept Chm 1978-83; OK Ed Assn, NEA 1976-; OK Coaches Assn 1978-, Asst HS Bsbl Coach of Yr 1988; Jr HS Coaches Assn Pres 1987-88; Amer Legion Bsbl Coach Majors Div; home: 1302 E Cleveland Guthrie OK 73044

YOUNG, VIVIAN B. CAVIEL, Retired 4th Grade Teacher; b: Glenflora, TX; w: James R. (dec); c: Camille Y. Young Baty; ed: (BA) Bus Admin, TX St Univ 1951; Rdng, Math 1964; Math Inst 1970-71; Staff Dev; Rdng Lecture Series; Prof Growth; Geography & Sci; Human Relation Ed; cr: 4th Grade Teacher B H Grimes Elem 1964-70, Windsor Village Elem 1970-87; Substitute Bus Teacher Sugarland HS; Elem Substitute Bus Teacher Sugarland HS; Elem Substitute Teach Houston Ind Sch Dist 1987-; ai: Volunteer Teacher Aide; Bus Womens Club; NEA, TX St Teachers Assn 1964-87; Houston Fed of Teachers 1980-87; Alpha Bettes Mem 1967-; Tx St Teachers Mem 1964-87; Houston Fed Teachers Mem 1980-87; Houston Teachers Assn Mem 1964-87;

Women of St Lukes Episcopal Church; Career Ladder Rating 1986-87; home: 3344 Rosedale Ave Houston TX 77004

YOUNG, WILLAM CHELSEA, Jr High Sci/Health Teacher; b: Greenville, OH; m: Brenda Jane Wuebker; c: Krista, Kaye, Dianne, Linda, Patricia; ed: (BA) Elem Ed, 1973, (MA) Curr/Supervision, 1978 Wright St Univ; cr: 5th Grade Teacher Arcanum Butler 1972-73; 5th/6th Grade Sci Teacher 1973-83, 7th/8th Grade Sci Dept Head 1983- Minster Local; ai: 8th Grade Boys Bsktbl & Jr HS Boys Track Coach; Coord 8th Grade Field Trip to Washington DC & World Wise Schls; Chm Sch Wide Discipline Comm; NEA, OH Ed Assn; Minster Teachers Assn Pres 1983-84; home: 230 S Cleveland St Minster OH 45865

YOUNG-ROBERTS, DEBRA KAY, Vocational Adjustment Coord; m: Bill Roberts; c: Jason, Justin; ed: (AA) Temple Jr Coll 1973; (BS) Health/Phys Ed/Eng, 1976, (ME) Admin, 1986, (ME) Generic Spec Ed, 1990 Univ of Mary Hardin Baylor; cr: 1st Grade Aide/7th Grade Bsktbl Coach Ferris Elem 1976-77; 7th-8th Grade Coach/Phys Ed Teacher Wilson Mid Sch 1977-82; Teacher for Regional Emotional Disturbed Class Bell Cty Coop for Exceptional Children 1982-83; 11th Grade Eng Teacher Taylor Ind Sch Dist 1983-88; Voc Adjustment Coord East Williamson Coop for Exceptional Children 1988-; ai: Coached; Soph Class Spon 1987; Jr Class Spon 1988; Sr Class Spon 1989; TX HS Coaches Assn 1977-82; TSTA 1977-88; Classroom Teacher Assn 1989; CEC 1988; TX Assn of Voc Adjustment Coord 1988-; BSA (Den Leader 1986-88, Asst Scoutmaster 1990-); Evangelical Luth Womens Assn 1989 Secy; office: Taylor HS 3101 N Main Taylor TX 76574

YOUNGER, DAISIANNE DAVIS, English/French Teacher; b: Mc Kinney, TX; m: Stephen Esten; c: Mark S., Meredith A.; ed: (BA) Eng/Fr/Scndry Cert - Magna Cum Laude, TX Chrstn Univ 1964; (MED) Ed/Counseling, N TX St Univ 1981; Great Books Leader Trng Course 1988; Wkshp for HS Teachers & Admin 1988-89; Keystone Project 1987; Ft Worth Ind Sch Dist Inservice Wkshps & Conferences; cr: Scndry Ed Teacher 1964-70, Adult Continuing Ed Teacher 1973-81 Ft Worth Ind Sch Dist; Base Ed/HS Teacher Carswell AFB 1976; Supvr/Cnslr/Certified Soc Worker Edna Gladney Center 1978-85; Scndry Ed Teacher Trimble Tech HS 1985-; ai: Fr Club; Advanced Placement Teacher Eng; Sr Class Spon 1988; NCTE, NEA, TX St Teachers Assn, Adult Ed Assn, Assn of Prof Educators, TX Assn of Continuing Ed for Adults; Natl Assn of Soc Workers; Amer Inst for Foreign Study (Teacher, Chaperone) 1967; Outstanding Teacher of Yr Polytechnic HS 1968; Columnist for Accent Youth Magazine 1976-77; Facilitator of Educl Wkshps 1973-81; home: 1820 Timber Line Dr Fort Worth TX 76126

YOUNG MAROHN, ANN, Language Arts Teacher; b: Decatur, IL; c: Richard, Kathryn Marohn Bartsch, Susan; ed: (BS) Speech/Eng, Marquette Univ 1957; (MA) Guidance/Counseling, NE IL Univ 1982; cr: Eng Teacher Brookfield HS 1957-59; Lang Art Teacher Emerson Jr HS 1973-; ai: Speech Coach; NCTE; Frank Lloyd Wright Home & Studio Fnd (Pres 1982-84, VP 1958-88); Academic Achievement Schlsp NE IL 1980; Coloring Book Author 1989; office: Emerson Jr HS 916 Washington Oak Park IL 60302

YOUNKIN, MARJORIE JANE (PRIEBE), 5th Grade Teacher; b: Crawfordsville, IN; c: Chance R., Chrade R.; ed: (BSED) Elem Ed, Ball St Univ 1967; Elem Ed, W MT Coll 1982; cr: Teacher Greeley Elem 1970-71, Longfellow Elem 1972-; ai: 6th Grade Girls Bsktbl & Longfellow Elem Track Coach; Butte Sch Dist Report Card, Onward to Excl Creating the Future Leadership Comm; Ed Articles Printed Monthly; office: Longfellow Elem Sch Wynne & Roosevelt St Butte MT 59701

YOUNT, BETTY DAVIDSON, Grade Chapter I Teacher; b: Goldust, TN; m: William H. Jr.; c: Rebecca T. Davidson; ed: (BS) Elem Ed, 1978; Early Chldhd Cum Laude Memphis TN Univ; cr: Chapter I Teacher Woodstock Elem 1978-; ai: Mentor & Research Person for Primary Dept; NEA; TEA, SCEA Political Rep for Sch 1986-; Goldstar Wives of Amer 1971-; office: Woodstock Elem Sch 5909 Woodstock-Cuba Rd Millington TN 38053

YOUNT, RUTH ANN (RHODES), Jr High Mathematics Teacher; b: Ironton, MO; m: Larry G.; c: Blake; ed: (AA) Elem Ed, Mineral Area Coll 1978; (BS) Elem Ed, SE MO St 1981; (MS) Ed, 1987; cr: Jr/Sr HS Math Teacher Valley of Caledonia R-6 1982-; home: Rt 1 Box 24A Belgrade MO 63622

YOUNT, WILLIAM G., Ethics/Philosphy Teacher; b: Dallas, TX; ed: (BS) Bible, Columbia Bible Coll 1982; (MED) Sch Admin, Reformed Seminary 1987; cr: Bible Teacher Cntrl Chrstn 1982-86; Bible Dept Head Ben Lippen Sch 1986-87; Asst Prin Northlake Chrstn 1987-; ai: Var Vlybl Coach 1982-; Var Tennis Coach 1982-88; office: Northlake Chrstn Schl 71104 Wolverine Dr Covington LA 70433

YOUNTS, LINDA TROTTER, English Teacher; b: Asheboro, NC; m: Baxter Paul Jr.; c: Lena T., Baxter P. III; ed: (BS) Eng, E Carolina Univ 1965; Grad Courses SC; cr: Teacher Graham HS 1965-66, Winder Elem 1967-68, Hart Cty HS 1968-69, Manning HS 1978-; ai: Manning HS Improvement, Clarendon Dist 2 Advisory Cncl & Materials Comm; Palmetto St Teachers Assn; Delta Kappa Gamma Secy 1988-; NCTE 1978; SC Cncl Teachers of Eng 1978; Manning United Meth Church Choir Mem; Manning HS Teacher of Yr; home: 101 Hillcrest St Manning SC 29102

YOVICH, SUZANN LUCY (SHIELD), 2nd Grade Teacher; b: Warren, PA; m: James E.; ed: (BS) Elem Ed, Murray St Univ 1971; cr: 4th Grade Teacher 1971-76; 2nd Grade Teacher 1976-78; 3rd Grade Teacher 1978-79; 2nd Grade Teacher 1979- Russell Elem; ai: PTA 1971-; Warren Cty Ed Assn 1971-; PA St Ed Assn

1971-; NEA 1971-; Delta Kappa Gamma Secy; Sugar Grove Rdng Club VP 1988-; Wacopse Credit Union-Bd of Dir; Spec Olympics Warren Cty Fair Volunteer; Church Chairperson of Worship Comm Secy & Trustee of Bd; home: RD 3 Box 38 Sugar Grove PA 16350

YRJO, DONALD ELVIN, Industrial Tech Teacher; b: Fosston, MN; m: Beverly Scheepstra; c: Melanie, Michael, Mark; ed: (AA) Worthington Jr Coll 1973; (BS) Industiral Art Ed, Bemidji St Coll 1975; (MS) Industrial Technology, Mankato St Univ 1985; NCN Machine Tool Programming; Industiral Cmptr Aided Drawing; cr: Industrial Art Teacher Linton HS 1975-77, Redwood Falls-Morton HS 1977-; ai: Var Asst Bsbl Coach; Rock Falls Ed Assn (VP, Pres) 1988-; MN Ed Assn, NEA 1988-; MN Technology Ed Assn 1977-; Birch Coulee Technology Ed Assn (Secy, Treas) 1980-82; Linton Jaycees Outstanding Young Educator Awd 1977; office: Redwood Falls-Morton HS 4th & Lincoln Redwood Falls MN 56283

YUKISH, DOROTHY KRECKER, Sixth Grade Teacher; b: Hazelton, PA; ed: (BA) Elem Ed, 1971, (MED) Curr & Instruction, 1985 Penn St Univ; cr: Elem Teacher Connellsville Area Schls 1971-; ai: PTG Prgm Comm; Sci Fair Coord; Environmental Scholastic Team Coach; NEA 1971-; Phi Delta Kappa 1985-; Delta Kappa Gamma Pres 1976-, Schlsp 1983; Church of God 1975-; Spec Project Grants; home: PO Box 370 Indian Head PA 15446

YUNKER, SHARON PORTER, Teacher/Eng Dept Chairperson; b: Springfield, OH; m: William F.; c: Kristen, Lisa; ed: (BA) Eng, Miami Univ 1964; (MED) His, Xavier Univ 1984; cr: 8th/11th/12th Grade Teacher St Bernard HS 1964-71; 11th/12th Grade Eng Teacher St Bernard-Elmwood Place HS 1977-; ai: Sr Class Spon; Tech Stage Mgr; TV Production; St Bernard-Elmwood Place Ed Assn Secy 1984-85, 1987-88; NDEA Grants OH Univ 1967 & Wittenburg Univ 1969; Natl Endowment for the Hum Summer Prgm Univ of DE 1987; 2 Equipment Grants for TV Equipment from Intercommunity Cable Regulatory Commission; office: St Bernard-Elmwood Place HS 4615 Tower Ave Saint Bernard OH 45217

YURKEWICZ, WILLIAM, Physics Teacher; b: Amsterdam, NY; m: Diane Valerio; c: Susan, Michael; ed: (BS) Sci, Union Coll 1964; (MS) Curr/Instruction, 1971, (EDD) Ed/Cognitive Dev, 1988 St Univ of NY Albany; Specialist Certificate in Curr & Instruction, St Univ of NY 1980; cr: Author Allyn & Bacon Incorporated 1980-85; Physics Teacher S Glens Falls Sr HS 1964-; Physics Lecturer SkidmorColl 1980-; Research Physicist Self Employed Consultant 1989-; ai: NSTA, AAPT 1984-; Sci Teachers Assn of NY St 1984-; S Glens Falls Faculty Assn (Building Rep, Exec Comm, Schlsp Comm) 1964-; Schenectady Swim Club Treas 1984-86; Sci Teachers Assn of NY St Excl in Sci Teaching Awd 1986; Presidential Awd for Outstanding Dissertation St Univ of NY Albany 1988; office: S Glens Falls HS Merritt Rd South Glens Falls NY 12803

YUST, ROGER ALBERT, Social Studies Teacher; b: Fond du Lac, WI; ed: (BST) Soc Sci, WI St Univ Oshkosh 1969; (MST) Soc Sci, Univ of WI Oshkosh 1975; Integrated Global Learning; cr: Teacher Washington Jr HS 1969-; ai: Manitowoc Ed Assn 1969-; office: Washington Jr HS 2101 Division St Manitowoc WI 54220

Z

ZABER, ALEC HENRY, Jr HS Science Teacher; b: St Louis, MO; m: Karen Blockyou; c: Jay, Eric, Kyle; ed: (BS) Phys Ed/Sci, S IL Univ Edwardsville 1967; Admin, Sci, Classroom Management; cr: Jr HS Sci Teacher Pontiac-William Holliday 1967-70, West Jr HS 1970-; ai: Athletic Dir; Grad Comm; AFT VP 1974; Belleville Parks & Rec (Bd of Trustees, Pres) 1990; St of IL Region IV B Memorial Hospital Belleville Elles Emergency Medical Services Peer Bd of Review; office: West Jr HS 820 Royal Heights Rd Belleville IL 62223

ZABILKA, ANITA HUGHES, Guidance Director; b: Charleston, IL; m: Anthony J.; c: Robert, Douglas, Laura Shaeffer; ed: (BS) Bio, 1971, (MS) Personnel/Guidance, 1975 E IL Univ; Certificate in Spec Ed, Natl Coll of Ed; cr: Instr Laboratory Sch E IL Univ 1970-71; Teacher Bryan Jr HS 1971-78; Teacher/Cnslr Monsignor Edward Pace HS 1978-; ai: Who Buddies; Wellness Comm Chairperson; Peer Counseling Coord; NABT, NSTA 1970-; FL Assn of Counseling & Dev, FL Sch Cnslr Assn, Dade Cty Assn of Counseling & Dev 1985-; Delta Zeta 1956-; Dade Cty Assn of Cath Cnslrs 1980-; Bd of Dirs Dev Resource Center 1988-; Research Grant OH St Univ to Produce Curr for Career Units 1973; office: Monsignor Edward Pace HS 15600 NW 32nd Ave Miami FL 33054

ZACCAGNA, MORJORIE CENSULLO, 10-12 Grade English Teacher; b: Union City, NJ; m: Richard G. Sr.; c: Richard Jr., Matthew; ed: (BA) Eng, Coll Misericordia 1965; (MA) Theater Ed, NYU New York 1969: Eng as 2nd Lang Cert St of NJ; cr: Eng Teacher Emerson HS 1965-; ai: Chrldr Adv 1966-75; Newspaper Adv 1967-69; NCTE 1975-; NJEA 1965-; UCEA 1965-; Union

City PTSA 1965-; FairfieLd PTA 1983-; Developed & Received NJ St Approval & Cert for Course Sr HS Level Entitled The Literary Theatre-A Survey of Modern Drama; *office:* Emerson H S 318 18th St Union City NJ 07087

ZACCARA, JACK J., Planetarium Director; *b:* New York, NY; *m:* Carol Ann; *c:* Patrick; *ed:* (AA) Liberal Arts, Concordia Coll 1968; (BA) His, Iona Coll 1970; (MS) Ed, West CT St Coll 1979; Certified Trainer West Cty Mental Health & Anti Defamation League; NASA Certified Lunar Sample Prgm; *cr:* Sci/Soc Stud Teacher Port Chester Mid Sch 1970-80; Planetarium Dir Port Chester Public Schls 1980-; *ai:* Chapter Leader Young Astronauts; Coach HS Academic Team; Host Ace Awd; Run Wkshps; Planetarium Shows; NSTA, NY Acad of Scis, Intnl Planetarium Assn, Planetary Society; PTA; Spaceshuttle Stu Involvement Prgm Judge 1985-86; Christa Mc Auliffe Fellow US Dept of Ed 1987; Applicant Teacher In Space Prgm; Author; *office:* Port Chester Public Schls Bowman Ave Port Chester NY 10573

ZACEK, MONICA WITTE, 1st Grade Teacher; *b:* Victoria, TX; *m:* Dennis Ray; *c:* Jill M., Jan M., Kali A.; *ed:* (BA) Eng, 1976, (MS) Rdng Concentration, 1982 Univ of Houston; *cr:* 3rd Grade Teacher Bay City Ind Sch Dist 1976-77; Kndgtn Teacher La Ward Elem 1977-78; 1st Grade Teacher Inez Elem 1978-80, 1988-; *ai:* Mid Coast Rdng Cncl (Secy 1988-89) 1987-; Cath Christian Mothers 1987-; Presented Inservice Palacios Ind Sch Dist 1982; Univ of Houston Victoria Lecturer 1982-87; Supvr Stu Teachers Univ of Houston Victoria 1987; *office:* Inez Elem Rt 1 Box 1-K Inez TX 77968

ZACH, MARY JANE GORDON, First Grade Teacher; *b:* Osage, IA; *m:* Jan; *c:* Sara, Aaron; *ed:* (BA) Elem Ed, Univ of N IA Cedar Falls 1977; Grad Stud; *cr:* 1st Grade Teacher Sidney Elem Sch 1977-; *ai:* Early Chldhd Needs Assessment, Develop a New Renewed Delivery System for Stu with Spec Needs Comm; Sidney Ed Assn (Pres 1987-88, Secy 1979-80); NEA; Percival Booster Club (Pres 1985-86, Secy 1987-88, VP 1984-85); Sunday Sch Teacher; Outstanding Young Women of America 1981; *office:* Sidney Elem Sch 1002 Illinois St Sidney IA 51652

ZACHARY, NINA (CHICOURAS), Social Studies Dept Chair; *b:* Clarksdale, MS; *m:* Nick A.; *c:* Constantine, Nick; *ed:* (BSED) Soc Sci, Delta St Univ 1974; Rdng/Cnslr Ed/Global Perspectives, Delta St, MS St Univ, Univ of Denver; Geography, Univ of AR; *cr:* Lang Art Teacher Oakhurst Elem 1976-77; Coll Prep/Choctaw His Teacher Choctaw HS 1984-85; Chairperson/Soc Stud Teacher Barton HS 1985-; *ai:* Citizens Bee Competition Coord; Gifted & Talented Competition Coach; Kappa Delta Pi, Pi Gamma Mu 1974-; Co-Editor of Books; *home:* 98 Mangrove Palm Starkville MS 39759

ZACHARY, PHILIP ALAN, Fourth Grade Teacher; *b:* Kingston, PA; *m:* Janet Irvin; *c:* David; *ed:* (BS) Elem Ed, E Stroudsburg Univ 1966; (MS) Elem Ed, Scranton Univ 1968; Grad Stud; *cr:* 5th Grade Teacher Shavertown Building 1967-68; 4th Grade Head Teacher Trucksville Elem 1968-82; 4th Grade Teacher Westmoreland Elem 1983-; *ai:* Dallas Ed Assn (Building Rep 1970-82) 1966-; PSEA, NEA 1966-; Little League 1980; Bk Mt Bsktbl 1985; *home:* 129 Jackson St Dallas PA 18612

ZACHEREL, RUTH COTTON, Sixth Grade Teacher; *b:* Seneca, PA; *m:* Arnold E. Sr; *c:* Deborah Blanchard, Robert, Pamela Bridges, Arnold Jr., James; *ed:* (BS) Elem Ed, Edinboro Univ 1954; Univ of MD; *cr:* 5th Grade Teacher Hasson Heights 1954-57; 6th Grade Teacher Riverdale Elem 1967-; *ai:* Testing Comm; Crisis Intervention Team; Prince Georges Cty Educl Assn; MD St Teachers Assn; NEA; Bladensburg Boys Club; Riverdale PTA; Eastminister Presbyn Church Youth Assn; *home:* 5530 Volta Avenue Bladensburg MD 20710

ZAHORAN, JOHN MICHAEL, English Teacher; *b:* Johnstown, PA; *m:* Pamela Langietti; *c:* Danielle M., Michol A., Jesse; *ed:* (BS) Eng, 1970, (MA) Eng, 1980 Clarion Univ; Amer Lit, Indiana Univ of PA; *cr:* Teacher Clarion Limestone 1970-; *ai:* Literary Journal; *office:* Clarion-Limestone Sch Rd 1 Box 205 Strattanville PA 16258

ZAHS, MICHAEL, Seventh Grade Teacher; *b:* Washington, IA; *m:* Julie Hartzler; *c:* Hannah, Adam; *ed:* (BA) Bio, 1969, (MA) Bio, 1971 Univ of N IA; Grad Stud NE MO St Univ; *cr:* HS Bio Teacher Mediapolis Cmmty Sch 1969-70; Jr HS Sci/Soc Stud Teacher Washington Cmmty Sch 1971-; His Teacher IA Wesleyan Coll 1989-; *ai:* Weight Lifting; NCA & Atrium Comms; Advanced IA His; IA Cncl for Soc Stud (St Pres 1988-, St VP 1986-87, Secy 1984-85); NCSS House of Delegates 1985-; Washington Cty Historical Society Pres 1984-; Numerous Preservation Groups Saving Numerous Historic Sites & Buildings; Kewash Nature Trail Pres 1989-; Blue Ribbon Task Force Teaching of IA His; Governors Awd for Volunteers IA His 1990; *home:* Haskins Rt 1 Ainsworth IA 52201

ZAK, JANET MARY, Eighth Grade Teacher; *b:* Chicago, IL; *ed:* (BA) Eng, Mundelein Coll 1969; (MA) Admin & Supervision, Roosevelt Univ 1980; *cr:* 3rd Grade Teacher Holmes Elem Sch 1969-70; 3rd/4th/8th Grade Teacher Hearst Elem Sch 1970-; *ai:* Young Authors Club Spon; Sch Improvement Comm; *office:* Hearst Elem Sch 4640 S Lamon Ave Chicago IL 60638

ZAKRAJSEK, JOYCE GNAT, 1st Grade Teacher; *b:* Warren, OH; *m:* Rudy Jr.; *c:* Daniel R., Matthew R.; *ed:* (BA) Early Childhd Ed, Kent St Univ 1977; *cr:* Kndgtn Teacher Warren City Schls 1977-78; 2nd/3rd/4th/5th Grade Teacher Farmington Local Sch 1978-88; 1st Grade Teacher Bristol Local Schls 1988- .

ZALETSKI, STEPHEN PAUL, Math Teacher; *b:* Pittsburgh, PA; *ed:* (BS) Ed/Math, IN Univ of PA 1966; (MED) Curr/ Supervision, Univ of Pittsburgh 1970; Post Grad Stud Math, Comm, Cmptrs, Ed; *cr:* Math Teacher North Hills HS 1966-; *ai:* Girls Tennis Coach; *office:* North Hills HS 53 Rochester Rd Pittsburgh PA 15229

ZALOSKI, ELLAMAE BALDELLI, Mathematics Teacher; *b:* Danbury, CT; *m:* Ted; *c:* Michael; *ed:* (BS) Elem Ed, 1971, (MS) Ed, 1979 Western CT St Univ; *cr:* Teacher Schaghticoke Mid Sch 1971-80, John Pettibone Sch 1980-84, Schaghticoke Mid Sch 1984-; *ai:* Math Curr; Teacher Adv & Evaluation Comm; Pi Lambda Theta 1980-; ATOMIC: New Milford Ed Assn (VP 1984-85, Pres 1985-86); Teaching Excl Awd; Cmptrs Spec Awds; Union Carbide Supt Awd; *office:* Schaghticoke Mid Sch 23 Hipp Rd New Milford CT 06776

ZAMARIPPA, RALPH M., JR., Band Director; *b:* San Angelo, TX; *m:* Adelina Valenzuela; *c:* Rae A., Ralph III, Ruben; *ed:* (BM) Instrumental Music, 1964, (MED) Music Ed, 1969 Sul Ross Univ; Prof Certificate Music Supervision, Mid-Management; *cr:* Band Dir Van Horn HS 1964-79; Asst Dir 1979-87, Dir of Bands 1987-89 Ft Stockton HS; *ai:* TX Music Educators Assn 1968-, Awd of Excl 1972; TX Music Adjudicators Assn 1975-; TX Band Masters Assn 1968-; Lions Club 1968-89; Jaycees 1969-72, Distinguished Service Awd 1972; Rotary Service Awd; UIL Sweepstakes 1968-69; Outstanding Class A Band Six Flags Over TX 1970; Outstanding Band Bucaneer Festival 1971; TMEA Honor Band Class A 1972, Class A Honor Band Finalist 1976; Outstanding Band Greater SW Music Festival 1974-76; *office:* Lincoln Mid Sch 1699 S 1st Abilene TX 79603

ZAMBO, CARL R., Counselor/Head Football Coach; *b:* Chicago, IL; *m:* Lynda L. J. Thede; *c:* Kristan L., Scott C.; *ed:* (BS) Phys Ed, S IL Univ; (MA) Guidance, NE IL Univ 1971; *cr:* Math Teacher 1966-75, Phys Ed Teacher 1975-78, Cnslr 1978- Hillcrest HS; *ai:* Head Ftbl Coach 1975-; Asst Bsbl Coach; Ftbl, Bsbl, Tennis Coach; NEA, IEA; South Sals Counseling Assn; *office:* Hillcrest HS 175th & Pulaski Rd Country Club Hills IL 60478

ZAMMIT, PAMELA SMITH, 8th Grade History Teacher; *b:* Brownsville, TX; *m:* John Timothy; *c:* Kimberly Keely; *ed:* (BA) Learning Disabilites Cert Elem Ed, Univ of SW LA 1976; Numerous Wkshps; *cr:* Resource Teacher New Iberia Frosh HS 1977-79, Prairie Elem 1979-80, New Iberia Frosh HS 1980-81; 7th/8th Grade Teacher Cathedral-Carmel 1981-; *ai:* Yrbk Adv; Odyssey of Mind Spon; LA Assn of Teachers of Math, NCEA; *home:* 121 Kensington Dr Lafayette LA 70508

ZANDER, DIANE SEDEVIE, 5th/6th Grade Teacher/Prin; *b:* Minot, ND; *m:* Timothy Lew; *c:* Danna M.; *ed:* (BS) Elem Ed, Minot St Univ 1979; Grad Stud Admin Coursework; *cr:* Elem Teacher/Prin Donnybrook Public Sch 1979-; *ai:* ND Elem Prin Assn; *office:* Donnybrook Elem Sch Donnybrook ND 58734

ZANDERS, DORIS DE VILLE, Physical Education Teacher; *b:* Dallas, TX; *m:* Donald Louis; *ed:* (BSED) Health/Phys Ed, Langston Univ 1965; (MED) Scndry Admin, Prairie View A&M 1979; TX A&M; *cr:* Phys Ed Teacher Langston Univ 1965-67, Neptune Public Sch 1967-69; Elem Phys Ed Teacher Huntsville Public Sch 1969-70; Phys Ed Teacher Oklahoma City Public Sch 1970-74; Eng/Phys Ed Teacher St Anthony Cath Sch 1974-75; Phys Ed Teacher Dallas Ind Sch Dist 1975-; *ai:* Pivoteers Dance Drill Team Dir; Sr Class Co-Chairperson; TX Assn of Phys Ed, Recreation, NEA 1975-; AAHPER 1965-; United Teachers of Dallas 1975; Delta Sigma Theta Scrapbook Chairperson 1979-81; Ladies Auxiliary Knights of Peter Cleaver Grandlady 1970-74; Future Homemaker of America Teacher of Month 1979; DECA Outstanding Service Awd 1978; Cornie Robinson Memorial Awd Schlsp 1964; Langston Univ Most Outstanding Stu in Health, Phys 1964-65; Purple Flash Drill Team Outstanding Service Plaque 1978-79; Outstanding Young Woman of America 1979; *home:* 9107 Windy Crest Dr Dallas TX 75243

ZANETTI, ROSANNE DERYNIOSKI, German Teacher; *b:* Southington, CT; *m:* Raymond F.; *c:* Mary E., Michael; *ed:* (BS) Ger/Scndry Ed, 1975, (MS) Elem Ed, 1983 S CT St Univ; Goethe Inst, Boppard W Germany *cr:* Ger Teacher Southington HS 1975-; *ai:* Yrbk & Ger Club Adv; SEA, NEA, CEA.

ZANGHI, PHYLLIS HAYES, First Grade Teacher; *b:* Mineola, NY; *m:* Joseph; *c:* Danielle, Joseph; *ed:* (BS) Ed, SUNY Cortland 1972; (MA) Ed, Adelphi Univ 1975; *cr:* Pre-K Teacher 1973, 1st Grade Teacher 1973-79, 1986-88, 2nd Grade Teacher 1979-84, Transitional 1st Grade Teacher 1988- John Street Sch; *ai:* Stu Evaluation Team; Grade Chairperson; Holy Trinity Church (Church Sch Dir 1985-, Choir 1980-); *office:* John Street Sch Nassau Blvd Franklin Square NY 11010

ZANNI, STEPHEN NICHOLAS, Science Dept Chair; *b:* Lawrence, MA; *m:* Janice M. Masoud; *c:* Jeffrey, Jana; *ed:* (BA) Ed, Curry Coll 1968; (MED) Sch Admin, Fitchburg St Coll 1975; Univ of Lowell, Northeastern Univ; *cr:* 5th/6th Grade Teacher 1968-69, 7th Grade Life Sci Teacher 1969-79, Sci Teacher/Dept Chm 1979- Hudson Memorial Sch; *ai:* 5th-8th Grade Flag Ftbl Coach; Weight Lifting Club; ASCD 1986-; NHTA; Lawrence Sch Comm Vice Chm 1971-79, Natl Sch Bd Awd 1975; St Alfio Society VP 1970-; Book Published 1975; Helped to Build Greenhouse at Sch 1985; *office:* Hudson Memorial Sch 1 Memorial Dr Hudson NH 03051

ZANONE, LUCIA R., 5th Grade Teacher; *b:* Kansas City, KS; *ed:* (AC) Bus, Kansas City Jr Coll 1950; (BA) Eng, 1965, (MA) Elem Ed, 1968 UMKC; *cr:* 5th Grade Teacher St Marys Elem 1964-67; 5th/6th Grade Teacher Spring Valley Elem 1967-; *ai:* MCREL Team for Sch Improvement; Lang Art Comm; MO St Teachers Assn 1967-; PTA (VP, Lifetime Membership 1988); St Thomas Mores Ladies Circle 1968-; Nom as Outstanding Teacher by Prin; *office:* Spring Valley Elem Schl 8838 E 83rd St Raytown MO 64138

ZANONI, ATTILIO JOSEPH, Retired Teacher; *b:* Milwaukee, WI; *m:* Barbara Lynn; *c:* David, Lisa Murray, Michael, Christopher, Patrick; *ed:* (BS) Upper Elem Ed, 1960, (MS) Curr/ Instruction, 1976 Univ of WI Milwaukee; Grad Stud; *cr:* Self Contained 6th Grade Teacher Willow Spring Sch 1961-68; 8th Grade Math Teacher Templeton Mid Sch 1968-89; *ai:* Mathcounts Team Coach; Kappa Delta Pi, WI Ed Assn Mem 1960-; WI Cncl Teachers of Math Mem 1988-89; NCO 84th Infantry Division Reserves 1950-58; WI Sch Masters Club 1960-75; 1st Church of Christ Scientist Sunday Sch Teacher; Miami Univ Natl Sci Fnd Summer Inst in Math; 1971; Univ of WI Milwaukee NDEA Advanced Study in Geography 1965; St of WI Mathcounts Team Coach 1986-87; *home:* 7700 W Clovernook Milwaukee WI 53223

ZAPPULLA, NANCY WADE, English Teacher; *b:* Norfolk, VA; *c:* Elizabeth; *ed:* (BS) Ed/Eng/Journalism, Radford Univ 1973; *cr:* 12th Grade Eng Teacher Amelia Cty Public Schls 1973-74; 7th-12th Grade Eng Teacher Portsmouth Chrstn Sch 1979-81, Alliance Chrstn Sch 1982-83, 1986-89; 7th-8th Grade Eng Teacher Atlantic Shores Chrstn Sch 1989-; *ai:* 7th Grade & Yrbk Spon; Sigma Tau Delta 1971-73; Univ of VA Study Grant to Folger Shakespeare Inst 1988; Published 4 Articles; *home:* 1116-A Hazel Ave Chesapeake VA 23325

ZARLING, DOUGLAS JAMES, 8th Grade Science Teacher; *b:* West Bend, WI; *m:* Kathryn L. Mowrer; *c:* Alex, Benjamin; *ed:* (BS) Elem Ed, UW Stevens Point 1974; (MS) Elem Ed, Natl Coll of Ed 1985; *cr:* 8th Grade Sci Teacher Silverbrook Mid Sch 1974-; *ai:* WBEA Prof Rights & Responsibilities Comm; WBEA Welfare Comm; WBEA Apple Awds Comm; Wamle 1984-; Planetary Society 1987; *office:* Silverbrook Mid Sch 120 N Silverbrook Dr West Bend WI 53095

ZARNICK, JUNE F., Kndgtn Teacher/Rdng Specialist; *b:* Kane, PA; *ed:* (BS) Elem/Early Chldhd, Edinboro St Coll 1974; (MA) Ed, Pittsburgh Univ 1978; Rdng Specialist, Edinboro St Coll 1981; *cr:* 1st Grade Teacher 1976-80, Rdng Specialist 1980-84, Kndgtn/ Rdng Specialist 1984- Kane Area Sch Dist; *ai:* Teacher Advisory; Faculty Rep Kane Area Teachers Assn; Kane Area Teachers Assn Faculty Adv 1984-; Cath Daughters of Americas 2nd Vice Regent 1987-.

ZAROB, VIRGINIA MARY, Social Studies Chair; *b:* Oak Park, IL; *ed:* (BA) His, 1966, (MA) Amer His, 1972, (PHD) Amer His, 1976 Marquette Univ; Cmmty Stud Newberry Lib Summer Instr; *cr:* His Chairperson St Hilary 1966-71; TA Instr Marquette Univ 1971-77; Hss Teacher Holy Cross 1978-82; His Chairperson Woodlands Acad 1982-; *ai:* His Honor Society; Greenpeace; Amnesty Intnl; Ed & Curr Comm; AHA, OAH 1971-; OAH HS Org 1988-; Soc Stud Research Cncl 1986-; Local Church Aid; Cyril Smith Fellowship; Articles Written; DAR Awd; Marquette Univ Teaching & Research Asst; Summer Schlsps; *office:* Woodlands Acad of Sacred Heart 760 E Westleigh Rd Lake Forest IL 60045

ZARRA, TONI MELE, Basic Skills Teacher; *b:* Newark, NJ; *m:* Joseph; *c:* Lisa, Lori; *ed:* (BS) Elem Ed, Jersey City St Coll 1957; Elem Ed, Montclair St, Jersey City St, Seton Hall; *cr:* 5th-6th Grade Teacher, Rdng/Math Coord, 6th Grade Teacher, Basic Skills Teacher Broadway Elem.

ZATEZALO, ROSE (EAGLEEYE), Former Teacher; *b:* Cleveland, OH; *m:* Albert W. Jr.; *c:* Shane M.; *ed:* (BA) Studio Art, Cleveland St Univ 1979; Graphic Design, Univ of Cincinnati 1967-70; Co-Op Prgm; Landscape Design, Polaris Voc Sch & OH St Univ Extension; *cr:* Graphic Designer Image Advertising Inc 1979-81; Art Teacher St Bartholomew Elem Sch 1982-87, St Bartholomew & Thomas More Sch 1986-87; Landscape Designer & Graphic Artist 1980-; Private Art Tutor 1985-; *ai:* New Organization For Visual Arts 1986-; Western Reserve Historical Society 1985-; Middleburg Hts Womens Club (Corresponding Secy 1989-, Recording Secy 1990); Ceramics Guild Mem 1985-87; Merit Schlsp Recipient from CSU; Journalist Parma Area Fine Arts Cncl Newsletter; Deans List 1976-79; *home:* 14741 Cherokee Trl Middleburg Heights OH 44130

ZAVADA, DEBRA GRABER, Basic Skills Teacher; *b:* Rolette, ND; *m:* Larry K.; *c:* Riley, Jeffrey; *ed:* (BS) Elem Ed, Minot St Univ 1981; Rdng Credential; *cr:* 5th-6th Grade Teacher 1981-83, Basic Skills Instr 1985- Wolford Public Sch; *ai:* PTO Pres 1987-88; *office:* Wolford Public Sch PO Box 478 Wolford ND 58385

ZAVADIL, MARTIN RICHARD, Band Director; *b:* New York City, NY; *m:* Sharon Lenore Silva; *c:* Carrie, Matthew, Amy, Daniel; *ed:* (BS) Music Ed, St Univ Coll Fredonia 1965; Grad Stud Numerous Univs; *cr:* Band Dir Hauppauge Public Schls 1966-71, Schalmont Schls 1971-77, Susquehanna Valley Cntrl Schls 1977-87, Shenendehowa Cntrl Schls 1987-; *ai:* Shenendehowa Plainsmen Marching & High Society Big Band; NY St Sch Music Assn, Intnl Trumpet Guild, NY St Band Dir Assn; Percussive Art Society; *office:* Shenendehowa HS 970 Rt 146 Clifton Park NY 12065

ZAVADSKY, NANCY BURNES, 8th Grade Lit/Eng Teacher; *b:* St Louis, MO; *m:* Thomas; *c:* Adam, Aaron; *ed:* (BA) Ed/Sociology, St Louis Univ 1971; (MS) Counseling, Univ of WI Oshkosh 1980; Working Towards Masters Ed, Univ of WI Stevens Point; *cr:* 3rd/4th/8th Grade Teacher Holy Family 1971-73; 7th/8th Grade Lit Teacher St Anns 1977-79; Guidance Cnslr Horace Mann Mid Sch 1980-81; 8th Grade Lit Teacher St Petes Mid Sch 1984-; *ai:* 8th Grade Unit Leader; Drama Coach; *office:* St Peters Mid Sch 708 1st St Stevens Point WI 54481

ZAVADSKY, NANCY BURNES, 8th Grade Teacher; *b:* St Louis, MO; *m:* Thomas J.; *c:* Adam, Aaron; *ed:* (BA) Ed - Magna Cum Laude, St Louis Univ 1971; (MA) Counseling - Summer Cum Laude, Univ WI Oshkosh 1980; Masters in Ed; *cr:* 8th Grade Teacher Holy Family Sch 1971-73; 7th/8th Grade Teacher St Anns 1973-75; Guidance Cnslr Horace Monn Jr Hs 1980-81; 8th Grade Teacher Stevens Point Cath Schls 1984-; *ai:* 8th Unit Team Leader; Drama Coach; Advisory, Rdng Comm; Magna Cum Laude St Louis Univ;Suma Cum Laude Univ WI Oshkosh; *office:* St Peters Mid Sch 708 1st St Stevens Point WI 54481

ZAZVRSKEY, MICHAEL EUGENE, Math Teacher/Bsktbl Coach; *b:* Phillipsburg, PA; *m:* Judy Kay Mc Cann; *ed:* (BS) Math/Phys Ed, Cedarville Coll 1969; (MS) Ed/Phys Ed, FL Atlantic Univ 1983; *cr:* Math Teacher/Coach OH Soliders & Sailors Orphange 1969-74, Westminster Acad 1975-87, Browley HS 1988-89, Chrstn HS 1989-; *ai:* Var Bsktbl & Weight Lifting Coach; Jr Class Adv; NCTM; *office:* Chrstn HS 2100 Greenfield Dr El Cajon CA 92019

ZECHA, LINDA MORSE, Fourth Grade Teacher; *b:* Plymouth, NH; *m:* Frederick P. Jr.; *ed:* (BED) Elem Ed, 1969, (MED) Elem Ed, 1973 Plymouth St Coll; *cr:* 4th Grade Teacher Huckleberry Hill Sch 1969-70; 3rd Grade Teacher Holderness Cntrl Sch 1970-81; 4th Grade Teacher Jaffrey Grade Sch 1981-; *ai:* Various Comms; Club Adv; NEA, NHEA, JRTA; *office:* Jaffrey Grade Sch 31 School St Jaffrey NH 03452

ZEHR, DENNIS JOE, Biological Science Teacher; *b:* Hutchinson, KS; *m:* Linda Kay Folk; *c:* Carrie J.; *ed:* (BS) Phys Ed, 1972, (MS) Spec Ed/EMH, 1974 Ft Hays St Univ; Grad Stud Biological Sci; *cr:* Teacher Salina Cntrl HS 1974-84; Grad Asst Ft Hays St Univ 1984-86; Teacher Horace Mann Mid Sch 1986-88, Wichita East HS 1988-; *ai:* Sci Club Co-Spon; Environmental Club Spon; Sch Building Comm; KS Ornithological Society 1982-; Audubon Society 1976-; KS Biological Teachers Assn 1987-; KS Assn Teachers of Sci 1985-; NEA Building Rep; *office:* Wichita East HS 2301 E Douglas Wichita KS 67211

ZEIGLER, EDWARD LYNN, 5th Grade Teacher; *b:* Decatur, IN; *m:* Karen Stauffer; *c:* Ryan, Craig; *ed:* (BS) Elem Ed, Univ of Indianapolis 1971; (MA) Elem Ed, Ball St Univ 1975; *cr:* 6th Grade Teacher Farmland Elem 1971-83; 5th Grade Teacher Monroe Cntrl Elem; *ai:* 8th Grade Boys Bsktbl; *home:* RR 1 Box 106 B Parker City IN 47368

ZEIGLER, KEVIN MARTIN, Science Teacher; *b:* Minot, ND; *m:* Cecilia M. Francis; *ed:* (BS) Bio, Minot St Univ 1984;: *cr:* Substitute Teacher Minot HS 1984; Sci Teacher Columbus HS 1984-85, Towner HS 1985-; *ai:* Jr/Sr Adv; Sci Olympiad Coach; Girls/Boys Bsktbl Coach; Bsbl Coach; Sci Fair Coord; Nd Edcl Assn 1984-; Towner Ed Assn Pres 1985-; N W Regional Sci Assn 1987-; ND Coaches Assn 1984-; *office:* Towner HS PO Box 270 Towner ND 58788

ZEIGLER, RITA ROOK, English Teacher/Dept Head; *b:* Mercersburg, PA; *m:* John Robt.; *c:* John A., Jeffrey R., Jared L.; *ed:* (BS) Eng Stud, 1961; (MS) Eng Stud, 1967 Shippensburg Univ; Seminars; Audited Stud; Supervisory Certificates St of PA; *cr:* Jr HS Eng Teacher Carlisle Sch Dist 1961-68; Dept Head/6th-12th Grade Teacher Big Spring Schl Dist 1968-; *ai:* Literary Magazine Adv; NCTE, PA Cncl Teachers of Eng, PA St Ed Assn, NEA 1961-; Big Springs Ed Assn 1968-; *home:* 48 Mt Rock Rd Newville PA 17241

ZEISLOFT, RUTH BOVAIRD, English Teacher; *b:* Philadelphia, PA; *m:* O. Samuel; *c:* Eric, Marc, Brian; *ed:* (BA) Amer Stud, Univ of PA 1959; (MED) Ed, Temple Univ 1962; Coe Fnd Fellow, Eastern Coll 1963; NW PA Writing Project Fellow, Gannon Univ 1987; In Service Trng in Writing Using Word Processor; *cr:* 7th Grade Core Teacher Darby-Colwyn Joint Sch Dist 1959-62; 9th-11th Grade Eng Teacher Upper Merion Sch Dist 1962-71; 11th/12th Grade Eng Teacher Millcreek Sch Dist 1986-; *ai:* Debate Team; Model United Nations; Inservice Trng Specialist; Curr Standardization & Revision Comm Eng Dept; PTSA Faculty Rep; NCTE 1962-71, 1988-; NW PA Cncl of Teachers of Eng Exec Bd 1988-; Shenandoah Meadows Home Owners Assn Treas 1980-; *office:* Mc Dowell HS 3580 W 38th St Erie PA 16506

ZEIT, NITA RUTH BRANT, 3rd Grade Teacher; *b:* Kansas City, MO; *m:* David Allen; *c:* Nathan, Adrienne, Marissa; *ed:* (BS) Elem Ed, Emporia St Univ 1976; (MS) Curr/Instruction KS St Univ 1985; *cr:* 3rd Grade Teacher Horton Elem 1977-; *ai:* Prof Dev Comm; Rdng Textbook Selection Comm; Brown Cty Teachers Assn; KS NEA; NEA; Modern Sunflowers 4-H Project Leader 1988-; Phi Delta Kappan; *office:* Horton Elem Sch 300 E 16th Horton KS 66439

ZEITZMANN, REBECCA JO, 7th Grade English Teacher; *b:* Washington, MO; *ed:* (BSE) Eng, 1984, (BS) Music 1984 Cntrl Mo St Univ; *cr:* 8th Grade Eng Teacher Publications HS/Pleasant Hill HS 1984-86; 7th Grade Eng/Literature Teacher Pleasant Hill Mid Sch 1987-; *ai:* Pleasant Hill Mid Sch Stu Cncl; Prof Dev Comm; Advisory Cncl; Staff Dev Team Mid Sch; Metropolitan Instructional Leadership Prgm Kansas City 1987-88; CTA Issues Comm 1989-; CTA Executive Comm 1988-89; PTA 1989-; *office:* Pleasant Hill Mid Sch 327 N Mc Kissock Pleasant Hill MO 64080

ZELENCIK, MARY JOAN, 4th Grade Teacher; *b:* Chicago, IL; *ed:* (BA) Ed, Purdue Univ Lafayette 1970; (MS) Ed, Purdue Univ Hammond 1974; *cr:* 1st-5th Grade Teacher Thomas A Edison Sch 1970-; *ai:* Girls Intramurals 1974-77, Bsktbl 1977-78, Vlybl 1979-81, Track 1978-80; Co-Spon Sch Newspaper 1975-; Chairperson Building Historical Comm; NEA 1967-78; AFT 1979-; PTA 1970-, Life Membership; Hammond Area Rdng Cncl 1985-; Amer Assn of Univ Women; Writing His of Thomas A Edison Sch; *office:* Thomas A Edison Sch 7025 Madison Ave Hammond IN 46324

ZELI, DORIS CONTI, Fifth Grade Teacher; *b:* Monessen, PA; *m:* William J.; *c:* Laura Reilly, William J. Jr.; *ed:* (BS) Elem Ed, 1971, (MED) Elem Ed, 1975 CA Univ of PA; *cr:* Teacher Belle Vernon Area Sch Dist 1971-; *ai:* Spelling Bee Coord; Kickball Tournament Organizer; Stu Teacher Directing Teacher; Phi Delta Kappa, Fed of Teachers Mem; PMET Teacher Trng 1987, Distinguished Service Awd; *home:* 204 Liberty Ave Belle Vernon PA 15012

ZELICOF, ERIKA F., Chemistry Teacher; *m:* Simon; *c:* Steven, Audrey; *ed:* (MS) Polymer Chem, Brooklyn Polytechnic Inst 1968; Grad Stud Ed; *cr:* Research Chemist Witco Chemical 1963-68; Chem Teacher Highland Sch 1979-84, HS for Hum 1984-; *ai:* Advanced Placement & Peer Tutoring Coord; Chem Team Coach; Amer Chem Society.

ZELINSKI, PAULA ANN, 8th Grade Mathematics Teacher; *b:* Milwaukee, WI; *ed:* (BA) Elem Ed, AZ St Univ 1983; (MA) Scndry Ed, N AZ Univ 1989; *cr:* Math Teacher Desert Sands Jr HS 1983-88; Grad Asst N AZ Univ 1988-89; Math Teacher Estrella Jr HS 1989-.

ZELJAK, THEODORE, 6th Grade Teacher; *b:* Rochester, PA; *m:* Diana; *c:* Pamela, Theodore; *ed:* (BS) Elem Ed, Clarion Univ 1969; (MED) Guidance/Counseling, Slippery Rock Univ 1974; *cr:* Elem Ed Teacher Aliquippa Sch Dist 1969-; Cnslr Beaver Cty Comm Coll 1980-; *ai:* Air Explorers Adv 1988-; *office:* Aliquippa Sch Dist Sheffield Rd & 21st St Aliquippa PA 15001

ZELLARS, FRANCES FAIR, Second Grade Teacher; *b:* Abbeville, SC; *m:* Barney C.; *ed:* (BS) Elem Ed, Allen Univ 1961; Univ of GA; *cr:* 7th Grade Teacher Ellison Elem Sch 1963-64; 2nd Grade Teacher Florence Chapel Elem Sch 1965-67, Washington Wilkes Primary Sch 1967-; *home:* 107 Norman St Washington GA 30673

ZELLE, DAVID ARTHUR, Mathematics Teacher; *b:* Champaign, IL; *ed:* (BA) Math, Wartburg Coll 1977; (MA) Math, Univ of SD 1987; *cr:* Math Teacher Washington HS 1977-; *ai:* Boys Tennis Coach; NEA & NCTM 1977-; MAA 1989-; *office:* Washington HS 600 W Bluff Cherokee IA 51012

ZELLER, ALLEN RAYMOND, 7th-12th Grade Dir of Bands; *b:* Fort Monmouth, NJ; *m:* Susan Diane Hays; *c:* Devon A.; *ed:* (BA) Music Ed, Azusa Pacific Coll 1976; Grad Stud CA St Fullerton, Chapman Coll; Music Ed, Univ of CA Los Angeles; *cr:* 2nd-12th Grade Substitute Teacher Imperial Valley Sch Dist 1977-78; Instrumental Music/Music Survey Teacher Wilson Jr HS 1980; Band/Orch/Math/Wrestling Teacher La Serna HS 1980-82; Dir of Bands Sequoia Intermediate Sch 1982-, Newbury Park HS 1984-; *ai:* Pageantry & Tall Flags Adv; Solo/Ensemble Competitions & Honor Band Auditions Brass, Woodwind, Percussion Coach; CA All St Band Audition Evaluator; Parade Adjudicator; S CA Drumline Circuit & Drum Major Competitions, SCSBOA Solo & Ensemble Festival Host; Performed USMC Public Relations Band 1968-72; CBDA, CODA, SSCBOA, CMEA, MENC 1982-; Intnl Trumpet Guild 1972-; USAF 562nd Band Mem; Sequoia Intermediate Sch Honorary Service Awd Certificate 1989; Newbury Park HS Meritorious Achievement Certificate 1989; 1st Baptist Church (Minister of Music, Youth Dir) 1979-80; Wrote Jr HS Instrument Music Curr Conejo Valley Unified Sch Dist 1987; Received Schlsp Music & Track 1972; *home:* 5363 Heather St Camarillo CA 93012

ZELLERS, JOSEPH MICHAEL, 6th Grade Teacher; *b:* Lorain, OH; *ed:* (BS) Elem Ed, Cleveland St 1975; Cmptr for Elem Ed; *cr:* 6th Grade Teacher St Joseph Sch 1975-; *ai:* Youth Sftbl Coach; Marathon Runner; Amherst Athletic Assn League Dir & Coach 1976-; *office:* St Joseph Sch 175 St. Joseph Drive Amherst OH 44001

ZELLHOFER, GREGOR F., 8th Grade Teacher; *b:* Kenosha, WI; *m:* Paula Saks; *c:* Eric Jacobson; *ed:* (BS) Pre-Law, 1962, (MED) Scndry Ed, 1964 Temple Univ; (PHD) His of Ed, Loyola Univ 1980; *cr:* Teacher Stoddart Fleisher Jr HS 1962-64, Burley Sch 1964-.

ZELLMANN, LUANN (LILLEVOLD), Vocal Music Teacher; *b:* Thief River Falls, MN; *m:* Lance; *c:* Peter, Mark, David; *ed:* (BA) Music Ed, Concordia Coll 1975; (MS) Curr & Instrtn, Mankato St Univ 1987; *cr:* Vocal Music Teacher Redwood Falls-Morton HS 1975-; *ai:* Musical Asst Dir; MMEA; ACDA; MEA; Childrens Church Choir Dir; Hand Bell Choir Dir; *office:* Redwood Falls-Morton H S 4th At Lincoln Redwood Falls MN 56283

ZELLNER, VIRGINIA ANNE (CORDASCO), K-5th Enrichment Sci Teacher; *b:* Philadelphia, PA; *m:* Errol W.; *c:* Scott A., Robin J.; *ed:* (BS) Elem Ed, W CT St Univ 1975; (MA) Environmental Stud, Fairfield Univ 1980; Classical Ballet, Sch of Performing Arts; *cr:* 2nd Grade Teacher 1976-79, 5th Grade Teacher 1979-80, 5th Grade Sci Teacher 1980-87, 4th-8th Grade Gifted/Talented Teacher 1980-, K-5th Grade Sci Enrichment Teacher 1987- Sherman Sch; *ai:* K-8th Grade Sci Team Leader, Curr 1990; Schoolhouse Company Performing Group Drama Coach 1980-; Yrbk Adv 1989-; Fine Arts 1980-; Teacher Evaluation Comm 1987-; CT Ed Assn, NEA; Sherman Ed Assn (Secy 1983-84) 1977-; NSTA 1987-; Friends of Performing Arts (Mem, Secy) 1984-; CT Teacher of Yr Conservation 1987-88; Assn of Sch Admins Gifted & Talented Prgm Exhibition 1989; Cornell Univ Natl Recognition Exemplary Prgms for Gifted & Talented 1989-; *office:* Sherman Sch RR 37 Sherman CT 06784

ZELLO, SUZANNA MARIE, Principal; *b:* Bridgeport, CT; *ed:* (BA) His/Elem Ed, Sacred Heart Univ 1973; (MS) Ed, Fairfield Univ 1981; *cr:* 6th Grade Teacher 1975-81, 7th/8th Grade Teacher 1981-89, Admin 1989- Blessed Sacrament/St Mary; *ai:* Religious Ed Teacher; NCEA; St Charles Parish Cncl Pres 1987-89; New England Cath Youth Ministers 1988-; Whos Who Among Amer Colls & Univs 1973; *office:* Blessed Sacrament/St Mary Sch 264 Union Ave Bridgeport CT 06607

ZELTKALNS, MARA, Second Grade Teacher; *b:* Parkersburg, West Germany; *m:* Peter; *ed:* (BS) Elem Ed, Monmouth Coll 1969; Monmouth Coll, Center Grad Coll, Society for Developmental Ed; *cr:* 3rd Grade Teacher 1969-84, 2nd Grade Teacher 1984- Sunnybrae Elem Sch; *ai:* Family Math; Career Ed; Math Comm; Learning Resource Center 1990; NJ Ed Assn, NEA, Hamilton Town Ed Assn Mem 1969-; PTA Mem 1969-, Certificate of Appreciation 1989; Red Cross (Sch Rep, Leader), 10 Yrs of Service; NJ 4-H Leadership Awd 1986; Governors Teacher Recognition Awd 1989; Served as Cooperating Teacher for Prospective Future Teachers; Presenter at Math & Rdng Wkshps.

ZEMAN, BARBARA ANN, 5th Grade Teacher; *b:* Milwaukee, WI; *ed:* (BED) Ed/Art, Univ of WI Whitewater 1968; (MED) Curr/Supervision, Natl Coll of Ed 1988; Grad Stud in Psych; *cr:* 2nd/3rd Grade Teacher Waterloo Cmmty Sch 1968-69; Head Start Teacher Joint Dist 1 Lake Mills 1968-69; 2nd Grade Teacher Elmbrook Sch System Dist 21 1969-70; Head Start Teacher Francis Parker Sch 1970; 2nd/3rd/5th Grade Teacher Union Ridge Sch Dist 86 1970-; *ai:* Adv to Commissioner of Finance Office for Stu Cncl; Counseling at Psychiatric Hospital Setting; PTA Faculty Rep 1987-; NEA VP 1987-89; STEP Sch Bd Mem 1981-83; Union Ridge Dist 86 Ed Assn Pres; Consultant Area Schls, Consultant/Co-Evaluator Univ of WI Team; *office:* Union Ridge Sch 4600 N Oak Park Ave Harwood Heights IL 60656

ZEMANSKY, ALEX JOHN, 8th Grade Eng Teacher; *b:* Aurora, IL; *ed:* (BA) Journalism/Comm, Coll of St Francis 1980; (MED) Curr/Instruction, Natl Louis Univ 1990; *cr:* 7th Grade Eng Teacher Jefferson Mid Sch 1985-86; 8th Grade Eng Teacher Hill Jr HS 1986-87, Gregory Mid Sch 1987-; *ai:* Outdoor Ed; Discipline Advisory Comm; Work Published 1990; *office:* Gregory Mid Sch 2621 Springdale Cir Naperville IL 60564

ZEMLOCK, LISA M., Band Director; *b:* Chilton, WI; *m:* Ronald L. Olson; *ed:* (BME) Music Ed, Univ of WI Oshkosh 1983; Working Towards Masters in Curr, Supervision & Music; *cr:* Band Dir Winneconne Mid Sch 1983-; *ai:* WI Natl Band Assn (Bd of Dir 1986-, Natl Cmmty Band 1986, 1988, 1990); Intnl Trumpet Guild 1978-; Natl Band Assn 1983-; Winneconne Cmmty Ed Assn VP 1990; Kiel Municipal Band 1977-; Article Published in Magazine 1985; Univ of WI Oshkosh Outstanding Sr Awd 1983; N Peter Nelson Schlsp 1983; Stu Music Educators Natl Conference Schlsp 1981; *office:* Winneconne Mid Sch 233 S 3rd Ave Winneconne WI 54986

ZENZ, CORNELIA RISATTI, Lang Art Teacher/Dept Chair; *b:* Chicago, IL; *m:* James Louis Sr.; *c:* James L. Jr., Susanne C.; *ed:* (BSEE) Elem Ed, De Paul Univ 1966; Coastal Bend Writing Project, Univ of TX Pan Amer; *cr:* Teacher Roosevelt Jr HS 1965-69, Travis Jr HS 1969-; *ai:* Natl Jr Honor Society, Univ Interscholastic League Ready Writing Spon; TX St Teacher Assn Mem 1969-; NCTE, TX Joint Cncl of Teachers of Eng Mem 1988-; TX Assn for Gifted & Talented Mem 1984-; Mc Allen Chamber of Commerce Mem; *office:* Travis Jr HS 2000 N 23rd St Mc Allen TX 78501

ZEPPERNICK, PATRICIA DERENE (DERY), Fifth Grade Teacher; *b:* Salem, OH; *m:* Kenneth Russell; *c:* Kevin R., Ryan A.; *ed:* (BA) Elem Ed, 1972, (MS) Elem Ed/Rdng Specialist, 1985 Kent St Univ; *cr:* 3rd Grade Teacher 1972-82, 5th Grade Teacher 1982- B L Miller Elem; *ai:* Elem Girls Bsktbl Coach; Young Authors Prgm Adv; Youngstown Vindicator Newspaper Advisory Panel; Sebring Local Ed Assn, OH Ed Assn, NEA, Mahoning Valley Rdng Assn, Intnl Rdng Assn, E OH Cncl Teachers of Math; Sebring Kids Incorporated Mem; Sebring Historical Society (Co-Founder, VP) 1989-; Martha Holden Jennings Scholar, Sebring Teacher of Yr 1981-82; *office:* B L Miller Elem Sch 506 W Virginia Ave Sebring OH 44672

ZERBAN, JOYCE A., 1st Grade Transition Teacher; *b:* Allegan Cty, MI; *m:* Don E.; *c:* Laurie, Scott, Jennifer, Rob, J. R.; *ed:* (BS) Elem Ed, Greenville Coll 1964; (MS) Elem Ed/Rdng, S IL Univ Edwandsville 1989; Elem Ed, Leadership Trng, Wkshp Seminars; *cr:* 1st Grade Teacher Bond Cty Comm Unit 2 1964-67; Substitute Teacher Bond & St Clair & Madison Ctys 1968-75; 1st Grade Teacher Highland Cmmty Unit Dist 5 1975-; *ai:* Rdng, Report Card, Supt Advisory, Textbook, Referendum, Sch Climate Comm Mem; Teachers Against Tax Incentive Financing; Highland Ed

Assn (Pres 1982-87, VP 1985, Building Rep, Public Chairperson, Negotiator); IL Ed Assn (Region Cncl, Personal, Prof Dev Comm); NEA; Phi Kappa Phi, Kappa Delta Phi; Jr Womens Club (Charter Mem, Pres, Santas House Chairperson, Chairperson Fund Raisers); PTA (Mem, Appropriations Comm); *office:* Highland Cmmty Schls 1800 Lindenthal Ave Highland IL 62249

ZERINGUE, SIDNEY PAUL, Eighth Grade Sci Teacher; *b:* New Orleans, LA; *m:* Laura Grace Kilgore; *c:* Benjamin, Amy, William, Andrew; *ed:* (BS) Animal Sci, SE LA Univ 1977; (MS) Dairy Nutrition, LA St Univ 1978; (BS) Bio Ed, SE LA Univ 1985; *cr:* Regular Teacher Franklinton Jr HS 1984-; *ai:* Ftbl Coach; Beta Club Spon; Drug & Alcohol Prevention Team; Parent Involvement Comm Chairperson; LA Assn of Educators (VP 1985-86, Building Rep 1987-); Holy Family Cath Church Pres Parish Cncl 1988-, St Louis Medallion 1989; Cath Youth Organization Youth Dir 1982-; Franklinton Jr HS Teacher of Yr 1986-; Parish Wide Jr HS Teacher; St Delegate LAE 1985-88; Natl Delegate LAE Washington DC 1989; *home:* 407 Main St Franklinton LA 70438

ZERKLE, MARGARET M. (ELLIOTT), Eighth Grade Health Teacher; *b:* Buffalo, NY; : John P.; *c:* John P., Sharon A., Cathleen M.; *ed:* (BS) Health/Phys Ed, St Teacher Brockport NY 1956; (MEQ) Counseling, Univ of Buffalo 1978; Grad Courses & Inservice Credits; Amer Red Cross Cardio Pulminary Resucitation & First Aid Instr; *cr:* Phy Ed Teacher Buffalo Sch Dist 1956-61; Heath Teacher Coatesville Area Sch Dist 1977-; *ai:* Home & Sch Teachers Liaison; People Reaching Out Stu Asst Prgm; Comm CPR Instr; Mentor New Teacher Assistance Prgm; PA St Ed Assn Mem 1977-; Faculty Rep Teachers Union Outstanding Service Awd; Golden Apple Awd; *home:* 931 Kingsway Dr Coatesville PA 19320

ZERN, JOHN FREDERICK, Sociology/Law Teacher; *b:* Albuquerque, NM; *m:* Donna Rumsey; *c:* Jason; *ed:* (BA) Poly Sci, Coll of Santa Fe 1970; (MA) His/Poly Sci, Highlands Univ 1976; Advanced Trng NM Law Related Ed; Relearning Teaching Seminars; Advanced Placement Seminars in US His and Amer Government; *cr:* Teacher Santa Fe HS 1971-; *ai:* Chess Club; Mock Trial Team; Curr Comm & Lib Ethics Comm; Part-Time Ftbl & Track Coach; Santa Fe Fed of Public Schls Pres 1980-87; Employees Amer Fed of Teachers NM Exec Cncl 1980-87; 1976 Bicentennial Grant Re Charro Horsemanship in NM; Produced Exhibition During Bicentennial; Provide Alternative Ed for at Risk Stus Comm; *office:* Santa Fe HS 2100 Yucca Rd Santa Fe NM 87505

ZETO, VICKI LYNN, Mathematics Teacher; *b:* Holden, WV; *m:* Phillip E.; *c:* Jonathan; *ed:* (AB) General Stud, S WV Comm Coll 1979; (BA) Elem Ed, 1981, (MA) Elem Ed, 1986 Marshall Univ; *cr:* Teacher Holden Elem 1982, Logan Jr HS 1982-; *ai:* Math Dept Chm; *office:* Logan Jr HS 500 University Ave Logan WV 25601

ZETZ, DONNA JEAN (NAN), Fifth Grade Teacher; *b:* Rochester, PA; *m:* Rudy Jr.; *c:* Rudy III; *ed:* (BA) Elem Ed, Edinboro Univ of PA 1969; *cr:* 5th Grade Teacher Hopewell Elem Sch 1962-82, Hopewell Jr HS 1982-; *ai:* Spon Vikingettes; Young Astronauts Chapter Leader & Trainer; Area Soc Stud Curr Coord Comm; PTSA Cultural Arts Appreciation 1985; Consultant/Adv WQED Weekly Televised Sci Prgm; *office:* Hopewell Jr HS Brodhead Rd Aliquippa PA 15001

ZEUSKE, DOREEN SYLVIA, Fifth Grade Teacher; *b:* Viking AB, Canada; *ed:* (BA) Ed, Pacific Luth Univ 1958; Grad Stud W OR St Coll & Williamette Univ; *cr:* 7th-9th Grade Teacher Puget Sound Jr HS 1958-60; 7th/8th Grade Teacher Milwaukie Jr HS 1960-64; 7th-12th Grade Teacher 1964-65, 7th/8th/10th Grade Teacher 1965-66 Overseas Dependent Schls; 5th/6th Grade Teacher Salem-Keizer Public Schls 1966-; *ai:* NEA, OR Ed Assn, Salem Ed Assn 1966-, Salem Teacher of Yr 1973; OR Cncl of Teachers Eng 1986-; *home:* 1745 Misty Pl NW Salem OR 97304

ZEVNIK, SHELLEY J., Social Studies Teacher; *b:* Tulsa, OK; *ed:* (BS) Ed/Soc Stud, OK St Univ 1983; Taft Inst for Two Party Government, OK City Univ; Summer Seminar Karl Marx Poly, Soc Thought, Dickinson Coll; Lions Quest Skills for Adolescence Trng; Impact-Drug Intervention Trng, Hillcrest Medical Center Tulsa; Working Towards Masters Ed/Curr OK St Univ; *cr:* Teacher Union Public Schls 1984-; *ai:* Stu Cncl, Cmmty Service Organization Spon; Dist Staff Dev Comm; Stu Support Group Facilitator; NEA, OK Ed Assn 1984-; Union Classroom Teachers Assn (Building Rep 1987-88, VP 1988-89); Natl Assn of Stu Act Adv, NCSS; Young Democrats of OK 1st Congressional Dist Dir 1989-; Tulsa Cty Young Democrats St Convention Comm 1990; Natl Endowment for Hum Fellowship; Union Public Schls Educator of Month 1989; Union Jr HS Teacher of Yr 1989-; *office:* Union Jr HS 7616 S Garnett Rd Tulsa OK 74137

ZEXTER, ELEANOR MARKS, French/English Teacher; *b:* Providence, RI; *m:* D. Ronald; *c:* Francine D., Judith B.; *ed:* (BA) Fr, 1958, (MAT) Fr, 1962 Brown Univ; Fr, Middlebury Coll; Eng, Univ of RI, Providence Coll, RI Coll; *cr:* Fr/Eng Teacher Cntrl HS 1959, Hope HS 1960-68; Fr Teacher Cntrl HS 1968-69; Fr/Eng Teacher Nathan Bishop Mid Sch 1969-; Consultant Brown Univ 1987-; *ai:* Grant Writer; Special & Substance Abuse Prgm Coord; Drop-In Center Cnslr; Trip Leader & Chaperone; Club Adv for Act Prgm; Creator of Author-In-Residence Prgms & Specialized Anti-Drug & Drop-Out Prgms; Educl Dev Center Consultant 1987-; AATF 1960-84; RIFLA 1975-; Pembroke Coll Club 1958-; Nathan Bishop PTO Faculty Liaison 1987-; Thomas Mc Clorin Awd; Citizen Citation; Teacher of Yr 1985, 1989-; *office:* Nathan Bishop Mid Sch 101 Sessions St Providence RI 02906

ZIARKO, PAULA AGNES (MURRAY), Second Grade Teacher; *b:* Worcester, MA; *m:* Francis Stanley; *c:* William; *ed:* (BS) Elem Ed, Worcester St Teachers Coll 1968; (MS) Early Chldhd Ed, St Coll at Worcester 1978; St Coll Worcester, Anna Maria Coll, Fitchburg St Coll; *cr:* 3rd Grade Teacher Center Sch 1967-72; 1st Grade Teacher Memorial Sch 1973-74; 2nd Grade Teacher Leicester Primary Sch 1975-; *ai:* Ed Assn of Leicester, MA Teachers Assn, NEA 1967-; French River Teachers Center 1982-; Intnl Rdng Assn, MA Rdng Assn, Cntrl MA Rdng Assn 1989-; Horace Mann Grant 1986-87; Leicester Arts Cncl Grant 1988-; Mothers Club Awd 1989-; *office:* Leicester Primary Sch Paxton St Leicester MA 01524

ZIBERT, SHIRLEY A., English Teacher; *b:* Washington, PA; *m:* John Jr.; *ed:* (BS) Comprehensive Eng, California Univ of PA 1970; *cr:* Scndry Eng Teacher Mc Guffey Mid Sch 1970-; *ai:* Mid Sch Act Spon; Mc Guffey Ed Assn 1970-; *office:* Mc Guffey Mid Sch R R 1 Box 219 Claysville PA 15323

ZICKLER, KAREN K. KING, Fifth Grade Teacher; *b:* Bandera, TX; *m:* Russell Lea Jr.; *c:* K. Wilynn, Russell L. III, Shandra K., Geoffrey A.; *ed:* (BS) Elem Ed, TX Tech Univ 1970; (MCI) Curr & Instruction, Univ of Houston 1975; Grad Stud; *cr:* 5th Grade Teacher 1971-73, 4th Grade Teacher 1973-78 Austin Elem; 4th Grade Teacher Bandera Elem 1979-86; 4th Grade Teacher 1986-89, 5th Grade Teacher 1989- Alkek Elem; *ai:* UIL Literary Coach; Textbook Comm; PTO Faculty Rep; Bandera Educators Secy 1979-; TX St Teachers Assn, NEA 1970-; Delta Kappa Gamma 1985; Bandera United Meth Church (Chairperson, Admin Bd 1989-, Musician, Teacher, Youth Choir Leader, Youth Leader) 1980-; Conducted Various Inservice Sessions Within Sch Dist & Private Schls; *office:* Alkek Elem Sch P O Box 727 Bandera TX 78003

ZIDANSEK, JANET STEINER, Mathematics Dept Chairman; *b:* Greensburg, PA; *m:* Anton; *ed:* (BS) Scndry Math, Clarion Univ 1972; (MED) Scndry Counseling, Indiana Univ of PA 1975; *cr:* Math Teacher Butler Intermediate HS 1972-82; Math Teacher/Dept Chm Marian HS 1984-; *ai:* Butler Intermediate Natl Jr Honor Society 1970-72; Detroit Area Cncl Teachers of Math (Treas, 1989-, Hospitality, Publicity 1987-89); Marion HS Teacher of Yr 1989; *office:* Marian HS 7225 Lahser Rd Birmingham MI 48010

ZIDBECK, WILLIAM EDWARD, Science/Journalism Teacher; *b:* Ancon Canal Zone, Panama; *m:* Jo Ann Marie Hill; *c:* William S., Suzann M.; *ed:* (BA) Bio, Stanford Univ 1954; (MS) Intnl Relations, Univ of S CA 1969; CA Teaching Credential, San Diego St Univ 1985; Naval War Coll, Sr Offocers Warfare Course Newport 1969; Industrial Coll Of Armed Forces 1977; Navy Flight Trng; *cr:* Rank Of Captain/Naval Officer/Pilot Us Navy Commanding Officer HS-5 Co Usnas Guantanamo Bay Cuba & Co Netscpac 1954-84; Bio Teacher 1987-, Journalism Teacher 1988- Castle Park HS; *ai:* Sch Newspaper Adv; Natl Chm Of Naval Helicopter Assn 1985-86, Bd Of Trustees 1975; Naval Inst Life Mem 1958-; Amer Defense Preparedness Assn Life Mem 1973-; Optimist Club Of Imperial Beach 1986-; Sino-Soviet Border Dispute, Naval War Coll; *office:* Castle Park HS 1395 Hilltop Ave Chula Vista CA 92011

ZIEBOLD, BARBARA M., Music Teacher/String Dept Head; *b:* Fremont, OH; *ed:* (MM) Music Performance/Ed, Bowling Green St Univ 1975; *cr:* Music Teacher Alliance City Schls 1975-77; Violin Instr Mt Union Coll 1976-77; Music Teacher/String Dept Head Fremont City Schls 1978-; *ai:* OH Music Ed Assn, Music Educators Natl Conference, Amer String Teachers Assn, OH String Teachers Assn, Natl Sch Orch Assn; OH Music Ed Assn Adjudicator; *office:* Fremont Ross Hs 1100 North St Fremont OH 43420

ZIEGENFUSE, BRUCE RICHARD, Mathematics Teacher; *b:* E Greenville, PA; *m:* Mary Ann Siegrist; *c:* Bryan, Megan; *ed:* (BS) Math Ed, Clarion St Coll 1967; Grad Stud Trenton St Coll, Glassboro St Coll; *cr:* Math Dept Chm 1976-80, Math Teacher N Burlington Cty Regional Jr/Sr HS 1967-; *ai:* NEA, NJ Ed Assn 1968-; ASCD 1989-; *home:* 3 Devonshire Ct Mount Laurel NJ 08054

ZIELINSKI, STEPHEN F., Secondary Mathematics Teacher; *b:* Buffalo, NY; *m:* Mary Louise Brady; *c:* Stephen, Michael, James, Linda, Peter; *ed:* (BA) Math, Univ of Buffalo 1963; (MS) Ed, Canisius Coll 1965; Cmptr Programming, Univ of Buffalo; *cr:* Jr HS Math Teacher Maryvale Jr HS 1965-71; Math Teacher Maryvale HS 1972-; *ai:* Var Bowling, Frosh Bsbl Coach; Maryvale Teachers Assn Treas 1970-73; Southline Athletic Assn Pres 1980-84; Niagara Frontier Girls Sftbl Assn Treas 1980-84; W NY Babe Ruth Traveling League Secy 1989-; Cheektowaga Chamber of Commerce Awd 1982; Erie Cty Interscholastic Coaching Awd 1980; Service to Youth Awd Cheektowaga Youth Bd 1986; Yrbk Dedication Maryvale HS 1988; *office:* Maryvale HS 1050 Maryvale Dr Cheektowaga NY 14225

ZIEMANN, JACK ELDOR, Jr HS Mathematics Teacher; *b:* Hazen, ND; *ed:* (BS) Chem/Math/Bio, Dickinson St Coll 1965; Various Courses; *cr:* Math Teacher Hazelton Public Sch 1965-68, Bowman Public Sch 1968-; *ai:* Coaching Mathcount; NDEA, NEA Mem 1965-; Bowman Ed Assn Treas 1985-; ND Cncl Teachers of Math Mem 1980-; Bowman Luth Church (Bd Mem 1980-85, Pres 1984-85); Bowman Golf Course Bd of Dir 1985-88; *office:* Bowman Public Sch Drawer H Bowman ND 58623

ZIEMBA, MARY JOANITA GERTRUDE, Mathematics-Religion Teacher; *b:* Reading, PA; *ed:* (BS) Elem Ed, 1969, (MA) Ed/Admin Supervision, 1983 Seton Hall Univ; *cr:* Kndgtn Teacher St Valentines Sch 1958-59, Holy Rosary Sch Baltimore MD 1959-69, Holy Rosary Sch Passaic NJ 1960-61; Kndgtn/1st/2nd Grade Teacher St Stanislaus Sch 1960-61; Kndgtn-3rd Grade Teacher 1961-62, 3rd Grade Teacher 1962-62 St Hedwigs Sch; 4th Grade Teacher 1962-64, 5th Grade Teacher 1964-65 Holy Rosary Sch Baltimore MD; 4th Grade Teacher St Francis Sch 1965-66, St John Sch 1966-67; 1st Grade Teacher St Hedwigs Sch 1966-67; 2nd Grade Teacher 1967-69, 6th Grade Teacher 1969-70 Holy Rosary Sch; 6th Grade Teacher Our Lady of Good Cncl 1970-71;6th-8th Grade Teacher St Anns Sch 1971-72, St Stephens Sch 1972-73; Prin Holy Rosary Sch Baltimore MD 1973-79; 6th-8th Grade Teacher St John Kanty Sch 1979-80; *ai:* After Sch Care; NCEA; Apostolic Services Comm; *home:* 6 Smalley Terr Irvington NJ 07111

ZIEMEK, DAVID W., Mathematics Teacher; *b:* Chicago, IL; *m:* Lela; *c:* James, Holly, Stacie; *ed:* (BS) Math, Culver-Stockton Coll 1960; (MS) Math/Ed, N IL Univ 1964; (MS) Admin, 1966, (MS) ADMIN, 1968 Univ of IL; *cr:* Math Teacher/Coach Ridgewood HS 1960-62, Prospect HS 1962-71; Dean/Dir of Stu Act 1971-72, Dir of Stu Act 1972, Math Teacher/Stu Cncl Adv 1985- Rolling Meadows HS; *ai:* Variety Show Dir; Class, Variety Club Spon; Ftbl, Wrestling, Bsbl Coach; IL Cncl Teachers of Math; NE Dist of IL Stu Cncl Adv of Yr 1985; IL Stu Cncl Adv of Yr 1986; Dist 214 Prin Awd 1988; *office:* Rolling Meadows HS 2901 Central Rd Rolling Meadows IL 60008

ZIETTLOW, JANICE L., Science Teacher; *b:* Billings, MT; *ed:* (BA) Bio, Westmar Coll 1968; (MAT) Botany, Duke Univ 1972; *cr:* 8th-10th Grade Sci Teacher North Rockland Sch Dist 1968-72; 10th Grade Bio Teacher Onslow Cty Sch Dist 1972-76; Jr/Sr HS Sci Teacher Des Moines Public Sch Dist 1978-; *ai:* NEA, ISTA 1968-; NSTA, NESTA, NABT; Natl Sci Fnd Grant Duke Univ; *office:* Cntrl Acad 1800 Grand Des Moines IA 50307

ZIEVE, SANDRA ANNE, 5th Grade Teacher; *b:* Cleveland, OH; *ed:* (BA) Elem Ed, OH St Univ 1965; (MA) Ed, Cleveland St Univ 1970; *cr:* 3rd Grade Teacher 1965-7,; 4th Grade Teacher 1972-80, 5th Grade Teacher 1981- Richmond Hts Elem Sch; *ai:* Facilitator Elem Stu Support Groups; Coord Femcom Project for 5th & 6th Grade Girls Cmptr Use; Pi Lambda Theta (Secy 1986-88/Newsletter Editor 1988- VP 1990-); Richmond Hts Teachers Assn; Martha Holden Jennings Grant Femcom Project to Integrate Cmptr Experience W/Research & Problem Solving for 5th-6th Grade Girls; East OH Gas Sunshine Esp Awd; *office:* Richmond Hts Elem Sch 447 Richmond Rd Cleveland OH 44143

ZILL, STEVEN E., Science Department Chair; *b:* Ann Arbor, MI; *m:* Julie Beth Priehs; *c:* Steven M., Elizabeth K., Michael S., Scott T.; *ed:* (AA) Liberal Art, Concordia Jr Coll 1974; (BA) Sci/Environmental Sci, Concordia Teachers Coll 1976; (MS) Geography/Remote Sensing, E MI 1982; Chem, Saginaw Valley St Univ; *cr:* 5th/6th Grade Teacher Mt Hope Luth Sch 1978-84; 7th Grade Teacher Trinity Luth Sch 1984-85; Admin Mt Hope Luth Sch 1985-87; Sci Dept Valley Luth HS 1987-; *ai:* Jr Class Adv; Var Girls & Boys Soccer Coach; Sci Club Coord; Drama Production; *office:* Valley Luth HS 3560 Mc Carty Rd Saginaw MI 48603

ZILLNER, KIM KREPS, Third Grade Teacher; *b:* Ontario, OR; *m:* Robert G.; *c:* Katie J., Jody K.; *ed:* (BS) Elem Ed, Univ of ID 1980; Post Grad Stud Boise St Univ, Coll of ID, Portland St Univ; *cr:* Summer Migrant Teacher 1980-89, 3rd Grade Teacher 1980- Butteview Elem; *ai:* Coached Hs Slowpitch Sftbl Team Phys Ed, Coord, Teacher for Grade Level; GCEA 1980-; IEA, NEA; *office:* Butteview Elem Sch 400 S Pine Emmett ID 83617

ZIMA, ELIZABETH M., 6th Grade Teacher; *b:* Philadelphia, PA; *ed:* (BS) Elem Ed, Temple Univ 1981; (MED) Elem Math Ed, Beaver Coll 1987; *cr:* 5th Grade Teacher 1981-88, 6th Grade Teacher 1988- Resurrection of Our Lord Sch; *ai:* Candidates Confirmation Dir; Schls Testing Coord 1984-; NCTM 1984-89; ATMOPAV 1985-89; *office:* Resurrection of Our Lord Sch 2020 Shelmire Ave Philadelphia PA 19152

ZIMBRO, ALBERT D., History Teacher; *b:* Baltimore, MD; *ed:* (BS) His, Towson St 1973; (MA) Univ of MD 1988; Ed Teaching Certificate Salisbury St 1978; *cr:* Teacher Baltimore City Lombard Jr 1978, Baltimore City Winston Mid 1978-82, Arundel Jr 1983-85, Glenburnie Sr 1985-; *ai:* Prgm Assist & Support Stus; Substance Abuse Prevention Comm 1989-; *office:* Glen Burnie Sr HS 7550 Baltimore-Annapolis Blvd Glen Burnie MD 21061

ZIMMER, CLARA ZULICK, First Grade Teacher; *b:* Pottsville, PA; *m:* George Richard; *c:* Sarah; *ed:* (BA) Elem Ed, West Chester Univ 1971; PA St Univ, Kutztown Univ; *cr:* 1st Grade Teacher Blue Mountain Sch Dist 1971-; *ai:* Disciplinary Comm; Blue Mountain Ed Assn Secy 1980-; Youth Group Adv 1987-; *home:* 622 N Warren St Orwigsburg PA 17961

ZIMMERMAKER, CHARLES S., Data Processing Teacher; *b:* Niagara Falls, NY; *m:* Lisa Guarino; *c:* Kristen, Chad, Sean; *ed:* (AS) Bus/Accounting, Niagara Cty Comm Coll 1964-66; (BS) Bus/Ed, Niagara Univ 1972-76; (MS) Spec Ed, Univ of S FL 1977-80; Additional Teaching Adult Ed, St Petersburg Jr Coll; *cr:* Military US Army 1974-76; Accountant Hooker Chemical Corporation 1967-76; Teacher Gibbs HS 1976-81, Tarpon Springs HS 1981-; *ai:* Former Ftbl & Track Coach; *office:* Tarpon Springs HS 1411 Gulf Rd Tarpon Springs FL 34689

ZIMMERMAN, ANNELLE GRIER, Science Teacher/Chair; *b:* Abbeville Cty, SC; *m:* Isaiah; *c:* Isaiah Jr.; *ed:* (MS) Bio Ed, 1979, (BS) Bio, 1971 SC St Coll; Univ of SC, SC St Coll; *cr:* Teacher Myrtle Beach HS 1971-72, Holly High HS 1973-74, Dantzler Mid Sch 1974-; *ai:* Charles Drew Sci Club & 8th Grade

Class Adv; Quiz Bowl Comm Mem; SC Sci Cncl; NSTA 1983-; NEA, SCEA, HHEA 1980-; Womens Missionary Society Asst Secy 1989-; Teacher of Yr 1986-87; *office:* Dantzler Mid Sch Rt 1 Holly Hill SC 29059

ZIMMERMAN, FRAN L. (SMITH), Sixth Grade Teacher; *b:* Oneonta, WI; *m:* Kenneth E. Sr.; *c:* Ken Jr., Kay L.; *ed:* (BS) Elem Ed, UW Plateville 1963; *cr:* 1st-8th Grade Teacher Nessa Sch 1955-58; 1st-8th Grade Teacher Plainview 1958-62; 6th Grade Teacher New Glarus Public Schls 1962-; *ai:* TAG Comm; Forensics; Public Speakg; Music; NEA; SWEA; NGEA Secy 1975; Swiss United Church Choir 1964-; Green County UCC Choir 1985-; Awd 25 Yrs Outdoor Ed 1988; 2 Poems Publ World Poetry 1989; Rcvd Golden Poet Awd; *home:* 108 14th Ave New Glarus WI 53574

ZIMMERMAN, JOYCE IRENE (BRETH), 5th Grade Teacher; *b:* Calumet, PA; *c:* Rhonda J. Zimmerman Householder, Beverly G. Zimmerman Reese, Doyle T., Lorena F.; *ed:* (BS) Elem Ed, Univ of Steubenville 1972; Grad Stud; *cr:* Teacher St Josephs Sch 1971-72, Richmond Elem 1972-; *ai:* Spelling Bee & Dist Inservice Comm; Early Chldhd Parent Wkshp Presenter; Edison Local Teacher Appreciation Banquet Chairperson; Edison Local Ed Assn, OH Ed Assn, NEA 1972-; 4-H Adv 1963-68, 1990; Lioness; Edison Local Ed Assn Building Rep; *office:* Richmond Elem Sch 386 Park St Richmond OH 43944

ZIMMERMAN, JUDITH DUNBAR, English Teacher; *b:* Russell Springs, KY; *m:* Ronnie G.; *c:* Jason; *ed:* (BA) Eng, 1970, (MA) Ed, 1974 W KY Univ; Writing Project W KY Univ 1988-89; *cr:* Eng/Sci Teacher Hiseville HS 1970-74; Eng Teacher Barren Cty HS 1974-; *ai:* Beta Club, Trojan Players, Sr Class Spon; Speech Club Coach & Spon; BCEA Treas 1986-88; KEA, NEA; Credit Union Rep Sch; Glenview Chrstn Church Mem; *home:* 263 Kino Rd Glasgow KY 42141

ZIMMERMAN, MARYBELLE (MC KIM), Fifth Grade Teacher; *b:* Hobart, OK; *c:* Kim E., Joy M.; *ed:* (BME) Voice, 1957, (MSED) 1974 Phillips Univ; *cr:* Elem Music Supvr Jefferson City MO 1957-58; 1st-12th Grade Vocal Music Teacher Wellsville MO 1958-60; Elem Music/6th Grade Teacher Okarche OK 1972-74; 5th Grade Teacher N Platte Public Schls 1975-79; *ai:* Coach HS Academic Team; Local Assn of Classroom Teachers Pres 1988-89; Delta Kappa Gamma 1988-; 1st Chrstn Church Choir 1950-; Kappa Kappa Iota; *home:* 1863 Surrey Dr Pryor OK 74361

ZIMMERMAN, NILA JEAN (POE), 6th Grade Teacher; *b:* Greencastle, IN; *m:* Donald Keith; *c:* Chad A. Fishero; *ed:* (BA) Elem Ed, 1978, (MS) Elem Ed, 1982 Univ of Indianapolis; *cr:* 5th/6th Grade His Teacher Neil A Armstrong Elem 1978-86; 6th Grade Teacher 1986-88, 5th Grade Teacher 1988-89 , 6th Grade Teacher 1989- Waverly Elem; *ai:* Summer Sch Teacher 1988-; After Sch Tutoring Prgm 1989-; Home Bound Teacher for Terminally Ill Stu 1984-86; Sunday Sch Teacher 1983-85; VFW Post IIII Schlsp Comm; Delta Kappa, Gamma Society (VP 1988-89, 1989-); Elem Sci Fair Judge 1988-89; *home:* 1600 Rooker Rd Mooresville IN 46158

ZIMMERMAN, RICHARD T., Fifth Grade Teacher; *b:* Danville, PA; *m:* Janet Wirtz; *c:* Thomas, Todd, Beth; *ed:* (BS) Elem Ed, Bloomsburg St Coll 1968; (MS) Elem Ed, Bloomsburg Univ 1973; Grad Stud Sci, Cmptrs, Soc Stud; *cr:* 6th Grade Teacher N Schuylkill Sch Dist 1968-69; 4th-6th Grade Teacher Crestwood Sch Dist 1969-72; Dist Exec BSA 1972; K-7th Grade Head Teacher 1972-82, 4th-6th Grade Teacher 1972- Crestwood Sch Dist; *ai:* Jr HS Boys Bsktbl, Girls Sftbl Coach; Creator & Dir Bow Creek Outdoor Environmental Ed Learning Center; Sci & Soc Stud Curr Comm; Crestwood Ed Assn (Building Rep 1972-84, Teacher Liaison Comm 1984-85); Mountaintop Mens Vlybl League (Pres 1971) 1968 ; Penn Lake Borough Cncl (Pres 1980) 1976-87; Mountaintop LittlE League Bsbl/Sftbl (Mgr/Coach) 1985-, Dist Champions Jr Babe Ruth 1987; Outdoor Environmental Ed Center Grant; Helped Write Grant Proposal for Penn Lake Park Dam Reconstruction; *office:* Crestwood Sch Dist Spruce St Mountain Top PA 18707

ZIMMERMAN, ROBERT GLEN, English/US His/Speech Teacher; *b:* Boise, ID; *m:* Rexann Jean Workman; *c:* Joseph L., Stephanie F.; *ed:* (BS) Ed, 1972, (MS) Guidance/Counseling 1989 Univ of ID; *cr:* Eng/His/Speech Teacher 1972-, Cnslr 1984- Salmon River HS; *ai:* Asst Ftbl, Head Girls Bsktbl, Track, Jr HS Bsktbl Coach; Guidance Counseling Assn; Riggins City Cncl Councilman 1989-; *office:* Salmon River HS Box 872 Riggins ID 83549

ZIMMERMAN, ROBERT L., History Teacher; *b:* Kingsport, TN; *m:* Joan Cowden; *c:* Brian A., Travis L., Les Chee; *ed:* (BS) His/Poly Sci, E TN St Univ 1969; (ME) Admin/Supervision, Univ of MS 1975; US Navy Comm Technician; *cr:* Soc Stud Teacher Blountville Mid Sch 1972-88; Government/His Teacher Sullivan Cntrl HS 1988-; *ai:* Stu Cncl Sullivan Cntrl HS, Photography Club Blountville Mid Sch Spon; NEA, TEA, SCEA 1972-; Indian Springs Ruritan Club VP 1988-89; Proofreader of TN His & Government Textbooks; *office:* Sullivan Cntrl HS 131 Shipley Ferry Rd Blountville TN 37617

ZIMMERMAN, ROGER EARL, 5th Grade Teacher; *b:* Lansing, MI; *m:* Darlene Marie Burby; *c:* Eric, Alicia; *ed:* (BA) Ger, Cntrl MI Univ 1968; Elem Cert, MI St Univ; *cr:* Permanent Substitute Teacher Lakeview Dist 1968; 5th Grade Teacher New Haven Elem Sch 1968-70; 6th-8th Grade Lang/Math Teacher 1970-75, 5th Grade Teacher 1975- New Haven Mid Sch; *ai:* Assertive Discipline Cncl; Pizza Hut BOOK IT; Educl Field Trip & Exit Exam Coord; New Haven Ed Assn Exec Bd (Pres 1980-85, VP 1979-80); Macomb Rdng Cncl 1980-; Cub Scouts of America (Webelo Leader, Asst Cub Master) 1981-83; Little League Coach 1982-84; Jaycees 1973-77; Macomb Cty Spelling Bee Judge.

ZIMMERS, GLORIA NANCY (KOEHLER), 5th Grade Teacher; *b:* St Louis, MO; *m:* William Edward; *c:* Nancee K.; *ed:* (AB) Elem Ed, Harris St Teachers 1974; *cr:* Teacher St George 1968-71, Delmar HS 1974-80, St Bernadette 1980-; *ai:* Camp Spon; Spelling Bee Adv; *office:* St Bernadette Sch 74 Kearney Saint Louis MO 63125

ZIMNY, BILLIE KATHRYN BOGGIO, English Teacher/Jr HS; *b:* Valier, IL; *m:* Joseph D.; *c:* Julianna Shpik, Kathryn, Joseph A.; *ed:* (BS) Elem Ed, 1958, (MS) Elem Ed, 1961 Southern IL Univ; Southern IL Univ 1967-71; *cr:* Classroom Teacher Carbondale Sch Dist 95 1958-63; Instr/Eng Breckinridge Job Corps Ctr 1964-65; Instr-Dept of Elem Ed Southern IL Univ-1965-73; Classroom Teacher Herrin Unit 4 Sch 1974-; Instr/GED John a Logan Coll 1988-; *ai:* Writing Talent Search; Unit Lang Arts Comm; Unit Assessment Comm; Supervise Stu Teachers; Southern IL CTE 1987-; NEA; IL Ed Assn; Easter Seal Society; St Francis Cath Womens Club; Headstart Consultant; Confrence Presenter Lang Arts; Confrence Presenter; IL Office of Ed; *home:* 400 S Dixon Carbondale IL 62948

ZINAMAN, HELAINE M., Talented & Gifted Prgm Coord; *b:* New York, NY; *ed:* (BA) Elem Ed, Amer Univ 1973; (MED) Gifted Ed/Spec Ed, Univ of MD 1979; Admin & Supervision Cert; Pre-Leadership Trng; Participation Math, Sci & Technology Network; *cr:* Resource Teacher John Eager Howard 1973-85; Coord for Talented & Gifted Glenarden Woods Elem 1985-; *ai:* Odyssey of Mind, Coach & Judge; Think Tank Teacher Univ of MD; ASCD 1987-; NAGC 1979-; NEA 1973-; WA Post Grants Ed Awd 1989; *office:* Glenarden Woods Elem Sch Glen Arden Pkwy Echols Ave Lanham Seabrook MD 20706

ZINGSHEIM, RONALD N., English Teacher; *b:* Sparta, WI; *m:* Debra Kay Kasper; *c:* Paxton, Gavin; *ed:* (BS) Bus Ed/Eng, Univ WI Whitewater 1971; Writing Process Approach, Univ WI Madison; *cr:* Teacher Boscobel Area Schls 1972-; Writer Boscobel Dial 1980-; Teacher Southwest Tech Coll 1989-; *ai:* Bsbl Coach; Bsktbl Announcer; Bsbl Class C St Champion 1987; Bsbl SWAL Coach of Yr 1986; *office:* Boscobel HS 300 Brindley St Boscobel WI 53805

ZINK, JOHN HENRY, Science Teacher; *b:* Cumberland, MD; *m:* Wanda Lee Hill; *c:* Misti Brandenburg, Johnna; *ed:* (BS) Ed, Frostburg St Univ 1960; (MS) Earth Sci, Univ of OK 1967; Univ of NC 1961; Univ of MD 1965; Amer Univ 1974; Frederick Comm Coll 1962, 1983; Hagerstown Jr Coll 1966; *cr:* Sci Teacher Thurmont HS 1960-64, Middletown Mid Sch 1964-; *ai:* NSTA, MD Assn Sci Teachers, NEA, MD St Teachers Assn; Braddock Heights Cmmty Assn Pres 1974-75; Greater Metropolitan Area Outstanding Earth Sci Teacher 1971; Nom Presidential Awd Excl Sci Teaching 1983; Search for Excl Sci Ed Finalist 1983; Frederick Cty Outstanding Teacher Awd 1984; Presidential Awd for Excl Sci Teaching Finalist 1986; *home:* 6727 Deer Spring Ln Middletown MD 21769

ZINKE, LAURA ALONSO, Spanish Teacher; *b:* Flagstaff, AZ; *m:* Franklin C.; *ed:* (BA) Span/Ed, N AZ Univ 1984; (MA) Span, Middlebury Coll 1990; *cr:* Span Teacher Mc Clintock HS 1984-; *ai:* Span NHS Spon; Jr Var & Frosh Cheer Coach; AATSP, AFLA 1984-; Kemper Goodwin Schlsp 1985; AZ Foreign Lang Assn Young Educator Awd 1985; Tempe Diablos Awd of Excl 1990; *home:* 1347 E Louis Way Tempe AZ 85284

ZINN, CARMINE RANIERI, Foreign Language Supervisor; *b:* Orange, NJ; *m:* James R.; *c:* Lisa; *ed:* (BA) Span, FL St Univ 1957; (MA) Foreign Lang Ed, FL St Univ 1974; (EDS) Supervision, Univ of S FL 1975; Civdad Universitaria Mexico; *cr:* Teacher Meadowlanw Jr HS 1957-62, Northeast HS 1963 76, Pinellas Park HS 1976-86; Supvr Curr & Instruction Center 1986-; *ai:* Intnl Club, Span Honor Society & Soph Class Spon; Head of Foreign Lang Dept; Teacher of Immersion Prgm; AATSP (Secy, Treas) 1970-74; FAATSP St Contest Spon 1982, Commissioners Awd 1971; Amer Assn Teachers of Foreign Lang 1965-; FL Span Teacher of Yr 1982; Accompany St Commissioner to Japan Stud Japanese Educl System 1989; *office:* Pinellas Cty Schls 205 4th St S W Largo FL 34640

ZINN, HOWARD STEPHEN, 4th Grade Teacher; *b:* Bronx, NY; *m:* Terrie Canelstein; *c:* David, Barrie; *ed:* (BA) Psych, City Coll of NY 1963; (MA) Pupil Personnel Services, Newark St Coll 1969; Grad Stud; *cr:* Teacher Manalapan-Englishtown Regional Schls 1965-67, PS 3 1967-73; Trainer Dist 31 Teacher 1973-75; Teacher PS 3 1975-; *ai:* United Fed of Teachers, NEA, AFT, NY St United Teachers; Bronx Cty Historical Society; Contributor to Diagnostic Prescriptive Arithmetic Book Published by Dist 31; *office:* Public Sch 3 80 S Goff Ave Staten Island NY 10309

ZINNA, FRANCES KLECAK, Kindergarten Teacher; *b:* Bayshore, NY; *m:* John J.; *c:* Meredith, Michelle; *ed:* (MA) Elem Ed, Adelphi Univ 1975; *cr:* 3rd Grade Teacher Tremont Elem 1972-79; 2nd Grade Teacher Bay Elem 1979-83, 5th Grade Teacher 1984-89, Kndgtn Teacher 1989- Tremont Elem; *ai:* Suffolk Rdng Cncl 1988-; Pilot Club of Sayville (Secy 1985-86, VP 1986-87); *office:* Tremont Elem Sch Tremont Ave Medford NY 11763

ZIPP, CYNTHIA BLANCHARD, Second Grade Teacher; *b:* Traverse City, MI; *m:* Thomas D.; *ed:* (BS) Elem Ed, N MI Univ 1977; Grad Classes, Cntrl MI Univ; *cr:* 2nd Grade Teacher Ottawa Elem Sch 1978-; *home:* 200 Fairview Ave Petoskey MI 49770

ZIRBEL, JANET WILSON, Mathematics Teacher; *b:* Springfield, MO; *ed:* (BS) Math/His, Sch of the Ozarks 1971; Grad Stud S MO St Univ Springfield, MO St Columbia; *cr:* 7th-8th Grade Teacher Ozark Public Schls 1972-74; 7th-12th Grade Math Teacher Sparta Public Schls 1975-76; 6th-8th Grade Math Teacher Mansfield Public Schls 1976-78; 6th-8th Grade Teacher Logan-Rogersville Mid Sch 1978-; *ai:* 5th/6th/8th Grade Math Teams Coach for Various Contests; Math Dept Chairperson; Home Bound Teaching Helper; Salary Comm; Mentor Teacher for Mentor Prgm for Beginning Teachers; St Judes Math-A-Thon Prgm Coord; MSTA, CTA 1988-89; Ozark Cncl Teachers of Math 1988-; Glendale Chrstn Church 1987-; Logan-Rogersville Mid Sch Outstanding Educator Awd 1988-89; *home:* 1101 Samuel J Ozark MO 65721

ZIRK, JEAN WILSON, Substitute Teacher; *b:* Moorefield, WV; *d:* Lee Wayne; *c:* Wayne E.; *ed:* (BA) Elem Ed/Health/Phys Ed, Fairmont St Coll 1954; Grad Courses, WV Univ Morgantown; *cr:* 1st-8th Grade Teacher Powers Sch 1946-47, Frosty Hollow 1947-48, Steel Run 1948-50; 1st-3rd Grade Teacher Burch Sch 1952-58; 1st/3rd Grade Teacher Moorefield Graded 1958-73; Summer Headstart 1965-69; 3rd Grade Teacher Consolidated Moorefield Elem 1973-89; *ai:* Report Card, Textbook Comm; Math Seminar; NEA, WV Educl 1957-78; Hardy Cty Ed Treas 1969-74; Auxiliary Bridgewater Home Mem 1989-; Amer Assn Univ Women Mem 1985-89; Cert Appreciation Dedication Service Church of Brethren; Plaque Appreciation 40 Yrs Service Hardy Cty Schls; *home:* 512 Winchester Ave Moorefield WV 26836

ZIRKELBACH, JOAN DIANE, 6th/8th Grade Health Teacher; *b:* Hornell, NY; *ed:* (BS) Health/Phys Ed, Bethel Coll 1970; (MS) Health, Univ of Buffalo 1975; *cr:* Health Teacher Iroquois Mid Sch 1970-; *ai:* Girls Var Tennis, Boys & Girls Cross Cntry Coach; Nationally Ranked Marathon Runner; *office:* Iroquois Mid Sch PO Box 32 Elma NY 14059

ZIRKLE, BARBARA JEAN, General Sci/Soc Stud Teacher; *b:* Piqua, OH; *ed:* (BA) His/Government, Otterbein Coll 1966; Course Work at UT St, Bowling Green; *cr:* 7th/8th Grade Teacher Plymouth Local Schls 1966-; *ai:* Ofcl Scorer Jr HS Girls Vlybl & Boys Bsktbl; NEA 1975-; OEA 1966-; PEA Grievance Comm Chm 1973-; Fletcher United Meth Church; *office:* Plymouth Local Schls Shiloh Mid Sch Shiloh OH 44878

ZIRKLE, JOHN WARREN, 5th Grade Teacher; *b:* Arlington, VA; *ed:* (BS) Elem Ed, Univ of VA 1972; (MS) Spec Ed-ID, Amer Univ 1977; *cr:* 3rd-6th Grade Teacher Markham Elem 1972-77; 5th/6th Grade Teacher Dogwood Elem 1977-; *ai:* Soc Stud Liason Teacher; VA Ed Computing Assn 1988-; Fairfax Ed Assn Faculty Rep 1986-; *office:* Dogwood Elem Sch 12300 Glade Dr Reston VA 22091

ZITLOW, DOROTHY PAPENFUSS, Jr HS Teacher; *b:* Fond du Lac, WI; *m:* Kenneth B.; *c:* Kevin, Lynn, Douglas, Daniel; *ed:* (BS) Elem Ed/Bio, Marian Coll 1968; *cr:* 3rd Grade Teacher Oakfield Public 1968-69; 2nd-7th Grade Teacher Consolidated Cath 1976-; *ai:* Building Coord; Sci Fair Judge & Coach; NCEA; *home:* N 2741 Kelly Rd Fond Dulac WI 54935

ZLOTNICKI, BOGDAN MICHAEL, Social Studies Dept Chair; *b:* Jaremeze, Poland; *m:* Gladys Middleton; *c:* Kristina, Michael; *ed:* (BA) Poly Sci, Univ of NC 1959; (MAT) Geography, Univ of SC 1983; Several Air Force & Army Schls; *cr:* Substitute Teacher Hillcrest HS 1980-84; Soc Stud Dept Chair St Jude Cntrl HS 1984-; *ai:* Stu Cncl Adv; Booster Club Mem; SC Soc Stud Assn 1983-; BSA Cncl Exec Bd 1975-, Silver Beaver 1990; St Jude Teacher of Yr 1989, Booster of Yr 1986, Yrbk Honoree 1988; *home:* 5806 Fish Rd Dalzell SC 29040

ZOANNI, RICHARD JAMES, Mathematics Department Chair; *b:* Sidney, MT; *m:* Kathleen Agnes Casey; *ed:* Michael, Ricky, Jeff, Angela; (BS) Math, Coll of Great Falls 1973; *cr:* Math/Phys Ed Teacher St Leos HS 1973-75, Math Teacher Malta HS 1975-76, Sidney HS 1976-; *ai:* MCTM 1980-; Teacher of Yr Lewistown Jaycees & Sidney Ed Assn; *home:* HC 69 Box 46 Culbertson MT 59218

ZOBAL, JULIE MILLER, 7th Grade Teacher of Eng/Rdng; *b:* Houston, TX; *m:* Arthur F.; *c:* Arthur F. Jr., Daniel C., Kathryn., Zobal Mc Mahan; *ed:* (BS) Elem Ed, Univ of North TX 1967; (MA) Med, TX Chrstn Univ 1979; *cr:* 3rd Grade Bi-Ling Teacher 1975-77, 5th Grade Teacher 1977-85 Fort Worth Sch Dist; 6th Grade Eng/Geography Teacher 1985-87; 7th Grade Eng/Rdng Teacher 1987- Trinity Valley Sch; *ai:* Kappa Delta Pi; Intnl Rdng Assn; NCTE; TX Joint Cncl Teachers of Eng; Assembly on Literature for Adolescents; 1st Presbyn Church Elder; *office:* Trinity Valley Sch 6101 Mc Cart Fort Worth TX 76133

ZOCCALLI, ANTHONY JOSEPH, Asst Principal; *b:* Youngstown, OH; *m:* Janet L. Toporcer; *c:* Anthony, John, Michael; *ed:* (BS) Soc Stud, 1968; (MS) Admin, 1972 Youngstown St Univ; Ed, Econ; *cr:* Teacher 1968-89, Stu Cncl Adv 1986-, Asst Prin 1989- Frank Ohl Mid Sch; *ai:* Ftbl & Track Coach 1969-74; Stu Cncl Adv 1986-; Mem Parish Cncl Elected to 4 Yr Post; Church Commemtator;TASC Mem; *office:* Frank Ohl Mid Sch 225 Idaho Rd Austintown OH 44515

ZODDA, PHILIP J., Teacher/Track & Field Coach; *b:* New York, NY; *ed:* (BS) Phys Ed, 1973, (MS) Ed, 1975 Niagara Univ; *cr:* Womens Athletic Dir Niagara Univ 1973-75; Recreation Dir NYC Housing Authority 1975-77; Teacher NYC Bd of Ed 1977-; Track/Field Coach South Shore HS 1985-; *ai:* NY City Empire St Games Team Track Coach; Kinney Natl HS Cross Cntry Championships NE Regional Asst Coord; Jr HS 51 Colgate

Womens Games Track Coach; United Fed of Teachers, Chapter Leader JHS 51; *office:* South Shore HS 6565 Flatlands Ave Brooklyn NY 11236

ZOKAI, ELLEN KAY (VIATOR), 6th-8th Grade Language Teacher; *b:* New Iberia, LA; *m:* Mansour; *c:* Olivia, Matthew; *ed:* (BA) Elem Ed, 1979, (MED) Elem Ed, 1988 Univ of Southwestern LA; Participant Prof Improvement Prgm; *cr:* Teacher New Iberia Jr HS 1979-82, Broussard Mid Sch 1982-83; Teacher-Gifted Prgm Paul Breaux Mid Sch 1983-; Teacher Univ of Southwestern LA 1989-; *ai:* Christmas Prgm Chairperson Spirit Comm Spon; Sch Newspaper; Yrbk Adv; Speech Team Coach; Coord Young Authors Contest; Stu Cncl Adv; Coord Kids in Th News; Mentorship Prgm; Faculty Study Chairperson; Chrldr Spon; NEA 1979-; LAE 1979-; Assn Gifted/Talented 1987-89; Phi Kappa Phi 1989; NEA 1979-; Religion Teacher 1987-; First Communion Prgm Coord 1987-; Religion Fair Co-Chairperson 1989; Girl Scout Troop Asst 1988-89; *office:* Paul Breaux Mid Sch 1400 S Orange Lafayette LA 70501

ZOLLICOFFER, JEAN THOMPSON, Third Grade Teacher; *b:* Florence, SC; *c:* Roselyn, Roderick; *ed:* (BA) Elem Ed, Benedict Coll 1968; Francis Marion Coll, Creighton Univ, Univ of SC; *cr:* Art Teacher Wilson Elem 1968-69; 3rd Grade Teacher Marrs Elem 1969-70; 4th Grade Teacher Carver Elem 1970-75, Spring Elem 1975-80; 3rd Grade Teacher Carver Elem 1980-; *ai:* 3rd Grade Level Chairperson; Sch Radio Show; Safety Patrol Adv; Retirement Comm; Staff Advisory Cncl; NEA, SC Ed Assn; Young Womens Auxiliary Pres 1988-; Teacher of Yr 1982; *office:* Carver Elem Sch 1001 Sumter St Florence SC 29501

ZORNOW, JOANN (SAPERSTEIN), Sixth Grade Teacher; *b:* Detroit, MI; *m:* Jay; *ed:* (BS) Elem Ed/Soc Stud 1967, (MA) Lit, 1974 Wayne St Univ; Mid Sch Endorsement, Wayne Univ 1980; *cr:* 5th/5th-6th/6th Grade Teacher Green Acres Elem 1967-; *ai:* Contest Coord; Dist Creative & Talented Comm Mem & Recording Secy; Curr, Mid Sch Soc Stud Planning, Mid Sch Health Curr Comm; MI Humane Society 1990; *office:* Green Acres Elem Sch 4655 Holmes Warren MI 48092

ZOTH, DIANA LYNN (SMART), Math/Cmptr Math Teacher; *b:* Wellington, KS; *ed:* (BS) Elem Ed, NW OK St Univ 1970; (MED) Spec Ed, OK Univ 1976; Psych & Math, Univ CA Los Angeles; Math, N TX St Univ; Cmptr & Math, Univ of TX Dallas; *cr:* Kndgtn Teacher Cherokee Public Schls 1970-72; Substitute Teacher Los Angeles Unified Sch Dist 1972-74; Spec Ed Teacher Hulcy Mid Sch 1977-79, June Shelton Sch 1976-77; Crisis Teacher Dallas Ind Sch Dist I & II 1979-84; Math/Cmptr Teacher Skyline HS 1984-; *ai:* CEC; NCTM 1987-; Whos Who in Amer Colls & Univs; *home:* 1811 Williams Way Dallas TX 75228

ZOTTOLA, MARTIN DOMENIC, English Teacher; *b:* Grants Pass, OR; *m:* Sherry Ann (Smith); *c:* Marcus D., Bartholomew D.; *ed:* (BS) Scndry Ed/Eng, S OR St Coll 1988; *cr:* Eng Teacher Ashland HS 1988-89, Grants Pass HS 1989-; *ai:* Asst Ftbl & Head Boys Tennis Coach; Educl Advisory Cncl; Establish Sr Project Comm; *office:* Grants Pass HS 522 NE Olive St Grants Pass OR 97526

ZOUCHA, DOUGLAS H., History Teacher; *b:* Platte Center, NE; *m:* Barbara Ann Rice; *c:* Joshua M., Lucas J.; *ed:* His, SD St Univ 1973-74; (BA) His, Wayne St Coll 1976; Working Towards Masters His, Wayne St Coll; *cr:* His Teacher Norfolk Cath & Sacred Heart 1977-; *ai:* Var Cross Country Coach Norfolk Cath HS; NE Coaches Assn, NCEA 1977-; *office:* Sacred Heart Sch 201 S 6th Norfolk NE 68701

ZRUBEK, MARCIA HOEVET, Mathematics Teacher; *b:* Omaha, NE; *m:* William E.; *c:* Valerie Zrubek Blair, Julie Zrubek Livingston, W. Scott; *ed:* (BA) Math, Univ of TX 1957; (MS) Math/Sci, Univ of Houston 1988; *cr:* Math Teacher Clear Lake HS 1973-; *ai:* Mu Alpha Theta/Jets Spon; NHS Co-Spon; NCTM; Calculus & Elem Analysis Teachers of Houston Bd of Dirs 1987-; Sch Leadership Awd 1987-88; Sch Nominee TX Excl Awd for Outstanding HS Teachers 1990; *office:* Clear Lake HS 2929 Bay Area Blvd Houston TX 77058

ZUBER, VINCENT HAROLD, Mathematics Teacher; *b:* Newton, IL; *m:* June Marie Keller; *c:* Ronald, Mark, Michael, Pamela, Steven, Thomas, Robert; *ed:* (BSED) Math, 1963, (MSED) Instructional Media, 1972 E IL Univ; *cr:* Teacher Assumption Jr-Sr HS 1963-; *ai:* NHS Spon; AEA, IEA, NEA Local Pres; ICTM, NCTM; St Mary Sch Bd Pres 1985-88; Assumption Park & Recreation Comm; Distinguished Teaching Awd W IL Univ 1987; *home:* 111 N St John Assumption IL 62510

ZUBKE, BILL, Computer Instructor; *b:* Webster, SD; *m:* Cathy Lewis; *ed:* (BS) Speech/Theatre, Moorhead St Coll 1971; Cmptr & Teaching Techniques; *cr:* Eng/Speech Teachers Fargo North HS 1971-72; Speech/Debate Teacher 1972-84, Cmptr Teacher 1984- Watertown Jr HS; *ai:* Sr HS Interpretation Coach; NEA, SDEA 1972-; SD Forensic Coaches Assn; Watertown Ed Assn Pres 1987-88; SD Pork Producers Pork Cookout King St Champ Natl Finalist; Outstanding Young Educator of Speech 1976; *home:* 417 N Broadway Watertown SD 57201

ZUECK, DEBRA LEE, First Grade Teacher; *b:* Pana, IL; *ed:* (BSED) Elem Ed, E IL Univ 1974; Educl Admin & Counseling Psych, Univ of IL Champaign; *cr:* 2nd Grade Teacher Sacred Heart Sch 1975-77; 1st Grade Teacher Washington Elem Sch 1977-; *ai:* Pana Ed Assn VP 1985-86; IL Ed Assn, NEA; Delta Theta Tau 1982-85; Articles in Educl Activity Newsletters; *office:* Washington Elem Sch 200 S Sherman St Pana IL 62557

ZUEHLKE, JANET ROLD, Chapter I Reading Teacher; *b:* Atlantic, IA; *m:* Alfred; *c:* Keith, Kevin, Kimberly; *ed:* (BA) Ed, Concordia Teachers Coll 1966; *cr:* 2nd Grade Teacher Trinity Luth 1966-68; 1st Grade Teacher Roselle Public Schls 1968-71; 3rd Grade Teacher 1975-81, Rdng Specialist 1981-85, 3rd Grade Teacher 1985-87, Chapter I Rdng Teacher 1987- Lewis Cntrl; *ai:* Chapter I Parent Teacher, At-Risk, Lang Art Comm, Stu Cncl, Sch Store Adv; Midlands of IA Rdng Cncl 1987-; IA Rdng Assn 1987-; Lakeview PTO Bd (Teacher Rep 1987-89, 2nd VP 1989-); NEA, LCEA 1975-; Aid Assn for Luth VP 1984-; *office:* Lakeview Elem Sch Wright & Piute Rds Council Bluffs IA 51501

ZUEHLKE, LARRY EUGENE, Mathematics Teacher; *b:* Ottumwa, IA; *m:* Susan Yvonne Sedore; *c:* Larry B., Todd D., Scott T.; *ed:* (AA) Liberal Arts, Indian Hills Comm Coll 1972; (BSE) Math, 1976, (MA) Admin, 1986 NE MO St Univ; Grad Stud; *cr:* Teacher Ottumwa Cmmty Schls 1977-; *ai:* Chess Club Adv; Girls Sftbl Coach; Boys Little League Mgr; Math Club & Sch Trip Spon.

ZUK, JOSEPH S., English Dept Chair; *b:* Battle Creek, MI; *m:* Carol Ann Zull; *c:* Stephanie, Sara, Andrew; *ed:* (BA) Eng, W MI Univ 1970; *cr:* Eng Dept Chm St Philip Cath Cntrl 1970-; *ai:* Asst Prin; Sr Class Adv; Asst Var Vlybl Coach; Eng Dept & Discipline Review Bd Chm; Natl Cath Ed Assn; *office:* St Philip Cath Cntrl Sch 20 Cherry St Battle Creek MI 49017

ZUKER, KATHY CAIN, 2nd Grade Teacher; *b:* Fredrick, OK; *m:* William J.; *c:* Stephane J.; *ed:* (BA) Elem Ed, 1980; (BA) Early Chldh Ed, 1980, (MS) Early Chldhd Ed, 1982 Cntrl St Univ; *cr:* 2nd Grade Teacher Prague Schls 1980-82; 5th Grade Teacher 1982-83, 2nd Grade Teacher 1983- Bristow Schls; *ai:* Textbook & Staff Dev Comm; NEA, OK Ed Assn 1982; Bristow Bus & Prof Womens Club Pres 1985-86; *home:* Rt 3 Box 144 Bristow OK 74010

ZUMBRUNNEN, KATHERINE ANDREA (MARNICH), Jr High School Band Instructor; *b:* Duluth, MN; *m:* Keith; *ed:* (BS) Instrumental Music, 1969, Masters Equivalency Scndry Ed, 1979 Univ of MN Duluth; Scndry Ed, Spec Ed; *cr:* Band Instr Pelican Rapids Jr Sr HS 1969-70; Elem Jr/Sr HS Band Instr Organ Park Jr/Sr HS 1970-82; Band Instr Morgan Park Jr HS 1982-87; *ai:* Intnl World Assn of Bands & Ensembles 1981-86; Woman Band Dir Assn 1971-85; Natl Band Assn 1975-85; Music Educators Natl Conference 1965-85; MN St HS League 1970-, Selected Mem of St Music Contest Revision Comm 1980-82, Certified Music Adjudicator for MN Dist Region & St Music Contests 1980-; N Cntrl Evaluation & Accreditation Assn Appointed Evaluation Team Mem 1986-; MN Ed Assn Nom MN Teacher of Yr 1986; *home:* 1259 92nd Ave W Duluth MN 55808

ZUPANCICH, ANTONIA, Principal; *b:* Pitston, PA; *m:* Victor W.; *c:* Gloria, Victoria; *ed:* (BA) His, Mt St Marys Coll 1969; (MA) Ed, Azusa Pacific Univ 1983; CA Sch Leadership Acad 1988; *cr:* Classroom Teacher 1974-82, Music Teacher 1982-84, Classroom Teacher 1984-87, Mentor Teacher 1985-87, Dist Resource Teacher 1987-89 Fontana Unified Sch Dist; Prin Virginia Primrose Elem 1989-; *ai:* TRA 1987-89; Arrowhead Rdng Cncl Treas 1987-88; *office:* Virginia Primrose Elem Sch 9680 Citrus Ave Fontana CA 92335

ZUTTER-BROCK, PAMELA J., Foreign Lang Dept Chair; *b:* Lima, Peru; *m:* Bruce; *c:* Eric; *ed:* (BA) Eng, Mc Kendree Coll 1973; Span & Fr Lang S IL Univ Edwardsville, Univ of MO St Louis, Maryville Coll, Universite De Geneve Switzerland; *cr:* Teacher/Eng & Foreign Lang Chairperson Wright City HS 1974-84; Teacher/Chairperson Francis Howell HS 1984-; *ai:* Span Club Spon; Cmmty Teachers Assn Pres 1980-81; Amer Assn of Teachers Span & Portuguese, MNEA, NEA 1985-; United Meth Church Nursery Bd 1985-87; *home:* 17 Novella Dr Saint Charles MO 63303

ZUZOV, ANN MARIE, Teacher of the Gifted; *b:* S Amboy, NJ; *m:* Michael E.; *c:* Michael T., Janice C.; *ed:* (BA) Eng/Bio/Elem, Montclair St 1959; (MA) Elem Ed, Trenton St Coll 1970; (Prin Cert) Supervision, Rider Coll 1976; *cr:* 3rd Grade Teacher Emma Arleth 1959-60; 5th Grade Teacher Trenton NJ Jr HS 2 1960-61; 2nd Grade Teacher Sunnybrae 1967-77; Teacher of the Gifted Hamilton Township 1977-; *ai:* Coach Future Problem Solving Team, Mock Trial Team; Key Club Adv; Phi Delta Kappa Fnds Dir 1987-; NEA, NJEA, HTEA, MCEA, HS Rep 1967-; Hamilton Society for Advancement of Gifted Children Inc Teacher Liason 1977-; Hamilton Township Kiwanis Membership Chairperson 1988-; NJ Bd of Key Club Dirs Zone Admin 1990; Teacher of Yr 1975, 1985; Mercer Cty Teacher of Yr 1986; NJ Cable Network Golden Apple Teacher Awd 1990; 2nd Grade Class Had Honeybee Designated Ofcl St Insect NJ St Legislature 1974; *office:* Nottingham H S 1055 Klockner Rd Hamilton Township NJ 08619

ZWERNER, WILLIAM GENE, Biological Science Teacher; *b:* Terre Haute, IN; *m:* Diana K. Duncan; *ed:* (BA) Life Sci, 1970, Teaching Cert, 1975 IN St Univ; (MS) Biological Sci, De Paul Univ 1979; *cr:* Sci Teacher South Vermillion HS 1975-; *ai:* Sci Dept Chm; Appreciation of Teacher Awd 1986, 1989; *office:* South Vermillion HS RR 1 Clinton IN 47842

ZWICK, WILLIAM ALLEN, Fifth Grade Teacher; *b:* Riverside, NJ; *m:* Judith A. Collinsworth; *c:* Carrie, Misty; *ed:* (BS) Elem Ed, Trenton St Coll 1973; *cr:* 4th Grade Teacher Aronson Bell Sch 1973-79; 5th Grade Teacher Millbridge Sch 1979-; *ai:* NJ Ed Assn 1973-; *office:* Millbridge Elem Sch Conrow Rd Delran NJ 08075

ZWIEFELHOFER, PATRICIA ANN (RUFF), Mathematics Teacher; *b:* Chippewa Falls, WI; *m:* Douglas Frank; *c:* Stacy; *ed:* (BS) Math, 1983, (MST) Math, 1988 UW Eau Claire; *cr:* Math Teacher Eau Claire Memorial HS 1984-; *ai:* Asst Track Coach; *office:* Eau Claire Memorial HS 2225 Keith St Eau Claire WI 54701

ZWILLICH, MARK ALAN, Business Teacher; *b:* Bronx, NY; *m:* Donna Joy Zoch; *c:* Alan C., Paula J.; *ed:* (BS) Bus Ed, Univ of Akron 1973; (MA) Bus Ed, NY Univ 1977; *cr:* Bus Teacher Cadiz HS 1973-74, Mt Vernon Public Schls 1975-77, Suffern HS 1977-78, Mamaroneck HS 1978-81, Spellman HS 1981-82, Port Chester HS 1982-; *ai:* Yrbk Adv 1987-; Delta Pi Epsilon, NBEA, E Bus Teachers Assn, NY Bus Teachers Assn, Westchester Cty Bus Teachers Assn; CT Jaycees (Region Dir 1987-88), 1986-89, Keyman Awd 1988; New Milford Bd of Ed 1988-89; Outstanding Young Men of Amer 1988; *office:* Port Chester HS Tamarack Rd Port Chester NY 10573

ZYLAK, RICHARD EDMUND, JR., Physics Teacher; *b:* Latrobe, PA; *m:* Cynthia Ann Petruso; *c:* Halley, Jordan; *ed:* (BSED) Math/Physics, 1976, (MSED) Earth Sciences, 1980, (BSGS) Geology, 1981 Edinboro St Univ; *cr:* Physics Teacher Meadville Sr HS 1976-80; Logging Engineer NL Basin Surveys & Eastern Well Surveys 1980-81; Physics Teacher Meadville Sr HS 1982-; *ai:* Sci Club Adv; AAPT 1982-; Astronomical Society of the Pacific 1986-; *office:* Meadville Sr HS North St Ext Meadville PA 16335

GEOGRAPHIC OCCUPATION INDEX

ALABAMA

ABBEVILLE
Kirkby, Helen Smith
  5th Grade Teacher
Lindsey, Barbara H.
  Headmaster

ADAMSVILLE
Beaudrie, Catharine D.
  Teacher of Gifted
Gossett, Lois Scoates
  Fifth Grade Teacher
Smith, Janet Warlick
  Spanish/English Teacher

ADDISON
Cleghron, Donna S.
  Second Grade Teacher
Gammon, Geraldine Crider
  Fourth Grade Teacher
Wilson, Patsy Denson
  Social Studies Teacher

ALBERTVILLE
Hall, Agatha Morton
  7th Grade English Teacher
Hayes, Sadie L.
  Second Grade Teacher
Johnson, Nelda Burroughs
  Third Grade Teacher
Taylor, Ann Montgomery
  Fifth Grade English Teacher
Terrell, Maryetta Van Devender
  5th Grade Mathematics Teacher

ALEXANDER CITY
Coley, Gwendolyn Darnell
  Chapter I Teacher
Humphrey, Gayle Corley
  8th Grade Soc Stud Teacher

ALICEVILLE
Russell, Thomas David
  Mathematics Teacher

ALTOONA
Moxley, Glenda Vaughn
  Fourth Grade Teacher

ANDALUSIA
Earnest, Bettie Oswald
  5th Grade Teacher
Mobley, Peggy Ham
  Mathematics Teacher

ANNISTON
Jackson, Glenda Serita
  5th Grade Teacher
Martin, Martha Hamilton
  Fifth Grade Teacher
Mc Daniel, Cynthia Lemley
  6th Grade Soc Stud Teacher
Perry, Sulane Stone
  Kindergarten Teacher
Rains, Dianne Dobbins
  Readiness Teacher
Rauch, Sharon Shinkle
  Mathematics Teacher
Robertson, Bettye Snead
  7th Grade English Teacher
Spurlin, Glenn E.
  Instrumental Music Teacher
Stahl, Caryl Lynn
  Second Grade Teacher
Willingham, Melissa Wolfe
  5th Grade Teacher
Woolsey, Robin Alicia
  2nd Grade Teacher

ARAB
King, Joan Black
  Third Grade Teacher

Trimble, Barbara Putman
  8th Grade Earth Sci Teacher

ARDMORE
Edge, Amy K.
  Biology/Chemistry Teacher
Hastings, Pamela Barron
  English Teacher

ARITON
Crawley, Olivia Prestwood
  Second Grade Teacher
Laney, Dorothy Hoover
  Fourth Grade Teacher

ASHFORD
Conway, Luverne Bowen
  Mathematics Dept Teacher
Kelley, Houston Dale
  Assistant Principal
Parker, Antoinette Boykin
  Science Teacher

ASHLAND
Riddle, Mary Morgan
  Teacher
Williams, Clara Jane
  Teacher

ASHVILLE
Arnold, Kellie Barton
  Teacher

ATHENS
Bailey, Bernice Mitchell
  Chapter I Reading Teacher
Bailey, Julia Tunstill
  Lang Art/Soc Stud Teacher
Beggs, Betty Croney
  Third Grade Teacher
Brooks, Anna Lois Staton
  Eng/Accounting/Typing Teacher
Clem, Ada Bee (Holt)
  First Grade Teacher
Craig, Dicie W.
  Math Teacher
Fowler, Pamela Gay Sayre
  Teacher of Elementary Gifted
Hubbard, Teresa Simpson
  Teacher of Gifted & Talented
Johnston, Mildred Schrimsher
  Kindergarten Teacher
Mc Shann, Doris Yarbrough
  Social Studies Teacher
Seibert, Cathy Malone
  Fourth Grade Teacher
Woodis, Dorthy Muecke
  Teacher

ATTALLA
DuPree, Dorothea Lewis
  8th Grade English Teacher
Hutchens, Patricia W.
  Biology Teacher
Samples, Brenda Darlene
  6th Grade Science Teacher

AUBURN
Branch, Tana Newman
  Art Teacher
Logan, Russell Mahlon
  Band Director
Niebuhr, Kitty Evans
  Counselor
Rubley, Todd Stephen
  Marketing Ed Teacher
Smith, Nancy L. (Lee)
  English Teacher

BAY MINETTE
Blosser, Lydia Holly
  9th Grade Teacher
Ford, Nancy Moore
  Mathematics Teacher
Jackson, Barbara Howard
  English Teacher

Rider, Carol Fleming
  1st Grade Teacher
Scott, Shirley Carroll
  Business Education Teacher
Strong, Florene Snipes
  Math Teacher

BAYOU LA BATRE
Sherlock, Betty Wilkinson
  5th Grade Teacher
Stanley, Karen Housman
  Physical Education Teacher

BESSEMER
Garzarek, Frank R. Jr.
  Mathematics Specialist
Johnson, Miller Jones
  Biology Teacher
Morgan, Debra Burroughs
  Second Grade Teacher
Morgan, Rosa Gaines
  English Teacher
Richardson, Lorenzo
  Fourth Grade Teacher
Strickland, Priscilla Burgess
  English Teacher

BIRMINGHAM
Baker, Shelby Mosley
  Second Grade Teacher
Bickford, Martha McLaurine
  Fifth Grade Teacher
Blanton, Mary Brown
  Kindergarten Teacher
Brown, Willie Albert Jr.
  Language Art Teacher
Charlton, Sandra Manning
  1st Grade Teacher
Classe, Jeanne Schaub
  French Teacher
Daily, Susie Bartley
  Seventh Grade Math Teacher
Derieux, Judy Killian
  Teacher
Fetner, Sandra Merrill
  Sixth Grade Teacher
Fillmer, Leslie Donald
  Advanced Placement Music Instr
Grissett, Gail Hamby
  6th-8th Grade Lit/Rdng Teacher
Hairston, Kathey Neely
  5th Grade Teacher
Halstead, Bettye Vines
  Counselor/French Teacher
Hammett, Mary Wein
  First Grade Teacher
Hutchinson, Gretchen Hudson
  History/Spanish Teacher
Kelly, Lillie Brown
  Science Teacher
King, Janice Morton
  Chairman of Music Department
Lee, Ronda F.
  Speech Teacher
Martin, Patricia Tyler
  Mathematics Teacher
Mc Swain, Martha Wait
  5th Grade Teacher
Morrison, Catherine Bryant
  Third Grade Teacher
Siler, Doris Griffin
  Science Teacher
Smith, Tyrone Wade
  Social Studies Teacher

BLOUNTSVILLE
Gobel, Debra Wright
  4th Grade Teacher
Meade, Velma Sue (Painter)
  6th Grade Teacher
Merchant, Rolaine Mann
  Sixth Grade Teacher
Simmons, Raymond Michael
  Fifth Grade Teacher

BOAZ
Donaldson, Kathleen Lovett
  Sixth Grade Teacher
Gillilan, Jerry Wayne
  Science Teacher
Langley, Carol Barkley
  Guidance Counselor
Patterson, Ellen Clay
  Math Department Chairperson

BREMEN
Pulliam, Shelia Duke
  First Grade Teacher

BRIDGEPORT
Freeman, Jeanette Lynn
  Third Grade Teacher
Hadley, Dorothy Evans
  4th Grade Teacher
Mc Coy, Rebecca Smith
  Chapter I/Science/Eng Teacher

BRILLIANT
Johnston, Shelia Powell
  Special Education Teacher
Myers, Ilean
  First Grade Teacher
Silas, Kayron Miles
  Fifth Grade Teacher
Walker, Wanda Benton
  Guidance Counselor

BROOKWOOD
Foster, Andrew Thomas
  History Teacher

BRUNDIDGE
Harden, Martha Ross
  History Teacher/Senior Sponsor
Helms, Nellie Sue
  English Department Chairman

BUTLER
Mc Bride, Betty Singley
  7th/8th Grade Math/Sci Teacher
Mc Kenzie, Suzan Martin
  4th-6th Grade Science Teacher
Nicholson, Margret Lee
  English/Journalism Teacher

BYNUM
Howard, Susan Cheyne
  Third Grade Teacher

CALERA
Cox, Marcia Smith
  Elementary Teacher

CAMDEN
Powe, Judy Pate
  Mid Sch Mathematics Teacher

CARBON HILL
Kirkland, Virginia Faye
  Third Grade Teacher
Nix, Euple Lee Baughn
  Third Grade Teacher

CENTRE
Abbott, Patricia Johnson
  Language Arts Teacher
Davis, Sherron Price
  Second Grade Teacher
Gladden, Lucy Emmalene
  1st Grade Teacher
Russell, Tony F.
  8th Grade Amer His Teacher

CENTREVILLE
Banks, Tommie Foster
  English & French Teacher
Forrest, Christopher Morton
  Health/History Teacher/Coach
Luker, Deborah Hooks
  English Teacher
Tate, Jo Ann Chism
  7th/8th Grade English Teacher

CHATOM
Ganus, Nelda Jeanette
  Sixth Grade Math Teacher

CHEROKEE
Rutland, Patricia Moody
  Science Teacher

CHICKASAW
Scott, Floretta P.
  Mathematics Department Chm

CHILDERSBURG
Limbaugh, Patricia Pepper
  6th Grade Teacher

CITRONELLE
Kubina, Beverly Powell
  Mathematics Teacher

CLANTON
Mc Kee, Sheri West
  Math & Physics Teacher
Mims, Judy Melton
  Fourth Grade Teacher
Smith, Arthur Herbert
  Social Studies Teacher

CLEVELAND
Cone, Dawn Clifton
  Sixth Grade Teacher
Harris, Rhonette Lyles
  Second Grade Teacher

CLIO
Stokes, Pearl Shipman
  7th-8th Grades Math Teacher

COFFEEVILLE
Donald, Karen Bumpers
  Kindergarten Teacher

CORDOVA
Stanley, Jimmy W.
  Sixth Grade Science Teacher
Watkins, Tony Irvin
  7th/8th Grade Math Teacher

CRAGFORD
Burton, Donna Walker
  Social Studies Teacher
Harris, Josie Evans
  English Teacher
Mattox, Sue Miller
  Fourth Grade Teacher

CRANE HILL
Waldrep, Mary Lorene
  First/Second Grade Teacher

CULLMAN
Brown, Judy Friedrick
  German & Mathematics Teacher
Christopher, Donna A.
  English Department Chairman
Cornelius, Donna Netherton
  First Grade Teacher
Heatherly, Charlotte Jasper
  Health Occupations Ed Teacher
Johnson, Elaine Simpson
  English Teacher
Shavers, Suzanne Richter
  Second Grade Teacher

DADEVILLE
Truitt, Susan Miller
  First Grade Teacher
Waters, Vicky Rhodes
  Science Teacher

DANVILLE
Pirtle, Harold N.
  Social Studies Teacher/Coach

DE ARMANVILLE
Prince, Kathy S.
  Mathematics Teacher

DEATSVILLE
Camp, Elizabeth A.
  Physical Ed Teacher/Coach
Earnest, Jacquelyn Hodges
  English Teacher

DECATUR
Cowart, Carol Jordan
  First Grade Teacher
Evans, Elizabeth Ann Mason
  Mathematics/History Teacher
Felts, Adele Gotthelf
  History Teacher
Tepper, Winnie Barnes
  Third Grade Teacher
Thrasher, Thomas Newton
  Mathematics Teacher
Wallace, Terry White
  Mathematics Teacher
Whitson, Marilyn Murphree
  Second Grade Teacher

DEMOPOLIS
Nelson, Carolyn Vick
  5th Grade Teacher

DOLOMITE
Cobb, Deidre Thompson
  Sixth Grade Teacher
Stanley, Brenda Cash
  Fifth Grade Teacher

DORA
Carden, Nancy Thelma (Roberts)
  Fourth Grade Teacher
Potts, Joe Vaughn
  History Teacher

DOTHAN
Andrews, Sara Nell
  Social Studies Teacher
Ash, Stephanie Baird
  Math Teacher
Mauldin, Lynda King
  American History Teacher
Mc Lendon, Steve
  Band Director
Oglesby, Jacqueline Jackson
  Teacher
Smith, Nellie Mae
  HS Counselor
Spears, Doris Arnold
  Fourth Grade Teacher
Still, Beverly Bryan
  Eighth Grade English Teacher
Watson, Margaret Lee
  Guidance Counselor

DOUBLE SPRINGS
Crumpton, Rebecca A.
  Mathematics Teacher
Curtis, Deborah A.
  Science Teacher

EAST TALLASSEE
Cassady, Barbara Hutchinson
  First Grade Teacher

ECLECTIC
Barnette, Beverley Boner
  Sr HS English Teacher

ELKMONT
Smith, Amelia Morris
  Home Economics Teacher

ELMORE
Smith, Margaret S.
  Mathematics Dept Chairman

ENTERPRISE
Baker, John Leslie
  Choral Director
Grimes, Mabel P.
  Retired 2nd Grade Teacher
Harding, Richard G. Jr.
  Sixth Grade Teacher
Jones, Freda Ikner
  Jr HS Mathematics Teacher
Saliba, Linda Guarin
  Spanish Teacher
Torres, Marco Jr.
  Earth Science Teacher

EUTAW
Morrow, Julia S.
  Fourth Grade Teacher

EVERGREEN
Bell, Mary Stinson
  English Teacher

FAIRHOPE
Ansell, Samuel Tilden III
  English Department Chair
Northrop, Diane Lennicx
  First Grade Teacher
Threadgill, Ollie Rix Jr.
  Teacher

FAYETTE
Jacobs, Reba I.
  English/Psychology Teacher

FLORALA
Peoples, Patricia Laird
  French/English Teacher

FLORENCE
Barfield, Kenny Dale
  Principal/Academic Dean
Barfield, Nancy Cordray
  Counselor/Home Ec Teacher
Bullard, Carl Edward
  Special Ed Teacher/Coach
Champion, James Edward
  Band Director
Dearin, J. D.
  French Teacher
Eddins, Judy Lovelace
  Third Grade Teacher
Graham, Shirley Cypert
  Business Teacher
Hudson, Jo Ellen Thorne
  Fourth Grade Teacher
Kea, Suzie Brewer
  English Instructor
Mc Inish, Betty Mc Kee
  Third Grade Teacher
Monceret, Millie Jo J. Liles
  Retired English Teacher
Pettus, Paula C.
  Sixth Grade Lang Art Teacher
Tillery, Cynthia R.
  Science Teacher
Wynne, Barbara Minor
  Fifth Grade Teacher

FORT DEPOSIT
Mc Dowell, Rosia Hall
  5th-6th Grade Reading Teacher

FORT MC CLELLAN
Little, Judy Butler
  Sixth Grade Teacher
Moncrief, Earl Douglas
  Fifth Grade Teacher

FORT PAYNE
Dean, Aubie Mae
  Retired Teacher
Leslie, Angela Mc Clain
  Migrant Education Teacher

FOSTERS
Trice, Amy Ruth
  Fourth Grade Teacher
Walker, Beverly Mc Graw
  1st-4th Grade Math Teacher

FRISCO CITY
Howard, Florastine Williams
  Math Department Chairman
Lett, Rosa Stanton
  6th Grade Teacher
Wilkins, Joan Saucer
  Third Grade Teacher

FULTONDALE
Marable, Mary A. Mc Call-Black
  Teacher

FYFFE
Brisendine, Linda Johnson
  Amer History/Phys Ed Teacher
Ellis, Elizabeth Henderson
  Third Grade Teacher
Shipp, Nadine H.
  Home Economics Teacher

GADSDEN
Boyd, Bettye Smith
  Science Teacher
Cranford, Rodney Lynn
  HS Mathematics Teacher
Davis, C Michael
  Principal/Mathematics Teacher
Firestone, Mary Mattox
  Math Teacher
Flannigan, Patricia Ruth
  Third Grade Teacher
Gregory, Kathy Rains
  Sixth Grade Teacher
Gurley, Charlotte Diane Mc Ginnis
  5th Grade Teacher
Hood, Maryann Cavender
  Middle School English Teacher
King, Nina Marrs
  3rd Grade Teacher
Lancaster, Lanny E.
  English Teacher
Lee, Jo Ann Moore
  Counselor
Logan, Judy Eaves
  Vocational Business Ed Teacher
Longshore, June Usry
  Principal
Pass, Lynn Thompson
  Special Education Resource

Turner, Diane Mc Brayer
  Mid Sch Band Director

GARDENDALE
Brown, C. Dwight
  Choral Director
Dixon, Barbara Nanette
  History Teacher & Dept Chair
Little, Mary Ann
  Biology Teacher
Mc Cay, Mary L.
  American History Teacher
Murray, Debra Montgomery
  Physical Education Teacher

GENEVA
Davis, Alice
  5th Grade Teacher

GERALDINE
Morgan, Tamela Houston
  Kindergarten Teacher
Wade, Donna Dobbs
  Jr High English Teacher

GORDO
Cowart, Rhonda Windham
  Fourth Grade Teacher

GREENSBORO
Chasteen, Sydney W.
  English/Spanish Teacher
Kelly, Bobby Lejuene Sr.
  Science Department Chairperson
Watson, Jean Woods
  Science Teacher

GREENVILLE
Barganier, Susan Cumbie
  English Lit/Amer His Teacher
Cumbie, Bobby Pope
  Fourth Grade Teacher
Pierce, Linda Talley
  7th Grade Life Science Teacher
Smith, Judy Thomas
  English Teacher

GROVE HILL
Foster, Terry
  Elementary Principal
Lanier, Willie Deloris Calhoun
  Fourth Grade Teacher
Mc Intyre, Brenda Kelley
  Science Dept Head/Teacher
Slayton, Linda Lindsey
  Advanced Math Teacher
Smith, Patricia Fleming
  First Grade Teacher

GUNTERSVILLE
Davis, Bertha Bridges
  7th Grade Soc Stud Teacher
Robinson, Glenyce Landers
  Mathematics Teacher
Sharit, Dianne Johnston
  Third Grade Teacher

HACKLEBURG
Cole, Winell
  Third Grade Teacher
Lynch, Carolyn Williford
  History Teacher
Morris, Brenda Pace
  Third Grade Teacher

HALEYVILLE
Fortenberry, Imagene (West)
  3rd Grade Teacher
Howell, Jack Marion
  Fifth Grade Teacher
Nix, Elizabeth K.
  Science Teacher

HAMILTON
Mc Cray, Liza Bates
  Fourth Grade Teacher

HANCEVILLE
Cason, Marie Moore
  2nd Grade Teacher

HARTFORD
Galloway, Norma S.
  Business & Health Teacher

HARTSELLE
Cochran, John Robert
  US/World History Teacher

HARVEST
Cochran, Betty Bates
  7th/8th Soc Stud/Lit Teacher

HAYDEN
Bowers, Sara Williams
  Retired Third Grade Teacher
Skeen, Terri Heer
  5th Grade Soc Studies Teacher

HAZEL GREEN
Towry, Linda Williams
  First Grade Teacher

HEADLAND
Griggs, Durwood Winston Jr.
  Mathematics Department Chair

HIGDON
Reeves, Joan
  Teacher

HOMEWOOD
Maxwell, Linda Elaine
  Fourth Grade Teacher
Palmer, Anne Caldwell
  French Teacher

HUEYTOWN
Hulgan, Charles Harold
  Band Director

HUNTSVILLE
Behnken, Donna D.
  Second Grade Teacher
Benefield, Marilyn Coots
  Eighth Grade English Teacher
Berry, Christophr Edward
  Social Studies Dept Chair
Booker, Wilma Tibbs
  Teacher
Brown, Elizabeth Ferebee
  Third Grade Teacher
Buffaloe, Ann Elizabeth
  Third Grade Teacher
Bullard, Beverly Loeb
  Third Grade Teacher
Butler, Sandra Hudson
  3rd & 4th Grade Teacher
Curry, Barbara C.
  Business Teacher
Drake, Mary James
  English Teacher
Edwards, Debi Sue
  6th Grade Mathematics Teacher
Henderson, Shirley Comus
  English Department Chairman
Hereford, Geraldine C.
  Third Grade Teacher
Highfield, Thomas Frank
  8th Grade Science Teacher
Hill, Roberta A.
  Chemistry Department Chair
Kauffman, Linda Sellers
  Sixth Grade Teacher
Lawson, Margaret Ariail
  AP English/German Teacher
Lewis, Bruce
  Guidance Counselor
Mc Million, Patricia Madar
  Fifth Grade Teacher
Mitchell, Karen Tatman
  French Teacher/Dept Chair
Mitchell, Thomas Steven
  Band Director
Moorehead, Lawrence Edward Jr.
  7th Grade Math/English Teacher
Moran, Barbara Carol
  First Grade Teacher
Murphy, Jeffry Wright
  European History Teacher
Naatz, Thomas John
  Jr High History Teacher
Owen, Gayle Grissom
  8th Grade Lead Teacher
Palmer, Deborah Taylor
  French Teacher
Palmer, James Gordon
  English Department Chair
Peck, Carolyn Childers
  Choral Director
Powel, M. Beth
  Biology Teacher
Rice, Michael De Leon
  Band Director
Sobotka, Kathleen Havrilla
  7th Grade English Teacher
Sumners, Penny Lenoir
  History Teacher/Dept Chairman
Thorne, James O.
  Mathematics Department Chair
Wilson, Cleveland Thaddeus
  Sixth Grade Teacher
Wright, Ruth E.
  Retired Teacher

JACK
Storey, Peggy Fuller
  1st Grade Teacher

JACKSONVILLE
Hulsey, Jerri Odell
  English Teacher
Hyde, Mary Angel
  Retired 5th/6th Grade Teacher
Mc Fall, Peggy Green
  Sixth Grade Teacher
Padgett, Sharon A.
  Mathematics Teacher
Pettit, Roland Lamar
  Mathematics Teacher

Sanford, L. G. G.
  Biology Professor
Smith, Pamela Marie
  Band Director

JASPER
Kiker, Ruth Blaylock
  Teacher
Manasco, Bobbie Mc Adams
  Fifth Grade Teacher
Sartain, Kerry L.
  Science Department Chair
Steelmon, Kenneth Martin
  7th/8th Grade Science Teacher
Steelmon, Sue Smith
  Mathematics Teacher

JOPPA
Dodd, Estel Mullinax
  2nd/3rd Grade Teacher

LACEYS SPRING
Whisenant, Sandra Walker
  Sixth Grade Teacher

LAFAYETTE
Brooks, Glenda A.
  English Teacher
Heard, Mary Combs
  5th Grade Mathematics Teacher

LANETT
Simms, Tanya Robertson
  Third Grade Teacher

LEEDS
Dawson, Beverly Joan Smithey
  4th Grade Teacher

LEESBURG
Hooper, Charlotte E. Inman
  Teacher/Assistant Principal
Morgan, Nina Perry
  Second Grade Teacher
Teat, Terri St. Clair
  English Teacher

LEIGHTON
Pace, Barbara Akin
  English Teacher

LESTER
Reece, Martha Brackeen
  First Grade Teacher

LEXINGTON
Cole, Georgia Echols
  Third Grade Teacher

LINCOLN
Britt, Sadie S.
  Fourth Grade Teacher
Johnston, Darrell L.
  Physical Ed/AL History Teacher

LINDEN
Huckabee, Gloria D.
  English Teacher
Kirkham, Mildred Jones
  Mathematics Teacher

LINEVILLE
Cooper, Tom W.
  Biology Teacher
Young, Jim E.
  Fifth Grade Teacher

LOUISVILLE
Helms, Erma B.
  Fifth Grade Teacher

LUVERNE
Wise, Roger David
  Mathematics Teacher

LYNN
Longshore, Mary Lyle
  English Teacher

MADISON
Allen, Dorothy Blakely
  8th Grade/Algebra/Math Teacher

MAPLESVILLE
Cox, Joyce Tucker
  K-12th Grade Counselor
Stange, Jo Ann Payton
  English & Commercial Teacher

MC CALLA
Cooley, Louise Arthur
  Mathematics Teacher
Spencer, Janice Green
  Sixth Grade Teacher

MIDFIELD
Pinkney, Lois Bradley
  Fifth Grade Teacher
Roy, Lu Ann Jackson
  Science Teacher
Sington, Sharon Crenshaw
  Mathematics Department Chair

MIDLAND CITY

Tarrant, Neecie
English Teacher
York, Sara Ellen
Mathematics Teacher

MILLPORT

Shambry, Geraldine Morgan
English/Spanish Teacher

MOBILE

Belue, Michael Allen
Chorus Teacher/Bsktbl Coach
Boykin, Regina Taylor
English/Literature Teacher
Burgett, David Robert
Science Teacher
Coleman, Verna White
Fifth Grade Teacher
Eason, Tonia Thompson
English Teacher/Dept Chair
Estes, Bobbie N.
Fourth Grade Teacher
Fairley, Ethel D.
Fifth Grade Teacher
Hamilton, Margaret Newcomer
Advanced Placement Teacher
Heath, Oliver N. Jr.
Mathematics/Science Teacher
Jeffries, Elizabeth Warren
Mathematics Teacher
Middleton, Betty Flowers
Fifth Grade Teacher
Moore, Nell Brackett
Sixth Grade Teacher
Powell, Clark Albright
Eng/Creative Writing Teacher
Powell, Gertrude
Third Grade Teacher
Richardson, Dorthy Smith
8th Grade Soc Stud Teacher
Sawyer, Earline Jordan
English Department Chair
Stephenson, Yvonne Newton
English Teacher
Stokes, Lois D. Penny
ABE Teacher
Straughn, Leo Richard Arnold
Math Teacher/Soccer Coach
Sullivan, Mary Doolittle
6th Grade Sci & Rdng Teacher
Thomas, Aurelia
Mathematics Teacher
White, Susan Walker
5th Grade Teacher

MONROEVILLE

Kelly, Cheryl Sawyer
First Grade Teacher
Lambert, Jimmy D.
Assistant Principal
Stacey, Paula Vick
English Teacher

MONTGOMERY

Barnes, Geneva Mc Ghee
US History Teacher
Boddie, Shirley Lyons
Math Teacher/Dept Chair
Butland, Belinda Buchli
Teacher Learning Disabilities
Dodd, Sandra (Whitten)
English Teacher
Eaton, Peggy Rudolph
Algebra/Computer Teacher
Fischer, Barbara Bushman
English Teacher
Gilchrist, Michael Reed
Science Supervisor
Hawkins, Yolanda Williams
Kindergarten Teacher
Hodges, Mary Napier
Third Grade Teacher
Hollinger, Curtis L.
Director of Bands
Johnson, Dennis Alan
Band Director
Johnson, Wanda Andrews
Math Dept/Computer Teacher
Maryland, Anna Lucile Patterson
Language Arts Teacher
Norton, Sammye Ruth
Mathematics Department Chair
Parma, Lisa Marie
Math/Computer Teacher
Sebring, Gwendolyn Allen
5th Grade Teacher
Shofner, Rebecca Lee
Choral Teacher/Music Chair
Smilie, Tade Lampley
History Teacher
Smith, Wanda J.
Mathematics Teacher
Star, Dianne Barnes
Learning Disabilities Teacher
Walker, Michael J.
Assistant Principal

Ward, Nita Andress
Second Grade Teacher
Young, Marion
4th/5th Grade Teacher

MOODY

Voelzke, Joyce Barttram
German & English Teacher

MORRIS

Campbell, Paulette Barnwell
English Teacher
Sprayberry, Melvin J.
Science Teacher

MOUNDVILLE

Mc Clelland, Rickey Leroy
Jr HS Science Teacher
Young, Inell Brown
6th Grade Elementary Teacher

MOUNT HOPE

Britnell, Don Franklin
Agribusiness Teacher
Butler, Deborah Long
Kindergarten Teacher

MOUNT OLIVE

Hudgins, Lynn
4th-6th Grade English Teacher

MUSCLE SHOALS

Jackson, Doris De Vaney
Mathematics Teacher
Kelly, Laura Jean
Jr HS Mathematics Teacher
Trotter, Jewel Wallace
Fifth Grade Teacher
Wheeles, Juanita Russell
Eighth Grade Math Teacher

NAUVOO

Cain, Nancy West
First Grade Teacher
Otwell, Brenda Kaye
Fifth Grade Teacher

NEW HOPE

Pearson, Selena Pollard
Third Grade Teacher
Walls, Karen Nancy
7th/8th Grade Lit Teacher

NEW MARKET

Knight, Jimmy
11th Grade Amer His Teacher

NEWBERN

Eubanks, Bettye Hall
English/Health/Phys Ed Teacher
Floyds, Carolyn Wilson
6th Grade Teacher

NORTHPORT

Bambarger, Bettye Stone
Mathematics Teacher
Mabry, Janis Melton
Chemistry Teacher
Suttle, Willie Mae Shirley
First Grade Teacher
Taylor, Glenn E.
Mathematics Teacher/Coach

OAKMAN

Smith, Cathy Suzanne
English Teacher

ODENVILLE

Layman, Jimmie Estes
5th Grade Teacher
Whitten, Gail Mc Geoch
5th Grade Teacher
Whitten, Joseph Lee
Media Specialist

ONEONTA

Ford, Carolyn Diggs
Fifth/Sixth Grade Lang Teacher
Williams, Mildred Weaver
Science Teacher

OPELIKA

Hannah, Charles Austin
Tenth Grade English Teacher
Hester, Suzanne Hooton
First Grade Teacher
Logan, Elizabeth Noll
Art Teacher

OPP

Moore, Norma Gaddie
Guidance Counselor

OWENS CROSS ROADS

Roberts, Roland D.
Language/Soc Stud Teacher
Sisk, Donna Clark
Second/Third Grade Teacher

OXFORD

Barnett, Pamela Joyce
Eng/Typing/Accounting Teacher

Curvin, Linda G.
Third Grade Teacher
Davidson, Connie M.
5th Grade Lang Art Teacher
Martin, Norma S.
English Teacher

OZARK

Byars, Dena Gibson
Science Teacher
Mikoda, Roslyn Anne
Second Grade Teacher
Schroeder, June Faulk
8th Grade Eng Teacher

PELHAM

Reynolds, Mary Wallace Byrd
English & Drama Teacher
Rigsby, Sallye Johnson
English Teacher
Walker, Linda Miller
English Teacher
Walls, Faye Drummond
AP American History Teacher

PELL CITY

Arnett, Jan Mc Allister
7th Grade Science Teacher
Harmon, Vicki Darough
Fifth Grade Teacher
Mc Carty, Mary S.
Mathematics Teacher
Threatt, Peggy F.
5th Grade Teacher
Winslett, Fred N.
Math Teacher

PHENIX CITY

Hudson, Maggie Jumper
Fourth Grade Teacher

PHIL CAMPBELL

Swinney, Jo Ann Wilson
Chapter I Reading Teacher

PINSON

Swann, Randall Harold
Drafting Teacher

PISGAH

Mc Fall, Daniel Scott
Advanced Curr Math Teacher
Mc Kenzie, Martha Faye
2nd Grade Teacher

PLANTERSVILLE

Mohprasit, Dianne Carter
History/Computer Teacher

PLEASANT GROVE

Johnson, Paula Parker
3rd Grade Teacher
Phillips, Barbara Hardie
American History Teacher

PRATTVILLE

Cranfield, Susan Bateman
English Department Chair
Scott, Nancy Keeton
7th Grade Soc Stud Teacher
Warnock, Glory Dean (Powell)
English/Science Teacher

PRICHARD

Baggett, Allen
Soc Stud/Amer His Teacher
Miller, Judith Bishop
Fourth Grade Teacher
Robbins, Linda De Witt
Counselor
Showers, Nadine Tolbert
Mathematics Teacher

RAINSVILLE

Ayers, William H.
Fifth Grade Teacher
Etherton, De Layne Newsome
Sixth Grade Teacher
Horton, Sarah Burks
First Grade Teacher
Peck, Martha Kirk
Third Grade Teacher

RAMER

Houlton, Janet Hannon
7th-8th Grade English Teacher

RED LEVEL

Kelley, Fred Jonathan
Science Teacher
Purnell, Michael
Math/Sci/Soc Stud Teacher
Wright, Rosayln C.
Kindergarten Teacher

ROANOKE

Henson, Philip Gerald
6th Grade Science Teacher

ROCKFORD

Griffin, Donald Lewis
Agribusiness Teacher
Hodge, Kay Blair
Counselor
Jacobs, Troy Max
Secondary Social Sci Teacher

ROGERSVILLE

Godsey, Linda Earnest
Fourth Grade Teacher

SALEM

Fields, Nancy French
Science Teacher/Dept Chair

SAMSON

Rials, Billie June
Vocational Business Teacher
Smith, Billie June
Fourth Grade Teacher
Wikel, Carol Iris
Fifth Grade Teacher

SCOTTSBORO

Patrick, Sandra F.
5th Grade Teacher
Stewart, Joanne Patterson
Third Grade Teacher

SEALE

Stringfellow, Ruthie H.
Health Occupations Instructor

SECTION

Hughes, Kathy Ann
Science Teacher
Stringer, Jan Webster
Amer History/English Teacher

SELMA

Adams, Dorothy Peoples
Government/Economics Teacher
Cook, Kenneth Herschel
7th-8th Grad Soc Stud Teacher
Grider, Carrie De Yampert
Home Economics Teacher
Jackson, Maldonia
English Teacher
Kelly, Teresa Baker
English Teacher
Ketton, Gloria Lawrence
K-6th Grade At-Risk Teacher
Morgan, Vanessa Goodwin
Kindergarten Teacher
Poole, Elaine Zetta
Third Grade Teacher
Redd, Patricia Moore
Assistant Principal
Scott, Julia Mc Intyre
Principal
Smitherman, Lynda Cooper
English Teacher
Twilley, Judy Kirk
Speech/History Teacher

SEMMES

Davis, Linda Powell
Algebra I Teacher
Davis, Rachael Brannon
Science Teacher
Ethridge, Iris Gay
Classroom Teacher
Harris, Aubrey Eugene
Assistant Principal
Hicks, Virginia Waggoner
1st Grade Teacher
Hill, Linda West
Science Dept Chm/Chemistry
Neal, Marie H.
Literature Teacher

SHORTER

Holmes, Ruth Richardson
Teacher
Sullen, Janet Thomas
Language Arts Dept Chair

SILAS

Mc Queen, Dorthy Turner
8th Grade Math/Soc St Teacher

SMITHS

Floyd, Bettye Byrd
English Teacher
Williams, Ronella Lazenby
Fifth Grade Teacher

SOMERVILLE

Estes, David Wayne
Algebra 1/Geometry Teacher
Latham, Andrew J.
Teacher/Coordinator
Moore, Ronnie Mitchell
Assistant Principal

STAPLETON

Thomas, Steve D.
6th Grade Teacher/Principal

STEVENSON

Blevins, James Raymond
Business Education Teacher
Moore, Sheila Gail
English Teacher
Thomas, Rubye Troxell
Science Teacher

SULLIGENT

Buckley, Lenora Green
Retired Jr HS English Teacher

SWEET WATER

Conner, Anne Rembert
Kindergarten Teacher
Glass, Nancy Caplinger
5/6 Grade Math Teacher
Hyman, Luanne K.
9th/10th Grade English Teacher

SYLACAUGA

Adair, Debbie Pearce
4th Grade Teacher
Andrews, Judy Craddock
Science Dept Chair/Bio Teacher
Brown, Laura Klinner
English Teacher/Academic Coach
Culp, Danny Ray
Fourth Grade Teacher
Hart, Inez Askew
Math Teacher
Ingram, Susan Patton
Science Teacher
Snyder, Janice Bussie
Third Grade Teacher

SYLVANIA

Townson, Patsy J.
Spanish Teacher

TALLADEGA

Adams, Shelley Brooks
Third Grade Teacher
Hinton, Evelyn S.
Coordinating/Resource Teacher
Patterson, Joyce Ann
Tenth Grade English Teacher

TARRANT

Hobby, Linda H.
Kindergarten Teacher

THEODORE

Hill, Nancy Schear
French Teacher
Owens, Henry Cleamon
Sixth Grade Teacher

TONEY

Ibezim, Hedy Smith
8th Grade Science Teacher

TOWNLEY

Pike, Ruby Crump
Fourth Grade Teacher

TOXEY

Mosley, Patricia Roberts
Sixth Grade Teacher

TRINITY

Crump, Joann Whisenant
First Grade Teacher
Webster, Doris Perry
7th-9th Grades Counselor

TROY

Hixon, Betty Dickinson
History Teacher

TRUSSVILLE

Hara, Monita G.
Teacher of Hearing Impaired
Mc Intosh, Hal Winston
Soc Stud/Theatre Arts Teacher

TUSCALOOSA

Byrne, Richard Porter
Teacher, Science Dept Chairman
Cummins, Curtis Leigh Jr.
Earth Science Teacher
Fletcher, Erin Briggs
7th Grade Soc Stud Teacher
Jones, Alma Wyatt
Social Studies Teacher
Lee, Theba Hodges
Drama Teacher
Martin, Linda Fleenor
Fourth Grade Teacher
Ouderkirk, Kim Audrey
Science Department Chair
Perteet, Sandra Plenty
English Teacher
Richardson, Jocqueline Killings
Choral Music Teacher
Southern, James Terry
English Teacher

TUSCUMBIA

Allan, Mary Ann (Mackey)
Science/English Teacher

TUSKEGEE
Matthews, Bettye Ruth
  6th Grade Teacher/Sci Dept Chm

TUSKEGEE INSTITUTE
Graham, Laura Williams
  Teacher

UNIONTOWN
May, Bessie Hill
  Social Studies Dept Chair

VALLEY
Booker, Mae Julia
  Sixth Grade Math/Sci Teacher
Huguley, Elsie Wanda
  AP English Teacher/Counselor
Meadows, Gail T.
  Assistant Principal

VERBENA
Pelham, Romie Mc Daniel
  Social Studies Teacher

VERNON
Abston, Carol Ruffin
  5th Grade Teacher
Arnold, James Austin
  Band Director
Hudson, Beverly Sledge
  4th Grade Teacher

VINEMONT
Haynes, Heidi Smith
  English/French Teacher

WARRIOR
Davis, Celia Mc Clellan
  5th/6th Grade Teacher
Hardiman, Michael Kirby
  7th/8th Grade English Teacher

WEAVER
Deerman, Van Michael
  Eng/Physical Education Teacher
Shipp, Francus Ruth
  Biology/Physiology Teacher

WEDOWEE
Bunn, Betty Taylor
  English Teacher

WEST BLOCTON
Braxton, Linda Sherer
  Third Grade Teacher
Burr, Esther Saunders
  English Teacher
Major, Clarence Lee
  History Teacher
Martin, Dorothy Ayers
  Business Education Teacher
Williamson, Joan Brewer
  English Teacher

WETUMPKA
Crum, Theresa Lee
  Biology Teacher
Mills, Pamela Bolton
  6th Grade Teacher
Pendergast, Sallie Brown
  Fourth Grade Teacher

WHISTLER
Greene, Brenda Chestang
  Fifth Grade Teacher

WILMER
Alsup, Sarah Williams
  Kindergarten Teacher
Calderone, Nancy Richardson
  Second Grade Teacher
Williamson, Carolyn Bedsole
  Kindergarten Teacher

WOODLAND
Burns, Lucille Minnifield
  First Grade Teacher
Cantrell, Sylvia Jean
  5th/6th Grade Math Teacher
Layman, Hattie Cynthia
  Science Department Teacher
Perrigin, Barbara Wallace
  English Teacher

WOODVILLE
Givens, Ronald Lee
  Assistant Principal
Simmons, Gillie Gilmore
  Sixth Grade Teacher

YORK
Edmonds, Linda W.
  Science Department Chair
Vaughn, Nell Jones
  Fourth Grade Teacher
Watkins, Ruth Cocke
  Retired

ALASKA

ANCHORAGE
Andersen, John Willy
  6th Grade Teacher
Arians, H Arthur
  Biology Teacher
Benson, Patricia Cameron
  6th Grade Elementary Teacher
Chesler, Karen L. (Rady)
  Social Studies Teacher
Decker, Marilyn Louise
  Foreign Lang Dept Head-French
Dexter, Sondra Diane
  Science/Health Teacher
Duvall, Judith M.
  1st Grade Teacher
Fellenberg, James E.
  Technology Teacher
Gaal, Zoltan Jr.
  7th/8th Grade Science Teacher
Grabowski, Kathy Lundahl
  Fifth Grade Teacher
Horton, Garry Curninza
  Mathematics Teacher
Hosken, Melba Prator
  First Grade Teacher
Johnstone, Mary K.
  3rd/4th Grade Teacher
Kauffman, Patricia Wolfe
  6th Grade Teacher
Little, Del Doucet
  Mathematics Teacher
Mc Clay, Bruce Edward
  His/Religion/Eng/Sci Teacher
Montgomery, Michael Joe
  Physical Education Teacher
Sabato, Michael Joseph
  7th Grade Science Teacher
Sanders, Jo Mc Connell
  German/Russian Teacher
Schmidt, Jan A.
  6th Grade Teacher
Snowden, Elaine W.
  Lang Art Teacher/Consultant
Stevens, Kathryn W.
  First-Second Grade Teacher
Wright, Glenn A.
  Language Art Dept Chairperson

DELTA JUNCTION
Aillaud, Cindy Lou Virginia (Petett)
  4th/5th Grade Teacher
Beito, Howard Dean
  Social Studies/Phys Ed Teacher
Mc Cowan, Michael O'Melia
  Sixth Grade Teacher

EAGLE RIVER
Johnson, Clifford F.
  Science Department Chair
Lepak, Norma Griffith
  5th Grade Teacher
Mundy, Twyla G.
  Math Teacher

ELMENDORF AFB
Jeffryes-Rose, Billie Scott
  5/6 Grade Teacher

ENGLISH BAY
Kriens, Jill Anne Churchill
  4th-8th Grade Teacher

FAIRBANKS
Colling, Mark Eugene
  6th Grade Teacher
Hull, Linda Du Puis
  Art Teacher
O'Bryan, Virginia Lois
  English Department Chair
Olsen, Robert Stephen
  Orchestra/Choir Director
Purcell, John Christopher
  Reading Specialist
Saiz, Michele Loban
  Junior HS Science Teacher

FORT WAINWRIGHT
Austin, Terri L.
  Sixth Grade Teacher

GLENNALLEN
Goozen, Barbara
  German/Mathematics Teacher

KAKE
Loges, La Vella Ann (Schultz)
  Eng/Sci/Home Ec Teacher

KENAI
Besch, Dorothy Ruth
  3rd Grade Teacher
Dixon, Patrick Stewart
  Photography Teacher

KETCHIKAN
Knapp, Donald E.
  Social Science/Drama Teacher
Ulrich, David Richard
  High School Generalist

KLAWOCK
Chapman, G. Diane Trotter
  Substitute Teacher

KODIAK
Nuttall, Jane E.
  Third Grade Teacher
Smedley, Patricia Zaveson
  Social Studies Teacher

NOME
Thomas, Teresa E.
  HS Business Education Teacher

PALMER
Alexander, Susan Katrin
  English Teacher
Roper, Ronald Wayne
  Language Art Teacher

SITKA
Hammons, Gayle L.
  English Teacher
Mc Gregor, Robert G.
  6th Grade Science/Math Teacher

SOLDOTNA
Mc Guiness, Sherry G.
  Business Education Teacher
Nolden, Patrick Daniel
  PC & Basic Biology Teacher
Stenal, John L.
  Biology Teacher
Waisanen, Richard A.
  Department Chair/Counselor

SUTTON
Brown, Carol Bruton
  5th/6th Grade Teacher

VALDEZ
Garrison, Larry Gaines
  Rdng/Creative Writing Teacher
Richardson, Steven Paul
  Fourth Grade Teacher
Taylor, William Andrew
  Science Teacher

WASILLA
Crabbs, Catherine Louise
  7th Grade Language Art Teacher
Kabatznick, Joel Max
  English Teacher
Mc Mullen, M. Sharon
  Reading/English Teacher

ARIZONA

AJO
Lopez, Leonard M.
  Sixth Grade Teacher/HS Coach

APACHE JUNCTION
Rye, Judy Celine
  Fifth Grade Teacher

ASH FORK
Tesdahl, Jill Kristine
  Phys Ed Teacher/Asst Principal

AVONDALE-GOODYEAR
Schilling, Dawn Diane
  English Teacher

BULLHEAD CITY
Fermon, Benjamin Franklin
  US/Arizona History
Greene, Kevin Robert
  English Teacher

CAMP VERDE
Mc Intrye, John Thomas
  High School Art Teacher
White, David Michael
  5th Grade Teacher

CASA GRANDE
Boone, Libby Sue
  Sixth Grade Teacher
Fossen, Susan Francyne
  English Teacher
Hindman, Paul D.
  Mathematics Teacher
Ivins, George Anthony
  English Teacher
Rowe, La Verne Marcy
  Retired Elementary Teacher

CAVE CREEK
Dalton, Paula Schoonover
  8th Grade Science Teacher

CHANDLER
Martin, Jeffrey Jay
  General Music, Band Teacher
Peterson, Stephanie Josephine
  Mathematics Teacher
Rossiter, Daphne Anne
  Mathematics Teacher
Weiss, Iris Gershon
  English Teacher

CHINO VALLEY
Shoop, Scott Lane
  English Department Chair

COTTONWOOD
Hodous, Kimberly Tucker
  History Teacher
Kirby, Kit Chadwick
  Math Teacher

DOUGLAS
Halverson, Jack E.
  Science Teacher

DUNCAN
Gaddy, Connie S.
  2nd Grade Teacher

EHRENBERG
Fahy, Leslie Lein
  Third Grade Teacher

ELOY
Bellafiore, John Albert
  Mathematics/Civics Teacher
Brassea, Nancy Cramer
  Fifth Grade Teacher
Dean, Howard Stokes
  Soc Stud Teacher/Athletic Dir

FLAGSTAFF
Brown, Thomas Allen
  Math Teacher
Campbell, Barbara Frances
  Sixth Grade Teacher
Heal, Helen Ortega
  English Teacher
Phillips, William Lee
  Social Studies Teacher
Riddle, Douglas Stephen
  Choral Music Instructor

FLORENCE
Smith, Shirley Lynch
  Second Grade Teacher

FORT DEFIANCE
Jasmer, Alice Guyton
  Mathematics Teacher

FORT HUACHUCA
Iachetti, Rose Maria Anne
  Fourth Grade Teacher

GILA BEND
Tavernaro, Gerald E.
  Classroom Instructor

GILBERT
Mc Namara, John Robert
  Social Studies Teacher

GLENDALE
Balthazor, Roberta I.
  3rd Grade Teacher
Barnes, Christopher Raymond
  Sci Teacher/Ftbl & Bsbl Coach
Brewka, Nattalie Lakos
  Junior High Teacher
Brubeck, Judith Ann
  Physical Education Teacher
Cota, Lisa Foley
  Amer History/Sociology Teacher
Coughanour, Sara Ann Hall
  English/Journalism Teacher
Houpt, Diane Lee
  English/Journalism Teacher
Jensen, Sara O.
  Second Grade Teacher
Rosenbaum, Mary Louise (Quam)
  Second Grade Teacher
Smith, Emmett Ray
  English Teacher/Coach
Spencer, Madge Anderson
  Third Grade Teacher

GLOBE
Harder, Romy Deitch
  English Teacher
Salas, Mary (Neufelder)
  Fourth Grade Teacher

HOLBROOK
Sands, Dan J.
  English Teacher

KAYENTA
Hart, Orrin Michael
  Student at Risk/Dept Chm
Shewmaker, Joyce A.
  Sci Dept Chm/Chemistry Teacher

KEARNY
Ponwith, Mark C.
  English Teacher

KINGMAN
Burden, Jack William
  English/History Teacher
Dolan, Teresa J.
  Junior HS Gifted Teacher
Kocher, Stephen L.
  Arts & Crafts Instructor
Minkler, Sandra Lynn
  Phys Ed & Home Arts Teacher

LAKE HAVASU CITY
Hollis, Joyce Eileen
  English Teacher
Malay, Gail T.
  Third Grade Teacher
Mc Afee, Susan J.
  Language Arts Teacher

LAKESIDE
Oliver, William Herverus
  Mathematics Teacher
Peterson, Judy Renee
  English Teacher/Dept Chair

LITCHFIELD PARK
Lock, Jo Ellyn Bidner
  4th Grade Teacher
Ross, Judy L.
  7th/8th Grade Teacher

MANY FARMS
Gruschow, Margaret
  Bio/Chem/Physics Teacher

MARANA
Beach, Carol A. Baker
  Fifth Grade Teacher
Coxon, Robin C.
  English Department Chair

MESA
Bischel, Leonard F.
  Science Teacher
Coleman, Vicky Lynn
  Fourth Grade Teacher
Cox, Dale Soren
  History/English Teacher
Frankel, Carole
  Mathematics Teacher
Hardert, Linda Blalock
  Extended Learning Prgm Teacher
Haws, Kayle E.
  Math Teacher
Mc Clellan, Michael Charles
  Eng Teacher
Mc Clure, D. Lance
  6th Grade Teacher
Mc Eachen, Avis R.
  ELP Teacher
Quick, Kevin Foster
  Biology Teacher

NOGALES
Barajas, Maria Lourdes
  6th Grade Teacher & Coord
Clark, Marcia Ivory
  Second Grade Teacher
Jones, Mary Longoria
  Third Grade Teacher
Mayer, Celina Karam
  Second Grade Teacher
Morales, Nancy Lee
  Home Ec Teacher

PAGE
Shorthair, Betty Barlow
  Business Teacher

PARADISE VALLEY
Swingler, Michael G.
  Upper School Science Teacher

PATAGONIA
Cardieri, Alexander Mario
  Music Teacher
Fagergren, Peter Jones
  Science Department Chair

PEORIA
Corrigan, Wendy Cotton
  HS Mathematics Teacher
Dye, Carol Lee (Horton)
  7th/8th Grade Reading Teacher
Gradillas, Gilbert F.
  6th Grade Teacher
Mc Guire, Eileen R.
  Learning Center Director
Rosalez, Alex L.
  Computer Teacher
Rosenbaum, Mitchell D.
  Social Studes Department Chair

PHOENIX
Acosta, Jesse J.
  Principal

PHOENIX (cont)
Andrade, Jeanette Marie
  Fourth Grade Teacher
Barnard, Kathryn Ann
  Dance/Business Teacher
Belden, Stanley L.
  6th Grade Teacher
Corbin, Neil W.
  Biology Teacher
Cornell, Paul Robert
  Mathematics Dept Chair
Cox, Frank William
  Spanish Teacher
Davenport, Alena Clark
  Mathematics Teacher
Engel, Marlene Marie (Cleland)
  First/Second Grade Teacher
Forcier, Helene F.
  English Teacher
Frazier, Janet Frances Lynch
  Retired Kindergarten Teacher
Garman, Howard D.
  Jr High Teacher/Admin Asst
Grandinetti, Barbara Ann
  Teacher of Gifted Lang Art
Harris, Don F.
  7th-8th Grade Teacher Gifted
Hepting, Karen Byram
  9th-11th Grade English Teacher
Hughes, Robert Edward
  5th Grade Teacher
Jones, Paula Laraine
  Science Teacher
Lambie, Robert Brooks
  Head Ftbl Coach/Math Teacher
Lowery, Jacqueline Lee
  Physical Education Teacher
Lutz, Tom V.
  7th Grade Science Teacher
Macrina, Denise Rose
  7th-8th Grade Lang Art Teacher
Mercer, Maryilyn Sylvester
  Fifth Grade Teacher
Metzger, John Mathias
  Mathematics Teacher
Miller, Steve
  Mathematics Teacher
Mooningham, Laura J.
  Sr English/Journalism Teacher
Myers, Bertha
  Teaching/Asst Principal
Palsma, Mary (Jacobson)
  Math Dept Chair & Teacher
Satton, Saralou (Combs)
  Second Grade Teacher
Schneider, Elaine Rose OSF
  Eighth Grade Teacher
Sharp, Bruce William
  Mathematics Teacher
Shelton, Sammie Lee
  4th Grade Teacher/Chairman
Shepp, Claire Canny
  6-8th Grade Math Teacher
Sherrill, Jean W. (Williams)
  Jr HS Teacher
Smiley, Diana Gayle
  Fourth Grade Teacher
Starks, Rosalyn June
  Physical Education Teacher
Walton, Claudia Mae Edwards
  Marketing/DECA Teacher
Zelinski, Paula Ann
  8th Grade Mathematics Teacher

PICACHO
Carino, Richard S.
  Migrant Teacher/Fed Coord

PIMA
Anger, Shirley Alder
  3rd Grade Teacher
Larson, Lynn J.
  5th Grade Teacher

PRESCOTT
Groom, Carla Ann (Rastello)
  Fifth Grade Teacher

QUEEN CREEK
Robinson, Amy Lynn
  History/Science Teacher

SAFFORD
Cranch, Cedric Daryl
  Reading/English Teacher

SAHUARITA
Miller, Leonard M.
  Mathematics/Computer Chair
Shiba, Katherin Lynn
  Chapter I Teacher
Stautz, Daniel F.
  English Teacher

SAINT JOHNS
Borg, Andrea Jean (Billy)
  English/Speech/Drama Teacher

SCOTTSDALE
Albertson, Kenneth A.
  Sci Teacher/Math Dept Chair
Cozort, Elden Mann
  Mathematics Teacher
Fitzsimmons, John Thomas
  Social Studies Teacher
Lamer, Joseph
  US History/ESL His Teacher
Mc Clure, Sandie Ruth
  6th Grade Teacher
Ortiz, Lilly Ortega
  Teacher
Thompson, Lois Drinkwater
  Mathematics Teacher

SEDONA
Adams, Eve
  Mathematics Teacher

SELIGMAN
Curley, Joanne C.
  Kindergarten Teacher
La Chat, Robert Joel
  Science Dept Chair

SHOW LOW
Lopeman, Linda Rae
  Dept Chair/Vocational Dir

SIERRA VISTA
Askew, Thomas Milton
  Principal/Teacher
Bealer, Jonathan Miles
  Science Department Chair
Gucciardo, Permilla Covington
  Retired Eng Teacher
Hudson, Laura Lorene
  8th Grade Science Teacher

SNOWFLAKE
Cocks, Margaret C.
  Third Grade Teacher
Evans, Dennis Michael
  Principal
Farr, Lois Whiting
  Teacher Lang Arts Vice Prin

STANFIELD
Kunz, Pamela
  2nd Grade Teacher
Whelchel, Gary L.
  Phys Ed Teacher, Dean Students

TEMPE
Benedict, Deborah Anklam
  English Teacher
Edington, Darl E.
  Jr HS Mathematics Teacher
Glass, Steven Michael
  Business Teacher
Green, Janet Cavett
  Math Teacher
Hall, Gary O.
  Business Department Chairman
Helm, Michelle I.
  Science Teacher
Jimenez, Olivia M. T. G.
  Eng/Span/Jrnlsm Teacher
Jude, Gretchen Wolfe
  High School English Teacher
Mack, Polly Annmarie
  1st Grade Teacher
Mac Lean, Mary Ann (Duffy)
  6th Grade Teacher
Mirizio, Frank P.
  History Teacher
Newton, Charles Willard
  Journalism/Eng/Photo Teacher
Pease, Sophia Andrychuk
  Sixth Grade Teacher
Peshall, Deborah Duncan
  1st Grade Teacher
Shahan, Gary B.
  Social Studies Teacher
Taysom, Douglas Lee
  Science Teacher
Thompson, Doris E. Young
  Business Dept Chairperson
Veeh, Alan Bruce
  Social Studies Teacher
Whitehead, Sharon S. (Young)
  Secondary Mathematics Teacher
Wood, Leo Milton
  Chemistry Instructor
Zinke, Laura Alonso
  Spanish Teacher

THATCHER
Montierth, Constance Overall
  First Grade Teacher

TOMBSTONE
Beaty, Gloria King
  Third Grade Teacher

TUBA CITY
Calsoyos, Judith Ann
  Language Art/Lit Teacher

Hatchett, Louise Glasby
  First Grade Teacher
Matthews, Ronald Burdett
  5th Grade Teacher
Schmidt, Stephen
  Science Teacher/Dept Chair
Tuchawena, Eddie E.
  Mathematics Teacher

TUCSON
Anderson, Peter John
  English Teacher
Angulo, Cecilia Patricia
  2nd Grade Teacher
Applebee, Terri Korman
  5th Grade Teacher
Bejarano, Michael Anthony
  Social Studies Teacher
Bohme, Virgnia Ann
  Mathematics Teacher
Campsen, Theresa Estrada
  Counselor
Close, Grace Ann
  English Teacher
Cossel, Donna Ann
  Fifth Grade Teacher
Cummings, Sharyl Virginia
  Mathematics Teacher
Day, Gloria Jeanne
  Music Specialist
Donnelly, Robert Lowell
  Science Teacher
Eggen, Paulann K.
  5th Grade Teacher
Espinoza, Kathleen Fannin
  Physical Education Teacher
Figueroa, Rosemarie Armijo
  Business Teacher
Foust, Ruth Ellen (Brumit)
  English Teacher
Fregoso, Manuel Jesus
  Soc Stud/Bi-ling Teacher
Freiman, Lela Linch
  Drama Teacher
Friedman, Kathleen Maher
  Earth Science Teacher
Groman, Jean Baugh
  Advisor
Hess, John Lawrence
  Chemistry Teacher
Hopkins, Pamela Lee
  English Teacher
Kershner, Paul Russell
  HS Physical Education Teacher
Kirk, Sarah Elaine
  English Teacher
Kotofskie, James W.
  English/Humanities Teacher
Krompasky, Renate Maria
  Principal
Leek, Richard John
  Orchestra Teacher
Matz, Henry Richard
  Chemistry/Phys Science Teacher
Montgomery, Rosalie Mertz
  Resource Teacher
Motley, Anna Ashlock
  Substitute Teacher
Olivas, Eduardo R.
  6th Grade Teacher
Parra, Dorothy Lee Holmberg
  Language Art/Soc Stud Teacher
Ratajczak, John Michael
  Industrial Arts Teacher
Reed, Carolyn Wise
  Fifth Grade Teacher
Reff, Steven M.
  Economics Instructor
Rhodes, Solveig Haugsjaa
  World Geography Teacher
Roberts, J. Berry
  Math Dept Chair/Teacher
Saxon, Vicki Kidwell
  COE/Business Education Teacher
Smith, Carol Ann
  Band/Orchestra Director
Sobkoviak, Carol Jo
  English Dept Chair/Teacher
Starr, Eileen Kagan
  Elementary Teacher
Thomas, Lorelyn Garbini
  5th Grade Teacher
Treiber, Alice Powers
  Third Grade Teacher
Vallentine, Roxann Elizabeth
  Mathematics Teacher
Velasco, Edidtsa R.
  Spanish/Mathematics Teacher
Vermillion, Greg J.
  Second Grade Teacher
Wacker, Ronnie Louise
  4th Grade Teacher
Wolpa, Brenda Ann
  Chemistry Teacher

WENDEN
Tillpaugh, Herbert Allan
  Head Teacher

WHITERIVER
Pahl, Randall Lee
  Mathematics Department Chair
Voss, David John
  Social Studies Chair

WILLCOX
Patterson, Michael Donald
  Mathematics/Science Teacher

WINDOW ROCK
Egnatuk, Mary Ann
  Junior High School Teacher

WINSLOW
Essary, Mack Ray
  Jr High Science-Dept Chairman

YOUNG
Sheffer, William Albert
  Vocational Agriculture Teacher

YUMA
Arviso, Ronnie Joseph
  7th/8th Mathematics Dept Chair
Badgley, Judeth Birdwell
  Learning Consultant
Breck, Barbara Askew
  7th Grade Teacher
Coffman, Louise Winward
  English Teacher
Hickok, Alice Marie
  Reading Specialist
Johnston, Cheryl Curry
  Mathematics Teacher
Laguna, Billy N.
  Health Teacher
Lichtenberg, Gloria Blazvick
  Fourth Grade Teacher
Meharg, Carrie Noland
  Chemistry Teacher
Mota, Edmundo
  7th Grade History Teacher
Neece, Anna M.
  6th Grade Teacher
Pancrazi, Michael J.
  Health Teacher
Patterson, Constance Lee
  Scndry English/Drama Teacher
Raebel, Martin Glen
  Mathematics Dept Chair
Schmidgall, Cary Prince
  Kindergarten Teacher
Strickland, Carol Ann
  Business Teacher
Thomas, D. R. Bob
  Mathematics Teacher

ARKANSAS

ALMA
Blasingame, Rosemary Christello
  Earth Science Teacher

ASHDOWN
Gentry, William Lechliter
  Business Education Teacher
Mc Kay, Mary Frances
  English & Art Teacher
Miller, Kay Smith
  Second Grade Teacher
Pennington, Dixie Goza
  History Teacher

ATKINS
Hays, Betsy Bauer
  GT Teacher/Coordinator
Warren, Mary Coffman
  Third Grade Teacher

AUGUSTA
Davis, Charlene Peebles
  Retired Teacher

BARTON
Zachary, Nina (Chicouras)
  Social Studies Dept Chair

BATESVILLE
Edwards, Cathy Reynolds
  Second Grade Teacher
Spurlin, David L.
  Consultant

BEEBE
Drennan, Ninette Burns
  Second Grade Teacher

BENTON
Garrett, Patricia Ann (Van Winkle)
  Counselor/Secondary School
Mc Adow, Sherrie Fite
  Mathematics/Physics Teacher

BENTONVILLE
Harmon, Jane E. Shores
  Third Grade Teacher
Hayes, Donald Paul
  Calculus/Physics Teacher
Witcher, Cheryle Turner
  Earth Science Teacher

BERGMAN
Howard, Corky
  Computer Coordinator

BLEVINS
Krudwig, Geraldine Zachry
  English/French/Speech Teacher
Ward, Catherine
  Substitute Teacher

BLYTHEVILLE
Harris, Linda Gilmore
  5th Grade Teacher

BOONEVILLE
Card, Geraldine Louise
  Gifted & Talented Coordinator
Hocott, Jerry Dale
  Mathematics Department Chair

BRANCH
Kirby, Jimmy Ray
  Mathematics Teacher

BRIGGSVILLE
Hill, Brenda G.
  Voc Business Teacher/Cnslr

BRINKLEY
Wilkins, Helen Jennings
  First Grade Teacher

BROOKLAND
George, Marie Ann (General)
  Jr/Sr High Art Teacher
Montgomery, Diane E.
  Teacher of Gifted & Talented
Shelton, Claudia Province
  Fourth Grade Teacher

BRYANT
Fugitt, Donna Riley
  Science Teacher
Hearn, Jerry B.
  Physical Science Teacher
Pennington, Judith Dianne
  9th Grade Civics Teacher
Smith, Mary Miller
  Gifted/Talented Facilitator

CABOT
Bell, Dorothy Ann
  Span/Amer Government Teacher

CAMDEN
Beard, Shelia Jones
  Mathematics Teacher
Blair, Omie Tidwell
  Counselor
Butler, Sonja Darby
  Fourth Grade Teacher
Johnson, Peggy Johnson
  Third Grade Teacher
Lowery, Donna Thomas
  4th Grade Teacher
Quarles, Rodney Deane
  Soc Stud Dept Chair/Teacher
Tolley, Betty Ruby
  Chairperson Foreign Language
Webb, John Clark
  Band Director

CARLISLE
Kittler, William H.
  Junior Science Teacher
Treadway, George Edward
  Math Teacher/Dept Chair

CASA
Holliman, Sherry Rainey
  K-12th Grade Resource Teacher

CAVE CITY
Edwards, Martha Amos
  Kindergarten Teacher

CEDARVILLE
Cottrell, Douglas E.
  4th Grade Instructor
Pendergrass, Linda Jo (Williams)
  Teacher of Gifted & Talented

CLARENDON
Johnson, Christene Earnest
  Third Grade Teacher
Whitehorn, Sue Webster
  4th-6th Grade Math Teacher

CLARKSVILLE
Blackard, Larry Paul
  Mathematics Department Chair
Cline, Sandra Park
  4th Grade Teacher

CLARKSVILLE (cont)
Usery, Gwen R.
  12th Grade English Teacher
CLINTON
Wolfe, Venita (Bates)
  Second Grade Teacher
CONWAY
Weeks, Pat Havens
  Guidance Counselor
CORNING
Harley, Nadi Williams
  Mathematics Teacher
Schatzley, Bill
  Boys Basketball Coach
CROSSETT
Lovell, Mary Lou (Bingham)
  Junior HS Principal
DARDANELLE
Orsburn, Deborah Crow
  Second Grade Teacher
DE QUEEN
Godwin, Jamie Key
  Fifth Grade Teacher
DERMOTT
Berry, Doria Neal
  8th Grade English Teacher
Gray, Annette
  7th Grade English Teacher
Herring, Phillip David
  General Cooperative Ed Coord
DES ARC
Fennig, Frederick Mark
  Science Teacher
Holloway, Ramona Carlock
  Mathematics Teacher
DONALDSON
Mc Daniel, Brenda Sebren
  5th/6th Grade Lang Art Teacher
EL DORADO
Harris, Vicki Henry
  Business Education Teacher
Littleford, Stanley David
  Math Teacher/Coach
ELAINE
Parker, Paulette Byars
  Speech/Drama/English Teacher
EUREKA SPRINGS
Mc Guire, Rod L.
  Sixth Grade Teacher
EVENING SHADE
Sample, Patty Lou
  Science Teacher
EVERTON
Phelps, Carolyn Sue
  English/Reading/Speech Teacher
Stokes, Vicki Graham
  Guidance Counselor
FAYETTEVILLE
Pudlas, Charles Floyd
  Marketing Ed Coordinator
Waldren, Patricia J.
  Sixth Grade Teacher
FORDYCE
Langford, Belinda Hall
  Kindergarten Teacher
Meador, Betsy Lowe
  French/Journalism Teacher
Ponder, Ted Lamar
  English Teacher
FOREMAN
Latson, Jacqueline Morgan
  2nd Grade Teacher
Smith, Karen Neal
  English Teacher
Stewart, Gary Lyndon
  Math Teacher
FORREST CITY
Barry, Peggy Steinbeck
  11th Grade English Teacher
Cranor, Els Grijseels
  Geography Teacher
Crumbly, Johnetta Williams
  Business Teacher
Petty, Veneta La Fluer
  Kindergarten Teacher
Sain, Lloyd
  7th Grade English Teacher
Wheat, Nurline Johnson
  Rdng/Eng Teacher
FORT SMITH
Brown, Rita Rachel
  English/Social Studies Teacher

Collett, Betty (Green)
  Kindergarten Teacher
Kern, Randy L.
  History Teacher
Kilpatrick, Sandra F.
  Biology/A P Biology Teacher
Long, Janet Taff
  Business Teacher
Rhodes, Richard G.
  6th Grade Teacher
Walker, Martha Lawton
  3rd/4th Grade Teacher
Wells, Robert B.
  Jr HS Band/Sr HS Bible Teacher
FOX
Thomas, Pamela Risner
  Fifth Grade Teacher
GENTRY
Burnside, Minnie P.
  Mathematics Teacher
Melton, Ramona June Bayley
  Business Teacher/Librarian
GREEN FOREST
Rose, Harvey Franklin
  Mathematics Teacher
GREENBRIER
Kellar, Dianna Davis
  English Teacher
Wilcox, Rosemary
  Third Grade Teacher
GREENWOOD
Bilyeu, Debra Calhoun
  Chem/Earth Sci Teacher
GRIFFITHVILLE
Henson, Franklin Delano
  K-12th Grade Counselor
GUY
Padgett, Brenda Reed
  Fourth Grade Teacher
Ward, Suellen Glover
  Home Economics Teacher
HACKETT
Hundley, Ruby Lee Ellis
  Second Grade Teacher
HARDY
Blaxton, Daryl Lee
  Mathematics Teacher
HARRISBURG
Faulkner, Johnita Henderson
  6th Grade Reading Teacher
Nance, Wilma Laretta
  Fifth Grade Teacher
HATFIELD
Christensen, Riley Eugene
  Jr/Sr HS Science Teacher
HECTOR
Pruitt, Pamela Hays
  2nd Grade Teacher
HELENA
Freemyer, Patsy Bennett
  9th/10th Grade English Teacher
HERMITAGE
Gates, Debbia Jenkins
  5th Grade Teacher
HOPE
England, Sheryl Kaye
  Science Teacher
Purtle, James Carroll
  Principal
HOT SPGS NATL PK
Collum, Janet Fisher
  Theatre Art & Eng Teacher
Hildreth, Barbara Paschal
  7th Grade English/Rdng Teacher
Hooks, Willie Hugh
  Mathematics Department Chair
HUGHES
Allen, Betty Rea
  Mathematics Teacher/Dept Chair
Coldren, Dorathy Ann
  Fourth Grade Math Teacher
JACKSONVILLE
Vines, Gean Weatherly
  Sixth Grade Teacher
JESSIEVILLE
Bremer, Janis Knipmeyer
  English Teacher
Mauch, Marilyn Tullar
  Secondary Mathematics Teacher
Williams, David P
  English/Journalism Teacher

JONESBORO
Chambers, Mary Lucille
  Commercial Art Teacher
Ewing, Sherry J. (Bryant)
  7th-9th Grade Math Teacher
Neeley, Patricia Cross
  Retired English Teacher
Richmond, Velmar Singleton
  Biology Teacher
JUNCTION CITY
Endel, Elizabeth Allene (Emerson)
  10th Grade English/Lit Teacher
KENSETT
Dawkins, Terry Allen
  Math/Geography Teacher
KINGSLAND
Burnside, Anne Owens
  Social Studies/English Teacher
LAKE VILLAGE
Cain, Betty Robertson
  Fourth Grade Teacher
Robinson, Gail Morgan
  Vocational Business Teacher
LESLIE
Adams, Jimmy D.
  Science Teacher
LINCOLN
Soules, Bobby Jean
  3rd Grade Teacher
LITTLE ROCK
Betton, Ira Brewer
  Reading Specialist
Carr, Marcelline Carthan
  Algebra II/Geometry Teacher
Croom, Lorene Payne
  Retired Elementary Teacher
Duncan, Edward Allison
  Band Director
Eskola, Patricia Meyer
  6th Grade Teacher
Finn, William F.
  Elementary Principal
Flemmons, Mari Robertson
  Journalism/Photography Teacher
Johnson, Ivria Jr.
  Science Teacher
Lamb, Carolyn Fisher
  Health/Physical Ed Teacher
Privitt, James Stephen
  Algebra Teacher
Smith, Brett Kendall
  Physical Education Head
Sullenger, Beverly Canaday
  Spanish Teacher
Webber, Kelly Robinette
  English Teacher
Williams, Grace Twining
  First Grade Teacher
LOCKESBURG
Jackson, Sandra Cobb
  Sci Teacher/Sci Dept Chairman
LONOKE
Byrd, Phyllis Denise (Waller)
  5th Grade Teacher
MABELVALE
Maddox, Cynthia Jernigan
  Reading Specialist
Swinney, Joyce Jeanne
  Choral Music Teacher
MALVERN
Buttrum, Harlan Ray
  Principal
Clements, Karen Mc Daniel
  Second Grade Teacher
Mc Guire, Betty Jones
  Social Studies Teacher
Sampson, Mary Catherine (Moore)
  First Grade Teacher
MARIANNA
Coleman, Lela Dukes
  Social Studies Teacher
Key, Marvellia Mc Fadden
  Kindergarten Teacher
Patterson, Jo Troxell
  Mathematics Department Chm
Vaccarp, Elaine Bullock
  Librarian
MARKED TREE
Hale, Dorothy L.
  Third Grade Teacher
MARMADUKE
Cooper, Virginia Turberville
  Retired 3rd Grade Teacher
Willis, Larry Lee
  Social Studies/Health Teacher

MARVELL
Washburn, Elizabeth Brown
  English Teacher/Counselor
MC CRORY
Burkett, Carole Bone
  1st Grade Teacher
Ferguson, Diane
  7th/8th Grade Math Teacher
Kidwell, Rodney Eugene
  10th/11th Grade Eng Teacher
Mc Gee, Donna Elizabeth
  Fifth Grade Math Teacher
MC GEHEE
Spence, Jada Sue (Cox)
  Kindergarten Teacher
Stobaugh, Ann Siever
  Mathematics Teacher
MENA
Lankford, Curtis Mitchell
  Science Teacher
Steele, Sharon Kay Mc Ghee
  Second Grade Teacher
MORRILTON
Humphreys, Betty Farris
  Teacher of Gifted & Talented
Jamell, Virginia Sheppard
  Third Grade Teacher
MOUNT PLEASANT
Blevins, Richard Lindle
  Health Teacher/Bsktbl Coach
MOUNT VERNON
Shock, Cheryl Holt
  Sixth Grade Teacher
MOUNTAIN HOME
Baker, Alice J.
  Third Grade Teacher
Jasen, Elizabeth Grace
  Fourth Grade Teacher
Johnson, Stanley Eugene
  9th Grade Phys Science Teacher
MOUNTAINBURG
Holcomb, Sue Cagle
  6th Grade Teacher
MULBERRY
King, Katie Johnson
  School Counselor
Medlock, Angela Hight
  Business Teacher
MURFREESBORO
Minton, Sarnia Murphy
  Jr/Sr Social Studies Teacher
NASHVILLE
Lewis, Cardie Bradley
  6th Grade Soc Stud Teacher
Spigner, Mary Frances
  Mathematics Teacher
Wilson, John J. Jr.
  Mathematics Dept Teacher
NEWPORT
Massey, Alma Moore
  Business Teacher
Western, Kim Stacy
  English Teacher
NORTH LITTLE ROCK
Alexander, Richard Clayton
  Phys Ed Teacher/Coach
Eudy, Russell D.
  Athletic Dir/Science Chair
Humphrey, Charles Edward
  Science Teacher
Keough, Katherine Nelson
  Fifth Grade Teacher
Martin, Catherine Roberts
  Principal
Ritchie, Suzanne
  Eng/Speech/Journalism Teacher
OLA
Kunkel, Donald Ray
  Science Department Chair
OMAHA
Bryant, Anna Sue
  1st Grade Teacher
OSCEOLA
Ammes, Patty Alder
  Headmaster & 3rd Grade Teacher
Beall, Rebecca Brown
  Special Education Teacher
Gathen, Emma York
  English Teacher
Willis, Purdy
  8th Grade Science Teacher
PANGBURN
Moore, Larry Eugene
  Math Teacher/Asst Principal

Sharpless, Beverly J.
  5th & 6th Grade Math Teacher
PARAGOULD
Beerly, Sandra Kay Greninger
  Elementary Aide
Fullen, Brenda (Smith)
  Business Teacher
Howard, Jane Elizabeth (Goins)
  Third Grade Teacher
Livingston, Dean Richard
  Bio Teacher/Boys Bsktbl Coach
Wilson, John Everett
  Science Teacher
PEARCY
Burch, Bobby Joe
  Physics/Biology HS Teacher
Hollingshead, Cheryl Rodgers
  Sci Dept Chairperson-Teacher
Lively, Judy Sanderson
  Teacher of Gifted/Talented
Matthews, Sandra K.
  Gifted & Talented Facilitator
Walker, Cheri Duncan
  4th Grade Language Art Teacher
PERRYVILLE
Chitwood, Bobbie Joan (Stone)
  Soc Stud/Remedial Teacher
PIGGOTT
Self, Danny Mack
  Math Department Chair
Vangilder, Alvin Jay
  7th & 8th Grade Sci Teacher
PINE BLUFF
Burton, Gregory Robert
  Band Director
Clark, Pattye Chandler
  Social Studies Teacher
Currie, Juanita
  Teacher/Counselor
Gray, Gwendolyn Jill
  Sixth Grade Teacher
Jackson, Alma Rose
  5th Grade Teacher
Jones, Rosie Dunn
  Third Grade Teacher
Pierce, Iris Langley
  Chem/Advanced Biology Teacher
Sadler, Rebecca Mc Afee
  Chemistry Teacher
Ward, Nancy Benson
  English Teacher
POTTSVILLE
Duvall, Margaret Harelson
  Chapter I Reading Teacher
Fryer, Jean Murdoch
  Fifth Grade Teacher
PRAIRIE GROVE
Dalmut, Frank Jr.
  Social Studies Teacher
PRESCOTT
Noesser, Vincent Paul
  Girls Basketball Head Coach
QUITMAN
Beene, Sherron Bradke
  Fifth Grade Teacher
Shaw, Joan Stroud
  English/Speech Teacher
RECTOR
Smith, J. Frank
  Science Dept Chair
RISON
Almond, Donald E.
  Guidance Counselor
ROGERS
Brugman, Carol Lee
  Sixth Grade Teacher
Eckard, M. Lana Mc Neal
  Gifted & Talented Facilitator
Langenegger, Frankie Hughes
  Eighth Grade English Teacher
ROHWER
Blevins, Betty Henley
  6th Grade Teacher
Gunn, Edna Jean
  Counselor
King, Gracie M.
  Junior High English Teacher
ROSSTON
Lively, Linda Reece
  English & French Teacher
RUSSELLVILLE
Daniels, Lee Ann
  Biology/Phys Sci Teacher
Mathis, Pam Martin
  6th Grade Science Teacher

RUSSELLVILLE (cont)
Mc Elroy, Lisa Card
  Second Grade Teacher
SCRANTON
Brewster, Lillie Grenwelge
  Fourth/Fifth Grade Teacher
SEARCY
Bass, Carolyn June
  Kindergarten Teacher
Gentry, Mary Sutton
  Second Grade Teacher
Nielsen, Lorraine Jeannette
  Spanish Teacher
SHERWOOD
Church, Beth Moore
  First Grade Teacher
Hindman, Nellie Wayland
  Counselor
SPRINGDALE
Mc Duffie, Catherine De Mara
  Teacher of Gifted & Talented
Ryan, Joye Moorman
  Mathematics Teacher
Shrader, Mary Hearn
  Fourth Grade Teacher
STAMPS
Morris, Caron Camp
  Gifted/Talented Coordinator
TEXARKANA
FitzRandolph, Robert E.
  Science Department Chair
VALLEY SPRINGS
Harness, William Wyatt
  10th/12th Grade Eng Teacher
VILONIA
Cauthen, Melba Moseley
  Math Teacher
Ragland, Sandra Horton
  Art Teacher/Department Head
WALDO
Cheatham, Martha Lee (Smith)
  Fifth/Sixth Grade Teacher
De Loach, Mary Elaine (Essner)
  Mathematics/Science Teacher
WALDRON
Hill, Carolyn Hale
  Science Teacher
WALNUT RIDGE
Tribble, Paula B.
  Fourth Grade Teacher
WARREN
Gathen, Barbara Ann
  9th Grade English Teacher
Ligon, Marianne Wynne
  Foreign Language Chairperson
Martin, Sue Swearingen
  First Grade Teacher
Mc Clellan, John L.
  Science Teacher/Chair
Montgomery, Bobbye Key
  Second Grade Teacher
WEINER
Cassidy, Judith Ward
  English Teacher
Norris, Mary Kathryn (Baker)
  Chapter 1 Coord/Teacher
WEST FORK
Merrill, Judy Kever
  Chapter I Supervisor
WEST HELENA
Graznak, Stephanie Ann
  Theatre Teacher
Greenberry, Tanya Thornton
  English Teacher
Lindsey, Harry Lee
  Mathematics Teacher
WEST MEMPHIS
Smith, Cathy G.
  English Teacher
WHITE HALL
Williams, Karmen Petersen
  English Teacher

CALIFORNIA

ADELANTO
Heldreth, Jackie Brooks
  Computer Laboratory Instructor
AGOURA HILLS
Hill, Patrick Lewis
  Soc Sci Teacher/Dept Chair

Kotal, Edith Marie
  Second Grade Teacher
Lasnik, Jerry L.
  Biology Teacher
ALBANY
Breault, Lois Brelsford
  Fifth Grade Teacher
Brill, Fred S.
  English Teacher
Uchiumi, Gerald M.
  Phys Ed Teacher/Athletic Dir
ALHAMBRA
Blais, Debora Lynne
  Teacher
Burns, Marie Paratore
  8th Grade Language Art Teacher
Gaskill, Julia Regan
  6th/7th/8th Grade ESOL Teacher
Heinrich, Sharron Lynne
  US History Teacher
Hill, Margaret Louise
  First Grade Teacher
Knowles, Clifton D.
  Science Department Chair
Kubal, Cynthia Canlas
  English Teacher
Salcido, Delores Jones
  6th Grade Teacher
Schofield, James Thomas
  English/Communications Teacher
Schwartz, Kathryn Ann
  Social Studies Chairman
ALTA LOMA
La Rochelle, Donna Smith
  Student Adv/Lang Art Teacher
Oxarart, Julianne Scandura
  Mathematics Teacher
ALTADENA
Bowman, Suellen Whitson
  Kindergarten Teacher
Guintu, Ramona Dabu
  Fifth Grade Teacher
ALTURAS
Thayer, Margaret May (Acord)
  First Grade Teacher
ANAHEIM
Edwards, Ronald Eugene
  Senior English Teacher
Mc Cance, Mary Susan
  Assistant Principal
Polley, Karen Thornton
  5th Grade Teacher
Sullivan, Timmerie Rose
  Athletic Dir/Coach/Teacher
Tozzie, James J.
  Social Studies Teacher
Vandesteeg, Marie Pansy
  Science Teacher
ANDERSON
Handel, Anne Kenyon
  6th Grade Teacher
ANTIOCH
Burkholtz, Maryann Korch
  Performing Arts Dept Chair
Creese, Jeri Lynne
  5th Grade Teacher
Rossi, Theresa Rose
  Teacher/Performing Arts Dept
Widener, Larry Dean
  Band Director
APO SAN FRANCISCO
Kelts, David William
  Fifth Grade Teacher
APPLE VALLEY
Cataneso, James J.
  Social Studies Teacher
Milton, Mark Glenn
  Math Teacher
APTOS
Doe, Nicholas K.
  Chemistry Teacher
ARCADIA
Keltner, Barbara Liss
  Third Grade Teacher
Morris, Ronald Scott
  Social Science Teacher
ARCATA
Hart, Bruce W.
  Seventh/Eighth Grade Teacher
Lundeen, Samuel
  5th Grade Teacher
Williams, Joan L.
  English Teacher
ARROYO GRANDE
Moore, Gary Lee
  Assistant Principal

ARTESIA
Ashker, Loretta Quimino
  6th Grade Teacher
ATASCADERO
Burrell, Michael P.
  Social Studies Teacher
Hames, Lynn Viel
  Fifth/Sixth Grade Teacher
Pry, Daniel Elvin
  Health/Science Teacher
ATWATER
Atkinson, Paul Gerald
  Mathematics Dept Teacher
Bell, Gregory E.
  Advanced Placement Bio Teacher
Browning, Joanna Jacobsen
  Language Art/Soc Stud Teacher
Candelaria, Dale Dean
  Sr Govt & A P History Teacher
Johnson-Russell, Jane Margaret
  Spanish Teacher/Dept Chairman
O'Bara, Carrie L. Sullivan
  First Grade Teacher
Sullivan, John Thomas
  Junior High Math Teacher
Wright, Harold C.
  Fourth Grade Teacher
AUBURN
Morgan, Kimberly Brown
  Art & Photography Teacher
AZUSA
Brower, Charlene Barnum
  Third Grade Teacher
Cooke, Jennifer Haines
  6th Grade Teacher
BAKERSFIELD
Bernal, Henry Paul
  Spanish Teacher
Bernstein, Beverly Chuchian
  6th Grade Teacher/Chairman
Bucklen, Jo Lynn Burress-Henderson
  Fourth Grade Teacher
Clark, Richard George
  Curriculum Specialist
Conley, Elaine Higgins
  English Teacher
David, Lisa Johnson
  Physical Education Teacher
Fillmore, Alva Rubert
  Fourth/Fifth Grade Teacher
Goetjen, Linda Jeanne
  Mathematics Dept Chairperson
Keller, Janie Cumberford
  5th Grade Teacher
Pena, Estefana S.
  7th-8th Grade Lang Art Teacher
Radley, Marilyn Yvonne (Kounter)
  7th/8th Grade Teacher
Thompson, Judy Jane Carpenter
  Math Teacher
Todd, William Eric
  Auto Technology Instructor
BALDWIN PARK
Atchley, Tina Kay
  English Teacher
Becker, Ann Stanton
  Science Teacher
Edwards, June M.
  English Teacher
Hill, Karen Gail
  Kindergarten Teacher
Humble, Susan Lorraine
  7th Grade Teacher
Koch, Judith Miller
  Mathematics Teacher
Sloper, Lorraine Obata
  Math Teacher
BELL
Cook, Beverly Anne
  Government & History Teacher
Phillips, Carol R.
  Physical Education Teacher
BELLFLOWER
Modlin, James Kenneth
  Retired Mathematics Teacher
Perry, Joseph Albert
  6th Grade Teacher
Sears, Russell Todd
  Physical Education Teacher
BELMONT
Cicero, Dorothy Wallach
  Sixth Grade Teacher
Dean, William Albert
  English Teacher
Downey, Michael John
  English Teacher
Merta, David Joseph
  Social Studies Teacher
Yager, Bryan C.
  American History Teacher

BENICIA
Garrett, James Michael
  Social Science Depart Teacher
Mullikin, Michael Craig
  5th Grade Teacher
Williams, Dalt B.
  Band Director
BERKELEY
Choulett, Harry E.
  Chemistry Teacher
Jukes, Marguerite A. V. Esposito
  Third Grade Teacher
BLOOMINGTON
Holmes, Delight (Anderson)
  Kindergarten Teacher
BLYTHE
Lester, Lou Ann (Wight)
  Fifth Grade Teacher
Steadman, Richard John
  Head Counselor
BRAWLEY
Ortiz, Diane Jablonski
  Resource Teacher
Sandoval, Janette Graham
  Spec Projects Resource Teacher
BREA
Hufferd, Dorcas A.
  English Teacher
BRENTWOOD
Del Chiaro, Didi J.
  Third Grade Teacher
Thornhill, Denise Bacchini
  Math/Phys Ed Teacher
BRIDGEVILLE
Grady, Michael John
  Superintendent/Principal
BUENA PARK
Chapman, Doris Kathleene
  5th/6th Grade Teacher
Hamilton, Barbara Ann (Vargo)
  Religion/History/Lit Teacher
BURBANK
Campbell, Steve
  English & Journalism Teacher
Kolpas, Sidney J.
  Mathematics Teacher
O'Dwyer, Mary Catherine
  Science/Computer Instructor
Olken, Diana
  Teacher
Perlis, Roberta Marcia
  6th Grade Teacher
Robertson, Neal Alonzo
  Teacher
BURLINGAME
Devincenzi, John Michael
  Social Science Dept Chair
Harrison, Adolph Charles Jr.
  American Government Teacher
BURNEY
Isbell, David Whitney
  Mathematics/Science Teacher
Riley, Dennis Paul
  Principal
CALABASAS
Azhar, Asif Ali
  Math/Physics/Hum Teacher
CALIENTE
Hill, Diane Lusara
  1st/2nd Grade Teacher
CALIFORNIA CITY
Weston, Carol Schmiel
  Fourth Grade Teacher
CAMARILLO
Craig, Pat M.
  Reading/English/Speech Teacher
CAMPBELL
Hill, Kenneth Duane
  Theatre/Fine Art Chair
CANOGA PARK
Newton, Helen Jones
  Mathematics Teacher
CANTUA CREEK
Cayme, Victorio Martinez
  Science/Mathematics Teacher
Cowan, Mosdal
  Second Grade Teacher
CANYON COUNTRY
Beiser, Julie Sue
  French Teacher
Soskin, Laurie Wechter
  Language Art Resource Teacher

CARLOTTA
Mc Henry, Paula L.
  Kindergarten-1st Grade Teacher
Newmaker, Dorothy Marie
  Fifth-Sixth Grade Teacher
CARLSBAD
Barker, Jacquelyn Ann
  Mathematics Teacher
CARMEL VALLEY
Smith, Phillip Lyn
  Fifth Grade Teacher
CARMICHAEL
Blau, Beatrice Brainin
  Retired 8th Grade Teacher
Ford, Thomas Alfred
  6th Grade Teacher
Kindrick, Milton E.
  Biology/Spanish Teacher
Maple, Beverly Ann
  7th Grade History Teacher
CARPINTERIA
Lindsay, Robert Bruce
  Science Teacher
CARSON
Bryant, Jan Johnson
  5th-8th Grade Teacher
CARUTHERS
Callaghan, Richard Michael
  8th Grade Humanities Teacher
CASTRO VALLEY
Menke, Georgiann
  Fourth Grade Teacher
Orluck, Debbie
  1st Grade Teacher
CERES
Engstrom, Susan Rivers
  Language Arts Teacher
Mays-Bukko, Debra
  English Instructor
CERRITOS
Brent, Dennis Michael
  English Teacher
Brunk, Lon Russell
  Teacher/Computer Coordinator
El Moussa, Dominique Angelique
  French/Spanish Teacher
Swann, Marjean Dorothy
  Math Department Teacher
Tanaka, Kristine Uragami
  Math Teacher
CHICO
Crandall, David C.
  5th/6th Grade Teacher
Davis, Janice Kay
  6th Grade Teacher
Lathrop, Janice Katherine
  Third Grade Teacher
CHINO
Atilano, Jesse J.
  HS Biology Teacher
Calkin, Mary Jane
  Special Education Dept Chair
Hunt, Miyuki Tyler
  4th Grade Teacher
Meador, Connie Jean
  Fifth Grade Teacher
Struve, Richard Dale
  Scndry Math Mentor/Dept Chair
Swangel, Patricia Arlene (Engelhard)
  English Teacher
Vaniman, Richard R.
  Psychology Teacher
CHUALAR
Sugahara, Tei Ann
  6th/7th Grade Teacher
CHULA VISTA
Berrian, James Edwin
  Biology Teacher
Bornhorst, Carol Ann
  Science Teacher/Dept Chair
Bullock, Nancy Cato
  English Teacher
Howarth, Douglas
  Counselor
Roth, Patricia Ann
  Principal
Sobel, Joy F.
  English/Communications Teacher
Wallace, Nathan
  Secondary Teacher/Adminstrator
Zidbeck, William Edward
  Science/Journalism Teacher
CITRUS HEIGHTS
Arellanes, Joanne Elaine
  5th/6th Grade Teacher

CLAREMONT
Gallagher, Ann Rawlins
  Mathematics/Science Teacher

CLAYTON
Rackow, Russel J.
  Fifth Grade Teacher

CLEARLAKE
Sullivan, Cheryl Pinto
  1st-2nd Grade Teacher

CLOVIS
Bitters, Conrad L.
  Biology/Zoology Teacher
Farris, Donald Herach
  Resource Teacher
Herrington, Diana L. (Slater)
  Mathematics Teacher
Pietro, John D.
  Math/Computer Science Teacher
Turner, Kristin Malia
  Spanish Teacher
Wylie, M. Elizabeth Conners
  Sixth Grade Elementary Teacher

COARSEGOLD
Porter, Valerie A.
  7th/8th Grade Teacher

COLTON
Clark, Ron Alan
  Sixth Grade Teacher
Geary, Dorothy Ann (Glynn)
  Fourth Grade Teacher

COMPTON
Ichikawa, Dorothy Seki
  French Teacher
Van Buren, Barbara Bachemin
  8th Grade Homeroom/Sci Chair

CONCORD
Hagerstrand, Allen Frank
  Physical Education Teacher
Kraetsch, Carolyn Jones
  Teacher of Gifted & Talented
Lee, Byron
  Teacher
Vigus, Daniel Leonard
  Band Dir 3rd Grade Teacher
West-Hodge, Rosemarie
  Teacher

COOL
Woodall, Drew David
  Counselor

CORNING
Deromedi, Eddi Zacharin
  Elementary Principal
Perry, Roberta Devaurs
  Science Department Chair

CORONA
Lister, Leilani Letwin
  Computer/Algebra Teacher
Yates, Mariko Lynn
  Mathematics Teacher

CORONA DEL MAR
Ternes, Linda (Woodworth)
  Mathematics Teacher

CORONADO
Clark, Kathleen Stevens
  8th Grade English Teacher

COSTA MESA
Barraclough, Jean Campbell
  Principal
Schroeder, Janice Ellenberger
  Language Arts Teacher/Chair

COTTONWOOD
Brown, Ronald Joseph
  Third Grade Teacher

COVELO
Lim, Donna
  Kindergarten/Strings Teacher

COVINA
Deal, Patricia Jean
  HS Counselor
Schlitt, David Alan
  Creative Dramatics Instructor
Sweger, Glenda Lee
  English Teacher & Mentor
Tiemann, Patricia (Schiele)
  Sixth Grade GATE Teacher

CRESCENT CITY
Nuszkiewicz, Dorothy Westfall
  Kindergarten Teacher

CULVER CITY
Kemp, Kathleen Bernadette
  Social Studies/Art Teacher
Ott, Charles Cearley
  Social Studies Teacher

CUPERTINO
Alwell, Mariana Francesca
  6th Grade Teacher
Stimson, Susan
  English Teacher
Wild, Janice L.
  6th Grade Teacher

CYPRESS
Lee, Mary Hong
  3rd Grade Teacher

DALY CITY
Delaney, Betty G.
  Chapter 1 Resource Teacher
Kaldahl, Jean Clark
  3rd Grade Teacher
White, Edna Meisekothen
  Computer/English Teacher

DANA POINT
Prerost, Patricia L. (Milnes)
  7th & 8th Grade Math Teacher
Rouse, Milton B.
  English Teacher

DANVILLE
Endicott, Jill Mc Kinnon
  Kindergarten Teacher
Estrada, Sylvie Caplier
  French Teacher
Hornbeck, Janel Monique
  Mathematics Department Chair
Krug, June
  Teacher/Student Activities Dir
Maxwell, Mike A.
  Leadership/Activities Advisor
Moore, Thomas Edward III
  Chemistry Teacher
Simonds, Richard Bruce
  Social Studies Teacher

DAVIS
Gill, Martin Kent
  Junior HS English Teacher
Kraemer, Kristi
  Eng Teacher/Stu Teacher Supvr

DELANO
Moore, Amanda Louise Owens
  5th Grade Teacher
Stahl, Karen E. (Pedersen)
  HS Physical Education Teacher

DENAIR
Wallace, Cynthia Kay (Jones)
  Third Grade Teacher

DIAMOND BAR
Hunter, Charlotte Williams
  1st Grade Teacher

DINUBA
Derderian, Violet E.
  Fifth Grade Teacher
Perales-Rubin, Albert
  Spanish Teacher
Williams, Kathleen S. Brouse
  Fifth Grade Teacher/Mentor

DOWNEY
Claiborne, Carolyn Palmer
  6th Grade Soc Stud Teacher
De Bois, Thelma Ingram
  English Teacher
Shimoda-Jung, Elaine
  Fifth Grade Teacher
Uthoff, Antoinette Maria
  English Teacher

DUARTE
Boehm, Stanley Eric
  Science Teacher

DUBLIN
Holloway, Linda Morgan
  Math/Computer Teacher
Iijima, Mike
  Biology & Anatomy Teacher
Vinella, Paul Victor
  6th Grade Teacher

DUNSMUIR
Swift, Linda A. (Lutz)
  6th Grade Teacher/Counselor

EL CAJON
Bennett, Tom Regan
  Mathematics Teacher
Bikson, Bruce E.
  Drama/Public Speaking Teacher
Elliott, Barbara Ann
  Fifth Grade Teacher
Hernandez, Gilbert Mendez
  Spanish Teacher
Mc Millan, Ann Eleanor (Barnes)
  Second Grade Teacher
Ostermeyer, Maryann
  GATE English & History Teacher

CUPERTINO (cont.)
Smith, Andrew G. III
  English Teacher
Zazvrskey, Michael Eugene
  Math Teacher/Bsktbl Coach

EL CERRITO
Williams, Loni R.
  Counselor

EL MONTE
Bonsey, Nancy K.
  Sixth Grade Teacher
Gonzales, Mario Richard
  7th-8th Grade Teacher

EL SOBRANTE
Sonaggera, Alan A
  Teacher

EL TORO
Brizzi, Madalyn Frost
  Retired Elementary Teacher
Rainer, Patricia C.
  Instrumental Music Teacher

ELK GROVE
Almas, Alana A.
  Spanish Teacher
Johnson, Gale Peirce
  6th Grade Teacher
Kaneko, Kimi Yokoyama
  Elementary School Principal
Schottle, Brad Lee
  Mathematics Teacher

ELSINORE
Ince, Susan M.
  English Teacher

EMPIRE
Dambrosio, Ellen Christensen
  Computer Teacher

ENCINITAS
Harvie, William Stuart
  Physics Teacher
Law, Suzanne Louise
  Junior High School Teacher
Marinello, Fred R.
  Visual/Performing Arts Teacher
Robertson, Jon C.
  English Teacher

ESCALON
Blixt, Elizabeth Haines
  Teacher/Administrator
Moreno, Leslie Ann (Harvey)
  7th/8th Grade Health Teacher

ESCONDIDO
Hutchinson, John Steve
  5th Grade Teacher
Steck, Bonnie F.
  8th Grade Math Teacher

EUREKA
Diaz, Sue A.
  Music Teacher
Feist, Eugene P.
  Mathematics Department Chair
Myers, Darrell Richard
  History Teacher
Quinby, Lucy Santino
  Spanish Teacher

EXETER
Caldwell, Steven De Witt
  Learning Opportunity Instr

FAIR OAKS
Dunkim, William Edward III
  Mathematics Teacher

FAIRFIELD
Boyd, Georgina Marie (Mello)
  4th Grade Teacher
Carpino, Clyde Phillips
  Student Activities Director
Hargro, Oretha Wilson
  Mathematics Mentor Teacher
Johnson, Glenda L. Farrer
  Kindergarten Teacher
Millward, Jack Mikel
  Anatomy & Physiology Teacher
Munoz, Loretta Lee
  K-6th Grade Math Teacher
Oren, Frederic Lynn
  Math Dept Chair & Teacher
Schulz, Janice Cox
  5th Grade Teacher
Winthrop, Jerauld Samuel
  English Teacher
Woodie, Coretha Boykin
  6th Grade Teacher

FELTON
Candia, Anne Katherine
  Fifth Grade Teacher
Umstead, Terry Lynn
  Jr HS Mathematics Teacher

FILLMORE
Cotsis, Virginia Mary
  English Department Chair
Lee, Janet Hiebert
  Bilingual Elem Teacher
Mittan, Kenneth D
  Jr HS Math GATE Teacher

FIVE POINTS
Mc Carthy, Joann Busch
  Fourth Grade Teacher
Perry, Susan De Masters
  Eighth Grade Teacher/Mentor

FONTANA
Berard, Joseph Alton
  Math Teacher
Zupancich, Antonia
  Principal

FOUNTAIN VALLEY
Chamberlain, Susan Rederus
  English Teacher
Rawhouser, James Austin
  Mathematics Teacher
Selich, Judith Ann (Jeffers)
  English & Amer History Teacher
Vander Meer, Peter Cornelius
  7th/ 8th Grade Teacher
Walcott, Judy Engstrom
  Kindergarten Teacher

FREMONT
Molander, Judy Schondelmayer
  5th Grade Teacher
Ratledge, John Eric
  Mathematics Teacher
Sanders, Adrian Lionel
  Gifted & Talented Ed Teacher

FRENCH CAMP
Fidler, Daniel Ross
  7th/8th Grade Teacher

FRESNO
Andersen, Sharon Rahnke
  Teacher
Aramburu, Michael Joseph
  5th-6th Grade Teacher
Blue, Mark La Mont
  Supervising Principal
Cardwell, Douglas William
  Computer Mentor Teacher
Costello, Daniel
  US History Teacher
Fleming, Cozett Cowan
  US History Teacher
Flint, George Jr.
  7th/8th Grade Teacher
Hagenzieker, Willem Peter
  Academic Block Teacher
Handley, Robert W.
  Eng Dept Chair/Mentor Teacher
Haynes, Oscar
  History/Government Teacher
Kehlenbeck, Anthony Paul
  English Teacher
Locker, Holland A.
  Principal
Mediavilla, Rosario
  Fourth Grade Teacher
Neumeier, Thomas C.
  Phys Ed/Religion Teacher
Paden, Cynthia Lee
  8th Grade Eng/Core His Teacher
Pettengill, Timothy Owen
  Spanish Teacher
Ratcliffe, Bruce Allen
  Science Teacher
Scoville, Robert Charles
  Social Science Teacher
Sharkey, Peter Michael
  Mathematics Teacher
Sherry, Elaine Claudette
  Sixth Grade Teacher
Stalis, Rachel Helen
  Third Grade Teacher
Stark-Olson, Jeanie Carroll
  Resource Teacher
Williams, Sharon Child
  7th Grade Life Science Teacher
Woods, Mattie Smith
  Third Grade Teacher

FULLERTON
Bailey, James W.
  Vocational Agriculture Teacher
Denton, Olga Gresh
  2nd/3rd Grade Teacher
Mc Clung, Karen Thorsen
  French Teacher
Nelson, Jeffrey Owen
  Biology Teacher
Pappas, Harry James
  Mathematics Dept Lecturer
Ringer, Sherry L.
  Physical Education Teacher

GARDEN GROVE (cont.)
Sprague, Belle B.
  Language Art Teacher
Thompson, Caroline Sue
  English Teacher

GARDEN GROVE
Beebe, Sandra E.
  English Teacher
Bertain, Karl Peter
  Bio & Advanced Bio Teacher
Brattstrom, Martha Ann
  Science Department Teacher
Olson, Randall Howard
  Mathematics Teacher
Steege, Dorothy Schaefer
  Teacher of Gifted/Talented
Stormer, Eugene E.
  APH English Instructor
Ulriksen, Janice
  Chemistry & Physics Instructor

GARDENA
Duffer, Jodeane Pataki
  Fourth Grade Teacher
Trudnich, Sheri Lynn
  Sixth Grade Teacher

GILROY
Ayala, Ronald Paul
  Teacher of Gifted & Talented

GLENDALE
Beers, Peter K.
  Music Department Chair
Burghdorf, Harry Paul
  English Teacher
Samaniego, Robert Jerry
  Sixth Grade Teacher

GLENDORA
Hooven, Sandra J.
  English Teacher

GONZALES
King, Loren Dennis
  Math Department Chairman

GRANADA HILLS
Stock, Malcolm
  Health Instructor/Dept Chair
Yagoobian, Jerilynn Hewey
  Kindergarten Teacher

GRASS VALLEY
Estin, Joan M.
  Teacher
Hinman, Barbara Jean
  Language Arts Dept Chairperson
King, Lois Ellen
  Kindergarten Teacher
Mc Daniel, Carolyn Marie Peterson
  English Teacher
Ramirez, Kenneth William
  Science Teacher/Coach

GRIDLEY
Haft, Carolyn Jean (Call)
  Fourth Grade Teacher
Jensen, Steven H.
  Teacher

GROVER CITY
Keyte, Nancy Madison
  3rd Grade Teacher

HACIENDA HEIGHTS
Gombos, Angela Karady
  Social Science/Scndry Teacher
Nicholson, Patricia Onodera
  Mathematics Teacher
Odama, Kuniye
  Mathematics Teacher
Pate, James Edward
  Mathematics Dept Chair
Smith, Mary Lewis
  English/Reading Teacher

HANFORD
O'Neal, Michael Lee
  Life Skills Teacher

HAWTHORNE
Baggelaar, Linda Miller
  7th Grade Teacher
Bradley, Betty Aloha
  Vice Principal
Dicus, Julianne
  Counselor
Ishibashi, Andrew Wayne
  Music Director
Kruse, Linda Humphrey
  Third Grade Teacher

HAYWARD
Doxey, Jo Anne Arrigoni
  Teacher of Gifted & Talented

HEALDSBURG
Chapman, Lynden Ray
  Social Studies Teacher

HEMET
Bowles, Larry Clark
  Soc Sci Teacher & Dept Chair
Conway, Beverly Fluth
  5th Grade Teacher
Delgado, Lorenzo Araiza
  Spanish Teacher
Mac Millan, Martha Smalley
  Mathematics Teacher
Slawson, Craig Lewis
  Teacher of Gifted & Talented

HESPERIA
Bables, Mary Hill
  Teacher
Dickinson, Gregory Dennis
  Mathematics Teacher
Harper, Peggy Mary
  10th Grade Honors Eng Teacher
Johnson, Janice
  Jr HS Teacher
Kirk, Robert Fred
  Science Teacher
Pope, Debra Saugstad
  Physical Education Teacher
Starbuck, Robert William
  Audio-Visual Teacher
Yee, James C.
  Math Teacher

HOLLISTER
Holland, Geoffrey Craig
  History Department Chairman
Holsapple, Louise Hernandez
  Kindergarten Teacher
Martinez, Sergio Lorenzo
  Mathematics Teacher
Schiavo, Susan G.
  Activities Director

HOLTVILLE
Wommack, Victoria Anne
  Vocational Agriculture Teacher

HOOPA
Contreras, Dave
  Social Studies Chair

HUNTINGTON BEACH
Broccolo, Patricia Ann
  Kindergarten Teacher
Campos, Jelica Zirojin Petkovic
  Science Teacher
D'Amico, Sandra Marie
  Business Education Teacher
Jennings, Jeanne Carlson
  Third Grade Teacher
Jordan, Mercedes Kronfeld
  7th/8th Grade Jr HS Teacher
Komanapalli, Sam Bob
  Science Teacher
Moore, Robert
  Health Teacher
Nettleton, Sue Nancy
  History/Language/Art Teacher
Schuesler, Mary M.
  Science/Math Teacher
Scudder, Catherine Patricia Genthner
  Teacher of Gifted/Talented

INDIO
Cardona, Lois Byllesby
  K-2nd Grade Substitute Teacher
Jenkins, Susan
  8th Grade Teacher

INGLEWOOD
Hughes, Wrelda Virginia
  US History Teacher

IRVINE
Brooks, William Robert
  Sixth Grade Teacher
Dyer-Forkasdi, Elizabeth Ann
  English Teacher
Henry, Carolyn Hahn
  2nd/3rd Grade Teacher
Mamer, James Michael
  History/Social Science Teacher
Matta, Ann Atkins
  Third Grade Teacher
Nakaue, Michael
  Science Department Chairperson
Nelson, Gretchen Gildemeister
  Social Studies Teacher
Nichols, Virginia Shields
  English/Social Science Teacher
Terry, Bruce David
  K-8th Grade Principal

KINGSBURG
Sears, William Russell
  7 & 8 Grade Ind Arts Teacher
Stevens, Carolyn B.
  French & Publications Teacher
Troisi, Barbara Jacobsen
  First Grade Teacher
Wall, Alicia Anderson
  7th/8th Grade English Teacher

Willems, Shirley J.
  Learning Director

LA CANADA
Arlow, Barbara
  Social Studies Teacher

LA HABRA
Baeder, Albert Philip
  Science Department Chairman
Baltes, Sandra Villelli
  Resource Teacher/SID Coord
Manzo, Nadele Stewart
  Seventh Grade Team Leader
Oliver, Robin L.
  Science Teacher

LA MESA
Barlow-Gillis, Jody
  Special Consultant to Gifted
Mote, Olga Jean
  Retired Jr High School Teacher
Ortiz, Carol Mauch
  4th/5th Grade Teacher
Piemme, Betty
  Fourth Grade Teacher

LA MIRADA
Farber, Marian Clark
  Business Education Dept Chair

LA PALMA
Aborne, Morris Michael
  History Teacher
Jantolak, Laura Jean
  6th Grade Teacher

LA PUENTE
Belak, Theodore Allan
  Math/Soc Stud Teacher
Dusbiber, Kathleen Small
  Physical Education Teacher
Gover, Maria Ramos
  English Teacher
Graff-Ramirez, Rosann
  Honors World His/Psych Teacher
Herron, Gail Sondergard
  Science & Health Teacher
Penrose, Patricia Wolters
  English Department Chair
Peters, Patricia Alsup
  English Department Chair
Slakey, Stephen Louis
  Social Science Teacher
Smith, Russell
  English Teacher

LA SELVA BEACH
Baerg, Elizabeth Slocum
  Mathematics Teacher

LA VERNE
Ransom, Marguerite Mitchell
  English Teacher
Tidwell, Harvey Eugene
  Physical Education Teacher

LAFAYETTE
Finn, Gordon Stephen
  Science/Mathematics Teacher
Searle, C. David
  Retired Teacher

LAGUNA BEACH
Englhard, Kathryn Fuller
  Spanish Teacher

LAGUNA NIGUEL
Armstrong, Amy Laurel
  First Grade Teacher

LAKE ELSINORE
Brown, Edward James Jr.
  English/Mentor Teacher
Engelhardt, Patricia Ann (Sisco)
  5th Grade Teacher
Jennings, Wanda Douglas
  Social Studies Dept Chairman

LAKE ISABELLA
Priddy, Jerry
  Mathematics Department Chair

LAKEPORT
Alakzay, Margaret Kern
  Fifth Grade Teacher

LAKESIDE
Fenton, Evelyn Lee (Zurcher)
  Second Grade Teacher
Goldstein, Barbara Mae Figler
  Third Grade Teacher
Waddell, Robert Johnson
  Fifth Grade Teacher

LAKEWOOD
Palladino, Stephen D.
  Advanced Mathematics Teacher
Parks, George Thomas
  Mathematics Teacher

Simons, Sue Lynn
  English Department Chair
Smith, Teri Hellman
  English Teacher
Valois, Rick
  Mathematics Department Chair
Walsh, Bonny Trent
  English as Second Lang Teacher

LANCASTER
Andrepont, Catherine Garzotto
  Chapter I Gifted Specialist
Lalicker, Beverly Sue Sells
  Kindergarten Teacher
Parks, Kathleen Montgomery
  English Teacher
Rogers, Mary Ann Piseck
  Teacher of Gifted & Talented
Smith, Cynthia Lewis
  Music Director
Tropp, Perle Ryave
  4th Grade Teacher
Underwood, Susan Gebstadt
  Mathematics Department Chair
Wayland, Joann Laflin
  Business Teacher/Dept Chairman
Wright, Raleigh K.
  Math Teacher/Dept Chm

LATON
Gregory, Kathy L.
  6th Grade Teacher

LE GRAND
Crawford, Tracey C.
  Mathematics Department Chair
Welsh, Terry Randall
  English Teacher
Wills, Gail Douglas
  6th Grade Teacher

LEMOORE
King, Morris Wayne
  Science Teacher

LENNOX
Arias, Marilyn Hasbun
  Literature/Lang Art Teacher

LINCOLN
Butler, Linda Charlene (Edgar)
  Fifth Grade Teacher
Crabtree, Carolynn Keeny
  Lang Art/Computer Sci Teacher
Eliopulos, Betty
  Spanish & French Teacher

LINDEN
Faussett, Russell Wayne
  History Teacher

LITTLEROCK
Beardlsey, Judy Mae
  Math/Sci Teacher/Math Chair

LIVE OAK
Jackson, Lynn Mc Clure
  3rd Grade Teacher

LIVERMORE
Bradley, Judy E.
  Mathematics Dept Chair/Teacher
Dyer, Eric B.
  6th-8th Grade Art Teacher

LODI
Finos, Marles Anne
  3rd Grade Teacher
Hatch, Samuel Mark
  English Teacher
Reid, Marjorie Follis
  Literature Librarian Teacher
Shreve, Donna Swagerty
  Math Specialist
Thompson, Julie Lorraine
  English Teacher

LOMPOC
Hutchinson, Mary Christene Dean
  Kindergarten Teacher
Lawrence, Robert Kent
  English Department Chair
Ryan, Lorna L.
  Resource/Program Specialist
Spilman, James B.
  Science Department Chair

LONE PINE
Kritz, Irene Bedford
  7th/8th Grade Math/His Teacher

LONG BEACH
Bacon, Ron
  Mathematics Teacher/Dept Chair
Blenderman, Joseph E.
  Drawing/Painting Teacher
Boos, Erin Lee
  5th Grade Teacher
Gilbert, Dean Craig
  Biology Teacher/Sci Dept Chair

Grace, Elizabeth Mills
  ESL Teacher/Department Chair
Hoffman, Valerie Jean (Bradley)
  Eng/Span/Lang Dept Chair
Padilla, Rochelle Le Kus
  Social Studies Teacher

LOOMIS
Jones, Ronald E.
  Student Activities Director

LOS ALAMITOS
Currie, Kathryn Martyn
  Science Dept Chair/Teacher
Schlatter, John Wayne
  Drama Teacher

LOS ALTOS
Kawamoto-Combes, Barbara Kikue
  Health/Guidance J H Teacher
Mc Cormack, M. Kathleen Thomas
  IHM
  Junior High School Teacher

LOS ANGELES
Armstrong, Alice Faye
  5th Grade Teacher
Ausby, Donna D.
  Mathematics Teacher
Bass, Robert Carl
  Mathematics/Phys Ed Teacher
Chappelle, Galen Rodney
  Eighth Grade Teacher
Chisholm, Claire Lang
  Gifted & Talented Teacher
Cimino, Jeanette Rose
  6th Grade Teacher of Gifted
Clark, Beverly Goodloe
  Second Grade Teacher
Costello, Aquinas Richard OP
  Religion Department Chair
Crawford, Theresa F.
  Third Grade Teacher
Deering, Hilary J.
  Science Department Chair
Duenas, Cecilia Marie
  Physics Teacher
Escalante, Jaime Alfonso
  Mathematics Instructor
Feinstein, Michael Irwin
  Economics Teacher
Fenton, Daniel Joseph
  Science Department Chair
Frechman, Alan D.
  Mathematics Teacher
Gutierrez, George Albert
  Spanish Teacher
Harberts, William
  Science Dept/Biology Teacher
Henderson, Wanda (Phillips)
  2nd Grade Teacher
Jensen, Rhiner Christen
  Social Studies Teacher
Jimenez, Benjamin Soto
  Mathematics Teacher
Kuhn, Deanna Jenkinson
  Third Grade Teacher
Lang, Jacklyn Harris
  French Teacher/Lang Dept Chm
Lee, Jennifer Morita
  Sixth Grade Teacher
Lee, Randal E.
  High School English Teacher
Morrison, Anne Marie
  5th Grade Teacher Gifted Prgm
Norton, Oakley L.
  Honors Mathematics Teacher
Oviatt, Ted
  English Teacher
Primus, Irma Britt
  Counselor
Roe, Michel M.
  Attendance Counselor
Salgado, Emma Eugenia
  Spanish Teacher
Spencer, Constance Eileen
  Categorical Program Advisor
Stahly, Marlene Wilson
  English Teacher/Dept Chair
Toeque, Sanubo
  Curriculum Director
Toy, Kailim
  History Teacher

LOS GATOS
Hammack, William Steven
  Physics/AP Biology Teacher
Ringsted, Nancy Hoyle
  5th Grade Teacher

LOS OSOS
Lovtang, Prudence Elaine
  Guidance/English Teacher

LYNWOOD
Eldridge, Penny Singleton
  Teacher of Gifted & Talented

Skinner, Laurence
  5th/6th Grade Teacher
Williams, Earl Louis
  Graphic Arts Teacher

MACDOEL
Cochrane, Judith Anne Ekstrand
  Teacher/Designated Principal

MADERA
Deniz, Natalie Cruz Rodriguez
  Counselor
Seybold, John Francis
  7th Grade Teacher/Vice Prin

MANHATTAN BEACH
Jacobson, Diana R.
  English Teacher

MANTECA
Newburg, Edwin E. Jr.
  Science Teacher

MARICOPA
Duquette, Edward John
  Science Department Chair

MARIPOSA
Hinojosa, Tom
  Science/Mathematics Teacher

MARTINEZ
Pruitt, Lewis Wilson
  Biology Teacher

MAYWOOD
Schutt, Michele Camille
  3rd Grade Teacher

MC FARLAND
Bowman, Cindy Lynn
  Home Economics Teacher

MC KINLEYVILLE
Brunson, Nancy Ann (Comstock)
  Home Economics Teacher
Dakis, Mike Nick
  Vice-Principal/P E Instructor
Smith, Kathleen (Cafer)
  Third Grade Teacher

MENLO PARK
Schwarz, Janet
  8th Grade Science Teacher
Taylor, Janet Irene
  7th Grade Teacher

MERCED
Ellett, Donna George
  Retired Teacher
Goddard, F. Howard
  Retired Teacher

MILPITAS
Carty, Lorenda Wong
  Computer Teacher
Forte, Geraldine Cynthia
  Language Art/Soc Stud Teacher
Lobdell, James Marston
  Social Studies Teacher
Lott, Tamara Neufeld
  English/Speech Teacher
Robertson, Bernie Taylor
  Mathematics Teacher

MISSION VIEJO
Akins, Val L.
  Science Teacher
Dargan, Mary Kay Macken
  Advanced Placement Eng Teacher
Herbert, Michael K.
  Mathematics Teacher
Houston, David George
  7th Grade Science Teacher
Sayles, Kenneth Lynn
  Social Science Teacher

MODESTO
Aguilera, Leopold Benjamin
  HS English Teacher
Azevedo, Clara Margaret
  HS Bilingual Counselor
Brown, Jeffrey Steven
  5th Grade G.A.T.E.
Changnon, Dianne Lynn
  Health Educator
Eaton, Margaret Ann
  English/ESL Teacher
Gilroy, Gary Patrick
  Dir of Bands/Music Dept Chair
Granderson, Mary F.
  Fifth Grade Teacher
Harris, Daniel Joseph
  Mathematics Teacher
Holmes, Gerry A.
  US History Teacher
Johnson, Susan Rykert
  Science Teacher
Kadani, Linda Hae
  Educator-English Teacher

MODESTO (cont)
Kennedy, Michael John
 Science Teacher
Magner, Philip Stevenson
 Mathematics Teacher
Marla, Lois Mac Leod
 English/Social Studies Teacher
Philpot, David L.
 6th Grade Teacher
Priest, Joe Ellen
 HS Counselor
Raingruber, Robert John
 Math Teacher
Riley, Mary Ann (Roe)
 Fifth Grade Teacher

MONROVIA
Dagne, Donald Ray
 Act Dir/Soc Sci Dept Chm
Pollock, Joan Crawley
 Elementary Reading Teacher

MONTCLAIR
Cronin, James Thomas
 English Teacher

MONTEBELLO
Haggerty, Christine Louise
 Physical Education Teacher
Serra, Michael G.
 Social Studies Teacher
Shragg, Mike Sidney
 Director of Activities

MONTEREY
Di Girolamo, Rosina Rena
 English Teacher/Dept Chm
Kendall, Susan Shinnick
 English Teacher

MOORPARK
Chung, Norman
 Biology Teacher
Cohen, Morley Jay
 Science Co-Chair
Donley, Will
 U S History Teacher/Dept Chair

MORAGA
Danielli, Lola Lynne
 Spanish Teacher
Thomas, Katherine Erin Ross
 French & English Teacher

MORENO VALLEY
Bogan, Cyndie
 Counselor-Dept Chairperson
Flinn, Rebecca Ann
 Teacher/Program Facilitator
Langley, Robert E. Jr.
 Biology Teacher
Payne, William C.
 History Teacher
Steele, Archibald Featherston Jr.
 Mathematics Teacher
Titus, Valerie Pellum
 High School Guidance Counselor
Twedell, Lester Ralph Jr.
 Teacher/Mathematics Dept Chair

MORGAN HILL
Rubino, Michael John
 Music Teacher

MORRO BAY
Wright, Sherry
 English & Theatre Teacher

MOUNTAIN VIEW
Comfort, Rosanne Elizabeth (Dorsey)
 Retired English Teacher
Devine, Dennis Thomas
 United States History Teacher
Kilmer-Garrido, Carol Louise
 Spanish Teacher
Miyano, Steven Clifford
 Biology/Marine Biology Teacher

NAPA
Grassmann, Donald Roger
 Fifth/Sixth Grade Teacher
Stittsworth, Marie Adele
 Second Grade Teacher
Wyckoff, Sandra Swearingen
 Bus Department Chair/Bus Instr

NAS LEMOORE
Good, Karleen Wagner
 8th Grade Teacher

NATIONAL CITY
Corrales, Marina
 Social Science/Spanish Teacher
Cruz, Maria Reynoso
 Sixth Grade Mentor Teacher
Gretler, Mary-Ellen Nichols
 Fourth Grade Teacher

NEWARK
Coaston, George Ellis
 Science Teacher

NEWBURY PARK
Zeller, Allen Raymond
 7th-12th Grade Dir of Bands

NORCO
Lowry, Lois Charles
 Kindergarten Teacher
Rhinehart, Laura Cleo
 English Teacher

NORTH HOLLYWOOD
Booth, Nancy Knowlton
 English Department Chair
Gantley, Judy Eckert
 Music/English Teacher
Jurman, Larry H.
 5th/6th Grade Teacher
Sontag, Vivian C.
 5th Grade Teacher

NORTHRIDGE
Mattner, Janice Carolyn
 Math/Eng/His/Art Teacher
Shaffier, Carolyn Howard
 8th Grade Teacher/Vice Prin

NORWALK
Adams, Darryl Rodney
 Journalism Dept Chair
Duffee, Beverly Ann
 English Dept Chair/Instructor
Hergesheimer, John H.
 Social Science Dept Chair
Perry, Janice O'Connell
 Kindergarten & 1st Grade Tchr
Sutterfield, Mona Armstrong
 7th Grade Teacher

NOVATO
Castro, Roberto Garcidueñas
 Vice Principal
Jagow, Beverly Sievert
 Computer Teacher

OAKHURST
Moore, Barbara Camp
 Principal/Teacher
Robison, Sara (Francis)
 5th Grade Teacher
Thomas, Constance Beth Tompkins
 Fourth Grade Teacher

OAKLAND
Andrews, Jerrell Dwaine
 Physical Education Teacher
Ansell, Joan Green
 Graphic Design Teacher
Barnett, Dana
 English Teacher/Dept Chair
Calderwood, John Carver
 Social Science Dept Chairman
Dinelli, Donald Ray
 Social Science Teacher
Gertler, Evelyn Fineberg
 Sixth Grade Teacher
Morrison, Mary Napoleon
 Choral/Piano Teacher
Palley, Beverly Hall
 Mathematics Teacher
Tyler, Shirley Tudas
 Third Grade Teacher

OCEANO
Montano, Robert A.
 4th Grade Teacher

OCEANSIDE
Leverette, Jannie Lee (Smith)
 Mathematics Dept Chairman

OILDALE
Horack, Larry
 5th Grade Teacher

OLIVEHURST
Morgan, Patricia M.
 Eng, Drama, Bus Law Teacher

ONTARIO
Arquieta, Joseph Jr.
 Social Sciences Teacher
Hammon, John B.
 6th Grade Teacher
Heald, Cameron R.
 HS Driver Education Teacher
Heath, Brent Edward
 Social Studies Dept Chair
Thompson, Wanda Cairncross Adams
 6-8th Grade Soc Stud Teacher
Vasquez, Anthony Jude
 History Teacher

ORANGE
Matthews, Irene Lynch
 English/Journalism Teacher

ORANGEVALE
Cooper, Leslie Ellen
 English/Spanish Teacher

OROVILLE
Goodes, Janice Wild
 Business Teacher
Light, Tina Rae
 Second Grade Teacher

OXNARD
Akune, Jane Elizabeth
 English Teacher
Cox, Lee Randolph
 English Literature Teacher
Fontes, Patricia Sanders
 7th Grade Teacher
Hayashi, Alan T.
 Mathematics Teacher
Held, Dennis Louis
 First Grade Teacher
Kinney, Cordelia Rose
 First Grade Teacher
Short, James Lester
 Mathematics Teacher
Terrazas, Bill Jr.
 Teacher

PACIFIC GROVE
Casas, John Thomas
 Social Studies/History Teacher

PALM DESERT
Strom, Lois Eleanor
 1st Grade Teacher

PALM SPRINGS
Cote, Letha J.
 Latin Teacher
Luckey, Jeanie Hugo
 Social Studies Teacher

PALO ALTO
Attig, John Clare
 History Teacher

PALOS VERDES PNSLA
Kelly, Joe B.
 English Teacher
Lieberman, Libby Shull
 First Grade Teacher

PANORAMA CITY
Gorman, Angela Clare SP
 English Teacher

PARADISE
Eisele, Darryl J.
 English Teacher
Watts, Jerry L.
 5th Grade Teacher

PARAMOUNT
Holland, Mark Robert
 Mathematics Teacher
Jones, Calvin Milton
 Soc Sci Teacher
Makin, Steve
 Social Science Teacher
Plourde, Martin Joseph
 Counselor

PARLIER
Gaitan, Edward W.
 7th Grade Teacher
Palacios, Lydia Cuellar
 4th Grade Span/Bi-ling Teacher
Whitworth, Bryan Truman
 Teacher/Science Dept Chairman

PASADENA
Crew, Mary Helen Sims
 3rd/4th Grade Teacher
Dumbauld, James Eldon
 Sociology & Psychology Teacher
Fraser, Elsie Williamson
 8th Grade English Teacher
Riherd, Shirley Benedict
 Spanish Teacher/Dept Chair
Saccoman, Stefanie Ann
 Science Teacher/Dept Chair
Scott, Doretha Hollins
 Math/Sci Mentor Teacher
Sterling, Gary C.
 English Teacher
Van Beek, Richard Ray
 Administrator
Wilcox, Marjorie Sherrill Johnson
 Math Dept Chm/7th Gr Teacher

PENN VALLEY
Lake, Joelle Bonham
 Third Grade Teacher

PENRYN
Campbell, Tom
 4th Grade Teacher

PERRIS
Van Dyke, Patricia Westra
 Teacher/Guidance Counselor

PHELAN
Walker, Scott M.
 Music Director/Spanish Teacher

PICO RIVERA
Pakradouni, Roubine M.
 Kindergarten Teacher
Sandoval, Anthony Joseph
 GATE Algebra/Science Teacher

PINE VALLEY
Abood, Richard Michael
 Social Science Teacher

PINOLE
Causey, Nina C.
 English Department Chairman
Ito, Teruyo Shiraki
 English Teacher

PIRU
Arundell, James Edward
 5th & 6th Grade Teacher

PITTSBURG
Atchison, Beth Tillotson
 First Grade Teacher

PLACENTIA
Jones, Gai Laing
 Theatre Instructor
Kimble, Dottie Martin
 Third Grade Teacher
Murphy, Josephine Tagle
 Bilingual Second Grade Teacher
Oakley, Othniel
 Jr HS Math Teacher/Chairperson
Shaffer, Don
 Activities Director

PLACERVILLE
Cohen, Janet Sambucetti
 Science Teacher
Todd, Larrie Ann
 Consultant

PLEASANT HILL
Boylan, Burton Lyle
 Gifted Eng/US His Teacher
Pardi, Robert Paul
 Social Science Teacher
Sihler, Camille Carso
 Third Grade Teacher

POLLOCK PINES
Chappell, Roger Bernt
 7th/8th Grade Science Teacher
Hoffman, Elizabeth Anne
 Music Director

POMONA
Bell, Wilzetta Mable Burns
 Counselor
Milant, Jacqueline
 Third Grade Teacher
Speakman, J. David
 Mathematics Department Chair

PORTERVILLE
Merryman, Jane Merigian
 Kindergarten Teacher
Schultz, Andrew Nathan
 6th-8th Grade Teacher
Sidwell, Marlene Ahner
 Third Grade Teacher

PORTOLA
Ross, Brenda J.
 6th Grade Teacher

POWAY
Davis, Sprigg Dix
 Biology Teacher
Easter, Robert Wesley
 Spanish Teacher
Tilles, Rebecca Wynn
 9th-12th Grade English Teacher

QUINCY
Davis, Kathryn Walker
 Third Grade Teacher
Stoddard, Wesley D.
 Vocational Education Teacher

RAMONA
Solis, Linda Kathleen
 8th Grade Teacher

RANCHO CORDOVA
Cardwell, David Emmanuel
 Earth Science Teacher
Davidson, Alice Saari
 Mathematics Department Chair
Kotrlik, Helen G.
 Mathematics Teacher/Dept Chair
Swan, Linda Parker
 5th Grade Teacher

RANCHO CUCAMONGA
Rebeck, Diana Powell
 First Grade Teacher
Wright, Cora B. Judy
 5th & 6th Combination Teacher

RED BLUFF
Albright, Syrie Lance
 3rd Grade Teacher
Schwabauer, John Anthony
 Mathematics Teacher
Wilson, Sharon Crossan
 Second-Third Grade Teacher

REDDING
Armstrong, Debra A.
 Math Teacher,Dept Chair
Thompson, Sandra Lee
 Mathematics Teacher

REDLANDS
Butler, Paul L.
 Social Science Instructor
Harvard, William K.
 Mathematics Teacher
Leonard, Ann Burdett
 High School English Teacher
Mendoza, Charles Phillip
 Biology/Phys Science Teacher
Scharer, Juley Ann
 6th Grade Teacher

REDONDO BEACH
Maturko, Joan Imperati
 Kindergarten Teacher

REDWOOD CITY
Liner, Rodney Wade
 History Teacher

REDWOOD VALLEY
Platt, William G.
 Science Teacher

REEDLEY
Netzer, Frank L.
 Sixth Grade Teacher

RESEDA
Braaten, Glenn Orlen
 Science Teacher

RIALTO
Bell, Dotsie M. (St. Julian)
 English Department Chairperson
D'Souza, Edward John
 Science Department Chairman
Gold, Mitchell L.
 Social Studies Teacher
Howard, Steven Phillip
 Mathematics Teacher
Johnson, Ruth Floyd
 Social Studies Teacher
Lowrance, Yvonne Mathiasko
 Assistant Principal
Madison, Vera Johnson
 Independent Study Teacher
Montgomery, John David
 Sixth Grade Teacher

RICHMOND
Close, Sofia
 English Department Chair
Jonas, Jeffrey Stephen
 Science Teacher & Coach

RIVERDALE
Fritz, Tommy G.
 Mathematics Department Chair

RIVERSIDE
Gray, Charles Joseph
 Director of Bands
Hert, Theresa Marie
 Mathematics Teacher
Meade, Robert
 Math/Science Chair
Robinson, Nancy L.
 Third Grade Teacher
Valdez, Maxine Clemmer
 Spanish Teacher

ROLLING HILLS ESTS
Mc Gehee, John Hiram
 Physics Teacher

ROSEMEAD
Cazier, Patricia Allen
 Third Grade Teacher
Girard, Char
 Reading/Language Arts Teacher
Masiello, Don Carl
 Mathematics Department Chair
Spann, Samuel Cleotho
 Music/Art Teacher
Stark, Margaret C.
 4th Grade Teacher/Mentor

ROSEVILLE
Newton, Deborah Ward
 4th-6th Grade Music Teacher
Rath, William Edward
 Government Teacher/Dept Chair

ROSSMOOR
Ketchum, Nelline Delhousay
 Second Grade Teacher

ROWLAND HEIGHTS
Orrin, Kathy Garner
  Principal
Underberger, Carol R.
  English Teacher
Whitson, Mary M.
  Fifth Grade Teacher

SACRAMENTO
Andersen, Brian C.
  Spanish Teacher
Bersola, Gertrudes Apilado
  ESL/Lang Arts/Math Teacher
Bryant, Doreen Marie
  Mathematics Teacher
Calcagno, Frank W.
  US History/Geography Teacher
Coonrod, Larry D.
  Drafting Department Chairman
Elliott, Judith Carol
  HS English Teacher
Engilis, Sarah Shelburne
  English Teacher
Evans, Don L.
  English Teacher
Hauger, James R.
  Math Dept Chair & Teacher
Hitomi, Jennifer M.
  Kindergarten Teacher
Hodgins, Alec Terence
  French/Ceramics Teacher
Honda, Robert K.
  Counselor/Coach
Ikemoto, Atsushi
  Social Science Teacher
Schenk, Judy Fisher
  Teacher/Vice Principal
Wong, Janice Sasaki
  Mathematics Teacher

SAINT FRANCISVILLE
Hartness, Robert Arnold Jr.
  Science Teacher

SALINAS
Babczak, Nancy Elizabeth
  English Teacher
Dresner, Daniel August
  Biology Teacher
Felice, John Steven
  Mill Cabinet Instructor
Harryman, F. Allen
  Mathematics Department Chair
Roach, Nancy Cauble
  English Teacher
Thure, Rheta V.
  Mentor Teacher
Velasquez, Albert Lee
  6th Grade Teacher
Yee, Elizabeth Ann
  English Teacher

SAN BERNARDINO
Escobar, Patrick Fredrick
  Fine Arts Teacher
Martin, Catherine Verge
  Computer Teacher
Quinteron, Socorro Gomez
  Counselor
Sherman, Daryl Edith
  6th Grade Teacher
Stockard, Pamela D. Hopkins
  English Teacher

SAN DIEGO
Anthony, Elizabeth Mosby
  French Teacher
Bowers, Barbara Jeanne
  3rd-4th Grade Teacher
Conaway, Trudi
  7th Grade Basic Ed Teacher
Englund, Linda Trumbull
  English Department Chair
Garcia, Norma Lucia (de los Cobos)
  Sixth Grade GATE Teacher
Hammock, Maureen Burke
  English Teacher
House, Kay Marie Tuttle
  History/English Teacher
Krug, Brenda Illene (Ohm)
  5th Grade Teacher
Lux, Thomas David
  Chemistry Teacher
Montague, Jacqueline Minor
  Special Education Teacher
Negus, Irene Bertha
  Fifth Grade Teacher
Parks, Rena Elizabeth Lacey
  7th & 8th Grade Teacher
Petro, Gordon Lawrence
  Military Science Teacher
Petties, Joan Esmeralda Woods
  Spanish Teacher/Dept Chair
Scott, T. Michael
  English Teacher
Scranton, Walter M.
  Head Counselor

Shepard, Dorothy Hartense
  English Teacher
Smith, Joan Biddle
  Kindergarten Teacher
Spahn, Ethel Parkllan
  Cont. Family Studies Teacher
Trent, Joyce Tourangeau
  Language Art Specialist
Tuttle, Mark F.
  English Teacher
Webb, Gerald Edwin
  Military Science Teacher
Weiss, Brett Hirth-Vinik
  English Teacher/AVID Coord
Winbury, John
  English/History Teacher
Yost, Joan Foster
  English Teacher

SAN DIMAS
Armandan, Alan Anthony
  Fifth Grade Teacher

SAN FERNANDO
Dick, Jean Bertram
  Substitute Teacher
Hernandez, Diane
  ESL/Soc Stud/Mentor Teacher

SAN FRANCISCO
Chow, Homer Quon
  Biological Science Teacher
Choy, Patsy H. Q. Young
  Program Resource Teacher
Dickenson, Mary Margaret P.
  Junior HS Teacher
Ernster, Thomas Joseph
  English Teacher
Graham, Ruby
  Social Studies Dept Chair
Grear, Carl C. Jr.
  Soc Stud/His/Science Teacher
Harless, Susan Louise
  Seventh Grade Teacher
Heinz, Gerald F.
  English Department Head
Himberg, Glen R.
  Science Teacher
Hood, Sheila Chisholm
  Eighth Grade Teacher
Hsue, Betty Locke
  English/Reading/Math Teacher
Johnson, Gwendolyn Ann
  Math/Sci/ESL Teacher
Laygo, Teresito Marquez
  Mathematics Teacher
Lew, Ann R.
  English Teacher
Loo, Diana Lynne
  Mathematics Teacher
Lucas, Alice R.
  History/English Teacher
Mc Govern, Vincent John
  Chemistry Teacher
Pan, Nancy S.
  3rd Grade Teacher
Ruane, James Joseph
  English Teacher
Schnitzer, Robert Jay
  English/Drama/ESL Teacher
Spellicy, James Paul
  Social Studies Teacher
Steinberg, Harold Sylvan
  English Teacher

SAN GABRIEL
Goulard, Marilynn Heidenreich
  Second Grade Teacher
Killebrew, Catherine Denise Anderson
  Kindergarten Teacher

SAN JACINTO
Horney, Robert R.
  Elem Music/Mid Sch Chorus

SAN JOSE
Alcazar-Chavez, Gloria M.
  9-12 ESL Reading Teacher
Alessandri, Thomas Paul
  English/Theatre Arts Teacher
Bell, Catherine Ann
  7th/8th Grade Reading Teacher
Buchanan, Robert Bruce
  Sixth Grade Teacher
Bullock-Barnhill, Kathy Jo
  Performing Art Teacher
Cang, Paul
  French Teacher
Church, Robert W.
  Sci Chair/Physiology Teacher
Clute-Hill, Patricia Dione (Wade)
  Second Grade Teacher
Crane, Elizabeth Ann
  Third Grade Teacher
Dal Porto, David N.
  Teacher
Gilbeau, Jeanette Barnes
  Retired Teacher

Healy, William Joseph
  English Teacher
Hopes, Nancy Jean
  Fourth Grade Teacher
Jackson, Keith D.
  Sixth Grade Teacher
Kegley, Sandra Ann (Pettit)
  Third Grade Teacher
Lorenz, Virgil Glenn
  Social Science Teacher
Lugo, Josephine Reyes
  Mentor-Resource Eng Teacher
Lynch, Dennis M.
  Mathematics Instructor
Mariant, Philip J.
  Science Teacher
Martin, Loren Edward
  Math/Computer Science Teacher
Maurer, John Robert
  Music Director & Dept Chair
Miller, Edna Garcia
  Math Teacher
Orlando, Sal
  English Teacher
Simpson, Roberta Jean
  English Teacher
Sinclair, Steve James
  English Teacher
Sousa, Maria
  Fourth Grade Teacher
Sullivan, Connie Betts
  Gate Teacher
Tanton, Carol Leyh
  Eighth Grade CORE Teacher
Turner, Angeline Nease
  Science Teacher
Uyeda, Sharon
  Resource Specialist/Spec Ed
Wight, Linda Elaine (Rush)
  ESL Teacher
Williams, Mary Young
  English Teacher Mentor

SAN JUAN CAPISTRNO
Filzen, Kevin Joseph
  Phys Ed/Sci Teacher

SAN LEANDRO
Dolder, Karen Jones
  English Teacher

SAN LUIS OBISPO
Balfour, Linda Gracia
  English/Journalism Teacher
Kaufman, Jon Michael
  Math & Phys Ed Dept Chair
Olson, Brian
  Third Grade Teacher

SAN MARCOS
Garrett, Beckie Cole
  English Teacher
Hamilton, James Eugene
  Science Teacher
Preyss, Leonard Thor
  English Department Chair

SAN MARINO
Brown, Claudia Anne
  Mathematics/Journalism Teacher
Hall, Kevin Barry
  Social Science Dept Chair

SAN MATEO
Beltrame, Irvin Francis
  History-Economics Teacher

SAN PABLO
Kennedy, Ernest James
  Spec Ed Resource Specialist

SAN PEDRO
Addison, Claire K.
  Social Studies Teacher
Fisher, Glenn Loe
  Teacher
Haan, Candace Ann
  Fifth Grade Teacher
Henkel, Susan Diane
  English Teacher
Lenhardt, Kathleen Hannemann
  English & Speech Teacher

SAN RAFAEL
Hourigan, Don T.
  HS Mathematics Teacher
Skinner, Patrick F.
  English Teacher

SAN RAMON
Bensley, Heidi Lehto
  Spanish Teacher
Carroll, Kenneth L.
  Sci Dept Chair/Chem Teacher
Irwin, Robert Mowry
  History/Drivers Ed Instructor

SANTA ANA
Cody, Thomas Geraldine CSJ
  3rd Grade Teacher

Douglas, Mark Todd
  Chemistry Teacher
Green, Sabrina Sercombe
  Music Department Chair
Pichler, Laura O'Dell
  Advanced Placement His Instr
White, Sharon Anglin
  Principal

SANTA CLARA
Britschgi, Doris Walker
  Fifth Grade Teacher
Stuefloten, Jerry Telford
  Science Department Chair

SANTA CLARITA
Voeltz, Diane Fiello
  Assistant to Principal

SANTA CRUZ
Martinez, George Luis
  Mathematics Teacher

SANTA MARGARITA
Gee, Cheryl Mac Donald
  2nd Grade Teacher

SANTA MARIA
Flores, Jana Sue
  6th Grade Teacher
Freckleton, Janet Ellen
  Sixth Grade Teacher
Stephens, Dorothy Foreacre
  Teacher

SANTA MONICA
Dickey, Teresa Alice
  English Teacher
Platis, Margaret F.
  English Department Chair

SANTA PAULA
Hall, Cynthia Jean
  Music Teacher Chairperson

SANTA ROSA
Hogan, Katherine Louise (Vukovich)
  English Teacher
Mc Kenna, Eileen Marie
  Sixth Grade Teacher
Monroe, Beverly Jeanne
  9th Grade English Teacher
Orr, Deborah Wester
  8th Grade Teacher
Van Noy, Betty Alden
  Choral Music Teacher

SANTEE
Freedman, Andrea Sue
  Third Grade Teacher

SARATOGA
Bertaccini, Jo Pistarino
  8th Grade Teacher
Bissonnette, Veva Karlene
  Speech Teacher/Dir Of Forensic
Garcia, Ronald James
  Industrial Arts Chairman

SAUGUS
Bruins, Olive (Upton)
  English Teacher

SEBASTOPOL
Bertsche, Nancy L.
  Spanish Teacher
Parmenter, Harley James
  Science Teacher

SELMA
Hushek, Joseph Charles
  Math/Science Div Chairperson

SHAFTER
Guterez, Carole Lynn Bausano
  Fourth Grade Teacher
Martinez-Meeler, Kathleen
  High School Counselor

SIMI VALLEY
Davenport, Bill
  History Teacher
Hill, Lorraine Theresa
  7th/8th Grade Math/Eng Teacher
Tamoto, Janice Carlson
  Spanish Teacher

SOLANA BEACH
Eastwood, Myrna Lois
  Science Teacher
Pasarilla, Michael David
  Mathematics Department Teacher
Stine, Kathy
  Second Grade Teacher

SOLEDAD
Flint, Rodney Lewis
  6th Grade Teacher
Williams, Nancy Beatrice
  Second Grade Teacher

SONOMA
Hale, Eileen V.
  4th Grade Teacher
Weir, Gay Brewington
  Kindergarten Teacher

SONORA
Lindgren, Russell Edmund Jr.
  Soc Sci Dept Chair
Sieben, Patrick Timothy
  Music Instructor

SOQUEL
Daniele, Neil Anthony
  5th Grade Teacher

SOUTH EL MONTE
Menendez, Oscar
  Second Grade Teacher

STOCKTON
Avila, Herlinda Sandoval (Lopez)
  Bilingual Teacher
Bisagno, Eugene Jr.
  Biology Teacher
Conrad, Brian Lynn
  Mathematics Teacher
Dayap, Juanita Valoria
  Fifth Grade Bilingual Teacher
Hanlon, Robert John
  English/Latin Teacher
Hines, Kathleen Carson
  Math Dept Chair/Teacher
Jones, Tom
  Social Science Teacher
Mazzoula, Sandra Lee
  7th Grade Teacher of Gifted
Platti, Rita Jane Stranglo
  7th Grade Math Teacher
Sethasang, Veronica Directo
  Bilingual Teacher-Dept Chair
Wade, Jenny Schaffer
  Biology Teacher

STRATFORD
Alconcher, Caroline Bernades
  Third Grade Teacher
Weigand, James Paul
  8th Grade Teacher

STRATHMORE
Truman, Norris Wesley
  Director of Counseling

SUN VALLEY
Bradley, Nicholas Holt
  English Teacher/Eng Dept Chair
Chapman, David L.
  English Teacher
Davis, Daniel Robert
  Teacher
Markham, E. Lynda Jameson
  Coord/Instr/Mentor Teacher
Perry, Raymond Y.
  Junior High School Teacher

SUNNYVALE
Birley, Dorothy Wallenstien
  Kindergarten Teacher
Sherman, Eleanor O. (Stone)
  Kindergarten/1st Grade Teacher
Stewart, Cheryl Larson
  Math Teacher/Academic Advisor

SUSANVILLE
Mc Cann, John Leo Jr.
  Social Sci Dept Chairperson

SYLMAR
Howard, William Cameron
  English Teacher

THERMAL
Riggs, Bessie Barnes
  6th Grade ESL Teacher

THOUSAND OAKS
Baker, Lareen Skogi
  Kindergarten Teacher

THREE RIVERS
Lebsock, Richard Dale
  7th Grade Teacher

TIPTON
Pharis, Michael M.
  8th Grade Teacher

TOLLHOUSE
Duwe, Cynthia Kay
  Spanish Teacher

TORRANCE
Lewis, Eric Stephen
  8th Grade Teacher
Oghigian, Jeanette Linda
  Teacher
Porter, Carol Kiernan
  English/Eng 2nd Lang Teacher

TRACY

Christman, Deborah Robertson
Project Asst/Resource Teacher
Traina, Diane Ciarlo
English Teacher

TULARE

Caetano, David Frank
Agricultural Instructor
Hillman, Sue Ann (Elliott)
Math Teacher/GATE Teacher
Jensen, John A.
US History Teacher
Kusserow, James Vernon
Band Director
Levine, Ronald Stuart
Superintendent/Prin/Teacher
Maness, Joan Jensen
Second Grade Teacher
Rinker, Mary E.
5th/6th Grade Teacher
Robinson, Edward A. Jr.
Teacher

TUOLUMNE

Atkins, Thomas Wilson
6th Grade Lang Art Teacher
Courtney, Alma L.
7th/8th Grade Teacher
Paquette, Mary Grace
French/Spanish Teacher

TURLOCK

Keennon, Carol Colleen
5th & 6th Grade Teacher
Marshall, Wilbur Lane
Counselor
Mc Donough, Robert R
Jr HS Soc Stud/Phys Ed Teacher
Ohman, Jerome C.
Mathematics Department Chair
Pellegrini, Carolyn Ann
4th Grade Teacher

TUSTIN

Marshall, Donald Kenneth
Drama & Speech Teacher
Weisz, Del
His Dept Chair/US His Teacher

TWAIN HARTE

Anderson, Gary Louis
7th/8th Lit Based His Teacher
Moore, Donald R.
Principal

TWENTYNINE PALMS

Lockwood, Nolan D.
Mathematics Teacher
Luke, Carolyn Haycock
United States History Teacher
Meyer, Elizabeth Hatch
Spanish Teacher

UKIAH

Boynton, Philip Henry
Social Science Dept Chairman
Falgout, Marshall
Mathematics Teacher
Graves, John Cyrus
Social Studies Teacher
Harris, Jerilyn Rolinson
Biology Teacher

UNION CITY

Kukulica, Ann Perreira
Teacher/Curriculum Leader

UPLAND

Craig, Lana Robb
Spanish Teacher
Guilfoyle, Marge Mary
English Teacher
Lubarsky, Marilyn E.
Social Studies Teacher
Sweetland, Greta Woods
Second Grade Teacher
Thompson, Valerie Hamilton
English/History Teacher
Yamamoto, Paul Akira
Science Teacher/Dept Chair

VACAVILLE

Blair, Judy Willis
1st-6th Grade Music Specialist
Wong, Anthony Martin
Science Instructor

VALLEJO

Bigoski, Frank Paul III
Music Instructor
Carmichael, Marilyn Zuppan
8th Grade Teacher
Harris, Rosemary Silvestri
Kindergarten Teacher

VALLEY SPRINGS

Spitzer, Mary Elizabeth
Fifth Grade Teacher

VAN NUYS

Bonyhady, Elizabeth M.
Teacher
Dent, Berdine Cloud
Sixth Grade Teacher
Dunlop, J. Catherine Biggs
English Teacher
Steele, Walter Daniel
Mathematics Dept Chairman

VENTURA

Diehl, Gary Edward
Eng/Creative Writing Teacher
Jones, Patsy Lee
English/Physical Ed Teacher
Mikles, Christine Methorn
Math Teacher/Coach

VICTORVILLE

Crenshaw, Melvin L.
Curriculum Coordinator
Dale, Robert Eugene Jr.
Sixth Grade Teacher
Lentz, Jerry Duane
English Department Chair
Pettinger, Ann Richards
Honors English Teacher
Shibata, Kirk Michael
Mathematics Teacher

VISALIA

Boucher, Ronald H.
Business Teacher
Hungerford, Richard Ray
Teacher/Coach
Loyd, Rondald
Teacher/Department Head
Mc Ninch, Stacy H.
Mentor/Eng/Rdng/His Teacher
Powell, Nancy Ann
6th Grade Teacher
Sylvia, John D.
Agriculture Teacher/Dept Chair
Westra, Roger Dean
Business Teacher
Wheatley, Patricia Spagel
4th Grade Teacher
Williams, Sara Sally Coburn
Lang Art Teacher/Dept Chairman
Winterton, Victoria Thompson
Chemistry Teacher
Wollenman, Maxine Michelle (Veyna)
7th/8th Grade English Teacher

VISTA

Lacey, David Steven
Assistant Principal

WALNUT

Van Wagoner, Jane Ellen (Schobe)
Home Economics Teacher

WALNUT CREEK

Engel, Twyla Joy
Third Grade Teacher
Johnson, Elizabeth A.
French Teacher/Dept Chair
Thomas, Keith A.
Computers Chair/Instructor

WARNER SPRINGS

Morris, Marcia Humphrey
First Grade Teacher

WASCO

Grisso, Miriam Louise
Band Director

WATSONVILLE

Guynn, Rod K.
Assistant Principal
Halfwassen, Bill
Band Instructor

WEAVERVILLE

Wallace, John Wayne
Eighth Grade Teacher

WELDON

Carroll, Ruth A.
7th/8th Grade Language Teacher

WEST COVINA

Elder, Shirley Brown
8th Grade Eng/Soc Stud Teacher
Fitzgerald, Margaret Lou
Math/Art Teacher

WEST PITTSBURG

Baker, Marlene Pallotta
Core Department Chair
Tilford, Barbara L.
8th Grade Core/Drama Teacher

WEST SACRAMENTO

Green, Sandra Ackerman
English Department Chairman

WESTLAKE VILLAGE

Robertson, James H.
Principal

WESTMINSTER

Fairchild, Alice Zack
Third Grade Teacher
Fielder, Linda Sims
Second Grade Teacher
Gardner, John Goodenough
Fifth Grade Teacher
Matza, Nathan
Health Teacher
Smith, David Walter
Freshman Science Teacher

WHITTIER

Lawrence, Marjorie Julie
7th-8th Grade Eng-Lit Teacher
Running, Jolene
English/Mathematics Teacher
See, Robert Harold
Science Teacher

WILLIAMS

Gobel, Cynthia
4th Grade Teacher

WILMINGTON

Briscoe, Michele Loeffel
French Teacher
De La Cal, Lourdes
Bilingual 4th Grade Teacher
Mannion, Angela
Jr HS Religion/Family Minister
Thompson, Sherril
3rd Grade Mentor Teacher
Ward, Vincent
Math/Physics/Chem Teacher

WOODBRIDGE

Potts, Nancy Tennant
Eng/Lang Arts Dept Chairperson

WOODLAKE

Burris, Hope Ainley
Kindergarten Teacher

WOODLAND

Daugherty, Mary E. (Howe)
6th Grade Teacher
Gouley, Janice Wadley
First Grade Teacher
Helvick, Linda A.
Phys Ed Teacher/Dept Chairman
Parker, Margaret Elaine (Thorburn)
Science Teacher

WOODLAND HILLS

Anderson, Kieth John
Mathematics Department Chair
Duke, Tobi
Music Department Chair
Harper, Shirley Louise
Social Science Teacher
Malik, Shagufta Adeeb
9-12th Grade Math Teacher
Spiro, Jonathan Peter
Social Studies Teacher
Van Velzer, Sharon Thill
Second Grade Teacher

YORBA LINDA

Horn, Jeanette Reed
Second Grade Teacher
Hudson, Trudy Castrup
Math/Language Art Teacher

YUBA CITY

Berri, Kenneth James
Mathematics Teacher
Briones, Max Jr.
Sixth Grade Teacher

YUCAIPA

Hayden, Kent Kane
Amer Govt/His HS Teacher
Mathers, Daniel Joseph
6th Grade Teacher
Watkins, Mark N.
English Teacher

YUCCA VALLEY

Barton, Bruce Andrew
World History Teacher
Downing, Wayne
History Teacher
Walker, Michael M.
Mathematics Instructor

COLORADO

ALAMOSA

Hay, Sandee Gilletti
Special Programs Director
Stegman, Joyce Lynn (Cramb)
Special Education Teacher

ANTON

Hayes, Annika Ellen
Mathematics-Art Teacher

ARVADA

Hinton, Janice M.
First Grade Teacher
Horst, John Russell
Latin & Classics Teacher
Hudspeth, Janet (Mauck)
Language Arts Teacher
Miller, Barbara Jean
Teacher of Handicapped
Rennels, V. Beth
Sixth Grade Teacher

AULT

Broeder, Iola Irene
Math Teacher

AURORA

Angelich, David Lawrence
Physical Education Teacher
Bergles, Matthew Paul
Social Studies Teacher
Bess, Barbara Kennedy
English Teacher
Budy, Betty Anne (Short)
Second/Third Grade Teacher
Busch, Phoebe Wood
European His/German Teacher
Carrier, Barbara Austin
Fifth Grade Teacher
Coble, Eric Clayton
Social Studies Teacher
Corby, Timothy Richard
Seventh Grade Soc Stud Teacher
De Conna, Thomas
English Teacher
Gaumer, Betty Jean
Chef Instructor
Grey, Linda Joy
Sixth Grade Teacher
Huffman, Betty L. Laursen
Mathematics Teacher
Medvig, Kay Johnson
3rd Grade Teacher
Ott, William L.
Mathematics Department Chair
Rinaldo, Angie Raicevich
Social Studies Teacher
Roaten, Diane L.
Third Grade Teacher
Smith, Blanche V. (Linville)
8th Grade Teacher
Williams, Elaine R.
5th Grade Teacher

BASALT

Matherly, Melissa Diane
Middle School Teacher
Palmer, Judy Bowlin
4th Grade Teacher

BAYFIELD

Horton, Thomas J.
Physical Ed/Health Teacher
Layton, Jesse J.
English/History Teacher

BERTHOUD

Rude, Debbie Mirich
Third Grade Teacher

BETHUNE

Schaff, Deanna K.
Mathematics/Science Teacher

BOULDER

Briggs, Roger Paul
Physics Teacher
Dolan, Maureen Therese
Sixth Grade Teacher
Henson, Earlene Viola (Ovletrea)
Jr HS Special Ed Teacher

BROOMFIELD

Blakemore, E. Jane Rush
Fourth Grade Teacher
Knight, Josephine Morrison
French Teacher
Meier, Beverly Loeffler
Science Curriculum Dir/Teacher
Schipper, Elis-Barbara Woeschka
German Teacher

BRUSH

Hess, Mark Steven
English Teacher

BURLINGTON

Fearon, Frederick David
6th Grade Math/Sci Teacher

CALHAN

Carter, Dennis R.
Athletic Dir/Phys Ed Teacher
Clark, Rose Mary
English Teacher

CAMPO

Cramer, Lynn
Math Teacher, Admin Assistant

CANON CITY

Cuppy, Barbara Ellis
Mathematics Teacher
Dean, Julie Ann
Dir Of Dramatics & Lang Arts
Hardin, Susan Royce
English Teacher

CARBONDALE

Cretti, Bonnie Elizabeth Birmingham
Social Studies Teacher
Hughes, Ronald D.
8th Grade English Teacher

CASTLE ROCK

Kissler, Jodene (Bartolo)
Mathematics Teacher
Mc Donnell, Sue S.
Substitute Teacher
Wigdahl, Matthew John
English Teacher

CHERAW

Martin, James David
Science Teacher

COLORADO SPRINGS

Abeyta, Raymond Lee
Sixth Grade Teacher
Anderson, Linda Maria
Science Teacher
Boggs, Lynne Alison
Science Teacher
Bowman, Jed R.
Science/Mathematics Teacher
Buck, Jana Ostrom
Latin Teacher
Callahan, Cathleen Anne
Phys Ed Teacher/Coach
Crumb, Candace Hertneky
English Teacher
Darpino, Victoria Gnojek
Elementary Vocal Music Teacher
Davies, Linda Petersen
Soc Stud Department Teacher
Downey, Douglas Franklin
Instrumental Music Chairman
Haberkorn, Jeanette InnToa
Eng-Drama Forensics Teacher
Hall, Susan Jane
Fifth Grade Teacher
Hood, Frank Richard
Phys Ed/Soc Stud Teacher
Jones, Dennis Lee
American History Teacher
Knoepke, Robin Mc Comes
English Teacher
Lartique, Chaurice Ransom
2nd Grade Teacher
Lucero, Melvin O.
Assistant Principal
Lupton, Ron E.
Art Teacher
Marshall, Kevin Karr
Science/Health Teacher
Mullins, Delores Williams
8th Grade Algebra/Math Teacher
Nuccio, Edward Anthony
Instrumental Music Teacher
Pacheco, Catherine De Rosa
6th Grade Teacher
Palmer, Ruth Banta
English Teacher/Eng Dept Chair
Passanete, Carl Jess
Jr High Counselor
Patterson, Richard John
Instrumental Music Department
Pell, Stafanie A.
English Teacher
Pitcher, Danny Francis
7th Grade Reading Teacher
Roberts, Wilma Juanita Mitchell
Choral Music Teacher
Sainer, Paul Anthony
Director of Bands
Singer, Karla Ann
8th Grade Lang Arts Teacher
Stevens, Ted
Art Dept Representative
Stewart, Sally
English Teacher
Warner, Marylin S.
English Teacher
Weed, Patricia Ann White
French Teacher
Williams, Edna Rene Middleton
Second Grade Teacher

COMMERCE CITY

Fuller, William Horace
Retired Teacher

CORTEZ

Kasper, Phil B.
5th/6th Grade Head Teacher
Reed, Ella Jeannetta Woolsey
Sixth Grade Teacher

DELTA

Colson, Charla Ruth
4th Grade Teacher
Crick, Wayne Dale
Science Teacher
Hansen, Dorothy Elizabeth
English Teacher
Smith, Veronica Rose
HS Mathematics/History Teacher

DENVER

Alcorn, Joan T.
Elementary Challenge Teacher
Angell, Elissa Becker
Librarian
Arriaga, Maricela
Span, French, Sci Teacher
Arthur, Mollie Sue
Political Science Teacher
Carey, Marty E.
English Department Chair
Dinh, Van Phuc
Teacher
Dorhout, Marlene Sue (Van Leeuwen)
Middle School English Teacher
Dugger, Mark Randal
Mathematics & Science Teacher
Garrisson, F. Terry
Social Studies Teacher
Gatewood, Patricia A.
Social Studies Teacher
Gray, Olga R.
Retired Third Grade Teacher
Greenberg, Roberta L. (Wolf)
English Department Chair
Hendricks, Bill L.
Math Teacher/Chairperson
Kile, Carol A.
Business Teacher
Lamle, Jack Duane
JROTC Instructor
Lewis, Andrea Deoria
Fourth Grade Teacher
Marsh, Robert Amil
Technical Education Teacher
Mc Daniel, Dennis Michael
Assistant to Superintendent
North, Carol Kay (Urban)
Teacher/Elementary Supervisor
Pope, Shirley Virginia
Retired Middle School Teacher
Saltar, Mary M. Robert
6th Grade Soc Stud Teacher
Schaefer, Lyle Loren
History Department Chairman
Shelton, Cheryl Ann
English Teacher
Simones, Marie Dolorosa
Social Studies/Eng Lit Teacher
Stansberry, Elizabeth Raby
Fifth Grade Teacher
Sullivan, Jean Stream
Retired Teacher
Thomas, William Corbin
English Teacher
Van Deman, Brenda Teter
7th/8th Grade Teacher

DOLORES

Argo, Brett L.
Music Director
Kratz, Janie Adams
Principal

DURANGO

Martinez, Susan Williams
6th Grade Teacher

EATON

Egloff, Diane Marie
Third Grade Teacher

EDGEWATER

Jordan, Gerald Eugene
English Teacher

ELBERT

Schoonover, Mary Ellen Ellen
Roseboom
English Department Head

ELIZABETH

Van Horn, Kareen L.
2nd Grade Teacher

ENGLEWOOD

Amberg, Patricia L.
Biology Teacher, Science Chair

Engel, Fred H.
Social Studies Teacher
Gavin, Twila Emge
Mathematics Teacher
Trelfa, Eugenia Henderson
Sixth Grade Teacher

ERIE

Avery, James B.
Kindergarten Teacher
Bledsoc, Robert Troy
Math Teacher

ESTES PARK

Day, Ann (Nagle)
English Teacher
Johnson, Robert Bruce
Reading/Writing Teacher
Kemmer, Jacquelyn J.
Language Arts Teacher

EVERGREEN

Ingram, Marjorie Mary
Counselor

FALCON

Oppermann, Marcia Evelyn (Nutt)
Foreign Language Teacher

FLAGLER

Harwick, Larry K.
6th Grade Teacher

FLORENCE

Caricato, Josephine Amanda (Gemma)
7th/8th Grade English Teacher

FORT CARSON

Coonfield, James Dee
Art Instructor

FORT COLLINS

Bachman, Wen
Electronics Instructor
Brown, Sally Jane
Language Arts Teacher
Duncan, Marlene Vaughn
Univ Supervisor-Stu Teachers
Greenwood, Tinka Kathleen Ann
Sixth Grade Teacher
Lane, Judith Ann
AP Hum/British Lit Teacher
Newlands, Donna Hull
Kindergarten Teacher
Payne, Maggie Ann
Applied Human Sciences Teacher

FORT LUPTON

Dailey, June Sauer
Retired Second Grade Teacher
Everitts, Donna Lee
High School English Teacher

FORT MORGAN

Kokes, Mark D.
Vocational Agriculture Teacher
Miller, Jack Richard
Chapter I/Cmptr Teacher

FOUNTAIN

Mueller, Janie Schieffelin
Chemistry Teacher

FRUITA

Allen, Judith Ann
History/Humanities/Lit Teacher
Arnett, Georgia Lee (Herring)
Math/Computer Literacy Teacher
Fox, David R.
Anatomy/Biology Teacher
Hunter, Nancy Crocker
English Teacher
Keller, Virginia Dority
Fifth Grade Classroom Teacher

GATEWAY

Mayhugh, Patsy Maria
3rd-5th Grade Teacher

GOLDEN

Thompson, Byron Keith
6th Grade Teacher

GRAND JUNCTION

Born, Frances Hollick
Art/Reading Teacher
Darnell, Barbara Kennedy
3rd-12th Grade Reading Teacher
Dexter, Coen Raye
Chemistry Teacher
Dickensheets, Patricia Lambert
Fourth Grade Teacher
Edmonds, Joan Marie
Phys Ed Teacher/Dept Chair
Gugat, Terry Michael
Social Studies Dept Chairman
Keithley, Ila May
Fifth Grade Elem Teacher
Provenza, Sam James
Physical Education Teacher

Waid, Louise Raber
Retired Teacher

GREELEY

Anderson, Christian Edward
Social Studies Teacher
Dennehy, Carolyn Ann
Bio Teacher/Scndry Sci Coord
Hanson, Kathleen Ann
Mathematics Teacher
Helwick, Virginia Dare
Fourth Grade Teacher
Patrick, Suzanne T. (Robinson)
Mathematics Teacher
Trautner, Brenda Kay
Second Grade Teacher

GROVER

Karlovetz, Marilyn Waythe
Business Teacher

GUNNISON

Wood, Rod A.
Social Studies Teacher

HOEHNE

Macaluso, Mark J.
History Teacher/Coach

HOLLY

Toth, Mary Ann A.
Second Grade Teacher

HOTCHKISS

Curtice, Brent Allan
Physical Education Dept Chair

IDAHO SPRINGS

Fredell, Conradt H.
Biology Teacher

IDALIA

Chamberlain, Dixie R.
Sixth Grade Teacher
Mansfield, Gail Wingfield
Art & English Teacher

ILIFF

Brandsted, Janice Torkelson
Mathematics/Computer Teacher

KARVAL

Nickell, Larry Arthur
Social Studies Teacher

KEENESBURG

Eisenman, Joann L.
Mathematics Teacher
Johnson, Linda L.
5/6th Grade Sci/Eng Teacher
Knies, William Stanton
Principal/Teacher

KIOWA

Balcerovich, Marjorie Ann
3rd Grade Elementary Teacher

LA JUNTA

Lowe, Betty Burtis
5th Grade Teacher
Tyler, Edwin A.
Band Director

LA SALLE

Kratzer, Dorothy Johnson
Second Grade Teacher
Lockhart, Jone E. (Tibbetts)
Art Teacher

LAFAYETTE

Henson, Bud
Art Teacher

LAKEWOOD

Berger, Sue Anne
Chemistry Teacher
Breidert, Dennis Dean
Teacher, Athletic Dir
Deuth, Allen
Social Studies Teacher
Johnson, Richard Orland
Language Arts Teacher

LAMAR

Setter, Alan Michael
Physical Science Teacher

LITTLETON

Anderson, Rahn E.
Language Art Instructor
Brown, Sandra J.
8th Grade Teacher
Condon, Patricia Elizabeth Heaton
French Teacher/Dept Chair
Crona, James Edward
Sixth Grade Teacher
Larrabee, Luann E.
7-8th Grade Teacher
Mikesell, Christine Louise
Mathematics Teacher
Miller, Bruce Gerard
Science Teacher

Ogden, Sally Northway
French/Psychology Teacher

LONGMONT

Adams, Derith Stoner
4th Grade Teacher
Block, Juliette Arline
Dept Chairperson-Sci Teacher
Brunner, Patricia Hain
English Teacher
Heiby, Edward C.
Chemistry Instructor
Mitchell, Mary Margaret
English Teacher
Sandmeier, Katherine K.
Social Studies Teacher
Small, Michelle Holcomb
AP Eng Teacher/Dept Chair
Stricklin, Patricia Naples
English Teacher
Suppe, Georgiana
5th Grade Teacher
Underwood, Robert Dean
English Teacher
Wunsch, Joan Martin
6th Grade Teacher

LOVELAND

Dittmar, Deborah John
Lang Art Teacher/Dept Chair
D'Orazio, Joseph
HS Spanish/Mathematics Teacher
Gatti, Cheryl G.
Mathematics Teacher
Mc Naney, Wendy Sue (Jochim)
First Grade Teacher

MANCOS

Newlin, Terry Ryan
Jr & Sr HS Phys Ed Teacher

MC CLAVE

Grasmick, Patty A.
9th&12th Eng/Spanish I Teacher
James, Renny
Art/Chemistry Teacher

MEAD

Elmquist, Gary Ray
Mathematics Teacher

MERINO

Johnson, Patsy June
Fourth Grade Teacher

MOFFAT

Kershner, Caren Doncaster
Science Teacher

MONTE VISTA

Davis, Helen Anderson
Sixth Grade Teacher

MONTROSE

Harris, Sandra Traver (Aeberli)
6th Grade Teacher/Team Leader

NORTHGLENN

Coolman, Rand William
Marketing Teacher/Coordinator
Renicker, John L.
Industrial Art Teacher
Talmage-Bowers, Kent Lee
English Department Chairman
Young, Doris Mussey
Third Grade Teacher

NORWOOD

Mc Kinney, Joan Mary Altgilbers
Substitute Teacher
Neisen, Thomas P.
Science/History Teacher

OLATHE

Adams, Nanette Alice
4th Grade Teacher
Perkins, Kathy Metts
Counselor

ORDWAY

Broadbent, Lorene (Riley)
High School Counselor

OURAY

Fagrelieus, Eric Walter
Science/Math Teacher

PALISADE

Settle, Virginia Martinez
English/Spanish Teacher

PAONIA

Cotten, Shirley Ann (Ayer)
Second Grade Teacher

PARKER

Mc Gee, Pamela Jo
English Teacher/Dept Chair
Ochsenbein, Dorothy Zirkle
Geometry/Algebra II Teacher
White, Sheri De Lue
4th Grade Teacher

PEETZ

Carlile, Jerry Don
Counselor/Coach
Schmale, Ruby Mae Wende
First Grade Teacher

PENROSE

Clear, Nancy Reed
Fourth Grade Teacher

PLATTEVILLE

Wallace, Robert Scott
Social Studies Teacher

PUEBLO

Aronofsky, Suzanne
Biology Teacher
Bonacquista, Joseph Martin
Social Studies Teacher
Guerrero, Gloria Teresa
Science Teacher/Dept Chair
Lee, Betty June (Swanson)
Mathematics Dept Chair
Lindquist, Sandra Skodack
Fourth Grade Classroom Teacher
Lindskog, Marjorie O.
Fifth Grade Teacher
Lockart, Susan Malony
2nd/3rd Grade Teacher
Meek, Connie Marie
Business Education Teacher
Miketa, Constance Genova
Mathematics Teacher
Pusatory, Katherine Ann
English/Drama Teacher
Sherman, Mary Jo
Reading Teacher
Stinchcomb, Marie Conty
Social Studies Teacher
Stutzman, Randal Grier
Social Studies Teacher
Takara, Brit S.
Fourth Grade Teacher
Taulli, Frank Vincent
Elementary Principal

RIFLE

Coleman, Marta Jo
English Teacher
Rosette, Lottie Stiers
Retired 2nd Grade Teacher

RUSH

Keller, George Ray
Phys Ed/Social Studies Teacher

RYE

Grey, Marilyn Cron
Retired Elementary Teacher

SAGUACHE

Lovato, Lori Goehl
Jr HS English/Science Teacher

SALIDA

Lambert, Edward Eugene
English/Social Studies Teacher
Meythaler, Eric Lanz
2nd Grade Teacher
Tessitore, Nick Jr.
1st Grade Teacher

SANFORD

Maestas, Ella Mary Montoya
4th Grade Teacher
Rudder, Bennie Jack
Industrial Arts Teacher

SECURITY

Cornils, Jay Albert
English Teacher
De Felice, Michael Joe
Phys Ed Teacher/Dept Chair
Hoffmann, Carmelita Languit
2nd Grade Teacher
Versaw, Francis Earl
Math Dept Chair/Teacher

SHERIDAN LAKE

Fees, Ruth
English Teacher

SPRINGFIELD

Chenoweth, Margaret Louise Quick
GED-ABE Teacher

STEAMBOAT SPRINGS

Campbell, Mike
High School Counselor

STERLING

Busteed, Patrick Lee
Geography/Psych/Cmptr Teacher
Eves, Donna Rae Dal Ponte
Science Teacher
Frank, Virginia Berkey
Third Grade Teacher
Hunter, Frank A.
Speech Teacher & Theater Dir

STERLING (cont)
Kautz, Robert Duane
Crafts Teacher
Mathis, Bernard Duane
Art/Indstrl Technolgoy Chair

STRASBURG
Shipley, Christopher Jon
7-12th Grade Soc Stud Teacher

THORNTON
Hyland, Marie Gargarella
Language Arts Teacher
Korn, J. David
English/Latin/History Teacher
Noah, Thelma Ann (Cage)
5th Grade Teacher
Robb, Don G.
Mathematics Teacher

TRINIDAD
De Bono, Carl Anthony
English Teacher
Maio, Norma Giardino
Retired Third Grade Teacher

USAF ACADEMY
Lundberg, Douglas T.
Science Teacher
Newburn, Mary Lou
English/Amer History Teacher

VAIL
Treat, Thomas Paul
Fourth Grade Teacher

WALDEN
Carlstrom, Claudia Jean
2nd Grade Teacher
Hodgson, Randy Lloyd
Physical Education Teacher

WALSENBURG
Hamilton, Deidre Lenzini
Language Arts Chair
Sharp, Tonya
Secondary Math/Science Teacher

WESTMINISTER
Thorton, Lisa Harper
Spanish Teacher

WHEAT RIDGE
Miller, Curtis H.
Physics Teacher

WINDSOR
Kisselman, Kenneth L.
4th Grade Teacher
Kula, Murray Robert
Health/Phys Ed Teacher
Kvamme, Mo Lloyd
Mathematics Department Chair
Weinmeister, Marilyn Schaefer
6th Grade Math Teacher

WOODLAND PARK
Black, Larry A.
7th/8th Grade Soc Stud Teacher
Dodds, Stan W.
Athletic Director
Hoffman, Marta S.
Chemistry/Science Teacher

WRAY
Evans, Richard A.
Mathematics Department Chair
Kolling, Nola Rae
Kindergarten Teacher

YUMA
Noble, Barbara Severin
Classroom Teacher
Wingfield, Jolene K.
4th Grade Teacher

CONNECTICUT

ANSONIA
Calabrese, Mario
Fifth Grade Teacher

BETHANY
Prezioso, Arlene Gorman
Mathematics Teacher

BETHEL
Pjura, Mary Madonna
1st Grade Teacher

BRANFORD
De Caprio, Judith La Vorgna
Social Studies Teacher

BRIDGEPORT
Bergeron, Thomas Ernest
Teacher of Hearing Impaired

Brooks, Evanne Sinclair
Fourth Grade Teacher
Listorti, Robert V.
Mathematics Specialist
Russell, Michele Taf
Mathematics Teacher
Zello, Suzanna Marie
Principal

BRISTOL
Lumpkin, Douglas E.
6th Grade Teacher

BROOKFIELD
Grenier, Kenneth L.
7th/8th Grade Math Teacher
Lohmann, Mary G.
Teacher/Academically Talented
Newell, Eugene L.
Teacher of Gifted/Talented
Smith, Carole L.
English Teacher

BROOKLYN
Socquet, Dianne Falardeau
Teacher

CENTRAL VILLAGE
Hadfield, Cornelia Ann (Czajkowski)
7th-12th Grade Math Consultant
Robbins, Carol Allen
English Department Chair
Sweatt, Linda Espinola
Mathematics Teacher/Dept Chair

CHESHIRE
Andrews, Valerie Warner
Foreign Lang Dept Chair
Chute, Allen Francis
English Teacher
Richard, Kathleen S. Maffucci
Volunteer Teacher
Teator, Robert H.
Industrial Arts Teacher

CLINTON
Fragola, Anthony Donald
Biology-Chemistry Teacher

COVENTRY
Matson, Joan Buckley
Third Grade Teacher

CROMWELL
Baron, Donald C.
Mathematics Teacher/Curr Coord

DANBURY
Arconti, Joseph Aldo
7th Grade Earth Sci Teacher
Hipp, Kenneth T.
4th Grade Teacher
Mc Cauley, David A.
Social Studies Teacher
Proudfoot, Harold B.
Teacher
Sanches, Clemente Vaz
Spanish/Portuguese Teacher
Skelly, Linda Brigid O'Keefe
English Teacher
Smigala, Theodore Francis
US History Teacher

DEEP RIVER
Judd, Edward Emil
Business Education Teacher

EAST HAMPTON
Badolato, Nicholas Francis
Art Teacher
Winters, Lisa Schuerholz
Soc Stud Teacher/Team Leader

EAST HARTFORD
Turner, Alexander L.
Art Teacher

EAST HAVEN
Gilbert, Marie Brady
Transitional Teacher
Ryan, Maureen Holman
5th-8th Grade Science Teacher

EAST LYME
Woudenberg, Thomas John
Biology Teacher

ELLINGTON
Arnore, Janet (Laterra)
Mathematics Teacher

ENFIELD
Brown, William Morgan
4th Grade Teacher
Falicki, Mary Noel (Anna S.)
Teachers Aide
Mc Carthy, Donna Kanner
Spanish Teacher

FAIRFIELD
Andrade, Donna Marie
Dir/Stu Support Services

Giegengack, Edward Thomas
Mathematics Teacher
Honey, John H.
Biology Teacher
Mitchell, Joan Betar
First Grade Teacher
Rivers, Nancy L.
4th Grade Teacher
Sakal, Wayne
Physics Teacher
Yost, Debra Ann
Home Economics Instructor

GRANBY
Glowacki, Walter M.
Geography Teacher
Smith, Raymond Kevin
English Teacher

GREEN FARMS
Caputi, J. Gary
Science & Economics Teacher

GROTON
Christie, Louise T. Berard
Fourth Grade Teacher

GUILFORD
Cassidy-Smith, Mary Elizabeth
Second Grade Teacher
Cinotti, Daniel A.
Science Chair/Teacher
Garbar, Joan Hayes
English Teacher
Larson, B. Kaye
Health/Phys Ed Teacher
Pallenberg, Jane Stamler
Social Studies Teacher
Smith, Frederick Samuel
Social Studies Teacher

HAMDEN
Annunziata, Adelaide De Lucia
Chapter I Teacher
Bass, Susan Fedele
English Teacher
Farley, John Gilbert Jr.
Science Teacher
Shinko, Rosemary Ellen
European History Teacher

HARTFORD
Anthony, Billie C.
Teacher of Gifted & Talented
Colvin, Ruth
Resource Teacher
Hodges, Walter O.
4th Grade Head Teacher
Kurns, Brenda Salowitz
Science Teacher
Lyons, Judith C.
English Teacher
Niles, Rhonda Rucker
Reading/English Teacher
Rusell, Douglas Thomas
8th Grade US History Teacher
Tallman, Patrick H.
Guidance Counselor
Welch, Mary Passamano
Teacher

HARWINTON
Janovic, Susan Gillette
Third Grade Teacher

HUNTINGTON
Purciello, Terri Mich
2nd Grade Teacher

JEWETT CITY
Whitford, Patricia Anne
Spanish Teacher

LAKEVILLE
Tames, Sarah
Head of English Dept

LITCHFIELD
Fowler, Phillip Henry
Advanced Biology Teacher

MADISON
Rylander, Janet F.
English Dept Chair

MANCHESTER
Moore, Edward F.
Science Department Chair
Norman, Michael David
Fourth Grade Teacher
Wooldridge, William Henry
Science Teacher/Athletic Dir

MERIDEN
Erazmus, Cynthia
Second Grade Teacher
Holian, Jack Francis
Math Teacher

MIDDLEFIELD
Quinn, Judy Cavalier
First Grade Teacher

MILFORD
Antonio, Robert John
7th/8th Grade Math Teacher
Jahnke, Susan Alice
First Grade Teacher
Marottoli, Ralph Thomas Jr.
6th Grade Teacher

MONROE
Sondergaard, Joan Rumble
5th Grade Soc Stud Teacher

MOOSUP
Burns, Virginia Zimmerman
Teacher
De Loge, Alice (Stradczuk)
Principal
Hall, Ethel Stevens
8th Grade Teacher

NAUGATUCK
Guarino, Susan Santoro
5th-8th Grade Math Teacher

NEW BRITAIN
Petterson, Evelyn Elizabeth
Fifth Grade Teacher
Phair, Sandra Chaet
Univ Supervisor & Lecturer
Sagraves, Mary Anne (Bokan)
Language Art Teacher

NEW CANAAN
Appleton, Julia Elizabeth
Director of Public Relations
Poltrack, Leslie D.
5th Grade Teacher
Schneider, Ann Lenore
Teacher

NEW FAIRFIELD
Beeler, Patricia S Brooks
6th Grade Teacher
Bielizna, Judy Foley
Math Teacher/Team Leader
Olander, Mark G.
Seventh Grade Math Teacher
Russell, Gail Roberts
7th Grade Eng/Rdng Teacher
Rypka, Stephanie G.
Teacher of Academically Gifted

NEW HAVEN
Ayres, Audrey Johnson
Reading Teacher
Fadus, Marie Iadarola
High School English Teacher
Sullivan, Christine Anne
Spanish Teacher
Wilson, Dorothy Batts
Third Grade Teacher
Young, Audrey King
Fourth Grade Teacher

NEW MILFORD
Bigham, Robert John
5th Grade Teacher
Zaloski, Ellamae Baldelli
Mathematics Teacher

NORTH GROSVENORDAL
Sideris, Kathleen Sheehan
First Grade Teacher

NORTHFORD
Girard, Linda Ann
Transitional 1st Grade Teacher

NORWALK
Doeberl, Gail L.
Foreign Language Teacher
Wolfe, Sheila Anne
Art Teacher

NORWICH
Aleskiewicz, Isabelle Twomey
Second Grade Teacher
Campbell, Hugh
Economics Teacher
English, Mary Elizabeth
11th/12th Grade US His Teacher
Fields, John Thomas
Math Teacher
Krieger, Morton Irwin
Math Teacher
Leta, Frances Banas
Asst Headmaster for Humanities
Nardone, Marianne Wlodkowski
Assistant Superintendent

OAKDALE
Kaczor, Charles S.
8th Grade History Teacher
Lamperelli, Robert Nicholas
Social Studies Dept Chair

Rawn, Kenneth H.
Social Studies Teacher
Sullivan, Lorna Nybakken
Fourth Grade Teacher

ORANGE
Burkus, Jean Casale
Biology Teacher/Sci Dept Chair
Pollins, John Anthony
Social Studies Teacher
Riordan, Michael J. Jr.
5th Grade Teacher

OXFORD
Cesaroni, Ellen K.
Spanish Teacher
Morrow, Adrienne Vida
Third Grade Teacher
Sponheimer, Elizabeth Joy
Language Art Teacher
Stopper, Virginia Sweet
Home Economics Teacher

PLAINFIELD
Imbriaco, Dianna Rose
Business Teacher
Marchesseault, Marian Sammataro
Kindergarten Teacher

PLAINVILLE
De Thomas, Carolyn R.
Science Department Chairman
Thompson, Carroll Richard
Mathematics Teacher

RIDGEFIELD
Bollenback, Dirk
Soc Stud Teacher/Dept Chm
Gaumer, Jean Erickson
English Teacher
Larson, Eric A. Jr.
Band Director/Music Teacher

ROCKY HILL
Rawski, Barbara Anne
2nd Grade Teacher

SEYMOUR
Giannone, Carolyn Weselcouch
Second Grade Teacher

SHELTON
Martin, Susan Simmons
Social Studies Teacher
Yolish, Kathleen T.
Second Grade Teacher

SHERMAN
Chapin, Donna Williams
4th Grade Teacher
Zellner, Virginia Anne (Cordasco)
K-5th Enrichment Sci Teacher

SIMSBURY
Domin, Paul P.
5th Grade Teacher

SOMERS
Roberts, Steven Ernest
Food Service Teacher

SOUTH MERIDEN
Carley, Rose Nigri
5th Grade Teacher
Toifl, Karlyn J.
4th Grade Teacher

SOUTHBURY
Griffin, Margaret M.
Spanish Teacher

SOUTHINGTON
Cipollini, Joseph G.
Gifted, Sci, Math Teacher
Freitag, Walter Fred
4th Grade Teacher
Remirez, Ellen Scadden
Foreign Lang Chm/Span Teacher
Zanetti, Rosanne Derynioski
German Teacher

STAMFORD
Antonowicz, Raymond C.
Teacher of Gifted & Talented
Pipping, Charlotte Helen SSMI
Director
Puglisi, Susan
Science Dept Chair
Sponaugle, Don Lee
Science Teacher
Tibbetts, Lutitia Bowen
3rd Grade Teacher

STRATFORD
Ewing, James G
History/Social Studies Teacher
Karst, Teri Susan
Fifth Grade Teacher
Moore, Marilyn Joyce Walluk
Third Grade Teacher

STRATFORD (cont)
Schueler, Maria Cavalieri
  French Teacher
Sutherland, Suzanne C.
  Sixth Grade Teacher
THOMASTON
Christianson, J. Dean
  Chemistry/Biology Teacher
Holbrook, Mary Lou Coffey
  Coordinator of Gifted/Talented
TORRINGTON
Gervasini, Marie Constance
  Fourth Grade Teacher
Porto, Louise C.
  Counselor
Royals, Raymond John
  Vocational Trade Instructor
TRUMBULL
Bair, James F.
  English Teacher
Berkman, Martin Lewis
  Social Studies Teacher
Crisanti, Gary A.
  Chemistry/Physics Teacher
Davis, Robert Joseph
  Biology Instructor
De Marco, Richard John
  Social Studies Teacher
Green, Rita R.
  English Chairman
Henry, Teresa M. CSJ
  Mathematics Teacher
Hunt, Laura Erickson
  Art Instructor
Jonassen, Linda Jean
  6th Grade Teacher
VERNON-ROCKVILLE
Spare, Patricia Kania
  Fifth Grade Teacher
WALLINGFORD
Baldelli, Larry Albert
  Science Teacher
Corbett, Cozette P.
  Third Grade Teacher
Costa, John Joseph
  Technology Education Teacher
Hetzel, Nancy K.
  German Teacher
Sylvestro, Philip Joseph
  Social Studies Teacher
Taylor, Irene L. Jellon
  Vocational Ed Dept Chairperson
WATERBURY
Barnes, Patricia Quinn
  French Teacher
Blancato, Patricia Ciarlone
  Spanish Teacher
Coss, Barbara Joan Atwood
  Kindergarten Teacher
Fraser, Brian Stephen
  Eighth Grade Teacher
Hudson, Pennie Dianne
  Fifth Grade Teacher
Hurdle, James Walter
  7th Grade English Teacher
Laudati, Edmund A.
  Mathematics Teacher
Navage, Raymond G.
  Business Education Teacher
Polzella, Louis Vincent Sr.
  English Teacher
Samela, Lorraine Ann
  5th Grade Teacher
Verrastro, Carmella S.
  English Teacher
WEST HARTFORD
Guyon, Nancy Lent
  Social Studies Teacher
Price, Kathleen Kriscenski
  6th-8th Grade Teacher
WEST HAVEN
Avallone, Patricia Liberatore
  Sixth Grade Teacher
Bidney, Kathleen Mary
  Art Teacher
Farrands, Denise Ann
  Science & Religion Teacher
Grey, Marian Perkins
  5th Grade Teacher
Hoye, Presentation CSJ
  Jr HS Teacher
Parkinson, William Henry
  Religious Studies Teacher
Raffone, Rudy Jr.
  Mathematics Teacher
WESTPORT
Morrison, Edward James
  Teacher
Rhodes, Stanley Williams
  Sci/Industrial Arts Coord

WETHERSFIELD
Evanisky, Joan
  Fifth Grade Teacher
WILLIMANTIC
Anthony, Beverly Bellavance
  Gifted & Talented Prgm Teacher
Fausey, Janis P.
  Social Studies/Latin Teacher
WINDSOR
Sullivan, Mary Brackett
  Teacher of Gifted
Williams, Mark C.
  History Teacher
WINSTED
Higgins, John Michael
  Latin Teacher
WOODBRIDGE
De Nicola, Richard Vincent
  Chemistry Teacher
Gibbons, Vicenta Calzadilla
  Spanish Teacher
Ginnetti, Anthony Joseph
  Fifth Grade Teacher
Hunt, Dennis Charles
  History Teacher
Shinkman, Karen L.
  Math Teacher/Dept Chair

DELAWARE

BEAR
Wissinger, Carolyn Crawford
  Teacher
BRIDGEVILLE
Carey, Peggy Marie
  English Teacher
Smith, Robin W.
  Secondary Business Teacher
CAMDEN-WYOMING
De Long, David Clarence
  Dir of Bands/Music Dept Chair
Johnson, Jeffrey Scott
  Social Studies Teacher
CLAYMONT
Krieder, Harry Moyer
  Biology Teacher/Sci Dept Chm
DELMAR
Baione, James Anthony
  Band Director
DOVER
Cauff, Deborah Lee
  Mathematics Teacher
Eaton, Jerren Unruh
  1st Grade Teacher
Hartnett, Elizabeth Anne Hutchison
  English/History Teacher
Kirk, Jan Baechler
  Biology Teacher
O'Brien, Janie C.
  First Grade Teacher
Patosky, Edward Joseph
  6th Grade Sci & Math Teacher
Ricks, Annie Echols
  6th Grade Science Teacher
Thompson, Patricia Campbell
  English/Journalism Teacher
Villa, Hector E.
  Spanish Teacher
ELSMERE
Gibbons, Joanne D.
  English Teacher
FELTON
Fields, Rachel Ouellette
  French Teacher
Ward, Randall Lee
  5th Grade Teacher
Wood, Judith Croft
  Business Teacher
GEORGETOWN
Moore, Judy Davis
  Sixth Grade Teacher
HARTLY
Riser, Jamila Q.
  Mathematics Teacher
HOCKESSIN
Ahlborn, Patricia Lee (Horn)
  Mathematics Department Head
LAUREL
Morris, Margo Lane
  Phys Ed/Health Teacher/Coach
Phillips, Ruth Ann
  Language Arts Chair

Sizemore, Emilie J.
  Guidance Counselor
LEWES
Eisenhour, Michael U.
  Mathematics Department Chm
Walls, Judith A.
  3rd Grade Teacher
MILFORD
Short, Margaret Carol
  English Teacher
MILLSBORO
Basara, Judith S.
  Kindergarten Teacher
Mitchell, Margaret Shockley
  English/Literature Teacher
MILTON
Jenkins, Elizabeth Mc Daniel
  Mathematics Teacher
Miller, Shirley Phillips
  Mathematics Teacher
Wilkinson, Sara Dill
  Fourth Grade Teacher
NEW CASTLE
Kuehlwein, Robert Elvir
  Social Studies Teacher
Moran, Melody Joy
  English/Speech Teacher
Oren, Rosemary Broome
  6th-8th Grade Grammar Teacher
NEWARK
Bowen, Lewellyn Murphy
  English/Gifted Teacher
Ciminello, Susan Mary
  Kindergarten Teacher
Hammonds, Jay A.
  Department Chair, Teacher
Huff, Charles Carlton
  Soc Stud Dept Chair/Teacher
Mc Fann, Jane Catherine
  English Teacher
Mc Vaugh, Charles P. Jr.
  US History Teacher
Perry, Patsy Pipkin
  Business Education Teacher
Pulliam, Dolores Anna Swiggett
  Third Grade Teacher
Remsburg, Charles Doug
  English Teacher
Rumsey, Robert Charles
  Technology Teacher
Shaw, Andrewetta Anderson
  7th Grade Science Teacher
Talley, Geraldine Anne
  Language Art/Reading Teacher
SEAFORD
Briddell, Deborah Ambrosia
  Teacher of Visually Impaired
Hancock, Stephen Paul
  History Department Chair
SMYRNA
Davis, Georgia Ann
  Second Grade Teacher
Knotts, Edith Priestley
  Third Grade Teacher
Myers, Michael Lynn Sr.
  Social Studies Teacher
Shotzberger, George Lee
  Art Teacher
WILMINGTON
Denney, Sandra Lee
  6th Grade Teacher
Eshleman, Ronald Eugene
  Chemistry Teacher
Ford, Thomas Lee
  Mathematics Instructor
Godt, Frances Wilson
  Science/Reading Grades Teacher
Grandell, Sara Mc Laughlin
  8th Grade Teacher
Harasika, Elena Lopatka
  6th Grade Gifted Teacher
Hutson, Carrie M. (Simpers)
  Mathematics Teacher
Kleier, Catherine Boone
  Mathematics Teacher
Matusoff, Seymour Bernard
  Mathematics Department Chair
Miller, Mark Leroy
  Soc Stud Teacher/Team Leader
Mullins, Robert S.
  Dir of TV Services/His Teacher
Scheu, Grace Marie
  Third Grade Teacher
Sechler, Louise Brusca
  Mathematics Teacher
Shanley, Deanna Genua
  European/World History Teacher
Thomas, Benjamin L.
  English Teacher

Wiesel, Mary Helen
  English Teacher
Wittman, Jonathan R.
  HS Band Director
Wright, Carol S.
  Social Studies Teacher
Wright, Therese Louise
  2nd Grade Teacher

DISTRICT OF COLUMBIA

WASHINGTON
Anderson, Barbara Mills
  Guidance Counselor
Battle, Beverly Cheryl
  Second Grade Teacher
Bell, Betty E.
  History Teacher
Berry, Renee Redonia
  Chemistry Teacher
Bishop, Jane Dodson
  Home Economics Teacher
Botta, Kenneth Marie
  Fourth Grade Teacher
Brown, Iona Burke
  Mathematics Teacher/Dept Chair
Brown, Nathaniel N.
  Social Studies Teacher
Carter, Jeanette Walker
  Assistant Principal
Chriss, Sandra Walker
  English Teacher
Cooke, Nellie
  English Teacher
Daly, Sally Louise
  7th Grade His/Lit Teacher
Davenport, Cullen Bruce
  Social Studies Dept Chairman
Epps, Lee Hamilton
  Eng Teacher/Asst Dept Chair
Faison, Ethel Speight
  Teacher
Ferris, Lorraine Catherine
  English Teacher
Hill, Amy P.
  Fourth Grade Teacher
Jackson, Regina B.
  9th Grade English Teacher
Johnson, Stanley Francis
  ESL Span Teacher/Frn Lang Chm
Knox, Barbara A.
  Mathematics Teacher
Lippmann, Richard D.
  Social Studies/Hum Teacher
Little, Linda Blackmon
  Teacher
Lucas, Barbara Logan
  Third Grade Teacher
Martin, Muriel Lea
  Social Studies Teacher
Marvin, James Paul
  Theatre Instructor
Merchant, Beatrice Byrd
  English Teacher
Moore, Marilyn Bracey
  Employability Skills Teacher
North, Carol Ann
  English Teacher
Pearce, Hollis (Edney)
  Fourth Grade Teacher
Reidy, George Hughes
  Mathematics Department Chair
Robinson, Martha Allie Moe
  4th Grade Teacher
Savoy, Doris Jean Hurd
  Spanish Teacher
Taylor, Roberta Cookie
  8th Grade Teacher
Turner, William Davis
  Band Director
Wilkins, Pamella Turner
  English Teacher
Williams, Frances Elizabeth
  Soc Stud Teacher/Dept Chair

FLORIDA

ALACHUA
Biggs, Cynthia Gardner
  8th Grade Soc Stud Teacher
Campbell, Janet Ernst
  2nd Grade Team Teacher
Huckstep, Alice Damin
  Art/Humanities Teacher
Randolph, Gloria J.
  Life Management Skills Teacher
Whittle, Dorothy Douglas
  8th Grade English Teacher

ALTAMONTE SPRINGS
Erickson, Sandra Valerie
  Gifted English Teacher
Fawcett, Virginia Carroll
  Gifted Teacher
Nieto, Shirley Bridgman
  Anatomy/Biology Teacher
Sciortino, Maria
  Jr High Math Teacher
APALACHICOLA
Kelley, Beverly Cashul
  Reading/World History Teacher
Simmons, Elinor Mount
  4th Grade Educator
APOPKA
Carswell, Deborah Bell
  Teacher of Gifted
Kirton, Timothy Lee
  English Department Chair
Wehr, Donald Lee
  Teacher
ARCADIA
Aceto, Cheryl L.
  7th Grade Mathematics Teacher
Russell, Peggy Boggess
  Social Studies Dept Chairman
Simmons, Pamela Auger
  Assistant Principal
AUBURNDALE
Gano, Janet Anne
  English Teacher
Hinegardner, Barbara Hartman
  Home Economics Teacher
Johnson, Denise Clary
  Fourth Grade Teacher
Sterling, Sandra Elaine
  English Teacher
AVON PARK
Claussen, Van Earle
  Elementary Teacher
BAKER
Barton, Mary Beth
  History Dept Chairman
Bryan, Janet Smith
  Mathematics Dept Chm/Teacher
BARTOW
Allison, Eleanor Adele
  Anatomy/Physiology Teacher
BELL
Powers, Allen Weston
  Mathematics Teacher
BELLE GLADE
Williams, John E.
  Fifth Grade Teacher
BELLEVIEW
Walton, Lorene Kiner
  Fifth Grade Teacher
BLOUNTSTOWN
Hanna, Enoch Hamilton
  6th Grade Math/Science Teacher
BOCA RATON
Baum, Susan Diane
  Guidance Coordinator
Darman, Laurie Thayer
  Sixth Grade Teacher
Giarrusso, Jean A.
  Mathematics Teacher
Goldsmith, Richard Iles
  History Teacher
Newnam, Cindy Lynn
  Director of Public Relations
BRADENTON
Casey, John Patrick Jr.
  Mathematics Teacher
Hill, Glen Roy
  Chemistry Teacher
Murphy, Patricia Elizabeth
  Social Studies Dept Chair
Wade, Afra Brouwer
  Mathematics Teacher
BRANDON
Dever, Annie Grace
  5th Grade Teacher
BRISTOL
Strickland, Charlotte D.
  Language Arts Teacher
BRONSON
Hastings, Robert Olin
  Principal
Spivey, Cheryl Sims
  Second Grade Teacher
BROOKSVILLE
Foster, Sayde P.
  English Department Chair

BROOKSVILLE (cont)
Thompson, Donald Neal
  Mathematics Teacher

BRYCEVILLE
Braxton, Gwendolyn C. Jackson
  2nd Grade Teacher

BUNNELL
Noble, Fran Zuckerman
  Marketing Teacher

BUSHNELL
Thompson, Nancy Wagner
  Vocational Home Ec Teacher

CAPE CORAL
Maxwell, Steven Robert
  Social Studies Instructor
Nolff, Dale Charles
  Financial Planner
Propert, Sue Ann Scimenes
  English Teacher

CASSELBERRY
Christiana, Joseph John
  8th Grade Amer History Teacher
Johnson, Amy Ballantyne
  7th Grade Geography Teacher

CHATTAHOOCHEE
Mauck, Dolores Gerzina
  Kindergarten Teacher
Rodgers, Janice Duke
  Social Studies Teacher

CHIEFLAND
Barnes, Marie Matern
  Social Studies Dept Chairman
Swilley, Deborah Rivers
  Fifth Grade Teacher

CHIPLEY
Barber, Betty R.
  Third Grade Teacher
Porter, Gail Godfrey
  Science Department Chair

CLEARWATER
Clark, Martha E.
  Anthropology Teacher
Cummings, Mary Voigt
  Guidance Coordinator
Gasper, William Joseph
  Math & Science Teacher
Haselschwerdt, Rosanne Guttrich
  English/Speech Teacher
Hayward, Samuel L.
  Band Director
King, Wanda (Bailey)
  Fourth Grade Teacher
Mc Combs, Judith Anne
  Religious Education Director
Yarbrough, Douglas B.
  AP English/Philosophy Teacher

CLEWISTON
Huss, Johanna C.
  Mathematics Teacher

COCOA
Lavinghousez, William Evan Jr.
  Magnet Program Director
Patton, Fern (Durham)
  Kindergarten Teacher
Perdue, Daniel Stephen
  Music & Athletic Director

COCONUT CREEK
Jones, Barbara Pierce
  Chemistry Teacher

COOPER CITY
Boykins, Kathy Lynette
  Assistant Principal

CORAL GABLES
Salas, Lucia M.
  English Teacher
Willis, Valerie B.
  10th/12th Grade Eng Teacher

CORAL SPRINGS
Cain, Robert B.
  Teacher

CRESTVIEW
Bolton, Dorothy Roberts
  Guidance Counselor
James, Jeanette Love
  Retired 4th Grade Teacher

CRYSTAL RIVER
Bacon, George Sewell
  Science/Health Teacher

DADE CITY
Jackson, Teron D.
  Science Teacher/Coach
Stout, Carol Touchton
  Math Teacher

DAVIE
Carrigan, Michelle Reed
  Mathematics Teacher

DAYTONA BEACH
Anderson, Robert Les
  Biology Teacher
Blood, Marie Alisa
  Exceptional Stu Educ Teacher
Bolden, Willie Frank
  Fourth Grade Teacher
Bowden, Denny Russ
  Process Writing Specialist
Eckoff, Ralph Richard
  Theology Teacher
Gamache, Dale N.
  Spanish Teacher
Mobley, Sonya Collins
  2nd Grade Teacher/Chair
Perry, Ophelia Jackson
  Fourth Grade Teacher
Still, Rosemary Woolfolk
  8th Grade American His Teacher

DE FUNIAK SPRINGS
Wilkerson, Mildred Thomas
  Science Teacher

DE LAND
Christiansen, Evan Carl
  Aerospace Sci Dept Teacher
Reese, Idella Keeley
  Third Grade Teacher

DEERFIELD BEACH
Burns, Robert D.
  Physical Education Instructor
Finnegan, Joann Salvino
  Social Studies Teacher
Johnson, Henry Eugene III
  Mathematics Dept Chairperson
Traynor, Barry
  Science Department Chairperson

DELRAY BEACH
Foxworthy, Becky J.
  French Teacher
Timberlake, Carolyn P.
  10th Grade English Teacher
Willis, Steven Cabot
  Studio Instructor

DELTONA
Badina, Valerie W.
  Computer Department Chair
Leasor, Charlene Janet
  6th-8th Grade Phys Ed Teacher

DUNEDIN
Bytheway, Charlotte Ann (Bragg)
  English Teacher/Dept Chairman
Graham, Martha King
  Fourth Grade Teacher
Long, Nancy Triffon
  Language Arts Teacher
Walker, Elizabeth Moore
  Mathematics Dept Chairperson

DUNNELLON
Northsea, Steven George
  English/Journalism Teacher

EAGLE LAKE
Davis, Thaddeus Leonard
  Sixth Grade Teacher
Moore, Yvonne Mathews
  Kindergarten Teacher

EDGEWATER
Avery, Donna Wynn
  4th Grade Teacher

EGLIN AFB
Austin, Sally Ann (Baldwin)
  Kindergarten Teacher

ELFERS
Milne, Gloria J.
  4th Grade Teacher

ENGLEWOOD
Lock, Frank Daniel
  Chemistry/Physics Teacher

EUSTIS
Boulden, George Robert III
  Band Director
Comer, Maxine Ray
  Choral Director
Cunningham, David Earl
  Dean
Curtis, James William
  Teacher
Hooks, Claudia Moore
  Social Studies Dept Chair
Metz, Barbara Dotson
  4th Grade Teacher
Wright, Barbara Louise
  6th Grade Teacher

FERN PARK
Merkergen, Carletha Loper
  3rd Grade Teacher

FERNANDINA BEACH
Albert, Charles L.
  Science Teacher

FORT LAUDERDALE
Culmer, Ollie Miller
  Fourth Grade Teacher
De Sadier, Deanaie Titus
  Health/Social Studies Teacher
Gardner, Sandra Jones
  Primary Specialist
Guerrero, Maria P.
  3rd Grade Teacher
Kroeger, Janet Garris
  Guidance Director
Mercer, Donald J.
  English Teacher
Palmaccio, Richard John
  Math Department Chairman
Ruhlman, Susan Lynn
  Mathematics Teacher

FORT MYERS
Daniels, Aubrey Lavon
  Assistant Principal
Dickey, Roxann Sarlo
  Second Grade Teacher
Dolan, Kristy Wiik
  7th-10th Grade Teacher
Eberle, Susanne Fisher
  Social Studies Chair
French, Kristin Jennifer
  Mathematics Teacher
Kennedy, Alan L.
  Chemistry Teacher
Nadeau, Beverly M.
  Mathematics Teacher
Renfroe, Jane Vincent
  11th Grade English Teacher
Smith, Janice Nelson
  Business Education Instructor
Sushil, Catherine
  Social Studies Teacher

FORT PIERCE
Biedenharn, Jane A.
  English Teacher
Brenner, Gwen Applegate
  English Teacher
Hutchinson, Carolyn Burney
  Third Grade Teacher

FORT WALTON BEACH
Britt, Thomas Milton
  Mathematics Teacher/Ftbl Coach
Glowa, Dodie Scherf
  Social Studies Teacher
Griffith, Jan Printup
  Elementary Teacher
Oates, Janice Smith
  Business Education Teacher
Wooten, Monta Faye
  Team Leader Soc Stud Dept Chm

FREEPORT
Anderson, Gloria Jackson
  Elementary Resource Teacher
Sloan, Anita Joyce
  Mathematics/Chemistry Teacher

GAINESVILLE
Keller, Corinne Conlon
  English Teacher
Kynast, Gregory Joseph
  Spanish Teacher
Speed, Wilhemina Hawkins
  Home Economics Teacher
Wright, Philoron A.
  Assistant Principal

GIBSONTON
Mc Kee, Hazel Grace
  Business Education Dept Head
Richards, Janet Laudano
  Marketing Teacher

GREEN COVE SPRINGS
Hanson, Toni Dracos
  English Teacher

GREENVILLE
Dean, Annie Blake
  8th Grade Reading Teacher

GULF BREEZE
Adams, Laura Wise
  Fifth Grade Teacher
Pritchett, Beverly Bacon
  Guidance Counselor

HAVANA
Bolton, Thomas Walter
  Athletic Director/HS Teacher

HIALEAH
De Leon, Jorge G.
  Spanish Teacher
Felice, Lucy Ann
  11th Grade English Teacher
Humes, Gloria Perry
  Home Ec Dept Chairperson
Jolley, Bethany Ellen
  Second Grade Teacher
Leggins, Carl Joseph
  Marine Biology Teacher
Miller, A. Nell
  English Teacher
Sandiford, Anderson Patrick
  English Teacher/Assoc Prin
Thomas, Annie Scott
  Fourth Grade Teacher
Weiss, Michael Howard
  Physics Teacher

HIGH SPRINGS
Burley, Therese Katherine
  Social Studies Teacher

HOBE SOUND
Deckard, Linda M.
  Kindergarten Teacher
Niemiec, Virginia A
  Fifth Grade Teacher

HOLLYWOOD
Di Pasquale, Sherry Fader
  Guidance Counselor
Sweet, Lynda Lee
  American History Teacher
Warren, Audrey Ann
  Fifth Grade Teacher

HOMESTEAD
Neville, Carolyn L.
  6th Grade Language Art Teacher

HUDSON
Byrd, Lisa Ohlemacher
  Earth Science Teacher
Mills, Jeanne M.
  1st/3rd Grade Teacher
Wolbert, Elin Virginia Eagleston
  Social Studies Teacher

INDIALANTIC
Bugense, Nancy (Miller)
  Art Teacher/Yearbook Advisor

INTERLACHEN
Mathe, Iris Suzanne
  5th Grade Teacher/Dept Chair

INVERNESS
Clifford, Dorothy F.
  Teacher
Ignico, Bonnie Lynn
  Teacher of Gifted
Trescott, Eugene Hyer Jr.
  Science Department Teacher

JACKSONVILLE
Camp, Rachel Scruggs
  Mathematics Teacher/Dept Chair
Cortez, James A.
  Science Teacher
Courreges, Jean May
  Fifth Grade Teacher
Groos, Patricia Smith
  Gifted Teacher
Guzzone, Lucille Pauline
  English Teacher
Harrell, Martha Ann
  12th Grade Lang Art Teacher
Herbert, Diane Holmes
  Foreign Lang Dept Chair
Hugget, Ann Moore
  4th Grade Lang Art Teacher
Jordi, Rebecca Haddock
  Jr/Sr High School Teacher
Lewe, Christopher Keller
  Fourth Grade Teacher
Lott, Dianetra Ruth
  Fifth Grade Teacher
Martin, Blandie J. Stewart
  Teacher
Mills, Sharon Ellis
  5th Grade Teacher
Orlando, Todd Martin
  History Teacher
Pardue, Una Howell
  Fifth Grade Teacher
Perry, Maggie Ola
  Social Science Department Chm
Petty, Flora Renshaw
  Third Grade Teacher
Sharp, Karen Whitlow
  Mathematics Teacher
Smith, Franklin La Vaughn
  Student Activities Director
Smith, Glenda Wells
  Elem Prin/6th Grade Teacher
Stewart, Carole Keys
  Fifth Grade Teacher

Stewart, Mary N. (Hand)
  Fifth Grade Teacher
Troup, Veronica Murphy
  Advanced Geography Teacher
Williams, Maria-Cristina Halley
  Spanish Teacher
Williamson, Carmen Oliver
  English Teacher

JASPER
Lowe, Jane Tyree
  His Teacher/Soc Stud Chair
Selph, Rhonda Kay
  8th Grade Soc Stud/Eng Teacher

JAY
Allred, Laura Gail Luker
  6th Grade Teacher/Art Teacher
Sheppard, Marcia (Wyche)
  Kindergarten Teacher

JENNINGS
Blair, James Billy
  Science, Physical Ed Teacher

KEY LARGO
Davis, Laura White
  Music Specialist

KEY WEST
Davis, Norman Alan
  7th Grade Team Leader
Kremer, Gregory Lawrence
  Social Science Teacher/Coach
Wise, Judd A.
  Life Management Skills Teacher

KISSIMMEE
Baker, Bob Louis
  Social Studies Teacher
Redgrave, Pat B.
  2nd Grade Teacher
Seddon, Karen Cullinane
  5th Grade Teacher

LAKE BUTLER
Bracewell, Mark Andrew
  Vocational Agriculture Teacher
Powell, Martha Armstrong
  Kindergarten Teacher

LAKE CITY
Chamberlin, Joan Crews
  World History Honors Teacher
Hunter, Nancy Sue
  Math Department Chairperson
Joye, Larry G.
  Biology Teacher

LAKE MARY
Beavers, Deborah Ward
  Mathematics Teacher
Coursey, Charles Chesnut
  Social Studies Teacher
Mc Neal, Mary Martindill
  Geography Teacher
Schiffer, Mark R.
  Science Department Chairman
Snaders, Ann Crews
  English Teacher
Wade, Jacqueline Marie
  Science Teacher
White, Marjorie Ann
  5th Grade Teacher/Team Leader

LAKE PLACID
Griffin, Vivian Ann
  Geography Teacher
Hammond, Nellie Viera
  ESOL Tutor/Clerk I
White, Troy Wade Sr.
  Social Studies Chm/Teacher

LAKE WORTH
Thew, Frances Marion
  HS Computer Teacher

LAKELAND
Baldwin, Jacquelyn Albrecht
  5th Grade Teacher
Grimes, Elaine Evans
  Gifted Teacher
Karns, Jeffrey Dean
  Math, Physical Ed Teacher
Moon, Patricia Anita (Hammond)
  3rd Grade Teacher
Peterson, James Parley
  Biology/Bible Teacher

LAND O'LAKES
Clark, Chenell Melanie
  Chemistry Teacher

LANTANA
Martin, Patricia Mc Keon
  Kindergarten Teacher

LARGO
Chapman, Barbara Williams
  Fifth Grade Teacher

LARGO (cont)
Di Lello, Annette J.
  Mathematics Teacher
Sweetman, Clarence James
  Fourth Grade Teacher
Zinn, Carmine Ranieri
  Foreign Language Supervisor

LAUDERDALE LAKES
Brady, Kathleen Mary
  Mathematics Teacher

LAUDERHILL
Thompson, Margaret Mary (Welton)
  English Teacher

LECANTO
Dickey, Kristen Alesiani
  Kindergarten Teacher

LEESBURG
Berry, Agnes Stevens
  Kindergarten Teacher
Brown, Janet Corinne
  Second Grade Teacher
Daniels, Nancy Dianne
  Spanish Teacher
Good, Sandra Marie
  Science Dept Chair
Mullen, Sue Moore
  Health Teacher
Parker, Virginia Bell
  English Teacher
Wright, Kathryn Ann Jones
  Teacher of Gifted/Eng

LEHIGH ACRES
Rock, Helen Dennis
  Elementary Music Teacher

LIVE OAK
Anderson, Janice Jordan
  6th Gr Math/Soc Stud Teacher
Holmes, Patricia Palmer
  Peer Counseling Teacher
O'Connor, Dale Leggett
  Computer Ed Teacher/Dept Head
Richmond, Roberta Thompson
  4th Grade Teacher
Roy, Lynne Elizabeth
  English Teacher

LONGWOOD
Broome, Ronald Allen
  5th Grade Teacher
Finke, Frederick John
  Science Teacher
Gruber, Barbara Rowlands
  Mathematics Dept Chairman
Gunderson, Margaret Haas
  Business Education Teacher
Salley, Glenda Grittman
  8th Grade English Teacher
Schreffler, Pamela Hicks
  Second Grade Teacher

LYNN HAVEN
Conrad, Rhonda Morgan
  Mathematics Teacher
Napier, Ronnie
  Industrial Art Teacher
Pipkin, Gloria Treadwell
  English Teacher

MADEIRA BEACH
Allcorn, Sundy
  Reading Teacher

MADISON
Mc Williams, Jean Phillips
  Real Estate Associate
Moore, Rhonda Aikens
  English Teacher
Parker, Eloney Williams
  6th Grade Teacher

MAITLAND
Clark, Sandy K.
  English Teacher

MALONE
Bellamy, Clarence
  Social Studies Teacher

MARATHON
Keeney, Arlene Ann
  Chapter I Teacher

MARIANNA
Burleson, Jeanie Ball
  Fifth Grade Teacher
Pforte, Dorothy E.
  5th Grade Teacher
Williams, Barbara Holmes
  Fourth Grade Teacher

MAYO
Mc Cray, Mary Anne
  Language Art Chair

MELBOURNE
Ascher, Hope Schneider
  Gifted Studies Teacher
Earhart, Brenda Jean
  12th Grade English Teacher
Harlow, June Bailey
  English & Journalism Teacher
Pittman, Mary Lou
  Personal Fitness Teacher
Potter, Julie A.
  English/Humanities Teacher
Smock, Thomas Maynard
  Physics/Sci Research Teacher

MERRITT ISLAND
Elebash, Marie Blackburn
  Gifted Social Studies Teacher
Gray, Wanda Lowery
  Teacher of Gifted

MIAMI
Alexander, Dimitry Nicholas
  Professor
Bermudez, Florinda Leonor
  Principal
Blessing, Lewis Harold
  Mathematics Teacher
Bolyard, Mattie Avice James
  Retired Teacher
Branch, Diana L.
  Business Ed Teacher/Dept Chair
Brown, Barbara Bowler
  Third Grade Teacher
Cartaya, Pedro Pablo
  Spanish Teacher/Counselor
Clark, Thelma Oliff
  3rd Grade Teacher
Conner, Marjorie Fletcher
  Fifth Grade Teacher
Cox, Estella Meggett
  3rd Grade Teacher
De La Cova, Gloria Grana
  Math Department Chairperson
Dudley, Debra Bass
  Advance-Placement Biology
Engram, Marvin C.
  English Teacher
Fischer, Kevin E.
  Computer Teacher
Fontani, Carol Geffner
  High School Art Teacher
Gardiner, Elsadia Delores
  First Grade Teacher
Haatvedt, Leslie Blair
  Dir of Guidance & Counseling
Hargrove, Thomasina Graham
  6th Grade Teacher & Chair
Hartfield, Charles Vernon
  Mathematics Department Chair
Hazelton, Carolyn Easley
  Fifth Grade Teacher
Hollinger, Martha Reese
  Mathematics Teacher
Hughes, Lee Thomas
  Director of Bands & Orchestra
Jensen, Jay W.
  Drama Director/Teacher
Jones, Katie Mae
  Language Arts Teacher
Kuebler, Karen L.
  Science Teacher
Lawrence, Keitha Denise
  High School History Teacher
Magidson, Carol Bickford
  5th Grade Teacher
Mansfield, Joanne Hutchison
  Language Arts Teacher
Martinez-Ramos, Alberto
  History Teacher
Matthews, Lona Bethel
  Language Arts Teacher
Mc Carthy, Judith M.
  Social Studies Teacher
Misitis, Jan H.
  History/Geography Teacher
Piscitelli, Steven Anthony
  Assistant Principal
Quintero, Barbara Maria
  Computer Teacher
Roberts, Charlene Felten
  First Grade Teacher
Robinson, Gloria Mc Crary
  Mathematics Teacher
Rodriguez, Sylvia Maria
  Social Studies Teacher
Rolle, Josephine Davis
  Sixth Grade Teacher
Rosenbluth, Helen Oliver
  Science Teacher
Sanson, Rick G.
  History Teacher/Athletic Dir
Sarraff, Mercedes Ayala
  Third Grade Teacher
Schachter, Linda (Zemon)
  Business Education Teacher

Seigel, Joyce Bratter
  English Teacher
Silva, Neva Jane Moore
  Fifth Grade Teacher
Sloan, Thelma Williams
  5th Grade Teacher
Stegall, Pamela Jane
  Jr High Science Teacher
Surrency, Joann Thomas
  4th & 5th Grade Teacher
Swift, Ruby Wilder
  Sixth Grade Teacher
Tavel, Norma Lugo
  Spanish Teacher
Thomas, Betty Alexander
  Student Services Chair
Thompkins, Edna Butler
  Librarian/Media Specialist
Wagener, William Ludwig III
  Earth Science Teacher
Walden, Linda L.
  Teacher
Washington, Jannette Maxine
  Fifth Grade Teacher
Williams, Dianne Theresa B.
  Psychology Teacher
Williams, Flossie K.
  First Grade Teacher
Williams, Lizzie Mitchell
  English Teacher
Wills, Billie S.
  ESOL Department Chair
Wolf, Joanne Shostack
  Alternative Education Teacher
Wooden, Jacquelyn Lumpkin
  English Teacher
Zabilka, Anita Hughes
  Guidance Director

MIAMI BEACH
Heller, Beverly Buxbaum
  Sixth Grade Teacher

MIDDLEBURG
Gilbert, Mary Jane
  English Teacher
Miller, Michelle Murray
  English II & III Teacher

MILTON
Allen, Joyce Ivy
  Second Grade Teacher
Cock, Bonnie Kearley
  4th Grade Teacher
Jones, Carol Cranford
  Home Economics Teacher
Mc Williams, Edna Plant
  Lang Art/Mathematics Teacher
Melton, Cynthia Blackwell
  Mathematics Teacher
Oser, Barbara S.
  Foreign Language Dept Chair
Von Axelson, Codylene Simmons
  Guidance Counselor
Walish, Myrna Mead
  Social Studies Teacher

MIMS
Hortert, Ruth Ellen
  Fifth Grade Teacher

MIRAMAR
Mc Roberts, Dennyse
  Guidance Counselor

MOUNT DORA
Jackson, Marjorie Tancimore
  Fifth Grade Teacher

NAPLES
Rutledge, James Joseph
  Mathematics Teacher

NEPTUNE BEACH
Jefferys, Glenn William
  5th Grade Teacher

NEW PORT RICHEY
Aeppel, Roswitha Maria
  German Teacher
Bellak, Sharon Lee
  Mathematics Teacher
Detlefsen, Wanda Kelly
  Teacher
Johnson, Melody Wallace
  Elementary Phys Ed Teacher
Lively, Gene D.
  Language Art Teacher
Procko, Grace Smilnak
  Fourth Grade Teacher
Rebensky, Raymond A. Jr.
  Journalism Teacher
Selfe, Robert Wilson
  Senior English Teacher
South, Lucinda Mary
  Sociology Teacher
Young, Rebecca
  Drama Teacher

NEW SMYRNA BEACH
Kent-Wohlrab, Jill E.
  Gifted Consultant Teacher
Sperber, Carol Heffner
  Media Specialist
Valerius, Linda Heitman
  English Teacher

NEWBERRY
Martin, Donna Wolfe
  DCT Coordinator
Roberts, Georgan Grady
  Mid Sch Lang Art Dept Chairman
Spangler, Harriet Caldwell
  Mathematics Teacher/Dept Chair

NICEVILLE
Eiriksson, Sandra Burns
  Science Teacher
Hobby, Douglas A.
  History Teacher
Leatherwood, Mary Leora (Morris)
  8th Grade Math/Team Leader
Richardson, Dorothy Jean Lauderdale
  Dept Chair/Science Teacher
Rupert, Louis C.
  Junior ROTC Commander

NORTH MIAMI BEACH
Thurmay, Brenda Gorick
  Science/Social Science Teacher

NORTH PALM BEACH
Guiliano, Virginia A.
  4th Grade Teacher

OAKLAND PARK
Anderson, Cynthia M.
  Educl Alternatives Teacher

OCALA
Cantrell, Kathleen Peironnet
  American History Teacher
Parker, Linda Nadine
  Business Teacher
Saxon, Ben L.
  Social Studies Teacher

OKEECHOBEE
La Penna, James Paul
  Fifth Grade Teacher/Dept Chair
Van Deman, James Edward
  History Teacher

ORANGE PARK
Belcher, Clark
  World History Teacher
Chasey, Virginia Wilbanks
  Science Teacher
Richardson, Katie Jones
  Mathematics Teacher
Taylor, Jim Conrad
  Athletic Director
Thompson, Bertina Satterfield
  Teacher/Business Dept Head

ORLANDO
Armstrong, Faye Patricia
  First Grade Teacher
Bowers, John Arthur
  Computer Instructor
Boyd, Ernest Alphonso
  Band Director
Brissey, Ronald Croel
  NJROTC Teacher/Instructor
Brown, James Alton
  4th Grade Teacher
Campbell, Frank De Guerre
  Administrative Dean
Caswell, Josephine Lauteria
  Reading Teacher
Chapman, Patricia J.
  7th Grade Soc Stud Teacher
Conger, Robert Brian
  Band Director
Curtin, Gloria Marie
  Jr HS Social Studies Teacher
Elliott, Shirley Nichols
  English Teacher
Fivush, Georgette Cynthia
  English Department Chairperson
Friederich, Gail Miller
  Curriculum Resource Teacher
Furman, Cheryl Bridges
  Fifth Grade Teacher
Goshen, Kathryn F.
  Government Teacher
Hagy, Wini Olson
  Third Grade Teacher
Hilley, Mary Martha Sawaya
  English Teacher
Holt, Kenneth A.
  Sci Dept Chair/Chem Teacher
Kochar, Karlen Bernet
  Mathematics Teacher
La Fountaine, Glenn Michel
  5th Grade Teacher
Lawson, James Henry
  Administrative Dean

Meyer, Lloyd Eugene
  7th/12th Grade Bible Teacher
Richardson, Ada Katherine
  5th Grade Teacher
Rivers, Constance Williams
  4th Grade Teacher
Rubin, Michael Scott
  Social Studies Teacher
Sorice, William Charles
  Asst Principal/Reading Teacher
Taylor, Lydia Spence
  Art Teacher
White, Eldred C.
  Principal-Owner
Wilson, James Copeland
  English Teacher/Yearbook Adv

ORMOND BEACH
Lapointe, Karen Margaret (Anderson)
  First Grade Teacher

OVIEDO
Davenport, Charlene Fox
  Third Grade Teacher
Fred, Charles Patrick
  6th Grade Mathematics Teacher
Lovett, Marva Norton
  Science Teacher
Pence, Jackie S.
  US History Teacher
Sidlik, Steven Rudolph
  Social Studies Department Chm
Williams, Susan Mary
  English Teacher

PACE
Hines, Betty Burnham
  Fifth Grade Teacher
Lambert, Opal Kimbriel
  Science Teacher
Norton, George R.
  Social Studies Teacher
Riddles, Howard Carlton
  English Instructor

PALATKA
Barron, Deborah Stokes
  6th Grade Teacher
Dixon, M. Todd
  Social Studies Teacher
Hickenlooper, Linda Lee
  Third Grade Teacher
Romay, Mary Hurst
  5th Grade Teacher
Shoeman, Diane Wallschlag
  Science Teacher

PALM BAY
Bonar, Judy Ann (Rataiczak)
  Third Grade Teacher
Holder, Carolyn Adcock
  Science Research Teacher

PALM BEACH GARDENS
Franklin, Alfred Brian
  Science Teacher

PANAMA CITY
Cox, Maudry Joyner
  Primary Specialist
Garner, Carolyn Larkins
  5th Grade Teacher of Gifted
Mc Kenzie, Patricia Roberts
  5th Grade Teacher
Moore, Roberta Dossie
  Prep Specialist
Thompson, Gayle Hood
  Mathematics Teacher

PENSACOLA
Billingsley, Barbara Ann
  English/Drama Teacher
Brittain, Norma Jean
  Fifth Grade Teacher
Buchanan, Bonnie M.
  English Teacher
Coats, Barbara Blackburn
  High School Math Teacher
Drake, Katherine Ann
  5th Grade Teacher
Howie, Mary Sue
  6th Grade Lang Art Teacher
Martin, William Henry
  9th-12th Grade Math Teacher
Montgomery, Karen Jeanette
  4th & 5th Grade Alternative Ed
Roach, Patsy Williams
  English Teacher/Dept Chairman
Sellers, Judith Anne Park
  Language Arts Teacher
Shores, Elaine Marie
  Phys Ed Teacher/Coach
Smith, Ronald Gene
  Music Teacher
Terrell, Kathy Zych
  Chorus & Music Teacher
Terrell, Sophia Brown
  English/Gifted Ed Teacher

PENSACOLA (cont)
Whitney, Michael Stephen
  English Teacher
PINELLAS PARK
Fillyaw, Mary Kathleen Fredrick
  5th Grade Teacher
PINETTA
Bishop, Doris Bass
  Language Art Teacher
PLANT CITY
Jones, Bernita Moir
  Social Studies Teacher
PLANTATION
Highstreet, John L.
  Social Studies Teacher
POMPANO BEACH
Mackifield, Barbara Davis
  First Grade Teacher
Siren, Anne Hanby
  Journalism/English Teacher
Stack, Evelyn A.
  Language Arts Teacher
PONTE VEDRA BEACH
Hansburry, Kathleen Haas
  Assistant Principal
PORT CHARLOTTE
Coleman, Edrel
  Retired Teacher
PORT ORANGE
Cargill, Carol Lohmann
  Voc Home Economics Teacher
Degler, Judith Huckaby
  1st Grade Teacher
Spence, Steven Laurence
  7th Grade Math Teacher
PORT RICHEY
Lee, Harry M.
  History/Geography Teacher
PORT SAINT JOE
Anchors, Betty Smith
  Fifth Grade Teacher
Howell, Myrtle Elizabeth (Hanna)
  Fourth Grade Teacher
Stone, Mazie Anne
  English/His/Geography Teacher
PORT SAINT LUCIE
Bromley, Linda Ann
  English Teacher
Dawson, Betty Ruth Wallace
  Elementary Teacher
PRINCETON
Ballard, Frances Porter
  Kindergarten Teacher
Serrott, Beverly Mann
  Sixth Grade Teacher
Witbeck, Randall S.
  Guidance Cnslr/Bible Dept Head
PUNTA GORDA
Crenshaw, Jeannine Claire
  Math Teacher
Thomas, Charlie A.
  Home Economics Teacher
QUINCY
Gunn, Pauline Levon
  English Department Chair
Robinson, Arthur Mc Gue
  6th Grade Teacher/Chair
Scott, Pearl Roberts
  Third Grade Teacher
RIVERVIEW
Jeffery, Maryetta M. Loftus
  Guidance Counselor
RIVIERA BEACH
Burke, Myrtis Edgecombe
  6th Grade English Teacher
ROCKLEDGE
Cahill, Joan
  Principal
Hines, Anthony Alan
  Social Studies Dept Chairman
Winters, Betty A.
  3rd/4th Grade Teacher
ROYAL PALM BEACH
Leonhardt, Rose Marie Leonardo
  Drama Teacher
SAFETY HARBOR
Potter, Rosemary Lee
  Reading Teacher
SAINT AUGUSTINE
Adams, Barbara Follette
  Art Teacher
Hellier, Audrey Lewis
  Third Grade Teacher

Holt, Shara Wigginton
  Eng Teacher/Dual Enrollment
Lietz, Cassandra Lin
  Art Teacher
Preysz, Claudia Karpowitz
  English Teacher
Stansel, Harold Luther
  5th Grade Teacher
SAINT PETERSBURG
Axt, Joan S.
  Economics/History HS Teacher
Barnum, Debra Louise
  Drama Teacher/Dept Chair
Baumner, Eleanor Deininger
  6th Grade Teacher
Brown, Harry Thomas Jr.
  Social Science Teacher
Drafahl, Robert L.
  5th Grade Teacher
Figley, Sandra Lea Skabo
  Biology Teacher
Fischer, Debbie Rotstein
  Bus Cooperative Ed Teacher
Fricke, Geraldine Spencer
  Kindergarten Teacher
Glass, Linda L.
  First Grade Teacher
Henderson, Richard Scott
  Interim Assistant Principal
Hicks, Steven Paul
  English/Computer Teacher
Hunnicut, Warren IV
  Biology Teacher
Jouret, Carolyn Skelton
  Language Arts/English Teacher
Pittman, Keturah Drayton
  Guidance Coordinator
Sinclair, Cecelia Ann
  Spanish/French Teacher
Slomback, Ronald George
  8th Grade Science Teacher
Stitt, Nancy Sneed
  Science Teacher
SANFORD
Brown, Betty Louise
  7th Grade Math Teacher Chair
Radford, Marie Rhodes
  Business Education Teacher
Woodruff, Arthur Devlin
  Physics/Journalism Teacher
SARASOTA
Ansley, Katherine Clark
  Fifth Grade Teacher
Bradley, Milton
  Theatre Instructor
Counts, Jeannine Graham
  Fourth Grade Teacher
Frank, Nancy Taylor
  Social Studies Teacher
Mc Cracken, William James
  Social Studies Chair
Risley, Cathy H.
  2nd Grade Teacher/Team Leader
Schlatter, Judith Bahr
  Substitute Elementary Teacher
Schleifer, Neal H.
  English Teacher/Lab Admin
SATELLITE BEACH
Blanchard, Glenn A.
  World History Teacher
Breithaupt, Keith Alton
  Mathematics Dept Chairman
Ramsay, Millicent E.
  4th Grade Teacher
Windsor, Jeanette Laura
  Physical Education Teacher
SEBASTIAN
Mills, James Owen
  History Teacher
Scott, Michelle Williams
  Sixth Grade Teacher
SEBRING
Ashford, Loma Morrison
  Fourth Grade Teacher
Ellis, Loretta Lindsey
  First Grade Teacher
Francke, Dorothy J. Dinkelmeyer
  Substitute Teacher
Russ, John Robert
  Assistant Principal
White, Sandra Parrish
  Choral Director/Fine Art Chm
SEFFNER
Allen, Magnolia Galloway
  English Teacher
Cochran, Janice Marie
  First Grade Teacher
Thie, Genevieve Ann
  Mathematics Department Chm

SEMINOLE
Alfaro, Aimee de la Concepcion
  Spanish/French Teacher
Dunn, Carol M.
  Language Art Chair
Gay, Catherine Elizabeth
  Home Economics/English Teacher
Haight, Thomas C.
  Bus Ed Instructor/Swim Coach
Jenrette, Dale William
  Fourth Grade Teacher
Walker, Terry L.
  United States History Teacher
SNEADS
Rose-Baxley, Peggy C.
  Social Studies Teacher
SOUTH DAYTONA
Atty, Janice Elizabeth
  First Grade Teacher
SPRING HILL
Callahan, Diane Clepper
  Fourth Grade Teacher
Cote, Richard G.
  Mathematics/Physics Teacher
Major, Jacqueline Davis
  Guidance Counselor
Wagner, Clifford
  Science Teacher
STARKE
Neighbors, Janet Caruso
  Second Grade Teacher
Smith, M. Sandra
  Science Department Chair
STUART
Haubert, Michelle Re
  Mathematics Teacher
Hogan, Durley Howard
  Spanish Teacher
Klett, Kathryn V.
  Mathematics Teacher
Krueger, Albert R. IV
  Science Teacher/Team Leader
Luckhardt, Alice Kershaw
  World Geography Teacher
SUMMERFIELD
Noxon, Deborrah Chapin
  Reading/Writing Teacher
SUNRISE
Basford, Philip
  Classroom Teacher
Romano, Christopher J.
  US History Teacher
TAFT
King, Joan Dean
  Reading Resource Teacher
TALLAHASSEE
Blanche, Scott Adam
  Mathematics Teacher
Bradwell, Sylvia Wynette (Clary)
  Social Studies Teacher
Butler, Carolyn Kelly
  4th/5th Alternative Ed Teacher
Densmore, Virginia Nolting
  Elementary Music Teacher
Giolightly, Peggy Sue Riggs
  9 & 11th Grade English Teacher
Henry, Isadora Williams
  Language Arts Teacher
Jackson, Angela Neda
  6th Grade Teacher
Mc Guire, Rose Mary
  Science Teacher
Monroe, Beatrice Hill
  English/Language Arts Teacher
Nims, Rosalind Myles
  English Teacher
Nour, Margaret Adams
  7th Grade Life Science Teacher
Obrecht, Steven E.
  English Teacher
Ouimet, Janice M.
  Biology Teacher
Register, Victoria Rich
  8th Grade Mathematics Teacher
Rice, Debra Ann
  7th Grade English Teacher
Robertson, Marylee Baskin
  Gifted Science Teacher
Rollins, Jennie Brown
  Choral Director
Simpson, Patricia Warner
  First Grade Teacher
Stephens, Janet Sue
  Mathematics Teacher
Stevenson, Jim
  Science Teacher
Wells, Darlene Adelle
  Physical Education Teacher

TAMPA
Baker, Betty Thomas
  Sixth Grade Teacher
Bruns, Patricia Morse
  Physical Education Instructor
Chesnut, Gail A.
  Agriculture Teacher
Churchill, Norman Clifford
  Social Studies Teacher
Coleman, Jacqueline B. Wiggins
  Social Studies Teacher
Flowers, Linda Doezema
  Eng Dept Chair/A P Coord
Furman, George A.
  Teacher
Gowdy, Valerie Bollensen
  Teacher of Gifted & Talented
Jones, Ann Elizabeth Giblin
  Junior High English Teacher
Jordan, Thomas Adam
  Physics Teacher
Lambert, Katherine Davies
  Religion & Mathematics Teacher
Lynch, James Patrick
  Language Art Teacher
Rodriguez, William A.
  Instrumental Music Teacher
Speed, Oryan Riley
  Fifth Grade Teacher
Surrency, Frank C.
  Agriculture Education Teacher
TARPON SPRINGS
Clark, Cenia Brown
  Retired Elementary Teacher
Haley, Priscilla Lemnertz
  Language Arts & Speech Teacher
Svabek, Joyce
  Math Department Chair
Van Dyke, Peter John
  Social Studies Teacher
Zimmermaker, Charles S.
  Data Processing Teacher
TAVARES
Bordenkircher, Dave
  Director of Music
Sprague, Betty Teece
  English Teacher
TAVERNIER
Chustz, Leta Hunter
  Science Teacher
Swango, Bruce E.
  Mathematics Department Chair
TITUSVILLE
Abdel-Al, Fayek H.
  7th-8th Grade Math Teacher
Andritz, Leah Daley
  Art Teacher
Blankenship, Geraldine Vickers
  Soc Stud/Lang Art Elem Teacher
Blanner, Deborah Ellen
  Foreign Lang Dept Chair
De Voss, Angela Cicanese
  AP Calculus Teacher
Hossley, Henry Fielding
  Middle Ed Learning Specialist
Mc Cord, Scott Anthony
  Honors/AP Chemistry Teacher
Metz, Gloria L. Beltzner
  Social Studies Teacher
Whitson, Ellisa Frank
  Teacher of Gifted
TYNDALL AFB
Sparks, Katherine Jackson
  Third Grade Teacher
VALRICO
Lelm, Stan
  English/Teacher of Gifted
VENICE
Billups, JoAnne Elizabeth
  Reading Laboratory Director
Jones, Corrine B.
  Social Studies Teacher
Lewis, Sharen C.
  Lang Art Teacher & Curr Coord
Wilson, Cheryl Diane
  Mathematics Teacher
VERNON
Primm, John Thomas
  Social Studies Teacher
VERO BEACH
Bramonte, Patricia P.
  5th Grade Teacher
Cassara, Cricket F.
  4th/5th Grade Science Teacher
Douglas, Lydia Davis
  9th Grade English Teacher
Powell, Jennifer S. (Thomas)
  English Teacher

WEST PALM BEACH
Anclade, Bruce Michael
  Bio/Work Experience Teacher
Down, Joyce IHM
  Fifth-Grade Teacher
Ghirardini, Carol H.
  Mathematics Teacher
Richer, Patricia Casey
  8th Grade English Teacher
Taylor, Jacquelyn Elaine
  4th Grade Teacher
Wilson, Cynthia Oliver-Baumann
  High School English Teacher
WIMAUMA
Fernandez, Shirly Wagner
  Sixth Grade PEP Teacher
WINDERMERE
Fisher, Rosalyn Wheeler
  Elem/Special Education Teacher
WINTER GARDEN
Gillespie, Kathryn Lee
  Chemistry Teacher
Harris, Juanita King
  Fourth Grade Teacher
WINTER HAVEN
Paullin, Robert L.
  6th Grade Teacher
WINTER PARK
Bouch, Cecily Hopkins
  Math Teacher
Ellman, Elaine Newland
  Teacher of Gifted
Fiorica, Carolyn J.
  Social Studies Teacher
Lickteig, Sharon Warren
  English Teacher
Sechrist, Carolyn
  Psychology Teacher
ZEPHYRHILLS
West, Shelia Anderson
  Fifth Grade Teacher

GEORGIA

ADAIRSVILLE
Silvers, Joan Renee
  Social Science Teacher
ADEL
Postell, Aurelia Tillman
  Lang Art & Reading Teacher
Shiflett, Bernice Mc Eachern
  First Grade Teacher
AILEY
Burns, Sara Elaine
  Science & Government Teacher
Wadley, Barbara Franklin
  Language Arts Teacher
ALBANY
Barker, Wiley Richard
  Social Science Teacher
Bryant, Carla A.
  Reading Teacher
Crews, Tammy Thompson
  American History Teacher
Davis, Valencia La Shon
  Mathematics Teacher
Drawdy, Patricia Wilson
  English Teacher
Fortson, Barbara Crawford
  Math Teacher/Dept Chairperson
Hodge, Linda S.
  History Teacher
Holiday, Delorise Reese
  Mathematics Teacher
Hoover, Sharon Pope
  Sixth Grade Teacher
Johnson, Allene P.
  English Department Chair
Joiner, Jo Williamson
  Science Teacher
Kennedy, Jan Harris
  4th Grade Teacher
Krummel, Betty Sanders
  High School English Teacher
Mikes, Janice (Coats)
  English Teacher
Miller, Lillian Crawford
  Science Teacher
Mott, Elizabeth Lavurn
  First Grade Teacher
Murphy, Charlotte V.
  Business/Mathematics Teacher
Poole, Donald Kenneth
  Health/Physical Ed Teacher
Rambeau, Janie Culbreth
  French Teacher

ALBANY (cont)
Reddick, Gladys Thompson
  Sixth Grade Teacher
Roberts, Rosa Lumpkin
  Mathematics/Cmptr Sci Teacher
Tate, Norma Faye
  Media Specialist
Tutcher, Larry Clifford
  Mathematics Instructor

ALMA
Boatright, Marsena Wheeler
  English Teacher/Dept Head
Hall, Sherman E.
  Science Teacher
Sykes, Betty J. Brown
  6th & 7th Grade Teacher
Sykes, Betty J. Brown
  Middle Grades Teacher

ALPHARETTA
Alhadeff, Barry S.
  8th Grade Science Teacher
Caswell, Ted C.
  Science Department Chairman
Gilden, Patricia Gagne
  Advanced Placement Teacher
Masters, Libby Woods
  Teacher of Gifted Education

AMERICUS
Battle, Geneva Polite Jr.
  Retired-Fifth Grade Teacher
Burnette, Gay E.
  Spanish Teacher
Green, Alice
  Social Sci Dept Chairperson
Hicks, Berda Whitehead
  Third Grade Teacher
Lockett, Emma Walters
  Seventh Grade Lead Teacher
Maxwell, Willie Pickren
  Science Dept Chairperson
Norman, Donna Vickery
  Asst Principal for Instruction
Poole, Nancy Roberts
  Second Grade Lead Teacher
Roland, Connie Bostick
  Lead 8th Grade Math Teacher
Welch, Sheila Greene
  Science Teacher
Welch, Susan Parker
  History Teacher
Wisham, Janice Wiggins
  Social Science Teacher

APPLING
Moore, Geniene Carter
  Second Grade Teacher

ASHBURN
Kennedy, Michelle Pitts
  Biology Teacher

ATHENS
Arthur, Terry Mc Nabb
  Counselor
Chappell, Katie Jones
  4th Grade Teacher
Daniels, Shirley Andrews
  HS Social Studies Teacher
Le Blanc, Barry Edward
  Music Teacher/Band Director
Mays, O'Joy Oaks
  2nd Grade Teacher
Meech Jr., Paul Collins
  Science Teacher
Patterson, Richard Johnston
  Science Teacher/Dept Head
Price, Michael Edward
  History Teacher
Rafal, Sam Allen
  Social Studies Teacher
Vipperman, Reginald Graham
  Seventh Grade Science Teacher
Walker, Lynda Binns
  Fourth Grade Teacher

ATLANTA
Abron, Christine Boddie
  Math Department Contact
Adams, Frances Danette
  Co-op Voc Ed Coordinator
Anderson, Joe L. Jr.
  Industrial Arts/Sci Teacher
Anthony, Sallie Sheffield
  Third Grade Teacher
Aughtry, Marsha Ann
  First Grade Teacher
Batiste, Wendall Hardy
  Second Grade Teacher
Childress, Christine Tankersley
  Biology Teacher
Clark, Ruth Wesley
  Science Teacher
Clemon, Beatrice Hargrove
  2nd Grade Teacher/Chairperson

Cohen, Joan Halleen
  Mathematics Teacher
Colbert, Natalie Fisher
  Orchestra Teacher
Copney, Barbara Louise
  Elementary Teacher
Cotton, Helen Manago (Stovall)
  Teacher
Daniel, Roberta Stinson
  Mathematics Lab Teacher
Dixon, Rickey
  Band Director
Dobbs, Darlene Johnson
  Fifth Grade Teacher
Fields-New, Susan Craige
  English Teacher
Griggs, Gloriadine D.
  Kindergarten Teacher
Harden, Bettie M.
  Counselor
Harris, Louise Taylor
  Kindergarten Teacher
Hayes, Darrell Rayfeal
  Graphic Art Teacher
Hogan, Ernestine Dearing
  Mathematics Teacher
Horner, Carol Elizabeth
  Mathematics Teacher
Hudson, George Walker Jr.
  Social Studies Dept Chair
Johnson, Bertha Hickman
  2nd Grade Teacher
Johnson, Winnie Scott
  7th Grade Mathematics Teacher
Jones, Angela Denise
  History Teacher
Lynum, Bettye H. Head
  Teacher/Mathematics Chair
Maddox, Betty Jessie
  Language Art Teacher
Rhodes, Eugene
  Social Studies Teacher
Richardson, Robert
  Mathematics Teacher
Romeo, Veola Taylor
  Chapter 1 Teacher
Sabbatini, Toni Elen
  Spanish Tutor
Sampson, Andrew James
  Science Teacher
Sanders, Pearlie Orr
  Teacher
Scott, Brenda Foster
  English Teacher
Shaheed, Stanley F. H.
  Mathematics Department Teacher
Sims, Jean Tyler
  Fourth Grade Teacher
Singletary, Polly Baker
  School Social Worker
Smith, Gloria Johnson
  Second Grade Teacher
Somerville, Bertha Olgetree
  Second Grade Teacher
Swinson, Sue Whitlow
  Latin Teacher
Waddy, Susanne Willis
  Bible/Latin Teacher
Washburn, Viola J.
  4th Grade Teacher
Welch, Thelma Favors
  First Grade Teacher
Yancey, Gloria S.
  Third Grade Teacher

AUGUSTA
Barnes, Charles
  Teacher/Basketball Coach
Bean, Linda Dacus
  Fifth Grade Teacher
Carpenter, Mildred Clark
  1st Grade Teacher
Hancock, Finetta Graves
  Social Studies Teacher
Holt, Geraldine Fay (Groth)
  Challenge Class Teacher
Mahaffie, Rick Lewman
  Social Studies Teacher
Mc Elreath, Mary Helen
  Health/Phys Ed Teacher/Coach
Mc Gahee, Barbara Ann
  Social Studies Teacher
Postell-Gee, Joy M.
  English & German Teacher
Price, Michael William
  HS Citizenship Teacher
Stewart, Frances Valaries Ward
  Language & Science Teacher
Thomason, Jon Keith
  English Teacher
Vanover, Joan Hurst
  1st Grade Teacher
Wallis, Alberta J.
  English Teacher
Waters, Vernon Edward
  Social Studies Teacher

Wilkerson, Ida Oglesby
  Math Teacher & Dept Chair

AUSTELL
Adair, Jerry Dwain
  Biology Teacher
Auchenpaugh, Ellen Hayes
  4th Grade Teacher
Davis, Gail Stewart
  Business Education Teacher
Denning, Lynda Walker
  3rd Grade Teacher
Gillham, Harriett Mc Daniel
  English Teacher
Laframboise, Joan C.
  Eighth Grade Teacher
Wheeler, Virginia Ann
  Choral Director
Wierengo, Sarah Jane
  Art Teacher

BAINBRIDGE
Cox, Linda Marie
  Sixth Grade Teacher
Grimsley, Nancy Tyson
  First Grade Teacher

BALDWIN
Churchwell, Richard Bruce
  Fourth Grade Teacher
Kimbrell, Charlotte Wade
  Fifth Grade Teacher

BAXLEY
Dominy, Sandy Taylor
  Social Studies Teacher
Massey, Jesse Lee
  Mathematics Teacher/HS Coach
Mc Kinney, Geneva Vaughn
  Sixth Grade Teacher
Morris, Angela Mc Daniel
  5th Grade Teacher
Rump, Robert Erwin
  Science Department Chairman
Stephens, Elaine Thomas
  English/Journalism

BELLVILLE
Sollosi, Tom R.
  HS Mathematics Teacher

BLACKSHEAR
Lott, Buffi Lee
  Mathematics Teacher

BLAIRSVILLE
Adams, Betty Johnson
  Fourth Grade Teacher
Decker, Eva
  Fourth Grade Teacher
Phillips, Revonda Lee
  6th Grade Teacher
Souther, Doris Hunter
  Second Grade Teacher

BLAKELY
Carmon, Donna Mc Arthur
  Fourth Grade Teacher
Crowdis, Rhonda Naramore
  HS English & French Teacher
Harrelson, Ann
  English Teacher
Hattaway, Anne Drake
  Learning Disabilities Teacher
Kuczynski, Evelyn Kathleen
  Mathematics Teacher
Lewis, Ozie Powell
  Teacher
Miller, Ellen Tinson
  Special Education Teacher
Powell, Willowdean Wims
  Fifth Grade Teacher
Smith, David Wiley
  Choral Director

BLUE RIDGE
Payne, Eddie A.
  Social Studies Chair

BONAIRE
Scott, Doretha Jackson
  4th Grade Teacher

BOWDON
Robinson, Dianne Y.
  Fourth Grade Teacher
Stanford, June Smith
  Fourth Grade Teacher

BREMEN
Burrell, Regina Holbrook
  1st Grade Teacher
Hughes, Ophelia Ann
  Assistant Principal
Mc Cain, Melissa Smith
  Fourth Grade Teacher
Sampler, Debra Bass
  Third Grade Teacher

BRUNSWICK
Brown, June Pilcher
  Business Teacher
Canady, Shirley Melissa
  Mathematics Teacher
Ervin, Wayne D.
  Social Studies Teacher
Haywood, Dorothy Carswell
  Eighth Grade Lang Arts Teacher
Holloway, Jane Crow
  Language Arts Teacher
Kemp, Mary Ann
  Sixth Grade Math Teacher
Kline, Vicki Sullins
  9th Grade English Teacher
Lee, John Wesley Jr.
  Social Studies Teacher
Lewers, Sharon Fae
  Fifth Grade Teacher
Lyde, Catherine Erlene
  Chemistry Teacher
Mac Leod, James Lewis
  Teacher of Gifted
Metz, Ingrid C.
  Latin Teacher
Murphy, Mary Dean
  English Teacher
Savage, Frances Buchan
  Volunteer Teacher

BUFORD
Burel, Bonita Pass
  Teacher/Math Dept Chair
Nash, Patricia Roebuck
  Junior High English Teacher

CALHOUN
Brooks, Mary Ann W.
  Span Teacher/Fine Art Dept
Burton, Susan Schollenberger
  Social Studies Teacher
Burton, William Speight
  Social Studies Department Head
Carroll, Teri Cowin
  First Grade Teacher
Davis, Wanda Sue
  Mathematics Dept Chairperson
Kleeman, Ruth S.
  Counselor
Knight, Terry Lynn
  Art Teacher
Reynolds, Phyllis E.
  Health/Physical Ed Teacher
Willis, Barbara Cummings
  Business Education Director

CANTON
Butterworth, Diane D.
  English Teacher
Hopkins, Jackie Jones
  Instructional Computer Coord
Murphy, Vivian Ingram
  7th Grade Geography Teacher
Porch, Brenda Kay Savage
  Fifth Grade Teacher
Rich, Lucille H.
  Lang Art Teacher/Dept Chair

CARNESVILLE
Stewart, Tim Edward
  French Teacher
Wilkes, Sarajo Owens
  Reading Teacher

CARROLLTON
Eason, Robin J.
  Math Teacher
Gentry, Rita B.
  Social Studies Dept Chairman
Geter, Nettie A.
  Mathematics Teacher/Dept Chair
Knapp, Brenda S.
  Performing Arts Teacher
Sullivan, Rebecca Hammock
  English/Latin Teacher

CARTERSVILLE
Ashworth, Dovie Hardin
  5th Grade Mathematics Teacher
Howell, Sarah Sawyer
  Social Studies Teacher
Kimsey, Virginia Wisnom
  Business Education Teacher

CEDARTOWN
Criswell, Melvin Daniel
  6th Grade Math Teacher
Noble, Ralph B.
  Fifth Grade Teacher
Orr, Charles Warren
  8th Grade History Teacher
Williams, Helen Hayes
  Second Grade Teacher

CENTERVILLE
Bryant, Pearleen Williams
  Third Grade Teacher

CHAMBLEE
Burley, Sandee Chilton
  Computer Coord/Math Teacher

CHATSWORTH
Beasley, Troy Daniel
  English Department Chairman
Jones, Floyd B.
  Teacher
Loyd, Linda Long
  Third Grade Teacher
Smith, Johanna (Terry)
  2nd Grade Teacher

CHESTER
Bailey, Elaine Moore
  6th-8th Grade English Teacher

CHESTNUT MOUNTAIN
England, Katie Irene
  Second Grade Teacher

CLAXTON
Lewis, John Stephen
  English Department Chair

CLEVELAND
Aiken, Sandra Wallis
  Chairman Science Department
Curtis, Joan Allen
  4th Grade Teacher

COCHRAN
Edwards, Dorothy F.
  1st Grade Teacher
Haupt, Brenda Pritchett
  Kindergarten Teacher
Porter, Charles Franklin
  Science Teacher

COHUTTA
Lowe, Sandra Houston
  Fourth Grade Teacher

COLLEGE PARK
Allums, Brenda Lea
  Counselor
Chappelle, Karen Lorraine (Randall)
  5th Grade Teacher
Dietz, George A.
  Chem Teacher/Asst Prin
Hankins, Susan Satterfield
  English Teacher
Kramlich, Carolyn Walz
  Middle School English Teacher
Rogers, Rebecca Wallace
  Mathematics Teacher
Smith, Nellie Manda
  Mathematics Teacher
Wilson, Joan Nelson
  10th Grade English Teacher

COLLINS
Nagle, Sharlene Mc Intyre
  Soc Studies/Lang Art Teacher

COLUMBUS
Andrews, Carmella Marie
  Reading/Math Teacher
Bickerstaff, Ellen Rambo
  Second Grade Teacher
Cargal, Eric Michael
  Sr Programmer/Analyst
Cason, Kimberly
  English/Drama/Debate Teacher
Chuites, Shepherd Johnston
  French Teacher
Dysick, Doris Byrd
  Social Studies Chairperson
Griffin, Robert Jim
  PECE Coordinator
Hinson, Peggy Mildred
  English Department Head
Ison, Walter S.
  Soc Stud/Phys Ed Teacher
Jenkins, Linda H.
  5th Grade Mathematics Teacher
Kirkland, Cathy Trigg
  English Teacher
Lyons, James Everett
  History & Spanish Teacher
Nolan, Elizabeth Max
  Fifth Grade Teacher
Pate, Nan R.
  History Department Chair
Pate, Steve C.
  Teacher of Gifted
Patrick, Carol Crosby
  First Grade Teacher
Pedersen, Nancy Ann
  Kindergarten Teacher
Rodgers, Helen Byrne
  English Teacher
Scott, Martha S.
  8th Grade Soc Stud Teacher
Sheffield, Lucille Lemons
  Third Grade Teacher
Shumate, Evelyn Smith
  English Teacher

COLUMBUS (cont)
Steed, Harriet Moore
  5th Grade Teacher
Thomas, Betty J.
  English Teacher
Wise, Elaine Vann
  English Teacher

COMMERCE
Prickett, Jefferson Bolton
  History Teacher

CONYERS
Anderson, Sheila Wade
  Mathematics/Computer Teacher
Bryan, Joseph W.
  English Teacher
Downing, John Michael
  History Teacher
Flynt, James Purks
  Fourth Grade Teacher
Hall, Sara B.
  Science Teacher
Melton, Louise Mc Clain
  Home Economics Teacher
Tutman, Guinnetta Mixon
  Lang Art/Soc Stud Teacher
Williams, Linda Ann (Davis)
  Sixth Grade Teacher

CORDELE
Brooks, Donald James
  Middle School Band Director
Calvert, Renna Biggers
  Science Teacher
Lucas, Dorothy
  Eighth Grade Reading Teacher
Spires, Denise Tate
  Mathematics Teacher

CORNELIA
Bates, Nancy H.
  Teacher of Gifted Math Courses
Cunningham, George S.
  Physical Education Teacher
Tench, Lynn Barnett
  Media Specialist

COVINGTON
Carnes, Marcia Lynn
  Second Grade Teacher
De Gay, Jeannine Chipoulet
  French Teacher
Denman, Dannette Daniel
  Third Grade Teacher
Greer, Pamela Peppers
  English Teacher
Harwell, Louise Drummond
  8th Grade Earth Sci Teacher
Johnson, Judith Hill
  Language Art Teacher
Kesler, Sue Potter
  Business Education Teacher
Racheff, Kathryn Foley
  Third Grade Teacher
Russell, Julia Thomas (Jackson)
  Middle School Teacher

CUMMING
Cole, Samuel Landis
  Technology Teacher
Money, Norman Allen
  Technology Teacher
Roughead, Rosalie Valeria
  English Department Chair

CUTHBERT
Curry, Wylene Fendley
  Physical Education Chairperson
Drew, Cecelia Hale
  Science Teacher

DAHLONEGA
Conner, Jenny Elaine (Tate)
  Health Teacher

DALLAS
Cochran, Shirley Davis
  Instructional Aide
Dodd, Kenneth Le Roy
  Middle Grades Teacher
Power, Samuel Eugene
  Science Dept Chairperson
Still, Candace Tyson
  Choral/Assistant Band Director

DALTON
Boyatt, Louis
  Health/Phys Ed Teacher/Coach
Brandt, Orpah Jean
  8th Grade Mathematics Teacher
Callahan, Reva Phelps
  Fifth Grade Teacher
Derrick, Sandra Whaley
  Teacher
Durham, Edna Brock
  Fourth Grade Teacher
Marsh, Patricia Marshall
  Sixth Grade Teacher

Powell, Wanda Lee
  Fifth Grade Teacher
Watkins, Brenda Kilpatrick
  Spanish Teacher
Whittenbarger, Bianca M.
  Math Department Chairperson

DAMASCUS
Dozier, Martha Hoover
  Art Dept Chair/English Teacher

DANIELSVILLE
Bond, Joan
  First Grade Classroom Teacher
Craig, Clifford
  Team Leader Phys Ed Dept
Davis, Barbara Colvard
  Teacher
Engel, Jeffrey L.
  Chemistry/Physics Teacher
Piedilato, Barbara Seymour
  7th Grade Mathematics Teacher
Scarborough, Karol Andrea
  Soc Stud Teacher & Dept Chair

DANVILLE
Shinholster, James Edward
  Science Teacher
Wiley, Dorothy Stewart
  Fourth Grade Teacher

DARIEN
Davis, Charles Hamilton
  Mathematics Teacher
Jackson, Flo Whitfield
  Science Department Head
Rogers, Joseph Leroy
  Third Grade Teacher

DAWSONVILLE
Kirton, Charlotte Marie
  Life Science Teacher

DECATUR
Connerley, Harold Allen
  Mathematics Teacher
Crowley, Beth M.
  Mathematics Dept Head/Teacher
Dail, Edith Jacqueline
  7th Grade Teacher
D'Ambra, Joseph Salvatore
  Fifth Grade Teacher
Daniel, Kelly Jane (Kuester)
  4th Grade Teacher
Doner, Judy Parker
  Sixth Grade Teacher
Freeman, K. Helen
  9th Grade English Teacher
Holbert, Mary Lou Collins
  Retired Teacher
Huckaby, Scott Allan
  Science Dept Chair/Asst Prin
Miller, Holland Lee
  Mathematics Teacher
Pelletier, Nancy (Dickey)
  Fifth Grade Teacher
Scott, Jeffrie Glenn
  Mathematics Teacher
Woods, Cheryl Denise
  Jr HS English-Science Teacher

DIXIE
Wright, Dorothye Harris
  4th Grade Teacher

DOERUN
Bridwell, Bobbie Clark
  Social Studies Teacher

DONALSONVILLE
Cannon, Gloria Roberts
  English Teacher
Guterman, Kaye Canington
  Media Specialist
Register, Martha H.
  Science Dept Chair/Teacher

DORAVILLE
Ault, Debra Marie
  Social Studies Teacher
Lapin, Gloria Codner
  First Grade Teacher
Leeks, Alexis Bryant
  6th Grade Teacher

DOUGLAS
Hodge, Lisa Chancey
  Mathematics/Reading Teacher
Jackson, Carolyn Denise (Jackson)
  Mathematics/Reading Teacher
Shrouder, Janice M.
  Mathematics Teacher
White, Cathrine Griffin
  5th Grade Teacher

DOUGLASVILLE
Behrman, Michael William
  Physical Education Teacher
Crawford, Jenell M.
  5th Grade Teacher

Gill, Maria Marla
  Biology Teacher
Prickett, Harvard Pittman Jr.
  Social Studies Teacher
Silverstein, Jaclyn Marcia
  7th Grade Math Teacher
Steadham, Zan Stallings
  Social Studies Dept Chair
Whittenburger, Nancy Gulley
  Music Consultant/Instructor
Yates, Brenda Carroll
  Language Arts Department Chair

DUBLIN
Darsey, Joseph Luther
  Teachers Aide
Jackson, Clarence Jr.
  In-Sch Suspension Supervisor
Jefferson, Maudine
  6th/7th Grade Reading Teacher
Kennedy, Terry R. Mc Millan
  Science Teacher/Dept Head

DUDLEY
Bishop, Kathryn
  Second Grade Teacher

DULUTH
Jordan, Carol Morgan
  Choral Director
Vaughn, Linda Sue (Seaton)
  6th Grade Teacher

DUNWOODY
Austin, Kenneth Sr.
  English Teacher
Lofgren, Carol Webb
  Latin Teacher
Rockett, Julia Elizabeth
  English Teacher

EAST POINT
Cranfill, Jeffrey Hamilton
  Director of Bands
Lynn, Lula Hale
  8th Grade Mathematics Teacher
Phillips, Mari Ann
  6th Grade Mathematics Teacher
Reeves, Kitty Hanson
  Fifth Grade Teacher

EASTANOLLEE
Williams, Donny Lee
  7th & 8th Grade Sci Teacher

EASTMAN
Dennis, Melinda Mullis
  Sophomore English Teacher
Dyal, Brenda Faye
  Math Teacher
Harrington, Catherine Rouse
  Third Grade Teacher
Long, Susan White
  English/Speech Teacher
Screws, Donald G. Jr.
  8th Grade Science Teacher
Walker, Patricia Ann
  English Teacher

EATONTON
Davis, Isabel Kinnett
  English Teacher
Griffin, Jo Beth Ritchie
  Gifted-Teacher
Hill, Joyce Holt
  7th Grade Soc Stud/Eng Teacher
O'Steen, Sandra Mains
  Third Grade Teacher

EDISON
Cherubini, Phyllis Foy
  Secondary English Teacher

ELBERTON
Crittendon, Mary Tom
  Social Studies Teacher
Glidewell, Joseph William
  History Teacher
Mc Call, Marguerite Dye
  Fifth Grade Teacher
Mc Lendon, Barbara Giles
  Science Teacher/Science Chair
Thornton, Sarah P.
  English Teacher/Chm Eng Dept
Ward, Iris Frazier
  5th Grade Teacher
Wilson, James Larry
  Mathematics Teacher

ELLENWOOD
Scott, Madelyn Cohen
  6th Grade Teacher
Trippe, Carol Elizabeth
  Chapter I Reading Teacher

ELLERSLIE
Taft, Lora Jane (Baker)
  5th Grade Teacher

ELLIJAY
Burnette, Linda Anderson
  7th Grade Lang Arts Teacher
Pritchett, Lynne Gheesling
  Home Economics Teacher
Rainey, Anne Thompson
  Third Grade Teacher
Sanford, Dorris Orene
  English Teacher
Worley, Daniel Osborn
  Sixth Grade Teacher

EMERSON
Rutland, Peggy Blenis
  Science Department Chairman

EVANS
Braid, Sara Roberts
  Biology Teacher
Crislip, Dianna Brickle
  English Teacher
Mc Gee, Sara G.
  First Grade Teacher
Shiplett, Susan Tillman
  Chorus Teacher

FAYETTEVILLE
Beard, Kenneth Franklin
  Band Director
Brackin, Eva Lee Russell
  Fifth Grade Teacher
Collins, Linda Butler
  Science Teacher
Flowers, Linda Kay
  Jr HS English/History Teacher
Harlan, Dale Jay
  Assistant Principal
Hooten, Norma Whitton
  Middle School Science Teacher
Paladino, Peggy S.
  Physical Sci Teacher

FITZGERALD
Resta, Barry A.
  English Teacher

FLINTSTONE
Guerrero, Nancy Gilbreath
  Fifth Grade Teacher

FOLKSTON
Crews, Jesse Andrew Jr.
  Physical Education Chair

FORSYTH
Crim, Janet Falk
  English Department Head
Evans, Sonja Hester
  English Teacher/Dept Chair
Gantt, Rosemary Faulkner
  First Grade Teacher
Lancaster, Fran Mitchell
  6th, 7th, 12th Grade Teacher

FORT GAINES
Morgan, Elaine King
  Title I Reading & Math Teacher
Salary, Georgia
  Reading Teacher

FORT OGLETHORPE
Souders, James A.
  Band Director/Dept Head

FORT VALLEY
Freeman, Woody Rumph
  6th Grade Mathematics Teacher

FRANKLIN
Barber, Wanda June
  History Teacher
Nelms, Sherry Stringer
  Sixth Grade Teacher
Smith, Phillip Ballard
  5th Grade Science Teacher

GAINESVILLE
Bennett, Marie
  First Grade Teacher
Cooper, Eleanor Jackson
  First Grade Teacher
Cope, Mary Elizabeth Cash
  First Grade Teacher
Dunn, Mark D.
  Social Studies Chairperson
Evans, Ronald James
  Band Director
Gillespie, Emily H.
  Biology Teacher
Higgins, Gordon Wesley
  English Teacher
Hulsey, Dorothy Lee
  Fourth Grade Teacher
Ingram, Gail Loggins
  English Teacher
Lawson, Kathy Fleeman
  Kindergarten Teacher
Mc Call, Margaret Carter
  Mathematics Teacher

Tanner, Martha Martin
  Second Grade Teacher
Veatch, Sara O.
  Science Teacher
Weaver, Russell Anthony
  English Teacher
Westmoreland, Allyson B.
  Marketing Education Teacher

GEORGETOWN
Taylor, Catherine Steele
  Third Grade Teacher

GIBSON
Reeves, Boyd Arrington
  English Teacher

GRAY
Rogers, Vicki Moore
  Data Processing Coordinator

GRIFFIN
Beaton, Richard Joseph
  Latin Teacher
Calloway, Christine
  English Teacher
Champion, Lottie M.
  First Grade Teacher
Cofield, Laura Jean
  Biology/Chemistry Teacher
Colwell, Patricia T.
  Second Grade Teacher
Goodson, Harold Glenn
  Electronics Instr
Kelly, Paula Ramsey
  Biology Teacher
Mathis, Larry Boynton
  Band Director/Supervisor
Morris, Sue Juanita Perteet
  English Dept Chairman
Peeples, Elizabeth Sotelo
  First Grade Teacher
Prince, Suzanne Attaway
  Second Grade Teacher
Stuckey, Wanda Mc Dearis
  English Teacher
Taylor, Diane Daniel
  Fifth Grade Teacher
Weldon, Cherri Ison
  2nd Grade Teacher
Whalen, Jan Shelnutt
  Choral Dir/Gen Music Teacher

GUYTON
Saturday, Janice Morgan
  Lead Teacher

HAHIRA
Lamon, Janet Gunter
  Language Arts Teacher

HAMILTON
Brown, Carol Carmel
  Business Education Teacher
Henderson, Russell Gene
  Social Studies Teacher
Hubbard, Carla Ingalls
  Social Studies Teacher
Mc Namara, Patricia Sandera
  Chapter I Teacher

HARLEM
Black, Joy Lowman
  8th Grade Earth Sci Teacher
Mitchell, A. Diane Dorn
  Advanced English Teacher
Shearouse, Margaret Mc Knight
  Fine Arts Dept. Head & Teacher

HARTWELL
Allen, Hazel
  4th Grade Teacher
Black, Sue Bannister
  First Grade Teacher
Marett, Cecil Dan
  Science Teacher
Marsh, Marylou Smith
  Fourth Grade Teacher
Swilling, Marjorie Craft
  Teacher

HAZLEHURST
Beecher, Rhonda
  5th Grade Teacher
Grimes, Howard Lee Jr.
  Band Director
Hurley, Martha Carol
  English Teacher
Lytle, Tamra Mc Lendon
  Fourth Grade Teacher
Mc Leod, Bonita Yvonne
  7th Grade Math Teacher
Mc Pherson, Linda Austin
  Fourth Grade Teacher
Simmons, Constance Hilga
  5th Grade Teacher

HEPHZIBAH
Adams, Gina Werrick
  Science Teacher

HEPHZIBAH (cont)
Caneda, Frances Richardson
 Social Studies Teacher
Cunningham, Jennifer Biel
 English Teacher
Jones, Sarah A.
 Sixth Grade Teacher
Kendrick, Joretta Brewton
 Seventh Grade Teacher
Mc Kie, Rosalyn Anita
 Second Grade Teacher
Myles, Rosa Thompson
 Second Grade Teacher
Sowell, Joyce Banks
 Social Studies/Reading Teacher

HINESVILLE
Garrison, Lona M.
 8th Grade Lang Arts Teacher

HIRAM
Abbey, Linda Lee
 Team Leader
Vollenweider, Betty H.
 6th Grade Teacher/Chairperson

HOGANSVILLE
Denney, Elisabeth Bishop
 2nd Grade Teacher
Drake, Beth Williams
 Social Science/Spanish Teacher

JACKSON
Alling, Mark Thomas
 Biology Teacher
O'Dell, Faye Loftin
 7th Grade Teacher

JASPER
Culbreth, Gail Ritcey
 Mathematics Teacher
Grotefend, Telete Richards
 First Grade Teacher
Neville, Patsy H.
 Third Grade Teacher

JESUP
Garbutt, Patricia Leaphart
 Physical Education Teacher
Voyles, Denise Dukes
 Mathematics Teacher

JONESBORO
Blevins, Andrea Elizabeth
 Social Studies/English Teacher
Marchman, Judith B.
 AP English Teacher
Rayburn, Betty Beck
 English Department Chairperson
Stokes, Gloria Bryant
 Latin Teacher
Wilson, Daniel Thomas
 Director of Bands

KENNESAW
Morrisson, Linda Uram
 Social Studies Teacher
Newton, Russell E.
 Mathematics Department Chair

KINGSLAND
Vincent, Sandra Lynn (Rainey)
 Music/Choral Director

KINGSTON
Ely, Debra G.
 Third Grade Teacher

LA FAYETTE
Benson, Emily R.
 Fourth Grade Teacher
Crews, Vicki Jeanes
 Third Grade Teacher
Jackson, Delores Lyon
 Remedial Education Teacher
Mahan, Gary Douglas
 English Teacher
Pope, Margie G.
 Home Economics Teacher
Rushing, Virginia Minor
 Social Studies Teacher
Thomas, Lanny E.
 Health/Physical Education
Tucker, John Larry
 High School Math Teacher

LA GRANGE
Bonner, Grady Clark
 Enrichment Teacher
Cook, Sandy Guy
 World Studies Teacher
Greenwood, Claudine Johnson
 8th Grade Math Teacher
Hendrix, Beasey Samuel III
 Developmental Guidance
Humphries, James Hunter
 5th Grade Soc Stud Teacher
Jackson, Cynthia Childers
 Biology Teacher

Korytoski, Wanda Joyce Brogdon
 English/GA History Teacher
Paul, Alexis White
 First Grade Teacher
Pino, Lee Jack
 Biology Teacher
Reimer, Patricia Alice
 Home Economics Teacher
Sivell, Brenda Mc Clurg
 5th Grade Teacher
Woodward, Ann Johnson
 Fourth Grade Teacher

LAKELAND
Brantley, Gloria Alexander
 5th Grade Teacher

LAVONIA
Holland, Jan Crump
 4th Grade Teacher

LAWRENCEVILLE
Koch, Linda Ouimette
 Eighth Grade Teacher
Mc Locklin, Melanie Neal
 Home Economics Dept Teacher
Stripling, Charles Mitchell
 Assistant Principal

LEESBURG
Kidd, Mary Grace
 Graphic Arts Instructor
Rials, Jackie S.
 8th Grade Matematics Teacher
Shiver, Missy Chester
 Business Teacher
Singletary, Katy Adkins
 2nd Grade Teacher
Stephens, Laura Marble
 6th Grade Teacher
Vann, Sylvia Scarborough
 Mathematics Teacher

LEXINGTON
Howeth, John Travis
 Science Teacher

LILBURN
Blasch, Barbara Renk
 Learning Disabilities Teacher
Collins, Doris Talley
 Math Teacher
Mc Guire, Julia Lynn
 Mathematics Teacher
Minick, Mitzi Knight
 5th Grade Teacher
Smith, Bonnie Bracewell
 English Teacher
Smith, Bonnie Douberley
 8th Science Teacher/Dept Chm
Terry, Nancy Keith
 Spanish Teacher

LITHIA SPRINGS
Smith, Darci Ann
 4th-12th Grade Supervisor

LITHONIA
Puckett, A.
 Science Teacher
Sullivan, Janene Collum
 French Teacher

LOGANVILLE
Ford, Hope Ann
 Third Grade Teacher
Goble, Betty Morin
 6th Grade Teacher
Greene, Gina Minton
 Foreign Language Chair
Helms, Charline Rigney
 Seventh Grade Teacher
Martin, Kathy Milano
 English Teacher
Rutter, Karen Lord
 Home Economics Teacher

LOOKOUT MOUNTAIN
Johnston, Virginia Montgomery
 6th Grade Teacher

LOUISVILLE
Camp, Angela H.
 Algebra Teacher
Spells, Sherry Robinson
 Kindergarten Teacher

LUDOWICI
Brock, Bill
 Social Science Teacher
Poland, Mary Nell
 Language Arts Teacher

LYERLY
Cook, Joel Edwin
 Lang Arts/Math Teacher

LYONS
Bryson, Brenda Smith
 6th Grade Soc Stud Teacher

Dees, Robbin Margarette
 Home Economics Teacher
Flanders, Doris Simmons
 First Grade Teacher

MABLETON
Murphy, Zelma Daves
 4th Grade Teacher/Admin Asst
Pike, Catherine Brown
 Special Education Dept Chair
Poole, Carolyn Meredith
 Third Grade Teacher

MACON
Baker, Jane Clark
 4th Grade Teacher
Bass, Gloria Bailey
 Mathematics Department Chair
Bass, Mary Cunningham
 Kindergarten Teacher
Bivins, Barbara Jones
 Teacher
Booker, Gwendolyn Stroud
 Biology Teacher
Childers, Rita (Wilson)
 4th Grade Teacher
Curry, Mattie Elizabeth
 Remedial Reading Teacher
Derreberry, Lynda Ann
 Science Teacher
Echols, Jeanetta Smith
 Social Studies Teacher
Faircloth, Margaret Wingate
 Math Dept Chairperson/Teacher
Felder, Ishmell
 Asst Chair-Soc Stud Teacher
Gregory, Sharon Mc Whirter
 Teacher/Counselor
Hill, Willie D. Jr.
 Social Studies Teacher
Hollis, Peggy D.
 Principal
Hudson, Elizabth Grayer
 Third Grade Teacher
Jackson, Oscar R.
 Director of Bands
Kimberly, Renee Geiger
 Choral Director
Scott, Linda Jordan
 6th Grade Teacher
Singleton, Lynda King
 Sixth Grade Teacher
Spyies, Gladine Hunter
 Teacher
Ussery, Sally Dominey
 Fifth Grade Teacher
Wheeler, Carole M.
 Chairperson/Kndgtn Teacher
Williams, Willena Smith
 K-5th Grade Teacher

MADISON
Ashburn, Barbara Schrimscher
 Eighth Grade Teacher
Bell, Amy Massey
 French & English Teacher

MANCHESTER
Smith, Roselyn Miller
 5th Grade Reading Teacher

MARIETTA
Back, James Michael
 Assistant Band Director
Bohacek, Cheo M.
 Spanish Teacher
Boler, Tran Charlton
 Health Educator
Bourg, Helen Ott
 English Teacher
Brooke, Anna J.
 Science/Biology Teacher
Buck, Jeannine Strange
 English Department Chair
Cheshire, Janice Adair
 Science Teacher
Connelly, Patricia Swain
 English Teacher
Eastman, Sally Schell
 Second Grade Teacher
Ellis, Robert Edward Jr.
 Social Studies Teacher
Evans, Sheila Hullinger
 Drama/English Teacher
Hopper, Barbra Anne
 Advanced Learning Teacher
Howell, Nancy Ward
 Teacher of Gifted
Landers, R. Michael
 Mathematics Teacher
Martin, Suzanne Spradling
 Science Teacher
Moss, Stephen S.
 Art Teacher
Reece, James Randall
 Asst to the Deputy Supt
Reynolds, Norma (Jennings)
 Mathematics Department Chair

Richard, Larry Andre
 English Teacher
Young, Georganne Mc Kenzie
 Social Studies Dept Chair

MC DONOUGH
Amis, Jerome
 Social Studies Chair
Childs, Elaine Compton
 English Teacher
Meadows, Betty Foster
 Spanish Teacher
Nutter, Lloyd Jr.
 History Teacher

MC RAE
Hall, Gladys Marie
 Business Education Teacher
Howard, Marvin Jerome
 Teacher
Shuman-Riley, Brenda Barton
 Assistant Principal

METTER
Hall, Julie Trapnell
 First Grade SIA Teacher
Lanier, Louise Bird
 Fifth Grade Teacher
Thrift, Rebecca Mallard
 6th Grade Teacher
Williams, Stephen Ray
 Social Studies Teacher

MILLEDGEVILLE
Coleman, Mary Sue Vaughn
 7th Grade Lang Arts Teacher
Jones, Judy Brown
 Mathematics Teacher
Taylor, Sol Yvonne (Noble)
 6th Grade General Sci Teacher
Weaver, Cheryl Everidge
 Fourth Grade Teacher
Wilkes, Paul Michael
 Science/Soc Stud/Rdng Teacher

MINERAL BLUFF
Edster, Paulette Evonne
 5th Grade Teacher

MONROE
Colbert, Larry D.
 Music Teacher & Band Director
Dinwiddie, Susan Mc Dowall
 Band Director
Hector, Donald
 5th Grade Teacher
Norton, Patrick Kevin
 Mathematics Teacher
Pope, Tamela Lee
 English Teacher
Poss, Allison Maughon
 Fourth Grade Teacher

MONTICELLO
Caldwell, Mary Pittard
 Fourth Grade Teacher
Mc Clelland, Linda Morgan
 6th-8th Grade Jr HS Teacher
Mock, Martha Thornton
 Latin/English Teacher

MORROW
Baker, Wylie James Jr.
 Chemistry Teacher
Bennett, Billie Ann
 English Teacher
Bennett, James Pierce
 Youth Pastor
Biffle, Ronald Edwin
 Band Director
Carden, Terry Lee
 Electronics Instructor
Feld, David Albert
 Aerospace Science Inst
Gilreath, Drue Williams
 Third Grade Teacher
Johnson, Ernestine Letice
 Foreign Language Dept Chair
Leader, Virginia Wright
 8th Grade English Teacher
Mc Queen, Gwen
 Business Teacher

MORVEN
Scott, Roger Wilkins Sr.
 7th Grade Teacher

MOULTRIE
Bledsoe, Mary Jo
 English Teacher
Caldwell, William M.
 Choir Director
Graham, Vickie Lyn (Register)
 Mathematics Dept Chair/Teacher
Mc Lendon, Richard Charles
 Band Director
Meadows, Annette
 Social Studies Teacher

Rinehart, Sharon Jones
 Fourth Grade Teacher
Smith, Joanne Watts
 Assistant Principal
Taylor, Cora Jean Norman
 Eng Teacher/Yrbk Journalism
Venet, Teresa Mims
 4th Grade Teacher

MOUNT ZION
Spruill, Shirley R.
 Social Studies Dept Teacher

NASHVILLE
Dove, Martha Pelle
 First Grade Teacher
Tomberlin, Carol Rowan
 Mathematics Teacher

NEWNAN
Hall, Peggy Tinsley
 Mathematics Teacher
Lang, Beverly Smith
 Science Teacher
Smith, Susan Powers
 Chemistry Teacher
Wright, Gladys Smith
 Second Grade Teacher
Wunner, Janet Hill
 Instructional Lead Teacher

NORCROSS
Burnett, Cassie Wagnon
 Sixth Grade Teacher
Duncan, Wendy Stanford
 1st Grade Teacher
King, Michael Dana
 8th Grade Soc Stud Teacher
Lammons, Leisa Scoggins
 Language Arts Teacher
Mankin, Patricia Stiger
 4th Grade Teacher
Nichols, James Neil
 Social Studies Teacher
Overman, Misty M.
 Mathematics Teacher
Pharris, William J.
 Band Director

ODUM
Odum, Lanette Barron
 First Grade Teacher

PALMETTO
Hammack, Judy V.
 English Department Chair

PATTERSON
Cooper, Jessie Blake
 Fourth Grade Teacher
Murray, Donna Boyette
 Second Grade Teacher
Newton, Nancy Walker
 Third Grade Teacher

PEACHTREE
Buckle, Charles Stewart
 History Teacher
Snider, Cynthia Deniston
 Senior HS English Teacher
Taylor, Shirley Jean
 Mathematics Teacher

PEACHTREE CITY
Bullock, Karen Faye
 Assistant Principal
Clower, Cheryl Smith
 Home Economics Teacher
Kirkland, Michael Wayne
 Life Science Teacher
Mullins, Catherine Thaxton
 First Grade Teacher
Richardson, Magalene Allen
 Third Grade Teacher
Teribury, Thomas Mott
 5th Grade Teacher
Wilde, Mary Kaythren
 Science Teacher/Dept Chairman

PEARSON
James, Rosemary W.
 Language Arts Teacher
White, Sue Evelyn (Mc Donald)
 Second Grade Teacher

PELHAM
Humphries, La Donnia V. Boutwell
 Jr HS Math Teacher

PERRY
Brooks, Joyce Holder
 Fourth Grade Teacher
Cook, Charles Waymon
 Math/Science Teacher
Cook, La Verne Young
 Fifth Grade Teacher
Langston, Barbara Rice
 7th Grade Mathematics Teacher
Marshall, Jacquelyn Ward
 Biology Teacher

PERRY (cont)
Pearson, Deborah Richardson
Third Grade Teacher

POOLER
Burkett, Gail Zettler
Resource Teacher for Gifted

POWDER SPRINGS
Barber, Dean Newton
First Grade Teacher
Langley, Dorothy Fincher
Fifth Grade Teacher
Paul, Deborah Anne
Teacher of the Gifted
Yates, Angelia Gwen
Spanish Teacher

QUITMAN
Keith, Effie Melton
Curriculum Director
Lane, Sylvia Bristow
Fifth Grade Teacher

RABUN GAP
Mc Cracken, Judy Garland
First Grade Teacher

REIDSVILLE
Hill, Beverly Arnold
Teacher/Science Dept Chair
Jeffers, Henry Byron
Physical Education Teacher
Mc Clellan, Beverly Sue
English Teacher

REX
Benefield, Mary Amberly (Whisnant)
6th Grade Teacher

RICHLAND
Alexander, Rushia Hall
Teacher
Dunaway, Sandra Hurst
4th Grade Teacher

RICHMOND HILL
Dismukes, Beth Cantrell
Kindergarten Teacher
Manigo, Carrie B.
5th Grade Teacher

RIVERDALE
Bean, Susan Montgomery
English Teacher
Torbush, Libby Martin
Gifted Resource Teacher

ROCK SPRING
Smith, Shirley Hall
Second Grade Teacher

ROCKMART
Cobb, Phillip H.
Mathematics Department Chair
Hatcher, Linda Dean
Science Dept/Science Teacher

ROCKY FACE
Malone, Sandra Elaine
Seventh Grade Teacher
Sorrell, Mark Stephen
8th Grade His Teacher/Coach

ROME
Amos, Patricia Cook
Latin/Spanish Teacher
Bragg, Christopher Lamar
Social Studies Teacher
Brumbeloe, Jean Jackson
Second Grade Teacher
Crawford, Elizabeth Webb
Eng Teacher/Forensics Coach
Curtis, Hilda Virginia (Finley)
6th Grade Teacher
De Angelus, Glenda Simpson
Physical Education Dept Chair
Johnston, Deborah Roper
4th Grade Teacher
Lingerfelt, Charlene Head
7th Grade Language Art Teacher
Mc Elveen, Terri Lynn
American History Teacher
Walton, Julie S.
Biology Teacher
Weatherford, Keitha Davis
Mathematics Teacher

ROOPVILLE
Duffey, Glenda Dianne
Teacher
Iverson, Frances Simpson
Fifth Grade Teacher

ROSSVILLE
Almany, Audrey Helvie
SIA Teacher/Kindergarten
Byrd, Teri J. Carter
English Teacher
Carroll, Carla Taylor
Choral Director

Gibbs, Carol Gaylor
Fourth Grade Teacher
Janeway, Wanda Brown
Sixth Grade Teacher
Ragon, Judith Ann
English Department Chairperson

ROSWELL
Sparrow, Mary Ellen
Teacher of Gifted

SAINT MARYS
Crumbley, Esther (Kendrick)
Mathematics Teacher
Kaiser, Mary Donna Linton
Biology/Chemistry Teacher
Steedly, Mae T.
First Grade Teacher

SAINT SIMONS ISL
Horton, Libby Martin
Second Grade Teacher
Pruett, Nancy Curtis
First Grade Teacher

SANDERSVILLE
Bryant, Ruby Huiett
Math Teacher
Clark, Wanda Kay
Second Grade Teacher
Daniel-Tyson, Camille
Soc Stud/Govrnmnt/Econ Teacher
Garnto, Angela B.
Kindergarten Teacher
Moore, Charline V.
Science Teacher
Williams, Terri Avant
Interrelated Spec Ed Teacher
Youmans, Mercedes Norris
8th Grade Lang Art Teacher

SAVANNAH
Formby, Jane Ford
Teacher of Hearing Impaired
Hardwick, Marietta Carter
Fifth Grade Teacher
Harms, M. Susan Arnold
First Grade Teacher
Johnson, Hugh James Jr.
Band Teacher
Johnson, Ronda Parker
English Teacher
King, Diane Duvall
History Teacher
Lang Brannen, William Langley
Business Teacher
Larcom, Lula Frances
Third Grade Teacher
Lucas, Marsha Gay
Science Dept Chairperson
Mantho, Henry Allen
Social Studies Dept Chair
Milner, Lynda Minor
Science Teacher
Mincey, Patricia Jenkins
English as Second Lang Teacher
Peebles, Patti Jones
French/Russian/Spanish Teacher
Rhodes-Pryor, Eunice Levy
Fifth Grade Teacher
Rushing, Sandra Splawn
Third Grade Teacher
Umbreit, Bonnie Muir
8th Grade Bible Teacher

SCREVEN
Collins, Lisa Royal
3rd Grade Teacher

SMYRNA
Cobb, Ann Weatherly
5th Grade Teacher
Harris, Virginia Robinson
8th Grade English Teacher
Howells, Ellen Scofield
7th Grade Mathematics Teacher
Jones, Stanley Alan
Social Studies Teacher
Lewis, Evelyn R.
Rdg/ESL Teacher
Patterson, Cynthia S.
Teacher of the Gifted K-5
Waller-Keoho, Barbara Elaine
Middle School Teacher

SNELLVILLE
Brodnax, Sarah Frances
8th Grade Mathematics Teacher
Haremski, Marcia J.
English Teacher
Kelly, Jolie Anne
Seventh Grade Teacher
Port, Kathleen Mc Leod
8th Grade Chair/Sci Teacher

SOCIAL CIRCLE
Grier, Olivia Banks
Teacher/GED Dir/Data Collector

SOPERTON
Byrd, Eloise Washington
Special Education Teacher

SPARTA
Cheely, Julia Elaine
Middle School English Teacher
Evans, Gwendolyn Sams
Kindergarten Teacher

SPRINGFIELD
Shellman, Willis
Guidance Counselor
Simmons, James William
World/European History Teacher

STATESBORO
Bonds, Lella Gantt
Laboratory School Instructor
Gerrald, Gwen Webb
11th Grade US History Teacher
Minick, Lisa Marsh
Language Arts Teacher
Mobley, Vivian Anderson
Geography Teacher
Moore, Stacey Lee
Spanish/German Teacher
Page, Jane Altman
Professor Foundations & Curr
Rushing, Nan Shealy
Seventh Language Art Teacher

STILLMORE
Moxley, Marie T.
English Teacher

STOCKBRIDGE
Coleman, Anne Jowers
English Department Chair
Daniel, Pat Lifsey
Spanish Teacher
Hainlin, Nancy Evans
4th Grade Teacher/Sci Chair
Mc Glone, Marsha Martin
English Teacher
Peabody, Debra Young
Drafting/Technology Teacher
Pickart, Jane Ann
English Teacher
Pierce, Martha Patton
1st Grade Teacher
Powers, Beverly Kos
Mathematics Department Chair
Shirley, George Russell Jr.
Teacher

STONE MOUNTAIN
Bennett, Lynn C.
1st Grade Teacher
Byrd, Bill
Teacher
Coto, Rene Anthony
4th Grade Mathematics Teacher
Daniel, Phyllis Edwards
Asst Principal/English Teacher
Foster, Linda Cavner
Second Grade Teacher
Mansour, Thomas John
History/Sociology Teacher
Mc Curdy, Carolyn Smith
Mathematics Teacher
Mc Guirt, Carolyn Joyce Sconiers
Kindergarten Teacher
Mote, Patricia Taylor
Senior High School Teacher
Reid, Richard Williams
Chemistry Teacher

SUCHES
Hamby, Joann Rich
Social Studies Teacher

SUMMERVILLE
Colwell, Gwendolyn D.
English Teacher
Osborne, Debra C.
8th Grade Teacher
Petitt, Wanda (Greeson)
Special Ed/Gifted & LD
Snow, Avis Cordle
Media Specialist

SWAINSBORO
Billups, Delores Richardson
7th Grade Teacher
Brown, Amanda R.
Mathematics Department Chair

SYLVANIA
Bennett, Kathleen D.
Second Grade Teacher
Inman, Carolyn
7th Grade Language Art Teacher

SYLVESTER
Goff, Geraldine Gibbs
3rd Grade Teacher
Park, Faye Whitley
Mathematics Teacher

Wooten, Kathryn Wilkerson
Speech-Language Pathologist

TALBOTTON
Ellison, Betty Daniel
Rdng Specialist/Fr Teacher
Flute, Eleanor Parker
Fifth Grade Teacher
Goolsby, Marilu Doster
Teacher of Gifted/Food Coord
King, Mary Alice
English Teacher

TALLAPOOSA
Smith, Joann Arnold
English Teacher

TENNILLE
Walden, Jerry Lee
Fifth Grade Teacher

THOMASTON
Adams, Janice Lynn (Thompson)
Fourth Grade Teacher
Gill, Gary
Soc Sci Dept Chair/Teacher
Olive, Ann Mc Farlin
5th Grade Teacher
Sharpe, Gwendolyn H.
Mathematics Teacher
Swift, Patricia Haynes
6th Grade Teacher

THOMASVILLE
Boykins, Rosemarye D.
Second Grade Teacher
Henderson, Candee Ferrera
Mathematics Teacher
Leas, Loyal Stapleton
English Teacher
Parker, Amy Hobbs
Third Grade Teacher
Trawick, Florence Hall
Retired
Walter, Judith Johnson
Science Teacher

THOMSON
Behrens, Virgina S.
English Department Chairperson
Brown, Christy Hawes
English/Speech Teacher
Dearstone, Janet Helm
6th Grade Teacher
Mc Neal, Ann Elizabeth
Science Department Chairperson
Van Sant, Brenda B.
Science Teacher

TIFTON
Murphy, Kenneth Michael
Science Teacher
Veal, Deanne Dodson
Gifted Stu Resource Teacher

TIGER
Burch, Daniel Scott
Cmptr Coord/Math Chair
Du Bois, Karen York
Business Education Teacher

TOCCOA
Broome, Tommie Fountain
English Teacher
Cheek, Jana Haley
Biology/Physical Sci Teacher

TRENTON
Ambrose, Kim D.
8th Grade Team Leader
Emmett, William Elton
Mathematics Department Head

TUCKER
Kern, Teresa N.
Instructional Lead Teacher
Robinson, Sarah Ragin
Third Grade Teacher
Sessions, Zenobia Deliyanni
French Teacher

TUNNEL HILL
Collins, Susan E.
Language Arts Teacher
Payne, Judith Kay (Felton)
4th Grade Teacher

TWIN CITY
Bowen, Melany Hagan
English & French Teacher
Greenway, Roy Wayne
Science Teacher
Mills, Joy Boatright
Fifth Grade Teacher

TYRONE
Wenning, Karolanne Pierce
Sixth Grade Teacher

UNION CITY
Norwood, Cecelia Louise
7th Grade Teacher

UNION POINT
Hawk, Joyce L.
Chapter 1 Teacher

VALDOSTA
Barrett, Patricia Louise
Mathematics Teacher
Clemons, Owen
Mathematics Teacher
Evans, Marie Lister
Assistant Principal
Gandy, Sharron Griffin
French Teacher
Hayes, Billy
Science Teacher
Josey, Janeen (Curl)
Instructional Supervisor
Miles, Oma Velma
Team Leader
Teffeteller, Elaine Gilliland
Second Grade Teacher
Thrasher, John P.
Chemistry Teacher
Wilkes, Peggy Passmore
Mathematics Teacher

VIDALIA
Barfield, Jan Greene
Spanish Teacher
Clinton, Donald Carey
History and Computer Teacher
Eidson, Frances Poole
Mathematics Teacher
James, William Jr.
6th/7th Grade Phys Ed Teacher
Sharpton, Judy Sasser
Fourth Grade Lang Art Teacher

VIENNA
De Bruce, Michael Lawrence
Special Ed Dept Chair
Jordan, Margaret Taylor
7th/8th Grade Math Teacher

VILLA RICA
Turner, Rebecca Cole
Fourth Grade Teacher

WARNER ROBINS
Brown, Juanita Curtis
Sixth Grade Teacher
Carreker, Vicki Lynn
10th-12th Grade Bio Teacher
Crosby, Peggy Faye
4th Grade Teacher
Davis, Barbara Lee
Middle School Teacher
Dean, Deborah Nelson
7th Grade Teacher/Team Leader
Dyson, Silvonia Allen
Mathematics Teacher
Gregory, Winnie Stewart
Fourth Grade Teacher
Hinnant, Sherin Cook
Resource Teacher of Gifted
James, Lillie Maier Everson
Lead Science Teacher
Murchison, Susan Harper
English Teacher
Stanley, Kathy Lambert
Instructional Coordinator
Stupke, Sylvia Ann
3rd-4th Grade Teacher
Ten Hoor, Janice Heath
9th Grade English Teacher
Walsh, Vianney
Spanish/7th Grade Teacher

WARRENTON
Chapman, Jane Blair
Elementary Instructional Supv

WASHINGTON
Adkins, Chandra Power
English Teacher
Cowan, Brenda Mays
Fifth Grade Lang Art Teacher
Williams, Curtis
Health & Phys Ed Teacher
Zellars, Frances Fair
Second Grade Teacher

WATKINSVILLE
Adams, Myra Mc Gee
Physical Education Teacher
Epting, Tammye Nisewonger
Language Art/Reading Teacher
Fair, Linda Elois
Fourth Grade Teacher
Green, Patricia Huff
Seventh Grade Teacher
Hansen, Carolyn Parkerson
Gifted Social Studies Teacher
James, Dana Clifton
Mathematics Teacher

WATKINSVILLE (cont)
Marshall, Dane Hammons
  Mathematics Teacher
Rhoden, D. C.
  Music Teacher
Smith, Vivian Ann
  Science Teacher

WAYCROSS
Arnold, Deborah Hersey
  Science Teacher
Hall, Brenda Dickerson
  Fourth Grade Teacher
Montgomery, Lawanna Hargroves
  8th Grade Language Art Teacher
Parrish, Carmelita Beal
  English Teacher
Perkins, Roy Gary
  English Instructor
Rhodes, Robert Joseph
  Special Education Teacher
Taylor, Charles Edward
  Mathematics Department Chair

WHIGHAM
Halbgewachs, Cynthia H. Taylor
  8th Grade Teacher
Kynoch, Ann Overly
  4th Grd Rdng/Lang Arts Teacher

WINDER
Lassiter, Bobbye Burris
  Business Ed Dept Chairman
Marine, Steven Murphy
  English Teacher

WOODBINE
Rhodes, Jennie Richardson
  Third Grade Teacher

WOODBURY
Barnes, Kay Carroll
  Mathematics Department Chair

WOODSTOCK
Belk, Audrey
  7th Grade Teacher

YATESVILLE
Atwater, Cleophas Sr.
  JROTC Instructor

ZEBULON
Bartlett, Patricia Shy
  First Grade Teacher

GUAM

DEDEDO
Bautista, Ada Lacanglacang
  Sixth Grade Math Teacher
Flis, Julia Calvo
  7th Grade Life Science Teacher
GUAM MAIN FACILITY
Guzman, Shirley Patricia (Duke)
  English Teacher
TAMUNING
Anderson, Charleen
  Language Arts Dept Chair

HAWAII

AIEA
Kuwada, Hajime
  Band Teacher
EWA BEACH
Palmer, Ernest Elvin
  Eighth Grade Teacher
HICKAM AFB
Mostad, C J. Christiansen
  2nd Grade Teacher
HILO
Corella, Charlotte
  Teacher
Decker, Elizabeth
  Social Studies Teacher
Tanioka, Christine Nakama
  Fourth Grade Teacher
HONOLULU
Asato, Michael Kenez Tsugio
  8th Grade Mathematics Teacher
Castillo, Sharlene Urakawa
  English Teacher
Choy, Lucille Ching
  2nd Grade Teacher
Chun, Wendi M. Y.
  Physics Teacher

Ebesu, Dustin Y.
  Music Teacher
Hirai, Edean Leigh
  Third Grade Teacher
Ho, Robert K. F.
  Physical Education Teacher
Inouye, Judith Shizue
  Science Teacher
Kakugawa, Frances H.
  Third Grade Teacher
Kudo, Mae T.
  5th Grade Teacher
Lee, Gerianne C.
  US History Teacher
Leong, Rose Lee
  Second Grade Chairman
Lim, Lloyd M.
  Math/Rdng/Phys Ed Teacher
Nakama, Patricia Piilani Ono
  English/Journalism Teacher
Nakamichi, Jane Chieko
  Second Grade Teacher
Ono, Samuel Kiyoshi
  Social Studies Teacher
Oshiro, Edward Y.
  Science Department Chair
Phillips, Susan M.
  English Teacher
Sanger, Theresa Lukenich
  Phys Sci/Physics Teacher
Shiroma, Joel Isami
  8th Grade Teacher
Stanevich, Laurent Robert
  Eng/Fr/Cmptr Sci Teacher
Wee, Wesley Y. H.
  School Counselor
Weiskopf, Sherry Rose
  English Teacher
Wong, Frances J. C.
  English Teacher Jr HS Coord
Yogi, Kay Keiko (Oyama)
  Computer Literacy Teacher
Yokozawa, Takeshi
  Japanese Teacher/Lecturer
Young, Clayton Dathoong
  Science Teacher
KAHUKU
Mariteragi, Victoria N. K.
  Stu Act/Leadership Teacher
KAILUA KONA
Matsukawa, Nancy Fujikawa
  Math Teacher/Dept Chair
KAMUELA
Bogue, Eva Marie
  Assistant Head Teacher
LIHUE
Tanioka, Anne Tokuda
  Star Lab Pilot Teacher
MILILANI
Sugimoto, Lily Ogawa
  Third Grade Teacher
PAHOA
Bidal, Maring Gacusana
  Language Arts Teacher
Palea, Susan Yamanaka
  Art Teacher
PEARL CITY
Kawaguchi, Thelma Oda
  Fifth Grade Teacher
PUKALANI
Sanches, Margaret Livingston
  Fourth Grade Teacher
WAHIAWA
Fukumoto, Keith Makoto
  Music Department Chairman
Overman, Charles Sage
  Gifted/Talented Coord/Teacher
WAIALUA
Gorter, Gloria Calimpong
  Language Arts Teacher
WAILUKU
Botielho, Charlotte Abreu
  Language Arts Teacher
Kalehuawehe, Catherine Bishop
  Kindergarten Teacher
Shimabukuro, Grace Kuo
  7th Grade Mathematics Teacher
WAIPAHU
Saito, Nora Ishida
  Fourth Grade Teacher

IDAHO

ABERDEEN
Farnsworth, Margaret Marie
  Business Teacher/Secondary
Johnson, Gail Margaret (Flaig)
  3rd Grade Teacher
Pulliam, Rebecca Simms
  Mathematics Teacher
ALMO
Cahoon, Edna Mae
  1st & 2nd Grade Teacher
AMERICAN FALLS
Aldous, R. Gary
  Mathematics Teacher
Workman, Terry Radtke
  English/History Teacher
ARIMO
Hatch, Ivalve Nielsen
  English Teacher
Mc Farland, James Dale
  Government/History Teacher
Rumsey, Cheryl Rudd
  Spanish Teacher
Yearsley, Gary Stanton
  Vice-Prinicpal
BANCROFT
Mickelsen, Marva Ann
  First Grade Teacher
BLACKFOOT
Manwaring, Dolores Kunz
  Sixth Grade Teacher
Mickelsen, Kay Lynn Broadhead
  Colorguard Advisor
Southern, Alan Richard
  Science Teacher/Dept Chair
Stallings, Merle Rigby
  Fourth Grade Teacher
Wray, Farrell D.
  8th Grade English Teacher
BOISE
Baldwin, Allison Comstock
  Sixth Grade Teacher
Branton, Constance C.
  Junior High Choir Teacher
Cook, Connie Mendenhall
  Fourth Grade Teacher
Davis, Marilyn Jean
  Fourth/Fifth Grade Teacher
Durst, Susan Rae
  English Teacher
Gabert, Judy K.
  English Teacher
Harrigan, Ann Frances
  Secondary Science Teacher
Keilty, Carla Lee
  Fourth Grade Teacher
Kroos, Judith Truell
  Asst Principal of Academics
Larson, Sheila Fife
  1st Grade Teacher
Madson, Susan K.
  6th-8th Language Art Teacher
BUHL
Schroeder, Maxine A. (Paschen)
  1st & 2nd Grade Teacher
BURLEY
Bailey, Douglas Vincent
  American Government Chair
Reas, Joyce Hill
  Health Teacher
CALDWELL
Choy, Margarita Lozano
  Second Grade Teacher
Nettleton, Gwen K.
  High School Biology Teacher
Rickenbach, Kristine
  4th Grade Classroom Teacher
Sasaki, Michael Duaine
  Sixth Grade Teacher
Slane, Jacqueline Marie (Gage)
  Second Grade Teacher
Smithers, James R
  District Computer Director
CASTLEFORD
Gandiaga, Beverly Reeves
  English/Reading/Art Teacher
COEUR D'ALENE
Couser, Carl Andrew
  Sixth Grade Teacher
Everson, Barbara Benner
  Spanish Teacher
Kraus, Patricia Brenda (Born)
  Language Arts Teacher
Stanosch, Sharlene Ramey
  Kindergarten Teacher

Ter Hark, Jean (Mack)
  Chorus Teacher
DAYTON
Christensen, Claudia Glynn
  Head Teacher
DRIGGS
Hill, Jerelyn R.
  Physical Education Teacher
EAGLE
Mapp, M. Lynn
  Fourth Grade Teacher
EMMETT
Kassens, Zola I.
  Third Grade Teacher
Presley, Judene C.
  5th Grade Teacher
Welberg, Dorothy Holverson
  Arts Teacher
Zillner, Kim Kreps
  Third Grade Teacher
FIRTH
Smith, Lane Drew
  English Teacher
FRUITLAND
Lake, Frederick Nelson
  Third Grade Teacher
Strough, Cathy Faye (Carter)
  Business Educator
Walton, Terri Polkinghorn
  Fifth Grade Teacher
GENESEE
Fabricius, Teresa (Tesnohlided)
  English/Communications Teacher
GRANGEVILLE
Agee, Christine Kathryn
  Business Education Teacher
Fox, Susan Crea
  Speech/English Teacher
GREENLEAF
De Vries, James H.
  English/Social Studies Teacher
Stands, Susan Hoffman
  Language Arts Teacher
HAGERMAN
Werth, Edna Reetz
  2nd Grade Teacher
HAYDEN LAKE
Shamberg, Robert A.
  5th Grade Teacher
HAZELTON
Cochran, Philip Clark
  6th Grade Teacher
Hammond, Dale Harley
  Science Teacher
Rudolph, Becky J.
  Eng Speech/Debate Teacher
HEYBURN
Tilley, Darrell Glen
  4th Grade Teacher
IDAHO FALLS
Anderson, Lisa M.
  Sixth Grade Teacher
Barrett, Justin James
  Fourth Grade Teacher
Benedikt, Margie Sue Holland
  Third Grade Teacher
Bryan, Mike A.
  Spanish/English Teacher
Budge, Susette Fletcher
  Third Grade Teacher
Francis, James Michael
  History Teacher
Hoopes, Jewel Edwards
  Coord/Facilitator Gifted Prgm
Kakacek, Steven Jacob
  Band Director
Killian, Ellen Glenn
  Fourth Grade Teacher
Mays, Kelli Kathleen
  Reading Teacher
Orchard, Vicki G.
  English Teacher
Pancheri, Amy C.
  6th Grade Teacher
Puskas, Deborah Denise
  Choir Teacher
Rowberry, Connie Lynn
  Geography Teacher
Schooler, John
  Band Director
Siems, Stanley Wayne
  Vocational Drafting Teacher
Solecki, Marcy (Kozacki)
  Sixth Grade Teacher
Waite, Randy Glen
  Physics/Chemistry Teacher

INKOM
Lish, Paul Evan
  Kindergarten Teacher
Robinson, Virginia Feider
  6th Grade Teacher
JEROME
Golding, Pearl Ann
  Second Grade Teacher
James, Karen Lavens
  English IV Teacher
JULIAETTA
Parks, DeAnn Mielke
  Chapter 1 Teacher
KAMIAH
Kirsch, Patricia Ann Pickering
  Kindergarten Teacher
Squires, Robert Larry
  Jr High Mathematics Teacher
KELLOGG
Claymore, Mary Kay Hunt
  6th Grade Math teacher
Cobb, Mary Stout
  Librarian
Costa, Renae Margaret (Egge)
  Chapter One Teacher
Godwin, Valorie Dawn
  English/Speech Teacher
Haller, Ann Cordwell
  Science Teacher
KENDRICK
Eldrich, Michael K.
  English Chair
KIMBERLY
Hall, Jan Standley
  Physical Education Dept Chair
Hogan, Gordon C.
  Mathematics Teacher
Mc Adams, George Alan
  History Teacher/Chairman
KOOSKIA
Smith, George Michael
  6th Grade Teacher
Weeks, Steve Wesley
  Fifth Grade Teacher
Wicks, Leann Gehrke
  Librarian
KUNA
Croy, Ann Strucher
  Kindergarten Teacher
Delaney, Terrence P.
  Mathematics Teacher
Nixon, Kimberlee Anne (Pardon)
  Third Grade Teacher
Snider, Toni Arnold
  2nd Grade Teacher
LEWISTON
Caudron, Cordell Robert
  English Teacher
Forge, Kathy Haye
  Math Teacher
Hutcheson, Kirk Steven
  Science Teacher
MACKAY
Barnhard, Joann R.
  Business Teacher
MALTA
Barnes, Evelyn Wrigley
  Third Grade Teacher
MARSING
Barr, Bill Ray
  Sci/Health/Phys Ed Teacher
MERIDIAN
Atlwood, Paul Robert
  Spanish Teacher
Beckwith, Robert E.
  Biology Teacher
Henckel, Nancy Irene
  Spanish Teacher
Henley, Sheryl Bergstrom
  9th-12th Grade French Teacher
Jones, William Arthur
  Science Teacher/Coach
Murakami, Vicki Anne
  Fourth Grade Teacher
Paige, Rhea Hansen
  Retired Elem Music Teacher
Reynolds, Marilyn Diane
  Business Education Instructor
Selvig, Linda Kay (Sipila)
  Earth Science Teacher
Toney, Patricia Northrop
  Senior English Teacher
Waters, Ginger Kay
  Science Teacher

MONTPELIER

Arnell, Dallas Hodges
  8th Grade Mathematics Teacher
Grandy, Barbara Curtis
  Retired

MORELAND

Yamada, Frances S.
  2nd Grade Teacher

MOSCOW

Anderson, Catherine Wilkinson
  Third Grade Teacher
Anderson, Elinor C.
  Third Grade Teacher
Carnell, Michael Ordraine
  English Teacher
Hughes, Carole A. Hurley
  English Department Chair
Milligan, Constance Fry
  Mathematics Teacher

MOUNTAIN HOME

Crawford, Mary Randleman
  Fourth Grade Teacher
Roberts, Vivian Freeman
  Fifth Grade Teacher
Starkey, Patricia South
  English/Science Teacher

NAMPA

Boeder, Curtis Iver Jr.
  Principal/6th Grade Teacher
Booth, Lola A.
  English Teacher
Boyd, Bruce Gregory
  5th Grade Teacher
Childers, Margaret Anne
  Biology Teacher/Sci Dept Chair
Friesen, Marlene Maude
  Music/English/Drama Teacher
Hill, Fred Allen
  Science Teacher
Long, Leon H.
  English Teacher

NEW PLYMOUTH

Decker, Arlo A.
  Sci/Health Teacher/Admin Asst
Pero, Dan Leonard
  Principal Sendry Athletic Dir

OROFINO

Lee, Joanne Mae (Hoffman)
  2nd Grade Teacher

PARMA

Leigh, Nathan A.
  Fifth Grade Teacher

PAUL

Brown, Shannon D.
  Industrial Technology Teacher

PAYETTE

Cain, Gerre M.
  Sixth Grade Teacher
Heater, Suzan Riddlemoser
  First Grade Teacher
Raynor, Patricia D. Astorquia
  Spanish Teacher

PINGREE

Mc Pherson, Ruth Rich
  Retired Primary Teacher

POCATELLO

Anderson, Marianne Bieniek
  Science & Mathematics Teacher
Dudley, Carolynn
  Sixth Grade Teacher
Durante, Tom
  Director of Bands
Green, Dan G.
  AP Calculus/Physics Teacher
Middleton, Cindy Sanders
  Mathematics Dept Chairperson
Owens, Grace Wittig
  Spanish Teacher
Stenson, Ed
  English Teacher

POST FALLS

Porter, Christine Anne
  Special Education Teacher

PRIEST RIVER

Barker, Shirley Monroe
  Third Grade Teacher

RATHDRUM

Ackerman, David Lawrence
  7th-9th Grade Math Teacher
Rogers, Pat J.
  Co-Chair, English Department

REXBURG

Beesley, Judy K.
  English Teacher
Clements, Louis J.
  Social Studies Dept Chair

RIGBY

Ward, Jon Clesmer
  German/English Teacher

RIGGINS

Zimmerman, Robert Glen
  English/US His/Speech Teacher

RIRIE

Holman, Helen H.
  First Grade Teacher

SAINT ANTHONY

Albaugh, Pauline Howard
  Second Grade Teacher
Davenport, DelRay S.
  Spanish/English Teacher

SHELLEY

Anderson, Jarvis
  6th Grade Teacher
Hansen, Darrel Chancy
  Earth Sci/Geography Teacher
Weist, Lamont Eugene
  Vice Prin/5th Grade Teacher

SODA SPRINGS

Hendricks, Cora Lee
  1st Grade Teacher
Morgan, Cleve
  Social Science Dept Chair
Summers, Bonnie Manwill
  Fourth Grade Teacher

TWIN FALLS

Stover, Kathy Anderson
  Mathematics Teacher

WALLACE

Paroni, Genevieve Swick
  Chem/Physics/Computers Teacher

WEISER

Huck, Barbara Ralph
  Comm Disorder Specialist

WILDER

Easley, Janet Lue
  Second Grade Teacher

WORLEY

Meyer, Douglas B.
  Science Teacher

ILLINOIS

ADDISON

Angelina, Jamine
  Jr HS Literature Teacher
Borchardt, Kathleen Marie
  Reading Department Chairperson

ALBION

Endsley, Vickie Enlow
  6th-8th Grade Math Teacher
Lowe, Linda Diane (Hadsall)
  Jr HS Science Teacher

ALEDO

Kaempfer, Lee Magill
  Mathematics Department Chair

ALEXANDER

Kingston, Dee Ann Stice
  Third Grade Teacher

ALGONQUIN

Bumbales, Charles J.
  Dean of Students

ALPHA

Wells, Mary H.
  Elementary Principal

ALTAMONT

Janota, Christine Anne
  Band Director

ALTON

Bollini, Connie O'Connor
  Kindergarten Teacher
Clouse, Mary Maher
  Kindergarten Teacher
Conrad, Joan Hollenbeck
  History Government Teacher
Cook, Denny Gene
  Algebra Teacher
Drillinger, David Wayne
  High School Band Director

ANDALUSIA

Rodgers, Ken
  Fifth Grade Teacher

ANNA

Bailey, William O.
  Physics/Chemistry Teacher
Miller, Bill
  Junior High Science Teacher

ARLINGTON HEIGHTS

Ahlberg, Grant W.
  Social Studies Dept Chair
Bellito, Michael John
  English/Speech Teacher
Javurek, Jeffrey J.
  Mathematics Teacher
Navin, John Patrick
  Social Studies Dept Chairman
Purves, Norman Duane
  Lang Arts/Soc Stud Teacher
Van Wiel, John Edward
  Chemistry Teacher

ASSUMPTION

Zuber, Vincent Harold
  Mathematics Teacher

AUBURN

Barton, Kirk E.
  Sixth Grade Teacher
Young, Raymon Dwaine
  Language Arts Teacher

AURORA

Abhalter, Peggy J.
  Spanish Teacher/Dept Chair
Bejec, Lilia Santiago
  Elementary Teacher
Calamaras, Jami Janice
  4th Grade Teacher
Copple, Priscilla Susan
  Phys Ed/Health Teacher
Engelhardt, Gerald J.
  Physical Education Dept Chair
Evert, Colleen Finnerty
  Social Studies Chair
Ferguson, Marian Brown
  Jr High History Teacher
Frieders, Carol Moenning
  4th Grade Teacher
Goodman, Dana Richard
  English Faculty Teacher
Grosshuesch, Clayt Emerson
  Guidance Counselor
Heintz, Karen Ann
  Jr HS Science Teacher
Holak, Thomas
  Social Studies Teacher
Jackson, Anjeanette Benefield
  Social Studies Teacher
Johnson, Gary Leonard
  Science Department Chairman
Kaler, Margie Woolcock
  English Teacher
Lopez, Elia
  Foreign Language Dept Coord
Mc Glynn, Jacqueline Marie
  Mathematics Teacher
Nardone, Nancy E.
  Sixth Grade Teacher
Plachetka, Beth Benjamin
  6th-8th Grade Lang Art Teacher
Porto, Carolyn J.
  5th Grade Teacher
Rozanski, Norbert Anthony
  Religion/Music Teacher
Schindel, Richard H.
  Bus Ed Dept Chair
Spencer, Kathryn Curran
  Latin & World History Teacher
Stevens, Carol SSSF
  Music Director
Sweeney, Jane L.
  6th Grade Teacher
Thompson, John Tyrus
  Biology Instructor
Weiss, Dorothy Marie
  Sixth Grade Teacher

AVON

Banta, Robert Ora
  Mathematics Teacher
Davis, Roberta Lee (Cowling)
  Second Grade Teacher

BARRINGTON

Littwin, James Patrick
  English Teacher
Munao, Jan Frank
  Jr High English Teacher
Offutt, Michael Lee
  Chemistry Teacher
Sandburg, Jo Ellen Maurer
  French Teacher

BARTLETT

Schroeder, Mary Mc Dougal
  5th Grade Teacher

BATAVIA

Cox, James Dale
  Science Department Chairman

BATH

Mitchell, Patricia Hamilton
  7-12th Grade English Teacher

ARLINGTON HEIGHTS (cont.)

Morgan, Rebecca L. (Stephens)
  5th/6th Grade Teacher

BEACH PARK

Meissner, Donald Wayne
  Life Science Teacher

BEARDSTOWN

Dalpiaz, Nancy K. (Rinehart)
  Business Ed Teacher
Dunham, Verna Bunnell
  Second Grade Teacher
Lacey, Craig Terhune
  4th Grade Teacher

BECKEMEYER

Hilmes, Charles Edward
  Jr High Teacher
Kreke, Loretta Marie
  Fifth-Sixth Grade Teacher
Wutzler, Linda Kay (Smith)
  Sixth Grade Teacher

BELLEVILLE

Crouse, Dale
  Business Education Teacher
Karban, Mary Felts
  First Grade Teacher
Phillips, Aaron W.
  Mathematics Teacher
Zaber, Alec Henry
  Jr HS Science Teacher

BELVIDERE

Clementz, Diane Rose Kwiecinski
  3rd Grade Teacher
Groh, Patricia Ann
  English/German Teacher

BENSENVILLE

Ayers, Terrance L.
  Social Studies Teacher
Green, Frederick T.
  Mathematics Teacher
Speers, John Keith
  Math Dept Chairman/Teacher

BENTON

Woodfin, Susan Rains
  Department Chair

BERWYN

Perepechko, Ann Virruso
  First Grade Teacher

BETHALTO

Downing, Phyllis L.
  First Grade Teacher
Huff, Sherry Lynn (Brueggeman)
  4th Grade Teacher

BETHANY

Henricks, Jane White
  English Teacher

BLOOMINGTON

Cavitt, Roger Nelson
  Guidance Dept Chairperson
Lang, Judith K.
  First Grade Teacher
Morkin, Sharon Bryson
  Second Grade Teacher
Otto, Stanley Alan
  Social Science Teacher
Vadala, Joseph D.
  5th Grade Teacher

BLUE ISLAND

Kuh, Elaine E. (Otto)
  Teacher
Stewart, Margaret Harvey
  8th Grade Soc Stud Teacher

BLUFORD

Blevins, Susan Lowe
  Math Teacher
Peacock, Melvin Leon
  Sixth Grade Teacher

BOLINGBROOK

Acton, Sara Jane Adams
  Fourth Grade Challenge Teacher
Alico, Robert J.
  5th Grade Teacher
Ivnik, Kathryn (Davisson)
  Physical Education Teacher
Rutledge, Curtis E.
  Social Studies/Reading Teacher
Shaw, Richard Ellis
  Teacher

BONFIELD

Monferdini, Susan Schultz
  Third Grade Teacher
Scholl, Linda Lee (Wenzelman)
  Physical Education Teacher

BOURBONNAIS

Harris, Retta Irene (Bryant)
  First Grade Teacher

Oswalt, Dale Allen
  Fifth Grade Teacher
Warke, Helen Jarosch
  English Teacher

BRADLEY

Blanchette, Michelle Marie
  Mathematics Teacher
Oberto, Alan James
  Teacher of Gifted/Talented
Sharp, Mary A.
  Science Teacher
Tracy, Charles Lee
  Math Teacher

BREESE

Kottmeyer, Georgine
  1st/2nd Grade Teacher
Sedlacek, Robert C.
  English Teacher
Smith, Judy Leith
  3rd/4th Grade Teacher

BRIDGEPORT

Paddock, Sandra Staley
  First Grade Teacher

BRIMFIELD

Flickinger, May O. Huber
  Third Grade Teachers Aide
Warner, Dennis Jay
  Mathematics Department Chair

BROADWELL

Hewitt, Michael Dennis
  6th/7th/8th Grade Teacher

BROWNING

Page, Edward Lewis
  Head Teacher

BROWNSTOWN

Rohlfing, Tracy Dolores
  English Teacher

BUFFALO GROVE

Abraham, Robert Paul
  Assistant Principal
Kern, Sandy G.
  Reading/Language Teacher
Loeb, Wendy Gartenberg
  Math Teacher

BURBANK

Bayless, Beverly Blue
  Fourth Grade Teacher
Bill, Kenneth George
  English Teacher/Dean
Caton, Joan Hinrichs
  English Teacher
Haskins, Elizabeth Parker
  History Teacher
Laude, Maureen Hanafin
  Mathematics Teacher
Miller, Carol Sacks
  First Grade Teacher
Murphy, Kathleen Rita Sullivan
  HS Mathematics Teacher
Ondrla, Thomas Joseph
  History Teacher/Principal
Sarther, David J.
  Jr HS Literature/Rdng Teacher
Scott, Mark Stonewall
  Theology/Art Teacher
Werner, Patricia Ann
  6th Grade Teacher/Asst Prin

BURLINGTON

Conro, James Philip
  Mathematics Teacher

BURR RIDGE

Martin, William J.
  5th Grade Teacher

BUSHNELL

Pyle, Anita Loraine
  Mathematics/Physics Teacher

CAHOKIA

Baker, Barbara Jean (Montgomery)
  3rd Grade Teacher
Davis, Donna K.
  Life Science Instructor

CAIRO

Sanders, Martha L.
  Second Grade Teacher

CALEDONIA

Wheeler, Cynthia Connor
  Fifth Grade Teacher

CALUMET CITY

Grenchik, George J.
  Junior High School Teacher

CAMBRIA

Schaefer, Sherry Williford
  Fourth Grade Teacher

CAMP POINT

Houston, Rodney Dean
 Math Department Chairman
Moody, Paul H.
 Fourth Grade Teacher

CANTON

Grimm, Patricia
 Sixth Grade Teacher
Harms, Nancy Ellen (Gunn)
 Second Grade Teacher
Havens, Sherrill Jane (Lynch)
 Third Grade Teacher
Kohler, Jaki
 English Department Chair
Patterson, Kimberly Kay
 Jr High Physical Ed Teacher
Phillips, Everett
 7th Grade Science Teacher

CARLINVILLE

Knetzer, Kathleen Hopper
 Mathematics Teacher
Priest, Rhonda Carol
 Fourth Grade Teacher

CARMI

Gaines, Judy Davidson
 Language Arts Teacher

CAROL STREAM

Beggs, William Thomas
 Math & Cmptr Science Teacher

CARPENTERSVILLE

Capps, Cindy Cohen
 Assistant Principal
De Long, James William Jr.
 4th Grade Teacher
Eck, Albert John
 Earth Science Teacher/Advisor
Lackey, Sue Andra
 Music Teacher/Advisor
Miller, Kenneth R.
 Instrumental Music Director

CARRIER MILLS

Dillard, Vickie Ann (Daniels)
 Third Grade Teacher

CARROLLTON

Meyer, Margaret
 Third Grade Teacher

CARTERVILLE

Church, Connie Hooker
 English Department Chair

CARTHAGE

Scheuermann, Kenneth Lee
 Teacher

CHAMPAIGN

Klimek, Patricia Everett
 Spanish Teacher

CHARLESTON

Chapman, Judith (Logan)
 Mathematics Teacher
Darding, Alverta Louise (Evans)
 First Grade Teacher
Mc Collum, Timothy David
 Science Instructor
O'Brien, D. Sue Nichols
 Sixth Grade Teacher

CHICAGO

Agenlian, Murad
 Teacher
Alexander, Ann Lorraine Romanchek
 First Grade Teacher
Ambrosio, Anthony Louis
 Principal
Aquino, Carmen Lopez
 ESL & Spanish Teacher
Baker, James L.
 7th Grade Teacher/Asst Prin
Barnes, Lorene Taylor
 English Teacher
Battle, Isaac L.
 4th Grade Teacher
Battles, Betty J. Mc Gehee
 Language Arts Teacher
Bean, Pamela Owens
 Asst Phys Ed Dept Chair
Benford, Gloria True
 8th Grade English Teacher
Bennett, Solomon Frederick
 7th-8th Grade Teacher/Gifted
Biddulph, Jean Koch
 Mathematics Teacher
Bishop, Charles
 5th Grade Teacher
Brereton, Gerard A.
 Spanish Teacher
Brown, Ann Butler
 6th Grade Teacher
Brown, Larry Jerome
 8th Grade Teacher

Brown, V. K.
 Physics Teacher
Brunson, Barbara Crofton
 6th Grade Hmrm Rdng Teacher
Caldwell, Barbara Noel
 Fourth Grade Unit Leader
Churchill, Anthony Peter
 Mid Sch Teacher & Coach
Collazo, Jose Alfonso
 Bilingual Biology Teacher
Colletti, Helen Perino
 Second Grade Teacher
Conway, Carol M.
 English Teacher
Cooney, Joan C. (Daleiden)
 8th Grade Math/Religion
Costopoulos, John Theodore
 Biology Teacher
Cunningham, James Joseph
 Geography/History Teacher
Dakewicz, Helene Powarzynski
 5-6th Grade Soc Stud Teacher
Delaney, Stella O'Connor
 Mathematics Teacher
Deutch, Janet Lee
 Sixth Grade Teacher
Dundek, Jeffrey M.
 Biology Teacher
Enders, Christine Kester
 English Teacher
Erazmus, Janet
 8th Grade Teacher
Fanning, Doris Grant
 Asst Prin & 6th Grade Teacher
Fitzsimons, Patricia K.
 5th Grade Teacher
Fogg, Rosa Yelling
 Library-Computer Resource
Foley, Mary Elizabeth
 Fourth Grade Teacher
Fontana, Jane Sarlas
 Kindergarten Teacher
Foxwell, Betsy M.
 7th/8th Grade Teacher
Fransen, Christine Irene
 HS Mathematics Teacher
Gans, John Thomas
 Teacher
Gantt, Randi Tolmaire
 8th Grade Lang Arts Teacher
Geers, Diane
 6th Grade Teacher/Asst Prin
Giusti, Vincenza Banducci
 Biology Teacher
Glenn, Georgia Starnes
 Biology Teacher
Glennon, Owen G.
 Math Teacher
Goldman, Robert Craig
 Social Studies Teacher
Goodrich, Louise Lyons
 Teacher of Phys Handicapped
Greaney, Donald Elias
 Social Studies Dept Chair
Green, William Harry
 History Teacher
Greig, Catherine Berg
 English Teacher
Hale, Patricia Jean
 Fourth Grade Teacher
Hammond, Stephen E.
 Jr HS Science Teacher
Hankin, Annette E.
 English-Drama Teacher
Heller, James Michael
 4th-8th Grade Lit Teacher
Hernquist, Dorothy Baum
 Lang Art Specialist Teacher
Hicks, Bobbie Conley
 2nd Grade Teacher
Higgins, Thomas Joseph
 Jr HS American History Teacher
Hirdler, Kenneth Edward
 Social Studies Dept Chair
Hoffman, Lillian E. Kubala
 Third Grade Teacher
Holbrook, Sheila Mary
 Jr HS Teacher
Hooks, James Byron Jr.
 English Literature Teacher
Hudson, Christine
 Social Studies Teacher
Humphrey, Brenda Lae Adair
 Teacher
Hunter, Marilyn Enyard
 Fourth Grade Teacher
Hurckes, Dorene Allen
 Principal
Ing, Terry Lee
 Second/Third Grade Teacher
Ingram, Adrienne Elaine
 State Pre-Kindergarten Teacher
Jamen, Donna Lee Loretta (Martin)
 6th & 7th Grade Teacher
James, Lillie Pearl
 Seventh Grade Teacher

Johnson, Carolyn Crawford
 Teacher
Johnson, Laurence Weldon
 Upper Grade Science Teacher
Johnson, Sadie Robinson
 2nd Grade Teacher
Juillard, Edward David
 Religious Studies Teacher
Kateeb, Linda
 Language Art Teacher
Kendall, Arnold Van
 8th Grade Science Teacher
Kincaid, Verlinda Bradley
 Physical Education Teacher
Klock, Frank C.
 Religion Dept Chairperson
Koller, Catherine Mary
 Seventh Grade Teacher
Krajewski, Joan F.
 English Department Chair
Lanier, Dorothy Hill
 Sixth Grade Teacher
Laskowska, Mary Loyola
 Clerical Assistant
Lech, Patricia Elizabeth
 4th Grade Teacher
Lee, Esther White
 Seventh Grade Science Teacher
Lee, Jay W.
 Social Science Teacher
Lemon-Anderson, Sheila E.
 Science Teacher
Lennon, Thelma Gordon
 Supply Teacher
Levant, Charlene Schwartz
 Primary Teacher of Gifted
Lewis, Babe Elaine
 8th Grade Teacher
Liberson, Shirley Alter
 First Grade Teacher
Lill, Michael Francis
 Music Teacher
Linnerud, Mark A.
 Chemistry Teacher
Longo, Michael Sharkey
 High School Teacher
Maccagnano, Vincent Philip
 Physics/Chemistry Teacher
Manuel, Harriette E.
 Earth Science Teacher
Maragh, Mae Ramey
 5th Grade Teacher
Markett, Mary Chilton
 Fourth Grade Teacher
Martin, Michelle Margaret (Klitz)
 Fourth Grade Teacher
Matthews, Mary Bush
 5th Grade Teacher
Mauersberger, Yudita G. Yunkeris
 Foreign Lang Dept Chair
Mazur, Diane Quinn
 Physical Ed/Health Dept Chair
Mc Ghee, Debra Nowels
 Second Grade ESEA Teacher
Mc Ghee, Leslie Lonnie
 African-Amer History Teacher
Meariewether, Patricia
 8th Grade Teacher
Messiah, Henry Robert
 Graphic Arts Teacher
Miller, Annie Blackwell
 Business Dept Chm/Teacher
Miller, Betty Jean
 English Department Chairperson
Mims, Vernon Eugene Jr.
 English Teacher
Minkoff, Sandra Rita (Cohen)
 Counselor
Modesto, Robert
 English Department Chair
Moore, Eurydice Ann
 Vocational Education Teacher
Moore, John Brendan
 Latin/Religion Teacher
Moore, Lillie M.
 9th Grade English Teacher
Morris, Alice M.
 High School Math Teacher
Muller, Ricard Charles
 Math & Cmptr Sci Teacher
Naddy, Candace Freyer
 7th Grade Science Teacher
Neeley, Cynthia Tillman
 8th Grade Teacher/Coordinator
Neveles, Paula Walker
 5th/6th Grade Teacher
Nicholson, Rosann Cicchetti
 Jr High/Language Arts Teacher
Nolan, Carol Murphy
 5th Grade Teacher
Oleszkiewicz, Karen Gembara
 Elementary Education
Olson, Margaret Ann
 High School Math Teacher
Orman, Judith D. (Jaffe)
 8th Grade Teacher

Pappin, Charlene Patricia
 Professor & Math Dept Chair
Pedryc, Rose Marie Holbrook
 7th Grade Teacher/Asst Prin
Perlman, Bella Beach
 4th-6th Grade Lang Art Teacher
Pero, Paula Kemmeel
 7th & 8th Grade Teacher
Perry, Edna Burrell
 Principal
Phillips, Evelyn Mosley
 Head Teacher
Pollard, Darlene
 Reading Teacher
Pols, Donna Innis
 English Teacher
Ramsey, Gayle Richardson
 Physical Ed/Driver Ed Teacher
Rawis, Sharon Gavin
 Fifth Grade Teacher
Reichel, Margaret Grant
 Mathematics Teacher
Richardson, Irving Roosevelt
 Sixth Grade Teacher
Richter, Erma Lee Perry
 Reading Resource
Rick, Norman Russell
 Mathematics Instructor
Roberts, John Joseph
 Social Studies Teacher
Rood, Mary A.
 English Teacher
Ross, Harry John
 Teacher of Eng/Dir Stu Act
Rottman, Mary Rose
 Fourth Grade Teacher
Rouse, Velma Spates
 Math Teacher
Rozak, Kathleen Marie
 Jr HS Teacher
Ryan, Kathleen A.
 Social Studies Teacher
Ryan, Suzanne Polmear
 English Teacher
Sailes, Micheal Edward
 Business Department Chairman
Sampson, James Edward
 8th Grade Teacher
Sanders, Beverly Isidore
 Rdng/Math Laboratory Teacher
Schaffer, Hannah Loeb
 Second Grade Teacher
Schanel, Mary J.
 Mathematics Department Chair
Schroeder, Carol (Studt)
 Mathematics Teacher
Schultz, Nancy E.
 5th Grade Teacher
Schwab, Nancy Ann
 First Grade Teacher
Schwarzkopf, Gloria Grossenbacher
 Former Teacher
Sehlinger, Carol Ann (Casper)
 5th-8th Grade Math Teacher
Seputis, Thomas John
 Business Department Chair
Shanahan, Richard Stephen
 6th Grade Teacher of Gifted
Sharpe, Alfrances Lyman
 English Teacher
Sidlik, Stan A.
 Drama & Theater Arts Teacher
Smith, Cheryl Armstrong
 Assistant Principal
Smith, Janet V.
 Sixth Grade Teacher
Sobucki, Andrew Joseph
 Science Teacher
Spell, Dana C.
 High School English Teacher
Strzalka, Alice Glowacki
 Mathematics Teacher
Swanson, Marcia Kay
 2nd Grade Teacher
Sweeney, James Martin
 Bilingual Teacher/Coordinator
Sylvester, Thelma Kingston
 English Teacher
Theodore, Jo Anna Mc Gee
 Lang Arts/Soc Stud Dept Chair
Thomas, Sarah Bell
 8th Grade Reading Teacher
Thompson, Edna Waits
 English Teacher
Thompson, Mary K. (Jones)
 Social Studies Teacher
Tibbett, Robert Anthony
 English Teacher
Turner, Patricia Sayles
 High School Counselor
Valone, Katherine G.
 Sixth Grade Teacher
Venckus, Meg
 Teacher/Coach
Walker, Gloria Edwards
 Teacher/Mathematics Dept Chair

Warren, Kenneth M.
 Chemistry Teacher
West, Micheal
 Counselor
White, Lucille Watkins
 Principal
Williams, Luvenia Reed
 English Coordinator
Wozniak, Stanley John Jr.
 Fourth Grade Teacher
Yancy, Regina Moore
 3rd & 4th Grade Teacher
Zak, Janet Mary
 Eighth Grade Teacher
Zellhofer, Gregor F.
 8th Grade Teacher

CHICAGO HEIGHTS

Colangelo, Janet Wszolek
 1st Grade Teacher
Newgard, Robert David
 Gifted-Enrichment Prgm Teacher
Overheidt-Smith, Sheryl
 English Teacher
Rayon, Marshall Singleton
 English Teacher

CHICAGO RIDGE

Dahlberg, Patricia Toczek
 Jr HS Reading Teacher

CHRISMAN

Anglen, Donald Edgar
 Mathematics Department Chair
Mason, Annette Marie
 Mathematics/Phys Sci Teacher
Means, Eleanor Webb
 First Grade Teacher

CHRISTOPHER

Senka, Frank Michael
 JTPA-Tutorial Representative

CIARO

Chambers, Mark Edward
 Reading/Language Art Teacher

CICERO

Antus, Robert Lawrence
 English Teacher
Pyzik, Glenna Magee
 Cooperative Education Coord
Schiddell, Betty L.
 Dean of Instruction Math/Sci
Schuett, Arthur George
 Social Science Teacher

COAL CITY

Lenig, Steven Dale
 General Science Teacher

COLCHESTER

Phillips, Sherry Brandt
 7th/8th Grade Lang Art Teacher
Rings, Diana St. John
 Fifth Grade Teacher

COLLINSVILLE

Nelson, Mark William
 Fine Arts Department Chair
Schefft, Walter Robert
 Principal

COLUMBIA

Anderson, Dale Michael
 4th-8th Grade Teacher
Stechmasser, Diane Schoenhoff
 Third Grade Teacher

COULTERVILLE

North, Gayle Fozard
 Mathematics Teacher

COUNTRY CLUB HILLS

Cappel, Thomas Joseph
 Social Studies Teacher
Shaffer, Bonnie J.
 Music Teacher
Zambo, Carl R.
 Counselor/Head Football Coach

CRETE

Chmielewski, Patricia Cavanaugh
 Fifth Grade Teacher
Kent, Sue Katherine Wyatt
 Learning Disabilities Resource
Sage, Linda Mary
 Spanish Teacher

CREVE COEUR

Cannon, Joy Fry
 Retired

CRYSTAL LAKE

Korus, Paula Sawyer
 History Teacher
Scheel, Leonard G.
 Science Department Chairman
Shea, Gerald J.
 Language Art Teacher

CRYSTAL LAKE (cont)
Walter, Georgia Hill
Fifth Grade Teacher

CUBA
Schoonover, Barbara Bennett
Science-Mathematics Teacher

DALE
Phillips, Juanita
Third Grade Teacher
Simich, Suzanne
Second Grade Teacher

DANVILLE
Bonomo, Donald E.
Mathematics Teacher
Pascal, Freddie Jean (Stewart)
2nd Grade Teacher
Stauder, Phillip J.
Third Grade Teacher
Turner, Jai B.
Fourth Grade Teacher

DARIEN
Kindlon, Timothy Mark
5th-6th Grade Teacher/Adm Asst
Lyman, Treasa Kate
7th/8th Grade Lang Art Teacher

DE KALB
Abrams, Barbara Krohner
4th Grade Teacher
Trautvetter, Leslie C.
8th Grade Math & Sci Teacher

DECATUR
Bryant, Janice L.
7th & 8th English Teacher
Buttz, Jean Haher
English Teacher & Dept Chair
Elson, Donna Ruth
Sixth Grade Teacher
Force, Charles E.
Mathematics Teacher
Glenn, Helen J.
4th Grade Teacher
Hayes, Peggy Ann
6th Grade Teacher
Hensler, Susan Jean
Principal
Lauderdale, B. Jo Putt
English Teacher
Milleville, Brenda Sturm
7th Grade Teacher
Moore, Cynthia Lynn
Chapter I Mathematics Teacher
Propst, Marilyn Lewis
Math Dept Chair/Instructor
Rayhill, Susan Caroline Mueller
Life Planning Skills Coord
Scott, Walter Lee
Dean of Students
Thacker, Randall
HS Social Studies Teacher

DEERFIELD
Baxter, Richard Llewellyn
English Teacher
Herr, Gerry
3rd Grade Teacher
Hugh, Donna S.
4th Grade Teacher
Samuels, Lynne Stone
Teacher of Gifted & Reading
Wason, Judith Nasers
Mathematics Teacher

DELEVAN
Carr, Sanish La Ray
Mathematics Teacher

DES PLAINES
Bizar, Doreen Sharon
Chapter I Reading Specialist
Borchardt, Cindy Jean (Roehl)
English Teacher
Daiberl, Richard Joseph
Jr HS Social Studies Teacher
Eigenfeld, Peter Bill
Eighth Grade Teacher
Hennessey, Donna Gleason
Third Grade Teacher
Schueler, Mary Ellen Beckman
Gifted Resource Teacher

DIVERNON
Wilmarth, Shelli Zimmer
Fifth Grade Teacher

DIXMOOR
Lindsay, Verniece Oliver
Math Teacher/Math Dept Chair
Peoples, Dorothy Sneed
Third Grade Teacher

DIXON
Clevenger, Wendy Ward
4th Grade Teacher

Healy, Jacqueline Ann
2nd Grade Teacher
Lafferty, William Patrick
Social Studies Teacher
Morss, Wayne
History Instructor
Vivian, Shirley Frances
Language Arts Teacher

DOLTON
Baker, Suzanne Markvart
Mathematics Teacher
Kreidler, Kathleen Ridges
Chemistry Teacher
Mc Cullagh, Nancy Jones
Third Grade Teacher

DOWNERS GROVE
Hlavacek, Paula J.
Mathematics/Science Teacher
Johnson, Gaile D.
Spanish Teacher
Mc Cracken, Richard E.
Science Teacher
Nasca, Diana Lynn (Hospodar)
Mathematics Teacher
Novak, Ronald F.
Science Teacher
Smith, Madonna Tucker
English Teacher
Wollenburg, Nancy A.
Reading/Language Teacher

DOWNS
Pearson, Barb Schaefer
History/Government Teacher
Roberts, Robin Louis
Social Studies/Phys Ed Teacher

DU QUOIN
Barrett, Janet Anne
Driver Education Teacher
Ferrari, Patricia Ann
Asst Principal/Bus Teacher
Karnes, Pat Ann (Leach)
5th Grade Science Teacher

DUNLAP
Arney, Helen Troisi
English Teacher
Bethel, Michael Brad
Administrative Assistant
Hutton, Gary Kent
8th Grade English Teacher
Stortz, G. Barry
Mathematics/Computer Teacher

DWIGHT
Rosenbaum, Linda
2nd Grade Teacher

EAST ALTON
Hart, Joyce Elaine
Fifth Grade Teacher
Hierman, Sally Ann
5th Grade Teacher
Northrop, Arlene Little
Fifth Grade Teacher
Pendt, Diana Burris
3rd Grade Teacher

EAST MOLINE
Ertel, Constance M. Skahill
Jr HS Social Studies Teacher
Foehrkolb, Sue Balkan
Lang Art/Rdng Dept Chairperson
Hanske, Robert William Jr.
Eng Teacher/Coord Gifted Prgms
Nelson, Dennis E.
Mathematics Teacher
Verlinden, Robert L.
5th Grade Teacher

EAST PEORIA
Ballard, Marcia Doran
Fifth Grade Teacher
Dunn, Rita E.
English Department Chair
Joos, Janet Westra
English Instructor
Melvin, Dorothy Eileene
Physical Education Teacher
Resutko, Larry
Jr HS Teacher

EAST SAINT LOUIS
Aldrige, Alice Jordan
Third Grade Teacher
Brimm, Wardell C.
French/English Teacher
Cooper, Lenora Ann Bonner
6th Grade Teacher
Curry, Janet
Teacher
Joiner, Sharon Marie
Language Arts Teacher
Lofton, Mary (Campbell)
Reading Teacher

Mayes, Mary Ann Kovachich
English Teacher
Swift, Angela Nelson
English Teacher
Thomas, Elizabeth Archibald
Fourth Grade Teacher
Wells, Rosalind Lenette
Language Arts Teacher

EDWARDSVILLE
Lybarger, Susan Elaine
Sixth Grade Teacher
Motley, Kate Richards
English Teacher
Royuk, Brent Ronald
Advanced Placement Teacher

EFFINGHAM
Brown, Kent D.
Speech/Drama Teacher
Hawkins, Phil
English Teacher
Koester, Irene Schmidt
Band Director
Pickett, Steven Harold
8th Grade Lang Art Teacher
Shull, Sharon Mc Mechan
French Teacher

ELDORADO
Simpson, Linda Bundren
5th Grade Teacher

ELGIN
De Vazquez, Nancy Ann Lindert
Spanish Teacher
Hood, Rosemary Grennan
English Teacher
Ismail, Abed M.
Teacher

ELIZABETHTOWN
Wiman, David W.
Director of Guidance

ELK GROVE VILLAGE
Haas, Constance Morrissey
English Teacher
Kropp, John Frederick
5th Grade Teacher

ELMHURST
Carr, Lorraine Grandys
Third Grade Teacher
Franz, Genevieve Mae Vander Tuin
4th Grade Teacher
Inman, Thomas James
Physical Education Teacher
Power, Donald Robert
4th Grade Teacher
Triezenberg, Henry J.
Science Dept Chairperson

EMDEN
Struebing, Donna Gail (Wagner)
1st/4th Grade Reading Teacher

ERIE
Ludwig, William Charles III
English Teacher/Dept Chairman

EVANSTON
Clark, Sara Elizabeth Young
2nd Grade Teacher
Collins, Jennifer
Volleyball Coach
Gawrusik, Pamela J.
6th Grade Teacher
Mims, Sandra Dianne
Spanish Teacher
Simon, Margaret Miller
4th Grade Teacher
Willson, John Paul
Health Teacher

EVERGREEN PARK
Hoke, Ardeen Denise
Kindergarten Teacher
Tierney, Noreen T. (Kennedy)
Eighth Grade Teacher
Wax, Marilyn
Phys Ed/Health Teacher/Coach

FAIRBURY
Costa, Joanne Marie
Computer Teacher
Erdman, Waneta Callahan
Fifth Grade Teacher

FAIRFIELD
Adams, Joyce Ann
Kindergarten Teacher
Drake, Ina Rae (Nees)
8th Grade Lit/Eng Teacher
Hill, Vicki L.
Sixth Grade Teacher
Kanady, Freeda Mae
Fifth Grade Teacher
Queener, Mary Julian
Fifth Grade Teacher

Robbins, Pamela S.
Parenting/Mathematics Teacher
Thomason, Diane Lynn (Clark)
Business Teacher
Wood, Jaquelyn E.
Mathematics Teacher

FAIRMONT CITY
Williamson, Carol Honer
1st Grade Teacher

FISHER
Elkins, Thelma Lucille
Social Studies Teacher
Obrecht, Roger Alan
Principal

FOREST PARK
Benke, Robert John
Youth/Evangelism Pastor
Kruse, Donna Mae (Hasse)
Second Grade Teacher
Schifo, Nancy Vesely
Gifted Education Coordinator
Waldron, Mark Allen
Media Teacher/Music Dir

FORRESTON
Dillavou, Robert L.
Social Studies Teacher

FOX LAKE
Beyer, Judith Ann
Fifth Grade Teacher
Chvatal, Marian Koskuba
Gifted Coordinator
Lomas, William Thomas Jr.
Principal

FOX RIVER GROVE
Knapp, Richard Laurence
2nd Grade Teacher

FRANKLIN
Morris, Johnathan E.
Agriculture Instructor
Smith, Rick Wallace
Mathematics Dept Chairman

FRANKLIN PARK
Swinden, Larry Allen
Special Education Teacher

FREEBURG
Ayers, MaryAnne (Smith)
4th Grade Teacher
Hawkins, Rob
Social Studies/History Teacher
Meggs, Katherine Nolan
English/Dramatics Teacher

FREEPORT
Cole, James Richard
Social Studies Dept Chair
Firebaugh, Douglas B.
Chemistry/Astronomy Teacher
Krueger, Joan Carol (Whalen)
Fifth Grade Teacher
Vorthmann, Marlene Haibeck
Speech & English Teacher

FULTON
Koehn, Ronald H.
HS Social Studies Teacher
Van Zuiden, Joy Ann
Kindergarten Teacher

GALENA
Corbett, Sue-Ann
Physical Education Teacher
Koester, Carole (Moon)
English-Speech Teacher

GALESBURG
Clark, Elane Janet
2nd Grade Teacher
Devena, Barbara Ann
High School Bus Teacher
Devore, D. Hal
Teacher/Department Chair
Gohring, Patricia M.
Social Studies Teacher
Hinrichs, Linda Claire
Coordinator
Lindsay, Donna Jeanne
Physical Ed/Health Teacher
Rinehart, Elizabeth Ann
Principal
Spencer, Bruce Edward
Science Department Chairman

GALVA
Bronny, Christopher Michael
7-8th Grade Science Teacher
Murray, Sharon Scott
7th-8th Grade Lang Art Teacher
Nodeen, Erma Farquer
4th Grade/Gifted Care Teacher

GARDNER
Lauterbach, Karen Elaine (Holliday)
Math/Chemistry Teacher

GEFF
Dye, Sally J.
Jr High Teacher
Pond, Anita Kay
Third & Fourth Grade Teacher
Spicer, Linda J.
5th/6th Grade Teacher

GENESEO
Pollard, Leslie Ann
First Grade Teacher
Steele, Thomas Michael
Social Studies Chair

GENOA
Perry, Donald Paul
Science Teacher

GEORGETOWN
Van Camp, Paul Samuel
Science Department Chair
Wellman, Debra Baker
Social Stud/Lang Art Teacher

GIFFORD
Roberts, Judy Poyner
Second Grade Teacher

GLEN ELLYN
Murray, Thomas George
High School Teacher

GLENVIEW
Hayes, Preston T.
Chemistry Teacher
Pasquini, David P.
History Teacher
Roschmann, Dennis E.
Teacher of Gifted Coordinator

GLENWOOD
Clutts, Lois Mary
Language Arts Teacher
Fields, Diana Maria
3rd Grade Teacher

GODFREY
Sommars, Edna M.
Fourth Grade Teacher

GOREVILLE
Kaeser, Romelle
Jr HS Teacher

GORHAM
White, Judith Maes
Third-Fourth Grade Teacher

GRAFTON
Grimes, Jean Jones
Librarian

GRANITE CITY
Brodzinski, Andrea Tharp
Home Economics Teacher
Forrest, R. Imogene Smith
Fourth Grade Teacher
Larsen, Deborah S.
Spanish Teacher
Lybarger, Len W.
Health Teacher
Pinnell, Thomas H.
Biology Teacher
Rehg, Robert L.
Biology Teacher
Rongey, Marilyn Francis
Fifth Grade Teacher
Schroeder, Edward Marshall
English Department Chair
Sich, Ann Catherine (Dye)
Library-Media Teacher
Sikora, John H.
Head Science Dept
Velloff, Michael M.
Fifth Grade Teacher

GRANT PARK
Koelling, Shirley (Johnson)
Mathematics Dept Chair

GRAYSLAKE
Martin, Lawrence Clyde
Physical Education Instructor
Robinson, Janet Mayberry
Secretarial Instructor

GREEN VALLEY
Summar, Sharon Kay
4th Grade Teacher/Cmptr Coord

GREENFIELD
Weller, Robin Ford
7th/8th Grade Lang Art Teacher

GREENVIEW
Rodgers, Larry Joe
Intermediate Math Teacher

GREENVIEW (cont)
Steinhauser, Judith Wilkinson
English Department Chair
GREENVILLE
Bowman, Beverly Hatfield
English Teacher
Harnetiaux, D. Mike
6th Grade Teacher
Potthast, Patricia Varel
Fifth/Sixth Grade Teacher
GURNEE
Neal, James Edward
8th Grade Lit/Drama Teacher
Paulus, Jayson John
Science Teacher
HAMILTON
Dion, David Arthur
Business Teacher
Heagy, Paula Jo
First Grade Teacher
Kinman, Richard James
7th/8th Grade Science Teacher
HARRISBURG
Hull, Stanley W.
6th Grade Teacher
Yahne, Dan L.
Media Specialist
HARVARD
Jordan, Dennis R.
Social Studies Teacher
HARVEY
Davis, Anne Parham
Sixth Grade Teacher
Jackson, Doris Hope
Science Teacher
Kidd, Kimberly Scott
Mathematics Teacher
HARWOOD HEIGHTS
Anderson, Ann Marie
Band/Chorus Dir/Music Teacher
Zeman, Barbara Ann
5th Grade Teacher
HAVANA
Pokorny, Susan Medhurst
4th Grade Teacher
HAZEL CREST
Candia-Bonner, Veronica
Sixth Grade Teacher
Lewis, Mary Lorean (Turner)
5th Grade Teacher
Lloyd, Edna Marie/Banks
Science Department Teacher
Spokas, Robert Alex
Counselor
HECKER
Hodapp, Leo John
7th & 8th Grade Teacher/Prin
HENRY
Bazyn, Richard W.
Physics/Mathematics Teacher
Mc Cracken, Jay Kent
5th Grade Teacher
HERRIN
Mc Cabe, Beverly Kelley
8th Grade Math/English Teacher
Mc Entire, Joyce A. Nava
6th Grade Teacher
Proctor, Joanna W.
Kindergarten Teacher
Zimny, Billie Kathryn Boggio
English Teacher/Jr HS
HERSCHER
Newsom, Angela Kae
Special Education Teacher
Splear, Wanda K.
Business Education Teacher
Thomas, Michael D.
Guidance Counselor
HIGHLAND
Brueggemann, Dennis W.
Business Manager
Monken, Susan Mary
5th Grade Teacher
Schaefer, Joseph M.
Assistant Principal
Scogin, Helen L.
Fourth Grade Teacher
Zerban, Joyce A.
1st Grade Transition Teacher
HIGHLAND PARK
Hershenson, Martha Bradford
5th Grade Teacher
HILLSBORO
Albracht, Robert D.
Jr High Social Studies Teacher

Morgan, Betty Delamarter
4th Grade Teacher
HINSDALE
Radcliff, Evelyn Deborah Lawrence
7th Grade History/Fr Teacher
HOFFMAN ESTATES
Hill, Frank P.
English Teacher
Mc Donald, Judith Ann
Social Studies Teacher
Wandro, Kathleen O'Rourke
Eng/Performing Arts Teacher
HOOPESTON
Preston, Sandra Umbanhowar
5th Grade Teacher
HUMBOLDT
Gebben, Christopher James
4th Grade Teacher
INGLESIDE
Michalski, Camille Buck
Jr High Social Studies Teacher
ITASCA
Harper, Almeta Powell
First Grade Teacher
Lesher, Ann Winter
Music Educator
Tison, Roy Frederick
History/Geography Teacher
JACKSONVILLE
Boudreau, Robert Richard
Elementary Music Teacher
Jolly, Donald T.
6th Grade Teacher
Manker, Robin C.
Mathematics Teacher
JERSEYVILLE
Mattis, Christine Morettini
Mathematics/English Teacher
JOHNSTON CITY
Eli, Paul Steve
High School Art Teacher
Jenkins, Dorris Hamby
Retired 3rd Grade Teacher
Koontz, Patricia Shaeffer
8th Grade Lang Arts Teacher
JOLIET
Baltz, Virginia Ruth
First Grade Teacher
Benson, Ann Elizabeth
Fifth Grade Teacher
Lippari, Russell Joseph
Music Coordinator
Mc Cawley, Kathleen Ann
Sci/Religion/Spanish Teacher
Okos, Mary Ann
Third Grade Teacher
Sefcik, James Richard
GED Teacher
JONESBORO
Bailey, Evelyn Rider
Fifth Grade Teacher
Schramka, Lawrence P.
Social Studies Teacher
KANKAKEE
Argadine, Pennie Lea
Junior High Reading Teacher
Cinnamon, Joan Peterson
Language Teacher
Clupper, Jo Ann
2nd Grade/Elem Supervisor
Dewitt, Helen Reeves
Math/Sci/Computer Teacher
Edwards, Richard C. Jr.
English Teacher
Feller, Emma Victoria
Fifth Grade Teacher
Frogge, James Lewis
Science Department Chairman
Gergen, Robert Dumont
Social Studies Dept Chair
Grams, Joan Lehnus
Fifth Grade Teacher
Hill, Jane Elaine
Jr HS Teacher
Reddick, Donald
Band Dir/Fine Art Dept Chair
Segert, Richard Ray
Jr High School Teacher
Yonke, Linda Carmitchel
Dean of Students
KANSAS
Kelly, Nancy Sue (Pierson)
English/Media Teacher
KENILWORTH
Sallas, Amelia Stefanos
Fifth Grade Teacher

KEWANEE
Mann, Jean Price
4th Grade Teacher
Mann, Roger
Mathematics/Computer Teacher
Sheahan, Anna L.
Spanish Teacher
KINDERHOOK
Ward, Dixie Kroencke
Jr HS Language Arts Teacher
White, Marilyn Meyer
Business Teacher
KIRKLAND
Benson, Marie Guidice
Jr & Sr HS Mathematics Teacher
KNOXVILLE
Engebretson, Timothy William
Health/Phys Ed Teacher
Shelly, John Benjamin
4th Grade Teacher
Tarochione, James Mason
Seventh Grade English Teacher
West, Lynne J.
English/Speech Teacher
LA MOILLE
Ehmen, Harlan George
Science Teacher
LA SALLE
Jordal, David L.
Biology/Chemistry Teacher
LADD
Coulter, Mary Rauh
First Grade Teacher
Lehning, E. Jane
Teacher Learning Disabilities
LAKE FOREST
Bryngelson, Shirley Johnson
Fourth Grade Teacher
Krouse, Ann Wolk
High School English Teacher
Wollman, Barbara Lewis
Librarian
Zarob, Virginia Mary
Social Studies Chair
LAKE IN THE HILLS
Bandelin, Lillian Salmela
5th Grade Teacher
LAKE VILLA
Bock, Judith Katherine
Teacher of Gifted & Talented
Foss, Martha Wager
First Grade Teacher
LANSING
Widstrand, Christine (Boardman)
Nursery School Teacher
Wynsma, Becky Krygsheld
Home Economics Teacher
LAWRENCEVILLE
Alsman, Philip Richard
Principal
LEBANON
Fertig, Sylvia Korte
Second Grade Teacher
Kottkamp, G. Michael
Jr HS Mathematics Teacher
LELAND
Johnson, Christine H.
Counselor
Travis, Marcia Helaine
History-Social Studies Teacher
LEMONT
Freehauf, Deanna Splitt
Fourth Grade Teacher
Staudt, Mary M.
Fourth Grade Teacher
Svoboda, Beverly R.
Science Department Teacher
LEWISTOWN
Rhodes, Janet Wilcoxen
US His/Amer Government Teacher
LINCOLN
Haning, Janet Mc Donald
5th Grade Teacher/Head
LIVINGSTON
Blastenbrei, Sherry Lynn (Early)
Spanish/English Teacher
Lamore, David L.
Jr High School History Teacher
LOMBARD
Bonde, Rowena M.
Fifth Grade Teacher
Grumbles, Carl E.
6th Grade Teacher

LONG GROVE
Smith, Susan D.
2nd Grade Teacher
MACOMB
Kessler, Virginia Anne
Second Grade Teacher
MALTA
Mc Millan, Elizabeth Worth
6th Grade Teacher
MANSFIELD
Summers, James L.
Social Studies Teacher
MAPLE PARK
Carlson, Darryl Rodney
Drivers Education Teacher
MARINE
Schuette, Richard C.
4th Grade Teacher
MARION
Forbes, Dana A.
Math/Phys Ed Teacher
MARISSA
Mc Guire, Patricia Ruth
Learning Disabilities Teacher
MARKHAM
Potempa, Roman Paul
5th Grade Teacher
MARQUETTE HEIGHTS
Sherwood, Lorna Joyce
8th Grade Lit/Rdng Teacher
MARSEILLES
Fennessey, L. Colleen
Kindergarten/Chapter I Teacher
Riley, Peggy (Adams)
Social Studies Teacher
MARSHALL
Smith, Daralea Harlow
Second Grade Teacher
MASCOUTAH
Henkel, Janice Mayfield
Business Teacher
Roy, John Dennis III
Adjunct Prof/Soc Stud Teacher
MASON CITY
Myers, Zac David
Speech, Physical Ed Teacher
MATTESON
Arkow, Debra Mary
Library Science & Math Teacher
Mc Burrows, Frances Jackson
Physical Education Teacher
MATTOON
Epperson, Rochelle S.
Scndry Science Teacher
Self, Clyde Craig
Sixth Grade Teacher
MAYWOOD
Brewer, Ann Bush
Teacher
Denton, Louise Willis
7th-8th Grade Math Teacher
Freelon, Gladys Ward
Fourth Grade Teacher
Freyman, Mary Therese BVM
Eighth Grade Teacher
Lindstrom, Gordon T.
Science Teacher
Morelli, Albert
Social Studies Teacher
Osborne, Rhonda Lynn
English Teacher
MC HENRY
Chamberlin, Roy A.
Math/Science/Computer Teacher
Roth, James H.
Third Grade Teacher
Sabatka, Carrie Mortell
Math/Social Science Teacher
MC LEANSBORO
Julian, Thelma Ray
Spanish Teacher
Winemiller, Jean Corn
2nd Grade Teacher
MELROSE PARK
Du Boise, Rosetta Jennings
7th & 8th Grade Teacher
Gluss, Jacquelyn S.
4th Grade Teacher
Ross, Sharon Lynn
Second Grade Teacher
Trotta, Carmen Leyva
Physical Education Teacher

Wos, Evelyn Muzika
Jr High/Language Arts Teacher
MENDON
Kreinberg, Timothy Lee
History Teacher
Tournear, Susannah M.
Spanish/English Teacher
MENDOTA
Anderson, Constance Cramer
Third Grade Teacher
Miller, Mary C. Lipke
Secondary Physical Ed Teacher
MEREDOSIA
Franklin, Janet M. Waitkus
Jr HS Science Teacher
Wilson, Terry
History Teacher
METROPOLIS
Rudolph, Jan Cockerill
Second Grade Teacher
MIDDLETOWN
Boward, Henrietta Kruse
Retired Fourth Grade Teacher
MIDLOTHIAN
Vechiola, Donald Francis
Business Teacher
MILAN
Williams, Nanette Smith
5th Grade Teacher
MILLSTADT
Hotz, Carol Poe
Junior HS Sci/Cmptr Teacher
MINOOKA
Maas, Kenneth
Mathematics Teacher
Skwarczynski, Nancy A.
Math Teacher
Smith, Glenda Rogene
Social Studies Dept Chair
Watson, Craig
English Teacher
MOLINE
Bell, Anne Brown
French Teacher
Brunner, Leo Robert
7th Grade Geography Teacher
Day, Edwin Louis
Sixth Grade Teacher
Swords, Jay
Social Studies Teacher
MOMENCE
Wood, Bette Hiatt
Guidance Counselor
MONMOUTH
Vicare, Gerald L.
Earth Science Teacher
MONTGOMERY
Barajas, Anthony Thomas
Third Grade Teacher
Boynton, Thomas Edwin
Sixth Grade Teacher
Mc Carron, James P.
Fifth Grade Teacher
MONTICELLO
Reinhart, Charles Phillip
Mathematics Teacher
MORRIS
Cinto, Ron
Teacher/Coach/Math Dept Chm
Eaton, Melinda Ringer
English Teacher
MORRISON
Campbell, Patricia Tierney
Eighth Grade English Teacher
MORTON
Corey, Judith Ann Springston
Fifth Grade Teacher
Grusy, Elizabeth Bond
Fifth Grade Teacher
Knoblauch, Susan Evans
Speech Teacher
Lievens, Grace Sineni Bunn
5th Grade Teacher
Reiser, Carol Kepner
Grammar/Literature Teacher
MORTON GROVE
Berger, Ronald Vincent
Eighth Grade Teacher
Pierson, Guy Robert
Fifth Grade Teacher
MOUNDS
Mc Neil, Jesse A. Jr.
6th Grade Teacher

MOUNT CARMEL
Gruca, Deborah Hatfield
Mathematics/Soc Stud Teacher
Moade, Mary James (Holsen)
Retired Substitute Teacher
Spruel, Richard Owen
Mathematics Department Chair

MOUNT ERIE
Wolfe, Ellen M.
Third Grade Teacher

MOUNT MORRIS
Mullin, Patsy Donohue
Spanish Teacher

MOUNT OLIVE
Battuello, Rosalie Ann
3rd Grade Teacher

MOUNT PROSPECT
Hickey, Lois May
4th Grade Teacher
Krupa, Carol Connery
Junior High Unit Chairman
Mitchell, Douglas S.
French Teacher

MOUNT VERNON
Ham, Bertie Mateer
Substitute Teacher
Pulley, Paula Jean
Math Teacher
Wilkinson, Carol E.
Art/Mathematics Teacher

MOUNT ZION
Browning, David Robert
Science Teacher
Flinspach, Ursula R.
Math Teacher
Hogan, Sheila Maureen (Krotz)
Biology Teacher
Marshall, Victoria (Addison)
Mathematics Teacher

MUNDELEIN
Ghilarducci, Beth Conroy
Math Teacher

MURPHYSBORO
Worley, David Wayne
Principal

NAPERVILLE
Grover, Ardith Gaylord
8th Grade English/Rdng Teacher
Hoppenrath, Patricia J.
Physical Ed Teacher/Coach
Zemansky, Alex John
8th Grade Eng Teacher

NEOGA
Brandenburg, Sheryl Whitaker
Fourth Grade Teacher

NEW LENOX
Bernhard, David C. Sr.
Mathematics Teacher
Miller, Joseph Alvin
History & Anthropology Teacher
Mostyn, Margie Irwin
Algebra/Geometry Teacher

NEWARK
Jorstad, Priscilla Kmiecik
6th-8th Lang Arts/Rdng Teacher

NEWMAN
Allen, I. Dianna
Mathematics Teacher
Lawless, Sheryl Bohn
2nd Grade Teacher

NEWTON
Deibel, Paula M.
2nd Grade Teacher
Geier, Russell Lee
Soc Stud/Govrnmnt/Econ Teacher
Nichols, Sandra Bailey Clark
English Teacher

NILES
Nalaski, Carol J.
English Department Chairman

NOBLE
Davis, Wiletha Bushart
Fifth Grade Teacher

NOKOMIS
Reuschel, Susan E.
Mathematics Teacher

NORMAL
Bollmann, David J.
Social Studies Teacher
Brown, Norma Jane (Bray)
English Teacher
Eaton, James D.
5th Grade Teacher

Giamette, Nancy J.
English Teacher
Kusmaul, Gerald Joseph
Biology Instructor
Leh, Ruth (Nelson)
First Grade Teacher
Willan, Janyth Sue (Walters)
English/Science Teacher

NORRIDGE
Cassettari, Nanette
Science Teacher

NORTH AURORA
Mc Lin, Anne Williams
Developmental Teacher

NORTH CHICAGO
Triolo, Joseph John
Counselor

NORTHBROOK
Roschmann, Joanne Goldberg
6th Grade Reading Teacher
Rosholt, Richard M.
Social Studies Teacher

NORTHFIELD
Kubera, Mary Beth
English Teacher/Hum Chair

NORTHLAKE
Ahbe, Dottie Rebokas
Fifth Grade Teacher
Anderson, Helen Salata
7th & 8th Grade Math Teacher
Barnes, Catherine E.
Lang Arts/Reading Teacher
Sremaniak, Mary Jean Munaretto
Spanish Teacher
Strauss, John W.
English Teacher
Swies, Ann Eddy
First Grade Teacher
Weiss, Nancy L.
Fourth Grade Teacher

O'FALLON
Curry, Eric Omar
Physics Teacher
Fulton, Karen E.
4th Grade Teacher
Grogan, Nila
Spanish Teacher
Hooker, Linda M.
Mathematics Teacher
Nute, Barbara Brown
5th Grade Teacher

OAK FOREST
Barker, Patricia Ann
US His/7th Gr Religion Teacher
Beer, Esther Rae
Sixth Grade Teacher

OAK LAWN
Scott, Dorothy Person
Third Grade Teacher
Turek, Henry John
6th Grade Teacher/Asst Prin

OAK PARK
Arellano, Andrew Michael
Speech Teacher
Baloun, Charlene Mary
Kindergarten Teacher
Langenderfer, Duane Lee
English Teacher
Smitherman, Betty Clark
Sixth Grade Teacher
Young Marohn, Ann
Language Arts Teacher

OAKLAND
Duzan, Sue Hearn
2nd Grade Teacher

OBLONG
Britton, Jennalee Stewart
Fourth Grade Teacher
Livingston, Donna Sue (Howard)
Fourth Grade Teacher

OHIO
Ehmen, M. Gwen
Junior High School Teacher
Mead, Toni Dierstein
Second Grade Teacher
Vaughan, Sharon R.
English Teacher

OKAWVILLE
Fox, Joy Bohleber
1st/2nd Grade Teacher

OLNEY
Czemski, Margaret Ann Stanley
6th Grade Teacher
Sterchi, Brenda S. (Mc Knight)
Fifth Grade Teacher

OLYMPIA FIELDS
Pluta, Maria E.
Physics Teacher

OREGON
Feazel, Brenda Kaye Mc Casky
Chemistry Teacher
Pravidica, Susan Shanley
First Grade Teacher

ORION
Chelstrom, Stephen Dean
Sixth Grade Science Teacher
Kessel, Catherine Heath
3rd Grade Teacher
Kron, Rebecca Ann
5th Grade Teacher
Nicholson, Tom C.
Director of Career Education
Parry, James Keith
8th Grade Math Teacher

ORLAND PARK
Brott, Barbara Berry
Gifted Language Art Teacher
Cutforth, Nancy Bohne
Reading Teacher/Gifted Program
Dalton, Patricia Lynch
Jr HS Eng/Amer His Teacher

OSWEGO
Hayner, George William
Fourth Grade Teacher
Mitchell, Gail Britt
Eng Dept Chair/AP Coordinator
Page, Jean Kendall
7th/8th Grade Teacher

PALATINE
Bachrodt, Michael P.
Chemistry Teacher
Keehn, Kevin B.
8th Grade Science Teacher
Martina, Joseph Philip
Mathematics Teacher
Ortman, Dorothy Klupping
4th Grade Teacher
Sofianos, Judith Jacobson
Fourth Grade Teacher

PALMYRA
Wagner, Elizabeth Ann
English/Reading Teacher

PALOS HILLS
Sikaras, Helene
4th Grade Teacher

PALOS PARK
Pehanich, Patricia M.
6th Grade Teacher

PANA
Casner, Sharon Ade
Math Instructor
Eilers, Barbara Ruth
Second Grade Teacher
Zueck, Debra Lee
First Grade Teacher

PARIS
Seals, Billie Ann
First Grade Teacher

PARK FOREST
Raftery, Michael Patrick
English Teacher
Rodey, Robert Alan
History Teacher

PARK RIDGE
Bauch, Gloria Jean (Meyer)
Third Grade Teacher

PAWNEE
Richardson, Gail Routzahn
Kindergarten Teacher

PAYSON
Morgan, Mary Helen
Fourth Grade Teacher
Morrison, Carla Nelson
History Teacher

PEARL CITY
Mc Ginness, J B
Teacher

PEKIN
Clark, Linda Kay (Riley)
Fourth Grade Teacher
Cole, David Eugene
Fourth Grade Teacher
Grodjesk, Kenneth B.
Science Teacher
Paulons, Janet Leigh (Jones)
World History Teacher
Peckham, Diana Maurer
English/Publications Teacher
Pfeffinger, Charla (Dumville)
Kindergarten/Chapter 1 Teacher

PEORIA
Bales, Marylee
Social Studies Teacher
Bright, Mollye Hunt
French Teacher
Clark, Nancy A.
Mathematics/Chemistry Teacher
Efinger, Marilyn Louise (Gilbert)
Jr High Science & Dept Head
Fabish, Charles Edmond
Physics Teacher
Geurin, Ronald E.
Mathematics Dept Chair
Glynn, Violet Martino
Third Grade Teacher
Jobe, Donna Jaree
6th Grade Teacher
Kelly, Susan Marie
5th-8th Grade Science Teacher
Link, Barbara Marie
Social Studies Teacher
Mack, Bonnie Jean (Gibson)
7th & 8th Grade Teacher
O'Connell, Barbara June
Social Studies & Lit Teacher
Rada, Eileen Glickley
Religion Teacher
Rouse, Ruth Dennis
Fourth Grade Teacher
Sallee, Vivian G. (Sanders)
Special Education Teacher
Seacrist, Marilyn Huber
Language Arts/Computer Teacher
Weiss, Sharon Martin
French Teacher
Wojcikewych, Joan Harris
Admin/Language Art Teacher

PEOTONE
Gardner, Beth Emerson
Computer Coordinator
Schranz, Bonnie Simonton
English/Journalism Teacher

PERU
Marquardt, Toni Lynn
Mathematics & English Teacher
Morel, Donna Wahl
Jr High School Teacher
Rosenkranz, Josephine OSF
4th Grade Teacher

PHOENIX
Jamrock, Maureen S.
Science Department Chair

PINCKNEYVILLE
Lovel, Susan Gaye
Guidance Counselor
Mc Pheeters, George Madison Jr.
Science Instructor
Rodgers, Debbie Hawkins
Fifth Grade Home Ec Teacher

PITTSFIELD
Dunn, Kathleen Rose
English/Business Teacher
Ring, Bob
English Teacher

PLAINFIELD
Coleman, Linda Kay
Chorus Teacher
Ellis, Lawrence William
Mathematics Teacher

PLEASANT PLAINS
Bensko, Diane Graham
4th-6th Grade Gifted Teacher

POLO
Cheek, Deborah Lynn
Mathematics Teacher

PONTIAC
Mehlberg, John Eldon
Head Fifth Grade Teacher
Raube, Dee Dee Carls
6th Grade Teacher/Asst Prin
Rutter, Jeanne Barron
Physical Ed Teacher/Coach
Schindlbeck, David John
Principal

POPLAR GROVE
Troller, Christine Loveland
Jr HS Social Studies Teacher

PORT BYRON
Lundahl, Christy Breckle
2nd Grade Teacher
Maccabee, Sara Kathryn
English Teacher

PRAIRIE VIEW
Dagro, Caryl Jo
Jrnlsm/English/Reading Teacher
Gregorin, Thomas S.
Scndry Mathematics Teacher

Mattucci, Frank Anthony
Educator/History Teacher
Nowicki, John S.
Business Education Instructor
Singer, Susan Jacobs
H S English Teacher

PRINCETON
Laesch, Phillip L.
German Instructor

PRINCEVILLE
Mansfield, Luther Albert Jr.
Junior High Teacher
Smith, Diane Mac Millan
1st Grade Teacher
Stahl, Alana June
Mathematics Teacher

QUINCY
Wagner, La Wanda Joyce
6th Grade Teacher

RAMSEY
Mc Clure, Joy Alexander
Fifth Grade Teacher

RANTOUL
Mc Elwain, Robert Douglas
Social Studies Teacher
Wilson, Janet Mc Cord
First Grade Teacher

RED BUD
Belter, James Edward
Fourth Grade Teacher
Letcher, Gail Edward
Fifth Grade Teacher
Pautler, Vera Mae (Laufer)
First Grade Teacher

REDDICK
Wancho, Amy Ann (Clark)
Third Grade Teacher
Williamson, Marilyn Joyce (Burrus)
General Music/Band/Chorus Dir

RICHTON PARK
Bukovsky, Diane Herbold
Teacher of Gifted

RIVER FOREST
Crnkovich, Rose A.
English Teacher
Heidloff, Dale R.
Jr HS Teacher/Sci Dept Chair
Jarzab, Arlene Roberta
ATP Humanities Teacher
Lindberg, Lois Ruth (Scharsich)
Fifth Grade Teacher

RIVERDALE
Matson, Karen Kramer
Third Grade Teacher
Tritt, Terry Lee
Music/Band/History Teacher

RIVERSIDE
Costopoulos, Leonard
Social Science/English Teacher
Unger, Lolita Seghetti
Fourth Grade Teacher

RIVERTON
Koger, Jeffrey Paul
Fifth Grade Teacher
Mulvany, Byeta M.
English Teacher
Stone, Virginia Lee
6th Grade Teacher

ROBBINS
Miller, Ronald Dale Sr.
Fourth Grade Teacher

ROBINSON
Bennett, Carolyn J. Richart
Fifth Grade Teacher
Johnson, Wayne Keith
HS Biology Teacher
Roche, Lynne Ann
7/8th Grade Lang Arts Teacher

ROCK FALLS
Anderson, Judy Mehl
Librarian/Cmptr Coord
Clementz, Betty May
French Teacher
Gadient, Elizabeth L.
7th & 8th English Teacher

ROCK ISLAND
Freers, Gary W.
English Teacher
Johnson, Janet Jo Lockhart
6th Grade Language Art Teacher
Krick, Paul Brian
Health Teacher
Lindmark, Marie Nelson
Elementary Teacher of Gifted

ROCK ISLAND (cont)
Marsoun, William J. Jr.
  Mathematics Teacher
O'Brien, Katherine Jean (Doty)
  Eng Teacher/Speech/Drama Coach
Sailer, Philip Patrick
  Social Studies Teacher

ROCKFORD
Austin, Jane S.
  6th Grade Teacher
Fisher, Joyce Hockman
  Fifth Grade Teacher
Gerrond, M. Carol Miller
  Business Education Teacher
Gunn, Melody Ann
  English Department Chair
Janssen, Robert E.
  Sixth Grade Teacher
Jenson, Jane Elizabeth
  Third Grade Teacher
Johnson, Richard Lewis
  Sixth Grade Teacher
Koenigsberger, Thomas G.
  Science Teacher Dept Chair
Layng, Constance Twietmeyer
  Business Education Teacher
McNamara-Eliseo, Nancy Tesmer
  5th Grade Teacher
Primuth, Andrea L.
  Counselor
Rinedollar, Thalia Nungezer
  Elementary Teacher
Scandroli, Lynn Essington
  2nd Grade Teacher
Sharp, Jean Stewart
  Math Teacher/Math Dept Chair
Steely, Allen M.
  Science Teacher
Wallens, Thomas J.
  English Teacher/Yearbook Adv
Weckerly, Ronald Roy
  4th Grade Instructor

ROLLING MEADOWS
Buob, Patricia Andersen
  2nd Grade Teacher
Monahan, Dennis P.
  Spanish Teacher/Coordinator
Nestor, Daniel E.
  Mathematics Teacher
Robertshaw, Rick
  Mathematics/Science Teacher
Ziemek, David W.
  Mathematics Teacher

ROMEOVILLE
Irwin, Thomas Joseph
  Instructor
Krblich, Edith Levering
  Fifth Grade Teacher
Magruder, Gary L.
  English Teacher

ROODHOUSE
Martin, Ronald D.
  Mathematics Teacher

ROSCOE
Novota, Marlene R.
  English/Language Arts Teacher
O'Connell, Thomas John III
  7th/8th Grade Soc Stud Teacher
Riemer, Martha Helen
  Fifth Grade Teacher
Williams, Sally Burden
  4th Grade Teacher

ROSELLE
Dwyer, Barbara Mitchell
  English Teacher
Kapes, Charles Peter
  5th Grade Teacher
Walthouse, Frances J. (Novak)
  Math Teacher

ROSSVILLE
Tracy, Christina Goekler
  Science/Computer Teacher

ROUND LAKE
Shepard, Carla (Eastman)
  Third Grade Teacher
St. Aubin, Sheila Katherine
  Principal

ROXANA
Barton, Bette Smith
  Sixth Grade Teacher
Hamelmann, Norma Ruth
  Math Teacher
Hunt, Sharon (Myers)
  English/Speech Teacher
Pitt, Judy Kay Rushton
  Second Grade Teacher
Skelton, Sandra Kay (Sunberg)
  Jr HS Mathematics Teacher

RUSHVILLE
Phillips, Rick
  Mathematics Teacher

SAINT ANNE
Owens, Jacqueline Hoekstra
  Fifth Grade Teacher
Wojnowski, Suzanne Dick
  English/Phys Ed Teacher

SAINT CHARLES
Koeppl, Gretchen Louisa Scherzer
  8th Grade Reading Teacher
Lindgren, Mona G.
  Social Studies Teacher
Perkins, Candace M.
  Journalism Teacher

SAINT JACOB
Jackson, Charles Borden
  History Teacher

SALEM
Dye, Lynette Marie (Hobell)
  Rdng Teacher/Chapter 1 Tutor
Roberts, John W.
  Mathematics Teacher

SANDWICH
Blackwell, Samauel M.
  Amer History/Pol Sci Teacher
Pax, Robert
  Physical Education Teacher

SAUK VILLAGE
Trelinski, Patricia Olson
  Learning Disability Teacher
Tripp, Paul Clark
  5th Grade Teacher

SAVANNA
Ferris, Jean Mace
  Kindergarten Teacher

SCHAUMBURG
Anderson, James Howard
  Math Department Chairman
Blenner, Peggy Dewane
  Jr H S Language Arts Teacher
Grapethin, Jennifer Anne
  Spanish Teacher
Moore, Rebecca Lenegar
  Sixth Grade Teacher
Tyler, June Parker
  Third Grade Teacher
Vergoth, Marilyn Johnson
  5th Grade Teacher
Walter, Judith Van Dyck
  Mathematics Teacher

SENECA
Keech, Tanya Mendenhall
  Science Teacher
Robinson, Joseph Allen
  Mathematics Teacher

SHAWNEETOWN
Harmon, Jane Schmitt
  Second Grade Teacher

SHOBONIER
Meseke, F. Gale
  Principal

SIBLEY
Goembel, Betty Louise
  Fifth Grade Teacher

SILVIS
Ross, David Michael
  Social Studies Teacher

SKOKIE
Batts, James Clark
  English Teacher
Gamm, Esther
  4th Grade Teacher
Savage, Patrick Joseph
  Teacher/Head Coach

SOUTH HOLLAND
Deutmeyer, Mary A.
  Mathematics Teacher/Dept Chair

SOUTH WILMINGTON
Micetich, Joel Phillip
  Jr HS Teacher
Naretto, Jean Trotter
  First Grade Teacher

SPARTA
Bourner, Oleta Carlyle
  Retired
Cox, Gary Wayne
  4th Grade Teacher
Williams, Patty L.
  Mathematics Teacher/Coach
Woodworth, Laura Grah
  6th Grade Language Art Teacher

SPRINGFIELD
Ames, Kathie Neill
  Kindergarten Teacher
Bretz, William Franklin
  Social Science Dept Chairman
Drew, Bonnie W.
  Business Dept Chairperson
Green, Julia A. (O'Connell)
  Retired Second Grade Teacher
Lookis, Jill Estelle
  Language Art & French Teacher
Richter, Nancy J.
  Sr English Teacher/Dept Chair
Stonecipher, Brenda (Vallowe)
  Family Support Specialist

STERLING
Chapman, Carol Jean (Michel)
  Mathematics Teacher

STILLMAN VALLEY
Lorbinenko, Nina
  French Teacher
Meves, Sharon Bromley
  Eng Lang Art Teacher

STOCKTON
Harmston, Terry Michael
  Teacher/Coach
Rankin, Linda Lou (Peterson)
  High School English Instructor

STRASBURG
Oyer, Donald Ray
  Sixth Grade Teacher

STREAMWOOD
Ericson, Eugene
  Business Education Teacher
Kamerlander, Richard Lee
  Social Studies/US His Teacher
Keck, Robert F.
  Honors Biology Teacher
Meade, Glenn Louis
  English Teacher

STREATOR
Cave, Jo Ann Hatzer
  8th Grade Teacher
Le Rette, Jacqueline Ann (Schmitt)
  Fourth Grade Teacher

STRONGHURST
Bavery, William Floyd
  Math and Science Teacher
Clifton, Richard W.
  Elementary & HS Principal
Davis, Lois Ann Brouse
  2nd Grade Teacher

SUMNER
Czemski, Anthony Joseph
  Social Studies Teacher

SYCAMORE
Bazeli, Marilyn Weerts
  4th Grade Teacher
Johnson, Yvonne A.
  5th Grade Teacher
Kouba, Sharon Shachter
  Fifth Grade Teacher
Roche, Margaret Ann Storer
  7th Grade Soc Stud Teacher

TAMMS
Mc Gowin, Jim Allen
  Fifth Grade Teacher
Reid, Alfreda Vines
  Language Arts Teacher
Shumaker, Linda Mc Cain
  High School Science Teacher

TAMPICO
Kolis, Jeanne Eileen
  Science Dept Chairperson

TAYLOR RIDGE
Brown, Jean Vander Linden
  Home Economics Teacher
Clayton-Davis, Ruth
  English Teacher
Ontiveros, Ranelle Downey
  Spanish Teacher
Redlinger, Laurie Felgenhauer
  7th Grade Soc Stud Teacher

TEUTOPOLIS
Lindvahl, Craig A.
  Director of Bands

THAWVILLE
Tammen, Linda Brown
  Kindergarten Teacher

TINLEY PARK
Adams, Patricia Kiewicz
  Dean of Students
Anderson, Ellen Marie
  English Teacher
Condon, Linda Lee
  Reading/French Teacher

Dima-Ferguson, Deborah
  Language Arts Teacher
Halpin, Dee
  5th Grade Teacher
Magnuson, Gayle Glascock
  School Social Worker
Polley, Phillip James
  English Teacher
Weil, Gayle Greenburg
  Fourth Grade Teacher

TOLEDO
Stone, Sidney P.
  7th/8th Grade Lang Art Teacher
Wilson, Harrietta Montgomery
  Third Grade Teacher

TOLUCA
Durham, Alta Hoerbert
  Science Teacher
Heck, Janis Lorraine (France)
  English/Home Ec Teacher

TREMONT
Moyers, Debby Ann (Warner)
  English Teacher
Strifler, Pete
  Social Studies Teacher

TRENTON
Kunz, Dianne Patricia (Ohl)
  5th Grade Teacher
Stalcup, Donald Soule
  Sixth Grade Teacher

TROY
Rees, Dorothy June
  Fifth Grade Teacher
Schwehr, Harold John
  7th/8th Grade Soc Stud Teacher

TUSCOLA
Eiben, Warner G.
  English Teacher

ULLIN
Cross, Linda Gordon
  Second Grade Teacher
Shumaker, Betty Richardson
  English Teacher
Thompson, Carmen (Wright)
  Jr/Sr English Teacher

URBANA
Mc Loughlin, Patrick Joseph
  Mathematics Teacher

VANDALIA
Diekroeger, Kimberly Ann
  7th/8th Social Studies Teacher
Donaldsofn, Susan J.
  Home Economics Teacher
Dugan, Billyanna Poe
  Chapter I Reading
Meseke, Helen Stephens
  Mathematics Teacher

VERNON HILLS
Arendsen, Ruth Neuman
  Third Grade Teacher

VILLA GROVE
Hoffman, Sharon Kile
  Jr. HS English Teacher
Landeck, Joe John
  Phys Ed & Drivers Ed Teacher

VILLA PARK
Stiffler, Elsie Marshall
  English Teacher

VIRDEN
Bruce, Beverly
  Social Studies Chair

WARRENSBURG
Ryterski, Camella (Parrett)
  Middle School Science Teacher

WARSAW
Finton, Esther Schafer
  Second Grade Teacher
Short, Linda Blackwood
  Social Studies Teacher

WASHINGTON
Huser, Billie
  Fifth Grade Teacher

WATERLOO
Schmuck, Judy Kuergeleis
  First Grade Teacher

WATERMAN
Harris, Brian Lloyd
  Social Studies Chair

WAUCONDA
Shenassa, Ann J.
  Assistant Principal

WAUKEGAN
Grisham, Trudy Christakis
  6th Grade Gifted Teacher

WAVERLY
Tolsdorf, Margaret Ann Wright
  French/English Teacher
Yocom, Ellen Stahr
  7th-12th Grade English Teacher

WEST CHICAGO
Masquelier, Gary L.
  English Teacher/Dept Head

WEST FRANKFORT
Blackwood, Shiela Kay
  Mathematics Department Chair
Darden, James Melton
  Principal/Math/Sci Teacher
Hopkins, George Edward Jr.
  Principal/Dist Fed Prgms Dir
Varis, Linda Treece
  Spanish/English Teacher
Wade, Peggy Joyce (Bradshaw)
  Chapter I Reading

WEST HARVEY
Jackson, Rita Eileen Hamilton
  Fifth Grade Teacher

WEST SALEM
Arvin, Gail Annette
  Language Arts Teacher

WESTERN SPRINGS
Cordes, John Bruce
  Fifth Grade Teacher/Asst Prin

WESTMONT
Hackbrush, Jerrilyn Kunze
  Science Department Coordinator

WHEATON
Gora, Patrick John Sr.
  English Teacher
Leimbach, Judith Hanagan
  Teacher of Gifted

WHEELING
Ratay, Gregory W.
  Psychology/Sociology Teacher
Sundquist, Suzanne Kathleen
  Fifth Grade Teacher

WHITE HALL
Rendleman, Billie Dean
  Social Studies Teacher

WILLIAMSVILLE
Barnes, Ken Lee
  Mathematics Dept Chair

WILMETTE
Speer, Judith Ann
  Fine Arts Dept Chair

WINDSOR
Herdes, Marie (Pickens)
  Biology Teacher
Hilligoss, Elizabeth Welch
  1st Grade Teacher

WINNETKA
Harper, Antony J. D.
  Science Teacher

WINTHROP HARBOR
David, Peggy Spitzig
  5th Grade Teacher
Morzuch, Robert Eugene
  Sci Teacher/Dept Chairperson
Scherman, Terry R.
  Principal

WITT
Irvine, Margie Yeske
  4th Grade Teacher

WOOD RIVER
Clugsten, Melody Shiff
  Vocal Music Teacher

WOODSTOCK
Connor, Judy Bartelt
  6th Grade Reading Teacher
Mielnik, Georgeann Passialis
  7th Grade Teacher

YORKVILLE
Nelson, Chris Allen
  Mathematics Teacher
Phillips, Mary Martha
  Business Education Teacher

ZION
Curtin, Brian Michael
  High School English Teacher
Fisher, Gail E. (Stringer)
  3rd Grade Teacher
Gilbert, Roxane
  English Teacher

ZION (cont)
Lee, Timothy Raymond
  Social Studies Teacher
Mors, Christine K.
  Third Grade Teacher
Ramlose, Herbert V. Jr.
  English Instructor
Rymer, Victoria Annette (Beem)
  5th Grade Teacher

INDIANA

ANDERSON
Beck, John Bernard
  4th Grade Teacher
Bush, Helen M.
  Elementary Montessori Teacher
Hatley, Ginger Kay
  Mathematics Teacher/Dept Chair
Hitz, Barbara J.
  3rd/4th Grade Algebra Teacher
Johnson, Eleanor Hartman
  Second Grade Teacher
Knaus, Betty Kose
  Third Grade Teacher
Moore, Jerry Joe
  Physical Education Teacher
Roby, Peggy May
  Mathematics Teacher
Rooks, Barbara Jean
  English Teacher
Sweeney, Mary Lou Isaacs
  Teacher
Welch, Michael G.
  6th Grade Teacher

ANGOLA
Wright, Tony Gene
  Chemistry Teacher

ARCADIA
Herndon, Richard L.
  Mathematics Dept Chairman
Stone, Mary Kohns
  2nd Grade Teacher

ARGOS
Wampler, Portia Spitler
  First Grade Teacher

ASHLEY
Mayberry, Latha Mc Kuin
  Fourth Grade Teacher

AURORA
Bressert, Robert T.
  5th Grade Teacher
Duerstock, Sabra Carmack
  6th/7th Grade Lang Art Teacher
Murray, Londalea
  First Grade Teacher

AUSTIN
Deaton, David F.
  5th Grade Teacher

BEECH GROVE
Williams, Alice Bramlett
  6th-8th Grade Phys Ed Teacher

BLOOMFIELD
Johnson, Debbie Carol (Abel)
  Junior High & HS Art Teacher
Riddle, Michael H.
  Mathematics/Writing Teacher

BLOOMINGTON
Kinzer, Mary Grise Forester
  Theatre/English Teacher
Lumbley, William D.
  Science Department Chairman
Witten-Upchurch, Gwendolyn
  Choral Director

BLUFFTON
Babcock, Mary Elizabeth (Steiner)
  Retired Primary Teacher
Biggs, Karen Sue
  Third Grade Teacher
Lux, Douglas Craig
  Math Teacher
Plummer, Kathi Careins
  Health Occupations Teacher

BOONE GROVE
Belegal, Porfirina Brucal
  Second Grade Teacher
Flood, Jerry Neil
  Business Education Teacher
O'Boyle, Timothy F.
  English Teacher
Snow, Kenneth
  Biology Teacher

BOONVILLE
Baker, Fred C.
  Retired Teacher

Ewin, Bill E.
  Mathematics Department Chair
Reinitz, Jane Ann
  Foreign Lang Chair/Cnslr

BORDEN
Istre, Gaynell Satterfield
  5th Grade Teacher

BOURBON
Smith, Ronald George
  Mathematics Department Chair

BRAZIL
Mc Cullough, Nancy Killion
  English Teacher
Mogan, Gregory Lee
  Science Teacher/Dept Chair

BROOKSTON
Wallmann, Billie Gomez
  Spanish/English/Lit Teacher

BROOKVILLE
Lamb, Ruth Bowen
  English Teacher
Mc Lane, Mark Dennis
  English Department Chairman
Renaker, Loretta Hartung
  3rd Grade Teacher
Seiter, Bonnie Wulber
  Fifth Grade Teacher

BROWNSBURG
Corn, Randall A.
  English Teacher
Holmes, Kathy Ann
  First Grade Teacher
Reynolds, John William
  History Teacher/Asst Admin
Swango, Colleen Jill
  Science Teacher
Tidball, Dee Oakes
  Science Teacher

BROWNSTOWN
Van Liew, Janet Craddock
  Social Studies Teacher
Williamson, Theda G.
  Fifth Grade Teacher

BUNKER HILL
Oatess, Janet Sue
  English Department Head
Smith, Nancy L (Mc Elwrath)
  Elementary Science Teacher

BUTLER
Bowman, Connie Jo (Howard)
  Math Teacher/Math Dept Chair

CAMBY
Hammonds, Marylyn R.
  Third Grade Teacher

CANNELTON
Jarboe, Sharman (Mulzer)
  Art Teacher
Lawalin, Edward Alan
  Fifth Grade Teacher

CARMEL
Branch, Kirby Todd
  Teacher
Clark, Mary Beth Brumfield
  Marketing Education Teacher
Swain, Sally Ann
  Physical Ed/Health Teacher

CAYUGA
Henderson, John Franklin
  English Teacher

CEDAR LAKE
Maybaum, Kay Lynn Reicher
  Third Grade Teacher

CHANDLER
Hassel, Helen Feulner
  Third Grade Teacher

CLAYTON
Flint, Diane
  English/Latin Teacher

CLINTON
Zwerner, William Gene
  Biological Science Teacher

CLOVERDALE
Cherry, Jeffrey Allen
  Earth Science Teacher

COLUMBIA CITY
Beck, Kenneth Lee
  3rd Grade Teacher
Lambert, Debbe Kilby
  Physical Education Teacher
Oliver, Jayne Mullendore
  English Teacher
Steill, Laurel Carlson
  English Teacher/Dept Chair

Taylor, Margaret Auer
  Third Grade Teacher
Young, Joan (Geiger)
  First Grade Teacher

COLUMBUS
Echsner, Mary
  Spanish Teacher
Fribley, David K.
  US History Teacher
Greene, Rita J.
  Social Studies Teacher
Haro, Rosemary Meier
  Spanish Teacher
King, Thomas Folger
  7th/8th Social Studies Teacher
Martin, David H.
  5th/6th Grade Teacher
Scherschel, Peggy Jo
  Sixth Grade Teacher
Schwenk, Arthur
  German Teacher

COMMISKEY
Miller, Julie Morin
  Third Grade Teacher

CONNERSVILLE
Blair, Wayne
  Science Teacher
Judd, Randal Glen
  Social Studies Dept Teacher

CONVERSE
Bennett, Mary Tobin
  History & English Teacher
Hendricks, Louann De Well
  Spanish/French Teacher

COVINGTON
Hughes, Joyce Ellen
  English Teacher

CRAWFORDSVILLE
Pyle, Larry Wayne
  Science Teacher
Williams, Karey Lynn
  English Teacher

CROWN POINT
Highsmith, Stephen W.
  6th Grade Teacher
Kernagis, Ruth
  Teacher
Shipley, Carol Mc Nabney
  Physical Education Teacher
Wolseley, Carrie Hofherr
  Substitute Teacher
Wool, Debra Lynn
  Fourth Grade Teacher

CULVER
Middleton, Sandra Sue
  Third Grade Teacher

DALE
Neukam, Carla Kay
  Fifth Grade Teacher

DALEVILLE
Lyon, Thomas Edward
  Earth Science/Biology Teacher
Unger, Cynthia Jane (Brandt)
  Fourth Grade Teacher

DECATUR
Germann, Kenneth Ralph
  Learning Disabled Resource
Moffett, David Ward
  Social Studies Chair

DELPHI
Freeman, Susan Maxwell
  2nd Grade Teacher

DEMOTTE
Frederich, Thomas Joe
  Fourth Grade Teacher
Shank, John F.
  5th Grade Teacher/Asst Prin
Swart, Joanne M.
  Second Grade Teacher

DENVER
Pippenger, Janice Rapp
  5th Grade Teacher
Whittlesey, Howard L.
  Music Dept Head/Choral Instr

DUBOIS
Acuff, Karen
  French/English Teacher
Mathena, Richard D.
  English/History Teacher
Mauntel, Margaret Schluter
  6th Grade Rdng/Sci Teacher
Schroeder, James Anthony
  Mathematics/History Teacher
Werne, Maureen Rose (Seger)
  Second Grade Teacher

DYER
Whitcombe, Roxann Robin
  Reading Department Chair

EAST CHICAGO
Beres, Betty Rose
  Fourth Grade Teacher

EDINBURGH
Barker, Maysel Royce (Schwartz)
  2nd Grade Teacher of Gifted
Snyder, Brenda Sue
  Teacher of Gifted & Talented

ELKHART
Copp, William Frederick
  Fourth Grade Teacher
Fields, Susan Michael
  Home Economics Teacher
Harness, Tim D.
  Fourth Grade Teacher
Lacy, Martha A.
  Science Teacher
Nelson, Ronald
  Music Department Chair
Polk, Sandra Lea
  Third Grade Teacher
Stork, Janice A.
  English Teacher

ELLETTSVILLE
Mitchell, Kenneth O.
  Science Teacher
Reagan, Michael L.
  Middle School English Teacher
Smith, Dorothy Small
  Music Teacher/Choral Director

EVANSVILLE
Baldwin, Mary Joyce Shaw
  Third Grade Teacher
Boyd, Glenda Lorney (Riney)
  Vocational Home Ec Teacher
Brown, Norman Allen
  Mathematics Teacher
Currier, Nancee Clark
  Head of Lower School
De Muth, Reno Ben
  Speech Teacher
Holste, Robert W.
  Eighth Grade Teacher
Jones, Jerry I.
  Mathematics Teacher
Kattau, Eva J.
  Speech/Theatre Teacher
Middleton, Donna Rahm
  Language Art Teacher
Motz, Steffanie
  Social Studies Teacher
Parker, Nadine Tompkins
  6th/8th Grade English Teacher
Reynolds, Paulette Angrick
  Fifth Grade Teacher
West, Robin Robert
  History Teacher

FAIRMOUNT
Earnest, Martin Leon
  Chem Teacher/Sci Dept Chair
Pickering, Dennis Richard
  7th Grade Science Teacher

FERDINAND
Hoppenjans, Diane Gogel
  5th/6th Grade Math Teacher

FISHERS
Leonard, Elizabeth V. Adams
  Science Department Chairman
Roberts, Melinda Jane
  Third Grade Teacher

FLORA
Dillman, Glen Dean
  Social Studies Teacher

FLOYDS KNOBS
Davids, Cheryl Eve
  Third Grade Teacher
Gullet, Sharon Odella
  American History Teacher

FORT BRANCH
Byrum, Rita (Cantrell)
  Language Arts Teacher
Mills, Charles E.
  Chemistry Instructor
Stansberry, Donald Wayne
  English Teacher

FORT WAYNE
Birkhold, Linda Horner
  Second Grade Teacher
Blose, Patrick Allen
  Biology Teacher
Boyer, Joan Graffis
  Social Studies Department Head
Burgan, Diane (Fuelling)
  Home Economics Teacher

Epple, Dorthy M.
  First Grade Teacher
Garvin, Madeline Marcelia
  English Teacher
Griffin, Roderic B. Jr.
  Spanish Teacher
Grimes, Johnnie Kennie
  Learning Disabilities Teacher
Imhoff, Calvin Paul
  Math/Phys Ed/Health Teacher
Imler, Mary Elizabeth
  Science Department Chairperson
Kanning, Marie Toepfer
  Kindergarten Teacher
Kennedy, Patricia E.
  Director of Choral Activities
Kidd, Stephanie Foster
  Mathematics Teacher
Kiefer, Sheila Diane
  Second Grade Teacher
Kleinscmidt, Marlene (Colicho)
  First Grade Teacher
La Fontaine, Patricia Jo
  French Teacher
Lipp, Evelyn M.
  World History Teacher
Opihory, Kathleen Ann
  Fourth Grade Teacher
Peterson, Cherry Boyer
  Teacher/Coach
Schmidt, Jeanette Price
  Language Arts Teacher
Seculoff, Florence Ann
  6th-8th Departmental Teacher
Trammel, Robert Wayne
  Mathematics Department Chair
Wodock, Rebecca Barnett
  Math Teacher
Wudy, Jim Robert
  3rd-8th Grade Phys Ed Instr

FORTVILLE
Fischer, Ellen Thompson
  Sixth Grade Teacher

FOUNTAIN CITY
Showalter, Catherine Lynn (White)
  1st Grade Teacher

FOWLER
Ballard, Elaine Robertson
  Fifth Grade Teacher

FRANCESVILLE
Heath, Bruce Williams
  6th Grade Science Teacher

FRANKFORT
Hughes, Larry M.
  Industrial Art Dept Chair
Peterson, Michael John
  Vocal Music Dir/Lang Teacher

FRANKLIN
Mattick, Gloria Palacios
  Chem Teacher/Sci Dept Head

FREETOWN
Rouse, Theresa Elaine (Murphy)
  Fifth Grade Teacher

FRENCH LICK
Harris, William H.
  Math Teacher/Math Dept Chm

FULTON
Berdine, Cedric
  Vocal Music Teacher

GARRETT
Neal, David Michael
  Area Supvr Math, Math Teacher

GARY
Bailey, Lillie C.
  Chapter I Resource Teacher
Burnette, Ella Bradley
  Third Grade Teacher
Butcher, Frances Mc Kee
  First Grade Teacher
Chandler, Barbara Houston
  Mathematics Teacher/Dept Chair
Conde, Veronica (Gurauskas)
  Multi-lingual Cultural Teacher
Diamond, Elaine Diane
  Social Studies Teacher
Fisher, Ethel Page
  Third Grade Teacher
Hargrove, Willie Charles
  Language Arts Teacher
Henrichs, Martin William
  Social Studies Teacher
Kerns, Yolanda Candelaria
  4th Grade Teacher
May, Ernestine M.
  Kindergarten Teacher
Peterson, Everne Horace
  Speech Teacher
Pierce, Carmen Maria
  Spanish Teacher

GARY (cont)

Pratt, Beverly Dority
Social Studies Teacher
Pryor, J. E.
Mathematics Tutor
Rainge, Thelma Gilliam
6th Grade Reading Teacher
Rouse, Doretha Stirgus
Elementary Mathematics Teacher
Saulsberry, Willie Louis Jr.
7th/8th Grade Soc Stud Teacher
Smith, Gloria Sharpe
Language Arts Teacher
Smith, Treacie Bradley
Spanish Instructor
Spindler, Davidanne M. SSCM
8th Grade Teacher
Steele, Charles Walter
History Teacher
Vincent, Juanita Parsons
Choir Teacher/Music Dept Chair
Watts, Augustine Smith
Business Education Teacher
Williams, Delores
English Teacher
Wilson, Eugena Elizabeth (Perry)
English Teacher
Wilson, Patricia Ann
Human Resource Specialist

GAS CITY

Breedlove, Jane Martin
7th/8th Grade Lang Art Teacher
Griffith, Minerva Jo
Mathematics Teacher
Woodard, Lloyd Ervin
Art Instructor

GASTON

Meier-Fisher, Pamela Sue (Beiser)
Mid Sch/High Sch Teacher
Washburn, Beverly Ann
English/Literature Teacher

GOSHEN

Fiandt, Janet Louise
3rd Grade Teacher

GRAYSVILLE

Baker, Kathy Mc Fadden
First Grade Teacher

GREENCASTLE

Evans, Sharon C.
4-6th Soc Stud Teacher/Homerm
Van Rensselaer, Michael Jeffrey
Mathematics Dept Chair

GREENFIELD

Bradway, Jimmy L.
8th Grade Mathematics Teacher
Frist, Bonnie Mae
4th Grade Teacher
Griggs, Nancy Ann Walker
First Grade Teacher
Murphy, Vera Branscum
First Grade Teacher
Overstreet, F. Traxler
Third Grade Teacher
Potter, Craig Edward
English Teacher/Coach
Reder, Constance Kleindorfer
5th Grade Teacher
Wilkinson, Mark James
English Teacher

GREENSBURG

Bohall, William David
Eng/Teacher of Gifted/Talented
Field, John Samuel III
5th Grade Teacher
Fortner, Nancy Kaye
1st Grade Teacher
Haggard, Sylvia Lee (Bohall)
Sixth Grade Teacher
Hayden, Connie Placke
Sixth Grade Teacher
Hickey, Jean Wesley
6th Grade Teacher
Hime, Scott A.
Social Studies Teacher
Sell, David Alan
Fourth Grade Teacher
Vernon, Sharon Rosemary
First Grade Teacher

GREENTOWN

Bryan, Diane (Klepfer)
5th Grade Lang Art Teacher
Maggart, Monty Cliff
Math/Science/Health Teacher

GREENWOOD

Brown, Susan Stephens
Elementary Music Teacher
Ray, Diana Providence
First Grade Teacher
West, Teresa Anne (Whitaker)
5th Grade Mathematics Teacher

GRIFFITH

Hodor, Frances R.
3rd Grade Teacher
Lukmann, Lynn Frances
Science Teacher
Marcinek, Julie Ann
Journalism Advisor

HAGERSTOWN

Diercks, Daniel Paul
English/Journalism Teacher

HAMILTON

Mihocko, Janice N.
French Teacher

HAMLET

Underwood, Marilyn Sue
6th Grade Teacher

HAMMOND

Collins, Amy Berniece Marcum
Principal
Crawford, Ann Jones
7th/8th Grade Teacher
Daronatsy, Aram R.
English Teacher
Evans, Richard Allen
8th Grade Teacher
Harker, Jay L.
Industrial Arts Teacher
Huber, George Richard
Mathematics Department Chair
Klisiak, Janice Gescheidler
First Grade Teacher
Reinke, Frances Kasperek
Science Dept Chairperson
Sherfey, Geraldine Richards
Sci Teacher/Stu-At-Risk Coord
Stum, Lisa Michele
Spanish/Psych/Math Teacher
Volbrecht, Richard E. Jr.
Mathematics Teacher
Wilson, Laura Kessler
German Teacher
Zelencik, Mary Joan
4th Grade Teacher

HAUBSTADT

Michel, Steven Harold
Science/Phys Ed Teacher
Williams, Julie Fisher
Third Grade Teacher

HAYDEN

Sargent, Terri Creech
Fourth Grade Teacher
Sullivan, Patrick L.
Sixth Grade Teacher

HEBRON

Snodgrass, Gerri A. (Marley)
4th Grade Teacher
Williams, Sandra S. Hanna
4th Grade Teacher

HENRYVILLE

Lovins, Dorothy Hoessle
Second Grade Teacher
Mc Intyre, Amy Bedell
English Teacher

HIGHLAND

Buxton, Alice I.
Junior High English Teacher
Chick, Tina M.
Science Dept Chairperson
Poropat, Josefina Lazaro
Spanish Teacher
Wozniak, Kathleen Louise
Fifth Grade Teacher

HOAGLAND

Knopf, Donald Henry
Third Grade Teacher
Lee, Calvin C.
Teacher

HOBART

Deal, Janet Plyler
Language Arts/Soc Stud Teacher
Smriga, Gayle (Vincent)
Third Grade Teacher
Thompson, Victoria Chiarelli
Art Teacher

HOLLAND

Stenftenagel, Claudia Ann (Rothring)
Third Grade Teacher

HOPE

Trotter, Rosemary Holder
Second Grade Teacher

HOWE

Akey, Kenneth Dee
Sixth Grade Teacher

HUNTINGBURG

Corn, Darrel Lee
Social Studies Teacher

Evans, Lindsey (Shelton)
English Teacher
Novak, William
Elementary Teacher

HUNTINGTON

Fields, Fred R.
Accounting Teacher/Coach
Fuhrman, Ervin Lester
4th Grade Teacher
Kline, Arthur Harold
Science Teacher
Mc Elhaney, Thomas A.
Band Director
Stoffel, Wallace James
Mathematics Department Teacher

INDIANAPOLIS

Allen, Virginia Jeanne (Walters)
Teacher of Gifted & Talented
Baker, Donna Maled
5th Grade Teacher
Beaty, Mary R.
Third Grade Teacher
Bedwell, Ralph K.
Hum/Performing Arts Dir
Bridgewater, Michael K.
Director of Performing Arts
Brown, Evelyn Erelene
Fifth Grade Teacher
Brown, Linda Lawrence
Resource/Special Ed Teacher
Burns, Vicki Bartlett
4th Grade Teacher
Burroughs, Jon Paul
8th Grade English Teacher
Busch, Karen Lee (Schmidt)
Mathematics Teacher
Carey, Dorothy J.
Mathematics Teacher
Clark, John David
Industrial Technology Teacher
Conner, Paulette A.
Principal
Coulston, Jane Needler
3rd Grade Teacher
Cravens, Dorcas Williams
English Teacher
Crosslin, Rick
4th Grade Teacher
Cunningham, Ronald Keith
US History Teacher
Davidson, Anne R. (Fisher)
Spanish Teacher
Dever-Miles, Marilyn Ann
Eng/Speech/US His Teacher
Dietrich, Judith Morgenstern
Spanish/Comm Skills Teacher
Edwards, Lois Jean
Fifth Grade Teacher
Eherenman, Christie E.
English Teacher
Everett, Deborah Stuart
Dir of Comm Soc Teacher & Adv
Fidler, Marcia Light
History Teacher
Finnell, Rudolph Eric
Instrumental Music Teacher
Gentry, Carsey Edward
Spanish Teacher
Glenn, Ann (Etsler)
Dir of Childrens Ministries
Hanna, Marlyce Elam
Kindergarten Teacher
Hard, Jody Plotner
4th-5th Grade Teacher
Hessong, Greg Alan
Biology Teacher
Hon, Timothy Dane
Science Teacher
Humphreys, Stephen W.
Instrumental Music Teacher
Jones, Harvey Wayne
Science Department Chair
Keller, Carol Skierkowski
Middle School Teacher
Kelley, Gwendolyn Julia
Second Grade Teacher
Kenworthy, Cheryl Lee
3rd Grade Teacher
Kerr, Linda Brown
English/Mathematics Teacher
Knight, Diane Dyer
Spanish Teacher
Lang, Marlene Wegehoft
4th Grade Teacher
Lewis, Carla Ross
Language Arts Teacher
Lewis, Deborah Hoyland
Science Teacher
Mc Cain, Jean Geipel
Fourth Grade Teacher
Meares, Cheryl Hootman
Fifth Grade Teacher
Medve, Eleanora Evans
First Grade Teacher

Meyer, Sue Ann
Music Teacher
Milhon-Cress, Candace Lynn
Assistant Principal
Minks, Stanley Jay
English Teacher
Morris, Jon Phillip
Assistant Principal
Park, Howard Walter
Retired Teacher
Parsons, Janis Annette (Mickelson)
Fifth Grade Teacher
Pfeiffer, Melvyn L.
6th Grade Elementary Teacher
Rebber, Mary Lee
English Teacher
Richardson, Ronald D.
Mass Communication Teacher
Robbins, Kathleen L.
2nd/3rd Grade Lang Art Teacher
Rocap, Joan Marie
Mathematics Teacher
Rose, Mary Etta
Director
Rottmann, Barbara Behrmann
Third Grade Teacher
Spargur, Lora Reeves
Grade 5/6 Academically/Talentd
Speckman, Julia A.
Foreign Language Dept Chairman
Stein, Alan
Fourth Grade Teacher
Stewart, Carolyn B.
2nd Grade Teacher
Strange, Wanda Jacobs
English & Journalism Teacher
Taylor, Wilma (Rugh)
English Teacher
Todd, John Philip
G/T Resource Teacher
Walpole, David Bunch
Mathematics Teacher
Walsh, Michael Paden
Mathematics Dept Chair/Teacher
Wolfe, Elaine Claire (Daughetee)
Science Teacher

IRELAND

Miller, Sandra Ann (Sternberg)
Second Grade Teacher
Yaggi, Connie Hoffman
Fourth Grade Teacher

JAMESTOWN

Blankenship, Joyce
Second Grade Teacher

JASONVILLE

Gerber, Elena Harden
Third Grade Teacher
Wardell, Marian Lisman
Sixth Grade Teacher

JASPER

Ahlbrand, Donna Jean
8th Grade Lang Art Teacher
Clark, Frederick J.
8th Grade Soc Studies Teacher
Rohleder, Linda Lou
7th/8th Grade Math Teacher
Seger, Susan Wagner
Second Grade Teacher

JEFFERSONVILLE

Bentley, Linda (Cavins)
8th Grade Lang Art Teacher
Hawn, Ronald Dale
Biology Teacher
Knoop, Faye Brewer
Third Grade Teacher
Mead, Barbara Gale (Winnett)
5th Grade Teacher
Wheeler, Judy G.
Sixth Grade Teacher

KENDALLVILLE

Nixon, James Russell
Elementary Principal
Rawlins, Jeffery Alan
English Teacher

KENTLAND

Bohanan, Rita Diane
Fifth Grade Teacher
Molter, Karen S.
English Teacher
Trowbridge, Cathy L.
8th Grade Lang Art Teacher

KINGSFORD HEIGHTS

Meyer, Deborah Lynn (Bain)
Fourth Grade Teacher

KNIGHTSTOWN

Maley, Mary Camplin
First Grade Teacher

KNIGHTSVILLE

Nichols, Donald Eugene
Third Grade Teacher

KNOX

Blubaugh, Deborah Sue
Mathematics Teacher
Hajek, Margaret Ashcraft
Fourth Grade Teacher
Sellers, Arlene Seltenright
Second Grade Teacher
Shank, Elizabeth A.
5th Grade Teacher
Tow, Gladys Mae (Duley)
Kindergarten Teacher

KOKOMO

Atkins, Gary Lee
8th Grade Language Art Teacher
Belcher, Sherri Richmond
Science/Mathematics Teacher
Crites, Barbara Grothouse
Learning Disabilities Teacher
Harshbarger, Arlene Record
Guidance Counselor
Hinkle, Barbara Stoneking
First Grade Teacher
Koloszar, Jan Lee
Gifted Ed Resource Teacher
Langevin, Patty Thomas
English Teacher
Slaughter, Keith Alan
Marketing Ed Teacher/Coord
Thomas, M. Monica Hilton
Third Grade Teacher

LA PORTE

Casto, Diane Williamson
Eighth Grade Reading Teacher
Feikes, Edward Lee
Social Studies Teacher
Frankinburger, Patricia Jean
English Teacher
Gower, Dortha Sue
Fourth Grade Teacher
Organ, Renee Harris
Second Grade Teacher
Thornburg, Joanne Canary (Shephard)
English Instructor

LAFAYETTE

Conner, Dennis W.
Sci Teacher/ Sci Dept Chair
Eberle, Jacqueline Leah
Mathematics Teacher
Fusiek, Bonita Payne
Writing Center Dir/Eng Teacher
Rifner, Philip J.
English Teacher/Department Chm

LAGRANGE

Anstett, Cheryl Ann (Williams)
Third Grade Teacher
Campbell, Kristy Ann
Speech/English Teacher
Newman, Stephen D.
Science Teacher
Parker, Stephen Gregg
Social Studies Dept Chair
Severson, Sherry Anne
Science Teacher/Coach

LAKE STATION

Cripliver, Thomas L.
English Teacher
Johnson, Kevin Lee
7th Grade Science Teacher

LAKE VILLAGE

Doffin, Sheri Lynn (Cook)
First Grade Teacher

LAKEVILLE

Dennie, Lee D.
Earth Science/US His Teacher
Downs, Michael William
First Grade Teacher
Downs, Suzanne (Stultz)
Kindergarten Teacher
Pickerell, Walt Devon
Arts/Technology Teacher
Taylor, Margaret Shoup
Fourth Grade Teacher

LAPEL

Baker, Johanna E.
2nd Grade Teacher
Davis, Deborah Layton
Third Grade Teacher
Eisenbise, Janet Mercer
2nd Grade Teacher
Hersberger-Gray, Denise Anne
Math Teacher

LAUREL

Mehlon, Michael A.
Jr HS Mathematics Teacher

LAWRENCEBURG

Bowell, Gerald Carr
Biology Teacher
Stevenson, James K.
8th Grade Lang Art Teacher

LEAVENWORTH

Ade, Deborah Moe
Second Grade Teacher

LEBANON

Feller, Susan Karlene
Fifth Grade Teacher
Polston, Donald Lee
Social Studies Chairman

LEO

Divelbiss, Ronald E.
Biology Department Head

LINCOLN CITY

Blessinger, Timothy L.
Language Art Teacher
Lifke, James Michael
Substance Abuse Coordinator
Schriefer, Michael Carl
Mathematics Teacher

LINTON

Woodruff, Linda Dee
Third Grade Teacher

LIZTON

Wilson, Mary Lou Lou (Feltner)
Home Economics Teacher

LOOGOOTEE

Jahn, Diane Sue
Language Arts Teacher
Johnson, Gregory O.
Speech/English Teacher
Kavanaugh, David Bernard
Mathematics Chairman

LYNN

Marker, Larry Duane
Asst Principal/Athletic Dir

LYNNVILLE

Cornelius, Cathy Suhrheinrich
Teacher/Counselor
Gregory, Annette
Music/Phys Ed/Health Teacher
Knight, Michael W.
Fourth Grade Teacher
Oxley, Kevin Ray
English Teacher

MADISON

Risk, Dianna Scott
Elementary Teacher

MARION

Abbott, Brian Ray
Jr HS Math Teacher
Fletcher, Betty Rains
Fourth Grade Teacher
Johnson, Jere
Phys Ed/Athletic Director
Miller, Nancy Mc Cord
Kindergarten Teacher
Moore, John Morton
Biology Teacher/Computer Prof
Moore, Rebecca Sue (Harvey)
4th Grade Teacher
Record, Linda Marlene
First Grade Teacher
Resler, Susanna Nation
5th Grade/Math/Science Teacher
Young, Dominic G.
Religion Teacher

MARSHALL

Veach, Gloria White
Fourth Grade Teacher

MARTINSVILLE

Levell, Sue King
Social Studies Teacher
Payne, Phyllis Smith
Third Grade Teacher
Tidd, Beckie Kain
Principal
Zimmerman, Nila Jean (Poe)
6th Grade Teacher

MAXWELL

Beagle, Terry Ann (Garrison)
Social Studies Teacher

MERRILLVILLE

Cole, Grace Nance
7/8th Soc Stud/Science Teacher
Lanzalaco, Joseph Michael
Dean of Students
Morgan, Sally (Burrows)
Biology/Science Teacher

MICHIGAN CITY

Crouse, Catherine S.
Second Grade Teacher

Cunningham, Earl Guy
Bus Law & Marketing Teacher
Gresham, Lynn E.
1st Grade Teacher
Kahn, Steven P.
Physical Education Teacher
Tilden, Byron Dennis
Mathematics Teacher

MIDDLETOWN

Brown, David Edward
German & English Teacher
Chambers, Pamela Sue
Fifth Grade Teacher
Grace, Alice Carol
Home Economics Teacher
Mc Coy, Mary Lou Lou (Baughn)
4th Grade Teacher

MISHAWAKA

Szumski, Carolyn Ann
8th Grade Teacher

MITCHELL

Mc Cracken, Eugene Keith
Business & Drivers Ed Teacher

MODOC

Barhorst, Sandra Elizabeth
6th Grade Teacher

MONON

Malchow, Janice Hopkins
Fine Arts Chair

MONROE

Arnold, Alan D.
Mathematics Teacher
Inniger, Cindy (Zeigler)
School Counselor

MONROE CITY

Cary, Debra Marie (Graman)
Fifth Grade Teacher

MONROVIA

Reeves, Devota Jean
English Teacher

MONTGOMERY

Gallagher, Thomas A.
Mathematics & Physics Teacher

MONTPELIER

Strickland, Sandra Ellsworth
Fourth Grade Teacher

MOORESVILLE

Graves, Sylvia Mills
Music Teacher
Snapp, Clarissa Sumners
Social Studies Teacher

MORRISTOWN

Myer, Dee Ann
Language Quest Teacher

MOUNT SUMMIT

Evans, Donna Harter
1st Grade Teacher

MOUNT VERNON

Kloeck, Vera Sr.
Religion/Math/Reading Teacher

MUNCIE

Greenwood, Theresa Winfrey
Asst Professor Elem Ed
Mc Peck, Charles Lee
5th Grade Teacher
Miller, Brice Hyman
Fourth Grade Teacher
Pope, Georgia Neihardt
Second Grade Teacher
Reason, David Verle
Math Department Chairman
Talbert, Linda Absher
Teacher
Waddell, Marvene (Fritzen)
English Teacher

NAPOLEON

Einhaus, Sandra Lynn (Green)
Fourth Grade Teacher

NAPPANEE

Anglemyer, Roma Kathleen (Wyman)
Fourth Grade Teacher
Baumgartner, Brenda B. Hurd
Kindergarten Teacher
Tobias, Deanna White
Fourth Grade Teacher
Yeager, James Wendell
5th Grade Teacher

NASHVILLE

Merkel, Terry M.
Sixth Grade Teacher
Ryan, Dorothy Ann
French Teacher

NEW ALBANY

Goldstein, Irvin L.
Intermediate Levels Teacher
Hoffmeister, Wesley Keith
Science Teacher
Sims, Damon Anderson Jr.
Social Studies Teacher

NEW CARLISLE

Miller, Linda Rueter
Eighth Grade Science Teacher
Schroeder, Gail Lynn
Third Grade Teacher
Tolmen, Patricia Stephens
Language Arts Teacher
Wade, Steve
Mathematics Teacher

NEW CASTLE

Koger, Janet M. (Frazier)
First Grade Teacher
Scott, Donald Mark
Social Studies Teacher
Walden, Jerry Lee
Drafting Teacher

NEW HAVEN

Glossenger, Carolyn Sue (Webb)
Business Computer Ed Teacher
Hostetler, Stanley R.
Biology Teacher
Lake, Diane Kay
Phys Ed & Health Teacher

NEW MIDDLETWN

Greenfield, Deborah Hall
6th-8th Grade Teacher

NEW WASHINGTON

Bowen, Jacqueline Lee
Music & Art Teacher

NEWBURGH

Harris, H. David
Social Studies Teacher
Lacer, Robert Lee Jr.
Counselor
Meyer, Ginny Merrell
Third Grade Teacher
Skinner, Kathy A.
Spanish Teacher

NOBLESVILLE

Cantlon, Delora Sue
First Grade Teacher
Chandler, Larry Floyd
8th Grade Math-Algebra Teacher
Emmert, Charles Leon
Physics Teacher

NORTH SALEM

Jensen, Patricia A.
Sixth Grade Teacher
Sims, Gayle A.
Chapter I Reading Teacher

NORTH VERNON

Howe, Robert W.
Mathematics Teacher/Coach
Moore, Sherida Burgmeier
English Teacher

OSGOOD

Westerman, Gene L.
Math/Chemistry/Physics Teacher

OSSIAN

Harkless, Judith Ann Dietrich
Third Grade Teacher
Waters, Ted A.
Mathematics Teacher/Dept Chair

OTTERBEIN

Garrett, Nancy Fromme
Second Grade Teacher

OWENSVILLE

Benson, Reba Emerson
Mid Sch Lang Arts Teacher
Johnson, Kermit Webb
Teacher

OXFORD

Purcell, Ronald Roy
Science Teacher/Dept Chair

PAOLI

Stuckwisch, Thomas Joe
Mathematics Department Chair

PARKER CITY

Davis, John Leo
Sixth Grade Science Teacher
Jackson, Ginger Kay (Jackson)
Kindergarten Teacher
Lee, Barbara Jean Robison
Mathematics & Science Teacher
Mills, Karen (Brewer)
First Grade Teacher
Mitchell, Larry Alan
Fourth Grade Teacher

Zeigler, Edward Lynn
5th Grade Teacher

PATRICKSBURG

Robbins, Megan Price
Art/Physical Ed Teacher

PENDLETON

Eversole, Margaret (Thomas)
Librarian/Media Specialist
Hall, Nancy Elizabeth Skinner
First Grade Teacher
Koch, Janet (Goff)
French Teacher
Simerly, Judith Gail (Price)
Second Grade Teacher
Sporinsky, Susan Donaldson
English Teacher

PERU

Boswell, Joy M.
Sixth Grade Teacher
Casper, Lynn Dee (Hullinger)
Womens Phys Ed Teacher
Cawood, Kenneth E.
Mathematics Teacher/Dept Chair
Coblentz, Michael James
Teacher of History/Government
Ellis, Arthur Fobes
English Teacher
Johnson, Paula Lauer
2nd Grade Teacher
Murphy, Carolyn Marie
6th Grade Teacher
Vollmer, Fred L.
Drafting Teacher

PETERSBURG

Hill, Vesper Lee
Middle School Math Teacher
Klipsch, Karen Trelinski
Second Grade Teacher
Krause, William Edward
Drafting Instructor
Whitten, Michael Vern
Mathematics Teacher

PLAINFIELD

Cavanaugh, Patrick Sean
Teacher-Learning Disabilities

PLYMOUTH

Leland, Roger Wayne
Soc Stud Teacher, Dept Chm

PONETO

Reiff, Linda Sue (Cherry)
4th Grade Teacher
Reinhard, Deborah (Betz)
Kindergarten Teacher

PORTAGE

Abbott, Jo Ann Becker
4th Grade Teacher
Baker, Carolyn Hall
Second Grade Teacher
Carnahan, Terry L.
Second Grade Teacher
Davis, Nancy Hallberg
Mathematics Teacher
Ohlfest, Sherry Vermilion
English Teacher
Wheeler, James William
American History Teacher

PORTLAND

Cole, Jane Elizabeth Switzer
Soc Stud Teacher/Dept Chm

POSEYVILLE

Anderson, James Edward
Math Dept Chairperson
Baysinger, Ronald Anthony
6th Grade Teacher

PRINCETON

Mason, Dale A.
Fifth Grade Teacher
Mc Connell, Jill Gentry
English Teacher
Pirkle, Lyndon Elmo
7th-12th Grade History Teacher

RICHMOND

Hellrung, Joseph E.
Teacher of Gifted & Talented
Koger, Kay Jo
Mathematics Teacher
Ronald, Pauline Carol
Art Department Head
White, Edna Dotson
Fifth Grade Teacher

ROACHDALE

Brothers, Jana Porter
5th/6th Grade Teacher

ROCKVILLE

Campbell, Russell Lee
Physics/Math/Cmptr Teacher

Cowan, Gary Alan
Latin/English Teacher
Engerski, Cheryl Justice
Elementary Counselor
Frederick, Sue Hazlett
5th Grade Teacher
Lohrmann, Patricia Poling
English/Composition Teacher

ROSEDALE

Woodard, Phyllis Sue
English Teacher

ROSELAWN

Lawson, Becky J. (Williamson)
First Grade Teacher
Ruwersma, Viviann Buchanan
Sixth Grade Teacher

ROYAL CENTER

Scheffer, Cheryl Ann
Mathematics Department Chair

RUSSIAVILLE

Adams, Beverly Chism
Second Grade Teacher
Brown, Phyllis Ann (Stitt)
Sendry Business Ed Teacher
Suffield, Judith Kreutz
English Teacher

SAINT JOHN

Dernay, Dorothy J. (Fedor)
Reading Tutor
Meyer, Charita
Sixth Grade Teacher

SAINT MEINRAD

Vinson, Betsy
1st Grade Teacher

SALEM

Duffy, Doris Reeves
Spanish Teacher
Medlock, Linda Sue
Physical Education Teacher

SCHERERVILLE

Du Bois, Nola Jane
First Grade Teacher
Hackett, Joseph Le Roy Jr.
World His Teacher/Band Dir
Olsen, Robert Allen
English/Music Teacher

SELLERSBURG

Hammond, Ralph Jeffrey
Science Teacher
Risk, Larry E.
Assistant Superintendent

SEYMOUR

Bean, Dietra Sears
2nd Grade Teacher
Clodfelter, Anne Eyler
English Teacher
Goodman, Sharon Leach
Second Grade Teacher
Hague, Elsie Ann Cordes
Third Grade Teacher
Haper, Kathryn Ann
First Grade Teacher
Huddleston, Wayne Scott
Math Teacher/Football Coach
Lasater, Mary Jane
1st Grade Teacher
Noelker, Cecily Niebank
Third Grade Teacher
Prange, Gregory Vernor
Science Teacher
Silver, Stewart H. Jr.
6th Grade Teacher

SHELBYVILLE

Benson, William Edward
Sixth Grade Teacher
Berner, Marcia
Spanish/English Teacher
Chesser, John W.
Science Teacher
Davis, Thomas William
Latin Teacher
Gray, Richard Allen
K-12th Grade Choral Director
Rice, Jerry Ken
Foreign Language Dept Chair
Roupp, Gary Wayne
Sixth Grade Teacher
Sugden, Nancy L.
Music Dept Chair/Choral Dir

SHERIDAN

Childers, Sandra Kay
Third Grade Teacher

SILVER LAKE

Schilling, Alice Marie (Foust)
5th Grade Teacher

SOUTH BEND
Brewer, John William
  7th Grade Science Teacher
Chambers, Joyce Eileen (Mc Cay)
  Fourth Grade Teacher
Harris, Michelle Geoffroy
  French Teacher
Hoffman, Jerome Michael
  Math & Foreign Lang Teacher
Hoffman, Norma Jean
  English Teacher
Hunkeler, Margaret Louise
  Third Grade Teacher
Klaybor, Stanley J.
  Retired Biology Teacher
Mc Kibbin, Karen Mc Clure
  Chemistry Teacher
Miller, Milvern Jordan
  Second Grade Teacher
Morningstar, Larry Michael
  Mathematics Teacher
Perry, Willie Frank Jr.
  Foreign Lang Dept Chair
Powell, Carol Davis
  5th Grade Teacher
Stalzer, Hildegard
  Ger/Fr/Span Language Teacher

SOUTH WHITLEY
Grant, Kevin
  Computer Coord/Math Teacher

SPEEDWAY
Bourke, Kevin Michael
  6th Grade Teacher/Asst Prin
Harrison, Nancy Thompson
  Health/Phys Ed Teacher
Helmink, C. Noel
  Mathematics & Computer Teacher

SPENCER
Anderson, Theresa Anne
  Art Teacher
Brighton, Kenneth Lyle
  6th Grade Teacher/Dept Chair
Hartman, Arnold Richard
  Chemistry Teacher
Hitchings, Linda (Flebotte)
  6th Grade Teacher
Simmerman, Jack Ray
  Agricultural Education Instr
Uhlhorn, Scott David
  7th/8th Grade Science Teacher

SPICELAND
Fisher, Karen Stonerock
  Third Grade Teacher

STRAUGHN
Kinser, Jennifer Bowman
  4th Grade Teacher
Metroka, Elizabeth R.
  Mathematics Dept Chair

SULLIVAN
Barrett, Theresia Ann
  4th Grade Teacher
Clodfelter, Margaret E.
  Science Teacher
Krieg, John Mark
  Chemistry Teacher
Thrasher, James Stanley
  Fourth Grade Teacher

SULPHUR SPRINGS
Hornaday, Theresa (Wilson)
  Fourth Grade Teacher

SWAYZEE
Green, Vera (Brower)
  Kindergarten Teacher

SWITZ CITY
Gragg, Lynda D.
  7th/8th Grade Teacher

SYRACUSE
Bokhart, Elaine Ann (Hoopingarner)
  Phys Ed/Health Teacher
De Hart, Scott David
  Physical Ed Teacher/Coach
Koble, Carol F.
  Fifth Grade Teacher
Metcalf, Philip Leslie
  HS Mathematics Teacher

TERRE HAUTE
Aird, Debra Walls
  Social Studies Teacher
Baxter, Linda L.
  English Teacher
Bingham, Jude Boyll
  Science Department Chairperson
Eder, Frances Aline
  First Grade Teacher
Lowdermilk, Donna J.
  History Teacher
Maehling, Shirley Raye
  Third Grade Teacher

Moore, Stephen Wayne
  Science Teacher
Sipes, Stuart Michael
  Fourth Grade Teacher
Stephens, Richard Eugene
  Anatomy & Physiology Teacher
Thacker, Della Kay
  Math Dept Chair/Asst Professor
Townsend, Marcia Ellen
  6th Grade Co Dept Chairperson
Turner, Donald Eugene
  Art Teacher

THORNTOWN
Engle, Amy L.
  HS Mathematics Teacher

TIPTON
Orr, Gordon Dale
  7th/8th Grade English Teacher

UNION CITY
Bortner, Margaret Mikesell
  Second Grade Teacher
Hirsch, Janet
  Business Teacher

UNIONVILLE
Powell, Marion S.
  3rd Grade Teacher

VALPARAISO
Allmon, Steven Charles
  J H Dept Chair/Soc Stud Chair
Blastick, Phyllis Jane
  2nd Grade Teacher
Folk, Joyce Ann (Libb)
  HS Coordinator/Math Teacher
Massoth, Ruth Pettet
  4th Grade Teacher
Punter, Robert Alan
  Math Teacher
Webster, Gary Scott
  Fifth Grade Teacher
Yelkovac, Penny
  Third Grade Teacher

VERSAILLES
Avedissian, Janice Aikens
  5th/6th Grade Science Teacher
Ester, Beverly Jean Farrow
  Business/Secretarial Teacher
Wilson, Ruth Waldrop
  Retired
Wygant, Pam Mc Coy
  Second Grade Teacher

VEVAY
Cole, M. Martha Furnish
  Jr HS Language Arts Teacher

VINCENNES
Battles, Marion Ishmael
  Social Studies Teacher
Campbell, Janice Eleanor (Dunford)
  Kindergarten Teacher
Lane, La Donna C. (Gartner)
  4th Grade Teacher
Letts, Cindy J. (Laue)
  5th Grade Teacher
Roark, Brenda Spanger
  Third Grade Teacher
Tucker, Brad
  Head Bsktbl Coach/Bus Teacher
Wyant, Richard Lee
  Teacher/Mathematics Chairman

WABASH
Herbert, Cornelia Mc Leod
  English Teacher/Academic Coach
Morris, Peggy L.
  5th & 6th Grade Teacher
Showalter, Diana Mc Kinney
  Principal
Woodward, Ronald Lee
  Social Studies Teacher

WADESVILLE
Arnold, Irma Ruth
  First Grade Teacher
Schapker, Thomas Joseph
  5th Grade Teacher

WAKARUSA
Cline, Sally Myers
  Home Economics Teacher

WALKERTON
Brown, Gerry Eugene
  General Science Teacher
Umbaugh, Joyce Ann
  English Teacher

WALTON
Ayers, John E.
  Social Studies Chairman
Engle, Stuart L.
  English-Journalism Teacher
Krug, Don Lee
  Jr High Band Director

Sisson, Marilyn Jean
  Second Grade Teacher
Thompson, Sandra Kay
  Kindergarten Teacher

WARSAW
Callighan, David Eugene
  Social Studies Teacher
Horton, Linda Jean
  Business Teacher/Chairman
Kuhn, Daniel Franklin
  Social Studies Teacher

WASHINGTON
Bradley, Dennis Lee
  Teacher
Etienne, Yvonne
  Kindergarten Teacher
Wade, Gordon Lee
  Social Studies Dept Chair

WEST LAFAYETTE
Dall, Cameron Mitchell
  Director of Bands
Dunwoody, Susan Penelope
  English Teacher
Foerster, Robert Steven
  Principal
Merkel, Graceann (Caesar)
  Second Grade Teacher

WESTFIELD
Denari, Robert John
  Biology Department Teacher
Everline, Jeri Louise
  English Teacher
Snyder, Linda Bradley
  Fifth Grade Teacher

WHEATFIELD
Brown, Carol Jane
  6th Grade Mathematics Teacher
Crosby, Kathy Jean
  English Department Chairperson
Green, Walter
  7th Grade English Teacher
Helms, Jack E.
  Science Teacher
Hostetler, Herald Edward III
  Mathematics Teacher
Savich, Julie Hackman
  6th Grade Science Teacher
Slaby, Kristi Lynn
  Biology Teacher
Woolever, Gail Waluk
  Elementary Art Teacher

WHITELAND
Loop, Martha A.
  English Teacher
Price, John G.
  6th Grade Teacher/Ath Director

WHITING
Bachmann, Don
  Mathematics Teacher
Bobby, Rosalie Skertich
  English/Literature Teacher
Haydock, Sherwood Iorweth
  Business Teacher
Howard, Seretha Sibley
  Counselor
Peschke, Patricia Anna
  Business Education Teacher
Ridgley, Gary Michael
  Math Teacher

WINCHESTER
Fulton, Krista Jan (Trimble)
  Third Grade Teacher
Pflasterer, Stephanie Barnes
  Second Grade Teacher

WINSLOW
Aust, Brenda Rominger
  Third Grade Teacher

WOLCOTT
Baer, Jennifer K. (Hughes)
  Fourth Grade Teacher
Streitmatter, Rebecca Lynn (Rupe)
  English Teacher

YORKTOWN
Lucas, Carolyn A.
  Chemistry Teacher

ZIONSVILLE
Orr, Adrianne Burr
  Third Grade Teacher

IOWA

ADEL
Anderson, Lorraine Lee
  High School Art Teacher

AFTON
Mc Neill, Stephanie Sloan
  Spanish/English Teacher
Rose, Lois Ann
  Secondary English Teacher
Wurster, Dorothy Fox
  Kindergarten Teacher

AGENCY
Smith, Shirley Wilson
  7th-8th Grade English Teacher

AINSWORTH
Curley, Mary Hendricks
  Sixth Grade Teacher

ALBIA
Coram, Mary A.
  Second Grade Teacher
Walker, James Daniel
  8th Grade Lang Arts Teacher

ALGONA
Burrow, David Michael
  Head Dept of Mathematics
Skyles, Mary
  5th Grade Teacher

ALLISON
Van Raden, Hinderene
  Retired

ALTA
Weinert, Sheldon Keith
  Mathematics/Science Teacher

ALTON
Ricke, Mary Galles
  7th/8th Grade Teacher

ANDREW
Burrow, John Randolph
  English Dept Head Teacher

ANKENY
Crabtree, Roy H.
  Life Science Teacher
Plantz, Jan Berg
  6th Grade Teacher
Renner, Biff Gregory
  Math Teacher

ANTHON
Pope, Richard Bramley
  5th & 6th Grade Teacher

ATKINS
Andersen, Dawn Anderson
  Fifth Grade Teacher
Demmel, Sheila Wright
  4th Grade Teacher
Frimml, Marlys Werning
  Kindergarten Teacher

ATLANTIC
Neary, Jo Ann Johnson
  5th Grade Lang Arts Teacher

AUDUBON
Davis, Frances Mc Kibbin
  Retired Elementary Teacher
Kristensen, Sandy Jacobs
  Voc Home Economics Teacher
Mc Laughlin, Russell Lowell
  Retired Science Teacher
Severin, Esther Mc Donald
  Third Grade Teacher

BANCROFT
Foth, Mary Gengler
  Second Grade Teacher

BATTLE CREEK
Forthum, Sharon Ann Mc Manus
  Second Grade Teacher

BELLEVUE
Brecht, Kenneth A.
  Social Studies Head/Teacher
Feller, Carol Scott
  Fourth Grade Teacher

BELMOND
Pollitt, Amy L. Johnson
  K-6th Vocal Music Teacher

BETTENDORF
Castro, Susan L.
  Teacher
Marcek, Marianne Galitz
  Teacher of Gifted Students
Marske, Kay Merrette (Detlefsen)
  Third Grade Teacher

BODE
Gruber, Janette Ashmore
  Spanish Teacher
Spaulding, David L.
  Science/Mathematics Teacher

BONAPARTE
Marsh, Arletta Jannings
  Third Grade Teacher

BONDURANT
Looft, Thomas Allan
  Mathematics/Algebra Teacher
Orsland, Kathy Rogers
  First Grade Teacher

BOONE
Gard, Jeff Richard
  Second Grade Teacher
Hora, Linda Beaton
  Sixth Grade Teacher

BROOKLYN
Collum, Mary Jo Rhoads
  Fourth Grade Teacher
Kriener, Robert Peter
  Jr HS Mathematics Teacher
Wallace, Kurt Alison
  Math/Computer Prog Teacher

BUFFALO CENTER
Dotseth, Ervin Richard
  Math Dept Chair/Cmptr Coord

BURLINGTON
Fenton, Theodore J.
  8th Grade Amer Studies Teacher
Huppenbauer, Patricia Breuer
  Home Economics Teacher
Mayle, Patricia Woolsey
  Kindergarten Teacher

CAMANCHE
Letchford, Roy L.
  Mathematics Teacher

CARLISLE
Grooters, Kathy Rhoten
  Second Grade Teacher
Rothfus, Laura Lowther
  2nd Grade Teacher

CASCADE
Sallade, Susan Jane
  English Teacher
Takes, Larry L.
  Mathematics Department Chair

CEDAR FALLS
Husmann, Lu Ann Fink
  Second Grade Teacher
Mark, Steve K.
  Band Director
Vance, Margaurite De Moss
  English Teacher

CEDAR RAPIDS
Brietbach, Paul Stephen
  K-8th Grade Phys Ed Teacher
Cammack, Roene Burghardt
  7th Grade Teacher
Conrad, Richard Lee
  Math Teacher/Team Leader
Eells, Gloria Louise
  History/Government Teacher
Haines, Cathy Moore
  Orchestra Director
Jackson, Jack Dean
  7th Grade Teacher
Mc Namara, Kathleen Marie
  Music Educator
Rinderknecht, Pricilla Anne
  Fourth Grade Teacher
Santee, Leslie R.
  8th Grade Social Stud Teacher
Schultz, Gerald Lee
  Industrial Technology Teacher
Strilich, William Thomas
  Industrial Technology Teacher
Svoboda, Ruth C. Ganske
  4th/5th Grade Teacher
Tackleson, Jon Scott
  Guidance Counselor
Wilson, Barry Robert
  Industrial Tech Teacher
Wilson, Patricia Ann
  Social Stud Prgm Facilitator
Young, Jo Ann R.
  6th Gr Teacher/Multidis Team

CENTER POINT
Stulken, Sharyl Lee
  HS Social Studies Teacher

CENTERVILLE
Campbell, Roger Allen
  Social Studies/PE H S Teacher
Clark, Ronald Richard
  8th Grade History Teacher

CENTRAL CITY
Haigh, Shirley Ball
  Third Grade Teacher

CHARITON
Hall, Va Donna C.
High School Counselor
Masters, Morgan L.
Science Instructor

CHARLES CITY
Kelly, Shirley Tatro
Mathematics Teacher
Myers, Jo An Buch
Jr & Sr High School Counselor

CHEROKEE
Kruse, Tomas R.
Director of Instrumental Music
Zelle, David Arthur
Mathematics Teacher

CLEAR LAKE
Schumacher, Beth Ann
Soc Stud Teacher & Dept Chair

CLINTON
Bukta, Mary P.
5th Grade Teacher

COGGON
Blin, Jackie Kay (Caryl)
Third Grade Teacher

COLLEGE SPRINGS
Bennett, Eula Damewood
4th Grade Elementary Teacher
Irvin, Connie Adams
Kindergarten Teacher

COON RAPIDS
Kult, Deborah Long
Vocal Music Director
Schwenk, Margie Maud
Teacher of Gifted & Talented
Waddle, John Lenord
HS Mathematics Instructor

CORNING
Field, Katherine Marie (Fuhr)
3rd Grade Teacher
Hook, Tracy William
7th-12th Grade Teacher
Kohlhoff, Carlene (Burmeister)
Kindergarten Teacher
Shipley, Patricia K.
Jr HS Language Arts Teacher

COUNCIL BLUFFS
Basch, Ronald Arthur
5th Grade Elementary Teacher
Crouse, Charles Franklin
Lead Teacher of Mathematics
Fox, Ronald John
Mathematics Department Chair
Graber, Howard S.
Mathematics Teacher
Koch, Sheryl Jarze
7th Grade English Teacher
Krivokucha, Elizabeth W.
Vocal Music/Art Instructor
Whitney, Phyllis Louise (Heckman)
Choir/General Music Teacher
Zuehlke, Janet Rold
Chapter I Reading Teacher

CUMBERLAND
Davidson, Rosemary Pearson
2nd Grade Teacher

DAVENPORT
Bates, Bruce Monroe
6th Grade Lang Art Teacher
Bolich, Margaret Vanderkarr
4th-6th Grade Math Teacher
Chernetsky, Marilyn Ann
9th Grade Speech Teacher
De Vilbiss, Betsy Korb
Mathematics Teacher
Deyo, Paul Arthur
Academic Dean
Donovan, Donna Lea CHM
Biology/Earth Science Teacher
Girlus, Kathleen Shuman
1st Grade Teacher
Hasso, Susan Marie
English Teacher
Hermie, Marie Ann
English Department Chair
Laake, Gary Edward
Business Education Instr/Chair
Miller, Kathleen Hayes
English/Speech/Drama Teacher
Reese, Jamie L.
Special Education Teacher
Vandeventer, Linda Marie
Social Studies Specialist

DENISON
Franken, Joleen Schneider
First Grade Teacher
Kollman, James Peter
Chemistry/Biology Teacher

DES MOINES
Coenen, Matthew John
6th-8th Grade Math Teacher
Gaines, Ruth Ann
Drama Teacher
Mattern, David Bruce
Fifth Grade Teacher
Mc Laughlin, Frederick Arthur
Band Director
Neufeld-Price, Nancy Ann
Second Grade Teacher
Nilius, Tim Paul
Music Teacher
Smith, Janet Meyer
Ger Teacher/Foreign Lang Chair
Vlassis, Sophie Pargas
Social Science Teacher
Williams, Janet Steensma
Reading Teacher
Winterberg, Carol Mc Kay
4th Grade Teacher
Ziettlow, Janice L.
Science Teacher

DOUDS
Peacock, Dolores Imogene Hootman
Lang Art/Soc Stud Teacher

DUBUQUE
Connolly, Connie Arlen
Mathematics Teacher
Gibbs, Dorothy Burbach
Language Arts Teacher
Gill, J. Scott
Science Department Chair
Kray, Patricia Pauly
Computer Teacher
Potts, Joseph Patrick
English Teacher
Scharringhausen, Julie
German Teacher

DUNLAP
Peterson, Virgil Richard
4th-6th Grade Math Teacher

DURANT
Moore, Nancy Lee (Madsen)
7-8th English Teacher
Pitz, Paul Nicholas
English/German Teacher

DYERSVILLE
Lehmann, Patricia Ernst
English Teacher

DYSART
Scott, Donnell Lynn
Third Grade Teacher

EAGLE GROVE
Becker, Jerry K.
History Teacher

EARLING
Gaul, Yvonne Marie
Kindergarten Teacher

EDDYVILLE
Harper, Mary Recktenwald
Spanish Teacher
Hogenson, Thomas E.
Guidance Counselor
Morrissey, Margaret Ann
Choral Director
Sheesley, Connie Ray
Fourth Grade Teacher

EDGEWOOD
Forkenbrock, James Joseph
English Teacher

ELDON
Coffman, Priscilla Chapman
5th Grade Teacher

ELDRIDGE
Birkhofer, Donald Dean
Math Teacher & Dept Chair
Brown, Ronald Lee
HS Mathematics Teacher
Green, Chris Ehrecke
Sixth Grade Teacher
Pfaff, Ann Brimm
Fifth Grade Teacher
Roesler, Lynda I.
Sixth Grade Teacher
Smith, Marya Booth
French Teacher

ELKADER
Anderson, Kevin Mark
Educational Consultant
Billings, Kay M. (Sanders)
Spanish Teacher
Newbern, Arma Jean
Second Grade Teacher
Reimer, Arlene E. (Johnson)
5-6th Grade Reading Teacher

Wildman, Mary A. (Rathert)
Second Grade Teacher

EPWORTH
Schmidt, Gerald Joseph
English Teacher

EXIRA
Erickson, M. Deane (Guy)
Third Grade Teacher
Payne, Beverly Nymand
Retired Teacher

FAIRFIELD
Freeman, Lezlie Eland
Pre-1st Grade Teacher

FARLEY
Noonan, James Edward
Jr HS Mathematics Teacher

FARMINGTON
Brune, David Joseph
Science Teacher

FONDA
Schmitt, Randal L.
Lang Art/Foreign Lang Teacher
Wells, Kellie Wessels
English Teacher

FONTANELLE
Wollenhaupt, Jan K.
Business Teacher

FORT DODGE
Goedken, Keith A.
Language Arts Dept Chairman
Gustafson, Betty Jeane (Ryder)
Retired Teacher
Prorok, John R.
Social Studies Teacher
Streit, Candis Derrig
Reading Teacher
Vogt, Melanie Polking
English Teacher
Williams, Dennis Ralph
Counselor/Cmmty Service Coord

FORT MADISON
Osborn, Marjorie Lynn
Second Grade Teacher

FREDERICKSBURG
Bailey, Beverly Sudol
Fifth Grade Teacher

GALVA
Christensen, James William
Science Teacher
Nook, Eula Anderson
Language Arts Teacher

GEORGE
Martens-Rosenboom, Marcia A.
Eng/Speech/Drama/TAG Teacher

GILBERT
Holtan, Donna Charlson
Third Grade Teacher

GILMORE CITY
Wiemers, Donna Frank
First Grade Teacher

GLADBROOK
Acton, April Mayer
English Teacher
Luehring, Terri Hyndman
Ath Dir/Social Studies Teacher

GLENWOOD
Harding, Edward Wayne
Mathematics Instructor
Swanson, Patricia M. Parks
Fourth Grade Teacher

GLIDDEN
Thelin, Diane (Patch)
English Teacher

GOOSE LAKE
Fey, Phyllis Lamp
Retired First Grade Teacher

GRAETTINGER
Millea, Betty Tindall
3rd Grade Teacher

GRANDVIEW
Hammer, Suzanne Chamberlin
Fifth Grade Teacher

GRANVILLE
Hamil, Lynn Ray
Science Department Chairman
Schueder, Jean
4th Grade Teacher

GRINNELL
Schneider, Leroy Paul
Science & Chemistry Teacher

GUTHRIE CENTER
Beck, Dolores Marie
5th & 6th Grade Math Teacher
Wessling, Sharon Walstrom
Math & Physics Teacher

GUTTENBERG
Bockenstedt, Diane Linn (Roth)
Upper Elem Mathematics Teacher

HARLAN
Barry, Jeffrey Anthony
English Teacher
Christiansen, Judy Robertson
4th Grade Teacher
Harrington, Phil J.
Physics Teacher
Klein, Dorris Ahrenholtz
Kindergarten Teacher
Koos, P. Kay Thomas
First Grade Teacher
Kumm, Kathryn Jane
Biology Teacher

HARTLEY
Magnussen, Macel J.
5th/6th Grade English Teacher

HILLS
Porter, Nancy Lefgren
First Grade Teacher

HOLY CROSS
Roling, Duane Joseph
7th & 8th Grade Teacher

HOPKINTON
Mc Donald, Mary June Hennessey
Kindergarten Teacher

HULL
Thorson, Pam Agrimson
English Teacher

HUMBOLDT
Holste, Daniel Paul
Physics/Chemistry Teacher

INDIANOLA
Brown, Arlan K.
Science Teacher/Department Chm
Dittmer, Linda Dillard
6th Grade Math Teacher
Mahlstadt, Kathy Shupe
Retired Kindergarten Teacher
Nunn, Curtis Eugene
Mathematics Teacher
Pullen, Carl W.
German Teacher

INWOOD
Lawton, Neil Edward
History/Psychology Teacher
Moen, Pamela Neuharth
Kindergarten Teacher

IOWA CITY
Beatty, Kristin Loghry
Band Director
De Salme, John William Sr.
Music Department Chair
Dwight, Timothy John
Social Studies Teacher

IOWA FALLS
Davidson, Vervon Eugene
HS Speech/English Teacher
Merz, Frank J.
Middle School Reading Teacher

JESUP
Emick, Kraig Robert
Dir of Bands

JOHNSTON
Busby, Gary Lloyd
Asst Athletic Dir/Sci Teacher

KANAWHA
Kobes, Betty J.
First Grade Instructor
Trautman, Diane Doreen
Language Art Teacher

KEOKUK
Meyer, Mary Dickinson
Kindergarten Teacher
Templeton, Marjorie Cooper
Retired

KEOSAUQUA
Harryman, Marilyn Burns
Home Economics/Health Teacher

KEOTA
Winter, Esther Joanne
Sixth Grade Teacher

KINGSLEY
Hodnefield, Elaine Marie
Third Grade Teacher

KNOXVILLE
Phillips, Lloyd Keith
9th Grade Science Teacher
Schultz, Geoffrey Allen
Jr/Sr HS Band Teacher
Stults, Gregory Lee
English Teacher/Dept Chair

LA PORTE CITY
Wigg, Bruce Jay
Soc Sci Department Chair

LAKE PARK
Read, Richard M.
Mathematics Instructor
Richardson, Gary A.
Principal

LAWTON
Herbold, Judith Hodoway
English/Speech Teacher

LE MARS
Stratton, Dorothea Hess
Chapter I/Reading Teacher

LEON
Helton, Ronald L.
Chemistry/Physics Teacher
Howell, Katherine Collins
Second Grade Teacher

LETTS
Mc Ferren, Clark David
English Teacher/Dept Chair
Yost, Bill
Mathematics Teacher

LITTLE ROCK
Peters, Sandra Eeten
K-8th Grade Resource Teacher

LONE TREE
Prizler, Mary Lou
Second Grade Teacher

LONG GROVE
Duda, Mima M.
4th Grade Teacher
Schmidt, Aaron L.
6th Grade Teacher

LU VERNE
Stripling, Margaret Kollmann
English Teacher

MADRID
Pierce, Linda Allene
English Teacher

MANCHESTER
Greve, Kathy Tegeler
Music Teacher
Struble, Ronald Ray
Technology Education Teacher
Walston, Kathleen Barnhart
4th Grade Teacher

MANNING
Shannon, Lori Ann (Hekter)
English Teacher

MAQUOKETA
Casabal, Melecia Luna
Fourth Grade Teacher
Triplett, Steven Mark
Associate Principal

MARBLE ROCK
Bruggeman, Geraldine Reints
6th Grade Teacher

MARION
Altenhofen, Rosanne Martin
Kindergarten Teacher
Kupka, Janice Houlahan
Second Grade Teacher
Van Deusen, Robert Moon
Technology & Assessment Coord

MARSHALLTOWN
Bell, Robert Laverne
Industrial Technology Teacher
Kesterson, Charles E.
Social Studies Teacher
Lang, Julie Jontz
Fourth Grade Teacher
Nuss, Deborah Hahn
Music Specialist
Stattler, Gary L.
Art Instructor

MARTENSDALE
Butcher, Marian Vivian
Business Education Teacher

MASON CITY
Johnson, Karen Boldt
Fourth Grade Teacher
Johnson, Robert Wayne
Science/Reading Teacher

MASON CITY (cont)
Stahl, Geraldine Ann
  4th & 5th Grade Teacher
MAYNARD
Niggemeyer, Janice Rea
  Fourth Grade Teacher
Niggemeyer, Steven Wayne
  6th Grade Mid Sch Teacher
MC GREGOR
Cowell, Severna (Johnson)
  5th Grade Teacher
Smalley, Pamela Diane
  Mid Sch Rdng/Geography Teacher
MECHANICSVILLE
Sadeghpour, Margaret Plattenberger
  4th-6th Grade Science Teacher
MEDIAPOLIS
Boal, Marilyn Rae
  Sixth Grade Teacher
Moehle, Ellen Miller
  Third Grade Teacher
MONROE
Bauer, Joyce Marie
  1st Grade Teacher
Grier, Jacqueline Ann
  English/Journalism Teacher
Herrema, Kathy Allen
  Spanish/Geography Instructor
Johnson, Delores Ann (Amoss)
  Kindergarten Teacher
MONTICELLO
Balster, Barbara May
  3rd Grade Teacher
Friedman, Madonna
  Third Grade Teacher
White, Scott E.
  History/Ind Arts Teacher
MORNING SUN
Hewitt, Barbara Yakle
  Jr HS Language Arts Teacher
Rhinehart, Jo Ann
  Mathematics/Computer Teacher
MOUNT AYR
Kimble, Larry L.
  Jr HS Science Instructor
MOVILLE
Chartier, Tom D.
  Health/Phys Ed/Drvr Ed Teacher
MUSCATINE
Thornton, Nancy Jean
  Classroom Teacher/Elem Prin
NEVADA
Ficken, Theresa Louise
  Coord of Gifted & Talented
Osmundson, Marcelline Marie Oakland
  Sixth Grade Teacher
Schneider, William Lee
  Mathematics Department Chair
NEW HARTFORD
Jaquis, Maurine White
  Second Grade Teacher
NEW MARKET
Roman, Stephen James
  5th-8th Grade Science Instr
NEW VIRGINIA
Van Every, Barbara E.
  Jr HS Language Arts Teacher
NEWELL
Kier, Joelle Anderson
  Kindergarten Teacher
NEWTON
Birkenholz, Jeanne Marie
  Elementary Guidance Counselor
Helfrich, Kathrine Hale
  6th Grade Teacher
Planer, Marilyn Stauffer
  English Department Chair
Prahl, Ronald H.
  English Teacher
ODEBOLT
Bloom, Barbara Kyle
  Fifth Grade Teacher/Dept Head
Schmidt, Alan Lee
  High School Science Teacher
OELWEIN
Arthaud, Patricia Dibble
  Fourth Grade Teacher
Schwemm, Steven James
  Social Studies Teacher
ONAWA
Kingsbury, Vicki Cose
  English & Speech Teacher

Mussack, Mark D.
  English/US History Instructor
Wright, Gary Keith
  5th Grade Teacher
ORANGE CITY
Cosgrove, Donna Kolb
  Secondary School Counselor
Miedema, Andrew Henry
  Counselor
Smiens, Doyle Gene
  English/Drama/Speech Teacher
OSCEOLA
Boldon, Eileen J.
  First Grade Teacher
Kelso, Sandra Edwards
  HS Mathematics Teacher
OSKALOOSA
Burrichter, Lorene E.
  5th Grade Teacher
De Groot, Donna Van Roekel
  Fifth Grade Teacher
Dieleman, Edwin Dean
  8th Grade Mathematics Teacher
Johnson, Thomas William
  Mathematics Teacher-Dept Chm
Stout, Russell L. Jr.
  English Teacher
OTTUMWA
Fisher, Collette Crotty
  Health/Home Economics Teacher
Gardener, Kathleen Carol
  2nd & 3rd Grade Teacher
Graziano, John M.
  Teacher
Zuehlke, Larry Eugene
  Mathematics Teacher
PACKWOOD
Kelly, Carol J. Bigg
  Kindergarten Teacher
PARKERSBURG
Cosner, Margaret Garnas
  Third Grade Teacher
PAULLINA
Golden, Lynn Mc Intosh
  Second Grade Teacher
Ulven, Bonnie
  Lang Art/Soc Sci Teacher
PELLA
De Jong, C. Marie Nikkel
  First & Second Grade Teacher
Graber, Ann Markee
  English/Journalism Teacher
POCAHONTAS
Olwell, Laurence Edward
  Mathematics Teacher
POSTVILLE
Campbell, Mona A. (Van Steenberger)
  Mid Sch Mathematics Teacher
PRAIRIE CITY
Bird, Michelle Frank
  Language Arts Teacher
PRESTON
Behrend, Louie Daniel
  6th Grade Teacher
Melvin, Linda Jean
  Science Teacher
PRIMGHAR
Klink, Marlene Groener
  7th Grade English/Sci Teacher
Larson, David Jon
  Mid Sch Social Studies Teacher
REINBECK
Messerly, Larry L.
  Business & Computer Ed Teacher
REMSEN
Groetken, Alan Leo
  Jr HS Instructor
Kane, Mary Kerwick
  Third Grade Teacher
RICEVILLE
Gilbertson, Donna (Schmidt)
  Sixth Grade Teacher
Mans, Ellen Marie Grady
  Second Grade Teacher
Recker, Mary A.
  High School English Teacher
Sprung, Della Johnson
  Retired First Grade Teacher
ROCKFORD
Weigand, Marie Catherine Trettin
  7th/8th Classroom Teacher
ROWLEY
Wheatley, Margery Mc Cright
  5th Grade Teacher

RUDD
Huisman, Peggy Jane
  2nd Grade Teacher
RUNNELLS
Brill, Kirk L.
  Biology & Study Skills Teacher
Tremble, Joyce Adams
  English Department Head
RUTHVEN
Graettinger, Janet Kay (Thurber)
  Vocal Music Director
Swanson, Janice Kay
  Third Grade Teacher
SABULA
Dickinson, Rae Ann Mc Lean
  Fourth Grade Teacher
SEYMOUR
Choponis, Richard Justin
  Jr/Sr HS Mathematics Teacher
SHEFFIELD
Bunting, Suzanne M.
  Instrumental Music Teacher
SHENANDOAH
Henderson, Linda Lee (Turner)
  8th Grade Language Art Teacher
SIBLEY
Earll, Mike Dean
  Agriculture Education Instr
SIDNEY
Schmale, Leigh A.
  Social Studies Teacher
Zach, Mary Jane Gordon
  First Grade Teacher
SIOUX CENTER
Overman, Dee Ann Schryver
  Third Grade Teacher
SIOUX CITY
Behlers, Geraldine Havekost
  Mathematics Teacher
Busker, Jean A.
  Choral Music Director
Chapman, Dennis Earl
  Administrator
Dahlkoetter, Debra Dykstra
  Biology Teacher
Engstrand, Margaret Ann
  Phase III Coordinator
Flom, Larry James
  Soc Stud Chm/History Teacher
Gallup, Cynthia E.
  Biology/Phys Sci Teacher
Iverson, Jon R.
  Chemistry Instructor
Martyn, Harry Allen
  Science Teacher
Stone, Gayle Kloeppel
  5th Grade Teacher
Towns, Rex L.
  Vocal Music Teacher
Woolworth, Judy A. (Goettel)
  5th Grade Teacher
SOLON
Meyer, Joette Ann Krall
  Kindergarten Teacher
SPENCER
Ohms, Diane Marie
  Sixth Grade Teacher
STACYVILLE
Reisch, Mary Lou
  Third-Fourth Grade Teacher
STEAMBOAT ROCK
Fox, David D.
  English Teacher
STOCKPORT
Conrad, Carol Ruth
  1st Grade Teacher
STORM LAKE
Brostad, John Charles
  8th Grade Math Teacher
Ingram, Marsha Cox
  Eighth Grade Teacher
Langenfeld, Thomas Edward
  History & Government Teacher
Lewis, Dee Dunham
  Fourth Grade Teacher
Nicholson, A. Dean
  8th Physical Science Teacher
Peterson, Dave Eric
  6th Grade Teacher
TABOR
Allgood, Marilyn Tynon
  Math/Computer Teacher
Botts, Susan Tibben
  Second Grade Teacher

TAMA
Davis, Melody Tjossem
  Second Grade Teacher
THORNTON
Langlitz, Nancy (Hill)
  Fifth Grade Teacher
TOLEDO
Mc Coy, Marybeth Halvorson
  6th Grade Language Art Teacher
TRIPOLI
Goudschaal, Roger Dean
  Business Teacher/Coach
UNION
Vorba, Jed Harold
  Science Teacher
UTE
Neumann, Wilma Ione (Klaus)
  Third Grade Teacher
VAN HORNE
Demmel, Wayne E.
  US History Teacher
Lieb, Jay Edward
  Middle School Teacher
Logan, Donald Dean
  Guidance Counselor/Psychology
VAN METER
Jones, Delores M.
  Kindergarten Teacher
WALCOTT
Mc Collam, Robert Lee
  4th-6th Grade Math Teacher
Siegel, Marcella Jean
  Fourth Grade Teacher
WAPELLO
Richers, Lois Jack
  First Grade Teacher
WASHINGTON
Beezley, Sally Risser
  Vocational Education Coord
Zahs, Michael
  Seventh Grade Teacher
WATERLOO
Clary, Martha Mae (Miller)
  Gifted/Talented Teacher
Gemar, Marie Elain
  Biology Teacher
Jacob, Nancy L.
  English Teacher
Smits, Anjean Elizabeth
  Kindergarten Teacher
WAUKON
Gourley, Mary Meineke
  English Teacher/Dept Chairman
WAVERLY
Cook, William Lee
  Social Studies Teacher
Gohlke, Barb Calhoun
  7th-8th Grade Teacher
Howard, Curt S.
  6th Grade Teacher
Hurley, James Ray
  Chemistry/Physics Teacher
Verdon, H. John
  Science Teacher
West-Lentz, Teresa Lynn
  English Teacher
WELDON
Warren, S. Imogene (Reinier)
  First Grade Teacher
WELLSBURG
Ascher, Mary Rops
  Fourth Grade Teacher
Harms, Meg Steinkamp
  Kindergarten Teacher
Meyer, Karen Schroeder
  Sixth Grade Teacher
WEST BEND
Kehoe, Steven Edward
  Agriculture Education Teacher
Metzger, Mary Fouts
  Fourth Grade Teacher
WEST BURLINGTON
Schach, Ann Wilcox
  Science Teacher
WEST DES MOINES
Cookman, Jay Preston
  Guidance Counselor
Hanzelon, Lee Ruth Peterson
  5th Grade Teacher
Hendel, Marc E.
  Mathematics Teacher

WEST LIBERTY
Elder, Barbara Ann
  5th Grade Math Teacher
Maylone, Linda Spinden
  Second Grade Teacher
Severson, Robert Keith
  7th & 8th Math Teacher
WILLIAMSON
Dawson, Patricia Merchant
  6th Grade Elementary Teacher
WILTON
Feuerbach, Tona Bailey
  Music Teacher
Frisch, Dennis D.
  7th/8th Grade Science Teacher
Hampson, Sharon K. Gibson
  Counselor
WINTERSET
Corkrean, John Patrick
  4th Grade Teacher

KANSAS

ALLEN
Powell, A. Elwin
  Social Studies Chairman
ALMENA
Smith, Glenda Schalansky
  First Grade Teacher
ANDOVER
Wilson, Robert Earl
  8th Grade Math Teacher
ANTHONY
Dills, Linda A.
  High School Business Teacher
ARKANSAS CITY
Day, Judith Weigand
  4th Grade Teacher
O'Hair, Steven Lee
  Soc Sci Teacher/Dept Chair
ASHLAND
Culver, Carlene Schroeder
  Third Grade Teacher
ATCHISON
Anthony, Elizabeth Ann (Green)
  6th Grade Reading Teacher
Dickson, John R.
  English Department Chairman
Krone, James Lawrence
  Social Studies Teacher
Mc Intyre, Velma Lucille
  5th-8th Grade Math Teacher
ATTICA
Bonham, Carol E.
  Science/Mathematics Teacher
ATWOOD
Kastens, Dianna (Hurst)
  5th Grade Teacher
BAXTER SPRINGS
Krokroskia, Karen Lee
  7th/8th Grade Soc Stud Teacher
Nichols, Carolyn Krueger
  English/Journalism Teacher
BELOIT
Fischer, Kenneth J.
  5th Grade Teacher
Long, Charles L.
  Sixth Grade Teacher
Rowh, Jay Allen
  Mathematics Instructor/Coach
BIRD CITY
Beougher, Barbara A.
  Language Arts Instructor
BONNER SPRINGS
Henry, Connie
  Latin & English Teacher
BROOKVILLE
Scuitte, Lorene Michelle
  English Teacher
BUHLER
Lohrentz, Vicky Sue
  Special Education Teacher
BURLINGAME
Farver, Helen Schenck
  Chapter I Reading Teacher
Kehler, Joyce Ann
  3rd Grade Teacher
CANEY
Collins, Betty Gower
  5th Grade Teacher

CANEY (cont)
Faulkenberry, Kathy Dalley
  Speech/Debate Teacher
Schultheiss, Karen
  Teacher and Coach

CARBONDALE
Mayes, Arlene Faye (Matney)
  Jr HS Language Arts Teacher

CENTRALIA
Bloom, Frances Ray
  Third Grade Teacher

CHANUTE
Pennington, B. Jolene Stolfus
  4th Grade Teacher

CHENEY
Brohammer, Martha S.
  Art/Spanish Teacher

CHERRYVALE
Pefley, Stephen Arlin
  6th Grade Teacher
Thompson, Sharon Ann
  Math Teacher
Wadman, Sharon Renee
  Biology/Physical Ed Teacher

CIMARRON
Conant, Grace Arlene
  4th Grade Teacher
Voth, Marla Sue (Rowe)
  Third Grade Teacher

COFFEYVILLE
Evans-Lombe, Judith Erroll
  Counselor
Murdock, Larry G.
  Accounting Instructor
Richards, Shari
  English Teacher & Dept Chair
Staudt, Joseph
  Science Department Chair
Thomas, Janet (Hendrix)
  4th Grade Teacher
Traxson, Timothy Lee
  8th Grade Science Teacher

COLBY
Anschutz, Geraldine Sundelius
  Mathematics Teacher
Schrag, Arnold Lee
  6th Grade Teacher

COLDWATER
Allen, Janis M. Oyler
  3rd Grade Teacher

COLWICH
Moon, Elizabeth Jean (Guddle Moore)
  Retired Mathematics Teacher

CONWAY SPRINGS
Means, Shirley Lacy
  First Grade Teacher

CUBA
Woodside, Sharon A.
  Business/Computer Teacher

DERBY
Mc Niel, Rae Cochrane
  Gifted Consultant
Morris, Debora Lynn Kounovsky
  Math Teacher
Owens, Helen M.
  Teacher
Villines, Sandra Dawn Halbrook
  Fifth Grade Teacher
Wilkerson, Gary Dwaine
  Kindergarten Teacher

DEXTER
Bradley, Jessie Ann
  Fourth Grade Teacher

DIGHTON
Ball, Amanda Lorretta
  9th-12th Grade Math Teacher
Hadley, Debra Lynn
  Jr High Language Arts Teacher
Timken, Judith Huffman
  Kindergarten Teacher

DODGE CITY
Chipman, Deborah (Gray)
  Kindergarten Teacher
Dryden, Susannah Rodenberger
  Director of Orchestras
Honish, Richard A.
  Professor of Music
Schuler, Janet Kay (Rosson)
  Elementary Vocal Music Teacher
Smith, Charlen Wycoff
  Voc Home Economics Instr
Wiley, Bennie K.
  Elementary Counselor

EASTON
Harmon, Kevin Webster
  Social Studies Teacher
Murphy, Jeanine Schwinn
  Kindergarten Teacher
Norris, Carol Elizabeth
  First Grade Teacher

EDNA
Hammett, Vickie Stamps
  6th Grade Teacher

ELDORADO
Gardner, James Clark
  Social Studies Chairman
Irwin, Denise Hiebert
  Gifted Education Teacher

ELKHART
Adams, Forrest Eugene
  Mathematics Teacher

ERIE
Skaggs, Jo Lynn
  Bio/General Sci Teacher

EUDORA
Clinton, Jane Elizabeth (Swartz)
  Business Teacher
Dymacek, Merilee Neis
  Vocal Elem Music Teacher
Sailler, Robert J.
  English Teacher

EUREKA
Collinge, Pamela Jean
  4th Grade Teacher
Jackson, Dan Adrian
  English Teacher
Mc Guire, Rosemary Gilkison
  5th Grade Teacher
Mc Guire, Rosemary Gilkison
  5th Grade Teacher
Osger, Deloris Jean
  Lang Arts & Geography Teacher
Powell, Marton Lee Jr.
  Math/Computer Science Teacher
Russell, Barbara Baird
  7th Grade Lang Art Teacher

FORT LEAVENWORTH
Campbell, Pamela Sue
  2nd Grade Teacher

FORT RILEY
Sanchez, Nicole Geraud
  French & Gifted Ed Teacher

FORT SCOTT
Regan, David Lee
  Health/Sci/Basic Skill Teacher
Sprecher, Doris Werner
  Retired
West, Carolyn Campbell
  3rd Grade Teacher

GALENA
Jones, Nedra Good
  Retired 1st Grade Teacher
Mc Daniel, Randy Glenn
  Biology Teacher
New, Penny Louise
  Fourth Grade Teacher
Outt, Dennis Brent
  Earth & Life Science Teacher

GARDEN CITY
Beene, Richard Glen
  HS Social Studies Teacher
Blickenstaff, Nancy (Greenlee)
  Language Art Teacher
Fear, Mary Sue Pollard
  Soph Language Arts Teacher
Graff, Dan L.
  Coach/Math Teacher
Powell, Donald K.
  Math Teacher/Dept Chairman
Pracht, Willis Charles
  Principal
Richardson, Jane Winders
  Fourth Grade Teacher

GARDNER
Cooper, Ramona S.
  Second Grade Teacher
Singer, Sonny Miriam (Gorin)
  Reading Specialist

GARNETT
Bauck, Melvin Robert
  Business Teacher
Fursman, Jacqueline Hibbs
  Kindergarten Teacher
Hughes, Susan Bremer
  Fourth Grade Teacher

GODDARD
Dimick, Patricia Buerki
  Jr HS Home Economics Teacher

Goates, Wayne
  Science/Communications Teacher

GREAT BEND
Chilcott, Ruth Swilley
  Fourth Grade Teacher
Eveleigh, Lorrayne
  Kindergarten Teacher
Gowdy, Charley J.
  Constitution Teacher

HALSTEAD
Kraisinger, Margaret Beller
  Business Teacher

HARPER
Hadsall, Martha Krus
  Third Grade Teacher

HAYS
Clough, David Otis
  Computer Studies Teacher
Fleischacker, Donna M.
  Health & Physical Ed Teacher
Gnad, Leroy P.
  Mathematics Teacher
Kellogg, Lorena M.
  5th Grade Teacher
Meagher, Thomas Walter
  Music Dept Chair/Orch Dir
Washburn, Cindy Karlin
  Kindergarten Teacher

HAYSVILLE
Lott, Mary Louise
  Language Arts Teacher
Pope, George Kirk
  Principal

HEALY
Clouse, Tracie Renee
  Business Teacher

HESSTON
Herrold, Jacqueline S.
  Journalism/English Teacher

HIAWATHA
Brooks, Wanda Jean
  English Teacher

HIGHLAND
Thompson, Marian Louise (Weber)
  Learning Disabilities Teacher

HILL CITY
Crippen, Doris Binder
  Chapter I Reading Teacher

HOLTON
Massey, Linda Bacon
  English Teacher
Oxandale, Doris Mae (Sourk)
  8th Grade Mathematics Teacher

HOLYROOD
Gish, Phyllis N.
  First Grade Teacher

HORTON
Cash, Anne Peterson
  Kindergarten Teacher
Zeit, Nita Ruth Brant
  3rd Grade Teacher

HOXIE
Hageman, Donald E.
  Social Science Chairman
Heim, William A.
  Fourth Grade Teacher

HUTCHINSON
Boggs, Jennalee Sue
  Language Art Teacher
Johnson, Deborah Leslie
  Eighth Grade English Teacher
Mc Kinnell, Marcie L.
  7/8th Grade Sci/Health Teacher
Randles, Dorthie A.
  Sixth Grade Teacher
Schroeder, Dave J.
  7-8th Grade Soc Stud Dept Chm
Siegrist, Evelyn Loeppke
  2nd Grade Teacher
Strong, Linda Mahan
  Elementary Guidance Counselor

INDEPENDENCE
Douglas, Alice Henry
  Mathematics Teacher
Harding, Lloyd Emery
  Chemistry, Physics Teacher
Nelson, Jo Ann Harlin
  K-8th Grade Gifted Ed Teacher

IOLA
Houser, Raymond E.
  Social Science/Reading Teacher

JUNCTION CITY
Ludlum, Ted Warren
  American History Teacher

Smith, Denise (Davidson)
  Business Teacher
Wells, B. R.
  Calculus Instr/Gifted Ed Coord

KANSAS CITY
Austin, Gwendolyn Hollinshed
  Home Economics Teacher
Barnes, Sharon Kraus
  Spanish Teacher
Beachly, Meredith Jan
  Life Science Department Head
Broderick, Eleanor A. Scott
  Fourth Grade Teacher
Carroll, Joy Yvonne
  5th Grade Teacher
Dodd, Linda Weinert
  8th Grade Math/Algebra Teacher
Estrada, Vickie
  7th Grade Geography Teacher
Everhart, Madge Cole
  Fourth Grade Teacher
Gallagher, Sheila Ann
  Fifth Grade Teacher
Gonzales, Mary Linda
  6th Grade Teacher
Hassig, Robert M.
  Social Studies Teacher
Helvey, Susan Kimberlee
  Freshmen Science Teacher
Hobick, Laurel D.
  Phys Ed/Driver Ed/Coach
Ishum, Marcella Luckett
  6th Grade Teacher
Johnson, Mary Bonds
  English Teacher
Lewis, Wesley Clyde
  Art Teacher
Martinat, Jeanne Marie
  Spanish Teacher
Mc Donald, Barbara Davidson
  Home Economics Dept Chair
Metz, Susan Lynn
  Second Grade Teacher
Mosley, Charles William
  Chem/Math/Physics Teacher
Ramsey, Donna Scott
  Sixth Grade Teacher
Smith, Stephen A.
  Social Studies Teacher
Spencer, Kimberly Lowe
  Computer Studies Teacher
Strimple, Clyde William
  Mathematics Teacher/Dept Chm
Venard, Doris Ferson
  4th Grade Teacher
Williams, Marlene Graves
  4th Grade Teacher
Wills, Gwendolyn Williams
  Secondary Counselor

KINSLEY
Korf, Lona Dell Conley
  Science Teacher

KIRWIN
Fall, Diana Lynne
  Fourth Grade Teacher

LAKIN
Berning, Larry Dean
  Third Grade Teacher

LANSING
Lo Presti, Priscilla Anschutz
  Fourth Grade Teacher
Mathison, Lorna Willard
  GED Instructor

LARNED
Cooper, Norman L.
  6th Grade Teacher
Howell, Beverly Salmans
  Grammar & Art Teacher

LAWRENCE
Ball, Shirley Marie (Galinski)
  6th Grade Teacher
Binns, Donald Victor
  Amer History & English Teacher
Glenn, Dorothy Tharp
  Office Ed Coordinator
Hess, Michael Henry
  Physics Teacher/Sci Dept Chm
Huntsinger, Jo Annette
  Teacher/Coach
Montgomery, Margaret Mei Mei Rogers
  4th Grade Teacher

LEAVENWORTH
Nowlan, Helen Chatburn
  Mathematics Teacher

LEOTI
Johnston, Johnny Ben
  Social Studies Chairman

LIBERAL
Binns, Geraldine Horton
  2nd Grade Teacher
Clark, Barbara June
  Fourth Grade Teacher
Flores, Jean Agee
  Sixth Grade Math Teacher

LONGTON
Currier, Arlene Marian
  HS His/Government Teacher

LYONS
Feldman, Rhonda Ann
  Second Grade Teacher

MAIZE
Ashby, Kathleen Ann
  German/English Teacher
Elliott, Deb K.
  Counselor
Kaufman, Susan Bland
  6th Grade Teacher

MANHATTAN
Adams, Carol Hoffman
  Eng Teacher/Eng Dept Chair
Coleman, James Joseph
  8th Grade English Teacher
Featherstone, Lila Nilson
  Chemistry Teacher
Penner, Diana Christine
  Scndry Level English Teacher
Schwinn, Myron E.
  Zoology/Botany Teacher

MARION
Case, Jean Hagans
  4th Grade Teacher
Willhite, Gary L.
  English Teacher/Dir of Curr

MAYETTA
Brunken, Laurel King
  School Counselor
Frazier, Vera Stevens
  Fourth Grade Teacher
Morris, Sandra Nelson
  First Grade Teacher

MC PHERSON
Lankford, Jerry Dale
  5th Grade Teacher
Stenzel, Howard Karl
  Mathematics Teacher

MEADE
Wiens, Waldo K.
  4th Grade Teacher

MEDICINE LODGE
Ferguson, Max Eugene
  7th/8th Grade Soc Stud Teacher
Rickard, Billie Lou (Sharkey)
  Language Arts Teacher

MERIDEN
Deiter, Bonita K.
  Biology/Chemistry Teacher
Di Zerega, Edward D.
  Choral Music Dept Director

MONTEZUMA
Lupton, Mary Doreen (Evans)
  Fifth Grade Teacher

MULVANE
Bolton, Shirley Woods
  4th Grade Teacher
Webster, Jennifer Bryson
  Home Economics Teacher

NESS CITY
Amrein, Allan G.
  Phys Ed/Amer His Teacher
Parker, Juanita Kay (Pember)
  Business Education Instructor

NEWTON
Adams, Timothy Clark
  Gifted Education Teacher
Graber, Robert Charles
  Teacher/Bsktbl Coach
Jones, Karen Mae
  Vocational Home Ec Teacher
Sieg, Rosemary
  First Grade Teacher
Whillock, Arthur Dwyane
  6th/7th Grade Sci/Math Teacher

NORTON
Jilka, Kevin Joe
  7th & 8th Grade Math Teacher
Morel, Philip E.
  Fourth Grade Teacher

OLATHE
Adams, Mark R.
  Natural/Computer Sci Teacher
Banks, Maryellen Cline
  7th Grade Unified Stud Teacher

OLATHE (cont)

Barnes, Keith E.
  Science Instructor
Cargill, Rodney Eugene
  Mathematics Dept Teacher
Finn, David Hal
  Teacher of English
Kruger, Gary L.
  Teacher of Behavior Disorders
Krusen, Hank E. Jr.
  Science Department Teacher
Limes, William E. Jr.
  Science Instructor
Reynolds, Delpha Ann
  Fifth Grade Teacher
Riley, Dixie D.
  Elem Visual Art Consultant
Spotts, Larry Lee
  French Teacher
Staudenmaier, Andrea Meyer
  Mathematics Teacher/Dept Chair

OSBORNE

Hutchison, Pamela Jean
  English And Spanish Teacher

OSKALOOSE

Fleming, Vickie L.
  Chapter 1 Teacher

OSWEGO

Ward, Charles Robert
  Sixth Grade Teacher

OTTAWA

Baylor, Nancy H.
  Developmental Teacher
Boch, Patrick John
  Physical Education Teacher

OVERLAND PARK

Brewer, Marilyn Juanice
  Language Arts Teacher
Brown, Charlotte Ann (Gunselman)
  5th & 6th Grade Band Teacher
Dawson, Richard Glen
  Biology/Futuristics Teacher
Ewing, C Craig
  English Teacher
Keiter, William J.
  World Geography Teacher
Koehler, Michael H.
  Math Teacher/Dept Chairperson
Murphy, Rebecca Harrison
  American History Teacher
Pribyl, Rick R.
  English Teacher
Spencer, Judith K. (Crabtree)
  English/Humanities Teacher
Unruh, Mary Anne
  3rd Grade Teacher
Waisner, Betty Darlene (Tersinar)
  4th Grade Teacher

OXFORD

Taylor, Sherra Slaughter
  English Teacher
Wagner, Barbara Ellen (Simmons)
  2nd Grade Teacher

PAOLA

Gray, Kevin Lawrence
  Publications Advisor

PARSONS

Viranda, Karla Kay
  7th/8th Grade Teacher/Coach
Wolverton, Deborah Leann (Couch)
  Art Instructor

PERRY

Riley, Marcia Gale
  Fifth Grade Teacher
Wealthall, Bill
  Music Teacher/Asst Principal

PHILLIPSBURG

Ludwig, Stephen M.
  Secondary English Teacher

PITTSBURG

Barberich, Linda Kay (Kovacic)
  7th Grade Lang Arts Teacher
Fleming, Peggy Sue (Fry)
  7th Grade Teacher
Hight, Betty Mc Lane
  Second Grade Teacher
Normand, Marcel Henry
  Soc Sci/Religion Teacher

PLAINVILLE

Thummel, Wanda Deges-Thyfault
  Fifth Grade Teacher

PROTECTION

Park, Lois Roberta-Allen
  1st Grade Teacher
Puderbaugh, Joyce Baldwin
  5th Grade Teacher

RANDALL

Burgess, Kelly Vinton
  Seventh Grade Teacher

RANDOLPH

Cramer, Vicki Marie (Logan)
  Mathematics Department Chair

RANSOM

Tillitson, Mary Lou
  5th Grade Teacher

RILEY

Whitesell, Mary Clarice Crispin
  7th/8th Grade Math Teacher

ROBINSON

Hankins, Robert M.
  Science Teacher

ROSSVILLE

Keller, Mary
  English Teacher

RUSSELL

Willson, Margaret Sue
  Vocal Music Teacher

SAINT JOHN

Williams, Arlene Van Galder
  Facilitator of Gifted

SALINA

Banninger, Loren Lynn
  6th Grade Teacher
Bassett, Arlene Rollins
  4th Grade Teacher
Fishel, Pauline Dean
  Mathematics Teacher
Hay, Barbara Barker
  First Grade Teacher
Mc Millen, Gayle Conner
  Band Director
Scheffer, James David
  Mathematics Teacher
Stegman, Bernadette
  Kindergarten Teacher

SCOTT CITY

Clare, Nanon Bird
  English IV Teacher
Rutledge, Janice Gayle
  English Teacher

SEDAN

Boulanger, Shirley J.
  Mid Sch Language Arts Teacher
Hadley, Dan Edward
  Industrial Art Teacher
Smith, Doran Eugene
  Science Teacher

SEVERY

Perkins, Catherine Kolterman
  Sixth Grade Teacher
Taliaferro, Mary Margaret
  Third Grade Teacher

SHAWNEE MISSION

Berroth, Rhondalyn Helen
  8th Grade English Teacher
Bolton, Carl Harper
  Social Studies Teacher
Cochran, Marilyn Lerner
  7th Grade Life Science Teacher
Friedman, Laura Louise
  English Teacher
Greene, Teresa Donnelly
  3rd Grade Teacher
Sinha, David Kumar
  Gifted Education Teacher
Spaith, Karen Conklin
  Facilitator Gifted Education

SILVER LAKE

Cunningham, Alan Lee
  Mathematics Department Head
Martinek, Dennis Eugene
  Seventh Grade Language Teacher
Wolf, Joann E. (Lilley)
  Second Grade Teacher

SOLOMON

Hansmann, Patricia J.
  Vocal Music Instructor
Veal, Jane F. (Zey)
  Third Grade Teacher

SPEARVILLE

Mc Daniel, Tim V.
  Language Arts Teacher
Morrisey, Rebecca Walker
  Mathematics/History Instructor

SUMMERFIELD

Argo, Janet Eileen
  6th Grade Math/Sci Teacher

SYLVAN GROVE

Karlin, Larry
  Scndry Eng/Soc Stud Teacher

TECUMSEH

Van Petten, Jackie Baker
  Journalism Teacher

THAYER

Minor, Donna Samuels
  Second Grade Teacher

TOPEKA

Braun, Wesley
  Secondary Counselor
Burris, Susan Mary
  1st Grade Teacher
Ebadi, Del M.
  Mathematics Teacher
Edmonds, Beth Samuelson
  Sixth Grade Teacher
Gregory, Mary Jane
  Soc Stud Teacher/Dept Chair
Hoge, Susan Marie
  Spanish Teacher/Dept Coord
Humston, Sandra Jean (Jevons)
  Kindergarten Teacher
Johnston, Pamela Warner
  English Teacher
Kelly, Darlene Warren
  3rd-4th Grade Teacher
Muilenburg, Margo A. (Moet)
  Elem Facilitator of Gifted
Olmstead, Linda Trobough
  Kindergarten Teacher
Thompson, Beverly Caruthers
  Fourth Grade Teacher
Waldo, Janice Curtis
  French Teacher
Weekly, Jenay Atkinson
  Gifted Education Teacher
Wiley, Linda Gail
  Biology Teacher/Dept Chm
Woolf, Stephen D.
  Civics/English Teacher
Wuenstel, Karen Fox
  6th-8th Grade Math Teacher

TROY

Cash, Don M.
  Social Studies Teacher
Harter, Donald L.
  Principal

ULYSSES

Brom, Joyce A.
  English Teacher
Mills, Pamela D'eon
  Senior English Teacher
Waldron, David L.
  Sixth Grade Instructor

UNIONTOWN

Chambers, Virginia Marie (Salmon)
  Retired Remedial Rdng Teacher
Goodno, Debra (Hudson)
  7th/8th Grade English Teacher
Herrmann, Gary Lee
  Sixth Grade Teacher
Jackson, Alicia Annette (Walker)
  Spanish/English Teacher
Ramsey, Debra Townsend
  Second Grade Teacher

VALLEY CENTER

Agnew, Patricia Andregg
  Fifth Grade Teacher
Sublett, Dawna (Sparks)
  English Teacher
Svaty, Monica Sue (Miller)
  Algebra/Geometry Teacher

VICTORIA

Werner, Ivan E.
  Mathematics & Computer Teacher

WALLACE

Pearce, Louise Evans
  1st-6th Grade Teacher

WAMEGO

Rush, Judy Duncan
  English Teacher

WESTMORELAND

Sumners, Robert Dean
  7th-9th Grade Math Teacher

WESTWOOK

Bourdess, Peter Lesue
  History/Art Teacher

WICHITA

Austin-Fresh, Gina S.
  Drama Teacher
Brown, Patricia S.
  HS Language Arts Teacher
Chapman, Donna Jean
  English Teacher
Cheatham, Val R.
  Teacher of Gifted
Curfman, Barbara Thayer
  French/Spanish Teacher
Davis, Gail Osborne
  Fifth Grade Teacher
Ellis, Ruth Anne (Olive)
  Fourth Grade Teacher
Firestone, Barbara Jane
  Fifth Grade Teacher
Franz, Donald L.
  Science Teacher
Fredin, John
  Literature/Composition Teacher
Frye, Tom R.
  Theatre Instructor
Gandy, Connie K.
  Phys Ed/Head Basketball Coach
Gross, Diane
  Mathematics Teacher
Guiltner, Bonnie Ivalene Johnson
  Retired 3rd Grade Teacher
Jacobs, Carla M.
  6th Grade Science Teacher
Jefferson, Willie L.
  Social Studies Teacher
Kerschen, Lucille Rita ASC
  Elementary Teacher
Lindsey, Wanda J. Goldsmith
  Computer Teacher/Coordinator
Mc Gaugh, Polly Poling
  First Grade Teacher
Mc Gilbray, Shirley Ann (Small)
  Third Grade Teacher
Riedel-Matthews, Holly
  English Teacher
Weber, Damon Franklin
  Fine/Performing Art Coord
Wesley, Betty Jane Slaughter
  1st & 2nd Grade Comb Teacher
Zehr, Dennis Joe
  Biological Science Teacher

WILLIAMSBURG

Bond, Forest Elwin
  Retired Teacher

WINCHESTER

Strickler, Karen Sue (De Poy)
  English Dept Chairperson

WINDOM

Raleigh, Susan Cordell
  6th Grade Teacher

WINFIELD

Eis, Terry
  English/Social Science Teacher

YATES CENTER

Solomon, Debbie Entz
  Fifth Grade Teacher

KENTUCKY

ALBANY

Shelton, Charles W.
  Retired 6th Grade Teacher

ALEXANDRIA

Blair, Ruth Hedges
  Teacher

ASHLAND

Blackburn, Krista Davis
  Science/Math Teacher
Blevins, Brenda Shelton
  English & Reading Teacher
Cline, Jeffrey L.
  English Teacher
Huntzinger, June Clifford
  Second Grade Teacher
Mc Dowell, Linda Guyette
  Math Teacher
Mc Glothlin, Betty Foley
  Teacher/Vocational Dept Chair
Miller, Neucedia Ison
  Fourth Grade Teacher
Moore, Ronald Lewis
  Social Studies Teacher
Pratt, Ellen
  Math & Algebra Teacher
Thornbury, Sandra Kay
  English & Latin Teacher
Wellman, Joyce Riddle
  German/English Teacher

AUBURN

Clark, Betty Deberry
  Science Teacher
Nole, Lois Rae
  3rd Grade Teacher
Rich, Shirley Freeman
  Second & Third Grade Teacher
Woodall, Aubrietta Newton
  7th/8th Grade Lang Art Teacher
Wright, Earl Ray
  Middle School Science Teacher

BANDANA

Chandler, Judy Stevens
  Fourth Grade Teacher

BARBOURVILLE

Bennett, Delores Ann
  7th/8th Grade Lang Art Teacher
Betancourt, Celina
  Spanish Teacher
Bingham, Mary Ann Cornett
  Social Studies Teacher
Buchanan, Joyce Campbell
  Mathematics Department Teacher
Elliott, Carolyn Sue (Bennett)
  Science Teacher
Fox, Joyce Grant
  Second Grade Teacher
Hammons, Burnetta Hubbard
  5th Grade Teacher
Pope, Susan Joe
  English Teacher

BARDSTOWN

Allen, Donna Hall
  Life Science Teacher
Berry, Patricia Reed
  Choral Department Chair
Brown, Emma Carol
  Social Stud Teacher-Hist Instr
Buffin, Brenda (Bunch)
  Business Teacher & Dept Chair
Crenshaw, Marcella Mattingly
  Second Grade Teacher
Hawkins, Ann Jones
  Home Economics Dept Teacher
Moore, David Wayne
  Technology Education Teacher
Peake, Jacqueline Stiles
  Chemistry/Biology Teacher
Wilson, Bridgett Hamilton
  Chemistry Teacher

BARDWELL

Thompson, Denise Gupton
  6th Grade Teacher

BATTLETOWN

Coyle, Rita Stevens
  4th/5th Grade Teacher

BEAVER DAM

Mayes, Debbie Duncan
  Fifth Grade Teacher
Minton, Tony Ray
  Sixth Grade Teacher

BEDFORD

Bell, Allison Tyler
  Spanish Teacher

BELFRY

Lester, J. David
  Mathematics Department Chair
Rutherford, Elaine Blackburn
  Business Education Teacher

BELLEVUE

Klopp, William A. Jr.
  Teacher/Mathematics Dept Chair
Lail, Viola
  Third Grade Teacher
Lewis, Joan Carol
  Science Department Chairman
Lykins, Beulah Davis
  Guidance Counselor
Smithers, Joyce Wanda
  Fourth Grade Teacher
Webber, David Eric
  Band Director

BENTON

Bushart, Debra Wyatt
  English Teacher
Edwards, David
  Mathematics Teacher
Lewis, Martha Cunningham
  Remedial Reading Teacher
Robichaud, Carolyn Wommack
  English Teacher
Sammons, Martha L.
  Biology/Anatomy Teacher
Shelton, Lester Thomas
  Science Teacher
Wood, Phyllis Park
  7th-8th Grade English Teacher

BEREA

Halstead, Judy C.
  Business Teacher
Mc Aninch, Vivien Durham
  Biology Teacher
Stewart, Marsha Devere
  Third Grade Teacher
Warren, Bettie Murphy
  2nd Grade Teacher
Wowk, Patricia Diane
  English Teacher

BEVINSVILLE
Johnson, Roger
7th/8th Grade Teacher

BLAINE
Edwards, Arnold
Retired
Elliott, Donna Fleming
Kindergarten Teacher
Sparks, Carolyn Jean
Second Grade Teacher

BOONEVILLE
Bowman, Phyllis Duff
English Teacher
Deaton, Gary
Jr HS Language Arts Teacher

BOWLING GREEN
Bertuleit, Nancy Liudahl
Teacher/Counselor
Duncan, Sandy Westerman
Mathematics Teacher
Ellison, Jesse Floyd
Health Teacher
Halbman, Robert Alan
Chair Military Science
Inman, Tracy Ford
English Teacher
Karrick, Brant Gilmore
Instrumental Music Teacher
Peterie, Stanley Taylor
Seventh Grade History Teacher
Romagnoli, Donna Grant
English Teacher
Sartin, Anita Joyce
4th-6th Grade Teacher
Thomas, Donita Bush
7th Grade English Teacher
Townsend, Angela Alexander
English Teacher

BRANDENBURG
Eskridge, Bettye Irving
Second Grade Teacher
Garris, Karl Jerome
US History Teacher
Jenkins, Mary Louise Barnett
Second Grade Teacher
Lyons, Kimberly Peveler
Business Education Instructor
Meadows, Jeffrey T.
Assistant Band Director
Melloy, Samuel H.
English Department Chair
Miller, Joyce Thomas
Mathematics Teacher
Wix, Janice Hope (Perry)
Coord/Teacher of Gifted Prgms

BREMEN
Doll, Barbara Romero
Junior HS Mathematics Teacher

BROOKSVILLE
Clayton, Connie Haley
2nd Grade Teacher
Markey, Eugenia Woodward
First Grade Teacher
Morgan, Barbara Korner
5th Grade Science Teacher
Teegarden, Sharon Mc Clanahan
English Teacher

BROWNSVILLE
Coates, Lucille
Teacher
Dardin, Basil Maxwell
Fourth Grade Teacher
Webb, Anna Manco
Fifth Grade Teacher
Williams, Sherry Webb
Literature Teacher

BUCKNER
Beasy, William Bryan III
Science Teacher
Bickel, Ted Jr.
Teacher
Culpepper, Jacquelyn Mc Clain
English/Speech Teacher

BURGIN
Akins, Gary Wade
7th/8th Grade Teacher
Yates, Bobbi Jo
Third Grade Teacher

BURKESVILLE
Frodge, Pauletta Smith
4th Grade Teacher
Huddleston, Charles Ray
Science Teacher
Radford, Dorothy L.
Math Teacher

BURLINGTON
Otte, Lindsay Owen
5th Grade Teacher

Powers, Imogene Skeen
First Grade Teacher
Tungate, Vicky Maddox
Third Grade Teacher

BUTLER
Henderson, Kay Ewing
Fourth Grade Teacher
Hickey, Michele Schultz
Third Grade Teacher
Mains, Pamela Schlueter
3rd Grade Teacher
Owen, Bill Carl
Physical Education Teacher

CADIZ
Bridges, Deborah Jane
7th Grade Mathematics Teacher
Dunn, Andrea Curtis
HS Mathematics Teacher
Hawks, Gary R.
4th Grade Teacher

CALVERT CITY
Brown, Sharon Webb
Art Teacher
Grizzard, Barbara Solomon
Science/Health Teacher
Parish, Carla Williams
7th/8th Grade Science Teacher
Vaughn, Janice Chilcutt
Math/Soc Stud Mid Sch Teacher

CAMPBELLSVILLE
Akridge, Jacqueline Louis Wilson
English/Journalism Teacher
Beal, Linda Eastridge
Mathematics/Computer Teacher
Browning, Catherine Schwartzmiller
Fifth Grade Teacher
Gaddie, Wilma Lester
Third Grade Teacher
Gorin, Betty Mitchell
US/World History Teacher
Gumm, Michael Lynn
8th Grade Sci/Math Teacher
Raikes, Sarah Minor
Home Economics Teacher

CAMPTON
Fugate, Peggy Chenault
Second Grade Teacher

CANEYVILLE
Edwards, Ruby Young
K-6th Grade Substitute Teacher

CARROLLTON
Jarmola, Christine
Spanish Teacher
May, Sandra Weaver
Elementary Principal
Shelton, Carol Louden
English Teacher

CARTER
Fultz, Barbara (Richardson)
Sixth Grade Teacher

CECILIA
Franklin, Thomas Lee
Language Art Teacher
Hayes, Linda Kays
Language Arts Department Chair
Kimberlain, Carol Bosley
Language Arts Teacher
Kral, Michael Emil
Science/Mathematics Teacher
Lee, Daniel Owen
Soc Stud Teacher/Dept Chair
Mattingly, Anna Catherine
Lang Art/Soc Stud Teacher
Van Zant, Carol Salato
6th-8th Grade Math Teacher
Williams, Karen Raub
1st Grade Teacher

CENTRAL CITY
Cosby, Anna Marie
Mathematics Teacher

CHAPLIN
Armstrong, Elaine Risk
Head Teacher

CLAY CITY
Everman, Nina Neal
LBD Special Ed Teacher
Salyer, Brenda Everman
2nd Grade Teacher

CLINTON
Armbruster, Robert Eugene
Jr High Hist/English Teacher
Brawley, Joan P.
6th Grade Teacher
Byers, Sarah Ellena
Fifth Grade Teacher
Hazlewood, Kathy Edwards
3rd Grade Teacher

Roberts, Sheri Hurd
9/10th Grade English Teacher
Thomas, Nancy Dixon
Kindergarten Teacher

COLUMBIA
Bradshaw, Judy Fann
Kindergarten Teacher
Coomer, Bobbie Powell
First Grade Teacher
Curry, Gary Vernon
7th Grade Soc Stud Teacher
Durham, Joyce Goodin
Business Ed Dept Chairman
Goodin, Judith Ann
6th Grade Teacher
Mc Cloud, Susan Willis
Sci/Math/Soc Stud Teacher
Roach, William Russell
7th Grade Teacher
Taylor, Samuel Dwight
Social Studies Teacher

CORBIN
Bowlin, Mary Patrick
Second Grade Teacher
Foley, Linda Joan
English Teacher
Garlich, Mary Martha CDP
Typing Teacher
Mitchell, Diane Miller
English/Journalism Teacher
Nicklson, Sherry Allen
1st Grade Teacher
Simpson, Freda Cox
2nd Grade Teacher

CORYDON
Draper, Yvonne Duncan
Second Grade Teacher
Mattingly, Sharon
Third Grade Teacher

COVINGTON
Gray, Bonita Lynne
Fifth Grade Teacher
Jackson, Garry Dale
Assistant Principal
Roenker, Patricia Hopkins
Business & Office Teacher

COXS CREEK
Fitzpatrick, James C.
6th Grade Teacher

CRAB ORCHARD
Brown, Susan Miracle
7th/8th Grade English Teacher

CRESTWOOD
Heid, Sharon Reece
8th Grade Health Teacher
Miller, Karen Austin
8th Grade Lang Arts Teacher
Pollock, Sue Hobgood
Second Grade Teacher

CUMBERLAND
Leach, Linda Sue
English IV Teacher
Morris, Victor Lewie
American History Teacher

CUSTER
Childers, Harold Dean
Principal/Science Teacher

CYNTHIANA
Brunker, Jerry
Assistant Principal
Fuller, Jimmy Lee
Fifth Grade Teacher
Howard, Sandra Reid
8th Grade Mathematics Teacher
Judy, Beverly G.
Middle School Gifted Program
Kearns, Johnetta Geoghegan
7th Grade Science Teacher
Kuster, Sylvia Lewis
4th Grade Teacher

DANVILLE
Baker, Patricia Votaw
English Teacher
Conner, Larry Walter
Elementary Media Specialist
Godby, Giovanna Burks
English Teacher
Mc Kee, Ralph K. II
Life Science Teacher

DEWITT
Hubbard, Michael Lane
Remediation Teacher
Ledford, Glenna Helton
Remedial Reading Teacher
Wahlstedt, Wilma Ann
7-8th Grade Teacher

DIXON
Gibson, Janice Mc Clain
Business Ed/Computer Instr
Gillaspie, Janice Bryant
Mathematics Teacher/Dept Chair
Tucker, E. Carolyn
Language Arts Instructor

DRAKESBORO
Houghland, Debbie Johnson
Math/Cmptr Sci Teacher
Tatum, Carlos Dale
Biology Teacher

DRY RIDGE
Lillard, Sandra Lynn Dozier
English/Spanish Teacher
Reed, Dianne Eckler
Science Department Chair
Spaulding, Mary Mc Glone
4th Grade Teacher

EASTERN
Watson, Joyce O'Quinn
Mathematics/German Teacher

EDDYVILLE
Buchanan, Ruth Etta
Vocational Home Ec Teacher
Burgdolf, Marilyn Timmons
Business Chairperson

EDGEWOOD
Wonderling, Kathleen Mc Killip
Computer/Mathematics Teacher

EDMONTON
Shirley, Ruby Thomas
Fourth Grade Teacher
Smith, Jill Wade
7th/8th Grade English Teacher

EKRON
Greenwell, Diana Gartin
First Grade Teacher

ELIZABETHTOWN
Baker, La Neil Powell
Fourth Grade Teacher
Barnard, Gayla Pfeiffer
Counselor
Buckles, Benita Highbaugh
Reading Coordinator
Hoskinson, Marjorie Leah
Collaborating Teacher
Lindsey, Janet Chaudoin
First Grade Teacher
Scott, Bobby Ray
Fifth Grade Teacher
Smith, Elvin Estil Jr.
Fifth Grade Teacher
Williams, Julie Foushee
First Grade Teacher
Wortham, David
Social Studies Chairman

ELKTON
Davis, Linda Hyams
First Grade Teacher
Kirkman, Carol Jones
Math Teacher/Dept Chairperson
Odum, Viola Roper
6-8 Computer Science Teacher
Wells, Carolyn Louise
English Teacher/Dept Chair

EMINENCE
Van Meter, Donald Ray
Science Teacher/Chair

EUBANK
Leigh, Anna Lee (May)
Fourth Grade Teacher
Livesay, Jayne Sandidge
Second Grade Teacher

EWING
Mc Glothlin, Mary Kathryn Ruark
Sixth Grade Teacher
Stevens, Sylvia Bailey
2nd Grade Teacher

EZEL
Wilson, Janet Sue
5th Grade Teacher

FAIRDALE
Lawson, Charlotte Pennebaker
Art/Photography Teacher
Prather, Ella Frances Dodson
Third Grade Teacher

FALMOUTH
Appel, Janis Marie
Mathematics Teacher
Bertram, Janice King
First Grade Teacher
Case, Sue Sanders
Speech-Language Pathologist
Naylor, Ann Mc Kinney
Eighth Grade Math Teacher

Seever, Shirley Miller
Fifth Grade Teacher
Van Landingham, Wanda Showalter
8th Grade Science Teacher

FARMINGTON
Gibbs, Sherry Hamlin
7th-8th Grade Teacher

FEDSCREEK
Hunt, Barbara J.
English Teacher

FLATGAP
Bowen, Woody
Mathematics & Science Teacher

FLATWOODS
Johnson, Eleanor Taylor
Retired Fifth Grade Teacher

FLEMINGSBURG
Beckett, Mona Carpenter
Third Grade Teacher
Combs, Lana Sutton
HS & Mid Sch Choral Director
Cox, Debra C.
Mathematics Teacher
Dials, Rita Thompson
Home Ec Teacher/Dept Head
Gold, Rosemarie
Teacher of Gifted
Gooding, Joy Tackett
Language Art Teacher
Mc Cord, Emma Mc Ginnis
Language Art Teacher
Peterson, Gene Mark
7th Grade Reading Teacher

FLORENCE
Akers, Dixie Greene
Music Teacher
Dunn, Ann Rose
English Teacher
Kohl, Virginia Nestor
Speech/Drama/Yearbook Teacher
Martin, Debra Goley
Guidance Counselor
Powell, Ben C.
English Teacher
Sullivan, Richard William
Elem/Phys Ed Teacher

FORT CAMPBELL
Cacal, June Mary
Business Teacher
Lange, Leon I.
Biology Teacher/Dept Head
Tutt, Mary Louise
Mathematics Teacher

FORT KNOX
Aubrey, Anne Wright
7th Grade Soc Stud Teacher
Washington, Joe Iva Jr.
Physical Education Teacher

FORT MITCHELL
Kirchner, Gene
Guidance Counselor
Saunders, Stephen Douglas
Science Teacher
Wolfe, Susan Sloan
Second Grade Teacher

FOUNTAIN RUN
Copass, Barbara Gumm
4th & 5th Grade Teacher

FRANKFORT
Adams, Sally Brown
High School English Teacher
Bowker, Linda W.
Head English Dept
Chase, Jerald L.
Mathematics Department Chair
Collins, Caroline Cleveland
Fourth Grade Teacher
Phelps, Randal Robert
English Teacher
Thomas, James A.
8th Grade Teacher
Wylie, Paula Cox
Kindergarten Teacher

FRANKLIN
Berry, Donna Alspaugh
4th Grade Teacher
Kummer, Rebecca Dinwiddie
Retired Substitute Teacher
Raines, Betty Jane
8th Grade History Teacher

FRENCHBURG
Thomas, Lola Mills
4th Grade Teacher

GAMALIEL
Collins, Teresa Wood
Instrumental Music Teacher

GEORGETOWN

Kleinhenz, Emma Amerson
Mathematics/Physics Teacher
Lee, Beth L.
English Teacher
Moore, Janice A.
5th Grade Teacher
Pollock, Mary Katherine
School Counselor
Travis, Billie Ann
7th/8th Grade Math Teacher

GIRDLER

Hammons, Janet Trudeau
First Grade Teacher

GLASGOW

Coomer, Joan Calvert
Spanish Teacher
Ritter, Joan Antle
English Department Chair
Russell, Helen Bull
Soc Stud Teacher/Dept Chair
Sturgeon, Patricia Doyle
Home Economics Teacher
Wyatt, Danny S.
Health Teacher
Zimmerman, Judith Dunbar
English Teacher

GLENDALE

Bell, Connie S.
Teacher
Chick, Gregory Dean
Language Arts Teacher
Cruse, Sharon Jones
Business Teacher
Kinney, Michael Walton
Social Studies Teacher

GRAHAM

Johnson, Madeline Stubblefield
Second Grade Teacher
Wright, Donna Lou
Science Dept/Russian Teacher

GRAYSON

De Santis, Mary Will Hall
Biology Teacher
Marshall, Teresa Flaugher
Biology Teacher
Mc Coy, Patricia Gallion
Fourth Grade Teacher
Meenach, Deborah Lewis
Home Economics/Science Teacher
Plummer, Lisa Graves
HS Home Economics Teacher
Steele, Ada Shaffer
Science Teacher
Wilcox, Verla Shaffer
Reading Teacher

GREENSBURG

Curnutte, Della Mather
Health Services Teacher
Edwards, Beverly Bloyd
Mathematics Teacher
Williams-Monson, Peggy Joyce Ellis
8th Grade Teacher

GREENVILLE

Adams, Nancy Cansler
Mathematics Dept Chairman
Eaves, Deborah Vincent
English Teacher
Heltsley, Guyla Bethel
Fifth Grade Teacher

HALLIE

Smith, Janice M.
Retired

HANSON

Turner, Linda Merrell
2nd Grade Teacher

HARDINSBURG

Gray, Homer Russell Jr.
Teacher/Coach
Harrison, Patricia
Science Teacher

HARDYVILLE

Burks, Linda S.
Fourth Grade Teacher

HARLAN

Jones, Catherine Glockner
Junior High School Teacher
Sargent, Sandra Owens
Fifth Grade Teacher

HARNED

Henderson, Patrick M.
Agriculture Teacher
Smiley, Betty Sue
Business Teacher

HARRODSBURG

Cole, Cecilia Sanders
6th Grade Teacher
Culp, Evelyn Bennett
5th Grade Teacher
Downey, Sandra Lee
English Teacher
Hudson, Rita Gilliland
2nd Grade Teacher
Moore, Marcella Coe
Fourth Grade Teacher
Semone, Elzurah Brashear
3rd Grade Teacher
Sharp, Joyce Cook
First Grade Teacher
Young, Brenda Long
English Teacher

HARTFORD

Daniel, Carol Barrass
Math Teacher
King, Kittye Barnes
Mathematics Teacher
Sapp, Paula Richey
6th Grade Teacher

HEBRON

Hartman, Brenda W.
Social Studies Teacher
Hudson, Michelle Terlau
English Teacher
Martin, John Lewis
Biology/Chemistry Teacher

HENDERSON

Ellis, Robert H.
Choral Director
Ettensohn, David Adrian
Art Teacher/Fine Arts Coord
Green, Linda Rowland
4th Grade Elementary Teacher
Guess, Glenda Alexander
Math Dept Coord/Math Teacher
Hedgespeth, Cathe Mc Ginnis
Mathematics Teacher
Jenkins, Robert
English Teacher
Key, Deborah Galloway
Elem/Family Life Skills Coord
Lindauer, Patricia Carroll
Elementary Teacher
Luebbert, Dianne Key
English Teacher
Meuth, Sally Williams
English Teacher
Mueller, Susan Jane
Science Teacher/Science Coord
Pullam, Roy N.
Social Studies Teacher
Reese, Randy
Teacher/Football Coach
Siewert, Mary Margaret
Third Grade Teacher
Todd, Dolores Adkins
Teacher
Watkins, Anthony Keith
Teacher/Lang Art Dept Chair

HERNDON

Giles, Ann Stivers
Fifth Grade Teacher
Haney, Bonnie Bastin
5th/6th Grade Teacher

HICKMAN

Black, David Albert
Ag/Horticulture Instructor

HINDMAN

Couch, Deborah Karen
Business & Office Teacher
Meade, Priscilla Gail Combs
Social Studies Teacher

HISEVILLE

Bauer, Deborah Newman
Elementary Librarian

HITCHINS

Kouns, Harriett Susie
Lang Art/Hlth/Phys Ed Teacher
Porter, Mrytle Slone
5th Grade Teacher

HODGENVILLE

Craft, Linda Clark
Mathematics Teacher

HOPKINSVILLE

Cochran, Dot Martin
Marketing Teacher/Coordinator
Everett, Elizabeth Lilly
Biology Teacher
Hancock, Connie Staude
1st Grade Teacher
Hill, Ophelia West
Retired Teacher
Lyon, Donald J.
Mathematics Teacher

Perrin, James Adison
Teacher/Coach
Peterson, Margaret Geraldine
English Teacher
Rust, Melva Gorrell
Home Economics Teacher
Tipton, Valery Sullivan
Elementary Teacher
Winn, Shirley Griffy
Fourth Grade Teacher

HORSE CAVE

Murray, Renee Logsdon
Language Arts Teacher

HUSTONVILLE

Coffey, Donna Hoskins
7th/8th Grade Lang Art Teacher
Smith, Philip R.
Math/Science Teacher

INDEPENDENCE

Cain, Jacqueline Malone
French/Spanish Teacher
Smith, Carolyn
Spanish Teacher
Snellen, Susan Moore
7th Grade Science Teacher
Vittetoe, Rebecca Kinman
Fourth Grade Teacher

INEZ

Collier, Vicky G.
Chemistry Instructor

IRVINGTON

Decker, William L. Jr.
English Teacher

JACKSON

Bellamy, Agnes Maria
Eng/Communications/Jrnlsm
Edmonds, Connie Campbell
First Grade Teacher
Napier, Donald Green
English Department Chairperson
Runion, Sally Chapman
Language Arts Teacher
Watts, Brenda Turner
4th-6th Grade Reading Teacher

JAMESTOWN

Barnes, Clara Thrasher
Fifth Grade Teacher
Cooper, Linda Witham
Third Grade Teacher
Johnson, Verta Norris
First Grade Teacher

JEFF

Klinglesmith, Kendra Colwell
English/Spanish Teacher
Shepherd, Phyllis Carol
English Teacher

KIMPER

Belcher, Jeanette
First Grade Teacher
Ford, Paul Roger
Jr HS Math/Soc Studies Teacher

KONA

Hall, Danita Tubbs
Third Grade Teacher
Ison, Carol Fields
Middle School English Teacher

LANCASTER

Francis, Marie Terry
Retired-Third Grade Teacher
Moore, Barbara Holton
5th Grade Teacher
Moore, Kenneth Dale
Social Studies Teacher
Purcell, Mildred M.
Second Grade Teacher

LANGLEY

Webb, Patricia L.
7th/8th Grade Teacher

LAWRENCEBURG

Stevens, Deborah Cornett
First Grade Teacher
Vaughn, Eva K.
5th Grade Teacher

LEITCHFIELD

Bennett, Georgena Fentress
4th Grade Teacher
Davis, Mary Leslie (Sarver)
3rd Grade Teacher
Gentry, William Park
Social Studies Teacher
Lee, Donald H.
Mathematics/Physics Teacher
Mc Call, William P. II
Life Science Teacher
Stikeleather, Lavonne Bruce
Second Grade Teacher

LETCHER

Back, Sandra Ann
Fourth Grade Teacher
Wright, Anna Belle
2nd Grade Teacher

LEWISBURG

Bailey, Joe Kenneth
Mathematics/Art Teacher

LEXINGTON

Black, Gretchen Zimmer
Fifth Grade Teacher
Caldwell, Rose Hill
Mathematics Teacher
Fee, Thomas Charles
Social Studies Teacher
Hays, Ellen Dee Dee Gordon
Mathematics Teacher
Hughes, Donna Beverly
Fifth Grade Teacher
Locker, Linda Sue
First Grade Teacher
Simandle, Stanton Anthony
Principal
Sloan, Mary Jane Enochs
Science Department Chair
Welch, Scott Warren
Social Studies Teacher
Wood, Rebecca Adelle
Mathematics Dept Chair

LIBERTY

Banks, David Wayne
Coord/Teacher of Gifted Ed
Douglas, Imo Jane (Rodgers)
Business Education Teacher
Hamilton, Barbara Jo Raley
5th/6th Grade Teacher
Payne, Susan Price
Health Teacher
Price, Maxine Rodgers
Business Education Teacher

LINEFORK

Bradley, Reneva Sparkman
Lang Arts/Math Teacher

LIVINGSTON

Cash, Katreka Fowler
4th Grade Teacher
Eversole, Martha Leach
Kindergarten/Chapter 1 Teacher
Graves, La Joy Lynn (Parrett)
6th Grade Teacher
Robbins, Miachel L.
Fifth Grade Teacher

LONDON

Gregory, Carolyn Ruth (Wells)
English Dept Head
Scott, Phyllis Jean
Sixth Grade Teacher
Wagers, Lois Brown
Business Teacher

LORETTO

Bugg, Patsy Wooley
Fifth Grade Teacher
Rowlett, Herman Elliott Jr.
Principal

LOST CREEK

Marshall, Dorothy Marie
Sixth Grade Teacher
Murr, Carol Van Kuiken
7th/8th Grade Teacher

LOUISA

Copley, Wanda Sue
Fifth Grade Teacher
Frazier, Anna Marie Wells
Fifth Grade Teacher
Salyer, Laura L.
Mathematics Teacher
Shannon, Marsha K. Rice
Mathematics Dept/Art Teacher
Ward, Debra Lee (Wood)
Computer Teacher
West, Ruth Graham
7th Grade Soc Stud Teacher
Young, Glenna Blevins
English Teacher

LOUISVILLE

Bainbridge, Anne Luking
5th Grade Teacher
Baughman, Harry Hill
Air Force Junior ROTC Instr
Bright, Dorothy Brown
7th Teacher/Co Chm Eng Dept
Bruner, Rebecca Beard
Basic Skills Teacher
Cooley, Margie Elaine (Burton)
Second Grade Teacher
Denoncourt, Leo Paul
Principal/Teacher
Drexler, Theresa Rembold
Language Art Teacher

Evans, Robert Carl
Exceptional Chldhd Ed Teacher
Fleming, Norton B.
5th Grade Teacher
Ford, Michael Dale
Geography/English Teacher
Freeman, Rachel Moody
Resource Teacher
Gamble, Sally Miller
4th & 5th Grade Teacher
Ghent, Robert Mitchell
Physical Education Chair
Gray, Becky Aarvig
HS Mathematics Teacher
Hallman, Nancey Ford
Rdng/Lang Art/Math Teacher
Hardin, Mary Lue
Counselor
Harvey, Vicki Bachman
2nd Grade Teacher
Hazen, Elizabeth Frances Mc Dowell
6th Grade Learning Disab
Heizer, Carol Goodman
Substitute Teacher
Heuke, Martha Pierce
First Grade Teacher
Hinds, Anne Hutchinson
7th Grade Science Teacher
Inderhees, Carol Louise RSM
Jr HS English Teacher
Johnson, Mary Etta
4th Grade Teacher
Karem, Kenny
Junior HS Teacher/Writer
Leighton, Bill Dodge Munro
Middle School Teacher
Lovett, V. Troy
Algebra II/Calculus Teacher
Mahoney, Paul Julian
Physics/Chemistry Teacher
Mangus, Dan Carl
HS English/Mathematics Teacher
May, Karen Cain
World History Teacher
Mc Culloch-Vislisel, Susan
English Dept Chair/Teacher
Mc Hugh, Phyllis Meadows
Mathematics Teacher
Mc Nabb, William Michael
Biology Teacher
Milby, Patricia Bell
Senior Counselor
Montgomery, Ronald Clell
Teacher/Family Leader
Nedros, Charlotte Hobbs
5th Grade Teacher
Nicholas, Sharon Anderson
Teacher of Gifted & Talented
Oesch, Ruth Asher
8th Grade Language Art Teacher
Olliges, George R.
Marketing/Bus Law Teacher
Pirtle, Retha Raymer
3rd Grade Gifted Stu Teacher
Rapley, Gay Mairson
English Teacher
Ricketts, David C.
English Dept Chair
Schuster, John Paul
Athletic Director/Math Teacher
Seay, Carol Rose
Psychology Teacher
Shively, Ann Hawkins
Assistant Principal
Shrader, Jan Munn
Medicine/Allied Health Coord
Simpson, Nancy P. Jean
8th Grade Science Teacher
Spiegelhalter, William Robert
Band Director
Unseld, Barbara King
Social Studies Teacher
Voelker, Sharon Buetenbach
6th/7th Grade Math Teacher
Wallshield, Ernest Matthew Jr.
Social Studies Dept Chair
White, Tom
Hi-Technology Teacher/Spec
Wold, Jerri Bowman
Advanced Spanish Teacher

LUCAS

Foster, Jeffrey Thomas
Principal
Woodcock, Linda Birge
Math Teacher

LUDLOW

Geimeier, Thomas Edwin
Social Studies Teacher/Chair
Mc Cormick, Gary Alan
English/Amer History Teacher
Smith, Tamara Benge
Art Teacher

MACKVILLE

Coulter, James Donnie
4th Grade Teacher

MADISONVILLE

George, Joyce W.
Science Teacher
Gipson, Vernon
US History AP Teacher
Hobgood, Gale Wilson
1st Grade Teacher
Niswonger, L. Carol
English/Drama Teacher
Rhye, Patsy Crowley
Gifted Coord & Lang Arts
Rowans, David Lee
7th Grade Language Art Teacher
Walters, Patricia Harris
English Department Chair

MANCHESTER

Hounchell, Monte Slater
Tenth Grade History Teacher
House, Alma F.
Third Grade Teacher

MANNSVILLE

Bates, Winfrey Phelps
Librarian/Reading Teacher
Grant, Rebecca Frankum
2nd Grade Teacher
Smith, Earldeen Atwood
Third Grade Teacher

MARION

Hatfield, Bonita Mattingley
Science Teacher
Hodges, Mary H.
Mathematics Teacher
Myrick, Linda Kirk
First Grade Teacher

MAYFIELD

Brown, Alicia Reaves
Media Director
Dobson, Charlotte Mc Pherson
First Grade Teacher
Rowland, Emma Lee
Guidance Counselor

MAYSVILLE

Huss, Sally Hutchinson
Jr HS Mathematics Teacher
Iery, Robert Leroy
7th Grade Lang Arts Teacher
Manley, Gay Brothers
Fourth Grade Teacher
Shortt-Ross, Ann Burnette
Spanish Teacher
Staggs, Diana Meadows
Social Studies Department Chm

MC DANIELS

Whitworth, Betty Allen
6th Grade Teacher

MC DOWELL

Caldwell, Joan C.
Biology/Chemistry Teacher
Miller, Sally Shannon
English Teacher

MC KEE

Anderson, Judy Mc Queen
Spanish/English Teacher
Clark, Brenda Harrison
Soc Stud Dept Chairperson
Estridge, Vickie Spurlock
Math Teacher
Gay, Gary L.
7-8th Language Arts Teacher
Harris, Doris Ann
Business Dept Chairman
Thesing, Teri A.
Mathematics Teacher/Dept Chair

MC KINNEY

Rancy, Charlotte Queener
Reading Teacher

MIDDLESBORO

Lane, Mary Winston
Teacher
Lewis, Dorothy Hoerter
English Teacher
Spangler, Stephen Ray
6th Grade Teacher

MIDDLETOWN

Hagan, Timothy Charles
Band Director/Department Chair

MILTON

Hereford, Lounita May Luckett
Third Grade Teacher
Woodward, Jill Renee Jenkins
Fourth Grade Teacher

MONTICELLO

Bell, Gwenave
Sixth Grade Teacher
Brewerton, Elizabeth Wells
English & Spanish Teacher
Casada, Betty Tucker
Math Teacher
Dick, Barbara B.
Elementary Music Teacher
Owens, Gary Wayne
English Teacher
Radford, Gale S.
Biology Teacher
Shearer, Peggy Young
English Teacher

MORGANFIELD

Greenwell, Robin Quinn
Mathematics Teacher
Long, Gary Edward
HS Social Studies Teacher

MORGANTOWN

Phelps, Eyelean D.
Retired Teacher

MOUNT STERLING

Brown, Lucy Goodpaster
Mathematics Teacher
Clemons, Mary Gay
7th Grade Language Art Teacher
Durham, Elsie Marie
Retired
Letton, Geraldine Ashton
2nd Grade Teacher
Mc Glothin, Pat O'Donnell
Fourth Grade Teacher
Owen, Oweney Elias
Health Education Teacher
Reeder, Daniel M.
6th Grade Teacher Team Coord
Ricker, Viola Mae Willoughby
Fourth Grade Teacher
Tackett, Jean Blanton
7th Grade Math/Eng Teacher

MOUNT VERNON

Cooke, Joy Darvel
Geometry Teacher
Lynch, William Junior Jr.
His/Psych Teacher-Chairperson

MOUNT WASHINGTON

Adams, Iona L.
Kindergarten Teacher
Cofer, Cathy Smiley
8th Grade Lang Arts Teacher
Curtis, Nancy S.
7th Grade Language Art Teacher
Dawson, Betty Gail
Second Grade Teacher
Ellis, Thelma Lambdin
Fourth Grade Teacher
Taylor, Edith L.
Second Grade Teacher

MULDRAUGH

Hinkle, Russell Ray Sr.
Principal/Chapter I Teacher

MUNFORDVILLE

Beams, Bobby Gene
Social Studies Teacher
Butler, Raybon
History/Drama/Spec Ed Teacher

MURRAY

Coleman, Lynda Kelso
English Department Chairperson
Lassiter, Patricia Jones
English Teacher

NANCY

Daulton, Sherill Hobgood
Chapter I Reading Teacher
Todd, Sheila Wood
Chapter I Reading Teacher

NEON

Adams, Cathy Floyd
English Teacher/Dept Chair
Furby, Cheryl Belinda
Biology Teacher/Science Chair
Nelson, Norma Addington
2nd Grade Teacher
Vance, Harold
7th & 8th Math Teacher

NEWPORT

Brown, Robert Grady
7th-8th Grade Science Teacher
Dornheggen, Nancy Rosenbloom
2nd Grade Teacher
Enos, Deborah H.
Science Teacher
Johnson, Wanda Fae
Remedial Reading Teacher
Lanham, William L.
Social Studies Dept Chairman

Stephens, Betty Louise
Mathematics Teacher
Turner, Garlene Raleigh
Remedial Reading Teacher

NICHOLASVILLE

Ison, Louis Charles
Chemistry/Physics Teacher

NORTH MIDDLETOWN

Wyatt, Judy Gay
Second Grade Teacher

NORTONVILLE

Brooks, David Gene
6th-8th Grade Eng/His Teacher
Gamblin, Brenda Fork
Mathematics Teacher

OIL SPRINGS

Hall, Carolyn Sue
Fourth Grade Teacher
Sparks, Catherine Jane
Kindergarten Teacher

OLIVE HILL

Stamper, Patricia G.
Counselor

OLMSTEAD

Miles, Janet Finch
Third Grade Teacher

ONEIDA

Burns, Richard P.
Band/Choral Dir/Fine Art Chair
Powell, Ruth Ann
5th/6th Grade Teacher
Travis, Melissa Jane
Mathematics/Chemistry Teacher

OWENSBORO

Adkisson, Bonnie Ramsey
Academic Intern Teacher
Berry, Glenn Patricia
Soc Stud Teacher/Dept Chair
Bouvier, Fumie (Nakaguki)
Teacher
Danhauer, Mary T.
Mathematics/Science Teacher
Duke, Jim Wayne
Chemistry & Physics Teacher
Hardy, Sam R.
Fourth Grade Teacher
Kingsley, Linda C.
English Teacher
Kurz, Thomas E.
Soc Stud Dept Chairman
Mountain, Patricia L. (Kurth)
Social Studies Teacher
Nall, Donald E.
US History Teacher
Parks, Dorothy Coffey
Mathematics Teacher
Preuss, Linda Smith
Teacher of Gifted & Talented
Reeves, David Michael
Social Studies Teacher
Riddle, Carole Goode
Fifth Grade Teacher
Rowe, Mark Anthony
Physical Education Teacher
Settle, Marsha Hunter
Fourth/Fifth Grade Teacher
Tingle, Phyllis Irene
6th Grade Teacher
Wigton, Terry Lee
Mathematics Teacher
Williams, Henry Woodson III
6th Grade Teacher

OWINGSVILLE

Apel, Carmie C.
Retired Business Teacher
Beck, Sue Rawlings
Mathematics Teacher
Church, Janet Couch
4th Grade Teacher
Huber, Judy S.
English Teacher
Stacy, Esther Catterton
Guidance Counselor
Thompson, Barbara Preston
Lang Arts & Journalism Teacher

PADUCAH

Boyd, Catherine Garrett
Fourth Grade Teacher
Edwards, Judith Rose Short
Gifted-English Teacher
Foster, Patricia H.
11th Grade English Teacher
Hovekamp, Robert Neil
Guidance Counselor
Jackson, Dennis Murl
8th Grade History Teacher
Mc Groarty, Tony Thomas
Biology Chair

Miller, Barbara Ann Feast
Fifth Grade Teacher
Reed, Diane Thompson
4th Grade Teacher
Reeves, Sharon Kay
8th Grade English Teacher
Werner, Lynn Boyd
Soc Stud/Teacher of Gifted
Wood, Pearl Bottoms
Teacher

PAINTSVILLE

Bailey, Mary Rose (Hall)
Sixth Grade Teacher
Jones, John Paul
9th Grade Science Teacher
Patrick, Henry Allen
Marketing Education Teacher

PARIS

Day, Betty June Reed
6th-8th Grade Art Teacher
Price, Jerry Lynn
Social Studies Teacher
Wagoner, David Lee
Fourth Grade Teacher

PARK CITY

Adams, Susan Mc Gloin
Sixth Grade Teacher
Cornwell, Nancy Landrum
Guidance Counselor
Turner, Zelma Turley
Fourth Grade Teacher

PARK HILLS

Timmerding, Diana Wilbers
English Teacher

PERRYVILLE

Moore, Margaret Henderson
2nd Grade Teacher

PHILPOT

Blandford, Mark Alan
Science Department Chairman
Montgomery, John Ray
Mathematics Teacher

PHYLLIS

Adams, Lucille
Retired Kindergarten Teacher

PIKEVILLE

Birchfield, Vivian Ford
Jr High English Teacher
Coleman, Margarette Candi
First Grade Teacher
Cunningham, Lesley Elder
Sixth Grade Teacher
Ford, Jeff Dale
7th Grade Sci/Phys Ed Teacher
Maynard, Brenda Stanley
English Teacher
Rice, Susan Poe
5th Grade Teacher
Smith, Rosalee Reynolds
Vocational Business Teacher

PINE KNOT

Anderson, Glenna (Trammell)
Second Grade Teacher
Thomas, Bruce Gordon
Social Studies Teacher

PINEVILLE

Carnes, Lois H Asher
Social Studies Teacher
Hufstedler, Shirley Lewellen
Social Studies Teacher
Poore, Toby Ann
Biology Teacher/Dept Chair

PLEASANT VIEW

Fox, Donnie Lee
Sixth Grade Teacher

PLEASUREVILLE

Hackett-Smith, Janeie Dale
5th Grade Teacher

PRESTONSBURG

Allen, Janice Blackburn
8th Gr Math/Lang Arts Teacher
Brown, Aleene
History Teacher
Carter, Judith Howard
7th-8th Grade Teacher
Dingus, Ralph Waldo
8th Grade Teacher
Dye, Patricia Balsley
Junior High Science Teacher
Hale, Bobby Jean
3rd Grade Teacher
Jones, Edith Hopkins
Sixth Grade Teacher
Robinson, Ronald
Mathematics Department Chair

PRINCETON

Anderson, Roy Jr.
Retired Substitute Teacher
Hankins, A. C.
Mathematics Teacher
Tichenor, Glenda Hill
French & English Teacher

RADCLIFF

Carter, Donna Graham
Mathematics Teacher
Hodge, Iris Davis
Social Studies Teacher
Koontz, Ronald Douglas
History Teacher
Morrison, Brian Lee
Assistant Band Director
Van Zant, Donna Johnson
French Teacher

RICHMOND

Cummins, Janet Leigh
8th Grade Lang Art Teacher
Gallicchio, Bertille Cole
HS English Teacher
Irwin, Victoria Del Vecchio
6th Grade Teacher
Lane, Priscilla A.
Assistant Professor
Moretz, Virginia Bridges
8th Grade Science Teacher

ROCKHOLDS

Stanley, Billy Ralph
4th Grade Teacher

ROUSSEAU

Hounshell, Janet Banks
6-8th Grade Teacher

RUSH

Davis, Barbara Calvert
Jr HS Lang Arts/Soc Stud Tchr
Miller, Elizabeth Hogan
Retired
Whitt, Shirley Ann Robinson
Reading Teacher

RUSSELL

Thompson, Alice Kay
Mathematics Teacher

RUSSELL SPRINGS

Antle, Tracey Roy
Advanced English Teacher
Baldock, Judy Lee
7th & 9th Grade Sci Teacher
Barnes, Margie Rigsby
English Teacher
Edwards, Charles H.
Social Studies Dept Chair
Emerson, Larry Douglas
8th-9th Grade Soc Stud Teacher
Hale, Charlene Aaron
Second Grade Teacher
Holt, Brenda Bottom
Chapter Math Teacher
Keene, Janice Wheat
Chemistry/Physics Teacher
Troutman, Elizabeth Lee
7th/8th Grade Lang Art Teacher

RUSSELLVILLE

Atkins, David W.
Mathematics Teacher
Collier, Jane Wright
Mathematics Department Head
Smith, Algie Ray
Eighth Grade Reading Teacher
Wilkins, Kaye Warren
5th Grade Dev Reading Teacher
Woodall, Gary H.
Biology Teacher
Wright, Nancy Brown
Math Teacher

SALYERSVILLE

Williams, Judy
Chapter I Math Teacher

SANDY HOOK

Adkins, Teresa Simmons
Teacher of Gifted & Talented

SCOTTSVILLE

Woodward, William Perry
Science Teacher

SHELBIANA

Matney, Kaye Varney
First Grade Teacher
Williams, Lojean Morris
8th Grade Eng/His Teacher

SHELBYVILLE

Cook, Cathy Brown
Second Grade/Contact Teacher
Hall, Deborah A.
Social Studies Teacher

SHELBYVILLE (cont)
Kendall, Sarah Brooks
  Third Grade Teacher
Waits, Donna Bottom
  4th Grade Teacher

SHEPHERDSVILLE
Davidson, Tom
  6-8th Grade Teacher of Gifted
Fleitz, Pamela Jean
  Choral Director
Navert, Mary Perpetua
  First Grade Teacher
Rishor, Patrick F.
  JROTC Instructor

SIDNEY
Stafford, Mary Ann Ann Mullins
  7th Grade Lang Art Teacher

SILER
Sears, Naomi Smith
  2nd/4th & 5th Grade Teacher

SMITHLAND
Calhoun, Ronnie Ford
  Teacher
Hodges, Cheryl Robertson
  English Teacher

SOMERSET
Adams, Kathy Gover
  Fifth Grade Teacher
Bales, H. G.
  Health/Phys Ed Teacher
Deitz, Martha M.
  Mathematics Teacher
Dugger, Susan E.
  Business Education Teacher
Gillum, Frances Sanders
  Social Studies Dept Chair
Hail, J. Sharon
  Psychology Teacher
Hale, Mary Auxier
  English Teacher
Holder, Elaine Thornton
  7th Grade Lang Arts Teacher
Hollars, Ann Moody
  Media Librarian
Hollars, Roger G.
  School Counselor
Mayne, John Robert
  Assistant Principal & Teacher
Nichols, Henrietta Scalf
  Sixth Grade Teacher
Popplewell, Kathy Koger
  Mathematics Teacher
Post, Kathy Angela
  Mathematics Teacher
Price, Marian Dunaway
  Third Grade Teacher
Sewell, Joanna Compton
  Language Arts Teacher
Vaught, Audean Thornton
  Business & Health Teacher

SONORA
Summers, Loretta Jump
  Mathematics Teacher

SOUTH SHORE
Rice, Floretta L.
  6th/7th/8th Grade Math Teacher

SOUTH WILLIAMSON
Collins, Phyllis Varney
  8th Grade Teacher

SPRINGFIELD
Beckham, Lillian Ann Lawson
  Chemistry Teacher
Lawson, Patricia B.
  English Teacher
Newton, Annelle Noel
  7th/8th Grade Math Teacher
Spaulding, Mary Jane
  Fourth Grade Teacher
Tatum, Nancy Roberts
  High School English Teacher

STANFORD
Mc Laren, Harold Winfred
  Assistant Principal
Petrey, Scena Ann (Goetz)
  English Teacher
Swope, Charline Whitaker
  Retired Fourth Grade Teacher

STANTON
Blanton, Annalene Spencer
  Social Studies Teacher
Brewer, Fern Smallwood
  Fourth Grade Teacher
Mc Cutcheon, Emogene S. Small
  Retired Science Teacher/Chair

STEARNS
Van Over, Gilbert Lee Jr.
  A P History Teacher & Instr

STEPHENSBURG
Gott, Tim
  Mathematics Teacher
Sweat, Nora Vaillancourt
  Home Economics Teacher

STURGIS
Littrell, Richard Lee
  Fifth Grade Teacher

SWEEDEN
Fitzpatrick, Sue Carol Johnson
  5th Grade Teacher

TAYLORSVILLE
Palmer, William Lee
  Social Studies Teacher

TOLLESBORO
Ferguson, Bonnie Meyer
  1st Grade Teacher
Harrison, Randell Edward
  US History Teacher
Tucker, Larry Gene
  Guidance Counselor

TOMPKINSVILLE
Carter, Louis Lee
  Math & History Teacher
Walden, Patricia
  Special Education Counselor

UPTON
Cruse, Edna M.
  Third Grade Teacher

UTICA
Hayden, Judith Marshall
  1st/2nd Grade Teacher
Mischel, Karen Wilderman
  Librarian

VANCEBURG
Claxon, Jacalyn Esham
  Mathematics Teacher

VERSAILLES
Haynes, Paula Clotfelter
  Gifted Language Arts Teacher
Roberts, Patricia Morris
  3rd Grade Teacher

VILLA HILLS
Whitten, Effie
  Creative Writing Teacher

VINE GROVE
Bickett, Agnes Irene
  Part-Time School Librarian
Green, Terri Rains
  Band Director

VIPER
Brashear, Beatrice Banks
  Retired Elementary Teacher
Brashear, Sandra Combs
  Language Arts Teacher

WALTON
Reeves, Rhonda La Follette
  7th-12th Grade Spec Ed Teacher

WARFIELD
Murphy, Emma Jean
  Fifth Grade Teacher

WAYNESBURG
Buis, Dianna Lovins
  5th Grade Teacher
Deatherage, Ronnie Wayne
  7th/8th Grade His/math Teacher
Horton, Judy Rector
  Fifth Grade Teacher

WEST LIBERTY
Collett, Eunice Jane Mosley
  Business Dept Chairperson

WHEELWRIGHT
Osborne, Doris Bird
  Bio/Anatomy/His Teacher

WHITE MILLS
Dawson, Judy Raizor
  Classroom Teacher
Hayse, Anna J.
  4th Grade Teacher

WHITE PLAINS
Byrum, George Daniel
  Middle School Humanities
Johnson, Gaynell
  1st & 2nd Grade Teacher

WHITESBURG
Halcomb, Bobbie S.
  6th-8th Grade Reading Teacher
Kuracka, Lorraine Banks
  First Grade Teacher

WHITESVILLE
Adams, Carroll Haydon
  7th/8th Grade Teacher

Clark, James Russell
  Mathematics & Religion Teacher
Howard, Alice Aud
  Second Grade Teacher
Hurm, Judy (Payne)
  Fourth Grade Teacher

WHITLEY CITY
Duncan, James Harding
  8th Grade Lang Arts Teacher

WILLIAMSBURG
Bowlin, Anna Shelley
  Sixth Grade Teacher
Falin, Carolyn Murray
  Teacher
Lawless, James Randall
  Mathematics Teacher
Owens, Constance Renfro
  HS Special Education Teacher
Wilson, Carolyn S.
  Spanish/English Teacher
Wilson, Ronald Preston
  English Teacher

WILLIAMSPORT
Chandler, Doris Ann (Holbrook)
  8th Grade Math Teacher

WILLIAMSTOWN
Simpson, Shirley Roland
  Third Grade Teacher

WINCHESTER
Atkinson, Nancy Jo Harrison
  7th Grade Science Teacher
Castle, James Langley
  Biology Teacher
Christiansen, David Jon
  Advanced Placement Bio Teacher
Coyle, Linna Ann
  8th Grade Earth/Space Science
Harrell, Gloria Seale
  8th Grade Reading Teacher
Jones, Anne W.
  Retired English Teacher
Jude, Cassandra Joy
  Elementary Music Teacher
Leary, Catherine Wilson
  Third Grade Teacher
Lowe, Richard Thomas
  Science Teacher
Rice, Karyn S. Mc Caslin
  First Grade Teacher
Sallee, Claude Douglas
  Phys Ed, Health Teacher
Snell, Mamie La Vonne Adams
  Fourth Grade Teacher
Van Sickle, Reecy Mason
  Fifth Grade Teacher
Volz, Phyllis Chaney
  Freshman English Teacher
White, Douglas Dale Jr.
  Social Studies Teacher
White, Sue Hobbs
  Secondary English Teacher

WINGO
Oldham, Donald G.
  Science/Health Teacher
Woodson, Lelia Myatt
  Third Grade Teacher

WORTHINGTON
Miracle, Kay Huffman
  6th Grade Teacher

WURTLAND
Scott, Vera Sargent
  Counselor
Yancey, Anita Archey
  Fifth Grade Teacher

LOUISIANA

ABBEVILLE
Langlinais, Jacqueline Smith
  Mathematics Department Chair
Leggette, Paula Boudreaux
  Bio Teacher/Sci Dept Chair

ALEXANDRIA
Arnold, Katharine Bennett
  Fifth Grade Teacher
Gaines, Frankie M.
  Vocal Music Teacher
Ortego, Jane Mattis
  Fourth Grade Teacher
Renegar, Linda Kay
  Gifted Program Developer
Rundell, Judy L.
  Instructor

AMITE
Brumfield, Herbert
  Biology Teacher

Hart, Marilyn Landry
  Jr HS Language Arts Teacher

ARABI
Orillion, Cheryl Saunee
  8th Grade Teacher/Asst Prin

ARCADIA
Crain, Cathey Mc Guire
  Second Grade Teacher

ATLANTA
Hollingsworth, Doris Walker
  5th Grade Teacher

BALDWIN
Abraham, Delores Madison
  English Teacher
Armelin, Dale Benjamin
  2nd Grade Teacher

BASILE
Miller, Brenda Manuel
  Third Grade Teacher
Ortego, Kayren Fontenot
  English Teacher
Spell, Betty Knight
  Second Grade Teacher

BASTROP
Stevens, Lynda Henderson
  English Teacher
Tubbs, Katherine Yates
  Kindergarten Teacher
Winston, Mable Williams
  8th Grade Reading Teacher

BATON ROUGE
Barton, Gaylyn Williams
  Chapter II Mathematics Teacher
Bosch, Linda Weber
  Mathematics Department Chair
Corroa, Anthony John
  Band Director
Day, Pamela June
  Drama Teacher
Frank, Cortez B.
  Math Dept Co-Chair/Asst Prof
Frost, Frances Miles
  Chemistry Teacher & Dept Chm
Harrison, Sandra June
  Fifth Grade Teacher
Hook, Elise A.
  English Teacher/Gifted Program
Kuhlmeier, Sandra Gellert
  4th Grade Teacher
Lemoine, Virginia Mary
  Second Grade Teacher
Lynch, Debbie Mix
  Fourth Grade Teacher
Mc Lean, Christine Fiona
  Civics & Geography Teacher
Milligan, Valerie Gayle Jones
  Biology Teacher
Nolan, Patricia Lavelle
  4th Grade Math/Science Teacher
Oulton, Grace Dieter
  English Teacher/Vice Principal
Rainey, Patricia Aston
  Social Studies Dept Chairman
Ratliff, Phyllis Knighten
  Sixth Grade Teacher
Roberts, Faimon Austin
  Middle Sch Science Instructor
Rochester, Clare Blagg
  Magnet 6th Grade Teacher
Roddy, Paula Merrick
  Mathematics Teacher
Stentiford, Alan George
  Social Studies Teacher
Theriot, Judine
  History Teacher
Welborn, Laura Lancaster
  Middle School Teacher
Williams, Lyndia Moses
  Vocal Music Teacher
Yglesias, Audry Hill
  Rdng Spec/Art Teacher/Prin

BIENVILLE
Rushing, Murline Robinson
  7th/8th Grade Teacher

BOGALUSA
George, Jennifer Germany
  6th-8th Grade Math/His Teacher
Keil, Chinese Amelia
  6th Grade Teacher
Knight, Kathy Humphrey
  4th Grade Teacher
Mc Cants, Lillian Gayle
  Gifted/Talented Teacher

BOSSIER CITY
Jackson, Richie
  Civics/Free Enterprise Teacher
Salinas, Dominic
  Assistant Principal

BREAUX BRIDGE
Cormier, Eddie Joseph
  Mathematics Teacher
Duncan, Donella Collet
  Reading/Social Studies Teacher

BRIDGE CITY
Howard, Mary Kathleen
  4th/5th Grade Teacher

BROUSSARD
La Fontaine, Mary Louis
  Teacher

BUCKEYE
Hathorn, George Gunter
  Science Department Chairman
Lawton, Diane Bives
  Elementary Phys Ed Teacher
Lucas, Clifford Joseph
  Mathematics Dept Chairman

BUNKIE
Benton, Jo Ann Hall
  Language Art Teacher
Bradley, Mary Jackson
  Teacher
Lambert, Judith Bergeron
  Mathematics/French Teacher
Welch, Susan Ducote
  Mathematics/Science Teacher

CAMPTI
Oliphant, Annie Jackson
  7th/8th Grade Eng/His Teacher

CARENCRO
Heidbrink, Betty Patterson
  Science Teacher

CARLISLE
Stallworth, Jacquelyn Ann (Blackwell)
  Language Arts Teacher

CASTOR
Nelson, Glenda Guest
  K-6th Grade Enrichment Teacher
Warren, Betty Wood
  Kindergarten Teacher

CECILIA
Calais, Alma Moreau
  Third Grade Teacher
Kidder, Jewell Landry
  7th-8th Grade English Teacher
Thibodaux, Charlie Janet
  Curriculum Coordinator

CHALMETTE
Dugger, Thomas Frederick
  English Teacher
Huie, Roland Eugene Jr.
  Band Director
Scott, Rose Misuraca
  Physical Education Teacher

CHATHAM
Graham, Micheal Mc Comb
  Vocational Agriculture Teacher

CHAUVIN
Foret, Gloria Kreamer
  Assistant Principal

CHOUDRANT
David, Betty Aswell
  First Grade Teacher
Lutes, Merlene S.
  7th/8th Grade Math Teacher

CONVERSE
Richardson, Linda Powers
  Business Education Teacher
Rivers, Shirley Le Duff
  English Teacher

COVINGTON
Yount, William G.
  Ethics/Philosphy Teacher

CROWLEY
Benoit, Cindy Perrodin
  Fourth Grade Teacher
Cain, Mary L.
  Religion Teacher
Cormier, Beaulah Edwards
  7th Grade Eng/Rdng Teacher
Wilkerson, Linda Tarver
  Guidance Counselor

CROWVILLE
Martin, Donna Rushing
  English Teacher
Steven, Cheryl Brooks
  Fourth Grade Teacher

DE QUINCY
Treme, Lynne Mitchell
  Math Teacher
Yellott, Jody Hyatt
  Social Studies Teacher

DE RIDDER
Cooley, Timothy Jack
 English Teacher/Coach
Herrington, Carolyn Peterson
 7th & 8th Grade Band Director
Manuel, Rose Miller
 6th Soc Stud/7th Lib Arts

DELHI
Doles, Glenda Coleman
 French/English Teacher

DESTREHAN
Bruce, Rickie
 English/Fine Art Teacher

DONALDSONVILLE
Pizzolato, Agnes Newchurch
 8th Grade Teacher
Waguespack, Royce G.
 Science-Mathematics Teacher

DUBACH
Pylant, Judy P.
 1st Grade Teacher

DUSON
Thibodeaux, Mary Lou Borel
 5th Grade Teacher

EDGARD
Mitchell, Brenda J. R.
 English Department Head

ELMER
Dezendorf, Jeannine Gay
 Kindergarten Teacher

ELTON
Allen, Helen Louise
 First Grade Teacher

ENTERPRISE
Blaney, James Martin Jr.
 Agriculture Teacher
Henry, Audrey Porter
 Kindergarten Teacher

EUNICE
Mc Gee, Susan Montelaro
 Third Grade Teacher
Menard, Clay Anthony
 Physics Teacher

EVANS
Smith, Cynthia Mc Bride
 Home Economics Teacher

FERRIDAY
Davis, Annie Paul
 6th Grade Teacher

FORT NECESSITY
Ensminger, Bobby
 Science Teacher

FORT POLK
Orgain, Gloria Jean Grace
 4th Grade ESL Teacher

FRANKLIN
Armelin, Sylvia Jean
 4th Grade Teacher
Lewis, Dora Jean-Jacob
 8th Grade English Teacher

FRANKLINTON
Bennett, Patricia Anglin
 English Teacher
Crain, Louise Kemp
 Second Grade Teacher
Zeringue, Sidney Paul
 Eighth Grade Sci Teacher

GIBSLAND
Douglas, Sheila Holland
 Science Teacher

GLENMORA
Graslie, Peter James
 English/Social Studies Teacher
Sutton, Michael Roy
 Science Department Chairman

GOLDEN MEADOW
Adams, Louise Ordoyne
 Chapter I Reading Teacher
Boudreaux, Peggy Estay
 Second Grade Teacher
Duet, Norma Faucheux
 6th Grade Teacher/Admin Asst

GONZALES
Moak, Lynn Davies
 English Teacher
Smith, Marian J.
 5th Grade Lang Art Teacher

GRAMBLING
Wesley, Lula Bradford
 Supervising Teacher

GRAND COTEAU
Eaglin, Marie Melancon
 Kindergarten Teacher

GRAY
Schiro, Edgar Louis
 Instrumental Music Teacher

GREENSBURG
Henry, Charles D.
 Mathematics Teacher
Stringer, Louise Smith
 Secondary English Teacher

GRETNA
Allen, Drema Ray
 6-8th Grade Lang Arts Teacher
De Armas-Ducros, Elizabeth Rosa
 Sixth Grade Teacher
Stelly, Noelie M.
 Mathematics/French Teacher

GUEYDAN
Heard, Frederick Ronald
 Mathematics/Science Teacher

HACKBERRY
Baker, Mary Hickman
 Business Teacher
Billedeaux, Ruth Sanner
 First Grade Teacher
Gray, Ann Byler
 Third Grade Teacher
Ross, Sherry Duplechain
 Mathematics Teacher

HARVEY
Washington, Prince Hall
 Principal

HAUGHTON
Hardwick, Dorothy Chandler
 Third Grade Teacher
Prunty, Lee Ann Sibley
 Third Grade Teacher

HAYNESVILLE
Garner, Anna P.
 Counselor/Assistant Principal

HICKS
Elkowitz, Angela Bradford
 Business Teacher
Folse, Raphael James III
 English Department Chairman

HOUGHTON
Thomas, Charles Michael
 Mathematics Teacher

HOUMA
Adams, Terri Reed
 First Grade Teacher
Crochet, Suzanne Therese
 Fifth Grade Teacher
Hebert, Wanda Ann
 5th Grade Teacher
Jones, Sherry Boyles
 Social Studies Teacher
Rogers, Barbara Bergeron
 Third Grade Teacher

IOTA
Bristow, Elwana Pearl
 Mathematics Teacher
Cart, Elizabeth Martin
 5th Grade Teacher

IOWA
Authement, Nancy Gennuso
 Third Grade Teacher

JEANERETTE
Gibson, Ray C.
 7th Grade Lit/Eng Teacher
Washington, Lue Pearl Robinson
 English/Reading Teacher

JENA
Russell, Nelda Roark
 Kindergarten Teacher

JONESVILLE
Krahn, Ann Christiansen
 English Teacher
Williams, Mary Jo
 Reading Teacher/Librarian

KAPLAN
Greene, Lovelace John Jr.
 Vocational Agriculture Teacher

KENNER
Ellis, Lenary G.
 English Teacher

KENTWOOD
Alford, Cecile Linton
 Fourth Grade Teacher
Oxholm, Wilda Fay Grace
 4th Grade Teacher

Peterson, Patricia Simmons
 Business Teacher/Asst Prin

LAFAYETTE
Chustz, Susan Rice
 LD Mathematics Teacher
Comb, Darrel Wayne
 High School Band Director
Ford, Cynthia Richard
 Math Teacher
Greig, Rebecca Lynne
 Mathematics Department Chair
Kresse, Margaret Fletcher
 Guidance Counselor
La Grange, Sandra Landry
 English Teacher
Marks, Johnnie Mae
 Assistant Principal
Miller, Mary Jane
 Chemistry/Physical Sci Teacher
Orgeron, Richard Keith
 Science Dept Chair/Bio Teacher
Patin, Keith James
 8th Grade Soc Stud Teacher
Reese, Lorelle Leonard
 Fourth Grade Teacher
Robin, Aaron James
 Band Director
Sharpe, Linda Stevens
 Language Art Teacher
Thibodeaux, Brenda Bertrand
 Teacher of Gifted Students
Touchet, Diane Roberts
 Gifted English I & II Teacher
Waguespack, Gerald Edward
 Director of Bands
Welcome, Preston M. Jr.
 Principal
Zammit, Pamela Smith
 8th Grade History Teacher
Zokai, Ellen Kay (Viator)
 6th-8th Grade Language Teacher

LAFITTE
Noel, Amelia Gail M.
 Fourth Grade Teacher

LAKE ARTHUR
Broussard, Evelyn Baudoin
 Bus/Fr/Cmptr Literacy Teacher
Broussard, Ida L.
 7th/8th Grade Lang/Sci Teacher
Linscombe, Ruth David
 5th Grade Teacher

LAKE CHARLES
Darnutzer, Debra Hebert
 Second Grade Teacher
Dent, Eunice Simmons
 Reading Teacher
Foster, Karen King
 English & Reading Teacher
Harrell, Frank Barnes
 Assistant Principal
Le Maire, Roselyn
 Sixth Grade Teacher
Mc Knight, Gladys Gwendolyn
 Choral/Keyboard Music Teacher
Orphey, Eary Goins
 Science Teacher
Rogers, W. R.
 Math Dept Chairman/Teacher
Sandford, Janice Mayfield
 Jr HS Social Studies Teacher
Vincent, Esther Davis
 Middle School Counselor
Wilkinson, Juanita S.
 Home Economics Teacher

LAROSE
Arcement, Sylviane Benaim
 Third Grade Teacher
Briscoe, Ronald Malcolm
 English Department Chair
Gautreaux, Camile A.
 Math/Cmptr Literacy Teacher

LECOMPTE
Jones, Rosa Scott
 Assistant Principal

LEESVILLE
Anderson, Tammy Laborde
 8th Grade English Teacher
Lambright, Kevin David
 Social Studies Teacher

LOCKPORT
Martin, Marjorie Parr
 Sixth Grade Teacher

LOGANSPORT
Coles, Mellissa Kneece
 English-History Teacher
Land, Debra Lynn Pogue
 English/Speech Teacher
Marshall, Osie Roberson
 Fourth Grade Teacher

LONGVILLE
Hornsby, Nancy Gary
 Elementary Teacher
McGee, Carl Owen
 Social Studies Teacher/Coach

MANDEVILLE
Reynolds, Victoria Anne
 Social Studies Teacher
Thompson, Linda Guarino
 Seventh Grade Science Teacher

MANGHAM
Handy, Ruby Hudson
 7th-8th Grade Reading Teacher
Knapp, Linda Singley
 English/Spanish Teacher

MARKSVILLE
Barbin, Geraldine Marie
 Science Teacher

MARRERO
Barbe, Susan Moley
 Mathematics Teacher
Bonham, Lane E.
 Teacher of Gifted/Talented Sci
Eugene, Marion Lee
 8th Grade English Teacher
Fiegel, Colleen Georgette
 Biology Teacher

MARTHAVILLE
Jordan, Kathy Foshee
 Junior High Math Teacher

MAURICE
Campbell, Carolyn Marceaux
 English Teacher

MELVILLE
Sanders, Jessie
 Kindergarten Teacher

MERRYVILLE
Mc Keivier, James A. III
 Teacher/Coach/Athletic Dir

METAIRIE
Adams, Cindy L.
 Reading & Religion Teacher
Arceneaux, Patricia Shannon
 Social Studies Teacher
Brady, Erin
 Third Grade Teacher
Cheek, Gayle Gulotta
 Counselor
Frigo, Anthony T.
 Band Director
Goldsby, Dianne Simpson
 Math Coordinator
Guajardo, Charles
 Fine Arts Chairman
Kropog, Susan Resor
 Assistant Principal
Lewis, Donna Bethune
 Director of Admissions
Maguire, Martha Ellen
 English Teacher
Nettleton, Lucetta Corley
 Fifth Grade Teacher
Rosenbaum, William Leopold
 Counselor & Psychology Teacher
Schaefer, Karen Koster
 4th Grade Teacher
Tadlock, Susan Melady
 Mathematics Teacher

MIDLAND
Leger, Bradley A.
 Voc Agriculture Instructor

MINDEN
Overstreet, Sarah Colvin
 Mathematics Department Chair

MONROE
Collins, Rubie M. (Brown)
 Science Teacher
De Tiege, Frank J.
 Sixth Grade Teacher
Fisher, Pat Twiner
 Chem Teacher/Sci Dept Chair
Fletcher, Carol Anne
 Business Teacher
Harrison, Gwendolyn Greer
 Social Studies Teacher
Mc Carter, Tamra Paul
 Gifted Math/English Teacher
Ricks, Mary Heflin
 First Grade Teacher
Rogers, James Robert
 Mathematics Teacher/Chair
Taylor, Ollie Mae
 English Teacher
Trevillion, Janis Pepper
 English Teacher
Tucker, Mary Helen (Price)
 English Teacher

Turner, Shirley Ann Thompson
 2nd Grade Teacher
Underwood, Peggy Sue (Carter)
 Advanced English I Teacher

MONTGOMERY
Kaufman, Cynthia Bagwell
 Spanish/English Teacher

MORGAN CITY
Alfred, Kenneth Edward
 Principal
Boudreaux, Wilbert
 Accounting Teacher
Holley, Mildred Norris
 High School Teacher
Lamunyon, Kelly Broussard
 Jr HS Home Economics Teacher
Myers, Susanne Dupuis
 Bio Teacher/Sci Dept Coord
Nails, Raymond Fulton
 English Department Chairman

NATCHITOCHES
Findley, James Lee
 Humanities Faculty
Methvin, Koleta Giles
 2nd Grade Teacher

NEW IBERIA
Marceaux, Raymond Joseph
 Chemistry Teacher

NEW ORLEANS
Bloom, Giselda Dill
 Third Grade Teacher
Boyd, Patricia Quarels
 Science Department Chair
Cherrie, Lolita V.
 Third Grade Teacher
Chighizola, June Fey
 Computer Science/Math Teacher
Costa, Alicia Christina SSF
 Mathematics Dept Chairperson
Davis, Morris Anthony Jr.
 Teacher/Head Coach
Douglas, Leroy
 Social Studies Teacher
Foucher, Joycelyn Ogle
 Sixth Grade Teacher
Hayden, Helena
 Teacher
Henry, Betty Gauthreaux
 Retired Teacher
Hicks, Gloria Prevost
 Kindergarten Teacher
Irvin, Leah Clark
 Sixth Grade Teacher
King, Donna Foster
 5th Grade Chairperson
Knight, Showalter Alton
 Classics Teacher
Layman, Charles Clifton Jr.
 Communications Teacher
Le Blanc, Loree
 English Teacher
Leonard, Barbara Ballard
 Science Teacher
Lew, Linda Chin
 Teacher of Gifted Math
Magnuson, Frank Earl
 Math Teacher
Metoyer, Kathy Bradley
 Special Education Teacher
Mitchell, Carol Lacinak
 Mathematics Department Chair
Mitchell, Jimmie Eugene
 Science Teacher
Phipps, Lois Ewell
 English Teacher
Piglia, Jacqueline M.
 Eighth Grade Teacher
Proctor, Linda Jean
 Science Teacher/Coach
Rovaris, Katie Moore
 English Teacher
Sander, Stephanie Ann
 5th Grade & Ranking Teacher
Sneed, Barara Follins
 French/Spanish Teacher
Stierwald, Marlene Lydia
 Rdng, Eng, Soc Stud Teacher
Tedesco, Janet Roux
 Math/Computer Dept Chair
Washington, Brenda Crockett
 Fifth Grade Teacher
Welch, Eli Jr.
 Physical Education Dept Chair
Young, Linda Auzout
 Fifth Grade Teacher

NEWELLTON
Doyle, Connie Mason
 3rd Grade Teacher
Williams, Robert Earl
 Social Studies Teacher

OAK GROVE
Nagem, Evelyn Trichell
First Grade Teacher

OAKDALE
Carraway, Laura D.
1st & 2nd Grade Teacher
Coleman, Linda Marie Citizen
1st-4th Grade Phys Ed Teacher
Yarbrough, Ruth E.
French/Spanish/English Teacher

OBERLIN
Jefferson, Hazel
Language Art Teacher

OPELOUSAS
Chenier, Eva Picou
Science & Physical Ed Teacher
Cortez, Mildred S.
Fifth Grade Teacher
Kimble, Rita Broussard
1st Grade Teacher
Mayer, Jeannie Bercier
2nd Grade Teacher
Reynolds, Beverly Ann Handy
8th Grade Eng/Rdng Teacher
Summers, Oren Charles
Advanced Math/Physics Teacher

PATTERSON
Rabalais, Robert Paul
Music Department Chair

PAULINA
Bourgeois, Catherine Waguespack
Fourth Grade Teacher

PEARL RIVER
Boone, James Raymond
Biology 1 & 2 Teacher
Delcarpio, Kathryne Cooper
English/Spanish Teacher
Le Blanc, Margaret Jumonville
Director/Elementary School

PINEVILLE
Sanders, Cynthia Casselmann
First Grade Teacher

PLAQUEMINE
Borruano, Susie P.
Business Teacher

PONCHATOULA
Felder, Paulette Maurin
Third Grade Teacher
Harper, Karin Williams
Science Dept Chairperson
Muscarella, Louis Monistere
Science Teacher
Settoon, Kathy R.
Elementary Teacher
Todd, James William
7th Grade Soc Stud Teacher

PRAIRIEVILLE
Ourso, Charlene Gomez
7th Grade Social Studies

PROVENCAL
Hoffpauir, Frances Miller
First Grade Teacher

RAYNE
Dubus, Charlene Mouton
Home Economics Teacher
Guillory, Ted Dwaine
8th Grade Science Teacher
Kahn, Marguerite K.
Librarian

RESERVE
Greenland, Gaynor Draper
Math/Science Teacher

ROANOKE
Brown, Raymond Eugene
Assistant Principal
Pierce, Donna Breaux
Librarian

ROSEPINE
Berry, Jack G. W. II
Elementary Phys Ed Teacher

ROUGON
Robertson, Gary P.
Social Studies Teacher

RUSTON
Boyd, Barbara Liner
Second Grade Teacher
Bullock, Patsy Pesnell
7th/8th Grade Math Teacher
Dick, Linda Wright
Teacher of Gifted & Talented
Gaulden, Beatrice Gilliam
Elementary Teacher
Hammock, Mamie Brown
Physical Education/Coach

Hay, Patrice Hilton
Kindergarten Teacher

SAINT AMANT
Davis, Kathy Mc Waters
Chemistry & Phys Sci Teacher

SAINT BERNARD
Rodi, Linda M.
Fourth Grade Teacher

SAINT JAMES
Scieneaux, Deloris Jackson
English Teacher

SAINT JOSEPH
Blanche, Tonya Lewis
5th/6th Grade Teacher

SCHRIEVER
Landry, Linda Dugas
Reading Lab Teacher

SCOTT
Andrus, Mary Patricia Hymel
Home Economics/Science Teacher
Cormier, Irene Watson
Third Grade Teacher

SHREVEPORT
Austin, Diane Cooper
Counselor
Baker, Dorothy Moore
7th-8th Grade Reading Teacher
Benjamin, Margaret Hutton
Biology Teacher/Chairperson
Carter, Gloria Stratton
Fifth Grade Teacher
Chandler, Renae Havard
Third Grade Teacher
Dinkins, Glenda Allums
Third Grade Teacher
Fair, William R.
Drama Teacher
Fuller, Ola Patterson
Fourth Grade Teacher
Gholson, John Samuel
Curriculum Coordinator Teacher
Henderson, Ronald W.
Chemistry Teacher
Mashell, Linda Cooper
Third Grade Teacher
Meredith, David Earl
Mathematics/Geometry Teacher
Newberry, Jane Leslie
Eighth Grade Teacher
Parrish, Pamela Knight
English Teacher
Pope, Connie Roach
Third Grade Teacher
Qualey, Barbara Wyche
1st Grade Teacher
Sloan, Nellwyn Delores Lee
Teacher
Timmons, Sandra Groves
English Teacher
Whitehead, Barbara Ann
Soc Stud/Amer His Dept Head

SIMSBORO
Ferrel, Sherri Barfield
Science Teacher
Woodard, Judy Fallin
Jr HS Language Arts Teacher

SLIDELL
Boudreaux, Darnell Noonan
Soc Stud Dept Chm/Teacher
Culotta, Joseph Jr.
Chemistry & Physics Teacher
Glaser, Louise Wagner
First Grade Teacher
Kopfler, Judith Hall
Director/Founder
Myers, Gloria Hay
Second Grade Teacher
Wade, Gwen Elaine
Principal

SPEARSVILLE
Post, Claire Bennett
Kindergarten Teacher

SPRINGFIELD
Foster, Paulette Hebert
Teacher

STARKS
Miller, Vivian Arlene
Kindergarten Teacher
Young, Ginger Eilene
Mid Sch English Teacher

START
Cooper, Barbara Mayo
5th Grade Teacher

STONEWALL
Graham, Robert Taylor Jr.
Agriculture Science Teacher

SULPHUR
Andreyk, Alice Hulls
Fifth Grade Teacher
Bailey, Patricia Hensley
Mathematics Teacher
Jackson, Timothy
Biology Teacher
Woods, Joyce Hewitt
Fifth Grade Teacher

SUNSET
Richard, Dudy Stelly
Business Teacher/Voc Coord

THIBODAUX
Bonvillain, Shirley K.
Business Teacher
Bouterie, Karen Hebert
5th Grade Lang Arts Teacher
Sargent, Lloyd Lionel
7th/8th Grade Science Teacher

TICKFAW
Lavigne, Deborah Mc Donald
Junior High Science Teacher

TIOGA
Sanders, Patricia Smith
English Teacher

TRANSYLVANIA
Hill, Frances Jones
Language Arts Teacher

VILLE PLATTE
Boudreaux, Kathleen Duplechain
Second Grade Teacher
Joseph, Rella Marie
6th Grade Elem Teacher

VINTON
Johnson, Myra La Combe
English Teacher

VIOLET
Eckerle, Beryl B.
Fourth Grade Teacher

WELSH
Derouen, Deborah Webster
2nd Grade Teacher

WEST MONROE
Foster, Betty V.
Sophomore English Teacher
Kiper, Nancy Cooper
Gifted Mathematics Teacher
Owens, Christine C.
5th Grade Teacher
Saulsbury, Sammie Fowler
Guidance Counselor
Stringer, Delilah Roark
Librarian
Traweek, Kathryn Shaver
English Teacher

WESTLAKE
Mc Ginnis, Judith Mc Clelland
Fifth Grade Teacher
Waller, Robert Benjamin
Algebra II Teacher

WESTWEGO
Le Blanc, Linda Marie
4th & 5th Grade Math Teacher

WHITE CASTLE
Osborne, Marilyn
Second Grade Teacher

WINNFIELD
Walker, Helene Byrnes
English & Reading Teacher

WINNSBORO
Lee, John Woodie
Fifth Grade Teacher

WISNER
Caldwell, Jo Meredith
First Grade Teacher

YOUNGSVILLE
Le Doux, Rita Tate
Math Teacher

ZACHARY
Anderson, Vivian Norsworthy
Speech Teacher
Washington, Carnell S.
History/Law Teacher

ZWOLLE
Cole, Rita R.
English Teacher

MAINE

AUGUSTA
Jackson, Michael Bryant
Industrial Arts Teacher

BERWICK
Thompson, Mary Pamela
10th Grade English Teacher

BETHEL
Melville, Beverly Lurvey
English Teacher
Pooley, Bonnie I.
English Teacher

BIDDEFORD
Mac Phail, Marion Jane
First Grade Teacher/Asst Prin

BOOTHBAY HARBOR
Lunt, John S.
Computer Coordinator
O'Connell, Eugenie Waugh
Choral Dir & Music Teacher

BRUNSWICK
Lieke, Richard Frederick
Chemistry Teacher

BUCKSPORT
Clapp, Kathleen Lyons
Mathematics Teacher

CAMDEN
Read, Harry Wilson
Health Coordinator/Educator
Seymour, Charles O.
Band Director

CARIBOU
Perreault, Stephen Mark
Science/Social Studies Teacher
Thibodeau, Carol H.
Biology Teacher

CARMEL
Stewart, Harold F.
Principal

CLINTON
Hatch, Stephen Daniel
5th Grade Teacher

CORINNA
Darrah, Vicki-Anne R.
First Grade Teacher

DOVER-FOXCROFT
Mac Pherson-Allen, Dawn
Honors English/AP Coordinator

EAST LEBANON
Lister, Roger Edward
Fourth Grade Teacher

EAST MILLIONCKET
Michaud, David R.
Business Teacher

FAIRFIELD
Jonassen, Lars Eric
7th Grade Teacher

FORT KENT
Gardner, Paula Lynn
Seventh Grade Lang Art Teacher

FRYEBURG
Barker, Durland B.
Accounting Instructor
Carpenter, Barbara Y.
English Teacher
Fredrick, Patrick J.
Art Teacher

GEORGETOWN
Goodman, Charles Christopher
Principal

GORHAM
Applebaun, Leslie Jill
Secondary English Teacher
Jenkins, Kevin A.
Mathematics Teacher
Mountain, Lillian Tierney
Third Grade Teacher
Roy, Deborah Couture
Spanish Teacher/Dept Chair

HOULTON
Blanchette, Donald James
Fourth Grade Teacher

JONESPORT
Reed, Gwendolyn Hartford
6-8th Grade Lang Arts Teacher
Robinson, Barbara Chamberlain
Kindergarten Teacher

KENNEBUNK
Evanoff, Jacqueline Lembree
2nd Grade Teacher

KINGFIELD
Clarke, Jeffrey Keith
Dean of Students & Teacher
Juers, Douglas H.
Mathematics/Science Teacher

KINGMAN
Roach, Jacquelyn Boutot
Kindergarten Teacher

LEWISTON
Ricker, Geraldine Margaret
Fourth Grade Teacher

LIVERMORE FALLS
Wallace, Frances C.
Business Education Teacher

MACHIAS
Walls, Vivian Burgess
First Grade Teacher

MARS HILL
Broad, Sharon Mersereau
Fifth Grade Teacher
Norsworthy, Remillie Ann (Good)
French/English/Art Teacher

OLD TOWN
Lucas, Bernie A. Jr.
Fourth Grade Teacher

OXFORD
Sturdivant, Brenda Adams
Fourth Grade Teacher

PALERMO
Glidden, Betty Tibbetts
Language Art/Soc Stud Teacher
Robbins, Marjorie Gilmartin
Second & Third Grade Teacher

PORTLAND
Beal, Pamela Louise
Fifth Grade Teacher
Mc Garry, Cynthia Knight
Religious Education Director
White, Richard Carlton
Mathematics Department Teacher

RUMFORD
Hayes, Duane Cole
4th Grade Teacher

SABATTUS
Blais, Armand
Third Grade Teacher

SACO
Wood, Frances M.
Language Department Chair

SANFORD
Lamoreau, Susan Beverly
Business Teacher

SCARBOROUGH
Snow, John O.
7th/8th Grade Science Teacher

SOUTH BERWICK
Burnell, Gerald William
Asst Prin/Soc Studies Teacher
Downey, John Francis III
Latin Teacher/Coach
Raposa, Daniel George Jr.
Civics Teacher/Athletic Dir

SOUTH PORTLAND
Small, Peter Van
Science Department Chairman

WALDOBORO
Flanagan, Rosemary Devaney
Chemistry Teacher

WATERBORO
Gamage, Jane Ellen
English Teacher

WEST BUXTON
Darling, Mary Jarema
7th Grade Soc Stud Teacher

WEST PARIS
Turk, Peggy Ann (Beagle)
1st-4th Grade Teacher

WINDHAM
Nickerson, Richard George
Director of Choral Music

WINTER HARBOR
Rudolph, Mark Helmut
5th Grade Teacher

YARMOUTH
Sorenson, Barbara Kay
3rd Grade Teacher

MARYLAND

ACCIDENT
Boord, James Edward II
Music Teacher/Fine Arts Chair
Dye, Mary Jane Trenum
6th Grade Soc Stud Teacher
Farrar, Richard B. Jr.
Biology Teacher
Jackson, Jeffrey Maxwell
Computer Teacher
Langley, Denise Blank
Mathematics Department Head
Law, Barbara Doyle
Home Economics Teacher
Miller, Maxine Klink
Fifth Grade Teacher
Warne, Sandra Parish
Language Arts/Reading Teacher

ADELPHI
Palmer, Pamela Elyn
US History Teacher

ANNAPOLIS
Christy, Rachel Taylor
Fourth Grade Teacher
Crane, Brian William
Mathematics Dept Chair
Radosevich, Linda Long
English Teacher
Rey, Nancy Spurlin
Third Grade Teacher
Solano, Louis Emil
Fifth Grade Teacher

ARBUTUS
Cheek, Judith Anne
Third Grade Teacher

ARNOLD
Vahsen, Faustena Fradd
Science Teacher

BALTIMORE
Anderson, Helen Griffin
Fifth Grade Teacher
Boston, Beverly Danielle
Mathematics Department Head
Boyd, Nikie Johnson
Science Teacher
Butler, Ann Pollard
Pre-School Teacher
Corson, Janet L. (Smith)
Foreign Lang Dept Chairperson
Drummond, James William Jr.
Fifth Grade Teacher
Duncovich, Mark Richard
Social Studies Teacher
Fearrington, Priscilla Epps
Second Grade Teacher
Fischer, Ted F.
Fifth Grade Teacher
Freeman, Dorothy Lee
Principal
Gudenius, Barbara Hamaker
English Department Head
Hill, Shirley Butler
Mathematics Teacher
Horowicz, Richard Edmund
History Teacher
Jack, Winifred Bookhout
Social Studies Dept Chair
Katzbeck, Raeann Getty
Teacher/Coordinator
Kolb, Mary L.
Mathematics Dept Chairperson
Kuchta, Linda Zaccari
Sixth Grade Teacher
Lindsey, Marie Evon Poe
3rd Grade Teacher
Luca, Mary Kay Minehart
ASWAS Teacher
Mc Cullough, Fannie Rogers
Fourth Grade Teacher
Moore, Prentiss II
Health/Science Teacher
Petrosino, Vincent Joseph
Foreign Languages Dept Head
Pope, James O.
Band Instructor
Posey-Hooper, Bettye Mc Cullough
Mathematics & Religion Teacher
Pruce, Gloria Forshlager
Teacher
Rasinski, Kathleen Stundick
Mathematics Teacher
Reese, Alan Carroll
English Teacher
Stauffer, David Brian
Music Instrumental Teacher
Thompson, Debruah Abruette Green
French & Latin Teacher
Wagner, Henry Vincent Jr.
Assistant Principal

Westray, Sharon Smith
Fifth Grade Teacher
Yaniger, Marilyn Trinkle
Guidance Counselor

BEL AIR
Boni, Mary Helterline
5th Grade Teacher
Gradishar, Susan Clor
9th-12th Grade Math Teacher
Greene, Richard Lee
Assistant Principal
Miller, Edward Hohman
Russian Lang & History Teacher
Minderlein, Philip Joseph
Social Studies Dept Chairman
Oswald, Joseph Steven
Science Teacher

BELTSVILLE
Bartlett, Susan D.
Instrumental Music Teacher
Beier, Alan M.
Chemistry Teacher
Braxton, Sheila Melinda
English Teacher
Hanka, Deborah Rae (Heironimus)
8th Grade US History Teacher
Minor, Eleanor True
Vocal/General Music Teacher
Starr, Wilfred Eugene
English & Soc Stud Teacher
Young, Raymond L.
Math Teacher

BERLIN
Carey, Thomas Kenny
Social Studies Teacher
Kuhn, Kathryn Erna
Highly Able Special Enrichment
Larimore, Dora Trader
Math Teacher
Vathis, James B.
World History Teacher

BETHESDA
Audilet, Devereux Oldfield
Chemistry/Biology Teacher
June, Deana
First Grade Teacher
Mc Geehin, Cynthia Marie Sears
Science Department Chair
Walsh, Irene C. Plisko
Science Dept Chair

BLADENSBURG
Bernache, Carolyn
Resource Specialist - ESOL
Klapper, Margery Mahler
English/Journalism Teacher
Kovach, Sandra Mary
Health Occupations Instructor
Leigh, Gary Andre
Math Teacher
Russell, Barbara A.
English Teacher

BOONSBORO
Eves, Adair
Reading Department Chair
Parks, K.
English Teacher
Scott, Dwight Lewis
Phys Ed Chair/Athletic Dir
Sturiolo, Janice Fiedor
Mathematics Teacher

BOWIE
Dove, Thomas Leland
Computer Coordinator
Durelli, Monique Juana
Spanish Teacher
Hayes, Myra Dunlap
Chapter I Home/School Teacher
Pearl, Lauren F
Foreign Lang Dept Chair
Rainville, Kathleen (Sullivan)
Latin/French Teacher
Snipes, Jessica Johnson
Fifth Grade Teacher
Walch, Shirley Casto
First Grade Teacher

BROOKLANDVILLE
Durfee, Sandra Sundquist
English Department Chairperson
Mc Fadden, Mary Clare Romans
Physical Education Teacher
Midura, Patricia Mulhall
Mass Media Chair/Lit Teacher

BRUNSWICK
Crone, Kathy Elizabeth
Third Grade Teacher
Powell, Jennifer Anne
7th Grade Soc Stud Teacher
Stevens, Teresa Rice
Ag/Horticulture Teacher

Thomas, Charles P.
8th Grade Team Leader

CAPITOL HEIGHTS
Henry, Michael Scott
International Studies Coord

CECILTON
Kedziora, Helene J.
4th Grade Teacher

CHESAPEAKE CITY
Casper, Carol Staats
Language Art Classroom Teacher

CHESTERTOWN
Vansant, Anne Burton
Third Grade Teacher

CHILDS
Reppert, Nelda G.
English & Music Teacher

CHURCHVILLE
Davis, Martha Demeter
Teaching Assistant Principal
Puckett, Anne Dukes
Second Grade Teacher

CLEAR SPRING
Swisher, Charles E. Jr.
School Counselor
Tabler, Debra Griffith
Math Department Chairperson

CLINTON
Harris, Emma Williams
Fifth/Sixth Grade Teacher
Stubbs, Thomas Albert
History/English Teacher

COLLEGE PARK
Mc Grath, Patrick Carrel
Teaching Assistant
Prior, Richard Edmon
Latin/Teaching Assistant

COLUMBIA
Frnech, Jacqueline Marie
Elementary Teacher

CUMBERLAND
Grimm, Angela Irene
Social Studies Teacher
Humbertson, Bonnie R.
8th Grade Reading Specialist
Winterberg, James Joseph
6th Grade Teacher

DENTON
Dize, Joan Fountain
Third Grade Teacher

DUNDALK
Carl, Richard David Jr.
Mathematics Teacher

EASTON
Hren, Diane Copelton
Science Department Chair
Murphy, Hope Stewart
Mathematics Teacher

EDGEMERE
Thanner, James Frederick
English Department Chair

ELKTON
Artinger, John
Social Studies Teacher
Verratti, Michele Gawel
Mathematics Teacher
Wesley, Thomas Gregory
Guidance Counselor

FEDERALSBURG
Andrew, Donna Lomax
Mathematics Teacher
Henry, Tina Geneva
Physical Science Teacher

FORESTVILLE
Kearns, J. Timothy
History/Geography Teacher
King, Linda Marie
French/Spanish/English Teacher
Nelson, Sandra Lucas
Mathematics Teacher
Spitzer, Joseph Lawrence
Third Grade Teacher
Steel, Narissa
English Teacher

FORT GEORGE MEADE
Hall, Carolyn Ruth
Sixth Grade Teacher

FREDERICK
Campagnoli, Kathy J.
English Teacher
Haller, Norma Rae
Third Grade Teacher

La Croce, Julianne Bainbridge
English Teacher/Guidance Cnslr
Miller, Tony
Social Studies Teacher
Waggoner, Laura Noel
Math Teacher
Wallace, Linda Kay
5th Grade Teacher

FRUITLAND
Frey, Nancy Brubaker
First Grade Teacher

GAITHERSBURG
Conger, Ronald Jesse
NJROTC Associate Instructor
Krayer, William Reed
Science Teacher
Lawrence, Barbra Jean (Bitto)
Fourth Grade Teacher
Vanderfrift, Mavis Johnson
3rd Grade Teacher

GARRISON
Parker, Mary Louise
Chemistry/Physics Teacher

GERMANTOWN
Early, Gilbert Neal
Social Studies Teacher

GLEN BURNIE
Carson, Sharon Farley
Spanish Teacher
Sayre, Cathy
Third Grade Teacher
Talarigo, Kim M.
Administrative Trainee
Zimbro, Albert D.
History Teacher

GLENELG
Godwin, William Joseph Jr.
Advanced History Teacher
Kincaid, Ginger Lee
Physical Education Dept Chair
Mundy, James Patrick
Social Studies Teacher

GLENWOOD
Du Bois, Ann Forgie
5th Grade Teacher/Team Leader
Kelly, Mary Lou
Science Teacher

GREENBELT
Elliott-Banks, Janice Dunlap
8th Grade English Teacher

GREENSBORO
Cook, Barbara Helms
Kindergarten Teacher

HAGERSTOWN
Beard, Robert Joseph Jr.
English Teacher/Administrator
Brewer, Gilbert Lee Jr.
Math/Science/Cmptr Sci Teacher
Carmel, Carol Feeley
Third Grade Teacher
Cline, Roland Douglas
Math Dept Chair/Math Teacher
Grove, Douglas Edward
Math Teacher
Hamberger, Nan Marie
11th Grade English Teacher
Kreiger, Frederick Donald Jr.
Govt Teacher/Coach
Priest, John Michael
History Teacher
Rotz, Duane L.
English Teacher

HAMPSTEAD
Errickson, Robin Rae
7th Grade Soc Stud Teacher

HANCOCK
Golden, Melinda Barnhart
Chemistry/Science Teacher
Higgins, Susan Stanley
4th Grade Teacher

HAVRE DE GRACE
Gregory, Ann H.
5th Grade Teacher
Horner, William Alvie
6th Grade Science Teacher

HILLCREST HEIGHTS
Bloyce, Ezekiel Alphonso
8th Grade Science Teacher
Rosenblatt, Marjorie Baker
Reading Specialist

HYATTSVILLE
Allison, Nancy Lee (Morrow)
First Grade Teacher
Conway, Donald Purnell
Elem Phys Ed Teacher/Coach

Mace, Myra Annette
Phys Sci/Gen Math/Life Sci
Morris, Crystal James
10th Grade English Teacher
Price, Joseph William
7th/8th Grade Phys Sci Teacher

INDIAN HEAD
Henry, Marie Dodson
Mathematics Teacher
Stine, James M. Jr.
Social Studies Teacher
Wisniewski, Lisa Klares
English/Work Study Teacher

JOPPA
Hodges, Janet Kennedy
6th Grade Math Teacher

LA PLATA
Coen, Lawrence Arthur
English Teacher
Gray, Susan Elizabeth
6th/7th Grade Science Teacher
Horsey, Geraldine E. Warren
Teacher
Howard, Margaret Burch
Vice Prin/5th Grade Teacher
Jameson, Phyllis Morrow
2nd Grade English Teacher
Lyons, Sara K.
6th/7th Grade Math Teacher
Olson, Polly (Leona) Ellis
Science Dept Chairman

LANHAM SEABROOK
Honecker, David Warren
Social Studies Teacher
Randolph, Kevin William
Social Studies Teacher
Stein, Barbara Linda
Sixth Grade Teacher
Terry, Betty Davis
5th/6th Grade Lang Art Teacher
Zinaman, Helaine M.
Talented & Gifted Prgm Coord

LAUREL
Herrington, Umbrenda
Fourth Grade Teacher
Hunt, Emilie Winifred
French Teacher/Dept Chair
Kidd, Carol (Winston)
French Teacher
Pavlacka, James Anthony
Science/Mathematics Teacher
Strong, Priscilla Tull
Second Grade Teacher

LINTHICUM HEIGHTS
Meeks, Francine Celeste (Garrett)
4th-6th Grade Science Teacher

LONACONING
Montgomery, Rose Winner
Second Grade Teacher
Smith, Marcia Babcock
Business Education Teacher

LOVEVILLE
Gabbert, Kay Dill
2nd Grade Teacher

LUSBY
Gensor, Lynne Mary (Wink)
Language & Reading Teacher

MIDDLETOWN
Wise, Marsha Shober
8th Grade Lang Arts Teacher
Zink, John Henry
Science Teacher

MILLINGTON
Potts, Charlotte Jeffers
First Grade Teacher

MOUNT AIRY
Scalzi, Louise Herrera
6th/7th Grade Science Teacher

MOUNT SAVAGE
Hughes, Irene Mary
English Dept Chair
Taylor, Mona Bridges
Social Studies Chairperson

OAKLAND
Beard, David C.
Civics Teacher
Fitzwater, Helen Cotrill
3rd Grade Teacher
Fleming, Linda Teets
Chapter I Resource Teacher
Freyman, William David
Vocational Drafting Teacher
Hinebaugh, Debra Kay
Fifth Grade Teacher
Martin, Patricia Ann
Fifth Grade Teacher

OAKLAND (cont)
Milburn, Debra Gianniny
Biology/Earth Science Teacher
Ryscavage, Mary Mc Cleskey
Language Arts/Soc Stud Teacher
Spiker, Shirley F.
Social Studies Teacher

OLDTOWN
Henson, Kim Allen
Social Studies Teacher

OWINGS
Cage, Candace Anne
Social Studies Teacher
Michael, Kevin Lee
Math/Computer Science Teacher
Vanderveen, Eric William
English Teacher

OWINGS MILLS
Rubin, Brenda
Judaic Studies Teacher

OXON HILL
Bell, Dianne Gardiner
Reading Specialist

PASADENA
Jepsen, Kathleen Hagerty
7th-8th Grade Eng Teacher
Moberg, Martha Jane Tully
6th Grade Science Teacher
Wilfong, Deborah June
Language Arts Teacher

PERRYVILLE
Connelly, Kevin Mark
Computer Science Teacher

POMFRET
Rogers, Carolyn Mc Daniel
Child Care Instructor
Shamdani, Rosa Nelson
French/Spanish Teacher

POOLESVILLE
Reichenbaugh, Thomas Merle
Social Studies Teacher

PORT REPUBLIC
Hammersla, Jeffrey Ward
2nd Grade Teacher

POTOMAC
Dvorsky, Victor F.
Mathematics Teacher/Chair
Morris, Claire Ann
Third Grade Teacher

PRESTON
Sturtz, Agnes Leonard
6th Grade Teacher/Admin Asst

PRINCE FREDERICK
Keosseian, Ellen Jane
English/Journalism Teacher
Keosseian, John Mark
Eng Teacher/Dir Mentor Prgm

PRINCESS ANNE
Herzins, Frank James Jr.
Social Studies Teacher

PYLESVILLE
Grub, John George
Social Studies Teacher
Starnes, David Edgar
Social Studies Teacher

RANDALLSTOWN
Wroten, Melvin Franklyn
Technology Ed Dept Chm

RISING SUN
Baker, Teresa Moore
Music Teacher
Erbe, Lewis M.
US History Teacher
Smith, Martin Robert
Sixth Grade Teacher

RIVERDALE
Hearle, Deanna Rose
Earth Sci/Bio/Chem Teacher
Martin, Joseph Andrew
Social Studies Teacher
Palmer, Linda Marie
Elem Special Education Teacher
Zacherel, Ruth Cotton
Sixth Grade Teacher

RIVIERA BEACH
Williams, Joan Monser
4th/5th Grade Lang Art Teacher

ROCKVILLE
Boucher, Charlotte Chakan
Inter Resource Instructor
Lyon, Dianne Francesconi
Social Studies Chair

Seidel, Katherine Vukelic
Eng Teacher/Honors Pgrm Coord
Seymour, Donna Carol
Fourth Grade Teacher
Wehrle, John George
Teacher-US History

ROSEDALE
Karwacki, Margaret Wolski
First Grade Teacher

SALISBURY
Householder, Brenda Jane
Health Occupations Instructor
Mac Leod, Joan Conrad
Social Studies Chair/Vice-Prin
Pratt, Joanne Phillips
Math Dept Chairperson
Vaughn, Elizabeth Cane
English Teacher

SEABROOK
Flynn, Gayle Gussman
7th Grade English Teacher
Joseph, Betty Parker
English/Reading Teacher

SEAT PLEASANT
Baccus, Amelia Diane Dunham
Third Grade Teacher

SEVERN
Bosica, Anna Marie
Religion Teacher

SEVERNA PARK
Latham, Patricia Ann
Mathematics Teacher

SILVER SPRING
George, Anne S.
Science Teacher
Wolfe, Pamela Kline
Social Studies Chairperson
Woods, Christopher Wildrick
Anatomy & Physiology Teacher

SMITHSBURG
Robertson, Earl Thomas
Biology Teacher-Sci Dept Chair
Shanholtz, Shirley Day
First Grade Teacher

SNOW HILL
Conaway, Rebecca Golt
Third Grade Teacher
Conrad, Darlene Joyce
History Teacher
Pruitt, Peggy P.
Enrichment Teacher
Smith, Warren Lee
Instructor/Professor

STEVENSVILLE
Bolyard, Paul David Jr.
7th/8th Grade US His Teacher
Honeycutt, Ava Kelley
Kindergarten Teacher

SUDLERSVILLE
Henckel, George Lee
Reading/Language Arts Teacher
Lenigan, Howard Edward
Principal
Milam, Dale Eric
Math/Sci/Religion/Phys Ed

SUITLAND
Noel, Trevia Griffin
Mathematics Teacher
Wadas, Frank Casmier Jr.
Fine Arts Department Chair

SYKESVILLE
Schnechagen, Ruth Gorey
Second Grade Teacher

TAKOMA PARK
Beach, Michele Raymonde
English Department Chair
Dunbebin, Anna Mae (Gulinello)
1st-3rd Primary Unit Teacher
Melbourne, Cavel Andrea (Beckford)
Social Studies Teacher
Rodenberg, Barbara Reid
Jr HS Sci/Math Teacher
Waller, David Lee
Vice Principal

UNION BRIDGE
Bloom, Dolores Shifler
Second Grade Teacher
Hibberd, Granville Haines
Social Studies Teacher

UPPER MARLBORO
Anderson, Cynthia S.
Physical Education Teacher
Hyde, Kathleen Scully
Health Education Teacher

Ludes, Ildiko Tunde
Art Teacher/Fine Arts Chair
Sipe, Lynn Garrison
Third Grade Teacher
Smith, Scott
Social Studies Teacher

WALDORF
Blizzard, Nancy Snyder
Gifted Ed Resource Teacher
Brown, Deborah Mc Allister
Second Grade Teacher
Fisher, William Peter
5th Grade Teacher
Fluharty, Barry Lee
Testing Coordinator
Illick, Marilyn Anita
Elementary Music Teacher
Jones, Irean V. Buckley
Third Grade Teacher
Wilson, Susan Ruth
Social Studies Teacher

WALKERSVILLE
Mummert, Michael Alvin
Business/Computer Dept Chair

WESTERNPORT
Riley, Joan Lorraine (Kidwell)
Retired

WESTMINSTER
Dotterweich, Patrick Timothy
7th Social Studies Teacher
Fogerty, Charles Vincent III
8th Grade Soc Stud Teacher
Harner, Louella Sauble
Third Grade Teacher
Kemp, Patricia
Language Arts Teacher
Lewis, Claudia Chapman
Science Teacher
Mathias, Marsha A.
Vocal Music Teacher

WHITE HALL
Wimer, Sharon Childers
5th Grade Teacher

WILLIAMSPORT
Hultslander, Jo A.
Spanish Teacher

WORTON
Fox, H. June
FM Broadcasting Teacher

MASSACHUSETTS

ACUSHNET
Foster, Nancy Morris
Second Grade Teacher
Kowalczyk, Joanne Grace
Third Grade Teacher
Santos, Sally Ross
8th Grade Mathematics Teacher

ADAMS
Getty, Ella Naberezny
Home Ec Department Team Leader

AGAWAM
Joseph, Richard Henry
Biology/Physics Teacher
Morrill, Emmet Francis
6th Grade Teacher

ANDOVER
Evans, Richard Mark
English Teacher
Finnigan, Patrick J.
Social Studies Teacher

ASHBURNHAM
Rogers, Rena (Perreault)
Fourth Grade Teacher

ASHBY
Adamowitch-LaPorte, Caryl
6th Grade Teacher

ATTLEBORO
O'Neill, Carole J.
Sixth Grade Math/Sci Teacher
Simnett, Joyce Le Claire
Third/Fourth Grade Teacher

AUBURN
Loosemoore, Marie K.
Science Teacher

BARRE
Grandone, Roberta Maki
Foreign Lang Dept Chairperson

BEDFORD
Reynolds, John Dennis
Social Studies Teacher

BELCHERTOWN
Pagos, Paula Ann
English Teacher

BEVERLY
Fonns, Matthew Charles
Humanities Instructor
Gauthier, Rhonda J.
7th Grade Math Teacher

BILLERICA
Callahan, James Francis
Science Teacher
Richards, Lucille Sawyer
Special Needs Teacher
Severo, Tom
English Teacher

BOLTON
Dugan, Maureen J.
Biology Teacher
Santagate-Sutton, Cheryl
Science Teacher

BOSTON
Chesbro, David C.
Social Studies/English Teacher
Chestnut, Sandra Eggleston
Physics Teacher
Giancristiano, Thomas F.
Social Studies Teacher
Powers, Mary Patricia
Third Grade Teacher
Salterio, Paul William
Department Head-Classics
Seyon, Patrick L. N.
US History Teacher

BOYLSTON
Barry, Irene Murray
Foreigh Language Teacher
Wentzell, Janet Marie (Freel)
6th Grade Language Art Teacher

BRAINTREE
Bandarra, Gilbert
Biology/Physiology Teacher
Grigas, Deborah Duran
6th Grade Science Teacher

BRIDGEWATER
De Lutis, Evelyn Ekberg
Kindergarten Teacher
Voto, James A.
Band Director

BRIGHTON
Dobbins, Marina
Business Dept Chairperson

BROCKTON
Campbell, Nellie Quan
Mathematics Teacher
Colvin, Rosemary Moosburner
Fifth Grade Teacher
Delaney, Phyllis Elizabeth
English Teacher
Jordan, Linda Colby
Math Resource Specialist
Rando, Jane Olson
High School English Teacher

BROOKLINE
Wiggin, Robert T.
Scndry Curriculum Coordinator

BURLINGTON
Dibella, Margaret Tompkins
8th Grade Science Teacher
Nash, Mildred Leonard
Teacher of Gifted & Talented
Vinecombe, Brenda
5th Grade Teacher

BYFIELD
Ausamara, David Swaydan
French & Spanish Teacher

CAMBRIDGE
Barrett, Mary June
First Grade Teacher
Brooks, Carol R.
Spanish Teacher
Ferolito, Joseph Anthony
Math Teacher/Advisor/Tutor
Kessler, Marcia Field
Adjunct Faculty
Larson, Lorna May
Eighth Grade Teacher
Patterson, Joyce Beatrice
2nd Grade Teacher
Payack, Christine Anne
4th/5th Grade Head Teacher
Pingree, Allison
Teaching Fellow Dept of Eng
Sumner, Donna Cellucci
Mathematics Department Chair

CARVER
Fernandes, Teresa Ann
Mathematics Teacher

CHATHAM
Ethier, Diane M.
6th Grade Teacher

CHELMSFORD
De Marais, Norman Charles
English Department Head

CHELSEA
Mietus, Maryann
4th Grade Teacher

CHICOPEE
Dawson, Sandra Louise
Vice Principal
Le Beau, Paul Anthony
Foreign Language Dept Head
Mathieu, Bernard Charles
Business Teacher
Osetek, Fred Leon
Science Teacher
Rahilly, Irene Patricia
Third Grade Teacher
Reardon, R. Purves
Principal

CLINTON
Gorman, Patricia Ann (Starr)
Third & Fourth Grade Teacher

CONCORD
Cussen, Anne
Primary Class Teacher

DANVERS
White, Brian Joseph
Biology Teacher

DARTMOUTH
Codieux, Thomas Henry
7th Grade Sci/Math Teacher

DEDHAM
Binnette, Ursula
Latin Teacher
Tomase, Carol Alessandri
English/Music Teacher

DORCHESTER
Nicholson, David Andrew
4th Grade Elem Sch Teacher
Rivers, Mary Francis White
6th Grade Teacher

DOVER
Cannon, Donald Edward
English Department Head

EAST BOSTON
Doran, Anne Marie
Fifth Grade Teacher
Maynard, Jerilyn Ouimette
Guidance Counselor

EAST BRIDGEWATER
Gagnon, Susan Miller
Teacher
Johnson, Robert Arthur
Literature & Geography Teacher

EAST LONGMEADOW
Francis, Richard T.
Specialist of Gifted Education
O'Hearn, James Brendan
English Department Chair

EASTHAMPTON
Parent, Robert Charles
6th Grade Teacher

FALL RIVER
Amiot, Claire P.
5th Grade Teacher
Barnaby, Anne Marie Fayan
Mathematics Dept Teacher
Furze, Cheryl Clarke
2nd Grade Teacher
Martel, Paul R.
Spanish/French Teacher
Rose, Nancy Silvia
French Teacher
Sullivan, Paul M. SJ
History Teacher/Assoc Prin

FEEDING HILLS
Hatheway, Margaret Coffey
Third Grade Teacher
Hegarty, Dorothy Lepore
Orchestra Director

FITCHBURG
Belli, Josephine
5th Grade Teacher
Brodeur, Loraine Ann (Candelet)
1st-5th Grade Music Teacher
Chakemian, K. Kenneth
Foreign Language Instructor

FITCHBURG (cont)
Dorsey, Jeff
Vice Principal
Dyer, Barbara Anita (O'Mara)
High School Science Teacher
Fitzpatrick, Karen A. Boudreau
Kindergarten Teacher
Grautski, Ronald Paul
Anatomy/Physiology Teacher
Morrilly, Elizabeth Jeffers
Elementary Guidance Counselor

FOXBORO
Myers-Pachla, Diana M.
Social Studies Teacher

FRANKLIN
Geysen, Thomas Francis
English Teacher
Menize, Elena Orvani
Math Teacher

GARDNER
Moriarty, Lucy Catherine
English Teacher

GRAFTON
Malkasian, Claire Tashjian
Reading/English Teacher

GRANBY
O'Neill, Patricia Cuff
3rd Grade Teacher

GROTON
Beck, Maureen Vincent
Social Services Prgms Director
Chadwick, Alden Carpenter
Science Teacher
Rutherford, Kathleen A.
Retired

HADLEY
Tudryn, Elaine Mary
Fifth-Sixth Grade Teacher

HATFIELD
Steinglein, Barbara
Second Grade Teacher

HAVERHILL
Ghee, Myrta Ramirez
5-8th Grade Bilingual Teacher
Gorski, Linda Urbalonis
Kindergarten Teacher
Quinney, Carol A.
7th/8th Grade English Teacher
Silveria, John F.
English Teacher

HILLCREST HEIGHTS
Smalls, Curtis Marie Forte
Social Studies Dept Chair

HINGHAM
O'Neill, Marylee Ritter
History Department Chairman

HOLBROOK
Tanner, Phyllis (Satter)
English/Reading Dept Chair

HOLDEN
Komenda, Alison B.
Mathematics Teacher

HOLYOKE
Jonker, Jean E. (Borowski)
English Teacher
Mc Donough, Mary T.
First Grade Teacher

HOPEDALE
Packard, Lee Edward
Sixth Grade Teacher

HOPKINTON
Krause, Jan Geist
English Teacher/Dept Chair

HYANNIS
Gardner, Ruth Ann Marshall
Assistant to Band Director

JAMAICA PLAIN
Green, Ernest A.
Mathematics Teacher

KINGSTON
Hopkins, Bonnie Clapper
Sixth Grade Teacher
Record, Luci Lagarto
English Teacher
Sorrento, Charles Robert
Art Teacher

LAWRENCE
Brooks, Ralph Gordon
English as Second Lang Teacher
Mc Cue, Leo Francis Jr.
Social Studies Dept Chair
Payano, Pedro
Eighth Grade Teacher

LEICESTER
Soojian, Paul Krikor
Grade 7 Science Teacher
Ziarko, Paula Agnes (Murray)
Second Grade Teacher

LEOMINSTER
Andrews, Anne C.
Teacher
Kenney, Clifford Orrin
4th Grade Teacher
Wennerberg, Carl Lawrence
7th Grade Math Teacher
Whittemore, George Charles
Physics Teacher

LEXINGTON
Daileanes, Kostas
English Teacher
Kollen, Vicki L. (Simms)
Spanish/French Teacher

LINCOLN
Como, Florence J.
Fifth Grade Teacher

LONGMEADOW
Dudley, Ann Austin
Foreign Language Chairperson

LOWELL
Hersey, Judith Tracy
Sixth Grade Teacher

LUDLOW
Yando, Raymond A.
Mathematics Teacher

LUNENBURG
Bennett, Larry James
Fourth Grade Teacher
Daukantas, Cynthia Pochini
Assistant Principal
Diamantopoulos, Dale Mitchell
Phys Ed/Health Teacher
Giesman, Beth A.
Fourth Grade Teacher

LYNN
Bernardo, Carolan Penkul
Math Teacher
De Amato, Lorraine Theresa
Science Teacher
Flamer, Celeste Althea
Fifth Grade Teacher
Griffen, Carol M.
Math-Algebra/Cluster Leader
Hegan, Donna Jane
Jr HS Mathematics Teacher
O'Brien, Gerald Leo
English Teacher
Smithers, Delores Lorraine
Principal/French Teacher

LYNNFIELD
Naylor, Gail E. Doherty
5th Grade Teacher
Needham, Marjorie Louise
3rd Grade Teacher

MALDEN
Bari, Flavia
Fourth Grade Teacher
Brown, Dana Francis
Teacher/Peer Leader Advisor
Chaplick, Virginia (Goodhue)
English Teacher
Kassabian, Nancy Bazarian
Spanish/French Teacher
Sasso, Patricia Ann Valente
Eng as Second Lang Teacher

MANCHESTER
Mentus, L. Tammy
Sci/Youth Challenge Teacher

MANSFIELD
Knowles, Beatrice Milliken
Fourth Grade Teacher
Vintro, Richard Allen
6th Grade Soc Stud Teacher

MARBLEHEAD
Cormier, Madeleine Tufts
Fourth Grade Teacher
Goldstein, Audrey R. (Gordon)
English Teacher
Le Clerc, Donald Robert
Phys Ed/Cmptr Teacher
Orlen, Gerald L.
Social Studies Teacher
Patach, Richard Charles
Physics Teacher
Towle, Donald Alan
Science Teacher

MARSHFIELD
Courchesne, Robert Eugene
Fr Teacher/Foreign Lang Coord

MATTAPAN
Robertson, Josephine Angela
English/Reading Teacher

MAYNARD
Klepadlo, Shirley J.
Chemistry Teacher

MEDFORD
Ritchie, Thomas Joseph Jr.
Electrical Shop Teacher
Rutstein, Barbara Lerner
Mathematics Department Teacher

MELROSE
Squatrito, Francis Paul
Assistant Director of Fine Art

METHUEN
Gibson, Kathleen Hammond
5th Grade Teacher

MIDDLEBORO
Denise, Robert Joseph
Business Education Teacher
Smith, Bonnie (Mac Aulay)
Fifth Grade Teacher

MILFORD
Campbell, Harriet Laverne
8th Grade Math Teacher
Coffey, Francis G.
Fifth Grade Teacher
Longo, Ann Marie
French-Spanish Teacher
Mobilia, Maria De Palma
Fifth Grade Teacher
Niro, Antonio M. Jr.
Teacher

MILTON
Mc Cabe, Frank James
Sales & Sales Trng

MONSON
Matrow, Peter Francis
5th Grade Teacher
Spear, Gail W.
French Teacher

MONTAGUE
Libby, Sophia Mary
Social Studies Teacher

NATICK
Baggs, Cheryl A.
German Teacher

NEEDHAM
Altman, Leslie Joan
Director Lower Sch/Eng Teacher
Ingraham, Paul Anderson
English Teacher
Mc Phee, Sharon Whiteis
English Teacher
Neal, Sarah Wright
Latin Teacher

NEW BEDFORD
Costa, Mary-Ellen
Health Teacher
De Pina, Barbara L.
Teacher
Foster, Robert W.
History Teacher
Goodfellow, George Edwin
Chemistry Teacher
Lavallee, Marie Theresa Guimond
Pre-Kindergarten Teacher
Murphy, Cynthia
Home Economics Teacher
Peccini, Robert
English Teacher
Salk, Harvey Leon
Fourth Grade Teacher
Smith, Marilyn Elizabeth
7th Grade Teacher
Sweeney, Virginia Mary RSM
First Grade Teacher
Veronneau, Donald Dennis
Guidance Counselor

NEWBURYPORT
Laffie, Lynne P.
English Teacher

NEWTON
Di Gregorio, Mary Gervasi
Third Grade Teacher/Religion

NEWTONVILLE
Jones, Christopher Arlen
Science Teacher
Rosenthal, Milton Eugene
7th Grade Science Teacher
Schreider, James Quint
Mathematics Teacher

NORFOLK
Gallerani, Paul Peter
American History Teacher

NORTH ADAMS
Estes, John Joseph
Junior High School Teacher

NORTH ANDOVER
Fitzpatrick, Michelle Massicotte
4th/5th Grade Science Teacher

NORTH ATTLEBORO
Robert, Earlene Miller
Mathematics Teacher

NORTH BROOKFIELD
King, Barbara A. Dembski
6th Grade English Teacher

NORTH CHELMSFORD
Meidell, Stephen Jacob
English Department Chairperson

NORTH DARTMOUTH
Baggarly, Bruce David
Social Studies Teacher
Charest, Lorraine Beaulieu
French Teacher

NORTH EASTON
Lessard, Lois P.
Fifth Grade Teacher

NORTH QUINCY
Crump, Bernadette CSU
Retired Mathematics Teacher
Manoli, Cheryl Ellen
Mathematics Teacher

NORTH READING
Scanzani, Frank R.
Science Teacher

NORTHAMPTON
Meunier, Frances Vitali
2nd Grade Teacher

NORTHBOROUGH
Dwyer, Richard S.
Social Studies Teacher

NORWOOD
Assad, Hellas M.
Spanish Teacher
Jacobs, William Michael
Head Teacher
Jenkins, David Gerard
English Department Head
Parks, Yvette Lorraine
Foreign Language Dept Head
Smelstor, Thomas W.
History Teacher
Tibert, Priscilla Church
Third Grade Teacher
Wheatley-Dyson, Elizabeth
French/German Sp Teacher

OTIS AFB
Fuller, Mary E.
Principal

OXFORD
Gardella, Paul Robert
Mathematics Teacher
Strachan, Martha Veronica
Fourth Grade Teacher

PALMER
Patterson, Mary Louise
First Grade Teacher

PEABODY
Apostolides, Catherine Angelakis
3rd Grade Teacher
Dobbins, James J. Jr.
Earth Science Teacher
Hague, Michalene E. Patti
English Teacher

PEPPERELL
Dube, Ronald Norman
Science Teacher
Sampson, Jeannette Wasznicky
Fourth Grade Teacher
Toomey, Carol J. Blood
Third Grade Teacher
Wilmot, Barbara Klein
Social Studies Teacher

PITTSFIELD
Antil, Stephen Gilles
Science/Theology Teacher
Breslin, Pamela Conroy
Spanish Teacher
Cooper, Robert Lewis
Mathematics Teacher
Coudert, Donald Jules Jr.
Mathematics Dept Chair
De Rita, Janet A.
Social Studies Teacher
Marinaro, Vincent Paul
Fifth Grade Science Teacher

PROVINCETOWN
Burhoe, Gloria T.
English Teacher

QUINCY
Walsh, Lucille Niles
Reading Teacher
Whitehouse, Raymond Charles
Biology Teacher

RANDOLPH
Brennan, Thomas G.
Science Teacher
Edwards, Thomas Broderick
Computer Tech Chair
Israel, Marcia Solon
Reading Specialist
Wortzman, Marilyn B.
5th Grade Teacher

ROSLINDALE
Rogers, Ann Hanlon
Social Studies Teacher

SALEM
Seeley, James Leo
English Teacher

SCITUATE
Berman, Christine Morin
English Teacher
Nord, Peter D.
English Teacher
Rinella, A. James
Fifth Grade Teacher

SEEKONK
O'Donnell, James Peter
5th Grade Teacher

SHARON
Brown, Cheryl Beshke
English Teacher
Dow, Clista Mary Etta
6th Gr Gifted & Talented Tchr

SHELBURNE FALLS
Wells, Lawrence Arthur
Fifth Grade Teacher

SOMERSET
Goulart, Edmond Jr.
Economics Teacher
Joynt, Marilyn C.
Second Grade Teacher
Mc Namara, Donald Joseph
Physics Teacher
Pelagio, Reginald Matthew
Business Department Chair
Vieria, Brian M.
Instrumental Music Teacher

SOMERVILLE
Damian, Patricia Re
English Teacher/Eng Dept Chair
Gorman, Marjorie Mary
Second Grade Teacher
Mc Laughlin, Mary Frances
Assistant Principal

SOUTH ASHBURNHAM
Von Deck, Joseph Francis
Social Studies Dept Chair

SOUTH GRAFTON
Borci, Priscilla Mac Donald
Fourth Grade Teacher

SOUTH YARMOUTH
New, John Emmett
Instrumental Music Director

SOUTHWICK
Connors, Patrick James
8th Grade Science Teacher

SPRINGFIELD
Cook, Mary Jane (Glover)
English Teacher
Davis, Zehline Rush
4th Grade Teacher
Ellis, Mary Frances
French/Spanish Teacher
Hurley, Ellen Marie
4th Grade Teacher
Superson, Susan J.
Religion Teacher
Tougas, Caroline A.
Reading Teacher
Walmer, Ellen K. (Glazier)
3rd Grade Teacher
Watson, Jean (Balboni)
Mathematics Teacher

STONEHAM
Chase, Peggy Ann
8th Grade Science Teacher

STOUGHTON
Camacho, Roberta Agnes
Head Science Teacher

SUDBURY
Wallis, Barbara Prince
  Second Grade Teacher

SWANSEA
Kirkman, Jeff
  5th Grade Teacher
Smith, E. Sheldon III
  Science Dept Head

TAUNTON
Bezanson, Charles A.
  Science Teacher
Boreri, Robert John
  History Teacher
Burns, Mary Catherine
  Mathematics/Physics Teacher
Furtado, Maureen Fahey
  Third Grade Teacher

TOWNSEND
Blunt, Bess
  Eighth Grade English Teacher
Day, Robert John
  Mathematics Dept Chairman
Goldberg, Fred Howard
  Fifth Grade Teacher
Mastandrea, Diane Marie
  Spanish Teacher
Mickson, Sandra Wiswell
  Biology Teacher
Philbin, Paula Jean
  Social Studies Teacher
Richard, Lee Twarog
  English Teacher
Rosa, Susan Frederick
  Third Grade Teacher

TYNGSBORO
Skirven, Shirley Berberian
  Math Department Chairperson

WAKEFIELD
Mc Donough, Susan Cotter
  English Teacher

WALES
Ferraro, Joan Hoarle
  Third Grade Teacher

WALPOLE
Hall, Robert Gerard
  Spec Ed/Math/English Teacher

WARE
Kade, Deborah Ann (Kalentek)
  4th Grade Teacher
Niedzwiecki, Barbara (Desjardins)
  Jr HS Soc Stud/Eng Teacher

WAREHAM
Starkie, Ilda B.
  Business Teacher

WATERTOWN
Aubin, Patricia A.
  Director of English
Delaney, Kathryn Golden
  English Teacher

WEBSTER
Ducharme, Janice A.
  English Teacher
Lango, Paul Joseph
  Computer Science Teacher
Loosemore, William James
  History Teacher
Marcotte, Joseph A.
  Pastor/Headmaster
Neiman, Marjorie A.
  Counselor

WELLESLEY HILLS
Li Calsi, Lynn
  Latin Teacher

WEST NEWBURY
Belanger, Albert Edward
  7th Grade English Teacher

WEST ROXBURY
Amiro, Barbara Di Santi
  Sixth Grade Teacher

WEST SPRINGFIELD
Shea, Sandra Thompson
  First Grade Teacher

WESTFIELD
Cauley, Mary Lou Griffin
  Sixth Grade Teacher

WESTWOOD
Balaschi, Kimberly Healy
  Spanish Teacher
Scribner, Susan Ann
  6th Grade Teacher/Team Leader

WILLIAMSTOWN
Bradley, Lucinda Rostollan
  English Teacher

WILMINGTON
Girouard, Yolanda Dorothy
  5th Grade Teacher
Hayes, Linda Ann (Battista)
  Social Studies Teacher

WINCHESTER
Sweeney, Therese A. (Sobocinski)
  8th Grade Teacher

WOBURN
Celi, Janet Lyn
  Spanish Teacher
Gregory, Barbara Brunckhorst
  English Teacher
Murphy, Barbara Breslin
  Latin Teacher
Wilkinson, Harry L.
  History Teacher

WORCESTER
Casey, Robin Bahr
  English/Journalism Teacher
Kirk, Kevin Edward
  Teacher/English Dept Chair
Riordan, Mary Murphy
  Principal

MICHIGAN

ADDISON
Brown, Susan Marie
  Mathematics & Science Teacher

ADRIAN
Parton, Daniel Richard
  Assistant Pastor/Bible Teacher

ALANSON
Liederbach, Kathy Reef
  Mathematics Teacher
Raiche, Cynthia Clark
  4th Grade Teacher

ALBION
Kernish, Edward S.
  Speech & Theatre Teacher
Offerman, Richard Allen
  Math/Cmptr Programming Teacher
Patrick, Joyce Elaine (Karger)
  Business Teacher
Taffs, Jean Vance
  English Teacher/Chair

ALGONAC
Edie, Wanda Beal
  Mathematics Teacher

ALLEN PARK
Haber, Scott A.
  Soc Stud Teacher/Dept Chair
Picklo, David Micheal
  Science Department Chair
Sharkey, Ellen M.
  Physical Education Teacher

ALMA
Smith, Shirley Ann
  Chapter I Reading Teacher

ALPENA
Lewis, Carol S.
  English Teacher
Phillips, Roger Bruce
  Journalism Teacher
Robinette-Bouchard, Eleanore T.
  (Wikaryasz)
  Third Grade Teacher
Roznowski, Marie De Caire
  Junior High Teacher

ANN ARBOR
Drake, Dee E.
  Science Teacher

ARMADA
Finley, Patricia J.
  6th Grade Mathematics Teacher
Landeck, Doreen Rae
  Language Art/Art Teacher

AUBURN
Grocholski, Leo N.
  Business Teacher
Schmidt, Shirley A. Siebrasse
  Fifth Grade Teacher
Smiley, Mary Alice Dawson
  Fourth Grade Teacher

AVOCA
Dailey, Barbara Bentley
  2nd/3rd Grade Teacher
Klaus, Richard Ralph
  Retired Fifth Grade Teacher

BANGOR
Hills, Kathleen Vincent
  4th Grade Teacher

BATTLE CREEK
Baltutat, Salli Poat
  Second Grade Teacher
Behnke, Karl K.
  Government Teacher
Burise, Barbara Lancaster
  Elementary Teacher
Cook-Johnson, Janice Marie
  College Life Director
Dearring, Gloria Delores
  5th Grade Teacher
Durkin, Mike
  English Dept Chair/Teacher
Evans, Jenny (Poot)
  10th Grade Eng/Rdng Teacher
Kelly, Stephan A.
  Ind Arts/Technology Teacher
Perry, Roxie Ella (Taylor)
  Fourth Grade Teacher
Richmond, Kathryn A.
  English Teacher
Rubel, Noman Ray
  Biology Teacher
Sutton, Cynthia L.
  Spanish Teacher
Vandenboss, Ardis Mary (Ellis)
  Jr HS English Dept Teacher
Wilburn, Marva J. (Protho)
  8th Grade English Teacher
Zuk, Joseph S.
  English Dept Chair

BAY CITY
Gatza, Julie SC
  1st Grade Teacher
Reno, Janet Scott (Wiles)
  Kindergarten Teacher
Sandow, Deborah Ranae Billingsley
  Mathematics Department Chair
Skinner, Margaret Sweeney
  Spanish Teacher
Talbot, Marjorie Anne Baumann
  Science Teacher
Vanden Brooks, Kathryn G.
  Teacher of Gifted/Reading

BELDING
Stiles, Robert William
  Director of Music Education

BELLEVILLE
Mulliga, Reginia
  Earth Science Teacher
Struble, Karen (Vandecar)
  6th Grade Teacher

BENTON HARBOR
Dorgelo, Carolyn Evans
  4th-6th Grade Science Teacher
Giegerich, Elisabeth
  Vocal Music Teacher
James, Olivia Ellis
  Sch Dev Teacher Consultant
Scott, Evelyn M.
  Teacher
Scott, Wilbur Winston Jr.
  6th Grade Teacher

BERRIEN SPRINGS
Hoge, Michael E.
  Band Director
White, Cleon Eugene
  Mathematics/Chemistry Teacher

BIG RAPIDS
Ludwig, Sheryl Ann
  7th/8th Grade Teacher
Nielsen, Lauri A. (Frizzell)
  Third Grade Teacher

BIRCH RUN
Davis, Linda Kay
  Accounting/Eng/Yrbk Teacher
Jenkins, Deann S.
  7th-8th Grade Math Teacher
Solinski, Dawn Marie
  2nd Grade Teacher

BIRMINGHAM
Coucke, Henry Radford
  6th-8th Grade Teacher
Kozlowski, David
  Asst Principal
Lessenberry, Karen Oxley
  Social Studies Teacher
Meyer, Herbert Theodore
  2nd-3rd Grade Teacher
Priskorn, Gary J.
  6th-8th Grade Science Teacher
Ryan, Judith Belknap
  Third Grade Teacher
Stevenson, Margaret Meagher
  Retired Teacher
Zidansek, Janet Steiner
  Mathematics Dept Chairman

BLANCHARD
Judd, Marilyn Dorothy
  First and Second Grade Teacher

BLISSFIELD
Charlefour, Peggy Lynn
  Fifth Grade Teacher
Grasley, Kevin Logan
  English Teacher
Niemi, Warren Richard
  Social Science Teacher

BLOOMFIELD HILLS
Finn, Ellen Brady
  English/Latin/History Teacher
Millett, Kate Sanderoff
  Social Studies Teacher
Travis, Dennis
  Teacher/Science Coordinator

BRIDGEPORT
Bowns, Jane Ann
  Mathematics Coordinator

BRIGHTON
Herbst, David L.
  7th-8th Grade Teacher
Martin, Gary James
  Language Arts Instructor

BRIMLEY
Smith, Douglas Ross
  Math/Science Teacher

BRONSON
Elkins, Patricia Ann Laferly
  Fourth Grade Teacher
Griffin, Catherine Elizabeth
  Mathematics Teacher
James, Betty Ann Winters
  Third Grade Teacher
Sineni, Frank Joseph
  Sixth Grade Teacher

BROWN CITY
Kreiner, Sheryl Lynn
  Social Studies Teacher

BYRON CENTER
Schippers, Robert John
  5th Grade Teacher
Terpak, Dorothy Ann
  First Grade Teacher
Vander Moere, Franklyn J.
  Social Studies Teacher

CADILLAC
Bunnell, Kathryn Collins
  5th Grade Teacher
Poag, Lois M.
  Kindergarten Teacher
Roberts, Susan Marie
  Mathematics/Science Teacher

CALEDONIA
Lewis, Luann
  7th Grade Eng/Rdng Teacher

CALUMET
Durocher, Clyde Francis
  6th Grade Science Teacher

CAMDEN
Bonnau, Ruth Snyder
  Fourth Grade Teacher
Briner, Kay Jeannine
  Fifth Grade Teacher
Cook, Kelly L.
  English/Spanish Teacher
Hinman, Donald Rex
  Social Studies Teacher
Murphy, Eldon E.
  Industrial Art/Phys Ed Teacher
Vallieu, Kenneth S.
  Science Teacher

CANTON
Hilfinger, Janyne Hladis
  Teacher
Marlow, Linda May (Murphy)
  German/French Teacher

CEDAR SPRINGS
Horowitz, Steven Abraham
  4th Grade Instructor
Welch, Herbert Timothy
  English Teacher/Dept Chairman

CHARLEVOIX
Henne, Betty M.
  English Teacher/Chair

CHARLOTTE
Dawson, Linda Lee
  6th Grade Mathematics Teacher
Smith, Glenn Graham
  5th Grade Teacher
Whitaker, Donis Ilene
  Fourth Grade Teacher

CHASSELL
Hill, Martha E. (Mattila)
  Second Grade Teacher

CHEBOYGAN
Scott, Randall Jay
  Science/Computer Teacher

CHELSEA
Turok, Linda Carlton
  Home Economics Teacher

CLARE
Feneley, Kenneth Howard
  Band Director

CLARKSTON
Denstaedt, Linda Mitchell
  English Teacher/Dept Chair

CLAWSON
Bruce, Barry Anthony
  Social Studies Teacher

CLIO
Hammer, Christine Ann
  English Teacher
Schipper, William Robert
  History Teacher

COLEMAN
Beamish, Sharon K.
  Yearbook Advisor
La Fleur, Kristi Jean
  Physical Ed/Health/Sci Teacher
Spalding, Allen Carl
  5th Grade Science Teacher

CONCORD
Hessler, David Robert
  Art Department Teacher/Head
O'Masta, Shirley Conway
  Chapter I Teacher/Director

CONSTANTINE
Boeschenstein, Sally (Penzotti)
  English Teacher

COOKS
White, Susan Marie
  Band Director/Computer Teacher

COOPERSVILLE
Christrup, Eric Lee
  Science Teacher

CORUNNA
Buysse, Bruce Lee
  Biology Teacher/Sci Chairman
Gazella, John Michael
  English Teacher
Johns, Margaret Riggs
  3rd Grade Teacher
Radcliffe, Merri Ann Baker
  English Teacher/Dept Chair

CROSWELL
Mueller, Vivian Santrock
  8th Grade English Teacher

CRYSTAL FALLS
Slater, Pamela Gue
  French/English Teacher

DANSVILLE
Thorburn, Stuart C.
  Social Studies Teacher
Whipple, Myron Charles
  Fifth Grade Teacher
Wood, Katherine A.
  Math Dept Chairman

DAVISBURG
Durnan, Charles Dennis
  6th Grade Teacher

DAVISON
Mac Lean, Ray Donald
  Instrumental Music Director
Potter, Jim Russell
  Speech & Drama Teacher
Yoder, Terry Robert
  Social Studies Teacher

DEARBORN
Astourian, Rosalind
  History Teacher
Davis, Keith Jerry
  Sixth Grade Teacher
Gaikowski, Patricia Ostrowski
  Science Teacher
Lamerato, Janet
  Teacher
Lesnau, Gary Stephen
  HS Social Studies Teacher
Sechrist, Dorothy Mc Donald
  Fourth Grade Teacher
Sullivan, Thomas William
  English Teacher

DEERFIELD
Beland, Jane Marie
  Fifth Grade Teacher
Parsons, Barbara Ann (Karcsak)
  Secondary Math Teacher
DELTON
Goebel, Nancy Lou
  Third Grade Teacher
Wojciechowski, Micheal Joseph
  U S History 8th Grade Teacher
DETROIT
Albert, Jack Constantine
  Biology Teacher
Apter, Katherine Barnes
  English Teacher
Atlas, Arthurlean Johnson
  Vocal Music Teacher
Barton, Bettie
  Reading Lab Teacher
Black, Connie Butler
  Business Teacher
Blake, Tomi Mc Campbell
  English Teacher
Blakely, Robert Thomas
  Physics Teacher
Booth, May Y.
  Reading/Language Arts Teacher
Brown, Peggy Mildred
  Social Studies Teacher
Calloway, Stella R. (Whittler)
  Typing/Quest Teacher
Cayce, Velma Snow
  English/Reading Teacher
Celer, Mary Beth
  Fifth Grade Teacher
Chaney, Willie Moore
  Mathematics Teacher
Clinkscale, Chelita Ann
  5th Grade Teacher
Dogariu, Janice Giroux
  6th Grade Teacher
Duhoski, John Vincent
  Religion Teacher
Fisher, Leona Kent
  Music/Performing Arts Teacher
Ford, Pamela Hunter
  Language Arts Teacher
Gandy, Mary Ann Smith
  4th Grade & Homeroom Teacher
Goldman, Jules A.
  Marketing Education Coord
Gugala, Lottie Winiarski
  Vocal Music Teacher
Gunn, Francene Ambrose
  English Teacher
Hatton, Cheryl Denise
  Spec Ed Resource Rm Teacher
Hester, Blondy Jean Burris
  Business Education Teacher
Hill, Fannie Wilson
  Fourth Grade Teacher
Horst, Brenetta Dukes
  Instrumental Music Teacher
Issa, Aswad Hashim Asim
  Social Studies Teacher
Jarrell, Margaret Ann
  Teacher of Oral Expression
Johnson-Lowe, Delores Kathleen
  Home Ec Teacher
Jones, Marceline Yvonne
  Mathematics Teacher
Jones, Patricia A.
  6th Grade Mathematics Teacher
Kittrell, Pamela Ann
  Special Education Teacher
Landrum, Ada Powell
  6th Grade Homeroom Teacher
Lawson, Marian Boyd
  5th Grade Lang Art Teacher
Lott, Lue B.
  9th Grade World His Teacher
Love, Adrienne Davis
  English Teacher
Lynch, Dorothy G. Clark
  Primary 1 Teacher
Manciel, Deborah Fay
  Sixth Grade Writing Teacher
Mandeville, Leonard
  Mathematics Department Chair
Mayes-Robinson, Debora
  English Teacher
Mueller, Michael John
  Math/English Teacher
Oldham, Mignon Hayes
  English Teacher
Oleksy, Debra Ann
  Mathematics Teacher
Otulakowski, Ronald James
  Drama Teacher
Owens, Patricia Mc Afee
  Mathematics Teacher
Peart, Joslyn Kristina
  Seventh Grade Math Teacher

Peart, Ronald Norman
  Math Instructional Specialist
Pettapiece, Bob
  Teacher
Russell, Mary Louise Smith
  3rd Grade Teacher
Seacord, Margaret Anne
  Teacher of Grade 8
Sheppard, Johnnie Frank
  Unit Head/Teacher
Spinner, Cozette Regena (Bell)
  5th Grade Language Arts
Stanley, Jacquelyn Cheryl
  Third Grade Teacher
Summers, Grace Davis
  Math Teacher
Talley, Delores Mc Griff
  Kindergarten Teacher
Turner, James Walter
  English Teacher
Waltz, Carolyn Jean
  Spanish Teacher
Wasik, Camille S.
  Jr HS Teacher
Watson, Sharon Denise
  8th Grade Lang Arts Teacher
Wheeler, Judy Delores
  AP English/Journalism Teacher
White, Margaret Woods
  Extended Day Kndgtn Teacher
Williams, Almeta
  6th/7th Grade Math Teacher
DIMONDALE
Scott, Suzanne De Turk
  5th Grade Teacher
DOWAGIAC
Jones, Judy Ann
  5th Grade Teacher
Shaffer, Paula Lynn
  English Teacher
Short, Robert Charles
  7th/8th Grade Health Teacher
EAST DETROIT
Green, Jayne Denton
  Spanish/English Teacher
Passarelli, Agnes Mary
  First Grade Teacher
EAST GRAND RAPIDS
Belfer, Claire Jean
  History, English Teacher
EAST LANSING
Ball, Richard Joseph
  7th/8th Grade Soc Stud Teacher
Rambo, Jean Adele (Cavanaugh)
  Math/Sci/Soc Stud Teacher
EATON RAPIDS
Fox, Charles Daniel
  Social Studies Teacher
Linsemier, Gerri A.
  Language Arts Teacher
EDMORE
Burdick, Kathy Bullard
  7th/8th Grade English Teacher
ELKTON
Gage, Sandra Lynn (Taylor)
  Third Grade Teacher
EVART
Bandlow, Richard Frank
  Eng Dept Chair/Cmptr Coord
FAIRVIEW
Diener, Larry Linford
  K-12 Vocal Music Teacher
Troyer, Genevieve Lee Yoder
  K-6 Elementary Principal
FARMINGTON HILLS
Morden, Joette Marie
  Life Management Teacher/Chair
FARMINGTON HLLS
Maxwell, Jerry H.
  History Teacher
FARWELL
Laverty, Larry Lee
  Science Teacher
FENNVILLE
Price, Patrick Shannon
  Health Education Teacher
FENTON
Wedel, Gerald Bradley
  Business Education Teacher
FERNDALE
Grady, Jim Jr.
  Government Teacher
FLAT ROCK
Norwood, Doreen Jeanne Penniman
  Home Economics Teacher

FLINT
Baab, Linda Jeanne (Kirkbride)
  6th Grade Teacher
Campeau, Janet Marie
  Guidance Department Chair
Debevec, Gary Raymond
  Mathematics/Science Teacher
Garnsey, Janet Jo
  Third Grade Teacher
Harris, Bettye Hannah
  Business Department Chair
Hennon, Joyce Ann
  HS Hearing Impaired Teacher
Lingenfelter, Mary Reinhardt
  7th Grade Math Teacher
Lundy, Barbara Ann
  2nd Grade Teacher
Massey, Donald R.
  Zoology/Earth Science Teacher
O'Neill, Willa Joyce
  Teacher
Rosborough, Robert
  English Teacher
Rutledge, Eugene
  4th/5th Language Arts Teacher
Sack, Ronald P.
  Marketing/Co-Op Teacher
Samec, Jayne Miller
  9th/10th Grade English Teacher
Simmons, Robert Randolph
  Elementary Principal
FLUSHING
Gillam, Gregory Alan
  Science Teacher
FOWLER
Shauver, Annette Hannula
  English & Reading Teacher
FOWLERVILLE
Frazier, Susan Grunn
  English Teacher
FRANKFORT
Pratley, Michael B.
  English/Social Studies Teacher
FREELAND
Bowen, James Dennis
  Science Teacher
Brink, Beverly Ann
  Fourth Grade Teacher
Compton, Marcia Robertson
  Second Grade Teacher
Kraycsir, Andrew Jr.
  Sixth Grade Teacher
Wren, Lois Jean (Leininger)
  4th Grade Teacher
FREMONT
Schwartz, Nancy S.
  Marketing Instructor
Scott, Chester Eugene
  Instructional Mgr Auto Service
FRUITPORT
Mellema, Thomas E.
  Math/Science Teacher
GALESBURG
Hill, Brenda Burgess
  Retired Second Grade Teacher
Morgan, Robert Keith
  High School Guidance Counselor
GARDEN CITY
Okins, Joan Pfleger
  4th Grade Teacher
GLADSTONE
Danforth, Robert Max
  HS Social Studies Teacher
GLADWIN
Gilliam, Kernie
  Social Studies Chair/Teacher
GLEN ARBOR
Karner, Robert F.
  Senior Master
GRAND BLANC
Steininger, Patricia Ponitz
  Third Grade Teacher
GRAND HAVEN
Mousseau, Andy W.
  HS Mathematics Teacher
Persing, Edith Elaine Klenk
  Senior Teacher of Psychology
Prelesnik, Barbara Cooper
  Fourth Grade Teacher
GRAND LEDGE
Foster, Judy Weber
  English Teacher
GRAND RAPIDS
Balas, Carol Budry
  First Grade Teacher

Bow, Amen Yvon
  English/Drama Teacher
Echtinaw, James R.
  Math Dept Chair/Cmptr Teacher
Engelsma, Daniel Lee
  Industrial & Tech Teacher
Khan, Mariama Joshua
  Mathematics Teacher
Lee, Laura A.
  Sixth Grade Teacher
Letherby, Frank Edward
  6th Grade Teacher
Luyk, David Martin
  Language Arts Teacher
Mc Knight, Norma Lynch
  Retired Teacher
Pratt, Sandra K.
  Bible Teacher/Acad Counselor
Rupinski, Marilyn Joyce (Holland)
  6th Grade Teacher
Saldino, Margot Luce
  Jr HS Math & Science Teacher
Scholten, Becky Treur
  German Teacher
Sheets, Daniel D.
  Mathematics & Computer Teacher
Smalligan, Charles Lee
  Science Teacher
Ver Merris, Donald Alan
  3rd Grade Teacher
GRANDVILLE
Weick, Dave Lee
  Computer/Math Jr High Teacher
GRASS LAKE
Poertner, Larry Paul
  Math Dept Chair & Teacher
GREENVILLE
Lutkus, Lynne (Adams)
  4th Grade Teacher
GROSSE ILE
Maunu, John Raymond
  Social Studies Instructor
GROSSE POINTE FARM
Lopez, Phyllis Ruth
  6th Grade Teacher
GWINN
Barto, Donna Marie Rigoni
  Fourth Grade Teacher
Dobrzenski, Darryl Thomas
  Vocational Auto Teacher
Filizetti, Ricky M.
  Industrial Tech Teacher
La Fave, Richard Edward
  Mathematics Teacher
Lasich, Vivian E. (Layne)
  8th Grade Eng Lang Teacher
Leppaluoto, Mikael Edward
  6th Grade Teacher
HALE
Reasner, Susan Lamphier
  Teacher
Shellenbarger, Nelson Lyle
  Secondary Science Teacher
HAMTRAMCK
Karpinsky, Bo
  Teacher
Traverso, Teresa Bollella
  High School English Teacher
HARBOR SPRINGS
Huffman, Carole Barden
  4th Grade Teacher
HARPER WOODS
Gore, Marguerite Florence Bardy
  Social Stud Dept Chairperson
Graham, Patti Mussill
  Spanish Teacher/Counselor
Heymes, Shirley
  Teacher
Hutton, Jo Anne Wolf
  8th Grade Eng/Math Coop Coord
Loewen, Mary Louise
  Religious Studies Teacher
Miller, Priscilla Soumis
  1st Grade Teacher
Smith, Elsa Aicheler
  High School Counselor
HARRISON
Chadwick, William Robert II
  Mathematics/Science Teacher
HARTFORD
Shoemaker, Thomas David
  Math Teacher/Computer Coord
Washburn, Margaret Elaine
  Kindergarten Teacher
HARTLAND
Mishler, Daniel J.
  Chem Teacher/Sci Dept Chair

HAZEL PARK
Hall, Johnnie Melvin
  Fourth Grade Teacher
Riley, Brenda Joyce (Ferguson)
  4th Grade Teacher
Silvasi, Louis Alex
  Journalism/Economics Teacher
HEMLOCK
Earle, Beverly Ann
  Kindergarten Teacher
Wilson, James Robert
  Earth Science Teacher
HESPERIA
Arbogast, Michael Ronald
  5th Grade Teacher
Blieler, Steven Mark
  Mathematics Department Chair
Fick, Beverly J.
  Language Arts/Reading Teacher
Godfrey, Carol A.
  2nd Grade Teacher
Porter, Mary Graff
  First Grade Teacher
HIGHLAND PARK
Blasco, John S.
  Teacher
Burns, Birdie Boyd
  4th Grade Teacher
Canfield, Patti Lee
  Eng Teacher/Choral Conductor
Carson, Charlotte Ann Agee
  8th Grade Lang Art Teacher
Richardson, Gloria Elaine Savage
  Science Teacher
Sullivan, Jerome Michael
  Social Studies Teacher
HILLMAN
Herbek, Melba Ellen
  4th Grade Teacher
HILLSDALE
Bell, Kathryn Tamblyn
  English/Journalism Teacher
Murphy, Kathleen A.
  Gifted & Talented Teacher
HOLLAND
Andree, Robert G.
  Sixth Grade Math Teacher
Mulder, Jon
  English Dept Chair/Teacher
HOLLY
Hetherington, David A.
  Biology Teacher/Sci Dept Chm
HOLTON
Van Lue, Marion I. (Marshall)
  6th Grade Teacher
HOMER
Welch, Arthur Glen
  English & History Teacher
HOPKINS
Mac Arthur, Thomas Pierce
  Mathematics Teacher
Rademacher, Mary Jane
  Fourth Grade Teacher
HOWARD CITY
Roberts, Jean Hitchcock
  Fourth Grade Teacher
Scholten, James Kent
  Mathematics Teacher
HOWELL
Packard, Lois M.
  Fifth Grade Teacher
Reinke, Mary Ellen Marcellus
  English/Journalism Teacher
Schwarz, Catherine E.
  HS Writing/Literature Teacher
HUDSONVILLE
Davis, Cynthia Rose (Westafer)
  English/Spanish Teacher
Reimink, Ronald L.
  Biology Teacher
IDA
Brunt, Kay L.
  Kindergarten Teacher
Eipperle, Ruth E.
  4th Grade Teacher
Radsheid, John E.
  Mathematics/Science Chair
INKSTER
Clark, Evelyn Lawrence
  Mid & Elem Cmptr Teacher
INTERLOCHEN
Gaede, Jean Maraldo
  Chair-Liberal Arts Division

IONIA
Palmer, Bernice Helen (Kappe)
Kindergarten Teacher

IRONWOOD
Belmas, Bruce J.
Elementary Principal
Bianchi, Darlene Anderson
Third Grade Teacher
Miklesh, Robert Louis
Biology Teacher

ITHACA
Gritzmaker, Craig Calvin
6th Grade Teacher
Mc Nabb, Bettyann Abbe
Third Grade Teacher

JACKSON
Fitzgerald, Pamela Jean Coffelt
English/Journalism Teacher
Garrison, Phillip E.
Computer Science Teacher
Glaser, Karen Wolf
Coordinator of Gifted/Talented
Graziadei, Raphaelle A.
Religion Dept Coordinator
Jackson, Sharon Powers
Teacher of Gifted & Talented
Johnson, Doris Marie
3rd Grade Elementary Teacher
Norris, Maynard R.
Teacher & Elementary Principal
Packer, Jon O.
Fifth Grade Teacher
Patton, Susan Stowell
Preschool Teacher
Pepper, Thomas Andrew
Science Department Chair
Pitts, Shirley Ann
English Teacher
Straayer, Carole Kerr
Fourth Grade Teacher
Tumey, Rita Marie
English Teacher

JENISON
Hansen, Thorval A.
4th Grade Teacher

KALAMAZOO
Arnson, Marcy M.
English Teacher
Caro, Frank
Mathematics/Business Teacher
Carper, Anne Webb
Retired
Emmons, Reva Loretta
Business Teacher
Mc Neal, Bertha Barbee
Vocal Music Teacher
Pearson, Charles Steven
Elementary Teacher
Smith, Richard L.
English Teacher
Wunderlin, Kitty Thomas
First Grade Teacher

KENT CITY
Dickerson, Bernadine Marie
7th Grade English Teacher
Lang, Barbara Ann (Knox)
5th Grade Teacher

KENTWOOD
Bacon, Michael C.
English Teacher
Brown, Rebecca Anne
1st Grade Teacher
Jongekrijg, Allen J.
Teacher
Magennis, Daniel Charles
Science Teacher

KINGSFORD
Richmond, Kim Ann Crago
English Teacher
Riverside, Inez Thornberry/Peterson
3rd Grade Teacher

KINGSTON
Rea, Michael L.
Asst Prin/Eng Teacher

L'ANSE
Simonsen, Randall Wayne
Director of Bands

LAKE CITY
Baker, Kurt Micheal
History Teacher

LAKE LINDEN
Christopherson, Mary Beth Bartter
Second Grade Teacher
Codere, Lois Bailey
Math Teacher

LAKE ORION
Lohr, Gail Ann (Stickney)
Middle School Science Teacher

LANSING
Bassett, Judith Ann
Early Childhood Director
Farnsworth, Constance Kay
5th Grade Teacher
Gambill, Verne W.
7th Grade Science Teacher
Gibbs, Ronald Kenneth
Government/History Teacher
Gregory, Worsie Taylor
4th And 5th Grade Teacher
Henry, Cleveland
Planning Specialist
Hutchinson, Marilyn E.
English Dept Chair/Teacher
Krutschewski, Penelope L.
4th Grade Teacher
Mehaffey, Mark E.
Secondary Art Teacher
Partlow, Kathleen Lawler
His Dept Chair/Teacher
Radtke, Nancy B.
French Teacher
Utter, Patricia Weigel
Business Department Chair

LAWTON
Everly, Calvin James
Sixth Grade Science Teacher

LINCOLN PARK
Roulo, Sherry Tanguay
Principal

LINWOOD
Lamberti, Carlo
Fifth Grade Homeroom Teacher

LIVONIA
Anselm, Diane Moran
1st Grade Teacher
Freeman, Daniel Lee
Gifted Math Program Teacher
Rada, Rose Ann
Art Teacher
Sypher, Mary Beth (Bellant)
French Teacher

LOWELL
Pike, Mary E.
Elementary Music Teacher
Pratt, Rita Hamilton
7th-8th Grade English Teacher

LUDINGTON
Catt, Richard K.
6th Grade Teacher/Gr Level Chm
Donley, Ross Wendell
Explorationist Teacher

MADISON HEIGHTS
Seaglund, Sharon Trader
French Teacher
Sobocienski, Patricia Sue (Sears)
Mathematics Department Chair
Wieleba, Frances Arlene
5th Grade Teacher

MANISTEE
Anderson, Robert Edward
8th Grade US History Teacher

MARCELLUS
Mason, Patricia Ann (Walther)
Middle School Teacher

MARINE CITY
Kaufman, Brian Russell
Fifth Grade Teacher
Webb, Colleen Johnson
Business Education Teacher

MARION
Brumels, Doris Taylor
Fifth Grade Teacher
Suomi, Maria Ann
Spanish/English Teacher

MARLETTE
Shadley, Lorri Ebert
French/Physical Ed Teacher

MARQUETTE
Clement, Ellen Thoren
HS Choral Director
Donckers, Judith Luoma
Spanish Teacher

MARSHALL
Coleman, Jerry
5th Grade Classroom Teacher

MARTIN
Boender, Karen Hellenga
Math Teacher

MARYSVILLE
Marshall, Thomas Robert
Mathematics Department Teacher
Montgomery, Deborah (Skinner)
Counselor

MASON
Campbell, William Edward Jr.
Life Science Teacher
Fry, Wallace Samuel
Science Teacher

MAYVILLE
Campbell, Marilyn Dean
Band Director
La Graff, John Martin
English Teacher

MENDON
Griner, Lynn Ann
6th Grade Teacher
Hollenbeck, Jan K.
Jr High Math Teacher

MENOMINEE
Brunelle, Edward Jay
Science Teacher
Malechuk, Edward Frank
English-Speech Teacher

MERRILL
Galbraith, Nancy E.
Mathematics & Chem Teacher
Haley, Judy Ann (Patterson)
Kindergarten Teacher

MICHIGAN CENTER
Kinch, Kathleen Ann (Golombek)
Secondary EMI Teacher
Yoell, Martha Bonfiglio
5th/6th Grade Teacher

MIDLAND
Young, Jan Elaine (Meredith)
Consultant of Gifted/Talented

MILFORD
Ewers, James Lee
8th Grade Teacher

MONROE
Dusseau, Beth LaBeau
Eighth Grade Teacher
Ellerbrock, Sondra Marie
5th/6th Grade Teacher
Gartz, Suzanne M.
Mathematics Teacher
Jukuri, Eldred W.
Seventh Grade Teacher
Kauza, Beverly
8th Grade Teacher
Krueger, Joyce M.
English Teacher
Le Duc, Esther Mary
Clinical Social Worker
Linkfield, Diane Jane (Crumm)
5th Grade Teacher
Pursley, Steven Neale
Third Grade Teacher
Reed, Eullalee
Sixth Grade Teacher
Stresman, Shirley Marie
3rd/4th Grade Teacher
Terrasi, Robert Michael
Counselor
Turnbull, Kathleen Ann
Science & Reading Teacher
Tyner, John Charles
Music Coordinator
Van Houten, Jacquelyn Lou
(Brumbaugh)
Fifth-Sixth Grade Teacher

MONTAGUE
De Long, Marjorie Louise
English Teacher

MONTROSE
Hitchcock, Patricia Ruth
First Grade Teacher
Kitts, James William
History Teacher
Masser, Peggy Birdena (Haven)
5th Grade Teacher

MORENCI
Tursak, Rosemary K.
English Teacher

MOUNT CLEMENS
Jacobson, Robert Paul
Chemistry Teacher
Miller, Marc Howard
4th Grade Teacher
Pickelman, Maureen R.
Fifth Grade Teacher
Pleger, Carolyn J.
Third Grade Teacher
Ponichter, Nadia Annette (Robidoux)
Drama/Eng/Spec Ed Teacher

Sanders, Patricia (Muehrer)
Span Teacher/Foreign Lang Head
Weiss, Jared L.
Eighth Grade Teacher
Welch, Daniel R.
Sci & Human Sexuality Teacher
Young, Susan Alice
Biology/Chemistry Teacher

MOUNT MORRIS
Craig, William Gordon Jr.
Jr HS Science Teacher
Ford, Mary Losey
English Teacher
Hughes, Cecilia Ann Smith
6th Grade Teacher
Lillie, Kay
English Teacher
Paquette, Anne IHM
7-8 Grade Religion/Eng Teacher
Shieck, Adrienne Griffin
Science/Social Studies Teacher

MOUNT PLEASANT
Cooper, Richard H.
Mathematics Teacher/Dept Chair
Ferguson, Dean Thornburg
Social Studies Teacher
Mc Halpine, Cathy Nightengale
Health Education Teacher
Seiter, Patricia Ragley
English Teacher
Sieffert, Ronald Lee
Sixth Grade Teacher
Tucker, Allan Lee
Drafting Teacher

MUSKEGON
Baker, Marie Raymond
Piano Teacher
Barber, Sharon Noble
Fifth Grade Teacher
Borchert, Cheryl
Visual Arts Instructor
Helmus, Donald Lee
Foreign Language Chairperson
Mackay, Dennis J.
Teacher
Matthews, Leslie G.
Business Education Teacher
Mc Kinney, Martha Ann (Morley)
First Grade Teacher
Monette, Lyle Gaylyn
Business Teacher
Nichols, Venus Londreau
5th Grade Teacher

MUSKEGON HEIGHTS
Buikema, Shirley Ann
English Teacher

NEW BALTIMORE
Hagemann, Nancy Jean Rickel
Kindergarten Teacher

NEW BUFFALO
Hartley, John F. Jr.
7th Grade Reading Teacher
Tomoske, Roger L.
English Teacher

NEW HAVEN
Arft, Elaine E.
1st Grade Teacher
Zimmerman, Roger Earl
5th Grade Teacher

NEW LOTHROP
Dvorak, Janeen Ann
Fifth Grade Teacher
Lahmann, James Victor
Sixth Grade Teacher
Wood, Bonnie Lou (Tullar)
Phys Ed/Health Ed Teacher

NILES
Demko, Olive Sutton
Kindergarten Teacher
Dennison, Terry King
World Geography Teacher
Herbel, Le Anna Rodie
1st-3rd Grade Teacher
Langmeyer, Douglas Frederick
Biology/Science Teacher
Weaver, Pamela Ann
Chapter 1 Reading Teacher

NORTH BRANCH
Lott, Robert Grodon
Science Teacher/Athletic Dir
Wallace, Thomas Charles
English Department Chairman

NORTHVILLE
Heist, Debra (Zubok)
First Grade Teacher

NOVI
Gervasi, Gina Antonia
Mathematics Teacher

OAK PARK
Mc Ginnis, Shirley A.
5th Grade Teacher

OAKLEY
Kinsey, Joyce Archambault
Primary Kindergarten Teacher

OKEMOS
Brown, Edward J.
Science Teacher
Miller, David Kell
Social Studies Teacher
Rae, Bruce A.
Art Teacher

OLIVET
Barkley, Mary Piepkow
First Grade Teacher
Mestemaker, Karen Wisnieski
Lang Arts Chairperson/Teacher

ONAWAY
Abshagen, Charles Eugene
World History Teacher
Pitts, Miss J.
Business Education Teacher

ONSTED
Van Meer, Debra Joyce
Sixth Grade Teacher

ORCHARD LAKE
Stoppa, Thomas M.
History/Science Teacher

ORTONVILLE
Falkenburg, Liane M. R.
Third Grade Teacher

OSCODA
Spencer, Jewelene Singleton
Third Grade Teacher

OTISVILLE
Carroll, Gretchen Reimann
Assistant Principal

OTTAWA LAKE
Scott, Nicholas
History & Journalism Teacher

OWOSSO
Craft, Rose Mary Damore
Science & Physical Ed Instr
Hoefling, Judy Elaine
4th Grade Teacher

OXFORD
Kisor, Margaret Ayres
Social Studies Teacher
Ott, Mark Ott Steven
English/Reading/Quest Teacher

PECK
Ferguson, Judith Gordon
Health Occupations Instructor
Grifka, Dale Joseph
Mathematics Department Chair

PELLSTON
Passino, June M. (Spray)
5th Grade Teacher

PENTWATER
Mousel, Ronald E.
Principal

PERRY
Fitts, David William
Director of Instrumental Music
White, Sandra Kay (Austin)
Bio Teacher-Staff Developer

PETERSBURG
Loy, Susan Guenther
Mathematics Teacher

PETOSKEY
Fralick, Mark D.
8th Grade History Teacher
Oelke, Debbi A.
Third Grade Teacher
Zipp, Cynthia Blanchard
Second Grade Teacher

PEWAMO
Rademacher, Carol Bogard
Business/Journalism Teacher

PINCONNING
Winkler, Catherine Anna (Lobocki)
Kindergarten-1st Grade Teacher

PLAINWELL
Whitney, Joan Betty (Le Roy)
Fourth Grade Teacher

PLYMOUTH
Grisius, Sharon Teahan
Third Grade Teacher

PONTIAC
Grant, Dorothy Elcan
  Social Studies Dept Chair
Orfale, Linda Shelton
  High School English Teacher
Paterra, Jane Ferguson
  Language Art Teacher/Dept Head
PORT HURON
Assaf, Alice Warr
  Spanish Teacher
Barrett, Janet Lane
  English Teacher
Dell, John Robert
  Fifth Grade Teacher
Faust, Richard F.
  Assistant Principal
Hart, Clare
  Fourth Grade Teacher
Johnson, Paul Douglas
  Electronics Teacher
Knapp, Patricia Anne
  Activities Dir/Bus Teacher
Lill, William H.
  5th Grade Teacher
Winters, Charles Stuart
  7th/8th Grade Math Instructor
Young, Gary J.
  Civics Teacher
PORTAGE
Nichols, Sharon Emily
  4th Grade Teacher
PORTLAND
Schrauben, Alan James
  Social Studies Teacher
Thompson, Betty Lawless
  3rd Grade Teacher
POTTERVILLE
Wood, Joseph Allen
  English Teacher/Dept Head
QUINCY
Stewart, Robert Thomas
  History/Civics Teacher
QUINNESEC
Westman, Linda Nelson
  3rd Grade Teacher
READING
Dillon, Patrick Joseph
  English Teacher/Eng Dept Chair
REDFORD
Adams, Gerard Earl
  English Teacher
Gugala, Kay Irene
  Spanish Teacher
La Londe, Janet Arndt
  Kindergarten Teacher
Makurat, Celine
  Junior High School Teacher
Weed, Ruth Kohlmorgan
  6th Grade Teacher
REED CITY
Britten, Patrick James
  5th Grade Mathematics Teacher
Jacobs, Pat Kempter
  6th Grade Teacher
Long, Allene Stolt
  Retired Teacher
Palmer, Curtis M.
  Mathematics Teacher
Schneider, Barbara Baumgart
  7th Grade Reading Teacher
REESE
Jaremba, Marc Allen
  Principal
REMUS
Yarrick, James A.
  Director of Bands
Yarrick, Nancy J.
  History Teacher
RICHMOND
Curtis, Peter M.
  Mathematics Teacher
Francisco, Leslie Stuart
  Earth Science Teacher
Haley, Marilyn Wagoner
  7th Grade Science Teacher
Wood, Virginia Reed
  Chemistry/Physics Teacher
ROCHESTER
Marleton, Lois Troast
  Fifth Grade Teacher
ROCHESTER HILLS
Mason, Carol A.
  Media Specialist
ROCKFORD
Carter, Tom F.
  Administrator

Owen, Linda Lee
  Kindergarten Teacher
ROMULUS
Kruse, Richard August
  Head Music Dept/Band Director
ROSCOMMON
Murray, William P.
  Mathematics Department Chair
Yorty, Rollin Dale
  Retired Teacher
ROSE CITY
Lee, Sandra Ann
  English/Literature Teacher
ROSEVILLE
Fite, Robert William
  His/Geography Teacher
Hoerauf, Kenneth A.
  Counselor
Maksym, Jeanne Mary Hurley
  Kindergarten Teacher
Schmidt, Mildred Westrup
  Sixth Grade Teacher
ROYAL OAK
Elmleaf, James R.
  Teacher
Golombisky, Linda Carol Minchey
  Reading Teacher
Louis-Prescott, Lee Ann
  Religion Department Chairwoman
Louis-Prescott, Lee Ann
  Religion Department Chair
Minch, David L.
  Social Studies/English Teacher
Skalski, Marie Pauline
  Reading Teacher
RUDYARD
Bickel, Kenneth Lee
  World Geography Teacher
SAGINAW
Barker, Gary Keith
  Mathematics/Sci Dept Teacher
Bowman, Beaulah Turner
  Elementary Teacher
Call, Thomas Robert Jr.
  His/Ged Soc Stud/Sci Teacher
Chaney, Betty A. (Reeder)
  English Teacher
Crevia, Debra Sonefeld
  Junior High Reading Teacher
Deford, Jo Ann
  French/Spanish Teacher
Dixon, Danette V.
  6th Grade Teacher
Enszer, Gary W.
  3rd Grade Teacher
Garcia, Maria Esther
  Fourth Grade Teacher
Gase, Mary Ellen
  Music Teacher
Goodell, Victoria Bernice
  Math/Science Teacher
Jones, Cora M.
  5th Grade Teacher
Kaul, Tim Herman
  Business Teacher/Co-Op Dir
Mc Afee, Beatrice Fowler
  English Teacher
Mc Laughlin, Ted I.
  Mathematics Teacher/Dept Chair
Nickodemus, Rose Marie
  Mathematics Teacher
Pastor, June L.
  Spanish Teacher
Smith, Michael George
  Dept Chair, Cmptr Sci Teacher
Torrey, Vicki Susan
  History Teacher/Asst Principal
Williams, Donald Woodrow
  Art Teacher
Zill, Steven E.
  Science Department Chair
SAINT CHARLES
Hunt, Joyce Arlene (Olney)
  Retired Teacher
Mroz, James F.
  Technology Education Teacher
SAINT CLAIR
Albrecht, Vernon L.
  7th Grade English Teacher
Appleford, Lynn Allyson
  Third Grade Teacher
Okoren, Frances M.
  Mathematics Teacher
SAINT CLAIR SHORES
Carrico, Ann Zulick
  4th/5th Grade Teacher
Metz, Carolynn E. (Wojcik)
  First Grade Teacher

Sinda, Roberta Martin
  American History Teacher
SAINT HELEN
Brown, Virginia Potter
  5th Grade Teacher
SAINT JOHNS
Mc Enaney, Judy Anderson
  Teacher
SALINE
Kiraly, Kathleen Mc Donough
  Health/Physical Ed Teacher
SAND CREEK
Walsh, Yvonne Katheryn
  4th Grade Teacher
SANFORD
Edwards, Gary Dale
  Social Studies Teacher
Mc Carty, Linda Jean
  First Grade Teacher
SARANAC
Coulson, Karen Peterson
  Third Grade Teacher
La Monica, Frank Anthony
  HS Mathematics Teacher
SAULT SAINTE MARIE
Faunt, Sharyn L.
  English Teacher
SAWYER
Gnodtke, Sandra Kay (Dahlen)
  Kindergarten/Preschool Teacher
Haughey, Cynthia Dawn (Holmes)
  Fifth Grade Teacher
SCHOOLCRAFT
Haas, Terry Michael
  Science Teacher
SHELBY
Near, Jacqueline Anne (Lankfer)
  2nd Grade Teacher
SHEPHERD
Dinkfeld, Robert Christopher
  Elem Phys Ed Teacher
Powers, Nancy Johnson
  4th Grade Teacher
SHERIDAN
Sanders, Thomas William
  Fifth Grade Teacher
SOUTH LYON
Haag, Dorothy M. (Barbour)
  Retired Elementary Teacher
SOUTHFIELD
Hoffenbacher, Susan E. (Beardsley)
  Business Education Teacher
Thomas, Lorraine Mary (Saour)
  Sci Dept Head/Teacher
SPARTA
De Braber, Leonard David
  Soc Stud Teacher & Dept Chm
Higgins, Mar
  4th Grade Teacher
Mc Callum, Brian Neil
  6th Grade Math/Sci Teacher
SPRINGPORT
Mohr, Marjorie Jean (Jackson)
  3rd Grade Teacher
STANTON
Leitch, Christina Lee
  7th Language Arts Teacher
STANWOOD
Morey, Norita A. (Morford)
  2nd Grade Teacher
STEPHENSON
Kaufman, Joseph Robert
  Biology Teacher
STERLING HEIGHTS
Boss, Chet W.
  Mathematics Teacher
Clements, Barry William
  Mathematics Teacher
Clippert, Richard John
  6th Grade Teacher
Greenway, Ruth Ann Sturgell
  1st Grade Teacher
Heft, Edward A. Jr.
  4th Grade Teacher
Hogan, Shirley A. Van Aelst
  Sixth Grade Teacher
Iskra, Donald
  Counselor
STEVENSVILLE
Feenstra, David Wayne
  High School Science Teacher

Kern, Denny Lee
  5th & 6th Grade Teacher
STURGIS
Caywood, Kathleen R.
  Reading Coordinator
Tufts, Frank Edward
  American History Teacher
TAWAS CITY
Decker, Drew LeRoy
  Physical Ed/Math Teacher
Jacob, Elizabeth Ann
  Fifth Grade Math Teacher
Reasner, Ann L.
  English Department Chairperson
Stoll, William David
  Mathematics Teacher
Wajda, Mary J. Derocher
  5th Grade Teacher
TECUMSEH
Novak, Carl Maxwell
  Mathematics Teacher
TEMPERANCE
Bell, James Gary
  Science Teacher/Dept Chair
Kreft, Bonnie Rae (Bellville)
  High School English Teacher
Self, Norma J.
  English & History Teacher
Smith, Mark F.
  Choral Director
THREE OAKS
Chesnut, Alice Smith
  Fourth Grade Teacher
TRAVERSE CITY
Gaines, Wendy Wittig
  Second Grade Teacher
Kurtz, Christine Marshall
  Communication Arts Teacher
Nelson, Harold
  Biology Teacher
Pratt, Mary Sanborn
  Sixth Grade Teacher
Sears, Judy E. Gribler
  First Grade Teacher
Visser, Konrad John
  German Teacher
TRENTON
Barbantini, Robert Louis
  Middle School Teacher
Lilly, Beverly Lynn
  Kindergarten Teacher
Lipinski, Helen Kolakowski
  5th Grade Teacher
Poindexter, James E.
  Science Teacher
Wiseman, Randy L.
  Sixth Grade Teacher
TROY
Clinton, Joe
  English Teacher
Hunter, Jon Robert
  Social Studies Teacher
Manfredi, Krista
  Theatre Teacher/Director
Maurer, Peter James
  Science Teacher
Midcalf, Randall W.
  English Department Chair
Rosenman, Deborah Bohm
  4th Grade Teacher
Smilnak, Andrew Joseph
  Mathematics/Quest Teacher
TWINING
Devereaux, Stewart Trent
  Industrial Art Teacher
UBLY
Holdship, Candice Kay (Golding)
  Sixth Grade Teacher
UNION LAKE
Monroe, Joy Ann Sauerbrun
  Retired Teacher
UTICA
Charles, Raleigh Glenn
  Biology/Computer Instructor
Fencyk, Edward W. Jr.
  8th Grade Counselor
Konnie, James Gerard
  Physics Instructor
Stoneking, Nancy Marie
  Administrative Asst to Supt
VARMONTVILLE
Spencer, Lonnie L.
  Biology Teacher/Science Chair
VASSAR
Mc Ardle, Martin Walter
  Secondary Mathematics Teacher

VERMONTVILLE
Acker, Norma Jean
  English Teacher
VESTABURG
Barnes, Michael L.
  Social Studies Chair
WALDRON
Donovan, Karen Manzel
  Business Dept Chairperson
WALKER
Niemi, Lois Lillibridge
  Fifth Grade Teacher
WALLED LAKE
Apap, Chuck Robert
  Math Teacher/Head Ftbl Coach
Losh, Daryl Russell
  5th Grade Teacher
WARREN
Cencich, David Joseph
  Mathematics Instructor
Garwood, Dianne Thornton
  Business Education Teacher
Moore, Neal F.
  Chemistry & German Teacher
Reed, Nancy C.
  Teacher/Lang Art Dept Chair
Zornow, Joann (Saperstein)
  Sixth Grade Teacher
WATERVLIET
Dongvillo, Darlene C.
  Elementary Principal
Hammond, Faith Louise
  English Teacher
Polaskey, Joan Cullitan
  Principal
WAYLAND
Jensen, Jon Christian
  Principal
WAYNE
Assenmacher, Sue Tomaszewski
  Junior High Teacher
Short, Carleen Lucke
  Seventh & Eighth Grade Teacher
WEBBERVILLE
Gruber, Mary Gettings
  Fifth Grade Teacher
West, Darrell A.
  Mathematics Teacher
WELLS
Wilson, Hazel Geraldine
  Sixth Grade Teacher
WEST BRANCH
Money, Jack Alan
  History Teacher
WESTLAND
Harmon, Gerald Edward
  Math & Computer Teacher
Kliza, Nancy G.
  English Teacher
Meyers, Linda Sue
  Science Teacher
Stresman, Diane K. (Schulz)
  English Teacher
WHITE CLOUD
McHattie, Tony Arthur
  English Teacher
Smith, Roger Raymond
  6th Grade Teacher
WHITE PIGEON
Hocevar, Elizabeth Ann
  French Teacher
Kohler, Daniel Richard
  Chemistry/Physics Teacher
Matthews, Kevin W.
  Director of Bands
WHITEHALL
Woods, Susan E.
  4th Grade Teacher
WHITTEMORE
Gillings, Gary Lee
  Social Studies Teacher
WOODHAVEN
Daniels, Bonnie Jean
  Composition Teacher
Di Biase, Jan B. De Waelsche
  English/Composition Teacher
Pretty, Susan Kamalay
  8th Grade Science Teacher
WYANDOTTE
Abercrombie, William I.
  Science Teacher
Clark, Nancy A.
  Third Grade Teacher

WYANDOTTE (cont)
Stieler, Beverlyann
  Elementary Teacher
Wehner, David Joel
  Bio/Microbiology/Dept Chair

WYOMING
Courter, James Robert
  5th Grade Teacher
Moulder, Joseph A.
  Chem/Physics/Earth Sci Teacher
Pullen, Elizabeth Bush
  Spanish/Communications Teacher
Schmidt, Suzanne Farnsworth
  Second Grade Teacher

YALE
Presnell, John
  Social Studies Teacher

YPSILANTI
Woolley, Judith Roxey
  Fifth Grade Teacher

MINNESOTA

ADAMS
Tipton, Dean D.
  Business Education Teacher

ADRIAN
Rother, Ronald Anthony
  Vocal Music Teacher Dept Chm

ALBANY
Nohava, Paulette Marie (Serbus)
  1st Grade Teacher

ALBERT LEA
Larson, Paul Theodore
  6th Grade Teacher
Peterson, Richard Kurt
  Band Director

ALEXANDRIA
Merkord, Lanny Dean
  Science, Phys Ed, Math Teacher

ANOKA
Bestul, Susan Kay Semling
  Special Education Teacher
Golyer, Larry Wes
  5th Grade Teacher
Rowbotham, Roger Kim
  Health Education Teacher

APPLE VALLEY
Egstad, Michael C.
  Social Studies Dept Coord
Pepera, Michael Gerard
  Geography Teacher

APPLETON
Makepeace, Terry Joseph
  Mathematics Instructor
Massey, Richard Ellsworth
  English Teacher

ARLINGTON
Hoops, Judith Ann
  Third Grade Teacher

ASHBY
Peterson, Lee Ella Mae Schmidt
  English Teacher

ATWATER
Rubis, William M.
  Language Art Teacher

AVON
Helling, Nancy Taylor
  First Grade Teacher
Kurilla, Joan Heurang
  5th/6th Grade Teacher

BARNESVILLE
Hilgers, Steven Francis
  Mathematics Teacher/Dept Chair

BARNUM
Peterson, Karen Winje
  1st Grade Teacher

BEARDSLEY
Harrison, Mildred Garner
  First Grade Teacher

BEMIDJI
Fausher, Juliann Marie Lundquist
  Third Grade Teacher
Galarneault, Thomas Richard
  World/American History Teacher
Grimes, Carol Jean
  Fifth Grade Teacher
Nichols, Ken E.
  History Teacher
Schultz, Darlene Lindseth
  Third Grade Teacher

BENSON
Hamann, Emil Elmer
  Science Instructor
Lilleberg, Darrell Eugene
  Math & Computer Sci Teacher

BIGFORK
Carlson, David Charles
  Mathematics Department Teacher
Lester, Joan (Nikolai)
  Sendry Social Studies Teacher

BLAINE
Anderson, Joan C.
  7th Grade Health Teacher
Dahl, Roger John
  World History/Soc Stud Teacher
Parks, Robin Dee (Platte)
  6th Grade Teacher

BLOOMING PRAIRIE
Amundson, Norma Jean
  Sixth Grade Teacher
Nelson, Le Mar Arden
  English/Journalism Teacher
Schwartz, Richard Henry
  Sixth Grade Teacher

BLOOMINGTON
Bradovich, Constance J.
  Media Director/Admin Asst
Fatchett, Patricia Angell Thomas
  Lang Art Teacher/Dept Chair
Goolsbey, Mary Ann
  Sixth Grade Teacher
Lyons, Earl James
  English Department Chair
Porter, Roger James
  Fourth Grade Science Teacher

BLUE EARTH
Grant, Robert S.
  5th Grade Teacher

BORUP
Haglund, Roger E.
  Mathematics Teacher

BRAINERD
Dambowy, Rosella
  Third Grade Teacher

BRICELYN
Beck, Marilyn Larson
  4th Grade Teacher

BROWNSDALE
Gillette, Grace Schnirring
  2nd Grade Teacher

BROWNTON
Popp, Brenda La Londe
  Fifth Grade Teacher

BURNSVILLE
Storlie, Willard Stanley
  Fifth Grade Teacher

CALEDONIA
Dahlen, Jeffrey John
  Sixth Grade Teacher
Engrav, Nancy Gaustad
  First Grade Teacher
Markegard, Beverly Lee
  5th Grade Teacher
Mc Cormick, Gail Lynn
  Physical Ed/Health Teacher

CANBY
Hoyme, Deborah J.
  Sixth Grade Teacher

CANNON FALLS
Hadler, Sally Lorraine
  Kindergarten-4th Grade Teacher
Hjermstad, Roslyn (Flaten)
  Sixth Grade Teacher
Severson, John Byron
  Science Instructor

CEDAR
Baumann, Marolyn Dorothy (Colness)
  Second Grade Teacher
Pearson, Helen Marie
  2nd Grade Teacher
Toll, Luverne Franzman
  Fourth Grade Teacher

CEYLON
Ballanger, Albert O.
  Mathematics/Computer Teacher
Cardille, Kevin Scott
  Science Teacher
Swenberg, Leila Ruth
  Elem Prin/3rd Grade Teacher

CHAMPLIN
Forrest, Martha L.
  Jr High School Counselor
Modec, Thomas Jack
  Math Dept Chair/Math Teacher

Ohlgren, Sandra Shuey
  Learning Disabilities Teacher

CHASKA
Kinkel, Merlyn Riley
  Biology Teacher
Schwermann, Betty Knutson
  Teacher of Gifted

CHISHOLM
Debevec, Mary Sullivan
  Soc Stud/Home Ec Teacher
Maki, Russell William
  Computer Coordinator

COHATO
Johnson, Melba J.
  Fifth Grade Teacher

COLD SPRING
Clark, Ronald Dean
  Social Studies Teacher
Holsinger, Dee (Lynn)
  Middle Sch Gen Music Teacher
Meyer, James George
  Fourth Grade Teacher

COSMOS
Card, Todd Thomas
  Business Teacher

COTTAGE GROVE
Ascher, Kathleen Anne
  Spanish Teacher
Ryan, Corinne English
  Home Economics Teacher/Coord

CROMWELL
Eliason, Oscar R.
  Science Teacher

DEER RIVER
Erzar, James Stephen
  Mathematics Teacher

DELANO
Keller, Sharon Kay (Dukatz)
  Fifth Grade Teacher
Litfin, Jerry Glen
  Physical Education Chair

DULUTH
Lundberg, Vinson
  Chemistry Teacher
Urbick, Robert J.
  6th Grade Teacher
Zumbrunnen, Katherine Andrea
  (Marnich)
  Jr High School Band Instructor

EAGAN
Sagen, Judy
  Vocal Music Teacher

EDGERTON
Butson, Randy Lee
  6th Grade Teacher

EDINA
Holm, Phillip Donald
  Music Director
Sharping, Alice Rayette
  English Teacher

EGAN
Gunville, Lawrence John
  5th Grade Teacher

ELLENDALE
Pelzl, Theodore A.
  Mathematics Department Chair
Stone, Marianne E.
  Second Grade Teacher

ELLSWORTH
Bruns, Gayle Anderson
  Business Ed/Library Instr
Roetman, Lois Mae Romberg
  Second Grade Teacher

ELY
Stefanich, George Matthew
  4th Grade Teacher

EVANSVILLE
Hutchings, DonaLou Nelson
  Sendry Eng/Rdng Teacher

EYOTA
Lindow, Bradley T.
  Mathematics Teacher
Pollema, Dorothy Anne
  First Grade Teacher

FARIBAULT
Waarvik, Janice L.
  Science Teacher

FERGUS FALLS
Anderson, Cris Michelle (Kling)
  Secondary Language Art Teacher
Larrivy, Jean Marie Scott
  4th Grade Teacher

Mesker, Glen E.
  Biology Teacher
Undseth, Steven Paul
  English Dept Chairman

FINLAYSON
Baustian, Bradley Kevin
  4th Grade Homeroom/1-5 Phys Ed

FLOODWOOD
Johnson, Cory Jordan
  Phys Ed Teacher/Coach

FOLEY
Bang, Timothy Donald
  English Teacher/Dept Chair
Brand, Carol Marie
  English Instructor

FRAZEE
Houdek, Allen J.
  US His/Span/Psych Teacher

FRIDLEY
Erickson, Rodney Eugene
  Social Studies Teacher

GARY
Nelson, Betty Liebenow
  5th Grade Teacher
Westhed, Mark Nils Oscar
  Science Teacher

GIBBON
Brelje, Sandra G.
  3rd Grade Teacher

GOLDEN VALLEY
Hefte, Arthur William
  Third/Fourth Grade Teacher

GOODRIDGE
Dahlen, Dave W.
  Mathematics Teacher
Johnson, Patti L.
  Science Instructor

GRAND MEADOW
Davidson, Nathan Royal
  General Music/Band Director

GRAND RAPIDS
Miner, John Ralph
  Science Teacher

GREENBUSH
Penas, Maxine Sluka
  Bio/Chem/Physics Teacher

GRYGLA
Jelle, Berniece Jeanette
  6th Grade Teacher

HASTINGS
Carlson, Karen Jane
  Fourth Grade Teacher
Teigland, John B.
  6th Grade Teacher

HENNING
Hermanson, Diane Bratlie
  Second Grade Teacher
Kantrud, Larry Harley
  Business Teacher
Twaddle, Donald D.
  German/Russian Teacher

HIBBING
Hanson, Herbert Harold
  Social Studies Chair
White, Leah Eskola
  2nd Grade Elementary Teacher

HOLDINGFORD
Noskowiak, Peggy Killoren
  English/Speech/Drama Teacher
Schoon, Steven Ray
  Mathematics/Physics Teacher

HOPKINS
Gieseke, Sharon Jean (Guggisberg)
  Math Dept Chm/Physics Teacher

HUTCHINSON
Carls, Michael A.
  American Government Teacher
De Bruyckere, Arlyn Matthew
  Chemistry/Physics Teacher

ISANTI
Anderson, Michael Ray
  Math Teacher/Computer Coord
Fischer, Joel Bruce
  Third Grade Teacher

ISLE
Searles, Jeffrey
  High School English Teacher

JORDAN
Dresow, Joan Rita
  Fourth Grade Teacher

Senske, Howard Victor
  Science Teacher

KELLIHER
Becwar, Mary Meyer
  Title I Teacher
Carlson, John Curtis
  Math/Computer Specialist
Hendrickson, Curtis Louie
  Third Grade Teacher

LAKE CITY
Gilman, Gregory Jay
  Math/Computer Sci Teacher
Pederson, Thomas Anthony
  Fifth Grade Teacher

LAKE ELMO
Gall, Steve R.
  Geography Teacher/Dept Chair

LAKEVILLE
Griebenow, Keith C.
  5th Grade Teacher
King, Timothy Brent
  Sixth Grade Teacher
Kurz, Jerold M.
  6th Grade Teacher/Chairperson

LAMBERTON
Amundson, Maxine (Killeaney)
  Vocal Music Teacher

LE ROY
Rachlisberger, Russell Neil
  Band Teacher

LE SUEUR
Powers, Brina Snyder
  3rd Grade Teacher

LITCHFIELD
Brix, Wayne A.
  English Teacher
Meyer, Edwin C.
  Technology Department Chair

LITTLE CANADA
Grengs, Barbara Krause
  8th/9th Grade English Teacher

LITTLE FALLS
Bauman, Albert O.
  Math Teacher/Department Chm
Hoglin, Jay Vaughn
  Math/Computer Dept Head
Lynch, Nancy Tancabel
  High School Math Teacher
Nagel, Lisa Wilkening
  K-8th Vocal Music Teacher
Spofford, Gregory Byron
  1st Grade Teacher

LYLE
Dahlquist, David Allen
  English Department Chair

MANKATO
Brown, Nadine Kollmann
  Sixth Grade Teacher
Gallup, Janice Ellen
  Physical Education Teacher
Peterson, Eldon Oren
  8th Grade History Teacher
Van Slyke, Linda Lee
  Spanish/Mathematics Teacher

MAPLE GROVE
Schweiger, David Frank
  Science Teacher
Seavert, Kathleen E.
  1st Grade Teacher

MAPLE LAKE
Anderson, Karleen Leiseth
  English Teacher
Gleason, Doris Matsuo
  1st Grade Teacher
Horstman, Jo Ann Elizabeth
  6th Grade Teacher
Leiseth, Keith M.
  Science Teacher
Mc Brady, Mary Siefert
  Kindergarten Teacher

MAPLEWOOD
Stolen, Hannelore M. A.
  Jr HS Teacher

MAYER
Lane, David Marland
  Mathematics Dept Chm/Teacher

MC GREGOR
Cummings, Steven Walter
  History/Social Studies Teacher
Geving, Bernis Flatjord
  Sixth Grade Teacher

MEADOWLANDS
Ohman, James Keith
  Fourth Grade Teacher

MEDFORD
Emerson, Steven John
  English Teacher/Coach
Hamner, Steve Carl
  5th Grade Teacher
Slifka, Jim Anthony
  Industrial Arts Teacher
Swenson, Catherine Wagner
  Second Grade Teacher

MENALIGA
Wolff, Marsha Berg
  English Teacher

MENDOTA HEIGHTS
Hollenbeck, Bonnie Morris
  Language Art Teacher
Marzolf, Richard Arthur
  Mathematics Teacher

MILACA
Sorenson, Janice Ekman
  Language Art Teacher

MINNEAPOLIS
Andrews, James Michael
  Assistant Principal
Dunning, Susan Arlene (Gibson)
  K-8th Grade Teacher
Dunphy, Helene Elaine
  6th Grade Teacher
Harris, Sandra Kaufman
  Elementary Classroom Teacher
Hendrickson, Lynne Nichols
  2nd Grade Teacher
Kauls, Guido Percy
  Ger Teacher/World Lang Chair
Nordgren, Lynn Lizbeth
  Fourth Grade Teacher
Roberts, George Albert
  Writing & English Lit Teacher
Strobel, Harold C.
  Biology Teacher

MINNETONKA
Chapman, Sue Manther
  Spanish Teacher

MONTICELLO
Forsberg, Dann Glenn
  Fifth Grade Teacher

MOORHEAD
Argent, Buzz Reed
  Mathematics Department Teacher
Beeson, Janice Thorwaldsen
  Teacher
Mickley, Arlene Williams
  Kindergarten Teacher
Rothlisburger, Rodney John
  Music Instructor

MORGAN
Kral, Gerald David
  Science Department Chair

NEW BRIGHTON
Grunke, John Herbert
  Mathematics Teacher

NEW HOPE
Schober, Albert Gustav
  Chemistry Teacher

NEW RICHLAND
Cyr, Paul Turgeon
  Jr/Sr HS Mathematics Teacher

NEW ULM
Gerasch, Inez Just
  Retired Substitute Teacher
Mc Namee, John Raymond
  Mathematics Teacher
Pickus, James Paul
  Industrial Technology Teacher

NEW YORK MILLS
Askew, Rita Geraldine
  5th Grade Teacher

NORTH BRANCH
Ahlm, Doniver Ray
  6th Grade Teacher
Brain, Patricia Anne
  English Teacher
Jones, Al Charles
  4th-5th Grade Teacher
Leland, Jeanne Carol
  Community Education Director

NORTH SAINT PAUL
Bettenberg-Pohl, Maria (Van Erp)
  Computers/Mathematics Teacher

NORTHFIELD
Giebel, Catherine Mc Gil
  Language Art Teacher

NORWOOD
Connell, Julie Holland
  Mathematics Teacher

Fasching, Jane Herrmann
  First Grade Teacher
Kroells, Sandra L.
  Kindergarten & ECSE Teacher

OGEMA
Ballard, Cecil Merle
  Fifth Grade Teacher

OGILVIE
Brennan, Deborah Ann
  Phys Ed & Health Teacher

OSSEO
Bigalke, Greg Eugene
  Economics Teacher
Larson, Robert Wayne
  Mathematics Teacher
Spangler, Pamela Karen
  Spec Admin Assignment Teacher

OWATONNA
Tillmann, Michael L.
  Staff Development Coordinator
Wacek, Susan (Nass)
  Mathematics/Computer Teacher

PELICAN RAPIDS
Mc Millen, John Charles
  Fourth Grade Teacher

PEQUOT LAKES
Schneider, Mary Jo Kelly
  Chapter I Teacher

PILLAGER
Pietz, Rose Marie Carlson
  4th Grade Teacher

PRINCETON
Erickson, Sondra Koering
  English/Journalism Teacher
Vaillancourt, Howard V.
  English Teacher

RANDALL
Stavish, Doris J. Martin
  3rd Grade Teacher

RED LAKE FALLS
Matzke, Cheryl Glaser
  Scndry Eng Teacher/Dept Chair

RED WING
Gaustad, Richard Harley
  Psych Teacher/Soc Stud Chm
Gustafson, Mary Bailey
  Second Grade Teacher

REDWOOD FALLS
Nieland, Joni Lange
  Chemistry Teacher
Yrjo, Donald Elvin
  Industrial Tech Teacher
Zellmann, Luann (Lillevold)
  Vocal Music Teacher

REMER
Welk, Sonia Sue
  Home Economics Teacher

RENVILLE
Peterson, S. Wayne
  Science & Phys Ed Teacher

RICHFIELD
Isherranen Abele, Marie Alena
    Maunula
  Language Art Teacher
Shimkus, Marjorie Monson
  Retired Teacher

RICHMOND
Bennett, Geralding Delores (Ward)
  4th Grade Teacher
Klaverkamp, Diane M.
  4th Grade Teacher

ROCHESTER
Brehmer, Steven Lester
  Physics Teacher
Deines, Judy Snell
  French Teacher
Greenberg, C. Sue (Bock)
  3rd & 4th Grade Teacher
Workman, Julia Geweke
  Orchestra Director

ROSEMOUNT
Brooks, Charles William
  High School English Teacher
Chandler, Katherine Mone
  First Grade Teacher
Gillund, Dennis Lee
  English Teacher
Gundacker, Rosemary Nigon
  Mathematics Teacher/Dept Chair
Hunter, Cynthia Lee
  Home Economics Teacher
Jaye, Pamela Youmans
  6TH Grade Eng/Soc Stud Teacher

Moen, Diana
  French Teacher
Price, John A.
  6th Grade English/Soc Teacher

ROSEVILLE
Cleary, Kathleen Ellen
  Teacher
Coury, Audrae Rochelle
  Eng as Second Lang Teacher

RUSH CITY
Hennen, Barb Ann
  Business Education Teacher
Proulx, Beverly Sue
  English Teacher

RUSHFORD
Dean, Maryellen
  Third Grade Teacher
Pettit, Jonathan Michael
  Sixth Grade Teacher

SAINT CHARLES
Smith, Judith Murrell
  Lang Art Teacher/Curr Dir

SAINT CLOUD
Jopp, Harlan V.
  Science/Agricultural Teacher
Niebur, Barbara E.
  6th Grade Teacher
Nohner, Shirley E.
  Campus Minister
Rotto, Judy Carol (Erickson)
  Kindergarten Teacher

SAINT FRANCIS
Dergantz, Susan Kaye
  Language Art Teacher
Fox, Mark Allen
  Life Science Teacher
Scott, Diane M.
  Kindergarten Teacher

SAINT LOUIS PARK
Bodin, Wesley James
  Social Studies Teacher
Dallmann, Carol Sundry
  Kindergarten Teacher
Getty, Joseph Charles
  7th/8th Grade English Teacher
Lane, Janice M.
  Chemistry Teacher
Skay, Margaret Nelson
  Third Grade Teacher

SAINT MICHAEL
Jordahl, Gina Marie
  Spanish Teacher
Loftus, Joyce Brenke
  5th Grade Teacher
Skogen, Darrell Lee
  Social Studies Chairperson

SAINT PAUL
Adams, Carol Jean
  A P European History Teacher
Andahazy, Marius Joseph
  K-12th Grade Dept Ballet Dir
Docherty, Gary James
  English Teacher
Erickson, Roy Richard
  Social Studies Teacher
Esselman, Barbara Munro
  Fourth Grade Teacher
Evensen, Elisabeth Hildegard
  Kindergarten Teacher
Graham, Curtis R.
  English Department Chair
Hopen, Dianne Brown
  French Teacher/Intnl Specialty
Jacobson, Gregory Douglas
  Language Arts Instructor
Kachel, Beth Johnsen
  Mathematics Teacher
Kerwin, Barbara Mary
  First Grade Teacher
Keyes, Mary Palcich
  English Teacher
Klein, Rhonda Mary
  Teacher
Lindman, Robert Allan
  Sixth Grade Teacher
Lorenzen, Robin Deborah
  Choral Music Educator
Magnuson, John David
  Teacher/Coach
Mc Cambridge, Elizabeth Turbes
  Soc Stud Dept Chairperson
Olson, Terry Robert
  Math & Computer Teacher
Sharp, Donna Jean
  Design Research Specialist
Weiss, Marilyn Peterson
  Home Economics Dept Chair
Wise, Linda L. (Horrisberger)
  English Teacher Dept Chair

Wood, Lu Ann
  Religion Teacher

SAINT PAUL PARK
Tschida, Sheila M. Jerikovsky
  8th Grade English Teacher

SANBORN
Walker, Brian Luvern
  Fifth Grade Teacher
Warning, Gerald Paul
  6th-8th Grade Teacher/Prin

SANDSTONE
Johnson, Susan Anderson
  Behavior Learning Teacher

SAUK CENTRE
Bakko, Barbara Allen
  English Teacher
Malevich, Sandra Rosnell (Stimac)
  4th Grade Teacher
Mayer, Mary K.
  English Teacher
Nelson, Kenneth E.
  Social Studies Teacher
Oberg, Thomas Carl
  7th Grade Math Teacher
Trutna, Tom Charles
  4th Grade Teacher

SEBEKA
Brown, Ann Marie
  4th Grade Teacher
Carlson, Bradley Paul
  Math/Geography Teacher

SHOREVIEW
Peterson, Verilyn Roxane (Potthoff)
  Vocal Music Teacher

SILVER LAKE
Collins, Wanda Abbott
  English Teacher
Woods, Mariel Gander
  Third Grade Teacher

SPRING LAKE PARK
Horns, David H.
  6th Grade Teacher
Wojciechowski, Donald Ray
  Mathematics Teacher

SPRINGFIELD
Kosiak, Kevin Jon
  Vocal Music Instructor

STAPLES
Trout, Lorraine M. Smith
  Retired 5th Grade Teacher

STARBUCK
Hanson, Shirley Jean
  Music Teacher

STILLWATER
Erickson, Merlyn S.
  Physics Teacher

TAYLORS FALLS
Anderson, David Carl
  Physical Education Teacher
Thimm, Joseph O.
  History Teacher

THIEF RIVER FALLS
Dunning, Dale John
  Mid Sch Geography Teacher

TRACY
Landman, Jane Sheimo
  English Teacher

VERNDALE
Hess, Joan C.
  Second Grade Teacher

VIRGINIA
Eskola, Robert Edwin
  Geography Teacher
Froehlingsdorf, Joseph C.
  HS Teacher
Gerchman, Leroy Fredrick
  Elementary Science Teacher
Pepelnjak, Joyce Cardoni
  Third Grade Teacher
Salmi, Nancy Peterson
  Social Studies Teacher
Turk, Tony
  English Teacher

WABASHA
Grimley, Mark James
  7th-8th Grade Soc Stud Teacher

WADENA
Waldahl, Baldy Jerome
  7th/8th Grade Math Teacher
Wegscheid, Nellie Hendrick
  5th Grade Teacher

WARREN
Anderson, Carol J.
  Fourth Grade Teacher

WASECA
Ayres, Charles Louis
  High School English Teacher
Chamberlain, Gary
  Second Grade Teacher
Smith, Mary Dobmeyer
  Fourth Grade Teacher

WATKINS
Geislinger, Robert Alfred
  Social Studies Teacher

WAUBUN
Dretch, Marie Mae
  6th Grade Teacher
Garmen, Greggory David
  Science Teacher Coach
Harstad, Lois Anderson
  Fourth Grade Teacher

WAYZATA
Traxler, Mary Therese
  First Grade Teacher

WELLS
Raimann, Linda J.
  Fifth Grade Teacher
Vincent, Franklin Anderson
  Fourth Grade Teacher

WHITE BEAR LAKE
Larson, Bill Martin
  6th Grade Teacher
Wiik, Susan Merrick
  English Teacher

WILLMAR
Beauvais, Herbert Lee Jr.
  Mathematics Instructor
Cole, Don
  6th Grade Teacher
Grewe, Connie Jean (Kemnitz)
  Ninth Grade English Teacher

WINDOM
Klosterbuer, Mary Sue
  Fourth Grade Teacher

WINONA
Manley, Patricia E.
  Instructor

WOODBURY
Kandler, Dorothea Helen
  2nd Grade Teacher

WORTHINGTON
Timm-Knuth, Lora Lee
  Home Ec Dept Chair & Teacher

WRIGHT
Thudin, Randy Carl
  Elementary Principal

YOUNG AMERICA
Balzum, Mary Jean Prochnow
  Fourth Grade Teacher

MISSISSIPPI

ABERDEEN
Carter, Melody Baker
  Mathematics Teacher/Dept Chair
Walker, Opal Cooperwood
  7th & 8th Grade Sci Teacher

ACKERMAN
Anderson, Gerry
  Social Studies Teacher
Cornish, Charlotte Young
  Teacher of Gifted
Wood, William Boyd
  Social Studies Teacher

AMORY
Carpenter, Sandra Kay (Petty)
  Language Art/Reading Teacher
James, Tyrone
  Chemistry Teacher/Sci Chair
Mc Call, Vera Mitchell
  Teacher

ASHLAND
Bostick, John Henry
  Eighth Grade Math Teacher

BASSFIELD
Hathorn, Carolyn Watts
  English Teacher
Hitt, Marty Thomas
  Fifth Grade Teacher
West, Mary J.
  Remedial Reading Teacher

BATESVILLE

Benson, Patricia Ann Barnhill
1st Grade Teacher
Butts, Robbie Harrison
Fifth Grade Teacher
Grantham, Rebecca Shumaker
Mathematics Instructor
Hentz, Emma Kay
Eighth Grade History Teacher

BAY SAINT LOUIS

Harder, Kenneth J.
Math Department Chairperson

BAY SPRINGS

Denson, Sharon Kay
English & Journalism Teacher
Mc Neer, Beverly King
Social Studies Teacher
Ordway, Janie Read
2nd Grade Teacher

BEAUMONT

Hinton, Ina Henderson
Fifth Grade Teacher

BECKER

Willis, Samuel E. Jr.
Elementary Administrator

BELMONT

Alexander, Lucretia Ann
Guidance Counselor
Banks, Alice Hall
4th Grade Teacher

BELZONI

Brown, Marion Louise Shamblee
9th-12th Grade Math Teacher
Hall, Frances Jackson
Third Grade Teacher
Proby, Ernestine Griffin
Third Grade Teacher
Ross, John
Reading Teacher

BENTON

Ruschewski, Woodson Earle
Mathematics Dept Chairman

BILOXI

Bogard, Margo Wilson
5th Grade Teacher
Estrada, Jane Morris
Sixth Grade Science Teacher
Gottsche, Myra M.
AP & Excel US History Teacher
Hill, Charlie Gaines
Metal Trades Instructor
Howat, Sandra Wilson
Second Grade Teacher
Hughes, Betty Jean
Latin Teacher
Kiefer, Yvonne Baker
First Grade Teacher
Killebrew, Loree Simpson
Second Grade Teacher
Layton, Carolyn Hollingsworth
Vocational Skills Instructor
Neaves, Tracey Black
6th Grade Science Teacher
Powers, Sue L.
Teacher
Roberts, Carlene Copeland
6th Grade Teacher
Shirley, Ann Cerra
6th Grade Teacher
Stafford, G. Sue Eldridge
2nd Grade Teacher
Todd, Marcia Friedrich
Sixth Grade Teacher
Veal, Mary Sue
English Teacher

BOGUE CHITTO

Hux, Barbara Smith
Business Education Teacher

BOONEVILLE

Jackson, Carolyn Wallis
English Teacher
Spain, Marie Robertson
Teacher of Gifted

BRANDON

Bender, Susan Arlyce
A P Bio/Adv Bio/Chem Teacher
Brister, Ramona Butler
Kindergarten Teacher
Buckhaulter, Barbara Harper
Social Studies Teacher
Hollis, June Davidson
Social Studies Dept Chair

BROOKHAVEN

Britt, Ruthie Juanita
Third Grade Teacher
Kelly, Flora M.
Kindergarten Principal

Lucas, Jeanette Lowe
First Grade Teacher
Martin, Ellen C.
English Department Chairman
Smith, Barbara J. Nelson
8th Grade Amer His Teacher
Spiller, Andrew
Social Studies Teacher
Spiller, Betty Mc Beth
Home Economics Teacher
Warren, Linda Henderson
Social Studies Teacher
Whittier, Jennifer Jackson
English/Spanish Teacher

BROOKLYN

Green, Yvonne Daniel
Rdng/Math/Soc Stud Teacher
Lee, Mary Ann Ann Hickman
Home Economics Teacher
Minter, Barbara Tims
Advanced Placement Eng Teacher
Pearce, Helen Gelling
First Grade Teacher
Whitworth, Breck Howard
Science Teacher/Football Coach

BRUCE

Parker, Donna Neal
Senior English Teacher
Yarbrough, Mark Anthony
Bio Teacher/Head Ftbl Coach

BURNSVILLE

Hall-Locke, Teddie
Media Specialist
Wood, James Walker
Social Studies Teacher

CALHOUN CITY

Parker, Martha Harrelson
Fourth Grade Teacher

CANTON

Baaree, Gloria Najeebah
Asst Prgm Devlpr/Pre-Sch Coord
Bonds, Jonas L.
English Teacher
Hayes, Freida Rochelle
English/Home Economics Teacher

CARRIERE

Harris, Ruby Nell Thrash
Third Grade Teacher

CARTHAGE

Moore, Gary Ann (Sistrunk)
Mathematics Teacher

CHARLESTON

Young, Joanne Adams
Sixth Grade English Teacher

CLARKSDALE

Catchings, Shirley Anderson
English Teacher
Tedford, Toni Gail
Biology Teacher

CLEVELAND

Bass, Debbie Hunt
Fifth Grade Teacher
Cooper, Jan Morrison
Teacher-Coordinator
Fitzgerald, Anita Bell
Fifth Grade Teacher
Mc Cool, Brenda Bell
English Teacher

CLINTON

Browning, Bennie Perry
Fifth Grade Teacher
Reynolds, Judith M.
English Teacher
Watson, Vera Dolores (Banks)
Social Studies Teacher

COLLINS

Norris, Barbara Ann
Second Grade Teacher

COLLINSVILLE

Murphy, Clarie Lisenbe
4th Grade Teacher

COLUMBIA

Abram, Mary Kathryn
Teacher
Bailey, Victoria Seirsdale
Fourth Grade Teacher
James, Carrie Marshall
Home Economics Teacher
Mann, Karl
Mathematics Teacher

COLUMBUS

Atkins, Joan Burkhart
5th Grade Teacher
Doty, Lillie Carson
Chemistry Teacher

Elmore, Maria Elizabeth
Mathematics Teacher
Freize, Arbra Celeste
Kindergarten Teacher
Hickman, Belle Shelton
Business Education Teacher
Holloman, Mary Alice Jackson
Mathematics Dept Chairman
Mitchell, Marie Shamburger
Mathematics Dept Chairperson
Norris, Linda Fleming
First Grade Teacher
Reece, Toni Bernheim
Band Director
Sanders, Lynn Catlette
Teacher
Weems, Mary Anne Paulk
Mathematics Teacher
Wicks, Nancy Ingram
4th Grade Teacher

CORINTH

Scott, Gladys Suitor
Third Grade Teacher

CRYSTAL SPRINGS

Derrick, Annie
Biology Teacher
Harris, Theresa Smith
4th Grade Teacher
Trim, David T.
English/Journalism Teacher

D'IBERVILLE

Paulson, Jean O'Neal
Chem Teacher/Sci Dept Chair

DE KALB

Brown, Joy Mc Lelland
Social Studies/Fr I Teacher
Eldridge, Edna Boren
Fifth Grade Teacher

DECATUR

Pearce, Kathy Hill
Mathematics Dept Chair/Teacher
White, Velma Lou Lewis
Science Teacher

DURANT

Logan, Argie Peters
First Grade Teacher

ECRU

Brown, Timothy Stephen
Science Teacher/Coach
Martin, Linda Dowdy
3rd Grade Teacher
Moore, Brenda Huffstatler
HS Social Studies Teacher

ELLISVILLE

Hinshaw, Kathy Kittrell
Third Grade Teacher
Morris, Beverly Wilson
7th & 8th Grade Eng Teacher

ENTERPRISE

Dunnam, Bobbye Lynne
History and French Teacher

FALKNER

Gunn, Linda Childs
Fourth Grade Teacher
Martindale, Linda Thompson
Third Grade Teacher

FAYETTE

Trimble, Mary Marie
Social Studies Teacher

FLORA

Hardy, Ada Harrell
2nd Grade Teacher/Elem Prin

FLORENCE

Byrd, Lisa Alford
Mathematics Teacher
Derryberry, Sylvia Gail
7th Grade Teacher
Tucker, Frances
Fourth Grade Teacher

FOREST

Garvin, Marsha Jean
First Grade Teacher

FRIARS POINT

Smith, Willie B. Willis
5th/6th Grade Science Teacher

FULTON

Bishop, Hilda Holcomb
10th/12th Grade Eng Teacher
Moore, Patsy Martin
Fourth Grade Teacher

GALLMAN

Ashley, Charlotte Pigg
English Teacher
Batton, Ann Burney
2nd Grade Elem Head Teacher

GAUTIER

Gaunce, Dronda White
8th Grade English Teacher

GLEN

Hill, Maudella M.
Second Grade Teacher
Young, Margie F.
Head Teacher

GOLDEN

Clayton, Brenda Young
Kindergarten Teacher
Odom, Sandra Darlene
Jr HS Science Teacher
Whitehead, Debbie Killen
English Teacher

GREENVILLE

Blaine, Susan Scott
Mathematics Teacher
Collins, Cynthia Guillory
English I Teacher
Cook, Sarah W.
English Teacher
Smith, Brenda Scott
9th Grade English Teacher
Thompson, Reba Denley
First Grade Teacher
Wilcox, Phillip Daniel
Science Department Chair

GREENWOOD

Barnwell, Anne Carter
Mathematics Teacher
Clark, Kathryn Murphey
Math Dept Chair & Teacher
Evans, Mattie Harris
English I Teacher
Hayes, Willie Lewis
Mathematics Teacher
Mc Coy, Hannah Littles
Social Studies Teacher
Norwood, Mack M.
Teacher/Coach
Scales, Lois L.
1st Grade Teacher
Simmons, Elizabeth Hill
Bio & Human Physiology Teacher
Webb, Bonita Dabbs
Elementary Principal

GRENADA

Brown, Willie Ola
Social Studies Teacher
Collins, Joyce Morrow
Business Teacher
Cox, John Rogers
MS His/Amer His Teacher
Estes, Robbie D.
Fourth Grade Teacher
Harrison, Rosetta
Fourth Grade Math Teacher
Mc Rae, Carol Reeves
8th Grade Teacher
Orrell, Sarah Evans
Third Grade Teacher
Scarborough, Delores (Barber)
Secondary Math Teacher
Spears, Lucille Coleman
Health & Physcial Ed Teacher
Watson, Nez
Social Studies Teacher

GULFPORT

Cain, Susan K.
Third Grade Teacher
Cook, Elizabeth Ann (Bandy)
English, Govt, Comp Teacher
Drake, Paulette Boudreau
Chemistry Teacher
Herbert, Karen Grigsby
Social Studies Dept Chair
Hertz, Peggy Ladner
Home Ec Teacher
Holley, Mary Shaw
English Department Chair
Lawrence, Vicki Lass
Eng Teacher/Dept Chairperson
Marsh, Harriet Redd
Social Studies Teacher
Mc Gee, James Willis
Mathematics Teacher
Modenbach, Patricia Fulkerson
English Dept Chair/Dev Dir
Moran, Sheryl Lee
Drafting Instructor
Randall, Elizabeth Jo
Second Grade Teacher
Rogers, Debra T.
Marketing Teacher/Coordinator
Shaw, Gisele Jackson
Secondary Math Teacher
Thomas, Barbara Jean
Chapter I Coordinator

HATTIESBURG

Barnes, Rebecca Ann
Fourth Grade Teacher
Bauer, Laurie Koenig
Science Educator
Blake, Debrah F.
Social Studies Teacher
Brown, Christine Husband
Teacher
Bryant, Yvonne
Assistant Principal
Byrnes, Rose Marie
Rural Mail Carrier
Dunn, Margaret Carter
History & Government Teacher
Emerson, Kay Lewis
Gifted & Talented Teacher
Hughes, Paul Buckner
Biology Teacher
Johnson, Terry Grant
7th Grade Soc Stud Teacher
Moore, Connie De Long
Teacher
Naylor, Sandra Payton
Second Grade Teacher
Sullivan, Ann Martin
Chemistry Teacher
Tebo, Mike O'Dell
Eng/Creative Writing Teacher
Thorne, Arneda Ellis
Chapter I Teacher

HAZLEHURST

Barden, Lillie Chase
Third Grade Teacher
Dorsey, Dorothy
Mathematics Teacher
Haynie, Vera Foster
First Grade Teacher
Mc Coy, Mae Taylor
High School Reading Teacher

HEIDELBERG

Lofton, Vernell Thigpen
Phys Ed Teacher/Coach/Chair
Page, Annie Grace (Tatum)
Third Grade Teacher

HERNANDO

Downing, Sharon S.
Teacher of Gifted
Flynn, James Benjamin
History Teacher & Coach

HICKORY FLAT

Bennett, Kathy Thompson
Sixth Grade Teacher
Massengill, Belinda Barber
Science Teacher

HOLLY SPRINGS

Belk, Linda Moore
Third Grade Teacher
Burton, Lillian Stephenson
Teacher
Hood, Fergenia Harrison
English Teacher/Dept Chair
Mc Crosky, Carolin Skyden
Kindergarten Teacher
Niknahad, Coral Garmon
Sr HS Social Studies Teacher
Robinson, James Bernard
Math Teacher/Basketball Coach
Schmidtknecht, Ramona Ann
Home Economics/Math Teacher
Stewart, Phoebe
Mathematics Teacher

HORN LAKE

Arnold, Mary Ann Barnett
Mathematics Dept Chairman
Guyer, Anita Massey
Kindergarten Teacher
Lott-Shelby, Lemoyne
1st Grade Teacher
Shannon, Sylvia Hence
Fourth Grade Teacher
Smith, Claudette Hence
Third Grade Teacher
Sublett, Mary Katherine
History Teacher

HOULKA

Cothran, Russell Randle
6th Grade Teacher

HOUSTON

Bonds, Shirley Atkinson
Fourth Grade Teacher
Smith, Denna Lantrip
Fifth Grade Teacher

INDIANOLA

Barner, Lillie Petty
Mathematics Teacher
Hutchinson, Susan Thomas
Math Dept & Cmptr Sci Chair
Kennedy, Alberta Thomas
4th Grade Teacher

INDIANOLA (cont)
Triplett, Gwendolyn Byrd
World History Teacher
Ware, Sarah R.
5th Grade Teacher
Wilson, Clifford Don
Assistant Principal/Teacher

ITTA BENA
Hilliard, Betty Cantrell
1st Grade Teacher
Porter, Anne Wait
Computer Literacy Teacher
Walker, Elsie Pittman
6th Grade Teacher

IUKA
Bruce, Robert Alan
Band Director
Lowrey, Bobby Wayne
Science Department Chairperson
Mc Clung, Diane Dean
Fourth Grade Teacher
Mc Neely, Becky Payne
Sixth Grade Teacher

JACKSON
Alexander, Mary Randolph
History Teacher
Allen, Polly Hope Bell
Substitute Elementary Teacher
Anglin, Linda Mc Cluney
5th Grade Teacher
Baker, Sherry M.
Curriculum Coordinator
Bender, Geraldine Smith
French/German Teacher
Bolian, Ida May
Fourth Grade Teacher
Bowie, Geraldine R. Basley
Principal
Bracey, Jerry Alexander
Director of Bands
Brown, Patricia
Social Studies Teacher
Clarkson, Betty Weems
Fourth Grade Teacher
Cora, Spiro Pete
His Teacher/Soc Stud Chair
Crosland, Barksdale Johnston
First Grade Teacher
Davis, James E.
Science Department Chair
Davis, Nancy Surratt
Mathematics Teacher
Gaston, Ardella D.
Biology/Chemistry Teacher
Gentry, Bessie Frazier
6th Grade Teacher
Hilliard, Barbara Thompson
English/Journalism Teacher
Holcomb, Elizabeth Turner
English Teacher
Howard, Peggy Moore
English Teacher
Irvin, Marina Badgett
English Teacher
Land, Excell
Fifth Grade Teacher
Lee, Mary Harrison
6th Grade Math Teacher
Lurate, Lauren Millette
Chemistry I Teacher
Manning, Dorothy Johnson
Mathematics Teacher/Dept Chair
Martin, Yolanda Alexandra
Eng, Span & Writing Teacher
Mc Sparin, Phillip A.
English Teacher
Moorehead, Stanley Leon
Fifth Grade Teacher
Page, Joycie Coleman
1st Grade Teacher
Robinson, Lovie Vinson
Fourth Grade Teacher
Robinson, Walter
Social Studies Teacher/Coach
Smith, Etta Evans
Principal
Sutton, Lillian Robinson
6th Grade Teacher
Sylvester, Nancy Wilcher
Academic Counselor
Vinson, Charlotte A.
Mathematics Teacher
Walker, Mae Charlotte Jones
Fourth Grade Teacher
West, Barbara Bruce
Mathematics Teacher
Westerfield, Barbara Gregory
Economics/Government Teacher
Winkler, Bradley Mason
8th Grade Amer History Teacher

KOSSUTH
Atkins, Betty Gwyn
English Teacher

Dunn, Elizabeth Joyce
Fifth Grade Teacher

LAKESHORE
Weiler, Frances Baird
English Teacher

LAUREL
Austin, Gladys
Science Teacher/Sci Dept Chair
Coleman, Alma James
English Resource Specialist
Collins, Katie Norton
Seventh Grade Science Teacher
Gable, Frances B.
Eng/Spelling/Soc Stud Teacher
Glaze, Bobby Glenn
Mathematics Teacher
Holifield, Terry Lynn
Biology Teacher
Martin, Andrea Mae
4th Grade Teacher
Morgan, Gay Davis
English Teacher
Rogers, Virginia Faye
Second Grade Teacher
Windham, Diana Doris
Science Dept Chairperson

LEAKESVILLE
Pulliam, Linda D.
English Teacher
Smith, Hilda Smith
1st Grade Teacher

LEARNED
Downing, Ina Womack
4th Grade/Piano/Music Teacher

LELAND
Cartlidge, Helen King
Kindergarten Teacher
Dantzler, Sharon Ann
Fifth Grade Math Teacher
Quinn, Ellen Ellis
Second Grade Teacher

LEXINGTON
Brown, Charles Edward
8th Grade Math Teacher
Ellis, Hattie Mae
6th Grade Reading Teacher
Montgomery, Betty J.
3rd Grade Teacher

LIBERTY
Moore, Yvonne
Third Grade Teacher

LITTLE ROCK
Leach, Judy Ann
English Teacher
Odom, Martha Mc Kenzie
4th/5th/6th Grade Lang Teacher
Sanders, Rosa Anne
Science Teacher

LONG BEACH
Bentz, Kathryn De Bord
4th Grade Teacher
Kramer, Jane B. (Hartsfield)
Social Studies Teacher
Ladner, Anne Brown
Fifth Grade Teacher
Mann, Perri Roberts
English Teacher

LOUISVILLE
Ballard, Beverly Sullivan
Social Studies/French Teacher
Bane, Ricky L.
Science Teacher
Eaves, Emily P.
Jr HS Math/Eng Teacher
Mitchell, Virginia Dale
Fourth Grade Teacher
Sinclair, Brenda Arnett
Sixth Grade Teacher

LUCEDALE
Brown, Frances Cooley
Assistant Principal
Henderson, Josie Ratliff
Jr HS Math & Reading Teacher
Parkinson, Brenda Joyce
9th-11th Grade English Teacher
Sellers, Jo Ann Coxwell
US History/Journalism Teacher
Tanner, Becky Eubanks
Third Grade Teacher

LUMBERTON
Harvey, Donald Leroy
Science Department Chairperson

LYON
Luster, Delores Catchings
Fourth Grade Teacher

MABEN
Crowley, Sherry
Library Media Specialist

MACON
Adams, Pam L.
1st Grade Teacher

MADDEN
Howell, Faithe Boatner
English/Speech Teacher

MAGEE
Hodum, Ellen Cliburn
First Grade Teacher
Nelson, Joyce Ann
Sixth Grade Teacher
Sanders, Mertha Rankin
Social Studies Chairman

MAGNOLIA
Coney, Elaine Marie
Span, French & Latin Teacher
Du Bose, Janet Hayes
4th Grade Teacher
Holbrook, Helen Andrews
Mathematics Teacher
Mc Cray, Willie James
Math Department Chairperson
Patterson, Geneva Nero
Middle School Librarian
Pollan, Cecil Barrett
English Teacher

MANTACHIE
Rieves, Joyce Sheffield
First Grade Teacher
Turner, Sarah Hill
4th Grade Teacher

MATHISTON
Ray, Lynda Turner
3rd Grade Teacher

MC COMB
Brock, Betty Pope
Mathematics Department Chair
Hensarling, Nancy Garland
8th Grade English Teacher
Simmons, Barbara B.
English/Speech Teacher

MC NEILL
Kellar, Tracy Prather
English/Language Arts Teacher

MEADVILLE
Cain, Vergie Williams
2nd Grade Teacher
Carraway, Linda Shell
Business Education Teacher
Graves, Mary Ann
8th Grade English Teacher
Guice, Michael David
8th Grade Soc Stud Teacher
Laird, Brenda Ratcliff
Biology Instructor
Mc Gehee, Judy Danner
Mathematics Teacher
Tillman, Carol Smith
Teacher
Tyson, Laura Boggan
Reading Teacher Chapter I

MENDENHALL
Dear, Linda Barlow
Bsktbl Coach/8th Grade Teacher
Perkins, Doris Wilson
4th Grade Mathematics Teacher

MERIDIAN
Brookshire, Kathy Langford
Teacher of Gifted & Talented
Cornwell, Jeannie Duke
Humanities Teacher
Davidson, Nelda M.
Fashion Merchandising Teacher
Harper, Patricia Smith
5th Grade Teacher
Keene, Lucy M.
Counselor
King, Diane
Third Grade Teacher
Little, Douglas David
Chemistry/Biology Teacher
Perry, Mary Annie Vernell
Fourth/Fifth Grade Teacher
Porter, Ivria J.
Third Grade Teacher
Reynolds, Jerry Robert
Social Studies Teacher
Roberson, Bebe Hayden
Fifth/Sixth Soc Stud Teacher
Wilson, Vinie Ann
Science Teacher

MONTICELLO
Deavers, Betty Lou Brister
4th/5th Grade English Teacher

MORTON
Boyd, Daisy White
3rd Grade Teacher
Johnson, John C.
6th-8th Grade Teacher/Coach
Lathem, Skip J.
Mathematics Teacher
Purvis, Edgar Lee
8th Grade Soc Stud Teacher
Purvis, Marcia Beard
2nd Grade Teacher

MOSELLE
Shows, Nancy Lindley
4th Grade Teacher
Sumner, Jennette C.
Third Grade Teacher

MOSS POINT
Anglin, Barbara Gayle (Hawthorne)
Art Teacher
Collins, Nettie Holloway
History Teacher
De Shields, Inez Dent
Mathematics Teacher/Dept Chair
Mitchell, Mary Elizabeth
8th Grade US History Teacher
Moorer, Lisa Willis
Senior English Teacher
Peresich, Mark Lee
History Teacher
Sanders, Lena Marbra
Government/Economics Teacher
Tanner, Peggy P.
Sixth Grade Teacher
Wood, Rebecca Jolly
Food Service Teacher

MOUND BAYOU
Carter, Ivy Richardson
Kindergarten Teacher
Harris, Emily C.
Third Grade Teacher
Langdon, Everette Wims
Fourth Grade Teacher

MYRTLE
Greer, Betty H.
5th-8th Grades Eng Teacher
Owen, Charles B.
Mathematics Department Teacher

NATCHEZ
Bowman, Barbara Stovall
Third Grade Teacher
Kirkwood, Janet Marion
7th/8th Grade Science Teacher

NETTLETON
Mc Daniel, Joann Pettigrew
Principal

NEW ALBANY
George, Leanne Tate
Teacher of Gifted & Talented
Kirkland, Kathi Henry
8th Grade Teacher
Nanney, Joan Bates
First Grade Teacher

NEW AUGUSTA
Lott, Jacquelyne Marie
8th Grade Mathematics Teacher

NICHOLSON
Breland, Larry Eugene
5th Grade Teacher

OCEAN SPRINGS
Baggett, Kay Bryan
Biology/Life Science Teacher
Belvel, Richard
Teacher
Blakeney, Doug B.
Gifted/Talented Instructor
Cacibauda, Joseph Anthony Jr.
Music Department Chairman
Harrison, Debra Ann (Young)
Secondary English Teacher
Poss, Elayne Knox
Guidance Counselor

OLIVE BRANCH
Reid, Susan Quarterman
7th/8th Grade Algebra Teacher
Sewell, Marie Finley
4th Grade Lang Arts Teacher

OXFORD
Jordan, Linda Golden
Fifth Grade Teacher
Logan, Sam T.
Social Studies Teacher
Whitwell, Martha Veazey
Chemistry/Physics Teacher

PACHUTA
Davis, Mary Sartor
Retired

PASCAGOULA
Arrington, Helga Przewosny
German & French Teacher
Beard, Gwendolyn Marx
6th Grade Teacher
Milstead, Virginia Lucas
Counselor
Murphy, Glen
Athletic Dir/His Teacher
Proctor, Edna Jackson
5th Grade Teacher
Ros, Eva Voncile (Livaudais)
Substitute Teacher
Trahan, Motie Gail Longo
English Teacher/Dept Chair
Turner, Natalie Welborn
Soc Stud/Journalism Teacher
Walton, Bobbie Nowell
Business Coordinator
Watts, Joyce Ann (Morgan)
Computer Department Chairman

PASS CHRISTIAN
Allen, Betty Gray
Math-Computer Science Teacher
Lain, Deborah Reynolds
JTPA Teacher

PEARL
Lee, Alexander H.
8th Grade Math Dept Chairman
Rogers, Patricia Reed
4th Grade Teacher
Wells, Irma Carter
Fifth Grade Teacher

PEARLINGTON
Spell, Gay Cain
Fifth Grade Teacher

PELAHATCHIE
Breland, Earlene Mc Cullum
English/French Teacher
Williams, Fannie Randolph
First Grade Teacher

PETAL
Boler, Barry Kemp
Biology Teacher/Coach
Carter, Lillian Ishee
4th-7th Grade Math Teacher
Carter, Vudger Mc Gilvery
4th-7th Science Teacher
Creel, Margarett Sanford
Third Grade Teacher
Huey, Carolyn Cook
7th Grade Math Teacher
Kendrick, Margaret Buxton
Chemistry Teacher/Science Dept
Lott, Jackie Rutland
4th Grade Teacher
Smith, William Todd
History Teacher/Ftbl Coach

PHEBA
Dobbs, Linda Carol
Mathematics Dept Chairman
Jones, Cora Lee
Jr HS English Teacher

PHILADELPHIA
Hall, Genie Callahan
Second Grade Teacher
Hardy, Valerie Walters
Social Studies Teacher
Luke, Sue Huff
Music & Piano Teacher
Mc Nair, Vikki Jenkins
Secondary Math Dept Teacher

PICAYUNE
Franklin, Melonee Seal
English Teacher
Ramsdale, Portia Rissler
Sixth Grade Reading Teacher
Tate, Diane Mitchell
English Teacher
Williams, Luddia Chatman
Second Grade Teacher
Young, Eddie
Health/Phys Ed Teacher

PONTOTOC
Burchfield, Curtis Dean
Amer His Teacher/Soc Stud Chm
Duke, Conwell
Principal
Galloway, Maria Cox
English IV & Spanish I Teacher
Griffin, Linda B.
1st Grade Teacher
Parker, Stella Bagwell
English-Business Teacher

PORT GIBSON
Watson, Gladys Juanita
5th Grade Teacher

PRENTISS
Gray, Patricia Ann Dampier
Mathematics Teacher
Laird, Shirley Barnes
Chapter I Lead Teacher
PUCKETT
Burnham, Lyda Alice
English Teacher
QUITMAN
Baldwin, Edea Pitre
English Teacher
Hailes, Kay S.
Reading/Language Arts Teacher
Mc Arthur, John Erwin
Director of Bands
RALEIGH
Lofton, Jimmy L.
State Government Teacher
Taylor, Sandra D.
English Teacher
RAYMOND
Gordon, Ann Sudduth
English Teacher
RICHLAND
Harpe, Betty Vance
Fifth Grade Teacher
Lewis, Marvin
History Teacher/Coach
Sullivan, Ellen Butler
Third Grade Teacher
Usry, Jackie Neely
8th Grade Math & His Teacher
RIPLEY
Braddock, Rita Clemmer
Fifth Grade Eng/Rdng Teacher
Breland, John O.
History Teacher
Brooks, Curtis
Science Teacher/Coach
Chapman, Janie Copeland
English Teacher
Elder, Nell Elizabeth
Fourth Grade Teacher
Locke, Linda J.
First Grade Teacher
White, Sylvia Yarbrough
Second Grade Teacher
ROSEDALE
Williams, LaVarne
5th/6th Grade Science Teacher
RULEVILLE
Miller, Charlis
Business Teacher
SALTILLO
Boutwell, Janice Cooper
Second Grade Teacher
SARDIS
Long, Etoyil F.
English Teacher
SEMINARY
Hughes, Glinder Flowers
Sixth Grade Teacher
Sanford, Patricia Bullock
Fifth Grade Teacher
SENATOBIA
Lowrie, Myrna Wallace
1st Grade Teacher
Sinquefield, Jo Ann Martin
Business Teacher
Young, Ann Miller
Third Grade Teacher
SHANNON
Danforth, Sandra Dobbs
English Teacher
SOSO
Tillman, Marion Ingram
Second Grade Teacher
SOUTHAVEN
Harvey, Nancy Cash
3rd Grade Teacher
Pope, Diane Davis
7th & 8th Pre-Algebra Teacher
Pryor, Laverne Hill
English Teacher
Rodgers, Martha Rackley
Third Grade Teacher
Tatum, Pamela Hurdle
Mathematics Teacher
STARKVILLE
Estes, Betty Berry
2nd Grade Teacher
Gholston, Nanette Nasif
Teacher
O'Bannon, Brenda Caraway
Mathematics Teacher/Dept Chair

Saucier, Linda Allen
Second Grade Teacher
Smith, Cindy Mc Minn
Junior High Science Teacher
Turner, Diana Leatherwood
Science Teacher
Warren, Sally Kennedy
Eng/Creative Writing Teacher
STURGIS
Dewberry, Dottie Maxey
Jr HS English & Math Teacher
SUMNER
Curtis, Delores Anderson
Science Teacher
SUMRALL
Dawsey, Kim Barattini
Band Director
Henderson, Nell Aultman
5th Grade Teacher
Miller, Nancy Lynn (Schaefer)
Fourth Grade Teacher
Patterson, Brenda Vance
Jr HS Mathematics Teacher
Shivers, Janice Polk
High School Principal
Turner, Patricia Curry
English & Spanish Teacher
Waters, Mary Burwell
Mathematics Teacher
TAYLORSVILLE
Moore, Rhonda Grafton
Science Dept Chair/Teacher
Robinson, Lou Ann (Wilder)
5th/6th Grade English Teacher
Roney, Barbara Holifield
Teacher
Wiltshire, Sherry Brown
Jr HS Mathematics Teacher
TUNICA
Williams, Lana M.
Business Technology Teacher
TUPELO
Elmore, Deborah Leathers
Fifth Grade Teacher
Smith, Conzella Prude
8th Grade Math Teacher
TYLERTOWN
Ervin, Cynthia Fortenberry
4th-6th Grade English Teacher
Fortenberry, Betty P.
Reading Teacher
Newman, Dorothy Phillips
Business Education Teacher
Watts, William Henry
Amer His Teacher/Soc Stud Chm
Wood, Henry Albert Jr.
Chemistry/Physics Teacher
UTICA
Brown, Johnnie Ruth Johnson
6th Grade Math/Science Teacher
Mason, Roy
Social Studies Teacher
VICKSBURG
Hale, Sharon Freeman
First Grade Teacher
Pinkston, Clara Booth
English Teacher
Wells, Susan T.
Social Studies Teacher
Yates, Gwendolyn Draper
Mathematics Teacher
WALLS
Bullock, Barbara Weatherly
Third Grade Teacher
WALNUT
Hudson, Ora Hollis
Elementary Teacher
WATER VALLEY
Beard, Gayle Spradling
8th&11th Grade Engish Teacher
Cox, Dee M.
6th Grade Math Teacher
WAVELAND
Bellone, Harriet Ann
Science-Mathematics Teacher
WAYNESBORO
Blakeney, Jo Anne Sellers
First Grade Teacher
Bohannon, Annie Gladis
English Teacher
Dyess, Jeffrey Keith
Geometry/Physics Teacher
Evans, Sundial (Strickland)
Third Grade Teacher
Kendrick, Patricia G.
First Grade Teacher

Staten, Bobby D.
Science/Health Teacher
Williamson, Donna Lizet
Secondary English Teacher
Woods, Sylvia Maufield
Fourth Grade Teacher
WEIR
Balentine, Ora Mae Ray
Third Grade Teacher
Cutts, Jessie B.
Business Teacher
WESSON
Clark, Wanda W.
Home Economics Teacher
Hawkins, Stella Louise Smith
Fourth Grade Teacher
Ishee, Rhonda Wilson
English Teacher
Mc Gee, V. Wayne
Mathematics Teacher
WEST
Ellard, Sandra Gandy
History Teacher
WEST POINT
Bounds, Elizabeth Randle
Kindergarten Teacher
Dobbs, Zelda Patterson
Mathematics Teacher
Hairston, Eleanor Swoope
Jr High English Teacher
West, Faith Craig
English Teacher
WHEELER
Murphy, Lonnie Joe
Math Teacher/Assistant Prin
YAZOO CITY
Buckley, Kenneth Welch
Math Dept Teacher/Chairman
Huddleston, Ruth Moore
Second Grade Teacher
Jones, Jessie Walker
6th Grade Teacher
Reid, Sandra Grayson
Senior English Teacher

MISSOURI

ALMA
Holden, Cynthia Anne
Social Studies Teacher
Lebold, Virginia Ann
English Teacher
ALTON
Barton, Carolyn Sanders
Sixth Grade Teacher
Cates, Nancy Bartholomew
Teacher
Hall, Lloyd Kenneth
Social Studies Teacher
Kauffman, Ellen Ganfield
Mathematics/Physics Teacher
ARNOLD
Andrus, Shirley M.
5th Grade Teacher
Bannecker, Susan Lynn
Primary Teacher
Glore, Marilyn Hill
Guidance Counselor
Herman, Sally Aubuchon
Jr HS Vocal Music Teacher
Kozlen, Diana Lato
Spanish Teacher
Morris, Gwen A.
Business Teacher/Coordinator
Warren, Frances
First Grade Teacher
ASHLAND
Lacy, Janine Dawn
Kindergarten Teacher
Morefield, Barbara Ruth (Harmon)
6th Grade Teacher
AURORA
Greer, Philip Edwin
5th Grade Teacher
AUXVASSE
Galloway, Mary
Kindergarten Teacher
BALLWIN
Buschmann, Judith D'Amico
Eng Teacher/Writing Lab Dir
Fixman, Robert Charles
Teacher
Garcia, L. Dianne Norwood
Social Studies Chair

Van Dyke, Margaret Marie Kraft
5th Grade Teacher
BARNHART
Curtis, Dorothy Marie
Retired Elem Music Teacher
BELLE
Edwards, Ann Simpson
5th Grade Teacher
Evans, Timothy Fitzgerald
Biology Department Chairman
BELTON
Kopp, Sandy Glavin
Social Studies Teacher
BENTON
Grossheider, Donna Glueck
Resource Teacher of Gifted
BERKELEY
Winter, Suzanne
5th Grade Teacher
BERNIE
Hawley, Jerry Wayne
Science Teacher
Sparks, Wanda Hodges
Sixth Grade Teacher
Tanner, Jeanice Beacham
English Teacher
BLAND
Vogt, Steven F.
Science Teacher
BLUE EYE
Beard, Ruth Cox
Second Grade Teacher
Martin, Nancy Lea (Brown)
Third Grade Teacher
Sims, Ricky Rhea
Science Teacher
BLUE SPRINGS
Bretz, Rosemary Sparks
Second Grade Teacher
Brock, Linda M.
English/Journalism Teacher
Cumberford, Starla Kenton
1st Grade Teacher
Dunn, Bradley P.
Mathematics Teacher
El-Hosni, Nina Bond
Substitute Teacher
Hurd, Michael Don
US History Teacher
Quackenbush, Carol Ann
Math Department Chairperson
Theroff, Marv W.
Biology Teacher
Woolley, Viki (Walker)
Teacher
BOLIVAR
Glidwell, Delrae Backus
Vocal Music Instructor
BOWLING GREEN
Mallory, William K.
Retired Teacher
BRADLEYVILLE
Stafford, Gary Lee
Mathematics Dept Chairman
BRASHEAR
Crockett, Georgia Madeleine
Librarian
Erwin, Kathy Ann (Chandler)
English/Phys Ed Teacher
BRAYMER
Brinkley, Martha Johnson
English/Speech/Drama Teacher
Goers, Sandra Lou
Eng, Span & Reading Teacher
Jones, Joni Gilliland
Second Grade Teacher
BRONAUGH
Antle, David Kent
Phys Ed/Social Studies Teacher
Brockmeyer, Dale L.
Science Teacher
Irwin, Evelyn Marie
Retired Elementary Teacher
BROOKFIELD
Hahn, Lynn D.
Mathematics Teacher
Mc Mains, Stuart Allen
Science Teacher
St. Clair, Mary Alice
2nd Grade Elementary Teacher
BRUNSWICK
Ousley, Ann Mc Ketchen (Wright)
Vocational Business Teacher

BUCKLIN
Ware, Valeta Ruth
6th Grade Teacher
BUFFALO
Hatfield, Sandra Ballard
Music Teacher
Phillips, Ray Dean
French & English Teacher
BUNCETON
Monk, George Edward
Science Teacher
BUTLER
Smith, Linda Kay
Second Grade Teacher
CADET
Parson, Joan Scott
English Teacher
CAINSVILLE
Skroh, Vanya (Carothers)
7th-12th Grade Math Teacher
CALEDONIA
Yount, Ruth Ann (Rhodes)
Jr High Mathematics Teacher
CALIFORNIA
Porterfield, Cox
English Teacher
CALLAO
Brown, Glenda Allen
5th and 6th Grade Teacher
CAMDENTON
Rector, Gerry Tomlinson
4th-6th Grade Teacher
Yaeger, Curtis Leroy
HS Mathematics Teacher
CAPE GIRARDEAU
Blanchard, Barbara Chaplin
5th Grade Teacher
Hekmat, Susan Rustige
English/Speech Teacher
Woods, Bonnie Hurley
English Teacher
CARDWELL
Clester, Rosemary Durham
Sixth Grade Teacher
George, Karen Rena
English Teacher
Patton, Brenda G.
Fourth Grade Teacher
CARL JUNCTION
Letner, Al C.
Art Teacher
Mc Griff, Georgiana Menapace
Lang Art/Journalism Teacher
Sutton, Ann Probert
Business Teacher
Twombly, Patty David
Third Grade Teacher
Wilks, Jane Ann
Fourth Grade Teacher
CARROLLTON
Anderson, Thomas Jefferson
HS Social Studies Teacher
CARTHAGE
Buchanan, Melfin Lee
Mathematics Teacher
Hinson, Norma Elaine Smith
6th Grade Teacher
CARUTHERSVILLE
Sorrell, Charlotte Prichard
History Teacher
CEDAR HILL
Talbott, Sherri Katherine
Art Teacher
CHADWICK
Morrill, Connie Nell
Cnslr/Home Economics Teacher
CHARLESTON
Ferrell, Pamela
5th Grade Teacher
CHESTERFIELD
Hoffmann, Joan Ellen
Guidance Counselor
Thomas, Rose Annette
French & Spanish Teacher
CHILLICOTHE
Jackson, Susan Bailey
Fouth Grade Teacher
CLIFTON HILL
Okruch, Thomas Michael
Language Art Instructor

CLINTON

Stillwell, James Thomas
  Soc Stud Teacher/Dept Chair
Ward, Steven Edward
  Mathematics Teacher

COFFEY

Price, Ethel May (Holcomb)
  Retired

COLE CAMP

Crenshaw, Margaret Alice
  Fifth Grade Teacher
Tuggle, Myra Williams
  Sixth Grade Teacher

COLUMBIA

Landry, Hank
  Social Studies Teacher/Coord
Nixon, Carolyn Sue
  Doctoral Student
Powderly, Rosemary Sheeran
  5th Grade Teacher
Schmitz, Elizabeth Ann (Zydervelt)
  Principal
Sergent, Ronald Lee
  8th Grade Amer His Teacher
Underdown, Joy
  Third Grade Teacher

CREIGHTON

Hon, Dianne Hess
  Home Economics Instructor

CREVE COEUR

Wehling, Thomas Matthew
  English Department Co-Chair

DE KALB

Osborn, Margaret Warren
  Jr HS Language Arts Teacher

DE SOTO

Hoffee, Betty C.
  Teacher/Department Chairperson
Stewart, Patricia Robinson
  Vocal Music Teacher

DELTA

Burton, Drenna Lee (O'Reilly)
  Kindergarten Teacher

DEXTER

Beard, Joan Thompson
  Vocal Music Teacher
Brickhaus, Patricia Kay
  7th Grade Math Teacher
Cox, Shirley Ann
  Fourth Grade Teacher

DIAMOND

Augustine, Larry Joe
  6th Grade Teacher

DORA

Gillam, Kenneth
  Math/Physics Teacher
Spencer, Rosa Leah (Story)
  Business Teacher
Wallace, Bonnie June Hambleton
  Third Grade Teacher

DREXEL

Eggleston, Mary Ann
  Computer/Math Teacher

DUENWEG

Greco, Linda Winn
  Second Grade Teacher

EAST LYNNE

Peoples, Darlene Arey
  Elementary Teacher

EDGAR SPRINGS

Washausen, Victoria Elaine (Parker)
  Social Studies Teacher

EL DORADO SPRINGS

Adams, Ralph Edward
  Social Studies Teacher
Fast, Pamela G.
  English/Journalism Teacher

ELDON

Caine, Brenda Clinkingbeard
  Social Studies Chairman
White, Betty Ruth
  8th Grade English Teacher
Wyrick, Constance Helen
  Biology/Chemistry Instructor

ELLINGTON

Bales, Wanda Ford
  6th Grade Teacher

ELLSINORE

Shoat, William Richard
  Junior High Sci/P E Teacher
Slicer, George William
  Science Teacher, Dept Chair

Thurman, Jo Ann Truax
  Mathematics Department Chair

ELSBERRY

Crozier, Nancy Joyce (Milliken)
  Third Grade Teacher

ELVINS

Helm, Beverly J.
  4th Grade Teacher

EMINENCE

Cook, Judy Hood
  Sixth Grade Teacher

ESTHER

Jones, Frank
  Physical Education Teacher

EUREKA

Brown, William Lee Jr.
  Social Studies Teacher

EWING

Casper, Annabelle De Vries
  Substitute Teacher
Myers, Debra Scoggin
  Art Teacher
Sykes, Marcia Morgan
  English/Speech/Drama Teacher

EXCELSIOR SPRINGS

Bates, Willa Charlene
  Third Grade Teacher
Mc Carroll, Norma Campbell
  6th Grade Reading Teacher
Mc Cullough, Diane R.
  Social Studies Chair
Schmidt, Diane Kay
  3rd Grade Teacher

FARMINGTON

Bauche, Kurt Douglas
  Director of Bands
Giesselmann, Duane Lyle
  7th & 8th Grade Teacher
Huck, Linda A.
  Assistant Band Director
Stewart, Katharine Straughan
  6th Grade Teacher

FAUCETT

Campbell, Louise Cable
  6th Grade Mathematics Teacher

FAYETTE

Biesemeyer, John H.
  English Teacher

FERGUSON

Quigley, William Richard
  Physical Education Teacher

FESTUS

Ebert, Jo Ann Schmidt
  Language Arts Teacher
Habibullah, Gemma W.
  Mathematics Dept Chair
Purcell, Virginia M. Roberson
  Music Teacher
Watin, Gemma B.
  Mathematics Dept Chairperson

FLAT RIVER

Carlyon, Mary Ann
  First Grade Teacher

FLORISSANT

Carnagey, Russell Dean
  Instructor-Vice President
Frede, Ronald L.
  Music Dept Chair/Band Dir
Gain, Betty Hamm
  Third Grade Teacher
Groaning, Joseph Glenn
  Chemistry Teacher
Mueller, Michael
  Physical Education Teacher
Rohr, Carol Ann (Hudson)
  First Grade Teacher
Schoch, Ray
  Social Studies Teacher
Shew, Janet Burke
  2nd Grade Teacher

FREDERICKTOWN

Dees, Ruth Sample
  Retired Fifth Grade Teacher
Huff, Donald Dean II
  Physical Education Teacher

GALLATIN

Sprague, Jeanette (Hill)
  Vocational Business Teacher

GALT

Shipley, Melody Lea Jackson
  HS Mathematics Instructor

GLADSTONE

Durham, Marilyn Fairchild
  American History Teacher

Nistendirk, Virginia Di Maggio
  5th Grade Teacher
Painter, Robin Lee (Eppes)
  Physical Education Teacher

GOODMAN

Gideon, Florene A.
  Retired Teacher

GRAHAM

Smith, Susan Elisabeth (Schmidt)
  English/Journalism Teacher

GRANBY

Andris, Diane Hobbs
  Guidance Counselor

GRANDVIEW

Hoeper, Connie Kay
  Fifth Grade Teacher
Schildberg, Peggy Sue (Gossett)
  5th Grade Science Teacher
Wilks, Nadine O.
  Retired Elementary Teacher

GRANT CITY

Hiatt, Rochelle Lynn
  Third Grade Teacher

GREENFIELD

Landers, Becky Lynne
  Vocational Home Ec Teacher

GREENVILLE

Froman, Mitchell Lee
  Jr High School History Teacher

GREENWOOD

Nielsen, Ginger Mae
  Kindergarten Teacher

GUILFORD

Scott, Linda Hilsabeck
  3rd Grade Teacher

HALLSVILLE

Clark, Mary Beth
  English Teacher

HANNIBAL

De Luca, Joseph August
  Spanish Teacher
Hams, Betty Rosser
  Teacher of Gifted & Talented
Paschal, Adele Mae
  6th Grade Science Teacher
Root, Maurice Richard
  4th Grade Teacher

HARRISONVILLE

Cockrill, Lee J.
  English Dept Chairperson

HERCULANEUM

Buchheit, Velda F.
  Eighth Grade Educator
Funston, Bonnie Sue (Hale)
  Music Teacher

HERMANN

Draper, Doris King
  4th Grade Teacher
Neale, William Christopher
  Computer/Music Teacher
Sargent, Kathryn Marie
  8th Grade Earth Sci Teacher

HIGGINSVILLE

Sheehan, Helen (Fuller)
  Counselor/Teacher
Tilly, Melody A.
  Fourth Grade Teacher

HIGH RIDGE

Murphy, Kathleen A.
  Eighth Grade Teacher

HILLSBORO

Alsobrook, Lynn Kneedler
  First Grade Teacher
Cowle, Paul Bernard
  Physical Education Teacher
Etchason, Rebecca Ann (Brockmann)
  Business Education Teacher
Linderer, Robert Joseph
  Guidance Counselor
Raspberry, James Roland
  Choral Director/Dept Chair
Schultz, Frank A.
  Social Studies Teacher
Steighorst, Pamela Weiss
  Phys Ed/Health Teacher

HOLCOMB

Blackman, Kent
  Agriculture Education Teacher
Henson, Bonnie Anderson
  Second Grade Teacher
Pery, Sherri Wright
  5th-8th Math Teacher

HOLDEN

Maupin, Diane C.
  Language Arts Teacher

HOLLISTER

Loftis, Leman Dean
  English Teacher

HOUSE SPRINGS

Stovall, Ellen Hartman
  Kindergarten Teacher
Wagner, Juanita Theriot
  3rd Grade Teacher
White, James Clay
  Science Department Chairman

HUMANSVILLE

Vernon, Rae Anne Anne (Cook)
  Mathematics Dept Chair/Teacher

IMPERIAL

Joyce, Jerald L.
  5th Grade Teacher
Moore, Linda Ann Weilitz
  Sci Dept Head/Biology Teacher
Wegmann, Linda Kaye
  Band Director

INDEPENDENCE

Adams, William Francis
  Business Teacher
Brock, Sammy Joe
  Teacher
Bunch, Alan Bret
  Vocal Music Director
Childers, Cindy Marie (Monroe)
  5th Grade Teacher
Coleman, Jerry Lee
  Physical Education Teacher
Craig, Denise Suzanne
  Teacher
Cummings, Margaret Jones
  Department Chair/Teacher
Fore, Donald Lee
  Algebra II Teacher
Graupner, Sheryll Ann
  Fifth Grade Teacher
Griffith, Shirley Miller
  Second Grade Teacher
Kim, Elizabeth Ann (Allen)
  Kindergarten Teacher
Leabo, Barbara Dickeson
  6th Grade Tchr/Science Spclst
Lotz, Sharon Hogan
  Business Department Chair
Ray, Nancy Roberta (Helton)
  8th Grade Soc Stud Teacher
Robinson, Darlene Faye
  Kindergarten Teacher
Schlagle, Donald E.
  Business Teacher
Spangler, Daniel Leroy Jr.
  History Teacher/Athletic Dir
Stewart, Dennis Marshall
  Biology Teacher
Swisher Kievet, Penny
  Drama Teacher/Director
Theiss, Kathryn Barker
  6th Grade Teacher
Whitaker, Linda R.
  Life Science Teacher
Willis, Nancy Joe
  Third Grade Teacher
Wilson, Ardis Krueger
  Mathematics Teacher

IRONTON

Adams, Donna Bock
  6th Grade Teacher
Branstetter, Melinda Kaye (Miller)
  Third Grade Teacher
Petersen, Nancy Sutton
  Science/Biology Teacher

JASPER

Salsman, Robert L.
  Industrial Arts Teacher

JEFFERSON CITY

Allen, Saundra Eileen (Mc Gruder)
  Art Instructor
Bardwell, Rosemary Ann (Wingate)
  5th-8th Grade English Teacher
Hentges, Ray Charles
  Science/Religion Teacher
Hoelscher, Judith C. (Bax)
  4th-6th Grade Science Teacher
Johnsen, Marilyn Thornby (Snelling)
  Teacher
Kempker, Lori Ann
  Business Education Teacher
Kollars, Catherine Anne
  8th Grade Teacher
Stegall, Nancy Blakemore
  4th-6th Grade Teacher
Thoenen, Rose Ann
  Science/Amer History Teacher

Wilson, Thomas Joseph
  Social Studies Teacher/Chair

JENNINGS

Akers, Dennis Lee
  Dean of Students
Shaw, Mary Jean
  Elem Administrative Intern

JOPLIN

Ideker, Susan Jarvis
  Vocal Director
Miles, Annette (Bigbee)
  English Teacher
Sterratt, Sue L.
  Enrichment Resource Teacher

KAHOKA

Stammeyer, Jacquelyn Winter
  7th Grade Soc Stud Teacher
St.Clair, Albert Lee
  Math Teacher
Wirsig, Gregory V.
  English Teacher

KANSAS CITY

Black, Charles Reed
  American History Teacher
Boothe, Judi Ann
  World History Teacher
Buford, Ronetta Coursey
  Fine Arts Chairperson
Corse, Ralph William
  K-12th Grade Science Coord
Crockett, Ann Graham
  English Teacher
Cunningham, Alsia Saulsberry
  Curriculum Coordinator
Don Carlos, Rosanna Payson
  Chemistry Teacher
Flournoy, James Alan
  Science Teacher
Forbes, Carla L.
  Counselor
Gasaway, Zenova Scott
  Second Grade Teacher
Halsey, Julie Michelle
  French Teacher
Hayman, Mamie (Dove)
  English Teacher
Higgins, Maureen Therese
  Mathematics/French Teacher
Kaplan, Jo Ann
  Elem/Substitute Teacher
Ketcher, Ronald Lorenz
  8th Grade Teacher
Koutsoumpas, Harriet CSJ
  Science Dept Chairperson
Lampton, C. Diane
  English & Writing Teacher
Le Blanc, Katherine Vennard
  English Teacher
Lindsey, James Robert
  Vocal Music Instructor
Long, Margaret Walker
  Science Teacher
Love, Alyce Marie
  Social Science Teacher
Mc Creary, Richard Oliver
  Head Teacher
Mc Eniry, John T.
  Cmptr Programming/Math Teacher
Omecene, Mary M.
  7th Grade Math/Science Teacher
Pickens, Cathy Joan
  Science/Social Studies Teacher
Saulet, Bobbie Jean (Grayson)
  Fifth Grade Teacher
Spungen, Albert M.
  Social Studies Instructor
Super, Bruce H.
  Social Studies Teacher
Ward, Thelma Mae
  Third Grade Teacher
Williams, Mary Carr
  First Grade Teacher

KEARNEY

Meder, Delores Ballew
  Gifted/Talented Prgm Teacher

KING CITY

Ficken, Connie R.
  English Teacher

KINGDOM CITY

Logan, Linda Nutter
  Business Education Teacher

KIRKSVILLE

Bahr, Sandra
  Science Teacher/Dept Chair
Mikel, Jeffrey Todd
  Elem Phys Ed Teacher
Morrow, Cheryl Bindseil
  8th Grade Math Teacher
Mudd, Maggie Weber
  Retired

KIRKWOOD
Frank, Julia Diane
  Health/Physical Ed Teacher
Harris, Ethel Switzer
  Retired
Hawley, William Donald
  Asst Prin/8th Grade Teacher
Hoffmann, Robert Louis
  History Teacher
Mendelsohn, William L.
  Social Studies Dept Chair

KNOB NOSTER
Miller, Wayne C.
  Counselor

LADDONIA
Kolzow, David Alan
  Phys Ed/Health Teacher

LAMAR
Gordon, Patricia Ann
  Second Grade Teacher
Thieman, Cynthia Jean (Strodtman)
  Third Grade Teacher
Williams, Robert Lee
  HS Mathematics/Science Teacher

LANCASTER
Dixon, Julinda Lea
  5th-12th Grade Band Director
Watkins, E. Maureen Shepherd
  Eng/Lang Art/Comm Teacher

LAQUEY
Grosvenor, M. Ildean
  Fifth Grade Teacher
Schowengerdt, Janet C.
  Lang Art Dept Chairperson

LATHROP
Barrett, Virginia G.
  Teacher of Gifted Program
Colvin, Lorraine Walters
  Third Grade Teacher
Martz, Laurie Jane
  English Teacher

LEBANON
Burnett, Barbara Beard
  Science Teacher
Copling, Donald Raleigh
  Physical Ed Teacher/Coach
Eaton, O. Lee
  Jr High Social Studies Teacher
Greenwood, Geanine Kay
  First Grade Teacher
Kinkead, Millard Clay Jr.
  Social Studies Teacher
Martin, Ellen K.
  Biology Teacher
Maskey, David Lee
  Mathematics Teacher

LEES SUMMIT
Mc Coy, Carol L.
  Teacher
Smith, Patricia A.
  Mathematics Teacher
Ware, Christine G. Showalter
  English Teacher/Dept Chair

LESTERVILLE
Wayne, Martha (Morrison)
  English Teacher/Dept Chair

LEXINGTON
Bollmeyer, Deborah Kay Singleton
  Third Grade Teacher

LIBERAL
Spurgeon, Kenneth William
  Soc Stud Teacher/Principal
Tahhan, Nancy Brisbin
  Kindergarten Teacher

LIBERTY
Dinsmore, Betty Ann (Wilson)
  6th Grade Teacher

LICKING
Barnes, Wanda Faye
  Elementary Math Teacher

LINCOLN
Cox, Jeana K.
  Elem Music/Jr HS Math Teacher
Huenemann, Linda Nicholas
  Senior English Instructor
Lewis, Carolyn Maurine (Woolery)
  Business Education Teacher
Smith, Karen Kaye
  2nd Grade Teacher

LINN
Baker, Bonnie Huot
  4th Grade Teacher
Humphrey, Janice Brennan
  Mathematics Teacher
Schmiedeskamp, Roger William
  Mathematics Teacher

LUTESVILLE
Lax, Donald Lionel
  Industrial Arts Instructor
Shrum, Lois I.
  Jr HS Language Arts Teacher

MADISON
Mowery, Brenda Lee
  Sixth Grade Teacher

MANCHESTER
Beckmann, Nancy Bourke
  Second Grade Teacher
Broyles, Elizabeth Ann
  Counselor
Mc Creary, Peter W. Jr.
  Mathematics Teacher
Tanner, John William
  Social Studies Teacher
Worley, David H.
  Unified Studies Teacher

MANSFIELD
Dimos, Sheri Bishop
  English Department Chair
Smith, Leslie Anne
  Chemistry/Biology Teacher

MAPLEWOOD
Rohlfing, Albert F.
  Social Studies Teacher

MARBLE HILL
Barks, Shirley Lou (Hoxworth)
  Third Grade Teacher
Schlief, Dan Ray
  HS Math & Science Teacher

MARCELINE
Cavanah, Delain Simmons
  First Grade Teacher
Mc Glothlin, Brian H.
  HS Social Studies Teacher
Sheerman, Joyce Johnston
  Third Grade Teacher
Shelman, Michael David
  Sixth Grade Teacher

MARQUAND
Schwarz, Sharon Ann
  Mathematics Teacher

MARYLAND HEIGHTS
Kaley, Reann Allyn
  Social Studies Teacher
Kramme, Theodore W.
  Math Teacher
Richardson, Linda Diane
  Health Teacher

MARYVILLE
Derks, Pauline Meyer
  Fourth Grade Teacher
From, Lorna Sue
  First Grade Teacher
Henry, Carolyn Schacht
  Sixth Grade Teacher
Lade, Diane Morley
  5-8th Grade Math Teacher
Marion, Jo Ann Stamm
  Associate Professor
Matthews, Don W.
  7th Grade Soc Stud Teacher
Posten, Kermitt Lee
  Science Dept Chair/Bio Teacher
Webb, Deana Hodgin
  Fourth Grade Teacher
Weichinger, David C.
  Fifth Grade Science Teacher

MAYSVILLE
Gaiser, Janice Walker
  Second Grade Teacher
Harwood, Peggy Mohr
  First Grade Teacher

MAYVIEW
Haney, Elizabeth Hifner
  5th Grade Teacher

MENDON
Cook, Carol Eileen Grile
  3rd Grade Teacher
Daugherity, Wanda Bolinger
  Language Arts Teacher
Holderieath, Evelyn Stoner
  Business Teacher

MEXICO
Oldvader, Larry L.
  English Teacher

MILAN
Hollon, Dorothy Marie (Kearns)
  Third Grade Teacher

MOBERLY
Ehrhardt, Virginia Mc Cowan
  Teacher of Gifted/Talented

MOKANE
Warner, Kenneth Emil
  Mathematics Teacher

MONROE CITY
Woodall, Jo Ann (Gibbs)
  Third Grade Teacher

MONTGOMERY CITY
Barley, George M.
  Mathematics/Computer Instr
Noe, Wanda Dean
  Retired Elementary Teacher

MOSCOW MILLS
Primeau, Ruth Anne
  2nd Grade Teacher

MOUNT VERNON
Newcomer, Saundra Kaye
  Journalism & English Chair

MOUNTAIN GROVE
Clark, Judy Borden
  Teacher/Soc Stud Dept Chair
Killgore, Connie Bowling
  Journalism/English Teacher
Lizotte, Chris
  Director of Bands
Peterson, Bonnie Rae
  Chemistry/Physics Teacher

MOUNTAIN VIEW
Coldwell, Louise Dennington
  Physical Education Teacher

NAYLOR
Spease, Deborah Lynn (Ray)
  Kindergarten Teacher

NEELYVILLE
Skaggs, Patricia Karon (Ward)
  Business Education Teacher

NEOSHO
Cole, Shirley Daniels
  Fourth Grade Teacher
Goade, Charles Edward
  Social Studies Teacher
Graham, James Franklin
  Science Teacher
Kraft, Marsha LeAnn
  Kindergarten Teacher
Sale, Margaret Lee Hyde
  Kindergarten Teacher Retired

NEVADA
Grooms, Ed Ray
  Gifted/Drama Teacher

NEW FRANKLIN
Hoefer, Sharon M.
  7th-8th/Social Studies Teacher
Mc Carthy, Edna Davis
  Retired
Whalen, Nancy B.
  HS Mathematics Teacher

NEW HARTFORD
Howell, Julie Belle Hudson
  Elementary Teacher Retired

NEW MADRID
Mc Keel, Jim Webb
  Physics/Chem Teacher/Dept Head
Shy, Mary Louise
  Fourth Grade Teacher

NIXA
Trippe, Vicky Lynn
  English Dept Chair/Teacher

NORTH KANSAS CITY
Sherbo, John Willard Jr.
  Science Department Chairman

NOVINGER
Goucher, Norma Lou (Reese)
  Third Grade Teacher
Moore, Beverly Jones
  Sixth Grade Teacher
Schmidt, Michelle Marie
  Mathematics Teacher

O'FALLON
Dralle, Peggy Ann
  Mathematics Teacher
Mc Guire, Georgette Marie
  Fifth Grade Teacher

OAK GROVE
Bozarth, Kathy Dye
  1st Grade Teacher

OAK RIDGE
Koeberl, Mary Marie Kranawetter
  First Grade Teacher
Lemons, Doris Bowden
  K-12th Grade Art Teacher

ODESSA
Borland, Cynthia Keck
  Second Grade Teacher
Holman, Gay Louise
  Business Department Instructor
Holman, Larry Kenneth
  Health/Physical Ed Teacher

ORRICK
Battagler, Jo Ann
  Math/Reading Teacher
Greer, Connie Battagler
  Third Grade Teacher
Koerner, Karen Sue
  6th Grade Teacher
Wrisinger, Rick S.
  Business Department Teacher

OVERLAND
Crowder, Kenneth Robert
  8th Grade Soc Studies Teacher
Goatley, Brenda Penn
  8th Grade Reading Teacher
Hirst, Richard Lee
  Vocal Music Director
Kofsky, Jacquelyn Goldman
  Teacher of Gifted
Venn, Robert Allen
  Physics Teacher

OZARK
Burns, Robert D.
  Mathematics Teacher
Peters, Susan Stephens
  Elementary Music Teacher

PACIFIC
Adams, Robert Patrick
  First Grade Teacher
Russell, Judith Ann
  Third Grade Teacher

PALMYRA
Mette, Patsy Ann
  Mathematics Teacher

PECULIAR
Brandt, Carol Voelker
  English Teacher
Genge, Jean Ann (Eidson)
  Business Teacher
Gunter, Horace Edward
  World History Teacher
Markley, Lois Holzhauser
  English Teacher
Ross, Janette Cipolla
  5th Grade Teacher
Sportsman, Roy
  Mathematics Teacher

PERRYVILLE
Beilharz, Cathy L.
  Mathematics/Chemistry Teacher
Fulton, Linda Dowdy
  Guidance Counselor
Paulus, Mick
  Social Studies Dept Head
Reisenbichler, Nancy Miesner
  Business/Mathematics Teacher
Schnurbusch, Virginia (Linebarger)
  Teacher/Counselor

PIERCE CITY
Schnake, Phyllis Stewart
  Fifth Grade Teacher
Williams, Debra Peters
  Eng/Speech/Drama Teacher

PLATTSBURG
Evans, Nancy Williams
  2nd Grade Teacher
Foster, H. Eugene
  History Department Chair
Irle-Kelly, Lisa
  Speech/Drama/Lang Art Teacher

PLEASANT HILL
Crawford, Carol Ruth (Holle)
  Kindergarten Teacher
Sherman, Ramona (Prewitt)
  Parent Educator
Strait, Darrell L.
  6th Grade Science Teacher
Zeitzmann, Rebecca Jo
  7th Grade English Teacher

POPLAR BLUFF
Clark, Laura Spencer
  Spanish Teacher
Heimsoth, Elroy Leslie
  Administrator
Schlimpert, Thomas Lee
  Assistant Principal

PORTAGEVILLE
Fritts, Janet Hicks
  English Teacher

POTOSI
Allen, Rebecca Foster
  Third Grade Teacher
Branstetter, Carmen E.
  Reading Teacher
Mowry, John Charles
  Speech/Language Pathologist
Mowry, Lou (Gillean)
  Learning Disabilities Teacher
Tweedie, Mary Jo (Sutton)
  Counselor

PURDIN
Guyer, Janis Mayre (Johnson)
  Second Grade Teacher
Knifong, Dyle Dean
  Counselor/Athletic Dir

PURDY
Oberbeck, Richard Dean
  Science Teacher

QUEEN CITY
Rowland, Geraldine Schmitter
  English Teacher

RAVENWOOD
Henry, Kila Ann
  Science Instructor

RAYMONDVILLE
Allen, Sharon Kay (Tennison)
  Third Grade Teacher

RAYTOWN
Alderson, Cyrla Jan
  Science Dept Chair
Schroer, Michael Allen
  Science Teacher/Biology Instr
Zanone, Lucia R.
  5th Grade Teacher

REEDS SPRING
May, Norma Lea (Hinkle)
  Elementary Music Teacher

REPUBLIC
Huson, Jim E.
  Freshman US History Teacher
Kendrick, Dorothy Jean
  Fifth Grade Teacher
Mounts, Daniel Charles
  Sixth Grade Teacher

RICHMOND HEIGHTS
Latragna, Sam
  Principal

RISCO
Fortner, Alice (Stobaugh)
  Second Grade Teacher

ROGERSVILLE
Alexander, Rebecca Lea (Holt)
  2nd Grade Teacher
Blakeney, Diana (Schroder)
  Health/Phys Ed Teacher
Crandall, Ronald W.
  History Teacher/Dept Head
Hetherington, John Scott
  Assistant Principal/Coach
Hurst, Susan Heinrich
  6th Grade Rdng/English Teacher
Long, Myrtice Carr
  Second Grade Teacher
Zirbel, Janet Wilson
  Mathematics Teacher

ROLLA
Knapp, Donald Lee
  Earth Sci/Astronomy Teacher
Miller, Amy (Kipp)
  Second Grade Teacher
Pierson, Ossean Eugene
  Mathematics Teacher
Schath, Imolee Joy Brown
  Fourth Grade Teacher
Strandberg, Berniece (Kirch)
  5th/6th Grade Music Teacher

ROSEBUD
Nichols, E. Susan Cowan
  Fifth Grade Teacher

ROSENDALE
Snyder, Jane Hyder
  English Teacher

RUSSELLVILLE
Morrow, Marjorie
  Second Grade Teacher

SAINT CHARLES
Bell, Sharon Rochelle Hicks
  Mathematics Teacher
Berthold, Sandra Jean (Bush)
  Soc Stud Teacher/Dept Chair
Blatt, Hilla Guzder
  Dept Chair/English Teacher
Boschert, Carol LeRoy
  Second Grade Teacher

SAINT CHARLES (cont)

Duchek, Mary K.
  First Grade Teacher
Greenberg, Lewis Anthony
  Art Department Chair
Horn, Gayle Patricia
  Peer Teacher/Counselor
Johnson, Marian Ruth
  3rd Grade Teacher
Kennedy, Alice Louise (Freese)
  Music Teacher
Kulage, Richard Henry
  Science Teacher
Lay, Dorothy Hoekman
  Fifth Grade Teacher
Muenstraman, Kathy Joyce (Hill)
  6/7th Grade Reading Teacher
Roach, Barbara Brunner
  Science Teacher/Dept Chair
Staude, Edmund David
  Mid Sch Eng/Math Teacher
Sternfels, Leonard Lee
  Science Teacher
Taylor, Jane Ann Dolan
  Physics Teacher
Timmons, Teri Downard
  Guidance Counselor
Wall, Sharon Pavoggi
  Jr HS Physical Ed Teacher
Whelan, Thomas Michael Jr.
  Social Studies Teacher
Zutter-Brock, Pamela J.
  Foreign Lang Dept Chair

SAINT CLAIR

Evans, Patricia Lee
  English/History Teacher/Supvr

SAINT JAMES

Davis, Bobbie Morton
  First Grade Teacher

SAINT JOSEPH

Darnell, Karen Fenelon
  Speech/Drama Teacher
Evans, Paul M.
  Speech/Debate Teacher
Gardner, Ginger
  Third Grade Teacher
Hoecker, Richard Vincent
  Elementary Teacher
Mahlandt, Louise Ann
  Speech & Forensics Teacher
Mc Fadin, Juanita Jones
  8th Grade Amer History Teacher
Schoenlaub, Elizabeth Cornman
  Remedial Reading Teacher
Voltmer, Renee
  Home Economics Teacher

SAINT LOUIS

Alden, Donna Scherrer
  Third Grade Teacher
Banks, Sandra C. (Peavie)
  Teacher
Baur, James Christopher
  Theology Teacher
Beatty, James Joseph III
  Spanish Teacher
Belcher, William Joseph
  Mathematics Department Chair
Bingaman, Rose A.
  Kindergarten Teacher
Black, Alma Jean
  Fourth Grade Teacher
Boettcher, Blase Ward
  English Department Chair
Bosch, Gerda M. Gross
  Chemistry/Physics Teacher
Brown, Irma King
  5th Grade Teacher of Gifted
Cannon, Theresa
  Language Arts Teacher
Chappelle, Barbara Wooten
  10th & 12th Grade Eng Teacher
Clark, Marie Isabel
  6th/7th Grade Science Teacher
Clem, Sandra Sue (Sandage)
  High School English Teacher
Cole, Yvonne E.
  Biology Teacher
Coleman, Gayle D.
  Mathematics Teacher
Cook, Sarah
  2nd Grade Teacher
Egleston, Gail Ruth
  Language Arts Teacher
Feick, Raymond R.
  Biology Teacher
Flynn, Jeanne Webb
  4th Grade Teacher
Fuller, Charles Henry
  4th Grade Teacher
Gorsuch, Bellvia L.
  English Teacher
Greer, Betty Vannatta
  4th Grade Teacher

Gregory, Janet Faye (Daubs)
  3-4th Grade Classroom Teacher
Grimley, Charles Michael
  English, Speech Teacher
Hall, Clarice
  First Grade Teacher
Holliday, Robert Doc
  World History/Cultures Teacher
Holloman, Anna Ruth Minter
  Mathematics/Science Teacher
Hubbard, Bill M.
  8th Grade Mathematics Teacher
Johnson, Gail Anna
  English/Journalism Teacher
Kalcic, Lynn Ann Dwiel
  Mathematics/Computer Teacher
Kassing, Sharon F. SL
  5th-8th Grade Science Teacher
Kehres, Donna Girard
  5th & 6th Grade Teacher
Knueppe, Sharon L.
  7th/8th Grade Art Teacher
Lechner, Margaret A.
  District Science Coordinator
Mahnken, Charlotte Blanke
  1st-8th Grade Art Teacher
Mana, Dave Paul
  English Department Chairman
Mayer, Heloise (Carr)
  English/Drama Teacher
Mc Caine, Gloria Moore
  7th Grade Soc Studies Teacher
Mc Daniel, William Matthew
  Physical Ed/Health Teacher
Meyers, Dorothy Pazdernik
  Sixth Grade Teacher
Myles, Glenda Jean (Mitchell)
  English Teacher
Null, Cherie Stapfer
  Fourth Grade Teacher
O'Connell, Judith Helen
  Modern Language Dept Chair
Palisch, Barbara Elaine
  Second Grade Teacher
Papas, Carolyn Russell
  4th Grade Teacher
Parham, Alice Marie
  Teacher Third Grade
Quinn, Agnes Grimes
  Guidance Counselor
Ray, Sandra R.
  Physical Education Teacher
Reichert, Celeste Marie
  Fourth Grade Teacher
Robinson, Carol Dierkes
  Spanish Teacher
Robinson, John Philip
  Coll Amer His/Psych Teacher
Rockel, Stephanie C.
  Second Grade Teacher
Rumbold, Paula Lathrop
  Second Grade Teacher
Russell, Lawrence P.
  Mathematics Department Chair
Schaefer, Carol Ramming
  Biology Teacher
Schibig, James Michael
  Principal
Schmitt, Linda Sue
  Fifth Grade Teacher
Shaw, Andrew Dwight
  Science Department Chair
Sinks, Jo Ann
  Third Grade Teacher
Smith, Al Joseph
  Social Studies Teacher
Smith, Richard Leonard
  HS Band Director
Smith, Valerie Lynn
  Instrumental & Vocal Instr
Starks, Vivian Mc Cadney
  7th/8th Grade Lang Art Teacher
Staufenbiel, Deborah Miller
  Sixth Grade Teacher
Suttmoeller, Joan M.
  Business Teacher
Terry, Lorraine Ann
  Fifth Grade Teacher
Vallar, Mary Ancilla OP
  Retired Teacher
Vaughn, James Harold
  Mathematics Teacher
Walleman, Daryl
  Social Studies Teacher
Walters, Melvina Jo Refine
  5th Grade Teacher
Wich, John Joseph
  Computer Science/Math Teacher
Williams, Ruth Ann (Reeves)
  Third Grade Teacher
Young, Beverly Jean
  Elementary Reading Specialist
Zimmers, Gloria Nancy (Koehler)
  5th Grade Teacher

SAINT PETERS

Busalacchi, Patrice Taaffe
  Kndgtn Teacher/Grade Level Chm
Willey, Debra Jane
  3rd Grade Teacher

SAINTE GENEVIEVE

Holland, David Joseph
  Assistant Manager
Jansen, Eulogia
  1st/2nd Grade Teacher/Prin
Willrett, Michele J.
  11/12th Grade English Teacher

SALEM

Jones, Beverly Brown
  8th Grade Science Teacher
Maledy, Cindy Rueter
  Counselor

SAPPINGTON

Krebs, Mary Schaeffer
  Fifth Grade Teacher

SARCOXIE

Frost, Sharon Anne (Dawald)
  First Grade Teacher

SAVANNAH

Anderson, Larry Wayne
  English/Literature Teacher
Luce, William Oliver
  History Teacher
Lund, Jackie Dale
  Mathematics Teacher
Wampler, Catherine Phillips
  Second Grade Teacher
Wendhausen, Dana Renee
  Science Teacher

SCOTT CITY

Eaker, Sally Blaylock
  Kindergarten Teacher
Mayo, Sherry Ellis
  Social Studies Teacher

SEDALIA

Bahner, Richard John
  Math Department Chair
Dey, Sharon L.
  Math/Computer Teacher
Harris, Carole Briscoe
  5th Grade Teacher
Harter, Charlotte Ann Kassabaum
  Fifth Grade Teacher
Turner, Marcia Miller
  Eng, AP Amer His Teacher

SENECA

Stephens, Maxine Miller
  Retired English Teacher

SEYMOUR

Smikle, Patricia Ann
  4th Grade Teacher
Thomas, Carmen Jeanine
  Physical Education Teacher

SIKESTON

Buck, Judith Kennemore
  Instructor/Dept Chairperson

SLATER

Buglovsky, Bonnie Mc Clain
  Third-Fourth Grade Teacher

SMITHTON

Hudson, Hazel (Eckles)
  HS Mathematics Teacher

SMITHVILLE

Miller, Pamela Hart
  School Psychologist

SPRINGFIELD

Adams, Joyce Mc Cracken
  Kindergarten Teacher
Baker, Kevin D.
  8th Grade US History Teacher
Barker, Pauline Pack
  Second Grade Teacher
Drye, Bonnie Tidwell
  Sixth Grade Teacher
Earls, Betsy Burk
  2nd Grade Teacher
Gates, Mary Scott
  Organist/Choir Accompanist
Gettle, Diane Bruens
  Mathematics Teacher
Gideon, Mark Allen
  Director of Theatre
Guinn, Ruth Ann Ann Marion
  Substance Abuse Counselor
Hall, Tommy A.
  English Teacher
Harris, Beverly Mc Glassion
  5th/6th Grade Math Teacher
Holden-Mc Querter, Dana
  7th & 8th Grade Math Teacher

Kester, Paula Watson
  Fifth Grade Teacher
Loudis, Anthony Alan
  Broadcast Journalism
Mc Carter, Larry Dan
  Mathematics Department Teacher
Mc Carty, Cheryl Ann
  English Teacher
Miesner, Stan
  Social Studies Teacher
Nickell, D.
  Theatre Art Teacher
Reynolds, Deana Nimmo
  Speech & Debate Instructor
Shantz, Sally Copper
  Fourth Grade Teacher
Smith, Cherlyn M.
  Earth Science Teacher
Teters, Peggy L.
  Elementary Science Supervisor
Wilson, Judith Ann
  Journalism Teacher/Advisor

ST LOUIS

Cross, Versia Williams
  Sixth Grade Teacher

STANBERRY

Marlow, Sandra Schumann
  Third Grade Teacher

STEELVILLE

Ruether, Michael Keith
  Music Director

STOCKTON

Miller, Mary Jane (Ellis)
  Third Grade Teacher
Newton, Helen A.
  Sixth Grade Teacher

STRAFFORD

Breedlove, Pamela S. (Gilbert)
  4th Grade Teacher
Johnson, Ruth Ann (Tilley)
  Guidance Counselor
Royston, Colleen Conway
  7th-12th Grade Span/Fr Teacher
Wilson, Freda Ann (Schreffler)
  English/Speech/Drama Teacher

STRASBURG

Braby, Jack Rollin
  Elementary Principal
Snyder, Treca Yocum
  Fourth Grade Teacher

STURGEON

Conrad, Tracey Branson
  Science Teacher
Hutshinson, Julie Smith
  Teacher

SULLIVAN

Wilkinson, Judy A. (Blanton)
  3rd-4th/7th-8th Grade Teacher

SUMMERSVILLE

Blumenstock, Beth Marie
  Choir Director

TARKIO

Parsley, Jaylene Wehmeier
  College Mathematics Teacher

TRENTON

Hannaford, Buddy
  Director of Instrumental Music
Hurst, Marsha Owings
  Third Grade Teacher
Provance, Susan Elin
  Kindergarten Teacher
Sager, Norman Eudean
  Science Teacher
Spencer, Barbara Higdon
  English/Speech Teacher

TROY

Pohlman, Larry Lynn
  Band Director
Roth, Audrey Stanek
  6th Grade Teacher
Whitworth, Cathy Mason
  Jr/Sr HS Vocal Director

TUSCUMBIA

Tharpe, Deborah C.
  English Teacher

UNION

Olszowka, Kathy Niemel
  Mathematics Teacher
Ridder, Jane Berger
  Third Grade Teacher

UNIONVILLE

Gibson, Donna Jean Stice
  Third Grade Teacher
Mitchell, Barbara
  Fourth Grade Teacher

Quigley, Dorothy Lorraine Robb
  Jr HS Social Studies Teacher
Sanders, Mary J.
  Junior High Teacher
Venzor, Sherl Ann (Daniels)
  Mathematics Teacher

UNIVERSITY CITY

Ackerman, David
  Principal
Lane, Daniel S.
  Chemistry Teacher
Minner, Frederick
  Soc Stud Teacher, Chairman
Waugh, Suzanne Mary
  Tutor

URBANA

Edwards, Kathryn Stone
  History Teacher

VALLEY PARK

Stokes, Daniel C.
  Mathematics Teacher

VANDALIA

Burniski, Thomas William Jr.
  Social Studies Teacher
Hoehn, Sharon Gillum
  Fourth Grade Teacher
Pitts, Dan L.
  Math Teacher

VERSAILLES

Akin, Sue Garber
  Third Grade Teacher
Hutchison, Adelia Cairns
  Social Studies Chairman

VIBURNUM

Mc Burnett, Stephen Ware
  Jr HS Science Teacher

WALKER

Burch, Jenise K.
  Voc Home Economics Teacher
Forsythe, Terry A.
  Counselor

WALNUT GROVE

Harris, Georgia Jean (Hoff)
  Mathematics Teacher

WARRENSBURG

Collins, Morris Lynn
  Art Teacher
Henry, Ann Connor
  Grad Assistant
Williams, Maria A. Lara
  Spanish Teacher

WASHBURN

Banks, Janeth Casper
  Soc Stud/Language Arts Teacher
Burnette, Treasa Ann
  Music Teacher
Cheek, Donna Matthews
  Vocational Home Ec Teacher

WASHINGTON

Mutert, Dinah Ruth
  Sixth Grade Teacher
Noelker, Ruth Connor
  First Grade Teacher
Schroeder, Glenda Renick
  Math/Computer Literacy Teacher

WAYNESVILLE

Gisselbeck, Eula Gibbs
  Fourth Grade Teacher
Hardman, Lula Mae
  Social Studies Instructor

WEBB CITY

Brown, Deanna F. (La Fevers)
  6th Grade Teacher
Pittman, Marti Robins
  Social Studies Teacher

WEBSTER GROVES

Sippel, Georgia Loesch
  Kindergarten Teacher

WELLINGTON

Bratton, Patricia Ann (Seibert)
  Science Teacher
Upton, Barbara Lynne
  Jr HS Mathematics Teacher

WENTZVILLE

Engelage, Melna Jean Bueneman
  Fifth Grade Teacher
Hendricks, Ellen Jean
  6th-8th Grade Art Teacher

WEST PLAINS

Dillard, Jack David
  Science Department Chair

WESTON

Benner, Patricia Lee
  Eng & Amer Lit/Spanish Teacher

WESTON (cont)
Pearson, James Greg
  History Teacher
WHEATON
England, Zona Mae
  First Grade Teacher
Fiene, Jeanne Rae
  High School Principal
Lacey, Sue
  Counselor
WILLARD
Swearengin, Carol H.
  Fifth Grade Teacher
WILLOW SPRINGS
Hicks, Barbara Jean
  Fifth Grade Teacher
WINDSOR
Sanders, Connie Fay (Call)
  Fourth Grade Teacher
WINFIELD
Byington, Mary Frances
  5th Grade Teacher
Sadlo, Mary Hemker
  4th Grade Teacher
WRIGHT CITY
Stetson, Robyn
  Computer Middle/HS Teacher
WYACONDA
Edgar, Judith Benson
  Social Studies Teacher
Feldkamp, Mary Goodwin
  Science Department Chair

MONTANA

ABSAROKEE
Arthun, Thale Marie Scott
  Third Grade Teacher
Eckstein, Amelia Madison
  Study Skills Teacher
ANACONDA
Alexander, Sonnia Moscolic
  Chemistry/Mathematics Teacher
Blaz, Stan L.
  Principal Intern
Kaney, Lanor Eccleston
  6th Grade Teacher
AUGUSTA
Carter, Jeanette Yvonne (Ropp)
  Business Teacher
BAINVILLE
Smith, Gennet M. L.
  Fifth-Sixth Grade Teacher
BIG TIMBER
Bassett, F. Charles
  Jr HS Social Studies Teacher
Tulley, Kathleen Crosbie
  English Department Chair
BIGFORK
Pulcini, Elinor De Lancey
  Science Teacher
BILLINGS
Bokum, Charlie W.
  4th Grade Teacher
Brownson, Wayne Darrel
  Vocal Music Director
Henry, Steven R.
  Sixth Grade Teacher
Kendall, Maria Perico
  Spanish Instructor
Marsh, Stephen David
  World/American History Teacher
Miller, John William
  Science Teacher
Peterson, Grover A.
  Band Teacher
Phillips, Gene F.
  Mathematics Teacher
Richau, Deborah L.
  Sixth Grade Teacher
Simmons, Richard Lee
  History Teacher
Tieggs, Ruth Streeb
  Principal
BOX ELDER
Capps, James Preston
  Mathematics Teacher
BOZEMAN
Comer, Les
  6th Grade Teacher
Johnson, Jon W.
  4th Grade Teacher

Mc Nellis, Marjorie Kathleen
  Asst Dir Bilingual Project
Newbury, Russell Dean
  Band Director
Pierre, Michael Joseph
  6th-8th Grade Math Teacher
Reisig, Jerry L.
  Mathematics/Physics Instructor
Rognrud, Gordon Allen
  Marketing Education Teacher
Strohmeyer, Judith Bishop
  Teacher
BRADY
Keith, Janice Dickey
  6th-8th Grade Teacher
Larson, Carol J.
  Second & Third Grade Teacher
Perry, Debby L.
  Home Economics Teacher & Cnslr
BROADUS
Goodwin, Kit D.
  Mathematics Teacher
BROWNING
Holbrook, Charles D.
  Mathematics Teacher
BUTTE
Groff, Shirley Hand
  Fifth Grade Teacher
Johnson, Diane Louise
  7th/8th Grade Math Teacher
Ronning, Kenneth Michael
  Economics & History Teacher
Younkin, Marjorie Jane (Priebe)
  5th Grade Teacher
CASCADE
Robbins, Roger Leo
  6th Grade Teacher/Elem Prin
CHESTER
Van Dessel, Don
  Jr HS Phys Ed/Sci Teacher
CIRCLE
Lala, Clarence Max
  Mathematics Teacher
O'Brien, Judy E. Scholl
  Third Grade Teacher
COLSTRIP
Conroy, Lyndon R.
  History Teacher
George, Sallie J.
  Business Education Teacher
Shreeve, David William
  Activities Director
COLUMBUS
Grossheider, Koenning
  1st Grade Teacher
CONRAD
Makelky, Jeff A.
  History Teacher
CUT BANK
Nelson, Marjorie Carlson
  5th Grade Teacher
DILLON
Pelletier, Roger Joseph
  Fifth Grade Teacher
Thomas, Dan B.
  Language Arts Teacher
DRUMMOND
Anderson, Donald Joseph
  Soc Stud/Health Teacher
DUTTON
Ashworth, Rick Alan
  Principal
EUREKA
Henderson, Robert G.
  Science Teacher
FAIRFIELD
Bremer, Cheryl Bowers
  4th Grade Teacher
Carlson, Marge Reiquam
  Retired K & 1st Grade Teacher
Fleming, Frank Joseph
  Science Teacher
FAIRVIEW
Taylor, Robby G.
  Fifth Grade Teacher
GLASGOW
Yoakam, Mark William
  English Teacher
GLENDIVE
Carpenter, Verna Vassler
  8th Grade Science Teacher

GREAT FALLS
Kunka, James Charles
  8th Grade Math Dept Chair
Mader, Jan Landis
  Physics Teacher
Parke, H. Lynn
  First Grade Teacher
Wallace, Gary Donald
  US History Teacher
HAMILTON
Bleibtrey, Karen Ann Pronovost
  Summer Program Director
HARDIN
Harlin, Bob F.
  Principal
O'Dell, Julie Myers
  HS Business Instructor
HAVRE
Hyke, Douglas Dwayne
  Sci Dept Chm/Bio Teacher
HELENA
Dawes, Edward Allen
  Auto Mech/Small Engine Teacher
Kukes, Patrick J.
  Orchestra Director
La Faver, Carol Ledbetter
  6th Grade Teacher
Logan, David Michael
  Spanish Teacher
Lund, Debra K.
  Earth Science Teacher
Mazanec, Thomas Paul
  Music Teacher
Sinnott, Danna Hintz
  Spanish Teacher
Spieker, Joseph
  English Teacher/Coach
HOBSON
Denton, Cynthia Dillon
  Business Education Chair
Denton, J. Larry
  History Teacher
HOT SPRINGS
Jolma, Barbara Heidegger
  First Grade Teacher
JUDITH GAP
Lemmon, Patti Else
  Mathematics Department Teacher
KALISPELL
Barragan, Jean Kellar
  Social Studies Teacher
Carver, Gary Lee
  9th Grade Eng/Speech Teacher
Chase, Sharon Lynne (Harris)
  5th Grade Teacher
Glenn, Katherine
  Membership Representative
Pond, Maxine Lister
  7th Grade Teacher Plus
Quigley, Susan Dianne
  Chapter I Jr HS Tutor
Ross, Nancy S.
  7th Grade Lang Arts Teacher
LAMBERT
Ligon, Diane (Shamley)
  Former Match Instructor
Vaira, Mary Rehbein
  4-6th Grade Science Teacher
LAUREL
Langager, Harvey James
  Business Education Teacher
LEWISTOWN
Borgreen, James Carl
  High School Art Teacher
Byrne, Judy Susanne
  English/French Teacher
Garcia, Richard Orlando
  Bands Director
LIBBY
Anderson, Alice Wekander
  Retired Teacher
Benda, Russell Bruce
  Science Teacher
Kelsch, Brad James
  4th Grade Teacher
Reckin, Gene
  Science Teacher/Dept Chair
LODGE GRASS
Anderson, Della J.
  Business/Computer Instructor
MALTA
Denson, Jenette Lee (Mathiot)
  Substitute Teacher
MILES CITY
Hosbein, Ann Buss
  Dir Religious Education

Stone, Alieda Mae
  Second Grade Teacher
MISSOULA
Braun, Cyndy
  Latin & French Teacher
Brown, Vicki C.
  Health & Physical Ed Teacher
Johnson, Edward Matthew
  Fifth Grade Teacher
Lyons, Michael Lawrence
  8th Grade English Teacher
Mc Enaney, Nicholas William
  English Teacher
Stengel, Roberta Zupan
  5th Grade Teacher
Wilson, David William
  Mathematics Teacher
MOORE
Barta, Marilyn Lerum
  First Grade Teacher
PLAINS
Beals, Dallas Layne
  Art Teacher/Counselor
RED LODGE
Bradshaw, Sandra Cummings
  Third Grade Teacher
ROUNDUP
Brower, Mary Sweeney
  Spanish/French Teacher
RYEGATE
Burgess, Lyle D.
  Bus/Phys Ed Teacher Admin Asst
SAINT REGIS
Mattheis, Dolores (Reese)
  Teacher/Librarian
SAINT XAVIER
Stewart, Doris M.
  Teacher
SHELBY
Bashor, Michael E.
  6th-7th Grade History Teacher
Mc Phillips, Bernice Boyum
  Second Grade Teacher
Stevens, Penny Lynn
  Third Grade Teacher
SHEPHERD
Thaut, Gerald Edward
  Junior High Science Teacher
SIDNEY
Arnold, Gary Peter
  8th Grade English Teacher
Zoanni, Richard James
  Mathematics Department Chair
STEVENSVILLE
Fisher, Nancy Anne
  Third Grade Teacher
TROY
More, James E.
  Counselor
TURNER
Malone, Ronald James
  Math Dept Chair
VALIER
Boumans, Randall Joseph
  Industrial Arts Teacher
VAUGHN
Frost, Frank Steven
  Mathematics/Science Teacher
WEST YELLOWSTONE
Christensen, Carolee Cunningham
  Fifth Grade Teacher
Etzwiler, Linda Fairweather
  Third Grade Teacher
Lynn, Peggy Ann
  Mathematics/Computer Teacher
Morris, Clifford William
  Business & Physical Ed Teacher
WHITEFISH
Heinrich, Joaquenia Shaw
  Sixth Grade Teacher
Helgath, Nancy L. (Wilson)
  English/Literature Teacher
WIBAUX
Capp, Karen Cossey
  Chapter I Teacher
Gerving, Herman Jerome
  Mathematics Teacher & Chairman
Hansen, Edward William
  7th-8th Grade Science Teacher
WILSALL
Forsyth, John P.
  English Teacher

WISE RIVER
Gneiting, Barbara Gould
  Kindergarten-4th Grade Teacher
WORDEN
Thorpe, Eileen Aaberge
  Business Teacher

NEBRASKA

ADAMS
Harrold, Margaret Spellman
  Math Teacher/Spanish Teacher
Hottovy, Thomas R.
  Mathematics/Computer Teacher
ALLEN
Furness, Doris Troth
  Retired
Rastede, Marcia Stamp
  English/Social Studies Teacher
ALLIANCE
Cummings, Iris Reece
  Mathematics Teacher
Hubbard, Leon David Jr.
  1st-5th Grade Phys Ed Teacher
Lawrence, Becky Russell
  1st Grade Teacher
Nelson, Patricia Way
  English Teacher
Schlattmann, Janet L. (Libal)
  Middle School Math Teacher
Schmeits, Sheila Ann
  Mid Sch Math/Sci Teacher
Schnell, Pamela Jane
  Science Teacher
ARLINGTON
Ludwig, Janet E. (Niebaum)
  2nd Grade Teacher
BELLEVUE
Hartel, Gregory John
  Biology/Ecology Teacher
Moore, Mary B.
  7th/8th Grade Religion Teacher
Williamson, Susan Ahrens
  Third Grade Teacher
BELLWOOD
Jahde, Tom
  Physical Education Teacher
Matulka, Yvonne M.
  8th Grade Teacher
Mc Donald, Shirley Brogan
  Third Grade Teacher
BENKELMAN
Haines, Donna Belle Wilson
  Substitute Teacher
BENNINGTON
Harshman, Stephen Douglas
  Scndry Social Studies Teacher
BLAIR
Kolb, Paul Stephen
  Social Studies Teacher
Laughery, Gwen Marie
  Third Grade Teacher
Weeces, Terri (Vander Stoep)
  Science Teacher
BRAINARD
Struebing, Dave Dean
  Physical Ed/History Teacher
BRUNING
Meyer, Betty Easton
  Kindergarten/Elem Music Tchr
Volkmer, Rona K.
  English Teacher
BYRON
Hoops, Yvonne Helene (Seybold)
  First/Second Grade Teacher
CAIRO
Eriksen, Donna L.
  Jr/Sr HS Soc Stud Teacher
Young, Donna Mae (Marcellus)
  Second Grade Teacher
CHAPMAN
Vipperman, E. June
  Retired Teacher
CLARKSON
Maliha, Sheryl Elizabeth Ditter
  Business Education Teacher
COLUMBUS
Boyle, Betty Harvey
  Seventh Grade Teacher

CRAWFORD
Gibbons, Elizabeth Weber
  Substitute Teacher All Grades
CREIGHTON
Crosley, Eloise Wiese
  Second Grade Teacher
CRETE
Conrad, Jill Kay
  Mathematics Teacher
Lingle, Muriel Ellen Anderson
  Fourth Grade Teacher
Prokop, Debra L. Rethmeier
  4th Grade Teacher
Wagner Georgi, Mary
  Eng/Journalism/Speech Teacher
CULBERTSON
Kershaw, John Darren
  Jr High/High School Teacher
CURTIS
Rue, Karon S.
  English Instructor
Witt, Elaine M.
  4/5th Grade Lang Arts Teacher
DAKOTA CITY
Hubbard, Beverly Flack
  Third Grade Teacher
DAVID CITY
Portrey, Leon Paul
  Business Teacher
DESHLER
Mroczek, David J.
  Social Science Teacher
DWIGHT
Chmelka, Rosalyn M.
  Retired Teacher
EDISON
Sawyer, Polly Kentfield
  Retired Elem Teacher
ELGIN
Sweem, Terence Allen
  English, Speech Dept Chair
ELKHORN
Hartman, Julie L.
  Physical Education Teacher
Windhorst, Julie Ann (Cover)
  Fifth Grade Teacher
ELM CREEK
Gunderson, Jim Allen
  Science/Mathematics Teacher
ELMWOOD
Shrader, Kurk Vann
  Business Teacher
EWING
Coy, Elsie May Cooper
  4th-8th Grade Head Teacher
Kurpgeweit, Joline (Smith)
  Fifth Grade Teacher
Lowe, Edward Paul
  7th-12th Grade Principal
FAIRBURY
Holloway, Amaryllis Barber
  Retired Elem Music Teacher
FALLS CITY
Masonbrink, John J.
  Science Teacher
FORT CALHOUN
Skrdla, Jerome J.
  Biology Teacher
Thomas, Lola (Shreves)
  Spanish/English Teacher
FREMONT
Bolton, Gary L.
  Jr HS Principal
Mruz, Linda Rolfsmeyer
  Physiology & Chemistry Teacher
Nissen, Beverly Ann
  Reading Teacher
Raasch, Michael Dean
  English Teacher/Dept Chair
FRIEND
Edwards, Willa L.
  Elementary Teacher
GENEVA
Mannel, Karen Ruth
  Second Grade Teacher
Trumper, Roger K.
  Guidance Director
GERING
Alvarez, Manuel Junior
  Mathematics Department Chair
Smith, Michael Lee
  Math Teacher

GRAND ISLAND
Arrants, Donald L.
  6th-8th Grade Phys Ed Teacher
Casteel, Nancy Kay (Hendrix)
  Fourth Grade Teacher
Kral, Elmer A.
  English Instructor
Mc Cue, Kermit Clare
  English Department Chairperson
Mc Gahan, James Eugene
  Science Department Chairman
Obermier, Duane A.
  Communicative Arts Dept Chair
Rempe, Doris
  English Teacher
Riggert, Kevin Lynn
  Elementary Principal
Wells, Joe
  7th English/Soc Stud Teacher
Wieck, Elaine Hodges
  Rdng/Latin/Japanese Teacher
GREELEY
Williams, Bradley C.
  Business Teacher
GRETNA
Pratt, Eleanor M.(Koke)
  Chapter I Teacher
HARTINGTON
Schroeder, Mary Elizabeth
  Biology Instructor
HOLDREGE
Jeffrey, Richard James
  History Teacher
HOWELLS
Prusa, Marla Mc Coy
  Home Economics Teacher
HUMBOLDT
Fraser, Madelyn C.
  Third Grade Teacher
Huffman, Calvin D.
  Chem/Physics/Sci Teacher
IMPERIAL
Cox, Jeannine Zurelda (Leach)
  2nd Grade Teacher
Heckenlivley, Rex J.
  Math Teacher
KEARNEY
Schrack, Norma Jean (Moors)
  2nd Grade Teacher
LAUREL
Manganaro, Carol Jean (Dittrich)
  Mathematics Teacher
LEBANON
Clinebell, Sabrena Gibbs
  Science Teacher
LEXINGTON
Ver Maas, Janelle Huss
  2nd Grade Teacher
LINCOLN
Buss, Eileen Chapman
  5th-6th Teacher
Carpenter, William Henry
  Piano Instructor
Deemer, A. Lisette Perez
  Music Teacher
Dunham, Sally Elizabeth
  5th/6th Grade Teacher
Hagele, Elaine (Stickle)
  Accounting Teacher
Hrnicek, Noreen Therese
  Chemistry Teacher
Johnson, Barbara Berger
  Retired 3rd/4th Grade Teacher
Lorenzen, Jeanne Marie Niemeier
  3rd Grade Teacher
Simpson, Deloise Lysgaard (Perry)
  Classroom Teacher
Uhing, Russ
  Business Instructor
Wingrove, M. Lynn (Grosscup)
  English Teacher
LINDSAY
Buhl, Mary Jo Kadavy
  K-6th Grade Elementary Teacher
Meredith, Joyce Adams
  Fourth Grade Teacher
LODGEPOLE
Soucie, Elizabeth Ann (Frantz)
  Spanish/Soc Stud Teacher
LYONS
Brown, Floyd Ivan
  History Teacher/Dept Chair
Toalson, Bobette Curry
  English/Speech Teacher

MADRID
Lee, Patti Hazzard
  English/History Teacher
MASON CITY
Skeen, Reva Jean
  5th/6th Grade Teacher
MAXWELL
Kraus, Patrick J.
  Industrial Arts Teacher
MC COOL JUNCTION
Patitz, Iva M. (Wright)
  Kindergarten/Chapter I Reading
MITCHELL
Blehm, Shirley R. (Settles)
  English Teacher
MULLEN
Volentine, Roger Wilbur
  Mathematics Instructor
MURRAY
Shields, Karen Kay (Smith)
  Elementary Principal
NEBRASKA CITY
Kernes, Ben O.
  Mathematics Teacher
Little, Sue Marie (Plugge)
  5th Grade Elementary Teacher
Sunderman, Joel Thomas
  Band Dir/Fine Art Dept Head
NELSON
Spirk, Jaynie Sue (Hansen)
  Mathematics Teacher
NEWMAN GROVE
Seier, Mark Jerome
  Biology Teacher
NORFOLK
Eden, Deanna Mae
  Phys Ed Instructor/Coach
Henre, B. Vauri
  English Instructor
Henriksen, Penelope Pearson
  First Grade Teacher
Hess, Anne Heusinger
  Music/Speech Teacher
Jessen, Jane Smith
  Fifth Grade Teacher
Zoucha, Douglas H.
  History Teacher
NORTH BEND
Allgood, Tony Allan
  Art Teacher
Feurer, Robert E.
  Science Teacher/Dept Chair
Phelps, Ann
  English/Journalism Dept Chair
NORTH PLATTE
Boerner, Ronald R.
  Chemistry Teacher
Gaipl, Linda L.
  6th Grade Mathematics Teacher
Gulzow, Steve Kenneth
  Amer His Teacher/Soc Stud Chm
Nielsen, Shirley Folker
  Seventh/Eighth Grade Teacher
Shandera, Joe R.
  Physical Education Teacher
OAKDALE
Petersen, Marlene Wood
  Fifth Grade Teacher
OMAHA
Bateman, Joseph G.
  Physical Education Teacher
Bitzes, John G.
  Teacher
Cobbs, Jo Barsh
  Third Grade Teacher
Dalton, Lois Eggert
  5th Grade Teacher
Davis, Ruby Mae (Mount)
  Fifth Grade Teacher
Delahanty, Eileen M.
  Social Sciences Teacher
Eickelman, Colleen Erin
  Soc Science/Eng Teacher
Galusha, Wesley Jay
  Art Teacher/Project Coord
Garofolo, Ronald Joseph
  Architectural Drafting Teacher
Gaul, Rita
  Sixth Grade Teacher
Glogowski, David Gerard
  English Teacher
Jaros, Sherry (Green)
  Second Grade Teacher
Johnson, Paula Larsen
  Third Grade Teacher

Lang, Charles Richard
  Physics Teacher
Miller, Lewis William
  7-9th Grade German Teacher
Mullen, Janelle Alderson
  Jr HS Administrator
Neumann, Clarice Turco
  Fifth Grade Teacher
Novak, Tommy James
  Fourth Grade Teacher
Olson, David Brian
  Chemistry Teacher
Peters, David John
  Building Principal
Phister, Carla Rust
  Reading Teacher
Reynolds, John Michael
  8th Grade Core Teacher
Robson, Carol Garnaas
  Fourth Grade Teacher
Rose, Terese Ann
  First Grade Teacher
Salberg, Jeff A.
  Social Studies Teacher
Starmer, Gene D.
  Mathematics Teacher
Swanson, Constance Ann (Kawa)
  Fifth Grade Teacher
Tingelhoff, Suzanne M. (Wortman)
  Fifth Grade Teacher
ORD
Lola, Charlene Helen Nekuda
  Fourth Grade Teacher
OSMOND
Manzer, Beth M.
  Business Educator
OXFORD
Luther, Brian Douglas
  English/Media Teacher
PAPILLION
Langabee, Joanne Marie
  Physics Instructor
Linse, Dee Ann (Dishman)
  Science Teacher
PERU
Adams, Maryon Thomas
  Retired
PETERSBURG
Rinas, Michelle Jane
  Principal/Science Teacher
Wies, Bonnie Braun
  First/Second Grade Teacher
PIERCE
Carlson, Dale Louis
  6th Grade Teacher
PLATTE CENTER
Ernesti, Dona J.
  K-8th Grade Resource Teacher
PLATTSMOUTH
Campbell, Sharon K. (Miner)
  Phys Ed Dept Head/Teacher
Kull, Kenneth K.
  Band Director
Watt, Betty J.
  8th Grade Earth Sci Teacher
PRIMROSE
Walrath, Pat Ann (Collins)
  K-3rd Grade Elementary Teacher
RALSTON
Taylor, Daryl Lee
  English Department Chair
RAVENNA
Stubbs, Gary Le Roy
  Business Teacher
ROSELAND
Cercle, Dean Frank
  Science Teacher
RUSHVILLE
Baker, Noelle Dora (Strang)
  English & Mathematics Teacher
SARGENT
Hays, Debra Lynn England
  English Teacher
Woracek, Clara Ann (Windels)
  Second Grade Teacher
SCOTTSBLUFF
Barker, James Richard
  7th Grade Soc Stud Teacher
Lane, Derek Ray
  Speech/Drama/Debate Teacher
SOUTH SIOUX CITY
Ebel, Linda Harms
  8th Grade Teacher
Huff, Patsy Jo Hernandez
  Fourth Grade Teacher

Koch, Helmut John
  Chemistry Teacher
SPRINGVIEW
Budnick, Thomas
  Business Department Teacher
STELLA
Luther, Susan Jayne
  Media Director
STROMBRUG
Lamoree, Barbara J.
  Fourth Grade Teacher
STROMSBURG
Alms, Paula J.
  French/English Teacher
Hengelfelt, Delores Harless
  Third Grade Teacher
SUMNER
Clark, Carolyn Cramer
  Third Grade Teacher
SUPERIOR
Stubbs, Patricia Gifford
  French Teacher
TALMAGE
Peterson, Dianne Dietrich
  Fifth Grade Teacher
TAYLOR
Harden, M. Jean
  6th Grade Teacher
TECUMSEH
Muller, Marcee Maree
  Mathematics Teacher/Dept Chm
TEKAMAH
Barnard, Janice M.
  Kindergarten/Chapter I Teacher
TRUMBULL
Strasheim, Patricia Ann
  5th Grade Teacher
TRYON
Miller, Alan Eugene
  Social Science Teacher
Neal, Elnora May
  Elementary Teacher
Wilkie, Margaret Anne
  English Teacher
VALLEY
Nordell, Geraldine Thompson
  Third Grade Teacher
VALPARAISO
Lorenz, Paul H.
  6th Grade Teacher
Martin, Patricia L.
  Third Grade Teacher
WALTHILL
Whisenhunt, Betsy Ann
  English Teacher
WAYNE
Swarts, Cyndi Sims
  Teacher
WEST POINT
Wegmann, Clare M.
  First Grade Teacher
WYMORE
Anderson, Shirley Le Ann (Paus)
  Science Teacher

NEVADA

BOULDER CITY
Johnson, Mary Serrano
  Teacher
Phoenix, Eleanor Crisp
  English Teacher
CARLIN
Blinn, Jon Mark
  Phys Ed-Math Teacher
Grube, David Quinn
  Social Studies Instructor
CARSON CITY
Glanzman, Duane Allan
  Mathematics Teacher
Rowley, Genine Mary
  Mathematics/Computer Teacher
EAST ELY
Sanborn, Cyndi M.
  2nd Grade Teacher
ELKO
Barrett, Scott Ray
  Physical Education Teacher

ELKO (cont)

Neitz, Helen Burr
8th Grade Home Ec Teacher

Williams, Gerald Lee
Electronics Teacher

FALLON

Hansen, Steve Gordon
Third Grade Teacher

Heck, Patricia Ogilvie
PACE Cor/Teacher

Hinz, Paul L.
History/Lang Arts Teacher

Olson, Clara Jean (White)
First Grade Teacher

Ranson, Steven Robert
English Department Chairman

HENDERSON

Brown, Helga Seinsoth
Foreign Language Teacher

Rishovd, Paula De Shaw
Industrial Art Teacher

Treanor, Marilyn J. (Parker)
High School Math Teacher

JACKPOT

Roberts, Billie Crooks
5th Grade Teacher

Strom, Michael John
6th Grade Teacher

LAS VEGAS

Andolina, Nancy Jean
Oral Lang Study Skills Teacher

Barclay, Donald L. Jr.
Social Studies Dept Chairman

Blomstrom, Lars
Third Grade Teacher

Boucher, Judy Elaine
Reading Specialist

Burleson, Joy Concannon
Physical Education Teacher

Gaydosh, Geri
Instructor/Gifted & Talented

Granese, Judith Ann
English Teacher

Hair, Kittie Ellen
World History Teacher

Hammelrath, Catherine Blackman
Spanish Teacher

Jensen, Jocelyn Reid
Fine Arts Dept Chairman

Karstedt, Julie Ann Greenfield
Mathematics/Science Dept Chair

Keairnes, William Paul
5th Grade Teacher

Lane, Marcella Ann
Eng/Advanced Placement Teacher

Leggett, Shirley Brassell
5th Grade Teacher

Mc Quaig, Meriam Randall
Fifth Grade Teacher

Parker, Leroy Neal
School Counselor

Partier, Joan Hansen
Fourth Grade Teacher

Paulucci, Phillip Samuel
Master English Teacher

Pina, Nena Harrison
English/Spanish Teacher

Ryan, Richard D.
Principal/Mathematics Teacher

Sassenberg, Gary R.
English Teacher

Snyder, John H.
Computer Science Instructor

Tarr, Jeanie Ann
Fifth Grade Teacher

Thomas, William Henry
Military Science Instructor

Thompson-Dunn, Robert Lynn
English/Journalism Teacher

Wasinger, John Robert
Reading Teacher/Dept Chair

Yarberry, Terry Lyle
Fourth Grade Teacher

LOVELOCK

Meyers, Cindy Lu
2nd Grade Teacher

MINDEN

Brandt, B. Shirley
English Teacher

Doherty, Barbara Sykes
HS English/History Teacher

NORTH LAS VEGAS

Bennett, Juanita Alexander
Sixth Grade Teacher

RENO

Baro, Elizabeth Mac Gregor
5th Grade Teacher

Elston, Jo Ann Foster
5th Grade Teacher

Lindstrom, Roselynn Mary
Mathematics Department Chair

Menicucci, Jill Marie
Sixth Grade Teacher

Monroe, Duncan Allen
Social Studies Lead Teacher

SPARKS

Eckdall-Estabrook, Karen Christine
6th Grade Teacher

Hausauer, Denise Flynn
Business/Mathematics Teacher

Kuhles, Billie Louise
5th Grade Teacher

Norris, Jeffrey A.
Social Studies Teacher

Young, Ginny (Keller)
Social Studies Teacher

TONOPEH

Brawley, Patricia Lynne
English Teacher/Dept Head

VIRGINIA CITY

Gladding, Karin Morghen
Special Education Teacher

Murkovich, Sally Anne
Fourth Grade Teacher

WINNEMUCCA

Hendrix, Margo Ward
Principal

NEW HAMPSHIRE

AMHERST

Dubreuil, Patrick Roland
French/Spanish Teacher

AUBURN

Kursewicz, Lynn Marie
Second Grade Teacher

Pinard, Cynthia Best
Third Grade Teacher

BELMONT

Garneau, John Michael
7th Grade History Teacher

Makely, Daniel Lavergne
Sixth Grade Teacher

BERLIN

Favreau, Anne-Marie
1st Grade Teacher

Provencher, Jane Bryant
Second Grade Teacher

BETHLEHEM

Frizzell, Everett Ray
HS Chemistry/Physics Teacher

Hixon, William Roy
4th Grade Teacher

CANDIA

Stathos, Donna Bohle
7th & 8th Math Teacher

Thurston, Marlene Gillen
Second Grade Teacher

CENTER STRAFFORD

Plante, Maryellen Childs
2nd Grade Teacher

CONCORD

Damour, Blithe Reed
English Teacher

Grenert, Beverly Diane
Curriculum Supervisor

Hennessey, Clare
Fourth Grade Teacher

CONTOOCOOK

Bickford, Lawrence Alan
Computer Coordinator

CONWAY

Hamlin, Michelle Sparre
Mathematics Teacher

DOVER

Falcione, Arnold M.
History Teacher

Ripa, Ronald Anthony
Theology Department Chair

EXETER

Arnold, David Hamlin
Math Teacher/Dir of Studies

Lennox, Angela Jane
Biology Teacher

FRANKLIN

Andrews, Susan Spiridondes
Third Grade Teacher

Colby, Gary Allan
Social Studies Teacher

HAMPTON

Mc Clain, Elizabeth Lee
Second Grade Teacher

Savage, Edgar Osborne
Physical Education Teacher

Talas, Toni Gail
Mathematics Teacher

HILLSBORO

Mansor, Susan Marie
Social Studies Teacher

HOLLIS

Lyle, Barry William
US/World History Teacher

HUDSON

Blanchard, Sandra Malette
Fourth Grade Teacher

Demyanovich, Karen Berlin
Eng Teacher

Hodgkins, John W.
Science Department Chairman

Landry, Beverly A. (Cluff)
President/Kindergarten Teacher

La Perriere, Paul Frederick Jr.
9-12th Grade Soc Stud Teacher

Matson, Heather Mitchell
Social Studies Teacher

Mc Coy, Bernadine Marie (Heck)
3rd Grade Teacher

Miller, Leonard M.
English Teacher

O'Shaughnessy, William James
7th Grade Social Stud Teacher

Poole, Elizabeth H.
Business Education Teacher

Turner, Richard W.
8th Grade Soc Studies Teacher

Zanni, Stephen Nicholas
Science Dept Chair

JAFFREY

Kaminski, Gloria Lebel
6th Grade Teacher

Zecha, Linda Morse
Fourth Grade Teacher

KEENE

Lammela, Robert J.
Chemistry Teacher

LEBANON

Fiske, John F. III
Mathematics Teacher

MANCHESTER

Ball, Patricia Marylyn
English Teacher & Curr Coord

Banks, Joan E.
English Teacher

Benson, William Farnum
Social Studies Teacher

Burgatti, Joseph C.
Social Studies Teacher

Dufour, Jay
Social Studies Teacher

Dugan, Carolyn Jane
English Teacher/I TV Coord

Fallu, Lesley Weldon
Mathematics Teacher

Hurley, Carol Provost
Business Education Teacher

Kenney, Michelle D. St. Hilaire
Social Studies Teacher

Kenney, W. Bruce F.
Science Teacher

Messier, David Charles
Principal

Morgan, Bonnie Lee
Counselor

O'Keefe, Donna Darrah
Level Coord/Lang Arts & Lit

Valade, Edmond Joseph
11th-12th Grade His Teacher

Van Houten, Constance Lafond
English Teacher

MEREDITH

Foster, Elaine Peterson
French Teacher

Meledandri, Caesar Francis
High School English Teacher

MERRIMACK

Bachand, Wayne Rene
7th Grade Mathematics Teacher

Blank, Raymond Henry
Mathematics/Computer Teacher

Gotsill, Thomas William
English Teacher

James, Lisa Handwerger
Math/Computer Teacher

Lavallee, Carol Ann
1st Grade Teacher

Leavitt, Laurel Elgart
Second Grade Teacher

Watkins, Louis Ralph
Science Teacher

MILFORD

Bailey, Arnold B.
Computer Coordinator

Castro, Luis Alfonso
Spanish Teacher

MILTON

Brown, Bruce Bailey
Mathematics Department Chair

NASHUA

Argencourt, Roger George SC
History Teacher/Dept Chm

Rizos, Eleanor Cachiona
Spanish Teacher

White, Richard W.
English/Journalism Teacher

NEW LONDON

Kocsis, Daniel John
English Teacher

NEWPORT

Barton, Nancy Niemi
First Grade Teacher

NORTH SUTTON

Ragazzo, Robert
Industrial Art/Voc Ed Coord

PEMBROKE

Johnson, Jeannie S.
Mathematics Teacher

Todd, Judith Ann (Murdock)
4th Grade Teacher

PLAISTOW

Binaghi, Giulio Paul
Spanish Teacher

Hill, Jeff W.
Mathematics Teacher

Hodgkins, Patricia Marion
Foreign Language Dept Chair

PLYMOUTH

Boisvert, Janet Claire
4th Grade Teacher

Drown, Timothy John
Athletic Trainer/Health Instr

PORTSMOUTH

Burns, Martin Breaden
6th Grade Teacher

Milotte, Jane L.
4th Grade Teacher

Robbins, Mary Ann
Fourth Grade Teacher

Theille, Anthony
English Teacher

RAYMOND

Scantlin, Euphemia E.
English Teacher

ROCHESTER

Hendryx, Wendy Glassner
Guidance Counselor

Pecor, Marcy Johnson
Fifth Grade Teacher

SALEM

Butler, Charlotte C.
8th Grade Soc Stud Teacher

Hummel, Daniel
School Counselor

Kublbeck, Jane Ann
Home Economics Teacher

Lake, Albert Clark Jr.
Science Teacher

Russo, Paulette Carro
Fourth Grade Teacher

Sinibaldi, Carol Chase
Fifth Grade Teacher

SANBORNVILLE

Eggleston, Cindy L.
Science Teacher

SUNAPEE

Rich, Pearl M.
Art Education Teacher

SUNCOOK

Jones, Duke Greg
Music Instructor

TEMPLE

Gregoire, Barbara Manning
First Grade Teacher

WEARE

Parker, Kathleen Howard
Teacher of Gifted & Talented

WEST LEBANON

Mills, Mary Lynn
Third Grade Teacher

NEW JERSEY

ABSECON

Collins, Deborah Jung
English Department Chair

Evans, David Alonzo
History/Philosophy Teacher

Pfeifer, David Alan
Social Studies Teacher

ALLAMUCHY

Cramer, Deborah Jean Henris
Primary Spec Ed Teacher

ALLENDALE

Haftel, Sandra
7th/8th Grade Soc Stud Teacher

ALLENWOOD

Gunther, Janice Morrissey
Third Grade Teacher

ALPINE

Nigohosian, Elsie Tatoian
Kindergarten Teacher

AMBERDEEN

Adler, Frances M.
COE Coord/Business Dept Chair

ANNANDALE

Lockart, David Royce
Vocal Music Teacher

ASBURY PARK

Brown, Victoria Colston
First Grade Teacher

Peters-Wynn, Zara
NI/PI Special Ed Teacher

ATCO

Blatherwick, Charles A.
9th Grade Science Teacher

Bubb, Georganne H.
English Teacher

Patterson, Marilyn Amy
English Teacher

Phillips, Timothy Edward
Teacher of Gifted & Talented

Young, Robert Wendell
Athletic Trainer

BARNEGAT

Laney, Charles Austin
5th Grade Teacher

BAYONNE

De Filippo, Cydney Zylo
Social Studies Teacher

Kane, Dolores Solan
1st Grade Teacher

Lynch, Michael P.
6th-8th Grade Math Teacher

Miesnik, Alice J.
English Instructor

Murphy, Thomas Michael
Social Studies Dept Chair

BAYVILLE

Cooper, Herman William
Teacher-Dept Head

Vignevic, Carol A.
Secondary Mathematics Teacher

BEACHWOOD

Downing, Linda A. Le Compte
First Grade Teacher

Heffernan, Linda Marascio
Language Arts Teacher

BELFORD

Donavan, Deborah
Fourth Grade Teacher

BELLE MEAD

Deluccia, Lynne Lenches
Social Studies Teacher

BELLEVILLE

Albanese, Linda Borella
Spanish Teacher

Kierney, Robert James
Social Studies Teacher

BELMAR

Burns, Jo Anne Smith
Basic Skills Teacher

Hoverter, Charlene Mokos
7th/8th Grade Teacher

Pullen, Carol Vayda
French Teacher

BELVIDERE

Amato, Anthony T.
Vice Principal

McDonald, Donna J. S.
Teacher of Human Ecology

Tshudy, Dean Jon
7th Grade Teacher

BERKELEY HEIGHTS
Balsam, Barbara Carol
Latin/English Teacher

BLACKWOOD
Benash, Kathleen Serafinelli
Physical Sci/Reading Teacher
Damico, Anthony Paul
8th Grade Language Art Teacher
Esposito, Dennis Joseph
Elementary Guidance Counselor
Fallon, Thomas Tracey
Sixth Grade Teacher
Keating, Mary Malan
6th Grade Teacher, Team Leader
Mc Call, Charlene N.
French Teacher
McKee, Thomas John
English Teacher
Richards, Janet Fischer
Chemistry Teacher

BLAIRSTOWN
Acker, Roger
5th & 6th Grade Teacher
Browse, Carolyn (Conforti)
English Teacher
Gladd, Gloria Belstra
English Teacher
Hough, Cheryl Moore
Fine Arts Teacher
Merrifield, Robert Paul
Biology Teacher

BLOOMFIELD
Cucolo, Nicholas Fred
HS English Teacher

BOGOTA
Swier, Susan A.
Business Education Teacher

BOONTON
Angilly, Beth R.
7th & 8th Grade Teacher
Retano, Vivien Maita
Third Grade Teacher

BORDENTOWN
Tenner, Frank Harrison
6th Grade Teacher/Science/Math
Walker, Harriet Nelms
7th Grade Science Teacher

BRANCHVILLE
Rigo, Barbara Henkel
5th Grade Teacher

BRICK
Antonacci, Denise Centrella
School Social Worker
Boyle, Susan
English Teacher
Clifford, Maureen
English Teacher
Genco, Stephen H.
Science Teacher
Morone, Leon A.
English Teacher/Drama Director

BRICK TOWN
Bocchetti, Richard William
2nd Grade Teacher

BRIDGETON
Bauer, Constance Joan
English Teacher
Coyne, James Michael
Principal
Hendricks, Nina Turman
English Teacher
Lewis, Donna Poloff
Teacher of Gifted & Talented

BRIDGEWATER
Iazzetta, John H.
Earth Science Teacher
Kopil, Joan Damms
First Grade Teacher
Ryor, Rita Millsom
6-8th Grade Rdng/Lit Teacher

BRIGANTINE
Revelle, Kathleen Ann
Fourth Grade Teacher

BROWNS MILLS
Emmons, Barbara R.
Basic Skills Teacher

BUDD LAKE
De Voe, Thomas Elliott
History Teacher

BURLINGTON
Newman, Robert Hausman
Guidance Counselor
Slagle, Elaine Sanderson
Second Grade Teacher

BUTLER
Kempson, G. Tim
Science Teacher

CALIFON
Schuetz, Alan Lee
5th-8th Grade Science Teacher
Sullivan, Dorothy Decker
Fourth Grade Teacher

CAMDEN
Filson, Johanna Varallo
7th/8th Grade Math Teacher
King, Richard William Jr.
12th Grade English Teacher
Mahan, Mozell Anita
Teacher of Social Studies
Malasky, Ronald K.
Chemistry Teacher
Massey, Sharon Fisher
First Grade Teacher
Mc Mullin, John Joseph
French Teacher

CAPE MAY
Swanson, Margaret Hannah
Teacher of Gifted & Talented

CAPE MAY CRT HSE
Conlin, James Donald
Business Department Chair
Lomax, Ellen Boeckel
Teacher of Gifted

CARLSTADT
Motto, Mary Lou (Muller)
5th-6th Grade Science Teacher

CARNEYS POINT
Hummel, Carole Devlin
Health/Physical Ed Teacher
Peak, Ann G.
3rd Grade Teacher

CEDAR GROVE
Jaeger, Jean Vandemark
1st Grade Teacher
Mattesky, Virgina Johnson
5th/6th Grade Teacher

CHATHAM
Cooke, Rosemary Reilly
Writing Process Teacher
Watkins Schorr, Christine Smith
English & History Teacher

CHERRY HILL
Bradney, Helen H.
Fourth Grade Teacher
Cutler, Gayle A.
English Teacher
Grubb, David G.
Chemistry Teacher
Quinn, Susan Joan
Theology Dept Chairperson

CHESTER
Lichatin, Rosanne Stango
Social Studies Teacher

CINNAMINSON
Callahan, Marjorie Floyd
Second Grade Teacher
Faber, Freddie James Jr.
7th/8th Grade Science Teacher
La Cerra, Margaret L.
6th Grade Teacher

CLAYTON
Grasso, Jean Grochowski
Second Grade Teacher

CLIFTON
Hartmann, Sandra Hornby
Social Studies Teacher
La Duke, Richard Martin
Physical Education Teacher
Okarma-Tkacz, Joyce M.
Mathematics Dept Teacher
Retalis, Christina F.
First Grade Teacher

COLONIA
Parsons, Patricia Marie
Science Teacher
Uszenski, Walter
Special Ed Teacher

COLTS NECK
Carhart, Carol A.
6th Grade Mathematics Teacher
Glemming, Patricia Reynolds
English Teacher
Pesce, Linda D.
Spanish/FLEX Teacher

COLUMBUS
Birkmire, Joanne
7th Grade English Teacher
Ziegenfuse, Bruce Richard
Mathematics Teacher

CRESSKILL
Bellina, Loretta
Principal

DELRAN
Krastek, Robert Anthony
Social Studies Teacher
Zwick, William Allen
Fifth Grade Teacher

DELRANCO
Godfrey, Edward J.
Mathematics/German Teacher
Maniglia, Ronald Joseph
AP Physics/Chemistry Teacher
Vahey, Regina Grant
Mathematics Department Chair

DENVILLE
Taormina, Geraldine Maupai
Science Teacher

DOVER
Sager, Rena
4th Grade Teacher

EAST HANOVER
Wiggin, Barbara Jones
Language Arts Teacher

EAST ORANGE
Alford, Martha Evans
Special Assignment Teacher
Jones, Vanessa Ann (Dillahunt)
Teacher of Gifted & Talented
Sepelyak, Carol Wallace
Spanish Teacher
Simmons, Robert Thomas
High School English Teacher
Tutt, Shirley Epps
Gifted/Talented Teacher

EAST RUTHERFORD
Fischer, Theodore
Guidance Counselor

EDISON
Bodnar, Helen
Honors Biology Teacher
Fisher-Glatt, Jill Meyerson
6th Grade English Teacher
Kurtiak, Carl Allan
History Teacher
Mc Clardy, Alice R.
First Grade Teacher
Nolan, Joseph A.
Language Department Chair
Thompson, Robert Rosedon Jr.
Biology Teacher

ELIZABETH
Aklonis, Raymond John
History Teacher
Fiano, Pilar Maria
Reading/Lang Arts Teacher
Maddock, Catherine
5th Grade Teacher
Paterek, Pamela Sigloch
US History/English Teacher
Ranhofer, Joan B.
Science Instructor
Sakowicz, Edward F.
Science Teacher
Schuster, Lory Zeidel
4th Grade Teacher

ELMER
Johnson, Nedd James
Guidance Counselor
Knudsen, Maryanne Ackley
Spanish Teacher
Pierangeli, Stephen Joseph
Social Studies Teacher
Travis, Claudia J.
Mathematics Teacher

ELMWOOD PARK
Niclaus, Gail Gardiner
3rd Grade Teacher

ENGLEWOOD
Maldonado, Beatriz
Math Teacher
Schwartz, Roberta Hellerman
Biology Teacher
White, Janis B.
Spanish Teacher

ENGLISHTOWN
Di Caro, Dianna M.
Mathematics Teacher

ERMA
Cherry, Alice Hiers
Geography/Related Art Teacher

FAIR LAWN
O'Neill, Thomas Eugene
Art Teacher

FLORENCE
Di Martino, Julia
Math Teacher

FORDS
Klubenspies, Claude Salerno
Third Grade Teacher
Mc Ginnis, Gertrude Williamson
8th Grade English Teacher

FORKED RIVER
Ciganek, Paulette Jacob
Mathematics Teacher

FORT LEE
Barbara, Fortunata J.
Social Studies Teacher

FRANKLIN
Manailovich, Adele C.
Kindergarten Teacher
Richards, Betty Jean (Van Riper)
Gifted/Talented Coord/Teacher

FRANKLINVILLE
Capizola, Grace Sylvester
Language Art Teacher
King, Wayne H.
Mathematics Teacher
Sparacio, Celia
Spanish Teacher

FREEHOLD
Janssen, Elaine Whitmore
Fourth Grade Teacher
Koba, Stanley J.
Social Studies Teacher
Mc Crohan, Roseann Strange
Reading Teacher

FRENCHTOWN
Petty, William Arthur
Industrial Technology Teacher

GARFIELD
De Graaff, Helen Goydich
Kindergarten Teacher
Khoury, Carol G.
Fifth Grade Teacher
Sciacca, Anna Degliomini
Seventh Grade Teacher

GLASSBORO
Swenson, Joanne R.
Third Grade Teacher

GLOUCESTER CITY
Danze, Nicholas Anthony
Theology Teacher
Di Vaccaro, Mary Dietrich
6th Grade Teacher
Genzano, Kathleen Sheldon
Mathematics Department Chair
Groff, Guy Robert
6th Grade Teacher
Higginbotham, Alfred J. Jr.
7th Grade Soc Stud Teacher
Mc Kibban, Joseph L. III
English Teacher
Young, Blanche
Second Grade Teacher

HACKENSACK
Foschini, Rosalie Brancato
Bilingual Education Teacher

HACKETTSTOWN
Nitto, Joseph Anthony
Computer/Health Teacher

HADDON HEIGHTS
Lavery, Mary Louise Jones
English Teacher

HADDONFIELD
Schlosser, Debra Stuart
Spec Ed/Resource Room Teacher

HAMBURG
England, John Mark
Science Teacher

HAMILTON SQUARE
Latini, Jane Cairo
Vice Principal

HAMILTON TOWNSHIP
Zuzov, Ann Marie
Teacher of the Gifted

HAMMONTON
Fucetola, Marie Grace
Mathematics Teacher
Thompson, Mary Lea
Gifted/Talented Teacher
Volpe, Teckla Anne
English Teacher

HAWTHORNE
Banks, Patricia Ann
Jr HS English Teacher

Lakefield, Bradley Ronald
Sci/Math/Computers Supervisor
Patella, Marie R.
English & Foreign Lang Teacher

HAZLET
Bagileo, Gerald James
Teacher/Admin Assistant
Neri, Anthony Joseph
Biology Teacher
Vitale, Carol Cottone
Mathematics Teacher

HIGHLAND
Rollins, Ann Johnston
Vocal Music Teacher

HIGHTSTOWN
Garrison, Phyllis Palombi
Social Studies Teacher

HILLSDALE
Hard, Susan Schott
Math & Computer Sci Teacher

HILLSIDE
Robinson, Sara Lucas
Business Education Teacher

HOBOKEN
Batistich, Evalee M.
4th Grade Teacher
Enrico, Gary
Band Director
Keller, William J.
Elementary School Teacher
Mason, Elizabeth Marie OP
Vice Prin & 8th Grade Teacher

HOLMDEL
Carnevale, Diane D.
Eighth Grade Math Teacher
Whitten, Sandra Elaine
English Teacher

HOPATCONG
Horvat-Lelling, Arlene Fogelson
1st Grade Teacher

HOWELL
Freitas, Maria
Fourth Grade Teacher
Lashley, Barbara Reiner
2nd Grade Teacher

IRVINGTON
Davis, Shelva Jones
History Teacher
Deutsch, Gerald David
Science Teacher
Hatch, Donald J.
Computer Science Teacher
Moxley, Warren Donald
Science Teacher/Coach
Ziemba, Mary Joanita Gertrude
Mathematics-Religion Teacher

ISELIN
Hansen, Helen Stefura
7th Grade Dev Lang/Reading

JACKSON
Darton, Robert Joseph
Social Studies Teacher
Kossmann, John Charles
Math Teacher

JERSEY CITY
Alvarez, Migdalia Roman
8th Grade Bilingual Teacher
Banks, Stella Perry
Typing Teacher
Barrett, James Joseph
French Teacher
Barrett, Kathleen Anne
4th Grade Teacher
Boyer, Margaret Zanor Kenny
4th Grade Teacher
Delo, Donald A.
English Teacher
Gavin, Allene S.
8th Grade Teacher
Gibney, Ellen
English Department Chair
Kaliades, Debra Kimmish
Second Grade Teacher
Kellers, Anne O'Neill
English Teacher
Kenny, Joanne Patrice
English Teacher
Mc Lean, Mary Ann
Jr HS Coord/7-8 His Teacher
Nestor, Kathy Gutch
English Teacher
Palladino, Nicholas S.
8th Grade Math Teacher
Ricci, Michael
English Teacher
Rose, Linda J.
Eighth Grade Math Teacher

JERSEY CITY (cont)
Santuoso, Madeline Claire
First Grade Teacher
Tadros, Nabila
Mathematics Teacher
Torrens, Alejandrina
Mathematics Teacher
Valentine, Carolyn Wright
Gifted & Talented Teacher
Warus, June Marie
Eighth Grade Reading Teacher
Williams, Lillian Pope
English Chairperson/Teacher

KEANSBURG
Loversidge, Patricia Cohill
Third Grade Teacher
Priolo, Charlene Sangiuolo
8th Grade Teacher
Van Deuenter, William Robert
Science Teacher

KEARNY
Feliciano, Blanca
Science Teacher
Hanf, Richard W.
English Teacher
Markey, Frances Janczyk
Third Grade Teacher
Robertson, Dolores Eckert
Fourth Grade Teacher
Whimpenny, Walter George
Mathematics Teacher

KENDALL PARK
Michie, Jean Strohmetz
First Grade Teacher

KENILWORTH
Baton, Nancy Leigh
Director of Gifted & Talented
Savage, Patricia Ann
Mathematics Teacher

KEYPORT
Schneider, Joan A.
Kindergarten Teacher

KINNELON
Grozalis, Mary Carolan
Latin & English Teacher

LAKEHURST
Coyle, Nancy Tomasso
7th Grade Teacher
Di Cicco, Barbara Anne
Basic Skills Teacher
Roche, Michael Terence
HS Sci Teacher/AV Coord

LAKEWOOD
Bryce, Helen Repko
English Teacher
Collins, Carol J.
Spanish/French Teacher
Frank, Rosemarie Elizabeth
Kindergarten Teacher
Hassler, Arlene Izzi
Fourth Grade Teacher of Gifted
Noack, Herbert A.
Science Teacher
Rauth, Virginia A.
4th Grade Teacher
Reed, Constance Lorraine
Sixth Grade Teacher

LANOKA HARBOR
De Simone, Louis J.
Science Teacher
Grant, Diane C.
Basic Skills Teacher
Graziano, Anthony Vincent
7th Grade Science Teacher
Saxton, Joseph James Jr.
English Teacher
Tranz, Eileen Mary Newton
Kindergarten Teacher
Wedding, David John
Health & Phys Ed Teacher

LAWRENCEVILLE
Liptak, Mary Ann Elizabeth
Dean of Academic Affairs
Mittnacht, Katherine L'Hommedieu
High School English Teacher

LINCROFT
Fili, Joseph D.
English Teacher

LINDEN
Boyd, Edith J. Major
8th Grade Soc Stud Teacher
Garbowski, Sabina Pruszynski
Algebra I & II Teacher
Klunder, Francine M.
Business Education Teacher
Lorenzetti, Gerard D.
Director of Bands

LINWOOD
Loper, Robert George
Mathematics Teacher
Shields, John J.
Teacher

LITTLE FALLS
Beyer, Patricia S.
English Teacher
Sayegh, Robert
English Teacher

LITTLE SILVER
Gance, Gerald A.
Chemistry Teacher

LIVINGSTON
La Belle, Michael Maurice
7th Grade Science Teacher
Wasserman, Honi
Media Specialist

LONG BRANCH
Borelli, Vincent J.
Speech/Theater Teacher
Dalessio, Elizabeth A. MPF
8th Grade Computer Teacher
Pabst, William F.
Eighth Grade English Teacher

LONG VALLEY
Dickinson, Janet Keroher
English Teacher

LYNDHURST
Lees, Richard Lawrence
Science Supervisor/Teacher

MAHWAH
Van Derbeek, Sharon Donohue
Third Grade Teacher

MANAHAWKIN
Fulkerson, Barbara Ann
11th-12th Grade His Teacher
Poorman, Ronald J.
Concert & Jazz Band Director

MANALAPAN
Dabbs, Loretta Young
Fourth Grade Teacher
Hagany, Judith Ann
7th/8th Grade Math Teacher
Stevens, Lois Katz
Third Grade Teacher

MANASQUAN
Bolderman, Mary Fox
Fifth Grade Teacher
Kirk, Richard Kenneth
7th & 8th Grade Sci Teacher

MANVILLE
Brunn, Herman Philip
6th Grade Elementary Teacher

MAPLE SHADE
Hill, Arthur R.
Mathematics/Science Supervisor
Rutan, Lawrence Richard
Mathematics Instructor
Toczylowski, Constance Morris
6th Grade Teacher

MAPLEWOOD
Dynan, William John
Social Studies Teacher
Krempasky, Matthew Francis
Music Teacher
Leuchs, John James Jr.
Elementary Teacher-Gifted

MARGATE CITY
Bobbins, Stephen Gerald
6th Grade Mathematics Teacher

MARLBORO
Castellucci, Joseph Alexander
Social Studies Teacher
Giebas, J. Michael
English/Latin Instructor
Robinson, Kathleen Anne
Computer Lab Teacher

MARLTON
Di Donato, Jeanette Serabian
Vocal Music Teacher
Malcom, Marianne Venuti
Mathematics Teacher
Mc Hale, Kathleen Anne
Sixth Grade Teacher
Mitchell, Robert Edward
Computer Science Teacher

MARTINSVILLE
Lane, Barbara T.
English Teacher
Szeles, Frederick John Jr.
Science Teacher

MATAWAN
Ruhe, Mary Ann Gallagher
Biology Teacher

MAYWOOD
Bernarducci, Matthew Daniel
7th Grade Language Art Teacher

MC GUIRE AFB
Gregory, Rubie Johnson
Elem Basic Skills Teacher
Stronstorff, Bert H.
Drug Education Instructor

MEDFORD
Carney, Rodger Dale
Supervisor Humanities Dept
Levin, David
3rd Grade Teacher
Page, Linda A.
Social Studies Teacher

MENDHAM
Cronin, Mary Lippincott
5-7th Grade Math Teacher
Di Battista, Anthony Paul
History Teacher
Jerris, Carol Ann (Rousseau)
Third Grade Teacher
Mills, Doris Ann
K-8 Dist Guidance Counselor
Shilakes, Carol H.
Sixth Grade Teacher

METUCHEN
Fischer, Wayne Thomas
Mathematics Department Chair
Moccia, Regis SC
English Department Chm/Teacher
Wallwork, Anne E. Sonnenschein
Kindergarten Teacher

MIDDLETOWN
Caldaro, Marie Dorio
History Teacher
Cusick, Thomas Patrick
Guidance Counselor
Demareo, Mark
Music Director
Haworth, Jeanne Ciaramelli
Physical Education Teacher
Steller, Robert Edward
History/Politicial Sci Instr

MILFORD
Stull, Frank Walter
8th Grade Soc Studies Teacher

MILLBURN
Barkovitz, Robert Walter
Physics Teacher
Selman, Carol
High School History Teacher

MILLINGTON
Gambatese, Lillian Piazza
4th Grade Teacher
Longo, Mary Tassielli
Fourth Grade Teacher

MILLTOWN
Carrato, Raymond Joseph
8th Grade Science Teacher

MILLVILLE
Baccile, Lawrence
Latin Teacher
Gius, Jo Anne Lynskey
Business Education Teacher

MONTAGUE
Buda, Karen Leckey
Fourth Grade Teacher

MONTCLAIR
Taylor, Zenobia Davis
Music Teacher

MONTVILLE
Drozd, Stanley J. Jr.
Social Studies Teacher
Van Lenten, Mary Shaw
8th Grade Math Teacher

MOORESTOWN
Marshall, Ruby J. Bennefield-Smith
Science Teacher

MORRIS PLAINS
Emmer, Agatha De Pinto
Dist Math Coord/Math Teacher

MORRISTOWN
Bertelli, Patricia Cortez
Educational Consultant
Cucozzella, Josephine Mary
7th Grade Teacher
Kim, Edward
AP Physics Teacher
Kroll, Gregory Edward
7th-12th Grade Phys Ed Teacher

Meaney, Peter Joseph
Guidance Cnslr & Math Teacher

MOUNT HOLLY
Grocott, Doreen
Departmental English Soc Stud
Gullo, Annette Norene
Third Grade Teacher

MOUNT LAUREL
Cutts, Pearl
3rd Grade Teacher
Saunders, Geraldine Barbara
School Librarian

MOUNTAINSIDE
Omilian, Michael
Dean of Students

NEPTUNE
Beard, Irene Landwehr
4th Grade Teacher
Mixson, Patricia Smith
Spanish Teacher
Soles, LaVerne Tufarelli
7th Grade Science Teacher

NEW BRUNSWICK
Costello, Katherine Najaim
Sixth Grade Teacher

NEW PROVIDENCE
Haness, Rosemary
Art Teacher
Iatesta, Susan Frisk
Band Director

NEWARK
Battle, Saundra Snyder
6th Grade Teacher
Chesley, Merrill L.
Kindergarten Teacher
Cicalese, Frances Ann
Mathematics Teacher
Cunningham, Edward John
English Teacher
D'Angelo, Richard Louis
Basic Skills Teacher
Delaney, Maureen Anne OP
Science Teacher
Estey, Bethany J.
1st Grade Teacher
Farina, Maritza
Seventh Grade Bi-ling Teacher
Gaynor, Sharon Elizabeth
2nd Grade Teacher
Greenaway, Millicent Dickenson
Principal And Founder
Huntley, Anona Savage
Science Teacher
Jefferson, Frances Malone
2nd Grade Teacher
Law, Hattie Wynn
Guidance Counselor
Matarazzo, Marion
English Teacher
Pasternack, Bonnie Greenwald
Fourth Grade Teacher
Piera, Susan G.
Seventh Grade Teacher
Richardson, Deborah Joy
5th Grade Teacher/Math Teacher
Stridacchio, Donna Marie
Mathematics Teacher
Torres, Eladio
Science Teacher IPS
Tortorello, Anthony L.
Social Studies Teacher
Tucker, Shirley Thompson
7th Grade Teacher
Waltz, James Roland
Science Teacher
Ware, Helen
3rd Grade Rdng & Math Teacher
Williams, Rita Majette
8th Grade Teacher
Zarra, Toni Mele
Basic Skills Teacher

NEWFIELD
Cavagnaro, Susan Van Hook
History Teacher
Kourtalis, Beatrice
Teacher of Gifted & Talented

NEWTON
Dunker, Lucy Mac Nulty
5th/6th Grade Lang Art Teacher
Haug, Mary Ann Schoettly
Sci Dept Chair/Biology Teacher
Wielechowski, Anita H.
Latin Teacher

NORTH ARLINGTON
Boyle, Alice T.
English Teacher

NORTH BERGEN
Dean, George Xavier
English/Writing Teacher

Terranova, Louis James
Sixth Grade Teacher

NORTH BRUNSWICK
Marquez, Elizabeth Lockhoven
Mathematics Teacher

NORTH CALDWELL
Monroe, Heidi Kurbjeweit
7th Grade Phys Science Teacher

NORTH HALEDON
Ciarlo, Jo Anne Hubbard
Eng/Theology/History Teacher
Van Loo, Joan Meire
US History Teacher/Dept Chair

NORTH PLAINFIELD
Wolliard, Lorraine J.
First Grade Teacher

NUTLEY
Metallo, Joan Ann P. Laratta
8th Grade Math/Eng Teacher
Nahirny, Dolores M.
Teacher

OAK RIDGE
Hardy, Brooke D.
Fifth Grade Teacher
Matthews, Daniel Joseph
First Grade Teacher

OCEAN
Christopher, George Joseph
Fifth Grade Teacher

OCEAN CITY
Jesperson, Kim Marie (Carneglia)
Mathematics Teacher
Mac Ewan, M. Bruce
7th Grade Soc Stud Teacher
Mazzarella, Mary Guokas
Jr HS English Teacher
Moreland, William Thomas Jr.
Mathematics Teacher
Mulvaney, Patrick Robert
Teacher of Gifted & Talented
Ogle, Patricia J.
Fifth Grade Teacher
Robinson, Nancy Zwart
Principal
Rogers, Betty Atzenweiler
Biology Teacher

OGDENSBURG
Kibildis, John Francis
Social Studies Teacher

OLD BRIDGE
Fischer, Lynda Pandozzi
English Teacher
Gill, Robert J.
Learning Disability Teacher
Higgins, Joanne Maguire
Spanish Teacher
Irish, Nancy Hatter
Lang Arts Teacher/Coordinator
Liebowitz, Relly Rosellen
Fourth Grade Teacher
Lopes, Rudy J.
Social Studies Teacher
Merenda, Robert F.
Principal
Stelevich, Ann Elizabeth
Home Economics Teacher

OLD TAPPAN
Maurino, Joseph
Teacher
Pilarcek, Barbara A.
Spanish Teacher

ORADELL
Munro, John Joseph
History Teacher
Stevenson, Robert George
Social Studies Instructor

ORANGE
Coleman, Charmaine Yanek
Language Arts Teacher/Chairman
Crawford, Janet Williams
Guidance Counselor
Hunt, Shirley
Spanish Teacher
Ostapiej, Michelle Theresa
Compensatory Education Teacher
Snack, Ronald
Teacher & Dept Chair Ind Ed

OXFORD
Kern, Robert F.
Eighth Grade Teacher

PALISADES PARK
Sinopulos, Ann M.
Third Grade Teacher

PALMYRA
Marron, Bettyanne A.
 1st Grade Teacher
PARAMUS
Fisher, William F.
 8th Grade Math/Science Teacher
Geisler, Harry S.
 English Teacher
PARK RIDGE
Langer, Norbert J. III
 German Teacher
Teagno, Marjorie
 Sixth Grade Teacher
PARLIN
Kawalec, Walter M. Jr.
 English Teacher
Kwiatkowski, Christine A.
 Spanish Teacher
Termini, Josephine
 5th Grade Teacher
PARSIPPANY
Campbell, Sylvia Smith
 Social Studies Teacher
Curnow, Gary William
 Fifth Grade Teacher
Flynn, William Joseph
 Reading/Writing Teacher
Foreso, Ronald F.
 Social Studies Teacher
Furlong, Richard Andrew
 Guidance Counselor
Garion, Gail Beatty
 Second Grade Teacher
Job, Patricia Forrest
 English Teacher
Kidd, John Edward
 Teacher/Department Chairman
Pollack, Charles
 Mathematics Dept Head
Popek, John Joseph
 Choral Director
Schenck, Theresa Young
 Foreign Language Dept Head
Vasile, Judith Glover
 Mathematics Teacher
PATERSON
Kayne, Stephen G.
 Eighth Grade Teacher
Pardine, Joseph Jr.
 Mathematics Teacher
PAULSBORO
Neal, Jannie M.
 Teacher of Gifted & Talented
PEMBERTON
Farner, Thomas Patrick
 US History Teacher
PENNS GROVE
Fithian, Gary D.
 8th Grade Science Teacher
Sama, Francis Bruno
 Assistant Principal
Smith, Elizabeth R.
 5th-8th Grade Lang Art Teacher
Vitanza, Beatrice Sepulveda
 Bilingual Teacher
PENNSAUKEN
Fitzgerald, Patricia Eileen
 Business/Marketing Chairperson
Lange, William John
 History Teacher/USI Coord
PENNSVILLE
Lowid, Joseph K.
 6th Grade Science Teacher
PERTH AMBOY
Bilbow, Ida Tamargo
 Biling Rdng/Lang Art Teacher
Degenhardt, Elizabeth Ann (Mullen)
 8th Grade Reading Teacher
Picchini, Margaret A. Magdon
 First Grade Teacher
Velazquez, Maria Torres
 Guidance Counselor
PHILLIPSBURG
Nixon, William
 Industrial Arts Dept Chair
Sbriscia, Donna Pizano
 5th Grade Teacher
PINE HILL
Gwalthney, Helen (Mac Kay)
 Latin/English Teacher
Mc Namara, Edward Eugene
 AP American History Teacher
PISCATAWAY
Halsted, Natalie Kowalski
 Social Studies Teacher

Impagliatelli, Leonard N.
 Sixth Grade Teacher
Kennedy, Miguelina Roura
 Spanish Teacher
Marano, Christopher John
 Biology Teacher
Regina, Fred Anthony
 6th Grade Teacher
Seeland, Thomas William
 Instrumental Music Teacher
Sullivan, M. Trinitas OP
 Associate Principal
PITMAN
Lohmann, Judith Leith
 8th Grade Reading Teacher
PLAINFIELD
Howell, Barbara Brown
 Sixth Grade Teacher
Schmidt, Anne Kathryn
 Health/Phys Ed Coordinator
POINT PLEASANT
Goldstein, Judy Lynne (Moncrief)
 Health/Physical Ed Teacher
POMPTON LAKES
Bistany, Sonia M.
 Teacher
Chamberlain, Horace
 Social Studies Teacher
Nurik, Margy Paula
 Social Studies/Spanish Teacher
Tyndall, William Alan
 Mathematics/Computer Teacher
PRINCETON
Johnson, Nancy O.
 Second Grade Teacher
Kruegel, Linda A.
 Chemistry Teacher
RAHWAY
Farrell, Kenneth M.
 US History Teacher
RAMSEY
Cantisano, Richard J.
 9th-12th Grade History Teacher
Marble, Anne
 2nd Grade Teacher
RANDOLPH
De Palma, John
 Mathematics Teacher
Steiner, Katherine Elizabeth (Haslett)
 Cheerleading Coach
RARITAN
Hicken, Baron B.
 Physics Teacher
Komarek, Ann L.
 Business Teacher
READINGTON
Hollowell, Elaine F.
 6th Grade English Teacher
RED BANK
Callahan, Regina Marie RSM
 Religion Teacher
Gruber, Fred
 5th Grade Teacher
RIDGEFIELD PARK
Boyle, Mary Ann
 Eighth Grade Teacher
RINGWOOD
Kroncke, Thomas John
 3rd Grade Teacher
Landy, Karen Ann
 6th Grade Teacher
Scutti, Paul N.
 Mathematics Teacher
RIVER EDGE
Milligan, Michael III
 Third Grade Teacher
ROCHELLE PARK
Loukas, Roberta Beyer
 4th Grade Teacher
ROCKAWAY
Fitzpatrick, Rosemary
 English Teacher
La Flamme, Pamela
 English Teacher
Nixon, George E.
 Mathematics Teacher
Selden, Monica Schuftan
 Seventh Grade Math Teacher
ROEBLING
Tapper, Carol L.
 Second Grade Teacher
ROSELLE
Friedman, Hyman Alexander
 Art Teacher

Grayson, Carole Hammer
 Mathematics Teacher
Harper-Giardina, Janet Carlson
 Psychology Teacher
Mayner, Edith
 Teacher of Gifted & Talented
Mc Craw-Orlando, Ann
 Science Coordinator/Teacher
ROSELLE PARK
Truncellito, Carolyn
 First Grade Teacher
RUNNEMEDE
Bada, Nancy L. (Moench)
 5th Grade Teacher
Natale, Marian Bowers
 Social Studies Teacher
Neuschafer, Julie Sullivan
 Mathematics Teacher
RUTHERFORD
Brown, Ethele Harvin
 Business Dept Chairperson
Laguna, Rolando A.
 Mathematics & Physics Teacher
SALEM
Evans, Gertrude Alice
 V-Principal/4th Grade Teacher
Smith, Sally L.
 Fifth Grade Teacher
Wood, Dolores Ann
 8th Grade Teacher
SAYREVILLE
Lichtenstein, Bernadine Czernikowski
 2nd Grade Teacher
Sienko, Janet Ferriol
 7th/8th Grade Science Teacher
SCOTCH PLAINS
De Vito, Marie Casciano
 Third Grade Teacher
Spring, Jeff S.
 Mathematics Teacher
SECAUCUS
Costello, Frank Thomas
 Music Teacher
Dreiss, Elenore Orocchi
 Second Grade Teacher
Germann, Michael
 Mathematics Teacher
Kuchar, Alex N.
 Sixth Grade Teacher
SEWELL
Barnshaw, Robert Gary
 History Teacher
Crane, Thomas Richard
 9th Grade Soc Stud Teacher
Crispin, George Atwood
 English Teacher
Detofsky, Louis Bennett
 Geology & Biology Teacher
Gorski, Robert Frank Jr.
 History Teacher
Meyer, Norma Weintraub
 Orchestra Director
Miamidian, Madelyn Borrelli
 Business Teacher
Moncreif, Cathy Peterka
 Spanish Teacher
Shaw, J. Michael
 Mathematics Teacher
Wright, David Brian
 Physics Teacher
SHORT HILLS
Mistretta, Philip J.
 5th Grade Teacher
SOMERSET
Hill, Melvin J.
 Life Science Teacher
Mac Dowell, Karen Chonka
 Reading & English Teacher
Rice, Lynn V.
 English Teacher
Sapala, Laurene Jane
 Kindergarten Teacher
SOMERVILLE
Celko, Anna Marie Slaight
 K-5th Grade Writing Teacher
Gesek, Linda Triola
 Social Studies Teacher
Gorton-Horan, Ann Hilbert
 English/Reading Teacher
Gottlieb, Carolee Mc Neill
 English Teacher
Martin, Judith Klein
 Fifth Grade Teacher
SOUTH RIVER
Carney, Patricia Leeds
 Soc Stud/Enrichment Teacher
Mondrone, Louis Anthony
 Seventh Grade English Teacher

Satterthwaite, Karen Lynn Mc Ilvaine
 5th Grade Teacher
SPARTA
Filitor, Veronica Lapetina
 2nd Grade Teacher
Holovacs, Mary Connors
 Special Needs Teacher
Leach, William Gordon Jr.
 Vocational Electricity Teacher
Shope, Gloria Dziewiatek
 Foreign Language Teacher
SPOTSWOOD
Ruela, Kathleen A.
 Business/Marketing Teacher
SPRING LAKE HTS
Muhlenbruck, Richard Owen
 7th/8th Grade Sci/His Teacher
STANHOPE
Charney, William James
 Language Arts Teacher
Lasky, Phyllis Mc Nair
 Third Grade Teacher
STILLWATER
Rice, G. Randall
 Science & English Teacher
STIRLING
Yankowitz, Colette Gaborit
 French Teacher
SUCCASUNNA
Jegge, Thomas C.
 Social Studies Teacher
Raffay, Charles V.
 Physics Teacher
TEANECK
Schwartz, Patricia B.
 Fourth Grade Teacher
TENAFLY
Ditzel, Thelma Bradford
 Retired/Assistant Principal
TINTON FALLS
Duerbig, Zina Patricia
 Teacher of Eng/Gifted/Talented
TOMS RIVER
Adams, Louise Bartik
 Fifth Grade Teacher
Duff, Victoria Burkholder
 Third Grade Teacher
Forster, Ardena Louise
 4th Grade Teacher
Grill, Robert George
 Mathematics Teacher
Hammonds, Mary Ellen
 4th Grade Teacher
Hepsley, Bonnie K.
 Second Grade Teacher
Kaszuba, Jill Elizabeth (Monaghan)
 English Teacher
Kiel, Alice
 English Teacher
Mc Cutcheon, Constance Thomas
 Social Studies Teacher
Mc Kee, Patrick Russell
 Social Studies Teacher
Miller, Jill D. Tormey
 6th Grade Teacher
Moreau, Barbara Obrig
 Third Grade Teacher
O'Dea, Timothy John
 Guidance Counselor
Parks, Frank
 Fifth Grade Teacher
Penna, Cecilia A. P.
 Biology Teacher
Rankin, Neil F.
 5th Grade Teacher
Reynolds, Sally Genovino
 First Grade Teacher
Sirianni, Frank Joseph
 English Teacher
Stout, Charles Robert
 6th Grade Teacher
Vandenberge, Donald Robert
 5th/6th Grade Music Teacher
Vandenbulcke, Nora Jane
 First Grade Teacher
Vescovi, James Craig
 Mechanical Drawing Instructor
Wolff, Judith Cassidy
 8th Grade Lang Arts Teacher
TOTOWA
Grato, Maria
 Mathematics Teacher
Ianzano, Arlene Marone
 Second Level Teacher
TOTOWA BOROUGH
Den Herder, Barbara Ann
 First Grade Teacher

TRANQUILITY
Fisher, Timothy Hyland
 5th/6th Grade Teacher
TRENTON
Burke, Jacqueline T.
 Chem/Earth Sci Teacher
Casey, Margaret Austina
 8th Grade Teacher
Cutter, Saula Leslie
 Sixth Grade Teacher
De Jesus, Christopher
 Mathematics Teacher
Dippolito, April Fish
 Second Grade Teacher
Di Via, Richard
 English Teacher
Foy, Eleanor Dolton
 2nd Grade Teacher
Jennings, K. Alfonso
 Phys Ed/XC/Track Coach
May, Joyce Volpe
 English Teacher
Mirando, Lucille Garofalo
 Computer Teacher
Murphy, Marie Klein
 Seventh Grade Teacher
Nath, Garie Ann Marie
 English Teacher
Pugliese, Domenick
 8th Grade Teacher
Robotin, Barbara Zielinski
 First Grade Teacher
TUCKERTON
Young, George E.
 Science Teacher
TURNERSVILLE
Buff, Anita S.
 Fifth Grade Teacher
UNION
Holmes, Josephine Sara
 Mathematics Teacher
Urciuoli, Robert John
 Science Teacher
UNION CITY
Andriano, Theresa
 Fifth Grade Teacher
Aprile, V. MPF
 Eighth Grade Teacher
Treanor, Ronald James
 Curriculum Resource Teacher
Wendelken, Robert Joseph
 American History Teacher
Wentworth, Caroline Smith
 Eighth Grade Science Teacher
Wilson, Veronica Mary
 Kindergarten Teacher
Zaccagna, Morjorie Censullo
 10-12 Grade English Teacher
UPPER MONTCLAIR
Wiegel, A. Jeanne Crines
 Language Art Teacher
UPPER SADDLE RIVER
Gardner, Alan William
 6th Grade Teacher
VERGA
Sillars, Joyce Ann Marshall
 6th-8th Grade Teacher
VERNON
Boltz, Frances Spell
 Gifted & Talented Teacher
Caporoso, Nancy Kogan
 1st Grade Teacher
Franklin, Ilene Greenberg
 Science Teacher
Marr, Grace Halsey
 Fourth Grade Teacher
VINELAND
Antale, Andrew F.
 Mathematics Teacher
Barbetti, Robert R.
 Sixth Grade Teacher
Crovo, Nila J.
 Fourth Grade Teacher
Danziger, Aileen Joan
 English Teacher
Hickman, Joan Sheppard
 7th/8th Grade Language Teacher
Horin, Leon W.
 Mathematics Teacher
Kopreski, Kathleen J. Rochetti
 Mathematics Teacher
Milana, Viola P.
 Language Art Department Chair
Miller, Dennis Eugene
 6th Grade Teacher
Mulligan, Maxine Rogers
 9th/10th Grade Coll English
Smith, Patricia Ann
 7th/8th Grade Science Teacher

VINELAND (cont)
Wittman, Louann (Blandino)
Junior High English Teacher

VOORHEES
Taylor, Mary Hudock
Mathematics Teacher

WALDWICK
Raleigh, William Patrick
4th & 5th Grade Teacher
Reynolds, Richard R.
Chemistry Teacher

WALL
Doyle, Charles F.
Science Teacher

WALLINGTON
Persico, Angela
English Teacher

WANAQUE
Cesa, Glenn James
Social Studies Teacher
Lynch, Eileen Schumacher
Reading Specialist

WARREN
Abella, John Anthony
Industrial Arts Teacher
Brooks, Bonnie G.
Mathematics Teacher
Holmes, William H.
Choral Director
Wilkening, Lorraine
Fourth Grade Teacher

WASHINGTON TOWNSHP
Provost, Susan M.
Spanish Teacher

WAYNE
Coleman, Diane S.
Fifth Grade Teacher
De Martino, Linda Don Diego
Mathematics Teacher
Ferrito, Oresta Mary
Science Teacher
Galle, Adele Cutler
English Teacher
Gavin, Suzanne
Fine, Perform Arts Chairperson
Hansen, Kathleen Black
Mathematics Teacher
Kraus, Roberta M.
First Grade Teacher
Mandel, Michael Walter
English Teacher
Mc Keon, Elaine Elizabeth
Math Teacher
Wintle, Jessie Osbun
Mathematics/English Teacher

WEEHAWKEN
Colasurdo, Anthony P.
English Dept Coordinator

WEST LONG BRANCH
Palaia, Joann
English/Theatre Arts Teacher
White, Carol Benz
Science Teacher

WEST MILFORD
Donegan, Mary E.
English Teacher

WEST NEW YORK
Silvestri, Vincent
English Teacher
Weiss, Mary Ann
Seventh Grade Teacher

WEST ORANGE
Kivlon, Barbara O' Toole
Staff Development Trainer
Piegaro, Kathleen Brannigan
Mathematics Teacher
Tropello, Daria Fennimore
Mathematics Teacher

WEST PATERSON
Ciccone, Jane Elizabeth Ann
8th Grade English/Rdng Teacher
Palma, Raymond Joseph
Teacher

WESTFIELD
Balcerski, Frank James
7th & 8th Grade Teacher
Kahn, Camille Minnicino
Basic Skills Teacher

WESTVILLE
Earnest, Jane Canal
5th Grade Teacher
Konyak, Daniel Michael
Social Studies Teacher

WESTVILLE GROVE
Burnham, Barbara M.
Math Teacher/Math Curr Dir

WESTWOOD
Lindemann, Regina Michelle
(Gwozdecka)
4-8th Grade Lang Arts Teacher
Randazzo, Elisa Gelices
Foreign Lang Chair

WHIPPANY
Greene, Joe
English Teacher
Guzo, Doreen Kuzminski
Language Art Teacher

WHITING
Donovan, Noreen
Special Education Teacher

WILDWOOD
Hubbs, Timothy L.
Religion Teacher/Chaplain

WILLIAMSTOWN
Ash, Donna Stillwell
Art Teacher
Brewer, Mark Richard
Social Studies Teacher

WILLINGBORO
Caiazzo, Robert James
6th Grade Science Teacher
Hagenbaugh, Frank Val
World History Teacher
Kervitsky, Carol Diane
English Teacher
Mc Nair, Linda A.
English Teacher
Richards, Christie Crais
5th Grade Teacher
Winsett, Ron
Fourth Grade Teacher

WOODBRIDGE
Bertagna, Rita Annette
Science Teacher
Stankewicz, Mary Christine
7th Grade Geography Teacher

WOODLYNNE
Cowen, Jill Dobie
Careers/Computers Teacher

WYCKOFF
Dunn, Timothy J.
Social Studies Teacher
Hogan, Marie Gloria (Phillip)
Third Grade Teacher
Knapp, Helen M.
Reading Specialist
Sikkema, Wilma Bonnema
3rd Grade Teacher

YARDVILLE
Zeltkalns, Mara
Second Grade Teacher

NEW MEXICO

ALAMOGORDO
Goodrich, Sara Jane Johnson
English Department Chair
Hathorn, E. Joan Ingerham
Third Grade Teacher
Hill, Joyce Blanton
Educational Diagnostician
Jackson, Loren E. Jr.
8th Grade Soc Stud Teacher
Martin, Matthew Dale
Biology Teacher
Pattison, Joseph Nelson
Industrial Art Teacher
Pattison, Marsha Teri
Teacher
Smith, Cecilia Spoleti
5th & 6th Grade Teacher
Stringfield, Joannabelle Holcomb
6th Grade Teacher
Thorp, Don G.
Choir Director
Young, Clifford Craig
English Teacher

ALBUQUERQUE
Alarid, Elaine Herrera
Spanish Teacher/Dept Chair
Altman, Lynda Susan
English Teacher
Apodaca, Richard Stephen
6th Grade Life Sci Teacher
Attleson, Mimi Barbour
French/English Teacher
Brodeur, Helen Sanchez
Third Grade Teacher

Buckner, Debra K.
Drama Director
Caffo, John A.
Math/Physics Teacher/Chair
Chase, Christopher Lockwood
English Teacher
Chavez, Lorraine Veronica
3rd Grade Teacher
Dai Zovi, Lonnie Gault
Spanish Teacher
Delgado, Hector
Social Studies Teacher
Douglas, Bennye Mc Nair
Lang Art/Lit Teacher
Douglas, Joan Barlow
Second Grade Teacher
Dover, Barbara Ellms
Teacher of Gifted Students
Elkins, Hollis L.
English Humanities Teacher
Espinosa, Peter Damian
5th Grade Teacher
Gallegos, Tony Alex
Teacher
Gerhart, Mary E.
Science Teacher
Gonzalez, Richard David
Mathematics Teacher
Harrison, Jesse William
Fourth Grade Teacher
Hicks, Don R.
CAD/CAM Instructor
Humphreys, La Fuan E.
ECO/Enriched US His Teacher
Jercinovic, Eugene
Teacher Mid Sch Honors Seminar
Jungbluth, Shirley Anne
Teacher of the Gifted
Knoll, Malva Ann
Chemistry Teacher
Kravitz, Merryl Leslie
Language Arts Teacher
Lucero, A. Eugene
5th Grade Teacher
Martinez-Broome, Miquelita
6th Grade Lit/Lang Art Teacher
Martinez, Andrew William
5th Grade Teacher
Martinez, Raymond Israel
Fourth Grade Teacher
Matthews, Sandra J.
Mathematics Teacher
Mc Carthy, Diane Elizabeth
Health Education Teacher
Mc Murray, Sandra K.
US History/Journalism Teacher
Mena, Manuel R.
Mathematics Dept Chairperson
Mills, Susan Weber
English/Psychology Teacher
Mills, Sylvia Anne
5th Grade Teacher
Minck, Stuart James
Health & Anatomy Teacher
Montoya, Sally Triviz
Consultant & Adv for Teachers
Moreno, Lydia Martinez
Fifth Grade Teacher
Nelson, Jean Bailey
English Teacher
O'Connor, John S.
7th-11th Grade English Teacher
Ogilvie, Cora Lucero
5th Grade Teacher
Papp, Gregory John
Educator/Soc Stud Teacher
Penn, Mary Jane
English/Language Art Teacher
Peterson, Jeannette Stanton
2nd Grade Teacher
Pinkel, Kathryn Marie
8th Grade English Teacher
Pinto, Walt Herman
Photography Teacher
Ramirez, Angela Castoria
8th Grade English Teacher
Reasor, Kevin Arthur
7th/8th Grade Teacher/Prin
Roybal, Steven E.
Art/Photography Teacher
Ruscetti-Kay, Nancy Hagarman
Teacher of Gifted
Sacoman, Patricia J. Gonzales
Math Teacher
Sanchez, Clara Castillo
English Honors Teacher
Sanchez, Robert A.
8th Grade US His, Span Teacher
Schallert, Gary T.
Director of Bands
Stockton, Jolene Hogrefe
Third Grade Teacher
Stuart, Stephan A.
Counselor
Tapia, Carmen Lobato
7th Grade Lang Arts Teacher

Templeton, Allen
Science Teacher
Torgerson, Mary Jo Joe Calloway
English Teacher
Torres, Raquel Lilly Duran
Second Grade Teacher
Treibel, Karen Zlotkowski
Reading Teacher/Consultant
Vigil, Laura
Business Teacher
Watts, Patricia Ann
English Teacher
Welder, Polly Anne Whitten
8th Grade Humanities Teacher
Wong, Stanley
Mathematics Teacher
Wright, Dan L.
Secondary Math Teacher
Wright, Ivan C.
Art Teacher

ALCALDE
Peralta, Patricia La Vern
First Grade Teacher

ANTHONY
Aber, Tomasine Dawn
Fourth Grade Teacher
Licona, Miguel M.
Science Department Chair
Long, Patrick Henry
Agriculture Ed Teacher

ANTON CHICO
Lucero, Eduardo E.
5th Grade Teacher
Maestas, Julia Montano
6th Grade Teacher

ARTESIA
Barron, Mary Lea Mc Afee
Fifth Grade Teacher
Branch, Vicki Hall
Second Grade Teacher
Gallegos, Jose E.
Elementary School Teacher
Horner, Elaine Carmichael
Math & Algebra Teacher
Surface, Patricia Gail (Mitchell)
Music Teacher
Surfaces, William Dean
Band Director
Trujillo, Lorena J. Betancur
Fifth Grade Teacher

AZTEC
Lee, Farrelyn Mankin
Second Grade Teacher
Longwell, Zella Ruth Welch
Retired Teacher
Smith, N. Marliene
3rd Grade Teacher

BAYARD
Crumbley, Vera H.
English Department Chairman

BELEN
Benavidez, Annette Aragon
Mathematics Teacher
Douglas, Serena E. Yates
Librarian
Goucher, Judith A.
US History Teacher
Haworth, Cindy Heisler
Math Teacher
Padilla, John Edward
Sixth Grade Teacher

BERNALILLO
Bashore, Frank M.
Mathematics Teacher
Bolinger, John Allen
Science Department Chair
Pennington, Carmen Gonzales
Teacher/Fine Arts Dept Chair

BLOOMFIELD
Brown, Dorothy Frances
First Grade Teacher
Reider, June Kerns
Chapter I Teacher

CAPITAN
Hammontre, Sidney Jean
Science/Latin Teacher
Shanks, Mary Ella (Fore)
Second Grade Teacher

CARLSBAD
Becker, Johnnie Cole
4th & 5th Grade Eng Teacher
Calvani, Josephine Eckert
Fifth Grade Teacher
Faircloth, Carol Sutherland
Special Education Teacher
Gist, Juanita Shearer
4th & 5th Grade Math Teacher
Price, Willie J.
Mathematics/Computer Teacher

Schiel, Joseph Bernard Jr.
Biology Teacher
Singleton, Ronald Kenneth
Physical Ed Teacher/Coach
Walker, Mary V.
Teacher/English Dept Chair
Woodfield, Darrill R.
Industrial Art Teacher

CARRIZOZO
Caster, June A Jones
Third Grade Teacher
Richmond, J.C. C. (I.O.)
Social Studies Teacher
Schwartz, Evelyn Noon
Eng/Accounting/Psych Teacher
Wilmore, Winimeril Vonderslice
5th Grade Teacher

CIMARRON
Rogers, Harl F.
Phys Ed/Health Teacher
Schneider, Dennis Ray
Band Director

CLAYTON
Alford, Barbara Ann (Skipper)
5th/6th Grade Art Director
Longwill, Robert M.
Science Teacher

CLOVIS
Brooks, Cheryl Christine
Science Teacher
Ingram, Peggy Weiss
Science Teacher/Dept Chair
Jacobs, Teresa Horton
English Teacher
Kilmer, Eddie J.
English Teacher/Coach
Spikes, Jan Edwards
2nd Grade Teacher
Tipton, Charles Lee
Choral Activities Director

DEMING
Bowman, Mary Evelyn
Second Grade Teacher
Stallard, Vincent A.
Business Dept Chairperson
Talley, Larry Gene
4th Grade Teacher

DEXTER
Salazar, Rozan Cruz
Social Science Teacher

DORA
Powell, Larry D.
Science Teacher

ESPANOLA
Atencio, Bernice Archuleta
8th Grade Lang Arts Teacher
Moore, Kathryn Warren
Resource Teacher
Quintana, Leo Genaro
Pre-Calculus Teacher
Williams, Avis Feiring
5th Grade Teacher

EUNICE
Goodman, Wallace Andrew
Retired Mathematics Teacher

FAIRVIEW
Velasquez, Josie Martina
English Teacher

FARMINGTON
Boognl, Mary Hoar
Teacher
Hoskins, Karen Boesel
Soc Stud Teacher/Dept Chair
Kannard, Susan Diane (Monk)
Third Grade Teacher
Mc Lamore, Tom J.
Science Teacher
Richardson, James Milam
Social Studies Teacher
Vincent, Jo Ann De Salle
Third Grade Teacher
Ward, Diana Lynn (Elmore)
Physical Ed Teacher/Coach
Whitney, Deborah L.
English Teacher

FLOYD
Jones, Joyce M.
5th Grade Teacher
Rippee, Linda Lou (Smith)
English/Speech Teacher

FORT SUMNER
Haynes, Lynda Morgan
Math & Computer Teacher
Hughes, Robert D.
Mathematics Teacher
Wertheim, Sandra Lydia
Lang Art & Spanish Teacher

GALLUP

Cowdrey, John Lee
Stu Assistance Cnslr
Kinsel, Gloria Ann
First Grade Teacher

GRANTS

Alexander, Shelby L.
Biology Teacher/Science Dept
Edwards, Arlene Ruth
3rd Grade Teacher
Miller, Loretta Dowling
6th Grade/Head Teacher/Prin
Quinn, James C.
Elementary Teacher
Savacheck, Mary Gates
Sixth Grade Teacher

HATCH

Bouvet, Steven Bernard
Vocational Agriculture Teacher
Le Noir, Jennifer Tomlin
English Teacher
Lopez, Frank D. Jr.
Social Studies Teacher/Coach

HOBBS

Allen, David Gene
Junior HS Band Director
Bryant, Gail
6th Grade Teacher
Dellinger, Helen Eddleman
Retired Teacher
Gage, Maryna Morris
6th Grade Teacher
Girton, Barbara Carolyn (Mahan)
Fourth Grade Teacher
Harper, Wilma Faye Craig
4th Grade Teacher
Harris, Mary Roush
Teacher of Gifted Education
Hobbs, Edith Mc Creavy
2nd Grade Teacher
Hobbs, Nina Marion
Math Teacher
Knight, Pam
Language Arts Teacher
Nichols, Sam E.
Assistant Principal
Roberson, Mary Grace
Band Director
Rodriguez, Orlando Andrew
Band Director
Sosa, Gracie
Mathematics Teacher
Swift, Violet Ann (Elder)
Third Grade Teacher

HOLLOMAN AFB

Lind, Johanna Sheryl (Smith)
Chapter I Reading Teacher

LAGUNA

Brown, Alberta Concho
2nd Grade Teacher
Thomas, Dorothy Rosanne
Fifth Grade Teacher

LAS CRUCES

Andrews, James Robert
Mathematics Teacher
Black, Harriet Martin
Director-Instructor
Bryant, Lynn Ann
Special Education Coordinator
Campbell, Frances M.
Second Grade Teacher
De la Pena, Julio
Fifth Grade Teacher
Estrada, S. D.
History Teacher
Flickinger, Terri C.
History/Civics Teacher
Hackney, Calleen J.
Physical Ed Dept Chairperson
Hackney, Gary D.
High School English Teacher
Hayes, Barbara Myers
Bio Teacher
Hout, Jay W.
5th Grade Teacher
Kirby, Rosemary Estrada
English Teacher
Marble, Judy Perschbacher
Third Grade Teacher
Martin, Sue M.
English Teacher
Smith, Stan Gordon
Science & Math Instructor
Sullivan, Billie Anderson
Retired Second Grade Teacher
Van Pelt, Barbara Ann
Social Studies Chair
Vermeer, Connie Lee
English Teacher

LAS VEGAS

Garduno, Yolanda Rita Gonzales
Music Teacher
Guenther, Patricia J. Maestas
9th-12th Grade English Teacher
Gutierrez, Angel Juliana
Business Education Teacher
Hernandez, Florence Theurer
English Teacher
King, Eddie
English/Journalism Instructors
Lucero, Connie T.
2nd Grade Teacher
Mares, Kenneth E.
Music Teacher & HS Band Dir
Martin-Maestas, Mary L.
English Teacher & Chairperson
Mc Elroy, Steve Charles
History Department Chair
Romero, Donald E.
Music Instructor
Sampson, Gary David
English Department Chair
Sanchez, Angela R.
Third Grade Teacher
Thornton, Norma Barbero
Third Grade Teacher
Torres, Priscilla Chacon
Spanish Teacher
Vanalek, George Joseph
Biology Teacher

LOGAN

Carter, Debra Lou Parman
First Grade Teacher
Fortner, Mary Merritt
Home Economics Teacher
Lees, Robert Michael
Mathematics Dept Instructor
Perez, Connie Lynn (Kuper)
Science/Physical Ed Teacher

LOS ALAMOS

Alexander, Melissa Justin
4th-6th Grade Teacher
Houfek, Gary William
United States History Teacher
Humphrey, Edward John
7th Grade Geography Teacher
Johnston, Julie Ann
Mathematics Teacher
Johnston, Stan W.
English Teacher
Lucht, Kathleen A.
Gymnastics Coach

LOS LUNAS

Chavez, Mildred Hernandez
Lang Arts/Speech/Drama Teacher
Fernandez, Priscilla Paig
Sixth Grade Teacher
Martinez, Erlinda Robertson
Middle School Principal
Storey, Johnna Vaughan
8th Grade Lang Arts Teacher

LOVING

Cosand, Sandra Ray
5th Grade Teacher

LOVINGTON

Lynn, Joyce Mc Minn
Kindergarten Teacher
Page, Michael Frederick
Fifth Grade Teacher
Palomo, Joe R.
Sixth Grade Bilingual Teacher

MORA

Cassidy, Robert Mark
History/Phys Ed Teacher
Laumbach, Belinda Pacheco
Fifth Grade Teacher

MORIARTY

Driver, Brenda Johns
Business Education Teacher
Goodman, Mary Kay
High School Teacher
Mosier, Earlene A.
Mathematics Teacher
Munck, Miriam Hoffman
Science Teacher

NAVAJO

Bennett, Fern Arthur
2nd Grade Teacher
Watchman, Paulina Yellowhair
Language Arts Teacher

OJO CALIENTE

Gurule, Joe Jr.
Phys Ed Teacher/Principal
Rodriguez, Ernest Anthony
Guidance Cnslr/Phys Ed Teacher

PENASCO

Gurule, Maximo
Mathematics Teacher/Dept Chm

PORTALES

Bollinger, Darrel Lane
Industrial Arts Instructor
Greathouse, Betty Toliver
Fifth Grade Teacher
Johnstn, Brion D.
Band Director

QUESTA

Jaramillo, Marilyn
Third Grade Teacher

RAMAH

Gibbons, D. Mark
Business/Music Teacher

RATON

Jackson, Linda L.
American Literature Teacher
Veltri, Patricia Ann (Christy)
First Grade Teacher
Wingo, Brenda Nixon
Chapter I Reading Teacher

RESERVE

Macdonald, Jennifer Lee
English Instructor/Dept Chair

ROSWELL

Beauchemin, Mary Waide
Art Teacher
Brownfield, Nancy Reeves
English/Language Arts Teacher
Carrell, Donna M. (Nelson)
Retired
Casey, Barbara Ann (Perea)
Spanish Teacher
De Los Santos, Rudy M.
500 W Hobbs
Dwyer, Shirley Vineyard
8th Grade Math Teacher
Eaton, Elizabeth Hope
English Teacher
Henderson, Carol Jane Roberts
Marketing Ed Instr/Coord
Jenkins, Edna Selman
6th Grade Teacher
Massey, Gail Whealton
Math Teacher
Massey, Norman
World History/English Teacher
Padilla, Orlando
6th Grade Teacher
Purcella, Les Allen
Agriculture Education Teacher
Samson, Tammina O.
1st Grade Teacher
Seale, Jerry Nelle (Ward)
8th Grade English Teacher
Whalen, Steve P.
Physical Education Teacher

RUIDOSO

Branum, Jacquelyn Murray
8th Grade Science Teacher
Cannella, Margaret (Krefft)
Kindergarten Teacher
Hawthorne, Linda Douglas
Student Services Director
Hopkins, Jody Jahna
Phys Ed Teacher/Coach
Skellett, Linda Marlene Jenkins
3rd Grade Teacher
Wierwille, Nancy Chapman
Fifth Grade Teacher

SANTA FE

Armendariz, George Ann
6th Grade Teacher
Beckmon, Tim A.
Chemistry Instructor
Devoti, Janis A.
Sixth Grade Teacher
Garcia, Evelyn Bell
5th Grade Teacher
Gonzales, David Fidel
8th Grade Reading Teacher
Graham, Betty Blue
Science/Health Teacher/Coord
Hill, Robert Kermit
Social Studies Teacher
Jimenez, John Fred
Sixth Grade Teacher
Johnson, Jayne Ann
7th-8th Grade Soc Stud Teacher
Juarros, Elaine Padilla
3rd Grade Teacher
Manning, Thomas Ray
Physical Education Teacher
Martinez, Thomas Jacob
7th/8th Grade Soc Stud Teacher
Mier, Joe A.
Chemistry Teacher
Ortiz, Beatrice C.
4th Grade Bilingual Teacher
Pacheco, Elizabeth Legits
Counselor

Pearson, Allan N.

German Teacher
Peters, Fritz S.
Social Studies Chairman
Quintana-Mier, Therese
5th Grade Teacher
Sandoval, Bertha V.
Spanish Teacher
San Miguel, Mary L.
Business Instructor
Sternberg, Milton H.
US History Teacher
Vaisa, Theresa Lobato
Home Ec Teacher/Dept Chair
White, Marie V.
Head of Middle School
Zern, John Frederick
Sociology/Law Teacher

SANTA TERESA

Phillips, Betty Jean Jackson
Guidance Counselor

SHIPROCK

Hendricks, Anna Belle Hasley
Eighth Grade English Teacher
Nelson, Martha R. Mc Caw
8th Gr Earth Science Teacher
Pagano, Lynn M.
Jr HS Social Studies Teacher
Vigil, Adelmo
Second Grade Teacher

SILVER CITY

Lewis, Betty Ritz
6th Grade Science Teacher
Miller, Steven Dennis
Science Department Chairman
Rydeski, Donald A.
Science Teacher/Sci Dept Chair
Stevens, Nancy Smith
Fourth Grade Teacher

TATUM

Adams, Mary Holladay
5th Grade Teacher
Luce, Reba D.
Mathematics Teacher/Dept Head

THOREAU

Pina, Rosamond Perry
Math Dept Chairperson
Wilson, Jeannette
Third Grade Teacher

TIJERAS

Burch, Shirley Anne
5th Grade Teacher

TRUTH OR CONSEQUEN

Cain, Emma Grace
Fifth Grade Teacher
Morrow, Tommy
Mathematics Dept Chair

TUCUMCARI

Carter, Peggy Lewis
Third Grade Teacher
Clark, Barbara Jean
English Teacher
Dowell, Sue York
Eng/His/Skills for Adolescence
Johnson, Barbara D. Kilgore
Language Arts Chair
Morper, Sheri Rae (Mathis)
4th/5th/6th Grade Teacher
Nials, Lucinda Chavez
HS Home Economics Teacher

TULAROSA

Basham, Austin E.
English Teacher

NEW YORK

ACCORD

Haber, Catherine
First Grade Teacher
Meoli, Patricia Ann
10th & 11th English Teacher
Thorn, Jean E.
Home Careers Teacher

ADAMS

Thornton, Barbara Ann
French & German Teacher

ADDISON

Brucie, Karen Ann (Gabic)
Third Grade Teacher
Gordon, Michele Ann (De Remer)
Elementary Teacher
• Hurd, Barbara Stevens
Mathematics Teacher/Dept Chair

AFTON

Power, Paul F.
English Department Chairperson

ALBANY

Fitzgerald, William Francis
French Teacher
King, Janet Marcia
First Grade Teacher
Kondratowicz, Ninette Waldo
Science/Health Teacher
Kretzler, Mary Jane Hunter
5th Grade Math/Science Teacher
Manning, Nancy Joan (Rizzi)
Math Department Chair/Teacher
Mathias, Neelam Adiel
2nd Grade Elementary Teacher
Rose, Linda Jamison
7th/8th Grade Science Teacher

ALBION

Sodoma, Karen J.
Math Teacher

ALEXANDER

Hollwedel, Robert Mark
Teacher/Department Chair
Phillips Good, Susan Gerth
Sixth Grade Teacher

ALMOND

Manske, Tad Peter
Social Studies Teacher
Shultz, Ellen L.
English Teacher/Drama Director

AMHERST

Matthews, Cynthia Ann
Sales Representative

AMITYVILLE

Monitto, Maryann
English Teacher

AMSTERDAM

Steward, Donna Marie
Spanish Teacher

ANDOVER

Witherow, Catherine Saslawsky
English Teacher

ANGOLA

Herlihy, Thomas M.
Music Teacher
Valvo, Frances Andolino
Sixth Grade Teacher

APALACHIN

Brougham, Joseph Harry
5th Grade Teacher
De Feo, Barbara A.
Third Grade Teacher
Redolphy, Lenore Jacobson
6th Grade Teacher
Wiggins, Mary Jean (Algar)
Fourth Grade Teacher

APO NEW YORK

Alce, Margaret Rose
Teacher
Ballard, Bruce Bolling
Physical Education Teacher
Baxter, Richard Keith
Science Teacher/Sci Dept Chm
Bonnaviat, Barbara Ann
French/Soc St/Lang Art Teacher
Bourland, Margaret Jean
English & Journalism Teacher
Brunelle, Charles David
Soc Studies Teacher/Chairman
Donovan, James Thomas
HS Social Studies Teacher
Dotson, Judy L.
Fifth Grade Teacher
Drake, John Richard
Teacher/Coach
Evanson, Clifford George
Air Force JROTC Teacher
George, Marcus Allen
Counselor
Hawkins, Donna-Marie Nelsonea
Sixth Grade Teacher
Hummer, George Barton
A P English Teacher/Dept Chair
Osgood, Maureen Reddy
English Teacher
Provinsal, John Stephen
Cooperative Work Experience
Sommer, Elfriede
Host Nation Teacher
Spaulding, Roberta Klimaski
Teacher/Sci Department Head
Toth, Larissa Muiznieks
English/German Teacher
Wickkiser, John D.
English/Phys Ed Teacher
Wood, Claudia Jane
HS Social Studies Teacher

ARDSLEY
Jackson, Robert Walter
  English Teacher
ARGYLE
Caulfield, John F.
  Fifth Grade Teacher
Fleury, Rick Lee
  Art Teacher/Art Dept Chair
Galough, Jamie Pereau
  Human Resource Teacher
ARKPORT
Troy, Melody Mc Intyre
  5th/6th Grade Teacher
ASTORIA
Kapusta, Olga (Skrenta)
  Fifth Grade Teacher
Malon, Patricia Glaser
  Social Studies Teacher
Mc Cartin, Brian
  Social Studies/Science Teacher
Nomikos, Sylvia Anna
  High School Math Teacher
AUBURN
Blair, Thomas Clark
  Health Education Teacher
Gargiul, Bella DeLuca
  Fourth Grade Teacher
Harris, Ernest C.
  Social Studies Teacher
Kany, Ronald E.
  Teacher
Messina, Patricia Hart
  First Grade Teacher
BABYLON
Drance, Daniel A.
  Teacher/Math Dept Chair
Gellert, Thomas Neil
  Director of Bands
Goitia, Daniel
  Admin Asst & Math Teacher
Kaplowitz, Marsha Lois
  First Grade Teacher
Morrow, Kathleen Smith
  Second Grade Teacher
BAINBRIDGE
Flack, Christine Hall
  4th Grade Teacher
Ives, Judith C.
  Fifth Grade Teacher
BALDWINSVILLE
Baker, Sarah Jane
  Social Studies Teacher
Bechard, Rebecca Jean
  9th Grade Mathematics Teacher
Dunham, Duane Donald
  Sixth Grade Teacher
Lewien, Karen Woodman
  Third Grade Teacher
Magnarelli, Thomas J.
  Social Studies/History Teacher
Nevid, Barbara Gail (Rothman)
  Spanish Teacher
BALLSTON LAKE
Hancock, Marie A.
  Kindergarten Teacher
BALLSTON SPA
Fletcher, Donald F.
  Retired
Shepalavy, Julie Nowadly
  Chemistry Teacher
BARKER
Haak, Kenneth J.
  Social Studies Teacher
BATAVIA
Edwards, John L.
  5th Grade Elementary Teacher
Galliford, George William
  4th/5th Grade Teacher
BATH
Galvin, Geraldine D.
  Third Grade Teacher
Hagadorn, Thomas W
  Mathematics Teacher
Jansen, Michael Marion
  Business Teacher
Le Ray, June Smith
  Dept Chair of Languages
Robbins, Peter
  Science Department Chairman
BAY SHORE
Doody, Janice Marie
  8th Grade Mathematics Teacher
Kaplar, Denise Balbi
  Biology Teacher
Richardson, Ray
  Law Studies Teacher

Robertson, Ann
  5th/6th Grade English Teacher
BAYSIDE
Belfi, Mary Grace
  Art Teacher
Fuchs, Susan May
  Third Grade Teacher
Matzner, Barbara J.
  HS English Teacher
Rosenfeld, Marcia
  Spanish Teacher
BEAVER FALLS
Eger, Gail Essenlohr
  Second Grade Teacher
BEDFORD
Fitzgerald, Kathleen
  Fourth Grade Teacher
BELLEVILLE
Bingle, Carl A.
  German/French Teacher
BELLMORE
Fleishman, Alan Richard
  Social Studies Teacher
Folkman, Barbara Bachner
  Mathematics Teacher
Petersen, Janet Evelyn (Korn)
  Social Studies Teacher
BEMUS POINT
Conroe, Jane E.
  Science Teacher
Edgerton, Judi L.
  Business Teacher
Gregory, Sarah Lodestro
  Fourth Grade Teacher
Isaacson, Matthew Oke
  Sixth Grade Teacher
Lewellen, Scott Jay
  Earth Science Teacher
Plyler, Robert W.
  Social Studies/English Teacher
Prindle, Kathryn
  Mathematics Dept Chair
Rollinger, Mary Elizabeth
  Secondary English Teacher
BERGEN
Chrzanowski, Ronald F.
  Social Studies Teacher
Mac Connell, Marsha A.
  Kindergarten Teacher
BERLIN
Schultz, Jeanne Demick
  Principal
BETHPAGE
Hager, Arthur F.
  Social Studies Teacher
Hartmann, Dolores O'Connor
  Teacher of Gifted & Talented
James, Carol A.
  Home & Career Skills Teacher
BINGHAMTON
Card, Joseph Robert
  Social Studies Teacher
Clapper, Kevin Matthew
  Sr HS Mathematics Teacher
Demaree-Cohen, Cott
  Home Economics Teacher
DeRitis, Joyce Marie
  Head School Nurse/Teacher
Fisher, Howard B.
  Biology Teacher
Foglia, Kim Bianca
  Science Teacher
Gill, David P.
  Mathematics Teacher
Irving, John Henry
  History Teacher
Mc Crea, Philip R.
  Sixth Grade Teacher
Mullineaux, Jeanne H.
  Fourth Grade Teacher
Steeves, Robert Burns
  5th Grade Teacher
Yocum, Timothy Allen
  Phys Ed Teacher/Athletic Dir
BLASDELL
Lilley, Joan Catanzaro
  Kindergarten Teacher
BOHEMIA
Martinsen, Eric Laurence
  English Teacher/Drama Dir
BOICEVILLE
Ostoyich, Matthew John
  Social Studies Dept Chair
BOLIVAR
Wolcott, Jane Austin
  Second Grade Teacher

BOONVILLE
Bennett, Mary Ellen Metzger
  1st Grade Teacher
BRADFORD
Grodis, Donald Anthony
  Teacher
BRANT LAKE
Fabian, Deborah Engle
  First Grade Teacher
BREESPORT
Oldroyd, Carolyn A.
  Mathematics/Spanish Teacher
Wyse, Toby Dean
  Music Department Teacher
BRENTWOOD
Bannon, Michael
  Science Teacher
Fasano, Joseph Anthony
  Career Education Coordinator
Governale, Joseph Anthony
  English Teacher
Hagan, Frances Theresa
  Religion Teacher
BREWSTER
Clare, Michele Di Mantova
  Foreign Language Teacher
Reed, Peter Martin
  Special Education Teacher
BRIARWOOD
Diorio, John V.
  American Government Teacher
BROCKPORT
Dumas, Robert Frank
  7th Grade Soc Stud Teacher
Reedy, David J.
  Physics Teacher
Sutton, James R.
  Eighth Grade Math Teacher
BRONX
Antinore, David
  Math Teacher
Bantz, John Peter
  Guidance Cnslr/Math Teacher
Barber, Janis Shapiro
  Resource Room Teacher
Berens, Edward Steven
  Educational Evaluator
Cohn, Howard Martin
  Social Studies Teacher
Connolly, Carmel
  First Grade Teacher
Engel, Judith S.
  Mathematics Teacher
English, Elizabeth Shell
  Business Education Teacher
Garguilo, Maria Theresa
  Social Studies Teacher
Guzman, Arturo David
  Theology/Science Teacher
Imundi, Janice Bonanno
  Assistant Principal
Kerins, Stephen Joseph
  Business Teacher
Kozuck, John
  Physical Education Teacher
Lotakis, Katina Cabinos
  Assistant Principal
Mc Carthy, Glenn A.
  Math Teacher/Asst Principal
Mc Carthy, Joseph R.
  Social Studies Teacher
Mc Laughlin, Thelma Gooch
  6th Grade Teacher
Murphy, Miriam
  Biology Teacher
Payson, Martin Saul
  7th Grade Math Teacher
Phillips, Barbara Gibney
  Teacher
Rhem-Tittle, Yvonne Shirley
  7th/8th Math & Science Teacher
Rivlin, Timothy Bennett
  History Teacher
Roesner, Stephen Joseph
  Social Studies Teacher
Schifini, Patricia Marie
  Religion Teacher
Semple, Deborah Oslyn
  Mathematics Teacher
Shook, Denise Eggleston
  Assistant Principal
Sunshine, Helen Albaum
  Second Grade Teacher
Tarangelo, Denise Marie
  First Grade Teacher
Warren, Russell E. Jr.
  Principal
Woodruff, Hyla
  Educational Director

Young, Daryle Ann Williams
  Staff Developer
BRONXVILLE
Jouas, Linda Mazzola
  French/Spanish Teacher
Saul, Mark E.
  Computer Coordinator
BROOKFIELD
Pugh, Nancy Lee
  Science Chair/Physics Teacher
BROOKHAVEN
Bergel, Steven Peter
  Earth Science Teacher
BROOKLYN
Abato, Barbara
  Jr HS Mathematics Teacher
Andersen, Theresa Nuzzo
  7th/8th Grade Math Teacher
Auguste, Gabriel J.
  Mathematics Teacher
Bernbach, Carolyn Ann
  Cultural Enrichment Teacher
Bileta, Grace Elena
  Italian Teacher
Blau, Arthur David
  Guidance Counselor/Coll Adv
Bloomfield, Stanley
  English Teacher
Brenner, Joel H.
  Physics Teacher
Byrne, John James
  Curriculum Coordinator
Corbett, Joan P.
  Kindergarten Teacher
Craig, Edna Brown
  Word Processing/Cmptr Teacher
Crosby, Rose (Ranieri)
  Mathematics Teacher
Doctor, Abby T.
  Mathematics Teacher
Echauri, Anita Therese
  6th-8th Grade Science Teacher
Edelstein, Eleanor
  English Teacher/Computer Coord
Edwards, Ransford George
  Math Teacher
Fannon, Adrian
  Social Studies Chairman
Fernandez, Nicholas Joseph
  HS Social Studies Teacher
Filene, Myron
  English Teacher Staff Coord
Fulton, Rebecca James
  Dean of Students
Grassi, Gloria G.
  4th&5th Gr Math/Soc St Teacher
Harrington, Charles Edward
  7th Grade Biology Teacher
Hickey, Georgiana Hayes
  7th/8th Grade Science Teacher
Hinchen, Thomas M.
  6th Grade Jr High Teacher
Isom, George Hemingway
  8th/9th Grade English Teacher
Jaffe, Carren Gerb
  Art Teacher
Joseph-Pernambuco, Lynette Barbara
  Chairperson Science Dept
Kantor, Karen Diane
  2nd Grade Teacher
Kartaginer, Marilyn
  Mathematics Teacher
Kaufman, Rosanne
  Thinking Skills Coordinator
Kay, Harvey Peter
  Lang Arts Teacher/Librarian
Keller, Ellen Freedkin
  English Teacher
Kitover, Mary Jane Mc Garry
  Eng as Second Lang Teacher
Kriss, Phyllis S.
  Third Grade Teacher
Lane, Michele J. F.
  Chairwoman Language Dept
Levine, Arlene Gay
  Teacher of Gifted Education
Loftus, Claudia Burnham
  Guidance Counselor
Mackiewicz, Barbara Theresa
  Sophomore Guidance Counselor
Maiorca, Grace Lercara
  Language Art Teacher
Olitsky, Eleanor Rosinsky
  Retired 6th Grade Teacher
Osterweil, Elaine Kuhn
  Teacher
Parker, Delorise
  Elementary Teacher
Quattrocchi, Ciro Anthony
  Italian & Spanish Teacher
Revinskas, Diane D.
  Mathematics Teacher

Ribaudo, Catherine Martine
  English Teacher
Russo, Nube Cabezal
  6th-8th Grade Math Teacher
Turnbull, Diane Lucas
  English Teacher
Volpe, Tina Maria
  Enrichment Teacher
Warden, Kenneth Bruce
  Guidance Counselor
Weissman, Adrienne Y.
  English Teacher
Wishnow, Elaine
  6th Grade G/T Teacher
Zodda, Philip J.
  Teacher/Track & Field Coach
BRUSHTON
Holmes, David Asa
  Secondary Mathematics Teacher
BUFFALO
Acevedo, Amelia
  4th Grade Bilingual Teacher
Bouton, Paula Velazquez
  Remedial English Teacher
Davis, Lynn Comstock
  French Teacher
Dietrich, Dennis Edward
  Social Studies Teacher
Diffine, Suzanne Michele
  Curriculum Resource Specialist
Elardo, Robert Anthony
  Soc Studies/Eng Teacher
Erker, Carmela Montagna
  Retired
Falkner, William Jackson
  Special Educ Coordinator
Frey-Mason, Patricia
  Mathematics Dept Chairperson
Gruber, James F.
  Program Coordinator
Jones, Alicia Davila
  Two-Way Bilingual Prgm Coord
Korvne, Erik P.
  Academic Advisor
Krist, Betty Jane
  Assoc Professor Mathematics
Lawler, Michael Joseph
  Sixth Grade Teacher
Lewandowski, Robert Gerald
  Teacher/Program Coordinator
Lo Vullo, Angelo M.
  Jr High Social Studies Teacher
Luczowski, Thomas Andrew
  5th Grade Teacher
Mc Kenzie, Denise
  Campus Minister/Instructor
Morton, Ruth Yvonne (Mungo)
  English Teacher
Mosner, Ann La Russo
  Vocal Music Teacher
Palisano, James Thomas
  History Teacher
Shinners, Paula Elizabeth Barnes
  Jr HS Exceptional Ed Teacher
Streit, Norman Joseph
  Technical Teacher
Thomas, Penelope April
  Business Admin Educator
White, Annette Ann (Burrell)
  Science Teacher
Wilhite, Dorothy Wielbon
  Sixth Grade Teacher
Yellen, Fred Lee
  7-9th Grade Math Teacher
BURNT HILLS
Doyle, Mary Anne Campanella
  Mathematics Teacher
Wagner, Joan S.
  Science Teacher
CALEDONIA
Brewster, Diane Layland
  5th Grade Teacher
CAMBRIA HEIGHTS
Church, Thalia Carolyn
  Dean
Kelly, Hazel E.
  Jr HS Math Teacher
CAMBRIDGE
Crowe, Clements
  Social Studies Teacher
Vitello, Joseph John
  Mathematics Teacher
CAMDEN
Schremph, Howard R. Jr.
  Math Department Chairperson
CANAJOHARIE
Hammersmith, Dorothy C.
  Sixth Grade Teacher

CANANDAIGUA
Bertino, Anthony J.
A P Biology Instructor

CANASTOTA
Di Prima, Florence Marie
English Teacher

CANDOR
Czerenda, Julie Ann
Art Teacher-Art Chairperson
Hynes, Cyndy
Physical Education Teacher
Parks, Dawn C. Beebe
6th Grade Teacher

CANISTEO
Chase, Alonzo O.
5th Grade Teacher
Mc Inroy, Richard Oliver
HS Mathematics Teacher

CARMEL
Goldberg, Jonathan B.
Social Studies Teacher
Kirk, Dianna Marie
High School English Teacher

CARTHAGE
Coffman, Terry Richard
Soc Stud Teacher/Ftbl Coach
Price, Alma M.
Teacher
Vermeulen, Nancy Irene
Project Charlie Teacher

CATO
Bartholomew, Robin Lane
HS Physical Education Teacher
Jordan, Edward Hill
Mathematics/Science Teacher
Russell, Lee Talbott
First Grade Teacher

CATTARAUGUS
Humphrey, Eileen Ross
4th Grade Teacher

CENTEREACH
Brisson, Donald Paul
English Teacher

CENTRAL ISLIP
Libert, Nancy Porta
6th Grade Teacher

CENTRAL SQUARE
Lindsley, Joyce Wickham
7th/8th Grade Music Teacher
Love, Scott Scott
English Teacher/Coach

CHADWICKS
Lindberg, Diane Marie
7th Grade Mathematics Teacher

CHAMPLAIN
Dawson, John Francis
Mathematics Department Chair

CHAPPAQUA
Houser, Steven Douglas
Social Studies Teacher
Lynch, Edward J.
Social Studies Teacher

CHEEKTOWAGA
Dee, Richard R.
Biology Teacher
Downey, Maryann Giordano
Spanish Teacher
La Sota, Gloria
Business Department Chairman
Pezzino, Esther Mae Falcone
Early Childhood Educator
Sesnie, Thomas Charles
Social Studies Teacher
Simonetta, Stefanie Gasbarre
French Teacher
Zielinski, Stephen F.
Secondary Mathematics Teacher

CHERRY PLAIN
Cary, Thomas David
Mathematics Department Chair
Comerro, John Burns
English Department Chairman
Miller, Robert Cassius
English Teacher

CHESTERTOWN
Davran, Ann
Social Studies Teacher

CHITTENANGO
Lebiedzinski, Carol Susan
Science Teacher

CHURCHVILLE
Hosenfeld, Martha Watt
English Teacher

Seidel, Don
Staff Development Coordinator
Talbott, Linda Mullens
Sendry Soc Stud Teacher
Wheaton, Mark G.
Instrumental Music Teacher

CICERO
Baker, Sandra Acker
English Teacher
Deuel, Ned
Social Studies Teacher
Riter, Constance
Math Teacher/Department Chair

CINCINNATUS
Ferguson, Terri Smith
First Grade Teacher

CLARENCE
Martin, June Sophia
French/Spanish Teacher
Walleshauser, Barbara Mary
Mathematics Instructor

CLAY
Tassa, Linda Evelyn
7th Grade Music Teacher

CLIFTON PARK
Conway, Ann F.
Social Studies Teacher
Fadgen, Sherolyn Goodrich
Sixth Grade Teacher
Zavadil, Martin Richard
Band Director

CLIFTON SPRINGS
Cook, Laura Catherine
English Teacher
Tuffy, Jean M.
HS Physical Ed Teacher

CLINTON
Duink, Marie Jones
Third Grade Teacher
Kelly, Nicholas Justin
Fifth Grade Teacher
Lee, Mary Ann Hamlin
French Teacher/Lang Chairman

COBLESKILL
Pendergrass, M. Eileen
Sixth Grade Teacher

COEYMANS
Palmer, Joann Linda (Iatauro)
Fifth Grade Teacher

COHOCTON
Robinson, Stephen Edward
HS English/Soc Stud Teacher

COHOES
Stephenson, Joan Sadowski
Fifth Grade Teacher

COLD SPRING
Scecina, Patricia A.
Nursery School Teacher

COLLEGE POINT
Cardone, Patricia Brennan
Religious Studies Teacher

COMMACK
Gulick, William D. Sr.
Science Teacher

CONKLIN
Bucchioni, Larry Paul
7th Grade Soc Stud Teacher
Burke, Michael J.
Mathematics Teacher
Searing, Kathleen Carden
English Teacher

COPIAGUE
Hazelton, Alex
Social Studies Teacher
Mahoney, James Joseph
Chemistry Teacher
Torns, Robert Louis
Music Teacher

CORFU
Dressel, Carol M.
Third Grade Teacher

CORINTH
Moynihan, Michael Francis
English Teacher
Rivette, Miriam Snyder
4th Grade Teacher
White, Ronald I.
Guidance Counselor

CORNING
Siegler, Irving
4th Grade Teacher

CORNWALL ON HUDSON
Ramsay, Colin M.
Asst Headmaster/Chm Soc Stud

COXSACKIE
Becker, Walter Siegfried
History Teacher
Fedoryszyn, Edward Alexander
Sixth Grade Teacher
Magee, Raymond Charles
7th Grade Science Teacher
Magee, Rita Matthews
Physical Education Teacher

CROFTON
Robinson, Mary Boitnott
Retired Teacher

CROSS RIVER
Croteau, Gale Harper
Secondary Sod Stud Teacher

DALTON
Montgomery, Marie Trescott
First Grade Teacher

DE RUYTER
Chaplin, Patricia Smith
1st Grade Teacher
Ludwig, Edmund Bruce
Biology/Physics Teacher
Mc Manus, Lois Tierney
Spanish Teacher
Smith, Carole Lynn
6th Grade Teacher

DEER PARK
Clancy, Jo Ann Corso
Fifth Grade Teacher

DELANSON
Greene, Denise M. (Patryk)
Fifth Grade Teacher
Sleeper, Joyce Elaine
Fourth Grade Teacher

DELEVAN
Kiec, Patricia Mc Carthy
First Grade Teacher

DELHI
Kruser, Edward
Social Studies Teacher

DELMAR
Feldmann, Jane Rogers
7th Grade Science Teacher
Yeara, James Carroll
English/Drama Teacher

DEPEW
Caruana, Anthony Francis
English Teacher
Troutman, Barbara Jane
(Rothenberger)
2nd Grade Teacher
Wetzel, Joan Ann
Third Grade Teacher

DEPOSIT
Stever, Deborah June
Teacher/Asst Prin

DIX HILLS
Silber, Marcia Liepper
2nd Grade Teacher

DOBBS FERRY
Singer, Mary Theresa
Social Studies Teacher

DOLGEVILLE
Foreman, Margery Doxtator
English Teacher
James, Sharon J. Sue
Business Teacher

DOVER PLAINS
Tierney, Michael Patrick
Social Studies Teacher

EAST AMHERST
Parisi, Ellen W.
History Teacher

EAST AURORA
Karg, Kathleen Elizabeth
1st Grade Teacher/Asst Prin

EAST ELMHURST
Corvasce, Frances Diane
English Teacher
Rumsey, Rosella Franca
Math/Computer Teacher

EAST GREENBUSH
Weinlein, Gregg Thomas
Alternative Ed Supervisor

EAST MEADOW
Kavett, Paula D.
Sixth Grade Teacher

EAST NORTHPORT
Moran, James Patrick
Bio & Marine Ecology Teacher

EAST NORWICH
Garone, Frank
English Teacher

EAST SYRACUSE
Fox, Susan C.
3rd Grade Teacher
Kirkwood, Richard M.
5th Grade Teacher
Meltzer, Michael R.
Physics Teacher
Novak, Susan Munro
1st Grade Teacher
Schwab, Richard Alan
Mathematics Teacher
Seeloff, Robert Carl
4th Grade Teacher
Willcox, Joanne Sassi
AP US History Teacher

EDEN
Lauricella, Mary Ann Spallino
6th Grade Teacher

EDINBURG
Frasier, Cynthia Ann (Smith)
Third Grade Teacher

ELLENVILLE
Mirra, Frank A.
English Teacher/Curr Coord
Roosa, Mark Edward
Earth Science Teacher
Spada, Richard E.
Social Studies/ESL Teacher

ELMA
Zirkelbach, Joan Diane
6th/8th Grade Health Teacher

ELMIRA
Bennett, Gary A.
Chemistry-Biology Teacher
Hall, Thomas J.
English Teacher
Hillman, John M.
Social Studies Teacher
Sheer, Rodney Nathan
Mathematics Teacher

ELMONT
Baade, Mary Ann A.
Business Education Teacher
Ferraro, Lorraine
6th Grade Teacher
Goldstein, Jack Leon
Art Teacher
Mc Dounough, Joseph Peter
Mathematics Teacher

ENDICOTT
Angeline, Francis Joseph
Latin/German Teacher
De Bonis, Michael Joseph
History Teacher
Materese, Richard Angelo
8th Grade Social Stud Teacher
Smith, William Stephen
Language Art Teacher
Truillo, James Nicholas
Math Teacher

ENDWELL
Perricone, John Michael
Health Educator

FABIUS
Magnani, Geoffrey Steven
Dir of Elem Instrumental Music
Marisco, Ronnie Wallace
Fifth Grade Teacher

FAIRPORT
Balzano, John G.
Mathematics Teacher

FALLSBURG
Cumbie, Carol Gavin
English Teacher

FARMINGDALE
Krell, Susan Becker
English Teacher
Maurer, Selma Cherny
Third Grade Teacher
Perez, Marta Bofill
Spanish Teacher
Tomko, Margarita Ossandon-Duncan
English Teacher

FARMINGVILLE
Bevelander, Nancy Weeks
5th Grade Teacher

FAYETTEVILLE
Broadbent, Peggy Sue (Mc Creery)
First/Second Grade Teacher

O'Gavaghan, John Albert
Sixth Grade Teacher

FILLMORE
Frasier, Linda Marie
English/French Teacher
Mullen, James L.
Secondary English Teacher

FISHKILL
Hale, Jack E.
4th Grade Teacher
Powers, Charles Andrew
5th Grade Teacher
Topf, Virginia Veronica
Fifth Grade Teacher

FLORAL PARK
Carlson, Paula Geraldine
Art Coordinator
Daniels, Catherine Loprete
Science Teacher
Palladino, Anthony
Third Grade Teacher
Schneiderman, Etta M.
Mathematics Teacher
Seely, Steven A.
English Teacher

FLORIDA
Searing, Virginia Mary
Mathematics/Computer Teacher

FLUSHING
Pallotta, Joseph J.
Director of Music

FONDA
Bellinger, Laura Jean
Secondary Bus Ed Teacher
Cox, Paulyn M.
Third Grade Teacher
Depuy, Cynthia Parker
6th Grade English Teacher
Di Caprio, Elizabeth Anne Gargiulo
5th Grade Reading Teacher
Emanuele, Joseph Robert III
Mid Sch Mathematics Teacher
Headwell, Robert Jr.
Dept Chair Technology
Mahon, Ann B.
English Department Chair

FOREST HILLS
Bluestone, Fran Schwartz
Social Studies Teacher
Nici, John Bartholomew
High School English Teacher

FORT ANN
Alverson, Georgia Hoffis
Science Teacher

FORT EDWARD
Mulchay, Noranne
Biology/Chemistry Teacher

FORT PLAIN
Gilday, Frederick John
Mathematics Teacher
Hunt, M. Elizabeth Murray
English Teacher
Nassen, Christine Elizabeth
Math/Computer Literacy Teacher
Nellis, Mary Ann
English/French Teacher
Offenborn, Katherine Christa
Second Grade Teacher
Simmons, Douglas R.
Science Teacher
Urbin, Christine A.
Art Teacher

FRANKLIN SQUARE
Bergbom, Joanne Piccarella
Teacher/Director of Stu Act
Cannava, Marie Cruz
English Teacher
Erreger, Charles John
Social Studies Teacher
Fern, Tami Lynne
Teacher of Gifted/Talented
Hoger, Grace Kathryn
Vocal Music Teacher
Suhovsky, Tracy Barnett
Chemistry Teacher
Zanghi, Phyllis Hayes
First Grade Teacher

FRESH MEADOWS
Castellano, Joseph Philip
English Teacher

FREWSBURG
Dull, Frederick John
Fifth Grade Teacher
Edwards, Mary Lou Jimison
English Teacher

FRIENDSHIP

May, Patricia A.
2nd Grade Teacher
Stanton, Beverly (Say)
Spanish & Computer Sci Teacher

GAINESVILLE

Bannister, Kathleen Beardsley
Mathematics Teacher
Driscoll, Ann Harrington
4th Grade Teacher
Lawrence, Ernest Joseph
Physics Teacher/Sci Dept Coord
Robbins, Wayne Russell
Sendry Social Studies Teacher
Thomas, Jeffrey M.
Health Coordinator

GALWAY

Cervenka, Barbara Ellen
Music Teacher
Goodemote, Barbara Holmberg
6th Grade Teacher/Dept Head
Kalinkewicz, Denise Filion
English Teacher

GARDEN CITY

Caruso, Penny M.
Kindergarten Teacher
Schenkel, Thomas Francis
Mathematics Teacher

GARRISON

O'Dell, Ralph
Librarian/Teacher

GENEVA

Gorgonzola, Gale Teresa
Mathematics Teacher/Dept Chair
Hudson, Richard Lee
Math Teacher
Johnson, Philip Roy
American History Teacher
Khoury, Anthony John
Social Studies Teacher
Morrow, Elaine Stolp
Principal
Ryan, Anne B.
4th Grade Teacher

GILBOA

Bagnardi, Kathyanna Marshall
4th Grade Teacher
Banks, Lorraine Miles
Third Grade Teacher

GLENS FALLS

Davis, Edward L.
Retired Phys Ed Coach
Hussa, Edwin F.
Mathematics Department Teacher

GLOVERSVILLE

Borkowski, Barbara A.
Mathematics Dept Chairperson

GOSHEN

Blaine, John Michael
Instructor-Culinary Food Trade

GOUVERNEUR

Amberg, Carol Scott
English Teacher
Kingsley, Joan B.
Kindergarten Teacher
Matejcik, Christine Cassidy
Fourth Grade Teacher

GOVERNORS ISLAND

Shestak, Joan Carole
5th Grade Teacher

GOWANDA

Kilian, Anne E.
Third Grade Teacher
Perdue, Sharon M.
Fifth Grade Teacher
Sutter, Frances Rowicki
Retired 4th Grade Teacher

GRAND ISLAND

Jewett, Everell W.
Biology Teacher

GRANVILLE

O'Brien, Felcia Sheloski
Second Grade Teacher
Smith, Herbert James
Fifth Grade Teacher
Wescott, Diane Blake
Mathematics Teacher

GREENE

Cline, William R.
English Department Chair

HAMBURG

Cichocki, Sharon A.
Mathematics Teacher
Decsi, Rita
Second Grade Teacher

Dollmann, Marilynn Zaccarine
Business Teacher
Dujanovich, Deborah Ann
6th Grade Teacher
Falkner, Noreen Margaret Roman
English Teacher/Dept Chair
Goodremote, Cecil J. Jr.
Jr HS Science Teacher
Gourlay, Linda Marie Strobel
Level Four Teacher
Gross, William Fredric
English Teacher
Henry, Diane Lazzelle
Instructional Coach
Hobart, Michael James
Instrumental Music Teacher
Schultz, Diane Obersheimer
English Teacher
Sipos, John F. Jr.
Math Teacher & Dept Chairman
Taneff, Teresa Ann Leitten
Biology Teacher
Turkasz, Edward Stephen Jr.
7th Grade Biology Teacher
Wiatrowski, Jo Ann Gauthier
French/English Teacher

HAMMONDSPORT

E., Mary
Math Teacher

HANNIBAL

Patane, Samuel Vincent
Social Studies Teacher

HARPURSVILLE

Hennessey, Radcliffe William
10th Grade Global Stud Teacher

HARTFORD

Friday, Susan Graves
English Teacher

HASTINGS ON HUDSON

Eckleman, Michael Arnold
7th/8th Language Art Teacher
Marcus, Jacqueline Pollak
4th Grade Teacher

HAUPPAUGE

Alio, Al
English/Computer Teacher
Schomaker, Anne Marie
5th Grade Teacher

HEMPSTEAD

Kennedy, Eileen Nevins
English Teacher
O'Neill, Kathleen Quinlan
English Teacher

HENRIETTA

Leary, Edward William
Teacher

HERKIMER

Stulmaker, Richard M.
Social Sciences Teacher

HEUVELTON

Allen, Joyce Elaine
First Grade Teacher
De Luca, Deborah Santamont
Business Teacher

HEWLETT

Merchant, Leslie Carol
English Teacher
Myers, Charles F.
Latin Teacher
Pesca, Joseph G.
Math/Soc Stud Teacher
Rosenblatt, Ina Barbara
Spanish Teacher

HICKSVILLE

Criscolo, John Thomas
Regents Biology Teacher
Owens, William Jude
9th Grade Soc Stud Teacher
Sparaccio, Kathleen
English Teacher
Sparaccio, Kathleen Malone
English Teacher

HILTON

Williams, Nicholas M.
Vocal Music Teacher

HOLBROOK

Farnum, George William
Fifth Grade Teacher
Oakes, Norman C.
Remedial Mathematics Teacher
Reynolds, Susan Stange
Fourth Grade Teacher
Sarakos, Joanne Esposito
Mathematics/Computer Teacher
Schubert, Barbara Emily
5th Grade Teacher

HOLLAND

Buono, Lawrence J.
Social Studies Teacher
Franczak, William J.
English Department Chairman
Klahn, Norma Jean
Social Studies Teacher
Poliseno, Carol Seel
Third Grade Teacher

HOLLAND PATENT

Hierholzer, Pernina Capanna
Kindergarten Teacher

HOLLISWOOD

Silberman, Barbara Ann
Kindergarten Teacher

HOLTSVILLE

Blasko, Carol Ann
6th Grade Teacher
Failla, Dorothy Charapata
5th Grade Teacher
Knapp, John P.
4th Grade Teacher

HOMER

Cecconi, Richard Alan
Science Teacher
Taube, Joan Marie (Lortscher)
Third Grade Teacher

HONEOYE

Blackmer, Sally
Global Studies Teacher

HOPEWELL JUNCTION

Licata, Guy Thomas
Biology Teacher
Lovelock, Patricia Anne
Language Arts Teacher
Schoen, William Joseph
Chemistry Teacher
Williams, Sheila Kelly
Second Grade Teacher

HORNELL

Baker, Barbara Allen
6th Grade Science Teacher
Libordi, Francis Andrew
American History Teacher
Loree, Joan Murphy
Pre-First Grade Teacher
Mastin, Eugene Arthur
Guidance Counselor
Pauly, Virginia A. Crozier
2nd Grade Teacher
Piper, W. Stephen
Health Teacher
Van Scoter, Maryann Cicero
Fifth Grade Teacher

HORSEHEADS

Conklin, Warren George
Econ/Criminal Justice Teacher
Davis, Margaret Ridall
Teacher of Gifted
Mc Inerney, Judith Strausbaugh
Math Teacher
Peckally, John A.
Fifth Grade Teacher
Roemmelt, Josephine Pastirik
Third Grade Teacher
Sanders, Bea Betty Garver
English Teacher

HUDSON FALLS

Clear, Gloria Lewis
Second Grade Teacher
Grieser, Wendy Sue
Second Grade Teacher
Mac Donald, Craig Lindsay
Teacher

HUNTINGTON

Borrelli, Jerry F.
Science Teacher
Friedman, Sandra Goldman
Resource Room Teacher
Shoemaker, Linda L.
Director of Bands

HUNTINGTON STATION

Lasky, Marsha Somer
Social Studies Teacher
Mc Cann, Lorraine Dorothy-Jean
4th Grade Teacher

HUNTINGTON STN

Carman, Lina T.
Science Teacher

HYDE PARK

Briggs, Rembert
English Teacher
Wiehe, Karl Stephen
Teacher

ISLAND PARK

Hester, Barbara Olszewski
Pre-Kindergarten Teacher

ISLIP

Backman, Carol Ann
7th Grade Math Teacher
Baranec, Diana Paternoster
Mathematics Teacher

JACKSON HEIGHTS

Bernardo, Alice
Teacher
Shubin, Joanna T.
Science Dept Chm & Teacher

JAMAICA

Harnett, Joan M. OP
Director of Programming
Schlesinger, Barbara Groveman
First Grade Teacher

JAMESTOWN

Boerst, William James
English Teacher
Cotten, Richard L.
Mathematics Teacher
De Francisco, Michael Anthony
Counselor
Falk, Charles William
English Teacher
Heppler, Linda Joyce
French Teacher
Kimbal, Richard Allen Jr.
Academic Supervisor
Lombardo, Joseph Paul
Fifth Grade Teacher
Luke, Dorothy Harrington
First Grade Teacher
Martin, Margaret Gately
First Grade Teacher
Munsee, Sandra Nupp
Math Teacher
Nelson, Nancy Poore
Second Grade Teacher
Peters, Gary R.
5th Grade Teacher
Peterson, George E.
English Teacher
Quackenbush, Barbara Barlow
5th Grade Teacher
Taylor, Beverly Ihle
4th Grade Teacher
Thompson, Clifton C.
Math Dept Chm/Dist Cmptr Coord
Thurber, Robert Evan
12th Grade Economics Teacher
Whitehead, Carolyn Taft
High School English Teacher
Wise, Teresa Andrews
5th Grade Teacher

JAMESVILLE

Sorkin, Neal B.
Social Studies Teacher

JEFFERSONVILLE

Brey, Eileen
1st Grade Teacher
Wooddell, P. Glenn
Fine Arts Department Chair

JOHNSON CITY

Coston, Gene Armstrong
4th Grade Teacher
Fisk, David James
History Teacher
Hill, Teresa Ellen
12th Grade English Teacher
Meyers, Bernard L.
Assistant Principal
Munley, Elizabeth Ann
Latin/Spanish Teacher
Patch, Lorraine Shoemaker
Fourth Grade Teacher

KENDALL

Henschel, Sandi
Teacher of English
Pollock, Gary John
Mathematics Teacher
Richards, Carl Ann (Fleck)
K-6 Remedial Math Teacher

KENMORE

Brege, Karen Elizabeth
Fifth Grade Teacher
Granger, Joanne G.
Biology/Chemistry Teacher
Kelley, Gary Stewart
Mathematics Teacher
Ostwald, Faith Ann
Mathematics Teacher

KINGS PARK

Brennan, Neil
Computer Science/Math Teacher
Pletz, Meredith Anne Gilmour
6th Grade Teacher

Polin, Patricia Young
Spanish Teacher
Porcelli, Stephanie (Adamowicz)
English Teacher

KINGSTON

Chin, Betty Lee
Secondary Mathematics Teacher

LA FAYETTE

Besten, John Joseph
Instrumental Music Teacher
Fox, William Raymond
5th Grade Teacher

LACKAWANNA

Galante, Paolina
Spanish Teacher

LAGRANGEVILLE

Usifer, Peter Joseph
Science Teacher

LAKE RONKONKOMA

Belli, Peter S.
Guidance Counselor
Cavalea, Joseph Anthony
Director of Orchestras
Genova, Eugene G.
Science Dept Chairman
Williamson, Ellen Mc Kernan
Guidance Counselor

LARCHMONT

Mc Cabe, Robert
5th Grade Teacher

LATHAM

Bartlett, Alan Paul
Science Teacher

LAURENS

Wenck, Romona Nellis
K-12th Grade Phys Ed Teacher

LEVITTOWN

Siewert, Sandra K.
Home & Career Skills Teacher

LINCOLNDALE

Herity, K. Joan Kelly
Social Studies Teacher

LINDENHURST

Koza, Burt T.
7th/8th Grade Soc Stud Teacher
Lederer, Emma Cincinnato
Spanish/Italian Teacher
Murphy, Josephine Strukel
6th-8th Grade Science Teacher
Nicholas, Ida Marie
Second Grade Teacher

LISBON

Masters, Elizabeth Mc Martin
Secondary English Teacher
Mc Guire, Patrick Michael
Fifth Grade Teacher
Turbide, Janet Chamberlain
Fifth Grade Teacher

LITTLE FALLS

Mahoney, Jane Mc Evilly
Retired Teacher

LIVERPOOL

Mitchell, Joseph Charles
Fourth Grade Teacher
Mouton, Patricia Penland
English Teacher
Potrikus, Susan Frances
Mathematics Teacher

LOCKPORT

Battaglia, Frank Louis
Social Studies Teacher
Cassart, Irene Chamberlain
6th Grade Teacher
Gately, James Mathew
Social Studies Teacher
Olick, Steven Andrew
Social Studies Dept Chairman
Stanley, Frederick Guy
6th-8th Grade Art Teacher

LOCUST VALLEY

Hodgson, Janice Mariarossi
Mathematics Teacher

LONG ISLAND CITY

Barone, Anthony John
7th/8th Grade History Teacher
Pender, Karen I. (Franz)
7th-8th Grade Lang Art Teacher
Powell, Gloria J.
Assistant Principal
Vodola, Catherine M.
Fifth Grade Teacher

LOUDONVILLE

Berggren, Carol Humphrey
Sixth Grade Teacher

LOUDONVILLE (cont)
Camilleri, Bruce Thomas
  Physical Education Teacher

LYNDONVILLE
Houseman, Terry E.
  Fifth Grade Teacher
Townsend, Nancy May
  Sixth Grade Teacher

MADISON
Saulsgiver, Daniel Scott
  Science Teacher

MAHOPAC
Del Campo, Christopher
  English Teacher
Di Cioccio, Joseph N.
  Mathematics Teacher
Hansen, Judith C.
  Sixth Grade Teacher

MANHASSET
Gorin, Robert Murray Jr.
  Social Studies Teacher
Segulji, Ann H. IHM
  Math Teacher

MANHATTAN
Streitferdt, Carolyn Chestnut
  Asst Principal-Teacher

MARATHON
Donald, Cathy M.
  Science Teacher
Funk, Karen Cornell
  Physical Education Teacher
Hines, Patricia Parker
  Third Grade Teacher
Loomis, Gail Ashcroft
  Spanish Teacher
Tei, Catharine May (Brown)
  Second Grade Teacher

MARION
Miller, Mary Alice
  First Grade Teacher

MARLBORO
Ratau, Sylviane Lubelski
  French Teacher
Rosengarten, Henry Alan
  Language Arts Teacher

MASPETH
Teel, Elizabeth
  English Teacher

MASSAPEQUA
Collom, Bette Gibson
  English Teacher
Garvey, Ann
  1st Grade Teacher

MASSENA
Bellor, Susan J.
  Spanish Teacher
Geagan, Sandra D'Arienzo
  Teacher of Gifted Children
Herman, Linda Sue
  Art Teacher/Dept Chair
Jock, Sue Mercurio
  Sixth Grade Teacher
Matthews, Virginia Woodard
  Kindergarten Teacher
Perez, Loretta Bronchetti
  7th/8th Grade Eng/Math Teacher
Rotonde, Albert Robert
  Music Teacher

MAYFIELD
Hugo, Judy A.
  Guidance Counselor
La Due, Stuart R.
  Dean of Stus/Soc Stud Teacher
Rovito, Eileen Buehler
  7th-12th Grade Phys Ed Coach

MECHANICVILLE
Holmes, Diane Ward
  1st Grade Teacher

MEDFORD
Squires, George Winston
  Fr, Span, Latin Teacher
Zinna, Frances Klecak
  Kindergarten Teacher

MEXICO
Rossman, Terry Michael
  8th Grade Social Stud Teacher
Skora, Shirley Jeanette
  Instrumental Music Teacher

MIDDLE ISLAND
Rose, Patricia Ann (Galea)
  English Teacher
Rosenblum, Hope Carol (Lisell)
  Teacher
Werner, Richard
  Fourth Grade Teacher

MIDDLE VILLAGE
Byrne, Veronica F.
  Social Studies Chair

MIDDLETOWN
Sauter, Cindy Elissa (Berg)
  Spanish Teacher

MILLBROOK
Riva, Jeffrey Francis
  Social Studies Teacher

MINOA
Wilkie, Eileen Kelley
  4th-6th Grade Teacher

MOHEGAN LAKE
Cassidy, John Francis
  Math Teacher

MONTGOMERY
Gridley, Gayle M.
  English Teacher
Sussdorff, Jay D.
  12th Grade English Teacher
Walton, Michael Ira
  Fifth Grade Teacher

MONTICELLO
Johnson, Harold G.
  5th Grade Teacher

MORAVIA
Garguil, Joseph A. Jr.
  Social Studies Teacher

MORRIS
Boyd, Norma Schultz
  Second Grade Teacher

MORRISVILLE
Russock, Helen Lodor
  Sixth Grade Teacher

MOUNT MARION
Popowicz, Sandra Mae
  Sixth Grade Teacher

MOUNT SINAI
Bautz, William F.
  Fifth Grade Teacher

MOUNT VERNON
Blackman, Elise Paul
  5th Grade Teacher
Collins-Cole, Vivian Joyce
  Mathematics Teacher
Costello, Georgiana M.
  Math Specialist
Dolce, Linda V.
  4th Grade Humanities Teacher
King, Rhonda Michele
  7th/8th Grade English Teacher
Stephens, Deloris K.
  Sixth Grade Teacher
Trotta, Laura
  English Teacher
White, Wanda M.
  First Grade Teacher

NANUET
Niblock, Patricia OP
  8th Grade Teacher

NEDROW
Garvey, Sharon Waltz
  Mathematics Teacher

NESCONSET
Bright, Theresa J.
  2nd Grade Teacher
Madonia, Diane (Lopipero)
  Mathematics Teacher
Wilson, B. Beth
  Second Grade Teacher

NEW BERLIN
Haley, Richard John
  Director of Instrumental Music
Stowell, William R. Sr.
  5th Grade Teacher

NEW CITY
Larkin, Susan M.
  5th Grade Teacher

NEW HARTFORD
Bliss, Sharon Cusworth
  Health Occupations Teacher
Donnelly, James David Jr.
  Dean of Students

NEW HYDE PARK
Filose, Elaine
  Third Grade Teacher
Wilson, Dolores M.
  English Teacher

NEW ROCHELLE
Armstrong, Veronica May-Lamb
  English Teacher

Brown, Leonette Taylor
  Fifth Grade Teacher
Einhorn, Kenneth Mark
  Health Teacher
Fullerton, Georgine Bonacci
  Second Grade Teacher
Mc Neil, Martin D.
  4th Grade Teacher
Turnbull, Joanne Tate
  Pre-School Teacher
Weiner, Berta Meltzer
  Mathematics Teacher

NEW YORK
Anker, Morten
  Teacher
Balog, Sharon Lewin
  Mathematics Teacher
Barassi, Louis W.
  History Teacher
Baskind, Bruce Phillip
  HS Social Studies Teacher
Baumel, Abraham
  Principal
Brown, Harry Ross
  Math Teacher
Carter, Sandra Mc Intyre
  Educational Director
Cooper, Kenneth Peter Russell
  His/Religion Teacher Chair
Curran, Matthew Charles
  Campus Minister
Diaz, Jose M.
  Spanish Teacher
Douglas, Violet Aaron
  5th/6th Grade Teacher
Edwards, Madeline Mosiello
  8th Grade Teacher/Asst Prin
Fodor, Mariana Duarte
  Sr Practical Nursing Coord
Gandolfo, Joseph E.
  English Teacher
Gerety, Shawn Francis
  English Teacher
Gottlock, Wesley George
  6th Grade Teacher
Hammill, Cleo M. Black
  Second Grade Teacher
Horowitz, Evelyn
  English Teacher
Jacobs, Bruce Richard
  English Teacher
Koller, Catherine A.
  Social Studies Dept Chair
Kolsky, Helen Paula
  English Teacher
Langford, Myra A. (Wilson)
  Assistant Principal
Liben, David Mark
  Mathematics Teacher/Grade Head
Ling, Larry K.
  Spanish/French Teacher
Maldonado, Milagros
  Secretarial Studies Teacher
Meade, Hazel Helen (Heastie)
  K-8th Grade Teacher/Director
Paces, Miloslav Josef
  Social Studies Teacher
Peteanu, Gertrude Dolores
  Coordinator of Cosmetology
Pickell-Ridley, Donna Marie
  PCEN Math Lab Facilitator
Ramirez, Rene George
  Assistant Professor
Sandomir, Lawrence Philip
  6th Grade Teacher/Writing Adv
Sassoon, Ingrid Anny Von Siemering
  Kindergarten Teacher
Schiff, Alison Goodwin
  Art Teacher
Schrader, Diana Lee
  8th Grade Teacher
Schultz, Warren Thomas
  Assistant Principal
Sievers, Cecil Norman
  Language Art Teacher
Simpson, Joyce Ann
  Secondary Eng & Span Teacher
Smith, Helaine L.
  English Teacher
Wallace, Donna M.
  Fifth Grade Teacher
Walters, Barbara J.
  English Grammar & Literature
Webb, John Badgley
  French Teacher & Dept Chair
Weithers, Merille G.
  English Department Chairman
Williams, Michael C.
  7th Grade Teacher/Principal
Wilson, Thomas M.
  Head of Humanities
Wolle, Selamtaw
  IB Economics Teacher
Zelicof, Erika F.
  Chemistry Teacher

NEW YORK MILLS
Fragetta, Frank Anthony III
  Fifth Grade Teacher
Simmons, Michael Lawrence
  Physical Education Teacher

NEWARK
Pritchard, Lori Williams
  8th Grade Reading Teacher
Russell, Theodore Edward
  Lang Art Coord/Eng Teacher

NEWBURGH
Calley, Thomas Peter
  Social Studies Teacher
Weiss, Barbara M.
  Social Studies Teacher

NEWFIELD
Longest, Ethel Brown
  First Grade Teacher

NIAGARA FALLS
Burnett, Barry Clinton
  Scndry Social Studies Teacher
Connell, Laura Burns
  Social Studies Teacher
De Munda, Richard
  Mathematics Teacher
Hughey, William Walker
  Fifth Grade Teacher
Johnson, Rosaire Regina
  8th Grade Homeroom Teacher
La Duca, Francis
  6th Grade Teacher
Pero, Judith G. Goss
  English Teacher

NORFOLK
Connelly, Margaret Margittny
  6th Grade Teacher
Sutter, Sally Ann Campbell
  Fifth Grade Teacher

NORTH BABYLON
Calderone, Jodi A.
  Kindergarten Teacher
Sharp, Neil F.
  Guidance Counselor

NORTH BALDWIN
Lebby, Gloria J.
  Fifth Grade Teacher

NORTH MASSEPEQUA
Feder, Helen
  Mathematics Specialist

NORTH SYRACUSE
Crabtree, Robert Allen
  Fourth Grade Teacher
Czirr, Mary Stengle
  Fourth Grade Teacher
Romano, Mary Grace Fiore
  Fourth Grade Teacher
Simone, Elizabeth Butterworth
  Retired Reading Specialist

NORTH TONAWANDA
Anker, Beverly Elaine
  4th Grade Teacher
Bowman, Jeanne Kraemer
  Third Grade Teacher

NORTH TROY
Kennedy, Cathal Halloran
  Kindergarten Teacher

NORTHPORT
Begley, James Walter III
  Social Studies Teacher
Eder, James M.
  Social Studies Teacher

NORWICH
Davis, Thomas John
  5th Grade/Elem Science Coord

NORWOOD
Hamrick, Christina Ann
  Sophomore English Teacher
Hinkley, Gregory C.
  Elementary Teacher
Ver Schneider, Constance W.
  English Teacher

OAKDALE
Drzal, Robert
  English Teacher
Lilie, Geraldine J.
  6th Grade Teacher

OAKFIELD
Miller, Edna A.
  9th Grade English Teacher

OCEANSIDE
Luisi, Frank A.
  English Teacher/Football Coach
Sheehan, Kevin Patrick
  Director of Student Projects

ODESSA
Vona, Beverly Jean
  Fifth Grade Teacher

OGDENSBURG
Ebberts, Theodore Edward Jr.
  Chem Teacher/Sci Dept Chair

OLEAN
Brace, Myra Booth
  Sixth Grade Teacher
Looker, Robert James
  6th Grade Teacher

ONEONTA
Campbell, Joseph Paul
  Sixth Grade Teacher

ONTARIO CENTER
Snyder, Wayne
  Physics Teacher

ORCHARD PARK
Kuss, Kathleen D. Clemente
  6th Grade Science Dept Teacher
Wallace, George West
  5th Grade Teacher

OSWEGO
Altman, Thomas C.
  Physics Teacher
Nix, Sue Jacoby
  6th Grade Elementary Teacher
Sullivan, Michael John
  English Teacher

OYSTER BAY
Siegelman, Richard Jay
  Third Grade Teacher

PAINTED POST
Laubach, Elizabeth De Marte
  English Department Chair

PALMYRA
Russell, Gregory D.
  History Dept Chair/Teacher

PARISHVILLE
Claus, Pamela Jeanne
  Elem Principal/Program Coord
Mandigo, Craig Martin
  4th Grade Teacher

PATCHOGUE
Albert, Charles William
  Teacher
Hickey, Elizabeth Anne (Sweeney)
  4th Grade Teacher

PEARL RIVER
Mangini, Rosanne Campanella
  7th & 8th Grade Teacher

PENFIELD
Maher, Daniel Patrick
  Superintendent
Peterson, Marjorie Brown
  Second Grade Teacher
Richardson, Carol Ann
  Second Grade Teacher
Rogers, Kathleen Kelly
  Mathematics Department Chair

PENN YAN
Baldwin, Jon Roger Eric
  Elementary Band
Gleason, Elaine Champlin
  Third Grade Teacher
Johnson, Kelley Sue
  1st Grade Teacher
Miles, John Raymond
  Math Dept
Nester, Dortha Holland
  Third Grade Teacher
Scher, Nancy Earlley
  Kindergarten Teacher
Smith, David Lawrence
  Sixth Grade Teacher

PERRY
Carter, George Ann
  Social Studies Teacher
Exton, William Thomas
  Math Department Chairman

PHELPS
Bolan, Linda Grinnell
  6th Grade Teacher
Herry, D. Mark
  6th Grade Teacher
Ruggles, Mary Frederick
  Kindergarten Teacher
Scott, Kay Keller
  English Teacher
Shappee, Donna Jones
  Sixth Grade Teacher
Van Der Linden, Sherrie L.
  5th Grade Teacher

PHILADELPHIA

Drake, Allen Terrance
  5th Grade Teacher
Fabrizio, Patricia
  English Teacher

PHOENICIA

Druffner, Jean Marie
  5th Grade Teacher
Nadler, Estelle Epstein
  Sixth Grade Teacher

PINE BUSH

Golden, Roger Joel
  Middle School Counselor
Proestopoulos, Ellen Chambers
  11th Grade English Teacher

PINE PLAINS

De Putron, David B.
  4th Grade Teacher

PITTSFORD

Hahn, W. Todd
  4th Grade Teacher
Hertweck, Gerard Anthony
  Spanish Teacher

PLATTSBURGH

Beaudin, Christopher
  English Teacher
Carroll, Gale (Lapham)
  Mathematics/Computer Teacher
Donnelly, Mark J.
  Physical Education Teacher
Gagnon, Ray
  English Teacher
Marcil, Joy Demarse
  English Teacher
Mockry, Jean Wade
  12th Grade English Teacher

PORT BYRON

Dominick, Roger E.
  7th Grade Mathematics Teacher

PORT CHESTER

De Rose, Agnes Joan
  Second Grade Teacher
Harper, Barbara Jean
  Second Grade Teacher
Waite, Edward R.
  Social Studies Teacher
Zaccara, Jack J.
  Planetarium Director
Zwillich, Mark Alan
  Business Teacher

PORT JEFFERSON

Dayton, Constance E.
  Language Arts Teacher

PORT JEFFERSON STN

Gold, Iris
  Special Education Teacher

PORT JERVIS

Patterson, Joyce T.
  Third Grade Teacher
Semerano, Ronald J.
  Health Teacher

PORTVILLE

Foust, Barbara Edson
  Second Grade Teacher
Scott, Linda L.
  6th-8th Remedial Rdng Teacher
Wood, Marylou Donovan
  English Teacher

POTSDAM

Ford, Lorraine M.
  2nd Grade Teacher
Ham, Thomas E.
  French Teacher

POUGHKEEPSIE

Grassia, Anthony Joseph
  Mathematics Teacher
Martin, H. Noreen Mills
  Social Studies Chairperson
Van Ackooy, Howard John
  6th Grade Soc Stud Teacher
Wohl, Judith R.
  Middle School English Teacher

PULASKI

Delaney, Elaine Heilig
  Third Grade Teacher
House, Frank Charles
  Principal
Lawrence, Kim Chontosh
  Math Department Chairperson
Warren, Betty Jane
  Third Grade Teacher

PUTNAM VALLEY

Campbell, Gerald
  Computer Coordinator

QUEENS

Rafter, Joseph Patrick
  6th Grade Teacher

QUEENSBURY

Foust, J'aime L. (Meyer)
  Social Studies Teacher
Mc Dowell, Sally Fitzgerald
  Social Studies Teacher
Morrissey, Stephen A.
  Retired 6th Grade Teacher
Porter, Edith M.
  3rd Grade Teacher

RANDOLPH

Crosby, Emily Jean Harris
  Retired Teacher
Klee, Kathleen M.
  Math Dept Chair/Cmptr Coord

RED CREEK

Gill, Daniel Patrick
  Fifth Grade Teacher
Williamson, Mildred Ellison
  First Grade Teacher

RED HOOK

May, Martha
  Math Dept Chm/Cmptr Coord

RENSSELAER

Gumbs, Marion Louise
  Sixth Grade Teacher
Kennedy, Linda Havens
  Secondary Math Teacher

RETSOF

Fusco, Andrew A.
  Mathematics Dept Teacher
Kelley, Karen Miller
  Sixth Grade Teacher

RICHBURG

Harkenrider, Carla Packer
  Sr HS English Teacher

RICHMONDVILLE

Lawyer, Aranka Vincze
  English Teacher

RICHVILLE

Done, Cathy Jean
  Mathematics/Science Supvr

RIVERHEAD

Brown, Gerald David
  5th Grade Teacher
Cohen, Meryl
  Science/Chemistry Teacher
Euell, Thomas Edwin III
  Fifth Grade Teacher
Hagen, Patricia Langsdorf
  Third Grade Teacher
Mc Killop, David J.
  Social Studies Teacher
Moravek, George Michael
  Music/Strings/Vocal Teacher

ROCHESTER

Augustine, James Philip
  Essential Skills/Math Teacher
Cowett, Mark
  Head of Upper School
Currie, John N.
  English Teacher
Fenton, Christina M.
  6th Grade Teacher
Finnegan, Kathleen Anne
  Mathematics Teacher
Frierson, Cassandra W.
  Human Resources Director
Gillis, Carol Ann
  Math Teacher/Dept Chairperson
Guido, Lisa Maria
  French/Italian Teacher
Hart, Rose (Coletta)
  First Grade Teacher
Hutchins, Carol E.
  Third Grade Teacher
Martina, Camille Anne
  Communications/English Teacher
Povero, Mary Borromeo
  Latin Teacher/Lang Dept Chair
Riesenberger, David Anthony
  Mathematics Teacher
Ritz, Veronica Toole
  Mathematics Teacher
Riviere, Barbara Scanlon
  Social Studies Teacher
Savella, Karen Noelle
  English Teacher
Scarfia, James Michael
  Soc Stud/Theology Teacher
Schwendy, Donna Merrill
  English Teacher
Swift, Kathy Hallock
  English Teacher
Welch, Jean Catherine
  Fifth Grade Teacher

Welch, Sharon R.
  Math Teacher

ROCKAWAY BEACH

Dwyer, Margaret Mary
  Third Grade Teacher

ROCKAWAY PARK

Mc Namara, Clare Agnes
  English Teacher
Pagano, Marianne B.
  Spanish Teacher

ROCKVILLE CENTRE

Strumeyer, Arline Z.
  Social Studies Teacher

ROME

Messick, Timothy B.
  English Department Chair
Santaferrara, James Phillip
  Sixth Grade Teacher
Wenz, Michael F.
  Business Department Chair

ROMULUS

Maleski, Theresa S.
  Mathematics Dept Chair/Teacher
Midey, Michael John
  7th-8th Grade Science Teacher
Prave, Karen Fairchild
  Science Teacher

RONKONKOMA

Boyle, Michael Warner
  English Teacher

ROOSEVELT

Collins, Jaqueline Wight
  Sr HS Guidance Counselor
Rogers, Helen Georgiana
  9th-12th Biology/Sci Teacher
Smith, Jerrie Lean
  7th Grade Soc Stud Teacher

ROSLYN

Easton, Joan S.
  Fifth Grade Teacher

RUSSELL

Harmer, Richard M.
  5th/6th Grade Math Teacher

SACKETS HARBOR

Sweeney, Michael Lawler
  Social Studies Teacher

SAINT ALBANS

Gaynor, Joseph Patrick
  Science Teacher

SAINT BONAVENTURE

Worth, Helen R.
  Student Teacher Supervisor

SAINT JAMES

Crandall, Arlene B.
  School Psychologist
Dunn, Arthur James
  Science & Mathematics Teacher
Gallo, John Christopher
  Social Studies Teacher
Mlinarich, John Joseph
  Social Studies Teacher
Stanton, Virginia Dlugos
  Kindergarten Teacher
Wiegand, Judith Lapen
  Mathematics Department Chair

SAINT JOHNSVILLE

Ortlieb, Cheryl B.
  Mathematics Teacher

SAINT REGIS FALLS

Eells, Murray M.
  Biology Instructor
Johnson, Karleen Martin
  Kindergarten Teacher

SANBORN

Gornicki, Henry A.
  History/Law Teacher
Rycombel, Thomas James
  7th Grade English Teacher

SANDY CREEK

Fenn, Charles G.
  Technology Teacher
Mc Kown, Jeanne Young
  3rd Grade Teacher

SARANAC LAKE

Fisch, Thomas Michael
  8th Grade Soc Stud Teacher
Fogarty, Emily St. Clair
  Mathematics Teacher
Kalinowski, Jacqueline Impero
  English/Drama Teacher

SARATOGA SPRINGS

Blaauboer, Peter R.
  Teacher & Dept Head

Fairchild, Francine Smith
  Third Grade Teacher
Gapczynski, James Joseph
  Sixth Grade Teacher
J., David
  African/Asian Cultures Teacher
Johns, Richard A.
  3rd Grade Teacher/Tennis Coach
Johnson, Charles Andrew
  Art Teacher
Kish, Charles Nicholas
  Science Teacher
Ohmstedt, Diana M. Bustillo
  Spanish Teacher
Patrei, Gregory L.
  Mathematics Teacher
Sova, Joyce Sprague
  Fifth Grade Teacher

SAUGERTIES

Rubenstein, David Miles
  English Teacher

SAUQUOIT

Talbot, Thomas Elbert
  Director of Choral Music
Winnicki, Maryann Keida
  First Grade Teacher

SCARSDALE

Salvaterra, Richard J.
  Physical Education Teacher

SCHENECTADY

Adler, Randee Hartz
  Teacher of Gifted and Talented
Causey, Richard T.
  Math Teacher/Chairman
Cavallaro, Donna Zelesnikar
  Teacher
Howard, John Whitney Sr.
  Science Teacher
Jones, Beatryce Lewis
  Retired Second Grade Teacher
Lotano, Ernest Joseph
  Social Studies Teacher
Westfall, Adrienne E.
  4th/5th Grade Teacher

SCHUYLERVILLE

Hammond, Constance Carpenter
  Retired Teacher
Nichols, Patricia K.
  2nd Grade Teacher
Sackman, Joan V.
  Third Grade Teacher

SCIO

Cleary, Catherine Powell
  Fifth Grade Teacher
Estabrook, Karen J.
  English Teacher
Gibbs, Timothy Robert
  Mathematics Department Chair
Lewis, Barbara Sloan
  Third Grade Teacher
Schroeder, Rose Sturdevant
  Kindergarten Teacher
Walker, Ella Hyslip
  Sixth Grade Teacher
Wood, Sandra Lee
  Third Grade Teacher

SELDEN

Glass, Margaret R.
  English Teacher
Welcome, Allen J.
  Biology Teacher

SENECA FALLS

Avery, Douglas Alan
  Music Department Chairman
Blanchard, M. Joan
  Home Economics Teacher
Wagener, John Andreas Jr.
  Earth Science Teacher

SETAUKET

Comerford, Daniel J. III
  7th Grade Soc Stud Teacher
Packey, Betty Baran
  Second Grade Teacher
Young, Ellen Wiesinger
  Sixth Grade Teacher

SHARON SPRINGS

Bader, Conrad F.
  Jr HS Soc Stud/Math Teacher
Cechnicki, Doreen L. Brown
  Home Economics Teacher
Handy, Barbara Bucciferro
  Business Teacher
Harding, Dorothy Hollely
  4th-6th Grade Science Teacher
Lauzon, Sally
  Science Department Chair
Toomey, Nancy S.
  Second Grade Teacher

SHERBURNE

Kleinstuber, Margaret Mason
  2nd Grade Teacher

SHERMAN

Brown, David Stuart
  5th/6th Grade Math Teacher
Swanson, Melford Carl
  5th/6th Grade Science Teacher

SHOREHAM

Gantt, Lloyd James Jr.
  Social Studies/Math Teacher

SHORTSVILLE

Gillern, Burdella Bitterman
  Third Grade Teacher

SHRUB OAK

Robinson, Dennis S.
  Physical Education Instructor

SIDNEY

Colvard, Mary Page
  Science Teacher/Chairperson

SINCLAIRVILLE

Armstrong, Morton Charles
  English Teacher
Rich, Donald F.
  6th Grade Teacher

SKANEATELES

Cangemi, Richard Anthony
  HS Instrumental Teacher
Capelli, Mary Grell
  Language Arts Teacher
Rehrl-Ruggio, Carmen Antoinette
  German/French Teacher

SLATE HILL

Barnett, Russell Clyde
  Social Studies Teacher
Budd, Richard Douglas
  Technology Chair
Mc Ginnity, Helene Carey
  3rd Grade Teacher
Teabo, Glenda Patterson
  First Grade Teacher

SLOAN

Odrobina, Peter Martin
  Physical Education Instructor

SMITHTOWN

Fitz Morris, Mary Malone
  Fifth Grade Teacher
Franco, Nancye (Hodges)
  Sixth Grade Teacher
Makris, George J.
  French & Spanish Teacher

SNYDER

Carter, Kenneth A.
  English/Soc Stud Teacher
Mikulec, Jo Ann Marie (Graziano)
  English Teacher

SODUS

Mac Dougall, Donald K.
  6th Grade Teacher

SOLVAY

Simiele, Carol A.
  4th Grade Teacher

SOMERS

Sherman, Carol Simpson
  Mathematics Dept Chair

SOUTH GLENS FALLS

Clough, James William
  6th Grade Teacher
Jenkins, Lowell Parker
  6th Grade Teacher
Yurkewicz, William
  Physics Teacher

SOUTH HUNTINGTON

Gillespie, Linda
  English Teacher
Reiter, Marjorie Ann
  Fifth Grade Teacher
Sella, Joseph J.
  Math Teacher

SOUTH KORTRIGHT

Yost, Sandra L.
  First Grade Teacher

SOUTH NEW BERLIN

Bliss, Joyce Mowry
  2nd Grade Teacher
Borden, Frances Elberta
  English Teacher
O'Donnell, Patricia A.
  Kindergarten Teacher

SPENCERPORT

Kennard, Bernice Vieau
  6th Grade Teacher/Math Coord

SPRINGVILLE

Bartkowski, Henry S.
English Coordinator
Benning, Karen Ann
Teacher of Gifted & Talented
Schlageter, Robert Leo
Math Teacher/Math Dept Chair

STAMFORD

Weeks, Nancy Heck
English & Writing Teacher

STATEN ISLAND

Agostino, Joseph Patrick
Religion Teacher/Coord
Ahern, Roger J.
Science Teacher
Calamera, Fran Fichera
Biology Teacher
Cappucci, Marie Circo
Mathematics Teacher
Cody, Michele L.
Seventh/Eighth Grade Teacher
Cummings, Josephine Scotto
English Teacher
Estreicher, Albert
Third Grade Teacher
Ferragano, Dolores M.
Principal Intern
Ferrando, Angela Amantea
Assistant Principal
Kurzon, Paul W.
Accounting Teacher
Liozzi, Bruce Nicholas
5th Grade Teacher
Milza, Jo Ann Bradley
Fifth Grade Teacher
Minichelli, John A.
Social Studies Teacher
Mohlenhoff, Bruce R.
Eighth Grade Teacher
Perrino, John Anthony
Mathematics Teacher
Riordon, Ann Marie Barbara
Kindergarten Teacher
Russo, Daniel M.
Social Studies Teacher
Sheehy, Virginia Cadan
8th Grade Teacher
Spinetta, Virginia A.
Kindergarten Teacher
Udell, Judith A.
5th Grade Teacher
Zinn, Howard Stephen
4th Grade Teacher

STELLA NIAGARA

Schug, Maureen Daly
6th-8th Grade Teacher

STILLWATER

Carney, Maureen
Fourth Grade Teacher
Mondoux, Marvin Joseph
Sixth Grade Teacher
Winchell, Jo-Ann Patterson
1st Grade Teacher

STONY POINT

Jaslow, Barbara Fechter
Language Art Teacher

SYOSSET

Campisi, Phyllis Perretta
Coordinator of Gifted/Talented
Clarson-Kruse, Nancy
Fourth Grade Teacher

SYRACUSE

Fennessy, Virginia Everett
Gifted English Teacher
Gigante, Domenico Antonio
Italian/French Teacher
Hayes, Mary Ann
Sixth Grade Teacher
Kasberger, Kay Mary
English Teacher
Lehtonen, Roseann (Bond)
Health Teacher/Dept Chair
Leonardo, Michael Joseph
Mathematics Teacher
Moon, Barbara Jean
Mathematics Teacher
Paolotto, Patricia Marie
Private Tutor
Phipps, Dianne M.
Spanish Teacher
Seymour, Sharon Anne
Sixth Grade Teacher
Trotty-Selzer, Thelma
Social Science Dept Teacher

TARRYTOWN

King, Julie Dean
His Teacher/Asst Dir Admission

TICONDEROGA

Curri, Theta Swinton
Retired Teacher

Tubbs, Kathleen Huchro
Physical Education Teacher

TIOGA CENTER

Rogers, Warren C.
Principal

TONAWANDA

Barnard, Carole Camp
Math Teacher
Disorbo, Ronald Jack
8th Grade Mathematics Teacher
Mroz, Roger W.
Director of Music
Pirrone, Frank John
Science Teacher
Roberts, Joan Carol (Smith)
High School English Teacher

TROY

Bitley, Charles Warren
8th Grade Math Teacher
Dow, Patricia K.
English Teacher
Legasse, Kenneth J.
Business Department Chair
Reuter, Ronald Edward
Soc Stud Teacher/Dept Chair
Strang, M. Janice Green
6th Grade Teacher

TUPPER LAKE

Kenniston, Michael Robert
Science Teacher

TURIN

Ventura, Jo Ann
Mathematics Teacher

UNION SPRINGS

Tanner, Dean N.
Fourth Grade Teacher
Tolomay, Lawrence Joseph
Mathematics Teacher

UNIONDALE

Frankel, Yitzchok David
Jewish Studies Teacher
Hargrove, Doris Elaine Hutchings
Guidance Counselor

UTICA

Brooks, Angela Camardo
Head Math Dept
Chwazik, Thaddeus Paul
Social Studies Teacher
Custodero, Theresa La Fache
Fifth Grade Teacher

VALATIE

Allen, Nancy Leffingwell
1st Grade Teacher

VALHALLA

Ballesty, Peter Joseph
Soc Stud/Cmptr Teacher
Caparelli, Frank Peter
Mathematics Coordinator
Reich, Steve
Social Studies Teacher

VALLEY STREAM

Adams, Richard Thomas Jr.
Teacher
Pantason, Dorothy I.
Enrichment Resource Teacher
Wade, Barbara Hartung
Spanish Teacher

VERONA

Hirsh, Kathy
Music Dept Chairperson
Nasutowicz, Frank Martin
English Teacher

VESTAL

Bartos, Joanna Osif
Russian Teacher
Colavito, Barbara J.
Fifth Grade Teacher
Jason, Ernst W.
Science Dept Chairman
Johnson, Terri Bernhardt
Mathematics Dept Chairperson
Stuart, Michon Michael
Fifth Grade Teacher

WALWORTH

Ginnane, Lynne Beardsley
Business Teacher

WANTAGH

Kalman, Richard
Math Teacher

WAPPINGERS FALLS

Dvorkin, Robert I.
6th Grade Science Teacher
Lynch, Isabel (Lampe)
Mathematics Teacher

Robisch, Natalie Lemoine
English Teacher
Santisteban, Maria Cristina
Math/Computer Teacher
Sherman, Douglas Allen
Sixth Grade Teacher
Skora, Dennis John
8th Grade Soc Stud Teacher

WARRENSBURG

Hubert, Kathleen Anne (Mitchell)
Third Grade Teacher
Kusnierz, Anne Donnelly
Fourth Grade Teacher
Marquardt, Katharine Turley
Biology Teacher

WARWICK

Carton, James M.
6th Grade Teacher
Leporati, Debra Ann
English Teacher

WASHINGTONVILLE

Diesenhouse, Arlene Pasternack
Mathematics Teacher
Eikhof, Kathleen Jane
Sixth Grade Teacher
Forsberg, Dale R.
5th Grade Teacher

WATERLOO

Boudreau, Cecelia Mary
3rd Grade Teacher
Doyle, Wendy Warren
K-5th Grade Computer Teacher
Sposato, Joseph
Math Teacher/Athletic Dir

WATERTOWN

Krayenvenger, Dave E.
6th Grade Teacher
Pooler, Bernard E.
Business Teacher
Ringwald, Edward Charles
Social Studies Teacher
Seaman, Ruth E.
Sixth Grade Teacher
Towne, Linda Winnie
Jr HS Health Teacher

WATERVILLE

Arthur, Karen R.
Fourth Grade Teacher

WATERVLIET

Hart, Judith Ann
Second Grade Teacher

WAYLAND

Sobiesiak, James John
Counselor

WEBSTER

Hamm, Joann Ellis
Eng & Public Speaking Teacher
Linder, Raymond Anderson
Mathematics Teacher
Meisch, Katherene Tuttle
Chemistry Teacher
Wilder, Gertrude
Mathematics Teacher

WEEDSPORT

Davis, Keith
Social Studies Teacher

WELLS

Howard, Gary Wayne
Social Studies Dept Chairman

WELLSVILLE

Dahlgren, Denis Andrew
3rd Grade Teacher
Filkins, Alice Jean
Retired 7th Grade Math Teacher
Tyson, Beth Milner
Mathematics Department Chair

WEST HEMPSTEAD

Beyer, Rita Berardi
2nd Grade Teacher
Indiviglio, Kaye Gould
Orchestra Director
Verdi, Kevin James
8th Grade English Teacher

WEST ISLIP

Hodgson, Gordon B.
HS Social Studies Teacher
Kovar, Rita (Andersen)
Sixth Grade Teacher
Murphy, Julia Mary OP
Social Studies/Science Teacher

WEST NYACK

Collins, Maria Colasuonno
Life Science Teacher
Padmore, Vivian Younger
Fourth Grade Teacher

Wilson III, Samuel Earl
Science Teacher

WEST SAND LAKE

Viens, Charles Henry
5th Grade Teacher

WEST SENECA

Behrns, Gary M.
French/Spanish Teacher
Deni, Roseann Perrello
Band Director
Lesinski, Jerome Carl
Teacher
Rayner, Kenneth C.
Technology Instructor
Rodgers, Viola Gamble
4th Grade Teacher
Seel, Nancy Koubik
Choral Director
Tingue, Mary Lou Burlage
Third Grade Teacher
Wenerski, Lou Anne
Business & Marketing Teacher

WESTBURY

Ambrose, John W.
Social Studies Teacher
O'Sullivan, William Peter
English Teacher

WESTFIELD

Bertges, Marilyn Ann
Sixth Grade Teacher
Seymour, Steven Paul
Sixth Grade Teacher

WESTHAMPTON BEACH

Mead, Gretchen Zaloga
3rd Grade Teacher

WESTMORELAND

Bradbury, C.Joyce Rogerson
Pre-First Grade Teacher
Fedor, Celia Majka
4th Grade Teacher
Franklin, Joan Jacobson
Kindergarten Teacher
Walker, Jean Gennaro
Fourth Grade Teacher

WHITE PLAINS

Bolling, Imani
School Social Worker
Potocki, Kathleen Penson
Art Teacher

WHITEHALL

Cote, Leo F.
Social Studies Teacher

WHITESBORO

Goodman, William Bennett
Social Studies Teacher

WHITESVILLE

Loughlin, Judy Buchholz
Kindergarten Teacher

WILLSBORO

Latford, James Nelson
Science Teacher
Lopez, Michael Paul
Jr High Math Teacher

WILSON

Brasure, Wendy Raven
5th Grade Teacher

WINDHAM

Valenti, John Michael
Science Teacher

WINDSOR

Northwood, William Campbell
5th Grade Teacher
Yonchuk, Linda Jean
Soc Stud Teacher/Dept Coord

WINGDALE

Freebern, Janet Flynn
Third Grade Teacher

WOLCOTT

Palmer, Elizabeth Imperator
Fourth Grade Teacher
Sobierajski, Frank
Math Teacher

WOODSIDE

Candelaria, Myrna
English Teacher
Mc Namara, Louise
Eighth Grade Teacher

WYANDANCH

Berger, Steven
Director of Mathematics

WYNANTSKILL

La Liberte, Lois De La Mater
Fifth Grade Teacher

YONKERS

Buonocore, Anna Odoardi
Mathematics Teacher
Di Carlo, Rosemarie Iannucci
Kindergarten Teacher
Di Lello, Antoinette Marie
Vice Prin & 5th Grade Teacher
Halpern, Jean Kammen
English Teacher
Halpern, Linda Ann
Mathematics Teacher
Hibbard, Jeannette Marie
Mathematics/Religion Teacher
Muckelvany, Sylvia A.
5th Grade Teacher
Nyahay, Janice Gleitsmann
ESOL Chairperson
Skoog, Judith Stahl
4th Grade Teacher
Ward, Christohper William
Medical Magnet Chairman

YORKSHIRE

Van Valkenburg, Edris Owsley
Mathematics Teacher
Wood, Diane Allen
8th Grade Lang Art Teacher
Wood, Wendy L.
English Teacher

YORKTOWN HEIGHTS

Bogdanoff, Stewart
Head Teacher
Madeux, George James
Fifth Grade Teacher
Maiden, Ula K.
7th Grade English Teacher

YORKVILLE

Breckel, Jill
Social Studies Teacher

YOUNGSTOWN

Gonzalez-Hogan, Gwendolyn
Spanish Teacher

NORTH CAROLINA

ABERDEEN

Swann, Rudolph
6th Grade Teacher

AHOSKIE

Dacus, Martha Barnette
English Teacher
Faulcons Blount, Freya Falucon
Business Teacher
Herman, Marione Jackson
Fr, Span Teacher/Dept Chair

ALBEMARLE

Lampley, Gordon Brooks
Middle Grades Teacher

ALBERTSON

Faison, Pearlene Miller
4th Grade Teacher

ANDREWS

Shepherd, Billy Hugh Jr.
Phys Ed Teacher/Coach
Stewart, Andrea Mays
Biology Teacher
Wilson, Jeanette West
Fifth Grade Teacher

APEX

Armfield, Judith Mc Manus
English Department Chairperson
Bigham, Lamar Bragg
Teacher
Griggs, John Richard
Mathematics Teacher
Hardison, Gray Maynard
1st Grade Teacher
Norton, Margaret Craig Hedgepeth
Biology Teacher
Richardson, Janet Ketz
Science Teacher

ASHEBORO

Bingham, Glenda Freeman
Lang Art & Soc Stud Teacher
Boone, Marie Cross
5th Grade Teacher
Carroll, Aileene Caviness
Mathematics Teacher
Ledwell, Victoria Lee
Biology Teacher

ASHEVILLE

Brown, Ann Wilson
6th Grade Math & Sci Teacher

ASHEVILLE (cont)
Carter, Mary Kilpatrick
2nd Grade Teacher
Crawford, Charlotte Ayers
Sixth Grade Teacher
Dolan, Patricia Ann
Audio-Visual Coordinator
English, Maxie June Fox
Sci Teacher & Sci Chairperson
Gudz, Brigitte Worden
Mathematics Teacher
Henley, Mary Helen Hughes
5th Grade Teacher
Hillyer, Martha Flynn
Science Teacher/Dept Chair
Morrison, Jack Harley
Electronics Teacher
Murray, Michael Lee
Assistant Principal
Tsiros, Anastacia Hanzas
Kindergarten Teacher
Van Horn, Regina Renee
Director of Choral Activities
Wilson, John Douglas
Math & Social Studies Teacher

ATKINSON
Peay, Sarah Ann
7th-8th Grade Teacher

AULANDER
Bowen, Kenneth Ray
Language Arts Teacher

BAHAMA
Arrington, Deitra Eaton
Fifth Grade Teacher

BAILEY
Finch, Jean
Teacher of Academically Gifted

BAKERSVILLE
Atwood, Stephen James
Chemistry/Biology Teacher
Miller, Kathy B.
Music Teacher

BATTLEBORO
Lyons, Regina Nadine
Lang Art Teacher/Dept Chair

BAYBORO
Murphy, Gwendolyn Gibbs
Sixth Grade Teacher
Potter, Wendy Ireland
10th/11th Grade Eng Teacher

BELMONT
Cohen, Nicki Horowitz
Social Studies Teacher
Deaton, Robert Allen
Band Director
Greemon, Joyce Benfield
Business Teacher

BETHEL
Carson, Kathryn Lewis
Soc Stud/Lang Art Teacher

BEULAVILLE
Grady, Mary Anna
Science Teacher & Dept Chair
Thigpen, Mary Powers
Retired Teacher

BLACK CREEK
Barnes, Janice Taylor
Second Grade Teacher

BLACK MOUNTAIN
Greene, Susan
8th Grade Mathematics Teacher

BLADENBORO
Baldwin, John Kelly
Vocational Agriculture Teacher
Coleman, James Bernis
Assistant Prin of Instruction
Morris, Elizabeth Ann Roberts
First Grade Teacher
Russ, Barbara Hester
4th Grade Mathematics Teacher

BLOWING ROCK
Pace, Cherye Scott
4th Grade Teacher

BOONE
Benson, Barbara Peterson
English Teacher

BOONVILLE
Hobson, Freddie Catherine
10th Grade English Teacher
Key, Connie Wilkins
English Teacher

BOSTIC
Hopper, Marty Luke
Eighth Grade Teacher

BREVARD
Ideker, Joan Fensterman
English Teacher
Tinsely, Janet Murray
Third Grade Teacher

BRYSON CITY
Proctor, Kathy Holden
8th Grade Reading Teacher

BUNNLEVEL
Bailey, Kathy Carvalho
Third Grade Teacher

BURGAW
Arnold, Lee Pugh
English Department Chairperson
Bannerman, Willie Mc Koy
Fifth Grade Teacher
Graham, Celestine Moore
Third Grade Teacher
Robbins, Susan Meyers
Mathematics Teacher/Dept Chair

BURLINGTON
Bolden, Gail Cox
4-8th Writing Resource Teacher
Harviel, Jolete Fuquay
Language Arts Teacher
Roane, Bonnie Campbell
English Teacher/Drama Advisor
Walker, Dennis Dee
Assistant Principal

BURNSVILLE
Bledsoe, Marilyn Weaver
Math Dept Chairperson/Teacher
Branch, Barbara June
8th Grade Language Art Teacher
Johnson, Dwight Harvey
Teacher of Special Education
Shaw, Nancy Sexton
Health Occupations Teacher

BUXTON
Finnegan, Michael Phillip
Fourth Grade Teacher
Hall, Braxton B.
History & Government Teacher

CAMDEN
Leary, Judy Lynette
Fifth Grade Teacher
Overman, Susan Johnson
Second Grade Teacher
Wescott, Gwendolyn Stanley
English Dept Chairman

CANDLER
Keever, Patricia Rouzer
8th Grade Teacher Lang Arts
Mc Curry, Cheryl Foster
Health & Physical Ed Teacher
Piercy, Mary Peters
Teacher
Sproul, Dianne Payne
Kindergarten Teacher
Wave, Kim Fisher
Sixth Grade Teacher

CANTON
Slaughter, Danny Lee
Reading/Soc Stud Teacher

CARY
Reid, Joanne Cameron
French Teacher

CASAR
Earl, Peggy Peeler
Fourth Grade Teacher

CERRO GORDO
Hammond, Joanne Kellihan
Biology Teacher
Stephens, Lorie Ann
Home Ec Teacher

CHAPEL HILL
Bell, Oscar Larkin
Social Studies Teacher
Haven-O'Donnell, Randee P.
Sixth Grade Teacher
Hebdon, Stephanie
Third Grade Teacher

CHARLOTTE
Alston, Betty Jean (Bruner)
Second Grade Teacher
Amos, Hazel Peace
English Teacher
Brazil, Hughlene Hall
Mathematics Teacher
Campbell, Paul D. Jr
French/Biology Teacher
Garcia, Jose Aurelio
Spanish Teacher
Gilmore, Martha Moore
6th Grade Teacher

Gulledge, Emily Coggin
Second Grade Teacher
Helm, Dianne M.
Physical Science Teacher
Johnson, Debra Anita
Language Art Teacher
Kessie, Alan I.
Business Ed & Computer Teacher
Lee, Janice Barton
Latin Teacher
Lucia, Geoffrey Allen
Mathematics Teacher
Mc Cauley, Jacqueline Robinson
English Teacher
Mc Clure, Jean Summers
5th Grade Teacher
Mc Cullough, Dekota Grier
Lang Art/Soc Stud Teacher
Mc Koy, Alvin L.
6th Grade Teacher
Mitchell, Verna Jean (Cole)
English Teacher
Morgan, Patricia Deese
Math/Science Teacher
Owen, Joan Whisnant
4th Grade Teacher
Park, Jack Edwards
Health-Physical Ed Teacher
Payne, Ronald Dean
Director of Bands
Pittard, Michael Larry
Choral Director
Roberson, Anne H.
Media Specialist
Sams, Sue Williamson
Mathematics Dept Chair
Terlizzi, Richard Samuel
Observer/Evaluator
Thorp, Carol Crossley
Spanish Teacher
Washington, Mildred Chisholm
French Teacher
Watson, Joseph Leland
Drama Teacher
Williamson, Arthur Wayne
Sports Medicine Teacher
Wittmann, Charles Michael
Mathematics Teacher
Woods, Martha Stone
First Grade Teacher

CHINA GROVE
Behrooz, Judy Graham
Kindergarten Teacher
Schenk, Sandra Bousman
9th Grade Mathematics Teacher
Trexler, Judy H.
English Dept Chair
Walton, Elizabeth Blanton
English Teacher

CHOCOWINITY
Bartik, Thomas Frank
Sci Teacher/Dir of Sports Med
Mc Roy, Rebecca Peoples
Fourth Grade Teacher

CLAREMONT
Dotson, Harriet Oliver
6th Grade Teacher
Harrison, Sheila Britt
Spanish & English Teacher
Phillips, Mary Adair
Eng Teacher/Spch/Debate Coach

CLAYTON
Allen, Mary Thompson
Third Grade Teacher
Ennis, Jennifer Edwards
4th Grade Teacher
Hatcher, Betty Joe
Science Teacher
Parrish, William Kenneth II
Science & Math Teacher/Coach
Tripp, Elizabeth Harris
Fourth Grade Teacher

CLEVELAND
Townsend, Paul Keith
Lang Arts Acad Gifted Teacher
Warner, Jeffrey Myron
8th Grade Science Teacher

CLIFFSIDE
Powell, Linda Ledford
Sixth Grade Teacher

CLINTON
Cooper, Shirley Brown
Business Teacher
Cooper, Valeria Frederick
English Department Chairman
Hudson, Janice Britt
Fourth Grade Teacher
Stokes, Lillie Ballard
Teacher Math Dept Chairperson
Williams, Joyce Smith
Fourth Grade Teacher

CLYDE
Cooke, Nada Garber
Sixth Grade Teacher

COATS
Brown, Deborah Byrd
7th Grade Math/Science Teacher
Roberts, Alice Jackson
6th Grade Teacher
Stewart, Polly Norris
4th Grade Teacher

COLLETTSVILLE
Haigh, Nancy Clark
8th Grade Teacher

COLUMBIA
Cowan, Penny Taylor
Mathematics Department Chair

COMFORT
Teal, Linda Sue (Andrews)
Principal

CONCORD
Brawley, Pam A.
English Teacher
Savage, Linda Juanene Phelps
English Teacher
Vanderburg, Timothy Warren
Asst Prin/Athletic Director
Wittmann, Mary Evelyn
Sixth Grade Teacher

CONWAY
Winfrey, Elsie Balmer
Mathematics-Science Teacher

CORDOVA
Cox, Hazel Croft
Teacher

CREEDMOOR
Perry, Patsy Emory
7th Grade Lang Arts Teacher

CRESWELL
Furlough, Vickie Bowman
7th-9th Grade Science Teacher

CRUMPLER
Bare, Diana Absher
Second Grade Teacher

CURRITUCK
Kulhanek, Jeffery Morgan
Science Teacher/Dept Head

DALLAS
Lee, Barron Wilson
History Teacher

DEEP RUN
Dickens, Dolly Clark
English/Spanish Teacher

DENTON
Futrell, Glenda J.
1st Grade Teacher

DENVER
Atchley, Teresa Finger
English Teacher

DOBSON
Coe, Sexton Earlie
7th/8th Grade Teacher
Kirby, Sandy Swift
8th Grade Teacher
Vestal, Donald Charlie
Agriculture Teacher

DUBLIN
Revels, Katherine Jones
Sixth Grade Teacher

DUDLEY
Daniels, Deborah Keen
Biology/Physics Teacher
Williams, Reba King
Kindergarten Teacher Assistant

DUNN
Benson, Beverly Norris
7th Grade Lang Art Teacher
Bradham, Charles Hugh
8th Grade Soc Stud Teacher
Eldridge, Hortense Bass
5th Grade Lang Art Teacher
Hutaff, Flora Gilbert
Teacher
Ralph, Daniel Thomas
Counselor

DURHAM
Bost, Janie P.
Fourth Grade Teacher
Cameron, Pamela Mc Adoo
Mathematics Teacher
Chapin, Jean Hunt
5th Grade Teacher

Crandall, Claude Jr.
Social Studies Teacher
Darnell, Virginia Willets
8th Grade Mathematics Teacher
Dixon, Janice Carol
Teacher
Duffner, Nancy Marie
H S English Teacher
El-Khouri, Barbara Ann
Math Teacher
Fisher, Elizabeth Grant
French/History Teacher
Fochler, Kathryn S.
3rd Grade Teacher
Hampton, Mina Mayton
Retired
Hartwell, Eileen Atkinson
Teacher of Academically Gifted
Haynes, Luisa Perera
Spanish Teacher
Herbin, Shirley Taborn
Business Teacher/Dept Chair
Hill, Dianne Mangum
6th Grade Teacher
Long, Amelia Graham
Mathematics Teacher/Dept Chair
Love, Mariah Davis
English/Social Studies Teacher
Marriott, Lori Shea
A G Teacher K-3
Miller, Patricia Wilson
English Teacher
Mull, Shirley Sutton
7th Soc Stud Teacher/Dept Chm
Oakley, Barry Lewis
Mathematics Department Chair
Scagnelli, Elaine Fitch
Science Teacher
Scott, Tonya Pendergraft
Math Teacher
Shields, Elnora Joyner
English Dept Chm/Teacher
Vincent, Carolyn H.
Language Arts Teacher

EAST BEND
Grit, Rachel Smith
Home Economics Teacher
Hicks, Janice Poindexter
Language Art Teacher
Mangum, Evelyn Lee
Third Grade Teacher
Matthews, Karen Hodges
6th Grade Teacher
Matthews, Kim K.
Assistant Principal
Mc Collum, Dorothy Hoots
2nd/3rd Grade Teacher

EAST SPENCER
Rambo, Betty Burner
Language Arts Teacher

EDEN
Sechrist, Lonnie R.
Principal

ELIZABETH CITY
Banks, Rita Carver
7th Grade Mathematics Teacher
Britt, Patricia Smith
Third Grade Teacher
Brown, Susan Horton
Home Economics Educator
Butcher, Linda Hodnett
9th Grade English Teacher
Gibson, Marion Spencer
Fifth Grade Teacher
Lane, Ina Dungan
English Teacher
Morris, Mary Daniels
Second Grade Teacher
Rogers, Michael Carter
8th/9th Grade Band Director
Sass, Melinda Tuttle
Social Studies Teacher
Shannon, Juanita Billups
8th Grade Mathematics Teacher
Spence, Christopher Lowry
Government & Economics Teacher
Trotman, Beverly Barrett
Principal
Walton, Yvonne Staton
Fifth Grade Teacher

ELIZABETHTOWN
Britt, Katherine Savage
Teacher/Math Dept Chair
Dowless, Mary Byrd
8th Grade History Teacher
Elks, Ann Pharr
Elementary Supervisor

ELK PARK
Johnson, Peggy Sharon
Kindergarten/1st Grade Teacher
Young, Dana Dean
7th & 8th Grade Teacher

ELON COLLEGE
Henderson, Buckner L.
  Third Grade Teacher

ENFIELD
Frederick, Elease
  Sixth Grade Teacher

ENKA
Kopp, Charles F.
  Civics Teacher
Lawrance, Ann H.
  Mathematics Teacher

ENNICE
Lyon, Barbara Brooks
  Eighth Grade Teacher

ERWIN
Currin, James H.
  History Teacher
Henderson, Florence Brown
  Teacher
Hudson, Marian Smith
  Kindergarten Teacher
Matthews, William Brooks
  Biology Teacher
Mc Cants, Dessie Mae Neill
  Bus/Office Education Teacher
Mc Pherson, Oscar Milton
  Business & Office Ed Teacher

ETOWAH
Carnes, Daris Taylor
  Kindergarten Teacher

EVERETTS
Daniels, Edith Council
  Kindergarten/1st Grade Teacher

FAIRMONT
Ellison, Annie Easterling
  7th Grade Teacher
Page, Geneva Ford
  Fourth Grade Teacher

FAISON
Turner, Elizabeth Tart
  6th Grade Teacher

FALLSTON
Patterson, Katherine Beam
  Fourth Grade Teacher

FAYETTEVILLE
Babb, Judy Ingram
  Mathematics Teacher
Beard, Wanda Carter
  Academically Gifted Teacher
Creek, Bondelyn Ann
  Fifth Grade Teacher
Daniels, John W.
  Assistant Principal
Evans, Annette Barnes
  Fifth Grade Teacher
Fipps, Brian Williamson
  Mathematics/Cmptr Prgm Teacher
Guy, Elaine Kelly
  English Teacher
Johnston, Catherie Byrd
  8th Grade Science Teacher
Matthews, Susan B.
  Teacher of Academically Gifted
Mills, Sonia Rose Vidal
  Foreign Language Chair
Morgan, M. Sue
  School Psychologist
Orr, Pauline Bengs
  Third Grade Teacher
Suggs, Nancy J.
  Mathematics Teacher
Worrel, Mary Jo White
  Third Grade Teacher

FOREST CITY
Blanton, Sally Stroud
  Kindergarten Teacher
Carver, Alan Clark
  Government/Economics Teacher
High, Judson Vipperman
  8th Grade History Teacher
Johnson, Donnis Kay
  Math Department Chairman
Norman, Charlotte Parris
  English Teacher
Wall, Deborah Williams
  English Teacher

FORT BRAGG
Wylly, Emily Ryals
  First Grade Teacher

FRANKLIN
Berger, Lee Hollingsworth
  HS English Teacher
Brogden, Zena P. Rickman
  5th Grade Teacher
Margan, David Wallace
  Health/Phys Ed Teacher

Taylor, Emma Jean Downs
  Fifth Grade Teacher
Vinson, Alan Karr
  8th Grade Teacher

FRANKLINTON
Mc Leod, Joyce Lee
  5th Grade Teacher

FRANKLINVILLE
Lednum, Shirley Lineberry
  Third Grade Teacher
Nixon, Mary Louise Rich
  5th Grade Teacher

GASTON
Lowe, Karen Louise
  World Studies Teacher
Ramsey, Louis G.
  7th-8th Grade Science Teacher

GASTONIA
Blackwelder, Joel David Jr.
  6th Grade Teacher
Calhoun, Nancy S.
  Fourth Grade Teacher
Cole, Sharon Carrickhoff
  6th Grade Teacher
Dogan, Mary Kadel
  Sci Teacher/Department Chair
Friend, Craig Thompson
  9th Grade Soc Stud Teacher
Grice, Susan Broome
  5th/6th Grade Teacher
Mc Kenzie, Sharon K.
  Teacher
Rhoton, Patricia T.
  Band Director
Rudisill, Linda Harrill
  Healthful Living Teacher
Simpson, Marie Webber
  Sixth Grade Teacher
Singleton, John Lee
  Science Teacher
White, David Phillips Jr.
  Assistant Principal
Wiggins, Jan Stamey
  Health/Physical Ed Teacher
Wiggins, Robert Wayne
  Physical Education Teacher

GASTONIANOCK
Hanna, Robert Conrad
  English Dept Chairman

GOLDSBORO
Ballance, Sylvia Marie
  English Teacher
Griffin, Susan
  Health & Phys Ed Dept Teacher
Gurganus, Marty Crosswell
  Jr HS Physical Ed Teacher
Jackson, La Rose Blackman
  9th Grade English Teacher
Smith, Jane Peele
  Elementary Counselor
Smith, Vernetta L. T.
  Lang Art/Teacher of Gifted
Uzzell, Melba Smith
  First Grade Teacher Chair

GRAHAM
Eason, John Francis Jr.
  Fifth Grade Teacher
Fuqua, David Berkley
  Accounting Teacher/Vice Prin
Holdren, Robert Earl
  Music Teacher/Department Chair
Loy, Linda Mann
  Lang Art Demonstration Teacher
Miller, Alice Blackmon
  5th Grade Teacher
Pleasant, Elizabeth Hoffman
  5th Grade Teacher
Sue, Elizabeth
  Spanish Teacher

GRANITE FALLS
Gersch, Diann
  Teacher
Smith, Dan R.
  Fourth Grade Teacher

GREENSBORO
Auman, Lynn Everage
  Instrumental Music Teacher
Brandon, Genua O'Neal
  6th Grade Soc Stud/Eng Teacher
Feeney, Thomas R.
  Ag Science/Biology Teacher
Hackett, Carolyn Ebhardt
  Language Arts Teacher
Harris, Gwendolyn Tipp
  First Grade Teacher
Jacobs, Elsie Lee
  Fifth Grade Teacher
Johnson, Angela Sharpe
  English Department Chair

Lenna, Brenda Williams
  5th/6th Grade Teacher
Light, Bette Hendrix
  Kindergarten Teacher
Lowry, Pamela Tucker
  8th Grade Teacher
McKinney, William Anthony
  Supervisor
Outlaw, Martha Bullock
  Eng as Second Language Teacher
Patnaud, Mary Chisholm
  Language Arts Teacher
Shook, Brucie Anne Parcell
  Media Specialist
Somers, Kathleen Snyder
  Commercial Foods Teacher
Wallace, Valeria Hedrick
  Third Grade Teacher
Williams, Sandra Jackson
  Counselor

GREENVILLE
Fowler, William Newton Jr.
  English Teacher
Pearce, James Alan
  English Teacher
Phillips, Randy S.
  Health/Phys Ed Teacher
Powers, Margaret Swaim
  Mathematics Department Chair

GRIFTON
Bullock, Shelby Vann
  Kindergarten Teacher
Coward, Earlene Ward
  Sci Dept Chm/8th Grade Teacher
Rice, Shirley Exum
  4th Grade Teacher

HALLSBORO
Sellers, Linda Baysdon
  5th Grade Teacher
Stines, Susan Munn
  Mathematics Teacher

HAMLET
Phelan, Andrew C. Jr.
  Mathematics & History Teacher

HAMPTONVILLE
Davis, Judy Crews
  Fifth Grade Teacher

HARKERS ISLAND
Beasley, Hannah Nelson
  8th Grade Mathematics Teacher
Guthrie, Frankie
  Math Teacher

HAVELOCK
Joyner, Patricia Fennessey
  Counselor
Siler, David C.
  Math Teacher/Athletic Trainer
Wilder, Barbar Gaskin
  Third Grade Teacher

HAYESVILLE
Anderson, Betty Davis
  Kindergarten Teacher

HENDERSON
Bullock, Annie Powell
  Science Department Chairperson
Faucette, Carolyn Chavis
  English Teacher
Fuller, Henrietta Cheek
  Fifth Grade Teacher
Hargrove, Glendora Small
  Team Leader/Math Teacher
Price, Peggy Reavis
  Kindergarten Teacher
Sadler, John Wavley Jr.
  Teacher of Academically Gifted
Terry, Michael Darnell
  7th Grade Physical Ed Teacher

HENDERSONVILLE
Brewer, Carolyn Groover
  Third Grade Teacher
Carter, Lynn Davis
  English Teacher
Jarrin, Mariano
  Spanish Teacher
Jones, David L.
  Third Grade Teacher

HERTFORD
Felton, Lloyd S.
  Science Teacher

HICKORY
Crooks, Evelyn Isenhour
  Fifth Grade Teacher
Elder, Margo Mitchell Lawson
  Seventh Grade Teacher
Hudson, Julia Treece
  Mathematics Teacher
Reinhardt, Jennifer Robin Taylor
  3rd/4th Grade Teacher

Williams, Trina Cornwell
  Scndry Bus Ed Teacher

HIDDENITE
Norton, Elaine Connolly
  7th/8th Grade Lang Art Teacher

HIGH POINT
Arnold, Don George
  French Teacher/Lang Dept Chair
Bobb, Katherine Jean Rudnicki
  First Grade Teacher
Bragoz, Lloyd Thomas
  English & Humanities Teacher
Meachum, Tony Franklin
  History Teacher
Moffitt, Terry Ervin
  Government/Ec/Academic Dean
Tate, Elizabeth Deal
  Mathematics Teacher
Yokley, W. Keith
  English Dept Chair

HIGHLANDS
Bryson, Margaret Vinson
  Language Arts Teacher
De Wolf, Margaret Jane Evans
  Mathematics Department Chair

HILLSBOROUGH
Braddy, Esqurido Bradsher
  English Teacher
Hamlin, Elizabeth Forrest
  Fr Teacher/Foreign Lang Chair
Rector, Melody Herman
  Marketing Teacher
Watters, Linda Brooks
  Fourth Grade Teacher
Williams, Jocelyn Jones
  Reading Teacher

HOLLY RIDGE
Garvey, Polly Foster
  10th Grade English Teacher

HOPE MILLS
Carter, Edna Melvin
  Fifth Grade Teacher
Daris, Patricia Jackson
  English I/Drama Teacher
Faucett, Sharon Lee
  Orchestra Director
Hall, Denise Dove
  Media Coordinator

HORSE SHOE
Poole, Rebecca Ingram
  Sixth Grade Teacher

HUDSON
Carson, Arden C.
  Band Director
Reese, Jasper Bernie
  Math Department Teacher
Wilson, Anita Freeze
  4th Grade Teacher

HUNTERSVILLE
Deal, Shirley Mayberry
  Marketing Ed Teacher

ICARD
Hefner, Rory Pruette
  Math Teacher
Mc Daniel, Janet Barber
  8th Grade Science Teacher
Nichols, Wynelle Whisnant
  Social Studies Chairperson

IRON STATION
Detter, Carla Renee
  Lang Arts/Soc Stud Teacher

JACKSONVILLE
Alexandar, Linda Fioriti
  Third Grade Teacher
Batchelor, Cathie Dieckmann
  Fifth Grade Lang Arts Teacher
Connolly, Alice Langston
  Retired Teacher/Substitute
Guthrie, Sheila Baysden
  Teacher/Math Dept Chairperson
Mc Clain, Bobby L.
  Teacher/Soc Stud Dept Chairman
Moore, Jacqueline Gray
  4th Grade Teacher/Chairman
Raynor, Dolores Lanier
  English/Reading Teacher
Rohner, Emma Lou Newman
  Kindergarten Teacher/Chair
Warren, Martha Melton
  Career Exploration Teacher
White, Deloris Elizabeth
  7th Grade English Teacher

JAMESTOWN
Patterson, Samuel Latham Jr.
  Lang Art/Soc Stud Teacher

JAMESVILLE
Wilson, Gail Purvis
  English Department Chairman

JEFFERSON
Blevins, Maxine Weaver
  Sixth Grade Teacher
Hurley, Ina Worth
  Fifth Grade Teacher
Phipps, Harold W.
  English Teacher

JONESVILLE
Drum, Sue Martin
  Fourth Grade Teacher
Swaim, Gary G.
  7th-8th Grade Teacher

KANNAPOLIS
Bowman, Amy Harris
  Math Teacher
Goodnight, Judy Davis
  Sixth Grade Teacher
Harwood, Carolyn Fite
  Fifth Grade Teacher
Rebhan, Dottie Ann
  6th Grade Teacher

KENANSVILLE
Alphin, Ann Byrd
  Fifth Grade Teacher
Outlaw, Nancy Marion
  8th Grade Teacher

KING
Boyles, Cynthia King
  Social Studies/Science Teacher
Goldsmith, Mary Gillespie
  Second Grade Teacher
Joyce, Janet M.
  Language Arts Teacher/Chair
Shaw, Michael Irving
  Science Teacher

KINGS MOUNTAIN
Clark, Alton Bruce
  10th-12th Grade His Teacher
Gibson, Judy B.
  Mathematics Teacher
Wood, Julia Woods
  Gifted English Teacher

KINSTON
Brown, Betty Lou Williams
  Kindergarten Teacher
Cousins, Catherine Worthington
  Seventh Grade Math Teacher
Hamm, Billy M. Jr.
  8th Grade Soc Stud Teacher
Hardy, Mary Civils
  1st Grade Teacher
High, Dorothy Jean
  5th Grade Teacher
Hill, Jean Carolyn
  First Grade Teacher
Jenkins, Thelma Miller
  Home Economics Teacher
Moseley, Cassandra Lane
  Fourth Grade Teacher
Parks, Mary Patrick
  Fourth Grade Teacher
Vernon, Jane Harper
  Music Teacher
Williams, Rainelle Tilley
  8th Grade Science Teacher

LAKE TOXAWAY
Kirby, Carrie Hutchinson
  Media Coordinator

LAUREL HILL
Salzer, Deborah Davis
  8th Grade English Teacher

LAURINBURG
Busko, Sarah Watson
  Second Grade Teacher
Lee, Gail B.
  Lead Reading Teacher
Mc Dougald, La Verne Lomax
  10th Grade Counselor

LAWNDALE
White, Connie Cook
  Science Teacher

LENOIR
Anderson, Jackie Refoar
  7th Grade Lang Art Teacher
Miller, Dorothy Freeman
  Fifth Grade Teacher
Seaver, Danny Wade
  Mathematics Teacher
Whitener, R. Edgar
  Director of Bands
Whitman, Jill Triplett
  Kindergarten Teacher

LEXINGTON

Craver, Judy Foster
Mathematics Teacher
Everhart, Stephen Daniel
Mathematics/Algebra I Teacher
Gobble, Jeffrey S.
8th Grade Soc Stud Teacher
Goodrich, Timothy Ward
His/Drafting/Chem Teacher
Johnson, Walter Bruce
Spanish Teacher
Myers, Rebecca Coppley
Lang Art/Soc Stud Teacher
Norred, Nora Hawkins
Social Studies Teacher
Sink, Leona Owens
Soc Stud/Phys Ed Teacher
Swicegood, Nancy Parnell
Algebra & Geometry Teacher
Tonsor, Diana Thomas
Phys Ed-Health Teacher

LIBERTY

Brooks, Mary Earline Alston
Kindergarten Teacher

LINCOLNTON

Cornwell, Debra Hoover
First Grade Teacher
Cornwell, Diane Andersen
6th Grade Math/Science Teacher
Micol, Raymond Thomas
7th Grade Sci/Health Teacher
Poe, Cindy Mullen
Principal
Wise, Elizabeth Leonard
7th Grade Mathematics Teacher

LITTLETON

Anderson, Margaret Page
Counselor
High, Barbara Jean
English/Journalism Teacher
Wells, Angelus Bracey
Third Grade Teacher

LOUISBURG

Harris, Pamela Burnette
5th-6th Grade Teacher

LUMBERTON

Britt, Nancy Carolyn Burns
First Grade Teacher
King, Shirley Deberry
Primary Reading Teacher/Asst
Simmons, Lucy Barker
Fifth Grade Teacher
Smith, Jacqueline Kay
3rd Grade Teacher

MAIDEN

Van Hoy, Nan Nichols
Science/Mathematics Teacher

MANTEO

Basnight, Stephen G. III
Amer His Teacher/Ftbl Coach
Overstreet, Catherine Marshall
Mathematics & Biology Teacher

MARION

Hardy, Debra Ross
Science Department Chairperson
Mc Entire, Merrill Joe
Arts Chairperson
Rabb, Ann Coleman
Science Department Chair

MARS HILL

Ballard, Betty Peek
3rd Grade Teacher
Briggs, Jamie Redmon
Kindergarten Teacher
Kramer, Connie Noblin
Seventh Grade Teacher
Thomas, Peggy Ammons
Eighth Grade Teacher

MARSHALL

Christie, Marla Cox
English/Journalism Teacher
Karpenko, Jennifer Perry
French Teacher
Sprinkle, Mary Elizabeth Chandler
Biology Teacher

MARSHVILLE

Cannon, Jerome Edward
Social Studies Teacher
Hyatt, Donna Fowler
Chemistry/Physics Teacher
Smith, Elizabeth Faulkner
Third Grade Teacher
Stegall, Ruby Waters
First Grade Teacher
Wiesendanger, Betty Griffin
English/Language Arts Teacher
Yarbrough, Hazel Hill
Lang Art/Soc Stud Coordinator

MATTHEWS

Greene, Wanda Ross
Math Teacher
Hemby, Sarah Dickens
8th Gr Math/Pre-Algbra Teacher
Williams, Deborah Anderson
First Grade Teacher

MAYSVILLE

Tabor, Janice Hinson
6th Grade Language Art & Sci

MICRO

Wooten, Pamela Johnson
Science, Math, Health Teacher

MILLERS CREEK

Benton, Richard Haze
Fourth Grade Teacher
Brooks, James Anthony
Eng/Latin/Journalism Teacher

MOCKSVILLE

Corriher, Carolyn Treece
Honors English Teacher
Everett, Eva Savage
Kindergarten Teacher
Leagans, Wanda Kitchings
Second Grade Teacher
Steele, Darrell Grant
History Teacher

MONROE

Baker, Janet Teague
Sixth Grade Teacher
Bateman, Rosanne Cunningham
Curriculum Specialist
Elliot, Mary Williams
6th-8th Grade Reading Teacher
Fisk, Nancy Dupuy
8th Grade Lang Arts Teacher
Hawkins, Robert Neil
Asst Principal/Science Teacher
Medlin, Wanda Hinson
5th Grade Teacher
Trull, Sharon Rollins
Business Education Teacher

MOORESVILLE

Brawley, Vicki Davis
1st Grade Teacher
Cooke, Mary Lois
Fifth Grade Teacher

MOREHEAD CITY

Kight, Laurie Ann
Soc Stud Dept Chairperson

MORGANTON

Freeman, Georgia Ann
6th Grade Teacher
Gober, Deborah Ann
Mathematics Teacher
Harris, Michael Alonzo
HS Mathematics Teacher
Keller, Christina Harris
First Grade Teacher
Miller, Mattie Elinora Brittain
Third Grade Teacher
Walsh, Mary Rheta
Fourth & Fifth Grade Teacher
Ward, Blenda Richards
Observer/Evaluator

MORVEN

Caudle, Cornelia Gaddy
1st Grade Teacher

MOUNT AIRY

Corder, Julie Fleck
Fourth Grade Teacher
Kirkman, Joseph Roy
Teacher of Academically Gifted
Lynch, Robert Stephen
Mathematics Department Teacher
Poore, Mitzi Draughn
Business Teacher
Williamson, Scarlet Doirk
Third Grade Teacher

MOUNT GILEAD

Greene, Erie L.
Job Placement Teacher/Cnslr
Sanders, Ruby Cowand
English IV Teacher
Sells, Barbara Holt
English Teacher
Thompson, Linda Baxter
Elementary Spanish Teacher
Williams, Billy Craig
Health/Phys Ed Teacher

MOUNT HOLLY

Reese, Mark Allen
Band Director
Sigmon, Nancy Cound
Spanish Teacher

MOUNT OLIVE

Mc Donald, Norma Summerlin
Math Teacher & Dept Chairman

MOUNT ULLA

Whisonant, Mary Dawkins
Third Grade Teacher

MURFRESBORO

Pierce, Linda Davis
7th Grade Lang Arts Teacher
Wilder, Dorothy Bunche
Eng/Soc Stud/Rdng Teacher

MURPHY

Bailey, Tamala Graham
Eighth Grade Teacher
Hedrick, Jeanette Farmer
Fifth Grade Teacher
Skomp, Lisa Hassfurder
Third Grade Teacher

NASHVILLE

Dew, Ida Louise
Social Studies Teacher
Weaver, Deborah Parris
Kindergarten Teacher

NEW BERN

Burkett, Judith Maides
Sixth Grade Teacher
Chesson, Nan Gardner
Mathematics Teacher
Queen, Diane Sutton
Fifth Grade Teacher

NEWPORT

Baugus, Sharon Pharis
5th Grade Teacher

NEWTON

Carmack, Debbie Everhart
Sixth Grade Teacher
Dillard, Kim Zebulun
Tennis Director
Early, Carla Thompson
Math Teacher
Lambert-Scronce, Katherine L.
English Teacher
Long, Deborah Lynn
Mathematics Dept Chairwoman
Paysour, Michael Glenn
7th-8th Grade Soc Stud Teacher
Ponti, Karen Trivett
Spanish Teacher

NEWTON GROVE

Herring, Patricia Wilson
Third Grade Teacher

NORTH WILKESBORO

Allen, Susan Smith
Language Art Teacher
Mc Gee, Judy Rhodes
Lang Art & Soc Stud Teacher
Mc Grady, Betty Shumate
Fifth Grade Teacher
Pardue, Wanda Mathis
4th Grade Teacher

NORWOOD

Almond, Jackie Lowder
K/1st Grade Teacher

ORRUM

Canady, Joyce Locklear
Jr HS Language Arts Teacher

OTTO

Cabe, Josephine Roper
4th Grade Teacher

PEMBROKE

Emanuel, David Jr.
Mathematics Teacher
Hicks, Annie Mae
Fifth Grade Teacher
Watts, Dennis W.
English Teacher

PIKEVILLE

Mann, Robert Wayne
English Dept Chm/Teacher

PILOT MOUNTAIN

Boyles, Carolyn Sue
Cmptr Science/Soc Stud Teacher
Frans, Charlotte Cox
Lang Art/Soc Stud Teacher

PINETOWN

Owens, Rebecca Foote Smith
Chemistry-Physics Teacher
Rogers, Ann H.
Teacher of Academically Gifted

PITTSBORO

Foust, Henry O.
Spanish Teacher

POPLAR BRANCH

Bowden, Virginia Gallop
5th & 6th Grade Teacher

PRINCETON

Godwin, Gregory Sheldon
Science Department Chairman

PROCTORVILLE

Sanders, Doris Jackson
Third Grade Teacher

RAEFORD

Butler, Joann Mc Cormic
Fourth Grade Teacher
Coleman, Belinda La Verne
Third Grade Teacher
Mc Grady, C. Nadine Sehl
Chemistry/Physics Teacher

RALEIGH

Barker, Judith Stevens
Mathematics Teacher
Brock, Lucy Brannen
Head Science Dept
Carter, Diantha Thomas
6th Grade Teacher
Cazin, Julia A.
Teacher
Frahm, Leslie Edward
7th Grade Math Teacher
Fulcher, Margaret Klein
First Grade Teacher
Jendro, Linda Cowser
Business Education Teacher
Kelly, Amy Addison
Science Teacher/Team Leader
Kennedy, James E. Jr.
11th Grade Eng Paideia Teacher
Kornemann, Anne Chandler
Fourth Grade Teacher
Moore, Tracey La Fevers
Mathematics Teacher
Perry, Joan Gregory
Second Grade Teacher
Potter, Mary Ann Ann Sikkema
English Teacher
Steger, Jan K.
Choral Director
Sturdivant, Betty Mills
Team Leader/7th Grade Teacher

RAMSEUR

Johnson, Louis Howard
Mathematics/Physics Teacher
Mc Lanahan, Bruce David
Bible/History Teacher
Moffitt, Judi Lynn Craven
7th/8th Grade Lang Arts/Soc St
Young, Susan Wentworth
English Teacher

RANDLEMAN

Brooks, Vanessa Payne
7th Grade Teacher
Linthicum, Terry Blaine
English Teacher

RED OAK

Ennis, Lottie Strum
5th Grade Teacher

RED SPRINGS

Huggins, Carla Adams
Language Arts Teacher
Sessoms, Margaret Johnson
Science Teacher

REIDSVILLE

Citty, Gay Smith
5th Grade Teacher
Hill, Larry Thomas
Mathematics Teacher
King, Patricia Everette
Reading Lab Teacher
Rountree, Sherry Hill
Second Grade Teacher
Whitlow, Wanda Chambers
Mathematics Teacher

RICHLANDS

Moore, B. Jeannette
Phys Ed & Health Teacher

ROANOKE RAPIDS

Parker, Nancy S.
Math Teacher

ROBBINSVILLE

Davis, Sara Rogers
Elementary Music Teacher
Haney, David Allan
Science Teacher
Nelson, Douglas Rodney
Physical Education Teacher

ROBERSONVILLE

Bentley, Annie Bond
Lang Art/Soc Stud Teacher

ROCKINGHAM

Deane, Myra Upchurch
Health Occupations Teacher
Garner, Nancy Campbell
Mathematics Teacher
Holland, Jeffrey Dean
Spanish Teacher
Seymour, Ashleigh Mood
Drafting Teacher
Wright, Darrell Lewis
Health, Phys Ed Teacher

ROCKWELL

Wall, Sue Lingle
First Grade Teacher

ROCKY MOUNT

Butler, Marshall E. Jr.
Choral Music Teacher
Harris, Alcester Bryant
Fifth Grade Teacher
Nettnin, Theresa Stubbs
Kindergarten Teacher
Pitt, Dina Cofield
Mathematics Teacher
Read, Sharon Lockwood
Music Teacher

ROCKY POINT

Quinn, Susan Brandt
3rd Grade Teacher

ROLESVILLE

Scarboro, Dolores Alford
Fifth Grade Teacher

ROPER

Bradshaw, Mary Kay Allsbrook
4th-8th Grade Ag Teacher
Bragg, Judith Harrison
Mathematics/Science Teacher

ROSMAN

Henson, Exie Wilde
Third Grade Teacher

ROXBORO

Betterton, Bonnie Harris
Second Grade Teacher
Blanks, Joanne Wade
Social Studies Dept Chairman
Brooks, Angeline Nelson
History/Social Studies Chair
Burke, Deborah Edmundson
Sixth Grade Teacher
Kincaid, Lori Tuck
Social Studies Teacher
Newell, Donna Blaylock
6th Grade Teacher
Spencer, Esther Faulkner
5th/6th Grade Teacher
Tillett, Harriett Jones
Chemistry Teacher

RUTHERFORDTON

King, Joan Edwards
Biology Teacher
Robbins, Sandra Kay Stanley
Science Teacher

SAINT PAULS

Koon, Anne Mitchell
English Teacher/Dept Chair

SANFORD

Berliner, Nancy Kane
Art Instructor
Cope, Nancy R.
Social Studies Teacher/Chair
Denton, Elizabeth Wimberly
Mathematics Teacher
Driggs, Peggy Easton
First Grade Teacher
Ingram, Kathy Durden
History Teacher
Lawson, Ramona Ascough
6th Grade Teacher
London, Regina Martin
Secondary Mathematics Teacher
Maddox, Sharen Ellis
Mathematics Teacher
Martin, Lucille Mumford
Sixth Grade Teacher
Smith, Carol C
Co-op Teacher/Coordinator
Smith, Stuart Davis
English Teacher
Willet, Romona Coggins
Mathematics Teacher

SEVEN SPRINGS

Mozingo, Anne Lynch
7th/8th Grade Teacher

SHALLOTTE

Chandler, Diane F.
Third Grade Teacher

SHELBY

Brown, Anita Long
Spanish Teacher
Elmore, Cara Adrienne
English Teacher
Price, Thomas Fredrick
2nd Grade Teacher
Weathers, Gerald Lee
Mathematics Teacher

SILER CITY

Morris, Judy Weaver
Fifth Grade Teacher

SMITHFIELD

Batten, Jenny Lou
Lang Art/Soc Stud Teacher
Creekmore, Henrietta Hood
Math/Sci/Pre-Algebra Teacher
Deaton, Mary Louise Attayek
Mathematics Teacher/Dept Chair
Jackson, Thomas Roland Jr.
Computer Science Teacher

SNOW HILL

Beaman, Susan Marie
8th Grade Math/Soc St Teacher
Beamon, Claudia Grantham
Third Grade Teacher
Norris, Andrea Harris
Social Studies Teacher/Chair
Welch, Renea Ginn
Counselor
Wyatt, Lorena Moseley
First Grade Teacher

SOUTHERN PINES

Brock, Phyllis Wooten
Business Education Teacher
Currie, William Ronald
6th-7th Grade Teacher
Lampros, Sandy Brewer
Teacher of Academically Gifted

SOUTHPORT

Brooks, Catherine Cabaniss
8th Grade Math Teacher
Furpless, Cathy Segraves
Academically Gifted Teacher
Laugisch, Helen Page
English Teacher

SPARTA

Bare, Mary Dancy
Fourth Grade Teacher

SPENCER

Kennedy, Jean Boyd
English Department Chairperson

SPRING HOPE

Brower, Pat Howard
Kindergarten Teacher
Harris, Charles Benson Jr.
Mathematics/Science Teacher
Wiggs, Christie Early
Ag-Lang Arts/English Teacher

SPRING LAKE

Barefoot, Sallie Holley
Third Grade Teacher
Cashwell, Janice Rogers
Science Department Chair
Pearce, Nancy Beckwith
Orchestra Director

SPRUCE PINE

Myres, Shelley Boone
Fourth Grade Teacher

STANLEY

Bonnell, Sandra Gaye (Horton)
8th/9th Grade Soc Stud Teacher
Mullis, Melanie Hovis
Sixth Grade Teacher
Reese, E. Annette Robertson
Band Director

STATESVILLE

Carter, Virginia Wood
Mathematics Teacher
Dowell, Kelly Johnson
Theatre Arts Teacher
Hamilton, Joseph Elroy
Jr/Sr HS Bible Teacher
Hartsoe, Sherrie Dianne
English Teacher
Lackey, Sherry Harwell
Third Grade Teacher
Lentz, Anne Stone
Fifth Grade Teacher
Lunsford, Betty Templeton
4th/5th Grade Teacher
Moses, Jeanne Kerr
First Grade Teacher
Reep, Linda Cook
7th Grade Lang Art Teacher
Sherck, Linda Carol
Mathematics Teacher

Strickland, Mary Lou
5th Grade Teacher

STONEVILLE

Chambers, Tanis Knight
2nd/3rd Grade Teacher/Coord

SUNBURY

Rountree, Jane Daniels
Second Grade Teacher

SWANNANOA

Talbert, Benjamin Murray
8th Grade English/Lit Teacher
West, Donna Pate
English Teacher
Whittington, Lorin Dale
Choral Dir/Cultural Arts Chair

SWANSBORO

Robinson, Joyce Vinson
First Grade Teacher

SYLVA

Bell, Teresa N.
7th Grade English/Lit Teacher
Burnette, Janice Barnes
Fifth Grade Teacher
Cowan, Linda Barnett
Seventh Grade Teacher
Henke, Kenneth Edward
Assistant Principal
Sutton, Jo Anne Henson
Sixth Grade Teacher

TAR HEEL

Thompson, Susan Kinlaw
Mathematics Teacher

TARBORO

Alexander, Frances Bizzell
Second Grade Teacher

TAYLORSVILLE

Comer, Gary Lynn
Mathematics Department Teacher

THOMASVILLE

Baity, Jane Trimnal
8th Grade Lang Arts Teacher
Bell, Carolyn Robertson
Mathematics Teacher/Dept Chair
Bowser, Nancy Everhart
First Grade Teacher
Crotts, Judy E.
Chapter I Reading Teacher
Drye, Yvonne C.
Business Education Teacher
Eddinger, Harold Wayne
Teacher of the Gifted
Kiger, Judy Calhoun
5th Grade Teacher
Leonard, Jeanne Ebelein
6th Grade Teacher
Minner, Sidney Rodd
Mathematics Teacher
Stephenson, Denise (Lackey)
English Teacher

TOPTON

Bateman, Angelia Morgan
Media Coordinator
Brown, Wanda Stamey
Phys Ed & Health Teacher
Cross, Ronald Gary
Science/Phys Ed Teacher

TRINITY

Canoy, Lisa Scotton
7th Grade Soc Stud Teacher

TROY

Poole, Susan Taylor
Kindergarten Teacher

TUXEDO

Le Var, Pearl Ann (King)
6th Grade Teacher/Librarian

VALDESE

Garrou, Jan Underwood
5th Grade Teacher

VALE

Gladden, Hope Wells
Third Grade Teacher

VANCEBORO

Foster, Nancy Parker
English Teacher

VASS

Frye, Ruth Chilton
Fourth Grade Teacher

VAUGHAN

Rowlett, Barbara Russell
Kindergarten Teacher

WADESBORO

Mabry, Terry Throneburg
Drafting Teacher

WALLBURG

Sink, Diane Williams
Kindergarten Teacher

WALNUT COVE

Cockerham, June W.
English Teacher

WARRENTON

Meek, Janis Gayle (Paynter)
Home Economics Teacher
Stephens, Dexter
7th Grade Lang Art Teacher

WASHINGTON

Chance, Kay Wilson
9th Grade English Teacher
Davis, Barbara Sutton
Mathematics Teacher/Dept Chair
Reddick, Iris Lodge
Fourth Grade Teacher
Swann, Marie Mc Keel
Physical Science Teacher

WAXHAW

Myers, Shannon Kirby
5th Grade Teacher

WAYNESVILLE

Breece, Carolyn Miller
Mathematics Teacher
Conard, Billie Boyd
Health/Physical Ed Teacher
Crouse, Debra Smith
Third Grade Teacher
Ethridge, Linda Kanas
4th Grade Teacher
Hooker, Carolyn Susie
Ag Language Arts Teacher
Howard, Charles Ronald
HS Mathematics Teacher
Painter, Ruth Elizabeth Mincey
First Grade Teacher
Smith, Rebecca-Lynn Swanson
8th Math Teacher
Stamey, Bonnie Matthews
Reading Specialist
Stamey, Eva Carolyn
Sixth Grade Teacher

WEAVERVILLE

Brantley, John Flake
Agriculture Teacher
Bruce, Barbara Cargile
Fourth Grade Teacher
Morgan-Hill, Charlene M.
English/Journalism Teacher
Wyatt, Gary Russell
7th Grade Science Teacher

WELCOME

Sides, Harriet Hartley
Fifth Grade Teacher

WENDELL

Burns, Robert William
Biology Teacher
Lanier, Cheryl Gay
Teacher
Miller, Fanny Knight Gaillard
History Teacher

WENTWORTH

Mabe, Linda Fulton
English Teacher

WHITEVILLE

Barefoot, Farley
Physics Chemistry II Teacher
Paschal, Patricia Kornegay
English/Literature Teacher
Simmons, Kivie Mc Ray
7/8th Grade Lang Arts Teacher
Tedder, Mollie Stevens
Fifth Grade Teacher

WHITTIER

Stillwell, Elizabeth Nell
7th & 8th Grade Teacher

WILKESBORO

Tedder, Gail H.
4th Grade Teacher

WILLARD

Briggs, Eva Mae
Kindergarten Teacher

WILLIAMSTON

Andrews, Mary Roberts
Elementary School Principal

WILMINGTON

Bryant, Doris Jackson
5th Grade Math Teacher
Burnett, Nancy Hanks
Speech/English Teacher
Du Bose, Diane Moore
Second Grade Teacher
Johnson, Myrtle Reasons
Social Studies Teacher

Keifer, Linda Lehr
First Grade Teacher
Koonce, Vonnie Yeager
8th Gr Sci/Cmptr Sci Teacher
Lennon, Vickie Davis
English Teacher
Lucas, Paul LeRoy Jr.
Social Studies Teacher
Mc Millan, Jeanette Mc Glohon
Third Grade Teacher
Murray, Henrietta Underwood
7th Grade Teacher/Soc Stud Dep
Ostby, Nell Mauney
Staff Administrator

WILSON

Darden, Martha Batts
Mainstream Public Sch Teacher
Howard, Ann R.
Biology Teacher
Humphrey, Mary Sue F.
Teacher of the Deaf
Massey, Jo Ann Anne
Soc Stud Teacher/Chairperson
Mercer, Karen Moore
Speech/Lang Pathologist/Coord

WILSONS MILLS

Gemmell, Emma Alice Avera
Kindergarten Teacher

WINDSOR

Byrum, Kaye M.
7th/8th Grade Teacher
Rascoe, Camille Holmes
Business Education Teacher

WINFALL

Meads, Sarah Agnes (Ownley)
Fifth Grade Teacher
Morring, Dorothy Wilson
Kindergarten Teacher

WINGATE

Hume, Marian Ruby
Fifth Grade Teacher

WINSTON-SALEM

Bernheim, David Mayer
Theatre Arts Director/Teacher
Caesar, Jeannene Farrow
Third Grade Teacher
Davis, Inez
Mathematics Instructor
Jenkins, Sylvia L.
Third Grade Teacher
Kimbrough, Valinda Carter
Mathematics Teacher
Muse, Michael G.
Physical Education Teacher
Tow, Shellie W.
7th/8th Grade Science Teacher
Woodle, H. Loraine
7th-8th Grade Math Teacher

WINTON

Powell, Elsie Hall
Fifth Grade Teacher

YADKINVILLE

Allred, Kathryn Redmon
6th Grade Math/Science Teacher
Miller, Wanda Haire
Third/Fourth Grade Teacher
Rooks, Brenda Hamby
Teacher
Shermer, Ruth Dobbins
7th & 8th Grade Math Teacher

ZEBULON

Wilder, Peggy Lee
Fourth Grade Teacher

NORTH DAKOTA

ANAMOOSE

Burckhard, Rhonda Britsch
English Teacher/Librarian

BALTA

Johnson, Dawn Renee
Math/Computer Dept Chair

BELCOURT

Davis, Steve
Fifth Grade Teacher
Leonard, Margaret Jean
Business Teacher
Palm, Violet Elaine
Science Teacher

BERTHOLD

Debertin, Richard Harold
Agricultural Education Teacher

BISMARCK

Fricke, Donna Nadeane Silbernagel
Marketing Teacher
Halling, Stanley D.
Life Science Teacher
Hruby, Dale
Vocational Agriculture Instr
Laches, Robert Duane
Electronics Technology Instr
Ohm, Betty T.
3rd Grade Elementary Teacher
Reimers, Faye Neil
Second Grade Teacher
Roth, Duane
6th Grade Teacher
Souther, Neil Clifford
Latin Teacher

BOTTINEAU

Caroline, Phyllis Elaine
2nd Grade Teacher
Johnson, Lynette Eileen (Geizler)
Fourth Grade Teacher
Nelson, Debra Lynn (Mc Nea)
7th/8th Grade Science Teacher

BOWMAN

Beyer, Sara La Setta (Schutz)
Spanish & English Teacher
Meschke, Dorothy Domagala
5th/6th Grade Lang Art Teacher
Ziemann, Jack Eldor
Jr HS Mathematics Teacher

BURLINGTON

Petrik, Rebecca Calvert
Music Teacher

CANDO

Fuchsgruber, Bernice Dahl
Retired 2nd Grade Teacher

CARRINGTON

Frahm, Kristi
English Teacher

CENTER

Kuehn, Remae L.
Bus/Office Education Teacher

CROSBY

Buck, Connie Seiffert
2nd Grade Teacher
Redlin, Robert P.
Junior High Teacher

DEERING

Andrist, Johanne Wright
3rd/4th Grade Teacher

DEVILS LAKE

Stein, Shirley Tatley
First Grade Teacher

DICKINSON

Derner, Janet Mary
English Teacher/Dept Head
Ficek, Ernest Joseph
Phys Education/Health Teacher
Jacobsen, Susan Kay (Ness)
5th Grade Teacher
Rafferty, Larry Dean
Mathematics Teacher
Reep, Vincent Scott
6th Grade Teacher

DONNYBROOK

Zander, Diane Sedevie
5th/6th Grade Teacher/Prin

DUNSEITH

Good, Randal Dean
Social Science Teacher/Chair

EMERADO

Quick, Wayne S.
3rd Grade Teacher

FARGO

Bullard, Susan Lee
TV Production Teacher
Kiesz, Margaret (Swenson)
Retired Teacher
Murie, Craig Robert
Mathematics Teacher
Scott, Kathlyn Jane
Spanish Teacher
Sullivan, Thomas E.
Science Teacher

GACKLE

Seymour, Stephen Franklin
Science Educator

GARRISON

Schneider, Duane Le Roy
Science Teacher

GOLDEN VALLEY

Beckwith, Maxine Huber
Secondary Prin/Bus Teacher

GOODRICH
Erdmann, La Donna Lynn (Benge)
　Mathematics/Computer Teacher
Faul, Audrey Ann (Kerr)
　Chapter I Teacher/Elem Prin
Olson, Doug James
　Soc Stud/Physical Ed Teacher

GRAND FORKS
Cameron, Bonnie Rose
　6th Grade Teacher
Janes, Allen L.
　Mathematics Teacher
Kulack, Robert John
　Social Studies Dept Chair

HARVEY
Bartz, Laurie Gunlikson
　Business/Phys Ed Teacher

HAZELTON
Weiser, Sharon Deseth
　Teacher

HAZEN
Rohde, Charlotte Schettler
　Second Grade Teacher

HETTINGER
Albert, Pamela Jo
　5th Grade Teacher
Smith, Bonnie M.
　English/Drama Teacher
Wilz, Gary Allan
　Science Teacher

HILLSBORO
Freeland, Judith M.
　5th & 6th Grade Dept Teacher

JAMESTOWN
Nannenga, Donna Mae Coombs
　Orchestra Teacher
Wilson, Eileen Lilleoien
　4th Grade Teacher

KENMARE
Munson, Alan W.
　Math/Computer Science Teacher

KINDRED
Dybing, Myron Jay
　HS Music/Math Teacher

LISBON
Bjerke, Marie Bot
　English Instructor/Dept Chair

MANDAN
Appert, Leo Stephen
　Sixth Grade Teacher
Batterberry, Shawn Norman
　Social Studies Teacher
Hanson, Donald Christian
　Mathematics Teacher
House, Leon Harold
　Science Teacher
Kary, Leon James
　Social Studies Teacher
Lacher, Mary Sue Sadowsky
　2nd Grade Teacher
Rogers, Debra Blanc
　Vocal Music Teacher
Stockdill, Owen Wayne
　5th Grade Teacher
Thiel, Marion Marquart
　4th-6th Grade Teacher

MANVEL
Rose, Barbara L.
　Third Grade Teacher

MENOKEN
Kiser, Glenda Walters
　Teacher/Principal

MINOT
Berve, Leslie Jo Jenkinson
　English/Theatre/Speech Teacher
Bredahl, Roger D.
　6th Grade Teacher/Asst Prin
Feist, Kathy Ross
　Fourth Grade Teacher
Hanson, Linda Hoppe
　First Grade Teacher
Hunsaid, Ann Berg (Nagel)
　Language Art Teacher
Jaeger, Julie D.
　Math/Language/Rdng Teacher
Jorgenson, Pat S.
　Fifth Grade Teacher
Sande, Sandra Lee (Norton)
　8th Eng Teacher & Dept Chair

NAPOLEON
Hilzendeger, Maggie
　Third Grade Teacher

NEW ENGLAND
Warbis, Meda Catchpole
　Math/Cmptr Sci Teacher

NEW LEIPZIG
Gruebele, Shirley Ann (Heim)
　3rd/4th Grade Teacher

NORTONVILLE
Hehr, La Rae Kay (Schulz)
　4th-6th Grade Teacher/Prin

OAKES
Kendall, James E.
　English Teacher
Weseloh, Vivian Unseth
　3rd Grade Teacher

PARSHALL
Grueneich, Mark Elliot
　Principal/Teacher/Coach

PEMBINA
Defoe, Nancy L.
　Second Grade Teacher/Elem Prin
Rohloff, Arnold James
　Sixth Grade Teacher

PETERSBURG
Graupe, Mark D.
　Physical Ed/Math Teacher

PLAZA
Kjos, Doug Glen
　Science/Computer Sci Teacher

SHERWOOD
Keith, Arlyn Dale
　Science Teacher
Morris, Timothy L.
　Math/Cmptr Sci/Physics Teacher
Pearson, Nancy Mollins
　Communications Teacher

STANLEY
Enget, Maureen Salo
　Home Economics Instructor
Solberg, Barbara Varberg
　7-8th Eng/9th Grade Teacher

STEELE
Webster, Bradley Newman
　English Teacher

STRASBURG
Eiseman, James John
　High School Principal

SURREY
Homsey, Thomas
　Phys Ed/Drivers Ed Teacher
Mc Conn, Mable Balinda Narum
　Second Grade Teacher

TOLNA
Forde, Roger Dean
　6th Grade Teacher

TOWNER
Zeigler, Kevin Martin
　Science Teacher

TRENTON
Rasch, Kelly Lynn
　HS Principal/Business Teacher

VALLEY CITY
Birchem, Maureen Goggin
　Teacher
Birchem, Ronald Nicholas
　History Teacher
Bultema, Harlan G.
　Fifth Grade Teacher
King, Nancy Kay
　Coord Health Occupations Instr
Rowekamp, Cheryl L. (Foss)
　5th-6th Grade Teacher
Schmidt, Jo Ann Irene
　LD Teacher
Stanford, Madonna Boehm
　Substitute Teacher

WAHPETON
Mc Daniel, Judith E.
　Office Technology/Bus Instr
Reubish, Gary Richard
　7th Grade Lang Arts Teacher
Wilson, Patrice Berhow
　Fourth Grade Teacher

WALHALLA
Benjaminson, Connie Anderson
　Third Grade Teacher
Nilsson, Gary Duane
　Jr/Sr HS Principal
Von Ruden, Denise Kay
　Mathematics/Computer Teacher

WASHBURN
Phillips, Lesley A. (Romanick)
　HS Mathematics Instructor

WEST FARGO
Olson, Betty Elmer
　Chapter I Teacher/Asst Prin

Simmons, Marti J. J.
　Coordinator of Gifted/Talented

WESTHOPE
Gullicks, Kristine Ronning
　First Grade Teacher

WILLISTON
Anderson, Loren C.
　English Teacher
Greutman, Richard Paul
　Social Studies Teacher
Healy, Dennis F.
　Social Studies/PE Teacher
Kraft, Judy A.
　English Teacher
Larsen, Larry Duane
　Futurism Teacher
Lobsinger, Beverly J. (Olson)
　2nd Grade Teacher
Moore, Linda Mae (Jenner)
　First Grade Teacher
Morgan, Shelly J.
　7th Grade English Teacher
Vossler, James Alan
　Mathematics Teacher

WILTON
Johnson, Erling Roger
　Guidance Counselor

WIMBLEDON
Goehring, Rebecca Susan
　Elementary Principal
Richards, Roleen Ussatis
　Fourth Grade Teacher

WING
Michelsen, William C.
　HS Mathematics Teacher

WOLFORD
Zavada, Debra Graber
　Basic Skills Teacher

ZAP
Becker, James J.
　Mathematics/Computer Teacher

ZEELAND
Bruning, Harold
　Jr HS Teacher

OHIO

ADA
Berger, Myra Sue
　2nd Grade Teacher
Hawkins, Charles H.
　History Teacher
Straub, Marybob Hogenkamp
　Spanish Teacher

ADENA
Elliott, Jane Ann
　First Grade Teacher

AKRON
Austin, Alice Blackman
　English Advisor/Communications
Frola, Cynthia Cipolloni
　English Teacher
Goffee, Kimberly Dawn (Thornton)
　Mathematics Teacher
Johnson, Beverly Annise Butler
　Reading Teacher
Kee, Mary V.
　7-8th Grade Teacher
Lindgren, Nina B.
　English Teacher/English Chair
Masidonski, Beverly Bendure
　President
Pletikapich, Penny Callas
　6th Grade Teacher
Sanders, Wayne II
　Sixth Grade Teacher
Taylor, Nancy Wakeman
　5th Grade Teacher

ALLIANCE
Berube, Janice Lee (Wood)
　Senior English/Speech Teacher
Campbell, Jean Marie
　English Teacher
Hempstead, Linda R.
　French Teacher
Hobbs, Rebekah
　5th Grade Teacher
Whetstone, Paula Gligor
　Retired Elementary Teacher

AMANDA
Musser, Antoinette Louise Angle
　Third Grade Teacher
Snoke, Sheila Hardie
　5th/6th Grade Teacher

Tilley, W. Carolyn Hughes
　6th Grade Teacher

AMHERST
Zellers, Joseph Michael
　6th Grade Teacher

ANNA
Davies, Beverly Jean
　2nd & 3rd Grade Teacher
Putnam, Keith Lee
　Science Teacher

ANSONIA
Hemer, Nancy Pearson
　4th Grade Teacher
Hemmerich, Carol Jean
　7th/8th Grade English Teacher
Lumpkin, Darlene Scholl
　5th Grade Teacher
Spencer, Rex L.
　Soc Stud Teacher & Dept Chmn

ANTWERP
Tavierne, Debra Marie (Driver)
　Special Education Teacher

ARCANUM
Brunswick, Lori Ann
　Social Studies/Health Teacher
Delk, Jennie Lee Groff
　Fourth Grade Teacher
Gruell, Todd
　US History Teacher
Handshoe, Garry
　Teacher
Judy, Lois Jean
　6th Grade English Teacher
Kelly, Martha Jean (Mc Coy)
　Science Teacher

ARCHBOLD
Keim, Margret Aughbaugh
　5th Grade Lang Art Teacher

ARLINGTON
Rader, Rachel Oman
　Mathematics/Computer Teacher

ASHLAND
Cutrer, Kenneth E.
　Social Studies Teacher
Edmondson, Joe-Ann
　First Grade Teacher
Green, Loren R.
　Sixth Grade Teacher
Henikman, Robert Harold
　Jr High Art Teacher
Rinehart, Janet Klingensmith
　6th Grade Teacher
Spellman, Peggy Price
　3rd Grade Teacher
Whitmore, Craig Steven
　8th Grade English Teacher

ASHTABULA
Cooley, Blanche B.
　Third Grade Teacher
Coxe, Eloise Amenta
　Supervisor Enrichment/Gifted
Edixon, Frances Aileen
　English Teacher
Fazenbaker, Allen R.
　Science Teacher
Ferritto, Dora Turano
　Second Grade Teacher
Kortyka, Dennis L.
　Art Teacher
Mc Gill, Darlene Jo (Dean)
　Reading Teacher
Patterson, Cindy Lou
　Foreign Language Teacher

ASHVILLE
Pickering, James Leslie
　8th Grade Amer History Teacher
Truex, Patty Ankrom
　6th Grade Teacher

ATTICA
Binninger, Patricia Baker
　English Teacher
Lamoreaux, Frank C.
　English Teacher

ATWATER
Hadinger, Donna Ruth
　Fourth Grade Teacher
Harcar, Raymond Andrew
　Instrumental Music Teacher

AUGUSTA
Perry, Ruth Queen
　Third Grade Teacher

AURORA
Dyer, Daniel Osborn
　English Teacher

AUSTINTOWN
Machuga, Sharon Rose
　Second Grade Teacher
Zoccalli, Anthony Joseph
　Asst Principal

AVON
Herbst, Helen Gertrude
　Music/Liturgy Coordinator

AVON LAKE
Kloc, Sheila Schweitzer
　Second Grade Teacher

BALTIMORE
Perdue, Nancy Crockett
　English Teacher

BARBERTON
Hurbean, Jean Mary
　Second Grade Teacher
Irish, Alice Mc Cloud
　Science/Gifted Teacher
Sitzlar, Denise Elaine
　6th Grade Teacher

BARNESVILLE
Davis, Darrell Edward II
　Business Education Teacher

BASCOM
Cramer, Ann M.
　Social Studies Teacher
Rouser, Sandra Mae (Baker)
　Business Education Teacher
Sendelbach, Nova Madeline (Haugh)
　Art Teacher
Steyer, Robert Eugene
　Mathematics Teacher
Warrington, Gloria Bodell
　First Grade Teacher

BATAVIA
Lewis, Lawrence R.
　Science Teacher
Richmond, Camm Halladay
　Social Studies Teacher
Steidle, Laura Stocker
　8th Grade Reading Teacher

BAY VILLAGE
Firich, Jean
　English Teacher
Nemec, Beverly Louise
　Elementary Principal
Starr, Joan of Arc HM
　Retired Teacher

BEACHWOOD
Hirschfeld, Margaret Abt
　5th-8th Grade Lang Art Teacher

BEALLSVILLE
Eikleberry, Janet Kauskey
　Third Grade Teacher
Venick, John Joseph
　Social Science Department Chm

BEAVERCREEK
Dearwester, James Edward
　HS Soc Stud Teacher
Fisher, Michael
　Teacher
Little, Richard William
　Fifth Grade Teacher
Starrett, William Grant
　Social Studies Teacher

BELLAIRE
Jepson, Mary Jo Meyers
　Secondary English Teacher
Kyanko, Carolyn Marie
　Principal
Mc Vey, Phyllis Jane
　Chapter I Teacher
Rataiczak, Thomas Edward
　Engish Teacher & Dept Chm

BELLE CENTER
Sheeley, Sharon K. (Grunden)
　Second Grade Teacher

BELLEFONTAINE
Harman, Beth
　5th Grade Teacher
Henry, Kathryn Ann (Marsh)
　Chapter I Reading
Ramsey, Kathryn Bradley
　4th Grade Teacher
Reames, Spencer Eugene
　Science Department Chair
Shaffer, Frankie Watkins
　Business Education Instructor

BELLEVUE
Lochotzki, Mary Paula SND
　8th Grade Jr HS Teacher
Sarty, Mary Jane (Loparo)
　Second Grade Teacher
Westerhold, Patricia (Rupp)
　Science Department Chair

BELMONT
Bartels, Michael Stanley
  Jr HS Soc Stud Chairperson
Miller, Stuart Earl
  7th/8th Grade Science Teacher
Sketel, Amie Lynn (Nelms)
  Mathematics Teacher
BELOIT
Fox, Shirley Myers
  Third Grade Teacher
BELPRE
Arnold, June King
  Sixth Grade Teacher
Hughes, Debbie A.
  7th Grade Rdng/Soc Std Teacher
BEREA
Bettendorf, Victoria
  English/Math/Reading Teacher
Thomas, Faye E. Johnson
  Fifth Grade Teacher
BERLIN CENTER
Owen, Harry David
  Science Teacher
BETHEL
Hauke, William A.
  6th Grade Mathematics Teacher
Herald, Imogene
  Social Studies Teacher
Wenzel, Patricia Ruggles
  6th Grade Lang Art Teacher
BETTSVILLE
Barth, Debra Jayne
  English Teacher
BEVERLY
Bahen, Dennis M.
  7th-8th Grade Soc Stud Teacher
Mc Cormick, Nancy Sands
  4th-6th Grade Elem Teacher
Miller, Nancy A.
  Mathematics Teacher
Moegling, Lawrence Anthony
  Spanish Teacher
Spearman, Teresa Foland
  Language Arts/Speech Teacher
BEXLEY
King, Thomas C.
  Teacher of Gifted
BLANCHESTER
Winkle, Alice Marie
  Jr HS Reading Teacher
BLOOMDALE
Ault, Diane Anderson
  Mathematics Teacher
Gross, Richard Allen
  Science/Health Dept Chair
BOARDMAN
Bender, Yvonne Nevada
  English Teacher
Darnell, Rosalind Michele Dolovy
  Third Grade Teacher
Nybell, Carolyn A.
  8th Grade English/Rdng Teacher
Patterson, Roger L.
  Mathematics Teacher
Sampson, Sally Ann Sweesy
  French/English Teacher
Shively, M. Scott
  Biology Teacher
Sullivan, Edward Lawrence
  Guidance Counselor
BOTKINS
Heitbrink, Margaret Wenning
  High School Science Teacher
BOWERSTON
Lada, Judson Ray
  Guidance Counselor
BOWERSVILLE
Gross, Roxie Marcum
  Third Grade Teacher
Gross, Roxie Marcum
  Third Grade Teacher
BOWLING GREEN
Diehl, Alta A.
  Second Grade Teacher
Laukhuf, Betty L.
  4-6th Grade Tlnted/Gft Teacher
St Clair, Jo (Diaz)
  8th Grade English Teacher
BRADFORD
Marker, Kathy Lynette
  Science, Biology Teacher
BRECKVILLE
Schoenlein, Karen Klemencic
  Fourth Grade Teacher

BRIDGEPORT
Marty, George Allan
  HS Mathematics Teacher
Myers, Roger William
  Mathematics Department Teacher
BRISTOLVILLE
Diehl, John L.
  Business Education Chair
Hiestand, Larry D.
  Jr HS & High School Teacher
Richards, Joan Shrodek
  2nd Grade Teacher
BRUNSWICK
Cox, Patricia Lee Stavrakis
  Teacher/Mentor-English
Mc Fadden, Pamela Echols
  8th Grade English Teacher
Mc Intyre, Sheila (Himmel)
  Teacher
Nabinger, Carol Ann Brown
  English/Chinese Teacher
Perz, Erva K.
  Fifth Grade Teacher
Regas, Mary
  First Grade Teacher
BRYAN
Moog, Helene Opdycke
  Fourth Grade Teacher
Snider, Mary Beth
  6th Grade Teacher
Wiles, Gary Caven
  Business Teacher
Wisniewski, Sharon Ann (Sullivan)
  2nd Grade Teacher
BUCYRUS
Ransom, Roger Lyle
  4th Grade Teacher
Widman, Connie Marie
  First Grade Teacher
BYESVILLE
Sokol, Leisa Lynn Du Beck
  Third Grade Teacher
CADIZ
Dennis, Mary Lou Spring
  First Grade Teacher
Swartz, Jane Lee
  Spanish Teacher
CALCUTTA
Marshall, Shirley Howell
  Third Grade Teacher
CALDWELL
Morris, Jeff Blake
  Mathematics Teacher/Dept Head
Peoples, Joyce Lee (Dennis)
  Fifth Grade Teacher
CALEDONIA
Taylor, Jacqueline Strine
  Fourth Grade Teacher
CAMBRIDGE
Charleston, Deborah Joan
  Fourth Grade Teacher
Hronec, Suzanne Kovalchik
  Reading Teacher
CAMDEN
Garland, Elizabeth Adams
  Fourth Grade Teacher
Shoemaker, Matthew L.
  5th-12th Grade Band Director
CANFIELD
Martin, Sue Marie
  Fourth Grade Teacher
Murphy, William Joseph
  Fourth Grade Teacher
Reel, Kenneth Alan
  American History Teacher
CANTON
Bailey, Ann
  Home Economics Teacher
Breen, Gary R.
  Seventh Grade Teacher
Burlingame, Virginia Jones
  Mathematics Teacher
Cheviron, Denise Lynne
  Counselor
Christie, Tina Marie
  Mathematics Teacher
Dudra, Ted E.
  Science Teacher/Team Leader
Ecenbarger, Gloria Jean
  Home Economics Teacher
Fisk, William Alan
  Science Teacher
Hickey, Mary Alice Cimmons
  5th Grade Teacher
Holm, Dale William
  Sixth Grade Teacher

Johnson, Doris (Larson)
  Retired Third Grade Teacher
Kiefer, Patricia (May)
  First Grade Teacher
Loughry, Richard Bernard
  Spanish Teacher
Love, Thomas Eugene
  Mathematics Dept Chairman
Mailat, Joanne Marie (Urdea)
  French Teacher
Mancini, Rick Guy
  6th Grade Teacher
Mc Natt, Donna Jean
  Mathematics Department Chair
Meunier, Carol Ann
  Teacher & Math Team Leader
Nelson, Howard E.
  Mathematics Teacher/Dept Chair
Peterman, Lucinda (Sheil)
  Jr HS Teacher
Putnam, Joseph Hector
  Cnslr/Chm Soc Stud Dept
Rametta, Samuel John Jr.
  Latin Teacher/Team Leader
Ramos, Robert Pedro
  Spanish Teacher
Spurgeon, Larry Dayton
  Art Teacher
Trovich, Donna Sergi
  3rd/4th/5th Grade Teacher
Tschantz, Dwight Alan
  Prescriptive Math Teacher
CARDINGTON
Hall, Jamie L.
  English Teacher
Miller, Hazel Henry
  4th Grade Teacher
CARLISLE
Bray, Elouise Kaye
  7th Grade Eng Teacher/Chair
Richardson, Shirley Mc Intosh
  Second Grade Teacher
CARROLL
Briggs, Jane Ellen
  Business Teacher
Lear, Douglas Gordon
  Instrumental Music Director
CARROLLTON
Ankrom, Nilah Walker
  Social Studies Teacher
Emerick, Karen Crawford
  Teacher of Gifted
Shuman, Julie Ann (Lumley)
  Cty Coordinator of Gifted Ed
CASSTOWN
Haupt, Peggy Ann (Eidemiller)
  Art Teacher
Summers, Fredia White
  English Teacher
CASTALIA
Gerold, Donna Jean (Johnston)
  Elem Teacher/Computer Coord
Kleckner, Roger Eugene
  Mathematics Teacher
Michalik, Peggy Ann
  6th Grade Teacher
Oatley, Linda Gerhardstein
  English Teacher
Schoenegge, Paul William
  Spanish Teacher
CEDARVILLE
Barber, Frances Noel
  Eng Dept Chair/Teacher
Evans, Debora Kershner
  Third Grade Teacher
Vaughn, C. Dennis
  6th Grade Teacher
CELINA
Franzer, Patricia Severt
  Math/Computer Teacher
Gunter, Diane M.
  3rd Grade Teacher
Pittsenbarger, Douglas Edward
  8th Grade Earth Sci Teacher
Schelich, Robert Dean
  Eighth Grade English Teacher
Smith, Page A.
  Social Studies Instructor
CENTERVILLE
Flaum, Steve M.
  Social Science Teacher
Jensen, Carolyn
  English Teacher
Laughlin, Debra J. (Pummill)
  Marketing Education Teacher
Maddox, Sandra J.
  6th Grade Teacher
Vogt, Sandra Josette
  English/Reading Teacher

CHAGRIN FALLS
Parmalee, Eileen M.
  Resource Teacher/Math Dept
CHARDON
Bretschneider, Frederick Edward
  Science Instructor
CHAUNCEY
Allen, Marilyn Sue (Abdella)
  Third Grade Teacher
CHESAPEAKE
Brammer, Granvil R.
  Vice Principal
Lang, Sharon Smith
  Fourth Grade Teacher
Murdock, Thomas Melvin
  Business Department Chairman
Sexton, Colleen Linda
  English Teacher
CHILLICOTHE
Alexander, Linda Bierbower
  Jr/Sr High English Teacher
Angles, Bess M.
  Elementary Principal
Ater, Terry David
  Language Art Teacher
Cottrill, Ruth Holt
  Mathematics Teacher
Curtis, Timothy J.
  Physics/Chemistry Instructor
Davis, Patricia Britton
  Sixth Grade Teacher/Coord
Davis, Terry Alan
  7th/8th Social Studies Teacher
Greene, Judy
  English Teacher
Hamilton, Rosa Lee
  Second Grade Teacher
Henry, Jo Ann Sarah
  Retired 4th Grade Teacher
Marshall, Charles R.
  Mathematics Dept Chairman
Neff, Don E.
  Science Teacher
Ray, Dennis Robert
  Mathematics Teacher
Sterwerf, Mary Peter
  Pastoral Minister
Swan, Steven R.
  Social Studies Chairman
Vaughn, Robert Lewis
  Sixth Grade Teacher
Wallace, Charles Robert
  American Government Teacher
CINCINNATI
Ahrens, Gerard Joseph
  Junior High School Teacher
Alexander, Stephen Paul
  Math Teacher/Math Dept Supvr
Borman, Barry J.
  Science Dept Chairman
Brandt, June Kathleen (Bieler)
  5th & 6th Grade Math Teacher
Brown, Philip Eugene
  Phys Ed/Science Teacher
Buquo, David Scott
  Bio/Anatomy/Physiology Teacher
Bush, Gwyn Fleming
  Teacher/Science Dept Chair
Carey, William Patrick
  English Department Chair
Cordrey, Lee O.
  Science Teacher
Crouch, Constance Ratleff
  Language Arts/Soc Sci Teacher
Crowe, Anne Evard
  Assistant Principal
Dennie, Edna Pinkston
  Third Grade Teacher
Derrick, Kathryn Fisk
  Media Center Director
Dienger, Joseph Edward
  Seventh Grade Teacher
Dukes, Marion
  5th Grade Teacher
Emmett, Patricia Driehaus
  Third Grade Teacher
Etter, Dana Vern
  Mathematics Teacher
Eve, Theresa Owlett
  Science Teacher
Fernandez-Dunn, Paula Kathryn
  Spanish Teacher
Fernandez, Otilia Janes
  Foreign Languages Dept Chair
Frank, Neil Howard
  Spanish Teacher/Dept Chair
Galvin, Jene Maurice
  Dean
Handler, Lori Allen
  Curriculum/Staff Dev Coord
Hausman, Michael L.
  Biology Teacher

Holy, Jo Alice Crenshaw
  6th Grade Teacher
Joachim, John Richard
  Biological Science Teacher
Jordan, Mary Ellen Haupt
  Fourth Grade Teacher
Kasper, Linda Haller
  Teacher
Kelemen, Elizabeth
  Mathematics Department Teacher
Kittenbrink, Lana Jo Beaber
  1st/2nd Grade Teacher
Krieg, Barbara Nicely
  Gifted Education Teacher
Krueger, Daniel William
  Vocal Music Director
Lienhart, Patricia Flynn
  First Grade Teacher
Long, Larry Chris
  Jr High Teacher/Asst Principal
Luckey, Mary Jean (Shannon)
  5th Grade Teacher
Lyons, Sharon M. (Anderson)
  Sixth Grade Teacher
Martin, Dennis John
  English/History/Gifted Teacher
Matthews, Samuel
  9th-12th Grade History Teacher
Mc Cormack, Thomas Huston
  Teacher
Mc Crea, Debi Catucci
  Teacher/Comm Facilitator
Mc Laughlin, Paul Francis
  Mathematics Teacher
Merkel, David Paul
  Business Education Teacher
Michael, Melinda Vogel
  AP Math Teacher
Morgan, Melba Caldwell
  8th Grade English Teacher
Mortsolf, Gayle J.
  2nd Grade Teacher
Mueller, Ollie Watts
  6th Grade Teacher
Novotni, Carol A.
  ESEA Reading Teacher
Oswald, Jo Ann Bauer
  Physical Education Teacher
Parks, Margaret La Verne
  Teacher
Pelzel, Michael J.
  Third Grade Teacher
Pfetzing, Deborah Schneuer
  English Teacher
Rains, Martha M.
  5th Grade Teacher
Reif, Barbara Ann (Cottingham)
  Kindergarten Teacher
Richards, Rebecca Watson
  English Teacher
Ross, Joan Heitz
  Science Teacher
Samuel, Ray Gyora
  English/Reading Co-Chair
Schlomer, Thelma
  Sixth Grade Teacher
Starkey, Daniel Edwin
  Counselor/Phys Ed Teacher
Stoll, Ken
  Latin Teacher
Traxler, David Edward
  Physics Teacher
Turner, Norma Foley
  Literature Teacher
Vissing, Pamela Ann
  Director of Student Activities
Washington, La Vonne Caise
  English/Reading Teacher
Wichmann, Joan Vesper
  5th Grade Teacher-Math Dept
Williams, Robert B. R.
  English/Social Studies Teacher
Woestman, Nancy Kay
  5th Grade Teacher
Yates, Gwen Edwards
  Supervisor of Elem Teachers
CIRCLEVILLE
Barkley, Phyllis M. Gifford
  5th Grade Teacher
Brisker, Paul Owen
  Science Teacher
Burke, Mary E.
  Physical Education Teacher
Hedges, Mollie Peters
  Fourth Grade Teacher
Logan, Sheryl Wood
  Fourth Grade Teacher
Martin, Natalie Ann
  Mid Sch Mathematics Teacher
Petty, Tamara Sue
  Music Teacher
Skidmore, Judy L.
  Vocational Home Ec Teacher
Weigand, Carolyn Stout
  Fifth Grade Teacher

CLARKSVILLE

Mc Carty, Susan Wertz
  Biology Teacher
Wellman, John B.
  6th Grade Sci/Health Teacher

CLAYTON

Oldham, Pamela S.
  Legal Secretary Instructor
Self, Candace Carmean
  Spanish & English Teacher

CLEVELAND

Anderson, Tayloria Stroud
  Retired Substitute Teacher
Apana, James L.
  English Department Chair
Bolek, Sheila Born
  Eighth Grade Teacher/Asst Prin
Dunning, Kevin Michael
  8th Grade Teacher/Principal
Dwyer-Kueller, Mary Therese
  Theology Teacher/Chairperson
Hackenberg, Elizabeth Mae
  Foreign Language Dept Chair
Hunte, Ruth Alice
  Science Dept Chairperson
Husband, Claudine Clark
  Science Teacher
James, Gwendolyn Raines
  Early Childhood Teacher
Johnson, Barbara Louise (Strauder)
  9th Grade English Teacher
Jordan, Vivian Du-Bose
  Retired/Substitute Teacher
Kennedy, Carolyn Barr
  Biology Teacher
Key, Helen Elaine
  Business Education Teacher
Kovats, Elizabeth A.
  4th Grade Teacher
Macken, Ita L.
  Sci/His/Rdng Teacher
Martin, Lydia Russell
  Fifth Grade Teacher
Monaco, Don
  English Teacher
Paglio, Constance Orosz
  Jr High Mathematics Teacher
Pierce, Ruthanne Caughey
  English Dept Chair/Teacher
Pritchard, David Ivan
  English Teacher
Sesso, Carol Ann
  Jr HS Teacher
Sims, Yvonne Nichols
  Guidance Counselor
Smith, Anne Marie Barnes
  Sixth Grade Teacher
Smith, Judith Hardaway
  Principal
Stacho, Linda S. Notman
  English Teacher
Stewart, Zelma Brown
  Fifth Grade Teacher
Wyman, Patricia Kathleen
  Language Art Teacher
Zieve, Sandra Anne
  5th Grade Teacher

CLEVES

Howard, Edward Frank
  Elem Instrumentl Music Teacher

COAL GROVE

Haney, Charles
  7th Grade Science Teacher

COLDWATER

Schmeising, Sam A.
  4th Grade Teacher
Severt, Marilyn Ann
  Third Grade Teacher
Weber, Eugene John
  Retired Teacher

COLLINS

Fraelich, Donna Phyllips
  5th Grade/8th Grade Reading

COLUMBIA STATION

Koharik, Wilomene Mole
  Retired Jr HS Math Teacher

COLUMBIANA

Renkenberger, Linda Hendricks
  Business Teacher

COLUMBUS

Beck, Nancy Ann
  5th Grade Teacher
Britton, Jill
  French Teacher
Claytor, Ernest F.
  7th Grade Math Teacher
Cole, Charles Everett Jr.
  Jr HS History/English Teacher
Denton, Sandra Elizabeth
  English Teacher

Diez, Margo Wilson
  Spanish Teacher
Ekleberry, Lee Edward
  Art Teacher
Elander, Rodger F. Jr.
  Mathematics Teacher
Everetts, Daniel Ernest
  Mathematics Teacher
Foreman, M. Jeanne
  COE Coordinator
Hainer, Carolyn Cornelius
  Sixth Grade Teacher
Hann, Edwin Craig
  5th Grade Teacher
Huff, C. Michael
  Social Studies Teacher
Jackson, John Charles
  Ohio & US History Teacher
Koons, Paula Jenyk
  6th Grade Teacher
Maiberger, Elizabeth Ann
  Home Economics Teacher
Maughmer, Lois Giles
  Mathematics Teacher
Mc Glocklin, Mary Burgoyne
  Science Department Chair
Meister, Linda S.
  English & Reading Teacher
Meserol, Hannah Kathleen
  Science/Health Teacher
Mohr, Carolyn Hupp
  Work Adjustment Coordinator
Orr, Charles Wesley
  Teacher
Reiter, Richard William
  HS History Teacher
Rembert, Errole Donnard
  Discipline Teacher
Rice, Gary L.
  Fifth Grade Teacher
Riggs, Robert Joseph
  Seventh Grade Teacher
Scott, Sheila E.
  Marketing Education Teacher
Sidner, Anne C.
  English Teacher & Dept Chair
Singer, Barbara J.
  English Teacher
Spencer, Betty Jean Scott
  5th Grade Teacher of Gifted
Sponaugle, Robert Lloyd
  English Teacher
Stebbins, Barry Steven
  Science Teacher
Thompson, Virginia R.
  Gifted/Talented Teacher
Trotier, Audrey Priscilla
  Gifted Education Teacher
Tucker, Bonita Frazier
  Third Grade Teacher
Vogel, Ruthanne Gaugh
  Sixth Grade Teacher
Watts, Jaqueline Mc Neil
  French Teacher
Weirick, Maria Cianflona
  Eighth Grade Teacher
Woods, Cindy Lee
  4th Grade Teacher

CONNEAUT

Young, Mary Cebasek
  Fourth Grade Teacher

COOLVILLE

Vogt, Jeffrey Von
  6th Grade Teacher

COPLEY

Barrett, Rebecca Ann
  Spanish Teacher/Dept Chair

CORTLAND

Cickelli, James A.
  Social Studies Teacher
Kostraba, Patricia Ferko
  English Teacher

COSHOCTON

Nagle, Douglas Raymond
  Social Studies Instructor

COVINGTON

Apwisch, Madeline T.
  First Grade Teacher
Hudson, Joan Lehman
  7th/8th Grade Teacher
Hutchins, Tera L.
  Science Teacher
Schwamberger, Jack Allen
  Phys Science/Health Teacher

CRIDERSVILLE

Doll, Ruth M
  Fourth Grade Teacher

CROOKSVILLE

Behrendt, Barbra Jane
  Second Grade Teacher

CROTON

Atwood, Juanita E. (Downey)
  Seventh & Eighth Grade Teacher
Layman, Mary Jo Fletcher
  6th Grade Teacher

CROWN CITY

Collins, Joyce Kitchen
  5th-6th Grade Math Teacher
Nogle, Georgia Yvonne (Fulks)
  Science Teacher
Scarberry, Timothy Lee
  Social Studies Chairman

CUYAHOGA FALLS

Gill, Joyce Ann
  6th Grade Teacher
Glowski, Norma Kay (Brininger)
  American History Teacher
Haas, Paul Thomas
  Social Studies Teacher
Kreiner, Sandra Beckwith
  Social Studies Teacher
Rodefer, Jan Shetler (Fillmore)
  G/T Resource Teacher

DALTON

Rohr, Richard Joseph
  Adv Composition/Eng XI Teacher
Shammo, Leah M.
  Third Grade Teacher
Vacha, Faye Rebman
  6th Grade Teacher
Walton, Kevin Deane
  American History Teacher

DANVILLE

Holmes, James Robert
  Social Studies Teacher

DAYTON

Andrews, Michael R.
  5th-6th Grade Teacher
Andrews, Miriam C.
  Reading Specialist
Brown, Clarence Harold
  Band Director
Clifford, Lawrence Paul
  Mathematics Teacher
Eloe, Laura Jane (Schneider)
  Mathematics Teacher
Eshbaugh, Patricia Boam
  4th Grade Teacher
Flaum, Carol J
  German Teacher
Gates, Paul E.
  Spanish Teacher
George, Kay A.
  Jr HS Teacher
Gilbert, Jean H.
  Fourth Grade Teacher
Hebb, Betty Ann Casto
  Second Grade Teacher
Hobbs, Lucille Blake
  6th Grade Teacher
Hodges, Sue Carr
  Fourth Grade Teacher
Kendrick, Earlene Watkins
  Communication Arts/Unit Leader
Kerr, Donald L.
  French Teacher
Lacy, Mary Frances Lewis
  Sixth Grade Teacher
Mc Guire, Kimberley Kaye
  Secondary Teacher
Minor, Tom W.
  Chemistry/Physic Teacher
Moore, Marva Ann (Rucker)
  Guidance Counselor
Ochsenbein, John Thomas
  Guidance Counselor/Dept Chm
Putnam, Carole Ann
  Learning Disability Teacher
Pyle, Paul William
  Bible Dept Chair
Shaw, Donna Lynne (Beckman)
  Second Grade Teacher
Swart, John Scott
  German Teacher
Tolliver, James Edward
  4th Grade Teacher
Webb, Linda Singletary
  Fourth Grade Teacher
Wise, Brenda Ogletree
  Third Grade Teacher

DEFIANCE

Fruth, Kirk Allen
  5th Grade Teacher/Elem Cnslr
Gerken, Joan Nicely
  3rd Grade Teacher
Jones, Mary Ann Deitrick
  Fourth Grade Teacher
Mack, Jill Elaine
  6th Grade Teacher
Reid, Pamela B.
  German Teacher

Saylor, Jackie L.
  7/8th Grade Rdng/Eng Teacher
Slocum, Lori Sue
  English/Reading Teacher

DELAWARE

Counts, Arthur William
  Art Instructor/Dept Chairman
Hesse, Thomas Ried
  Mathematics Department Chair
Nesselroad, Michael Alan
  Chemistry Teacher
Semon, Carl William
  Aerospace Science Instructor
Shisler, Richard Lee
  Eighth Grade Teacher
Steward, Larry Dean
  6th Grade Sci/Health Teacher

DELPHOS

Hasselschwert, Mary
  1st Grade Teacher

DILLONVALE

Boroski, Naomi L.
  Sixth Grade Teacher
Fisher, Robert Douglas
  Sci Teacher/Guidance Cnslr

DOVER

Doutt, Terry Ann (Teynor)
  Third Grade/Music Teacher
Hare, Robert S. Jr.
  7th-8th Grade Math/Sci/Cmptr

DRESDEN

Denton, Thomas Johns
  Social Studies Teacher
Welch, Larry Dean
  Mathematics Teacher.
Wiczen, Linda Whiting
  Third Grade Teacher

DUBLIN

Damian, Carol G.
  Physics Teacher
Niemie, Philip E. Jr.
  Fifth Grade Teacher
Rogers, Dennis Edwin
  Teacher

DUNCAN FALLS

Harper, Donald Dean
  Seventh Grade English Teacher

EAST CLEVELAND

Clayton, Karen Darlene
  Physical Education Teacher
Elizey, Georgia Robinson
  Chemistry Teacher
France, Natalie O. S.
  8th Grade Soc Stud Teacher
Prest, Maryellen (Yank)
  Guidance Counselor
Robinson, Michael Charles
  5th Grade Teacher
Senor, Virginia L.
  Spanish Teacher
Shy, Terri Rawls
  Biology Teacher
Turk, Maria Norma (Schembri)
  Chemistry & Science Teacher
Whelan, John Joseph
  Principal
Williams, Van Oliver
  Special Education Teacher

EAST LIBERTY

Sullinger, Joan Foos
  Fourth Grade Teacher

EAST LIVERPOOL

Adney, Carolyn Rose
  History Teacher
Arzberger, Mary Mc Bee
  Fourth Grade Teacher
Patterson, Beverly May
  Fifth Grade Teacher
Wetzel, Nancy Howell
  English Teacher

EAST PALESTINE

Lynch, Barbara A.
  Social Studies Coordinator

EASTLAKE

Hostetter, Katherine Balsley
  English Teacher
Prince, Robert M.
  English Teacher

EATON

Kochensparger, Kevin Philip
  Mathematics Teacher/Dept Chair
Rhoden, Linda Donohoe
  Sixth Grade Teacher
Straszheim, Cindy Blakeman
  5th Grade Teacher

EDGERTON

Hulbert, Lu Ann
  Social Studies Teacher
Huner, Rita A.
  Home Economics Dept Chair
Pahl, Karen Bernath
  Fifth Grade Teacher

EDISON

Maslar, Nancy Jolley
  Kindergarten Teacher
Sample, Roberta Klingel
  2nd Grade Teacher

EDON

Hall, Lanna Pendleton
  Art Teacher

ELIDA

Glickstein-Sandy, Barbra
  6th Grade Teacher

ELYRIA

Gehman, Judy Kay
  9th-12th Grade English Teacher
Hoover, Beverly Marie (Kirk)
  6th Grade Teacher
Hoy, Steven Wayne
  English/Reading Teacher
Russ, Laurence Starr
  6th Grade Teacher
Trbovich, Helen
  Third Grade Teacher
Wilkinson, Mary Ann (Heavner)
  Third Grade Teacher

ENGLEWOOD

Delk, Darrell D.
  7th Grade Soc Stud Teacher
Veres, Marguerite
  6th Grade Teacher

ENON

Arnold, Barbara Studebaker
  Reading/Communications Teacher
Tully, Deborah Imri
  Teacher of Lit/Comm/Quest

EUCLID

Hoffert, Frank
  Social Studies Department Chm
Mohoric, Franklin Joseph
  Third Grade Teacher
Molinaro, Ruth Ann Swarner
  6th Grade Teacher
Serra, Paul Thomas
  Mathematics Teacher
Syracuse, Anthony Vetus
  Science Teacher
Von Benken, William David
  Chemistry Teacher

FAIRBORN

Frank, Catherine Durfee
  Teacher of Gifted
Jones, Robert Edward
  Teacher
Moss, Relda Ann
  2nd Grade Teacher
Persensky, Mary Ann Still
  6th Grade Teacher
Seewer, Michael L.
  AP His & Lit Teacher

FAIRFIELD

Dillard, Samuel O.
  Physical Education Teacher
Hanby, Donna (Weiss)
  Teacher of Talented & Gifted
Hartley, Christine V.
  Mathematics Teacher of Gifted
Nichols, Danny Maddox
  Band Dir/Music Coordinator

FAIRLAWN

Monroe, Janet M.
  Principal

FAYETTE

Lash, Pamela Pattison
  English/Social Studies Teacher
Short, James B.
  Science Teacher

FAYETTEVILLE

Johnson, Louis B.
  7th-10th Grade Teacher

FELICITY

Mc Williams, Kelly Lynn
  English Teacher

FINDLAY

Lowery, Kathryn Johnston
  Third Grade Teacher
Musser, Saundra J.
  Vocal Music Teacher

FOREST

Taylor, Jackie Lee
  Sixth Grade Teacher

FOREST PARK
Bahner, Paul David
 Science Teacher
FOSTORIA
Clay, Doyle Ellis Jr.
 Physical Education Teacher
Clouse, Jane Marie
 Fifth Grade Teacher
Earl, Richard Jon
 8th Grade English Teacher
Justice, Penelope Harpley
 4th Grade Teacher
FRANKLIN
Noland, Patti M.
 Bio/Psych Teacher Dept Chair
Termuhlen, Helen Forrest
 4th Grade Teacher
FREDERICKTOWN
Ackerman, Loretta Ann
 HS Soc Stud Teacher/Sr Advisor
Dearth, Ruth Ann
 Fifth Grade Teacher
Dremann, Beverly Henwood
 Kindergarten Teacher
FREMONT
Ackerman, Ruth A.
 Sixth Grade Teacher
Czech, Marya
 Science Teacher/Academic Dean
Holcomb, Kathy Marie
 Fifth Grade Teacher
Logsdon, Gary William
 4th Grade Teacher
Plihall, Michele Reardon
 Sixth Grade Teacher
Vaffis, Carol Feick
 Third Grade Teacher
Ziebold, Barbara M.
 Music Teacher/String Dept Head
GALLIPOLIS
Howell, Donald Rick
 Social Studies Teacher
GARFIELD HEIGHTS
Jambor, Glenn John
 English Teacher/Chair
Pokorski, Claire Nemec
 Sci Dept Teacher/Chairperson
GARRETTSVILLE
Foster, Connie Van Camp
 Third Grade Teacher
Walker, Iva Louise
 Social Studies Teacher
Wetzel, Pat Ryan
 Home Economics Teacher
GATES MILLS
O'Malley, Mary Kay
 Fourth Grade Teacher
GENEVA
Pizon, Jeff A.
 High School Biology Teacher
Spiesman, John Michael
 6th Grade Teacher
GENOA
Terry, Diane Dunn
 4th Grade Teacher
Williams, Elizabeth Ann
 Sixth Grade Teacher
GERMANTOWN
Benton, Rose Mary
 Mid Sch Teacher/Counselor
Gordon, Loyd Huston
 Mathematics Teacher
GETTYSBURG
Shepard, R. Jean
 First Grade Teacher
GIRARD
Archer, Thomas L.
 7th Grade Life Science Teacher
Medicus, Julia Ann (Kallenbaugh)
 8th Grade Eng/Rdng Teacher
Radza, Joseph Edward
 5th Grade Sci/Hlth/Gft Teacher
GNADENHUTTEN
Goforth, Mary Davey
 English Teacher
GOSHEN
Moesker, Martha Garland
 English Teacher
GRAND RAPIDS
Mohr, Norma Jean (Bateson)
 Sixth Grade Teacher
GREENSBURG
Collier, Lawrence Richard
 7th Grade Life Science Teacher

O'Connor, Barbara Blough
 Third Grade Teacher
Taylor, Norma Lehman
 Social Studies Chair
GREENVILLE
Hart, Brenda Lee
 Mathematics/Science Teacher
Kensinger, Grace Willetts
 6th Grade Quest Teacher
Mc Kim, Louise Wooton
 English Teacher
Steffen, Carol Marie
 Fourth Grade Teacher
Ulrich, Sharon Ann
 5th/6th Grade & French Teacher
Westfall, David Lee
 4th Grade Teacher
GREENWICH
Hord, Cheryl Snapp
 Fourth Grade Teacher
Kreais, Mary L.
 Math/Cmptr Science Teacher
GROVEPORT
Hilbert, Jean Ann
 4th Grade Teacher
Morris, Ellen L.
 Social Studies Teacher
GYPSUM
Hudak, Joan Kristenak
 Chapter 1 Reading
HAMERSVILLE
Witten, Susan Carol
 Pre-First Grade Teacher
HAMILTON
Aufranc, Gary Lee
 Ninth Grade Science Teacher
Bauman, Ronald E.
 Art Teacher
Blair, Barbara Elaine (Bahl)
 Second Grade Teacher
Carbary, Eleanor S.
 Art/Social Studies Teacher
Heiser, James Scott
 High School Principal
Hornsby, Judith Bennett
 Teacher Visually Handicapped
Kuykendall, Patricia Wogenstahl
 4th/5th Grade Teacher
Matthews, Irene B.
 Principal
Owen, Thomas S.
 Religion Department Chair
Sheriff, Vivian Sharp
 Fourth Grade Teacher
Sloneker, Marlene Gesell
 Kindergarten Teacher
Smith, Carol Ann (king)
 Second Grade Teacher
Vido, Fay Wagner
 English Teacher
HAMLER
Bloor, Ruth Davison
 Mathematics Teacher
Brown, Diann Ellen
 Social Studies & Eng Teacher
Pennington, Lillian Doris
 German/Spanish Teacher
HAMMONDSVILLE
Lundquist, Karen Blom
 Health/Phys Ed Teacher/Coach
Tedeschi, Pamela Ann (Crowe)
 5th Grade Teacher
HARRISON
Bihr, Shirley Ann
 Lang Arts & Religion Teacher
Brater, Kathie Rolfes
 2nd-6th Substitute Teacher
Meeks, Dan
 Instrumental Music Teacher
Sandman, Susan Richards
 Third Grade Teacher
HARROD
Parks, Margaret Cecil (Hershberger)
 4th Grade Teacher
HARTFORD
Hendryx, Phyllis J. (Roth)
 2nd Grade Teacher
HARTVILLE
Johnson, Phillip Lee
 7th Grade Soc Stud Teacher
Richards, Jeanette M. (Willis)
 5th Grade Teacher
Wolf, Kathy Santoro
 5th Grade Teacher
HEATH
Coleman, Penny Martin
 Second Grade Teacher

England, Timothy Edward
 Social Studies Teacher
Johnson, Linda Bayliss
 Social Studies Teacher
Jones, Joseph Alan
 English Teacher
Ryan, Susan Anderson
 Third Grade Teacher
Staley, Lorrie Belcher
 Reading/Mass Media Teacher
Steinbrook, Russetta Lynn
 Fourth Grade Teacher
HEBRON
Connor, Steven Morley
 English Teacher
HICKSVILLE
Baringer, Deborah Ann Shreve
 Health & L D Teacher
De Long, Shayna J.
 Business Teacher
Fabian, Carol Flory
 First Grade Teacher
Mc Pike, Karlyn Korsgaard
 German/French Teacher
HIGHLAND HEIGHTS
Flaisig, Carol Popa
 Junior High School Teacher
HILLIARD
Knickel, Karen Lenora
 Fourth Grade Teacher
Nonnemacher, Clarence Martin
 Social Studies Teacher
HILLSBORO
Benson, Mary Elmore
 5th Grade Teacher
Bihl, Leone Meredith
 Spanish I & II/Latin I & II
Griffith, Julia K.
 Second Grade Teacher
Mathews, Marilyn Jo-Fauber
 8th Grade Life Science Teacher
West, Nancy Rae Palmer
 1st Grade Teacher
HOLLAND
Miller, Carol Braun
 5th Grade Teacher
Slough, Elaine Ann (Sonnichsen)
 German Teacher
HOLLANSBURG
Hottle, Nanette Seybold
 Fifth Grade Teacher
Nordstrom, Jeanne Bolyard
 Sixth Grade Teacher
HOPEDALE
Campanizzi, Louis Domonic
 Social Studies Chairman
HOWARD
Frere, Kathy J.
 English & Physical Ed Teacher
Owens, Crystal J.
 Spanish Teacher
HUBBARD
Carbone, Barbara J.
 Instrumental Music Teacher
Modarelli, Marianne Orlando
 Kindergarten Teacher
HUBER HEIGHTS
Ferraro, Anthony John Jr.
 Sixth Grade Teacher
Frum, Robert Harold
 6th Grade Teacher
Mullins, Jimmy J. Sr.
 Air Force Junior ROTC Instr
Murray, Ted William
 Marketing Education Coord
HUDSON
Isler, William Conrad
 Science Teacher
Radie, Ken Neal
 Sixth Grade Teacher
HUNTSBURG
Doyle, Kathleen Kozar
 Sixth Grade Teacher
IRONTON
Bare, David J.
 Director of Instrumental Music
Bell, Janice Dolin
 Fifth Grade Teacher
Blair, Doris Starr
 English Teacher
Conley, Melaine Ann
 Middle School Science Teacher
Cramblit, Sharon Parnell
 5th Grade Soc Stud Teacher
Massie, Annette Alban
 3rd Grade Teacher

Washburn, Florence Kathryn
 Teacher of Gifted & Talented
Wipert, Jimmy Dalton
 Principal
JACKSON
Altherr, Fred B.
 Occupational Work Teacher
Armstrong, Denise Lynn (Perkins)
 Spanish Teacher
Chapman, Pauline Mc Williams
 English/Psychology Teacher
Cooper, Cathy Marie
 Mid Sch Math Teacher
Donley, Marlin Buckley
 History Teacher/Guidance Cnslr
Eisnaugle, Michael Lee
 Science Teacher
Erwin, Paula W.
 Elem Phys Ed Teacher
Fults, Nanetta
 Curriculum Director
Heflin, Douglas Miller
 Director of Vocal Music
Jones, Suzanne Grillo
 2nd Grade Teacher
Loxley, Kathryn Harleman
 5th Grade Teacher
Plummer, Martha W.
 6th Grade Teacher
Riegel, Mary Christman
 Second Grade Teacher
Sites, Mary Ramsey
 Rdng & Performing Art Teacher
Williams, Victoria Howell
 Jr HS Dev Handicapped Teacher
Young, Jeff A.
 8th Grade Science Teacher
JAMESTOWN
Thomas, Linda Denger
 Second Grade Teacher
JEFFERSON
Carlson, David E.
 Retired Teacher
Hall, Linda Lipps
 2nd Grade Teacher
Havens, Richard Harley
 Mathematics Department Chm
Lewis, Patricia A. (Crothers)
 English Teacher
Pluff, Darrel A.
 Information Processing Instr
KENT
Lowe, Loretta Bond Allred
 Third Grade Teacher
Moledor, Elizabeth Winnefeld
 Third Grade Teacher
Rippey, Sandra N.
 Second Grade Teacher
Sargi, Terrie Anderson
 Fifth Grade Teacher
KENTON
Baker, Jane Eileen
 7th Grade Life Science Teacher
Hughes, Ronda L.
 First Grade Teacher
KERNERSVILLE
Carpenter, Elizabeth Meggs
 English Teacher
KETTERING
Gibbs, Dorothy Scott
 Latin Teacher
Raonick, Patricia A.
 Fifth Grade Teacher
Rykoskey, Carol Kleber
 Third Grade Teacher
KINGSTON
Eveland, June Wolf
 Third Grade Teacher
KINGSVILLE
Rust, James Eugene
 Fifth Grade Teacher
KINSMAN
Samball, Loretta
 Grade 8 Social Studies Teacher
KIRKERSVILLE
Frey, Melody Bascom
 Third Grade Teacher
KUNKLE
Whalen, Priscilla Kirtland
 Jr HS Reading Teacher
LAFAYETTE
Dellifield, Dennis L.
 Conductor of Bands
Eyl, David E.
 Business Teacher

LAKEVIEW
Van Horn, Patricia Lynn (Baer)
 First Grade Teacher
LAKEWOOD
Denicola, Marian P.
 English Teacher
Elrick, Donald
 English Teacher
Harrington, Kathleen M.
 Spanish Teacher/Foreign Lang
Jones, Thomas Edward
 7th Grade Life Science Teacher
Mulling, Arthur L.
 Teacher
Wilgus, John Peter
 Math Teacher
LANCASTER
Duffy, Kathleen Morris
 First Grade Teacher
Hedges, Sara Fraker
 English Teacher
Mc Clurg, Joseph Allen
 Cmptr Lab Coord/Math Teacher
Mc Conville, Edward Joseph
 Third Grade Teacher
Reall, Judith Spurgeon
 6th Grade Teacher
Stoner, James Frederick Jr.
 6th-8th Grade Science Teacher
LANSING
Blush, Ruth Ann (Terrell)
 First Grade Teacher
LAWTON
Wilson, Mary L.
 Guidance Counselor
LEAVITTSBURG
Crook, Juanita Marie Yoho
 Teacher
LEBANON
Bryant, Deborah Palmer
 Spanish Teacher
Foster, Sally Young
 Kindergarten Teacher
LEETONIA
Candle, Gladys M.
 English Teacher
De Rosa, Patricia Leason
 Teacher of Disabilities
Sherwood, William Curtis
 Fifth Grade Teacher
LEIPSIC
Frick, Elizabeth Stechschulte
 Fourth Grade Teacher
Walls, Jill K.
 Business Teacher
LIMA
Lawrence, Cheryl Lynn
 Fourth Grade Teacher
Leonard, Janet Edinger
 Fifth Grade Teacher/Cmptr Chm
Mann, Virgil Charles
 Advanced Placement Eng Teacher
Plaskey, Theresa Mrugala
 Retired Teacher
Stemen, Judith (Bahr)
 First Grade Teacher
LISBON
Arnold, Jennifer J. (Mason)
 Biology Teacher
Mack, Robert D.
 Senior Marine Instructor
LITTLE HOCKING
Alkire, Rose Marie
 Fourth Grade Teacher
LOCKLAND
Stewart, Donna F.
 Math & Science Teacher
LOGAN
Morgan, Roberta Leonard
 Fourth Grade Teacher
LORAIN
Fadale, William F.
 Fifth Grade Teacher
Jones, Gara French
 English Teacher
Jones, Loretta Hall
 Fifth Grade Teacher
Kachur, Betty Rae
 1st Grade Teacher
Kasprowski, Jacqueline Bollerhey
 English Department Chairperson
Morton, Sheila Annette
 Mathematics/Computer Teacher
Nowicki, Mary Mc Dermott
 5th Grade Teacher

LORAIN (cont)
Vitale, Janet L.
5th Grade Teacher

LORE CITY
Birney, Barb Virginia
1st Grade Teacher
Muffet, Janet Brown
English/Drama Teacher

LOUDONVILLE
Kick, Stephen P.
American History Teacher

LOUISVILLE
Baker, Jeffrey L.
Fifth Grade Teacher
Bole, Lisa M.
Eighth Grade Teacher
Boon, Susan Bartow
Science Teacher
Ciraci, Sandra Roberto
Kindergarten Teacher
Harold, Joseph E.
Geography Teacher
Jentes, Ralph Emerson
Social Studies Teacher
Leuenberger, Robert Charles
Sixth Grade Teacher
Rand, Michael Gene
Visual Arts Teacher
Snyder, Carol Lynn
Language Art Teacher
Thomas, Patricia Ann
3rd Grade Teacher
Wolpert, Debra Ann (Betz)
Mathematics Teacher

LOWELL
Beck, Jeanne Ann
Sixth Grade Teacher

LUCAS
Hendrickson, Jean Parto
English & Reading Teacher
Mattes, Frances Brockman
English Teacher
Mc Kown, Joan Louise Heffelfinger
History Teacher
Wable, Raymond A.
Fifth Grade Teacher

LUCASVILLE
Adkins, Donald Todd
French/World History Teacher
Thompson, Frank Ralph
English Instructor

LYNDHURST
Banasik, Carmela Mugnano
Junior High Teacher

LYONS
Rupp, Linda (Himelhan)
First Grade Teacher

MACEDONIA
Devore, Janice Fichtner
English Teacher

MADISON
Curkendall, Susan Merriam
Mathematics Teacher

MAGNOLIA
Marcoaldi, Joseph John
Junior High School Teacher

MALINTA
Meyer, Konnie Eickhoff
Third Grade Teacher

MANSFIELD
Giffin, Philip Cooke
Ohio History/Geography Teacher
Grim, Herschel A.
Content Specialist
Lesher, Curtis Alan
Guidance Counselor
Miefert, Dianne Weber
Third Grade Teacher

MAPLE HEIGHTS
Rusk, Frances Caesar
7th Grade Teacher

MARIETTA
Berentz, William C.
Social Studies/Science Teacher
Luthy, Jim E.
Chemistry Teacher
Matheny, Joseph Charles
Mathematics Teacher
Santini, Martin Edward
Social Studies/Cmptr Teacher
Stone, Kristen Patricia
3rd/4th Grade Tag Teacher
Weber, Bonnie Lee
Science/Health/English Teacher

MARION
Brown, Rebecca Ann (Schulte)
French Teacher
Fitch, Shirley Clanton
Fifth Grade Teacher
Kile, Douglas L.
English Teacher
New, Robert Charles
English Teacher
Pezley, Priscilla Diehl
Guidance Counselor
Rhoades, Cathie Bolen
Mathematics Teacher
Van Riper, N. Lynn
7th/8th Grade Art Teacher
Webb, Robert Okey
English Teacher

MARTINS FERRY
Beck, Lillian Mae (Mattingly)
Second Grade Teacher
Delande, Daniel Dale
Seventh Grade Teacher
Downie, Gordon L.
Bus Education Teacher
Hartenstein, Patricia Ann
First Grade Teacher
Krupnik, Thomas Edward
5th/6th Grade Science Teacher
Little, Linda Circosta
Second Grade Teacher
Minder, Judith Mowry
Jr HS Social Studies Teacher
Patterson, Mary Jane-Ruthers
Fifth Grade Teacher
Ramser, Barbara Judith
Geography & Science Teacher
Rippey, Betty Thompson
Advanced Mathematics Teacher
Sarratore, Anthony A.
6th/7th Grade Elem Teacher
Wagner, William Glenn
Science Teacher
Yardley, Janet Ellen (Harvey)
6th-7th Grade Math Teacher

MARYSVILLE
Coder, Susan Brubaker
3rd Grade Teacher

MASSILLON
Calabrese, Donna Carlise
English Teacher/Dept Chair
Gifford, Patricia Marie
English Teacher
Heist, Keith Douglas
Mathematics Teacher
Hewer, Barbara Ellen
3rd Grade Teacher
Higgins, Judith Girard
8th Grade Math/Algebra Teacher
Mattachione, Louie E.
Speech/Theatre Dept Chair
Murphy, Michael H.
10th-12th Grade Eng Teacher
Nielsen, Karen E.
English/Vocabulary Teacher
Prato, Marilyn Leah
6th Grade Math Teacher
Riffle, Margaret Jean
Elem Teacher of Gifted
Rubin, Marcia Orwick
Spanish Teacher
Schaaf, Karen Anne
Jr High Language Arts Teacher
Simon, Bonnie M.
US History & Civics Teacher
Turkal, Thomas George
Physics Teacher
Wise, James R.
Fifth Grade Teacher

MC ARTHUR
Graham, Shirley De Pue
Junior High Guidance Counselor
Stover, Louella Marie (Halley)
Business Education Teacher
Toon, Pam J.
6th Grade Language Art Teacher

MC CONNELSVILLE
Moore, Ronald Lee
Lang Arts/Jr High Teacher
Schubert, Blythe Gallaway
English Teacher

MC DERMOTT
Baker, Gary Neil
Art Instructor
Travis, Ellen M.
Language Arts Teacher

MC DONALD
Dolsak, Donna Millik
Algebra/Geometry Teacher
Franko, Susan Marie
7th/8th Grade English Teacher

Gadd, Roselyn Simini
Fourth Grade Teacher
Morris, Constance Elizabeth Barth
5th Grade Teacher

MC GUFFEY
Dudek, Sandra Lou
English Teacher
Dunson, Jackie Lee (Eibling)
Health/Physical Ed Teacher
Ries, Hilma Elizabeth
French/German Teacher

MEDINA
Bender, Hildegard (Groseclose)
Eng Teacher/Writing Lab Co-Dir
Cooksey, Alan R.
Social Studies Teacher & Chair
Gerspacher, Denise Eileen (Perzy)
Early Chldhd Ed Instr/Coord
Gunkleman, Barbara Ann
Teacher of Gifted Grades 3-6
Hadgis, Thomas
Science Teacher

MEDWAY
Burgess, Brenda Kay (Tope)
Fifth Grade Teacher
Martin, Phyllis Jean
Third Grade Teacher

MENDON
Bowling, Alice Marie (Daniels)
First Grade Teacher
Schwartz, Gloria Jean (Ringwald)
5th Grade Teacher
Scott, Julia Arlene
Junior High School Teacher
Snyder, Lee Ann A
Music Teacher

MENTOR
Gerard, Rebecca Hudak
First Grade Teacher

MESOPOTAMIA
Newcomb, Kathy Palmer
First Grade Teacher

METAMORA
Flickinger, Jodie Nephew
High School Science Teacher
Huskins, Catherine Joan
English Teacher

MIDDLETOWN
Aldridge, Lawrence Yewell
6th Grade Teacher
Baldwin, Patricia Ann
Vocational Home Ec Teacher
Childers, Diane Glei
Jr High Teacher
Lethgo, Linda Daye
Fifth Grade Teacher
Mc Gee, Betty Ann Benson
Retired Third Grade Teacher
Way, Wanda Strickland
English Teacher

MILFORD CENTER
Lowry, Susan Schaffner
English Teacher

MILLBURY
Bosl, Thomas Michael
Sixth Grade Teacher
Peiffer, George Edward
Fifth Grade Teacher

MILLERSBURG
Findley, David Martin
Guidance Counselor
Martin, Bruce Edward
Business Education Teacher

MINERAL RIDGE
Blaney, Virginia Briggs
Mathematics Teacher

MINERVA
Hubbard, Connie Harless
Science Teacher/Sci Dept Chair

MINFORD
Bailey, Gary D.
Mathematics Department Teacher
Gampp, Pamela Sue
Social Studies Teacher

MINGO JUNCTION
Lenzi, Linda Jean
Teacher of Talented & Gifted

MINSTER
Baumer, Patrick A.
5th/6th Grade Science Teacher
Meyer, William Joseph
7th/8th Grade Math Teacher
Voskuhl, Dianne P.
2nd Grade Teacher

Young, Willam Chelsea
Jr High Sci/Health Teacher

MOGADORE
Brawley, Dennis M.
7th-8th Grade Soc Stud Teacher

MONTPELIER
Meyers, Debbie Boetz
8th Grade English/Rdng Teacher
Stinehelfer, James Daniel Jr.
6th Grade Science Teacher
Wilson, Robert John
English Teacher

MORAINE
Billman, Diane Pendrey
Kindergarten Teacher

MORRAL
Bayless, Christine Pezoldt
7th/8th English Teacher
Sheets, George William
Language Art Teacher

MORRISTOWN
Parker, Chris
Second Grade Teacher

MORROW
Bird, Terry Woods
Fr Teacher/Foreign Lang Chair

MOUNT BLANCHARD
Whetstone, Emilee Anne
French/Spanish Teacher

MOUNT GILEAD
King, Cris
7th/8th Grade Soc Stud Teacher

MOUNT ORAB
Murphy, Marguerite J.
7th & 8th Grade Teacher

MOUNT VERNON
Baby, Brian Christopher
Art Teacher
Davenport, Stephanne Allen
Spanish Teacher
Dininger, Edward Lowell
Mathematics Department Teacher
Humphrey, Barbara Jones
Vocational Home Ec Teacher
Kahrl, Susan Thompson
6th Grade Teacher

NAPOLEON
Benedict, Joyce Arendosh
Third Grade Teacher
Downey, Timothy Joseph
Mathematics Teacher
Gubernath, Kathleen Gail
Fifth Grade Teacher
Nelson, Beverly Jean
English Teacher

NASHPORT
Reese, Marjorie Wilson
Fourth Grade Teacher

NAVARRE
Triner, Susan Laurie
Seventh Grade Teacher

NELSONVILLE
Mc Vey, Marjorie M.
Business Teacher

NEW ALBANY
Morrison, Nancy Stupp
Second Grade Teacher
Peddicord, Jane Stephan
6th Grade Math/Science Teacher
Polzin, Roxann Welborn
2nd Grade Teacher
Smith, Deborah N.
7th/8th Grade Soc Stud Teacher

NEW CARLISLE
Horstmann, Judy Benton
Fourth Grade Teacher
Ross, Bette Elaine
Fifth Grade Teacher
Sabo, Cynthia L.
Art Teacher

NEW CONCORD
Grubb, A. Jill
8th Grade Science Teacher
Rogers, Marsha Anne (Britton)
7th Grade Lang Arts Teacher

NEW KNOXVILLE
George, Janice Dreyer
Lang Art/Phys Ed Teacher
Henschen, Ruth L.
5th Grade/Gifted/Cmptr Teacher

NEW LEXINGTON
Albanese, Beth Kullman
Social Studies Teacher

Lollo, Michael Anthony
Jr HS & HS Spanish Teacher
Wallace, Neil D.
Science Teacher
Welch, William Dennis
8th Grade Amer History Teacher

NEW MADISON
Dubbs, Shirley Ann Miller
Social Studies Teacher

NEW MATAMORAS
Elder, Vincent K.
Mathematics Teacher
Mason, Amelia Jane
6th-8th Grade Teacher

NEW MIDDLETOWN
Bestic, Barbara Nelson
Fifth Grade Teacher
Williams, Pamela Eileen
Fourth Grade Teacher

NEW PARIS
Brower, Barbara Jean (Reid)
First Grade Teacher
Evans, Joanne Vogelsang
Mathematics Teacher

NEW PHILADELPHIA
Kovreg, Marie Ann
Principal
Riker, Carol Wherley
Kindergarten Teacher
Stein, Ann Weese
8Th Grade Reading Teacher

NEW WASHINGTON
Rarick, Craig Alan
Social Studies Teacher

NEWARK
Cousins, Jackie Hatcher
Reading/Language Arts Teacher
Gall, Janet Karen
3rd Grade Teacher
Low, Sharon Ruth
1st Grade Teacher
Thomas, Debbie Unternaher
Teacher
Woolard, Linda Ann
Fifth Grade Teacher

NEWCOMERSTOWN
Nigro, Ardath Hagan
Fourth Grade Teacher

NEWTON FALLS
Freisen, Edward Michael
Ohio History Teacher
Nogay, Joseph F. Jr.
7th-8th Grade Science Teacher

NILES
Augustine, Anthony James
Science Teacher
Hackett, Cynthia Lee
Chemistry Teacher
Kauffman, Carol Annuzzi
First Grade Teacher
Watkins, Jacqueline C. (Klein)
5th Grade Elementary Teacher

NORMANDY
Farmer, Shirley Ellen
Kindergarten Teacher

NORTH BALTIMORE
Weith, Fran Good
English Teacher
Whiteleather, Denise Marie
Second Grade Teacher

NORTH CANTON
Berrodin, Robert L.
Science/Health Teacher
Glock, Doris P. Hand
English Teacher
Neiss, Carole L.
8th Grade English Teacher

NORTH JACKSON
Kuzma, Barbara A.
Teacher

NORTH KINGSVILLE
Barnes, Mary Fraley
First Grade Teacher
Loomis, Colleen S.
First Grade Teacher
Pallo, Janet Lee
5th Grade Teacher
Peters, Cheryl Janet Hall
Third Grade Teacher

NORTH LEWISBURG
Mabry, Linda Arment
6th Grade Teacher
Mc Daniel, Barbara Marie
3rd Grade Teacher

NORTH RIDGEVILLE

Giovannazzo, Daniel Ellis
7th Grade English Teacher
Hase, James Robert
United States History Teacher
Maczuzak, Jane Bricker
Sci Teacher/Outdoor Ed Coord
Mansbach, Arthur Craig
Teacher of Learning Disabled
Soucy, Barbara J. (Stone)
Fourth Grade Teacher

NORTH ROBINSON

Everett, Constance Powers
Mathematics Teacher
Huber, Norman C.
Biology Teacher
Huggins, Charles Wade III
6th Grade Math Dept Chairman
Johnson, Joyce Yancey
English Teacher/Eng Dept Chair
Snyder, Alice (Kleinman)
High School French Teacher

NORTHFIELD

Allen, Kimberly Ann
Middle School Art Teacher
Morehead, Jeannette Eileen
6th Grade Teacher

NORTHWOOD

Sanders, Richard J.
4th Grade Teacher
Susor, Marianne Phillips
Fourth Grade Teacher

NORWALK

Emmons, Jerry
Mathematics Teacher
Ford, Scott Clinton
English Teacher
Hord, Randy Lee
Bio/Life Science Teacher
Opper, Nancy Okolish
Fifth Grade Teacher
Seaman, Deborah Louise
Second Grade Teacher
Sellers, Brent Lee
Elementary Principal

NORWOOD

Bretz, William Thomas
6th Grade Soc Stud/Team Leader
Fey, Rose M.
Art Teacher
Martin, Allan David
Music Teacher
Westlund, Margaret Webb
Elementary Music Teacher

OAK HARBOR

Damschroder, Louis G.
Agriculture Ed Instructor
Floro, P. Thomas Jr.
Social Studies Teacher
Peters, Carol Kaiser
5th Grade Teacher

OAK HILL

Evans, Marlene Crabtree
Third Grade Teacher

OBERLIN

Mc Mullen, Carol (Pancost)
Food Service Instructor
Randall, John A.
English Teacher
Reeder, Jessie La Ruth Holley
4th-12th Grade Music Teacher
Walzer, Michaelene Ann (Baker)
6th Grade Teacher

OLD WASHINGTON

Altvater, Phyllis A.
6th Grade Teacher

OLMSTED FALLS

Sayers, John Wallace
1st-3rd Grade Phys Ed Teacher

OREGON

Pasztor, William Michael Jr.
Adapted Phys Ed Specialist
Routson, James L.
Mathematics Teacher
Schwartz, Louise Warns
Health/Phys Ed Teacher

ORRVILLE

Gill, Caroline Ruth (Dawsey)
4th Grade Teacher
Marr, Lynette Hahn
Teacher of Gifted
Nicholas, Eleanor Ann
Kindergarten Teacher
Stuckey, Shari Taylor
English Teacher
Warner, Patricia Ann
English Teacher

ORWELL

Shoaf, Joseph Bernard
Soc Studies Teacher/Dept Head

OTTOVILLE

Hoersten, Thomas J.
6th Grade Teacher
Knott, Mark A.
Sch Counselor/Business Teacher

PAINESVILLE

Loucks, Richard D.
English Teacher

PARMA

Cosiano, Gaytana Iacano
3rd Grade Teacher
Coughlin, Maureen Elizabeth
Theology Teacher
Montgomery, Ernest David
English Teacher
Perrigo, Janis Houck
Fourth Grade Teacher
Pizon, Lawrence John
Social Studies Teacher
Riha, Joan (Johnson)
English Department Chairperson
Schweitzer, John H.
Social Studies Teacher
Sorace-Thomas, Karen Kaye
Art Department Chairman
Sroda, Sophie Urbanick
First Grade Teacher

PARMA HEIGHTS

Pankiw, Mary
Foreign Language Dept Chair
Sharp, Charles K. (Kirkwood)
Honors Biology Instructor

PATASKALA

Starn, Nancy Geiger
Biology Teacher

PATRIOT

Luman, Carolyn Sue
Teacher

PAULDING

Boesling, Sue Ann Siler
Third Grade Teacher
Foltz, Madeline Carol
Home Economics Teacher
Fry, Marilyn Van Cise
Biology/Physiology Teacher
Hibbard, Max Albert Jr.
English Teacher
Hughes, Barbara Hutchinson
Home Economics Instructor

PAYNE

Hook, Elizabeth Ann (Price)
First Grade Teacher

PEMBERVILLE

Sheets, Nedra Ellen (Jacobs)
1st Grade Teacher

PENNSVILLE

Jarvis, Rebecca Maikranz
Fourth Grade Teacher

PERRY

Kylmanen, Ruth Hilma
Retired Elementary Teacher

PERRYSBURG

Brown, Kathleen Rose
Third Grade Teacher

PERRYSVILLE

Spreng, David L.
Science Department Teacher

PIKETON

Crawford, David Paul
Dept of Eng-Teacher/Counsel
Miller, Lavonna Faye (Rose)
Business Education Teacher
Shepherd, Greg
Physical Education Teacher

PIQUA

Mc Allister, Lesia Jean
Fifth Grade Teacher
Williams, Timothy Harmon
Sr Data Processing Instructor

PLAIN CITY

Brown, D. Robin Linsenmann
1st/5-8th Grades Rdng Speclst

PLEASANT HILL

George, Mary Beth Benham
First Grade Teacher

POLK

Johnston, Cynthia Faith
Fourth Grade Teacher

PORT CLINTON

Carr, Karen Lang
Kindergarten Teacher
Farris, John Ben
Physical Education Teacher
Greer, Victoria Lee (Burr)
Life Science Teacher
Gulas, Marlene Sue (Adrick)
Reading Teacher
Rasmussen, Gary L.
Computer/OH History Teacher
Sherick, Philip Lyle
German/English Teacher

PORTSMOUTH

Conley, Betty Newland
Language Arts Teacher

POWHATAN POINT

Buff, Judy M.
Third Grade Teacher
Kuzio, Janice Church
Home Economics/Science Teacher
Longstaff, Dannielle Kasprowski
Language Arts Teacher

PROCTORVILLE

Joseph, Audrey Jenkins
Second Grade Teacher

QUINCY

Blair, Cinda J.
Sixth Grade Teacher

RANDOLPH

Culbertson, Candace K.
Math & Computer Sci Teacher

RAVENNA

Busher, Janice J.
English Teacher/Dept Chair
Gillis, Vera Etling
Kindergarten Teacher
Mc Burney, Donald Evans
Science Teacher
Sarver, Vicki Bost
1st Grade Teacher
Senseman, Douglas Charles
Social Studies Teacher
Tontimonia, Guy C.
8th Grade Amer History Teacher

RAWSON

Bauman, Joan Lou Clymer
3rd Grade Teacher
Leuthold, Christopher John
Mathematics Dept Chairman

REEDSVILLE

Tillis, Gina R.
English Teacher
Weber, Grace Pickens
Retired Teacher/Admin
Williams, Rita Peer
French/English Teacher

REPUBLIC

Schlick, Jerome Francis
Language Arts/Health Teacher

REYNOLDSBURG

De Gennaro, Anthony Ray
Chemistry/Physics Teacher
Husto, Diann Jane Williamson
High School Art Teacher

RICHMOND

Lamatrice, Louis F.
Counselor
Neptune, Larry Edward
Science Teacher
Zimmerman, Joyce Irene (Breth)
5th Grade Teacher

RICHMOND DALE

Easterday, Dannie Dean
History/Geography Teacher

RISINGSUN

Livoti, Stephen J.
World Geography Teacher

RITTMAN

Mason, Terri Gilmore
US His/World Geography Teacher
Sabo, Judity M. (Burger)
Biology Teacher

ROCKFORD

Collins, Lora Chaffins
Kindergarten Teacher
Masser, Mary Virginia (Grams)
German Teacher

ROCKY RIVER

Motz, Karen Zabell
French Teacher

ROOTSTOWN

Fetzer, Karen Nelson
Mathematics Teacher

ROSSFORD

Weirich, Phillip O.
7th Grade Science Teacher

SABINA

Davis, Juanita Bernard
Third Grade Teacher
Hargrave, Virginia English
8th Grade Teacher

SAINT BERNARD

Yunker, Sharon Porter
Teacher/Eng Dept Chairperson

SAINT CLAIRSVILLE

Evick, John Allan
Mathematics Teacher & Coach
Fithen, Donna S.
Spanish/French Teacher
Lollini, Dorothy Logonoveach
7th-8th Grade Rdng Lit Teacher
Mc Call, David L.
Spanish Teacher
Phillips, Charles Lewis
Geography & Reading Teacher
Phillips, Emma Jo Lambros
Teacher
Ritter, Stacey Georges
First Grade Teacher
Shane, Penny Frohnapfel
Business Education Teacher
Teliga, Darlene Annette
English Teacher
Verba, Steven Joseph
8th Grade Science Teacher
Wolfson, Eloise Symons
Retired Teacher

SAINT HENRY

Broering, Donald Lawrence
Agricultural Education Teacher
Summers, Charles Alan
Science Teacher

SAINT MARYS

Grindrod, John James
English Department Chair
Gruber, Larry Lee
Science Teacher
Johns, Fern (Leffel)
Retired First Grade Teacher
Meinerding, Allen August
7th-8th Grade Soc Stud Teacher

SALEM

Craig, Jeffery Alan
5th Grade Teacher
Esposito, William Michael
English Teacher
Kaufman, Jean Garlock
Sixth Grade Teacher
Paxson, Ila Jeanne
Third Grade Teacher

SALINEVILLE

Beatty, Helen Gail
Mathematics Dept Chairperson
Dunham, Dennis James
6th/8th Grade Health Teacher
Gill, Jeff W.
Mathematics Teacher

SANDUSKY

Armstrong, Lorene Stark
2nd Grade Teacher
Colatruglio, Kenneth Anthony
English Department Chairman
Hempel, Judith Gilmore
Second Grade Teacher
Schrader, Rita J. (Zeller)
Kindergarten Teacher
Wagner, Mary Eileen
Retired Mathematics Instructor
Wagner, Mary Jon
Principal

SARDIS

Wright, David Walter
American History Teacher

SCIOTOVILLE

Boyd, Naomi C. Craft
Fourth Grade Teacher

SEAMAN

Carter, Sharon Ann (Simmons)
Third Grade Teacher

SEBRING

Garrity, Debbe Anne
Jr HS Math/Eng Teacher
Jones, Ronald A.
Jr HS Science/Health Teacher
Myers, Kathy Abmyer
English Teacher
Thomas, Laurie Henderson
First Grade Teacher
Zeppernick, Patricia Derene (Dery)
Fifth Grade Teacher

SEVEN HILLS

Kittleberger, Frederick William
Mathematics Teacher/Dept Chm
Sedlak, Rose Marie Assad
New Direction At Risk Teacher

SHADYSIDE

Durant, Jeffry Lynn
Fifth Grade Teacher
Jones, Helen Kane
Fourth Grade Teacher

SHAKER HEIGHTS

Johnson, William Richard
English/Social Studies Teacher
Krogness, Mary Mercer
English/Language Arts Teacher
Lane, Donna-Marie M.
Sixth Grade Teacher
Miller, Fay Brownlee
Third Grade Teacher
Salkin, Joan Cheryl
6th Grade Teacher

SHELBY

Bell, Pamela Kay (Weirich)
Business Teacher
Fugate, Robert Jr.
Science Teacher
Kettering, Donald R.
6th Grade Teacher
Terman, Ken L.
Chemistry Teacher/Tennis Coach

SHERWOOD

Rhodes, Marjorie L.
Sixth Grade Teacher

SHILOH

Briggs, Ethel Louise
Fifth Grade Teacher
Follett, Charles Michael
Health & Physical Ed Teacher
Steinmetz, Kevin Lee
Mathematics Teacher/Dept Chair
Zirkle, Barbara Jean
General Sci/Soc Stud Teacher

SIDNEY

Gilfillen, Rita (Enders)
Science, Math Teacher
Mc Alexander, Charlotte Duer
English/Vocal Music Teacher
Rittenhouse, Deborah Boblit
Sixth Grade Teacher
Thompson, Terri Snavley
6th Grade Teacher

SMITHVILLE

Frizell, Daniel
High School English Teacher
Mc Gowan, Charles Clinton
History/Earth Science Teacher

SOMERSET

Burkhart, Mary Melinda
First Grade Teacher
Simmons, Jonn Louis
Principal
Wolf, Catherine Rose
Sixth Grade Teacher

SOUTH AMHERST

Buehner, Richard Andre
8th Grade US History Teacher

SOUTH CHARLESTON

Banion, Suzanne Wilt
7th & 8th Grade Lit Teacher

SOUTH EUCLID

Hart, Linda J.
4th Grade Teacher
Kirby-Becker, Maureen Therese
(Kibry)
Biology Teacher
Thomson, Zina
7th/8th Grade Soc Stud Teacher

SOUTH SALEM

Drummond, Mabel S.
Fourth Grade Teacher

SPRINGBORO

Conde, A. Richard
Spanish Teacher
Kuhn, Vicki Sue (Akers)
Mathematics Teacher
Lawson, Jean Elizabeth
7th Grade Earth Sci Teacher

SPRINGFIELD

Bennett, Barney Lea
Music Teacher
Hickinbotham, David Lee
7th/8th Grade Math Teacher
Love, Diane Louise
7th Grade Eng & Rdng Teacher
Rugh, Matthew Shealy
Health & Pre-Algebra Teacher

SPRINGFIELD (cont)
Sheridan, Elaine S. (Fisher)
  Spanish Teacher
Taylor, Thomas Edward
  Science Teacher
Wilson, Thomas Linn
  7th Grade Teacher/Chairperson

STERLING
Renninger, Lillian Marie (Lance)
  4th Grade Teacher

STEUBENVILLE
Lydick, Donald Howard
  Fifth Grade Teacher
Thomas, Pat Mehringer
  8th Grade Teacher

STOCKPORT
Ryan, Jane F.
  6th-8th Grade Soc Stud Teacher
Stall, Patricia Kelly
  Second Grade Teacher

STOUTSVILLE
Henderly, Elaine Ann
  Jr HS Reading Teacher
Williams, Sandra Ankrom
  Third Grade Teacher

STOW
Senuta, Suzanne
  Level 6 Teacher

STREETSBORO
Volk, Deborah J.
  French Teacher

STRONGSVILLE
Anderson, Sandra L.
  Second Grade Teacher
Ring, Lucy M.
  Spanish Teacher

STRUTHERS
Dama, Jo Ann Adams
  Second Grade Teacher
Kapsulis, Dulcie J.
  Kindergarten Teacher
Martz, Beverly Dobos
  English Teacher

STRYKER
Carey, Carolyn Deann (Shankster)
  4th Grade Teacher
Luthy, Brian Howard
  Science Teacher
Swanger, Kathy Lynn
  Soc Stud Teacher/Chairperson

SUGAR GROVE
Schlosser, Ruthe Palmer
  Fifth Grade Teacher

SULPHUR SPRINGS
Wagner, Joyce C.
  4th Grade Teacher

SUMMITVILLE
Sparre, Mary
  Third Grade Teacher

SUNBURY
Mc Canney, Terra Baker
  Spanish Teacher/Chair

SYLVANIA
Hill, William Frank
  History Teacher
Van Horn, Ellen McGrane
  Second Grade Teacher

THE PLAINS
Chapman, Karen Russell
  4th Grade Teacher

THORNVILLE
Glade, Karen Trunick
  Senior English Teacher
Koehler, Janet Hursey
  Business Education Teacher
Steen, Karen Sue (Keister)
  Business Instructor

TIFFIN
Alfred, Judith Saltzman
  Mathematics Teacher
Foy, Jan Miller
  Fourth Grade Teacher
Hampp, Michael Allan
  Band Director
Hart, Joyce Elchert
  Second Grade Teacher
Johns, Rita Mae OSU
  Jr HS Math/Science Teacher
Mass, Anthony James
  Soc Stud Teacher/Athletic Dir

TILTONSVILLE
Durbin, Jeffrey Allen
  Biology/Chemistry Teacher

Snodgrass, Snowe Stilwell
  Visual Arts Teacher

TIPP CITY
Welbaum, Margarat Ann
  Spanish Teacher

TOLEDO
Asendorf, Sheila Griffin
  Art/Chemistry Teacher
Black, Neil James
  Health/Phys Ed Teacher
Blakeman, Beverly Kurtz
  Kindergarten Teacher
Boblitt, Edmond Ray
  Assistant Principal Curriculum
Bragg, Kathleen Kae (Hall)
  K-12th Grade Music Teacher
Brister, Bonnie Arendale
  Fifth Grade Teacher
Carey, Eloise
  Third Grade Teacher
Carmony, James Walter Jr.
  Teacher/Sr Class Advisor
Czerniak, Charlene M.
  Assistant Professor
Davis, Joanne Quetschke
  Kindergarten Teacher
Demarkowski, Carl John
  English Teacher
Dewey, Paulette Baker
  English Teacher/Dept Chair
Dieball, Judith Cole
  4th Grade Teacher
Donaldson, Annelle R.
  Choral Director
Duty, Lynn Ann (Miller)
  Sixth Grade Teacher
Feltner, Harold
  English Department Chairman
Ford, Avearn
  6th Grade Teacher
Green, Leola
  Elementary Teacher
Hamrick, Virgie Louise Watson
  Behavioral Intervention Coord
Harley, Joyce Lee
  Language Art Teacher
Hipp, Marynette Myers
  Second Grade Teacher
Hoag, Ronald George
  Science Teacher
Jordan, Andrew Lee
  Business Education Instructor
Lewinski, Patricia Ann
  Mathematics Teacher
Lutz, Regan Ann (Richardson)
  Social Studies Dept Chair
Mayesky, Gary John
  Mathematics Teacher
Monto, Marilyn Ann
  Fifth Grade Teacher
Napieralski, Valerie A.
  Business Teacher
Pruden, Mary A.
  English Teacher
Puglisi, Teresa Marie
  School Counselor
Simon, Cynthia Mc Mullen
  Mathematics Teacher
Simon, William
  Music/Band Teacher
Slane, Michael Leroy
  Social Studies Teacher
Walasinski, Alice Joyce Dziewiatka
  Jr High Teacher

TONTOGANY
Scott, Bernard James
  Agriscience Instructor

TORONTO
Fithen, Pamela Meyer
  Third Grade Teacher

TRENTON
Titkemeyer, Ramona Swanson
  Kindergarten Teacher

TROTWOOD
Boike, Dorothy Roberts
  Teacher
Devers, Thomas Oliver
  4th Grade Teacher
Harris, Antoinette Maceo
  English Teacher
Mc Kinney, John Huston
  Math/Social Studies Teacher
Meeks, Darrell James
  Mathematics Teacher

TROY
Callagher, Rita Davis
  Substitute Teacher
Campbell, Robert J.
  Elementary Physical Ed Teacher
Fushimi, Cindy
  Biology Teacher

Sloan, Ann Henderson
  6th-8th Grade Math/Sci Teacher

TUPPERS PLAINS
Perine, John Vincent
  Fourth Grade Teacher

TWINSBURG
Brownfield, Robert Beaumont Jr.
  Fourth Grade Teacher
Denges, Ethel Lynn Krumme
  American History Teacher
Dye, Richard Alan
  Guidance Counselor
Harrell, Virginia Persinger
  Mathematics Teacher/Dept Chair

UNIONTOWN
Jones, Anna Heckel
  Second Grade Teacher
Simmons, Patricia Reese
  Rdng Recovery-Remedial Teacher

UNIVERSITY HEIGHTS
Nemeth, Rosemary Leone
  4th Grade Teacher
Rodman, Loretta Frattzolino
  Special Education Teacher
Schweitzer, Debra Ann (Perry)
  Teacher of Gifted & Talented

URBANA
Hackenbracht, Josephine
  Fourth Grade Teacher
Harlamert, Mary Jo Wallace
  English Teacher
Johnson, Marion Crist
  Mathematics Teacher
Rosset, Emily Jean Jeffries
  High School Supervisor

UTICA
Schetzsle, Barbara Ann
  World His/Civics/Rdng Teacher

VAN BUREN
Rader, John Edward
  Mathematics/Computer Teacher
Rhoten, Linda Dutton
  Fifth Grade Teacher

VAN WERT
Hetrick, Mary Hurrelbrink
  First Grade Teacher

VANDALIA
Hempel, James A.
  Latin Teacher

VIENNA
Webb, Susan Kay
  French/English Teacher

WADSWORTH
Franz, Susan Tolson
  Third Grade Teacher
Ott, Mary Lou
  8th Grade English Teacher
Toth, Twila Stone
  English Teacher
Van Steenberg, Suzanne J. Richards
  Third Grade Teacher

WAKEMAN
Schedley, Holly Jean
  7th Grade Lang Art Teacher

WAPAKONETA
Frame, Jane Thuma
  Third Grade Teacher
Porcher, Connie Mitchell
  Spanish Teacher
Taubken, Christine Crawford
  3rd Grade Teacher
Warner, Debora Payne
  Physical Education Teacher

WARREN
Bailey, Richard Lee
  English Teacher
Dalrymple, Dorothy Moran
  Retired Second Grade Teacher
Grischow, A. Lynne Steffen
  Sociology Teacher
Koski, Barbara Ann
  Teacher/Coord of Gifted
Loomis, Stan Lee
  Math Teacher
Lubert, Rose Angela (Moran)
  Fourth Grade Teacher
Petschel, Sally Jane Neff
  Fourth Grade Teacher

WARRENSVILLE HTS
Capes, Jay Franklin
  4th Grade Teacher
Cardwell, Debra Jeanne (Holloway)
  Fourth Grade Teacher
Talley, Sandra Knowles
  8th Grade Eng Teacher/Coord

WARRINGTON HEIGHTS
Brown, Billie Carmichael
  Retired Teacher

WARSAW
Mc Millan, Viola Brown
  Mathematics Teacher
Stocker, Joyce Ann
  English Teacher

WASHINGTON CRT HSE
Lewis, Mary Statt
  Mathematics Teacher

WATERFORD
Beardmore, Nellie Hess
  Biology/Mathematics Teacher

WATERLOO
Hale, Janet Bennett
  Reading Recovery Teacher
Lunsford, Johnna Miller
  Elementary Principal

WATERVILLE
Amos, Nancy Stockwell
  Kindergarten Teacher

WAUSEON
Brothers, Mary Beth Beth (Keil)
  Fourth Grade Teacher
Croninger, Cathy Le
  Kindergarten Teacher
Oberski, Ann Miller
  English/Reading Teacher

WAVERLY
Murrell, Susan Smith
  Sixth Grade Soc Stud Teacher
Peters, Jamie (Sue) Ward
  2nd Grade Teacher
Vansant, Ann M.
  Fifth Grade Teacher

WAYNESVILLE
Campbell, Ellen L. (Earhart)
  Fifth Grade Teacher
Leist, David P.
  Music/Drama Teacher

WELLINGTON
Stevens, Douglas Alan
  8th Grade Science Teacher

WELLSTON
Downard, James Robert
  8th Grade English Teacher
Shumard, Sally L.
  High School Art Teacher
Smith, Frieda Sue
  1st Grade Teacher

WELLSVILLE
Acerra, Barbara Thomas
  4th Grade Teacher
Calhoun, Esther Bryan
  English Department Chairperson
Chamberlain, Judith Lynn
  Fifth Grade Teacher
Logston, Stephen Kenneth
  Sixth Grade Teacher
Mc Cutcheon, Joie C.
  Third Grade Teacher

WEST CARROLLTON
Alexander, Gary F.
  6th Grade Teacher
Shafer, Thomas Russell
  English/Literature Teacher
Wilson, L. Alvine
  English & Literature Teacher

WEST CHESTER
Hendricks, Willis Aileen Farmer
  Fifth Grade Teacher
Noble, Linda A.
  Physics Teacher/Sci Dept Chair

WEST ELKTON
Immel, Cheryl Ann Pendell
  5th Grade Teacher
Roberts, Linda Carol (Brady)
  First Grade Teacher

WEST FARMINGTON
Holderbaum, Suzanne Bartley
  4th Grade Teacher
Zakrajsek, Joyce Gnat
  1st Grade Teacher

WEST JEFFERSON
Hayes, Sharon Miller
  Third Grade Teacher
Reynolds, William Taylor
  Biology Teacher

WEST MANCHESTER
Clark, Ronald Lee
  Science/Phys Ed Teacher
Reck, Nancy Jane
  5th Grade Teacher

Thompson, Earline Kay (Miller)
  Sixth Grade Teacher

WEST SALEM
Krajcik, Jackie Harter
  Guidance Counselor

WEST UNION
Kramer, Joseph John
  Business Teacher

WESTERVILLE
Donofrio, Daniel Joseph
  Science Teacher
Hiser, Mark Charles
  English/Humanities Teacher
Potts, Becky Ann
  Gifted Teacher
Volpe, Deborah Love
  HS Mathematics Teacher

WESTLAKE
Thompson, Jon Steven
  7th Grade English Teacher

WHARTON
Hemmerly, Audrey Switzer
  Language Arts Teacher

WHEELERSBURG
Branon, Jack Kent
  Social Studies Teacher
Butts, Brenda (Horner)
  Fourth Grade Teacher
Fenimore, Patricia Flannery
  Kindergarten Teacher
Gleim, Carol Jane (Hill)
  English Teacher

WHITEHALL
Bradshaw, Serena Moody
  Social Studies Teacher
Easter, Judith Rae
  7th Grade Eng/Soc Stud Teacher
Farry, Melinda (Heuer)
  English Teacher
Frazier, Steven Lee
  Sixth Grade Teacher

WHITEHOUSE
Johnson, Valerie K.
  Biology/Physiology Teacher
Nolder, Daala Ames
  5th Grade Teacher

WILLIAMSPORT
Cochenour, Shara Lee
  English Teacher
Crites, Charlotte Barnes
  Home Economics/Reading Teacher
Riley, Beverly Hamric
  Business Teacher
Riley, Virginia Ann (Hamric)
  English Teacher

WILLOUGHBY
Schmidt, Kathleen Louise Turner
  5th Grade Teacher

WILMINGTON
Adams, Judith Myers
  Social Studies Chairperson
Rupp, Sherry L.
  Third Grade Teacher

WINDHAM
Mitchell, Wilma Duffield
  Teacher of Gifted/Talented
Pozsgai, Bill
  Health/Phys Ed/Psych Teacher

WINTERSVILLE
France, Roberta Payne
  4th Grade Teacher
Herrick, Alberta Elaine (Lugano)
  English Teacher
Hocking, Melanie E.
  Chemistry Teacher
Rathbun, Donna Louise Hester
  1st Grade Teacher
Sells, D. Randall
  Asst Dir Learning Skills Lab

WOODSFIELD
Christman, R. Todd
  Business Teacher

WOOSTER
Fischer, Max W.
  6th Grade Teacher
Topovski, Shirley Elser
  First Grade Teacher

WORTHINGTON
Davis, Roberta
  7th Grade Science Teacher
Dove, Timothy Mark
  7th Grade Soc Stud Teacher
Turner, Cheryl Young
  Pre-School Teacher

XENIA
Nichols, Louise
  Fifth Grade Teacher
White, Betty Canty
  Sixth Grade Teacher

YELLOW SPRINGS
Christopher, Mary Ann Lacour
  Mathematics/English Teacher
Robey, John Samuel
  Mathematics Teacher

YORKVILLE
Kopral, Irene Kuntupis
  5th Grade Teacher
Signorini, Daniel Albert
  English/Language Arts Teacher

YOUNGSTOWN
Bokesch, Daniel J.
  Principal
Clark, Carol Sue
  Orchestra Director
Coleman, Karen Hulburt
  English Department Chair
Collier, Janet Owen
  7th Grade Language Arts
Collins, Kathy L.
  Elementary Guidance Counselor
Conti, Jacklyn Marie
  Kindergarten Teacher
De Toro, James P.
  Eighth Grade Math Teacher
Di Pillo, Marylou Dutko
  Middle Grade Teacher
Dougherty, Elaine
  Seventh/Eighth Grade Teacher
Elias, William Edward
  Spanish Teacher
Fritchey, Judd E.
  Band Director
Gonda, Mary Garcar
  Third Grade Teacher
Hamrock, Angela Salreno
  Fourth Grade Teacher
Heri, Barbara A.
  6th Grade Teacher
Huff, Denise Horad
  Second Grade Teacher
Jeswald, Marcia A.
  7th Grade Reading Teacher
Kapusinski, Marianne Walls
  Math/Physical Ed Teacher
Loree, Susan Diane
  English Teacher
Macejko, Ruby Marie
  Fourth Grade Teacher
Minghetti, Rita Ann
  Theology Teacher/Dept Chair
Novello, Doris Jean
  Honors English Teacher & Chm
Novello, Rita Mae (Romeo)
  Spanish Teacher
Pappas, Maria Cougras
  Coord Gifted & Talented Prgms
Perry, Wayne A.
  7th Grade Mathematics Teacher
Popio, Joan Kish
  Language Arts Teacher
Reed, Gretchen Keefer
  Third Grade Teacher
Sims, Carl Walker
  Fifth Grade Teacher
Villella, Kathleen Lynn (Coppola)
  8th Grade Teacher
Wagner, Yvonne D.
  English Department Teacher
Wolford, Mildred Lozier
  Seventh Grade Teacher

ZANESFIELD
Ortli, Patricia Grayatt
  General Science Teacher
Swartz, Jon C.
  English Teacher

ZANESVILLE
Davis, Edna Mc Court
  Retired Elementary Teacher
Duncan, Joanna Mihok
  6th Grade Teacher
Gibson, Jerry Edson
  Vocal Music Teacher
Good, Linda Moore
  2nd Grade Head Teacher
Henderson, Robert F.
  French/English Teacher
James, Anita Marie Young
  8th Grade English/Rdng Teacher
Koncar, George Alan
  Mathematics Teacher
Newman, Vicki Elaine
  Social Studies Teacher

OKLAHOMA

ACHILLE
Anders, Kay
  Business Education Teacher
Thornburg, Donola Pannell
  Science Teacher
Winnett, Cheryl Onstott
  Kindergarten-5th Grade Teacher

ADA
Bledsoe, D. Coleen Murray
  Fifth Grade Teacher
Green, Trudy Coffey
  Business Teacher
Hisle, Claudia Parker
  Science/Computer Teacher
Looper, Sandra Kay (Savage)
  Elementary Principal
Martin, Gae Vonne Rue
  Fifth Grade Teacher
Stewart, Jana (Richardson)
  Reading Teacher
Sweatt, Martha Bullard
  Third Grade Teacher
Thompson, Lola Beatrice (Rush)
  Fifth Grade Teacher
Tipton, Judy Ann
  Speech Teacher
Vandewalker, David Richard
  Band Director
White, Ila Faye
  2nd Grade Teacher

ADAMS
Farmer, Deanna Louise
  3rd & 4th Grade Teacher

ALBERT
Ingram, Tomisene Mc Alister
  Vocational Home Ec Teacher

ALLEN
Turpin, Jimmie Nell
  Fifth Grade Teacher

ALTUS
Bailey, Shirlee Storm Freeman
  Vocal Music Specialist
Crawford, Ruby Barker
  Kindergarten Teacher
Grimes, David Lee
  Elementary Principal

ALVA
Bradt, Charlene Susan
  Teacher
Holder, Lisa Dozier
  Language Arts Instructor
Koehn, Karen Leigh
  High School Counselor

AMBER
Anderson, Melody Lynn (Treat)
  English/Science Teacher
Sanders, Dickie Dee
  Mathematics Teacher

ANADARKO
Matlock, Debra Lynn
  Math Teacher

ANTLERS
Latham, Billy Randall
  Industrial Arts & Art Teacher

ARDMORE
Brumley, Leann Louise
  2nd Grade Teacher
Jones, Dorothy Hellen
  Second Grade Teacher
Riner, Susan Mason
  1st Grade Teacher
Roberts, Taujuanna Lynn
  8th Grade Lang Arts Teacher
Thompson, Mary Lou
  Third Grade Teacher
Willis, Becky Jane (Estes)
  Mathematics Teacher

ARKOMA
Pope, Rita Jean (Conrad)
  Business Education Teacher

ARNETT
Knowles, Linda K.
  Mathematics Teacher

ATOKA
Crow, Clifteen J.
  Vocational Business Teacher

BALKO
Weeks, Phyllis Erlene
  Second Grade Teacher

BARTLESVILLE
Anduss, Janet Fleming
  Mathematics Teacher

Austerman, Donna Lynne
  Spanish Teacher
Barclay, Karen Mc Kinley
  Kindergarten Teacher
Burpo, Joyce Swartz
  Business Education Dept Chair
Conover, Mitsuye Hamada
  Social Studies Teacher
Culver, Marilyn Ann (Buck)
  Chapter I Math Teacher
Goetzinger, Carolyn Mc Kinney
  Mathematics Teacher
Mc Intosh, Beverly A. (Wortz)
  Biology Teacher
Wheeler, Thomas Lee
  Economics/Amer History Teacher

BENNINGTON
Knight, Mary Ann (Phillips)
  Kindergarten/Elem Principal

BETHANY
East, Patricia Rae Going
  Elementary Classroom Teacher
Lankford, Nancy
  Fourth Grade Teacher
Lyon, Judee (Rowland)
  Art Teacher/Fine Arts Chairman

BILLINGS
Carter, Patricia Worrell
  First Grade Teacher

BIXBY
Brown, Julia Stimson
  Sixth Grade Teacher
Coffman, Anna Marie
  Music Specialist
Coleman, Gary L.
  Counselor
Ketchum, Wanda Marie Morrow
  Fourth Grade Teacher
Maxey, Eloise Evelyn
  Director of Gifted/Talented Ed
Schauer, Larry D.
  Teacher/Assistant Dept Head
Schmitt, Claudia K. (Galusha)
  English Teacher/Dept Head
Shipman, Judy Capehart
  High School Counselor

BLACKWELL
Brandt, Tim James
  Director of Bands

BLAIR
Mc Millin, Judith Ann (Osborn)
  Fourth Grade Teacher

BLANCHARD
Turner, Kathryn Butler
  Guidance Counselor
Wood, Cassie Coggins
  History-Government Teacher

BOISE CITY
Miller, Gladys (Wilson)
  Reading Teacher

BOKCHITO
Iker, Joan White
  Mathematics Teacher

BRISTOW
Dill, Rick
  Social Studies Teacher/Coach
Matthews, Patti Duncan
  First Grade Teacher
Thompson, Kathryn Holcomb
  7th Grade English Teacher
Zuker, Kathy Cain
  2nd Grade Teacher

BROKEN ARROW
Blackburn, Betty Lou (Martin)
  Voc Home Economics Teacher
Burns, Elizabeth Jayne
  Communicative Skills Teacher
Jack, Rebecca G.
  French/Spanish Teacher

BURBANK
Gauger, Irene Vaughn
  First & Second Grade Teacher
Sherrill, Nancy Goucher
  Teaching Principal

BUTLER
Roberts, Marian Ruth
  Jr/Sr HS Trigonometry Teacher

CADDO
Thornton, Francille Taylor
  Chapter I Teacher

CALVIN
Lindley, Deloris Rae (Orr)
  Business Teacher

CANTON
Stevenson, Phylls Janet (Lee)
  Fourth Grade Teacher

CASHION
Beaty, Monty Quade
  Technology Education Teacher

CATOOSA
Rinaldi, Margaret Hussey
  Mathematics Teacher

CHICKASHA
Verhines, Steve Edward
  Elementary Teacher

CHOCTAW
Harris, Sharon A.
  Mathematics Dept Chairperson
Holland, Linda Westfall
  Sixth Grade Teacher
Hoover, Sarah Lynda
  Vocal Music HS Teacher
Pruett, Dale Alden
  Computer Literacy Teacher
Sanders, Barbara Brown
  Science Teacher
Sloan, Linda (Klingstedt)
  Vocational Home Ec Teacher
Torbett, C. Jolene
  Teacher
Uselton, Bill W.
  European History Teacher
Wafford, Francis Catherine
  First Grade Teacher
Ward, Teresa J.
  English Teacher

CHOUTEAU
Holland, Connie Enyart
  Social Studies Dept Chair

CLAREMORE
Batty, Linda L.
  Gifted/Talented Teacher
Butler, Deborah Dolmovich
  Counselor

CLINTON
Mc Murry, Doyle Ray
  Science Teacher
Scarlett, Annie Brown
  2nd Grade Teacher

COLBERT
Wallace, Ronnie Glenn
  Language Arts Teacher

COLEMAN
Jemison, Linda Joy (Ogle)
  5th-6th Grade Teacher

COLLINSVILLE
Dortch, Ellen Garner
  1st Grade Teacher of Gifted

COMANCHE
Mc Gowen, Billie Jo
  Mathematics Teacher
Phillips, Jerry H.
  Business Education Instructor
Spears, Pat (Sitz)
  Fourth Grade Teacher

COMMERCE
Morrison, Scott R.
  4th Grade Teacher
Morrison, Sue
  Fifth Grade Teacher

COPAN
Diehl, Penny Sue (Ruch)
  Science Teacher
Radebaugh, Charlene Sallee
  Second Grade Teacher

COUNCIL HILL
Whitman, Harley Wayne
  Principal/Eng Teacher/Coach
Whitman, Robin Anne
  English Teacher

COVINGTON
Peacock, Carolyn L. Elliott
  2nd Grade Teacher

CROWDER
Banks, Jan Sue (Rogers)
  Remedial Reading Teacher
Lambert, Sheryl Darlene
  HS Mathematics Teacher

CUSHING
Swindell, Nelle Fuller
  English Teacher

DEL CITY
Calaway, Norman Hardy
  History Teacher
Cloud, Donna Leach
  5th Grade Teacher

Dawkins, Rick
  Assistant Principal
Goodwin, Gary Lynn
  Fifth Grade Teacher
Harris, James D.
  Physical/Life Science Teacher
Moore, Thomas Freeman
  On-Campus Supervisor
Rasberry, L. Darlene
  Mathematics Teacher
Santa Cruz, Oscar Roberto
  Computer Science Teacher
Sutton, Bill L.
  Social Studies Teacher

DEWEY
Santine, Ann (Donnelly)
  7th/8th Grade Math Teacher

DILL CITY
Cunningham, Nancy Ann Mather
  4th Grade Teacher

DRUMMOND
Hill, Nola Hedges
  Retired Teacher
Hughes, Anita Anderson
  Social Studies/English Teacher

DRUMRIGHT
La France, Ernestine Christine Gettys
  Biology/Computer Teacher
Miller, Maria Joy Mc Corkle
  Business Teacher

DUNCAN
Brancich, Mary Hodgson
  Fourth Grade Teacher
Coleman, Patricia Ann
  6th Grade Teacher
Drake, Robin Annear
  Eng Teacher
Haxton, Judith Ann
  Fifth/Sixth Grade Teacher
Hornick, Jeri Lyn
  3rd Grade Teacher
Hughes, Jack Hobart
  Retired Mid Sch Teacher
Sayers, Billye Burrough
  Mathematics Teacher

DURANT
Dunham, Janice Flynt
  Retired Teacher
Gaither, Gayle Caldwell
  English Department Chairperson
Hartin, Haljean Ward
  English Teacher
Hunnicutt, Nettie O'Donley
  Reading/Math Lab Teacher
Lilley, Melissa Dawson
  English Teacher
Peoples, James Wendell
  Math Teacher

EAGLETOWN
Puckett, Beverly Klein
  High School English Teacher
Sloat, Harold Wayne
  Social Studies Teacher

EDMOND
Bath, Marsha Patterson
  7th Grade Geography Teacher
Bundrick, Elizabeth Ann Henthorn
  Second Grade Teacher
Eckel, Robert J.
  Principal
Fine, Joe Thomas
  Band Director
Riggs, Steven Wayne
  Phys Ed/Health Teacher
Roberts, Sonja Ramona (Davis)
  Fourth Grade Teacher
Teague, Rebecca Slade
  Chem Teacher/Sci Dept Chair
Thomas, Pat
  Mathematics Teacher/Dept Chair
Tippin, Mark T.
  Mathematics Teacher
Young, Cynthia Boyle
  Fifth Grade Teacher

EL RENO
Carter, Rocky K.
  Social Studies Teacher

ENID
Druiett, Nancy Jean
  Third Grade Teacher
Gay, Marjorie Rose
  Reading Specialist
Mayfield, Donna Elliott
  Spanish Teacher
Mc Creary, Beth Christine
  1st Grade Teacher
Peck, Steven Randal
  Fifth Grade Teacher

ENID (cont)
Roberts, Gary Gray
5th Grade Teacher
Stuever, Vicki Leslie
Honors Eng/Psych Teacher
Williams, Lois Geraldine Phipps
6th Grade Teacher

EUFAULA
Flud, Sherrie Nunn
5th Grade Teacher
Kiener, Sharon June (Burns)
English Teacher

FAIRFAX
Long, Carolyn Gillispie
Fifth Grade Teacher

FAIRLAND
Gardner, Sharon Marie
Vocational Home Ec Teacher
Smith, Win V.
History Teacher

FAIRVIEW
Haworth, Denice Kay
4th Grade Sci & Math Teacher
Sacket, Billy Ray Jr.
6th/7th Grade Science Teacher

FARGO
Johnson, Rick Joe
6th Grade Teacher

FORT COBB
Wall, Linda Beth
Fourth Grade Teacher

FORT GIBSON
Corley, Larry Dale
Mathematics Department Chair

FOX
Bruner, Virginia Jane (Dunlap)
HS English Teacher
Gossvener, Penny Sturgeon
Second Grade Teacher

FOYIL
Hendrickson, Robert Dean
Science Teacher

GARBER
Daniel, Delbert L.
Elementary Principal
Eggers, Donna Backhaus
Jr HS English Teacher
White, Marilyn Kennedy
Fourth Grade Teacher

GLENCOE
Nichols, Charles Lloyd
Fifth Grade Teacher

GLENPOOL
Barnes, Tammy Kaye
8th Grade English Teacher
Brown, Paula Halfast
French/Spanish Teacher

GRAHAM
Crosthwait, Linda (Conner)
1st/2nd Grade Teacher

GUTHRIE
Clinton, Linda Kay (Morgan)
8th English Teacher/Dept Chair
Hanson, Mary Lou Caldwell
Second Grade Teacher
Thomas, Francis J.
2nd Grade Teacher
Young, Thomas Wilfred
Teacher/Athletic Director

GUYMON
Mc Clenagan, Brenda Howell
1st Grade Teacher
Tuttle, John G.
6th Grade Teacher

HAMMON
Powers, Renita Elaine
Vocational Home Ec Educator
Redd, Betty Jo (Miller)
Kindergarten Teacher

HARDESTY
Stump, Kathy Gibson
5th & 6th Grade HS Art Teacher

HARRAH
Givens, Gary Franklin
Principal
Harris, Roger Alan
First Grade Teacher
Stravlo, Willo Dean
First Grade Teacher

HARTSHORNE
Hunt, Donna Monks
Sixth Grade English Teacher

HEALDTON
Chase, La Veta Young
Teacher
Feldmann, Randy G.
Science Teacher/Coach
Porterfield, Anita La Verne
Reading Teacher

HELENA
Redman, Amanda Schoeb
Kindergartn/Elem Music Teacher

HENDRIX
Proctor, Cindy Ann (Blackburn)
7th & 8th Grade Teacher
Terrell, Terry Ray
5th/6th Grade Teacher

HENRYETTA
Cook, Chelsea Carroll
Principal

HITCHITA
Duvall, Mary Louise Hood
Fourth Grade Teacher

HOMINY
Worthy, Christine Dare (Swords)
K-5th Grade Teacher

HULBERT
Baker, Linda K. (Mc Niel)
English, Civics & Geo Teacher
Sly, Johnny Richard
Social Studies Teacher

HYDRO
Brown, Helen Ottinger
Teacher/Counselor of LD

IDABEL
Hill, John Bruce
9th-10th Grade History Teacher
Stevenson, David Roy
Science Teacher/Dept Chair

INDIANOLA
Blessing, Delores Elaine
Secondary English Teacher

JAY
Cunningham, Rhonda Fryer
Kindergarten Teacher
Maynard, Phelecia Jane
5th Grade Teacher
Robbins, Nancy (Phillips)
Developmental Teacher
Thornton, Mary Hardin
Jr-Sr Counselor

JENKS
Cepurniek, Joy Price
Fifth Grade Teacher
Langford, Stephen Ray
Chemistry Teacher
Robinson, Esther Martin
Social Studies Dept Chair
Rogers, Keith Rodney
Director of Speech Activities
Spencer, Diana Blake
Biology Teacher

JONES
Kline, Patricia Fletcher
Middle School Teacher
Lucas, Randy Joe
Mathematics Department Chm
Mc Adoo, Lisa Gail
Mathematics Teacher
Sisco, Linda Marie (Ray)
2nd Grade Teacher

KELLYVILLE
Lowry, Marilyn Denham
Jr HS Speech/English Teacher
Nelson, Kenneth John
Director of Bands

KEOTA
Alderson, Niki Adcock
English/Speech Teacher

KETCHUM
Campbell, Sue Raines
H S Business Education Teacher

KINGFISHER
Stolz, Anna Maples
Kindergarten Teacher

KINGSTON
Corbett, Gerri M.
Middle School Math Teacher
Goldsmith, Bill W.
Fourth Grade Teacher

KREBS
Dunbar, Debbie Lynn
Sixth Grade Teacher
Griffith, Mary Carano
Third Grade Teacher

Richardson, Carol Denise
7th Grade Teacher/Coach

LAWTON
Hagen, Nanette Chestnut
2nd Grade Teacher
Hightower, Ernestine Rollins
Third-Fourth Grade Teacher
Kaigler, Anquanita Madden
6th Grade Reading Teacher
Kuchynka, Randall G.
World His/US His Teacher
Schoonover, Wayne Keith Jr.
Sixth Grade Teacher
Stewart, Lynn Eugene
Counselor
Talley, Joe L.
Teacher
Washington, Danny J.
Drivers Ed Teacher/Coach
Weryavah, Dana Andrew
High School Counselor
White, Daniel W.
Physical Education Teacher
Wiginton, Vickie (Mc Gee)
Drama/Debate Teacher

LOCUST GROVE
Cowan, Frances (Jones)
English Teacher

LONE WOLF
Hohmann, Darrell R.
Science Computer
Howard, Nancy Carole (Arnold)
Fifth Grade Teacher

MANGUM
Bull, Ruby Jane
Mathematics Teacher

MARLOW
Julian, Carolann Simpson
Third Grade Teacher
Layn, Shena Cooper
9th Grade English Teacher
Wood, Katheryn Jane
Fourth Grade Teacher

MAYSVILLE
Deviney, Susan Kay Silcott
First Grade Teacher

MC ALESTER
Horne, Don Clayton
Social Studies Teacher
Johnson, Kelly Kirkes
Business & Office Instructor
Loy, Delila Vickery
2nd Grade Teacher
Woodward, Rita Lamirand
Sixth Grade Teacher

MC CURTAIN
Warren, Sue (Kennedy)
Fifth Grade Teacher

MC LOUD
Shive, Janice Monger
6th Grade Teacher

MEEKER
Hendrickson, Patricia (Roach)
English Teacher
Spencer, Buel
5th Grade Teacher

MIAMI
Barker, Jimmie Dean
6th Grade Teacher
Beggerly, Harry D.
Science Teacher
Essex, Carol Allton
Fifth Grade Teacher
Goodrich, Linda A.
Third Grade Teacher
Mangus, Thomas Eugene
Band Director
Wall, Joyce Ann
Physical Education teacher

MIDWEST CITY
Aylor, Suzanne Marley
Vocal Music Teacher
Barker, Patricia Yvonne
First Grade Teacher
Crain, Pamela K.
Business Teacher
Diehl, Clarence Harold
Retired Teacher
Hinton, Linda Courtnay
First Grade Teacher
Hodge, Linda Gail
English Teacher
Kirk, Silvya A.
History Department Chair
Mc Clure, J. Scott
5th Grade Teacher
Merkx, Kathryn C
11th Grade English Teacher

Porter, Myra Wade
English Teacher/Chair
Sullivan, Joy Jean
Fourth Grade Teacher

MINCO
Frisbie, Ann Hern
Vocational Home Ec Teacher

MOORE
Ferguson, Celinda Yunger
Mathematics Teacher/Dept Chair
Nichols, Phyllis Newsom
Counselor
Park, Lori Rhae
High School Choral Director
Rickets, Peggy Ort
Physics/Earth Science Teacher
Whatley, Theresa Paige
Fourth Grade Teacher

MORRIS
Bearden, Susan (Roulston)
Mid Sch Eng/Speech Teacher
Harris, Martha Jane (Burke)
7th-8th Grade Rdng/Sci Teacher
Todd, Cleda Latta
Third Grade Teacher

MORRISON
Cartmell, David Dwayne
Mathematics-Science Teacher

MULDROW
Cassady, Darleen Hail
Third Grade Teacher
Secratt, Sharon Eileene
8th Grade Science Teacher

MULHALL
Daniels, Norma Jean (Listen)
Third Grade Teacher

MUSKOGEE
Allen, Dorothy Jeanne
7th Grade Amer His/Civics
Arnold, Patsy R.
Second Grade Teacher
Bolding, Melanie Hagerdon
First Grade Teacher
Hyde, Donna Thrower
Business Teacher
Mehew, Deborah Eskridge
Debate/Drama Coach
Palmer, Betty Bonham
Fourth Grade Teacher
Whitaker, Henry Washington
English Teacher

MUSTANG
Bridges, Karen Sue Packer
8th Grade Teacher
Mc Elhaney, Jody Patrick
7th Grade Science Teacher
Mouse, Melani Marque
Bio/Anatomy Physiology Teacher
White, Rhonda Chapin
Reading Teacher

NEWCASTLE
Burchel, Pat
7th/8th Grade English Teacher
Dunsworth, Deborah Ellen
Geometry/Math Analysis Teacher
Wedel, Deborah Lynn (Smith)
Science Teacher

NICOMA PARK
Frosch, Carol Snow
Soc Stud Department Chair

NOBLE
Bugg, Cathey Clarke
6th Grade Teacher
Fields, Susan Ercanbrack
Speech & Drama Coach

NORMAN
Asbury, Barbara Anne Smith
Mathematics Teacher
Askey, David Mall
Chemistry Teacher
Ballard, Elizabeth Lyons
Eng/Debate/Acting Teacher
Bounds, David Alan
History/Geography Teacher
Burns, Joanna Crisp
Fourth Grade Teacher
Christian, Polly Gaebe
Elem Physical Educ Teacher
Maloney, Susan Ann
5th Grade Teacher
Matlick, Pamela Shepherd
Vocal Music Teacher
Minshall, Melinda S.
French Teacher
Odom, Carol Wood
Third Grade Teacher
Rust, Elizabeth Annie Moorhead
Home Economics Teacher

St.John, Gayle Mullen
English Teacher
Ward, Marion S.
English Teacher

NORTH ENID
Harvey, Peggy S. Herbert
Third Grade Teacher

OKAY
Dunn, Joseph Irving
History Department Chair
Hughes, Charles Evans Jr.
HS Mathematics Teacher

OKEMAH
Johnston, Doris Clark
Language Art Teacher
Wilbourn, Martha Jean
5th/6th Math/Sci/Rdng Teacher

OKLAHOMA CITY
Adams, Sue Pulley
4th Grade Teacher
Adkins, Paul Michael
Social Studies Teacher
Anderson, Barbara Boling
Language Arts Dept Chair
Brock, Marilyn F. (Morris)
7th/8th Grade English Teacher
Brogan, Carol Jenke
Administrative Intern
Brown, Donna
Drama Coach
Campbell, Steven V.
Instrumental Music Director
Cox, Kaye
Mathematics/Computer Teacher
Crosby, Frances Mc Cord
5th Grade Science Teacher
Dean, Larry Clyde
5th Grade Teacher
Engel, Al E.
Social Studies Teacher/Coach
Fellenstein, Terry Allan
Teacher
Frazier, Etta Brown
Science Teacher
Goodwin, Jamie Lynne
Third Grade Teacher
Haraughty, Candy Gonzalez
Sixth Grade Lang Art Teacher
Holloway, June French
Fifth Grade Teacher
Horton, Barbara Taylor
4th Grade Teacher
Howe, Bruce Vincent de Paul
Human Anatomy Instructor
Kenney-Franzese, Laurette Diane
English Dept Chair
Kerr, Janis Garrett
Science Teacher
King, Martin W.
Band Director
Mc Curtain, Rita Jane
Teacher
Michel, Sharon Lantz
Sixth Grade Teacher
Morton, David L.
Counselor/Coach
Noakes, Betty La Vonne-Hawkins
Teacher
O'Brien, Patrick Antony III
Social Studies Dept Teacher
Ogle, Clifton Robert
Science Teacher/Sci Dept Chair
O'Rourke, Nancy Foree
12th Grade English Teacher
Pantlik, Jean
Cosmetology Teacher
Perkins, Wheatie Baldridge
First Grade Teacher
Piland, Barbara Raymond
2nd Grade Classroom Teacher
Pratt, Paul Edward
Phys Ed Teacher/Coach
Rainey, Nancy Jean Caldwell
First Grade Teacher
Reynolds, Kathlyn Roberts
Vocal Music Teacher
Richmond, Kim L. (Miller)
Lang/Music/Band Teacher
Rosander, Dean Leroy
Science Teacher
Ruby, Nancy Eddleman
6th Grade Teacher
Standafer, Judy Lynn
6th Grade Teacher
Sullivan, Sue
American History Teacher
Swanson, Barbara Jean
Fourth Grade Teacher
Taylor, Edward E.
Assistant Principal
Taylor, James Edgar
3rd Grade Teacher

OKLAHOMA CITY (cont)
Tufford, Rawlins Dale
Science Teacher
Walton, Janetta Elizabeth
Learning Disabilities Teacher
Weiner, Kathy Cross
English/Russian Teacher
Williams, Ruby Anna Tepe
Math Teacher/6-8 Dept Chm
Willingham, Janice Darrah
Chem Teacher/Sci Dept Head
Wong, Victor Alexander
Vocal Music Teacher
Wright, Betty Jean Croom
Teacher of the Gifted Gr 1-5
Wright, June Alderson
Kindergarten Teacher
Wylie, M.Sue Haggard
Ath Director/ICAN Teacher
Young, Juanita Bachle
Mathematics Teacher

OOLOGAH
Ford, Kelly Curtis
English Teacher
Hougardy, Daniel Allen
Science Education Specialist

ORLANDO
Dunn, Cynthia Lynn
7th Grade Teacher
Raupe, Ruth Reeves
English Teacher

OWASSO
Casey, Brenda Vaughn
Elementary Counselor
Johnson, Sandra B.
Social Studies Chair
Payne, Martha Anderson
Mathematics Teacher
White, Steven Loy
9th Grade Algebra Teacher

PANOLA
Jones, Judy Kay
Business Education Teacher
Paulk, Carla Faye
English Teacher

PAULS VALLEY
Grimmett, Mickie Diane
6th Grade Teacher
Johnson, Floyd William
Life Science Teacher

PAWHUSKA
Holloway, Sharon Sossamon
Vocational Business Teacher

PAWNEE
Miller, Donald Bruce
Mathematics Department Chair

PERKINS
Hallman, Norma Troxel
Remedial Rdng/Lang Art Teacher

PERRY
Breshears, Joan Reed
English Teacher
Pense, Dorene Sands
First Grade Teacher

PIEDMONT
Butorac, Marylin Marie
Director of Bands & Chorus

PITTSBURG
Crandell, Sharon Marie
5th-8th Grade Math/Cmptr Sci

POCASSET
Davidson, Joetta Mae (Garrett)
Third Grade Teacher
Townley, Steven Henry
5th/6th Grade Teacher

PONCA CITY
Arner, Mel Glenn
Band Director
Jackson, Kenneth Aubrey
8th Grade English Teacher
Powers, Linda Waltermire
Dept Chairman/Eng Instructor
Williams, Shirley Ann (Tanquary)
Elementary Science Teacher

POTEAU
Anderson, James Enoch
Geography Teacher

PRAGUE
Terrell, Kathy (Quary)
2nd Grade Teacher

PRESTON
Snowden, Pamela Ann (Evans)
Business Education Teacher

PRYOR
Zimmerman, Marybelle (Mc Kim)
Fifth Grade Teacher

QUINTON
Lockwood, Ronnie Lewis
4th-6th Grade Science Teacher

RATTAN
Shockey, Rita Lynne Smith
Second Grade Teacher
Work, Betty Anli
Elementary Teacher

RED OAK
Morris, Margarett Sue
6th Grade Teacher

RED ROCK
Johnston, Elizabeth J.
Home Economics Teacher

REYDON
Mc Cauley, Kathi Clay
Teacher
Thomas, Melba Carter
Art/English Teacher

ROLAND
Hall, Mary Anita Tibbits
Spanish-English Teacher
Henson, Lenna Perceful
English/Language Art Teacher

RUSH SPRINGS
Crabb, Betty Carnes
6th-8th Grade Math Teacher
Pelley, Oreta M.
3rd Grade Teacher

RYAN
Ninman, Larry Ray
High School Principal
Northrip, Arvella (Pitmon)
English Teacher

SALINA
Robison, Beverly Ann
Phys Ed Teacher/Coach

SALLISAW
Johnson, Doris Luella (Walker)
First Grade Teacher

SAND SPRINGS
Anderson, Jane Israel
6th Grade Teacher
Geier, Margaret Evelyn
Fifth Grade Teacher
Greenfeather, Laura Faye
4th Grade Teacher
Mendenhall, Deanna Dudley
Third Grade Teacher
Miller, Judith Ann (Stocklin)
Gifted Coordinator/Librarian

SAPULPA
Mc Reynolds, Mary Frances
Spanish/French Teacher
Simpson, Sondra Renee (Garrison)
Mathematics Department Teacher
Whillock, Tom L.
English Teacher

SEMINOLE
Cowart, David Mike
Teacher/Sci Dept Chm

SHADY POINT
Terry, Ilene Sweeten
7th Grade Civics

SHAWNEE
Adams, Charles Leslie
Principal/English Teacher
Homer, Willie
Gifted/Talented Teacher
Morris, Nancy Drinkwater
4th Grade Teacher
Rich, Jane (Biles)
Calculus/Physics/Math Teacher
Totty, Thixe Kay (Henderson)
Mathematics/Bible Teacher

SNYDER
Mosley, Gloria Aline
Language Art Teacher/Librarian

SPENCER
Hargrove, Joe C.
English/Reading Teacher
Wright, Barbara Roberson
Math Dept Chair/Math Teacher

SPERRY
Kennedy, Daniel Coffey
English Teacher

SPIRO
Hopper, Ellen Real
Third Grade Teacher

STIGLER
Duncan, Jennifer Lynn
8th Grade English/Lit Teacher
Mann, Cheryl Scott
3rd Grade Teacher
Perryman, Judy Kay (Fowler)
First Grade Teacher

STILLWATER
Tipps, Sherry S.
Biology/Botany/Zoology Teacher

STONEWALL
Elliot, Sherlene (Johnson)
Business Teacher

STRATFORD
Coatney, Patricia Adams
Fifth Grade Teacher
Sullivan, Patrick Shannon
Sixth Grade Teacher

STROUD
Harwood, Sherry Johnson
1st Grade Teacher
Harwood, William Henry
Science Teacher
Navrath, Joe
Voc-Ag Instructor
Wood, Alice Nichols
Kindergarten Teacher

STUART
Tipton, Deborah Diekmann
Math/Spanish Teacher

SULPHUR
Mc Cullah, L. Dolphyne
Librarian
Payne, Alfred Derrel
Special Education Teacher

TAHLEQUAH
De Steiguer, Mary Jo Jo (Deem)
8th Grade Lang Arts Teacher
Isaac, Marvin D.
Principal
Lawrence, Janet Marie
Science Teacher
Poteete, Darryl
Physical Education Teacher

THOMAS
Claussen, Donald Gordon
Sixth Grade Teacher
Hoskins, Loy Mac
Second Grade Teacher

TINKER AFB
Byrd, Connie Johnson
Second Grade Teacher

TISHOMINGO
Cothran, Susan Walker
Mathematics Teacher

TULSA
Bernardine, Kilian FSC
Mathematics Teacher
Bowman, Janice Pauline
English Teacher
Bradshaw, Carolyn Tannehill
Mathematics Teacher
Carlson, Katherine Leigh
Fifth Grade Teacher
Collier, Viola Christine
Fourth Grade Teacher
Compton, Cleo Richardson
Retired Elem Supvr
Crafton, Gary Wayne
World History Teacher
Crowder, Pamela Mc Crory
Fifth Grade Teacher
Dewees, Alice Baldwin
Social Studies Teacher
Elder, Joseph David
World/Amer History Teacher
Gimlim, Wanda Lou Floyd
11th/12th Grade Teacher
Hancock, Kenneth Lee
Computer Education Teacher
Harris, Carol L.
Middle School Teacher
Huntzinger, Penney Maria (Diolordi)
Language Art Dept Chair
Johnson, Ruth Elaine
Social Studies Dept Chairman
Klassen, James Reed
Mathematics Teacher/Dept Chair
Logan, Leila F.
Kindergarten Teacher
Marshall, Richard Lee
History Teacher
Merrill, Suzanne E.
Spanish & English Teacher
Miller, Steven J.
United States History Teacher
Murta, Philip H.
Asst Prin/Science Teacher

Nelson, Zelda Carroll
Fifth Grade Teacher
Pollard, Rebecca Rae (Kreisher)
Cmptr Teacher/Coord of Gifted
Powell, Gerald King
Counselor
Pribram, John G.
Social Studies Teacher
Reid, Jacqueline Hope
French Teacher
Shaffer, Janet Eileen
Mathematics Teacher
Slemons, Suella Swales
English Department Chair
Speer, Tony A.
Mathematics Teacher
Stauffer, John Dave
Science Teacher
Stone, Carolyn Spencer
Third Grade Teacher
Townsend, Joyce C. Gordon
Algebra/Personal Dev Teacher
Treece, Pamela Kay
6th Grade Science Teacher
Tyde, Cherry Conrad
Mathematics Teacher
Walker, Raydene Lewis
Counselor
Zevnik, Shelley J.
Social Studies Teacher

TUPELO
Crow, V. Estell Mc Leroy
Remedial Math/Reading Teacher
Mantooth, Sandra Rae
Head of English and Spanish

TUTTLE
Frenzel, Victoria Eberle
Mathematics/Soc Stud Teacher
Mc Pherson, Deborah Standridge
English Department Chair

TWIN OAKS
Hix, Sandra Elaine
Third Grade Teacher
Strong, Mary Helen (Hix)
Kindergarten Teacher

TYRONE
Arnold, Cathy Elaine
1st Grade Teacher
Harke, Bonita
5th Grade Teacher
Reed, Jerry Ray
Mathematics/Science Teacher
Wetzbarger, Nora Amy (Di Fulco)
Fourth Grade Teacher

VELMA
Linke, Donna Karlin
Third Grade Teacher
Pierce, Joyce Shrader
Elem/EMH Special Ed Teacher
Pruitt, Mike Dan
Math Department Chairperson
Romine, Joanne
HS Social Studies Teacher
Sandlin, Cheryl Watson
Third Grade Teacher

VERDEN
Barnett, Donna Voyles
Sixth Grade Teacher

VIAN
Konemann, Shonda Layne
English/Spanish Teacher
Lemmon, Gene
Technology Education Instr

VICI
Herzer, Charlene Been
Second Grade Teacher
Hopper, Peggy Mc Pherson
Art/Reading/Spelling Teacher
Peoples, Leila Osborn
Third Grade Teacher
Ward, Rayburn Wesley
Language Arts Teacher

VINITA
Frisby, Donna Stevens
Fourth Grade Teacher
Humble, Catherine S.
3rd Grade Teacher

WAGONER
Altaffer, Glenda Faye
2nd Grade Teacher
Blair, Odema Gail
Reading/English Teacher
Hughes, Marjorie Leanna
Fifth Grade Teacher
Johnson, Gayla Ann
12th Grade English Teacher

WAUKOMIS
Hampton, Joan Markes
HS Mathematics Teacher

WAYNE
Doty, Debbie Sargent
Mid Sch Mathematics Teacher
Martin, Frankie G.
Asst Principal/Bus Teacher

WAYNOKA
Percival, Cindy Miller
Mathematics Teacher

WEATHERFORD
Leonard, Cheryl L.
Mathematics Teacher

WELEETKA
Womack, Monte Charles
Agriculture Education Teacher

WELLSTON
Becker, Phyllis Jeanne
2nd Grade Teacher
Humphrey, Janet Rae (Kimbrell)
4th Grade Teacher
Rogers, Sheila Bryant
HS Social Studies Teacher

WETUMKA
Hill, Wana Bryant
Retired Teacher

WILBURTON
Lawrence, Peggy L.
English Department Teacher
Vogt, M. Wayne Jr.
Instrumental Music Director

WILSON
Chatham, Edward Allen
History Teacher

WISTER
Hollan, Sherry Ann
8th Grade Math/Sci/Eng Teacher
Shipman, Verla Sue
First Grade Teacher

WOODWARD
Bassett, Mary Jane
Science Teacher-Dept Chair
Hicks, La Dawn Ann
Third Grade Teacher
Irving, Diana Williamson
5th Grade Teacher
Servis, Mary Carmichael
Science Teacher

WYANDOTTE
Armstrong, Judith Patricia
Kindergarten Teacher

WYNONA
Berry, Viola Kay
HS Language Arts Teacher

YALE
Wilson, Mike V.
Social Studies Teacher/Coach

YUKON
Grimes, Charlotte Susan
7th Grade English Teacher
Karn, Cherrie Annette
2nd Grade Teacher/Director
Lee, Janet Kay Ledford
Principal
LoBaugh, Glenda G.
Fifth Grade Teacher
Schimmer, Deborah Ann (Hart)
5th Grade Teacher
Shultz, Robert Michael
Mathematics Dept Chair
Williams, Carolyn Gayle
Pre-Algebra/Algebra I Teacher

OREGON

ALBANY
Eicher, Roma Jean (Diller)
Piano/Voice/Choral Teacher
Fisk, Judith Elizabeth
Principal
Gould, James Douglas
Science Teacher/Dept Co-Chair
Miller, Harvey James
Teacher

ALOHA
Schlegel, Laurie Sheridan
6th Grade Teacher

ASHLAND
Thacker, Charles Ernest
Fourth Grade Teacher

AURORA
Huffman, Susan E.
Language Art Teacher

BAKER CITY
Long, Viginia
1st Grade Classroom Teacher
BANDON
Handley, Richard Dale
Social Studies Teacher
BEAVER
Marvis, Bryan Edward
7th/8th Grade Lang Art Teacher
BEAVERTON
Almeter, Marsha Lynn
Sixth Grade Teacher
Falk, Candy L.
3rd Grade Teacher
Mautner, Meg W.
Science Teacher
Paranto, Steve A.
Physical Education Specialist
Robbins, David G.
Literature/Composition Teacher
BEND
Thomason, William Dale
Sixth Grade Teacher & Coach
Van Paepeghem, A. Quinn
Teacher
BONANZA
Dysert, L. Darylene
1st Grade Teacher
BORING
Dunn, Thomas Michael
Admin Asst/Math Dept Chairman
BROOKINGS
Dillenburg, Michael David
Phys Ed & Health Dept Chair
CANBY
Crawford, Anthony D.
History Teacher/Athletic Dir
Jones, Bob Lloyd
Director of Forensics
Ricksger, Darrell L.
Vocational Agriculture Teacher
Robins, Gregory J.
Fourth Grade Teacher
Wright, Lawrence Alfred
Principal
CENTRAL POINT
Hayes, Marvin U.
Craft Instructor
Le Fever, Lloyd Wilson
Social Studies Teacher
COOS BAY
Bowden, James E.
Fifth Grade Teacher
Hoffer, Howard William
Science/Mathematics Teacher
Hoy, Harold Arthur
Wood Shop Teacher
Kelly, Gladys Bernice (Weber)
Second Grade Teacher
Kotsovos, Jerry Frank
Social Studies Teacher
COQUILLE
Taylor, Helen Valentine
6th/8th Grade Lang Art Teacher
CORVALLIS
Cochran, Brenda Quinn
Home Economics Teacher
La Vietes, Anne Sherr
Spanish Teacher/Dept Liason
CRESWELL
Gant, Morris Clyde
Fourth Grade Teacher
DAYS CREEK
Graham, Irwin William
Wood Processing Teacher
Watson, Roger Everett
Math/Physics/Computer Teacher
DAYTON
Bridges, Jon Patrick
Mathematics Dept Chair
Heimbach, Arnold Mark
Fifth Grade Teacher
EAGLE POINT
James, Lamarr
Mathematics Instructor
Milne, Jane Marie
Physical Ed/Health Teacher
ENTERPRISE
Hager, William Alan
Head Teacher
EUGENE
Bliss, Kenneth O.
History/Global Issues Teacher

Hodges, James Melvin
Guidance Counselor
Mc Cauley, Kevin James
Biology Teacher
Purcell, Ron A.
Biology Department Head
Rodgers, Sharon L.
Chemistry Teacher
Stephenson, Kathryn Claska
Fourth Grade Teacher
Temple, Michael Edward
Fifth Grade Teacher
Thompson, Lee Ann Lefler
Mathematics Teacher
GILCHRIST
Catania, Roger
History/Government Teacher
GRANTS PASS
Bickle, Julie Rae Chamberlain
Scndry Art Education Teacher
Brown, Wayne Russell
Science Teacher
Hoover, Norma Tharp
English/Literature Teacher
Weyand, Bradford
6th Grade Teacher
Zottola, Martin Domenic
English Teacher
GRESHAM
Carpenter, Nancy Robbins
Supervisor
Kim, Kandice Kay
Third Grade Teacher
Renz, Heather Reekie
Mathematics Teacher
Schnell, Arnold Hamilton
Sixth Grade Teacher
Suter, William Henry
Mathematics Teacher
HALSEY
Hawkins, Joy Leanne
7th-8th Lang Arts/Lit Teacher
Peters, Marcee Shriver
Secondary Vocal Music Teacher
HARRISBURG
Mills, Donna Maeda
1st/2nd Grade Teacher
HERMISTON
Martin, Ione
1st Grade Teacher
HILLSBORO
Farr, Jerry William
Health/Phys Ed Teacher
Green, Kathryn Parrott
Biology Teacher
O'Donnell, Hugh John Jr.
Social Studies/Cmptrs Teacher
Thomas, Verity Petre
Language Arts Teacher
HINES
Durheim, Larry Robert
Computer Science Teacher
IRRIGON
Edinger, Sally J.
Media Specialist/Teacher
JUNCTION CITY
Simone, Mary Jo
Elementary Vice Principal
Stanley, Sally Seaver
Interdisciplinary Teacher
KLAMATH FALLS
Bailey, Mary Lou
Social Studies Teacher
Griffiths, Darlene Mullek
Fourth-Fifth Grade Teacher
O'Boyle, Michael Kevin
Chemistry Instructor
Scanlon, Mary (Harris)
Third Grade Teacher
Van Fleet, Byron
Science Teacher
LA GRANDE
Berry, Raymond Harvey
8th Grade Soc Stud Teacher
Nicholson, Larry Dean
Social Studies Teacher
Yoshioka, Vernon Kosuke
6th Grade Head Teacher
LAKE OSWEGO
Byerly, Larry A.
Science Teacher
Samuelson, Sahni Weinhardt
Theatre Arts Teacher
LAKEVIEW
Thomas, Clair Oliver
Biology Teacher

LEBANON
Bruno, Mary E. Kelso
Teacher
Knapp, Gloria Maurice (Buchfink)
Health/Ch Dev Teacher
Mc Ewen, Ralph Edwin
HS Literature/Drama Teacher
MAUPIN
Wong, Sandra
Math Department Chairperson
MEDFORD
Hutchings, Faye Marie
Kindergarten Teacher
Morse, Jennifer June
Science Teacher/Chairperson
Roehl, Terry Lee
Jr HS Teacher/Athletic Dir
MILWAUKIE
Cooper, Sherry Dahrens
Jr HS Counselor
Diaz, Grace Salas
Tutoring
Wilkins, Larry Dean
Mathematics Teacher
MYRTLE CREEK
Larson, James E.
Social Studies Teacher
NEWBERG
Phillips, Ken A.
Physics Teacher
NEWPORT
Bertun, Mary Croff
First Grade Teacher
Fitzpatrick, Al
Teacher
Matzke, Norma Jean
8th Grade Teacher
Mc Pherson, Doris Jean Madison
Sixth Grade Teacher
NORTH BEND
Calhoun, John C.
5th Grade Teacher
NYSSA
Bullock, Barbara Stafford
Mid Sch Language Art Teacher
ONTARIO
Berry, Gregory Wayne
English/Drama Instructor
Snyder, Doyal B.
Elementary Principal
OREGON CITY
Cottle, Michael Wade
Teacher & Principal
Love, Karl W.
His/Eng/Geography Teacher
Miller, Diane
6th Grade Teacher
Otto, Dorothy Hunter
Retired Choir Director
PENDLETON
Thompson, Margaret Duff
Retired Teacher
Wimberly, Robert James
AP US History/US Hist Teacher
PLEASANT HILL
Jackson, Jeanette Henry
Soc Studies Teacher/Counselor
Rasmussen, Harry
Mathematics & Science Teacher
PORTLAND
Brooks, Geoffry Neil
Social Studies Teacher
Harlan, John S.
Chairman Science Department
Hunsdon, Linda Boshears
Mathematics Teacher & Coord
Jury, Margaret Teller
Third Grade Teacher
Kanyid, Ann Marie
Team Leader
Kopra, Gregory Thomas
Religion Teacher/Retreat Dir
Lebaron, Edwin Ivan
High School Teacher
Othus, Marcella Mc Lean
Honors Eng/Soc Stud Teacher
Radick, Gregory Joseph
Refugee ESL Teacher
Romans, Paul Bernard
Science Department Chair
Rosene, Harold Lawrence
5th & 6th Grade Teacher
Staub, William R.
Humanities Teacher

REDMOND
Gardner, Mike Don
Mathematics Department Chair
ROSEBURG
Clark-Tyler, Ann Lorena
French Teacher
Copeland, Alfred Lee
Art & Ceramic Teacher
Garrow, Sheila May (Kandt)
3rd/4th Grade Teacher
Heaton, Robert Main
American Studies Teacher
Kamerer, Richard Daniel Jr.
Mathematics/Physics Teacher
Wickham, Brian L.
Mathematics Teacher
SAINT HELENS
Turner, Marc Morgan
Fourth Grade Teacher
SALEM
Anderson, Loren Charles
Chem Physics IPS Teacher
Bulen, Steve
4th Grade Teacher
Gantz, Marilyn Kay
English Teacher
Hercher, Wendi Smith
Science Teacher
Philips, James Gray
German/History/English Teacher
Ulrey, Donald Glenn
Education Specialist
Wilson, Douglas Kent
English Teacher
Zeuske, Doreen Sylvia
Fifth Grade Teacher
SANDY
Barr, Patricia Ann
English/Journalism Teacher
SEASIDE
Hummasti, Neil W.
English Teacher
SISTERS
Summerfield, Steven Lyle
School Counselor
SPRINGFIELD
Albright, Patrick D.
Publications Advisor
Moore, Carol Smith
Third Grade Teacher
Schaufler, Mary Ruth (Murr)
Media Specialist
Sharp, Betty Burkart
High School French Teacher
SWEET HOME
Eddy, Shirley Kathryn (Idso)
Literacy Program Director
Nowlin, Dan
Retired
Wright, Janet Carol
School Counselor
THE DALLES
Ameling, Glenn Alan
Foreign Language Teacher
TIGARD
Wolf, Wendy
Career Education Director
TILLAMOOK
Fetzer, Cathie Marie (Rouse)
6th Grade Teacher
Nash, Donna Schilling
Business Education Teacher
TRAIL
Walloch, Lawrence Ray
Third Grade Teacher
TUALATIN
Bonica, Diane Mc Nicholas
Pre-School/Lead Teacher
TURNER
Godfrey, Ernest E.
Biology Instructor
UNION
Mc Craw, Sally
Reading Teacher
VALE
Allegre, Darlene Elaine
Phys Ed/Health Teacher
Gardner, Daniel Wayne
Mathematics & Science Teacher
WEST LINN
Funk, Susan Schuppel
Middle School Teacher

WINCHESTER
Bartholomew, Dixie Ann (Stovall)
Sixth Grade Teacher
YAMHILL
Dickson, James Howard
Literature Teacher
Trachsel, Margaret Copping
Vice Principal

PENNSYLVANIA

ALBION
Cryder, Carol Meerhoff
Kindergarten Teacher
Johnston, Sandi Rae
Assistant Principal
ALEXANDRIA
Kyper, Nancy Vaughn
Mathematics Teacher
Mc Kee, Diane K.
Fourth Grade Teacher
Smith, Gene Anthony
World Cultures Teacher
ALIQUIPPA
Byrne, Eileen
Language Arts Chairperson
Cronin, Margaret Abayes
2nd Grade Teacher
Grippa, Ardith Crespi
Science Teacher
Kanitra, Edmund Andrew
Social Studies Teacher
Mason, Garry R. II
Chemistry/Physics Educator
Mazur, Richard Joseph
Mathematics Teacher
Mendenball, Jack Leonardo
Biology Instructor
Morris, Sonya K.
5th Grade Teacher
Pierce, Richard James
English/Gifted English Teacher
Pulcini, Diane Mary
Fourth Grade Teacher
Watkins, Ronald
5th Grade Teacher
Zeljak, Theodore
6th Grade Teacher
Zetz, Donna Jean (Nan)
Fifth Grade Teacher
ALLENTOWN
Benning, Jane Mack-Adamson
Fifth Grade Teacher
Brommer, Wanda Marshall
Dept Chair/French Teacher
D'Arconte, Jean Ann
Business Dept Chairperson
Donchez, Robert J.
Social Studies Teacher
Facchiano, Vincent Anthony
Fifth Grade Teacher
Fellencer, Mary Louise George
5th Grade Homeroom Teacher
Glascom, Patricia Hertz
Fifth Grade Teacher
Gutierrez, Kathleen Gallagher
5th Grade Teacher
Krivak, John A.
Religion Teacher
Maciag, George
Biology Teacher
Mikovich, Theodore J.
Fifth Grade Teacher
Steckel, Mary Catherine
Third Grade Teacher
Tannery, Charles N. Jr.
7th Grade English Teacher
ALLISON PARK
Carr, Katherine N.
Fourth Grade Teacher
ALTOONA
Cristillo, Frank D. Jr.
Computer Programming Instr
Dusza, Constance T.
Math Dept Chair/Math Teacher
Frank, Stephen Eugene
9th Grade Math Teacher
Helinski, David Allen
Secondary English Teacher
Killian, William Clarence
5th Grade Teacher
Matthews, Kenneth Lee
Social Studies Teacher
Mc Cullough, Claudia Elissa
English Teacher
Miller, Irma Jean (Imler)
8th Grade Math & Sci Teacher

ALTOONA (cont)

Piper, William Carl II
 English Teacher
Rentz, Helen (Hartman)
 First Grade Teacher
Swalga, Frank Michael
 Biology Teacher Sci Dept Chm
Traficante, Michael Francis
 Reading Teacher

ALVERTON

Clara, Erika E.
 Language Arts/English Teacher
Kraisinger, Karen Stoner
 Fourth Grade Teacher

AMBRIDGE

Finnegan, Dawn Turney
 Fifth Grade Teacher
Whitford, Linda Treantafellow
 English Department Chair

ANNVILLE

Bugden, Joseph Edward
 Science Department Chair
Marisa, Mary Lou Spang
 Nursery Sch Teacher
Wood, Dennis R.
 Sixth Grade Teacher

APOLLO

Petrarca, Frances Ferrero
 Retired 7th Grade Teacher

ARENDTSVILLE

Bushey, Linda K.
 6th Grade Teacher
Kane, Cynthia Ann
 First Grade Teacher

ARMAGH

Plyler, Darlene J.
 Mathematics Teacher

ASTON

Grassano, Charles A.
 Language Arts Teacher

ATGLEN

Disipio, Anthony Joseph Jr.
 8th Grade Science Teacher
King, Wanda Dawn
 6th Grade Teacher
Rentz, Jean Magee
 First Grade Teacher

ATHENS

Bean, Bonnie L.
 5th Grade Teacher

BADEN

Biskup, Susan Lynn
 Chemistry Teacher
Muny, Robert Gaylord
 5th Grade Teacher

BALLY

Kurcz, Mary Ann Herhal
 5th-8th Grade Science Teacher
Little, Kathleen D. (Schmidt)
 Elementary Teacher

BARNESBORO

Kirsch, Laura Jean Mc Anulty
 First Grade Teacher

BATH

Falstich, William B.
 Administrative Intern
Steiner, Doris Snyder
 Fourth Grade Teacher

BEAVER

Giannette, Helen
 1st Grade Teacher
Riggs, Richard E.
 Social Studies Teacher
Roe, Yvonne Heath
 Senior High English Teacher

BEAVER FALLS

Raybuck, Annie Farrell
 7th Grade Teacher

BEDFORD

Wertz, David E.
 4th Grade Teacher

BELLE VERNON

Studnicki, Henry Thomas
 7th/8th Grade Math Teacher
Zeli, Doris Conti
 Fifth Grade Teacher

BELLEFONTE

Miller, Gary Allen
 Acting Principal

BELLWOOD

O'Connor, Mary Kay Conley
 Home Economics Teacher

Ross, Ruth A.
 POD/Economics Teacher
Rupert, Nancy Gottshall
 Developmental Reading Teacher

BENSALEM

Bernabei, Alan J.
 Principal
Burtt, James
 Humanities Teacher
Ditchkofsky, Michael Patrick
 English Department Chair
Frazier, Gerry Lewis
 Physical Education Teacher
Johnson, Jay M.
 6th Grade Mathematics Teacher
Kirby, Joseph Francis
 Aquatic Director
Marcella, Teresa Ann Cardone
 Business Ed Dept Chairperson
Reinhart, Katrina Schumacher
 Reading Teacher

BENTLEYVILLE

Cole, Irene Lanik
 Kindergarten Teacher

BENTON

Roberts, Beatrice Hess
 Fourth Grade Teacher
Watson, Carolyn Cauffman
 Sixth Grade Teacher

BERNVILLE

Leininger, Ralph E.
 Social Studies Teacher
Ravert, Christie Allen
 Third Grade Teacher

BERRYSBURG

McMillan, Bonnye Brink
 Second Grade Teacher

BERWICK

Barski, Margaret Bittner
 7th & 8th Grade Teacher
Kile, Diana Lynne
 Kindergarten Teacher
Learn, Nelson R.
 8th Grade Math/Algebra Teacher

BERWYN

Calabrese, Marylyn Jones
 English Department Chairperson
Jones, Louise Linnemeier (Cubbler)
 8th/9th Grade English Teacher
Rosenberger, Nancy Louise
 High School English Teacher

BESSEMER

Benson, Donald Eugene Jr.
 English Teacher
Donofrio, Archie
 Mathematics Teacher/Coach
Ernst, Evan G.
 Mathematics Teacher
Jones, William H.
 Biology Teacher
Kerr, Harold R.
 Social Studies Teacher
Majors, Terri B.
 Teacher of Gifted
Oden, Hartley Calvin
 Math Dept Chairman
Randolph, Eunice Sproul
 Teacher
Steinheiser, Glenn Wayne Lamont
 4th Grade Teacher

BETHEL PARK

Alisesky, David John
 Instrumental Music Teacher
Georgiana, Samuel Thomas
 Chemistry/Science Teacher
Kalocay, Mary Lee
 Science Teacher
Siverts, Ann Harvey
 English Teacher
Toretti, Margaret Ann
 First Grade Teacher

BETHLEHEM

Bauer, Eileen M. Doyle
 English/History Teacher
Fox, Linda Lencalis
 Science Teacher
Fulmer, Kathleen A. (Gallagher)
 Mathematics Teacher
Kreitz, Carol Jane (Smith)
 Fourth Grade Teacher
Mancusi, Michael Mary CRSP
 Amer Government Teacher
Miller, Jody Robert
 English Teacher
Perrett, Leonard Anthony
 English Teacher
Pulcini, Barbara
 7th Grade Teacher

Ross, L. Patrick
 Social Studies Teacher
Rotondo, Michael Dennis
 Reading Teacher
Shermetta, Kathleen E. (Barna)
 5th Grade Teacher
Tylenda, Donna Marie (Ressler)
 Fourth Grade Teacher
Walter, Valerie Ceccherelli
 Earth Science Teacher

BIG RUN

Stuby, Gordon William
 Fifth Grade Teacher

BIGLERVILLE

Bucher, Michael Kermit
 Math Dept Chairman
Fox, Jane (Boyer)
 Business Ed/Department Chair

BIRDSBORO

Heimel, Helen Miller
 Mathematics Teacher
Murphy, Mary Catherine
 Third Grade Teacher

BLAIN

Conaway, Dianne E.
 4th Grade Teacher/Dept Chm

BLAIRSVILLE

Inge, Gregory E.
 History Teacher
Rippel, Patricia Black
 Fifth Grade Teacher

BLOOMSBURG

Gaughenbaugh, Kathleen Williams
 Fifth Grade Teacher
Huntley, James Bryan
 Social Studies Teacher
Stone, John Randall Jr.
 Music Teacher/Band Director

BLOSSBURG

Retorick, Mary E. Sterling
 First Grade Teacher

BOBTOWN

Mc Intire, Carolyn Jean (Metcalf)
 Fourth Grade Teacher

BOILING SPRINGS

Grove, Nila F.
 Reading Teacher
Roden, Keith T.
 Jr/Sr HS Music Teacher

BOSWELL

Coughenour, Sallie (Foust)
 Chemistry/Mathematics Teacher
Smith, Victor H.
 Fifth Grade Teacher
St Clair, Thomas Arthur
 Second Grade Teacher

BOYERTOWN

Beck, Sandy Neiman
 Spanish Teacher

BRADFORD

Danielson, Barbara
 9th Grade English Teacher
Kervin, Shirley Dieter
 5th Grade Teacher

BRIDGEVILLE

Rodrigues, Robert Manuel
 Civic Education Teacher
Snavely, Robert Bradley
 Secondary Mathematics Teacher

BRISTOL

Boyd, Andrea Padgett
 English Teacher

BROCKWAY

Cherubini, Robert Matthew
 Computer Specialist
Reckner, Raymond E. Jr.
 Sixth Grade Teacher
Starr, Faith Brumberg
 2nd Grade Teacher

BRODHEADSVILLE

Brown, Judy Ann
 Math Teacher
Kresge, William Eugene
 8th Grade Physical Sci Teacher
Martin, Richard Neal
 Sixth Grade Teacher
Moran, Mary
 Mathematics Department Chair

BROOKVILLE

Briggs, Carole A.
 Elementary Enrichment Teacher
Kutz, William Craig
 Social Studies Teacher
Ohl, Kay Bish
 Third Grade Teacher

Plyler, Peggy Brewster
 4th Grade Teacher
Ramolt, Ronald Charles II
 Communication Arts Teacher
Smith, Larry Hudson
 5th Grade Head Teacher

BROOMALL

Dye, Robert Joseph
 Eng Teacher/Rdng Specialist
Williams, S. Jerome
 Math Teacher/Dept Leader

BRYN MAWR

Schleyer, Johanna Weissinger
 Second Grade Teacher

BUCKINGHAM

Wallis, Michaell James
 Technical Graphics Instructor

BURGETTSTOWN

Carson, David Emerson
 Science Teacher
Eannace, Rebecca S.
 Math Teacher/Gifted Coord
Gavazzi, Mary Margaret
 Seventh Grade Teacher
Howard, Ken R. Z.
 Kindergarten Teacher
Mc Wreath, Cynthia L.
 English Teacher
Vukotich, Dorothy
 French Teacher

BUTLER

Bealles, Mary Jo Wolfgong
 Fourth Grade Teacher
Crytzer, Lynn Carol (Brozenick)
 Choral Director, Music Teacher
Holman, Christine (Keefer)
 English Teacher
Kenderes, George Steven
 German/History Teacher
Knechtel, Victoria Lynn (Ashe)
 Chemistry/Physics Teacher
Malis, Lucy Ellen
 Second Grade Teacher
Megnin, Julia King
 Elementary Teacher of Gifted
Okeson, Richard Gary
 6th Grade Teacher
Swigart, Deborah Calvin
 Music Teacher
West, Dorothy H.
 Social Studies Teacher
Williams, Leah Ann Rieg
 Science Teacher
Woods, Douglas Elliot
 English/Writing Teacher

CABOT

Montag, Mary Jean
 1st/2nd Grade Teacher

CAMBRIDGE SPRINGS

Higgins, Dorothea Busche
 2nd Grade Teacher

CANONSBURG

Bellicini, Elizabeth R. (Adams)
 Fifth Grade Teacher
Breon, Tisana Maria
 6th Grade English Teacher
Burr, Martha Ann Morris
 Teacher/Dean of Students
Resinol, Marsha M.
 Physical Education Teacher
Trozzi, Janet G. (Kiski)
 Gifted Education Instructors

CARBONDALE

Sabina, Frank James
 English/French Teacher
Smith, Robert Paul
 History/Spanish/Psych Teacher

CARLISLE

Auxer, Cathy Wedo
 First Grade Teacher
Brymesser, Connie Clevenger
 Third Grade Teacher
Diehl, Mary Jane
 Physical Education Teacher
Mc Carter, Margaret Anne (Mains)
 Kindergarten Teacher
Schorpp, Janice Finkey
 Fourth Grade Teacher

CARLISLE BARRACKS

Carrol, Verma L.
 6th Grade Soc Stud Teacher
Cook, Ann Shackelton
 Gifted Education Specialist

CARMICHAELS

Smalara, Ann Valla
 Fourth Grade Teacher

CARNEGIE

Cumo, Philomena Ann
 French Teacher
Esterburg, Arlene Catherine
 5th Grade Teacher
Freed, Sharon Lynn
 First Grade Teacher
Jones, Lawrence Arthur
 Mathematics Teacher
Mistro, Nancy Nesta
 Sixth Grade Teacher

CARROLLTOWN

Ankeny, Virginia Daley
 5th Grade Computer Teacher

CECIL

Raymer, Andrea A. Coleman
 4th Grade Teacher

CENTER VALLEY

Weaver, Walter Robert
 8th Grade Teacher

CHAMBERSBURG

Barr, David B.
 Third Grade Teacher
Branham, Anne Kinney
 Creative Writing/Eng Teacher
Dickinson, Donald C.
 English Teacher
Hallock, Donald James
 Mathematics Teacher
Peron, Evelyn L.
 Spanish Teacher
Shull, Kenneth H.
 Mathematics Teacher

CHARLEROI

Ritacco, Joseph Sylvester
 Middle School Principal
Smolick, Diane Marie (Kruell)
 Kindergarten Teacher
Stasicha, Barry Robert
 Middle School Math Teacher
Tomayko, Mary Ann
 Business Education Teacher

CHELTENHAM

Glickman, Marsha
 2nd Grade Teacher

CHESTER

Arthur, Denise Ashby
 Fifth Grade Teacher
Wiley, Carolyn
 English Department Head

CHURCHVILLE

Sfarnas, Evangeline Litsa
 Sixth Grade Teacher

CLARIDGE

Baugh, Richard Allen
 Mathematics/Reading Teacher

CLARION

Bruner, Judith Venturella
 Kindergarten Teacher

CLARKS SUMMIT

Armezzani, Anne Mc Donnell
 7th Grade English Teacher
Caboot, Blair Edward
 Mathematics Teacher
Frutchey, James Arthur
 Social Studies Coordinator
Fueshko, Stephen
 Fourth Grade Teacher
Heckman, Pauline Bartleman
 8th Grade Mathematics Teacher
Schultheis, Eugene Richard
 Teacher

CLAYSBURG

Eckley, Mona Nelson
 Sixth Grade Teacher
Oeffinger, Cheryl K.
 Fourth Grade Teacher
Royer, William M.
 Fourth Grade Teacher
Woodring, Mark Edwin
 Social Studies Teacher

CLAYSVILLE

Berry, Marilyn Blake
 English Teacher
Flanigan, James Robert
 English Teacher
Hughes, W. Herbert
 English Teacher
Malesic, Dona Group
 Librarian
Marasco, Floyd C.
 Mathematics/Computer Sci Instr
Zibert, Shirley A.
 English Teacher

CLEARFIELD

Ardary, Kelly Vincent
English Instructor
Billotte, Donald Duane II
Social Studies Teacher
Blake, Ella Jane
1st Grade Teacher
Meckey, Marylynne Learish
9th Grade English Teacher
Watson, Randall Gregg
5th Grade Teacher

CLYMER

Duke, C. James
5th Grade Teacher
Fetterman, Joyce Carney
Sixth Grade Teacher

COATESVILLE

Assetto, Henry John
Soc Stud Teacher/Dept Head
Renfrew, William Howard
Biology Teacher
Smith, Crystal Perry
World Cultures Teacher
Zerkle, Margaret M. (Elliott)
Eighth Grade Health Teacher

COLLEGEVILLE

Hersh, John
Third Grade Teacher
Panetta, Mary Chaffee
Fourth Grade Teacher
Underkoffler, Terry Marvin
Teacher/Computer Coordinator

COLUMBIA

Martin, Jolene Hohenadel
Mathematics Department Chair

COMMODORE

Buchanan, William George Sr.
Social Studies Dept Chairman
Lord, George E.
Driver Education Instructor

CONCORDVILLE

Gatchell, Susan Jean
Business Teacher

CONNEAUTVILLE

Baker, Arlene Taylor
English Teacher
Baker, Donna Chalovich
English Teacher
Coon, Mary Lemme
2nd Grade Teacher
Taylor, Karen Woodward
Fifth Grade Teacher

CONNELLSVILLE

Lloyd, Barbara Shirey
English Teacher
Lynn, Sara Sally Estille
5th Grade Teacher
Manns, Virginia Keller
Third Grade Teacher
Mc Luckey, Robert Allen
Principal
Premoshis, Gregory Francis
Chaplain/Religion Instr
Severin, Arlene M.
English Teacher/Dept Chair

COOPERSTOWN

Rupert, Joyce O'Neill
Third Grade Teacher

COPLAY

Frederick, Jane (Fink)
6th Grade Teacher

CORAOPOLIS

Aaron, Woodrow V. Jr.
Middle School Math/Sci Teacher
Baca, George Jr.
Biology/Science Teacher
Colella, Phillip James
Retired
Corwin, Norma Baum
Band Director
Coulson, Barbara Sale
Third Grade Teacher
Dwyer, Susan L.
High School Guidance Counselor
Kooi, Warren James
Biology/Computer Teacher
Mc Vicker, Linda Janssens
English Teacher
Napierski, William
Science Teacher

CORNWALL

Rhoads, Sarah Gross
Retired 3rd Grade Teacher

CORRY

Alexander, Gene Dennis
5th Grade Teacher

Foster, Nancy P.
English Teacher

COUDERSPORT

Oviatt, Dona Daugherty
Fifth Grade Teacher
Troy, Thomas James
Fourth Grade Teacher

CREEKSIDE

Jones, Patricia Warren
Kindergarten Teacher

CRESSON

Mc Cool, Deborah Joyclyn
Chemistry Teacher
Myers, Kenneth J.
5th Grade Teacher
Pollino, James Anthony
English-Drama Teacher

CURWENSVILLE

Decker, George Russell
English Teacher
Keely, Michael Lane
Science Teacher
Kendrick, Joseph Robert
Mathematics Teacher
Maholtz, Mickey
Sci Dept Head/Physics Teacher
Neff, Ann Rougeux
Fourth Grade Teacher
Wetzel, Sally Ann
Spanish Teacher

DALLAS

Amesbury, Norine Mary
English Teacher
Liput, Pricilla Reese
Third Grade Teacher
Reilly, Barbara Cohen
Fourth Grade Teacher
Zachary, Philip Alan
Fourth Grade Teacher

DALLASTOWN

Johnston, Barbara Dessler
Substitute Teacher

DANVILLE

Bower, Jack R.
Instrumental Music Teacher
Burke, Maria T. Mirocke
Reading Specialist
Gaugler, Penny Moyer
Reading Teacher
Harter, Mollie Haas
English Teacher
Marrara, Carl John
High School Counselor

DAVIDSVILLE

Bowman, Jan Albright
English Teacher
Grisin, Suzette Aline
Jr/Sr HS Band Director
Volk, Herbert Jay
Business Education Teacher

DAWSON

Natale, James A.
Elementary Science Teacher

DAYTON

Watterson, Dawn Zellefrow
6th Grade Teacher

DENVER

Small, Ann Louise
7-8th Grade Lang Arts Teacher
Willig, Lois (Hilcker)
Third Grade Teacher

DILLSBURG

Boreman, E. Daniel
Sixth Grade Math Teacher
Hagenbuch, Mark Odis
Elementary Principal

DIMOCK

Aten, Irvin
Fifth Grade Soc Stud Teacher
Hall, Betty Jane Waltz
Mathematics Teacher

DOVER

Arendt, Donald M.
Social Studies Dept Chair
Bishard, Lois Burd
5th Grade Teacher
Dockey, Joan Elizabeth
3rd Grade Teacher
Justh, Darrel R.
Music Teacher
Kaltreider, Carolyn Ann
8th Grade English Teacher
March, Richard Paul II
English & History Teacher
Smith, Sheryl Jeanne (Curran)
HS Mathematics Teacher

Snyder, Jeffrey L.
Music Teacher/Suprv of Music

DOWNINGTOWN

Austin, Neville Perry
Social Studies Teacher
Fennelly, Robert E.
8th Grade Mathematics Teacher
French, Mary
English Department Chair
Gaskins, John David
Biology/Chemistry Teacher
Meade, Francis J.
Business Education Teacher
Murtaugh, Marianne Santarelli
Social Studies Teacher
Rao, Sara S.
Sixth Grade Teacher
Sigle, Susan Vance
Counselor

DREXEL HILL

Funk, Frederick James
8th Grade Teacher
Wieners, Charles J.
Social Stud Department Chair

DRUMS

Harrington, Robert Paul
Sixth Grade Teacher

DU BOIS

Pifer, Eloise Jane
Music Teacher
Rensel, Aileen Mc Elhattan
English Teacher

DUNCANNON

Wiehe, James Michael
History Teacher

DUNMORE

Brown, Patricia Lawrence
Art Teacher
Wetter, Janine Teresa
English Teacher

DUQUESNE

Bush, Aralessa Davis
3rd Grade Teacher
Leggin, Julia Anne (Yadack)
Eighth Grade Teacher

EAST BERLIN

Firestone, Marvel A.
Third Grade Teacher

EAST GREENVILLE

Bates, Susan Elizabeth
Social Studies Teacher
Farkas, Richard David
5th Grade Teacher

EAST MCKEESPORT

Howard, Constance Rose Davane
8th Grade Teacher

EAST PETERSBURG

Pisano, Mary Anne Cassidy
K-8th Grade Reading Specialist

EAST SPRINGFIELD

Porter, Mary Ann
Third Grade Teacher

EAST STROUDSBURG

Gormley, John Denis
Algebra/Physics Teacher

EASTON

Bogdan, Barry Louis
Mathematics Teacher
Case, Rhea Parsons
8th Grade Eng Teacher/Dept Hd
Evans, Melvin James
Third Grade Teacher
Frankenfield, Robert Barry
4th Grade/Head Teacher
Leyshon, Deborah Daneker
Music Teacher
Pettit, Germaine
Biology Teacher
Rider, William Scott
Guidance Counselor
Skrobak, Joanne Slivko
Third Grade Teacher
Williams, Michael Thomas
7th Grade Life Science Teacher

EBENSBURG

Biter, Miriam Rita
Business Teacher
De Yulius, Salvatore
4th Grade Teacher
Guinee, Patricia Ann
French/English Teacher
Karwoski, Joseph Paul
Computer Coordinator
Mastrine, Diana Nedock
Second Grade Teacher

Poole, H. John
Mathematics Dept Chairman
Solomon, Allen
Mathematics Department Chair

EDDYSTONE

Horne, Bruce Arthur
Fifth Grade Teacher

EDGEWORTH

Sklarsky, Thomas
Fourth Grade Teacher

EDINBORO

Donche, Louis Jr.
6th/7th Grade Science Teacher
Jenkins, Lon W.
English Teacher
Ward, Suanne Strand
3rd Grade Teacher
Wise, James Lewis
Science/Mathematics Teacher

EIGHTY FOUR

Chimento, Deborah Ann
Third Grade Teacher

ELDERSVILLE

Cowden, Marjorie Robertson
4th Grade Teacher

ELIZABETH

Artis, Arthur
Mathematics Teacher
Gasdick, Mary Elizabeth Sheppard
Fourth Grade Teacher
Greenewald, Betty Lee Whitacre
Life Science/Teacher of Gifted
Hartle, Sallie Nolf
English Teacher
Skomra, Jean Gealy
Reading Teacher

ELIZABETHTOWN

Bradley, Christine Owen
English Teacher
Brown, Dennis Jay
Mathematics Teacher
Clouser, Ralph Charles Jr.
HS Mathematics Teacher
Cox, Carol W.
English Teacher
Foor, Corinne Elaine
Instrumental Music Instr
Renoe, N. Lawrence
Math/Sci/His Teacher
Romanowski, Michael H.
Social Studies Dept Chair

ELIZABETHVILLE

Hamme, Ronald Edward
Fine Arts/Humanities Teacher
Williams, Evan Price
English Department Chairman

ELLIOTTSBURG

Neely, Fred Eugene
Biology Teacher

ELLWOOD CITY

Atkins, Marjorie Ann
Mathematics Teacher
De Fonde, Agnes Murphy
Third Grade Teacher
Fisher, Arlene K.
Science Teacher
Flick, Marjorie Eberle
Computer Coordinator
Hazen, Rita Ann
Mathematics Department Chair

ELMORA

Frontino, Dolly
Elementary & Head Teacher

ELVERSON

Dewalt, Karen Sue
Computer Coordinator

EMMAUS

Hamm, Deborah Joy Reyher
Math Teacher
Meyer, Josepha
Third Grade Teacher
Smartschan, Carl Ernest
Biology Teacher

ENOLA

Donovan, Michael E.
Fourth Grade Teacher
Young, Bonnie Evans
Third Grade Teacher

EPHRATA

Nestlerode, Carol Louise (Demmy)
Fourth Grade Teacher
Nolt, James L.
6th Grade Teacher
Vazquez, Elaine C.
6th Grade Teacher

Young, Betsy Wright
Fourth Grade Teacher

ERDENHEIM

Inman, Vernon Kerry
English Teacher
Sorkness, Thomas John
Secondary Soc Studies Teacher

ERIE

Annegan, Siri Kessinger
Secondary English Teacher
Barringer, Charlene Day
Kindergarten Teacher
Brothers, Mary Ann
Sixth Grade Teacher
Colvin, Clarence Leroy
English Teacher
Drexler, Nora Lee Bjalme
4th Grade Teacher
Griffin, Janet Kramer
Fourth Grade Teacher
Halquist, Shawn Allen
Director of Instrumental Music
Hinchman, Myron Craig
Chemistry Teacher
Huegel, Darlene Marie
German Teacher
Lee, Clarence A.
Math/Science/Computer Teacher
Maraden, David E.
Reading Teacher
Meleason, Geralyn Uhl
7th Grade Soc Stud Teacher
Miller, Sandra G.
Mathematics Teacher
Nowakowski, Pamela A.
Business Education Teacher
Nutter, Donna Bohrer
Reading Teacher
Pfisterer, Diane Smith
Reading Teacher
Pilewski, Margaret Ann OSB
7th/8th Grade Teacher
Roddy, Robert Conlin
English Teacher
Scanzillo, Janet Packo
Third Grade Teacher
Sluga, Craig Charles
6th Grade Mathematics Teacher
Swanson, Kathrine Elma
Science Department Chairperson
Trambley, Marlene Krug
Science Department Chair
Trautman, Ned R.
Music Teacher
Villa, Mary Ruska
5th Grade Teacher
Westcott, Shirley Dalglish
French & English Teacher
Wilson, Agnes Jackson
Science Teacher
Zeislolt, Ruth Bovaird
English Teacher

ESSINGTON

Bondarchuk, Lois Ash
Mid Sch Mathematics Teacher
Davis, Benjamin Franklyn Jr.
Principal

EVANS CITY

Brady, Nancy Ann (Carl)
6th Grade Teacher

EVERETT

Barker, Betty Lane Jarvis
Kindergarten Teacher
Dodson, Linda Mae
Secondary Math Teacher
Karns, Mary Buckey
7th/11th Grade Eng Teacher
Reed, Emily Foore
Mathematics/Gifted Instructor

EXETER

Harmanos, Stephen Andrew
Social Studies/AP Instructor
Stocker, Joyce Saunders
8th Grade Teacher English Comp

FACTORYVILLE

Thomas, Kenneth
Business Teacher/Dept Chair

FAIRLESS HILLS

Cahill, Jean Shatto
Reading Teacher
Crosby, Anne Seward
English Teacher
Firda, Emma Minemier
Second Grade Teacher
Foley, Judith H.
French Teacher
Griffiths, Linda Liedke
Sixth Grade Teacher
Micir, Sylvester Mark
8th Grade Math Teacher

FAIRLESS HILLS (cont)
Shea, Sandra Barnes
Social Studies Dept Chair
FAIRVIEW
Weislogel, Orville Wallace
Science Teacher
FAIRVIEW VILLAGE
Emery, David Roland
Mathematics Teacher
Ulrich, Kurt S.
English/Gifted Teacher
FAIRVIEW VLG
Di Giovanni, Mary Lou A.
Second Grade Teacher
FARRELL
Foust, Frances Napolitan
First Grade Teacher
FEASTERVILLE
Rogers, Mary Teresa
Seventh-Eighth Grade Teacher
FENELTON
Hinchberger, Terry Dale
Sixth Grade Teacher
FINLEYVILLE
Cochenour, Linda Feick
Sixth Grade Teacher
Kuvinka, Eric William
Mathematics/Science Teacher
Mancinelli, Kathleen Elizabeth
Fifth Grade Teacher
FISHERTOWN
Collier, Patricia Ann
Third Grade Teacher
Deremer, Emily Moorhead
5th Grade Teacher
Iagulli, Thomas Louis
8th Grade English Teacher
FLEETVILLE
Pardue, Jane Ellen
2nd Grade Teacher
FLINTON
Burmeister, Richard
Science Department Chair
Rainey, Diane B.
1st Grade Teacher
Vesnesky, Karen Sue
Social Studies/Quest Teacher
FLOURTOWN
Donohoe, Francis X.
English Teacher
FOLSOM
Clevenstine, Richard Francis
Biology Teacher
FORD CITY
Oleksak, William L.
5th Grade Science/Rdng Teacher
Serene, Joyce E. Mc Mahon
Senior High School Art Teacher
FOREST CITY
Kerl, Thomas J.
5-6th Grade Reading Teacher
Soete, Bernadine Pleviak
5th/6th Grade Math Teacher
Templeton, M. Ardis Possanza
Reading/English Teacher
FORT WASHINGTON
Probert, Edwin Nightingale II
English Teacher
Wood, Denise
9th/10th Grade Teacher
FRACKVILLE
Chrin, Ted S.
5th Grade Teacher
FRANKLIN
Bliss, Sally M.
Third Grade Teacher
Henderson, Carl M.
Business Ed/English Teacher
Mc Nutt, Patricia Mc Cune
Mathematics Teacher
FREDERICKSBURG
Etchberger, Robert David
Sixth Grade Teacher
Messinger, Kathleen Fugate
Fifth Grade Teacher
Rusen, Gary Vladimir
Visual Arts Teacher
Whitlow, Fay Righter
3rd Grade Teacher
FREEDOM
Sklack, Elizabeth Lauretta (Mc
Curdy)
Kindergarten Teacher

FREELAND
Stiller, David W.
Chemistry Teacher
FREEPORT
Akins, Christine Warriner
Life Science Teacher
Krugle, Max E.
Civics/Psychology Teacher
Rea, Jerry Cree
Fourth Grade Teacher
Sproull, Barbara L.
Mathematics Teacher
FRIEDENSBURG
Zimmer, Clara Zulick
First Grade Teacher
GALETON
Salvadge, Gay Evans
Sixth Grade Teacher
GALLITZIN
Baacke, Timothy Allen
Director of Instrumental Music
Inman, John George
English Teacher
GAP
Lauchnor, Deborah Rund
Second Grade Teacher
GETTYSBURG
Edwards, Barbara Jean
Spanish Teacher
Warner, Drusilla Deitch
5th Grade Teacher
GIBSONIA
Dittrich, Julie Ann
Biology Teacher
Mc Candless, Elizabeth M.
4th Grade Teacher
GILBERTSVILLE
Dietz, Elizabeth Ann
Junior HS Vocal Music Teacher
GLEN ROCK
Spang, James Charles
English Teacher
GLENOLDEN
Duffy, Rosemary Frattaroli
Teacher
Kimble, Betty Crockett
8th Grade Lang Art Teacher
GRATERFORD
Cestrone, Dianne Turner
Home Economics Teacher
Wiser, Susan Virginia
Span/Eng 2nd Language Teacher
GREENCASTLE
Bender, Kenneth E.
Contemporary World Cultures
Black, Keith Donald
Fifth Grade Teacher
Reinwald, Sherri Ritz
Coord of Commonwealth Classrm
GREENSBORO
Novak, William Andrew
English/Language Arts Teacher
GREENSBURG
Brisbane, Gene Dennis
Sixth Grade Teacher
Henry, Louise Elvira (Seibel)
Spanish Teacher
Kardash, Patricia Ann (Cunningham)
Fifth Grade Teacher
Loya, Eugene S.
Latin/English Teacher
Schildkamp, R. Joseph
Secondary Art Teacher
Smith, Delver B.
English Teacher
Steve, Michael G.
Mathematics Teacher
Stewart, James C.
Mathematics Teacher
Talamo, Yolanda Marie
Spanish Teacher/Chairperson
Tucci, Maria
English Teacher/Journalism Adv
Wansor, Collin Terrance
English Department Chair
Wilburn, Jean Ann
Elementary Librarian
GREENVILLE
Duffy, Joan Clara
4th Grade Teacher
Emswiller, Marsha Mc Entire
Kindergarten Teacher
Mc Elhinny, Mary Gertrude SC
Fifth Grade Teacher
Nagel, Doris (Saul)
4th Grade Teacher

Renwick, Marlene A. (Gutowski)
11th Grade English Teacher
GRINDSTONE
Williams, Tammie Rouse
Secondary Mathematics Teacher
GROVE CITY
Hazy, Mark
Industrial Technology Teacher
Mills, Judith Zilla
Chair-Language Arts Teacher
Noel, Shelly Conway
4th Grade Teacher
Phillips, Rose Duschek
5th Grade Teacher
Pollock, Kaye Teare
English Teacher
GUYS MILLS
Eriksen, Ted Don II
English Department Chair
GWYNEDD VALLEY
Carusi, Maria Pia
History Department Chair
HALIFAX
Harman, Scott James
5th Grade Teacher
HAMBURG
Althouse, Robert Lee
Soc Stud Teacher/Dept Chairman
Crandall, Maurice Emil
Secondary English Teacher
Hertzog, Judith Ann (Tobias)
English Teacher
Kramer, Nancy Kauffman
English Teacher
HAMLIN
Peet, Jane Elizabeth (Guy)
4th Grade Teacher
HARBORCREEK
Arnold, John Charles
5th/6th Grade Science Teacher
Hargest, Christine Ackelson
Fourth Grade Teacher
Rose, Paul Frederick
Physics/Calculus Teacher
HARMONY
De Polo, Robert John
Chemistry Teacher
Kappeler, Shirley Simons
Spanish Teacher
O'Neill, Daniel H.
Jr HS Science Teacher
Stephenson, Susan M.
English Teacher
HARRISBURG
Bush, Carole Scott
English/Humanities Teacher
Cobb, Dolorez
6th Grade Teacher/Team Leader
Cochran, Jeanne Taylor
Spanish Teacher
Duzen, Suzanne SSCM
Principal
Engle, Karen Elaine
Sixth Grade Teacher
Hawkins, Patricia Avera
English 2nd Language Teacher
Kegerreis, Phyllis Knudsen
First Grade Teacher
Rockey, Susan May
Latin Teacher
Wagner, Edward Demmy
Sixth Grade Teacher
HARRISON CITY
Loughner, Helen L.
Chemistry Instructor
HASTINGS
Anna, Dorothy (Bearer)
English Teacher
Hicks, Robert Allen
Math & Computer Teacher
Kochinsky, Robert John
History/Civics Teacher
HATBORO
Touchton, Gary D.
Social Studies Teacher
HAVERTOWN
Flounders, Margaret R. Mc Farland
6th Grade English/Rdng Teacher
Hulse, Raymond Burrell
Chemistry Teacher
HAZLETON
Edmondson, Adam Russel Sr.
AP Chemistry Teacher
Foran, Lawrence F.
Head Teacher/Soc Stud Teacher

Lopashanski, Barry L.
Inter Elem Math & Sci Teacher
Matteo, Alicia
First/Second Grade Teacher
Murphy, John Patrick
Chemistry Teacher
Podczaski, Catherine Ann
Director of Religious Ed
Rattigan, Mary Elizabeth
Latin Teacher
Steber, Ronald J.
Power Technology Instructor
Van Eeden, Cecilia Fazzi
Foreign Language Dept Chair
HELLERTOWN
Singer, Gwendolyn Keiper
Second Grade Teacher
HEREFORD
Slack, Emily Fox
3rd Grade Teacher
HERMINIE
Bateman, Joan Kushnir
Accounting & Typing Teacher
Lucarelli, Dianne Kapanak
Business Teacher
Merdian, Patricia V.
Language Arts Department Chair
Sann, Deborah J. Balentine
English Teacher
HERMITAGE
Wright, William Mc Kinley
Social Studies Teacher
HERNDON
Deppen, David M.
5th Grade Teacher
Madara, Linda Louise
Business Teacher & Chairperson
Wiest, Karen Machtley
Gifted Ed/English Teacher
HERSHEY
Pavone, Vicki Lynn
Fifth Grade Teacher
Pfeiffenberger, Eleanor Charlotte
Ackalusky
5th-8th Grade Eng Teacher
Strait, Larry H.
Biology Teacher
HOLLAND
Duaime, Robert E.
Mathematics Teacher
Wolverton, Carolyn Cestra
English/Speech/Drama Teacher
HOLLIDAYSBURG
Mc Donald, John William
Mathematics Teacher
Miller, Milton Maxwell
Fifth Grade Teacher
Olsavick, Kim Wilt
Third Grade Teacher
HOLLSOPPLE
Dibert, Ann Elizabeth (Rosko)
Business Education Teacher
Furda, Alice
English Teacher
HOMER CITY
Finotti, Roger C.
5th Grade Teacher
HOMESTEAD
Dithrich, Marie
4th/5th Grade Math/Cmptr Instr
Florian, Elsie Keady
Religion Teacher
HOOKSTOWN
Deep, Annora Rodgers
Fourth Grade Teacher
D'Eramo, Margaret Mary
Counselor
HORSHAM
Heaton, Kenneth Robert
6th Grade Teacher
HOUSTON
Mc Cullough, Sophia Agoris
Kindergarten Teacher
HOUTZDALE
Marcinko, Thomas John
Science Teacher/Dept Chair
HUMMELSTOWN
Bartholomew, Timothy Alan
5th Grade Teacher
Schankweiler, Robert Daniel
Bus Ed Dept Chairperson
HUNTINGDON
Coppes, Jeffery Wayne
Teacher of the Gifted

Hindeman, Donald Frank
Science Department Chairman
HUNTINGDON VALLEY
Parry, Ritchard George
Chemistry Teacher
IMPERIAL
Dalmolin, Jo Ann Dell
Spanish Teacher
Smith, Sandra Lee (French)
Librarian
INDIANA
Lowman, Karen Montgomery
7th Grade Science Teacher
IRWIN
Gesalman, Jack W.
Mathematics Teacher
Mango, Antonia Marie
First Grade Teacher
Michel, Antonia La Rosa
5th Grade Teacher
Pavlik, Jeffrey C.
Sixth Grade Teacher
Plank, Mary Catherine
3rd Grade Teacher
JAMESTOWN
Michalyk, Catherine J.
Spanish/English Teacher
Piroga, James Francis
Math & Computer Teacher
JEANNETTE
Freed, Karen Ann
Second Grade Teacher
JENNERSTOWN
Kowalczyk, Stephanie Jacqueline
Kindergarten Teacher
Wylie, Charlotte Lee
5th Grade Teacher
JERMYN
Bonacci, Jean Leonard
Music Teacher
Doud, David M.
English Department Chairman
JERSEY SHORE
Daneker, Marlene M.
Teacher of Gifted
Maines, Donna Rode
English/Enrichment Teacher
Rohe, Patti Jane (Brown)
8th Grade English Teacher
Teufel, George William
Social Studies Teacher
JOHNSONBURG
Breakey, Curtis Emery
Social Studies Teacher
Frank, Donald E.
Guidance Counselor
JOHNSTOWN
Alwine, Judith S. (Weigle)
Third Grade Teacher
Claar, Lori L.
Mathematics Teacher
Colbert, David Charles
Fourth Grade Teacher
Fetchko, John D.
Physics Teacher
Gresh, Carol Stephenie (Long)
Second Grade Teacher
Higgins, Dona Slobozien
Reading/Literature Teacher
Hillard, Samuel Marc
7th/8th Grade Soc Stud Teacher
Kush, David John
Fourth Grade Teacher
Remick, Karen Noreen
Horticulture Instructor
Roberts, Marlene B.
Business Education Teacher
Simmons, Paula Riggi
Fourth Grade Teacher
Swank, Elaine
Fourth Grade Teacher
Yanity, Lynne (Patterson)
7th Grade Teacher
JONES MILLS
Emert, Lorna Jones
5th & 6th Grade Teacher
JONESTOWN
Ebersole, Ruth Longenecker
Sixth Grade Teacher
Olff, Sharon Faith Gettel
Third Grade Teacher
KANTNER
Dickey, Jack S.
Middle School Principal
Shank, Walter Glenn Jr.
7th Grade Mathematics Teacher

KENNETT SQUARE
Beck, James Walter
Mathematics Teacher
Roselle, Deborah Muhlenberg
English Teacher
KERSEY
Miller, Margaret Gallagher
Second Grade Teacher
KINGSTON
Everhart, Carol H.
6th Grade Sci/Health Teacher
Germak, George A.
English/Latin Teacher
Makravitz, Carol A.
Biology/Accel Physics Teacher
Mebane, Nancy L.
English Teacher
Morgan, Mary Ann
Second Grade Teacher
Nenni, Irene Yastremski
First Grade Teacher
Ondash, Madonna L.
Span Teacher/Lang Dept Chair
Shurnicki, Roberta
Teacher of Gifted & Talented
Sirak, Anita Bogusko
Math Dept Chairperson
KINTNERSVILLE
Greenhalgh, Judith Byrnes
German Teacher
Smith, Valerie Moritz
English Teacher Dept Chair
KITTANNING
Mc Kee, Teresa Lee (Smith)
Chemistry Teacher
KNOXVILLE
Doan, Winifred Snyder
Fifth Grade Teacher
KULPMONT
Repko, Sherry Lynn
Sixth & Seventh Grade Teacher
KUTZTOWN
Schearer, Miriam J.
Third Grade Teacher
LAKE ARIEL
Davis, Jeanne Marie (Ball)
8th Grade Social Stud Teacher
Neri, Maria Ann
6th Grade Teacher
Stedenfeld, Michelle Coury
Art Teacher
LANCASTER
De Graaff, Erwin
1st-8th Grade Head Teacher
Garbrick, George Richard
Language Arts Teacher
Lapp, Jessica W.
English Teacher
Mc Cormack, William Daniel
History Department Chair
Metzler, C. Lehman
Ag Teacher/Dept Chairperson
Pugh, Lucia Ann
Spanish Teacher
Woodcock, Thomas C.
Fourth Grade Teacher
LANGHORNE
Bauer, Douglas George
Science Department Chair
Hanlon, Daniel P.
Physics Teacher
Upton, Lorraine Cohen
Third Grade Teacher
LANSDALE
Eckfeldt, Fred W.
Chemistry & Astronomy Teacher
Wolper, Timothy M.
Social Studies Dept Chairman
LANSFORD
Reinbold, Marian
5th Grade Teacher
LAPORTE
Hoffman, Gerald Victor
Third Grade Teacher
Laidacker, Larry M.
Fourth Grade Teacher
Ruhl, Randall Wayne
Mathematics Teacher
LARKSVILLE
Alichnie, Connie Spatz
First Grade Teacher
LATROBE
Bates, Dawna Richards
Health/Physical Ed Teacher
Billett, Lynda Laudig
Kindergarten Teacher

Billett, Marc Lindsey
Health/Physical Ed Teacher
Ebert, Patricia Marshall
Language Arts Teacher
Miller, Deborah Ruth (Mock)
7th-8th Grade Spanish Teacher
Romano, Sandra A.
Teacher-Language Arts Dept
Thurn, Julie K.
Art Teacher
LAURELDALE
Killian, Bonnie Bean
Learning Lab Instructor
LEBANON
Beazley, Thomas R.
Social Studies Chair
Darrenkamp, Michele Anne
Mathematics Teacher
Granger, Deborah Ann (Wile)
Fifth Grade Teacher
Herneisey, Curtis Lee
Second Grade Teacher
Kohl, Gordon Sr.
Mathematics Department Supvr
Nunemacher, Julia Martin
Mathematics Teacher
Pennypacker, Harry Byron
History Teacher
Richwine, Harry Thomas III
5th Grade Teacher
Rife, Elaine Moyer
Sixth Grade Teacher
Strauss, Thelma Hauer
Sixth Grade Teacher
Weddle, Harry
7th Grade Soc Studies Teacher
LEECHBURG
Olshansky, Patricia Joan (Oldfield)
Science/Computer Teacher
LEESPORT
Miller, Robert Fulton Jr.
6th Grade Social Stud Teacher
LEETSDALE
Andrews, Jeffrey Jay
Social Studies Teacher
LEHIGHTON
Maher, Terence R.
Director of Pupil Services
Mychaliszyn, Kim M.
Business Education Teacher
Sabol, Lucinda Maholick
First Grade Teacher
Sowden, Eileen L.
2nd Grade Teacher
LEHMAN
Frank, Helen C.
Mathematics Teacher
Glogowski, Marilyn Cigarski
5th Grade Teacher
Kopcho, Christine A.
Biology Teacher/Science Chair
Langan, Robert Michael
HS Social Studies Teacher
Lipski, Jean Johnson
English Teacher
Malpass, Mary Hourigan
Mathematics Teacher
Toole, Marietta Resio
First Grade Teacher
LEMOYNE
Gates, James Edward
Computer Training Specialist
LEVITTOWN
Hammond, Patricia Jean
Elementary Librarian
Harre, James H.
Tech Physics Teacher
Schein, Eileen Hoffman
Spanish Teacher
Schneider, Linda M.
6th Grade Teacher
LIBERTY
Mitstifer, Arwood E.
4/5/6 Grade Soc Stud Teacher
Morgan, Terry Lee
Language Arts Teacher
Reith, Sandra Isabel
English Teacher
LINESVILLE
Chesko, Richard Lee
History Teacher
LITITZ
De Perrot, Lucy Musselman
3rd Grade Teacher
Lefever, Harold M. Jr.
Technology Education Teacher
Pillion, Richard Joseph
Mathematics Teacher

Roggie, Bertha
6th Grade Reading Teacher
Wagaman, Craig Carpenter
5th Grade Teacher
LITTLESTOWN
Bowersox, David F. A.
Health/Physical Ed Teacher
James, Sue Miller
First Grade Teacher
Kittinger, Thomas William
Vocal Music Instructor
Smyers, Dennis D.
Language Art Dept Chairperson
LOCK HAVEN
Bowers, Gloria Mills
Art Teacher
Greninger, Richard Delano
7th & 8th Grade Math Teacher
Kling, Ann Roush
Kindergarten Teacher
LOGANTON
Berry, Ruth Smith
3rd Grade Teacher
LOWER BURRELL
Conroy, Catherine Funkhouser
Teacher of Gifted
Corey, Michele
Spanish Teacher
Nykiel, Janet
English/Reading Teacher
Turowski, Donald Alex
Computer/Mathematics Teacher
LOYSBURG
Over, Edward N.
6th Grade Teacher
LYKENS
Caffas, Mary Ellen Golden
7th/8th Grade Eng Teacher
MAHANOY CITY
Babatsky, Angeline Carrato
Kindergarten Teacher
Horan, Martha Ann
French Teacher
Kaye, Stephanie Romanison
Spanish Teacher
MALVERN
Coghlan, Rosemarie M.
English Teacher
Lovejoy, Dawn DeDolf
AP Biology & Chemistry Teacher
MANCHESTER
Cabott, Sandra Miller
6th Grade Mid Sch Teacher
Dougherty, Clarence Clark
Fourth Grade Teacher
Gingerich, William John
Social Studies Teacher
Haag, Alana Z.
French Teacher
Owen-Goodling, Susan Gail
Third Grade Teacher
Plappert, William F.
Mathematics Teacher
MANHEIM
Acaley, Philip B.
History Teacher
MARIENVILLE
Beichner, Linda Graham
Second Grade Teacher
MARION CENTER
Mc Ginnis, Linda (Frye)
4th Grade Teacher
Mogle, Nancy Francis
Math Teacher
Null, Marjorie Murray
English Dept Chairperson
Receski, Stanley Joseph
Fourth Grade Teacher
MARS
Austen, Marcy Kathleen
Elem Teacher-Remedial Math
Clingensmith, Donald
Mathematics Teacher
MC ALISTERVILLE
Spade, Larry Edwin
Intermediate Math Teacher
MC CLELLANDTOWN
Marchelletta, Janet Lynne (Kovach)
Third Grade Teacher
Martin, Denise Marie (Blazek)
Principal
MC CONNELLSBURG
Christophel, Paul William
Science Teacher

MC DONALD
Abdulavic, Peter
6th Grade Teacher
Arbore, Beverly
Spanish Teacher
Deichler, James Kenneth
Mathematics Teacher
Korchnak, Karen H.
Business Teacher
Stewart, Gary Wayne
5th Grade Teacher
MC KEES ROCKS
Dines, Alan John
History Teacher
MC KEESPORT
Gorman, Gene Francis
Science Teacher
Maksin, Patricia Lickert
Sixth Grade Teacher
Markosky, Rita Whetsell
Spanish Teacher
Mc Dermott, Tara Zetler
4th Grade Teacher
Palmer, Patricia (Faix)
Jr-Sr High School Librarian
Vranish, Jane
String Teacher
MC MURRAY
Noel, Karyl Lynne
Health/Physical Ed Teacher
MEADVILLE
Hootman, Daniel Winfield
Teacher
Kane, Sybil K.
Earth Science Teacher
La Scola, Linda L.
Pre-School Owner/Teacher
Smith, Paul M.
5th Grade Teacher
Zylak, Richard Edmund Jr.
Physics Teacher
MECHANICSBURG
Bowser, Karen Wilson
English Teacher
Lacey, Rebecca Rumberger
Teacher of Gifted
Murdocca, Lorraine Yanno
Mathematics Teacher
Schaffstall, Robert Dale
5th Grade Teacher
MEDIA
Mac Donald, Linda Ann
8th Grade Lang Arts Teacher
MERCER
Smith, Mary Ann Todorich
5th Grade Teacher
MERCERSBURG
Cornelious, Bonnie Martic
7th Grade English Teacher
Malone, James Leland Jr.
Science Department Chair
Treml, Millie Yurchik
7th Grade Reading Teacher
MERION STATION
Small, Rita
Latin Teacher
MEYERSDALE
Gnagey, Patricia Ann (Zamer)
Business Teacher
Kinsinger, H. Lee
Reading Specialist
Smaila, John
Athletic Director
Troutman, Carol E.
Fourth Grade Teacher
Whitford, Jeannie Ellen
Sixth Grade Teacher
MIDDLETOWN
Kutz, Harvey J.
6th Grade Math/Reading Teacher
MIFFLINTOWN
Houtz, Curtis Lynn
World Cultures/US His Teacher
Hummel, Suzanne DeForrest
Ninth Grade English Teacher
Schaaf, Mary Lou (Amole)
English/Speech Teacher
Trego, Michael Robert
Instrumental Music Teacher
MILFORD
Merow, Craig Banks
District Mathematics Coord
MILL HALL
Decker, Daniel E.
Head Football Coach

Livingston, Carole Ann
Fifth Grade Teacher
Randecker, Charles Henry
Fifth Grade Teacher
MILLERSBURG
Burris, Betty Thompson
4th Grade Teacher
Higgins, Alice F.
6th/8th Grade Science Teacher
Ryan, Angela Udovich
Spanish/French Teacher
Sheaffer, John Clarence
Middle School Science Teacher
Sheaffer, William A.
HS Science/Psychology Teacher
MILLERTON
Pazzaglia, Susan Butcher
First Grade Teacher
MILLVILLE
Baney, Todd Michael
Sixth Grade Teacher
Bowen, James William
Chemistry Teacher
Sherlinski, Mark
5th Grade Teacher
MILTON
Hartley, Margaret D.
Math Teacher
MINERSVILLE
Sabaday, Joseph Andrew
7th/8th Grade Math/Sci Teacher
MONACA
Babich, Ivan Paul
Mathematics Dept Chairman
Halsac, Cynthia K.
Teacher
Policastro, Ellen (Stanik)
German Teacher
MONONGAHELA
Bellamy, Jon P.
English Teacher
Frederick, L. Scott
Amer & World Cultures Teacher
Mancinelli, Joseph Albert
Mathematics Teacher
Robinson, Lynda K.
Mathematics Teacher
Rodriguez, Manuel Robert
Mathematics Instructor
MONROEVILLE
Koller, John Albert
Elementary Phys Ed Teacher
Machen, Gary Lee
American History Teacher
Shafer, James W.
4th Grade Teacher
Vassilaros, Constantine George
Anatomy/Physiology/Bio Teacher
MONTANDON
Murray, Catherine Louise
4th Grade Teacher
MONTOURSVILLE
Bauer, Friederike Barbara
German Teacher
Hopkins, Michelle Lee
English Teacher
Schreiter, Rhonda Reppert
Third Grade Teacher
Williams, Gary Bennett
Chemistry Teacher
Young, David Allen
5th/6th Grade Math Teacher
MOOSIC
Symuleski, Diane M. Barycki
5th Grade Elementary Teacher
MORRISDALE
Houser, Jacalyn Carol
Third Grade Teacher
MORRISVILLE
Yetto-Reichard, Lynette
Teacher of Gifted/Talented
MOSCOW
Benjamin, Lee J.
Physics/Meteorology Teacher
Grudis, Carol Ann Fogliani
Third Grade Teacher
Harvey, Keith R.
6th Grade Teacher
Hennigan, Alexandria
5th Grade Eng/Lang Art Teacher
Lisandrelli, Elaine Slivinski
7th Grade English Teacher
Moore, Joseph
Chemistry Teacher

MOUNT CARMEL
Litchko, Joseph Michael
  Science Teacher
Shrawder, Antoinette Fierro
  First Grade Teacher

MOUNT JEWETT
Zarnick, June F.
  Kndgtn Teacher/Rdng Specialist

MOUNT JOY
Sener, Scott T.
  Sixth Grade Teacher

MOUNT PLEASANT
Blank, Gail L.
  Fifth Grade Teacher
Bosdosh, Stephanie Suzanne
  Third Grade Teacher
Kelly, Anne M.
  Fifth Grade Teacher
Lesko, Joseph P.
  English Teacher
Queer, Linda Caruso
  First Grade Teacher
Randolph, Kathleen Patricia
  Third Grade Teacher
Rega, Georgene Roberta
  Second Grade Teacher
Schroll, Beverly Lohr
  English Teacher
Smail, Samuel James
  Head Teacher 6th Grade Teacher

MOUNTAIN TOP
Ronan, Joan Smith
  First Grade Teacher
Zimmerman, Richard T.
  Fifth Grade Teacher

MUNCY
Sheptock, Colleen Collins
  Guidance Counselor

MUNHALL
Barnes, George John
  Science Teacher
Farkal, George Edward
  Fourth Grade Teacher
Manfred, Rosemary Pusatere
  Math Dept Chair/Teacher

MURRYSVILLE
Reese, Okey Leonard
  Mathematics Teacher
Wolfe, Helen H.
  Fourth Grade Teacher

MYERSTOWN
Bomberger, Brenda White
  Business Education Teacher
Rank, Sherilyn Smith
  Drama Coach/Dir of Guidance
Witter, John H.
  Mathematics Teacher

NANTICOKE
Argento, Santina J.
  Fourth Grade Teacher

NANTY GLO
Leonard, Carole Austin
  Mathematics Teacher

NATRONA HEIGHTS
Arbutiski, Mary Harenski
  English/German Teacher

NAZARETH
Altemose, Constance S.
  First Grade Teacher
Hallman, Robert Richard
  Eng/Creative Writing Teacher

NEMACOLIN
Bandish, Elizabeth Cerjanec
  1st Grade Teacher

NEW BETHLEHEM
Moore, Morna Ruth Wright
  3rd Grade Teacher

NEW BLOOMFIELD
Kaseman, Ray William Henry
  Health Phys Ed Teacher

NEW BRIGHTON
Petruska, Sharon Ann
  Fourth Grade Teacher
Sinclair, E. Mardele (Field)
  Kindergarten Teacher
Thiessen, Paul G.
  Music Director

NEW CASTLE
Angert, Mary Catherine
  Mathematics Teacher
Black, Eleanora Louise Schmidt
  Fourth Grade Teacher
Deal, Edwin E.
  English Teacher

Genkinger, A. Bruce
  4th Grade Teacher
Getchy, Eleanore Flowers
  Biology Teacher
Wertz, Joan P.
  Third Grade Teacher

NEW CUMBERLAND
Axsom, Glenda Yingling
  Fifth Grade Teacher
Knepper, Kathleen Allwein
  8th Grade Mathematics Teacher

NEW FLORENCE
Kelly, R. Maxine
  Fifth Grade Teacher
Ritenour, Jay K.
  Fifth Grade Teacher

NEW HOLLAND
Davis, Susan Lynn
  Art Teacher

NEW KENSINGTON
Birkmeyer, Stephanie
  Chemistry Teacher
Glock, Carol Thomas
  French Teacher
Lockett, Marjorie Anderson
  Third Grade Teacher
Matyas, Eileen Heiles
  Spanish Teacher

NEW RINGGOLD
Fritz, Leah Wertman
  First Grade Teacher

NEW STANTON
Mc Cauley, Ronald James
  Electronics Instructor

NEW TRIPOLI
Hough, John T.
  6th Grade Teacher

NEW WILMINGTON
Hill, Phyllis M.
  Retired English/Span Teacher

NEWTOWN
Carroll, Frances Marie
  French Teacher
Chapman, Gertrude Welsh
  Social Studies Teacher
Culp, Carolyn M.
  Spanish Teacher
Kervick, Irene Therese
  8th Grade Teacher
Lanfrey, James Frederick
  Federal Programs Coordinator
Rabberman, Anna Maria Lehner
  Social Studies Teacher

NEWTOWN SQUARE
Bannar, Dorothy Kemble
  Mathematics Teacher
Lake, Peter John
  6th Grade Mid Sch Teacher
Scott, William Conway
  Social Studies Chair
Subers, Stephen Edward
  Mathematics Teacher
Warkentin, Rose Marie
  4th Grade Teacher

NEWVILLE
Baker, Ruby Reeder
  Business Education Teacher
Smith, Thomas George
  Life Science Teacher
Stover, Ronna Lee Price
  Health & Physical Educator
Zeigler, Rita Rook
  English Teacher/Dept Head

NORMALVILLE
Yukish, Dorothy Krecker
  Sixth Grade Teacher

NORRISTOWN
Anders, Carol Petrilla
  6th-8th Grade Home Ec Teacher
Hillegas, Donald Lee
  Social Studies Teacher
Miller, Henry A.
  English Teacher
Petruso, Ronald Thomas
  Chemistry Instructor
Wagner, Robert James
  Mathematics Professor

NORTH EAST
Baniszewski, David Edmund
  1st-12th Grade Lead Teacher
Spacht, Irene OSB
  8th Grade Teacher

NORTH HUNTINGDON
Bluhm, John M.
  Chemistry Teacher

Cornali, Robert Louis
  Social Studies Teacher
Falcocchio, Maryanna
  Upper Elem Mathematics Instr
Hancock, Louis Joseph
  Dir of Bands/Music Dept Chair
Krist, Catherine A.
  Second Grade Teacher
Lynn, Albert Charles III
  6th Grade Teacher
Mc Clain, Theresa Nalepa
  Science Teacher
Mc Corkle, Cecelia Russak
  Home Ec Teacher/Dept Chair
Polivka, John B.
  History Teacher
Rovesti, Randy
  Physical Ed & Science Teacher
Salsi, Bonnie Chappell
  5th Grade Teacher

NORTHAMPTON
Anthony, Debra Dietrick
  Health & Physical Ed Teacher
Bryant, Robert John
  HS Social Studies Teacher
Fertig, Ralph A. III
  Fourth Grade Teacher
Glessner, Theresa Ann
  English/Journalism Teacher
Jessamine, Vicki Lee
  English Teacher
Keglovits, Michael J.
  History Teacher
O'Donnell-Smith, Patricia
  Science Teacher
Vulcano, Pat Jr.
  Teacher/Coordinator

OAKDALE
Gilden, Robin Elissa
  Fourth Grade Teacher

OBERLIN-STEELTON
Dorn, Robert David
  Technology Education Teacher

OIL CITY
Guth, Nancy English
  6th Grade Teacher
Moran, Frances Russell
  4th Grade Teacher
Murray, R. Eileen Williams
  Intermediate Lang Arts Teacher
Stevens, Richard K.
  Chemistry Teacher
Wenner, Douglas Keith
  English Teacher

OLEY
Gundrum, Elsa May
  Business Teacher
Ranieri, Ronald David
  Reading Teacher
Wildermuth, Larry Guy
  World Cultures Teacher

ORBISONIA
Hummel, Cheryl Ann
  Business Education Teacher

OREFIELD
Dimmich, Kathleen Brobst
  Librarian-HS/Scndry Lib Coord
Lindenmuth, Douglas D.
  Mathematics Teacher
Longenberger, Sally S.
  Chemistry Teacher

ORWIGSBURG
Gross, James R.
  Science Teacher
Herb, Mark Ray
  7th Grade Science Teacher
Jones, Lorraine Snyder
  Elementary Gifted Teacher

PALMERTON
Olivia, Susan (Rehrig)
  Sixth Grade Teacher
Wallace, Anna Smacchi
  English Teacher

PALMYRA
Boltz, Gerald Michael
  Sixth Grade Teacher
Miller, John P.
  Social Studies Teacher
Snyder, William Birch
  9th Grade Lang Arts Teacher
Vance, Amee M. Lewis
  Kindergarten Teacher

PATTON
Bilko, A. Daniel
  Chemistry Teacher
Hoover, Patricia Zerbee
  1st Grade Teacher
Thomas, Carol Mercedes (Clews)
  First Grade Teacher

PENNSBURG
Moyer, Linda D.
  Spanish Teacher

PEQUEA
Brown, Sandra Lee
  Seventh Grade Reading Teacher

PHILADELPHIA
Barnett, Barbara Williams
  Teacher
Basara, Judy Belcak
  Mathematics Department Chair
Bess, Sylvia Renee
  Spanish/French Teacher
Brandt, Paul Charles
  Religion Teacher
Brennan, David W.
  Dir of Dev/Alumni
Bryan, Henry Collier
  Math Teacher
Bullock, June Odom
  Counselor
Burns, Eleanor M.
  Third Grade Teacher
Calciano, Marie Frances
  8th Grade Teacher/Sci Coord
Cardano, Regina Marie
  6th Grade Teacher
Cohen, Joan S.
  Teacher of Mentally Gifted
Cooke, Eileen Francis Marie
  Religion Teacher
Costello, Michael John
  English Teacher/Dept Head
Cuff, Alvin J.
  Science Dept Chm/Teacher
Darden, Mary Palmer
  5th Grade English Teacher
De Biase, Jean M.
  Mathematics Teacher
Di Cicco, Rosemarie Teresa
  8th Grade English Teacher
Di Giesi, John Vincent
  Eighth Grade Teacher
Di Santis, Geraldine Ann
  Second Grade Teacher
Donohie, John M.
  College/Career Counselor
Eibell, Marilyn
  4th Grade Teacher
Gannon, John Joseph
  Social Studies Teacher
Gigliotti, Lisa Ann
  Science Chair & Teacher
Heintz, Susan M.
  8th Grade English Teacher
Herens, Denise Clark
  Mathematics Teacher
Herman, Christine
  Fifth Grade Teacher
Hershman, Alan R.
  Teacher of Gifted & Talented
Hobbs, Debra Cathey
  Program Liaison
Holliday, Diane Jones
  English Teacher
Huber, Barry Robert
  Choral Music Teacher
Jackson, Cynthia Thomas
  First Grade Teacher
Joftis, Frank Jay
  8th Grade Teacher
Johnson, Celeste C. (Nicholson)
  12th Grade Teacher
Johnson, June Thurston
  First Grade Teacher
Kaporch, Moya Regina
  English Teacher/Lecturer
King, Rosemary
  Fourth Grade Teacher
Knapper, Patricia Tarrant
  Teacher
Kruvczuk, Sandra DeWolff
  English/Reading Teacher
Leise, Maureen Wilkinson
  Teacher/Forensics Moderator
Levin, Victor S.
  English Teacher
Lieber, David Thomas
  Physical & Health Ed Teacher
Lotz, Vivian Evelyn
  Counselor
Madden, Theresa Marie
  8th Grade Math Teacher
Marshall, Delores Nichols
  Second Grade Teacher
Mc Cafferty, Eileen Patricia
  2nd Grade Teacher
Mc Clelland, Phyllis Dittman
  German/Spanish Teacher
Mc Mahon, Mary Smith
  Teacher of Mentally Gifted
Mc Peak, Patricia Rappucci
  English Teacher

Meroney, Richard Francis
  History Teacher
Metelits, Melvin
  6th Grade Retired Teacher
Mosley, Barbara Galloway
  Mathematics Teacher
Nejman, Gerard John
  English Teacher
Oberholzer, Cecilia Garvin
  Chemistry Teacher
Poteat, Kathryn Marlou Joyner
  Mathematics Teacher
Reichman, David Michael
  Music Department Chair
Ronzoni, Arnold David
  English Teacher
Russo, Deborah Marie
  Fifth Grade Teacher
Russo, Lila Ammeen
  Third Grade Teacher
Scartozzi, Cheryl Cevoli
  8th Grade Teacher
Schug, John Russell
  English Teacher
Scott, Linda Simkins
  2nd Grade Teacher
Smith, Helen Gabriel
  7th Grade Math/Soc Std Teacher
Sowri, Arokiadoss
  Science Teacher
Staniec, Victor G.
  Chemistry/Physics Teacher
Stickney, Phyllis
  Mathematics Teacher
Strong, Elminor Morris
  5th Grade Teacher
Trendler, Gerald J.
  5th Grade Teacher
Vass, Susan J.
  Reading Teacher
Vignola, Eileen Young
  8th Grade Teacher
White, Miriam Recker
  Chemistry Teacher
Young, Marilyn S.
  Science Teacher
Zima, Elizabeth M.
  6th Grade Teacher

PHILIPSBURG
Veronesi, Peter D.
  Physical Science Teacher

PHOENIXVILLE
Good, Vivian D. (Dye)
  Eng/Theatre/Comm Teacher
Kelly, William David Jr.
  Social Studies Teacher
Michalski, Donna L.
  Art Teacher 8-9/Dept Chair
Ponisciak, Lenora T.
  6th Grade Teacher
Wright, Jean Norman
  Sixth Grade Teacher

PINE GROVE
Hikes, Barbara Luckenbill
  Remedial Reading Teacher

PIPERSVILLE
Senderling, Susan G.
  Fifth Grade Teacher

PITTSBURGH
Baker, Patricia CDP
  Director of Liturgy
Baumbach, David E.
  Humanities Teacher
Binz, Marian Cuccaro
  8th Grade Teacher
Brozick, James R.
  English Teacher
Fialkovich, Stephen Gerard
  Religion Teacher
Finseth, Constance E. (St John)
  Math Teacher
Frederick, Karen Susan (Adiutori)
  Director of Choirs
Grode, Linda Downing
  5-8th Grade Math Teacher
Lobaugh, Donna Pascarella
  6th Grade Teacher
Martin, Carol Louise
  Health/Physical Ed Teacher
Martin, Donna
  Social Studies Teacher
Moriarty, Brigid
  Teacher
Nardozzi, Kathleen S.
  English Teacher
Nardozzi, Ronald J.
  Social Studies Teacher
Norkus, Patricia Lynn
  High School Art Teacher
Och, Sandra
  6th Grade Reading Teacher
Perriello, Joseph E.
  4th Grade Teacher

PITTSBURGH (cont)
Pfeffer, Inez Gatte
  Jr HS Social Studies Teacher
Preston, Thomas William
  8th Grade Science Teacher
Roberta, M. SDR
  Jr HS Religion Teacher
Ross, Charles Daniel
  6th Grade Elementary Teacher
Schleicher, Ann W.
  Scndry English/Speech Teacher
Signore, Richard A.
  Spanish & Latin Teacher
Spencer, Gloria Kirkmon
  English Teacher & Dept Chair
Stanczak, Richard Joseph
  Gifted Program Coordinator
Sumpter, Sarah Davis
  English Teacher
Suvak, Dolores Clougherty
  Advanced English II Teacher
Tambucci, Sarah
  Art Teacher-Department Chair
Thomas, Richard N.
  5th Grade Teacher
Thomas, Robert John
  High School Science Teacher
Wentzel, Howard Scott
  Social Studies Teacher
Wilkinson, Catherine Jelensky
  8th Grade Teacher/Math Chair
Zaletski, Stephen Paul
  Math Teacher

PITTSTON
Adonizio, Robert Joseph
  6th Grade Science Teacher
Myers, Mary Kathryn Toole
  Second Grade Teacher

PLAINS
Kordek, Charlotte Crawford
  Biology Teacher

PLEASANT HILLS
Pavlak, Patricia Mc Ginty
  English Teacher

PLUMSTEADVILLE
Otto, Nancy Kushmider
  Biology/Scndry Sci Teacher

PLYMOUTH
Marko, Andrew Paul Jr.
  Advanced Placement Eng Teacher
Tarantini, Mary Jean Delycure
  World Cultures Teacher
Wilski, Christopher Joseph
  Orchestra Director

PORT ALLEGANY
Bennett, Thomas Lee
  Social Studies Teacher

PORT TREVORTON
Wagner, Maureen Schaeffer
  Fourth Grade Teacher/Principal

PORT VUE
Cardarelli, Paula Mihalko
  Fifth Grade Teacher
Kalocay, Bernard Andrew
  Elementary School Principal
Slafka, Stephen Michael
  6th Grade Teacher

PORTERSVILLE
Duncan, George Ernest
  5th Grade Teacher

POTTSTOWN
Albert, Elizabeth E.
  Biology Teacher
Rheel, Ruth Ann Ross
  Language Arts Teacher
Ruth, Thomas Griswold
  History Instructor

POTTSVILLE
Sabol, David
  Mathematics Dept Chair
Wagner, Miriam Davis
  Mathematics Teacher

PULASKI
Lyons, Portia Nicely
  First Grade Teacher

PUNXSUTAWNEY
Bowser, Anita Quinlisk
  6th-8th Grade Science Teacher
Conti, Judtih Hogan
  7th Grade Art Teacher
Henry, Lois E.
  Spanish Teacher
Hughes, D. Keith
  Technology Education Teacher
Reitz, Margaret L.
  Third Grade Teacher

Swanson, Caryn A.
  English/Journalism Teacher

QUARRYVILLE
Deibler, R. Blake
  Middle School Mathematics

READING
Ambrose, Joseph Eugene
  Social Studies Teacher
Calabria, Rosarita Mary
  Fifth Grade Teacher
Frymoyer, Dennis Clayton
  English Teacher
Hamilton, Richard Curtis
  Mathematics Teacher/Dept Chair
Leinbach, Jay P.
  Teacher
Simcik, William Andrew
  English Teacher/Team Leader

RED LION
Brown, Marilyn J.
  8th Grade Soc Stud Teacher
Keener, Deborah Ann (Roseman)
  Mathematics Teacher
Nauman, Mary Ann (Finkbiner)
  7th Grade Soc Stud Teacher

REYNOLDSVILLE
Kriner, Leon Dale
  Data Processing Teacher

RHEEMS
Daub, Louise Wenger
  4th Grade Teacher

RICHBORO
Judice, Anthony Dominic
  English & Computer Teacher

RICHFIELD
Niemond, Stephen W.
  Social Studies Teacher

RIDGWAY
Shaw, Scott O.
  7th Grade Geography Teacher
Wildnauer, Marcia Mascioni
  2nd Grade Teacher

ROCHESTER
Gill, Pamela Sieger
  Chapter I Dir/Elem Rndg Coord
Mohr, David
  Science Department Chair

ROCHESTER MILLS
Neely, Teresa Yackuboskey
  First Grade Teacher

ROSEMONT
Gaul, Marion Malley
  4th Grade Teacher

ROSLYN
Greenawalt, Ethel M.
  Second Grade Teacher

ROYERSFORD
Kodish, Nancy Whiteside
  Health/Physical Ed Teacher
Rowe, Xandra Kay
  Third Grade Teacher

RUSSELL
Carberry, H. Robert
  Science Department Chairman
Yovich, Suzann Lucy (Shield)
  2nd Grade Teacher

SAEGERTOWN
Clark, Robert Donald
  Biology Teacher
Hayes, Sharon (Bird)
  Fifth Grade Teacher
Monteforte, Stephanie Lupo
  1st Grade Teacher

SAINT MARYS
Cartwright, Mary Lou Santiso
  5th Grade Teacher
Evans, Nancy King
  Spanish & French Teacher
Fedorko, John Charles
  Math Department Chairman
Florig, Sandra Mary (Hauber)
  Jr HS Sci & Health Teacher
Gaskill, Jeanne Dippold
  Sixth Grade Teacher
Hasselman, Sharon Minnick
  6-8th Grade Soc Stud Teacher
Kronenwetter, Salome Marie Lion
  Third Grade Teacher
Nekuza, Kathleen Marie Breindel
  4th Grade Teacher
Pfeufer, Bernice Marie (Salter)
  Mathematics/Reading Teacher
Scilingo, William James
  Physics Teacher

Snelick, Gregory Leonard
  Mathematics Teacher
Steele, Mary Kopp
  English/Computer Teacher
Straub, Aaron John
  Athletic Director

SAINT THOMAS
Beeler, Richard William
  5th Grade Elementary Teacher
Bender, Kimberly Pensinger
  Fifth Grade Teacher

SALTSBURG
Bower, William Richard
  Math Teacher/Swimming Coach
Johnson, Lorrie
  4th Grade Teacher
Murphy, Janet Compton
  Fifth Grade Teacher
Schirf, Martha
  First Grade Teacher
Szilagyi, Tamas
  History Teacher
Weimer, Carol Logan
  Home Economics Teacher

SARVER
Bly, Clifford L.
  Mathematics Teacher

SAXONBURG
Callender, Evelyn Mae (Windows)
  Music Teacher/Choral Director
Greco, Raymond Louis
  Science Teacher
Hoovler, Lee W.
  Chemistry Teacher

SAXTON
Satterfield, James Albert
  Mathematics Teacher/Dept Chair

SCHAEFFERSTOWN
Bicher, Stephanie Ann (Keeney)
  Third Grade Teacher

SCHUYLKILL HAVEN
Roberts, Robert William
  English Teacher/Dept Chair
Santee, Gladys (Snyder)
  Kindergarten Teacher
Ulsh, E. Jane
  Social Studies Teacher

SCRANTON
Buckley, William F.
  Social Studies Teacher
Burke, Carol Connolly
  4th Grade Teacher
Cooke, Patricia Kucha
  Learning Disabilities Teacher
Gilhooley, James W.
  Vice Principal
Gowell, Cynthia Ann
  5th Grade Teacher
Higgins, Sabine M.
  Assistant Production Mgr
Holmes, Linda K.
  Science Teacher
King, William Francis
  Industrial Arts Teacher
Mc Andrew, Mary Jordan
  Third Grade Teacher
Nee, Sharon Codick
  Home Economics Teacher
Walsh, Marion Wyworski
  Science Department Chair

SELINSGROVE
Lauer, David Charles Sr.
  6th Grade Health Teacher

SENECA
Clark, Mary Proper
  English/Reading Teacher

SEWICKLEY
Iacobucci, Nancy Beard
  English Teacher
King, Helen
  Retired Third Grade Teacher
Nichols, Mary Butler
  Third Grade Teacher
Rose, Patrica Stallings
  Head Middle School Teacher

SHAMOKIN
Bamford, Terrie (Maurer)
  Mathematics Teacher
Stellfox, Jean Louise
  English Teacher

SHARON
Alford, Margaret Mahood
  Science Teacher
James, Diane Marie
  2nd Grade Teacher
Mc Math, Josephine Rosa
  Fourth Grade Teacher

SHARON HILL
Cantrell, Cheryl L.
  Science Teacher
Clements-Cobb, Cynthia A.
  Business Teacher/Dept Chair
Dent, Sheldon Ralph
  Business Education Teacher

SHEATOWN
Sokolowski, Ted S.
  Fifth Grade Teacher

SHELOCTA
Simon, Pamela S.
  Teacher/Consultant Grades K-6

SHENANDOAH
Babatsky, Joseph John
  English Teacher

SHICKSHINNY
Sorber, Barbara Ann
  Computer/Mathematics Teacher

SHIPPENSBURG
Basler, Lawrence Edward
  Principal
Rebuck, Richard Hugh
  Physics Teacher
Riester, Connie Ainslee
  2nd Grade Teacher

SIDMAN
Billings, Robert A.
  Music Teacher
Goncher, Thomas James
  Fifth Grade Teacher

SIMPSON
Luchonok, Regina Marie (Gatto)
  Second Grade Teacher

SLATINGTON
Hicks, Bernice Rauch
  German Teacher
Mack, Ruth Kern
  Retired

SLIPPERY ROCK
Ellis, Janet De Corte
  Chapter I Reading Specialist
Taylor, Brenda Joyce
  Health/Physical Ed Teacher

SOMERSET
Hay, Nancy Ann (Landis)
  Girls Physical Ed Teacher

SOUDERTON
Hamilton, Kenneth Lee
  Science Teacher
Saile, Roberta Charlton
  Special Education Teacher

SOUTHAMPTON
Dennis, Donald A.
  Science Teacher
Kedersha, Lucille R.
  English Teacher

SPARTANSBURG
Hopkins, Gary A.
  6th Grade Teacher

SPRING CHURCH
Bonello, Robert L.
  Secondary Gifted Ed Teacher
Steinback, Tim J.
  Science Teacher

SPRING GROVE
Jackson, J. Donald
  9th Grade Teacher
Jennerjohn, Marilyn Rinker
  English Teacher
Snyder, Ray A.
  Art Teacher/Department Chair

SPRINGFIELD
Brown, John
  English & Poetry Teacher
De Curtis, Anthony Phillip
  English Teacher
Dugan, Alice Bernice (Farris)
  Cmptr Resource/Math Teacher
Miller, Susan Teresa
  7th & 8th Grade Math Teacher

STATE COLLEGE
Burkhardt, Beverly Adams
  3rd & 4th Grade Teacher
Lima, Sally Murphy
  Sixth Grade Teacher

STEELTON
Good, Michael Scott
  6th Grade Social Stud Teacher

STRATTANVILLE
Zahoran, John Michael
  English Teacher

STROUDSBURG
Kramer, Marla J.
  8th Grade Science Teacher

SUGARGROVE
Fitzsimmons, Kenneth R.
  Elementary Principal

SUNBURY
Groce, Becky Gilbert
  Mathematics Teacher
Kashuba, Cynthia Teater
  First Grade Teacher
Reaser, James Robert
  Vocal Music/Choral Director
Sanders, Gerald David
  Teacher/Principal

SUSQUEHANNA
Escandel, Thomas Raymond
  Fourth Grade Teacher

SWIFTWATER
Dorati, Henry M.
  Sr HS Math Teacher

TAMAQUA
Finley, Carolyn B.
  Language Arts Teacher
Mettler, John H.
  Fifth Grade Teacher

TARENTUM
Heasley, William W.
  Elementary Principal
Nickols, Mitchel Antoine
  Pastor/TV Teacher

TAYLOR
Joyce, Patrick Francis
  Language Art Teacher
Kosek, John K.
  Art Teacher/Observatory Dir

THORNDALE
Mc Feely, Edward Cary Jr.
  Fifth Grade Teacher
Trimble, Victoria Monko
  Second Grade Teacher

THROOP
Spinosi, Barbara A.
  Sixth Grade Teacher
Walker, William Martin
  Sixth Grade Teacher

TIONESTA
Schlentner, Eliza Calderwood
  English & History Teacher
Shirey, Michael R.
  Business Education Teacher

TITUSVILLE
Campasino, Ellen Marie
  Third Grade Teacher

TOPTON
Hillegass, Cynthia Reichard
  Social Studies Teacher
Jones, Jean Marie (Naydock)
  Middle School Art Teacher
Orlando, Jean M.
  Fourth Grade Teacher
Slick, Kim Joel
  Chemistry/Computer Sci Teacher

TOWER CITY
Cickavage, William John
  Math/Computer Science Teacher
Coleman, Anna Rodichok
  Biology Teacher
Kiraly, Barbara Jean (Mrazek)
  Third Grade Teacher
Miller, James Edward
  Social Studies Teacher
Potlunas, John Francis
  Instrumental Music Teacher

TOWNVILLE
Murphy, James Edward
  English/History Teacher
Sackett, Beverly A. Stevens
  Sixth Grade Teacher

TRAFFORD
Clair, Daryl Richard
  Reading/Language Art Teacher

TROY
Hess, Donna Maloney
  Second Grade Teacher
Myfelt, Carol Jean
  5th Grade Lang Arts Teacher
Rogers, Patricia Ann
  English Teacher

TRUCKSVILLE
Kirk, Patricia Edwards
  First Grade Teacher

TUNKHANNOCK
Delinsky, Nancy Davidson
  Spanish Teacher
Griggs, Howard G. Jr.
  Business Education Chairperson
Hudak, Alice Ide
  Elementary Teacher
Kaufer, Larinda Dyson
  First Grade Teacher

TYRONE
Bloom, Fracis A.
  Mathematics Teacher
Friday, Susan Fresh
  1st Grade Teacher
Heidel, Charles Franklin
  4th Grade Teacher
Moore, Melissa Kowalski
  English Teacher
Strong, Linda Davidson
  6TH Grade Teacher
Tate, John L.
  Elementary Art Teacher

UNIONTOWN
Bubonovich, Carol Hines
  Sixth Grade Teacher
Ciarrocchi, Julia Grace (Agostini)
  Economics Teacher
Clark, Janet E.
  Fourth Grade Teacher
Florkevich, Jerry
  7th/8th Grade English Teacher
Helms, David Craig
  Chemistry/Computer Teacher
Lemansky, Arlene Gondek
  7th Grade Teacher
Martina, Mary Louise
  Chair/Business Ed Teacher
Molk, Bonnie Jean
  Spanish Teacher
Whetzel, Elaine
  Science Teacher
Wilson, John Alan
  4th Grade Teacher

UNIONVILLE
Angelo, Clevio Albert
  US History Teacher/Team Leader

UNITED
Dzuba, Johnette
  Third & Fourth Grade Teacher

UPPER DARBY
Kijewski, Edward John Jr.
  Social Science Teacher
Maxwell, Richard Russell
  Physics Teacher
Nath, Nancy Lee
  Fourth Grade Teacher
Pagliara, Michael D.
  Computer Coordinator

VANDERGRIFT
Answine, Iloa Adametz
  English Teacher
Lambing, Margaret Louise
  Kindergarten Teacher
Mc Clelland, John W.
  Choir Director
Musselman, Susan Edens
  English Teacher
Rusnak, Mary Liska
  K-6th Grade Substitute Teacher

VENUS
Marsh, Carolyn Lucille
  Third Grade Teacher

VILLA MARIA
Leslie, Margaret Mary HM
  Mathematics Teacher

WALNUTPORT
Colarusso, Katherine M.
  Physical Education Teacher

WARMINSTER
Almeida, Roderick R.
  Mathematics Teacher

WARREN
Clough, Dixie Louise
  Third Grade Teacher
Mc Cann, Nancy Miller
  Retired Elem Teacher
Waldeck, Eileen T.
  Math Department Chairperson

WARRINGTON
Pagel Bewley, Mary Jane
  Theology Teacher

WASHINGTON
Berty, Mary Ann (Yoskey)
  Scndry English/Speech Teacher
Booher, Rebecca Jeanne Rea
  English Teacher

Gallagher, Penny Cox
  Physical Ed Teacher/Coach
Haines, Gaylord W. Jr.
  Social Studies Teacher
Mc Cabe, Sandra Petika
  French Teacher
Pavella, Charlotte Katherine
  6th Grade Science Teacher
Richardson, Arthur Patrick
  History Department Chairman
Riddle, Carol Linton
  TELLS Remedial/Cmptr Teacher
Sagona, Barbara Joan Sepashe
  6th Grade Mathematics Teacher
Strennen, James
  Elem Math Department Chairman
White, Judith Dougherty
  English Teacher

WATERFALL
Cromer, Freda Warthin
  First Grade Teacher
Cutchall, Craig Clarton
  Fifth & Sixth Grade Teacher
Helsel, Byron Lee
  5th/6th Grade Teacher
King, Deborah (Bookheimer)
  HS English Teacher

WATERFORD
Cyterski, Norbert A.
  5th-8th Grade Guidance Cnslr
Dinsmore, Judith Szall
  8th Grade Math Teacher
Seymour, Christine Graff
  Kindergarten Teacher

WAYNE
Springer, Mark A.
  7th Grade Watershed Teacher

WAYNESBORO
Herr, Judith Ann (Gorndt)
  Elementary Teacher of Gifted
Shearer, G. Michael
  Guidance Counselor
Shockey, Mark Bruce
  American Cultures Teacher
Spence, Brenda Sue Romaine
  English Teacher
Walter, Dorothy Ralsten
  Bio Teacher/Staff Dev Trainer

WAYNESBURG
Allinder, Richard O.
  Geography Teacher
Augustine, Carolyn
  1st Grade Teacher
Baniecki, Patricia Krajnak
  Language Art Teacher
Braddock, Charlene Knapik
  First Grade Teacher
Cole, Terry R.
  Physical Education Instructor
Cook, Joseph H.
  Social Studies Teacher
Hoover, Lynn A.
  Math Teacher/Math Dept Chair
Knight, Diana Smith
  4th Grade Teacher
Mc Collum, Mark
  Band Director
Muzichuck, Jack F.
  Welding Teacher

WEATHERLY
Hill, Carol Ann
  Home Economics Teacher
Jemo, David Nicholas
  Social Studies Chairman
Kelshaw, Ronald H.
  Guidance Counselor

WEEDVILLE
Duttry, Cynthia Yohe
  Second Grade Teacher

WEST CHESTER
Eadie, Mary Ellen
  Communications Teacher
Galloway, Joan K.
  Biology/Chemistry Teacher
Kupsis, David C.
  5th Grade Teacher
Meshey, Edward Franklin
  Bible Teacher

WEST HAZELTON
Milot, John L.
  History Department Chair

WEST HAZLETON
Clark, Joseph Richard
  Latin & Psychology Teacher
Nocchi, Martin C.
  English Teacher

WEST LAWN
Magala, John Fred Jr.
  Mathematics Teacher

WEST MIFFLIN
Ahern, Judith M.
  Senior Counselor
Di Rocco, Anthony John
  European/AP Amer His Teacher
Forsyth, John W
  Teacher, English Dept Chairman
Piontek, Anne Kazimer
  Third Grade Teacher

WEST NEWTON
Fedrow, Linda L.
  Gifted Ed/Elementary Teacher

WEST READING
Fagan, S. Margaret IHM
  Eighth Grade Teacher

WEST SUNBURY
Duke, Joann D.
  Gifted Coordinator
Morton, Thomas Richard
  5th Grade Teacher/Head Teacher

WESTFIELD
Bollinger, Gail Eick
  Third Grade Teacher
Heyler, Constance Collum
  6th Grade Teacher
Stuart, F. Kay Staples
  Computer Science Teacher

WEXFORD
Fleischaur, Michael J.
  History Teacher

WHITE OAK
Giglio, Marsha Zamosky
  Upper Elementary Teacher
Ulakovic, Loretta M.
  Fourth Grade Teacher

WHITEHALL
Fister, Michael Jon
  Music Teacher
O'Connor, Carol Kurnig
  Science/Social Studies Teacher

WILKES-BARRE
Ashton, Robert William
  7th/8th Grade Science Teacher
Cardoni, Agnes A.
  English Teacher
De Polo, Carol Davenport
  First Grade Teacher
Evans, Ned John
  5th Grade Teacher
Mainwaring, John Rosser
  Music Teacher
Moore, Thomas Edward
  Sixth Grade Teacher
Shafer, Joseph Francis
  Social Studies Teacher
Spagnuolo, John Ralph
  Biology Teacher
Stehur, Peter
  Science Dept Chair
Vasile, Mary Ann R.
  Second Grade Teacher
Yenchik, John A.
  Spanish Teacher/Dept Chair

WILLIAMSPORT
Clark, John Franklin Jr.
  World Geography Teacher
Straiton, Walter James
  Director of Orchestras

WILLIAMSTOWN
Wright, Sandra Lee
  Fourth Grade Teacher

WILLOW GROVE
Cassady, Linda E.
  Social Studies Teacher
Werner, David Gary
  Science Supervisor

WILMERDING
Wells, Karen Keating
  Third Grade Teacher

WINGATE
Houck, C. Bruce
  Business Education Teacher

WOMELSDORF
Becker, David Ernest
  Fourth Grade Teacher
Bennick, Brenda Corl
  6th Grade Teacher
Greenich, Karl Edward Jr.
  Sixth Grade Teacher

WRIGHTSTOWN
Hauler, Lawrence Albert
  3rd Grade Teacher

WRIGHTSVILLE
Lefever, Frances H.
  4th Grade Teacher

White, Kerry Allen
  American History Teacher

WYALUSING
Fox, Michael Alan
  Sixth Grade Teacher

WYNCOTE
Comer, Rosalyn Sue
  Mathematics Teacher
Mc Kenna, Mary Kay
  Religion/English Teacher
Reim, George David
  Social Studies Department Chm

WYOMISSING
Sheetz, Jane Hernley
  Kindergarten Teacher

YATESVILLE
Schillaci, Patricia Ann
  Mathematics Teacher

YEADON
Rabatin, Mildred Bruce
  Seventh Grade Teacher
Realer, Wendy
  4th Grade Teacher

YORK
Adams, Paul Edwin
  7th-8th Grade Science Teacher
Chronister, Kay Landis
  5th Grade Teacher
Cochran, Patsy Burns
  Sixth Grade Teacher
Fickes, Kay Ness
  Second Grade Teacher
Goodling, John Melvin
  Science Teacher
Mc Afee, Charles Hamilton Jr.
  Fifth Grade Teacher
Mc Donald, Barbara Louise
  4th Grade Teacher
Moyer, Edward Llewellyn Jr.
  7th Grade World His Teacher
Seitz, Sandra Stump
  Kindergarten Teacher
Straw, Robert Eugene
  Elem Art Teacher
Warner, Michelle Butler
  Chairman English Department
Warner, Robert Eugene
  HS Social Studies Teacher
Wert, Dorothy Golden
  Mathematics Teacher

ZELIENOPLE
Paul, Alice Lee Craig
  Kindergarten Teacher

PUERTO RICO

BAYAMON
Santos, Yakelin D.
  History Teacher

CABO ROJO
Lespier, Leyinska
  English Teacher
Maya, Maryln
  Marketing & Distributive Coord

CAGUAS
Cintron, Norma H.
  Spanish Teacher
Tirado, Carmen M.
  Third Grade Teacher

CIDRA
Ortiz, Eneida
  Elementary School Teacher

COTO LAUREL
Ortiz, Nora Irizarry
  English Teacher

FORT BUCHANAN
De Hernandez, Frances Nochera
  Art/English Teacher
Franco, Aida Coriano
  Fourth Grade Teacher

HUMACAO
De Arroyo, Mercedes M.
  School Director

JAYUYA
Cancel, Luz Neida
  Emeritus Teacher

MAYAGUEZ
Hunt, Susan Conway
  English Teacher

MOROVIS
Efrain, Aviles Lopez
  6th Grade Mathematics Teacher

PONCE
De Quintero, Myriam
  Elementary School Teacher
Nieves Caraballo, Angel L.
  Social Studies Teacher
Pagan, Elba I
  Sci Teacher/Sci Dept Chair

RIO PIEDRAS
Cancel, Myriam Martinez
  Science Professor
Santiago, Edna
  7th/8th Grade English Teacher

SAN JUAN
Castro, Victor S.
  Industrial Arts Teacher
Nieves, Noris Colberg
  Mathematics Teacher

SANTURCE
De Pantiga, Maricel Hernandez
  Science Teacher

RHODE ISLAND

CENTRAL FALLS
Andrade, Clara
  Physical Education Teacher
Laramee, Paula Webber
  Teacher of Gifted/Talented
Nunn, Joyce Marie Lawrence
  5th/6th Grade ESL Teacher

COVENTRY
Hargraves, Lucy A.
  English Teacher
Pothier, Bernadette Ann
  Mathematics Teacher
Price, Ronald Gordon
  Math Teacher
Roberts, Sylvia L. Reed
  Art Teacher
Sharkey, Marcia Goulet
  Fifth Grade Teacher
Spaziano, Carol Murphy
  Mathematics Teacher
Storti, Daniel Anthony
  Mathematics Teacher/AV Coord

CRANSTON
Burns, Barbara Ann
  Mathematics Department Chair
Donahue, Martha M.
  5th Grade Teacher

EAST PROVIDENCE
Dwyer, James Patrick
  Mathematics Teacher
Morel, Diane (Capone)
  Social Studies Teacher

JOHNSTON
Cross, Marcia A.
  Reading Consultant
Mandeville, Anne M.
  Italian/Spanish Teacher

NARRAGANSETT
Flynn, Leslie M.
  Third Grade Teacher
Leonard, Judith Essex
  6th Grade Teacher

PAWTUCKET
Connolly, Michael James
  Eighth Grade History Teacher
Costa, Carol Anne
  History/Economics Teacher
Forrest, Kathleen Poholek
  Spanish Teacher
Hayes, Patricia Silva
  Foreign Lang Dept Chair
La France, Raymond Joseph
  Religious Studies Chairperson
Mahoney, Susan Sullivan
  2nd Grade Teacher
Meglio, Norma-Jean J.
  High School Teacher
Robert, Victor Paul Jr.
  Social Studies Dept Chair
Walsh, Jacqueline M.
  Director of Elem Education

PORTSMOUTH
Mc Cann, Ann Marie Cox
  First Grade Teacher
Mc Carthy, David R.
  Daniel Sargent Master of Eng

PROVIDENCE
Blanchard, Walter Joseph
  English Teacher
Cullen, Mary Anne
  Fifth Grade Teacher

PROVIDENCE (cont)

Dietrich, Betsy B.
English as 2nd Lang Teacher
Koshgarian, Eileen Mc Cormick
Elementary School Principal
Shafran, Avi
Religious Studies/His Teacher
Zexter, Eleanor Marks
French/English Teacher

WARWICK

Lytle, Patricia (Lukowicz)
Mathematics Teacher
Pannone, Alfred
Spanish/Italian/French Teacher
Ventura, Louis A.
Science Teacher/Dept Chair

WEST WARWICK

La Plante, Cynthia Ann PM
4th Grade Teacher

WOONSOCKET

Akucewich, Paula Bert
Health Occupations Instructor
Connor, Pauline Dumas
Classroom Teacher
Eagan, Claudia A.
English Teacher
Gagnon, Denise Lacroix
French Teacher
Gentili, Dennis Richard
Principal
Jzyk, Linda Zonfrillo
Biology Teacher
Lamansky, Constance Maryann
Fourth Grade Teacher
Menard, Albert Ernest
Fourth Grade Teacher
Ouimette, Clare M.
Second Grade Teacher

SOUTH CAROLINA

ABBEVILLE

Dunlap, Crystal Bonds
Biology Teacher
Fernandez, Rebecca Bond
Home Economics Teacher
Morgan, Nancy Epting
5th Grade Teacher

AIKEN

Carter, Karen Diane
Physical Education Dept Chair
Morgan, Betty Jean Wiliams
Mathematics Teacher

ALCOLU

Jordan, Sue Allen
5th Grade Teacher

ANDERSON

Cauthen, Kathy (Vargo)
Art Teacher
Floyd, William Arthur
Assistant Principal
Hawkins, Mary Jane Shirley
Fourth Grade Teacher
Kaiser, Louise M.
4th Grade Teacher
Mc Alister, Mary Terrell
English Teacher/Dept Chair
Singleton, Mae Joyce (Burke)
6th Grade Social Stud Teacher
Smith, Lottie Lee
Fourth Grade Teacher
Spaid, Joseph S.
Government/Economics Teacher
Speight, Rosemary Cynthia
5th Grade Teacher
Swinger, De Lois Yvonne Carter
Mathematics Teacher

ANDREWS

Shealy, Bettye Tylee
2nd Grade Teacher
Solomon, Paul Hampton
English Teacher

BAMBERG

Grambling, Flora G.
First Grade Teacher
Raysor, Rosa M.
Classroom Teacher

BARNWELL

Holiday, Vivian Whisnant
English Teacher/Dept Chair
Hunter, Jane Gray
4th Grade Lang Arts Teacher
Sanders, Yvette La Londe
Guidance Counselor

Shealy, Kelly
Mathematics Teacher/Coord

BEAUFORT

Hipp, Sarah Olmert
3rd Grade Teacher
Scott, Benjamin Jr.
Math Teacher

BELVEDERE

Holland, Elizabeth Griffin
Retired Teacher

BENNETTSVILLE

Bedenbaugh, Cynthia Brown
Soc Stud Teacher/Dept Chair
Curry, Virginia Harrington
Sixth Grade Language Teacher
Thompson, Beverly Hoover
English/Mathematics Teacher

BETHUNE

Hall, Gail West
6th-12th Grade Music Teacher

BISHOPVILLE

Davidson, Mark Daniel
Physics/Science Teacher/Coach
Welch, Kathryn Latimer
First Grade Teacher
Wilson, Cythnia George
English Teacher

BLACKSBURG

Edwards, Sharon Ann
English Teacher
Miller, Jetanna Huskey
Sci Dept Chairperson

BOWMAN

Fludd, Leon
JROTC Instructor

BRANCHVILLE

Thompson, Jenny Mc Alhany
Sixth Grade Teacher

BRUNSON

Stewart, Anne Reynolds
5th-8th Grade English Teacher

BURTON

Brown, Charlotte Pazant
English Department Chair
Deans, Barbara James
Science Teacher
Holliday, Barbara Gayle Overby
5th Grade Teacher

CAMPOBELLO

Barnwell, Betty Atkins
Social Studies Teacher

CAYCE

Tomlin, Carol Garrison
Mathematics Teacher

CENTRAL

Holstead, Charles
US History Teacher
Wainscott, Susan Brod
Mathematics Teacher

CHAPIN

Mc Million, Madeline Carley
Seventh Grade Teacher

CHARLESTON

Brown, Sadie Thompson
English Teacher
Etheredge, Vanetta Bing
Fifth Grade Teacher
Finley, Bernadette De Voe
4th Grade Teacher
Forsberg, Renie Pappas
2nd Grade Teacher
Gadsden, Margaret
Fifth Grade Teacher
Haynsworth, Susan B.
English Teacher
Jordan, Nancy Youngblood
3rd Grade Teacher
Long, Charles Harold Jr.
5th Grade Teacher
Morris, Elizabeth Ann (Bartlett)
History Teacher
Raymond, Jeanne Warren
7th Grade Mathematics Teacher
Richardson, Ted Robert
Middle School Principal
Scott, Linda Brown
Sixth Grade Teacher
Shifflette, Marjorie Joan B.
7th Grade English Teacher
Trapalis, Sylvia
World His/Church His Teacher
White, Jack Kenneth
Fourth & Fifth Grade Teacher
Young, Naomi Sheares
4th/5th Grade Science Teacher

CHESTER

Ezell, Doris Amurr
7th Grade Lang Art Teacher

CLEARWATER

Hicks, Barbara Mileur
Kindergarten Teacher

CLEMSON

Horton, Elaine Austin
First Grade Teacher/Admin Asst
Robinson, Helen S.
Second Grade Teacher
Ryan, Connie M.
6th Grade Lang Art Teacher

CLINTON

Bridgeman, Jane Ray
Fifth Grade Teacher

CLOVER

Bennett, Valerie Williams
English Teacher
Burrell, Sarah Curry
Mathematics Teacher/Dept Chair
Falls, Marianne Barnett
3rd Grade Teacher
Harvey, Anita Bennett
English Teacher
Moses, Nell Johnson
First Grade Teacher
West, Gail Mc Carter
Keyboard Teacher

COLUMBIA

Brown, Janice Watson
Mathematics Teacher
Fergusson, Dianne Smith
English Teacher
Hoffmeyer, Thompson Price Jr.
Mathematics Teacher
Kinney, Claire Mullen
Guidance Counselor
Minor, James Beauregard Jr.
Social Studies Teacher
Mulkey, Judith Mullis
8th Grade Language Arts
Plummer, Marsha Anderson
Fifth Grade Teacher
Rauch, Elizabeth Monts
8th Grade Mathematics Teacher
Riddick, Lynne Russell
5th Grade Teacher
Savitz, Philip Barth
Physical Education Teacher
Wehman, Karen Kirkegard
English Teacher

CONWAY

Campbell, Andean Booth
Third Grade Teacher
Cecile, Marcia Bunn
8th Lang Art/Reading Teacher
Hedgepath, Doris S.
English Department Chair
Huggins, Betty Ford
8th Grade Mathematics Teacher
Lamson, Roberta Taniser
7th Grade Math Teacher
Nobles, Wayne
6th Grade Teacher
Ricks, Edna (Hinson)
6th Grade Lang Art Teacher
White, Mark Edward
Fifth Grade Teacher

CORDOVA

Covington, Judith Livingston
Fifth Grade Teacher
Fogle, Debora Hendrix
First Grade Teacher
Johnson, H. Wade
Band Director
Mosley-Jenkins, Shirlan Woodbury
Mathematics Teacher
Watts, Sandra Kay (Broome)
Sci Teacher Dept Chairperson

COWARD

Mc Elveen, Donna Nell (Mc Allister)
Fifth Grade Teacher
Nestico, Jane Matthews
Principal

COWPENS

Bland, Sarah Bell
Fifth Grade Teacher

CROSS

Banks, Rosalind Moyd
Mathematics & Science Teacher
Bryant, Pauline Prioleau
Math & Science Teacher
Wilson, Michelle Bonita (Aiken)
Fourth Grade Teacher

DALZELL

Frierson, Delaney Walker
Business Education Teacher

Reeves, Gerald Archie Jr.
Industrial Tech Teacher

DARLINGTON

Bacote, Eugene Charlie Jr.
Mathematics Teacher
Middleton, Margaret Ann
English Teacher
Robbins, Claudia Wilson
English Department Chair

DILLON

Bass, Marjorie Long
English Teacher
Carlson, Randolph Jay
Social Studies Teacher
Freitas, Mary Cumbee
Social Studies Teacher
Hamilton, Lorraine Myers
English Teacher
Taber, Maxine Fore
Retired
Webb, Larry Lee
Band Director

DONALDS

Frasier, Martha M.
Fourth Grade Teacher

DUE WEST

Davis, Monica Denise
Phys Ed/Phys Sci Teacher
Stackhouse, Vivian Hawthorne
Science Teacher

DUNCAN

Miller, Gina Monteleone
4th Grade Teacher
Moss, Wanda (Ussery)
English Teacher

EASLEY

Petersen, James Dennis Sr.
Principal/Business Teacher
Welborn, Lisa
English/French Teacher
Werntz, Helen Sharkey
Fourth Grade Teacher

ELLOREE

Brunson, Josephine Gadsden
7/8th Grade Lang Arts Teacher
Hopkins, Ada R. Young
1st Grade Teacher

ESTILL

De Loach, Louise J.
Even Start Director
Johnson, John W. Jr.
Mathematics Dept Chairman

FLORENCE

Barber, Sandra Walker
Mathematics Teacher
Carter, Kay Stephens
Kindergarten Teacher
Clements, Carrie Ann
4th-6th Grade Lang Arts & Math
English, Lena Cokley
Science Teacher
Felder, Betty G.
Earth Science Teacher
Finklea, Coleen Woodham
Principal
Fore, Jo Anne Monson
Fifth Grade Teacher
Greene, Levester
Mathematics Teacher
Le Master, Linda Dantzler
Choral Director
Mc Lean, Emily Leigh
English Teacher
Scales, Frances Williams
Fifth Grade Teacher
Skoko, Paul Ivan
English Teacher
Turner, Deborah L.
Soc Stud/Geography Teacher
Waddell, Debra Hobbs
Language Art Teacher
Zollicoffer, Jean Thompson
Third Grade Teacher

FORT MILL

Murphy, Barbara White
Fourth Grade Teacher

FOUNTAIN INN

Blighton, Richard Dean
Teacher of Gifted/Talented/Sci
Drummond, Julia Butler
English & Drama Teacher
Gamble, Laura Christine
Music Teacher
Helms, Debra Rene
Industrial Arts Teacher
Thombs, Hattie Clement
Fifth Grade Teacher
Vassey, Connie Lynn
7th/8th Grade Soc Stud Teacher

GAFFNEY

Childers, Harold Van
Fifth Grade Teacher
Loftis, Ann Ellison
Compensatory Teacher
Marett, Paula Barnhill
Science Department Chairperson
Mc Culloch, Becky Clary
6th Grade Teacher
Miller, Louise Quilliam
French Teacher
Parris, Anna E.
English Teacher
Perry, Deborah Watts
Elementary Teacher
Smith, D. Brooks
Industrial Technology Teacher

GASTON

Kleckley, Patricia Johnson
Fourth Grade Teacher

GEORGETOWN

Alston, Ruthena Alston
7th Grade Math Teacher
Gordon, Sharon Young
English Department Chairperson
Greene, Sadie
Fourth/Fifth Grade Teacher
Hunt, Sandra Lee (Ciotti)
Spanish/French/German Teacher
Plexico, Pamela Arden
6th Grade Language Art Teacher
Staggers, Michelle Green
English Teacher

GILBERT

Screen, Elizabeth James
Science Department Chairperson

GOOSE CREEK

Ethridge, Cheryl (Coker)
Mathematics Dept Chair
Griswell, Elaine Moses
English Teacher
Haynes, James Walter
Band Director/Arts Dept Chair
Mc Bride, Judith Lewis
Instrumental Music Teacher
Mole, Laura A.
English Teacher
Morton, Deborah Criddle
Reading Dept Chair/Teacher
Rogers, Robert Woodrow III
Social Studies Teacher
Swafford, Maxine Smith
Social Studies Teacher/Chair

GRAY COURT

Traynham, Carroll
Fourth Grade Teacher

GREAT FALLS

Holladay, Anne Bouknight
Social Studies Dept Chair

GREELEYVILLE

Hilton, Francis King
Science Dept Chair/Bio Teacher
Jonte, Elizabeth Odom
Language Art Teacher

GREEN SEA

Strickland, Debra Gwen
Language Arts Teacher

GREENVILLE

Austin, Sallie Boyd
Psychology Teacher
Block, Bonney Georgia (Rudd)
Algebra Teacher
Gallivan, Therese Thomson
8th Grade Teacher
Hawkins, Thelma Taylor
8th Grade History Teacher
Kennedy, Annie Ruth
4th Grade Teacher
Mc Coll, Carolyn Walker
Latin Teacher
Owens, Karen Neal
English Teacher
Parillo, Terri Mary Teresa
Third Grade Teacher/Vice Prin
Peavy, Becca Hazel Mc Graw
5th Grade Teacher
Ray, Barbara Moran
Fourth Grade Teacher
Sizemore, Georgia Montgomery
Fifth Grade Teacher
Varnadore, Videra Koogler
Remedial Math & Rdng Teacher

GREENWOOD

Daniel, Jackie Louise
Third Grade Teacher
Morrison, Beverly Jane
English Teacher
Partain, Cynthia
Assistant Professor

GREENWOOD (cont)
Pyles, Maria Mc Alister
  10th Grade Government Teacher
Sligh, Louise Beaudrot
  8th-9th Grade Algebra Teacher
Watson, Annie Lites
  Second Grade Teacher
Wilson, Joyce Garrett
  English Teacher/Dept Chair

GREER
Beason, Karl Cason Jr.
  AP Eng/Latin Teacher
Blakely, Anne Price
  French Teacher/Dept Chair
Cooke, Patricia Bridwell
  English Teacher
Crowley, Margie Ross
  8th Grade Earth Sci Teacher
Farmer, Michael H.
  Science Department Chairman

HAMPTON
Atkins, Janet Tuten
  English Teacher
Crawford, Linda Carter
  Literature/Reading Teacher
Kemmerlin, Stephen Kearse
  Driver Education Teacher
Miller, Betty Jane
  English Teacher
Woods, Ruth Anne Guerry
  Mathematics/Science Teacher

HANAHAN
Gooding, Linda Chabers
  6th Grade Soc Stud Teacher
Nicholson, Kathrine Tilton
  Fr/Soc Stud/Eng Teacher
Saner, Elizabeth Lesley
  Second Grade Teacher

HARTSVILLE
Anderson, John Wayne
  Spanish/Science/Phys Ed
Fisher, Teresa Haywood
  High School English Teacher
Hewitt, Pat A.
  Phys Ed Dept Chair
Segars, Cooper Lee Jr.
  Soc Studies Teacher/Ftbl Coach
Taylor, Martha Ann
  Mathematics Teacher

HEATH SPRINGS
Bradley, Janice Robinson
  2nd Grade Teacher

HOLLY HILL
Brown, Penelope Weeks
  Secondary Sch English Teacher
Zimmerman, Annelle Grier
  Science Teacher/Chair

HONEA PATH
Ashley, Regina Broome
  Math Department Chairperson

HOPKINS
Brown, Barbara Hammett
  7th Grade Mathematics Teacher
Pittenger, Ann Cunningham
  English Teacher

INMAN
Mc Clure, Sandra Davis
  Spanish Teacher
Necker, Pauline Knowles
  5th Grade Mathematics Teacher
Poteat, Shirley Page
  4th Grade Teacher
Shealy, Karen Susan
  Fifth Grade Teacher

IVA
Stokes, Albert B. III
  10th-12th Grade His Teacher

JACKSON
Minolfo, Andrea Susan
  6th Grade Math Team Leader
Risher, Deanne Phillips
  2nd Grade Teacher

JOHNS ISLAND
Dudley, Angela Maxine
  Home Arts Teacher

KERSHAW
Izzard, Marilyn Jones
  Kindergarten Teacher
Plyler, Millie Mc Elwee
  Business Teacher
Plyler, Nannie Williams
  Retired 4th Grade Teacher
Wall, Ronnie L.
  Science Teacher
Welch, Lynn Byrd
  Language Arts Teacher

KINGSTREE
Council, Janie Mae Mabray
  1st Grade Teacher/Chairperson

LADSON
Furnari, Elaine Dodge
  8th Grade Mathematics Teacher

LAMAR
Dove, Mildred Allene Powers
  Fifth Grade Teacher/Dept Chair
Howell, Janie Lloyd
  8th Grade Lang Art Teacher

LANCASTER
Cauthen, Gennell Mingo
  Guidance Counselor
Cooper, Jane Kizer
  Sixth Grade Teacher
Hough, Francis Madison Jr.
  English Dept Chairman
Petroski, Carolyn Taylor
  Special Education Teacher

LANGLEY
Mc Kie, Gerald
  Phys Sci Ecology Teacher
Rhodes, Janet Marie
  Science Teacher & Dept. Chair

LATTA
Strickland, June Smith
  7th Grade Teacher/Lang Art Chm

LAURENS
Crawford, Libby Byars
  1st Grade Teacher
Howell, Ann Pridgen
  Eng Teacher/Guidance Counselor
Love, Sally
  English & Reading Teacher
Moss, Paula Allen
  Band Director
Prescott, Edwin William II
  Math/Phys Ed Teacher/Coach

LEXINGTON
Chubbuck, Janice Fulcher
  Physical Ed Dept Chairperson
Cox, Doris Ann Pate
  General Music Teacher
Hartley, Jeanne Shull
  Science Teacher Dept Chair
Kleckley, Rayna Waites
  8th Grade Soc Studies Teacher

LIBERTY
Babb, Mary Finley
  Math Teacher/Curr Asst

LORIS
Edwards, Vivian Skipper
  Social Studies/Chair
Fore, Deborah Shelton
  Business Education Teacher
Springs, Sylvia Hooks
  12th Grade English Teacher

LYMAN
Suttles, Nancy Hawkins
  6th Grade Teacher

LYNCHBURG
Dickey, Rosa Lee
  Retired

MANNING
Gibson, Premuel Louise (Crosby)
  Physical Education Instructor
Hudson, Gwendolyn Elease
  Earth Science Teacher
Younts, Linda Trotter
  English Teacher

MARION
Cartrette, Mary Coleman
  6th Grade Lang Art Teacher

MAULDIN
Barron, Debra Bulger
  English Teacher/Debate Coach
Gault, Rebecca Pearson
  English Teacher
Kaplan, Lorraine Steiner
  Third Grade Teacher
Reid, Benjamin David
  Target 2000 Teacher
Snoad, Gregory Thomas
  HS Social Studies Teacher

MC CLELLANVILLE
Gadsden, Benjamin Dan
  Band & Choral Director

MC CORMICK
Hensley, Vicky Moyer
  English Teacher

MONCKS CORNER
Cooper, Patricia Sanders
  Talented/Gifted Teacher

Huxford, Pamela Wilson
  Compensatory Reading Teacher
Mitchum, Fulton J.
  Soc Stud Teacher/Dept Head

MOUNT PLEASANT
Biggs, Bailey Elwood
  Physical Education Teacher
Boseski, Martha Anne
  Latin Teacher
Herron, Jane Ellen Lawton
  Teacher/Department Head
Reilly, Thomas Eugene
  Psychology Teacher

MULLINS
Grainger, William
  Earth Science Teacher
Hodge, Cynthia Brown-Woodson
  English Teacher
Johnson, Arlene Brown
  Physical Science/Chem Teacher

MYRTLE BEACH
Nadeau, Susan Norris
  4th Grade Teacher
Woodward, Dianne Gibson
  Social Studies Teacher

NEWBERRY
Crawford, Jane Thrower
  Reading Teacher/Dept Chairman
Miller, Jackie Mercer
  English Teacher

NICHOLS
Williams, Peggy Alford
  Mathematics Department Chair

NINETY SIX
Bridgers, Linda Brothers
  Advanced Placement Eng Teacher
Robinson, Mildred Spearman
  English Teacher
Scurry, Betty Jo
  1st Grade Teacher
Willingham, Anne Simpson
  Chapter I Reading Teacher

NORTH AUGUSTA
Anderson, Sara Jones
  English Teacher
Davidson, Cecelia Anne
  Principal

NORTH CHARLESTON
Ford, Mary Octavia (Brown)
  Mathematics & Science Teacher
Polley, Christine M.
  English Department Chair
Varner, Betty R.
  5th Grade Teacher
Wilkerson, Donna Watkins
  2nd Grade Teacher

NORWAY
Russ, Faye R.
  English Department Chairman

ORANGEBURG
Arrington, Gloria Burney
  Teacher
Autry, Shirley Langston
  5th Grade Teacher
Caldwell, Emma Louise
  1st-4th Grade Math Teacher
Finney, Geneva B.
  French-Spanish Teacher
Fulton, Nadine Hall
  Fourth Grade Teacher
Goodwin, Sharon Frinks
  Teacher
Haywood, Ida T.
  Science Teacher
Jacques, Verline Jamison
  Pre-Kindergarten Teacher
Mitchell, Janelle Sistrunk
  6th/8th Grade Math Teacher
Ott, Linda Fleming
  English Teacher
Walters, Georgia Cato
  English Teacher

PAMPLICO
Swinton, Ella Hughes
  6th Grade Language Art Teacher

PAULINE
Smith, April Flowers
  5th Grade Teacher

PELZER
Kramer, Jane
  Third Grade Teacher

PENDLETON
Dyar, Fonda Williams
  English Teacher/Dept Head
Shabazz, Doris Blackwell
  Guidance Counselor

Valentine, Leroy
  Social Studies Teacher

PICKENS
Gilstrap, Rebecca Ann
  Second Grade Teacher
Gramblin, Elizabeth Ann
  6th Grade Lang Arts Teacher
Jones, Suzanne Ryals
  Science Teacher

PIEDMONT
Blighton, Margie A.
  7th Grade Mathematics Teacher
Campbell, Sandra Thrasher
  Language Art Dept Chair
Ferrell, Alice Lavon (Thomas)
  Teacher
Mc Gee, Diane Chiariello
  Mathematics Teacher
Nance, Margaret Peggie Oeland
  Language Arts & Literature
Smith, Rex Alan
  8th Grade Earth Sci Teacher
Stenhouse, Linda Jackson
  In-School Suspension Teacher

PINEVILLE
Mallard, Ida R.
  Retired Elem School Teacher

PROSPERITY
Lovelace, Dorothy L.
  English Teacher/Eng Dept Chair

REMBERT
Toney, Patricia Rembert
  4th-5th Grade Lang Art Teacher

RIDGELAND
Dickerson, Belinda Gail
  English/Journalism Teacher

ROCK HILL
Alt, Patricia Worsham
  Science Teacher
Coppedge, Penny S.
  English/Geography Teacher
Keeling, Brenda Walker
  6th Grade Teacher
Kirkland, Karen Elizabeth
  First Grade Teacher
Pratt, Anne Smith
  Chemistry Teacher
Siglin, Ralph Dwaine
  6th Grade History Teacher

ROEBUCK
Thompson, Peggy S.
  Home Arts Teacher

RUFFIN
Hudson, Carolyn Feder
  Soc Stud Teacher/Dept Chair

SAINT MATTHEWS
Chastain, Margaret Stokes
  Third Grade Teacher
Hubbard, Emma Mack
  Business Teacher

SAINT STEPHEN
Williams, Linda Darby
  First Grade Teacher

SENECA
Hunsucker, Clara Broyhill
  4th Grade Teacher
King, Rosalie C.
  Retired Third Grade Teacher
Sears, Charlotte Bowen
  English Teacher

SIMPSONVILLE
Allen, Catherine Fleming
  Fourth Grade Teacher
Ammons, David Franklin
  Fifth Grade Teacher
Ammons, Sherilyn B.
  Fourth Grade Teacher
Barefoot, Pamela Blackwelder
  8th Grade Soc Stud Teacher
Burnham, Ellen Edwards
  Retired Teacher
Dukas, George John
  Chemistry/Physics Teacher
Edwards, Linda Lee Boyles
  Chemistry/Mathematics Teacher
Holman, Cole Albert
  6th Grade Science Teacher
Lentz, Barbara Geressy
  Science Teacher/Dept Chair
Stuckey, Vanessa
  English/Lit Teacher/Dept Chair

SPARTANBURG
Brown, Elizabeth Ann
  Mathematics Dept Chm
Combs, Jack E.
  Physical Education Teacher

Combs, Mary-Jo Cudd
  Business Education Teacher
Dunn, Cathy Hoefer
  Jr HS Social Studies Coord
Johnson, Danny James
  Algebra I & II Teacher
Killian, Ronald Vernon
  History Teacher
Leary, Linda Hughes
  English Teacher
Sloan, Mary Page T.
  English Teacher

SUMMERTON
Hall, Shirley Dantzler
  Second Grade Teacher

SUMMERVILLE
Barnes, Yvette
  Mathematics Teacher
Dingle, Becky Barbour
  8th Grade Soc Studies Teacher
Dufford, Kelly Jo
  English Teacher
Plexico, Helen Moore
  Mathematics Teacher
Talley, Harriette Whitworth
  Mathematics Teacher
Townsend, Frances Wilder
  US His/Broadcasting Teacher
Walker, Carol U.
  Mathematics Dept Chairman

SUMTER
Brush, Lea
  Mathematics Teacher
Cousar, Tarah Faith
  English Teacher/Dept Chair
Hamptom, Margaret Moses
  7th/8th Grade Teacher
Huth, Frederick Lloyd Jr.
  Bible Teacher
Leach, Barry Douglas
  5th Grade Teacher
Mitchell, Betty Goodman
  5th Grade Teacher
O'Hara, Gene Paul
  8th Grade Science Teacher
Richardson, Dale Folsom
  Social Studies Teacher
Rollerson, Mary Howard
  Language Arts Teacher
Swartz, Randy Mark
  Junior High Supervisor
Zlotnicki, Bogdan Michael
  Social Studies Dept Chair

TAYLORS
Hughes, Marie Grace
  Science Teacher
Smith, Gail Evans
  Second Grade Teacher

TIMMONSVILLE
Jackson, Rudelle Williams
  Third Grade Teacher
Jordan, Ruth Williams
  English Teacher

TRAVELERS REST
Cottingham, Walter Lee Jr.
  8th Grade His & Lit Teacher
Gaines, William Henry
  Social Studies Teacher/Chair
Hart, Suzanne Casgrain
  Retired French Teacher

UNION
Brock, Karen Whitehead
  English Teacher
Gregory, Melissa Phillips
  Eighth Grade Science Teacher
Malone, Jeanie Blackwood
  Social Studies Teacher

WAGENER
Kitchings, Virginia Joan Hudson
  Social Studies Chairperson
Young, Le Myra Tyler
  Eng I/SC His/Home Arts Teacher

WALHALLA
Calhoun, Vicki Phillips
  Mathematics Teacher
Hopkins, Deborah L.
  Science Teacher
Morrah, Annette Herring
  5th Grade Teacher
Sinnett, Terry Brooks
  English Teacher

WALTERBORO
Blocker, Janis Kinsey
  AP/Honors/CP English Teacher
Bodison, Vera M.
  English Teacher
Simmons, Nell Mealing
  Retired

WARE SHOALS

Bouknight, Gail Anderson
  Second Grade Teacher
Nelson, Colleen Cothran
  Retired Science Teacher
O'Dell, Wanda Malone
  Mathematics & Algebra Teacher
Tisdale, Hazel Ann
  Third Grade Teacher

WEST COLUMBIA

Garner, H. Wayne
  Social Studies Teacher
Patterson, Jerald Wray
  Health/Soc Stud/PE Teacher
Price, Brenda Rawls
  Teacher
Smith, Anne Whitt
  Teacher Visually Handicapped

WESTMINSTER

Blackburn, Donna Trent
  English Teacher
Bryant, Joseph Marion
  American History Teacher
Garvin, Linda D.
  Spanish Teacher

WHITMIRE

Oswald, Ann K.
  Fifth Grade Teacher
Patridge, Carolyn H.
  Remedial Math/Lab Teacher

WILLISTON

Sheppard, Diane Robertson
  2nd Grade Teacher

WINNSBORO

Ingram, Marie Horton
  Math Teacher
Richmond, Plumie Shannon
  Elementary Guidance Counselor

WOODRUFF

Penn, Marsha Barrs
  World Geography Teacher
Thomas, Paul Lee II
  English Dept Chair
Williams, Francis Richard Jr.
  History Teacher/Coach
Young, Gloria Byrd
  Fourth Grade Teacher

YONGES ISLAND

Bligen, Alvin Earl
  Chapter I Math Teacher

YORK

Blough, Doris Browder
  English Teacher
Cruz, Debra Smith
  Fifth Grade Teacher
Guerry, Patricia Moss
  5th Grade Teacher
Moore, James Glenn
  Science Teacher
Sherer, Jane Scott
  Math Teacher

SOUTH DAKOTA

ABERDEEN

Caron, Steven Edward
  Mathematics Teacher
Fischer, Donna Pool
  4th Grade Teacher
Kienow, Evelyn Angerhofer
  5th Grade Teacher
Maas, Dorothy Hauck
  Fourth Grade Teacher
Pelkofer, Shirley Jenniges
  Third Grade Teacher
Whitley, James
  Social Studies Teacher
Wuertz, Carol Krueger
  English Teacher

ARTESIAN

Whitney, Linda Hansen
  Guidance Counselor/Band Dir

BALTIC

Murphy, John E.
  Fourth Grade Teacher
Seely, Anna M. Erickson
  Kindergarten Teacher

BERESFORD

Mitchell, William Donald
  Eng/Literature Dept Teacher

BLACK HAWK

Stoltz, Sylvia A.
  3rd Grade Teacher

BRANDON

Helm, Nancy Schiefelbein
  5th Grade Teacher
Mehlbrech, Terrance L.
  Chemistry Instructor

BROOKINGS

Barkus, David William
  Choral Director
Mc Daniel, Joyce Nollmann
  Spanish Teacher

CHESTER

Beyer, Betty J. (Mc Laughlin)
  Reading/English/Art Teacher

DEADWOOD

Fundaun, Kim
  8th Grade Science Teacher

DELL RAPIDS

Mergen, Cheryl Kay (Aker)
  Third Grade Teacher
Pierret, Madonna Mary
  Mathematics & Computer Teacher

ELK POINT

Neblesick, Gary Daniel
  Mathematics Teacher

ELKTON

Fredriksen, Beth A. (Mc Keown)
  K-7 Grade Chap I Rdng Teacher
Swenson, Terry Dean
  Soclgy/Psych/Soc Stud Teacher
Vincent, C. Terry
  History Teacher/Coach

ELLSWORTH AFB

Shearer, Patricia Watson
  Reading Specialist

EMERY

Hanssen, Ruth M.
  Retired Teacher

ESTELLINE

Taylor, Gwen Ann (Juntunen)
  Mathematics/Computer Teacher

ETHAN

Wall, Peggy Lea (Ells)
  Business Education Teacher
Weigandt, Dorothy Mae
  Kindergarten Teacher
Weigandt, Larry Edward
  Math & Sci Dept Chair

EUREKA

Bauer, Ann Marie (Streifel)
  Sixth Grade Teacher
Billotto, Robert John
  Ger/Social Studies Teacher

FLORENCE

Remien, Roger Allen
  Soc Sci/Phys Ed Teacher/Coach

FORT PIERRE

Cummings, Jo Ann (Bely)
  Jr HS Math/English/Art Teacher

GEDDES

Dolejsi, Rose A. Soukup
  Retired

HARTFORD

Feldhaus, Kathy L.
  Third Grade Teacher

HAYES

Hosack, William Dale
  Mid Sch Industrial Art Teacher

HAYTI

Likness, Arlin Elsworth
  US History/Government Teacher

HECLA

Ruenz, Carma Hoines
  English/Journalism Teacher

HIGHMORE

Klebsch, Shirley Goldsmith
  Fourth Grade Teacher
Mc Girr, Harriet Gladine (Vaughn)
  Retired Substitute Teacher

HILL CITY

D'Hont, Kim Wallior
  Spanish/English Teacher
Jordan, Bruce Alan
  High School Principal
Knapp, John Dawain
  Math & Social Science Teacher

HITCHCOCK

Johnson, David Lee
  Business Teacher

HOT SPRINGS

Klukas, Myrt Blasey
  Spanish and Debate Teacher

HURON

Wendelgass, Mark L.
  Social Studies Teacher

IROQUOIS

Lemon, Ruth Marie
  German/Eng/Tutoring Teacher
Wallmann, Evelyn Tschetter
  2nd Grade Teacher

LEAD

Calabro, Patricia Ann Winderlin
  2nd Grade Teacher
Peterson, Dean E.
  Vocal Music Teacher

LETCHER

Rothenberger, Gwendolyn Olene
  Elem Prin/Kndgtn Teacher

LONGVALLEY

Graupmann, Kenneth H.
  6th-8th Grade Teacher

LYONS

Bambas, Steve W.
  7th/8th Grade Science Teacher

MADISON

Struwe, Merle Eugene
  8th United States His Teacher

MARION

Preheim, Joyce Richert
  1st Grade Teacher

MARTIN

Anderson, Rodney Gene
  Biology-Physiology Teacher
Kohel, Rhonda Marthena (Grooms)
  Home Economics Teacher

MARTY

Loken, Wilma Audrey (Ringen)
  Mathematics Teacher

MILLER

Sivertsen, David LaVern
  Chem/Cmptr Science Teacher
Waters, Patricia Jeanne (Yost)
  1st Grade Primary Teacher

MISSION

Sazama, Noma Larson
  Middle School Teacher

MITCHELL

Aslesen, Terry Lynn
  Assistant Principal
Mc Lean, Donald Jess
  History Teacher

MONTROSE

Vermeulen, Vicky Lynn
  Social Science Teacher

NEWELL

Vissia, Larry Dean
  English Teacher

OELRICHS

Britain, Maynard Dryden
  7th & 8th Grade Teacher
Cope, Lou Ann J.
  Science/Biology Teacher
Peterson, Juanita L. (Cole)
  Math/Computer/Art Teacher

PARKER

Hintz, Marlene Joan
  Fourth Grade Teacher
Hoover, Clarke Hutchison
  Senior English Teacher
Sisson, Esther
  First Grade Teacher

PHILIP

Mahoney, Daniel James
  Physical Education Teacher

PIERRE

Johnson, Laurence Thomas
  Jr HS Band Director
Mickelson, Edward Jay
  Latin/German Teacher

PINE RIDGE

Podhaisky, Patricia Jean
  Spanish/Theology Teacher

RAPID CITY

Brandt, Gloria Jean
  7th-9th Grade Choral Music
Gill, Jo (Mc Dougall)
  Science Teacher
Houska, Mary Kay (Kelley)
  7th Grade English Teacher
Murphy, Carol Jenison
  Mathematics Teacher/Dept Chair
Pagel, Lyle Wayne
  Biology Teacher

Purcell, Michael James
  Science Teacher/Coach
Richardson, Kim A.
  Math Teacher
Semrock, Harold Reynold
  Bible Teacher/Principal
Smith, Jonel Rene
  Civics Teacher
Wolff, Roger Dennis
  Fifth Grade Teacher

ROSCOE

Flannery, Bernita Lynn
  Music Instructor

SIOUX FALLS

Berglin, Brian Kelly
  Mathematics Department Teacher
Carlson, Kevin Scott
  Mathematics Instructor
Hagedorn, Julie Ann
  5th Grade Teacher
Hansen, Carol Ann
  Art Supervisor/Art Teacher
Keill, John Henry
  9th World Geography Teacher
Kranzler, Linda Terveen
  3rd Grade Teacher
Peters, Patricia Henning
  Home Economics Department Rep
Strand, Patricia Anderson
  Business Education Teacher

SISSETON

Block, Betty L. Treffry
  2nd Grade Teacher
Gangle, Gary J.
  Business Teacher

SPEARFISH

Noble, Frank James
  Fifth Grade Teacher
Schleleway, Norma Jean Hansen
  Third Grade Teacher

STURGIS

Hines, Larry Theodore
  Mathematics Teacher/Dept Chair

VERMILLION

Kephart, Helen Orr
  Mathematics Teacher
Wood, Elizabeth Gunhus
  3rd Grade Teacher

VOLGA

Skogen, Daniel Lee
  Fifth & Sixth Grade Teacher

WAGNER

Schoepf, Lorean O.
  English Teacher

WALL

Anderson, Terri Rae Harris
  Third Grade Teacher
Eisenbraun, Iva Albin
  Elementary Substitute Teacher
Leier, Julie M.
  Agriculture Education Teacher
Walker, Lori Lenette
  8th Grade Teacher

WATERTOWN

Lange, Iris Nelson
  Fourth Grade Teacher
Zubke, Bill
  Computer Instructor

WHITE

Trewatha, Robert Alan Hershel
  Mathematics Teacher

WHITE RIVER

Sharp, Lisa Ann
  English Department Chair

WILLOW LAKE

Meyer, Junia Marie (Schlinkert)
  Home Ec Teacher

WILMOT

Peacock, Maryline Ann
  5th Grade Teacher

WINNER

Brozik, Donna Jean (Roedl)
  Rural Elm Grades 3-5 Teacher
Johnson, Betty Lloyd
  Middle School Teacher
Nollmann, Jean Louise
  Fourth Grade Teacher
Streifel, Jo Marie
  Business Teacher

TENNESSEE

ADAMSVILLE

Rodman-Downing, Mary Ann
  Media Specialist
Sims, Joyce Mitchell
  Third Grade Teacher

AFTON

Neal, James Kenny
  Mathematics Teacher

ALAMO

Bailey, Jane
  English Teacher
Barker, Martha Carol
  Mathematics Dept Chairman
Reddick, Brenda Carol Ligon
  Fourth Grade Teacher
Turnage, Sandra Ann
  Language Arts Teacher
Warmbrod, David Edward
  Phys Sci/Phys Ed Teacher

ANTIOCH

Lamar, Sue Bean
  Mathematics Teacher
Parkinson, Nancy Owens
  7th Grade Science Teacher

ARLINGTON

Finley, William Henry
  American History Teacher
Glenn, Deborah Lynn
  Social Studies Teacher
Mc Intyre, Mike E.
  Phys Sci/Health Teacher
Sheesley, Betty Jo
  8th Grade Science Teacher

ASHLAND CITY

Argevine, Betty Gray
  English Teacher/Yrbk Sponsor
Dodson, Darlee D.
  Kindergarten Teacher

ATHENS

Akins, Stephen Michael
  Pre-Algebra/Math Teacher
Conar, Lucy C.
  5th Grade Teacher
Cummings, Olivia Cox
  Third Grade Teacher
Hall, Reita Jane
  English Department Chairperson
Harrill, Peter John
  K-6th Grade Phys Ed Teacher
Haynie, James Roy
  Economics Teacher
Hicks, Diane Trotter
  Fourth Grade Teacher
Hudson, Andrew D.
  Guidance Counselor
Ivens, Deborah Russell
  Chemistry-Physics Teacher
Lamb, Georgia Morris
  Teacher/Department Chair
Parks, Linda Ingle
  English Teacher
Parks, Roger Dale
  Physical Education Instructor

ATWOOD

Williams, Rutha C.
  Mathematics Teacher

BARTLETT

Gooch, Joyce Smith
  Third Grade Teacher
Mc Cullar, Mary M.
  Spanish Teacher
Smith, Jonathan Kennon Thompson
  Curriculum Coordinator

BAXTER

Fletcher, Barbara Ann
  5/6th Grade English Teacher
Pierce, Sarah Faith
  6th Grade Soc Stud/Chairperson
Tucker, Linda Gail
  English Teacher

BEAN STATION

Day, William Douglas
  Social Studies Teacher
Livesay, Dennis Lon
  6th Grade Teacher
Scheick, Eyvonne Livesay
  First Grade Teacher

BEECH BLUFF

Johnson, Barbara Maness
  5th Grade Teacher
Matthews, Cheryl Butler
  Sci/Eng/Home Ec Teacher

BELLS
Kail, Sherry Freeman
  Fifth Grade Teacher
BENTON
Barnett, Laura Harbison
  First Grade Teacher
Moss, Cynthia Boggs
  Mathematics Dept Chairperson
Pippenger, Wilma Jean (Cochran)
  Teacher, Department Chair
BETHPAGE
Crampton, Frank Rotz
  5th Grade Teacher
BLOUNTVILLE
Darden, Judy Bass
  Teacher
Zimmerman, Robert L.
  History Teacher
BLUFF CITY
Combs, Betty Jo
  Elementary Teacher
Harkleroad, Charlotte Dalton
  Business Teacher
Harr, Ramona Gaminde
  Mathematics Teacher
Rasnake, John Samuel II
  English Teacher
BOLIVAR
Stevens, Patricia
  K-6th Grade Art Teacher
Watson, Rebecca Hooper
  First Grade Teacher
BRADYVILLE
Heath, Charley Mack Sr.
  Principal
BRENTWOOD
Fox, Martha Sue
  Biology/Physiology Teacher
Stockton, Judith Beeler
  Sixth Grade Teacher
BRICEVILLE
Mc Ghee, Marshall Larry
  Fourth Grade Teacher
BRISTOL
Booner, Anna Louise Carr
  American History Teacher
Dodson, Brenda Lou
  Second Grade Teacher
Ensor, Mary Catherine Grace
  Sixth Grade Teacher
Francis, Margaret Alexander
  Fifth Grade Teacher
Jennings, Deborah Crawford
  Math/Computer Teacher
Jurs, Barbara Mendes
  Visiting Spanish Professor
King, William Rigby III
  English Teacher
Stickley, Betty Windle
  Sixth Grade Teacher
BROWNSVILLE
Bond, Dorothy Jean Mann
  5th Grade Teacher
Silvia, Thomas A.
  Government Teacher
Smith, Sylvia Mc Caleb
  4th Grade Teacher
BULLS GAP
Southerland, Ginny Kite
  English Teacher
CAMDEN
Allen, Wanda Waller
  English/Social Studies Teacher
Hawkins, Paula Covington
  Spanish/Language Art Teacher
Lumpkin, Cynthia Rawls
  7th/8th Grade English Teacher
Lumpkin, John Wayne
  Science Teacher
Pafford, Ronald Everett
  7th/8th Grade Soc Sci Teacher
Presson, Anita Myracle
  1st Grade Teacher/Asst Prin
CARTHAGE
Dowell, Steven Gaines
  Music/Band Director
CELINA
Buford, Phyllis Gwenn (Browning)
  Social Studies Teacher
Strong, Linda N.
  4th Grade Teacher
CENTERVILLE
Bridges, Karen Ford
  5th Grade Teacher
Cherry, Faye Harber
  History & Government Teacher

Copley, James Wilson
  Language Arts Teacher
Evans, Shirley Gossett
  8th Grade Lang Art Teacher
Hamilton, Eleanor Aydelott
  English/Accounting Teacher
Hansford, Jeannie Marie (Dillingham)
  Substitute Teacher
Murphree, Marietta Jones
  First Grade Teacher
CHARLESTON
German, Nancy Cheatham
  Kindergarten Teacher
Studdard, Cynthia Lynne
  High School Science Teacher
CHATTANOOGA
Browning, Lynne Schneider
  Teacher of 3 Yr Olds
Callahan, Joy Purtee
  English Teacher
Collins, Charles Jr.
  Piano & Vocal Music Teacher
Dance, Nobel Sylvester
  Chapter I Math Teacher
Downer, Rita Heard
  First Grade Teacher
Lott, Marvin James
  Band Teacher
Mackey, Cheryl Bryan
  6th Grade Language Art Teacher
Neff, Nancy L.
  Social Studies Teacher
Shannon, Jerry Wayne
  Mathematics Department Chair
Smith, David Paul
  His./Civics/Geography Teacher
Vickery, Joyce Jarvis
  Fifth Grade Teacher
Weiss, Debra (Steranko)
  Mathematics Teacher
CHUCKEY
Gray, Karen Rhea
  Third Grade Teacher
Wagner, Nancy Brown
  7th & 8th Grade Teacher
Wright, Nancy Barkley
  7th/8th Language Arts Teacher
CHURCH HILL
Anderson, Dennis Earl
  Teacher/Coach
Birchfield, Gary H.
  Biology Teacher
Dykes, Jim Byron
  Seventh Grade Science Teacher
Livesay, Glenda Kaye
  6th Grade Math Teacher
CLARKRANGE
Little, Patrick Lee
  6th Grade Teacher
CLARKSVILLE
Baggett, Kerry J.
  Mathematics Teacher
Corley, Barbara Purcell
  Speech/Drama Teacher
Covington, Juanita Crawford
  Biology Teacher
Giles, George Hulon
  Mathematics Teacher
Harris, Dianne B.
  English III Teacher
Houde, Janet Lynne
  8th Grade Soc Stud Teacher
Jones, Nina Clare
  Spanish Teacher/Dept Chairman
Meacham, Karen Vickrey
  Vocational Office Educ Teacher
Moss, Linda Faye
  English Teacher
Ramsey, Gordon Edward
  7th Grade Soc Stud Teacher
Smith, Clara Owens
  First Grade Teacher
Vertrees, Kaye Rogers (Kelley)
  Third Grade Teacher
CLEVELAND
Bancroft, Connie Melinda
  Third Grade Teacher
Carroll, Jannuth Gatlin
  3rd Grade Teacher
Coggin, Danny Keith
  Director of Bands
Dent, Wanda Pressley
  English Teacher
Dunn, Carolyn Matthews
  6th Grade Teacher
Leffew, Robert Joe
  Eng/Foreign Lang Teacher/Chair
Maupin, Mildred Lee
  English Teacher
Rose, Cathy Carol
  Fifth Grade Teacher

Samples, Edith Leona
  6th Grade Math/English Teacher
Smiddy, Gloria Watkins
  Business Teacher
Warren, George Clayton
  Mathematics Dept Chair
Wojcik, Norman Thomas
  Guidance Counselor
Yates, Joy O'Dell
  Elementary Guidance Counselor
CLIFTON
Cook, Sarah Ann
  Fifth Grade Teacher
Davis, Sherry Kidd
  7th/8th Grade Lang Art Teacher
Franks, Carolyn Dicus
  4th/5th/6th Grade Teacher
CLINTON
Scroback, Jo Ann Kopp
  Mathematics Teacher
Stults, Dallas M.
  Biology Teacher
Taylor, Diane Walsh
  Kindergarten Teacher
COLLEGEDALE
Stanaway, Barbara Colleen (Sears)
  5th/6th Grade Teacher
Swafford, Carleton Lee
  Science Teacher
COLLIERVILLE
Boston, Florence Ann (Wilkins)
  9th/10th Grade English Teacher
COLUMBIA
Fowler, Sally Keith
  7th-9th Grade Lit Teacher
Ivey, Leon Enlo
  Chemistry Teacher
CORDOVA
Baker, Dee
  Algebra Teacher/Coach
Bierbrodt, Patsy Milford
  Spanish Teacher
CORNERSVILLE
Lee, Dorothy Richardson
  Fourth & Fifth Grade Teacher
CORRYTON
Tarvin, Terri Lynn
  Music Teacher
Whitehead, Brenda Judy
  8th Grade Science Teacher
COSBY
Knittel, Maretta Wheeler
  Language Arts Teacher
Nelson, John F.
  Math & Economics Teacher
COUNCE
Jones, Susan Claunch
  2nd Grade Teacher
COVINGTON
Barton, Thomas Witherington
  Physical Science Teacher
Hazlerig, Bonnie Shelley
  English/French Teacher
Heaston, Russell
  Seventh Grade Science Teacher
Jones, Mary Francis
  Sixth Grade Teacher
Lawler, Martha Lynn
  Science Teacher
Murray, Carolyn Johnson
  Kindergarten Teacher
Murray, William Leroy
  Jr HS Social Studies Teacher
Parker, Joseph Vincent
  Mathematics Teacher
Rone, Theta Kelley
  7th Grade Mathematics Teacher
COWAN
Langley, Katrina Juannell
  Retired Teacher
Young, Kim B.
  Kindergarten Teacher
CRAWFORD
Phillips, Roxie Ramsey
  2nd Grade Teacher
CROSS PLAINS
Lamb, Jimmy G.
  History/Economics Teacher
Wright, Jama Covington
  1st Grade Teacher
CROSSVILLE
Kerley, Ruth Davis
  Language Arts Teacher
Ramey, Kathy
  Chapter Reading/Math Teacher

CUNNINGHAM
Dinsmore, Joetta Carol
  English Department Chair
DANDRIDGE
Murray, Shirley Jones
  Reading Teacher
Patterson, Janice Whitlaw
  Chemistry Teacher
DAYTON
Eastman, Marie Maxine
  Mathematics Dept Chair
Marler, Brenda Kelly
  7th-8th Grade English Teacher
Sarr, Clarence Arthur
  Mathematics-Science Head
Tallent, Susan Anderson
  4th Grade Teacher
DECATUR
Hunt, Patricia Ann
  Bio/Chem/Physics Teacher
DEL RIO
Ball, Connie
  Principal
DICKSON
Bledsoe, Judy Rowland
  Vocational Guidance Counselor
King, Mary Kay
  Business Law Teacher
Maynard, Susan Smith
  Coord/Lead Teacher
Sullivan, Randall Jay
  Speech & Drama Teacher
DOVER
Baggett, Connie Edlin
  Business Education Teacher
Borens, Betty T.
  Jr HS Math Teacher
Crockarell, Mary Trinkle
  Third Grade Teacher
DRESDEN
Brann, Carol Pentecost
  Home Economics Teacher
Gearin, Dawn Davidson
  English Teacher
Gilbert, Amelia Rambo
  Fifth Grade Teacher
Stooksberry, Mary Ellen Nielsen
  English/Drama Teacher
DYER
Harris, Paulette Abbott
  Second Grade Teacher
Mc Farland, William
  Eng/Bus/Journalism Teacher
Palmer, Joe Delano
  English Teacher
Patterson, Steven Lynn
  Mathematics Teacher/Coach
DYERSBURG
Burks, Judy Hall
  5th Grade Math Teacher
Clift, Brenda Crabtree
  Third Grade Teacher
Green, Ann Spence
  7th Grade Reading Teacher
Hopper, Martha Ketchum
  5th Grade Reading Teacher
Jones, Mickey Tubbs
  Second Grade Teacher
Logan, Shirley Ann (Hilliard)
  Guidance Counselor
Pressler, Linda Hooton
  Interim 1st Grade Teacher
EAST RIDGE
Mullins, Kimberly Wright
  English/Speech Teacher
ELIZABETHTON
Birchfield, Jennifer Goddard
  Chemistry Teacher
Brown, Floyd Ernest
  Mathematics Teacher
Buck, Nancy Slagle
  Science Teacher
Buckles, Hugh Frederick
  Social Studies Teacher
Cates, Teresa Jill
  Biology/Chemistry Teacher
Cox, Nancy Orren
  Sixth Grade Teacher
Ferguson, Carolyn Odom
  First Grade Teacher
Fulwider, Cindy Walker
  Physical Ed/Health Teacher
Guinn, Lisa Garland
  Chemistry/English Teacher
Laws, Martha Fair
  Third Grade Teacher
Payne, Linda Mc Kinney
  Vocational Office Ed Teacher

Rogers, Carolyn Rector
  Drivers Ed/Health Teacher
Stout, Judy Wilson
  First Grade Teacher
Williams, Kathryn Thelma
  Retired
Wilson, Jonnie Lewis
  Second Grade Teacher
Wilson, Kent
  English/Social Studies Teacher
ELKTON
Mc Clure, Joe Rivers
  Math Instructor
ERWIN
Correll, Kenneth Robert
  Sixth & Seventh Grade Teacher
Eller, Lisa Ogle
  Math Teacher
Jackson, Mickey Steven
  Elementary Counselor
ESTILL SPRINGS
Shasteen, Lynda Clark
  6th Grade Teacher
ETHRIDGE
Lopp, Stan Edward
  English Teacher
ETOWAH
Nichols, John Michael
  Eighth Grade Teacher
EVENSVILLE
Garrison, Mary Sue Fischesser
  Assistant Principal
Rankin, Marquetia Fisher
  Art Teacher I & III
FAIRVIEW
Anderson, Linda Smith
  4th Grade Soc Stud/Art Teacher
Gipson, Patricia Moore
  6th Grade Science Teacher
Stewart, William Charles Jr.
  Teacher/Math Department Head
FAYETTEVILLE
Beasley, Elma M.
  Second Grade Teacher
Holloway, Womack
  Social Studies Dept Chair
Jean, Jack Allen
  English Teacher
Williams, Linda Faye
  Vocational Office Ed Teacher
Wolf, Martha E.(Van Lantschoot)
  Asst Prin/2nd Grade Teacher
FLINTVILLE
Reid, Robbie Vance
  5th Grade/Adjunct Eng Coll Ins
FOWLKES
Bishop, Betty F.
  4th Grade Teacher
Parr, Margeret Welch
  Second Grade Teacher
Weakley, Sybil Lee
  7/8th Grade Lang Arts Teacher
FRANKLIN
Bishop, Pamela A.
  Social Studies Teacher
Gore, Sharon Lanier
  Sixth Grade Teacher
Green, Pearlette Kinnard
  6th Grade Teacher
Harned, Melissa Farmer
  Science Teacher
Redmon, Alice Pressgrove
  8th Grade Lang Arts Teacher
Santymire, Earl B.
  History Teacher
Smith, Joyce Watson
  3rd Grade Teacher
Taylor, Ethel Burns
  Fourth Grade Teacher
FRIENDSVILLE
Hill, Frances French
  Kindergarten Teacher
GALLATIN
Bubb, Terry Lee
  Spanish Teacher
Roth, Nancy Ann
  Sixth Grade Teacher
Webster, Linda Scott
  7th Grade Life Science Teacher
Wright, Ann Prosser
  Sixth Grade Teacher
GATLINBURG
Norville, Flo P.
  4th Grade Teacher
Peine, Marie Elaine
  Teacher of Gifted

GERMANTOWN

Gilland, Angela Poindexter
 English Teacher
Hankins, Elizabeth Porter
 AP English/Spanish Teacher
Hardin, Barbara Anne
 Latin Teacher
Hawkins, Delores Merritt
 Kindergarten Teacher
Herr, Arthur Lynn
 Physics Teacher
Patrick, Cecelia Celeste
 Science Teacher
Rich, Janet L.
 7th Grade Language Art Teacher
Russell, Ann Martin
 6th Grade Soc Stud Teacher
Terrell Jr, Goldie Jackson
 9th Grade English Teacher
Windsor, Lyn Menzie
 AP English Teacher

GLEASON

Hudson, Anita Kay (Sanders)
 Language/Spelling Teacher
Melton, Beverly Dunn
 5th Grade Teacher

GOODLETTSVILLE

Miles, Rebecca Harrison
 First Grade Teacher

GRAY

Davis, Deanna H.
 English Teacher & Dept Chair
Dykes, Ronald A.
 History/Biology II Teacher
Garrett, Jewell Johnson
 American Government Teacher
Harwood, Jean De Votie
 Guidance Counselor
Robinson, Linda Gay Graybeal
 Fifth Grade Teacher
Winebarger, Mary Tester
 Language Arts Teacher

GREENBACK

Wolfe, Violet Kirkpatrick
 First Grade Teacher

GREENBRIER

White, Lex
 Spanish Teacher

GREENEVILLE

Baxter, Helma Coriece
 2nd Grade Teacher
Davis, Phyllis Murdock
 English Teacher

HALLS

Adcock, Patricia W.
 English/Art Teacher
Avery, Joyce Cannon
 Third Grade Teacher

HARRIMAN

Jackson, Jayne Russell
 5th Grade Teacher

HARRISON

Perdue, Deborah Williams
 History Teacher
Smith, Deborah B.
 Assistant Principal

HARTFORD

Strange, James Estle
 Retired Teacher

HARTSVILLE

Haynes, Thena Byrd
 2nd Grade Teacher

HENDERSONVILLE

Clark, Martha Frances
 Latin & Spanish Teacher
Deering, Gale Powell
 Sixth Grade Teacher
Demarest, Sonja Ann
 Third Grade Teacher
Edgin, Beverly Winn
 Mathematics Department Chair
Greer, Peggy Garner
 Fourth Grade Teacher
Isenberg, Olivia Lassiter
 Assistant Principal
Jett, Willis Warren III
 Science/Mathematics Teacher
Jones, David Marcus Sr.
 World History Teacher
Kandros, Sandra L. (Jones)
 10th-12th Grade Art Teacher
Lilly, Donna Wojahn
 5th Grade Teacher
Mc Cormick, Karen E.
 Spanish I & II Teacher
Roach, Ralph Ann Eblen
 Third Grade Teacher

Rogers, Lile Ellis
 Psychology/Sociology Teacher
Stein, Sue T.
 Office Technology Teacher
Stubblefield, Sandra C.
 Business Education Teacher
Taylor, Barbara Nabors
 8th Grade Reading Teacher
Towe, Linda Miller
 Music & Choral Teacher

HERMITAGE

Duke, Robert Ellis
 Art Teacher

HILHAM

Langford, Lizzie Holt
 Retired Teacher

HILLSBORO

Johnson, Linda Davis
 Fifth Grade Teacher
Thomas, Eva M.
 6th Grade Teacher

HIXSON

Dunnigan, Debra Denice
 Mathematics Teacher

HORNBEAK

Huff, Jettie CLenney
 Fourth Grade Teacher
Lynn, Richard Arthur
 7th & 8th Grade Sci Teacher
Roberson, Janice Hooper
 Third Grade Teacher
Short, Peggy Mingle
 Jr High Reading Teacher

HUNTINGDON

Hill, Bettie Sue
 8th Grade Lang Arts Teacher
Stallings, Debbie Finley
 Kindergarten Teacher
Tedford, Wayne John
 7th Grade Teacher

HUNTLAND

Brim, Ruth Bright
 Second Grade Teacher
Pack, Bobbie Sue
 Guidance Counselor
Reynolds, Pat Mathews
 Sixth Grade Teacher
Spaulding, Diana Lynn
 Math Teacher

HUNTSVILLE

Stanley, Sharon
 English/Drama Teacher

HURON

Emison, Julia Reves
 7th/8th Lang Arts Teacher
Fesmire, Joyce Nell (Hays)
 Fourth Grade Teacher
Hatley, Melanie Renee
 First Grade Teacher

JACKSBORO

Douglas, Linda Gale
 Science/Reading Teacher
Mc Farland, Jane Ann Teague
 Fourth Grade Teacher
Ridenour, Michael W.
 Secondary Teacher
Stout, Jerry Lynn
 Physical Science Teacher
Templin, Don Lynn
 Mathematics Department Chair
Wood, Louise
 4th Grade Teacher

JACKSON

Barnes, Callie Bond
 1st Grade Teacher
Deberry, Sharis Kymble
 Social Studies Teacher
Hayes, Jerry Wayne
 Amer His Teacher/Coach
Kee, Lisa Lange
 English Teacher/Academic Coach
Luna, Teresa Long
 History Teacher
Luther, Donald Stephen
 Social Studies Teacher
Neisler, Frances Weaver
 English Department Chairman
Pettit, Nancy Kemp
 English II Teacher
Piercey, James Nelson
 Assistant Principal
Roland, June Hardin
 Algebra Teacher/Math Dept Chm
Wilson, Martha Boyd
 Science Teacher

JASPER

Alder, Virginia Barger
 7th Grade English Teacher

Austin, Martha Elizabeth
 First Grade Teacher

JEFFERSON CITY

Jones, S. Diane Hodge
 6th Science Teacher
Lindsey, Reva Stallings
 Second Grade Teacher
Queen, H. Eugene
 Math Teacher

JELLICO

Archer, George Eddie
 Fifth Grade Teacher

JOHNSON CITY

Buck, Carolyn Janette
 5th Grade Eng/Lang Art Teacher
Curd, Connie Sue
 Third Grade Teacher
De Bord, Harold Webb
 6th Grade Soc Stud/Rdng Teachr
Dosser, Marcia Edgeworth
 1st Grade Teacher
Hall, Mildred Johnson
 Health Occupations Teacher
Joy, Henry Francis III
 Language Art Teacher
Lyons, Karen Sue (Miller)
 Third Grade Teacher
Mc Gee, Brenda K. Humphrey
 4th Grade Teacher
Mc Graw, Nancy Simone
 7th Grade Teacher
Pike, Cora Sue
 1st Grade Teacher
Voitlein, Michael Lee
 Biology Teacher

JONESBORO

Barnes, Dorothy Maden
 Kindergarten Teacher
Silvers, Mary Lo
 Social Studies Teacher

JONESBOROUGH

Lewis, Patsy Jane Shanks
 Fourth Grade Teacher

KENTON

Dunn, Ella Jean (Martin)
 First Grade Teacher
Harding, Marita Moseman
 Fourth Grade Teacher
Stephens, Linda Lane
 Second Grade Teacher

KINGSPORT

Daugherty, Edwin Lee
 Mathematics Teacher
Derrick, Alice Meade
 French/Spanish Teacher
Fletcher, Wanda Sutherland
 Fifth Grade Teacher
Ford, Phyllis Hughes
 First Grade Teacher
Hamm, Douglas Wayne Sr.
 Computer Instructor
Hickam, Jeffrey Brown
 7th Grade Tennessee History
Murrell, Reba R.
 5th Grade Teacher
Prince, Betty Jo Woodson
 Fifth Grade Teacher
Redmond, Alan D.
 General Science Teacher
St Clair, Gerri Gilbert
 Chemistry Teacher
Stidham, Pam Hicks
 Math Teacher
Thompson, Steve A.
 Teacher
Thornton, Jane Lysbeth
 4th Grade/Admin Asst
Welch, James Monroe
 Soc Stud Teacher/Dept Chair

KINGSTON

Blevins, Shaune Dallett
 Director/Owner
Delaney, Judith Lyle
 Science Department Chair
Suits, John Michael
 English Teacher

KNOXVILLE

Anders, Bonnie Fawcett
 Rdng Teacher/Lang Art Chair
Ashworth, Thomas David
 Fifth Grade Teacher
Atkins, Franklin George
 Social Studies Teacher
Beard, Jo Ann
 Business Teacher
Beeler, Susan Lynne
 English Department Chair
Benedict, Karen Robey
 Teacher

Boney, Martha Marlene Ogle
 Fourth Grade Teacher
Bryson, Patricia Gragg
 Russian/German/Spanish Teacher
Clark, John D.
 6th Grade Math Teacher
Comeaux, Barbara W.
 Biology Teacher
Danner, Larry Clinton
 8th Grade Instrumental Teacher
Davis, Jennifer Webster
 High School English Teacher
Evridge, Robert Joseph
 8th Grade Soc Stud Teacher
French, Elizabeth Jane (Mosley)
 7th Grade Mathematics Teacher
Galbraith, Frank P. III
 7th Grade Soc Stud Teacher
Guard, Marsha R.
 Mathematics Teacher
Handly, Linda Phillips
 Guidance Counselor
Hatcher, Barbara K.
 Sixth Grade Teacher
Heins, Sue Culbertson
 Third Grade Teacher
Hill, Phylis Davis
 5th Grade Teacher
Kennedy, Lynda Herndon
 Traveling Mathematics Teacher
Ketron, Mildred F.
 Science Teacher
Kirkland, Dorothy Yater
 Business Dept Chair
Lozano, Robert Catano
 Assistant Principal
Mc Cullough, Bunderlai Souto
 Spanish Teacher
Mc Daniel, Georgia Cockerham
 5th Grade Teacher
Mixon, Lisa Edens
 Spanish Teacher
Napier, Ellen Ruth
 3rd Grade Teacher
Neuhaus, Darlene Chambers
 Fourth Grade Teacher
Simerly, Mary Alice Baldwin
 Cosmetology Instructor
Smith, Frederick Dale
 History & English Teacher
Smith, Hugh David
 Science/Bible Teacher
Wilson, Dora Clinkscales
 English/Reading Teacher

KODAK

Harwell, Rebecca Duncan
 7-8th Grade/Lang Arts Teacher
Porter, Robert Chris
 5th/6th Grade Math Teacher

LA FOLLETTE

Herron, Elizabeth L. England
 7th/8th Grade English Teacher

LA VERGNE

Cathey, Jacqueline Watson
 Physical Education Teacher
Essary, Patricia Ann (Connell)
 Head Librarian
Feuerbacher, John William
 Science/Computer Sci Teacher
Royal, Brenda C.
 Science Department Chair
Sullivan, Elizabeth E.
 7th Grade Social Stud Teacher
Vaughan, Nancy Bryson
 Social Studies Teacher

LAFAYETTE

Clairborne, Paulette Smith
 Fifth Grade Reading Teacher
Eller, Brenda Duncan
 Fourth Grade Teacher
Fitzpatrick, Robert John
 Math Department Teacher
Langford, Joy Ann
 8th Grade Mathematics Teacher
Morris, Judy Carver
 Spanish Teacher

LASCASSAS

Garvin, Mava Shelton
 Librarian/Teacher

LAWRENCEBURG

Joiner, Marion Fowler
 English Teacher
White, Mary Alice Robinson
 Mathematics Teacher

LENOIR CITY

Allen, Brenda Faye
 Reading Teacher
Jones, Reta Morton
 Fifth Grade Teacher
Laughlin, Teresa Ann
 7th Grade English Teacher/Chm

Peters, Sandra Fiechter
 Fifth Grade Teacher
Scott, Roger Dale
 8th Grade Science Teacher
Trotter, Sharon Calvert
 Second Grade Teacher
Tuck, Darrell Alan
 7th Grade Soc Stud Teacher

LEWISBURG

Bishop, Mike
 Mathematics Teacher
Patterson, Ann Hester
 Office Technology Teacher
Rickman, Judy Green
 First Grade Teacher

LEXINGTON

Beal, Jo Ann
 2nd Grade Teacher
Foster, Richard Wayne
 History Teacher, Coach

LIBERTY

Mullinax, Carolyn Vandergriff
 Third Grade Teacher
Parkerson, Robert D. Jr.
 Teacher

LIVINGSTON

Byers, Janie Beaty
 Fourth Grade Teacher
Dale, Alberta Dixon
 Elem Cnslr & Gifted Ed Teacher
Peterman, Deborah M.
 Sixth Grade Teacher

LORETTO

Davis, Larry Andrew
 7th Grade English/His Teacher
Geise, Donna Mashburn
 English/Art Teacher
Jones, Ricky Elwin
 Eighth Grade Science Teacher
Simbeck, Don K.
 Biology & German Teacher

LYLES

Damico, Wayne Gillespie
 8th Grade Science Teacher

LYNNVILLE

Moore, Pamela Edwards
 7th/8th Grade Teacher

MADISON

East, Robbie Ezell
 Fifth Grade Teacher
Stanczak, Allan Michael
 High School Science Teacher

MADISONVILLE

Mc Culloch, Carol Stamey
 Third Grade Teacher
Pennington, Kimberley Watson
 7th Grade English Teacher

MANCHESTER

Blessing, Stephen Wayne
 Mathematics Department Chair
Bush, Judy Banks
 English Teacher
Clark, Jennifer Wells
 Science Teacher
Coats, Janelle Layne
 Reading Teacher
Daniel, Carolyn Mc Clure
 8th Grade Lang Art Teacher
Enos, James Thomas
 Fifth Grade Teacher
Jarell, Stanley Mc Clure
 Assistant Principal
Lockhart, Teresa Ann
 English Teacher
Mc Cullough, Joyce Ann
 English Teacher
Rose, Iva Messick
 Second Grade Teacher

MARTIN

Boyte, Cheryl James
 English/French Teacher
Conley, Jerrie Childress
 K-1st Grade Music/Art Teacher
Graves, Glenda Cole
 Fourth Grade Teacher

MARYVILLE

Campbell, Eula Faye (Skidmore)
 Science Teacher
Dickinson, Cathy Jones
 Third Grade Teacher
Ferguson, Penny Blackwood
 English Department Chair
Moser, C. Steve
 Science Teacher
Parrish, Sandra Y.
 English Teacher
Rutherford, Joseph Douglas
 English/Health Teacher

MARYVILLE (cont)

Tullock, Vendeda H.
Chair Sci Dept/Teacher
Williamson, Mark Anthony
Marketing Teacher

MASCOT

Denton, Linda Alice
Fourth Grade Teacher

MASON

Marshall, Ida Degrafinried
Language Arts Teacher

MAYNARDVILLE

Goforth, D. Wayne
Guidance Counselor
Grim, Richard David
Science & Biology Teacher
Ray, Kate Lee
Fourth Grade Teacher
Williams, Loretta Foust
Sixth Grade Teacher

MC MINNVILLE

Allen, Deborah Jill
3rd Grade Teacher
Clark, Melba Dean
7th Grade Soc Stud Teacher
Eades, Ann Jacobs
Secondary Teacher/H S Coach
Greer, Haskell Harrison
US History Teacher
Long, Tim L.
Sociology/Psychology Teacher
Northcutt, Steven Wayne
High School History Teacher
Smith, Elizabeth Ann (Hill)
3rd Grade Teacher
Tilton, Craig Robert
Amer & Modern History Teacher
Williams, James C.
11th Grade Guidance Counselor

MEDINA

Nelson, John L.
Middle School Science Teacher
Roberts, Sandra Bell
6th-8th Grade Lang Art Teacher

MEMPHIS

Ames, Jennie M.
English Teacher
Avey, Dixie Watson
Teacher
Bailey, Patti A.
Science Lab Instructor
Balton, Sheila Vaden
Fourth Grade Teacher
Bennett, Josephine Adams
Advanced Placement/Bio Teacher
Bolden, Charles C.
9th Grade Physical Sci Teacher
Boldreghini, Mike
Health Teacher
Boyd, Doris Godwin
English Teacher
Bradley, Dolores Jordan
English Teacher
Branyan, Carole L.
Honors English 12 Teacher
Caldwell, Earline Gilland
Reading Teacher
Callicoat, Elizabeth Ann
Biology Teacher
Carr, Elizabeth Malmo
Spanish/English Teacher
Cate, Alfred B. Jr.
American History Teacher/Coach
Chapleau, Elizabeth Ann
English/French Teacher
Clagett, Mildred Winter
Retired 12th Grade Eng Teacher
Clark, Annette Renfro
2nd Grade Teacher
Coleman, Olivia Patricia Jackson
Spanish Teacher
Crawford, Marilyn Long
Guidance Counselor
Culp, Margaret A. Tramel
6th Grade Teacher
Cutliff, Barbara Davis
Fifth Grade Teacher
Cutter, Portia L. Greene
Geometry/Algebra Teacher
Davis, Edna Thompson
English Teacher
Dawson, Georgia Murphy
Supervisor
Day, Wanda Hunter
Teacher of Gifted & Talented
Ditto, Florence Jean
6th Grade Teacher/Elem Supvr
Doss, Barbara Mull
Biology Teacher
Dowell, Olivia Sprunt
Director of Admissions

Draper, Claire Perry
Health Teacher
Dunn, Janice Elizabeth
Phys Ed/Health Teacher & Coach
Edwards, James Ray
Math Teacher
Falls, Cherry Varee
3rd Grade Teacher/Math Coord
Fentress, Ruby P.
Mathematics Teacher/Dept Chair
Gilliam, Florence Collins
5th Grade Teacher
Glenn, June Betton
Choral Director
Gossett, Robert Breen
English Teacher
Grant, Marsha W.
Computer Programming Teacher
Griffith, Helene
Counselor
Hightower, Sharron Yarbrough
Health Occupations Teacher
Jackson, Bessie Anderson
English Teacher
Johnson, Catherine M.
Chairperson of English Dept
Johnson, Joyce Tate
5th Grade Teacher
Joy, James Russell
Supvr Certificated Personnel
Joyner, Lea W.
Bus Data Processing Dept Chair
Kirby, Kimberly Cobb
English Teacher
Knight, Carol Bucy
Teacher/Principal
Lawson, Annie Brownlee
English Chair
Ledbetter, Patricia Nann
Business Dept Chairperson
Loeber, Ed R.
AP American History Teacher
Markart, Dana Trayler
Mathematics Teacher
Massey, Lorraine Mc Neil
Mathematics/Science Teacher
Mattox, Debra Elaine
Soc Stud Dept Chairperson
Mc Hugh, Steve
Social Studies Dept Chairman
Meacham, Grace Austin
English Teacher
Miller, Dianne Ewing
Second Grade Teacher
Moore, Rita Faye
Science Teacher
Mullins, Jacqualin Grubbs
English/Spanish Teacher
Murray, Jane Roudebush
English Teacher
Nabers, Vicki L.
Sixth Grade Teacher
Nelson, Aline Collins
5th Grade Teacher
Newman, Dorothy P.
Sixth Grade Teacher
Nichols, Alice Jo Daves
5-kindergarten Teacher
Parker, Lois Hawkins
Coordinator of Gifted Programs
Pellman, Jeanette (Thornton)
English Teacher
Pratt, Marcie Beardain
5th Grade Teacher
Seratt, Nancy White
Biology Teacher
Seymour, Elphreda Brittenum
Sixth Grade Teacher
Smith, Jacqueline Jones
Mathematics Teacher
Smith, Octavia Hawkins
Business Teacher
Stallworth, Barbaris Moore
Fourth Grade Teacher
Stansbury, Claudine
Biology Teacher/Sci Dept Chair
Stephenson, John Wm.
Teacher
Stigall, Rhoda Mays
Kindergarten Department Chair
Stokes, Bobbie Vaulx
Sixth Grade Chair
Teague, Joyce Ann (Matthews)
Director
Thomas, Ginny A.
English Teacher
Thomson, Judith Ann Van Camp
5th Grade Supervising Teacher
Whitaker, Barbara Lindsay
Health & Physical Ed Teacher
White, Gaynell Reeves
Fifth Grade Teacher
Williams, Elizabeth C.
Spanish Teacher
Wright, Bernadine Tyler
Teacher/Math Department Chair

MICHIE

Avery, Vicki West
Chapter I Rdng & Math Teacher

MIDDLETON

Shelly, Sue V.
3rd/4th Grade Teacher

MILLINGTON

Bonds, Ronetta Jones
Fifth Grade Teacher
Crawford, Carol Veazey
Science Teacher
Dickson, John Robert III
4th Grade Teacher
Fulwood, Betty Cross
First Grade Teacher
Miller, Lorraine Craig
8th Grade English Teacher
Timbs, Diana Forbes
Lang Art & Math Teacher
Todd, Donnie Mae
Substitute Teacher
Wilson, Linda Martin
Assistant Principal
Yount, Betty Davidson
Grade Chapter I Teacher

MOHAWK

Carpenter, Patricia Carver
Jr High Math & Science Teacher
Carter, Cindy Nanette
4th Grade Teacher

MONTEAGLE

Brookman, Geneva Kilgore
Second Grade Teacher

MORRISTOWN

Bain, Angela Charlene (Weston)
Fifth Grade Teacher
Baker, Barbara Simpson
Spanish Teacher
Bolton, Lois Strange
8th Grade Math Teacher/Chm
Buergler, Betty Hess
Teacher
Carroll, Errin
Math Teacher
Claborn, Jim W.
8th Grade Soc Stud Teacher
Gass, Carol Davis
Kindergarten Teacher
Grigsby, Leslie Buchanan
Fifth Grade Teacher
Helton, Kenneth Ray
Principal
Hurst, Larry Wade
8th Grade English Teacher
Inman, Paula Kay (Hickey)
Third Grade Teacher
Kaylor, Martha Bullman
Kindergarten Teacher
Mills, Ronald Michael
Math Teacher
Mitchell, Brenda Dearing
Fourth Grade Teacher
Owens, Patty Deel
Second Grade Teacher
Pearson, Perry Alan
Sixth Grade Science Teacher
Reitz, Pamela Cribb
6th Grade Math/Cmptr Teacher
Stroup, James Earl
English Teacher
Tullock, Vicki Watson
Fifth Grade Teacher
Turner, Sharon Clark
First Grade Teacher
Wilder, Betty Ann
Fourth Grade Teacher
Wolfe, Josephine
Retired Third Grade Teacher
Woodroffe, Marcia Frederico
Biology/Phys Science Teacher

MOSHEIM

Couch, Eya
Second Grade Teacher

MOUNT JULIET

Brooks, Jamie Carver
History Teacher
Kitchen, Kathryn Hunt
Mathematics Teacher
Ladd, Ann Newman
Math Department Chairperson
Ray, Emily Camille
Kindergarten Teacher
Sharpe, Beverly Adams
Mathematics Teacher

MURFREESBORO

Dunn, David Mitchel
Bible Dept Chair/Teacher
Foster, Rebecca Hodges
English Teacher

Lane, Cheryl Joyce
Third Grade Teacher
Long, Karen Burrell
Remedial Reading Teacher
Malone, Sarah Gooch
Teacher/Instructor
Mayberry, Betty Pate
Algebra Teacher
Mayercik, John Edward
JROTC Instructor
Monroe, Karen Kinslow
Fourth Grade Teacher
Mullins, Mary Jane (Neal)
First Grade Teacher
Potter, Nancy Moudy
Fourth Grade Teacher
Stanczak, David John
Mathematics Teacher
Tackett, Marion Bradley
Mathematics Teacher
Thompson, Joe Earl
Assistant Principal
Thompson, Kay Van Zant
Third Grade Teacher
Weeks, Terry M.
Asst Professor of Education
Wilson, Patricia R.
Mathematics/Algebra Teacher

NASHVILLE

Askew, Barbara Ellen (Dixon)
Third Grade Teacher
Bain, Patrica Gilley
High School Teacher
Bell, Judi Williams
Career Ladder Evaluator
Black, Sandra Ledbetter
VOE Data Processing Teacher
Blankenship, Robert Roy
Eighth Grade Science Teacher
Bowen, June Gudmanson
Retired English Teacher
Bradshaw, Mary Catherine
AP Amer His/Amer Lit Teacher
Brasher, Sharon Davis
US History/Civics/Span Teacher
Clark, Brenda M.
11th Grade Guidance Counselor
Claxton, John R.
Physics, Bio, Phys Sci Teacher
Flannery, Amanda Talley
Second Grade Teacher
Foster, Mary Linda Grissom
Mathematics Department Chair
Gafford, Youlanda K.
Physical Education Teacher
Hagewood, William Lowell
Social Studies Dept Chair
Hall, Deborah Jean
Mathematics/Chemistry Teacher
Howell, Nancy Irene
Latin Teacher
Hyde, Bonnie Forehand
Sixth Grade Teacher
Jones, Norman Hooper
Eng as Second Lang Teacher
Kendrick, Kay Wilson
English/History Teacher
Marsh, Jean Thompson
Graduate Research Assistant
Mayernick, Arthur Michael
Assistant Principal
Middleton, Rosalie Row
6th Grade Teacher
Mosier, Rosemary Johnson
5th Grade Teacher
Reece, Shirley Johnson
Fifth Grade Teacher
Reynolds, Ellen Clarissa
English Teacher
Skavron, George Joseph Jr.
Mathematics/Science Teacher
Snider, James Henry
Teacher & Team Leader
Startup, Nancy Hancock
Physical Education Teacher
Stocks, Stephanie Rose
Science/Bible/Phys Ed Teacher
Sullivan, Marsha Celeste
4th Grade Teacher
Therber, Marvin Kent
Department Chair
Weaver, Fay Benson
French Teacher
White, N. Gale
English Teacher
White, Pamela J.
English Teacher

NEW TAZEWELL

Leonard, Gail Mc Daniel
2nd Grade Teacher
Minton, Jacquelyn Beeler
Eighth Grade Teacher

NEWBERN

Larkin, Rosemary Sue Tillman
English Teacher
Van Vickle, Connie Sue
English Teacher

NEWPORT

Anders, Glenn Kale
Biology Teacher/Sci Dept Chair
Burchette, Sandra White
Kindergarten Teacher
Costner, Stephen Monroe
Chemistry/Biology Teacher
Davidson, Linda Johnson
Kindergarten Teacher
Davidson, Steve Alan
Principal
Drinnon, Bobbie (Neatherly)
Consumer & Homemaking Teacher
Dunn, Carwin Vinson
Elementary Counselor
Inman, Sandra Hillard
7th Grade Language Art Teacher
Miller, Odus James
Mathematics Teacher
Parks, Trena La Shea
Earth Science Teacher
Proffitt, Jan S.
Seventh Grade Teacher
Sutton, Kathleen Humberd
Retired
Williams, Gary
Business Teacher
Williamson, Lynette Coggins
Fifth Grade Teacher

OAK RIDGE

Burkey, Thomas Lynn
Social Studies Dept Chair
Campbell, Gordon Dee
5th Grade Teacher
Colglazier, Catherine Clark
English Teacher
Ellis, Karen Floren
Mathematics Teacher
Finane, Naida Karoly
English Teacher
Geren, Wanda Hope
Fourth Grade Teacher
Greene, Sylvia Woods
English Teacher
Krushenski, Barbara Gouge
Second Grade Teacher
Sutton, Donna Hurst
English & Gifted Teacher
Volk, Louis J.
Sixth Grade Teacher
White, Betty Jean
Music & Chorus Teacher

OAKLAND

Whitaker, Amelia Batts
3rd Grade Teacher

OLDFORT

Ellis, Cynthia Jane
Sixth Grade Teacher
Frazier, Thomas Gilbert
Sixth Grade Teacher

OLIVER SPRINGS

Boyd, Gorman Franklin
7th/8th Grade Science Teacher
Heacker, Thelma Weaks
Fourth Grade Teacher
Tate, James Roger
Band/Math/Social Stud Teacher

ONEIDA

Chambers, Martha Lominac
High School Guidance Teacher
Clayton, Charles
6th/7th Grade Soc Stud Teacher
Kyle, Maxine W.
4th Grade Teacher
Lewis, Jann R.
Fifth Grade Teacher
Marlow, Linda Sue
Fine Arts Department Chairman
Scott, Sharon Terry
Kindergarten Teacher

OOLTEWAH

Brown, Sharon Cary
US History Teacher/Dept Chair
Lumpkin, Betty Stewart
Librarian
Tate, Donna Marsh
6th Grade Soc Stud Teacher
Wilson, Rebecca Lovell
High School English Teacher

PARROTTSVILLE

Blazer, Dolores H.
Kindergarten Teacher

PARSONS

Crosby, William Larry
Math Teacher

PARSONS (cont)
Quinn, Rhonda Conder
 8 Grade Math/Drama/Spl Teacher
Spence, Philip Gary
 5th Grade Teacher
PEGRAM
Conatser, Marguerite Holland
 5th Grade Teacher
PELHAM
Oliver, Michael Clinton
 History Teacher
PETERSBURG
Wilson, Janine Marks
 K-8th Grade Principal
PIGEON FORGE
Trotter, Jimmie Faye
 Language Arts Teacher
PIKEVILLE
Cagle, Warner Redmond
 4th Grade Teacher
Wheeler, Patricia Ann Rose
 Kindergarten Teacher
PINSON
Fuller, Lizzie Loraine
 Fifth Grade Teacher
PLEASANT VIEW
Buttrey, Susanne Fort
 Fifth Grade Teacher
Harris, Linda Richardson
 7th Grade Math/Science Teacher
PORTLAND
Woodward, Shirley Ann Mc Carroll
 6th Grade Science Teacher
POWELL
Crosby, Judy Gibbs
 Art/Math Teacher/Librarian
Thomas, Joanne Duke
 Kindergarten Teacher
PULASKI
Bryan, Jean Young
 Chemistry Teacher
Cosby, Jean Burns
 Second Grade Teacher
Forsythe, Charles Wayne
 Administrator
Sims, Susan Blackman
 First Grade Teacher
RAMER
Pearson, Patsy Johnson
 6th/7th/8th Grade Math Teacher
READYVILLE
Cox, Annie May
 1st Grade Teacher
RED BOILING SPRING
Clements, Nelda R.
 Second Grade Teacher
Greer, Nancey Newlin
 English Teacher
Trent, Robbie West
 Kindergarten Teacher
RICEVILLE
Buckley, Gail Guthrie
 6th Grade Teacher
Mullins, Brenda McKeehan
 2nd Grade Teacher
Purdy, Douglas E.
 6th Grade Math/Science Teacher
Woods, Martha Cate
 Fifth Grade Teacher
RICKMAN
Harris, James Louis
 Fifth Grade Teacher
Poston, Diann Neal
 Third Grade Teacher
Smith, Betty S.
 Kindergarten Teacher
RIDGELY
Fraley, Judy Roberson
 Grammar Rules Teacher
Morgan, Billie Sue Moore
 Kindergarten Teacher
RIPLEY
Carmack, Stephen S.
 Math Teacher
Langley, Sheila Pilcher
 Marketing Coordinator
Toles, Sue Lattimore
 9th/10th Grade English Teacher
RIVES
Webb, Paula Sue Jones
 7th/8th Grade Lang Art Teacher

ROAN MOUNTAIN
Morgan, Roger James
 Lang Art/World His Teacher
Oaks, Garry Gene
 Soc Stud & English Teacher
ROCKWOOD
Kirkham, Betty Jane
 8th Grade Literature Teacher
ROGERSVILLE
Cope, Linda Onks
 9th Grade English Teacher
Welch, Mildred Bailey
 Third Grade Teacher
ROSSVILLE
Johnson, Rose Marie Storm
 3rd Grade Teacher/Elem Prin
Spencer, Sally Bailey
 Senior HS English Chairperson
RUSSELLVILLE
White, Jane Yount
 Mathematics Teacher
RUTLEDGE
Ledford, Gwen Green
 Guidance Counselor
Morgan, Patty Myers
 Language Art Teacher
SCOTTS HILL
Dyer, Margaret Goff
 10th & 11th Grade Eng Teacher
Tucsnak, Joseph Frank
 7th Grade Teacher
SELMER
Blakely, Paul Edward
 Social Studies Dept Chairman
Bradley, Teresa Willis
 Computer Teacher
Day, Gail Armstrong
 Teacher
Dickey, Ronald Neal
 History Department Chairman
Durr, Sheila Ann Avery
 6th Grade Soc Stud Teacher
Redding, Helen Alford
 Choral Director
Turner, Judith Forsyth
 Assistant Principal
Wilkerson, Betty Etheridge
 Second Grade Teacher
SEVIERVILLE
Berrier, Harriet Louise
 Second Grade Teacher
Book, Stephen Mark
 8th Grade Science Teacher
Chambers, Dennis Earnest
 8th Grade Soc Stud Teacher
Enloe, John Taylor
 Principal
Fuller, Patricia Lucile Davenport
 7th/8th Grade Teacher
Haggard, Gail Welch
 Kindergarten Teacher
Mc Farland, Robert J.
 Math Teacher
Walker, Richard Walter
 6th Grade Teacher
SEYMOUR
Hancox, Gregory Lee
 Mathematics Department Chair
Hyder, Edna Ruth
 History Teacher
Mosher, David Byron
 Spanish/Eng 2nd Lang Teacher
Ogle, Charles A.
 Fifth Grade Teacher
SHADY VALLEY
Howard, Capriece Cole
 4th Grade Teacher
SHARON
Capps, Debbie Penick
 Kindergarten Teacher
Claybrooks, Beverly Caldwell
 5th Grade Teacher
Thompson, William Anthony
 Sixth Grade Teacher
SHARPS CHAPEL
Sharp, Allena H.
 Third Grade Teacher
Tolliver, Wilma Cole
 5th/6th Grade Teacher
SHELBYVILLE
Bobo, Dawn Swing
 4th Grade Teacher
Donegan, Deborah Mealer
 English Teacher
Gill, Teresa Wheeler
 7th Grade Mathematics Teacher

Kimery, Roseanna Clark
 8th Grade US History Teacher
SIGNAL MOUNTAIN
Waller, Carol
 Third Grade Teacher
SMITHVILLE
Bennett, Jane Ellen
 English Teacher
Franklin, Linda Early
 6th Grade Science Teacher
Groom, Dorothy Jane (Frazier)
 Third Grade Teacher
SMYRNA
Chavez, Deborah Lee
 Second Grade Teacher
Jones, Wanda Donell
 Kindergarten Teacher
Young, Lynda B.
 Reading Teacher
SNEEDVILLE
Dodson, Danita Joan
 English and Spanish Teacher
Jones, Fred L.
 Fifth Grade Teacher
Southern, E.R. Jr.
 Counselor
SODDY-DAISY
Beavers, Joyce Jenkins
 7th Grade Social Stud Teacher
Campbell, Donna Wood
 English Teacher
Levi, Judy Stewart
 Sixth Grade Teacher
Raulston, Dorothy Driver
 Math Teacher
SOMERVILLE
Jordan, Vashti
 Teacher
Montague, Arnett Glenn
 Teacher
SOUTH FULTON
Dunavant, Mary Wall
 5th Grade Teacher
SPARTA
Kidd, Sharon Elaine
 Soc Stud Dept Chair & Teacher
Mc Ghee, Wanda Roberts
 Sixth Grade Teacher
Roberts, Patricia Hancock
 1st Grade Teacher
SPEEDWELL
Ausmous, Pauline
 Kindergarten Teacher
Russell, Jo Ann
 Business Education Teacher
Treece, June Evans
 Retired
Vannoy, Ron L.
 Health Teacher/Coach
SPRINGFIELD
Bargatze, Stephen Ray
 8th Grade Teacher
Felts, Katherine Clinard
 Substitute Teacher
Morris, Elizabeth Goetz
 Teacher/Coordinator of Gifted
Moulton, Gladys Mayo
 Retired
Nicholson, Nancy Bagwell
 Third Grade Teacher
Reedy, Charlotte Edwards
 Spanish Teacher
Webb, Cynthia Womack
 7th/8th Grade English Teacher
STRAWBERRY PLAINS
Bailey, John Wallace Jr.
 Social Studies Teacher
Smith, Steve A.
 Middle School Art Teacher
SURGOINSVILLE
Fairchild, Lowell Thomas
 Eighth Grade Teacher
Thurman, Mary Nancy Miller
 Fourth Grade Teacher
TAZEWELL
England, Carolyn Mc Cray
 Albebra/Geometry Teacher
Munsey, Neta Kimbrough
 Science Teacher
TELLICO PLAINS
Best, Carolyn Jeanette
 6th-8th Grade Soc Stud Teacher
Cole, Norman William
 5th Grade Teacher
Stehens, Edna Mitchell
 Teacher

Tallent, Sara Blair
 Third Grade Teacher
TEN MILE
Herd, Dorothy Parks
 3rd & 4th Grade Teacher
TENNESSEE RIDGE
Clemmons, Dixie Jane
 2nd Grade Teacher
TIPTONVILLE
Vaughn, Georgianne C.
 5th/6th Grade Reading Teacher
TRACY CITY
Mc Daniel, Rhonda Gwen
 VIP English/Math Teacher
TRENTON
Scott, Mary Jane
 8th Grade English Teacher
TREZEVANT
Carter, Travis Lee Jr.
 Mathematics/Computer Teacher
TROY
Blackley, Mary Sue Summers
 1st Grade Teacher
Jones, Doris Andrews
 Second Grade Teacher
Parker, Donna Paschall
 World Geography/Econ Teacher
TULLAHOMA
Stopinski, Pamela Ingle
 Fourth Grade Teacher
UNICOI
Benedetto, Sheila Horne
 Fifth Grade Teacher
UNION CITY
Cunningham, Deborah Wright
 7th Grade Mathematics Teacher
Davis, Sandra Bell
 Math & Social Studies Teacher
Moyers, Patti Hixson
 4th Grade Teacher
UNIONVILLE
Carlton, Lana Cartwright
 Math Dept Chair/Teacher
Garner, Karen Snelson
 English/Drama/Art His Teacher
VANLEER
Ragan, Kim Monday
 Second Grade Teacher
VONORE
Lovingood, Darlene Shell
 Chapter 1 Reading Teacher
Lowry, Michael Louis
 Social Studies Teacher
WARTBURG
Frazier, Janet Lee
 Kindergarten Teacher
WATERTOWN
Simpson, Lynda Sue Harris
 Fifth Grade Teacher
WAVERLY
Brazzle, Janice Marlene
 Teacher
Bullington, Joyce Enochs
 Social Studies Teacher
Collier, Crystel S.
 1st Grade Teacher
Evans, Carlton Webb
 Biology Teacher
Phillips, Adrienne Hatcher
 7th Grade Soc Stud Teacher
Sparks, Edwin Claude Jr.
 6th Grade Science Teacher
WAYNESBORO
Price, Michael J. (Price)
 Principal/Vocational Director
WESTMORELAND
Honeycutt, James Allen
 Biology Teacher/Football Coach
Law, Jean Smith
 7th Grade Mathematics Teacher
WHITE BLUFF
Buttrey, Darlene Brown
 English Teacher/Dept Chair
WHITES CREEK
Beem, Laura Robinson
 English Teacher
Metzgar, Vicki Hopkins
 Biology Teacher
WHITWELL
Gravitt, Dorothy Boyd
 Retired Second Grade Teacher

WINCHESTER
Edens, Deborah Brown
 Marketing Education Teacher
Fernander, William Robert
 English Teacher
Fraley, Betty Newman
 Business Education Chairperson
Fuller, Angie Prince
 Health & PE Teacher
Groves, Diana Collins
 Social Studies Teacher
Jolley, Alton Roger
 Social Studies Dept Chairman
WOODBURY
Ledford, Teresa Ann
 Band/Choral Director
Melton, Anita
 7th-8th Grade Teacher/Prin
Nichols, Barbara Darlene
 English Teacher
Patterson, Bonnie Hoover
 6th/7th Language Arts Teacher
WOODLAWN
Boothe, Clarissa Busse
 Second Grade Teacher
Buckhart, Margaret Graves
 Third Grade Teacher

TEXAS

ABILENE
Bacon, Marylan K.
 Fourth Grade Teacher
Bowden, Glenda Edwards
 Mathematics/Science Teacher
Bowens, George Austin
 Mathematics Teacher
Boyd, Cindy Huskin
 Math Teacher
Drennan, Peggy Hollis
 Music Teacher
English, Judy Beth
 Second Grade Teacher
Herrington, Don Alan
 Industrial Technology Chair
Hogg, Farrell F.
 Mathematics Teacher
Mc Clellan, Carol
 Music Teacher
Nelson, Angie Juarez
 Mathematics Teacher
Ortiz, Sallye (Hartt)
 Business Dept Chairman
Petty, Carole Felts
 Sixth Grade Reading Teacher
Pickens, Jimmy Burton
 Earth Science Teacher
Popelka, La Verne D.
 English Teacher
Snow, Veronica Dickenson
 Computer Science Teacher
Swanner, Darla C.
 English Teacher
White, Sharon Janet
 4th Grade Mathematics Teacher
Zamarippa, Ralph M. Jr.
 Band Director
ADDISON
Gump, Linda Ann
 Spanish Teacher Foreign Lang
Pendleton, Kent Lund
 Mathematics Department Chair
ALBANY
Heatly, Lynda Killingsworth
 1st Grade Teacher
ALICE
Garcia, Celina Hinojosa
 Business Teacher
Sanchez, Gus Michael
 Teacher
Waldrum, Dolores Moore
 Science Chair
ALIEF
Dallas, James Robert
 Counselor/Science Teacher
Kraloskey, George Michael
 English Teacher
ALLEN
Long, Sondra Foster
 8th/Rding Advisory Coord
Moore, Lynda Stroud
 Third Grade Teacher
Parker, Philip A.
 Teacher
Vrba, Glenn William
 Health Teacher/Coach
Whitaker, Carol Dunagin
 3rd Grade Teacher

ALPINE
Reesing, Jo Christian
  Second Grade Teacher

ALVARADO
Bankston, David Bruce
  8th Grade US History Teacher
Shaffer, Kathy Elaine Goldring
  Eng/Hist/Spanish Dept Chair

ALVIN
Ansel, Stehanie Wilson
  Physical Education Teacher
Baker, Cynthia
  English Teacher
Mercer, James Louis
  Life Skills Coord
Nichols, Donna Kennedy
  History Teacher & Chair

AMARILLO
Cobb, Jaketta Mangold
  Biology Teacher
Day, M. Jo Ann
  Fourth Grade Teacher
Des Pain, Arvia Smith
  Fifth Grade Teacher
Dominguez, Rosa Martha
  Second Grade Teacher
Elam, Reba J.
  English Teacher
Frazer, Jeff Clark
  Government/US History Teacher
Gill, Dee Gifford
  High School Science Teacher
Godfrey, Susan Gayle
  History Teacher
Hall, Jerre Jackson
  7th/8th Grade Eng/Rdng Teacher
Horner, Karen Mathews
  First Grade Teacher
James, Rebekah Markee
  Phys Ed Teacher/Coach
Jones, Charles T.
  5th Grade Teacher
Lummus, Carl Russell
  History Teacher/Coach
Moore, Anne Russell
  Mathematics Teacher/Dept Chair
Stewart, Jerome Lex
  History Teacher
Stone, Kathie Dorman
  Health Occupations Coordinator
Tillotson, Billie Marie (Ford)
  6th Grade Math Teacher
Trader, Richard Eugene
  Office Administration Coord

ANDERSON
Boehm, Gloria Schaffer
  Elementary Physical Ed Teacher
Burzynski, Loukattie Kroll
  Fifth Grade Classroom Teacher
Lavender, Mary Macha
  Sixth Grade Teacher

ANDREWS
Jones, Billie Porter
  Fifth Grade Teacher
Marquez, Linda
  English Teacher

ANGLETON
Gilbert, Sharon Brunt
  Fourth Grade Teacher
Hejl, James George
  Director of Bands
Lewis, Donna Spoor
  5th Grade Mathematics Teacher

ANNA
Childress, Linda S.
  Fifth Grade Teacher

ARANSAS PASS
Smith, Linda Knesek
  High School Counselor

ARLINGTON
Battle, Mary Catherine Bush
  8th Grade English Teacher
Bourque, Mary Jo
  Third Grade Teacher
Carlon, Beth Nordin
  5th Grade Lead Teacher
Crum, Katherine Gonis
  Third Grade Teacher
David, Connie Jene
  Physical Education Teacher
Davis, Patricia Ann
  Phys Ed Coach/Health Dept Chm
Elrod, Peggy Martin
  Fourth Grade Teacher
Everett, Sherry Allen
  Teacher
Fisher, La Juan Martin
  Mathematics Teacher/Dept Chair
Haas, Tracey Bristow
  History Teacher

Lightfoot, Janet Y. (French)
  Sixth Grade Teacher
Linderman, Judy Ann
  Principal
Miles-Hutcheson, Beatrice
  Physical Education Teacher
Moore, Vickie Lorene (Owen)
  English/French Teacher
Scott, Linda Hall
  Math Teacher/Level Leader
Scribner, Jane Ann
  English Dept Chairperson
Soncrant, Robert Leo
  7th Grade Math Teacher
Thompson, Barbara L.
  4th Grade Teacher
Villemaire, Maureen Frain
  Fifth Grade Teacher
Wood, Lynda Susan
  9th Grade Algebra Teacher

ARP
Mackey, Barbara Ellis
  1st-5th Grade Computer Teacher
Rieken, Margaret Wages
  7th/8th Grade Math Teacher
Shuttlesworth, Newana Goolsby
  Business Teacher
Svoboda, Patricia Newby
  English/Cmptr Sci Teacher

ASPERMONT
Walling, Gregory Allen
  Science Teacher/Play Director

ATHENS
Bailey, Carol Albright
  7th Grade English Teacher
Ferrell, Janice Rene
  Director of Choral Music
Hart, Penny Warren
  Mathematics Teacher
Mc Natt, Carol Dowdy
  English Teacher
Peacock, Francyse Spitler
  Art/English Teacher
Presley, Jeanne Hale
  Teacher
Saylors, Michael Evan
  Social Studies Dept Chairman
Smith, Alice Harlan
  4th Grade Teacher
Tidmore, Zan E.
  English Teacher
Weatherford, Lisa Marlene
  Anatomy and Biology Teacher

ATLANTA
Harper, Arlister Washington
  Mathematics Teacher
White, Debbie Dodson
  US His/Government Econ Teacher
White, Michael Joseph
  Mathematics Teacher/Coach

AUBREY
Fuller, Jackie Balthrop
  Social Studies Teacher

AUSTIN
Baethge, Sam J.
  Mathematics Teacher
Balusek, Melissa Jane
  Fifth Grade Teacher
Beaver, Donald W.
  Mathematics Teacher
Bell, Patricia Banks
  English Department Chair
Clark, Glenn E.
  English Teacher
Craycroft, Peter Rambicur
  Journalism Teacher
Crayon, Darrell Keith
  Mathematics Teacher
Crittenden, Terrie Ann (Webb)
  Teacher/Assistant Principal
Du Perier, Susanna Currie
  Kindergarten Teacher
Ellison, Jo Ella Johns
  Typing Teacher
Flatau, Susie Kelly
  English Teacher
Franzetti, Robert Joseph
  Government Teacher
Furtado, Robert A.
  Biology Teacher
Garrett, Elisa Daniel
  United States History Teacher
Gerlach, Rob K.
  Mathematics/Music Teacher
Grayson, Laura Vela
  World History Honors Teacher
Harrell, Barbara L.
  Business Department Chair
Hatch, Hazel Ratcliff
  First Grade Teacher
Henry, Mixon Lee
  Third Grade Teacher

Hiller, Marla Strickland
  Dance Teacher/Drill Team Dir
Jackson, Henry Hoyt
  Counselor
La Cour, Michael Edward
  Band Director
Lockwood, Vickie Jane
  Lang Art Teacher/Dept Chair
Mokry, Patricia Raesener
  Science Teacher/Chairperson
Nethercut, Jane Swann
  Latin and English Teacher
Norris, Denise Kelbaugh
  8th Grade Earth Sci Teacher
Ochoa, Albert Richard Jr.
  Art Instr/Var Tennis Coach
Perez, Alberto Zuvia
  8th Grade English Teacher
Potter, Rose M.
  Spanish Teacher/Dept Chair
Robertson, Jacquelyn Davis
  7th & 8th Grade Rdng Teacher
Russell, Helen Helm
  HECE Teacher/Coord
Russell, Marsha K.
  English/Social Studies Teacher
Shank, Nancy Trojanoski
  4th Grade Teacher
Speier, Patricia M.
  English Department Chairperson

AVERY
Deaton, Marsha Grant
  2nd Grade Teacher

AXTELL
Linton, Beverlay Morgan
  Junior High School Teacher

BALCH SPRINGS
Gullion, James Madison II
  History Department Chair
Peters, Renia Fulce
  HS Eng/Algebra Teacher/Prin

BANDERA
Zickler, Karen K. King
  Fifth Grade Teacher

BARTLETT
Butler, Joe L.
  English Teacher
Weeks, James Douglas
  Third Grade Teacher

BASTROP
Travis, Jane Anderson
  English/Language Arts Teacher
Wright, Ellen E.
  VOE Teacher/Coordinator

BAY CITY
Battle, Patricia Ann
  Art Teacher
Ryan, Barbara (Boyd)
  Social Studies Teacher
Ussery, Evelyn Guest
  8th Grade Math Teacher

BAYTOWN
Borah, William Bryan
  English Teacher
Culp, Barbara Clark
  Mathematics Teacher
Cunningham, Hunter Du Bois
  Jr HS Band Director
Ethridge, Mary Jane
  2nd Grade Teacher
Guidry, Kay Moreau
  Second Grade Teacher
Kellner, Laura Ward
  Algebra Teacher

BEAUMONT
Dallison, Belva Ann
  Kindergarten Teacher
Gaston, Carolyn Dupree
  Spanish/French Teacher
Graves, Belinda Jordan
  High School/Jr High Librarian
Hebert, Billie Street
  Fourth Grade Teacher

BECKVILLE
Maher, James Patrick
  Phys Ed/Health Teacher/Coach
Wilson, Robert Clements
  Science Teacher

BEDFORD
Gunn, Joe E.
  Director of Bands
Kean, Beth
  Elementary School Counselor

BEEVILLE
Garcia, Kathrine Lazarine
  Counselor
Hoffman, Karen A.
  7th/8th Grade Reading Teacher

Martinez, Teresa Guzman
  1st Grade Teacher/Chairman
Todd, Darlene Lawrence
  Spec Ed Learning Disabilities

BELLAIRE
Gay, Martha Newport
  Mathematics Dept Chairman
Mc Lendon, Elizabeth Lee
  Russian Department Chair
Pass, Susan Jeanette
  PIB US History

BELTON
Bartek, Ava Lynne (Poncik)
  6th Grade General Sci Teacher
Kurtz, Cedalia Latham
  Third Grade Teacher

BEN BOLT
Garcia, Janie
  Counselor

BEN WHEELER
Chambers, Dorothy J.
  Second Grade Teacher
Mc Intyre, Mike Wayne
  Scndry Sch Math/Sci Teacher

BENAVIDES
Garcia, Azalia Oliveira
  Social Studies/Science Teacher
Salinas, Joe Jr.
  Spanish Teacher

BIG LAKE
Drennan, Mitzi Jan
  English Teacher
Harris, Rita Dell Petty
  Science Teacher
Mc Reavy, Sharon Treadwell
  First Grade Teacher

BIG SPRING
Adams, Deanna Boles
  Life Science Chairperson
Calhoun, Peggy Darlene
  English/Phys Ed/Teacher/Coach
Gladden, Lyndon K.
  Math Department Chairman
Hayes, Kristy Denise (Jasek)
  Choral Director
Rhoton, Patricia Rudd
  6th Grade Science Teacher

BISHOP
Moon, Norma Nilda (Martinez)
  English Teacher

BLACKWELL
Schoen, Allie B. (Landers)
  7-12th Grade Science Teacher

BLOOMBURG
Bricker, Patsy Smith
  English Teacher
Gennings, Barbara Jean (O'Kelley)
  Fifth Grade Teacher

BLOOMING GROVE
Ross, Linda Cochran
  Biology/Earth Science Teacher

BLOOMINGTON
Jimenez, Sandra Kay
  History Teacher
Mayer, George J. Jr.
  Math/Cmptr Literacy Teacher

BOERNE
White, Faye Porter
  First Grade Teacher

BOGATA
Gunter, Brenda Kay
  English Teacher
Hays, Pamela Verner
  Spanish/English/Drama Teacher

BONHAM
Whisenhunt, Audrey Elaine
  Span Teacher/Foreign Lang Head

BORGER
Brink, David Ernest
  Physics Teacher
Denton, Elizabeth Bass
  Home Economics Teacher
Johnston, Marsha Gregg
  Second Grade Teacher
Lowe, Janet Sutton
  Mathematics Teacher
Maupin, Vicki Tollison
  Computer Literacy Teacher

BOVINA
Willard, Frances Totty
  Math Teacher

BOWIE
Gray, Claudette Gann
  Kindergarten Teacher

BRADY
Graves, William Lamar
  Social Studies Dept Chair
Munden, Lynn K.
  8th Grade Lang Art/G T Teacher

BRAZORIA
Wathen, Harriet Seabrook
  Fourth Grade Teacher

BRECKENRIDGE
Cummings, Sharee Ann (Creagh)
  Biology Teacher/Coach
Edwards, Weldon Lynn
  English Department Chair

BRENHAM
Doherty, Gary
  Music/Band Director
Guentert, Marylou Harris
  9th Grade English Teacher
Hathaway, Lana Krause
  Seventh Grade Reading Teacher
Morgan, Dorothy Marie (Broz)
  Government & Economics Teacher

BRIDGE CITY
Nicotre, Sherri Sheffield
  Third Grade Teacher

BROOKELAND
Henson, Rebecca Ann (Mc Claw)
  Business/Computer Teacher

BROWNFIELD
Geron, Sylvia F.
  8th Grade Soc Stud Teacher
Harlan, Tanya Price
  3rd Grade Teacher
Martin, Mercie L.
  Kindergarten Teacher

BROWNSVILLE
Campos, Celina Estrada
  Assistant Principal
Castillo, German
  Assistant Principal
Cavazos, Christina Doria
  Journalism Advisor/Eng Teacher
Champion, Celina
  Health/Quest Teacher
Foltz, Emily J.
  English Teacher
Funkhouser, Linda Jahns
  English Teacher
Garcia, Juan Diego
  Sixth Grade Teacher
Garcia, Mary Lou
  Social Studies Teacher
Garza, Victor Islas
  Computer Literacy Teacher
Gomez, Sandra Corkill
  Reading Teacher
Guzman, Jose R.
  Business Teacher/Bsktbl Coach
Hammons, Merrill R.
  English Teacher
Iyer, Malini K.
  Mathematics Dept Chair
Jahan-tigh, Batul Lavon
  11th Eng Honors/GT & Advanced
Laredo, Delfino
  6th Grade Teacher
Luna, Bella Pena
  Sixth Grade Teacher
Mac Nelly, Annie Sue Lope
  Bus Office Services Teacher
Mascola, Corinne Anderson
  Counselor
Montemayor, Martina Longoria
  Teacher
Muniz, Frances Garcia
  Kindergarten Teacher
Padilla, Carlos
  Reading Teacher
Parson, Paula T. (Mukai)
  Reading Instructor/Eng Dept
Perez, Blanca Dina
  Journalism Advisor
Seguin, James William
  English Teacher
Shands, Mary Jane (Hale)
  Science Department Chair
Sidoroff, Diane Doreen
  Reading Teacher
Sierra, Elsa
  First Grade Teacher
Tegarden, Jackson Eaves
  Commercial Drafting Instructor
Trevino, Irma
  Life Science Teacher

BROWNWOOD
Blackburn, Margaret Young
  Teacher & Supervisor
Cravens, Mickey B.
  Teacher

BROWNWOOD (cont)
Eoff, Debbie Milburn
  8th Grade English Teacher
Fine, Marjorie Louise
  Chemistry/Phys Science Teacher
Horner, Tanya Evon (Fedora)
  Mathematics Teacher
Horner, Tonya Evon (Fedora)
  Mathematics Teacher
King, Rebecca Collier
  English Department Teacher
Larner, Patricia Black-Locks
  Vocational Counselor
Morlan, Pamela P.
  English Teacher
Nuss, Bobbye Byrd
  Second Grade Teacher
Reynolds, Simmie Colene
  Chapter I Math Teacher
Stewart, Joan N.
  7th Grade Life Science Teacher
Wheeless, Linda Coppic
  Elementary Music Teacher
Wheelis, Ruth Lasater
  Mathematics Teacher
Wilcox, Brenda Ratliff
  First Grade Teacher
Wilson, Marvin Rick
  US & World History Teacher

BRYAN
Carter, Johnnie Petty
  Third Grade Teacher
Paris, Rodney Melvin
  Mathematics Teacher
Robison, Mary Gilland
  Second Grade Teacher

BUCKHOLTS
Dusek, Thomas Clayton
  History Teacher

BUDA
Babbitt, Gerald Allen
  Band/Music Director
Mc Clendon, Marcia Kay (Siecko)
  Computer Teacher
Reich, Shirley Ann
  American History Teacher

BUFFALO
Harcrow, Dortha (Stone)
  Jr HS Science Teacher
Van Nostrand, Terry Lynne
  Science Teacher/Chairperson

BULLARD
Braly, Suzanne
  American His/Health Teacher
Callison, Dirk F.
  Teacher/Vocational Coordinator
Lester, Virginia Masters
  Fifth Grade Teacher

BUNA
Mc Adams, Tina Burks
  Eighth Grade Earth Sci Teacher
Noyes, Ginger Williamson
  7th Grade Life Science Teacher

BURKBURNETT
Bohuslav, Diana Awtrey
  English/Sociology Teacher
Moody, Camille Rose
  Span/Life Management Teacher
Roberts, Diane (Burden)
  7th/8th Grade Math Teacher
Stonner, Kathy Dodd
  Kindergarten Teacher
Wright, James Edwin
  Biology Teacher

BURNET
Berryhill, Roy H.
  Band/Choir/Theatre Art Teacher
Chiles, Jerold Dee
  Earth Sci/Amer His Teacher
Grill, Richard Wayne
  Agricultural Science Teacher

CADDO MILLS
Williams, Anna Kathleen
  9th/11th/12th English Teacher

CALDWELL
Stefka, Deborah Ann
  Mathematics Teacher
Tharp, Patricia Cordell
  6th Grade Teacher

CAMERON
Rosson, Susan Coleman
  English IV Teacher

CANYON
Bigham, Marsha Ellis
  Social Studies Teacher
Weber, Joan M.
  Choral Director

CARRIZO SPRINGS
Majek, Linda
  History Teacher
Valdez, Mary Alice Murray
  Reading/Lang Arts Teacher

CARROLLTON
Bradley, Jacqueline Diane
  English Teacher
Gallo, Christine Johnson
  Educational Coordinator
Helton, Bronnie Loyd
  TX History Teacher
Miller, Colette Mary
  6th Grade Teacher
Sunthimer, Lennie Clark
  Chemistry Teacher/Science Dept
Trout, Danny Joe
  Sixth Grade Teacher
Womble, Evelyn Crouch
  Gifted Education Facilitator

CARTHAGE
Burchette, Fatha Lee (Roberts)
  6th Grade Soc Stud Teacher
Duke, Carolyn Holland
  4th Grade Mathematics Teacher
Everett, Glenda Mc Gee
  5th Grade Soc Stud Teacher
Reeder, Eloise Jennings
  Third Grade Teacher
Tinkle, Jeanette Stanley
  Office Education Coordinator

CEDAR HILL
Farmer, Gina Kay
  English Teacher
Knagg, Kathryn Lynn
  World History Teacher

CHANNELVIEW
Barber, Kitty Sue
  10th Grade English Teacher
Murray, Millie Cooley
  Teacher

CHANNING
Blaut, Connie Marlene (Cope)
  Second Grade Teacher
Noles, James Carl
  Teacher-Counselor
Thomas, Laurel Gracey
  Math/English Teacher

CHILLICOTHE
Stone, Emily Wall
  English Teacher

CHILTON
Phelps, Ann Jones
  Math Dept Chair/Teacher

CHINA
Bruce, Sue A.
  Teacher/Administrator
Green, Catherine Walker
  Reading Teacher
Kirkland, Geraldine
  Kindergarten Teacher
Martin, Candye Patricia
  8th Grade Earth Sci Teacher

CHRISTOVAL
Luce, Marilyn Carothers
  Language Arts Teacher

CIBOLO
Hamblin, Edna Hendricks
  Retired-Vice Principal
Miller, Bonnie Ruth (Max)
  Fourth Grade Teacher

CISCO
Maxwell, Nanette West
  Fourth Grade Teacher

CLARKSVILLE
Bryant, Pamela Powell
  Kindergarten Teacher
Cagle, Walter Neal (Buck)
  Teacher/Coach
Cochran, Patricia Mann
  Secondary Mathematics Teacher
Ewing, Betty Linton
  5th Grade Teacher
Ewing, Dickie Harold
  Science Teacher

CLAUDE
Douglass, James Gary
  Social Studies Teacher
Weller, Dianna Friemel
  Mathematics Teacher
Whitaker, Cynthia Lizabeth (Jones)
  Third Grade Teacher

CLEVELAND
Chesson, Kay Mylene
  Spanish/French Teacher

Simpson, Wesley Allen
  Social Studies Teacher

CLINT
Lugo, Robert L.
  English Teacher
Martinez, Rebecca Parada
  Reading Teacher

COAHOMA
West, Kent
  Computer Science Teacher

COLDSPRING
Lewis, Laura Goffney
  Elementary Teacher
Moldenhauer, Marlene Latham
  Science Department Chairperson
Sewell, Beth Locke
  8th Grade US History Teacher

COLEMAN
Childress, Howard B.
  Social Studies Teacher
Strawn, Charlotte Edwards
  Retired

COLLEGE STATION
Angel, Travis L.
  Fine Arts Chairman/Choral Dir
Hess, Adana Creel
  Bio/Environmental Sci Teacher

COMANCHE
Brannan, Reitha Frances
  Second Grade Teacher
Sharp, Susan Warren
  11th Grade English Teacher

COMMERCE
Carter, Nelda Alderman
  Science Teacher
Garret, Jennifer Stoll
  7th & 8th Grade Math Teacher

CONROE
Anderson, Lavina Kip
  Physical Education Teacher
Buchner, Betty A.
  English Teacher/Drill Team Dir
Butler, Samuel D. De Lyra
  Spanish Teacher
Eikenberg, Babette Metcalf
  Principal
Giesinger, Imogene Mock
  Consultant
Joiner, Lana Faye (Bagen)
  Language Art/5th Grade Teacher
Kamman, Sue Ellen
  Second Grade Teacher
Reece, Froncell
  Ag-Science Technology Teacher
Sellars, Cindy Holmes
  Math Teacher
Spell, Ava Bargmann
  Biology I & II Teacher

CONVERSE
Bicklein, Ronald Roy
  Geography/Soviet Stud Teacher
Collins, Karen Kropinicki
  5th Grade Teacher
Gough, Terry Jo
  Spanish Teacher
Keltner, Marc E.
  Mathematics Department Teacher
Miller, Bill Wayne
  Biology Teacher
Price, Douglas
  Science Teacher
Reichenbach, Debra Sue
  Mathematics Teacher

COPPERAS COVE
Canales, Judith Martin
  5th Grade Reading Teacher
Kelly, Rubye M.
  French/Eng Teacher of Gifted
Roy, Angelika A.
  Foreign Language Dept Chair
Taylor, Malcom Gordon
  Science Department Chairman
Turner, Nancy Draper
  Reading Department Chair

CORPUS CHRISTI
Burk, Sandra Wallen
  English Chairperson
Casler, Deanna Vincent
  Chapter I Supervising Teacher
Chegwidden, Dorothy C.
  Honors English IV Teacher
Crowder, James David
  Dept Chairman/Ag Sci Teacher
Evans, Ann Marie
  English Teacher
Garza, Severo
  Asst High School Band Director
Kehoe, Coleen Rice
  6th Grade Science Teacher

Kennard, Frances Lewis
  Third Grade Teacher
Kiolbassa, Elizabeth Rising
  Chem Teacher, Sci Dept Chair
May, Dennis Keith
  Teacher/Coach
Mc Carty, Patricia Lobpries
  High School Math Teacher
Pickett, J. Michael
  Teacher/Soc Stud Chair
Robeau, Sally Garwood
  History Dept Chair
Roberts, Shirley Adams
  Teacher
Tuley, Herschiel D.
  Science Department Chair

CORRIGAN
Reed, Carrel Josey
  English/Journalism Teacher
Seago, Anita Renee
  English Teacher

CORSICANA
Carroll, Eleanor Mosley
  Fifth Grade Elementary Teacher
Cummins, Norma Gries
  6th Grade Study Skills Teacher
Henson, Glenda Gayle
  8th Grade English/Lit Teacher
Isbell, Vivian Ann Bogart
  5th Grade Teacher
Jenkins, Leila Don
  Fourth Grade Teacher
Mc Kinney, Wanda Mewbourn
  2nd Grade Teacher
Parker, Teresa O'Neal
  English Teacher
Shugart, Theresa Lively
  English/Latin Teacher
Tekell, Christie Dianne
  Fifth Grade Teacher
Wilson, Leanna Zay
  Mathematics Teacher

COTULLA
Jones, Elizabeth Schulze
  English Coordinator

CRANE
Beverly, Diana Chubb
  Physical Education Instructor
Hamilton, Mary Elizabeth (Cain)
  Kindergarten Teacher
Roberson, Jody Dodd
  Mathematics Teacher
Taylor, Debra Lea
  English Teacher

CROCKETT
Bear, Janice Gilson
  English IV Teacher

CROSBY
Waihman, Lisa Girard
  Mathematics Teacher

CROSBYTON
Weaver, Madge Yvonne
  4th Grade Teacher

CROSS PLAINS
Barclay, Thomas Adison
  Mathematics Department Chair

CROWLEY
Hull, Helen Lester
  Mathematics/Geometry Teacher
Mc Lean, Sara Cunningham
  World History Teacher
Newberry, Kay Kinne
  Theatre/English Teacher
Perry, David Max
  Gifted & Talented Sci Teacher
Szedeli, Brenda Blair
  Eng Teacher of Gifted/Talented

CRYSTAL CITY
Castillo, George S.
  5th Grade Math/Sci Teacher

CUERO
Colman, Linda Kuester
  Chemistry Teacher
Madden, Joyce Jemelka
  Fifth Grade Teacher

DALHART
Green, Jon J.
  Mathematics Dept Chm/Teacher
Johnson, Randy Scott
  His/Psychology Teacher/Coach
Matthews, Debbie Lynne
  2nd Grade Teacher
Przilas, Catherine Clara (Koch)
  5th & 6th Grade Teacher

DALLAS
Ahne, John Paul
  English Teacher

Anderson, Betty Smith
  Teacher
Baker, A;eme Ingram
  Mathematics Teacher
Ballard, Dana Jean
  Mathematics Teacher/Coach
Barnett, Velda Nickerson
  Public Speaking Teacher
Beal, Willie Roy
  9th-12th Grade US His Teacher
Behrend, Elisabeth Kugel
  7th/8th Grade Soc Stud Teacher
Bender, Leslie Sue
  Counselor
Blomquist, Jean Carlson
  Mathematics Teacher
Bowles, Gayle Eileen Long
  6th Grade Mathematics Teacher
Bozarth, Paul Gene Jr.
  United States History Teacher
Brooks, Mary Kathleen
  US History Teacher
Brown, Alice Bennett
  Second Grade Teacher
Carter, Lana Read
  Sixth Grade Teacher
Castillo, Beatrice
  Third Grade Bilingual Teacher
Cloman, Rita Nell (Lincoln)
  Algebra Teacher
Coleman, Michelle Clay
  Speech/Theatre Arts Teacher
Cook, Frances Lowery
  Mathematics Department Chair
Cooper, Dennis Allen
  7th/8th ESOL/Spanish Teacher
Cowart, Melinda Trice
  ESOL Teacher/Asst Professor
Crawford, Doris Greer
  Teacher of Gifted
Currier, Barbara (Shappard)
  Mathematics Teacher
Da Silva, Geraldine Mary CSFN
  Religion & Fine Art Teacher
Dawson, Dorothy Jean Smith
  5th Grade Teacher
De Boer, Karen L.
  History Teacher
Dietze, Judy Huffhines
  Third Grade Teacher
Diffie, John Edward
  Physics/Physical Sci Teacher
Ennis, Linda Larche
  Mathematics Teacher
Fitzgerald, Davanel
  Second Grade Teacher
Freeman, Lina Lewis
  Special Ed Dept Chair/Teacher
Gammage, Susan Carol
  Science Teacher
Gengelbach, Frances Harding
  Science Teacher
Gilbert, Margaret Mead
  Teacher of Gifted Education
Gilmore-Smith, Evelyn Elizabeth
  Gilmore
  English Teacher
Greimann, Steven Paul
  Math/Religion Teacher
Hamm, Teresa Terrell
  8th Grade English Teacher
Hammert, Marian Dieckman
  Kindergarten Classroom Teacher
Hannon, Elizabeth Jane
  Anatomy & Physiology Teacher
Harbaugh, Lois Jensen
  Science Department Chair
Hauglie, Joseph W.
  ESOL/Foreign Lang Dept Chm
Heard, Felda C.
  9th Grade English Teacher
Henard, John C.
  Social Studies Teacher
Hiemann, Sharon Blanks
  3rd Grade Teacher
Huerta, Juan M.
  Language Arts Teacher
Jacques, Talmadge Molett
  US History Teacher
Jolly, Donna Marie Skipper
  6th Grade Teacher/Chairperson
Jonas, Karen Elaine
  4th-6th Grade Gifted Teacher
Jordan, Nellie L. Howard
  Gifted Education Teacher
Kallus, Frank Theodore
  Science Teacher
Kinney, Elyria Oakley
  Fourth Grade Teacher
Kraus, Colette
  Third Grade Teacher
La Roe, Katherine Van Story
  English Department Chair
Leeman, Peggy Ann Moore
  English Department Chairman

DALLAS (cont)

Leventhal, Sheila Smith
  4th Grade Teacher/Team Leader
Lorentz, Teresa Aldera
  English Teacher
Malone, Camille Shields
  Mathematics Dept Chairperson
Manuel, Lewis Alfred
  Sixth Grade Math Teacher
Mc Call, Janice Lynne
  Speech Teacher
Mc Dermott, Carol Keck
  Math Teacher/Department Chair
Millner, Ruth Raibon
  Middle School Choral Director
Mitchell, A. Maria
  English Teacher
Moore, Cyndia Dunevant
  2nd Grade Teacher
Moore, Odie
  Director
Morrow, Jeffery Dale
  Math Teacher
Nelson, Miriam
  Biology I Teacher
Oakley, Virginia Allbritton
  Fourth Grade Teacher
Parker, Rose Dawn
  Teacher
Peal, Shirley Ann
  Advanced Reading Teacher
Perez, Lindy Willett
  Choir Director/Department Head
Prager, Linda M.
  HS English Teacher
Ramos, Josue
  Spanish Teacher
Reed, Juanita Virginia
  French Teacher
Renner, Cooper Bryan
  9th Grade Librarian
Rogers, Emily Warner
  4th-6th Grade Lead Teacher
Roland, Shirley Bryant
  Special Education Teacher
Rose, Daniel Alan
  Spanish Teacher
Scott, Allen Wayne
  Math/Computer Teacher
Shoemaker, A. T. Jr.
  6th Grade Teacher
Smith, David Paul
  History Teacher
Stribling, Vernell D.
  4th Grade Teacher
Temme, James Joseph
  American History Teacher
Thomas, Barbara Overton
  Fifth Grade Teacher
Thomas, F. Kay (Westbrook)
  Special Ed Teacher
Tucker, Glynn
  Bio Teacher/Sci Dept Chm
Turner, Gail Wheeler
  Second Grade Teacher
Uland, Larry Lee
  Science Teacher
Volk, Elizabeth Ann
  Choral Dir
Walker, Eric Michael
  English Instructor
Walker, George Randy
  Biology Teacher/Coach
Warren, Mary Louise
  Third Grade Teacher
Weaver, Jo Nell (Bryant)
  4th Grade Teacher
Webb, Wonda Gale Johnson
  Math Teacher
Williams, Jomargaret
  Orchestra/Music Teacher
Wilson, Bessie Ball
  Language Arts Department Head
Young, Felecia Dian
  Consumer & Home Ec Teacher
Zanders, Doris De Ville
  Physical Education Teacher
Zoth, Diana Lynn (Smart)
  Math/Cmptr Math Teacher

DANBURY

Jurek, Kenneth J.
  English Department Chairman

DARROUZETT

Robertson, Charmaine (Brown)
  Mathematics/Phys Ed Teacher
Schoenhals, Ruth Faye
  Jr HS Language Art Teacher

DAWSON

Mitcham, Betty Taylor
  Sixth Grade Teacher
Sutcliffe, Harry Franklin
  Social Studies/English Teacher

DAYTON

Thomas, Kerry Don
  U S History Teacher

DE KALB

Benton, Jenna Shavers
  2nd Grade Teacher
Crawford, Wallie M.
  Science Teacher
Germany, James L.
  Teacher

DE LEON

Koonce, Patricia Bagley
  Chapter I Reading Teacher
Lesley, Sharon Knipstein
  Lang Art/Gifted Teacher

DE SOTO

Valdez, Jannay Parkins
  Government Teacher

DEER PARK

Fuchs, Gerald R.
  Science/Social Studies Teacher
Hambrick, Penny Sharp
  Senior English Teacher
Harrison, Linda Guidry
  Language Arts Teacher
Laird, Connie Chrestman
  First Grade Department Chair
Middleton, Jimmy
  Teacher
Neathery, Madelyn Faye (Wilson)
  Fifth Grade Teacher

DEL RIO

Avalos, Irma Elda
  Fifth Grade Teacher
Bailey, Deborah M.
  Science Teacher
Brijalba, Jesse V.
  Freshman Band Director
Gomez, Blanca Lydia
  Elementary School Counselor
Hanson, Edward Allan
  Aerospace Science Instructor
Leyva, Luis E.
  Art Teacher
Meza, Raymond P.
  Principal
Mota, Lydia
  Special Education Teacher
New, Walter
  Honors & AP English Teacher
Torres, Bertha Noyola
  Art Teacher

DENISON

Johnson, Janice Warwick
  5th Grade Teacher
Lakey, Glenda De Vore
  Second Grade Teacher
Wilburn, Avonell Utterback
  Second Grade Teacher
Wilson, Karen Gerdes
  English Teacher

DENTON

Boynton, Madge Boucher
  History Teacher
Brentzel, Marylnn Hopkin
  5th Grade Teacher
Carlton, Betty Blair
  Teacher
Ephraim, Norma Louise
  History Teacher
Grindle, Deborah White
  Counselor
Hartline, Betty Magill
  First Grade Teacher
Jones, Diane Garcia
  5th Grade Teacher
Long, Loreace Hopkins
  World History Teacher
O'Rear, Susan Adams
  Music Teacher
Rektorik-Sprinkle, Patricia Jean
  Latin Teacher
Smith, Keith Elliott
  Math Teacher
Waldo, Nancy (Allen)
  Biology Teacher

DENVER CITY

Milligan, John David
  Biology Teacher
Rahn, Patricia Roberts
  5th Grade Teacher

DEPORT

Davis, Juanita (Rhodes)
  History Teacher
Rhoades, Gail Williams
  Fifth Grade Teacher

DETROIT

Lewis, Colleen Tomlin
  Secondary Bus/English Teacher

DEVINE

Buckles, Guy
  Computer Literacy Teacher
Lorraine, William Vinson
  HS Science Coordinator
Mc Anelly, Linda Burleson
  English Department Chairperson

DIANA

Lancaster, Judy E.
  1st Grade Teacher
Mc Luckie, Gloria Lindsey
  Theatre Teacher

DIMMITT

Cleveland, Libby Leigh
  Teacher/Mathematics Dept Chair

DONNA

Mena, Rosa Natalia
  Third Grade Teacher
Perez, Josie Mendoza
  4th Grade Teacher

DOUGLASS

Killam, George Robert
  History Teacher/Coach
Walters, Billie Spencer
  Fifth Grade Teacher

DRISCOLL

Garcia, Timotea Pruneda
  1st-5th Grade Phys Ed Teacher
Hernandez, Guadalupe R.
  6th-8th Grade Math Teacher

DUBLIN

Stafford, Edwin Charles
  Junior High Science Teacher

DUMAS

Hawkins, Alan Ray
  Texas History Teacher

DUNCANVILLE

Davis, Annette Corder
  English Teacher
Ketron, Carrie Ogden
  Teacher
Mc Hargue, Jackie Rushing
  History Teacher
Meadows, Judith Sandra
  Girls Athletic/Phys Ed Coord
Smith, Marilyn Moffett
  7th/8th Grade Typing Teacher
Thiebaud, Shirley Weaver
  Vocal Music Teacher 6-8

EAGLE PASS

Macias, Herminia
  Counselor
Moses, Lilian
  Mathematics Teacher

EARLY

Bledsoe, Ione Allgood
  Fifth Grade Teacher
Christmas, Lora Pinkerton
  English Teacher

EDCOUCH

Cortez, David
  Mathematics Teacher

EDDY

Beard, Janis Miller
  Second Grade Teacher
Carter, Connie J.
  Third Grade Teacher
Murrey, Mary (Armstrong)
  Jr HS Language Arts Teacher
Whatley, Calvin Arthur
  Retired Teacher/Principal

EDGEWOOD

Cates, Grace Williams
  Fifth Grade Teacher
Edwards, Phillip Wilson
  High School Math Teacher
Shellnutt, Jack G.
  Athletic Director/Teacher

EDINBURG

Aaron, Brenda Colleen
  Coach & Phys Ed Teacher
Alvarado, Lucy Anna Lopez
  8th Grade Counselor Dept Chair
Bonura, Luke Joseph
  English Teacher & Chairman
Christian, Elda Ramos
  Math/Science Teacher
Garza, Alberto Jr.
  Theatre Arts Instructor
Gorena, Anibal
  Physical Science CP Teacher
Hinojosa, Dora
  English Teacher/Dept Chair
Pena, Leocadita
  Fourth Grade Teacher

Perez, Graciela D.
  Junior High Counselor
Prestia, Laurette Riggio
  English Teacher

EL CAMPO

Alexander, Bernice C.
  Second Grade Teacher
Anderson, Patricia A.
  Second Grade Teacher
Parencia, Shirley Marie
  English Teacher/Coach

EL PASO

Acosta, Minerva Corona
  6th Grade Teacher
Bartram, Anne Laux
  Science Teacher
Bobbey, E. Jean
  Learning Center Monitor
Burton, Sharon Smith
  Fifth Grade Teacher
Buss, Robert Allen
  Mathematics Teacher
Cervantes, Gloria Varela
  Eighth Grade Teacher
Chavez, Avelardo Antonio
  Health & Physical Ed Teacher
Cheney, Jonathan Edwin
  Mathematics Teacher
Choate, Carolyn Hannah
  English Teacher
Cramer, Laura Shelley
  Principal
De Lacretaz, Cheryl Diane
  English Teacher
Del Toro, Dolores Travis
  Fifth Grade Teacher
De Santis, James Lee
  History Teacher
Figueroa, Margarita P.
  Physical Education Teacher
Frady, Tonda Murr
  8th Grade US History Teacher
Garcia, Ana M. (Meza)
  7th Grade Math Teacher
Gragg, Diane Garman
  5th Grade G T Teacher
Gresham, Margaret Patterson
  Soc Stud/Psych Teacher
Griffing, Betty V.
  Communications Dept Chair
Helm, Michael W.
  English/Psychology Teacher
Hernandez, Dolores Cadena
  Business Education Teacher
Jaraba, Martha Donaldson
  ESOL Teacher
Jennings, Patricia Sue
  7th/8th Grade Math Teacher
Jones, Kenneth Earl
  Seventh Grade English Teacher
Kvapil, Donna Lee Trujillo
  Business Education Dept Chair
Leiman, Ronald Lee
  Athletic Supervisor
Leiman, Rosemary N.
  Student Activity Director
Licona, Katherine Lupton
  English Teacher
Lowenberg, Georgina Orellana
  Third Grade Teacher
Mc Connell, Lori Anne
  Special Education Teacher
Melanson, Lynda Garrett
  Speech/Debate Coach
Melendez, Mary Alice
  Honors English I Teacher
Mendez, Lorelena
  Eng as Second Lang Teacher
Misenhimer, Linda Spieler
  Student Project Coordinator
Molix, Willie Mae
  Math Teacher & Dept Chair
Panke, Jacqueline L.
  Sixth Grade Teacher
Patty, Sandra Marlin
  Third Grade Teacher
Perales, Arturo
  Mathematics Teacher
Petranto, Lisa Ann
  4th Grade Teacher
Pieplow, Sharon Vise
  Third Grade Teacher
Salquero, Arthur Raymond IV
  Sixth Grade Teacher
Sanchez, Milton
  5th Grade Bilingual Ed Teacher
Serros, Charles
  Math Department Chairperson
Stone, Sandra Louise
  Assistant Principal
Torres, Irene Calderon
  Spanish/Portuguese Teacher
Valdez, Lydia Cardenas
  4th & 5th Grade Teacher

Velez, Esperanza
  Honors Chemistry Teacher
Vigil, Irene Richardson
  Science Teacher
Vogel, Charlene Sue
  Sixth Grade Teacher
Weick, Sue
  Fifth Grade Teacher
Williams, Michael Kevin
  Honors English Teacher

ELKHART

Watkins, Joan Moore
  HS Mathematics Teacher

ENNIS

Clay, Priscilla Bradley
  First Grade Teacher
Cooper, Jack E.
  Science Teacher
Hyde, Harryette Burden
  Language Arts Teacher
Kallus, Sybil Marks
  Retired Fourth Grade Teacher
Lapic, Terry Mark
  Mathematics Teacher
Moore, Bettye Griffis
  Teacher Elem Gifted/Talented
Webb, Andrea Ivie
  Honors English Teacher

EULESS

Hickman, Dorita Dodd
  American History Teacher
Mitchell, Jolette
  Band Director

EUSTACE

Cain, Julia O.
  English Teacher

EVERMAN

Geno, Dorthy Darmer
  Mathematics Teacher/Tutor
Jones, Charles Alan
  US Government/Econ Teacher
Jones, Sharon Gaye
  Spanish & French Teacher
Ritchie, Larry Ross
  Chemistry/Physics Teacher

FAIRFIELD

Robbins, Nancy Taylor
  Teacher of Gifted & Talented

FALFURRIAS

Arredondo, Anna Gloria
  English Teacher
Guerrero, Carlos Esteban
  Math/Cmptr Math Teacher

FALLS CITY

Kotara, Dorothy Moy
  Science Teacher
Wiatrek, Deborah Kotara
  Speech/English Teacher

FARMERSVILLE

Reavis, Lo Etta Bates
  Second Grade Teacher
Toombs, Marion Moore
  Science Teacher
Truemper, Mary Anne Cooke
  Spanish/English Teacher

FERRIS

Perkins, Jack H.
  US History/Soc Stud Teacher

FLORENCE

Bauer, James Francis
  Teacher
Gillespie, Robert Nicholas
  Social Studies/English Teacher

FLORESVILLE

Haverlah, Douglas Gerald
  5th Grade English Teacher

FLOWER MOUND

Callahan, Daniel F.
  Science Teacher

FORT HANCOCK

Whittington, Lona Teresa
  English/Drama Teacher

FORT STOCKTON

Blanco, Linda Sue
  Second Grade Teacher
Davis, Lee Allen
  Math Teacher
Tavarez, Rachel Ramos
  Mathematics Teacher

FORT WORTH

Adams, Leann Cox
  Humanities Teacher
Bone, Donna Pryor
  Science & 5th Grade Teacher

FORT WORTH (cont)
Braudaway, Gary Wayne
  English Teacher
Browning, Sandra Williams
  Sixth Grade Teacher
Burke, Joyce Henderson
  5th Grade Teacher
Buyden, Juanita Easley
  8th Grade Advanced Eng Teacher
Carter, Jessie Anita
  Mathematics Teacher
Corder, Gail Singleton
  French Teacher
Culpepper, Julia Gaye
  Computer Lab Teacher
Eklund, Janelle M.
  English Teacher
Estes, Carolyn Hull
  Fifth Grade Teacher
Foster, Sharon V.
  Science Teacher
Foust, Daniel G.
  Mathematics Department Chair
Freeman, Marcia Dale
  Teacher
Gay, Bobbie Jean Moore
  Kindergarten Teacher
Henning, Kent S.
  Upper School Principal
Hittle, Susan Haesly
  Homemaking Teacher
Housewright, Roy L.
  Texas History Teacher
Howard, Jimmy Bruce
  Science Department Chair
Jackson, Valetta Byrdsong
  1st Grade ESL Teacher
Justice, Laraine Cass
  7th Grade Math Teacher
Kern, Ellen Cornell
  Third Grade Teacher
Lanningham, Karen Kuenstler
  Math Department Chairman
Maddux, Charles E.
  Social Studies Teacher
Marut, Janice Beverley
  5th-8th Grade Language Teacher
Matney, Charles T.
  Band Director
Mc Alister, Kathryn Joyce Freeman
  Chairperson/Reading Department
Michael, Cynthia Kennedy
  11th Grade Soc Stud Teacher
Miller, Walter Robert Jr.
  Ath Director/Math Teacher
Moody, Frank Cozby
  Biology Teacher
Moore, Harriett Powell
  Kindergarten Teacher
Mosley, Clarence Marlon
  Principal
Pekurney, Tuell Ann
  Language Art/Soc Stud Teacher
Powell, Mary
  English Teacher
Rankin, Linda Kay
  7th Grade Life Science Teacher
Reed, Bob
  English Department Chair
Riffee, Billy Jackson
  Math Dept Key Teacher
Selking, Barbara Wharton
  Teacher of Three Year Olds
Shelton, William Allen
  History Department Chairman
Simpson, Jeanne Gillette
  Second Grade Teacher
Sizemore, Lloyd Wayne
  Social Studies Chairperson
Slater, Jack James
  Reading & English Teacher
Spooner, Janice Sue
  Spanish Teacher
Valentine, Peggy Joyce
  Mathematics Teacher
Von Rosenberg, Gary Marcus Jr.
  Science/Math Teacher
Watson, Johnnie Jean (Small)
  Teacher-Medical
Webb, Jean Hefner
  3rd Grade Teacher
Williams, Ingrid Harvey
  English/Journalism Teacher
Wilson, Evelyn Funderhurk
  Honors English Teacher
Younger, Daisianne Davis
  English/French Teacher
Zobal, Julie Miller
  7th Grade Teacher of Eng/Rdng

FRANKSTON
Taylor, Judy Jaggers
  Fourth Grade Teacher

FREDERICKSBURG
Bonn, Terry Walter
  Math Teacher

Brookshire, Don Wayne
  Teacher/Coach
Culver, Barbara Rhea Britton
  4th Grade Teacher
Hannemann, Janalee Ann (Smith)
  1st Grade Develpmnt Teacher
Ohlenburg, Diane Cato
  English Teacher
Smith, Natalie R.
  English Teacher
Treibs, Glen R.
  Texas History Teacher
Wahrmund, Janice Evelyn Klein
  Fourth Grade Teacher
Whitewood, Lois Burns
  English Department Chairperson
Wille, Shelley Vaughn
  HS English/German Teacher

FREEPORT
Bacica, Cristina Garcia
  Mathematics/Chemistry Teacher
Bernzen, John F.
  Band Director
Casey, Beth Baldwin
  Director of Choirs
Kaspar, Kenneth Wayne
  American History Teacher

FREER
Garcia, Arturo
  Mathematics Department Chair
Roberts, Y. Ann
  Pre-Kindergarten Teacher
Uribe-Cano, Gracie
  Fifth Grade Teacher

FRIENDSWOOD
Johnson, Donna Lee
  Kindergarten Teacher
Mayo-Albrecht, Karen
  9th/10th Grade English Teacher
Ray, Darla Dunlap
  Drama Teacher/Director
Roberts, Barbara Blum
  Fifth Grade Teacher
Stone, Donna Christine
  English/Leadership Teacher

FRIONA
Carr, Thomas Bryan
  Industrial Technology Teacher
Richards, Janice
  Mathematics Teacher

FRITCH
Anderson, Sandra Kay
  Mathematics Teacher
Jacobs, Donis L. Heider
  Business Teacher

FRUITVALE
Mc Enturff, Arie Putraie Faulk
  4th Grade Teacher
Nations, Cathy Mills
  Science/Ag Science Teacher

GAIL
Copeland, Beverly Jones
  Kindergarten Teacher

GAINESVILLE
Mc Gahey, Elizabeth Ann Hunt
  Fourth Grade Teacher
Middlebrooks, Diane Solomon
  Principal
Schalk, Joybell Die
  Algebra Teacher
Wilson, Marlene E.
  5th Grade Teacher

GALENA PARK
Gilbreath, Jackie Beaird
  Speech-Drama Teacher
Lauderdale, Riona Sue (Stacy)
  Mathematics Teacher
Price, Johnnie Andrew
  6th-8th Grade Coach
Travis, Patricia Ann (Avington)
  English Teacher

GALVESTON
Badger, Christine Steding
  6th-8th Grade Grammar Teacher
Kirschner, Patricia Gray
  Chemistry Teacher
Merchant, Diane Bowers
  7th Grade Reading Teacher
Pena, Diane Macaluso
  Fifth Grade Teacher
Ward, Gwendolyn Hanna
  Instructor
White, Noemi Lopez
  Mathematics Teacher

GARLAND
Beam, Gay Osburn
  English Teacher
Brackeen, Joan Bryer
  Fifth Grade Teacher

Burks, Carrie Stout
  Sixth Grade Teacher
Cortez, Gerre L.
  History Teacher/Coach
Crouch, Wanda Faye
  Mathematics Teacher
Donnell, Lark Williams
  Math Teacher/Dept Chair
Hallmark, Lawanta M.
  Fifth Grade Teacher
Hammerle, Stephen Helms
  Govt Teacher/Activity Director
Harper, Sherry Edwards
  Language Arts Dept Chair
Hodges, Marcella Valdez
  5th Grade Classroom Teacher
Johnson, Alice Fae
  Vocational Home Ec Teacher
Kerbel, Carol Susan (Lauck)
  Home Ec/Career Invst Teacher
Kirk, Kathleen Annette
  Biology Teacher
Lane, Marcy Dickson
  Mathematics Teacher
Mc Gill, Stan Alan
  Choir Director
Singh, Kabul
  Algebra Teacher
Wickersham, Hubert Elton Jr.
  Social Studies Teacher

GARWOOD
Boenisch, Cynthia Brehm
  First Grade Teacher

GATESVILLE
Powell, Diana Spiva
  Kindergarten Teacher

GEORGETOWN
Read, Jennifer Jones
  ESL/PALS Teacher

GIDDINGS
Rost, Loree Polansky
  6th Grade English Teacher
Smith, Helen Fox
  Fifth Grade Teacher

GILMER
Turner, Jerry Donald
  Science Teacher/Coach

GLADEWATER
Bridges, Rhonda Reynolds
  Mathematics Teacher
Byrd, Tanye Carroll
  8th Grade Math Teacher
Till, Suzanne Weatherall
  4th Grade Teacher

GOLIAD
Hausmann, John W.
  Social Studies Dept Chairman

GONZALES
Marek, Colleen Jones
  Teacher
Saldana, Genaro Alonzo
  Spanish Teacher

GRAHAM
Mullin, Rita Mc Alister
  Fifth Grade Teacher
Slaton, Mary Lois
  Teacher

GRANBURY
Alaha, Nancy Sifford
  Fourth Grade Teacher
Anderson, Brad Scott
  American History Teacher/Coach
Brawner, Lynnell (Fouts)
  First Grade Teacher
Grantham, Sharon
  Language Arts Dept Chair
Kunkel, Marcia Lee
  Fifth Grade Teacher
Mullen, James Elwin
  Head Band Director
Pigg, Cynthia Stroud
  Science Teacher
Reed, L. Ray
  Marketing Education Teacher
Reid, Jana Jones
  English Teacher/Drill Team Dir
Yarborough, Paula Hamilton
  First Grade Teacher

GRAND PRAIRIE
Collins, Ida Lou Berly
  First Grade Teacher
Fisher, Virginia Starr
  Science Teacher/Dept Chair
Heimann, Susan Jan
  Second Grade Teacher
Mattern, Margarette Albarran
  Science Teacher
Rogers, Lynn Willner
  Honors Biology/Psych Teacher

Tidwell, Merlene Presley
  English Department Chairperson
Valenzuela, Victor Hugo
  Sr English Teacher/Yrbk Adv
Walsh, John Allen
  Assistant Principal

GRAND SALINE
Ellis, Mozelle Whiteside
  Soc Stud/Language Arts Teacher
Fisher, Beth Swint
  Kindergarten Teacher
Horton, V. Marie Knight
  7th Grade Language Art Teacher

GRANDFALLS
Brooks, Stephen Marion
  Speech/English Dept Chair

GRAPEVINE
Annis, Angela Barnes
  Computer Science Teacher
Breed, Freda Annette
  Director of Choral Music
Cook, Janice J.
  English Chair/Jr Eng Teacher
Slade, Kenneth Lee
  History Teacher
Swinney, Sarah Elizabeth (Johnson)
  Chapter I Rdng/Math Teacher
Symon, Bill Harold
  Honors Chemistry Teacher/Coach
Tidmore, Linda June Hill
  Counselor
Wilson, Nancy Morris
  Senior English Teacher

GREENVILLE
Baker, Karen Cline
  Chapter 1 Reading Teacher
Davenport, Judith Scott
  Team Leader-Teacher
Gilbert, Patricia Preston
  Principal
Gilstrap, Ila M.
  4th Grade Teacher
Goodson, Jo Brown
  English Teacher
Rice, Melva Powell
  Retired
Rosenbalm, Jan Duran
  Math Teacher
Sanders, Ralph Lee
  Mathematics Department Chair
Tave, Charlie Frank
  Mathematics Team Leader
White, Laurie Ann
  Spanish/Photo/Yearbook Teacher

GROVETON
Dalton, Cary J.
  Director of Bands

GRUVER
Dahl, Brenda Sue
  First Grade Teacher

HALE CENTER
Bizzell, Nancy Robnett
  5th Grade Teacher

HALLETTSVILLE
Hale, Sherry Hoffer
  Third Grade Teacher
Timm, Bettye
  Curriculum Coordinator

HALLSVILLE
Slate, Kay Lasater
  High School English Teacher

HALTOM CITY
Dilks, Edwin Kelvin
  History Teacher/Activity Dir
Loomer, Shari Lynn
  Science/Phys Ed Teacher

HAMILTON
Andrews, Brenda Gail (Stephens)
  Secondary Business Teacher
Krempin, L. Jean Stanley
  Computer/Geometry Teacher

HAMSHIRE
Sachitano, Shelia Louviere
  English/French Teacher

HAPPY
Null, Gail Knox
  Mathematics Teacher

HARKER HEIGHTS
Moore, Deborah Joan
  Third Grade Teacher
Runnels, Peggy Joyce (Roth)
  Basic Skills Math Teacher

HARLETON
White, Brenda Cookson
  Language Arts Teacher

HARLINGEN
Chamberlain, Elva Duran
  English Teacher
Holland, Carolyn Cernosek
  1st Grade Teacher
Jaeger, Bonnie Longmore
  Second Grade Teacher
Metke, Donna Rawlings
  English Teacher
Sluyter, Rebecca L.
  Health Occupations Coordinator
Stirzaker, Thomas Duncan
  Scndry Instrumental Music Inst
Theriot, Jane Harrington
  Teacher of Gifted & Talented

HART
Clinton, Deborah Berry
  Fourth Grade Teacher
Henry, Lanette Allison
  Secondary Business Teacher

HEARNE
Hudson, Mable Margaret Todd
  Third Grade Teacher
Jones, Patricia Linley
  English Teacher/Chair
Judie, Florine Waddleton
  6th Grade Teacher

HEMPHILL
Woods, Greta Gary
  Kindergarten Head Teacher

HENDERSON
Hall, Sally Gale
  6th Grade English Teacher
Haynes, Lillian Fae
  Fourth Grade Teacher
Pyle, Celia Conwell
  Biology Teacher
Robinson, Rosaline Janet
  Teacher

HENRIETTA
Maddox, Mary Harding
  Third Grade Teacher

HEREFORD
Chand, Nisar
  Composite Science Teacher
Gilbreath, Lynn Ann
  Biology Teacher/Coach
Kitchens, Wiley H. (Cuby)
  Retired Teacher
Sparks, Georgia Thompson
  Kindergarten Teacher

HIGGINS
Farris, Sharon Akers
  Langauge Art/Spanish Teacher
Meller, Paula Detrixhe
  Eng/Theatre Arts/Span Teacher

HIGHLAND VILLAGE
Krause, Linda Jones
  Fifth Grade Science Teacher

HIGHLANDS
Garey, Diana Jennings
  First Grade Teacher
Wadley, Barbara Anne Brophy
  8th Grade English Teacher

HILLSBORO
Knox, Lucinda Susan
  Mathematics Teacher

HOLLAND
Kneten, Dorothy Smith
  K-4th Music/4th Grade Teacher

HOLLIDAY
Elliot, Mary Ellen
  Kindergarten Teacher

HONDO
Aelvdet, Denise Spadafore
  Biology Teacher
Cowan, Renean Balke
  Algebra II Teacher
Wolff, Dorothy Weynand
  Home Economics Teacher

HONEY GROVE
Holt, Caryla Shadden
  Kindergarten Teacher
Lochridge, Pamela Ellis
  English/Speech Teacher

HOUSTON
Alexander, Carolyn Mc Clary
  Business Department Chair
Alsup, Linda Sue Patton
  English Teacher
Badeaux, Margaret Mary
  History Dept Chairperson
Barzilla, Sandra Good
  3rd Grade Teacher
Bennett, Frances Troha
  English Teacher

HOUSTON (cont)

Blackmon, Lola Bell
Fourth Grade Teacher
Bradford, Cheryl Rene
Var Sftbl/Soccer Coach/Teacher
Buelow, Judith Salisbury
English Department Chairperson
Burns, Herman Gene
English Teacher
Cain, Donald Wayne
Soc Stud/Public Spkng Teacher
Carrier, Charlotte Wright
Teacher
Clay, Willie Mae Thomas
Science Teacher
Cleveland, Elinor A.
Director of Bands
Clough, John L.
Fourth Grade Teacher
Collier, Sharon Anita (Risinger)
Speech Teacher
Collins, Hortense Davis
Pre-Kindergarten Teacher
Conrey, Patricia Ann
Biology I & II Teacher
Crabb, Virginia Lee Comstock
Business Ed/Voc Dept Chair
Day, Linda Lorraine
English Teacher/Dept Chair
Dean, Sandra Powers
English Teacher/Dept Chair
Dixon, Sharon Lynne
Learning Center Coordinator
Donato, Linda Wells
Eng as Second Lang Teacher
Egalnick, Deborah Shawd
Life Management/Skills Teacher
Elam, Pat Wayne
1st Grade Teacher
Ennis, Rebecca Lee
Teacher-Specialist
Fortune, Eddie Lee
7th Grade Mathematics Teacher
Fussell, Freddie M.
Kindergarten Teacher
Godso, Carol Brown
Mathematics Teacher
Granieri, Liliana L.
Spanish Teacher
Gray, Ira Jean Wafer
8th Grade English Teacher
Hahn, Willie Mc Cray
History Teacher
Hall, Daisy Ruth
Mathematics/Science Teacher
Hall, Jennie Anderson
Teacher
Hardy, Nelwyn A.
Home Economics Teacher
Hargett, Linda Larkan
English Teacher
Harris, Robert D.
Computer Instructor
Holmes, Val G.
Physical Education Teacher
Hruska, Cecilia Anne
First Grade Teacher
Jaehne, Julie Simon
Business/Office Ed Teacher
Janak, Bonnie Lowe
Math Teacher
Johnson, Ivonne M.
1st Grade Bilingual Teacher
Kearns, Michael Patrick
Eng/Photo Journalism Teacher
Kennedy, Roslyne (Dixon)
Mathematics Teacher
Knight, Roy Thomas
ROTC Instructor
Laird, Virginia Orr
Mathematics Teacher
Lanclos, Patsy Felt
Facilitator/Coord Instrl Tech
Le Maire, Elizabeth Griffin
6th-8th Grade Soc Stud Teacher
Lewis, Elaine Thibodeaux
Mathematics Teacher
Llewellyn, Peter Michael
English/Biology Teacher
Lockridge, Darrell Jay
Asst Principal/Algebra Teacher
Mauzy, Harriet Lynn
8th Grade Social Stud Teacher
Maxcy, William Patrick
American History Teacher
Mc Whirter, Patricia Webb
Third Grade Teacher
Meadough, Barbara George
Health/Phys Ed Teacher
Mercado, Lucy
Social Studies Chair/Teacher
Middleton, Carol De Vone
Physical Education Teacher
Mikulencak, Marsha Overton
8th Grade English Teacher

Miller, Kaye Graham
Science Department Chair
Milligan, June Moore
English Teacher
Mills, Mary Ann
Principal
Mills, Melinda Bozett
7th Grade Life Science Teacher
Mills, Milton Alexander
Math & Phys Ed Supervisor
Mitchell, Sarah L.
Biology/Science Teacher
Moore, Edward C.
Computer Literacy Teacher
Moore, Martine
Fifth Grade Teacher
Nanton, Ulmont Claudius
Senior ROTC Instructor
Nichols, Nancy Jo
Science Teacher
Null, Marsha Clary
Phys Ed Teacher/Track Coach
Oldham, Julia Jones
Office Education Coordinator
Oliver, Virginia Dakan
Pre-Kindergarten Teacher
Oswalt, Cheryl Roberts
Study Skills Teacher
Overstreet, Johanna
Assistant Principal
Pahlavan, Gholam H.
Science Department Chair
Perkins, Barbara Ann
12th Grade English Teacher
Petruzzi, Josephine A.
Retired Teacher
Ramsey, Mary Jeter
Mathematics Department Chair
Randle, Ladonia Carolyn
Transition Teacher
Rawson, Teresa A. (Ventura)
Adaptive Physical Ed Teacher
Rhodes, Jimmy Lee
History Teacher
Rowe, Glenda Raymond
Math Teacher
Rucker, Polly Grigg
Asst Principal/Lang Art Coord
Rushing, Shirley Ann
HPER Coach
Ryherd, Ann Collins
Computer/Science Teacher
Sanders, Brenda Graham
Fourth Grade Teacher
Silverthorn, Ernest Kasbaum
Mathematics/Science Teacher
Skweres, Audrey Carol (Ward)
Third Grade Teacher
Spiller, Carol Ann
Earth Science Teacher
Stauffer, Rick Alan
Mathematics/Soc Stud Teacher
Steele, Alice Lee Robberson
Orchestra & Fine Arts Teacher
Taylor, Ceola (Enard)
English Teacher
Taylor, Mildred Nero
Third Grade Teacher
Temperilli, John Robert
Biology Instructor
Thomas, Doris Davenport
Fifth Grade Teacher
Thomas, Gerald E.
American History Teacher
Thomas, Shirley Wesley
Mathematics Teacher
Threet, John Thomas
English Teacher
Villamagna, George
US History Teacher
Ward, Donald Webster
Biology Teacher
Wasson, Danny Alan
United States History Teacher
Weiss, Dolores Hamiter
Fifth Grade Teacher
West, Susan Kapczynski
Math Dept Chair/Admissions Dir
Williams, Gail Suzanne
Language Arts Teacher
Williams, Patrecia Annette Murphy
English Teacher
Willis, Paula Dee
Math Teacher
Wiseman, Mary Jane
Chapter I Teacher
Young, Jean Baker
5th Grade Teacher/ESL
Young, Vivian B. Caviel
Retired 4th Grade Teacher
Zrubek, Marcia Hoevet
Mathematics Teacher

HOWE

Beaty, Tracy Glen
Mathematics, Phys Ed Teacher

Jarma, Donna Marie
English/Spanish Teacher

HUBBARD

Kilgo, Jacquelyn Jarvis
Mathematics Teacher
Raymond, Max Edwin
Science Teacher

HUGHES SPRINGS

Cain, Cathie Jean
Band Director

HUMBLE

Bakke, Jean Black
Language Art Department Chair
Bartlett, Georgia Pasterchick
Language Arts Teacher
Devor, Robert Phillip
Science Teacher
Gardener, Bernetta Harris
English Teacher
Gustafson, Mary Ann Crutchfield
Language Arts Teacher
Jeanes, Lovelyn Tompkins
Science Teacher
Kukis, Gary
Mathematics Instructor
Marshall, Clarice Hairston
Extended Learning Teacher
Masters, Michael Lynn
World History Teacher
Steed, Dena Beth
Band Director

HUNTSVILLE

Eubanks, Susan Sadler
7th Grade Mathematics Teacher
James, Cora Gilford
Mathematics Teacher
Lively, Karen Mc New
2nd Grade Teacher
Marks, Colleen Mc Donald
Second Grade Teacher
Nash, Patricia Kay (Blew)
Mathematics Teacher/Dept Chair
Rohe, Cindy Dorrell
Choir Teacher
Spriggs, Marjetta Ragan
Fifth Grade Teacher

HURST

Brown, S. Ann Dodson
Fourth Grade Teacher
Carriger, Billy Joe
6th Grade Team Coordinator
Hodges, Gene
Biology/Anatomy Teacher

HUTCHINS

Wafer, Clarette S. Thomas
Vocational Education Chair

IMPERIAL

Holladay, Betty Phillips
Kindergarten Teacher

INEZ

Ardoin, Linda Garrison
Elementary Fine Art Teacher
Zacek, Monica Witte
1st Grade Teacher

INGRAM

Sawyer, Carmen Sanchez
Jr HS English Teacher

IRA

Hudgins, Rebecca
Business Teacher

IRVING

Anderegg, Terri L.
English Teacher/Coach
Birdsall, Gina Yvonne
9th Grade English Teacher
Etheredge, Janet Lynn Phillebaum
Third Grade Teacher
Fagan, Sharon Kae
Elementary Counselor
Fields, Carole Beth
8th Grade English Teacher
Garnier, Valerie Barnes
English/Honors English Teacher
Haaser, Robert Joseph
Social Studies Dept Chair
Hahn, Janis Stephens
World History Teacher
Hughs, Nancy Gracey
2nd Grade Teacher
Joslin, Joyce Ann
Fr/Eng as Second Lang Teacher
Kelbly, Norma Kay
Teacher
Kilday, Connie Cardwell
Mathematics Department Chair
Lade, J. W. Don
Counselor
Le Viseur, Virginia Louise
4th Grade Teacher/Chairperson

Montague, Nancy Jeanne
Theatre Director
Sisco, Patty Tingley
English Teacher
Steven, Sharon Sue
4th Grade Teacher
Ussery, Helen Outon
5th Grade Teacher
Vickrey, Peggy Church
English Department Chair
Wilson, Janice (Beal)
Math Teacher

ITALY

Shepard, Jan Price
2nd Grade Teacher
Tipping, William David
Mathematics Teacher

JACKSONVILLE

Folden, Joyce Woodham
Second Grade Gifted/Talented
Garner, Patricia Ann
Life Science Teacher
July, Felicia La Jean (Williams)
6th Grade Soc Stud Teacher
Mc Cown, Margaret Halbert
Retired Science Teacher
Mullican, Gail Brown
Teacher of Gifted & Talented
Sadler, Sheila Hudspeth
First Grade Teacher
Sharp, Pamela Ann (Corbell)
Teacher
Stine, Joyce Taylor
Math Dept Chair/Teacher
Tannert, William E.
Mathematics Teacher
Waller, Phil Ray
US History Teacher

JASPER

Barrington, Vivian Hansen Hancock
5th Grade Teacher

JEFFERSON

Abbott, Lori J. (Adams)
Business Education Teacher
Cerliano, Rebecca Ann
Spanish Teacher
Mauldin, Esther Lowery
7th Grade Mathematics Teacher
Shaw, Anna Elizabeth
Retired Teacher

JEWETT

Wilson, Carol Janeba
Sixth Grade Teacher

JONESBORO

Lightsey, Melva Jane
History/English Teacher
Shaw, Kathie Schraeder
First Grade Teacher

JOSHUA

Crocker, J. W. III
History Teacher

JOURDANTON

Wilson, Paul Wade
Social Science Teacher

KARNACK

Poole, Brenda Fulton
Spanish Teacher

KATY

Beck, Ellen Ruth Baker
Phys Ed Teacher/Coach
Chapman, Margaret Ann
Reading Teacher
Olson, Sandra Brennan
Physics Teacher/Sci Dept Chair
Sillavan, Christina
English Department Chair

KELLER

Coakley, Elizabeth Sutherlin
Special Education Teacher
Outlaw, Nina Stephenson
Science Teacher/Dept Chair
Reneau, Helen Owens
Office Admin Teacher

KENNARD

Loving, Nelda Fay
Second Grade Teacher

KENNEDALE

Barnfield, Rose Rene
US His/Elem Phys Ed Teacher
Ford, Theresa Gilliland
Health/General Bus Teacher
Pratt, Marilyn Keller
Gifted/Talented Teacher
Worley, Ruth
Social Studies Dept Chairman

KERMIT

James, Ruth Anderson
1st Grade Teacher
Stooksberry, Barbara Ann
Earth Science Teacher
Truelove, Tony Lee
Mathematics Teacher

KERRVILLE

Homilius, Louise Ann
Third Grade Teacher
Rushing, Laura Ellis
6th Grade Reading Teacher
Syers, Martha Katherine
Mathematics Teacher
Thompson, Jeanne A.
Mathematics Dept Chair

KILGORE

Baggett, Gloria Wix
US History Teacher
Fowler, Betty L. (Olney)
Home Economic Teacher
Gunn, Karlene Edmonds
First Grade Teacher
Mc Comic, John Alvis
American History Teacher
Melton, Martha Lawrence
Fifth Grade Teacher
Newsome, Ann L.
7th Grade TX History Teacher
Phipps, Patsy Eubanks
English Teacher
Pickett, Jo Brock
7th Grade Math Teacher
Sartor, Linda Nixon
Mathematics Teacher
Waller, Anne Bonds
5th Grade Teacher

KILLEEN

Armistead, Patricia Pettijohn
2nd Grade Teacher
Cunningham, Gina Marlene Strickland
7th/8th Grade TAG/Sci Teacher
Donahue, Sheila Edmonds
Elementary Music Teacher
Haigler, Rhonda Sue
Computer Teacher
Heron, Julie Anne
Spanish Teacher
Mc Kelvain, Tricia M.
Counselor
Mc Pherson, Katharyn Ann (Ross)
5th Grade Teacher
Midkiff, Richard Norman
Mathematics Department Teacher
Szeman, Edward Robert
Music Teacher

KINGSVILLE

Figueroa, Edna
Biology Teacher
Wright, Damon H.
Religion Teacher

KINGWOOD

Arnold, Nancy Creel
Mathematics Teacher
Maddox, Phyllis Mc Guill
Assistant Elementary Principal
Shepeard, Anna Palm
Texas History Teacher
Tracy, Janet Woodyard
Health Teacher/Dept Head

KIRBYVILLE

Brewster, Jerry Hilton
8th Grade Amer His Teacher

KLEIN

Grenfell, Mary Roberta Jarboe
Debate Coach
Raddin, Phillip Thomas
Director of Choirs

KYLE

Witte, Eula Ann
Kindergarten Teacher

LA MARQUE

Evans, Zora A. Outlaw
Retired 2nd-3rd Grade Teacher
Nelson, Jeanne Samuelson
5-6 Lang Arts/Soc Stud Teacher
Weddell, Alan
Athletic Director/Head Coach

LA PORTE

Kramer, Susie
Physical Education Coach

LA PRYOR

Hall, Sherry Davenport
Science Teacher
Salazar, Irma Teran
7th-12th Grade Counselor

LAMESA

Norman, Rick W.
  Earth Science Teacher
Vann, Melody Hicks
  Home Economics Instructor

LAMPASAS

Klose, Janice Kaye
  Fourth Grade Teacher
Knudson, Johnette Walker
  2nd Grade Teacher
Tompkins, Sandra Orr
  Elementary Art Teacher

LANCASTER

Brundage, Patsy O'Rear
  Cosmetology Teacher
Kersh, Tanya Jones
  Reading Teacher, Chair & Coord

LAREDO

Barrera, Sylvia Laura
  Phys Ed/Psychology Teacher
Batey, Andrea Cobos
  Reading Specialist
Carrillo, Rene L.
  French Teacher
Castaneda, Armando
  Fifth Grade Teacher/Chair
Coronado, Juanita Margarita
  Assistant Principal
Davila, Yolanda C.
  8th Grade English Teacher
Dominguez, Diana Gonzalez
  2nd Grade Head Teacher
Howard, Lupita Salazar
  Mathematics Department Chair
Jasso, Angela Cardenas
  Office Education Teacher
Jimenez, Felipe De Jesus Jr.
  English Teacher
Juarez, Pamela Rodriguez
  Science Teacher
Lopez, Herminia Vela
  Mathematics Teacher
Macomber, Kathy Davis
  Sixth Grade Teacher
Martinez, Felipe Vichareli
  English Teacher
Mc Dowell, Emily
  Choir Director
Montemayor, Elia Irene (Palos)
  Computer Literacy Teacher
Montemayor, Juan Jesus
  English Teacher
Pena, Cristina Gutierrez
  US/World History Teacher
Pena, Lina Villarreal
  Teacher
Perez, Ma Eugenia Santos
  Math Teacher
Ramirez, Amelda S.
  4th Grade Elementary Teacher
Tinajero, Sara Garcia
  English Dept Chair

LEAGUE CITY

Alexander, Sandra (Bingham)
  4th Grade Teacher
Campbell, Linda Rudolph
  English Teacher
Garza, Robert
  Mathematics Teacher
Johnson, Patricia Felkins
  Music Specialist
Senftleber, Jana Lynne
  French Teacher
Shannon, Michial Scott
  6th Grade Teacher
Stengler, Fay M.
  Language Arts Dept Chair
Willis, Edward William
  Science Department Chairman

LEANDER

Malone, Georgia Risner
  Bus Office Services Teacher
Roberts, Steven Paul
  6th Grade Soc Stud/Sci Teacher

LEFORS

Phillips, Pauline Allen
  English Teacher

LEGGETT

Jones, Vicki Galloway
  English Teacher

LEVELLAND

Lawson, Dick
  Third Grade Teacher
Leaf, Buster Carl
  Athletic Director
Tubb, Pat Bridges
  Special Education Supervisor

LEWISVILLE

Crivello, Michael Anthony
  AP English Teacher

Domer, James Allen
  Physical Education Teacher

LIBERTY

Chandler, Cynthia Sue (Cox)
  Theater/English Teacher

LINDALE

Black, Lynne Hartman
  7th Grade Mathematics Teacher
Stanley, Retha Thompson
  K-8th Grade Librarian

LINDEN

Roberts, Hattie Wetuski
  4th Grade Mathematics Teacher
Stewart, Gayle Washington
  Mathematics/Computer Teacher

LITTLE RIVER

Henson, Rhonda Harden
  Mathematics Teacher

LIVINGSTON

Burk, Paula Dickens
  Mathematics Department Chair
Wiegreffe, Tyba Gilliland
  Fifth Grade Teacher

LLANO

Ashley, Janeane Raesener
  English Teacher
Stovall, Robert Daniel Jr.
  US History Teacher
Thornton, Sidonie Simpson
  Chapter I Reading Teacher

LOCKHART

Cranford, Aaron Reese
  Earth/Life Sci Teacher/Coach
Ortiz, Mary Helen Castillo
  5th/6th Grade Phys Ed Teacher
Stedman, Mark A.
  Science Department Chair

LOCKNEY

Aufill, La Dora Ayres
  Mathematics/Computer Teacher

LOLITA

Hajek, William Anton
  Science/Computer Teacher
Mc Bryde, Mary Alice
  Mathematics Teacher/Coach
Stone, Peggy R.
  Gifted/Talented Coord

LONGVIEW

Bardwell, Suzanne Brown
  Social Studies Teacher
Beaty, Mary S. Belew
  Librarian
Dade, Vickey Gale
  Third Grade Teacher
Fetter, Sandra June (Kelble)
  Teacher & Coach
Maxey, Veronica Ann
  Third Grade Teacher
Pierce, Glen De Wayne
  Computer Science Teacher
Romines, Elizabeth Courtney
  Language Arts Teacher
Tucker, Alaine L.
  Dance Teacher
Wheeley, Bobby E.
  Middle/Upper School Admin

LORENA

Bischoff, Janet Buckner
  4th Grade Teacher
Blanchard, Gregory Allen
  Health Teacher/Coach
Penoli, Carol Harwell
  Band Director

LUBBOCK

Arnold, James Carl
  7th/8th Social Studies Teacher
Bloxom, Gayla Coffey
  3rd Grade Teacher
Brumley, Connie Sue
  Resource Teacher
Cates, Patrick
  English Department Chair
Covington, Carol Crews
  Mid Sch Admin/English Teacher
Crum, Jo Ann Cook
  Sixth Grade Teacher
Davis, Peggy Ruth
  Physical Education Teacher
Dunn, Joanna Starnes
  6th Grade Teacher
Garrett, Larry Eugene
  Band/Orchestra Director
German, James David
  Mathematics Teacher
Haynes, Sheri Lee
  Basketball Coach
Hutchens, Mike
  8th Grade English Teacher

Jackson, Debbie Hoffman
  Third Grade Teacher
Kramer, Lisa Brewer
  Science Teacher
Langdon, Wilma Joy
  Biology Teacher/Vlybl Coach
Locke, Jon David
  Director of Bands
Norman, Judy Carol
  7th-9th P E/9th Grade Coach
Parks, Julie Durbin
  Math Teacher
Poffenbarger, Judith Watkins
  English Teacher
Rhodes, Vikki Cheryl
  Latin Teacher/Act Dir
Richards, Virginia Fry
  Home Economics Teacher
Romero, Charlotte Marie (Aguilar)
  Counselor
Satterwhite, Diana Mc Clead
  History Teacher/Tennis Coach
Smith, Betty Hamilton
  5th Grade Teacher
Tabor, Debby Lynn
  History/Geography Teacher
Thompson, Ann Phillips
  Mathematics Dept Chairperson
Villalobos, Berta De Los Santos
  English Teacher
Wright, Ginger Connelley
  Physical Education Teacher

LUFKIN

Cloonan, Lisa Breazeale
  Third Grade Teacher
Haas, Sally Marie
  HS Mathematics Teacher
Harris, Patricia Pondant
  English/Speech/Lang Teacher
Mc Adams, June Allen
  Physical Science Teacher
Robinson, Bonnie Lenderman
  Fourth Grade Teacher
Ross, Thelma Williams
  Remedial Reading Teacher

LUMBERTON

Hartt, Jo Herrington
  Language Arts Teacher
Mc Cown, Joan M.
  Fifth Grade Teacher
Roberts, Patti Palmer
  Mathematics Teacher
Terry, Joycelyn Harris
  English II Teacher

LYFORD

Gorena, Jaime
  Earth Science Teacher

MABANK

Geddie, Judy Wallace
  Fourth Grade Teacher

MANOR

Sandoval, Nancy Wilson
  Spanish/ESL Teacher

MANSFIELD

Butler, Cathy Louise Brown
  Honors Science Teacher
Craig, Jennifer Mann
  11th Grade English Teacher
Gibbs, Trina Cramer
  8th Grade Amer His Teacher

MARFA

Rojo, Viola
  First Grade Teacher

MARION

Bielke, Mariann Jeanette Ohnheiser
  Homemaking Teacher
Machalec, Paul G.
  Biology Teacher

MARSHALL

Cox, Jon L.
  US History Teacher
Edwards, Theresa Tucker
  Educational Diagnostician
Farcas, Claudette Dusseault
  Spanish Teacher
Garcia, Robot Charles
  Earth Science Teacher
Hanes, Larry F.
  Mathematics Teacher
Jones, Annie Walton
  Business Education Instructor
Morris, Ruth F.
  Teacher

MART

Sawyers, Lynn Lewis
  3rd Grade Teacher

MASON

Schmidt, Mary Kothmann
  Science Teacher

Underwood, Glendene Kalerner
  5th/6th Grade English Teacher
Young, Barbara Henson
  7th-8th Grade English Teacher

MATHIS

Briscoe, Allene Vickers
  English/Speech Teacher

MAYPEARL

Blake, Beverly A.
  Teacher-Librarian
Restivo, Evelyn Darlene Brandt
  Science Teacher

MC ALLEN

Arellano, Oralia R.
  Science Teacher & Dept Chm
Castillo, Israel
  Health & PE Teacher
De Leon, Maria Elva Perez
  3rd Grade Teacher
Gindler, Paulette S.
  German Teacher
Kowalski, Nellie Lamas
  English Teacher
Kutch, Falma Anne
  Third Grade Teacher
Larson, Kathleen Karst
  Teacher of Gifted & Talented
Mills, Cynthia Alpers
  Math Department Teacher
Moss, Gloria Salinas
  7th/8th Grade Science Teacher
Soto, Joyce Ann
  Physical Education Teacher
Stone, Ellen Weaver
  Soc Stud Dept Chairperson
Zenz, Cornelia Risatti
  Lang Art Teacher/Dept Chair

MC CAMEY

Witcher, James Douglas
  Science Teacher

MC KINNEY

Swann, Karen Jones
  Dance/Drill Team Director

MEDINA

Chrisman, Wesley Steven
  Science Teacher/Coach

MERIT

Patterson, Paul Sebron
  English Teacher

MESQUITE

Allen, Ada Kay
  Business Teacher
Banks, Jon M.
  Science Department Chairman
Cross, Jo Ann Mathews
  Mathematics Department Chair
De Lamar, Mickey
  Head Coach/Government Teacher
Edwards, Glenda Vaughan
  English Teacher
Fergason, Nancy Snipes
  Teacher of 5th Grade Gifted
Grigsby, Julie (Buist)
  Head Math Dept/Math Teacher
Hagar, Lynne Marie
  English/History Teacher
Kirkindoll, Betty Fennel
  Fifth Grade Teacher
Lipsett, Wynona Wieting
  Choral Director
Lumpkin, Beverly Wright
  7th Grade Mathematics Teacher
Mayfield, Valarie Jean Ramsey
  Pre-Kindergarten Teacher
Maynard, Cathy Pike
  French/English Teacher
Middleton, Wanda Brewster
  Language Arts/Speech Teacher
Miller, Carolyn Jones
  6th Grade Teacher
Mohlman, Dean Gerald
  Life Science Teacher
Pruitt, James Donald Jr.
  Biology Teacher/Football Coach
Sanders, Beverly Ruth
  Language Arts Chair

MEXIA

Danner, Alice Mae
  Attendance Clerk/Secretary
Phillips, Mary Miller
  Retired First Grade Teacher
Plummer, Helen Holbrook
  American History Teacher
Rash, Deborah Jolly
  Spanish Teacher
Sims, Sheila M.
  Science Teacher/Sci Dept Chair
Stone, Bernadette Barkouskie
  English I Teacher

MIDLAND

Aldridge, Lauren Ham
  7th Grade Teacher
Armstead, Tressa Maddux
  English Teacher
Awtry, Gordon William
  Social Studies Teacher
Coombes, George William
  History Department Chairman
Dean, Buena Kay
  Instructional Consultant
Dulin, Joyce Wommack
  6th Grade Teacher
Evans, Una Merle
  Second Grade Teacher
Fitts, Milton Thomas
  Teacher Social Studies/Coach
Givhan, Rebecca Joyce (Curnutt)
  Office Ed Teacher
Huckabay, Paula
  English Teacher
Kinder, Mary Kathleen
  Reading Teacher

MIDLOTHIAN

Arnold, Cornelius Matthew
  Retired
Coleman, Jean Cherry
  Second Grade Teacher
Mar, Nancy
  High School Science Teacher
Rollins, Marilyn Thompson
  Math/Accounting Teacher
Thompson, Linda Bean
  English Teacher

MINERAL WELLS

Bilides, Linda Wheeler
  6th Grade Language Art Teacher
Ford, Joyce Eaves
  Honors Eng/Eng II Teacher
Fulkersin, Lorraine Fern (Alford)
  ESL Teacher & GT Span Teacher

MISSION

Alaniz, Adelina Bazan
  Mathematics Department Chair
Blair, Mary Helen Pickering
  Retired Teacher
Legge, Sharon Ann
  Fourth Grade Teacher
Sarinana, Cecilia
  5th Grade Teacher

MISSOURI CITY

Yaffie, David Scott
  Science/History Teacher

MONAHANS

Coffman, Ronna Large
  English/Journalism Teacher
Grant, Linda Wein
  Eng/Psych/Sociology Teacher
Greenfield, Vicki Richmond
  Fourth Grade Teacher
Hanna, Larry Joe
  Biology Teacher
Heuman, Jana Sullivan
  Office Education Teacher
Jones, Evelyn Rojean
  English Teacher/Dir of Theatre
Kidd, Lois Ellis
  Language Teacher
Linton, Lynda Heck
  Business Education Teacher

MONTGOMERY

Cahoon, Sandra Giesinger
  4th/5th Grade Math Teacher
Webster, Candace Lynn
  Pre-Kindergarten Teacher

MOODY

Belobrajdic, Patrice M.
  English Teacher
Cornforth, Ullah Delle
  Third Grade Teacher
Moffatt, G. Carrol
  Band Director
Stephens, William Avera Jr.
  HS Math/Cmptrs/Physics Teacher

MOULTON

Joiner, Caroline B.
  Social Studies Teacher

MOUNT PLEASANT

Sinclair, Micky Mercer
  Fifth Grade Teacher

MULESHOE

Costen, Joyeline Stearns
  4th Grade Teacher
Prather, Norma Jo
  Kindergarten Teacher
Turnbow, Shelly Dunham
  6th Grade Soc Stud Teacher
Watson, Patricia Morgan
  English Teacher

MUNDAY
Longan, Karen Crawford
Spanish/Theatre Arts Teacher

N RICHLAND HILLS
Coker, Onita Cobb
3rd Grade Teacher

NAVASOTA
Dacus, Julie
Computer Literacy/Math Teacher
Dorsey, Loraine
English Teacher
Rice, Susan Rowland
Business/Science Teacher
Woehler, Carol Anne (Nachtrab)
Fourth Grade Teacher

NEDERLAND
Dial, Carrol Wayne
Principal
Evans, Patricia Mahfouz
Fourth Grade Teacher
Reynolds, Helen Pate
English Teacher
Ross, Don L.
English Teacher
Trevey, Marilyn S.
8th Grade Eng/Rdng Teacher

NEEDVILLE
Virdell, Diana Wilde
Math Teacher

NEW BRAUNFELS
Baker, Patricia Ann
2nd Grade Teacher
Dry, Mary Jo Eilers
Honors & AP English Teacher
Dunn, Charlotte Lund
5th Grade Teacher
Engler, Gail P. (Weyel)
Mathematics Teacher
Odell, Wesley W.
Ag Science Teacher/Voc Dir
Poeck, Gary Ovid
Mathematics Teacher

NEW CANEY
Stout, Joanna Wheat
Art Teacher/Historian
Thompson, Marvin Russell
Theatre Arts Teacher

NEW DEAL
Tyson, Ronald Lynn
Science Instructor

NEW LONDON
Bradshaw, Jean Rayford
3rd Grade Teacher
Morrison, Michael G.
Athletic Director/Teacher

NIXON
Harvey, Linda Cook
Kindergarten Teacher
Schmoekel, Jerry Lee
Science Teacher

NOCONA
Coats, Russell Carl
Business Teacher & Coach
Gee, Glenda Miller
Mathematics Teacher
Haralson, Laura Jordan
Science Dept Chair/Teacher

OAKWOOD
Handsborough, Doris Jean
Teacher

ODEM
Butler, Deborah Fox
Teacher of Gifted/Talented

ODESSA
Barlau, Bess L.
8th/9th Grade Teacher
Baucom, Gregory Lee
US History Teacher
Bernhard, Paula Jordan
Teacher of Gifted & Talented
Birkhead, Reta Burnett
Third Grade Teacher
Briones, Paul Olivas
Biology Teacher
Brown, Beverly Snell
Choral Director
Collins, Gwen Williams
Fourth Grade Teacher
Cortez, Esperanza Hope
Elementary Counselor
Flores, Herminia Santiago
Spanish Teacher
Hargis, Debbie Price
U S History Teacher
Hartmann, Mara Zarins
Mathematics Teacher

Merkel, Elizabeth
First Grade Teacher
Nail, Charles E.
Supervisor of Music
Ragan, Arlyne Stokes
Mathematics Teacher
Ramsey, Carol J. (Ward)
Mathematics Teacher
Reed, Freda E.
English Teacher
Sadler, Sherard Michael
8th Grade History Teacher
Thompson, Milton Blair III
Biology Teacher/Coach
Weaver, La Donna Lewis
Biology/AP Teacher

OLNEY
Talbott, Virblene Foster
Third Grade Teacher

OLTON
Fewell, Becky J.
Mathematics Department Chair
Long, Helen Lucy Maruca
1st Grade Teacher
Nafzger, Georgana
2nd Grade Teacher

ORANGE GROVE
Torres, Elma De Santos
Gifted/Talented Teacher

ORE CITY
Butler, Johnnie Huel
Principal
Dossey, Joyce Walters
Resource Teacher
Handy, Raeann Ashley
Kindergarten Teacher

PADUCAH
Muston, Betty Ruth Atkins
Third Grade Teacher
Trent, Jane Wilson
English/Journalism Teacher
Trent, Kenneth Eugene
Mathematics Teacher
Truelock, Vicky Crupper
4th Grade Teacher

PAINT ROCK
Glasscock, Selma Nelle
Sci Dept Chairperson/Teacher
Phinney, Patsy E.
English/History Teacher

PALACIOS
Green, Cheryl Green
Secondary Choral Director
Joyce, Darlene R.
English Teacher/Dept Chair

PALESTINE
Asberry, Almeda V. Joiner
5th Grade Teacher
Beene, Virgil David
Director of Instrumental Music
Johnston, Arnold Wayne
Mathematics Dept Chair/Teacher
Liles, Kandi Kay
English & Art Teacher
Rhodes, William Don
Science Department Chair
Stroud, Kay Humphrey
Biology Teacher

PALMER
Bonner, Ida May (Spencer)
Fourth Grade Teacher

PAMPA
Case, Mary Lynn Stephens
English Teacher
Collins, Bruce Dwain
Band Director
Colwell, Carol Ann
Biology Teacher
Diller, Marcella M.
Teacher of Gifted/Talented/Eng
Gandy, Mary Drew
History Teacher
Jett, Sharon Adams
6th Grade History Teacher
Johnson, Charles
Band Director
Mc Anelly, Elizabeth Ann Bowyer
Bio Teacher/Chm Science Dept
Prock, Jo Ashworth
Math Teacher
Velez, Vickey
1st Grade Teacher

PANHANDLE
Bonner, Patsy Stone
4th Grade Teacher

PARIS
Anthony, Wanda Foster
Science Teacher

Davis, Clyde Newton
Earth Sciences Teacher
Oats, Mae Ellen
Fifth Grade Teacher
Smith, Kimberly Walker
Jr High Science Teacher

PASADENA
Cherry, Sharon Hallmark
6th Grade Lang Art Teacher
Christopherson, Steven Douglas
Math Teacher
Corbett, Joan Riddle
3rd Grade Teacher G/T
Crawford, Rebecca Ann
Consumer/Homemaking Dept Chair
Delaney, David Allan
Choir Director
Eubanks, Patricia Gale
6th Grade Art/Soc Stud Teacher
Freeland, Phyllis Letbetter
Computer Teacher
Gwin, Mary Jane Barnes
6th-8th Grade Eng Teacher
Johnson, Jimmie Young
4th Grade Teacher
Keeling, Wanda Ensey
Kindergarten Teacher
Klinar, Ann Elizabeth
Fifth Grade Teacher
Ligget, Noemi Castillo
American History Teacher
Padgett, Christine Montgomery
6th Grade Reading Teacher
Pitts, Larry Guinn
Assistant Band Director
Shannon, Steve O.
Teacher
Taylor, Trudy Ellen
Third Grade Teacher
Tumberlinson, Arlene R.
Fourth Grade Teacher

PEARLAND
Ellis, Barbara Huseman
Language/Reading Teacher
Robinson, Faye Johnson
2nd Grade Teacher/Grade Leader

PEASTER
Cockrell, Lisa Boone
English/His/Theater Teacher

PECOS
Mc Donald, Cora Edna (Poe)
8th Grade Sci Teacher/Dept Chm
Moore, Bennie Doris Teague
6th Grade Lang Art Teacher

PETTUS
Rabe, Richard Wayne
Agriculture Science Teacher

PFLUGERVILLE
Artz, Susan Whaley
English Teacher
Muery, Judy Orr
4th Grade Teacher
Peterson, Carol Curtis
Health Dept Chair & Teacher

PHARR
Resendez, Margaret Thelma
6th Grade Teacher
Santiago, Marie Gonzalez
High School Geology Teacher
Wood, Wilford Robert
Science Teacher

PILOT POINT
Church, Kellye Needles
Spanish Teacher
Murphy, Sharon Marr
Office Education Teacher
Pedigo, Pamela Jo
Fourth Grade Teacher
Whitley, Harriet Coker
Mathematics Teacher

PINELAND
Welch, Elizabeth Brown
4th Grade Teacher

PITTSBURG
Matthews, Anita Sue
Business Teacher
Robinson, Earlean Williams
Third Grade Teacher

PLAINVIEW
Bilbruck, Ann R. (Hamilton)
K/1st Benchmarks Teacher
Cross, Phyllis Ann (Garvin)
Mathematics Teacher
Green, Ruth Rlee Blythe-Mc Kinzie
Retired Fifth Grade Teacher
Job, Valerie Y'Llise
Spanish Teacher
Johnson, Patricia Turner
Social Studies Teacher

Manning, Paulette Cunningham
Mathematics Teacher
Mc Cormick, Joyce Worcester
Third Grade Teacher
Ross, Carolyn Henson
8th Grade Mathematics Teacher
Taylor, Becky Lawson
Government Teacher
Williams, Sandra Jane Brown
Social Studies Dept Head

PLANO
Bickle, Denise Smith
Fifth Grade Teacher
Brown, Rebecca Rector
Teacher of Gifted & Talented
Butler, Julia Brown
Sixth Grade Teacher
Engelbrecht, Lynn Moser
5th Grade Teacher/Team Leader
English, Charlotte Patrice (Strong)
Interpretation & Debate Coach
Gafford, Lynn (Roberts)
English Teacher
Gatzlaff, Caryl Stephenson
English Teacher
Harrison, Nadine Gillispie
Math Dept Chairperson-Teacher
Hassack, Judy Carol (Stevenson)
Office Education Teacher/Coord
Heiting, Joan Katherine (Jelinski)
Elementary Principal
Kariak, Judy M.
8th Grade Earth Sci Teacher
Kolb, Sheila S.
Physics Teacher
Ladis, Deborah J.
Speech Teacher/Debate Coach
Landman, Sheri Waters
English Department Chairperson
Navarre, Rick Lynn
Resource Teacher of Gifted
Rislov, George Ray
History Teacher
Robinson, James Wade
History Dept Chairman
Spencer, Sheila Frances (Walsh)
Dean of Students
Stiles, Nancy Jo Tennant
Fifth Grade Teacher
Thomas, James Lawrence III
English Teacher/Coach
Wussow, Rebeca Rousso
Biology Teacher/Dept Chair
Young, Frances Jeane Tatum
Business Department Chairman

PLEASANTON
Brown, Denice Johnston
English Teacher
Greene, Anna Holmes
Mathematics Teacher

POLLOK
Vann, Beverley Gay
7th Grade English Teacher

PORT ACRES
Beckham, Opal Carr
Fifth Grade Teacher
Cantu, Anna Maria
Middle School Lang Arts Supvr
Comeaux, Loyce Williams
English Department Chair
Hardy, Jena D.
Reading Teacher
Powers, Mary Ellen
5th Grade Teacher

PORT ARTHUR
Dozier-Bryant, Sharon Diane
Home Economics Teacher
Gaspard, Regina Bruno
Math/Computer Literacy Teacher
Henry, Billie Douglass
Home Ec Teacher-Coordinator
Knowles, Danny Lee
Life/Earth Science Teacher
Nelson, Richard Alan
Health Teacher/Athletic Trng
Sewell, Carolyn Hughes
Mathematics Teacher
Smith, Jayne Ruth
English Teacher
Washington, Michael James
Biology I Teacher

PORT LAVACA
Leadbetter, Lola M.
Fifth Grade Teacher

PORT NECHES
Bryant, Debbie L.
2nd Grade Teacher
Fitzgerald, Stephen M.
HS Mathematics Teacher

PORTLAND
Martinez, Alma Lydia
8th Grade Mathematics Teacher

POTEET
Cisnero, Betty Trevino
English Teacher

POTTSBORO
Whitehead, Norma Lea Luper
Fourth Grade Teacher

PRESIDIO
Hernandez, Irene Pineda
Jr High Language Art Teacher
Lymas, Ralph E.
History Teacher/Coach
Tavarez, Justina C.
2nd Grade Bilingual Teacher

PRIDDY
Barr, Karen Bryant
Resource/Bus/Phys Ed Teacher

PRINCETON
Banschbach, Thomas B.
Mathematics Department Chair
Chapman, La Vada Joan
Texas History Teacher
Kern, Stephanie Perry
Computer Science Teacher
Marquart, Mitzi Lynn
Mathematics Teacher
Talley, Dianne Bates
Third Grade Teacher
Washerlesky, Janet Johnson
Lead Teacher

PROGRESO
Dombi, Kathleen Kay
3rd-5th Grade Teacher
Ramirez, Gerardo
First Grade Teacher
Willingham, Reyna A.
Business Education Teacher

PROSPER
Barker, Michael Ray
Spanish/English Teacher

QUANAH
Mahoney, Sylvia Gann
English Teacher

QUINLAN
Divinia, Ethel Ann
Assistant Principal

QUITMAN
Butler, Mary Alice (Blackwell)
English Teacher
Johnson, Tomie L.
Business Teacher

RANKIN
Head, Deral Dean
Mathematics Teacher

RAYMONDVILLE
Carmichael, Kelly Daniel
Science Department Chairman

RED OAK
Cheshier, Carolyn Hancock
English Department Chair
Etter, Julie Marleen (Neie)
Mathematics Teacher
Morton, Charles Bradley III
Mathematics Department Chair

REDWATER
Clark, Jackie Cope
English Teacher
Markham, Lynn Kennedy
Third Grade Teacher
Scales, Linda Kay
4th Grade Teacher

RICE
Place, Rose Ella (Mc Coy)
6-8th Grade Lang Arts Teacher

RICHARDSON
Baily, Beth Filgo
Home Economics Teacher
Baker, Katherine June (Sherrill)
4th Grade Teacher
Besco, Janis Fennell
Calculus Teacher
Burton, Wilgus Jr.
Mathematics/Physics Dept Chm
Clay, Samantha Williams
12th Grade English Teacher
Cook, Nancy Stepan
Spanish Teacher
Findley, Kathryn Marlar
Math Teacher
George, Linda Burke
Math Department Chairperson
Greenwood, Yvonne Earl Boone
Business Dept Chairperson

RICHARDSON (cont)
Harp, Rose Marie
  Lead Government Teacher
Jackson, Donald Ray
  Physics/Mathematics Teacher
Johnston, Jeri Boulware
  Speech Department Chairperson
Lovett, Lois Elaine
  Second Grade Teacher
Mahan, Budd Powell
  Science Teacher
Manning, Deborah Lynn
  English Teacher
Mc Clendon, Lynn Price
  English Teacher
Morgan, Katherine Williams
  4th Grade Teacher/Chair
Ray, Michael Hoyal
  Mathematics Teacher
Seat, Marlene Staton
  9th Grade Mathematics Teacher
Taylor, Robin Darr
  Child Care/Guidance Teacher

RICHLAND SPRINGS
Smith, Melanie Maxted
  8-12 English/Theatre Teacher
Wood, Cynthia Mutz
  1st Grade Teacher

RICHMOND
Daniels, Helen Hicks
  Language Arts Teacher

ROBERT LEE
Ballew, Patricia Ann
  Jr HS Language Arts Teacher
Mauldin, Melba Rives
  Sixth Grade Teacher
Wright, Dorothea Helen
  Science Teacher

ROCKDALE
Hargrove, Barbara Ann
  Mathematics Teacher

ROCKWALL
Greenwalt, Joy Bounds
  7th Grade Language Art Teacher
Holland, Jan Ives
  Biology Teacher
Hyde, Constance Deane Crimmings
  English Instructor
Lamb, Patsy Hopkins
  Fourth Grade Teacher
Lewis, Patricia Money
  Mathematics Teacher
Rakow, Ursula H.
  Science Department Head
Sandknop, Jane K.
  9th Grade English Teacher
Smothermon, Debbie Kay
  Third Grade Teacher
Womack, Gail Werner
  Choir Director

ROMA
Villareal, Maria Teresa
  Second Grade Teacher

ROPESVILLE
Willis, Anniece Durham
  4th Grade Teacher

ROSCOE
Burke, Jancy Pollan
  English Teacher
Paty, Orville Britt
  Mathematics Teacher
Raughton, Cindy Ann
  Language Art Teacher

ROSEBUD
Randall, Daniel Lee
  American History Teacher

ROSENBERG
Boman, James Paul
  Theatre Arts Teacher
Buzek, Veta Williams
  Office Educ Teacher/Coord
Colihan, Barbara D.
  Math Dept Chair/Teacher
Davenport, Linda Carter
  4th Grade Teacher
Eaves, Virginia Stewart
  Mathematics Department Chair
Hill, Linda Lou
  History Department Chair
Jordan, Sundra Sykes
  Earth Science Teacher
Lanier, Mike Gregory
  Science Teacher/Coach
Melasky, Jeanette Beth
  Math Teacher
Tomas, Doris Davis
  Science Dept Chairperson

ROTAN
Mc Call, Melba June (Matney)
  Retired Teacher

ROUND ROCK
Cotter, Sue
  Fr Teacher/Foreign Lang Chair
Cromwell, Richard Lee
  Social Studies Teacher
Dusterhoff, Marilane G.
  Math Coordinator
Hilsabeck, Marcia Stewman
  English Teacher
Jansen, George F.
  Band Director
Komandosky, Susan White
  Journalism Teacher
Linville, Martin Richard
  Learning Center Teacher
Tidwell, Tommy Noel
  Science Teacher

ROXTON
Barnes, Jana Shepherd
  Vocational Homemaking Teacher
Humphries, Golda Vandygriff
  Principal

RUSK
Brooks, Barbara Walker
  English Teacher

SABINAL
Felts, Vaneta Lowery
  Third Grade Teacher
Smith, George Francis Jr.
  Mathematics Teacher/Coach

SAINT JO
Parker, Bernice M.
  Fourth Grade Teacher
Sperces, Delmer Troy
  History Teacher

SALADO
Bates, Melvin Dean
  Biology/History Teacher/Coach
Fiebig, Connie Shumate
  Counselor
Guess, Virginia Townsend
  Language Arts Teacher
Le Master, Beth Ann
  Science Teacher

SAN ANGELO
Clark, Ava Eakman
  Retired Teacher
Crain, Susan Kohutek
  Counselor & English IV Teacher
Doyle, Diane Lewallen
  Junior English Teacher
Halbert, Billie Mackey
  Honors World His Teacher
Hall, Deryl Ann (Dunagan)
  Third Grade Teacher
Hernandez, Elizabeth Ezra
  2nd Grade Teacher
Highsmith, Jamie Jones
  Counselor
Holden, Patsy Tucker
  6th Grade Teacher
Koehn, Kathy B.
  7th Grade English Teacher
Maedgen, Cynthia Beck
  English Teacher
Morgan, Judy A.
  English Teacher
Riley, Shari Bahlman
  Choral Music Director
Ripple, Karen Hoelscher
  Texas History/English Teacher
Shotts, Steven Landis
  Amer/TX History Teacher/Coach
Walker, Tony Alan
  Physical Education Teacher
Watts, Norma Hughes
  Theatre Arts Teacher
Wetzel, Coralie Ann
  English Teacher

SAN ANTONIO
Altfather, Miriam Garza
  Elementary Music Teacher
Aniol, Betty Sue Troutman
  Assistant Principal
Baucum, Beverly Gutelius
  10th Grade World His Teacher
Belcher, Jacqueline Ann
  Kindergarten Teacher
Bell, Sandy Morton
  English Teacher
Bigler, Virginia Graham
  Theatre Art/Speech Teacher
Brice, Sally Goodridge
  Fourth Grade Teacher
Brischetto, Barbara Palmieri
  Mathematics Teacher

Carroll, Margaret Wilkinson
  Third Grade Teacher
Casanova, David Ralph
  Chemistry Teacher
Chandler, Martha Emmott
  5TH Grade Teacher
Chidgey, Terri Wassmund
  Assistant Principal
Clark, Anne Marie
  Teacher of Gifted & Talented
Clay, Celia Anne
  Science Teacher
Compton, Penny Dornbusch
  Instrumental Music Teacher
Cooley, Martha Teinert
  English Teacher
Corbell, Berman Dalton
  Social Studies Teacher
Creech, Dee Mullins
  12th Grade English Teacher
Cummings, Joseph Michael
  Lang Art/Soc Stud Teacher
Davis, Daisy Campbell
  Teacher
De Kunder, Ella Jean
  Teacher of Gifted/Talented/Eng
Denice, Marcela Louise
  English II Teacher
Derderian, Michael James
  Earth Science Teacher
Domkowski, Alexander Joseph
  Physics/Biology Teacher
Ellebracht, Linda G. (Walker)
  Fifth Grade Teacher
Even, Shirley Ann (Johnson)
  Teacher of Gifted/Talented
Flores, Emily Loverde
  English Department Chair
Flowers, Roland E.
  5th Grade Teacher
Foust, Robin K.
  Teacher/Area Supervisor
Frazer, Andrea Wood
  Science Teacher
Freeman, Phyllis Anne
  Third Grade Teacher
Gallegos, Virginia Warzecha
  English IV/IVAPH Teacher
Garcia, Lucia Serna
  3rd Grade Teacher/Dept Chair
Garcia, Patricia Anne
  Math/Science Teacher
Garza, Delia Alcala
  8th Grade English Teacher
Glaze, Arthur Irvin Jr.
  Spanish Teacher/Dept Chair
Glodich, James Thomas
  Phys Ed Teacher/Coach
Gonzales, Juan Jose
  Computer Department Head
Granato, Connie
  Science Teacher
Graves, Rita Manzo
  8th Grade Teacher
Greenwood, Betty Mc Clure
  Second Grade Teacher
Gries, Larry Francis
  Teacher
Harrison, Philip Michael
  Health Department Chairman
Harvey, Sherrie Franklin
  Earth Science Teacher
Havel, Eddy
  History Teacher
Havel, Patricia Pepper
  Mathematics Teacher
Haynes, Alan Keith
  Assistant Principal
Hazard, Donald Maurice
  Fifth Grade Teacher/Adm Aide
Higgins, Dan J.
  Principal/Athletic Director
Hildebrand, Lou Ann Patterson
  Mathematics Teacher
Hitzfelder, Elaine Willmann
  Advanced Placement Eng Teacher
Holloway, Willie Mae (Smith)
  Government/History Teacher
Hooper, Marvin Ray
  Assistant Band Director
Horvath, Kathryn Corey
  German Teacher
Hummel, Pamela Biery
  Forensics Director
Johnson, Jo Anne Padgett
  Art Teacher
Jones, Brenda Yarbrough
  English Teacher
Kardon, Kathleen Rice
  Teacher of Gifted & Talented
Kejner, Marta
  Spanish Teacher/Chair
Keller, Carmen Joan
  Third Grade Teacher
Kenyon, Bobbye Akin
  Earth Science Teacher

Kirby, Gloria
  Reading Teacher
Kleiman, John Reeve
  English Teacher
Krueger, Barbra K. (Sellers)
  Phys Ed Teacher/Coach
Lane, Sandra Mullin
  Vocational Teacher
La Presto, Amy C.
  Theatre Arts Teacher
Lewis, Robert James Jr.
  Physical Education Teacher
Lynn, Anita Ford
  Pre-School Montessori Teacher
Mack, John Steven
  Agriculture Science Teacher
Malloy, Laurel M.
  Theatre Arts Teacher
Marin, Michele Harbin
  Foreign Language Dept Chair
Marks, Mary Brent Barbour
  Senior English Teacher
Marques, Steve Joseph
  Accounting & Computer Teacher
Matamoros, Mary Annette
  Theatre Director
Mc Connell, Brian Keith
  5th Grade Teacher
Mc Dougall, Nancy Brown
  Elementary Counselor
Mc Elveen, Gail Marie
  7th Grade/Life Science Teacher
Medford, Maisie Coon
  4th Grade Teacher
Miculka, James Ray
  Instrumental Music Dept Chm
Miller, Laurie Crouch
  Principal
Mitcham, Margret
  Health Teacher
Montano, Joseph Edward
  Mathematics Teacher
Morgenroth, Gerry Rohan
  Electives Department Chair
Mueller, Marlene Meyer
  2nd Grade Teacher
Nealon, Linda Ryan
  Russian & French Teacher
Osborne, Linda L.
  6th Grade Teacher
Palmer, Rebecca Anne
  Biology Teacher
Perez, Anna M.
  Kindergarten Teacher
Phalen, Mary Lucy Segura
  Mathematics Teacher
Plant, Sandra Dale
  Fourth Grade Teacher
Price, Sandra Smith
  English Teacher
Ramirez, Bernadine De La Cruz
  5th Grade At Risk Teacher
Ramos, Antoinette Toscano
  Kindergarten Teacher
Richbourg, John Allen Jr.
  Math Teacher
Rivera, Joseph Manuel
  Assistant Principal
Roberts, Michael Don
  Bible Teacher
Rodriguez, Carol Schuetz
  Journalism Teacher
Rodriguez, James Ernest
  8th Grade English Teacher
Rodriguez, Leonor A. Lara
  10th Grade English Teacher
Rodriguez, Patricia Ann (Gutierrez)
  Office Admin Lab Teacher
Rosas, David A.
  Fifth Grade Teacher
Ross, B. George
  Health Teacher/Dept Head/Coach
Ruiz, Juan Carlos
  Band Director
Ruston, Mary Nell Olfers
  Fifth Grade Teacher
Sacre, Ida Buppert
  Lang Art Teacher/Vice Prin
Sager, Donna L.
  French Teacher
Schmidt, Larry Lee
  Band Director
Schmidt, Sandra Smith
  English Teacher
Sekula, Dolores La Chepelle
  World Geography Teacher
Spellmon, Mercedes Phytalion
  Fifth Grade Teacher
Stephenson, Judy A.
  Choral Director
Terrell, Carolyn Wells
  Science Department Chair
Thomas, Carita Chapman
  Bio/Anat/Physiology Teacher
Thompson, James L.
  Air Science Teacher

Tothero, Melissa Le Beouf
  Physical Science Teacher
Trainor, Elizabeth Gaenslen
  Middle School Science Teacher
Turner, Rodell
  Biology Teacher
Wedin, Georgia Morgan
  Science Teacher/Coordinator
Whitley, Pamela Kaye
  English Teacher
Wilbanks, Randall Thomas
  Industrial Technology Teacher
Williams, Loretta Nieschwitz
  Mathematics Department Chair
Wilson, Betty King
  1st Grade Teacher

SAN AUGUSTINE
Garrett, Willie F. Biggers
  Third Grade Teacher

SAN BENITO
Senteno, Sylvia
  History Teacher
Tamez, Rick
  Health Teacher

SAN DIEGO
Lackey, Philip C.
  Science Teacher
Lopez, Grace Everett
  12th Grade English Teacher
Lopez, Janie Zamora
  World History Teacher
Perez, Ernesto Amadeo
  Mathematics Teacher
Torres, Yolanda V.
  6th Grade Teacher
Upchurch, Renee Joyaline
  Mathematics Department Chair

SAN ELIZARIO
Fleming-Foster, Ima Jean
  Social Studies Chairman

SAN MARCOS
Caffey, Deborah Hemperly
  Third Grade Teacher
Cavazos, Velia Rodriguez
  Counselor
Edwards, James E.
  Mathematics Department Chair
Gish, David M.
  Assistant Athletic Trainer
Henk, Mary Tidwell
  7th Grade Lang Art Teacher
Hoch, Margaret Ewing
  Fifth Grade Teacher
Palermo, Joseph Andrew
  English Teacher
Pate, Pamela
  French/English Teacher
Riley, Rick
  Athletic Coordinator
Rodriguez, Olivia
  English Teacher
Theisen, Teresa June
  English Teacher
Wolking, Paula Kelly
  Social Studies Teacher

SAN SABA
Schulze, Lesa A.
  5-6 Grade Soc Stud Teacher
Schulze, Ronald C.
  Social Studies Teacher/Coach

SANDERSON
Evans, Peter Michael
  Social Studies Teacher
Mc Clellan, Jessie Mc Donald
  Fifth Grade Teacher

SANGER
Bucklew, Mary Kathryn
  Kindergarten Teacher
Yeatts, Marian Sunny Smith
  Teacher

SANTA FE
Caltagirone, Janet Martin
  Second Grade Teacher
Chadwick, Vicki Elizabeth
  Early Childhood Education
Newbrough, Wilda R. F.
  Speech & English Teacher
Tubb, Nancy Williams
  Mathematics Teacher

SANTA MARIA
Garcia, Armando
  History Teacher

SANTA ROSA
Ramirez, Jose Jesus
  5th Grade Teacher

SAVOY
Francis, Janet Kay Rino
  Home Economics Teacher

SCHERTZ

Bellesen, David Anthony
Science Teacher/Tennis Coach
Schmidt, Carol Ann (Culley)
Science Teacher/Dept Chairman

SCHULENBURG

Havelka, Diane Marie
Mathematics Teacher/Coach
Hertel, Annette Jane Berger
4th-5th Grade Fine Arts/Health
Martin, Rumaldo Luna
Spanish Teacher
Venghaus, Phyllis Langhamer
Science Teacher

SEAGRAVES

Lacy, Darla Baker
Secondary Mathematics Teacher

SEALY

Hollis, Jimmie Annette Hicks
Second Grade Teacher
Kaminski, Allen Wayne
Agriculture Teacher
Rossler, Mary Louise
8th Grade Teacher

SEGUIN

Petrisky, Robert Franklin
Band Director

SEMINOLE

Aryain, Patricia Denton
Kindergarten Teacher
Mobley, Mike Colin
Choral Act/HS Choir Dir
Roberson, Betty Moore
4th Grade Teacher

SEYMOUR

Brown, Annabelle
Retired Teacher
Peters, Sandy Marcum
English Teacher

SHAMROCK

Potter, William T. II
Science Teacher
Shannon, Fleeta Carthel
Jr HS English Teacher

SHELBYVILLE

Carter, Mac T.
Mathematics Department Chair
Carter, Mavis Elizabeth
Kindergarten Teacher
Fitzgerald, Frankey Lynn
Third Grade Teacher
Harrison, Esther Cox
Fifth Grade Teacher
Helms, Jeannene Asken
Third Grade Teacher
Reed, Jerry Lewis
Head of Science Department

SHEPPARD AFB

Peterson, Thada Tinker
4th-6th Grade Science Teacher

SHERMAN

Allen, Linda (Honts)
Third Grade Teacher
Merideth, Duane Allen
Biology Teacher

SHINER

Riske, Joyce Meyer
Semi-Retired 1st Grade Teacher
Seidenberger, Sylvia Tupa
Third Grade Teacher
Turek, Patricia Beal
Elementary Teacher

SIDNEY

Nelson, Allan Dale
Science Department Teacher
Trosper, Ray Lynn
Soc Stud/Eng Teacher

SIERRA BLANCA

Lujan, James B.
Athletic Director/Teacher

SILSBEE

Coldren, Ida Flo
Teacher
Graves, Nelda
3rd Grade G/T Teacher
Mc Whorter, Carol Andess
6th Grade English Teacher

SILVERTON

Long, Michael Darwin
Science Teacher
Reynolds, Richard Duane
Retired Math/His Teacher

SINTON

Alaniz, Norma Linda
Fifth Grade Teacher

Bezoni, Peggie Thomasson
Third Grade Teacher
Fergerson, James Fredrick
Physics/Physical Sci Teacher
Karr, Rosemary Kenny
Kindergarten Teacher
Kay, Nancy
5th Grade Teacher
Price, Karen Stokes
Sophomore English Teacher
Ramirez, Rosalinda Saenz
Fifth Grade Teacher

SKIDMORE

Schlitzkus, Jolly Maddox
Instructional Facilitator

SLATON

Heathington, Linda Susan
Spanish Teacher

SLIDELL

Franklin, Carolyn Louise
English/Theatre Arts Teacher

SMITHFIELD

Hammond, James Michael
Mathematics/French Teacher

SMITHVILLE

Adamcik, Erwin F.
Mathematics Department Chm
Ingram, Denise Gupton
Kindergarten Teacher

SMYER

Graves, Tina Nichols
Mathematics & Health Teacher
Morrison, Sarah Elizabeth
K-12th Grade Counselor

SNOOK

Bedford, Theresa Louise
HS Science Teacher

SNYDER

Collier, Kim Jennings
English Teacher
Combest, Bobbie Reed
English/Reading Teacher
Echols, Kay Maner
First Grade Teacher
Gressett, Sue Cook
4th Grade Teacher
Hamby, Dale D.
Teacher
Peek, Ollie Louis
Mathematics Teacher
Vest, Theresa Kaye (Abbott)
8th Grade Teacher
Wesson, Janet Hunt
Counselor

SOUR LAKE

Marrou, Janice F.
World History Teacher
Peveto, Cynthia Holecek
English Teacher
Samuel, Doris L.
Chapter Reading Teacher
Van Noord, Ruth
Phys Ed Teacher/Coach

SOUTH HOUSTON

Doiron, Doris J. Robinson
Teacher of Fine Arts
Eads, Charlotte Elizabeth
Orchestra Director
Jordan, Fred
Director of Bands
Stringer, Jo Ann Harper
Honors Biology I & II Teacher
Taylor, Cathy Roby
Phys Ed Dept Chairperson
White, John Mark
Social Studies Teacher

SOUTH SAN ANTONIO

Nehr, L. Margaret
Retired Elementary Teacher

SOUTHLAKE

Lester, Bettye Plummer
Fourth Grade Teacher

SPEARMAN

Flowers, Karla Mc Carter
4th Grade Teacher

SPLENDORA

De Ford, Linda Ehrigson
Social Studies Chairperson
Findeisen, Ben Henry
Science Teacher
Weatherly, Elmina Donette
Elementary Principal

SPRING

Applegate, Todd Edward
Social Studies Teacher

Ditta, Frances Mary
Government Teacher
Humphrey, Linda Kay Cole
Physics Teacher
May, Karri E.
6th-8th Grade Art Teacher
Mc Clure, Michael Craig
Science Department Chair
Meissner, Barbara Graham
English Teacher
Miller, Kathryn Marie (Brown)
Latin Teacher
Stonaker, Ashley Shackelford
Fifth Grade Teacher

SPRING BRANCH

Dowdy, Hazel Brown
Teacher/VOE Coordinator
Marceax, Peggy Theresa
English Teacher
Tatum, Robert Lowell
History Department Chair
Thornton, Melanie Alford
Math Dept Chr/Teacher
Williams, Carl Glenn
Industrial Technology Teacher

SPRINGTOWN

Crawford, Cathy Jo
Mathematics Dept Head/Teacher
Peterson, Elaine Rone
8th Grade Amer His Teacher

STAFFORD

Lockley, Elizabeth Lou Rheinlander
Fourth Grade Teacher
Soliz, Yolanda
Spanish Teacher

STAMFORD

Pritchard, Betty Jo Ann (French)
Teacher

STEPHENVILLE

Buice, Janie
Mathematics Teacher
Campbell-Furtick, Cristy Lynn
English Teacher
Crouch, Nancy Lee
7th Grade TX History Teacher
Hampton, Carolyn Carr
First Grade Teacher
Larimore, Marilyn Miniard
6th Grade Lang Arts Teacher
Walton, Sandra Casper
English Teacher, Dept Chair

STERLING CITY

White, Larry Dwayne
Math/Computer Teacher

STRATFORD

Hauser, Linda Sutton
6th Grade Sci/Reading Teacher
Kautz, Viola E.
Counselor
Mc Clellan, Brenda Bouldin
English/Speech Teacher
Ragsdale, Sonja Guffee
Third Grade Teacher

SUGAR LAND

Alexander, Cybele Joyette
English Teacher
Brett, Judith Housekeeper
High School English Teacher
Chan, Eva Sim
Biology Teacher
Chiang, Suehing Woo Yee
Math/Sci/Soc Stud Teacher
Clark, Marjorie Trulan
Teacher
Davis, Larry Ray
Aerospace Sci Instr USAF JROTC
Hill, Dan Allen
Science Teacher
Hohnbaum, Daniel Lawrence
Science Teacher
Matthys, John William
Mathematics Teacher
Mc Cullar, Roger Mark
History Teacher
Prater, Roberta Louise (Cooke)
Industrial Technology Teacher
Pruitt, Nancy Shelton
Reading Department Chair
Turner, Joyce Gregor
Librarian

SULPHUR BLUFF

Murray, Vickie Harris
Elementary Mathematics Teacher

SULPHUR SPRINGS

Dennis, Kathleen Murphy
Spanish Teacher
Glenn, Sandra Kay
English Teacher

Jones, Annada Elliott
7th-8th Grade Hnrs Eng Teacher

SUNNYVALE

Holland, Karen Lynn
History Teacher

SUNRAY

Hazlett, Bud F.
History Teacher

SWEENY

Vermillion, Linda Dianne
Chemistry Teacher

SWEETWATER

Waddell, Gelene Williams
Physical Education Teacher

TAFT

Eleazer, Richard Elon
HS Mathematics Teacher

TAHOKA

Foster, Barbara Lou
English Teacher

TALPA

Bean, Athena Hafner
Counselor

TATUM

Farar, Vicki Bauske
Math/Typing Teacher/Drill Team
Villareal, Roxanne Beall
5th Grade Teacher

TAYLOR

Lumpkin, Sandra Barrier
Math & Computer Teacher
Rogers, Patricia Busby
Business Education Teacher
Simcik, Karen Dykowski
8th Grade Teacher
Volek, Dan R.
Speech/English Teacher
Young-Roberts, Debra Kay
Vocational Adjustment Coord

TEMPLE

Barganier, Grady Lynn
English Teacher/Coach
Barrganier, Grady Lynn
English Teacher/Coach
Boyd, Shirley Lock
8th Grade Science Teacher
Conner, Alma Gayle
Fourth Grade Teacher
Cornelius, Rose Angela
Psychology/Sociology Teacher
Downing, Gwenda Whatley
4th Grade Teacher
Popelka, Julia Stinson
Language Arts Teacher
Popelka, Julia Stinson
Language Art Teacher
Ratliff, Lela H.
Second Grade Teacher
Russell, Lois Ann
Second Grade Teacher
Schulze, Howard Dean
Science Department Chair

TERRELL

Lane, Caroline Dennehy
Second Grade Teacher
Thornton, Mark Mc Kinney
Principal

TEXARKANA

Sparkman, Carolyn Hopkins
5th Grade Soc Stud Teacher

TEXAS CITY

Byrd, Lynda Berryhill
Mathematics Teacher
Daniels, Charles Wesley
Eighth Grade English Teacher
Holt, Dorothy Holland
English Teacher
Pirtle, Deborah De Cuir
8th Grade Earth Sci Teacher
Schaper, Laurel T.
Reading/Spelling Teacher
Tasler, Margaret Goeke
Government/Economics Teacher

TEXHOMA

Nash, Joyce Sweeney
Mid Sch Language Arts Teacher

THE COLONY

Hames, Karen Luddeke
English Dept Chair
Precopia, Penny Anderson
Fourth Grade Teacher

THE WOODLANDS

Frazier, Barbara Lane (Parker)
Journalism Teacher

Leavelle, Martha Carole (Grayson)
Retired Teacher

TIVOLI

Pagel, Marilyn Gentry
5th Grade Teacher

TRENTON

Lowrey, Sandra Seraphine
7th/8th Grade English Teacher

TRINIDAD

Ashlock, Karen Brooks
1/2/3 Grade Lang Arts Teacher

TRINITY

Monroe, Pamela Turner
Social Studies Teacher

TROUP

Arwood, Barbara Cross
English Teacher
Smith, Travis Neil
Band Director

TULIA

Carlisle, Kathy A.
English Teacher

TYLER

Alden, Dennis J.
Teacher
Anderson, Ruth Finley
Fifth Grade Teacher
Bogue, Jan Crawford
English Teacher
Brown, Donna Maxwell
Career Investigation Educator
Busbee, Martha Murphy
English Teacher
Calloway, Ethel Warren
US His/Soc Stud Teacher
Delley, Vernell Violeta Henderson
4th Grade Teacher
Falzone, Shirley Revill
English Teacher
Gilbreath, Barbara Faseler
Middle School Counselor
Hitt, Deborrah Wood
English Teacher
Johson, Brett Alan
Band Director
Newton, Joanne Barron
Mathematics Teacher
Ray, Ruben L.
Electronics Instructor
Rollins, Christolyn Turner
6th-8th Grade Choral Director
Skelton, Diane Jones
9th Grade Teacher of G/T ENG
Wilson, James Austin
Fifth Grade Teacher
Yancy, Ruth Robertson
Fifth Grade Teacher

UNIVERSAL CITY

Schulze, Shirley Gail
Business Teacher

UVALDE

Cabada, Shirley A.
Eng Teacher/Jr HS Dept Chair
Hilderbran, Betty Frantzen
Mathematics Dept Chairperson
Rummel, Alvis Jay
8th Grade Science Teacher

VALLEY MILLS

Bailey, Emily Kattner
Math/Computer Teacher

VAN

Praytor, Beth Lyon
Business Teacher
Stephenson, Mary Anna
English II Teacher

VAN VLECK

Durham, David Craig
English/Speech Teacher
Grisham, Nancy Boden
Chapter I/Math/Rdng Teacher
Osina, Martha A.
English Teacher
Wiggins, Patrica Edison
Math & English Teacher

VEGA

Sunderman, Max Bryan
Secondary Science Teacher

VENUS

Coudert, Sharon
Phys Ed Teacher/Coach
Mc Clure, Sally Van Landingham
7th-8th Grade Science Teacher

VERIBEST

Johnson, Ruth Rebecca Seaborn
Fourth Grade Teacher

VERIBEST (cont)
Lindsay, Marcia A.
  English/Social Studies Teacher
VERNON
Byars, Kathryn Luanne
  Kindergarten Teacher
Dennis, Dorris Straughan
  Fourth Grade Teacher
Hamm, Frances Jayne (Mote)
  English/Art Teacher
Ramsey, Patsy Hainline
  Social Studies Teacher
VICTORIA
Cole, Donna Cope
  English Teacher
Cowan, Mel L.
  Band Director
Gray, Michael Bernard
  Mathematics Teacher
Hagel, Leona P.
  French Teacher
Laurence, Allan Hardee
  US History/Government Teacher
Maroney, James Thomas
  Social Stud Instr/Head Coach
Mendez, Deborah Sue
  Drill/Dance Team Director
Middleton, Luther Clay
  Asst Principal for Instruction
Murray, Anderson Oneal
  Retired
Slone, Joyce M. Wingate
  Social Studies Teacher
Witwer, William Frederick
  Director of Choral Activities
VIDOR
Absher, Faith Simpson
  Sixth Grade Soc Stud Teacher
Fairchild, Brenda Davis
  6th Grade Teacher/Group Leader
Miller, Wanda Sue
  8th Grade Soc Stud Teacher
Murphy, Vicki (George)
  Kindergarten Teacher
Spiers, Mary Carolyn
  English Teacher/Dept Head
Thomas, Linda F.
  Teacher/Coach/Dept Chair
WACO
Aman, J'Ann Payne
  Mentor Teacher/Eng Dept Chm
Cooper, Michael Howard
  Jr HS Principal
Darden, Robert Fulton Jr.
  Science Teacher
Emmet, Audrey Rigney
  Mathematics Dept Chairperson
Fulmer, Barbara Dell
  Third Grade Teacher
Goldsmith, Marvin Ray
  Science Teacher
Gross, Linda Bell
  Fifth Grade Teacher
Hopkins, Kathryn Harmon
  Science Teacher
Howard, Bobbie Jean (Thomas)
  Second Grade Teacher
Lichnovsky, Billy Joe
  8th Grade Mathematics Teacher
Mabry, Mary Huffman
  Third Grade Teacher
Mc Kenzie, Brenda Wylie
  Computer Math & Sci Teacher
Moore, Elsa Lutz
  Teacher
Pickens, Lee Fentress
  5th Grade Teacher
Pulattie, Jo Ann Boyd
  Journalism/English Teacher
Reese, Minesue Wright
  Kindergarten Teacher
Smith, Dorris Ann
  4th Grade Teacher
Strother, Phyllis Helms
  English Teacher
Vardeman, David A.
  English Teacher
WAELDER
Tresner, Roy Wayne
  English/Lang Art Teacher
WALL
Willman, Jay
  Computer Lit Teacher/Coach
WALLER
Bode, Harold
  Science Teacher
Craig, Verna Petry
  Home Economics Teacher
Dever, Patricia Simmons Brown
  Assistant Principal

WARREN
Hebert, James Clint
  Poly Sci/Ec/US His Teacher
Martin, Bobby Gene
  Math Dept Chair/Asst Prin
WATAUGA
Butler, Brad William
  Science Department Chairperson
Spurlock, Regina L.
  Phys Ed Teacher/Coach
WATER VALLEY
Ray, Homa Lee (Childress)
  Retired Third Grade Teacher
WAXAHACHIE
Ballard, Ruth Robinson
  Teacher/Dept Chair
Hastings, Ronnie Jack
  Physics & Adv Math Teacher
Hill, Carolyn Cole
  5th Grade Teacher
Jacoby, Charline
  8th Grade Math/Cmptr Teacher
Mullican, Dorothy Finley
  Mathematics Teacher
Nickols, John M.
  History Teacher/Bskbl Coach
White, Carrie Lee
  Mathematics Teacher
Winn, Susan Lewis
  Fifth Grade Teacher
WEATHERFORD
Yarnell, Jim
  Government Teacher/Coach
WEBSTER
Simsarian, Karen Ann
  6th Grade Teacher
WELLMAN
Pittman, Kay Fern (Elder)
  English Teacher
WESLACO
Brebner, Nancy Atteberry
  English Teacher
Mireles, Sylvia
  Biology Teacher
Ramirez, Inocente Jr.
  6th Grade Teacher
WEST
Shaw, Martha Amanda
  Fourth Grade Teacher
WEST COLUMBIA
Coleman, Wanda Joy
  Gifted/Talented/Eng Teacher
WHARTON
Boyar, Threasa Z.
  Mathematics Teacher
Munoz, Minerva Aguilar
  Kindergarten Teacher
WHITE DEER
Birkes, Darlene Prouse
  Journalism/English Teacher
WHITE SETTLEMENT
Fellers, Lynne Herthum
  Social Studies Chair/Teacher
WHITEHOUSE
Falls, Patricia Freeman
  English-Debate Teacher
WHITESBORO
Belcher, Cladene Landers
  Second Grade Teacher
WHITHARRAL
Duke, Doris Marion
  Fourth Grade Teacher
Everts, Michael Lea
  Math Dept Chairman
WICHITA FALLS
Anson, Marion Ann Higgins
  History Department Chair
Goodman, Deborah Kay (Chapman)
  Honors Government & Economics
Henderson, Steven Brent
  Biology Teacher
Himstedt, Tillie
  Mathematics Department Chair
Piper, Linda Gail
  Music/Spelling Teacher
Redding, Joseph Dwayne
  Band Director/Music Teacher
WILLIS
Lorimier, Lynde
  Physical Education Teacher
Wood, Jean Petrosus
  English Teacher

WILLS POINT
Brooks, Robert Samuel Jr.
  Teacher
Petillo, Bobby Dean
  Developmental Reading Teacher
WINNSBORO
Crow, Cheryl Annette
  8th Grade Math Teacher
Gode, Elizabeth Faye
  Soc Stud Dept Chair
Satterwhite, Deborah Conner
  Speech Therapist
WODEN
Curtis, Debra Dungan
  HS History & English Teacher
WOLFE CITY
Thomas, John Douglas
  Science Teacher
WOLFFORTH
Fletcher, Cathy Wilson
  Computer Teacher
Hudgins, Carolyn Sue Brewer
  1st Grade Teacher
Mc Larty, Karen Shepherd
  Mathematics Teacher
WOODVILLE
Santos, Rebecca Basil
  English Teacher
WORTHAM
Airheart, Debra Reed
  English/Spanish/Drama Teacher
Frazier, Linda Renee
  1st Grade Teacher
WYLIE
Eavenson, Marcia Whitten
  Fourth Grade Teacher
Mc Mullin, Craig
  Social Studies Teacher
Natale, Joseph Anthony
  English Teacher
YOAKUM
Raney, Paula Schmittgens
  Fourth Grade Teacher
YORKTOWN
Irvin, Diann F.
  Reading Teacher of Migrants
Karnei, Shirley Ann (Geffert)
  Journalism/English Teacher
Krause, Valeta
  Chapter I & Migrant Aide
Mc Ada, Dee-Dee
  Fifth Grade Teacher

UTAH

AMERICAN FORK
Anderson, Dona H.
  Health Education Teacher
Farr, Dierdri
  Social Studies Teacher
Miner, Sherl Max
  5th Grade Teacher
Peterson, Gail Winther
  English Teacher
BENNION
Marsh, Barbara Jane
  World Geography Teacher
BOUNTIFUL
Andersen, Marilyn Clay
  Math Teacher-Dept Chm
Campbell, Robert Henry
  Band Director
Johnston, F. Joan Stewart
  7th Grade English/Art Teacher
Lang, Debbie Carlson
  Home Economics Teacher
Muna, Mitri John
  Industrial Arts/Tech Dept Head
Weber, Jack Carl
  Fifth Grade Teacher
BRIGHAM
Goldsberry, Reid
  English Department Chairperson
BRIGHAM CITY
Cefalo, Ronald Gene
  Physics Instructor
Freeman, Ellen Reeder
  Second Grade Teacher
Nielsen, Judy Ann
  Mathematics Teacher
Nielsen, Vaughn S.
  Eng/Lang Art/Reading Teacher
Wilhelmsen, W. Grover
  Music Teacher

CEDAR CITY
Hileman, Beth Ann
  Drama Teacher
CENTERVILLE
Dame, Steven
  6th Grade Teacher
Michie, Helen S.
  6th Grade Teacher
Mills, Michael L.
  Sixth Grade Teacher
CLEARFIELD
Hirschi, Clark Hugh
  Fifth Grade Teacher
Keime, Al
  Social Studies Teacher
Mills, John G.
  German/AP European His Teacher
CLINTON
Lund, Brent E.
  Physical Education Teacher
Vander Does, Jerry R.
  Choral/Musical Theatre Teacher
Van Dyke, Rebecca Layton
  A P English Teacher
DELTA
Nielson, Marilyn Shuldberg
  Third Grade Teacher
ENTERPRISE
Bowler, Terry Wayne
  Spanish/History Teacher
Roper, Roddy Lee
  Retired
FARMINGTON
Adams, Paiger Parkin
  Algebra-Geometry Teacher
Robb, Donald George
  Sixth Grade Teacher
FILLMORE
Blad, Phil
  Science/Math/Phys Ed Teacher
GRANTSVILLE
Addy, Carol P.
  First Grade Teacher
GREEN RIVER
Hughes, Sharyn Burgess
  First Grade Teacher
HEBER CITY
Southerlin, Carolyn Rossi
  English Dept Chair
HOLLADAY
Wade, Reed Ashby
  5th Grade Teacher
HOOPER
Maddock, Leslie Garth
  3rd Grade Teacher
HUNTINGTON
Emfield, Scott Douglas
  Soc Stud Teacher/Dept Head
HYRUM
Culbertson, M. Jean
  Mathematics Teacher/Dept Head
KAYSVILLE
Bosch, Jeanine Thatcher
  5th Grade Teacher
Kunz, Melanie Roundy
  4th/5th Grade Teacher
Lochhead, Louise Keiser
  Business Dept Chairperson
KEARNS
Hurley, Diana Hunt
  6th Grade Teacher
Woffinden, Brent E.
  Teacher
KOOSHAREM
Torgersen, Tarval A.
  5th/6th Grade Teacher
LAYTON
Arnett, Shirley G.
  Teacher/Asst Principal
Rasmussen, Joyce Porter
  6th Grade Teacher
Seiter, Claudia Collier
  Social Studies Dept Chair
Wach, Douglass R.
  Mathematics Teacher
Wakefield, Lou Ann
  Third Grade Teacher
LOGAN
Anderson, La Mar Marvin
  Chemistry Instr/Lecturer Chem
Crane, William Bruce
  History Teacher

CEDAR CITY
Dobson, Dorothy Lynn Watts
  Fifth Grade Teacher
Kinzer, Carol Varner
  Spanish Teacher
MAGNA
Coombs, Earl S.
  Biology Teacher
Jones, Robert Allen
  History Teacher
MIDVALE
Brinton, Victoria Ruth
  AP European/World His Teacher
Huddleston, Robert Thomas
  Youth in Custody Dept Head
MORGAN
Nethercott, Mark A.
  Physical Science Teacher
Porter, Anna Bell Carter
  6th Grade Teacher
MORONI
Christensen, Perry Owen
  Elementary School Principal
Cook, Nanalee Larsen
  4th Grade Teacher
MURRAY
Ludlow, Dick
  Science Dept Chair
Meyer, Wil J.
  AP US His/Ger/Soc Stud Chair
Patterson, L. Ruth
  Mathematics Department Teacher
Pond, Nicholas J.
  Debate/Speech/Theatre Teacher
Taylor, Susan Anderson
  Third Grade Teacher
NORTH OGDEN
Haacke, Von K.
  Fifth Grade Teacher
OGDEN
Coleman, Ronald Earl
  Fourth Grade Teacher
Favero, Carol Ebert
  Language Arts Chairman/English
Hadley, Dennis B.
  Spanish/English Teacher
John, Ila Marlene
  Home Economics Teacher
Johnston, Mary H.
  English Teacher
Kersey, Michele L.
  Teacher
Kilts, Clair Theodore
  Social Studies Chairperson
Lamb, Max Suel
  Educator
Marriott, Connie Roberts
  2nd Grade Teacher
Smith, Trudy L.
  Language Art/French Teacher
Turner, Alan D.
  Drafting Instructor
Willmore, Leanna Read
  Choir Teacher
OREM
Hemond, Diane Robitaille
  Social Studies Chair
Johansen, William Carl
  English Dept Chairman
Reeder, James Rondell
  Chemistry Teacher
PARK CITY
Fleming, James Christopher
  8th Grade Soc Stud Teacher
PAYSON
Argyle, Dorothy M.
  3rd Grade Intern Coordinator
Dahlquist, David C.
  Choral Director
Houghten, Doug W.
  Eng Dept Chm/Coord Testing
Meldrum, Joseph Reuel
  Biology/Physiology Teacher
Nielson, Julie
  First Grade Teacher
Shenk, Warren R.
  Social Studies Dept Chair
Walter, Linda Larson
  Chemistry/Physics Teacher
PLAIN CITY
Johnson, Helen C.
  First Grade Teacher
PLEASANT GROVE
Cornell, Geneve Smith
  5th Grade Teacher/Director
PRICE
Milovich, Charlene M.
  Teacher/English Dept Chairman

PRICE (cont)
Morley, Diane Bean
  4th Grade Teacher
Romano, Edna M.
  Principal

PROVIDENCE
Wilkins, Ann Boston
  Eng/Rdng/Amer His Teacher

PROVO
Baker, Susan Leigh (Gilliat)
  Dance Teacher
Berner, Karen V.
  Library-Media Coordinator
Johnson, Ruth B.
  English/Great Lit Teacher
Larson, Anne Breinholt
  Sixth Grade Teacher
Nielsen, Patricia Terry
  2nd Grade Teacher
O'Bryant, Annette Barnes
  Mathematics Teacher
Snyder, Shannon Claire
  English/Hum/Drama Teacher
Ungerman, Rosanna Weeks
  Grade Drama Dept Chair
Wiscombe, Rem C.
  Fourth Grade Teacher

RICHFIELD
Anderson, Larry E.
  Science & Mathematics Teacher
Oldroyd, Jerald Todd
  Fifth Grade Teacher
Pace, Paula B.
  English/Resource Teacher

RIVERTON
Shirley, Sharon Elizabeth
  Math Department Chair

ROY
Andersen, Laurie
  Seminary Teacher
Boyson, Steve R.
  Eng Teacher
Grossenbach, Richard Taggart
  Social Studies Teacher
Jensen, Suzi M.
  CP English & Dance Teacher

SAINT GEORGE
Burr, David Jack
  Chemistry/Physics Teacher
Hunt, Roderick Joseph
  Biology Teacher
Wenzel, Marilyn Cole
  English/AP English Teacher

SALT LAKE CITY
Bernini, Linda J.
  Second Grade Teacher
Curry, Robert Alan
  Music Teacher
Gambles, Camille de St. Jeor
  Sixth Grade Teacher
Green, Kathleen Louise (Ely)
  Computer Sci Teacher/Leader
Hodges, Denise S.
  Business Teacher
Jensen, Lucy
  English Teacher
Lawrence, Patricia
  1st/2nd Split Grade Teacher
Ligget, Robert Cope
  History Teacher
Long, Christopher James
  English Teacher
Mule, Carol Jean Schmidt
  Fifth Grade Teacher
Olsen, Rebecca Jane
  A P European History Teacher
Parker, Blaine Ray
  Metals Instructor
Pray, Toni Hansen
  Library Media Teacher
Rees, Gordon T.
  English Teacher
Riet, Brenda Yorgason
  5th Grade Teacher
Rockwell, John W.
  Social Studies Teacher
Sain, Paul E.
  Sixth Grade Teacher
Snarr, Daniel Ray
  High School Teacher
Sorben, Geraldine A.
  English & Latin Teacher
Sturges, Carl Martin
  Assistant Principal
Sutton, Tom W. B.
  Social Studies Teacher
Teichert, V. Dalene
  Teacher of the Gifted
Wilson, Margaret West
  English Department Chair

SANDY
Allen, Kathryn Peterson
  6th Grade Teacher
Bauer, Karlene Humphrey
  Biology Teacher
Hansell, Bonnie Umberger
  Middle School Teacher
Kunz, Nadine Mash
  Fifth Grade Teacher
Piper, Karlene S. (Bailey)
  Third Grade Teacher
Ward, Barbara B.
  English Teacher

SMITHFIELD
Fife, Dell Scott
  Mathematics Department Chair
Jensen, Jalaine P.
  2nd Grade Teacher

SOUTH JORDAN
Carmichael, Argie Adondakis
  English Teacher
Conder, Ra Nae Naylor
  Fifth Grade Teacher
Crump, Scott
  Social Studies Teacher
Hageman, Colette Van Wagenen
  Sixth Grade Teacher
Page, Gwen
  Fourth Grade Teacher
Rasmussen, Randall Jay
  Youth in Custody Teacher
Sudbury, Albert Louis
  Social Studies Teacher/Coach
Taggart, Diana L.
  Math Teacher

SPANISH FORK
Cloward, Susan Lundell
  First Grade Teacher
Robinson, Ty S.
  Science Department Chairman

SPRINGVILLE
Boyer, Rebecca Turner
  English Teacher
Burdett, Beverly Jean (Cornett)
  Spanish/World History Teacher
Clements, Kelly Reed
  Social Studies Teacher/Coach
Johnston, Timothy James
  Fifth Grade Teacher
Leek, Priscilla F.
  History/Soc Psychology Teacher

SUNSET
Saunders, Peggy J.
  English Teacher

TOOELE
Howard, Sarah Lee Flowers
  Sixth Grade Teacher
Leslie, Lee K.
  Physical Education Teacher

TREMONTON
Deatry, Crystal Lee Campbell
  Art/Mathematics Teacher
Leyva, Charles B.
  Spanish Teacher

VERNAL
Baker, Kay
  Mathematics Teacher
Redden, Boyd J.
  Fourth Grade Teacher
Shipton, Sharon Michelle
  Business Teacher

WASHINGTON TERRACE
Wilson, Wilford Drew
  Science Teacher

WEST JORDAN
Hansen, Barry Bracken
  Sixth Grade Teacher
Soleimani, Liane Harding
  4th Grade Teacher

WEST VALLEY CITY
Linton, Mary Gourley
  Sixth Grade Teacher
Porter, Cornell Burr
  Religion Instructor
Rindlisbacher, Robert Fred
  Science Teacher/Chairman
Roach, Kathy Richins
  English/Reading Teacher
Rosvall, Patricia
  Biology Teacher
Strassburg, Jennifer Audentia
  Music Department Chairperson
Young, Donna Paulette
  French Teacher

VERMONT

ALBURG
Tower, Robert Howard
  Physical Ed/Health Teacher

BENNINGTON
Beriau, David L.
  English Teacher

BRADFORD
Mac Lean, Bruce Edward
  Social Studies Dept Chairman

BRANDON
Ketcham, Thomas Johnson
  7th Grade Lead Teacher

BRATTLEBORO
Heller, Daniel Alan
  English Department Chairman
Stone, Amelia Patricia
  English Teacher

CLARENDON
Lettierre, Angela Valente
  Third Grade Teacher

ENOSBURG FALLS
Bradford, Pamela Eyler
  Second Grade Teacher

FAIRFAX
Kuhn, Bernard Michael
  United States History Teacher

HUNTINGTON
Cozzens, Rebecca Austin
  Kindergarten Teacher

JERICHO
Porter, Linda Ravlin
  English Teacher

LYNDON CENTER
Prevost, Gerald H.
  Business Teacher

MIDDLEBURY
Kaplan, Paul William
  5th Grade Teacher

MORRISVILLE
Kristan, Linda Anderson
  Enrichment Coordinator

POULTNEY
Colomb, Irene Godzik
  5th Grade Teacher

RICHMOND
Mc Neil, James Michael
  7th Grade Soc Stud Teacher

RUTLAND
Costello, Patricia Pockette
  English Teacher
Hooker, George E.
  Bio/Health Teacher/Sci Chair
Justin, Mary Anne Bania
  Sixth Grade Teacher
Marcell, Phillip H.
  6th Grade Elementary Teacher

SAXTONS RIVER
Tinney, Donald Lewis
  English Department Chair

SOUTH BURLINGTON
Bourbeau, Carol Ann
  Mathematics Teacher

SPRINGFIELD
Carbonetti, Laurence S.
  Teacher of English
Robbins, Karin Leslie
  Physical Education Teacher

SWANTON
Babcock, Mary Shepard
  Elem Teacher/Asst Principal
Jette, Beth Hunter
  Mathematics Teacher

WEST RUTLAND
Johnson, Linda T.
  Math/Science/History Teacher

WILLISTON
Fleming, Bradley D.
  Admin/High School Teacher

WOODSTOCK
Paige, Virginia Zielinski
  Third Grade Teacher

VIRGIN ISLANDS

SAINT CROIX
Moross, Mark S.
  Senior High Literature Teacher

SAINT THOMAS
Hodge, Carolyn Leola
  Spanish Teacher
Hodge, Yvonne La Place
  Fourth Grade Teacher
Smith, William E.
  Bus Ed Teacher/Chair
Wallace, Muriel Orita
  Kindergarten Teacher

VIRGINIA

ABINGDON
Vestal, Brenda Lloyd
  7th Grade Lang Art Teacher

ALEXANDRIA
Beeby, Donald Mc Callen
  Social Studies Teacher
Casey, Terri Lynn
  Mathematics Teacher
Fetters, Claudia M.
  Earth Science Teacher
Fleming, Joan Vodoklys
  Third Grade Teacher
Grady, Elizabethann Erbin
  World Geography Teacher
Hylton, Nancy Nye
  Mathematics Teacher
Mc Mackin, Mary Brenda
  Third Grade Teacher
Melone, John Irvin Jr.
  Retired Physics Teacher
Patel, Manu V.
  Physics Teacher
Scully, David John
  French/Spanish/Chinese Teacher
Steele, Derrek Eugene
  Teacher/Coach
Teter, Janet T.
  Fourth Grade Teacher

ANNANDALE
Nawrotzky, Nicholas
  Mathematics Teacher

APPALACHIA
Brooks, Wilma Brewer
  Math Teacher/Dept Chair

APPOMATTOX
Berryman, Audrey Simms
  6th Grade Rdng/Math Teacher
Dickerson, Coty Darnell Jr.
  Health/Physical Ed Teacher
Fisher, Susan Grady
  English Teacher
Meadows, Victor Lyle
  US History Teacher
Mills, D. Jean
  Classroom Teacher

ARLINGTON
Baxter, Robert Marti
  Director of Choral Activities
Gaynor, Janice Marsh
  Teacher of Gifted & Talented
Greathouse, Claude Daniel
  Asst Aerospace Sci Instructor
Havens, Bonnie Worley
  Second Grade Teacher
Johnson, Steve
  English Teacher
Nasca, David Michael
  Mathematics Teacher
Nielsen, Sally Sue
  Sixth Grade Teacher
Peebles, Edward M.
  Physics Teacher
Revere, Ronald William
  Physics Teacher
Scott, Anita Knipling
  Writing Skills Teacher
Sipes, Carol Schrantz
  Mathematics Teacher
Taylor, Joshua Jr.
  Social Studies Specialist

ASHBURN
Bornarth, Norma L.
  English Teacher
Brinkley, Candace Lea
  Spanish Teacher

ASHLAND
Will, Angela M.
  French/Spanish Teacher

ATKINS
Pratt, Shirley Leonard
  Kindergarten Teacher

BASSETT
Byrd, Gerald Lee
  Eng/Advanced Placement Teacher
Collins, Pamela Wilson
  6th Grade Math & Sci Teacher
Critz, Janice Lackey
  5th Grade Teacher

BEALETON
Gredler, Peter Shepard
  Social Studies Dept Chairman

BEDFORD
Ramsey, Cynthia Burch
  Band Director
Wallace, Vickie Kinsley
  Kindergarten Teacher

BEN HUR
Newman, Nell Slemp
  Business Teacher

BERRYVILLE
Novak, Edward F.
  Technology Education Dept Head
Robinson, Elizabeth Ann
  Third Grade Teacher

BIG ROCK
Fuller, Jimmy Daryl
  6th-7th Grade History Teacher

BIG STONE GAP
Armentrout, Carolyn Bass
  Fr/Span/Eng/Rdng Teacher
Bloomer, Diane Bunch
  Second Grade Teacher
Daughtery, James Franklin
  Choral Director
Potter, Preston W.
  History Teacher

BIRCHLEAF
Colley, Kathleen Pittman
  Fourth Grade Teacher
O'Quinn, Patricia Sutherland
  Fifth Grade Teacher

BLACKSBURG
Brewbaker, Minnie Henderson
  Third Grade Teacher
Carr, Jane Winchester
  English Teacher
Dunford, Ina Farmer
  Kindergarten Teacher
Maddy, Teresa Helms
  Mathematics Teacher
Ogliaruso, Basila Elizabeth (Gallo)
  Second Grade Teacher
Wang, June Liang
  Business Education Teacher

BLUEFIELD
Green, Cherly Mason
  Fourth Grade Teacher
Louthan, Chuck
  Math/Science/Phys Ed Teacher
Whaley, Anne Backus
  Science Dept Chairperson

BOISSEVAIN
Horton, Mabel Marie Richmond
  4th Grade Teacher

BOONES MILL
Boitnott, Linda A.
  4th Grade Teacher

BOWLING GREEN
Griffin, Valerie Odessa
  Resource Teacher

BRISTOL
Andresen, Sherry Guynn
  7th/8th Grade English Teacher
Campbell, Wilda Jean
  Fourth Grade Teacher
Chafin, Hallie Henderson
  Language Arts Teacher
Duncan, Janice Taylor
  4th Grade Mathematics Teacher
Fanis, Judy Trantham
  Earth Science Teacher
Hart, Lacie Ann Lester
  Seventh Grade Teacher
Johnson, Sharon Denton
  French & Spanish Teacher
King, Julia Connie James
  L D Resource Teacher
Kirk, Dwight David
  5th Grade Teacher
Lambert, Harold Scott Jr.
  Band Director
Mc Daniel, Evelyn Hutton
  7th Grade Soc Stud Teacher

BRISTOL (cont)
Moore, Charles Michael
Biology Teacher
Owens, Kittye Easterly
Third Grade Teacher
Parker, Nancy Puckett
Mathematics Teacher
Ratliffe, Phyllis
English Teacher
Stone, Geraldine Mc Croskey
Third Grade Teacher
Thayer, Janice Ann
First Grade Teacher
BROADWAY
Funkhouser, Betty Driver
10th/12th Grade Eng Teacher
Wenger, Jo Ann Craun
Mathematics Dept Chairperson
BROWNSBURG
Kessinger, Kimberley Dawn
Reading/English Teacher
BUCHANAN
Markham, Barbara Abshire
Second Grade Teacher
BUENA VISTA
Whitesell, Joan Snider
Computer Teacher
CALLAWAY
Wray, Bessie Holland
Grade School Teacher
CENTERVILLE
Hankins, Hilda Moore
Tenth Grade Biology Teacher
CHANTILLY
Hankins, Barbara Small
Dept Chair/Business Teacher
Silliman, Benjamin D.
GUIDANCE DIRECTOR
CHARLOTTE CRT HSE
Bates, Pamela H.
Math Teacher
Hunter, Frances Ramsey
Science Teacher
Rowland, Rhonda Stockton
Mathematics Teacher
CHARLOTTESVILLE
Reardon, Patricia Miller
Physical Education Teacher
Ridenour, David Lee
Physics Teacher
Tevendale, Richard Michael
Science Department Chair
CHASE CITY
Puryear, Hilda Jones
Fifth Grade Teacher
CHATHAM
Bennett, Dorothy Harraway
7th-Math/Sci/Health-Teacher
Webb, William David
Science Teacher
CHESAPEAKE
Acker, Lora Lee Langan
French & Spanish Teacher
Adkins, Wanda Iona-Brown
5th Grade Teacher
Belcher, Julie Adams
Mathematics Teacher
Dezern, Kay Langley
Teacher
Elliott, Janice Haught
First Grade Teacher
Farley, Thomas Roscoe
World History Teacher
Gramlich, Penny Leigh
Assistant Principal
Haver, Deborah Todd
Mathematics Teacher
Hopkins, Linda Holt
Computer Literacy Teacher
Howell, Linda Creekmur
Biology Teacher
Johnson, Thomas Ernest
7th Grade Life Sci Teacher
Kent, Lydia Lawless
Spanish Teacher
Mizelle, Teresa K.
English Teacher
Moore, Nancy Jane
English Department Chairperson
Perkins, Muriel Yvette
English Teacher
Stone, Kay S.
English Teacher
Woolery, Martha Walling
English Department Head

CHESTER
Clark, Patch Lee
Theatre/English Teacher
Diebel, Muriel Davis
French Teacher
Randles, Oland
Guidance Director
Rogers, Charlotte A.
Mathematics Teacher
Woolard, David Eugene
Mathematics Teacher
CHESTERFIELD
Cormier, Steven A.
Social Studies Teacher
CHRISTCHURCH
Neilson, Charles Douglas
English Department Teacher
CHRISTIANSBURG
Basham, Betty Robertson
Third Grade Teacher
Bronaugh, Karen Dalton
Latin Teacher
Marks, Janet Wood
Teacher
CLIFTON FORGE
Strong, Edward Dickerson Jr.
Math Teacher
CLINCHCO
Deel, Cecil
Seventh Grade Teacher
COEBURN
Beverly, Sharon Wood
Fourth Grade Teacher
COLLINSVILLE
Gunter, Margaret Beeler
English Department Chairperson
COVINGTON
Cruise, Karen Ashby
Fourth Grade Teacher
Mansfield, Agnes Louise
Business Teacher
Pitzer, Dolores Barber
English Teacher
Saville, Shirley D.
Sixth Grade Teacher
CULPEPER
Brooks, Bessie Burrus
Sci Dept Chair/Bio Teacher
Lawson, Loudelia Serena
Second Grade Teacher
CUMBERLAND
Anderson, Judith Ruth
French Teacher
DANVILLE
Burnett, Dianne Creed
Math Teacher/Dept Chairperson
Kolendrianos, Carol Athans
Physical Science Teacher
Millner, Gwendolyn Dalton
Mathematics Teacher
Otersen, Jennie Beck
Substitute Teacher
Rawley, Debra Crawford
Kindergarten Teacher
Watson, Darlene Law
Resource Teacher for Gifted
Whisnant, Evelyn
Math/Science/Health Teacher
DAYTON
Miller, Joyce DeBolt Miller
Lang Art/Soc Stud Teacher
DENDRON
Wyatt, Wilma Holmes
Music Teacher
DINWIDDIE
Gunnels, Janet C.
French/English Teacher
DISPUTANTA
Fisher, Grace Kimberly
3rd Grade Teacher
DRAPER
Corder, Barbara Riggle
Second Grade Teacher
DRY FORK
Blalock, Dennis Warren
Science Department Chairman
Lindsey, Nina Atkinson
4th Grade Teacher
Lovelace, Sandra Stowe
Guidance Counselor
DUBLIN
Huffman, Jerry Alvin
Business Education Teacher

Meyer, Bill Richard
Social Studies HS Teacher
Pfaff, Alice Firebaugh
Fourth Grade Teacher
Powell, Marilyn Ash
Chapter I Reading Teacher
Roop, Mary Mc Daniel
Printing Instructor
Shelburne, Carolyn Jane
Sixth Grade Teacher
Sparks, Nancy Mustard
Health Occupations Teacher
Weikle, Mickey Gilley
Home Economics Teacher
Weschke, Bert E.
Drafting Teacher
DUMFRIES
Miller, Gloria Cash
French Teacher
Vaughn, Adrian J.
Speech/Language Therapist
EARLYSVILLE
Partin, Jane Carpenter
Second Grade Teacher
EMPORIA
Tucker, Cozy H.
Chapter I Reading Teacher
FAIRFAX
Alexander, Susan Horton
Choral Dir/Music Dept Chair
Askew, Virginia D.
5th Grade Retired Teacher
Barlow, Barbara Ann
Sixth Grade Teacher
Casagrande, John E.
Band Director/Music Dept Chm
Dow-Wilson, Kathryn
Orchestra Director
Henderson, Nancy Chilton
Home Economics Dept Chair
Joseph, Rose Marie
Fifth Grade Teacher
Mc Donald, Anne
Resource Teacher
Munday, Nancy Wyckoff
Third Grade Teacher
Salewski, Robert Joseph
Mathematics Department Chair
Spencer, Paula (Holt)
Social Studies Teacher/Chair
Thomas, William J. A.
Biology Teacher
Thompson, Eva Susong
Sixth Grade Teacher
Verbanic, Thomas Glen
US History Teacher
FALLS CHURCH
Almquist, Jon L.
Athletic Trainer/Teacher
Berard, Ulric Claiborne
Social Studies Teacher
Elder, Carlyn Lang
Social Studies Dept Chair
Gerardi, Duchere King
French/English/Lit Teacher
Margrave, Robert
Pre-Calculus/AP Eng Teacher
Mensh, Barry Alan
Biology Teacher
Singley, Marion R.
English Teacher
Terry, Janet E.
Fifth Grade Teacher
Thomas, Constance Terzopolos
Biology Teacher
Williams, Vern S.
Mathematics Teacher
Wilson, Eunice Navene
Social Studies Teacher
Winner, Kathleen Bernard
Fifth Grade Teacher
FALLS MILLS
Martin, Anita Pendry
Fifth Grade Teacher
FALMOUTH
Gosnell, Karen Ford
Social Studies Dept Head
Siegmund, Winona S.
English Teacher
Sudduth, Elizabeth Muirheid
Third Grade Teacher
FARMVILLE
Hazelwood, Frances Walthall
English Teacher
FIELDALE
Collins, Charles Allen
Soc Stud/Cmptr Sci Teacher
Joyce, Glenda Shelton
Fifth Grade Teacher

FINCASTLE
Blanchard, Janie Monday
7 Grade Math/Sci/Rdng Teacher
Hall, Rita Firestone
7th Grade Mathematics Teacher
FLEET BR NORFOLK
D'Abreu-Roddin, Deborah
English Teacher
FOREST
Cardwell, Virginia Langel
5th Grade Teacher
Stennette, Janice S.
Soc Stud Teacher/Dept Chair
FORT BELVOIR
Freund, Peggy G.
3rd Grade Teacher
FORT BLACKMORE
Quillin, Lois Gilmer
Principal
FORT DEFIANCE
Ball, Bonnie Mc Donald
French Teacher/Dept Chair
Huffman, Robert K. III
7th Grade Mathematics Teacher
Myers, Beverley Simmons
Mathematics Teacher
FREDERICKSBURG
Catlett, Marceline Rollins
Admin Asst/6th Grade Teacher
Cuddy, Meredith Fink
English Teacher
Ford, R. Denise Roberts
Math Teacher
Mc Kenney, Edward Garland II
6th Grade Teacher/Admin Asst
Tyler, Susan Carter
5th Grade Teacher
Warrick, Roberta Bergman
6th Grade Teacher
FRIES
Sumner, Cathy Jones
Mathematics/Science Teacher
Wheatley, Carol Nichols
3rd Grade Teacher
FRONT ROYAL
Porter, J. Craig
English Department Chair
GALAX
Chappell, Barbara Harmon
Guidance Counselor
Henderson, Mary Pugh
Third Grade Teacher
GATE CITY
Blalock, Marjorie Gilliam
Mathematics Teacher/Dept Chm
Coleman, Margaret Mc Connell
English Teacher
Quillen, Charles Case
Mathematics Teacher/Coach
GOOCHLAND
Allen, Majelle
Kindergarten Teacher
Beauchamp, Lucie
French Teacher
GOODE
Hurley, Carol Ann (Heller)
First Grade Teacher
GRETNA
Bailey, Cynthia Bond
French Teacher
Craig, Martha Elizabeth
Chemistry Teacher
Jones, Theodore Richard Jr.
Assistant Principal
Pierson, Patricia Watlington
First Grade Teacher
Royster, Mary Collis
Biology Teacher
GRUNDY
Barnett, De Anna Dawm
6th Grade Teacher
Smith, Dorsey Whetsil
English/Oral Comm Teacher
Smith, Kenneth Edward II
Social Studies Teacher
Swiney, James Marvin
Pres/Music/Choir/Guid Cnslr
HAMPTON
Bashaw, Craig Lee
English Teacher
Cheney, Lonnie E.
Computer Mathematics Teacher
Heldreth, Cynthia Holt
Mathematics Department Chair
Howell, Laura Cooley
Math Teacher

Hughes, Jeanine Benton
3rd Grade Teacher
Mac Donald, Richard Emerson
Science Teacher
Mc Cary, Diane Barnes
4th Grade Teacher
Parrish, Sandra Grigg
2nd Grade Teacher
Scott, Georgia Perry
8th Grade Mathematics Teacher
Sherrard, James Gleason
Calculus/Physics Teacher
Shobe, Charles Lee Jr.
7th Grade Lang Art Teacher
Shriver, Louis Marsh
Geometry Teacher/Athletic Dir
Sommer, Deborah Kelly
Spanish Teacher
Spicer, Selma Gwendolyn
Alternative Education Teacher
Wallace, Mary Kershaw
Social Studies Teacher
HARRISONBURG
Buhl, Henry Franklin
Chm/Soc Studies Teacher
Coffman, Janet Hollar
History Teacher
HEATHSVILLE
Tomlin, Lela Bouldin
Science/Computer Teacher
HENRY
Worley, Betty Quinn
2nd Grade Teacher
HERNDON
Carter, Deborah Savage
Business Teacher/Dept Chair
Hand, Bob Frederick
English Teacher
Smith, Franklin Foster
Sixth Grade Teacher
HILLSVILLE
Bunn, Ruth Brown
Teacher of Gifted & Talented
Horton, Hazel Bowman
Kindergarten Teacher
Mc Grady, Ruth Sue Gardner
Retired Elementary Teacher
Whittington, Shirley Morris
Chemistry Teacher
HIWASSEE
Hale, Patricia Bowling
Fifth Grade Teacher
HONAKER
Hale, Rita Lois
Second Grade Teacher
HOPEWELL
Bond, Mary Kathryn
Fourth 4th Grade Teacher
Bujakowski, Jane Sharp
Fourth Grade Teacher
Mitchell, Madie Washington
Third Grade Teacher
HURLEY
Dotson, Pamela Tester
7th Grade Math Teacher
Mc Clanahan, Donna Gail
English Teacher
INDEPENDENCE
Amburn, Maggie Taylor Frazier
English Teacher
Byrd, Ronald Paul
Agriculture Teacher
Holder, Amelia Babette
Bio I/Anatomy Teacher
Young, Mary Osborne
Mathematics Teacher
KEOKEE
Peters, Lynn Edwards
Third Grade Teacher
KEYSVILLE
Jones, Rhonda Fulghum
First Grade Teacher
KING GEORGE
Graves, Viola Marie
English Teacher
Miller, Jane Hoffman
Fifth Grade Teacher
LA CROSSE
Crutchfield, Katherine Moore
Third Grade Teacher
LANCASTER
English, Jennifer Sullivan
Math Teacher/Dept Chairperson
Luttrell, Jeanne M.
Bus Teacher/Chm Votec Dept

LAWRENCEVILLE
Bland, Bessie Carr
  8th/9th Grade English Teacher
Freeman, Juliana Lashley
  Business Education Teacher
Gill, Gretchen Moore
  8th Grade Science Teacher
Holman, Harry Stuart
  Social Studies Chairman
Jarrett, Gloria Barksdale
  Business Teacher
Miles, Geraldine Sykes
  Sixth Grade Teacher
Newson, Francis Davis
  8th-12th Grade Headmaster
Owen, Evelyn Bernadette
  English Teacher
Smith, Bessie Johnson
  Second Grade Teacher

LEBANON
Rainbolt, Leisa W.
  Geography Teacher

LEXINGTON
Ramsey, Elizabeth Courtney
  United States History Teacher

LURAY
Harden, Karen Entsminger
  English Dept Chair/Teacher

LYNCHBURG
Adkins, Elizabeth A.
  Fourth Grade Teacher
Anderson, James Carroll
  Instructor
Davis, Rachel Brown
  English Department Chair
Davis, Thurman Blanton
  Advanced Placement/His Teacher
Delong, Janice Ayers
  Assistant Professor
Fitzpatrick, Dona Fran
  Mathematics Teacher
Hopkins, Karen Payne
  Math Teacher
Lindeman, Cheryl De Wyer
  Biology Instructor/Advisor
Martin, Joan Thompson
  6th Grade Teacher
Reith, Kay T.
  Science Teacher
Roberts, Donna Rainey
  English Teacher
Witt, Cathy Brown
  Third Grade Teacher
Yeaman, Deloris Burks
  Fifth Grade Teacher

MANASSAS
Bell, Donna Cantwell
  Resource Teacher of Gifted Ed
Foley, Michael
  Marketing Ed Teacher
Futyma, Kathleen Walters
  Spanish Teacher/Dept Chairman
Hall, Harold David
  Biology/Chemistry Teacher
Soderberg, Marion Cook
  Elementary Guidance Counselor
Steele, Michael James
  Chem Teacher/Sci Dept Chairman
Switzer, Sandra G.
  9th-12th Grade Teacher

MARION
Beckett, Robin Lewis
  Earth Science/Biology Teacher
Francis, Margaret Thornton
  First Grade Teacher
Goodman, Nancy Fisher
  Chemistry/Physics Teacher
Richardson, Jeffrey Trent
  8th Grade Teacher

MARSHALL
Gaskins, Theresa Mae
  1st Grade Teacher
Thompson, Robyn Walker
  Fourth Grade Teacher

MARTINSVILLE
Martin, Linda Lackey
  Third Grade Teacher
Parks, Mary Tolbert
  Health/Physical Ed Teacher

MATHEWS
Anthony, David Bertram
  Social Studies Dept Chairman
Owen, Donna Pugh
  English Teacher
Register, Cynthia Lewis
  First Grade Teacher

MAX MEADOWS
Jones, Susan Hill
  French Teacher

Quesenberry, Connie Jackson
  Teacher
Williams, Robert Ellis
  Biology Teacher

MC LEAN
Sawyer, Mary Ellen Keeffe
  Social Studies Teacher/Chair

MEADOWVIEW
Alexander, Alice Faye
  First Grade Teacher

MECHANICSVILLE
Ellis, Gayle Mc Clymont
  4th Grade Teacher
Townsend, Kathleen Ashley
  French Teacher/Dept Chair
Weaver, Velma Moseley
  Science Teacher

MIDLOTHIAN
Cushing, Gale Keating
  Assistant Principal
Dobbs, Katherine Purinton
  6th Grade Mathematics Teacher
Ellis, Theresa Torregrossa
  Math Teacher & Computer Coord
Groves, Joan Bradley
  8th Grade Science Teacher
Lasswell, Juanita Glaspie
  Mathematics Teacher
Sumpter, Anne Graham
  English Teacher

MILFORD
Yerby, James Nathan
  7th Grade Mathematics Teacher

MINERAL
Anderson, Avis Mc Laughlin
  7th Grade Science Teacher
Coles, Deborah Calloway
  Language Arts Teacher
Hamilton, Suzanne D.
  English Teacher/Dept Chair
Havasy, Judith Esther
  Head Librarian
Pierce, Kathleen Mills
  Gifted Prgm Resource Teacher

NARROWS
Fraley, Charles Lee
  Psych Teacher/Athletic Dir
Margheim, Linda Hale
  Fifth Grade Teacher
Spencer, James Howard
  Science/Math Teacher

NARUNA
Seals, Ernest R. II
  6th Grade Teacher
Woodell, Peggy Anderson
  Special Education Teacher

NATHALIE
Thompson, Martha Barrett
  Sixth Grade Teacher

NATURAL BRIDGE STN
Hayslette, Amy Randall
  Mathematics Teacher/Dept Chair
Shoemaker, Rachel Joann
  Art Teacher
Starnes, Debra Hudspeth
  Home School Teacher

NEW KENT
Marsh, Donald Harry II
  Social Studies Teacher

NEWPORT NEWS
Ballard, Joyce Davis
  English Teacher
Bell, Margaret Shearin
  Assistant Principal
Brunson, Ethel D.
  Teacher
Carter, Joyce Scott
  Eng/Drama/Fine Arts Teacher
Coltrane, Patricia Branch
  Science Department Chair
Crittenden, Gaybrooke Garrett
  Reading Resource Teacher
Hespenhide, Rodney T.
  English Teacher
Holman, Patricia Hayes
  English Dept Chair/Teacher
Kenney, Valerie Denise
  Social Studies Teacher
Law, Robert Thomas
  Bible/Government Teacher
Morton, Sondra W.
  Teacher
Oney, Kay Prater
  Sixth Grade Teacher
Sharpe, Betty Delbridge
  Chemistry & Biology Teacher
Spencer, Alice Sims
  Eng/Speech Teacher/Dept Chair

NOKESVILLE
Derrickson, Denise A.
  Social Studies Teacher

NORA
Kirk, Rosa Whisenhunt
  Mathematics Teacher

NORFOLK
Barham, Jean H.
  Middle School Teacher
Becker, Mary Foxworth
  Fourth Grade Teacher
Brothers, Cheryl Patricia
  Mathematics Teacher
Carlisle, M. Averill
  7th Grade Teacher
Glasser, Jane Ellen
  English Teacher
Griffin, Edna Koonce
  Health/Physical Ed Teacher
Hook, Ellen Smith
  Mathematics Teacher
Jarvis, Edna B.
  Fifth Grade Teacher
Josephsen, Steven Arthur
  Director of Gifted Education
Martin, Victoria Boone
  English Teacher
Mendenhall, Sharon Lynch
  7th Grade Teacher
Mullin, Elizabeth Brownlow
  Retired Kindergarten Teacher
Nelson, Laura J.
  Chemistry Teacher/Track Coach
Parker, Thelma Robinson
  Social Studies Dept Chairman
Payne, Robert Lee III
  English Teacher
Pope, Stephanie Marie
  Latin Teacher
Rasmussen, Conni Calhoon
  Science Teacher
Riddell, Wilma Quinones
  Spanish/Foreign Lang Teacher
Roundtree, Carolyn
  7th Grade Teacher
Sergeant, Robert Stewart
  English Teacher/Admin Asst
Sheehan, Nancy Palaszewski
  Health/Physical Ed Teacher
Wilgus, Patricia Snipes
  Social Studies Dept Chairman
Wilson, Constantine Lowery
  Fourth Grade Teacher

NORTH ARLINGTON
Chang, Athena S.
  Kindergarten Teacher

NORTH TAZEWELL
Blevins, Betty Jennings
  Chapter I Mathematics Teacher
Crane, Merrell C. Jr.
  Third Grade Teacher

OAKWOOD
Kirby, Ruby Stiltner
  Assistant Principal

ONLEY
Jones, Christopher Michael Thomas
  English Teacher

PALMYRA
Brown, Jeanette Aderhold
  Teacher
Griffin, Jeri Lynn
  Teacher/Acting Asst Principal
Morris, Barry Sherman
  Mathematics Department Chair

PEARISBURG
Mann, Judy J.
  Health & Physical Ed Teacher

PETERSBURG
Barlow, Evelyn Faulcon
  Guidance Counselor
Hawkins, Cyril A. Jr.
  Assistant Principal
Robertson, Francine Watkins
  Sixth Grade Teacher
Summers, Janet Louise
  Fourth Grade Teacher
Taylor, June Stewart
  Chairperson/Kndgtn Teacher

PILGRIMS KNOB
Cole, Pamela Burress
  English Teacher

POCAHONTAS
Campbell, Nancy Kyle
  Math Teacher
Haun, Rita Nave
  English/Speech Teacher

POQUOSON
Goddin, Deborah Ellis
  English Teacher
Powell, Judith Mac Avoy
  Band Director

PORTSMOUTH
Ashley, Cheryl Lynn (Allemand)
  Mathematics Department Chair
Bolden, Naomi Jones
  Business Ed Teacher/Dept Chm
Bowers, Amy Lloyd
  Social Studies Dept Teacher
De Loatch, Elizabeth Robinson
  Bio Teacher & Sci Dept Chair
Garris, Catherine Tyner
  Kindergarten Teacher/Dept Chai
Hampton, Paula Schimmels
  English Teacher
Kersey, L. Wilbur
  Principal
Poteat, Carolyn Senter
  First Grade Teacher
Smith, Sandra Hargrove
  Guidance Counselor
Wall, Anna Morris
  English Teacher

POWHATAN
Meredith, Kay Gillum
  English Teacher

PRINCE GEORGE
Jones, Betty Wade Blanton
  Science Department Chair
Roberts, Anne Tinsley
  Computer Applications Teacher
Trexler, Debra Cain
  English Teacher

PULASKI
Dickerson, Ernest Richard Jr.
  Health/Phys Ed Teacher
Duff, Lee Belshee
  Sixth Grade Teacher
Gardner, Diann Strauser
  Language Art Teacher
Malcolm, Harold Edward Jr.
  6th Grade Teacher
Saul, Susan Powell
  4th Grade Teacher
Vipperman, Rebecca Hill
  Chapter I Teacher

RADFORD
Hendrix, Sally Slusher
  Art Teacher

RESTON
Zirkle, John Warren
  5th Grade Teacher

RICH CREEK
Sartin, Charlotte Stafford
  Kindergarten Teacher

RICHLANDS
Adams, Mary Gillespie
  US History/Adv History Teacher
Blevins, Rhonda Hess
  Health & Physical Ed Teacher
Blevins, Rickie Lee
  Biology Teacher
Chapman, Paul Eugene
  At-Risk Programs Coordinator
Davis, Hester Hagy
  French & Latin Teacher
Hayden, Judith Hillman
  Fifth Grade Teacher
Layne, Robert W.
  8th Grade Mathematics Teacher
Miller, Bobbie Tolliver
  Language Arts Teacher
Mullins, James Allison
  Social Studies Dept Chairman
Ramer, Faith Ellen
  French/Psych/Math Teacher

RICHMOND
Bachman, Connie Elizabeth
  Mathematics Teacher
Carter, Janet Fuller
  Health & Physical Ed Teacher
Crenshaw, Melvin Alexander Sr.
  Guidance Counselor
Eddleton, Susan Clark
  First Grade Teacher
Goldwasser, Janet Schneyer
  Judaic Studies Teacher
Shoemaker, Candace L.
  4th/5th Grades Gifted Teacher
Streagle, Jimmi Dineen
  Earth Science Teacher/Mentor
Tucker, Mckinley R. Jr.
  Teacher/Coach
Waldrop, Winifred Dale Preddy
  Fourth Grade Teacher
Welsh, Jeannette Mc Williams
  Mathematics Teacher

Wilson, Karen Garrett
  Math Teacher
Woody, Roslyn De Cordova
  Second Grade Teacher
Wright, Janet Jackson
  Third Grade Teacher

RIDGEWAY
Copeland, Harriett Martin
  Principal
Lillard, Herman Eugene
  7th Grade Teacher
Williams, Martha Sweitzer
  Social Studies Teacher

RINER
Brennan, Kathryn Altizer
  Science/Social Studies Teacher
Osborne, Gayle Ratliff
  6th Grade Lang Arts Teacher

RINGGOLD
Kidd, Gale Ricketts
  Chemistry Teacher

ROANOKE
Futrell, Terrie Brantham
  English Teacher
Gallion, Linda S.
  Teacher
Grayson, Margaret Mac Queen
  Latin Teacher
Iseminger, Robert Fletcher
  Teacher of Gifted/Talented
Little, Annette Martin
  Third Grade Teacher
Mc Michael, Edward John
  HS Bio/Chem/Marine Bio Teacher
Morgan, Sandra Kay Rader
  4th Grade Teacher
Moss, Marcia Stewart
  Third Grade Teacher
Wilder, Donna Bocock
  Mathematics Teacher/Dept Chair

ROCKY GAP
Henthorn, Joyce Brock
  Art/Home Economics Teacher

ROCKY MOUNT
Adkins, Gwendolyn Alice
  Assistant Principal
Anderson, Gloria Vickers
  First Grade Teacher
Angle, Lisa Deese
  Eng 10 Teacher/Dept Co Chm
Angle, Steve Carter
  Business Teacher
Fore, Linda Compton
  United States History Teacher
Furrow, Mary Catherine
  Fifth Grade Teacher
Guthrie, Donna Morter
  English/Journalism Teacher
Layman, Sandra Hall
  Business Department Chair
Martin, Ammie G.
  Third Grade Chapter I Teacher
Parcell, Emma Perdue
  Spanish Teacher
Smith, Clyde Timothy
  Health & Physical Ed Teacher
Woods, Deborah Powell
  Biology Teacher

RURAL RETREAT
Cole, Kady Eunson
  Sixth Grade Teacher
Walker, Charlene Elledge
  Fifth Grade Teacher

SALEM
Bradley, Larry Roy
  Social Studies Teacher
Garren, Sheila Johnston
  4th Grade Teacher
Gearhart, Rebecca Rhudy
  Third Grade Teacher
Ward, Charles Randolph
  Guidance Counselor
Wheeling, Daniel Francis
  Physical Education Teacher

SALTVILLE
Hess, Judy Frye
  Third Grade Teacher

SHACKLEFORDS
Brill, Martha Carter
  English Teacher

SKIPWITH
Hamilton, Deborah Ann Jennings
  Chemistry Teacher
Reamy, Ann Hines
  English/Social Studies Teacher

SMITHFIELD
Prow, Anna D.
  English Teacher

SOUTH BOSTON

Bosiger, Gail Witcher
Physics Teacher
Mc Caskey, Theodore John
Biology Teacher

SOUTH HILL

Mc Keathern, James Alvin
Dept Chm/Science Teacher

SPOTSYLVANIA

Gratzick, Gail Lentz
Mathematics Department Chair
Winn, David Ervin
Latin Teacher/Foreign Lang

SPRINGFIELD

Creneti, Frank Joseph
Assistant Athletic Director
Jewel, Beth Ann
Biology Teacher
Patton, Joan Cuccias
Mathematics Teacher
Picard, Mary H.
Fourth Grade Teacher
Pilley, Charles Franklin Jr.
Mathematics Teacher
Powers-Lotson, Francine
Counselor
Rosebrock, Genie B.
8th Grade English Teacher

STAFFORD

Payne, Wendy Howell
Physical Education Teacher
Schwartz, Helen Jeanne Lacell
Mathematics Teacher
Sutherland, Helen Robinson
Fourth Grade Teacher
Warner, Judith Knapp
German Teacher

STAUNTON

Didawick, Cynthia Finley
Sixth Grade Teacher
Rhoades, Shirley Fields
Fourth Grade Teacher

STERLING

Howard, Albert R.
Civics Teacher

STRASBURG

Gaidos, William Michael
Business Teacher
Taylor, Timothy Francis
Math Teacher/Computer Coord

STUART

Martin, Lisa Spencer
English Teacher
Pendleton, Paula Plaster
Third Grade Teacher

STUARTS DRAFT

Ellis, James F.
Health & Phys Ed Teacher

SUFFOLK

Boone, Ruth Lamb
Home Economics Teacher
Bowles, Deborah Beuth
Chemistry Teacher
Butler, Jane King
8th-12th Grade English Teacher
Byrum, Phyllis Collier
Social Studies Teacher
Carter, Mary Ward
Fourth Grade Teacher
Howell, Faye Joyner
Sixth Grade Teacher
Spencer, Helen M.
Vocational Dept Chairperson
Story, Billie Diane Tarkington
Reading Specialist

SWOOPE

Hollingshead, Bruce Leroy
Social Studies Teacher

SWORDS CREEK

Lester, Rodney Garnet
7th Grade Teacher
Rasnake, Jane Lloyd
Fourth & Fifth Grade Teacher

TABB

Hoskins, Charlotte Thompson
Math Teacher
Tylavsky, Gerry Baltes
English Teacher

TAZEWELL

Britton, Cathy Dillman
Fourth Grade Teacher
Brown, Kathy Jo
Driver Ed/Phys Ed Teacher
Hrovatic, Natalie Stansfield
Fourth Grade Teacher

Laney, Regina Ann Tatum
Kindergarten Teacher
Reid, Rodney Stephen
Mathematics Teacher
Whittaker, Susan Royall
English/Speech/Drama Teacher

VERONA

Ware, Leona Yelton
Fourth Grade Teacher

VIENNA

Beller, Elaine Cohen
Third Grade Teacher
Fomous, Cathy O'Donnell
Chemistry Teacher
Kirkman, Karen Kirkland
Biology Teacher/Sci Dept Chair
Scholz, Mary B.
English Teacher
Taylor, Mary Newcomb
English Teacher

VINTON

Dowdy, Milton Davis
7th Grade Lang Art Teacher
Sboray, Stephen Charles III
Chemistry Teacher

VIRGINIA BEACH

Boyd, Iona Vick
6th Grade Teacher
Branighan, Wendie
Sixth Grade Teacher
Davenport, Robin Douglas
4th Grade Teacher
Dunbar, Nancy Mc Kinley
2nd Grade Teacher
Emerson, Ella K.
Health/Phys Ed Teacher
Francis, Rebecca Jane
Art Department Chair
Frost, Sue London
Art Teacher
Fruit, Grace Tucker
Art Teacher
Gillikin, Carol Jones
5th Grade Teacher
Giorgi, Jacqueline Ann
English Teacher/Eng Dept Chair
Jones, Robert Clair
Social Studies Teacher
Karl, Robert John
Art Instructor
Kier, Vernice E.
Mathematics Teacher
Livesay, Kathy Ann
A P Chemistry Teacher
Rivet, Katherine Zimmer
5th Grade Teacher
Whitehurst, Barbara Woodhouse
Sixth Grade Teacher/Dept Chm
Zappulla, Nancy Wade
English Teacher

WARRENTON

Bailey, Phyllis Romans
US History Teacher
Benedusi, Lesley Ann
English Department Chairperson
Brown, Shirley Jean
US History Teacher
Burnham, Bonnie Lee Mayo
Latin Teacher
Coffin, Elizabeth Gring
Principal/Teacher/Dir/Owner
Rhodes, Betty Blair
3rd Grade Teacher
Wilson, James William
Social Studies Teacher
Wine, Patricia Shirley
English Teacher

WARSAW

Packett, Cynthia Bronner
8th Grade Mathematics Teacher

WAYNESBORO

Conyers, Lynn Hilton
3-D Art & Photography Teacher
Hullett, Arthur Joseph III
Social Studies Teacher
Luckett, Lillian Hodges
Kindergarten Teacher
Pittman, Wanda Luck
Third Grade Teacher
Robson, William Thurman Jr.
Sixth Grade Teacher
Sachlis, Constance Koger
Reading Specialist
Shirley, Jo Anne Coakley
Fourth Grade Teacher
Stover, Betty Jo Fainter
Reading Specialist Teacher
Stultz, Lucy Carole
5th Grade Teacher

WHITEWOOD

Hobbs, Kimberly Keen
Elementary School Librarian

WILLIAMSBURG

Cahill, Thomas M.
5th Grade Teacher
Fox, Reginald Alan
Choral Dir/Cmptr Sci Teacher
Richardson, Emily Hayden
Voc Dept Chair/Home Ec Teacher

WINCHESTER

Davis, Jane Schneider
7th Grade Mathematics Teacher
Mills, C. Edward
Biology Teacher
Nemeth-Barath, Anne (Collins)
English Teacher
Russell, Kristine Louise
First Grade Teacher
Sciegaj, Robert Allen
Mathematics Dept Chair
Shickle, Louise Marie (Grube)
Mathematics Teacher
Webb, Carol Woodworth
Ag Ed Teacher/Dept Chairman

WINDSOR

Gwaltney, Deloise G.
7th Grade Teacher
Jones, Verna M.
Sixth Grade Teacher
Laine, Nancye Allen
5th Grade Teacher
Mebane, Janice Harrison
Teacher
Richardson, Carita Jones
Mathematics Teacher

WIRTZ

Weddington, Cheryl Debra
Second Grade Teacher

WISE

Carter, Willie Charles
Sixth Grade Teacher
Swindall, Ronnie Edward
Chemistry Teacher

WOODBRIDGE

Bengier, Joseph Peter
7th-8th Grade Math Teacher
Butler, Gloria Fay
Fourth Grade Teacher
Cornwell, Mary Huddleston (Turner)
Fifth Grade Teacher
Engman, Gilta Casanova
Spanish Teacher/Chair
Fitzgerald, Rodger Pierpont
Guidance Counselor 9-12
Robertson, Toni Traylor
Mathematics Teacher
Shiring, Mark A.
Fifth Grade Teacher
Sills, Jane Huber
7th Grade Lang Arts-Team Ldr
Smuzynski-Penland, Bonnie Lane
6th Grade Teacher
Stuart, Lois Gloff
Orchestra Teacher

WOODLAWN

Goad, James Nelson
8th/9th Grade Ag Teacher

WOODSTOCK

Fox, Brenda Dix
Second Grade Teacher
Helsley, Martin Jacob Jr.
8th Grade Math/Science Teacher

YORKTOWN

Crossett, Becky Forbes
Dept Chair for Gifted Center
Eaton, Melinda Guth
High School English Teacher

WASHINGTON

ABERDEEN

Descher, John Daniel
Mathematics Teacher
Hunter, Robert Charles
Art Teacher

ARLINGTON

Everson, H. Lorraine Armstrong
3rd/4th Grade Teacher
Taylor, Virginia Ginger Lynn
4th Grade Teacher

AUBURN

Ewing, Kay Nozaki
Language Art Teacher

Fundingsland, Marsha Gayle
Fourth Grade Teacher
Hoffman, Christina Louise
Fourth Grade Teacher
O'Connor, Terry James
English Teacher
Stow, James William
9th Grade World His Teacher

BATTLE GROUND

Edgerly, Art Clinton
Remediation Coordinator
Pedersen, James Keith
8th Grade Math/Science Teacher
Windemuth, Millie K. Baran
Business Ed & English Teacher

BELFAIR

Nuttman, John Mark
Physical Science Teacher

BELLEVILLE

Lang, Eleanor
Chemistry Teacher

BELLEVUE

Darragh, Marion Ward
Teacher
Dion, Raymond L.
Health Teacher
Lowy, Rita Landweber
Mathematics Teacher
Sherrard, Edith Randal
English Teacher/Director
Sternoff, Diane Markrack
Mathematics Teacher
Vlahos, Pete A.
4th/5th Grade Teacher

BELLINGHAM

Dolmatz, Steven J.
English Teacher
Palmer, Jane Ellen
7th Core Rdng/Soc Stud Teacher

BENTON CITY

Gustafson, Doug Allan
6th Grade Teacher

BOTHELL

Shields, Charlotte Ann
Fourth Grade Teacher
Westvang, Saundra Lee Irwin
5th Grade Teacher
Wetta, Janet Ingrid
Third Grade Teacher

BREMERTON

Chase, Michael John
Physical Education Teacher
Kaech, Joe Jr.
Sixth Grade Teacher
Newell, Clinton Harrison
French Teacher
Triplett, Karen (Williamson)
6th Grade Gifted Ed, 6th House

BREWSTER

Moore, Kim Charlene
Third Grade Teacher

BUCKLEY

Kaelin, John Michael
Fifth Grade Teacher

BURLINGTON

Waetje, Kathryn Joyce
German Teacher

CARNATION

Barich, Michael Peter
Mathematics Teacher
Carlson, Dea Johnson
High School English Teacher
King, Karen Buff
Speech/Drama Instructor
Mejlaender, John Robert
English Teacher/Coach
Owen, Kelly Peters
5th Grade Teacher

CATHLAMET

Dennis, Sharon Mae
Math/Physics/Chem Instructor
Gilbertsen, Kayrene Marie
Correspondence Ed Director
Hedman, Audrey Jean
Third Grade Teacher

CHATTAROY

Marcuson, Robert Wade
Science Teacher
Mc Clure, Thomas Matthew
Mathematics Teacher
Miller, Barbara Vinciquerra
HS Special Education Teacher

CHEHALIS

Timpone, Joseph A.
Science Teacher-Dept Chair

CHELAN

Pierson, Walter Gerold
Vocational Agriculture Teacher

CHENEY

Urdahl, Karlyn Kessler
Home & Family Life Teacher

CLARKSTON

Adams, Samuel David
Mathematics Teacher/Coach
Hill, Bonnie J.
WA State/US History Teacher
Rotz, Glenn Eldon
Fifth Grade Teacher

COLBERT

Johnsen, Peggy Mac Gown
6th Grade Teacher
Rose, Debbie Karlson
Fourth Grade Teacher

DAVENPORT

Lyle, Karen L.
4th Grade Teacher/Tennis Coach

ELLENSBURG

Foote, Nanci Lee Cook
5th Grade Teacher
Hall, Steven Richard
Eighth Grade Teacher

ELMA

Garrett, Gloria G.
Fourth Grade Teacher

ENUMCLAW

Madden, Timothy Edward
Assistant Principal

EVERETT

Anderson, Kristin Osborn
English/Drama Teacher
Bittinger, John Matthew
Science Teacher
Dougherty, Jan Albert
4th Grade Teacher
Hurlbert, Michael Ray
Soc Stud/English/Rdng Teacher
Peeps, Richard Donald James
Computer Language/Math Teacher
Ruff, Sharon Thiege
English Department Chair
Smithson, Robert George Jr.
Health Instr/Head Bsbl Coach
Vittor, Nancy Ann
Lang Art/Soc Stud Teacher
Walter, James Coyne
Band Director

EVERSON

Edin, Marsha Rick
Librarian

FEDERAL

France, Robert Charles
World History/Sports Medicine

FEDERAL WAY

Baker, D. Joyce Baine
Math Teacher/Cmptr Dept Head
Best, Phyllis Jean Cravalho
Third Grade Teacher
Hosford, Shelby A.
English & Spanish Teacher
Metcalf, John
Volunteer History Teacher

GIG HARBOR

Malich, Theresa Marie
Language Arts Teacher
Settle, Linda K.
French Teacher

GRAHAM

Quick-Gunther, Kathleen Ann
5th Grade Teacher

HARRAH

Wilcox, Nancy Karen
Adm/Prin/5th,6th,7th Teacher

HOQUIAM

Crocker, Sherry Darlene
Teacher
Rabourn, Nancy Ann
Computer Teacher/Counselor
Tackett, Donald L.
Director of Vocal Music

ISSAQUAH

Petett, Ronald Delano
4th Grade Teacher
Schieber, Craig Evan
Gifted/Talented Prgm Coord

JOYCE

Maynard, Jim
5th Grade Teacher

KALAMA

Anacker, Robert John
Science/Mathematics Teacher
Trinneer, Judith Wyatt
1st Grade Teacher

KENNEWICK

Dimmick, Christina Fischer
8th Grade US History Teacher
Hansen, Sandra Louise
Sixth Grade Teacher
Hornberger, Patricia Orr
Kindergarten Teacher
Rawlins, Darryl Lee
Mathematics Teacher

KENT

Hukari, Karen (Hansen)
English Teacher
Leivestad, Carolyn Mc Gee
Fifth Grade Teacher
Owens, Sue Thompson
6th Grade Teacher

KETTLE FALLS

Bonstrom, G. Dana
Mathematics Dept Chairman
Bonstrom, Janet Johnson
Resource Room Teacher
Hayward, Karlene Gale
Business Teacher
Mathews, Bena Elizabeth
3rd Grade Teacher

KINGSTON

Morton, William Dunbar
Second Grade Teacher

KIRKLAND

Birkland, Leslie Okada
Japanese Teacher
Brannman, Ward Scott
Director of Bands
Cahill, Mary Ann
Mathematics Teacher
Higgins, John Franklin
Mathematics Teacher
Jones, Charles
English Teacher
Millard, Gary A.
Chemistry/Math Teacher
Ossewaarde, Debbie Radoll
English Teacher
Smith, Susan K.
Athletic Dir/Phys Ed Teacher
Terry, Kathee Gerde
Chemistry Teacher
Thomas, Joan M.
Kindergarten Teacher
Traisman, Andrew M.
Soc Stud/Lang Art Teacher

LACEY

Ebersole, Julie A.
Spanish Teacher
Mc Glamery, Nancy Ann (Chaney)
Teacher of Gifted Education

LAKEWOOD

Gann, Andrea Folsom
7th Grade Block Teacher
Gann, Ronald Wayne
Mathematics Department Chair
Taylor, Laurie A.
Fourth Grade Teacher

LONGVIEW

Byman, Larry D.
Science Teacher
Davis, Billie Jean (Pierce)
4th Grade Teacher
Gorman, Adrienne Toppila
Fifth Grade Teacher
Hayes, Wayne Ivan
Business Education Teacher
La Berge, Michael Ivan
6th/7th Grade Teacher
Le Monds, Jim Edward
English Teacher/Dept Chairman
Mezger, Gail Eileen (Mc Manus)
7th/8th Grade Math Teacher
Selby, Steven Gail
Mathematics Dept Chairman

LYNNWOOD

Barrett, Frances Patricia (Rodman)
Lang Arts/Soc Stud Teacher
Lee, Ronald Harrison
Social Science Instr

MABTON

Arrestouilh, Kimberlyn Halstead
6th Grade Teacher

MANSON

Moser, Melody (Phillips)
5th Grade Teacher

MARYSVILLE

Elder, Karen Ione (Sageman)
Earth Science Teacher
Tripp, Richelle Thaden
Vocal Music Teacher
Walsh, Richard Harold
Librarian

MEDICAL LAKE

Bates, Sharon Byram
Teacher of Gifted & Talented
Huffman, Sharon Mesmer
5th Grade Teacher

MENLO

Rockett, Robert Carl
Fourth Grade Teacher

MERCER ISLAND

Bragg, Marcy Pauline Nixon
Marketing Teacher/DECA Advisor
Lindquist, Tarry Clifton
5th Grade Teacher

MOSES LAKE

Brizendine, Wilma H.
Second Grade Teacher
Vander Wal, Velma Ann (Kilborn)
Third Grade Teacher

MOUNT VERNON

Mc Nulty, Molly Beth
7th/8th Grade Lang Art Teacher

MOUNTLAKE TERRACE

Buzitus, Betty Jean
Challenge Teacher

MUKILTEO

Mc Guire, Teresa K.
Health/Bio/Math Teacher

NAPAVINE

Mills, George W.
Teacher

NEWPORT

Anselmo, Harold Thomas
US History/Soc Stud Teacher
Bishop, Leroy James
5th Grade Teacher
Shawgo, Kate Wallman
2nd Grade Teacher

NORTHPORT

Guglielmino, Patricia Coulter
First Grade Teacher
Hunnicutt, Annabelle
Administrative Assistant
Wilson, Catherine Diane
7th Grade Teacher

OAK HARBOR

Moser, Charles Paul
Science Teacher

OAKESDALE

Grodt, Margaret Kilpatrick
Third Grade Teacher
Hansen, June Blank
First Grade Teacher

OKANOGAN

Clark, Jacquie C.
English Teacher
Garrison, Robert James
Science Department Chair
Sanborn, Robert Laurent
Spanish Teacher

OLALLA

Thomas, Patricia Moncure
Teacher

OLYMPIA

Barry, John Matthew
4th Grade Teacher
Mauer, Charles M.
5th Grade Teacher
Nielson, Larry D.
Physical Education Teacher
Rouse, Renard R.
4th Grade Teacher

ORTING

Kilby, Joe H.
Physical Education/Sci Teacher

PACIFIC

Fettig, Alfred
Sixth Grade Teacher

PASCO

Dong, Jeff Wing
History Teacher

PATEROS

Hagenbuch, Betty Johnson
Teacher

PORT ANGELES

Huber, Louis Anthony
Social Studies Teacher
Kays, John Beldon
Math Teacher/Department Chm
Licht, William Bret
Principal/Social Stud Teacher
Moore, Pamela Wetzel
Vocal Music Teacher
Thompson, Donna Marsh
5th/6th Grade/Jr HS Teacher

PORT ORCHARD

Mc Elyea, Wanda Hand
Fourth Grade Teacher

PORT TOWNSEND

Van Ackeren, John Leonard
AP Calculus/Physics/Dept Chair

POULSBO

Bressan, Anthony Mark
History Teacher
Frodel, Edward C.
History Department Chair
Hooper, Nancy Wells
Social Studies Teacher
Kuniyasu, Keith Kazumi
Comm Technology Facilitator
Rose, Charles Frederick
6th-8th Grade Math Teacher

PROSSER

Boyle, Steven Leonard
Instrumental Music Teacher
Schmidt, Herbert E.
Civics/US History Teacher

PUYALLUP

Duffy, Craig Stephen
Social Studies Teacher
Jansen, Joyce Akers
Home & Family Life Teacher
Storino, John Edward
Social Studies Teacher
Sullivan, Lisa (Herrold)
Social Studies Teacher

QUILCENE

Bennett, Naomi Ann (Hobbs)
Business Education Teacher
Wyatt, Nancy L.
5th Grade Teacher

QUINCY

Goble, Lyle
English Dept Chair/Teacher
Ohme, Gregory Alan
Music Teacher
Wolf, Earl Dudley
History/Physical Ed Teacher

REDMOND

Harrington, Mary Grace (Johnson)
Second Grade Teacher
Lundvall, Doug E.
Pres Lake Washington Ed Assn
Sypher, Beverly Anne
4th Grade Teacher

RENTON

Horne, Linda Ardis (Pitzen)
Teacher of Gifted
Kulle, Carlton David Jr.
Third Grade Teacher
Penton, Martha White
2nd Grade Teacher

RICHLAND

Castleberry, Jim A.
Sixth Grade Teacher
Makenas, Vickie Lynn (Swain)
Math/Computer Science Teacher
Nordsten, Michael John
German Teacher
Richardson, Karlyn Anderson
7th/8th Grade Lang Art Teacher
Smith, Merodee Buchanan
Mathematics Teacher

RIDGEFIELD

Jones, Patricia Ann
Eng & Teacher of at Risk Stu

SEATTLE

Andrews, Robert L.
History Department Chair
Bowie, Leeanne L.
English/Mathematics Teacher
Brockman, Frank William III
Mathematics Teacher/Dept Chair
Curtis, Ramona
Assistant Principal
Dominguez, Gloria Ann
Spanish/Honors Teacher
Dwyer, David William
Math Teacher/Team Leader
Grover, David Allen
Music Department Chair

PORT ANGELES

Hoekema, Bonnie Lou
Social Science Teacher
Mc Donald, Judith Iwen
Religion Teacher
Muckerheide, Paul Robert
Mathematics Teacher
Packard, Elaine Susan
Program Manager
Paulter, Edward Stephen
Social Studies Teacher/Coach
Robinson, Lucretia Metz
Eng/Hum/Journalism Teacher
Shadow, Marcelyn Hellbusch
IPP Teacher/Team Leader
Talbot, Frank K.
Social Studies Dept Chair
White, Mary Catherine
Humanities/World His Teacher

SELAH

Mills, Brenda (Lewis)
Elementary School Counselor

SHELTON

Smith, William Edward
Mathematics Teacher
Walker, Andrea Marie
7th Grade Lang Arts Teacher

SILVERDALE

Parkes, Sally Ann
Spanish Teacher
Story, Ray C.
Sixth Grade Teacher

SKYKOMISH

Hiatt, Vernetta Ness
Science Teacher

SNOHOMISH

Davis, Eileen P. (Schipper)
7th Grade Language Art Teacher

SPOKANE

Badinger, Tami Jo-Vigue
Spanish Teacher
Barnes, Stephen James
Sixth Grade Teacher
Bohlen, Marvin F.
Teacher
Coller, George Patrick
Science Teacher
Davis, Stanley John
English Teacher
Gould, Virginia Carol
Third Grade Teacher/Substitute
Hewitt, Janet Steinke
Third & Fourth Grade Teacher
Jenson, James Curtis
Physical Education Teacher
Johnson, Cheryl Ann
8th Grade English Teacher
Kostecka, Joe M.
Mathematics Teacher
Manfred, Gerald A.
Mathematics Instructor
Mc Cann, Josephine Anne
Principal
Mc Neill, Charles Bishop
Teacher/Mathematics Dept Chair
Meyers, Jacqueline Gunns
Seventh Grade Math Teacher
Schultz, Greg Wynne
History/Speech/Comm Teacher
Taylor, Nancy Jo
English/Phys Ed Teacher
Van Doren, Timothy Paul
Physical Education Specialist
White, Nancy Aplin
Second Grade Elem Sch Teacher

SPRAGUE

Culligan, Sharon Lee
Second Grade Teacher

SPRINGDALE

Bartlet, William Henry
Mathematics/Science Teacher

STANWOOD

Johnson, Paul Emanuel
Spanish Teacher

SULTAN

Hirst, Helen Carter
4th Grade Teacher

SUMNER

Ellwein, Betty Goetz
Fourth Grade Teacher
Percival, Dennis Lee
Social Studies Teacher
Thomsen, Timothy Scott
Teacher/Act-Athletic Dir/Coach

SUQUAMISH

Budd, Sharon Leighton
ASSIST Teacher

TACOMA

Barnett, Cheryl Anne
Jr High Choral Director
Buchholz, Clayton Grant
English-Literature Teacher
Catalinich, James Mark
History Teacher
Cherbas, Christy Andrew
Soc Stud Teacher/Dept Chm
De Vore, Linda Walters
Second Grade Teacher
Green, Wayne Gordon
5th Grade Teacher
Hanis, Kevin Charles
Mathematics/Phys Ed Teacher
Johnson, Gretchen Van Biber
German Teacher
Mc Neal, Evelyn Boyk
Teacher of Gifted Speech
Oliver, Ernest L.
Fourth & Fifth Grade Teacher
Parsons, Jan Marie
English Teacher
Rimbach, Linda M.
Biology Teacher
Rupert, Barbara Jean
Spanish Teacher
Shelton, John Antonio
Gifted Ed/Soc Stud Teacher
Smitherman, Karen Coach
Coordinator of Partnerships
Sole, Jim L.
English Teacher
Vinson, David Lloyd
English/History Teacher
Whitt, Arville Philip
Biology & Phys Science Teacher
Woltjer, John Gerard
History Teacher/Dept Chair
Wright, Ruth Nelson
Teacher
Wright, Sandra Lee
5th/6th Grade Teacher

TENINO

Cox, Casey Edvard
Agriculture Instructor

THORP

Butkovich, Jean Lanigan
5th-6th Grade Teacher

TOUCHET

Bussell, Merri L.
Special Education Teacher

TUMWATER

Haskin, Susan Alice
Sixth Grade Teacher

UNION GAP

Schwartz, Paula Fields (Varco)
7th-8th Eng/Rdng/Quest Teacher

VANCOUVER

Bowyer, Kathy Mc Phee
7th Grade Teacher
Dacus, Jeffrey Ray
8th Grade Teacher
Daltoso, Michael Joseph
Jr HS Teacher
Franklin, Jim William
Social Science Teacher
Gillingham, Dennis Ray
Attendance/Science Specialist
King, Pat Brian
Phys Ed-Sports Development
Mayfield, D. Donald
English Teacher
Moyers, Anne A.
Fifth Grade Teacher
Spear, George Gilbert
10th/12th Grade Eng Teacher

WAPATO

Gilman, Wallace Leroy
7th & 8th Grade Math Teacher
Plesha, John F.
Industrial Arts Teacher
Timmer, Dennis John
Mathematics Teacher

WENATCHEE

Benner, Scott Michael
Social Studies Teacher

WESTPORT

Cloud, Juliana Coleman
1st Grade Teacher

WINLOCK

Alongi, Claudia Knight
History Teacher

WOODINVILLE

Gulberg, E. Lawrence
Athletic Dir/Chem Teacher
Merril, G. Denise
Kindergarten Teacher

YAKIMA
Bennett, Pamela Jane
  2nd Grade Teacher
Marquett, Kathy Denise
  9th Grade English Teacher
Munson, Howard Adelbert III
  7th/8th Grade Teacher
Osburn, Lary
  6th Grade Teacher
Peterson, Donald Robert
  History & Philosophy Teacher
Rogers, Paul W.
  US History/Psychology Teacher

WEST VIRGINIA

ANAWALT
Bailey, Peggy Ann Presley
  Fourth Grade Teacher
Eanes, A. B. Brady
  Principal
Gillespie, Norma R.
  First Grade Teacher

ANSTED
Bickford, Vicky Lea
  Kindergarten Teacher

ARTHURDALE
Jenkins, Rhonda Lynne
  Language Art Teacher

ASHFORD
Hill, Delores Ann
  Second Grade Teacher

ATHENS
Lockhart, Doris Matherly
  Mathematics Dept Chair/Teacher
Mc Claugherty, Carol Thorn
  French/Spanish Teacher

AUGUSTA
Colebank, Sharon Tutwiler
  First Grade Teacher

AURORA
Durst, Hazel Wilt
  Retired

BARBOURSVILLE
Bowen, Hazel Anna
  Chemistry Instructor
Call, Delora Jean
  Third Grade Teacher
Hettlinger, Patricia Callicoat
  Spanish Teacher
Jeffords, Cynthia Mae
  Third Grade Teacher
Spencer, Joyce Cazad
  English Teacher

BEAVER
Allen, Rodney Lee
  9th Grade Health Teacher
Foust, Carol Lynn
  Teacher/Coach

BECKLEY
Blevins, Cynthia Ann Smith
  Social Studies Teacher
Gauldin, Alice Gallaway
  English 10 Honors Teacher
Harrison, Marion L.
  Psychology/Biology Teacher
Ketz, Joseph Patrick
  A P Chem & Chem I Teacher
Newcomb, Phyllis Jean Lyall
  Anatomy/Biology Teacher

BELINGTON
De Long, David Alden
  Fourth Grade Teacher
Dodds, Caroline Coleman
  Media Specialist
Proudfoot, Dana Evans
  Language Art Teacher

BELMONT
Coby, Reba Jan
  5th Grade Reading Teacher
Mc Dowell, David Samuel
  Life Science Teacher

BERKELEY SPRINGS
Burkhart, William Franklin Jr.
  Chapter I Math Teacher
Linaweaver, Julia Hovermale
  Third Grade Teacher
Lintz, Barbara Lee
  4th Grade Teacher
Mc Graw, Linda Largent
  Teacher
Messner, Larry Kent
  Principal

Sims, Kenneth
  Second Grade Teacher
Smith, Ann Moss
  2nd Grade Teacher

BIG CHIMNEY
Baldwin, Karen Sue
  Third Grade Teacher

BLACKSVILLE
Moore, Jacqueline Russell
  Library/Media Specialist
Van Meter, Mary Jane (Birch)
  Eng Dept Chairperson/Teacher

BLUEFIELD
Addington, Duard Gale
  Mathematics Instructor
Blevins, Frances Musolin
  Mathematics Teacher
Cromer, Frances Alba
  Sixth Grade Teacher
Smith, Pauline Campanello
  Business Teacher

BRADLEY
Bazzie, Beverly Mc Clung
  5th/6th Grade Lang Art Teacher

BRADSHAW
Chadwell, Deborah Darlene
  Math Dept Chair & Teacher
Maxey, Silas Otis
  5th/6th Math/Soc Stud Teacher
Rickman, Samuel Eugene
  Band Master
Smith, Donald Ray
  7-9 English Teacher

BRANCHLAND
Christian, Billy Joe
  3rd Grade Teacher/Principal

BRANDYWINE
Dahmer, Cheryl Lynn
  3rd Grade Teacher

BRENTON
Hall, Debbie Morgan
  Media Specialist
Mason, Judy Marie (Short)
  First Grade Teacher

BRIDGEPORT
Ball, Jackie Gaines
  Reading/Keyboarding Teacher
Barrick, Minetta Flint
  Fifth Grade Teacher
Jeffers, Martha Gaynelle (Nease)
  Fourth Grade Teacher
Kinard, Carole Wright
  Fourth Grade Teacher

BRUCETON MILLS
Forman, Mardelle Hopkins
  Second Grade Teacher
Hemler, Debra A.
  Science Department Chair

BUCKHANNON
Hackett, Roianne Miller
  Elementary Teacher of Gifted
Raffety, Cynthia (Kirby)
  Math Teacher/Dept Chairperson
Sharpalisky, Rebecca Williams
  Learning Disabilities Teacher

BUNKER HILL
Greenwalt, Susan Gess
  Fifth Grade Teacher

CAMERON
Bayza, Samuel Paul
  6th Grade Teacher
Kennedy, Sandra Hughes
  Honors Eng Teacher
Mc Cracken, Sharilyn Lyons
  Fourth Grade Teacher
Whipkey, Edith Marie (Yost)
  Retired Elementary Teacher

CAPON BRIDGE
Masters, Arleen Veronica
  7th-9th Grade Teacher

CEDAR GROVE
Barton, Jon Robert
  5th Grade Teacher
Kinsolving, Barbara (Wills)
  Science Teacher
Lorea, Nella Butta
  Mathematics/Science Teacher

CHAPMANVILLE
Freeman, Harry E.
  Social Studies Teacher
Gladkosky, Deborah Nagy
  Latin & English Teacher
Lucas, Marie Dawn
  Math Teacher

CHARLES TOWN
Kable, Janice Holpe
  Instructional Specialist
White, Wilson Henry Stout III
  Mathematics/Cmptr Science Chm

CHARLESTON
Cameon, Brian Keith
  Sixth Grade Teacher
Corbett, Peter Ramsay
  Drivers Ed & Phys Ed Teacher
Hill, Sharon Reed
  Second Grade Teacher
James, Sandra Beller
  French Teacher
Landers, Nell Johnson
  Art Teacher

CHESTER
Casini, Louis A.
  Band Director

CLARKSBURG
Bode, Gertrude Beth
  Fifth Grade Teacher
Boggs, Teresa June
  English/Journalism Teacher
Bucy, Lizabeth Leigh
  4th-6th Grade Curriculum Coord
Cann, Claudia
  Jr HS Gifted Teacher
Hansen, Andrea Susan
  Religion Department Chair
Oliverio, Rosanne Malfregeot
  Third Grade/Music Teacher

CLAY
Davis, Lowell Dale
  Teacher
Stephens, Norman Chase
  7th/8th Grade Math Teacher

COAL CITY
Acord, Kathryn Mace
  Business Department Chair
Hughes, Charles Leon
  Biology Teacher

COALTON
Stalnaker, Denise Gower
  Special Ed/Journalism Teacher

COWEN
Fletcher, Virginia Greene
  7th/8th Grade Lang Art Teacher
Nelson, Rex Otto
  K-8th Grade Art Teacher

CRAB ORCHARD
Shumate, O. Helen Horton
  Third Grade Teacher

CULLODEN
Arnold, Mary Vanater
  Fifth Grade Teacher

CYCLONE
Smith, Brenda Browning
  Language Arts Teacher

DELBARTON
Haney, Leonard Francis
  Mathematics Teacher/Chairman

DUNBAR
Dorcas, Carolyn Brown
  English Teacher

EAST LYNN
Maynard, Cleo
  Retired Substitute Teacher

ELIZABETH
Ball, Sheila Kay
  Sixth Grade Teacher
Davies, Linda Wilson
  Kindergarten Teacher
Egbert, Patricia Ann (Donham)
  Math Teacher
Reed, Connie Jeanette
  Chapter I Reading Lab Teacher
Winters, Phillip B.
  Vocational Agriculture Teacher

ELKINS
Baxa, Barbara Crumrine
  Third Grade Teacher
Beckwith, Robert Nicholas
  Phys Sci Teacher/Sci Dept Head
Dailer, Jay
  Biology Teacher
Louk, Leslie Kaye (Gainer)
  First Grade Teacher
Super, Deborah Harvey
  Gifted Program Teacher

ELKVIEW
Bird, Linda Burdette
  Fourth Grade Teacher

ELLENBORO
Walker, Stephen Michael
  1st Grade Teacher

ENTERPRISE
Lantz, Mary Lou Fittro
  Fifth Grade Teacher

FAIRDALE
Archie, Wilda Bowyer
  4th Grade Teacher

FAIRMONT
Cayton, Nancy M.
  Journalism Teacher
Cimino, James Allen
  French/German Teacher
Deadrick, Thomas Kent
  Sci Teacher/Sci Dept Chm
Leonard, Cynthia Cain
  Fourth Grade Teacher
Munza, Diana Johnson
  Mathematics Teacher
Richardson, Carolyn Daniel
  Vocational Home Ec Teacher
Robinson, Linda Kay
  4th Grade Teacher
Warren, Martha Morris
  Kindergarten Teacher

FAIRVIEW
Ammons, Marla Jean (Tennant)
  5th & 6th Grade Teacher
Linger, Martha Jane
  1st/2nd Grade Teacher
Swanson, Barbara Randeau
  English Teacher

FALLING ROCK
Burdette, Othel Davis
  Retired

FARMINGTON
Dean, Rhonda Shelene
  English Teacher

FAYETTEVILLE
Shaffer, James Lanty
  Mathematics Teacher

FLEMINGTON
Shriver, Teresa Burnside
  Bio/Sci Teacher/Dept Chair

FOLLANSBEE
Nolan, Susan Long
  4th Grade Teacher

FORT GAY
Thompson, Susan Bissett
  11th/12th Grade Eng Teacher

FRANKLIN
Propst, Karen Tackett
  Business Teacher
Waggy, Paula Jean (Dickerson)
  6th & 7th Grade Sci Teacher
Wagner, Donald Joseph
  Science Teacher

GALLIPOLIS FERRY
Long, Karen Sue
  4th Grade Teacher

GILBERT
Miller, Jerry D.
  Mathematics/Phys Ed Teacher

GLEN DALE
Eddy, Kathleen Ellis
  1st Grade Teacher
Fulton, Patricia Anne
  Biology Teacher

GLEN DANIEL
Ferris, Rachel De Mario
  Teacher of English Composition
Saunders, David Allen
  Mathematics Teacher

GLENVILLE
Woofter, Betty Langford
  Business Education Teacher

GRAFTON
Curry, Janet Edwards
  Correlated Lang Arts Teacher
Godwin, Kenneth O. Jr.
  Director of Choral Music
Hart, Jacqueline Eileen (Norris)
  School Counselor
Ludwick, Nancy Ann
  Fifth & Sixth Grade Teacher
Work, James Jay
  Music Teacher

GRANTSVILLE
Edwards, Michael Pain Sr.
  Spanish Teacher

GREEN BANK
Hoover, Diane Ervine
  1st Grade Teacher

HAMBLETON
Calhoun, Deby Chapman
  SLD Teacher
Usnik, Patricia Ann
  Mathematics Teacher

HAMLIN
Cummings, Audrey Jeane
  English-Social Science Teacher
Jones, Cynthia Lou Kundrat
  Second Grade Teacher
Nelson, Esther Louise (Mangus)
  7th/8th Grade Science Teacher
Salmons, Victoria Ann
  Business Teacher
Stapleton, Shelia Lucas
  Third Grade Teacher
Ward, Janet Rykoskey
  Basic Skills Remedial Teacher

HARMAN
Yokum, Nora G. (Harder)
  Retired Teacher

HARPERS FERRY
Hine, Linda Kay (Cook)
  Social Studies Teacher
Kidwiler, Betty Engle
  6th Grade Teacher

HARRISVILLE
Dumire, Pauletta Jean
  H S Social Studies Teacher

HARTS
Adkins, Peggy Ann (Johnston)
  Principal
Blair, Anna Brumfield
  Sixth Grade Teacher

HEDGESVILLE
Aberegg, Bernadine Erb
  First Grade Teacher
Fox, Mary Linn
  Second Grade Teacher
Scott, Charles R.
  HPER Teacher & Coach
Thomas, Cindy Funkhouser
  Mathematics Teacher

HERNDON
Graham, Lela Mc Kinney
  Business Teacher
Mills, Benny Ray
  Language Art Dept Chair

HINTON
Fleshman, Theresa Fazio
  Third/Fourth Grade Teacher
Lawrence, Susan Jane (Shanks)
  Business Education Teacher
Parmer, Barbara J.
  Teacher of Gifted

HUNDRED
Saban, Jo Ann Louise
  First Grade Teacher

HUNTINGTON
Boggess, James Frank
  General Supervisor
Cole, Patricia Ann (Aluise)
  Fifth Grade Teacher
Eagleston, Kenneth Lee
  Chemistry Department Head
Huffstutler, Phyllis Lewis
  Principal
Hughes, Sandra Jordan
  Teacher
Linn, Sandy Bias
  Oral Communications Teacher
Lycan, Shirley Dalton
  English/Humanities Teacher
Mc Dowell, Judith Ann
  Choral Music Teacher
Mc Lain, Katherine J.
  Band Director
Newlon, Carol Rowe
  Remedial Language Art Teacher
Ronan, Mary Michael
  Director of Religious Ed
Stacy, Geraldine Parcell
  Retired Teacher

HURRICANE
Fisher, Penny Summers
  Assistant Principal
Lusher, Pamela Clarkson
  Language Art Teacher

IAEGER
Perdue, Karen June
  Language Arts Teacher
Peters, Darnell
  6th Grade Teacher

JOLO
Breeding, Caroll Kennedy
Sixth Grade Teacher

JUMPING BRANCH
Cox, Mary Lou
Third Grade Teacher

JUNIOR
Bennett, Bonnie Clowser
Fourth Grade Teacher

KENOVA
Maynard, Delylia Gail (Ramey)
Fourth Grade Teacher
Turner, Jaylen Sperry
Phys Ed Chair/Intramural Dir
Veazey, Judith Beuhring
4th Grade Classroom Teacher

KEYSER
Morris, Dennis Elden
Third Grade Teacher
Nofsinger, Joan M.
Mathematics Teacher

KIRBY
Hott, Karen Sue
Teaching Principal

LASHMEET
Pratt, Carolyn K.
Sixth Grade Teacher/Dept Head

LESAGE
Floyd, Marilyn Louise
Substitute English Teacher

LEVELS
Larson, Linda Christian
Third Grade Teacher

LEWISBURG
Bryant, Jeff A.
Director of Bands
Fullen, Mary Mc Clung
6th Grade Teacher

LOGAN
Ball, Linda Ann
Art Teacher
Brannon, Patricia Ann
Language Art Teacher
Fortner, Charles R.
Spec Ed Dept Coordinator
Jones, Susan
7th Grade English Teacher
Maynard, Dianna Lynn
Athletic Trainer
Rogers, Judith Dianne
American History Teacher
Vance, Barbra Browning
Business Teacher
Zeto, Vicki Lynn
Mathematics Teacher

MABSCOTT
Smyre, Velma Whitlow
Fourth Grade Teacher

MAC ARTHUR
Cooper, Lois Moore
Fifth Grade Teacher

MADISON
Baisden, Geneva C. Hager
Retired Teacher
Bond, Virginia Frances
Sixth Grade Soc Stud Teacher

MALLORY
Cline, Sally Williams
6th Grade Teacher
Flannery, Carmel Thompson
Retired Teacher
Murray, Brookie Ann
Fourth Grade Teacher

MAN
Stowers, Patricia Justice
Third Grade Teacher

MANNINGTON
Edgell, Carol Ashcraft
Fourth Grade Teacher
Hays, Michael Alan
Sixth Grade Teacher

MARTINSBURG
Myers, James Howell
Social Studies Teacher
Pugh, Judy Miller
First Grade Teacher
Sigler, Gwen Light
Retired English Teacher
Taylor, Stanley K.
Reading Specialist

MATEWAN
Chafin, Lydia Estepp
Dean of Students

MAYBEURY
Williams, Audrey English
Fourth Grade Teacher

MAYSVILLE
Travis, Wanda Lee Muntzing
Third Grade Teacher

MC MECHEN
Angalich, Daniel Thomas
Math Teacher/Chairman
Rakay, Mathilde Miller
Retired 5th Grade Teacher

METZ
Roberts, Rita Carol
6th-8th Grade Reading Teacher
Snider, Jo Ellen Stewart
Fifth Grade Teacher

MIDDLEBOURNE
Stender, Diane Lynn
Rdng/Social Studies Teacher

MIDKIFF
Nelson, Bertha Brumfield
Sixth Grade Teacher

MILTON
Barrett, Margaret Minichan
Teacher of Gifted Eng
Harris, Ann Nyquist
English, Math Teacher
Ross, Glenda Davis
Fifth Grade Teacher

MINERALWELLS
Arrowood, Grace Blaschke
Elementary Music Specialist
Cline, Albina L.
Health Teacher 4-6/Phy Ed 1-6
Criss, Sharon Candace (Greenleaf)
5-6th Grade Eng/Spell Teacher
Hale, Janice J. (Adams)
Third Grade Teacher

MINNORA
Morris, Ronald Grover
Elementary Teacher

MOOREFIELD
Hammer, Sharon Ciccolella
Speech/Language Pathologist
Hines, Bonnie L.
Second Grade Teacher
Zirk, Jean Wilson
Substitute Teacher

MORGANTOWN
Colebank, Harriet Scott
Mathematics Teacher
Howat, Janet Michelle
Fifth Grade Teacher
Jackson, Joyce Ellen
School Counselor
Kimbrew, Paul Richard
Technology Teacher
Kirelawich, Margaret Reber
Math Teacher & Dept Chairman
Logar, Dianne L.
English/Writing Teacher
Navarra, Mary Jo
Second Grade Teacher
Swecker, Gary J.
Mathematics Teacher

MOUNDSVILLE
Strickling, Stella L.
Fourth Grade Teacher
Wilburn, William Joe
Bus Dept Head/Soc Stud Teacher

MOUNT HOPE
Billings, Jill Manon
Biology Teacher/Sci Dept Head
Harmon, Shirley Turner
Third Grade Teacher
Warden, Cecilia Harless
Mathematics Teacher

MOUNT STORM
Gardner, Daniel B.
Mathematics Teacher

MULLENS
Houck, Barbara Kaye
Life Science Teacher
Mc Kinney, Tammy Ann Canterbury
English/Reading Teacher
Smith, Terri Lea
5th Grade Teacher
Valentine, Annie Marion
Retired Teacher

NAOMA
Daniel, Linda Martin
Dean of Stu/Soc Stud Teacher

NEW CUMBERLAND
Olashuk, Leanora D. Gregorio
Instructor-Health Assistant

Ranhart, John David
Instrumental Music Teacher

NEW MARTINSVLLE
Figlar, Raymond Gregory
Social Studies Teacher
Richmond, Nancy Lee
Reading/English Teacher

NEWBURG
Knotts, Linda Marie (King)
Kindergarten Teacher

NEWELL
Martin, Verneta D. Hawkins
6th Grade Teacher

NITRO
King, Norma Lasure
Business Education Teacher

NORTHFORK
Jackson, Donna Hopkins
English/Business Teacher

OAKVALE
Alvis, Debra J.
Biology/Science Teacher Chm
Ball, Patricia Six
5th & 6th Grade Teacher
Buckner, Danny Keith
Sixth Grade Teacher

OCEANA
Crouse, Camellia Miller
Biology Teacher
Halsey, Betty Ritchie
Spanish/French Teacher
Powell, Elizabeth Pearl
Mathematics Dept Chair
Short, Karen Lee (Gunter)
Third Grade Teacher
Stowers, Mary Kathryn
English Department Chair

ONA
Legg, Wayne E.
Mathematics Teacher
Seaton, Judy Heffner (Elmore)
1st Grade Teacher

PARKERSBURG
Brannon, Randall Lanier
Band Director
Dennis, James L.
Social Studies Teacher
Durnell, Carol Justice
Math Lab-Chapter I
Gunchuck, Roberta Sue
Behavior Disorder Teacher
James, Daniel Douglas
World Cultures Teacher
Lacey, Vicky Shanklin
K-6th Grade Phys Ed Teacher
Lantz, Karen Sue
English Teacher
Lemley, Joan Rae
English Teacher
Mancini, Alphonse F. Jr.
6th Grade Teacher
Stout, James Edward
Retired
Swarr, Lora Holman
Gifted Education Teacher
Williams, Wendy Parker
English Teacher

PARSONS
Hebb, Cathy Markham
6th-8th Grade Math Teacher

PENNSBORO
Goff, Roberta Diane
Language Arts Teacher
Hardway, Alan Wayne
Social Studies Teacher
Jackson, H. Kenneth Jr.
5th/6th Grade Soc Stud Teacher

PETERSBURG
Bean, Edna Elizabeth
English Teacher
Goodall, Suzanne Hardy
9th/10th Grade English Teacher
Kite, Don Bradford
Jr High Language Arts Teacher
Moyers, John Russel
Social Studies Teacher
Propst, Angela
Jr HS Language Arts Teacher

PETERSTOWN
Bailey, Karen Campbell
5th Grade Teacher
Coburn, Barbara Ann (Mooney)
Chemistry Teacher
Fields, Dorothy Mann
5th Grade Teacher
Hazelwood, Linda Martin
Kindergarten Teacher

Hines, Beatrice Kaye Williams
English Dept Chair
Miller, Freda Dillon
Sixth Grade Teacher

PHILIPPI
Caplinger, Jeffrey Lynn
Director of Bands
Emigh, Charlinda Walker
Third Grade Teacher
Everson, David Paul
Biology Teacher
Golden, Jennie Dilly
Business Education Teacher
Hyde, Karen M.
6th Grade Science Teacher
Propst, Ellen Farley
Mathematics Teacher

PINEVILLE
Mayhew, Ronald Dale
Social Studies Teacher
Williams, Shirley Church
Business Education Teacher

POCA
Walters, William Monroe Jr.
Mathematics Dept Chair/Teacher

POINT PLEASANT
Miller, Rosalie Kay
Third Grade Teacher
Morse, Opal Marie (Rose)
Biology Teacher/Sci Dept Chair
Withers, Kimberly Denae
Biology/Physical Sci Teacher

PRATT
Harkins, Marjorie Davis
Fifth Level Teacher

PRINCETON
Benson, Max Eugene
Principal
Gaspersich, Mary Cecile
English/Speech/Drama Teacher
Hawks, Kathy June
5th Grade Teacher
Lewis, Robert Bruce Jr.
Sixth Grade Teacher
Taylor, Billie Dalton
Mathematics Dept Chair/Teacher
Wade, Mary Clow
English Teacher
White, Helen Camberos
English Teacher

READER
Aberegg, Joan Dulaney
Gifted-Teacher
Yeager, Robert Jay
Assistant Principal

RICHWOOD
Bailey, Alice W.
Mathematics Teacher
Barrett, Susan Manning
4th Grade Teacher
Bay, David L.
Fifth Grade Teacher
Coffman, Tim J.
Science Instructor

RIDGELEY
Clark, Leslie Ann (Myers)
Fourth Grade Teacher
Unger, Roberta Marie (Randolph)
Spec Ed Teacher

RIPLEY
Swisher, Pamela Reese
Sixth Grade Teacher

ROCK CREEK
Canterbury, Judith Brown
4th Grade Teacher

ROMNEY
Duckworth, Kelly Lee
6th Grade Teacher
Likins, Judith Ann
Choral Director
Prado, Donna (Puffinburger)
Mathematics Instructor
Staub, Linda Gurtler
Eng Journalism Speech Teacher

RONCEVERTE
Montgomery, Joyce Belle
Sixth Grade Teacher

RUPERT
Nutter, Glee Lelia
Reading Teacher

SAINT ALBANS
Bibbee, Lora W.
Sixth Grade Teacher
Dillman, Paul D.
Teacher/Ind Tech Chairman

SAINT MARYS
Armstrong, John Graham
Economics Teacher
Oliverio, Paula Jones
Special Education Teacher

SALEM
Kapphan, Elaine Dowling
Second Grade Teacher

SCOTT DEPOT
Kingery, Elizabeth Marie
English Teacher/Dept Chair

SETH
Ralston, Margaret Louise
English Teacher

SHADY SPRING
Prince, Rachella Stanley
Sixth Grade Teacher
Snuffer, Larry Preston
Economics/Government Teacher

SHENANDOAH JCT
Demchik, Michael Joseph
Chemistry/Physics Teacher
Walker, Susan M.
English Teacher
Williams, Salena Mae
Business Teacher
Woods, Vera Gail
English Teacher

SHINNSTON
Mitchell, John Gilbert Jr.
Science Teacher

SISTERSVILLE
Cavezza, Catherine Sperry
Mathematics Teacher
Lovell, Barbara (Skidmore)
Remedial Reading Teacher
Wilson, Carolyn Neely
Sixth Grade Teacher

SOUTH CHARLESTON
Drummond, Patricia Ferguson
English/Speech Teacher
Hamilton, James Clair
6th Grade Teacher

SPANISHBURG
May, Sharla Godfrey
English Teacher
Mc Mullin, Sheila Daniel
Sixth Grade Teacher

SPENCER
Anderson, Karen (West)
Kindergarten Teacher

STONEWOOD
Brown, Shirley Urtso
6th Grade Teacher

SUMMERSVILLE
Mowrey, Romilda Neal
Health/Phys Ed Teacher

SURVEYOR
Smith, Marsha Kay
Assistant Principal

SUTTON
Loudin, Jean Snyder
8th Grade Science Teacher

TALCOTT
Davis, Carol Salmons
English Teacher/Librarian

TERRA ALTA
Bowman, Rodger Lee
Mathematics Teacher
Williams, Susan Lynette Nine
First Grade Teacher

TROY
Butcher, Pamela Sue (Bush)
4th Grade Teacher
Foxworthy, Deanna Barnabo
Fifth Grade Teacher

TUNNELTON
Wolfe, Robert Jr.
Third Grade Teacher

UNION
Taylor, Doris Ann Lemons
6th Grade Teacher

UPPERGLADE
Gladwell, Gilbert Wesley
Biology Teacher
Mann, William Edward
French Teacher
Martin, Wanda Lee
Phys Ed/Health Teacher

VAN
Setser, Sherry Lynn
Social Studies Teacher

VIENNA

Hardin, Katie (Frazer)
  Third Grade Teacher
Mc Cullough, Barbara Zinn
  English Teacher
Thorpe, Rebecca Jean
  Fifth Grade Teacher

WADESTOWN

Elliott, Wilma Cooper
  Sixth Grade Teacher

WALTON

Williams, Don E. Sr.
  Teacher & Coach

WAR

Boyd, Joseph Lee
  Art Teacher
Linkous, Donna Hardy
  Mathematics Teacher

WAYNE

Mc Sweeney, Connie June (Ward)
  Mathematics Teacher
Mills, Anita Troxell
  Fourth Grade Teacher
Mitchell, Shirley W.
  9th Grade English Teacher
Prichard, Leona Adkins
  Physical Science Teacher
Warren, Rebecca Wright
  8th Grade Language Art Teacher

WEBSTER SPRINGS

Mc Coy, Delmas Boyd
  Physical Ed/Health Teacher

WEIRTON

Karpyk, Pete
  Chemistry Teacher

WELCH

Bateman, Linda Dumbauld
  Fifth Grade Teacher
Cortellesi, Debra Jean
  Educational Evaluator
England, Pamela Ann
  Secondary Mathematics Teacher
Perdue, Mary Kathryn (Clark)
  5th Grade Teacher

WELLSBURG

Ferrell, Jeanne Marie Andriano
  7th Grade Reading Teacher
Furioli, Helen Virginia (Wiseman)
  Fifth Grade Teacher
Harper, Sharon Murphy
  Teacher of the Gifted
Higgins, Paul Robert
  Econ/Contemp America Teacher
Javorsky, Ronald Joseph
  Social Studies Teacher
Rafa, Michael Joseph
  Biology Teacher
Waters, Sandra Carol
  English Teacher
Wojcik, Richard John
  Sr HS Language Arts Teacher

WEST HAMLIN

Wilkinson, Mary Alice Courts
  Fifth Grade Teacher

WEST MILFORD

De Fazio, Alice Barberio
  Kindergarten Teacher

WESTON

Sinnott, Eileen Marie
  Principal

WHARTON

Boyko, Thomas M.
  3rd Grade Teacher

WHEELING

Banco, John Harold
  Language Art/English Teacher
Baranowski, Crystal Meyer
  Spanish/Language Art Teacher
Campbell, Joan L.
  Fourth Grade Teacher
Grob, Richard Joseph
  Science Department Chairman
Grubler, Janet M. (Ciripompa)
  Spanish/English Teacher
Holden, Nancy Byrum
  Third Grade Teacher
Huggins, Alberta Petrie
  Teacher/Reading Specialist
Kachurik, Elizabeth M.
  Business Education Teacher
Mauck, Sandra Miller
  Language Arts Teacher
Morton, Patricia Howley
  Jr HS Language Arts Teacher
Paul, Anne Hatten
  Mathematics/Computer Teacher

Richardson, Dan Lynn
  Fifth Grade Teacher
Toland, Debra Yzenski
  German/English Teacher/Chair

WINFIELD

Crum, Avaflorence Powell
  Mathematics Teacher

WISCONSIN

ABBOTSFORD

Voss, Jeffrey Charles
  Third Grade Teacher

ADELL

Filemyr, Sara Walker
  Second Grade Teacher

ALTOONA

Gunderson, John Albert
  5th Grade Teacher
Schofield, Thomas Patrick
  7th/8th Grade Math Teacher
Traun, Carla Jean
  English Teacher

APPLETON

Bergen, Michael William
  Commercial Arts Teacher
De Broux, Richard Theodore
  8th Grade Science Teacher
Funk, Michael Lee
  US History Instructor
La Bar, William D.
  Sixth Grade Teacher
Lee, Gregory Robert
  English/Governments Teacher
Levorson, Ruth Helen
  First Grade Teacher
Maxwell, Dawn Leeal
  School-Age Parent Teacher
Weber, Linda Besch
  Spanish Teacher

ASHLAND

Be Beau, Stanley Bernard
  Jr HS Teacher
Junker, Constance Williams
  Librarian/Media Director

AUGUSTA

Stutzman, Randall Lynn
  Social Studies Dept Teacher

BALDWIN

Trahms, Alice Spooner
  Retired Elem 4th Grade Teacher

BALSAM LAKE

Schoess, Sandra Marie
  6th Grade Teacher
Swenson, Rhonna Mary
  Language Art Teacher

BARRON

Weghorn, Michael Steven
  English Teacher

BEAVER DAM

Hartl, Rosemary Schinderle
  Fifth Grade Teacher
Rabata, John J.
  5th Grade Teacher
Van Haren, Roger James
  Dir Stu Activities/Eng Instr

BELMONT

Gaulke, Glenn W.
  Phys Ed/Health Teacher
Harrison, Zita Ellen
  Third Grade Teacher

BERLIN

Dietrich, Michael Steven
  Mathematics Teacher
Lichtfuss, Frank George Jr.
  Middle School Science Teacher
Reif, Jody Ann
  Spanish Teacher

BIRCHWOOD

Harnisch, Robert W.
  English Teacher

BLACK CREEK

Hering, Carol Will
  Retired 3rd Grade Teacher
Thede, Audrey Steward
  7th-8th Grade Soc Stud Teacher

BLACK EARTH

Kiehl, James Robert
  Reading Specialist
Martinsen, Wanda Johnson
  Pre-1st Grade Teacher
Poch, Lisa Marie
  School Social Worker

BLOOMER

Allison, Janet Marie Pingel
  Bus Education Dept Chairperson
Lasocki, Ann Leslie
  First Grade Teacher
Paulson, Nancy (Novak)
  Fourth Grade Teacher

BLOOMINGTON

Myers, Colleen Brendemuehl
  Third Grade Teacher

BONDUEL

Hartman, Anita Mae
  English Department Chair

BOSCOBEL

Anderson, Cynthia R. Carlisle
  Home Economics Teacher
Houtchens, Karl J.
  Social Studies Teacher
Klesath, Julie Kay
  Chemistry/Physics Teacher
Stahlman, Steve W.
  High School Science Teacher
Zingsheim, Ronald N.
  English Teacher

BOYCEVILLE

Thompson, Carol Ann (Carlson)
  Health/Physical Ed Instructor

BRILLION

Bertrand, Harold Robert
  6th Grade Math/Sci Teacher
Schwartz, Shirley Ann
  First Grade Teacher

BRISTOL

Booth, Bertha E. Anduray
  4th Grade Teacher

BRODHEAD

Van Horn, Pamela Lee (Loudenbeck)
  Third Grade Teacher

BROOKFIELD

Caruso, Carolyn Thibault
  Religious Education Director
Reddemann, Sandra Lee (Sobel)
  9th-12th Grade English Teacher

BROOKLYN

Weigand, Mary Catherine (Sullivan)
  Fifth Grade Teacher

BRUSSELS

Dufek, Dan Matthew
  5th Grade Teacher

BURLINGTON

Foat, Sandy M.
  Sixth Grade Teacher
Hill, Barbara Kopack
  Gifted & Talented Coordinator
Mikulasch, Michael Peter
  Social Studies Teacher

CAMERON

Correll, Michael James
  5th Grade Teacher
Miller, Lois Mork
  Kindergarten Teacher

CAMPBELLSPORT

Baker, Mary Kay
  Business Educator
Palmer, Rebecca E.
  Junior High Science Teacher
Pelischek, Patti Lynn (Deglow)
  5th Grade Teacher
Vollendorf, Sharon Ann
  Phys Education/Health Teacher

CASCO

Secor, Marilyn M.
  Spanish & Lang Art Teacher

CECIL

Strei, Clarice Heier
  Retired

CEDARBURG

Cullman, Loretta L.
  8th Grade Language Teacher

CHETEK

Adams, James Charles
  Techonology Coord & Teacher

CHIPPEWA FALLS

Bissell, Harold Preston
  Social Studies Chair
King, Mary S.
  Third Grade Teacher

CLAYTON

Amundson, Sally Delong
  Voc Agriculture Teacher
Eggert, Eleanor (Moskal)
  First Grade Teacher

Kuntz, Karen F. (Merth)
  Junior Kindergarten Teacher

CLINTONVILLE

Akey, Craig A.
  English Instructor
Huftel, Monica Rose
  Kindergarten Teacher

COLBY

Braun, Albert Carl
  World History Teacher
Polzin, Donna Lynn
  Business Education Teacher

COLOMA

Dredske, Sharon Annette
  5th/6th Grade Teacher

CORNELL

Westerberg, Sonja Elizabeth
  Kindergarten Teacher

CUBA CITY

Harris, Anne Marie Egger
  Physical Ed & Health Teacher
Schultz, Ronald Matthew
  Science Department Chairman
Staver, Jill Leahy
  Third Grade Teacher

DARLINGTON

U Ren, Geri Palzkill
  Kindergarten Teacher

DE PERE

Aerts, Rita J.
  Fifth Grade Teacher
Gerrits, Marianne C.
  Sci/Cmptr Sci Teacher
Kirchman, Mary Kasal
  Language Art Teacher
Landreman, Kristine Marie
  1st-6th Grade Art Specialist
Molling, Thomas Clarence
  8th Grade Math Teacher
Paluch, Deborah Lane
  First Grade Teacher

DEERFIELD

Jacobson, Julie Johnson
  Middle School Teacher

DELAFIELD

Siebers, Perry James
  English Department Chair

DENMARK

Trousil, Jeanne Albers
  Mathematics Teacher

DOUSMAN

Hemschik, Terry Kahlert
  Reading Teacher/G T Coord

EAST TROY

Wappel, Louis C.
  Principal/Teacher

EAU CLAIRE

Bejin, Rozanna Marie Hanson
  English Teacher
Clark, Duane Robert
  English Teacher
Hagen, Kim A.
  Elementary Principal
Larson, Cherisma E. Myhers
  6th Grade Teacher
Nolting, Paul David
  Principal/Social Studies Chair
Poss, Frederick Maurice
  Dept Chair of Language Arts
Reetz, Michael Leon
  Sixth Grade Teacher
Scheible, Steven A.
  7th Grade Geography Teacher
Smieja, Debra Anne
  Mathematics Teacher
Zwiefelhofer, Patricia Ann (Ruff)
  Mathematics Teacher

ELMWOOD

Radtke, Delores Mc Keeth
  8th Grade Teacher

EVANSVILLE

Kerkenbush, Ann Hansmeier
  8th Grade Language Art Teacher
Loftus, Micheal K.
  Social Studies Teacher

FALL RIVER

Ducat, Christine A. (Weiner)
  Mathematics Department Teacher
Ladwig, Agnes Teeter
  Third Grade Teacher

FLORENCE

Valine, Ralph James
  Teacher/English Dept Chair

FOND DU LAC

Bond, James Joseph
  Fifth Grade Teacher
Britt, Jane Y. Wiemer
  6th Grade Teacher
Hackbarth, David G.
  Biology Teacher
Hayes, Wendy Sukow
  First Grade Teacher

FORT ATKINSON

Johnson, Carole Jo
  Fifth Grade Teacher
Looze, Richard C.
  Social Studies Teacher
Price, Nancy L.
  French Teacher

FOUNTAIN CITY

Florin, Suzanne M.
  Mathematics Teacher/Chair

FRANKSVILLE

Revolinski, Charlene Ruth
  First Grade Teacher

GALESVILLE

Christianson, Robert Peter
  History Teacher/Chair

GERMANTOWN

Altmayer, Robert C.
  Mathematics/Science Teacher
Champan, Louise Hable
  Science Teacher
Crump, Charles Winslow
  Retired English Teacher
Gosenheimer, Judi Thomas
  English Teacher
Held, Donna Teclaw
  Gifted Coordinator
Musloff, Keith Steven
  Reading Teacher

GLENDALE

Brockdorf, Jeanette Gurske
  Fourth Grade Teacher
Owens, Ruth Wilma Townsel
  English Teacher
Werner, Julia Stewart
  Humanities Teacher

GLENWOOD CITY

Holldorf, Cheryll Novotny
  Fifth Grade
Lindelof, Roger Hadley
  District Reading Coordinator
Wyss, Ardis Harvey
  Family & Consumer Ed Teacher

GRAFTON

Gruenwald, Deborah Anne
  Third Grade Teacher

GRANTSBURG

Solomonson, Betty Rydeen
  Retired Elementary Teacher

GREEN BAY

Brock, Richard Donald
  8th Grade Soc Stud Teacher
Dunlap, John H.
  Mathematics Teacher
Fischer, Lyman Dixon
  Mathematics Teacher
Kilmer, Bruce Norbert
  Science Teacher/Content Ldr
Kiser, Bernal Allen Jr.
  Chemistry Department Chair
Madden, Jerry Eugene
  Teacher/Mathematics Dept Chair
Mc Crary, Herdis W.
  Dept Chm-Lang Arts Teacher
Shupita, Harlan Harry
  Physics Teacher/Sci Dept Chair
Stein, James William
  Mathematics Teacher
Stock, Michael Robert
  Athletic Director/Teacher
Tobin, Pamela Patterson
  Mathematics Teacher

GREEN LAKE

Hanson, Polly Sue
  Physical Science Dept Chair

GREENDALE

Kemp, Patricia Mary
  Second Grade Teacher
Porter, Claudia Siehr
  Religion & Art Teacher

GREENFIELD

Black, Valerie Bendix
  Fifth Grade Teacher
Burrill, Gail Frances
  Mathematics Department Chair
Lind, William Robert
  Mathematics Teacher

GREENWOOD

Bushman, Constance Bauer
Bus Education Teacher/Chair

HALES CORNERS

Fons, Shirley Crane
Third Grade Teacher
Puschnig, Anne Eberhardy
Third Grade Teacher
Wallschlaeger, Joy Dorothy (Redlin)
6th-8th Grade History Teacher

HARTFORD

Biersack, Leslie Skumatz
Junior High School Teacher
Larkee, Mary Luchterhand
3rd Grade Teacher

HARTLAND

Borzykowski, Janis Thone
Math/English Teacher
Peterson, Richard A.
Mathematics/Computer Teacher
Schaefer, James John
English Teacher

HAWKINS

Cicha, Sharon Larson
2nd & 3rd Grade Teacher
Maday, Theodore F. Jr.
Middle Sch Teacher/Principal

HAYWARD

Aspenes, Mary Fabricius
Fourth Grade Teacher
Berner, Tom E.
Middle School Guidance Cnslr
Hnath, Kathleen Marie
English/Journalism Teacher
Kozak, Carl Eugene
Technology Education Teacher
Neff, Patricia Ann
Spanish Teacher

HELENVILLE

Manthe, Matthew Dan
Fifth & Sixth Grade Teacher
Wilke, Russell A.
6-8th Grade Principal

HIGHLAND

Benish, Ronald Eugene
Mathematics/Science Teacher
Doye, Joette Cheryl (Fault)
English/French Teacher

HILBERT

Kust, Joan Kay
K-12th Grade School Counselor

HOLCOMBE

Glaus, Perry L.
English Teacher

HOLMEN

Tangen, Jean Elizabeth
4th Grade Teacher

HORICON

Bemus, Alice Koepsell
Kindergarten Teacher

HORTONVILLE

Shekoski, Naomi CSA
Fourth Grade Teacher

HOWARDS GROVE

Bennin, Jeanelle Lenz
Second Grade Teacher
Goes, John Robert
7th Grade Science Teacher
Madlung, Paul David
Seventh Grade Teacher

IXONIA

Davidovich, Robert D.
Principal

JANESVILLE

Taylor, Chester William
Social Studies Teacher

JEFFERSON

Herbst, Richard Alan
Technology Education Instr

JOHNSON CREEK

Johnson, Ken L.
English Teacher
Liebmann, Donald Edward
Elementary Guidance Counsler
Mead, Isabel Delores
7th & 8th Soc Stud Teacher

KANSASVILLE

Bushing, Arthur Brown
5th-8th Grade History Teacher

KAUKAUNA

Farnum, Barbara L.
English Teacher

Novitske, Linda Sue (Kososki)
Learning Disabilities Teacher
Vandenberg, Ronald
Mathematics Teacher

KENOSHA

Becker, George L.
English Teacher
Lawler, Terry Lee
English Department Co-Chair
Moschell, Bonita Jones
Mathematics Dept Chairperson
Perry, Nancee Vaicelunas
Art Teacher
Romano, Charles Anthony
Biology Teacher
Shierk, Wilson Andrew
Principal
Warter, Shirley Ann (Nelson)
Fifth Grade Teacher

KEWASKUM

Dillman, David Kevin
Mathematics/English Teacher
Jacak, Judith Lavarda
English/Geography Teacher
Leader, Timothy Michael
Fifth Grade Teacher

KIEL

Mertens, Irene Medvecz
Seventh Grade Teacher

LA CROSSE

Ellingson, Nancy May
English Teacher
Garcia, Gloria B.
Teacher Primary Unit
Sahagian, Janet Helen
Vocal/Choral Music Director
Santos, Kathleen Joan (Ryan)
6th-8th Grade Soc Stud Teacher

LA FARGE

Stout, Garnet J. (Campbell)
Fourth Grade Elem Teacher

LADYSMITH

Ek, Karen Esther
Music Department Chair
Hoesly, Clarence L.
Science-Health-Algebra Teacher

LAKE GENEVA

Pankow, Sharon Johnson
1st Grade Teacher & Principal
Welch, Thomas R.
Reading/Social Studies Teacher

LAKE MILLS

Darnall, Gloria Meyer
6-12th Vocal Music Teacher
Shutters, Edward Earl
Science Teacher
Slauson, Susan Le Master
5th Grade Teacher

LITTLE CHUTE

Boogaard, Dorothy Jane
Second Grade Teacher
Bouressa, Ken D.
Vocal Music Teacher
Klozotsky, Robert John
Language Art Teacher

LOMIRA

Zitlow, Dorothy Papenfuss
Jr HS Teacher

LOYAL

Benz, Beth Ann
Mathematics Teacher

LUXEMBURG

Ehren, William James III
Cmptr/Chem/Physics Teacher
Werner, Thomas David
Fifth Grade Teacher

MADISON

Mann, Arthur Harold Jr.
Eng-Soc Stud 7th Grade Teacher

MANAWA

Hackbarth, Gerald Henry
Mathematics & Science Teacher

MANCHESTER

Kuehn, Alice Asplund
Third Grade Teacher

MANITOWOC

Benfield, Kenneth William
Sixth Grade Teacher
Helf, Linda L.
Fourth Grade Teacher
Henrickson, Majel Pinney
Chorus Teacher
Moen, Mona L.
Physical Education Teacher

Reinert, Phyllis Dorothy Galikowski
Teacher
Stammler, Julie Ann (Jackson)
Business Education Teacher
Stan, Trudy Louise (Reilly)
Third Grade Teacher
Yust, Roger Albert
Social Studies Teacher

MAPLE

Lundquist, Peggy Lynne Abrahamson
Kindergarten Teacher

MARION

Kjendalen, Dianne Marie
(Mierkiewicz)
Computer Coordinator/Teacher

MARKESAN

Hirschy, Russel Philip
Mathematics/Computer Teacher

MAUSTON

Gougeon, Raymond Joseph
Social Studies Instructor

MAYVILLE

Kaepernick, Kenneth Lee
Math/Computer Science Teacher
Persha, Susan R.
Fifth Grade Teacher

MC FARLAND

Mc Laughlin, Mark F.
AODA/SAP Coordinator

MEDFORD

Fuchs, Enid J.
First Grade Teacher

MELLEN

Schraufnagel, Patricia Louise
5th Grade Teacher

MENASHA

Hanson, Randall Jon
Coord of Gifted & Talented
Hughes, Marie Belongie
Middle Level Teacher
Long, John William
Mathematics Teacher/Dept Chair
Lundt, Karen Kronwall
Sixth Grade Teacher
Schatz, Gerene Aiko
Third Grade Teacher

MENOMONEE FALLS

Egan, Julane Barczak
English/Social Studies Teacher
Schmitt, Rosemary White
Fourth Grade Teacher

MERTON

Mc Cabe, Dennis Robert
Social Studies Teacher

MILWAUKEE

Bailie, Ann (Nesemann)
United States History Teacher
Bickel, David W.
English Teacher
Bristol, Susan Ellen
Gifted/Talented Coord/Teacher
Coles, Edward L.
6th Grade Teacher
Deines, Dixie Snyder
Eng as Second Lang Teacher
Drasch, Catherine M. Schueller
Mathematics Teacher
Ellis, Patricia Ann
Second Grade Teacher
Gustafson, Dennis Keith
Biology Teacher
Hanson, Jerrold S.
History Teacher
Hodgson, Nita Parcel
Teacher
Intravaia, James A.
Sixth Grade Teacher
Jadin, Rita
Fifth Grade Teacher
Korth, Jeffrey Gilbert
Teacher/Athletic Dir/Vice Prin
Kranedonk, Henry A.
Math/Computer Science Teacher
Krueger, Nancy L.
Business Education Dept Chair
Kukowski, Elizabeth Ann (Billo)
5th Grade Teacher
Piccicolo, Lea Zaidins
English Department Chair
Ross, Rebecca Harrell
Fifth Grade Teacher
Scardina, Philip A.
History Teacher
Slak, Daniel James
Mathematics Teacher
Slottke, Gloria Jane
Teacher

Thompson, Cliff Henry
Athletic Dir/Religion Teacher
Turner, Eliza M. Taylor
Fourth Grade Teacher
Wild, Thomas Richard
Psychology/History Teacher

MINERAL POINT

Bergenske, M. Diane
3rd/4th Grade Teacher
Erickson, Ellen Cox
First Grade Teacher

MISHICOT

Spevacek, Donna Munson
Fifth Grade Teacher

MONONA

Kaether, William Owen Jr.
English Teacher
Nesvacil, Sheila Dahmen
Marketing Teacher

MONTELLO

Atkinson, Peggy Schmitz
First Grade Teacher
Ellenbecker, Catherine Riedl
Art Specialist
Schultz, Karen (Whitney)
6th Grade Teacher

MOSINEE

Baltz, Janet Lucille
Third Grade Teacher
Kowalski, Marsha Marie
English Teacher
Morril, Lorraine Ann
Science Department Teacher

MOUNT CALVARY

Plale, Neal Anthony
Religion Teacher

MUKWONAGO

Adkins, Sandra Sizemore
Spanish Teacher
Burt, Lowell Richard
Art Teacher and Art Dept Chair
Davies, Marilyn
English Teacher
Joers, Carol Lipphardt
6th Grade Teacher
Nelson, Lynn A.
Science Teacher
Smith, David G.
English Teacher/Activities Adv
Tulius, Patricia Ponasik
First Grade Teacher

MUSKEGO

Fortmann, Candice J.
English Teacher
Toman, Vincent
Social Studies Teacher

NEENAH

Hardt, Sandra Kay (Rudie)
Kindergarten Teacher
Pogue, Mary A.
English Teacher
Weinmann, Donald John
7th Grade Soc Stud Teacher

NEW AUBURN

Johnson, Dennis D.
Science Department Chair

NEW BERLIN

Fickau, Barbara J.
1st Grade Teacher
Gutoski, Gerald Robert
Geology/Earth Sci Instructor
Miller, Agatha Louise
6th Grade Teacher

NEW GLARUS

Guldhaug, Violet M. (Hendrickson)
Retired Supervisor & Teacher
Zimmerman, Fran L. (Smith)
Sixth Grade Teacher

NEW HOLSTEIN

Flora, James Edward
Social Studies Teacher
Lodes, Mike G.
7th/8th Grade Math/Sci Teacher

NEW LONDON

Kafer, Catherine Ramharter
1st Grade Teacher
Peterson, Danny A.
Band Director/Fine Arts Chair

NIAGARA

Marinich, Marcia Lee Person
5th Grade Teacher

OAK CREEK

Keane, John Patrick
Eighth Grade Teacher

Ramstack, Kathleen Klein
Third Grade Teacher

OCONOMOWOC

Holtzmiller, Dan R.
Chemistry Teacher
Jensen, James H.
Science Teacher
Lee, Beverly Hanson
Business Education Teacher
Lewis, Diana R.
Rdng Teacher/Rdng Specialist
Mahnke, Glenn Ronald
Minister of Music/Teacher
Miksic, Robert Michael
English Teacher
Neary, Joann Rholl
Physical Science Teacher
Reynolds, Judy Kay
2nd Grade Teacher/Asst Prin
Schuster, Barbara Enters
6th Grade Teacher
Strong, Mark Christopher
Third Grade Teacher

OCONTO

Liefke, Mary Ann Mavis (Vorpahl)
Third Grade Teacher

OMRO

Gusick, Barbara Velin
Mid Sch/HS Reading Teacher
Knurr, Allen D.
Chemistry/Physics Instructor

ONALASKA

Buege, Deborah A.
Mathematics Teacher
Hurlburt, Ruth Hass
7th/8th Language Arts Teacher

OOSTBURG

Adams, Robert Vincent
Fifth Grade Teacher

OSCEOLA

Bents, Theodore Fredick
Mathematics/Science Teacher

OSHKOSH

Rathsack, Steven Angelo
5th Grade Teacher
Yana, Patricia (Huevler)
Kindergarten Teacher

PATCH GROVE

Neises, Barbara Horkheimer
4th-6th Grade Teacher

PLAINFIELD

Copas, Linda Brettmann
Fourth Grade Teacher
Mesyk, John
Mathematics Teacher/Dept Head
Robinson, Harlan Patrick
5th/6th Grade Soc Stud Teacher
Sierk, Janice A. (Losey)
First Grade Teacher

PLATTEVILLE

Ewing, Stanley E.
Mathematics Teacher

PORT EDWARDS

Penke, Darwin D.
Soc Stud/Driver Ed Teacher

PORT WASHINGTON

Campbell, Mary Ann
Phys Ed/Health Teacher
Taucher, John C.
Social Studies Teacher

PORTAGE

Coleman, Janine Marie
Spanish Teacher
Comstock, Verla Mae (Schroeder)
3rd/4th Grade Teacher
Molstad, Kerry Lynn
Health Education Teacher

POTOSI

Donahoe, Laureen Kay (Mc Donald)
First Grade Teacher
Lefeber, David D.
Sixth Grade Teacher

PRAIRIE DU SAC

Evarts, Lynn
English Teacher

PRAIRIE FARM

Appelholm, Robert Allan
Elementary Principal

PRESCOTT

Vortherms, David Lee
Business Teacher

RACINE

Anzalone, A. Carmen (Tower)
Sixth Grade Teacher

RACINE (cont)

Clouthier, Kathleen Joan (Mc Grath)
Mathematics Teacher
Hoskins, Euradell Epps
Third Grade Teacher
Kirby, Ozetta
Third Grade Teacher
Kizewic, Richard Donald
United States History Teacher
Kozleuchar, Barbara E.
Jr High School Teacher
Schultz, Judith Ann
5th Grade Teacher
Sprague, Susanne Furtek
Jr HS Science Teacher

RANDOM LAKE

Bertelsen, Terri Lynn
Elementary Music Teacher
Tenges, John William
Math/Computer Science Teacher

REEDSBURG

Parrott, Mark Alfred
Technology Education Teacher

REEDSVILLE

Meier, David G.
Math/Computer Science Dept Chm

RHINELANDER

Reiser-Antonuk, Ruth Ann
Spanish Teacher

RICHLAND CENTER

Mc Millin, Mary Zick
Fourth Grade Teacher

RINGLE

Augustine, Edward S.
3rd Grade Teacher

RIO

Easley, Sharon Ann (Welch)
English Teacher/Dept Chair

RIPON

Klapperich, Margaret R.
Art Teacher

RIVER FALLS

Elling, Ann Marie Eastman
Fourth Grade Teacher
Kenseth, Ted L.
7th Grade Lang Arts/Math/Rdng
Murphy, Teri M.
Art Teacher
Olson, Mary Louise
Language Art Teacher

ROBERTS

Helders, Dixie Lee
5th Grade Teacher
Mueller, Connie Frederick
Curr Coord/Rdng Teacher

ROSENDALE

Kennedy, Linda Gulmire
Second Grade Teacher
Kennedy, Terrance E.
Social Studies/Geo Teacher

ROSHOLT

Van Haren, Jane Marie Stodola
Middle School Teacher

SAINT FRANCIS

Bretzel, Milton James
Mathematics/Computer Teacher
Lutz, John Marvin
Fifth Grade Teacher

SAUK CITY

Aylward, William P.
8th Grade Soc Stud

SCHOFIELD

Rebischke, M. Jill Vogler
Physical Education Teacher

SENECA

Oldenburg, Miriam Kvigne
Third/Fourth Grade Teacher
Peterson, Gladys Hanson
7-8th Grade Lang Arts Teacher

SEYMOUR

Mullen, Evelyn (Kueter)
HS English Teacher/Dept Chair
Swett, Keith Ellsworth
English Teacher

SHARON

Jamka, Mercedes Henry
Jr High Science Teacher
Perenne, Lina G.
Fifth Grade Teacher

SHAWANO

Hoffmann, Richard Daniel
Social Studies Teacher

Hovey, Alfred Allan Jr.
Science Teacher Coordinator
Reinholz, Jeanne L.
4th Grade Teacher
Stuber, Isabell A. (Zittel)
Retired Teacher

SHEBOYGAN

Dekker, Gary
8th Grade Math/Algebra Teacher
Miotke, Cheri L.
Kindergarten Teacher
Niemuth, Roger Lawrence
Fifth Grade Teacher
Paulmann, Eleanor Marian
Retired 3rd Grade Teacher

SHELDON

Nichols, Darlene Anderson
5th-8th Grade Soc Stud Teacher

SHULLSBURG

Boyle, Robert Joseph
Social Science Scndry Teacher
Klein, David Joseph
Soc Sci/Jr H S/H S Teacher
Reitzner, Colleen Locy
K-12th Grade Art Teacher
Spillane, Margaret Schmitz
Third Grade Teacher
Swenson, Gloria Kathleen Lambert
English/Spanish Teacher

SOBIESKI

Martinson, Jerry Keith
Mathematics/Computer Teacher
Wesolowski, Germaine Velicer
Kindergarten Teacher

SOUTH WAYNE

Kaster, Cindi Lou (Stauffer)
Third Grade Teacher

SPARTA

Gatzke, Carol Ann (Morgan)
7th/8th Grade Science Teacher
Gleason, Paulette L. Finn
First Grade Teacher
Smith, Thomas Joseph
6-7 Science/8th Grade Teacher

SPRING GREEN

Bruhn, Julia Ann (Poad)
Science Teacher

STEVENS POINT

Nebel, Armin C.
Intermediate Teacher
Weller, Leone Hein
3rd Grade Teacher
Zavadsky, Nancy Burnes
8th Grade Teacher
Zavadsky, Nancy Burnes
8th Grade Lit/Eng Teacher

STOCKBRIDGE

Steinert, William Edward
English Teacher/Dept Chair

STONE LAKE

Cronk, Kathleen Cherry
Second & Third Grade Teacher

STOUGHTON

Hall, Richard D.
Mathematics Teacher/Coach

SULLIVAN

Stewart, Claire Hunold
Third Grade Teacher

SUPERIOR

Paulson, Eleanor F. Lamberg
1st Grade Teacher

SURING

Beschta, Patricia
English Teacher

SUSSEX

Eimermann, Frederick O.
Math/Computer Teacher
Hallick, Mary Paloumpis
Eighth Grade Teacher
Komatz, Penny R.
Mathematics Teacher
Metzelfeld, Kathleen McCartan
5th Grade Teacher
Mueller, Richard W.
4th Grade Teacher
Zanoni, Attilio Joseph
Retired Teacher

TAYLOR

Barka, Angela (Hong)
Learning Disabilities Teacher

TOMAH

Falkner, James William
7th Grade Geography Teacher

TOMAHAWK

Herbison, Nancy Rae (Johnson)
Guidance Counselor
Theiler, Tula Drivas
3rd Grade Elementary Teacher

TONY

Carlsen, Kenneth L.
Jr High School Science Teacher

TREMPEALEAU

Davis, Gaye Christianson
Home Economics Teacher
Lee, Scott Arlan
Fifth Grade Teacher

TWO RIVERS

Stapleton, Patrick Joseph
8th Grade Mathematics Teacher

UNION GROVE

Graf, Eileen M.
Junior HS Science Teacher

VIOLA

Marshall, Glòria J. (Bennett)
7th/8th Grade Eng/Rdng Teacher

VIROQUA

Guist, Maynard L.
Reading/Computer Teacher
Mack, Wes D.
Health Teacher/Coach

WATERFORD

Lewis, Larry George
Guidance Director

WATERTOWN

Reid, Harriet (Slack)
Kindergarten Teacher
Westphall, M. Diane
Jr HS Math/English Supervisor

WAUKESHA

Benner, Elouise Wright
5th Grade Teacher
Bralick, Anthony J.
US History Teacher
Fraid, Colette Nelson
7th Grade English Teacher
Frostman, Shirley G.
7th Grade Science Teacher
Gajafsky, Gloria Johnson
Science/Biology Teacher
Helgert, Mark James
Director of Bands
Jacobi, Allen Lee
Driver Education Teacher
Lantz, Alberta Busby
Fifth Grade Educator
Noe, Mary Ann Hentschel
English Teacher
Pless, Nancy Elizabeth (Artmann)
Business Teacher
Wolfe, Holly G.
Second Grade Teacher

WAUNAKEE

O'Neil, J. Peter
7th & 8th Grade Sci Teacher

WAUPACA

Knoepfel, Selma Esneault
7th Grade Life Science Teacher
Kottke, Carlyle Marvin
Fifth Grade Teacher
Shearer, Marilyn Ruth (Davis)
5th Grade Teacher

WAUPUN

Buteyn, Maureen Cheryl
Fourth Grade Teacher

WAUSAU

Fischer, Falton M.
Fifth Grade Teacher

WAUTOMA

Schmoldt, Clifford James
Program Director

WAUWATOSA

Minessale, Joanne Steffen
Second Grade Teacher

WAUZEKA

Finn, Janet L. (Guillett)
Science Teacher

WEST ALLIS

Buth, William Donald (Dex)
Physical Education Instructor
Christensen, Gail Marie Reisenauer
Guidance Counselor
Howard, Gladys Meier
Reading Teacher
Mazner, Violet M.
3rd/4th Grade Teacher

WEST BEND

Henkel, Ann Marie V.
Speech Communications Teacher
Safford, Eunice A.
5th Grade Teacher
Zarling, Douglas James
8th Grade Science Teacher

WEST MILWAUKEE

Walloch, Heidi M. (Hayduk)
Vocal Music Teacher

WEST SALEM

Kindchy, Errol Roy
Middle School Teacher

WEYAUWEGA

Anibas, Robert Anthony
Sixth Grade Teacher
Garnett, Cynthia S.
Fifth Grade Teacher
Reimann, Robert Henry
Fifth Grade Teacher

WHITE LAKE

Pence, Marjorie (Raisch)
English/Spanish Teacher
Syrjala, Debra (Orlich)
Second Grade Teacher

WILLIAMS BAY

Bechman, Michael Dean
Mathematics/Science Teacher

WIND LAKE

Uglow, Mary F.
4th Grade Teacher

WINNECONNE

Giddings, Roger Dean
Mathematics Teacher
Harrison, James Louis III
Biology Teacher
Hoppe, Susan Hanson
Third Grade Teacher
Krueger, Joanne Novak
2nd Grade Teacher
Zemlock, Lisa M.
Band Director

WINTER

Hale, Samuel Stephen
Sci/Social Studies Teacher
Olson, Linda Musser
5th Grade Teacher
Williams, Lloyd David
Social Studies Teacher

WISCONSIN RAPIDS

Marshall, Thomas A.
Student Services Director
Rosin, Mary Ann
Math Teacher/Math Dept Chair

WRIGHTSTOWN

Maki, Judith
English Teacher
Petermann, Alice Schwoerer
Seventh Grade Teacher

WYOMING

AFTON

Sessions, Billie Palmer
Art Teacher/Fine Arts Head

BIG PINEY

Brown, Thomas Loring
Physical Education Teacher

BUFFALO

Goodman, James D.
7th/8th Grade Math Teacher

CASPER

Axworthy, Betty Jean
3rd Grade Teacher
Horne, James D.
World History Instructor
King, Stanley Ewin
Science Department Chair
Mc Lellan, Judy Combes
Sixth Grade Teacher
Miller, Mary Lynn
Third Grade Teacher
Robertson, John W.
Science Teacher
Shaeffer, Brent H.
Social Studies Teacher
Stedillie, Michael Patrick
Theatre Director

CHEYENNE

Jasperson, J. Dan
English Teacher
Kelly, Mary Bille
Second Grade Teacher

Korthals, Tamera Ruhter
Transitional 1st Grade Teacher
Rice, Wallace William
Earth Science Teacher
Stowers, Linda L. (Scheer)
Administrative Assistant
Wacker, John M.
Band Director

CODY

Behrens, Jerry Leigh
Mathematics Instructor
Downing, Jack Russell
Physical Education Instructor
Pentila, Celeste Corinne
English Teacher

EVANSTON

Patzer, Ronald Lester
Chairman Social Studies Dept

GILLETTE

Chaney, Marget Lee Sollenberger
Third Grade Teacher
Cummings, Ernest L.
Elem Phys Ed Teacher
Geis, Carol Ann (Franciscotti)
Teacher/Lang Art Facilitator
Hanson, Peg Vangsnes
Choral Director
Keith, Dan K.
Science Department Chairman
Neyer, Sara Rose Felix
English Teacher
Reynolds, Lois A.
Third Grade Teacher
Schrupp, Thomas Dana
9th Grade Phys Ed Teacher
Wilson, Lindy B.
Mathematics Teacher

GLENROCK

Gray, Christopher A.
Activities Director/Adm Asst

GREEN RIVER

Davidson, Mike R.
Mathematics Instructor
Eklund, Nancy Raso
Elementary Phys Ed Specialist
Scheer, Catherine Marie
Science Teacher
Smith, Peggy Maurer
First Grade Teacher
Stark, Anne Green
Fourth Grade Teacher

HANNA

Reinbold, Philip Alan
Chemistry/Physics Teacher
Sanchez, Ruby Judy
Third Grade Teacher

JACKSON

Carruth, Ann Delaney
English Teacher

KAYCEE

Biggar, Paula Kay
7-12th Grade Eng/Span Teacher

KINNEAR

Scott, Beverly Jean
Science Teacher

LANDER

Crouch, Phil
Mathematics & Computer Teacher
De Witt, Susan Marie
Third Grade Teacher
Willhelm, Bonnie Belle
Mathematics/Science Teacher

LARAMIE

Rux, Jean Dixon
Fifth Grade Teacher
Schreckengost, Frank James Jr.
Mathematics Teacher
Stonehouse, Rick B.
English Teacher
Swierczek, Clinton Andrew
Health Teacher
Vaske, Mary Lou (Simmons)
Home Ec Teacher

LINGLE

Fullmer, Richard Lee
Math Teacher/Track Coach

LOVELL

Bischoff, Mable Ann
Second Grade Teacher
Brown, Vontella
Transition Teacher
Crosby, Josephine Mecham
English Teacher
Dixon, Patricia Frame
Sixth Grade Eng/Rdng Teacher
Gerhardt, Gus William
Social Studies Teacher

LYMAN

Copley, Laurens Windsor
  Science Department Chairman

NEWCASTLE

Dixon, Linda Lay
  Retired Teacher
Morrow, Scott A.
  Third Grade Teacher
Sample, Bette Jean Hart
  Second Grade Teacher
Thomas, Richard John
  German/Social Studies Teacher

PINE BLUFFS

Roeder, Kendra Leigh
  Science Teacher

PINEDALE

Ptasnik, Gregory D.
  Business Education Teacher

POWELL

Aguilar, Lee
  Spanish Teacher
Battershell, Barbara L.
  First Grade Teacher
Gonion, Leo Burl
  7th Grade Mathematics Teacher
Gracey, John J.
  5th Grade Teacher
Kidneigh, Jane Lisbeth
  Language Arts Teacher
Sapp, Anna Mae
  Remedial Reading Teacher

RAWLINS

Bohlender, Brad Alan
  Middle School Science Teacher
Kathan, Gary Otis
  Chemistry/Physics Teacher
King, Elaine Marie
  Third Grade Teacher
Miller, Beverly Johnson
  1st Grade Teacher

RIVERTON

Black, Eveleyn Irene (Klamm)
  Business Education Teacher
Flom, Sherman H.
  5th Grade Teacher
Yager, Julie K.
  Intermediate Lang Arts Teacher

ROCK SPRINGS

Chadey, Helen Putz
  Sixth Grade Teacher
Pribyl, Steven Douglas
  5th Grade Teacher

ROZET

Schell, Robert
  4th Grade Teacher

SARATOGA

Bensen, Pat Wilson
  Teacher of Gifted & Talented

SHERIDAN

Fessler, Edward John
  Social Studies Teacher
Nielsen, Lenus A.
  Chemistry Teacher

TORRINGTON

Williams, Sarah Loring
  7th Grade Reading Teacher

WORLAND

Groshart, Louise Jean
  3rd Grade Teacher
Mischke, Sandra Anne Mc Carty
  Language Arts Teacher

NABSE

National Alliance of Black School Educators

Committed to Eliminating the Effects of Racism in Education

All Children Can Learn

For Further Information:
National Alliance of Black School Educators
2816 Georgia Ave., NW
Washington, DC 20001
(202) 483-1549

Create the Climate for Today's Education Generation of the 90s

with Doorknob Hangers announcing . . .

"Teacher at Work — Future Under Construction"

A partnership message from NSPRA and Servicemaster ® . . . these bright yellow door hangers work as a constant reminder to everyone in your school of education's importance to our future.

We will provide one on request at no charge to teachers listed in WHO'S WHO AMONG AMERICA'S TEACHERS ™

National School Public Relations Association
1501 Lee Highway, Suite 201
Arlington, Virginia 22209
703/528-5840 — FAX 703/528-7017